- Schizophreniform Disorder
- Schizoaffective Disorder
- Delusional Disorder
- Brief Psychotic Disorder
- Shared Psychotic Disorder (Folie a Deux)
- Psychotic Disorder Due to a General Medical Condition
  - with delusions
  - with hallucinations
- Psychotic Disorder NOS

MOOD DISORDERS

Code current state of Major Depressive Disorder or Bipolar Disorder as follows:

unspecified, mild, moderate, severe without psychotic features, severe with psychotic features, in partial remission, in full remission

- Depressive Disorders
  - Major Depressive Disorder
    - single episode
    - recurrent
  - Dysthymic Disorder
  - Depressive Disorder NOS
- Bipolar Disorders
  - Bipolar I Disorder
    - single manic episode
    - most recent episode hypomanic
    - most recent episode manic
    - most recent episode mixed
    - most recent episode depressed
    - most recent episode unspecified
  - Bipolar II Disorder (Recurrent major depressive episodes with hypomania)
  - Cyclothymic Disorder
  - Bipolar Disorder NOS
- Mood Disorder Due to a General Medical Condition
- Mood Disorder NOS

ANXIETY DISORDERS

- Panic Disorder
  - Without Agoraphobia
  - With Agoraphobia
- Agoraphobia Without History of Panic Disorder
- Specific Phobia (Simple Phobia)
- Social Phobia (Social Anxiety Disorder)
- Obsessive-Compulsive Disorder
- Posttraumatic Stress Disorder
- Acute Stress Disorder
- Generalized Anxiety Disorder (Includes Overanxious Disorder of Childhood)
- Anxiety Disorder Due to a General Medical Condition
- Anxiety Disorder NOS

SOMATOFORM DISORDERS

- Somatization Disorder
- Conversion Disorder
- Hypochondriasis
- Body Dysmorphic Disorder
- Pain Disorder
  - Associated with Psychological Factors
  - Associated with Both Psychological Factors and a General Medical Condition
- Undifferentiated Somatoform Disorder
- Somatoform Disorder NOS

FACTITIOUS DISORDERS

- Factitious Disorder
  - with predominantly psychological signs and symptoms
  - with predominantly physical signs and symptoms
  - with combined psychological and physical signs and symptoms
- Factitious Disorder NOS

DISSOCIATIVE DISORDERS

- Dissociative Amnesia
- Dissociative Fugue
- Dissociative Identity Disorder (Multiple Personality Disorder)
- Depersonalization Disorder
- Dissociative Disorder NOS

SEXUAL AND GENDER IDENTITY DISORDERS

- Sexual Dysfunctions
  - Sexual Desire Disorders
    - Hypoactive Sexual Desire Disorder
    - Sexual Aversion Disorder
  - Sexual Arousal Disorders
    - Female Sexual Arousal Disorder
    - Male Erectile Disorder
  - Orgasm Disorders
    - Female Orgasmic Disorder (Inhibited Female Orgasm)
    - Male Orgasmic Disorder (Inhibited Male Orgasm)
    - Premature Ejaculation
  - Sexual Pain Disorders
    - Dyspareunia
    - Vaginismus
  - Sexual Dysfunctions Due to a General Medical Condition
  - Sexual Dysfunction NOS
- Paraphilias
  - Exhibitionism
  - Fetishism
  - Frotteurism
  - Pedophilia
  - Sexual Masochism
  - Sexual Sadism
  - Voyeurism
  - Transvestic Fetishism
  - Paraphilia NOS
- Sexual Disorder NOS
- Gender Identity Disorders
  - Gender Identity Disorder
    - in Children
    - in Adolescents and Adults
  - Gender Identity Disorder NOS

EATING DISORDERS

- Anorexia Nervosa
- Bulimia Nervosa
- Eating Disorder NOS

SLEEP DISORDERS

- Primary Sleep Disorders
  - Dyssomnias
    - Primary Insomnia
    - Primary Hypersomnia
    - Narcolepsy
    - Breathing-Related Sleep Disorder
    - Circadian Rhythm Sleep Disorder (Sleep-Wake Schedule Disorder)
    - Dyssomnia NOS
  - Parasomnias
    - Nightmare Disorder (Dream Anxiety Disorder)
    - Sleep Terror Disorder
    - Sleepwalking Disorder
    - Parasomnia NOS
- Sleep Disorders Related to Another Mental Disorder
  - Insomnia related to (Axis I or Axis II Disorder)
  - Hypersomnia related to (Axis I or Axis II Disorder)
- Other Sleep Disorders
  - Sleep Disorder Due to a General Medical Condition
    - Insomnia type
    - Hypersomnia type
    - Parasomnia type
    - Mixed type

IMPULSE CONTROL DISORDERS NOT ELSEWHERE CLASSIFIED

- Intermittent Explosive Disorder
- Kleptomania
- Pyromania
- Pathological Gambling
- Trichotillomania
- Impulse Control NOS

ADJUSTMENT DISORDERS

- Adjustment Disorder
  - With Anxiety
  - With Depressed Mood
  - With Disturbance of Conduct
  - With Mixed Disturbance of Emotions and Conduct
  - With Mixed Anxiety and Depressed Mood
  - Unspecified

AXIS II [PERSONALITY] DISORDERS

- Paranoid Personality Disorder
- Schizoid Personality Disorder
- Schizotypal Personality Disorder
- Antisocial Personality Disorder
- Borderline Personality Disorder
- Histrionic Personality Disorder
- Narcissistic Personality Disorder
- Avoidant Personality Disorder
- Dependent Personality Disorder
- Obsessive-Compulsive Personality Disorder
- Personality Disorder NOS

OTHER CONDITIONS THAT MAY BE A FOCUS OF CLINICAL ATTENTION

- (Psychological Factors) Affecting Medical Condition

Choose name based on nature of factors:

  - Mental Disorder Affecting Medical Condition
  - Psychological Symptoms Affecting Medical Condition
  - Personality Traits or Coping Style Affecting Medical Condition
  - Maladaptive Health Behaviors Affecting Medical Condition
  - Unspecified Psychological Factors Affecting Medical Condition
- Medication-Induced Movement Disorders
  - Neuroleptic-Induced [Parkinsonism, Malignant Syndrome, Acute Dystonia, Acute Akathisia, Tardive Dyskinesia]
  - Medication-Induced [Postural Tremor, Movement Disorder NOS]
- Adverse Effects of Medication NOS
- Relational Problems
  - Relational Problem Related to a Mental Disorder or
- General Medical Condition
  - Parent-Child Relational Problem
  - Partner Relational Problem
  - Sibling Relational Problem
  - Relational Problem NOS
- Problems Related to Abuse or Neglect
  - Physical Abuse of Child
  - Sexual Abuse of Child
  - Neglect of Child
  - Physical Abuse of Adult
  - Sexual Abuse of Adult
- Additional Conditions That May Be a Focus of Clinical Attention
  - Bereavement
  - Borderline Intellectual Functioning
  - Academic Problem
  - Occupational Problem
  - Childhood or Adolescent Antisocial Behavior
  - Adult Antisocial Behavior
  - Malingering
  - Phase of Life Problem
  - Noncompliance with treatment for a mental disorder
  - Identity Problem
  - Religious or Spiritual Problem
  - Acculturation Problem
  - Age-Associated Memory Decline

ADDITIONAL CODES

- Unspecified Mental Disorder
- No Diagnosis or Condition on Axis I
- Diagnosis or Condition Deferred an Axis I
- No Diagnosis on Axis II
- Diagnosis Deferred on Axis II

Abnormal Psychology and Modern Life

Ninth Edition

Robert C. Carson
Duke University

James N. Butcher
University of Minnesota

HarperCollins*Publishers*

Sponsoring Editor: Laura Pearson
Developmental Editor: Joanne M. Tinsley
Project Coordination, Text and Cover Design: Proof Positive/Farrowlyne Associates, Inc.
Cover Illustration/Photo: (front top) Hill Gallery, Burmingham, Michigan; (center, bottom, back cover, and spine) Collection de l'Art Brut, Lausanne
Photo Researcher: Leslie Coopersmith
Production Manager: Michael Weinstein
Compositor: Black Dot Graphics
Printer and Binder: R. R. Donnelley & Sons Company
Cover Printer: The Lehigh Press, Inc.

Abnormal Psychology and Modern Life, Ninth Edition

Library of Congress Cataloging-in-Publication Data

Carson, Robert C., 1930–
Abnormal psychology and modern life / Robert C. Carson, James N. Butcher.—9th ed.
p. cm.
Includes bibliographical references and index.
ISBN 0-673-46488-1 (student ed.)
ISBN 0-673-46617-5 (teacher ed.)
1. Pyschiatry. I. Butcher, James Neal, 1933– . II. Title.
[DNLM: 1. Mental Disorders. 2. Psychopathology. WM 100 C321a]
RC454.C275 1991
616.89--dc20
DNLM/DLC
for Library of Congress 91-20863
CIP

93 94 9 8 7 6 5 4 3

Contents in Brief

Contents

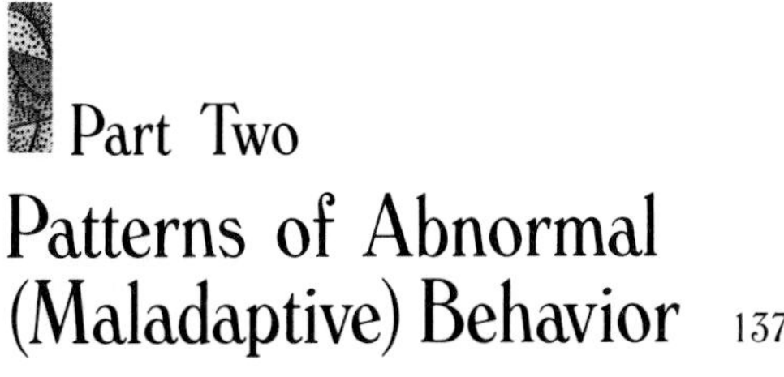

Chapter 10
Sexual Disorders and Variants 340

Chapter 11
Mood Disorders and Suicide 380

Chapter 12
The Schizophrenias and Delusional Disorders 426

Chapter 13
Organic Mental Disorders 476

Preface

As instructors who have used earlier versions of this text will readily perceive, the pace of developments in the field of abnormal behavior on both the conceptual and empirical fronts has accelerated substantially in recent years. This quickening pace requires an almost constant scanning of the pertinent literature in order to ensure that important milestones and trends will not be missed in the avalanche of information that the investigators and scholars of the field produce and place before us. As textbook authors committed to educating our readers comprehensively in the best that contemporary research and thinking has to offer, our involvement in this ninth edition of *Abnormal Psychology and Modern Life* has been a taxing enterprise. It has also been an enormously exciting one because the task has obliged us to immerse ourselves in this rapidly evolving field at a level we suspect would be unlikely under any less compelling circumstances.

The sheer density of new challenges and advances in the four years since we completed the eighth edition has required us to rethink and restructure our approach across a broad front. For example, concern with issues of taxonomy and classification of mental disorders, never far beneath the surface, has become a dominating theme recently as we struggle toward the creation of a new system, the fourth edition of the *Diagnostic and Statistical Manual of Mental Disorders* (DSM-IV). Meanwhile, we have witnessed the development of important new insights in numerous substantive areas, such as the pervasive character of posttraumatic stress disorders and the mechanisms underlying human adaptational failure in response to stress; the limitations of the genetic model of mental disorder; the nature of degenerative brain changes in Alzheimer's disease; the origins and consequences of drug abuse, particularly cocaine; and the profound impact of child abuse on the long-term adjustment of victims, to mention only a few.

In response to these developments as well as to reviewer input, the structure of the ninth edition has been extensively revamped. Most immediately apparent here is the addition of one chapter, expanding the total to 19. This addition was necessitated by our recognition that it was no longer possible to combine mental retardation and organic mental disorders in a single chapter and do justice to each of these topics. They now appear in separate chapters, enabling us to expand our coverage of both developmental (Axis II childhood) disorders, in which mental retardation is included, and the organic mental syndromes. In regard to the latter, we have more thoroughly examined the increasingly important problem of Alzheimer's dementia; we have also been able to introduce what we have learned to date about the newly recognized AIDS dementia complex, a widespread complication of AIDS infection.

A new chapter sequence was devised for Part Two (Patterns of Abnormal [Maladaptive] Behavior) of the ninth edition, one that better emphasizes conceptual relatedness as the various disorders of abnormal psychology are sequentially addressed. Thus, problems of behavioral medicine and the psychogenesis of physical disease are discussed immediately following the examination of stress and the anxiety-based disorders. Personality, substance-use, and sexual disorders are then taken up in an uninterrupted sequence involving conduct problems. We move next to the mood and schizophreniform disorders. The organic mental disorders then come into focus, followed by two chapters devoted to the specific types of psychopathology usually becoming manifest prior to adolescence.

Within chapters, all material has been updated with respect to new findings and developing trends at the conceptual level. Particular updating effort has been devoted to those disorders on which new and productive attention has been focused since the last edition, such as posttraumatic stress disorder (Chapter 5), multiple personality disorder (Chapter 6), and dementia of the Alzheimer's type (Chapter 13). Relating in particular to the first two of these, we have expanded at many points throughout the text our coverage of the etiologic significance of childhood trauma, in keeping with our dramatically enhanced recognition of the tragic dimensions of childhood abuse, both sexual and general, in our society.

We have also become even more critical of the too facile interpretations of the major disorders now increasingly offered to the general public—for example, that schizophrenia has been proven to be a unitary entity always caused by brain disease (usually of genetic origin), or that one can "cure" the profoundly human experience of depression by resorting to drugs. In each of these cases, as in many others, we invite the reader to weigh the evidence with us. Usually, as in these instances, it is found wanting.

For the first time in four decades the name of James Coleman is missing from the cover and title page of *Abnormal Psychology and Modern Life*. Although this change reflects the inevitability of change in human affairs, we cannot forego this opportunity to express our gratitude and admiration for the signal contribution our senior mentor made to higher education in the field of abnormal psychology. Like most psychologists of our generation, our own introduction to the field was enhanced by the scholarship, wisdom, and profound humanity of the man who brought this now classic text into being.

One of Coleman's abiding strengths, perhaps his major one, as a leading author in abnormal psychology was that he never succumbed to the temptation of oversimplification. This is an extremely challenging and complex field, as challenging and complex as are broader but intimately related questions pertaining to the fundamental origins of human behavior. While other authors in the field took "positions," and most to a greater or lesser extent reviewed evidence selectively and followed particular viewpoints, Coleman could be counted on to give every viewpoint its due and to emphasize an unbiased reporting of empirical findings—even when the "facts," as was often the case, led to no coherent, unqualified conclusions. A reputation for comprehensive analysis had thus been earned well before the present authors became involved with the text.

Much has changed in the field of abnormal psychology since we assumed major responsibility for this work, and indeed we can point to many areas where genuine advances in knowledge have been achieved. Nevertheless, it remains true that many basic issues are at least as puzzling now as they were when we began preparation for the sixth edition some 15 years ago. True to the tradition of this text, we have tried from the outset to be unstinting in identifying these areas of continuing perplexity and in rejecting premature closure on matters for which the empirical evidence remains equivocal. The ninth edition is in this essential respect no exception.

Our experience is that many more such unsettled questions remain than is commonly acknowledged. In this era of quick summaries, thumbnail sketches, and selectivity in reported evidence, our approach may seem to some unduly detailed and at times skeptical. Nevertheless, "telling it like it is" has remained one of our foremost objectives. We reject out of hand any notion that such an objective is inappropriate for a college textbook.

We do think this book will challenge students; the field, we reiterate, is itself challenging. We also hope it will inspire them to demand more of themselves, of the mental health professions, and of our society than has characterized our history in the area of coping effectively with mental disorder. Within the broad boundaries that we give to the study and treatment of abnormal behavior, a cogent argument can be made that nothing is more important to the advancement—even the survival—of humankind.

Ancillaries

The ancillaries for this text are many, and we will provide a brief overview here.

For the Student

A *Study Guide* by Mary Koss (University of Arizona) provides chapter overviews, key terms, learning objectives, and extensive study questions and self-tests.

SuperShell Computerized Tutorial by David Lutz (Southwest Missouri State University) is an interactive text-related program for IBM and compatibles, featuring multiple-choice, true-false, and completion quizzes, as well as chapter outlines and flash cards for key terms and concepts.

The *Brief Casebook in Abnormal Psychology* by Judith Rosenberger (Hunter College) and Edith Gould (Psychoanalytic Institute of the Post Graduate Center for Mental Health—New York City) provides a set of 13 case studies covering a wide range of psychological disorders.

Computerized Case Simulations by Matthew E. Lambert (Texas Tech University) is a new interactive program in which the student can take the role of a therapist to assess, diagnose, and treat fictional clients for various disorders.

For the Instructor

In addition to the ancillaries for students, a complete set of ancillary materials is available from our publisher for instructors who adopt this book.

An *Instructor's Manual* by Frank J. Prerost (Western Illinois University) gives overviews, lists of key terms, learning objectives, abstracts with discussion questions, recommended readings, discussion and lecture ideas, as well as activities and projects for each chapter.

Videos from "THE WORLD OF ABNORMAL PSYCHOLOGY," a new thirteen part telecourse, produced by the Annenberg/CPB Project in conjunction with Toby Levine Communications, Alvin H. Perlmutter, and HarperCollins Publishers, are available with accompanying literature on how to incorporate the videos into classroom lectures.

HarperCollins Video in Abnormal Psychology, features interviews with clients at the Western Missouri Mental Health Center, conducted by David S. Holmes (University of Kansas). The 80-minute video contains eight separate interviews and offers an exceptionally clear depiction of a wide range of symptoms covered in the text. Print materials are available with the video.

A *Test Bank,* written by David Lutz (Southeast Missouri State University) contains over 100 multiple-choice and essay questions per chapter. Questions are keyed to learning objectives in the study guide and instructor's manual, and are referenced according to difficulty level and cognitive type.

TestMaster, the computerized version of the test bank, is also available for IBM PC and MAC compatibles. The program allows you to customize your own tests on a built-in word processor that lets you delete, add, and revise questions as necessary.

GRADES is a classroom management program that lets you store data for up to 200 students and calculate average scores, grading curves and individual grades. For IBM PCs and compatibles.

For more information on the ancillaries and their availability, please contact your local HarperCollins representative or write the company at the address on the copyright page.

Acknowledgments

No project of this magnitude, which on this occasion included the coordinate development of a series of documentary videotapes, could be brought to fruition without the dedicated efforts of numerous talented people. We particularly note the gracious and competent reception we have received from our new publishers, HarperCollins. Those individuals making direct contributions are named in the following paragraphs. We want here to single out for a special note of praise and appreciation our developmental editor, Joanne Tinsley. Indeed, we believe that her editorial wisdom and taste and her unfailing organizational skill are central to whatever success the current edition enjoys, just as they have been for four of its predecessors.

Also at HarperCollins, we would like to thank Susan Driscoll, Editor-in-Chief; Laura Pearson, Acquisitions Editor; Michael Weinstein, Full Service Manager; Paula Cousin, Project Editorial Supervisor; and Otis Taylor, Marketing Manager, for their enthusiastic support of and attention to the development of the ninth edition. Our Photo Researcher Leslie Coopersmith delighted us with her sensitive graphic depictions of what we were trying to say. Bob Olander, Project Editor, and Ann Skuran, Designer, at Proof Positive/Farrowlyne Associates were superb and unflappable in the hectic and demanding role of managing, under pressured time constraints, the conversion of our sometimes chaotic manuscript copy into printed pages.

Numerous others also contributed materially to our efforts as authors. Carolyn L. Williams provided timely references and some of the case material used in the text. We also benefited significantly from the comments offered by reviewers of the previous edition and of various versions and parts of the manuscript for the current one. They are:

Lewis R. Aiken
Pepperdine University

G. Dale Baskett
Tuskeegee University

Ernest E. Beckham
University of Oklahoma

Lorna S. Benjamin
University of Utah

Ira H. Bernstein
University of Texas/Arlington

James F. Calhoun
University of Georgia

Lee Anna Clark
Southern Methodist University

Lorry J. Cology
Owens Technical College

Eric Cooley
Western Oregon State

Barry Edelstein
West Virginia University

Robert Emmons
University of California/Davis

Peter R. Finn
Indiana University

Sheila Fling
Southwest Texas State

Robert L. Gossette
Hofstra University

Robert Holmstrom
George Washington University

D. Lamar Jacks
Sante Fe Community College

Fred A. Johnson
University of the District of Columbia

Edward Katkin
State University of New York/Stony Brook

Karl G. Krisac
Delaware County College

Michael J. Lambert
Brigham Young University

Arnold LeUnes
Texas A&M University

Muriel Lezak
Oregon Health Sciences University

Patrick E. Logue
Duke University

James E. Maddux
George Mason University

Lisa McCann
Traumatic Stress Institute

Linda D. Nelson
University of California/Orange

Richard Neufeld
University of Western Ontario

Marcia Ozier
Dalhousie University

Robert W. Payne
University of Victoria

Harold A. Ries
California State University/Sacramento

Alexander Rosen
University of Illinois/Chicago

Michael J. Ross
St. Louis University

Dennis P. Saccuzzo
San Diego State University

John R. Schallow
University of Manitoba

Milton Simmons
University of Tennessee/Martin

Art Skibbe
Appalachian State University

Barry D. Smith
University of Maryland/College Park

T. Gale Thompson
Bethany College

Elliot S. Valenstein
University of Michigan

William Van Ornum
Marist College

Herman A. Walters
University of Montana

Charles Wenar
Ohio State University

Fred Whitford
Montana State University

Logan Wright
University of Oklahoma

Finally, we thank once again the members of both of our immediate families, who endured without complaint the substantial privations of presence, residual energy, and focused attention necessarily entailed in an authorship task of this magnitude.

R.C.C.
J.N.B.

To the Student

A number of features have been incorporated into this book to help you learn about abnormal psychology. Another goal is to enable you to develop a balanced yet critical perspective that should serve you well in future pursuits.

Chapter outlines introduce each chapter and provide an overview of what is to come. **Chapter summaries** provide a broad overview of the chapter and can be read for preview purposes before you read the chapter and for review purposes after you've read and studied the chapter.

Key terms appear in boldface type when first introduced and defined in the text. For each chapter, key terms are also placed after the summary in a page-referenced composite list; at the end of the text, the terms are again listed and defined in an expanded glossary.

Highlight boxes expand on or summarize important text content. An in-text reference to each box tells you when you should read each Highlight.

Unresolved Issues sections appear before the summary for each chapter. These sections bring the field alive by examining some of the challenges and dilemmas facing researchers. They are a great source for term paper topics or extra credit work.

The **DSM-III-R,** a classification system for abnormal behavior that you will read about in Chapter 1 and use throughout this book, is printed for ready reference on the back endsheets of your book.

Case studies of individuals with various behavior disorders appear throughout the book. These cases provide real-life examples of the clinical pictures of the many disorders you will read about. Some are brief excerpts; others are quite detailed analyses. In any case, they serve not only to make what you're reading about more real, but also to remind you of the human factor so intimately a part of the subject matter of this text. In scanning the text, you can spot case studies by the pale screen behind the type; cases also sometimes appear in Highlight boxes.

Patient art appears on the cover and in the chapter openers, with a brief biographical sketch of the artist. **Photos,** too, are used throughout to visually enhance the key concepts of the text; in many cases, these photos are of individuals who have actually been diagnosed as having a disorder. We hope the art and the photos will serve not only to instruct but also to humanize your study of abnormal behavior.

At the end of the book, you will find a **Glossary** that contains definitions to words that appear in boldface type in the text and to other terms commonly encountered in this or other psychology texts; you can use the glossary as a general reference tool and as a study aid for the course. You will find here, too, the **Subject** and **Name Indexes** in which you can find quickly any topic or individual discussed in the book. The boldface page numbers in the **Subject Index** indicate where key terms are first discussed in-depth. A listing of **References** appears at the end of the text; should you wish to further examine any of the citations that appear in the text proper, this is where you will find the information you need.

A ***Study Guide*** by Mary Koss can assist you in organizing and mastering the material you are studying. It includes chapter overviews, learning objectives, a list of key terms, study questions, and multiple-choice self-test quizzes that should prepare you for class exams. If the *Study Guide* is not available at the bookstore, ask the bookstore manager if he or she can order a copy for you.

A **Mailer** appears on the last printed page of your text. This is your opportunity to provide us with your thoughts on how this text has worked for you. We hope you will take time to complete this brief questionnaire; we have relied on student input over the years to improve each edition of *Abnormal Psychology and Modern Life.*

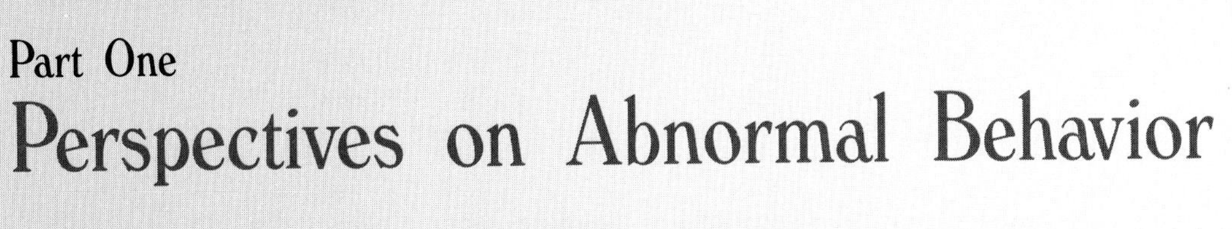

Part One

Perspectives on Abnormal Behavior

Chapter 1

Abnormal Behavior in Our Times

Miguel Hernandez, *Odalisques* (1947–1948). Hernandez (1893–1957), a Spaniard of working-class background, was interned in a concentration camp in France for fighting on the Republican side during the Spanish Civil War. He drew his first designs during his imprisonment in the camp. After his release, Hernandez began to work in oil, eventually to the exclusion of almost all other activities. He spent the last ten years of his life in Paris under a cloud of loneliness and spiritual exhaustion. This strikingly warm and harmonious painting is all the more remarkable for having been created by one who endured such difficult personal trials.

In studying abnormal psychology, we set our sights squarely on the worst that can happen when human beings find themselves confronted by challenges or demands that exceed their coping resources, by problems that are just too great. Consider the following cases:

Albert G., a 62-year-old university professor at a small college in the Midwest, was immensely popular and well regarded by everyone who knew him. Students flocked to his classes; his professional colleagues sought his consultation and scholarly views; and he wrote, when his moods permitted, with penetrating insight and unusual candor. With such high praise and with obvious success, why did he kill himself—a victim of deep personal despair? He had lived a tidy and conscientious life, always concerned about how he was viewed by others. Although dwelling alone, he had had several close friends, yet no one knew of the personal plight he apparently had experienced. No one around him, even his closest associates, had been aware of the depth of his despondent moods. The suicide left everyone in the community wondering about the psychological forces that could prompt someone as promising as Albert to end his life.

Many people live their lives, or episodes of their lives, in suffering and desperation, unable to cope with challenges that are too great. Abnormal psychology is concerned with these difficulties of human adaptation and with investigating ways in which they may be prevented or reversed.

Sue D., a 38-year-old attorney, acknowledged to her treatment group that she did not know how long she had had a problem with alcohol and tranquilizer abuse. She had become painfully aware of her problems when she had "hit bottom." She described the evening when she had gone to dinner with some friends and had lingered afterward in the restaurant bar to have a few drinks. She had drunk a great deal more than she had intended (as was often the case) and had gotten into a heated argument with other patrons and the manager of the bar. Sue explained how the situation had deteriorated. Objects had been thrown, the police had been called, and she had been arrested for public drunkenness and abuse of police officers. The police then had taken her to a detoxification center at the county hospital—the same hospital where she served as chief counsel for the law firm at which she worked. Sue told her group that the hospital administrator had been incensed, and the law firm partners had been embarrassed and outraged. Sue had been given the option of leaving the law firm or seeking treatment; she had chosen the latter and had begun a new phase of her life. She had entered a treatment program and was trying to understand how she had allowed her life to shatter as it had.

Manuel D., a 22-year-old Hispanic American, lived in a predominantly Spanish community in a large California city. One evening, after four teenagers in another car on the highway had allegedly made obscene gestures to him, he followed their car for some distance until they stopped. He then accosted the group and, with a revolver, killed one youth, and wounded another. What prompted him to engage in such destructive behavior? Although he lived in a tough neighborhood in which youth gangs were prominent, he was not a gang member. He had acted alone in the shooting. Drug and alcohol screening, conducted shortly after the incident, was negative. A search of his background showed that he had had several previous incidents of personal violence, a record of arrests, and a previous commitment to a psychiatric hospital for suspicious and threatening behavior. What factors underlaid his lack of impulse control and his violent acts toward other people?

To an extent, when we study cases such as these we see a distorted picture of human adaptation, one emphasizing the failings of psychological resourcefulness rather than the inspiring heights it more often attains. But in looking at these failings, we also learn something of their sources and the ways in which they may be prevented or reversed. We find that these failings are scientifically lawful; they are understandable and even, within reason, predictable and controllable. This knowledge about behavior problems allows us to expand our scientific understanding of abnormal psychology. Perhaps one day we may reach the point where irrational behavior that leads to persistent self-defeat and threatens group survival is no longer of serious concern. But before we reach that point, we have much to learn. We will begin our study of abnormal psychology by examining some popular views on the makeup of individuals with psychological problems.

POPULAR VIEWS OF ABNORMAL BEHAVIOR

Examples of mental disorders that we have heard or read about are apt to give us a distorted, perhaps even a chamber-of-horrors impression of abnormal behavior. In truth, less spectacular maladjustments are far more common. Popular beliefs about abnormal behavior thus tend to be based on atypical, exaggerated, and often unscientific descriptions.

Mental disorders of one kind or another have been a favorite topic of writers for many centuries, and the public's changing conceptions of mental disorders have been strongly influenced by popular literary and dramatic works. Though certainly not the first to explore this area, William Shakespeare is especially notable for having created a number of characters whose actions resemble certain behaviors we now associate with officially recognized clinical patterns—characters such as Lady Macbeth (obsessive-compulsive behavior), King Lear (paranoia), Iago (antisocial personality), Ophelia (depression/melancholy), and Othello (obsessive, paranoid jealousy).

The fascination with abnormal behavior has continued in modern writing, often in autobiographies. Examples include Mark Vonnegut's *The Eden Express* (1975), in which the author describes his own acute schizophrenic breakdown, and Hannah Green's *I Never Promised You a Rose Garden* (1964), which describes her treatment by a gifted therapist for a more chronic form of the same disorder. Stuart

In Shakespeare's play Hamlet the heroine Ophelia—driven mad with grief upon learning of the death of her father—drowns herself in a pond. Ophelia is one of a number of Shakespeare's memorable characters who suffer greatly from mental disorder and confusion.

Sutherland, a distinguished British psychologist, presents an account of his own psychotic episode in *Breakdown* (1977). An earlier autobiographical account of psychosis, *A Mind That Found Itself* (1908/1970) by Clifford Beers, played a significant role in the development of the mental hygiene movement in the United States. The Beers book, in part a chilling account of the conditions in mental hospitals around the turn of the century, foreshadowed equally disturbing modern accounts by Mary Jane Ward in *The Snake Pit* (1946) and by Ken Kesey in his fictionalized (but in many ways poignantly accurate) *One Flew Over the Cuckoo's Nest* (1962). Fortunately, the horrible conditions described by these writers have been rectified in many contemporary mental hospitals, although in many cases the problems may have been transferred unwittingly to the deplorable conditions of the many mentally ill who are homeless or who live in substandard community-based nursing facilities.

We seem to have an insatiable curiosity about bizarre behavior, and—in addition to accounts we read in books—most of us avidly seek and devour newspaper, radio, and TV accounts on the subject. Though we surely learn some things from these accounts, we also may be narrowing our perspective because the popular media typically simplify issues, appearing to give answers when, in fact, they barely succeed in posing the correct questions. The daily press regularly carries stories about seemingly demented people and often seeks to legitimize these stories by citing mental health professionals who more often than not have never examined these people. Such armchair diagnoses are useless (and probably unethical) in the majority of cases.

As a result of such exposure in literature and the media, you are likely to have a more than passing acquaintance with abnormal behavior. You may already have reached conclusions about its causes and its treatment. In most instances, however, we simply do not yet have sufficient information to permit valid conclusions about causal factors and treatment options, and the misinformation that is

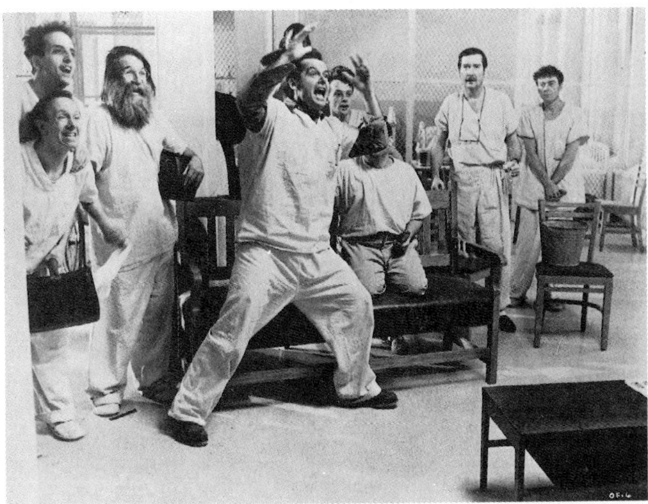

The public's changing conceptions of mental disorders have been strongly influenced by popular literary and dramatic works. Shown here is a still from the film version of Ken Kesey's One Flew Over the Cuckoo's Nest, a classic account of the disturbing, dehumanizing conditions in mental hospitals.

HIGHLIGHT 1.1

Some Popular Myths and Misconceptions Concerning Mental Disorder and Abnormal Behavior

Myth	Fact
Abnormal behavior is invariably bizarre.	The behavior of most individuals diagnosed with a mental disorder is usually indistinguishable from that of "normal" people.
Normal and abnormal behavior are different in kind.	Few if any types of behavior displayed by mental patients are unique to them. Abnormality consists largely of a poor fit between behavior and the situation in which it is enacted.
As a group, former mental patients are unpredictable and dangerous.	A typical former mental patient is no more volatile or dangerous than a "normal" person. The exceptions to this rule generate much publicity and give a distorted picture.
Mental disorders are associated with fundamental personal deficiencies and hence they occur because individuals fail to correct a deficit.	So far as we know, everyone shares the potential for becoming disordered and behaving abnormally.
Appropriate attitudes toward mental disorder include awe and fearfulness about one's own foibles and vulnerability.	Mental disorders are natural adaptive processes that are comprehensible within this context. The majority of people have an excellent chance of never becoming disordered and of recovering completely should the unlikely happen.

readily available can cloud one's perspective. Therefore it is wise to suspend any preconceived beliefs about abnormal psychology until we consider the evidence. Look, too, at *HIGHLIGHT 1.1* for an overview of the more common misconceptions people are likely to have about abnormal behavior.

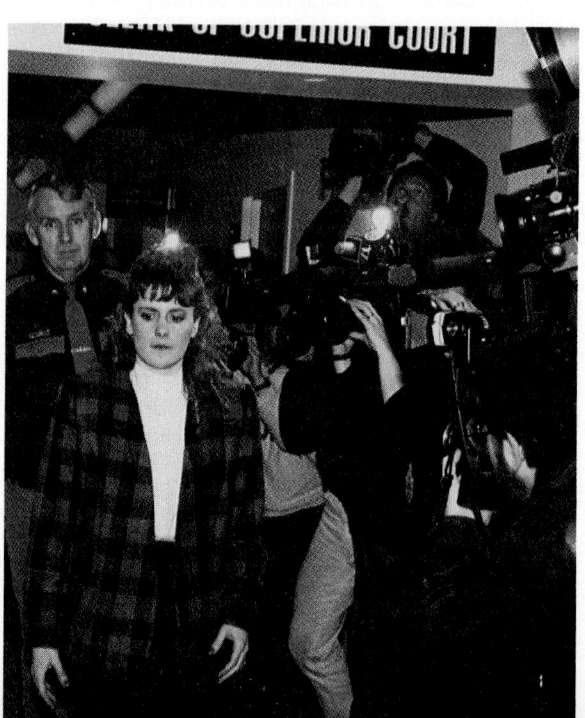

We tend to find sensationalistic accounts of bizarre behavior compelling. Witness the media furor over the recent case of 23-year-old Pamela Smart, found guilty of conspiring with her 16-year-old lover to murder her husband. The mixture of sex, scheming, and murder in the setting of a quiet New Hampshire town dominated news reporting for weeks. Cases such as these are likely to give us a narrow perspective of abnormal behavior because the information we get from press and TV stories may be simplified or distorted.

WHAT DO WE MEAN BY ABNORMAL BEHAVIOR?

To assess, treat, and prevent abnormal behavior, it is important to develop definitions of normal and abnormal and to specify criteria for distinguishing one from the other. Unfortunately, making such distinctions is not always easy to do. The word *abnormal* literally means "away from the normal," which implies deviation from some clearly defined norm. But what is the norm? In the case of physical illness, the norm is the structural and functional integrity of the body; here, the boundary lines between normality and pathology are usually (but not always) clear. For psychological disorder, however, we have no ideal model or even normal model of human functioning to use as a base of comparison. Thus we find considerable confusion and disagreement as to just what is or is not normal, a confusion aggravated by our changing values.

In the final analysis, any definition of abnormal must be somewhat arbitrary. Definitions tend to represent one of two broad perspectives. One view is that the concepts of normal and abnormal are meaningful only with reference to a given culture: abnormal behavior is behavior that deviates from society's norms. The other view—which is the one we advocate—is that behavior is abnormal if it interferes with the well-being of the individual and the group. Let us look more closely at each of these perspectives.

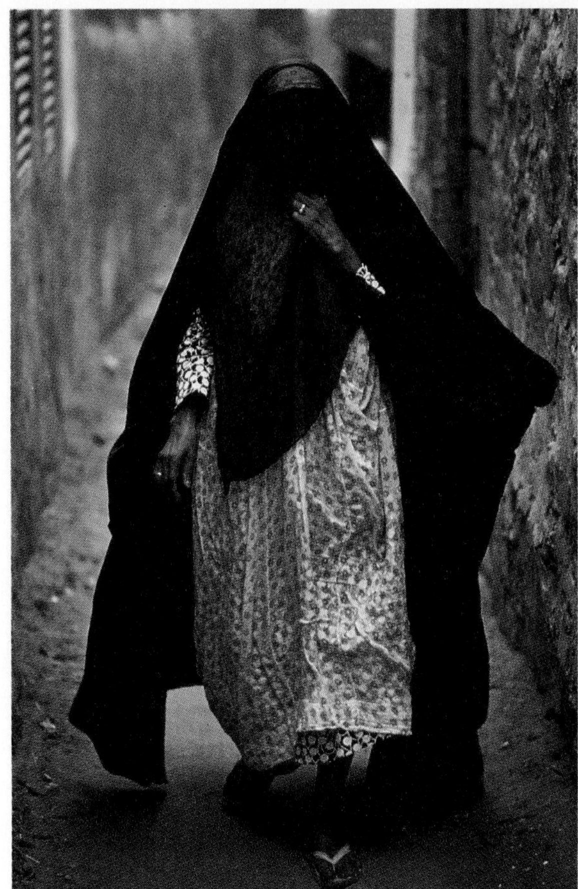

What is considered abnormal or deviant behavior in one society may be quite normal in another. We might consider this Arab woman's style of dress to be abnormal, but in her society it is the norm. What we consider normal may not be normal for everyone.

Abnormal Behavior as a Deviation from Social Norms

According to Ullmann and Krasner (1975), *abnormal* is simply a label given to behavior that deviates from social expectations. They maintain that behavior cannot be considered abnormal as long as society accepts it. As *cultural relativists,* they reject the concept of a sick society in which the social norms themselves might be viewed as pathological.

A critical example is whether an obedient Nazi concentration camp commander would be considered normal or abnormal. To the extent that he was responding accurately and successfully to his environment and not breaking its rules, much less coming to the professional attention of psychiatrists, he would not be labeled abnormal. Repulsive as his behavior is to mid-twentieth-century Americans, such repulsion is based on a particular set of values. Although such a person may be held responsible for his acts—as Nazi war criminals were—the concept of abnormality as a special entity does not seem necessary or justified. If it is, the problem arises as to who selects the values, and this, in turn, implies that one group may select values that are applied to others. This situation of one group's values being dominant over others is the fascistic background from which the Nazi camp commander sprang. (Ullmann & Krasner, 1975, p. 16)

The acceptance of complete cultural relativism simplifies the task of defining abnormality: behavior is abnormal if—and only if—the society labels it as such (Scheff, 1984). But serious questions can be raised about the validity of this definition. It rests on the questionable assumption that social acceptance makes behavior normal—that one set of values is as good as another for human beings to adopt. It then follows that the task of the psychotherapist is to ensure that patients conform to the norms their society views as appropriate, regardless of the values on which these norms are based.

Cultural relativists maintain that behavior cannot be considered abnormal as long as society accepts it. In this context, is the behavior of a concentration camp guard—such as these German guards leading Jewish prisoners to a Nazi concentration camp—abnormal if he is conforming to the norms of his environment?

Abnormal Behavior as Maladaptive

Although some degree of social conformity is essential to group life, we believe that the best criterion for determining the normality of behavior is not whether society accepts it, but whether it fosters individual and group well-being. When we use the term *well-being* we mean more than maintenance and survival. The term also implies growth and fulfillment—the actualization of potentialities. According to this criterion, **abnormal behavior** is *maladaptive behavior.* Even behavior that conforms to societal values is abnormal if it interferes with functioning and growth and if it is self-defeating.

So defined, abnormal behavior includes the more traditional categories of mental disorders—alcoholism and schizophrenia, for example—as well as prejudice and discrimination, wasteful use of natural resources, pollution of air and water, irrational violence, and political corruption, regardless of whether such actions are condemned or condoned by a given society. All of these actions represent maladaptive behavior that impairs individual or group well-being. Typically they lead to personal distress, and often they bring about destructive group conflict as well.

In defining abnormal behavior as maladaptive, we are making two value assumptions: (a) survival and actualization are worth striving for on both individual and group levels; and (b) human behavior can be evaluated in terms of its consequences for these objectives. As with the assumptions underlying cultural relativism, these value assumptions are open to criticism on the grounds that they are arbitrary. But unless we value the survival and actualization of the human race, there seems little point in trying to identify abnormal behavior or do anything about it. We can thus claim that our position is ultimately pragmatic.

In assessing, treating, and preventing abnormal behavior, mental health personnel are concerned not only with the maladaptive behavior itself, but also with the family, community, and society. From this perspective, therapy is defined not solely in terms of helping individuals adjust to their personal situations—no matter how frustrating or abnormal—but also in terms of alleviating group and societal conditions that may be causing or maintaining the maladaptive behavior.

Before we move on, you should be aware of several distinct but closely related professional fields concerned with the study of abnormal behavior and mental health. The distinction among them is often hard to draw precisely, for even though each has its own functions and areas of work, the discoveries in one field are constantly influencing and contributing to the thinking and work in others.

Abnormal psychology, or **psychopathology,** has long been referred to as that part of the field of psychology concerned with the understanding, treatment, and prevention of abnormal behavior. Within the area of applied psychology, **clinical psychology** is the discipline broadly concerned with the study, assessment, treatment, and prevention of abnormal behavior. **Psychiatry** is the corresponding field of medicine; it is thus closely related to clinical psychology, the chief difference being that psychiatrists tend to conceptualize abnormal behavior and its treatment in medical rather than behavioral terms. **Social work** is concerned with the analysis of social environments and with providing services that help individuals adjust in both family and community settings.

Most research in abnormal behavior is conducted by psychologists, in keeping with their primarily academic roots—the Ph.D. continues to be the most common degree among clinical psychologists. A relatively small proportion of psychiatrists, chiefly those in academic settings (such as medical schools), also do research, typically after obtaining specialized research training. Research activity is not usually conducted by social workers or other types of mental health professionals.

CLASSIFYING ABNORMAL BEHAVIOR

Traditionally, the study of abnormal behavior focuses on three distinct but often overlapping categories: (a) the nature of the abnormality, (b) the factors that cause or influence its occurrence, and (c) the methods developed for reducing or eliminating the behavior. As you will see, although much of the discussion in this text is organized around these categories, and although the categories are readily defined, it is still often difficult to understand completely the nature, causes, and treatment of abnormal behavior.

Describing the nature of abnormal behavior, also known as defining its **clinical picture,** is critical to understanding the cause and treatment of the behavior. Considerable attention has been paid to obtaining accurate clinical pictures because they serve as scientific guideposts, often pointing to important areas of needed research. For these descriptions to be helpful, they must organize the observed data in a systematic way, one that enables us to use the descriptions as diagnostic and treatment tools. In other words, good clinical pictures allow us to *classify* abnormal behavior.

Classification is important in any science, whether we are studying plants, planets, or people. With an agreed-upon classification system, we can be confident that we are communicating clearly. If someone says to you, "I saw a collie running down the street," you probably have an accurate idea of what the collie looked like—not from seeing it but rather from your knowledge of dog classifications.

In abnormal psychology, classification involves the delineation of various types, or categories, of maladaptive behavior. Classification is the necessary first step toward introducing some order into our discussion of the nature, causes, and treatment of such behavior. It enables communication about particular clusters of behavior in agreed-upon and meaningful ways. For example, we cannot conduct research on background causal factors in a given disorder unless we begin with a more or less clear definition of the behavior under examination. We need that clarity first of all to select proper research subjects. There are other reasons for "diagnostic" classifications, too, such as enabling adequate statistical counts of the incidence of various disorders or meeting the needs of medical insurance companies (which insist on having formal diagnoses before they will authorize payment of claims).

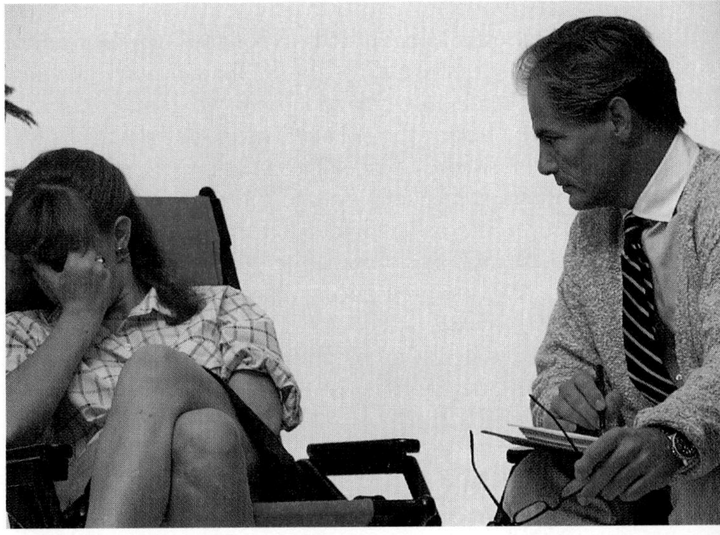

Mental health practitioners, in looking for the nature, causes, and treatment of maladaptive behavior, use diagnostic classifications. To diagnose a patient's problem, they must consider whether the patient shows a specific number of symptoms that fit a given diagnostic category.

It is important to keep in mind that all classification is the product of human invention—it is, in essence, a matter of making generalizations based on what has been observed. Even when observations are precise and carefully made, generalizations go beyond them by making inferences about underlying similarities and differences. In abnormal psychology, it is important to keep in mind that formal classification is accomplished only through precise techniques of psychological, or clinical, assessment—techniques that have been refined over the years. We will examine these techniques in Chapter 16, after we have looked thoroughly at the nature of abnormal behavior. In short, it is helpful first to understand the nature and causal factors underlying abnormal behavior before studying how to assess it.

Granting that all classification systems are fundamentally arbitrary, some of them are much better than others in helping us organize and discuss our observations. We base a classification system's usefulness on its reliability and validity. **Reliability** is the degree to which a test or measuring device produces the same result each time it is used to measure the same thing. In the context of classification, it is a measure of the extent to which different observers can agree that a behavior "fits" a given diagnostic category. If observers cannot agree, it may mean that the classification criteria are not precise enough to determine whether the disorder is present or absent. In contrast, **validity** refers to the extent to which a measuring instrument actually measures what it claims to measure. In the case of classification, validity is determined by whether the diagnostic category tells us something important or basic about the disorder. If, for example, we diagnose a person as schizophrenic, we should be able to infer from the classification information the characteristics that differentiate the person from others considered normal or from those suffering from different mental disorders, characteristics that go beyond the observations leading to the diagnosis. Validity presupposes reliability. We will encounter the important concepts of reliability and validity again when we discuss psychological assessment techniques in Chapter 16.

DSM Classification of Mental Disorders

The most widely used classification scheme for mental disorders in the United States is the *Diagnostic and Statistical Manual of Mental Disorders,* Third Edition Revised, put together by the American Psychiatric Association (1987). It is referred to in brief as **DSM-III-R.** There also exists a worldwide classification system called the *International Classification of Diseases,* Ninth Edition (World Health Organization, 1979), or ICD-9, which covers all diseases and disorders, both physical and mental. Both the American Psychiatric Association and the World Health Organization have worked closely over the years to ensure compatibility between their classification systems. For example, with the publication of DSM-III in 1980, a clinical modification of the mental disorders section of the ICD-9 was written to accommodate many of the DSM-III changes. Some differences remain, however; the ICD-9-CM (the CM was adopted to indicate the clinical modification) retains a number of categories that have since been dropped from DSM-III-R. These differences show that the process of classification is an ongoing search for a better, more effective system.

Each successive edition of DSM has sought to improve its clinical usefulness for professionals who diagnose and treat patients. Efforts have been directed specifically at overcoming the weaknesses in reliability and validity encountered with its predecessors. The distinctive innovation in DSM-III (and DSM-III-R) is its attempt to use only "operational" criteria for defining the different disorders included in the classification system. This innovation means that the DSM system specifies the exact behaviors that must be observed for a given diagnostic label to be applied. In a typical case, a specific number of signs or symptoms from a designated list must be present before a diagnosis can properly be assigned. In other words, efforts have been made to remove subjective elements from the diagnostic process.

To the extent this goal can be achieved, diagnostic reliability is substantially improved. On the other hand, the use of stricter criteria can cause much abnormal behavior to be assigned to "wastebasket" or residual categories such as "psychotic disorders not elsewhere classified." When this occurs, validity suffers, since a category so broad can give only generalities about disorders within it.

DSM-III-R evaluates an individual's behavior according to five dimensions, or *axes.* The first three axes assess an individual's present condition:

I. The particular maladaptive symptoms, or clinical psychiatric syndromes, such as schizophrenia
II. Any long-standing personality problems (adults) or specific developmental problems (children and adolescents)
III. Any medical or physical disorders that may also be present

More than one diagnosis may be recorded on Axes I and III and, in exceptional instances, on Axis II. A person may have multiple psychiatric symptoms or medical diseases (Axes I and III, respectively), and may have more than one personality disorder diagnosed on Axis II.

The last two DSM-III axes are used to assess broader aspects of an individual's situation, one dealing with the stressors that may have contributed to the current disorder and the other dealing with how well the individual has been coping in recent months.

IV. The severity of psychosocial stressors
V. The level of adaptive functioning

Axes I and II, which list the categories of mental disorders, are provided in full on the endsheets of this book. These categories may be regarded for purposes of clarity as fitting into several broad groupings, each containing several subgroupings:

1. *Organic mental disorders* refer to disorders involving gross destruction or malfunctioning of brain tissue (as in Alzheimer's disease) and a wide range of other conditions based on brain pathology. These disorders are described in Chapter 13.

2. *Substance-use disorders* involve problems such as drug and alcohol abuse. These are discussed in Chapter 9.

3. *Disorders of psychological or sociocultural origin* have no known brain pathology as a primary causal factor, as in anxiety (Chapter 6), psychophysiologic (Chapter 7), psychosexual (Chapter 10), and personality (Chapter 8) disorders. The **functional psychoses**—that is, severe mental disorders for which a specific organic pathology has not been demonstrated—such as major mood disorders (Chapter 11) and schizophrenia (Chapter 12), are also traditionally included here, although it appears increasingly likely that certain types of brain dysfunction sometimes help cause them.

4. *Disorders usually arising during childhood or adolescence* include mental retardation and special problems, such as early infantile autism and pervasive developmental disorders, that may occur in children and that warrant separate categorization (Chapter 14), as well as other problems of childhood, such as hyperactivity and conduct disorders (Chapter 15).

In referring to mental disorders, several qualifying terms are commonly used. **Acute** is a term used to describe disorders of relatively short duration, usually under six months. In some contexts, it also connotes behavioral symptoms of high intensity. **Chronic** refers to longstanding and usually permanent disorders, but the term can also be applied generally to low-intensity disorders since long-term difficulties are often of this sort. **Mild, moderate,** and **severe** are terms that describe the severity of a disorder. **Episodic** is used to describe disorders that tend to recur, as with some mood and schizophrenic patterns.

Axis III of DSM-III-R is often used in conjunction with an Axis I diagnosis of psychological factors affecting physical condition. An Axis III diagnosis, which requires a medical examination, is used when a diagnostician has reason to believe that a psychological factor is contributing in some way to a physical disease—for example, problems with dependency are often thought to be associated with gastric ulcers. Axis III itself can be used for any physical disorder that accompanies a psychiatric one, whether or not the two are related.

Axes IV and V were new to the DSM-III and revised in DSM-III-R. They provide a framework for assessing an individual's life situation (Axis IV) and recent ability to cope with it (Axis V). Axis IV (presented in *HIGHLIGHT 1.2*) has a six-point scale for rating the severity of psychosocial factors—either acute events or enduring circumstances—that may be placing an individual under stress and contributing to the current disorder. The scale can be used for both adults and children. Levels range from *none* at one end of the scale to *catastrophic* at the other. Axis V (presented in *HIGHLIGHT 1.3*) has a ninety-point scale for rating an individual's current global level of functioning. A clinician is also encouraged to use the same scale to rate the highest level of functioning in past years. Here the levels range from good functioning in all areas through levels of impairment to conditions considered dangerous. Both these scales can help ensure that when different clinicians talk about either stress severity or "good" adjustments, for example, they are talking about the same thing.

As an example of an extended DSM-III-R diagnosis, let us consider the case of Albert, the university professor described in the opening pages of this chapter. His diagnosis might be as follows:

Axis I
Major depressive disorder
Axis II
Compulsive personality disorder
Axis III
None
Axis IV
Level of psychosocial stressors: 3 (moderate)
Axis V
Global functioning: 60 (moderate difficulty)

Axes IV and V are significant additions. Knowing the demands that have been on an individual is important for understanding the problem behavior that has developed. Knowing an individual's general level of success in meeting these demands in the recent past can help a clinician make an appropriate and realistic treatment plan and can give him or her an idea of what to expect. Some clinicians, however, object to the routine use of these axes for insurance forms and the like on the grounds that such use unnecessarily compromises a patient's right to privacy. Because of such concerns, Axes IV and V are now considered optional for diagnosis and in fact are rarely used in most clinical settings.

The Development of DSM-IV

Discussion is currently underway to develop the next version of the diagnostic classification system (DSM-IV), which is planned for publication in 1993 (Frances, Widiger, & Pincus, 1989). One of the main goals of the revision is to coordinate the DSM diagnostic categorization system with the International Classification of Disease System (which is also in revision and to be designated ICD-10). Another reason for periodic revisions of the DSM is that using diagnostic systems reveals

HIGHLIGHT 1.2

Axis IV Scale for Rating the Severity of Psychosocial Stressors

Code	Term	Adult Examples	Child or Adolescent Examples
1	None	No apparent psychosocial stressor or enduring circumstances	No apparent psychosocial stressor or enduring circumstances
2	Mild	Break-up with boyfriend or girlfriend or child leaving home; family arguments; job dissatisfaction	Break-up with boyfriend or girlfriend; family arguments; overcrowded living quarters
3	Moderate	Marriage or marital separation; loss of job; marital discord; serious financial problems	Suspension from school; birth of sibling; chronic parental discord; disabling illness in parent
4	Severe	Divorce; birth of a child; unemployment; poverty	Divorce of parents; unwanted pregnancy; harsh or rejecting parents; multiple foster home placement
5	Extreme	Death of a spouse; serious illness; victim of rape; ongoing physical or sexual abuse	Sexual or physical abuse; death of a parent; recurrent sexual or physical abuse
6	Catastrophic	Death of a child; suicide of a spouse; hostage or concentration camp experience	Death of both parents; chronic, life-threatening illness
0	Inadequate information or no change in condition		

Adapted from DSM-III-R (APA, 1987, p. ii).

their inadequacies in terms of reliability and validity. Thus there is a need to incorporate refinements in the system that improve the understanding of patient problems and enable the communication of ideas and research findings through an agreed-upon language. One important goal in the revision of DSM-III-R is to incorporate an ongoing, multisite research program to make revisions in the system (Spitzer & Williams, 1988).

The Limitations of DSM Classifications

Not all writers and practitioners subscribe to the DSM classification system. Even the coauthors of this book view the DSM classifications from somewhat different perspectives and with different de-

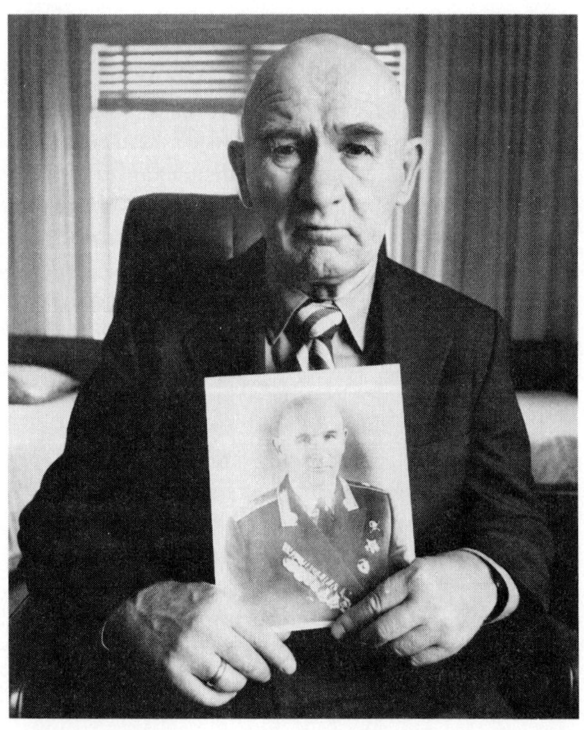

Pyotr Grigorenko is one of a number of Soviet dissidents who have been committed to mental hospitals because of their dissent. Grigorenko was a highly honored Red Army general before his dissent led Soviet doctors to incarcerate him. After finding asylum in America, Grigorenko was evaluated and found to be sane.

HIGHLIGHT 1.3

Axis V Scale for Rating the Global Level of Functioning

Code	Description	Examples
90	Good in all areas	Social, occupational (or school), and psychological functioning is without notable problems; absent or minimal symptoms
80	Slight impairment	Temporary inefficiency in occupational or school work; if present, symptoms are transient and normal for stressors experienced
70	Some difficulty	Acceptable overall functioning, but some problem in social, occupational, or school sphere; retains some meaningful interpersonal relationships; if present, symptoms are mild
60	Moderate difficulty	Social, occupational, or school gunctioning moderately disrupted; *or* symptoms of moderate severity, such as occasional panic attacks
50	Serious difficulty	Serious impairment in social, occupational, or school functioning; *or* serious symptoms, such as suicidal thoughts or severe compulsive rituals
40	Major impairments	Major impairment in several areas, such as work or school, family relations, judgment, thinking, or mood; *or* some impairment of judgment or communication
30	Unable to function	Inability to manage in almost all areas; *or* behavior considerably influenced by delusions or hallucinations; *or* seriously impaired judgment or communication
20	Some danger	Clinical status judged to be of some danger to self or others; *or* some failure to maintain minimal standards of personal hygiene; *or* gross communication impairment
10	Persistent danger	Person judged to be a persistent danger to self or others; *or* inability to maintain minimal standards of hygiene; *or* recent serious suicidal act having clear expectation of death

Adapted from DSM-III-R (APA, 1987, p. 12).

grees of respect for their utility (see the Unresolved Issues section at the end of this chapter for more on this issue). One of the major problems in the DSM classification system is that the categories *describe* rather than *explain.* It is all too easy to believe that something has been explained when, in fact, it has only been named. When we apply the term *schizophrenic* to an individual's behavior we have not said anything about how that pattern came into being—only that the person's behavior resembles that of individuals we have defined as schizophrenic.

A second limitation is that only individual behavior is covered. Disturbed families, delinquent subcultures, and violence-prone societies show maladaptive behavior that does not fit into a scheme made for classifying individuals. Classifying only individual behavior as abnormal implies that when individuals do not fit smoothly into their social milieu, it is the individuals who are at fault and must change. This attitude casts the mental health profession in the role of preserving the status quo, no matter how abnormal the status quo might be. The Soviet Union has made this possibility a terrifying reality by "diagnosing" dissidents as mentally disturbed and forcing "hospitalization" and "treatment" upon them.

As we examine specific disorders later in the text, we will try to overcome this limitation by examining the role that pathogenic families and other groups play in causing and maintaining maladaptive behavior. As you will see, this behavior does not occur in a vacuum but, in part, is a response to the social context in which an individual lives (Hooley, 1985; Weary & Mirels, 1982).

HIGHLIGHT 1.4

Mental Illness as a Myth

Psychiatrist Thomas Szasz (born 1920) has been an outspoken critic of current practices and labels within the field of abnormal psychology (Szasz, 1961, 1970). In his writings, Szasz contends that mental illness is a myth and that traditional treatment can be more harmful than helpful.

According to Szasz, most of the disorders treated by psychiatrists and other mental health professionals are not illnesses. Instead, he claims, they are simply individual traits or behaviors that deviate from what our society considers morally or socially normal. They are caused by problems in living—by unmet personal needs or by stressful relationships, for example.

Szasz believes that traditional psychiatric treatment harms many people by labeling them as ill. Not only does this labeling encourage these people to fulfill society's expectations and thus act in irresponsible ways, but it also implies that they must become patients and accept treatment in order to change. In Szasz's view, this means that they are being encouraged to think and behave in ways considered normal by psychiatrists rather than to attack the social causes of their problems.

More recently, Sarbin and Mancuso (1980) have developed a related attack on the specific concept of schizophrenia, thought by many to be the most serious of all mental disorders. These authors liken the concept of schizophrenia to that of the unicorn, a mythical animal of antiquity. Schizophrenia, they say, is not a proper medical diagnosis but instead is a moral label given to people who do not behave in prescribed ways.

The Problem of Labeling

Some researchers have pointed out another equally important limitation to diagnostic classification: a psychiatric diagnosis is nothing more than a label applied to a defined disorder. The label does not describe a *person,* but rather some behavioral pattern associated with that person's current level of functioning. Yet once a label has been assigned, it may close off further inquiry. It is all too easy—even for professionals—to accept a label as an accurate and complete description of an individual rather than of that person's behavior. It is hard then to look at the person's behavior objectively, without preconceptions about how he or she will act. These expectations can influence even the simplest interactions and treatment choices.

Once an individual is labeled, he or she may accept a redefined identity and play out the expectations of that role. ("I'm a substance abuser, therefore everyone expects me to take drugs.") This tendency can be harmful because of the pejorative and stigmatizing implications of many psychiatric labels—implications that have the power to transform social identities and "mark" people as second-class citizens with severe, often debilitating limitations (Jones et al., 1984; Sarbin & Mancuso, 1970). Obviously, the effects on a person's morale and self-esteem can be devastating. (For a look at how some psychologists have responded to these problems, see *HIGHLIGHT 1.4*).

Interestingly, other researchers have concluded that "labeling," per se, does not necessarily imply that people are going to act negatively toward a former patient simply because he or she has been mentally ill (Cockerham, 1981; Rabkin, 1972). In fact, some writers have stated that former mental patients can avoid negative reactions from people by simply behaving differently. In this view, labeling actually has little impact on people's attitudes toward mental illness (Segal, 1978). In opposition to this view and reaffirming the role of labeling on the social rejection of former mental patients, Link, Cullen, Frank, and Wozniak (1987) found that placing labels of mental illness on a person did influence others to judge that individual as "dangerous" and to seek social distance from the individual. The relative impact of labeling on views toward mental illness is an active debate within the field of abnormal psychology, and one can find considerable research and emotional commitment to both sides of the argument.

Clearly, it is important for professionals to be very cautious in the diagnostic process, in their use of labels, and in ensuring confidentiality with respect to both. A related change has developed over

Gladys Burr (shown here with her lawyer) is a tragic example of the dangers of labeling. Involuntarily committed by her mother (apparently because of some personalilty problems) in 1936 at the age of 29, Ms. Burr was diagnosed as psychotic and was later declared to be mentally retarded. Though a number of IQ tests administered from 1946 to 1961 showed her to be of normal intelligence, and though a number of doctors stated that she was of normal intelligence and should be released, she was confined in a residential center for the mentally retarded or in a state boarding home until 1978. Though a court did give her a financial award in compensation, surely nothing can compensate for 42 years of unnecessary and involuntary commitment.

the past 40 years regarding the person who goes to see a mental health professional. For years the traditional term for such a person has been *patient,* which is closely associated with a medically "sick" person and a passive stance, waiting for a doctor's cure. Today many professionals prefer the term *client* because it implies more responsibility and participation on the part of an individual for bringing about his or her own recovery.

The Extent of Abnormal Behavior

What is the rate of mental disorder in society today? Or, to put it another way, how many people actually have psychological disorders? The frequency or infrequency of particular disorders are important considerations for a number of reasons. For one, researchers in the mental health field need to have a clear understanding of the nature and extent of abnormal behaviors in order to conduct research into their causes. In addition, mental health practitioners need to know whether the problems they are dealing with are relatively common or rare in order to evaluate the appropriateness of treatment measures. Finally, mental health planners need to have a clear picture of the nature and extent of psychological problems being faced by society in order to determine how resources can be most effectively allocated.

Before we can discuss the extent of mental disorders in society we must clarify how psychological problems are counted. **Epidemiology** (specifically, mental health epidemiology) is the study of the distribution of mental disorders in a given population. A key component of an epidemiological survey is determining the magnitude of the problem being studied. There are several ways of doing this. The term **prevalence** refers to the rate of active cases that can be identified at a given point in time. It is to be distinguished from the term **incidence,** which is the occurrence rate of a given disorder in a given population. For example, "point" prevalence refers to the proportion of actual cases in a given population at a particular

Practitioners are concerned with how often various mental health problems occur in the population at large. Epidemiologists can provide answers because they study the distribution of mental disorders in a given population. Statistical information about the prevalence and incidence of disorders is important as a basis for devising appropriate interventions.

point in time—say on May 9, 1991. Incidence refers to the proportion of people in a population who have at some time been diagnosed as having the disorder and includes recovered cases. Incidence rates are normally reported as an individual's lifetime risk of contracting the disorder in question.

A large-scale epidemiological study sponsored by the National Institutes of Mental Health (NIMH) has provided us with perhaps the most reliable and valid information about the prevalence of mental disorders in contemporary society (Regier et al., 1988). The NIMH catchment area epidemiological study surveyed 18,571 individuals from five communities: Baltimore, New Haven, St. Louis, Durham, and Los Angeles. They found that about 15.4 percent of the population suffer from substance abuse problems or mental disorders in any given month. They also concluded that 33 percent of the individuals sampled are likely to have some psychological disorder or substance abuse problem in their lifetimes.

The NIMH study also provided information on specific issues or disorders:

1. There appear to be substantial differences in the lifetime prevalence for various disorders (the probability of a person ever having a certain disorder) in the five sites studied. For example, the prevalence rate for simple phobia in Baltimore was more than twice the rate in St. Louis and three times the rate in New Haven (Robins et al., 1984).

2. One-month prevalence studies show that disorders vary in frequency. The most common specific disorders were phobia (6.2%), dysthymia or depression (3.3%), major depressive episode (2.2%) and alcohol abuse or dependence (2.8%).

3. Rates of disorder differ between men and women. Men have a greater preponderance of substance abuse disorder (6.3% as opposed to 1.6% in women) and personality disorder (.8% as opposed to .02% in women); women appear to develop relatively more major mood disorder (6.6% as opposed to 3.5% in men), anxiety disorder (9.7% as opposed to 3.6% in men), and somatization disorder (.1% as opposed to an insignificant percentage in men).

Another recent epidemiological study provided important information about the development of mental disorders in "healthy" individuals. Vaillant and Schnurr (1988) conducted a follow-up study of 188 healthy men who had been studied for 50 years. They found that the incidence rates for mental disorders in this group were similar to the rates found in other studies—20 to 25 percent of the men had developed psychological disorders at some point. Fourteen percent were alcoholic and 6 percent had developed depressive disorders.

The decline in psychiatric populations in public mental health facilities has been linked to the current problems of homelessness in the United States.

Most individuals with psychological problems do not get hospitalized in a large state or county psychiatric institution. Recent information from the U.S. Department of Health and Human Services (1990) indicates that admission to mental hospitals has decreased substantially over the past 35 years. Inpatient hospitalization constituted 77 percent of all mental health episodes in 1955 but decreased to only 27 percent in 1986. Long-term psychiatric care in inpatient facilities has been steadily declining over the past decades, as noted in *HIGHLIGHT 1.5*. This trend, often referred to as *deinstitutionalization,* will be discussed more extensively in Chapter 19. Individuals experiencing psychological problems are more likely to receive treatment in outpatient facilities. However, evidence suggests that only about 25 percent of individuals with psychological problems actually receive any treatment at all (Robins et al., 1984).

RESEARCH IN ABNORMAL PSYCHOLOGY

The facts and ideas presented in this book are products of the powerful methods of research used to study maladaptive human behavior. You are

HIGHLIGHT 1.5

Changing Patterns of Mental Health Admissions

In 1986 one-third fewer patients were in America's large, isolated state and county mental hospitals than at the end of 1969. The trend toward fewer patients began shortly after the peak year for admissions, 1955. Fifty percent fewer patients are in state mental health facilities today than in 1955 (Lee & Goodwin, 1987). This dramatic decline in occupied state and county mental hospital beds is due to several factors, including (a) the introduction of a host of potent drugs that suppress severe mental symptoms; (b) the recognition of the debilitating and antitherapeutic effects of long-term hospitalization and the attendant deinstitutionalization movement; (c) the introduction of community health centers and related community facilities to care for individuals on an outpatient basis; and (d) the increased availability of alternate care facilities, such as nursing homes for the aged.

The decline in psychiatric populations in state and county facilities has been linked to the current problems of homelessness in the United States (see Chapter 19). This decline in admissions to traditional psychiatric hospitals has also been accompanied by an *increase* in admissions to other psychiatric facilities, such as private psychiatric hospitals, Veterans Administration facilities, and nonfederal general psychiatric services. The actual net effect has been a steady *increase* in overall hospital admissions during the past several decades. Data show that mental health problems continue to require a great deal of our health resources to manage. In 1985 most states spent daily between \$20.00 and \$40.00 per capita for mental health care. The daily per capita cost of mental health services varied, however, from \$10.51 in Iowa to \$90.12 in New York.

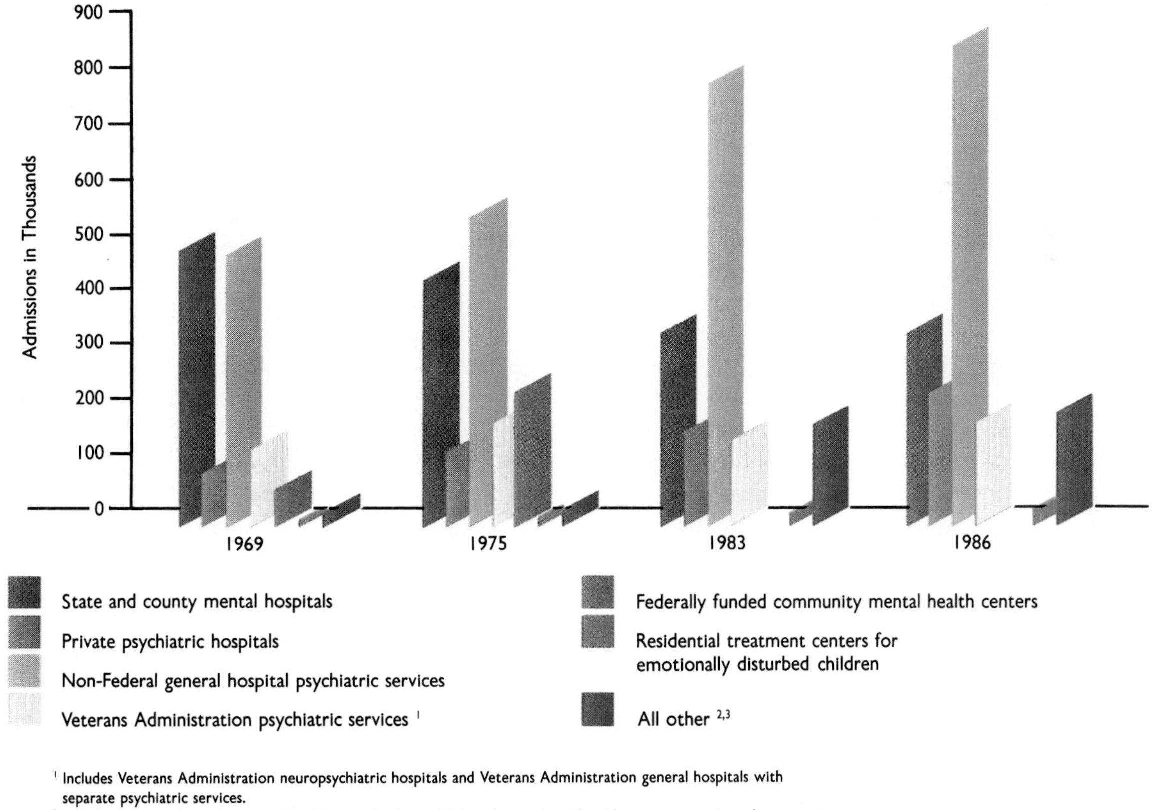

[1] Includes Veterans Administration neuropsychiatric hospitals and Veterans Administration general hospitals with separate psychiatric services.

[2] Includes other multiservice mental health organizations with inpatient and residential treatment services that are not elsewhere classified.

[3] Beginning in 1983 a definitional change sharply increased the number of multiservice mental health organizations while decreasing the number of freestanding psychiatric outpatient clinics.

probably already familiar with scientific methods in general and likely have been exposed to their uses in various areas of psychology. Certain issues and problems arise in applying these methods to understanding the nature, causes, and treatment of abnormal behavior; thus some review is appropriate before we move on. Our review will be organized around (a) direct observation of behavior, (b) sampling and generalization, (c) correlation and causation, (d) experimental strategies, (e) case studies, and (f) retrospective and prospective strategies.

Observation of Behavior

Whatever we are observing—be it the overt actions of an organism, certain of its measurable internal behaviors (e.g., its physiological processes), or verbal reports about human inner processes or events—the focus of psychology is always on observing behavior. Of course, all of us observe our own overt behavior and certain of our inner events, such as thoughts and feelings. But self-observation of one's inner processes has distinct limits as a data base for psychological science, in large part because the observations are one's own, hidden from direct confirmation by anyone else. Science normally demands such confirmation by others. This constraint has been a source of considerable difficulty for the discipline of psychology throughout its history.

The **observational method** is a systematic technique by which observers are trained to watch and record behavior without bias. This technique has helped to ensure the scientific integrity of observational research, but obstacles still remain.

In the field of abnormal psychology, psychologists must inevitably make use of a subject's verbal reports or "observations" of his or her inner experience; we cannot directly observe the subject's thoughts and feelings. In most situations, a subject will be cooperative and truthful. But even assuming a sincere attitude, often a subject will be unable to make crucial observations. The determinants of behavior are many, and they operate at many levels of functioning; not all of them are within the range of a person's conscious awareness.

To make sense of observed behavior, psychologists generate **hypotheses,** more or less plausible ideas to explain something—in this case, behavior. All empirical sciences use hypotheses, although these hypotheses appear to be more closely tied to observable phenomena in the more established physical sciences. For example, the concept of electricity is actually hypothetical. Scientists have only observed the effects of this presumed entity, but these effects are extremely reliable and predictable; hence we believe in the real existence of electricity. Most people have less confidence in a construct such as the ego.

One of the ways psychologists generate hypotheses about behavior and determine therapeutic approaches is through observation, a systematic technique for watching and recording behavior. Observing and making sense of behavior, however, is highly dependent on a practitioner's point of view. What one psychologist "observes" in watching a child, as in the photo here, may not be what another observes, and both may arrive at effective, if differing, treatments.

These considerations are particularly important in the study of abnormal behavior. For the most part, we understand the behavior of the people we meet, at least to the extent necessary to carry on ordinary social interactions. Even when we observe something unexpected in a person's behavior, we can usually empathize enough to have a sense of the factors that have contributed to the behavior. Almost by definition, however, abnormal behavior is unintelligible to the majority of persons observing it. Abnormal behavior does not seem governed by the same principles we generally understand, and our minds are therefore attracted to extraordinary explanations of it—to extraordinary hypotheses. Whether or not these hypotheses can account satisfactorily for abnormal behavior is open to question, but it is clear that we need them in order to begin to understand. Behavior never explains itself, whether it is normal or abnormal.

Several competing hypotheses exist to explain the highly complex behavior patterns we find in abnormal behavior. In fact, these hypotheses tend to cluster together in distinctive approaches or viewpoints. These general viewpoints are described in Chapter 3. For now, we wish merely to emphasize that all forms of psychological inquiry begin with observations of behavior, and that much of the subject matter of abnormal psychology is built on hypotheses that account more or less adequately for observed behavior. These hypotheses are important because they frequently determine the therapeutic approaches used to counter an abnormality. For example, suppose we are confronted with someone who washes his or her hands 60 to 100 times a day, causing serious injury to the skin and underlying tissues. If we conclude that this behavior is a result of subtle neurological damage, we would try to discover the nature of the individual's disease in the hope of administering a cure. If we view the behavior as the symbolic cleansing of sinful thoughts, we would try to unearth and address the sources of the person's excessive scrupulousness. If we regard the hand-washing "symptom" as merely the product of unfortunate conditioning or learning, we would devise a means of counterconditioning to eliminate the offending behavior. These different approaches are based on different conceptualizations of the causes of the abnormal behavior. Without such conceptualizations—if we are limited merely to observing behavior itself—we would be left with no means of grasping difficult-to-understand behavior.

Sampling and Generalization

Research in abnormal psychology is concerned with gaining enhanced understanding and, where possible, control of abnormal behavior. Although we can occasionally get important leads from the intensive study of a single case of a given disorder, such a strategy rarely yields enough information to allow us to reach firm conclusions. The basic difficulty with this strategy is that we cannot know whether our observations pertain to the disorder, to unrelated characteristics of the person with the disorder, to some combination of these factors, or even to characteristics of the observer. It is also possible that the particular abnormality might arise from different internal sources in different people, a circumstance that could be detected only by studying a number of people who exhibit the behavior.

For these reasons, we generally place greater reliance on research studies using groups of individuals who show roughly equivalent abnormalities of behavior. Typically, several people in such studies share one characteristic (the problematic behavior) while varying widely on others. We can then infer that anything else they have in common, such as excessively punitive parents, may be related to the behavioral abnormality—provided, of course, that the characteristic is not widely shared by people who do not have the abnormality. If the abnormality arises from different sources in different people (which might in itself be an important finding), we would probably have considerable difficulty identifying with precision the patterns underlying the abnormality. In fact, difficulties of this sort are impeding our progress in respect to several of the disorders we will consider in later chapters. For example, it seems increasingly likely that the disordered behavior known as schizophrenia has multiple patterns of causation that vary from one affected person to another.

If we wanted to research the problem of compulsive hand-washing, for example, a first step would be to determine criteria for identifying persons affected with the alleged condition. Presumably, these criteria would cover such areas as the frequency of hand-washing and the degree of impairment caused by it. We would then need to find people who fit our criteria. Obviously, we could never hope to study all of the people in the world who meet our criteria; we would use instead a technique called **sampling,** in which we would select as subjects a limited number of hand-washers who appear to be representative of the much larger group of compulsive hand-washers. From our study of this group, we would hope to generalize our findings to the larger group. To ensure validity, it is important that every person in the larger group have an equal chance of being included in the group we intend to study. Usually, we can only approximate this degree of rigor in choosing research samples.

As we have learned from the results of poorly designed public opinion polls, nonrepresentative sampling can produce erroneous conclusions about the larger group we wish to study. For example, if our research group of hand-washers did not adequately represent the socioeconomic statuses of compulsive hand-washers in general, we might attribute some characteristic to hand-washers that is in fact more true of persons in a given socioeconomic group.

Even if our study group were thoroughly representative, there would always be the possibility that our findings about, for example, the family backgrounds of our hand-washers would be similar to findings about other selected groups, or even about persons in general. If such were the case, we would have wasted our own and our subjects' time. Thus researchers use a **control group,** a sample of people who do not exhibit the disorder being studied but who are comparable in all other respects to the **criterion group,** members of which do exhibit the disorder. Typically, the control group is psychologically "normal" according to specified criteria. We can then compare the two groups in certain areas—such as reported parental punishment practices—to determine if they differ. They would in fact almost certainly differ because of chance factors, but we have powerful statistical techniques to determine whether or not such factors are truly significant. If we found, for example, that compulsive hand-washers had significantly more severe parental punishment in their backgrounds, as reported, than the "normals," we might conclude that severe parental punishment in childhood is associated with later compulsive hand-washing. This hypothesis, of course, assumes that the people in our study have reported their backgrounds accurately, a sometimes dubious assumption.

Though a dysfunctional family relationship may be a correlate of some form of abnormal behavior, this is not necessarily a causal factor because there may be many other ways of accounting for a particular mental disorder.

Correlation and Causation

The mere **correlation,** or association, of two or more variables can never by itself be taken as evidence of **causation,** that is, a relationship in which a preceding variable causes other variables. This is an important distinction to bear in mind, especially so in the field of abnormal psychology. Returning to our hypothetical hand-washing study, for instance, we could not legitimately conclude that severe parental punishment is a causal factor in the emergence of compulsive hand-washing among adults. There are simply too many alternative ways to account for such an association, including the possibility that hand-washers are more prone than others to exaggerate the level of punishment to which their parents subjected them.

Many studies in abnormal psychology show that two (or more) things regularly occur together, such as poverty and retarded intellectual development, or depression and reported prior stressors. Such variables may well be related to one another in some kind of causal context, but the relationship could take a variety of forms:

- Variable *a* causes variable *b* (or vice versa).
- Variable *a* and variable *b* are both caused by variable *c*.
- Variables *a* and *b* are both involved in a complex pattern of variables influencing *a* and *b* in similar ways.

Coming from a broken home, for instance, has been established as a significant correlate of many forms of abnormal behavior. Yet we cannot conclude that such families cause abnormality because many other potential causes of abnormality are statistically associated with parental separation or divorce—socioeconomic stress, marital disharmony, alcoholism in one or both parents, a move to a new neighborhood or school, the effort to adjust to a single parent's new love relationships, and so forth. Unfortunately, such complexity is the rule rather than the exception that we find when attempting to understand how abnormal behavior becomes established.

Recently developed statistical techniques (such as path analysis) that take into account how variables "predict" and are related to one another through time are frequently helpful in disentangling correlated factors. These techniques give us much greater confidence in our causal inferences. A relatively simple application of path analysis was made in a study by Mednick et al.(1978) of high-risk children. The study found that an adult outcome of schizophrenia was statistically linked with both obstetrical complications at birth and the presence of subtle autonomic nervous system impairment. Path analysis confirmed that the impact of the birth complications was dependent on the influence of the nervous system damage; in other words, obstetrical complications were involved with schizophrenia only to the extent that they were accompanied by nervous system impairment observed in childhood. This study strongly suggested a causal chain beginning with birth difficulties and leading to neurological dysfunction, which in turn increased the likelihood of schizophrenia.

However great their problems in pinning down causal relations, correlational studies can be a powerful and rich source of inference; they often suggest causal hypotheses and occasionally provide crucial data that confirm or refute these hypotheses. As a measure of their usefulness, we need only reflect on what the science of astronomy would be without correlational studies, since astronomers cannot manipulate the variables they study, such as stars and planets.

Correlational studies have been useful in many areas of abnormal psychology, but especially so in determining epidemiological patterns. Epidemiological research attempts to establish the pattern of occurrence of certain disorders (in our case, mental disorders) in different times, places, and groups of people. Where we find significant variations in the incidence or prevalence of a disorder, we ask why. In some cases, the answer will be obvious or trivial, as in the observation that the diagnosis of mental retardation increases suddenly among six-year-olds (i.e., children facing their first real intellectual challenge, in school). But in other cases, the question leads, if not to the unequivocal identification of causal factors, at least to promising avenues for investigation.

Observations that, for example, a particular disorder is highly associated with a particular causal factor but is uncorrelated with others may help us identify possible causal factors in other disorders; such observations make certain hypotheses more likely and others less so and thus maximize the efficiency with which the search for understanding continues. In the next section, we review methodological approaches that have a higher promise of exactitude than correlational studies as well as the enhanced problems and risks of actively intervening in people's lives.

Experimental Strategies

Scientific research is most rigorous, and its findings most reliable, when it employs the full power of the **experimental method.** In such cases, scientists control all factors, except one, that could have an effect on a variable or outcome of interest; then they actively manipulate that one factor. If the outcome of interest is observed to change as the manipulated factor is changed, the factor can be regarded as a cause of the outcome.

Unfortunately, the experimental method cannot be applied to many problems of abnormal psychology because of practical and ethical restraints. Suppose, for example, we wanted to use the experimental method to determine whether parental punitiveness causes compulsive hand-washing. But for ethical constraints, our ideal approach would be to choose at random two groups of young children for a longitudinal study (a study in which subjects are examined over an extended period of time). In one group, the children's parents would be taught to be highly punitive in their child-rearing practices; the other group of parents would be left to their own devices. We would carefully monitor the two groups of children until they reached an age considered beyond risk for the development of new cases of compulsive hand-washing. At that point, we would assess in a systematic way the prevalence of hand-washing compulsions in the two groups, hypothesizing that the ill-treated children would have a significantly higher rate of the disorder. Such a study would be good—although logistically demanding—science, but it would of course be ethically unacceptable to treat people in this callous and destructive way.

The ethical constraints on using the experimental method to search for causes can sometimes be circumvented or reduced by employing models of abnormal behavior. Experiments of this kind are generally known as **analogue studies**—studies in which a researcher attempts to simulate the conditions under investigation. These experiments establish the causes of maladaptive behavior by (a) inducing the behavior in subhuman species or (b) inducing the behavior in humans, if the behavior is of trivial import, temporary, or reversible (for example, inducing temporary depression by having normal subjects concentrate on negative thoughts). Apart from what many would regard as undiminished ethical problems in much research of this sort, the major scientific problem is of course to establish major commonality between the contrived behavior and the real thing as it occurs "naturally." By and large, such analogue studies have failed to make convincing connections.

A case in point is the hypothesis that learned helplessness is a cause of depression in humans (Seligman, 1975). Laboratory experiments with dogs demonstrated that, when subjected to repeated experiences of painful, unpredictable, inescapable shock, these animals lost their ability to learn a simple escape routine to avoid further shock; they just sat and endured the pain. Seligman argued from this observation that human depression (which he equated with the reaction of the "helpless" dogs) is a reaction to the experience of noncontingency between one's behavior and the outcomes of that behavior—that is, to learned helplessness. There ensued a large number of learned helplessness experiments on human subjects, all attempting to induce mild and reversible depressions, with results that can only be called disappointing. Subjects often did not respond with helplessness to noncontingency situations, many of them actually showing enhanced effort (facilitation) following the frustrating experiences (see the February 1978 issue of *Journal of Abnormal Psychology*, Volume 87).

Reacting to these disappointing results, Seligman and colleagues (Abramson et al., 1978) modified the learned helplessness theory of depression. They suggested that a noncontingency experience should have a depression-inducing effect only on those persons prone to interpret failure-to-cope

Analogue studies in which generalizations are made from laboratory models to the real world may fail to make convincing connections. Results of testing—using rats, mice, dogs, or monkeys, for example, in a laboratory setting—may not hold up when extended to humans.

experiences in a negative way—specifically by attributing them to personal (internal) characteristics that are pervasive (global) and relatively permanent (stable). Of course, it could be (and indeed has been) argued that people having such negative thoughts may already be depressed, experiences of helplessness notwithstanding. In fact, the possibility that depressed feelings precede and cause such negative attitudes, rather than the other way around, continues to be a viable alternative to the modified learned helplessness theory (Carson, 1989; Cochran & Hammen, 1985; Peterson, Villanova, & Raps, 1985).

This ongoing research on learned helplessness and human depression illustrates the hazards involved in generalizing from laboratory models to the real world. As is often the case, the learned helplessness analogue generated much research and thereby clarified certain aspects of an important psychopathological problem. For example, further research showed that mere noncontingency is not a cause of depression in otherwise "normal" persons; that people react differently than dogs; and that helplessness may be an effect rather than a cause of depression. To that extent, it has been a productive venture. At the same time, like many other analogue models in the field, it has proven to be flawed and even misleading.

If the role of the experimental method in establishing the causes of abnormal behavior must necessarily be a limited one, no such restriction applies to its role in the evaluation of treatment approaches. On the contrary, the sophisticated use of experimental techniques in determining the efficacy of different therapies for a given disorder remains an indispensable tool.

It is a relatively simple and straightforward matter to set up a study in which a treatment is given to a designated group of patients and withheld from a similar group of patients. Should the former group show significantly more improvement than the latter, we can have confidence in the treatment's effectiveness. Of course, special techniques must often be employed in such treatment research to ensure that the two groups are in fact comparable in every respect. Once a treatment has proved effective, it can subsequently be employed for members of the original control group, leading to improved functioning for everyone. When this *waiting list control group* strategy is deemed inadvisable, as it sometimes is for ethical and other reasons (Imber et al., 1986), a research design may call for a comparison of two or more treatments in different equivalent groups. Such comparative outcome research has much to recommend it (VandenBos, 1986) and is being utilized increasingly.

Fortunately, we have made great progress in the statistical control of variables that do not yield readily to the classic form of experimental control. Statistical controls, in effect, allow us to adjust for otherwise uncontrolled variables. For example, the incidence of certain mental disorders appears to vary with socioeconomic status. Using statistical controls, we can "correct" our results for any differences in socioeconomic status existing between our experimental and control groups. The same effect could be achieved by experimental control if we could ensure that socioeconomic statuses in our control group existed in exactly the same proportions as those in the pathological group we wish to study, but such a proportional distribution might be difficult to achieve. An additional problem could create difficulty. If we insist that socioeconomic statuses in our control group exactly mirror those in the experimental group rather than those in the general population, then our control group may no longer be representative of the general population.

Clinical Case Studies

Despite the growing use of experimental methods, most instances of a given disorder are still studied individually, using the traditional clinical case study method. A **case study** is an in-depth examination of an individual or family that draws from a number of data sources, including interviews and psychological testing. The clinical investigator, who is usually also a patient's therapist, intensively observes an individual's behavior and marshals background facts that may be pertinent when attempting to formulate the case. A case study includes a set of hypotheses about what is causing the problem and a guide to treatment planning. These hypotheses and therapies may be revised as necessary based on a patient's response to treatment interventions. This strategy is sometimes called an *N=1 experiment,* especially when the precise relationships between treatment interventions and patient responses are systematically monitored. While much can be learned when skilled clinicians use the case study method, the information thus acquired can also be seriously flawed, especially if one seeks to apply it to other cases involving an apparently similar abnormality. When there is only one observer, and when the observations are made in a relatively uncontrolled context, there is a distinct possibility that erroneous conclusions will be drawn.

Retrospective Versus Prospective Strategies

In one of the most important developments in recent years, the more or less standard **retrospective research** (research that looks backward from the present) has been supplemented by **prospective research** that focuses, before the fact, on individuals who have a higher-than-average likelihood of becoming psychologically disordered. As we saw in our example of compulsive hand-washers, there are certain difficulties in attempting to reconstruct the pasts of people already experiencing a disorder; it is hard to disentangle the effects of the present disorder from the effects of past events and to trace a clear cause-and-effect relationship. Nevertheless, this has been the standard method of causal investigation: we observe the behavioral abnormality and then comb the backgrounds of afflicted individuals for commonalities that might have caused it. Apart from the fact that a disordered person may not be the most accurate or objective source of information, such a strategy invites investigators to discover what they expect to discover about the background factors theoretically linked to a disorder. One way around these difficulties is to utilize documents and records dated before the emergence of the disorder. While this strategy has on occasion been productively employed, it obviously depends on the accidental availability of the precise information needed.

We can have much more confidence in our causal hypotheses when they look ahead instead of backward and when they correctly predict the individuals in a group who will develop a particular form of disordered behavior—or, alternatively, which of two groups will prove to have been at risk. It is logistically difficult, of course, to follow various unselected groups from childhood into adulthood in the numbers required to produce a suitable "yield" of various adult disorders. Hence, in a typical instance, children sharing a risk factor known to be associated with relatively high rates of subsequent breakdown are studied over the course of years. Those who do break down are compared with those who do not in the hope that crucial differentiating factors will be discovered. The method is not without certain difficulties, however, including uncertainties about what constitutes risk and how the selected risk factor may interact with other factors. In addition, prospective studies have so far failed to produce striking and unequivocal results. Despite these reservations, the very invention of the method and its widespread deployment in many long-term, ongoing research projects is probably indicative of a genuine maturing of the field (Garmezy, 1978c). Serious researchers in abnormal behavior are aware of the magnitude of the challenges facing them, and as a group they are no longer confident that easy answers are lying about ready to be discovered by an enterprising but impatient investigator. Such a high level of confidence was never justified in the first place, in that it seriously underestimated the complex nature of human behavior.

THE ORIENTATION OF THIS BOOK

Psychology is an unusual science in that the human mind is both the agent and the object of study. The difficulty is one of reflexivity: in our study we are using the very instrument—the mind—that we hope to understand. Keeping a proper perspective in such a situation is and will continue to be problematic. Can we fashion an approach to abnormal behavior that is scientific and humanistic in the best senses of both of these terms? This book is an attempt in that direction, but the course is to a large extent uncertain and uncharted.

In this text we will study abnormal behavior and its place in contemporary society. Although we will deal with all the major categories of mental disorders, we will focus on those patterns that seem most relevant to a broad, basic understanding of maladaptive behavior. While we will not hesitate to include the unusual or bizarre, our emphasis will be on the unity of human behavior, ranging from normal to abnormal.

Throughout this text we assume that a sound and comprehensive study of abnormal behavior should be based on the following concepts:

1. *A scientific approach to abnormal behavior.* Any comprehensive view of human behavior must draw upon concepts and research findings from a variety of scientific fields. Of particular relevance are genetics, biochemistry, neurophysiology, sociology, anthropology, and of course psychology. Common scientific concepts, such as causal processes, control groups, dependent variables, placebos, and theories, will figure in our discussion. Special emphasis will be placed on the application of learning principles to the understanding and treatment of mental disorders.

In this general context, you are encouraged to take a critical and evaluative attitude toward the research findings presented in this text and in other sources. When properly conducted, scientific research provides us with information that has a high probability of being accurate, but many research findings are subject to bias and open to serious questions. We must appreciate as well the special problems involved when we attempt to turn the light of scientific inquiry on ourselves. While science may not have all the answers, it is also true that we have not yet pushed science to its limits. The problems we face in moving toward the twenty-first century are too important to afford ourselves the luxury of ignorance and uncritical analysis.

2. *An awareness of our common human concerns.* Science cannot touch on many of the experiences and problems common to human existence. Insights into hope, faith, courage, love, grief, despair, death, and the quest for values and meaning are not obtainable in a laboratory. Rather, we must turn to literature, drama, autobiographical accounts, and even art, history, and religion to seek a greater understanding of these aspects of human psychological functioning. Although these sources of insight strike a common chord in all of us, it is important to distinguish the information gained through them from the information obtained through scientific observation.

3. *Respect for the dignity, integrity, and growth potential of the individual.* A basic orientation of this book is described well in the opening statement of the *Ethical Principles of Psychologists,* formulated by the American Psychological Association: "Psychologists respect the dignity and worth of the individual and strive for the preservation and protection of fundamental human rights" (1990, p. 390). Implicit in this statement is a view of individuals not merely as products of their past conditioning and present situation, but as potentially active agents as well—people who can develop and use their capacities for building the kind of life they choose and a better world for humankind.

In attempting to provide a perspective on abnormal behavior, we will focus not only on how maladaptive patterns are perceived by clinical psychologists and other mental health personnel, but also on how such disorders feel to and are perceived by the individuals experiencing them. In dealing with the major patterns of abnormal behavior, we will focus on four significant aspects of each: the *clinical picture, causal factors, treatments,* and *outcomes.* In each case, we will examine the evidence for *biological, psychosocial* (psychological and interpersonal), and *sociocultural* factors.

Since this is a psychology book, much of our focus will be on the psychosocial factors involved in abnormal behavior. This focus is apt as well because it is the psychosocial area that presents especially challenging adaptational problems for the future. We are less well equipped for rapid advance in this area than in the biomedical arena, which continues to develop at a rate more equal to that of the culture generally. Yet even in respect to our physical health, there are increasing signs that ultimate solutions will depend on a far greater sophistication about ourselves as psychosocial as opposed to biological entities. The advances in biomedicine to which we have become accustomed are not likely to bail us out—at least not in the foreseeable future. For example, it is not presently conceivable that a prescription medication or a brain operation might be fashioned that will convert a person lacking in both cognitive and social skills into one capable of effortlessly negotiating the complexities of modern life.

Most of this book will be devoted to a presentation of well-established patterns of abnormal behavior and to special problem behaviors of our time that are more controversial but directly relevant. Initially, however, we will trace the development of contemporary views of abnormal behavior from early beliefs and practices, outline several attempts to explain what makes human beings "tick," and review the general causes of abnormal behavior in modern life.

Later, after a series of chapters on various problem behaviors, we will devote four chapters to modern methods of assessment and treatment. These chapters will include a discussion of the potential of modern psychology and allied sciences for preventing mental disorders and for helping humankind achieve a more sane and harmonious world.

At the close of his journeys, Tennyson's Ulysses says, "I am part of all that I have met." It is the authors' hope that, at the end of your journey through this book, you will have a better understanding of human experience and behavior—and that you will consider what you have learned to be a meaningful part of your own life experience.

UNRESOLVED ISSUES on Classification

Of the several sources of potential confusion facing a student of abnormal psychology, none is likely to be more perplexing or fundamental than the manner in which abnormal behavior is segmented into various types. It will be of some comfort, we hope, to know that even the "experts" differ in the value they place on the current diagnostic classification scheme—the categories of DSM-III-R and what promise to be the quite similar ones of DSM-IV (Carson, in press-b; Widiger et al., in press).

Unfortunately, both reliability and validity have proven extraordinarily difficult to achieve in the classifications used in abnormal psychology. This is due in no small part to the enormous complexity of human behavior. But it is also due, according to some observers, to our having chosen an inadequate model for describing behavioral abnormalities. This model is essentially a medical or disease metaphor for conceptualizing abnormal behavior. By this we mean that abnormal behavior has been viewed as the outward manifestation of a corresponding type of illness or disease. But is it? While we are not troubled by the notion of a diseased brain, what possible meaning, on close examination, can we assign to the concept of a diseased mind? They are not, after all, the same thing.

Despite the fact that every genuine human disease shows a certain level of individual variation, it also has at its core a fundamental and invariant pathophysiology that can be described with increasing precision with advances in biomedical knowledge. Thus we know that the pain associated with the coronary heart disease known as angina is produced by an insufficient oxygen supply to the heart muscle, due to blocked coronary arteries. Armed with this knowledge, we can discriminate between two or more diseases even when their surface characteristics may share certain similarities—for example, between angina and indigestion.

To use another example, a fever of 101 degrees tells us that something is wrong with a physical organism, perhaps a flu infection; a fever of 104 degrees tells us that something is *very* wrong, such as pneumonia. A physician is usually able, by using various diagnostic signs and perhaps laboratory findings, to pinpoint with great accuracy the nature of the underlying pathophysiology.

Personal despondency at the level of a diagnosable mental depression also tells us that something is wrong, and in severe cases that something is *very* wrong. But what? Generally, we would be right in concluding that something has gone awry in the person's self-perceived ability to cope with some life dilemma. Consistent with this observation is the fact that serious depressive feelings often complicate many other forms of disorder, both mental and physical. Beyond that, however, the situation is notably clouded; despite occasional claims to the contrary, we have no laboratory test to give us a more reliable answer, nor is it obvious that a more precise answer is possible. From this perspective, one depression is pretty much like any other, except for minor variations in expression and, like fever, in severity. The DSM-III-R, however, specifies several separate categories of depression, largely based on surface characteristics—despite the fact that there is little convincing evidence of fundamental differences among them, apart from severity. (The severity dimension, incidentally, also has no obvious breaks, or discontinuities.) We know of no one who seriously suggests that it would be useful to designate fever to be itself a separate disease, or to try to discriminate among qualitatively different kinds of fever, yet this is what the DSM does with depression.

As the example of depression illustrates, the DSM attempts to treat mental disorder as consisting of a variety of discrete (discontinuous) categories. Implicit in this approach is the idea that each of the

DSM-III-R treats depression as consisting of a variety of discrete types, even though the evidence to support this view still eludes us. The question of whether efforts to differentiate disorders in this way are meaningful is an unresolved issue in the field of abnormal psychology.

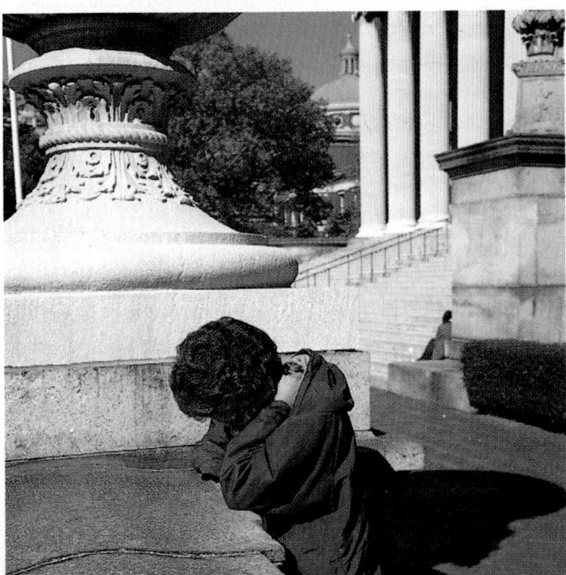

categories has a unique underlying core and a definable boundary separating it from other categories, as in the case of true diseases (Millon, in press). The fact that we cannot identify the features of the core except by uncertain inference from surface characteristics is attributed to a temporary lack of knowledge, a lack that supposedly will be overcome by future research. Meanwhile, the exact boundary of each category will remain uncertain and will have to be approximated by somewhat arbitrary rules to achieve a satisfactory separation from other categories.

There is considerable disagreement and doubt about the possibility of our ever finding such a precisely definable and constant array of causal factors at the core of each mental disorder included in the DSM classification. The only exceptions may be those relatively few disorders that are in fact related to brain diseases, the so-called organic mental disorders. Thus, lacking a constant core for each purported disorder, it becomes difficult to know if our efforts to differentiate one sort of disorder from another are in fact correct or even meaningful.

As noted by Widiger and Frances (1985a), there appear to be three basic approaches currently possible to classify abnormal behavior: the categorical, the dimensional, and the prototypal. A **categorical approach,** as we have seen, assumes that (a) all human behavior can be sharply divided into the categories *normal* and *abnormal,* and (b) there exist discrete, non-overlapping classes or types of abnormal behavior, often referred to as "mental" illnesses or diseases. The categorical approach bears a close affinity to the identification of diagnosable physical illnesses such as pneumonia, coronary thrombosis, diabetes, and so on. As already suggested, some professionals believe that this approach is inappropriate for most types of mental disorder, which do not seem to be discrete. It is, however, the one officially used.

The dimensional and prototypal approaches differ fundamentally in the assumptions they make, particularly in respect to the requirement of discrete classes of behavior. In a **dimensional approach,** it is assumed that a person's typical behavior is the product of differing strengths or intensities of behavior along several definable dimensions, such as mood, emotional stability, aggressiveness, gender identity, anxiousness, interpersonal trust, clarity of thinking and communication, social introversion, and so on. The important dimensions, once established, would be the same for everyone. In this conception, people differ from one another in their configuration or profile of these dimensional traits (each ranging from very low to very high), not in terms of surface indications of some presumed "illness." Normal could be discriminated from abnormal, then, by precise statistical criteria applied to dimensional intensities. Returning to our example of depression, a person's level of depression would probably need to be included as one of the basic trait measures in any serious attempt to use a dimensional strategy for organizing abnormal behavior and for "diagnosing" individual disorders.

DSM-III-R Axes IV and V are examples of dimensional scales. These axes, however, are not directed to the definition of types of disorders, but rather to certain qualifying features of disorders as diagnosed.

Of course, in taking a dimensional approach it would be possible—perhaps even likely—to discover that such profiles tend to cluster together in types, and even that some of these types are correlated, though imperfectly, with recognizable sorts of gross behavioral malfunctions, such as anxiety disorders or depression. It is highly unlikely, however, that any individual's profile would exactly fit a narrowly defined type, or that the types identified will not have some overlapping features. This brings us to the matter of a prototypal approach.

A *prototype* (as the term is used here) is a conceptual entity depicting an idealized combination of characteristics, ones that more or less regularly occur together in a less perfect or standard way at the level of empirical reality. Prototypes are actually an aspect of our everyday thinking and experience; we can all generate in our mind's eye a prototypal apple, while recognizing that we have never seen nor ever will see two identical apples. Thus no item in a prototypally defined group may actually have all of the characteristics of the defining prototype, although it will have many of the more central of them. It is also possible that a certain item may be an exemplar, in part at least, of more than one prototype within a given domain. A dog whose parents are, let us say, a purebred collie and a purebred golden retriever will show both prototypal organizations in its appearance. Unlike the often forced categorical separations of the DSM-III-R, prototypes are not mutually exclusive. A given prototype may blend into another with which it shares many characteristics—perhaps especially its more peripheral ones, such as redness in apples.

Some psychologists believe that by adopting a **prototypal approach** we could wed some of the advantages of the categorical and the dimensional approaches while avoiding the disadvantages of each (the dimensional approach, for example, is cumbersome and inconvenient for routine clinical use). Use of such a "hybrid" (Millon, in press) approach implies, however, that we should expect to find few if any pure exemplars of diagnostic groupings, as well as much blurring of the boundaries between them. This, of course, would make communication for researchers and clinicians more difficult. For advocates of a prototypal approach, however, this drawback is necessary to attain more validity and a classification system that better represents what mental disorder really involves.

There is reason to believe in fact that the more recent versions of the DSM, including the projected DSM-IV, *have* moved closer to a prototypal model without explicitly acknowledging this to be the case (Carson, in press). In the DSM-III-R, for example, multiple diagnoses within Axes I and II are not only permitted, but encouraged.

Though many psychologists have reservations about the prevailing classificatory and diagnostic procedures, most do not recommend that these procedures be summarily abandoned or ignored. While far from ideal, they constitute the standard language of the field for both formal (especially research-based) and informal communication. Familiarity with the system in use is thus vital for the serious student. We hope, however, that this discussion has given you a more sophisticated perspective on the classificatory issues facing the field.

SUMMARY

In our contemporary culture, people constantly face a bewildering assortment of challenges and pressures, many of which may stymie their efforts to live happy, fulfilling, and purposeful lives. Psychologists are ethically committed to helping people succeed in these efforts, but psychologists too must face certain obstacles, in particular those beliefs and preconceptions that impede progress in their understanding of mental disorder, its prevention, and its proper treatment.

Students beginning serious study of abnormal psychology are likely to hold preconceptions about the field that are widely shared by others. In part, this is due to certain popular images of mental disorders that have persisted over time, but it is also due to the great attention that the media has focused on the subject in recent years and to the willingness of mental health professionals to supply offhand accounts of behavior disorders and their treatment. Much of this exposure has accurately depicted limited aspects of the field, but some of it has distorted other aspects, causing widespread misconceptions about mental disorders and the people who suffer from them.

The most certain way to avoid misconception and error is to adopt a scientific attitude and approach to the study of abnormal behavior. This involves, among other things, the habit of suspending judgment until pertinent facts are known, the employment of objective and reliable methods of observation, and the development of a valid system for classifying the phenomena being studied. Progress has been made in all these areas, but abnormal psychology continues to be a complex and challenging field. Much work remains to be done, even in so basic an area as classification. We still lack even a universally accepted definition of abnormality, although we, the authors, argue for one that emphasizes outcomes of behavior in terms of the good that is accomplished for an individual or a group.

A scientific approach to abnormal behavior also involves a focus on research and research methods, including an appreciation of the distinction between what is observable and what is hypothetical, or inferred. Much of the content of abnormal psychology falls into the latter category. Research on abnormal conditions, if it is to produce valid results, must be done on people who are truly representative of the pathological groups to which they purportedly belong—a requirement that is often difficult to satisfy. We must also remain alert to the fact that mere correlation does not establish a causal relationship between the variables in question. Researchers use experimental methods and prospective research designs to resolve questions of causality, but these approaches are not always appropriate and may not always be effective. The individual case study method, despite its weaknesses, remains a frequently used investigative technique.

Science, of course, does not have all the answers. Any approach to the field must also recognize the significance of more simply human concerns, such as the feelings of despair or of hope that are such crucial elements in the total picture of normal and abnormal functioning.

Key Terms

abnormal behavior (p. 8)
abnormal psychology (p. 8)
psychopathology (p. 8)
clinical psychology (p. 8)
psychiatry (p. 8)
social work (p. 8)
clinical picture (p. 9)
reliability (p. 9)
validity (p. 9)
DSM-III-R (p. 10)
functional psychoses (p. 11)
acute (p. 11)
chronic (p. 11)
mild (p. 11)
moderate (p. 11)
severe (p. 11)
episodic (p. 11)
epidemiology (p. 15)
prevalence (p. 15)
incidence (p. 15)
observational method (p. 18)
hypotheses (p. 18)
sampling (p. 19)
control group (p. 19)
criterion group (p. 19)
correlation (p. 20)
causation (p. 20)
experimental method (p. 21)
analogue studies (p. 21)
case study (p. 22)
retrospective research (p. 23)
prospective research (p. 23)
categorical approach (p. 26)
dimensional approach (p. 26)
prototypal approach (p. 26)

Chapter 2
Historical Views of Abnormal Behavior

Baya, *Village au Palmier* (1950?). Baya (b. 1931) was born to a family in the Kabyle tribal group near the north African city of Algiers. Orphaned at the age of 5, she was taken to live in the city proper, where she began to paint and sculpt for her own amusement. In 1950 she married into a traditional Algerian family and immediately ceased her creative efforts. In 1963 a retrospective of her work at the national museum in Algiers induced Baya to begin painting again, but the pieces done since that time have been clearly influenced by popular Algerian art and so cannot be properly considered "Art Brut."

The history of our efforts to understand abnormal behavior is a fascinating one. Certainly, many of our misconceptions about mental disorders have their roots in the past, but it is equally true that many modern scientific concepts and treatments have their counterparts in approaches tried long ago. For example, free association—a technique used in twentieth-century psychoanalytic therapy to allow repressed conflicts and emotions to enter conscious awareness—is described by the Greek playwright Aristophanes in his play *The Clouds* (423 B.C.). Interestingly enough, the scene in which Socrates tries to calm and bring self-knowledge to Strepsiades is complete with a couch. Nineteenth-century psychiatrists attempted to use electricity to cure mental disorders almost a century before electroconvulsive therapy became an accepted form of biologically based treatment. (See Chapter 17 for more on early electrical stimulation instruments.)

In this chapter, we will trace the evolution of popular views and treatments of psychopathology from ancient times to the twentieth century. In a broad sense, we will see an evolution from beliefs we view today as superstition to those based on scientific awareness—from a focus on supernatural causes to a knowledge of natural causes. The course of this evolution has not been a steady movement forward; on the contrary, it has often been marked by brief periods of great advancement or unique individual contributions followed by long years of inactivity or unproductive backward surges. (A summary of many of the people we will discuss and their contributions appears later in this chapter.)

As we will see, current views of abnormal behavior have been shaped by the prevailing attitudes of past times and the advances of science. Each has contributed to the growth—and often the stagnation—of the other. For example, during certain periods in ancient Greece, the body was considered sacred. Researchers were thus prevented from performing human autopsies, which did little to advance understanding of human anatomy or biological processes. Much later, during the nineteenth and early twentieth centuries, the belief that a biological (medical) solution was needed to cure mental disorders thwarted investigation into psychological causes. Even today, with the renewed emphasis upon biological causes and treatments, the focus on psychological causation and treatment is sometimes undervalued.

The advances in understanding and treatment of abnormal behavior become all the more remarkable when viewed against a persistent resurfacing of ignorance, superstition, and fear. And if we think that we have today arrived at a knowledgeable and humane approach to treating the mentally ill, we should think again. We are still bound by many culturally conditioned constraints; for many, attitudes toward people who are different are still formed, at least in part, by superstition and fear.

ABNORMAL BEHAVIOR IN ANCIENT TIMES

Although human life presumably appeared on earth some 3 million or more years ago, written records extend back only a few thousand years. Thus our knowledge of our early ancestors is limited.

The earliest known treatment of abnormal behavior was that practiced by Stone Age cave dwellers some half-million years ago. For certain forms of mental disorders, probably those in which an individual complained of severe headaches and experienced convulsive attacks, a shaman (medicine man) appears to have treated the disorder by means of an operation that later came to be called **trephining.** This operation was performed with stone instruments and consisted of chipping away a circular area of the skull until it was cut through. The opening, called a trephine, presumably allowed the evil spirit that was causing the trouble to escape. In some cases, trephined skulls of primitive people show signs of healing, indicating that the patient survived the operation and lived for many years afterward (Selling, 1943).

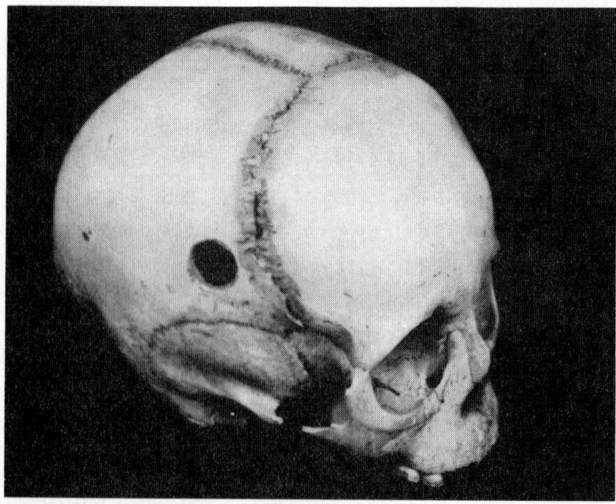

Stone Age cave dwellers used a technique called trephination to treat mental disorders. With a stone instrument, a medicine man would produce a hole in the skull of a patient, allowing the "evil spirits" causing the disturbance to be driven out.

Two Egyptian papyri dating from the sixteenth century B.C. have provided some of the earliest written evidence of the treatment of diseases and behavior disorders. The Edwin Smith papyrus (named after its nineteenth-century discoverer) contains detailed descriptions of the treatment of wounds and other surgical operations. In it, the brain is described—possibly for the first time in history—and the writing clearly shows that the brain was recognized as the site of mental functions. We may think this remarkable for the sixteenth century B.C.; it becomes even more remarkable once we realize that this papyrus is believed to be a copy of an earlier work from about 3000 B.C. The Ebers papyrus provides another perspective on treatment. It covers internal medicine and the circulatory system but relies more on incantations and magic for explaining and curing diseases that had unknown causes. Although surgical techniques may have been used, they were probably coupled with prayers and the like that reflected the prevailing view of the origin of behavior disorders, to which we now turn.

Demonology, Gods, and Magic

References to abnormal behavior in the early writings of the Chinese, Egyptians, Hebrews, and Greeks show that they generally attributed such behavior to a demon or god who had taken possession of an individual. This belief is not surprising if we remember that "good" and "bad" spirits were widely used to explain lightning, thunder, earthquakes, storms, fires, sickness, and many other events that otherwise seemed incomprehensible. It was a simple and logical step to extend this theory to peculiar and incomprehensible behavior as well.

The decision as to whether the "possession" involved good spirits or evil spirits usually depended on an individual's symptoms. If a person's speech or behavior appeared to have a religious or mystical significance, it was usually thought that he or she was possessed by a good spirit or god. Such individuals were often treated with considerable awe and respect, for it was thought that they had supernatural powers.

Most possessions, however, were considered to be the work of an angry god or an evil spirit, particularly when an individual became excited or overactive and engaged in behavior contrary to religious teachings. Among the ancient Hebrews, for example, such possessions were thought to

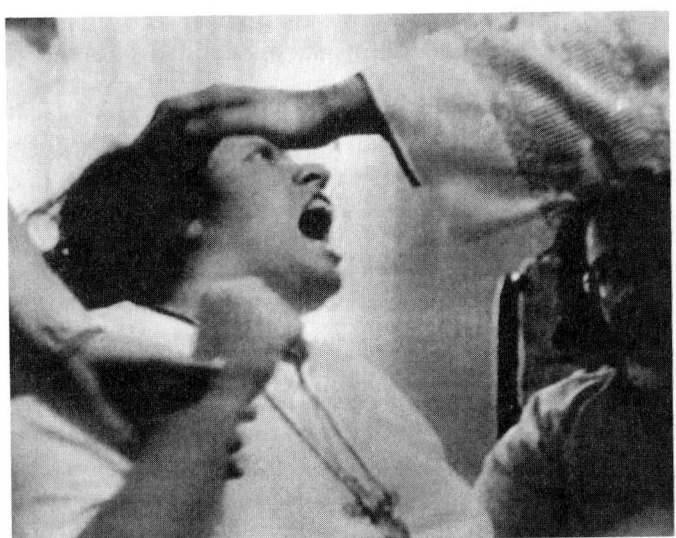

Exorcism as a treatment for mental illness still has appeal today, not only in fictionalized accounts, but even in practice. Amid much controversy, an exorcism performed on a 16-year-old emotionally disturbed girl, known as Gina, was recently shown on the television program "20/20." Gina can be seen here, being restrained, and having a cross pressed to her cheek during the exorcism. The state of her mental health after the exorcism is not known. This televised ritual underscored the deep-seated and powerful belief in demonology, even in contemporary society.

represent the wrath and punishment of God. Moses is quoted in the Bible as saying, "The Lord shall smite thee with madness." Apparently this punishment was thought to involve the withdrawal of God's protection and the abandonment of the individual to the forces of evil. In such cases, every effort was made to rid the person of the evil spirit. Jesus reportedly cured a man with an "unclean spirit" by transferring the devils that plagued him to a herd of swine who, in turn, became possessed and "ran violently down a steep place into the sea" (Mark 5:1–13).

The primary type of treatment for demonic possession was **exorcism,** which included various techniques for casting an evil spirit out of an afflicted person. These techniques varied considerably but typically included magic, prayer, incantation, noisemaking, and the use of various horrible-tasting concoctions, such as purgatives made from sheep's dung and wine. More severe measures, such as starving or flogging, were sometimes used in extreme cases to make the body of a possessed person such an unpleasant place that an evil spirit would be driven out. We will look more closely at exorcism as the treatment of choice in the Middle Ages later in this chapter. The continuing popularity of movies and books on possession and exorcism suggests that these primitive ideas still have appeal today.

The task of exorcising was originally in the hands of shamans, but was eventually taken over in Egypt and Greece by priests, who apparently served as holy people, physicians, psychologists, and magicians. Many of their cures remained based in magical rites. Although these priests typically believed in demonology and used established exorcistic practices, many of them began to treat people with mental disturbances in a more humane way. For example, in the temples of the god Asclepius in ancient Greece, the priests had patients sleep in the temple. Supposedly, the dreams they had there would reveal what they needed to do to get better. The priests supplemented prayer and incantation with kindness, suggestion, and recreational measures, such as plays, riding, walking, and harmonious music.

Early Philosophical and Medical Concepts

The Greek temples of healing ushered in the Golden Age of Greece under the Athenian leader Pericles (461–429 B.C.). During this time, considerable progress was made in the understanding and treatment of mental disorders. Interestingly, this progress was made in spite of the fact that Greeks of this time considered the human body sacred and thus little could be learned of human anatomy or physiology. During this period the Greek physician Hippocrates (460–377 B.C.), often referred to as the father of modern medicine, received his training and made substantial contributions to the field.

Hippocrates Hippocrates denied that deities and demons intervened in the development of illnesses and insisted that mental disorders had natural causes and required treatments like other diseases. His position was unequivocal: "'For my own part, I do not believe that the human body is ever befouled by a God'" (in Lewis, 1941, p. 37). Hippocrates believed that the brain was the central organ of intellectual activity and that mental disor-

Hippocrates' (460–377 B.C.) belief that mental disease was the result of natural causes and brain pathology was revolutionary for its time.

ders were due to brain pathology. He also emphasized the importance of heredity and predisposition and pointed out that injuries to the head could cause sensory and motor disorders.

Hippocrates classified all mental disorders into three general categories—mania, melancholia, and phrentis (brain fever)—and gave detailed clinical descriptions of the specific disorders included in each category. He relied heavily on clinical observation, and his descriptions, which were based on daily clinical records of his patients, were surprisingly thorough. Hippocrates considered dreams to be important in understanding a patient's personality. On this point, he not only elaborated on the thinking set forth by the priests in the temples of Asclepius, but also was a harbinger of a basic concept of modern psychodynamic psychotherapy.

The treatments advocated by Hippocrates were far in advance of the exorcistic practices then prevalent. For the treatment of melancholia, for example, he prescribed a regular and tranquil life, sobriety and abstinence from all excesses, a vegetable diet, celibacy, exercise short of fatigue, and bleeding if indicated. He also believed in the importance of the environment and often removed his patients from their families.

Hippocrates' emphasis on the natural causes of diseases, clinical observation, and brain pathology as the root of mental disorders was truly revolutionary. Like his contemporaries, however, Hippocrates had little knowledge of physiology and could still be far from the truth. He wrongly believed that hysteria (the appearance of physical illness in the absence of organic pathology) was restricted to women and was caused by the uterus wandering to various parts of the body, pining for children. For this "disease," Hippocrates recommended marriage as the best remedy. He also wrongly believed in the existence of four bodily fluids or *humors*—blood, black bile, yellow bile, and phlegm. In his work *On Sacred Disease,* he stated that when the humors were adversely mixed or otherwise disturbed, physical or mental disease resulted: "'Depravement of the brain arises from phlegm and bile; those made from phlegm are quiet, depressed and oblivious; those from bile excited, noisy and mischievous'" (in Lewis, 1941, p. 37). Although the concept of humors went far beyond demonology, it was too crude physiologically to be of much therapeutic value. Yet in its emphasis on the importance of bodily balances to mental health, it may be seen as a precursor of today's focus on the need for biochemical balances to maintain normal brain functioning and good health.

Plato and Aristotle The problem of dealing with mentally disturbed individuals who have committed criminal acts was studied by the Greek philosopher Plato (429–347 B.C.). He wrote that such persons were in some "obvious" sense not responsible for their acts and should not receive punishment in the same way as normal persons: ". . . someone may commit an act when mad or afflicted with disease. . . . [If so,] let him pay simply for the damage; and let him be exempt from other punishment." Plato also made provision for mental cases to be cared for in the community as follows: "If anyone is insane, let him not be seen openly in the city, but let the relatives of such a person watch over him in the best manner they know of; and if they are negligent, let them pay a fine . . ." (Plato, n.d., p. 56). In making these humane suggestions, Plato was addressing issues with which we are still grappling today—for example, the issue of *insanity* as a legal defense. **Insanity** is a legal term for mental disorder that implies a lack of understanding as required by law and therefore a lack of responsibility for one's acts and an inability to manage one's affairs. Even today the question of whether an individual's mental condition at the time of a crime is relevant to a legal defense is widely debated (we will return to this issue in Chapter 19).

In addition to his emphasis on the humane treatment of the mentally disturbed, Plato contributed to a better understanding of human behavior by pointing out that all forms of life, human included, were motivated by physiological needs, or "natural appetites." He viewed psychological phenomena as responses of the whole organism, reflecting its internal state. He also seems to have anticipated Freud's insight into the functions of fantasies and dreams as substitute satisfactions; he concluded that in dreams, a person could satisfy desires through imagery because the higher faculties no longer inhibited the "passions." In his *Republic,* Plato emphasized the importance of individual differences in intellectual and other abilities, pointing to the role of sociocultural influences in shaping thinking and behavior. He also included a provision for "hospital" care for individuals who developed beliefs that were contrary to the broader social order. These antagonistic individuals would be removed and housed separately so that their minds could be altered. These individuals would have periodic conversations analogous to psychotherapy to promote the health of their souls (Milns, 1986). Despite these modern ideas, however, Plato shared the belief of his time that mental disorders were in part divinely caused.

The celebrated Greek philosopher Aristotle (384–322 B.C.), who was a pupil of Plato, wrote extensively on mental disorders. Among his most lasting contributions to psychology are his descriptions of consciousness. He, too, anticipated Freud in his view of "thinking" as directed striving toward the elimination of pain and the attainment of pleasure. On the question of whether mental disorders could be caused by psychological factors such as frustration and conflict, Aristotle discussed the possibility and rejected it; his lead on this issue was widely followed. Aristotle generally believed the Hippocratic theory of disturbances in the bile. For example, he thought that very hot bile generated amorous desires, loquacity, and suicidal impulses.

Later Greek and Roman Thought Hippocrates' work was continued by some of the later Greek and Roman physicians. Particularly in Alexandria, Egypt (which became a center of Greek culture after its founding in 332 B.C. by Alexander the Great), medical practices developed to a high level, and the temples dedicated to Saturn were first-rate sanatoriums. Pleasant surroundings were considered of great therapeutic value for mental patients, who were provided with constant activities, including parties, dances, walks in the temple gardens, rowing along the Nile, and musical concerts. Physicians of this time also used a wide range of therapeutic measures, including dieting, massage, hydrotherapy, gymnastics, and education, as well as some less desirable practices, such as bleeding, purging, and mechanical restraints.

One of the most influential Greek physicians was Galen (A.D. 130–200), who practiced in Rome. Although he elaborated on the Hippocratic tradition, he did not contribute much that was new to the treatment or clinical descriptions of mental disorders. Rather, he made a number of original contributions concerning the anatomy of the nervous system. (These findings were based on dissections of animals; human autopsies were still not allowed.) Galen also maintained a scientific approach to the field, dividing the causes of psychological disorders into physical and mental categories. Among the causes he named were injuries to the head, alcoholic excess, shock, fear, adolescence, menstrual changes, economic reverses, and disappointment in love.

Roman medicine reflected the characteristic pragmatism of the Roman people. Roman physi-

Galen (A.D. 130–200) believed that psychological disorders could have either physical causes, such as injuries to the head, or mental causes, such as disappointment in love.

cians wanted to make their patients comfortable and thus used pleasant physical therapies, such as warm baths and massage. They also followed the principle of *contrariis contrarius* (opposite by opposite)—for example, having their patients drink chilled wine while they were in a warm tub.

Although historians generally consider the fall of Rome at the end of the fifth century to be the dividing line between ancient and medieval times, the "Dark Ages" in the history of abnormal psychology began much earlier, with Galen's death in A.D. 200. The contributions of Hippocrates and the later Greek and Roman physicians were soon lost in the welter of popular superstition, and though some exceptions can be found, most of the physicians of Rome returned to some sort of belief in demonology as an underlying factor in abnormal behavior.

Views During the Middle Ages

In Islamic countries during medieval times, the more scientific aspects of Greek medicine survived. The first mental hospital was established in Baghdad in A.D. 792; it was soon followed by others in Damascus and Aleppo (Polvan, 1969). In these hospitals, the mentally disturbed received humane treatment. The outstanding figure in Islamic medicine was Avicenna (c. A.D. 980–1037), called the "prince of physicians" (Campbell, 1926) and author of *The Canon of Medicine,* perhaps the most widely studied medical work ever written. In his writings, Avicenna frequently referred to hysteria, epilepsy, manic reactions, and melancholia. The following story shows his unique approach to the treatment of a young prince suffering from a mental disorder:

A certain prince was afflicted with melancholia, and suffered from the delusion that he was a cow . . . he would low like a cow, causing annoyance to everyone, . . . crying "Kill me so that a good stew may be made of my flesh," finally . . . he would eat nothing. . . . Avicenna was persuaded to take the case. . . . First of all he sent a message to the patient bidding him be of good cheer because the butcher was coming to slaughter him, whereat . . . the sick man rejoiced. Some time afterwards Avicenna, holding a knife in his hand, entered the sickroom saying, "Where is this cow that I may kill it?" The patient lowed like a cow to indicate where he was. By Avicenna's orders he was laid on the ground bound hand and foot. Avicenna then felt him all over and said, "He is too lean, and not ready to be killed; he must be fattened." Then they offered him suitable food of which he now partook eagerly, and gradually he gained strength, got rid of his delusion, and was completely cured. (Browne, 1921, pp. 88–89)

Islamic physician Avicenna (980–1037) approached the treatment of mental disorder with humane practices, unknown by Western medical practitioners of the time.

Unfortunately, most Western medical practitioners of Avicenna's time dealt with mental patients in a far different way. The advances made by the thinkers of antiquity had little impact on the ways most people approached abnormal behavior.

During the Middle Ages in Europe (about A.D. 500–1500), scientific inquiry into abnormal behavior was limited, and the treatment of psychologically disturbed individuals was more often characterized by ritual or superstition than by attempts to understand an individual's condition. In contrast to Avicenna's era or to the period of enlightenment during the seventeenth and eighteenth centuries, the Middle Ages can largely be characterized as void with respect to scientific thinking and the humane treatment of the mentally disturbed. A similar sequence of events occurred in other parts of the world, as can be seen in *HIGHLIGHT 2.1.*

Mental disorders were quite prevalent throughout the Middle Ages, especially so toward the end of the period, when medieval institutions, social structures, and beliefs began to change drastically. During this time, supernaturalistic explanations of the causes of mental illness grew. Within this environment, it obviously was difficult to make great

HIGHLIGHT 2.1

Early Views of Mental Disorders in China

Tseng (1973) traced the development of Chinese concepts of different mental disorders by reviewing their descriptions and recommended treatments in historical medical documents. For example, the following passage is taken from an ancient Chinese medical text supposedly written by Huang Ti (c. 2674 B.C.), the third legendary emperor. Historians now believe that the text was written at a later date, possibly during the seventh century B.C.:

The person suffering from excited insanity initially feels sad, eating and sleeping less; he then becomes grandiose, feeling that he is very smart and noble, talking and scolding day and night, singing, behaving strangely, seeing strange things, hearing strange voices, believing that he can see the devil or gods. . . . (p. 570)

Even at this early date, Chinese medicine was based on a belief in natural rather than supernatural causes for illnesses. For example, in the concept of Yin and Yang, the human body, like the cosmos, is divided into positive and negative forces that both complement and contradict each other. If the two forces are balanced, the result is physical and mental health; if they are not, illness will result. Thus treatments focused on restoring balance: "As treatment for such an excited condition withholding food was suggested, since food was considered to be the source of positive force and the patient was thought to be in need of a decrease in such force" (p. 570).

Chinese medicine reached a relatively sophisticated level during the second century, and Chung Ching, who has been called the Hippocrates of China, wrote two well-known medical works around A.D. 200. Like Hippocrates, he based his views of physical and mental disorders on clinical observations, and he implicated organ pathologies as primary causes. However, he also believed that stressful psychological conditions could cause organ pathologies, and his treatments, like those of Hippocrates, utilized both drugs and the regaining of emotional balance through appropriate activities.

As in the West, Chinese views of mental disorders regressed to a belief in supernatural forces as causal agents. From the later part of the second century through the early part of the ninth century, ghosts and devils were implicated in "ghost-evil" insanity, which presumably resulted from possession by evil spirits. The "Dark Ages" in China, however, were not as severe—in terms of the treatment of mental patients—nor as long lasting as in the West. A return to biological, somatic (bodily) views and an emphasis on psychosocial factors occurred in the centuries that followed.

strides in the understanding and treatment of abnormal behavior. However, as Schoeneman (1984) puts it, "Demonology did not triumph as a theory of insanity, but coexisted with naturalistic etiologies and treatments derived from Galenic humoural theory and folk medicine" (p. 301). Although the influence of theology was growing rapidly, "sin" was not always cited as a causal factor in mental illness. For example, Kroll and Bachrach (1984) examined 57 episodes of mental illness, ranging from madness and possession to alcohol and epilepsy. They found sin implicated in only 9 cases (16%).

To understand better this elusive period of history, let us look at two events of the times—mass madness and exorcism—to see how they relate to views of abnormal behavior.

Mass Madness During the last half of the Middle Ages, a peculiar trend emerged in abnormal behavior. It involved the widespread occurrence of group behavior disorders that were apparently cases of hysteria. Whole groups of people were affected simultaneously.

Dancing manias (epidemics of raving, jumping, dancing, and convulsions) were reported as early as the tenth century. One such episode, occurring in Italy early in the thirteenth century, was recorded by physicians of the time whose records were reviewed by medical historian H. E. Sigerist. He wrote the following:

[It] occurred at the height of the summer heat. . . . People, asleep or awake, would suddenly jump up,

In this painting, The Removal of the Stone of Folly, by Pieter Brueghel, we can see one of the more severe medieval methods of treating the psychologically disturbed. Patients were bound and holes were bored into their skulls in order to remove stones thought to be the cause of insanity.

feeling an acute pain like the sting of a bee. Some saw the spider, others did not, but they knew that it must be the tarantula. They ran out of the house into the street, to the market place, dancing in great excitement. Soon they were joined by others who like them had been bitten, or by people who had been stung in previous years. . . .

Thus groups of patients would gather, dancing wildly in the queerest attire. . . . Others would tear their clothes and show their nakedness, losing all sense of modesty. . . . Some called for swords and acted like fencers, others for whips and beat each other. . . . Some of them had still stranger fancies, liked to be tossed in the air, dug holes in the ground, and rolled themselves into the dirt like swine. They all drank wine plentifully and sang and talked like drunken people. . . . (1943, pp. 103, 106–107)

Known as **tarantism** in Italy, this dancing mania later spread to Germany and the rest of Europe, where it was known as **St. Vitus's dance.** The behavior was similar to the ancient orgiastic rites by which people had worshiped the Greek god Dionysus. These rites had been banned with the advent of Christianity, but they were deeply embedded in the culture and were apparently kept alive in secret gatherings (which probably led to considerable guilt and conflict). Then, with time, the meaning of the dances changed. The old rites reappeared, but they were attributed to symptoms of the tarantula's bite. The participants were no longer sinners but the unwilling victims of the tarantula's spirit. The dancing became the "cure" and is the source of the dance we know today as the *tarantella.*

Isolated rural areas were also afflicted with outbreaks of **lycanthropy**—a condition in which people believed themselves to be possessed by wolves and imitated their behavior. In 1541 a case was reported in which a lycanthrope told his cap-

This fifteenth-century engraving shows peasant women overcome by St. Vitus's dance.

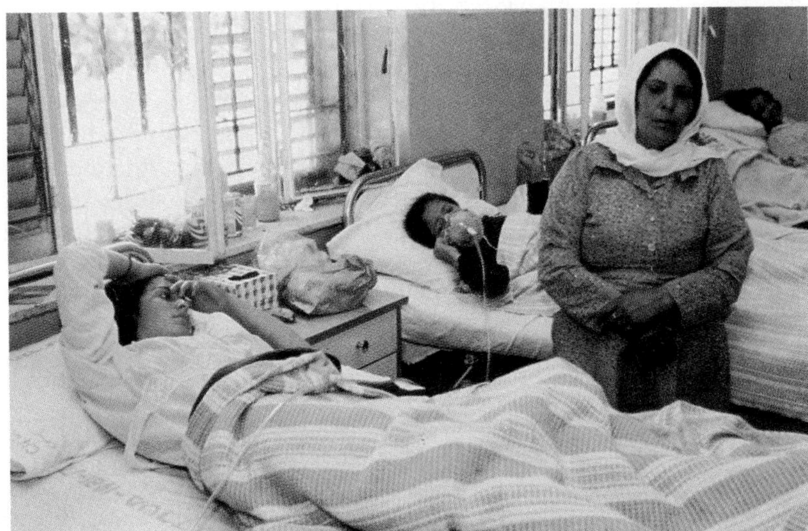

Mass disorders seem to occur during periods of widespread public fear and stress, such as that felt by these West Bank Palestinian schoolgirls, who developed the same mysterious physical symptoms in April of 1983. Although Arab leaders at first suspected the girls had been the victims of an Israeli poison plot, it was later thought that psychological factors had played an important role in the appearance of their symptoms.

tors, in confidence, that he was really a wolf but that his skin was smooth on the surface because all the hairs were on the inside (Stone, 1937). To cure him of his delusions, his extremities were amputated, following which he died, still uncured.

Mass madness occurred periodically into the seventeenth century but apparently reached its peak during the fourteenth and fifteenth centuries—a period noted for oppression, famine, and pestilence. During this period, Europe was ravaged by a plague known as the Black Death, which killed millions (some estimates say 50 percent of the population of Europe died) and severely disrupted social organization. Undoubtedly, many of the peculiar cases of mass madness were related to the depression, fear, and wild mysticism engendered by the terrible events of this period. People simply could not believe that frightening catastrophes such as the Black Death could have natural causes and thus could be within our power to control, prevent, or even create. On the other hand, many investigators today believe that mass madness during the Middle Ages was the result of ergotamine poisoning caused by bad grain.

So-called mass hysteria occasionally occurs today; the affliction usually mimics some type of physical disorder, such as fainting spells or convulsive movements. In 1982, after a nationwide story about some Chicago-area residents poisoned by Tylenol capsules, California health officials reported a sudden wave of illness among some 200 people who drank soda at a high school football game. No objective cause for the illness could be found, and officials speculated that most sufferers had been experiencing a kind of mass hysteria related to the Tylenol incident (UPI, 1982). Another case of apparent mass hysteria occurred among hundreds of West Bank Palestinian girls in April of 1983. This episode threatened to have serious political repercussions because some Arab and Israeli leaders initially thought that the girls had been poisoned by Israelis; health officials later concluded that psychological factors had played a key role in most of the cases. As in many such instances, the initial failure to control inflammatory reactions to the incident was due to a communications breakdown (Hefez, 1985; *Time* April 18, 1983, p. 52).

Exorcism In the Middle Ages, treatment of the mentally disturbed was left largely to the clergy. Monasteries served as refuges and places of confinement. During the early part of the medieval period, the mentally disturbed were, for the most part, treated with considerable kindness. "Treatment" consisted of prayer, holy water, sanctified ointments, the breath or spittle of the priests, the touching of relics, visits to holy places, and mild forms of exorcism. In some monasteries and shrines, exorcisms were performed by the gentle "laying on of hands." Such methods were often joined with vaguely understood medical treatments derived mainly from Galen, which gave rise to prescriptions such as the following: "For a fiend-sick man: When a devil possesses a man, or controls him from within with disease, a spewdrink of lupin, bishopswort, henbane, garlic. Pound these together, add ale and holy water" (Cockayne, 1864–1866).

As exorcistic techniques became more fully developed, emphasis was placed on Satan's pride, which was believed to have led to his original downfall. Hence, in treating persons possessed by a

As the notion spread in the Middle Ages that madness was caused by Satanic possession, exorcism became the treatment of choice.

devil, the first goal was to strike a fatal blow to the devil's pride—to insult him. This strategy involved calling the devil some of the most obscene epithets that imagination could devise, and the insults were usually supplemented by long litanies of cursing:

May all the devils that are thy foes rush forth upon thee, and drag thee down to hell! . . . May god set a nail to your skull, and pound it in with a hammer, as Jael did unto Sisera! . . . May . . . Sother break thy head and cut off thy hands, as was done to the cursed Dagon! . . . May God hang thee in a hellish yoke, as seven men were hanged by the sons of Saul! (*Thesaurus Exorcismorum*)

This procedure was considered highly successful in the treatment of possessed persons. A certain bishop of Beauvais claimed to have rid a person of five devils, all of whom signed an agreement stating that they and their subordinate imps would no longer persecute the possessed individual (A. D. White, 1896).

Interestingly, there has been a resurgence of superstition in contemporary society. Today one can find those who believe that supernatural forces cause psychological problems and that "cures" should involve exorcism to rid people of unwanted characteristics or "spells." Some practicing clinical psychologists actually incorporate exorcism into their treatment programs for some clients.

Witchcraft and Mental Illness: Fact or Fiction?

Fifteenth- and sixteenth-century Europe witnessed extensive witch-hunts in which many individuals were accused of and punished for deviating from the Christian faith. Possessed people were supposed to have made a pact with the devil, consummated by signing in blood a book presented to them by Satan, which gave them certain supernatural powers. It was believed that these people could cause pestilence, storms, floods, sexual impotence, and injuries to their enemies; could turn milk sour; and could rise through the air, ruin crops, and turn themselves into animals. In short, they were witches.

These beliefs were not confined to simple serfs but were held and elaborated on by most of the important clergy of the period. No less a man than Martin Luther (1483–1546), the German leader of the Protestant Reformation, came to the following conclusions:

The greatest punishment God can inflict on the wicked . . . is to deliver them over to Satan, who with God's permission, kills them or makes them to undergo great calamities. Many devils are in woods, water, wildernesses, etc., ready to hurt and prejudice people. When these things happen, then the philosophers and physicians say it is natural, ascribing it to the planets.

[People] are possessed by the devil in two ways; corporally or spiritually. Those whom he possesses corporally, as mad people, he has permission from God to vex and agitate, but he has no power over their souls." (*Colloquia Mensalia [Table Talk]*)

It has long been thought that, during this period, many mentally disturbed people were accused of being witches and thus were punished and often killed (e.g., Zilboorg & Henry, 1941). But more recent interpretations have questioned the extent to which this situation was the case. Schoeneman (1984), for example, in a review of the literature, points out that "the typical accused witch was not a mentally ill person but an impoverished woman with a sharp tongue and a bad temper [the majority of witches who were punished were women] . . ." (p. 301). He goes on to say that "witchcraft was, in fact, never considered a variety of possession either by witch hunters, the general populace, or modern historians . . ." (p. 306). To say "never" may be overstating the case; clearly, some mentally ill individuals were punished as witches. Otherwise, as you will see in the next section, why did some physicians

This French engraving of "moonstruck" women dancing in the town square illustrates the commonly held belief that the moon could affect behavior.

and thinkers go to great lengths to expose the fallacies of the connection? In the case of witchcraft and mental illness, the confusion may be due, in part, to a confusion about demonic possession. As can be seen in the quote from Luther's *Colloquia Mensalia,* there were two types of demonically possessed people—those corporally possessed were considered mad; those spiritually possessed were likely considered witches. With time, the distinctions between these two categories may have blurred in the eyes of historians, thus resulting in a less-than-accurate perception that witchcraft and mental illness were connected more frequently than was the case.

The changing view of the relationship between witchcraft and mental illness points up an even broader issue—the difficulties of interpreting historical events accurately. We will discuss this issue in more depth in the Unresolved Issues section at the end of the chapter.

THE GROWTH TOWARD HUMANITARIAN APPROACHES

During the latter part of the Middle Ages and the early Renaissance, scientific questioning reemerged and a movement emphasizing the importance of specifically human interests and concerns began—a movement (still with us today) that can be loosely referred to as ***humanism.*** Consequently, the superstitious beliefs that had retarded the understanding and therapeutic treatment of mental disorders began to be challenged.

The Resurgence of Scientific Questioning in Europe

Paracelsus, a Swiss physician (1490–1541), was an early critic of superstitious beliefs about possession. He insisted that the dancing mania was not a possession but a form of disease, and that it should be treated as such. He also postulated a conflict between the instinctual and spiritual nature of human beings, formulated the idea of psychic causes for mental illness, and advocated treatment by "bodily magnetism," later called hypnosis (Mora, 1967). Although Paracelsus rejected demonology, his view of abnormal behavior was colored by his belief in astral influences (*lunatic* is derived from the Latin word *luna* or "moon"). He was convinced that the moon exercised a supernatural influence over the brain—an idea, incidentally, that persists among some people today. Paracelsus defied the medical and theological traditions of his time; he often burned the works of Galen and others of whom he disapproved. Had he been more restrained and diplomatic in his efforts, he might have exerted more influence over the scientific thinking of his day. Instead, he became known more for his arrogance than for his scientific advances.

During the sixteenth century, Teresa of Avila, a Spanish nun who was later canonized, made an extraordinary conceptual leap that has influenced thinking to the present day. Teresa, in charge of a group of cloistered nuns who had become hysterical and were therefore in danger from the Spanish Inquisition, argued convincingly that her nuns were not possessed but rather were "as if sick" (*comas enfermas*). Apparently, she did not mean that they were sick of body. Rather, in the expression "as if," we have what is perhaps the first suggestion that a mind can be ill just as a body can be ill. It was a momentous suggestion, which apparently began as a kind of metaphor but was, with time, accepted as fact: people came to see mental illness as an entity, and the "as if" dropped out of use (Sarbin & Juhasz, 1967).

Teresa of Avila, a sixteenth-century Spanish nun, had a major influence on the conception of mental illness in her era when she insisted that the hysterical nuns in her care were not possessed, but were "as if sick." This argument paved the way for the view that the mind can be sick like the body.

Johann Weyer (1515–1588) wrote against the prevalent beliefs in witchcraft and decried the persecution of the mentally ill.

Johann Weyer (1515–1588), a German physician and writer who wrote under the Latin name of Joannus Wierus, was so deeply disturbed by the imprisonment, torture, and burning of people accused of witchcraft that he made a careful study of the entire problem. About 1563 he published a book, *The Deception of Demons,* which contains a step-by-step rebuttal of the *Malleus maleficarum,* a witch-hunters handbook published in 1486 for use in recognizing and dealing with those suspected of being witches. In it, he argued that a considerable number, if not all, of those imprisoned, tortured, and burned for witchcraft were really sick in mind or body and, consequently, that great wrongs were being committed against innocent people. Weyer's work received the approval of a few outstanding physicians and theologians of his time. Mostly, however, it met with vehement protest and condemnation.

Weyer was one of the first physicians to specialize in mental disorders, and his wide experience and progressive views justify his reputation as the founder of modern psychopathology. Unfortunately, however, he was too far ahead of his time. He was scorned by his peers, many of whom called him "Weirus Hereticus" and "Weirus Insanus." His works were banned by the Church and remained so until the twentieth century.

Perhaps there is no better illustration of the developing spirit of scientific skepticism in the sixteenth century than the works of the Oxford-educated Reginald Scot (1538–1599). Scot devoted his life to exposing the fallacies of witchcraft and demonology. In his book, *Discovery of Witchcraft,* published in 1584, he convincingly and daringly denied the existence of demons, devils, and evil spirits as the cause of mental disorders:

"These women are but diseased wretches suffering from melancholy, and their words, actions, reasoning, and gestures show that sickness has affected their brains and impaired their powers of judgment. You must know that the effects of sickness on men, and still more on women, are almost unbelievable. Some of these persons imagine, confess, and maintain that they are witches and are capable of performing extraordinary miracles through the arts of witchcraft; others, due to the same mental disorder, imagine strange and impossible things which they claim to have witnessed." (in Castiglioni, 1946, p. 253)

King James I of England, however, came to the rescue of demonology, personally refuted Scot's thesis, and ordered his book seized and burned.

The clergy, however, were beginning to question the practices of the time. For example, St. Vincent de Paul (1576–1660), at the risk of his life, declared: "Mental disease is no different to bodily disease and Christianity demands of the humane and powerful to protect, and the skillful to relieve the one as well as the other."

In the face of such persistent advocates of science, who continued their testimonies throughout the next two centuries, demonology and superstition gave ground. These advocates gradually paved the way for the return of observation and reason, which culminated in the development of modern experimental and clinical approaches.

The Establishment of Early Asylums and Shrines

From the sixteenth century on, special institutions called **asylums,** meant solely for the care of the mentally ill, grew in number. The early asylums were begun as a way of removing from society troublesome individuals who could not care for themselves. Although scientific inquiry into understanding abnormal behavior was on the increase, most early asylums, often referred to as *madhouses,* were not much better than concentration camps. The unfortunate residents lived and died amid conditions of incredible filth and cruelty.

Early Asylums In 1547 the monastery of St. Mary of Bethlehem at London was officially made into a mental hospital by Henry VIII. Its name soon was contracted to *Bedlam,* and it became widely known for its deplorable conditions and practices. The more violent patients were exhibited to the public for one penny a look, and the more harmless inmates were forced to seek charity on the streets of London in the manner described by Shakespeare: "Bedlam beggars, who, with roaring voices . . . Sometimes with lunatic bans, sometime with prayers Enforce their charity" (*King Lear,* Act II, Scene iii).

Such hospitals for the mentally ill were gradually established in other countries. The San Hipolito, established in Mexico in 1566 by philanthropist Bernardino Alvares, was the first mental hospital established in the Americas. The first such hospital in France, La Maison de Charenton, was founded in 1641 in a suburb of Paris. A mental hospital was established in Moscow in 1764, and the notorious Lunatics' Tower in Vienna was constructed in 1784. This structure was a showplace in Old Vienna, an ornately decorated round tower within which were square rooms. The doctors and "keepers" lived in the square rooms, while the patients were confined in the spaces between the walls of the rooms and the outside of the tower. The patients were put on exhibit to the public for a small fee.

These early asylums were primarily modifications of penal institutions, and the inmates were treated more like beasts than like human beings. The following passage describes the treatment of the chronically insane in La Bicêtre, a hospital in Paris. This treatment was typical of the asylums of the period and continued through most of the eighteenth century.

The patients were ordinarily shackled to the walls of their dark, unlighted cells by iron collars which held them flat against the wall and permitted little movement. Ofttimes there were also iron hoops around the waists of the patients and both their hands and feet were chained. Although these chains usually permitted enough movement that the patients could feed themselves out of bowls, they often kept them from being able to lie down at night. Since little was known about dietetics, and the patients were presumed to be animals anyway, little attention was paid to whether they were adequately fed or to whether the food was good or bad. The cells were furnished only with straw and

From the sixteenth century on, an accepted treatment for people with mental disorders was confinement in asylums like this, the Bethlehem Royal Hospital in London. The hospital's name was soon contracted to Bedlam, a synonym for the uproar and confusion within its walls. This view of Bedlam is from Hogarth's Rake's Progress. In the eighteenth century, it was considered entertaining to view the lunatics, as the two ladies of fashion shown here are doing.

were never swept or cleaned; the patient remained in the midst of all the accumulated ordure. No one visited the cells except at feeding time, no provision was made for warmth, and even the most elementary gestures of humanity were lacking. (Modified from Selling, 1943, pp. 54–55)

In the United States, the Pennsylvania Hospital at Philadelphia, completed under the guidance of Benjamin Franklin in 1756, provided some cells or wards for mental patients. The Public Hospital in Williamsburg, Virginia, constructed in 1773, was the first hospital in the United States devoted exclusively to mental patients. The treatment of mental patients in the United States was no better than that offered by European institutions. Zwelling's (1985) review of Public Hospital's treatment methods show that, initially, the philosophy of treatment involved the view that patients needed to choose rationality over insanity. Thus the treatment techniques were aggressive, aimed at restoring a "physical balance in the body and brain." These techniques were designed to intimidate patients; they included powerful drugs, water treatments, bleeding and blistering, electrical shocks, and physical restraints. For example, a violent patient might be plunged into ice water or a listless patient into hot water; frenzied patients might be administered drugs to exhaust them; or any patient might be bled in order to drain their system of "harmful" fluids. Early estimates of the cure rate for patients at the hospital were only about 20 percent.

Even as late as 1830, new patients had their heads shaved, were dressed in straitjackets, put on sparse diets, compelled to swallow some active purgative, and placed in dark cells. If these procedures did not quiet unruly or excited patients, more severe measures, such as starvation, solitary confinement, cold baths, and other torturelike methods, were used (Bennett, 1947).

The Geel Shrine There were a few bright spots in this otherwise bleak situation. Out of the more humane Christian tradition of prayer, laying on of hands (or holy touch), and visits to shrines, there arose several great shrines where treatment by kindness and love stood out in marked contrast to prevailing conditions. The shrine at Geel in Belgium, visited since the thirteenth century, is probably the most famous. Legend has it that hidden in the forest of Geel is the body of a young princess who, upon the death of her mother, had dedicated her life to the poor and mentally disturbed. She was later slain by her incestuous father. Years later, five lunatics who spent the night in the forest recovered their mental health. Villagers believed that the princess, reincarnated as St. Dymphna, was responsible for the cures. Pilgrimages to Geel were organized for the mentally sick; many of the patients stayed on to live with the local inhabitants (Karnesh & Zucker, 1945). The colony of Geel has continued its work into modern times (Aring, 1974, 1975b; Belgian Consulate, 1990). Today, a new psychiatric hospital has been built in Geel, and nearly 1000 mental patients live in private homes with "foster families," work in community-based centers, and suffer few restrictions other than not drinking alcohol. Many types of mental disorders are represented, including schizophrenia, affective disorder, antisocial personality, and mental retardation. Ordinarily, patients remain in Geel until they are considered recovered by a supervising therapist. It is unfortunate that the great humanitarian work of this colony—and the opportunity it affords to study the treatment of patients in a family and community setting—has received so little recognition.

Humanitarian Reform

Clearly, by the late eighteenth century, most mental hospitals in Europe and America were in need of reform. The humanitarian treatment of patients received great impetus from the work of Philippe Pinel (1745–1826) in France.

Pinel's Experiment In 1792, shortly after the first phase of the French Revolution, Pinel was placed in charge of La Bicêtre in Paris. In this capacity, he received the grudging permission of the Revolutionary Commune to remove the chains from some of the inmates as an experiment to test his views that mental patients should be treated with kindness and consideration—as sick people and not as vicious beasts or criminals. Had his experiment proved a failure, Pinel might have lost his head, but fortunately it was a great success. Chains were removed; sunny rooms were provided; patients were permitted to exercise on the hospital grounds; and kindness was extended to these poor beings, some of whom had been chained in dungeons for 30 years or more. The effect was almost

This painting shows Philippe Pinel supervising the unchaining of inmates at La Bicêtre hospital. Pinel's experiment represented both a great reform and a major step in divising humanitarian methods of treating disorders.

miraculous. The previous noise, filth, and abuse were replaced by order and peace. As Pinel said: "The whole discipline was marked with regularity and kindness which had the most favorable effect on the insane themselves, rendering even the most furious more tractable" (Selling, 1943, p. 65).

The reactions of these patients when all their chains were removed for the first time was telling. One patient, an English officer who had years before killed a guard in an attack of fury, tottered outside on legs weak from lack of use, and for the first time in some 40 years saw the sun and sky. With tears in his eyes he exclaimed, "Oh, how beautiful!" (Zilboorg & Henry, 1941, p. 323). When night came, he voluntarily returned to his cell, which had been cleaned during his absence, to fall peacefully asleep on his new bed. After two years of orderly behavior, including helping to handle other patients, he was pronounced recovered and permitted to leave the hospital. Pinel himself was once saved from a mob that accused him of antirevolutionary activities by a soldier whom he had freed from asylum chains.

Pinel was later given charge of La Salpêtrière hospital, where the same reorganization was instituted with similar results. La Bicêtre and La Salpêtrière hospitals thus became the first modern hospitals for the care of the insane. Pinel's successor, Jean Esquirol (1772–1840), continued Pinel's good work at La Salpêtrière and, in addition, helped establish ten new mental hospitals. These hospitals put France in the forefront of humane treatment for the mentally disturbed and "signalled the end of the indiscriminate mixture of paupers and criminals, the physically sick, and the mentally deranged" (Rosenblatt, 1984, p. 246).

Tuke's Work in England At about the same time that Pinel was reforming La Bicêtre, an English Quaker named William Tuke (1732–1822) established the York Retreat, a pleasant country house where mental patients lived, worked, and rested in a kindly religious atmosphere (Narby, 1982). This retreat represented the culmination of a noble battle against the brutality, ignorance, and indifference of his time. Some insight into the difficulties and discouragements he encountered may be gleaned from a simple statement he made in a letter regarding his early efforts: "All men seem to desert me." This statement is not surprising when we remember that the belief in demonology was still widespread and that as late as 1768 Protestant leader John Wesley declared that "the giving up of witchcraft is in effect the giving up of the Bible." The belief in demonology was too strong to be conquered overnight.

As word of Pinel's amazing results spread to England, Tuke's small force of Quakers gradually gained support from John Connolly, Samuel Hitch, and other great English medical psychologists. In 1841 Hitch introduced trained nurses into the wards at the Gloucester Asylum and put trained supervisors at the head of the nursing staffs. These innovations, quite revolutionary at the time, were of great importance not only in improving the care of mental patients but also in changing public attitudes toward the mentally disturbed.

Rush and Moral Management in America The success of Pinel's and Tuke's humanitarian experiments revolutionized the treatment of mental patients throughout the Western world. In the United States, this revolution was reflected in the work of Benjamin Rush (1745–1813), the founder of American psychiatry. While associated with the Pennsylvania Hospital in 1783, Rush encouraged more humane treatment of the mentally ill; wrote the first systematic treatise on psychiatry in America, *Medical Inquiries and Observations upon the Diseases of the Mind* (1812); and was the first American to organize a course in psychiatry. But even he did not escape entirely from established beliefs of his time. His medical theory was tainted with astrology, and his principle remedies were bloodletting and purgatives. In addition, he invented and used a

Benjamin Rush (1745–1813) founded American psychiatry and encouraged more humane treatment of the mentally ill. He was the first American to write a systematic treatise on psychiatry and to organize a course on the subject.

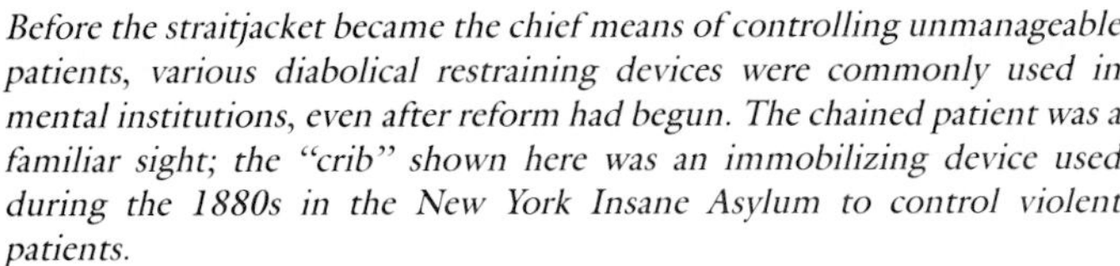

Before the straitjacket became the chief means of controlling unmanageable patients, various diabolical restraining devices were commonly used in mental institutions, even after reform had begun. The chained patient was a familiar sight; the "crib" shown here was an immobilizing device used during the 1880s in the New York Insane Asylum to control violent patients.

device called "the tranquilizer," which was probably more torturous than tranquil for patients. Despite these limitations, we can consider Rush an important transitional figure between the old era and the new.

During the early part of this period of humanitarian reform, the use of **moral management**—a wide-ranging method of treatment that focused on a patient's social, individual, and occupational needs—became relatively widespread. This approach, which stemmed largely from the work of Pinel and Tuke, began in Europe during the late eighteenth century and in America during the early nineteenth century. As Rees (1957) has described the approach:

The insane came to be regarded as normal people who had lost their reason as a result of having been exposed to severe psychological and social stresses. These stresses were called the moral causes of insanity, and moral treatment aimed at relieving the patient by friendly association, discussion of his difficulties, and the daily pursuit of purposeful activity; in other words, social therapy, individual therapy, and occupational therapy. (pp. 306–307)

Changes at Williamsburg's Public Hospital reflected this change in attitude. First, the hospital was renamed the Williamsburg Lunatic Asylum to reflect "the view that the mentally ill were innocent victims who required protection from society" (Zwelling, 1985, p. 30). Treatment regimens were also changed. There were fewer physical restraints, more open wards, and opportunities to practice positive activities such as farming and carpentry. Social activities, some involving members of the opposite sex, were incorporated into the daily activities of the patients.

Moral management achieved an almost incredible level of effectiveness—all the more amazing because it was done without the benefit of the antipsychotic drugs so prevalent today and because many of the patients were probably suffering from syphilis, the then-incurable disease of the central nervous system. In the 20-year period between 1833 and 1853, Worcester State Hospital's discharge rate for patients who had been ill less than one year prior to admission was 71 percent. Even for patients with a longer preadmission disorder, the discharge rate was 59 percent (Bockhoven, 1972).

Despite its relative effectiveness, moral management was nearly abandoned by the latter part of the nineteenth century. The reasons were many and varied. Among the more obvious ones were the ethnic and racial prejudice that came with the rising immigrant population, leading to tension between staff and patients; the failure of the movement's leaders to train their own replacements; and the overextension of hospital facilities, reflecting the misguided belief that bigger hospitals would differ from smaller ones only in size.

Two other reasons for the demise of moral management are, in retrospect, truly ironic. One was the rise of the **mental hygiene movement,** which advocated a method of treatment that focused almost exclusively on the physical well-being of hospitalized mental patients. Although the creature comforts of patients may have improved under the mental hygienists, the patients received no help for their mental problems and thus were condemned subtly to helplessness and dependency.

The use of moral management included less use of restraint and the practice of positive activities and socializing. This photo from the turn of the century shows male patients taking their leisure. Moral management had profoundly positive effects on a great many patients, and it was certainly a more humanitarian practice than the methods that had preceded it.

Advances in biomedical science also contributed to the demise of moral management and the rise of the mental hygiene movement. These advances fostered the notion that all mental disorders would eventually yield to biological explanations and biologically based treatments. Thus the psychological and social environment of a patient was considered largely irrelevant; the best one could do was keep the patient comfortable until a biological cure was discovered. Needless to say, the anticipated biological cure-all did not arrive, and by the late 1940s and early 1950s discharge rates were down to about 30 percent. We do better today, with discharge rates above 90 percent, but these improved rates are a recent development due to many factors, including advances in drug therapy and a trend to release many patients for continued care in their communities. The fact that the care in the community often does not meet acceptable standards is an issue we will address in Chapter 19.

Notwithstanding its negative effects on the use of moral management, the mental hygiene movement has accounted for many humanitarian accomplishments.

Dix and the Mental Hygiene Movement

Dorothea Dix (1802–1887) was an energetic New England schoolteacher forced into early retirement because of recurring attacks of tuberculosis. In 1841 she began to teach in a women's prison. Through this contact she became acquainted with the deplorable conditions in jails, almshouses, and asylums. In a "Memorial" submitted to the Congress of the United States in 1848, she stated that she had seen

> *more than 9000 idiots, epileptics and insane in the United States, destitute of appropriate care and protection . . . bound with galling chains, bowed beneath fetters and heavy iron bails attached to drag-chains, lacerated with ropes, scouraged with rods and terrified beneath storms of execration and cruel blows; now subject to jibes and scorn and torturing tricks; now abandoned to the most outrageous violations. (Zilboorg & Henry, 1941, pp. 583–584)*

As a result of her findings, Dix carried on a zealous campaign between 1841 and 1881 that aroused people and legislatures to do something

Dorothea Dix (1802–1887) was a tireless reformer who made great strides in changing public attitudes toward the mentally ill.

about the inhuman treatment accorded the mentally ill. Through her efforts, the mental hygiene movement grew in America: millions of dollars were raised to build suitable hospitals, and 20 states responded directly to her appeals. Not only was she instrumental in improving conditions in American hospitals, but she directed the opening of 2 large institutions in Canada and completely reformed the asylum system in Scotland and several other countries. She is credited with establishing 32 mental hospitals, an astonishing record considering the ignorance and superstition that still prevailed in the field of mental health. She rounded out her career by organizing the nursing forces of the northern armies during the Civil War. A resolution presented by the United States Congress in 1901 characterized her as "among the noblest examples of humanity in all history" (Karnesh & Zucker, 1945, p. 18).

Retrospective criticism of Dix's work has questioned the importance of her contributions and has attributed several negative consequences to her efforts (Bockhoven, 1972; Dain, 1964). Later critics have claimed that establishing hospitals for the mentally ill and increasing the number of people in them created overcrowded facilities and custodial care. Housing patients in institutions away from society, these critics have claimed further, interfered with the treatment of the day (moral therapy) and deferred the search for more appropriate and effective treatments for mental disorders (Bockhoven, 1972). These criticisms, however, do not consider the context in which Dix's contributions were made (see the Unresolved Issues discussion on page 50). Dix's advocacy of the humane treatment of the mentally ill should be considered in light of the cruel treatment common at the time (Viney & Bartsch, 1984), and we believe her efforts warrant considerable praise for their results.

THE FOUNDATIONS OF TWENTIETH-CENTURY VIEWS

It is difficult to partition modern views of abnormal behavior into discrete, uniform attitudes or to trace their historical precedents without appearing arbitrary and overly simplistic. Much that has happened in the nineteenth and twentieth centuries is the subject of the next chapter; however, a brief, selective overview here will bring us into the twentieth century and set the scene for Chapter 3.

Changing Attitudes Toward Mental Health

By the end of the nineteenth century, the mental hospital or asylum—"the big house on the hill"—with its high turrets and fortresslike appearance, had become a familiar landmark in America. In it, mental patients lived under semiadequate conditions of comfort and freedom from abuse. To the general public, however, the asylum was an eerie place, and its occupants a strange and frightening lot.

Little was done by the resident psychiatrists—then called *alienists,* in reference to treating the "alienated," or insane—to educate the public to reduce the general fear and horror of insanity. A principal reason for this silence, of course, was that early psychiatrists had little actual information to impart.

Gradually, however, important strides were made toward changing the general public's attitude toward mental patients. In America, the pioneering work of Dix was followed by that of Clifford Beers (1876–1943), whose book, *A Mind That Found Itself,* was published in 1908. Beers, a Yale graduate, described his own mental collapse and told of the bad treatment he received in three typical institutions of the day. He also explained his eventual recovery in the home of a friendly attendant. Although chains and other torture devices had long since been given up, the straitjacket was still widely

Clifford Beers (1876–1943) used his own experiences of incarceration in mental institutions to wage a campaign of public awareness about the need for changes in the attitudes toward and treatment of mental patients.

used as a means of "quieting" excited patients. Beers experienced this treatment and supplied a vivid description of what such painful immobilization of the arms means to an overwrought mental patient:

No one incident of my whole life has ever impressed itself more indelibly on my memory. Within one hour's time I was suffering pain as intense as any I ever endured, and before the night had passed that pain had become almost unbearable. My right hand was so held that the tip of one of my fingers was all but cut by the nail of another, and soon knife-like pains began to shoot through my right arm as far as the shoulder. If there be any so curious as to wish to get a slight idea of my agony, let him bite a finger tip as hard as he can without drawing blood. Let him continue the operation for two or three minutes. Then let him multiply that effect, if he can, by two or three hundred. In my case, after four or five hours the excess of pain rendered me partially insensible to it. But for nine hundred minutes—fifteen consecutive hours—I remained in that strait-jacket; and not until the twelfth hour, about breakfast time the next morning, did an attendant so much as loosen a cord. (Beers, pp. 127–128)

After Beers recovered, he began a campaign to make people realize that such treatment was no way to handle the sick. He soon won the interest and support of many public-spirited individuals, including the eminent psychologist William James and the "dean of American psychiatry," Adolf Meyer.

The Growth of Scientific Research

While the mental hygiene movement was gaining ground in the United States during the latter years of the nineteenth century, great technological discoveries were occurring both at home and abroad. These advances helped begin what we know today as the scientific, or experimentally oriented, view of abnormal behavior and the application of scientific knowledge to the treatment of disturbed individuals.

The most immediately apparent advances were in the study of the biological and anatomical factors underlying both physical and mental disorders. A major biomedical breakthrough, for example, came with the discovery of the organic factors underlying general paresis—syphilis of the brain—one of the most serious mental illnesses of the day. General paresis produced paralysis and insanity and typically caused death within two to five years. The investigation into the causes of paresis and the finding of a cure—in essence, infecting a sufferer with malarial fever—stretched over a period of nearly 100 years, as outlined in *HIGHLIGHT 2.2.* Though today we have penicillin as an effective, simpler treatment of paresis, the early malarial treatment represented, for the first time in history, a clear-cut conquest of a mental disorder by medical science. The field of abnormal psychology had come a long way—from superstitious beliefs to scientific proof of how brain pathology can cause a specific disorder. This breakthrough raised great hopes in the medical community that organic bases would be found for many other mental disorders—perhaps for all of them.

Despite the emphasis on biological causation, the scientific investigation into psychological factors and human behavior was progressing, too. In 1879 Wilhelm Wundt (1832–1920) established the first experimental psychology laboratory at the University of Leipzig. While studying the psychological factors involved in memory and sensation, Wundt and his colleagues devised many basic experimental methods and strategies. Early contributors to the empirical study of abnormal behavior were directly influenced by Wundt; they followed his experimental methodology and also used some of his research strategies to study clinical problems. For example, a student of Wundt's, J. McKeen Cattell (1860–1944), brought Wundt's experimental methods to the United States and used them to assess individual differences in mental processing. He and other students of Wundt's work established research laboratories throughout the United States.

HIGHLIGHT 2.2

Events Leading to the Discovery of Organic Factors in General Paresis

Scientific discoveries do not occur overnight; usually they require the combined efforts of many scientists over extended periods of time. In addition, such discoveries rarely proceed sequentially from point *a* to point *z*. Rather, they often result from an uncoordinated process in which many scientists pursue dead-end hypotheses, go off on tangents, refuse to accept "evidence," experience crises in their thinking, and so on.

Abbreviated descriptions of the events leading to scientific discoveries often fail to capture the excitement, intrigue, and frustration that enter the process. With this caution in mind, we identify here ten key steps in the long effort to find a cure for general paresis.

1. In 1825 French physician A. L. J. Bayle differentiated general paresis as a specific type of mental disorder. Bayle gave a complete and accurate description of the symptom pattern of paresis and convincingly presented his reasons for believing paresis to be a distinct disorder.
2. In 1857 Esmarch and Jessen reported on paretic patients known to have had syphilis and concluded that the syphilis caused the paresis.
3. In 1869 Argyll-Robertson in Scotland described the failure of the pupillary reflex (failure of the pupil to narrow under bright light) as diagnostic of the involvement of the central nervous system in syphilis.
4. In 1897 Viennese psychiatrist Krafft-Ebing conducted experiments involving the inoculation of paretic patients with matter from syphilitic sores. None of the patients developed secondary symptoms of syphilis, which led to the conclusion that they must previously have been infected. This crucial experiment established the relationship of general paresis to syphilis.
5. In 1905 Schaudinn discovered that *Spirochaeta pallida* is the cause of syphilis.
6. In 1906 von Wassermann developed a blood test for syphilis. This development made it possible to check for the presence of the deadly spirochetes in the bloodstream of an individual before the more serious consequences of infection appeared.
7. In 1908 Plant applied the Wasserman test to the cerebrospinal fluid to indicate whether or not the spirochete had invaded a patient's central nervous system.
8. In 1909 Ehrlich, after 605 failures, developed the arsenical compound arsphenamine (which he thereupon called *606*) for the treatment of syphilis. Although 606 proved effective in killing the syphilitic spirochetes in the bloodstream, it was not effective against the spirochetes that had penetrated the central nervous system.
9. In 1913 Noguchi and Moore verified that the syphilitic spirochete was the brain-damaging agent in general paresis. They discovered these spirochetes in a postmortem study of the brains of patients who had suffered from paresis.
10. In 1917 Wagner-Jauregg, chief of the psychiatric clinic of the University of Vienna, introduced the malarial fever treatment of syphilis and paresis. He inoculated nine paretic patients with the blood of a soldier who was ill with malaria and found marked improvement in three patients and apparent recovery in three others.

Wilhelm Wundt (1832–1920) established the first experimental psychology laboratory, which led others to use scientific methods to investigate psychological processes, including mental disorders.

It was not until 1896, however, that another of Wundt's students, Lightner Witmer (1867–1956), combined research with application and established the first American psychological clinic at the University of Pennsylvania. Witmer's clinic focused on the problems of mentally deficient children, both in terms of research and therapy. Other clinics were soon established. One clinic of note was the Chicago Juvenile Psychopathic Institute (later called the Institute of Juvenile Research), established in 1909 by William Healy (1869–1963). Healy was the first to describe juvenile delinquency as a symptom of urbanization and not as a result of inner psychological problems. In so doing, he was among the first to seize upon a new area of causation—environmental, or sociocultural, factors.

By the first decade of the twentieth century, psychological laboratories and clinics were burgeoning, and a great deal of research was being generated. The rapid and objective communication of scientific findings was perhaps as important in the development of modern psychology (or any science) as the collection and interpretation of research findings. This period saw the origin of many scientific journals for the dissemination of research and theoretical discoveries. Two notable publications in the field of abnormal psychology were the *Journal of Abnormal Psychology,* founded by Morton Prince in 1906, and *The Psychological Clinic,* founded by Lightner Witmer in 1907. As the years have passed, the number of journals has grown. The American Psychological Association now publishes over 20 scientific journals, many of which focus on research into abnormal behavior and personality functioning. The many avenues available for communicating new findings ensures that important discoveries will become widely known. Yet the very amount of information available can cause confusion and controversy, as we shall see in Chapter 3. We may have left supernatural beliefs behind, but we have moved into something far more complex in trying to determine the role of natural factors—be they biological, psychological, or sociocultural—in abnormal behavior. For a recap of some of the key contributors to the field of abnormal psychology, see *HIGHLIGHT 2.3*

UNRESOLVED ISSUES

on Interpreting Historical Events

One would think that trying to look back in history to get a picture of events that occurred long ago would not be all that difficult a task—that it would be a simple matter of reviewing some history books and some publications from the time in question. Any number of obstacles, however, can stand in the way of our gaining an accurate picture of the attitudes and behaviors of people who lived hundreds of years ago. This has certainly been the case with our views of the Middle Ages.

The foremost problem in retrospective psychological analysis is that we cannot rely on direct observation, a hallmark of psychological research. Instead, we must turn to written documents or historical surveys of the times. Though these sources are often full of fascinating information, they may not reveal directly the information we seek; we must therefore extrapolate "facts" from the information we have, which is not always an easy task. We are restricted in our conclusions by the documents or sources available to us; attempting to learn about a people's subtle social perceptions hundreds of years ago by examining surviving church documents or biographical accounts is less than ideal. First, we view these documents out of the context in which they were written. Second, we do not know whether the authors had ulterior motives or what they were—that is, what the real purposes were behind the documents. Kroll and Bachrach (1984), in their review of historical misinterpretations of the Middle Ages, point to the "propaganda element" that existed during the Middle Ages (as it still does today). For example, many historians have conclud-

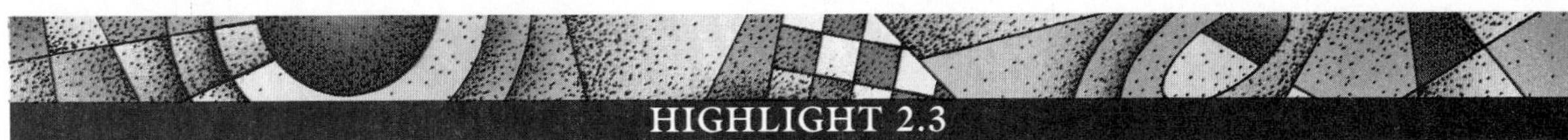

HIGHLIGHT 2.3

Major Figures in the Early History of Abnormal Psychology

The Ancient World

Hippocrates (460–377 B.C.) A Greek physician who believed that mental disease was the result of natural causes and brain pathology rather than demonology.

Plato (429–347 B.C.) A Greek philosopher who believed that mental patients should be treated humanely and should not be held responsible for their actions.

Aristotle (384–322 B.C.) Greek philosopher and pupil of Plato who believed in the Hippocratic theory that various agents, or humors, within the body, when imbalanced, were responsible for mental disorders. Aristotle rejected the notion of psychological factors as causes of mental disorders.

Galen (A.D. 130–200) A Greek physician and advocate of the Hippocratic tradition who contributed much to our understanding of the nervous system. Galen divided the causes of mental disorders into physical and mental categories.

The Middle Ages

Avicenna (980–1037) An Islamic physician who adopted principles of humane treatment for the mentally disturbed at a time when Western approaches to mental illness were the opposite.

Martin Luther (1483–1546) A German theologian and leader of the Reformation who held the belief, common to his time, that the mentally disturbed were possessed by the devil.

Paracelsus (1490–1541) A Swiss physician who rejected demonology as a cause of abnormal behavior. Paracelsus believed in psychic causes of mental illness.

The Sixteenth Through the Eighteenth Centuries

Teresa of Avila (16th century) A Spanish nun who argued that mental disorder was an illness of the mind.

Johann Weyer (1515–1588) A German physician who argued against demonology and was ostracized by his peers and the Church for his progressive views.

Reginald Scot (1538–1599) An Englishman who refuted the notion of demons as the cause of mental disorders and was castigated by King James I.

Philippe Pinel (1745–1826) A French physician who pioneered the use of moral management in La Bicêtre and La Salpêtrière hospitals in France, where mental patients were treated in a humane way.

William Tuke (1732–1822) An English Quaker who established the York Retreat, where mental patients lived in humane surroundings.

Benjamin Rush (1745–1813) An American physician and founder of American psychiatry who used moral management, based on Pinel's humanitarian methods, to treat the mentally disturbed.

The Nineteenth and Early Twentieth Centuries

Dorothea Dix (1802–1887) An American teacher who founded the mental hygiene movement in the United States, which focused on the physical well-being of mental patients in hospitals.

Clifford Beers (1876–1943) An American who campaigned to change public attitudes toward mental patients after his own experiences in mental institutions.

Wilhelm Wundt (1832–1920) A German scientist who established the first experimental psychology laboratory in 1879 and subsequently influenced the empirical study of abnormal behavior.

J. McKeen Cattell (1860–1944) An American psychologist who adopted Wundt's methods and studied individual differences in mental processing.

Lightner Witmer (1867–1956) An American psychologist who established the first psychological clinic in the United States, focusing on problems of mentally deficient children. He also founded the journal *The Psychological Clinic* in 1907.

William Healy (1869–1963) An American psychologist who established the Chicago Juvenile Psychopathic Institute and advanced the idea that mental illness was due to environmental or sociocultural factors.

ed erroneously that people of the Middle Ages considered sin as a major causal factor in mental illness. This wrong conclusion may have been due in part to writings that invoked God's punishment if the victims of illnesses were enemies of the authors. Apparently, historians did not take note of the fact that if the victims were friends of the authors, sin was typically not mentioned as a causal factor (Kroll & Bachrach, 1984). Such writings, of course, are biased, but we may have no way of knowing this. The fewer the sources surveyed, the more likely any existing bias may go undetected.

In other cases, concepts important to historical interpretation may have quite a different meaning to us today than they did in the past. Or the meaning may simply be unclear. Kroll and Bachrach (1984) point out that the concept of "possession"—so critical to our views of the Middle Ages—is

> *a very vague and complex concept for which we have no helpful natural models. Our language fails us, except for colourful analogies and metaphors. Just as the term "nervous breakdown" means different things to different people, so too "possession" means and meant many different things, and undoubtedly had a different range of meanings to medieval persons from what it has to us. (p. 510)*

This kind of uncertainty can make definitive assessments of the happenings during the Middle Ages difficult—if not impossible.

Bias can come into play during interpretation, also. Our interpretations of historical events or previously held beliefs can be colored by our own views of normal and abnormal. In fact, it is difficult to conduct a retrospective analysis without taking current perspectives and values as a starting point. For example, our modern beliefs about the Middle Ages have led, says Schoeneman (1984), to our contemporary misinterpretation that, during the fifteenth and sixteenth centuries, the mentally ill were typically accused of being witches. For most of us, this interpretation—albeit a wrong one—makes sense simply because we do not understand the medieval perspective on witchcraft.

Although reevaluations of the Middle Ages have minimized the views that demonology, sin, and witchcraft played a key role in the medieval understanding of mental illness, it is also clear that in some cases, these concepts *were* associated with mental illness. Wherein lies the truth? It appears that the last word has not been written on the Middle Ages, nor on any period of our history, for that matter. At best, historical views—and, therefore, retrospective psychological studies—must be held as working hypotheses that are open to change as new perspectives are applied to history or "new" historical documents are discovered.

SUMMARY

The development of modern views on psychopathology has not followed a straight evolutionary path. We can, however, trace a general movement away from superstitious and "magical" explanations of abnormal behavior toward more reasoned, scientific explanations.

Early superstitions were followed by the emergence of medical concepts in many places, such as Egypt and Greece; many of these concepts were developed and refined by Roman physicians. With the fall of Rome near the end of the fifth century A.D., most Europeans returned to superstitious views, which dominated popular thinking about mental disorders for over 1000 years. In the fifteenth and sixteenth centuries, it was still widely believed that mentally disturbed people were possessed by a devil.

During the latter stages of the Middle Ages and early Renaissance, a spirit of scientific questioning reappeared in Europe, and several noted physicians spoke out against inhumane treatments, arguing that "possessed" individuals were actually "sick of mind" and should be treated as such. With this recognition of a need for the special treatment of disturbed people came the founding of various "asylums" toward the end of the sixteenth century. However, with institutionalization came the isolation and maltreatment of mental patients; slowly, this situation was recognized, and in the eighteenth century, further efforts were made to help afflicted individuals by providing them with better living conditions and kind treatment.

The nineteenth and early twentieth centuries witnessed a number of scientific and humanitarian advances. The work of Philippe Pinel in France, William Tuke in England, and Benjamin Rush and Dorothea Dix in the United States prepared the way for several important developments in contemporary abnormal psychology. Among these developments were the gradual acceptance of mental patients as afflicted individuals who needed and deserved professional attention; the success of biomedical methods as applied to disorders such as general paresis; and the growth of scientific research into the biological, psychological, and sociocultural roots of abnormal behavior.

Understanding the history of viewpoints on psychopathology, with its forward steps and reverses, helps us understand the emergence of modern concepts of abnormal behavior. This knowledge also provides us with a perspective for understanding new and future advances.

Key Terms

trephining (p. 30)
exorcism (p. 31)
insanity (p. 32)
tarantism (p. 36)
St. Vitus's dance (p. 36)
lycanthropy (p. 36)
asylums (p. 41)
moral management (p. 45)
mental hygiene movement (p. 45)

Chapter 3

Biological, Psychosocial, and Sociocultural Viewpoints

Paul Goesch, *Dream Fantasy*. Goesch, a native of East Germany, made his name both as an architect and as a painter. After several years of successful architectural practice, he quit to devote all his time to painting. He was institutionalized in 1921 and lived in psychiatric institutions until 1940, when he was murdered by the Nazis.

We have a strong tendency to look for explanations, to seek final answers. Even in the most exact of the scientific disciplines, however, we rarely find ultimate answers. In the preceding chapter, for example, we examined many interpretations developed over the centuries to explain the sources of deviant behavior, from beliefs in supernatural possession to theories of naturally occurring factors. Alternative viewpoints of the causes and treatments of abnormal behavior emerge because no single existing approach sufficiently accounts for or explains abnormal behavior. Different perspectives develop in an effort to better explain the complex phenomena under study. Each of these viewpoints focuses on important facets of behavior, though each falls short of standing alone as the "complete" explanation. In this chapter, we will look at several viewpoints that dominate today's approaches to understanding abnormal behavior and that form the basis for the types of therapy we will discuss in Chapters 17 and 18. All these viewpoints derive from the events described in Chapter 2, and, since we can expect them to continue evolving to meet new ideas and discoveries, they may well represent tomorrow's "history."

Students are often perplexed by the fact that, in the behavioral sciences, there are several competing explanations for the same thing. In general, the more complex the phenomena being investigated, the greater the number of viewpoints that emerge, all attempting to explain the phenomena. Inevitably, not all these viewpoints will be equally valid. As you will see, the applicability of a viewpoint is often determined by the extent to which it helps an observer understand a given phenomenon.

Clearly, the viewpoints to be discussed here help many professionals explore abnormal behavior. They help people understand disorders on three broad fronts: their clinical pictures (the symptoms of the disorders), their causal factors, and their treatments. In each case, these orientations help people organize the observations they have made, provide a system of thought in which to place the observed data, and suggest areas of focus. They can also blind people to evidence that may call for a change of orientation.

Typically, theoretical orientations in science retain a strong hold over their adherents, even in the face of disconfirming evidence and alternative explanations of observable phenomena. They do so until some new insight is achieved that resolves the problems left unsolved by the conflicting interpretations of the empirical data. These new insights constitute *paradigm shifts,* fundamental reorganizations of how people think about an entire field of science (Kuhn, 1962).

Sigmund Freud, for example, was responsible for a major shift in the focus of abnormal psychology; later, as seems to be the ultimate fate of all such shifts, major aspects of Freud's theory came under attack. Though we cannot yet say with certainty where the next paradigm shift will take us, it appears likely that the biological viewpoint will have significant impact. Let us hope, however, that adherents of a biological perspective have learned from their predecessors. Recall that during the mental hygiene movement many believed that a biological cure-all for mental illness would be found; thus psychosocial or sociocultural efforts to treat abnormal behavior were put on the back burner. We are still waiting for this biological "cure." Though today we can be more certain that biology will play a major role in the treatment of many behavior disorders, we know, too, that if the biological viewpoint is to become a dominant force, its adherents need to incorporate into its tenets a variety of well-established findings in the psychosocial and sociocultural areas.

Many researchers and practitioners in abnormal psychology do not subscribe to a single view or theoretical perspective. Rather, they take an *eclectic* approach, drawing on what they see as the best principles or techniques from two or more viewpoints. This approach seems to work better in practice than in theory; regardless, it reflects a growing trend by some practitioners not to be bound to any one viewpoint. We will return to this issue in the Unresolved Issues section of this chapter.

But first we must understand the major viewpoints of abnormal behavior. Our survey will be descriptive, comprehensive, and, we hope, objective. We do not intend to advocate one viewpoint over another; rather, we will present information about the structure and ideology of each perspective. It will be up to you to decide on your particular preference, if any, as you become more knowledgeable about the field. We will first consider the biological viewpoint. From there we will move on to several psychosocial approaches, including the psychodynamic, behavioristic, cognitive-behavioral, humanistic, and interpersonal perspectives. We will look briefly, too, at the sociocultural viewpoint and the importance of accounting for traits that stem from being reared in a cultural background different from the majority culture. Finally, in this chapter's Unresolved Issues section, we will investigate avenues leading toward the integration of theories.

THE BIOLOGICAL VIEWPOINT

Many professionals in the field, especially those with biological backgrounds, focus on the biophysical processes that have gone awry in affected people. This approach represents the **biological viewpoint.** In its most extreme form, this viewpoint, also referred to as the **medical model,** focuses on mental disorder as a medical disease, the primary symptoms of which are behavioral rather than physiological or anatomical. Mental disorder is thus viewed as a disease of the central nervous system that is either inherited or caused by some brain pathology. Neither psychological factors nor the psychosocial environment of an individual are believed to play a causal role in the mental disorder. A less extreme version of the biological viewpoint allows for other causal factors but focuses on the biochemical processes that have become imbalanced (for whatever reason) and are disrupting the normal behavior of an individual. These two versions of the biological viewpoint mirror, respectively, the early and more recent developments in the field, which are discussed in the following sections.

The Roots of the Biological Viewpoint

We can look far back into our history (as we did in Chapter 2) and find individuals who suspected that organic factors played a role in psychopathology. To find the more direct roots of our current views, however, we need not look back very far.

The Establishment of Brain Pathology as a Causal Factor With the emergence of modern experimental science in the early part of the eighteenth century, knowledge of anatomy, physiology, neurology, chemistry, and general medicine increased rapidly. These advances led to the gradual identification of the biological, or organic, pathology underlying many physical ailments. Scientists began to focus on diseased body organs as the cause of physical ailments. It was only another step for these people to assume that mental disorder was an illness based on the pathology of an organ—in this case, the brain.

In 1757 Albrecht von Haller (1708–1777), in his *Elements of Physiology,* emphasized the importance of the brain in psychic functions and advocated postmortem dissection to study the brains of the insane. The first systematic presentation of this viewpoint, however, was made by the German psychiatrist Wilhelm Griesinger (1817–1868). In his textbook *The Pathology and Therapy of Psychic Disorders,* published in 1845, Griesinger insisted that all mental disorders could be explained in terms of brain pathology.

During this time, scientists discovered the organic cause of general paresis, which we discussed in Chapter 2. Other successes followed. The brain pathology in cerebral arteriosclerosis and in the senile mental disorders was established by Alois Alzheimer and other investigators. Eventually, the organic pathologies underlying the toxic mental disorders (those severe mental disorders caused by toxic substances such as lead), certain types of mental retardation, and other mental illnesses were discovered.

It is important to note here that although the discovery of the organic bases of mental disorders may have addressed the *how* behind causation, it did not, in most cases, address the question of *why.* This situation is sometimes true to this day. For example, although we know what causes certain "presenile" mental disorders—brain pathology—we do not yet know why some individuals are afflicted and others not. Nonetheless, we can predict quite accurately the courses of these disorders. This ability is due not only to a greater understanding of the organic factors involved, but also, in large part, to the work of a follower of Griesinger, Emil Kraepelin (1856–1926).

Emil Kraepelin (1856–1926), by integrating clinical data, worked out one of the first systematic classification systems, a forerunner of the modern DSM-III-R.

The Beginnings of a Classification System Kraepelin played a dominant role in the early development of the biological viewpoint. His textbook, *Lehrbuch der Psychiatrie,* published in 1883, not only emphasized the importance of brain pathology in mental disorders but also made several related contributions that helped establish this viewpoint. The most important of these contributions was his system of classification, which became the forerunner of today's DSM-III-R (discussed in Chapter 1). Kraepelin noted that certain symptom patterns occurred regularly enough to be regarded as specific types of mental disease. He then proceeded to describe and clarify these types of mental disorders, working out a scheme of classification that is the basis of our present system. The integration of the clinical material underlying this classification was a herculean task and represented a major contribution to the field of psychopathology.

Kraepelin saw each type of mental disorder as separate and distinct from the others and thought that the course of each was as predetermined and predictable as the course of measles. Thus the outcome of a given type of disorder could presumably be predicted even if it could not yet be controlled. Such conclusions led to widespread interest in the accurate description and classification of mental disorders.

Advances Achieved as a Result of Early Biological Views Although early biologically based thinking was perhaps too widely adopted before its limitations were recognized, it represented the first great advance of modern science toward the understanding and treatment of mental disorder. In turn, there was an enormous research effort to discover specific causes of disorders that would yield to specific medical treatments; researchers looked for damage or disease in particular sections of the brain to find the causes underlying different disorders. Such efforts necessarily involved differentiating various forms of abnormality, leading to a promising system for classifying separate disorders. These were substantial accomplishments.

Not all of the consequences of this early thinking were positive, however. Because the disorders best understood in terms of then-available knowledge were ones in which brain damage or deterioration were a central feature (as in general paresis), there naturally developed an expectation that all abnormal behavior would eventually be explained by reference to gross brain pathology. To be sure, organic mental disorders do occur (and we will describe them in Chapter 13), but the vast majority of abnormal behavior is not clearly associated with physical damage to brain tissue. Nonetheless, the medical model—a conceptual model that is inappropriate for much abnormal behavior—became stubbornly entrenched by these early but limited successes.

It is important to note that a medical-model orientation is not limited to biological viewpoints on the nature of mental disorder. It has also extended into psychosocial theorizing by adopting a *symptom/underlying-cause* point of view. This point of view assumes that abnormal behavior, even though it may be psychological (rather than biological) in nature, is a symptom of some sort of underlying, internal pathology or "illness"—just as a fever is a symptom of an underlying infection. As we will discuss later in the chapter, Freud, who was a physician, took this approach in developing his psychoanalytic theory of abnormal behavior.

Modern Biological Thinking

As we have discussed, the disorders first recognized as having biological or organic components were those associated with gross destruction of brain tissue. These disorders were *neurological diseases*—that is, they resulted from the disruption of brain functioning by physical or chemical means and often involved a psychological or behavioral aberration. We should distinguish between neurological diseases and the abnormal mental states (such as delusions) that sometimes accompany them; neurological damage does not necessarily result in abnormal behavior.

Likewise, bizarre thought content is probably never, in itself, the direct result of brain damage. Clearly, a neurologically damaged person will have many challenges to overcome, and these challenges will probably be all the more difficult because of his or her limited cognitive resources for coping with them. Such a person's behavioral *impairment* (such as memory loss) is readily accounted for by structural damage to the brain, but it is not so apparent how such damage produces the sometimes bizarre *content* of the person's behavior. For example, we can understand how the loss of neurons in general paresis could lead to difficulties in executing certain tasks, but the fact that an individual claims to be Napoleon is not likely to be the result simply of a loss of neurons. So far as we know, there are no "I am (or am not) Napoleon" neurons in the brain. Such behavior must be the product of some sort of functional integration of many different neural structures, some of which have been "programmed" by past experience.

In addition, many conditions temporarily disrupt the information-processing capabilities of the brain without inflicting permanent damage or death to the neural cells involved—for example, brain inflammation or high fever. In these cases, normal functioning is altered by the context (especially the chemical context) in which the neural cells operate. The most routine example here is alcohol intoxication. In this condition, behavior that would normally be inhibited is given free rein, only to be regretted the morning after.

In sum, we now realize that many processes short of brain damage can affect the functional capacity of the brain and thus change behavior. Adequate brain functioning is dependent on the efficiency with which an excited nerve cell, or neuron, can transmit its "message" across a synapse to the next neuron in an established pathway in the brain. These interneuronal (or transsynaptic) transmissions are accomplished by chemicals called **neurotransmitters** that are released into the synaptic gap by the presynaptic neuron (see *HIGHLIGHT 3.1* on page 61). Some neurotransmitters increase the likelihood that the postsynaptic neuron will "fire" (produce an impulse), while others inhibit the impulse. Whether or not the neural message is successfully transmitted to the postsynaptic neuron depends on the concentration of certain neurotransmitters within the synaptic cleft. This situation can be complicated by the fact that the cleft is normally bathed in various other biochemical substances that may or may not have transmitter properties. The belief that *biochemical imbalances* in the brain can result in abnormal behavior is the basic tenet of the biological perspective today. Some adherents of this view even suggest that psychological stress can bring on biochemical imbalances.

We will now look briefly at two key areas of research surrounding biochemical imbalances that are contributing to the resurgence of the biological viewpoint: (a) behavior genetics and (b) biophysical therapies. We will then discuss these topics in relation to causal factors in Chapter 4.

Behavior Genetics Genes affect biochemical processes and thereby the structure and physiologic functioning of organisms. Though behavior is never determined exclusively by genes, organisms are genetically programmed through biochemical processes to adapt, physically and behaviorally, to their environments. In general, the more complex the organism, the greater its built-in capacity to meet and overcome the challenges of its environment. It requires little imagination to suppose that because of genetic endowment, some humans have a greater or lesser adaptive capacity than others. This idea has many unfortunate sociopolitical and racial overtones, and it has occasionally been misused by both scientists and politicians. Nonetheless, substantial evidence shows that some mental disorders have a hereditary component. The genetic transmission of traits from one generation to the next is, by definition, a biological process. Thus, the many recent studies suggesting that heredity is an important causal factor in several disorders, particularly depression and schizophrenia (Neale & Oltmanns, 1980; Paykel, 1982a) and alcoholism (Cloninger et al., 1986; Li et al., 1987), support the biological viewpoint.

We are still far from understanding the extent to which genetically determined hormone levels influence human behavioral tendencies. Our most advanced knowledge in this area has to do with gender-related behaviors. Building on the earlier work of Money and Ehrhardt (1972), several investigators have convincingly reported that the brain pathways that determine behavior in males and females differ in certain ways because chromosomal differences cause each sex to produce different hormones or hormone levels (Ehrhardt & Meyer-Bahlburg, 1981; MacLusky & Naftolin, 1981; McEwen, 1981; Rubin, Reinisch, & Haskett, 1981).

It also seems possible that many broad temperamental features of newborns and children are genetically determined—for example, social introversion. Some characteristics also appear to be both familial and consistent over time. In an extensive study of identical twins reared apart being conducted at the University of Minnesota, Bouchard and his colleagues (1990) concluded that a great many psychological characteristics had a high genetic component. For example, their data suggested that about 70 percent of the variation in people's intelligence could be attributed to genetic endowment. Moreover, they also reported that personality characteristics had considerably more of a genetic basis than had been believed before. They concluded that

for almost every behavioral trait so far investigated, from reaction time to religiosity, an important fraction of the variation among people turns out to be associated with genetic variation. . . . We infer that the diverse cultural agents of our society, in particular most parents, are less effective in imprinting their distinctive stamp on the children developing within their spheres of influence—or are less inclined to do so—than has been supposed. (p. 227)

The idea that temperament affects mental health is an ancient one, and it is a key element in the modern biological approach to mental disorders. The importance of genetic factors in forming adult personality has been demonstrated in a study by Pogue-Geile and Rose (1985). They used a longitudinal research design with college-aged twins to study genetic factors in personality. The research group initially identified 203 same-sex

This set of identical twins from Bouchard's University of Minnesota study of the roles of genetics versus environment provides some striking support for the prominence of the genetic influence. Jim Springer (left) and Jim Lewis (right) were separated four weeks after their birth in 1940. They grew up 45 miles apart in Ohio. After they were reunited in 1979, they discovered they had some eerie similarities: both chain-smoked Salems, both drove the same model blue Chevrolet, both chewed their fingernails, and both had dogs named Toy. Further, they had both vacationed in the same neighborhood in Florida. When tested for such personality traits as sociability and self-control, they responded almost identically.

twins from the undergraduate population at Indiana University. The researchers then determined which twins were identical and conducted preliminary psychological testing, using the Minnesota Multiphasic Personality Inventory (MMPI), to assess their personalities. They initially tested 101 identical pairs and 102 nonidentical pairs. The researchers retested the twins 4½ years later to determine the consistency of personality factors over time. They were able to obtain complete follow-up MMPIs on 133 twin pairs (71 identical pairs of which 25 pairs were male, and 62 nonidentical pairs of which 24 pairs were male). The researchers found that genetic inheritance, as measured by the differences between the identical and nonidentical twins, was related to the performance of individuals on several personality dimensions (particularly social maladjustment, depression, unusual thinking, and anxiety). Even here, however, the biological factor did not operate alone. Different environmental experiences appeared to have important mediating effects on personality, shown by the similar results on personality measures for many pairs of both nonidentical and identical twins.

Biophysical Therapies With few exceptions, advances in the understanding and treatment of mental disorders languished during the first third of this century. At the same time, discharge rates from mental hospitals declined and resident populations of such hospitals rose at an alarming pace. These trends were due to a simple fact: the medical model of abnormal behavior had not fulfilled its promise. Biological interventions based on theories such as the nutritional or infectious basis of mental disorders had not proven successful at curing large numbers of patients (Valenstein, 1986).

Then, beginning in the 1930s, new therapies were introduced that produced significant behavioral changes in some patients. One of these then-revolutionary techniques, electroconvulsive therapy (ECT), is still in use today. ECT produces a convulsion in a patient by passing an electric current through his or her brain. In certain instances, this treatment results in a patient's prompt return to normal functioning. How electroconvulsive therapy works is still not fully understood, although some promising research has been done in this area (Abrams & Essman, 1982). It is generally believed that the loss of consciousness produced by the electrical current produces a confused state that disrupts previously disturbing thoughts, thereby allowing a patient to "reconstruct" his or her thinking along more adaptive lines. Biologically speaking, the electric current presumably disrupts the biochemistry of the brain and somehow returns it to a more appropriate biochemical balance. Though more will be said about ECT and other biological treatment approaches in Chapter 17, we should point out here that ECT is considered an extreme form of therapy and is quite controversial today.

More importantly, since the 1950s we have witnessed many new and often dramatic developments in the use of drugs to treat mental disorders —in particular, the more severe ones. In contrast to the situation with ECT, we have a good understanding of how these medications produce their beneficial effects. We know at least to some extent what biochemical changes are caused by taking these drugs, and we can evaluate those effects by noting behavioral changes that occur with a patient. For example, phenothiazines are known to reduce confused thinking and block intrusive thoughts. We can evaluate such changes by determining a patient's altered modes of thinking following various dosages of the medication. As we will see throughout this text, research on the mediating effects of medications have led to many intriguing hypotheses about the chemical imbalances that accompany, and may be causally related to, various disorders. Most of these hypotheses are concerned with the nature of neurotransmission, which is graphically depicted in *HIGHLIGHT 3.1.*

The Impact of the Biological Viewpoint

Biological discoveries have profoundly affected the way we think about human behavior. We now recognize the important role of biochemical factors and innate characteristics, many of which are genetically determined, in both normal and abnormal behavior.

The host of new drugs that dramatically and quickly alter the severity and course of certain mental disorders has brought renewed attention to the biological viewpoint, not only in scientific circles but also in the popular media. Biological treatments seem to have more immediate results than other available therapies, and the hope is that they may in most cases lead to a "cure-all"—immediate results with seemingly little effort.

However, we must remind ourselves again that few, if any, mental afflictions are independent of people's personalities or of the problems they face in trying to live their lives. We will examine viewpoints that emphasize these psychosocial and sociocultural considerations in the pages that follow. Keep in mind that many clinicians and researchers are eclectic in practice: they incorporate seemingly different

HIGHLIGHT 3.1

Neurotransmission and Abnormal Behavior

The synapse is the action site for several therapies used in combating abnormal behavior. The axonal endings of one neuron lie near the dendritic endings of the next neuron. As an impulse reaches the end of its axon, it stimulates the release of neurotransmitters. The neurotransmitters are released through the terminal portion of the axon into the space between the axon and the dendrite of the next neuron. The neurotransmitters thus stimulate that dendrite to initiate an impulse. The neurotransmitters are quickly destroyed by an enzyme, such as monoamine oxidase, or they are returned to storage vesicles in the axonal button by a "reuptake" mechanism, so that the second neuron does not continue firing in the absence of a real impulse. Certain medications act to increase or decrease the concentrations of pertinent neurotransmitters in the synaptic gap.

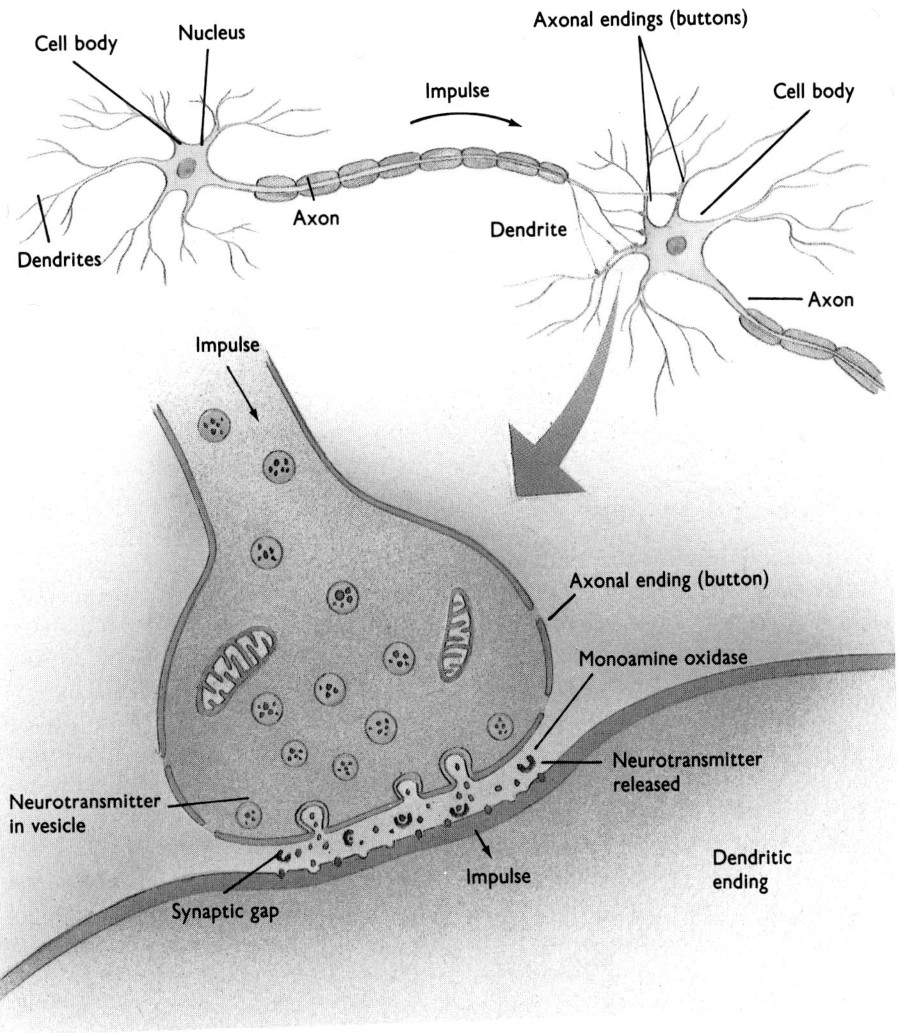

elements of biological, psychological, and sociocultural viewpoints in their work. One problem, however, is that eclecticism is easier in practice than in theory. The challenge remains to integrate these varying perspectives into a theoretically consistent general system of psychopathology. We will return to this challenge in more depth in this chapter's Unresolved Issues section.

THE PSYCHOSOCIAL VIEWPOINTS

There are many more psychosocial interpretations of abnormal behavior than biological ones, reflecting the difficulty of understanding humans as people and not just as biological organisms. The following sections will examine five perspectives on human nature and behavior: psychodynamic, behavioristic, cognitive-behavioral, humanistic, and interpersonal. Although these viewpoints represent distinct and sometimes conflicting orientations, they are in many ways complementary. All of them emphasize the importance of early experience and an awareness of social influences and psychological processes within an individual—hence the term **psychosocial viewpoints** as a general descriptive label.

The Psychodynamic Perspective

The first steps toward understanding psychological factors in mental disorders were taken by Sigmund Freud (1856–1939). During five decades of observation, treatment, and writing, Freud developed a theory of psychopathology that emphasized the inner dynamics of unconscious motives, called the **psychoanalytic perspective.** The methods he used to study and treat patients are called **psychoanalysis.** Over the last half century, other clinicians have modified and revised Freud's theory, resulting in new **psychodynamic perspectives.** These perspectives contain many of the same assumptions and viewpoints as Freud's original theory, but they differ from classical psychoanalysis in some important respects (for example, Adler rejected Freud's emphasis on sexuality in favor of social motivation). We will review some of these perspectives later in this section.

In reviewing the psychodynamic perspective, we will divide our discussion into an examination of (a) the roots of psychodynamic thought, (b) Freud and the beginnings of psychoanalysis, (c) the basic principles of psychoanalysis, (d) newer psychodynamic perspectives, and (e) the impact of the psychodynamic perspective on our views of human nature.

The Roots of Psychodynamic Thought

We find the roots of psychoanalysis in a somewhat unexpected place—the study of hypnosis, especially in its relation to hysteria. Hypnosis, an induced state of relaxation in which an individual is highly open to suggestion, first came into widespread use in late eighteenth- and early nineteenth-century France.

Mesmerism. Our story starts with Anton Mesmer (1734–1815), a German physician who further developed Paracelsus' ideas about the influence of the planets on the human body (see Chapter 2). Mesmer believed that the planets affected a universal magnetic fluid in the body, the distribution of which determined health or disease. In attempting to find cures for mental disorders, Mesmer concluded that all people possessed magnetic forces that could be used to influence the distribution of the magnetic fluid in other people, thus effecting cures.

Mesmer attempted to put his views into practice in Vienna and various other towns, but it was in Paris in 1778 that he gained a broad following. There he opened a clinic in which he treated all kinds of diseases by "animal magnetism." In a dark room, patients were seated around a tub (a *baquet*) containing various chemicals, and iron rods protruding from the tub were applied to the affected areas of the patients' bodies. Accompanied by music, Mesmer appeared in a lilac robe, passing from one patient to another and touching each one with his hands or his wand. By this means, Mesmer was reportedly able to remove hysterical anesthesias and paralyses. He also demonstrated most of the phenomena later connected with the use of hypnosis.

Eventually branded a charlatan by his medical colleagues, Mesmer was forced to leave Paris and he quickly faded into obscurity. His methods and results, however, were at the center of scientific controversy for many years—in fact, **mesmerism,** as his technique came to be known, was as much a source of heated discussion in the early nineteenth century as psychoanalysis became in the early twentieth century. This discussion led to a renewed interest in hypnosis itself as an explanation of the "cures" that took place.

The Nancy School. Liébeault (1823–1904), a French physician who practiced in the town of Nancy, used hypnosis successfully in his practice.

Anton Mesmer believed that the distribution of magnetic fluid in the body was responsible for determining health or disease. He further thought that all people possessed magnetic forces that could be used to influence the distribution of fluid in others, thus effecting cures. In this painting of Mesmeric therapy, Mesmer stands at the back, on the right, holding a wand. Mesmer was eventually branded a fraud by his colleagues, but he did demonstrate most of the phenomena later connected with the use of hypnosis.

Also in Nancy at the time was a professor of medicine, Bernheim (1840–1919), who became interested in the relationship between hysteria and hypnosis. His interest was the result of Liébeault's success in curing by hypnosis a patient who Bernheim had been treating unsuccessfully by more conventional methods for four years (Selling, 1943). Bernheim and Liébeault worked together to develop the hypothesis that hypnotism and hysteria were related and that both were due to suggestion (Brown & Menninger, 1940). Their hypothesis was based on two lines of evidence: (a) phenomena observed in hysteria, such as paralysis of an arm, inability to hear, or anesthetic areas in which an individual could be stuck with a pin without feeling pain (all of which occurred when there was apparently nothing organically wrong), could be produced in normal subjects by means of hypnosis; and (b) the same symptoms also could be removed by means of hypnosis. Thus it seemed likely that hysteria was a sort of self-hypnosis. The physicians who accepted this view ultimately came to be known as the **Nancy School.**

Meanwhile, Jean Charcot (1825–1893), who was head of the Salpêtrière Hospital in Paris and the leading neurologist of his time, had been experimenting with some of the phenomena described by the mesmerists. As a result of his research, Charcot disagreed with the findings of the Nancy School and insisted that degenerative brain changes led to hysteria. In this, Charcot was eventually proved wrong, but work on the problem by so outstanding a scientist did a great deal to awaken medical and scientific interest in hysteria.

The dispute between Charcot and the Nancy School was one of the major debates of medical history, during which many harsh words were spoken on both sides. The adherents of the Nancy School finally triumphed, representing the first recognition of a psychologically caused mental disorder. This recognition spurred more research on the behavior underlying hysteria and other disor-

It took some time before Jean Charcot (1825–1893), the leading neurologist of his time, believed that there might be a causal relationship between self-hypnosis and hysteria. Once convinced, however, he did much, through research and lectures about hypnosis, such as the one shown here, to promote interest in the role psychological factors may play in mental disorders.

ders. Soon the data suggested that psychological factors were also involved in anxiety states, phobias, and other psychopathologies. Eventually, Charcot himself was won over to the new point of view and did much to promote the study of psychological factors in various mental disorders.

The debate as to whether mental disorders are caused by biological or psychological factors continues to this day. The Nancy School/Charcot debate represented a major step forward for psychology, however. Toward the end of the nineteenth century, it was clear that mental disorders could have either psychological bases or biological bases, or both. With this recognition, a major question remained to be answered: How do the psychologically based mental disorders actually develop?

The Beginnings of Psychoanalysis The first systematic attempt to answer this question was made by Sigmund Freud. Freud was a brilliant young Viennese physician who specialized in neurology and received an appointment as lecturer on nervous diseases at the University of Vienna. In 1885 he went to study under Charcot and later became acquainted with the work of Liébeault and Bernheim at Nancy. He was impressed by their use of hypnosis with hysterical patients and came away convinced that powerful mental processes could remain hidden from consciousness.

On his return to Vienna, Freud worked in collaboration with another physician, Joseph Breuer (1842–1925), who had introduced an interesting innovation in the use of hypnosis with his patients. Unlike hypnotists before him, he directed his patients to talk freely about their problems while under hypnosis. The patients usually displayed considerable emotion, and on awakening from their hypnotic states felt considerably relieved. Because of the emotional release involved, this method was called **catharsis.** This simple innovation in the use of hypnosis proved to be of great significance: it not only helped patients discharge their emotional tensions by discussing their problems, but it also revealed to the therapist the nature of the difficulties that had brought about certain symptoms. The patients, upon awakening, saw no relationship between their problems and their hysterical symptoms.

Thus was made the discovery of **the unconscious**—that portion of the mind that contains experiences of which a person is unaware—and with it the belief that processes outside of a person's awareness can play an important role in the determination of behavior. In 1893 Freud and Breuer published their joint paper, *On the Psychical Mechanisms of Hysterical Phenomena,* which was one of the great milestones in the study of psychodynamics.

Freud soon discovered, moreover, that he could dispense with hypnosis entirely. By encouraging patients to say whatever came into their minds without regard to logic or propriety, Freud found that patients would eventually overcome inner obstacles to remembering and would discuss their problems freely. Two related methods allowed him to understand patients' conscious and unconscious

Sigmund Freud (1856–1939), the founder of psychoanalysis, emphasized the role of unconscious processes in the determination of behavior. He abandoned the use of hypnosis for the techniques of free association and dream analysis to help patients achieve insight into their problems.

Joseph Breuer (1842–1925) used the cathartic method to help patients discharge emotional tensions by discussing their problems. The discussion would usually reveal the nature of the difficulties that had brought about neurotic symptoms.

thought processes. One method, **free association,** involved having patients talk freely about themselves, thereby providing information about their feelings, motives, and so forth. A second method, **dream analysis,** involved having patients record and describe their dreams. These techniques helped analysts and patients gain insights and achieve a more adequate understanding of emotional problems.

Freud devoted the rest of his long and energetic life to the development and elaboration of psychoanalytic principles. His views were formally introduced to American scientists in 1909, when he was invited to deliver a series of lectures at Clark University by the eminent psychologist, G. Stanley Hall, who was then president of the university. These *Introductory Lectures on Psychoanalysis* created a great deal of controversy and helped popularize psychoanalytic concepts among scientists as well as the general public.

The Basics of Psychoanalysis The actual techniques involved in psychoanalysis are based on the general principles underlying Freud's theory of personality; they are very complex. We shall not attempt to deal with them in detail here. For our purposes, a general overview of the principles of classical psychoanalysis should suffice. For those wishing more information, good resources include Alexander's (1948) *Fundamentals of Psychoanalysis* or any of Freud's original works.

Id, ego, and superego. Freud theorized that an individual's behavior results from the interaction of three key parts or subsystems within the personality or psyche: the id, ego, and superego.

The **id** is the source of instinctual drives, which are inherited and considered to be of two opposing types: (a) *life instincts,* which are constructive drives primarily of a sexual nature, and which constitute the **libido,** the basic energy of life; and (b) *death instincts,* which are destructive drives that tend toward aggression, destruction, and eventual death. Freud used the term *sexual* in a broad sense to refer to almost anything pleasurable, from eating to painting. The id is completely selfish, concerned only with the immediate gratification of instinctual needs without reference to reality or moral considerations. Hence it is said to operate in terms of the **pleasure principle.** While the id can generate mental images and wish-fulfilling fantasies, referred to as the **primary process,** it cannot undertake the realistic actions needed to meet instinctual demands.

Consequently, a second part of the personality, as viewed by Freud, develops—the **ego.** The ego mediates between the demands of the id and the realities of the external world. The basic purpose of the ego is to meet id demands, but in such a way as to ensure the well-being and survival of an individual. This role requires the use of reason and other intellectual resources in dealing with the external world, as well as the exercise of control over id

During his only visit to the United States, in 1909, Freud delivered a series of lectures to American scientists at Clark University. Among those in the front row here are William James (third from the left), G. Stanley Hall (sixth from the left), Freud (seventh), and Carl Jung (eighth).

demands. The ego's adaptive measures are referred to as the **secondary process,** and the ego is said to operate in terms of the **reality principle.** Freud viewed id demands, especially sexual and aggressive strivings, as inherently in conflict with the rules and prohibitions imposed by society.

Since the id-ego relationship is merely one of expediency, Freud postulated a third key subsystem—the **superego.** The superego is the outgrowth of the taboos and moral values of society. It is essentially what we refer to as the *conscience;* it is concerned with right and wrong. As the superego develops, it becomes an additional inner control system that copes with the uninhibited desires of the id. The superego also operates through the ego system and strives to compel the ego to inhibit desires that are considered wrong or immoral.

Freud believed that the interplay of id, ego, and superego is of crucial significance in determining behavior. Often, inner conflicts arise because the three subsystems are striving for different goals. These conflicts are called **intrapsychic conflicts** and, if unresolved, lead to mental disorder.

Anxiety, defense mechanisms, and the unconscious. The concept of anxiety—generalized feelings of fear and apprehension—is prominent in the psychoanalytic viewpoint. Freud distinguished among three types of anxiety, or "psychic pain," that people can suffer: (a) *reality anxiety,* arising from dangers or threats in the external world; (b) *neurotic anxiety,* caused by the id's impulses threatening to break through ego controls into behavior that will be punished in some way; and (c) *moral anxiety,* arising from a real or contemplated action that is in conflict with an individual's superego and thus arouses feelings of guilt.

Anxiety is a warning of impending danger as well as a painful experience, so it forces an individual to take corrective action. Often, the ego can cope with anxiety through rational measures; if these do not suffice, however, the ego resorts to irrational protective measures that are referred to as **ego-defense mechanisms** and are described in *HIGHLIGHT 3.2.*

These defense mechanisms discharge or soothe anxiety, but they do so by helping an individual push painful ideas out of consciousness rather than by dealing directly with a problem. For the individual, this results in a distorted view of reality.

A key concept of psychoanalytic principles, as we have seen, is the *unconscious.* Freud thought that the conscious part of the mind represents a relatively small area, while the unconscious part, like the submerged part of an iceberg, is the much larger portion. In the depths of the unconscious are the hurtful memories, forbidden desires, and other experiences that have been *repressed*—that is, pushed out of consciousness. Unconscious material continues to seek expression when ego controls are temporarily lowered under hypnosis, or in fantasies, dreams, slips of the tongue, and so forth. Until such unconscious material is brought to awareness and integrated into the ego structure—for example, through psychoanalysis—it presumably leads to irrational and maladaptive behavior.

Psychosexual stages of development. Freud conceptualized five **psychosexual stages of development.** Each stage is characterized by a dominant mode of achieving libidinal (sexual) pleasure:

- *The oral stage.* During the first two years of life, the mouth is the principal erogenous zone; an infant's greatest source of gratification is sucking.
- *The anal stage.* From age 2 to age 3, the membranes of the anal region provide the major source of pleasurable stimulation.
- *The phallic stage.* From age 3 to age 5 or 6, self-manipulation of the genitals provides the major source of pleasurable sensation.
- *The latency stage.* In the years from 6 to 12, sexual motivations recede in importance as a child becomes preoccupied with developing skills and other activities.
- *The genital stage.* After puberty the deepest feelings of pleasure come from heterosexual relations.

Freud believed that appropriate gratification during each stage is important if an individual is not to be *fixated* at that level. For example, he maintained that an infant who does not receive adequate oral gratification may be prone to excessive eating or drinking in adult life.

In general, each stage of development places demands on an individual and arouses conflicts that must be resolved. One of the most important conflicts occurs during the phallic stage, when the pleasures of self-stimulation and accompanying fantasies pave the way for the **Oedipus complex.** Oedipus, according to Greek mythology, unknowingly killed his father and married his mother. Each young boy, Freud thought, symbolically relives the Oedipus drama. He has incestuous cravings for his mother and views his father as a hated rival; however, he also fears his father and especially is afraid that his father may harm him by removing his penis. This **castration anxiety** forces the boy to repress his sexual desire for his mother and his hostility toward his father. Eventually, if all goes well, the boy identifies with his father and comes to have only harmless affection for his mother.

The **Electra complex** is the female counterpart of the Oedipus complex. It is based on the view that each girl experiences penis envy and wants to possess her father and replace her mother. While the boy renounces his lust out of fear of castration, no such threat can realistically be posed for the girl. Her emergence from the complex is more mild and less complete than the boy's. She essentially settles for a promissory note: one day she will have a man of her own who can give her a baby—a type of penis substitute.

For either sex, resolution of this conflict is considered essential if a young adult is to develop satisfactory heterosexual relationships. In short, the psychoanalytic perspective holds that about the best we can hope for is a compromise among our warring inclinations, from which we will realize as much instinctual gratification as possible with minimal punishment and guilt. It thus presents a pessimistic and deterministic view of human behavior that minimizes rationality and freedom of self-determination. On a group level, it interprets violence, war, and related phenomena as the inevitable products of the aggressive and destructive instincts present in human nature.

The demands of the id are evident in early childhood. According to Freud, babies pass through an oral stage, in which sucking is a dominant pleasure.

HIGHLIGHT 3.2

Summary Chart of Ego-Defense Mechanisms

Mechanism	Example
Denial of reality. Protecting the self from an unpleasant reality by the refusal to perceive or face it.	A smoker concludes that the evidence linking cigarette use to health problems is scientifically worthless.
Fantasy. Gratifying frustrated desires by imaginary achievements.	A socially inept and inhibited young man imagines himself chosen by a group of women to provide them with sexual satisfaction.
Repression. Preventing painful or dangerous thoughts from entering consciousness.	A mother's occasional murderous impulses toward her hyperactive two-year-old are denied access to awareness.
Rationalization. Using contrived "explanations" to conceal or disguise unworthy motives for one's behavior.	A fanatical racist uses ambiguous passages from Scripture to justify his hostile actions toward minorities.
Projection. Attributing one's unacceptable motives or characteristics to others.	An expansionist-minded dictator of a totalitarian state is convinced that neighboring countries are planning to invade.
Reaction formation. Preventing the awareness or expression of unacceptable desires by an exaggerated adoption of seemingly opposite behavior.	A man troubled by homosexual urges initiates a zealous community campaign to stamp out gay bars.
Displacement. Discharging pent-up feelings, often of hostility, on objects less dangerous than those arousing the feelings.	A woman harassed by her boss at work initiates an argument with her husband.
Emotional insulation. Reducing ego involvement by protective withdrawal and passivity.	A child separated from her parents because of illness and lengthy hospitalization becomes emotionally unresponsive and apathetic.
Intellectualization (isolation). Cutting off affective charge from hurtful situations or separating incompatible attitudes by logic-tight compartments.	A prisoner on death row awaiting execution resists appeals on his behalf and coldly insists that the letter of the law be followed.

Newer Psychodynamic Perspectives In seeking to understand his patients and develop his theories, Freud was chiefly concerned with the workings of the id, its nature as a source of energy and the manner in which it could be channeled or transformed. Later theorists, notably including his daughter Anna Freud (1895–1982), were much more concerned with how the ego performed its central functions as the "executive" of personality. This second generation of psychodynamic theorists refined and elaborated on the ego-defense reactions.

Contemporary approaches focus on neither the nature of the id nor the ego, but rather on the objects toward whom the child has directed these impulses and which the child has introjected (incorporated) into his or her own personality. *Object* in this context refers to the symbolic representation of another person in the child's environment, most often a parent. The concept of **introjection,** a difficult one for most students, refers to an internal process in which the child incorporates symbolically, through images and memories, some person viewed with strong emotion. For example, the child might internalize the image of a parent's scowling face. Later, this symbol, or object, can influence how a person experiences events and behaves.

Mechanism	Example
Undoing. Atoning for or magically trying to dispel unacceptable desires or acts.	A teenager who feels guilty about masturbation ritually touches a doorknob a prescribed number of times following each occurrence of the act.
Regression. Retreating to an earlier developmental level involving less mature behavior and responsibility.	A man whose self-esteem has been shattered reverts to childlike "show-off" behavior and exhibits his genitals to young girls.
Identification. Increasing feelings of worth by affiliating oneself with a person or institution of illustrious standing.	A youth-league football coach becomes excessively demanding of his young players in emulation of an authoritarian pro football coach.
Overcompensation. Covering up perceived weaknesses by emphasizing a desirable characteristic or making up for frustration in one area by overgratification in another.	A dangerously overweight woman goes on eating binges when she feels neglected by her husband.
Acting out. Engaging in antisocial or excessive behavior without regard to negative consequences as a way of dealing with emotional stress.	An unhappy, frustrated sales respresentative has several indiscriminate affairs without regard to the negative effects of the behavior.
Splitting. Viewing oneself or others as *all* good or bad without integrating positive or negative qualities into the evaluations; reacting to others in an "all or none" manner rather than considering the full range of their qualities.	A conflicted manager does not recognize individual qualities or characteristics of her employees. Instead, she views them as all good or all bad, seeing most of them as all bad.
Sublimation. Channeling frustrated sexual energy into substitutive activities.	A sexually frustrated artist paints wildly erotic pictures.
Fixation. Attaching oneself in an unreasonable or exaggerated way to some person, or arresting emotional development on a childhood or adolescent level.	An unmarried, middle-aged man still depends on his mother to provide his basic needs.

Based on Anna Freud (1946); DSM-III-R (1987).

The earliest development of this **object-relations** emphasis in psychodynamic thought took place in the 1930s in England under the leadership of Melanie Klein, W. R. D. Fairbairn, and D. W. Winnicott. These theorists developed the general notion that internalized objects could have various conflicting properties—such as exciting or attractive versus hostile, frustrating, or rejecting—and moreover that these objects could split off from the central ego and maintain independent existences, thus giving rise to inner conflicts. For example, a child might internalize images of a punishing father; that image would then become a harsh self-critic. An individual experiencing such splitting among internalized objects is, so to speak, "the servant of many masters" and cannot therefore lead an integrated, orderly life.

The work of Margaret Mahler (1897–1985) in the United States complemented and added additional insights to this approach (see, for example, Mahler, 1976). Mahler pointed out that, for a very young child, objects are not differentiated with respect to self versus other. Only gradually does a child gain an internal representation of self as distinct from representations of other objects. Only gradually is object constancy achieved (in which, for

Anna Freud (1895–1982) elaborated the theory of ego-defense mechanisms and pioneered the psychoanalytic treatment of children.

Margaret Mahler (1897–1985) elaborated the object-relations approach, which many see as the main focus of contemporary psychoanalysis.

instance, the mother of yesterday is seen as the same object as the mother of today). This process involves a developmental phase of **separation-individuation,** the successful completion of which is essential for the achievement of personal maturity.

Many other American analysts have, in recent years, become advocates of the object-relations point of view. Among them is Otto Kernberg, noted especially for his studies of both borderline and narcissistic personalities (see Chapter 7). Kernberg's view is that the borderline personality, whose chief characteristic is instability (especially in personal relationships), is an individual who is unable to achieve a full and stable personal identity (self) because of an inability to integrate and reconcile pathological internalized objects.

These newer developments in psychodynamic therapy emphasize interpersonal relationships and how the quality of early relationships affects a person's subsequent ability to achieve fulfilling adult interactions. These ideas have developed largely independently of the psychodynamic mainstream and have assumed importance in their own right. They will be addressed further in a later section on the interpersonal perspective.

Impact of the Psychodynamic Perspective

In historical perspective, Freudian psychoanalysis can be seen as the first systematic, psychodynamic approach to show how human psychological processes can result in mental disorders. Much as the biological perspective had replaced superstition with organic pathology as the suspected cause of mental disorders, the psychoanalytic perspective replaced brain pathology with exaggerated ego defenses as the suspected cause of at least some mental disorders.

Freud greatly advanced our understanding of both normal and abnormal behavior. Many of his original concepts have become fundamental to our thinking about human nature and behavior. Two of Freud's contributions stand out as particularly noteworthy.

1. He developed techniques such as free association and dream analysis for becoming acquainted with both the conscious and unconscious aspects of mental life. The data thus obtained led Freud to emphasize (a) the dynamic role of unconscious motives and ego-defense processes, (b) the importance of early childhood experiences in later personality adjustment and maladjustment, and (c) the importance of sexual factors in human behavior and mental disorders. Although, as we have said, Freud used the term *sexual* in a much broader sense than usual, the idea struck a common chord, and the role of sexual factors in human behavior was finally brought out into the open as an appropriate topic for scientific investigation.

2. He demonstrated that certain abnormal mental phenomena occur in the attempt to cope with difficult problems and are simply exaggerations of normal ego-defense mechanisms. This realization that the same psychological principles apply to both normal and abnormal behavior dissipated much of the mystery and fear surrounding mental disorders. Patients could be mentally disordered, but could also have dignity as human beings.

The psychodynamic perspective has come under attack from many directions—from other perspectives as well as from theorists within the psychodynamic tradition. Two important criticisms of psychoanalytic theory center around its failure as a scientific theory to explain abnormal behavior. First, it fails to recognize the scientific limits of personal reports of experience as the primary mode of obtaining information. Second, there is a lack of scientific evidence to support many of its explanatory assumptions or the effectiveness of its therapy. Freudian theory in particular has been criticized for an overemphasis on the sex drive; for undue pessimism about basic human nature; for an exaggeration of the role of unconscious processes; and for failing to consider motives toward personal growth and fulfillment. The second generation of psychodynamic theorists did much to overcome these objections. Criticisms surrounding the scientific validity of psychodynamic approaches remain, however. In addition, today's psychodynamic therapies have been criticized for neglecting the role of cultural differences in shaping behavior and because they frequently take months, and even years, to complete, which is very expensive for a client.

The Behavioristic Perspective

While psychoanalysis dominated thought about abnormal behavior in the early part of this century, another school—behaviorism—was emerging to challenge its supremacy. Behavioristic psychologists believed that the study of subjective experience—through the techniques of free association and dream analysis—did not provide acceptable scientific data, because such observations were not open to verification by other investigators. In their view, only the study of directly observable behavior and the stimuli and reinforcing conditions that "control" it could serve as a basis for formulating scientific principles of human behavior.

The **behavioristic perspective** is organized around a central theme: the role of learning in human behavior. Although this perspective was initially developed through research in the laboratory rather than through clinical practice with disturbed individuals, its implications for explaining and treating maladaptive behavior soon became evident.

Roots of the Behavioristic Perspective

The origins of the behavioristic view of abnormal behavior and its treatment are tied to experimental work on the form of stimulus-response learning known as **conditioning.** This work began with the discovery of the conditioned reflex by Russian physiologist Ivan Pavlov (1849–1936). Around the

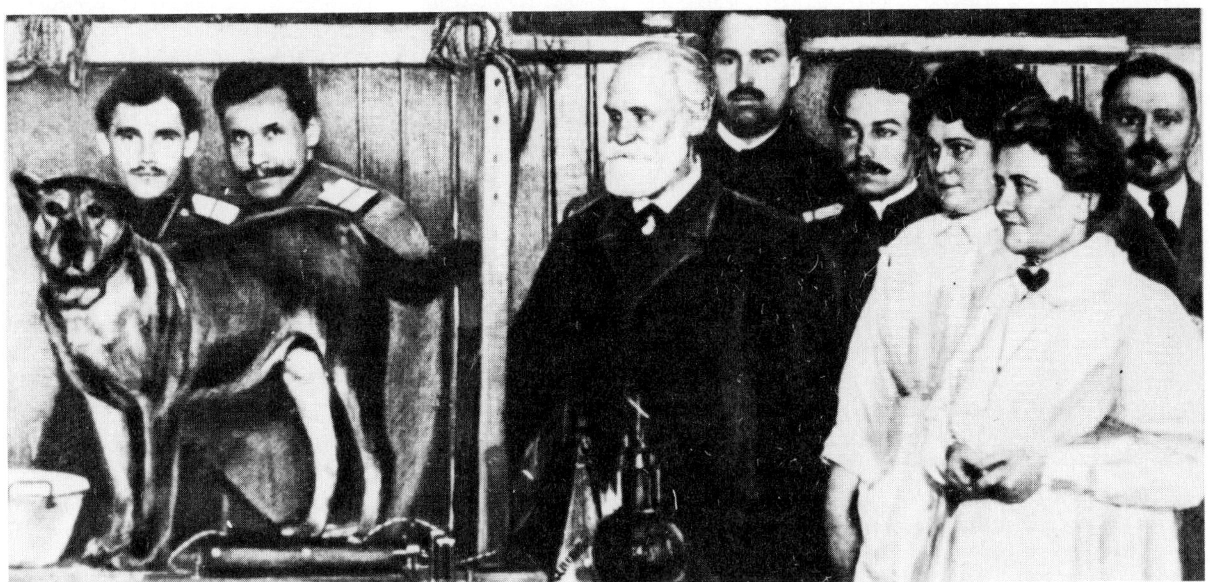

Ivan Pavlov (1849–1936), a pioneer in demonstrating the part conditioning plays in behavior, is shown here with his staff and some of the apparatus used to condition reflexes in dogs.

turn of the century, Pavlov demonstrated that a dog would learn to salivate to a nonfood stimulus, such as a bell, after the stimulus had been regularly accompanied by food.

Pavlov's discovery, which came to be known as *classical conditioning,* excited a young American psychologist, John B. Watson (1878–1958), who was searching for objective ways to study human behavior. Watson reasoned that if psychology were to become a true science, it must abandon the subjectivity of inner sensations and other "mental" events and limit itself to what could be objectively observed. What better way to do this than to observe systematic changes in behavior brought about simply by rearranging stimulus conditions? Watson thus changed the focus of psychology to the study of overt behavior, an approach he called *behaviorism.*

Watson, a man of impressive energy and demeanor, saw great possibilities in behaviorism, and he was quick to point them out to his fellow scientists and a curious public. He boasted that, through conditioning, he could train any healthy child to become whatever sort of adult one wished. He also challenged the psychoanalysts and the more biologically oriented psychologists of his day by suggesting that abnormal behavior was the product of unfortunate, inadvertent earlier conditioning and could be modified through reconditioning.

By the 1930s Watson had made an enormous impact on American psychology. Watson's approach placed heavy emphasis on the role of the social environment in conditioning personality development and behavior, both normal and abnormal. Today's behavioristically oriented psychologists still accept the basic tenets of Watson's doctrine, although they are more cautious in their claims.

While Watson was studying stimulus conditions and their relation to behavioral responses, E. L. Thorndike (1874–1949) and subsequently B. F. Skinner (1904–1990) were exploring the other side of the conditioning coin—the fact that, over time, the consequences of behavior tend to influence behavior. Behavior that *operates* on the environment is *instrumental* in producing certain outcomes, and those outcomes, in turn, determine the likelihood that the behavior will be repeated on similar occasions. This type of learning came to be called *instrumental* or *operant conditioning.*

The principles of conditioning had been worked out enough by 1950 that in that year John Dollard and Neal Miller published their classic work *Personality and Psychotherapy,* which essentially reinterpreted psychoanalytic theory in the terminology of learning principles. In essence they asserted that the ungoverned pleasure-seeking impulses of Freud's id were merely an aspect of the principle of reinforcement (the behavior of all organisms being determined by the maximization of gratification and minimization of pain); that anxiety was merely a conditioned fear response; that repression was

John B. Watson (1878–1958) changed the focus of psychology from the study of inner sensations to the study of outer behavior, an approach called behaviorism.

E. L. Thorndike (1874–1949) formulated the law of effect—a seemingly simple observation that rewarded responses are strengthened and unrewarded responses are weakened—which had implications for controlling human behavior.

B. F. Skinner (1904–1990) formulated the concept of operant conditioning in which reinforcers could be used to make a response more or less probable and frequent.

merely conditioned thought-stoppage; and so on. The groundwork was thus laid for a behavioristic assault on the prevailingly psychodynamic doctrines of the time. Early efforts to apply learning principles in the treatment of abnormal behavior, such as those by Salter (1949) and Wolpe (1958), were met with much resistance by the well-entrenched supporters of psychoanalysis; it was not until the 1960s and 1970s that behavioral therapy became established as a powerful way of viewing and treating abnormal behavior.

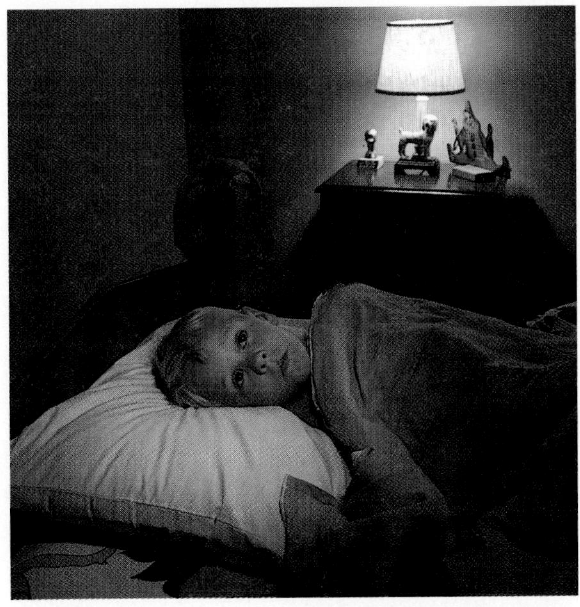

Fear, which is a response of the autonomic nervous system, can be conditioned. Fear of the dark, for example, can be learned if frightening encounters or experiences happen under conditions of darkness.

Basics of the Behavioristic Perspective As we have noted, **learning**—the modification of behavior as a consequence of experience—provides the central theme of the behavioristic approach. Since most human behavior is learned, the behaviorists have addressed themselves to the question of how learning occurs. In trying to answer this question, they have focused on the effects of environmental conditions (stimuli) on the acquisition, modification, and possible elimination of various types of response patterns—both adaptive and maladaptive.

Classical and operant conditioning. A specific stimulus may come to elicit a specific response through the process of **classical conditioning.** For example, although food naturally elicits salivation, any stimulus that reliably precedes the presentation of food will also elicit salivation. In this case, food is the *unconditioned stimulus,* and salivation is the *unconditioned response.* A stimulus that precedes food delivery and eventually elicits salivation is called a *conditioned stimulus.* Conditioning has occurred when presentation of the conditioned stimulus alone elicits salivation (called the *conditioned response*). Pavlov, for instance, sounded a tone (the soon-to-be conditioned stimulus) just before he presented food (the unconditioned stimulus) to his dogs. After several tone-food pairings, the dogs salivated (the conditioned response) to the tone (the conditioned stimulus) alone. The dogs had learned that the tone was a reliable predictor of food delivery. The hallmark of classical conditioning is that the response is elicited by the conditioned stimulus.

The chief importance of classical conditioning in abnormal psychology is the fact that many responses of the autonomic nervous system, including those relating to fear or anxiety, can be conditioned. Thus one can learn a fear of the dark if fear-producing stimuli (such as frightening dreams or fantasies) occur regularly during conditions of darkness.

In **operant (or instrumental) conditioning,** an individual learns how to achieve a desired goal. The goal in question may be to obtain something that is rewarding or to avoid something that is unpleasant. Here a response typically precedes the desired stimulus, as when an individual kicks a coffee machine that has failed to function. If the kick causes the machine to produce coffee, the next time it does not work, the person will probably kick it again. As we grow up, operant learning becomes an important mechanism for discriminating between what will prove rewarding and what will prove unrewarding—and for acquiring the behaviors essential for coping with our world.

Unfortunately, there is no guarantee that what we learn will be accurate or useful. Thus we may learn to value things that seem attractive but actually will hurt us; we may fail to learn techniques necessary for coping; or we may learn coping patterns such as helplessness, bullying, or other irresponsible behaviors that are maladaptive rather than adaptive.

Reinforcement. Essential to both classical and operant conditioning is **reinforcement**—the strengthening of a new response by manipulating its relationship with a particular stimulus. This stimulus can be either pleasant or aversive. In operant conditioning, a behavior is strengthened by being repeatedly associated either with a pleasant stimulus or with the avoidance of an aversive stimulus. For example, a child may learn a certain response if it has in the past produced a reinforcer (such as candy) or avoided a punisher (such as a spanking). Initially a high rate of reinforcement may be necessary to establish a response, but lesser rates are usually sufficient to maintain it. In fact, a learned response appears to be especially persistent when reinforcement is intermittent—when the reinforcing stimulus does not invariably follow the response—as demonstrated in gambling when occasional wins seem to maintain high rates of response. However, when reinforcement is consistently withheld over time, the conditioned response—whether classical or operant—eventually extinguishes. In short, the subject stops making the response; this process is known as **extinction.**

A special problem arises in extinguishing a response in situations where a subject has been conditioned to anticipate an aversive event and to respond by avoiding it. For example, a boy who has been bitten by a vicious dog may develop a *conditioned avoidance response* in which he consistently avoids all dogs. When he sees a dog, he feels anxious; avoiding contact lessens his anxiety and is thus reinforcing. As a result, his avoidance response is highly resistant to extinction. It also prevents him from having experiences with friendly dogs that could bring about reconditioning. In later discussions, we will see that conditioned avoidance responses play a role in many patterns of abnormal behavior.

Generalization and discrimination. In both classical and operant conditioning, when a response is conditioned to one stimulus or set of stimulus conditions, it can be evoked by other, similar stimuli; this process is called **generalization.** A person who fears bees, for example, may generalize that fear to all flying insects.

A process complementary to generalization is **discrimination,** which occurs when an individual learns to distinguish between similar stimuli and to respond differently to them. The ability to discriminate may be brought about through *differential reinforcement.* For example, since red strawberries taste good and green ones do not, a conditioned discrimination will occur if an individual has experience with both. According to the behavioristic perspective, complex processes like perceiving, forming concepts, and solving problems are all based on this basic discriminative process.

The concepts of generalization and discrimination have many implications for the development of maladaptive behavior. While generalization enables us to use past experiences in sizing up new situations, the possibility always exists of making inappropriate generalizations—as when a troubled youth fails to discriminate between friendly and hostile "joshing" from peers, or when a child of wealthy parents learns to regard all rich people with respect, whatever the source of their wealth. In some instances, a vital discrimination may be beyond an individual's capability—as when a bigoted person deals with others as stereotypes rather than as individuals—and may lead to inappropriate and maladaptive behavior.

Impact of the Behavioristic Perspective

By means of relatively few basic concepts, behaviorism attempts to explain the acquisition, modification, and extinction of all types of behavior. Maladaptive behavior is viewed as essentially the result of (a) a failure to learn necessary adaptive behaviors or competencies, such as how to establish satisfying personal relationships; or (b) the learning of ineffective or maladaptive responses. Maladaptive behavior is thus the result of learning that has gone awry and is defined in terms of specific, observable, undesirable responses.

For the behaviorist, the focus of therapy is thus on changing specific behaviors—eliminating undesirable reactions and learning desirable ones. For example, therapists can have considerable impact with the application of learning principles in the area of social skills training (Liberman, Mueser, & DeRisi, 1989). A number of *behavior-modification techniques* have been developed, based on the systematic application of learning principles, many of which are described in *HIGHLIGHT 3.3.* Additional examples of these techniques will be given in later chapters.

The behavioristic approach has been heralded for its precision and objectivity, for its wealth of research, and for its demonstrated effectiveness in changing specific behaviors. A behavioral therapist specifies what behavior is to be changed and how it is to be changed; later, the effectiveness of the therapy can be evaluated objectively by the degree to which the stated goals have been achieved. On the other hand, the behavioristic perspective has been criticized for being concerned only with symptoms, for ignoring the problems of value and meaning that may be important for those seeking help, and for denying the possibility of choice and self-direction.

The behavioristic tradition has been expanded to focus on human thought processes (as will be

Some Behavior-Modification Techniques Based on Learning Principles

Learning Principle	Technique	Example
Behavior patterns are developed and established through repeated association with positive reinforcers.	Use of positive reinforcement to establish desired behavior	Paul and Lentz (1977) successfully rehabilitated a group of chronic mental patients by providing them with tokens contingent on desirable behavior. The tokens could subsequently be used to "purchase" food, pleasant surroundings, etc.
The repeated association of an established behavior pattern with aversive stimuli results in avoidance behavior.	Use of aversive stimuli to eliminate undesirable behavior (aversive conditioning)	Rolider and Van Houten (1985) suppressed tantrum behavior in a 5-year-old psychotic boy and inappropriate behavior in a 10-year-old retarded boy through use of a delayed punishment procedure. Parents tape-recorded tantrums or inappropriate behavior that occurred in daily school settings, then later played back portions of the tape while administering punishment. Punishment consisted of response suppression (holding the child in a corner) and firm verbalizations. The tape-recorder-mediated procedure produced greater reductions in tantrums than verbal punishment alone.
When an established behavior pattern is no longer reinforced, it tends to be extinguished.	Withdrawal of reinforcement for undesirable behavior	Liberman and Raskin (1971) reported improvement in the treatment of depression by instructing family members of a depressed person to provide attention for constructive behavior but to ignore depressive behavior.
Avoidance behavior will be inhibited or reduced if the conditions that provoke it are repeatedly paired with positive stimuli.	Desensitization to conditions that elicit unreasonable fear or anxiety	Rimm and Lefebvre (1981) cited the successful treatment of phobias concerning loud noises and high places in a 45-year-old air force veteran. The treatment, known as systematic desensitization, consisted of having the man repeatedly imagine fearful scenes relating to his phobias while in a state of deep relaxation.
A specified behavior can be established gradually if successive approximations of the behavior are reinforced.	Shaping of desired behavior	Blount et al. (1984) successfully used shaping and modeling procedures to teach children to swallow pills required for their treatment. They used graduated sizes of candy, a vitamin pill, and a placebo capsule as training stimuli; and they used toys to reinforce the child to swallow a training stimulus. In the initial training session, the child was seen without parents present. The experimenter first modeled the swallowing behavior, then reminded the child of the correct steps to use in swallowing the pill. When the child successfully swallowed two training stimuli, the toy was given as reinforcement. After the child learned to swallow the pills, he or she was tested with the parents present. The child was followed-up in the home for three weeks immediately after training and again at three months. Five out of six children successfully learned to take their medications.
Reinforcement can operate to modify covert behavior (cognitions) as well as overt behavior.	Cognitive restructuring	Goldfried, Linehan, and Smith (1978) told highly anxious subjects to imagine being in an anxiety-arousing test situation and then presented them with instructions for reducing their anxiety. Subjects not only learned to react to test situations with less anxiety but reponded to other social circumstances with more adaptive attitudes.

discussed in the next section). Even with this trend, however, the most ardent behaviorists continue to emphasize the potential use of modern science and technology for planning a better world. In his famous novel, *Walden Two* (1948), and its nonfiction version, *Beyond Freedom and Dignity* (1971), Skinner depicted the utopian world he believed would result from the systematic application of learning principles and behavior-modification procedures to world problems. He (1974) stated the matter succinctly: "In the behavioristic view, man can now control his own destiny because he knows what must be done and how to do it" (p. 258). Skinner does not explain how people who have no choices could choose to exert such control.

Whatever its limitations and paradoxes, the behavioristic perspective has had and continues to have a tremendous impact on contemporary views of human nature, behavior, and psychopathology.

John Dollard (1900–1980) was a pioneer in shifting the focus on the nature of psychological functioning from overt behavior to the underlying cognitions assumed to be producing that behavior.

The Cognitive-Behavioral Perspective

The behavioristic perspective was a reaction to the subjectivism of an earlier era in psychology. It sought to banish private mental events from psychological study because they were unobservable and therefore unsuitable for scientific research. Some proponents of behaviorism even refused to use such terms as *mind* and *thought*. Although there were some who rejected behaviorism, it quickly gained wide acceptance among psychologists. As a result, the constraints imposed by the behavioristic point of view inhibited the development of cognitive psychology for three decades after the 1920s.

The Basics of the Cognitive-Behavioral Perspective Since the 1950s, psychologists, including some learning theorists, have focused on **cognitive processes**—the thoughts, images, and techniques involved with information processing—and their impact on behavior. In many respects, the current emphasis on the cognitive aspects of human behavior is a reaction to the mechanistic nature of the behavioral viewpoint.

Developments in clinical psychology have paralleled this reorientation of the larger field. In many instances, this reorientation has been led by individuals who were formerly identified with the behavioral tradition. A number of theorists have diverged from a somewhat mechanistic, purely learning-based approach to understanding abnormal behavior to an approach that incorporates human thought processes. This approach, referred to as the *cognitive* or **cognitive-behavioral perspective,** focuses on thought and information-processing processes as they apply to distorted thinking and maladaptive behavior. Unlike behaviorism's focus on overt behavior, the cognitive view treats thoughts as "behaviors" and thus brings them into focus as appropriate and relevant events from which to obtain empirical data.

The pioneering work of John Dollard (1900–1980) and Neal Miller (b. 1909), in their efforts to scientifically study and apply learning principles to psychodynamic processes, focused on cognitive concepts to explain abnormal behavior. They considered cognition—for example, using symbolic processes to visualize and label emotions and problems—an important process in gaining control over maladaptive behaviors.

Another pioneering theorist, George Kelly (1905–1966), contributed substantially to the cognitive viewpoint. Kelly developed a personality theory in which he postulated that people build **personal constructs**—uniquely individual ways of perceiving other people and events. People then use these personal constructs to interpret events around them. For example, the way a person describes or interprets a comment made by an acquaintance can produce emotional upset even though the comment was neutral and not intended to hurt. It is the meaning an individual attaches, filtered through his or her own personal constructs, that results in negative feelings and an emotional reaction.

Another learning theorist, Albert Bandura (b. 1925), has placed considerable emphasis on the

Neal Miller (b. 1909), along with John Dollard, reinterpreted psychoanalytic theory into the language of learning principles in their classic work, **Personality and Psychotherapy.**

George Kelly (1905–1966) was another cognitive-behavioral theorist who linked maladaptive behavior to the way people use personal constructs—how they interpret events around them.

Albert Bandura (b. 1925) stressed that people learn more by internal than external reinforcement; they can visualize the consequences of their actions and influence their environment rather than rely exclusively on environmental reinforcements.

cognitive aspects of learning. Bandura has stressed that human beings regulate their behavior by internal symbolic processes—thoughts. That is, they learn by ***internal reinforcement.*** We prepare ourselves for difficult tasks, for example, by visualizing what the consequences would be if we did not perform them. Thus we take our automobiles to the garage in the fall and have the antifreeze checked because we can "see" ourselves stranded on a road in the winter. We do not always require external reinforcement to alter our behavior patterns; with our cognitive abilities we can solve many problems internally. Bandura (1974) has gone so far as to say that human beings have "a capacity for self-direction" and that recognition of this capacity "represents a substantial departure from exclusive reliance upon environmental control" (pp. 861, 863).

The development of a cognitive-behavioral viewpoint distinct from behaviorism is not surprising. A hallmark of clinical behavioristic practice has always been the precise identification of specific problem behaviors, followed by the use of techniques directed specifically at those behaviors. This is in contrast to, for example, psychodynamic practice, which assumes that diverse problems are due to a limited array of intrapsychic conflicts (such as an unresolved Oedipus complex) and tends not to focus treatment techniques directly on a person's particular problems or complaints. Behaviorally oriented therapies, such as ***systematic desensitization*** (described in Chapter 18), have from the outset relied heavily on asking clients to conjure up images in their minds, certainly a process that is cognitive in nature. Cognitive-behavioral theoreticians and clinicians have simply shifted their focus from overt behavior itself to the underlying cognitions assumed to be producing that behavior. The issue then becomes one of altering the maladaptive cognitions.

Today many behaviorally-oriented clinicians and researchers are incorporating cognitive processes, including imagery and self-awareness, into their pictures of psychological functioning. To a large extent, cognitive-behavioral clinicians are concerned with their client's self-statements—with what these people say to themselves by way of interpreting their experiences. For example, people who interpret what happens in their lives as a negative reflection of their self-worth are likely to feel depressed. A cognitive-behavioral clinician would approach this situation with a variety of techniques designed to alter the negative cognitive bias the client harbors (see, for example, Beck, Emery, & Greenberg, 1985; Kendall & Braswell, 1985; Meichenbaum, 1977). The most widely used cognitive-behavioral therapies, Ellis' Rational Emotive Therapy and Beck's Cognitive-Behavioral Treatment, will be described in greater detail in Chapter 18.

The Impact of the Cognitive-Behavioral Perspective The cognitive-behavioral viewpoint has had a powerful impact on contemporary clinical psychology. Many researchers and clinicians support the principle of altering human behavior through changing the way people view or think about themselves and others. Many traditional behaviorists, however, are skeptical of the cognitive-behavioral viewpoint. Skinner (1990), in his last major address, remained true to his theories over the years. He questioned the move away from principles of operant conditioning and toward cognitive behaviorism. He reminded his audience that cognitions are not observable phenomena and cannot, as such, be relied on as solid empirical data. Though Skinner is gone, this debate will surely continue.

The Humanistic Perspective

The **humanistic perspective** focuses on freeing people from disabling assumptions and attitudes so that they can live fuller lives. Its emphasis is thus on growth and self-actualization rather than on curing diseases or alleviating disorders; its practitioners do not typically deal with individuals suffering from serious mental disorders.

The humanistic perspective has been influenced by both the behavioristic and the psychodynamic perspectives, but it is in significant disagreement with both. The behavioristic perspective, with its focus on the stimulus situation and observable behavior, is seen as an oversimplification that underrates the importance of an individual's psychological makeup, inner experience, and potential for self-direction. Humanistic psychologists also disagree with the negative picture of human nature presented by psychoanalytic theory and its stress on the overwhelming power of irrational, unconscious impulses. Instead, the humanistic perspective views basic human nature as "good," emphasizes present conscious processes—paying less attention to unconscious processes and past causes—and places strong emphasis on peoples' inherent capacity for responsible self-direction. Humanistic psychologists think that much of the empirical research designed to investigate causal factors is too simplistic to uncover the complexities of human behavior. Thus the humanistic perspective tends to be as much a statement of values—how we *ought* to view the human condition—as it is an attempt to account for human behaviors, at least among persons beset by personal problems.

Some psychologists have raised objections to the use of the term *humanistic* to describe the more experientially-oriented therapies because it implies that other approaches demean individuals or view humans as objects with which to tinker. All approaches, of course, ultimately aim at helping people to be happier and more effective; all approaches are "humanistic" in this sense, just as all are interested in changing behavior and thus recognize the importance of learning. Their labels indicate their special focuses but do not imply that they exclude all other factors.

The Roots of the Humanistic Perspective

The humanistic perspective has been heavily influenced by outstanding psychologists such as William James, Gordon Allport, Abraham Maslow, Gardner Murphy, Carl Rogers, and Fritz Perls. Although some of its roots extend deep into the history of psychology—as well as philosophy, literature, and education—others are of more recent origin. The humanistic approach emerged as a major perspective in psychology during the 1950s and 1960s when many middle-class Americans began to feel materially affluent and spiritually empty. (A related movement—the existential perspective—is described in *HIGHLIGHT 3.4.*)

The humanistic approach recognizes the importance of learning and other psychological processes that have traditionally been the focus of research, but, as noted above, it is optimistically concerned with an individual's future rather than his or her past. This perspective is also concerned with processes about which we have as yet little scientific information—love, hope, creativity, values, meaning, personal growth, and self-fulfillment. Inevitably, its formulations are less based on empirical observation than those of behaviorism. In essence, humanistic psychologists feel that modern psychology has failed to address many of the most significant problems of human existence.

The Basics of the Humanistic Perspective

Though not readily subject to empirical investigation, certain underlying themes and principles of humanistic psychology can be identified. These views are described in the following sections.

The self as a unifying theme. In the first comprehensive textbook on psychology, published in 1890, William James included a discussion of the consciousness of self. This concept was later dropped by the behaviorists because the self could not be observed by an outsider. Though the behaviorists have again incorporated cognitive aspects of human behavior into their perspective, it was the humanists of the 1950s and 1960s who focused their perspective on the concept of self.

Among humanistic psychologists, Carl Rogers (1902–1987) developed the most systematic formulation of the **self-concept,** based largely on his pioneering research into the nature of the psychotherapeutic process. Rogers (1951, 1959) stated his

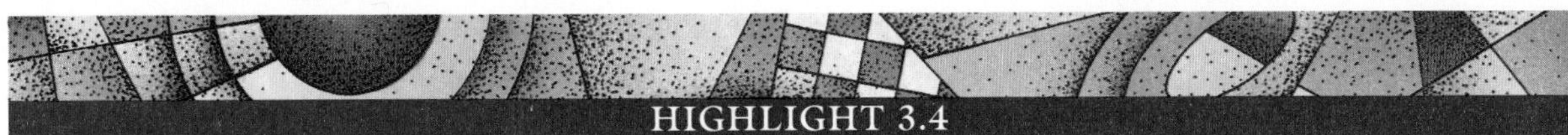

HIGHLIGHT 3.4

The Existential Perspective

During the middle part of this century, as the humanistic perspective was becoming an influential force in the field of psychology, a related intellectual movement (centered in Europe) was also beginning to have a notable impact. This movement was called *existentialism,* a philosophical outlook with roots in the work of such existential thinkers as Martin Heidegger and Søren Kierkegaard.

The existential perspective resembles humanism in its emphasis on the uniqueness of each individual, the quest for values and meanings, and the existence of freedom for self-direction and self-fulfillment. The existential perspective, however, represents a less optimistic view of human beings and places more emphasis on the irrational tendencies and the difficulties inherent in self-fulfillment—particularly in a modern, bureaucratic, and dehumanizing mass society. In short, living is much more of a "confrontation" for the existentialists than for the humanists. Existential thinkers also place considerably less faith in modern science, being more concerned with the inner experiences of an individual in his or her attempts to understand and deal with the deepest human problems. The following paragraphs summarize some of the basic tenets of existentialism:

1. *Existence and essence.* A basic theme of existentialism is that our existence is a given, but what we make of it—our essence—is up to us. An adolescent boy who defiantly blurts out, "Well, I didn't ask to be born," is stating a profound truth, but in existential terms it is completely irrelevant. Whether he asked to be born or not, he is in the world and answerable for himself—for one human life. What he makes of his essence is up to him. It is his responsibility to shape the kind of person he is to become and to live a meaningful and constructive life.

2. *Choice, freedom, and courage.* Our essence is created by our choices, because our choices reflect the values on which we base and order our lives. As Sartre said, "I am my choices." In choosing what sort of people to become, we have absolute freedom; even refusing to choose represents a choice. Thus the locus of value is within each individual. We are inescapably the architects of our own lives.

3. *Meaning, value, and obligation.* A central theme in the existential perspective is the will-to-meaning. This trait is considered a basic human characteristic and is primarily a matter of finding satisfying values and guiding one's life by them. As we have noted, this is a difficult and highly individual matter, for the values that give one life meaning may be quite different from those that provide meaning for another. Each of us must find our own pattern of values. This orientation should not be interpreted as purely nihilistic or selfish. Existentialism also places strong emphasis on our *obligations* to each other. The most important consideration is not what we can get out of life but what we can contribute to it. Our lives can be fulfilling only if they involve socially constructive values and choices.

4. *Existential anxiety and the encounter with nothingness.* A final existential theme, *nonbeing,* or *nothingness,* adds an urgent and painful note to the human situation. In its ultimate form, nothingness is death, which is the inescapable fate of all human beings. The awareness of our inevitable death and its implications for our living can lead to *existential anxiety*—a deep concern over whether we are living meaningful and fulfilling lives. We can overcome our existential anxiety and deny victory to nothingness by living a life that counts for something. If we must perish, we can at least resist our death—living in such a way that nothingness will be an unjust fate.

This philosophy has clear implications for students of abnormal psychology. Existential psychologists focus on the importance of establishing values and acquiring a level of spiritual maturity worthy of the freedom and dignity bestowed by one's humanness. It is the avoidance of such central issues that creates corrupted, meaningless, and wasted lives. Much abnormal behavior, therefore, is seen as the product of a failure to deal constructively with existential despair and frustration.

Before the turn of the twentieth century, William James (1842–1910) set the stage for the humanistic perspective by discussing the concept of self in his book, Principles of Psychology.

Gordon Allport (1897–1967) believed that personality traits were actual forces in a person that could be used to explain the consistency of his or her behavior.

Abraham H. Maslow (1908–1970) devoted more than two decades to showing the potentialities of human beings for higher self-development and functioning.

views in a series of propositions that may be summarized as follows:

- Each individual exists in a private world of experience of which the I, me, or myself is the center.
- The most basic striving of an individual is toward the maintenance, enhancement, and actualization of the self.
- An individual reacts to situations in terms of the way he or she perceives them, in ways consistent with his or her self-concept and view of the world.
- A perceived threat to the self is followed by a defense—including a tightening of perception and behavior and the introduction of self-defense mechanisms.
- An individual's inner tendencies are toward health and wholeness; under normal conditions, a person behaves in rational and constructive ways and chooses pathways toward personal growth and self-actualization.

In using the concept of self as a unifying theme, humanistic psychologists emphasize the importance of individuality. Because of the great human potential for evaluation and learning and the great diversity in genetic endowments and experience, each person is unique. In studying human nature, psychologists are thus faced with the dual task of describing the uniqueness of each person and identifying the characteristics that all people share.

A focus on values and personal growth. Humanistic psychologists emphasize values and the process of value choices in guiding our behavior and achieving meaningful and fulfilling lives. They consider it crucial that each of us develop values based on our own experiences and evaluations rather than blindly accepting the values of others; otherwise, we deny our own experiences and lose touch with our own feelings.

To evaluate and choose for ourselves requires a clear sense of our own identity—the discovery of who we are, what sort of person we want to become, and why. Only in this way can we become **self-actualizing,** meaning that we are achieving our full potential.

According to the humanistic view, psychopathology is essentially the blocking or distortion of personal growth and the natural tendency toward physical and mental health. Such blocking or distortion is generally the result of one or more of these causal factors: (a) the exaggerated use of ego-defense mechanisms that leave an individual increasingly out of touch with reality; (b) unfavorable social conditions and faulty learning; and (c) excessive stress.

A positive view of human nature and potential. In contrast to the psychoanalytic and behavioristic perspectives, the humanistic approach takes a much more positive view of human nature and potential. Despite the myriad instances of violence, war, and cruelty that have occurred since ancient times, humanistically oriented psychologists conclude that under favorable circumstances humans tend to be

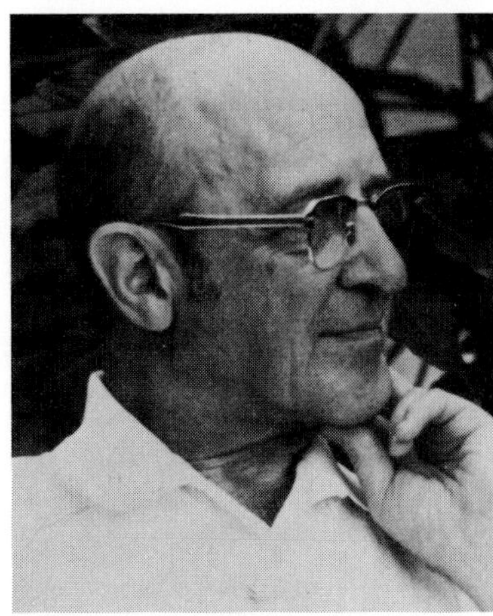

Carl Rogers (1902–1987) contributed significantly to the humanistic perspective with his systematic formulation of the concept of self, which emphasizes the importance of individuality and a striving towards what Rogers called self-actualization.

Fritz Perls (1893–1970) was influential in the development of therapeutic procedures for enhancing human experiencing and functioning, particulary in the context of confrontation groups.

friendly, cooperative, and constructive. Selfishness, aggression, and cruelty are viewed as pathological behaviors resulting from the denial, frustration, or distortion of basic human nature. Though people can be misled by inaccurate information, handicapped by social and economic deprivation, and overwhelmed by the complexity of human life, they still tend to be rational creatures. People try to find meaning in their experiences, to act and think in consistent ways, and to follow standards and principles they believe are good. According to this view, humans are not passive automatons but active participants in life with some measure of freedom for shaping their personal destinies and the destinies of their social groups.

The humanistic approach takes a positive view of human nature and potential. Humanistically oriented psychologists believe that under favorable circumstances, human propensities are in the direction of friendly, cooperative, and constructive behavior. According to this view, we are active participants in life with some measure of freedom for shaping our personal destiny.

Impact of the Humanistic Perspective

The major impact of the humanistic perspective has been its emphasis on our capacity for full functioning as human beings. In a sense, the humanistic perspective has introduced a new dimension to our thinking about abnormal behavior. Abnormality is seen as a failure to develop our tremendous potentials as human beings—as a blocking or distortion of our natural tendencies toward health and personal growth rather than as abnormality or deviance. In fact, Maslow (1962, 1969) has even expressed concern about the "psychopathology of the normal"—that is, the disappointing and wasteful failure of so many "normal" people to realize their potentialities as human beings.

Therapy, according to this way of thinking, is not a means of moving an individual from maladjustment to adjustment, but of fostering growth

Alfred Adler (1870–1937) was a student of Freud who took issue with psychoanalytic theory for its neglect of social factors as determinants of behavior. Adler believed that people were inherently social beings motivated primarily by the desire to belong to and participate in a group. His work laid the foundation for the interpersonal perspective.

Erich Fromm (1900–1980) focused on the orientations that people adopt in their interactions with others. He believed that these basic orientations to the social environment were the bases of much psychopathology.

Karen Horney (1885–1952) was trained in Freudian theory, but she rejected Freud's demeaning psychoanalytic view of women. She believed that "femininity" was a product of the culturally determined social learning that most women experience.

toward a socially constructive and personally fulfilling way of life. As might be expected, humanistic psychologists are keenly interested in encounter groups, awareness training, and other experiential techniques for promoting individual growth, building satisfying relationships, and finding effective methods of coping.

The humanistic perspective has been criticized for its diffuseness, for its lack of scientific rigor, and for its high expectations. Although some psychologists view its goals as grandiose, others see them as useful descriptions of the challenging long-range tasks that confront psychology today.

The Interpersonal Perspective

We are social beings, and much of what we are is a product of our relationships with others. It is logical to expect that much of psychopathology reflects this fact—that psychopathology is rooted in the unfortunate tendencies we have developed while dealing with our interpersonal environments. It is also true that abnormal behavior has its chief impact on our relationships with other people. Hence it should not be surprising that many theorists conclude that abnormal behavior is best understood by analyzing our relationships, past and present, with other people. This is the focus of the **interpersonal perspective.**

Roots of the Interpersonal Perspective

The roots of the interpersonal perspective lie clearly in the psychodynamic movement. The defection in 1911 of Alfred Adler (1870–1937) from the psychoanalytic viewpoint of his teacher, Freud, grew out of Adler's emphasis on social rather than inner determinants of behavior. Adler objected to the prominence Freud gave to instincts as the basic driving forces of personality. In Adler's view, people were inherently social beings motivated primarily by the desire to belong to and participate in a group.

Over time, a number of other Freudian theorists took issue with psychoanalytic theory for its neglect of crucial social factors. Among the best known of these theorists were Erich Fromm (1900–1980) and Karen Horney (1885–1952). Fromm focused on the orientations, or dispositions (exploitive, for example), that people adopted in their interactions with others. He believed that these basic orientations to the social environment were the bases of much psychopathology. Horney independently developed a similar view and, in particular, vigorously rejected Freud's demeaning psychoanalytic view of women (for instance, the idea that women experience penis envy). According to Horney, "femininity" was a product of the culturally determined social learning that most women experienced.

Erik Erikson (b. 1902) elaborated and broadened Freud's psychosexual stages into more socially oriented concepts. Erikson described conflicts that occurred at eight stages, each of which could be resolved in a healthy or unhealthy way.

The interpersonal model is based largely on the work of Harry Stack Sullivan (1892–1949), who believed that personality had meaning only in relation to interaction with others.

Erik Erikson (b. 1902) also extended the interpersonal aspects of psychoanalytic theory. He elaborated and broadened Freud's psychosexual stages into more socially oriented concepts, describing conflicts that occurred at eight stages, each of which could be resolved in a healthy or unhealthy way. For example, during the oral stage, a child may learn either basic trust or basic mistrust. Although these conflicts are never fully resolved, failure to develop toward the appropriate pole of each conflict handicaps an individual during later stages. Trust, for instance, is needed for later competence in many areas of life. A clear sense of identity is necessary for a satisfying intimacy with another person; such intimacy, in turn, is important for becoming a nurturing parent.

Contemporary psychodynamic thought has partially responded to the challenges leveled by these socially oriented theorists. The psychodynamic tradition has become much more interpersonal in focus, largely due to the influence of the object-relations approach. In fact many foresee the possibility of a harmonious integration of the psychodynamic with the more distinctly social and interpersonal viewpoints (Fine, 1979). Still, classical psychodynamic theory continues to emphasize the primacy of libidinal energies and intrapsychic conflicts, an emphasis that many interpersonally oriented theorists find objectionable.

Currently the dominant interpersonal theory is that developed by Harry Stack Sullivan (1892–1949), an American psychiatrist. The section that follows treats his theory in detail.

Sullivan's Interpersonal Theory While the thinking of many individuals had nourished the roots of interpersonal theory, Sullivan offered a comprehensive and systematic theory of personality that was explicitly interpersonal.

Sullivan (1953) maintained that the concept of personality had meaning only when defined in terms of an individual's characteristic forms of relating to others. He argued that personality development proceeded through various stages involving different patterns of interpersonal relationships. Early in life, for example, a child becomes socialized mainly through interactions with parents. Later, during a gradual emancipation from parents, peer relationships become increasingly important. In young adulthood, intimate relationships are established, culminating typically in marriage. Failure to progress satisfactorily through these various stages paves the way for maladaptive behavior.

In this developmental context, Sullivan was concerned with the anxiety-arousing aspects of interpersonal relationships during early childhood. Because an infant is completely dependent on parents and siblings, called **significant others,** for meeting all physical and psychological needs, a lack of love and care leads to insecurity and anxiety. Sullivan emphasized the role of early childhood relationships in shaping the self-concept, which he saw as constructed largely out of the appraisals of significant others. For example, if a little girl perceives that others are rejecting her, she may view herself in a similar light and develop a negative self-image that almost inevitably leads to maladjustment.

The pressures of the socialization process and the continual appraisals by others lead a child to label some personal tendencies as the *good-me* and others as the *bad-me.* It is the bad-me that is associated with anxiety. With time, an individual develops a **self-system** that protects him or her from such anxiety through the control of awareness —the person simply does not attend to elements of experience that cause anxiety. If severe anxiety is aroused by some especially frightening aspect of self-experience, the individual perceives it as the *not-me,* totally screening it out of consciousness or even attributing it to someone else. Such actions, however, lead to an incongruity between the individual's perceptions and the world as it really is, which may result in maladaptive behavior. Here we can see a similarity between Sullivan's views and those of Freud, Rogers, and the cognitive-behavioral psychologists.

The good-me and bad-me constructs are especially important aspects of a much broader and more profound idea—that all mental processing concerning ourselves, others, and our relationships with them is influenced by precedents, or prototypes, established in earlier relationships. These mental prototypes, which Sullivan called *personifications,* determine how we perceive current relationships. We each have our own ideas about the characteristics, behaviors, and interactions we expect of our moms, teachers, lovers, and friends. Unfortunately, this means that we may distort events involving important current relationships. When such distortions are severe, relationships become complicated and confusing. Because these distortions shape our behavior toward other people, they tend to become self-fulfilling. The result can be anxiety and, ultimately, dissolution of certain relationships.

Features of the Interpersonal Perspective

Many subdisciplines of the social sciences and psychiatry have contributed to the interpersonal perspective in recent years. Some of these contributions are described briefly in the following sections.

One way of viewing interpersonal relationships is in terms of social roles. In family relationships, each person has certain role expectations—in terms of obligations, rights, duties, and so on—that the others are expected to meet. If a member of the family significantly diverges from his or her expected role, interpersonal complications are likely to occur.

Social exchange and roles. Two ways of viewing our relationships with other people are helpful in understanding both satisfying and hurtful interactions. First, the **social-exchange** view, developed largely by Thibaut and Kelley (1959) and Homans (1961), is based on the premise that we form relationships with each other to satisfy our needs. Each person in a relationship wants something from the other, and the exchange that results is essentially like trading or bargaining. When we feel that we have entered into a bad bargain—that the rewards are not worth the costs—we may attempt to work out some compromise or simply terminate the relationship.

A second way of viewing interpersonal relationships is in terms of **social roles.** Whether we are teachers, or doctors, or patients, we subscribe to certain behaviors. While we each lend a personal interpretation to our roles, there are usually limits to the "script," beyond which we are not expected to go. Similarly, in intimate personal relationships, each person has certain role expectations—in terms of obligations, rights, duties, and so on—that the other person is expected to meet. If one spouse, for example, fails to live up to the other's role expectations, or if the husband and wife have different conceptions of what a "wife" or "husband" should be or do, serious complications are likely to occur.

Causal attribution in interpersonal relations. Another contribution to the interpersonal approach is **attribution theory** (Bem, 1972; Heider, 1958; Weary & Mirels, 1982), which simply refers to the process of assigning causes to things that happen. We may attribute external causes, such as rewards or punishments; or we may assume that the causes are internal—that they are traits within ourselves or others. These causes are not seen but are assumed to exist as underlying realities. Assuming them helps us explain our own or other people's behaviors and makes it possible to predict what we or others are likely to do in the future.

For example, if a person does something mean, we may assume that he or she has a quality of meanness and expect it to cause mean behavior in the future. Or if a person fails a test, he or she may attribute the failure to stupidity as a personal trait. On the other hand, if the person attributes the failure to ambiguous test questions or unclear directions, he or she is looking to the environment as a cause and not to his or her own abilities.

Attribution theorists say that attributions are important in relationships because they form the basis for continuing evaluations and expectations. However inaccurate the attributions may be, they become important parts of our view of the world and tend to become self-fulfilling. They can also make us see other people and ourselves as unchanging and unchangeable, leading us to be inflexible in our relationships. Obviously, these ideas are similar to Sullivan's notion of personifications.

Communication and interpersonal accommodation. **Interpersonal accommodation** is the process in which two people develop patterns of communication and interaction that enable them to attain common goals, meet mutual needs, and build a satisfying relationship. People use many cues, both verbal and nonverbal, to interpret what is really being said to them. If individuals in a close relationship have a tangle of unresolved misunderstandings and conflicts, they will probably have trouble communicating clearly and openly with each other. In fact, the final phase of a failing marriage is often marked by an almost complete inability of the partners to communicate. Sullivan believed that faulty communication is far more common than most people realize, especially in family interactions on an emotional level.

In addition to establishing and maintaining effective communication, interpersonal accommodation involves other adjustments, such as determining mutually satisfying role relationships, resolving disagreements constructively, and dealing adequately with external demands. Sullivan thought that interpersonal accommodation is facilitated when the motives of the individuals in a relationship are complementary, as when two people are strongly motivated to give and receive affection. When interpersonal accommodation fails and a relationship does not meet the needs of one or both partners, it is likely to be characterized by conflict, dissension, and eventually dissolution. The principles of interpersonal behavioral accommodation have been analyzed at length by Benjamin (1982), Carson (1969, 1979), Kiesler (1983), Leary (1957), and Wiggins (1982).

Impact of the Interpersonal Perspective

The interpersonal perspective views unsatisfactory relationships in the past or present as the primary causes of many forms of maladaptive behavior. Such relationships may extend back to childhood, as

Interpersonal accommodation is the process in which two people evolve patterns of communication and interaction that enable them to attain common goals, meet mutual needs, and build a satisfying relationship.

when a boy's self-concept is distorted by parents who tell him he is worthless or by rigid socialization measures that make it difficult to integrate the bad-me into his self-concept. Poor relationships may also result from self-defeating games that individuals learn to play, from uncomfortable roles they are given, from faulty assumptions about the causes of their own or others' behaviors, or from unsuccessful attempts to separate from parents and other adults in order to become a fully functioning adult.

In the area of diagnosis, many supporters of the interpersonal perspective believe that the reliability and validity of psychological diagnoses can be improved if a new system based on interpersonal functioning is developed. Some work and thinking underlying these efforts is described in *HIGHLIGHT 3.5*.

The focus of interpersonal therapy is on alleviating problem-causing relationships and on helping individuals achieve more satisfactory relationships. Such therapy is concerned with verbal and nonverbal communication, social roles, processes of accommodation, causal attributions (including those supposedly motivating the behavior of others), and the general interpersonal context of behavior. The therapy situation itself can be used as a vehicle for learning new interpersonal skills.

Like the humanistic viewpoint, the interpersonal approach is handicapped by incomplete information. As a result, many of Sullivan's concepts and those of later investigators lack adequate scientific grounding. Despite such limitations, the interpersonal perspective has focused attention on the key role an individual's close relationships play in determining whether behavior will be effective or maladaptive.

To review, each of the psychosocial perspectives on human behavior—psychodynamic, behavioristic, cognitive-behavioral, humanistic, and interpersonal—contributes to our understanding of psychopathology, but none alone seems to account for the complex variety of human maladaptive behavior. Each perspective has a substantial amount of evidence to support it, yet each one also depends on generalizations from limited events and observations. In attempting to explain a complex disorder such as alcoholism, for example, the psychodynamic principles focus on intrapsychic conflict and anxiety; the behavioristic principles focus on faulty learning and environmental conditions that may be exacerbating or maintaining the condition; the cognitive-behavioral principles focus on maladaptive thinking, including deficits in problem solving and information processing; the humanistic principles focus on the ways in which an individual's struggles with values, meaning, and personal growth may be contributing to the problem; and the interpersonal principles focus on difficulties in a person's past and present relationships.

Thus adopting one perspective or another has important consequences: it influences our perception of maladaptive behavior, the types of evidence we look for, and the way in which we are likely to interpret data. In later chapters, we will discuss relevant concepts from all these viewpoints, and in many instances, we will contrast different ways of explaining and treating the same behavior.

THE SOCIOCULTURAL VIEWPOINT

By the beginning of the twentieth century, sociology and anthropology had emerged as independent scientific disciplines and were making rapid strides toward understanding the role of sociocultural factors in human development and behavior. Early sociocultural theorists included such notables as Ruth Benedict, Ralph Linton, Abram Kardiner, Margaret Mead, and Franz Boas. Their investigations and writings showed that individual personality development reflected the larger society—its institutions, norms, values, ideas, and technologies—as well as the immediate family and other groups. Studies also made clear the relationship between sociocultural conditions and mental disorders—between the particular stressors in a society and the types of mental disorders that typically occur in it. Further studies showed that the patterns of both physical and mental disorders in a given society could change over time as sociocultural conditions changed. These discoveries have added another dimension to modern perspectives concerning abnormal behavior.

Uncovering Sociocultural Factors Through Cross-cultural Studies

The relationships between maladaptive behavior and sociocultural factors such as poverty, discrimination, or illiteracy are complex. It is one thing to observe that an individual with a psychological disorder has come from a harsh environment. It is quite another thing, however, to show empirically

HIGHLIGHT 3.5

Toward an Interpersonal Diagnostic System

While acknowledging that the DSM-III-R diagnostic system is an improvement over its predecessors, Clinton McLemore and Lorna Benjamin (1979; Benjamin, 1982) argue that it is fundamentally flawed in at least three ways: (a) it still requires a diagnostician to make impressionistic clinical judgments; (b) it still categorizes human beings by reference to certain broadly defined "illnesses"; and, especially, (c) it almost totally neglects the social context in which maladaptive behavior occurs. They note that abnormality is typically displayed by the way in which a person relates to others: "We submit that rigorous and systematic description of social behavior is uniquely critical to effective definition and treatment of the problems that bring most individuals for psychiatric or psychological consultation" (p. 18).

The solution, according to these authors, is to seek the careful and rigorous development of a diagnostic system organized around disordered forms of interpersonal functioning rather than alleged entities of mental disorder. Building on the work of earlier investigators, they suggest that the beginnings of such a system should incorporate dimensions of autonomy-interdependence, friendliness-hostility, and (where the situation is one of high interdependence between a person and others) dominance-submission. Since the most important and central of the behaviors associated with traditional (DSM) psychiatric diagnoses involve precisely these dimensions, they argue, it should be possible to include virtually all DSM-III-R diagnoses within this more systematic and potentially more meaningful framework. For example, the DSM-III-R diagnosis of major depression might, in interpersonal terms, be described as a position of appeasement (hostile submission) toward another person's stance of accusation and blame (hostile dominance), which leads to internalized self-accusation and blame (hostile domination of self). The narcissistic personality disorder, on the other hand, might be viewed as a hostile assertion of autonomy ("Ignore it, pretend it's not there"), which leads to a preoccupation with oneself and one's own affairs and a reversion to fantasy as a principal means of gratification.

and unequivocally that these circumstances were both *necessary* and *sufficient* conditions for producing the later disorder. The **sociocultural viewpoint** is thus concerned with the impact of the social environment on mental disorder.

Evidence that sociocultural factors have influenced personality adaptation or resulted in abnormal behavior is compelling but difficult to verify. It is virtually impossible to conduct controlled experiments. Both economic and ethical restraints prevent investigators from rearing children with similar genetic or biological traits in diverse social or economic environments in order to find out which variables, if any, play a part in the individual adjustment.

However, natural occurrences have provided laboratories for researchers. Groups of human beings have been exposed to very different environments, from the Arctic to the tropics to the desert. These societies have developed different means of economic subsistence and different types of family structures for propagating the species under different and often adverse conditions. Human groups have developed highly diverse social and political systems. Nature has indeed done social scientists a great favor by providing such a wide array of human groups for study.

Yet an investigator who attempts to conduct crosscultural research is plagued by numerous technological and methodological problems. Some of these are (a) the different languages and thought systems; (b) the political and cultural climates that prevent objective inquiry; (c) the difficulties in finding appropriately trained local scientists to collaborate in the research and prevent the researcher's ethnocentric attitudes or values from distorting the findings; and (d) the high costs of large scale crosscultural research.

In the earliest cross-cultural studies, Western-trained anthropologists observed the behavior of "natives" and considered those behaviors in the context of Western scientific thought. One of the

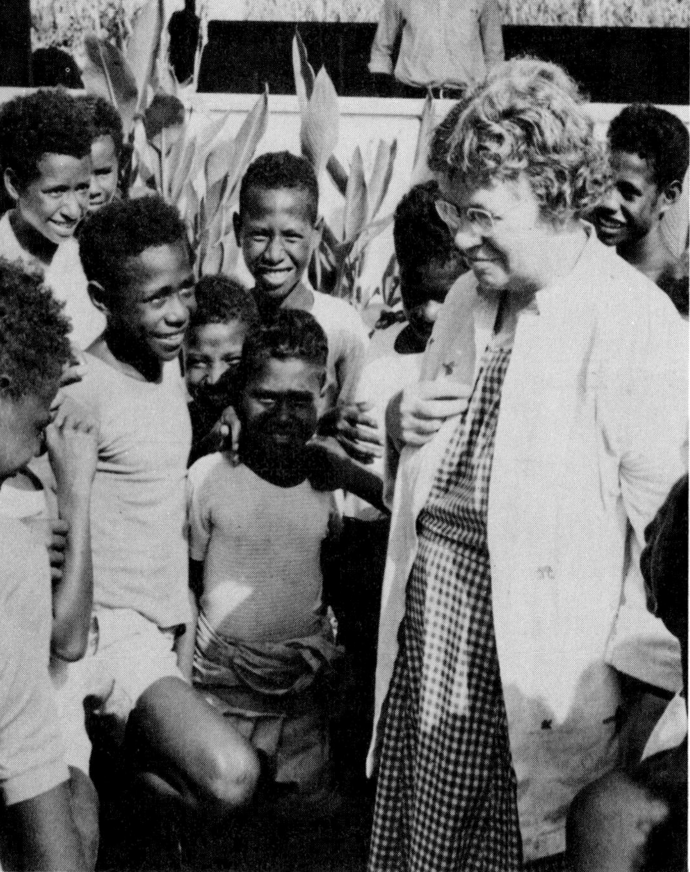

Margaret Mead (1901–1978), the world-famous anthropologist, spent years studying other societies and amassing cross-cultural data. Her Coming of Age in Samoa (published in 1928) gave a favorable picture of many aspects of life in a "primitive" society and was influential in establishing an attitude of cultural relativism among many scientists and thinkers. Here she is pictured meeting with schoolchildren in New Guinea.

earliest attempts to apply Western-based concepts in other cultures was the classic study of Malinowski (1927), *Sex and Repression in Savage Society.* In this work, he attempted to explain the behavior of "savages" through the use of the then dominant principles of psychoanalysis. Malinowski found little evidence among the Trobriand Islanders of any Oedipal conflicts as described by Freud. He concluded that the sexually based behavior postulated by psychoanalytic theory was not universal but rather was a product of the patriarchal family structure in Western society.

Shortly thereafter, Ruth Benedict (1934) pointed out that even the Western definitions of abnormality might not apply to behavior in other cultures. Citing various ethnographic reports, she indicated that behavior considered abnormal in one society was sometimes considered normal in another. For example, she noted that some cultures valued cataleptic and trancelike states. Thus she concluded that normality was simply a culturally defined concept.

Early research also found that some types of abnormal behavior occurred only in certain cultures. Several of these "culture-bound" behaviors are described in *HIGHLIGHT 3.6.*

These and other early anthropological findings led many investigators to take a position of **cultural relativism** concerning abnormal behavior. According to this view, one cannot apply universal standards of normality or abnormality to all societies. In fact, for a time many people accepted the anthropologist's veto: any general principle could be rejected if a contrary instance somewhere in the world could be demonstrated. For example, schizophrenia would no longer be viewed as abnormal if its symptoms were somewhere accepted as normal behavior.

This extremely relativistic view of abnormal behavior is not widely held (Strauss, 1979). As noted earlier, the biological viewpoint is the dominant force in the fields of psychiatry and abnormal psychology today. Whether this perspective is accepted or not, it is generally recognized that the more severe types of mental disorder described in Western psychology are found and considered maladaptive in societies throughout the world. When individuals become so mentally disordered that they can no longer control their behavior, perform their expected roles, or even survive without special care, their behavior is considered abnormal in any society.

Research supports the view that many psychological disturbances are universal, appearing in most cultures studied (Al-Issa, 1982; Carpenter & Strauss, 1979; Cooper et al., 1972; Murphy, 1976; World Health Organization, 1975). For example, although the incidences and symptoms vary, the behaviors we call schizophrenia can be found among almost all peoples, from the most primitive to the most technologically advanced. Recent studies have also shown that certain psychological symptoms, as measured by the Minnesota Multiphasic Personality Inventory (MMPI, see Chapter 16), were consistently found among similarly diagnosed clinical groups in other countries (in Turkey by Savacir & Erol, 1990; in China by Cheung & Song, 1989).

Sociocultural influences, however, cannot be disregarded. Although some universal symptoms appear, there is reason to believe that cultural factors influence abnormal behavior. The cultural relativists, though a minority voice, raise the unimpeacha-

HIGHLIGHT 3.6

Unusual Patterns of Behavior Considered to Be Culture-bound Disorders

Name of Disorder	Culture	Description
Amok	Malaya (also observed in Java, Philippines, Africa, and Tierra del Fuego)	A disorder characterized by sudden, wild outbursts of homicidal aggression in which an afflicted person may kill or injure others. This rage disorder is usually found in males who are rather withdrawn, quiet, and inoffensive prior to the onset of the disorder. Stress, sleep deprivation, extreme heat, and alcohol are among the conditions thought to precipitate the disorder. Several stages have been observed: typically in the first stage the person becomes more withdrawn; then a period of brooding follows in which a loss of reality contact is evident. Ideas of persecution and anger predominate. Finally, a phase of automatism or *Amok* occurs, in which the person jumps up, yells, grabs a knife, and stabs people or objects within reach. Exhaustion and depression usually follow, with amnesia for the rage period.
Anorexia nervosa	Western nations (particularly the U.S.)	A disorder occurring most frequently among young women in which a preoccupation with thinness produces a refusal to eat. This condition can result in death (see Chapter 8).
Latah	Malay	A fear reaction often occurring in middle-aged women of low intelligence who are subservient and self-effacing. The disorder is precipitated by the word *snake* or by tickling. It is characterized by *echolalia* (repetition of the words and sentences of others) and *echopraxia* (repetition of the acts of others). A disturbed individual may also react with negativism and the compulsive use of obscene language.
Koro	Southeast Asia (particularly Malay Archipelago)	A fear reaction or anxiety state in which a person fears that his penis will withdraw into his abdomen and he will die. This reaction may appear after sexual overindulgence or excessive masturbation. The anxiety is typically very intense and of sudden onset. The condition is "treated" by having the penis held firmly by the patient or by family members or friends. Often the penis is clamped to a wooden box.
Windigo	Algonquin Indian hunters	A fear reaction in which a hunter becomes anxious and agitated, convinced that he is bewitched. Fears center around his being turned into a cannibal by the power of a monster with an insatiable craving for human flesh.
Kitsunetsuki	Japan	A disorder in which victims believe that they are possessed by foxes and are said to change their facial expressions to resemble foxes. Entire families are often possessed and banned by the community. This reaction occurs in rural areas of Japan where people are superstitious and relatively uneducated.
Taijin kyofusho (TKS)	Japan	A relatively common psychiatric disorder in Japan in which an individual develops a fear of offending or hurting other people through being awkward in social situations or because of an imagined physical defect or problem. The excessive concern over how a person presents himself or herself in social situations is the salient problem.

Based on Kiev (1972), Kirmayer (1991), Lebra (1976), Lehmann (1967), Simons and Hughes (1985) and Yap (1951).

ble point that human biology does not operate in a vacuum. Cultural demands serve as primary causal factors and modifying influences in psychopathology. Fabrega (1989) recently questioned the pervasive biological reductionism used as an explanatory model, arguing that contemporary relativistic perspectives explain how physiological behavior results in part from an individual's experiences. The role a particular sociocultural factor plays in producing abnormal behavior largely depends on the amount of stress it creates for an individual (Al-Issa, 1982; Sue & Sue, 1987). For example, children growing up in an oppressive society that offers few rewards and many hassles are likely to experience more stress and thus be more vulnerable to disorder than children growing up in a society that offers ample rewards and considerable social support. Growing up during a period of great fear, such as during a war, a famine, or a period of persecution, can make a child vulnerable to psychological problems.

Sociocultural factors also appear to influence what disorders develop, the forms that they take, and their courses. How a disordered individual is treated and what is expected from a patient can influence whether the individual recovers or becomes chronically disordered (Murphy, 1982). A good example of this point is a comparison study of psychiatric patients from Italy, Switzerland, and the United States carried out by Butcher and Pancheri (1976). Patients grouped according to diagnostic categories produced similar general personality patterns on the MMPI. However, the Italian patients also showed an exaggerated pattern of physical complaints significantly greater than that of the Swiss and the American patients, regardless of clinical diagnosis.

This finding was consistent with earlier work by Opler and Singer (1959) and Zola (1966). For example, Zola examined symptom expression in two samples of second-generation American patients (Italian and Irish) at an ear-nose-throat clinic in Boston. When patients were matched on the basis of their actual physical illnesses, Zola found that the Italian patients made more complaints than the Irish. He attributed this difference to a defense mechanism, which he called *dramatization,* that led the Italian patients, once identified as ill, to exaggerate or dramatize their physical problems to a greater extent than the Irish patients.

In another study, Kleinman and Good (1985) surveyed the experience of depression across cultures. Their data show that important elements of depression in Western societies—for example, the acute sense of guilt typically experienced—do not appear in other cultures. They point out that the symptoms of depression (or dysphoria), such as

sadness, hopelessness, unhappiness, lack of pleasure with the things of the world and with social relationships has dramatically different meaning in different societies. For Buddhists, taking pleasure from things of the world and social relationships is the basis of all suffering; a willful dysphoria is thus the first step on the road to salvation. For Shi'ite Muslims in Iran, grief is a religious experience, associated with recognition of the tragic consequences of living justly in an unjust world; the ability to experience dysphoria fully is thus a marker of depth of person and understanding. Some societies, such as the Kaluli of Papua New Guinea, value full and dramatic expression of sadness and grieving. (p. 3)

Kleinman (1986) traced the different ways that Chinese people (in Taiwan and in the People's Republic of China) deal with stress compared to Western individuals. He found that in Western societies depression was a frequent reaction to individual stress. In China, on the other hand, he noted a relatively low rate of reported depression. Instead, the effects of stress were more typically manifested in physical problems, such as fatigue, weakness, and other complaints.

These findings illustrate an important point—the need for greater study of the cultural influences on psychopathology. This neglected area of research may yet answer many questions about the origins and courses of behavior problems (Draguns, 1979; Marsella et al., 1985). Yet, even with strong evidence of the cultural influences on psychopathology, many professionals may fail to adopt an appropriate cultural perspective when dealing with mental illness. Clark (1987) notes a reluctance of "mainstream" psychologists and psychiatrists to incorporate the cross-cultural perspective in their research and clinical practices even when their patients or subjects are from diverse cultures. In a shrinking world, with instant communication and easy transportation, it is crucial for our sciences and professions to take a world view. In fact, Kleinman and Good consider cultural factors so important to our understanding of depressive disorders that they have urged the psychiatric community to incorporate another Axis in the DSM diagnostic system to reflect cultural factors in psychopathology.

Sociocultural Influences in Our Own Society

As we narrow our focus to our own society, we find a number of early studies dealing with the relation of social factors to the nature and incidence of mental disorder. For example, in a pioneering 1939 study, Faris and Dunham found that a disproportionate number of the schizophrenic patients admitted to mental hospitals came from the lower socioeconomic areas of a large city. The rate of admission decreased according to how far patients lived from these deteriorating sections of the city. Later surveys have consistently found a relationship between social class and psychopathology (e.g., Dohrenwend & Dohrenwend, 1974).

Other researchers have investigated a wider range of subgroups (such as urban-rural, ethnic, religious, and occupational) in relation to mental disorders. An extensive study of mental disorders in Texas conducted by Jaco (1960) found that the incidence of psychoses was three times higher in urban than in rural areas and higher among the divorced and separated than among the married or widowed. Several studies found that the highest rates of mental disorders were in the areas of large cities that were undergoing rapid and drastic social changes (Blazer et al., 1985; Bloom, Asher, & White, 1978; Dooley & Catalano, 1980). It must be emphasized, however, that these are merely correlational findings and thus not evidence of causal relationships.

As was noted in Chapter 1, the study of the incidence and distribution of physical and mental disorders in a population (as in the research just cited) is called *epidemiology*. The epidemiological approach implicates not only the social conditions and high-risk areas that are correlated with a high incidence of given disorders, but also the groups for whom the risk of pathology is especially high—for example, refugees from other countries (Vega and Rumbaut, 1991). Throughout this text we will point out many high-risk groups with respect to suicide, drug dependence, and other maladaptive behavior patterns. This information provides a basis for formulating prevention and treatment programs; in turn, the effectiveness of these programs can be evaluated by means of further epidemiological studies.

With the gradual recognition of sociocultural influences, what was previously an almost exclusive concern with individual patients has broadened to include a concern with societal, communal, familial, and other group settings as factors in mental disorders. It is now clear that a person's maladaptive behavior might be caused not only by personal problems but also by abnormal conditions in the surrounding social environment.

Sociocultural research has led to programs designed to improve the social conditions that foster maladaptive behavior and to community facilities for the early detection, treatment, and long-range prevention of mental disorder. In Chapter 19 we will examine some clinical facilities and other programs—both governmental and private—that have been established as a result of community efforts.

UNRESOLVED ISSUES on Theoretical Viewpoints

The viewpoints described in this chapter are theoretical constructions devised to orient psychologists in the study of abnormal behavior. As a set of hypothetical guidelines, each viewpoint speaks to the importance and integrity of its own position to the exclusion of other explanations. Most psychoanalytically-oriented clinicians, for example, value those traditional writings and beliefs consistent with Freudian or later psychodynamic theory, and they minimize or ignore the teachings of opposing viewpoints; they would likely adhere to prescribed practices of psychoanalysis in their therapy and not use other methods, such as desensitization therapy.

Theoretical integrity and adherence to a systematic viewpoint has a key advantage: it provides a consistent approach to orient one's practice or research efforts. Once mastered, the methodology can guide a practitioner or researcher through the complex web of human problems. It can also provide direction and considerable reassurance that one's approach is relevant and effective. Theoretical adherence has its disadvantages, however. In excluding other possible explanations, it can blind researchers to other factors that may be equally important.

The fact is that none of the theories to date address the whole spectrum of abnormality—they are each limited by their focus. Two general trends have occurred as a result. The first involves *revisions* of an original theoretical doctrine by expanding or modifying some elements of the system. The second involves making use of two or more diverse approaches in a more general, *eclectic* approach. We will now examine how effectively each of these trends brings order to theoretical complexity.

1. *The revision of theoretical viewpoints.* The emergence of diverse viewpoints to explain abnormal behavior has led to criticisms of each viewpoint and thus to attempts to accommodate these criticisms. There are many examples of such corrective interpretations, such as Adler's or Jung's modification of Freudian theory or the more recent cognitive-behavioral approach in behavior therapy. But many of the early Freudian theorists did not accept the neo-

Freudian additions, and many classical behavior therapists today do not accept the revisions proposed by cognitive behaviorists. Therefore, theoretical viewpoints tend to multiply and coexist—each with its own proponents—rather than being assimilated into previous views. In effect, "revisions" of an original doctrine tend to survive as new, alternative interpretations of psychopathology. The result is a cumbersome backdrop of myriad theoretical viewpoints from which to study abnormal behavior. Of course, this situation complicates communication among psychologists who may hold to different perspectives. In addition, it is more difficult for a person to evaluate the scope and nature of any research or treatment because a complete understanding requires an awareness of the perspective from which the research or the treatment is initiated. With so many different perspectives, it is impossible to have a clear grasp of them all.

2. *The eclectic approach.* As the research engendered by different perspectives has gradually led to a better understanding of mental disorders, it has become increasingly apparent that explanations based on single viewpoints are likely to be incomplete. Usually, the interaction of several causal factors (biological, psychosocial, and sociocultural) produces the disorders that we see. For example, an individual may have a biological predisposition to severe mood swings but may function well until some severe crisis brings on a depressive state. Gradually, investigators have come to realize that even where brain damage is present, a patient's psychological reaction to it and to the resulting change in his or her life are of vital importance in determining an overall clinical picture. It is also apparent that the emotional support of family members—as well as the kind of situation to which a patient will return after discharge from the hospital—are significant factors in determining a favorable outcome. Likewise, research has found that the use of biological therapies—such as antidepressant drugs or electroconvulsive shock—sometimes produces dramatic results even for mental disorders that are apparently the result of psychological rather than biological factors. Finally, the symptoms, prognosis, and reaction to a treatment for a certain disorder may all vary somewhat for individuals from different cultural backgrounds.

In practice, many psychologists have responded to the existence of many perspectives by adopting an eclectic stance—that is, they accept working ideas from several existing viewpoints and use them all as practicable. For example, a psychologist using an eclectic approach might accept causal explanations from psychoanalytic theory while applying techniques of anxiety reduction derived from behavior therapy. Purists in the field—those advocates of a single viewpoint—are skeptical about eclecticism, claiming that the eclectic approach tends to lack integrity and produces a "crazy quilt" of activity with little rationale and inconsistent practice. This criticism may be true, but the approach certainly works for many psychologists.

Typically, those using an eclectic approach make no attempt to synthesize the theoretical perspectives. The approach seems to work best in practice rather than in theory; the underlying principles of many of the theoretical perspectives are incompatible as they now stand. Thus the eclectic approach still falls short of the final goal, which is to tackle the theoretical clutter and develop a single, comprehensive, internally consistent viewpoint that accurately reflects what we know empirically about abnormal behavior. It may be unrealistic to expect a single theoretical viewpoint to be broad enough to explain abnormal behavior in general and specific enough to accurately predict the symptoms and causes of specific disorders. Nevertheless, such a unified viewpoint is the challenge for the next generation of theorists in the field of abnormal psychology. Perhaps some reader of this chapter will confront this challenge and perform the necessary synthesis for a clearer conceptual picture of psychopathology.

SUMMARY

Abnormal psychology is a relatively young scientific discipline that contains many points of view on the interpretation and treatment of abnormal behavior. The early biological viewpoint focused on neurological brain damage as a model for the understanding of abnormality. We now see that model as limited even for the cases to which it most clearly applies. Modern biological thinking about mental disorders has focused on the biochemistry of brain functioning. Investigations in this area show much promise for advancing our knowledge of how the mind and the body interact to produce maladaptive behavior, particularly in respect to the more severe disorders.

The psychosocial viewpoints on abnormal behavior, dealing with human psychology rather than biology, necessarily are more varied than the biological perspective. The oldest of these perspectives is Freudian psychoanalysis. For many years this view has been preoccupied with questions about libidinal energies and their containment, but more recently it has shown a distinctly social or interpersonal thrust under the direction of object-relations theory. Psychoanalysis and closely related approaches are termed *psychodynamic* in recognition of their attention to inner, often unconscious forces. An integration of psychodynamic and interpersonal perspectives (as suggested by Sullivan's work) would seem possible as we move into the future.

The behavioristic perspective, which is rooted in the desire to make psychology an objective science, was slow in overcoming a dominant psychodynamic bias, but in the last 25 years has established itself as a significant force. Behaviorism focuses on the role of learning in human behavior, and views maladaptive behavior as a failure of learning. Its therapeutic methods have achieved excellent results, and its ability to accommodate itself to the current dominance of cognitive thinking in psychology ensures its continued growth and importance.

Initially a spinoff from (and in part a reaction against) the behavioristic perspective, the cognitive-behavioral viewpoint attempts to incorporate the complexities of human cognition in a rigorous, learning-based framework. This viewpoint attempts to alter maladaptive thinking and improve people's abilities to solve problems and to plan. As we will discuss in Chapter 18, the treatment procedures incorporating cognitive processes are highly effective in dealing with many behavioral problems.

The humanistic perspective does not chiefly concern itself with the origins and treatments of severe mental disorders. Rather, it focuses on the conditions that can maximize functioning in individuals who are just "getting along." It views abnormality as a failure to develop individual human potential. As such, it has to do with personal values and personal growth.

The originators of the interpersonal perspective were defectors from the psychoanalytic ranks who took exception to the Freudian emphasis on the internal determinants of motivation and behavior. As a group, interpersonal theorists have emphasized that important aspects of human personality have social or interpersonal origins. This viewpoint sees unsatisfactory relationships in the past or present as the primary causes of maladaptive behaviors. The most fully articulated and important interpersonal theories are those of Harry Stack Sullivan.

Any comprehensive approach to the study of human behavior—normal or abnormal—must take account of the sociocultural context in which a given behavior occurs. Cultural influences on psychopathology are important in understanding the origin and course of a behavioral problem. The sociocultural viewpoint is concerned with the social environment as a contributor to mental disorder.

Finally, we are still a long way from the goal of a complete understanding of abnormal behavior. The many theoretical perspectives that exist have given us a start, and a good one at that—but they fall short. To obtain a more comprehensive understanding of mental disorder, we must draw on a variety of sources, including the findings of genetics, biochemistry, psychology, sociology, and so forth. Clearly, none of the theories currently available is complete; we do not have an integrated, theoretically consistent view of abnormal behavior that is widely accepted. It rests upon future generations of theorists to devise a general theory of psychopathology, if indeed one is possible.

Key Terms

biological viewpoint (p. 56)
medical model (p. 56)
neurotransmitters (p. 58)
psychosocial viewpoints (p. 62)
psychoanalytic perspective (p. 62)
psychoanalysis (p. 62)
psychodynamic perspectives (p. 62)
mesmerism (p. 62)
Nancy School (p. 63)
catharsis (p. 64)
the unconscious (p. 64)
free association (p. 65)
dream analysis (p. 65)
id (p. 65)
libido (p. 65)
pleasure principle (p. 65)
primary process (p. 65)
ego (p. 65)
secondary process (p. 66)
reality principle (p. 66)
superego (p. 66)
intrapsychic conflicts (p. 66)
ego-defense mechanisms (p. 66)
psychosexual stages of development (p. 67)
Oedipus complex (p. 67)
castration anxiety (p. 67)
Electra complex (p. 67)
introjection (p. 68)
object-relations (p. 69)
separation-individuation (p. 70)
behavioristic perspective (p. 71)
conditioning (p. 71)
learning (p. 73)
classical conditioning (p. 73)
operant (or instrumental) conditioning (p. 73)
reinforcement (p. 73)
extinction (p. 74)
generalization (p. 74)
discrimination (p. 74)
cognitive processes (p. 76)
cognitive-behavioral perspective (p. 76)
personal constructs (p. 76)
humanistic perspective (p. 78)
self-concept (p. 78)
self-actualizing (p. 80)
interpersonal perspective (p. 82)
significant others (p. 83)
self-system (p. 84)
social exchange (p. 84)
social roles (p. 84)
attribution theory (p. 85)
interpersonal accommodation (p. 85)
sociocultural viewpoint (p. 87)
cultural relativism (p. 88)

Chapter 4

Causal Factors in Abnormal Behavior

Eddie Arning, *Untitled.* Arning (b. 1898), a native of Texas, was committed to a state mental hospital while in his mid-twenties because of his violent behavior and depression. At the age of 64, he was found mentally stable and was moved to a nursing home. It was at this point that Arning began to make highly schematic crayon drawings, first of recollections of his family life and later of images he saw in newspaper and magazine ads. Sadly, Arning's creative inspiration seemed to leave him when he was released from the nursing home at age 78, and he stopped drawing.

Abnormal behavior almost never arises suddenly, out of the blue, in a person with a faultless biological and psychological makeup—if any such person ever existed. Rather, we can usually see—although often only in retrospect—the pattern of factors that made an individual vulnerable to abnormality. At the very least, we can usually piece together a number of hypotheses about these background factors.

It is a reasonable assumption that all of us harbor **vulnerabilities,** factors that under certain circumstances make us susceptible to behaving abnormally. Whether or not we ever do appears to depend on the nature, number, and degree of these vulnerabilities; on the way they combine in any given individual and on the nature and severity of the life challenges we face. Commenting on the enormous complexity and widespread individual differences implied here, Meehl (1978, 1989) has suggested that severe mental breakdown is often the result of "bad luck." He notes, however, that such a conclusion does not justify the abandonment of our efforts to understand, prevent, and treat mental disorder.

In the preceding chapter, we described several *theoretical* viewpoints concerning abnormal behavior, each of which focuses on different origins or background events that contribute to maladaptive behavior. In brief, the biological viewpoint emphasizes various organic conditions that can impair brain functioning and lead to psychopathology. Of the psychosocial viewpoints, the psychodynamic focuses on intrapsychic conflicts that lead to anxiety; the behavioristic, on faulty learning; the cognitive-behavioral, on information processing processes involved in distorted thinking; the humanistic, on blocked or distorted personal growth; and the interpersonal, on unsatisfactory relationships. Finally, the sociocultural viewpoint focuses on pathological social conditions. In this chapter we will look at the *empirical* evidence concerning the origins, in general terms, of our human vulnerabilities, reviewing available research on the subject. Unfortunately, there is often little discernible relationship between theoretical perspectives and the sorts of causal or risk factors that can be studied using empirical methods. This situation results from the difficulty of formulating these theoretical propositions into terms clear enough to permit empirical investigation. Before proceeding with a review of the evidence, however, we must give some additional attention to the concept of causation in abnormal behavior.

PERSPECTIVES ON CAUSATION

Central to the field of abnormal psychology are questions about what causes some people to behave maladaptively in some situations for varying periods of time. These questions not only challenge us to deepen our appreciation of the human condition, but they also address practical considerations in prevention, assessment, and treatment. Equipped with a knowledge of the specific causes for given classes of disorder, we could more efficiently help to avoid conditions that lead to disorder and perhaps reverse those that maintain it. Somewhat less obviously, we could better classify and diagnose disorders if we clearly understood the causal sequences leading to diverse disordered outcomes rather than relying on clusters of apparently similar behavior, as we for the most part do now.

Although understanding the causes of abnormal behavior is clearly a desirable goal, it is enormously difficult to achieve because human behavior is so complex. Even the simplest of human behaviors, such as speaking or writing a word, is the product of literally thousands of prior events—only some of which are understood, and then frequently only in the vaguest of ways. Understanding a person's life in causal terms, even an utterly "adaptive" life, is an incomplete project of enormous magnitude; when the life is a maladaptive one, we can assume the task is even more difficult. As a result, many investigators now prefer to speak of *risk factors* (variables correlated with an abnormal outcome) rather than of *causes.* Nevertheless, causes remain the ultimate quarry.

In attempting to analyze the causal factors in abnormal behavior, it will be helpful to consider (a) the distinctions between primary, predisposing, precipitating, and reinforcing causes; (b) the problem of feedback and circularity in abnormal behavior; and (c) the concept of diathesis-stress as a broad causal model of abnormal behavior.

Primary, Predisposing, Precipitating, and Reinforcing Causes

Regardless of one's theoretical perspective, several terms can be used to specify the role a factor plays in the **etiology,** or causal pattern, of abnormal behavior. A **primary cause** is a condition that must exist for a disorder to occur—syphilis of the brain is an example in the case of general paresis. A primary cause is a necessary but not always sufficient factor in abnormality. Many recognized disorders appear not to have primary causes. A **predisposing cause** is a condition that comes before and paves the way for a later occurrence of disorder under certain conditions; an example is parental rejection, which could predispose a child toward difficulty in handling close personal relationships later. A **precipitating cause** is a condition that proves too much for an individual and triggers a disorder; an example is a crushing disappointment. Often a precipitating cause seems insignificant and related only tangentially, if at all, to a primary or predisposing cause. In short, it is the straw that breaks the camel's back. For example, leaving the cap off the toothpaste may be a minor annoyance in a basically well-adjusted family, but the same act can cause a full-fledged argument in a family already experiencing major difficulties in communicating. Finally, a **reinforcing cause** is a condition that tends to maintain maladaptive behavior that is already occurring. An example is the extra attention, sympathy, and removal from unwanted responsibility that often come when a person is "ill"; these pleasant experiences may contribute to a delay in recovery. Reinforcing causes have received a great deal of attention in recent years, especially among behaviorally-oriented psychologists.

In a given case, a primary cause may be either absent or unknown, or two or more factors may share primary responsibility. Likewise, the exact patterning of primary, predisposing, precipitating, and reinforcing causes may be far from clear; a given factor or event may contribute to a disorder in more than one way. For example, the death of a parent can be both a primary and a precipitating factor in a child's subsequent grief reaction; it might also predispose the child to severe reactions to losses in adulthood.

As this example suggests, serious adjustment challenges early in life, whatever their nature, may predispose a person toward specific difficulties later in life. In other words, all the causal factors just discussed (including primary, precipitating, and

Serious adjustment challenges, such as the death of a loved one, may predispose a person toward later difficulties in life.

reinforcing factors) can act as predisposing factors; that is, they may play important roles in increasing a person's vulnerability to disorder. (For our purposes, the terms *predisposition* and *vulnerability* can be used interchangeably.) A parent's overprotective behavior, for example, could become a reinforcing cause for fearfulness and timidity in a child, so that the child would be less well equipped than others to manage the rigors of adulthood. Such a child would be more predisposed, more vulnerable, to breakdown when his or her resources are seriously challenged.

Feedback and Circularity in Abnormal Behavior

Traditionally in the sciences, the task of determining cause-and-effect relationships has focused on isolating the condition X (cause) that could be demonstrated to lead to condition Y (effect). For example, when the alcohol content of the blood reaches a certain level, alcoholic intoxication occurs. Where more than one causal factor is involved, the term **causal pattern** has been used. Here conditions A, B, C, etc. lead to condition Y. In either case, this concept of cause follows a simple linear model in which a given variable or set of variables leads to a result either immediately after or later in time. Classical physicists had adopted this essential causal model until it was shown to be inadequate for the much more complex universe discovered by twentieth-century physicists.

In the behavioral sciences, and particularly in abnormal psychology, such simple cause-and-effect sequences are very rare. This rarity results not only because we usually must deal with a multitude of interacting causes, but also because we often have difficulty distinguishing between what is cause and what is effect. The concept of self-regulating systems can be applied here. A *self-regulating system* is one in which effects operate as causes for new effects, as when room temperature determines whether or not a home thermostat will signal the furnace to put out more heat. In abnormal behavior, the effects of feedback and the existence of mutual, two-way influences must be taken into account. Consider the following situation:

A husband and wife are undergoing counseling for difficulties in their marriage. The husband accuses his wife of drinking excessively, while the wife accuses her husband of rejecting her and showing no affection. In explaining her frustrations to the therapist, the wife views the situation as "I drink because my husband rejects me." The husband sees the problem differently: "I reject my wife because she drinks too much."

Over time, a vicious circle has developed in which the husband has increasingly withdrawn as his wife has increasingly lost control of her drinking. It is extremely difficult, if not impossible, to differentiate cause from effect. Rather, the problem has become a vicious circle: each person influences and maintains the behavior of the other.

Even more subtle confoundings of cause and effect are regularly encountered in the lives of disturbed people. Consider the following scenario:

A boy with a history of disturbed interactions with his parents routinely misinterprets the intentions of his peers as being hostile. He

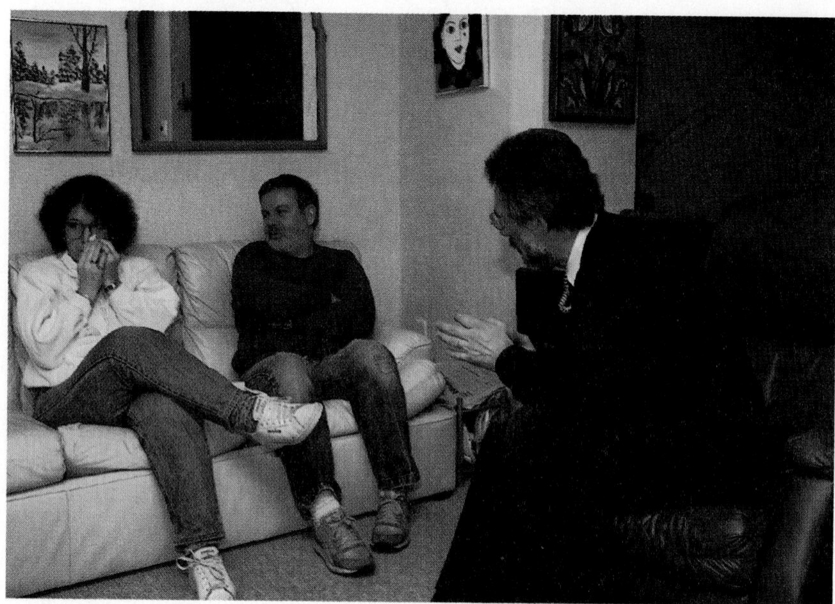

In abnormal psychology, we often have difficulty distinguishing between what is cause and what is effect. For example, in problems between marital partners, a vicious circle may develop in which each person influences and maintains the behavior of the other. A wife who feels her husband is rejecting her may become increasingly hostile, and the husband may become more withdrawn as his wife's hostility increases, making it virtually impossible to differentiate cause from effect.

develops defensive strategies to counteract the supposed malevolence of those around him, such as the surly rejection of others' efforts to be friendly, which efforts he misconstrues as patronizing. His behavior is difficult for others to deal with, even if those others in fact have benign intentions at the outset. Confronted by the boy's prickly behavior, however, they become defensive, hostile and rejecting, thus confirming and strengthening the boy's distorted expectations. In this manner, each opportunity for new experience and new learning is in fact subverted and becomes another encounter with a social environment that seems perversely and persistently hostile—exactly in line with the boy's expectations.

These not-so-hypothetical situations illustrate that our concepts of causal relationships must take into account the complex factors of feedback, information exchange (communication), patterns of interaction, and circularity.

The Diathesis-Stress Model

Throughout the rest of this chapter, we will deal chiefly with predispositional causes of maladaptive behavior in their biological, psychosocial, and sociocultural contexts. A predisposition toward developing a given disorder is termed a **diathesis.** Most mental disorders are conceived (probably rightly) as the product of stress operating on an individual who harbors a diathesis for the type of disorder that emerges. Hence we adopt here what is commonly known as a **diathesis-stress model** of abnormal behavior, which is little more than a recognition of the rather obvious fact that disorder results when a challenge exceeds a particular organism's capacity to meet it. The model should be viewed merely as a conceptual convenience. It has little analytical precision or predictive utility in individual cases of disorder, because it is usually impossible to identify pathogenic diatheses or stressors independently of one another or of an occurrence of maladaptive behavior.

Stress, the response of an organism to adjustive demands made upon it, will be the focus of Chapter 5. Inevitably, however, we will find ourselves referring to stress and *stressors* (the adjustive demands themselves) in our discussion of diatheses because these concepts are so closely related. Indeed, as already suggested, the presence of a diathesis often can be inferred only after some stressful circumstances have led to a breakdown of adaptive behavior. Often, the factors contributing to the development of a diathesis are themselves highly potent stressors, as when a child is physically abused by parents and thereby acquires a predisposition to become a child abuser later in life.

Since stress is the response of an organism to an adjustive demand, it follows that the consequences of stress depend on the coping resources available to

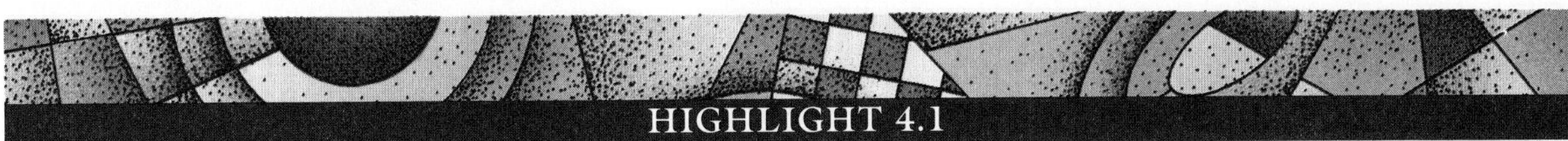

HIGHLIGHT 4.1

Predisposing Causes of Depressive Reactions to Rape

Atkeson et al. (1982) assessed depressive responses to rape in a group of 115 victims of sexual assault, following them for a period of 12 months after the occurrences of the crime. Most of these women experienced depressive emotions immediately following the assaults, but as a group, they were not significantly more depressed than a nonvictim control group at the 4-month follow-up. However, a subgroup of these victims continued to be depressed even at the 12-month follow-up. Demographic variables such as age and socioeconomic factors were found to be related to subsequent depression (older and poorer women being the more affected). Surprisingly, the levels of trauma experienced during the rapes had no detectable effect on long-term depressive symptomatologies. Adequate support immediately after the rapes did appear to lessen long-term effects.

The strongest determinants of adjustment in the long-term post-rape period were associated with the victim's level of prior functioning. Less functional individuals were much more vulnerable to depression after having been raped than were their more functional counterparts. Women who already had had psychological problems of one sort or another, especially including depression, anxiety, and obsessive-compulsive behavior, were slower to recover from rapes. Additionally, problems with sexual relationships generally and with physical health seem to have hampered rapid recoveries from the stress of rapes. Research on the general effects of rape on its victims (e.g., Koss, 1983) suggests that they may sometimes be exacerbations of preexisting tendencies.

an individual undergoing an adjustive challenge. Thus one way of viewing vulnerability is in terms of a lack of resources needed to overcome a challenge. This way of viewing vulnerability is general but does have merit, as can be seen in the research, described in *HIGHLIGHT 4.1,* on differential rates of recovery from the experience of rape.

The more specific concept of diathesis refers to a vulnerability to a particular disorder, or a tendency to respond in a particular way to adjustive failure. In other words, an individual is likely to be at special risk for developing the disorder in question should stress exceed current coping resources.

In sum, we can distinguish between causes of abnormal behavior that lie within and are part of the biological makeup or prior experience of a person—diathesis, vulnerability, or predisposition—and those that pertain to current challenges in a person's life, generally termed stressors. A reinforcing cause, for example, would be a special type of stressor. It will be useful to keep these distinctions in mind as we explore the sources of our vulnerabilities in the following sections. Although we will be discussing biological, psychosocial, and sociocultural factors separately, it will also be important to keep in mind that their interaction is critical.

BIOLOGICAL CAUSAL FACTORS

Biological factors influence all aspects of our behavior, including our intellectual capabilities, basic temperament, primary reaction tendencies, stress tolerance, and adaptive resources. Thus a wide range of biological conditions—such as faulty genes, diseases, endocrine imbalances, malnutrition, injuries, and other factors that interfere with normal development and functioning—are potential causes of abnormal behavior.

In this section we will focus on four categories of biological factors that seem particularly relevant to the development of maladaptive behavior: (a) genetic defects; (b) constitutional liabilities; (c) brain dysfunction; and (d) physical deprivations or disruptions. Each of these categories encompasses a number of conditions that influence the quality and functioning of our bodies. They are not necessarily independent of each other, and they may—and most likely do—occur in varying combinations in given individuals.

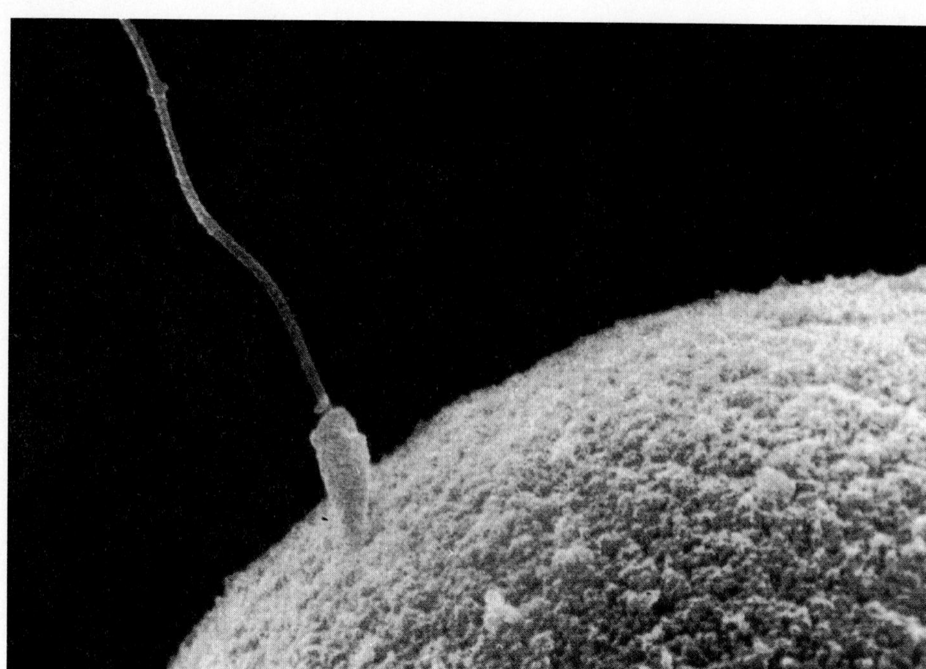

Inheritance begins at conception when the male sperm cell penetrates and fertilizes the female egg cell. The resulting embryo receives a genetic code that provides potentialities for development and behavior throughout a lifetime.

Genetic Defects

The essential characteristics of human inheritance are basically the same for all people of all racial and ethnic groups. The specific features of genetic endowment, however, vary widely. Except for identical twins, no two humans have ever begun life with the same endowment. Thus heredity not only provides the potentialities for development and behavior typical of the species, but it is also an important source of individual differences. In general, heredity determines not the specifics of human behavior but rather the ranges within which characteristic behavior can be modified by environmental or experiential influences.

Inheritance begins at conception, when the egg cell of a female is fertilized by the sperm cell of a male, and the resulting embryo receives a genetic code that provides potentialities for development and behavior throughout a lifetime. Since our behavior is inevitably influenced by our biological inheritance, it should hardly be surprising that certain vulnerabilities have their sources at this basic level. Some inherited defects cause structural abnormalities that interfere directly with the normal development of the brain. Other more subtle defects can leave a person susceptible to even the most severe mental disorders. These subtle influences are usually transmitted in the genetic code itself, showing up as metabolic or biochemical variations from an ideally functional norm. The form of mental retardation known as phenylketonuria (PKU), for example, is produced by a genetic error that prevents the adequate metabolization of a chemical compound present in many foods. Other genetic defects are believed to affect adversely the delicate regulation of brain biochemistry. In other words, the individual may inherit faulty genes.

Chromosomal Anomalies The chainlike structures within a cell nucleus that contain the genes are **chromosomes.** Advances in cellular biological research have enabled us to readily detect **chromosomal anomalies**—irregularities in the chromosomal structure—even before birth, thus making it possible to study their effects on future development and behavior. The first major breakthrough in this area was the discovery that most normal human cells have 46 chromosomes containing the genetic materials in which the hereditary plan—the overall guide for development—is encoded. When fertilization takes place, the normal inheritance consists of 23 pairs of chromosomes, one of each pair from the mother and one from the father. Twenty-two of these chromosome pairs are called **autosomes;** they determine by their biochemical action general anatomical and physiological characteristics. The remaining pair, the **sex chromosomes,** determine an individual's sex. In a female both of these sex chromosomes—one from each parent—are designated as **X chromosomes.** In a male the sex chromosome from the mother is an X, but that from the father is a **Y chromosome.**

Research in developmental genetics has shown that abnormalities in the structure or number of the chromosomes are associated with a wide range of malformations and disorders. For example, Down syndrome is a type of mental retardation in which there is a *trisomy* (a set of three chromosomes instead of two) in chromosome 21. Here the extra chromosome is the primary cause of the disorder. A predisposing cause in Down syndrome is parental age at conception; the probability of this defect rises sharply with the age of the mother (especially after 40) and less sharply but still significantly with the age of the father (Hook, 1980; Stene et al., 1981). Fortunately, this predisposing factor manifests itself only rarely in Down syndrome, but the risk reaches 1 in 50 for a mother in her 40s (Holvey & Talbot, 1972).

Anomalies may also occur in the sex chromosomes, producing a variety of complications that may predispose a person to develop abnormal behavior. For example, Klinefelter's syndrome also involves 47 chromosomes, but in this case the pathogenic element is an extra X chromosome. These XXY individuals have male body structures (although they are usually infertile) and a predominantly male gender identity. They are, however, far more likely than males with the usual 46 chromosomes to develop several kinds of psychopathology, such as juvenile delinquency and problems arising from gender identity confusion (Wright, Schaefer, & Solomons, 1979). Such individuals are said to be at high risk for these outcomes.

Studies by Sergovich et al. (1969) and Hanerton et al. (1975) indicate that the incidence of observable chromosomal abnormalities in newborns is approximately one half of 1 percent. The exact causes of chromosomal anomalies are not yet fully understood. Some have evidently been passed on from one or both of the parents; some apparently are due to errors that occur in the combining of egg and sperm at conception; and still others are caused by aberrant embryo development after conception.

A search for chromosomal irregularities in schizophrenia and other nonorganic psychoses has not proved fruitful, and none of the chromosomal anomalies thus far observed has been directly related to such disorders. Even in the case of Down syndrome, where a trisomy has been identified, it is estimated that 65 percent of the fetuses thus affected spontaneously abort (Creasy & Crolla, 1974). The potential effects of extreme chromosomal irregularities are largely unknown because they ordinarily result in an embryo's death. Nearly 50 percent of stillborn infants have such chromosomal abnormalities (Poland & Lowry, 1974).

One thing appears certain: females are less susceptible to defects from sex-linked disorders because they have two X chromosomes. If one proves faulty, the other member of the pair generally can handle the work of development. Nevertheless, females are sometimes born with a missing chromosome (XO, called Turner's syndrome) or an extra sex chromosome (XXX), either of which may produce abnormalities. Since males normally have a single X chromosome paired with a single Y chromosome, a defect in either may mean trouble. For a summary of some of the known chromosomal abnormalities that can occur, see *HIGHLIGHT 4.2.*

Faulty Genes It is important to distinguish between chromosomal irregularities, which can now usually be directly observed, and genetic faults (abnormalities of specific genes), which can exist in the absence of obvious chromosomal deviations. **Genes** are the long molecules of DNA (deoxyribonucleic acid) that form at various locations on a chromosome. Individual genes may contain information that causes bodily processes to malfunction, as in the PKU example cited earlier. Unfortunately, we cannot yet predict with any great certainty the occurrence of most such malfunctions.

Through the use of electron microscopes, however, we can study the internal structure of genes, and by complicated gene mapping techniques we can gain information concerning the code that regulates the development and functioning of an organism. This code is carried by the biochemical constituents of the DNA molecule's now-familiar spiraling ladder—the double helix (see *HIGHLIGHT 4.3*). Genes carry the instructions for specific body traits, such as eye color and blood type. They also provide the assembly instructions for organ development. Thus they are the specific units or bearers of an individual's biological inheritance.

Some genes are **dominant genes;** their instructions are activated even if the other member of the pair carries contradictory instructions. **Recessive genes** have instructions that are not carried out unless an individual has inherited two of them, one from each parent. In the field of abnormal psychology, however, genetic influences rarely express themselves in such simple, straightforward ways. This results because behavior, unlike some physical characteristics such as eye color, is not determined exclusively by genetic endowment: it is a product of the environment's interaction with the structural and functional characteristics of an organism.

HIGHLIGHT 4.2

Chromosomal Abnormalities

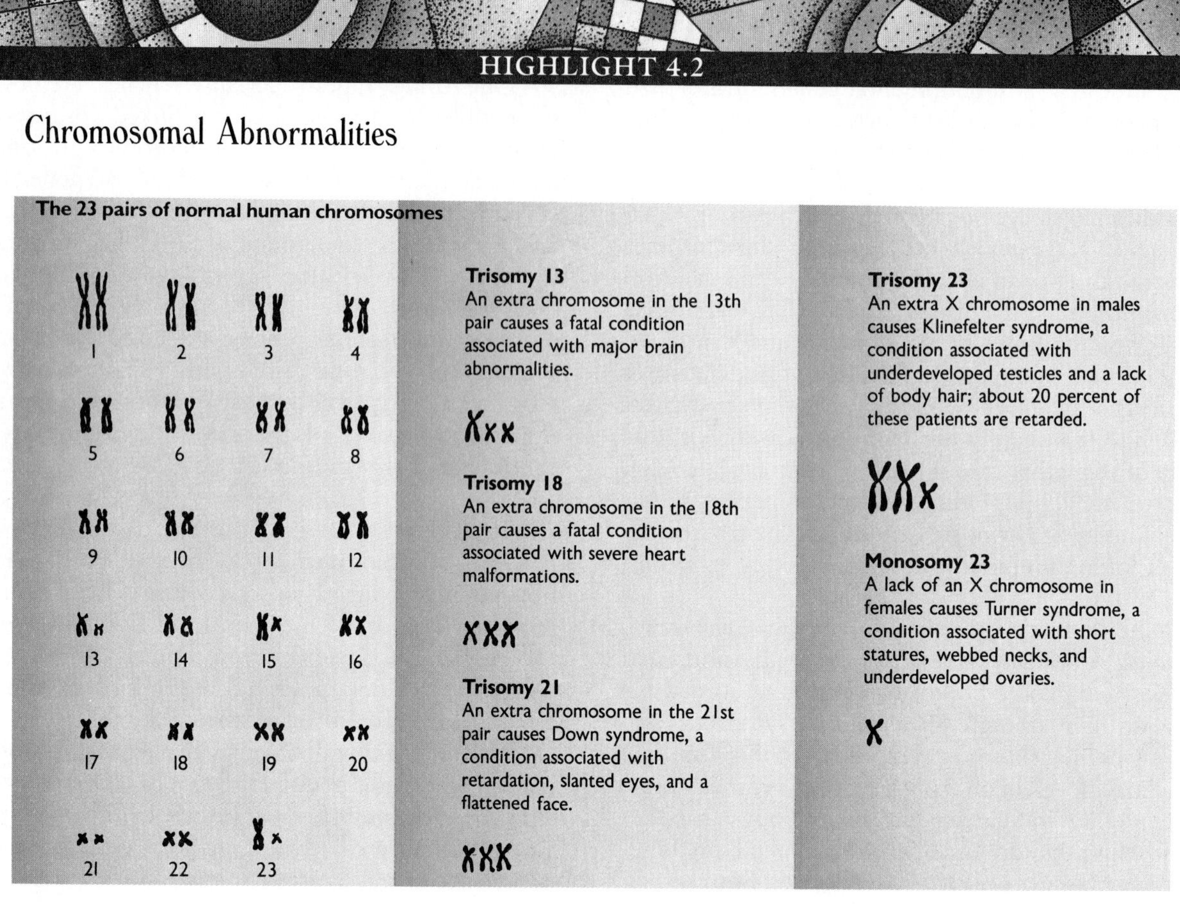

The 23 pairs of normal human chromosomes
1
2
3
4
5
6
7
8
9
10
11
12
13
14
15
16
17
18
19
20
21
22
23
Trisomy 13
An extra chromosome in the 13th pair causes a fatal condition associated with major brain abnormalities.
Trisomy 18
An extra chromosome in the 18th pair causes a fatal condition associated with severe heart malformations.
Trisomy 21
An extra chromosome in the 21st pair causes Down syndrome, a condition associated with retardation, slanted eyes, and a flattened face.
Trisomy 23
An extra X chromosome in males causes Klinefelter syndrome, a condition associated with underdeveloped testicles and a lack of body hair; about 20 percent of these patients are retarded.
Monosomy 23
A lack of an X chromosome in females causes Turner syndrome, a condition associated with short statures, webbed necks, and underdeveloped ovaries.

Adapted from a *Chicago Tribune* graphic; *Chicago Tribune,* February 6, 1983.
Data from "It's Not Too Late for a Baby: For Women and Men over 35" by Sylvia P. Rubin.

Genes can affect behavior only indirectly, through their influence on the physical and chemical properties of a body, whose development they regulate in concert with other factors in their environments. Gene "expression," therefore, is normally not a simple or direct outcome of the information encoded in DNA, but is rather the end product of an intricate and involved process that may be influenced by the internal (and likely the external) environment. Unqualified statements about the inheritance of certain mental disorders—sometimes made even by authorities who should know better—must therefore be viewed with a degree of caution; they are almost always untrue in any literal sense (Carson & Sanislow, 1992).

The few instances in which relatively straightforward predictions of mental disorders can be made on the basis of known laws of inheritance invariably involve gross neurological impairment. In such cases, abnormal behavior arises, in part, as a consequence of a central nervous system malfunction. Examples of these rare disorders include Huntington's chorea (a type of brain degeneration beginning in the young or middle adult years) and Tay-Sachs disease (a disorder of fat metabolism causing mental retardation and early death, found mostly among people of European Jewish ancestry). Generally, such disorders occur where there is a pairing of two recessive genes, each of which contains the faulty code.

It appears likely that many of the most interesting (if still largely obscure) genetic influences in abnormal behavior do not usually involve dominant and recessive relationships in one or only a few gene pairs. Rather, most researchers believe that pathogenic genetic influences typically operate *polygenically,* that is, through the action of many genes together in some sort of additive or interactive fashion (e.g., Faraone & Tsuang, 1985). A genetically vulnerable individual has inherited a large

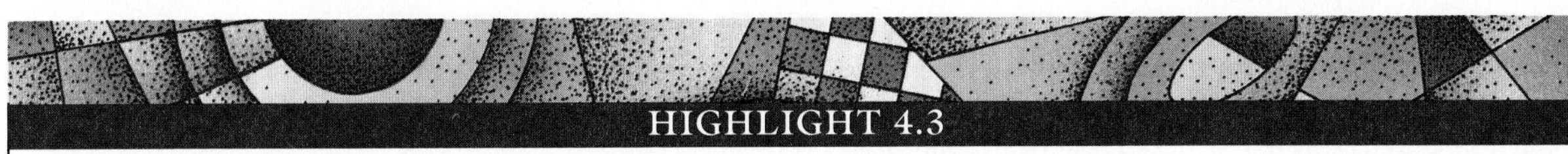

HIGHLIGHT 4.3

The Double Helix

The DNA double helix molecule is depicted in the figure below. The bases of the two strands point toward one another, joined by the "rungs" of the twisting ladderlike form. The helical form is stabilized because these rungs always consist of one purine (adenine [A] or guanine [G]) and one pyrimidine (thymine [T] or cystocine [C]) "base pair" of molecules, which form a hydrogen bond between them; every A is paired with a T, and every G is paired with a C. The genetic code itself depends on the sequencing of these base pairs of molecules. Though we do not know exactly how it occurs, aberrations in the pairing of the molecules result in biochemical malfunctioning, which may, in turn, affect bodily structure and function. The extremely small size of DNA's structure is indicated by scale in nanometers (nm). A nanometer is one-billionth of a meter. The diameter of the helix is maintained at 2 nanometers.

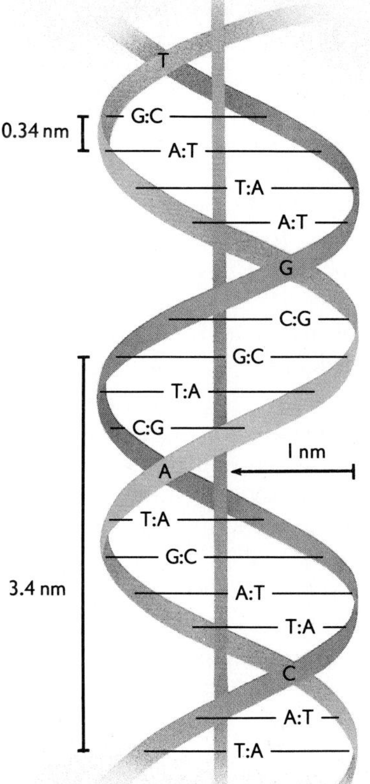

number of these genes that collectively represent faulty heredity. These faulty genes, in turn, may lead to errors in the regulation of brain chemistry that predispose the individual to later difficulties.

Although marked advances have been made in identifying faulty genetic endowment (including the location of the faulty genes responsible for certain physical anomalies), we are not yet able to isolate specific defects on the genes themselves. Therefore most of the information we have on the role of genetic factors in mental disorders is based not on studies of genes, but on studies of individuals genetically related to one another. This pedigree, or family history, method requires that an investigator observe samples of relatives of each ***proband*** or ***index case*** (the subject, or carrier, of the trait in question) in order to see whether the incidence increases in proportion to the degree of hereditary relationship. In addition, the incidence of the trait in a normal population is compared (as a control) with its incidence among the relatives of the index cases.

Such research is much more difficult and complicated to carry out than it may at first appear. The history of research in this area, particularly with regard to schizophrenia, is littered with exaggerated conclusions and biased reports. For example, many studies have been made of the rates at which schizophrenia in one monozygotic (genetically identical) twin predicts schizophrenia in the other (Gottesman & Shields, 1972). These rates are called **concordance rates.** Reports from such studies have varied between 6 percent and 86 percent. An accurate figure, it now appears, would be somewhat under 50 percent, but this figure is hard to interpret because twins, especially identical twins, almost always share similar environments as well as heredity. Even if identical twins are separated from birth they are likely to have more similar environments than, say, separated dizygotic (fraternal) twins because, being of the same sex, appearance, and so on, they affect the environment in more similar ways. Nevertheless, identical twins do have sufficiently different experiences to produce measurable effects on personality development (Baker & Daniels, 1990), which is consistent with the observation that many monozygotic twins are ***discordant*** for schizophrenia—that is, if one twin becomes schizophrenic the other does not necessarily become so as well. Thus firm and stable conclusions about the magnitude of genetic contribution to mental disorders are hard to come by.

The main point here is that in many instances of schizophrenia (and probably in certain other mental disorders), there seems to be a modest but inexactly quantified hereditary component—an innate vulnerability. As was noted in Chapter 3, evidence of this type supports the resurgent biological viewpoint. Whether an individual with this pathogenic makeup will develop schizophrenia is determined by many factors that operate after conception. We still do not know much about these other factors and how they interact with genetic endowment. In Chapter 12 we will address in greater detail this matter of genetic influences in schizophrenia.

Given a favorable life situation, an individual's inherited vulnerability to a certain disorder probably will never result in abnormal behavior. The evidence suggests that in a genetically predisposed person, the most likely outcome is nonoccurrence of the disorder, as is proven in the most conservaive possible fashion by routine findings of monozygotic twin concordance rates of under 50 percent. In the area of physical disease, there are also many examples of genetic predispositions that never become observable diseases; these include predispositions for diabetes, hypertension, coronary heart disease, and some forms of cancer (Bergsma, 1974; Kaiser Foundation, 1970).

Constitutional Liabilities

The term **constitutional liability** is used to describe any detrimental characteristic that is either innate or acquired so early—often in the prenatal environment—and in such strength that it is functionally similar to a genetic characteristic. Physique, physical handicaps, and basic reaction tendencies are among the many traits included in this category. Our focus will be on the role of these constitutional factors in the etiology of maladaptive behavior.

Physique Though some early research sought to establish a direct link between physique and psychopathology—for example, between muscular physique and criminal behavior (Glueck & Glueck, 1968; Sheldon, 1954)—most data suggest that the link, if any, is not primarily biological but is rather a product of social learning. A muscular person, for instance, may learn that aggression often pays off.

A look at everyday situations shows that physique and other aspects of physical appearance do play an important role in personality development and adjustment. Beauty, for example, is highly valued in our society. One need only attend a social gathering, watch television, or note the billions of dollars spent each year on cosmetics to see the influence of beauty on people's behavior and on their feelings about themselves and others. It is reasonable to assume that, on the whole, physically attractive people have advantages in life not shared by the less attractive; indeed, mental disorder has been found to be correlated with judged unattractiveness (Napoleon, Chassin, & Young, 1980).

Even the mistaken impression that one is unattractive may enhance the risk of disorder (Noles, Cash, & Winstead, 1985). Some data suggest that attractiveness may facilitate recovery from disorder (Farina et al., 1986). The power of this variable, neglected until recently in psychological research, is illustrated in an intriguing experiment by Snyder, Tanke, and Berscheid (1977). These investigators demonstrated that college males who believed they were talking on the telephone to an attractive female behaved quite differently from those who believed they were talking to an unattractive female. (The subjects had been shown false photographs of their "partners" that had previously been judged as to attractiveness.) Interestingly, the females as-

Beauty is highly valued in our society. Children, such as these young girls putting on makeup, understand at an early age that being physically attractive is an important advantage in life.

sumed to be attractive responded to the greater interest shown them and were rated by independent judges (listening to recordings of the conversations) as in fact being attractive, a good example of the circularity in causation mentioned earlier. On the other hand, the females assumed to be unattractive responded to their telephone partners' behavior in ways that led the judges to rate them as unattractive. What had been reality only in the minds of the male subjects became "reality" in the behavior of their unknown female partners.

This study suggests that other people's reactions to our real or imagined characteristics may determine our own behavior, often in ways that conform to their expectations. Further confirmation of this point has been provided by Christensen and Rosenthal (1982). Their study provided male and female college students with arbitrary expectations concerning strangers with whom they were asked to interact. The behavior of the strangers did indeed conform to the students' expectations. Interestingly, males tended to produce stronger conforming behaviors in their partners, while female partners were more likely to conform to expectations. As Jones (1990) has shown in a detailed examination of the entire field of person perception, effects of this kind are both widespread and subtle in human interactions. People are rarely aware of the extent to which their own expectancy-based behaviors produce the expected behavior in others. Biases or stereotypes about physical attributes (such as, "redheads have fiery tempers") therefore stand a better than chance likelihood of being confirmed.

Physical Handicaps Embryologic abnormalities or environmental conditions operating before or after birth may result in physical defects. A defect that a child is born with is called a **congenital defect.** Some time ago it was estimated that 5 out of every 100 babies born in this country had such defects (Wright et al., 1979). About a third of these defects were considered to be inherited; another sixth were thought to be due to drugs or disease; the causes of the rest—about half in all—were unknown, though an indeterminate proportion may also have been hereditary. It is likely that these figures have now changed somewhat in light of such factors as the increased use of cocaine by pregnant women. Some defects are apparent at birth, while others—such as brain anomalies, endocrine disturbances, and heart defects—may go undetected for months or years. Often such anomalies are minor, but more serious congenital defects constitute one of the five leading causes of death during childhood, accounting for over half a million deaths yearly. It is estimated that nearly half of the deaths occurring in pediatric hospitals are due to structural disorders with significant genetic components (Wright et al., 1979).

The most common birth difficulty associated with later mental disorders (including mental retar-

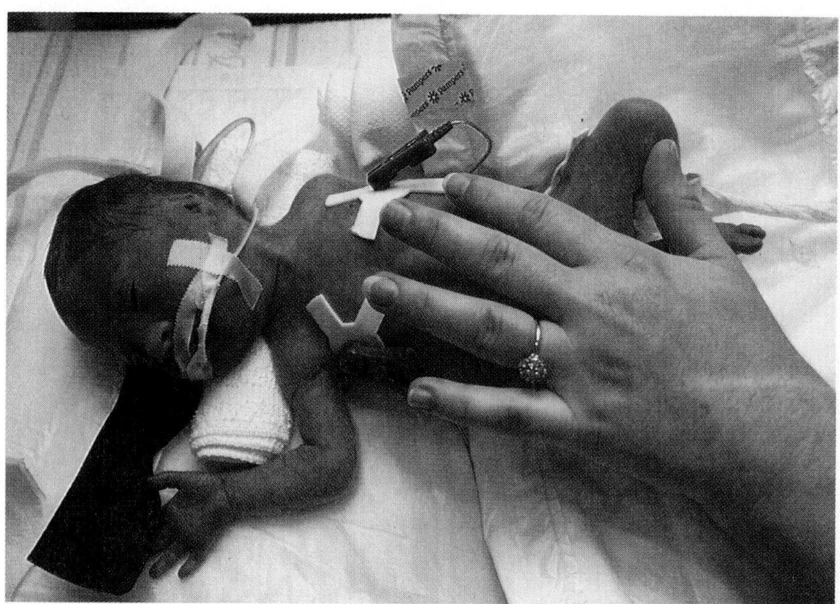

The most common birth difficulty associated with later mental disorders is low birth weight, which is defined as a birth weight in the range of 5 pounds or less. Low birth weight is most often a factor in premature births, but it can also occur in full-term babies. Some of the risk factors associated with low birth weight may be lessened if the infant is given special treatment, such as stroking and massage, in the first month after birth. Unfortunately, many such infants are not given this care because they tend to spend their early days in incubators.

dation, hyperactivity, and emotional disturbances) is low birth weight, which is defined as a birth weight in the range of 5 pounds or less. This problem is most often a factor in premature births, but can also occur in full-term births. Prenatal conditions that can lead to premature birth and to low birth weight include nutritional deficiencies, disease, exposure to radiation, drugs, emotional stress, or the mother's excessive use of alcohol or tobacco.

It appears that the risk factor associated with low birth weight may be lessened by special treatment of the infant, such as systematic stroking and massage, during the first postnatal month (Rice, 1977). Unfortunately, the likelihood that such treatment will occur is not high since high-risk infants tend to spend their early days mostly in incubators because of their uncertain viability.

Mothers who experience severe emotional stress during pregnancy appear to have a much higher incidence of premature deliveries. Even in the case of full-term babies, severe maternal stress seems to be associated with hyperactivity in the fetus during later pregnancy, and with feeding difficulties, sleep disorders, irritability, and other problems after birth (Blau et al., 1963; Sontag, Steele, & Lewis, 1969). As might be expected, socioeconomic status is related to fetal and birth difficulties, the incidence being several times greater among mothers on lower socioeconomic levels (Robinson & Robinson, 1976).

A fetus, and especially a fetal brain, is not so well protected as many investigators once thought; a variety of biological and psychological conditions affecting a mother during pregnancy can have profound effects on a child's development and adjustment. Considerable evidence suggests that children whose earliest development is thus compromised are at significant risk for a variety of later maladaptive behaviors (e.g., Rutter et al., 1970). Such difficulties may be the direct result of impaired brain function (Breslau, 1990), or they may reflect diminished abilities to handle life challenges.

Primary Reaction Tendencies Newborns differ in how they react to particular kinds of stimuli. Some are startled by slight sounds or cry if sunlight hits their faces; others are seemingly insensitive to such stimulation. These reactions differ from baby to baby and are examples of **primary reaction tendencies,** characteristic behaviors that appear to have been established prior to any extensive interaction with the environment. These behaviors are regarded as constitutional rather than genetic because they are likely due to more than genetic influences alone; prenatal environmental factors may also play a role in their development. They include such things as sensitivity to stimuli, temperament, and activity level (Rothbart, 1981). Longitudinal studies have shown that reaction tendencies are relatively enduring from infancy to young adulthood and beyond (e.g., Kagan et al., 1984).

Studies suggest that even the differences in behavior between men and women may be due in part to primary reaction tendencies caused by hormonal influences on the developing nervous system. Though we know that sex-typing and other social learning experiences may override such influences, vestiges of biological determination may yet remain and show up in gender-related primary reaction tendencies (Ehrhardt & Meyer-Bahlburg, 1981; Money & Ehrhardt, 1972; Pervin, 1978; Rubin, Reinisch, & Haskett, 1981). Sex differences that fall into this category may be cognitive, affective, or behavioral. After a careful review of the then-available evidence, Pervin (1978) concluded, in part, as follows:

In cognitive functioning, there is no evidence of overall differences in intelligence but considerable evidence suggesting differences in special abilities. Females tend to perform better than males on tests of verbal ability while males tend to perform better than females on tests of mathematical ability and the manipulation of spatial relationships. . . . The differences between the sexes tend to be small and the overlap between the sexes great.

[In] the realm of affective functioning . . . enough studies have reported differences in activity level [higher for males], fearfulness [higher for females], and emotional responses to frustration [higher for males] to suggest that basic differences in affective functioning may exist. . . .

In overt behavioral functioning, the evidence suggests that males are higher in aggression and dominance behavior while females are higher in dependence and nurturance behavior. . . . The evidence for a difference in aggression seems to be most reliable since it comes from a variety of sources—evolutionary, crosscultural, developmental, and biological-hormonal. . . . (pp. 176–177)

Since Pervin's review a variety of new evidence questions the suggestion of a basic gender difference in verbal versus mathematical-spatial abilities. Researchers have, however, raised no serious challenge to the notion of gender differences (on average) in affectivity or dominance and aggression.

Primary reaction tendencies also include characteristic ways of reacting to stress. Some infants react to changes in routine or other stressors by running fevers; others, by having digestive disorders; still others, by developing sleep disturbances. Several investigators have attempted to relate such primary reaction vulnerabilities to stress and maladaptive behavior.

In a classic longitudinal study of infant development, Chess, Thomas, and Birch (1965) found that 7 to 10 percent of all babies are "difficult"—they show irregular patterns of eating, sleeping, and bowel movement; tend to cry a great deal and to show predominantly negative moods; and are inclined to be irritable and have difficulty adjusting to changes. These researchers concluded that since mothers do not gain the satisfactions they expected from having such babies, the temperamental difficulties become overlaid and complicated by unsatisfactory mother-infant relationships. In recent follow-up work with adopted children, Maurer, Cadoret, and Cain (1980) confirmed the link between membership in the "difficult" group and later childhood adjustment difficulties. In extreme cases, a difficult child can contribute to its own abuse and maltreatment and thus increase its vulnerability. For example, in a study of infants who were either abused or neglected, Crittenden (1985) found that the abused children tended to be "difficult," contributing thereby to repetitive parental abuse.

Thomas, Chess, and Birch (1968) have made the important point that a poor "fit" between a child's temperament and the structure and flexibility of environmental demands, particularly those within the home, can lead to "dissonant stress." Such stress in turn can lead to a behavioral disturbance that may partly reflect the child's temperament. The problem is complicated if the child also suffers from developmental deviations such as mental retardation. Such deviations increase the likelihood of behavior disorders and thus make a "good fit" between temperament and environmental conditions even more crucial. A number of factors may thus help determine the links between constitutional features and subsequent behavior disorders (Buss & Plomin, 1975; Maziade et al., 1990; Thomas & Chess, 1977).

Other longitudinal studies (e.g., Mednick, Schulsinger, & Schulsinger, 1975) have followed children believed to be at high risk due to abnormal prenatal conditions or to parents with serious problems. As was noted in Chapter 1, such studies have potential advantages in clarifying causal patterns. They start with subjects who have not yet developed a disorder and try to predict which ones will succumb, or, as in the preceding case, they watch what actually happens and try to identify the conditions that seem to push a child in one direction or another. These studies are demanding and expensive, however, and can encounter many unforeseen difficulties. Thus most of our evidence still comes from research in which individuals who have already developed a disorder are studied, and the researcher must reconstruct a picture of the probable causes.

Incomplete though our knowledge is, we can conclude that childhood disturbance is often followed by adult disturbance. The specific form of childhood problem, however, does not clearly indicate the particular nature of adult difficulties (Fish,

1975; Hanson Gottesman, & Meehl, 1977; Meehl, 1978; Roff, 1960, 1963). To at least some extent, early manifestations of vulnerability seem to be diffuse and nonspecific; what later abnormality will result, in terms of the specific adult diagnosis, is hard to predict. For example, a child who shows delinquent behavior may later be diagnosed as a schizophrenic, but delinquency is not necessarily a predictor of schizophrenia.

Brain Dysfunction

The unique aspect of human inheritance is an immeasurably superior brain. It has been described as the most highly organized apparatus in the universe, consisting of some 10 billion nerve cells, or neurons, with countless interconnecting pathways as well as myriad connections with other parts of the body. The human brain provides a fantastic communication and computing network with tremendous capabilities for learning and storing experiences; for reasoning, imagining, and problem solving; and for integrating the overall functioning of the organism. The human brain makes possible our enormous adaptability to varied and changing conditions of existence, but it often does so at a price—a price being paid mostly by those people who live with mental disorders. The nervous systems of lower organisms are not nearly so flexibly adaptive, but they are also much less likely to go awry or lead to behavior that is maladaptive.

As we discussed in Chapter 2, a major scientific breakthrough in psychopathology came when researchers proved that general paresis was related to definite destruction of brain tissue. We now realize that significant damage or loss of brain tissue places a person at risk for psychopathology.

Gross brain pathology (that is, physical malformation of or damage to the brain) is a known causal factor in only about 25 percent of mentally retarded people who acquire the condition before or at birth. Likewise, severe brain injuries due to early childhood accidents are relatively infrequent. In fact, gross brain pathology in children or young adults is not a major factor contributing to psychiatric disorder (Eisenberg, 1990). The incidence of such damage increases notably among the elderly, owing chiefly to the aging process itself (often resulting in Alzheimer's disease) or to associated cardiovascular insufficiency, both of which will be discussed in Chapter 13. It is estimated that at least 17 percent of people above the age of 65 have significant brain damage (Kolata, 1981a). Brain damage sometimes leads to a demented condition and increases vulnerability by making a person less able to cope. At the same time, the person is often quite aware of his or her disability, and this awareness can be a significant source of stress. Thus it is not surprising that some 5 percent of people over age 60 develop distinctly psychopathologic symptoms, such as delusions, and are diagnosed as having organic mental disorders (Dohrenwend et al., 1980). These elderly patients typically occupy a substantial proportion (about 20 percent overall) of the beds in mental hospitals.

Gross brain pathology, in which there are observable defects in brain tissue, is only a small part of the brain pathology "story." Much research is currently under way to correlate specific neurotransmission irregularities (presumed diatheses) with certain mental illnesses, such as major mood disorders. Clearly, the normal functioning of the brain is dependent on a delicately balanced biochemical system. Some people may be genetically prone under stress to experience disruptions in this delicate balance; these disruptions, in turn, would make them vulnerable to brain malfunctions and therefore to serious psychopathologies. We will have much more to say about such matters in subsequent chapters.

Even more subtle deficiencies of brain function, such as those involved in attention deficit disorders and specific learning disabilities in children, may enhance vulnerability to subsequent disorders of a more serious and pervasive sort, particularly when a child's difficulties remain undiagnosed and remedial efforts are not undertaken. Too often in such cases these difficulties are attributed to intelligence or "character" defects in the child, such as stupidity or laziness, leading to severe impairments in self-esteem and a blunted desire to try new or challenging tasks. Such a child may have well-entrenched psychological problems by adolescence, by which point, ironically, the original disorder may no longer be in evidence. The occurrence of "soft" neurological signs (such as slightly abnormal reflexes), fairly common in these children, is a probable risk factor for even so severe a disorder as schizophrenia.

Physical Deprivation or Disruption

Although we do not fully understand the processes involved, we do know that digestive, circulatory, and other bodily functions work to maintain the body's physiological equilibrium and integration. The mechanisms for ensuring normal blood chemistry, for maintaining constant body temperature, and for combating invading microorganisms strive to preserve *steady states*—to maintain physiological activity within a range essential to efficient functioning and survival. This process is generally referred to as **homeostasis.** For example, if we are cold, we shiver; if we are too hot, we sweat.

Injuries and diseases that result in pain and infirmity strike all of us from time to time and upset our normal equilibrium. The psychological repercussions from such events, often underestimated, can be profound. Depressions, for example, frequently accompany significant physical illnesses, in part because illnesses painfully remind us of the limits of our control over our lives. Should a disability be permanent or a recovery long delayed, it may be difficult or even impossible for a person's body to become reorganized around a new steady state.

Also, obvious physical disabilities may result in social stigmatization that is itself demoralizing and destabilizing, leaving a person vulnerable to still other types of stress (Jones et al., 1984). Even without such unfortunate events, many people routinely experience challenges to their equilibriums. In the following sections, we deal with two such situations: deprivation of basic physiological needs and nonoptimal levels of stimulation.

Basic Physiological Needs The most basic human requirements are those for food, oxygen, water, sleep, and the elimination of wastes. In order to survive and meet adjustive demands, people must constantly renew themselves through rest and by taking in nutrients to replace materials used up in the process of living. Prolonged interference with such renewal weakens people's resources for coping with even normal demands and makes them vulnerable to special stresses. Prisoners have sometimes been "broken" by nothing more persuasive than the systematic prevention of sleep or deprivation of food over a period of several days.

Experimental studies of volunteers who have gone without sleep for periods of 72 to 98 hours show increasing psychological problems as the sleep loss progresses—including disorientation for time

The effects of sleep deprivation are obvious in the before and after photos of the subjects shown here. These subjects volunteered for an experiment in which they went without sleep for periods of 72 to 98 hours. The subjects showed increasing psychological problems as their sleep loss progressed, including disorientation for time and place and feelings of depersonalization.

and place and feelings of depersonalization. As Berger (1970) has summarized it, "One thing is sure . . . we must sleep in order to stay sane" (p. 70).

Studies of dietary deficiencies have pointed to marked changes in psychological functioning, the exact changes depending largely on the type and extent of the deficiencies. Some of these effects were demonstrated in a pioneering study of semistarvation carried out by Keys (1950) and his associates during World War II, a study that probably will never be repeated.

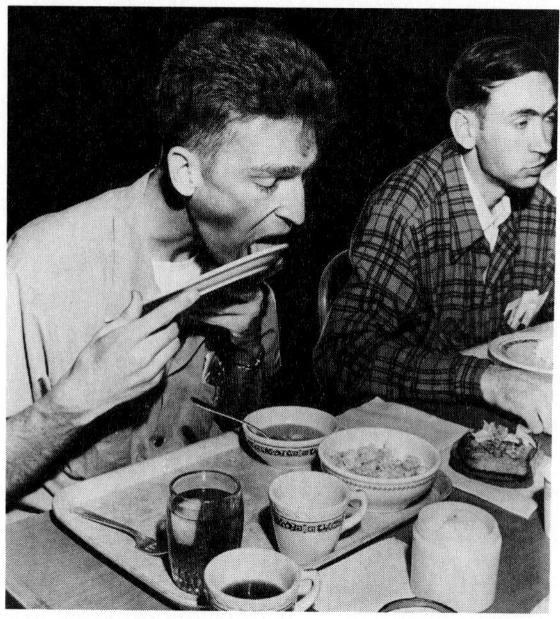

During the semistarvation period in the Keys et al. (1950) experiment, the hunger drive became the most important factor affecting the subjects' behavior. The men became unsociable, frequently ignoring such amenities as table manners.

Thirty-two conscientious objectors served as volunteer subjects. The men were first placed on adequate diets for three months. They were then given low-caloric diets characteristic of European famine areas for a period of six months, followed by a three-month period of nutritional rehabilitation.

During the six-month period of semistarvation, the men had an average weight loss of 24 percent. At the same time, they also showed dramatic personality and behavioral changes. They became irritable, unsociable, and increasingly unable to concentrate on anything but food. In some instances they resorted to stealing food from one another and lying in attempts to obtain additional food rations. Other psychological changes included apathy, loss of pride in personal appearance, and feelings of inadequacy. By the close of the experiment, there was a marked reduction or disappearance of their interest in sex, and the predominant mood was one of gloom and depression. Food dominated the men's thoughts, conversations, and even daydreams. They pinned up pictures of chocolate cakes instead of pretty women. In some cases, they went so far as to replan their lives in the light of their newly acquired respect for food. The investigators concluded that by the end of the twenty-fifth week, hunger had become the dominant influence in the men's behavior.

The long-term compromise of cognitive functioning has been demonstrated in a group of former World War II and Korean War POWs who had lost 35 percent or more of their original body weight while in captivity (Sutker, Galina, & West, 1990). In ordinary life, chronic deprivation may result in lowered resistance to stress. Insufficient rest, inadequate diet, or attempts to carry a full work load under the handicap of a severe cold, fatigue, or emotional strain may interfere with our ability to cope and predispose us to personality disorganizations.

Perhaps the most tragic deprivation is seen in young children who are malnourished. If they survive, the scars of vulnerability are likely to remain for life. Severe malnutrition, which is associated with a host of other potentially damaging variables such as parental neglect and limited access to health care (Brozek & Schurch, 1984), not only impairs physical development and lowers resistance to disease, but also stunts brain growth and results in markedly lowered intelligence (Amcoff, 1980; Cravioto & DeLicardie, 1975; Winick, 1976). Peterson (1978) has noted that thiamine, niacin, and vitamin B_{12} deficits may lead to organic brain syndromes.

In a postmortem study of infants who had died of malnutrition during their first year of life, Winick (1976) found the total brain cell content to be 60 percent below that of normal infants. Further research on animals showed a similar effect in the offspring of malnourished mothers (Winick & Rosso, 1973). Babies who undergo severe malnutrition but survive suffer the permanent stunting of brain growth because the brain's fastest growth

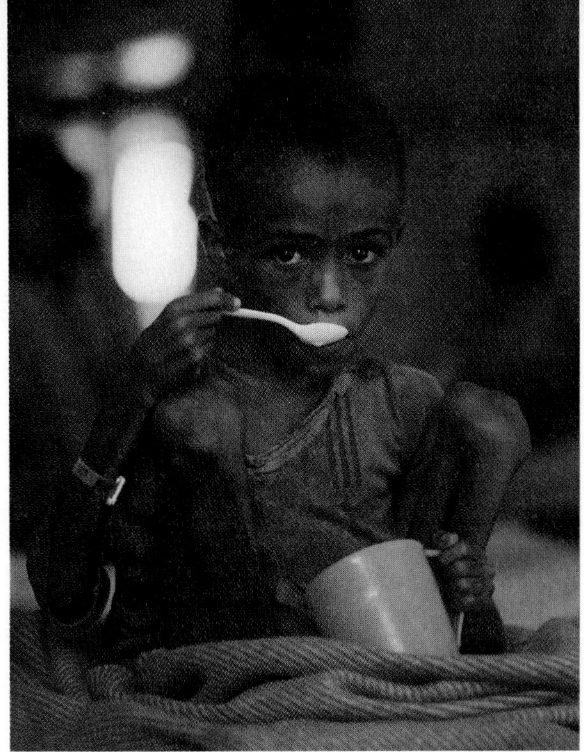

Severe malnutrition, which can be observed in this Ethiopian child, not only impairs physical development and lowers resistance to disease, but also stunts brain growth and results in markedly lowered intelligence.

occurs from about five months before until ten months after birth. In a random sample of areas in ten American states where 75 to 80 percent of the resident families were living either in poverty or close to it, the U.S. Public Health Service found that 15 percent of all children studied showed evidence of physical and mental retardation associated with malnutrition (reported in Winick, 1976).

Malnutrition because of faulty diet, resulting in a wide range of physical disorders and generally lowered resistance to stress, is found even in lower middle-income families (Reice, 1974). Among adults, Robinson and Winick (1973) have reported on the higher incidence of psychoses and other mental disturbances among individuals who follow crash diets to achieve rapid weight losses. In some cases, such reactions result from disappointed expectations: weight losses do not solve long-standing psychological and social problems (Knittle et al., 1982). Nevertheless, changes in mental status can be directly produced by severe nutritional deficiencies (Baker & Lyen, 1982).

Stimulation and Activity We have known for some time that healthy mental development depends on a child's receiving adequate amounts of stimulation from the environment. Since the 1940s (Spitz, 1945), a number of researchers have described a "hospitalism" syndrome among understimulated, institutionalized infants. The syndrome leads an alarming proportion of these children simply to waste away and die. Psychological vulnerabilities induced by too little stimulation clearly can be substantial; we shall explore these predispositions in the upcoming discussion of psychosocial factors. It also seems probable, however, that the physical development of the brain is adversely affected by an insufficient environment (Shapiro, 1968). Numerous animal studies demonstrate enhanced biological development produced by conditions of special stimulation (Wright et al., 1979), including positive changes in brain chemistry and anatomy (Diamond, 1988; Krech, 1966; Krech, Rosenzweig, & Bennett, 1962; Rosenzweig et al., 1968).

On the other hand, there are limits to how much stimulation is beneficial to a developing organism. We know that sensory overload can impair adult functioning (Gottschalk, Haer, & Bates, 1972) and that excessive life changes are correlated with physical illness. Although we might assume that infants and children are similarly affected, we unfortunately have no solid research on this issue.

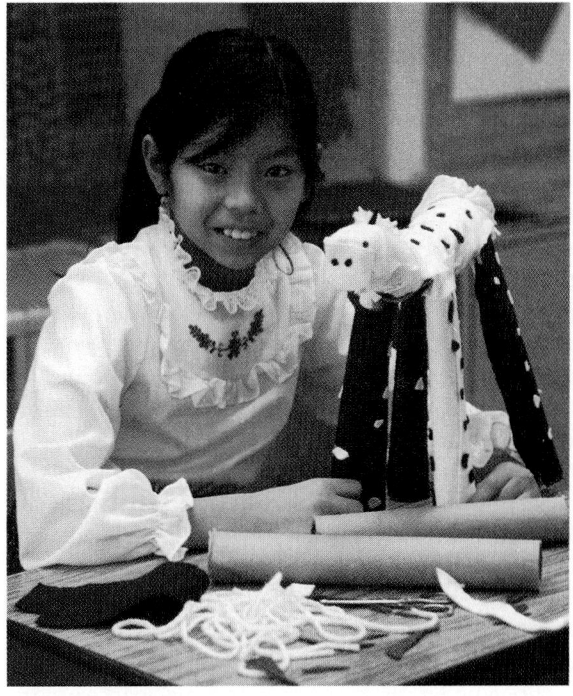

Healthy mental development depends on a child's receiving adequate amounts of stimulation from the environment. Providing enjoyable, creative, tactile activities for children, like the art project this young girl is involved in, can influence psychological development. Such stimulation may also enhance brain development.

In general each individual seems to have an optimal level of stimulation and activity that may vary over time, but that must be maintained for normal psychological functioning. Under excessive pressure, we may strive to reduce the level of input and activity. On the other hand, under some conditions—such as boredom—we may strive to increase the level of stimulation by doing something engaging. In Chapter 8, we will see that certain personality types, such as antisocial personalities, have higher than average needs for excitement.

PSYCHOSOCIAL CAUSAL FACTORS

We begin life with few built-in patterns and a great capacity to learn from experience. We may use our experiences to develop perspectives that can help us face challenges resourcefully and resiliently. Unfortunately, such a happy outcome is by no means guaranteed—not even for people who are biologically and constitutionally sound.

In this section we will examine the psychosocial factors that make people vulnerable to disorder. Psychosocial factors are those developmental influences that may handicap a person psychologically, making him or her less resourceful in the struggle to cope.

What we know about psychosocial causal factors is less precise and reliable than our knowledge of biological predispositions. Even though there are a host of psychosocially-based theoretical perspectives (as were summarized in Chapter 3), few of them are helpful in pinpointing the causal factors contributing to mental disorders in individual cases. It is much more difficult to measure and quantify the psychosocial aspects of an individual than the biological ones. Nonetheless, we will examine here what we do know about psychosocial factors, beginning with a brief examination of the central role played by our perceptions of ourselves and our world. From there we will move to a review of more specific influences that may distort the cognitive structures on which good psychological functioning is dependent. We will focus on early deprivation and trauma, inadequate parenting, pathogenic family structures, and maladaptive peer relationships. Such factors typically do not operate alone. They interact with each other and with other psychosocial factors; with particular genetic and constitutional factors; and with particular settings or environments.

Self-perception and Cognitive Maps

Fundamental to determining what we know, want, and do are some basic assumptions that we make about ourselves, our world, and the relationship between the two. These assumptions make up our frames of reference—our **cognitive maps,** or **schemas**—concerning the universe and our place in it. Because what we can learn or discern directly through our senses can provide, at best, only an inadequate representation of "reality," we need extensive cognitive frameworks to fill in the gaps and make sense out of what we can observe. Our personal cognitive maps are our guides, one might say, through the complexities of living in the world as we understand it. These maps include our views on what we are, what we might become, and what is important to us. Other aspects concern our notions of the various roles we occupy or might occupy in the social fabric, such as woman, man, student, parent, physician, American, older person, and so on. An individual's cognitive map also can be

Our cognitive maps—our frames of reference concerning our place in the world—are influenced by the roles we occupy. How we perceive ourselves in relation to these roles may result in effective behavior or may make us vulnerable to disorder. A key element of this young woman's cognitive map is likely to be her role as a skater. If she focuses on the grace, athleticism, and self-discipline required to be a skater, her cognitive map is a source of healthy functioning. If she views skating as something that is lonely and stressful, her cognitive map may be a source of psychological vulnerability.

construed as his or her **self-identity:** what that person is as distinguished from other persons; what he or she knows and believes; what he or she holds dear and reveres; what meaning his or her existence has. One aspect of these cognitive systems, the *love map* (Money, 1986; Money & Lamacz, 1989) is at the root of our sexual orientation and our erotic relationship to an idealized partner, as discussed in Chapter 10. Vital though they are to effective and organized behavior, our cognitive maps are also, regrettably, key sources of our psychological vulnerabilities, many of which can predispose us to abnormal behavior.

Parts of our cognitive maps may be valid, some invalid; other parts may be true for us but not for others; still other parts may be held with varying degrees of conviction, and they may be more or less explicit and conscious. Although our daily decisions and behavior are in large part shaped by our frames of reference, we may be quite unaware of the assumptions on which they are based—or even of having made assumptions at all. We think that we are simply seeing things the way they are. We do not often consider the fact that other pictures of the "real" world might be possible or that other rules for "right" might exist. Some people (e.g., Scheff, 1984) have even suggested we may be unable to achieve this level of detachment from our most fundamental assumptions. Thus many of our thoughts, actions, and feelings are based on internalized rules and ways of seeing the world that we would be hard-pressed to articulate or define.

On the one hand, the self can be seen as a set of rules for processing information and for selecting behavior alternatives; on the other hand, it can be seen as the product of those rules—a sense of selfhood, or self-identity (Vallacher, Wegner, & Hoine, 1980). Deficiencies or deviations in either aspect of the development of the self can make one vulnerable to disorder. For example, if a person's information-processing rules differ in major respects from those of his or her peers, then that person's "reality" will be correspondingly different and may lead to rejection, isolation, despair, and disorder. Similarly, should an individual's self-identity require propping up by membership in an eccentric cult, or should its perceived contents be so amorphous or fragmented that they must be continuously inferred from the intense reactions of partners in serial love relationships (as in many cases of borderline personality disorder, Chapter 7), the individual will be at serious risk of a breakdown.

As Vallacher et al. (1980) have put it, we look *through* the rules of the self—rarely *at* them. For this reason, the rules, once established, may be hard to identify, and it may be difficult to deliberately change them. New experiences tend to be **assimilated** into our existing cognitive frameworks, even if the new information has to be reinterpreted or distorted to make it fit. We tend to cling to existing assumptions and reject or change new information that is contradictory to them. **Accommodation**—changing our existing frameworks to make it possible to incorporate discrepant information—is more difficult and threatening, especially when important assumptions are challenged. Accommodation is, of course, a basic goal of psychosocial therapies—explicitly in the case of the cognitive and cognitive-behavioral variants, but deeply implicated in virtually all other approaches as well. This process makes major therapeutic change a difficult task.

An individual's failure to acquire appropriate principles or rules in cognitive organization can affect future vulnerability. Indeed, about 75 percent of so-called mentally retarded persons—who as a group are at high risk for mental disorder—are intellectually disabled not because of defective brain tissue, but rather because their neural tissue has been insufficiently "programmed" to manage the complexities of modern life. Failure at this level—whether the inadequate programming involves academic, employment, or social skills—results in a person's being less able than others to cope effectively with adjustive demands.

Essentially, these issues involve learning, and they grow in importance as children progress beyond the simple conditioning that characterizes the infancy period. Although children in a given culture show similarities in what they learn, they also show marked differences. Mischel (1973) has identified five learning-based differences that become apparent early in childhood: (a) children have acquired different levels of competency in different areas; (b) they have learned different concepts and strategies for coding and categorizing their experiences, and they thus "process" new information differently; (c) although they have all learned that certain things follow from certain others, what they have learned to expect is quite different, depending on their unique experiences; (d) they have learned to find different situations attractive or disagreeable and thus to seek quite different things; and (e) they have learned different ways of coping with impulses and regulating their behavior—they have developed a characteristic "style" of dealing with life's demands. Differences in these general areas continue through childhood and into the adult years and help shape later learning.

These learned variations make some children far better prepared than others for further learning and personal growth. The ability to make effective use of new experience depends very much on the degree to which past learning has created cognitive structures that facilitate the integration of the novel or unexpected. A well-prepared child will be able to assimilate or when necessary accommodate new experience in ways that will be productive of growth; a child with less adequate cognitive foundations may be confused, unreceptive to new information, and psychologically vulnerable. It is mainly for this reason that most theories of personality development emphasize the importance of early experience in shaping the main directions that an individual's coping style will take.

A good example is afforded by modern research on the cognitive antecedents of psychological depression. The onsets of most such depressions, including severely incapacitating ones, have been linked repeatedly with the prior occurrence of negative life events, such as illness, divorce, or serious financial setbacks. Negative events are inevitable in all of our lives, and most of us muddle through them in one way or another without becoming psychological casualties. Substantial evidence shows that people who respond to such events with clinically diagnosable depressions are in some sense "primed" to respond in this way because of the ways in which they process the negative happenings. While the details of such a negative "set" are still being researched, they seem to involve a kind of overreaction and overgeneralization as to the meaning of negative events, one that was learned much earlier and may have remained relatively dormant for many years. The ultimate source of these maladaptive learnings is often unclear, but some evidence suggests that traumatic experiences, such as the death of a parent in childhood, may encourage their acquisition.

The example just given reminds us that the events making up one child's experiences may be vastly different from those of another, and that many such events are neither predictable nor controllable. At one extreme are children who develop in stable and lovingly indulgent environments within families that buffer them, as far as possible, from the harsher realities of the world; at the other extreme are children whose developmental experiences consist of constant exposure to frightening events, sometimes including unspeakable cruelties. We see the effects of such different experiences in the corresponding cognitive maps of adults: some present a world that is uniformly loving, unthreatening and benign, which of course it is not; others resemble a jungle in which minimal safety and perhaps even life itself is constantly in the balance, also a distortion for most adults. Given a preference in terms of likely outcomes, most mental health professionals would opt for the former of these maps, but in fact neither is optimal as a blueprint for engaging the real world; both represent serious adaptive deficits.

Fear or *anxiety* (fear in the absence of objective danger) occupies a place close to the conceptual center of psychopathology; it is also the central problem in a number of the specific mental disorders to be discussed in later chapters of this book. While we are accustomed to viewing anxiety as an emotion or affect, recent research and thinking (e.g., Barlow, 1988; Beck, Emery, & Greenberg, 1985) have emphasized a substantial cognitive component in the genesis and experience of the crippling types of anxiety seen in clinical situations. Barlow (1988), in fact, characterizes anxiety as "a diffuse cognitive-affective structure" whose "essence is *arousal-driven apprehension*" (p. 235). Apprehension, of course, has a substantial cognitive component of expectation, the expectation that one is soon going to have an unpleasant experience—in the extreme, perhaps even the experience of dying.

In Barlow's well-researched model, arousal drives apprehension, but apprehension (expectation) also, importantly, drives arousal. While this model acknowledges the likely contribution of some sort of biological vulnerability to stressful circumstances, it stresses the importance of experience with negative outcomes perceived to be unpredictable and uncontrollable, based on a focused review of pertinent human and animal research. Restated in terms of the present discussion, a clinically anxious person is someone whose cognitive map includes strong possibilities that terrible things over which he or she has no control may happen unpredictably. It is not difficult to imagine developmental scenarios that would lead to a life map having these elements as prominent characteristics.

Finally, it appears that some uncontrollable experiences to which children are subjected are so overwhelming and contradictory that it is impossible to construct a coherent cognitive map within which they can be assimilated. This situation is perhaps seen most clearly in cases of multiple personality disorder (MPD), where the separate personalities develop separate cognitive maps that may be completely walled off from one another. Indeed, in one recently reported instance, the original "person," having been repeatedly raped by a stepfather at age 2, simply ceased to exist; she was "replaced" by a host of alter personalities that were better able to manage the bizarre and terrifying events of the child's life (Chase et al., 1990). We have in fact learned in recent years that MPD (discussed in Chapter 6) may be associated with repeated, traumatic sexual abuse in childhood. The main point here is that a fragmented selfhood, whatever its origin—and it is frequently traumatic—invites the development of abnormal behaviors.

Early Deprivation or Trauma

Fortunately, experiences of the intensity and persistence just noted, while more common than was thought only a decade ago, are nevertheless relatively rare. There are, however, other kinds of experiences that, while less dramatic and chilling, may leave children with deep and sometimes irreversible psychic scars. The deprivation of needed resources normally supplied by parents or parental surrogates is one such circumstance.

Parental deprivation refers to an absence of adequate care from and interaction with parents or their substitutes during the formative years. It can occur even in intact families where, for one reason or another, parents are unable (for instance, because of mental disorder) or unwilling to provide for a child's needs for close and frequent human contact. The children of parents experiencing severe depressions, for example, are at enhanced risk for disorder themselves (Downey & Coyne, 1990), at least partly because depression makes for inept parenting—notably including inattentiveness to a child's needs (Gelfand & Teti, 1990). The most severe manifestations of deprivation, however, are usually seen among abandoned or orphaned children who may either be institutionalized or placed in a succession of unwholesome foster homes.

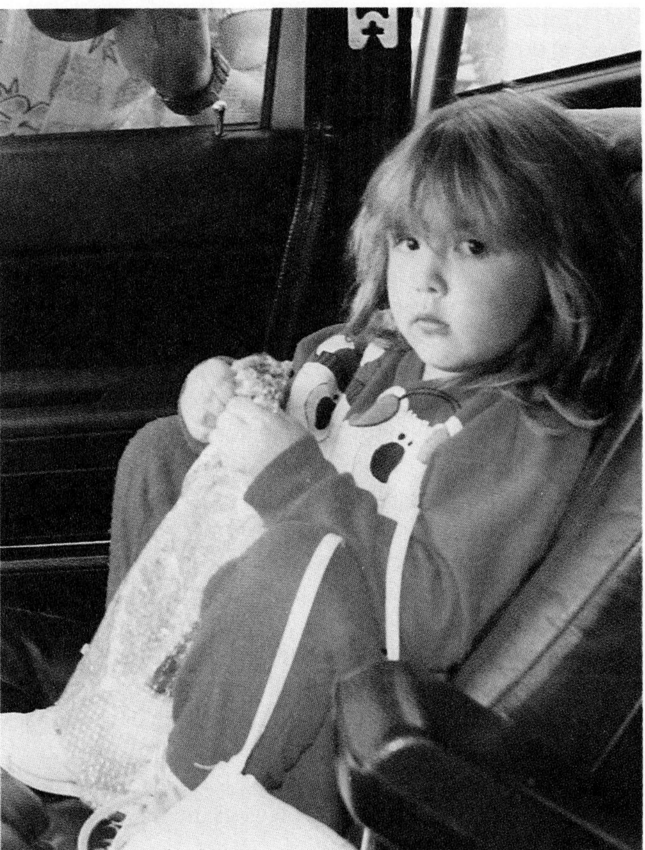

Parental deprivation refers to an absence of adequate care from and interaction with parents or their substitutes during the formative years. Its most severe manifestations are usually seen among abandoned or orphaned children. Parental deprivation can take other forms, however, as in the case of 4-year-old Rachel Rauser, whose father allegedly tried to sell her to her aunt and uncle. Rachel was turned over to her stepmother.

We can interpret the consequences of parental deprivation from several psychosocial viewpoints. Such deprivation might result in fixation at the oral stage of psychosexual development (Freud); it might interfere with the development of basic trust (Erikson); it might retard the attainment of needed skills because of a lack of available reinforcements (Skinner); it may preempt self-actualizing tendencies with maintenance and defensive requirements (Rogers, Maslow); or it might stunt the development of the child's capacity for relatively anxiety-free exchanges of tenderness and intimacy with others (Sullivan). Any of these viewpoints might in a given instance be the best way of conceptualizing the problems that arise, or some combination of them may be superior to any one in the insight it affords. Most generally, however, we see the victims of such experiences as acquiring dysfunctional cognitive maps. On such maps, the basic stability, trustworthiness, and affection of the world and of relationships are represented, if at all, to be uncertain and thus unworthy of serious investment or commitment.

From any viewpoint, the effects of parental deprivation can be serious. Faulty development has often been observed in infants experiencing deprivation. Many studies have focused on the role of the mother, but all such studies are essentially concerned with warmth and stimulation, whether it comes from the mother, the father, or institutional staff members.

Institutionalization In an institution, as compared with an ordinary home, there is likely to be less warmth and physical contact; less intellectual, emotional, and social stimulation; and a lack of encouragement and help in positive learning. A much-referenced study by Provence and Lipton (1962) compared the behavior of infants living in institutions with that of infants living with families. At 1 year of age, the institutionalized infants showed general impairments in their relationships to people, rarely turning to adults for help, comfort, or pleasure and showing no signs of strong attachments to any person. These investigators also noted a marked retardation of speech and language development, emotional apathy, and impoverished and repetitive play activities. In contrast to the babies living in families, the institutionalized infants failed to show the personality differentiation and learning that "can be thought of both as accomplishments of the first year of life and as the foundation upon which later learning is built" (p. 161). With more severe and pervasive deprivation, development may be even more retarded.

The long-range effects of severe early deprivation are suggested by the early findings of Beres and Obers (1950) in their study of 38 adolescents who had been institutionalized between the ages of about 3 weeks and 3 years. At the time of the study, 16 to 18 years after discharge from the orphanage, 4 were diagnosed as psychotic, 21 as having character (or "personality") disorders, 4 as mentally retarded, and 2 as neurotic. Only 7 were judged to have achieved satisfactory personal adjustments. In general, it appears that "affectionless psychopathy"—characterized by the inability to form close interpersonal relationships and often by antisocial behavior—is a syndrome commonly found among children who have been institutionalized at an early age, particularly before the age of 1 year.

These early findings have been confirmed in a review of more recent research on child abandonment by Burnstein (1981). Burnstein concludes that abandoned children are at high risk for psychological disturbances and that excessive levels of aggressiveness, rebelliousness, and disobedience are especially likely. Such behaviors suggest interpersonal anxieties that are defended against by the adoption of "antiweak," "antitrust" orientations to the world. The long-range prognosis for children suffering early and prolonged parental deprivation is considered unfavorable (Rutter, 1972; Tizard & Rees, 1975; Wolkind, 1974).

Although some earlier estimates of the pathological effects of such deprivation were exaggerated, it is now clear that many children deprived of normal parenting in infancy show maladaptive personality development. The extent to which early deprivation can be made up for by abundant love and attention at a later time is not yet known. It does appear, however, that attachment to a particular adult (typically the mother)—once considered the essential element in healthy development—may not, in fact, be the critical factor. Research by Leiderman and Leiderman (1974) comparing ***monomatric*** with ***polymatric*** (one mother versus multiple mother) households, and by Kagan, Kearsley, and Zelazo (1976) on the effects of early placement in quality day-care settings, failed to show any substantial deficits in multiple-mothered children. Belsky and Steinberg (1978) and Scarr (1984) reached a similar conclusion concerning quality alternate care settings. The operative word here is ***quality,*** however, and as many dual-career couples have learned to their dismay, it may be difficult to find quality day-care centers.

In sum, whether maladaptive personality development can be reversed probably depends on a number of factors, including the duration of prior deprivation and the quality and time of therapeutic enrichment efforts. It is clear that, if the deprivation continues, any movement toward more adaptive personality development becomes increasingly difficult as a child gets older (Freedman, Kaplan, & Sadock, 1976; Skolnick, 1986). After some period of time a child's cognitive map no longer accommodates new experiences, in part because the child's expectations of abandonment make it difficult for even well-meaning others to convincingly disconfirm them; most of us do not have an unending supply of patience in confronting persistent and surly mistrust.

An institutional environment may be detrimental to young children, but the defects of such settings can be overcome by the quality of care they provide. These children in a day-care center, judging by their surroundings, are in an enriched setting. Studies have shown that placement in quality day-care settings has no substantial impact on children's personality development.

Deprivation in the Home By far the greatest number of infants subjected to parental deprivation are not separated from their parents, but rather suffer from inadequate or distorted care at home. In these situations parents typically neglect or devote little attention to their children and are generally rejecting.

The effects of such deprivation may be devastating. The early work of Ribble (1944, 1945), for example, showed that rejecting, indifferent, or punishing mothers may cause tense, unsatisfied, and negative behavior in their infants at a very early age. In fact, Bullard and his associates (1967) delineated a "failure to thrive" (FTT) syndrome that "is a serious disorder of growth and development frequently requiring admission to the hospital. In its acute phase it significantly compromises the health and sometimes endangers the life of the child" (p. 689). In a follow-up study conducted eight months to nine years after the hospitalization of such children for treatment, Bullard found that almost two-thirds of the subjects showed evidence "either of continued growth failure, emotional disorder, mental retardation, or some combination of these" (p. 681).

The effects of deprivation vary considerably from infant to infant; in some societies, practices that we would expect to be permanently damaging are not. For example, Kagan (1973) compared the development of year-old Guatemalan Indian infants with that of American-raised infants. Due to the custom of the culture, Guatemalan Indian infants spend their first year in a psychologically impoverished environment. Kagan found that they were, by comparison, severely retarded in their development. After the first year, however, the environment of these infants was enriched, and by age 11, they performed as well or better than American children on problem-solving and related intellectual tasks.

Prolonged neglect may have serious long-term effects even where a child shows minimal immediate difficulties. For example, Roff and Knight (1981) conducted a follow-up study of individuals averaging 43.7 years of age who had had adjustment difficulties as children and who had become schizophrenic in young adulthood. They found that childhood parental neglect was significantly associated with relatively poor long-term outcomes. These outcomes also appeared to have been due to serious family disorganization and disruption, factors that we will discuss later.

Parental rejection of a child is closely related to deprivation and may be demonstrated in various ways—by physical neglect, denial of love and affection, lack of interest in the child's activities and achievements, harsh or inconsistent punishment, failure to spend time with the child, and lack of respect for the child's rights and feelings. In a minority of cases, it also involves cruel and abusive treatment. Parental rejection may be partial or complete, passive or active, or subtly or overtly cruel.

Parental rejection may underlie a child's attempt to run away from home. Other behaviors exhibited by children who are victims of parental rejection are a tendency to be overly aggressive and prone to impulsive behavior, diminished intellectual functioning, excessive fears, and an inability to form meaningful relationships.

Regardless of its specific nature or intensity, parental rejection has been associated with a more or less specific pattern of development in its victims. These children often have a tendency to be overly aggressive and prone to impulsive behavior (Lefkowitz et al., 1973; Patterson, 1979; Pemberton & Benady, 1973; Sears, Maccoby, & Levin, 1957). Pringle (1965) reported that adults who had experienced significant rejection in childhood had serious difficulty in giving and receiving affection, and Yates (1981) found that severely abused children lacked the capacity to form meaningful relationships, a trait common to adult narcissistic personalities (see Chapter 8). Wolfe, Gentile, & Wolfe (1989), in a follow-up study of 71 sexually abused children, have likened the outcomes observed to those of posttraumatic stress disorder (see Chapter 5). Other reported behaviors associated with parental rejection include diminished intellectual functioning (Hurley, 1965), excessive fears (Poznanski, 1973), and running away from home (Stierlin, 1973).

A large proportion of parents who reject or abuse their children have themselves been the victims of parental rejection (Kaplun & Reich, 1976; Wright et al., 1979), with corresponding effects on their cognitive maps. In this sense, lack of love has been referred to as a communicable disease. Rejection, of course, is not a one-way street; a child may also reject or otherwise cause unusual stress for his or her parents (Crittenden, 1985; Wolfe, 1985). This pattern sometimes occurs when the parents belong to a low-status minority group of which the child is ashamed. Although the results of such rejection have not been studied systematically, it appears that children who reject their parents deny themselves needed models, loving relationships, and other essentials for the healthy development of their cognitive maps.

Childhood Trauma Most of us have had one-time traumatic experiences that temporarily shattered our feelings of security, adequacy, and worth and influenced our perceptions of ourselves and our environment. The term **psychic trauma** is used to describe any aversive (unpleasant) experience that inflicts serious psychological damage on an individual. The following illustrates such an incident.

I believe the most traumatic experience of my entire life happened one April evening when I was 11. I was not too sure of how I had become a member of the family, although my parents had thought it wise to tell me that I was adopted. That much I knew, but what the term adopted *meant was something else entirely. One evening after my step-brother and I had retired, he proceeded to explain it to me—with a vehemence I shall never forget. He made it clear that I wasn't a "real" member of the family, that my parents didn't "really" love me, and that I wasn't even wanted around the place. That was one night I vividly recall crying myself to sleep. That experience undoubtedly played a major role in making me feel insecure and inferior.*

Traumas of this magnitude are apt to leave psychological wounds that never completely heal. As a result, later stress that reactivates these wounds may be particularly difficult for an individual to handle and often explains why one person has difficulty with a problem that is not especially stressful to another. Psychic traumas in infancy or early childhood are especially damaging for the following reasons:

1. *Children, almost by definition, have limited coping resources and are relatively helpless in the face of threat.* They are therefore more readily overwhelmed by traumas than an older person would be. Conditioned responses, which in cognitive terms are ***acquired expectancies*** that a particular event will follow from another, are readily established in situations that evoke strong emotions; such responses are often highly resistant to extinction. Thus one traumatic experience of almost drowning in a deep lake may be sufficient to establish a fear of water that endures for years or a lifetime.

2. *Conditioned responses stemming from traumatic experiences may generalize to other situations.* A child who has learned to fear water may also come to fear riding in boats and other situations associated with even the remotest possibility of drowning.

3. *Traumatic situations tend to result in strong and automatic conditioning that is relatively resistant to cognitive reappraisal.* Consequently, exposure to similar situations tends to reactivate an affective-cognitive structure of intense apprehension that usurps a person's attention and thereby prevents a rational review of the actual risk confronting the person. Young children are thus especially prone to acquiring intense anxieties that remain resistant to modification even as their resources for coping undergo tremendous growth during their subsequent development.

The aftereffects of early traumatic experiences depend heavily on the support and reassurance given a child by parents or other significant people. This support appears particularly important when the trauma involves an experience that arouses strong feelings of inadequacy and self-devaluation, such as being ridiculed for stuttering or clumsiness. For a look at the factors of vulnerability that may be involved when children are separated from their parents, see *HIGHLIGHT 4.4*

Many psychic traumas in childhood, though highly upsetting at the time, probably have minor long-term consequences. Some children are less vulnerable than others and show more resilience and recoverability from hurt (Crittenden, 1985). Not all children who experience a trauma—for example, a parent's death (Barnes & Prosen, 1985; Crook & Eliot, 1980)—exhibit discernible long-term effects. However, a child exposed to repeated early psychic traumas, such as physical abuse (Crittenden, 1985) or incestuous advances (Owens,

Separation from Parents as a Traumatic Experience

Bowlby (1960, 1973) has summarized the effects on children from 2 to 5 years old of being separated from their parents during prolonged periods of hospitalization. He cited three stages of their separation experiences:

1. *Initial protest*—characterized by increased crying, screaming, and general activity.
2. *Despair*—included dejection, stupor, decreased activity, and general withdrawal from the environment.
3. *Detachment*—followed discharge from the hospital and reunion with their mothers; characterized by indifference and sometimes even hostility toward their mothers.

The effects of long-term or permanent separation from one or both parents are complex. When the separation occurs as early as 3 months after birth, an infant's emotional upset seems to be primarily a reaction to environmental change and strangeness, and he or she usually adapts readily to a surrogate parent. But once attachment behavior has developed, the emotional hurt of separation may be deeper and more sustained, and a child may go through a period of bereavement and have greater difficulty adjusting to the change. It appears that the age at which an infant is most vulnerable to long-term separation or loss is from about 3 months to 3 years. The long-term consequences of such loss appear to depend not only on the time of its occurrence, but also on the child in question, the previous relationship with the parent, and the quality of subsequent parental care.

The magnitude of this problem is indicated by the statistic that well over 10 million children in the United States have lost at least one parent through separation, divorce, or death.

1984), is likely to show a disruption in normal personality development. Even though subsequent experiences may have a moderating influence, the detrimental effects of such early traumas may never be completely overcome, partly because experiences that would provide the necessary relearning are selectively avoided. A child whose cognitive map does not include the possibility that others can be trusted does not venture out toward others far enough to learn that some people in the world are in fact trustworthy.

Inadequate Parenting

All the psychosocial viewpoints on abnormal behavior focus attention on the behavioral tendencies a child acquires in the course of early social interaction with others—chiefly parents or parental surrogates. While their explanations vary considerably, all the viewpoints accept the general principle that certain deviations in parenting can have profound effects on a child's subsequent ability to cope with life's challenges.

You should keep in mind that a parent-child relationship is always bidirectional in respect to influence. As with any continuing relationship, the behavior of each person affects the behavior of the other. Some children are easier to love than others; some parents are more sensitive than others to an infant's needs. It is often hard to say which person was originally the most responsible for certain interactional patterns.

In occasional cases, we are able to identify characteristics in an infant that have been largely responsible for an unsatisfactory relationship between parent and child. One example is the difficult baby, described by Chess and her associates (see page 107), a baby whose irregularities may help establish a mutually unsatisfying relationship between parent and child.

Another example is the withdrawn, unresponsive, autistic child (described more fully in Chapter 14). It has been observed that the parents of such children often seem cold, emotionally reserved, and "intellectual." Early researchers had blamed this parental coldness and distance for their children's autism—thereby adding guilt to the problems these

Parents play a critical role in their children's growth toward physical and psychological competence. Though a parent-child relationship is bidirectional—the behavior of each person affects the behavior of the other—the influence of a parent on a child is likely to be more important in shaping the child's behavior than vice versa.

parents already were facing. Infantile autism is now recognized by most authorities as usually related to a congenital neurological deficit in children; evidently, parents restrict their emotional involvement, often unconsciously, as a way of coping with their profoundly unresponsive children (Schopler, 1978). Other evidence suggests that some of the disturbances commonly found in the parents of schizophrenic patients are a reaction to their children's disturbances, rather than the other way around (Carson, 1984).

In most cases, however, the influence of a parent on his or her child is likely to be more important in shaping a child's behavior than vice versa. Several specific patterns of parental influence appear with great regularity in the backgrounds of children who show certain types of faulty development that enhance the likelihood of adaptive breakdown. Some of these patterns will be discussed in the following sections.

Overprotection and Excessive Restriction Overprotective parents may watch over their children constantly, protect them from the slightest risk, overly clothe and medicate them, and make decisions for them at every opportunity. In essence, they smother their children's growth. With recent societal changes favoring dual-career parenting and the placement of young children in nursery schools or other day-care centers, the problem of overprotection probably occurs less frequently than it once did. It is doubtful, however, that it has disappeared from the scene, especially because overprotective parents most likely resist alternate care options.

Although fathers have been known to overprotect their children, the problem is probably more common among mothers (Weintraub & Frankel, 1977). Such maternal reactions represent a type of behavior in which a mother attempts, through contact with her child, to live out a cognitive map whose "mother" component has problematic features. She may, for example, attempt to gain satisfactions that are better pursued in relations with other adults or her husband. One common pattern, usually involving a male child, is the encouragement of excessive closeness and intimacy, to the extent that the father of the child may develop distinct feelings of resentment for playing "second fiddle." A corollary syndrome sometimes occurs between fathers and daughters.

In a study of the family backgrounds of children referred to a child guidance clinic, Jenkins (1968) found that those youngsters characterized as overanxious were likely to have an infantilizing, overprotective mother. Similarly, in his study of children with excessive fears, Poznanski (1973) found a dependent relationship on an overprotective mother to be a key reason for the fears. Roff and Knight (1981), in a longitudinal study (mentioned earlier) of middle-aged men who had experienced schizophrenic episodes, found that maternal overanxiousness and overprotectiveness, as well as maternal neglect, predicted poor outcomes.

In shielding a child from every danger, an overprotective parent fails to provide the opportunities the child needs for reality testing and the development of essential competencies. In addition, the overprotective behavior implies that the parent regards the child as weak, fragile, and incapable of coping with everyday problems, qualities that may then be incorporated in the child's emerging self-identity. A "sissy" reputation among the child's peers is a frequent complication of this pattern. It is not surprising that such children often reach adolescence and young adulthood feeling inadequate and threatened by a dangerous world.

Closely related to overprotection is restrictiveness. Here parents rigidly enforce unduly restrictive rules and standards and give a child little autonomy or freedom for growing in his or her own way. Parental restrictiveness is of course one of the most commonly heard complaints, whether justified or not, of adolescence—an age range whose major developmental task is the achievement (ambivalently desired) of autonomous selfhood. Restrictiveness may foster well-controlled, socialized behavior, but it can also nurture fearfulness, dependency, submission, repressed hostility, and some dulling of intellectual striving (Baumrind, 1971; Becker, 1964). Often, too, extreme behavior on the part of an adolescent is a way of rebelling against severe restrictions. In the overcontrolled hostility syndrome (Megargee, 1966), a history of extreme restrictions on anger and appropriate forms of aggression may lead to an impulsive, murderous attack.

Unrealistic Demands Some parents place excessive pressures on their children to live up to unrealistically high standards. For example, a child may be expected to excel in school and all other activities. If the child has the capacity for exceptionally high-level performance, things may work out; but even then the child may be under such sustained pressure that little room is left for spontaneity or development as an independent person.

Typically, however, such a child is never quite able to live up to parental expectations and demands. Nothing the child does seems good enough. If the child raises a grade of C to a B, rather than giving praise, the parents may ask why it was not an A. Effort only brings more painful frustration and self-devaluation. Those parents who promote feelings of failure by their excessive demands also tend to discourage further effort on the child's part. Almost invariably such a child feels hopelessly in the wrong league: "I can't do it, so why try?"

One need only observe a child's eager "Watch me, Daddy," while demonstrating some new achievement, to understand how important parental recognition for new skills is to healthy development. Research studies, such as the investigation of the antecedents of children's self-respect carried out by Coopersmith (1967), have shown that high parental expectations are both common and helpful for a child's development, particularly when they encourage reasonable achievement strivings. Such expectations, however, need to be realistically set for the capabilities and temperament of each child. A child who is repeatedly rebuffed in his or her efforts to gain approval and self-esteem is unlikely to develop effective coping techniques.

Often, unrealistic parental demands focus on moral standards—particularly with regard to sex, alcohol, and related matters. For example, parents may instill in a child the view that masturbation or any other sexual activity is sinful and can lead only to moral and physical degeneration. The child who accepts such parental standards, unmodulated by the influence of his or her peer group, may face many guilt-arousing and self-devaluating conflicts.

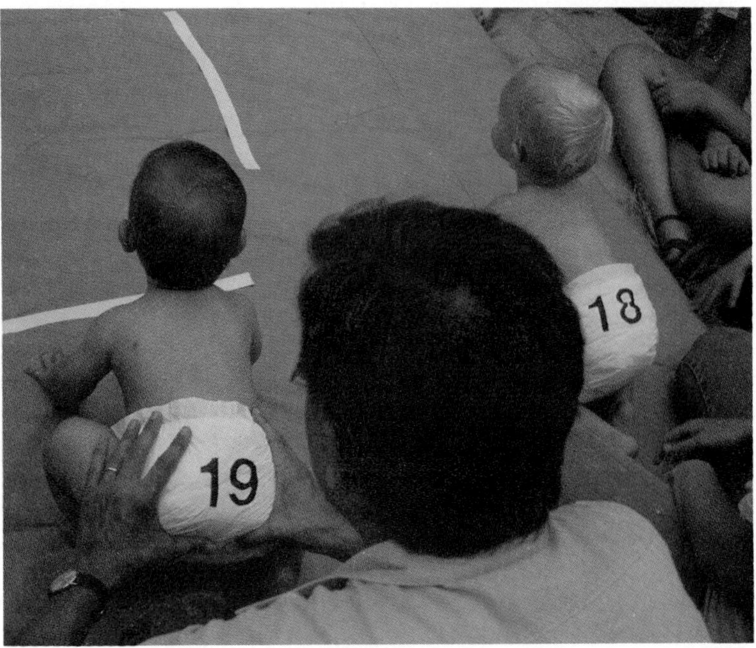

Parental expectations are common and helpful for a child's development, but they need to be realistically set for the capabilities and temperament of each child. A child who is repeatedly rebuffed in his or her efforts to gain approval and self-esteem is unlikely to develop effective coping techniques.

In still other instances, parental demands are unrealistically low; the parents do not care what happens as long as the child stays out of trouble. Coopersmith (1967) found that the children of such parents had significantly lower achievement and self-esteem levels than children whose parents had high but realistic expectations for them. Thus unrealistic expectations and demands—either too high, too low, or distorted and rigid—can help cause a faulty self-identity.

Overpermissiveness and Indulgence Sometimes one or both parents will cater to a child's slightest whims and, in so doing, fail to teach and reward desirable standards of behavior. In essence, the parent surrenders the running of the home to an uninhibited son or daughter. As noted in an amusing fashion by comedian Bill Cosby (1986), children seem to have a perverse tendency to exploit any such parental weaknesses.

Pollack (1968), for example, has quoted a permissive father who finally rebelled at the tyranny of his 9-year-old daughter, and, in a near tantrum, exploded with, "I want one thing clearly understood—I live here, too!" (p. 28). Similarly, one of the authors has observed a 3-year-old girl essentially demolish the living room of a neighbor's home in full view of her doting mother. When the mother finally intervened, she was repeatedly struck and kicked by this little tyrant, who was in turn not punished in any way for her behavior.

Overly indulged children are characteristically spoiled, selfish, inconsiderate, and demanding. Sears (1961) found that much permissiveness and little discipline in a home were correlated positively with antisocial, aggressive behavior, particularly during middle and later childhood. Unlike rejected, emotionally deprived children, indulged children enter readily into interpersonal relationships, but they exploit people for their own purposes in the same way that they have learned to exploit their parents. In dealing with authority, such children are usually rebellious because they have had their own way for so long. Overly indulged children also tend to be impatient, to approach problems in an aggressive and demanding manner, and to find it difficult to accept present frustrations in the interests of long-range goals (Baumrind, 1971, 1975). In short, they have cognitive maps with extended "entitlement" features.

The fact that their pampered status at home does not transfer automatically to the outside world may come as a great shock to indulged youngsters. Confusion and adjustive difficulties may occur when "reality" forces them to reassess their assumptions about themselves and the world. When they fail to do so in an adequate manner, as is often the case, their adult lives are littered with repeated interpersonal failures and eventual frustration and disillusionment.

Faulty Discipline Parenthood is one of the most important and demanding commitments adults undertake, yet they are usually ill prepared for it. Despite the increasing availability of special programs, such as parent effectiveness training, and a variety of sophisticated books on the subject, most parents still rely primarily on what they learned from their own parents, who may or may not have been ideal models (Wright et al., 1979). Disciplining children is a particularly controversial and confusing topic for most parents (Baumrind, 1975). Many simply abdicate the responsibility. In other cases, parents have resorted to excessively harsh discipline, convinced that if they "spare the rod" they will spoil the child. And in still other cases, parents behave inconsistently, punishing children one day and ignoring or even rewarding them the next for the same behavior. Depressed adults, as might be expected, have several deficiencies as parents, one of which is ineptness in disciplining their children (Gelfand & Teti, 1990).

There is no question that well-placed permissiveness can be good, encouraging a child's creativity. Overpermissiveness and lack of discipline, however, tend to produce a spoiled, inconsiderate, aggressive child—and an insecure one as well. On the other hand, overly harsh discipline may have a variety of harmful effects, including a fear and hatred of the punishing person, a lack of initiative or spontaneity, and a mistrust of others. When accompanied by rigid moral standards, overly severe discipline is likely to result in a seriously repressed child who lacks spontaneity and warmth and devotes much effort toward controlling impulses that are, in fact, natural. Such children often subject themselves to severe self-recrimination and self-punishment for real or imagined mistakes and misdeeds. They may also apply the same standards to the behavior of their peers, thus earning reputations as "prudes" or worse. Overly severe discipline, combined with restrictiveness, also may lead to rebellion and socially deviant behavior as children grow older and are subjected to outside influences that are incompatible with parental views and practices.

When severe discipline takes the form of physical punishment—as opposed to the withdrawal of approval and privileges—the result tends to be increased aggressive behavior on the part of a child (Eron et al., 1974; Faretra, 1981; Patterson, 1979). Apparently, physical punishment provides a model of aggressive behavior that the child emulates and incorporates into his or her own cognitive map. Researchers and clinicians, in only recently discovering the tragic proportions of physical child abuse, have also discovered that abusers were almost always abused themselves as children.

Inconsistent discipline makes it difficult for a child to establish stable values for guiding behavior. A child who is punished one time and ignored and rewarded the next time for the same behavior does not learn what behavior is appropriate. Deur and Parke (1970) found that children with a history of inconsistent reward and punishment for aggressive behavior were more resistant to punishment and to the extinction of their aggressive behavior than were children who had experienced more consistent discipline. This study supports earlier findings showing a high correlation between inconsistent discipline and later delinquent and criminal behavior.

In the past, discipline was conceived as a method for both punishing undesirable behavior and preventing or deterring such behavior in the future. Discipline is now thought of more positively as providing needed structure and guidance for promoting a child's healthy growth. Such guidance provides a child with a cognitive map that is richly representative of the outcomes actually meted out by the world, contingent on a person's behavior. The person thus informed has a sense of control over these outcomes and is free to make deliberate choices. For example, Baumrind (1975) has found that authoritative discipline is associated with children's development of general competencies for dealing with others and with their environments. When coercion or punishment is deemed necessary, it is important that a parent make clear exactly what behavior is considered inappropriate; it is also important that the child know what behavior is expected, and that positive and consistent methods of discipline be worked out for dealing with infractions. In general, a child should be granted autonomy commensurate with his or her level of maturity and ability to use it constructively. As competent parents would doubtless agree, this judgment is not always easy to make.

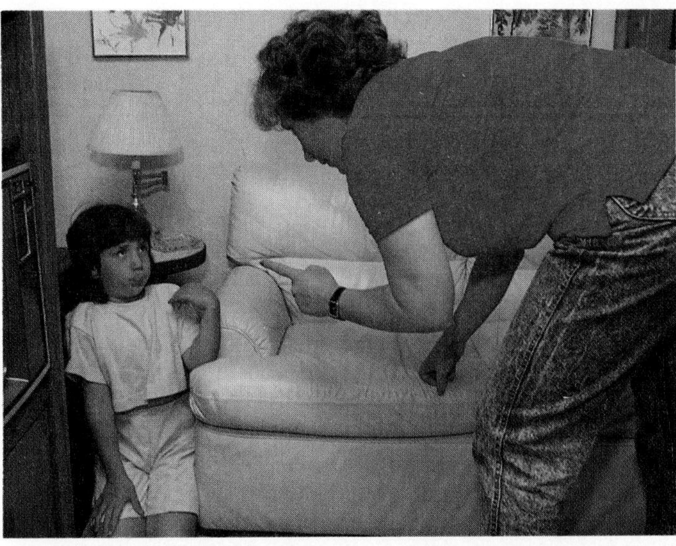

The question of disciplining children is a particularly difficult one for most parents. Inconsistent discipline makes it difficult for a child to establish stable values for guiding behavior. When punishment is deemed necessary, a parent should make it clear what behavior was considered inappropriate. The child should also be told what behavior is expected. Positive and consistent methods of discipline should be worked out for rewarding appropriate behavior and for dealing with infractions.

Inadequate and Irrational Communication

Parents sometimes discourage a child from asking questions and in other ways fail to foster the information exchange essential for helping the child develop essential competencies. Limited and inadequate communication patterns have commonly been attributed to economically disadvantaged families, but these patterns are not restricted to any socioeconomic level.

Inadequate communication may take a number of forms. Some parents are too busy or preoccupied with their own concerns to listen to their children and to try to understand the conflicts and pressures they are facing. As a consequence, these parents often fail to give needed support and assistance, particularly when there is a crisis. Other parents have forgotten that the world often looks different to a child or adolescent—rapid social change can lead to a communication gap between generations.

In other instances, faulty communication may take more deviant forms in which messages become completely garbled because a listener distorts, disconfirms, or ignores a speaker's intended meaning. The following case study is a good example of such pathological communication. The setting is a meeting in a hospital involving a schizophrenic young man, his parents, and his therapist. Prior to the meeting, the patient had sent his mother a Mother's Day card containing the inscription, "For Someone Who's Been Like a Mother to Me." We pick up the conversation following a confrontation between mother and son concerning the obliquely hostile inscription:

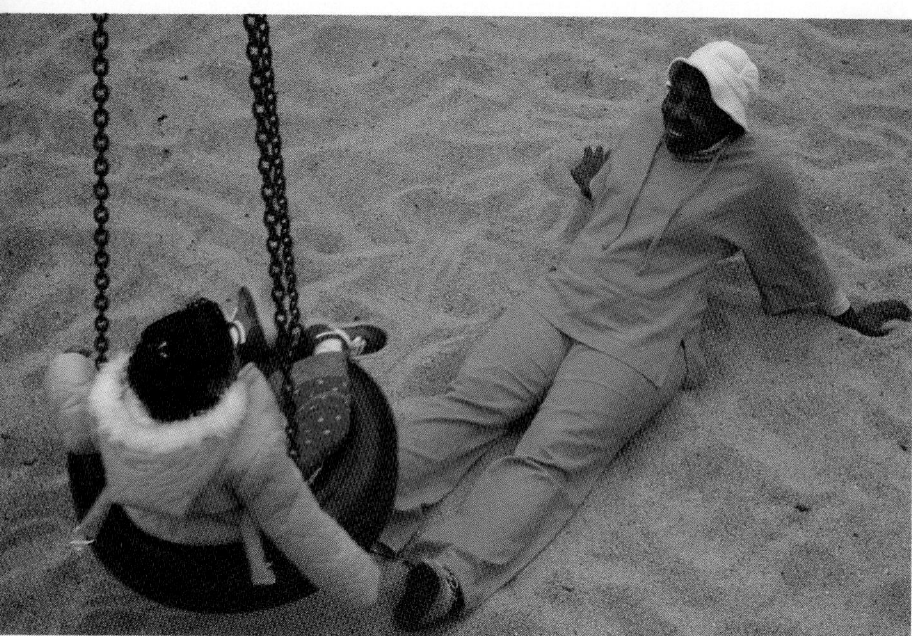

Encouraging children to ask questions, taking the time to listen to their concerns, and trying to understand the conflicts and pressures they are facing are important ways that parents—and in this photo, a grandparent—can help children to develop essential competencies.

Patient: *Well, I meant to sting you just a tiny bit by that outside phrase.*
Mother: *You see I'm a little bit of a psychiatrist too, Simon, I happen to be—(laughing). So I felt so—when you talked to [the therapist] I brought along that card—I wanted to know what's behind your head. And I wanted to know—or you made it on purposely to hurt me—well, if you did, I—I . . .*
Patient: *(interrupting) Not entirely, not entire . . .*
Mother: *(interrupting and overlapping) I'll take all—Simon, believe me. I'll take all the hurt in the world if it will help you—you see what I mean?*
Therapist: *How can you . . .*
Mother: *(continuing) Because I never meant to hurt you—Huh?*
Therapist: *How can you hurt anybody who is perfectly willing to be hurt? (short pause)*
Father: *What's that?*
Mother: *I uh—a mother sacrifices—if you would be—maybe a mother you would know too. Because a mother is just a martyr, she's sacrificing—like even with Jesus with his mother—she sacrificed too. So that's the way it goes on, a mother takes over anything what she can help . . .*
Therapist: *(interrupting) What mother?*
Mother: *(continuing) . . . her children.*
Patient: *(interrupting and overlapping) Well, uh, I'll tell you Ma—listen, Ma, I didn't mean to—to sting you exactly that outside part there.*
Therapist: *Well, you said so.*
Patient: *Oh, all right, but it—it wasn't that exactly. No, I'm not giving ground—uh—it's hard to explain this thing. Uh—uh—what was I going to say? Now I forgot what I was going to say (short pause). I mean I felt that this—this is what I mean, uh—that I felt that you could have been a better mother to me than you were. See there were things.*
Mother: *Uh . . .*
Father: *Well you said . . .*
Patient: *(interrupting) You could have been better than you were. So that's why—that's that—I felt—it was, uh—uh, was all right to send it that way.*
Mother: *Well, if you meant it that way that's perf—that's what I wanted to know—and that's all I care, you see. But I still say, Simon, that if you would take your father and mother just like they're plain people—you just came here and you went through life like anybody else went through—and—and don't keep picking on them and picking them to pieces—but just leave them alone—and go along with them the way they are—and don't change them—you'll be able to get along with everybody, I assure you.*
Patient: *(interrupting) I mean after all a card is a*

card—why I'd—it seems to me kind of silly (anguish in his voice and near weeping) to bring that thing in here—they have sold them at the canteen, Ma . . .
Therapist: *Are you anxious now . . .*
Patient: *Why . . .*
Therapist: *Are you anxious now because she said . . .*
Patient: *I shouldn't be blamed for a thing like that, it's so small . . .*
Mother: *(overlapping) I'm not blaming you.*
Patient: *(continuing) I don't even remember exactly what the thing was.*
Mother: *(overlapping) Well, that's all I wanted to know (laughs).*
Patient: *(continuing) I didn't want to—to—to —to blame you or nothing." (Haley, 1959, p. 360)*

This conversation continued in similar fashion until the patient conceded that what he had meant by the inscription was that his mother had been a *real* mother to him. This concession produced a considerable reduction in general tension, but it was, of course, at the expense of what might have proved a useful confrontation with reality.

Such deviant forms of intrafamilial communication are often found in the families of schizophrenic individuals. Although other types of unusual parent-child relations are also seen in such cases, many investigators believe that communication deviance has a special relevance for schizophrenia (Carson & Sanislow, 1992; Goldstein & Strachan, 1987). It is still not definitely established, however, that such communication patterns have causal significance; they may be only correlations. It is possible, for example, that the presence of a schizophrenic or preschizophrenic child in a household might induce parents to communicate in strangely ineffective ways.

In any event, the types of deviant communication often found in the households of schizophrenic individuals are quite varied. They include fragmented and amorphous ways of communicating, erotic overtones between parent and child, difficulties in maintaining a focus of attention, inability to establish closure about a topic, and undue amounts of hostile and critical attention focused on the member who is at risk for a schizophrenic episode (Liem, 1980). Before we move on to broader issues of family structure, *HIGHLIGHT 4.5* summarizes faulty parent-child relationships.

Pathogenic Family Structures

The pathogenic parent-child patterns so far described, such as parental rejection, are rarely found in severe form unless the total familial context is abnormal. Thus pathogenic family structure is an overarching risk factor that increases an individual's vulnerability to particular stressors. A parent's repeated incestuous assaults on a child, for example, can hardly escape a spouse's detection; somewhat incredibly, and very sadly, it is not at all unusual to discover that the spouse does not intervene. In the Roff and Knight (1981) longitudinal study of persons who became schizophrenic in early adulthood, two types of mothering—neglectful and overprotective—were found to be common among those individuals who had poor long-term outcomes. It was also demonstrated, however, that each of these patterns of mothering occurred in a particular type of disordered family structure. This finding confirmed earlier reports concerning two family patterns that had appeared especially predictive of a schizophrenic outcome in offspring. Maternal neglect was found to be associated with a *discordant* family pattern, whereas maternal anxiety and overprotectiveness was associated with a *disturbed* one. Each of these family structures is described in the following sections, including a description of the potential pathogenic effects of disrupted families.

Discordant and Disturbed Families In a **discordant family,** one or both of the parents is not gaining satisfaction from the relationship. One spouse may express feelings of frustration and disillusionment in hostile ways such as nagging, belittling, and doing things purposely to annoy the other person. Value differences, a common source of conflict and dissatisfaction, may lead to serious disagreements about a variety of topics, including sexual behavior and how money is spent. Whatever the reasons for the difficulties, seriously discordant relationships of long standing are likely to be frustrating, hurtful, and generally pathogenic in their effects on the adults and their children. Children who grow up in discordant families are likely to find it difficult to establish and maintain marital and other intimate relationships.

In a **disturbed family,** one or both of the parents behave in grossly eccentric or abnormal ways and may keep the home in constant emotional turmoil. Such families differ greatly, but it is common to find (a) parents who are fighting to maintain their own equilibrium and are unable to give children the love and guidance they need; (b) grossly irrational communication patterns as well as

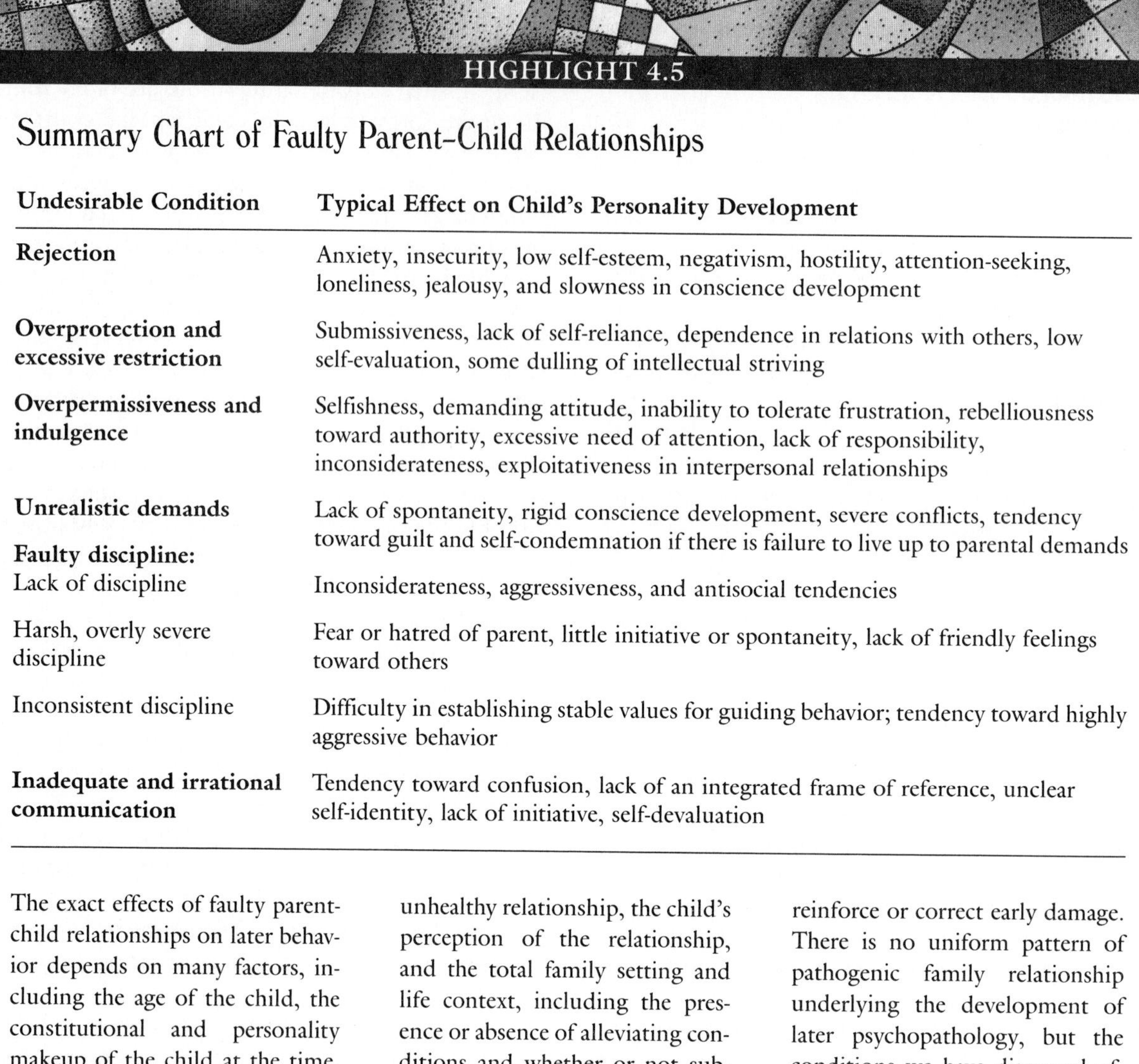

HIGHLIGHT 4.5

Summary Chart of Faulty Parent-Child Relationships

Undesirable Condition	Typical Effect on Child's Personality Development
Rejection	Anxiety, insecurity, low self-esteem, negativism, hostility, attention-seeking, loneliness, jealousy, and slowness in conscience development
Overprotection and excessive restriction	Submissiveness, lack of self-reliance, dependence in relations with others, low self-evaluation, some dulling of intellectual striving
Overpermissiveness and indulgence	Selfishness, demanding attitude, inability to tolerate frustration, rebelliousness toward authority, excessive need of attention, lack of responsibility, inconsiderateness, exploitativeness in interpersonal relationships
Unrealistic demands	Lack of spontaneity, rigid conscience development, severe conflicts, tendency toward guilt and self-condemnation if there is failure to live up to parental demands
Faulty discipline:	
Lack of discipline	Inconsiderateness, aggressiveness, and antisocial tendencies
Harsh, overly severe discipline	Fear or hatred of parent, little initiative or spontaneity, lack of friendly feelings toward others
Inconsistent discipline	Difficulty in establishing stable values for guiding behavior; tendency toward highly aggressive behavior
Inadequate and irrational communication	Tendency toward confusion, lack of an integrated frame of reference, unclear self-identity, lack of initiative, self-devaluation

The exact effects of faulty parent-child relationships on later behavior depends on many factors, including the age of the child, the constitutional and personality makeup of the child at the time, the duration and degree of the unhealthy relationship, the child's perception of the relationship, and the total family setting and life context, including the presence or absence of alleviating conditions and whether or not subsequent experiences tend to reinforce or correct early damage. There is no uniform pattern of pathogenic family relationship underlying the development of later psychopathology, but the conditions we have discussed often act as predisposing factors.

faulty parental models; and (c) almost inevitably, the entanglement of children in the parents' emotional conflicts.

Lidz et al. (1965) described two similar patterns in the family backgrounds of many schizophrenic patients they studied. They called these patterns (a) **marital schism,** in which both parents are constantly embroiled in deep-seated conflicts; and (b) **marital skew,** in which the healthier marital partner, in the interest of minimizing open disharmony, essentially accepts and supports the frequently bizarre beliefs and behaviors of his or her spouse. Marital schism and skew are roughly equivalent, respectively, to discordant and disturbed family patterns. In either instance, the children in such families are caught up in an unwholesome and irrational psychological environment.

Disrupted Families A third type of family pattern that may be pathogenic is the disrupted family. A **disrupted family** is incomplete as a result of death, divorce, separation, or some other circumstance. Due partly to a growing cultural acceptance of divorce, more than a million divorces now occur yearly in the United States, with a rate of increase averaging about 8 percent per year. These statistics provide a sobering commentary on the difficulties of maintaining extended intimate relationships.

Unhappy marriages are difficult, but ending a marital relationship can also be enormously stressful, both mentally and physically. Divorced and separated individuals are overrepresented among psychiatric patients, although the direction of the causal relationship is not always clear. In their comprehensive review of the effects of marital disruption, Bloom, Asher, & White (1978) concluded that such disruption is a major source of psychopathology, physical illness, death, suicide, and homicide.

Divorce can have traumatic effects on children, too. Feelings of insecurity and rejection may be aggravated by conflicting loyalties and, sometimes, by the spoiling the children receive while staying with one of the parents—maybe not the one they would prefer to be with. Some children, however, adjust quite well to the divorce of their parents, particularly those who were relatively well-adjusted or very young prior to the breakup (Kurdek et al., 1981; Wallerstein, 1984).

It has been commonly assumed that the loss of a father is more traumatic for a son than for a daughter, but some doubt has been raised about this assumption. It is now believed that the absence of a father has adverse effects on the formation of a secure gender identity for both girls and boys (Hetherington, Cox, & Cox, 1978). For example, Hetherington (1973) found that "the effects of father absence on daughters appear during adolescence and manifest themselves mainly as an inability to interact appropriately with males" (p. 52). Similarly, Roy (1985) has found a small but significant association of adult depression with permanent separation from either parent prior to age 17, irrespective of gender.

The long-range effects of family disruption on a child may vary greatly—they may even be favorable compared to the effects of remaining in a home torn by marital conflict and dissension (Hetherington et al., 1978). Detrimental effects may be minimized if a substitute for the missing parent is available, if the remaining family members compensate for the missing parent and reorganize the family into an effectively functioning group, or if a successful remarriage follows that provides an adequate environment for child rearing. Above all, the remaining parent (usually the mother) can help children work through the crisis by coping well with his or her own emotional upset while addressing the children's needs—an extremely demanding task that some divorced parents understandably cannot master.

Unquestionably, parental separation or divorce involves great stresses for children; it is hardly surprising that some succumb to these stresses and develop maladaptive responses. Delinquency and other abnormal behaviors are much more frequent among children and adolescents from disrupted homes than among those from intact families, although it may be that a contributing factor here is prior or continuing parental strife (Rutter, 1971, 1979). We are beginning to learn, however, that we are not always justified in inferring that a disrupted home has caused some maladaptive behavior. For example, since both broken homes and delinquency are more common among families in lower socioeconomic circumstances, it may be that disrupted homes and childhood deviance are each largely caused by the stresses of poverty and exclusion from society's mainstream.

Maladaptive Peer Relationships

Relationships with family members, particularly parents or parental surrogates, clearly have a profound effect on a child's coping resources that often continues into the adolescent and early adult years (and sometimes beyond). Another important set of relationships begins in the preschool years—those involving age-mates, or peers. Normally, these neighborhood or school relationships involve a much broader range of possible experiences than do the more constrained and established intrafamilial relationships, including sibling relations. When a child ventures into a world relatively bereft of adult monitoring and supervision, he or she is faced with a number of complicated and unpredictable challenges whose solution is largely in the child's own hands. The potential for failure is considerable.

Children at this stage are hardly masters of the fine points of human relationships or diplomacy. Empathy—the appreciation of another's situation, perspective, and feelings—is at best only primitively developed, as can be seen in a child who turns on and rejects a current playmate when a more favored candidate arrives. The child's own immediate satisfaction tends to be the preemptive goal of any interaction, and there is only an uncertain recognition that cooperation and collaboration may bring even greater benefits. The assessments a child makes

Juvenile socializing is a risky business in which a child's hard-won prestige in a group is probably perceived as being constantly in jeopardy. Actually, reputation and status in a group tend to be stable. Thus, in spite of deviations from characteristic behavior, popular youngsters will tend to remain "stars" and socially rejected ones will tend to remain "rejects."

of others in the juvenile society also tend to be centered on the other's potential contribution to the child's own sense of well-being. Should an assessment be negative, it is apt to be accompanied by actions whose directness, sometimes including physical assault, would affront the sensibilities of most adults. Even when physical retaliation is inconvenient or problematic, a resourceful youngster may recruit a coalition of peers who proceed to heap uncommonly cruel forms of social abuse and rejection on the offender, as when a victim is surrounded and taunted concerning some alleged shortcoming.

In short, juvenile socializing is a risky business in which a child's hard-won prestige in a group is probably perceived as being constantly in jeopardy. Actually, reputation and status in a group tends to be persistent, even in the face of substantial changes in characteristic behavior. We may surmise that this status inertia is a useful buffer for a child who, while occasionally lapsing into unacceptable behavior, has amassed considerable status "credits" in his or her peer group. But what of the child who has few or no credits, who has perhaps already become an object of ridicule, contempt, or unrelenting social rejection? Few options are available to such a youngster in this unforgiving social environment; the role of "goat" is as sticky as that of "star."

It requires but a moment's reflection on one's own childhood experience to recognize that such social casualties are by no means rare in the juvenile peer situation. A classic instance is that of the socially rejected girl who, in adolescence, becomes the neighborhood "easy make" in a desperate but ill-fated bid for attention and affection. This substantial minority of youngsters seems somehow ill-equipped for the rigors and competition of the school years, most likely by virtue of constitutional factors and deficits in the psychosocial climate of their families. Given the limited paths available, large numbers of them withdraw from their peers; others, also in large numbers (especially among males), develop intransigent hatreds and resentments, turn against their "tormenters," and adopt physically intimidating and aggressive life-styles. The neighborhood bully and the menacing schoolyard loner are examples. Neither of these routes, of course, solves such children's problems—quite the contrary—nor do they bode well for good mental health outcomes (e.g., Hartmann et al., 1984; Kupersmidt, Coie, & Dodge, 1990; Roff & Wirt, 1984).

Fortunately, there is another side to this coin. If peer relations have their developmental hazards, they can also be sources of key learning experiences that stand an individual in good stead for years, perhaps for a lifetime. For a resourceful youngster, the give-and-take, the winning and losing, the successes and failures of the school years provide superb training in coming to grips with the real world and with his or her developing self—its capabilities and limitations, its attractive and unattractive qualities. The experience of intimacy with another, a friend, has its beginning in this period of intense social involvement. A child reveals things to, and checks out things with, a friend that could never be revealed to any other person, thus laying the groundwork for intimate exchanges and the recognition of the commonalities and differences among people. In short, peer relations during the school years, in the best of circumstances, afford a marvelous opportunity for honing and rounding out a child's cognitive map.

If all has gone well in the early juvenile years, a child emerges into adolescence with a considerable repertoire of knowledge and skills relating to human interaction. Such a youth can effectively adapt his or her behavior to the requirements of a situation and communicate, as appropriate, his or her thoughts and feelings to others. Practice and experience in intimate communication with others makes possible a transition from attraction, infatuation, and mere sexual curiosity to genuine love and commitment. These and a multitude of other resources acquired while negotiating among peers can be strong bulwarks against frustration, demoralization, despair, and mental disorder. A youth who, for one reason or another, has not had access to the rich store of learning available in peer interactions during the school years will find it difficult to compensate for this experience deficit in later years and will be more vulnerable than those who participated fully.

Although the scenario just outlined seems reasonable, it lacked until recently a strong empirical research foundation. In fact, the developmental period it addresses had been largely ignored by the major personality theorists, Erickson and Sullivan being notable exceptions. In the last 25 years, however, research into the risk factors associated with youngsters' peer relations has been developing at an accelerating pace, and, as a result, we have been nailing down some significant facts. Some of the more important of these findings are briefly summarized in the following sections.

Popularity By far the most consistent correlate of popularity among juveniles is being seen as friendly and outgoing (Hartup, 1983). The causal relationship between popularity and friendliness is indeterminate and probably complexly involved with other variables, such as intelligence and physical attractiveness. The other side of the coin, peer rejection, is also only partly understood. One large factor is an excessively demanding or aggressive approach to ongoing peer activities, but this factor by no means characterizes the behavior of all children rejected by their peers. A smaller group of children is apparently rejected because of their own social withdrawal. The remaining large group is rejected for unknown reasons; evidently some of the antecedents of rejectability are quite subtle (Coie, 1990).

Status Invariance A child's sociometric position in a group tends, in the absence of intervention, to remain stable, especially by the fifth grade and beyond. Although there are exceptions to this general rule, "stars" tend to remain stars and "rejects," rejects (Coie & Dodge, 1983). Moreover, a child of given status in one group will tend to replicate that status in a new group in a relatively short time; childhood peer status, it appears, is portable (Coie & Kupersmidt, 1983).

Early Sources of Rejection A number of studies have attempted to identify why some children are persistently rejected by their peers. As already suggested, many of these children have poor entry skills in seeking to join ongoing group activities: they draw attention to themselves in disruptive, task-irrelevant ways; make unjustified aversive comments to others; and frequently become the focal point of verbal and physical aggression (Coie & Kupersmidt, 1983; Dodge, 1983; Putallaz & Gottman, 1983). More generally, Dodge and colleagues (1980; Dodge & Newman, 1981; Dodge & Frame, 1982; Dodge, Murphy, & Buchsbaum, 1984) have described these children as taking offense too readily and as unjustifiably attributing hostile intent to the bantering actions of their peers, escalating confrontations to unintended levels. In the end, rejection leads to social isolation, often self-imposed (Dodge, Coie, & Brakke, 1982; Hymel & Rubin, 1985; Ladd, 1983). Coie (1990) has recently pointed out that such isolation is likely to have serious consequences because it deprives a child of further opportunities to learn the "rules" of social behavior and interchange, rules that become increasingly

If all has gone well in childhood peer relationships, an adolescent has gained a considerable repertoire of knowledge and skills relating to human interaction. Such a youth can effectively adapt his or her behavior to the requirements of a situation and can appropriately communicate his or her thoughts and feelings.

sophisticated and subtle with increasing age. Repeated social failure is the usual result, with further damaging effects on self-confidence and self-esteem.

Adult Outcomes Both logic and research findings lead to a similar conclusion: a child who fails to establish a satisfactory relationship with peers during the developmental years is deprived of a crucial set of background experiences. We would expect such a child to have an increased likelihood of coping with failure and adaptive breakdown as the various challenges of the adult years present themselves. Again, the relevant research, recently surveyed by Kupersmidt, Coie, & Dodge (1990), supports this assumption. Peer social problems in childhood have been linked to a variety of breakdowns in later adaptive functioning, including schizophrenia, school dropout, crime, and increased general involvement with mental health services. While these correlational data do not in themselves permit strong causal inferences, they constitute important links in a highly plausible causal chain.

SOCIOCULTURAL CAUSAL FACTORS

As we discussed in Chapter 3, the sociocultural viewpoint grew out of observations on the varying value and behavior patterns among different cultural groups. These observations increased insight into the power of social and cultural forces to shape behavior and personality. We also noted that a number of cultures and subcultures seem to protect their members from the more serious forms of personal misery and disorganization, as shown by incidence rates that are markedly below worldwide averages. Other cultures—southern Ireland, for example—have above-average incidence rates for certain disorders (Torrey, 1979; Torrey et al., 1984). We can assume that these differences occur because the cultures themselves in some way either protect their members from disorder or instill within them a measure of vulnerability.

For reasons of temperament, conditioning, and other individual factors, not all people adopt the prevailing cultural patterns. These people may escape some of the culture's detrimental influences but may also miss the protection of the more adaptive ones. This situation is especially common in Western society, where we are exposed to many competing values and patterns. The following sections will emphasize that, in our society, several social and cultural influences may act to increase our vulnerabilities to the development of abnormal behaviors. We will begin by discussing the role of culture in determining an individual's behavior pattern. We will then turn to particular factors in the sociocultural environment that may increase vulnerability: low socioeconomic class, disorder-engendering social roles, prejudice and discrimination, economic and employment problems, and social change and uncertainty.

The Sociocultural Environment

In much the same way that we receive a genetic inheritance that is the end product of millions of years of biological evolution, we also receive a sociocultural inheritance that is the end product of thousands of years of social evolution. The significance of this inheritance was well pointed up by Aldous Huxley (1965):

The native or genetic capacities of today's bright city child are no better than the native capacities of a bright child born into a family of Upper Paleolithic cave-dwellers. But whereas the contemporary bright baby may grow up to become almost anything—a Presbyterian engineer, for example, a piano-playing Marxist, a professor of biochemistry who is a mystical agnostic and likes to paint in water colours—the paleolithic baby could not possibly have grown into anything except a hunter or food-gatherer, using the crudest of stone tools and thinking about his narrow world of trees and swamps in terms of some hazy system of magic. Ancient and modern, the two babies are indistinguishable. . . . But the adults into whom the babies will grow are profoundly dissimilar; and they are dissimilar because in one of them very few, and in the other a good many, of the baby's inborn potentialities have been actualized. (p. 69)

Because each group fosters its own cultural patterns by systematically teaching its offspring, all its members tend to be somewhat alike—to conform to certain basic personality types. Individuals reared among headhunters become headhunters; individuals reared in societies that do not sanction violence learn to settle their differences in nonviolent ways. In New Guinea, for example, Margaret Mead (1949) found two tribes—of similar racial origin and living in the same general geographical area—whose members developed diametrically opposed characteristics. The Arapesh were a kindly, peaceful, cooperative people, while the Mundugumor were warlike, suspicious, competitive, and vengeful. Such differences appear to be social in origin.

The more uniform and thorough the education of the younger members of a group, the more alike they will become. Thus in a society characterized by a limited and consistent point of view, there are not the wide individual differences typical in a society like ours, where children have contact with diverse, often conflicting, beliefs. Even in our society, however, there are certain core values that most of us consider essential.

Subgroups within a general sociocultural environment—such as family, sex, age, class, occupational, ethnic, and religious groups—foster beliefs and norms of their own, largely by means of **social roles** that their members learn to adopt. Expected role behaviors exist for a student, a teacher, an army officer, a priest, a nurse, and so on.

The extent to which role expectations can influence development is well illustrated by masculine and feminine roles in our own society and their effects on personality development and on behavior. In recent years, a combination of masculine and feminine traits (**androgyny**) has often been proclaimed to be psychologically ideal for both men and women. Many people, however, continue to show evidence of having been strongly affected by assigned masculine and feminine roles. Moreover, there is accumulating evidence that the acceptance of gender-role assignments has substantial implications for mental health. In general, studies show that low "masculinity" is associated with maladaptive behavior and vulnerability to disorder for either biological sex, possibly because this condition tends to be strongly associated with deficient self-esteem (Carson, 1989). Baucom (1983), for example, has shown that high-feminine-sex-typed (low masculinity) women tend to reject opportunities to lead group problem-solving situations. He likens this effect to learned helplessness, which, as we have seen, has in turn been suggested as a causal factor in anxiety (Barlow, 1988) and depression (Abramson et al., 1978).

An individual, being a member of various subgroups, is subject to various role demands. These social roles, of course, change as group memberships—or positions in various groups—change. In fact, an individual's life can be viewed as a succession of roles—child, student, worker, spouse, parent, and senior citizen. The various groups may allow a person considerable leeway in role behavior, but there are limits. Conformity to role demands is induced by the use of positive and negative reinforcers—money, prestige, status, punishment, or loss of membership in a group—as well as through instruction. When social roles are conflicting, unclear, or uncomfortable, or when an individual is unable to achieve a satisfactory role in a group, healthy personality development may be impaired —just as when a child is rejected by juvenile peer groups.

Each individual interacts with various people and groups, typically beginning with family members and gradually extending to peer group members and other significant people. Much of an

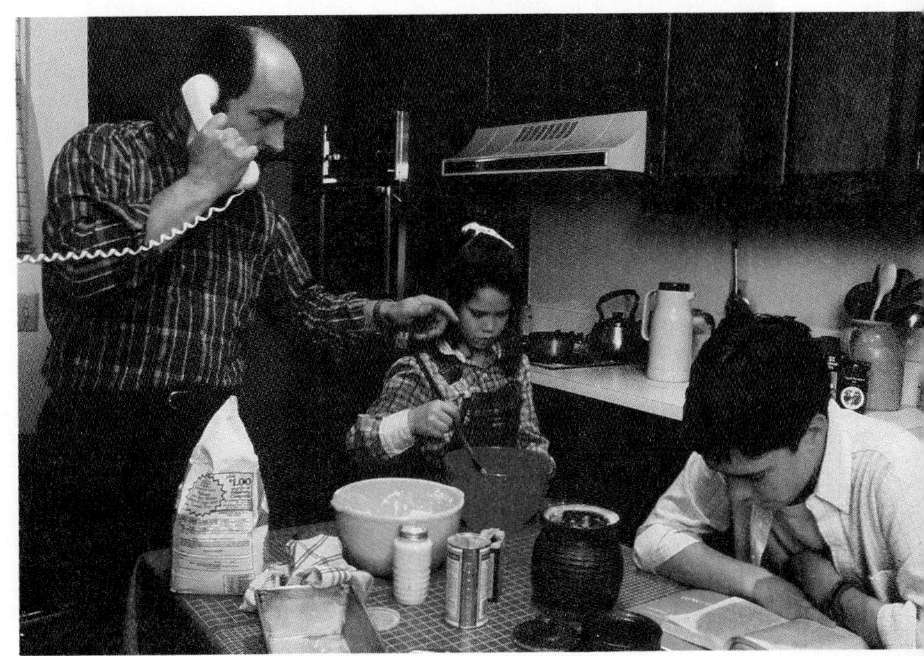

An individual's life can be viewed as a succession of roles—child, student, worker, spouse, parent, and so on. When social roles are conflicting, unclear, or uncomfortable, healthy personality development may be impaired. The extent to which role expectations can influence development is well illustrated by "masculine" and "feminine" sex roles in our own society and their effects on personality development and characteristic behavior.

individual's personality development reflects experiences with these key people. Relationships formed in a Boy Scout troop, for example, will likely have effects on development quite different from relationships formed in a delinquent gang. The behavior patterns children learn depend heavily on which models they observe, whose expectations they are trying to meet, and what rewards are forthcoming for their behavior.

Pathogenic Societal Influences

Since each of us belongs to different subgroups and experiences different interpersonal relationships, we each participate in the sociocultural environment in a unique way. In the situations that follow, different social roles and experiences can be seen as significant influences in the development of maladaptive behaviors.

Low Socioeconomic Status In our society, an inverse correlation exists between socioeconomic status and the prevalence of abnormal behavior—the lower the socioeconomic class, the higher the incidence of abnormal behavior (Eron & Peterson, 1982). The strength of the correlation seems to vary with different types of disorder, however. Some disorders may be related to social class only minimally or perhaps not at all. For example, the incidence of schizophrenia is inversely correlated with social class, while that of mood disorders bears a less distinct relationship to class and, if anything, may tend in the opposite direction.

We do not understand all the reasons for the more general inverse relationship. Undoubtedly some inadequate and disturbed people slide down to the lower rungs of the economic ladder and remain there; these people will often have inadequate and disturbed children. At the same time, more affluent people are better able to get prompt help or to conceal their problems.

In addition, it is almost certainly true that people living in poverty encounter more, and more severe, stressors in their lives than do people in the middle and upper classes, and they usually have fewer resources for dealing with them. As Kohn (1973) has pointed out, the conditions under which lower-class youngsters are reared tend to inhibit the development of the coping skills needed in our increasingly complex society. Thus the tendency for abnormal behavior to appear more frequently in lower socioeconomic groups may be at least partly due to predispositional coping deficits.

Disorder-engendering Social Roles An organized society, even an "advanced" one, sometimes asks its members to perform roles in which the prescribed behaviors are either deviant themselves or may produce maladaptive reactions. A soldier who is called upon by his superiors (and ultimately by his society) to deliberately kill and maim other human beings may subsequently develop serious feelings of guilt. He or she may also have

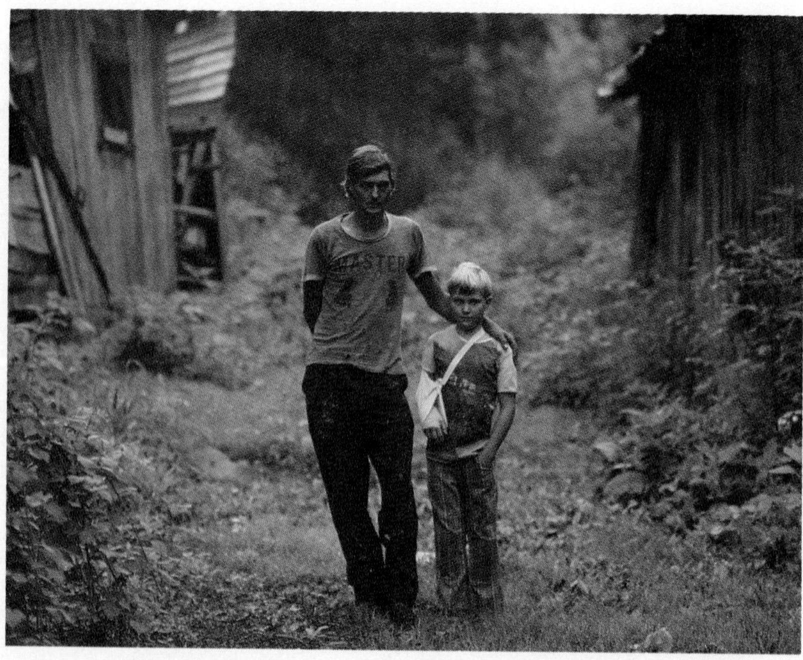

In our society, the lower the socioeconomic class, the higher the incidence of abnormal behavior. The conditions under which lower-class youngsters are reared tend to inhibit the development of coping skills. Many individuals, however, emerge from low socioeconomic environments with strong, highly adaptive personalities and skills.

latent emotional problems resulting from the horrors commonly experienced in combat and hence be vulnerable to disorder. As a nation, we are still struggling with the many problems of this type that have emerged among veterans of the Vietnam War, whose rates of abnormality have been well above national averages (Strayer & Ellenhorn, 1975). As a group, these veterans are expected to have continuing problems well into the future (Horowitz & Solomon, 1978). In fact, the DSM-III diagnosis of posttraumatic stress disorder was created largely in response to the problems of these veterans of the Vietnam War.

Militaristic regimes and organizations are especially likely to foster problematic social roles. Military and civilian officials in Germany during the Nazi Holocaust and in the Soviet Union during Stalin's collectivization of rural areas in the 1930s (Conquest, 1986) willingly participated in history's most heinous and cold-blooded mass murders. Some American street gangs demand extreme cruelty and callousness on the part of their members. Well-organized terrorist groups, feeling that the world is ignoring their just claims, train their members for hostage-taking, mass destruction, and murder.

In a famous experiment, Zimbardo and his associates (1975) demonstrated the power of "guard" and "prisoner" roles to quickly produce extremely maladaptive behavior in otherwise normal persons. As an unintended consequence, the study's subjects learned some things about themselves that they may have been better off not knowing. In fact, the study had to be prematurely ended because of its disturbing effects on the subjects.

There is, of course, no easy answer to the problems of violence and coercion in the modern world; people will often resort to force when other remedies fail, as demonstrated by the seemingly unending turmoil in the Middle East. As long as such actions are taken, many people will be subjected to conditions of extraordinary stress and will feel compelled to enact difficult and painful social roles. In some cases, the end result will be psychological disorder.

Prejudice and Discrimination Vast numbers of people in our society have been subjected to demoralizing stereotypes and overt discrimination in areas such as employment and education. We have made progress in race relations since the 1960s, but the lingering effects of mistrust and discomfort among various ethnic and racial groups can be clearly observed on almost any college campus. For the most part, students socialize informally only with members of their own subcultures, despite the attempts of many well-meaning college administrators to break down the barriers. The tendency of students to avoid crossing these barriers needlessly limits their educational experiences and probably contributes to continued misinformation about and prejudice toward others.

We have also made recent progress in recognizing the demeaning and often disabling social roles our society has historically assigned to women. Again, though, much remains to be done. Many more women than men seek treatment for various emotional disorders, notably depression; mental health professionals believe this fact is a consequence both of the vulnerabilities (such as passivity and dependence) intrinsic to the traditional roles assigned to women, and of the special stressors with which many modern women must cope (being full-time mothers, full-time homemakers, and full-time employees) as their traditional roles rapidly change.

Economic and Employment Problems
Economic difficulties and unemployment have repeatedly been linked to enhanced vulnerability and thus to elevated rates of abnormal behavior (Dooley & Catalano, 1980). Recession and inflation coupled with high unemployment are sources of chronic anxiety for many people. Unemployment has placed a burden on a sizable segment of our population, bringing with it both financial hardships and self-devaluation. In fact unemployment can be as debilitating psychologically as it is financially (Nelson, 1974). In recent years the economic plight of the nation's small farmers has produced widespread fear and discouragement in this group. Similarly, the changing economic situation of America's traditional major manufacturing industries has displaced tens of thousands of skilled workers for whom comparable employment simply does not exist. As a society, we have yet to solve the human problems such major economic shifts entail, and some would hold that we have not even begun to engage them. The philosophies of free enterprise and rugged individualism run deep in American culture and politics, and they are in fact shared by many of the victims of these displacements. The result is self-blame and personal demoralization.

Periods of extensive unemployment are typically accompanied by increases in certain types of maladaptive behavior, such as depression, suicide, and crime (Brenner, 1973). Hardest hit by economic and employment problems are those at the bottom of the social ladder, who are already handicapped by poor education, poor nutrition, broken or unstable families, inadequate housing, feelings of helplessness, and a sense of rejection by the larger society—all of this in the midst of a culture that indulges itself in crass displays of affluence. It is small wonder that some members of these groups are enticed by the dangerous but lavish life-style and elevated status afforded by the sale of illegal drugs.

Even for many people who are employed, a major source of demoralization is job dissatisfaction. Job dissatisfaction is related to anxiety, tension, and a wide range of psychophysiologic disorders. It has also been linked to impaired marital and family relationships.

Whatever the possibilities for job satisfaction in an increasingly complicated society, the demand for it seems to be increasing (Gartner & Riessman, 1974). People no longer see money alone as an adequate return for their investment of time and energy; they also desire meaningful employment and the integration of education, work, and leisure into a fulfilling life pattern. The difficulties of achieving this goal adds yet another frustrating dimension to the job picture: many people may realize their career ambitions and still find themselves unhappy or disillusioned with their work.

Environmental pollution is one aspect of contemporary life that is threatening to our sense of well-being. The uncertainty people feel about a future clouded by problems of such large magnitude can increase vulnerability to abnormal behavior.

Social Change and Uncertainty The rate and pervasiveness of change today are different from anything our ancestors ever experienced. All aspects of our lives are affected—our educations, our jobs, our families, our leisure pursuits, our finances, and our beliefs and values. Constantly trying to keep up with the numerous adjustments demanded by these changes is a source of constant and considerable stress. In fact, Toffler (1970) proposed the term *future shock* to describe the profound confusion and emotional upset resulting from too-rapid social change.

Simultaneously, we confront inevitable crises as the earth's consumable natural resources dwindle and as our environment becomes increasingly noxious with pollutants—while environmentalists vie with those who feel their jobs will be threatened by tighter controls. No longer are Americans confident that the future will be better than the past or that technology will solve all our problems. On the contrary, our attempts to cope with existing problems increasingly seem to create new problems that are as bad or worse. The resulting despair, demoralization, and sense of helplessness are well-established predisposing conditions for abnormal reactions to stressful events (Dohrenwend et al., 1980; Frank, 1978).

UNRESOLVED ISSUES on Causation

For people sharing particular forms of maladaptive behavior, we have made substantial progress in identifying certain background factors, often called *risk factors,* that they tend to have in common (usually with many exceptions). For example, persons diagnosed as schizophrenic are found, at a higher than normal rate, to have close relatives suspected of having the disorder—suggesting genetic predisposition as a possible causal element. In order someday to predict with accuracy who is at risk for and who will develop schizophrenia, we must discover as many of these relationships as possible, even if we do not yet know how they are causally related to the disorder.

Thus we know that individuals born to schizophrenic mothers are at a quantifiable risk for schizophrenia, but we do not know the mechanisms accounting for the increased probability of schizophrenia; a genetic connection is only one of several possibilities. Moreover, if we did have such knowledge, it would be of limited help in understanding the many schizophrenics who have no history of schizophrenia in their family backgrounds. And, of course, we would still have to account for the many people born to schizophrenic mothers who never develop the disorder. Evidently, there is more than one causal pathway that can lead to schizophrenia, and this situation appears to be the rule rather than the exception across the broad spectrum of behavioral abnormalities.

Thus in undertaking a causal analysis of an individual case of disorder, we rarely have any precise, reliable knowledge about how the person got from "there" to "here." Even the exceptions, largely limited to those disorders in which true primary causes have been established, can leave us baffled when observing diverse outcomes. For example, general paresis cannot occur in the absence of an untreated (or unsuccessfully treated) syphilitic infection; yet only a small percentage of people with advanced syphilis exhibit the full general paretic syndrome. What then are the additional conditions leading to the disorder? We can make educated guesses, but in the end, we often do not know.

Causal analysis is difficult in part because of our dependence on essentially *correlational* methods. The mere association of one variable with another cannot by itself establish a causal connection between them. Would the full use of *experimental* methods on etiological questions—ethical issues aside—be an assured way of gaining the information we need? Probably not.

In essence, investigators using the experimental method systematically vary one factor or variable (or at most a few) while controlling all others, and then observes the outcome in respect to the phenomena of interest—in our case, the occurrence of some type of abnormal behavior. The method derives from classical physics, where the task is to understand the behavior of matter, and in that context it has been fruitful. Increasingly, however, physicists are recognizing its limitations, as they probe more deeply into phenomena that do not yield to simple cause-and-effect analysis. Human behavior is probably even more complex.

We are thus coming to the conclusion that most disorders, especially beyond childhood, are the result of many causal factors—biological, psychosocial, and sociocultural—that for any person may be unique, or at least not widely shared in major groupings of other people. If this conjecture proves true in terms of future research findings, then we are faced with a truly intimidating task that we cannot solve with our currently available scientific tools. In brief, the problem is this: if common causal patterns cannot be found in individuals supposedly sharing the same disorder, then we have no obvious means of distinguishing between an attribute of an individual as opposed to an attribute of a disorder. Our considerable knowledge of the general factors correlated with one or another disorder at the group level provides clues about causal influences in individual cases, but it never completes the individual causal picture. A rather large array of "unexplained" influences almost always remains. Nor is it obvious at present what new methodology we need to move beyond this stymied position.

Meanwhile, we suspect that the individual case study method, for all its imprecision and shortcomings (described in Chapter 1), will remain an indispensable tool for assessing causal patterns and sequences. The absence—one might even say the inconceivability—of cookie-cutter, universally applicable patterns to account for most disorders also means that sound, experienced clinicianship is not likely to be replaced by technological advances.

SUMMARY

In most instances the occurrence of abnormal or maladaptive behavior is the joint product of an individual's vulnerability (diathesis) to disorder and of certain stressors that challenge an individual's coping resources. Such vulnerabilities are generally considered predisposing causes. Predisposing causal influences are the focus of this chapter, although other types of causes (primary, precipitating, and reinforcing) are discussed. In practice it is often difficult to make distinctions between these various types of causes.

Predisposing causes of mental disorder may be classified as biological, psychosocial, and sociocultural. While these three classes can interact with each other in complicated ways, certain known causes are especially related to each.

In examining biologically-based vulnerabilities, we must consider genetic endowment (including chromosomal irregularities), constitutional factors, primary reaction tendencies, and various disruptions of the biological system. All of these essentially physical disturbances can create conditions that make a person vulnerable to disorder.

For psychosocially determined sources of vulnerability, the situation is somewhat more blurred. It is clear, however, that a person's frame of reference, or cognitive map (including its *self*-identity component), plays a central role as both an information-processing system and as a collection of attributions and values concerning the world and that person's personal identity. The efficiency, accuracy, and coherence of a person's cognitive map appears to be an important bulwark against breakdown. Sources of psychosocially determined vulnerability include early social deprivation, severe emotional trauma, inadequate parenting, and dysfunctional peer relationships.

Sociocultural variables are also important sources of vulnerability, or, conversely, of resistance to it. The incidence of particular disorders varies widely among different cultures; unfortunately, we know little of the specific factors involved in these variations. In our own culture, certain prescribed roles, such as those relating to gender, appear to be more predisposing to disorder than others. Low socioeconomic status is also associated with greater risk for various disorders, possibly because it is often difficult for economically distressed families to provide their offspring with sufficient coping resources. Additionally, certain roles evolved by given cultures may in themselves be maladaptive, and certain large-scale cultural trends, such as rapid technological advance, may increase stress while lessening the effectiveness of traditional coping resources.

Finally, the intimidating nature of the search for a complete understanding of the causes of vulnerability leaves little room for complacency despite the very real progress made in identifying general factors at the group level. It is not clear how we will approach the problem of the individual patterning of these causal factors.

Key Terms

vulnerabilities (p. 95)
etiology (p. 96)
primary cause (p. 96)
predisposing cause (p. 96)
precipitating cause (p. 96)
reinforcing cause (p. 96)
causal pattern (p. 97)
diathesis (p. 98)
diathesis-stress model (p. 98)
chromosomes (p. 100)
chromosomal anomalies (p. 100)
autosomes (p. 100)
sex chromosomes (p. 100)
X chromosomes (p. 101)
Y chromosome (p. 101)
genes (p. 101)
dominant genes (p. 101)
recessive genes (p. 101)
concordance rates (p. 104)
constitutional liability (p. 104)
congenital defect (p. 105)
primary reaction tendencies (p. 106)
homeostasis (p. 109)
cognitive maps (schemas) (p. 112)
self-identity (p. 113)
accommodation (p. 113)
psychic trauma (p. 118)
discordant family (p. 125)
disturbed family (p. 125)
marital schism (p. 126)
marital skew (p. 126)
disrupted family (p. 126)
social roles (p. 131)
androgyny (p. 131)

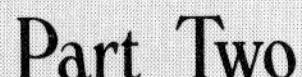

Part Two

Patterns of Abnormal (Maladaptive) Behavior

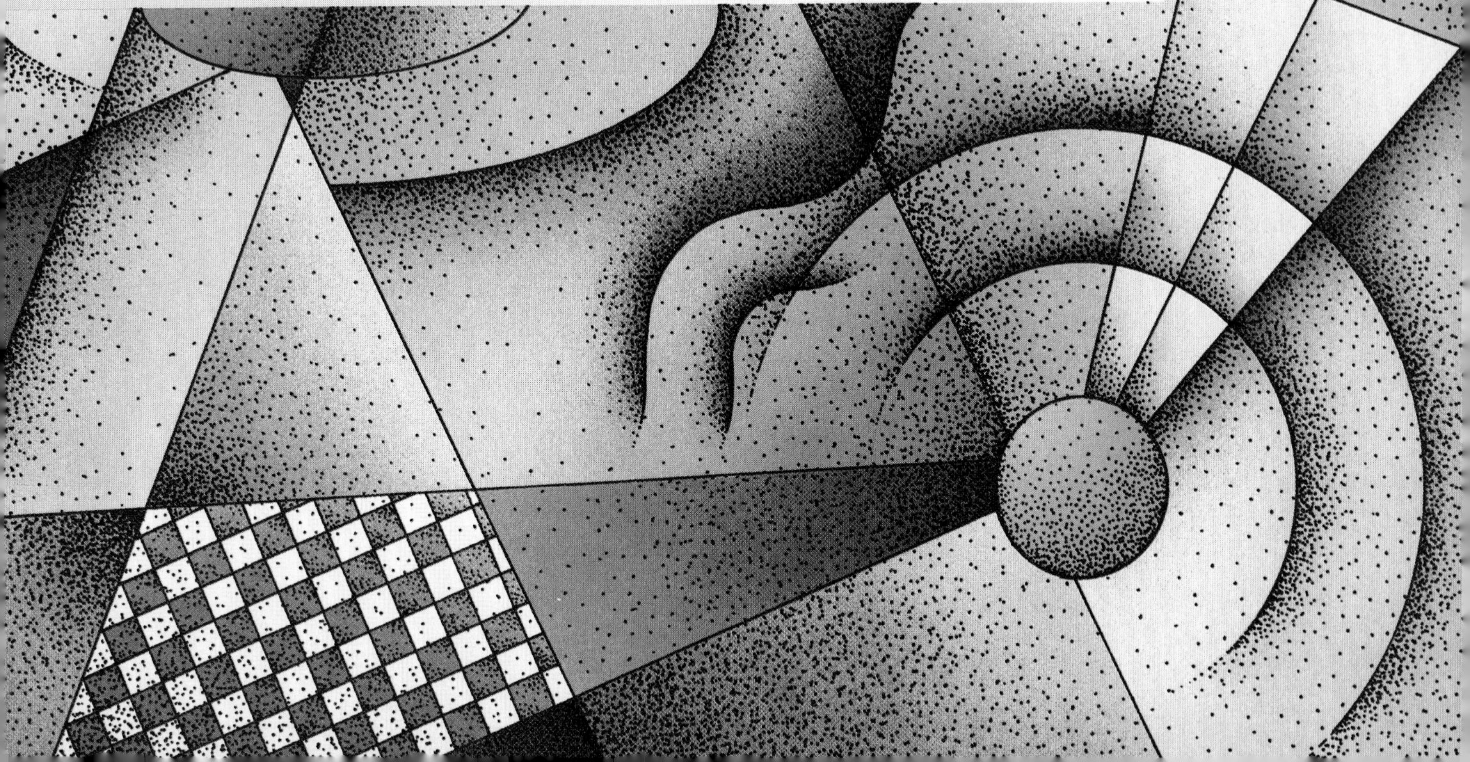

Chapter 5

Stress and Adjustment Disorders

Josef Schneller (Sell), *The Next World, Myriad-Resurrection.* Schneller (1878–?) was an architectural draftsman by trade. He was committed to a mental institution in 1907 with psychosis marked by delusions and hallucinations that involved his senses of smell and touch. Some of Schneller's work has sadistic-masochistic images of women in a setting that is part school, part prison, and part convent. Other works convey his interest in fantasy, magic, and architecture.

Any one of us may break down if the going gets tough enough. Under conditions of overwhelming stress, even a previously stable individual may develop temporary (transient) psychological problems. That is, the individual may experience a lowering or breakdown of integral, adaptive functioning. This breakdown may be sudden, as in the case of an individual who has gone through a severe accident or fire, or it may be gradual, as for a person who has been subjected to prolonged periods of tension and self-esteem loss culminating in a marital breakup. Usually a person recovers once a stressful situation is over, although in some cases there may be long-lasting damage to his or her self-concept and an increased vulnerability to certain types of stressors —today's stress can be tomorrow's vulnerability. In the case of an individual who is quite vulnerable to begin with, of course, a stressful situation may precipitate more serious and lasting psychopathology.

In Chapter 4 we focused on the diathesis, or vulnerability, half of the diathesis-stress model of abnormal behavior; we saw that our vulnerabilities can predispose us to abnormal behavior. In this chapter we will focus on the role of stress as a precipitating causal factor in abnormal behavior. We will see that, at times, the impact of stress depends not only on its severity, but on an individual's preexisting vulnerabilities as well. It is important to note here that a duality exists in the relationship between diathesis and stress: many of the factors that contribute to diatheses are also sources of stress. This duality is especially true of psychosocial factors, such as emotional deprivation, inadequate parenting, and the like. In this chapter our focus will be on the *precipitating* nature of stress; in Chapter 4 we focused on its *predisposing* nature.

We will first look at what stress is, the factors that affect it, and how we react to it. Then we will turn to some specific situations that result in severe stress and examine their effects on adjustment. We will then examine severe, catastrophic stress situations that predispose a victim to the development of posttraumatic stress disorders. In the last part of the chapter, we will look at attempts made by mental health workers to intervene in the stress process—either to prevent stress reactions or to limit their intensity and duration once they have developed.

STRESS AND STRESSORS

Life would be simple indeed if our needs were automatically gratified. As we know, many obstacles, both personal and environmental, prevent this ideal situation. Such obstacles place adjustive demands on us and can lead to stress. The term *stress* has typically been used to refer both to the adjustive demands placed on an organism and to the organism's internal biological and psychological responses to such demands. To avoid confusion, we will refer to adjustive demands as **stressors,** to the effects they create within an organism as **stress,** and to efforts to deal with stress as **coping strategies.** Note that separating these constructs is a somewhat arbitrary action; as Neufeld (1990) has pointed out, stress is a byproduct of coping. For the purpose of study, however, making the distinction can be of help. What is important to remember in the long run is that the two concepts—stress and coping—are interrelated and dependent on each other.

All situations, positive and negative, that require adjustment are stressful. Thus, according to Canadian physiologist Hans Selye (1956; 1976a), the notion of stress can be broken down further into positive stress, **eustress,** and negative stress, **distress.** (In most cases, the stress experienced during a wedding would be eustress; during a funeral, distress.) Both types of stress tax an individual's resources and coping skills, though distress typically has the potential to do more damage. In the following sections, we will look at (a) categories of stressors; (b) factors predisposing an individual to stress; and (c) the unique and changing stressor patterns that characterize each person's life.

Categories of Stressors

Adjustive demands, or stressors, stem from a number of sources. These sources represent three basic categories: frustrations, conflicts, and pressures. Though we will consider these categories separately, they are closely interrelated.

Frustrations When a person's strivings are thwarted, either by obstacles that block progress toward a desired goal or by the absence of an appropriate goal, frustration occurs. Frustrations can be particularly difficult for an individual to cope with because they often lead to self-devaluation, making the person feel that he or she has failed in some way or is incompetent.

A wide range of obstacles, both external and internal, can lead to frustration. Prejudice and discrimination, unfulfillment in a job, and the death of a loved one are common frustrations stemming from the environment; physical handicaps, lack of needed competencies, loneliness, guilt, and inadequate self-control are sources of frustration based on personal limitations.

Selye distinguished between two types of stress: eustress (positive stress) and distress (negative stress). The stress experienced during a wedding is eustress; during a funeral, distress. In general, distress has greater potential for causing difficulties in adjustment.

Conflicts In many instances stress results from the simultaneous occurrence of two or more incompatible needs or motives: the requirements of one preclude satisfaction of the others. In essence we have a choice to make, and we experience conflict while trying to make it. Conflicts with which everyone has to cope may be classified as approach-avoidance, double-approach, and double-avoidance types.

1. *Approach-avoidance conflicts* involve strong tendencies to approach and to avoid the same goal. Perhaps an individual wants to join a high-status group but can do so only by endorsing views contrary to his or her personal values; or a former smoker may want to smoke during a party but realizes that doing so may jeopardize his or her long-term status as a nonsmoker. Approach-avoidance conflicts are sometimes referred to as mixed-blessing dilemmas because some negative and some positive features must be accepted regardless of which course of action is chosen. Roth and Cohen (1986) point out that being inflexible in making these choices—that is, in always choosing an approach strategy or an avoidance strategy—can be maladaptive. When dealing with a stressor, sometimes the best method of coping is to approach it; at other times, the best thing to do is to avoid it.

2. *Double-approach conflicts* involve choosing between two or more desirable goals, such as which of two movies to see on one's only free night of the week. To a large extent, such simple plus-plus conflicts result from the inevitable limitations in one's time, space, energy, and resources; they are usually handled in stride. In more complex cases, however, as when an individual is torn between two good career opportunities or between present satisfactions and future ones, decision making can be difficult and stressful. Though the experience may cause more eustress than distress, the stress is still real and the choice difficult; in either case, the individual gives up something.

3. *Double-avoidance conflicts* are those in which the choices are between undesirable alternatives, such as either going to a party when you would rather stay home or being considered impolite if you cancel at the last moment. Neither choice will bring satisfaction, so the task is to decide which course of action will be least disagreeable—that is, least stressful.

Classifying conflicts in this manner is somewhat arbitrary, and various combinations among the different types are perhaps the rule rather than the exception. Thus a double-approach conflict between alternative careers may also have its approach-avoidance aspects because of the responsibilities that either will impose. Regardless of how we categorize conflicts, they represent a major source of stress that can often become overwhelming in intensity.

Pressures Stress may stem not only from frustrations and conflicts, but also from pressures to achieve specific goals or to behave in particular ways. In general, pressures force a person to speed up, intensify effort, or change the direction of goal-oriented behavior. All of us encounter many everyday pressures, and we often handle them without undue difficulty. In some instances, however, pressures seriously tax our coping resources, and if they become excessive, they may lead to maladaptive behavior.

Pressures can originate from external or internal sources. Students may feel under severe pressure to make good grades because their parents demand it, or they may submit themselves to such pressure because they want to get into graduate school. The long hours of study, the tension of examinations, and the sustained concentration of effort over many years result in considerable stress for many students (Bolger, 1990), as shown in *HIGHLIGHT 5.1.*

Occupational demands can also be highly stressful, and many jobs make severe demands in terms of responsibility, time, and performance.

Pressure is a significant source of stress. Certain occupations make severe demands in terms of responsibility, time, and performance. Workers who experience unusually high degrees of stress, such as air-traffic controllers, may have an increased vulnerability to disease or disorder.

HIGHLIGHT 5.1

Examinations and Anxiety

Many students preparing for important, career-determining examinations, such as the Graduate Records Exam (GRE) or the Medical College Admissions Test (MCAT), experience considerable anxiety as the examination date approaches. Bolger (1990) obtained self-reported anxiety ratings on 50 premedical students for 17 days before and 17 days after the MCAT examination. As shown in the following figure, the experience of anxiety was clearly greater in the days preceding the examination—with peak anxiety occurring as the examination day approached. Individuals who were prone to using maladaptive coping mechanisms, such as wishful thinking or self-blame, tended to show increased maladaptive behavior and increased anxiety under high stress. Performance on the examination, however, did not appear to be related to the use of various coping strategies to deal with the stress—that is, those students who used maladaptive behaviors did not appear to do worse on the exam.

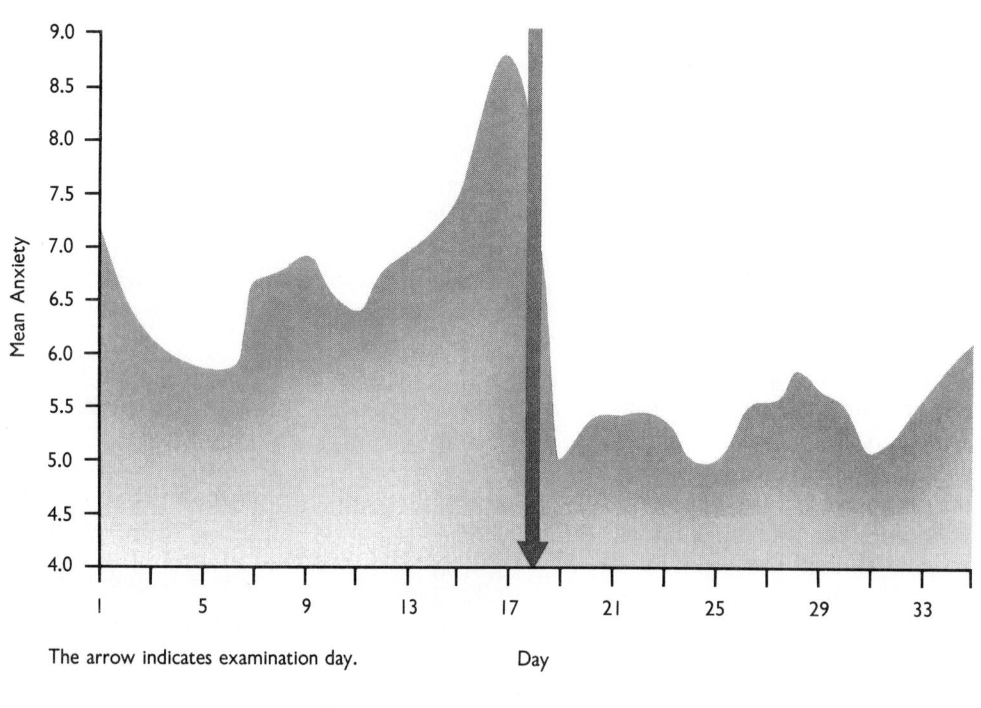

The arrow indicates examination day.

Carruthers (1980) has noted that some occupations, such as coal mining, airplane flying, or auto racing, apparently place individuals under unusually high levels of stress, which result in vulnerabilities to heart disease. Carruthers has pointed out that our "stone-age biochemistry and physiology has in several important respects failed to adapt to [our] present-age situation" (p. 11). In almost any job, if an individual is not interested in or well suited to the work, occupational demands are likely to be a major source of stress, regardless of the actual job demands. Pressures that people experience in times of economic recession can have considerable impact on their psychological adjustments. In a study on individual vulnerability to economic stress, Aldwin and Revenson (1986) interviewed workers who had been laid off from their jobs; they found, not surprisingly, consistent patterns of depressed moods and chronic frustration.

It appears that a given situation may involve elements of all three categories of stressors—frustration, conflict, and pressure. The following case illustrates this point:

A premed student whose lifelong ambition was to become a doctor received rejection letters from all the medical schools to which he had applied. This unexpected blow left him feeling depressed and empty. He felt extreme frustration over his failure and conflict over what his next steps should be. He was experiencing pressure from his family and peers to try again, but he was also overwhelmed by a sense of failure. He felt so bitter that he wanted to drop everything and become a beach bum or a blackjack dealer in Las Vegas. The loss of self-esteem he was experiencing left him with no realistic backup plans and little interest in pursuing alternative careers.

Although a particular stressor may predominate in any situation, we rarely deal with an isolated demand. Instead, we usually confront a continuously changing pattern of interrelated and sometimes contradictory demands.

Factors Predisposing an Individual to Stress

The severity of stress is gauged by the degree to which it disrupts functioning. For example, an individual will experience severe disruption of both physiological and psychological processes if deprived of food for a long time.

The actual degree of disruption that occurs or is threatened depends partly on a stressor's characteristics and partly on an individual's resources—both personal and situational—and the relationship between the two. The following sections examine the factors that predispose us to react poorly to external demands.

The Nature of a Stressor The impact of a stressor depends on its importance, duration, cumulative effect, multiplicity, and imminence. Although most stressors are dealt with as a matter of course, stressors that involve important aspects of an individual's life—such as the death of a loved one, a divorce, a job loss, or a serious illness—tend to be highly stressful for most people (Grant et al., 1981; Holmes & Rahe, 1967; Rahe & Arthur, 1978; Zilberg, Weiss, & Horowitz, 1982). Furthermore, the longer a stressor operates, the more severe its effects. Prolonged exhaustion, for example, imposes a more intense stress than does temporary fatigue. Also, stressors often appear to have a cumulative effect (Singer, 1980). A married couple may maintain amicable relations through a long series of minor irritations or frustrations only to dissolve the relationship in the face of one "last straw"—a precipitating stressor.

Encountering a number of stressors at the same time also makes a difference. If a man has a heart attack, loses his job, and receives news that his son has been arrested for drug abuse—all at the same time—the resulting stress will be more severe than if these events occurred separately.

In difficult situations, including those involving conflicts, the severity of stress usually increases as the need to deal with the demand approaches. In a classic study, Mechanic (1962) found that although graduate students thought about their examinations from time to time and experienced some anxiety during the three months prior to the tests, they did not demonstrate intense anxiety until the examinations were nearly upon them. Similar experiences have been reported by sports parachutists as the hour of their next jump approached (Epstein & Fenz, 1962, 1965). People anticipating other stressful situations—such as major surgery—have found that the severity of stress increased as the time for the ordeal approached (Janis & Leventhal, 1965).

Finally, the symptoms of stress intensify when a person is more closely involved in a traumatic situation. Pynoos et al. (1987) conducted an extensive investigation of children's symptoms and behavior one month after a shooting incident in a schoolyard (one child was killed and several others wounded when a sniper randomly fired into the playground). A total of 159 children from the school were interviewed. Depending on where they were—on the playground, in the school, in the neighborhood, on the way home, absent from school, or out of the vicinity—the children experienced different stress levels. Children on the playground, closest to the shooting, had the most severe symptoms, whereas children on vacation or who were not at school during the shooting experienced no symptoms.

An Individual's Perception and Tolerance of Stress Most of us are well aware that, in some cases, one person's stressor is another person's "piece of cake." The different reactions can be due to both a individual's perception of threat and his or her stress tolerance.

Perception of threat. If a situation is seen as threatening, it is highly stressful, especially if a person believes that his or her resources for dealing with the situation are inadequate—whether they really are or not. A person who is generally unsure of his or her adequacy and worth is much more likely to experience threat than a person who feels generally confident and secure (except, of course, in objectively stressful situations, such as rape, when all people would experience extreme stress).

Often, new adjustive demands that have not been anticipated and for which no ready-made coping strategies are available will place an individual under severe stress. To avoid this stress, the training of emergency workers, such as police and firefighters, normally involves repeated exposure to controlled or contrived stressors until coping patterns have become second nature. Likewise, recovery from the stress created by major surgery can be markedly facilitated when a patient is given realistic expectations beforehand (MacDonald & Kuiper, 1983). The same sense of adequacy and control can be achieved by choosing a stressful situation voluntarily, rather than having it be imposed by others or occur unexpectedly (Averill, 1973). The importance of having a sense of control has been noted by Paterson and Neufeld (1987): "Control appears to moderate the effects of stress by allowing the individual to alter the stress response directly or to select a response that will alter or avert the threatened event" (p. 413).

Understanding the nature of a stressful situation, preparing for it, and knowing how long it will last all lessen the severity of the stress when it does come. Of course, we continually create new stressors that make preparation and anticipation difficult at best. Two recent nuclear disasters are cases in point: the Chernobyl nuclear disaster in the Soviet Union in 1986 and the 1979 nuclear accident at Three Mile Island in Pennsylvania. Koscheyev (1990) reported high levels of stress and lowered psychological functioning among workers at the plant following the Chernobyl accident. Sixty percent of the workers were experiencing psychological symptoms a year after the accident. Victims of the Three Mile Island nuclear accident were showing physical effects from the experience, such as high blood pressure, more than a year after its occurrence (Baum, Gatchel, & Schaeffer, 1983).

Stress tolerance. If a person is marginally adjusted, the slightest frustration or pressure may be highly stressful. The term **stress tolerance** refers to a person's ability to withstand stress without becoming seriously impaired.

Stress tolerance may be increased by the environmental support of a prescibed course of action. Thus the training of emergency personnel, such as these Coast Guard trainees, often involves repeated exposure to controlled or contrived stressors until coping patterns have become second nature.

Both biologically and psychologically, people vary greatly in overall vulnerability to stressors. In addition, different people are vulnerable to different stressors. Emergencies, disappointments, and other problems that one person can take in stride may prove incapacitating to another. As we have seen, early traumatic experiences can leave an individual especially vulnerable to certain stressors.

External Resources and Social Supports

Considerable evidence suggests that positive social and family relationships can moderate the effects of stress on an individual and can reduce illness and early death (Monroe & Steiner, 1986). Conversely, the lack of external supports—either personal or material—can make a given stressor more potent and weaken an individual's capacity to cope with it. A divorce or the death of a person's mate evokes more stress if he or she is left feeling alone and unloved than if the person is surrounded by people he or she cares about and feels close to. Siegel and Kuykendall (1990), for example, found that widowed men who attended church or temple experienced less depression than those who did not. In this study spouse loss was related to depression more in the men than in the women. The reasons for this finding remain unclear, though others have found similar results as well (e.g., Stroebe & Stroebe, 1983). It could be that the women had more social resources available to them from the outset, which may have reduced their vulnerability to depression.

In other situations, an individual may be adversely affected by other family members who are experiencing problems. The level of tension for all family members can be increased if one individual experiences extreme difficulty, such as a chronic or life-threatening illness or a psychiatric disability. Yager, Grant, and Bolus (1984) concluded that the intensity of an individual's own psychological symptoms was related to that of his or her spouse; a person showed more emotional symptoms if his or her spouse was psychologically disturbed.

Environmental supports are a complex matter, however, and behavior by an individual's family or friends that is intended to provide support may actually increase the stress. In his study of graduate students facing crucial examinations, Mechanic (1962) compared the effects of different types of spousal behavior. Though the study was conducted 30 years ago, the findings are still relevant today:

In general, spouses do not provide blind support. They perceive the kinds of support the student wants and they provide it. The [spouse] who becomes worried about examinations also may provide more support than the spouse who says, "I'm not worried, you will surely pass." Indeed, since there is a chance that the student will not pass, the person who is supportive in a meaningful sense will not give blind assurance. . . . Often a statement to the effect, "Do the best you can" is more supportive than, "I'm sure you are going to do well." The latter statement adds to the student's burden, for not only must he fear the disappointment of not passing, but also the loss of respect in the eyes of his spouse. (p. 158)

Often the culture offers specific rituals or courses of action that support individuals as they attempt to deal with certain types of stress. For example, most religions provide rituals that help the bereaved through their ordeals, and in some faiths, confession and atonement help people deal with stresses related to guilt and self-recrimination.

In sum, the interaction between the nature of a stressor and an individual's resources for dealing with it largely determines the severity of stress. However great a challenge, it creates little stress if an individual can easily handle it.

Individual Stressor Patterns over Time

Each individual faces a unique pattern of adjustive demands. This fact is partly due to differences in the way people perceive and interpret similar situations, but also, objectively, no two people are faced with exactly the same pattern of stressors. Each person's age, sex, occupation, economic status, personality, competencies, and family situation help determine the demands he or she will face. The stressor pattern a child faces will differ in many ways from that of an older person, and the pattern faced by a carpenter will differ from that of a business executive.

Sometimes, key stressors in a person's life center around a continuing, difficult life situation. These stressors are considered *chronic,* or long-lasting. A person may be frustrated in a boring and unrewarding job from which there is seemingly no escape, suffer for years in an unhappy and conflictful marriage, or be severely frustrated by a physical handicap or a long-term health problem.

Stressor patterns often change with time—either predictably, as when we enter different life periods, or unpredictably, as when an accident, a death in the family, or a drastic social change makes new demands. Also, the type of stressors vary. Some of these changes bring only minor stress, while others place us under severe or excessive stress. Regardless of severity, the stressor patterns we face today are somewhat different from those we faced a week ago, and they will be different in the future from what they are now. The total pattern at any time determines the part any one stressor will play and how much difficulty we are likely to have coping with it—and the way that we cope with stressors over time shapes the course of our lives.

From time to time, most of us experience periods of especially *acute* (sudden and intense) stress. The term **crisis** is used to refer to times when a stressful situation approaches or exceeds the adaptive capacities of an individual or group. Crises are often especially stressful because the coping techniques we typically use do not work.

A crisis may center around a traumatic divorce, an episode of depression in which a person seriously considers suicide, or the aftermath of an injury or disease that forces difficult readjustments in a person's self-concept and way of life. Estimates of how

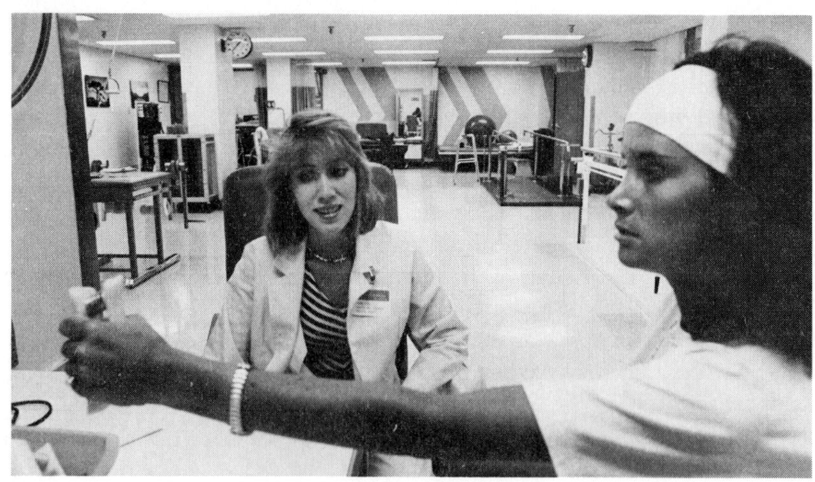

From time to time, most of us experience periods of intense stress brought on by some sort of crisis. The outcome of such crises can have a profound effect on a person's subsequent adjustment. Consider the case of Renee Katz (left). Ms. Katz, a music student who played the piano and flute, was pushed in front of a subway train and lost her right hand. Though the hand was reattached, she was not able to pursue her musical career. Instead, after undergoing physical and occupational therapy to regain some strength in her mangled hand, Ms. Katz became an occupational therapist in order to help those who, like her, needed some rehabilitative help. In this case, severe personal trauma was followed by a positive adjustment to a new situation.

often such crises occur in the life of the average person range from about once every ten years to about once every two years. In view of our complex and rapidly changing society, the latter estimate may be more realistic.

The outcome of such crises has a profound influence on a person's subsequent adjustment. An effective new method of coping developed during a crisis may be added to the person's repertoire of coping behaviors; the inability to deal adequately with the crisis may impair the person's ability to cope with similar stressors in the future because of the expectation of failure. For this reason **crisis intervention**—providing psychological help in times of severe and special stress—has become an important element in contemporary treatment and prevention approaches. We will discuss such intervention in more detail in Chapter 19.

It is important to remember that life changes, even some positive ones, place new demands on us and thus may be stressful. The faster the changes, the greater the stress. Early research efforts on life changes focused on developing scales that could measure the relationship between stress and possible physical and mental disorders. Holmes and his colleagues (Holmes & Holmes, 1970; Holmes & Rahe, 1967; Rahe & Arthur, 1978), for example, developed the Social Readjustment Rating Scale, an objective method for measuring the cumulative stress to which an individual has been exposed over a period of time. This scale measures life stress in terms of "life change units" (LCU): the more stressful the event, the more LCUs assigned to it. At the high end of the scale, "death of a spouse" rates 100 LCUs and "divorce" rates 73 LCUs; at the low end of the scale, "vacation" rates 13 LCUs and "minor violations of the law" rates 11 LCUs. Holmes and his colleagues found that individuals with LCU scores of 300 or more for recent months were at significant risk for getting a major illness within the next two years. In another effort, Horowitz and his colleagues (Horowitz, Wilner, & Alvarez, 1979) developed the Impact of Events Scale. This scale measures an individual's reaction to a stressful situation by first identifying the stressor and then posing a series of questions to pinpoint how he or she is coping.

In the past ten years, these life stress scales have been criticized for numerous methodological problems. For example, a number of criticisms have targeted the items selected for different scales, the subjectivity of the scoring, the failure to take into account the relevance of items for the populations studied, and the reliance on the subjects' memory of events (Monroe, 1983; Schroeder & Costa, 1984; Zimmerman, 1983). Perhaps the most problematic aspect of life events scales is that they provide only a general indicator of distress and do not assess specific types of disorders. This vagueness has not helped researchers gather specific information on various disorders. Another significant limitation of life event scales, and one that eats away the foundation of these studies, is that they tend to measure chronic problems rather than reactions to specific environmental events (Depue & Monroe, 1986). Despite these limitations, however, the weight of evidence supports the stressfulness of life changes (Maddi, Bartone, & Puccetti, 1987).

With an awareness that research in this area is sometimes flawed, let us examine, in the following sections, some of the ways individuals cope with stressful events.

COPING STRATEGIES

Evidence suggests that some particularly hardy individuals may be relatively immune to stressors that would impair most people's functioning (Kobasa, 1979). In general, however, increased levels of stress threaten an individual's well-being and produce automatic, persistent attempts to relieve the tension. Stress forces a person, in short, to do something. What is done depends on many influences. Sometimes inner factors—such as a person's frame of reference, motives, competencies, or stress tolerance—play the dominant role in determining his or her coping strategies; at other times, environmental conditions—such as social demands and expectations—are of primary importance. Any stress reaction, of course, reflects the interplay of inner strategies and outer conditions—some more influential than others, but all working together to make the individual react in a certain way. In the following section, we will consider some general principles of adjustive behavior and coping; then we will examine some characteristic stages that occur when an individual's adaptive functioning is threatened.

General Principles of Coping with Stress

In reviewing certain general principles of coping with stress, it is helpful to conceptualize three interactional levels. On a biological level, there are immunological defenses and damage-repair mechanisms; on a psychological and interpersonal level, there are learned coping patterns, self-defenses, and support from family and friends; and on a sociocultural level, there are group resources, such as labor unions, religious organizations, and law-enforcement agencies.

The failure of coping efforts on any of these levels may seriously increase an individual's vulnerability on other levels. For example, a breakdown of immunological defenses may impair not only bodily functioning, but psychological functioning as well; chronically poor psychological coping patterns may lead to peptic ulcers or other diseases; or the failure of a group on which a person depends may seriously interfere with his or her ability to satisfy basic needs.

In coping with stress, a person is confronted with two challenges: (a) to meet the requirements of the stressor, and (b) to protect the self from psychological damage and disorganization. When a person feels competent to handle a stressful situation, a **task-oriented response** is typical—that is, behavior is directed primarily at dealing with the requirements of the stressor. Typically, this response means the individual objectively appraises the situation, works out alternative solutions, decides on an appropriate strategy, takes action, and evaluates feedback. The steps in a task-oriented response—whether the actions turn out to be effective or ineffective—are generally flexible enough to enable an individual to change course.

Task-oriented responses may involve making changes in one's self, one's surroundings, or both, depending on the situation. The action may be overt—as in showing one's spouse more affection—or it may be covert—as in lowering one's level of aspiration. The action may involve retreating from the problem, attacking it directly, or trying to find a workable compromise. Any of these actions are appropriate under certain circumstances. For instance, if one is faced with a situation of overwhelming physical danger, such as a forest fire, the logical task-oriented response might well be to run.

When a person's feelings of adequacy are seriously threatened by a stressor, a **defense-oriented response** tends to prevail—that is, behavior is directed primarily at protecting the self from hurt and disorganization, rather than at resolving the situation. Typically, the person using defense-oriented responses has forsaken more productive task-oriented action in favor of an overriding concern for maintaining the integrity of the self, however ill-advised and self-defeating the effort may prove to be.

There are two common types of defense-oriented responses. The first consists of responses such as crying, repetitive talking, and mourning that seem to function as psychological damage-repair mechanisms. The second type consists of the so-called ego- or self-defense mechanisms introduced in Chapter 3 (p. 66). These mechanisms, including such responses as denial and repression, relieve tension and anxiety and protect the self from hurt and devaluation. They protect an individual from external threats, such as failures in work or relationships, and from internal threats, such as guilt-arousing desires or actions. They appear to protect the self in one or more of the following ways: (a) by denying, distorting, or restricting an individual's experience; (b) by reducing emotional or self-involvement; and (c) by counteracting threat or damage. Often, of course, a given defense mechanism may offer more than one kind of protection.

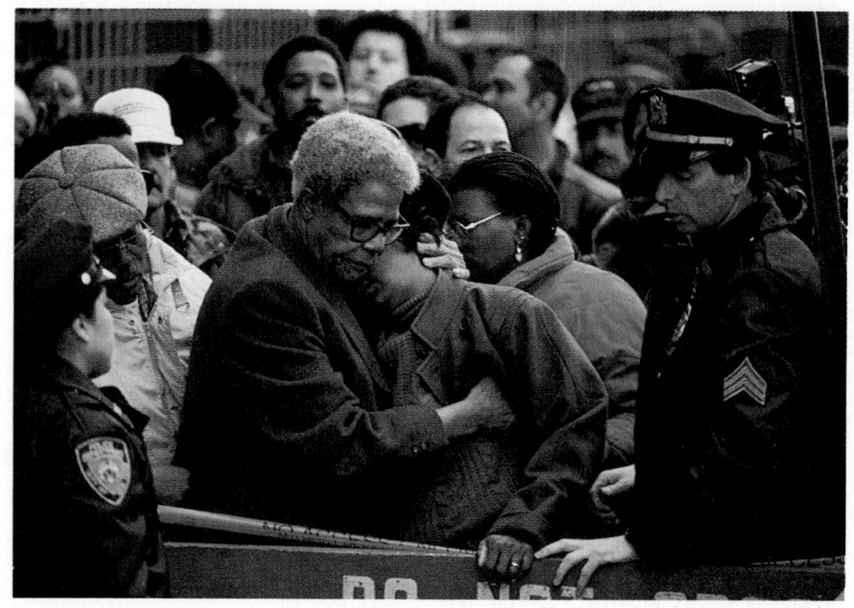

Two ways that we may choose to deal with a stressful situation are through task-oriented behavior, in which we try to resolve the situation, or through defense-oriented behavior, in which we protect ourselves from psychological damage and disorganization. The couple weeping and holding each other in this photo have witnessed a fire in a Bronx discotheque that left 87 dead. They cannot change or resolve the situation. Their reactions are defense-oriented, used to help them cope with the hurt of an overwhelming stressor.

These defense mechanisms are ordinarily used in combination rather than singly, and often they are combined with task-oriented behavior. We all use them to some extent for coping with the problems of living. In fact, Gleser and Sacks (1973) have concluded that we tend to be fairly consistent in the particular mechanisms we use. Ego-defense mechanisms are considered maladaptive when they become the predominant means of coping with stressors.

Decompensation Under Excessive Stress

As we have seen, stressors challenge a person's adaptive resources, bringing into play both task- and defense-oriented reactions. Most of the time these varied reactions are successful in containing a threat. When stressors are sustained or severe, however, a person may not be able to adapt and may experience lowered integrated functioning and eventually a breakdown. This lowering of adaptive functioning is referred to as **decompensation.** Whether stress becomes "excessive" depends, as we have seen, not only on the nature of a stressor, but also on an individual's tolerance for stress and available resources for coping with it. In the following section we will deal with some of the generalized effects of excessive stress. Then we will move on to specific forms of decompensation on biological, psychological, and sociocultural levels.

The Effects of Severe Stress Stress is a fact of life, and our reactions to stress can give us competencies we need and would not develop without being challenged to do so. Stress can be damaging, however, if certain demands are too severe for our coping resources or if we believe and act as if they are. Severe stress can exact a high cost in terms of lowered efficiency, depletion of adaptive resources, wear and tear on the system, and, in extreme cases, severe personality and physical deterioration—even death.

Lowering of adaptive efficiency. On a physiological level, severe stress may result in alterations that can impair the body's ability to fight off invading bacteria and viruses. On a psychological level, the perception of threat leads to an increasingly narrow perceptual field and rigid cognitive processes. It thus becomes difficult or impossible for the individual to see the situation objectively or to perceive the alternatives actually available. This process often appears to be part of suicidal behavior.

Our adaptive efficiency may also be impaired by the intense emotions that commonly accompany severe stress. Acute stage fright may disrupt our performance of a public speech; examination jitters may lead us to fail an exam despite adequate preparation. In fact, high levels of fear, anger, or anxiety may lead not only to impaired performance, but to behavior disorganization.

Depletion of adaptive resources. In using its resources to meet one severe stressor, an organism may suffer a lowering of tolerance for other stressors. Selye (1976b) demonstrated that successions of noxious stimuli can have lethal effects on animals. It appears that an organism's coping resources are limited: if they are already mobilized against one stressor, they are less available against others. This finding helps explain how sustained psychological stress can lower biological resistance to disease and vice versa. Interestingly, prolonged stress may lead to either pathological overresponsiveness to stressors—as illustrated by the "last straw" response—or to pathological insensitivity to stressors, as shown by a loss of hope or extreme apathy. In general, severe and sustained stress on any level leads to a serious reduction in an organism's overall adaptive capacity.

Wear and tear on the system. Most of us probably believe that even after a very stressful experience, rest can completely restore us. In his pioneering studies of stress, however, Selye has found evidence to the contrary:

> *Experiments on animals have clearly shown that each exposure leaves an indelible scar, in that it uses up reserves of adaptability which cannot be replaced. It is true that immediately after some harassing experience, rest can restore us almost to the original level of fitness by eliminating acute fatigue. But the emphasis is on the word* almost. *Since we constantly go through periods of stress and rest during life, even a minute deficit of adaptation energy every day adds up—it adds up to what we call aging. (1976, p. 429)*

When pressure is severe and long-lasting, adjustment problems such as excessive worry may become chronic and eventually lead to physical changes such as high blood pressure. Davidson and Baum (1986) studied the effects of stress over a five-year period. In a follow-up to the study mentioned earlier on p. 144, they found that individuals exposed to the March 1979 nuclear accident at Three Mile Island, even five years after the incident, showed symptoms of high stress such as elevated blood pressure and the presence of urinary noradrenaline (often associated with a persistent arousal state). These people also reported more intense psychological symptoms of stress, such as intrusive thoughts, than residents in the control community.

Biological Decompensation It is difficult to specify the exact biological processes underlying an organism's response to stress. A model that helps explain the course of biological decompensation under excessive stress is the **general adaptation syndrome,** introduced by Selye (1956; 1976b). Selye found that the body's reaction to sustained and excessive stress typically occurs in three major phases: (a) *alarm reaction,* in which the body's defensive forces are "called to arms" by the activation of the autonomic nervous system; (b) *stage of resistance,* in which biological adaptation is at the maximum level in terms of bodily resources used; and (c) *exhaustion,* in which bodily resources are depleted and the organism loses its ability to resist so that further exposure to stress can lead to illness and death. A diagram of this general adaptation syndrome is shown in *HIGHLIGHT 5.2.*

When decompensation does not run its entire course (resulting in the death of an organism), maintenance mechanisms attempt to repair damage and reorganize normal function. If the stress has resulted in extensive damage, this restorative process is often a matter of reorganizing remaining resources, but a permanent lowering of the previous level of integration and functioning remains.

Psychological Decompensation Personality decompensation under excessive stress is somewhat easier to specify. It appears to follow a course resembling that of biological decompensation and may, in fact, involve specific biological responses.

1. *Alarm and mobilization.* First an individual's resources for coping with a stressor are alerted and mobilized. Typically involved at this stage are emotional arousal, increased tension, heightened sensitivity, greater alertness (vigilance), and determined efforts at self-control. At the same time, the individual undertakes various coping measures—which may be task-oriented or defense-oriented or a combination of the two—in attempts to meet the emergency. During this stage, symptoms of maladjustment may appear, such as continuous anxiety and tension, gastrointestinal upset or other bodily diseases, and lowered efficiency—signs that the mobilization of adaptive resources is inadequate.

2. *Resistance.* If stress continues, an individual is often able to find some means for dealing with it and thus to resist psychological disintegration. Resistance may be achieved temporarily by concerted, task-oriented coping measures; the use of ego-defense mechanisms may also be intensified during this period. Even in the resistance stage, however, indications of strain may exist, including psychophysiologic symptoms and mild reality distortions. During the late phases of this stage, the individual tends to become rigid and to cling to previously developed defenses rather than trying to reevaluate the stressor situation and work out more adaptive coping patterns.

3. *Exhaustion.* In the face of continued excessive stress, an individual's adaptive resources are deplet-

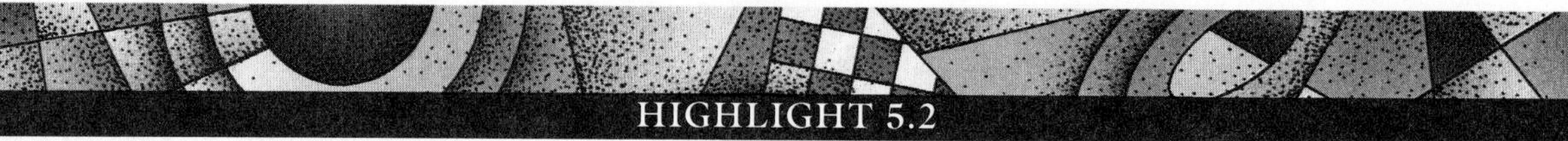

HIGHLIGHT 5.2

Selye's General Adaptation Syndrome (GAS)

The general adaptation syndrome (GAS), shown in the diagram below, graphically illustrates a typical individual's general response to stress. In the first phase (alarm reaction), the person shows an initial lowered resistance to stress or shock. If the stress persists, the person shows a defensive reaction or resistance (resistance phase) in an attempt to adapt to stress. Following extensive exposure to stress, the energy necessary for adaptation may be exhausted, resulting in the final stage of the GAS—collapse of adaptation (exhaustion phase).

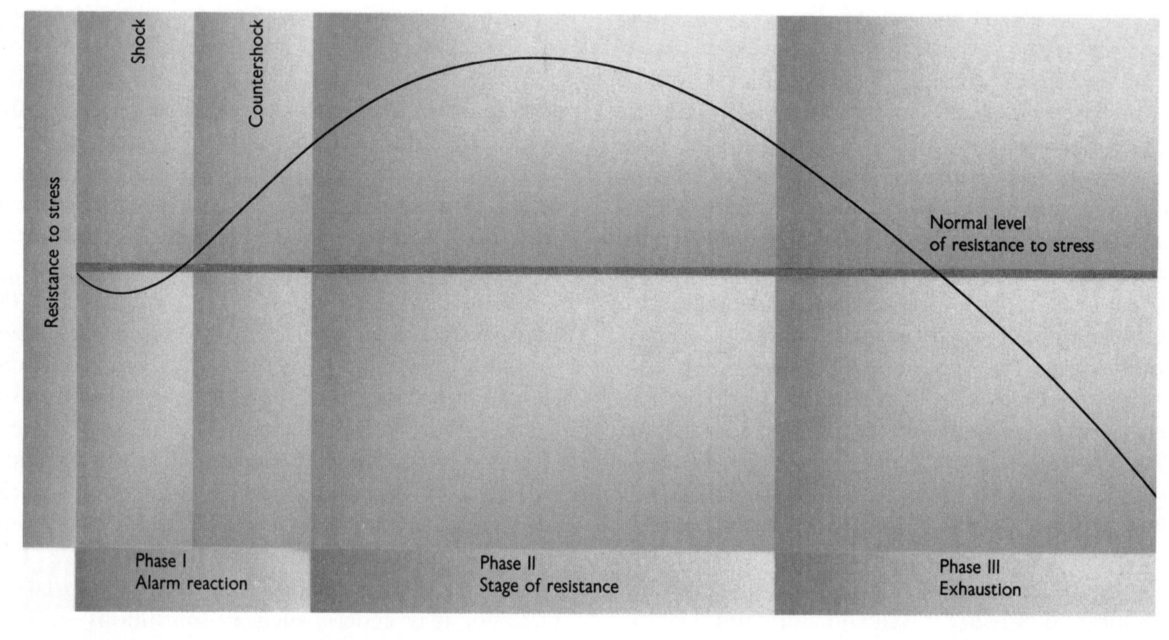

ed and the coping patterns called forth in the stage of resistance begin to fail. As the stage of exhaustion begins, integration is lowered and exaggerated and inappropriate defensive measures are introduced. The latter reactions may be characterized by psychological disorganization and a break with reality, involving delusions and hallucinations. These delusions appear to represent increasingly disorganized thoughts and perceptions along with desperate efforts to salvage psychological integration and self-integrity by restructuring reality. Metabolic changes that impair normal brain functioning may also be involved in delusional and hallucinatory behavior. Eventually, if the excessive stress continues, the process of decompensation proceeds to a stage of complete psychological disintegration—perhaps involving continuous uncontrolled violence, apathy, stupor, and eventually death. Siegel (1984) found this pattern among 31 hostage victims whose cases he analyzed. Those who had been held under conditions of isolation, visual deprivation, physical restraint, physical abuse, and threat of death typically experienced hallucinations.

As we will see, relatively severe psychological decompensation may be precipitated by sudden and extreme stress; but more often, decompensation is a gradual, long-term process. Typically, of course, treatment measures are instituted before decompensation runs its course. Such measures may increase an individual's adaptive capabilities or alleviate a stressor situation so that the process of decompensation is reversed.

Sociocultural Decompensation Although social science has made only modest inroads into the understanding of group pathology, it appears that the concept of decompensation is just as applicable here as on the biological and psychological levels. In the face of wars, economic problems, and other internal and external stressors that surpass their adjustive capabilities, societies may undergo varying degrees of decompensation. At such times societies often resort to extreme measures in their attempts to maintain their organization and resist disintegration. The historian Toynbee and other writers have depicted this process while describing the decline and fall of civilizations throughout history.

In completing our immediate discussion of decompensation, it should be emphasized that the outcome in a given situation—on biological, psychological, and sociocultural levels—depends on the extent to which any damage can be repaired and remaining resources reorganized. In some instances, an individual or group's functional level may be permanently lowered following excessive stress; in other cases, with successful problem resolution, the individual or group may attain a higher level of integration and functioning than before the episode.

ADJUSTMENT DISORDER: REACTIONS TO COMMON LIFE STRESSORS

Research literature and clinical observations on the relationship between stress and psychopathology are so substantial that the role of stressors in symptom development is now formally emphasized in diagnostic formulations (Brett, Spitzer, & Williams, 1988). In DSM-III-R, for example, a diagnostician can specify on Axis IV (shown on p. 12) the specific psychosocial stressors facing an individual. The Axis IV scale is particularly useful in relation to two Axis I categories: adjustment disorder and posttraumatic stress disorder (acute, chronic, or delayed). Both of these disorders involve patterns of psychological and behavioral disturbances that occur in response to identifiable stressors. The key differences between the two disorders lie not only in the severity of the disturbances, but also in the natures of the stressors and the time frames during which the disorders occur. In both disorders, the stressors supposedly can be identified as causal factors and specified on Axis IV.

An individual whose response to a common stressor—such as marriage, divorce, childbirth, or losing a job—is maladaptive *and* occurs within three months of the stressor can be said to have an **adjustment disorder.** The individual's reaction is considered maladaptive if he or she is unable to function as usual or if the person's reaction to the particular stressor is excessive. Usually, the individual's maladjustment lessens or disappears when (a) the stressor has subsided or (b) the individual learns to adapt to the stressor. Should the symptoms continue beyond six months, DSM-III-R recommends that the diagnosis be changed to some other mental disorder. As will be evident, the reality of adjustment disorders does not always adhere to such a strict time schedule.

We might well ask here, "What would be considered a normal response to a stressor?" The answer seems a bit elusive by DSM criteria. Clearly, not all reactions to stressors are adjustment disorders. What seems to push a reaction into this category is the inability to function as usual—and yet this criteria is true for many other disorders as well. We will not resolve this uncertainty any time soon; it is perhaps more important to recognize that *adjustment disorder* is probably the least stigmatizing and mildest diagnosis a therapist can assign to a client, and it is frequently used by therapists for insurance purposes.

We will look now at some of the stressor situations that typically cause adjustment disorders: unemployment, bereavement, and divorce or separation. We will then turn to stressor situations that can lead to posttraumatic stress disorder: major life problems such as life-threatening traumatic events, rape, military combat, imprisonment, being held hostage, and forced relocation.

Stress from Unemployment

Managing the stress associated with unemployment requires great coping strength, especially for people who have previously earned an adequate living. The negative impact of losing one's job and being unable to find suitable employment has been common in the last decade. The economic decline of the automobile, steel, oil, gas, electronics, and small-scale farming industries especially has transformed many thriving communities into depressed areas and many industrious employees into unemployed or underemployed individuals. In almost any community one can find numerous workers who have been laid off from jobs they had held for many years and who are facing the end of their unemployment compensation. The following case is typical of the problems that unemployment can bring:

David C., a 49-year-old construction foreman who was married and had two children attending college, had worked for a large building construction firm since he graduated from high school. One afternoon in May of 1982, his company, without warning, filed for bankruptcy, closed down its remaining job sites, and began to liquidate its resources.

David was stunned. The unexpected changes in his life were not easy for him to face. Early efforts to find other employment were met only with frustration because other construction companies were experiencing similar economic problems and layoffs.

After a few weeks his savings were depleted, and he took a step he never dreamed possible: he applied for unemployment compensation. This action was a tremendous blow to his self-esteem. He had always been self-sufficient and had taken great pride in being a hard worker and a good provider for his family. He was particularly upset at not being able to pay the tuition and living costs for his two sons in college and he felt a great sense of failure when they remained on their summer jobs rather than returning to school. His wife, who had never worked outside the home since their marriage, took a job in a local department store to meet some of the family's living expenses.

After some searching David seemingly gave up on finding a job and began to spend more time in bars. His drinking problems intensified. When he returned home in the evenings he sulked around the house and rebuffed most attempts by other family members to socialize or communicate. During this period family arguments were so frequent that Joel, his eldest son, felt that he couldn't tolerate the tension any more and enlisted in the army. In February, eight months after he lost his job, David saw a notice in the newspaper indicating that a local company was taking applications for 25 construction jobs the following Monday. He arrived at the company's employment office early on Monday morning only to find that there were about 3000 other applicants ahead of him—some who had arrived the day before and had stood in line all night in the bitter cold. He left the lot dejected. That same week the bank initiated foreclosure proceedings on his house because he had not made a mortgage payment in seven months. He was forced to sell his house and move into an apartment.

For the next year David still could not find work in his community. Finally, after he had exhausted his unemployment benefits, he and a fellow employee left their families and moved to another city in the Southeast to find work. David planned to have his wife follow him when he got settled. She, however, had by that time been enjoying some success on her job and refused to move away. After several months of living apart, David's wife filed for a divorce. No further information is available on David.

Unemployment is becoming a common experience in today's society—plant closings, layoffs, and hostile takeovers all result in work-force reductions, often in management-level positions. Some population subgroups—especially young minority males—live in a permanent economic depression, more pervasive and just as debilitating as the Great Depression was for the white majority. Unemployment among blacks (12.2%) is almost twice that for whites (6.3%) (Department of Labor, 1991). Indeed, for young black men, the unemployment rates today are over twice those for whites during the 1930s (Lebergott, 1964). The long-range psychological consequences of this situation can be great. Some people can deal with setbacks such as David experienced and can adapt without suffering long-range adjustment difficulties once the initial stressful situation has ended. For others, however, unemployment can have serious long-term effects.

The impact of chronic unemployment on an individual's self-concept, sense of worth, and feeling of belongingness is shattering—especially in an affluent society. The vulnerability of our population's lower socioeconomic segment to unemployment helps explain why this segment contributes a disproportionately high number of individuals to penal institutions and mental hospitals.

Recently, a number of employee-based intervention programs have been initiated to counsel and assist displaced workers. Maida, Gordon, and

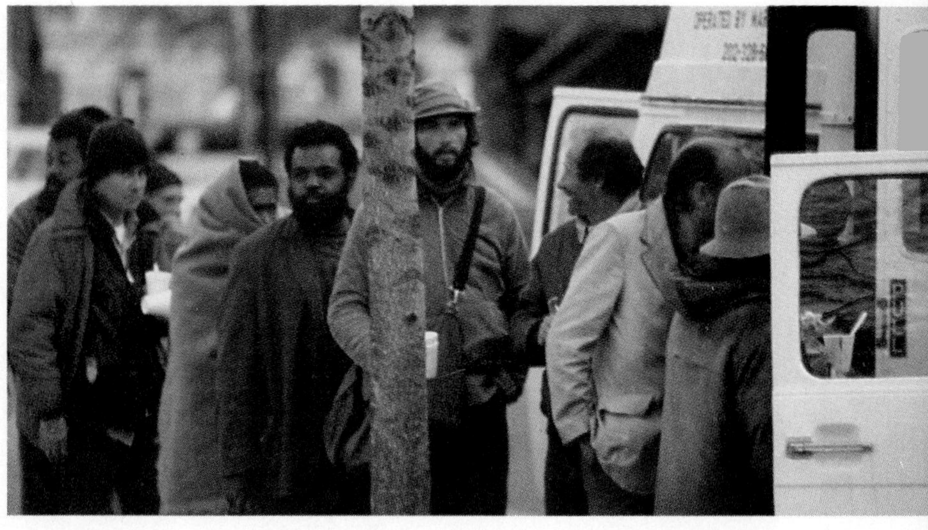

Managing the stress associated with unemployment requires great coping strength. Some people can deal with setbacks and can adapt without suffering long-range adjustment difficulties once the initial stressful situation has ended. The impact of chronic unemployment, however, can be shattering and can have serious long-term effects.

Farberow (1989) provide a valuable survey of the issues that affect these newly unemployed individuals and describe many problems resulting from transitional stress and chronic unemployment. They also explore several intervention strategies—such as increasing support networks, out-placement counseling, stress counseling, and more—that can reduce the psychological impact of job loss and promote more effective coping strategies.

Stress from Bereavement

When someone close to us dies, we are psychologically upended. Often the first reaction is disbelief. Then, as we begin to realize the significance of the death, our feelings of sadness, grief, and despair (even, perhaps, anger at the departed person) frequently overwhelm us.

Grief over the loss of a loved one is a natural process that allows the survivors to mourn their loss and then free themselves for life without the departed person. The following description of the normal grief process (*uncomplicated bereavement* in DSM-III-R terms) was provided by Janis et al. (1969):

Typically, the normal grief pattern following the loss of a loved one begins with a period of numbness and shock. Upon learning of the death, the person reacts with disbelief. For several days his feelings may be blunted and he may be in a semi-dazed state, punctuated by episodes of irritability and anger. In some instances the protest reactions take the extreme form of outbursts of impotent rage, as when adult brothers and sisters bitterly blame one another for having failed to do something that might have prolonged the life of their elderly parent. This initial phase usually ends by the time of the funeral, which often can release the tears and feelings of despair that had been bottled up in the grief-stricken person. Thereafter, a very intense grief reaction ensues: The mourner weeps copiously, yearns for the lost person, and wishes he had been more helpful and considerate while the loved one was still alive. . . . Attacks of agitated distress are likely to alternate with periods of more silent despair, during which the sufferer is preoccupied with memories of the dead person.

For many days and perhaps weeks the mourner remains somewhat depressed and apathetic, expresses a general sense of futility, and becomes socially withdrawn, although he still goes through the motions of carrying out his usual social obligations. During this period of despair, he is likely to suffer from insomnia, psychosomatic [psychologically induced] intestinal disorders, loss of appetite, restlessness, and general irritability. A tendency to deny the fact of the death may persist for many weeks; the mourner continues to think of the dead person at times as still alive and present in the house. There is also a tendency to idealize the dead person in memory and . . . to seek companionship mainly with persons who are willing to limit their conversation to talking about him.

The mourner is usually able to return to work and resume other daily activities, such as talking with friends and relatives, after about two or three weeks. But he may continue to withdraw from certain types of social affairs that used to give him pleasure. After a month or two the most acute

When someone close to us dies, we are psychologically upended. Our first reaction is often disbelief. Then, as we begin to realize what has happened, we are often overcome by feelings of sadness, grief, despair, and even anger. In general, grief over the loss of a loved one is a natural process that seems to allow the survivors to mourn their loss and then free themselves for life without the departed person.

symptoms begin to subside, but there may still be residual sadness, yearning, and attacks of acute grief during the ensuing months. (pp. 179–180)

Some individuals do not go through the typical process of grieving, perhaps because of their personality makeups or as a consequence of their particular situations. An individual may, for instance, be expected to be stoical about his or her feelings or may have to manage the family's affairs. Other individuals may develop exaggerated or prolonged depressions after their normal grieving processes should have ended (a normal grieving process should last no longer than one year). Such pathological reactions to death are more likely to occur in people who have a history of emotional problems or who harbor a great deal of resentment and hostility toward the deceased, thus experiencing intense guilt. They are usually profoundly depressed and may, in some instances, be suffering from major depression (see Chapter 11 for more on this). The following case illustrates an extreme adjustment disorder with withdrawal or pathological grief reaction (and, in this instance, a positive outcome):

Nadine, a 66-year-old former high school teacher, lived with Charles, age 67, her husband of 40 years (also a retired teacher). The couple had been nearly inseparable since they met—they even taught at the same schools during most of their teaching careers. They lived in a semirural community where they had worked and had raised their three children, all of whom had married and moved to a large metropolitan area about 100 miles away. For years they had planned their retirement and had hoped to travel around the country visiting friends. A week before their fortieth anniversary, Charles had a heart attack and, after five days in the intensive care unit, had a second heart attack and died.

Nadine took Charles's death quite hard. Even though she had a great deal of emotional support from her many friends and her children, she had great difficulty adjusting. Elaine, one of her daughters, came and stayed a few days and encouraged her to come to the city for a while. Nadine declined the persistent invitation even though she had little to do at home. Friends called on her frequently, but she seemed almost to resent their presence. In the months following the funeral, Nadine's reclusive behavior persisted. Several well-wishers reported to Elaine that her mother was not doing well and was not even leaving the house to go shopping. They reported that Nadine sat alone in the darkened house—not answering the phone and showing reluctance to come to the door. She had lost interest in activities she had once enjoyed.

Greatly worried about her mother's welfare, Elaine organized a campaign to get her mother out of the house and back to doing the things she had formerly enjoyed. Each of Nadine's children and their families took turns visiting and taking her places until she finally began to show interest in living again. In time, Nadine agreed to come to each of their homes for visits. This proved a therapeutic step since Nadine had always been fond of children and took pleasure in the time spent with her eight grandchildren—she actually extended the visits longer than she had planned.

The loss of a close family member can significantly affect a survivor's life for months. Over a period of two years, Shanfield and Swain (1984) studied parents who had lost an adult child in a traffic accident. They found that the parents continued to grieve intensely and had higher-than-expected emotional symptoms and physical complaints for months after their losses. Rinear (1988) studied the grief processes of parents who had lost one of their children through homicide and found severe, long-term effects, including lingering fears over what might happen to their other children.

Stress from Divorce or Separation

The deterioration or ending of an intimate relationship is a potent stressor and a frequent reason why people seek psychological treatment. Divorce, though more generally accepted today, is still a tragic and usually stressful outcome to a once close and trusting relationship. We noted in Chapter 4 that marital disruption is a major source of vulnerability to psychopathology: individuals who are recently divorced or separated are markedly over-represented among people with psychological problems.

Many factors make a divorce or separation unpleasant and stressful for everyone concerned: the acknowledgment of failure in a relationship important both personally and culturally; the necessity of "explaining" the failure to family and friends; the loss of valuable friendships that often accompanies the rupture; the economic uncertainties and hardships that both partners frequently experience; and, when children are involved, the problem of custody—including court battles, living arrangements, and so on.

After the divorce or separation, new problems typically emerge. The readjustment to a single life, perhaps after many years of marriage, can be a difficult experience. Since in many cases it seems that friends as well as assets have to be divided, new friendships need to be made. New opposite-sex relationships may require a great deal of personal change. Even when the separation has been relatively agreeable, new strength to adapt and cope is needed. Thus it is not surprising that many people seek counseling after the breakup of a significant relationship. The following case illustrates how the stress in a marital breakup can adversely affect a capable and generally well-functioning person.

Janice was a 33-year-old manager of an office that employed over 50 people. She had always been competent and had received a great deal of satisfaction from her career. For several months, however, she had been quite upset and depressed about her marital situation and had been unable to sleep. She had lost 12 pounds because of her poor appetite and was experiencing painful burning feelings in her stomach; she was worried about having ulcers.

Janice's marriage (her second) had begun to show signs of trouble almost from the start. Shortly after the wedding two years before, her husband's drinking had increased. He often stayed out late and on two occasions did not come home at all. Usually he lied about his whereabouts. For the first few months Janice was tolerant of his transgressions, trying to make this second marriage work. Her husband, who she regarded as a charming person that she "couldn't stay mad at," was always forgiven, and they "had a great time making up." In the most recent incident, however, he had returned late at night with "evident traces of another woman." This was the last straw, and Janice moved out.

The intense stress she was experiencing over the breakup of the marriage appeared to be directly related to her sense of failing in life for a second time. Her first marriage had ended in divorce after her husband of seven years developed a severe drinking problem, stayed away from home a great deal, and frequently abused her physically.

Janice's marital problems did not interfere with her performance at work, but, in addition to depression and physical problems, she began to experience problems with her teenage daughter. As a result she entered psychotherapy, hoping it would help her know herself better and understand why she had married two "losers."

Janice, diagnosed as having an adjustment disorder with anxious mood, was seen in cognitive-behavioral therapy for about six months. During that time she gained a great deal of insight into her motivation for marrying alcoholics: she wished to "save" them from themselves. Janice's father had been an alcoholic and had died when she was a teenager—from chronic drinking. During therapy Janice was able to "resist" taking her husband back and was able to feel more comfortable about living with her daughter.

POSTTRAUMATIC STRESS DISORDER: REACTIONS TO SEVERE LIFE STRESSORS

In **posttraumatic stress disorder (PTSD),** the stressor is unusually severe (that is, outside the realm of typical human experience) and is psychologically traumatic—for example, a life-threatening situation, the destruction of one's home, seeing another person mutilated or killed, or being the victim of physical violence. Posttraumatic stress disorder includes the following symptoms:

1. The traumatic event is persistently reexperienced by the individual—he or she may have intrusive, recurring thoughts or repetitive nightmares about the event.
2. The individual persistently avoids stimuli associated with the trauma; for example, he or she tries to avoid activities related to the incident or blocks out the memory of certain aspects of the experience. Situations that recall the traumatic experience provoke anxiety.
3. The individual may experience persistent symptoms of increased arousal, such as chronic tension and irritability, often accompanied by insomnia, the inability to tolerate noise, and the complaint that "I just can't seem to relax."
4. The individual may experience impaired concentration and memory.
5. The individual may experience feelings of depression. In some cases he or she may withdraw from social contact and avoid experiences that might increase excitation—commonly manifested in the avoidance of interpersonal involvement, loss of sexual interest, and an attitude of "peace and quiet at any price."

In DSM-III-R no separate category exists for stress disorders, and posttraumatic stress disorder is categorized under the anxiety disorders. Clearly, PTSD includes elements of anxiety—generalized feelings of fear and apprehension—but since PTSD bears such a close relationship to the experience of stress, we cover it here and follow in Chapter 6 with coverage of the more traditional anxiety disorders.

The diagnosis of posttraumatic stress disorder is not given unless the symptoms last for at least one month. The diagnosis can be further specified in terms of when the symptoms begin. If the symptoms begin within six months of the traumatic event, then the reaction is considered to be ***acute.*** If the symptoms begin more than six months after the traumatic situation, the reaction is considered to be ***delayed.*** The delayed version of PTSD is less well defined and more difficult to diagnose than disorders that emerge shortly after the precipitating incident. Some authorities have even questioned whether a delayed reaction should be diagnosed as a posttraumatic stress disorder at all; instead, some would categorize such a reaction as some other anxiety-based disorder. It is important to keep in mind that the criteria for posttraumatic stress disorder specify that the reaction last for at least one month; if the length of the reaction is less than that, it would be considered a "normal" stress reaction to a clearly threatening situation.

We will look now at some general principles underlying reactions to catastrophic events. Then we will turn to some specific stressor events that can cause posttraumatic stress.

Reactions to Catastrophic Events

With few exceptions, people exposed to plane crashes, automobile accidents, explosions, fires, earthquakes, tornadoes, sexual assaults, or other terrifying experiences show psychological "shock" reactions—transient personality decompensation. The symptoms may vary greatly, depending on the nature and severity of the terrifying experience, the degree of surprise, and the personality makeup of the individual. Consider the following examples: over half of the survivors of the disastrous Coconut Grove nightclub fire—which took the lives of 492 people in Boston in 1942—required treatment for severe psychological shock (Adler, 1943). When two commuter trains collided in Chicago in 1972, leaving 44 people dead and over 300 injured, the tragedy also left scores of people with feelings of fear, anxiety, and guilt; more than 80 of them attended a voluntary "talk session" arranged by the University of Chicago's psychiatric adult outpatient clinic (Uhlenhuth, 1973). Psychological evaluations of 8 of the 64 survivors of the collision of two jet planes on Santa Cruz de Tenerife Island in 1977,

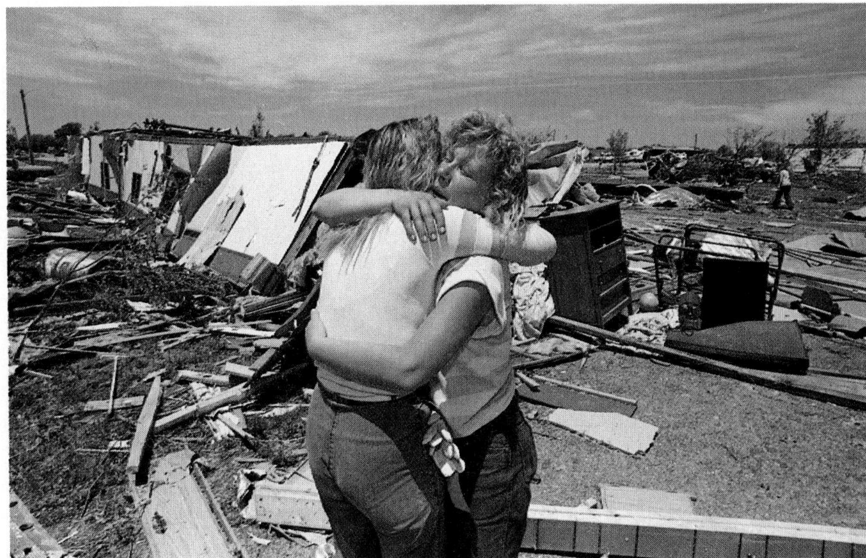

The aftermath of catastrophic events, such as the destruction of one's home by a tornado, may bring about psychological reactions including initial shock, passivity, repetitive retelling of the experience, and sometimes long-lasting or delayed symptoms of stress, such as recurrent nightmares.

in which 580 people died, indicated that all eight suffered from serious emotional problems stemming directly from the accident (Perlberg, 1979).

A **disaster syndrome** has been delineated that appears to characterize the reactions of many victims of such catastrophes (see *HIGHLIGHT 5.3*). This syndrome may be described in terms of the reactions during the traumatic experience; the initial reactions after it (the acute posttraumatic stress); and the long-lasting or late-arising complications (the chronic or delayed posttraumatic stress).

The Disaster Syndrome A victim's initial responses following a disaster typically involve three stages: (a) the *shock stage,* in which the victim is stunned, dazed, and apathetic; (b) the *suggestible stage,* in which the victim tends to be passive, suggestible, and willing to take directions from rescue workers or others; and (c) the *recovery stage,* in which the individual may be tense and apprehensive and show generalized anxiety, but gradually regains psychological equilibrium—often showing a need to repetitively tell about the catastrophic event. It is in the third stage that posttraumatic stress disorder may develop.

These three stages are well illustrated in the *Andrea Doria* disaster, in which 52 persons died and over 1600 were rescued.

On July 25, 1956, at 11:05 P.M., the Swedish liner Stockholm smashed into the starboard side of the Italian liner Andrea Doria a few miles off Nantucket Island, . . . During the phase of initial shock the survivors acted as if they had been sedated . . . as though nature provided a sedation mechanism which went into operation automatically. [During the phase of suggestibility] the survivors presented themselves for the most part as an amorphous mass of people tending to act passively and compliantly. They displayed psychomotor retardation, flattening of affect, somnolence, and in some instances, amnesia for data of personal identification. They were nonchalant and easily suggestible. [During the stage of recovery, after the initial shock had worn off and the survivors had received aid,] they showed . . . an apparently compulsive need to tell the story again and again, with identical detail and emphasis. (Friedman & Linn, 1957, p. 426)

In some cases, the clinical picture may be complicated by intense grief and depression. When an individual feels that his or her own personal inadequacy contributed to the loss of loved ones in a disaster, the picture may be further complicated by strong feelings of guilt, and the posttraumatic stress may last for months. This pattern is well illustrated in the following case of a husband who failed to save his wife in the jet crash at Tenerife in 1977.

Martin's story is quite tragic. He lost his beloved wife of 37 years and blames himself for her death, because he sat stunned and motionless for some 25 seconds after the [other plane] hit. He saw nothing but fire and smoke in the aisles, but he roused himself and led his wife to a jagged hole above and behind his seat. Martin climbed out onto the wing and reached down and took hold of his wife's hand, but "an explosion from within literally blew her out

HIGHLIGHT 5.3

Mount Saint Helens and the Disaster Syndrome

Can psychological responses to disasters result in diagnosable mental disorders, such as depression, generalized anxiety disorder, or schizophrenia? This point is debated among researchers. Dohrenwend and Egri (1981) are among those who find clear evidence of mental disorders among individuals who were "normal" prior to a stressful event. On the other side, Depue and Monroe (1986) and McFarlane (1986) have noted that psychological problems following stress tend to occur most frequently among individuals who were previously maladjusted or vulnerable to problems prior to the stress. Methodological problems and the absence of reliable predisposing personality measures on disaster victims limit research in this area; consequently, a definitive conclusion is difficult to reach. One recent field study by Shore, Tatum, and Vollmer (1986) provided some weight to the position that stress in response to a natural disaster can produce psychological disorder even in victims who were not at risk for developing disorder before the disaster. They conducted an epidemiological study of the Mount Saint Helens disaster victims in an effort to further understand the disaster syndrome—the dazed, confused state of victims following a disaster.

In May of 1980 Mount Saint Helens violently erupted, producing volcanic flow, ash fall, and flooding that resulted in great property damage and loss of life. This catastrophic situation placed many people in the surrounding Washington state area at great risk of property loss, injury, and even death for a time following the eruption. The researchers surveyed residents whose homes had suffered significant damage as determined through tax assessor records. The families who experienced the most damage as a result of the eruption were further subdivided, after the interviews, into *high-* (N = 138) and *low-* (N = 410) exposure-to-stress categories on the basis of the amount of damage suffered or whether loss of life was involved. They also surveyed residents from a control community (N = 477) in Oregon that was similar in demographic characteristics but had not been affected by the eruption or floods. In each case one household member (between the ages of 18 and 79) was interviewed in his or her home between 38 and 42 months after the disaster. The interviews were conducted by trained personnel following the diagnostic interview schedule based on DSM-III.

The researchers found that a significantly higher number of DSM-III diagnosable disorders occurred in individuals exposed to high levels of stress following the Mount Saint Helens eruption. Specifically, there was a greater prevalence of generalized anxiety, major depression, and posttraumatic stress disorder in the high-exposure subjects. The study also found some tendency for older females to be more vulnerable to disorder.

The results of this study do not unequivocally support the idea that disaster-related stress produces psychological disorders because the researchers had no prestress measures on the groups. Assuming that the two groups were in fact equal on psychopathology prior to the volcanic eruption, then these data do suggest that a natural disaster can produce psychological disorder among individuals who are not at risk for disorder on the basis of their prestress adjustment. Evidence did indicate that the *amount* of stress, in the form of high exposure, was associated with diagnosed clinical disorder.

of my hands and pushed me back and down onto the wing." He reached the runway, turned to go back after her, but the plane blew up seconds later. . . .

[Five months later] Martin was depressed and bored, had "wild dreams," a short temper and became easily confused and irritated. "What I saw there will terrify me forever," he says. He told [the psychologist who interviewed him] that he avoided television and movies, because he couldn't know when a frightening scene would appear. (Perlberg, 1979, pp. 49–50)

In some instances the guilt of the survivors seems to center around the belief that they deserved to survive no more or perhaps even less than those who died. As one flight attendant explained after the crash of a Miami-bound jet in the Florida Everglades that took many lives, "I kept thinking, I'm alive. Thank God. But I wondered why I was spared. I felt, it's not fair . . ." (*Time,* Jan. 15, 1973, p. 53).

Sometimes individuals who undergo terrifying experiences exhibit symptoms of stress that may endure for weeks, months, or even years. The experience of extreme posttraumatic symptoms is not uncommon. In a recent review and comparison of all published disaster research in which estimates of postdisaster psychopathology were included, the average effect was that 17 percent of individuals showed psychological adjustment problems in the aftermath of the disaster (Rubonis & Bickman, 1991). Shore, Vollmer, and Tatum (1989) studied the prevalence rates of posttraumatic stress disorder in two northwestern communities and found a lifetime prevalence rate of posttraumatic stress reaction, according to DSM-III criteria, to be about 3 percent for both men and women.

Recurrent nightmares and the typical need to tell the same story about the disaster again and again appear to be mechanisms for reducing anxiety and desensitizing the self to the traumatic experience. Tension, apprehensiveness, and hypersensitivity appear to be residual effects of the shock reaction and to reflect the person's realization that the world can become overwhelmingly dangerous and threatening. As we have seen, feelings of guilt about having failed to protect loved ones who perished may be quite intense, especially in situations where some responsibility can be directly assigned.

The posttraumatic stress may be more complicated in cases of physical mutilation that necessitate changes in one's way of life. It may also be complicated by the psychological effects of disability compensation or damage law suits, which tend to prolong posttraumatic symptoms (Egendorf, 1986; Okura, 1975).

Causal Factors in Posttraumatic Stress Most people function relatively well in catastrophes, and, in fact, many behave with heroism (Rachman, 1978). Whether someone develops posttraumatic stress disorder or not depends on a number of factors. Some research suggests that preexisting personality factors are more relevant at low and moderate levels of stress, and less relevant for more extreme traumatic experiences; for the latter, the nature of the traumatic stressor itself appears to account for most of the stress-response variance (for example, Ursano, Boydstun, & Wheatley, 1981). In other words, everyone has a breaking point, and at sufficiently high levels of stress the average person can be expected to develop some psychological difficulties (which may be either short-lived or long-term) following a traumatic event. Other researchers suggest that preexisting factors may play a greater role even at high levels of stress. For example, McFarlane (1988) studied fire fighters over a period of months after an intensely traumatic experience fighting a brushfire. He concluded that though an extremely traumatic event can trigger multiple psychiatric problems, the trauma is insufficient to explain the onset of disorder. The existence of posttraumatic symptoms can only be explained by considering the individual's biological makeup; preexisting psychological problems, such as low self-esteem; emotional insecurity; interpersonal skill deficits; and the social context of recovery.

In all cases of posttraumatic stress, conditioned fear—the fear associated with the traumatic experience—appears to be a key causal factor. Thus prompt psychotherapy following a traumatic experience is considered important in preventing conditioned fear from establishing itself and becoming resistant to change.

Treatments and Outcomes Supportive therapy and proper rest (induced by sedatives if necessary) usually can alleviate symptoms that lead to posttraumatic stress disorder. Repetitive talking about the experience and constantly reliving it in fantasies or nightmares may serve as built-in repair mechanisms to help an individual adjust to the traumatic event. As Horowitz has concluded from his own experimental findings and an early review of available literature,

> *A traumatic perceptual experience remains in some special form of memory storage until it is mastered. Before mastery, vivid sensory images of the experiences tend to intrude into consciousness and may evoke unpleasant emotions. Through such repetitions the images, ideas, and associated affects may be worked through progressively. Thereafter, the images lose their intensity and the tendency toward repetition of the experience loses its motive force. (1969b, p. 552)*

In general, the more stable and better integrated a personality and the more favorable an individual's life situation, the more quickly he or she will recover from a severe stress reaction.

Many people who experience a disaster benefit from at least some psychological counseling, no matter how brief, to begin coping with their experiences. Brom, Kleber, and Defares (1989) conducted a controlled study of the effectiveness of brief therapy with individuals experiencing PTSD and found that treatment immediately following the traumatic event significantly reduced the PTSD

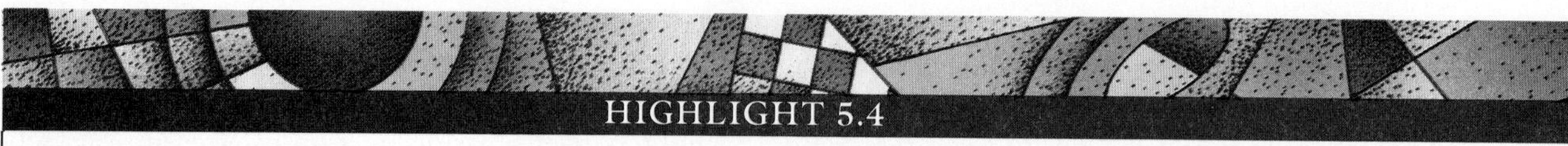

HIGHLIGHT 5.4

Counseling for Disaster Workers

In September 1978 an airliner collided with a private airplane in the vicinity of the San Diego airport, killing all 137 passengers aboard the two planes and 7 people on the ground. Unlike many other air disasters, the wreckage and remains of the victims were not scattered widely but were instead concentrated in an area smaller than a city block. The force with which the planes struck the ground left few recognizable aircraft parts or human beings.

Disaster workers called to the scene to give aid and clear away the debris were generally unprepared for the calamity they witnessed. One police officer reported that "it was like stepping suddenly into hell. . . . We were standing in a pile of human tissue mixed with tiny pieces of airplane" (Davidson, 1979a). Several hundred police officers and fire fighters worked five days in temperatures that soared over 100 degrees to clean up the area. Most of the people involved in the cleanup operation—even veterans of many years of police work—were stunned by the horrible circumstances. Apparently one reason why such experienced people were so adversely affected by the situation was that "it looked very different from what people expected a plane crash to look like—they had no frame of reference for such a calamity and really lost their equilibrium" (Davidson, 1979b). Many developed psychological symptoms—depression, loss of appetite, inability to sleep, and anxiety.

To help the disaster workers, a group of psychologists from the San Diego area offered free psychological counseling. Within a few days of the accident, over 30 police officers and fire fighters along with about 50 civilians sought counseling. Interestingly, few relatives or friends of people who perished in the crash sought

symptoms. Sixty percent of the treated individuals showed improvement while only 26 percent of the untreated group improved. They also found, however, that treatment did not benefit everyone and that some individuals maintained their PTSD symptoms even after therapy was terminated.

Treatment is often required, too, for disaster area workers, as can be seen in *HIGHLIGHT 5.4*. Many people called to the scene of a disaster to assist victims later experience posttraumatic stress disorder themselves. Bartone et al. (1989) found that workers who provide support to bereaved families of disaster victims are at risk for increased illness, psychiatric symptoms, and negative psychological well-being for up to a year following the disaster. They also reported a dose-response effect relating disaster intensity with later psychological symptoms in assistance workers following an air disaster. (That is, the closer one is to the disaster, the more intense and disabling the reaction is.) They found that social supports, including high morale and cohesive group relationships, lessen the amount and intensity of posttraumatic symptoms among disaster workers.

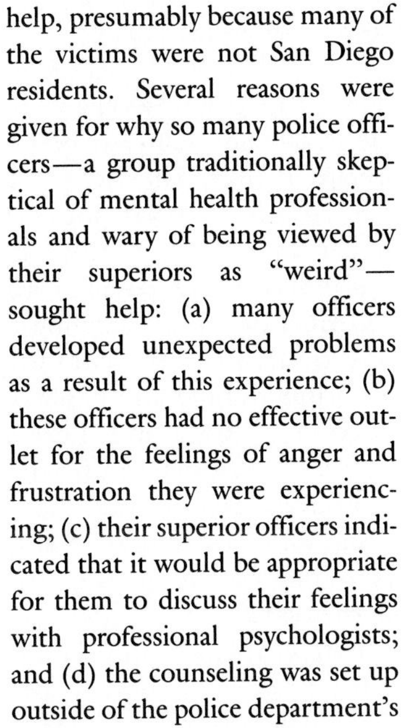

help, presumably because many of the victims were not San Diego residents. Several reasons were given for why so many police officers—a group traditionally skeptical of mental health professionals and wary of being viewed by their superiors as "weird"—sought help: (a) many officers developed unexpected problems as a result of this experience; (b) these officers had no effective outlet for the feelings of anger and frustration they were experiencing; (c) their superior officers indicated that it would be appropriate for them to discuss their feelings with professional psychologists; and (d) the counseling was set up outside of the police department's influence, thus assuring anonymity.

The counseling—crisis intervention therapy (see Chapter 18)—focused on providing support and reassurance and allowing individuals to vent their pent-up or unmanageable emotions. For most of the individuals involved, this brief crisis intervention was effective in providing symptom relief. A few individuals, however, required more extensive, long-term psychotherapy. The following description is of a 42-year-old police officer who suffered a severe reaction to the stress of the San Diego air crash.

Don had been a model police officer during his 14 years on the force. He was highly evaluated by his superiors, had a master's degree in social work, and had attained the rank of sergeant. While patrolling in a squad car, he heard that there had been an accident, and he quickly drove to the scene to give aid to any survivors. When he arrived he wandered around "in a daze" looking for someone to help—but there was only destruction. He later remembered the next few days as a bad dream.

He was quite depressed for several days after the cleanup, had no appetite, couldn't sleep, and was impotent. Images and recollections of the accident would come to him "out of nowhere." He reported having a recurring dream in which he would come upon an airplane crash while driving a car or flying a plane. In his dream, he would rush to the wreckage and help some passengers to safety.

Don decided that he needed help and sought counseling. Because of his deteriorating mood and physical condition, he was placed on medical leave from the police force. Eight months after the accident he was still in therapy and had not returned to work. During therapy it became apparent that Don had been experiencing a great deal of personal dissatisfaction and anger prior to the crash. His prolonged psychological disorder was not only a result of his anguish over the air crash but also a vehicle for expressing other problems. (Davidson, 1979a)

Based on Davidson, 1979a, 1979b; O'Brien, 1979.

We will explore now several instances of posttraumatic stress disorder, examining both the immediate and long-range effects of several debilitating situations: rape, military combat, imprisonment as a POW or in a concentration camp, detainment as a hostage, and displacement from one's homeland.

The Trauma of Rape

The experience of rape inflicts severe trauma on a victim. *Rape* is a criminal act of violence in which sexual relations, typically intercourse, are forced on one person by another. In most cases, the victim is a woman.

Our concern here is with a victim's response to rape, which can vary depending on a number of factors. In a "stranger" rape—one in which the victim does not know the offender—the victim is likely to experience strong fear of physical harm and death. In an "acquaintance" rape the reaction is apt to be slightly different (Ellison, 1977). In such a situation the victim not only may feel fear, but also may feel that she has been betrayed by someone she had trusted. She may feel more responsible for what happened and experience greater guilt. She may also be more hesitant to seek help or report the rape to the police out of fear that she will be held partially responsible for it.

The age and life circumstances of a victim may also influence her reaction (Notman & Nadelson, 1976). For a young child who knows nothing about sexual behavior, rape can lead to sexual scars and confusion, particularly if the child is encouraged to forget about the experience without thoroughly talking it over first (Browne & Finkelhor, 1986). For young adult women, rape can increase the conflicts over independence and separation that are normal in this age group. In an effort to be helpful, parents of these victims may encourage various forms of regression, such as moving back to the family home, which may prevent mastery of this developmental phase. Married rape victims with children face the task of explaining their experience to their children. Sometimes the sense of vulnerability that results from rape leaves a woman feeling temporarily unable to care for her children.

Husbands and boyfriends can also influence rape victims' reactions by their attitudes and behavior. Rejection, blaming, uncontrolled anger at the offender, or insistence on a quick resumption of sexual activity can increase victims' negative feelings.

In a recent formulation of the stress women experience following rape, McCann (1988) found empirical evidence of problems in five areas of functioning: (a) physical disturbances, including hyperarousal; (b) emotional problems, such as anxiousness, depressed mood, and low self-esteem; (c) cognitive dysfunctioning, including disturbed concentration and the experience of intrusive thoughts; (d) atypical behavioral acts, such as aggressive, antisocial actions and substance abuse; and (e) interference in social relationships, including sexual problems, intimacy problems, and further victimization.

Coping Behavior of Rape Victims The research on rape victims soon after their rapes has provided clear insights into the emotional turmoil and psychological processes they go through in coping with their experiences (Burgess & Holmstrom, 1974, 1976; Holmstrom & Burgess, 1975; McCombie, 1976; Meyer & Taylor, 1986; Roth & Lebowitz, 1988). The following sections summarize these findings and integrate the feelings and problems women experience at different points of their traumas.

Anticipatory phase. This period occurs before an actual rape when an offender "sets up" a victim and the victim begins to perceive that a dangerous situation exists. In the early minutes of this phase, the victim often uses defense mechanisms such as denial to preserve an illusion of invulnerability. Common thoughts are "Rape could never happen to me" or "He doesn't really mean that."

Impact phase. This phase begins with a victim's recognition that she is actually going to be raped and ends when the rape is over. The victim's first reaction is usually intense fear for her life, a fear much stronger than her fear of the sexual act itself. Symonds (1976) has described the paralytic effect of intense fear on victims of crime, showing that this fear usually leads to varying degrees of disintegration in the victim's functioning and possibly to complete inability to act. Roth and Lebowitz (1988) found that the sexual trauma "confronts the individual" with emotions and images that are difficult to manage and may have long-term adjustment consequences. When the victim later recalls her behavior during the assault, she may feel guilty about not reacting more efficiently, and she needs to be reassured that her actions were normal. Major physiological reactions such as vomiting sometimes occur during this phase, but victims who try to simulate such reactions in order to escape generally discover that they cannot produce them voluntarily.

Posttraumatic recoil phase. This phase begins immediately after a rape. Burgess and Holmstrom (1974, 1976) observed two emotional styles among the rape victims they interviewed in hospital emergency rooms. Some victims exhibited an *expressed style* where feelings of fear and anxiety were shown through crying, sobbing, and restlessness. Others demonstrated a *controlled style* in which feelings appeared to be masked by a calm, controlled, subdued facade. Regardless of style, most victims felt guilty about the way they had reacted to the offender and wished that they had reacted faster or fought harder. (Excessive self-blame has been associated with poor long-term adjustment [Meyer & Taylor, 1986].) Feelings of dependency were increased, and victims often had to be encouraged and helped to call friends or parents and make other arrangements. Physical problems, such as general tension, nausea, sleeplessness, and trauma directly related to the rape, were common.

Reconstitution phase. This phase begins as a victim starts to make plans for leaving the emergency room or crisis center. It ends, often many months later, when the stress of the rape has been assimilated, the experience shared with significant others, and the victim's self-concept restored. Certain behaviors and symptoms are typical during this phase.

1. Motor activity, such as changing one's telephone number and moving to a new residence, is common. The victim's fear is often well justified at this point because, even in the unlikely event that the offender has been arrested and charged with rape, he is often out on bail.
2. Frightening nightmares in which the rape is relived are common. As the victim moves closer toward assimilating the experience, the content of the dreams gradually shifts until the victim successfully fights off the assailant.
3. Phobias—including fear of the indoors or outdoors (depending on where the rape took place), fear of being alone, fear of crowds, fear of being followed, and sexual fears—have been observed to develop immediately following rape.

Counseling Rape Victims The women's movement has played a crucial role in establishing specialized rape counseling services, such as rape crisis centers and hotlines. Rape crisis centers are often staffed by trained paraprofessionals who provide general support for a victim, both individually and in groups. Crisis centers also have victim advocacy services in which a trained volunteer accompanies a victim to a hospital or police station, helps her understand the procedures, and assists her with red tape. The advocate may also accompany the victim to meetings with legal representatives and to the trial—experiences that tend to temporarily reactivate the trauma of the rape.

In a study of the counseling needs of rape victims, Mezey and Taylor (1988) reported that rape victims needed to better understand the trauma situation and desired information about how they could cope with their dramatically altered lives. They also found that rape victims wanted to talk with other women who had gone through similar experiences.

Long-term Effects Whether a rape victim will experience serious psychological decompensation depends to a large extent on her past coping skills and level of psychological functioning. A previously well-adjusted woman usually will regain her prior equilibrium, but rape can precipitate severe pathology in a woman with psychological difficulties (Atkeson et al., 1982; Meyer & Taylor, 1986; Santiago et al., 1985). Keep in mind that this general finding is not true in every case—clearly the nature of the crime and the adequacy of therapy are critical factors contributing to a victim's recovery. What we are saying is that research does point to a correlation between previous psychological functioning and recovery from a rape experience.

As for long-term effects, comparisons of women who have been raped with those who have not indicate that, though victims feel that their rapes have had and continue to have impacts on them, generally no significant differences in overall psychological adjustment exist between victims and nonvictims (Oros & Koss, 1978). When problems do continue, or when they become manifest later in a delayed posttraumatic stress disorder, they are likely to involve anxiety, depression, withdrawal, and heterosexual relationship difficulties (Gold, 1986; Koss, 1983; Meyer & Taylor, 1986; Santiago et al., 1985).

Rape crisis centers provide both psychological counseling and advocacy services with the intent of helping rape victims cope with their crisis and its aftermath. Such intervention can have a significant impact on psychological recovery from rape.

The Trauma of Military Combat

At any given time wars or armed conflicts are taking place in some parts of the world. Shaw (1990) recently noted that "war is a constant of history." War continues to take an incredible toll on human lives and economic resources, often leaving large numbers of victims in its wake. The consequences of war on survivors, both civilian and military, are often great. Many individuals who have been involved in war's turmoil can experience devastating psychological problems for months or even years following the conflict. Much research has accumulated on the psychological effects of war.

During World War I, traumatic reactions to combat conditions were called *shell shock,* a term coined by a British pathologist, Col. Frederick Mott (1919), who regarded these reactions as organic conditions produced by minute brain hemorrhages. It was gradually realized, however, that only a small percentage of such cases represented physical injury from the concussion of exploding shells or bombs. Most victims were suffering instead from the general combat situation, with its physical fatigue, ever-present threat of death or mutilation, and severe psychological shocks. During World War II traumatic reactions to combat passed through a number of classifications, such as *operational fatigue* and *war neuroses,* before finally being termed *combat fatigue* or *combat exhaustion* in the Korean and Vietnam wars.

Even the latter terms were none too aptly chosen, since they implied that physical exhaustion played a more important role than was usually the case. They did, however, serve to distinguish such disorders from other psychological disorders that happened to occur under war conditions but might well have occurred in civilian life—for example, among individuals showing histories of maladaptive behaviors that were aggravated by the stress of combat. Most soldiers who became psychological casualties because of combat had adjusted satisfactorily to civilian life and to prior military experiences.

It has been estimated that in World War II, 10 percent of Americans in combat developed combat exhaustion; however, the actual incidence is not known because many soldiers received supportive therapy at their battalion aid stations and were returned to combat within a few hours. Records were kept mainly on soldiers evacuated from the front lines who were considered the most seriously disturbed cases. Of the just over 10 million people accepted for military service during World War II, approximately 530,000—a little over 5 percent—were given medical discharges for neuropsychiatric reasons (including combat exhaustion, psychosis, neurosis, and other personality disorders that made them unsuitable for military life). In fact combat exhaustion caused the single greatest loss of personnel during that war (Bloch, 1969). During the Korean War the incidence of combat exhaustion dropped from an initial high of over 6

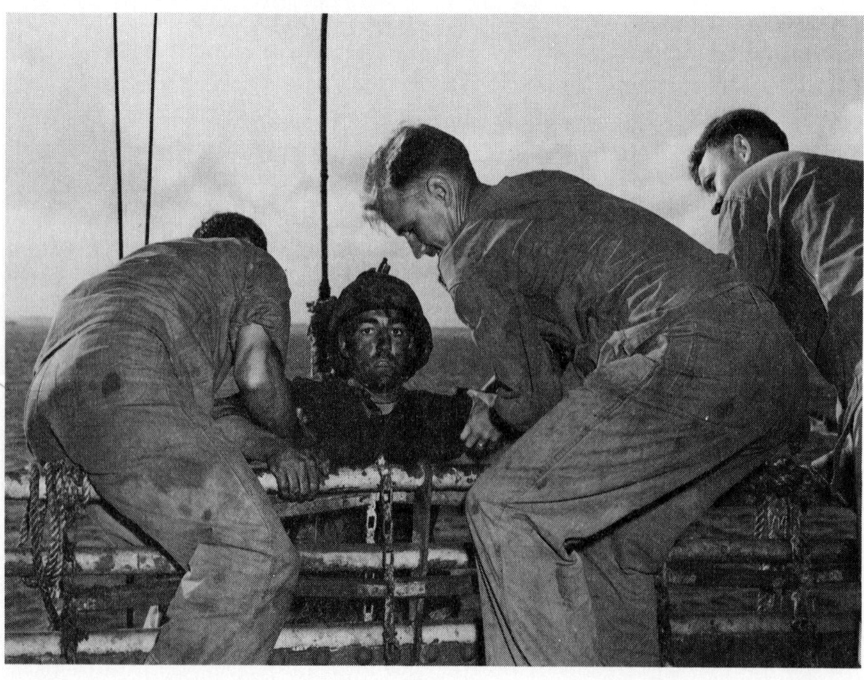

It has been estimated that in World War II, 10 percent of Americans in combat developed combat exhaustion. The stress of combat clearly took its toll on this Marine who had just finished two days of heavy fighting in the Pacific.

percent to 3.7 percent; 27 percent of medical discharges were for psychiatric reasons (Bell, 1958). In the Vietnam War the figure dropped to less than 1.5 percent for combat exhaustion, with a negligible number of discharges for psychiatric disorders (Allerton, 1970; Bourne, 1970).

Reasons advanced to explain the decrease in combat exhaustion during the Vietnam War include (a) better medical care near the front lines; (b) the sporadic nature of the fighting, in which brief intensive encounters were followed by periods of relative calm and safety—as contrasted with the weeks and months of prolonged combat that many soldiers went through in World War II and the Korean War; and (c) a policy of rotation after 12 months of service (13 months for Marines).

However, research has shown a high prevalence of posttraumatic stress disorder for Vietnam veterans. Though combat exhaustion was not as great a factor as in previous wars, combat-related stress apparently manifested itself later. Adopting research methodology developed in the study of genetic inheritance, Goldberg et al. (1990) studied identical twins who were in the military during the Vietnam War but who experienced different degrees of combat exposure. Some members of the twin pairs had served in Southeast Asia (SEA) and others had not; the latter served as the control group. Using military service records, the researchers identified 2092 pairs of male-male identical twins who agreed to cooperate in the study. These twins were surveyed to determine their exposure to stressful combat situations using an objective demographic and experience questionnaire. The researchers placed individuals into combat-exposure groups as follows: 950 twin pairs had not served in SEA; 427 twin pairs included two individuals who had served in SEA; 715 twin pairs included one twin who had served in SEA and one who had not. The presence or absence of PTSD symptoms was assessed by having each twin complete a health survey containing 12 items that dealt with their specific military experiences. The questionnaire followed the DSM-III-R PTSD symptom cluster and enabled the researchers to determine the presence of posttraumatic symptoms. The researchers based their determinations on the belief that PTSD can be diagnosed "when an individual reports a traumatic event outside the normal range of human experience and at least one symptom of reexperiencing the event, at least three symptoms of avoidance, and at least two symptoms of increased arousal." (p. 1228)

Marked differences in the prevalence of PTSD were found between the groups that had served in SEA and those that had not. The twin pair group that had not served in SEA reported low rates of PTSD symptoms (4.3 to 12.3 percent) compared with the group in which both pairs had served in SEA (14.4 to 28.2 percent). The most interesting comparison was in the discordant group in which one twin had served in SEA and the other had not. In this group the twins not serving in SEA reported low rates of PTSD (from 4.8 to 12.2 percent), similar to the group of twins that had not served in SEA. Those twins from the discordant pair who had actually served in SEA reported high rates of PTSD (from 15.8 to 30.6 percent), similar to the twin group in which both pairs had served in SEA.

A further analysis was conducted to assess the relationship between the degree of combat exposure and the later development of posttraumatic stress disorder. The researchers found a clear intensity effect in the later development of PTSD symptoms. Individuals who had experienced high levels of combat had a greater prevalence of posttraumatic stress symptoms than those who had had lower levels of combat exposure.

Clinical Picture in Combat-related Stress

The specific symptoms of combat-related stress vary considerably, depending on the type of duty, the severity and nature of the traumatic experience, and the personality of the individual.

A recent study evaluating different dimensions of posttraumatic stress disorder according to the type of war-related stress experienced was conducted by Laufer, Brett, and Gallops (1985). They surveyed 251 Vietnam veterans and, on the basis of the veterans' self-reports, grouped them according to three levels of experienced stress: (a) exposed to combat; (b) exposed to abusive violence in combat; and (c) participated in abusive violence in combat. They found that different degrees of stress symptoms were reported by individuals who had been exposed to different types of war trauma. Exposure to combat and exposure to violence were found to be associated with later experiences of posttraumatic symptoms, including intrusive imagery, hyperarousal, numbing, and cognitive disruption. Participation in abusive violence was most highly associated with more severe pathologies marked by cognitive disruptions, such as depression. The authors concluded that the clinical picture of posttraumatic stress disorder varies depending on the stressors experienced. Patients who have experienced particular types of war stress are likely to present specific types of symptoms, and not all PTSD patients present identical symptoms.

Despite variations in experience, however, the general clinical picture was surprisingly uniform for soldiers who had developed combat stress in different wars. The first symptoms had been a failure to maintain psychological integration, with increasing irritability and sensitivity, sleep disturbances, and often recurrent nightmares. The following diary covers a period of about six weeks of combat in the South Pacific during World War II and illustrates the cumulative effect of combat stresses on an apparently stable personality.

"Aug. 7, 1942. Convoy arrived at Guadalcanal Bay at approximately 4 A.M. in the morning. Ships gave enemy a heavy shelling. At 9 A.M. we stormed the beach and formed an immediate beachhead, a very successful landing, marched all day in the hot sun, and at night took positions and rested. Enemy planes attacked convoy in bay but lost 39 out of 40 planes.

"Aug. 8, 1942. Continued march in the hot sun and in afternoon arrived at airport. Continued on through the Jap village and made camp for the night. During the night Jap navy attacked convoy in battle that lasted until early morning. Enemy had terrific losses and we lost two ships. This night while on sentry duty I mistook a horse for a Jap and killed it.

"Aug. 19, 1942. Enemy cruiser and destroyer came into bay and shelled the beach for about two hours. The cruiser left and the destroyer hung around for the entire morning. We all kept under shelter for the early afternoon a flying fortress flew over, spotting the ship and bombed it, setting it afire we all jumped and shouted with joy. That night trouble again was feared and we again slept in foxholes.

"Aug. 21, 1942. The long awaited landing by the enemy was made during the night 1500 troops in all and a few prisoners were taken and the rest were killed. Bodies were laying all over the beach. In afternoon planes again bombed the Island [Here the writing begins to be shaky, and less careful than previously.]

"Aug. 28, 1942. The company left this morning in higgins Boats to the end of the Island, landed and started through thick jungle and hills. It was hot and we had to cut our way through. In afternoon we contacted the japs. our squad was in the assault squad so we moved up the beach to take positions the enemy trapped us with machine gun and rifle fire for about two hours. The lead was really flying. Two of our men were killed, two were hit by a hand greade and my corporal received a piece of shrampnel in back,—was wounded in arm, out of the squad of eight we have five causitry. We withdrew and were taken back to the Hospital.

"Sept. 12, 1942. Large jap squadron again bombed Island out of 35 planes sent over our air force knocked down 24. During the raid a large bomb was dropped just sevety yards from my fox hole.

"Sept. 13, 1942. At one o'clock three destroyers and one cruiser shelled us contumally all night. The ships turned surch lights all up and down the beach, and stopped one my foxhole seveal time I'm feeling pritty nervese and scared, afraid I'll be a nervas reack befor long. slept in fox hole all night not much sleep. This morning at 9:00 we had another air raid, the raid consisted of mostly fighter planes. I believe we got several, this afternoon. we had another raid, and our planes went out to met them, met them someplace over Tulagi, new came in that the aircraft carries wasp sent planes out to intersept the bombers. This eving all hell broke lose. Our marines contacted enemy to south of us and keep up constant fire. . . .

"Sept. 14, 1942. This morning firing still going on my company is scaduted to unload ships went half ways up to dock when enemyfire start on docks, were called back to our pososeion allon beach, company called out again to go after japs, hope were lucker than we were last time [part of this illegible]. Went up into hills at 4:00 P.M. found positions, at 7.00 en 8 sea planes fombed and strifed us, 151942 were strifed biy amfibious planes and bombed the concussion of one through me of balance and down a 52 foot hil. I was shaking likd a leaf. Lost my bayanut, and ran out of wathr. I nearves and very jumpy, hop I last out until morning. I hope sevearly machine s guns ore oping up on our left flank there going over our heads.

"Sept. 16. this morning we going in to take up new possissons we march all morning and I am very week and nerves, we marched up a hill and ran in to the affaul place y and z company lost so many men I hardly new what I was doing then I'm going nuts.

"Sept. 17. don't remember much of this day.

"Sept. 18. Today I'm on a ship leaving this awful place, called Green Hell. I'm still nearves and shakey." (Stern, 1947, pp. 583–586)

In the Vietnam War, soldiers were seldom exposed to prolonged periods of shelling and bombardment; combat reactions were typically more sudden and acute as a result of some particularly overwhelming combat experience.

The recorded cases of combat-related stress among soldiers in various wars show that the common sympton usually has been overwhelming anxiety. In comparison, it is interesting to note that most wounded soldiers have shown less anxiety or

Many factors may contribute to traumatic reactions to combat —constitutional predisposition, personal immaturity, compromised loyalty to one's unit, diminished confidence in one's officers, as well as the actual stress experienced. Thus, although combat situations completely undermine a person's ordinary coping methods, some soldiers can tolerate great stress without becoming psychiatric casualties, while others may break down under only slight combat stress.

fewer combat exhaustion symptoms—except in cases of permanent mutilation. Apparently a wound, in providing an escape from a stressful combat situation, removes the source of anxiety. A similar finding was reported among Israeli soldiers hospitalized during the Yom Kippur War. (The Yom Kippur War began on October 6, 1973, the Jewish Holy Day of Atonement [Yom Kippur], when Egyptian and Syrian forces attacked Israel in an effort to regain control of the Sinai Peninsula and the Golan Heights. A cease-fire was agreed to on October 23, and on November 11, a peace agreement calling for talks to resolve differences was signed.) Those soldiers hospitalized for physical injuries—even severe ones such as paralysis or loss of limb—showed no appreciable psychological disturbances. In contrast, those hospitalized because of psychiatric problems —such as severe depression, thought disorders, and obsessiveness—were quite disturbed about their physical symptoms, even minor ones (Merbaum & Hefez, 1976).

In fact it is not unusual for soldiers to admit that they have prayed to be hit or to have something "honorable" happen to them to remove them from battle. When approaching full recovery and the necessity of returning to combat, injured soldiers sometimes show prolonged symptoms or delayed traumatic reactions of nervousness, insomnia, and other symptoms that were nonexistent when they were first hospitalized.

Causal Factors in Combat Stress Problems

In a combat situation, with the continual threat of injury or death and repeated narrow escapes, a person's ordinary coping methods are relatively useless. The adequacy and security the individual has known in the relatively safe and dependable civilian world are completely undermined. However, we must not overlook the fact that most soldiers subjected to combat have not become psychiatric casualties, although most of them have evidenced severe fear reactions and other symptoms of personality disorganization that were not serious enough to be incapacitating. In addition, many soldiers have tolerated almost unbelievable stress before they have broken, while others have become casualties under conditions of relatively slight combat stress or even as noncombatants—for example, during basic training.

In order to understand traumatic reactions to combat, we need to look at factors such as constitutional predisposition, personal maturity, loyalty to one's unit, and confidence in one's officers—as well as at the actual stress experienced.

Biological factors. Do constitutional differences in sensitivity, vigor, and temperament affect a soldier's resistance to combat stress? They probably do, but little actual evidence supports this assumption. We have more information about the conditions of battle that tax a soldier's emotional and physical stamina. Add other factors that often occur in combat situations—such as severe climatic conditions, malnutrition, and disease—to the strain of continual emotional mobilization, and the result is a general lowering of an individual's physical and psychological resistance to all stressors.

Psychosocial factors. A number of psychological and interpersonal factors may contribute to the overall stress experienced by soldiers and predispose them to break down under combat. Such factors include reductions in personal freedom, frustrations of all sorts, and separation from home and loved ones. Central, of course, are the many stresses arising from combat, including constant fear, unpredictable circumstances, the necessity of killing, and prolonged harsh conditions.

An individual's personality is an important determinant of adjustment to military experiences. Personality characteristics that lower an individual's resistance to stress or to particular stressors may be important in determining his or her reactions to combat. Personal immaturity—sometimes stemming from parental overprotection—is commonly cited as making a soldier more vulnerable to combat stress. Worthington (1978) found that American soldiers who experienced problems readjusting after they returned home from the Vietnam War also tended to have had greater difficulties before and during their military service than soldiers who adjusted readily.

In their study of the personality characteristics of Israeli soldiers who had broken down in combat during the Yom Kippur War, Merbaum and Hefez (1976) found that over 25 percent reported having had psychological treatment prior to the war. Another 12 percent had experienced difficulties previously in the six-day Israeli-Arab war of 1967. Thus about 37 percent of these soldiers had clear histories of some personality instability that may have predisposed them to break down under combat stress. On the other hand, the other soldiers who broke down —over 60 percent—had not shown earlier difficulties and would not have been considered to be at risk for such breakdown.

A background of personal maladjustment does not always make an individual a poor risk for withstanding combat stress. Some individuals are so accustomed to anxiety that they cope with it more or less automatically, whereas soldiers who are feeling severe anxiety for the first time may be terrified by the experience, lose their self-confidence, and go to pieces. It has also been observed that sociopaths (antisocial personalities, according to DSM-III-R), though frequently in trouble during peacetime service for disregarding rules and regulations, have often demonstrated good initiative and effective combat aggression against the enemy. However, the soldiers who function most effectively and are most apt to survive combat usually come from backgrounds that fostered self-reliance, the ability to function in a group, and ready adjustment to new situations (Bloch, 1969; Borus, 1974; Grinker, 1969; Lifton, 1972).

Sociocultural factors. Several sociocultural factors play an important part in determining an individual's adjustment to combat. These general factors include clarity and acceptability of war goals, identification with the combat unit, esprit de corps, and quality of leadership.

An important consideration is how clear and acceptable the war's goals are to an individual. In general, war goals have a supportive effect on a soldier if they can be concretely integrated into the soldier's values in terms of his or her "stake" in the war and the worth and importance of what he or she is doing. Another important factor is a person's identification with the combat unit. The soldier who is unable to identify with or take pride in his or her group lacks the feeling of "we-ness" that helps maintain stress tolerance. Lacking this identity, a soldier stands alone, psychologically isolated and less able to withstand combat stress. In fact the stronger the sense of group identification, the less chance that a soldier will break down in combat. Feelings of esprit de corps influence an individual's morale and adjustment to extreme circumstances. Finally, the quality of leadership and confidence in one's unit are of vital importance in a soldier's adjustment to combat. If a soldier respects his or her leaders, has confidence in their judgment and ability, and can accept them as relatively strong parental or sibling figures, the soldier's morale and resistance to stress are bolstered. On the other hand, lack of confidence or dislike of leaders is detrimental to morale and to combat stress tolerance.

It also appears that returning to an unaccepting social environment can increase a soldier's vulnerability to posttraumatic stress. For example, in a one-year follow-up of Israeli men who had been psychiatric war casualties during the Yom Kippur War, Merbaum (1977) found that they not only continued to show extreme anxiety, depression, and extensive physical complaints, but in many instances they appeared to have become more disturbed over time. Merbaum hypothesized that their psychological deterioration had probably been due to the unaccepting attitudes of the community; in a country so reliant on the strength of its army for survival, considerable stigma is attached to psychological breakdown in combat. Because of the stigma, many of the men were experiencing not only isolation within their communities, but also self-recrimination about what they perceived as failure on their own parts. These feelings exacerbated the soldiers' already stressful situations.

Long-term Effects of Posttraumatic Stress

In some cases, soldiers who have experienced combat exhaustion may show symptoms of posttraumatic stress for sustained periods of time, as is graphically detailed in *HIGHLIGHT 5.5.* In cases of delayed

Residual Effects of Posttraumatic Stress Among Outpatients at a VA Clinic

Twenty years after the end of World War II, Archibald and Tuddenham (1965) conducted a follow-up study of the residual effects of posttraumatic stress in 62 combat exhaustion cases. The following chart compares the incidence of several symptoms in this group and in 20 veterans who had not suffered combat exhaustion during the war. In addition to the symptoms listed here, the more severe combat exhaustion cases revealed various other symptoms, including difficulties in work and family relationships, social isolation, and narrowing of interests. Alcoholism was a problem for about 20 percent of both groups.

In many cases symptoms had appeared to clear up when the stress was over, only to reappear in chronic form later. It seems evident that intense and sustained stress can lead to lasting symptoms even if the victims receive follow-up care. Although the combat exhaustion veterans were receiving assistance at a Veterans Administration outpatient psychiatric clinic, they were not receiving additional disability compensation as a result of their prolonged stress reactions.

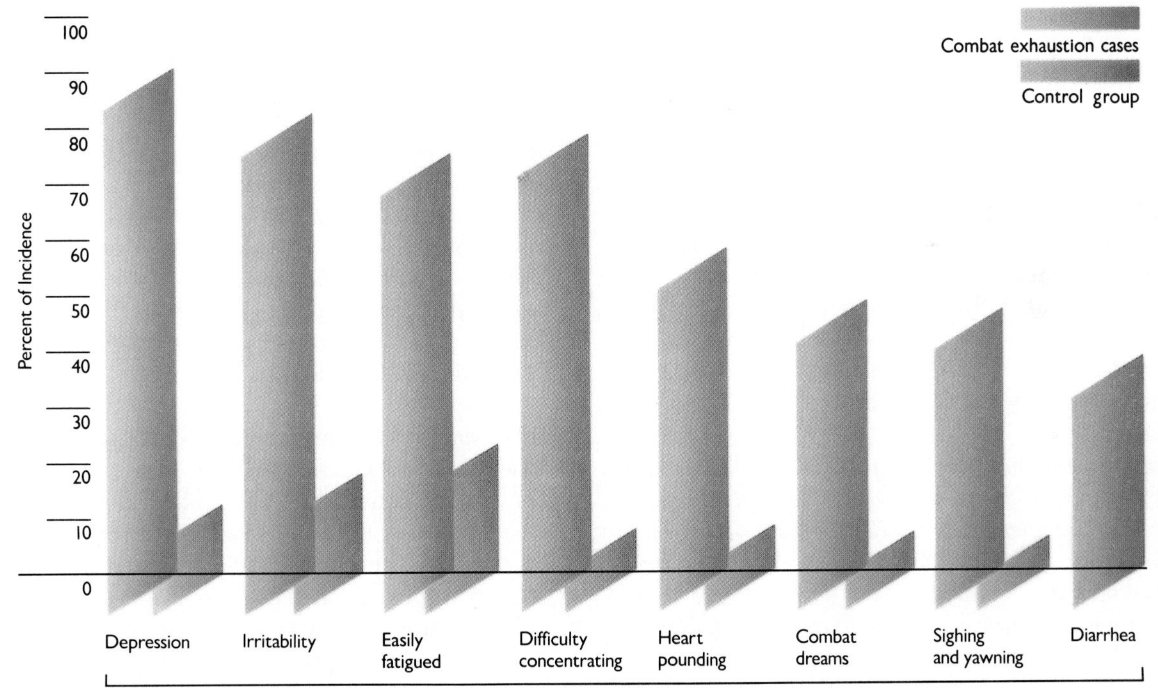

Chart adapted from Archibald and Tuddenham (1965), omitting statistics for noncombat psychiatric military cases.

In March 1986, Michael Dean, a Vietnam veteran, and the woman he lived with, Caroline Hull, fed sleeping pills to her three children. Hull then took sleeping pills herself. When Hull and her children were unconscious, Dean shot each of them in the heart and set the house on fire. He then shot himself. Letters from Dean and Hull described the deaths as an act of protest for the forgotten veterans of the Vietnam War and their families. Dean, who had been depressed and moody after his return from the war, was considered by many doctors to be a clear example of posttraumatic stress syndrome.

posttraumatic stress, some soldiers who have stood up exceptionally well under intensive combat situations have experienced posttraumatic stress only upon their returns home, often in response to relatively minor stresses that they had handled easily before. Evidently, these soldiers have suffered long-term damage to their adaptive capabilities, in some cases complicated by memories of killing enemy soldiers or civilians that are tinged with feelings of guilt and anxiety (Haley, 1978; Horowitz & Solomon, 1978; Polner, 1968).

Shatan (1978) illustrated the effects of posttraumatic stress disorder on Vietnam veterans with the story of Dwight Johnson, who had won the Medal of Honor in Vietnam:

Jon Nordheimer's front-page New York Times story [1971] sensitively described Sgt. Dwight Johnson's apathy and alienation, his demoralization by unemployment, and his suspicion that he was being exploited by the army, even when he was in the hospital. His government's highest martial honor weighed heavily around his neck each time he was praised for slaughter—and thereby forced to recall that he was the sole survivor of his tank crew, buddies during eleven months of warfare. While the army used him in recruiting drives, empty promise piled upon empty promise and his cynicism grew.

Johnson had been placed in restraints and narcotized for 24 hours immediately after his final day of combat—the action for which he received the supreme distinction. Yet, 48 hours later, he was back in the U.S. with a non-psychiatric discharge. His emotional difficulties received no official interest until he became a "hot property." His treatment began more than a year after his return home, at the Valley Forge Army Hospital. There he was diagnosed as suffering from "depression caused by post-Vietnam adjustment problems."

On several occasions, he asked his psychiatrist how society would react if he were to respond to the black dilemma in Detroit with the same uncontrolled ferocity that had earned him the highest recognition in battle. He found his ultimate answer, not in a distant jungle but on the floor of a hometown grocery. There he lived out his haunting fantasies and nightmares of being killed at point blank range. (pp. 46–47)

Similarly, the long-term effects of posttraumatic stress were shown in a follow-up study of 92 combat veterans of the Vietnam War. Polner (1968) cited a number of cases in which combat experiences continued to disturb the veterans after their returns to civilian life. In most instances the difficulties appeared to center around guilt feelings over killing. For example, one veteran said, "I can't sleep, I'm a murderer." He continued,

"We were outside Bac Lieu, out on an eight-man patrol along with 15 ARVNs [South Vietnamese soldiers]. Our orders were to move ahead and shoot at anything suspicious. My God, how I remember that damned day! It was hot and sticky. The mosquitoes were driving me crazy. And there was this boy, about 8 or 9. He had his hand behind his back, like he was hiding something. 'Grab him,' someone screamed, 'he's got something!' I made a move for

him and his hand moved again. 'Shoot!' I fired. Again and again, until my M-2 was empty. When I looked he was there, all over the ground, cut in two with his guts all around. I vomited. I wasn't told, I wasn't trained for that. It was out-and-out murder. . . .

"You know I killed nine people as an adviser." (p. 12)

Many of the other veterans interviewed by Polner, however, felt that they had simply done their duty in a worthwhile cause.

In another study of Vietnam returnees, Strange and Brown (1970) compared combat and noncombat veterans who were experiencing emotional difficulties. The combat group showed a higher incidence of depression and of difficulties in their close interpersonal relationships. They also showed a higher incidence of aggressive and suicidal threats but did not actually carry them out. In a later study of Vietnam veterans who were making a satisfactory readjustment to civilian life, DeFazio, Rustin, and Diamond (1975) found that the combat veterans *still* reported certain symptoms twice as often as the noncombat veterans. Based on a questionnaire obtained from 207 veterans who had been out of the armed forces for over five years, DeFazio et al. found the following percentages of combat veterans still reporting symptoms: (a) frequent nightmares —68 percent; (b) quick temper—44 percent; (c) many fears—35 percent; (d) worries about employment—35 percent; (e) difficulties with emotional closeness—35 percent; (f) quick fatigue—32 percent. In a more recent study, Solomon (1989) found that combat veterans reported more stress symptoms over a three-year period than did a control group. The symptoms of combat stress, however, diminished over time.

In some cases a significant incident may precipitate a chronic reaction. A case reported by Christenson et al. (1981) shows how a later event may trigger past traumas and result in serious adjustment problems.

Mr. A, a 55-year-old divorced man, was admitted with severe anxiety, multiple somatic complaints, feelings of hopelessness, somatovegetative signs of depression, and suicidal ideations. He had required psychiatric hospitalization for "nerves" shortly after his discharge from the service at the end of World War II. He subsequently had a good adjustment and a stable marriage and work history. Three years before this admission, Mr. A abruptly left his job as an emergency room technician and began drinking heavily. Eventually his wife left him, and the actual signing of divorce papers precipitated the symptoms that led to his admission.

It was only after another patient on the ward began talking of his difficulties during World War II that Mr. A revealed the following history. He had been stationed in the South Pacific and had survived two battles in which his ship had been destroyed and many people around him violently killed. Shortly after these events, his unit was instructed that island children were being wired as human bombs, and an order was issued to shoot all children approaching the camp. When Mr. A was on duty, he had been forced to shoot a 10-year-old boy. After this incident, Mr. A began having nightmares of exploding shells, violent scenes of people being killed, and scenes of himself killing the boy. These cleared over a period of a few years.

Mr. A's recent deterioration (3 years ago) came after an episode at work in the emergency room where he was told to clean up a child in one of the rooms. He was unaware that the child (a 9-year-old boy) was already dead when he was brought to the emergency room. When Mr. A discovered that the boy was dead, he was horrified, left work, and never returned. His nightmares resumed, but he felt unable to discuss these war episodes with his wife. At times, he would wake up screaming and throw his wife to the floor to "cover" her from exploding shells. It was this unexplained behavior that forced their separation.

During this hospital stay, Mr. A was able to talk about these war episodes for the first time in 35 years. He actively participated in a small therapy group of World War II veterans that focused on the veterans ventilating their feelings about traumatic war experiences. Mr. A was also treated with 150 mg h.s. of doxepin [an antidepressant administered at bedtime].

Gradually, Mr. A's depression cleared, and he claimed he was less anxious than at any time since the war. He was sleeping through the night without nightmares. Mr. A made appropriate arrangements to resume his most recent job and had an optimistic view of the future. He identified the opportunity to openly discuss his war experiences as the most important factor in his recovery. (p. 984)

The nature and extent of this delayed posttraumatic stress disorder are somewhat controversial (Burstein, 1985). Reported cases of delayed stress syndrome among Vietnam combat veterans are often difficult to relate explicitly to combat stress because these individuals may also have other significant adjustment problems. Individuals experiencing adjustment difficulties may erroneously attribute their present problems to specific incidents from their past, such as experiences in combat. The wide publicity recently given to delayed posttraumatic stress disorder has made it easy for clinicians to "find" a precipitating cause in their patients' backgrounds; indeed, the frequency with which this disorder has recently been diagnosed in some settings suggests that its increased use is as much a result of its plausibility and popularity as of its true incidence.

The Trauma of Being a Prisoner of War or in a Concentration Camp

Although some individuals adjust to the stress of being a prisoner of war or in a concentration camp (especially if part of a supportive group), the past shows us that the toll on most prisoners is great. About half of the American prisoners in Japanese POW camps during World War II died during their imprisonment; an even higher number of prisoners of Nazi concentration camps died. Those who survived the ordeal often sustained residual organic and psychological damage along with a lowered tolerance to stress of any kind.

Without question, reentry to society is difficult for former POWs and concentration camp survivors. They must adjust to the sudden and major changes in their lives and to the social changes that took place during their imprisonments.

The residual damage to survivors of Nazi concentration camps was often extensive and commonly included anxiety, insomnia, headaches, irritability, depression, nightmares, impaired sexual potency, and "functional" diarrhea (which occurs in any situation of stress, even relatively mild stress). Such symptoms were attributed not only to the psychological stressors but also to biological stressors, such as head injuries, prolonged malnutrition, and serious infectious diseases (Eitinger, 1964, 1969, 1973; Sigal et al., 1973; Warnes, 1973).

Among returning POWs, psychological problems were often masked by the feelings of relief and jubilation that accompanied release from confinement. Even when there was little evidence of residual physical pathology, however, survivors of prisoner-of-war camps commonly showed impaired resistance to physical illness, low frustration tolerance, frequent dependence on alcohol and drugs, irritability, and other indications of emotional instability (Chambers, 1952; Goldsmith & Cretekos, 1969; Hunter, 1978; Strange & Brown,

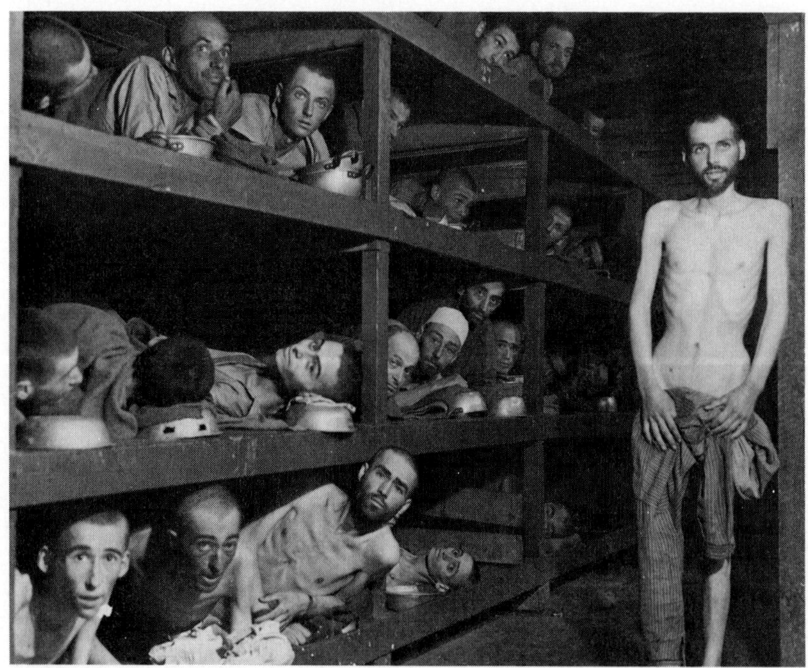

The physical and psychological stresses of life in Nazi concentration camps left permanent scars on many of those who survived the ordeal. When samples of concentration camp survivors who did not undergo psychotherapy have been studied, however, they have been shown to be resilient and well-functioning over time. Elie Wiesel, pictured here on the second tier of prisoners (the second man behind the man with the bandaged head), was liberated from Buchenwald and went on to win the Nobel Peace Prize in 1986.

HIGHLIGHT 5.6

Failure to Readjust After Captivity: A Case of Diathesis or Stress?

When the POWs held in North Vietnam were finally released in 1973, most Americans felt relieved that the Vietnam War was at last over. The prisoners who returned—some after many years of captivity—were welcomed back into society. A few of the returning prisoners, however, found the United States to be as hostile an environment as a North Vietnamese POW camp.

One such soldier, Jerry L., returned to the United States to find himself facing a possible court-martial on charges of collaboration with the enemy. His alleged behavior during captivity had received adverse publicity, and Jerry's friends and relatives reacted by treating him with coldness and suspicion. Shortly after his return, Jerry died of self-inflicted gunshot wounds.

Two psychologists were asked by the district attorney's office to construct a "psychological autopsy" to clear up the circumstances surrounding the unexpected death. In conducting their investigation, Selkin and Loya (1979) encountered resistance from Jerry's family and from the military. Jerry's wife and other family members believed that the government had mistreated Jerry and that his death was related to the military's lack of support and medical attention, plus the extreme anxiety caused by the collaboration charges. As a result the family was at first reluctant to provide information about Jerry's early life, though they later became more cooperative. Meanwhile, military officials initially refused to release Jerry's records—though they, too, finally decided to cooperate.

Selkin and Loya discovered that Jerry had been following what appeared to be a "suicidal life course that had begun long before the war in Vietnam" (p. 89). For years Jerry had tended to drink heavily when under stress and had a history of delinquency and other maladjustments. Despite this history the military had provided Jerry with little psychiatric attention after his release from the POW camp. Although he spoke briefly with a "partially trained" psychiatrist, he was not offered psychological help or a psychiatric follow-up after he returned home. It was apparent that "no one in any official capacity made an honest attempt to understand him or take a careful look at his life situation" (p. 90).

This investigation indicates both the relationship of prior psychological problems to adjustment after captivity and the importance of the environment to the successful repatriation of prisoners of war. A few days after the psychological autopsy was completed, the government dropped all charges against other POWs who had been accused of collaborating with the enemy.

1970; Wilbur, 1973). In a retrospective study of psychological maladjustment symptoms following repatriation, Speed et al. (1989) interviewed a large sample of former POWs and found that half of them reported symptoms that met DSM-III criteria for PTSD in the year following their releases from captivity.

Another measure of the toll taken by the prolonged stress of being in a POW or concentration camp is the higher death rate after return to civilian life. Among returning World War II POWs from the Pacific area, Wolff (1960) found that within the first six years, nine times as many died from tuberculosis as would have been expected in civilian life, four times as many from gastrointestinal disorders, over twice as many from cancer, heart disease, and suicide, and three times as many from accidents. Eitinger (1973) has reported comparable figures for concentration camp survivors. The case of one Vietnam POW is examined in *HIGHLIGHT 5.6.*

Aware that problems may show up years after release, military psychologists and psychiatrists have been following representative groups of Vietnam War POWs on a long-term basis with yearly checkups. These former POWs differ from those in earlier wars in that they were almost all flight crew personnel, which meant that they were officers and somewhat older than the rank-and-file combat personnel. In the examination made two years after their return, it was found that the longer the imprisonment, the more likely a person was to develop psychiatric problems (O'Connell, 1976). Other factors that seemed to predispose individuals to later problems were harsh POW treatment and isolation while captured (Hunter, 1976). The most frequent problems requiring psychological help were depression and marital difficulties (Hunter, 1978, 1981).

A great deal has been written about the long-term adjustment problems of concentration camp survivors. Some writers, for example Krystal (1968) and Niederland (1968) (who based their views on the survivors of death camps who later sought psychological treatment), have contended that concentration camp survivors carry psychological scars with them for the rest of their lives. Other writers have concluded that these emotional scars are so profound that they can be transmitted to the survivors' children (Epstein, 1979; Schneider, 1978). We must bear in mind, however, that most of the conclusions about the psychopathologies of concentration camp survivors and their children are based on people who are undergoing or have undergone psychotherapy. The observations that long-term adjustment problems persist, as noted by some writers, may be valid for particular individuals and may support the idea that some people do not deal effectively with life after experiencing severe life stress. These clinical studies, however, cannot be viewed as representative. The biased nature of their samples (psychotherapy patients) precludes generalizations about concentration camp survivors as a whole. In fact, when community (nonpsychiatric) samples of concentration camp survivors are studied they have been shown to be remarkably resilient and well functioning over time (Kahana, Harel, and Kahana, 1988; Leon et al., 1981).

The Trauma of Being Held Hostage

Hostage-taking seems to increase each year. Not only are politically driven hostage-taking situations becoming more frequent, but kidnappings in the United States for economic or other motives also seem on the rise. Clearly such situations can produce disabling psychological symptoms in victims (Danto, 1990). The following case reported by Sonnenberg (1988) describes a man who experienced a horrifying ordeal that left him with intense symptoms of anxiety and distress for months following the incident.

Mr. A. was a married accountant, the father of two, in his early thirties. One night, while out performing an errand, he was attacked by a group of youths. These youngsters made him get into their car, and took him to a deserted country road.

There they pulled him from the car and began beating and kicking him. They took his wallet, began taunting him about its contents (they had learned his name, his occupation, and the names of his wife and children), and threatened to go to his home and harm these family members. Finally, after brutalizing him for several hours, they tied him to a tree, one youth held a gun to his head, and after he begged and pleaded for his life, the armed individual pulled the trigger. The gun was empty, but at the moment the trigger was pulled this victim defecated and urinated in his pants. Then the youths untied him and left him on the road.

This man slowly made his way to a gas station he had seen during his abduction, and called the police. I was called to examine him, and did so at intervals for the next 2 years. The diagnosis was PTSD. He had clearly experienced an event outside the range of normal human experience, and was at first re-experiencing the event in various ways: intrusive recollections, nightmares, flashbacks, and extreme fear upon seeing groups of unsavory looking youths. He was initially remarkably numb in other respects: he withdrew from the members of his family and lost interest in his job. He felt generally estranged and detached. He expected to die in the near future. There were also symptoms of increased psychophysiologic arousal: poor sleeping, difficulty concentrating, exaggerated startle response, and when we first spoke about his abduction in detail, he actually soiled himself at the moment he described doing so during the original traumatic experience.

This man received treatment during the next 2 years from another psychiatrist, consisting of twice-weekly intensive individual psychotherapy sessions and the concurrent administration of a tricyclic antidepressant. The individual psychotherapy consisted of discussions that focused on the sense of shame and guilt this man felt over his behavior during his abduction. He wished he had been more stoic and had not pleaded for his life. With the understanding help of his psychotherapist, he came to see that he could accept responsibility for his behavior during his captivity, that his murderous rage at his abductors was understandable, as was his desire for revenge and that his response to his experience was not remarkable compared with what others might have done and

Being held hostage, like this blindfolded American in Iran, and subjected to both physical and mental abuse is an experience that seems to be on the rise. Victims of other traumatic situations outside the range of normal human experience may exhibit disabling psychological symptoms months and years after the ordeal is over.

felt. Eventually he began to discuss his experience with his wife and friends, and by the end of the 2 years over which I followed him, he was essentially without symptoms, although he still became somewhat anxious when he saw groups of tough-looking youths. Most importantly, his relationship with his wife and children was warm and close, and he was again interested in his work. (p. 585)

The Trauma of Forced Relocation

Being uprooted from home is a threatening event that violates a person's sense of security. In recent years at Love Canal in New York, at Times Beach in Missouri, at Bhopal in India, and at Chernobyl in the USSR, families found their homes and themselves exposed to deadly toxins that had contaminated the environment. The danger forced these families to relocate. It is not surprising that, in such circumstances, the accompanying stress can be severe.

Imagine, then, the trauma of refugees who are forced not only to leave their homes but also their homelands and to face the stress of adapting to a new and unfamiliar culture. For those who come to the United States, the "land of opportunity" may seem a nightmare rather than a haven. Such was the case for Pham, a 34-year-old Vietnamese refugee who killed his sons and himself. Because Pham had no past history of mental disorder and seemed to function reasonably well, it is likely that he was experiencing symptoms of poor adaptation to his new environment.

Pham's ordeal began with a comfortable life in a wealthy Vietnamese family and a good job as a Saigon pharmacist. It ended after six months in the United States in a small two-bedroom apartment in Washington, D.C. The county police called it a murder-suicide.

Police believe that the refugee, a lab technician in a local community college's work-study program, administered the poison to his own family and then took his own life. Only Pham's wife survived the administration of the poison.

Two seven-page suicide notes, one in Vietnamese and one in English, began, "To whom it may concern. We committed suicide by cyanide. The reason is that I lost my mind I cannot live here like a normal person. . . ."

Pham, according to relatives, had been depressed over what he considered his financial and social failures in America. He was despondent over having to study five years to become a pharmacist here and about his difficulties communicating in English.

Pham was a dutiful son who had never been away from home before leaving for Thailand. He was homesick for his native country and for the parents who remained behind.

"He had a lot of expectations about America," said one relative, "he just could not cope." (Adapted from the Washington Star, December 8, 1980)

Pham's suffering is not unique. It is estimated that more than 16 million refugees exist in today's world, mostly from third-world or developing countries, with only about 11 percent of them relocating in developed nations like the United States and Canada (Brandel, 1980). Most refugees move between third-world countries; for example, more than 1.5 million Kurdish refugees from Iraq have either fled to Iran or live near the Iraq-Turkey border in makeshift living quarters.

In the United States, recent refugees have come from many countries—Poland, the Soviet Union, Iran, Cuba, Haiti, Laos, Vietnam, and Cambodia. The largest group of refugees currently entering the United States is from the Soviet Union—over 40,000 immigrants a year (U.S. Committee for Refugees, 1990). The Southeast Asians who began arriving in America after 1975 perhaps had the most difficult adjustment. Although many of these individuals were functioning well in their homeland and, in time, became successful and happy American citizens, others have had difficulty adjusting (Westermeyer, Williams, & Nguyen, 1991). For example, in a 10-year longitudinal study of Hmong refugees from Laos, Westermeyer, Neider, and Callies (1989) found that many refugees had made considerable progress in their acculturation. Many had improved economically—about 55 percent were employed with incomes approaching those of the general population. The percentage of people initially living on welfare had dropped from 53 percent to 29 percent after ten years. As a group, psychological adjustment had also improved, with symptoms of phobia, somatization, and low self-esteem showing the most positive changes. Considerable problems remain, however. Many refugees still have not learned the language, some seemingly have settled permanently onto the welfare rolls, and some show symptoms—such as anxiety, hostility, and paranoia—that have changed little over the period studied. Although many refugees have adapted to their new culture, many are still experiencing considerable adjustment problems even after ten years in the United States.

PREVENTION OF STRESS DISORDERS

If we know that extreme or prolonged stress can produce maladaptive psychological reactions that have predictable courses, is it possible to intervene early in the process to prevent the development of emotional disorder? When an unusually stressful situation is about to occur, is it possible to "inoculate" an individual by providing information about

Being forced out of one's home is a threatening event that violates one's sense of security. The physical suffering of the Kurdish refugees from Iraq, recently forced to flee to Iran or to the mountains near the Iraqi-Turkish border because of Saddam Hussein's brutality, has been well-documented, but the psychological trauma can only be imagined.

likely stressors ahead of time and suggesting ways of coping with them? If preparation for battle stressors can help soldiers avoid breakdowns, why not prepare other people to effectively meet anticipated stressors?

One researcher, Janis, did just this with patients about to undergo dangerous surgery. His findings provide a substantial base for preventive efforts aimed at reducing the emotional problems of patients following their surgery (Janis, 1958; Janis et al., 1969).

Janis (1958) conducted interviews before and after surgery to determine the relationship between preoperative fear and adjustment after surgery. He found that patients with moderate fear did better than those with either extreme or little fear. Those who greatly worried about suffering pain or being mutilated by the surgery exhibited, after surgery, extreme anxiety, emotional outbursts, and fearfulness about participating in postoperative treatment. Those who showed very little anticipatory fear displayed afterward an acute preoccupation with their vulnerability and were often angry and resentful toward the staff for being "mistreated." Those patients who were moderately fearful before surgery were the most cheerful and cooperative during the postoperative treatment.

An important finding in Janis's work is that individuals who are outwardly calm and appear to feel invulnerable to real danger are likely to have more postcrisis problems than individuals who have been "part-time worriers" beforehand. Janis suggested that the "work of worrying" may involve processes similar to the "work of mourning" following bereavement. In this case, however, it is accomplished before a trauma, helping an individual understand and work through the dangerous and aversive situation and be emotionally ready to adjust to it when it comes. Later studies, too, have shown that when patients are prepared for surgery by being given accurate information about the procedures and a warning about the pain they will experience, they are less likely to have severe emotional reactions following surgery (Egbert et al., 1964).

Work in cognitive-behavioral therapy has focused on **stress inoculation training** to prepare individuals for difficult events (Beech, Burns, & Sheffield, 1982; MacDonald & Kuiper, 1983; Meichenbaum & Cameron, 1983). This training prepares individuals to tolerate an anticipated threat by changing the things they say to themselves before the crisis.

A three-stage process is employed. The first stage provides information about the stressful situation and about ways people can deal with such dangers. In the second stage, self-statements that promote effective adaptation—for example, "Don't worry, this little pain is just part of the treatment"—are rehearsed. In the third stage, the individual practices making such self-statements while being exposed to a variety of ego-threatening or pain-threatening stressors, such as unpredictable electric shocks, stress-inducing films, or sudden cold. This last phase allows the person to apply the new coping skills learned earlier. We shall discuss stress-inoculation training and the use of self-statements in greater detail in Chapter 19.

UNRESOLVED ISSUES on the Politics of Posttraumatic Stress Disorder

This chapter has addressed the role of stress in producing psychological disorders. A considerable amount of research has substantiated the link between severe stress or trauma and subsequent psychological problems. Individuals may react to stressful situations in ways that are quite disabling. Many symptoms of posttraumatic stress disorder can interfere with psychological functioning, at least for a time, and can require considerable adaptive effort to

In recent years, for better or for worse, psychological disability as a result of posttraumatic stress disorder has become a popular avenue of defense in both civil and criminal cases. Although this defense has been legitimately employed in many cases, it has also been misused by generously "broadening" the concept of posttraumatic stress disorder.

Posttraumatic stress is frequently used as a defense in court cases to justify criminal acts. A recent case illustrates the sometimes loose connection between PTSD and deviant behavior.

In January 1987 an employee of an air cargo company, who had been fired from his job the day before, returned to the office dressed in army fatigues and carrying a sawed-off shotgun. He chased several employees away from the office and took his former supervisor hostage. He held his supervisor at gunpoint for about 1½ hours, making him beg for his life. During this time he fired about 21 shots at desks, computers, and windows, destroying a great deal of property. Once the hostage-taking situation ended, the former employee was arrested on charges of property destruction and assault with a deadly weapon. He reportedly claimed that he was extremely distraught and was suffering a posttraumatic stress disorder. He explained that he had just viewed the movie Platoon, which brought back horrible memories of Vietnam and had resulted in his becoming enraged. However, a check of his background and military records showed that he had never been in Vietnam and had actually spent his service time in a low stress, noncombat environment.

The posttraumatic syndrome is also being increasingly used in civil court cases, such as those involving compensation and personal injury. For example, in one case (*Albertson's Inc.* v. *Workers' Compensation Appeals Board of the State of California,* 1982), a bakery employee was awarded damages because her boss's comments to her caused her great embarrassment. The court concluded that job harassment was a sufficient cause of psychological damage and stress, and it was thus compensable. In another case a police officer filed a compensation claim because his job had created a great deal of stress for him. The police officer was not awarded a stress-related disability; the court ruled that when a person accepts a job as a police officer, he or she accepts the stress that accompanies it. The court did, however, award compensation payments for his physical disability (ulcers) as a result of the stressful job (*Egeland* v. *City of Minneapolis,* 1984).

Establishing legal justification for the "stress defense" is an interesting exercise, often involving considerable imagination if not out-and-out mythmaking. Whether a stressor is causally linked to a specific psychological disorder—thereby warranting compensation in disability cases or commanding leniency in criminal trials—is often difficult to substantiate and usually involves expert witness testimony by psychiatrists or psychologists. In most situations both sides in a case rely on expert testimony to support their side. However, the most important factor, from the standpoint of legal precedent, is that there must be sufficient evidence that the alleged stressor was clearly related to the behavior in question.

When circumstances clearly involve a significant psychological stressor, the opposing side may attempt to lessen the perception of its responsibility for stress effects in order to reduce liability in the case. The most dramatic example of this tactic involves the litigation following the 1985 Delta Airlines crash in Dallas, which resulted from the pilot's inability to control the aircraft because of wind shear. In an apparent effort to limit the liability of claims against the airline, the legal staff employed by the airline's insurer conducted private investigations on many of the victims and survivors to show that their problems actually preceded the crash. For example, in the case of one passenger who was killed, the insurer's attorneys argued that the man and his wife had been having marital problems and that the baby born to his wife four days after the crash was not actually his. The lawyers concluded that, because the man's marriage was on the rocks, they shouldn't have to pay much for his death. In another trial the attorneys argued that another passenger who was killed in the crash was a homosexual who probably would have died of AIDS anyway—thus limiting their liability ("60 Minutes," Feb. 15, 1987). These tactics are certainly questionable, but we must keep in mind that our legal system requires a lawyer to do everything legally possible to defend his or her client. In the Delta Airlines cases, the lawyers' tactics may be more indicative of the fact that definitively proving the existence of posttraumatic stress disorder remains exceedingly difficult.

Seeking psychological damages for alleged stress, whether justified or contrived, will probably continue as a legal strategy in court cases. Because symptoms of stress disorders are not uniform, and disabilities following stressful events are not easily predictable, it is likely that the problem of clearly establishing causal links between stressors and claimed symptoms will continue to plague our courts.

SUMMARY

Many factors influence an individual's response to stressful situations. The impact of stress depends not only on its severity, but also on the individual's preexisting vulnerabilities. An individual's response to conflict situations may be viewed differently depending on whether the conflicts are approach-avoidance, double-approach, or double-avoidance. A wide variety of psychosocial stressors exists, and a person can respond to them in different ways. In attempting to deal with stressful events, for instance, an individual may react with task-oriented or defense-oriented responses. The effects of extreme or prolonged stress on a person can bring about extensive psychological problems.

The DSM-III-R classifies individual problems in response to stressful situations under two categories: adjustment disorders and posttraumatic stress disorder (included with the anxiety disorders). Several relatively common stressors (prolonged unemployment, loss of a loved one through death, and marital separation or divorce) may produce a great deal of stress and psychological maladjustment, resulting in adjustment disorder. More intense psychological disorders in response to trauma or excessively stressful situations (such as rape, military combat, imprisonment, being held hostage, relocation, or other disasters) may be categorized as posttraumatic stress disorder. These disorders may involve a variety of symptoms, including intrusive thoughts and repetitive nightmares about the event, intense anxiety, avoidance of stimuli associated with the trauma, increased arousal manifested as chronic tension, irritability, insomnia, impaired concentration and memory, and depression. If the symptoms begin six months or more after the traumatic event, the diagnosis is *delayed* posttraumatic stress disorder. Many factors contribute to breakdown under excessive stress, including the intensity or harshness of the stress situation, the length of the traumatic event, the individual's biological makeup and personality adjustment prior to the stressful situation, and the ways in which the person manages problems once the stressful situation is over. In many cases the symptoms recede as the stress diminishes, especially if the individual is given supportive psychotherapy. In extreme cases, however, there may be residual damage or the disorder may be of the delayed variety, not actually occurring until some time after the trauma.

The treatment of stress-related psychological problems is most effective when intervention is applied early. Crisis intervention therapy, a brief problem-focused counseling approach, may aid a victim of a traumatic event in readjusting to life after the stressful situation has ended. In some situations it may be possible to prevent maladaptive responses to stress by preparing an individual in advance to deal with the stress. This approach to stress management has been shown to be effective in cases where the individual is facing a known traumatic event, such as major surgery or the breakup of a relationship. In these cases a professional attempts to prepare the individual in advance to cope better with the stressful event through developing more realistic and adaptive attitudes about the problem.

Posttraumatic stress disorder has been used frequently in recent criminal and civil court cases to explain deviant behavior or to justify compensation for perceived damages. The extent to which this psychological disorder has been successfully used in court has varied. In some situations, especially when extreme trauma has been involved, the maladaptive behavior is readily explainable in terms of the traumatic event. In other situations, however, a causal link between maladaptive behavior and a traumatic event has been difficult to establish.

Key Terms

stressors (p. 140)
stress (p. 140)
coping strategies (p. 140)
eustress (p. 140)
distress (p. 140)
stress tolerance (p. 144)
crisis (p. 145)
crisis intervention (p. 146)
task-oriented response (p. 147)
defense-oriented response (p. 147)
decompensation (p. 148)
general adaptation syndrome (p. 149)
adjustment disorder (p. 151)
posttraumatic stress disorder (PTSD) (p. 156)
disaster syndrome (p. 157)
stress inoculation training (p. 177)

Chapter 6

Anxiety-based Disorders

Vojislav Jakíc, *Les Effrayants Insectes Cornus*. Jakíc (b. 1932), the son of a Montenegrin priest, was raised in a small town in Serbia. Ostracized as a boy by his peers because of his ethnic background, he developed an introverted personality. While at school, Jakíc became aware of his artistic ability. He began art studies in Belgrade at the age of 20. Thereafter, his life was marked by chronic illness, poverty, and lack of recognition, as well as by increasing paranoia.

In our discussion of stress and different reactions to it, we dealt primarily with stable people who had been subjected to excessive stressor demands. In this chapter we will look at disorders in which maladaptive reaction patterns—the beginnings of which are often evident early in life—have resulted in persistent vulnerability to experience fear or anxiety when facing *everyday* problems. In these cases ordinary methods of coping, including the "normal" use of ego-defense mechanisms, have proven inadequate, and an individual either experiences disabling anxiety or increasingly relies on more extreme defensive reactions. Although these defenses may help ward off acute feelings of threat, they exact a high price in ineffective and self-defeating behavior.

Neurotic behavior—the exaggerated use of avoidance behaviors and defense mechanisms—is clearly maladaptive. It does not, however, typically involve gross distortion of reality or marked personality disorganization, nor is it likely to result in violence to the individual or to others. Rather, we are dealing here with individuals who are typically fearful, ineffective, unhappy, and often guilt-ridden; they do not ordinarily require hospitalization but nevertheless are in need of therapy. Incidence rates are difficult to determine, but it has been estimated that between 8 and 25 percent of American adults—a reasonable guess is some 30 million people—suffer from one of the many variants of neurotic disorder (Dohrenwend et al., 1980; National Institute of Mental Health, 1985b; Robins et al., 1984).

The term **neurosis** was coined by Englishman William Cullen and first used in his *System of Nosology,* published in 1769, to refer to disordered sensations of the nervous system. It reflected the long-held belief that neurological malfunction must be involved in neurotic behavior. This belief endured until the time of Freud, himself a neurologist, who postulated that neurosis stems from intrapsychic conflict rather than a physically disordered nervous system. Specifically, Freud held that neurosis is the outcome of an inner conflict involving an unbearable wish (approach tendency of the id) and the ego's and superego's prohibitions against its expression (avoidance tendency). **Anxiety**—a general feeling of fear and apprehension—is central to this formulation. It is both a signal provided by the ego that a dangerous impulse has been activated and the motivational force behind the deployment of

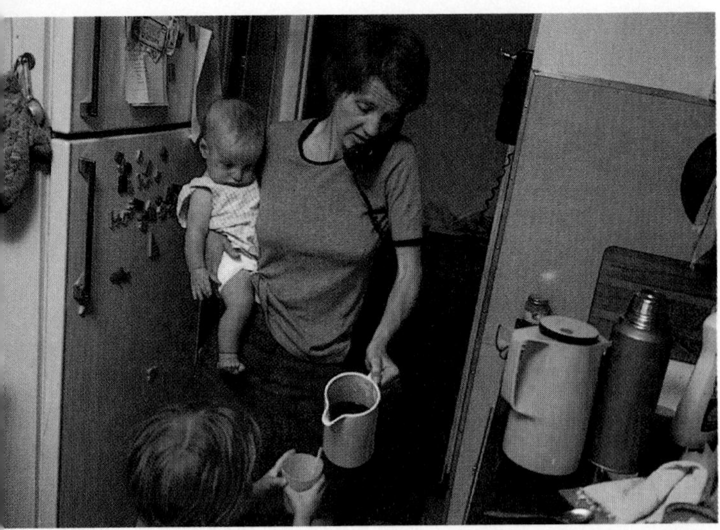

Most people handle everyday problems—such as the demands of their family—with a variety of "normal" ego-defense mechanisms. Individuals with anxiety-based disorders, on the other hand, experience disabling fear or rely on extreme defensive reactions in response to life stress.

defenses. Thus for Freud neurosis consists of an intrapsychic approach-avoidance conflict, psychological in nature. It is acquired during a developmental process involving excessive, impulse-generated anxiety and maladaptive efforts to cope with it. The symptoms traditionally ascribed to neurosis are the outward manifestations of the conflict raging within. Over time Freud's conception of neurosis has tended to become its definition.

As we will see, the prominence Freud gave to anxiety is readily understood when we consider the frequency and intensity with which anxiety is manifested in many of the disorders traditionally classified as *neurotic*. The other components Freud claimed as intrinsic to neurosis are typically much less obvious. As such, Freud's overall views on the nature of neuroses have come under attack as being too theoretical, referring as they do to essentially unobservable inner states and events. The original meaning of the term *neurotic* also became clouded as it entered the popular lexicon. Responding to these concerns, the authors of DSM-III and its 1987 revision (DSM-III-R) pursued the theoretically neutral course of abandoning (except in parenthetical phrases) the term *neurosis* and its derivatives. Instead, they favored descriptions of specific symptom syndromes, most of which had previously been considered as diverse manifestations of a generic "neurotic" condition. These syndromes are now grouped into three general classes according to the predominant symptoms overtly displayed: anxiety, somatoform, or dissociative.

The new DSM classification has provoked some controversy from those committed to a psychodynamic, especially Freudian, position because many consider the concept of neurosis the crowning achievement of psychoanalytic theory. That is, some have seen the change as a broad attack on their fundamental ideological tenets (Bayer & Spitzer, 1985; Millon, 1986). We will address this matter again in the Unresolved Issues section, but such questions ultimately must and will be settled, if at all, on the basis of superior empirical evidence. In the meantime these questions should perhaps not be co-opted by issues of nomenclature. By the same token, we find ourselves not quite ready to join in a fervent rejection of all things psychodynamic that we detect in some of our colleagues, as will be clear in this chapter. Our decision to retain the overarching term *neurosis* (and its derivatives) is in part a concession to this conservative bent but is also motivated by our lingering doubts that the disorders to be considered here are as discrete and discontinuous as current nomenclature suggests. In particular many of them seem to be driven and fueled by anxiety, even where anxiety may not be a striking or obvious element in their clinical pictures.

Given this hypothesis, we will begin by discussing the nature of anxiety as an emotional state to which humans seem all too vulnerable. We will then move to a description of the DSM categories subsumed under anxiety, somatoform, and dissociative disorders. From there we will consider whether or not less severe or asymptomatic forms of these disorders exist in the guise of neurotic styles. We will then look at specific causal factors in this range of disorders, typical methods of treatment, and treatment outcomes.

THE ANXIETY-RESPONSE PATTERN

The task of defining *anxiety* in explicit terms is a difficult one. Most of us have an intuitive appreciation of what anxiety is, based largely on direct experience with the obtrusive and usually quite unpleasant inner state the term signifies. The experience, including its perceived autonomic nervous system components, shares many properties with that of fear; in the case of the latter, however, the source or the instigating circumstances are normally quite clear to us and we know that the danger would be regarded as objectively real by most people. With anxiety, we frequently cannot specify clearly what the danger is, and if we can, we are painfully aware that others do not understand the "problem." It is as though we are anticipating some dreadful happening not objectively predictable from our actual circumstances, a quality recognized in the widespread use of the term *apprehension* to describe the state.

Animal experimentation going back many decades has established that the basic fear-response pattern is highly conditionable—that is, it can readily be transferred to previously neutral stimuli by promptly and repeatedly linking the occurrences of these stimuli with painful events, such as electric shocks. Of course, few human infants or children are subjected to electric shocks, but many have experiences that are inherently fear-inspiring; and, as we have increasingly discovered in recent years, some have unspeakably cruel and terrifying experiences visited upon them by disturbed parents or other adults. In such situations a wide variety of inherently non-noxious stimuli may come, accidentally as it were, to serve as cues that something threatening and unpleasant is about to happen. The stimuli thus become, themselves, fear-invoking. In addition, we have at the human level the enormously complicating feature of a richly elaborate mental life, such that fleeting impressions, thoughts, images, and indeed even acquired mental associations to them may (like the external stimuli in animal experiments) become capable of eliciting the fear-response pattern—or what in this case would be experienced as *anxiety*. In this scenario any type of stimulus, mental or physiological, regularly preceding a full-blown anxiety episode would be expected to acquire in itself the tendency to elicit anxiety.

This relatively straightforward and doubtless somewhat oversimplified account of the origins of human anxiety is consistent in its main outlines with the conclusions reached in a comprehensive analysis recently offered by David Barlow (1988). Barlow presents a model of the genesis of anxiety as involving biological, psychological, and environmental events that, when "lined up" in a mutually facilitative way, become a self-sustaining feedback system—an **anxiety-response pattern** of sorts. The cognitive and emotional core of this system, strengthened by repeated "alarm" experiences (physiological arousal cues) in contexts construed as unpredictable and uncontrollable, becomes stored in long-term memory. There it may undergo further pathological elaboration through the formation of new associative networks. Once the pattern is established, its automatic nature makes it immune to rational processing, and cognitive reappraisals based on new experiences are difficult to arrange. At an advanced stage, then, systematic therapeutic intervention to disrupt the feedback system becomes a challenging task. That task is complicated by the fact that, by this point, many severely anxiety-prone patients will have developed an array of avoidant-defensive behaviors, typically with redundant backups, that are in themselves maladaptive and that effectively defeat countermeasures. A phobic patient, for example, will usually have developed a multitude of behavioral strategies to make certain that he or she does not confront the anxiety-provoking circumstance, thus ensuring a lack of corrective experience regarding its benign nature. It will be useful to bear in mind these general features of the anxiety-response pattern as we proceed to examine the recognized clinical disorders of which it is the core element.

ANXIETY DISORDERS

An **anxiety disorder,** as the term suggests, has an unrealistic, irrational fear of disabling intensity at its core and also as its principal and most obvious manifestation. DSM-III-R recognizes seven basic types of anxiety disorder: panic disorder, agoraphobia, phobias of "social" or of "simple" type, obsessive-compulsive disorder, generalized anxiety disorder, and posttraumatic stress disorder. The last of these, basically a delayed reaction to traumatic stressors, was discussed in the preceding chapter and will not be considered here.

Anxiety disorders are relatively common. In the New Haven-Baltimore-St. Louis Epidemiologic Catchment Area program sponsored by the National Institute of Mental Health, phobia was the most common psychiatric disorder reported for women and the second-most common (behind alcohol abuse or dependence) for men. Among women, obsessive-compulsive disorder had a prevalence rate exceeded only by phobia and certain mood disorders (Myers et al., 1984; Robins et al., 1984). Projecting the figures for panic, phobic, and obsessive-compulsive disorders to the entire American population yields a combined estimate of about 15 million cases (National Institute of Mental Health, 1985).

Panic Disorder and Agoraphobia

Diagnostically, **panic disorder** is defined and characterized by the occurrence of one or more "unexpected" panic attacks not triggered by the sufferer's being the focus of others' attentions. The person must have experienced at least four attacks in a four-week period, or, in the case of fewer attacks, must have been fearful of recurrence for at least a month. An attack is defined in terms of a lengthy list of symptoms (such as shortness of breath, palpitations, sweating, dizziness, fear of dying, fear of "going crazy") of which the person must have at least four for the experience to qualify as a full panic episode. Such attacks are normally unexpected in the sense that they do not appear to be provoked by identifiable components of the immediate situation. Their initial appearance, however, often follows earlier-appearing feelings of distress (Lelliott et al., 1989) or some highly stressful life circumstance, such as the loss of an important relationship (Foa, Steketee, & Young, 1984; Pollard, Pollard, & Corn, 1989). A panic attack typically subsides within a few minutes, but the stark terror of those minutes normally precludes any reassurance of a quick end. These two features—the characteristic brevity and the marked intensity of the reaction—distinguish panic disorder from other types of anxiety problems.

The specific fear in **agoraphobia** is that of being in places or situations from which escape would be physically or psychologically difficult, or in which immediate help would be unavailable in the event of some untoward reaction, particularly a panic attack. In short, what agoraphobics fear is fear. They usually fear travel in general, and they commonly avoid cars, buses, airplanes, subway trains, and so on. These individuals are even apt to be uncomfortable venturing outside their homes alone. Other typical sources of difficulty include being in crowded situations or standing in lines.

Mary, the woman shown here, is riding an escalator as part of her therapy in overcoming her agoraphobia. The specific fear in agoraphobia is that of being in places or situations from which escape would be physically or psychologically difficult. Agoraphobic individuals typically avoid crowded situations, standing in line, and vehicles of transportation.

Agoraphobia is a frequent complication of panic disorder, but it can also occur in the absence of prior attacks whose intensity would merit the designation *panic*. In the latter instance a common pattern is that of a gradually spreading fearfulness in which more and more aspects of the environment outside the home acquire threatening properties, a condition informally referred to as *pan-phobia*. In severe cases agoraphobia becomes a terribly confining disorder in which an individual is unable to go beyond the narrow confines of home, or even particular parts of the home.

We consider panic disorders and agoraphobia together because accumulating research evidence suggests that they share some basic properties, including a possible genetic linkage (Noyes et al., 1986). Many people with an agoraphobic pattern report a history of repetitive panic attacks. It appears that in at least some cases agoraphobia develops as a secondary reaction to the experience of panic. That is, an individual fears being "out on the town," especially alone, because he or she is terrified of having a panic attack in public. The DSM-III-R recognizes this link by providing for diagnoses of agoraphobia with and without a history of prior panic attacks. In the former instance, in fact, the primary diagnosis would be that of panic disorder (with agoraphobia).

The case of Anne Watson is in many respects typical of panic disorder with agoraphobia:

Ms. Watson, married mother of two and age 45 at her first clinic contact, experienced her first panic attack some two years earlier, several months after the sudden death of an uncle to whom she had been extremely close while growing up. While returning home from work one evening she had the feeling that she couldn't catch her breath. Immediately thereafter her heart began to pound, she broke out in a cold sweat, and she had a sense of unreality. Feeling immobilized by a leaden quality in her legs, she became certain she would pass out or die before she could reach home. Soliciting help from a passerby, she was able to engage a cab, directing the driver to take her to the nearest hospital emergency room. Her ensuing physical examination revealed no abnormalities apart from a slightly elevated heart rate, which subsided to normal limits before the examination was completed. She regained composure rapidly and was able to return home on her own.

Four weeks later, after the incident had been all but forgotten, Ms. Watson had a second similar attack while at home preparing a meal. Four more occurred in the next several weeks, all of them surprises, and she began to despair about discovering their source. She also noticed that she was becoming anxious about the probability of additional attacks. Consultation with the family physician yielded a diagnosis of "nervous strain" and a prescription for antianxiety medication. The medication made Ms. Watson calmer, but seemed to have no effect on the continuing panics. She discovered alcohol was even more effective than the medication in relieving her tension and began to drink excessively, which only increased the worry and concern of her husband.

As the attacks continued, Ms. Watson began to dread going out of the house alone. She feared that while out she would have an attack and would be stranded and helpless. She stopped riding the subway to work out of fear she might be trapped in a car between stops when an attack struck, preferring instead to walk the 20 blocks between her home and work. She also severely curtailed her social and recreational activities—previously frequent and enjoyed—because an attack might occur, necessitating an abrupt and embarrassing flight from the scene. When household duties and the like required brief driving excursions, she surreptitiously put these off until she could be accompanied by one of the children or a neighbor. Despite these drastic alterations of life-style and her growing unhappiness and desperation, however, she remained her normal self when at home or when her husband accompanied her away from home.

On the advice of the family physician, Ms. Watson began psychotherapy sessions with a psychiatrist. While she found these sessions, which were entirely verbal and nonspecific in focus, helpful in a number of ways, they had no apparent effect on the frequency or intensity of her panic attacks. About a year later she read an article describing a clinic program for agoraphobia. She decided to apply.

The clinic program was engaged in an evaluation of the efficacy of antidepressant medication (imipramine [Tofranil]) in the treatment of panic disorder, encouraging reports of which had begun to appear in the professional literature. After some initial difficulties in establishing an optimal dosage level, Ms. Watson ceased reporting further panic attacks. Within eight months she had resumed all of her former activities, stopped drinking, and reduced her antianxiety medication to a minimal level. She was enjoying life again and reported being back to her "old self." (Adapted from Spitzer et al., 1983.)

It should be noted that the relatively rapid resolution of Ms. Watson's difficulties through the use of antidepressant medication is not necessarily typical. Although these drugs do sometimes suppress panic attacks, their precise mode of action in doing so is unknown. Also, troublesome side effects (such as blurring of vision) are common in such treatment, causing many patients to tolerate recommended dosages poorly and thus to stop taking the drugs (Mavissakalian & Perel, 1989). Many behaviorally oriented clinicians question the wisdom of using these potent medications as the initial treatment for difficulties of this sort; they point to the established efficacy of certain specialized programs that treat patients through controlled exposure to the avoided situations (e.g., Barlow & Waddell, 1985; Barlow & Cerny, 1988). We will have more to say about treatment issues in a later section.

Other Phobic Disorders

Traditionally, a **phobia** is a persistent and disproportionate fear of some specific object or situation that presents little or no actual danger to a person. Recalling our earlier discussion on the nature of the anxiety-response pattern, phobia victims literally but involuntarily "psyche" themselves into their problems. This traditional concept is most closely approximated by the DSM-III-R diagnosis of **simple phobia.** The clinical picture in this type of problem is described in the next few paragraphs.

The following list of the common phobias and their objects will give some hint of the variety of situations and events around which simple phobias may be centered:

Acrophobia—high places
Algophobia—pain
Astraphobia—storms, thunder, and lightning
Claustrophobia—closed places
Hematophobia—blood
Monophobia—being alone

Mysophobia—contamination or germs
Nyctophobia—darkness
Ochlophobia—crowds
Pathophobia—disease
Pyrophobia—fire
Syphilophobia—syphilis
Zoophobia—animals or some particular animal

Some of these phobias involve an exaggerated fear of things that most of us fear to some extent, such as darkness, fires, disease, spiders, and snakes. Others, such as phobias of open places or crowds, involve situations that do not elicit fear in most people. Some evidence (e.g., Cook, Hodes, & Lang, 1986; Tomarken, Mineka, & Cook, 1989) suggests that phobic reactions to objectively fearful objects are more readily acquired and less readily extinguished than those to more benign stimuli.

Phobic disorders are more common among adolescents and young adults than among older people. They are also, as earlier indicated, more frequently diagnosed in females than in males, possibly because strong fears have traditionally been more compatible with female roles than with male roles in our society. Of course, most of us have minor irrational fears, but in phobic disorders such fears are intense and interfere with everyday activities. For example, phobic individuals may go to great lengths to avoid entering a small room or passageway, even when they must. People who suffer from phobias usually admit that they have no real cause to fear the object or situation, but they say that they cannot help themselves. If they attempt to approach the phobic situation, they are overcome with anxiety, which may vary from mild feelings of uneasiness and distress to a full-fledged anxiety attack verging on panic.

Phobic individuals usually show a wide range of other symptoms in addition to their phobias, such as tension headaches, back pains, stomach upsets, dizzy spells, and fears of "cracking up." At times of more acute panic, such individuals often complain of depersonalization phenomena and of feelings of unreality, strangeness, and "not being themselves." Depression frequently accompanies phobias, and many patients report serious interpersonal difficulties, some of them doubtless the result of the impatience of significant others with the victims' irrational fears. In some instances, phobics also have serious difficulty in making decisions—a condition that Kaufmann (1973) somewhat facetiously called *decidophobia.* Here we may be touching on a seeming connection between phobias and obsessions.

The particular phobias that develop are often influenced by cultural factors. For example, a phobia of flying was quite unlikely until we entered the age of commercial air travel. In some cases, phobic

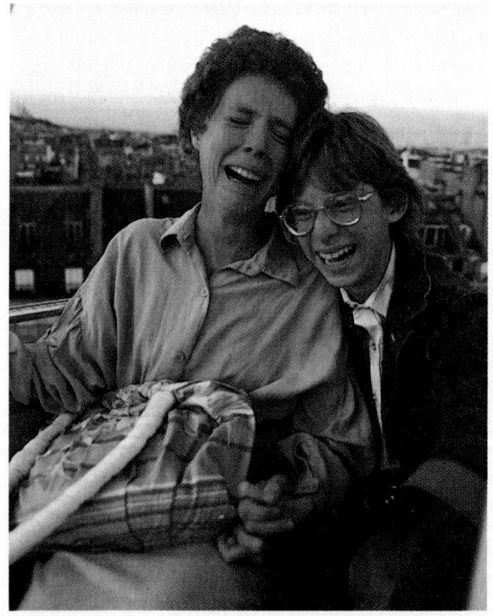

Phobias come in many shapes and sizes. Fear of flying is such a common phobia that a number of classes and programs have been developed to help aerophobics, such as the man shown here, overcome their fears. The woman on the ferris wheel is exhibiting the intense fear of height that is characteristic of acrophobia.

reactions may also be obsessive, as when a persistent, obsessive fear of contamination dominates a neurotic individual's behavior and consciousness. In such a case the DSM-III-R requires consideration of an *obsessive-compulsive* diagnosis (to be discussed in a subsequent section). In certain instances a phobia is a rather transparent displacement; a person substitutes a more "acceptable" fear-inspiring object or situation for one whose acknowledgment would be difficult or painful. The classic example here is that of a woman who develops a phobia of public places because of a fear that she may yield to the blandishments of men who may try to "pick her up."

Regardless of how it begins, phobic behavior tends to be reinforced by the reduction in anxiety that occurs each time an individual avoids a feared situation. In addition, phobias may be maintained in part by secondary gains (benefits derived from being disabled), such as increased attention, sympathy, and some control over the behavior of others. For example, a phobia of driving may enable a homemaker to escape from responsibilities outside the home, such as grocery shopping or transporting children to and from school. If the homemaker should also happen to feel chronic anger toward her unhelpful spouse, who must now pick up these chores, so much the better for phobia maintenance. Phobias, then, in addition to being primary manifestations of irrational, acquired fears, may sometimes serve the interests of seemingly remote objectives, although usually without the sufferer's awareness. Since the net effect of phobias, especially the more expansive ones, is to render the victim "helpless," they draw our attention in particular to a secondary gain hypothesis involving the avoidance of adult independence and responsibility. Our experience has frequently (but not always) confirmed such a hypothesis in careful clinical assessment, where it may also appear that other members of a family have a stake in maintaining the phobic individual's helplessness. The sometimes complicated ways in which phobic behavior may become involved in other personal and interpersonal issues is illustrated in the following case:

An intelligent, well-educated married woman in her mid-30s complained of marked fear, bordering on panic, of driving her auto in unfamiliar neighborhoods, riding in elevators, flying, and entering tall buildings and shopping centers. During the initial interview she revealed that she had had these fears for some 18 years. For this entire period, except since her marriage two years earlier, she had been in almost continuous treatment. A succession of reputable therapists had employed widely differing modes of intervention, including psychoanalysis and certain behavior therapy techniques. None of these measures had brought significant relief, and by this point the patient had become so adept at "managing" therapists that she could usually maintain their interest in "taking care of her" over considerable periods without seriously attempting to resolve her difficulties. At the outset, then, the situation appeared rather unpromising for a renewed attempt at therapy.

The history revealed a long series of dependent relationships, chiefly with males (including male therapists), culminating in marriage to an older, previously married professional man. Initially the husband had appeared "strong" although somewhat given to tyrannical outbursts; over time, this strength proved to be largely an illusion. As the husband's appearance of strength had evaporated, the wife's phobic symptoms had returned and increased in severity over time, driving her back into therapy once again. With the wife's increase in phobic symptoms, the husband's life had become more frantic and hectic, since he had had to assume many of the household responsibilities she could no longer perform. The marital relationship had deteriorated rapidly under the assault of these conflicting interests. This collapse was accelerated in the wife's case by the emergence of increasingly disabling symptoms and in the husband's by a return after long abstinence to excessive alcohol consumption, accompanied by verbal and moderate physical abuse of his now "helpless" wife.

A relatively clear understanding of the intermeshing of these contributory factors, together with some confidence (in light of her history) that standard treatment would almost certainly fail, encouraged the therapist to intervene forcefully into this complicated situation. For example, he largely ignored the patient's fears and insisted on discussing her relationship with her husband, who was also summoned to attend some therapy sessions. As was expected, the patient became markedly dependent on the therapist as her condition improved—to the extent that she continued to complain of phobias even after her phobic behavior had essentially disappeared. Meanwhile, her marital situation became more stable as she came to accept and even be sympathetic toward her husband's insecurities.

At the point where a relative marital tranquility and mutual support had been reestablished, the therapist, after weighing options and possible consequences, unilaterally terminated further therapy sessions; this unusual step was taken to abort the client's growing dependency on the therapist. He assured the surprised and doubtful client that there was no need for further therapy and that any remaining fears would clear up spontaneously. Several weeks later, the client telephoned to say cheerfully that, in fact, they had. Informal long-term follow-up indicates that this client continues to do well.

Although some phobias, once established, remain fairly circumscribed, others, as we have seen, tend to "spread" or generalize to additional situations, possibly because of an "incubation" effect that is thought to occur with some types of anxiety (Eysenck, 1976). The following case illustrates this spreading effect:

An 18-year-old woman had been given strict "moral" training concerning the evils of sex, and she associated sexual relations with vivid ideas of sin, guilt, and hell. This basic orientation was reinforced when she was beaten and sexually attacked by a young man on her fifteenth birthday. Nevertheless, when the young man she was dating kissed her and "held her close," it aroused intense sexual desires. These desires were extremely guilt arousing, however, and led to a chain of avoidance behaviors. First she stopped seeing the man in an effort to get rid of her "immoral" thoughts; then she stopped all dating; then she began to feel uncomfortable with any young man she knew; and finally she became fearful of any social situations where men might be present. At this point, her life was largely dominated by her phobias and she was so "completely miserable" that she requested professional help.

The case just described verges, in DSM terms, into **social phobia.** Criteria for this diagnosis emphasize (a) a fear of situations in which one is exposed to focused scrutiny by others, and (b) the corollary fear that one may do something or act in such a manner as to risk humiliation or embarrassment. Probably a far more common type of social phobia is what is commonly known as stage fright, which can mount to levels rendering performance impossible or at least markedly impaired. The following case is illustrative:

Social phobia consists of a fear of being in situations in which one is exposed to focused scrutiny by others and the corollary fear that one may do something or act in such a manner as to risk humiliation or embarrassment. The most common type of social phobia is probably stage fright, which can render performance virtually impossible in some cases.

An intelligent, recently-divorced mother of two young children sought consultation because she "froze" whenever asked to audition for membership in local orchestral groups. An accomplished cellist, performing with this instrument had been one of her few reliable sources of satisfaction, self-esteem, and genuine recreation during her adult years. She had tried various methods of self-help, including commercially available tape recordings purporting to teach relaxation, to no avail. On initial interview, she appeared unusually tense and anxious, and it rapidly became clear that she regarded the interview as another "performance" in which she was under scrutiny. A gently-framed invitation for her to consider this "hypothesis" produced confirmation but no discernible tension reduction.

The client suggested hypnosis as a treatment approach in an obvious effort to circumvent the discomfort she felt in relating to the therapist in normal conversation. The therapist was willing to consider this mode but suspected that the question of her hypnotizability would be experienced as another performance demand resulting in the characteristic disabling anxiety. A brief test of hypnotic responsivity confirmed this suspicion.

There was no change in situational anxiety level in a series of brief additional appointments deliberately planned to desensitize the client to the treatment situation; in fact, the client canceled and rescheduled several of these. Finally, the client was provided with a tailor-made (with the therapist as trainer) relaxation-training tape and instructions to practice on a regular basis at home, recontacting the therapist when she felt she had made some progress and was ready for the next step. She has not been heard from since.

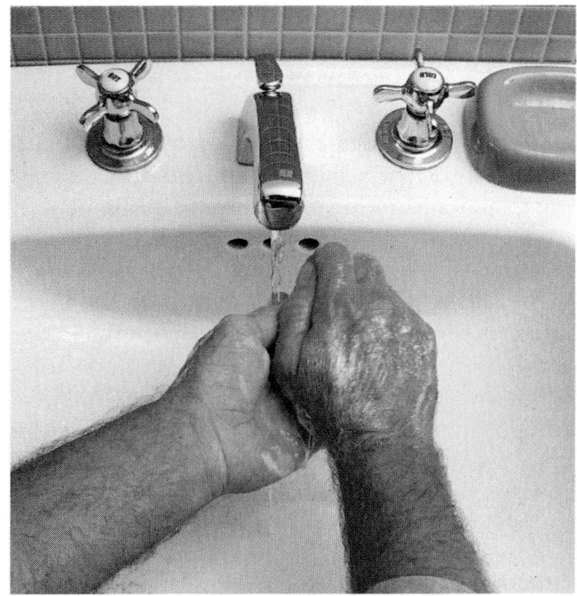

Many of us show some compulsive behavior, but people with compulsive disorders feel compelled to perform repeatedly some act that seems pointless and absurd even to them and that they in some sense do not want to perform, such as washing one's hands as often as six times each hour.

Fortunately, the type of treatment complication encountered here, where the client's principal difficulty negatively impacts the treatment process, is not especially typical for the treatment of social phobia. On the contrary, a relatively good treatment outcome for this disorder can normally be anticipated, although especially intense fears of negative evaluation, as in this case, may limit long-term treatment efficacy (Mattick, Peters, & Clarke, 1989).

Obsessive-Compulsive Disorder

An **obsession** is a persistent preoccupation with a certain mental content, typically an idea or a feeling. A **compulsion** is an impulse to engage in some behavior experienced as irresistible. Thus in **obsessive-compulsive disorder** (OCD) individuals feel compelled to think about something that they do not want to think about or to carry out some action, often pointlessly ritualistic, seemingly against their own will. These individuals, usually having high levels of manifest anxiety, realize that their behavior is irrational but cannot seem to control it. The DSM-III-R diagnosis requires that this involuntary behavior cause marked distress to an individual, consume excessive time, or interfere with occupational or social functioning.

Estimates from the Epidemiologic Catchment Area study, expanded to five widely dispersed American communities, indicate that obsessive-compulsive disorder is more prevalent than was once thought. Specifically, the lifetime prevalence rate (which somewhat underestimates the incidence rate because as yet unaffected younger subjects remain at risk) of OCD in this composite sample was 2.5 percent, with divorced (or separated) and unemployed people being somewhat overrepresented (Karno et al., 1988). This figure translates to a U.S. population estimate in excess of 6 million cases. Also contrary to earlier reports suggesting a preponderance of OCD among females, these newer figures show no gender difference after correcting for marital status. The disorder is not uncommon in children, where its symptoms are strikingly similar to those of adult cases (Swedo et al., 1989). As Nemiah (1967) has pointed out, obsessive-compulsive behaviors cover a wide range:

The phenomena may be manifested psychically or behaviorally; they may be experienced as ideas or as impulses; they may refer to events anticipated in the future or actions already completed; they may express desires and wishes or protective measures against such desires; they may be simple, uncomplicated acts and ideas or elaborate, ritualized patterns of thinking and behavior. . . . (p. 916)

Most of us have experienced minor obsessive thoughts, such as persistent thoughts about a coming trip or a haunting melody that we cannot seem to get out of our minds. In the case of obsessive reactions, however, the thoughts are much more persistent, appear irrational to the individual, and interfere considerably with everyday behavior. Neurotic obsessive thoughts may center around a variety of topics, such as a concern over bodily functions, committing immoral acts, attempting suicide, or even finding the solution to some seemingly unsolvable problem. Particularly common are obsessive thoughts of committing some immoral act. A wife may be obsessed with the idea of poisoning her husband; a daughter may constantly imagine pushing her mother down a flight of stairs.

Even though obsessive thoughts are usually not carried out in action, they remain a source of often excruciating torment to an individual. This pattern is well illustrated in a classic case described by Kraines (1948) of a woman who

complained of having "terrible thoughts." When she thought of her boyfriend she wished he were dead; when her mother went down the stairs, she "wished she'd fall and break her neck"; when her sister spoke of going to the beach with her infant daughter, the patient "hoped that they would both drown." These thoughts "make me hysterical. I love them; why should I wish such terrible things to happen? It drives me wild, makes me feel I'm crazy and don't belong to society; maybe it's best for me to end it all than to go on thinking such terrible things about those I love." (p. 183)

As is the case with obsessive thoughts, many of us show some compulsive behavior—stepping over cracks in sidewalks, checking to see that a door is locked immediately after having locked it, or making multiple backups of our computer files—but without the degree of compulsiveness of a neurotic individual. Most of us also resort to minor obsessive-compulsive patterns under severe pressure or when trying to achieve goals that we consider of critical importance. Many historical figures have shown an "obsessive-compulsive" adherence to their goals despite discouragement and ridicule: Columbus persisted for 18 years in his efforts to secure financial backing for his expedition to "India," and Darwin assembled evidence for 22 years before he would present his ideas on evolution. Goal-directedness is a distinguishing feature of such persistence.

In contrast, people with compulsive disorders feel compelled to perform repeatedly some act that seems pointless and absurd even to them and that they in some sense do not want to perform. These compulsive acts vary from relatively mild ritual-like behavior, such as checking to be sure that the free ends of a shoelace are exactly the same length, to more extreme behavior, such as washing one's hands as often as six times each hour. They can involve actual physical acts or can be essentially cognitive in nature, involving feelings and thoughts (see *HIGHLIGHT 6.1*). The performance of the compulsive act or the ritualized series of acts usually brings a feeling of reduced tension and satisfaction (Carr, 1971; Hodgson & Rachman, 1972). On the other hand, anxiety mounts if the person tries to resist the compulsion.

An obsessive-compulsive disorder is considered maladaptive because it represents irrational and exaggerated behavior in the face of stressors that are not unduly upsetting to most people. In addition, such patterns reduce the efficiency and flexibility of behavior and the capability for self-direction. Generally, people exhibiting such behavior are characterized by feelings of inadequacy and insecurity, rigid and perfectionistic conscience development, a tendency toward feelings of guilt, and high vulnerability to threat. In short, these people appear chronically overaroused, unable to relax (Turner et al., 1985).

As in all of the anxiety disorders, certain maladaptive personality characteristics show up at greater than expected rates in the backgrounds of affected people. Significantly, a large proportion of obsessive-compulsive individuals are found to have been unusually preoccupied with issues of control long before their symptoms appeared. These individuals often have histories suggesting marked discomfort in any situation in which they felt they were not in control of the events immediately around them. The following case is illustrative:

Prior to his hospitalization, this patient had his life ordered in minute detail. He arose in the morning precisely at 6:50, took a shower, shaved, and dressed. His wife had breakfast ready precisely at 7:10 and followed a menu that he worked out months in advance. At exactly 7:45, he left for the office where he worked as an accountant. He came home precisely at 5:55, washed, read

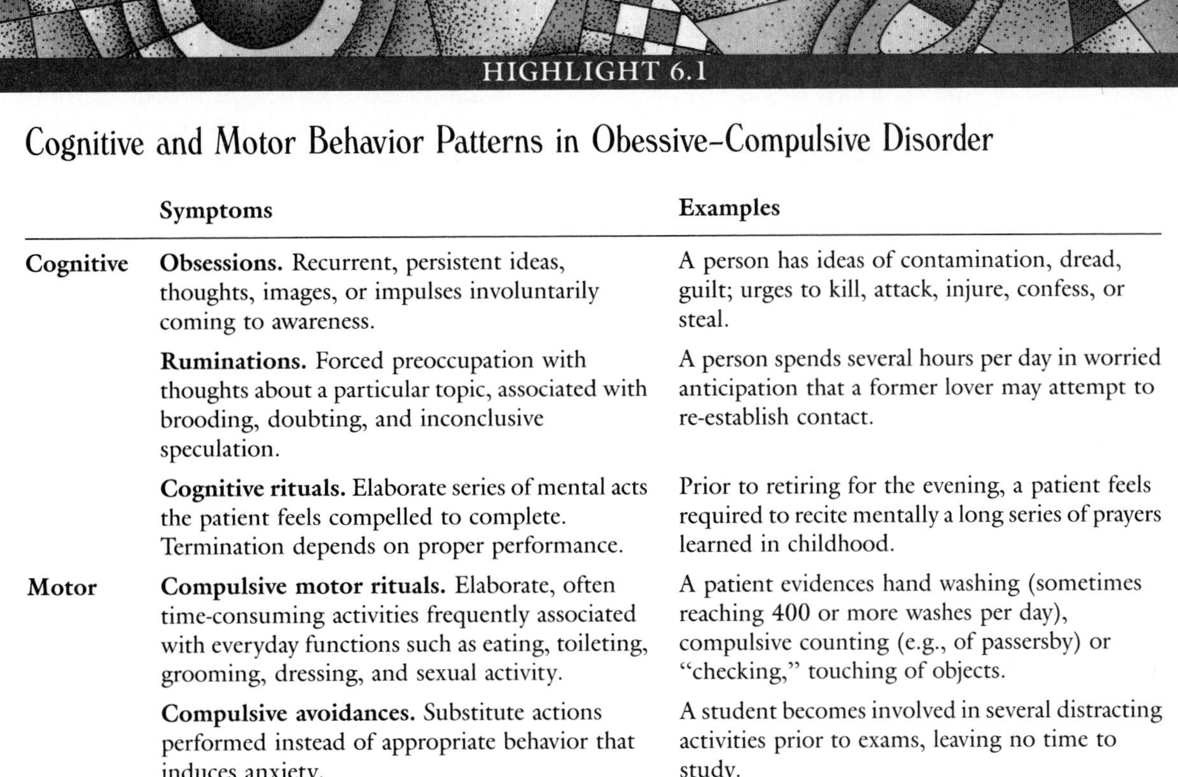

HIGHLIGHT 6.1

Cognitive and Motor Behavior Patterns in Obsessive-Compulsive Disorder

	Symptoms	Examples
Cognitive	**Obsessions.** Recurrent, persistent ideas, thoughts, images, or impulses involuntarily coming to awareness.	A person has ideas of contamination, dread, guilt; urges to kill, attack, injure, confess, or steal.
	Ruminations. Forced preoccupation with thoughts about a particular topic, associated with brooding, doubting, and inconclusive speculation.	A person spends several hours per day in worried anticipation that a former lover may attempt to re-establish contact.
	Cognitive rituals. Elaborate series of mental acts the patient feels compelled to complete. Termination depends on proper performance.	Prior to retiring for the evening, a patient feels required to recite mentally a long series of prayers learned in childhood.
Motor	**Compulsive motor rituals.** Elaborate, often time-consuming activities frequently associated with everyday functions such as eating, toileting, grooming, dressing, and sexual activity.	A patient evidences hand washing (sometimes reaching 400 or more washes per day), compulsive counting (e.g., of passersby) or "checking," touching of objects.
	Compulsive avoidances. Substitute actions performed instead of appropriate behavior that induces anxiety.	A student becomes involved in several distracting activities prior to exams, leaving no time to study.

the evening paper, and had dinner precisely at 6:30, again as per menu. His schedule was equally well worked out for evenings and weekends, with a movie on Tuesday, reading on Wednesday, rest on Monday and Thursday, and bridge on Friday. Saturday morning he played golf and Sunday morning and evening he attended church. Saturday evening usually involved having guests or visiting others. He was also fastidious in his dress. Each shirt had to be clean and unwrinkled, his suit pressed every two days, and so on. His demands, of course, also meant close supervision of his wife, who was inclined to be easygoing and was upset when he "blew up" at the smallest variation from established routine.

By means of his carefully ordered existence, the patient had managed to make a reasonably successful adjustment until he became involved in a business deal with a friend and lost a large sum of money. This loss proved too much for him and led to a severe anxiety reaction with considerable agitation and depression, necessitating hospitalization.

In this case we assume that the patient's need to be in utter control of his life was driven by anxiety over being controlled by something or someone else. When his ordered existence in fact failed to protect him from another's exploitation, he fell apart.

Quite often the intense concern with self-imposed control in a pre-obsessive-compulsive person takes the form of exaggerated perfectionism or concerns that his or her actions may lead to terrible consequences. The following case illustrates this characteristic and also indicates how intractable and persistent this disorder may become:

A 32-year-old high school cooking teacher developed marked feelings of guilt and uneasiness, accompanied by obsessive fears of hurting others by touching them or by their handling something she had touched. She dreaded having anyone eat anything she had prepared, and if students in her cooking class were absent, she was certain they had been poisoned by her cook-

ing. In addition, she developed the obsessive notion that a rash at the base of her scalp was a manifestation of syphilis, which would gnaw at her brain and make her a "drooling idiot."

Accompanying these obsessive fears were compulsions consisting primarily of repeated hand-washings and frequent returns to some act already performed, such as turning off gas or water, to reassure herself that the act had been done right.

In treatment the patient was self-centered but highly sensitive and conscientious. She had graduated from college with honors and considered herself highly intelligent. About three years before her present difficulties she had married a noncollege man of whom she had been ashamed because of his poor English, bad table manners, and lack of other characteristics she thought important to a good social showing. As a result she had rejected him in her thinking and behavior and had treated him in what she now considered a cruel manner. On one occasion she had also been unfaithful to him, which was directly opposed to her moral upbringing and values.

Over a period of time, however, she came to realize that he was a fine person and that other people thought highly of him despite his lack of social polish. In addition, she gradually came to the realization that she was very much in love with him. At this point she began to reproach herself for her cruel treatment. She felt that he was a truly wonderful husband, and that she was completely unworthy of him. She was sure her past cruelty and unfaithfulness could never be forgiven. "Heaven knows that every word he says is worth fifty words I say. If I were real honest and truthful I would tell my husband to leave me."

In some cases of obsessive-compulsive disorder, the preexisting behavior seems to involve problems in the control of aggression. Many parents, for instance, have fleeting thoughts and fantasies about harming their children. Fortunately, these thoughts are only rarely expressed in action, and most such parents are amused or at least not frightened by these impulses. Others are less successful in managing their hostility, as the following case illustrates:

A farmer developed obsessive thoughts of hitting his 3-year-old son on the head with a hammer. The father was completely unable to explain his "horrible thoughts." He stated that he loved his son very much and thought he must be going insane to harbor such thoughts. In the treatment of this case, it was revealed that the patient's wife had suffered great pain in childbirth and had since refused sexual relations with him for fear of again becoming pregnant. In addition, she lavished most of her attention on the son, and their previously happy marriage was now torn with quarreling and bickering.

It appears here that the farmer could not be sufficiently assertive either to allow himself to experience his resentment toward his son or to confront his wife on needed changes in their relationship. His feelings could emerge only in seemingly automatic, alien thoughts. As with neuroses in general, persons having OCD seem unable to take the direct steps needed to diminish or resolve their difficulties; on the contrary, they regularly dig deeper holes for themselves.

Generalized Anxiety Disorder

Unlike other neurotic patterns, generalized anxiety disorder does not include in its behavioral profile any effective anxiety-avoidance mechanisms. Thus although victims of other disorders to some extent allay their anxieties, feelings of threat and anxiety are the central feature of generalized anxiety disorder.

Generalized anxiety disorder is characterized by chronic excessive worry, traditionally described as free-floating anxiety. While the disorder is common, precise prevalence rates are unavailable. DSM-III-R criteria specify that the worry must last at least six months and not be confined to a single life circumstance. Its content may not be related to another, concurrent Axis I disorder, such as the possibility of a panic attack. The subjective experience of worry must also be accompanied by at least six of the following symptoms:

Motor tension

- Trembly, twitchy, "shaky" feeling
- Tense, aching, sore muscles
- Restlessness
- Easy fatigability

Vigilance and scanning

- "Keyed up," "on edge" feeling
- Exaggerated startle response
- Difficulty sleeping

- Concentration problems
- Irritability

Autonomic hyperactivity

- Shortness of breath, feeling of "smothering"
- Rapid pulse, palpitations
- Sweating, clammy hands
- Dry mouth
- Dizziness, lightheadedness
- Nausea, diarrhea, other gastrointestinal distress
- Hot flashes or chills
- Frequent urination
- Trouble swallowing, lump in throat

Although the diagnostic criteria in this clinical picture are silent about occasional flare-ups of intense anxiety (indistinguishable from "panic" as previously described), such attacks are known to be quite common—as indeed they are in the anxiety disorders generally (Barlow et al., 1985).

Individuals suffering from generalized anxiety disorder live in a relatively constant state of tension, worry, and diffuse uneasiness. They are oversensitive in interpersonal relationships and frequently feel inadequate and depressed. Usually they have difficulty concentrating and making decisions, dreading to make a mistake. The high level of tension they experience is often reflected in strained postural movements, overreaction to sudden or unexpected stimuli, and continual nervous movements. Commonly, they complain of muscular tension, especially in the neck and upper shoulder region, chronic mild diarrhea, frequent urination, and sleep disturbances that include insomnia and nightmares. They perspire profusely and their palms are often clammy; they may show cardiovascular changes such as elevated blood pressure and increased pulse rate. They may experience breathlessness and heart palpitations for no apparent reason.

No matter how well things seem to be going, individuals with generalized anxiety disorder are apprehensive and anxious. Their vague fears and fantasies—some examples of which are given in *HIGHLIGHT 6.2*—combined with their general sensitivity keep them continually upset, uneasy, and discouraged. Not only do they have difficulty making decisions, but after decisions have been made they worry endlessly over possible errors and unforeseen circumstances that may prove the decisions wrong and lead to disaster. They have no appreciation of the logic most of us use in concluding that it is pointless to torment ourselves about possible outcomes over which we have absolutely no control.

Generalized anxiety disorder is characterized by chronic unrealistic or excessive worry. Individuals suffering from generalized anxiety disorder live in a relatively constant state of tension, worry, and diffuse uneasiness.

The lengths to which they go to find things to worry about are remarkable; as fast as one cause for worry is removed, they find another, until relatives and friends lose patience with them.

Even after going to bed, people who suffer from generalized anxiety disorder are not likely to find relief from their worries. Often, they review each mistake, real or imagined, recent or remotely past. When they are not reviewing and regretting the events of the past, they are anticipating all the difficulties that may arise in the future. Then, after they have crossed and recrossed most of their past and future bridges and managed to fall asleep, they frequently have anxiety dreams—dreams of being choked, being stabbed with knives, falling from high places, or being chased by murderers, with the horrible sensation that their legs will move only in slow motion. *HIGHLIGHT 6.3* provides an idea of the frequency with which individuals experiencing this disorder report various symptoms.

Many of these individuals show mild depression as well as chronic anxiety (Barlow, 1988; Downing & Rickels, 1974; Prusoff & Klerman, 1974). This finding is not unexpected in view of their generally gloomy outlook on the world. Nor is it surprising that excessive use of tranquilizing drugs, sleeping pills, and alcohol often complicates the clinical picture in generalized anxiety disorder.

As the following two cases illustrate, this disorder often results from the breakdown of previously functional but fragile defensive systems:

HIGHLIGHT 6.2

Fantasies of Anticipated Harm in Anxiety Disorders

In a study of 32 anxiety-neurotic individuals, Beck, Laude, and Bohnert (1974) found unrealistic expectations and fantasies of harm associated with these patients' heightened levels of anxiety and with anxiety attacks. The degree of anxiety was related to the severity and the perceived likelihood of the anticipated harm.

These expectations and fantasies centered around both physical and psychological dangers—such as being involved in an accident, becoming sick, being violently attacked, failing, and being humiliated or rejected by significant others. In this context, the following examples are instructive.

Often the fantasies and images reported by a given patient were related to past personal experiences. For example, in the following cases, the homemaker had experienced the death of a close friend and the artist's mother had died of a heart attack. These investigators concluded that the expectations and fantasies of anxious patients "not only hold up mirrors to their psychopathology but provide entry points for treating it" (p. 325).

Patient	Fantasy of Anticipated Harm	Stimuli Triggering Anxiety
Physician Male, age 32	Fear of sudden death	Any gastrointestinal symptoms
Teacher Male, age 25	Fear of inability to function as a teacher and of ending up on skid row	Anticipation of giving lecture
Homemaker Female, age 30	Fear of physical catastrophe happening to member of family	Sirens, news of deaths, fires, accidents, etc.
Student Male, age 26	Fear of psychological harm, school failure, rejection of everyone, illness	Schoolwork, confrontation with people, any physical symptom
Laborer Male, age 35	Continuous visual fantasies of accident, fear of imminent death	Any noises that might suggest danger (e.g., traffic noises)
Psychologist Male, age 40	Fear of heart attack, cerebral hemorrhage, fainting in public and subsequent disgrace	Physical sensations in chest or abdomen, back pains, hearing about heart attacks
Artist Female, age 35	Fear of heart attacks	Exertion, anticipation of exertion, reading or hearing about heart attacks
Student Male, age 18	Fear of appearing foolish and subsequent rejection by others	Contact with or anticipated contact with others

Thomas G., a 44-year-old Protestant minister, upon discovery of his wife's infidelity, began to experience chronic anxiety. He was quick to take the blame for the failure of the marriage, sure that his inattentiveness to the needs of his wife and children had driven her away. Yet he was angry at her for creating a public embarrassment for him. He was contemplating a divorce, but such an action would violate his moral convictions. He was also torn by the feeling that because his marriage had failed, he had failed the church, and must resign from the ministry. He loved his work so much, however, that he could not imagine being without it.

During the week before he came for therapy, he had been unable to sleep, lying awake worrying about his problems. He could not eat and complained of a strong burning sensation in his stomach and feelings of being constantly choked up. He was unable to think clearly enough to prepare his sermon for Sunday or to follow through on several commitments he had previously made.

Rev. G.'s present stress only exaggerated problems he had had for many years. He reported that he had always been an insecure and dependent person who found a great deal of emotional support in the church and in his strong, indepen-

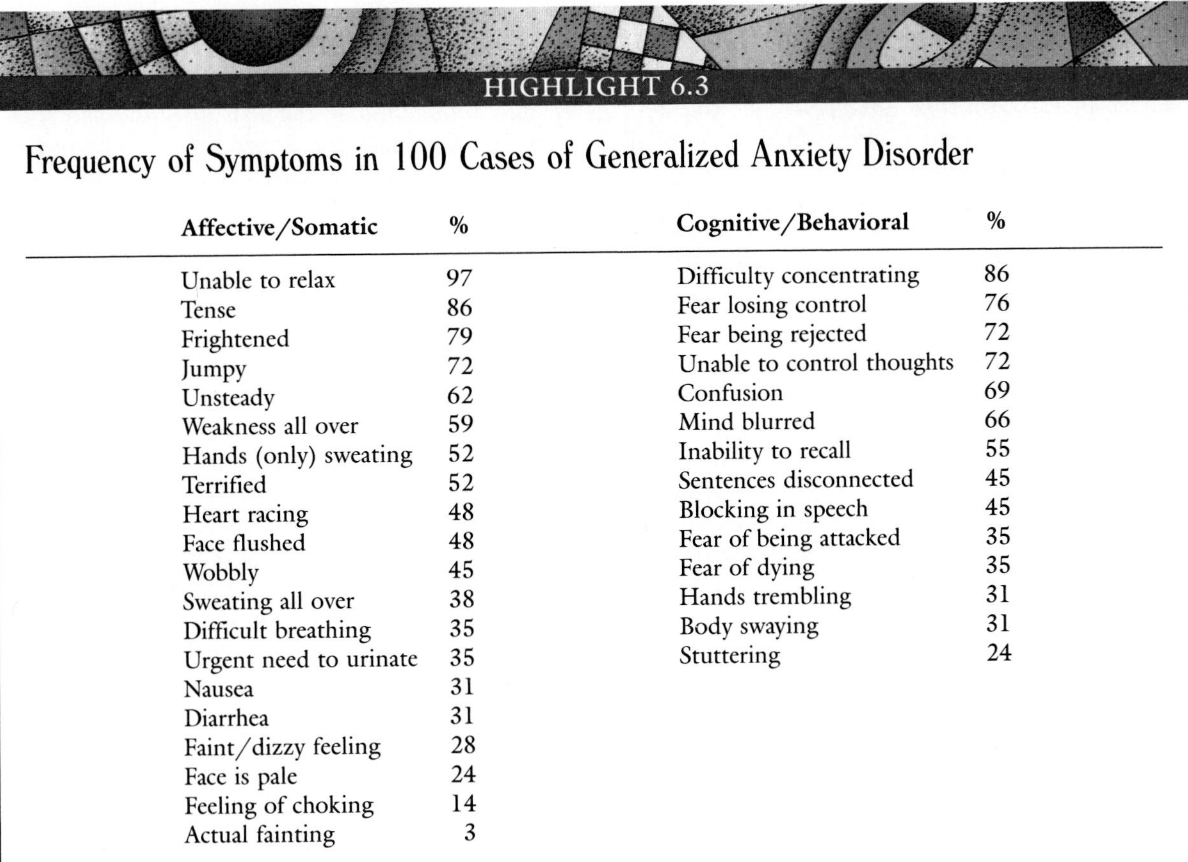

HIGHLIGHT 6.3

Frequency of Symptoms in 100 Cases of Generalized Anxiety Disorder

Affective/Somatic	%	Cognitive/Behavioral	%
Unable to relax	97	Difficulty concentrating	86
Tense	86	Fear losing control	76
Frightened	79	Fear being rejected	72
Jumpy	72	Unable to control thoughts	72
Unsteady	62	Confusion	69
Weakness all over	59	Mind blurred	66
Hands (only) sweating	52	Inability to recall	55
Terrified	52	Sentences disconnected	45
Heart racing	48	Blocking in speech	45
Face flushed	48	Fear of being attacked	35
Wobbly	45	Fear of dying	35
Sweating all over	38	Hands trembling	31
Difficult breathing	35	Body swaying	31
Urgent need to urinate	35	Stuttering	24
Nausea	31		
Diarrhea	31		
Faint/dizzy feeling	28		
Face is pale	24		
Feeling of choking	14		
Actual fainting	3		

Adapted from Beck and Emery (1985, pp. 87–88).

dent wife. She was a "take charge" person who had always handled all their personal matters, including shopping for his clothes. Any thought of an end to either his marriage or his position with the church made him extremely anxious and insecure—but now it seemed that continuing in the marriage and in his current position would be intolerable.

In short, the minister was able to function when surrounded by familiar supports but became overwhelmed when he was forced to face the necessity of leading a self-directed life. His reaction was an exacerbation of long-standing difficulties, not merely an adjustment disorder in response to a stressful event.

Specifically, we see in this case substantial evidence of a dependent personality organization preceding and in all likelihood contributing causally to Thomas G.'s anxiety disorder. The following case represents a pattern similar in basic structure, although involving a rather different type of preexisting personality organization:

Dr. H. J., a second-year resident in internal medicine at a major university medical center, referred himself for therapy in connection with his growing problems in coping with anxiety. He dated the onset of these difficulties to his acceptance of an invitation to join an elite cardiology team at the conclusion of his first year of postdoctoral training. The team consisted of a small, hand-picked group of senior resident physicians, two brilliant younger medical faculty members, and the leader, who was world famous for his basic discoveries in cardiovascular functioning and his innovations in the assessment and treatment of cardiovascular disease. The team collaborated in various cutting edge research projects and in managing the care of a large number of seriously ill patients. "Graduation" from this team was a virtual guarantee of a high-profile career in cardiovascular medicine, but the demands were great and the rate of attrition notoriously high for those who joined.

On initial assessment, Dr. J., who was manifestly tense, complained of never being entirely free of a sense of impending disaster, although he could not further specify the nature of this anticipated catastrophe. The thought of being involuntarily terminated from his envied position on the cardiology team, earlier a source of intense anxiety, had "on one or two occasions lately," he acknowledged, provided him momentary feelings of relief. He noted a number of signs of autonomic hyperarousal that he experienced on virtually a daily basis, emphasizing in particular excessive sweating, which had become a source of embarrassment. He was medicating himself for persistent attacks of diarrhea. He complained of an inability to attain a refreshing level of sleep even on those rare occasions when he could count on a few uninterrupted, off-duty hours, and his few waking "leisure" hours were filled with restless irritability. He was greatly concerned about his wife's growing complaints of loneliness, and he was fearful she would leave him; however, he expressed a sense of helplessness about being able to alter the situation.

Dr. J.'s request for therapy was precipitated by three additional concerns of more recent origin: (a) He had experienced his first panic attack several evenings ago and had fled from an intensive care unit for which he had been the sole responsible physician, an understanding nurse having had to cover for his absence. (b) He had noticed that the "requirement" (actually, a team expectancy) of remembering without recourse to notes the full background and updated details of every patient under the team's care, never easy, had lately become impossible. (3) He was concerned that his ever-increasing use of antianxiety medication (Valium) would be noticed or lead to drug dependency.

Exploration of Dr. J.'s background revealed he was the adopted child of an otherwise childless couple of modest circumstances. He had been adopted shortly after birth and knew nothing of his biological parentage. While his adoptive parents were extremely loving and had made him "the center of their world," Dr. J. vividly recalled the shock he had experienced when, in his early teens, he had been informed he was adopted. This information had mortified him and had engendered in him a vague, irrational, unshakable sense of being "different," "not quite right," and, in the final analysis, unacceptable as a human being. Apparently in consequence of this imagined basic flaw, Dr. J. thereafter had placed himself on a life course of unforgiving and ruthless pursuit of perfection.

A decidedly "average" young man, academically and otherwise, prior to learning of his adoption, J. had astonished his parents, his teachers, and his friends by his sudden transformation into a grim and dourly serious, incredibly organized, coldly efficient "nerd." As his social life had deteriorated, partly because he had had little time for anything other than his studies and partly because he had developed an annoying tendency to be bossy, critical, and aloof, his school performance had improved enough to place him at the head of his large high school class. He had been appointed valedictorian in his senior year, by which time he had determined he would become a physician.

Dr. J. had continued on essentially the same course through college and medical school. He had been somewhat resentful that financial constraints had precluded his matriculation at the most prestigious educational institutions, but he had consoled himself with the thought that, with his now customary relentless application, he could easily outdistance "the competition" in the schools he attended. And he had, receiving various academic honors and awards throughout. While working at a part-time service job in college, he had met the woman he would subsequently marry; although plain in appearance, she came from an extremely wealthy and socially prominent family. By Dr. J.'s account, this courtship had been remarkable for its decidedly unpassionate character.

Dr. J.'s performance as a medical student, possibly aided by his recently acquired family connections, had resulted in his being accepted into the highly acclaimed internal medicine residency of his choice. His unsparing diligence and exactitude in fulfilling duties during his first year had led to his being asked to join the elite cardiology team already described. Significantly, Dr. J. reported that, from the first, he never had felt "good enough" to be a member of this team.

Treatment of Dr. J. was made contingent on his agreeing to a programmed withdrawal from antianxiety medication. It involved a combined behavioral-interpersonal-cognitive approach, in the course of which he came to see that his "flaw" was no more a flaw than was his attempted compensation for it (being "super doc," as he put it) a true aspiration. In due course he resigned from the cardiology team, acknowledging that his former team colleagues might well be "better" than he in terms of their motivation and expertise in that particular field. He decided to complete his residency in internal medicine, however, because he felt it was a good basis for practicing family medicine. This new goal, he recognized, was related to his discovery of a need for "real contact" with people, including his wife. As his anxiety diminished and he began to permit himself the satisfactions of such contact, his compulsive ordering and organizing of the most minute details of his life gradually fell away. A long-suppressed passion for freshwater fishing (which he had enjoyed as a boy with his adoptive father) reappeared.

By mutual agreement between Dr. J. and his therapist, treatment was terminated 15 months following its initiation, at which point Dr. J. and his wife were anticipating the arrival of their first child. He was virtually free of all anxiety symptoms.

The cases of Reverend G. and Dr. J. raise an important and somewhat controversial issue. Prior to their anxiety disorder breakdowns, the personality organization of each may have qualified them for DSM-III-R, Axis II personality disorder diagnoses (to be considered in Chapter 8). Specifically, Reverend G. might have been considered to have had a *dependent* and Dr. J. an *obsessive-compulsive* personality disorder. The observation of Axis I disorders seeming to develop out of already existing Axis II disorders is extremely common, and is in fact an important reason why personality disorders are recognized in the diagnostic nomenclature. On the other hand, however, as in these two cases, the later-developing symptomatic difficulties (generalized anxiety disorder) could reasonably be conceived as part of and continuous with an underlying anxiety-driven personality disorder. In other words, what may look like (and even meet criteria for) an Axis II personality disorder might sometimes more profitably be conceived as part of an essentially anxiety-based process, one many would describe as neurotic in nature. We will address this issue further in the pages that follow.

As a group, the anxiety disorders, while clearly outside the normal range, rarely strike us as utterly strange or exotic—probably because we have all at one time or another experienced relatively strong fears or apprehensions that we could not rationally explain. And, as was noted, most of us are not even strangers to mild obsessive and compulsive phenomena. In the following sections we take up neurotic patterns that are more remote from the experience of most people.

SOMATOFORM DISORDERS

Soma means "body," and **somatoform disorders** involve anxiety-based neurotic patterns in which individuals complain of bodily symptoms that suggest the presence of physical problems, but for which no organic bases can be found. Such individuals are typically preoccupied with their state of health and with various presumed disorders or diseases of bodily organs. Though no organic bases exist, these individuals sincerely believe their symptoms are real and serious, and they should not be confused with people who feign physical illness (malingerers) in order to obtain some special treatment. "Functional" somatic symptoms, in which psychological problems are manifested in sincere complaints of physical dysfunction, are extremely common (Kellner, 1985); they represent a large proportion of the clientele of primary care physicians.

In our discussion, we will focus on four more or less distinct somatoform patterns: somatization disorder, hypochondriasis, somatoform pain disorder, and conversion disorder. Although all four involve the neurotic development or elaboration of physical disabilities, the patterns of causation and the most effective treatment approaches may differ somewhat. DSM-III-R includes a fifth syndrome, body dysmorphic disorder, in which there is a preoccupation with some imagined defect in one's physical appearance. While this problem doubtless occurs with significant frequency and sometimes with such severity as to approach delusion, it seems to be fundamentally different in character from the classic somatoform patterns. It will not be considered in this section.

Somatization Disorder

Somatization disorder is characterized by multiple complaints of physical ailments over a long period, beginning before age 30, that are inadequately explained by independent findings of physical illness or injury. A diagnostician need not be con-

HIGHLIGHT 6.4

Qualifying Symptoms for the Diagnosis of Somatization Disorder

DSM-III-R diagnostic criteria for somatization disorder include the specification that at least 13 of the 35 symptoms listed below have at some time been a focus of significant complaint by an individual. The items appearing in boldface may be used to "screen" for the disorder; the reported occurrence of any two of them establishes a high likelihood of the presence of the full syndrome.

Gastrointestinal symptoms

1. **Vomiting** (other than during pregnancy)
2. Abdominal pain (other than while menstruating)
3. Nausea (other than motion sickness)
4. Bloating (gassy)
5. Diarrhea
6. Intolerance of (gets sick from eating) several different foods

Pain symptoms

7. **Pain in extremities**
8. Back pain
9. Joint pain
10. Pain during urination
11. Other pain (not including headaches)

Cardiopulmonary symptoms

12. **Shortness of breath when not exerting self**
13. Palpitations
14. Chest pain
15. Dizziness

Conversion or pseudoneurological symptoms

16. **Amnesia**
17. **Difficulty swallowing**
18. Loss of voice
19. Deafness
20. Double vision
21. Blurred vision
22. Blindness
23. Fainting or loss of consciousness
24. Seizure or convulsion
25. Trouble walking
26. Paralysis or muscle weakness
27. Urinary retention or difficulty urinating

Sexual symptoms (occurring for most of the person's life following commencement of opportunities for sexual activity)

28. **Burning sensation in sex organs or rectum, *not* during sexual intercourse**
29. Sexual indifference
30. Pain during intercourse
31. Erectile dysfunction

Female reproductive symptoms (judged by the person to be more frequent or more severe than in most women)

32. **Painful menstruation**
33. Irregular menstrual periods
34. Excessive menstrual bleeding
35. Vomiting throughout pregnancy

vinced that these claimed illnesses actually existed in a patient's background history; the mere reporting of them is sufficient. The DSM-III-R provides a list of 35 symptoms (summarized in *HIGHLIGHT 6.4*) that qualify as possible indicators of somatization disorder. To qualify, the symptoms must be reported as having been severe enough to require medication, to require consulting a physician, or to cause an alteration in life-style.

The differences between somatization disorder and hypochondriasis (discussed in the following section), are none too clear in the DSM-III-R diagnostic manual, apparently because the two disorders (if they are in fact distinct) are closely related. The main differences seem to be that hypochondriasis may have its onset after age 30; that the abnormal health concerns characteristic of hypochondriasis need not focus on any particular set of symptoms nor on a profusion of them; and that a hypochondriacal person mostly focuses on the idea that he or she has a serious disease, claims of explicit symptoms or physical disabilities being secondary to this concern.

The somatization disorder diagnosis, new to DSM-III in 1980, has not as yet been subjected to the extensive clinical and research scrutiny characteristic of other somatoform disorders. It is apparently based on long clinical experience with a certain group of medical patients who seem almost never to be entirely "well," even though clear identification of specific organ malfunctions often (although not always) proves to be elusive. The pattern was earlier known as *Briquet's syndrome.*

Hypochondriasis

One of the most frequently seen somatoform patterns is **hypochondriasis,** which is characterized by an individual's multiple complaints about possible physical illness where no evidence of such illness can be found. Hypochondriacal complaints are usually not restricted to any physiologically coherent symptom pattern; rather, they express a preoccupation with health matters and unrealistic fears of disease. Although hypochondriacal people repeatedly seek medical advice, their fears are not in the least lessened by their doctors' reassurances—in fact they are frequently disappointed when no physical problem is found.

Individuals with this disorder may complain of uncomfortable and peculiar sensations in the general area of the stomach, chest, head, genitals, or anywhere else in the body. They usually have trouble giving a precise description of their symptoms, however. They may begin by mentioning pain in the stomach, which on further questioning is not really a pain but a gnawing sensation, or perhaps a feeling of heat, or of pressure, whose locus may now on more careful observation migrate to a neighboring portion of the abdomen, and so on. The mental orientation of these individuals keeps them constantly on the alert for new symptoms, the description of which may challenge the capacity of mere language to communicate.

Hypochondriacal patients are likely to be avid readers of popular magazines on medical topics and are apt to feel certain that they are suffering from every new disease they read or hear about. They are major consumers of over-the-counter (and often virtually worthless) remedies touted in ads as being able to heal vaguely described problems such as "tired blood" or "irregularity." Tuberculosis, cancer, exotic infections, and numerous other diseases are readily diagnosed by these individuals. Their morbid preoccupation with bodily processes, coupled with their often limited knowledge of medical pathology, leads to some interesting diagnoses. One patient diagnosed his condition as "ptosis of the transvex colon," and added, "If I am just half as bad off as I think, I am a dead pigeon."

This attitude appears to be typical: such individuals are sure they are seriously ill and cannot recover. Yet—and this is revealing—despite their exaggerated concerns over their health, they do not usually show the fear or anxiety that might be expected of those suffering from such horrible ills. In fact they are usually in good physical condition. Nevertheless, they are not **malingering,** that is, consciously faking symptoms; they are sincere in their conviction that their symptoms represent real illness, although an attentive listener may get the impression that something more is being communicated in these complaints.

A classic illustration of the shifting symptoms and complaints in a severe case of hypochondriasis is presented in the following letter that a hospitalized patient wrote to her anxious relatives:

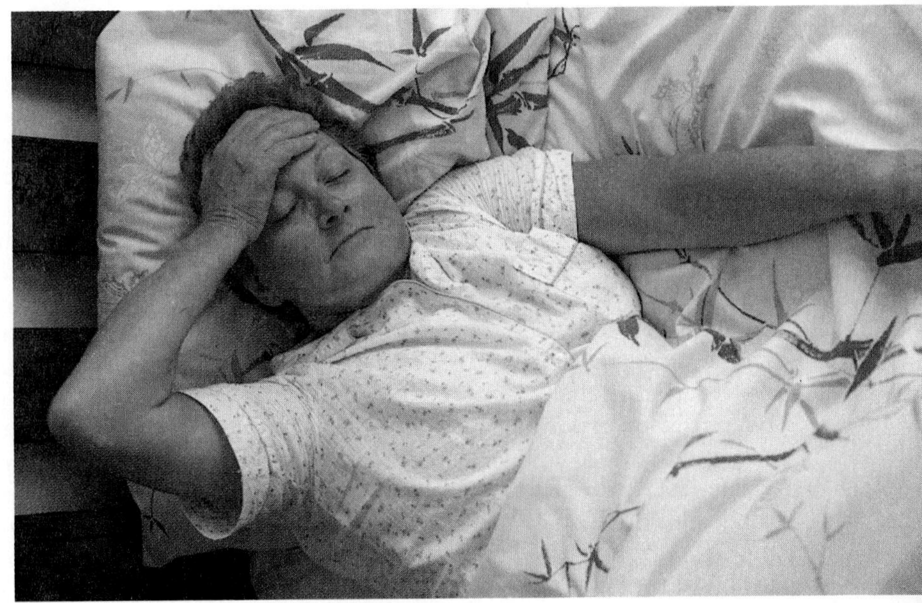

Hypochondriacal individuals are preoccupied with health matters and unrealistic fears of disease. They are convinced that they have symptoms of physical illness, but their complaints typically do not conform to any coherent symptom pattern, and they usually have trouble giving a precise description of their symptoms.

"Dear Mother and Husband:

"I have suffered terrible today with drawing in the throat. My nerves are terrible. My head feels queer. But my stomach hasn't cramped quite so hard. I've been on the verge of a nervous chill all day, but I have been fighting it hard. It's night and bedtime, but, Oh, how I hate to go to bed. Nobody knows or realizes how badly I feel because I fight to stay up and outdoors if possible. . . .

"The long afternoons and nights are awful. There are plenty of patients well enough to visit but I'm in too much pain.

"The nurses ignore any complaining. They just laugh or scold.

"Eating has been awful hard. They expect me to eat like a harvest hand. Every bite of solid food is agony to get down, for my throat aches so and feels so closed up. . . .

"My eyes are bothering me more.

"Come up as soon as you can. My nose runs terribly every time I eat.

"The trains and ducks and water pipes are noisy at night.

Annie"

(Menninger, 1945, pp. 139–140)

Hypochondriacal individuals often show a morbid preoccupation with digestive and excretory functions. Some keep charts of their bowel movements, and most are able to give detailed information concerning diet, constipation, and related matters. Many, as earlier suggested, use a wide range of self-medications of the type frequently advertised on television. However, they do not show losses or distortions of sensory, motor, and visceral functioning that occur in conversion disorder (to be discussed in a later section); nor do their complaints have the bizarre delusional quality—such as "insides rotting away" or "lungs drying up"—that typically occurs in psychotic disorders.

Most of us as children learn well the lesson that, when sick, special comforts and attention are provided and, furthermore, that one is excused from a number of responsibilities or, at least, is not expected to perform certain chores up to par. This lesson has proved exceptionally alluring and persistent for a hypochondriacal adult. Such an adult is in effect saying, (a) "I deserve more of your attention and concern," and (b) "You may not legitimately expect me to perform as a well person would." Typically these messages are conveyed with more than a touch of angry rebuke or whining, inconsolable demand. In short, hypochondriasis may be viewed as a certain type of interpersonal communication as well as a disorder involving abnormal preoccupation with disease. Treatment of the latter in the absence of an appreciation of the former frequently produces clinical frustration, if not exasperation.

Somatoform Pain Disorder

Somatoform pain disorder is characterized by the report of severe and lasting pain. DSM-III-R specifies a duration of at least six months. Either no physical basis is apparent, or the reaction is greatly in excess of what would be expected from the physical pathology. In approaching this phenomenon it is important to understand that pain is always a sensation registered in a patient's mental experience; there is in fact no perfect correlation between the occurrence or intensity of pain (as reported in the general population) and tissue damage or irritation. This partial independence of physical damage and psychological experience evidently makes possible the considerable effectiveness of purely psychological treatment for pain that has a definite physical basis (Keefe & Williams, 1989). Because, like all other experience, pain is ultimately always private, we have no way of gauging with certainty the actual extent of a patient's pain. This fundamental unclarity is wholly insufficient to justify the conclusion that a patient is faking or exaggerating his or her pain, although such a judgment is regrettably frequent among clinicians. Somatoform pain disorder is fairly common among psychiatric patients (Katon, Egan, & Miller, 1985) and is more often diagnosed among women.

The reported pain may be vaguely located in the area of the heart or other vital organs, or it may center in the lower back or limbs. (Tension headaches and migraines are not included here, since they involve demonstrable physiological changes, such as muscle contractions.) People with psychogenic pain disorders flirt with an invalid life-style. They tend to "doctor-shop" in the hope of finding both a physical confirmation of their pain and some medication to relieve it. This behavior continues even if several visits to doctors fail to indicate any underlying physical problem. Sadly enough, in many cases somatoform pain patients actually wind up being disabled—either through addiction to pain medication or through the crippling effects of surgery they have been able to obtain as treatment for their condition.

Although technically a disorder should be diagnosed as a somatoform pain disorder only when no adequate organic basis for the pain can be found, some vaguely related injury or physical problem may be discovered in a pain patient's medical history. Usually, however, the past incident serves more as perceived justification for the patient's physical concern rather than as a predisposing factor to it.

■ Conversion Disorder

Conversion disorder, earlier called *hysteria,* involves a neurotic pattern in which symptoms of some physical malfunction or loss of control appear without any underlying organic pathology. It is one of the most intriguing and baffling patterns in psychopathology, and we still have much to learn about it.

As we mentioned in Chapter 2, the term *hysteria* was derived from the Greek word meaning "uterus." It was thought by Hippocrates and other ancient Greeks that this disorder was restricted to women, and that it was caused by sexual difficulties, particularly by the wandering of a frustrated uterus to various parts of the body because of sexual desires and a yearning for children. Thus the uterus might lodge in the throat and cause choking sensations, or in the spleen, resulting in temper tantrums. Hippocrates considered marriage the best remedy for the affliction, and ironically—as Freud's subsequent experience with Victorian-era women showed—he may in some instances have been right. Freud used the term *conversion hysteria* for these disorders because he believed that the symptoms were an expression of repressed sexual energy—that is, the psychosexual conflict was seen as *converted* into a bodily disturbance. For example, a conflict over masturbation might be "solved" by developing a paralyzed hand. This was not done consciously, of course, and the person was not aware of the origin or meaning of the physical symptom.

In contemporary psychopathology, reactions of this type are no longer interpreted in Freudian terms as the "conversion" of sexual conflicts or other psychological problems into physical symptoms. Rather, the physical symptoms are now usually seen as serving a defensive function, enabling an individual to escape or avoid a stressful situation without having to take responsibility for doing so. The term *conversion* has been retained, however.

Conversion disorders were once relatively common in civilian and especially in military life. In World War I, conversion disorder was the most frequently diagnosed psychiatric syndrome among soldiers; it was also relatively common during World War II. Conversion disorder typically occurred under highly stressful combat conditions and involved men who would ordinarily be considered stable. Here, conversion symptoms—such as being paralyzed in the legs—enabled a soldier to avoid an anxiety-arousing combat situation without being labeled a coward or being subjected to court-martial.

During World War I, conversion disorder was the most frequently diagnosed psychiatric syndrome among soldiers. It enabled soldiers to avoid anxiety-arousing combat situations, the severity of which is evident in this scene on the western front.

Today conversion disorders constitute only some 5 percent of all neurotic disorders treated. Interestingly enough, their decreasing incidence seems to be closely related to our growing sophistication about medical and psychological disorders: a conversion disorder apparently loses its defensive function if it can be readily shown to lack an organic basis. In an age that no longer believes in such phenomena as being struck blind or suddenly afflicted with an unusual and dramatic paraplegia, the cases that occur now increasingly simulate more exotic physical diseases that are harder to diagnose, such as convulsive seizures or gastrointestinal ailments. Even psychologically sophisticated people have been known to develop conversion symptoms under stress, however, as the following case shows:

A 29-year-old physician in the first year of a psychiatric residency was experiencing a great deal of stress from problems in both his personal life and his hospital work. His marriage was deteriorating and he was being heavily criticized by the rather authoritarian chief of psychiatry for allegedly mismanaging some treatment cases. Shortly before he was to discuss his work in an important hospital-wide conference being conducted by the chief psychiatrist, he had an "attack" in which he developed difficulty in speaking and severe pains in his chest. He thought his condition was probably related to a viral infection, but physical findings were negative.

Here we see with particular clarity how a conversion symptom may serve the function of escape from unwanted responsibility.

The range of symptoms in conversion disorder is practically as diverse as for physically based ailments. In describing the clinical picture in conversion disorder, it is useful to think in terms of three categories of symptoms: sensory, motor, and visceral.

Sensory Symptoms Any of the senses may be involved in sensory conversion reactions. The most common forms are as follows:

Anesthesia—loss of sensitivity

Hypesthesia—partial loss of sensitivity

Hyperesthesia—excessive sensitivity

Analgesia—loss of sensitivity to pain

Paresthesia—exceptional sensations, such as tingling

You may be wondering why somatoform pain disorder, given its essential similarity to the symptoms just listed, is not included here as merely another form of sensory conversion disorder. Why is it a separate category? The DSM-III-R offers no satisfactory answer to this question. It may be that it was given separate status because it appears to occur far more frequently than other conversion phenomena.

Some idea of the range of sensory symptoms that may occur in conversion disorders can be gleaned from Ironside and Batchelor's (1945) study of hysterical visual symptoms among airmen in World War II. They found blurred vision, photophobia (extreme sensitivity to light), double vision, night blindness, a combination of intermittent visual failure and amnesia, deficient stereopsis (the tendency to look past an object during attempts to focus on it), restriction in the visual field, intermittent loss of vision in one eye, color blindness, jumbling of print during attempts to read, and failing day vision. They also found that the symptoms of each airman were closely related to his performance duties. Night fliers, for example, were more subject to night blindness, while day fliers more often developed failing day vision. The results of a later study of student military aviators who developed conversion disorders are reported in *HIGHLIGHT 6.5*.

The other senses may also be subject to a wide range of disorders. A puzzling and unsolved question in hysterical blindness and deafness is whether individuals actually cannot see or hear, or whether the sensory information is received but screened from consciousness (Theodor & Mandelcorn, 1973). In general, the evidence supports the latter hypothesis, that the sensory input is screened from consciousness.

Motor Symptoms Motor conversion reactions also cover a wide range of symptoms, but only the most common need be mentioned here.

Paralysis conversion reactions are usually confined to a single limb, such as an arm or a leg, and the loss of function is usually selective. For example, in "writer's cramp," a person cannot write but may be able to use the same muscles in shuffling a deck of cards or playing the piano. Tremors (muscular shaking or trembling) and tics (localized muscular twitches) are common. Occasionally, symptoms include contractures, which usually involve flexing of the fingers and toes, or rigidity of the larger joints, such as the elbows and knees. Paralyses and contractures frequently lead to walking disturbances. A person with a rigid knee joint may be forced to

HIGHLIGHT 6.5

Conversion Reactions in Student Naval Aviators

Mucha and Reinhardt (1970) reported on a study of 56 student aviators with conversion reactions who were assessed at the U.S. Naval Aerospace Medical Institute in Pensacola, Florida. In the group, representing 16 percent of a total population of 343 patients at the institute, four types of symptoms were found. These were, in order of frequency: visual symptoms (most common), auditory symptoms, paralysis or paresthesias (prickling sensations) of extremities, and paresthesia of the tongue.

Generally, the 56 students came from middle-class, achievement-oriented families. The fathers of 80 percent of them were either high school or college graduates and were either professional men or white-collar workers. Interestingly enough, 89 percent of the cases had won letters in one or more sports in high school or college; all were college graduates and presently were flight students, officer candidates, or officers.

Commenting on the relatively high incidence of conversion reactions among the patients at the institute, Mucha and Reinhardt emphasized three conditions which they considered of etiological significance:

1. *Unacceptability of quitting.* In the students' previous athletic training, physical illness had been an acceptable means of avoiding difficult situations, whereas quitting was not. Moreover, the present training environment tended to perpetuate this adaptation, since the military is also achievement-oriented and does not tolerate quitting as a means of coping with stress situations.

2. *Parental models and past experience.* Seventy percent of the parents of these students had had significant illnesses affecting the organ system utilized in the students' disorders; and a majority of the students had had multiple physical symptoms prior to enlistment—often as a result of athletic injuries.

3. *Sensitization to the use of somatic complaints.* As a result of their previous experience, the students were sensitized to the use of somatic complaints as a face-saving means of coping with stressful situations.

When faced with the real stress of the flight training program and with frequent life-or-death incidents they resorted to this unconscious mechanism to relieve the stress and to avoid admitting failure. To admit failure would be totally unacceptable to the rigid demands of their superegos. (p. 494)

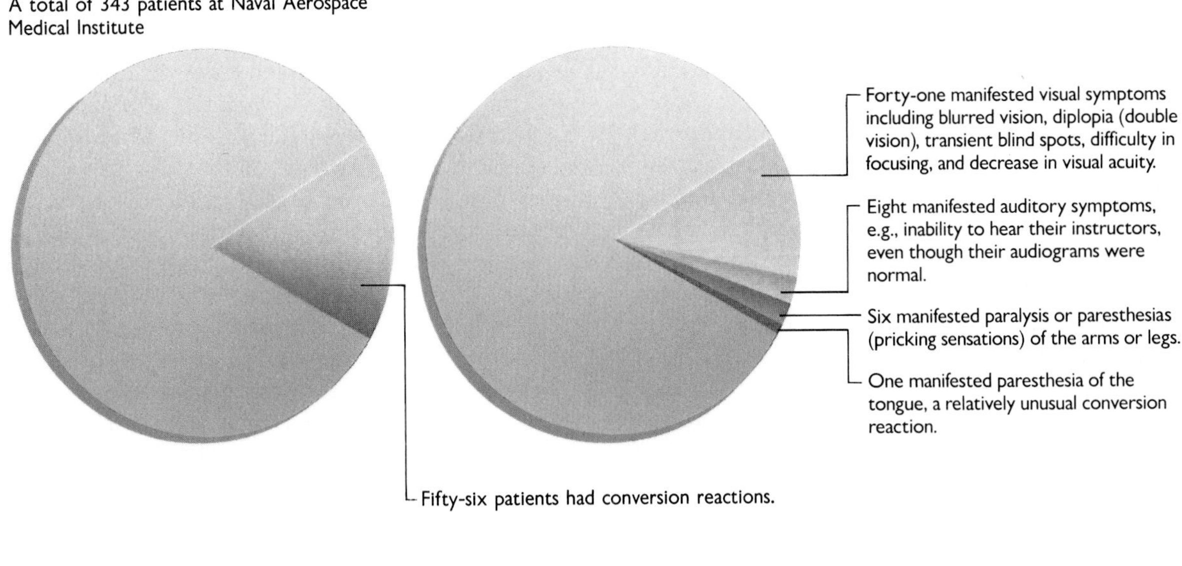
A total of 343 patients at Naval Aerospace Medical Institute
Fifty-six patients had conversion reactions.
Forty-one manifested visual symptoms including blurred vision, diplopia (double vision), transient blind spots, difficulty in focusing, and decrease in visual acuity.
Eight manifested auditory symptoms, e.g., inability to hear their instructors, even though their audiograms were normal.
Six manifested paralysis or paresthesias (pricking sensations) of the arms or legs.
One manifested paresthesia of the tongue, a relatively unusual conversion reaction.

throw his or her leg out in a sort of arc as he or she walks. Another walking disturbance is *astasia-abasia,* in which an individual can usually control leg movements when sitting or lying down, but can hardly stand and has a grotesque, disorganized walk, with both legs wobbling about in every direction.

The most common speech-related conversion disturbances are *aphonia,* in which an individual is able to talk only in a whisper, and *mutism,* in which he or she cannot speak at all. Interestingly enough, a person who can talk only in a whisper can usually cough in a normal manner. In true laryngeal paralysis both the cough and the voice are affected. Aphonia is a relatively common conversion reaction and usually occurs after some emotional shock, whereas mutism is relatively rare. Occasionally, symptoms may involve convulsions, similar to those in epilepsy. People with such symptoms, however, show few of the usual characteristics of true epileptics—they rarely, if ever, injure themselves in falls, their pupillary reflex to light remains unaffected, they are able to control excretory functions, and they do not have attacks when alone.

Visceral Symptoms Visceral conversion reactions also cover a wide range of symptoms, including headaches, "lump in the throat" (formerly known as *globus hystericus*) and choking sensations, coughing spells, difficulty in breathing, cold and clammy extremities, belching, nausea, vomiting, and so on. Occasionally, persistent hiccoughing or sneezing occurs.

Actual organic symptoms may be simulated to an almost unbelievable degree. In a pseudoattack of acute appendicitis, a person not only may evidence lower-abdominal pain and other typical symptoms, but also may have a temperature far above normal. Conversion-reaction cases of malaria and tuberculosis have also been cited in the literature. In the latter, for example, an individual may show all the usual symptoms—coughing, loss of weight, recurrent fever, and night sweats—without actual organic disease. Numerous cases of pseudopregnancy have been reported, in which menstruation may cease, the abdominal area and breasts may enlarge, and the woman may experience morning sickness.

Because the symptoms in conversion disorder can simulate almost every known disease, accurate diagnosis can be a problem. However, in addition to specialized medical techniques, several criteria are commonly used for distinguishing between conversion disorders and organic disturbances:

1. A certain *belle indifference,* in which the patient describes what is wrong in a rather matter-of-fact way, with little of the anxiety and fear that would be expected in a person with a paralyzed arm or loss of sight. Mucha and Reinhardt (1970) reported that all of the 56 student fliers in their study (p. 203) showed this pattern, seeming to be unconcerned about long-range effects of their disabilities. In itself, however, unconcernedness cannot be taken as a reliable sign of conversion; some stoic individuals having genuine organic pathology display a similar disregard.

2. The frequent failure of the dysfunction to conform clearly to the symptoms of the particular disease or disorder. For example, little or no wasting away or atrophy of a "paralyzed" limb occurs in paralyses that are conversion reactions, except in rare and long-standing cases.

3. The selective nature of the dysfunction. For example, in conversion blindness, an individual does not usually bump into people or objects; "paralyzed" muscles can be used for some activities but not others; and uncontrolled contractures usually disappear during sleep.

4. The interesting fact that under hypnosis or narcosis (a sleeplike state induced by drugs) the symptoms can usually be removed, shifted, or reinduced by the suggestion of the therapist. Similarly, if the individual is suddenly awakened from a sound sleep, he or she may be tricked into using a "paralyzed" limb.

Where conversion symptoms are superimposed on an actual organic disorder, making a diagnosis may become difficult. It is usually fairly easy, however, to distinguish between a conversion reaction and frank malingering. Malingerers are consciously perpetrating frauds by faking the symptoms of diseases, and this fact is reflected in their demeanors. Individuals with conversion disorders are usually dramatic and apparently naive; they are concerned mainly with the symptoms and willingly discuss them. If inconsistencies in their behaviors are pointed out, they are usually unperturbed. To the contrary, malingerers are inclined to be defensive, evasive, and suspicious; they are usually reluctant to be examined and slow to talk about their symptoms, lest the pretense be discovered. Should inconsistencies in their behaviors be pointed out, malingerers immediately become more defensive.

Thus conversion disorder and malingering are considered distinct patterns, although sometimes they overlap.

The phenomenon of *mass hysteria,* as typified by outbreaks of St. Vitus's dance and biting manias during the Middle Ages, is a form of conversion disorder that has become a rarity in modern times. As we saw in Chapter 2, however, some outbreaks do still occur (for some recent examples, see page 37). In all cases, suggestibility clearly plays a major role—a conversion reaction in one individual rapidly spreads to others.

In the development of a conversion disorder, the following chain of events typically occurs: (a) a desire to escape from some unpleasant situation; (b) a fleeting wish to be sick in order to avoid the situation (this wish, however, is suppressed as unfeasible or unworthy); and under additional or continued stress, (c) the appearance of the symptoms of some physical ailment. The individual sees no relation between the symptoms and the stress situation. The particular symptoms that occur are usually those of a previous illness or are copied from other sources, such as symptoms observed among relatives, seen on television, or read about in magazines. The symptoms may also be superimposed on an existing organic ailment, associated with anticipated secondary gains, or symbolically related to the conflict situation.

Sometimes, conversion disorders seem to stem from feelings of guilt and the necessity for self-punishment. In one case, for example, a female patient developed a marked tremor and partial paralysis of the right arm and hand after she had physically attacked her father. During this incident she had clutched at and torn open his shirt with her right hand, and apparently the subsequent paralysis represented a sort of symbolic punishment of the "guilty party," while preventing a recurrence of her hostile and forbidden behavior.

Conversion symptoms often develop following an accident or injury from which an individual hopes to receive financial compensation. These reactions usually occur after accidents in which an individual might have been seriously injured but is actually only shaken up or slightly injured. Later, in discussions with family or friends, it may be agreed that the individual would have had a strong legal case if there had been an injury. "Are you sure you are all right? Could you possibly have injured your back? Perhaps there is something wrong with it." Indeed, the recent advertising practices of some law firms have involved precisely this approach. With the aid of a "sympathetic" lawyer (whose fee often will be determined by the size of the monetary award), the individual may proceed to file suit for injury compensation.

In such cases it is especially hard to distinguish between a malingerer's deliberate simulation of injury and the unconscious deception of an individual suffering from conversion disorder (Lewis, 1974). It may well be that this dichotomy itself is misleading. Apparently many conversion disorder cases include a combination of the two, in which conscious acting is superimposed on unconscious acting or role playing. In any event, the patient in such cases often shows an amazingly rapid recovery once there has been "proper" compensation for the "injuries."

Whatever specific causal factors may be involved, however, the basic motivational pattern underlying conversion disorder seems to be to avoid or reduce anxiety-arousing stress by getting sick—thus converting an intolerable emotional problem into a face-saving physical one. Once this response is learned, it is maintained because it is repeatedly reinforced—both by anxiety reduction and by the interpersonal gains (in terms of sympathy and support) that result from being sick.

DISSOCIATIVE DISORDERS

Like somatoform disorders, **dissociative disorders** appear mainly to be ways of avoiding anxiety and stress and of gratifying secret needs. Both disorders also permit a person to deny personal responsibility for his or her "unacceptable" wishes or behavior. In the case of dissociative disorders, however, the person avoids the stress by dissociating—in essence by escaping from his or her own personal identity. Dissociative patterns include psychogenic amnesia and fugue states, multiple personality, and depersonalization. A generalized conception of these patterns appears in *HIGHLIGHT 6.6.* These patterns are generally not so well researched or understood as those already described; hence our coverage of them will be relatively brief.

Psychogenic Amnesia and Fugue

Amnesia is partial or total inability to recall or identify past experience. It may occur in neurotic

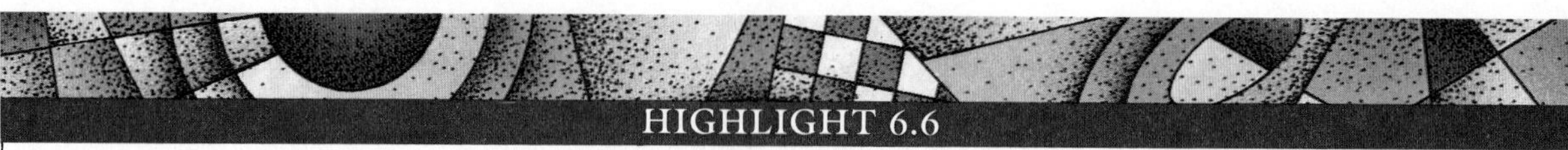

HIGHLIGHT 6.6

Continuum of Dissociative Processes and States

The following figure is a graphic representation of the manner in which Ross (1989, p. 80) conceives dissociation's fundamental role in mental disorders of varying types and severities. Thus a simple form of dissociative process is involved in normal dissociative states, whereas complex dissociation processes characterize MPD, all the more where many and changing alter personalities are poorly integrated with one another (called "polyfragmented" MPD). Notice that Ross includes conversion disorder on this continuum, the symptoms of which are also conceived to be dissociated parts of the self. While this idea is not prominent in contemporary writings on conversion disorder, much historical precedence exists for it.

SIMPLE								COMPLEX
	Normal dissociation	Psychogenic amnesia Conversion disorder	Psychogenic fugue Atypical dissociative disorder	Partial MPD	Dual personality	Complex MPD	Polyfragmented MPD	

Note: MPD = multiple personality disorder

and psychotic disorders and in brain pathology, including brain injury and diseases of the central nervous system. If the amnesia is caused by brain pathology, it usually involves an actual *retention* failure. That is, either the information is not registered and does not enter memory storage, or, if stored, it cannot be retrieved; it is truly and almost always permanently lost (Hirst, 1982).

Psychogenic amnesia, on the other hand, is usually limited to a failure to *recall.* The "forgotten" material is still there beneath the level of consciousness, as becomes apparent under hypnosis or narcosis interviews, and in cases where the amnesia spontaneously clears up. Four types of psychogenic amnesia are recognized: *localized* (a person remembers nothing that happened during a specific period—usually the first few hours following some traumatic event); *selective* (a person forgets some but not all of what happened during a given period); *generalized* (a person forgets his or her entire life history); and *continuous* (a person remembers nothing beyond a certain point in the past). The latter two types occur rarely.

As we have noted, psychogenic amnesia is fairly common in initial reactions to intolerably traumatic experiences, such as those occurring during combat conditions and immediately after catastrophic events. Some neurotically functioning individuals, however, develop such amnesias in the face of stressful life situations with which most people deal more effectively.

In typical psychogenic amnesic reactions, individuals cannot remember their names, do not know how old they are or where they reside, and do not recognize their parents, relatives, or friends. Yet their basic habit patterns—such as their abilities to read, talk, perform skilled work, and so on—remain intact, and they seem quite normal aside from the amnesia.

In this amnesic state, a person may retreat still further from real-life problems by going away in what is called a **fugue state.** A fugue reaction is a defense by actual flight—an individual is not only amnesic, but also wanders away from home, often assuming a partially or completely new identity. Days, weeks, or sometimes even years later, such

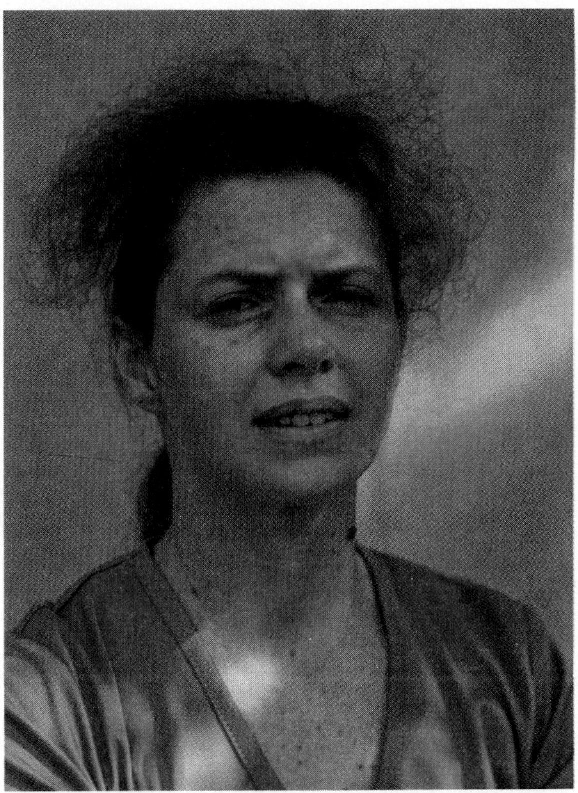

This woman, dubbed "Jane Doe," was emaciated, incoherent, partially clothed, covered by insect and animal bites, and near death when discovered by a Florida park ranger in September 1980. Her recovery was further complicated by a rare form of psychogenic amnesia, ***generalized amnesia,*** *in which she had lost the memory of her name, her past, and her ability to read and write. Judging from her accent, linguistic experts said the woman was probably from Illinois. Although interviews conducted under the effect of drugs revealed that the woman had apparently had a Catholic education, her few childhood memories were so common that they were meaningless. In a dramatic attempt to recover her past, Jane Doe and her doctor appeared on "Good Morning America" and appealed to her relatives to step forward. The response was overwhelming, and authorities came to believe that Jane Doe was the daughter of a couple from Roselle, Illinois, whose daughter had gone to the Ft. Lauderdale area to open a boutique. Their last contact with their daughter had been a phone call in 1976. Despite the couple's certainty, Jane Doe was never able to remember her past.*

individuals may suddenly find themselves in strange places, not knowing how they got there and with apparently complete amnesia for their fugue periods. Their activities during their fugues may vary from merely going on a round of motion pictures to traveling across the country, entering a new occupation, and starting a new way of life.

The pattern in psychogenic amnesia is essentially the same as in conversion disorder, except that instead of avoiding some unpleasant situation by getting sick, a person avoids thoughts about the situation or in the extreme leaves the scene. Apparently, virtually any type of inner conflict involving wishes that are unacceptable to a person and are therefore anxiety-arousing may serve as the basis of an amnesic reaction and its elaboration into fugue. The threatening information becomes inaccessible, owing either to some sort of automatic cognitive blockage or to deliberate suppression. In patterns involving suppression, individuals apparently tell themselves that they will not remember some traumatic event or situation; subsequently they try to believe and behave as though they actually are amnesic. For example, in a study of 98 amnesia cases, primarily among military personnel, Kiersch (1962) found 41 to be of this seemingly "feigned" ("factitious" in DSM-III-R terminology) type.

People experiencing psychogenic amnesia are typically egocentric, immature, highly suggestible individuals who are faced with extremely unpleasant situations from which they see no escape. Often, they previously had experienced conscious impulses to "forget" and run away but were too inhibited to accept that solution. Eventually, however, the stress becomes so intolerable that they suppress large segments of their personalities and all memory for the stressful situations, thus allowing more congenial patterns to carry on. As O'Neill and Kempler (1969) have pointed out, psychogenic amnesia is highly selective and involves only material that is basically intolerable or threatening to the self.

During a dissociative fugue reaction, an individual appears normal and is able to engage in complex activities. Normally the activities chosen reflect a rather different life-style from the previous one, the rejection of which is usually transparent. This behavior is well illustrated in the following case:

Burt Tate, a 42-year-old short-order cook in a small-town diner, was brought to the attention of local police following a heated altercation with another man at the diner. Questioned by the police, he gave his name as Burt Tate and indicated that he had arrived in town several weeks earlier. However, he could produce no official identification and could not tell the officers where he had previously lived and worked. No charges were proffered and no arrest made, but Burt was asked to accompany the officers to the emergency room of a local hospital so that he might be examined, to which request he agreed.

Burt's physical examination was negative for evidence of recent head trauma or any other medical abnormality, and there was no indication of drug or alcohol abuse. He was oriented as to current time and place, but manifested no recall of his personal history prior to his arrival in town. He did not seem especially concerned about his total lack of a remembered past. He was kept in the hospital overnight for observation and discharged the following day.

Meanwhile, the police instituted missing-person search procedures and discovered that Burt matched the description of one Gene Saunders, a resident of a city some 200 miles away who had disappeared a month earlier. The wife of Mr. Saunders was brought to the town and confirmed the real identity of "Burt," who, now noticeably anxious, stated that he did not recognize Mrs. Saunders.

Prior to his disappearance, Gene Saunders, a middle-level manager in a large manufacturing firm, had been experiencing considerable difficulties at work and at home. A number of stressful work problems, including failure to get an expected promotion, the loss through resignation of some of his staff, failure of his section to meet production goals, and increased criticism from his superior—all occurring within a brief time frame—had upset his normal equanimity. He had become morose and withdrawn at home, and had been critical of his wife and children. Two days before he had left he had had a violent argument with his 18-year-old son, who'd declared his father a "failure" and had stormed out of the house to go live with friends. (Adapted from Spitzer et al., 1989, pp. 215–216.)

Multiple Personality Disorder

Multiple personality is a dissociative reaction, usually with identifiable stressor precipitants, in which a patient manifests two or more complete systems of personality. Each system has distinct, well-developed emotional and thought processes and represents a unique and relatively stable personality. The individual may change from one personality to another at periods varying from a few minutes to several years, though shorter time frames are more common. The personalities are usually dramatically different; one may be carefree and fun-loving, and another quiet, studious, and serious. Needs and behaviors inhibited in the main or basic personality are usually liberally displayed by the others.

Dual and multiple personalities have received a great deal of attention and publicity in fiction, television, and motion pictures. Actually, however, they were until recently relatively uncommon in clinical practice. Prior to about the last 15 years, in fact, only slightly more than 100 cases could be found in the psychological and psychiatric literature. Their occurrence seems to have increased dramatically in recent years. No wholly satisfactory explanation exists for such a change in the occurrence base rate. Some of the increase, however, may be artifactual, the product of increased acceptance of the diagnosis by clinicians, who traditionally have been somewhat skeptical of the astonishing behavior these patients often display—such as undergoing sudden and dramatic shifts in personal identity before one's eyes. More females than males are diagnosed as having the disorder, with the ratio being about nine to one (Ross, 1989).

A more substantive and disturbing reason for the apparent increase in cases of multiple personality disorder (MPD) is offered by Ross (1989), who attributes it in part to an increasingly "sick" society in which child abuse, especially sexual abuse by adults, has become rampant. If Ross's suggestion about the deterioration of society is arguable, his observation that MPD is commonly preceded by childhood abuse is almost certainly not. While it is somewhat amazing that this connection was not generally recognized until about 1984, there is now no reasonable doubt about the reality of this association. Since childhood sexual abuse is a far more common occurrence for females than for males, there may be a relationship here with the gender discrepancy in diagnosis. The issue of abuse is addressed in further detail later in this section.

As already suggested, the question of malingering has dogged the diagnosis of MPD for at least a century. These doubts are reinforced by the suspicion that clinicians, by virtue of undue fascination with the problem and unwise use of techniques such as hypnosis, are sometimes responsible for eliciting these phenomena in highly suggestible patients. The latter criticism has a modest ring of truth, but it fails adequately to account for all of the observations reported—such as the elaborate pretreatment personal histories with which alternate personalities are commonly endowed. Cynicism about the concept of MPD has also been encouraged by the frequency with which it is used by defendants and their attorneys to escape punishment for crimes

("My other personality did it."). This defense was used in the famous case of the "Hillside Strangler," Kenneth Bianchi (Orne, Dinges, & Orne, 1984).

It is also true, as Spanos, Weekes, and Bertrand (1985) have clearly demonstrated, that normal college students can be induced by suggestion to exhibit some of the phenomena seen in MPD, including the adoption of a second personality. Such role-playing demonstrations are interesting in various ways, but they do not answer, nor even convincingly address, the question of the reality of MPD. That college student subjects might be able to give a convincing portrayal of a person with a broken leg would not, after all, establish the nonexistence of broken legs.

Our own view of the controversy surrounding MPD, as was suggested previously in our discussion of conversion versus malingering, is that it rests on a dichotomous way of thinking that is itself false. The increasing knowledge about normal mental and cognitive processes, such as the widespread evidence of separate (dissociated) memory subsystems and nonconscious active mental processing, strongly suggests that much highly organized mental activity is carried on in the "background," outside of awareness—analogous in some ways to computer multitasking (Hintzman, 1990). Accordingly, questions about whether a given behavior is consciously *or* unconsciously mediated, genuine *or* feigned, intended *or* unintended, deliberate *or* spontaneous, and so on are in the final analysis usually unanswerable as asked. So far as we can tell, the human mind does not operate in these dichotomous ways. In addition, such oversimplifications distract us from the task of understanding how it is that individuals go about solving the often difficult problems they have with managing and somehow integrating their extant mental contents with the challenges of their everyday lives. Is MPD "real?" Perhaps, but that is not to say we believe elements of theatrical pretense are never a part of this interesting and complex disorder.

The number of alter personalities in MPD varies, but in two substantial series of cases evaluated by questionnaire it averaged an amazing 15 (Ross, 1989). Alter personalities are usually strikingly different from the primary personality, suggesting that the alters express rejected parts of the original self. Alter characteristics are also highly varied, but certain "roles" are extremely common in the alter repertoires of MPD patients. These include the roles of Child, Protector, and Persecutor; an Opposite Sex alter, who may share one of these other roles, is also present in a majority of cases (Ross, 1989). These various types of role behaviors are discernible in *HIGHLIGHT 6.7,* which attempts to outline the kinds of cognitive structures regularly observed to be operating in cases of MPD. Normally, alters know of the existence of the primary personality and of each other, but the primary personality is not "permitted" knowledge of these others occupying his or her space, time, and body. Mutual and unidirectional amnesias among the alters also sometimes occur. Interestingly, very often one alter personality knows "everything" and, if cooperative, may be a valuable consultant for the therapist.

Wolfe, Gentile, and Wolfe (1989), in a recent study evaluating 71 sexually abused children, have likened their reactions to posttraumatic stress disorder. Evidence is building impressively in support of the notion that MPD is largely a type of posttraumatic dissociative disorder, one whose principal manifestation is the development of partially independent (dissociated) subsystems that constitute, in themselves, coherent personality organizations. The existence of these semiautonomous subpersonalities appears to serve important adaptive and coping functions for individuals who were severely and repeatedly traumatized as children, particularly (although not exclusively) by incestuous sexual abuse. Concerning the latter, 79.2 percent of Ross and colleagues' (1989) 236 cases, and 83.0 percent of Putnam and colleagues' (1986) 100 cases of MPD reported childhood abuse of a specifically sexual nature. The figures for other types of physical abuse were not far behind, suggesting that as children most of these individuals had lived in environments characterized by marked brutality. It is thought that the tendency to dissociate as a method of coping begins while victimization is in process—"This is not happening to *me.*"

The cruelty that some MPD patients suffered as children is almost unbelievable. A compelling illustration is the well-known case of Sybil, who was the subject of both a well-researched biography (Schreiber, 1973) and a feature motion picture. The case is briefly summarized here.

By the time of her adult years, Sybil reportedly had developed 15 alter personalities. Some of these were relatively minor characters, one was a baby, and two late developers were men. From infancy through late childhood, Sybil had been brutalized, sexually tortured, and nearly murdered by her psychotic (schizophrenic) mother,

HIGHLIGHT 6.7

Core Assumptions Characteristic of Multiple Personality Disorder and Associated Cognitive Distortions

Different parts of the self are separate selves.

- We have different bodies.
- I could kill (or slash, burn, force to overdose) her and be unaffected myself.
- Her behavior is not my responsibility.
- The abuse never happened to me.
- They're not my parents.

The victim is responsible for the abuse.

- I must be bad; otherwise it wouldn't have happened.
- If I had been perfect, it wouldn't have happened.
- I deserved to be punished for being angry.
- If I were perfect, I would not get angry.
- I never feel angry—she is the angry one.
- She deserves to be punished for allowing the abuse to happen.
- She deserves to be punished for showing anger.

It is wrong to show anger (or frustration, defiance, etc.).

- When I showed anger I was abused.
- If I never show anger, I will not be abused.
- I deserve to be punished for being angry.
- If I were perfect, I would not get angry.
- I never feel angry—she is the angry one.
- She deserves to be punished for allowing the abuse to happen.
- She deserves to be punished for feeling anger.

The past is present.

- I am 8 years old.
- The abuse is still happening.
- I am scared.
- The doctor is going to abuse me now.
- No one will protect me.

The primary personality can't handle the memories.

- We have to keep the memories.
- You can't tell her about us.
- If she has to remember, we will make her crazy.
- If she remembers, she won't like us.
- The abuse never happened.
- They must be sick to think those things happened.
- My parents are not like that.
- She is weak—I am strong.

I love my parents but she hates them.

- She is the bad one.
- You have to get rid of her.
- Nobody could ever be friends with her (or like her).
- She wants to hurt me.

The primary personality must be punished.

- It's her fault the abuse happened.
- She deserves all the bad things that happen to her.
- Everything bad that happens to her happens because she is bad.
- She has suffered enough—she would be better off if I killed her.
- I can punish her and be unaffected myself.
- I (the punishing alter) was never abused.
- Nobody would ever want to be close to me (persecutor alter).
- I am unlovable.

I can't trust myself or others.

- People have always abused me.
- I always end up choosing abusive relationships.
- I want to be abused.
- My parents were never consistent with me.
- Previous doctors wouldn't believe me (concerning abuse history and diagnosis).
- Whenever people get close to me, they leave.
- She trusted before and she got hurt.
- We won't let anyone get close to her.
- I can't trust her—she gets herself in situations she can't handle.

Adapted from Ross, 1989, pp. 126–130.

while her proper, hypocritical, and detached father managed persistently to convince himself—contrary to overwhelming evidence—that nothing untoward was happening in his family.

In the course of 11 years of ultimately successful treatment by a devoted and tenacious therapist, Sybil's extraordinary history—confirmed by her father when the outraged therapist forcefully confronted him—was gradually pieced together. The following are some highlights from that history:

The parents, engaging in extensive sexual activity nightly, made no obvious effort over the first nine years of her life to shield Sybil, who shared the same bedroom, from these experiences. In the daytime, neither parent was physically affectionate toward the other, and both held forth often and vociferously on the evils of sex. An additional twist on this bizarre situation was that Sybil frequently observed her mother molesting little girls she was supposedly baby-sitting, in the course of certain "games" she would suggest they play together. Also, on one occasion Sybil inadvertently discovered her mother engaged in mutual genital manipulation with three teenage girls in the neighborhood.

Beginning when Sybil was not yet a year old, her mother regularly performed certain morning rituals on her. These varied considerably but included such things as tying her up in various ways, suspending her from the ceiling by means of a light bulb cord, administering unneeded, adult-sized enemas to her with cold water, and forcing her to take potent laxatives with the prohibition that the child not use the bathroom; if she soiled herself she was beaten. The mother laughed during all of this; Sybil cried until she was 3½, then cried no more.

One morning ritual that her mother took great pains to carry out in an orderly fashion involved placing Sybil on the kitchen table and forcefully inserting various objects, including sharp metal ones, into her vagina. She explained to the child continuously from 6 months of age that she was only preparing her for "what men do to you." Needless to say, the child's vaginal canal was seriously injured by these ministrations, and permanent scarring of her genitalia to the point of probable sterility was observed in adult gynecological exams.

When Sybil's mother determined that actual punishment was in order because of misbehavior, she would become even more dangerous. The child would be slapped with enough force to knock her to the floor, or she might be flung across the room—on one occasion with such violence as to dislocate her shoulder. On another occasion Sybil's larynx was fractured with a blow delivered to her neck. She was also seriously burned with a hot flat iron and was nearly asphyxiated with a scarf tied tightly around her neck. In addition to these more deliberate inflictions of injury the child suffered many "accidents," such as a drawer violently closed on her hand. These numerous injuries were explained with vague references of the "kids will be kids" variety, a fabrication that was not seriously challenged by either Sybil's father or the family physician. Her mother's all-too-credible threats kept Sybil from revealing the truth to anyone.

On one occasion Sybil's mother nearly succeeded in killing her daughter. She placed her in a well-stocked wheat crib above her husband's shop "to play," and elevated the retractable stairs so that escape was impossible. Anyone with a rural background would know well the considerable danger of smothering in an entrapment of this kind, and in fact Sybil, buried in wheat and having difficulty breathing, thought she was going to die. She was saved by her father's unexpected return from work and his curiosity about the retracted stairs. Sybil's mother denied to her concerned husband any knowledge of how the child had got into the wheat crib, suggesting that it may have been done by a certain neighborhood bully, who of course also denied any knowledge of the incident.

The more recently publicized case of Truddi Chase and her "troops," a total of 92 separately identifiable personalities, is more typical in involving a male stepfather as the abuser, but no less revolting in its depiction of years of sadistic cruelty and heinous sexual victimization—beginning in this case at age 2. Frighteningly (but apparently of common occurrence in these cases), Truddi's mother did not effectively intervene to terminate the abuse for 14 years. Meanwhile, Truddi Chase, the original personality and the designated main author of the remarkable book, *When Rabbit Howls* (Chase et al. 1990), apparently ceased to exist; she has been "asleep" since age 2, having been replaced by "the troops."

The troops, the actual authors, are an astounding assortment of characters, many of them extremely talented and articulate, who participated in a program of treatment with psychotherapist Robert

One of the most well-known recent illustrations of multiple personality disorder is the case of Truddi Chase, who developed 92 personalities by the time she was an adult. Truddi's history of unspeakably brutal treatment by her stepfather and the subsequent manifestation of the "troops" is in keeping with the growing evidence that severe and repeated childhood trauma, both physical and sexual, is a significant factor in the occurrence of multiple personality disorder.

A. Phillips, Ph.D. The currently main personality is an employed adult woman, divorced and the mother of one child, a daughter. Prior to her treatment she had experienced continual dizziness, temper tantrums, and periods of blackout, but knew nothing of the others inhabiting her body. These other personalities include the following:

- Rabbit, mentioned in the book's title, who does not communicate except by howling in pain
- Mean Joe, the principal Protector, who is 11 feet tall
- Miss Wonderful, a model of human perfection
- Elvira, somewhat wild and irresponsible
- Twelve, a sensitive and artistic child
- Black Katherine, the assertive caretaker of Twelve and the other children
- Sewer Mouth, another woman who expresses rage in explicit language
- Ean the Irishman, who offers obscure commentary in a thick brogue
- The Front Runner, who keeps track of and reports on the other troops

The treatment undertaken by Dr. Phillips was apparently successful in achieving a workable "integration" of these diverse and fragmented personifications.

The question arises as to whether or not MPD occurs in the absence of a history of chronic childhood trauma. Ross (1989), who has had much clinical experience with MPD, allows that there may be such atraumatic cases of the disorder, but that he has personally never seen one where MPD was well-established and complexly organized. An unequivocal answer to the question is not easily obtained owing to an understandable and well-documented resistance among MPD patients to remembering events of this kind. In the absence of definitive information, our guess is that significantly disruptive MPD does occur in people whose backgrounds are unremarkable with respect to abuse. We would expect in such cases, however, to see evidence of other factors encouraging the development of dissociative tendencies.

Depersonalization Disorder

A relatively more frequent dissociative disorder that occurs predominantly in adolescents and young adults is **depersonalization disorder,** in which there is a loss of the sense of self. Individuals with this disorder feel that they are, all of a sudden, different—for example, that they are other people or that their bodies have drastically changed and have become, perhaps, quite grotesque. Frequently, the altered states are reported as out-of-body experiences in which individuals feel that they are, for a time, floating above their physical bodies and observing what is going on below. Mild forms of the experience are extremely common and are no cause for alarm. Reports of out-of-body experiences have included perceptions of visiting other planets or relatives who are in other cities. The disorder is often precipitated by acute stress resulting from an infectious illness, an accident, or some other traumatic event, as in the following case:

Charlotte D., a recently separated 19-year-old woman, was referred to an outpatient mental health service by her physician because she had experienced several "spells" in which her mind left her body and went to a strange place in another state. The first instance had occurred two months earlier, a few days after her husband had left her without explanation. Since then, she had had four episodes of "traveling" that had occurred during her waking state and had lasted for about 15 to 20 minutes. She described her experiences as a dreamy feeling in which her arms and legs were not attached to her body and other people around her were perceived as zombielike. Typically she felt dizzy and had pains in her stomach for hours after each spell.

Individuals who experience depersonalized states, and they are many, are usually able to function entirely normally between episodes. With more severe manifestations, as in the preceding case, the experience can be quite frightening and understandably causes a victim to become anxiously concerned about imminent mental collapse. Mostly such fears are unfounded, but the person might well profit from some professional help in dealing with the precipitating stressors and for reducing anxiety. A diagnostic problem may nevertheless arise because feelings of depersonalization sometimes are in fact early manifestations of impending decompensation and the development of frankly psychotic states of a schizophreniform type, discussed in Chapter 12.

NEUROTIC STYLES

As was earlier noted, the strategy employed in recent DSMs in creating discrete categories for the syndromes described above is probably a good one from a diagnostic perspective. Abandonment of the *concept* of neurosis may be premature on other counts, however. It has robust research and clinical support; it continues to be employed by numerous workers in the field; and it remains a useful way to conceptualize many of the behaviors described not only in this chapter but elsewhere in the text.

In this section we will explore the possibility that neurotic patterns can exist in the absence of the relatively dramatic symptom syndromes described in preceding sections. In this context, we will introduce the notion of neurotic "styles." Personal misery and ineffectiveness are not, after all, dependent on the presence of obtrusive "symptoms." We will illustrate this point with a brief consideration of the manner in which neurotic styles can influence interpersonal processes.

No precise equivalent to the concept of **neurotic style** has ever been included in the formal Axis I DSM categories. It is unlikely that one will be because these styles, as general "symptomless" ways of coping with anxiety, do not warrant the status of formally recognized mental disorders. By *symptomless,* we mean that neurotic styles do not entail disabilities that would be obvious to everyone. Rather, they involve general ways of behaving that interfere with an individual's effectiveness and ability to satisfy personal needs, and are in this sense somewhat akin to Axis II personality disorders. We include them here for two reasons: (a) many individuals who seek the services of mental health practitioners are less troubled by specific clinical symptoms per se than by unsatisfactory interpersonal relationships caused by neurotic styles; and (b) an understanding of neurotic styles should enhance our understanding of the established DSM categories of neurotic symptom disorders, since generalized neurotic behavior patterns often accompany these specific disorders (as a recall of several of the cases presented earlier will confirm). Concerning this point, Shapiro (1965) has written: "Every reader with clinical experience and, for that matter, every sensitive person will know that [neurotic] symptoms or outstanding pathological traits regularly appear in contexts of attitudes, interests, intellectual inclinations and endowments, and even vocational aptitudes and social affinities with which the given symptom or trait seems to have a certain consistency" (p. 3).

In other words, disabling neurotic symptoms are usually embedded within a broader context of related personal characteristics. As we will see, many of these characteristics seem to arise from the same sources as do the symptoms. An example at this point may help clarify.

A 30-year-old man, married and with two children, was referred to a psychologist because of a persistent paralysis of his left arm and hand. Though the paralysis had developed following an auto accident, no evidence of organic damage would account for it. It was diagnosed as a conversion disorder. The man's history revealed that he had been dependent on an aunt who had raised him but who had subsequently died when he was 15. He had responded by making a show of self-sufficiency, but his work history as an adult had been marred by a series of dissatisfactions and changes of employment—primarily because he invariably had grown to feel that not enough was being done for him by his employers. Prior to the accident, his marital relationship had also become disrupted because his wife, having become more independent, was spending less time at home. The patient had bitterly complained that she was not being a "good mother" for her children.

Despite making a somewhat halfhearted attempt to resolve his difficulties in psychotherapy, treatment progress was reported as slow. The paralysis continued, and the patient appeared to have settled comfortably into the role of helpless victim. (Adapted from Spitzer et al., 1983.)

We see here the interplay between the patient's life-style prior to the accident and the particular symptom he developed in response to increased stress and the "opportunity" the accident afforded. Dependency appeared to be the principal theme both before and afterward. As we will see, neurotic dependency of this sort is usually the product of the *inhibition,* by anxiety, of independent, autonomous behavior (Hine, 1971; Hine et al., 1972, 1983). We will now consider how inhibition functions in neurotic styles.

The Role of Inhibition in Neurotic Styles

As indicated earlier, a person can be conditioned to respond with anxiety (or fear) to certain non-noxious stimuli. The person may then respond in the same way to other stimuli having similar properties. Once the anxiety-response pattern is established, the individual will learn to avoid the stimuli that provoke it. In a neurotic process, certain of an individual's own *behaviors,* or even the person's thoughts of engaging in them, will evoke the anxiety response. These anxiety-inspiring behaviors are then avoided or inhibited. Should such behaviors be important or essential for good adjustment, the affected person may be deprived of the means to function effectively in the world.

Let us suppose, for example, that a child is born to parents who do not tolerate aggressive behavior in any form, so much so that they repeatedly threaten to abandon their child anytime she displays normal childhood levels of aggressive conduct. It is possible that such a child would learn to respond with strong anxiety to the more "aggressive" elements of her behavioral repertoire, or to any internal demand (motivational impulse) or external need to act aggressively. In other words, she would have pronounced inhibitions with respect to aggression and perhaps even related behavior, such as normal assertiveness. Here we may introduce the notion of an inhibited behavior *system*—a cluster of related behaviors that act as anxiety-eliciting stimuli. Insofar as aggressive or assertive behaviors are in some situations appropriate and adaptive, this child will have an important gap in her adaptive repertoire as she grows into adulthood.

The scenario given here is hypothetical, and we do not mean to suggest that all such anxieties are learned in this or comparable ways. In fact it is often difficult to determine precisely the sources of a neurotic person's special fears concerning the enactment of certain types of behavior. As suggested earlier, we certainly cannot rule out a constitutional element as a possibility, and indeed Shapiro's (1965) discussion of neurotic styles strongly hints at constitutional origins.

In any event, as the preceding example illustrates, one important characteristic of a person with a neurotic style is a deficit in behavioral repertoire. That is, certain types of behavior that seem adaptive and even expected in certain circumstances do not occur. They are blocked or inhibited by the anxiety their expression would cause. Dr. J., in the case described earlier, did not have egalitarian, easygoing, "passive" responses in his repertoire prior to his anxiety disorder breakdown. Two other characteristics often seen accompanying such deficits deserve brief mention, partly because of their importance as diagnostic clues:

1. A tendency for a person to behave, often in an inflexible and exaggerated manner, in ways that are the seeming opposite of the "missing" behaviors. Evidently, this is a defense used by the person to further lessen the likelihood of expressing, or perhaps even recognizing the existence of, the behavior system that is inhibited by anxiety. In the case of neurotic inhibition of aggressive behavior, for example, we might be struck by a person's extreme and unfailing agreeableness, even in situations that would seem to call for a vigorous defense of self—for example, in being unjustly humiliated by a bullying superior.

2. The failure of neurotic defenses to contain fully either the anxiety underlying them or some indirect evidence of the inhibited behavior system. Hence a person who develops a neurotic style will often show overt signs of anxiety, such as excessive sweating or muscular tension, while attempting to pursue his or her well-practiced defensive stance. Total success in blocking the expression of inhibited behavior systems is rarely, if ever, achieved. A trained observer, or even an especially sensitive layperson, will usually be able to detect in the person a tendency for the inhibited system to reveal itself, but normally only in indirect ways. The behavior of a client of one of the authors provides an instructive example. The client, a well-educated man who was a victim of severe aggression inhibition, repeatedly interrupted the therapist's comments with "respectful" requests that the therapist define the meaning of the relatively common words he was using, the client claiming to have a "poor vocabulary." The therapist's own increasing annoyance with these interruptions ultimately provided the clue to understanding. As subsequently confirmed by the client, his constant requests for interpretation of vocabulary items were his way of expressing his "aggressive" feelings that the therapist was acting like a "pompous ass." So much for the self-esteem hazards of the therapist's trade!

We will now briefly examine four inhibition patterns common to neurotic styles that can be seen in our own culture: aggression/assertion, responsibility/independence, compliance/submission, and intimacy/trust. Our illustrations should be considered as models or prototypes, much oversimplified for pedagogic reasons. They are based to a considerable extent on the analyses of Hine and colleagues (1971, 1972, 1983).

Aggression/Assertion Inhibition The problems associated with this form of neurotic style have been illustrated already. A person with this neurotic style is markedly uncomfortable in any situation in which aggressive, self-assertive actions would seem to be reasonable responses. Instead, the person rigidly clings to a typically cooperative, agreeable, and "forgiving" stance, showing little or no hostile response to even extreme provocation. The anger and hostility presumably felt at some levels are largely stifled, though their intensities may build over time in the face of continued provocation. Physical and psychological problems (such as hypertension or compulsive behavior) are common long-term results. Fortunately less common is the so-called overcontrolled hostility syndrome (Megargee, 1966), in which buried anger and resentment may lead to a sudden outburst of incredibly intense violence. Out of such circumstances are bred tales of, say, the much-admired Eagle scout who one day hacks his mother to death with an axe.

Responsibility/Independence Inhibition

Some individuals acquire in the course of their development a marked, anxiety-driven aversion to exercising personal independence or legitimate authority over others. Situations or events calling for assertions of independence or authority are, for these people, occasions of painful stress and anxiety. Hence such persons normally arrange their lives to minimize the likelihood they will be called on for displays of strength and autonomous action. They may, for example, prove to be incompetent at many of life's most simple tasks. Related to and normally accompanying these traits is a notable submissiveness and a clinging dependency on others. Few people can tolerate such childlike dependency indefinitely, and therefore such a person's relationships usually turn out to be unsatisfactory and short-lived. The development of symptoms consistent with this "helpless" state is a typical complication of this neurotic style.

Compliance/Submission Inhibition Individuals who fear tendencies to comply or submit constitute a significant proportion of the "rebels" within our own and other cultures. They tend to reject ready-made solutions to personal problems offered by various professional, religious, and media figures, and also solutions imposed by authorities, legitimate or not. Presumably, people with this form of anxiety have learned that reliance on "established" authorities, parental or otherwise, leads to far greater disasters than does reliance on themselves. Accordingly, they become anxious and rebellious when they are required (or are motivated) to obey or "go along."

Compliant, submissive, and dependent behaviors are appropriate to many life circumstances—such as when one has a serious physical illness or when a legitimate authority frustrates one's plans—but these responses exact an enormous cost in anxiety from an individual who fears submission. Such an individual may display intense, inappropriate "strength" in the form of defiance, noncompliance with legitimate authority, inability to accept help in adversity, dangerous risk taking, and exaggerated wariness about letting anyone else be in control.

Traits of this sort are of course highly valued in American folklore. For example, Butch Cassidy and

Compliant, submissive, and dependent behaviors are appropriate to many life circumstances, but an individual who fears submission may display defiance, noncompliance with established authority (parental or otherwise), dangerous risk taking, and exaggerated wariness about letting anyone else be in control.

the Sundance Kid enraptured sophisticated movie audiences of the 1970s as much as similar film cowboys had since virtually the beginnings of the movie industry. More recent versions are Augustus McCrae and Woodrow Call of the novel and television series *Lonesome Dove.* It is certainly true that, in moderation, such traits can be functionally adaptive. When they are based on unrealistic fears of submission, however, they rarely can be contained within the moderate range. The result is often behavior that is unsatisfying, self-defeating, and on occasion dangerous to health and physical survival. For example, a person who cannot submit, comply, and depend on others during the treatment period immediately following a heart attack will have a significantly diminished life expectancy.

Intimacy/Trust Inhibition People who feel unusually strong anxiety over establishing close personal attachments with others typically need relationships of mutual trust and intimacy at least as much as the rest of us. Indeed, they may spend inordinate amounts of time and energy in seeking them. However, at a crucial point in a relationship —perhaps when it seems to be going especially well or when an enhanced commitment is demanded— such a person suddenly becomes wary and retreats. Explicit suspiciousness and cynicism about the other's sincerity frequently enter the picture at this point, and the often bewildered other is more or less forcefully driven away. In cases of severe intimacy/trust inhibition, this sequence is played out rapidly, with the result that few if any potential relationships ever really get off the ground. When the problem is this severe, even more serious psychopathology tends to develop. In milder instances, a person can manage an occasional long-term relationship, although in such cases the person usually maintains a certain aloofness and distance.

As was mentioned earlier, neurotic styles often turn out to be similar in their manifest, overt aspects to certain of the DSM personality disorders, which are the subject of Chapter 8. In fact Horowitz and colleagues (1984) have used the term "personality styles" to refer to this class of problems. For example, the overt manifestations of neurotic intimacy/trust inhibition are as a practical matter often indistinguishable from those of the Axis II avoidant personality disorder. The distinction is at the conceptual level of imputed etiology; as we will see, "personality" disorders are conceived to be merely the aberrant developments of certain personality traits—not defensive behaviors driven by unrealistic fear (anxiety), as in neurotic styles.

Interpersonal Aspects of Neurotic Styles

As the preceding descriptions illustrate, individuals who develop neurotic styles can create not only frustration and misery for themselves, but also serious problems for people with whom they interact. Typically, people who behave neurotically do not have large networks of enduring relationships, and they tend to be quite dependent (although not necessarily in any obvious way) on the few they have. Consequently, most relatively non-neurotic people sooner or later find it unappealing to attempt to deal with the conflicting and unrelenting demands placed on them by their neurotic partners. For reasonably well-functioning individuals who are drawn to neurotically functioning people, it is literally a "no win" situation. For example, a man may find that a woman with compliance/submission inhibition is in many respects an "ideal" partner; she will "take charge" of all situations and will not allow herself or her mate to be taken advantage of or controlled. Yet the man in such a relationship might well find it difficult never to have his suggestions taken seriously, never to be allowed to take the lead. Hence the typical experience of a neurotic person is that relationships fall by the wayside, which may be yet another source of anxiety and insecurity.

Relationships need not turn out this way, however, particularly if the prospective friend or lover is also neurotic in a complementary way. For example, two people with aggression/assertion inhibitions may sustain a satisfying relationship because both are so frightened of aggression that neither presents a hint of provocation to the other. The relationship is characterized by a level of "understanding" and "niceness" that astounds external observers, although such observers may also be aware of a certain lack of zest and spontaneity in the interactions of the mutually inhibited pair. In effect they protect each other from their darker sides.

Other types of mutually neurotic, sustainable relationships readily come to mind. For example, a person with responsibility/independence inhibition married to a person with compliance/submission inhibition may find that the marriage results in a reasonably stable standoff. Of course, the relationship is apt to be punctuated by stormy episodes because, as we have seen, the inhibited portion of a neurotic individual's behavioral repertoire is unlikely to remain totally and permanently in abeyance. Thus even in cases of this kind of "perfect match," the upshot can often be a major crisis, sometimes ending in divorce court.

An obvious implication of these remarks is that relationships maintained on the basis of neurotic complementarity are vulnerable to disruption should one of the parties undergo therapy. Hafner (1984), for example, identified a group of husbands who experienced negative reactions when their wives, through therapy, overcame the "helplessness" of agoraphobia.

THE DEVELOPMENT AND MAINTENANCE OF NEUROTIC BEHAVIORS

In our preceding discussion we described the basic nature of neurotic disorders, noting that they may be manifested in certain characteristic symptoms, in general behavioral styles, or both. We presented a variety of specific neurotic patterns. Now let us focus more closely on relevant causal factors and give some attention to treatment considerations and to the outcomes that may be expected.

As we have seen, Freud considered anxiety to be the central problem in neurosis, a conclusion echoed over the years by many writers of widely differing theoretical persuasions. It is also basically the approach we have taken in seeking to conceptualize the varied behavioral phenomena traditionally classified as "neurotic." To understand these disorders, then, we need to understand the origins of relatively severe anxiety and of the inefficient and self-defeating modes often used to cope with it. We will approach these issues from biological, psychosocial, and sociocultural perspectives.

Biological Factors

The precise role of genetic and constitutional factors in neurotic behavior has not been delineated. Ample evidence from army records and civilian studies indicates that the incidence of neurotic patterns is much higher in the family histories of neurotic individuals than in the general population. The extent to which such findings reflect the effects of heredity is not known, however. Other explanations for these correlations are readily available, such as the likelihood that symptom modeling occurs among family members. For example, in the chronic multiple phobia case described earlier (page 187), the client's mother had also suffered lifelong phobic reactions and had sought actively to transmit her fears to her daughter.

In a study of concordance rates of neurotic disorders in identical and fraternal twins in the military, Pollin et al. (1969) found that among identical twins, the rate was only one and a half times as high as it was among fraternal twins. Since the environmental backgrounds of identical twins are likely to be more similar than those of fraternal twins, these investigators concluded that heredity plays a minimal role in the development of neurotic behaviors. After evaluating the evidence, Cohen (1974) came to a similar conclusion: "the concept of a genetically based disease or defect cannot provide a satisfactory explanation for the diversity and variability of most neurotic phenomena" (p. 473). Barlow (1988) has thoroughly reviewed the evidence on the heritability of the anxiety disorders, concluding that genetic factors seem modestly implicated, but only in the sense of contributing to some generalized vulnerability.

Sex, age, glandular functioning, and other physiological factors have also been investigated without clearly illuminating the causal picture. It is known, of course, that stress tolerance is lowered by loss of sleep, poor appetite, and increased irritability associated with prolonged emotional tension—but such conditions are by no means exclusive to the neurotic disorders. A more promising possibility centers around constitutional differences in ease of anxiety-response conditioning, as was suggested earlier. For example, extreme sensitivity and autonomic lability (instability) may predispose an individual to a "surplus" of conditioned fears and hence to avoidance behavior. Or it may be that some individuals are more prone biologically to experience the physiological disruptions underlying the anxiety experience.

Along these lines, several investigators have shown that infusions of sodium lactate or sodium bicarbonate (e.g., Gorman et al., 1989; Hollander et al., 1989; Liebowitz et al. 1984, 1985), or the inhalation of carbon dioxide (e.g., Woods et al., 1986, 1987), can produce panic attacks in panic disorder patients at a much higher rate than in normal subjects. While such observations are consistent with the notion that panic disorder patients have some sort of elevated biological vulnerability to evocation of the panic pattern, a much simpler explanation pertains to the subjective effects produced by these procedures. Namely, they mimic the physiological cues normally preceding a panic attack. Panic disorder patients, being familiar with these prodromal cues, apparently "misinterpret" the latter type of experience as beginning panic. As noted earlier in our discussion of anxiety-response dynamics, such a misinterpretation would be expected often to lead to a full-blown panic attack. In other words, sensitivity to lactate or CO_2 is more likely a *consequence* than a cause of the panic experience. Along somewhat similar lines, Ley (1988) has suggested that panic attacks are produced by physiological cues resulting from unnoticed hyperventilation in panic-prone patients.

In general it would be somewhat surprising to discover that innate features of physiologic reactivity and temperament have no role in predisposing individuals to the anxiety response or to particular ways of managing it when it occurs. As yet, however, the evidence is inconclusive; a great deal more research is needed to clarify the possible role of constitutional and other biological factors in the development of neurotic disorders.

Psychosocial Factors

The psychological and interpersonal causal factors that we reviewed in Chapter 4 as predisposing an individual to develop specific maladaptive behaviors are especially applicable to neurotic behaviors. Relevant here are early psychic trauma, pathogenic parent-child and family patterns, and disturbed interpersonal relationships.

Additionally, each of the psychosocial viewpoints summarized in Chapter 3 has posed a hypothesized origin of neurosis and neurotic behaviors. We list some of the more explicit of these in the following sections.

Anxiety-Defense As we have noted, neurotic disorders have traditionally been explained within the framework of anxiety-defense, as originally proposed by Freud and elaborated by later investigators. According to this view, threats stemming from internal or external sources elicit intense anxiety; this anxiety in turn leads to the exaggerated use of various ego-defense mechanisms and to maladaptive behaviors. Although today other causal factors, such as cognitive elaboration, are also taken into account, this view still has broad generality and explanatory power, as illustrated in earlier sections of this chapter. As we have already indicated, however, it is now thought that virtually any human propensity —not just primitive sexual and aggressive impulses —may become blocked or inhibited by anxiety, leading to essentially defensive (and ultimately maladaptive) behaviors. This view does not in itself address the *sources* of such maladaptive anxiety, but it seems likely that many of them relate to faulty conditioning and learning, to which we now turn.

Faulty Learning In more recent years, faulty learning, a major focus of the behavioral perspective, has become the most widely used explanation for both the development and the maintenance of neurotic behaviors. Faulty learning is seen in the acquisition of maladaptive anxiety responses and modes of coping with stressful situations. It is also

The fear associated with a stimulus such as a large dog may, through generalization, be associated with other similar stimuli, leading to a phobia of all dogs, big or small.

seen in the typical failure of neurotic individuals to learn the competencies and attitudes needed for dealing with normal life problems. For individuals who feel basically inadequate and insecure in a competitive and hostile world, making the effort to become competent is especially difficult; relying on defensive and avoidant life-styles is less threatening and brings enough short-term alleviation of anxiety to be repeatedly reinforced.

The principles of simple learning, or conditioning, may in certain instances account for the acquisition of irrational fears and anxieties in the first place. As noted earlier, the physiological arousal pattern associated with fear has been shown in countless experiments to be readily conditioned to previously neutral stimuli. These stimuli then act as expectancy cues signaling that painful events will follow. In fact, some evidence suggests that people who are already anxious overestimate the strength or reliability of contingencies of this kind; that is, a potentially threatening stimulus is perceived as more likely to be followed by an aversive event than is actually the case (Tomarken, Mineka, & Cook, 1989). Furthermore, through ***generalization,*** the newly acquired fear may spread to other, similar stimuli, including internal ones, such as motives to engage in certain actions. The generalization process seems especially pertinent to certain phobias in which there occurs a "displacement" of anxiety from one situation to another having similar elements or characteristics.

The powerful role of learning in the development of neurotic behaviors was supported in a survey by Ost and Hugdahl (1981). These investigators administered questionnaires to 106 adult phobic patients concerning, among other things, the purported origins of their fears. In describing the situations they considered as sources of their phobias, 58 percent cited conditioning experiences, and another 17 percent described situations that were based on indirect or "vicarious" learning. Such observations may be but an aspect of the more general problem of traumatic events sensitizing individuals to the unpredictable and uncontrollable nature of negative life events. Pollard, Pollard, and Corn (1989), for example, have shown the onset of panic attacks to be related to the prior occurrence of such events. Relatedly perhaps, Sanderson, Rapee, and Barlow (1989) have shown that a sense of control, even an illusory one, may decrease the likelihood of laboratory-induced panics.

An important point to consider in any discussion of acquired or learned fears (anxieties) is that, almost certainly, some stimuli more readily come to elicit fear than do others. This too is an aspect of a far more general principle that we have come to appreciate only in recent years: what can be learned efficiently is to a considerable extent limited and species-specific. The term ***preparedness*** has been used to refer to the likelihood that humans are biologically predisposed to develop certain types of fears (Cook, Hodes, & Lang, 1986; Seligman & Hager, 1972). For example, we seem much more likely to acquire a fear of snakes than a fear of grapefruits. Thus any listing of commonly observed types of phobias, while it is apt to be extensive, is also finite. Lelliott et al. (1989) note in this connection that 81 percent of the first panic attacks experienced by a series of agoraphobic patients occurred in places having strong "extraterritorial" (unfamiliar environmental) cues.

Conditioning is by no means the only way in which people can learn irrational fears. Abundant evidence exists that much human learning, including the learning of fears, is ***observational*** in nature. Frightening events in which a person in no way participates may nevertheless become the occasion for marked and persistent fear arousal. How many people have had their enjoyment of the beach marred by having seen the movie *Jaws* or one of its sequels? Similarly, as noted earlier, fears can be transmitted from one person to another by a ***modeling*** process: merely observing the fear of another in a given situation may cause that situation to become a fearful one for the observer. For example, if a child's parents prove to be more or less uniformly anxious in situations calling for assertive behavior, that child might well grow up with a similar maladaptive anxiety. Of course, the same result might be accomplished via a conditioning process if the parents routinely punish the child for any show of assertiveness.

Blocked Personal Growth We have noted the emphasis placed by the humanistic perspective on values, meaning, personal growth, and self-fulfillment; we have also seen how stressful one's life situation can become when it is devoid of meaning and hope, as depicted by reports of former inmates of concentration and POW camps. In any case, lack of meaning and blocked personal growth often appear to stem from a lack of needed competencies and resources or a feeling that duty requires one to remain in a self-stifling role. As a result, an individual's main efforts are devoted to simply trying to meet basic needs, rather than to personal growth and development. According to the humanistic perspective, such a life-style can ultimately bring feelings of anxiety, hostility, and futility—feelings that may inspire neurotic behaviors.

Pathogenic Interpersonal Relationships As we have seen, certain interactions within families and other early relationships can set the stage for children to develop neurotic life-styles in later life. For example, parents who overprotect or indulge their children may prevent them from developing the independent, effective coping techniques required in their adult years. Or insecure parents may instill their own excessive concerns with ailments into their children, which is a common background feature in somatoform disorders (Kellner, 1985). Much of what a person becomes in later life—attitudes, values, and often even particular symptoms—can be traced to interactions within the family during the formative years.

It is apparent that the preceding views of psychosocial causation are interrelated and may apply in varying degrees to a given case. This is an important point to remember. Though we may have focused at times on one or another feature of a person's behavior, in most cases all of the concepts discussed above are helpful in understanding the development of neurotic behavior.

Sociocultural Factors

Reliable data on the incidence of neurotic disorders in other societies is meager. Kidson and Jones (1968) failed to find classical neurotic patterns among the aborigines of the Australian western desert; but they did note that as these groups were increasingly exposed to modern civilization, hypochondriacal concerns and other somatic complaints occurred. In general, however, it appears that conversion disorder is more common among the people of underdeveloped countries, while anxiety and obsessive-compulsive disorders are more common in technologically advanced societies.

In our own society, neurotic disorders are found among all segments of the population. Significant differences, however, seem to exist in the incidence and types of patterns manifested by particular subgroups. In general, neurotic individuals from the lower educational and socioeconomic levels appear to show a higher than average incidence not only of conversion disorder but also of aches, pains, and other somatic symptoms. Neurotic individuals from the middle and upper classes, on the other hand, seem especially prone to anxiety and obsessive-compulsive disorders—with such subjective symptoms as "unhappiness" and general feelings of dissatisfaction with life. Phobias and the more serious dissociation disorder of multiple personality, as we have seen, are far more common in women than in men, although it is not yet certain that these differences are due to sociocultural variables.

Although there has been little systematic research on how specific sociocultural variables affect the development of neurotic disorders, it seems clear that the social environment influences both an individual's likelihood of developing a neurotic reaction and the particular form that reaction is most likely to take. Thus as social conditions continue to change in our own society and elsewhere, we can expect corresponding changes in both the incidence and prevailing types of neurotic behavior.

TREATMENTS AND OUTCOMES

The treatment of neurotic disorders may involve a wide range of goals and procedures. Treatment may be aimed at alleviating distressing symptoms, changing an individual's basically defensive and avoidant life-style, or both; it may include drug therapy or psychotherapy, or some combination of these approaches. Anxiety (excluding obsessive-compulsive), phobic, and conversion disorders usually respond more readily to treatment than do other more complex neurotic patterns, but the outlook here is, in general, favorable. Andrews and Harvey (1981) have reanalyzed the data on overall outcomes of psychosocial therapy specifically as these data relate to neurotic disorders. They have used a technique known as *meta-analysis* (Smith, Glass, & Miller, 1980), a description of which may be found in Chapter 18. Results from 81 controlled studies involving the treatment of neurotic individuals indicated that the average client who had received treatment was more functional than nearly 80 percent of comparably disordered, untreated control clients evaluated at the same time. Also, the relapse rate for treated clients during two years following therapy was insignificant.

For present purposes, we shall keep our discussion brief and focused on the aspects of treatment that are particularly relevant to neurotic behavior. These therapies will be more thoroughly examined in Chapters 17 and 18.

Pharmacological (Drug) Therapies

"Psychopharmacological agents are the most widely prescribed, widely misprescribed, most frequently abused, and probably the most advertised of all the pharmaceuticals available to the practicing clinician. They clearly occupy a role at or near the center of medical practice" (Levenson, 1981, p. xi).

As the preceding statement attests, many patients seen by medical practitioners are neurotic individuals seeking relief from their "nervousness" and their various functional (psychogenic) physical problems. Most often in such cases minor tranquilizing drugs such as Valium or Xanax are prescribed. These drugs are used—and misused—for tension relief and for relaxation; they also reduce subjective anxiety and may stabilize emotional reactivity. Neurotic individuals also frequently attempt to control their anxiety or other symptoms by self-medication with nonprescription drugs, including alcohol.

Available statistics indicate that some 70 percent or more of neurotic patients show some symptom relief following drug therapy, and most of them are able to function more effectively (Bassuk, Schoonover, & Gelenberg, 1983; Covi et al., 1974; Engelhardt, 1974; Prusoff & Klerman, 1974). These drugs, however, can have undesirable side effects—such as drowsiness—and in some cases a patient develops an increasing tolerance for and persistent dependence on a drug. In addition, many people expect too much of a treatment that is merely palliative, and the masking of their symptoms may discourage them from seeking needed psychotherapy.

We earlier took note in the case of Anne Watson of the use of antidepressant medication to control panics and agoraphobia. While the evidence is still somewhat fragmentary, this approach looks promising and has led to speculation (e.g., Breier, Charney, & Heninger, 1984) concerning a possible biological connection between depression and panic (and agoraphobic) disorders. As also noted earlier, antidepressant drug side effects can be a serious problem (Mavissakalian & Perel, 1989).

Recently the drug Clomipramine has been suggested as an effective biological treatment for obsessive-compulsive disorder (e.g., Benkelfat et al., 1989). It appears in fact to reduce the intensity of this disorder's symptoms, but we have not yet seen convincing evidence of marked and lasting therapeutic potency.

Psychological Therapies

Individual psychotherapies, behavior therapy, family therapy, and multimodal therapy have been used to treat neurotic disorders.

Individual Psychotherapies These therapies are oriented toward helping individuals achieve greater understanding of themselves, their problems, and their relationships, and toward developing healthier attitudes and better coping skills. The various types of therapy included in this general category differ somewhat in their specific goals and procedures—each reflecting the particular psychosocial perspective on which it is based—but all stress the need for self-understanding, a realistic frame of reference, a satisfying pattern of values, and the development of effective techniques for coping with adjustive demands.

These objectives sound deceptively easy to achieve—actually they share a number of stumbling blocks. First is the problem of creating a therapeutic situation in which neurotic individuals feel safe enough to lower their defenses; explore their innermost feelings, thoughts, and assumptions; and begin to recognize the possibility of other options. Second is the problem of providing opportunities for neurotic individuals to learn new ways of perceiving themselves and their world, and to see new ways of coping. Third is the problem of helping them transfer what they have learned in the therapy situation to real life; even when they understand the nature and causes of their self-defeating behavior and have learned that more effective coping techniques are available, they may still be "unable to risk the initial venture into the heretofore out-of-bounds area of living" (Salzman, 1968, p. 465). Fourth is the problem of changing the conditions in their life situations that may be reinforcing and thus maintaining the neurotic life-styles. For example, a domineering and egocentric husband who will not participate in a therapy program may tend to block his wife's efforts toward self-direction and make it more difficult for her to give up her insecure, neurotic behavior. He may even manage to sabotage the entire treatment program.

The behavior patterns we have called neurotic styles seem especially amenable to treatments emphasizing an interpersonal approach, since these conditions are manifested chiefly in interpersonal difficulties. Interpersonal therapies tend to be active and confrontative in focusing on how to alter maladaptive interpersonal behavior. Hence they tend to be efficient and relatively brief (Anchin & Kiesler, 1982; Carson, in press-a).

Behavior Therapies As we have seen, behavior therapies focus on (a) removing specific symptoms or maladaptive behaviors; (b) developing needed competencies and adaptive behaviors; and (c) modifying environmental conditions that may be reinforcing and maintaining maladaptive behaviors. In this last context, Bandura (1969) has stated, "A treatment that fails to alter the major controlling conditions of the deviant behavior will most certainly prove ineffective" (p. 50). In general, behavior therapy approaches have an excellent record of efficacy in the neuroses (Smith, Glass, & Miller, 1980).

The behavior therapy most commonly used in the treatment of neurotic behaviors is controlled exposure to anxiety-producing circumstances. Here clients are placed—symbolically or increasingly under "real life" conditions—in those situations they

Systematic desensitization is frequently used to help people overcome simple phobias, such as the fear of snakes. In this type of therapy, patients are placed in a series of situations, each closer to the situation that would provoke the most anxiety, while they practice relaxation techniques to counter their anxiety. Here, a number of patients have progressed from handling rubber snakes (upper left) and peering at snakes through glass (center top) to actually handling living but harmless snakes. Note that some patients first handle the snakes while wearing rubber gloves.

find most threatening. In the variant known as systematic desensitization, an attempt is made to associate the fear-producing situations with states that reduce anxiety, such as relaxation. Other forms of "guided exposure" to fear-producing stimuli also continue to show much promise (Barlow, 1988), perhaps particularly where a "self-efficacy" component is emphasized (Williams, S. L., Turner, & Peer, 1985). A combination of exposure and (compulsive) response prevention, illustrated in *HIGHLIGHT 6.8* may be the most effective approach to the difficult problem of obsessive-compulsive disorders (Steketee & Foa, 1985). In addition, Klosko et al. (1990) have recently reported a well-designed study showing that a particular behavior therapy program emphasizing exposure is significantly superior to antianxiety medication in the treatment of panic disorder.

As we saw in our discussion of specific types of neurotic disorders, some maladaptive behaviors—such as conversion paralyses—may be extinguished by removing reinforcements that have been maintaining the behavior, while simultaneously providing reinforcements for more responsible coping patterns. Other maladaptive behaviors can sometimes be removed by mild aversive conditioning (Bandura, 1969, 1973; Stern, Lipsedge, & Marks, 1973). Here, too, the conditioning works best when combined with reinforcements of more adaptive alternative behaviors (Sturgis & Meyer, 1981).

As noted in Chapter 3, many behaviorists in recent years have been using behavior therapy techniques to change cognitive behavior (Mahoney, 1974; Meichenbaum, 1977). Individuals who are experiencing neurotic problems, such as anxiety attacks, may be viewed as behaving anxiously in response to internal thoughts and beliefs (cognitions). Here a therapist attempts to change the neurotic behavior by changing the individual's inner thoughts and beliefs that may be causing or reinforcing the behavior. This process is called *cognitive mediation.* With encouraging preliminary results, Beck and colleagues (1985) have extended to the anxiety disorders their well-known work on the cognitive-behavioral treatment of depression. We will discuss cognitive-behavioral therapy in more detail in Chapter 18.

Although behavior therapy is usually directed toward changing specific "target behaviors"—such as removing phobias—it often seems to have more far-reaching positive results (Marks, 1978). A client who overcomes a specific phobia gains confidence in his or her ability to overcome other problems. Ultimately, the individual learns that coping effectively with adjustive demands is more rewarding than trying to avoid them. Thus although cognitive-behavioral therapies usually focus more on modifying a patient's internal cognitions and behavior therapy focuses more on the removal of specific target behaviors, the outcomes of these two forms of therapy (and others) are often comparable (Sloane et al., 1975; Smith et al. 1980; Stiles et al., 1986).

Often pathogenic family interactions maintain neurotic behaviors in individuals. Family therapy emphasizes treating family systems rather than focusing primarily on individuals.

Family Therapy Often pathogenic family interactions keep a neurotic individual in a continually "sick situation." As Melville (1973) has expressed it, "In a family there is no such thing as one person in trouble" (p. 17). As a consequence of such findings, increasing emphasis has been placed on treating family systems rather than focusing primarily on individuals (Fox, 1976; Gurman & Kniskern, 1978).

Multimodal Therapy As this term, coined by Lazarus (1981, 1985), implies, a combination of varied approaches may be used in the treatment of a given individual for neurotic behaviors. In fact increasing evidence (see, for example, Goldfried, 1980; Goldfried & Safran, 1986) shows that professional therapists are lessening their strong allegiances to particular therapies and are increasingly willing

HIGHLIGHT 6.8

Treatment of Obsessive-Compulsive Disorder with Exposure and Response Prevention

Steketee and Foa (1985) present the following case as an illustration of their recommended approach to the treatment of obsessive-compulsive disorders. The patient, June, was a 26-year-old recently married nursing graduate who complained of washing and cleaning problems so severe that she was unable to seek work in her profession. On initial evaluation she was agitated and distressed, feeling helpless to control her need to take at least two 45-minute showers daily and, in addition, to wash her hands some 20 times a day for five minutes. She also spent a great deal of time wiping various objects with alcohol. Inquiry soon determined that she was terrified of becoming "contaminated," particularly by bird, animal, or human feces, which she took great pains to avoid. She also had problems with garbage and with dead animals on the roadway. Previous treatment by systematic desensitization, tranquilizing drugs, and "cognitive restructuring" had been ineffective. Her marriage was now threatened owing to her husband's frustration with her excessive cleanliness.

Exposure treatment. The therapist and patient worked together to create a hierarchy of upsetting stimuli, rating them on a scale of 1 through 100 according to their capacities to evoke disgust and the impulse to wash. For example, the patient gave ratings of 100 to touching dog feces (if unable to wash immediately), 90 to automobile tires (which may have contacted a dead animal), and 40 to the outside doorknob of a public bathroom (the inside doorknob rated 80). Subsequently, in treatment sessions three times weekly, June was instructed to expose herself deliberately to these stimuli either in guided fantasy (in vitro) or directly (in vivo), beginning with those rated relatively low in the hierarchy and moving gradually to the more severely threatening ones.

In addition to the exposures conducted during therapy sessions, "homework" was liberally assigned. Subjective ratings of discomfort were carefully monitored during these encounters. On one occasion well into treatment, the therapist drove with the patient to a place where she had observed a dead cat on the roadside and insisted that the patient approach the "smelly" corpse and touch it with a stick. The stick and a pebble lying close by were presented to the patient with the instruction that she keep them in her pocket and touch them frequently throughout the day. The patient was also told to drive her car past the spot on subsequent days.

The therapist made "home visits" to assist the patient in facing her problems in that setting,

to learn and to employ techniques they formerly criticized. For example, a therapist could use an interpersonal therapeutic strategy to defeat a client's neurotic style while employing behavior therapy techniques to eradicate particular symptoms. In our judgment, this "ecumenical" trend in psychosocial treatment represents a maturing of the field, and we strongly applaud it.

No matter which therapeutic techniques are employed, it often requires a great deal of courage and persistence on a neurotic individual's part to face problems realistically and give up the defensive and avoidant life-style that has helped alleviate feelings of inadequacy, anxiety, and even stark terror. For some, this seems too great a task, and they present themselves in such a way as to put the whole responsibility for their immediate well-being and happiness on their therapists. For these individuals, palliative drug therapy may be the only recourse.

Despite the difficulties involved, however, powerful forces are aligned on the side of psychotherapy. For one thing, neurotic individuals who seek help are usually experiencing considerable inner distress, so they are motivated to change. When helped, in a supportive environment, to understand their problems and learn more effective and satisfying ways of coping with them, they usually find the

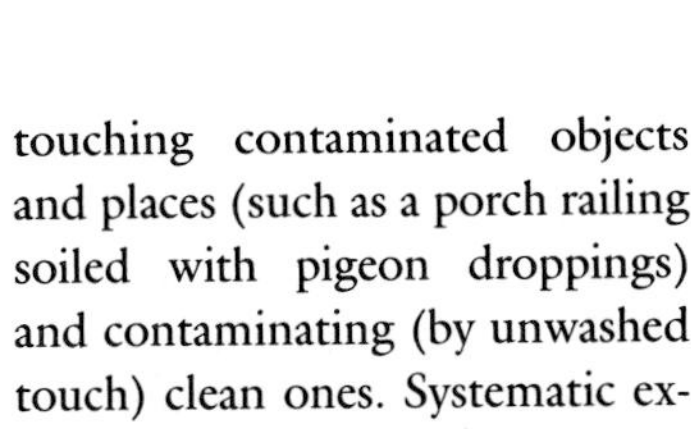

touching contaminated objects and places (such as a porch railing soiled with pigeon droppings) and contaminating (by unwashed touch) clean ones. Systematic exposure continued until the patient appeared at ease with a particular confrontation and her discomfort rating concerning it dropped to the 40 to 50 range.

Response prevention. After obtaining June's commitment to the full treatment procedure (which had previously been explained) in the fourth session, the therapist instituted a no washing rule. Specifically, the patient was to remain unwashed for a period of five days, after which she could take a ten-minute shower to be followed by another wash-free five days. As anticipated, June was notably upset by this proposed regimen and strongly doubted she could carry it off. The therapist was encouraging but insistent, promising support through the hard times, and the patient was successful in curbing her frequent impulses to wash. A transition to "normal washing and cleaning behavior" was instituted shortly before the end of the planned 15 therapy sessions. This plan consisted of one 10-minute shower per day and hand-washings not to exceed six per day at mealtimes, after bathroom use, and after touching clearly soiled or greasy objects.

Because June's discomfort ratings remained somewhat high (maximum 70, but only briefly) following the planned 15 sessions, a few additional follow-up sessions were given. In an evaluation nine months following the initiation of treatment, June described herself as "definitely a lot better . . . maybe 80 percent." She acknowledged that she still had obsessions "once every week or two" (such as "driving over someone"), but she was now employed and her relationship with her husband was much improved. She felt she was living a "normal life."

As Steketee and Foa pointed out, obsessive-compulsive disorders rarely remit completely; even a successfully treated patient will usually have some residual obsessive problems or rituals, as in June's case. The treatment undertaken here was of course direct and rigorous and was based on a behavioral formulation. It appears to have been the treatment of choice. One can only speculate on how June would have fared under the care of a psychoanalyst, particularly in view of the pronounced "anal" character (signalled by her preoccupation with dirt and feces) of her symptoms.

courage to see it through. Although outcomes vary considerably, it appears that from 70 to 90 percent of the people who receive appropriate kinds of help for their neurotic behavior benefit from it (Lambert, Shapiro, & Bergin, 1986).

In concluding our discussion of neurotic disorders, several additional points should be mentioned. Fear of committing suicide is a common neurotic symptom, but the actual incidence of suicide among neurotic individuals does not appear to be higher than for the general population. Nor do the life spans of these individuals appear to be adversely affected by their chronic tension and somatic disturbances, unless these disturbances result in pathologic organ changes (to be discussed in Chapter 8). As to whether neurotic behavior is likely to develop into psychotic behavior, the answer seems to be a definitive no. In only 5 percent or fewer of neurotic behavior cases does excessive stress lead to severe personality decompensation and psychotic patterns.

Finally, people often ask how a neurotic style affects creativity and productiveness. Many authors have described neurotic individuals as "pleasantly different," and more likely than a "normal" person to be innovative and productive. In general, however, the evidence indicates that by relying on defensive strategies, neurotic individuals reduce their potential for positive accomplishments as well as their enjoyment of life.

UNRESOLVED ISSUES
on the Anxiety-based Disorders

The framers of DSM-III (affirmed by those of DSM-III-R) dropped the category *neurosis* because they thought it had accumulated excess meaning beyond what could reliably be demonstrated regarding the clinical phenomena of anxiety, somatoform, and dissociative disorders. These disorders are now listed as distinct major categories in themselves. This conservative step leaves open for further investigation the questions of the natures and etiologies of these behavioral anomalies. While it has provoked considerable objection because it has been widely interpreted as an attack on psychodynamic thinking (to which the notion of neurosis is central), the move is defended by its protagonists as emphasizing a proper theoretical neutrality in respect to such matters as the etiologies of the disorders in question. As we have indicated, we find the latter reasoning sound and have no quarrel with the new taxonomy on this score.

The basic question of the validity and generality of the "neurosis" model remains, however; it cannot be dismissed or resolved by a change in terminology. Unfortunately, it seems unlikely that it will be resolved in a timely fashion by the preferable route of skillfully conducted empirical research. It is difficult, if not impossible, at present to conceive of a definitive study or program of studies that would establish the anxiety-defense internal-conflict interpretation of most of these disorders as incontrovertibly right or wrong. Hence it is a judgment call, and one on which serious, competent investigators and clinicians honestly differ.

While we find the anxiety-defense model a useful and heuristic one, our commitment to it is a loose and flexible one. Moreover, we think it fits to varying degrees such reliable empirical observation as we have in regard to the conditions described in this chapter. In general it appears to clearly apply in respect to neurotic styles and some anxiety disorders, such as obsessive-compulsive behavior. Its adequacy as an integrating model for the somatoform and dissociative disorders is also variable within these classes, but overall less certain. Presumably it was just such uncertainty that caused the authors of DSM-III to limit their approach to the descriptive level. Obviously we have much to learn in this area, including a more complete understanding of the predisposing factors that influence an individual's "choice" of maladaptive reaction pattern.

Finally, although we have made impressive progress in fashioning demonstrably effective treatment approaches to these conditions, there remains the puzzling question of why they do not, in effect, cure themselves. Inasmuch as they generate considerable misery for the persons affected, and inasmuch as we know behavior tends to maximize pleasant consequences and minimize pain, how is it that these usually self-defeating behaviors persist—often over many years? Freud was acutely aware of this paradox, although his attempted solution of it—a somewhat magical concept of "repetition compulsion" (a hypothesized drive causing persons to return to and relive traumas of the past)—did little to clarify the issue. Another attempted explanation involving a presumed prepotency of immediate over delayed consequences (for example, prompt anxiety reduction), while more promising, tends to founder on the routine observation that humans seem at least as much influenced by long-term as short-term satisfactions. Were it otherwise, indeed, we might have to close down our more demanding colleges. We suspect that the main answer lies in the often complex and distorted "feedback loops" a neurotic person tends to set up with a usually unwitting social environment, such that the environmental response in some way reinforces and maintains the maladaptive behavior. Obviously we are touching here on problems relating to therapy, and we shall return to this intriguing issue in Chapter 18.

SUMMARY

This chapter has been concerned with maladaptive behavior patterns that appear to have *anxiety* as their bases. Sometimes these patterns, while not involving disabling symptoms as such, act to inhibit behaviors that would be appropriate, effective, and adaptive in certain situations. We have termed these conditions *neurotic styles.* In other cases, anxiety, or defenses against it, gives rise to disabling symptoms. Formerly these symptom disorders were officially called *neuroses,* but recent versions of the DSM have largely abandoned this term. We have chosen to retain the term *neurotic* for its pedagogic and descriptive advantages, although acknowledging that the basic issue remains unresolved. Neurotic symptom disorders, on careful assessment, often turn out to be related to preexisting neurotic styles.

Of the neurotic symptom disorders, the anxiety disorders are those in which, for some reason, a person has been unable to develop means of controlling and containing relatively severe anxiety. The anxiety thus surfaces in overt, fearful behavior. In somatoform disorders, an individual "somatizes" anxiety (diverts it to the body), causing psychologically based disabilities, preoccupations with illnesses, or both. In dissociative disorders, anxiety causes aspects of an individual's personality to "split off" and function more or less independently of the core self. To a large extent, somatoform and dissociative symptoms are conceived as defenses against experiencing the full impact of anxiety.

Researchers have identified a number of neurotic styles. Four relatively common neurotic styles are those involving inhibition of aggression/assertion, responsibility/independence, compliance/submission, and intimacy/trust behaviors.

The experience of anxiety in neurotic disorders is indistinguishable from strong fear, and indeed some of these problems have their origins in terrifying circumstances. Most neurotic individuals, however, do not have identifiable, rational, realistic sources of current anxieties. Most such anxieties are believed to be acquired through conditioning or other learning mechanisms, although some people may be constitutionally predisposed to acquire such responses.

Many neurotic people are treated by physicians, often with drugs designed to allay anxiety. Such treatment is essentially palliative in nature, and it is not without dangers. A number of alternative means of achieving anxiety reduction are available. In general, psychosocial treatments, which typically aim at solving a person's problems, have a reasonably good record with the neurotic disorders. However, some neurotic people fail to achieve satisfactory benefits from any form of treatment. The persistence of neurotic disorders in the face of the miseries to which they give rise remains a puzzling paradox.

Key Terms

neurotic behavior (p. 181)
neurosis (p. 181)
anxiety (p. 181)
anxiety-response pattern (p. 183)
anxiety disorder (p. 183)
panic disorder (p. 183)
agoraphobia (p. 184)
phobia (p. 185)
simple phobia (p. 185)
social phobia (p. 188)
obsession (p. 189)
compulsion (p. 189)
obsessive-compulsive disorder (p. 189)
generalized anxiety disorder (p. 192)
somatoform disorders (p. 197)
somatization disorder (p. 197)
hypochondriasis (p. 199)
malingering (p. 199)
somatoform pain disorder (p. 200)
conversion disorder (p. 201)
dissociative disorders (p. 205)
amnesia (p. 205)
psychogenic amnesia (p. 206)
fugue state (p. 206)
multiple personality (p. 208)
depersonalization disorder (p. 212)
neurotic style (p. 213)

Chapter 7
Psychological Factors and Physical Illness

Carlo, *Personnage au Visage Vert et aux Cheveux Longs*. Carlo (b. 1916) grew up in the Italian province of Verona, where he was put to work as an agricultural worker at the age of 9. As a child, he showed evidence of a solitary nature, preferring in general the company of his dog to that of other people. During the war, he suffered a series of psychological shocks that undermined an already-fragile psychological condition. Subject to delirium and visions of persecution, Carlo entered a psychiatric hospital in 1947. Since 1957, working in a small artist's studio provided by the hospital, he has devoted himself to creating complex, stylized drawings of animals and humans.

Traditionally, the medical profession has concentrated clinical and research efforts on understanding and controlling anatomical and physiological factors in disease. In psychopathology, on the other hand, interest has centered primarily on the discovery and remedy of psychological factors that are associated with mental disorders. Today we realize that both these approaches are limited: although a disorder may be primarily physical or primarily psychological, it is always a disorder of the whole person—not just of the body or the psyche.

Fatigue or a bad cold may lower tolerance for psychological stress; an emotional upset may lower resistance to physical disease; maladaptive behavior, such as excessive alcohol use, may contribute to the impairment of various organs, like the brain and liver. Furthermore, an individual's overall life situation has much to do with the onset of a disorder, its form, duration, and prognosis.

Recovery is apt to be more rapid for a patient eager to get back to work and to accustomed interactions with significant others than for the one who will be returning to a frustrating job or an unpleasant home. In short, an individual is a biopsychosocial unit.

There seems little doubt, too, that sociocultural influences affect the types and incidences of disorders found in different groups. The ailments to which people are most vulnerable—whether physical, psychological, or both—are determined in no small part by when, where, and how they live.

Behavioral medicine is the broad interdisciplinary approach to the treatment of physical disorders thought to have psychological factors as major aspects of their causal patterns (Gentry, 1984a). The field includes professionals from many disciplines—including medicine, psychology, and sociology—who seek to incorporate biological, psychological, and sociocultural factors into a total picture. Its emphasis, however, is essentially on the role psychological factors play in the occurrence, maintenance, and prevention of physical illness.

Because we are dealing here with largely **psychogenic illnesses** (psychologically induced or maintained diseases), it is only natural that psychologists have found this an area of major interest. **Health psychology** is the subspecialty within the behavioral medicine approach and within the generic discipline of psychology that deals specifically with psychology's contributions to the diagnosis, treatment, and prevention of these psychological components of physical illnesses (Bradley & Prokop, 1981; Weiss, Herd, & Fox, 1981). Currently developing at a rapid pace, the field has already evolved some of the trappings of a new and independent profession (G. C. Stone et al., 1987).

A behavioral medicine approach examines the broad biopsychosocial context of the following problem areas (adapted from Gentry, 1984a):

1. *Etiology.* How do critical life events, characteristic behavior, and personality organization predispose an individual to physical illness?

2. *Host resistance.* How are the effects of stress reduced by resistance resources, such as coping styles, social supports, and certain personality traits?

3. *Disease mechanisms.* How is human physiology altered by stressors, particularly those arising from maladaptive behavior? What effects are produced in such systems as the immune, the gastrointestinal, and the cardiovascular?

4. *Patient decision making.* What are the processes involved in the choices individuals make with respect to such matters as hazardous life-styles, health care decisions, and adherence to preventive regimens?

5. *Compliance.* What factors—biomedical, behavioral, self-regulative, cultural, social, and interpersonal (for example, factors in the practitioner-patient relationship)—determine compliance with sound medical advice?

6. *Intervention.* How effective are psychological measures, such as health education and behavior modification, in altering unhealthy life-styles and in directly reducing illness and illness behavior at both individual and community levels?

From this perspective, then, *any* instance of physical illness should occasion a review of the context in which the specific pathogen or primary cause is operating. To do so is to use a behavioral medicine approach; properly applied, it multiplies the tools available for interventions whose efficacy often extends beyond any immediate crisis to conditions both prior and subsequent to such events.

We might, for example, ask whether emotional factors may have lowered the resistance of a tuberculosis patient and hence contributed to the onset of the disease. We might also ask how the individual will react to the life changes brought about by the disease. Some patients apparently give up when medically the chances seem good that they will recover. Others with objectively more serious organic pathologies recover or survive for long periods of time. Dunbar, a pioneer in the field, concluded that it is often "more important to know what kind of patient has the disease than what kind of disease the patient has" (1943, p. 23).

Before DSM-III, psychogenic illnesses were categorized as *psychophysiologic disorders* (and before that as *psychosomatic disorders*); the focus in these earlier times was on specific body system diseases, such as peptic ulcer, traditionally thought to have psychological origins. In 1980 (with the adoption of DSM-III), the category of psychophysiologic disorders was dropped (and it remained so in DSM-III-R), partly because of the newer perspective that emphasizes the psychological component of all physical illnesses. That is, the attempt to specify particular diseases as having psychological components in their etiology or maintenance came to be seen as both limiting and misleading, because it was increasingly understood that the absence of such components in any disease would be quite rare. As we have seen, in DSM-III-R patients are now rated separately on different axes for psychiatric symptoms (Axis I), developmental and personality disorders (Axis II), and accompanying physical disorders (Axis III). Thus there is no place on the first two axes for the classic psychosomatic disorders.

To permit some sort of psychiatric coding for the many diseases that we now recognize may involve psychological contributions, Axis I provides a category called *psychological factors affecting physical condition.* This category should be used when a physical disorder, coded on Axis III, involves psychological factors that have either definitely or probably played a significant role in initiating or exacerbating the illness. Obviously, this decision is intended to be left to the diagnostician's judgment, because no sharp line of demarcation exists between a significant and a less significant role for psychological factors.

In this chapter, after a broader consideration of the role of psychological factors in both health and illness, we will look at coronary heart disease and the eating disorders known as anorexia and bulimia, which have special contemporary significance. From there, we will move to brief considerations of other physical illnesses having strong psychological components. Then we will examine possible causal factors, and, finally, highlight several treatment approaches in this rapidly developing area.

GENERAL PSYCHOLOGICAL FACTORS IN HEALTH AND DISEASE

Research has repeatedly shown that mental and emotional processes are somehow implicated both in good health and in most physical diseases. Definitive proof of such relationships, however, and a beginning knowledge of what is happening in the body, are relatively recent accomplishments. The boundaries of this field seem virtually limitless. As Ader and Cohen (1984) have put it: "As a result of research in psychosomatic and behavioral medicine, it has become clear that there is probably no major organ system or [physical] homeostatic defense mechanism that is not subject to the influence of interactions between psychological and physiological events" (p. 117).

In this section we will outline the main phenomena relating to psychosocial influences on biological health in general, specifying, where possible, the mechanisms involved. We will begin our survey with observations on health, attitudes, and coping. We move from there to an examination of the autonomic nervous system and its potential effects on health. We then move to what may eventually be recognized as the most basic and general topic in this area—the immune system and the compromise of its functioning by psychological states and events. The section ends with a brief discussion of life-style and its implications for physical health maintenance.

Health, Attitudes, and Coping Resources

The sometimes devastating effects of hopeless and helpless attitudes on organic functioning have long been known, partly through anthropological research on voodoo deaths and similar phenomena. Today many surgeons will delay a major operation until they are convinced that a patient is reasonably optimistic about the outcome, and optimism in a more positive, everyday sense seems to buffer against disease (Scheier & Carver, 1987). Likewise, harboring an "explanatory style" of helplessness in the face of adversity is associated with poor health outcomes, as shown in an interesting study of hall-of-fame baseball players by Peterson and Seligman (1987). Such negative attitudes in this group of athletes (as assessed by their verbatim statements

The relationship between mental and emotional processes and good health is now well documented. Positive emotions may produce a certain immunity to physical disease. Likewise, chronic negative styles of coping with ordinary frustrations of life, such as being stuck in traffic, may enhance the risk of disease.

reported in newspapers and other sources) were significantly associated with health problems following their active playing years. In the literature, too, are numerous reports of apathy deaths in situations such as concentration and prisoner-of-war camps. Every year we hear reports of "unexplained" deaths among people who believed themselves to be in hopeless circumstances—for example, after having ingested poisonous substances in dosages that were actually too small to be lethal. Such phenomena have been extensively reviewed by both Seligman (1975) and Jones (1977).

Less dramatically but in many ways of equal or greater importance, the effects of multiple life changes on a variety of illnesses have been amply documented (e.g., Elliott, 1989), as outlined in Chapter 5. To cite only two examples, Rahe (1974) noted a study on the health status of physicians that demonstrates a marked correspondence between health problems experienced and the amount of change-related stress undergone in an immediately preceding period. Similarly, in a study of 192 men between the ages of 30 and 60, Payne (1975) found that long-standing physical and psychological health problems were related to larger degrees of life changes, even when the changes had been favorable. Some evidence suggests, however, that the negative health effects of positive life changes are limited, interestingly, to individuals having prior low self-esteem (Brown & McGill, 1989). Evidently, it is the amount of adjustment required following change that overtaxes such individuals' resources, and good things happening to people who do not expect them may constitute significant adjustment challenges.

In other instances, the particular nature of an individual's coping resources is itself suspect. The most familiar example here is the Type A behavior pattern. When certain ordinary frustrations of life (such as having to wait in line) habitually provoke extremes of behavior (such as rage), a person is designated "Type A." A large body of evidence, some of it reviewed later in this chapter, has implicated a component of this coping style as a significant risk factor for coronary heart disease. More generally, any type of chronic negative affect or emotion seems to enhance the risk of disease (Friedman & Booth-Kewley, 1987b).

Often it appears that any severe stress serves to facilitate, precipitate, or aggravate a physical disorder in a person already predisposed to it. This assumption is in keeping with the diathesis-stress model we discussed in Chapter 4. A person who is allergic to a particular protein may find resistance further lowered by emotional tension; similarly, as we will see, when an invading virus has already entered a person's body—as is thought to be the case in multiple sclerosis, for example—emotional stress may interfere with the body's normal defensive forces or immunological system.

In like manner, any stress may tend to aggravate and maintain certain disorders, such as migraine headaches (Levor et al., 1986). Day (1951), another pioneer in psychosomatic disorders, once pointed out, "To develop chronic active pulmonary tuberculosis a person needs some bacilli, some moderately inflammable lungs . . . and some internal or external factor which lowers the resistance to the disease." He noted further that unhappiness was among the stressors that could lower resistance.

The relationship between psychological factors and good health has also been well-documented (e.g., Jones, 1977); that is, positive emotions often seem to produce a certain immunity to physical disease or to be associated with speedy and uncomplicated recoveries when disease does strike (O'Leary, 1985). In fact, this reality complicates efforts to determine the true effectiveness of new treatment techniques, such as new drugs. A patient who *believes* a treatment is going to be effective has a much better chance of showing improvement than does one who is neutral or pessimistic—even when the treatment is subsequently shown to have no direct or relevant physiological effects. This reaction has become known as the **placebo effect,** and it accounts in part for the controversies that arise periodically between the scientific community and the general public regarding the efficacy of certain drugs or other treatments.

It has even been suggested that, had it not been for the placebo effect, the medical profession as we know it would not have survived to the present century, because until this century practitioners in fact had little else to offer disease sufferers; indeed, specific treatments were as often as not harmful. The profession's survival and prosperity from ancient times is to a large extent a demonstration of the power of "faith" in healing (Shapiro & Morris, 1978). Thus the fundamental intimacy of the mind and body is perhaps nowhere better documented than in health and illness.

Autonomic Excess and Tissue Damage

Our cave-dwelling ancestors had much need for organ systems that could rapidly prepare their bodies for the intense life-or-death struggles that were the daily fare of their existence. Nature provided these in the form of a rather elaborate apparatus for dramatically enhancing energy mobilization on a short-term basis. The pertinent physiological events, chiefly involving the autonomic nervous system, were termed the "flight or fight" pattern by Walter Cannon (1929), underscoring its apparent function either in fleeing danger or subduing an aggressor. In describing the pattern, Cannon noted that, with the advance of civilization, it has become to a degree obsolete; in fact he referred to certain psychosomatic disorders as "diseases of civilization." Because contemporary human beings rarely have the concrete options of either physically fleeing or attacking a threat, no effective avenue exists for the prompt discharge of high states of physiologic readiness to perform extraordinary physical feats. In Cannon's view (and the views of many contemporary investigators), this state of affairs, when unduly repetitive or long-continued, produces tissue breakdown—that is, disease, such as ulcers and hypertension.

Autonomic nervous system arousal involves many component processes, some of them subtle or even "silent" in terms of ready accessibility to observation. With increasing levels of arousal, we can see many of the more dramatic manifestations: increased breathing and heart rate, increased perspiration, increased muscle tone, and flushing; a keen observer will note pupillary dilation, enhancing vision. With adequate instrumentation, we could also observe, for example, increased blood pressure, the dumping of sugar reserves into the blood, redistribution of blood pooled in the viscera to the peripheral or "voluntary" musculature, and enhanced secretion of powerful neurotransmitter substances. All of these changes are sometimes referred to collectively as the *alarm reaction* (Selye, 1976b),[1] the first phase of the general adaptation syndrome (Chapter 5). They are the body's response to a "battle stations" signal from the brain. Such a system was not evolved for dealing with trifling circumstances, and it is hardly surprising that such widespread and potent effects, if not permitted to subside (and the system to remain for the most part at rest), might over time lead to organic structural alterations of a pathological sort.

Coming to a similar conclusion, the early psychosomatic theorists, notably including Flanders Dunbar (1943) and Franz Alexander (1950), reasoned that chronic *internal* sources of threat could place physical health in serious jeopardy. In other words, unremitting psychological conflict of the type found in anxiety-related disorders (Chapter 6), which by its very nature would preclude arousal discharge, might actually cause physical damage to vital organs. These early theorists appear to have been largely on the right track, although—as so often happens in psychology and in science generally—many of their more detailed conceptions have proven inaccurate or oversimplified.

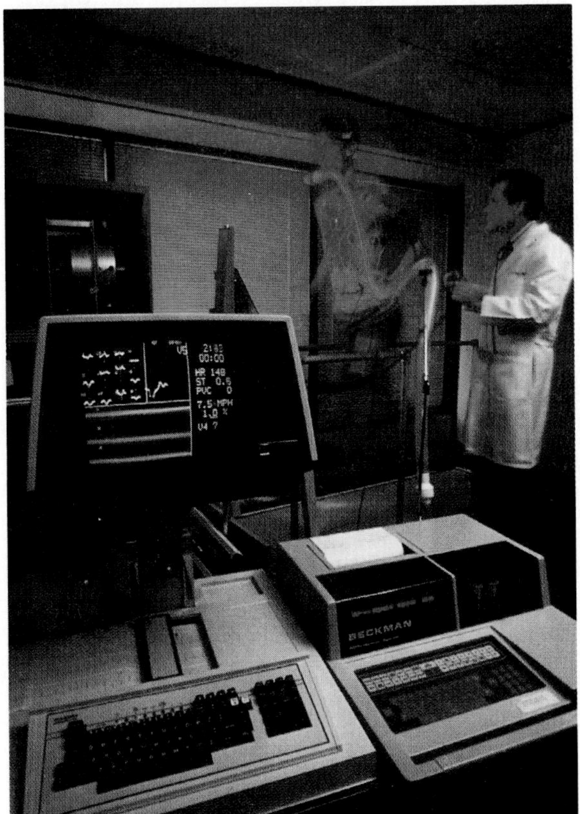

Internal bodily changes similar to those caused by stress can be induced by carefully monitored physical activity. This patient on a treadmill can be observed for such things as increased heart rate and blood pressure to determine how much arousal may be a threat to physical health.

Psychosocial Factors and the Immune System

Although autonomic nervous system events often dominate the alarm stage of the general adaptation syndrome, they are joined in due course, often quite rapidly, by a complex array of other bodily processes. These processes contain or, if possible, eliminate the threat posed. This reaction is the beginning of Selye's stage of resistance, where the protective resources of an organism are mobilized to detect the nature of a threat and to deploy countermeasures against it. To use a simple example, if you burn your finger while cooking, your "alarm" reaction is followed promptly by transport to the site of the injury of a variety of substances that tend to limit damage and initiate tissue repair. We say "tend" in the above sentence because in this instance, as in many other more important ones, the damage-control mechanism sometimes overshoots the mark, exceeding the requirements of adequate defense and producing new problems of its own making. Thus the recommended first aid of cold application for minor burns has as its purpose the *inhibition* of an excessive defense process. We do much the same thing, incidentally, when we take common-cold remedies to inhibit mucus production in the nasal and sinus passages.

The examples just cited illustrate an important point: just as the psyche's defensive resources can display "adaptiveness" without "intelligence," so too can the body's defensive resources be both marvelously attuned to protection and at the same time clumsy and self-defeating. This paradox has important implications in many areas of medicine, such as organ transplantation. Here the body's defenses against invasion by "foreign" protein may actually destroy the life-sustaining new organ.

Considered biomedically, a crucial component of an organism's resistance-stage equipment is the immune system, whose basic properties are outlined in the next section.

---

[1]This usage of the term is somewhat incorrect. In Selye's original formulation of the general adaptation syndrome, the alarm reaction is not necessarily observable, as when it occurs in response to an intruding infectious microorganism.

Elements of the Human Immune System

While much remains to be learned about the details of immunologic functioning, particularly in regard to psychosocial influences, certain broad outlines are now fairly well understood. What follows is a brief summary of the workings of the system insofar as they are known or strongly suspected, based on contemporary research.

The **immune system** is an organism's principal means of maintaining its integrity when faced with the intrusion of foreign substances, such as bacteria, viruses, or tumors. The primary components of the immune system are the blood, thymus, bone marrow, spleen, and lymph nodes. Of the blood's principal components, the serum (a soluble medium) and the white blood cells are especially important in immune function. The serum is made up of large protein molecules and water; it is the medium by which the body transports its defenses.

The white blood cells, also called leukocytes, contain much of the body's defense system. They can be further divided into subpopulations (each with specialized functions) and are found in the thymus, spleen, and lymph nodes and in the blood itself. White blood cell subpopulations include B-cells, T-cells, macrophages (literally, big eaters), and natural killer cells, which have inherent properties destructive to foreign protein. While the role of these cells in immune functioning is often quite direct, certain of them also secrete various chemical substances that have a more indirect effect in regulating, orchestrating, and enhancing the total immune response.

Immune function is traditionally divided into two branches, humoral and cellular. The humoral branch refers to the activity of B-cells and the antibodies they produce. Cellular immune function, on the other hand, is mediated by T-cells, whose effects, while widespread, do not include antibody production. When an organism is invaded by an **antigen**—that is, a substance recognized as foreign—B- and T-cells become activated and multiply rapidly, deploying the various forms of counterattack mediated by each type of cell. In the process of defense, a subset of memory cells becomes "programmed" to recognize the particular antigen (or substances that mimic it in important respects), the code being retained for any subsequent reexposure. Thus the organism is "sensitized" for future rapid deployment of specific defensive processes. This sensitization process can also go awry, as in the sometimes serious reactions certain people have to minimally threatening foreign substances to which they have previously been exposed. Bee stings are a good example of this type of reaction: for some people who have become sensitized to bee sting venom, subsequent exposure to it can produce a life-threatening condition known as anaphylactic shock.

B-cells, which are formed in the bone marrow, perform their defensive function by producing antibodies that circulate in the blood serum. B-cell (or humoral immune) functioning is involved chiefly with protection against the more common varieties of bacterial infection.

T-cells develop to maturity in the thymus and mediate immune reactions that, while slower, are far more extensive and direct in character. While T-cells do not produce or secrete antibodies, they are capable of secreting chemicals (lymphokines) that have toxic and other effects on other cells. These cells mainly generate an attack that is highly specific to a given invading antigen.

Particular types of T-cells, called helper cells, signal B-cells to turn on antibody production and other immune cells to seek and destroy the invading antigen. The T_4 helper cell, principal target of the AIDS (HIV-1) virus, plays a crucial early role in the detection and precise identification of foreign protein. Randomly circulating macrophages encounter such protein, fragments of which then become attached to the cells' surfaces. The immune response is initiated when a T_4 cell, marvelously equipped for analyzing the threat and alerting other components of the system to its presence, collides with one of these contaminated macrophages and "reads" the antigen code on its surface. The T_4 cell is thus a vital part of an organism's first line of defense against invaders, such as viruses, that escape antibody destruction by gaining access to the interior of host cells (McCutchan, 1990).

The devastating and unrelenting effects of AIDS, an unusually virulent disease, can be attributed to the fact that HIV-1, by invading the T_4 (also called Cluster Determinant$_4$) and certain other immune cells, participates in the cellular proliferation its own invasion sets off. Furthermore, the virus destroys or functionally impairs not only the cells it invades but other T_4 cells as well in some manner not yet understood. It also attacks the circulating macrophages essential to the T_4's immunological effectiveness. In due course the T-cell defense system is severely weakened by a drastic depletion of its component members. Hence a victim is rendered highly vulnerable to a multitude of potentially dangerous antigens that would promptly be detected and destroyed in an immunocompetent person. For this reason the infections and tumors acquired by AIDS patients are said to be "opportunistic."

Antibodies to the AIDS virus, which are detectable in the blood of exposed people, are compromised in their effectiveness because the virus lives in

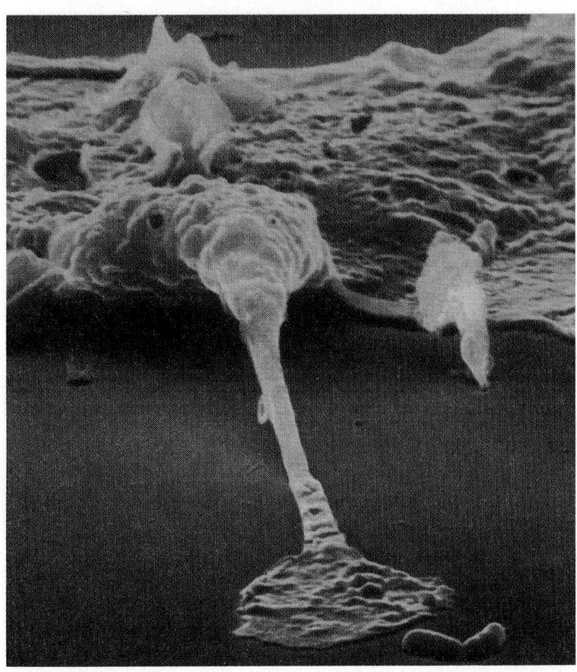

A macrophage reaches out to eat bacteria. Macrophages are important components of the immune system because they initiate the action of B-cells and T-cells against bacterial, or antigen, invasion.

a protected intracellular habitat. One can hardly imagine a killer entity better designed than HIV-1 to frustrate efforts to deter it by methods that are not in themselves dangerous to a victim. This awesome scourge underscores our utter dependence on a well-functioning immune system for health maintenance.

In summary, the front line of immune defense is contained within the highly differentiated system of white cells that circulate freely in the blood or remain as resident reinforcements in the lymph nodes. One of its two main divisions, the B-cell (or humoral), mediates the production of antibodies—circulating immunoglobulin substances of high specificity whose main role is detecting the presence of and destroying invading bacteria. The other and far more complicated main division—mediated by several descendant forms of the progenitor T-cell—includes the following among its functions: (a) direct and indirect (in concert with other elements such as macrophages) destruction of certain types of antigens, especially nonbacterial ones; and (b) regulation and in certain instances activation of the other, antibody-based division of the defense system. The immune system's response to antigen invasion is thus generalized and intricately orchestrated, requiring the intact functioning of numerous components. A much-simplified illustration of the system appears in *HIGHLIGHT 7.1*.

Psychosocial Compromise of the Immune Response The virulence of the AIDS virus is such that psychosocial factors were originally thought to play little or no role in the resultant immune breakdown and death. More recent research suggests that this conclusion may have been premature (Kiecolt-Glaser & Glaser, 1988). For example, Antoni et al. (1990) report preliminary results indicating that behavioral interventions, such as aerobic exercise, had positive psychological and immunocompetence effects among groups of uninfected high-risk and early-stage infected gay men. If such results can be maintained over time they may show how to prevent HIV from gaining a sustainable foothold after exposure, or to slow the progress of the disease following established infection. In light of the serious toxicity of the antiviral drugs known to deter the progress of HIV infection, the discovery of more benign, noninvasive (and less expensive) treatment methods would be of tremendous help in containing the disease's effects and improving the quality of life of infected individuals.

The role of psychosocial factors in respect to many other less fearsome disease-producing antigens may be considerable. Recent evidence from a wide variety of sources, reviewed by Antoni et al. (1990) and Geiser (1989), strongly suggests that psychosocial factors can have an important effect on the functional status of the immune system at any point in time. In particular, psychosocial stressors and the mental states associated with them may depress immune function to the point of enhancing vulnerability to virtually any antigen to which a person is concurrently exposed. It seems extremely likely, for example, that some such mediating mechanism is involved in the observed relationship between stressful life changes and subsequent physical illnesses (Geiser, 1989; Koranyi, 1989; Rogers, 1989; also see *HIGHLIGHT 5.2*, p. 150).

Obviously, the central nervous system would somehow be involved in mediating effects of this kind. These observations have led to the development of the relatively new field of **psychoneuroimmunology,** which explores psychological influences on the nervous system's control of immune responsiveness. Although still in its infancy and hampered for obvious reasons in mounting a full-scale experimental assault on some outstanding questions (such as the risks associated with purposely introducing antigens into the blood streams of experimental subjects), the field has developed in a rapid and impressive manner.

Fortunately for research progress, it is possible to estimate at least the earliest phases of immune responsiveness (for example, enhanced reproduc-

HIGHLIGHT 7.1

Star Wars in Microcosm: The Body's Exquisitely Organized Defense System

Below is a simplified schematic of the cellular functioning of the human immune system. The immune system is normally brought into action upon detection of the presence of a foreign, "nonself" substance—an *antigen* (An)—say the *Streptococcus* bacterium often responsible for sore throat. *Phagocytes,* or *macrophages,* eating cells that wander about in the blood serum, attempt to ingest the invader, leaving identifying parts of it embedded in their own membranes. In due course, one of these foreign-substance-containing phagocytes chances to make contact with a circulating *helper T-cell* (T_h) of the T_4 variety whose surface antibody code happens to match the foreign material captured on the phagocyte membrane. This chance meeting initiates the more dramatic phases of the immune response.

The helper T-cell with the matching molecule (and hence the essential information identifying the Streptococcal invader) begins to divide, as do succeeding generations of daughter cells. These distinctive cells, shortly numbering in the thousands and each containing essentially a copy of the invading antigen, migrate to various regions and mediate, in addition, the large-scale production of targeted *cytotoxic T-cells* (T_c) and *B-cells.* The latter in turn produces *antibodies* specifically coded to bind to the offending *Streptococci* and render them vulnerable to easy attack by other cells, such as macrophages.

Meanwhile, the antigen/antibody complex combines with a group of proteins known as *complements* to stimulate the secretion of histamine and the production of fever, both of which serve additional defensive functions but also make us feel ill.

If all goes well, and it usually does eventually even without antibiotic treatment, *suppressor T-cells* (T_s) assume a dominant role and turn off the system. If neither antibiotic medication nor the natural immune defense is successful in curbing the infection, serious medical consequences may ensue, even with so common an antigen as *Streptococcus.*

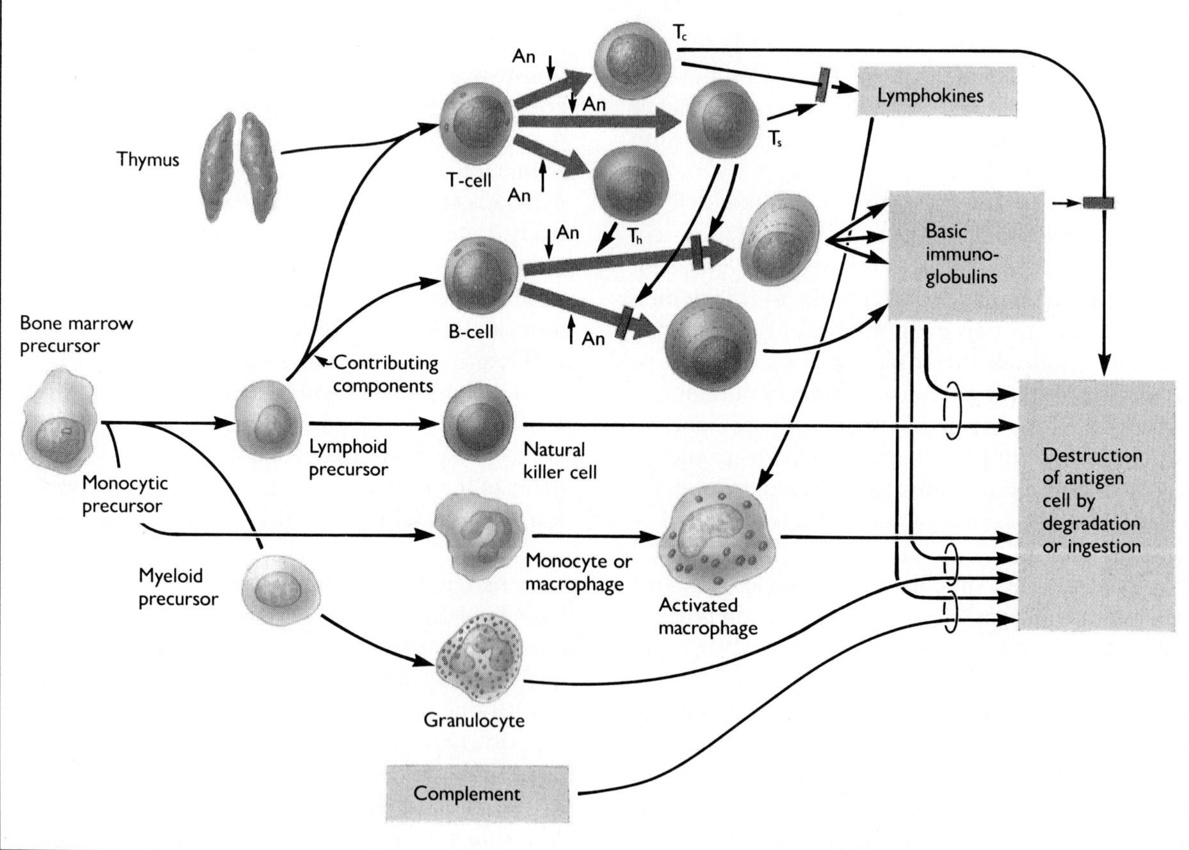

tion of various types of white cells) from laboratory examination of blood samples. This investigative strategy has been used effectively in demonstrating, for example, the suppression of white blood cell reproduction following sleep deprivation, marathon running, space flight, death of a spouse, and during psychological depression (Schleifer, Keller, & Stein, 1985; Schleifer et al., 1989; Vasiljeva et al., 1989). Immune responsiveness has been shown to vary with even normal, diurnal mood variations (A. A. Stone et al., 1987). A group of researchers at Ohio State University has repeatedly demonstrated the compromise of white blood cell proliferation, including diminished natural killer cell activity, among medical students undergoing stress (Glaser et al., 1985, 1987). Natural killer cells are believed to play a key role in tumor surveillance and the control of viral infections.

Granting the likelihood that stressors, in particular psychosocial or "mental" ones, can impair the immune response, a conclusion supported by the weight of evidence (Antoni et al., 1990; Jemmott & Locke, 1984), intriguing questions remain about the pathway or pathways of influence that may be involved. Until fairly recently, most researchers were convinced that the primary pathway was the hypothalamus-pituitary-adrenocortical (HPA) axis. According to this hypothesis, the processing of stressful events in the brain causes hypothalamic activation of the pituitary, which in turn stimulates the adrenal cortex to secrete excessive levels of adrenocortical hormones (steroids). Certain of the latter substances are known to have negative (as well as some positive) effects on immune functioning. Hence the hypothesis, while largely speculative, remains somewhat attractive.

Nevertheless, more recent research findings and conceptual refinements have turned up a host of strong competitors to the HPA interpretation. For example, we now know that a number of other hormone substances, including growth hormone, testosterone, and estrogen, are responsive to stressor conditions and also affect immune competence. The same is true of a variety of neuropeptides, including endorphins. The link between psychosocial stressors and the immune system may be even more direct, however. The discovery of nerve endings in thymus, spleen, and lymph nodes, tissues literally teeming with white blood cells, suggests the possibility of direct neural control of the secretion of immunologic agents. Along somewhat similar lines, it is now known that white blood cell surfaces contain receptors for circulating neurotransmitter substances (Rogers, 1989). We must assume that the presence of such structures on these cells is not a gratuitous freak of nature, but rather that the cells respond in some way to messages conveyed by the brain-regulated substances. Finally, and perhaps most unexpectedly, immunosuppression can be classically conditioned (Ader & Cohen, 1984)—that is, it can be *learned* as a response to previously neutral stimuli, just as Pavlov's dogs learned to salivate to a tone. Conceivably, even mental stimuli such as thoughts could thus come to activate immunosuppression if they were regularly paired with immunosuppressive events (operating as unconditioned stimuli).

In sum, we have a wealth of potential ways to eventually understand the relationship between psychosocial stressors and immunosuppression. Our guess is that such an understanding will turn out to be very complicated.

Much circumstantial evidence shows, in keeping with Selye's postulate of a state of exhaustion, that the resources of the immune system and other "resistance" mechanisms are not infinitely replenishable. In other words, these defensive resources apparently may under certain circumstances be used up at a rate faster than they can be replaced by the body's compensatory metabolism. Indeed, Selye held that this metabolic regulatory mechanism might itself become impaired as demands placed on it over a lifetime accumulate, resulting ultimately in aging and death. In any event, the weight of evidence strongly suggests that the adequacy of the immune response to a particular antigen diminishes proportionally with the quantity and intensity of other stressors simultaneously impinging on an organism, including other, unrelated illnesses. Among its other strengths, this conception nicely integrates the vast amount of data we have associating much physical illness, notably including infectious diseases, with the occurrence of antecedent stressful events (Elliott, 1989; Koranyi, 1989; Maddi, Bartone, & Puccetti, 1987).

Note that the stressful events referred to in the preceding sentence are largely psychosocial rather than physical in meaning and presumed impact on a recipient—for example, death of a spouse, change in employment status, marital difficulties, and so on. In short, we find the evidence compelling, if not conclusive, that psychosocial stressors temporarily impair the immune response and thereby contribute substantially to the development of many physical illnesses.

While efforts to relate specific stressors to specific physical diseases have not generally been successful, stress is becoming a key underlying theme in our understanding of the development and course of virtually all organic illness. Stress may serve as a predisposing, precipitating, or reinforcing factor in the causal pattern, or it may merely aggravate a condition that might have occurred anyway. Often stress appears to speed up the onset or increase the severity of a disorder, and to interfere with the body's immunological defenses and other homeostatic functions. Presuming we all have one organ system somewhere in our bodies that is at maximum relative vulnerability, a high, chronic level of stress puts us at risk for a breakdown of that organ system, and perhaps others, sooner or later.

Life-style as an Added Factor in Health Maintenance

Today a great deal of attention is being paid to the role of life-style in the development or maintenance of many health problems. Numerous aspects of the way we live are now considered influential in the development of some severe physical problems: diet—particularly overeating and consuming too many high-fat, low-fiber foods; lack of exercise; smoking cigarettes; excessive alcohol and drug use; constantly facing high-stress situations; and even ineffective ways of dealing with day-to-day problems are but a few of the many life-style patterns that are viewed as contributing causes. This growing awareness of the role individual factors play in susceptibility to disease, its impact and course, has resulted in more attention to life-style by both physicians and psychologists working in health care settings (Engel, 1977; O'Leary, 1985; Oldenburg, Perkins, & Andrews, 1985; Weiner, 1977). Particularly in this area of life-style factors, health psychology—which focuses heavily on prevention and health maintenance—is growing rapidly. New efforts are being made to determine more precisely what role personality or life-style factors play in the genesis and course of disease. Finding the answers becomes all the more important when we realize that life-style factors—habits or behavior patterns presumably under our own control—are believed to play a major role in three of the leading causes of death in this country: coronary heart disease, automobile accidents, and alcohol-related deaths (National Center for Health Statistics, 1982).

We cannot help but be struck by the rather sobering observation of Knowles (1977), who takes the position that most people are born healthy and suffer premature death and disability only as a result of personal misbehavior and unnecessarily pathogenic environmental conditions. He believes that most health problems could be drastically reduced if only

It is generally recognized that personal life-style influences psychophysiologic well-being.

> *no one smoked cigarettes or consumed alcohol and everyone exercised regularly, maintained optimal weight on a low-fat, low-refined carbohydrate, high-fiber content diet, reduced stress by simplifying their lives, obtained adequate rest and recreation, . . . drank fluoridated water, followed the doctor's orders for medication and self-care once disease was detected, and used available health resources. (p. 1104)*

Before anyone rushes to alter radically his or her life-style according to the rather Spartan regimen outlined by Knowles, it should be pointed out that the connection between many life-style habits or patterns and physical illness may not be as strong as some advocates suggest. In many cases the connection, though seemingly proven in a statistical sense, is relatively weak and usually one of correlation, with the force of the argument based more on common sense than definitive data. For example, the extent to which rates of physical diseases, such as coronary heart disease, can be controlled or reduced through such means as reducing dietary cholesterol has not been conclusively established. Nevertheless, the stakes are sufficiently high that it would seem imprudent to tempt fate by ignoring one's cholesterol intake.

Even in cases where virtual proof of causation exists, it is difficult for many individuals to alter significantly their life-styles to reduce their risk for disease—an incentive that may be remote for people not experiencing current health difficulties. Significant and lasting change is generally hard for people, and this is especially true where available rewards are immediate and powerful, as in the case of addictions (Chapter 9). The high and sustained motivation necessary to achieve reliable self-control often proves fragile. Some of the most well-established risk factors, such as cigarette smoking, are thus not easy habits to alter, even when the connection between the habit and the disease is direct and seemingly evident. After having two heart attacks and surgery to remove a cancerous lung, one man continued to smoke two and a half packs of cigarettes a day even though he frequently said, "I know these things are killing me a little at a time . . . but they have become so much a part of my life I can't live without them!"

PSYCHOSOCIAL FACTORS IN SPECIFIC DISEASE PROCESSES

The debilitating effects of stressful life circumstances and of harmful life-style habits tend to be relatively diffuse and nonspecific in terms of the organ systems adversely affected and the diseases for which risk is ultimately enhanced. Excessive autonomic activity, persistent negative emotional states, diminished immune competence, or even "bad habits" such as cigarette smoking typically compromise a person's functioning in several different ways and may therefore be implicated in a range of disease processes. Complementing such generalized influences are a host of more specific factors that help determine whether or not a given individual will acquire a particular illness or disease at some time. Most obvious among these are certain innate predispositions to develop a disease, often inherited ones, and levels of exposure to pertinent pathogenic agents, such as noxious chemicals in the workplace. In addition, contemporary research (see e.g., Friedman & Booth-Kewley's (1987b) quantitative review) increasingly implicates factors of personality and interpersonal functioning as having causal roles in the development of certain physical illnesses. The present section undertakes a selective survey of apparent instances of the latter.

As we have seen, the idea that personality traits might be causally related to the development of one or another type of physical illness is by no means new. Until fairly recently, however, evidence for such relationships was based mainly on unsystematic and often rather casual observations. This evidence has now been supplemented, at least in some instances, with quite rigorously developed data that render the implicated causal hypotheses highly plausible, if not compelling. In the following sections we will review in some detail certain widespread conditions that are the focus of much contemporary psychophysiologic research and theorizing—coronary heart disease and the eating disorders known as anorexia nervosa and bulimia. Then we shall move on to a brief survey of several other illnesses classically considered to have strong psychogenic aspects.

Coronary Heart Disease and the Type A Behavior Pattern

Coronary heart disease (CHD) is a potentially lethal blockage of the arteries supplying blood to the heart muscle, or myocardium. Its chief clinical manifestations are (a) angina pectoris, severe chest pain signalling that the delivery of oxygenated blood to the affected area of the heart is quantitatively insufficient for its current work load; (b) myocardial infarction, functionally complete blockage of a section of the coronary arterial system, resulting in death of the myocardial tissue supplied by that arterial branch; and (c) disturbance of the heart's electrical conduction consequent to arterial blockage, resulting in disruption or interruption of the heart's pumping action, often leading to death. Many instances of sudden cardiac death, in which victims have no prior history of CHD symptoms, are attributed to "silent" CHD (see *HIGHLIGHT 7.2*).

While deaths from CHD have declined dramatically in recent years, this decline has occurred at the end of a long period, comprising most of the twentieth century, of rising CHD-related mortality in the United States. CHD retains today the dubious distinction of being the nation's number one killer, despite spectacular advances in treatment (such as coronary artery bypass surgery) and markedly enhanced appreciation of risk factors, some of which (elevated serum cholesterol, smoking, lack of exercise, obesity, and hypertension, for example) are potentially reversible.

The known biological risk factors for CHD explain less than half of the CHD-related outcomes people actually experience. In other words, much of the causal pattern for CHD development (or, for that matter, for its failure to develop) remains shrouded in mystery. Noting this circumstance, cardiovascular researchers have increasingly turned their attention to possible nonbiological contributions to the disease's development—to psychosocial and personality factors—emulating in this respect some eminent forebears. Englishman William Harvey, the discoverer of circulation, was writing of "affections of the mind" that generate problems in heart function as early as 1628. The distinguished Canadian physician Sir William Osler, in landmark lectures on cardiology published in 1892, explicitly related the development of CHD to "the worry and strain of modern life" and "the high pressure" under which people live. Attempts to refine and precisely specify the psychological contribution to the disease's development continue to the present day, for the most part in the context of identifying the crucial components of what M. Friedman and Rosenman (1959) first labeled the **Type A behavior pattern.**

As conceptualized by Friedman and Rosenman, the Type A pattern is a complex set of behaviors that may be observed in certain individuals under appropriately stressful or challenging circumstances. The pattern, they said, involves excessive competitive drive in the absence of well-defined goals, impatience or time urgency, and hostility. It manifests itself in accelerated speech and motor activity. The

The Type A behavior pattern may be observed in certain individuals under stressful or challenging circumstances. The pattern involves excessive competitiveness, impatience, hostility, and accelerated speech and motor activity.

pattern is best assessed and measured, according to these investigators, by means of a structured interview devised for this purpose (Rosenman, 1978). The contrasting Type B pattern, to which little descriptive attention has been paid, is negatively defined in terms of the absence of Type A characteristics. Various questionnaire-type approaches to the assessment of Type A behavior have also been developed, of which the Jenkins Activity Survey for Health Prediction (Jenkins et al., 1971) has been most popular among researchers.

Unfortunately, the various assessment measures for the A/B typology are not as strongly intercorrelated as one might wish. This situation suggests continuing problems in the construct's definition and the likelihood that differing measurement approaches emphasize different components of the Type A pattern as originally described. This measurement problem may be the principal reason why a few studies have failed to find a Type A-CHD relationship (Fischman, 1987). Moreover, as Krantz and Glass (1984) have noted, some evidence shows that not all components of the Type A pattern are equally predictive of CHD or even of differing pathological manifestations within the CHD syndrome (for example, angina versus infarction). Overall, some consensus has developed that the pattern's hyperaggressivity/hostility component, perhaps in association with status insecurity and inhibition of overt expressions of anger, is the one most closely correlated with demonstrable coronary artery deterioration (M. Friedman & Ulmer, 1984; Krantz & Glass, 1984; Williams et al., 1980; Williams, Barefoot, & Shekelle, 1985; Wood, 1986).

However, considerable conceptual and empirical uncertainties remain regarding the measurement of the A/B-Type variable and identification of its most significant components. Booth-Kewley & H. Friedman (1987), after a careful review of the pertinent evidence, have suggested that anxiety and depression are as important as anger and hostility in the correlational network that includes CHD development. Further, a recent longitudinal study by Hearn, Murray, & Luepker (1989) tends to negate any role for hostility. These authors contacted, in 1985 through 1986, 1313 men, or their surviving relatives, who had completed the Minnesota Multiphasic Personality Inventory, or MMPI (see Chapter 16) as university freshmen in 1953. The MMPI can be scored for a special, relatively well-validated scale measuring subject hostility (Ho). The subjects, divided according to those scoring high and low on the Ho scale, or their relatives were interviewed (by telephone) about their intervening health statuses. Hostility, as measured by the Ho

HIGHLIGHT 7.2

Heart Attack

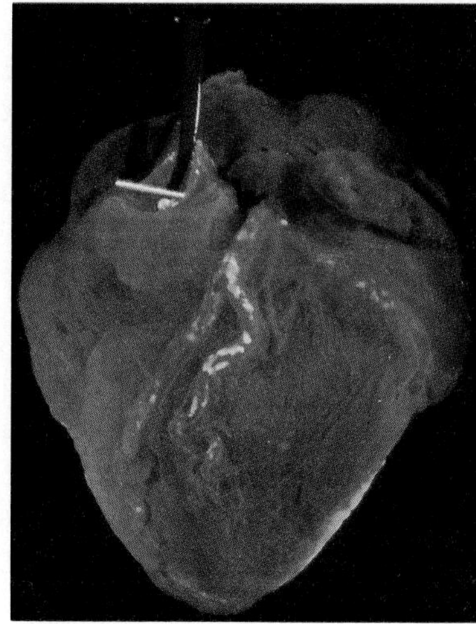

We have all heard the old story about the faint-hearted guard dog who, on being told "Attack," had one. *Attack* is now a common word in our vocabulary, as well it should be since heart attacks kill over half a million Americans each year. The incidence of heart disease among Americans is one of the highest in the world; about 30 million people are affected. (Some countries have a higher rate, including France, or a lower one, such as Japan.) But what is a heart attack? Technically, it is the result of a *myocardial infarction*—that is, a blockage of the arteries that feed the heart. (The lighter areas in the photo indicate blockage.)

When such an artery is blocked, the oxygen-starved muscles of the heart begin to die. Depending on how much of the heart is damaged and how badly, the results can vary from almost complete recovery to death. Blockage of the coronary vessels that feed the heart is usually caused by one of three things: a clot lodged in the vessel, a prolonged contraction of the vessel walls, or atherosclerosis.

Atherosclerosis is the result of the buildup of a number of substances, such as fat, fibrin (formed in clots), parts of dead cells, and calcium. These substances reduce the elasticity of the vessel, and by decreasing its diameter, they raise blood pressure, just as you raise the pressure in a garden hose by holding your thumb over the end. No one knows what causes atherosclerosis, but a number of things can speed its development, such as smoking cigarettes and, probably, eating animal fat and cholesterol. Other factors include age, hypertension, diabetes, stress, heredity, gender (males have more heart attacks), and a Type A behavior pattern.

The warnings of heart attack are often (but not always) (1) a pain that spreads along the shoulders, arm, neck, or jaw; (2) sudden sweating; (3) a heavy pressure and pain in the center of the chest; and (4) nausea, vomiting, and shortness of breath. The symptoms may come and go.

People who have not developed a strong and efficient cardiovascular system through exercise are particularly susceptible to *angina pectoris* (chest pain), which occurs when the heart fails to receive enough blood, particularly during times of stress or exercise. It should not be confused with a true heart attack, although it may forecast one in the future. The pain may be relieved by stopping the unusual exercise or by reducing the stress levels. Blood flow to the heart can be increased by an exercise program or by surgically inserting vessels from other parts of the body (a coronary bypass). Certain chemicals, such as nitroglycerin, also dilate the heart's vessels and increase the circulation of blood there.

Another form of heart attack results in a phenomenon called *sudden death*. The death may be due to chaotic and uncoordinated contractions of the ventricles, often brought on by an unanticipated myocardial infarction. The contractions do not move blood along and, after a few spasms, the heart may stop entirely. Many people afflicted in such a way mysteriously fall dead in their tracks. Some however, can be saved if they are helped in time.

In fact, victims of any form of heart attack stand a much greater chance of surviving if they are treated immediately. In many metropolitan areas, citizens are being trained in cardiopulmonary resuscitation (CPR) to help restore a victim's circulation in such emergencies. CPR continues the flow of blood to the brain, where sensitive tissues die quickly without oxygen. In Seattle, Washington, with an extensive citizen-training program, passersby have performed about one-third of the city's resuscitations. Their success rate is higher than that of professionals because they usually reach victims sooner.

Adapted from *Biology: The world of life,* Robert A. Wallace (Glenview, Ill.: Scott, Foresman and Company, 1987).

scale, did not in fact predict subsequent CHD-related illness, CHD mortality, or total mortality from all causes over the 33-year period involved.

In spite of these continuing conceptual and measurement uncertainties, it remains difficult to dispute the original evidence that the general cluster of reactions identified as the Type A pattern is a significant predictor of CHD, independent of other risk factors. While several studies support such a conclusion, two in particular stand out because their prospective designs circumvent many of the interpretation problems attending less powerful investigative strategies. (For example, inquiry about personality factors occurring after a diagnosis of CHD could lead to retrospective distortion based on preconceived notions of a coronary-prone personality type.) The first of these prospective studies is known as the Western Collaborative Group Study (WCGS) project, in which some 3150 healthy men between the ages of 35 and 59 on entry were typed as to A or B status and followed for a period of eight and a half years. Type As were found to be approximately twice as likely as Type Bs to have developed CHD (angina or myocardial infarctions) during the follow-up period. This differential remained even when other risk factors were statistically eliminated from consideration. When the data for a younger group of men (ages 39 to 49 on entry into the project) were considered separately, CHD was proportionately six times more prevalent among Type As than Type Bs (Rosenman et al., 1975). The findings also linked the Type A pattern to recurrent myocardial infarctions (Jenkins, Zyzanski, & Rosenman, 1976) and to sudden cardiac death (M. Friedman et al., 1973).

We should note in passing that Ragland and Brand (1988) have called into question the WCGS study's conclusions on the basis of their finding that people who died from a heart attack subsequent to their first ones were more likely to be Bs than As. It seems to us, however, that such a finding does not negate the original conclusions. Also to be noted is that those Type As who were maximally at risk were already dead when the data on subsequent attacks was analyzed, leaving behind a sample of subjects biased in favor of CHD deaths among Bs. Nobody ever held that A or B status was the only determinant of death from CHD.

The second prospective study to be considered here was an aspect of the well-known Framingham Heart Study, now in its fourth decade and involving long-term follow-up of a large sample of male and female individuals from that Boston suburb. Some 1700 coronary-free subjects were typed as to A or B status in the mid-1960s. Analysis of the data for CHD occurrence during an eight-year follow-up period not only confirmed the major findings of the WCGS project but extended them to women as well. In fact the two-fold increase in CHD risk reported for Type A men was almost exactly replicated for Type A women. Somewhat curiously, the CHD-Type A association among males in this study was limited to those of white-collar socioeconomic status (Haynes et al., 1980). See *HIGHLIGHT 7.3* for a graph summarizing these results.

Taken together, these and other studies meet most of the stringent criteria established by epidemiologists to justify the assumption of a cause-effect relationship in disease genesis. That is, the evidence overall suggests that some aspect of the Type A behavior pattern, possibly one involving general negative affect that remains unexpressed (Endicott, 1989; H. Friedman & Booth-Kewley, 1987a), is more or less directly implicated in the development of a potentially lethal organic deficit (CHD) among some individuals. It is important to note, too, however, that this area is under active investigation and heated debate. Clearly, many factors are involved in the causal chain of CHD.

The theoretical importance of the preceding findings for advancing our understanding of basic processes underlying CHD is considerable. Beyond that, they raise the possibility of saving lives by devising preventive therapeutic interventions to alter the Type A reaction pattern (or more precisely its negative affect component) in persons at risk. To date, however, little formal or systematic work in this area has been reported.

The Anorexic and Bulimic Syndromes

Anorexia nervosa and bulimia, which are normally considered separate syndromes, are coded (separately) as eating disorders of adolescence and adulthood in DSM-III-R. In fact neither syndrome occurs in appreciable numbers prior to adolescence, and onset after age 25 is rare. Also, the overwhelming preponderance of victims are female—on the order of 20 to 1. This figure suggests that, for reasons not yet fully understood, "femaleness" may be an intrinsic factor in these disorders. Further, it suggests that males exhibiting similar anomalies in eating behavior may therefore not represent true instances, in other essential respects, of these presumed clinical entities. In any event, little of a systematic nature is known about such males and hence we will confine ourselves here to typical cases involving girls or young women. Anorexia, in particular, is often an intractable and dangerous disorder, with a mortality rate near 5 percent (Szmukler & Russell, 1986).

HIGHLIGHT 7.3

The Type A Behavior Pattern and Coronary Heart Disease

The following graph depicts the percent incidence of coronary heart disease (CHD) over an eight-year period among subjects of the Framingham Heart Study. Subjects are distinguished according to age, sex, occupation (men only), and Type A versus Type B behavior pattern. Note the substantial rise in CHD among Type A women and men of white-collar occupations over their Type B counterparts. The failure to confirm this finding among blue-collar males remains unexplained.

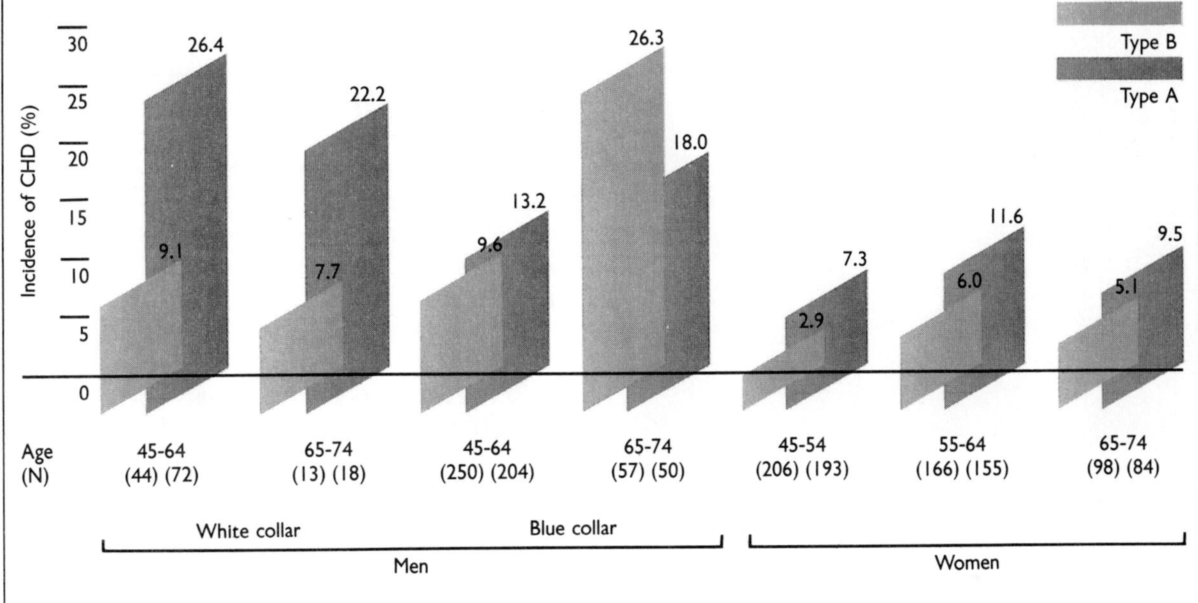

Anorexia nervosa has been officially recognized as a distinct disorder for at least a century. The central features of the syndrome are an intense abhorrence of obesity coupled with the often absurd complaint that one is "fat"; loss of at least 25 percent of original body weight (or, in those under 18, significant weight loss and a discrepancy from average projected weight gain that together constitute a 25 percent shortfall); and unremitting refusal to maintain weight within the lower limits of normal for age and height. Associated features that are usually present include cessation of menstruation and marked overactivity. Brief binges of overeating followed by self-induced vomiting or other purging practices are also common, constituting one of several links with bulimia.

Anorexic girls usually describe their mothers in unflattering terms: excessively dominant, intrusive, overbearing, and markedly ambivalent. We must register caution here, however, in light of the possibility that mothers respond in these ways to the self-starvation of their children. By contrast, anorexic girls usually describe their fathers as "emotional absentees." Most clinicians who work with anorexic individuals are in fact impressed with the extent to which family dynamics seem to contribute to the disorder. Along this line, Humphrey (1989) has analyzed the interactions of families with an anorexic daughter using the Structural Analysis of Social Behavior (SASB; Benjamin, 1974), a highly systematic, quantitative technique for measuring the nature of interpersonal relationships. The parents of these young women were found to communicate with their daughters in abnormally complicated ways, providing "double messages" that at once communicated both nurturant affection and disqualification of the daughters' attempts to express themselves. In turn, the anorexic daughters displayed behaviors that wavered between self-expression and submission to the leads provided by parents.

Anorexia often begins when life changes require new or unfamiliar skills concerning which the person feels inadequate, such as occurs when going off

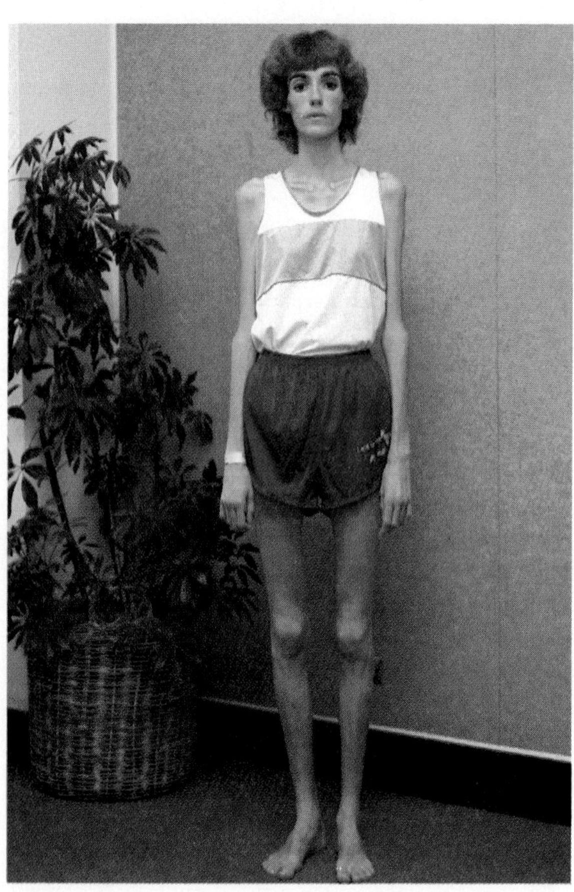

Though this anorexic woman's appearance is shocking to us, she is likely convinced that she is "fat." This distorted view of the true nature of one's body weight is a central feature of anorexia nervosa, along with a refusal to maintain weight within the normal limits for age and height. Anorexia often begins as an extension of normal dieting, but what distinguishes a normal dieter from one who converts dieting into a dangerous activity remains a mystery.

to college, getting married, or even reaching puberty. Often the disorder begins as an extension of normal dieting, which is common among young women. What distinguishes the normal dieter from the one who converts dieting into a dangerous flirtation with disaster remains a mystery. The case of Mary S., including her marked activity despite dwindling energy resources and her unfailing denial of the growing seriousness of her condition, is in most respects fairly typical of the anorexic syndrome:

Mary S., aged sixteen and one-half years, grew disgusted with a close friend who began to put on weight by eating candy. The two girls agreed to go on a reducing diet, although Mary weighed only 114 pounds. A year later she graduated from high school and obtained a job as a stenographer. She began to lead a very busy life, working every day, and going dancing at night with a young man who paid her attention. As her activities increased, her weight loss became more apparent, and soon her menses disappeared. Up to this time her dieting had been a voluntary control of eating, but now her appetite failed. Some months later one of the patient's sisters lured her boyfriend from her. Mary began to feel tired, and had to force herself to keep active. The onset of dizzy spells caused her to consult a doctor, who suggested a tonsillectomy. After the operation she refused to eat, but continued her active pace, including dancing every night. She now weighed 71 pounds. Two months later she became so dizzy and weak that she could no longer walk, and was finally brought to the hospital weighing 63 pounds. In three days, two and a half years after beginning her diet, Mary S. was dead of bronchopneumonia. (Nemiah, 1961, p. 10)

Recurrent episodes of seemingly uncontrollable binge eating, with full awareness of the pattern's abnormality and with much secrecy, shame, guilt, and self-deprecation concerning it, are the hallmarks of *bulimia,* now relabeled **bulimia nervosa** in DSM-III-R. Victims normally have pronounced fears that they will be unable to stop eating voluntarily; are preoccupied with weight gain; and engage in frequent attempts to lose weight by severe methods, such as fasting, self-induced vomiting, and overuse of laxatives and diuretics. While extreme weight fluctuations are common among bulimics, many successfully avoid obvious obesity and are able to conceal their problems from families, associates, and friends. Bulimia is thus a quite specific and distinctive syndrome and should be distinguished from the more common and demographically far less specific problem of overeating and obesity per se, which is discussed in Chapter 11. Unlike anorexia nervosa, its specific recognition as a psychiatric syndrome is relatively recent—it is not mentioned in the DSM-II of 1968.

The term *bulimarexia* was coined in 1976 by Boskind-White and White (1983) upon their discovering a large group of young women with distinctive dietary problems whose syndromes, they felt, differed significantly from either anorexia or bulimia, as these terms were then generally understood. These authors acknowledge (1986) that, with the inclusion of the purging phenomenon in the DSM-III bulimia definition, the terms *bulimia* and *bulimarexia* have become essentially interchangeable. While we have opted for the shorter term here, Boskind-White & White's (1983) rich clinical descriptions of the "bulimarexic" syndrome may be unsurpassed (see *HIGHLIGHT 7.4* for an example), and they add much to our understanding of these unfortunate young women. They emphasize a common core of psychological attributes involving perfectionism; obsessive concern with food and body proportions; low self-esteem; social withdrawal; and excessive preoccupation with pleasing others, if necessary to their own detriment.

Both anorexia nervosa (Strober, 1986) and bulimia (Boskind-White & White, 1986) have undergone a marked rise in incidence in the United States over at least the past three decades. Numerical estimations of incidence are therefore difficult to pin down. For females, onset of the disorder within the age range of 12 to 18 is probably in excess of 1 in 250. Foreyt (1986) estimates the incidence of bulimia to be "as high as" 15 percent in college-aged women.

Most authorities agree that these eating disorders have their origins in psychological problems that somehow become focused on food ingestion and body proportions. Many believe that our contemporary cultural preoccupation with an ideal of thinness encourages the rise in eating disorders we in fact seem to be experiencing. The fact that these syndromes are overwhelmingly more common in females than males is explained, in part, by the greater pressure for thinness experienced by females, as demonstrated in a clever study by Fallon & Rozin (1985). Using figure drawings as stimuli, these authors found that (a) women judged their "current figure" as too heavy; (b) men believed women liked heavier female figures than they in fact did; and (c) women believed men liked thinner female figures than they in fact did. Overall, men were satisfied and women dissatisfied with their own current figures as personally judged. While this self-devaluating perceptual bias in women hardly seems a complete explanation for their markedly disproportionate vulnerability to serious eating disorders, the likelihood is high of its making some contribution to that outcome (Hsu, 1989). Fashion magazines and the like, with their depictions of the ideal woman as malnourished in appearance, undoubtedly exacerbate the effect.

As Garner (1986) convincingly argues, the current trend of considering anorexia and bulimia to be psychologically dissimilar disorders may be seriously misleading. Not only do anorexic and bulimic individuals typically share many psychological traits, such as perfectionism and dysfunctional thought processes, they also share the same goal of maintaining suboptimal body weights. Moreover, a given patient may often move between the two syndromes at different times in her quest for ultimate thinness. Most anorexic and bulimic individuals come from socioeconomically advantaged backgrounds. The perfectionism and overachievement typical of anorexic patients were illustrated in a recent study by Dura and Bornstein (1989), who showed the school achievements of a group of hospitalized anorexic adolescents to be well above those predicted from their IQ scores.

Comparable underlying psychodynamics have also been described for anorexic and bulimic patients. The Humphrey (1989) study on family interactions in anorexia mentioned earlier contained a bulimic subject group. Disturbed family dynamics involving an undercutting of the daughter's autonomy (here within a context of excessive family enmeshment) were also observed for young women having this form of eating disorder. The general picture of family dysfunction in bulimia was also confirmed by Scalf-McIver and Thompson (1989) in a questionnaire study of college women showing bulimic eating patterns. In short, both anorexic and bulimic individuals seem deeply but ambivalently involved with their parents in power struggles concerning autonomy and identity.

Bruch (1986), who until her recent death was generally considered the world's leading authority on anorexia, saw the genuine anorexic person (she believed there were many "me too" facsimiles) as attempting to camouflage an undeveloped and amorphous selfhood by being different, even unique, in a special and fiercely "independent" way. She reportedly doubted that bulimia existed as a basic entity independent of anorexia or possibly even of some other unrelated syndrome (Foreyt, 1986). Boskind-White and White (1983, 1986), although seeing anorexic and bulimic individuals as struggling with similar personal and family issues, consider the typical bulimic person to be at a relatively more advanced stage of identity development, having achieved a measure of independence from family and been at least minimally successful in peer relations. The establishment of a truly autonomous selfhood, including a mature approach to sexuality, however, remains a difficult hurdle for both groups of women—although bulimic women as a group may be more likely to have had extensive sexual experiences (Coovert, Kinder, & Thompson, 1989).

Granting apparent psychological origins, persistent anorexia or bulimia leads eventually to serious

HIGHLIGHT 7.4

A Bulimic's Morning

Nicole awakens in her cold dark room and already wishes it was time to go back to bed. She dreads the thought of going through this day, which will be like so many others in her recent past. She asks herself the same question every morning: "Will I be able to make it through the day without being totally obsessed by thoughts of food, or will I blow it again and spend the day binge-ing?" She tells herself that today she will begin a new life, today she will start to live like a normal human being. However, she is not at all convinced that the choice is hers.

She feels fat and wants to lose weight, so she decides to start a new diet: "This time it'll be for real! I know I'll feel good about myself if I'm thinner. I want to start my exercises again because I want to make my body more attractive."

Nicole plans her breakfast, but decides not to eat until she has worked out for a half hour or so. She tries not to think about food since she is not really hungry. She feels anxiety about the day ahead of her. "It's this tension," she rationalizes. That is what is making her want to eat.

Nicole showers and dresses and plans her schedule for the day—classes, studying, and meals. She plans this schedule in great detail, listing where she will be at every minute and what she will eat at every meal. She does not want to leave blocks of time when she might feel tempted to binge.

"It's time to exercise, but I don't really want to; I feel lazy. Why do I always feel so lazy? What happened to the will power I used to have?"

Gradually, Nicole feels the binge-ing signal coming on. Halfheartedly she tries to fight it, remembering the promises she made to herself about changing. She also knows how she is going to feel at the end of the day if she spends it binge-ing. Ultimately, Nicole decides to give into her urges because, for the moment, she would rather eat.

Since Nicole is not going to exercise, because she wants to eat, she decides that she might as well eat some "good" food. She makes a poached egg and toast and brews a cup of coffee, all of which goes down in about thirty seconds. She knows this is the beginning of several hours of craziness!

After rummaging through the cupboards, Nicole realizes that she does not have any binge food. It is cold and snowy outside and she has to be at school fairly soon, but she bundles up and runs down the street. First she stops at the bakery for a bagful of sweets —cookies and doughnuts. While munching on these, she stops and buys a few bagels. Then a quick run to the grocery store for grano-

Boskind-White and White (1983, pp. 29–32).

physical problems relating both to starvation and the dire methods often employed to purge food following a binge. These patients routinely suffer from anemia; dehydration; deficiencies in essential vitamins, minerals, and electrolytes; chronic urinary and bowel difficulties; hypoglycemia; endocrine abnormalities; and potentially serious alterations in cardiovascular functioning. Amenorrhea is virtually always present in anorexia and is common in bulimia as well. At some point in the process, biological factors seem to develop their own demands, taking the behavior beyond conscious control and making it exceedingly difficult to reverse, as we will see later in the chapter in our discussion of treatment measures. One school of thought holds that hypothalamic functioning is altered by deliberate selfstarvation, resulting finally in autonomous dysregulation of both appetite and menstruation, and yielding the typical advanced clinical picture (Bemis, 1978; Walsh, 1980).

Like CHD, these disorders of the basic drive for nutritional sustenance are dangerous and have become commonplace in modern American society. Also like CHD, we have yet to devise a reliably effective means of preventing or reversing the psychological substrates that encourage their development and maintenance. As we will see later, however, progress is being made on both these fronts.

The main issues addressed thus far in this chapter have had a decidedly contemporary focus, and deliberately so. We have sought to introduce the topic of psychological influences on health by discussing some currently high-profile concerns in both the public and professional sectors. We have

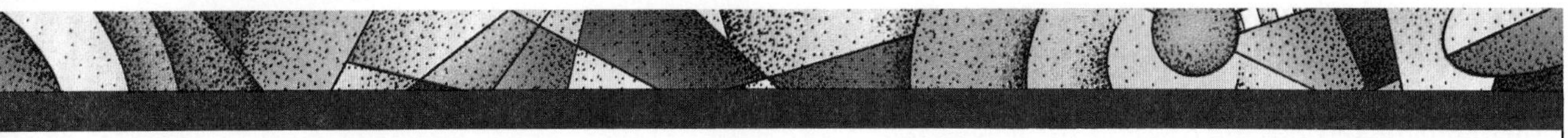

la and milk. At the last minute, Nicole adds several candy bars. By the time she is finished, she has spent over fifteen dollars.

Nicole can hardly believe that she is going to put all of this food, this junk, into her body; even so, her adrenaline is flowing and all she wants to do is eat, think about eating, and anticipate getting it over with. She winces at the thought of how many pounds all of this food represents, but knows she will throw it up afterward. There is no need to worry.

At home Nicole makes herself a few bowls of cereal and milk, which she gobbles down with some of the bagels smothered with butter, cream cheese, and jelly (not to mention the goodies from the bakery and the candy bars which she is still working on). She drowns all of this with huge cups of coffee and milk, which help speed up the process even more. All this has taken no longer than forty-five minutes, and Nicole feels as though she has been moving at ninety miles an hour.

Nicole dreads reaching this stage, where she is so full that she absolutely has to stop eating. She will throw up, which she feels she has to do but which repels her. At this point, she has to acknowledge that she's been binge-ing. She wishes she were dreaming, but knows all too well that this is real. The thought of actually digesting all of those calories, all of that junk, terrifies her.

In her bathroom, Nicole ties her hair back, turns on the shower (so none of the neighbors can hear her), drinks a big glass of water, and proceeds to force herself to vomit. She feels sick, ashamed, and incredulous that she is really doing this. Yet she feels trapped—she does not know how to break out of this pattern. As her stomach empties, she steps on and off the scale to make sure she has not gained any weight.

Nicole knows she needs help, but she wants someone else to make it all go away. As she crashes on her bed to recuperate, her head is spinning. "I'll never do this again," she vows. "Starting tomorrow, I'm going to change. I'll go on a fast for a week and then I'll feel better."

Unfortunately, deep inside, Nicole does not believe any of this. She knows this will not be the last time. Reluctantly, she leaves for school, late and unwilling to face the work and responsibilities that lie ahead. She almost feels as though she could eat again to avoid going to school. She wonders how many hours it will be until she starts her next binge, and she wishes she had never gotten out of bed this morning.

also tried to give due attention to the contextual, system-level thinking that is growing in the health field (for example, organ failure is not a discrete, isolated event). As we have seen, the behavioral medicine approach explicitly embodies such a far-reaching perspective, calling into question much of traditional medicine's exclusive concern with the pathophysiology of individual organs when (*after*) disease strikes (Weiner & Fawzy, 1989).

We have also seen, however, that various medical pioneers have from time to time called attention to the influence of psychosocial factors, chiefly emotional ones, in causing or maintaining physical illness. By the 1950s this thinking had become strongly wedded to the psychoanalytic tradition. As was noted earlier, these ideas involved quite specific causal hypotheses concerning certain diseases that came to be considered "psychosomatic" in nature—organic dysfunctions produced by aberrant emotional processes.

As a group, these early notions shared the joint problems of being both too specific and too general. They frequently specified the exact type of psychological "conflict" presumed to underlie a given disease, and they tended to assume that this alleged conflict was both necessary and sufficient in causing any instance of the disease. For example, asthma was conceived as "suppressed crying" caused by an impulse to cry joined with a need to inhibit it, both propensities relating in turn to a fear of abandonment. We now know that asthma can have many causes, that it probably does not occur in the absence of a biologically based predisposition, and that any emotional factors involved in precipitating an attack tend to be quite idiosyncratic to the victim (A. Alexander, 1977, 1981; Knapp, 1989). Comparable ideas relating a number of other illnesses to rather fanciful and specific psychogenic hypotheses also lost credibility when subjected to rigorous empirical evaluation.

Despite the general failure of this "psychosomatic specificity" approach, there were some exceptions—not so much in the sense of detailed confirmations as in that of establishing modest associations between certain illnesses and certain emotional states (much as in the relatively more recent case of CHD and some still imprecisely identified component of the Type A pattern). We will now briefly examine three illnesses that have continued to attract attention in this regard: essential hypertension or high blood pressure, peptic ulcers, and persistently recurrent headaches.

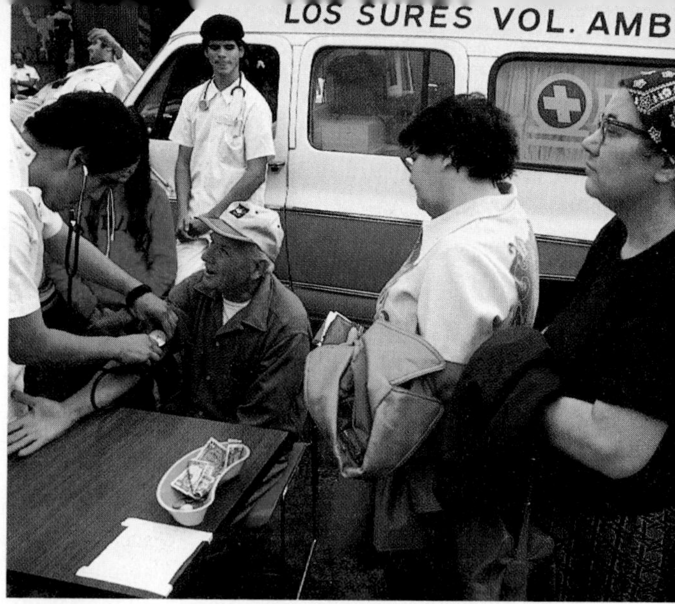

High blood pressure is an insidious and dangerous disorder, but it is easy and painless to detect by means of the familiar inflated arm cuff. It is common to see mobile units at shopping centers and the like, offering free blood pressure checks.

Essential Hypertension

During states of calm, the beat of the heart is regular, the pulse is even, blood pressure is relatively low, and the visceral organs are well supplied with blood. With stress, however, the vessels of the visceral organs constrict, and blood flows in greater quantity to the muscles of the trunk and limbs—part of the flight or fight pattern described earlier. With the tightening of the tiny vessels supplying the visceral organs, the heart must work harder. As it beats faster and with greater force, the pulse quickens and blood pressure mounts. Usually, when the crisis passes, the body resumes normal functioning and the blood pressure returns to normal. Under continuing emotional strain, however, high blood pressure may become chronic.

About 12 percent of Americans suffer from chronically high blood pressure, or **hypertension.** Preexisting organic factors account for only some 5 to 10 percent of hypertension cases (Byassee, 1977); the large remainder are given the designation **essential hypertension,** meaning no physical cause is known. Although Wing and Manton (1983) have reported a reduced incidence of deaths due to hypertension, it nevertheless is the primary cause of more than 60,000 deaths each year and a major predisposing factor in another 1 million or more deaths a year from strokes and cardiovascular diseases, including CHD (Coates et al., 1981). It is also a risk factor in kidney failure, blindness, and a number of other physical ailments. For reasons that are not entirely clear but apparently relate in part to diet, the incidence of hypertension is about twice as high among blacks as among whites (Anderson & Jackson, 1987; Edwards, 1973; Mays, 1974), making it a more serious health problem in this population than even sickle-cell anemia.

Unlike the other disease states we have dealt with, there are usually no symptoms to signal high blood pressure. Sufferers experience no personal distress. In severe cases, some people complain of headaches, tiredness, insomnia, or occasional dizzy spells—symptoms often easy to ignore—but most people suffering from hypertension receive no warning symptoms. In fact, Nelson (1973) reported on one survey encompassing three middle-class neighborhoods in Los Angeles that revealed that a third of the adults tested had high blood pressure; only half of them had been aware of it. As Mays (1974) has described the situation, "In most instances . . . the disease comes as silently as a serpent stalking its prey. Someone with high blood pressure may be unaware of his affliction for many years and then, out of the blue, develop blindness or be stricken by a stroke, cardiac arrest or kidney failure" (p. 7).

Since there is no such thing as benign hypertension, high blood pressure is an insidious and dangerous disorder. Ironically, it is both simple and painless to detect by means of the familiar inflated arm cuff, automatic versions of which are now widely available for self-testing at shopping centers and the like.

In some cases a physical cause of hypertension can be identified. For example, it may be attributable to a narrowing of the aorta or one of its arteries, to the excessive use of certain drugs, or to dietary factors. The normal regulation of blood pressure, however, is so complex that when it goes awry in a particular case, identifying the causal factors can be extremely difficult (Herd, 1984). Kidney dysfunction, for example, may be a cause or an effect of dangerously elevated pressures—or both.

Obesity, long suspected as an etiological factor, has emerged as a possible underlying factor in several other known correlates of hypertension, such as poor diet and lack of exercise (Ostfeld & D'Atri, 1977). Obesity, of course, can also be a factor contributing to the current level of experienced stress.

A number of investigators have shown that chronic hypertension may be triggered by emotional stress. For example, a highly stressful job markedly increases the risk of high blood pressure (Edwards, 1973). The stresses of inner-city life—as well as dietary factors such as excessive salt intake—have been identified as probably playing a key role in the high incidence of hypertension among black people (Anderson & Jackson, 1987; Mays, 1974).

The classical psychoanalytic interpretation of hypertension is that affected people suffer from "suppressed rage," and scattered evidence supports this hypothesis (Gentry et al., 1982; Spielberger et al., 1985; Stone & Hokanson, 1969). Although there is a high incidence of hypertension in the black inner-city population, among whom suppressed hostility might be expected to run high (Harburgh et al., 1973), the suppressed-rage hypothesis cannot be said to be firmly established in respect to all, or even necessarily a majority, of affected persons. Findings by Esler et al. (1977) suggest that, in the subgroup of hypertensive people who do show suppressed hostility, it is often accompanied by high levels of submissiveness, overcontrol, and guilt.

A variant of the suppressed-rage hypothesis has been proposed by McClelland (1979). According to this view, an affected individual is driven not so much by rage and the need to suppress it as by power motives and the need to inhibit their expression. Unexpressed anger is then a frequent accompaniment. In a well-conceived study designed to test these ideas, McClelland found that personality measures of "need for power" and "activity inhibition" were indeed jointly associated with elevated blood pressures. Moreover, he demonstrated that this inhibited power motive syndrome in men in their 30s accurately predicted elevated blood pressure and signs of hypertensive disease in these same men 20 years later.

Perhaps we will find that neither rage nor power motives per se are critical elements in essential hypertension. What is common to the findings of McClelland and earlier work is the inhibition or suppression of strong, emotion-laden urgings to perform certain acts that are poorly tolerated by polite society. The common factor, in other words, might be that of a poor match between individual drives and internalized societal restraints. Conflictual states of this sort were examined in some detail in our earlier discussion of neurotic processes (Chapter 6).

Peptic Ulcers

Peptic ulcers were first observed in Western culture during the early part of the nineteenth century. The term derives from *pepsin,* an important component of the acid stomach juices that aid in the early phases of digestion. These ulcerations of the stomach or upper intestine (the duodenum) were first found primarily in young women, but a shift occurred in the second half of the nineteenth century, and in the twentieth century men became far more prone to peptic ulcers than women. Today the sex ratio appears to be equalizing, and incidence and prevalence figures show a downward trend. The epidemiologic data suggest that incidence trends mirror the transformation from rural to urban living in different societies, declining in the posturbanization period (Thompson, 1982). Approximately 10,000 Americans die every year from peptic ulcers (Whitehead et al., 1982).

The ulcer itself results from an excessive flow of the stomach's acid-containing digestive juices, which eat away the lining of the stomach or duodenum, leaving a craterlike wound. Although dietary factors, diseases, and other organic conditions may also lead to ulcers, it is now recognized that worry, repressed anger, resentment, anxiety, dependency, and other negative emotional states may be causally involved in many cases. A high activity level, in particular, has been found to be a frequent correlate of gastric lesions (Weiss, 1984). Conceivably, any of these factors might contribute to a breakdown of the stomach's mucosal lining, which seems to be the immediate cause of ulcer formation. The result is that the stomach begins to digest itself.

It has long been believed that conflicts centering on dependency needs are especially likely to be found in individuals who develop ulcers. In support of this belief we have available a landmark study, the scope of which has not since been equaled (Weiner et al., 1957):

Relying on prior evidence of a high rate of gastric secretion in ulcer-prone individuals, as indicated in part by a high level of pepsinogen in the blood serum, Weiner and his colleagues tested a population of 2073 army draftees and chose for study those men found to be maximum and minimum gastric secreters. These were groups of men, in other words, who should be at maximum and minimum risk for ulcer formation by virtue of constitutional predisposition.

Membership in one or the other group did in fact predict the incidence of ulcer formation during the stress of basic training. Of perhaps even greater importance, however, is the fact that a battery of psychological tests also correctly predicted the pepsinogen-level group in which recruits would fall, and even correctly identified at an above-chance level which high-pepsinogen recruits would develop ulcers. These test results showed evidence of major unresolved dependency (in Freudian terms "oral") conflicts, with resultant frustration and suppressed hostility.

The most important point established by this study was that neither a high pepsinogen level nor dependency conflicts was alone responsible for peptic ulcer development. Taken together, however, they constituted a pathogenic predisposition that, on exposure to a special stressor (basic training), could be expected to challenge the equilibrium of an individual, thus producing an abnormally high risk of ulcer formation. Strang (1989), reviewed a variety of other research findings and found that they generally support dependency issues as having special relevance in the pathogenesis of ulcers.

The dependency of an ulcer-prone individual is not always obvious at the behavioral level. In fact such an individual may seem to be quite independent or autonomous, even excessively hard-driving in terms of surface behavior. We also have little doubt that psychological factors other than unresolved dependency conflicts can be involved in the development of ulcers. Animal experiments, for example, suggest that gastric lesions are most likely to occur when an organism's attempts to cope with a challenge produce little or no useful feedback to guide future responding (Weiss, 1984). Human situations having these characteristics are readily imagined, but as yet we have no solid evidence relating them to ulcer development.

Recurrent Headaches

Although headaches can result from a wide range of organic conditions, the majority of them—about nine out of ten—seem to be related to emotional tension. More than 50 million Americans suffer from tension or migraine headaches, with the overall incidence apparently being higher among women than men. In one survey, Andrasik, Holroyd, and Abell (1979) found that 52 percent of a large group of college students reported headaches at least once or twice a week.

Research in this area has focused primarily on **migraine,** an intensely painful headache that recurs periodically. Although typically involving only one side of the head, migraine is sometimes more generalized; it may also shift from side to side. Migraine was described extensively by medical writers of antiquity, but the cause of the pain remained a mystery until the 1940s, when interest was focused on the pain-sensitive arteries of the head. The typical migraine occurs in two phases. First, there is a markedly reduced flow of blood (and hence oxygen) to certain parts of the brain. Although this reduced blood flow is not associated with pain, many victims experience it as an "aura" that predictably leads to the painful second phase. This second phase is characterized by a sudden rush of blood to the previously deprived areas, causing rapid expansion of the affected arteries and stimulation of local nerve endings. This stimulation produces the distinctive migraine pain.

It has also been shown that a variety of experimentally induced stressors—frustrations, excessive demands for performance, and threatening interviews—cause vascular dilation among migraine sufferers but not among other people. *HIGHLIGHT 7.5* traces the course of a headache induced during a discussion that evoked hostile feelings in the subject—a migraine sufferer.

The vast majority of headaches are so-called **simple tension headaches.** These, too, involve stress and vascular changes, but the changes are thought to be different from those in migraine headaches. With simple tension headaches, emotional stress seems to lead to contraction of the muscles surrounding the skull; these contractions,

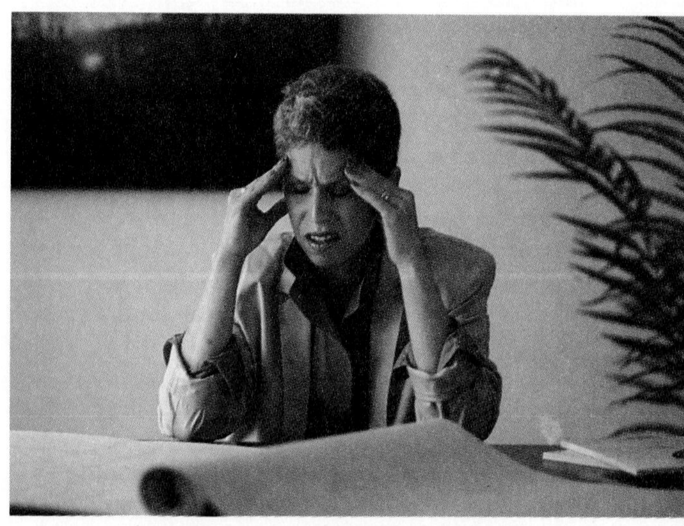

Emotional tension seems to be the cause of nine out of ten headaches. More than 50 million Americans suffer from tension or migraine headaches.

HIGHLIGHT 7.5

Migraine Headaches

The side-view drawing of the head below shows the location of pain-sensitive cranial arteries. The dotted lines mark the areas where a headache is felt as various parts of the arteries dilate.

The graph traces the course of a headache induced during a discussion that evoked feelings of hostility in the subject. Both the changes in the amplitude of the artery pulsations and the corresponding increase and decrease in the intensity of the pain reported are shown. The headache was completely relieved by means of an injection that the subject believed would end the suffering but which actually could have had no physical effect.

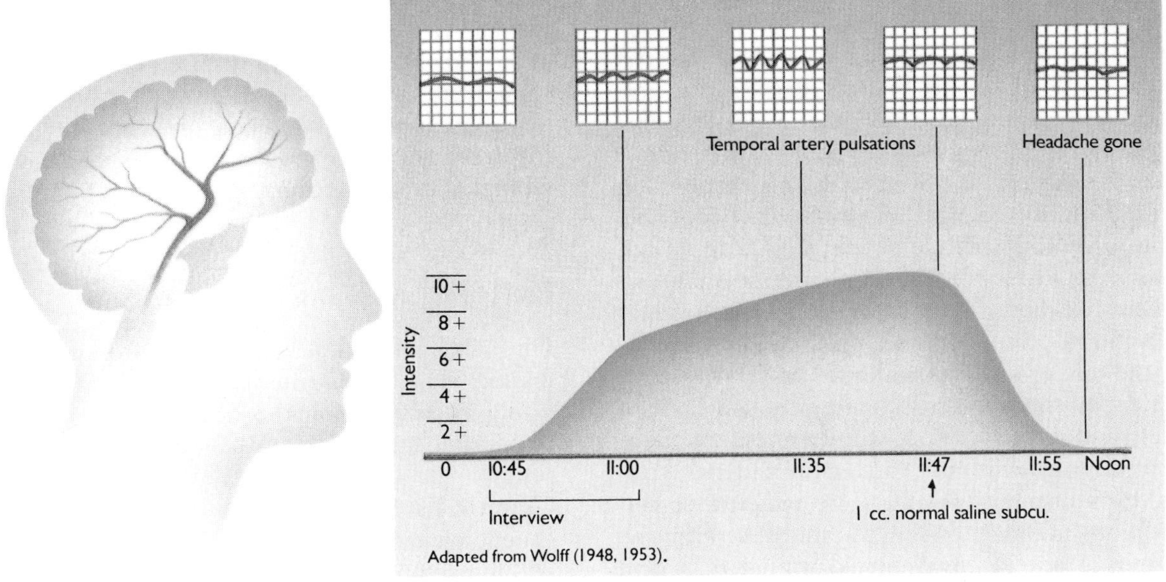

From *Wolff's headache and other head pain,* Fourth Edition, by Donald J. Dalessio. Copyright © 1980 by Oxford University Press, Inc. Reprinted by permission.

in turn, result in vascular constrictions, which cause headache pain. We should note here, however, that with the more precise measurement techniques now available, the evidence for the physiological differences between migraine and tension headaches is being drawn into question (Blanchard & Andrasik, 1982). Though further studies are needed, it may be that the physiological processes are similar for the two types of headaches and that the difference is rather one of degree, with migraine involving greater vascular disruption. Certainly it is true that many people suffer headaches that appear to have both vascular and muscular origins.

Both tension and migraine headaches usually appear during adolescence and recur periodically during stressful times. The pain can often be relieved with analgesics, with muscle-relaxant drugs, or with certain relaxation-inducing psychological procedures (Blanchard et al., 1990a). These latter procedures include **biofeedback,** a technique in which a person is taught to influence his or her own physiological processes (Blanchard et al., 1990b). Of the two types, migraine headaches are usually more painful and slower to respond to treatment than simple tension headaches.

The presumed psychological predispositions for psychogenic headaches are less clear than in the case of other disorders considered in this chapter. Also, the interaction of personality factors with particular types of stressors appears to be especially important for headache sufferers (Levor et al., 1986). However, clinicians increasingly seem to agree that it is important to the typical headache-prone person to feel in control of events impinging on him or her. Such individuals are usually described as highly organized and perfectionistic (Williams, 1977). In one instance, a highly skilled nurse, who specialized in the demanding field of cardiac emergencies, was subject to excruciatingly severe migraine attacks. She went to a clinic for therapy but was so bent on maintaining control of virtually every aspect of the therapeutic relationship that she managed to sabotage it with a regularity astonishing to both herself and her therapist.

In a study by Andrasik et al. (1982), the traditional belief that migraine sufferers show higher levels of depression, passivity, nonassertiveness, hostility, and high-achievement strivings was not supported. Psychological tests of migraine sufferers revealed psychologically normal profiles. Instead, the tension headache sufferers showed the greatest psychopathology. This finding suggests that tension headaches might be more indicative of psychological problems per se than migraine headaches.

In focusing, as we have in this section, on certain diseases in which a psychogenic contribution to etiology seems especially likely, we do not intend to exclude by omission the possibility—indeed likelihood—that other specific diseases may sometimes have identifiable psychogenic roots. As in the case of asthma mentioned earlier, however, we suspect that in most such instances, some sort of biological predisposition will turn out to be a necessary element in the total causal pattern. Within this constraint, the literature indicates several additional candidates for continued scrutiny in search of specific psychogenic mediators. These diseases include: certain allergies and skin eruptions; chronic diarrhea and ulcerative colitis; rheumatoid arthritis; Raynaud's disease (a potentially serious local vasoconstriction that may interrupt the blood supply to certain body parts); diabetes; menstrual irregularities and other endocrine disturbances (see, e.g., Levitan, 1989; Sandhu & Cohen, 1989); and chronic disturbances of the sleep cycle.

PSYCHOGENIC PHYSICAL DISEASE: ADDITIONAL ETIOLOGIC CONSIDERATIONS

In the foregoing pages we have explored at a general level the manner in which negative thinking and attitudes, autonomic excess, stressor-induced immunosuppression, and health-endangering life-styles can compromise a person's biological integrity. From there, we proceeded to discuss apparently specific psychogenic contributions, insofar as these are known, to the etiology of five extremely common and sometimes life-threatening physical conditions: coronary heart disease, eating disorders (anorexia and bulimia), essential hypertension, peptic ulcers, and recurrent headaches. We also noted that this listing is by no means exhaustive in cataloging the physical ills that may have psychogenic roots.

In this section we return to a more general level of analysis to complete our picture of psychological causation in physical illness. We will be particularly concerned with the problem of specificity—of why, under stress, one individual develops anorexia, another hypertension, and still another migraine headaches. For the sake of economy and convenience, we will generally refer to such stress-related conditions as psychogenic illnesses or diseases, even though it should be clear that other etiological factors, particularly predisposing biological ones, are inevitably involved. We begin the discussion at the level of biological predisposition.

Biological Factors

Obviously, biological factors are involved in all disease. We focus here on those factors likely to have a role in determining the adequacy of a person's response to stressor circumstances.

Genetic Factors In general, understanding of genetic contributions to diseases believed to have strong psychogenic origins remains limited (Kidd & Morton, 1989). The field involves many perplexities, including the mind-boggling difficulties of differentiating genetic contributions to (a) an underlying physical vulnerability for acquiring the disease in question; (b) the psychological makeup of the individual and his or her stress tolerance; and (c) the nature of any interaction between (a) and (b).

Research by Gregory and Rosen (1965) has demonstrated that the brothers of ulcer patients are about twice as likely to have ulcers as comparable members of the general population. Relatedly, Rotter et al. (1979) have presented evidence of genetic cotransmission of both high pepsinogen serum levels and peptic ulcers. Increased frequencies of hypertension, migraine, and other reactions have also been reported for close relatives of people with these disorders.

Although social learning (for example, children modeling the inadequate coping skills of their parents) could be a factor in such family resemblances, research evidence on this point is equivocal, and genetic factors cannot be ruled out. In fact it would probably be difficult to discover any human disease in which genetic factors could be ruled out entirely.

An interesting separation of genetic and psychological influences is contained in the findings of Liljefors and Rahe (1970), who studied the role of life stress in coronary heart disease among twins. The subjects consisted of 32 pairs of identical male twins between 42 and 67 years of age, in which only one twin in each pair suffered from coronary heart disease. The genetic contribution in such twinships is of course constant for each pair, thus controlling for this factor. The investigators found that the twins suffering from heart disease were more work oriented, took less leisure time, had more home problems, and in general experienced greater dissatisfactions in their lives than their healthier twin brothers. Such a finding represents a rather compelling case for psychosocial contribution to the development of CHD, but the study's design cannot rule out a genetic contribution as well. The latter could still be a *necessary,* but not *sufficient,* condition for CHD pathology. According to this scenario, both twins may have been at genetic risk for CHD—its actual "expression" then being determined by an excess of psychosocial disorganization in one of the pair's members. Interpretive complexities of this sort are the rule rather than the exception in trying to estimate the magnitude of genetic influences here as well as in other areas of psychopathology.

Differences in Autonomic Reactivity and Somatic Weakness In our earlier discussion (Chapter 4) of vulnerability and causal factors, we noted that individuals vary significantly in primary reaction tendencies. Even very young infants reveal marked differences in their sensitivities to aversive stimuli; some infants react to such stressors by developing fevers, others by digestive upsets, and still others by sleep disturbances. Such differences in reactivity continue into adult life and presumably help account for individual differences in susceptibility to psychogenic diseases, and for the types of diseases a given individual is most likely to develop.

In connection with the latter point, Wolff (1950) suggested that people can be classified as "stomach reactors," "pulse reactors," "nose reactors," and so on, depending on what kinds of physical changes stress characteristically triggers in them. For example, a person who has an inherited tendency to respond to stressors with increased cardiac output and vasoconstriction may be at special risk for chronic hypertension (Friedman & Iwai, 1976). A person who reacts with increased secretion of stomach acids will be more likely to develop peptic ulcers (Strang, 1989).

Sometimes a particular organ is especially vulnerable because of heredity, illness, or prior trauma. A person who has inherited or developed a "weak" stomach will be prone to gastrointestinal upsets during anger or anxiety. Presumably, the weakest link in the chain of visceral organs will be the organ affected. Caution must be exercised, however, to avoid ex post facto reasoning, because it would not be safe to conclude that when a particular organ system is affected it must have been weak to begin with. Also, as we will see, conditioning may play a key role in determining which organ system is involved.

Disruption of Corticovisceral Control Mechanisms Other biological explanations have focused on the role of central control mechanisms in regulating autonomic functioning. According to one hypothesis, the corticovisceral control mechanisms of the brain may fail in their homeostatic functions, so that an individual's emotional response is exaggerated in intensity and his or her physiological equilibrium is not regained within normal time limits (Halberstam, 1972; Lebedev, 1967; Schwartz, 1989). Such control failures might well be central to deficient hypothalamic regulation of *both* the autonomic nervous system and the adrenocortical hormones of the endocrine system, which may be involved in the body's immunity to disease. More generally, we have seen that breakdowns in a number of different pathways can compromise immune competence during the brain's processing of stressor events.

In assessing the role of biological factors in psychogenic diseases, most investigators would take into consideration each of the factors we have described. Perhaps the greatest emphasis at present would be placed on a person's characteristic autonomic activity, the vulnerability of affected organ systems, and possible constitutionally-based or acquired alterations in the control mechanisms of the brain that normally regulate autonomic and endocrinologic functioning.

Psychosocial Factors

Though evidence suggests that psychological factors play a prominent role in the causal picture of many diseases, it is still not altogether clear what factors are involved or how they exert their effects. Factors that investigators have emphasized include personality characteristics (including failure to learn adequate coping patterns), interpersonal relationships, and learning in the autonomic nervous system.

Personality Characteristics The work of Dunbar (1943, 1954) and a number of other early investigators raised the hope of identifying specific personality factors associated with certain psychophysiologic disorders—for example, noting that rigidity, high sensitivity to threat, and chronic underlying hostility are typical among those who suffer from hypertension. The ability to delineate ulcer types, hypertensive characters, and so on would, of course, be of great value in understanding, assessing, and treating the pertinent illnesses—and perhaps even in preventing them.

As we have seen, however, later research evidence has suggested that such an approach is oversimplified. For example, although Kidson (1973) found hypertensive patients as a group to be significantly more insecure, anxious, sensitive, and angry than a nonhypertensive control group, a sizable number of the control-group members also showed these characteristics. Similarly, the tendency for Type A behavior (or some limited component of it) to be associated with CHD and heart attacks must be tempered with the observation that most Type As do not have coronary problems, and some Type Bs do (see figures in *HIGHLIGHT 7.3*).

So even though personality makeup seems to play an important role, we still do not know why some individuals with "predisposing" personality characteristics do not develop a particular disease; nor can we account adequately for the wide range of personality makeups among individuals who suffer from that same condition. Usually, we can at best conclude only that particular personality factors are weakly but significantly correlated with the occurrence of certain illnesses.

Normally, when individuals are subjected experimentally to frustrating experiences, their blood pressures rise and their hearts beat more rapidly. If they are then given an opportunity to express physical or verbal aggression against the frustrator, their blood pressures and heart rates rapidly return to normal. If they are permitted only fantasy aggression or no aggression at all, however, their bodies return much more slowly to normal physiological functioning (Hokanson & Burgess, 1962). Thus, besides looking at people's abilities to cope with the stress of frustrations or conflicts or whatever, it seems necessary to consider their abilities to deal adequately with the accompanying emotional tensions.

Interpersonal Relationships In our previous discussions we have repeatedly noted the destructive effects that stressful interpersonal patterns—including marital unhappiness and divorce—may have on personality adjustment. Such patterns may also influence physiological functioning. In fact, death rates from varied causes, including physical disease, are markedly higher in people who have recently undergone marital problems or divorce than in the general population (Bloom, Asher, & White, 1978).

Loss of a spouse through death also puts the survivor at risk. In an extensive review of the literature, Stroebe and Stroebe (1983) concluded that men are slightly more adversely affected by the death of their wives than women are by the death of their husbands. For example, in an earlier study of widowers, Parkes, Benjamin, and Fitzgerald (1969) reported that during the six-month period following the death of their wives, the widowers' death rate was 40 percent above the expected rate. In fact the incidence of cardiac deaths among these men was so high that the investigators referred to this pattern as "the broken-heart syndrome."

Lynch (1977), in a book entitled *The Broken Heart,* argues convincingly that the relatively high incidence of heart disease in industrialized communities stems in part from the absence of positive human relationships. He notes that heart disease and other illnesses are more prevalent among individuals lacking human companionship and for whom loneliness is common. This group includes not only those people who have recently lost a spouse through death but also single or divorced individuals.

Other studies have focused on the role of pathogenic family patterns. For example, studies have found that the mothers of asthmatic patients have in many cases felt ambivalent toward these children and tended to reject them, while at the same time being overprotective and unduly restrictive of the children's activities (Lipton, Steinschneider, & Richmond, 1966; Olds, 1970). Because individuals coming out of such family backgrounds tend to be overdependent and insecure, it would hardly be surprising if they should react with chronic emotional mobilization to problems that do not seem threatening to most people. On the other hand, as we have seen, a strictly psychogenic interpretation of asthma is questionable. Severe asthma is a terrifying and life-threatening disorder. It would not be surprising on this basis alone to discover that asthmatic children are overdependent and insecure, or that their mothers tend to become ambivalent, protective, and restrictive after the asthma appears.

Complementing the work of Humphrey (1989) mentioned earlier, Kog and Vandereycken (1985) found substantial evidence of controlling relationships and parental discord in the families of eating disorder patients. They also noted a high incidence of physical illness, mood disorder (see Chapter 11), and alcoholism (Chapter 9) in these families.

Learning in the Autonomic Nervous System Although Pavlov and many subsequent investigators have demonstrated that autonomic responses can be conditioned—as in the case of salivation—it was long assumed that an individual could not learn to control such responses "voluntarily." We now know that this assumption was wrong. Not only can autonomic reactivity be conditioned involuntarily via the classical Pavlovian model, but operant learning in the autonomic nervous system can also take place.

Thus the hypothesis has developed that certain physical disorders may arise through accidental reinforcement of symptom and behavioral patterns. "A child who is repeatedly allowed to stay home from school when he has an upset stomach may be learning the visceral responses of chronic indigestion" (Lang, 1970, p. 86). Similarly, an adolescent girl may get little or no attention from being "good," but if she starves herself to the point of severe weight loss she may become the center of attention. If this pattern is continued, she might learn to avoid weight gain at all costs and correspondingly learn a profound aversion to food. The increasing alarm of her parents and others would presumably serve as a potent reinforcement for her to continue in her dangerous ways regarding food ingestion.

Although causal factors other than conditioning are now thought to play a role in most cases of psychogenic illness, it seems clear that regardless of how a physical symptom may have developed, it may be elicited by suggestion and maintained by the reinforcement provided by **secondary gains,** indirect benefits derived from the illness behavior. The role of suggestion was demonstrated by a study in which 19 of 40 volunteer asthmatic subjects developed asthma symptoms after breathing the mist of a salt solution that they were told contained allergens, such as dust or pollen. In fact, 12 of the subjects had full-fledged asthma attacks. When the subjects then took what they thought was a drug to combat asthma (actually the same salt mist), their symptoms disappeared immediately (Bleeker, 1968). This study clearly shows the effect of suggestion on an autonomically mediated response. Why the other 21 subjects remained unaffected is not clear.

In short, it appears that some physical disorders may be acquired, maintained, or both in much the same way as other behavior patterns. Indeed, this finding is a basic tenet of behavioral medicine and health psychology, one aspect of which examines how various behavior modification and psychotherapeutic techniques can alter overt and covert reactions to physical disease processes (Bradley & Prokop, 1982; Gentry, 1984b; G. C. Stone et al., 1987; Williams & Gentry, 1977).

Sociocultural Factors

As we have seen, the incidence of specific disorders, both physical and mental, varies in different societies, in different strata of the same society, and over time. In general, what Cannon (1929) called diseases of civilization do not occur among nonindustrialized societies like the aborigines of the Australian Western Desert (Kidson & Jones, 1968), the Navajo Indians of Arizona, or certain isolated groups in South America (Stein, 1970). As these societies are exposed to social change, however, gastrointestinal, cardiovascular, and other psychogenic diseases begin to make their appearances. There is evidence of change in the nature and incidence of such disorders in Japan paralleling the tremendous social changes that have taken place there since World War II (Ikemi et al., 1974). For example, the incidence of hypertension and coronary heart disease has increased markedly with the post-war westernization of Japanese culture.

After an extensive review of the literature within our society, Senay and Redlich (1968) found that psychogenic diseases did not respect social class or other major sociocultural variables. Similarly, Kahn (1969) found that, contrary to folklore, only a small number of executives develop peptic ulcers; in fact, blue-collar workers who are dissatisfied with their jobs are more likely to develop ulcers than successful business executives who are moving up the corporate ladder.

The phenomenon of eating disorders poses fascinating sociocultural questions for which answers are largely lacking. We still have no entirely satisfactory explanation of the seeming epidemic of eating disorders recently among young American women, although it appears likely that changing sociocultural factors are somehow implicated. It seems doubtful that the cultural preference for thinness, which for women was well-established at a time when eating disorders were quite rare, provides a complete answer. Although the combination of high achievement striving and middle-class socioeconomic origins is consistent from a sociocultural standpoint, it is not clear what role that combination, or either factor separately, plays in the increasing incidence and prevalence of dietary dyscontrol. For that matter, we do not have a confident understanding of the tremendous gender imbalance in the occurrence of these syndromes, although again sociocultural factors are likely to be involved. Perhaps the time has come for us to make a serious effort to unearth and eradicate the seemingly impossible demands we as a society have created for that now large group of young women who are at high risk for these dangerous disorders.

In general, it appears that any sociocultural conditions that markedly increase life stress tend to play havoc with the human organism and lead to an increase in disease as well as other physical and mental problems.

TREATMENTS AND OUTCOMES

Though a particular environmental stressor may have been a key causal factor in the development of a physical illness, removal of this stressor, even combined with learning more effective coping techniques, may be insufficient for recovery if organic changes have taken place; such changes may have become chronic and irreversible.

Treatment therefore begins by assessing the nature and severity of the organic pathology as well as the roles of psychosocial and organic factors in the total causal pattern. In hypertension, for example, the role of dietary factors may far outweigh that of current psychosocial stressors in causation and maintenance. Dietary patterns, however, reflect cultural patterns and attitudes—that all-important life-style—that also may have to be reckoned with. Thus a thorough assessment involving the past and present roles of biological, psychosocial, and sociocultural factors is essential to the development of an effective treatment program.

Except for conditions involving serious organic pathology, treatment methods are similar to those for anxiety-based disorders; the outcomes are likewise reasonably favorable. Instead of going into detail concerning the methods of treatment and the outcomes for each type of disorder, we shall briefly summarize the general treatment measures currently used. More detailed discussion of these therapies can be found in Chapters 17 and 18.

Biological Measures

Aside from immediate and long-range medical measures, such as emergency care for bleeding ulcers or bypass surgery for coronary heart disease, biological treatment can involve the use of mild tranquilizers aimed at reducing emotional tension. Such drugs, of course, do not deal with the stressful situation or the coping reactions involved. By alleviating emotional tension and distress symptoms, however, they may provide an individual with an opportunity to regroup his or her coping resources. Of course, health professionals must guard against too readily prescribing tranquilizers to insulate patients against everyday stress that they might be better off facing and resolving in some manner. Some patients may also come to rely too much on their prescriptions for easy "cures," and such palliative, symptomatic treatment may divert needed attention from a persistently destructive life-style.

Other drugs, such as those used to control high blood pressure, are prescribed on a more specific basis. Recent reports suggest that antidepressant medication may have a modest role in the treatment of bulimia (Hughes et al., 1986; Mitchell et al., 1990), although we are troubled by the absence of a convincing theoretical rationale to support this type of intervention. A change of diet may be indicated in certain of the psychogenic diseases, including peptic ulcers, migraine headaches, and hypertension. Acupuncture is still considered a largely experimental approach for alleviating certain types of symptoms (such as the pain of tension and migraine headaches) because of problems in disentangling specific from nonspecific placebo effects.

Psychosocial Measures

In treating psychosocially mediated physical diseases, one-on-one, verbally oriented psychotherapies—aimed at helping patients understand their problems and achieve more effective coping techniques—have been (with certain exceptions) relatively ineffective. The cognitive-behavioral therapy variant, however, has shown considerable promise in the treatment of bulimia (Agras et al., 1989) and psychogenic headaches (Blanchard et al., 1990a, 1990b). Bulimic individuals have also recently been found to respond quite positively to intensive, specifically structured group therapy

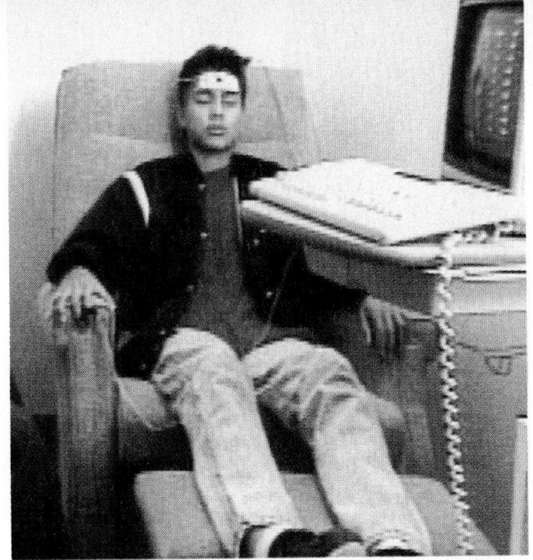

Dylan is a boy suffering from severe and throbbing migraine headaches that may last for days. Here he is receiving biofeedback treatment for his migraines. With biofeedback, people are taught to change and control internal bodily processes once thought to be involuntary. Though generally failing to live up to the hype it generated when first introduced two decades ago, biofeedback is showing modest success in treating migraine.

(Mitchell et al., 1990). As might be expected, family therapy has shown some promising results in the case of anorexia nervosa (Minuchin, 1974); rather than singling out the individual, family therapy examines the whole family structure and patterns of communication. Those structures that are thought to be preventing the individual from developing positive relationships within the family (resulting in personal maladjustment) are then targeted for change.

It is interesting to note here that, although classical psychoanalytic theory has emphasized associations between emotions and pathological visceral states, it has had little impact on the treatment of psychogenic physical disorders (Agras, 1982). That is, psychoanalytic approaches have not derived treatment methods that can reverse or prevent the disease process in predictable ways. Also somewhat ironically (in light of its focus on altering physiological states), biofeedback treatment for psychogenic diseases, though showing modest success (for example, in treating migraine [Blanchard et al., 1990b]), has generally failed to live up to the hype it generated when first introduced some two decades ago. In general, its effects are so small and transient as to lack substantial clinical significance, and they rarely exceed those that can be obtained in simpler (and cheaper) ways, as by providing systematic relaxation training (Reed, Katkin, & Goldband, 1986). In fact it is not clear that biofeedback is anything more than an elaborate means to teach patients to relax.

Behavior Therapy Behavior-modification techniques are based on the assumption that because autonomic responses can be learned, they can also be unlearned via extinction and differential reinforcement. In one rather famous case, the patient, June C., was a 17-year-old girl who had been sneezing every few seconds of her waking hours for a period of 5 months. Medical experts had been unable to help her, and Kushner, a psychologist, volunteered to attempt treatment by behavior therapy.

Dr. Kushner used a relatively simple, low power electric-shock device, activated by sound—the sound of June's sneezes. Electrodes were attached to her forearm for 30 minutes, and every time she sneezed she got a mild electric shock. After a ten-minute break, the electrodes were put on the other arm. In little more than four hours, June's sneezes, which had been reverberating every 40 seconds, stopped. Since then, she has had only a few ordinary sneezes, none of the dry, racking kind that had been draining her strength for so long. "We hope the absence of sneezes will last," said Dr. Kushner cautiously. "So do I," snapped June. "I never want to see that machine again." (Time, 1966, p. 72)

In a follow-up report, Kushner (1968) stated that a program of maintenance therapy had been instituted, and at the end of 16 months the intractable sneezing had not recurred.

Many studies have examined the effects of various behavioral relaxation techniques on selected psychogenic illnesses. Results obtained have been variable, though generally encouraging. For example, simple tension headaches have proven quite amenable to general relaxation treatment procedures (Blanchard et al., 1990a; Cox, Freundlich, & Meyer, 1975; Tasto & Hinkle, 1973). The same kinds of procedures have not been quite as effective when used to treat essential hypertension (Blanchard et al., 1979; Schwartz, 1978; Surwit, Shapiro, & Good, 1978), especially in comparison with medication (Wadden, et al., 1985).

The potential of behavior therapy alone in treating psychogenic physical disorders remains to be established. A great deal of work is continuing in this area, and it looks promising. It may turn out that the greatest contribution of behavioral approaches will be in the area of altering self-injurious "habits," such as smoking and excessive alcohol use, in systematic programs that teach self-control and life-style alteration (Blanchard & Andrasik, 1982; Goldfried & Merbaum, 1973; Weisenberg, 1977). Such programs may have particular importance in recovery from heart attack (Oldenburg, Perkins, & Andrews, 1985). Relatedly, some success has been reported in modifying Type A life-styles using a group therapy approach (Fischman, 1987).

In sports, behavioral relaxation techniques are used as a means of reducing stress and enhancing performance. Here the University of Wisconsin football team goes through a relaxation exercise before a game.

Cognitive-Behavioral Treatment Some cognitive-behavioral techniques have also been used to treat stress-related illnesses. In one study, these techniques were shown to be effective at reducing maladaptive behaviors—such as rushing, impatience, and hostility—characteristic of Type A personalities (Jenni & Wollersheim, 1979). In two studies designed to teach patients how to cope better with life stresses that precipitated headaches, researchers showed that stress-management techniques could decrease the frequency of headaches (Holroyd & Andrasik, 1978; Holroyd, Andrasik, & Westbrook, 1977). More generally, Kobasa (1985) and colleagues are experimenting with cognitive-behavioral methods to increase "hardiness," the ability to withstand stressful circumstances and remain healthy. Though we will look at these techniques in more detail in Chapter 18, they basically involve teaching individuals to use more effective coping skills to lower their experiences of stress and thus reduce the occurrences of symptoms.

Combined Treatment Measures

To be treated successfully, psychogenic diseases usually require prompt medical attention for physical symptoms combined with psychosocial therapeutic intervention to alter or reduce the maladaptive behavioral factors underlying the disorder. The treatment for anorexia nervosa clearly illustrates the need for combined medical and psychological measures. If an anorexic individual's condition becomes life-threatening, extreme measures must be taken to nourish the patient. Typically, hospitalization is necessary in an emergency of this sort. The patient may initially be fed intravenously, but because the disorder is apparently under voluntary control, therapy must ultimately focus not only on weight gain but also on the psychological factors underlying the patient's refusal to eat.

Several treatment approaches have been successful in promoting weight gain among anorexic patients. One includes making a patient stay in isolation, earning privileges—such as time for socializing—only as she gains weight. Leon (1983) describes this scenario:

Given the compliant, perfectionistic behavioral characteristics of many anorexics, it might not be surprising that once the youngster has made the decision to eat in order to gain relief from isolation or to gain a variety of social and other reinforcers, she compliantly follows the daily weight gain criteria set up for her and systematically gains weight. It has been my experience, however, in viewing charts of the weight histories of many treated anorexics, that their weight precipitously plummets once they are released from the hospital. Thus, compliance with the treatment regimen has brought relief from the aversiveness of the hospital situation and has also affected hospital discharge. (Leon, 1983)

As Leon suggests, then, in many cases therapy achieves no significant long-term normalization in eating patterns, even when drastic measures are taken in response to life-threatening crises. This major drawback results if the therapy focuses single-mindedly on just the immediate need to gain weight. Leon goes on to say,

The crucial issue of the regulation of food intake as one of several treatment goals is under-scored by the fact that some anorexics after release from the hospital continue eating until the point of obesity or develop bulimia-vomiting patterns to control their weight. Thus, treatment should also address the personal concerns about self-control over one's body and one's environment, and other difficulties related to family interactions that the anorexic might be attempting to cope with through self-starvation.

This conclusion seems related to an earlier finding by Halmi, Falk, and Schwartz (1981) in which data suggested that treatment choice did not seem to be a factor in successful weight gain for hospitalized patients: they typically gained weight regardless of the treatment technique employed.

Though the obvious goal, both short- and long-term, is to get an anorexic patient to gain weight, therapy for psychological adjustment may be far more important and far more elusive for long-term success. In the end, as Bruch (1988) has noted in a posthumously published book on the subject, lasting therapeutic results in anorexia may involve nothing less than a patient's rediscovery of *herself*. Such a goal is unlikely to be achieved by merely technical interventions that cause the patient temporarily to put on a few pounds.

Lucas, Duncan, and Piens (1976) reported on an interesting therapeutic setting developed at the Mayo Clinic and designed to deal with both the physiological and psychological needs of an anorexic patient. Their approach was a combined medical-psychiatric effort, with a coordinated team of professionals who focused on the problems of malnutrition as well as on the psychological family problems in each case. The first step in their treatment efforts was to remove the anorexic person from the home. The individual was placed in an inpatient ward where the nutritional problems were dealt with by staff members who monitored food intake. The patient was given social rewards—such as time with peers—for appropriate food consumption. Group psychological treatment with a supportive orientation was provided, in which the patient was allowed to express her thoughts, concerns, and fears. While the inpatient treatment program was in progress, the staff also worked with the family in an effort to resolve the family behaviors that might be encouraging the patient's anorexic behavior. This approach thus combined medical efforts with individual and family therapy.

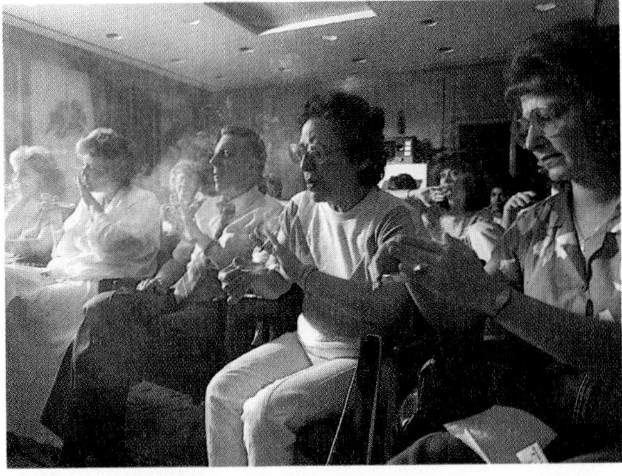

Behavioral approaches to health maintenance are important in systematic programs that teach self-control and life-style change. The stop-smoking class pictured here helps smokers break their habit by holding their cigarettes in an uncomfortable way.

Sociocultural Measures

Sociocultural treatment measures are targeted more toward preventive efforts and are typically applied to selected populations or subcultural groups thought to be at risk for developing disorders. Within these groups, efforts are made to alter certain life-style behaviors to reduce the overall level of susceptibility to a disorder. For example, cigarette smoking is associated with increased risk for lung cancer and heart disease; to reduce the general risk of these scourges, efforts might be made to reduce or prevent cigarette smoking in groups that are vulnerable to the smoking habit—such as adolescents. Similarly, some correlation appears to exist between high-cholesterol diets and coronary heart disease; at high risk here are middle-aged men, and efforts might be made to alter their diets to reduce the rate of coronary heart disease in the total population. Obviously, such intervention efforts involve substantial amounts of persuasive appeal—often employing the media and, in the case of smoking, even restrictive changes in quasi-legal federal regulations (such as airline passenger smoking policies).

An excellent example of a community-based, prevention-oriented program aimed at reducing the incidence of atherosclerotic disease (a predisposing factor in coronary heart disease) comes from Finland. The North Karelia Project, named after the province in which it was conducted, was a large-scale effort that included 60,000 "subjects" (the province residents) and involved several types of community intervention efforts.

The overall goal was to promote greater public awareness of the high-risk factors—especially cigarette smoking and high serum cholesterol levels thought to be caused by eating high-fat foods—in atherosclerotic disease. Then the effort was made to get individuals to reduce these risk factors by smoking less and eating low-fat foods. Project staff (a) provided information through the mass media—such as a seven-session TV course aimed at reducing smoking—and through public meetings; (b) organized existing health-care services and initiated new ones to focus on eliminating high-risk factors by forming self-help groups; (c) trained community leaders, such as teachers, to work on the program; (d) promoted the distribution and sale of healthy, low-fat foods; and (e) devised a method by which they could measure the effects of the program (McAlister et al., 1980; Puska, 1983; Puska et al., 1979).

Early results were encouraging. The intervention program was shown to lower effectively the coronary heart disease risk in the population: death from heart disease fell 27 percent for men and 42 percent for women. A self-report survey on smoking behavior indicated that participants had reduced their cigarette consumption; significant reductions were also found in serum cholesterol levels.

As we learn more about the role of biological, psychosocial, and sociocultural factors in the etiology of disease, it becomes increasingly possible to delineate high-risk individuals and groups—such as heart-attack-prone personalities with chronic negative affects and groups living in precarious and rapidly changing life situations. This ability, in turn, enables treatment efforts to focus on early intervention and prevention. In this context, counseling programs—aimed at fostering changes in maladaptive life-styles of individuals and families and at remedying pathological social conditions—seem eminently worthwhile.

UNRESOLVED ISSUES on Psychological Factors and Illness

The many reports in the research literature of severe illnesses or deaths attributed to the *attitudes* of hopelessness or helplessness, including documented cases of apparent voodoo deaths, continue to puzzle and confound us. If we assume the reliability of the primary observations, we might account for some of these events on the basis of a possibly lethal autonomic system "storm" provoked by severe fright, or, in more delayed reactions, by reference to immunosuppression and the compromise of defenses against virulent antigens present in the body or the local environment. Neither of these proposed mechanisms, however, can reasonably be invoked to explain every reported case. To further complicate matters, there are many seemingly reliable reports of instances in which unexplained remissions of terminal illnesses have occurred following attitude changes emphasizing patients' mastery and control over their pathological processes.

Most of us remain somewhat skeptical concerning phenomena of this type, but our skepticism is in large part the product of our continuing ignorance concerning the fundamentals of mind-body interaction. We still find ourselves struggling, for example, with the problem of how an *idea,* such as "I am going to master my illness," might be transformed into the *physical processes* that must underlie, let us say, tumor regression. None of the proposed solutions to this age-old philosophical dilemma can claim to be proven, and in fact the question may be fundamentally insoluble within a scientific context.

Closely related and equally vexing are a host of other psycho-physical interactions entailed in the notion of psychogenesis. Among the foremost is the issue of the control of immunocompetence by events that may be stressors to one person but not to another. The designation "stressor" is not as a general rule inherent in an event itself but is rather assigned somehow by a stressed person as he or she cognitively processes the event. To put it another way, the person, in reacting stressfully, is responding to the *meaning* the event is perceived to have, not to its objective, physical characteristics. We need therefore ultimately to understand how this subjective meaning somehow produces the multitude of physical events we must assume are involved in immune-reaction inhibition. The task promises to be a formidable one.

The discovery of the conditionability of immunosuppression, which may appear promising in this regard, is probably a different case. Although the procedure involved may be viewed as one in which the occurrence of a conditioned stimulus acquires the "meaning" that ingestion of an immunosuppressant substance is soon to follow (as tone signified the arrival of food to Pavlov's dogs), the use of an immunosuppressant substance as the "unconditioned stimulus" may make the demonstration irrelevant to our everyday trials and tribulations. We say "may" here because we are not completely certain. We assume, however, that stress normally *is* the unconditioned stimulus for immunosuppression, which still leaves us with the problem of idiosyncracy in what are perceived as "stressors."

Moving now to a more mundane level, our rapidly developing knowledge concerning psychological influences in health and illness is not matched by equally impressive advances in the areas of prevention and treatment of psychogenic disease. While some strides have been made in limited areas, our overall impression is that, thus far, our efforts in this arena have been feeble and to a large extent unimaginative. We have not, for example, figured out reliable ways of getting people to alter life-styles we know to be unhealthy. Though our species has had eons of experience with the bereavement process, now known to be a substantial risk to physical health, we have not yet devised effective means of easing the enormous stress of this common experience. Indeed there is little evidence that we have even tried to solve this problem on a scientific basis, apparently owing to the unproven assumptions that such stress is inevitable, and that nothing effective could ever be found to alleviate it.

SUMMARY

Research has clearly established that emotional factors influence the development of many physical disorders and play an important role in the course of disease processes. The official Axis I diagnosis, Psychological Factors Affecting Physical Condition (new to the DSM-III and unchanged in DSM-III-R), is an acknowledgment of our enhanced appreciation of the widespread nature of such effects. Likewise, the relatively new field of behavioral medicine has its origins in the general recognition of these influences and seeks to extend our conceptions of disease beyond the traditional medical preoccupation with the physical breakdown of organs and organ systems.

At the most general level, the influence of psychological variables on health is seen in excessive autonomic nervous system responses to stressor conditions, sometimes resulting directly in organ damage. It is also seen in the increasing evidence that psychosocial challenges can impair the immune system's ability to respond, leaving a person more vulnerable to disease-producing agents. Damaging habits and life-styles are also known to enhance risk for physical disease.

Psychogenic vulnerability to particular diseases may be somewhat specific in nature, although not so specific as early doctrines implied. The distressingly common coronary heart disease and the increasingly common eating disorders known as anorexia nervosa and bulimia nervosa seem to be cases in point. The Type A behavior pattern, or rather one or more of its components, is now well-established as an independent risk factor for CHD, and the two eating disorders have been somewhat less compellingly associated with deficiencies in achieving autonomy. Evidence relating to specific psychosocial factors in the etiology of other physical diseases—notably hypertension, peptic ulcers, and recurrent headaches—continues to show promise.

Biological factors, including genetic vulnerabilities, excessive autonomic reactivity, and possible organ weaknesses, must of course continue to be given prominent attention in the search for etiological patterns. They must also be a part of treatment considerations whenever physical disease occurs, regardless of strong evidence of psychological contributions to its development.

A common factor in much psychosocially mediated physical disease is inadequacy in an individual's coping resources for managing stressful life circumstances. Our own culture seems particularly rich in providing these challenges, whereas we have made only limited progress in learning how to instill hardiness in our citizenry and thereby prevent many needless physical breakdowns. Psychosocial treatment measures, typically used (if at all) only after illness is discovered, are showing considerable promise. However, the more exciting challenge will be to devise more, and more effective, psychosocial interventions that prevent breakdowns in the first place.

Key Terms

behavioral medicine (p. 229)
psychogenic illnesses (p. 229)
health psychology (p. 229)
placebo effect (p. 232)
immune system (p. 234)
antigen (p. 234)
psychoneuroimmunology (p. 235)
coronary heart disease (CHD) (p. 239)
Type A behavior pattern (p. 240)
anorexia nervosa (p. 243)
bulimia nervosa (p. 244)
hypertension (p. 248)
essential hypertension (p. 248)
peptic ulcers (p. 249)
migraine (p. 250)
simple tension headaches (p. 250)
biofeedback (p. 251)
secondary gains (p. 255)

Chapter 8
Personality Disorders

Gaston Duf, *Pâulîhinêle gânsthêrs vitrês-he* (1949). As a child, Duf (b. 1920) was frequently terrorized by his father, often seeking the protection of his mother. When his parents finally married, Duf, then 18, reacted violently. After two suicide attempts, he was institutionalized in 1940. He began his artistic career while in the asylum, painting strange, powerful animals, as well as comically proportioned, motley human figures like this one.

It is probably meaningless to speak of an end product in the developmental process; people continue to change throughout their lives. Healthy adjustment through the life cycle is, after all, chiefly a matter of flexibly adapting to the changing demands, opportunities, and limitations associated with different life stages. Nevertheless, a person's broadly characteristic traits, coping styles, and ways of interacting in the social environment emerge during development. These traits normally crystalize into established patterns by the end of the adolescent years. They represent the individual's **personality**—the unique pattern of traits and behaviors that characterize the individual.

For most of us, our adult personality is attuned to the demands of society. In other words, we readily comply with societal expectations. In contrast, there are certain individuals who, although not necessarily displaying obvious symptoms of disorder, nevertheless seem somehow ill-equipped to become fully functioning members of society—any society. For these individuals, personality formation has been so warped that they are unable to perform adequately the varied roles expected of them by their societies. These people might be diagnosed as having **personality disorders,** or **character disorders.**

Personality disorders typically do not stem from debilitating reactions to stress, as in posttraumatic stress disorder, nor from disabling defenses against anxiety, as in the neurotic disorders. Rather, the disorders to be examined here stem largely from the development of immature and distorted personality patterns, which result in persistently maladaptive ways of perceiving, thinking about, and relating to the world. These maladaptive approaches usually significantly impair functioning and in some cases cause subjective distress. Often these patterns of personality and behavior are recognizable by adolescence and continue into adult life.

The category of personality disorders is broad, with behavioral problems that differ greatly in form and severity. On the mildest end of the spectrum we find individuals who generally function adequately but would be described by their relatives or associates as troublesome or eccentric. They have characteristic ways of approaching situations and people that make them difficult to get along with, yet they are often quite capable or even gifted in some ways. At the other end of the spectrum are individuals

We might consider Michael Jackson eccentric because of the unusual way he dresses or his rumored multiple plastic surgeries, but eccentric behavior alone does not necessarily indicate a personality disorder. People with personality disorders tend to be at the extreme of a continuum of unusual behavior; they live aberrant lives that others find confusing, exasperating, unpredictable, and unacceptable. Their behavior typically causes at least as much difficulty in the lives of others as in their own lives.

whose extreme and often unethical "acting out" against society makes them less able to function in a normal setting; many are incarcerated in prisons or maximum security hospitals, but some are able to manipulate others and keep from getting caught.

The prevalence of personality disorders is unknown, since many individuals with such disorders never come in contact with mental health or legal agencies. Estimates of the prevalence of one personality disorder, antisocial personality, were reported in an epidemiological study to be 2.1 percent, 2.6 percent, and 3.3 percent in the three study sites (Robins et al., 1984). Many individuals become identified through the correctional system or through court-ordered psychological evaluations stemming from family problems such as physical abuse. Others eventually show up in alcohol treatment programs. Although we have no accurate estimates as to what percentage of incarcerated individuals would be classified as having personality disorders, it is believed that the figure would be quite high. Reich, Yates, and Nduaguba (1989) reported an 11.1 percent prevalence rate for DSM-III-R personality disorders in prison inmates.

Personality disorders are an area of active research in the field today. To support this statement we need only point out that Gorton and Akhtar (1990) surveyed articles on personality disorders published between 1985 and 1988; they found over 1000 articles on the subject. In this chapter, we will consider several types of disordered personalities that have been identified and then examine one of them—antisocial personality—in greater detail to give you an idea of the extensive research in this area.

Personality disorders are often a factor in several disorders that will be considered in other chapters, such as alcoholism (Chapter 9), sexual deviations (Chapter 10), and delinquency (Chapter 15). Although conduct disorders and juvenile delinquency do in fact sometimes represent the early stages of a lifelong process of personality disorder, they often do not; much of the acting-out behavior of adolescence, including much delinquency, is limited to the adolescent years. Thus we will discuss conduct disorders and delinquency with the other special disorders of childhood and adolescence. Finally, the behavioral patterns associated with personality disorders can be similar to those determined primarily by the residual effects of head injuries or other brain pathologies. In such cases, these behaviors are evidence of organic brain disorders, which we consider in Chapter 13. These qualifications aside, let us move on to an examination of personality disorders.

PERSONALITY DISORDERS

Personality disorders are chiefly, although not exclusively, characterized by problems in which individuals typically cause at least as much difficulty in the lives of others as in their own lives. Such people live aberrant lives that others find confusing, exasperating, unpredictable, and, in varying degrees, unacceptable—although rarely as bizarre or out of contact with reality as those people with psychotic disorders (to be discussed in Chapters 11 and 12). People with personality disorders do not suffer unduly from anxiety or depression. Their persistent behavioral deviations seem to be intrinsic to their personalities; for one reason or another they develop in an aberrant manner and do not learn to take part in mutually respectful and satisfying social relationships.

In the past, these persistent disorders were thought to center around personality characteristics referred to as **temperament** or **character traits,** suggesting the possibility of hereditary or constitutional influences. More recently, environmental and social factors, particularly learning-based habit patterns, have been receiving more attention as possible causal elements. The possibility of genetic transmission of these disorders, however, particularly antisocial personality, has been once again receiving strong support in the research literature.

The definition of personality disorders in DSM-III-R is as follows:

Personality traits are enduring patterns of perceiving, relating to, and thinking about the environment and oneself, and are exhibited in a wide range of important social and personal contexts. It is only when personality traits are inflexible and maladaptive and cause either significant functional impairment or subjective distress that they constitute Personality Disorders. The manifestations of Personality Disorders are often recognizable by adolescence or earlier and continue throughout most of adult life, though they often become less obvious in middle or old age.

The diagnostic criteria for the Personality Disorders refer to behaviors or traits that are characteristic of the person's recent (past year) and long-term functioning since early adulthood. The constellation of behaviors or traits causes either significant impairment in social or occupational functioning or subjective distress.

The diagnosis of a Personality Disorder should be made only when the characteristic features are typical of the person's long-term functioning and are not limited to discrete episodes of illness. (American Psychiatric Association, 1987, p. 335)

The behavior patterns of personality disorders are rather new to clinical texts and diagnostic manuals; they were not clearly described until the publication of the American Psychiatric Association's first *Diagnostic and Statistical Manual* (DSM-1) in 1952. Before that, they were regarded as "disorders of character" found in people who were otherwise essentially normal—problems "without psychosis" (Murray, 1938).

In the DSM-III-R, the personality disorders are coded on a separate Axis II because they are regarded as being different enough from the standard psychiatric syndromes (which are coded on Axis I) to warrant separate classification. Axis II represents long-standing personality traits that are inflexible and maladaptive and that cause social or occupational adjustment problems or personal distress. The traits included on Axis II are reaction patterns so deeply embedded in the personality structure (for whatever reason) that they are extremely resistant to modification. Though an individual might be diagnosed on Axis II only, he or she could instead be diagnosed on both Axes I and II, which would reflect the existence of both a currently active mental disorder and a more chronic, underlying personality disorder.

A special caution is in order regarding the personality disorders. Perhaps more misdiagnoses occur here than in any other categories. There are a number of reasons for this problem. One is that personality disorders are not as sharply defined as other diagnostic categories; no clear set of criteria exists for them. To ensure the reliability of the diagnosis, more precise operational criteria are needed for each disorder (Tyrer, 1988).

A second reason is that the diagnostic categories are not mutually exclusive: often an individual will show characteristics of more than one type of personality disorder, which makes diagnosis difficult (Blashfield & Breen, 1989; Gorton & Akhtar, 1990; Widiger & Frances, 1985). For example, an individual might show the suspiciousness, mistrust, avoidance of blame, and guardedness of paranoid personality disorder, along with the withdrawal, absence of friends, and aloofness that characterize schizoid personality disorder.

A third reason for diagnostic problems is that the personality characteristics that define personality disorders are dimensional in nature—that is, they range from normal expressions to pathological exaggerations and can be found, on a smaller scale and less intensely expressed, in many normal individuals (Frances, 1980). For example, liking one's work and being conscientious about the details of one's job does not make one an obsessive-compulsive personality, nor does being economically dependent automatically make a spouse a dependent personality. Applying diagnostic labels to people who are functioning well enough to be outside a hospital setting is always risky; it is especially so where the diagnosis involves judgment about characteristics that are also common in normal individuals.

A fourth reason is that personality disorders are defined by inferred traits or consistent patterns of behavior rather than by objective behavioral criteria. On Axis I, for example, there are objective behavioral criteria for drug intoxication or somatization disorder, but on Axis II dependent or compulsive personality patterns are inferred from consistencies in behavior. Personality disorders thus require more judgment in classification than do many Axis I disorders.

These problems can lead to unreliability of diagnoses and in fact they often do (Gorton and Akhtar, 1990). Someday a more objective scheme for the personality disorders may be devised that accounts for the problems described here. In the meantime, however, the categorical system of symptoms and traits will continue to be used with the recognition that it is more dependent on the observer's judgment than one might wish. Several theorists have attempted to deal with the problems inherent in categorizing personality disorders (Cloninger, 1987; Millon, 1981; Tyrer, 1988; Widiger & Frances, 1985); however, no clearly consistent theoretical view on the classification of personality disorders currently exists. With these cautions, we will look now at the elusive and often exasperating clinical features of the personality disorders.

Clinical Features of Personality Disorders

The several special types of personality disorders are classified according to the particular characteristics (dependence, avoidance, and so on) that are most prominent, although, as we have seen, in given cases these dividing lines are often unclear. These characteristics, in turn, predict what kind of disordered relationships can be expected. Although we will look individually at the several types of personality disorders that have been delineated, let us look first at a number of features they all seem to have in common:

1. Perhaps most characteristic is a pattern of disrupted personal relationships. Whether narcissistic or dependent or passive-aggressive, individuals with personality disorders usually leave a trail of disturbed personal relationships marked by difficulties they have caused others.

2. Personality disorders are generally long-standing and marked by behaviors that are considered troublesome to others. There are not usually "episodes" of pathological behavior that can be identified, but rather persistent patterns of recurring problems.

3. Personality disorders are often associated with other negative life outcomes, such as addictive disorders and criminal or illegal behaviors. For example, Khantzian and Treece (1985) found that the entire range of personality disorders was represented among individuals who became addicted to narcotics.

4. Whatever the particular trait patterns affected individuals have developed (obstinacy, covert hostility, or suspiciousness, for example), these patterns color each new situation and lead to a repetition of the same maladaptive behaviors. For example, a dependent person may wear out a relationship with someone, such as a spouse, by incessant and extraordinary demands; after that partner leaves, the person may go immediately into another dependent relationship and repeat the behavior. Thus personality disorders are marked by considerable consistency over time, with no apparent learning from previous troubles.

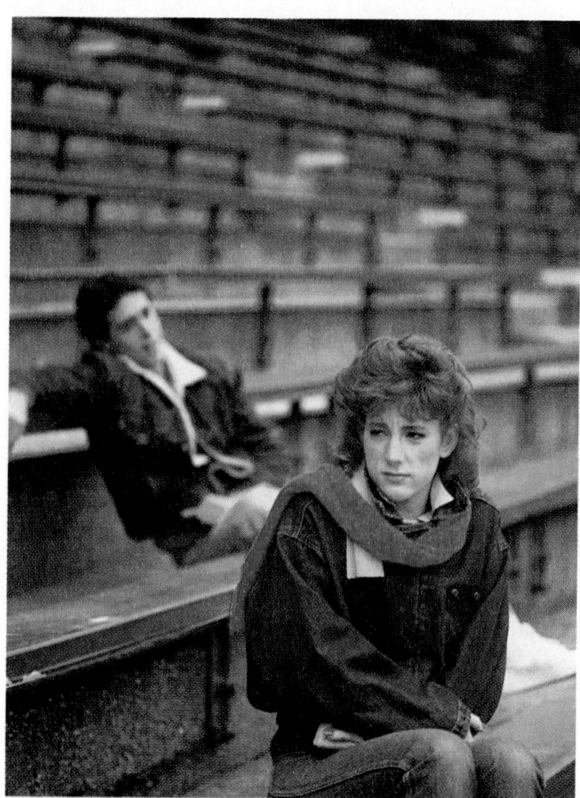

One common feature of personality disorders is a pattern of disturbed personal relationships.

5. It follows from the preceding feature that many of these disorders are in a sense disorders of reputation: they are marked by the imprints they make on others rather than by any psychic pain felt by the affected individuals. In many cases, these individuals are known not by what they have reported to clinicians but by the reports of others. People with certain disorders, such as antisocial personality disorder, rarely take the initiative in seeking therapy and, when referred for therapy by others, have little or no motivation to profit from it. Instead, they are likely to disrupt or sabotage it—or leave it if possible.

6. Finally, the behavioral patterns reflected in personality disorders are highly resistant to change. Many of these individuals neither seek to change nor to accommodate the demands other people place on them to alter their behaviors.

All these characteristics lead to the fractured relationships that are the hallmark of the personality disorders.

Types of Personality Disorders

The DSM-III-R personality disorders are grouped into three clusters on the basis of similarities among the disorders. Many people meet the criteria for more than one personality disorder.

Cluster I includes paranoid, schizoid, and schizotypal personality disorders. Individuals with these disorders often seem odd or eccentric, although their unusual behavior takes quite different forms.

Cluster II includes histrionic, narcissistic, antisocial, and borderline personality disorders. Individuals with these disorders have in common a tendency to be dramatic, emotional, and erratic. Their impulsive behavior, often involving antisocial activities, is more colorful, more forceful, and more likely to get them into contact with mental health or legal authorities than the behaviors characterizing disorders in the first cluster.

Cluster III includes avoidant, dependent, obsessive-compulsive, and passive-aggressive personality disorders. Unlike in the other clusters, anxiety and fearfulness are often part of these disorders, making it difficult in some cases to distinguish them from anxiety-based disorders. Because of their anxieties, individuals suffering from these disorders are more likely to seek help.

Two new personality disorders—self-defeating and sadistic personality disorders—are listed in DSM-III-R in the appendix under the heading *proposed diagnostic categories needing further study.* Individuals with these disorders are typically involved in interpersonal interactions that are characterized by abusiveness. These disorders, as we will see, are controversial because there is some potential for misuse or misapplication and because some professionals have considered them inappropriate and biased toward women. A summary of the personality disorders and their characteristics is presented in *HIGHLIGHT 8.1.*

Paranoid Personality Disorder Individuals with **paranoid personality disorder** typically are suspicious, hypersensitive, rigid, envious, and argumentative. They tend to see themselves as blameless, instead finding fault for their own mistakes and failures in others—even to the point of ascribing evil motives to others. Such individuals are constantly expecting trickery and looking for clues to validate their expectations, while disregarding all evidence to the contrary. They are keenly aware of power and rank, envious of those in high places, and disdainful of those who seem weak or soft. It is important to keep in mind that paranoid personalities are not psychotic; that is, they are in clear contact with reality. Another disorder, paranoid schizophrenia, to be discussed later in the book, may have some symptoms found in paranoid personality. Paranoid schizophrenics have additional problems, however, including loss of reality contact and extreme behavioral deterioration, such as delusions and hallucinations.

The following case demonstrates well the behaviors characteristic of paranoid personality disorder:

A 40-year-old construction worker believes that his coworkers do not like him and fears that someone might let his scaffolding slip in order to cause him injury on the job. This concern followed a recent disagreement on the lunch line when the patient felt that a coworker was sneaking ahead and complained to him. He began noticing his new "enemy" laughing with the other men and often wondered if he were the butt of their mockery. He thought of confronting them, but decided that the whole issue might just be in his own mind, and that he might get himself into more trouble by taking any action.

The patient offers little spontaneous information, sits tensely in the chair, is wide-eyed and carefully tracks all movements in the room. He reads between the lines of the interviewer's questions, feels criticized, and imagines that the interviewer is siding with his coworkers. He makes it clear that he would not have come to the personnel clinic at all except for his need for sleep medication.

He was a loner as a boy and felt that other children would form cliques and be mean to him. He did poorly in school, but blamed his teachers—he claimed that they preferred girls or boys who were "sissies." He dropped out of school, and has since been a hard and effective worker; but he feels he never gets the breaks. He believes that he has been discriminated against because of his Catholicism, but can offer little convincing evidence. He gets on poorly with bosses and coworkers, is unable to appreciate joking around, and does best in situations where he can work and have lunch alone. He has

HIGHLIGHT 8.1

Summary of Personality Disorders

Personality Disorder	Characteristics
Cluster I	
Paranoid	Suspiciousness and mistrust of others; tendency to see self as blameless; on guard for perceived attacks by others
Schizoid	Impaired social relationships; inability and lack of desire to form attachments to others
Schizotypal	Peculiar thought patterns; oddities of perception and speech that interfere with communication and social interaction
Cluster II	
Histrionic	Self-dramatization; overconcern with attractiveness; tendency to irritability and temper outbursts if attention seeking is frustrated
Narcissistic	Grandiosity; preoccupation with receiving attention; self-promoting; lack of empathy
Antisocial	Lack of moral or ethical development; inability to follow approved models of behavior; deceitfulness; shameless manipulation of others; history of conduct problems as a child
Borderline	Impulsiveness, inappropriate anger; drastic mood shifts; chronic feelings of boredom; attempts at self-mutilation or suicide
Cluster III	
Avoidant	Hypersensitiveness to rejection or social derogation; shyness; insecurity in social interaction and initiating relationships
Dependent	Difficulty in separating in relationships; discomfort at being alone; subordination of needs in order to keep others involved in a relationship; indecisiveness
Obsessive-compulsive	Excessive concern with order, rules, and trivial details; perfectionistic; lack of expressiveness and warmth; difficulty in relaxing and having fun
Passive-aggressive	Lack of assertiveness expressed through indirect hostile means, such as procrastination, intentional forgetting, and stubbornness
Provisional Categories	
Self-defeating	Avoidance of pleasurable experiences; persistent involvement in disappointing or punishing relationships
Sadistic	Intimidation of others through infliction of pain, humiliation, embarrassment, or cruelty

switched jobs many times because he felt he was being mistreated.

The patient is distant and demanding with his family. His children call him "Sir" and know that it is wise to be "seen but not heard" when he is around. At home he can never comfortably sit still and is always busy at some chore or another. He prefers not to have people visit his house and becomes restless when his wife is away visiting others. (Spitzer et al., 1981, p. 37)

This pervasive suspiciousness and mistrust of other people leave a paranoid personality prone to numerous difficulties and hurts in interpersonal relationships. These difficulties typically lead the individual to be continually "on guard" for perceived attacks by others.

Schizoid Personality Disorder Individuals with **schizoid personality disorder** usually show an inability to form social relationships and a lack of interest in doing so. Such individuals are unable to express their feelings and are seen by others as cold and distant; they often lack social skills and can be classified as *loners,* with solitary interests and occupations.

Early theorists considered a schizoid personality to be a likely precursor to the development of schizophrenia. This viewpoint has been challenged in recent times, however (Seiver, 1986). Research studies on the possible genetic transmission of schizoid personality have failed to establish either a link between the two disorders or the hereditary basis of schizoid personality (Kety et al., 1975; Slater, 1953). Seiver (1986), in his theoretical comparison of the schizoid and schizotypal personality disorders (to be considered in the next section), considered the schizotypal personality to be more closely linked genetically to schizophrenia; however, as we will see, the evidence for this linking is also contradictory.

The following case of a schizoid personality illustrates a fairly severe personality problem in a man who had been functioning adequately as judged both by occupational criteria and by his own standards of "happiness." When he sought help, it was at the encouragement of his supervisor and his physician.

Bill D., a highly intelligent but quite introverted and withdrawn 33-year-old computer analyst, was referred for psychological evaluation by his physician, who was concerned that Bill might be depressed and unhappy. At the suggestion of his supervisor, Bill had recently gone to the physician for rather vague physical complaints and because of his gloomy outlook on life. Bill had virtually no contact with other people. He lived alone in his apartment, worked in a small office by himself, and usually saw no one at work except for the occasional visits of his supervisor to give him new work and pick up completed projects. He ate lunch by himself and about once a week, on nice days, went to the zoo for his lunch break.

Bill was a lifelong loner; as a child he had had few friends and always had preferred solitary activities over family outings (he was the oldest of five children). In high school he had never dated and in college had gone out with a woman only once—and that was with a group of students after a game. He had been active in sports, however, and had played varsity football in both high school and college. In college he had spent a lot of time with one relatively close friend—mostly drinking. However, this friend now lived in another city.

Bill reported rather matter-of-factly that he had a hard time making friends; he never knew what to say in a conversation. On a number of occasions he had thought of becoming friends with other people but simply couldn't think of the right words, so "the conversation just died." He reported that he had given some thought lately to changing his life in an attempt to be more "positive," but it never had seemed worth the trouble. It was easier for him not to make the effort because he became embarrassed when someone tried to talk with him. He was happiest when he was alone.

In short, the central problem of the schizoid personality is an inability to form attachments to other people. It is as though the needs for love, belonging, and approval fail to develop in these individuals—or if they do, they are somehow obliterated at an early stage. The result is a profound barrenness of interpersonal experience.

Schizotypal Personality Disorder Individuals with **schizotypal personality disorder** are seclusive, oversensitive, and eccentric in their communication and behavior. They tend to be egocentric and frequently see chance events as related to themselves. Though both schizotypal and schizoid personalities are characterized by behavioral patterns of isolation and withdrawal, the two can be distinguished in that schizotypal personality—but not schizoid personality—also involves oddities of thought, perception, or speech. Though reality contact is usually maintained, highly personalized and superstitious thinking are characteristic of individuals with a schizotypal personality. Their oddities in thinking, talking, and other behaviors are similar to those often seen in more severe forms in schizophrenic patients; in fact, they are sometimes first diagnosed as exhibiting simple or latent schizophrenia. Widiger, Frances, and Trull (1987) found that the cognitive malfunctioning symptoms included in schizotypal personality disorder, such as cognitive perceptual problems, magical thinking (for example, belief in telepathy and superstitions), ideas of reference (the belief that conversations or gestures of others refer to oneself), recurrent illusions (the distortion of a person or event) odd speech, and suspicious beliefs were more useful in making a clinical diagnosis than social isolation, inadequate rapport, and social anxiety. A genetic association with schizophrenia is widely suspected (Seiver, 1986); in fact the term *schizotypal* is an abbreviation for "schizophrenic genotype" (Rado, 1956). However, evidence for a genetic link with schizophrenia is not conclusive (Neale & Oltmanns, 1980). The following case is fairly typical:

A 41-year-old male was referred to a community mental health center's activities program for help in improving his social skills. He had a lifelong pattern of social isolation, and spent hours worrying that his angry thoughts about his older brother would cause his brother harm. He had previously worked as a clerk in civil service, but had lost his job because of poor attendance and low productivity.

On interview the patient was distant and somewhat distrustful. He described in elaborate and often irrelevant detail his rather uneventful and routine daily life. He told the interviewer that he had spent an hour and a half in a pet store deciding which of two brands of fish food to buy, and explained their relative merits. For two days he had studied the washing instructions on a new pair of jeans—Did "Wash before wearing" mean that the jeans were to be washed before wearing the first time, or did they need, for some reason, to be washed each time before they were worn? He did not regard concerns such as these as senseless, though he acknowledged that the amount of time spent thinking about them might be excessive. When asked about his finances, he could recite from memory his most recent monthly bank statement, including the amount of every check and the running balance as each check was written. He knew his balance on any particular day, but sometimes got anxious if he considered whether a certain check or deposit had actually cleared. He was very sensitive to questions put by the interviewer, reading in criticism where none was intended. (Spitzer et al., 1981, p. 234)

The distinguishing feature of a schizotypal person is peculiar thought patterns, which are in turn associated with a loosening—although not a complete rupture—of ties to reality. The individual appears to lack some key integrative competence of the sort that enables most of us to "keep it all together" and move our lives toward some personal goals. As a result, many basic abilities, such as being able to communicate clearly, are never fully mastered, and the individual tends to drift aimlessly and unproductively through the adult years.

Histrionic Personality Disorder Individuals with **histrionic personality disorder** typically show immaturity, excitability, emotional instability, a craving for excitement, and self-dramatization (an attention-seeking device that is often seductive in nature). Sexual adjustment is usually poor and interpersonal relationships are stormy. These individuals often exhibit dependence and helplessness and are quite gullible. Usually they are self-centered, vain, and overconcerned about approval from others, who see them as overly reactive, shallow, and insincere. The following case illustrates the histrionic personality pattern:

Attention-seeking tactics are common in histrionic behavior.

Pam, a 22-year-old secretary, was causing numerous problems for her supervisor and co-workers. According to her supervisor, Pam was unable to carry out her duties without constant guidance. Seemingly helpless and dependent, she would overreact to minor events and job pressures with irritability and occasional temper tantrums. If others placed unwanted demands on her, she would complain of physical problems, such as nausea or headaches; furthermore, she frequently missed work altogether. To top it off, Pam was flirtatious and often demandingly seductive toward the men in the office.

As a result of her frequent absenteeism and her disruptive behavior in the office, Pam's supervisor and the personnel manager recommended that she be given a psychological evaluation and counseling in the Employee Assistance Program. She went to the first appointment with the psychologist but failed to return for follow-up visits. She was finally given a discharge notice after several incidents of temper outbursts at work.

Both Pam's physical complaints and her seductive behavior are examples of attention-seeking tactics commonly found in the histrionic personality pattern. When these tactics fail to bring about the desired result, irritability and temper outbursts typically follow.

Narcissistic Personality Disorder Individuals with **narcissistic personality disorder** show an exaggerated sense of self-importance and a preoccupation with receiving attention. Ronningstam and Gunderson (1989) reported that grandiosity was the most stable and generalizable criterion for diagnosing narcissistic patients. They reported that the common components of narcissistic personality included a search for recognition, disregard for society's values and rules, and crimes committed because of rage or to avoid defeat. Individuals with narcissistic personality disorder have a chronically fragile, low self-esteem (Svrakic, 1990) and a strategy for asserting their own self-worth so that they and others do not recognize their own basic frailities. Their sense of entitlement is frequently a source of astonishment to others, although they themselves regard their lavish expectations as merely their just dues. By and large, they do not permit others to be genuinely close to or to become dependent on them. They behave in stereotypical ways (for example, with constant self-references and bragging) to gain the acclaim and recognition that feeds their grandiose expectations. These tactics, to those around them, appear to be excessive efforts to make themselves look good.

Akhtar (1989) considers six areas of functioning to be central to narcissistic personality disorder: (a) a narcissistic individual has a basic sense of inferiority, which underlies a preoccupation with fantasies of outstanding achievement; (b) a narcissistic individual is unable to trust and rely on others and thus develops numerous, shallow relationships to extract tributes from others; (c) a narcissistic individual shows a superficial commitment to excellence—instead he or she has an aimless orientation toward superficial interests. Such a person is often socially charming and successful, however, and is preoccupied with appearances; (d) a narcissistic individual has a shifting morality—always ready to shift values to gain favor. He or she may, however, show to the outside world a calculated sense of modesty; (e) a narcissistic person is unable to remain in love, showing an impaired capacity for a committed relationship. Consequently, marital instability and promiscuity are prominent; (f) although he or she may impress others with knowledge and decisiveness, a narcissistic person's information base is often limited to trivia. Such a person characteristically shows "headline intelligence," knowing only sketchy details, yet is able to use language to enhance his or her self-esteem and impress others.

Narcissistic personalities share another central element—they are unable to take the perspective of others, to see things other than "through their own eyes." In more general terms, they lack the capacity for empathy, which is an essential ingredient for mature relationships. In this sense all children begin life as narcissists and only gradually acquire a perspective-taking ability. For reasons that are far from entirely understood, some children do not show normal progress in this area, and indeed, in extreme cases, show little or none. The latter grow up to become adult narcissistic personalities. The following case is illustrative:

A 25-year-old, single graduate student complains to his psychoanalyst of difficulty completing his Ph.D. in English Literature and expresses concerns about his relationships with women. He believes that his thesis topic may profoundly increase the level of understanding in his discipline and make him famous, but so far he has not been able to get past the third chapter. His mentor does not seem sufficiently impressed with his ideas, and the patient is furious at him, but also self-doubting and ashamed. He blames his mentor for his lack of progress, and thinks that he deserves more help with his grand idea, that his mentor should help with some of the research. The patient brags about his creativity and complains that other people are "jealous" of his insight. He is very envious of students who are moving along faster than he and regards them as "dull drones and ass-kissers." He prides himself on the brilliance of his class participation and imagines someday becoming a great professor.

He becomes rapidly infatuated with women and has powerful and persistent fantasies about each new woman he meets, but after several experiences of sexual intercourse feels disappointed and finds them dumb, clinging, and physically repugnant. He has many "friends," but they turn over quickly, and no one relationship lasts very long. People get tired of his continual self-promotion and lack of consideration of them. For example, he was lonely at Christmas and insisted that his best friend stay in town rather than visit his family. The friend refused, criticizing the patient's self-centeredness; and the patient, enraged, decided never to see this friend again. (Spitzer et al., 1981, pp. 52–53)

The narcissistic personality disorder is more frequently observed in men than in women (Akhtar & Thompson, 1982). Individuals with narcissistic personality patterns may not seek psychological treatment because they view themselves as nearly perfect and in no need of personal change. Those who do enter treatment often do so at the insistence of another person, such as a husband or wife, and may terminate therapy prematurely—particularly if their therapist is confrontational and questions their self-serving behavior. Most of what is known about narcissistic personality disorder has emerged from psychoanalytic therapy and later egoanalytic writings (Kernberg, 1984; Kohut & Wolff, 1978). The psychodynamic treatment approach appears to be the most viable therapy because a long-term treatment relationship seems needed to bring about changes in these patients' persistent self-oriented patterns (Kernberg, 1989).

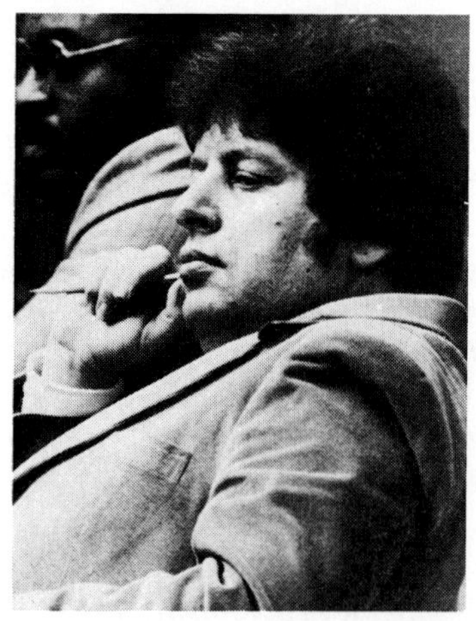

Antisocial personalities violate the rights of others through aggressive behavior and seldom show any loyalty toward others or remorse for cruel behavior. They may have enough charm and intelligence to carry out elaborate schemes for conning people. Such behavior is typified by Giovanni Vigliotto, who was convicted of defrauding one of his 105 wives. Vigliotto would allegedly marry a lonely, middle-aged woman, get control of her assets, and then, setting a date for a rendezvous in another city, disappear. Several of his wives said of him that he was charming, friendly, and warm. Though he admitted to marrying 105 women over a 33-year span, Vigliotto denied swindling anyone.

Antisocial Personality Disorder Individuals with **antisocial personality disorder** continually violate the rights of others through aggressive, antisocial behavior, without remorse or loyalty to anyone. Some antisocial personalities have enough intelligence and social charm to devise and carry out elaborate schemes for conning large numbers of people. Impostors fit into this category. Because this pattern has been studied more fully than the others, it will be examined in some detail later in this chapter. A brief clinical description should suffice here.

Mark, a 22-year-old, came to a psychology clinic on court order. He was awaiting trial for car theft and armed robbery. His case records revealed that he had a long history of arrests beginning at age 9, when he had been picked up for vandalism. He had been expelled from high school for truancy and disruptive behavior. On a number of occasions he had run away from home for days or weeks at a time—always returning in a disheveled and "rundown" condition. To date he had not held a job for more than a few days at a time, even though his generally charming manner enabled him to readily obtain work. He was described as a loner, with few friends. Though initially charming, Mark usually soon antagonized those he met with his aggressive, self-oriented behavior.

Mark was generally affable and complimentary during the therapy session. At the end of it, he enthusiastically told the therapist how much he'd benefited from the counseling and looked forward to future sessions.

Mark's first session was his last. Shortly after it, he skipped bail and presumably left town to avoid his trial.

Borderline Personality Disorder Individuals with **borderline personality disorder** show a pattern of behavior that resembles features of both the personality disorders and some of the more severe psychological disorders, particularly the affective disorders (Chapter 11) and schizophrenia (Chapter 12). The designation of "borderline" personality is applied because the symptoms fall on the border between the personality disorders and the more extreme mood disorders and schizophrenia. Although they are usually aware of their circumstances and surroundings, borderline personalities may have short episodes in which they appear to be out of contact with reality and experience delusions or other psychotic-like symptoms, such as recurrent illusions, magical thinking, and paranoid beliefs (O'Connell et al., 1989).

Individuals with borderline personalities are frequently impulsive and unpredictable, angry, empty, and unstable. They have chronic feelings of boredom and a low tolerance for frustration. Their extreme instability is reflected in drastic mood shifts and erratic, self-destructive behaviors, such as binges of gambling, sex, alcohol use, eating, or shoplifting. They commonly have a history of intense but stormy relationships, typically involving overidealizations of friends or lovers that later end in bitter disillusionment and disappointment (Gunderson & Singer, 1986). They typically display intense anger outbursts with little provocation, and they may show disturbances in basic identity that preoccupy them and produce a basically negative outlook. Feeling slighted, they might, for example, become verbally abusive toward loved ones or might threaten suicide over minor setbacks. Suicide attempts, often flagrantly manipulative, are frequently part of the clinical picture (Fine & Sansone, 1990), and self-mutilation is one of the most discriminating signs for borderline personality (Widiger et al., 1986). The following case illustrates the frequent risk of suicide and self-mutilation among borderline personalities:

A 26-year-old unemployed woman was referred for admission to a hospital by her therapist because of intense suicidal preoccupation and urges to mutilate herself by cutting herself with a razor.

The patient was apparently well until her junior year in high school, when she became preoccupied with religion and philosophy, avoided friends, and was filled with doubt about who she was. Academically she did well, but later, during college, her performance declined. In college she began to use a variety of drugs, abandoned the religion of her family, and

The women shown here have been diagnosed as having borderline personalities. They have been in some kind of therapy for at least five years and have made enormous progress. Nonetheless, in this therapy group, Linda (center) describes how at times she gets so angry that she cuts herself. Self-mutilation is one of the most discriminating signs for borderline personality.

seemed to be searching for a charismatic religious figure with whom to identify. At times massive anxiety swept over her and she found it would suddenly vanish if she cut her forearm with a razor blade. Three years ago she began psychotherapy, and initially rapidly idealized her therapist as being incredibly intuitive and empathic. Later she became hostile and demanding of him, requiring more and more sessions, sometimes two in one day. Her life centered on her therapist, by this time to the exclusion of everyone else. Although her hostility toward her therapist was obvious, she could neither see it nor control it. Her difficulties with her therapist culminated in many episodes of her forearm cutting and suicidal threats, which led to the referral for admission." (Spitzer et al., 1981, pp. 111–112)

Clinical observation of people whose behavior meets the criteria of borderline personality disorder points strongly to a problem of achieving a coherent sense of self as a key predisposing causal factor. These people somehow fail to complete the process of achieving an articulated self-identity and hence do not really become individuals. This lack of individualization leads to complications in interpersonal relationships.

Avoidant Personality Disorder Individuals with **avoidant personality disorder** are hypersensitive to rejection and apprehensive of any sign of social derogation; such individuals readily see ridicule or disparagement where none was intended. Lifelong patterns of limited social relationships and reluctance to enter into social interactions are common. These individuals are too fearful of criticism and rebuff to seek out other people, yet they desire affection and are often lonely and bored. Unlike schizoid personalities, they do not enjoy their aloneness: their inability to relate comfortably to other people causes acute distress and low self-esteem, as shown by the following case:

Sally, a 35-year-old librarian, lived a relatively isolated life and had few acquaintances and no close personal friends. From childhood on, she had been very shy and had withdrawn from close ties with others to keep from being hurt or criticized. Two years before she entered therapy, she had had a date to go to a party with an acquaintance she had met at the library. The moment they had arrived at the party, Sally had felt extremely uncomfortable because she had not been "dressed properly." She left in a hurry and refused to see her acquaintance again. It was because of her continuing concern over this incident that—two years later—Sally decided to go into therapy, even though she dreaded the possibility that the psychologist would be critical of her.

In the early treatment sessions, she sat silently much of the time, finding it too difficult to talk about herself. After several sessions, she grew to trust the therapist, and she related numerous incidents in her early years in which she had been "devastated" by her alcoholic father's obnoxious behavior in public. Though she had tried to keep her school friends from knowing about her family problems, when this had become impossible she instead had limited her friendships, thus protecting herself from possible embarrassment or criticism.

When Sally first began therapy, she avoided meeting people unless she could be assured that they would "like her." With therapy that focused on enhancing her assertiveness and social skills, she made some progress in her ability to approach and talk with people.

Sally's extreme need to avoid situations in which she might be embarrassed is the keynote of the avoidant personality. Life is full of risks, yet such individuals cannot face even the slightest risk of embarrassment or criticism. They want guarantees of success before they will participate—and if they cannot have them, they just will not play the game.

The diagnosis of avoidant personality is not without its critics, particularly with regard to how well it can be distinguished from schizoid personality disorder (Livesley, West, & Tanney, 1985). The diagnostic criteria for avoidant personality have been thought to blend imperceptibly with two other categories—schizoid and dependent personalities. Trull, Widiger, and Frances (1987), however, in a diagnostic study of personality disorder in an inpatient facility, found that these disorders were clearly distinguishable. The key difference is that avoidant personality is associated with being hypersensitive, shy, and insecure, while schizoid personality is characterized by being indifferent, aloof, and cold. The more difficult distinction is between dependent and avoidant personalities. In this case, a dependent personality has great difficulty separating in relationships, while an avoidant personality has problems initiating them.

Some research (e.g., Alden & Capp, 1988) suggests that an avoidant personality may be a biologically based disorder that is reinforced by environmental factors to become a highly stable and chronic behavioral pattern (Kagan, Reznick, & Snidman, 1988). However, efforts to modify avoidant personality behaviors have recently been undertaken with some success; this success calls into question the nature of any biological causal factor. Alden (1989), for example, reported on a controlled study of structured behavioral treatment in which the treated group of avoidant clients showed significant improvements in terms of self-esteem and a reduction in social reticence. However, in spite of their noticeable improvements, the avoidant clients, at the end of treatment, still had not achieved normal levels of social functioning. This limited success of treatment and poor prognosis for behavioral change was confirmed in a recent study by Stravynski et al. (1989). They found that social skills training was not effective in reducing avoidant behavior.

Dependent Personality Disorder Individuals with **dependent personality disorder** show extreme dependence on other people and acute discomfort—even panic—at having to be alone. These individuals usually build their lives around other people and subordinate their own needs to keep these people involved with them. They lack self-confidence and feel helpless even when they have actually developed good work skills or other competencies. They function well as long as they are not required to be on their own. The following case is one in which a woman with a dependent personality experienced such distress following desertion by her husband that she sought help:

Sarah D., a 32-year-old mother of two and a part-time tax accountant, came to a crisis center late one evening after Michael, her husband of a year and a half, abused her physically and then left home. Although he never physically harmed the children, he frequently threatened to do so when he was drunk. Sarah appeared acutely anxious and worried about the future and "needed to be told what to do." She wanted her husband to come back and seemed rather unconcerned about his regular pattern of physical abuse. At the time, Michael was an unemployed resident in a day treatment program at a halfway house for paroled drug abusers that taught abstinence from all addictive substances through harassment and group cohesiveness. He was almost always in a surly mood and "ready to explode."

Although Sarah had a well-paying job, she voiced great concern about being able to make it on her own. She realized that it was foolish to be "dependent" on her husband, whom she referred to as a "real loser." (She had had a similar relationship with her first husband, who had left her and her oldest child when she was 18.) Several times in the past few months, Sarah had made up her mind to get out of the marriage but couldn't bring herself to break away. She would threaten to leave, but when the time came to do so, she would "freeze in the door" with a numbness in her body and a sinking feeling in her stomach at the thought of "not being with Michael."

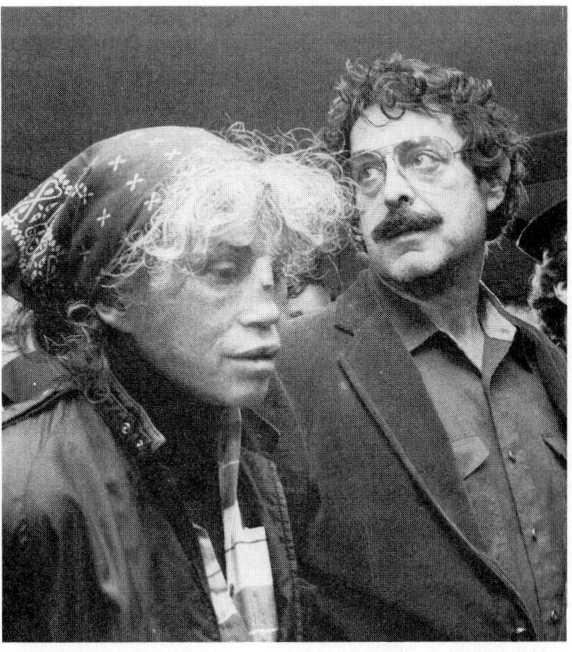

Dependent personalities may tolerate emotional or physical abuse in order to avoid being abandoned. Their lack of self-confidence is so extreme that they passively allow other people to take over the major decisions in their lives. Hedda Nussbaum exhibited such behavior in her relationship with her lover Joel Steinberg. He physically abused Hedda and their illegally adopted daughter Lisa for years. On the last night of 6-year-old Lisa's life, when Steinberg beat her and left her comatose on the bathroom floor all night, Hedda did nothing to help Lisa. Hedda testified against Joel at the trial for the murder of Lisa in exchange for not being prosecuted herself. Once a competent person with a job as a children's book editor, Hedda had become so unable to function without Joel, though he abused her, that she tolerated the abuse of Lisa as well, ultimately sharing the responsibility for her death. Steinberg was convicted of first-degree manslaughter and is currently serving his sentence.

As a result of their lack of confidence, dependent personalities passively allow other people to take over the major decisions in their lives—such as where they will live and work, what friends they will have, and even how they will spend their time. These individuals typically appear "selfless" and bland, since they usually feel they have no right to express even mild individuality.

Obsessive-Compulsive Personality Disorder Individuals with **obsessive-compulsive personality disorder** show excessive concern for rules, order, efficiency, and work, coupled with an insistence that everyone do things their way and an inability to express warm feelings. Such individuals tend to be overinhibited, overconscientious, overdutiful, and rigid, and to have difficulty relaxing or doing anything just for fun. They are usually preoccupied with trivial details and poor allocations of time.

The behavior patterns of this disorder are somewhat similar to those of neurotic compulsive disorders. In obsessive-compulsive disorder, however, an individual suffers from the persistent intrusion of particular undesired thoughts (obsessions) or actions (compulsions) that are a source of extreme anxiety because the individual recognizes that they are irrational but cannot seem to control them. Obsessive-compulsive personalities have whole lifestyles characterized by obstinacy and compulsive orderliness. Although they may be anxious about getting all their work done in keeping with their exacting standards, they are not anxious about their compulsiveness itself (Pollack, 1979). An example of obsessive-compulsive personality is reflected in the following case:

Alan appeared to be well suited to his work as a train dispatcher. He was conscientious, perfectionistic, and attended to minute details. However, he was not close to his coworkers and, reportedly, they thought him "off." He would get quite upset if even minor variations to his daily routine occurred. For example, he would become tense and irritable if coworkers did not follow exactly his elaborately constructed schedules and plans. If he became tied up in traffic, he would beat the steering wheel and swear at other drivers for holding him up.

In short, Alan got little pleasure out of life and worried constantly about minor problems. His rigid routines were impossible to maintain, and he often developed tension headaches or stomachaches when he couldn't keep his complicated plans in order. His physician, noting the frequency of his physical complaints and his generally perfectionistic approach to life, referred him for a psychological evaluation. Psychotherapy was recommended to him, although the prognosis for significant behavioral change was considered questionable. He did not follow up on the treatment recommendations because he felt that he could not afford the time away from work.

Other people tend to view obsessive-compulsive personalities as rigid, stiff, cold, and even disorganized—in spite of their frequent and extensive preoccupation with the details in their lives.

Passive-Aggressive Personality Disorder One of the most controversial of the personality disorder diagnoses is that of **passive-aggressive personality disorder.** The reasons for this controversy are twofold. First, the diagnosis is conceptually ambiguous: that is, a person is considered both passive and actively aggressive at the same time—two seemingly contradictory behaviors. Second, empirical support of the reliability and validity of this diagnosis is limited (Penna, 1986). Individuals with this disorder typically express hostility in indirect and nonviolent ways, such as procrastinating, pouting, "forgetting," or being obstructionistic, stubborn, or intentionally inefficient. Passive-aggressive individuals resent and manage not to comply with demands others make on them; the behavior is most apparent in their work situations but also occurs in their social relationships. Resentment of authority figures, coupled with a lack of assertiveness, is typical.

The passive-aggressive personality pattern is shown in the following case of marital therapy. Though the marital problems were the major focus of the initial sessions, Wanda's adjustment difficulties required additional attention.

David and Wanda had met through a singles travel club and had been initially attracted to each other because of their mutual interest in travel and dancing. After a brief courtship, they had married. Two successive pregnancies had left them with two lovely children but little time or money to pursue their interests.

In the early sessions, David, a 29-year-old sales representative, complained that Wanda, a

28-year-old homemaker, was a "great procrastinator" and that she kept the house a "shambles." Apparently, Wanda also often "forgot" to cook, sometimes because she became preoccupied with a book or a puzzle. She was often unaware of the time and fed the children late; in addition, she often did not have dinner ready when David came home. On the other hand, after some prodding, Wanda revealed that she found herself in an intolerable situation. She was unhappy with her marriage; she saw her husband as a selfish, picky person who was obsessive about the cleanliness of the house and the preparation of the meals, and who was unaware of the difficulties of caring for two young children. It was clear from these early sessions that David and Wanda were frustrated in their marriage and each harbored great resentments toward the other.

In subsequent therapy sessions, it became apparent that Wanda's problems were consistent with a lifelong pattern and not just the result of her present situation. She was a rather passive and nonassertive person who had difficulty making her objections known to others. She had great difficulty making her feelings known to David about her disappointments in the marriage. Instead, she dealt with her frustration through indirect means—intentional inefficiency. She related several incidents in her life in which she had had periods of ineffective functioning or, as she called it, stubbornness. Inevitably, these periods had occurred during times of frustration. For example, her parents had hoped she would pursue a career in music, as they had; rather than tell them she had no desire to be a musician, she instead could "just never seem to complete" her university assignments and eventually had flunked out of school.

In addition to the marital therapy sessions, it was recommended that Wanda also be seen in individual psychotherapy to explore further her personal adjustment problems. As for the maintenance of the house, it was recommended that, for the time being at least, they hire outside help.

In sum, we can see in a passive-aggressive personality a pattern of never confronting a problem situation directly. This characteristic way of reacting to a problem is really no solution at all. It is frustrating for others, who must deal with the inefficient behavior usually without knowing the real reason for it; and it is frustrating for the individual, because it typically does not productively resolve the problem.

Self-defeating Personality Disorder The **self-defeating personality disorder** (often called masochistic personality disorder) is an extensive pattern of behavior characterized by an individual's avoidance of pleasurable experiences and persistent involvement in disappointing relationships. Individuals with this disorder seemingly choose relationships or situations that lead to disappointment, failure, or mistreatment even though better options are available. These individuals appear to be almost magnetically drawn to punishing relationships and seemingly discourage or reject the attempts of others to help them extricate themselves from these painful experiences.

Self-defeating personalities fail to accomplish tasks or goals that are crucial to their personal objectives in spite of the fact that they have the ability to perform them. If they do achieve personal recognition or accomplishments, these individuals might react by feeling depressed or guilty or by engaging in some inappropriate behavior rather than feeling self-enhanced as most people would. They avoid opportunities for pleasure or success and are reluctant to admit to enjoyment.

Self-defeating individuals elicit rejecting responses from others and then feel hurt or scorned by them. For example, a man who makes fun of his wife in public may provoke her to make a negative response. He then feels devastated over the spouse's rejection.

Self-defeating personality disorder is a provisional diagnostic category that is included in the appendix of DSM-III-R. It is there because many clinicians believe that no other personality disorder is adequate to describe this pattern of personality disturbance in which an individual is drawn to relationships in which he or she will suffer. Reich (1989) found that the behavioral and symptomatic criteria for self-defeating personality disorder were somewhat difficult to apply because of clear overlap with other disorders, such as avoidant, dependent, and especially borderline personalities. Reich also concluded, however, that diagnosis, though difficult, could be applied effectively.

Fuller and Blashfield (1989) evaluated whether the proposed personality disorder—the self-defeating, or masochistic, personality disorder—was needed to classify the behaviors in question, or whether patients with these problems could be classified using another DSM-III-R category. They found that the behaviors in question did not fall into an existing category and thus suggested that the proposed category was needed.

The authors of DSM-III-R attempted to incorporate criteria that would distinguish self-defeating personality disorder from normal reactions to being victimized or abused (Kass et al., 1989). Nevertheless, the category of self-defeating personality disorder has met with considerable objection from vocal critics, particularly some feminist action groups, which view it as having antifemale biases. For example, representatives of Women in Psychology have made the point that the diagnostic label *self-defeating personality disorder* misplaces the blame for abusive relationships onto women who are actually the victims of abuse (Fisher, 1986). Fuller & Blashfield (1989) evaluated the question of whether this proposed disorder might be vulnerable to gender bias when applied as a diagnosis. They found no evidence for bias, but the extent to which the usefulness of the diagnosis in clinical practice outweighs the criticism of bias has yet to be determined. It is likely that additional research will be required to assure critics of the objectivity of this proposed disorder.

Sadistic Personality Disorder Another proposed diagnostic category in the appendix of DSM-III-R is **sadistic personality disorder,** which is defined by a pervasive pattern of cruel, demeaning, and aggressive behavior toward other people. It is usually evident by early adulthood. Individuals with this disorder have a history of using physical cruelty to inflict pain on other people, usually for the satisfaction of seeing them suffer. They might humiliate, demean, or embarrass other people in social situations, or they might attempt to get other people to do what they want by intimidation. Sadistic individuals tend to restrict the autonomy of other people with whom they are involved in close relationships; they will, for example, not let others go out unaccompanied. They are characteristically fascinated with violence, weapons, martial arts, or torture.

As with the self-defeating disorder, some critics have expressed concern that the sadistic disorder might be used to disadvantage women. For example, having a diagnostic label *sadistic personality disorder* for individuals who have committed violent crimes against women may tend to excuse these abusive individuals by attributing their behavior to their being disordered.

An additional argument advanced by Women in Psychology in response to the new diagnostic categories, which they consider antiwomen, is that they are not based on scientific research and do not represent advances in our understanding of behavior disorders. Whether these proposed diagnostic categories will eventually be fully substantiated by research is yet to be determined.

Causal Factors in Personality Disorders

Establishing the causal factors in personality disorders has not progressed far, partly because such disorders were not even included in the official diagnostic classifications before 1952 and partly because they are less amenable to thorough study. Many individuals with these disorders are never seen by clinical personnel. Typically, those who do come to the attention of clinicians or legal authorities have already developed a full-blown disorder, so that only *retrospective* study is possible—that is, going back through what records may exist in an effort to reconstruct the chain of events that may have led to the disorder. As we have seen, researchers have more confidence in *prospective* studies, in which groups of individuals are observed before a disorder appears and followed over a period of time to see which individuals develop problems and what causal factors have in fact been present.

Research on causal factors in disordered personalities is also made difficult by the fact that, for the most part, general personality traits rather than specific behavioral patterns are being studied in the personality disorders. It is hard to identify the point at which, for example, great attention to detail ceases to be within the normal range and becomes characteristic of compulsive personality.

Of possible biological factors, it has been suggested that the constitutional reaction tendencies that infants display (high or low vitality, special sensitivity, and so on) may predispose them to the development of particular personality disorders. In addition, some research suggests that genetic factors may be important for the development of paranoid personality (Kendler & Gruenberg, 1982) and borderline personality (Loranger et al., 1982). The constitutional basis for the personality disorders remains largely hypothetical, however, with the possible exception of antisocial personality, to be discussed later in this chapter.

Among psychological factors, early learning is usually assumed to contribute the most in predisposing an individual to develop a personality disorder, yet the "data" in support of this belief are based largely on speculation and inference. Some research has suggested that abuse in childhood may be related to the development of personality disorders. Ogata et al. (1990) found that 71 percent of borderline patients reported having been abused as children, while only 22 percent of depressed patients reported having been abused. However, except for antisocial personality, research has simply not sufficiently established particular antecedents for these disorders.

Sociocultural factors contributing to personality disorders are even less well defined. We do know that the incidence and form of psychopathology in general vary somewhat with time and place, and some clinicians believe that personality disorders have increased in American society in recent years (Smith, 1978). If this claim is true, we can expect to find the increase related to changes in our culture's general priorities and activities. Is our emphasis on impulse gratification, instant solutions, and pain-free benefits leading more people to develop the self-centered life-styles that we see in more extreme forms in the personality disorders? Only further research can clarify this issue.

Treatments and Outcomes

Personality disorders seem especially resistant to therapy. For example, speaking of antisocial personalities, Ellis (1977) pointed out that

[they] are exceptionally difficult to treat with psychotherapy. They only rarely come for treatment on a voluntary basis; and when they are treated involuntarily, they tend to be resistant, surly, and in search of a "cure" that will involve no real effort on their part. Even when they come for private treatment, they are usually looking for magical, effortless "cures," and they tend to stay in treatment only for a short period of time and to make relatively little improvement. (p. 259)

In many cases, people with personality disorders who are seen clinically are there as part of another person's treatment—as, for example, in couple counseling, where a partner identified as the "patient" has a spouse with a personality disorder. Or a child referred to a child guidance center may have a parent with a personality disorder. In these cases, of course, the problems of the so-called patient may be due in no small measure to the great strain caused by the family member with severe personality disorder. A narcissistic father, who is so self-centered and demanding of attention from others that family relationships are constantly strained, leaves little room for small children to grow into self-respecting adults. Likewise, a mother whose typical manner of responding to others is through passive-aggressive maneuvers, such as procrastination, obstruction, and pouting, may create an unhealthy family atmosphere that distorts a child's development.

A child subjected to such extreme, inescapable, and often quite irrational behavior on the part of one or both parents may become the weak link that breaks, bringing the family into therapy. Many a child or family therapist has quickly concluded after seeing a child in a family context that psychological attention, if it is to be effective at all, must be focused on the parental relationships. The following case clearly illustrates this problem:

Mrs. A. brought her 7-year-old son, Christopher, to a mental health center for treatment because he was fearful of going out and recently had been having bad nightmares. Mrs. A. sought help at the recommendation of the school social worker after Chris refused to return to school. She voiced a great deal of concern for Chris and agreed to cooperate in the treatment by attend-

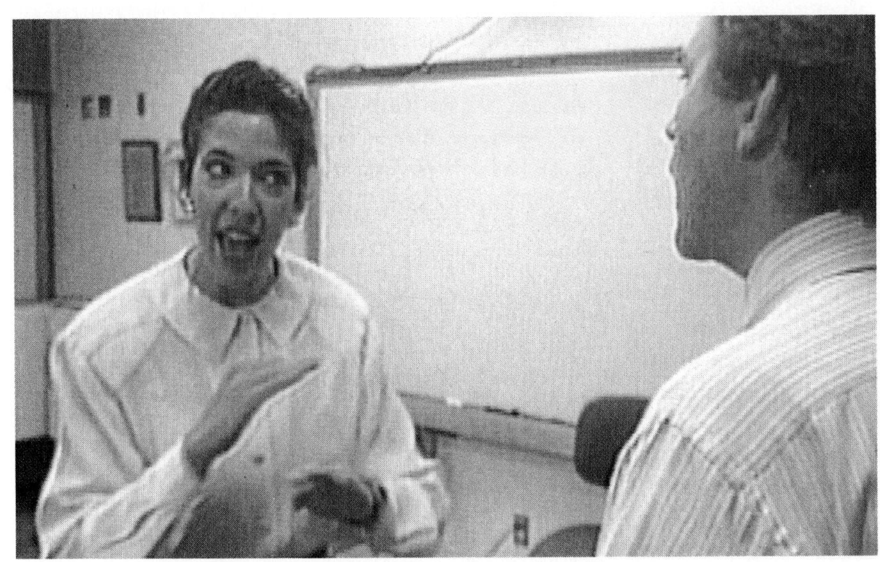

As part of an interesting training program for psychotherapists, the actress shown here is being trained to behave in ways characteristic of an individual with narcissistic personality, for example, by being self-centered and demanding of attention. She will then act out her role in mock therapy sessions with would-be psychotherapists.

ing parent effectiveness training sessions. However, she seemed quite reluctant to talk about getting her husband involved in the treatment. After much encouragement, she agreed to try to bring him to the next session, but he adamantly refused to participate. Mrs. A described him as a "very proud and strong-willed man" who was quite suspicious of other people. She felt that he might be afraid people would blame him for Chris's problems. She reported that he had been having a lot of problems lately—he had seemed quite bitter and resentful over some local political issues and tended to blame others (particularly minorities) for his problems. He refused to come to the clinic because he "doesn't like social workers."

After several sessions of therapy, Mrs. A. confessed to her therapist that her husband's rigid and suspicious behavior was disrupting the family. He would often come home from work and accuse her of, for example, "talking with Jewish men." He was a domineering person who set strict house rules and enforced them with loud threats and intimidation. Both Mrs. A. and Chris were fearful of his tyrannical demands, but his suspicious nature made it difficult for them to explain anything to him. Mrs. A. also felt a great deal of sympathy for her husband because she felt that deep down inside he was frightened; she reported that he kept numerous guns around the house and several locks on the doors for protection against outsiders, whom he feared.

Because they usually enter treatment only at someone else's insistence and do not believe that they need to change, individuals with personality disorders typically put the responsibility for treatment on others and are adept at avoiding the focus of therapy themselves. In addition, the difficulties they have in forming and maintaining good relationships generally tend to make a therapeutic relationship stormy at best. The pattern of acting out, typical in their other relationships, is carried into the therapy situation, and instead of dealing with their problems at the verbal level, they may become angry at their therapist and loudly disrupt the sessions. Goldberg et al. (1986) reported high dropout rates for some types of personality disordered patients. These patients may also behave in socially inappropriate ways outside the sessions to show their therapist that the therapy is not working.

When questioned about such behavior, these individuals often drop out of treatment or become even more entrenched in their defensiveness. In some cases, however, confrontation can be quite effective. For individuals who become identified with their therapy group, or who are sufficiently "hooked" into couple therapy not to flee the sessions when their behavior comes under scrutiny, the intense feedback from peers or spouse often is more acceptable than confrontation by a therapist in individual treatment (Gurman & Kniskern, 1978; Lubin, 1976).

In some situations, therapeutic techniques must be modified. For example, recognizing that traditional individual psychotherapy tends to encourage dependency in people already too dependent, Leeman and Mulvey (1974) developed a treatment strategy in individual outpatient therapy for altering a dependent individual's basic life-style instead of fostering it. First, they would inform a patient at the outset that the therapy would be brief. Next, they made it clear that they "would not assume responsibility for managing the patient's life" (p. 36) and that they expected strength on the part of the patient "both to tolerate feelings and to behave in more adaptive and self-satisfying ways" (p. 36). Therapy sessions were then kept focused on relationships outside of therapy rather than on the treatment relationship, and demands were made on the patient to *change* his or her behavior—not just to understand it. Several highly dependent patients, including one "veteran" of ten years of individual psychotherapy, responded favorably to this treatment, and most reported that they were doing much better two and a half years later.

In general, therapy for individuals with severe personality disorders may be more effective in situations where acting-out behavior can be constrained. Outpatient treatment is often not promising because severe acting out can disrupt the course of treatment. The tenacity of these disorders and the failure of individuals either to profit from ordinary therapy or to learn from their life experiences is shown in the following case of an individual diagnosed as a passive-aggressive personality:

Charles, age 29, appeared to be a highly successful salesperson in a large retail shoe store. He was a handsome, friendly, and outgoing person who quickly impressed customers and gained ready admirers. His relationships with coworkers and employers, however, were an entirely different matter. He was a disorganized person who couldn't keep the bookkeeping and stock in order. He was a procrastinator who promised everything but delivered nothing. He responded to criticism by his employers with smiles and promises but was never able to get organized. He never expressed anger toward his supervisor or disgruntled customers but seldom fulfilled their demands.

One evening, after he had been criticized for his sloppiness, he was directed to straighten out his "mess" and lock up the store after everyone else had left. He failed to comply and actually left the store open with the lights on. This was the last straw for his employers, and Charles was fired.

Over the years, his stubborn and passive-aggressive actions had lost him several other jobs. In each situation, he had been able to secure a sales position quite readily, but in short order his behavior had angered his employers and the ensuing criticisms had made him even more intractable.

Finally, he entered therapy at his wife's insistence because of marital problems. His behavior toward his wife was similar to his behavior in other personal relationships: he was obstinate and unyielding even though he always smiled and never lost his temper. After only two weeks in therapy, he began to miss sessions until, after a month, he stopped coming altogether because "he had to look for work."

Treatment prognosis (outcome) for borderline personality disorder patients is typically considered to be guarded because of their long-standing problems and extreme instability. Because borderline patients are usually difficult to manage due to their behavioral problems and acting out tendencies, treatment often involves a judicious use of both psychological and biological treatment methods (Swenson & Wood, 1990). Cowdry and Gardner (1988) found that some borderline personality patients can be effectively treated with the drug tranylcypromine (Parnate), an MAO inhibitor for use in treatment of depression (see *HIGHLIGHT 17.3)*, as an adjunct to psychological treatment. They concluded that pharmacotherapy aided in the reduction of mood and behavior in borderline patients. Treatment of borderline patients typically requires optimal flexibility on the part of a therapist to shift from a psychological to a medications-based treatment approach (Stone, 1990).

As might be expected, research comparing treatment outcomes for borderline, bipolar mood disorder, and schizophrenic patients found significantly better results for the bipolar and borderline patients than for the schizophrenic patients (McGlashan, 1986). Adjustment after discharge from the hospital was, nevertheless, rocky for the borderline patients, and they frequently required further hospitalization.

ANTISOCIAL PERSONALITY

As we have seen, the outstanding characteristics of antisocial personality disorder are a marked lack of ethical or moral development and an apparent inability to follow approved models of behavior. Basically, these individuals are unsocialized and seemingly incapable of significant loyalty to other people, groups, or social values. These characteristics often bring them into repeated conflict with society. The terms **psychopathic personality** and **sociopathic personality** are also commonly used in referring to this disorder.

The category called *antisocial personality* includes a mixed group of individuals: unprincipled business people, shyster lawyers, quack doctors, high-pressure evangelists, crooked politicians, impostors, drug pushers, a sizeable number of prostitutes, and assorted criminals. Few of these individuals find their way into community clinics or mental hospitals. A larger number are confined in penal institutions, but a history of repeated legal or social offenses is not sufficient justification for assuming that an individual is sociopathic. In point of fact, a large number of sociopathic individuals manage to stay out of correctional institutions, although they tend to be in constant conflict with authority (see *HIGHLIGHT 8.2)*.

The prevalence of antisocial personality disorder—as reported in one large-scale epidemiological study (Robins et al., 1984)—is between 3.9 and 4.9 percent for males and less than .07 percent for females. Onset is in early childhood for males but typically not until puberty for females.

The Clinical Picture in Antisocial Personality

Often intelligent, spontaneous, and likeable on first acquaintance, antisocial personalities are deceitful and manipulative, callously using others to achieve their own ends. Often they seem to live in a series of

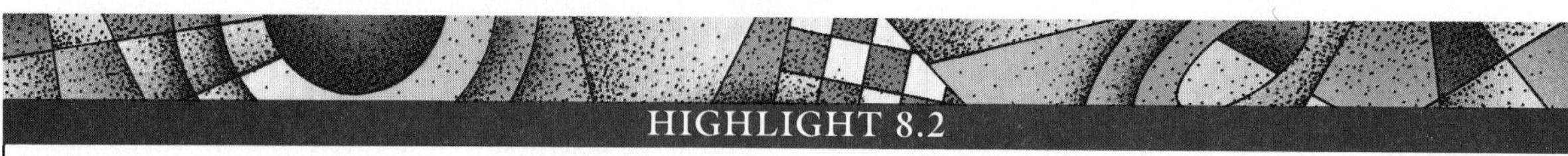

HIGHLIGHT 8.2

Wanted: Everyday Psychopaths

Most studies of antisocial personalities have been conducted on institutionalized individuals, leaving us ignorant about the far larger number who never get caught. Widom (1977) tried an ingenious approach for reaching this larger group. She ran advertisements in the local newspapers which read:

Are you adventurous? Psychologist studying adventurous, carefree people who've led exciting, impulsive lives. If you're the kind of person who'd do almost anything for a dare and want to participate in a paid experiment, send name, address, phone, and short biography proving how interesting you are to. . . . (p. 675)

Widom had hoped to attract antisocial individuals and apparently did just that. When given a battery of tests, those who responded turned out to be similar in personality makeup to institutionalized psychopathic individuals. Although she did not go further than a personality assessment of these individuals, her method suggests a way of making contact with samples of uninstitutionalized antisocial personalities.

present moments, without consideration for the past or future. The following example is illustrative:

Two 18-year-old youths went to visit a teenager at her home. Finding no one there, they broke into the house, damaged a number of valuable paintings and other furnishings, and stole a quantity of liquor and a television set. They sold the TV to a mutual friend for a small sum of money. On their apprehension by the police, they at first denied the entire venture and then later insisted that it was all a "practical joke." They did not consider their behavior particularly inappropriate, nor did they think any sort of restitution for damage was called for.

Also included in the general category of antisocial individuals are hostile, sociopathic people who are prone to acting out impulses in remorseless and often senseless violence. In other cases, antisocial individuals show periods of reliability and are capable of assuming responsibility and pursuing long-range goals, but they do so in unethical ways with a complete lack of consideration for the rights and well-being of others.

Only individuals 18 or over are diagnosed as antisocial personalities. According to the DSM-III-R classification, this diagnosis is made if the following criteria are met: (a) at least three instances of deviant behavior, such as theft, vandalism, or unusually aggressive actions, occur before age 15; (b) at least four behavioral problems, such as financial irresponsibility, illegal occupation, ineffective functioning as a parent, or poor work history, occur after age 15, with no period longer than five years without such a problem; (c) the antisocial behavior endures, with no "remission" lasting longer than five years (unless the person is incapacitated or imprisoned); and (d) the antisocial behavior is not a symptom of another mental disorder.

To fill in the clinical picture, let us begin by summarizing characteristics that antisocial personalities tend to share. We will then describe a case

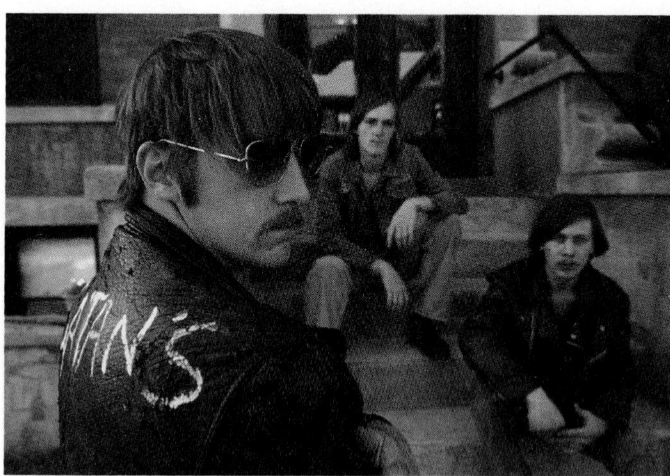

Delinquency can sometimes be a prelude to the development of antisocial personality disorder in adulthood. In many cases, however, delinquent behavior ends with adolescence.

that illustrates the wide range of behavioral patterns that may be involved.

Common Characteristics While all the characteristics examined in the following sections are not usually found in a particular case, they are typical of antisocial personalities in general.

Inadequate conscience development. Antisocial personalities are unable to understand and accept ethical values except on a verbal level. They make glib verbalizations and claims of adherence to high moral standards that have no apparent connection with their behavior. In short, though their intellectual development is typically normal or above, their conscience development is severely retarded or nonexistent.

Antisocial personalities tend to "act out" tensions and problems rather than worry them out. Their apparent lack of anxiety and guilt, combined with the appearance of sincerity and candor, may enable them to avoid suspicion and detection for stealing and other illegal activities. They often show contempt for those they are able to take advantage of—their "marks."

Serial killer Ted Bundy, here shown on a TV monitor outside Florida State prison, exhibited antisocial behavior at its most extreme and dangerous. He had considerable good looks, charm, and intelligence, which masked violent impulses, manipulativeness, and a total lack of remorse for his victims. Bundy's clean-cut image, which he used to get close to his victims—all young women whom he sexually abused and then murdered—was so convincing as to be chilling when the magnitude of his acts became apparent. Bundy was electrocuted in Florida in 1989.

Irresponsible and impulsive behavior. Antisocial individuals generally have a callous disregard for the rights, needs, and well-being of others. They have learned to take rather than earn what they want. Prone to thrill seeking and deviant and unconventional behavior, they often break the law impulsively and without regard for the consequences. They seldom forego immediate pleasure for future gains and long-range goals. They live in the present, without realistically considering either past or future. External reality is used for immediate personal gratification. Unable to endure routine or to shoulder responsibility, they frequently change jobs. Several studies have shown that antisocial personalities have high rates of alcoholism (Lewis, Robins, & Rice, 1985; Lewis, Cloninger, & Pais, 1983).

Ability to impress and exploit others. Often antisocial individuals are charming and likeable, with a disarming manner that easily wins friends. Typically, they have a good sense of humor and an optimistic outlook. Though frequent liars, they usually will seem sincerely sorry if caught in a lie and promise to make amends—but not do so. They seem to have good insight into other people's needs and weaknesses and are adept at exploiting them. For example, many psychopathic individuals engage in unethical sales schemes in which they use their charm and the confidence they inspire in others to make "easy money." They readily find excuses and rationalizations for their antisocial conduct, typically projecting the blame onto someone else. Thus they are often able to convince other people—as well as themselves—that they are free of fault.

Rejection of authority. Antisocial individuals behave as if social regulations do not apply to them: they do not play by the rules of the game. Frequently they have a history of difficulties with educational and law-enforcement authorities. Yet although they often drift into criminal activities, they are not typically calculating, professional criminals. Despite the difficulties they get into and the punishments they may receive, they go on behaving as if they are immune from the consequences of their actions.

Inability to maintain good relationships. Although initially able to win the liking and friendship of other people, antisocial personalities are seldom able to keep close friends. Irresponsible and egocentric, they are usually cynical, unsympathetic, ungrateful, and remorseless in their dealings. They seemingly cannot understand love in others or give it in return. As Horton, Louy, and Coppolillo (1974) have expressed it, the psychopathic personality "continues to move through the world wrapped in his separateness as though in an insulator, touched rarely and never moved by his fellow man" (p. 622).

Antisocial personalities pose a menace not only to chance acquaintances but also to their family and friends. Violence toward family members is common. Herman (1986) reported that antisocial personality was the only clinical diagnosis found to be unusually frequent among males who were abusive toward others.

Manipulative and exploitive in sexual relationships, antisocial individuals are irresponsible and unfaithful mates. Although they often promise to change, they rarely do so for any considerable length of time.

Many of the preceding characteristics may be found in varying degrees in maladjusted individuals, in those dependent on drugs, and in those showing other maladaptive behavior patterns. In the case of antisocial personalities, however, these characteristics are extremely pronounced and occur apart from other "symptoms" of psychopathology. Whereas most maladjusted individuals, for example, are beset by worry and anxiety and have a tendency to avoid difficult situations, antisocial personalities act on their impulses fearlessly, with little or no thought for the difficulties they may be incurring.

Patterns of Behavior The antisocial personality disorder is illustrated in the following case study published by Hare (1970):

Donald S., 30 years old, has just completed a three-year prison term for fraud, bigamy, false pretenses, and escaping lawful custody. The circumstances leading up to these offenses are interesting and consistent with his past behavior. With less than a month left to serve on an earlier 18-month term for fraud, he faked illness and escaped from the prison hospital. During the ten months of freedom that followed he engaged in a variety of illegal enterprises; the activity that resulted in his recapture was typical of his method of operation. By passing himself off as the "field executive" of an international philanthropic foundation, he was able to enlist the aid of several religious organizations in a fund-raising campaign. The campaign moved slowly at first, and in an attempt to speed things up, he arranged an interview with the local TV station. His performance during the interview was so impressive that funds started to pour in. However, unfortunately for Donald, the interview was also carried on a national news network. He was recognized and quickly arrested. During the ensuing trial it became evident that he experienced no sense of wrongdoing for his activities. He maintained, for example, that his passionate plea for funds "primed the pump"—that is, induced people to give to other charities as well as to the one he professed to represent. At the same time, he stated that most donations to charity are made by those who feel guilty about something and who therefore deserve to be bilked. This ability to rationalize his behavior and his lack of self-criticism were also evident in his attempts to solicit aid from the very people he had misled. Perhaps it is a tribute to his persuasiveness that a number of individuals actually did come to his support. During his three-year prison term, Donald spent much time searching for legal loopholes and writing to outside authorities, including local lawyers, the Prime Minister of Canada, and a Canadian representative to the United Nations. In each case he verbally attacked them for representing the authority and injustice responsible for his predicament. At the same time he requested them to intercede on his behalf and in the name of the justice they professed to represent.

While in prison he was used as a subject in some of the author's research. On his release he applied for admission to a university and, by way of reference, told the registrar that he had been one of the author's research colleagues! Several months later the author received a letter from him requesting a letter of recommendation on behalf of Donald's application for a job.

Donald was the youngest of three boys born to middle-class parents. Both of his brothers led normal, productive lives. His father spent a great deal of time with his business; when he was home he tended to be moody and to drink heavily when things were not going right. Donald's mother was a gentle, timid woman who tried to please her husband and to maintain a semblance of family harmony. When she discovered her children engaged in some mischief, she would threaten to tell their father. However, she seldom carried out these threats because she did not want to disturb her husband and because his reactions were likely to be dependent on his mood at the time; on some occasions he would fly into a rage and beat the children and on others he would administer a verbal reprimand, sometimes mild and sometimes severe.

By all accounts Donald was considered a willful and difficult child. When his desire for candy or toys was frustrated he would begin with a show of affection, and if this failed he would throw a temper tantrum; the latter was seldom necessary because his angelic appearance and artful ways usually got him what he wanted. Similar tactics were used to avoid punishment for his numerous misdeeds. At first he would attempt to cover up with an elaborate facade of lies, often shifting the blame to his brothers. If this did not work, he would give a convincing display of remorse and contrition. When punishment was unavoidable he would become sullenly defiant, regarding it as an unjustifiable tax on his pleasures.

Although he was obviously very intelligent, his school years were academically undistinguished. He was restless, easily bored, and frequently truant. His behavior in the presence of the teacher or some other authority was usually quite good, but when he was on his own he generally got himself or others into trouble. Although he was often suspected of being the culprit, he was adept at talking his way out of difficulty.

Donald's misbehavior as a child took many forms including lying, cheating, petty theft, and the bullying of smaller children. As he grew older he became more and more interested in sex, gambling, and alcohol. When he was 14 he made crude sexual advances toward a younger girl, and when she threatened to tell her parents he locked her in a shed. It was about 16 hours before she was found. Donald at first denied knowledge of the incident, later stating that she had seduced him and that the door must have locked itself. He expressed no concern for the anguish experienced by the girl and her parents, nor did he give any indication that he felt morally culpable for what he had done. His parents were able to prevent charges being brought against him. Nevertheless, incidents of this sort were becoming more frequent and, in an attempt to prevent further embarrassment to the family, he was sent away to a private boarding school. . . .

When he was 17, Donald left the boarding school, forged his father's name to a large check, and spent about a year traveling around the world. He apparently lived well, using a combination of charm, physical attractiveness, and false pretenses to finance his way. During subsequent years he held a succession of jobs, never staying at any one for more than a few months. Throughout this period he was charged with a variety of crimes, including theft, drunkenness in a public place, assault, and many traffic violations. In most cases he was either fined or given a light sentence.

His sexual experiences were frequent, casual, and callous. When he was 22 he married a 41-year-old woman whom he had met in a bar. Several other marriages followed, all bigamous. In each case the pattern was the same: he would marry someone on impulse, let her support him for several months, and then leave. One marriage was particularly interesting. After being charged with fraud Donald was sent to a psychiatric institution for a period of observation. While there he came to the attention of a female member of the professional staff. His charm, physical attractiveness, and convincing promises to reform led her to intervene on his behalf. He was given a suspended sentence and they were married a week later. At first things went reasonably well, but when she refused to pay some of his gambling debts he forged her name to a check and left. He was soon caught and given an 18-month prison term. As mentioned earlier, he escaped with less than a month left to serve.

It is interesting to note that Donald sees nothing particularly wrong with his behavior, nor does he express remorse or guilt for using others and causing them grief. Although his behavior is self-defeating in the long run, he considers it to be practical and possessed of good sense. Periodic punishments do nothing to decrease his egotism and confidence in his own abilities, nor do they offset the often considerable short-term gains of which he is capable. However, these short-term gains are invariably obtained at the expense of someone else. In this respect his behavior is entirely egocentric, and his needs are satisfied without any concern for the feelings and welfare of others. (Hare, 1970, pp. 1–4)

The repetitive behavior pattern shown by Donald is common among individuals diagnosed as having an antisocial personality. Interestingly, many antisocial individuals do eventually settle down to responsible positions in their community. Furthermore, Brantley and Sutker (1984), in reviewing the literature on people with an antisocial personality, point out that—although much of the literature has focused on their negative aspects—these individuals also have positive qualities; as a group they seem to be

> *robust, socially facile and ingenious in many situations. . . . In fact, there are . . . data on which to build a case for their capacity to respond with appropriate emotional expression in most interpersonal situations. Certainly, the extreme cases among groups in which individuals are diagnosed as antisocial personality or sociopathic may represent the epitome of distaste for authority as well as disregard for the wishes of significant others in their lives. Among their ranks, however, are daring, adventuresome, resourceful persons who may have capabilities to outperform so-called normals when the going gets rough.*

It is interesting to note that though high intelligence is characteristic of antisocial personality disorder, intelligence also seems to serve as a protective factor for most individuals at risk for antisocial behavior. Kandel et al. (1988), for example, found that many individuals predisposed to antisocial personality never get involved in criminal behavior because they become more reinforced by schooling. Thus they presumably focus their energies on more socially accepted behaviors.

■ Causal Factors in Antisocial Personality

As is the case with all the personality disorders discussed here, the causal factors in antisocial personality are still not fully understood. Our perspective is complicated by the fact that the causal factors involved appear to differ from case to case, as well as from one socioeconomic level to another. However, more research has been conducted on the antisocial personality than on any of the other personality disorders, so we do at least have a broader basis of data on which to draw. Contemporary research in this area has variously stressed the causal roles of constitutional deficiencies, the early learning of antisocial behavior as a coping style, and the influence of particular family and community patterns.

Biological Factors Because an antisocial individual's impulsiveness, acting out, and intolerance of discipline tend to appear early in life, several investigators have focused on the role of biological factors as causative agents in antisocial behaviors. The following sections focus on some of these biological factors.

Deficient emotional arousal. Research evidence indicates that a primary reaction tendency typically found in antisocial individuals is a deficient emotional arousal; this condition presumably renders them less prone to fear and anxiety in stressful situations and less prone to normal conscience development and socialization.

In an early study, for example, Lykken (1957) concluded that antisocial individuals have fewer inhibitions about committing antisocial acts because they suffer little anxiety. Similarly, Eysenck (1960) concluded that antisocial individuals are less sensitive to noxious stimuli and have a slower rate of conditioning than normal individuals. As a result, antisocial individuals presumably fail to acquire many of the conditioned reactions essential to normal avoidance behavior, conscience development, and socialization. Support for this viewpoint is found in a study by Chesno and Kilmann (1975), who concluded that sociopathic individuals, unlike normal people, "were relatively unsuccessful in acquiring active avoidance responses" (p. 150).

Hare (1970) and other later investigators have reported comparable findings with respect to antisocial individuals' lack of normal fear and anxiety reactions and failure to learn readily from punishments. The latter point merits qualification, however. Schmauk (1970) confirmed earlier observations that such individuals were less adept than nonantisocial individuals in learning to avoid physical and social punishments, but found them to be more adept than normal people in learning to avoid the loss of money—a type of punishment that was apparently *meaningful* to them. These findings are more understandable when it is added that the individuals observed in the experiment were inmates of a penal institution where physical and social punishments were relatively mild for most forms of misbehavior, whereas money was both hard to come by and valuable for obtaining niceties beyond the grim prison fare.

In addition, it should be noted that although the lack of normal emotional arousal may be based on constitutional deficiencies, it may also be based partially on learning. Antisocial individuals often manage to avoid the full consequences of their antisocial behavior by such devices as lies and plausible excuses, dramatic shows of remorse, and empty but convincing promises of "good" behavior in the future. In fact, the absence of anxieties attributed to these individuals has been questioned by Vaillant (1975), who believes that they have simply learned to handle their anxieties differently. In Vaillant's view, rather than succumb to their anxieties like individuals with anxiety-based disorders, they conceal them and in most cases find ways to escape from them. When they cannot flee, they may experience anxieties, but they hide their feelings. Vaillant believes that this concealment of anxieties was learned because the parents could not tolerate their own anxieties. He points out that escaping from anxiety-arousing situations is an immature behavior, such as is found in adolescence.

Stimulation seeking. In his study of criminally antisocial individuals, Hare (1968) reported that they operate at low levels of arousal and are deficient in autonomic variability. He considered these characteristics—together with their lack of normal conditioning to noxious and painful stimuli—indicative of a "relative immunity" to stimulation, which in turn would likely prompt them to seek stimulations and thrills as ends in themselves. In a study comparing antisocial and normal individuals, Fenz (1971) also found that the former seemed to have an insatiable need for stimulation. Several other investigators, using Zuckerman's sensation-seeking scale (a scale that measures such characteristics [Zuckerman, 1972, 1978]), have noted that individuals involved in antisocial behaviors—such as prison escapes (Farley & Farley, 1972), drug use (Kilpatrick et al., 1976), and recurrent arrests among skid-row alcoholics (Malatesta, Sutker, & Treiber, 1981)—have higher sensation-seeking scores and low tolerances for boredom.

Such findings support the earlier view of Quay (1965), who concluded that antisocial behavior is, in essence, an extreme form of stimulation-seeking behavior:

The psychopath is almost universally characterized as highly impulsive, relatively refractory to the effects of experience in modifying his socially troublesome behavior, and lacking in the ability to delay gratification. His penchant for creating excitement for the moment without regard for later consequences seems almost unlimited. He is unable to tolerate routine boredom. While he may engage in antisocial, even vicious, behavior, his outbursts frequently appear to be motivated by little more than a need for thrills and excitement. . . . It is the impulsivity and the lack of even minimal tolerance for sameness which appear to be the primary and distinctive features of the disorder. (p. 180)

Such extreme stimulation seeking does not bode well in the total context of a personality also characterized as impulsive, lacking in judgment, deficient in inner reality and moral controls, and seemingly unable to learn from punishment and experience. Though further investigation is needed, it seems plausible that stimulation seeking "unchecked by conditioned fear response is a two-edged sword for antisocial behavior" (Borkovec, 1970, p. 222).

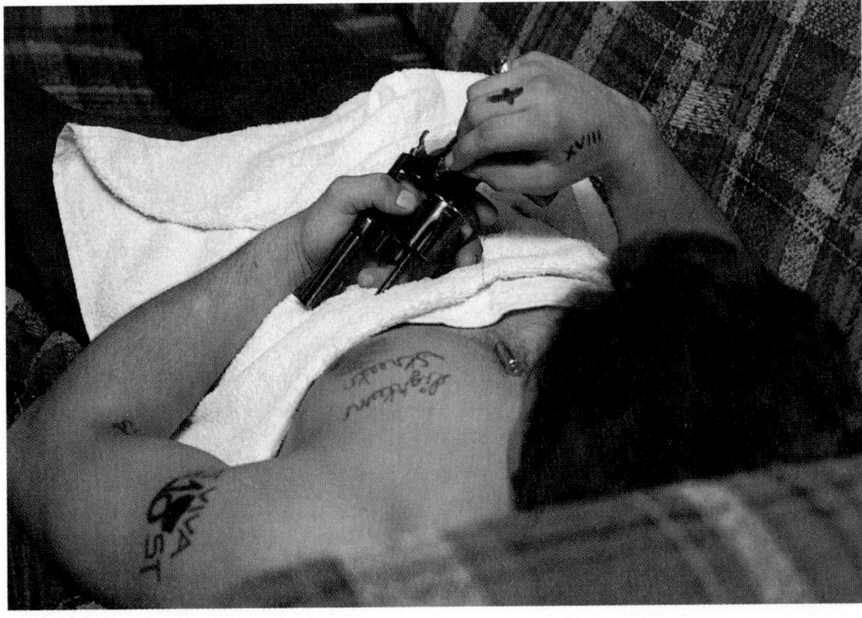

There is evidence that individuals involved in antisocial behaviors, such as playing with dangerous weapons, have an insatiable need for stimulation.

Deficits in cognitive functioning. Gorenstein (1982) raised the possibility that antisocial individuals have deficits in cognitive processes, such as attention to detail, reflecting dysfunctioning in the frontal-lobe area of the brain. He found that antisocial individuals tested in a psychiatric setting performed poorly on several cognitive measures of frontal lobe functioning compared to nonantisocial individuals. However, Hare (1984) disputed these results on grounds that the particular diagnostic procedures were inappropriate for testing frontal lobe functioning. In an attempt to replicate the Gorenstein study using similar procedures to test frontal-lobe functioning in a prison population, Hare did not find differences between antisocial and nonantisocial individuals. Hare suggested that narcotics abuse among antisocial individuals could explain the discrepant results. Gorenstein (1987), in a reanalysis of his data, found that the original findings held when narcotics abuse was controlled. Until more conclusive findings are available, the most appropriate conclusion appears to be that antisocial individuals in psychiatric settings exhibit cognitive or neurological deficits although many such individuals in prison do not.

Genetic influence. MacMillan and Kofoed (1984) provided an interesting sociobiological theory as a causal explanation for antisocial personality. Their view assumes a genetic influence on predispositions for particular behaviors. They maintain that because the goal of natural selection involves the spreading of genes into the next generation, an individual who maximizes the number of his or her offspring by "courting and copulating with multiple mates" is demonstrating the general characteristic of the "most fit" (in the Darwinian sense) of the species. In this scheme, antisocial personalities, especially males, are likely to be most successful in propagation. They are charming, have a lack of guilt and remorse, and are usually promiscuous. Moreover, they are likely to misrepresent themselves, in terms of status and resources, to quickly impress others in forming relations. MacMillan and Kofoed refer to this behavior as the "cheating strategy" and suggest that many individuals with antisocial personality disorders are generally adept at manipulating women for their own purposes. The validity of this viewpoint has not been studied; however, it provides some interesting leads for researchers to follow in further studies of antisocial personality. For example, it might be fruitful to assess the interpersonal attraction and "cheating" skills of antisocial personalities and relate these findings to other known aspects of antisocial behavior.

Family Relationships Perhaps the most popular generalization about the development of an antisocial personality is the assumption of some form of early disturbance in family relationships. The following sections explore some of these disturbances.

Early parental loss and emotional deprivation. A number of early studies reported that an unusually high number of antisocial individuals had experienced the trauma of losing a parent at an early age—usually through the separation or divorce of their parents. For example, Greer (1964) found that 60 percent of one group of antisocial individuals he studied had lost a parent during childhood, as contrasted with 28 percent for a control group of other psychologically maladjusted individuals and 27 percent for a control group of normal subjects.

Because many normal people have experienced the loss of a parent at an early age, it seems that considerably more than parental loss is required to produce an antisocial personality. In reviewing the available evidence, Hare (1970) suggested that the factor of key significance was not the parental loss per se, but rather the emotional disturbances in family relationships created before the departure of a parent.

This point is supported by Wolkind (1974), who found a high incidence of "affectionless psychopathy" in a group of 92 institutionalized children. In many of these cases, the antisocial disorder seemed to have been caused by pathogenic family situations prior to the children's being placed in an institution.

Parental rejection and inconsistency. A number of studies have attempted to relate parental rejection and inconsistent discipline to inadequate socialization and antisocial personality. After an extensive review of the available literature, McCord and McCord (1964) concluded that severe parental rejection and lack of parental affection were the primary causes of antisocial personality.

Another aspect of this theory has been pointed out by Buss (1966), who concluded that two types of parental behavior foster antisocial personality. In the first, parents are cold and distant toward a child and do not allow a warm or close relationship to develop. A child who imitates this parental model will become cold and distant in later relationships;

although the child learns the formal attributes and amenities of social situations, he or she does not develop empathy for others or become emotionally involved with them.

The second type of parental behavior involves inconsistency, in which parents are capricious in supplying affection, rewards, and punishments. Usually they are inconsistent in their own role enactments as well, so that a child lacks stable models to imitate and fails to develop a clear-cut sense of self-identity. Often these parents reward not only "superficial conformity" but also "underhanded nonconformity"—that is, nonconformity that goes undetected by outsiders. Thus they reinforce behaviors that lead to antisocial behavior. Similarly, when parents are both arbitrary and inconsistent in punishing a child, avoiding punishment becomes more important than receiving rewards. Instead of learning to see behavior in terms of right and wrong, the child learns how to avoid blame and punishment by lying or other manipulative means.

In Chapter 4, we noted that slow conscience development and aggression are among the damaging effects of parental rejection and inconsistent discipline. We also noted that children subjected to inconsistent rewards and punishments for aggressive behavior were more resistant to efforts to extinguish the behavior than were children who experienced more consistent discipline. It seems desirable, however, to exercise caution in using parental rejection and inconsistency as basic explanations of antisocial personalities. For one, these same conditions have been implicated in a wide range of later maladaptive behaviors. In addition, many children coming from such family backgrounds do not become antisocial personalities or evidence other serious psychopathology. Thus further explanation is needed.

Faulty parental models and family interactions. In an early study of 40 male antisocial personalities, Heaver (1943) emphasized the influence exerted by faulty parental models—typically a mother who overindulged her son and a father who was highly successful, driving, critical, and distant.

Greenacre (1945) added a number of details that have been supported by later studies of antisocial individuals from middle-class families. The father is typically a successful and respected member of the community and is distant and fear inspiring to his children. The mother, on the other hand, is indulgent, pleasure loving, frivolous, and often tacitly contemptuous of her husband's importance. When such families are heavily dependent on the approval and admiration of their communities—as in the case of some clergy and politicians—it is crucial that they maintain the illusion of a happy family by concealing and denying any evidence of bickering or scandal. Thus the children learn that appearances are more important than reality, and they, too, become part of the show-window display, where a premium is put on charm and impressing others rather than on competence and integrity. This need to please and to win social approval for their parents' sake seems to bring out a precocious but superficial charm in some of these children, together with great adroitness in handling people for purely selfish ends.

A son in such a family cannot hope to emulate his successful and awe-inspiring father, but, aware that the high evaluation that is placed on his father extends to himself, he develops a feeling of importance and of being exempt from the consequences of his actions. Frequently the prominence of the father does, in fact, protect the child from the ordinary consequences of antisocial behavior. If we add one additional factor—the contradictory influence of a father who tells his son of the necessity for responsibility, honesty, and respect for others, but who himself is deceitful and manipulative—we appear to have a family background capable of producing a middle-class antisocial personality.

Supporting this explanation is Hare's (1970) finding of a high incidence of psychopathic personalities—particularly fathers—in the families of children who later manifest such behavior themselves. In this context, Hare concluded that "at least part of a psychopath's behavior results from modeling another individual's psychopathic behavior" (p. 107).

The intermittent reinforcement of short-term gains and success in avoiding punishment also make the antisocial life-style especially resistant to change. With relative freedom from anxiety, guilt, and remorse, little motivation exists to learn different patterns.

Sociocultural Factors Antisocial personality is thought to be more common in lower socioeconomic groups. Although we have emphasized the part played by constitutional and family factors, it appears that social conditions such as those found in our urban ghettos also produce their share of antisocial individuals. An environment characterized by the breakdown of social norms and regulations,

An environment characterized by the breakdown of social norms, disorganization, undesirable peer models, and alienation may produce antisocial personalities.

disorganization, undesirable peer models, and pervasive alienation from and hostility toward the broader society seems to produce inadequate conscience development, lack of concern for others, and destructive behavior. On a family level, the picture is often aggravated by broken homes, parental rejection, and inconsistent discipline. These family situations lead to distrust, a confused sense of personal identity, self-devaluation, and feelings of hurt and hostility. The end result may be overtly aggressive behavior, directed especially at the representatives of "conventional" society.

In one high school in a disadvantaged area, two youths held a teacher while a third poured gasoline over him and set him on fire. Fortunately, another teacher came to the rescue and was able to extinguish the flames before the teacher was seriously burned. The youths were apprehended and detained in a juvenile facility because they were under 18 years of age. Interviewed by a social worker, they showed no remorse for their act, did not consider it wrong, and were disappointed that they had not succeeded in killing the teacher. The youths were not in any of his classes, nor did they know him personally. The apparent leader of the group stated that "Next time we'll do it right, so there won't be nobody left around to identify us."

Melges and Bowlby (1969) have pointed out that such individuals believe other people cannot be counted on and see their own futures as out of their hands. In essence, they feel helpless and hopeless—as well as resentful and hostile—in relation to their aversive life situations. Seeing no possible way they can make it, they lash out to make others suffer too.

Another possible explanation for the development of an antisocial personality has been suggested by Smith (1978). Smith believes that antisocial orientations are encouraged and rewarded by the materialistic, competitive, marketplace values of our capitalistic society. Antisocial individuals, he feels, simply carry these prevalent tendencies to extremes. While this view offers a plausible explanation for some typically antisocial behaviors, such as manipulativeness, superficial charm, and concern only for outward appearances, it does not seem sufficient to explain the extreme lawlessness and destructive behaviors that also accompany this disorder.

Although some cultural groups appear to have a relatively high rate of antisocial personality among their members, others have relatively low rates. Among the Hutterites, members of a relatively isolated religious sect who live on large communal farms in the Midwest, there is a negligible incidence of antisocial personality disorder. Perhaps the close-knit social structure with its strong emphasis on traditional values punishes or fails to reinforce the expression of antisocial behaviors. In addition, the adults to whom this group's children are exposed during their early development provide nonpsychopathic role models. The low rate of antisocial disorders among the Hutterites may also result from a natural selection process in which individuals who have deviant social characteristics leave the group so that neither they nor their offspring contribute to the statistics.

In summary, antisocial personalities are a mixed group of individuals who nevertheless have certain characteristics in common. Although the causal factors are not clear and may differ from case to case, varying combinations of biological, psychosocial, and sociocultural factors appear to be involved.

Treatments and Outcomes in Antisocial Personality

Because most individuals with antisocial personalities do not exhibit obvious psychopathology and can function effectively in many respects, they seldom come to the attention of mental hospitals or clinics. Those who run afoul of the law may participate in rehabilitation programs in penal institutions, but usually they are not changed by them. Even if more and better therapeutic facilities were available, effective treatment would still be a challenging task.

In general, traditional psychotherapeutic approaches have not proven effective in altering antisocial personalities. For example, in a treatment program for opiate addicts, those individuals with diagnosed personality disorders were the most difficult to treat and had the most negative outcomes—that is, they got worse or failed to improve (Woody et al., 1985). Factors inherent in antisocial individuals' personalities—the inability to trust, to feel as others do, to fantasize, and to learn from experience—apparently make the prognosis for psychotherapy very poor (Charney, 1979). Nor have biological treatment measures for psychopathic personalities—including electroconvulsive therapy or drugs—fared any better.

Perhaps the most promising treatment approach for antisocial personalities is behavioral therapy. Behavioral therapists have dealt successfully with specific antisocial behaviors, and their techniques appear to offer promise of more effective treatment (Bandura, 1969; Sutker, Archer, & Kilpatrick, 1979).

On the basis of a now-classic review of research findings, Bandura (1969) suggested three steps that can be used to modify antisocial behavior through the application of learning principles: (a) the withdrawal of meaningful reinforcements for antisocial behavior, and, where appropriate, the use of punishment for such behavior; (b) the modeling of desired behavior by *change agents*—the therapist and other behavioral models who are admired—and the use of a graded system of rewards or reinforcers for imitating such behavior; and (c) the reduction of material incentives and rewards as the individual's behavior is increasingly brought under the control of self-administered, symbolic rewards. Essentially, the objective is to effect the gradual transfer of evaluative and reinforcement functions from the environment to the antisocial individual by helping him or her develop inner controls that minimize the need for external ones.

An important facet of this approach is providing situations in which one individual's improved behavior becomes a model for others in treatment. Patients can thus function as change agents for each other while furthering the long-range modification of their own behaviors. Such a program requires a controlled situation in which the therapist can administer or withhold reinforcement and the individual cannot run away.

The necessity of having a controlled situation seems paramount for greater success in treatment. When treating antisocial behavior, we are dealing with a total life-style rather than with a specific maladaptive behavior, like a phobia, which can be targeted for treatment. Without a controlled situation, the intermittent reinforcement of short-term gains and successful avoidance of punishments, combined with a lack of anxiety and guilt, leave an antisocial individual with little motivation to change.

Vaillant (1975), for example, believes that antisocial individuals can be effectively treated *only* in settings where behavioral control is possible—in other words, treating sociopaths on an outpatient basis is doomed to failure. He has found control necessary, also, to prevent self-destructive behaviors and to overcome these individuals' fears of intimacy. Like other investigators, he has concluded that punishment is ineffective for controlling antisocial behavior and that severely antisocial individuals "should work for liberty, not pay for past mistakes."

Vaillant also pointed out that one-to-one therapeutic relationships (even meeting several times a week) were rarely adequate to change sociopathic behavior. What seemed to work best was group membership that provided both an opportunity to learn to care for others and a place to be accepted by peers.

Fortunately, many antisocial personalities improve after the age of 40 even without treatment, possibly because of weaker biological drives, better insight into their self-defeating behaviors, and the cumulative effects of social conditioning. Such individuals are often referred to as "burned-out psychopaths." Hare, McPherson, and Forth (1988) recently confirmed the hypothesis that antisocial individuals tend to burn out over time. They followed up a group of male antisocial personalities and tracked their criminal careers beyond age 40. They found a clear and dramatic reduction in criminal behavior after age 40. They were quick to note, however, that even with this reduction in criminal behavior, over 50 percent of these individuals continued being arrested after age 40. Even with the prospect that they might eventually engage in less destructive behavior, antisocial individuals can create a great deal of havoc before they reach 40—as well as afterward if they do not change. In view of the distress and unhappiness they inflict on others and the social damage they cause, it seems desirable—and more economical in the long run—to put increased effort into the development of effective treatment programs.

UNRESOLVED ISSUES on Axis II of DSM-III-R

While reading this chapter, you may have had some difficulty in capturing a clear, distinctive picture of each of the personality disorders. Possibly, as you studied the descriptions of the different disorders, the characteristics and attributes of some of them, say the schizoid personality disorder, seemed to blend with other conditions, such as the schizotypal or avoidant disorders. You certainly are not alone in this difficulty. Even expert clinicians often disagree and will arrive at different conclusions about an Axis II diagnosis on the same patient. In other words, Axis II diagnoses are considerably less reliable than diagnoses made for Axis I disorders.

Axis II diagnoses are unreliable for several reasons. One major difficulty lies in the classification process used in grouping the disorders. As noted in Chapter 1, some aspects of the diagnostic process are best thought of in terms of dimensions of behavior rather than categories of behavior. The personality processes classified on Axis II are dimensional in nature; that is, the data on which Axis II classifications are made are underlying personality traits that vary in individuals in terms of degree. For example, the trait of suspiciousness, central to paranoid personality disorder, can be viewed as a personality dimension on which essentially all people can be rated or given scores. The scores might range, on an illustrative "scale of suspiciousness," as follows:

Extremely Low		Low		Average		High		Extremely High		
0	10	20	30	40	50	60	70	80	90	100

It is rather arbitrary to take the presence of "suspiciousness" as a criterion of paranoid personality disorder since it exists, to some extent, as a trait in virtually everyone. No attempt is made in the DSM-III-R categorization to quantify this trait or provide a means of grading the degree of suspiciousness; instead, all traits are forced into discrete categories or types.

A second problem inherent in Axis II classifications involves the fact that traits that are highly correlated with other traits may be seen as symptoms and treated as though they are mutually exclusive behaviors for a personality disorder. However, the same or other correlated traits may be used in the classification of other, different diagnoses. For example, suspiciousness, a defining characteristic of paranoid personality, may be correlated with avoidance, which is a defining characteristic of avoidant personality disorder. The DSM-III-R personality disorders are thus not based on mutually exclusive criteria.

Both researchers and clinicians are somewhat dissatisfied with Axis II. This situation is due, in part, to the difficulties in applying the system and to its relative unreliability. Penna (1986), for example, called Axis II "one of the most unsatisfactory links in DSM-III." He concluded that the specificity of the criteria for disorders varies widely and results in low confidence in the application of some personality disorder categories. Moreover, in actual clinical practice, the multiaxial system is seldom applied to its fullest. While Axis I is usually recorded on patients' charts (because it is required for insurance and administrative purposes), other axes, including Axis II, are frequently omitted because their concepts are vague and because they are viewed as inessential to the immediate classification requirements.

The developers of DSM-III made an important theoretical leap when they recognized the importance of weighing premorbid personality factors in the clinical picture and thus developed the second axis. Practiced employment of the Axis II concepts can lead to a better understanding of a case, particularly with regard to treatment outcomes. Strong, ingrained personality characteristics can work against treatment interventions. The use of Axis II forces a clinician to attend to these long-standing and difficult-to-change personality factors in planning treatment.

What can be done to resolve the difficulties with Axis II? One possible solution involves the psychiatric community's giving up on the typological approach to classification in favor of a dimensional approach and developing rating methods that would take into account the relative "amounts" of given traits shown by patients. It is not likely, however, that the dimensional approach to personality measurement will supplant the present categorical system, because sound quantitative rating would likely involve far too much time for most busy clinicians to apply it. In addition, as we saw in Chapter 1, medically oriented practitioners have a pronounced preference for categorical diagnosis.

If the present categorical classification system continues to be used, a clearer set of classification rules is needed to make the categories more accurate and more mutually exclusive. The classification rules should be made more exhaustive and incorporate behaviors that do not overlap with other categories. Such an undertaking, while scientifically desirable, would doubtless be extremely difficult—perhaps, in the final analysis, impossible. There appear to be few if any "pure" clusters for grouping people's behaviors into the type of neat pigeonholes ideally required by the categorical approach.

In sum, the ultimate status of Axis II in future editions of the DSM is uncertain. Many problems inherent in using typological classes for essentially dimensional behavior (traits) have yet to be resolved. Whether Axis II will survive in its present form and remain an integral part of future diagnosis is, according to some predictions, open to debate.

SUMMARY

Personality disorders, in general, appear to be extreme or exaggerated patterns of personality traits that predispose an individual to troublesome behavior—often of an interpersonal nature. A number of personality disorders have been delineated in which there are persistent maladaptive patterns of perceiving, thinking, and relating to the environment. Three general clusters of personality disorders have been described. Individuals with paranoid, schizoid, and schizotypal personality disorders seem odd or eccentric; individuals with histrionic, narcissistic, antisocial, and borderline personality disorders share a common tendency to be dramatic, emotional, and erratic; and individuals with avoidant, dependent, obsessive-compulsive, and passive-aggressive personality disorders, unlike those with the previous disorders, show fearfulness or tension as in anxiety-based disorders. Two new and somewhat controversial personality disorders are listed for further study in the appendix of DSM-III-R: the self-defeating and sadistic personality disorders. The acceptability and utility of these disorders by practicing clinicians has not yet been determined. Each of these disorders reflect characteristics such as immaturity, self-centeredness, lack of feeling for others, manipulativeness, and a tendency to act out and to project blame for problems and frustrations onto others.

For many of the personality disorders, little research into causality has been conducted. One of the most notable of the personality disorders is the antisocial, or psychopathic, personality. In this disorder, an individual is callous and unethical, without loyalty or close relationships, but often with superficial charm and intelligence. Both constitutional and learning factors seem to be important in causing the disorder. Some evidence suggests that genetic factors may predispose an individual to develop this disorder. Unlike the anxiety-based disorders described in Chapter 6, an antisocial individual does not appear to experience anxiety. The disorder often begins and is recognized in childhood or adolescence, but only individuals who are 18 or over are given the diagnosis of antisocial personality.

Treatment of these individuals is difficult, because they rarely see any need for self-change and tend to blame other people for their problems. Traditional psychotherapy is typically ineffective, but where control is possible, as in institutional settings, newer methods incorporating meaningful reinforcement and behavioral modification have had some success.

Key Terms

personality (p. 263)
personality disorders (character disorders) (p. 263)
temperament (character traits) (p. 264)
paranoid personality disorder (p. 267)
schizoid personality disorder (p. 268)
schizotypal personality disorder (p. 269)
histrionic personality disorder (p. 270)
narcissistic personality disorder (p. 271)
antisocial personality disorder (p. 272)
borderline personality disorder (p. 273)
avoidant personality disorder (p. 274)
dependent personality disorder (p. 275)
obsessive-compulsive personality disorder (p. 276)
passive-aggressive personality disorder (p. 276)
self-defeating personality disorder (p. 277)
sadistic personality disorder (p. 278)
psychopathic personality (sociopathic personality) (p. 281)

Chapter 9

Substance-Use and Other Addictive Disorders

Guillaume Pujolle, *Les Aigles—La Plume d'Oie* (1940). Pujolle (1893–?) was born in the Haute-Garonne area in France. A joiner by trade, he was torn by emotional conflicts and was eventually admitted to a hospital in Toulouse. He began to draw in 1935. His pictures (such as the one here) have a dream-like, fluid appearance, composed as they are of a mosaic of broad, undulating strips of color.

Cambyses, King of Persia in the sixth century B.C., has the dubious distinction of being one of the first alcoholics on record. People of many other early cultures, including the Egyptian, Greek, and Roman, made extensive and often excessive use of alcohol. Beer was first made in Egypt around 3000 B.C. The oldest surviving wine-making formulas were recorded by Marcus Cato in Italy almost a century and a half before the birth of Christ. About 800 A.D., the process of distillation was developed by an Arabian alchemist, thus making possible an increase in both the range and the potency of alcoholic beverages.

Addictive behavior, behavior based on the pathological need for a substance or activity, may involve the abuse of substances, such as alcohol or cocaine, or the excessive ingestion of high-caloric food, resulting in extreme obesity. Addictive behavior is one of the most pervasive and intransigent mental health problems facing our society today. Addictive disorders represent disorders of self-control and can be seen all around us: in extremely high rates of alcoholism, in tragic exposés of cocaine abuse among star athletes and entertainers, and in reports of the "epidemic" proportions of eating disorders.

The most commonly used problem drugs are the **psychoactive drugs,** those drugs that affect mental functioning: alcohol, barbiturates, minor tranquilizers, amphetamines, heroin, and marijuana. Some of these drugs, such as alcohol, can be purchased legally by adults; others, such as the barbiturates, can be used legally under medical supervision; still others, such as heroin, are illegal.

The diagnostic classification of addictive or psychoactive substance-use disorders is divided into two major categories. First, psychoactive substance-induced organic mental disorders and syndromes (the latter of which are included within the organic mental disorders) are those conditions that involve *organic impairment* resulting from the ingestion of psychoactive substances. These conditions involve such factors as **toxicity,** the poisonous nature of the substance (leading to, for example, amphetamine delusional disorder, alcoholic intoxication, or cannabis delirium), or physiologic changes in the brain due to vitamin deficiency (resulting in, for example, alcohol disorder involving amnesia, also known as Korsakoff's syndrome).

A number of addictive disorders are covered in the second category, which focuses on the maladaptive *behaviors* resulting from regular and consistent use of a substance and includes psychoactive substance-abuse and -dependence disorders. This category is further subdivided into two general groups: substance abuse and substance dependence. **Psychoactive substance abuse** generally involves a pathological use of a substance resulting in potentially hazardous behavior, such as driving while intoxicated, or in continued use despite a persistent social, psychological, occupational, or health problem. **Psychoactive substance dependence** includes more severe forms of substance-use disorders and usually involves a physiological need for a substance. Dependence in these disorders means that an individual will show either **tolerance** for a drug or **withdrawal symptoms** when the drug is unavailable. (Tolerance refers to the need for increased amounts of a substance to achieve the desired effects; withdrawal symptoms are physical symptoms, such as sweating, tremors, and tension, that accompany abstinence from the drug.)

The increasing problem of substance abuse and dependence in our society has drawn both public and scientific attention. Although our present knowledge is far from complete, investigating these problems as maladaptive patterns of adjustment to life's demands, with no social stigma involved, has led to clear progress in understanding and treatment. Such an approach, of course, does not mean that an individual bears no personal responsibility in the development of a problem; the widespread notion that drug dependence and abuse can be viewed as forms of "disease" does not imply that the individual is a passive participant in the addiction process. Individual life-styles and personality features are thought by many to play important roles in the development of addictive disorders and are central themes in some types of treatment.

In addition to the abuse and dependence disorders that involve particular substances, there are disorders that have all the features of an addictive condition, such as excessive eating, but do not involve substances with chemically addicting properties (Orford, 1985). Two of these disorders, excessive overeating and pathological gambling, are discussed in this chapter because the maladaptive behaviors involved and the treatment approaches shown to be effective suggest that they are quite similar to the various drug-use and drug-induced disorders.

ALCOHOL ABUSE AND DEPENDENCE

The terms *alcoholic* and *alcoholism* have been subject to some controversy and are used differently by various groups. The World Health Organization, for instance, uses the term *alcoholic* to refer to any person with life problems related to alcohol. The National Council on Alcoholism, on the other hand, uses a more restrictive definition; certain diagnostic signs delineating the extent and severity of abuse must be present for an individual to be classified as an alcoholic. Some behavioral researchers recommend a still more restrictive definition; they prefer to use the term *problem drinker* for most alcohol abusers, conceptualizing drinking as a continuum, with alcoholics constituting a small subgroup at one extreme and nondrinkers at the other (Miller, 1979; Miller & Caddy, 1977). In this chapter we will use the definition of The President's Commission on Mental Health (1978), which uses the term **alcoholic** to refer to an individual with a serious drinking problem, whose drinking impairs his or her life adjustment in terms of health, personal relationships, and occupational functioning. Likewise, the term **alcoholism** refers to a dependence on alcohol that seriously interferes with life adjustment.

However defined, alcoholism is a major problem in the United States. Per capita alcohol consumption increased nearly 50 percent over the past generation (Heckler, 1983). Alcohol is the most commonly abused substance in the United States; approximately 7 percent of all adults age 18 or older, about 10 million people, are problem drinkers (Smith, 1989). Yet only about 1 million of these individuals currently receive treatment for their drinking problems.

The potentially detrimental effects of excessive alcohol use—for an individual, his or her loved ones, and society—are legion. The life span of the average alcoholic is about 12 years shorter than that of the average citizen, and alcohol now ranks as the third major cause of death in the United States, behind coronary heart disease and cancer. Over 37 percent of alcohol abusers suffer from at least one coexisting mental disorder (Rovner, 1990). Organic impairment, including brain shrinkage, occurs in a high proportion of alcoholics (Lishman, Jacobson, & Acker, 1987).

About 10 percent of alcoholics commit suicide (Miles, 1977), and over 18 percent are found to

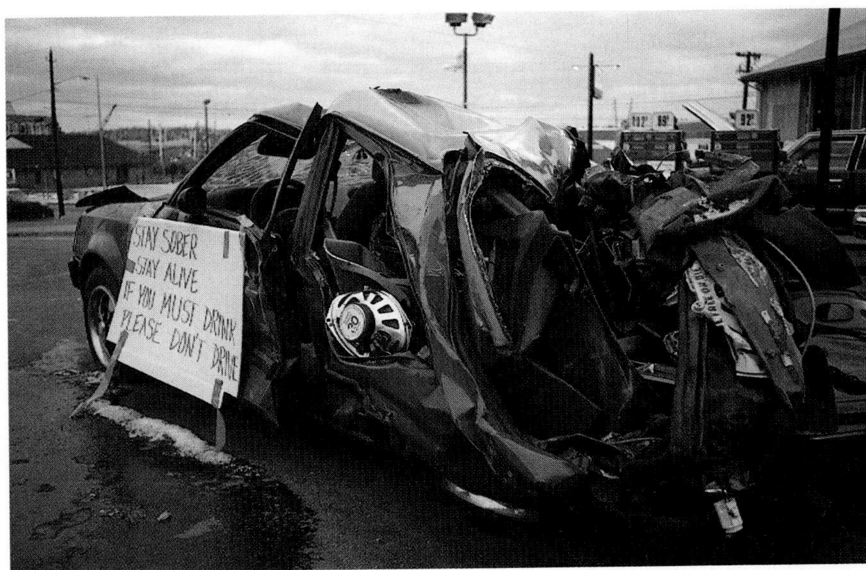

Alcohol is associated with over half of the deaths and serious injuries suffered in automobile accidents in the United States each year.

have a history of suicide attempts (Black et al., 1986). Recent research (Murphy, 1988; Rich et al., 1988) has reaffirmed the strong relationship found between substance abuse and suicide. The increased suicide rates among the young during the 1970s and 1980s have been tied to alcohol and drug abuse. Gomberg (1989) reported that, of women experiencing psychological difficulties, a significantly higher percentage with alcohol problems (40%) had attempted suicide than had women without alcohol problems (8.8%). In a follow-up study of mortality in psychiatric outpatients, Martin et al. (1985) found that alcoholics were in the group of disorders with highest mortality rates. Bengelsdorf (1970a) has pointed out that ". . . its abuse has killed more people, sent more victims to hospitals, generated more police arrests, broken up more marriages and homes, and cost industry more money than has the abuse of heroin, amphetamines, barbiturates, and marijuana combined" (p. 7).

In addition to the serious problems they create for themselves, excessive drinkers pose serious difficulties for others. About 10 percent of all deaths each year are related to alcohol abuse (Smith, 1989). Alcohol abuse is associated with over half the deaths and major injuries suffered in automobile accidents each year, and with about 50 percent of all murders, 40 percent of all assaults, 35 percent or more of all rapes, and 30 percent of all suicides. About one out of every three arrests in the United States are related to alcohol abuse. Alcohol-related accidents are, in fact, the leading cause of death among college-age people (NIDA, 1981). The financial drain imposed on the economy by alcoholism is estimated to be over $49.4 billion a year, in large part composed of losses to industry from absenteeism, lowered work efficiency, accidents, and the costs involved in the treatment of alcoholics. Alcohol use has also been found to play a role in victimization. A recent study showed that 46 percent of homicide victims in the city of Los Angeles had detectable blood-alcohol levels, and in 30 percent of the victims, the count of alcohol in their blood qualified them as legally drunk (Goodman et al., 1986). The authors hypothesized that alcohol could increase the likelihood of risk taking and could result in provocative behavior on the victim's part. In a follow-up study of alcoholics, Polich, Armor, and Braiker (1981) found that 14.5 percent of their subjects had died during the 4½-year period since the study began. These deaths were attributed to alcohol-related conditions, such as cirrhosis, suicide, gastrointestinal hemorrhage, and automobile accidents.

Alcoholism in the United States cuts across all age, educational, occupational, and socioeconomic boundaries. It is considered a serious problem in industry, in the professions, and in the military; it is found among such seemingly unlikely candidates as priests, airline pilots, politicians, surgeons, law enforcement officers, and teenagers. The once popular image of the alcoholic as an unkempt resident of skid row is clearly inaccurate. Further myths about alcoholism are noted in *HIGHLIGHT 9.1.*

The great majority of problem drinkers are men and women who are married and living with their families, who hold jobs—often important ones—and who are accepted members of their communities. Although alcoholism has traditionally been considered to be more common among males than females, alcohol abuse among women appears to be

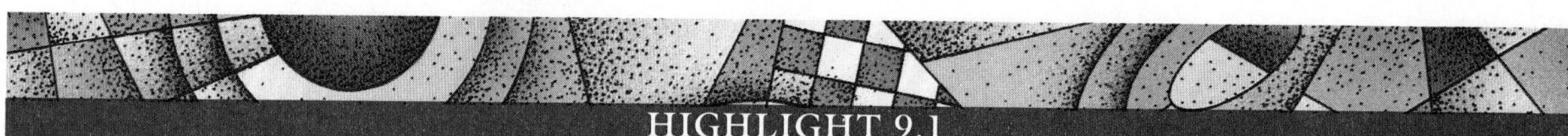

HIGHLIGHT 9.1

Some Common Misconceptions About Alcohol and Alcoholism

Fiction	Fact
Alcohol is a stimulant.	Alcohol is actually a nervous system depressant.
You can always detect alcohol on the breath of a person who has been drinking.	It is not always possible to detect the presence of alcohol. Some individuals successfully cover up their alcohol use for years.
One ounce of 86-proof liquor contains more alcohol than two 12-ounce cans of beer.	Actually two 12-ounce cans of beer contain *more* than an ounce of alcohol.
Alcohol can help a person sleep more soundly.	Alcohol may actually interfere with sound sleep.
Impaired judgment does not occur before there are obvious signs of intoxication.	In fact, impaired judgment can occur long before motor signs of intoxication are apparent.
An individual will get more intoxicated by mixing liquors than by taking comparable amounts of one kind—e.g., bourbon, Scotch, or vodka.	It is the actual amount of alcohol in the bloodstream rather than the mix that determines intoxication.
Drinking several cups of coffee can counteract the effects of alcohol and enable a drinker to "sober up."	Drinking coffee does not affect the level of intoxication.
Exercise or a cold shower helps speed up the metabolism of alcohol.	Exercise and cold showers are futile attempts to increase alcohol metabolism.
People with "strong wills" need not be concerned about becoming alcoholics.	Alcohol is seductive and can lower the resistance of even the "strongest will."
Alcohol cannot produce a true addiction in the same sense that heroin can.	Alcohol has strong addictive properties.
One cannot become an alcoholic by drinking just beer.	One can consume a considerable amount of alcohol by drinking beer. It is, of course, the amount of alcohol that determines whether one becomes an alcoholic.
Alcohol is far less dangerous than marijuana.	There are considerably more individuals in treatment programs for alcohol problems than for marijuana abuse.
In a heavy drinker, damage to the liver shows up long before brain damage appears.	Heavy alcohol use can be manifested in organic brain damage before liver damage is detected.
The physiological withdrawal reaction from heroin is considered more dangerous than is withdrawal from alcohol.	The physiological symptoms accompanying withdrawal from heroin are no more frightening or traumatic to an individual than alcohol withdrawal.

growing. The commonly used incidence figure of 5 males to 1 female is considered a conservative estimate (Smith, 1989). A survey by Celentano and McQueen (1978) showed that of 81 percent of the men who drank alcohol, 26 percent considered themselves heavy drinkers; of 68 percent of the women who drank, 8 percent considered themselves heavy drinkers. It appears, too, that problem drinking may develop during any life period from early childhood through old age. Mann, Chassin, and Sher (in press) report that 64.9 percent of their sample of high school students indicated a moderate use of alcohol and 18.8 percent of these reported a misuse of alcohol. Some evidence also indicates that the rates of alcoholism among rural populations, particularly rural blacks, is higher than among urban dwellers. Blazer, Crowell, and George (1987) recently conducted an epidemiological survey showing that adults living in rural communities disclosed almost twice as many alcohol-related problems as a matched sample of urban residents.

The Clinical Picture of Alcohol Abuse and Dependence

The Roman poet Horace, in the first century B.C., wrote lyrically about the effects of wine: "It discloses secrets; ratifies and confirms our hopes; thrusts the coward forth to battle; eases the anxious mind of its burthen; instructs in arts. Whom has not a cheerful glass made eloquent! Whom not quite free and easy from pinching poverty!" Unfortunately, the effects of alcohol are not always so benign or beneficial. According to a Japanese proverb, "First the man takes a drink, then the drink takes a drink, and then the drink takes the man."

Alcohol is a depressant that affects the higher brain centers, impairing judgment and other rational processes and lowering self-control. As behavioral restraints decline, a drinker may indulge in the satisfaction of impulses ordinarily held in check. Some degree of motor incoordination soon becomes apparent, and the drinker's discrimination and perception of cold, pain, and other discomforts are dulled. Typically the drinker experiences a sense of warmth, expansiveness, and well-being. In such a mood, unpleasant realities are screened out and the drinker's feelings of self-esteem and adequacy rise. Casual acquaintances become the best and most understanding of friends, and the drinker enters a generally pleasant world of unreality in which worries are temporarily left behind.

When the alcohol content of the bloodstream reaches 0.1 percent, the individual is considered to be intoxicated. Muscular coordination, speech, and vision are impaired, and thought processes are confused. Even before this level of intoxication is reached, however, judgment becomes impaired to such an extent that the person misjudges his or her condition. For example, drinkers tend to express confidence in their ability to drive safely long after such actions are in fact quite unsafe. Although it differs somewhat between individuals, when the blood-alcohol level reaches approximately 0.5 percent, the entire neural balance is upset and the individual passes out. Unconsciousness apparently acts as a safety device, because concentrations above 0.55 percent are usually lethal. *HIGHLIGHT 9.2* provides additional information on alcohol levels in the blood and their effects on individual behavior.

In general, it is the amount of alcohol actually concentrated in the bodily fluids, not the amount consumed, that determines intoxication. The effects of alcohol, however, vary for different drinkers, depending on physical condition, gender, amount of food in the stomach, and duration of the drinking. In addition, alcohol users may gradually build up a tolerance for the drug so that ever-increasing amounts may be needed to produce the desired effects. Drinkers' attitudes are important, too: although actual motor and intellectual abilities decline in direct ratio to the blood concentration of alcohol, many people who consciously try to do so can maintain ***apparent*** control over their behavior, showing few outward signs of being intoxicated even after drinking relatively large amounts of alcohol.

Exactly how alcohol works on the brain is not yet fully understood, but several physiological effects are common. One is a tendency toward increased sexual stimulation but, simultaneously, lowered sexual performance. As Shakespeare wrote in ***Macbeth,*** alcohol "provokes the desire, but it takes away the performance."

Second, an appreciable number of problem drinkers also experience blackouts—lapses of memory. At first these occur at high blood-alcohol levels, and individuals may carry on rational conversations and engage in other relatively complex activities but have no trace of recall the next day. For heavy drinkers, even moderate drinking can elicit memory lapses.

A third curious phenomenon associated with alcoholic intoxication is the hangover, which many drinkers experience at one time or another. Some

Drinkers' attitudes can influence the effects of alcohol. At BARLAB, a mock bar used as part of a University of Washington class, students feel and act drunk even though they are unknowingly drinking beer that does not contain alcohol.

HIGHLIGHT 9.2

Alcohol Levels in the Blood After Drinks Taken on an Empty Stomach by a 150-pound Male Drinking for One Hour

Effects	Time for Alcohol to Leave the Body (Hours)	Alcohol Concentration in Blood (Percent)	Amount of Beverage
Slight changes in feeling	1	0.03	1 highball (1½ oz. whiskey) *or* 1 cocktail (1½ oz. whiskey) *or* 5½ oz. ordinary wine *or* 1 bottle beer (12 oz.)
Feeling of warmth, mental relaxation	2	0.06	2 highballs *or* 2 cocktails *or* 11 oz. ordinary wine *or* 2 bottles beer
Exaggerated emotion and behavior—talkative, noisy, or morose	4	0.07	3 highballs *or* 3 cocktails *or* 16½ oz. ordinary wine *or* 4 bottles beer
Clumsiness—unsteadiness in standing or walking	6	0.12	4 highballs *or* 4 cocktails *or* 22 oz. ordinary wine *or* 6 bottles beer
Gross intoxication	10	0.15	5 highballs *or* 5 cocktails *or* 27½ oz ordinary wine *or* ½ pint whiskey

Calories

5½ oz. wine	115
12 oz. beer	170
1½ oz. whisky	120

Note: Blood-alcohol level following given intake differs according to a person's weight, the length of the drinking time, and the person's sex.

Time, April 22, 1974, p. 77.

observers consider the hangover to be a mild form of withdrawal. As yet, no one has come up with a satisfactory explanation or remedy for the symptoms of headache, nausea, and fatigue characteristic of the hangover.

Development of Alcohol Dependence Excessive drinking can be viewed as progressing insidiously from early- to middle- to late-stage alcoholism, although some alcoholics do not follow this progressively developing pattern. (*HIGHLIGHT 9.3* presents some of the common early warning signs of excessive drinking.) Alcohol dependence is reached when symptoms of alcohol tolerance or alcohol withdrawal can be identified. Some investigators view alcohol dependence as recognizable through a number of related symptoms of alcohol use. In their extensive study of the "natural course of alcoholism," Polich et al. (1981) evaluated the presence of alcohol-dependence symptoms among drinkers in their sample of identified alcoholics and found the following percentages of individuals reporting the occurrence of certain symptoms in a 30-day period:

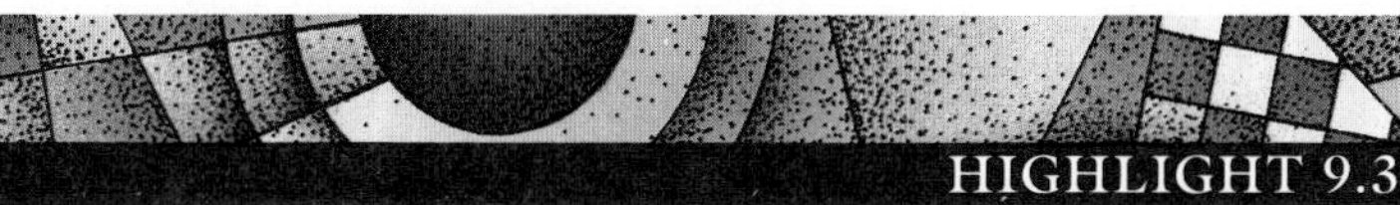

HIGHLIGHT 9.3

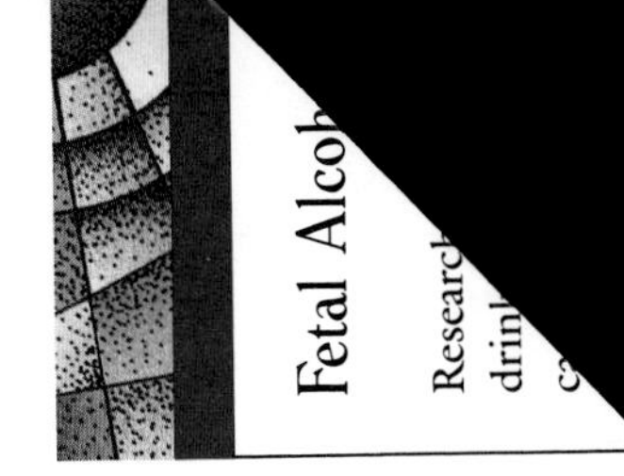

Early Warning Signs of Drinking Problems

1. *Frequent desire*—increase in desire, often evidenced by eager anticipation of drinking after work and careful attention to maintaining supply.
2. *Increased consumption*—increase that seems gradual but is marked from month to month. An individual may begin to worry at this point and lie about the amount consume
3. *Extreme behavior*— mission of various that leave an indivi feeling guilty and en rassed the next day.
4. *"Pulling blanks"*—in ity to remember what pened during an alcol bout.
5. *Morning drinking*—either as a means of reduc-

spouse, job situation, or sociocultural setting.

- Tremors (had the "shakes") 31
- Morning drinking (had a drink as soon as they woke up) 41
- Loss of control (tried to stop drinking but couldn't) 32
- Blackouts (memory lapses) 29
- Missing meals (missed a meal because of drinking) 42
- Continuous drinking (12 hours or more) 37
- One or more of the above symptoms 64

The researchers concluded that these secondary symptoms of dependence could not be viewed as isolated events but rather as related problems.

Chronic Alcohol Use and Dependence

Although many investigators have maintained that alcohol is a dangerous systemic poison even in small amounts, in moderate amounts it is not harmful to most people and may actually be beneficial to reduce the tensions of everyday life (HEW, 1974). For pregnant women, however, even moderate amounts are believed to be dangerous; in fact, no safe level has been established, as is discussed in *HIGHLIGHT 9.4*.

For individuals who drink immoderately, the clinical picture is highly unfavorable. For one, the alcohol that is taken in must be assimilated by the body, except for about 5 to 10 percent that is eliminated through breath, urine, and perspiration. The work of assimilation is done by the liver, but when large amounts of alcohol are ingested, the liver may be seriously overworked and eventually suffer irreversible damage. In fact, over time, an excessive drinker has a 1-in-10 chance of developing cirrhosis of the liver, a pathological condition in which liver cells are irreparably damaged and replaced by fibrous scar tissue. This results in the death of over 63,000 people each year (Smith, 1989).

Alcohol is also a high-calorie drug. A pint of whiskey—enough to make about 8 to 10 ordinary cocktails—provides about 1200 calories, which is approximately half the ordinary caloric requirement for a day. Thus consumption of alcohol reduces a drinker's appetite for other food. Because alcohol has no nutritional value, the excessive drinker often suffers from malnutrition. Furthermore, heavy drinking impairs the body's ability to utilize nutrients, so the nutritional deficiency cannot be made up by popping vitamins. The excessive intake of alcohol also impairs the activity of the white blood cells in fighting disease and is associated with a greatly increased risk of cancer (HEW, 1974).

In addition to the other problems, an excessive drinker usually suffers from chronic fatigue, oversensitivity, and depression. Initially, alcohol may seem to provide a useful crutch for dealing with the stresses of life, especially during periods of acute stress, by helping screen out intolerable realities and enhancing the drinker's feelings of adequacy and worth. The excessive use of alcohol becomes counterproductive, however, resulting in lowered feelings of adequacy and worth, impaired reasoning and judgment, and gradual personality deterioration. Behavior typically becomes coarse and inappropriate, and the drinker assumes increasingly less responsibility, loses pride in personal appearance, neglects spouse and family, and becomes generally

HIGHLIGHT 9.4

ol Syndrome: How Much Drinking Is Too Much?

indicates that heavy king by expectant mothers n affect the health of unborn babies. Newborn infants whose mothers drank heavily during pregnancy have been found to have frequent physical and behavioral abnormalities. For example, such infants are lighter and smaller than average and sometimes show facial and limb irregularities (Jones & Smith, 1975; NIMH, 1978a; Jones, Smith, & Hansen, 1976; and Streissguth, 1976). In fact, *The Third Report on Alcohol and Health* (HEW, 1978) reports that alcohol abuse in pregnant women is the third-leading cause of birth defects (the first two being Down syndrome and spina bifida, the latter referring to the incomplete formation and fusion of the spinal canal).

How much drinking endangers a newborn's health? The HEW report warns against drinking more than one ounce of alcohol per day or the equivalent (two 12-ounce cans of beer or two 5-ounce glasses of wine, for example). The actual amount of alcohol that can safely be ingested during pregnancy is not known, but it is clear that existing evidence for fetal alcohol syndrome is strongest when applied to heavy alcohol users rather than light to moderate users (Kolata, 1981b). Nonetheless, the American Medical Association (1982) has approved a report recommending that pregnant women abstain from using alcohol as the "safest course" until safe amounts of alcohol consumption can be determined.

touchy, irritable, and unwilling to discuss the problem.

As judgment becomes impaired, an excessive drinker may be unable to hold a job and generally becomes unqualified to cope with new demands that arise. General personality disorganization and deterioration may be reflected in loss of employment and marital breakup. By this time, the drinker's general health is likely to have deteriorated, and brain and liver damage may have occurred. For example, Golden et al. (1981) found significant structural changes in the left hemisphere of the brains of chronic alcoholics. Lishman (1990) indicated that evidence is beginning to show that an alcoholic's brain could be accumulating diffuse organic damage—even in cases in which no extreme organic symptoms are evident. Goldman, Williams, and Klisz (1983) found that alcoholics over age 40 failed to recover from visual-spatial brain dysfunction as readily as did younger alcoholics, and they were less able to compensate for impairments. Svanum and Schladenhauffen (1986) found extensive alcohol consumption to be associated with an increased amount of neurological deficit in later life.

Psychoses Associated with Alcoholism Several acute psychotic reactions fit the diagnostic classification of substance-induced disorders. These reactions may develop in individuals who have been drinking excessively over long periods of time or who have a reduced tolerance for alcohol for other reasons—for example, because of brain lesions. Such acute reactions usually last only a short time and generally consist of confusion, excitement, and delirium. They are often called alcoholic psychoses because they are marked by a temporary loss of contact with reality. Two commonly recognized psychotic reactions will be briefly described.

Among those who drink excessively for a long time, a reaction known as ***alcohol withdrawal delirium*** (formerly known as ***delirium tremens***) may occur. This reaction can happen during a prolonged drinking spree or on the withdrawal of alcohol after prolonged drinking. The delirium usually is preceded by a period of restlessness and insomnia during which a person may feel generally uneasy and apprehensive. Slight noises or sudden moving objects may cause considerable excitement and agitation. The full-blown symptoms include (a) disorientation for time and place in which, for example, a person may mistake the hospital for a church or jail, no longer recognize friends, or identify hospital attendants as old acquaintances; (b) vivid hallucinations, particularly of small, fast-moving animals like snakes, rats, and roaches, which are clearly localized in space; (c) acute fear, in which these animals may change in form, size, or color in terrifying ways; (d) extreme suggestibility, in which a person can be made to see almost any animal if its presence is

The effects of fetal alcohol syndrome can be both dramatic and long-lasting. This child suffers from permanent physical abnormalities because his mother drank alcohol while pregnant.

The subject was broug
psychiatric ward of a general h
fired his shotgun at 3:30 A.M.
repel an invasion of cockroache
he was confused and disorient
ing hallucinations involving "
lions" of invading cockroaches. He leaped from his bed and cowered in terror against the wall, screaming for help and kicking and hitting frantically at his imaginary assailants. When an attendant came to his aid, he screamed for him to get back out of danger or he would be killed too. Before the attendant could reach him, he dived headlong on his head, apparently trying to kill himself.

The subject's delirium lasted for 3½ days, after which he returned to a state of apparent normality, apologized profusely for the trouble he had caused everyone, stated he would never touch another drop, and was discharged. On his way home, however, he stopped at a bar, had too much to drink, and on emerging from the bar, collapsed on the street. This time he sobered up in jail, again apologized for the trouble he had caused, and, extremely remorseful, was released with a small fine. What happened to him beyond that time is unknown.

merely suggested; (e) marked tremors of the hands, tongue, and lips; and (f) other symptoms, including perspiration, fever, a rapid and weak heartbeat, a coated tongue, and foul breath.

The delirium typically lasts from three to six days and is generally followed by a deep sleep. When a person awakens, few symptoms—aside from possible slight remorse—remain, but frequently the individual is badly scared and may not resume drinking for several weeks or months. Usually, however, drinking is eventually resumed, followed by a return to the hospital with a new attack. The death rate from withdrawal delirium as a result of convulsions, heart failure, and other complications once approximated 10 percent (Tavel, 1962). With newer drugs such as chlordiazepoxide, however, the current death rate during withdrawal delirium and acute alcoholic withdrawal has been markedly reduced. The following is a brief description of a 43-year-old male withdrawal delirium patient:

A second alcohol-related psychosis is the disorder referred to as ***alcohol amnestic disorder*** (formerly known as *Korsakoff's psychosis*). This condition was first described by the Russian psychiatrist Korsakoff in 1887. The outstanding symptom is a memory defect (particularly with regard to recent events), which is sometimes accompanied by falsification of events (confabulation). Individuals with this disorder may not recognize pictures, faces, rooms, and other objects that they have just seen, although they may feel that these people or objects are familiar. Such people increasingly tend to fill in their memory gaps with reminiscences and fanciful tales that lead to unconnected and distorted associations. These individuals may appear to be delirious, delusional, and disoriented for time and place, but ordinarily their confusion and disordered actions are closely related to their attempts to fill in memory gaps. The memory disturbance itself seems related to an inability to form new associations in a manner that renders them readily retrievable. Such a reaction usually occurs in older alcoholics, after many years of excessive drinking.

The symptoms of this disorder are now thought to be due to vitamin B (thiamine) deficiency and f dietary inadequacies. Although it has been nerally believed that a diet rich in vitamins and minerals generally restores a patient to more normal physical and mental health, recent evidence suggests otherwise. Lishman (1990) reported that Korsakoff's psychosis did not respond well to thiamine replacement. Some memory functioning appears to be restored with prolonged abstinence. However, some personality deterioration usually remains in the form of memory impairment, blunted intellectual capacity, and lowered moral and ethical standards.

Recently, the American Public Health Association *(The Nation's Health,* 1986) has proposed that vitamin B be added to all alcoholic beverages to prevent these deficiencies. Concentrations of thiamine to prevent malnutrition would not adversely affect the taste or the appearance of alcoholic beverages yet would help prevent the occurrence of alcohol amnestic disorder. Whether this measure will eventually be approved is uncertain.

Alcohol abuse knows no age, educational, occupational, or socioeconomic boundaries. Bill Shoemaker's outstanding career as a jockey—with the most wins in horse-racing history—ended with an automobile accident that left him paralyzed. Shoemaker was alone in the car and driving drunk.

Causes of Alcohol Abuse and Dependence

In trying to identify the causes of problem drinking, some researchers have stressed the role of genetic and biochemical factors; others have pointed to psychosocial factors, viewing problem drinking as a maladaptive pattern of adjustment to the stress of life; still others have emphasized sociocultural factors, such as the availability of alcohol and social approval of excessive drinking. As with most other forms of maladaptive behavior, it appears that there may be several types of alcohol dependence, each with somewhat different patterns of biological, psychosocial, and sociocultural causal factors. Recently, a committee of experts from the National Academy of Sciences (Institute of Medicine, 1990) concluded that identifying a single cause for all types of alcohol problems is unlikely.

Biological Factors In an alcohol-dependent person, cell metabolism has adapted itself to the presence of alcohol in the bloodstream and now demands it for stability. When the alcohol in the bloodstream falls below a certain level, withdrawal symptoms occur. These symptoms may be relatively mild—involving a craving for alcohol, tremors, perspiration, and weakness—or more severe—with nausea, vomiting, fever, rapid heartbeat, convulsions, and hallucinations. The shortcut to ending them is to take another drink. Once this point is reached, each drink serves to reinforce alcohol-seeking behavior because it reduces the unpleasant symptoms. An unusual craving could result from a genetic vulnerability. The possibility of a genetic predisposition to developing alcohol-abuse problems has been widely researched. Cotton (1979)—in a review of 39 studies of families of 6251 alcoholics and 4083 nonalcoholics who had been followed over 40 years—reported that almost one third of alcoholics had at least one parent with an alcohol problem. More recently, a study of children of alcoholics by Cloninger et al. (1986) reported strong evidence for the inheritance of alcoholism. They found that, for males, having one alcoholic parent increased the rate of alcoholism from 11.4 percent to 29.5 percent, and having two alcoholic parents increased the rate to 41.2 percent. For females with no alcoholic parents, the rate was 5.0 percent; for those with one alcoholic parent, the rate was 9.5 percent; and for those with two alcoholic parents, it was 25.0 percent. However, it should be kept in mind that the majority of individuals in the study did not have alcoholic parents. Also, such studies do not rule out environmental influences, such as modeling.

An interesting problem for researchers in the search for causal factors in substance abuse is how to determine if the behavior being investigated is antecedent to the drinking or caused by the drinking itself. One approach to understanding the precursors to alcoholism is to study the behavior of individuals who are at high risk for substance abuse but who are not yet affected by alcohol—prealcoholic personalities. An alcohol-risk personality has been described by Finn (1990) as an individual (usually an alcoholic's child) who has an inherited predisposition toward alcohol abuse and who is impulsive, prefers taking high risks, is emotionally unstable, has difficulty planning and organizing behavior, has problems in predicting the consequences of his or her actions, has many psychological problems, finds that alcohol is helpful in coping with stress, does not experience hangovers, and finds alcohol rewarding.

Research has shown that prealcoholic men show different physiological patterns than nonalcoholic men in several respects. Prealcoholic men are more sensitive to stress-response dampening (lessened experience of stress) with alcohol ingestion than nonalcoholic men (Finn & Pihl, 1987; Finn, Zeitouni, & Pihl, 1990). They also show different alpha wave patterns on EEG (Stewart, Finn, & Pihl, 1990). Prealcoholic men as defined by the personality characteristics described in the preceding paragraph were found to show larger conditioned physiological responses to alcohol cues than were individuals who were considered at a low risk for alcoholism, according to Earlywine and Finn (1990). These results suggest that prealcoholic men may be more prone to develop tolerance for alcohol than low risk men.

In support of possible genetic factors in alcoholism, some research has suggested that certain ethnic groups, particularly Orientals and American Indians, have abnormal physiological reactions to alcohol. Fenna et al. (1971) and Wolff (1972) found that Oriental and Eskimo subjects showed a hypersensitive reaction, including flushing of the skin, a drop in blood pressure, and nausea, following the ingestion of alcohol. The relatively lower rates of alcoholism among Oriental groups are tentatively considered to be related to a faster metabolism. Schaefer (1977, 1978), however, questioned these and other metabolism studies as a basis for interpreting cultural differences in alcoholism rates. Using more explicit criteria of metabolism rate, he found no differences in alcohol metabolism between a group of Reddis Indians and a group of northern European subjects. He concluded that further research into metabolism rate differences and sensitivity to alcohol needs to be integrated with studies focusing on relative stress in various cultures.

The role genetics play in the development of alcoholism remains unclear. We will return to this topic in the Unresolved Issues section at the end of the chapter.

Psychosocial Factors Not only do alcoholics become physiologically dependent on alcohol, they develop a powerful psychological dependence as well. Because excessive drinking is so destructive to an individual's total life adjustment, the question arises as to why psychological dependence is learned. A number of psychosocial factors have been advanced as possible answers.

Psychological vulnerability. Is there an "alcoholic personality"—a type of character organization that predisposes a given individual to turn to the use of alcohol rather than to some other defensive pattern of coping with stress? In efforts to answer this question, investigators have reported that potential alcoholics tend to be emotionally immature, to expect a great deal of the world, to require an inordinate amount of praise and appreciation, to react to failure with marked feelings of hurt and inferiority, to have low frustration tolerance, and to feel inadequate and unsure of their abilities to fulfill expected male or female roles. Morey, Skinner, and Blashfield (1984) have shown that individuals at high risk for alcoholism development were significantly different in personality, especially in terms of showing more impulsivity and aggression, from those at low risk for abusing alcohol.

The two psychopathological conditions that have been most frequently linked to addictive disorders are depression (Lutz & Snow, 1985; Weissman et al., 1977; Woodruff et al., 1973) and antisocial personality (Cadoret et al., 1985; Seixas & Cadoret, 1974; Stabenau, 1984). By far, most of the research has related antisocial personality and addictive disorders, with about 75 to 80 percent of the studies showing an association between the two (Alterman, 1988; Grand et al. 1985).

While such findings provide promising leads, it is difficult to assess the role of specific personality characteristics in the development of alcoholism. Certainly many people with similar personality characteristics do not become alcoholics, and others with dissimilar ones do. The only characteristic that appears common to the backgrounds of most problem drinkers is personal maladjustment, yet most maladjusted people do not become alcoholics. An alcoholic's personality may be as much a result as a cause of his or her dependence on alcohol—for example, the excessive use of alcohol may lead to depression, or a depressed person may turn to the excessive use of alcohol, or both.

Stress, tension reduction, and reinforcement. A number of investigators have pointed out that the typical alcoholic is discontented with his or her life and is unable or unwilling to tolerate tension and stress. In this view, anyone who finds alcohol to be tension-reducing is in danger of becoming an alcoholic, even without an especially stressful life situation. If this were true, however, we would expect alcoholism to be far more common that it is, since alcohol tends to reduce tension for most people who use it. In addition, this model does not explain why some excessive drinkers are able to maintain control over their drinking and continue to function in society while others are not.

At the opposite end of the spectrum are investigators who reject the view that alcoholism is a learned maladaptive response, reinforced and maintained by tension reduction. They point out that the long-range consequences of excessive drinking are too devastating, far outweighing its temporary relief value. However, as Bandura (1969) has pointed out, "This argument overlooks the fact that behavior is more powerfully controlled by its immediate, rather than delayed, consequences, and it is precisely for this reason that persons may persistently engage in immediately reinforcing, but potentially self-destructive behavior . . ." (p. 530).

Cox and Klinger (1988) describe a ***motivational model of alcohol use*** that places a great deal of responsibility on the individual. According to this view, the final common pathway of alcohol use is motivation; that is, a person decides, consciously or unconsciously, whether to consume a particular drink of alcohol. Alcohol is consumed to bring about affective changes, such as the mood-altering effects, and even indirect effects, such as peer approval. In short, alcohol is consumed because it is reinforcing to the individual.

Finally, much data in the literature suggest that for certain individuals, alcohol reduces the magnitude of response to stressful situations, thereby reinforcing the drinking of alcohol. Levenson et al. (1980) found that alcohol had a dampening effect on an individual's feeling of immediate stress. It thus seems that alcoholics drink to feel better at a particular moment, even though they may know they will feel worse later.

Marital and other intimate relationships. Excessive drinking often begins during crisis periods in marital or other intimate personal relationships, particularly crises that lead to hurt and self-devaluation. For example, in an important early study of 100 middle- and upper-class women who were receiving help at an alcoholism treatment center, Curlee (1969) found that the traumas that appeared to trigger the women's drinking problems were related to changes or challenges in their roles as wives or mothers, such as divorce, menopause, or children leaving home (the so-called empty-nest syndrome). Many women appear to begin their immoderate drinking during their late thirties and early forties when such life-situation changes are common.

A husband who lives with an alcoholic wife is often unaware of the fact that, gradually and inevitably, many of the decisions he makes every day are based on the expectation that his wife will be drinking. In a case such as this, the husband is becoming "drinking-wife oriented." These expectations, in turn, may make the drinking behavior more likely. Thus one important concern in many treatment programs today involves identifying ***codependency*** in alcohol-abusing relationships. That is, such programs try to identify the personality or life-style factors in a relationship that serve to promote, maintain, or to justify the drinking behavior of an alcoholic. Eventually an entire marriage may center around the drinking of an alcoholic spouse. In some instances, the husband or wife may also begin to drink excessively, possibly through the reinforcement of such behavior by the drinking mate or to blank out the disillusionment, frustration, and resentment that are often elicited by an alcoholic spouse. Of course, such relationships are not restricted to marital partners but may also occur in those involved in love affairs or close friendships.

Excessive use of alcohol is the third most frequent cause of divorce in the United States (and often a hidden factor in the two most common causes—financial and sexual problems). People who abuse alcohol are about seven times more likely to be divorced or separated than nonabusers (Levitt, 1974). The deterioration in such people's interpersonal relationships, of course, further augments the stress and disorganization in their life situations.

Sociocultural Factors In a general sense, our culture has become dependent on alcohol as a social lubricant and a means of reducing tension. Thus numerous investigators have pointed to the role of sociocultural as well as physiological and psychological factors in the high rate of alcohol abuse and dependence among Americans. It is of interest to note here the conclusions of Pliner and Cappell (1974) concerning the reinforcing effects of social

Drunken college students on spring break have become a symbol of springtime. Our society reinforces the role of alcohol in promoting gaiety and fun—witness any beer commercial—but the reinforcement of social drinking can lead some people to excessive alcohol use.

drinking in our society, in which liquor has come to play an almost ritualistic role in promoting gaiety and pleasant social interaction.

According to the present results, if it is the case that much of the early drinking experience of . . . individuals takes place in such convivial social settings, drinking will be likely to become associated with positive affective experiences. This reinforcing consequence may in turn make drinking more probable in the future. Thus, to the extent that a social context can enhance the attraction of alcohol, for some individuals it may play a crucial role in the etiology of pathological patterns of alcohol consumption. (p. 425)

Bales (1946), in a classic study, outlined three cultural factors that play a part in determining the incidence of alcoholism in a given society: (a) the degree of stress and inner tension produced by the culture; (b) the attitudes toward drinking fostered by the culture; and (c) the degree to which the culture provides substitute means of satisfaction and other ways of coping with tension and anxiety. This outline has been borne out by cross-cultural studies.

The importance of the stress level in a given culture is shown in studies of preliterate societies. In a pioneering study of 56 such societies, Horton (1943) found that the greater the insecurity level of the culture, the greater the amount of alcohol consumption—due allowance having been made for the availability and acceptability of alcohol.

Rapid social change and social disintegration also seem to foster excessive drinking. For example, the U.S. Public Health Service's Alaska Native Medical Center reported excessive drinking to be a major problem among Eskimos in many places in rural Alaska (*Time*, April 22, 1974). This problem was attributed primarily to rapid change in traditional values and ways of life, in some cases approaching social disintegration.

The effect of cultural attitudes toward drinking is well illustrated by Muslims and Mormons, whose religious values prohibit the use of alcohol, and by orthodox Jews, who have traditionally limited its use largely to religious rituals. The incidence of alcoholism among these groups is minimal. In comparison, the incidence of alcoholism is high among Europeans, who comprise less than 15 percent of the world's population yet consume about half the alcohol (Sulkunen, 1976). Interestingly, Europe and six countries that have been influenced by European culture—Argentina, Canada, Chile, Japan, the United States, and New Zealand—make up less than 20 percent of the world's population yet consume 80 percent of the alcohol (Barry, 1982). The French appear to have the highest rate of alcoholism in the world, approximately 15 percent of the population. France has both the highest per capita alcohol consumption and the highest death rate from cirrhosis of the liver (Noble, 1979). Thus it appears that religious sanctions and social customs can determine whether alcohol is one of the coping methods commonly used in a given group or society.

In sum, we can identify many reasons why people drink—as well as many conditions that can predispose them to do so and reinforce drinking behavior—but the combination of factors that result in a person's becoming an alcoholic are still unknown.

Treatments and Outcomes

Unfortunately, many alcoholics refuse to admit they have a problem or to seek assistance before they "hit bottom"—which, in many cases, is the grave. When alcoholics are confronted with their drinking problem they may react with denial or become angry at the "messenger" and withdraw from this person. At times, however, such a confrontation has the desired effect, as in the case of Don Shelby, a Minneapolis television newscaster, who described in the following manner the day, March 31, 1980, when he went on the air drunk:

> *"I had done that before, so you at home didn't know, but there was no hiding this," Shelby said. "Incomprehensible. It was incredibly embarrassing to me, but I want to tell you the kind of embarrassment Ron Handberg suffered.*
>
> *"Ron Handberg is the general manager of the television station, the man who hired me. He was humiliated beyond words that I had done that to him and his television station. Ron Handberg wanted to fire me and I wanted to be fired. I didn't want to be forced to walk down the street and have people see my face and realize what I had done," Shelby said.*
>
> *"Mr. Handberg invited me into his office and complained that he could not fire me, because under certain rules and regulations he was forced to offer me treatment, and he despised my guts.*
>
> *"He told me that the company would pay for my treatment, and I'd be given some time off and I could come back to work and resume my duties.*
>
> *"Mr. Handberg said he was also authorized to tell me that if I refused treatment I would be fired and he would spend the rest of his natural life seeing to it that I was never employed in television again," Shelby said.*
>
> *"I decided to enter treatment and the rest is history, as they say. Six years later, I am co-anchor of the 10 p.m. news. That's a remarkable story, a story of recovery, and a story of Ron Handberg," Shelby said.*
>
> *Since Shelby's recovery, eight other people at the station were identified and helped "short of humiliation," and each one of those individuals has climbed either the reportorial or executive ladder. (Bloomington Sun Current, June 16, 1986)*

A multidisciplinary approach to the treatment of drinking problems appears to be most effective because the problems are often complex, thus requiring flexibility and individualization of treatment procedures. Also, an alcoholic's needs change as treatment progresses.

Formerly it was considered essential for the treatment of a problem drinker to take place in an institutional setting, removing the individual from a probably aversive life situation and making possible more control over his or her behavior. However, an increasing number of problem drinkers are now being treated in community clinics, especially drinkers who do not require hospitalization for withdrawal treatment. In fact, one survey of treatment facilities (ADAMHA, 1982) found that most alcoholics are treated on an outpatient basis, which appears to be as effective as inpatient treatment (Miller & Hester, 1986). When hospitalization is required, the length of the hospital stay is often short—an average of roughly 28 days. (In some treatment programs, stays are now being limited to 7 to 14 days.) Halfway houses are also being used increasingly to bridge the gap between institutionalization and return to the community and to enhance the flexibility of treatment programs.

Treatment program objectives include physical rehabilitation, control over alcohol-abuse behavior, and development of an individual's realization that he or she can cope with the problems of living and lead a much more rewarding life without alcohol. Although traditional treatment programs usually include the goal of abstinence from alcohol, some current programs are attempting to promote controlled drinking as a treatment goal for some problem drinkers.

Biological Approaches Biological approaches include a variety of treatment measures ranging from detoxification procedures to medication use. In acute intoxication, the initial focus is on detoxification (the elimination of alcoholic substances from an individual's body), on the treatment of withdrawal symptoms, and on a medical regimen for physical rehabilitation. These steps can best be handled in a hospital or clinic, where drugs, such as chlordiazepoxide, have largely revolutionized the treatment of withdrawal symptoms. Such drugs overcome motor excitement, nausea, and vomiting, prevent withdrawal delirium and convulsions, and help alleviate the tension and anxiety associated with withdrawal. Concern is growing, however, that the use of tranquilizers at this stage does not promote long-term recovery. Accordingly, some detoxification clinics are exploring alternative approaches, including a gradual weaning from alcohol instead of a sudden cutoff.

Medications are also used in the treatment of alcoholism. Maintenance doses of mild tranquilizers are used at times on patients withdrawing from alcohol to reduce anxiety and help them sleep. Such use of tranquilizers may be less effective than no treatment at all, however. Usually patients must learn to abstain from tranquilizers as well as from alcohol, because they tend to misuse both. Further, under the influence of tranquilizers, they may even return to alcohol use.

Disulfiram (Antabuse), a drug that causes violent vomiting when followed by ingestion of alcohol, may be administered to prevent an immediate return to drinking. However, such deterrent therapy is seldom advocated as the sole approach, because pharmacological methods alone have not proven effective in treating alcoholism. For example, since the drug is usually self-administered, an alcoholic may simply discontinue the use of Antabuse when he or she is released from a hospital or clinic and begin to drink again. In fact, the primary value of drugs of this type seems to be their ability to interrupt the alcoholic cycle for a period of time, during which therapy may be undertaken. Uncomfortable side effects may accompany the use of Antabuse; for example, alcohol-based after-shave lotion can be absorbed through the skin, resulting in an individual becoming ill.

Psychosocial Approaches Detoxification is optimally followed by psychosocial measures, including family counseling and the use of community resources relating to employment and other aspects of an individual's social readjustments. Although individual psychotherapy is sometimes effective, the focus of psychosocial measures in the alcoholism treatment more often involves group therapy, environmental intervention, behavioral therapy, and the approach used by Alcoholics Anonymous.

Group therapy. In the rugged give-and-take of group therapy, alcoholics are sometimes forced to face their problem and recognize its possible disastrous consequences, but they also begin to see new possibilities for coping with it. Often, but by no means always, this double recognition paves the way for learning more effective methods of coping and other positive steps toward dealing with their drinking problem.

In some instances, the spouses of alcoholics and even their children may be invited to join in group therapy meetings. In other situations, family treatment is itself the central focus of therapeutic efforts. In the latter case, an alcoholic individual is seen as a member of a disturbed family in which all the members have a responsibility for cooperating in treatment. Because family members are frequently the people most victimized by the alcoholic's addiction, they often tend to be judgmental and punitive, and the alcoholic, who has already passed harsh judgment on himself or herself, tolerates this further source of devaluation poorly. In other instances, family members may unwillingly encourage an alcoholic to remain addicted, as, for example, when a wife with a need to dominate her husband finds that a continually drunken and remorseful spouse best meets her needs.

Environmental intervention. As with other serious maladaptive behaviors, a total treatment program for alcoholism usually requires measures to alleviate a patient's aversive life situation. As a result of their drinking, alcoholics often become estranged from family and friends and either lose or jeopardize their job. Typically the reaction of those around them is not as understanding or supportive as it would be if they had a physical illness of comparable magnitude. Simply helping alcoholics learn more effective coping techniques may not be enough if their social environment remains hostile and threatening. For alcoholics who have been hospitalized, halfway houses—designed to assist them in their return to family and community—are often important adjuncts to their total treatment program.

Relapses and continued deterioration are generally associated with a lack of close relationships with family or friends, or with living in a stressful environment. In general, it appears unlikely that an alcoholic will remain abstinent after treatment unless the negative psychosocial factors that operated in the past are dealt with.

Behavioral therapy. One interesting and often effective form of treatment for alcohol-abuse disorders is behavioral therapy, of which several types exist. One is *aversive conditioning,* involving the presentation of a wide range of noxious stimuli with alcohol consumption in order to suppress drinking behavior. For example, the ingestion of alcohol might be paired with an electrical shock. The Romans used a similar technique by placing a live eel in a cup of wine; forced to drink this unsavory cocktail, an alcoholic presumably would feel disgusted and from then on be repelled by wine.

Today a variety of pharmacological and other deterrent measures can be used in behavioral therapy after detoxification. One approach involves an intramuscular injection of emetine hydrochloride, an emetic. Before experiencing the nausea that results from the injection, a patient is given alcohol, so that the sight, smell, and taste of the beverage become associated with severe retching and vomiting. With repetition, this classical conditioning procedure acts as a strong deterrent to further drinking—probably in part because it adds an immediate and unpleasant physiological consequence to the more general socially aversive consequences of excessive drinking.

These paintings were done by W., a 40-year-old male with a history of alcoholism, loss of employment, and hospitalization for treatment. His interest in painting, which gradually became the key aspect of his treatment program at an alcoholism treatment center, also led to a new way of life following his discharge. In the painting on the left, W. depicted alcoholism as a magnetlike vise that drew and crushed his consciousness. He symbolized his feelings in sober periods between drinking sprees as the chained tree, and the nebulous higher power to which he looked for help as a descending dove. The egg and the eye, a motif W. used in earlier work to depict his unrealistic view of alcohol, are merged into a straining muscular arm reaching back to the more placid past and unattainable dream castles—that is, futile quests with which W. associated his past abuses of alcohol. In the painting on the right, the overriding concept is of constructive action. Three portals are depicted, one leading to a world "blown to hell" (left); another with two entrances (right), one leading downward to an abyss, the other to barrenness; and a third in the shape of a cross (middle), symbolic of hope, that leads upward to a pleasant landscape, representing a goal or purpose.

Mild electrical stimulation is another of the aversive-conditioning techniques. This method presumably enables a therapist to maintain more exact control of the aversive stimulus, reduces possible negative side effects and medical complications, and can even be administered by means of a portable apparatus that can be used by a patient for self-reinforcement. Using a procedure that paired electrical stimulation with drinking-associated stimuli, Claeson and Malm (1973) reported successful results—no relapses after 12 months—in 24 percent of a patient group consisting mostly of advanced-stage alcoholics.

Another aversive approach, called *covert sensitization,* involves extinguishing drinking behavior by conditioning an individual to associate it with noxious mental images (Cautela, 1967). Positive results have been reported, with reduction of drinking for a time. The long-term effects of covert sensitization, however, generally have not been impressive. To expect stimuli such as images (which are under an individual's control) to change a deeply ingrained life pattern is perhaps unrealistic. Covert sensitization procedures might be effectively used as an early step, with other treatment procedures then employed while a person remains abstinent. The most important effect of any type of aversion therapy with alcoholics seems to be this temporary extinction of drinking behavior, making it possible for other psychosocial methods to be used effectively (Davidson, 1974).

One of the most promising contemporary procedures for treating alcoholics is the cognitive-behavioral approach recommended by Marlatt (1985) and Lang and Marlatt (1983). This approach combines cognitive-behavioral strategies of intervention with social-learning theory and modeling of behavior. The approach, often referred to as a *skills-training procedure,* is usually aimed at younger problem drinkers who are considered to be at risk for developing more severe drinking problems because of alcoholism in their family history or their heavy current consumption level. This approach relies on such techniques as imparting specific knowledge about alcohol, developing coping skills in situations associated with increased risk of alcohol use, modifying cognitions and expectancies, and acquiring stress-management skills.

Other behavioral techniques have also received attention in recent years, partly because they are based on the hypothesis that some problem drinkers need not give up drinking altogether but can learn to drink moderately (Gottheil et al., 1982; Lang & Kidorf, 1990; Miller, 1978). Several approaches to learning controlled drinking have been attempted (Lloyd & Salzberg, 1975), and research has suggested that some alcoholics can learn to control their alcohol intake (Miller, 1978; Miller & Caddy, 1977). Miller et al. (1986) evaluated the results of four long-term follow-up studies of controlled-drinking treatment programs. They reported a clear trend of increased numbers of abstainers and relapsed cases at long-term follow-up. However, a consistent percentage (15 percent) of individuals across the four studies controlled their drinking. The researchers concluded that controlled drinking was more likely to be successful in individuals with less severe alcohol problems. The finding that some individuals are able to maintain some control over their drinking after treatment (and not remain totally abstinent) was also reported by Polich and colleagues (1981). They found that 18 percent of the alcoholics they studied had reportedly been able to drink socially without problems during the six-month follow-up of treatment.

One promising approach to teaching alcoholics self-control over drinking was reported by Lovibond and Caddy (1970). They conducted blood-alcohol discrimination training sessions, which were aimed at getting alcoholics to control drinking by becoming aware of intoxicating levels of alcohol in their blood. Miller and Munoz (1976) and Miller (1978) used behavioral self-control training to teach alcoholics to monitor and reduce their alcohol intake. Patients kept records of their drinking behavior, and the therapy sessions focused on determining blood-alcohol concentration based on their intake. Strategies for increasing future intake control were discussed along with identifying alternatives to alcohol consumption. Self-control training techniques, in which the goal of therapy is to get alcoholics to reduce alcohol intake without necessarily abstaining altogether, have a great deal of appeal for some drinkers. It is difficult, of course, for individuals who are extremely dependent on the effects of alcohol to abstain totally from drinking. Thus many alcoholics fail to complete traditional treatment programs. The idea that they might be able to learn to control their drinking and at the same time enjoy the continued use of alcohol might serve as a motivating element (Lang & Kidorf, 1990).

Whether alcoholics who have learned to recognize intoxicating levels of alcohol and to limit their intake to lower levels will maintain these skills in the long run has not been sufficiently demonstrated. Most workers in the field still assume that total abstinence should be the goal for all problem drinkers. Some groups, such as Alcoholics Anonymous, are adamant in their opposition to programs aimed at controlled drinking for alcohol-dependent individuals.

Alcoholics Anonymous. A practical approach to alcoholism that has reportedly met with considerable success is that of Alcoholics Anonymous (AA). This organization was started in 1935 by two individuals, Dr. Bob and Bill W. in Akron, Ohio. Bill W. recovered from alcoholism through a "fundamental spiritual change," and immediately sought out Dr. Bob, who, with Bill's assistance, achieved recovery. They in turn began to help other alcoholics. Since that time, AA has grown to over 10,000 groups with over 1 million members. In addition, AA groups have been established in many other countries.

Alcoholics Anonymous operates primarily as a nonprofessional counseling program in which both person-to-person and group relationships are emphasized. AA accepts both teenagers and adults with drinking problems, has no dues or fees, does not keep records or case histories, does not participate in political causes, and is not affiliated with any religious sect, although spiritual development is a key aspect of its treatment approach. To ensure anonymity, only first names are used. Meetings are devoted partly to social activities, but consist mainly of discussions of the participants' problems with alcohol, often with testimonials from those who have recovered from alcoholism. Recovered members usually contrast their lives before they broke their alcohol dependence with the lives they now live without alcohol. We should point out here that the term *alcoholic* is used by AA and its affiliates to refer either to individuals who currently are drinking excessively or to people who have recovered from such problems but must, according to AA philosophy, continue to abstain from alcohol consumption in the future. That is, one is an alcoholic for life, whether or not one is drinking—one is never "cured" of alcoholism.

An important aspect of AA's rehabilitation program is that it lifts the burden of personal responsibility by helping alcoholics accept that alcoholism, like many other problems, is bigger than they are. Henceforth, they can see themselves not as weak-willed or lacking in moral strength, but rather simply as having an affliction—they cannot drink—just as other people may not be able to tolerate certain types of medication. By mutual help and

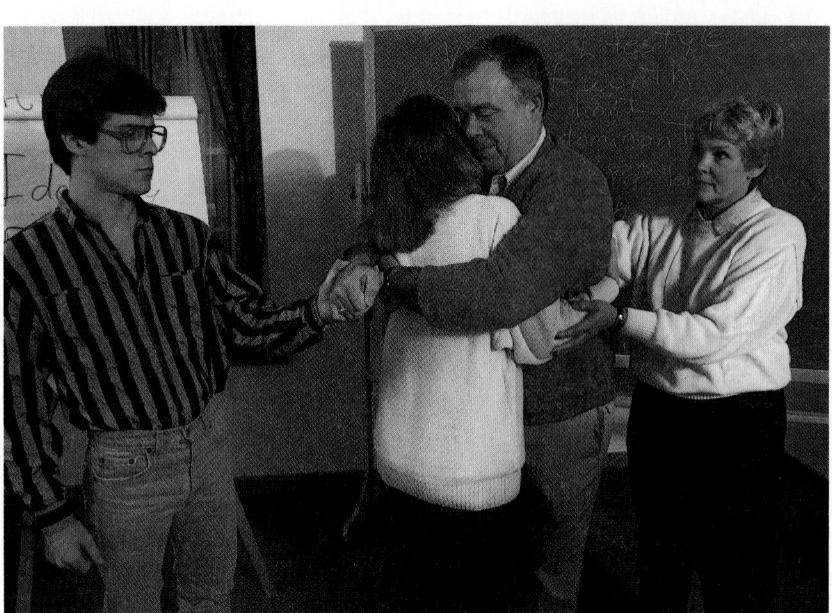

Family relationships are severely threatened by an alcoholic family member. In some instances, the spouses and children of alcoholics may be invited to join in therapy, and family treatment may itself be the central focus of therapeutic efforts. Because family members are frequently the people most victimized by an alcoholic's addiction, they often tend to be judgmental and punitive. They also may unknowingly encourage an alcoholic to remain addicted. Therapy can help them to gain an understanding of the nature of alcoholism and to learn ways of helping an alcoholic family member deal with his or her problem.

reassurance through a group composed of others who have shared similar experiences, many alcoholics acquire insight into their problems, a new sense of purpose, greater ego strength, and more effective coping techniques. Continued participation in the group, of course, helps prevent the crisis of a relapse.

Affiliated movements, such as Al-Anon family groups and Ala-Teen, are designed to bring family members together to share common experiences and problems, to gain understanding of the nature of alcoholism, and to learn techniques for helping an alcoholic individual deal with his or her problem.

The generally acknowledged success of Alcoholics Anonymous is based primarily on anecdotal information rather than objective study of treatment outcomes. Brandsma et al. (1980), however, included an AA program in their extensive comparative study of alcoholism treatments. The success of this treatment method with severe alcoholics was quite limited. One important finding was that the AA method had high dropout rates compared to other therapies. Apparently many alcoholics are unable to accept the quasi-religious quality of the sessions and the group testimonial format that is so much a part of the AA program. The individuals who were assigned to the AA group subsequently encountered more life difficulties and drank more than individuals in other treatment groups.

Results of Treatment Statistics on the long-range outcomes of alcoholism treatments vary considerably, depending on the population studied and on the treatment facilities and procedures employed. They range from low rates of success for hard-core alcoholics to recoveries of 70 to 90 percent where modern treatment and aftercare procedures are used. Rounsaville et al. (1987) reported that psychopathology was influential in treatment outcomes for alcoholics. Individuals who were also diagnosed as having a personality disorder or affective disorder tended to have poorer outcomes in alcohol treatment than those for whom the diagnosis was simply alcoholism.

In their extensive four-year follow-up of a large group of treated alcoholics, Polich et al. (1981) found that the course of alcoholism after diverse treatment methods was variable:

There is no single pattern, and no definite path, characterizing the 4-year history of alcoholics in this study. Instead, we find remission, frequent relapse, and diverse forms of behavior among alcoholics. Our conclusions about the course of alcoholism depend upon recognizing these multidimensional and highly diverse features of alcoholic behavior. (p. 201)

In some respects, the findings of this study were not encouraging and seemed to point to the difficulty of treating alcoholics. Only 7 percent of the total sample (922 males) abstained from alcohol use throughout the four-year period, and 54 percent continued to show alcohol-related problems. (In addition, 36 percent of the sample demonstrated alcohol-dependence symptoms, and another 18 percent showed adverse consequences—such as arrests—from drinking.)

On the positive side, however, the Polich et al. study can be viewed as demonstrating a clear beneficial effect of treatment for some individuals. Although 54 percent showed drinking problems at follow-up, over 90 percent of the subjects had had serious drinking problems at the beginning of treatment—a significant reduction. Interestingly, although only 7 percent of the alcoholics had been able to abstain from drinking for the full four-year period, others had abstained for shorter periods. For example, 21 percent had abstained for one year or more, and an additional 7 percent had abstained for six months. An impressive finding, and one that will fuel the controlled-drinking versus total-abstinence controversy, was that 18 percent of the alcoholics had been able to drink without problems during the six-month period before follow-up.

The outcome of treatment is most likely to be favorable when an individual realizes that he or she needs help, when adequate treatment facilities are available, and when alcohol-use reduction (as opposed to strict abstinence) is an acceptable treatment goal. However, Fontana and Dowds (1975) reported a "honeymoon effect" following treatment of severe alcohol abuse. They found a frequent pattern of decreased alcohol consumption with a return to initial drinking levels at a six-month follow-up.

Great progress has been made in alcoholism treatment by the introduction of employee programs in both government and industry. Such programs have proven highly effective in detecting drinking problems early, in referring drinkers for treatment, and in ensuring the effectiveness of aftercare procedures. When we realize that an estimated 5 percent of the nation's work force are alcoholics, and an additional 5 percent are considered alcohol abusers, it is apparent that such programs can have a major impact on coping with the alcohol problem in our society (Alander & Campbell, 1975).

In their study of various treatments of chronic, severe alcohol problems, Brandsma et al. (1980) found that direct treatment—whether professional or paraprofessional, insight-oriented or rational-behavior therapy—was more effective than an untreated control condition. The investigators randomly assigned chronic alcoholics to treatment groups—insight-oriented therapy, rational behavior therapy, Alcoholics Anonymous, self-help (paraprofessional) therapy—or to a nontreatment control group. One important finding was that professional treatment was more effective than nonprofessional treatment, although either of the two major therapeutic orientations (insight-oriented versus rational-behavior therapy) was equally effective. As noted above, Alcoholics Anonymous was the least effective, partly due to a high dropout rate.

Clearly no miracle cure for alcoholism is available. Nevertheless, it appears that the great majority of alcoholics may find a treatment program that can be tailored to their needs and provide a good chance for recovery.

Relapse Prevention One of the greatest problems in the treatment of addictive disorders, such as alcoholism or any of the conditions described in this chapter, is maintaining abstinence or self-control once the behavioral excesses have been checked. Most alcohol treatment programs show high success rates in "curing" the addictive problems, but many programs show lessening rates of abstinence or controlled drinking at various periods of follow-up. Many treatment programs do not pay sufficient attention to the important element of maintaining effective behavior and preventing relapse into previous maladaptive patterns.

In recent years, some researchers have been focusing on the problem of relapse prevention by examining the thought processes that lead an abstinent individual back into the self-indulgent patterns that originally got him or her in trouble. The cognitive-behavioral approach to relapse prevention by Marlatt and his colleagues (Cummings, Gordon, & Marlatt, 1980; Marlatt & Gordon, 1980, 1985) shows great promise in this area.

The cognitive-behavioral view holds that the definition of relapse behavior should be broadened beyond the previously held notion that people resume drinking because of a "craving" based on vaguely understood physiological needs. Instead, the behaviors underlying relapse are "indulgent behaviors" and are based on an individual's learning history. When an individual is abstinent or has an addiction under control, he or she gains a sense of personal control over the indulgent behavior. The longer the person is able to maintain this control, the greater the sense of achievement—the self-efficacy or confidence—and the greater the chance that he or she will be able to cope with the addiction and maintain control.

However, according to Marlatt, an individual may violate this rule of abstinence through a gradual, perhaps unconscious, process rather than through the sudden "falling off the wagon" that constitutes the traditional view of craving and relapse. In the cognitive-behavioral view, an individual may inadvertently make a series of mini-decisions, even while maintaining abstinence, that begin a chain of behaviors making relapse inevitable. For example, an abstinent alcoholic who buys a quart of bourbon just in case his friends drop by or a dieting obese woman who changes her route to work to include a pass by the bakery are both unconsciously preparing the way for relapse. Marlatt refers to these minidecisions that place an individual at risk as "apparently irrelevant decisions." These decisions are easy for the individual to make, since they do not appear to be related to the abstinent behavior; however, they lead the individual into a situation in which some form of relapse is likely to occur.

Another type of relapse behavior involves the "abstinence violation effect," in which even minor transgressions are seen to have drastic significance by the abstainers. The effect works this way: an abstinent individual may hold that he or she should not, under any circumstance, transgress or give in to the old habit. Abstinence-oriented treatment programs are particularly guided by this prohibitive rule. What happens, then, when an abstinent man becomes somewhat self-indulgent and takes a drink offered by an old friend? He may lose some of the sense of self-efficacy, the confidence needed to control his drinking. Since the vow of abstinence has been violated, he may feel guilty about giving in to the temptation and rationalize that he "has blown it and become a drunk again, so why not go all the way?"

Marlatt and his colleagues recommend a cognitive-behavioral treatment program for preventing relapse. Clients are taught to recognize the apparently irrelevant decisions that serve as early warning signals of the possibility of relapse. High-risk situations are targeted, and the individuals learn to assess their own vulnerability to relapse. Clients are also trained to be prepared for the abstinence violation effect, and, if they do relapse, not to become so discouraged that they lose their confidence. Some cognitive-behavioral therapists have employed a "planned relapse" phase in the treatment to supervise an individual's cognitive behavior and to help the client through this important problem area.

DRUG ABUSE AND DEPENDENCE

Aside from alcohol, the psychoactive drugs most commonly associated with abuse and dependence in our society appear to be (a) narcotics, such as opium and its derivatives; (b) sedatives, such as barbiturates; (c) stimulants, such as cocaine and amphetamines; (d) antianxiety drugs, such as benzodiazepines; and (e) hallucinogens, such as LSD and PCP. (These and other drugs are summarized in *HIGHLIGHT 9.5*.) Caffeine and nicotine are also drugs of dependence, and disorders associated with tobacco withdrawal and caffeine intoxication are included in the DSM-III-R diagnostic classification system; we will deal with them briefly in our present discussion.

Though they may occur at any age, drug abuse and dependence are most common during adolescence and young adulthood (Smith, 1989). Clinical pictures vary markedly, depending on the type, amount, and duration of drug use; the physiological and psychological makeup of the individual; and, in some instances, the social setting in which the drug experience occurs. Thus it appears most useful to deal separately with some of the drugs that are more commonly associated with abuse and dependence in contemporary society.

It should be noted that the most common action of all drugs—even those that are medically prescribed—is the alteration of cell metabolism. Typically, this change in cellular action is a temporary one designed to help combat a patient's problem. Nevertheless, the changes that drugs bring about in target cells are in a direction *away* from normal functioning. Thus medication does not result in cells performing "better than ever." Of course, some drugs, such as hormones, do replace or supplement substances that are normally present in the body, and in this sense they may improve the normal functioning of various organs and cells; but in general, drugs tend to block some important function of cells. Hence it is best to keep drug use to a minimum.

Opium and Its Derivatives (Narcotics)

People have used opium and its derivatives for over 5000 years. Galen (A.D. 130–201) considered theriaca, whose principal ingredient was opium, to be a panacea:

It resists poison and venomous bites, cures inveterate headache, vertigo, deafness, epilepsy, apoplexy, dimness of sight, loss of voice, asthma, coughs of all kinds, spitting of blood, tightness of breath, colic, the iliac poisons, jaundice, hardness of the spleen, stone, urinary complaints, fevers, dropsies, leprosies, the trouble to which women are subject, melancholy and all pestilences.

Even today, opium derivatives are still used for some of the conditions Galen mentioned.

Opium is a mixture of about eighteen nitrogen-containing agents known as *alkaloids*. In 1805 the alkaloid present in the largest amount (10 to 15 percent) was found to be a bitter-tasting powder that could serve as a powerful sedative and pain reliever; it was named **morphine** after Morpheus, god of sleep in Greek mythology. The hypodermic needle was introduced in America about 1856, allowing morphine to be widely administered to soldiers during the Civil War, not only to those wounded in battle but also to those suffering from dysentery. As a consequence, many Civil War veterans returned to civilian life addicted to the drug, a condition euphemistically referred to as "soldier's illness."

Scientists concerned with the addictive properties of morphine hypothesized that one part of the morphine molecule might be responsible for its analgesic properties (that is, its ability to eliminate pain without inducing unconsciousness) and another for its addictiveness. Thus at about the turn of the century, it was discovered that if morphine were treated by an inexpensive and readily available chemical called *acetic anhydride,* it would be converted into another powerful analgesic called **heroin.** Heroin was hailed enthusiastically by its discoverer, Heinrich Dreser (Boehm, 1968). Leading scientists of his time agreed on the merits of heroin, and the drug came to be widely prescribed in place of morphine for pain relief and related medicinal purposes. However, heroin was a cruel disappointment, for it proved to be an even more dangerous drug than morphine, acting more rapidly and more intensely and being equally if not more addictive. Eventually, heroin was removed from use in medical practice.

As it became apparent that opium and its derivatives—including codeine, which is used in some cough syrups—were perilously addictive, the United States Congress enacted the Harrison Act in 1914. Under this and later acts, the unauthorized sale and distribution of certain drugs became a federal offense; physicians and pharmacists were held accountable for each dose they dispensed. Thus, overnight, the role of a narcotic user changed from that of addict—which was considered a vice, but tolerated—to that of criminal. Unable to obtain drugs through legal sources, many turned to illegal ones, and eventually to other criminal acts as a means of maintaining their suddenly expensive drug supply. The number of addicts in the United States declined, however, and stayed near 40,000 for several decades.

During the 1960s, there was a rapid increase in heroin use. An estimated 150,000 or more addicts lived in New York City alone, with some 300,000 in the country as a whole—and public attention was focused on the "heroin epidemic" (Bazell, 1973; Greene & Dupont, 1974). Fortunately, the actual number of heroin users has diminished steadily since 1975 (Smith, 1989). Heroin-related hospital admissions have decreased in recent years from 47 percent of total drug-related admissions to 37 percent.

Effects of Morphine and Heroin Morphine and heroin are commonly introduced into the body by smoking, snorting (inhaling the powder), eating, "skin popping," or "mainlining," the last two being methods of introducing the drug via hypodermic injection. Skin popping refers to injecting the liquefied drug just beneath the skin, and mainlining to injecting the drug directly into the bloodstream. In the United States, a young addict usually moves from snorting to mainlining.

Among the immediate effects of mainlined or snorted heroin is a euphoric spasm (the rush) lasting 60 seconds or so, which many addicts compare to a sexual orgasm. This rush is followed by a high, during which an addict typically is in a lethargic, withdrawn state in which bodily needs, including needs for food and sex, are markedly diminished; pleasant feelings of relaxation, euphoria, and reverie tend to dominate. These effects last from 4 to 6 hours and are followed—in addicts—by a negative phase that produces a desire for more of the drug.

The use of opium derivatives over a period of time usually results in a physiological craving for the drug. The time required to establish the drug habit varies, but it has been estimated that continual use over a period of 30 days is sufficient. Users then find that they have become physiologically dependent on the drug in the sense that they feel physically ill when they do not take it. In addition, users of opium derivatives gradually build up a tolerance to the drug so that even larger amounts are needed to achieve the desired effects.

When people addicted to opiates do not get a dose of the drug within approximately 8 hours, they start to experience withdrawal symptoms. The character and severity of these reactions depend on many factors, including the amount of the narcotic habitually used, the intervals between doses, the duration of the addiction, and especially the addict's health and personality.

Contrary to popular opinion, withdrawal from heroin is not always dangerous or even very painful. Many addicted people withdraw without assistance. Withdrawal can be an agonizing experience for some people, however. Initial withdrawal symptoms usually include a running nose, tearing eyes, perspiration, restlessness, increased respiration rate, and an intensified desire for the drug. As time passes, the symptoms become more severe, usually reaching a peak in about 40 hours. Typically a feeling of chilliness alternates with vasomotor disturbances of flushing and excessive sweating, vomiting, diarrhea, abdominal cramps, pains in the back and extremities, severe headache, marked tremors, and varying degrees of insomnia. Beset by these

HIGHLIGHT 9.5

Psychoactive Drugs Commonly Involved in Drug Abuse

Classification	Drugs	Effects
Sedatives	Alcohol (ethanol)	Reduce tension Facilitate social interaction "Blot out" feelings or events
	Barbiturates Nembutal (pentobarbital) Seconal (secobarbital) Veronal (barbital) Tuinal (secobarbital and amobarbital)	Reduce tension
Stimulants	Amphetamines Benzedrine (amphetamine) Dexedrine (dextroamphetamine) Methedrine (methamphetamine)	Increase feelings of alertness and confidence Decrease feelings of fatigue Stay awake for long periods
	Cocaine (coca)	Decrease feelings of fatigue Increase endurance Stimulate sex drive
Narcotics	Opium and its derivatives Opium Morphine Codeine Heroin	Alleviate physical pain Induce relaxation and pleasant reverie Alleviate anxiety and tension
	Methadone (synthetic narcotic)	Treatment of heroin dependence
Psychedelics and hallucinogens	Cannabis Marijuana Hashish	Induce changes in mood, thought, and behavior
	Mescaline (peyote)	
	Psilocybin (psychotogenic mushrooms)	"Expand" one's mind
	LSD (lysergic acid diethylamide-25)	
	PCP (phencyclidine)	Induce stupor
Antianxiety drugs (minor tranquilizers)	Librium (chlordiazepoxide) Miltown (meprobamate) Valium (diazepam) Others, e.g., Compōz (scopolamine)	Alleviate tension and anxiety Induce relaxation and sleep

In reviewing this list, it is important to note that it is by no means complete; for example, it does not include new drugs, such as Ritalin, which are designed to produce multiple effects; it does not include the less commonly used volatile hydrocarbons, such as glue, paint thinner, gasoline, cleaning fluid, and nail-polish remover, which are highly dangerous when sniffed for their psychoactive effects; and it does not include the antipsychotic and antidepressant drugs, which are

discomforts, an individual refuses food and water, and this, coupled with the vomiting, sweating, and diarrhea, results in dehydration and a weight loss of as much as 5 to 15 pounds in one day. Occasionally, symptoms may include delirium, hallucinations, and manic activity. Cardiovascular collapse may also occur and can result in death. If morphine is administered, the subjective distress experienced by an addict ends, and physiological equanimity is restored in about 5 to 30 minutes.

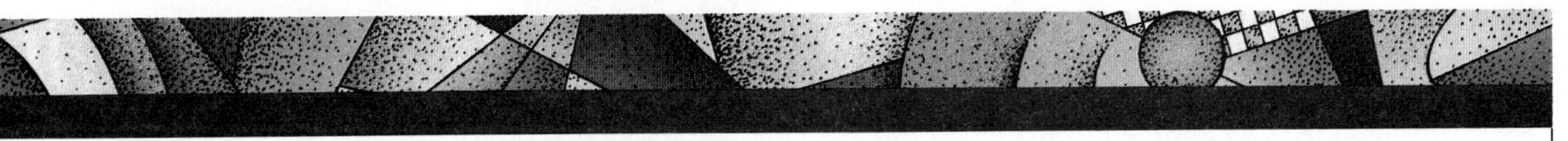

Medical Usage	Tolerance	Physiological Dependence	Psychological Dependence
No	Yes (reverse tolerance later)	Yes	Yes
Yes	Yes	Yes	Yes
Yes	Yes	No	Yes
No	No (minimal)	No	Yes
Yes, except heroin	Yes	Yes	Yes
Yes	Yes	Yes	Yes
No, except in research	No—possible reverse tolerance (marijuana)	No	Yes
No	No	No	Yes
Yes	Yes	Yes	Yes

abused, but relatively rarely. We shall deal with these and the anti-anxiety drugs in our discussion of drug therapy in Chapter 17. It also should be emphasized that abuses of various kinds can occur with both prescriptive and non-prescriptive drugs, and with both legal and illegal drugs. In all cases, drugs should be used with great care.

If an addict stops taking heroin, the withdrawal symptoms will usually be on the decline by the third or fourth day, and by the seventh or eighth day will have disappeared. As the symptoms subside, the individual resumes normal eating and drinking and rapidly regains lost weight. An additional hazard exists now in that after withdrawal symptoms have ceased, the individual's former tolerance for the drug also disappears, and death may result from taking the former large dosage.

Several investigators have reported a stable pattern of controlled heroin use (Harding et al., 1980; Zinberg, 1980). These researchers have found that some users tend to both limit and control their use of the drug.

In some cases, individuals may have enough self-control to use opiates without allowing them to interfere with their work and ruin their life; but the danger in the use of such drugs—especially heroin—is great. Kirsch (1974) noted that occasional, not hard-core, narcotics users were overrepresented to a great degree among heroin overdose cases treated in the emergency room of a New York hospital. In general, tolerance builds up so rapidly that larger and more expensive amounts of the drug are soon required, and withdrawal treatments are likely to do little to end the problem. Most addicted individuals—even after withdrawal—find it extremely difficult to break their dependence. Biochemical alterations appear to be at least partly responsible for an individual's continued craving for the narcotic even after completion of a withdrawal treatment.

Typically the life of a narcotic addict becomes increasingly centered around obtaining and using drugs, so the addiction usually leads to socially maladaptive behavior as the individual is eventually forced to lie, steal, and associate with undesirable companions to maintain a supply of drugs. Many addicts resort to petty theft to support their habits, and some female addicts turn to prostitution as a means of financing their addictions.

It should be noted that narcotic drugs introduced during pregnancy can have seriously damaging effects on the development of infants after birth. Householder et al. (1982) reviewed the effects of narcotics addiction in mothers and the subsequent problems of their offspring. They concluded that in later childhood these children showed increasingly frequent disturbances of activity level, attention span, sleep pattern, and socialization.

Along with the lowering of ethical and moral restraints, addiction has adverse physical effects on an individual's well-being. An inadequate diet, for example, may lead to ill health and increased susceptibility to a variety of physical ailments. The use of unsterile equipment may also lead to various problems, including liver damage from hepatitis and, in some groups, transmission of the AIDS virus. In addition, the use of such a potent drug without medical supervision and government controls to assure its strength and purity can result in fatal overdosage. Injection of too much heroin can cause coma and death. In fact, over 10,000 heroin addicts have died through heroin overdose (Smith, 1989), and in one short period between January and June 1988, more than 867 deaths associated with heroin overdose were reported in the United States (Project DAWN, 1988).

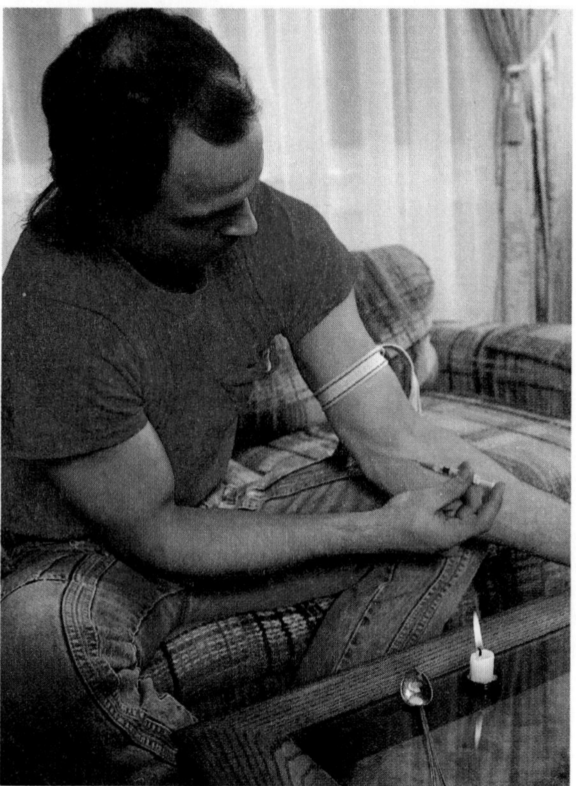

Mainlining heroin, or injecting it with a needle, gives an immediate "rush," often compared to a sexual orgasm, followed by a high lasting from 4 to 6 hours in which feelings of relaxation, euphoria, and reverie are prominent.

Usually, however, addiction to opiates leads to a gradual deterioration of well-being. The ill health and general personality deterioration often found in opium addiction do not result directly from the pharmacological effects of the drug, but are usually products of the sacrifice of money, proper diet, social position, and self-respect as an addict becomes more desperate to procure the required daily dosage. For example, Westermeyer (1982b), in a book detailing his experiences treating opium addicts in Southeast Asia during the 1960s, concludes that long-term opium use has clear dangers in terms of a person's health and the social and economic deprivation it can bring to the user's entire family. On the other hand, a narcotic addict with financial means to maintain both a balanced diet and an adequate supply of drugs without resorting to criminal behavior may maintain his or her drug dependence over many years without the usual symptoms of physical or mental disorder.

Causal Factors in Opiate Abuse and Dependence No single causal pattern fits all addictions to narcotic drugs. A study by Fulmer and Lapidus (1980) concluded that the three most frequently cited reasons for beginning to use heroin were pleasure, curiosity, and peer pressure. Pleasure was the single most widespread reason—given by 81 percent of addicts. Other reasons, such as life stress, personal maladjustment, and sociocultural conditions, also play a part (Bry, McKeon, & Pandina, 1982).

Alexander and Hadaway (1982) argued convincingly that opiate addiction could be more sufficiently explained by an "adaptive" orientation than by the traditional view that people become addicted by being "exposed" to opiates. They cited evidence that simply using heroin or other opiates for a period of time is not sufficient cause for continued, addictive use of the substance—many people have not, even after prolonged use, been compelled to continue. Alexander and Hadaway concluded that "opiate users are at risk of addiction only under special circumstances, namely, when faced with severe distress and with no more salubrious way of coping than by habitual use" (p. 367).

Although the following categorization of causal factors is somewhat artificial, it does provide a convenient means of ordering our discussion.

Neural bases for physiological addiction. Research teams have isolated and studied receptor sites for narcotic drugs in the brain (Goldstein et al., 1974; Pert & Snyder, 1973). Such receptor sites are specific nerve cells into which given psychoactive drugs fit like keys into the proper locks. This interaction of drug and brain cells apparently results in a drug's action, and in the case of narcotic drugs, may lead to addiction. Research shows that there are different neurotransmitter receptor sites that produce the various effects of these drugs—for example, pleasurable euphoria or painkilling and tranquillizing action (Bloom, 1983; Gold & Rea, 1983).

The human body produces its own opiumlike substances, called **endorphins,** in the brain and pituitary gland. These substances are produced in response to stimulation and are believed to play a role in an organism's reaction to pain (Akil et al., 1978; Bolls & Fanselow, 1982). Some investigators have suspected that endorphins may play a role in drug addiction, speculating that chronic underproduction of endorphins may lead to a craving for narcotic drugs. Hollt et al. (1975) experimented on animals to determine whether drugs like heroin or methadone influence endorphin production by causing actual changes in the receptor sites; they found only transient changes and no modification of the underlying receptor mechanisms. Research on this issue has not yet been extensive; however, some indication that endorphins may be a factor in addiction was suggested in a study by Su et al. (1978). These researchers attempted to block methadone withdrawal by administering endorphins and found that endorphins were moderately effective in reducing withdrawal symptoms.

Research on the role of endorphins in drug addiction has generally been inconclusive and disappointing. According to Watson and Akil (1979), before the anatomical and physiological bases of addiction and drug tolerance can be understood, many complex problems of measurement must be resolved.

Addiction associated with pain relief. Many patients are given narcotic drugs, such as morphine, to relieve pain during illness or following surgery or serious injury. The vast majority of such patients never develop an addiction, and when their medication is discontinued, they do not again resort to the use of morphine. Those narcotic addicts who blame their addiction on the fact that they used drugs during an illness usually show personality deficiencies that may have predisposed them to drug use—such as immaturity, low frustration tolerance, and the ability to distort and evade reality by way of a flight into drug-induced fantasy.

Addiction associated with psychopathology. A high incidence of antisocial personalities has been found among heroin addicts. In a comparison between a group of 45 young institutionalized male addicts and a control group of nonaddicts, Gilbert and Lombardi (1967) found that distinguishing features were "the addict's antisocial traits, his depression, tension, insecurity, and feelings of inadequacy, and his difficulty in forming warm and lasting interpersonal relationships" (p. 536). Similarly, in a study of 112 drug abusers admitted to Bellevue Psychiatric Hospital in New York, Hekimian and Gershon (1968) found that heroin users usually showed antisocial personality characteristics. Meyer and Mirin (1979) found that opiate addicts were highly impulsive and showed an inability to delay gratification. Kosten and Rounsaville (1986) reported that about 68 percent of heroin abusers were also diagnosed as having a personality disorder. As in the case of alcoholism, however, it is essential to exercise caution in distinguishing between personality traits before and after addiction; the high incidence of psychopathology among narcotics addicts may in part result from, rather than precede, the long-term effects of addiction.

Addiction associated with sociocultural factors. In our society a so-called narcotics subculture exists in which addicts can obtain drugs and protect themselves against society's sanctions. Apparently the majority of narcotics addicts participate in this drug culture. The decision to join this culture has important future implications, for from that point on addicts will center their activities around their drug-user role. In short, addiction becomes a way of life.

With time, most young addicts who join the drug culture become increasingly withdrawn, indifferent to their friends (except those in the drug group), and apathetic about sexual activity. They are likely to abandon scholastic and athletic endeavors and to show a marked reduction in competitive and achievement strivings. Most of these addicts appear to lack good sex-role identification and to experience feelings of inadequacy when confronted with the demands of adulthood. While feeling progressively isolated from the broader culture, their feelings of group belongingness are bolstered by continued association with the addict milieu; at the same time, they come to view drugs both as a means of revolt against authority and conventional values and as a device for alleviating personal anxieties and tensions.

Treatments and Outcomes Treatment for heroin addiction is initially similar to that for alcoholism in that it involves building up an addict both physically and psychologically and providing help through the withdrawal period. Addicts often dread the discomfort of withdrawal, but in a hospital setting it is less abrupt and usually involves the administration of a synthetic drug that eases the distress.

After withdrawal has been completed, treatment focuses on helping a former addict make an adequate adjustment to his or her community and abstain from the further use of narcotics. Traditionally, however, the prognosis has been unfavorable. Despite the use of counseling, group therapy, and other measures, only about 13 percent of people discharged from government rehabilitation programs in England did not become readdicted (Stephens & Cottrell, 1972). These and comparable findings from studies in the United States have led to the hypothesis that withdrawal does not remove the craving for heroin and that a key target in treatment must be the alleviation of this craving.

An approach to dealing with the physiological craving for heroin was pioneered by a research team at the Rockefeller University in New York. Their approach involved the use of the drug methadone in conjunction with a rehabilitation program (counseling, group therapy, and other procedures) directed toward the "total resocialization" of addicts (Dole & Nyswander, 1967; Dole, Nyswander, & Warner, 1968). **Methadone hydrochloride** is a synthetic narcotic that is related to heroin and is equally addictive physiologically. Its usefulness in treatment lies in the fact that it satisfies an addict's craving for heroin without producing serious psychological impairment, if only because it is administered as a "treatment" in a formal clinical context.

As a result of impressive preliminary findings, the federal government in 1972 agreed to a licensing program for physicians and clinics using methadone in the treatment of narcotics addicts. As methadone treatment has become more widely employed, however, the question as to whether methadone alone is sufficeint to rehabilitate narcotics addicts has been raised. Research on whether providing psychological treatment along with methadone contributes to a successful outcome has been contradictory. A recent, well-controlled study to evaluate the effectiveness of providing psychotherapy in addition to methadone maintenance found that psychotherapy added little to treatment outcome. Patients randomly assigned to the methadone treatment group with no psychotherapy were doing as well at follow-up over 2½ years later as patients who had received psychotherapy along with methadone (Rounsaville et al., 1986). The researchers found that many former addicts improved in social (73 percent) and psychological (61 pecent) functioning with little ancillary treatment.

The practice of weaning an addict from heroin only to addict him or her to another narcotic drug that may be required for life is also questionable. Methadone advocates might respond that addicts on methadone can function normally and hold jobs—not possible for most heroin addicts. In addition, methadone is available legally, and its quality is controlled by government standards. Nor is it necessary to increase the dosage over time. In fact, some patients can eventually be taken off methadone without danger of relapse to heroin addiction. Many heroin addicts can undergo methadone treatment without initial hospitalization, and during treatment they are able to hold jobs and function in their family and community settings (Newman & Cates, 1977).

Improvements in methadone maintenance treatment over the past few years have increased its attractiveness for treating heroin abusers and have improved its overall success rates. Milby (1988) reported that consistent gains have been made in the improvement rates for methadone maintenance over the past 20 years: from 39.7 percent reported in studies from 1970 to 1975, 54.9 percent in studies during the years between 1976 and 1980, and 76.3 percent in studies reported since 1980. The increased success rates for methadone treatment have been attributed to the use of additional drugs like clonidine (an antihypertensive drug used to treat essential hypertension and prevent headache), which aid in the detoxification process and reduce the discomfort of withdrawal symptoms.

Barbiturates (Sedatives)

In the 1930s, powerful sedatives called **barbiturates** were introduced. Although barbiturates have legitimate medical uses, they are extremely dangerous drugs commonly associated with both physiological and psychological dependence and with lethal overdoses.

Effects of Barbiturates Barbiturates are widely used by physicians to calm patients and induce sleep. They act as depressants—somewhat like alcohol—to slow down the action of the central nervous system. Shortly after taking a barbiturate, an individual experiences a feeling of relaxation in which tensions seem to disappear, followed by a physical and intellectual lassitude and a tendency toward drowsiness and sleep—the intensity of such feelings varies depending on the type and amount of the barbiturate taken. Strong doses produce sleep almost immediately; excessive doses are lethal because they result in paralysis of the brain's respiratory centers.

Excessive use of barbiturates leads to increased tolerance as well as to physiological and psychological dependence. It can also lead to a variety of undesirable side effects, including sluggishness, slow speech, impaired comprehension and memory, extreme and sudden mood shifts, motor incoordination, and depression. Problem solving and decision making require great effort, and an individual usually is aware that his or her thinking is "fuzzy." Prolonged, excessive use of barbiturates can lead to brain damage and personality deterioration. Unlike opiates, tolerance of barbiturates does not increase the amount needed to cause death. This fact means that users can easily ingest fatal overdoses, either intentionally or accidentally. Indeed, barbiturates are associated with more overdoses and suicides than any other drug.

Causal Factors in Barbiturate Abuse and Dependence Though many young people experiment with barbiturates, or downers, most do not become dependent. In fact, the individuals who do become dependent on barbiturates tend to be middle-aged and older people who often rely on them as "sleeping pills" and who do not commonly use other classes of drugs (except, possibly, alcohol and the minor tranquilizers). Often these people are referred to as *silent abusers* because they take the drugs in the privacy of their homes and ordinarily do not become public nuisances. Barbiturate dependence usually seems to occur in emotionally maladjusted individuals who seek relief from feelings of anxiety, tension, inadequacy, and the stresses of life.

Barbiturates are commonly used with alcohol. Some users claim they can achieve an intense high—a kind of controlled hypersensitivity—by combining barbiturates, amphetamines, and alcohol. However, one possible effect of combining barbiturates and alcohol is death, because each drug *potentiates* (increases the action of) the other. This situation was true in the case of Judi, described in *HIGHLIGHT 9.6*.

Treatments and Outcomes As with many other drugs, it is often essential in treatment to distinguish between barbiturate intoxication, which results from the toxic effects of overdosage, and the symptoms associated with drug withdrawal. With barbiturates, withdrawal symptoms are more dangerous, severe, and long-lasting than in opiate withdrawal. A patient going through barbiturate withdrawal becomes anxious and apprehensive and manifests coarse tremors of the hands and face; additional symptoms commonly include insomnia, weakness, nausea, vomiting, abdominal cramps, rapid heart rate, elevated blood pressure, and loss of weight. Between the sixteenth hour and the fifth day, convulsions may occur. An acute delirious psychosis often develops, which may include symptoms similar to those found in withdrawal delirium.

For individuals used to taking large dosages, the withdrawal symptoms may last for as long as a month, but usually they tend to abate by the end of the first week. Fortunately, the withdrawal symptoms in barbiturate addiction can be minimized by administering increasingly smaller doses of the barbiturate itself or another drug producing similar effects. The withdrawal program is still a dangerous one, however, especially if barbiturate addiction is complicated by alcoholism or dependence on other drugs.

Amphetamines and Cocaine (Stimulants)

In contrast to barbiturates, which depress or slow down the action of the central nervous system, amphetamines and cocaine have chemical effects that stimulate or speed it up.

Amphetamines The earliest **amphetamine** to be introduced—Benzedrine, or amphetamine sul-

HIGHLIGHT 9.6

One Girl Who Gambled with Barbiturates and Lost

Judi A. was a young, attractive girl from a middle-class family who apparently was seeking something that eluded her. She died of an overdose of barbiturates. The newspaper account of her death began with a statement from the autopsy report:

"The unembalmed body for examination is that of a well-developed, well-nourished Caucasian female measuring 173 cm. (68 inches), weighing 100–110 pounds, with dark blonde hair, blue eyes, and consistent in appearance with the stated age of. . ."

Judi A. had lived only 17 years, 5 months and 27 days before her nude body was found on a grimy bed which had been made up on the floor of a rundown apartment in Newport Beach [California].

The inside of her mouth and her tongue were a bright red. The fingers of both hands were stained with the same color. . . . A small pill was found on the bed near the body, another was discovered on the floor.

Judi's death was classified as an accident because there was no evidence that she intended to take her own life. Actually it was about as accidental as if she'd killed herself while playing Russian roulette.

Judi didn't intentionally take too many reds. She was familiar with them, had taken them before, knew what to expect. She'd even had an earlier scare from a nonfatal overdose.

But her mind, clouded by the first few pills, lost count and she ingested a lethal number. She was dying before she swallowed the last pill. . . . (Hazlett, 1971, p. 1)

A complete investigation was ordered, in which it came to light that Judi had taken drugs when she had been unhappy at home, apparently often feeling unloved and unwanted. Following her parents' divorce, she had lived with her grandparents—who seemed to have been unaware of her drug problem and hence had not attempted to help her with it.

Judi had escalated the odds against herself by combining barbiturates with alcohol. Her friends said she had not been particularly different from the other girls they knew, most of whom also took pills in combination with beer or wine. In Judi's case, however, the combination had been lethal. She had not been able to find the something that had eluded her, but she had ultimately found death.

fate—was first synthesized in 1927 and became available in drugstores in the early 1930s as an inhalant to relieve stuffy noses. However, the manufacturers soon learned that some customers were chewing the wicks in the inhalers for "kicks." Thus the stimulating effects of amphetamine sulfate were discovered by the public before the drug was formally prescribed as a stimulant by physicians. In the late 1930s two newer amphetamines were introduced—Dexedrine (dextroamphetamine) and Methedrine (methamphetamine hydrochloride, also known as speed). The latter preparation is a far more potent stimulant of the central nervous system than either Benzedrine or Dexedrine and hence is considered more dangerous. In fact its abuse is lethal in an appreciable number of cases.

Initially these preparations were considered to be "wonder pills" that helped people to stay alert and awake and to function temporarily at a level beyond normal. During World War II, military interest was aroused in the stimulating effects of these drugs, and they were used by both Allied and German soldiers to ward off fatigue (Jarvik, 1967). Similarly, among civilians, amphetamines came to be widely used by night workers, long-distance truck drivers, students cramming for exams, and athletes striving to improve their performances. It was also discovered that amphetamines tend to suppress appetite, and they became popular with people trying to lose weight. In addition, they were often used to counteract the effects of barbiturates or other sleeping pills that had been taken the night before. As a result of their many uses, amphetamines were widely prescribed by doctors.

Today amphetamines are used medically for curbing the appetite when weight reduction is desirable; for treating individuals suffering from narcolepsy—a disorder in which people cannot prevent themselves from continually falling asleep during the day; and for treating hyperactive children. Curiously enough, amphetamines have a calming rather than a stimulating effect on many of these youngsters. Amphetamines are also sometimes prescribed for alleviating mild feelings of depression, relieving fatigue, and maintaining alertness for sustained periods of time.

Since the passage of the Controlled Substance Act of 1970 (DEA, 1979), amphetamines have been classified as Schedule II controlled substances—that is, drugs with high abuse potential that require a prescription for each purchase. As a result, medical use of amphetamines has declined in recent years, and they are more difficult to obtain legally. Nevertheless, it is apparently easy to find illegal sources of amphetamines, which thus remain among the most widely abused drugs.

Causes and effects of amphetamine abuse. Despite their legitimate medical uses, amphetamines are not a magical source of extra mental or physical energy, but rather serve to push users toward greater expenditures of their own resources—often to a point of hazardous fatigue. In fact athletes have damaged their careers by using speed to try to improve their stamina and performance (Furlong, 1971). Although amphetamines are psychologically but not physiologically addictive, the body does build up tolerance to them rapidly. Thus habituated users may consume pills by the mouthful several times a day, whereas such amounts would be lethal to nonusers. In some instances, users inject the drug to get faster and more intense results. To get high on amphetamines, people may give themselves from 6 to 200 times the daily medical dosage usually prescribed for dieters.

For a person who exceeds prescribed dosages, amphetamine consumption results in heightened blood pressure, enlarged pupils, unclear or rapid speech, profuse sweating, tremors, excitability, loss of appetite, confusion, and sleeplessness. In some instances the jolt to body physiology from "shooting" (injecting) Methedrine can raise blood pressure enough to cause immediate death. In addition, the chronic abuse of amphetamines can result in brain damage and a wide range of psychopathology, including a disorder known as amphetamine psychosis, which appears similar to paranoid schizophrenia. Suicide, homicide, assault, and various other acts of violence are associated with amphetamine abuse. In the United States, Ellinwood (1971) studied 13 people who committed homicide under amphetamine intoxication and found that, in most cases, "the events leading to the homicidal act were directly related to amphetamine-induced paranoid thinking, panic, emotional lability (instability), or lowered impulse control" (p. 90). A study of 100 hospital admissions for amphetamine intoxication revealed that 25 of the subjects had attempted suicide while under the influence of amphetamines (Nelson, 1969).

Treatments and outcomes. Withdrawal from amphetamines is usually painless physically, because physiological addiction is absent or minimal. In some instances, however, withdrawal on a cold turkey basis from the chronic, excessive use of amphetamines can result in cramping, nausea, diarrhea, and even convulsions (AMA, 1968a).

Psychological dependence is another matter, however, and abrupt abstinence commonly results in feelings of weariness and depression. The depression usually reaches its peak in 48 to 72 hours, often remains intense for a day or two, and then tends to lessen gradually over a period of several days. Mild feelings of depression and lassitude may persist for weeks or even months after the last dose. If brain damage has occurred, residual effects may also include impaired ability to concentrate, learn, and remember, with resulting social, economic, and personality deterioration.

Cocaine Like opium, **cocaine** is a plant product discovered and used in ancient times. It was widely used in the pre-Columbian world of Mexico and Peru (Guerra, 1971). It has been endorsed by such diverse figures as Sigmund Freud and the legendary Sherlock Holmes. Because of its exorbitant price, cocaine has become known as the "high" for the affluent. Its use increased significantly in the United States during the 1980s to the point that it was considered epidemic, especially among middle- and upper-income groups. Hospital admissions for cocaine abuse nearly doubled between 1978 and 1981 (NIDA, 1981). In a recent follow-up study of young adults (ages 15 to 16) who had been surveyed nine years earlier about drug use, Kandel et al. (1986) found that 37 percent of males and 24 percent of females surveyed had tried cocaine. Recent statistics (NIDA, 1990) suggest that the number of Americans who are "occasional cocaine users" is declining: 45 percent in the last two years and 72 percent since 1985. It may be that drug use is becoming unfashionable in the health-conscious middle- and upper-socioeconomic classes. The number of hardcore cocaine users, however, especially those in poverty-ridden inner-city neighborhoods, is increasing.

Like the opiates, cocaine may be ingested by sniffing, swallowing, or injecting. Also like the opiates, it precipitates a euphoric state of four to six hours' duration, during which a user experiences feelings of confidence and contentment. However, this blissful state may be preceded by headache, dizziness, and restlessness. When cocaine is chronically abused, acute toxic psychotic symptoms may occur, similar to those in acute schizophrenia—a user encounters frightening visual, auditory, and tactual hallucinations, such as the "cocaine bug" (Post, 1975).

Unlike the opiates, cocaine stimulates the cortex of the brain, inducing sleeplessness and excitement as well as stimulating and accentuating sexual processes. Consequently, some individuals have been known to administer cocaine to others as an aid to seduction. To complicate matters, Rolfs, Goldberg, and Sharrar (1990) found that cocaine abusers, because of their high sexual promiscuity, were at risk for contracting syphilis.

Dependence on cocaine also differs somewhat from dependence on opiates. It was believed until recently that tolerance was not increased appreciably with cocaine use. However, acute tolerance has now been demonstrated, and some chronic tolerance may occur as well (Fischman & Schuster, 1982; Jones, 1984). The previous view that cocaine abusers did not develop physiological dependence on the drug also has been changing. Recently, Gawin and Kleber (1986) demonstrated that chronic abusers who become abstinent develop uniform, depression-like symptoms, but the symptoms are transient. These states are usually followed by a period of dysphoria. Kleinman et al. (1990) reported that 47 percent of cocaine abusers were found to be clinically depressed, and many also reported symptoms of phobic behavior.

The psychological and life problems experienced by cocaine users are often great. In a 2½-year follow-up study of cocaine users and nonusers, Kosten, Rounsaville, and Kleber (1988) found that users (particularly those whose use increased over the span of the study) had significantly more psychosocial problems than nonusers. These problems included employment, family, psychological, and legal matters. Many life problems experienced by cocaine abusers result, in part, from the considerable amounts of money that are required to support their habits. Kleinman et al. (1990) reported that most of the cocaine abusers in their sample were spending in excess of $1000 per month to buy the drug.

Finally, cocaine use can be fatal—a recent study showed that cocaine-related deaths almost tripled between 1985 and 1988, with a total of 1033 deaths nationwide in the first six months of 1988, excluding New York City (Project DAWN, 1988). This point was dramatically illustrated during a period of ten days in the summer of 1986 when two well-known athletes, Len Bias, an all-American basketball player, and Don Rogers, a star running back for the Cleveland Browns, died after taking cocaine.

Psychological dependence on cocaine, like addiction to opiates, often leads to an obsession with procuring the drug, concurrent with a loss of social approval and self-respect. The following case illustrates this pattern:

The subject was a strikingly pretty, intelligent woman of 19 who had divorced her husband two years previously. She had married at the age of 16 and stated that she was terribly in love with her husband but he had turned out to be cruel and brutal. The woman was too ashamed of her marital failure (her parents had violently opposed the marriage and she had left home against their will) to return to her home. She had moved away from her husband and had gotten a job as a cocktail waitress in the same bar where her husband had been accustomed to taking her. She had been severely depressed, and several of his friends had insisted on buying her drinks to cheer her up. This process had continued for almost a year, during which she drank excessively but managed to hold her job. Following this, she had met a man in the bar where she worked who had introduced her to cocaine, assuring her that it would cheer her up and get rid of her blues. She stated that it both "hopped me up and gave me a feeling of peace and contentment." For a period of several months, she had purchased her cocaine from this same man until she had become ill with appendicitis and had been unable to pay the stiff prices he asked. Following an appendectomy, she had been induced to share his apartment as a means of defraying her expenses and ensuring the supply of cocaine, which she had now become heavily dependent on psychologically. She stated that she had felt she could not work without it. During this period, she had had sexual relations with the man although she had considered it immoral and had severe guilt feelings about it. This pattern had continued for several months until her "roommate" had upped his prices on the cocaine, on the excuse that it had been getting more difficult to obtain. He had suggested that she might be able to earn enough money to pay for it if she were not so prudish about whom she slept with. At this time, the full significance of where her behavior was leading seems to have dawned on her and she had come voluntarily to a community clinic for assistance.

Many celebrities—actors, musicians, politicians, sports figures—have become involved in cocaine use. Tragically, the activities of many of these individuals have led to drug-related problems and drug abuse. Former Mayor Marion Barry of Washington, D.C., made headlines for months after he was arrested while using cocaine in a hotel room with a young woman who had turned FBI informer. Through her, the FBI was able to videotape the encounter; we can clearly see Barry smoking crack in the portion of the tape shown here. His prominence as a public figure put the pervasive use of cocaine in the spotlight; about one million other, less prominent, Americans have also tried crack.

A new "supercharged" variety of cocaine, with the street names of *crack* and *rock,* made its appearance in the United States during the mid-1980s and became an immediate sensation among drug users. The high from crack is immediate and intense. It is estimated that over 1 million Americans have tried crack. The resulting human problems have been dramatic. Crack is believed to be one of the most dangerous drugs introduced to date because of its immediate addicting properties and its health risks (Smith, 1989). The devastation this drug can cause to a user is illustrated in the following case:

Eva is a 16-year-old patient at New York City's Phoenix House drug rehabilitation center who got hooked on crack two years ago. The product of a troubled middle-class family, she was already a heavy drinker and pot smoker when she was introduced to coke by her older brother, a young dope pusher. "When you take the first toke on a crack pipe, you get on top of the world," she says.

She first started stealing from family and friends to support her habit. She soon turned to prostitution and went through two abortions before she was 16. "I didn't give a damn about protecting myself," she said. "I just wanted to get high. Fear of pregnancy didn't cross my mind when I hit the sack with someone for drugs." (Time, 1986)

The modifications in DSM-III-R diagnostic classification reflect a significant increase in our knowledge of cocaine's addictive properties. A new disorder, cocaine withdrawal, is described, which involves symptoms of depression, fatigue, disturbed sleep, and increased dreaming.

Treatment for psychological dependence on cocaine does not differ appreciably from that for other drugs that involve physiological dependence. Kosten (1989) reported that effective cocaine-abuse treatment includes the use of medications, such as desipramine, to reduce cravings and the use of psychological therapy to insure treatment compliance. The feelings of tension and depression that accompany absence of the drug have to be dealt with during the immediate withdrawal period.

LSD and Related Drugs (Hallucinogens)

The **hallucinogens** are drugs whose properties are thought to induce hallucinations. In fact, however, these preparations do not so often "create" sensory images as distort them, so that an individual sees or hears things in different and unusual ways. These drugs are often referred to as *psychedelics.* The major drugs in this category are LSD (lysergic acid diethylamide), mescaline, and psilocybin. Not long ago, PCP, or "angel dust," became popular as well. Our present discussion will be restricted largely to LSD because of its unusual hallucinogenic properties.

LSD The most potent of the hallucinogens, the odorless, colorless, and tasteless drug **LSD** can produce intoxication with an amount smaller than a grain of salt. It is a chemically synthesized substance first discovered by the Swiss chemist Hoffman in 1938. Hoffman was not aware of the potent hallucinatory qualities of LSD until some five years after his discovery, when he swallowed a small amount. This is his report of the experience:

Last Friday, April 16, 1943, I was forced to stop my work in the laboratory in the middle of the afternoon and to go home, as I was seized by a peculiar restlessness associated with a sensation of mild dizziness. On arriving home, I lay down and sank into a kind of drunkenness which was not unpleasant and which was characterized by extreme activity of imagination. As I lay in a dazed condition with my eyes closed (I experienced daylight as disagreeably bright) there surged upon me an uninterrupted stream of fantastic images of extraordinary plasticity and vividness and accompanied by an intense kaleidoscope-like play of colors. This condition gradually passed off after about two hours." (Hoffman, 1971, p. 23)

Hoffman followed up this experience with a series of planned self-observations with LSD, some of which he described as "harrowing." Researchers thought LSD might be useful for the induction and study of hallucinogenic states or "model psychoses," which were thought to be related to schizophrenia. About 1950, LSD was introduced into the United States for purposes of such research and to ascertain whether it might have medical or therapeutic uses. Despite considerable research, however, LSD has not proven therapeutically useful.

After taking LSD, a person typically goes through about eight hours of changes in sensory perception, lability of emotional experiences, and feelings of depersonalization and detachment. The peak of physiological and psychological effects usually occurs between the second and fourth hours. Physiological effects include increased heart rate, elevation of blood pressure, and faster and more variable breathing.

An LSD "trip" is not always pleasant. It can be extremely traumatic, and the distorted objects and sounds, the illusory colors, and the new thoughts can be menacing and terrifying. For example, Rorvik (1970) has cited the case of a young British law student who tried to "continue time" by using a dental drill to bore a hole in his head while under the influence of LSD. In other instances, people undergoing "bad trips" have set themselves aflame, jumped from high places, and taken other drugs that proved lethal in combination with LSD.

An interesting and unusual phenomenon that may occur following the use of LSD is a **flashback,** an involuntary recurrence of perceptual distortions or hallucinations weeks or even months after taking the drug. These experiences appear to be relatively rare among individuals who have taken LSD only once—although they do sometimes occur. One recent study found that continued effects on visual function were apparent at least two years following LSD use. Abraham and Wolf (1988) reported that individuals who had used LSD for a week were shown to have reduced visual sensitivity to light during dark adaptation and showed other visual problems compared to control individuals who had never used the drug.

Despite the possibility of adverse reactions, LSD was widely publicized during the 1960s, and a number of relatively well-known people experimented with it and gave glowing accounts of their "trips." In fact, during this period, an "LSD movement" was under way, based on the conviction that the drug could "expand the mind" and enable one to use talents and realize potentials previously undetected. No evidence exists that LSD enhances creative activity: no recognized works of art have been produced under the influence of the drug or as a consequence of a psychedelic experience. Although several artists have claimed improved creativity stemming from their LSD experiences, objective observers recognize few, if any, improvements in the work of these artists (AMA, 1968a). It should be pointed out, too, that though users of LSD do not develop physiological dependence, some chronic users have developed psychological dependence in the sense that they focus their life around LSD experiences.

For acute psychoses induced by LSD intoxication, treatment requires hospitalization and is primarily a medical matter. Often the outcome in such cases depends heavily on an individual's personal stability prior to taking the drug; in some cases, prolonged hospitalization may be required. Fortunately, brief psychotherapy is usually effective in treating psychological dependence on LSD and in preventing the recurrence of flashbacks that may still haunt an individual as a result of a bad trip. As in the case of trauma experienced in combat or civilian disasters, therapy is aimed at helping the individual work through the painful experience and integrate it into his or her self-structure.

Mescaline and Psilocybin Two other well-known hallucinogens are mescaline and psilocybin. **Mescaline** is derived from the small, disclike growths (mescal buttons) at the top of the peyote cactus; **psilocybin** is obtained from a variety of "sacred" Mexican mushrooms known as *Psilocybe mexicana.* These drugs have been used for centuries in the ceremonial rites of native peoples living in

Mexico, the American southwest, and Central and South America. In fact, they were used by the Aztecs for such purposes long before the Spanish invasion. Both drugs have mind-altering and hallucinogenic properties, but their principal effect appears to be enabling an individual to see, hear, and otherwise experience events in unaccustomed ways—transporting him or her into a realm of "nonordinary reality." As with LSD, no definite evidence shows that mescaline and psilocybin actually "expand consciousness" or create new ideas; rather, they seem primarily to alter or distort experience.

Marijuana

Although **marijuana** may be classified as a mild hallucinogen, there are significant differences in the nature, intensity, and duration of its effects as compared with those induced by LSD, mescaline, and other major hallucinogens. Marijuana comes from the leaves and flowering tops of the hemp plant, *Cannabis sativa.* The plant grows in mild climates throughout the world, including parts of India, Africa, Mexico, South America, and the United States. In its prepared state, marijuana consists chiefly of the dried green leaves—hence the colloquial name *grass.* It is ordinarily smoked in the form of cigarettes (reefers, or joints) or in pipes, but it can also be baked into brownies and other foods. In some cultures the leaves are steeped in hot water and the liquid is drunk, much as one might drink tea. Marijuana is related to a stronger drug, **hashish,** which is derived from the resin exuded by the cannabis plant and made into a gummy powder. Hashish, like marijuana, may be smoked, chewed, or drunk.

Both marijuana and hashish use can be traced far back into history. Cannabis was apparently known in ancient China (Blum, 1969; Culliton, 1970) and was listed in the herbal compendiums of the Chinese emperor Shen Nung, written about 2737 B.C. Until the late 1960s, marijuana use in the United States was confined largely to members of lower socioeconomic minority groups and to people in entertainment and related fields. In the late 1960s, however, its use among the youth of our society dramatically increased, and during the early 1970s it was estimated that over half the teenagers and young adults in America had experimented with marijuana in social situations, with about 10 percent presumably going from occasional to habitual use. Recently, Kandel et al. (1986) reported that among 24- and 25-year-old subjects, about 78 percent of males and 69 percent of females had tried marijuana.

Effects of marijuana The specific effects of marijuana vary greatly, depending on the quality and dosage of the drug, the personality and mood of the user, the user's past experiences with the drug, the social setting, and the user's expectations. However, considerable consensus exists among regular users that when marijuana is smoked and inhaled, an individual gets high. This state is one of mild euphoria distinguished by increased feelings of well-being, heightened perceptual acuity, and pleasant relaxation, often accompanied by a sensation of drifting or floating away. Sensory inputs are intensified. Often a person's sense of time is stretched or distorted, so that an event lasting but a few seconds may seem to cover a much longer span. Short-term memory may also be affected, as when one notices a bite taken out of a sandwich but does not remember having taken it. For most users, pleasurable experiences, including sexual intercourse, are reportedly enhanced. When smoked, marijuana is rapidly absorbed and its effects appear within seconds to minutes but seldom last more than two to three hours.

Marijuana may lead to unpleasant as well as pleasant experiences. For example, if an individual takes the drug while in an unhappy, angry, suspicious, or frightened mood, unsavory feelings may be magnified. With higher dosages and with certain unstable or susceptible individuals, marijuana can produce extreme euphoria, hilarity, and overtalkativeness; it can also produce intense anxiety and depression as well as delusions, hallucinations, and

Group counseling is a common treatment for psychological dependence on drugs. In the give and take of group therapy, individuals may be able to face the consequences of their addiction and to see new possibilities for coping with it.

other psychotic-like behavior. Recent evidence (Tien & Anthony, 1990) suggests a strong relationship between daily marijuana use and the occurrence of self-reported psychotic symptoms.

Marijuana's short-range physiological effects include a moderate increase in heart rate, a slowing of reaction time, a slight contraction of pupil size, bloodshot and itchy eyes, a dry mouth, and an increased appetite. Furthermore, Braff et al. (1981) reported that marijuana induces memory dysfunction and a slowing of information processing. Continued use of high dosages over time tends to produce lethargy and passivity. In such cases marijuana appears to have a depressant and a hallucinogenic effect. The effects of long-term and habitual marijuana use are still under investigation, although a number of possible adverse side effects have been related to the prolonged, heavy use of marijuana.

Marijuana has often been compared to heroin, but the two drugs have little in common with respect either to tolerance or to physiological dependence. Marijuana does not lead to physiological dependence, as heroin does, so discontinued use is not accompanied by withdrawal symptoms. Marijuana can, however, lead to psychological dependence, in which an individual experiences a strong need for the drug whenever he or she feels anxious and tense.

Caffeine and Nicotine

Two quite common addictions to legally available and widely used substances, caffeine and nicotine, are included in the DSM III-R. Although these addictions do not represent the extensive and self-destructive problems found in the drug and alcohol disorders previously described, they are important physical and mental health problems in our society for several reasons: (a) These drugs are easy to abuse. It is easy to become addicted to them because they are widely used and most people are exposed to them early in life. (b) These drugs are readily available to anyone desiring to use them; in fact, it is usually difficult, because of peer pressure, to avoid using them in our society. (c) Both caffeine and nicotine have clearly addictive properties; use of them promotes further use, until they become a needed commodity in one's daily life. (d) It is difficult to quit using these drugs both because of their addictive properties and because they are so embedded in the social context (nicotine use, however, is falling out of favor in many settings). (e) The extreme difficulty most people have dealing with the withdrawal symptoms when trying to "break the habit" often produce considerable frustration. (f) Finally, the health problems and side effects of these drugs have been widely noted. One in seven deaths in the United States is associated with cigarette consumption (USDHHS, 1988).

Because of their tenacity as habits and their contributions to many major health problems, we will examine each of these addictions in more detail.

Caffeine **Caffeine** is a chemical compound found in many commonly available drinks and foods. Although the consumption of caffeine is widely practiced and socially promoted in contemporary society, problems can occur as a result of excessive caffeine intake. The negative effects of caffeine involve intoxication rather than withdrawal. Unlike with other drugs, such as alcohol or nicotine, withdrawal from caffeine does not produce severe symptoms, except for headache, which is usually mild.

Caffeine-induced organic mental disorder (also referred to as Caffeinism), as described in DSM-III-R, involves symptoms of restlessness, nervousness, excitement, insomnia, muscle twitching, and gastrointestinal complaints. It follows the ingestion of caffeine-containing substances, such as coffee, tea, cola, or chocolate. The amount of caffeine that results in intoxication differs among individuals; however, consumption of over 1 gram of caffeine could result in muscle twitching, cardiac arrythmia, agitation, and rambling thinking. Consumption of 10 grams of caffeine can produce seizures, respiratory failures, and death.

Nicotine **Nicotine** is a poisonous akaloid that is the chief active ingredient in tobacco; it is found in such items as cigarettes, chewing tobacco, and cigars, and is even used as an insecticide.

Strong evidence indicates a nicotine dependency syndrome (USDHHS, 1988). Nicotine-induced organic mental disorder, as it is called in DSM-III-R, results from ceasing or reducing the intake of nicotine-containing substances after an individual has acquired physical dependence on them. The diagnostic criteria for nicotine withdrawal include (a) the daily use of nicotine for at least several weeks; and (b) the following symptoms after nicotine ingestion is stopped or reduced: craving for nicotine; irritability, frustration, or anger; anxiety; difficulty concentrating; restlessness; decreased heart rate; and increased appetite or weight gain. Several other physical concomitants are associated with withdrawal from nicotine, including decreased metabolic rate, headaches, insomnia, tremors, increased coughing, and impairment of performance on tasks requiring attention.

These withdrawal symptoms usually continue for several days to several weeks, depending on the extent of the nicotine habit. Some individuals report a desire for nicotine continuing for several months after they have quit smoking. In general, nicotine withdrawal symptoms operate in a manner similar to other addictions—they are "time limited and abate with drug replacement or gradual reduction" (Hughes, Higgins, & Hatsukami, 1990, p. 381).

Treatment of nicotine withdrawal Over the past 25 years, since the Surgeon General's report that detailed the health hazards of smoking cigarettes, numerous treatment programs have been developed to aid smokers in quitting (Lando, in press; Schwartz, 1987; USDHHS, 1989). Quit-smoking programs use many different methods, including social support groups; various pharmacologic agents, which replace cigarette consumption with other safer forms of nicotine, such as candy or gum; self-directed change, which involves giving individuals guidance as to how they can change their own behaviors (Abrams et al., in press); and professional treatment using psychological procedures such as behavioral or cognitive-behavioral interventions (Lando, in press).

In general, tobacco dependency can be successfully treated (USDHHS, 1989), and most of the quit-smoking programs enjoy some success, averaging about a 20 to 25 percent success rate, when evaluated by objective criteria. Lando (in press) concluded that "no *single* treatment suitable for all smokers has emerged," and Schwartz (1987) found that smokers tend to prefer self-help and minimal-contact treatments over more intensive treatment programs.

OTHER ADDICTIVE DISORDERS: HYPEROBESITY AND PATHOLOGICAL GAMBLING

Not all addictive disorders involve the use of substances with chemical properties that induce dependency. People can develop "addictions" to certain activities that can be just as life-threatening as severe alcoholism and just as damaging, psychologically and socially, as drug abuse. We include two such disorders in this chapter—hyperobesity and pathological gambling. They are similar to other addictions in their behavioral manifestations, their etiologies, and their resistance to treatments.

Hyperobesity

To get an idea of how extensive the problem of obesity is, just look around and count the number of individuals who are seriously overweight. Weiss (1984), defining hyperobesity as 20 percent in excess of desirable weight, estimates that from 15 to 16 million Americans fall into this category. In addition, Weiss reports that obesity is a serious but often overlooked health problem in the United States today. Stewart and Brook (1983) found, in a survey of 5817 Americans aged 14 to 61, that 10 percent were moderately overweight and 12 percent severely overweight.

In this discussion, we are concerned with **hyperobesity**—often called morbid obesity—which we define as being 100 pounds or more above ideal body weight. Such obesity is not simply unattractive; it can be a dangerous, life-threatening disorder, resulting in such conditions as diabetes, musculoskeletal problems, high blood pressure, and other cardiovascular diseases that may place an individual at high risk for a heart attack. Although some cases of extreme obesity result from metabolic or hormonal disorders, most obese individuals simply take in more calories than they burn off.

Obesity, as a disorder, may be placed in several diagnostic categories, depending on which characteristics are being emphasized. If we focus on the physical changes, for example, we may view obesity as having both psychological and physical components. Many clinicians, however, view the central problem not as the excessive weight itself, but as the long-standing habit of overeating. Thus obesity resulting from gross, habitual overeating is considered to be more like the problems found in the personality disorders—especially those involving loss of control over an appetite of some kind (Kurland, 1967; Leon et al., 1978; Orford, 1985).

Causes of Persistent Overeating What prompts people to overeat to the point of obesity, despite an awareness of the detrimental health effects and a consciousness of the strong social prejudice in favor of the "body beautiful"? Several potential causal factors have been explored; although results are not conclusive, biological and learning factors seem to be of great importance.

Biological factors. Some people seem able to eat high-calorie foods without significant weight gain, while others become overweight easily and engage in a constant struggle to maintain their weight. Most people gain weight with advancing age, but this gain could be related to reduced activity and to the fact that older people are likely to continue their earlier eating habits even though they need fewer calories. As already indicated, some individuals have metabolic or endocrine anomalies that can produce obesity at any age, though these cases seem to be relatively rare.

Adult obesity is related to the number and size of the adipose cells (fat cells) in the body (Weiss, 1984). Individuals who are obese have markedly more adipose cells than people of normal weight. When weight is lost, the size of the cells is reduced, but not their number. Some evidence suggests that the total number of adipose cells stays the same from childhood on (Crisp et al., 1970). It is possible that overfeeding infants and young children may cause them to develop more adipose cells and may thus predispose them to weight problems in adulthood.

Psychosocial factors. Factors other than biological endowment play an important role in obesity (Newman et al., 1990). In many cases the key determinants of excessive eating and obesity appear to be family behavior patterns. In some families, the customary diet or an overemphasis on food may produce obesity in many or all family members. In such families, a fat baby may be seen as a healthy baby, and there may be great pressure on infants and children to eat more than they want. In other families, eating (or overeating) becomes a habitual means of alleviating emotional distress.

Several psychological views address the causes of gross habitual overeating. Some of these views are discussed in the following paragraphs:

1. According to the psychodynamic view, obese individuals are fixated at the oral stage of psychosexual development (Bychowski, 1950). They are believed to orient their lives around oral gratification (through excessive eating) because their libidinal energies and psychological growth have not advanced to a more mature level.

This view has been elaborated by Bruch (1973), who distinguishes between developmental obesity and reactive obesity. She sees developmental obesity as a childhood response to parental rejection or other severe disturbances in the parent-child relationship. Supposedly, the parents compensate for their emotional rejection by overfeeding and overprotecting the child. Such children never learn to distinguish different internal signals because their parents respond to all signs of distress by giving them food. Bruch sees this pattern as leading to a distorted perception of internal states—that is, not knowing when enough food has been ingested.

Reactive obesity is defined by Bruch as obesity that occurs in adults as a reaction to trauma or stress. Here, individuals are thought to use the defense mechanism of overeating to lessen their feelings of distress or depression. Though this view may be depicted as "truth" in countless cartoons and sitcoms, the research findings are inconclusive.

2. According to the *externality hypothesis,* eating is under the control of external cues rather than an individual's internal state. Whereas hunger and its satisfaction dictate the eating patterns of most people, obese people are seen as being at the mercy of environmental inducements. Regardless of how recently or amply they have eaten, they may be prompted to eat again simply by the sight or smell of food. This reliance on external cues is pointedly illustrated in the complaint of an obese 29-year-old patient:

I crave food . . . everywhere I go, whatever I do, I am reminded of food. Today after breakfast, I rode to work on the bus. The advertisements made me so hungry that I had to stop at the coffee shop for rolls before I went into the office. When I watch TV, I find myself constantly eating—I want everything. I can't stop. My big downfall is "munchies"—peanuts, potato chips, brownies. Going to the grocery store, I lose control and before you know it I have to get another grocery cart—and the first one is just full of junk. I can sit down in the evening to write a letter and before I know it the jar of peanuts is completely gone!

Other investigators, however, reject the externality hypothesis. Rodin (1974) found obese people no more sensitive to external cues than people of normal weight. Leon and Roth (1977), too, in a review of research on this hypothesis, found the evidence highly equivocal.

3. The simplest explanation—and therefore the easiest to accept—seems to be found in the behavioral view. According to this view, a person's weight gain and his or her tendency to maintain excessive weight can be explained quite simply in terms of learning principles (Jordan & Levitz, 1975; Leon & Chamberlain, 1973; Stuart, 1971b).

For all of us, eating behavior is determined in part by conditioned responses to a wide range of environmental stimuli. For example, people are encouraged to eat at parties and movies, while watching TV, and even at work. Eating is reinforced in all these situations, and it is difficult to avoid the many inducements to eat. Thus a wide assortment of seemingly avoidable reinforcers and conditioned stimuli enter the lives of most Americans.

Obese people, however, have been shown to be conditioned to more cues—both internal and external—than people of normal weight. Anxiety, anger, boredom, and social inducements all may lead to overeating. Eating in response to such cues is then reinforced because the taste of good food is pleasurable and the individual's emotional tension is reduced. This reinforcement increases the probability that overeating will continue and worsen.

With such frequent overfeeding, obese people may then learn not to respond to satiety cues, no longer feeling full when they have had enough. Meanwhile, physical activity, because its short-term effects are often aversive rather than pleasant, tends not to be reinforced, especially as pounds accumulate. Thus obese individuals may become less and less active.

Sociocultural factors. Different cultures have different concepts of human beauty. Some value slimness; others, a rounded contour. In some cultures, obesity is valued as a sign of social influence and power. Within our own society, obesity seems to be related to social class, occurring six times as often in lower-class adults and nine times more often in lower-class youngsters. (Stunkard et al., 1972). Obesity may be related to high-carbohydrate diets in lower-class families, however.

Treatment of Hyperobesity Losing weight is a preoccupation of many Americans; diet books, dietary aids, and weight-loss programs are big business. Diet plans abound, with new programs emerging as often as clothing fads. The success rates of most of these devices and programs are quite low. In fact Stuart (1967) reported that the average outcome from diets is a regaining of 105 percent of the weight lost (Stuart, 1967). Cyclic loss and regaining can even be dangerous because it may do serious damage to the cardiovascular system, further compounding the problem.

Most obese patients who seek professional help have failed on many diets in the past. Some of the most successful dietary programs are the self-control behavioral management programs, conducted in groups and including follow-up booster sessions (Kingsley & Wilson, 1977).

A number of weight-loss group programs are conducted by commercial organizations like TOPS (Take Off Pounds Sensibly) and Weight Watchers (Bumbalo & Young, 1973). These programs provide strong group pressures to reduce weight by public praise of weight losses and public disapproval and "punishments" for failures. Thus they provide community support and encouragement to maintain better eating habits. Individuals who remain with these group programs lose about 14 pounds on the average (Garb & Stunkard, 1974); however, less than a third of those who begin the programs stay for 24 months.

Fasting or starvation diets under medically controlled conditions generally produce weight losses in hyperobese patients—with some studies reporting losses of over 100 pounds (Leon, 1976). This method of rapid weight loss, however, may involve several dangerous potential complications, such as hypertension, gout, and kidney failure (Munro & Duncan, 1972; Runcie & Thompson, 1970). Two eating disorders, anorexia nervosa and bulimia (discussed in Chapter 7), involve an excessive preoccupation with weight loss.

Another questionable medical treatment of hyperobese patients has centered on the use of *anorexigenic drugs* to reduce appetite. Diet pills, such as amphetamines, suppress the desire for food and, as a result, have been used extensively. Again, however, maintenance of weight loss once the diet pills are gone often becomes a problem.

Moreover, diet pills often present an additional problem of their own. As we have seen, amphetamines are addicting substances and are particularly dangerous when used in combination with other substances, such as alcohol. The general ineffectiveness of amphetamines for long-term weight control plus their high abuse potential has made these drugs of doubtful value in weight-reduction programs.

The most effective psychological treatment procedures for extremely obese patients are behavioral management methods, which teach individuals to take off weight gradually through reduced food intake and exercise (Jeffery, Wing, & Stunkard, 1978). A number of methods using positive reinforcement, self-monitoring, and self-reward can produce moderate weight loss over time. In general these procedures, based on positive reinforcement, are more effective than classical conditioning procedures, such as aversive conditioning in which shock or unpleasant thoughts may be paired with eating behavior (Leon, 1976).

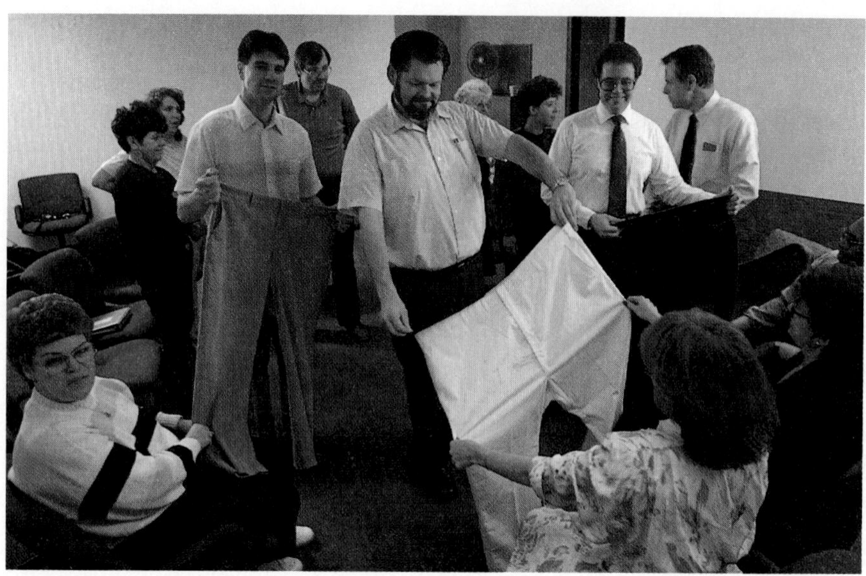

Some of the most successful dietary programs are the self-control behavioral management programs, conducted in groups. Here dieters show how much weight they have lost by proudly displaying pants they can no longer wear. Programs like this provide strong group pressures to lose weight through public praise of successes and support and encouragement for maintaining better eating habits.

The treatment of extremely obese patients is often a difficult and frustrating task for all concerned. Even with the most effective treatment procedures, failures abound, partly due to the necessity of self-motivation in treatment.

In one case involving a 15-year-old high school student named Beth, a variety of treatment and counseling approaches were used, including a token reward system for eating balanced meals with smaller portions. Though she reportedly complied with the point system and earned rewards for the first three weeks, she nevertheless lost little weight. She said that she had cut down on high-calorie snacks but was still eating large portions at mealtimes. The treatment sessions focused on problems occurring in her school and with her family that were related to her eating habits. Ways of maintaining her diet were explored, as were issues concerning the decision to eat and her commitment to change. The primary emphasis was on self-control and self-management techniques. She was also taught a system of self-monitoring of her food intake. After 16 treatment sessions over a period of five months, Beth had only decreased her weight from an original 208½ pounds to 207¼ pounds. The therapist confronted her with her apparent lack of commitment and pointed out the difference between wanting to lose weight and wanting to change her eating style. Two weeks later, Beth came to the final session having decided that the freedom to eat what she wanted was more important to her at that point in her life than changing her eating patterns.

The poor outcome in this example illustrates the tenacity of extreme obesity. As in Beth's case, many patients lose interest in their remote goal and choose to remain obese rather than make the difficult and persistent effort required to lose weight and keep it off.

A promising cognitive-behavioral treatment approach for eating disorders has been explored by Garner (1986). This approach emphasizes how the symptom pattern of obesity logically follows from faulty assumptions individuals make and their beliefs about their bodies. The cognitive-behavioral approach is not incompatible with other treatment approaches and allows exploration of early developmental issues, interpersonal conflicts, faulty family interaction patterns, and biological factors. In this approach a patient (a) is taught to monitor his or her own thinking, especially the pattern of faulty beliefs; (b) is helped to recognize the connection between faulty thoughts and maladaptive eating behaviors; (c) is taught to seek evidence for the faulty beliefs underlying the overeating; and (d) is taught to gradually substitute more realistic and appropriate views of his or her own behaviors based on objective evidence.

Garner's cognitive-behavioral approach follows two "tracks" in assisting a patient to alter his or her eating patterns. The first track involves normalizing the patient's eating behavior and physical condition; the second track involves assisting the patient to assess his or her faulty thoughts and actions (Garner, 1986). Evidence on the effectiveness of this approach awaits further research.

Pathological Gambling

Gambling is usually defined as wagering on games or events in which chance largely determines the outcome. In modern societies, money is typically the item of exchange; in other societies, seashell currency, beads, jewelry, and food are often used. The ancient Chinese frequently wagered hairs of their heads—and sometimes even fingers, toes, and limbs—on games of chance (Cohen & Hansel, 1956). Regardless of the item of exchange, gambling seems to be an enduring human proclivity. Judging from written history and the studies of anthropologists, gambling has occurred and continues to occur almost universally and among all social strata.

Pathological gambling, also known as compulsive gambling, is an addictive behavior in which gambling disrupts an individual's life. Although this behavior pattern does not involve a chemically addictive substance, it can be considered an addictive disorder because of the personality factors that tend to characterize compulsive gamblers, the difficulties attributable to compulsive gambling, and the treatment problems involved. Like other addictions, pathological gambling involves behavior maintained by short-term gains despite long-term disruption of an individual's life.

Clinical Picture in Pathological Gambling

Gambling in our society takes many forms, including casino gambling, betting on horse races (legally or otherwise), numbers games, lotteries, dice, bingo, and cards. The exact sums that change hands in legal and illegal gambling are unknown, but it has been estimated that habitual gamblers in the United States lose more than 20 billion dollars each year.

If one were to define gambling in its broadest sense, even investing in the stock market might be considered a game of chance. Sherrod (1968) has pointed to the need for a clearer definition of terms: "If you bet on a horse, that's gambling. If you bet you can make three spades, that's entertainment. If you bet cotton will go up three points, that's business. See the difference?" (p. 619).

In any event, gambling appears to be one of our major national pastimes, with some 50 percent of the population gambling at one time or another on anything from Saturday night poker games to the outcome of sporting events. Usually, such gambling is a harmless form of social entertainment; an individual places a bet and waits for the result. Win or lose, the game is over. But while most people can gamble and then get on with their life, an estimated 6 to 10 million Americans get "hooked" on gambling (see *HIGHLIGHT 9.7*). Whatever an individual gambler's situation, a recent survey confirmed that compulsive gambling significantly affects the social, psychological, and economic well-being of the gambler's family (Lorenz & Shuttlesworth, 1983). In fact, a recent study by Blaszczynski, McConaghy, and Frankova (1989) found that a high proportion of pathological gamblers commit crimes that are related to gambling.

Causal Factors in Pathological Gambling

Although a few psychologists and psychiatrists have dealt with the topic of pathological gambling, little systematic research has been done, and the causal factors are not yet well understood. Pathological gambling seems to be a learned pattern that is highly resistant to extinction. Often a person who becomes a pathological gambler won a substantial sum of money the first time he or she gambled; chance alone would dictate that a certain percentage of individuals would have such "beginner's luck." Bolen and Boyd (1968) considered it likely that the reinforcement an individual received during this introductory phase is a significant factor in later pathological gambling. Because anyone is likely to win from time to time, the principles of intermittent reinforcement could explain an addict's continued gambling despite excessive losses. Bolen and Boyd were struck particularly by the similarity between slot-machine players and Skinner's laboratory pigeons; the latter, placed on a variable reinforcement schedule, "repetitively and incessantly pecked to the point of exhaustion and eventual demise while waiting the uncertain appearance of their jackpot of bird seed" (1968, p. 629).

Despite their awareness that the odds are against them, and despite the fact that they rarely or never repeat their early success, compulsive gamblers continue to gamble avidly. To "stake" their gambling, they often dissipate their savings, neglect their families, default on bills, and borrow money from friends and loan companies. Eventually, they may resort to writing bad checks, embezzlement, or

HIGHLIGHT 9.7

A Case of Pathological Gambling

John was a 40-year-old, rather handsome man with slightly graying hair who managed an automobile dealership for his father. For the previous two years, he had increasingly neglected his job and was deep in debt as a result of his gambling activities. He had gambled heavily since he was about 27 years old. His gambling had occasioned frequent quarrels in his first marriage and finally a divorce. He had married his second wife without telling her of his problem, but it eventually had come to light and had created such difficulty that she had taken their two children and had returned to her parents' home.

John joined an encounter group in the stated hope that he might receive some assistance with his problem. In the course of the early group sessions, he proved to be an intelligent, well-educated man who seemed to have a good understanding of his gambling problem and its self-defeating nature. He stated that he had started gambling after winning some money at the horse races. This experience convinced him that he could supplement his income by gambling judiciously. However, his subsequent gambling—which frequently involved all-night poker games, trips to Las Vegas, and betting on the races—almost always resulted in heavy losses.

In the group, John talked about his gambling freely and coherently—candidly admitting that he enjoyed the stimulation and excitement of gambling more than sexual relations with his wife. He was actually rather glad his family had left because it relieved him of certain responsibilities toward them and alleviated his guilt for neglecting them. He readily acknowledged that his feelings and behavior were inappropriate and self-defeating, but he stated that he was "sick" and that he desperately needed help.

It soon became apparent that although John was willing to talk about his problem, he was not prepared to take constructive steps in dealing with it. He wanted the group to accept him in the role of a pathological gambler who could not be expected to "cure" himself. At the group's suggestion, he attended a few meetings of Gamblers Anonymous but found them "irrelevant." It was also suggested that he try aversive therapy, but he felt this would not help him.

While attending the group sessions, John apparently continued to gamble and continued to lose. After the eighth encounter group session, he did not return. Through inquiry by one of the members, it was learned that he had been arrested for embezzling funds from his father's business, but that his father had somehow managed to have the charges dropped. John reportedly then left for another state and his subsequent history is unknown.

other illegal means of obtaining money, feeling sure that their luck will change and that they will be able to repay what they have taken. Whereas others view their gambling as unethical and disruptive, they are likely to see themselves as taking "calculated risks" to build a lucrative business. Often they feel alone and resentful that others do not understand their activities.

In a pioneering and well-controlled study of former pathological gamblers, Rosten (1961) found that as a group they tended to be rebellious, unconventional individuals who did not seem to fully understand the ethical norms of society. Half of the group described themselves as "hating regulations." Of 30 men studied, 12 had served time in jail for embezzlement and other crimes directly connected with their gambling. Rosten also found that these men were unrealistic in their thinking and prone to seek highly stimulating situations. In the subjects' own words, they "loved excitement" and "needed action." Although the men admitted that they had known objectively the all-but-impossible odds they faced while gambling, they had felt that these odds did not apply to them. Often they had the unshakable feeling that "tonight is my night"; typically, they had also followed the so-called Monte Carlo fallacy—that after so many losses, their turn was coming up and they would hit it big. Many of the men discussed the extent to which they had "fooled" themselves by elaborate rationalizations.

For example, one gambler described his previous rationalizations as covering all contingencies: "When I was ahead, I could gamble because I was playing with others' money. When I was behind, I had to get even. When I was even, I hadn't lost any money" (Rosten, 1961, p. 67).

It is of interest to note that within a few months after the study, 13 of Rosten's 30 subjects either had returned to heavy gambling, had started to drink excessively, or had not been heard from and were presumed to be gambling again.

Later studies strongly support Rosten's findings. They describe pathological gamblers as typically immature, rebellious, thrill seeking, superstitious, and basically psychopathic (Bolen & Boyd, 1968; Bolen, Caldwell, & Boyd, 1975; Custer, 1982; and Graham, 1978a). The most comprehensive study is that of Livingston (1974), who observed, interviewed, and tested 55 mostly working-class men who had joined Gamblers Anonymous to try to stop gambling. Livingston found that these men often referred to their "past immaturity" in explaining their habitual gambling. They also described themselves as having a "big ego" and acknowledged a strong need for recognition and adulation from others.

Although these men had usually been able to cover their losses early in their gambling careers, the course was downhill, leading to financial, marital, job, and often legal problems. Eventually, things got so bad that it seemed the only way out of their difficulties was the way they got into them—by gambling.

A study by Graham (1978a) compared the psychological test performance of pathological gamblers with that of alcoholics and heroin addicts. The three groups of addicts showed many similar characteristics. The individuals in each group were self-centered, narcissistic, tense, nervous, and anxious; they overreacted to stress and were pessimistic and brooding. They were characterized by acting out, impulsive behavior; they had periodic outbursts of anger, were frustrated with their own lack of achievement, were reluctant to open up emotionally for fear of being hurt, often showed superficial remorse, and were passive-dependent and manipulative. They stated a desire to "turn over a new leaf" but showed a poor prognosis for behavioral change in traditional therapy. These similarities suggest that common personality characteristics may be involved as predisposing factors in the three disorders.

Cultural factors also appear to be important in developing gambling problems. Recently reported research with Southeast Asian refugee populations highlights the role of cultural influences in gambling. Pathological gambling is one of the most serious, yet most common, problems shown by Southeast Asian refugees, particularly those from Laos, in adapting to resettlement countries. The problem of out-of-control gambling among refugees has been underestimated in the past because health-service-needs surveys have been typically directed at surveying participation in mental health programs. New surveys of mental health problems that have focused on ***key informants***—that is, knowledgeable, concerned, and observant leaders in refugee communities—have reported almost epidemic problems with gambling (Aronoff, 1987; Ganju & Quan, 1987). For example, Aronoff (1987) reported that 54 percent of informants in the Laos group reported gambling as a significant problem. This

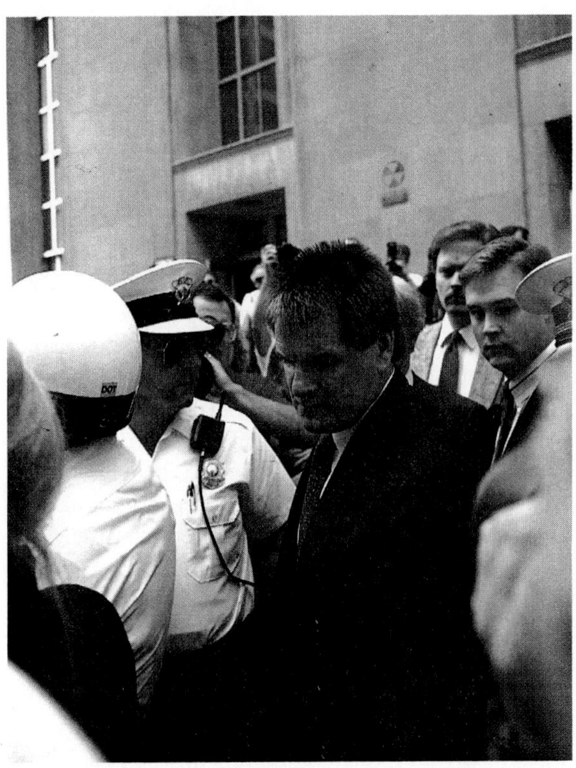

A famous case of the destructive nature of gambling is that of Pete Rose, whose long and record-breaking career in baseball was tarnished when he was convicted for betting on the sport. It is difficult to fathom why someone with such fame, talent, and success would be so careless as to risk it all by gambling. The causal factors in pathological, or compulsive, gambling are not well understood, but we do know that compulsive gamblers will continue to gamble avidly, even at risk of personal disasters; their thinking is unrealistic and their behavior is sensation-seeking and oblivious to ethical norms.

problem is among the most serious adaptation difficulties for refugees because family members who gamble away the limited resources available to them (for example, food stamps) can place even greater pressure on their efforts to adapt to a new culture.

Pathological gambling problems are not new to Southeast Asians because gambling is reportedly common among these groups in their own cultures. However, these problems have apparently become more intensified and more widespread in this country. Reasons for these increased gambling problems include the following: (a) social sanctions that worked to control excessive gambling in Southeast Asia appear no longer to operate; (b) the stress levels that refugees experience are high, and gambling serves temporarily to relieve cares; reportedly, when they are in their gambling houses or "casinos," many refugees feel, at least temporarily, as though they are still in their native lands; (c) many individuals have a great deal of time on their hands because they are unable to find employment, and gambling helps pass the time; and (d) finally, of course, gambling lures refugees with the possibility of great rewards and the opportunity to regain all they lost during migration.

Professionals working in refugee mental health programs have become increasingly concerned with the extent of gambling problems in refugee families. Because these problems are not brought to the mental health clinics, they are often not dealt with in treatment.

Treatments and Outcomes Treatment of pathological gamblers is still a relatively unexplored area. However, Boyd and Bolen (1970) have reported on a study in which eight pathological gamblers and their spouses were treated together through group psychotherapy—an approach based on the finding that a pathological gambler's marital relationship is generally chaotic and turbulent, with the spouse frequently showing seriously maladaptive behavior patterns also. Gambling ceased in three of these cases and almost completely stopped in the other five. The extent to which changes in the gamblers' marital relationships influenced the treatment outcomes can only be surmised—six of the eight couples showed significant improvements. Other treatment approaches, including aversion therapy and covert sensitization (Cotler, 1971) and cognitive-behavioral therapy (Bannister, 1975) have been tried with individual cases, but further studies are needed before we can evaluate the potential effectiveness of psychotherapy in treating this disorder.

Some pathological gamblers who want to change find help through membership in Gamblers Anonymous. This organization was founded in 1957 in Los Angeles by two pathological gamblers who found that they could help each other control their gambling by talking about their experiences. Since then, groups have been formed in most major American cities. The groups are modeled after Alcoholics Anonymous, and they view those who gamble as personally responsible for their own actions. The only requirement for membership is an expressed desire to stop gambling. In group discussions, members share experiences and try to gain insights into the irrationality of their gambling and to realize its inevitable consequences. As with Alcoholics Anonymous, members try to help each other maintain control and prevent relapses. Unfortunately, only a small fraction of pathological gamblers find their way into Gamblers Anonymous. Of those who do, only about 1 in 10 manages to overcome the addiction to gambling (Strine, 1971).

A novel inpatient treatment program for pathological gamblers has been developed at the Brecksville, Ohio, Veterans' Administration Medical Center (1981). This program, initiated in 1972, has helped many individuals and has served as a model for many other hospitals.

The Brecksville treatment program for pathological gamblers, which lasts for a minimum of 28 days, is integrated into the alcohol treatment program. Five inpatient beds in the 55-bed unit are set aside for pathological gamblers. Alcoholics and gamblers are housed together and share many common program elements because their problems are viewed as quite similar.

It may seem that inpatient hospital treatment for a "social" problem such as pathological gambling is an overly drastic and unwarranted measure. In a number of circumstances, however, such measures seem necessary. For example, a gambler might be depressed or be experiencing severe panic or desperation and may present a possible suicide risk; or the individual may have allowed his or her health to deteriorate; or the individual's legal situation might require confinement; or in some areas of the country, the individual may not have access to outpatient attention for his or her gambling behavior (for example, there may not be a local chapter of Gamblers Anonymous).

The treatment goals for these pathological gamblers include abstinence from gambling, major life-style changes, participation in Gamblers Anonymous programs, and, because gambling behavior is viewed as "trivial" and of no social value, the acquisition of more adaptive forms of recreation.

A variety of treatment approaches are used during an individual's hospital stay: (a) the ward is managed according to strict rules of discipline and any deviation from the rules may result in discharge from the hospital; (b) group therapy is provided; (c) workshops devoted to helping the resident learn more adaptive living skills are offered; (d) educational lectures related to gambling problems are given; (e) attendance at AA and Gamblers Anonymous meetings is required; and (f) the individual is expected to get involved in planned recreational activities.

Pathological gambling, as an addictive disorder, is on the increase in the United States (Custer, 1982). Furthermore, liberalized gambling legislation has permitted state-operated lotteries, horse racing, and gambling casinos in an effort to increase state tax revenues. In the context of this apparent environmental support and "official" sanction for gambling, it is likely that pathological gambling will increase substantially as more and more people "try their luck." Given that pathological gamblers are resistant to treatment, it is likely, too, that our future efforts toward developing more effective preventive and treatment approaches will need to be increased as this problem continues to grow.

UNRESOLVED ISSUES on the Genetics of Alcoholism

Several recent research efforts suggest a possible genetic predisposition toward alcoholism (Tarter, 1988). One source of evidence has come from studies of alcoholics' children who were placed for adoption early in life and did not come under the environmental influences of their biological parents. Several such studies can be found to support the genetic viewpoint. For example, Goodwin et al. (1973) found that children of alcoholic parents who had been adopted by nonalcoholic foster parents had nearly twice the number of alcohol problems by their late twenties as did a control group of adopted children whose real parents were not alcoholics. In another study, Goodwin and his colleagues (1974) compared the sons of alcoholic parents who were adopted in infancy by nonalcoholic parents with those raised by their alcoholic parents. Both adopted and nonadopted sons later evidenced high rates of alcoholism—25 percent and 17 percent respectively. These investigators concluded that being born to an alcoholic parent, rather than being raised by one, increased the risk of a son's becoming an alcoholic.

Another approach to exploring a possible genetic basis in alcoholism has focused on finding underlying mechanisms for the transmission of alcohol abuse or susceptibility to alcoholism. For example, researchers have attempted to determine if individuals who have a genetic "risk" for alcoholism—such as children of alcoholics—show signs of a predisposition toward alcoholism. Evidence for increased alcoholism risk includes such factors as a decreased intensity of subjective feelings of intoxication, a decrease in motor performance, and less body sway after alcohol ingestion. Along with these behavioral indices, increases in prolactin (a pituitary hormone) levels after low doses of alcohol has been thought to occur in individuals with a predisposition to alcohol-abuse disorders. Research into these risk factors in alcohol predisposition typically involves obtaining a sample of highly susceptible individuals, such as children of alcoholics, and a sample of controls, and then determining if certain variables (one or more of the risk factors) distinguish the groups. Recent research by Schuckit and Gould (1988) has reported that alcohol susceptibility indicators significantly separate sons of alcoholics from matched controls.

The evidence on the genetic basis of alcoholism continues to be debated, however, and other experts are not convinced of the primary role of genetics in alcoholism development. Searles (1988) points to the ambiguous evidence for the genetics of alcoholism and cautions against interpreting genetics as a causal factor in the development of alcoholism. Negative results have been found in both adoptive studies and in studies designed to follow-up the behavior of high-risk individuals. It is clear that the great majority of children who have alcoholic parents do not themselves become alcoholics—whether or not they are raised by their real parents. The successful outcomes—that is, children of alcoholics who make successful life adjustments—have not been sufficiently studied (Heller, Sher, & Benson, 1982). In one study of high-risk children of alcoholics, a group of young men 19 to 20 years of age who were presumably at high risk for developing alcoholism were carefully studied for symptoms of psychopathology. Schulsinger and colleagues (1986) found no differences in psychopathology or alcohol-abuse behavior from a control sample similar to the general population. In another study of high-risk individuals, Alterman, Searles, and Hall (1989) failed to find differences in drinking behavior or alcohol-related symptoms between a group of high-risk subjects (those who had alcoholic fathers) and a group of non-high-risk subjects.

We do not know the possible role genetic factors play in the etiology of alcoholism. Available evidence suggests that they might be important as predisposing causes, or that they might contribute to constitutional factors in alcoholism development. Of course, a constitutional predisposition to alcoholism could be acquired as well as inherited. It is not known whether acquired conditions, such as endocrine or enzyme imbalances, increase an individual's vulnerability to alcoholism.

The evidence for a genetic basis of alcoholism is ambiguous at best. At present, it appears that the genetic interpretation of alcoholism remains an attractive hypothesis; however, additional research is needed for us to hold this view with confidence.

SUMMARY

Addictive disorders—such as alcohol or drug abuse, extreme overeating, and pathological gambling—are among the most widespread and intransigent mental health problems facing us today. Alcohol- and drug-abuse problems can be viewed as psychoactive substance-induced organic mental disorders and syndromes or as psychoactive substance-abuse and -dependence disorders. Many problems of alcohol or drug use involve difficulties that stem solely from the intoxicating effects of the substances. Dependence occurs when an individual develops a tolerance for the substance or exhibits withdrawal symptoms when the substance is not available. Several psychoses related to alcoholism have been identified: idiosyncratic intoxication, withdrawal delirium, chronic alcoholic hallucinosis, and dementia associated with alcoholism.

Drug-abuse disorders may involve physiological dependence on substances, such as opiates—particularly heroin—or barbiturates; however, psychological dependence may occur with any of the drugs that are commonly used today—for example, marijuana or cocaine.

A number of factors are considered important in the etiology of alcoholism. Although the data are not conclusive, it appears that genetic factors may play some role in causing susceptibility, as may other biological factors, such as metabolic rates and sensitivity to alcohol. Psychological factors—such as psychological vulnerability, stress, and the desire for tension reduction—and marital and other relationships are also seen as important etiologic elements in alcohol-use disorders. Although the existence of an "alcoholic personality type" has been disavowed by most theorists, personality factors apparently play an important role in the development and expression of addictive disorders. Finally, sociocultural factors may predispose individuals to alcoholism.

Possible causal factors in drug abuse include the influence of peer groups, the existence of a so-called drug culture, and the availability of drugs as tension reducers or as pain relievers. Some recent work has explored a possible physiological basis for drug abuse. The discovery of endorphins, morphinelike substances produced by the body, has raised speculation that a biochemical basis to drug addiction may exist.

The treatment of individuals who abuse alcohol or drugs is generally difficult and often fails. Many reasons can be found for this poor prognosis: the abuse may reflect a long history of psychological difficulties; interpersonal and marital distress may be involved; and financial and legal problems may be present. In addition, all such problems may be operating on an individual who denies that problems exist and is not motivated to work on them.

Several approaches to the treatment of chronic alcoholism or drug abuse have been developed. Frequently, the situation requires biological or medical measures—for example, medication to deal with withdrawal symptoms and withdrawal delirium, or dietary evaluation and treatment for malnutrition. Psychological therapies, such as group therapy and behavioral interventions, may be effective with some alcoholic or drug-abusing individuals. Another source of help for alcoholics is widely available through Alcoholics Anonymous; however, the extent of successful outcomes with this program has not been sufficiently studied.

Most treatment programs show high success rates in "curing" addictive problems, but show lowered success rates at follow-up. Recent work in the area of relapse prevention has contributed new insights into the problems of self-control once addictive behaviors have been checked. Part of this approach involves making an individual aware of factors that can lead to relapse and preparing him or her to deal with these phenomena. Most treatment programs require that an individual remain abstinent; however, over the past 15 years, research has suggested that some alcoholics can learn to control their drinking while continuing to drink socially. The controversy surrounding controlled drinking remains unresolved.

Not all addictive disorders involve the use of substances such as alcohol or drugs. Some individuals eat to excess, endangering their health. Others gamble to such an extent that they wreck their lives and damage or destroy their family relationships. These disorders—hyperobesity and pathological gambling—involve many of the same psychological mechanisms that seem to underlie chronic alcoholism or drug addiction. Treatment approaches found to be effective for alcoholism and drug abuse appear to work about the same with obese clients and pathological gamblers. Many of the same difficulties, especially concerning response to treatment and relapse, also plague the treatment of obese individuals and compulsive gamblers.

Key Terms

addictive behavior (p. 295)
psychoactive drugs (p. 295)
toxicity (p. 295)
psychoactive substance abuse (p. 296)
psychoactive substance dependence (p. 296)
tolerance (p. 296)
withdrawal symptoms (p. 296)
alcoholic (p. 296)
alcoholism (p. 296)
opium (p. 314)
morphine (p. 314)
heroin (p. 315)
endorphins (p. 319)
methadone hydrochloride (p. 320)
barbiturates (p. 321)
amphetamine (p. 321)
cocaine (p. 323)
hallucinogens (p. 325)
LSD (p. 325)
flashback (p. 326)
mescaline (p. 326)
psilocybin (p. 326)
marijuana (p. 327)
hashish (p. 327)
caffeine (p. 328)
nicotine (p. 328)
hyperobesity (p. 329)
pathological gambling (p. 333)

Chapter 10

Sexual Disorders and Variants

Gaston Teuscher, *Dessin* (1976). The son of a soldier in the Swiss army and a midwife of French ancestry, Teuscher (1903–?) at an early age developed an ambivalent attitude toward women, an attitude that he traced back to his parents' strong desire to have a girl. He never married, and devoted much of his life to esoteric mathematical and philosophical pursuits. Teuscher began producing sketches and drawings in 1974. He worked at a prodigious rate on bits of crumpled paper, stained tablemats—that is, on whatever materials came immediately to hand.

At the lower levels of the evolutionary scale, animal reproductive processes are not sexual and seem to be essentially preprogrammed and more or less "automatic." The individuals of a species show little variation in their reproductive functioning.

As we move up the scale, reproduction becomes sexual in nature, and by the time we reach the higher animals, we see the reproductive process richly infused with behavioral distinctiveness. Organisms differ considerably in their sexual behaviors and selectively choose mates. Sexual functioning also incorporates other behavioral characteristics, such as a dominance hierarchy and aggressiveness in the case of males.

This expanding repertoire of reproductive behavior continues up to the human level, but the gap between humankind and even the highest of the other animals is huge. It is paralleled only in the advantage humans enjoy in intellectual power by their possession of conceptual language.

Several dimensions of variation underlie this evolutionary progression in reproductive behavior. The most important of these, for our concerns, is the increasing freedom from rigidly programmed, instinctual, stereotyped forms of sexual behavior. For example, the human female is free from recurrent, biologically based cycles of heat and nonreceptivity. Of perhaps even greater importance is the enormously increased adaptability in human sexual needs themselves. With a loosened connection between sex and procreation, human sexual behavior is no longer simply the expression of instinct but has become at least as much a matter of *learned* patterns of attraction, activity, and consummation. To put it another way, human sexuality has largely come under the control of "higher" neural processes. It is primarily recreational and only incidentally procreational for most people.

As in numerous other areas of human activity, these gains in flexibility and adaptability, while having unquestioned species advantages, have come at some cost. Although human sexuality has much more variety than that of any other species, sexuality at the human level is also more likely to go awry. While much sexual variation adds zest and richness to our lives, enhances our happiness, and may intensify our bonds to each other, it may also cause profound misery or worse for the individuals involved, for those close to them, and, in the case of certain deviations, for countless victims.

Money (1986) has suggested the concept of the **lovemap** to refer to the pattern of an individual's own erotic attachments and preferences, his or her idealized scenario for sexual fulfillment. Some lovemaps become distorted or "vandalized" (Money & Lamacz, 1989) in the course of development, leading to a variety of maladaptive outcomes. We will be employing this useful concept in some of the discussion that follows. It is formally defined as

> *. . . a developmental representation or template, synchronously functional in the mind and the brain, depicting the idealized lover, the idealized love affair, and the idealized program of sexuoerotic activity with that lover, projected in imagery and ideation, or in actual performance." (Money & Lamacz, 1989, p. 43)*

The lovemap is analogous to a person's native language in its developmental and cognitive representational qualities. Its basic properties are thought to be largely settled prior to puberty and, once settled, highly resistant to change. Lovemaps vary on a number of dimensions, of which an important one is relative simplicity versus complexity.

This chapter is concerned with "abnormalities" of human sexuality. They fall naturally into two distinct classes. The *sexual dysfunctions* involve inhibitions in sexual desire or problems with psychophysiological functioning in the sexual response cycle; premature ejaculation in males is an example. The *sexual variants* or *deviations* include those forms of sexual behavior that fall outside the range of generally accepted sexual activity, such as exhibitionism or sexual sadism. In our discussion, we make a further distinction between victimless sexual variants and those that involve injury, force, or nonconsent.

It should be noted that not all forms of sexual abnormality, especially those in which no one is victimized, are considered disorders requiring treatment. Neither are all sexual disorders seen as inevitably causing additional difficulties in other aspects of a person's personal life. Conversely, some abnormalities, such as incest, are considered crimes rather than psychological disorders and thus do not appear in the official (that is, the DSM) classification system, presumably because manifestations of disorder are not legally punishable. Obviously, however, many behaviors can be both crimes and manifestations of disorder, and because we need not here concern ourselves with such legal niceties, we will discuss some disorders that are also crimes by statutory definition.

Human societies have generally exhibited a kind of "double vision" regarding sexual behavior. On the one hand, they typically have rather elaborate systems, often legally codified, limiting sexual behavior and directing that sexual acts shall encompass only certain narrowly defined "proprieties" with partners having specified characteristics—that is, one's opposite-sex spouse. On the other hand, societies have informal expectations that these limits will be regularly and routinely exceeded by at least the more venturesome of their members. It is only in recent times, thanks largely to the pioneering work of Kinsey and his associates (1948, 1953), that we have come to understand that personal problems with sexuality and deviations from formal propriety are widespread and at times extreme within our own culture.

As is implied in these observations, issues pertaining to sexual behavior tend to arouse strong emotional and attitudinal responses and inspire much concern about public regulation and control of individual behavior. In our own culture public concern about sexual matters is never far beneath the surface, a fact that can be and has been exploited by shrewd political campaign managers. It is difficult in such a climate to maintain a scholarly, objective approach to matters of human sexual behavior and its abnormalities. Nevertheless, that is our intent in this chapter. We are not so arrogant as to assume complete success in this intention, nor so naive as to imagine we can avoid offending some readers.

Issues pertaining to sexual behavior, such as sex education in the schools, tend to arouse strong emotional and attitudinal responses and inspire much concern about the public regulation and control of individual behavior.

SEXUAL DYSFUNCTIONS

The term **sexual dysfunction** refers to impairment either in the desire for sexual gratification or in the ability to achieve it. With some exceptions, such impairments occur in the absence of anatomical or physiological pathology and are based on faulty psychosexual adjustment and learning. They vary markedly in degree and, regardless of which partner is alleged to be dysfunctional, the enjoyment of sex by both parties in a relationship is typically adversely affected; both are prevented from approximating the conditions of their respective lovemaps. Certain types of sexual dysfunction, such as erectile disorder, occur with significant frequency in homosexual relationships, but research in this domain is seriously lacking. Thus we will focus on the heterosexual context.

Like sexuality in general, sexual dysfunctions were until recently either ignored entirely by polite society or—if discussed at all—were the subject of turgid medical treatises written by authors who were usually as ill-informed and prejudiced as their readers. Then, with the popularization of Freudian thought, an era gradually developed in which all manner of difficulties in sexual functioning (and some that were not even "difficulties" in the normally accepted sense) were said to be the result of unconscious conflicts of childhood origin—requiring years of psychoanalytic treatment to resolve. We now know, thanks again to precedent-breaking and courageous work—chiefly by Masters and Johnson (1966, 1970, 1975)—that the common sexual dysfunctions are both more numerous and less complex and mysterious than had once been believed. We will first describe several of the most common ones and then discuss issues of causation and treatment. *HIGHLIGHT 10.1* summarizes the dysfunctions we will be covering here.

Dysfunctions Affecting Males

Here we will briefly discuss several dysfunctions that may affect men: erectile insufficiency, premature ejaculation, and inhibited male orgasm.

Male Erectile Disorder Inability to achieve or maintain an erection sufficient for successful sexual intercourse—formerly known as *impotence*—is known clinically as *erectile insufficiency,* or in DSM terms, **male erectile disorder.** In **primary erectile insufficiency,** a man has never been able to sustain an erection long enough to accomplish a satisfactory duration of penetration—usually defined as including intravaginal ejaculation. In **secondary erectile insufficiency,** a man has had at least one successful attempt at coitus but is presently unable to produce or maintain the required level of penile rigidity. Primary insufficiency is a relatively rare disorder, but it has been estimated that half or more of the male population has experienced the secondary variety of erectile insufficiency on at least a temporary basis, especially in the early years of sexual exploration.

Prolonged or permanent erectile insufficiency before the age of 60 is relatively rare and is often due to psychological factors, notably anxiety-induced interference by distracting, dysfunctional thoughts concerning "performance" (Barlow, 1986, 1988). In fact, according to the findings of Kinsey and his associates, only about one-fourth of males become impotent by the age of 70 and even here many cases have psychological components in their causal patterns. More recent studies have indicated that men and women in their 80s and 90s are quite capable of enjoying intercourse (Burros, 1974; Kaplan, 1975; Masters & Johnson, 1975). It appears that in some cases men who experience difficulties in their later years may simply be complying with the societal expectation of declining performance (Tollison & Adams, 1979). On the other hand, the vascular, neurological, and hormonal factors that support adequate erectile functioning do undergo impairment with advancing age in many men (Mohr & Beutler, 1990). The lessened reliability of the erectile response may lead to the type of dysfunctional cognitions already noted, thus exacerbating the difficulty. Erectile problems are notoriously self-perpetuating, with every "failure" psychologically enhancing the likelihood of further ones.

We have probably underestimated in recent years the proportion of erectile problems having some pathophysiologic involvement, formerly considered to be as low as 15 percent (Kaplan, 1975). More recent data suggest that the figure may actually be close to 50 percent (Mohr & Beutler, 1990; Tiefer & Melman, 1989), which at a minimum implies the necessity of a thorough assessment of contributory medical conditions. Thus a diagnosis of psychogenic causation does not by itself rule out an element of physiologic malfunction, or vice versa. These organic conditions can be quite varied and can include certain types of vascular disease, diabetes, neurological disorders, kidney failure, hormonal irregularities, and excess blood levels of certain drugs, including alcohol (Tiefer & Melman, 1989; Wagner & Green, 1981).

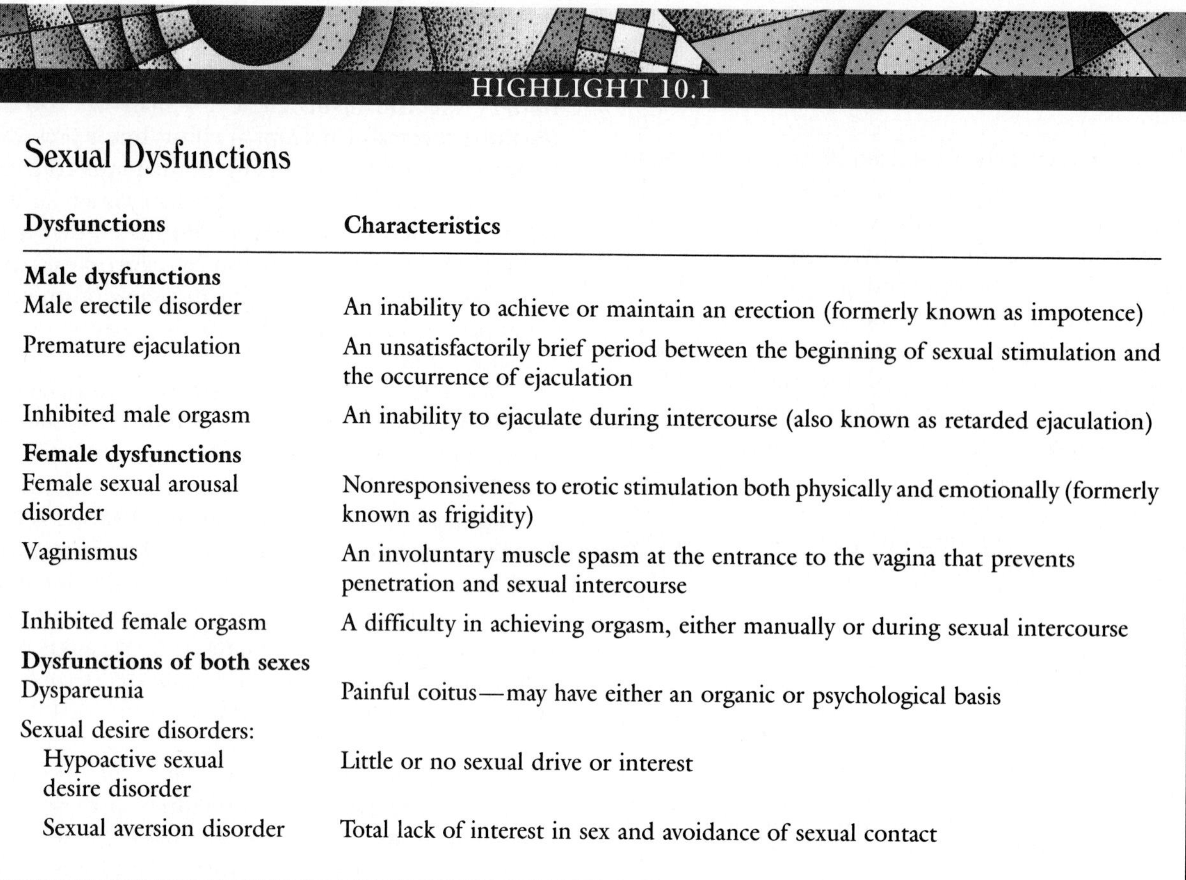

HIGHLIGHT 10.1

Sexual Dysfunctions

Dysfunctions	Characteristics
Male dysfunctions	
Male erectile disorder	An inability to achieve or maintain an erection (formerly known as impotence)
Premature ejaculation	An unsatisfactorily brief period between the beginning of sexual stimulation and the occurrence of ejaculation
Inhibited male orgasm	An inability to ejaculate during intercourse (also known as retarded ejaculation)
Female dysfunctions	
Female sexual arousal disorder	Nonresponsiveness to erotic stimulation both physically and emotionally (formerly known as frigidity)
Vaginismus	An involuntary muscle spasm at the entrance to the vagina that prevents penetration and sexual intercourse
Inhibited female orgasm	A difficulty in achieving orgasm, either manually or during sexual intercourse
Dysfunctions of both sexes	
Dyspareunia	Painful coitus—may have either an organic or psychological basis
Sexual desire disorders:	
Hypoactive sexual desire disorder	Little or no sexual drive or interest
Sexual aversion disorder	Total lack of interest in sex and avoidance of sexual contact

Distinguishing between psychogenic and organically caused insufficiency for diagnostic purposes is at best a complicated process. The normal male has several erections per night, associated with periods of REM (rapid eye movement) sleep. Some researchers have suggested that organically based insufficiency can be distinguished from psychogenic by noting an absence of these nocturnal erections. However, it now appears that many other factors must also be evaluated in order to establish a proper diagnosis, because the nocturnal penile tumescence (NPT) procedure has been found, by itself, to produce both false positive and false negative results that are unacceptably high (Mohr & Beutler, 1990; Wagner, 1981). An important implication of these assessment difficulties is that we have probably, once again, made the common error of assuming a mutually exclusive dichotomy (organic versus psychogenic), where such pure cases may in fact be the exception rather than the rule (Tiefer & Melman, 1989).

Premature Ejaculation Often psychologically related to erectile insufficiency, **premature ejaculation** refers to an unsatisfactorily brief period between the commencement of sexual stimulation and the occurrence of ejaculation. The consequences include failure of the female partner to achieve satisfaction and, often, acute embarrassment for the male with disruptive anxiety about recurrence on future occasions. An exact definition of prematurity is not possible, however, partly because of pronounced variations in both the likelihood and the latency of female orgasm in sexual intercourse. LoPiccolo (1978) suggested that an inability to tolerate as much as four minutes of stimulation without ejaculation is a reasonable indicator that a man may be in need of sex therapy. This suggested guideline is subject to numerous qualifications, however, including the age of a client—the alleged "quick trigger" of the younger male being more than a mere myth (McCarthy, 1989). Not surprisingly, premature ejaculation is most likely when previous abstinence has been lengthy (Spiess, Geer, & O'Donohue, 1984). This fact suggests the use of masturbation as a form of self-treatment for the difficulty, but, somewhat curiously, few premature ejaculators discover or make use of this coping method.

In sexually normal men the ejaculatory reflex is to a considerable extent under voluntary control. They monitor their sensations during sexual stimulation and are somehow able, perhaps by judicious use of distraction, to forestall the point of ejaculatory inevitability until they decide to "let go" (Kaplan, 1987). Premature ejaculators are for some reason unable to use this technique effectively, probably in many cases because their anxiety prevents adequate monitoring of their current stage in the sexual response buildup leading to orgasm. As in the case of erectile difficulties, failures in control lead to increased anxiety in subsequent opportunities, and thus increased likelihood of failures.

Inhibited Male Orgasm It is interesting that, while problems of female orgasmic dysfunction have received wide attention in the popular press, one rarely hears public mention of the corollary problem in males. It is not a topic high on the locker room agenda, and indeed sexually active women seem to have a more realistic appreciation of its prevalence than do most men. As a result, many males suffering from **inhibited male orgasm**—that is, retarded ejaculation or the inability to ejaculate during intercourse—are condemned to worry needlessly about their supposedly unique defect, a type of worry likely to worsen the problem. In fact, relatively few cases of inhibited male orgasm are seen by sex therapists, but our own clinical experience suggests that the problem is much more widespread than this observation would seem to indicate, a conclusion shared by Apfelbaum (1989) and by Kaplan (1974). It appears that many men are too embarrassed by the problem even to contemplate therapy for it.

Instances of complete ejaculatory incompetence are rare. Most men who have difficulty ejaculating intravaginally during intercourse can nevertheless achieve orgasm by other means of stimulation, notably through solitary masturbation. In milder cases a man can ejaculate in the presence of a partner, but only by means of manual or oral stimulation (Kaplan, 1987). Retarded ejaculation may even be partner-specific; that is, it occurs only with a particular partner but not with others (Apfelbaum, 1989). The problem is therefore largely one of psychological inhibition or overcontrol, and it appears relatively specific to the circumstance of vaginal containment of the penis. It thus seems obvious that substantial "symbolic" and interpersonal elements exist in the typical instance of this dysfunction.

Dysfunctions Affecting Females

Female sexual dysfunctions somewhat parallel the male sexual dysfunctions. The following sections will discuss arousal insufficiency, vaginismus, and orgasmic dysfunction.

Female Sexual Arousal Disorder Formerly and somewhat pejoratively referred to as *frigidity,* **female sexual arousal disorder** is in many ways the female counterpart of erectile insufficiency (DSM-III-R lists both as *sexual arousal disorders*). It is often accompanied by an absence of sexual arousal feelings and an unresponsiveness to most or all forms of erotic stimulation. Its chief physical manifestation is a failure to produce the characteristic swelling and lubrication of the vulva and vaginal tissues during sexual stimulation, a condition that may make intercourse quite uncomfortable.

Fortunately, true primary nonresponsiveness to erotic stimuli (where a woman has never experienced arousal to any form of stimulation) is rare; it may also be untreatable in terms of currently available intervention techniques. Most often, then, we are dealing here with a dysfunction that, while it may be stubbornly entrenched, is at least to some minimal extent situational. A woman with this disorder is not so much lacking in the capacity for sexual responsiveness as she is inhibiting for some reason a responsiveness that might otherwise be full and gratifying. The possible reasons for this inhibition run the gamut from early sexual traumatization to excessive and distorted socialization about the evils of sex to dislike of or disgust with a current partner's sexuality.

Vaginismus An involuntary spasm of the muscles at the entrance to the vagina (not due to a physical disorder) that prevents penetration and sexual intercourse is called **vaginismus.** Evidently these muscles are readily conditionable to respond with intense contraction to stimuli associated with impending penetration. In some cases, women who suffer from vaginismus also have arousal insufficiency, possibly as a result of conditioned fears associated with earlier traumatic sexual experiences. In other cases, however, they are sexually responsive, but are still afflicted with this disorder. It is not always possible to identify the "unconditioned stimuli" presumed to have been involved in the acquisition of vaginismus (Kaplan, 1987), probably because the disorder is sometimes "overdetermined" in the sense of having multiple causal links (Leiblum, Pervin, & Campbell, 1989). This form of sexual dysfunction is relatively rare, but, when it occurs, it is likely to be extremely distressing for both an affected woman and her partner (Leiblum et al., 1989; Tollison & Adams, 1979).

Inhibited Female Orgasm Many women who are readily sexually excitable and who otherwise enjoy sexual activity nevertheless experience **inhibited female orgasm**—greater or lesser difficulty in achieving orgasm, whether manually or through intercourse. Of these women, many do not routinely experience orgasm during sexual intercourse without direct supplemental stimulation of the clitoris; indeed this pattern is so common that it can hardly be considered dysfunctional. A small percentage of women are able to achieve orgasm *only* through direct mechanical stimulation of the clitoris, as in vigorous digital manipulation, cunnilingus (oral stimulation), or the use of an electric vibrator. Even fewer are unable to have the experience under any known conditions of stimulation; this condition is called **primary orgasmic dysfunction,** analogous to primary erectile insufficiency in males.

The diagnosis of orgasmic dysfunction is complicated by the fact that the subjective quality of orgasm varies widely among women, within the same woman from time to time, and depending on mode of stimulation. Thus precise evaluations of occurrence and quality are difficult (Singer & Singer, 1978). The criteria to be applied are also unclear in the vast middle range of orgasmic responsiveness. Most clinicians agree that a primary anorgasmic woman needs treatment, and that a woman at the other extreme who routinely climaxes with relatively brief intercourse, or perhaps even with only breast stimulation or fantasy, does not. Differences of opinion become notable, however, as we move away from these extremes into the range in which most women's experiences actually fall (Kaplan, 1987). Our own view is that this question is best left to a woman herself to answer; if she is dissatisfied about her responsiveness, and if there is a reasonable likelihood that treatment will help, then it should be provided on request.

Dysfunctions Affecting Both Sexes

Certain dysfunctions are, at least on surface presentation, common to both sexes. Their underlying causes, however, may differ somewhat between men and women.

Dyspareunia Painful coitus, or **dyspareunia,** can occur in males but is far more common in females (Lazarus, 1989). This is the form of sexual dysfunction most likely to have an organic basis—for example, in association with infections or structural pathology of the sex organs. It often has a psychological basis, however, as in the case of a woman who has an aversion to sexual intercourse and experiences her displeasure as intense physical discomfort; in such cases the designation *functional* is used. Understandably, dyspareunia is often associated with vaginismus. This form of sexual dysfunction is rare.

Sexual Desire Disorders Researchers have delineated two types of sexual desire disorders. The first is **hypoactive sexual desire disorder.** As distinguished from sexual arousal disorder (male erectile disorder or female arousal disorder), it is a dysfunction in which either a man or a woman shows little or no sexual drive or interest. It is assumed in most cases that the biological basis of the sex drive remains unimpaired, but that for some reason sexual motivation is blocked. These people usually come to the attention of clinicians only at the request of their partners, who typically complain of an insufficient frequency of sexual interaction. This fact exposes one problem with the diagnosis, because it is known that preferences for frequency of sexual contact vary widely among otherwise "normal" individuals. Who is to decide what is "not enough"? DSM-III-R explicitly indicates that this judgment is left to the clinician.

Nevertheless, there do appear to be some people who are almost totally lacking in sexual desire. In extreme cases, sex actually becomes psychologically aversive, and warrants a diagnosis of **sexual aversion disorder,** the second type of sexual desire disorder. Formerly considered rare and largely limited to females, sexual desire disorder diagnoses have in recent years become fairly common and are applied relatively often to males (Rosen & Leiblum, 1989). Doubtless this change is due at least in part to changing role expectations, of which more will be said later.

Causal Factors in Sexual Dysfunctions

Both sexual desire and genital functioning may be affected by a wide range of organic conditions, including injuries to the genitals, disease, fatigue, excessive alcohol consumption, and abuse of certain drugs, such as tranquilizers. Most cases of sexual dysfunction, however, are more likely due to psychosocial rather than physical causes. Although specific causal factors may vary considerably from one type of sexual dysfunction to another, the following psychosocial factors are commonly found.

Faulty Learning In some nonindustrialized societies, older members of a group instruct younger members in sexual techniques before marriage. In our society, though we recognize that sexual behavior is (with certain proscriptions) an impor-

In our society, the learning of sexual techniques and attitudes is too often left to chance, which may include such sources as X-rated video shops. As a result, a great number of people acquire faulty information and expectations that can impair their sexual enjoyment and adequacy. Sexual dysfunction is a problem for many different kinds of people from all walks of life.

tant aspect of life, the learning of sexual techniques and attitudes is too often left to chance. The result is that many young people start out with faulty expectations and a lack of needed information or harmful misinformation that can impair their sexual adequacy and enjoyment. In fact, Kaplan (1974) has concluded that couples with sexual problems are typically practicing insensitive, incompetent, and ineffective sexual techniques; this conclusion is readily endorsed by most investigators in the field (Leiblum & Rosen, 1989a; LoPiccolo & LoPiccolo, 1978; Tollison & Adams, 1979).

In our society, many people, but especially women (being at risk for pregnancy), have been subjected to early training that depicts sexual relations as lustful, dirty, and evil. The attitudes and inhibitions thus established can lead to a great deal of anxiety, conflict, and guilt about sexual relations, whether in or out of marriage. Faulty early conditioning may also have taken the form of indoctrination in the idea that a woman has a primary responsibility to satisfy a man sexually—and therefore to suppress her own needs and feelings. Masters and Johnson (1970) considered such faulty learning to be the primary cause of orgasmic dysfunction in females. In vaginismus, a somewhat different conditioning patterning has occurred, leading a female to associate vaginal penetration with pain—either physical, psychological, or both. This conditioned defensive reflex comes into operation when penetration is attempted by a sexual partner (Kaplan, 1975; Leiblum, Pervin, & Campbell, 1989).

Although males may also be subjected to early training emphasizing the evils of sex, such training apparently is in general a far less important factor for them. However, another type of faulty early conditioning may be a key factor in premature ejaculation: males typically have their first and often extensive sexual experiences in solitary masturbation, and such masturbatory sessions are likely to be highly efficient in the achievement of orgasm and ejaculation. A young male may thus train his sexual response cycle in this mode of rapid, direct, and altogether "impersonal" discharge, thereby paving the way for prematurity in his later love relationships (McCarthy, 1989).

Researchers have also observed the seemingly opposite pattern in which premature ejaculators report markedly subnormal masturbatory activity on moral or religious orthodoxy grounds. Such young men are also unlikely to have alternative outlets other than involuntary nocturnal emissions, and may thus experience lengthy periods of ejaculatory inactivity. Since it is known that a lengthy interval following the last ejaculation increases the likelihood of a precipitous emission, these men are at high risk for an awkward incident should an acceptable opportunity for sexual experience present itself.

In other instances, initial difficulties in sexual functioning have led to conditioned anxieties that in turn have impaired subsequent performances. We will elaborate on this point in the section that follows.

Feelings of Fear, Anxiety, and Inadequacy

In a study of 49 adult males with erectile disorders, Cooper (1969) found anxiety to be a contributing factor in 94 percent of the cases and the primary problem for those whose erectile problems had started early. Many subsequent investigators have confirmed this essential observation. Similarly, Kaplan (1974) concluded from her studies that "a man who suffers from impotence is often almost unbearably anxious, frustrated, and humiliated by his inability to produce or maintain an erection" (p. 80). Males who suffer from premature ejaculation may also experience acute feelings of inadequacy—and often feelings of guilt as well—stemming from their lack of control and inability to satisfy their sexual partners via intercourse.

Females may also feel fearful and inadequate in sexual relations. A woman may be uncertain whether her partner finds her sexually attractive, and this may lead to anxiety and tension that interfere with her sexual enjoyment. Or she may feel inadequate because she is unable to have an orgasm or does so infrequently; we have seen many women who have permitted such problems to undermine severely their sense of themselves, their identities as complete women. Sometimes a woman who is not climaxing will pretend to have orgasms to make her sexual partner feel fully adequate. The longer a woman maintains such a pretense, however, the more likely she is to become confused and frustrated; in addition, she is likely to resent her partner for being so insensitive to her real feelings and needs. This in turn only adds to her sexual difficulties.

From a more general viewpoint, Masters and Johnson (1975) concluded that most sexual dysfunctions are due to crippling fears, attitudes, and inhibitions concerning sexual behavior, often based on faulty early learning and then exacerbated by later aversive experiences. In a more recent review of the accumulated evidence, Beck and Barlow (1984) played down the role of anxiety per se—which can actually enhance sexual performance in males—emphasizing instead the cognitive distractions frequently associated with anxiety in dysfunctional people. A follow-up laboratory study (Abrahamson, Barlow, & Abrahamson, 1989) confirmed that dysfunctional men with erectile problems differ from their more functional counterparts chiefly in being readily and specifically distracted by cues about their performance, resulting in decreased penile rigidity during erotic stimulation. These self-defeating thoughts about performance encourage the adoption of a "spectator role" in sexual relations, making wholehearted participation impossible.

Interpersonal Problems Interpersonal problems may cause a number of sexual dysfunctions. Lack of emotional closeness can lead to erectile or orgasmic problems. An individual may be in love with someone else, may find his or her sexual partner physically or psychologically repulsive, or may have hostile feelings from prior misunderstandings, quarrels, and conflicts. A one-sided interpersonal relationship—in which one partner does most of the giving and the other most of the receiving—can lead to feelings of insecurity and resentment with resulting impairment in sexual performance (Friedman, 1974; Leiblum & Rosen, 1989a; Lobitz & Lobitz, 1978; Simon, 1975).

For a female, lack of emotional closeness often appears to result from intercourse with a partner who is a "sexual moron"—rough, unduly hasty, and concerned only with self-gratification. As Kaplan (1974) pointed out,

> *Some persons have as much difficulty giving pleasure as others do in receiving it. These individuals don't provide their partners with enough sexual stimulation because they lack either the knowledge and sensitivity to know what to do, or they are anxious about doing it. (p. 78)*

In other instances, an individual may be hostile toward and not want to please his or her sexual partner. This situation seems to occur rather frequently in unhappy marital or other intimate relationships. In such relationships, channels of communication have largely broken down and sexual relations continue as a sort of habit or duty or simply to gratify one's own sexual needs.

Physiologically, people are capable of experiencing orgasm with any personally acceptable partner. However, Switzer (1974) aptly pointed to a generally agreed-on conclusion: "Orgasm has especially delightful overtones when you're with a person whom you love and when you can abandon yourself" (p. 36).

Changing Male-Female Roles and Relationships An increase in erectile problems was reported during the 1970s that a number of investigators have related to two phenomena occurring during that period: (a) the increasing changes being achieved by the women's movement in our society, and (b) the growing awareness of female sexuality (Burros, 1974; Heiman & Grafton-Becker, 1989; Leiblum & Rosen, 1989b). These trends have led women to want and expect more from their lives, including their sexual relationships. Women no longer accept the older concept of being the passive partner in sex, and many are taking a more assertive and active role in sexual relations.

This new role appears to threaten the image many men have of themselves as the supposedly "dominant" partner who takes the initiative in sexual relations (Steinmann & Fox, 1974). In fact some men appear to regard sexually assertive women who play an active role in sex as "castrating females" (Kaplan, 1974). In addition, the greater assertiveness and expectancy of women makes many men feel that they are under pressure to perform. As Ginsberg, Frosch, and Shapiro (1972) expressed it early on, "This challenge to manhood is most apparent in a sexually liberated society where women are not merely available but are perceived as demanding satisfaction from masculine performance" (p. 219). The distracting thoughts such a challenge may inspire in an insecure man may result not only in impaired male performance but even in erectile failure.

Changing male-female roles in sexual relationships also place greater demands on women. The expectation of taking an active rather than a passive role may cause a woman to make unrealistic demands on her own sexual responsiveness—such as expecting to have a highly pleasurable orgasm each time she engages in sexual relations. Such demands are likely to lead to some degree of unfulfilled desires, confusion, and self-devaluation, which in turn impair actual sexual performance. This situation seems especially true when a female assumes a "spectator's role" and almost literally monitors her own sexual performance, thus depriving it of spontaneity and naturalness.

Finally, our enhanced awareness of sexually transmitted diseases—fueled by the seemingly relentless advance of the deadly AIDS virus—has added an increment of anxiety to many sexual encounters both casual and otherwise (Leiblum & Rosen, 1989b). The relatively carefree promiscuity of the 1960s and 1970s has increasingly and wisely given way to concerns about "safe sex" with partners whose sexual (and drug-use) histories place them outside of the known high-risk groups. Monogamy and sexual exclusivity have made dramatic comebacks. The adolescent's sense of invulnerability and immortality has been not so gently shaken, probably for the better. The condom, once widely rejected as inhibiting spontaneity (or the appearance of it) and decreasing pleasure, is now heralded as essential equipment for many prudent adolescents and young adults—male and female—who still "cruise." In short, we are clearly in the midst of a new sexual revolution, one involving life and death decisions, and thus one whose constraints all but the foolhardy will heed. It is still too early to tell what effect these dramatic changes will have on the incidence and prevalence of sexual dysfunctions. Conceivably, the added anxiety and suspicion created by the AIDS epidemic will be counterbalanced by the positive effects that may come with expectations of more enduring and committed relationships.

Treatments and Outcomes

The treatment of sexual dysfunctions, too, has undergone nothing less than a revolution during the lifetime of today's young adults. Once regarded as difficult and intractable therapeutic challenges, most instances of sexual dysfunction are now readily treated with new techniques that are still being developed and improved. Generally, these techniques include direct methods of attack on the dysfunctions themselves, usually with high levels of gentle and affectionate partner participation. For example, a couple may be given instruction and guided practice in overcoming, by vigorous stimulation, orgasmic inhibition in one of the partners; or vaginismus may be treated with intravaginal insertion, by the male partner, of cylindrical objects of gradually increasing circumference until the excessive vaginal contractions cease. As a result of these newer approaches, success rates approaching 90 percent or more for some dysfunctions have become quite routine (Andersen, 1983; Kaplan, 1987; Leiblum & Rosen, 1989a; LoPiccolo & Stock, 1986; Tollison & Adams, 1979; Zilbergeld & Kilmann, 1984).

The turning point in sex therapy is uniformly considered to be the publication in 1970 of Masters and Johnson's *Human Sexual Inadequacy,* the product of an eleven-year search to develop truly effective treatment procedures for the common dysfunctions, both male and female. The success rates claimed by this team of dedicated clinical researchers astonished the professional community and rapidly led to the widespread adoption of their general approach, which combined elements of traditional and behavioral therapy in a framework emphasizing, as already noted, direct intervention aimed at the dysfunctions themselves.

Although the early confidence inspired by Masters and Johnson's reported results has waned somewhat (Leiblum & Pervin, 1980; Leiblum & Rosen,

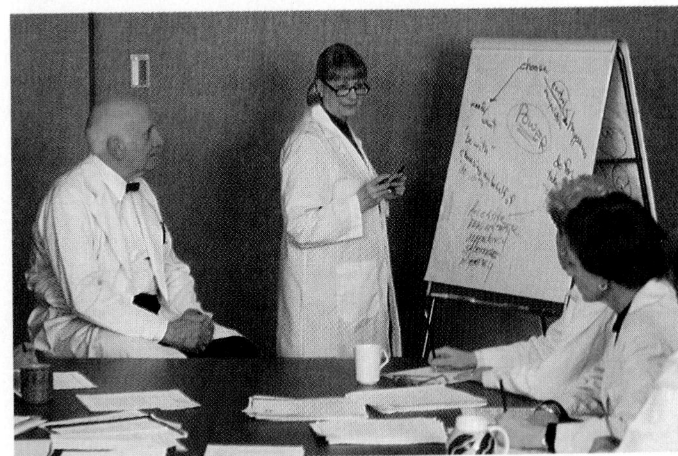

Masters and Johnson, pioneers in the treatment of sexual dysfunction, emphasize the importance of removing crippling fears, misconceptions, and inhibitions about sex and fostering attitudes toward and participation in sexual behavior as a pleasurable, natural, and meaningful experience.

1989b; LoPiccolo & Stock, 1986; Vandereycken, 1982; Zilbergeld & Evans, 1980), their work has unquestionably unleashed a ground swell of new therapeutic techniques. Despite differences in emphasis and methods, there seems to be general agreement on the importance of removing crippling misconceptions, inhibitions, and fears, and on fostering attitudes toward sexual behavior as a pleasurable, natural, and meaningful experience.

Because of the manner in which sexual dysfunctions are presented and described by those suffering from them, it is easy to lose sight of a crucial issue emphasized by Masters and Johnson and by virtually all those who have followed in their footsteps. That is, sexual dysfunctions are not normally disorders of individuals, but rather of relationships between individuals. Thus the new treatments for sexual dysfunctions typically involve *both* parties to a relationship in which a disorder manifests itself. Joseph LoPiccolo (1978) put it this way:

It must be stressed that all sexual dysfunctions are shared disorders; that is, the husband of an inorgasmic woman is partially responsible for creating or maintaining her dysfunction, and he is also a patient in need of help. Regardless of the cause of the dysfunction, both partners are responsible for future change and the solution of their problems. (p. 3)

With competent treatment, success rates vary between approximately 30 and 100 percent, depending in part on the individual or couple and on the nature of the problem. For example, Masters and Johnson (1970) and Kaplan (1975) have reported success rates approaching 100 percent for the treatment of premature ejaculation and vaginismus, but considerably lower rates for male erectile and female orgasmic dysfunctions. More recent reviews (Andersen, 1983; Leiblum & Rosen, 1989a; LoPiccolo & Stock, 1986; Zilbergeld & Kilmann, 1984) essentially confirm these relative outcome expectancies but make an important distinction between primary and secondary female orgasmic dysfunction. Treatment of the former, typically beginning with instruction and guided practice in masturbating to orgasm, has a high likelihood of success, while "situational" anorgasmia (where a woman may experience orgasm in some situations, with certain kinds of stimulation, or with certain partners, but not under the precise conditions she desires) often proves intractable.

The more treatment-resistant erectile disorders probably reflect underlying contributory medical problems, the prevalence of which were until recently seriously underestimated. As noted by Mohr & Beutler (1990), the only available recourse for these disorders may be the use of some sort of mechanical aid. Inflatable penile prostheses often prove preferable to implanted prostheses that maintain a constant rigidity, despite the potential disruption the need to inflate them may entail. The combination of a vacuum device (which draws blood into the spongy tissue of the penis) and

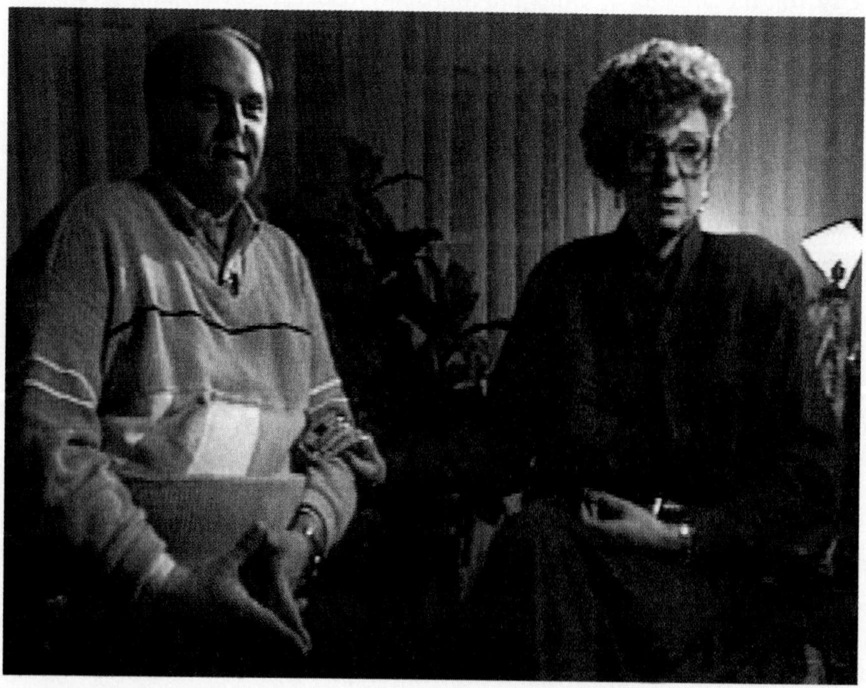

This couple has had successful sex therapy. They are able to laugh now that they have worked out some of their problems. With competent treatment, success rates for the treatment of sexual dysfunctions vary between approximately 30 and 100 percent, depending in part on an individual or couple and on the nature of the problem.

constricting rubber or plastic rings at the base of the penis (which keeps it there under pressure) shows considerable promise for some men whose erectile problems prove resistant to psychological or medical treatments.

The term *competent treatment* should be stressed in any discussion of sex therapy, because the quality of treatment in the several thousand American sex clinics may range from sophisticated psychotherapy to outright charlatanism. Indications are strong, in fact, that unqualified practitioners have entered this field in abundance recently, often charging astronomical fees for their decidedly inexpert services.

VARIANT SEXUAL BEHAVIORS

Human sexual interest may take many channels, especially when for some reason the usual patterning has become blocked. It is hardly surprising then that many people find their principal sexual interests and satisfactions in practices outside the range of what is considered acceptable or normal in a given culture. The sexual drive, which is functionally inseparable from the lovemap in which it is manifested, is normally sufficiently powerful to override all but the most severe social sanctions; thus we see variant sexual needs frequently erupting into variant sexual behavior.

Variant sexual behavior is behavior in which satisfaction is dependent persistently and primarily on something other than a mutually desired sexual engagement with a sexually mature member of the opposite sex. So defined, the domain encompasses a vast array of behavior patterns of arousal and sexual consummation in which the sexual development of an affected individual has for some reason deviated from the standard, adult heterosexual course.

As already observed, the specter of these sexual variants seems peculiarly threatening to many people in our society, and expressions of tolerance for such behavior as homosexuality, for example, can arouse intense emotion. It is certainly true that some forms of sexual variation, such as rape and child molestation, are contrary to the welfare of society and its members. Other forms, however, are in themselves generally victimless and thus constitute no obvious, rationally based threat to the public order—provided of course due precaution is taken to avoid sexually transmitted infections. For this reason, we make a distinction between *victimless* sexual variants—in which the acts involved do not infringe on the rights of noninvolved others and are engaged in by mutually consenting adults who do no physical harm to each other—and sexual deviations that involve nonconsent or assault. In the former category, we place gender identity disorders, uncomplicated male and female homosexuality, most cases of fetishism, and transvestism. The more problematic sexual variants, from the standpoint of the welfare of society, include voyeurism, exhibitionism, sexual sadism and masochism, pedophilia, incest, and rape. In most jurisdictions, laws against acts in this category not only exist but are actively enforced.

It is important to reiterate that we have chosen *not* to follow the lead of DSM-III-R in respect to the categories of variant behavior. Specifically, that document excludes incest and rape from consideration as mental disorders. We include these variants because they clearly fall within our definition of abnormal behavior, irrespective of whether they are officially considered to be psychiatric disorders. Our position is that the criminal and the abnormal are separate domains having no necessary relationship to one another; some behaviors, such as rape and incest, can be considered both crimes and abnormalities, while others may be one of these without being the other. Homosexuality, which remains a crime in many jurisdictions and a subject of intense controversy regarding its "abnormality," represents a special case to be discussed in a later section.

A key point—one particularly emphasized by Adams and Chiodo (1984) and Barlow (1974)—deserves mention here. In considering these behaviors, we tend to focus our attention on the variant arousal patterns themselves to the exclusion of other, perhaps equally important, factors that may help cause or maintain variant behaviors. These other factors often include (a) the absence of a normal level of arousal to adults of the opposite sex; (b) significant deficits in the social skills normally needed for initiating successful adult heterosexual relationships (Overholser & Beck, 1986; Segal & Marshall, 1985); and (c) failure to establish a firm psychological gender identity, which in males often manifests itself in concerns about dominance and power.

The importance of this broadened view for both understanding and therapy is illustrated in findings of several studies on therapy for homosexual individuals who wanted to change their sexual orientations. Adams and Sturgis (1977), reviewing the evidence, concluded that multiple-target treatment procedures aimed at the three factors just mentioned plus the variant arousal pattern greatly enhanced the likelihood of successful sexual reorientation therapy, as compared with approaches that focused only on suppression of the variant sexual arousal pattern.

Gender Identity Disorders

As has just been noted, individuals manifesting sexually variant behavior are often to a degree confused, uncertain, or disorganized in their concepts of themselves as males or females. This confusion is seen most explicitly in cases of **gender identity disorder** and in some cases of transvestism (dressing in the clothes of the opposite sex) and homosexuality. But even where outward behavior appears to conform to societal expectations and norms, many people will prove on careful assessment to have unclear or unstable gender identities and to lack appropriate repertoires of gender-role behaviors (Adams & Chiodo, 1984).

Gender Identity Formation The formation of gender identity and the acquisition of culturally prescribed gender-role behaviors are obviously matters of great complexity, and our understanding of the processes involved is limited. Research by Money and colleagues (1980; Money & Ehrhardt, 1972; Money & Lamacz, 1989), among others, has established that outcomes in this area are powerfully determined by learning—that is, by adapting to a host of psychosocial forces that are normally quite effective in "shaping" a person to be psychosocially male or female. But of course, differing social environments will on occasion produce blends or blurrings of the cultural concepts of maleness and femaleness, and the impact of these environments on a developing child will likely be very strong. Many of the most functional men and women in our society seem to have highly developed masculine *and* feminine traits, as conventionally conceived. Conversely, many of the least functional lack a strong identification with *either* side of this traditional behavioral dichotomy and appear confused or "undifferentiated" with respect to psychosocial gender (Carson, 1983; Orlofsky & O'Heron, 1987; Spence & Helmreich, 1978).

While psychosocial influences seem paramount in determining gender identity and role, mounting evidence from both human and animal studies shows that biological factors are also importantly involved, both generally and in respect to specific preferences for differing forms of sexual expression and satisfaction (Bell, Weinberg, & Hammersmith, 1981; Ehrhardt & Meyer-Bahlburg, 1981; MacLusky & Naftolin, 1981; Money, 1980; Money & Lamacz, 1989; Rubin, Reinisch, & Haskett, 1981). Considering the incidence of sexually variant behaviors such as transsexualism or homosexuality in the light of a historically strong societal rejection of them, such findings give us a potentially valuable insight into why some individuals remain strongly driven to adopt variant behaviors despite the vigorous and continuing condemnation these behaviors often inspire. It may in fact be that they have little choice in the matter (see *HIGHLIGHT 10.2).*

This apparent absence of choice seems especially true of gender identity disorders, as defined in the DSM-III-R, which recognizes separate adult and childhood forms of a profound rejection of one's anatomical sex. Individuals with this disorder feel themselves to be the victims of some grotesque error of fate in being forced to occupy a body that is alien to their gender-related sense of self.

Often this anatomically discrepant gender identity is accompanied by role behaviors and dress that affirm the desired identity, and, in sexually active adults, by a "homosexual" orientation and partner choice; of course, in this context such a choice (for example, a male transsexual choosing a male partner) is the psychological equivalent of a heterosexual one. Many of these individuals feel driven to seek and submit to surgical and endocrinological interventions that hold some promise of bringing them anatomically closer to their gender identities—a venture that is much more likely, for technical/surgical reasons, to have an objectively satisfactory outcome if the desired conversion is male-to-female rather than the opposite. In children, the disorder may be accompanied by stubborn, irrational beliefs that their anatomies will undergo future changes in the desired direction.

The DSM-III-R also recognizes a type of gender identity disorder among adults that is not accompanied by preoccupation with sex change. Rare in incidence, it is designated as ***nontranssexual cross-gender disorder.***

Gender identity disorders are quite rare overall. Their incidence in males is estimated to be somewhat less than 3 per 100,000 and in females just under 1 per 100,000 (Walinder, 1968). These figures do not include children, who typically manifest the disorder before the age of 4, and many of whom yield to pressures and adopt sex-appropriate behavior; the few who do not become adult transsexuals (Adams & Chiodo, 1984).

While the hypothesis of biological causation seems plausible, it is also possible that reverse-gender identity and behavior could be learned. Green (1974) has noted certain psychosocial factors that appear to be common in the backgrounds of transsexual boys, among them parental indifference to or encouragement of "feminine" behavior dur-

HIGHLIGHT 10.2

Transsexualism and a Tangled Relationship

After a lengthy courtship, Bob and Mae Sylvester married in 1972, Mae having concluded that Bob had overcome, through therapy, his wish to dress in women's clothing. Bob knew better, but was so attached to Mae that he tried to tell himself he was "cured" of his transvestism. After a brief period, the urge to cross-dress became so strong that Bob told Mae he wished occasionally to wear women's clothing at home. Mae responded by telling him it made her "physically sick" to see him dress in that manner. Nevertheless, on the advice of a second therapist, Bob resumed regular cross-dressing—but never in Mae's presence. At about this time, Bob successfully ran for election to the St. Paul, Minnesota, city council. During a four-year term as a member of this body, Bob distinguished himself as an effective and dynamic leader.

Meanwhile, Bob and Mae tried, with essentially no success, to establish a satisfactory sexual relationship. Both agreed that their sex life was a disaster. Their relationship was strained further with the emergence of Bob's second identity, an adolescent girl named Susan. Susan was petulant and demanding, and Mae resented the maternal role into which she was now cast. As Susan developed, she wanted more and more "time" and resisted being Bob for an evening at home. Susan demanded, and got, an adolescent girl's bedroom, decorated in pink and mauve with birds, flowers, ribbons, and a pink canopy over the bed. This was apparently the last straw for Mae, and shortly thereafter, in 1981, the couple separated. Bob could not bear to lose the bedroom, so Mae moved out.

Bob had been aware since childhood of his wish to be female. A life-threatening event in February 1982 brought home to him forcefully his wish "just once" to make love as a woman. The next week he initiated procedures to undergo a sex change. On March 28, Bob legally became Susan Elizabeth Kimberly. Surgery to provide her with female genitalia was scheduled for 1984. Before the surgery, Ms. Kimberly transformed her social identity exclusively to that of a woman.

Mae Sylvester's initial reaction to these events was similar to grieving—indeed, for her, her husband Bob *had* died. Nevertheless, she maintains an active friendship with Susan Kimberly. The two continue to see each other and to share the (nonsexual) activities both had enjoyed before the divorce and Susan's reversal of gender identity. Mae says that Susan has retained many of the qualities she had found attractive in Bob.

Based on *Minneapolis Tribune,* May 1, 1983, pp. 1A, 4A–6A.

ing the first year, maternal overprotection and domination, being dressed in female clothes by a female family member, and a lack of male friends in the early years. Obviously, some of these factors could be secondary accommodations to a child's displaying effeminate behavior from an early age, and hence are not inconsistent with a biological hypothesis. Of incidental interest, Green (1985) followed up these identity-reversed youngsters and found some 70 percent of them to be homosexually or bisexually oriented as adults.

Sex Reassignment Surgery Efforts to alter gender identity by means of behavior therapy and other psychotherapeutic procedures have generally proven unsuccessful. As a consequence, transsexuals who feel a complete inability to accept their assigned sex identity have requested surgical sex change in increasing numbers during recent years.

The first transsexual operation is said to have been performed by F. Z. Abraham in the 1930s. Although occasional reports of similar operations were forthcoming the next two decades, it was not until 1953, when Hamburger reported the case of Christine Jorgensen, that surgical sex change became well known. Currently, medical centers that offer this service receive numerous requests per year from transsexual individuals to undertake evaluation and management of their cases.

In anatomical males, modern surgical procedures accomplish sex conversion through removal of male organs and their replacement with an artfully designed vagina that apparently works satisfactorily in many cases, sometimes even enabling an individual, now a woman, to achieve coital orgasm. Weekly injections of sex hormones stimulate breast development, give more female texture to the skin, and also lessen beard growth, though electrolysis is usually needed to remove excess hair. Surgery for anatomically female transsexuals generally has been less successful, for although surgeons can remove the breasts, ovaries, vagina, and uterus, and can attach a penis constructed from rib cartilage, plastic, or other material, the makeshift penis does not function normally. Nevertheless, many receiving this surgery report satisfaction with the outcomes (Blanchard, Steiner, & Clemmensen, 1985). Transplants of reproductive organs are not yet possible in either males or females, and the individual will be sterile after surgery.

Various evaluative studies of the outcomes of such operations have been reported. One of the best-known early studies is that of Benjamin (1966). This investigator questioned 50 transsexuals who had crossed the sex line from male to female. Their ages at the time of surgery ranged from 19 to 58, with an average age of 32. Of these subjects, 44 reported contentment sexually and socially with their new roles as women; 5 complained either about their abilities to perform sexually or about their appearances; and 1 was totally dissatisfied with the results. In another study, Pauly (1968) reviewed the postoperative courses of 121 male transsexuals who had received sex-reassignment surgery and found that satisfactory outcomes outnumbered unsatisfactory ones at a ratio of 10 to 1. He also reported previous unsuccessful attempts by psychotherapy to help these patients achieve male gender identities. Comparable results were reported by Green (1974). In a more recent and relatively rigorous assessment, Abramowitz (1986) estimated the psychosocial outcome success rate for transsexual surgery to be about two-thirds overall, the female-to-male variety actually showing a slight advantage; some 10 percent of male-to-female interventions were said to produce serious complications, usually associated with the surgery.

Considerable controversy has raged about sex-conversion surgery, and many physicians as well as other professionals remain opposed to it. Newman and Stoller (1974) have pointed out that occasionally schizophrenics and other mentally disturbed individuals seek sexual reassignment, but that their desire is only transitory. For this and related reasons, it is recommended that those considering sex-reassignment surgery undergo a trial period first during which they receive hormone therapy and live in their new roles to get a clearer understanding of the many psychological and social adjustments that will be required. Based on his considerable clinical experience with this group, Lothstein (1982, 1983) is also impressed with the prevalence of serious mental disturbances, recommending psychotherapy as the initial treatment of choice. In general, it appears that strict criteria are needed for selecting surgical reassignees (Lothstein, 1982).

Dr. Richard Raskin, a physician and professional tennis player, became Renee Richards through transsexual surgery.

The Paraphilias

The **paraphilias** are a group of persistent sexual behavior patterns in which unusual objects, rituals, or situations are required for full sexual satisfaction. While mild forms of these activities probably have occurred in the lives of many normal people, a paraphilic person is distinguished by the insistence and relative exclusivity with which his or her sexuality focuses on the acts in question—without which orgasm is often impossible. Paraphilic individuals may or may not have persistent desires to change their sexual preferences.

As described by Money and Lamacz (1989), paraphilic lovemaps tend to be quite stable within individuals but quite variable in character among people having paraphilic tendencies. Some such lovemaps are organized in a quite simple, straightforward manner, while others are complex and richly elaborated, calling for extraordinary preparation and "staging." The playing out of a lovemap may be complete on the first and every subsequent occasion in which it appears, or it may unfold in a series of stages. Some paraphilias require interpersonal formats, and a fortunate paraphilic individual may discover another person with a reciprocally paraphilic lovemap—as in sexual sadomasochism—which may then lead to a lasting although by conventional standards somewhat bizarre love affair. Fairly common is a situation in which a sexually normal person becomes unwittingly involved in a paraphilic person's ritualized sexual program, only gradually discovering that he or she is a mere accessory, a sort of stage prop, in the latter's sexual drama.

The DSM-III-R recognizes nine paraphilias: fetishism, transvestic fetishism, voyeurism, exhibitionism, sexual sadism, sexual masochism, pedophilia, zoophilia (sexual attraction to animals), and frotteurism (rubbing against a nonconsenting person). Of these, we will discuss all but zoophilia, a rare disorder, and frotteurism, a category that is relatively new and not yet satisfactorily researched.

Fetishism In **fetishism,** sexual interest typically centers on some body part or on an inanimate object, such as an article of clothing. As is generally true for the paraphilias, males are most commonly involved in cases of fetishism; reported cases of female fetishists are extremely rare. The range of fetishistic objects includes hair, ears, hands, underclothing, shoes, perfume, and similar objects associated with the opposite sex. The mode of using these objects to achieve sexual excitation and gratification varies considerably, but it commonly involves kissing, fondling, tasting, or smelling the objects. Fetishism is a victimless sexual variant because, although it sometimes involves crimes such as thievery, its basic nature does not normally interfere with the rights of others, except in an incidental way.

To obtain the required object, a fetishistic person may commit burglary, theft, or even assault. Probably the articles most commonly stolen by fetishistic individuals are women's underthings. One young boy was found to have accumulated over 100 pairs of panties from a lingerie shop when he was apprehended. In such cases the excitement and suspense of the criminal act itself typically reinforce the sexual stimulation and sometimes actually constitute the fetish—the stolen article being of little importance. For example, one youth admitted entering many homes in which the entering itself usually sufficed to induce an orgasm. When it did not, he was able to achieve sexual satisfaction by taking some "token," such as money or jewelry.

Frequently, fetishistic behavior consists of masturbation in association with a fetishistic object. Here, of course, it is difficult to draw a line between fetishistic activity and the effort to increase the sexual excitation and satisfaction of masturbation through the use of pictures and other articles associated with a desired sexual object. Using such articles in masturbation is a common practice and not usually considered pathological. Where antisocial behavior, such as breaking and entering, is involved, however, the practice is commonly referred to as fetishistic. For example, Marshall (1974) reported a rather unusual case of a young university student who had a "trouser fetish"; he would steal the trousers of teenagers and then use them in physical contact during masturbation. A somewhat different, but not atypical, pattern of fetishism is illustrated by the case of a man whose fetish was women's shoes and legs.

The fetishist in this case was arrested several times for loitering in public places, such as railroad stations and libraries, watching women's legs. Finally he chanced on a novel solution to his problem. Posing as an agent for a hosiery firm, he rented a large room, advertised for models, and took motion pictures of a number of women walking and seated with their legs displayed to best advantage. He then used these pictures to achieve sexual satisfaction and found that they continued to be adequate for the purpose. (Adapted from Grant, 1953)

Another type of fetishism involves setting fires. Although people who set fires are a mixed group, a sizable number of fires—including some involving loss of life—are set by fetishistic individuals who have come to experience relief of sexual tension from setting and watching fires burn. Such fires include brush and forest fires as well as building fires. Diagnostically, fetishistic fire-setting is included in the DSM-III-R rubric of pyromania, an impulse control disorder.

In approaching the causal factors in fetishism, we should again note that, through learning, many stimuli can come to be associated with sexual excitation and gratification. Probably most people are stimulated to some degree by intimate articles of clothing and by perfumes and odors associated with potential sexual partners. Thus the first prerequisite in fetishism seems to be a conditioning experience. This original conditioning may be quite accidental, as when sexual arousal and orgasm—which are reflexive responses—are elicited by a strong emotional experience involving some particular object or part of the body. More commonly, probably, the conditioning occurs during masturbatory fantasies.

In some instances, however, the associations involved in fetishism are not easy to explain. Bergler (1947) cited an unusual case in which a man's sex life was almost completely absorbed by a fetishistic fascination with automobile exhaust pipes. Nor would just any exhaust pipe do; it had to be in perfect shape, undented and undamaged, and it had to emit softly blowing gases. This fetish became far more attractive to him than sexual behavior with women.

Fetishistic patterns of sexual gratification usually become the preferred patterns only when they are part of a larger picture of maladjustment, at least in the far more common cases involving males; such maladjustment typically involves doubts about one's masculinity and potency, and fear of rejection and humiliation. By fetishistic practices and mastery over an inanimate object—which comes to symbolize a desired sexual object—a man apparently safeguards himself and also compensates somewhat for his feelings of inadequacy.

Transvestic Fetishism The achievement of sexual arousal and satisfaction by "cross-dressing," that is, dressing as a member of the opposite sex, is called **transvestic fetishism.** It is an uncommon condition in which an individual, usually a male, enjoys excursions into the social roles of the other sex or is markedly distressed by urges to do so. Although a transvestic male, for example, regards himself as a man when dressed as a man, he may have feelings of being a woman when dressed in women's clothing. A medical researcher and transvestite himself for 35 years expressed it this way: "The transvestite finds that he is both a 'he' and 'she' together—at the same time or alternating from one to the other when opportunity permits or desire compels" (*Los Angeles Times,* September 30, 1973). Because transvestism usually does not directly involve anyone but the cross-dressing individual, it can be considered a victimless sexual variant.

Little is known about transvestism, especially as practiced by females, in whom it appears to be extremely rare. Most reports are based on studies of single male cases, and most of those studied have been in therapy, which may make them an unrepresentative group. Buckner (1970), however, has formulated a description of the "ordinary" male transvestite from a survey of 262 transvestites conducted by the magazine *Transvestia.*

He is probably married (about two-thirds are); if he is married he probably has children (about two-thirds do). Almost all of these transvestites said they were exclusively heterosexual—in fact, the rate of "homosexuality" was less than the average for the entire population. The transvestic behavior generally consists of privately dressing in the clothes of a woman, at home, in secret. . . . The transvestite generally does not run into trouble with the law. His cross-dressing causes difficulties for very few people besides himself and his wife. (p. 381)

The most extensive studies to date of male transvestites' personalities are those of Bentler and Prince (1969, 1970) and Bentler, Shearman, and Prince (1970). These investigators obtained replies

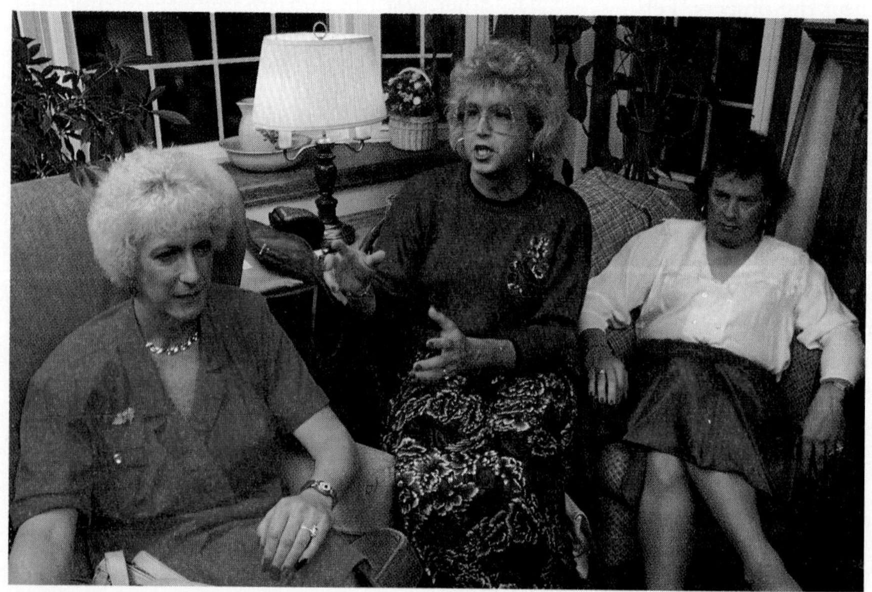

Studies have shown that men who cross dress may actually feel less anxiety and shyness when in their female roles. Though an individual may therefore enjoy excursions into the social roles of the other sex, he may also be markedly distressed by urges to do so, and, if married, his transvestism may also cause difficulties for his wife. Cross dressers are seeking out others of their kind to deal with their special problems in support groups like the one shown here.

to a standardized psychological inventory from a large sample of transvestic people through the cooperation of a national transvestite organization. The transvestic individuals, compared to matched control groups, showed no gross differences on neurotic or psychotic inventory scales. They did, however, present themselves as being more controlled in impulse expression, less involved with other individuals, more inhibited in interpersonal relationships, and more dependent.

Interestingly, it appears that cross-dressing may reduce the strength of some of these aberrant tendencies. Gosslin and Eysenck (1980) asked transvestic males to take a personality test while functioning in regular male clothing and while cross-dressed. "Neuroticism" and "introversion" both declined in the cross-dressed condition. This finding was consistent with subjects' reports of less anxiety and shyness when in their female roles.

It appears that much transvestism can be explained in terms of a simple conditioning model. A male child may receive attention from females in his family who think it is cute for him to dress in feminine attire and hence reinforce this behavior with attention and praise. Such a conditioning process is well portrayed in the case of an adult transvestite studied by Stoller (1974):

"I have pictures of myself dressed as a little girl when I was a small child. My mother thought it was cute. She was right. I was a pretty little girl.

"The highlights of my life as a girl came when I was between the ages of 10 and 17. I had an aunt who was childless and wanted to take me through the steps from childhood to young womanhood. She knew of my desires to be a girl. I would spend every summer at her ranch. The first thing she would do was to give me a pixie haircut, which always turned out pretty good since I would avoid getting a haircut for two months before I went to her ranch. She then would take me into the bedroom and show me all my pretty new things she had bought me. The next day, dressed as a girl, I would accompany her to town and we would shop for a new dress for me. To everyone she met, she would introduce me as her 'niece.'

"This went on every year until I was 13 years old. Then she decided I should start my womanhood. I will never forget that summer. When I arrived I got the same pixie haircut as usual but when we went into the bedroom there laid out on the bed was a girdle, a garter belt and bra, size 32AA, and my first pair of nylons. She then took me over to the new dressing table she had bought me and slid back the top to reveal my very own makeup kit. I was thrilled to death. She said she wanted her 'niece' to start off right and it was about time I started to develop a bust.

"The next morning I was up early to ready myself for the usual shopping trip to town, only this time it was for a pair of high heels and a new dress. I remember I stuffed my bra with cotton, put on my garter belt, and slipped on my nylons with no effort. After all, I became an expert from practice the night before. My aunt applied my lipstick because I was so excited I couldn't get it on straight. Then off to town we went, aunt and 'niece.' What a wonderful day. I shall never forget it." (pp. 209–210)

The adult transvestite who marries faces problems that are well brought out in another case reported by Stoller (1974):

"We fell in love and as soon as I felt we could we were married. We have been as happy as two people can be and the best part of it is that she knows all about me and not only accepts me as I am but assists in my transformation and then admires me. . . ."

This is the way the relationship looks at first, when the wife is pleased to see her husband's femininity. She does not know yet that as he becomes a more successful transvestite her enthusiasm will wane. Then he will be hurt that she is no longer interested in his dressing up, his sexual needs, his work. The fighting will start, neither will understand what has happened, and they will divorce. (p. 212)

As we have indicated, transvestic fetishism, like fetishism, causes harm to others only when accompanied by such illegal acts as theft or destruction of property. This is not always the case with the other paraphilias, many of which do contain a definite element of injury or significant risk of injury—physical or psychological—to one or more of the parties involved in a sexual encounter. Typically these practices have strong legal sanctions against them. We shall consider only the most common forms of these paraphilias: voyeurism, exhibitionism, sadism, masochism, and pedophilia.

Voyeurism The synonymous terms **voyeurism, scotophilia,** and **inspectionalism** refer to the achievement of sexual pleasure through clandestine peeping. Although children often engage in such behavior, it occurs as a sexual offense primarily among young males. These Peeping Toms, as they are commonly called, usually concentrate on females who are undressing or on couples engaging in sexual relations. Frequently they masturbate during their peeping activity.

How do males develop this pattern? First, viewing the body of an attractive female seems to be quite stimulating sexually for many, if not most, males. In addition, the privacy and mystery that have traditionally surrounded sexual activities have tended to increase curiosity about them.

Second, if a boy with such curiosity feels shy and inadequate in his relations with the other sex, it is not too surprising for him to accept the substitute of voyeurism. In this way he satisfies his curiosity and to some extent meets his sexual needs without the trauma of actually approaching a female, and thus without the failure and lowered self-status that such an approach might bring. In fact voyeuristic activities often provide important compensatory feelings of power and secret domination over an unsuspecting victim, which may contribute materially to the maintenance of this pattern. Also, of course, the suspense and danger associated with voyeurism may lead to emotional excitement and a reinforcement of the sexual stimulation. A voyeur does not normally seek sexual activity with those he observes.

If a voyeur is married, as many are, he is rarely well-adjusted sexually in his relationship with his wife.

A young married college student had an attic apartment that was extremely hot during the summer months. To enable him to attend school, his wife worked; she came home at night tired and irritable and not in the mood for sexual relations. In addition, "the damned springs in the bed squeaked." In order "to obtain some sexual gratification" the youth would peer through his binoculars at the room next door and occasionally saw the young couple there engaged in erotic activities. This stimulated him greatly, and he thus decided to extend his peeping to a sorority house. During his second venture, however, he was reported and apprehended by the police. This offender was quite immature for his age, rather puritanical in his attitude toward masturbation, and prone to indulge in rich but immature sexual fantasies.

Although more permissive laws concerning "adult" movies, videos, and magazines have probably removed much of the secrecy from sexual behavior and also have provided an alternative source of gratification for would-be voyeurs, their actual effects on the incidence of voyeurism is a matter of speculation. For many voyeurs these movies and magazines probably do not provide an adequate substitute for secretly watching the sexual behavior of an unsuspecting couple or the "real-life" nudity of a woman who mistakenly believes she enjoys privacy.

Although a voyeur may become somewhat reckless in his behavior and thus may be detected and assaulted by his subjects, voyeurism does not ordinarily have any serious criminal or antisocial aspects. In fact many people probably have rather strong inclinations in the same direction, which are well checked by practical considerations, such as the possibility of being caught, and ethical attitudes concerning the right to privacy. On the other hand, strong voyeuristic tendencies are sometimes accompanied by other, more bizarre elements in a peeper's lovemap that might signal deeper and far more serious problems. For example, one of the authors is involved at this writing in the assessment of a chronic voyeur who preserves over long periods, in plastic baggies, his ejaculate from masturbation. There is a possibility in this case of psychotic disorder.

Exhibitionism The word **exhibitionism** (*indecent exposure* in legal terms) describes the intentional exposure of the genitals to others in inappropriate circumstances and without their consent. The exposure may take place in some secluded location, such as a park, or in a more public place, such as a department store, church, theater, or bus. In cities an exhibitionist often drives by schools or bus stops, exhibits himself while in the car, and then drives rapidly away. In many instances the exposure is repeated under fairly constant conditions, such as only in churches or buses, or in the same general vicinity and at the same time of day. In one case, a youth exhibited himself only at the top of an escalator in a large department store. The sex object too is usually fairly consistent for an individual exhibitionist. For a male offender, this ordinarily involves a young or middle-aged female who is not known to the offender.

In some instances, exposure of the genitals is accompanied by suggestive gestures or masturbatory activity, but more often there is only exposure. Although it is considered relatively rare, a hostile exposer may accompany exhibitionism with aggressive acts and may knock down or otherwise attack a victim. In fact some research indicates a subclass of exhibitionists who may best be considered antisocial personalities, as described in Chapter 8 (Forgac & Michaels, 1982).

Despite the rarity of assaultive behavior in these cases, and the fact that most exhibitionists are anything but the aggressive and dangerous criminals they are often made out to be, an exhibitionistic act nevertheless takes place without the viewer's consent and may be emotionally upsetting, as is indeed the perpetrator's intent. This intrusive quality of the act, together with its explicit violation of propriety norms respecting "private parts," assures condemnation. Thus society considers exhibitionism a criminal offense.

Exhibitionism is the most common sexual offense reported to the police in the United States, Canada, and Europe, accounting for about one-third of all sexual offenses (Rooth, 1974). Curiously enough, it is rare in most other countries. For example, in Argentina only 24 people were convicted of exhibitionism during a five-year period; in Japan only about 60 men are convicted of this offense each year. In still other countries, such as Burma and India, it is practically unheard of.

Exhibitionism is most common during the warm spring and summer months, and most offenders are young adult males. Practically all occupational groups are represented. Usually exhibitionism by males in public or semipublic places is reported to the police, although some women simply ignore such incidents.

Among women, exhibiting the genitals for noncommercial, erotic purposes is so rare that instances sometimes prompt the publication of full case reports in the professional literature (for example, Grob, 1985). Furthermore, these rare occurences are less likely to be reported to the police. Because so little is known about female exhibitionism, the following discussion of causal factors will be limited to male offenders.

In general, cases of exhibitionism appear to fall into one of three categories. These categories are described in the sections that follow.

Personal immaturity. Witzig (1968) found that about 60 percent of male exhibitionism cases referred by courts for treatment fall into the category of personal immaturity. Here the exhibitionism seems to be based on inadequate information about sex, feelings of shyness and inferiority in approaching potential sexual partners, and puritanical attitudes toward masturbation. Commonly, such exhibitionists have strong bonds to overly possessive mothers. Often an exhibitionist states that he struggled against the impulse to expose himself in much the same way that an adolescent may struggle against the impulse to masturbate; as sexual or other tensions increased, however, he felt compelled to carry out his exhibitionistic activities. Often an exhibitionist feels guilty and remorseful afterward, particularly if he has achieved ejaculation.

Although over half of all exhibitionists are married, they usually fail to achieve satisfactory sexual and personal relationships with their wives. Witzig (1968) pointed out the following:

> *These men almost never like to discuss sexual matters with their wives and frequently avoid undressing before them. The idea of living in a nudist colony is a repulsive thought to most exhibitionists, although they are periodically willing to show off their genitals in quite public places. (p. 78)*

Many of these offenders state that they married only because of family pressure, often at a late age. Thus we are dealing here with individuals who are essentially immature in their sex-role development, even though they may be well-educated and competent in other life areas.

Closely related to a male exhibitionist's personal immaturity appears to be a second factor: doubts and fears about his masculinity, combined with a strong need to demonstrate masculinity and potency. Apfelberg, Sugar, and Pfeffer (1944), for example, cited the case of an exhibitionist who achieved sexual satisfaction only when he accompanied the exposure of his genitals with a question to his victim as to whether she had ever seen such a large penis. On one occasion, the woman, instead of evidencing shock and embarrassment, scornfully assured him that she had. On this occasion, the defendant stated, he had received no sexual gratification. In general, it appears that the lovemap of an exhibitionist is one that requires the victim to be intimidated by the "awesome" display to which she is an involuntary witness.

It is worth noting that exhibitionism normally takes place in a setting that would not be conducive to having sexual relations—for example, the parking lot of a busy shopping mall. An exhibitionist attempts to elicit a reaction that confirms his masculine "power" without entailing the risk of having to perform adequately in a mutual sexual encounter. Some exhibitionists, to be sure, fantasize that their victims will "take the first step" and approach them for sexual services (Adams & Chiodo, 1984). Because such a reaction is exceedingly unlikely to occur, an exhibitionist is protected from any such real confrontation; most would probably flee were this unlikely event to materialize.

In reviewing the role of personal immaturity and sexual ignorance in exhibitionism, it is interesting to note the conclusion of Rooth (1974) that the "sexual revolution" of the 1960s and 1970s in the Western world may have made matters worse for male exhibitionists: the growing assertiveness of women may make them even more insecure while at the same time they are being bombarded by sexually suggestive material from the "emancipated" mass media, thus increasing their frustration. The impact of these changes on women, both as victims and as potential exhibitionists themselves, has not been studied.

Interpersonal stress and acting out. Another causal factor is suggested by the high incidence of precipitating stress (Blair & Lanyon, 1981). Often a married exhibitionist appears to be reacting to some conflict or stress situation in his marriage, and his behavior is like a regression to adolescent masturbatory activity. In such instances, an exhibitionist may state that exhibiting himself during masturbation is more exciting and tension-reducing than using pictures of nude women.

An interesting example of stress-induced exhibitionism was published a number of years ago in the autobiography of a prominent National Football League player. Intellectually and physically talented, attractive, wealthy, famous, and married to one of the most beautiful women in the entertainment field, this individual was nevertheless arrested on two occasions for exhibiting himself to preadolescent girls. By his own account, these incidents occurred only during periods of intense pressure, when he felt he was failing in those aspects of his life he most valued—his athletic career and his marriage (Rentzel, 1972).

Exhibitionism without genital arousal may take place following a period of intense conflict over some problem—often involving authority figures—with which an individual feels inadequate to cope.

For example, a Marine who wanted to make a career of the service was having an experience with a superior that made it impossible for him to reenlist. He could not admit to himself that he could be hostile to either the corps or the superior. For the first time in his life, he exposed himself to a girl on the beach. Arrested, he was merely reprimanded and returned to the scene of conflict. A short time later he displayed his genitals to a girl in a parking lot. This time he was placed on probation with the stipulation that he seek treatment, and his enlistment was allowed to terminate in natural sequence. He never repeated the act. He was happily married and seemed to be acting out in this instance a vulgar expression of contempt. (Witzig, 1968, p. 77)

These cases of exhibitionism as expressions of anger and contempt may be partly viewed as a product of societal expectations that men express masculinity by dominating women.

Other psychopathology. Like other paraphilias, exhibitionism may occur in association with more pervasive forms of psychopathology. Severely mentally retarded youths—both male and female—may exhibit themselves, being apparently unaware or only partially aware that society disapproves of their behavior. Some exhibitionists are older men with senile brain deterioration who evidence a lowering of inner reality and ethical controls.

In other cases, as we have seen, exhibitionism is associated with antisocial personality disorder. Here individuals usually have histories of poor school adjustment and erratic work records; often they have had difficulties with authorities as a consequence of other antisocial acts. Their exhibitionism appears to be just one more form of antisocial behavior, from which they may or may not achieve sexual excitation and gratification. In some instances, exhibitionism is associated with manic or schizophrenic reactions. For example, the only woman in a group of offenders studied by Witzig (1968) typically exposed herself prior to the onset of a full-blown psychotic episode.

Sadism The term **sadism** is derived from the name of the Marquis de Sade (1740–1814), who for sexual purposes inflicted such cruelty on his victims that he was eventually committed as insane. Although the term's meaning has broadened to denote cruelty in general, we will use it in its restricted sense to mean the achievement of sexual stimulation and gratification by inflicting physical or psychic pain or humiliation on a sexual partner. The practice of "bondage and discipline" (B & D) to enhance sexual excitation and pleasure is a closely related pattern. These elements of a sadist's erotic interest suggest a psychological association with rape (Marshall, Laws, & Barbaree, 1990a), discussed in a later section. The lovemaps of sadistic individuals are thus heavily infused with the inflic-

Mild degrees of sadism and masochism are involved in the sexual foreplay customs of many cultures, and some couples in our own society—both heterosexual and homosexual—regularly engage in such practices. In some cases sexual gratification is obtained from the sadistic practice alone. Sadomasochistic services are even sold in places like the one shown here, complete with racks, pillories, cages, whipping posts, and shackles. Here, people pay $40 to be whipped and abused, and for $20 per half-hour counseling session, can be taught how to practice B & D safely at home.

tion of suffering, or the appearance of it, on their partners.

The pain may be inflicted by such means as whipping, biting, or pinching; the act may vary in intensity, from fantasy to severe mutilation and even murder. Mild degrees of sadism (and masochism) are involved in the sexual foreplay customs of many cultures, and some couples in our own society —both heterosexual and homosexual—regularly engage in such practices. The "golden showers" ritual, for example, in which partners urinate on one another, is a form of foreplay among male homosexuals. Males are ordinarily the "aggressors" in sadistic heterosexual relations, although Krafft-Ebing (1950) early reported a number of cases in which sadists were women; likewise, some contemporary prostitutes specialize in the B & D trade as "dominatrixes." In one unusual case, a wife required her husband to cut himself on the arm before approaching her sexually. She would then suck the wound and become extremely aroused.

In some cases, sadistic activities lead up to or terminate in actual sexual relations; in others, full sexual gratification is obtained from the sadistic practice alone. A sadist, for example, may slash a woman with a razor or stick her with a needle, experiencing an orgasm in the process. The peculiar and extreme associations that may occur are shown by the case of a young man who entered a strange woman's apartment, held a chloroformed rag to her face until she lost consciousness, and branded her on the thigh with a hot iron. She was not molested in any other way.

Sometimes sadistic activities are associated with animals or with fetishistic objects instead of other human beings. East (1946) cited the case of a man who stole women's shoes, which he then slashed savagely with a knife. When he was in prison, he was found mutilating photographs that other prisoners kept in their cells by cutting the throats of the women in them. He admitted that he derived full sexual gratification from this procedure.

In other instances, gratification is achieved only if mutilation is performed directly on a victim. Chesser (1971) refers to such offenders as ***pathological sadists*** and notes that they are often extremely dangerous. The following is such a case:

The offender, Peter Kursten, was 47 years old at the time of his apprehension in Düsseldorf, Germany, for a series of lust murders. He was a skilled laborer, well groomed, modest, and had done nothing that annoyed his fellow workers.

Peter came from a disturbed family background, his father having been an alcoholic who had been sent to prison for having intercourse with Peter's older sister. Peter's own earliest sexual experiences were with animals. When he was about 13 years old, he attempted to have intercourse with a sheep, but the animal would not hold still, and he stabbed her with a knife. At that moment he had an ejaculation.

After this experience, Peter found the sight of gushing blood sexually exciting, and he turned from animals to human females. Often he first choked his victim, but if he did not achieve an orgasm, he then stabbed her. Initially he used scissors and a dagger, but later he took to using a hammer or an axe. After he achieved ejaculation, he lost interest in his victim, except for taking measures to cover up his crime.

The offender's sexual crimes extended over a period of some 30 years and involved over 40 victims. Finally apprehended . . . he expressed a sense of injustice at not being like other people who were raised in normal families. (Adapted from Berg, 1954)

The news media have reported more recent cases in which victims have been mutilated and killed in association with sadistic sexual practices. In the early 1970s, a horror story broke concerning the sadistic homosexual murders of 27 teenage boys in Texas. More recently, but prior to the AIDS epidemic, the San Francisco city coroner found it advisable to meet with leaders of the local homosexual community to discuss means of curbing serious injuries and deaths due to sado-masochistic practices within that group (*Time,* May 4, 1981). We do not, however, have enough available case material on which to base definitive conclusions concerning the actual clinical picture or the causal factors involved in cases of sadism reported by the media.

The causal factors in sadism appear roughly comparable to those in fetishism. These factors are listed in the following paragraphs:

1. *Experiences in which sexual excitation and possibly orgasm have been associated with the infliction of pain.* Such conditioned associations may occur under a variety of conditions. In their sexual fantasies many children visualize violent attacks by men on women, and such ideas may be strengthened by newspaper accounts of sadistic assaults on females. Perhaps more directly relevant are experiences in which an individual's infliction of pain on an animal or another person has given rise to strong emotions and, unintentionally, to sexual excitement. We have noted elsewhere the connection between strong emotional stimulation and sexual stimulation, especially during adolescence. Just as in fetishism—where simple conditioning seems to make it possible for almost any object or action to become sexually exciting—conditioning can also be an important factor in the development of sadistic tendencies.

2. *Negative attitudes toward sex.* Sadistic activities may protect individuals with negative attitudes toward sex from the full sexual implications of their behaviors. At the same time, such activities may help certain people express their contempt for and punishment of their partners for engaging in sexual relations. Several early investigators described male sadists as timid, passive, undersexed individuals; they described sadistic behavior as apparently designed to arouse strong emotions in a sex object which, in turn, arouses a sadist and makes orgasm possible. The sadist apparently receives little or no satisfaction if the victim remains passive and unresponsive to the painful stimuli. In fact the sadist usually wants the victim to find the pain exciting, and may even insist that the victim act pleasurably aroused when being stuck with pins, bitten, or otherwise hurt.

For many sexually inadequate and insecure individuals, the infliction of pain is apparently a "safe" means of achieving sexual stimulation. Strong feelings of power and superiority over a victim may for the time shut out underlying feelings of inadequacy and anxiety.

3. *Association with other psychopathology.* In schizophrenia and other severe forms of psychopathology, sadistic rituals and sexual behavior may result from the lowering of inner controls and from pathologically convoluted symbolic processes. Wertham (1949) cited an extreme case in which a schizophrenic individual with puritanical attitudes toward sex achieved full sexual gratification by castrating young boys and killing and mutilating young girls. He rationalized his actions as being the only way to save them from later immoral behavior.

Masochism The term **masochism** is derived from the name of the Austrian novelist Leopold V. Sacher-Masoch (1836–1895), whose fictional characters dwelt lovingly on the sexual pleasure of pain. As in the case of the term *sadism,* the meaning of *masochism* has been broadened beyond sexual connotations, so that it includes deriving pleasure from self-denial; from expiatory physical suffering, such as that of the religious flagellants; and from hardship and suffering in general. As we saw in Chapter 8, the recent proposal to incorporate this pattern as an Axis II personality disorder in DSM-III-R provoked a storm of controversy, resulting in the banishment of the diagnosis (now changed to self-defeating personality disorder) to a DSM-III-R appendix of questionable scientific or professional status. Here we will restrict our discussion to the sexual aspects of masochistic behavior.

The clinical picture of masochism is similar to that in sadistic practices, except that the pain is inflicted on the self instead of on others (Sack & Miller, 1975). For example, East (1946) cited the case of a young woman who frequently cut herself on the arms, legs, and breasts; she also inserted pins and needles under her skin. The woman experienced sexual pleasure from the pain and from seeing the blood from the incisions.

Patterns of masochistic behavior may come about through conditioned learning: as a result of early experiences, an individual comes to associate pain with sexual pleasure. For example, Gebhard (1965) cited the case of an adolescent boy who had the fractured bones in his arm hurriedly set without an anesthetic. To comfort the boy, the physician's attractive nurse caressed him and held his head against her breast. As a consequence, he experienced a "powerful and curious combination of pain and sexual arousal," which led to masochistic—as well as sadistic—tendencies in his later heterosexual relations.

Such sayings as "crushed in his arms" or "smothered with kisses" reveal the association commonly made between erotic arousal and pain or discomfort. Thus it is not surprising that many individuals resort to mild sadomasochistic acts, such as biting, in an attempt to increase sexual excitement. For most people, however, such behavior does not result in serious physical injury, nor does it serve as a substitute for normal sexual relations. In actual masochism, by contrast, an individual experiences sexual stimulation and gratification from the experience of pain and degradation in relating to a lover.

In the case of both sadism and masochism, it should be noted that gratification in many instances requires a shared, complementary interpersonal relationship—one sadist and one masochist or, in milder forms, one superior "disciplinarian" and one obedient "slave." Such arrangements are not uncommon in both heterosexual and homosexual relationships (Tripp, 1975). One of the authors has treated a promiscuous male homosexual whose exclusive desire was to be aggressively penetrated anally. Through this act the man sought to relive an exquisitely painful experience in which, as a boy, his father had administered an enema to him, by far the "closest" and most intimate experience he had ever had with this profoundly rejecting man. Here we see an instance in which the lovemap evidently was enormously affected by a single, overwhelmingly powerful experience.

Pedophilia In **pedophilia** the preferred sex object is a child; the intimacy usually involves manipulation of the child's genitals. Occasionally the child is induced to manipulate the pedophile's sex organ or to engage in fellatio (mouth-genital contact). Sexual intercourse is apparently rare (Adams & Chiodo, 1984), although it is attempted by some pedophiles and often results in injury to the child.

The sexual exploitation and abuse of children might be said to have a long past but a brief history. The ancient Greeks are known to have valued pedophilia, particularly the male homosexual variety, and to have practiced it with considerable enthusiasm. In modern Western culture, until very recently, pedophilic interests have mostly been seen as only moderately "quirky," sometimes amusingly

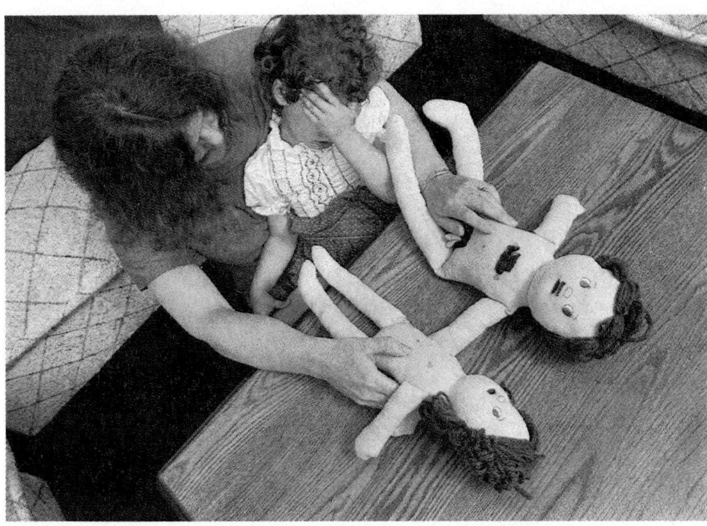

Young children who have been sexually exploited and abused may not be able to verbalize what they have experienced. One way that therapists work with such children is to allow them to demonstrate how they were abused with the use of anatomically correct dolls.

so, as in the novel and motion picture *Lolita*. In general, these activities have been remarkably well tolerated owing to the widespread myths that children suffer no lasting consequences from such encounters, and may indeed benefit from them in some obscurely reasoned way. Organizations and support groups for pedophiles have been open and sometimes quite strident in advocating adult-child sexual relations (Plummer, 1980). This permissiveness even extended only a few years back to the professional and scientific literature on pedophilia, which often emphasized children's seductiveness and their willing and active participation (Stermac, Segal, & Gillis, 1990). Such an observation reminds us of the common legal defense of blaming rape victims for having been raped, and in our judgment merits equal and exceptionless rejection as a factor supposedly mitigating the guilt of the offender.

Over about the past decade a growing body of evidence has suggested the long-term ill effects of subjecting children to the confusion, exploitation, and powerful emotionality of too-early and abrupt sexual engagements with genitally mature people—people occupying other roles as parents, family members, caretakers, and "adults" (who are to be "respected"). We have finally awakened to the terrible psychological scars that may be sustained by these children (Browne & Finkelhor, 1986). Childhood sexual abuse is turning up as a significant risk factor for a substantial proportion of the many mental disorders described in this text—including, ironically, pedophilia involving chiefly male victims (Becker et al, 1989; Herman, 1990). We are not, therefore, dealing with a "fun and games" issue, as some pedophilic propaganda suggests, and the mounting public awareness and outrage concerning the sexual victimization of children seems to us well justified—if more than a bit late in coming.

Offenders are diverse in terms of the act committed; in the intentionality of and general circumstances surrounding the act; and in age, education, and developmental history. Most pedophiles are men, but women occasionally engage in such practices. The average age of these offenders is about 40 years. Many of them are or have been married, and many have children of their own. Indeed, some choose their own children as victims, although there is an increasing trend to differentiate this incest pattern from pedophilia per se (Lanyon, 1986). In an early study of 836 pedophilic offenders in New Jersey, Revitch and Weiss (1962) found that older offenders tended to seek out immature children, while younger offenders preferred pubescent girls between 12 and 15. Girls outnumbered boys as victims more than two to one. Concerning this last observation, more recent data (Abel & Rouleau, 1990) have indicated a higher proportion of male victims. We suspect the discrepancy is due to pedophile sample differences in the two studies, the crucial upshot being that neither girls nor boys can be considered especially "safe" relative to the other sex.

In most cases of pedophilia, a victim is known to an offender, and the sexual behavior may continue over a sustained period of time. Usually no physical coercion takes place, but this can by no means be considered the rule (Abel & Rouleau, 1990). Although in some cases an offender may be encouraged or even "seduced" by his or her victim (a concept we find doubtful, as already noted), Swanson (1968) found provocation or active participation by the victim in only 3 of the 25 cases he studied. Whether or not there is an element of alleged provocation by a victim, the legal onus is quite properly always on an adult offender.

Since pedophiles may subject children to highly traumatic emotional experiences as well as physical injury, legal safeguards to protect children need to be explicit and uncompromising. A serious problem exists, however, in cases where the evidence concerning the occurrence of molestation is equivocal. An alleged offender is sometimes considered guilty until proven innocent, in fact, and a number of people have served time in penal institutions because children or their parents interpreted simple affection as attempted intimacy or molestation. On the other hand, many cases of sexual assault on children undoubtedly go unreported to spare the children further ordeals (Sgroi, 1977).

Researchers have made several attempts to arrive at subtype classifications of pedophiles or of pedophilic activity, but none to date has proved sufficiently reliable or productive of new insights to achieve overall acceptance. The latest of these attempts, so far as we are aware, is one by Knight & Prentky (1990; Knight, Carter, & Prentky, 1989). Their general model is in part hierarchical, having a structure that sometimes branches in proceeding from higher to lower levels.

According to Knight and Prentky, pedophiles and their paraphilic lovemaps vary on a number of dimensions that are to some extent independent of one another. The most important of these dimensions are listed in the following paragraphs:

1. *High versus low fixation.* For those pedophiles considered fixated, sexual activity with children of one or the other sex is virtually their only sexual interest. Others engage in a range of sexual activities and fantasies, both normal and abnormal, and molest children only as another sexual diversion or as the opportunity presents itself.

2. *High versus low social competence.* Regardless of their fixation levels, some pedophiles show little or no deficit in social skills, including those "heterosocial" skills involved in the initiation and maintenance of adult heterosexual relationships. Other pedophiles, evidently the larger group, show deficits that are quite characteristic of paraphiliacs in general. For these pedophiles, the choice of children as love objects usually has obvious compensatory and self-protective features. Many acts of pedophilia are precipitated by events that call into question the perpetrator's adult heterosexual adequacy.

3. *High versus low amount of contact with children.* People with pedophilic interests often arrange their occupational and recreational lives so as to ensure a high degree of contact with children, who of course become potential victims. Thus in recent years the media have reported a rash of arrests and convictions of alleged child molesters who operate alternative child-care facilities. Unfortunately, as a result, innocent individuals have come under unwarranted suspicion. Parents, however, are wise to err on the safe side and to use caution in selecting their child-care arrangements. Some pedophiles, on the other hand, show no particular interest in child-centered activities and appear to choose their victims on other, more opportunistic bases.

4. *Interpersonal versus narcissistic meaning of contact.* In instances of high contact with children, some pedophiles' motives are not exclusively sexual in nature. These individuals (designated "interpersonal" in type) appear genuinely to like children and to enjoy interacting with them in various modes; the sexual contact in these cases is an inappropriate extension of this affectional bonding. Narcissistic high-contact offenders show little evidence of enjoying relations with children for other than the opportunities they may provide for sexual exploitation.

5. *Low versus high physical injury.* According to this scheme of classification, the question of child injury does not normally arise in high-contact pedophilia, probably because such pedophiles usually use seduction instead of force. Low-contact pedophiles, on the other hand, may engage in greater or lesser force or other physically assaultive behaviors with their victims.

6. *Sadistic versus nonsadistic infliction of injury.* Physical injury to a child, mild or serious, may occur unintentionally and incidentally to pedophilic sexual acts, or it may be purposeful and deliberate in character where a pedophile's lovemap requires explicit victim suffering. This suffering might be relatively mild and involve low physical injury but substantial humiliation; it might also be physically dangerous or even fatal. In either case it is likely to leave the surviving victim seriously traumatized psychologically.

In a case known to one of the authors, an offender's sexual satisfaction was uniquely dependent on hearing his boy victims' screams of terror and pain as he violently sodomized them. This man, physically large and of intimidating demeanor, would patrol neighborhoods on a motorcycle in search of victims, who were then frightened into accompanying him to a remote area where the acts would be consummated. Using the scheme just outlined, this case of pedophilia would be described as one involving high fixation, low social competence, low contact, and high physical injury, sadistically motivated.

A number of investigators have also pointed to other severe psychopathology in pedophilic offenders. Some are alcoholic or schizophrenic. Many are older individuals in whom brain deterioration has led to a weakening of normal inhibitory controls. In fact pedophilia and exhibitionism are the most common sexual offenses committed by individuals suffering Alzheimer's or arteriosclerotic brain damage and displaying organic personality syndromes (Chapter 13).

Incest and Rape

In certain respects, the DSM-III-R is a quite conservative document, while in others it may exceed proper boundaries (for example, in the Axis II diagnosis of *developmental arithmetic disorder* in children, which would seem to describe more an educational than a psychiatric problem). Certain sexual deviations, such as incest and rape, are unaccountably (in the authors' judgment) missing from the DSM-III-R classification; this absence seems too conservative. Accordingly, as noted earlier, these two "disorders" are included in what follows even though they are not presently a part of the official psychiatric nomenclature.

Incest Culturally prohibited sexual relations (up to and including coitus) between family members, such as a brother and sister or a parent and child, are known as **incest.** Although a few societies have approved incestuous relationships—at one time it was the established practice for Egyptian pharaohs to marry their sisters to prevent the royal blood from being "contaminated"—the incest taboo is virtually universal among human societies.

An indication of the risks involved in such inbreeding has been provided by Adams and Neel (1967), who compared the offspring of 18 nuclear-incest marriages—12 brother-sister and 6 father-daughter—with those of a control group matched for age, intelligence, socioeconomic status, and other relevant characteristics. At the end of six months, 5 of the infants of the incestuous marriages had died, 2 were severely mentally retarded and had been institutionalized, 3 showed evidence of borderline intelligence, and 1 had a cleft palate. Only 7 of the 18 infants were considered normal. In contrast, only 2 of the control-group infants were not considered normal—one showing indications of borderline intelligence and the other manifesting a physical defect.

A number of investigators have also maintained that the incest taboo serves to produce greater variability among offspring, and hence to increase the flexibility and long-term adaptability of the population (Schwartzman, 1974).

In our own society, incestuous behavior does occur, but its actual incidence is unknown because it mostly takes place in a family setting (Peters, 1976)

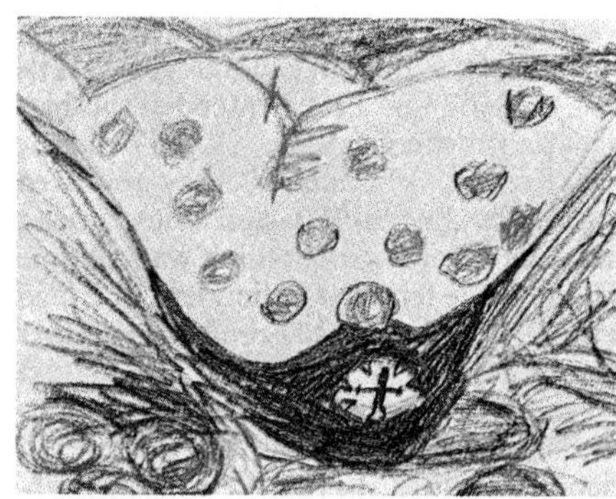

The drawings shown here are all the work of incest victims. Left: a 7-year-old girl engulfed by a maelstrom. Middle: a 9-year-old boy caught in a trap in the middle of a country landscape. Right: a teenage girl threatened by a snake.

and comes to light only when reported to law enforcement or other agencies. It is almost certainly more common than is generally believed, partly because many of the victims do not consider themselves victimized (De Young, 1982; Maisch, 1972). The incidence of "intrafamilial sexual abuse" coming to the attention of professionals approached 100,000 in 1985 (Williams & Finkelhor, 1990). Meiselman (1978) estimated the incidence at 1 or 2 per every 100 people. Kinsey et al. (1948, 1953) reported an incidence of 5 cases per 1,000 people in a sample of 12,000 subjects, and Gebhard et al. (1965) found 30 cases per 1,000 subjects in a group of 3,500 imprisoned sex offenders. In both these latter studies, brother-sister incest was reported as being five times more common than the next most common pattern—father-daughter incest. Mother-son incest is thought to be relatively rare.

In a study of 78 cases of incest, which excluded the brother-sister variety, Maisch (1972) found that the father-daughter and stepfather-stepdaughter varieties accounted for fully 85 percent of the sample; mother-son incest accounted for only 4 percent. Summit and Kryso (1978) estimated that some 36,000 cases of father-daughter incest occur each year in the United States. This estimate may seriously underestimate the actual occurrence (Herman, 1981). In occasional cases, multiple patterns of incest may exist within the same family, and some incestuous fathers involve all of their daughters serially as they become pubescent.

For an understanding of incestuous behavior, it should be noted that incestuous fantasies and desires are common during the adolescent period, and it is not uncommon for fathers to have such feelings toward their daughters. Social mores and prohibitions, however, are usually so deeply ingrained that the desires are not often acted out. When they are, no single-factor explanation seems to account for it; no characteristic appears universal or near-universal among incestuous fathers, and, contrary to widespread belief, they have usually *not* themselves been sexually abused in childhood (Williams & Finkelhor, 1990).

Bagley (1969) has suggested that several different causal patterns may be involved where incestuous behavior occurs. The following list represents a slight modification of his schema.

1. *Situational incest.* When brothers and sisters share the same bedroom during the preadolescent or adolescent period (which is not uncommon among poorer families), they may tend to engage in sexual exploration and experimentation. In some cases older siblings seduce their younger siblings without any apparent understanding of the social prohibitions or possible consequences.

2. *Incest associated with severe psychopathology.* In the case of psychopathic parents, the incest may simply be part of an indiscriminate pattern of sexual promiscuity. In other individuals, such as alcoholics and psychotics, the incestuous relations may be associated with a lowering of inner controls. Overall, however, only a small minority of incestuous fathers have diagnosable psychiatric disorders, although many show antisocial tendencies of insufficient magnitude to bring them into direct conflict with the law (Langevin et al., 1985; Williams & Finkelhor, 1990).

3. *Incest associated with pedophilia.* Some parents have intense sexual cravings for young children, including their own. It is evident, however, that

HIGHLIGHT 10.3

Sexual Molestation of Young Children

While most incestuous contacts between parents and their children occur after a child has attained puberty, young children—even infants—have been subjected to sexual molestation and abuse by parents or other adults. According to Sgroi (1977), these cases, like those involving adolescents, are markedly underreported. Even in the face of overwhelming evidence, this researcher claims, physicians are extremely reluctant to conclude that a child has been sexually attacked. Apparently it is considered "in bad taste" professionally to draw such a conclusion.

The cases Sgroi uses to illustrate the magnitude of the problem are truly disconcerting. She writes of one city's youngest known rape victim, a child 2 months old; of a 2½-year-old boy and his 4-year-old sister, both of whom acquired acute gonorrhea from their father; of a 17-month-old girl with a torn anus, dead of asphyxiation, with semen in her mouth and throat. In the face of such horror, one can only applaud Sgroi's attempt to break through the secrecy and "discretion" too often associated with this "last frontier" of child abuse.

Because many cases remain unreported, the actual incidence of child abuse of all types—and especially of sexual abuse—is unknown. In Connecticut, during fiscal years 1973 and 1974, approximately 10 percent of all cases of reported abuse were suspected to involve sexual assault or impropriety—a total of 248 separate incidents. The suspected perpetrators were most often fathers, male relatives, or boyfriends. This finding corroborates an earlier study by DeFrancis (1969). Assuming Connecticut to be representative of the United States as a whole, many thousands of young children are sexually assaulted or abused each year, and all too often the damage is inflicted by their own parents. As indicated in a review of the pertinent research evidence (Browne & Finkelhor, 1986) and our only recently acquired understanding of multiple personality disorder (Chapter 6), the long-term consequences of such abuse can be both extensive and severe. One of the authors is acquainted with the case of a preschool-aged girl who became psychotic, apparently in consequence of her father's protracted sexual molestation. The father, a well-educated and successful middle-level manager, committed suicide when he could no longer successfully deny his culpability.

Sgroi and other advocates for sexually abused children can claim a measure of success in their efforts to direct a spotlight on this long-neglected problem. In recent years a number of states have enacted laws that compel a professional person, under severe penalty, to report to authorized agencies his or her suspicion that child abuse may have occurred. Regrettably, this judgment is often difficult to make, and many cases doubtless still go unreported.

pedophilic motivation is not a primary cause of incest, in that most victims are beyond puberty. (A discussion of disturbing exceptions appears in *HIGHLIGHT 10.3.*)

4. *Incest associated with a faulty paternal model.* A father may set an undesirable example for his son by engaging in incestuous relations with his daughters and may encourage his son to do so as well—either at the time with his sisters, or later in life with his own daughters.

5. *Incest associated with family pathology and disturbed marital relations.* In some instances a rejecting wife may actually foster father-daughter incest. Most (but not all) cases of father-daughter incest, in fact, occur in a setting of marked family disorganization (Lanyon, 1986; Williams & Finkelhor, 1990). Many mothers of father-daughter incest victims have been observed clinically to show incredible levels of inattentiveness in the maintenance of their "ignorance" about the sexual intimacy between their husbands and daughters.

In general, incestuous fathers who come to the attention of authorities do not have a history of sexual offenses or other criminal behavior, nor do they show a disproportionate incidence of prior hospitalization for mental disorders. In fact such fathers tend to restrict their sexual activity to family members, not seeking or engaging in extramarital sexual relations. For example, in his early, intensive study of 12 fathers convicted of incestuous relations with their daughters, Cavillin (1966) reported that only 2 of the 12 had resorted to extramarital relations, despite uniform feelings that they were unloved and rejected by their wives. Such a pattern suggests a certain passivity and lack of venturesomeness among many of these fathers, a picture that has been confirmed fairly regularly in subsequent research (Williams & Finkelhor, 1990). The typical incestuous father's lovemap is thus somewhat paradoxical; it is on the one hand rather cautious and restrictive but on the other does not contain the usual exclusion concerning his own children.

Cavillin further reported that the youngest father in the group was 20 and the oldest 56, with an average age of 39. The average age of the daughters was 13, the youngest being 3 and the oldest 18. Five of the 12 fathers had had a relationship with more than 1 daughter, usually beginning with the oldest; in 11 of the cases the relationships had gone on for some time—from 3 months to 3 years—before being reported by the daughters. In all cases, too, the father felt rejected and threatened by his wife. Cavillin's findings are generally confirmed by Maisch (1972), who studied 78 cases of incest that came to the attention of officials in the Federal Republic of Germany, and by Dixen and Jenkins (1981), Lanyon (1986), and Williams and Finkelhor (1990) in pertinent literature reviews.

Most of us feel a profound repugnance when we hear of fathers seducing, or in rare instances being seduced by, their daughters. Our disgust is certainly appropriate, especially when we consider the future adjustment difficulties many of these girls must face in trying to come to terms with their experiences (Browne & Finkelhor, 1986; Gold, 1986; Owens, 1984). Offit (1981), however, offers us a different, more compassionate view of a father's situation. She described her work with a depressed and lonely man who felt grief for the loss of his married daughter, a daughter who had been the center of his life and his love for 15 years. Like many incestuous fathers, the man described by Offit does not seem, apart from his "perversion," to be a monstrous or evil man. Such descriptions remind us that in our haste to condemn incestuous behavior, we should not assume that all such relationships are tawdry or utterly lacking in genuine feeling or affection. Needless to say, we do not in making this observation intend to convey any tolerance for such profound lapses in parental responsibility.

The psychological effect of an incestuous relationship on a daughter appears to depend on her age at the time of the relationship and on how much anxiety and guilt she experiences. Most girls studied who were still adolescent expressed feelings of guilt and depression over the incestuous behavior. Some girls in this situation turn to promiscuity; others run away from home to escape the stressful environment, and some of these become prostitutes. Later difficulties in adult heterosexual adjustment are extremely common, and incestuous involvement with a father or stepfather appears to inflate the risk of several adult disorders, including multiple personality disorder (Chapter 6) and borderline personality disorder (Chapter 8). It also enhances the likelihood of revictimization by sexual assault or rape (Koss & Dinero, 1989). In some instances no apparent long-range ill effects can be detected (Dixen & Jenkins, 1981; Gold, 1986). Interestingly, in a case treated by one of the authors, a young woman had been continually molested by her father during her childhood and adolescence. She resolutely refused all further sexual contact with him after he provoked her first orgasm. Up to that time, as is apparently often the case, she had not fully grasped the implications of this type of interaction with her father.

Rape The term **rape** describes sexual activity that occurs under actual or threatened forcible coercion of one person by another. In most states, legal definitions restrict *forcible rape* to forced intercourse or penetration of a bodily orifice by a penis or other object. *Statutory rape* is sexual activity with a person who is legally defined to be under the age of consent (18 in most states). Statutory rape is considered to have occurred regardless of the apparent willingness of an underage partner.

In the vast majority of cases, men rape women. The incidence of forcible rape has increased more rapidly in the last 15 years than that of any other violent crime. Part of the rise, however, as measured by the FBI and other law enforcement agencies, may merely reflect increased reporting by victims and an enhanced likelihood that sexual assaults meeting the definition of "rape" will in fact be recorded as such within local police departments. Even so, the actual incidence of rape is considered to be as much as ten times higher than that reported in FBI *Uniform Crime Report* statistics, which in recent years has approximately 100,000 cases annually.

Many sexually assaulted women remain, for various reasons, reluctant to file complaints with the police and (in the case of students) school officials. Some want to put the whole sickening and degrading experience behind them and not be reminded of it. Others, particularly victims of date rape or where the offender is otherwise known to the victims, have a misguided sense of protecting their attackers or find the role of principal accuser in a major felony very uncomfortable. Still others wish

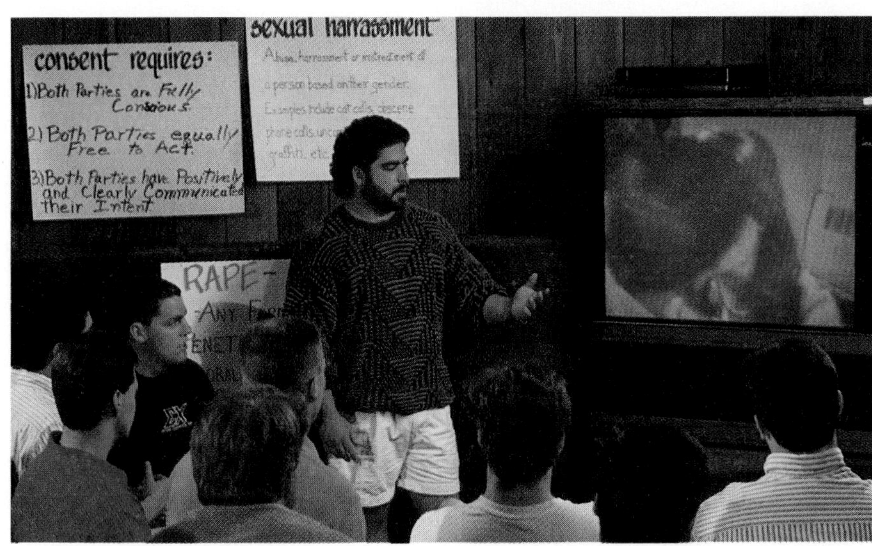

In an effort to raise awareness about date rape and sexual harrassment on college campuses, schools are beginning to offer rape-prevention programs, such as this one at Hobart College in New York, in which young men and women are counseled on understanding and avoiding sexual victimization.

to avoid the unfortunate consequences that in the past have often followed a rape complaint. These include social stigmatization and, regrettably, crude and insensitive treatment by some police jurisdictions. There is hope that the gap between actual and reported rapes has been narrowed in recent years as women have banded together to call attention to these widespread assaults, and to protect themselves by doing everything possible to keep rapists from preying on them.

Based on information gathered by the FBI about arrested and convicted rapists, rape, relatively speaking, is a young man's crime. Forty-five percent of all rapists arrested in 1985 were under 25 years of age, and the greatest concentration was in the 18-to-24 age group, accounting for 30 percent of the total. Of the rapists who get into police records, about half are married and living with their wives at the time of the crime. As a group, they come from the low end of the socioeconomic ladder. Typically they are unskilled workers with low intelligence, low education, and low income. How representative they are of all rapists we do not know. The substantial numbers of a certain type of college male who is excessively and sometimes physically coercive (Kanin, 1985; Koss, Gidycz, & Wisniewski, 1987; Koss & Oros, 1982; Lisak & Ross, 1988; Rapaport & Burkhart, 1984) suggests that the basic propensity is not limited to the disadvantaged. One of the authors has assisted in the college expulsion of a student with a history of four documented date rapes; as is apparently typical of the type, he saw nothing wrong with these acts.

Rape tends to be a repetitive activity rather than an isolated act, and most rapes are planned events. In fact, a strong case can be made that rape should be considered a category of paraphilia—not different in its essentials from the paraphilias already discussed (Abel & Rouleau, 1990). Another interesting view is that of Herman (1990), who considers it an addiction—with all that this implies in terms of its repetitive nature and the difficulty of treatment. About 80 percent of rapists commit the act in the neighborhoods in which they reside; most rapes take place in an urban setting at night. The specific scene of the rape varies greatly, however. The act may occur on a lonely street after dark, in an automobile in a large shopping center's parking lot, in the elevator or hallway of a building, and in other situations where a victim has little chance of assistance. Rapists have also entered apartments or homes by pretending to be deliverers or repairpersons. In fact, rapes most often occur in the victim's home.

About a third or more of all rapes involve more than one offender, and often they are accompanied by beatings. The remainder are single-offender rapes in which the victim and the offender may know each other; the closer the relationship, the more brutally the victim may be beaten. When a victim struggles against her attacker, she is likely to receive more severe injuries or in rare cases to be killed. On the other hand, one study found that when the victim was able to cry out and run away, she was more likely to be successful in avoiding the rape (Selkin, 1975).

In addition to the physical trauma inflicted on a victim, the psychological trauma may be severe (see Chapter 5, pp. 161–163). One especially unfortunate factor in rape is the possibility of pregnancy; another is the chance of contracting a sexually transmitted disease. A rape may also impact negatively on a victim's marriage or other intimate relationships. The situation is likely to be particularly upsetting to a husband or boyfriend if he has been forced to watch the rape, as is occasionally the case when a victim is raped by the members of a juvenile gang.

The concept of "victim-precipitated" rape, a favorite of defense attorneys and of some police and court jurisdictions, turns out on close examination to be a myth. According to this view, a victim, though often bruised both psychologically and physically—if not worse—is regarded as the *cause* of the crime, often on such flimsy grounds as the alleged provocativeness of her attire, her past sexual behavior, or her presence in a location considered risky (Stermac, Segal, & Gillis, 1990). The attacker, on the other hand, is treated as a brain-dead organism, unable to quell his lust in the face of such irresistible provocation—and therefore not legally responsible for the act. A society as threatened as is ours by rampant sexual assault can ill-afford this type of nonsensical and myth-based jurisprudence; in more than 60 years of combined clinical practice neither of the authors has ever encountered a woman who desired to be raped, nor have we ever heard a convincing account of any such case. Evidence to the contrary notwithstanding, however, the pernicious and dangerous concept that women *want* to be forced into sex is persistent and widespread (Segal & Stermac, 1990).

Women who are repeated victims of rape are especially likely to be suspected of provoking the attacks. In fact such women tend to be significantly dysfunctional in many areas of their lives, and they tend also to be victims in situations other than rape, perhaps including other forms of sexual traumatization (Koss & Dinero, 1989). Far from being the seductresses of popular folklore, they are often more like chronic "losers" with insufficient personal resources to fend off those who would exploit them (Ellis, Atkeson, & Calhoun, 1982; Myers, Templer, & Brown, 1985). It should be pointed out in this context that many college women report having experienced strong unwanted advances from men; such encounters do not imply a special vulnerability to rape (Koss & Oros, 1982).

Rape is a complex act in its antecedent conditions, involving at least factors creating motivation, factors of cognitive distortion, factors influencing inhibitory processes, and factors relating to opportunity (Barbaree, 1990; Darke, 1990; Laws & Marshall, 1990; Malamuth, 1986; Marshall & Barbaree, 1990; Segal & Stermac, 1990). As a group, rapists seem to find violence against women sexually arousing (McFall, 1990; Murrin & Laws, 1990; Quinsey, Chaplin, & Upfold, 1984). Several typologies of rapes and rapists have been proposed, most of them based on inadequate data of questionable representativeness. The system proposed by Groth, Burgess, and Holmstrom (1977) is not only well documented, but apparently has the additional virtue of being able to subsume the types identified in earlier as well as more recent work (e.g., Knight & Prentky, 1990). It is based on the accounts of 133 convicted male rapists and 92 victims of rapes occurring during a limited time period in Massachusetts.

Groth and colleagues, in agreement with many others (e.g., Darke, 1990), noted that rape attacks combine psychological elements of power and anger as well as sexuality. Their strategy was to rank these elements in terms of their apparent prominence for each of the 225 separate accounts of rape available to them. In doing so, they discovered no case in which sexual satisfaction appeared to be the dominant motive of the rapist; that is, all the rapes were characterized as involving either power motives or anger expression more than sexuality on the part of the rapists (see *HIGHLIGHT 10.4)*. Evidently a rapist's lovemap has undergone such contortion that "love" is not its most prominent component. Groth et al. also noted that predominantly power- or anger-inspired rapes could each in turn be divided into two subtypes. These subdivisions form the basis of their classification scheme, as described in the following paragraphs:

1. *Power-assertive type.* The essence of a rape in which power motives predominate is that of establishing control over a victim through intimidation; the mode of intimidation used may involve a weapon, physical force without severe injury, or simply threats of harm. The achievement of sexual penetration is regarded as a "conquest." The rape is frequently preceded by fantasies that the victim, once overpowered, will willingly participate with wild abandon. Because reality never matches this fantasy, the rapist is frustrated and is likely to repeat the act compulsively on another occasion. A power-assertive rapist tends to have a history of "hypermasculinity," striving always to assert power and domination over those with whom he comes in contact. We may surmise, of course, that such people in fact have serious questions about their manhood. In Groth and colleagues' sample, 44 percent of the rapes were of the power-assertive variety.

2. *Power-reassurance type.* Like his power-assertive counterpart, a power-reassurance rapist seeks to intimidate and conquer his victim. In this case, however, the underlying sense of weakness, inadequacy, and indistinct gender identity is much more obvious. As in some cases of exhibitionism and pedophilia, the act commonly takes place following some blow to the rapist's fragile ego; the rape is an attempt to repair the damage. Rapes of the power-

HIGHLIGHT 10.4

The Power, Hostility, and Humiliation Dimensions of Rape

Levine and Koenig (1980) have published transcripts of their interviews with ten incarcerated rapists. The following are verbatim selections from these interviews that reveal the nonsexual components of their assaults on victims.

"It's mostly humiliating the victim, but not hurting or any heavy violence." (p. 25)

"When I was becoming angry . . . I felt I had to have sex at any cost as a reversal of caring. To go as far as I could away from that caring, to cheapen that person." (p. 46)

"I made hate to her." (p. 51)

"I know that I purposely degraded them." (p. 59)

"I fantasized about stabbing her with a knife in the anus—of all places. Just a degrading thought. Put her down and put her in her place for challenging me." (p. 66)

"I think the reason we used to do this [gang rape] was because I like to lower the chicks to me, that's the way I used to think, that I was lowering them and making them look cheap . . . and making them look like dirty tramps. . . . She [the victim] was really humiliated; she was really put down." (pp. 71, 75)

Darke (1990) adds the following rape accounts derived from an analysis of reports to police by victims, witnesses, and offenders:

The assailant used physical violence to subdue his victim. During the assault he said, "Thirteen other guys want to screw you." He also indicated that he was raping her because he couldn't go to a "whorehouse."

The assailant referred to his victim as a "white squaw" and his "slave."

Following physical and sexual assault, the assailant told his victim that she wasn't "worth a shit."

Using physical violence to subdue his 15-year-old victim the assailant then said, "Look at the mess you've gotten yourself into. It was dumb to take a ride from someone you don't know. . . . Have you ever been fucked before?" The victim responded "yes" and the assailant stated, "You should have said no. Are you going to let this happen? Don't you have any respect for yourself?" (p. 64)

reassurance type accounted for 21 percent of Groth and colleagues' sample.

3. *Anger-retaliation type.* In comparison with power-oriented rapists, who rarely inflict severe physical damage on their victims, predominantly anger-driven rapists are exceedingly dangerous—sometimes to the point of murdering the women they attack. In such cases, rage, contempt, and hatred dominate the assault, which is usually brutal and violent. Sexual satisfaction, if it occurs at all, is minimal. In fact many anger-dominated rapists view normal sex with revulsion and disgust. Here the rape is an expression of hate toward women in general, and the predominant motive is one of revenge for real or imagined slights suffered at the hands of females. Derogation and humiliation are prominent features of this type of attack. Of the rapes studied by Groth et al., 30 percent were of the anger-retaliation type.

4. *Anger-excitation type.* More than any other, this type of rapist fits the category of ***pathological sadist.*** His attack is one of eroticized aggression; he derives sexual pleasure, thrills, and excitement not from the sexual elements of his assault but from the suffering of his victim. The anger-excitation type accounted for only 5 percent of Groth and colleagues' sample.

It might seem from the preceding descriptions that rapists as a group are a disturbed segment of the population and that potential rapists should therefore be easy to recognize. This would be an erroneous and possibly dangerous conclusion, however. Although it is true that a certain proportion of rapists are obviously abnormal on a chronic basis—some even being blatantly psychotic—the literature in this area abounds with instances of rape in which, prior to an attack, the rapist had given no hint to the victim of being a sexually assaultive person (Gager & Schurr, 1976; Medea & Thompson, 1974). The apparently widespread occurrence of attempted (and completed) date rape, particularly on college campuses, underscores the same point (Kanin, 1985; Koss, Gidycz, & Wisniewski, 1987; Koss & Oros, 1982; Rapaport & Burkhart, 1984). Whatever rape prevention involves, it is not a matter of informal psychodiagnostic predictions. We know of one university in which women students have taken to listing the names of excessively coercive male dates on dormitory bathroom walls, but of course such a procedure lacks certain safeguards for the falsely accused.

Conviction rates for rape are low and most men who have raped are free in the community. In fact one study of rapists who were in the community found that the men had raped anywhere from 5 to 100 times (Abel et al., 1978). In a more recent study, Abel and colleagues (reported in Abel & Rouleau, 1990) found that 907 separate acts of rape were reported by only 126 nonincarcerated offenders, an average of 7 per offender. Rape, even at its least violent, is a bullying, intrusive violation of another person's integrity, selfhood, and personal boundaries that deserves to be viewed with more gravity—and its victims with more compassion and sensitivity—than is usually the case (Gager & Schurr, 1976; Medea & Thompson, 1974). Much still remains to be done in providing services to these victims (Koss, 1983), many of whom suffer from moderately severe posttraumatic stress disorder (see Chapter 5).

In recent years, new rape laws have been adopted by a majority of states, many of them based on the "Michigan model," which describes four degrees of criminal sexual conduct, with different punishment levels for different degrees of seriousness. In calling the offense *criminal sexual conduct* rather than *rape,* the Michigan law also appropriately places the emphasis on the offender rather than the victim. Unfortunately, the majority of sexual assaults are not reported, and of those that are, less than 10 percent result in conviction (Darke, 1990). Convictions often bring light sentences, and a jail term does not dissuade a substantial number of offenders from repeating their crimes (Furby, Weinrott, & Blackshaw, 1989). The upshot, we reiterate, is that the large majority of rapists are out among us.

Treatments and Outcomes

Research concerning the effective treatment of variant sexual behavior has not progressed as far or as rapidly as with the dysfunctions, but there are encouraging signs of progress. As we noted at the beginning of this discussion, we now know that most sexually variant acts are not simply aberrations of sexual arousal. In most instances, we also need to look at an individual's response level to adult heterosexual stimuli, overall social skills with potential and appropriate sexual partners, and adult gender identity development. An important principle embedded in such a program is that it is unrealistic to anticipate an offender giving up an important source of gratification without gaining something comparable in return. Only by taking all these factors into account is it possible to assess a given client's difficulties and fashion treatment procedures for intervening on a broad enough front (Marshall, Laws, & Barbaree, 1990b).

Even when taking all these steps, however, sexually deviant behavior is enormously difficult to treat or to manage if the goal is (as it certainly should be) long-term relapse prevention. Minimally, it may require long-term monitoring and supervision similar to the parole model used by prison administrations. Follow-up data from one study using this approach (Pithers, 1990) is so far encouraging, with a recidivism rate of only 4 percent for combined groups of rapists and pedophiles.

To date, unfortunately, such cutting-edge intervention has been the exception rather than the rule in therapeutic attempts to change variant sexuality, and most treatment efforts still focus on the sexual arousal aspects. Aversive conditioning procedures, in which unpleasant or painful stimuli are paired with the arousal state, though controversial, have proven effective in suppressing problematic arousal variants. Similarly, we know something of how to develop or strengthen arousability to appropriate sexual stimuli (Barlow & Abel, 1976). Surely, we will be able to find ways to teach appropriate social skills where they are lacking; an impressive analysis of what seems needed in this respect, such as enhanced ability to read accurately the "cues" emitted by potential sexual partners (for example, whether a woman is encouraging or discouraging an advance), has recently been contributed by McFall (1990).

Two remaining obstacles appear to exist, both of them major. The first is learning how to strengthen an adult client's gender identity, not necessarily in an exclusively "masculine" or "feminine" direction but more in terms of overcoming amorphousness and immaturity in the individual's sense of being a man or a woman. This promises to be a difficult challenge for clinical research. Having delineated the problem, however, we are in a much better position now than we were even a few short years ago. The second difficult obstacle is that of discovering means to maintain therapeutic gains

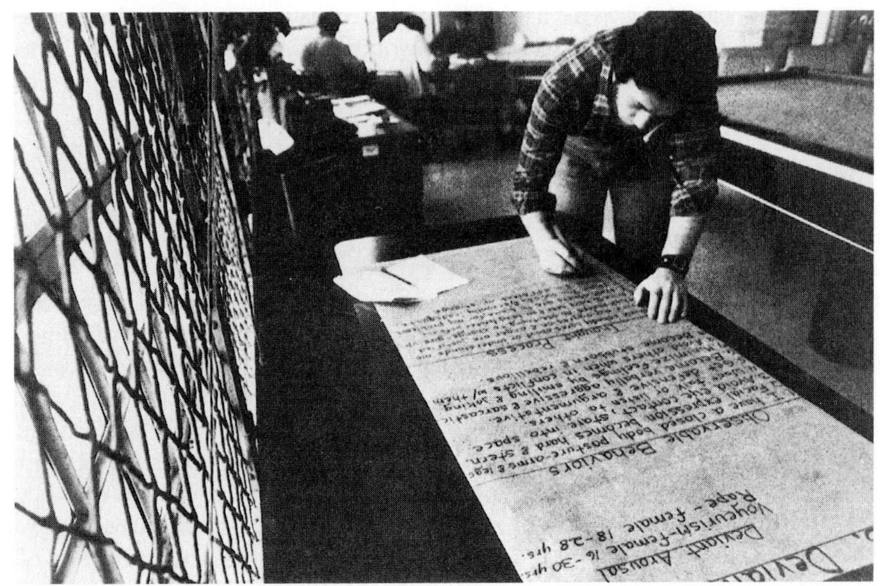

The long-term relapse rate for untreated sex offenders released from prison is about 80 percent. At Oregon State Hospital, a voluntary inpatient treatment program for sex offenders is having some success at reducing this rate through intensive treatment, including psychotherapy and social skills training, various types of behavioral therapy (such as aversive conditioning techniques), and drug therapy to inhibit sexual functioning. Clients continue to be monitored for 18 months after release from prison. This program claims about a 10 percent recidivism rate among offenders who have completed treatment. Here, in one phase of treatment, prisoners must write scenarios of their behavior preceding an assault.

that are made, or prevent relapse. If a more efficient and less costly method than indefinite supervisory contact cannot be devised, we have grave doubts that our society will be willing to bear the expense. Certainly the prison parole system, with its overburdened caseloads and frequent changes of poorly paid and "burned out" personnel, provides little cause for optimism on this front. At least, however, we now understand that the problem of recidivism is central to the reduction and ultimate prevention of sexual victimization.

In the final analysis, of course, the best long-range solution for our society is the eradication or prevention of those conditions that lead to the development of problematic sexual variants. We will address this matter in the Unresolved Issues section at the end of this chapter.

THE HOMOSEXUALITIES

The authors acknowledge some ambivalence about addressing the issue of homosexuality in a text whose title includes the term *abnormal*. This is a sensitive point among some members of the homosexual community, who sincerely feel that in doing so we inevitably contribute to their stigmatization and provide ammunition to "homophobics" and others intent on suppressing homosexual activity and punishing those who engage in it. Indeed, we have been accused of being homophobic ourselves in correspondence from readers of earlier editions. In the final analysis, we think it would be unwise and perhaps professionally irresponsible to intentionally exempt certain behaviors from consideration solely on the grounds that their inclusion generates an unusual degree of unpleasantness. We do think there are serious questions in this area deserving of open discussion.

Dilemmas of Classification

On December 14, 1973, by vote of the trustees of the American Psychiatric Association, **homosexuality** (a tendency to direct sexual desires and activities toward people of the same sex) was removed from the list of officially recognized mental disorders. Whatever the motives behind this action—and they appear to have been principled and ethical ones—the voting of a disorder out of existence raises questions concerning the fundamental value of applying a medical perspective to personal and sociobehavioral issues, as was discussed in Chapter 1. We are not here supporting the position that homosexuality should be considered a "mental illness"—quite the contrary, we are pointing up a certain capriciousness sometimes involved in the "diagnosis" of human behavior.

Additional developments have further complicated the situation. First, the intended removal of psychiatric stigma from homosexuality was incomplete. The original version of DSM-III, adopted in 1980, continued to list *ego-dystonic homosexuality* as a mental disorder. This category referred to a situation in which a homosexual orientation was persistently unwanted by a person who had it. The inclusion of subjective distress about one's condition as the defining characteristic of a disorder is a questionable premise. As Adams and Chiodo

(1984) have pointed out, discrepancies between one's values and one's behavior are common aspects of life, but we do not ordinarily think of such discrepancies as deciding, or even raising, questions of mental disorder. In the DSM-III-R of 1987 the picture changed once again. Here what had been called ego-dystonic homosexuality was relegated to an "example" under the category *sexual disorder not otherwise specified,* a sort of wastebasket for various additional deviant behaviors; the intent, it appears, was chiefly cosmetic.

We have some sympathy for the catalogers of official psychiatric disorders, who are faced with highly charged issues that are not resolvable by appeal to either logic or unequivocal evidence—and certainly not in our era by appeal to the old standby of professional authority. We also sympathize with the millions of homosexual people who resent having to defend themselves against attributions of psychiatric illness based on sexual preference, although—as the long list of "paraphilias" indicates—their situation is not unique in this particular respect. It seems clear that we have not heard the last word on the controversy, which, as *HIGHLIGHT 10.5* illustrates, extends to the question of treatment. We suspect that any ultimate resolution will require a substantial reformulation of psychiatry's proper domain as it relates to nonmedical, sociobehavioral issues.

As we have indicated both implicitly and explicitly from the outset, our own notion of abnormal behavior does not always mirror the official psychiatric nomenclature, although the two must obviously overlap at numerous points. Rather, we define abnormality in terms of behavioral maladaptiveness, broadly conceived, and intend thereby no *necessary* attribution of internal psychological derangement to a maladaptively behaving person. We reject, likewise, any pejorative connotations that anyone would attach to abnormality per se when so defined.

Homosexuality has existed throughout history. This ancient Greek wall art showing two male lovers at a drinking party is from the tomb of the Diver, at Paestum, near the Gulf of Salerno.

Homosexual Heterogeneity

We have used the plural form of *homosexuality* in the title of this section on The Homosexualities because we believe the psychological organization of homosexuality to be extremely heterogeneous, not only between men and women homosexuals but also within these gender categories. That is, we find the evidence inconsistent with the notion that, beyond the obvious same-gender partner choice, one can assign valid attributions to "homosexuals," "gay men," or "lesbian women" considered as classes of people sharing other major psychological commonalities. For example, the relative mix of "nature" (genetic/constitutional) versus "nurture" (environmental) in the causal patterns leading to homosexual orientations appears to vary considerably for both men and women (see, for example, the pertinent work of Money and his associates, 1969, 1972, 1974, 1980, and that of Bell & Weinberg, 1978). At the behavioral level, researchers also note marked variation in the extent to which sexuality per se plays a prominent role in identifying oneself as "homosexual," although in general sexuality is more emphasized among gay men than among lesbian women. In short, the roads leading to homosexuality and the needs served by this mode of sexual expression appear to be many and varied.

Research on homosexual populations has concentrated on gay men. As a result, much less is known about the biopsychosocial correlates of lesbianism. Due to this imbalance, we will here concentrate on homosexuality in males. As will be seen, we do regard certain manifestations of male homosexuality—certain male homosexual lovemaps—to be plainly maladaptive, hence "abnormal."

The issue of **bisexuality** is an interesting one theoretically. As is well known, Freud held that we are all bisexual in the sense of having some basic propensity toward the achievement of sexual satisfaction with partners of either sex. Kinsey and colleagues' (1948) early study seemingly confirmed this view in showing that a significant proportion of the men surveyed admitted to having had homosexual wishes or experiences after the onset of adolescence; 37 percent of male responders, in fact, indicated they had had such a homosexual experience to the point of orgasm.

In interpreting such figures, one must bear in mind that young unmarried American men of the

HIGHLIGHT 10.5

Should Homosexuality Be "Treated"?

The question of whether homosexual people should receive therapy to change their sexual orientations has been one of the key issues in the intense controversy over whether homosexuality is a personality or paraphilic disorder or only a normal sexual variant. In recent years, a number of therapy programs have been developed in which the explicit purpose is that of "reorienting" the sexual needs of homosexual individuals; many of these programs employ aversive conditioning techniques to suppress or eradicate the homosexual arousal pattern. Because the existence of treatment strongly implies that the condition being treated is undesirable, if not pathological, many supporters of the gay liberation movement object to these treatment programs.

This issue was forcefully brought to the attention of psychologists and other mental health professionals by Davison (1976, 1978), a leading researcher in the development of new therapies for sexual difficulties. Davison argues that the very existence of sexual reorientation treatment programs strengthens prejudices against homosexual individuals and increases their self-hatred and embarrassment. Therefore, he concludes, the only ethical course is to stop offering this type of treatment—even to those individuals who voluntarily seek it.

Sturgis and Adams (1978) take the opposing position, arguing that the question of whether homosexuality is abnormal is entirely irrelevant to the question of whether an individual seeking treatment should have access to it. Sturgis and Adams charge that Davison's position will cause therapists to impose their own values —in this case, the belief that homosexuals should not receive treatment—on clients who may not share these values. For Sturgis and Adams, then, the primary issue is that of the "right to treatment" of those homosexual individuals who desire reorientation therapy. Davison (1978) acknowledges that his position is value-based, but he contends that values are the central consideration in the controversy. He also states that therapists have no absolute responsibility to provide what clients may request.

As seemed likely when this exchange of views first appeared in the professional literature, many sexual reorientation programs have continued to be offered to those who request such treatment. In the meantime, this spirited dialogue between researchers has sharpened the issues and has provoked a wide-ranging and, we think, positive reexamination of attitudes about homosexuality within the professional community.

pre-1960s era had few outlets for their abundant sexual energies, and that opportunities for orgasmic experiences with their female peers were severely limited. We suspect, therefore, that the overwhelming majority of these homosexual encounters were ones in which young men submitted passively to the sexual blandishments, usually offers to perform fellatio, of the few openly and aggressively gay men who were well known in virtually every community of any size. It was unusual for the recipients of these acts to consider that *they* were engaging in homosexuality; they were simply, in their conceptions of it, permitting themselves to be serviced by "queers" who for unfathomable reasons liked to do this sort of thing. It is our view therefore that Kinsey and colleagues' figures do not confirm the universality of bisexuality as some sort of fundamental libidinal gender neutrality. What they do suggest, as is now well known from research on prison populations and the like, is that many men denied sexual access to women can and do "make the best of it" by having sexual relations with other men.

While most people appear capable of engaging in and enjoying homosexual activity at some point in their lives, the overwhelming majority of people, given a choice, prefer heterosexual forms of satisfaction. Among "true" bisexuals—those who are consistently active in both heterosexual and homosexual relationships—some question arises about which, if either, arousal pattern is the more fundamental. Laboratory studies of the arousal patterns of self-designated bisexuals have shown that they in fact respond with stronger arousal to homosexual than to heterosexual stimuli, a finding that holds for both men (Tollison, Adams, & Tollison, 1979) and women (Lamson, 1980). To these findings may be added the observation of Altshuler (1984) that only 1 of 13 self-identified "bisexuals" met reasonable criteria for claiming this designation—these criteria being an approximately equal and random choice in the sex of partners and approximately equal distribution of experienced pleasure with partners of either sex. The exception in Altshuler's sample proved (on independent grounds) to be psychotic. Although much remains to be clarified in this area, the available evidence thus suggests that "bisexuality" is more a label that certain homosexually oriented people apply to themselves than it is a valid description of an equal arousal to both genders.

One of the most poignant and sobering memorials to AIDS victims is the AIDS quilt on exhibit around the United States, in which each square of the enormous quilt represents someone who died from AIDS. Many of those victims were homosexuals. Responsible members of the gay community have responded vigorously and tirelessly to the threat of AIDS with efforts to provide vital information, to promote changes in life-style, and to advocate "safe sex." The result has been a leveling off of new cases of HIV infections among gay men, though the disease continues to escalate in other groups.

Gay Promiscuity

It is obvious to any but the most prejudiced eyes and minds that being gay does not preclude competence, accomplishment, and significant societal contribution across a vast array of human activity. In particular fields, such as the arts, homosexuality may indeed be associated with extraordinary talent. Much research (Bell, 1974; Bell & Weinberg, 1978; Freedman, 1975; Hooker, 1957; Thompson, McCandless, & Strickland, 1971; Weinberg & Williams, 1974) also clearly demonstrates that gay people as a group do not have disproportionate general psychopathology, especially when we discount problems that are reactive to membership in a sometimes persecuted and despised minority. Many gay individuals lead exemplary, ethical lives of quiet service to humankind, while often maintaining stable, committed, and sexually faithful relationships with their lovers.

Another gay life-style, however, includes problematic features that have escalated immeasurably with the AIDS epidemic in the 1980s. We refer to the preference among some gay men for frequent, largely anonymous, uncommitted, multiple-partner (sometimes in a single evening) sex. Among a certain large subgroup of gays, the value of such casual, multiple-partner sex had become practically a matter of ideologic allegiance prior to the early 1980s, when the connection was definitely made between this life-style and infection with the HIV-1 (AIDS) virus. One of Hooker's (1962) subjects described the life-style poignantly and succinctly: "To be gay is to go to the bar, to make the scene, to look, and look, and look, to have a one-night stand, to never really love or be loved, and to really know this, and to do this night after night, and year after year" (p. 9).

Although pre-1980s adherents to this life-style had, for obvious reasons, much exposure to sexually transmitted diseases (STDs), such as gonococcal infections and syphilis, and although significant numbers of them contracted these diseases, easy access to highly effective antibiotic drugs, such as penicillin, made the risk tolerable. Then, with remarkable suddenness, HIV-1 appeared—having no cure, a fatal outcome, and a transmission profile that made unprotected (condomless) anal intercourse extremely dangerous for the receptive partner. Ironically and tragically, the appearance of the virus, manifested in large numbers of not-yet-diagnosable infections, coincided with major triumphs of the gay liberation movement. The outcome has been sobering, if not frightening. According to Glasner & Kaslow (1990), prevalence rates of infection (as assessed by blood samples positive for HIV-1) were at 20 to 50 percent in one San Francisco community in 1984; another sample from clientele at an STD clinic had an astounding 70 percent seropositive rate for the period 1978 through 1987.

Once the connection with AIDS became clear, responsible members of the gay subculture responded vigorously and tirelessly with efforts to provide vital information, to promote changes in life-style, and to advocate "safe sex." Their efforts have been rewarded in a definite leveling off of new cases of HIV infections among gay men. Unfortunately, the disease, having gained an established foothold, continues to escalate out of control in other groups.

Evidence also shows that the allures of irresponsible sex are sufficiently strong for some notably immature gay young men that they have modified their behavior little, if at all. For example, Kelly et al. (1990) conducted a recent field study in gay bars in three cities and found that 37 percent of the 526 patrons questioned admitted to engaging in unprotected anal intercourse during the prior 3 months. Of the various risk factors associated with this potentially fatal behavior, such as relative youth, perceived peer pressure, and ignorance of the facts, knowledge of whether or not one had the infection was *not* significantly involved; that is, this knowledge—or the lack of it—made no discernible impact on the decision to engage in condomless anal intercourse. Such findings are, to say the least, deeply disconcerting.

The seemingly compulsive and apparently continuing unprotected sexual promiscuity of a significant group of gay men in this age of literal "fatal attraction" gives us little pause in declaring this behavior to be abnormal, as defined in this text. We should add that we also have no hesitation in coming to exactly the same conclusion about heterosexual behavior that is equally unrestrained as to the known risks, about which more is said in this chapter's Unresolved Issues section.

Homosexuality and Society

The centuries-old laws against homosexuality in England were repealed by Parliament in 1967, making private homosexual acts between consenting adults none of the law's business. In the United States, Illinois in 1961 was the first state to repeal existing statutes against private homosexual acts between consenting adults. Many, but not all, other states have since followed suit. Unfortunately, the emergence of AIDS in the 1980s and its original localization in the male homosexual community threatens to halt or even reverse this climate of increased tolerance for gay life-styles.

Certainly, it is in the interest of all to discourage those sexual practices implicated in the spread of the virus, whether in homosexual or heterosexual contexts. It would be tragic, however, if our tendency to "blame the victim" were to result in renewed or more virulent persecution of homosexuals, thereby driving many of them back into the "closet" of secrecy and shame. Apart from the psychological damage that would be inflicted, such a reaction would almost certainly result in an *increased* spread of AIDS. History teaches that the eradication of homosexuality is not a realistic goal for any society, even if it were a worthy one. No evidence suggests that the social gains heretofore made by "gay liberation" have led to a significant increase in homosexuality or have proven in themselves to be detrimental to the general welfare. In addition, heterosexual interests seem to remain alive and well, so we need have little fear that our species will be decimated by rampant homoeroticism. It could well be decimated by rampant HIV infection. This distinction will be of crucial importance as we face an uncertain future in respect to controlling this deadly threat.

UNRESOLVED ISSUES
on Sexual Disorders and Variants

The unprecedented advances of the past two decades in the treatment of what were previously stubborn problems in sexual functioning should not blind us to the fact that tens of thousands of men and women continue to experience frustration and demoralizing difficulties. Along this line, some researchers suggest that failures to replicate in more recent work the extraordinarily high success rates originally achieved with our new, direct treatment approaches reflect a continuing core of problematic cases; the "easy" ones have now all been successfully resolved, many perhaps even through informed self-help techniques, and hence do not show up in treatment outcome statistics. Whatever the explanation, the search for more effective therapies continues, particularly in the areas of male erectile dysfunction and situational or secondary female anorgasmia. Unfortunately, from a strictly clinical and scientific standpoint, the search must take into account certain societal tolerances and constraints, such as, for example, the controversial and potentially legal consequences of using trained surrogate partners (of *both* sexes) in programs of sex therapy.

Even more difficult and baffling problems continue to plague us, of course, in respect to sexually variant behavior. Of these, perhaps none is more crucial than the relationship between sexuality and aggression, of which we have only the vaguest understanding. The phenomena of rape and sadomasochism, observations of the sexual behavior of some subhuman species, and a growing number of human laboratory studies (e.g., Yates, Barbaree, & Marshall, 1984) suggest that, for males at least, we cannot dismiss the possibility of some sort of synergism being involved at a basic level in these two motivational systems. That is, sexual arousal may enhance the likelihood of aggression, and vice versa. Needless to say, we are not here offering a possible apology or excuse for sexual assault or victimization. To be civilized, after all, is to have control over many urgings of primal origin. Nor do we intend to convey a particular conclusion on the controversial matter of pornography inciting violence, one almost completely confounded by the aggressive or violent themes in much sexually explicit media material. While we are inclined to find censorship repugnant in any form, we think the legally enforced removal of violent, aggressive, sadomasochistic themes from erotica probably would reduce to a measurable extent the prevalence of sexual assaults.

Whatever the origins, it is plain that as a society we are failing in efforts to curb sexual exploitation, victimization, and assault. The extent of our failure becomes all the more agonizing in the face of numerous recent research findings on the often serious short- and long-term consequences for many victims, both child and adult. Apart from enforced physical separation of an offender from his or her victim or potential victims, satisfactory solutions are badly wanting. Surely, at least, we can find ways to improve our services to victims, such as ensuring access to expert counseling. Much work in this area is already underway.

On the offender side, psychotherapeutic intervention may be promising if an offender acknowledges a "problem" and is motivated to work on its resolution, neither of which can be taken for granted. Therapy initiated on court order seems unpromising without an offender's genuine commitment to the process. Radical solutions, such as offender castration, although having a certain emotional appeal for some outraged by these crimes, are often based on fundamental misconceptions about etiology and would, we suspect, more often compound than alleviate the menace. Close monitoring of past offenders shows promise, but it may be too costly on the scale required. We have sound reasons to believe that eliminating child abuse, particularly sexual abuse, would have significant impact in this area. Unfortunately, the time frame for achieving such an objective is generations rather than years. Meanwhile, it seems that we are entitled to a more vigorous form of law enforcement in these areas than has been characteristic of the recent past.

As of February 1989, 85,590 cases of AIDS had been reported in the United States alone; because the average survival period following diagnosis is approximately 11 months, most of these people are already dead. The number of HIV-infected individuals (who, without some dramatic breakthrough in medical research, will acquire AIDS in an average of 8 years following infection) is difficult to estimate, in part because of wide variations in different risk groups and even in different locales. For example, 57 percent of female prostitutes tested in metropolitan (New York) cities in New Jersey were seropositive for HIV-1, whereas this rate was only 1 percent among Atlanta prostitutes. Although rates of seroconversion (that is, new infections) have been declining among gay men, they remained unacceptably high in the latest figures available, and—with the notable exception of transfusion-induced infections—there is little evidence of such decline in other high-risk groups (Glasner & Kaslow, 1990). We are thus dealing with a threat of staggering proportions, one inextricably linked to the manner in which we manage our sexuality.

Such evidence as we have—and it is chiefly anecdotal and informal—indicates that many people have in fact modified their sexual choices and behavior and thus substantially reduced their risk. The increased availability (for example, in college dorm coin dispensers) and use of latex condoms, which have a demonstrated record of prevention (Detels et al., 1988; Fischl et al., 1987), is an encouraging sign of wisdom and maturity. As the history of sexually transmitted diseases painfully reminds us, however, some people will neglect or even refuse to take reasonable precautions. For example, a sexually active undergraduate male recently told one of us in conversation that he would "never" use a condom on the grounds that it "interfered" with his pleasure. What does one do or say in the face of such density and self-indulgence, of such a dangerous denial of common sense, of such *abnormality?*

SUMMARY

In contrast to lower animals, human sexuality is remarkably free of biological constraints and is therefore highly plastic and subject to acquired inhibitions and appetites. The inhibitions are associated chiefly with psychosexual dysfunctions—varied inabilities to achieve satisfaction or to provide it for one's partner. Sexual appetites may involve psychosexual variants or deviations, in which an individual's preferred modes of arousal and gratification are different from conventionally accepted heterosexual patterns and, in some instances, are thought to threaten a group's welfare.

Some such variants, however, are victimless and cause no great harm either to individuals or to society in general.

Some psychosexual dysfunctions involve inhibited sexual desire in either sex. Other dysfunctions are more gender-specific: for males, erectile insufficiency, premature ejaculation, and ejaculatory retardation or incompetence; for females, arousal insufficiency (analogous to erectile insufficiency in a male), vaginismus, orgasmic dysfunction, and dyspareunia. Great strides have been made recently in the treatment of psychosexual dysfunctions in both sexes. Contrary to the situation a quarter-century ago, many people experiencing dysfunctions can now be reassured that, in all likelihood, they will be able to overcome their difficulties with competent professional help.

Of the sexual variants, one of the least understood is gender identity disorder, in which a person feels trapped in a body of the wrong gender. This disorder often results in efforts to have the body altered so as to conform to the person's internal sense of maleness or femaleness. Neither the male nor female pattern is well understood at this time, but it seems likely that both biological and psychosocial factors are implicated in most cases.

The paraphilias are a group of disorders in which sexual satisfaction becomes persistently focused on some unusual object, ritual, or situation. We distinguish between victimless varieties, such as transvestism, and those deviations involving assault or nonconsent, such as exhibitionism. Other paraphilias include fetishism, voyeurism, sadism, masochism, and pedophilia. A persistent rapist may best be conceived as a paraphiliac. Little is known about the development of these deviant practices, but it is strongly suspected that, for the most part, they are due to faulty learning and an inadequate sense of self.

Discussions of incest (especially of the father-daughter type) and rape are also included here, even though neither behavior is recognized in the DSM-III-R. The chief importance of incest, from an abnormal psychology standpoint, is that the child-victim often suffers serious adjustment difficulties in adolescence and adulthood. Contrary to most public opinion, sexual gratification is not the dominant motive in the overwhelming majority of rapes. A desire for power and aggression against women are far more likely to instigate incidents of rape. Many rape victims also sustain long-term reactions that compromise adaptive functioning.

Therapy for the sexual dysfunctions has developed at an impressive pace since the 1970s. The prognosis for the sexual variants and deviations is, in general, far less optimistic—although, even here, treatment successes do occur, especially where a comprehensive treatment approach is planned and effected.

The DSM-III-R recognizes one type of disorder involving homosexuality—called ego-dystonic homosexuality—in which an individual persistently wishes to change his or her variant sexual orientation. Homosexuality itself is a complex and heterogeneous phenomenon. Both homosexual and heterosexual potentials exist to varying degrees in virtually everyone, but it cannot be said that everyone is fundamentally bisexual. Unlike a "normal" bell-shaped distribution curve, few "bisexuals" are found in the middle portion in terms of behavioral choices made or, probably, satisfaction experienced. Many people claiming to be bisexual are probably homosexual.

Although homosexuality is itself no longer diagnosable as a mental disorder, the authors take the position that one form of the gay life-style emphasizing sexual promiscuity and relative partner anonymity is definitely abnormal within their definition of the term, especially in this age of AIDS.

Unresolved issues in this area include certain dysfunctions, chiefly male erectile and female secondary orgasmic problems, that are proving relatively difficult to treat, and questions of both theoretical and practical import concerning the relationship of sexuality to aggression. Finally, the effect of the growing AIDS crisis on societal attitudes toward sexuality has involved some adaptive life-style changes, but with disturbing exceptions.

Key Terms

lovemap (p. 342)
sexual dysfunction (p. 343)
male erectile disorder (p. 343)
primary erectile insufficiency (p. 343)
secondary erectile insufficiency (p. 343)
premature ejaculation (p. 344)
inhibited male orgasm (p. 345)
female sexual arousal disorder (p. 345)
vaginismus (p. 345)
inhibited female orgasm (p. 345)
primary orgasmic dysfunction (p. 346)
dyspareunia (p. 346)
hypoactive sexual desire disorder (p. 346)
sexual aversion disorder (p. 346)
gender identity disorder (p. 352)
paraphilias (p. 354)
fetishism (p. 355)
transvestic fetishism (p. 356)
voyeurism (p. 357)
scotophilia (p. 357)
inspectionalism (p. 357)
exhibitionism (p. 358)
sadism (p. 360)
masochism (p. 362)
pedophilia (p. 363)
incest (p. 365)
rape (p. 368)
homosexuality (p. 373)
bisexuality (p. 374)

Chapter 11
Mood Disorders and Suicide

Heinrich Müller, *The Fly-Man and the Snake*. Müller (1865–1930), a Swiss vineyardist and amateur inventor, was institutionalized as a mental patient at the age of 41. In the hospital, he occupied his time by "experimenting" with bizarre, homemade machines and by drawing disturbing hallucinatory sketches like the one shown here.

Mood disorders are so named because they involve states of positive or negative emotion, or *affect,* that are intense and persistent enough to be clearly maladaptive for significant periods of time. Consider the following case:

A nationally prominent businesswoman in her middle years, noted for her energy and productivity, was unexpectedly deserted by her husband for a younger woman. Following her initial shock and rage, she began to have uncontrollable weeping spells and serious doubts about her business acumen. Decision making, in particular, became an enormous ordeal. Her spirits worsened over a relatively brief period of time, and she began to spend more and more of her time in bed, refusing to deal with anyone. Simultaneously, her alcohol consumption increased to the point that she was seldom entirely sober. Within a period of weeks, serious financial losses were incurred owing to her inability, or refusal, to keep her affairs in order. She felt she was a "total failure," a self-attribution that was entirely resistant to alteration by a review of her considerable achievements; indeed, her self-abnegation gradually spread to all aspects of her life and her personal history. Finally, having become alarmed, members of her family essentially forced her to accept an appointment with a clinical psychologist.

How was the psychologist to deal with this situation? Was something "wrong" with the woman, or was she merely experiencing normal human emotions due to her husband's departure? The psychologist concluded that the woman was suffering from a mood disorder, and treatment was initiated. The diagnosis, based on the severity of the symptoms and the degree of impairment, was major depression. As we shall see, mood-related reactions to distressing events are not limited to relatively mild forms of "adjustment disorder," but may and frequently do include the emergence of the full major depressive syndrome. This source of potential confusion will be further discussed in a later section.

When a mood change, because of its extent, brings about behavior that seriously endangers the affected person's welfare, psychologists and other mental health professionals conclude that the person is disordered. Mood disorders are conceived to be heterogeneous, as is suggested by the many types of depression recognized in the DSM-III-R, listed in *HIGHLIGHT 11.1* Whether or not such elaborate differentiation of depressive disorder is justified is open to question, as we will see in later sections.

In all mood disorders (formerly called *affective disorders*), extremes of *emotion*—soaring elation or deep depression—dominate the clinical picture. By contrast, the schizophrenic and paranoid disorders discussed in the next chapter are predominantly disturbances of thought, or *cognition,* although often they have some distortion of affect, too. In severe cases of any of these disorders, disturbances of both thought and affect may involve **psychotic behavior** (or **psychosis**)—a loss of contact with reality to the extent that a person harbors delusional beliefs or reports bizarre perceptions (hallucinations). Most, but not all, instances of mood disorder fall short of this level of disorganization.

Disordered thought processes are not typical in mood disorders, except where a disorder reaches extreme intensity; even here, though, the disturbed thinking is often circumscribed and seems in some sense "appropriate" to the emotional extremes that the person is experiencing. For example, the delusional idea that one's internal organs have totally deteriorated—an idea sometimes held by severely depressed people—ties in with the mood of a despondent person; in contrast, the idea that one has been chosen by the Deity for a special mission to save humankind is inconsistent with the self-abnegation normally seen in depression. The former type of disordered thinking is termed **mood-congruent thinking,** which means that it is consistent with the predominant mood.

The two key states of mood disorder are **mania,** characterized by intense and unrealistic feelings of excitement and euphoria, and **depression,** which involves feelings of extraordinary sadness and dejection. These states are often conceived to be at opposite ends of a single mood continuum, with normal mood occupying the middle portion. While accurate to a degree, this conception cannot be taken too literally in trying to understand every instance of mood disorder, because in rare cases a patient appears to be both manic and depressed at the same time. Such an observation suggests the aptness of a model involving two independent dimensions, each ranging from mood normality at one pole to either extreme mania or extreme depression at the other.

Depressions of mild intensity are so much a part of our lives that incidence and prevalence figures for them would be difficult to estimate and would probably be meaningless anyway. Of the two types of major mood disorders, **major depression** (a *unipolar* form of disorder in which only depressive episodes occur) is much more frequent, and its occurrence has apparently increased in recent years. The other type, **bipolar disorder** (in which both manic and depressive episodes occur), has decreased. In fact, estimates indicate that some 8 to 10 people in 100—about 25 million Americans—will experience a severe depressive episode at some time in their lives (Brown, 1974). More than 2 million of these will suffer profound depressions (President's Commission on Mental Health, 1978).

Though the great majority of mood disorder cases occur between the ages of 25 and 65, such reactions may occur anytime from early childhood to old age. Lefkowitz and Tesiny (1985) reported a point prevalence rate (cases at a particular point in time) for depression of 5.2 percent among some 3000 third to fifth graders. Poznanski and Zrull (1970) described significant depressive reactions among children ranging from 3 to 12 years of age, and depressions meeting the criteria for designation as *major* have been observed in preadolescent youngsters (Puig-Antich et al., 1985; 1989). A possible early manifestation of the syndrome has recently been observed in the infants of mothers depressed at postpartum (Whiffen & Gotlib, 1989). The occurrence of mood disorders apparently has no upper age limit, and, as we will see, females are considerably more at risk than males.

Fortunate indeed (and probably nonexistent) is the adult who has never experienced at least mild depression from time to time. Research suggests that we can conceive such mild mood disturbances as being largely on the same continuum, at least at the clinical level (what we can actually observe), as the more severe disorders on which this chapter will focus. The differences seem chiefly to be of degree, not of kind, a conclusion supported in a recent review of the pertinent evidence by Free and Oei (1989). At some point along this continuum, however, as we encounter the more extreme or even psychotic phenomena, subtle biological factors likely become implicated, rendering a person in many instances less amenable to psychological treatment approaches. Interestingly, antidepressant medication, the most common biologically-based treatment for depressions, is not particularly useful in treating milder depressions, including milder "major" depressions (Elkin et al., 1989), unless these depressions are accompanied by panic attacks (Stewart et al., 1985).

Our discussion will start with the milder mood disturbances, which are regarded as "normal." From there, we will move to disorders of affect in

HIGHLIGHT 11.1

Varieties of Depression According to DSM-III-R

Diagnosis	Main Features
Organic mood disorder, depressed Primary degenerative dementia with depression Multi-infarct dementia with depression Hallucinogen mood disorder, depressed	The person has notably depressed mood, including symptoms associated with major depression, whose primary cause is considered to be interference with normal brain functioning by some organic process. Where the organic process is known (e.g., multi-infarct dementia), it is specified in the diagnosis on Axis I or III.
Major depression	The person has one or more major depressive episodes in the absence of any manic episode. Symptoms include prominent and persistent depressed mood, accompanied by symptoms such as poor appetite, insomnia, psychomotor retardation, decreased sex drive, fatigue, feelings of worthlessness or guilt, inability to concentrate, and thoughts of death or suicide.
Bipolar disorder, depressed	The person experiences a major depressive episode (as in major depression) and has had one or more manic episodes.
Dysthymia	For the past two years, the person has been bothered all or most of the time by a depressed mood, but not of sufficient severity to meet the criteria for major depression.
Cyclothymia, depressed	At present or during the past two years, the person has experienced episodes resembling dysthymia, but also has had one or more periods of hypomania—characterized by elevated, expansive, or irritable mood not of psychotic proportions.
Adjustment disorder with depressed mood	The person reacts with a maladaptively depressed mood to some identifiable stressor occurring within the past three months. "Uncomplicated bereavement" does not qualify. It is assumed the reaction is temporary.

which an individual's functioning is clearly impaired but in which little or no evidence suggests a pervasive personality breakdown or loss of contact with reality. Finally, we will deal with moderate to severe mood disorders, a group of conditions currently undergoing intensive scientific investigation. Throughout, we will focus primarily on depression, which is much more common than mania.

Suicide is a distressingly frequent and almost always possible outcome of relatively significant depressions. In fact, such episodes are undoubtedly the most common of the predisposing causes leading to suicide. The latter part of this chapter includes a discussion of the varieties, causes, and prevention of suicidal behavior.

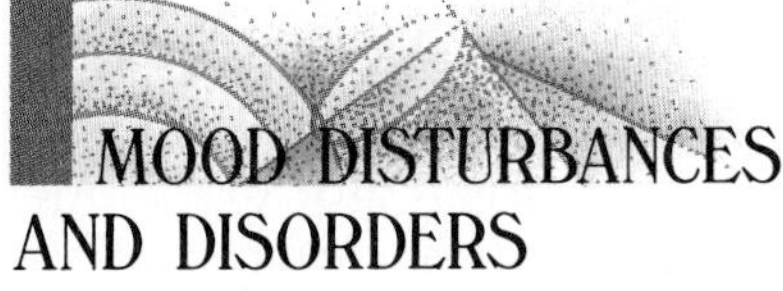

MOOD DISTURBANCES AND DISORDERS

Sadness, discouragement, pessimism, and hopelessness about being able to improve matters are familiar feelings to most people. Most of us are prone to move in and out of these states throughout our lives. Depression is unpleasant, even noxious, when we are in it, but it usually does not last long. Sometimes it seems almost to be self-limiting, turning off after a period or after a certain intensity level has been exceeded. As we come out of it, we often experience it as having been in some sense useful: we were stuck, and now we can move on; the former situation was easier to get out of than we thought it could be, and our new perspective encompasses all sorts of possibilities.

This familiar scenario contains certain hints that may be significant to depression generally, including its more severe forms. The more important of these hints are that (a) depression, in its mild form, may actually be adaptive in the long run; (b) much of the "work" of depression seems to involve self-exposure to images, thoughts, and feelings that would normally be avoided; and (c) depression may, at least under some circumstances, be self-limiting. All of these considerations suggest that the capacity to experience depression may be normal—even desirable—provided of course that it is maintained within certain limits of time and intensity. They also suggest the idea of *normal* depressions—depressions we would expect to occur in anyone undergoing certain traumatic but common life events, such as significant personal, interpersonal, or economic losses.

Normal Depression

Though the often problematic distinction between "normal" and "abnormal" is especially fuzzy here, any reasonable estimate would suggest that normal depressions far surpass abnormal ones in terms of the numbers of people affected at a given time. Most people suffering from normal depression will not seek or need the specialized services of a mental health professional—although, in doubtful cases, it is certainly better to err on the conservative side and seek such assistance.

Normal depressions are almost always the result of recent stress. In fact, some depressions are considered adjustment disorders (in response to stressors) rather than mood disorders. We discuss such reactions here as well as in Chapter 5 because we doubt such sharp demarcations are justified by the facts. As already noted, many depressions meeting criteria as "major" are clearly related to the prior occurrence of obvious stress (Hammen et al., 1989; Harder et al., 1989; Hirschfeld et al., 1985; Shrout et al., 1989; Winokur, 1985), although this fact tends to be understated or ignored by some biologically-oriented investigators. We will consider some of the milder forms of normal depression in the following sections.

Grief and the Grieving Process We usually think of grief as the psychological process one goes through following the death of a loved one—a process that, we have noted, appears to be more damaging for men than women (Stroebe & Stroebe, 1983). Though this may be the most common and intense form of grieving, many other types of loss will give rise to a similar state in an affected person. Loss of a favored status or position (including one occasioned by promotion), separation or divorce, financial loss, the breakup of a romantic affair, retirement, separation from a friend, absence from home for the first time, or even the loss of a cherished pet may all give rise to the symptoms of acute grief.

Whatever the source, this condition has certain characteristic qualities beyond the virtually omnipresent weeping spells. A grieving person will normally "turn off" in response to events that would usually provoke a strong response; figuratively, he or she seems to roll up in a ball, fending off any and all possibilities of additional involvement and hurt by the simple expedient of losing interest in nearly all external happenings. At the same time, the griever often becomes actively involved in fantasies that poignantly depict the now unavailable former situation of satisfaction and gratification. Initially painful, these fantasies, if only by sheer repetition, gradually lose their capacity to evoke pain—a process of response extinction or, as Sullivan (1956) called it, "erasure."

In the typical instance, after a variable interval of a few weeks or months, the ability to respond to the external world is gradually regained, sadness

We usually think of grief as the psychological process one goes through following the death of a loved one. We see grief in the face of this grandmother attending the funeral of her grandson, who died in the Gulf War. Grief may accompany other types of loss as well, such as separation or divorce, romantic break-up, retirement, loss of a job, or even loss of a pet.

abates, zest returns, and a person moves out again into a more productive engagement with the challenges of life. This is the normal pattern. Some people, however, become stuck somewhere in the middle of the sequence, in which case they enter into a more serious psychological status to be described in a later section. P. J. Clayton (1982) estimated that the process of grieving following bereavement is normally completed within one year, during which time a grieving person may experience the "full depressive syndrome" (that is, major depression, to be examined later). If depressive symptoms persist beyond the first year after loss, therapeutic intervention may be called for.

Ignoring for the moment such potential complications, it is easy to see grief as having an adaptive function. In fact the lack of grief under conditions in which it seems warranted would generally be of some concern to a mental health professional. On the other hand, as we discussed in Chapter 7, a prolonged sense of hopelessness may endanger physical health, and eventual recovery and resolution following loss is not a guaranteed outcome (Wortman & Silver, 1989).

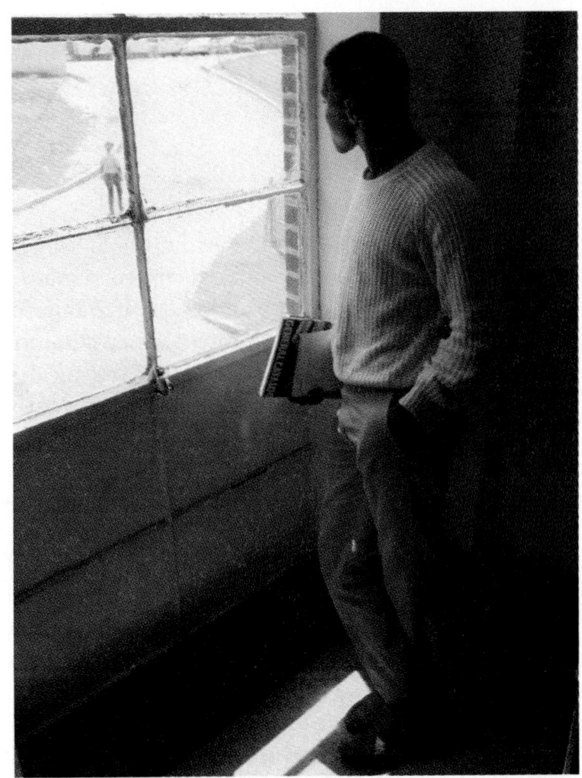

Many college students experience bouts of depression during their college years. The internal and external pressures to get good grades and to achieve can sometimes cause those students who don't make the grade to devalue themselves and to see their lives as having no meaning.

Other Normal Mood Variations Many situations other than obvious loss can provoke depressive feelings, and as we will see, some people seem especially prone to develop depressive responses. It is a commonplace observation, for example, that some doctoral candidates in various fields, including those in clinical psychology, undergo pronounced depressive reactions soon after completion of their final oral exams. A seemingly similar phenomenon is the so-called postpartum depressive reaction of some new mothers (and sometimes fathers) on the birth of a child. Pitt (1982) indicated that as many as 50 percent of women experience at least a mild attack of "the blues" following childbirth, 10 percent of them having reactions of moderately severe depression. Clearly, hormonal readjustments and the like are a key factor here (except for fathers). It is obvious that a psychological component is present as well: it may reflect a letdown after sustained effort and anticipation; or perhaps a person's expectations had failed to include certain realities about the more challenging (overwhelming?) aspects of infant care and dependency, leading to depression rather than to joy; or it may be a feeling of loss—that is, of missing that constant companion in the womb who is now a separate entity.

Many college students experience bouts of mild or serious depression during their college years of supposed freedom and carefree personal growth. Normal depressions among college students were studied by Blatt, D'Afflitti, and Quinlan (1976) in an effort to determine the basic dimensions of the experience. In brief, they found that depression was similar for males and females, and that it involved chiefly three main psychological variables: (a) *dependency*, the sense that one is in dire need of help and support from others; (b) *self-criticism*, the tendency to exaggerate one's faults and to engage in self-devaluation; and (c) *inefficacy*, the sense that events in the world are independent of—not contingent on—one's own actions or efforts. In subsequent work, Blatt and colleagues (1982) focused on the first two of these dimensions, suggesting that there may be two basic types of depressive experience organized around themes of either dependency or self-criticism, inefficacy being common to both. Other investigators, such as Hammen et al. (1985, 1989) and Nietzel and Harris (1990), have contributed independent evidence that such subgroups may indeed exist; that is, some depressed people seem primarily involved with the state of their interpersonal relationships, while others' concerns focus on achievement issues. Because dependency and self-criticism are commonplace among the more severely depressed, these observations lend support to the notion of a continuous severity dimension.

Mild to Moderate Mood Disorders

The point on the severity continuum at which mood *disturbance* becomes mood *disorder* is a matter of clinical judgment. Unfortunately, though criteria exist for exercising this judgment, they are not precise enough to guarantee consensus among different clinicians, and—perhaps more importantly—it is decidedly unclear that any such sharp demarcation would meet the requirement of *validity*—in other words, that it could actually reflect a meaningful point of transition between clinical and nonclinical depression. Although the more severe forms of mood disorder are obviously abnormal to even the casual observer, a gray area exists where a distinction between normal and abnormal is difficult to establish or defend.

It is customary to differentiate the mood disorders along three principal dimensions: (a) *severity*—the number of dysfunctions experienced in various areas of living and the relative degree of impairment evidenced in those areas (for example, sexual performance and satisfaction); (b) *type*—whether depressive, manic, or mixed symptoms predominate; and (c) *duration*—whether the disorder is acute, chronic, or intermittent, with periods of relatively normal functioning between the episodes of disorder. The following discussion reflects these customary divisions, as do the DSM-III-R categories.

DSM-III-R includes three main categories for mood disorders of mild to moderate severity: cyclothymia, dysthymia, and adjustment disorder with depressed mood. Each of these is considered in the following sections.

Cyclothymia As we have noted, mania is in some ways the mood or affective opposite of depression; it is a state involving excessive levels of excitement, elation, or euphoria, often liberally admixed with components of domination and the assumption of great powers. In its milder forms it is known as **hypomania.** It has long been recognized that certain people are subject to cyclical mood alterations with relative excesses of hypomania and depression that, though substantial, are not disabling. These, in essence, are the symptoms of **cyclothymia.**

Many clinicians feel that cyclothymia is but a milder variant of bipolar disorder (to be discussed later in this chapter), and evidence for this view has in recent years become quite compelling. For example, Depue and his colleagues have identified a subsyndromal (that is, showing few symptoms) cyclothymic personality organization that is predictive of serious mood disorder episodes (Depue et al., 1981; Goplerud & Depue, 1985; Klein & Depue, 1984, 1985; Klein, Depue, & Slater, 1985, 1986). Specifically, these investigators developed a hypomanic personality inventory scale that postdicted (that is, identified those individuals who had had) not only hypomanic episodes but other maladaptive patterns, including depression, among a group of college undergraduates. This study is significant because it suggests that an identifying personality component is present independent of hypomanic episodes.

Changes in the DSM classification reflect current thinking about cyclothymia. In DSM-I and DSM-II, this pattern was included under the category of personality disorders and was not related to mood disorders per se. The DSM-III-R definition of cyclothymia makes the pattern sound a bit like a junior-grade version of major bipolar disorder, minus certain extreme symptoms and psychotic features, such as delusions. In the depressed phase of cyclothymia, a person's mood is dejected and he or she experiences a distinct loss of interest or pleasure in usual activities and pastimes. In addition, the individual may exhibit sleep irregularity (too much or too little); low energy level; feelings of inadequacy; decreased efficiency, productivity, talkativeness, and cognitive sharpness; social withdrawal; restriction of pleasurable activities, including a relative disinterest in sex; a pessimistic and brooding attitude; and tearfulness.

The hypomanic phase of cyclothymia consists essentially of the opposites of these characteristics, except that the sleep disturbance is invariably one of an apparent decreased need for sleep. As in the case of bipolar disorder, no obvious precipitating circumstance may be evident, and an affected person may have lengthy periods between episodes in which he or she functions in a relatively adaptive manner. In cyclothymia, however, the diagnostic criteria specify at least a two-year span of disturbance for adults and one year for adolescents and children. The following case is illustrative:

A 29-year-old car salesman was referred by his current girl friend, a psychiatric nurse, who suspected he had an Affective [i.e., Mood] Disorder, even though the patient was reluctant to admit that he might be a "moody" person. According to him, since the age of 14 he has experienced repeated alternating cycles that he terms "good times and bad times." During a "bad" period, usually lasting four to seven days, he oversleeps 10–14 hours daily, lacks energy, confidence, and motivation—"just vegetating," as he puts it. Often he abruptly shifts, characteristically upon waking up in the morning, to a three-to-four-day stretch of overconfidence, heightened social awareness, promiscuity, and sharpened thinking—"things would flash in my mind." At such times he indulges in alcohol to enhance the experience, but also to help him sleep. Occasionally the "good" periods last seven to ten days, but culminate in irritable and hostile outbursts, which often herald the transition back to another period of "bad" days. He admits to frequent use of marijuana, which he claims helps him "adjust" to daily routines.

In school, A's and B's alternated with C's and D's, with the result that the patient was considered a bright student whose performance was mediocre overall because of "unstable motivation." As a car salesman his performance has also been uneven, with "good days" canceling out the "bad days"; yet even during his "good days" he is sometimes perilously argumentative with customers and loses sales that appeared sure. Although considered a charming man in many social circles, he alienates friends when he is hostile and irritable. He typically accumulates social obligations during the "bad" days and takes care of them all at once on the first day of a "good" period. (Spitzer et al., 1981, pp. 31–32)

In short, cyclothymia consists of mood swings that, at either extreme, are clearly maladaptive but of insufficient intensity to merit the major disorder designation.

Dysthymia The symptoms of **dysthymia** are essentially identical to those indicated for the depressed phase of cyclothymia; they include sleep disturbance, low energy level, low self-esteem, concentration difficulties, and pessimism. The main difference is that dysthymically disordered people evidence no tendency toward hypomanic episodes in their life histories. Rather, they exhibit moderate, nonpsychotic levels of depression over a chronic period—that is, at least two years (one year for children and adolescents) of more or less uninterrupted duration. Normal moods may briefly intercede, but they last at most from a few days to a few weeks. As in the case of cyclothymia, no identifiable precipitating event or condition need necessarily be present, though such circumstances are frequently observed for depressions of this general type. Indeed, a depressed person tends to elicit reactions from the social environment that will bring about "bad" feelings on a continuous basis (Strack & Coyne, 1983). The following case, which includes obvious self-sustaining features, is typical of this disorder:

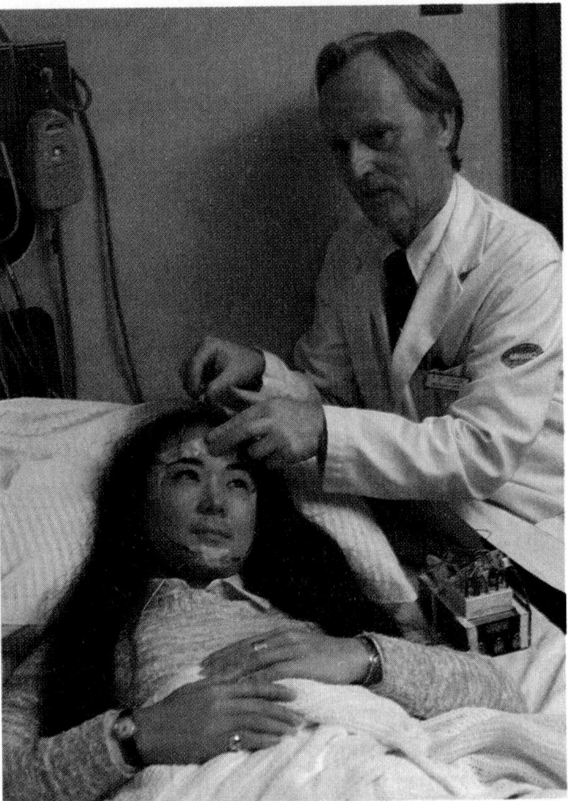

Sleep disturbances are common in both cyclothymia and dysthymia. Studying the brainwave patterns of sleeping cyclothymic and dysthymic patients has helped researchers discover some of the basic patterns underlying these disorders.

A 28-year-old junior executive was referred by a senior psychoanalyst for "supportive" treatment. She had obtained a master's degree in business administration and moved to California a year and a half earlier to begin work in a large firm. She complained of being "depressed" about everything: her job, her husband, and her prospects for the future.

She had had extensive psychotherapy previously. She had seen an "analyst" twice a week for three years while in college, and a "behaviorist" for a year and a half while in graduate school. Her complaints were of persistent feelings of depressed mood, inferiority, and pessimism, which she claims to have had since she was 16 or 17 years old. Although she did reasonably well in college, she constantly ruminated about those students who were "genuinely intelligent." She dated during college and graduate school, but claimed that she would never go after a guy she thought was "special," always feeling inferior and intimidated. Whenever she saw or met such a man, she acted stiff and aloof, or actually walked away as quickly as possible, only to berate herself afterward and then fantasize about him for many months. She claimed that her therapy had helped, although she still could not remember a time when she didn't feel somewhat depressed.

Just after graduation, she married the man she was going out with at the time. She thought of him as reasonably desirable, though not "special," and married him primarily because she felt she "needed a husband" for companionship. Shortly after their marriage, the couple started to bicker. She was very critical of his clothes, his job, and his parents; and he, in turn, found her rejecting, controlling, and moody. She began to feel that she had made a mistake in marrying him.

Recently she has also been having difficulties at work. She is assigned the most menial tasks at the firm and is never given an assignment of importance or responsibility. She admits that she frequently does a "slipshod" job of what is given her, never does more than is required, and never demonstrates any assertiveness or initiative to her supervisors. She views her boss as self-centered, unconcerned, and unfair, but nevertheless admires his success. She feels that she will never go very far in her profession because she does not have the right "connections" and neither does her husband, yet she dreams of money, status, and power.

Her social life with her husband involves several other couples. The man in these couples is usually a friend of her husband. She is sure that the women find her uninteresting and unimpressive, and that the people who seem to like her are probably no better off than she.

Under the burden of her dissatisfaction with her marriage, her job, and her social life, feeling tired and uninterested in "life," she now enters treatment for the third time. (Spitzer et al., 1981, pp. 10–11)

Adjustment Disorder with Depressed Mood Basically, **adjustment disorder with depressed mood** is behaviorally indistinguishable from dysthymia or the depressed phase of cyclothymia. It differs from the latter two conditions in that it does not exceed six months in duration, and it requires the existence of an identifiable (presumably precipitating) psychosocial stressor in the client's life within three months prior to the onset of depression. The justification for making a clinical diagnosis is that the client is experiencing impaired social or occupational functioning, or that the observed stressor would not normally be considered severe enough to account for the client's reaction. There is a difficulty here, of course, because assessing stressor severity is a highly subjective matter. Also, the diagnosis assumes that the person's problems will remit when the stressor ceases or when a new level of adjustment is achieved. This assumption causes further difficulties, because it calls for the diagnostician to predict a benign future course; if enhanced adjustment does not occur, we must assume a continuation of the stressor or a failure of the client to make the "new" adjustment. Presumably, chronic cases of this sort would need to be rediagnosed as dysthymia.

Despite evident problems with this particular set of formal diagnostic criteria, there are doubtless many cases of relatively brief but moderately serious depression (involving definitely maladaptive behavior) that occur in reaction to circumstances generally regarded by most as stressful. (Uncomplicated bereavement, by the way, would not be included under this diagnosis.) The following excerpt from a clinical interview is illustrative of an adjustment disorder with depressed mood.

Patient: *Well, you see, doctor, I just don't concentrate good, I mean, I can't play cards or even care to talk on the phone. I just feel so upset and miserable, it's just sorta as if I don't care any more about anything.*

Doctor: *You feel that your condition is primarily due to your divorce proceedings?*

Patient: *Well, doctor, the thing that upset me so, we had accumulated a little bit through my efforts—bonds and money—and he (sigh) wanted one half of it. He said he was going to San Francisco to get a job and send me enough money for support. So (sigh) I gave him a bond, and he went and turned around and went to an attorney and sued me for a divorce. Well, somehow, I had withstood all the humiliation of his drinking and not coming home at night and not knowing where he was, but he turned and divorced me and this is something that I just can't take. I mean, he has broken my health and* *broken everything, and I've been nothing but good to him. I just can't take it, doctor. There are just certain things that people—I don't know—just can't accept. I just can't accept that he would turn on me that way.*

It should be noted that few, if any, depressions—including milder ones—occur in the absence of significant anxiety. In fact the distinction between depression and anxiety, at clinical levels, may be difficult. In a recent study involving 470 patients of mixed diagnoses, their cognitive and symptom profiles for anxiety and depression did in fact show up as distinct and separable factors, but a fairly substantial group of patients had mixtures of these profiles (Clark, Beck, & Stewart, 1990). The frequent "comorbidity" (co-occurrence) of anxiety and depression has also been found in children (Kovacs et al., 1989). Whatever may turn out to be the reason for this connection between anxiety and depression—an interesting question theoretically—a depressed person is often notably fearful and anxious. Perhaps the person becomes frightened as a consequence of observing the mentally and physically paralyzing effects of his or her own developing depression. Alternatively, perhaps a more intrinsic relationship exists between anxiety and depression, even at the neurophysiological or neurochemical level (Roth & Mountjoy, 1982). Some investigators, such as Seligman (1975) and Brown and Harris (1978), believe that depression may be a naturally occurring consequence of anxiety, particularly under conditions interpreted as hopeless. In any event, because of this close association, the treatment of depression often includes specific treatment for anxiety as well.

In the range of mild to moderate mood disorders, there are no officially recognized manic or hypomanic counterparts to dysthymia or adjustment disorder with depressed mood. The implicit assumption appears to be that all mania-like behaviors must be part of a cyclothymic or bipolar disorder, or perhaps must exist along a continuum on which these two conditions fall. Considering behavior alone, however, any such assumption is readily challenged. Most clinicians are familiar with a type of person who is chronically overactive, dominating, counterdependent, deficient in self-criticism, perhaps excessively optimistic concerning the outcome of various plans and schemes, and yet shows no pronounced history of depressive episodes; such people are by no means rare. It is unfortunate to assume automatically that this pattern is related to the classic bipolar syndrome. On the contrary, such people are most often found to have underlying anxiety that they are attempting to manage by overactivity in the standard fashion of neurotic defense, and their problems are perhaps best considered manifestations of what we have called compliance/submission inhibition (see Chapter 6, page 215).

Incidentally, the individuals just described are unlikely to present themselves initially for treatment at a psychological or psychiatric clinic. The more common pattern is for them to show up in medical clinics with a stress-related physical disease, perhaps as Type A patients with coronary problems (see Chapter 7).

Moderate to Severe Mood Disorders

We have noted that mood disorders seem to array themselves along an unbroken continuum of severity; there are no discernible gaps in this continuum that allow us to distinguish different basic types of disorder. We must now add a qualification to this general proposition; the continuum does not quite tell the whole story. Mood disorders differ, as we have seen, along the dimensions of severity, type, and duration. Both severity and type, however, are often hard to pin down: the *profile,* or pattern, of symptoms (for example, sleep disturbance, psychomotor retardation or agitation) may vary greatly from individual to individual and may exist at least somewhat independently of severity. An obvious distinction, for example, can be drawn between manic- and depressive-symptom profiles; but even within different instances of either mania or depression, different symptom profiles can occur at varying levels of intensity. Far more research attention has been directed to possible differing types of depression than mania, and some of the findings are discussed below.

Major Depression To a large extent, the diagnostic criteria for major depression involve merely more intense forms of the symptoms for dysthymia or the depressive phase of cyclothymia. An affected person may experience marked sadness of mood, fatigue, insomnia or hypersomnia (that is, too little or too much sleep), loss of interest in pleasurable activities, diminished cognitive capacity, and self-denunciation to the point of claiming worthlessness or guilt out of proportion to any past indiscretions. In addition, the person will often show a decreased appetite and significant weight loss (or, much more rarely, their opposites), a slow-down—or, less often, agitation—of mental and physical activity, and a preoccupation with death and suicide. A majority

Pulitzer Prize–winning novelist William Styron suffered an episode of depression so severe that it completely disrupted his life for about 9 months. He couldn't concentrate enough to write; couldn't sleep more than four hours a night; lost interest in eating and other activities he had previously found pleasurable, such as walks through the hills around his Connecticut home; believed his life was worthless; and thought about suicide—all symptoms of major depression. When his suicidal impulses became overwhelming, Styron agreed to enter a psychiatric hospital, where his recovery began. He has recounted his experiences in a book titled Darkness Visible. He likens the disorder to "unimaginable pain—not like the pain of a fractured limb, yet every bit as severe."

(at least five, including either sad mood or loss of pleasure response) of these symptoms must be present all day and nearly every day for two consecutive weeks before the diagnosis is applicable. Psychotic features, such as delusions, hallucinations, or depressive stupor (a mute and unresponsive state), may or may not accompany the other symptoms. Normally, any delusions or hallucinations present are mood-congruent; that is, they involve themes of personal inadequacy, guilt, deserved punishment, death, disease, and so forth. The following conversation between a therapist and a patient illustrates a major depression of moderate severity:

Therapist: *Good morning, how are you today?*
Patient: *(Pause) Well, okay I guess, doctor. . . . I don't know, I just feel sort of discouraged.*
Therapist: *Is there anything in particular that worries you?*
Patient: *I don't know, doctor . . . everything seems to be futile . . . nothing seems worthwhile any more. It seems as if all that was beautiful has lost its beauty. I guess I expected more than life has given. It just doesn't seem worthwhile going on. I can't seem to make up my mind about anything. I guess I have what you would call the "blues."*
Therapist: *Can you tell me more about your feelings?*
Patient: *Well . . . my family expected great things of me. I am supposed to be the outstanding member of the family . . . they think because I went through college everything should begin to pop and there's nothing to pop. I . . . really don't expect anything from anyone. Those whom I have trusted proved themselves less than friends should be.*
Therapist: *Oh?*
Patient: *Yes, I once had a very good girlfriend with whom I spent a good deal of time. She was very important to me. . . . I thought she was my friend but now she treats me like a casual acquaintance (tears).*
Therapist: *Can you think of any reason for this?*
Patient: *Yes, it's all my fault. I can't blame them—anybody that is. . . . I am not worthy of them. I have sinned against nature. I am worthless . . . nobody can love me. I don't deserve friends or success. . . .*
Therapist: *You sinned against nature?*
Patient: *Well . . . I am just no good. I am a failure. I was envious of other people. I didn't want them to have more than I had and when something bad happened to them I was glad. Now I am being repaid for my sins. All my flaws stand out and I am repugnant to everyone. (Sighs) I am a miserable failure. . . . There is no hope for me.*

For this patient, the most prominent clinical feature—aside from the general mood depression—is self-denunciation, which may have a certain cultural specificity, as we will see.

The most severe form of major depression is the *depressive stupor,* which is characterized by marked psychomotor underactivity. This disorder is illustrated in the following case:

The patient lay in bed, immobile, with a dull, depressed expression on his face. His eyes were sunken and downcast. Even when spoken to, he would not raise his eyes to look at the speaker. Usually he did not respond at all to questions, but sometimes, after apparently great effort, he would mumble something about the "scourge of God." He appeared somewhat ema-

ciated, his breath was foul, and he had to be given enemas to maintain elimination. Occasionally, with great effort, he made the sign of the cross with his right hand. The overall picture was one of extreme vegetative-like immobility and depression.

Two basic subcategories of major depression have been defined: (a) *single episode* (no previous episode of the disorder), and (b) *recurrent* (one or more previous episodes). The type descriptor *melancholic,* described below, may be applied to either. The diagnosis of major depression cannot be made if a patient has ever experienced a manic episode; in such a case, the current depression is viewed as a depressive episode of bipolar disorder. Accordingly, major depression is also known as **unipolar disorder.**

As was suggested earlier, there has been considerable interest recently in attempting to differentiate various types of depression—especially major depression—according to the particular symptom patterns displayed. Such efforts are driven mostly by the hope of discovering differentially effective treatment methods. Thus DSM-III-R requires a specification as to whether or not a major depression is of "melancholic" type. This designation is applied where (in addition to meeting the criteria for major depression) a patient complains of a loss of interest or pleasure in almost all activities, of early morning awakenings, and of increased bad feelings in the morning; shows no evidence of personality disturbance prior to the first major depressive episode; or has had a good response to antidepressant, biologically based therapies in any prior episodes. The chief theoretical importance of the melancholia concept is that it is strongly linked in the psychiatric literature to the idea of *endogenous* causation—that is, to the notion that certain depressions are caused "from within," so to speak, and are unrelated to any events that may currently be impacting a patient's life. We will have more to say about this idea in a later section.

Discriminating major depression from other forms of depressive disorder is not as easy as might be hoped. One complication here is the suggestion that major depression may coexist with dysthymia or other milder forms in some individuals, a condition given the designation "double depression" (Keller & Shapiro, 1982; Keller et al., 1983). The actual data here are more consistent with the notion that some people who are moderately depressed on a chronic basis undergo increased problems from time to time, during which they manifest "major" symptoms. Also, and perhaps contrary to what one might expect, a major depression is not necessarily a disorder of marked severity. DSM-III-R coding provides for diagnosing major depression where severe (that is, psychotic) features are not present and even—by use of the qualifying phrase *in remission*—where there are currently no notable symptoms at all. Tentatively, then, we doubt the validity of the notion of double depression.

It is plain, in any event, that the diagnostic term *major depression* does not necessarily refer to something observable in the current behavior of a diagnosed person, but possibly to some inferred behavior potential. In current practice, in fact, use of the term normally implies a biological defect or aberration that purportedly renders a person vulnerable to episodes of more or less severe depressive disorder. It is therefore possible to have a major depressive disorder with only mild current symptoms, provided a person has a history of past major depression. By contrast, severe symptoms are almost always considered outward manifestations of a "major" disorder. The concept of major depression is therefore quite problematic because it rests on a pattern of inferences that have been, in our judgment, insufficiently examined.

Overall, we remain unconvinced that there in fact exist several varieties of depression or of major depression representing distinct psychopathological entities. Such differentiation, when it can be accomplished on sound and meaningful grounds, is obviously desirable. We are far from certain, however, that we gain a great deal from the types of differentiations we are presently able to make, limited as they are to certain gross observations about the context, symptom pattern, and severity of the dysphoric mood state.

We think it is reasonable to suggest, for example, that psychological depression may best be conceived as analogous to fever in general medicine. Its occurrence tells us that something is wrong, and with extreme deviation that something is very wrong, but it does not in itself tell us *what* is wrong. Depression in mental dysfunction, like fever in physical dysfunction, is a common phenomenon with a high degree of co-occurrence across many more specifically defined syndromes. Like fever, it should always be taken seriously; but we know of no medical researcher who would advocate mounting a large-scale research effort to discriminate *types* of fever, as opposed to types of pathologic processes with which its occurrence may be associated. Though granting that it is often necessary to treat depression as a problem in and of itself, this is in fact also true of fever; the difference is that with fever we are never entirely satisfied until we have discovered and eradicated its source, whereas with depression we are encouraged to conclude that when it abates the "problem" is solved. If this analogy to fever has any validity, we should find that depression, when successfully treated in a purely symptomatic fashion (that is, without eradicating its cause), has a tendency to recur. Unfortunately, that is too often exactly what happens.

The proportion of patients exhibiting a recurrence of major depression is difficult to estimate reliably because of wide variations in the results of different studies. Coryell and Winokur (1982) tabulated data from the then-available work in this area and reported recurrence figures ranging from 39 to 95 percent of cases, averaging about 63 percent. In an epidemiologic, community-based study, 19.1 percent of subjects having major depression on initial contact were depressed when contacted a year later, whereas 62.2 percent were considered recovered—the remainder of the original sample having been lost. In addition, a history of prior depression predicted depression recurrence or continuance (Sargeant et al., 1990). Probably the best data we have on the question of recurrence has been published recently by Lewinsohn, Zeiss, and Duncan (1989). These investigators interviewed 2046 unipolar depressives concerning previous episodes. Of these subjects, 1130 (55%) reported at least one prior episode, and 173 (8%) reported as many as three. Again, the probability of relapse was a function of the number of prior episodes, and also of the severity of the current episode. Women showed a stronger pattern of recurrence than did men, echoing the gender-related incidence and prevalence figures for depressive disorder.

Different outcomes for depressive disorders also depend importantly on their particular manifestations and several other predictor variables (Gonzales, Lewinsohn, and Clarke, 1985). Despite the variable results from different studies, it is clear that the risk of having additional episodes of major depression is considerable for an individual experiencing a first one. The duration of a given episode is estimated, on average, to be about four months (Perris, 1982).

The traditional view has been that between episodes, a person suffering from a recurrent major mood disorder is essentially normal. This view has been increasingly called into question as more and better research data have become available (Coryell & Winokur, 1982). Indeed, given the frequently devastating effects such episodes have on a person's life circumstances, it would be surprising to find no lasting compromises in personal adjustment. Presumably, such compromises increase with successive episodes. In this connection, Akiskal and Simmons (1985) describe a chronic, residual type of low-grade depression affecting some 10 to 15 percent of people who recover from acute major depressive episodes.

The prospects for "complete recovery" (that is, no recurrence of an episode for a period of five years) from major depression are not particularly encouraging, probably being somewhere around 40 percent (Coryell & Winokur, 1982). As we learn more about managing depression, however, definite possibilities appear for limiting both the severity and the duration of attacks, and increasingly for preventing recurrences. For example, we now know that marital distress—especially as manifested in perceived criticism from the spouse—is a substantial predictor of short-term relapse (Hooley & Teasdale, 1989), and it should prove possible to fashion intervention techniques that lessen the impact of such risk factors.

Bipolar Disorder As we have seen, depression and mania—despite their seeming opposition—are sometimes closely related. Cyclothymia, described earlier, is a case in point, but a far more dramatic example is the full bipolar syndrome. The sixth-century physician Alexander Trallianus may have been the first to recognize recurrent cycles of mania and melancholia in the same person, thus anticipating by several hundred years Bonet's (1684) "folie mania mélancolique" and Falret's (1854) "folie circulaire." It remained for Kraepelin, however, in 1899, to introduce the term manic-depressive psychosis and to clarify the clinical picture. Kraepelin described the disorder as a series of attacks of elation and depression, with periods of relative normality in between and a generally favorable prognosis.

Bipolar disorder is distinguished from major depression by at least one episode of mania; it is classified as depressive, manic, or mixed, according to the predominant pattern. Even though a patient is exhibiting only manic features, it is assumed that in fact a bipolar disorder exists. Substantial manic or mixed patterns are much less common than the depressive pattern.

The features of the depressive form of bipolar disorder are clinically indistinguishable from those of major depression (Perris, 1982), and we will therefore not describe them in detail here. The essential difference is that these depressive episodes alternate with manic ones, either closely or separated by intervals of relatively normal functioning.

As in the case of the relationship between depressive symptoms of major depression and of cyclothymia, manic symptoms in bipolar disorder tend to be extreme forms of the symptoms associated with the hypomanic phase of cyclothymia. A person who experiences a manic episode has a markedly elevated, euphoric, and expansive mood, often interrupted by occasional outbursts of irritability or even violence—particularly when others refuse to go along with the manic person's antics and schemes. A notable increase in activity occurs, which may appear as an unrelievable restlessness. Mental activity, too, speeds up, so that the individual may evidence a "flight of ideas" and may experience thoughts that "race" through the brain. High levels of verbal output in speech or in writing are common features. Inflated self-esteem is a constant element and at the severe level becomes frankly delusional, so that the person harbors feelings of enormous grandeur and power. The person sleeps only briefly, and in extreme cases hardly at all. Typically, personal and cultural inhibitions loosen, and the individual may indulge in foolish ventures, ignore personal hygiene, make crude and inappropriate sexual advances, or otherwise indicate contempt for conventional restraints and standards of conduct.

The following conversation illustrates a manic episode of moderate severity. The patient is a 46-year-old woman.

Doctor: *Hello, how are you today?*
Patient: *Fine, fine, and how are you, Doc? You're looking pretty good. I never felt better in my life. Could I go for a schnapps now. Say, you're new around here, I never saw you before—and not bad! How's about you and me stepping out tonight if I can get that sour old battleship of a nurse to give me back my dress. It's low cut and it'll wow 'em. Even in this old rag, all the doctors give me the eye. You know I'm a model. Yep, I was number one—used to dazzle them in New York, London, and Paris. Hollywood has been angling with me for a contract.*
Doctor: *Is that what you did before you came here?*
Patient: *I was a society queen . . . entertainer of kings and presidents. I've got five grown sons and I wore out three husbands getting them . . . about ready for a couple of more now. There's no woman like me, smart, brainy, beautiful, and sexy. You can see I don't believe in playing myself down. If you are good and know you're good you have to speak out, and I know what I've got.*
Doctor: *Why are you in this hospital?*
Patient: *That's just the trouble. My husbands never could understand me. I was too far above them. I need someone like me with savoir faire you know, somebody that can get around, intelligent, lots on the ball. Say, where can I get a schnapps around here—always like one before dinner. Someday I'll cook you a meal. I've got special recipes like you never ate before . . . sauces, wines, desserts. Boy, it's making me hungry. Say, have you got anything for me to do around here? I've been showing these slowpokes how to make up beds but I want something more in line with my talents.*
Doctor: *What would you like to do?*
Patient: *Well, I'm thinking of organizing a show, singing, dancing, jokes. I can do it all myself but I want to know what you think about it. I'll bet there's some schnapps in the kitchen. I'll look around later. You know what we need here . . . a dance at night. I could play the piano, and teach them the latest steps. Wherever I go I'm the life of the party.*

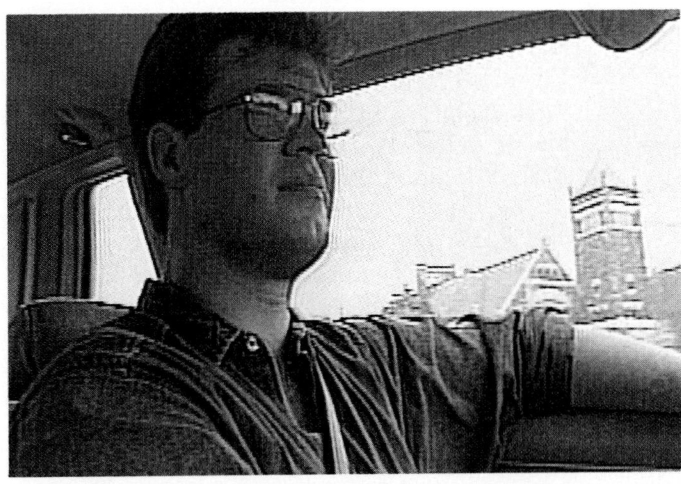

During a manic episode, Rodney, shown here, drove his car 120 miles per hour, hit two cars, crashed, stripped off his clothes, and began preaching to passing traffic, thinking he was Christ. He now controls his bipolar disorder with lithium and group therapy.

This case is particularly illustrative of the inflated self-esteem characteristic of a manic individual. The erotic suggestiveness and impatience with routine seen here are also common features of manic episodes.

The following case description is interesting in its simultaneous and interactive portrayal of two manic patients, one severely disturbed and the other less so. The former, in particular, provides an illustration of the extreme excitement that can occur during a manic episode. The scene is the courtyard of a public mental hospital in the days prior to the advent of effective antimanic medication.

A manic patient had climbed upon the small platform in the middle of the yard and was delivering an impassioned lecture to a number of patients sitting on benches surrounding the platform. Most of the audience were depressed patients who were hallucinating and muttering to themselves and not paying a bit of attention to the speaker. The speaker, however, had an "assistant" in the form of another manic patient who would move rapidly around the circle of benches shaking the occupants and exhorting them to pay attention. If anyone started to leave, the assistant would plump him or her back in a seat in no uncertain terms. In the background were a number of apparently schizophrenic patients who were pacing a given number of steps back and forth, and beyond was a high wire fence surrounding the yard.

The speaker herself was in a state of delirious mania. She had torn her clothing to shreds and was singing and shouting at the top of her voice. So rapidly did her thoughts move from one topic to another that her "speech" was almost a complete word hash, although occasional sentences such as "You goddamn bitches" and "God loves everybody, do you hear?" could be made out. These points were illustrated by wild gestures, screaming, and outbursts of song. In the delivery of her talk, she moved restlessly back and forth on the platform, occasionally falling off the platform in her wild excitement. Her ankles and legs were bleeding from rubbing the edge of the platform during these falls, but she was completely oblivious of her injuries.

Fortunately, the degree of excitement in manic disorders can now be markedly reduced by various drugs, and scenes such as this need no longer occur. The typical stages in a manic episode are summarized in *HIGHLIGHT 11.2.*

Bipolar disorder, like major depression, is typically an intermittent or episodic phenomenon, although with both forms of disorder a relatively small number of patients who otherwise meet diagnostic criteria remain disturbed over long periods of time, even years, and sometimes despite the successive application of all the standard treatment techniques. It is not known whether or not these "refractory" cases represent fundamentally different psychopathological entities (Akiskal & Simmons, 1985).

The diagnostic subcategories for bipolar disorder—mixed, manic, and depressed—refer to particular, present episodes. The latter two of these are self-explanatory; the "mixed" is something of an anomaly. Mixed cases are those in which the full symptomatic picture of both manic and depressive episodes occur, either intermixed or alternating every few days. Such cases do indeed occur, although they are rare.

As we have seen, a person who appears to be depressed cannot be diagnosed as bipolar unless he or she has exhibited at least one manic episode in the past. This means that many people with bipolar disorder whose initial episode or episodes are depressive in nature will be misdiagnosed, at least at the outset and possibly (if no manic episodes are observed) throughout their lives. On the other hand, misdiagnosis is automatically prevented if a person presents distinctly manic symptoms: by DSM-III-R definition, this would be a bipolar disorder, even though some researchers have noted the probable existence of a unipolar type of manic disorder (Andreasen, 1982; Nurnberger et al., 1979). The sometimes arbitrary nature of diagnosis is quite clear in this instance.

People affected with a bipolar disorder seem in many ways to be even more unfortunate than those who suffer from recurrent major depression. On average, they have their first episode at a younger age (25–30 versus 40–45); they suffer from more episodes during their lifetimes (although these episodes tend to be about a month shorter in duration); and they have a substantially higher mortality rate from suicide and other "unnatural" causes (Perris, 1982). The long-term outcomes for the two forms of disorder, however, do not appear to differ greatly, and the probabilities of "full recovery" (that is, being symptom-free for a period of five years) are about equally discouraging—about 40 percent (Coryell & Winokur, 1982). In one recent follow-up study of 73 hospitalized manic patients, 40 percent of them had experienced another manic episode within 1.7 years after discharge, many of them in spite of maintenance lithium therapy (Harrow et al., 1990).

In contrast to the gender neutrality of most types of maladaptive behavior, mood disorders at all levels of severity are more prevalent among women than among men, at a ratio approaching two-to-one overall (Wing & Bebbington, 1985). Though this gender discrepancy is quite marked in the case of major depression, it is less but still discernible for bipolar disorder (Boyd & Weissman, 1982). The diminished discrepancy in bipolar disorder may be related to an apparent tendency for specifically manic episodes to occur less frequently in females (Angst, 1980).

In any event, the finding of a sex differential may have considerable theoretical importance. At

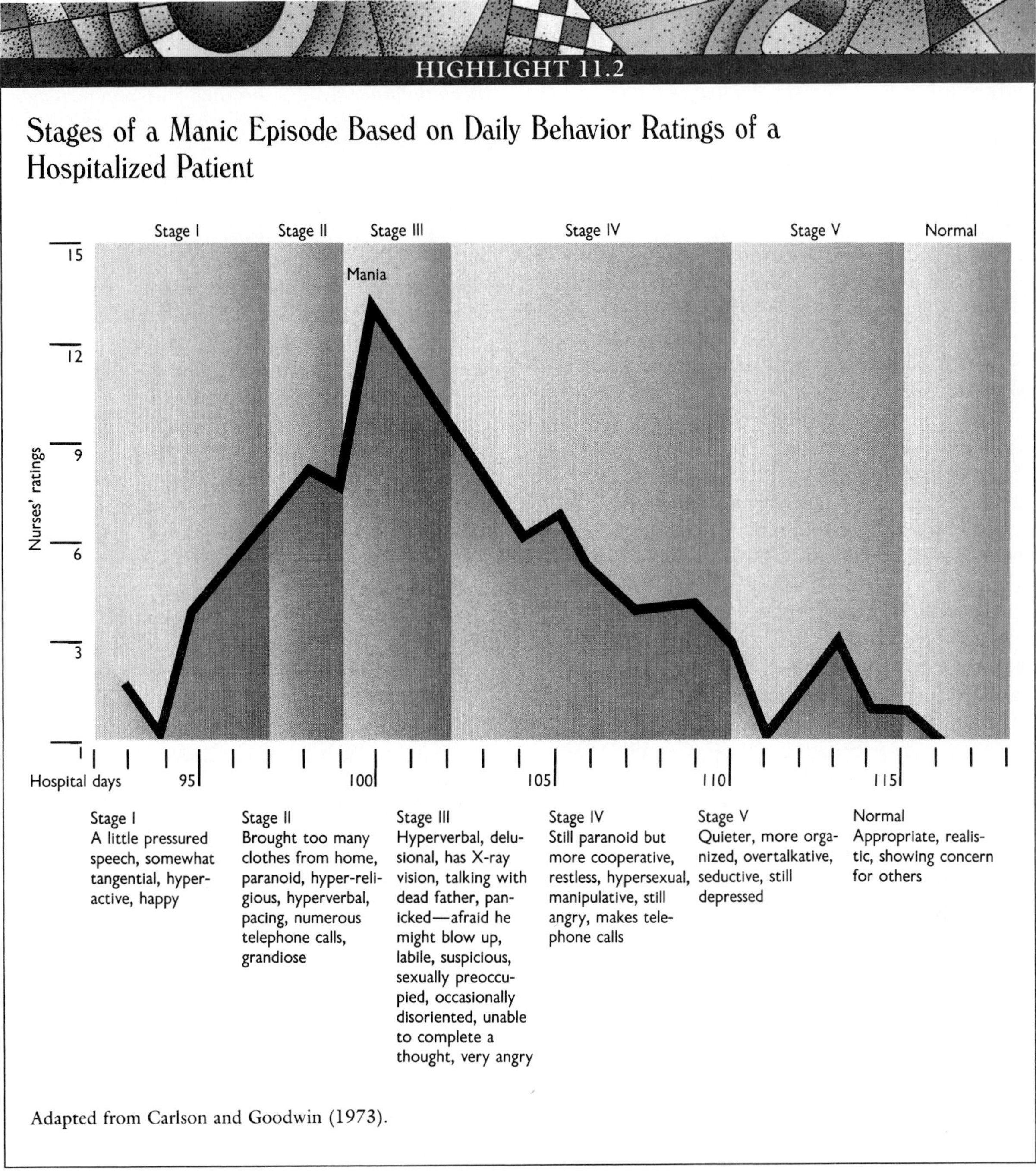
HIGHLIGHT 11.2
Stage I
Stage II
Stage III
Stage IV
Stage V
Normal
Mania
Nurses' ratings
15
12
9
6
3
Hospital days
95
100
105
110
115
Stage I
A little pressured speech, somewhat tangential, hyperactive, happy
Stage II
Brought too many clothes from home, paranoid, hyper-religious, hyperverbal, pacing, numerous telephone calls, grandiose
Stage III
Hyperverbal, delusional, has X-ray vision, talking with dead father, panicked—afraid he might blow up, labile, suspicious, sexually preoccupied, occasionally disoriented, unable to complete a thought, very angry
Stage IV
Still paranoid but more cooperative, restless, hypersexual, manipulative, still angry, makes telephone calls
Stage V
Quieter, more organized, overtalkative, seductive, still depressed
Normal
Appropriate, realistic, showing concern for others

Stages of a Manic Episode Based on Daily Behavior Ratings of a Hospitalized Patient

Adapted from Carlson and Goodwin (1973).

least with respect to unipolar depression, the discrepancy appears to be neither artifactual nor a product of differential psychosocial advantage for men versus women (Amenson & Lewinsohn, 1981; Nolen-Hoeksema, 1987). Though women, especially married ones, frequently report a greater sense of well-being than men (Wood, Rhodes, & Whelan, 1989), they are also for some reason much more prone to experience repeated depressive attacks. It appears that women have more extreme reactions at both ends of this continuum than do men. In fact being unmarried, employed, and without young children at home are factors that may *reduce* female risk for depression (Wing & Bebbington, 1985). The latter factors would seem to implicate the traditional feminine gender role as possibly pathogenic for depression. This gender role may also contribute to a tendency to ruminate about problems rather than to find ways of distracting oneself from them, as males are more prone to do. The former mode of coping tends to encourage depressive reactions and to be far more common in women than in men (Morrow & Nolen-Hoeksema, 1990; Nolen-Hoeksema, 1987). Although this line of thought is intriguing and consistent with much evidence, we cannot rule out a biological contribution at this time; neither, however, can we positively confirm it.

Schizoaffective Disorder Occasionally, clinicians are confronted with a patient whose mood disorder is the equal of anything seen in the major depressive or bipolar disorders but whose mental and cognitive processes are so deranged as to suggest the presence of a *schizophrenic* psychosis (see Chapter 12). Such cases are quite likely to be diagnosed as **schizoaffective disorder** under the DSM-III-R category of *psychotic disorders not elsewhere classified.*

The often severe disturbances of psychological functioning seen in these cases, such as mood-incongruent delusions and hallucinations, are indeed reminiscent of schizophrenic phenomena. Unlike schizophrenia, however, the schizoaffective pattern tends to be highly episodic, with a good prognosis for individual attacks and with relatively lucid periods between episodes. The traditional view has also been that schizoaffective patients have a relatively good prognosis for full recovery under the five-year criterion. Recently published follow-up data on these patients, however, cast considerable doubt on such a benign outlook (Coryell et al., 1990a, 1990b). The following case illustrates the mixed picture one sees in this type of disorder:

The patient, Mr. Nehru, is a 32-year-old single, unemployed male who is hospitalized for the fourth time in approximately five years, each episode having had essentially the same features. On interview he is markedly euphoric in mood and his speech is so rapid it is hard to follow. He does much pacing on the hospital ward, where he appears preoccupied with certain religious insights involving the idea that he is the new Messiah—in fact some sort of combination of Jesus, Moses, Vishnu, and Krishna. "Voices" repeatedly confirm to him this extraordinary new identity. His attempts to explain the new religion to others are interrupted by irrelevant distractions that momentarily capture his attention, such as the color match of a doctor's shirt and tie. When limits are placed on his excessively enthusiastic and intrusive behavior, he becomes loud and angry. He states that the hospital is part of a conspiracy to suppress his promulgation of the new religious order, which God has directly inspired him to do.

A native of India, Mr. Nehru migrated to the United States at the age of 13. Recently he had been living with his brother and sister-in-law, who report that his behavior had begun to deteriorate some four weeks prior to hospitalization. Specifically, he was waking up his brother at all hours of the night to discuss religious matters, and he had stopped bathing or changing his clothes. His rehospitalization was precipitated when neighbors complained that he was harassing them in the street with his religious messages.

Mr. Nehru admits that he has been troubled by voices, which he has been hearing throughout the day almost continuously for about five years. Several different voices comment, generally without evaluation, on his ongoing behavior, discussing him in the third person. On occasion they have become insulting, suggesting that he is a fool or a person of limited understanding. The patient states that he is unable to work at a regular job because the voices distract him and prevent him from concentrating on the work to be done. He thus appears to be significantly dysfunctional even in the interludes between his more flagrant episodes.

Between these episodes the patient is described by others as a quiet and somewhat withdrawn person with no remarkable mood deviations. While he reads occasionally, he rarely watches television because of a conviction that television programs often make direct reference to him and his affairs; these references upset him. He is popular in the neighborhood because of his habit of offering help to elderly people in such matters as shopping and yard work.

(Adapted from Spitzer et al., 1989, pp. 64–65)

Mr. Nehru's case actually has an interesting diagnostic twist. Between episodes he meets DSM criteria for schizophrenia, chiefly because of his prominent nonmood-related hallucinations. Within episodes, on the other hand, he consistently presents a classically manic picture that would yield an unqualified diagnosis of bipolar disorder were his interepisode behavior unremarkable or unknown.

As the common diagnostic perplexities of the above case may suggest, the diagnosis of schizoaffective disorder is a controversial one. Some clinicians believe these individuals are basically schizophrenic; others believe they are suffering primarily from mood disorder psychoses; and still others consider their affliction a distinct entity unto itself (Lehmann, 1985). The suggestion that a person might be both schizophrenic and mood disordered concurrently is not generally accepted, apparently owing to the belief that reliability of diagnosis will suffer without sharp discriminations among Axis I disorders. Of course, by attempting to ensure reliability here, we may well be sacrificing validity. It does not strike us as unreasonable to suppose that the co-occurrence of two or more psychiatric disorders is in fact a rather common phenomenon.

Causal Factors in Mood Disorders

In considering the development of major mood disorders, we again find it useful to examine the possible roles of biological, psychosocial, and sociocultural factors.

Biological Factors A biological basis for severe manic and depressive disorders is suggested by the fact that, once a disorder is underway, it often seems to become relatively autonomous until it runs its course or is interrupted by drugs or other interventions. Attempts to establish a biological basis for these disorders have run the familiar gamut from genetic and constitutional factors through neurophysiological and biochemical alterations. Even various related considerations, such as disturbances in the normal cycles of brain activity during sleep or the seasonal variations in ambient light and darkness, have been implicated.

Hereditary predisposition. The incidence of mood disorders is considerably higher among the blood relatives of individuals with clinically diagnosed mood disorders than in the population at large. Because of the difficulties of disentangling hereditary and environmental influences, however, mere familial concordance can never in itself be taken as conclusive proof of genetic causation. In an early study, Slater (1944) found that approximately 15 percent of the brothers, sisters, parents, and children of "manic-depressive" patients had developed the same disorder, as compared to an expectancy of about 0.5 percent for the general population.

Kallmann (1958) found the concordance rate for these disorders to be much higher for identical than for fraternal twins. Other studies have supported these earlier findings (Mendlewicz, 1985; Perris, 1979).

Twin-based studies such as those just cited have proven useful in many areas of psychological research. Various difficulties with the twin method, however, make it problematic to draw reliable conclusions from them about genetic factors. Among the most basic problems is the fact that identical twins (because they are of the same gender and share similar physical characteristics and appearances, such as physical attractiveness) are likely to *create* more similar environmental reactions to themselves than are fraternal twins or people having any other type of familial relationship. Hence high concordance in psychopathological outcome could as much reflect environmental as genetic commonalities.

Recognition of the inherent problems of twin-based studies led a number of years ago to the *adoption method* of genetic research. This method involves the psychiatric evaluation of people who were adopted out of their biological families at an early age and the comparison of their disorders with those of their biological and adoptive family members. If a predisposition to develop a given disorder is inheritable, it should show up (so the logic goes) more often among biological, as opposed to adoptive, relatives of the affected adoptees.

Of the limited number of adoption studies on mood disorders published thus far, the most adequate is one contributed by Wender et al. (1986). Beginning with Danish samples of 71 mood-disordered subjects and 71 matched normal control adoptees, the close biological and adoptive relatives of these individuals were independently assessed for psychiatric status. With respect to major mood disorders (that is, major depression and bipolar disorder), unipolar depression was eight times more likely to occur among the biological relatives of the depressed subjects as compared with control cases; suicide was fifteen times more likely among biological relatives. By any standard, these are impressive figures.

Based on statistics like these, the case for some hereditary contribution in the causal patterns of at least the major mood disorders is quite strong. The risk for blood relatives of people with bipolar disorders (including an enhanced risk for unipolar disorder) appears to be greater than for relatives of people who suffer from unipolar disorders (Mendlewicz, 1985), but this may merely reflect the likelihood that unipolar disorder is a more diffuse and heterogeneous category (Carson & Carson, 1984). Some researchers have suggested a genetic connection between mood and anxiety disorders, especially agoraphobia and panic disorder (Breier, Charney, & Heninger, 1984; Weissman et al., 1984). A relationship may indeed exist here with the finding that panic attacks are sometimes successfully treated with antidepressant drugs (Stewart et al., 1985).

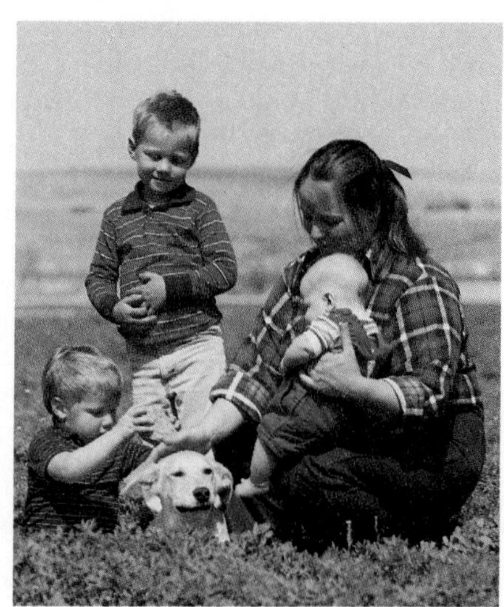

The incidence of mood disorders is considerably higher among the blood relatives of individuals with clinically diagnosed mood disorders than in the population at large. This family has a history of bipolar disorder spanning four generations, from a woman to her daughter, granddaughter, and a great-grandson, who was diagnosed at only three years of age.

The disproportionately high number of female cases of mood disorder has been cited by some as evidence for genetic predisposition. On the basis of findings indicating higher concordance among female than male members of families, Winokur, Clayton, and Reich (1969) proposed that the gene or genes in question might be located on the X chromosome. If this were universally true, there would be no evidence of father-to-son transmission, because the X chromosome in males can only be inherited from the mother. The investigators in this early study found precisely this anomaly. Since then, however, numerous cases of apparent father-to-son transmission have been reported. The overall picture, reviewed by Nurnberger and Gershon (1982), has thus become somewhat murky and includes at least one confirmation of the Winokur et al. father-son anomaly (Mendlewicz, 1980, 1985). As of this writing, the question remains unresolved.

Finally, we should mention recent work on genetic linkage studies and attempts by gene mapping techniques to locate the chromosomal site of the purportedly implicated gene or genes. One such study, which was widely reported in the popular press several years ago, presented what appeared to be compelling evidence for genetic transmission of a bipolar disorder diathesis. The population involved was the tightly knit Amish community of Lancaster County in southern Pennsylvania (Egeland et al., 1987). Identifying 32 active cases of bipolar disorder in this community of 12,500 members, all of them descendants of a small number of couples immigrating to the area in the early eighteenth century, the investigators were able to document, for *every* case, instances of the disorder in ancestors going back several generations. The 26 documented cases of suicide occurring since 1880 were all traced to just *four* families. Perhaps most importantly, the gene involved was traced to a specific region on chromosome 11, using rather complicated recombinant DNA techniques. Some 63 percent of individuals carrying this gene were said to show at least minimal signs of the disorder.

Reactions to the publication of this study constitute a veritable case history in the premature acceptance of preliminary scientific findings. In fact two other studies (Detera-Wadleigh et al., 1987; Hodkinson et al., 1987) published in the same issue of the same journal in which the Egeland et al. (1987) study was published presented data contradicting the notion of a single gene locus for bipolar disorder. These discrepant studies were almost uniformly ignored at the time by both the media and numerous professional commentators. In any event, it is now clear that daunting methodological problems must be overcome before we can look forward to the effective use of genetic linkage studies to identify specific genes for bipolar disorder, or indeed *any* of the mood disorders (Merikangas, Spence, & Kupfer, 1989). Most importantly, linkage studies are highly dependent on the existence of homogeneous diagnostic groupings. Of the various mood disorders, bipolar disorder is doubtless the best candidate for study in this respect; unfortunately, the precision with which it can at present be delineated appears to fall short of the requirements of this approach.

Overall, no consistent support exists for any specific mode of genetic transmission of the mood disorders, according to a recent comprehensive review by Faraone, Kremen, and Tsuang (1990). These authors do note, however, the continuing possibility of an X-chromosome-linked variant of bipolar disorder.

Biochemical factors. Kraepelin considered manic-depressive psychoses to be toxic, and a good deal of research effort has been directed toward finding possible metabolic alterations and pathologic brain chemistry in individuals with these disorders. Increasingly prominent since the 1960s has been the view that depression and mania both may arise from disruptions in the delicate balance of biochemical substances that regulate and mediate the activity of the brain's nerve cells, or neurons. Certain of these substances, called ***neurotransmitters,*** mediate the transfer of nerve impulses across the synaptic cleft from one neuron to the next one in a particular neuronal pathway. Emitted by the activated presynaptic neuron, neurotransmitters may either stimulate or inhibit the firing of the next neuron in the chain.

A growing body of evidence suggests that various biological therapies often used to treat severe mood disorders—such as electroconvulsive therapy, potent antidepressant drugs, and lithium carbonate—may affect the concentrations of transmitter substances at the synapse and thus determine the extent to which particular brain pathways are relatively volatile or sluggish in conducting messages. In fact the largely happenstance discovery of these treatments (particularly the antidepressant drugs) and the growing understanding of how they work are what encouraged and now sustain the dominant biochemical conceptions of the etiology of the major mood disorders. They are due, according to this general view, to faulty communication between neurons, caused by disruption of the transmission process.

A bit of history is in order here. Early attention in the 1960s and 1970s focused on two substances of the monoamine class, ***norepinephrine*** and ***5-hydroxytryptamine*** (also known as serotonin), because researchers observed that antidepressant medication had the uniform effect of increasing their concentrations at synaptic junctions. This observation led to the theory that depression was due to a depletion and mania to an excess of one or both of these neurotransmitters. It is now clear, based on the known complexity of brain biochemical functioning, that no such straightforward mechanism is likely to provide the answers we need (Thase, Frank, & Kupfer, 1985; Zis & Goodwin, 1982). Unfortunately, the demise of this theory has not been accompanied by the introduction of a compelling alternative. Recently, research attention in this area has been shifting to a concern with possibly abnormal receptor systems (that is, the large molecules on a postsynaptic neuron to which neurotransmitters bearing the appropriate chemical codes selectively bond) in the major mood disorders (McNeal & Cimbolic, 1986; Sedvall et al., 1986). The yield from such studies, however, as yet provides no firm etiological conclusions.

Though biochemical approaches have not thus far established the case for a primary biological role in the causation of major mood disorders, as many had hoped, biological causation in general remains a viable hypothesis. The case rests essentially on three facts that are beyond reasonable dispute: (a) a predisposition to these disorders may be genetically transmitted; (b) the behavioral symptoms of the disorders often abate promptly with certain biological interventions; and (c) certain profound alterations of bodily function, such as changes in the sleep cycle, often accompany the affective symptoms.

Neurophysiologic and neuroendocrine factors. A collateral goal of biochemical researchers has been to identify subtypes of mood disorder within this heterogeneous domain by establishing differences in treatment effectiveness for different drugs having known effects on various biological systems (e.g., Akiskal, 1979). The success of this line of investigation has so far not been especially impressive. To an extent in fact it has even been overshadowed by developments in other areas of biological research, notably the possible neurophysiologic and neuroendocrine (hormonal) correlates of some distinguishable forms of mood disorder (Thase, Frank, & Kupfer, 1985). For example, it is now clear that some depressed people show disturbances in their electroencephalographic (brain-wave) sleep rhythms, especially in an abnormally brief delay in onset of REM sleep (sleep characterized by rapid eye movements, as well as other organismic changes).

These findings on electroencephalographic indicators of sleep irregularities may be related to a growing body of evidence that some mood disorders are to an extent under seasonal control—that is, that they are responsive to the total quantity of available light in the environment (Rosenthal et al., 1984). More specifically, these individuals, said to have ***seasonal affective disorder*** (SAD), tend to be depressed in the fall and winter and normal or even hypomanic in the spring and summer (Wehr et al.,

1986). The DSM-III-R acknowledges such seasonal effects by requiring the designation *seasonal pattern,* where appropriate, as a supplement to the diagnosis of bipolar disorder or recurrent major depression. No specification of particular seasons need be involved, however; this appears to have been a wise omission, because it is now known that a minority of SAD patients are reactive to summer rather than winter conditions (Kasper et al., 1989; Wehr & Rosenthal, 1989), a fact that complicates etiologic speculation.

Studies evaluating the potential therapeutic use of controlled exposure to light, even artificial light, for patients with a winter SAD pattern have shown considerable promise (Blehar & Rosenthal, 1989; James et al., 1985; Rosenthal et al., 1984, 1986; Sack et al., 1990; Wehr et al., 1986). In fact a small industry has already developed around the production and sale of therapeutic lighting devices. Though the phenomenon appears genuine and reliable, just how therapeutic light works remains shrouded in controversy (Blehar & Rosenthal, 1989).

With the modern technology of positron emission tomography (PET) scans, it has even proven possible to visualize an anticipated variation in brain metabolic rates, subnormal to supernormal, for depressed and manic states, respectively (Baxter et al., 1985). Findings in this physiological area tend to be scattered, however, and have not yet yielded a coherent conceptual integration or meaning.

Ideas about hormonal influences on mood have a long history. Contemporary thinking (e.g., Stokes & Sikes, 1987) in this area has focused on the hypothalamus-pituitary-adrenocortical influence chain, and in particular on the hormone *cortisol,* which is excreted by the cortex (covering mantle) of the adrenal glands. Blood plasma levels of this substance are known to be elevated in from 50 to 75 percent of seriously depressed patients, suggesting a possible clue of etiological significance. Even more intriguing, however, is the finding that a potent suppressor of plasma cortisol in normal individuals, *dexamethasone,* either fails entirely to suppress or fails to sustain suppression in one- to two-thirds of seriously depressed patients.

These findings, in themselves essentially undisputed, have given rise to the widespread use of the dexamethasone suppression test (DST) in assessing depressed individuals. From this point, however, the issues become murkier. It has been suggested that DST nonsuppressor patients constitute a distinct subgroup among depressed individuals, namely the group sometimes referred to as having the "endogenous" or melancholic form of depression (Carroll, 1982; Kalin et al., 1981). Considerable evidence shows that nonsuppression is in fact correlated with clinical severity and retarded response to treatment (Arana, Baldessarini, & Ornsteen 1985). Also, depressed nonsuppressor patients tend to be older, have better premorbid histories, and have been subject to fewer prior stressors of the more obvious sort than those who show suppression (Zimmerman, Coryell, & Pfohl, 1986). As reviewed by Thase et al. (1985), however, numerous other groups of psychiatric patients exhibit high rates of nonsuppression, calling into question the specificity and hence ultimate diagnostic utility of the DST.

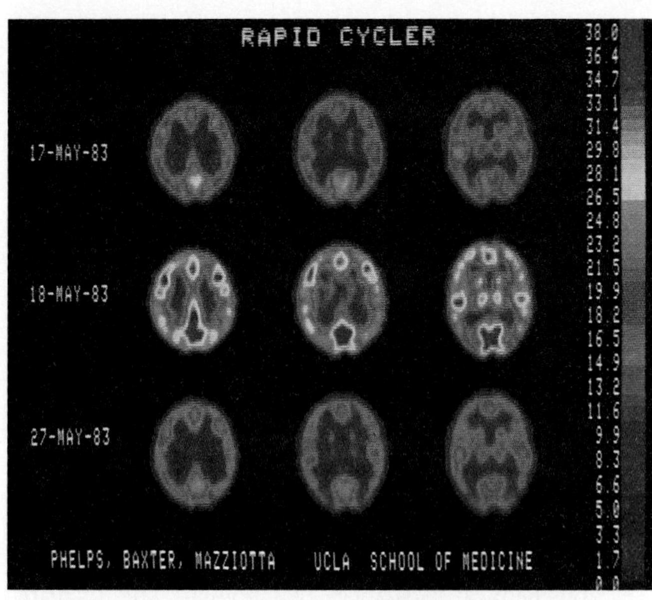

Shown here are positron emission tomographic (PET) scans of identical planes of the brain of a rapid-cycling bipolar patient. The top and bottom sets of planes were obtained on days in which the patient was depressed; the middle set was obtained on a hypomaniac day. Colors of scans correspond to glucose (sugar) metabolic rates in the respective brain areas, the reds and yellows representing high rates and the blues and greens lows.

The accuracy, reliability, and validity of the DST are subject to numerous variables that are difficult to control. Ritchie et al. (1985), for example, suggested that many of the conflicting results reported may be traced to poor assessment techniques for estimating plasma cortisol levels. Meanwhile, other reports (e.g., Uhde, Bierer, & Post, 1985) show that cortisol nonsuppression may be due to excessive coffee consumption. It is also possible that nonsuppression is merely a nonspecific indicator of generalized mental distress, an idea supported by the finding that it occurs somewhat routinely in baboons who are socially subordinate (Sapolsky, 1989). As of this writing, the jury is still out on the question of the DST's ultimate value, particularly as it relates to the question of etiology. In their comprehensive review, Arana et al. (1985) cautioned against either excessive enthusiasm or excessive skepticism regarding this line of research. Though this still seems good advice, enthusiasm for the hypothesis has in fact diminished appreciably in the interim.

Psychosocial Factors Growing awareness of biological factors in the etiology of affective disorders does not, of course, imply that psychosocial factors are irrelevant. In Chapter 4, we outlined various ways in which biological influences may interact with life experience to produce an observed behavior. In the present case, evidence for an important psychological element in most mood disorders is at least as strong as evidence for biological factors. Most likely, then, we are dealing with a complex interaction between the two.

Stress as a causal factor. In Chapter 7, we learned something of the ways in which psychosocial stressors may lead to altered bodily functioning. We are now in a position to suggest that such stressors may also affect biochemical balances and other conditions in the brain, at least in predisposed people.

Barchas and his colleagues (1978), in a summary of research in this area, suggest that psychosocial stressors may cause long-term changes in brain functioning and that these changes may play a role in the development of mood disorders. Essentially the same point has been made by other leading researchers in the field, notably Akiskal (1979) and Kupfer (Thase, Frank, & Kupfer, 1985).

There is no basic incompatibility between biochemical and psychosocial approaches to understanding the mood disorders. In fact, evidence of interactions between biological and psychosocial factors of the kind described here represent a breakthrough of enormous importance in enhancing our understanding of the age-old problem of mind-body interaction. At the same time, this evidence should not blind us to the probability that in some mood disturbances—certainly the milder ones—the contribution of an abnormal biological factor will turn out to be minimal or nonexistent. Pertinent here is the fact that the biological forms of treatment are typically of no value in such conditions. We have also seen that the milder depressions almost always have clear stressor antecedents; the occurrence of depression following significant losses, for instance, would seem understandable on psychological grounds alone—without the postulation of extraordinary changes in the brain's physical state.

In the case of the more severe mood disorders, too, many investigators, as already noted, have been impressed with the high incidence of aversive life events that apparently serve as precipitating factors. Harder et al. (1989) in fact found no difference between more and less severely depressed patients in regard to the magnitude of prior life stressors. Beck (1967) provided a broad classification of the most frequently encountered precipitating circumstances in depression: (a) situations that tend to lower self-esteem; (b) the thwarting of an important goal or the posing of an insoluble dilemma; (c) a physical disease or abnormality that activates ideas of deterioration or death; (d) single stressors of overwhelming magnitude; (e) several stressors occurring in a series; and (f) insidious stressors unrecognized as such by an affected person.

Paykel (1982b) comprehensively reviewed the earlier literature on life events occurring before episodes of mood disorder and arrived at conclusions generally in agreement with Beck's. In particular, and perhaps not surprisingly, separations from people important in one's life (through death, for example) are strongly associated with the emergence of depressive states, although such losses tend to precede other types of disorder as well. A more recent study by Phifer & Murrell (1986) involving older people (ages 55 and over) confirmed that loss events were associated with the onset of depression but pointed to health problems and minimal sources of social support as having even greater depression-inducing effects in this group.

It may be noted in connection with the last-mentioned finding that the nature of depression-inducing stressors is likely to change over a lifetime, conforming with changing levels of exposure to them and with changing beliefs as to which interests and concerns are more and less vital. Stressors are also likely to differ within age ranges depending on values, needs, personality characteristics, and the like. Hammen et al. (1989), for example, showed that "autonomous" unipolar depressives were more reactive to negative events involving issues of achievement, whereas their more "sociotropic" counterparts reacted mostly to negative events in their relationships with others.

Research data on life events preceding specifically manic attacks are contradictory and inconclusive (Dunner & Hall, 1980). *HIGHLIGHT 11.3*

HIGHLIGHT 11.3

Stressors Preceding Severe Depression

In an intensive study of 40 depressed patients, Leff, Roatch, and Bunney (1970) found that each patient had been subjected to multiple stressful events prior to early symptoms and to a clustering of such events during the month preceding the actual breakdown in functioning. The chart shows the ten types of stressors most frequently involved.

Strikingly similar to the findings of Leff and her associates are those of Paykel (1973). In this study, which involved 185 depressed patients, it was found that comparable stressful events preceded the onset of the depressive breakdown. In order of significance, these events were categorized as (a) marital difficulties, (b) work moves or changes in work conditions, (c) serious personal illness, and (d) death or serious illness of an immediate family member. Paykel's (1982) more recent review of findings in this area is generally confirmatory.

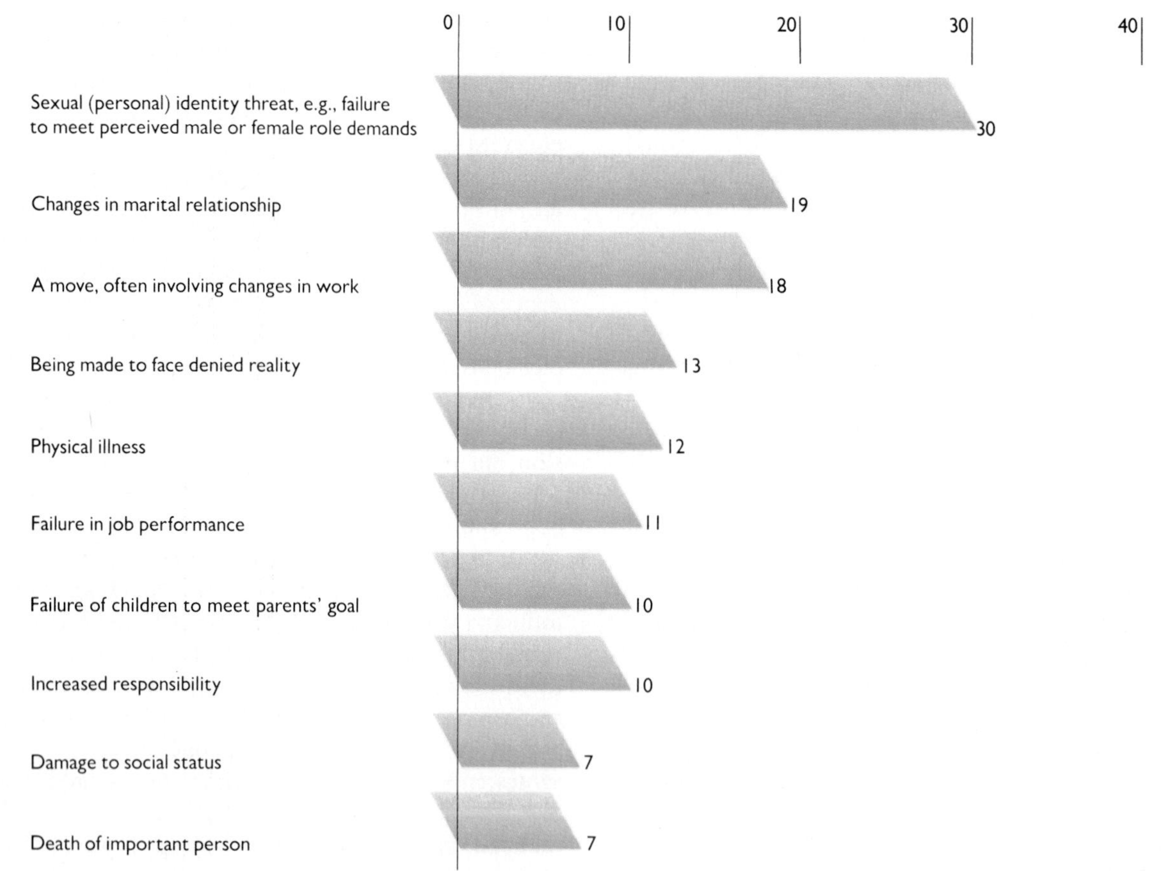

summarizes the stressors that had most often preceded severe depression in one study. An interesting example of the apparent role of aversive life events as precipitating causes in alternating bipolar attacks has been described by Hartmann (1968):

A patient had six severe manic episodes between the ages of 44 and 59, all of which required hospitalization. The patient also had a number of depressive episodes, two of which required hospitalization. Typically this patient tended to be overactive in his general functioning, but during the early autumn he usually either ran for a political office himself or took an active role in someone else's campaign. In the process, he would become increasingly manic; when the ventures led to defeat—which they almost invariably did—he would become depressed in November or December.

Some descriptions of major mood disorders imply that they typically occur *de novo*—out of the blue, so to speak—in the absence of either notable personal distress or significant psychosocial antecedents. This implies that such episodes must be *endogenous*—caused entirely from within—rather than precipitated by life events and circumstances. The idea of endogenous causation is more compatible with the currently strong biomedical model, although instances of major disorder with substantial "situational" components are, as we have seen, quite routine (e.g., Hirschfeld et al., 1985). Because the issue is an important one, we will take a closer look at the evidence to the contrary.

Estimates of the proportion of significant mood disorders that are preceded by precipitating stressors vary from almost none (Winokur & Pitts, 1964) to almost all (Leff, Roatch, & Bunney, 1970; Paykel, 1973). In general, studies that adhere most closely to meticulous background search (e.g., Leff et al., 1970) tend to produce the highest estimates of antecedent stress. A rigorously conducted study of 409 matched pairs of normal and unipolar depressive subjects by Billings, Cronkite, and Moos (1983) provides convincing evidence not only of a greater frequency of prior stressor "events" but also of more chronic sources of psychosocial strain in the depressed group. The "spontaneous" occurrence of mood disorders seems to be at best an infrequent phenomenon, and even where that seems to be the case, we may have overlooked a stressor that was not obvious.

If we take the position—and the available research data seem to justify doing so—that some people are constitutionally more prone than others to develop mood disorders, then it would seem reasonable to suppose that such high-risk individuals would react more intensely to subtle, easily overlooked stressors than would individuals less at risk for these disorders. In addition, if a threshold exists beyond which biological factors play an important role in increasing the intensity of progressive mood deviation, then these high-risk, low-stress cases would exhibit relatively severe symptoms. Unfortunately, there are no data that permit us to evaluate this hypothesis directly and unequivocally.

Predisposing personality and cognitive characteristics. Beck (1967) argues convincingly that psychosocial stressors provoke severe depressive reactions only in people who already have a negative cognitive set, consisting of negative views of the self, the world, and the future. According to this hypothesis, a stressor merely serves to activate negative cognitions that have heretofore been dormant. The result is an abnormally extreme negative affect. Obviously, Beck's "negative cognitive set" is in the nature of a psychological predisposing variable.

Among factors that might be expected to produce such an underlying negativity would be early parental loss (through death or permanent separation), which Beck in fact reported in his original patient series. Scattered confirmations (and an occasional disconfirmation) of this observation have occurred in research and clinical literature going back many years. Two additional confirmations of a link between adult depression and childhood parental loss have more recently been reported by Barnes and Prosen (1985) and Roy (1985). The weight of evidence appears rather strongly on the positive association side, suggesting that such loss leaves in its wake a long-lasting vulnerability to depression for some individuals. Parental loss through suicide doubtless adds an additional layer of problems for child survivors. Though systematic research on this subject is lacking, moving accounts of the effects of parental suicide on children have recently been presented by Lukas and Seiden (1990), the first author having been himself exposed to such trauma.

We might also expect that exaggerated mood swings in a child would be fostered by observations of similar emotional patterns in his or her parents, and that such behavior would then persist as learned maladaptive response patterns. The high incidence of mood disorders in the families of manic and depressive patients provided greater than average opportunity for such learning.

In their study of 14 depressed children, Poznanski and Zrull (1970) reported that five of the children's parents were depressed at the time of the child's referral; one father had committed suicide, apparently during an episode of depression. Beardslee et al. (1983) and Puig-Antich et al. (1989) have confirmed that parental depression puts children at high risk for many problems, but especially for depression. Finally, Keller et al. (1986) have reported a study on 72 children from families in which at least one parent had a severe mood disorder but no other psychosis. They found that the severity and chronicity of the parents' (especially the mothers') disorders were uniformly associated with adaptive failure and psychiatric diagnoses, including depression, among the children. Of course, a confirmed skeptic could argue that studies such as these merely prove that these disorders are genetically transmitted, but such an argument strains credulity. It seems more likely, in the light of current knowledge, that psychosocial influences would be the deciding factor in such cases, with possibly some contribution from a genetically determined vulnerability.

Attempts to delineate a typical personality pattern for adults who later suffer serious mood disorders have met with limited success. In general, however, manic patients—whatever their childhood backgrounds may have been—are described as ambitious, outgoing, energetic, sociable, and often highly successful, both prior to their breakdown and after remission. As contrasted with members of control groups, they tend to place a higher conscious value on achievement, are conventional in their beliefs, and are deeply concerned about what others think of them. Depressive patients share these characteristics, but they appear to be more obsessive, anxious, and self-deprecatory. They also tend to show an unusually rigid conscience development, which prevents the overt expression of hostile feelings and makes them particularly prone to feelings of guilt and self-blame when things go wrong. A recent finding of low premorbid emotional strength and resiliency (Hirschfeld et al., 1989) suggests that predepressive individuals tend not to take an active approach to problem resolution.

People suffering from bipolar disorder—those destined to experience affective swings between mania and depression—might be expected to share the personality characteristics of both groups, perhaps in alternating phases. Depue et al. (1981) present strong evidence suggesting that this is the case. It must be noted, however, that all such findings are subject to numerous qualifications. Many people who exhibit the traits described will never have a serious mood disorder, and many who do not will develop such a disorder.

Feelings of helplessness and loss of hope. Investigators of widely differing theoretical orientations have emphasized that feelings of helplessness and hopelessness are basic to depressive reactions. In what is considered the classic treatment of the subject, Bibring (1953), a psychoanalyst, held that the basic mechanism of depression is "the ego's shocking awareness of its helplessness in regard to its aspirations . . . such that the depressed person . . . has lost his incentives and gives up, not the goals, but pursuing them, since this proves to be useless" (p. 39). A sense of hopelessness may be central in the considerable prevalence of depression among the aged (Fry, 1984). Other investigators have referred to "learned helplessness" in severe depression; presumably an individual, perceiving no likelihood that coping efforts will remove the source of stress, eventually stops fighting and gives up (Hiroto & Seligman, 1975; Seligman, 1973, 1975; Weiss, 1974). Recall that a sense of basic inefficacy does seem to characterize the depressed state. As was discussed in Chapter 1, laboratory experiments have identified conditions that can lead to "learned helplessness," but attempts to relate such conditions directly to clinical depression have not fared well.

Feelings of helplessness and hopelessness and their behavioral consequences have been dealt with from an operant learning standpoint by several investigators. Lazarus (1968) concluded that "depression may be regarded as a function of inadequate or insufficient reinforcers . . . some significant reinforcer has been withdrawn" (pp. 84–85). Similarly, Lewinsohn (1974) concluded that feelings of depression—along with other symptoms of this clinical picture—can be elicited when an individual's behavior no longer results in accustomed reinforcement or gratification. The failure to receive "response contingent positive reinforcement" (RCPR) in turn leads to a reduction in effort and activity, thus resulting in even less chance of coping with aversive conditions and achieving need gratification. The question here, however, is not whether depressed people have low rates of RCPR—they certainly do, almost by definition—but rather whether this is a cause or an effect of the depressed state. The evidence, reviewed by Carson and Carson (1984), suggests that it is an effect, thus illustrating once again the hazards of confusing cause with correlation.

Although the behavioristic perspective seems potentially helpful in understanding depressive reactions, it would seem at first glance less applicable to manic reactions. One might speculate, however, that the manic behavior represents attempts to obtain needed reinforcers via an indiscriminate increase in activity level. As in the case of depressive reactions, however, such reinforcers are not forthcoming. Here the conclusion of Ferster (1973) seems applicable: "It seems likely . . . that any factor which causes a temporary or long-term reduction in positively reinforced ways of acting . . . will also produce bizarre or irrational behavior as a byproduct" (p. 859). Not adequately accounted for in this explanation, however, are the feelings of euphoria that characterize manic reactions.

Extreme defenses against stress. Manic and depressive disorders may be viewed as two different but related defense-oriented strategies for dealing with severe stress.

In the case of mania, individuals try to escape their difficulties by a "flight into reality"—that is, they try to avoid the pain of their inner lives through outer world distractions. In less severe form, hypomania, this type of reaction to stress is shown by a person who goes on a round of parties to try to forget a broken love affair or tries to escape from a threatening life situation by restless action, occupying every moment with work, athletics, sexual affairs, and countless other activities—all performed with professed gusto but with little true enjoyment.

In true mania, this pattern is exaggerated. With a tremendous expenditure of energy, a manic individual tries to deny feelings of helplessness and hopelessness and to play a role of domineering competence. Once this mode of coping with difficulties is adopted, it is maintained until it has spent itself in emotional exhaustion, for the only other alternative is an admission of defeat and inevitable depression. This pattern is well brought out in the following case of a moderately disturbed manic patient:

He neglected his meals and rest hours, and was highly irregular, impulsive, and distractible in his adaptations to ward routine. Without apparent intent to be annoying or disturbing he sang, whistled, told pointless off-color stories, visited indiscriminately, and flirted crudely with the nurses and female patients. Superficially he appeared to be in high spirits, and yet one day when he was being gently chided over some particular irresponsible act he suddenly slumped in a chair, covered his face with his hands, began sobbing, and cried, "For Pete's sake, doc, let me be. Can't you see that I've just got to act happy?" (Masserman, 1961, pp. 66–67)

Unfortunately, as manic disorders proceed, any defensive value they may originally have had is negated, for thought processes are speeded up to a point where an individual can no longer process incoming information with any degree of efficiency. In a manner of speaking, the operator loses control of the computer, resulting in behavior that is highly erratic at best and incomprehensible at the extreme.

In the case of depression, a person apparently gains some relief from an intolerable stress situation by admitting defeat and withdrawing psychologically from the fight. Also, the slowing down of thought processes may serve to decrease suffering by reducing the sheer quantity of painful stimuli to be processed. Any such feelings of relief, however, are gained at the expense of a sense of adequacy and self-esteem and thus are accompanied by marked guilt and self-accusation. Like a soldier who panics and flees from combat, a depressed individual may feel relieved to be out of an intolerable situation but may also feel guilty and devalued.

Because depressive patients tend to blame themselves for their difficulties, they often go over the past with microscopic detail, picking out any possible sins of omission or commission and exaggerating their importance in relation to the present difficulties. They may even accuse themselves of selfishness, unfaithfulness, or acts of hostility that witnesses say did not occur. These self-accusations seem to be attempts to explain and find some meaning for their depression and at the same time achieve some measure of expiation and atonement. The entire process has a certain paradoxical quality: on the one hand, a depressive individual feels unable to determine events that might occur and, on the other hand, tends to accept personal responsibility for all negative events that do occur. Clearly, this pattern requires a degree of cognitive distortion, which is seen even in relatively mild cases.

It may be that the remission of depressive disorders even without treatment occurs because the effort at expiation and atonement has been successful. In such cases, there may be a gradual working through of feelings of unworthiness and guilt in which an individual pays the price for past failures by self-punishment and is thereby cleansed and ready for another go at life.

In bipolar reactions, the shift from mania to depression may tend to occur when the defensive function of the manic reaction breaks down. Similarly, the shift from depression to mania may tend to occur when an individual, devalued and guilt-ridden by inactivity and an inability to cope, finally feels compelled to attempt some countermeasure, however desperate.

Although the view of manic and depressive reactions as extreme defenses seems plausible up to a certain point, it is becoming difficult, as we have seen, to account satisfactorily for the more extreme versions of these states without acknowledging the importance of contributory biological involvement. It seems likely that aberrant biological mechanisms become involved as some level of severity is exceeded, and thereafter the disorder assumes an autonomous course. The effectiveness of biological treatment in alleviating severe episodes lends support to this hypothesis. And yet there remain questions in this area, if only because the impact of manic and depressive behavior on others is so notable and may contribute to the maintenance of this behavior.

Interpersonal effects of mood disorders. Manic individuals apparently feel that wishing to rely on others or to be taken care of is threatening and unacceptable. Instead, such an individual maintains self-esteem and feelings of adequacy and strength by establishing a social role in which control of other people is possible (Janowsky, El-Yousef, & Davis, 1974).

On the other hand, a depressed individual tends to adopt a role that attempts to place others in the position of providing sympathy, support, and care—and thus reinforcement (Ferster, 1973; Janowsky et al., 1970). Positive reinforcement does not necessarily follow, however. Depressive behavior can, and frequently does, elicit negative feelings and rejection in other people (Coyne, 1976; Gurtman, 1986; Hammen & Peters, 1977, 1978; Hokanson et al., 1989; Howes & Hokanson, 1979). These reactions may remain covert (Stephens, Hokanson, & Welker, 1987). Moreover, such negative reactions are often correctly anticipated by a depressed person (Strack & Coyne, 1983). In fact merely being around a depressed person may induce depressed feelings in others (Howes, Hokanson, & Loewenstein, 1985).

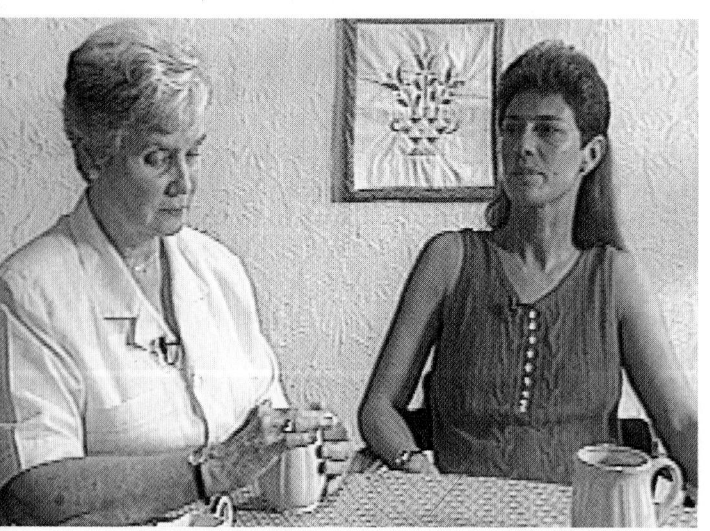

Jan (right), shown here with her mother, Phyllis, described her mother's depression this way: "I had really reached the point where I was tired of it all. . . . I didn't want to hear it anymore. . . . You talk about a love-hate relationship, that's exactly what—what I remember feeling. . . ."

Coyne (1976) has suggested that the presence or absence of support may depend on whether a depressed individual is skillful enough to circumvent and turn to advantage the negative affect he or she tends to create in other people. Especially if the other people are prone to guilt feelings, a skillful depressive patient may be able to extract considerable sympathy and support, at least over the short term. More commonly, one suspects, the ultimate result is a downwardly spiraling relationship from which others finally withdraw, exacerbating the instigator's depressive state.

Observations such as these raise questions about the extent to which depressive symptoms function as a sort of inept and defeated attempt to exert power over other people. We do not as yet have reliable answers to such questions, although the casual experience of most of us in interacting with depressed people is that of feeling "under pressure," as though we were being accused of lacking in some fundamental empathic quality. Because we usually have no ready response to the vague hint, "So what have you done for me lately?" we are apt to have an unpleasant sense of helplessness ourselves. It is known that depressed people can be quite sensitive about power cues and that they are not averse to the use of power in interpersonal situations (Hokanson et al., 1980).

These and other considerations discussed earlier in the chapter may mean that we should look more closely at issues of power in depression and conceivably in mania as well. Arieti (1982; Arieti & Bemporad, 1980) suggested the existence of two types of depression, one involving submission to a dominant personality (and the consequent failure to thrive as a person), the other concerned with failure to achieve unattainable goals. As already noted, Blatt et al. (1982) presented data supporting such a dichotomy, identifying dependent and self-criticizing depressive modes that correspond to the Arieti subtypes, a characterization in turn supported by other researchers (e.g., Hammen et al., 1989; Nietzel & Harris, 1990). The theme of dominance versus submission is one that may have special import in our attempts to understand those depressions where dependency appears central.

Depressive reactions can often be seen as an individual's attempts to communicate, in pantomime as it were, feelings of angry discouragement and despair—to say, in effect, "I have needs that you are failing to meet." Too often, however, this communication goes unheeded. Thus in failing marriages, which are commonly associated with depressive reactions, we may see one partner trying to communicate his or her unmet expectations, distress, and dependency and then becoming increasingly depressed and disturbed when the other partner fails to make the hoped-for response. Indeed, probably as often as not, the spouse is observed to respond with increased contempt for what he or she sees as the other's "weakness."

General Sociocultural Factors The incidence of mood disorders seems to vary considerably among different societies: in some, manic episodes are more frequent, while in others, depressive episodes are more common. In some cultures, particularly China, rates of depression are low but appear to be manifested as somatic symptoms (Kleinman, 1986).

In early studies, Carothers (1947, 1951, 1959) found manic disorders to be fairly common among the East Africans he studied, but depressive disorders relatively rare—the opposite of their incidence in the United States. He attributed the low incidence of depressive disorders to the fact that, in traditional African cultures, individuals have not usually been held personally responsible for failures and misfortunes. The culture of the Kenya Africans, Carothers observed, may be taken as fairly typical in this respect:

Their behavior in all its major aspects is group-determined. Even religion is a matter of offerings and invocations in a group; it is not practiced individually, and does not demand any particular attitude on the part of the individual. Similarly, grief over the death of a loved one is not borne in isolation, but appropriate rites are performed amid great public grieving. In these rites, widowed persons express their grief dramatically in ways prescribed by custom and then resume the tenor of their life as if no bereavement had occurred.

Psychologically speaking, Kenyans receive security because they are part of a larger organism and are not confronted with the problems of individual self-sufficiency, choice, and responsibility that play such a large part in our culture. They do not set themselves unrealistic goals, and they have no need to repress or feel guilty about "dangerous" desires. Their culture actively discourages individual achievement of success, does not consider sexual behavior as evil, and is tolerant of occasional outbursts of aggressive hostility.

In addition, Kenyans feel a great humbleness toward their natural environment, which is often harsh in the extreme. They always expect the worst, and hence can accept misfortunes with equanimity. Here too, responsibility and blame are automatically placed on forces outside themselves. Although they attempt to counteract misfortune and assure success in their ventures by performing appropriate rituals, the outcome is in the hands of the gods. They are not personally responsible and hence do not ordinarily experience self-devaluation or the need for ego-defensive measures. When excessive stress and decompensation do occur, there tends to be a complete disorganization of personality—as in the hebephrenic type of schizophrenia, which is the most common type of psychotic reaction. (Adapted from Carothers, 1947, 1951, 1953)

Needless to say, much has changed in Africa since Carothers made these observations, and more recent data suggest a quite different picture. In general, it appears that as societies take on the ways of Western culture, their members become more prone to the development of what might be called Western-style mood disorders (Marsella, 1980).

Even in those nonindustrialized countries where depressive disorders are relatively common, they seem less closely associated with feelings of guilt and self-recrimination than in the "developed" countries (Kidson & Jones, 1968; Lorr & Klett, 1968; Zung, 1969). In fact, among several groups of Australian aborigines, Kidson and Jones (1968) found not only an absence of guilt and self-recrimination in depressive reactions, but also no incidence of attempted or actual suicide. In connection with the latter finding, they stated, "The absence of suicide can perhaps be explained as a consequence of strong fears of death and also because of the tendency to act out and project hostile impulses" (p. 415).

These conclusions are generally supported in Marsella's (1980) comprehensive review of the cross-cultural literature concerning depression. Though various methodological problems make it inadvisable at this time to say with certainty that depression occurs less frequently in cultures other than our own, there is little doubt that it generally takes a different form from that customarily seen here. For example, in some non-Western cultures, symptoms of depression lack substantial psychological components, being limited to the so-called vegetative manifestations, such as sleep disturbance, loss of appetite, weight loss, and loss of sexual interest. Interestingly, in some such cultures there is not even a concept of depression that would be reasonably comparable to our own.

In our own society, the role of sociocultural factors in mood disorders is clarifying gradually. It appears that conditions that increase life stress—

such as being a homemaker-mother with young children at home—lead to a higher incidence of these as well as other disorders. In an early study, Jaco (1960) found that although psychotic mood disorders were distributed more evenly in the population than schizophrenia, the incidence was significantly higher among the divorced than among the married, and that it was about three times higher in urban than in rural areas. Subsequent work, such as that by Blazer et al. (1985) on the rural-urban difference and Bloom, Asher, and White (1978) on marital status, has generally confirmed these findings. Some evidence also suggests that the incidence of psychotic depression is higher in the upper socioeconomic classes (Bagley, 1973), though this effect appears limited to bipolar disorder (Boyd & Weissman, 1982). The reasons for this effect are open to speculation, but the elevated depression rates among people of high educational and occupational status has been confirmed in a carefully controlled study (Monnelly, Woodruff, & Robins, 1974). Finally, it should be mentioned that the relatively high percentage of women who suffer from mood disorders may not be universal in all cultures (Rao, 1970).

Treatments and Outcomes

Antidepressant, antipsychotic, and antianxiety drugs are all used with more severely disturbed manic and depressive patients. The role of medication in the mild and moderate forms of depression, as we have seen, is minimal, and such patients are likely to benefit more from appropriate psychological therapies (Beckham & Leber, 1985a; Klerman, 1982).

Lithium carbonate, a simple salt of the lightest elemental metal, was first successfully tried for the treatment of manic disorders in the late 1940s by Cade of Australia, but it was found to have adverse and even dangerous side effects that delayed its acceptance in the United States for nearly 20 years. Thanks to refinements in monitoring blood levels and determining appropriate dosages, however, lithium therapy has now become widely used in the treatment of manic episodes and, more recently, in the treatment of some major depressions as well (Coppen, Metcalfe, & Wood, 1982; Depue & Monroe, 1978; Kramlinger & Post, 1989; Noll, Davis, & DeLeon-Jones, 1985). Some believe that lithium is effective in depression only where the underlying disorder is bipolar in nature.

Lithium therapy is often effective in preventing the cycling between manic and depressive episodes, and susceptible patients are frequently maintained on lithium therapy over long time periods. Until recently lithium was considered an effective preventative for approximately 75 percent of patients suffering repeated bipolar attacks, but some new follow-up data suggest that this figure may be unduly optimistic (Harrow et al., 1990). Unfortunately, too, lithium therapy has some unpleasant side effects, such as lethargy, decreased motor coordination, and gastrointestinal difficulties in some patients. Long-term use has also been associated with kidney malfunction and sometimes permanent kidney damage (Bassuk, Schoonover, & Gelenberg, 1983).

For most seriously depressed patients, the drug treatment of choice is one of the standard antidepressants (called tricyclics because of their chemical structure), such as Tofranil (imipramine). Increasingly, physicians are choosing "second generation" antidepressants from a growing list of such products. One of these, Prozac (fluoxetine), is now extremely popular among physicians in various specialties, and prescriptions for it are being written at a rate that seems clearly excessive; modest distress or unhappiness should not, we think, be an occasion for taking drugs but rather for rigorously examining one's life. When properly prescribed, these drugs are often effective in prevention as well as treatment for patients subject to recurrent episodes (Hollon & Beck, 1978; Mindham, 1982; Noll, Davis, & DeLeon-Jones, 1985).

Unfortunately, antidepressant drugs usually require a week or more to manifest their effects. Thus electroconvulsive therapy (ECT) is often used with patients who present an immediate and serious suicidal risk (Brown, 1974; T. D. Hurwitz, 1974). When selection criteria for this form of treatment are carefully observed (which is by no means guaranteed), a complete remission of symptoms occurs after about four to six convulsive treatments in some 70 to 80 percent of the cases treated (Noll, Davis, & DeLeon-Jones, 1985). Maintenance dosages of antidepressant and antianxiety drugs ordinarily are then used to maintain the treatment gains achieved, until the depression has run its course. If necessitated as a last resort, however, electroconvulsive therapy should be used sparingly because of its distressing side effects, including temporary memory loss and disorientation. Furthermore, compelling evidence shows that, in some cases, ECT produces irreversible brain damage (Breggin, 1979).

In the best of circumstances, the treatment of depression is not confined to drugs or drugs plus electroconvulsive therapy, but is combined with individual and group psychotherapy directed at helping a patient develop a more stable long-range

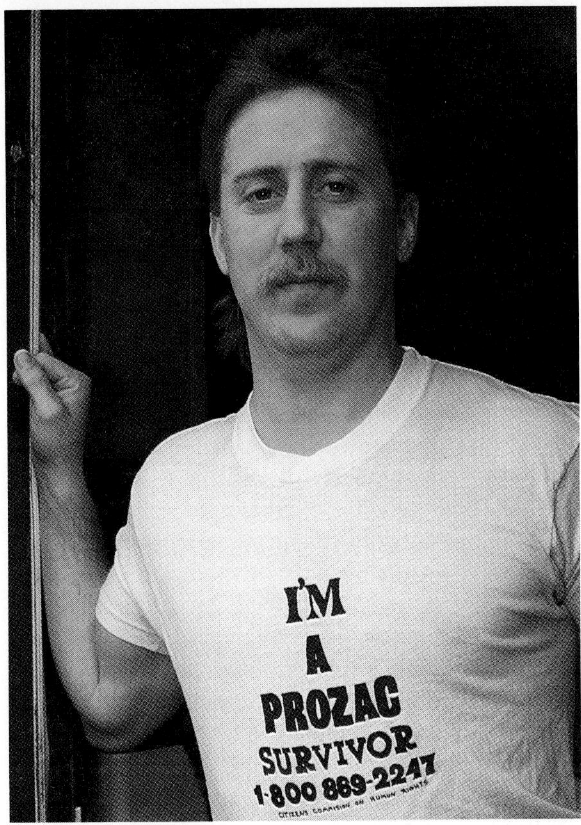

This man claims that he became suicidal after treatment with the antidepressant drug Prozac. Whether or not the drug actually precipitates suicidal impulses in susceptible individuals, the point to be underscored here is that antidepressants are powerful drugs that must be prescribed and used carefully. When care is taken with them, they are said to be effective in prevention as well as treatment for patients subject to recurrent depressive episodes.

adjustment. Studies on the efficacy of the drugs-psychotherapy combination have been reviewed by Klerman and Schechter (1982), Beckham and Leber (1985a), and Conte et al. (1986). The conclusions are most encouraging; apparently, the two broad types of therapy make independent but complementary contributions when combined. Considerable evidence, reviewed by Hollon and Garber (1990), also suggests that appropriate psychotherapy for depression, alone or in combination with drugs, significantly decreases the likelihood of further depressive episodes.

Proposed psychosocial treatments for depression have proliferated at an extraordinary rate over the past few years. In the comprehensive *Handbook of Depression,* edited by Beckham and Leber (1985b), no fewer than seven chapters are devoted to various psychotherapeutic approaches, versus one each for biological-somatic and combined treatments. In addition to depression-focused modifications of classical therapies, a number of specialized systems of psychotherapy have been developed that specifically address the problem of depression. By and large, these psychosocial therapies are intended for outpatient (nonpsychotic) treatment, but they are increasingly applied in inpatient settings as well (e.g., Salkovskis & Westbrook, 1989).

Two of the best known of these depression-specific psychotherapies are the ***cognitive-behavioral approach*** of Beck and colleagues (Beck et al., 1979) and the ***interpersonal therapy (IPT)*** program developed by Klerman, Weissman, and associates (Klerman et al., 1984). Both are relatively brief approaches that focus on here-and-now problems rather than remote causal issues. For example, the cognitive-behavioral technique consists of a highly structured, systematic attempt to reeducate a patient in regard to the aberrant cognitions presumed to underlie a depressed state. The Beck approach has amassed an impressive record of success, even as competitively compared with drug treatment, especially for long-term follow-up (Blackburn et al., 1981; DeRubeis, 1983; Murphy et al., 1984; Rush et al., 1977, 1982; Simons et al., 1986). These conclusions were confirmed in a recent quantitative review (using meta-analysis) of virtually all the pertinent research literature (Dobson, 1989).

The IPT approach, being relatively new, has not been subjected as yet to as extensive an evaluation. The efficacy of both of these psychosocial treatments for depression, however, recently received strong support from the findings of a carefully-designed, multisite study sponsored by the National Institute of Mental Health. In competitive comparison with immediate posttherapy outcomes from antidepressant drug treatment, both these psychosocial treatment approaches proved equally effective for milder cases of major depression, and in some instances even severe ones (Elkin et al., 1989; this important study is further described in Chapter 18). Based on the earlier research mentioned already, we anticipate a distinct advantage for at least the cognitive-behavioral approach over drug therapy when long-term follow-up of these patients is completed.

The more strictly behaviorist approaches have also spawned a number of innovations in the treatment of depression (T. Carson & Adams, 1981; Hoberman & Lewinsohn, 1985). A good example of one such technique, the manipulation of reinforcement contingencies, is presented in the following case study. The patient was a 37-year-old homemaker who had been depressed since the recent death of her mother. The therapist began by observing the patient in her home.

The therapist recorded each instance of "depressive-like" behavior, such as crying, complaining about somatic symptoms, pacing, and withdrawal. He also noted the consequences of these behaviors. Initially, she had a high rate of depressive behaviors and it was noted that members of her family frequently responded to them with sympathy, concern, and helpfulness. During this time, her rate of adaptive actions as a housewife and mother were very low, but she did make occasional efforts to cook, clean house, and attend to the children's needs. . . .

The therapist, in family sessions, instructed her husband and children to pay instant and frequent attention to her coping behavior and to gradually ignore her depressed behavior. They were taught to acknowledge her positive actions with interest, encouragement, and approval. Overall, they were not to decrease the amount of attention focused on the patient but rather switch the contingencies of their attention from "sick woman" to "housewife and mother." Within one week, her depressed behavior decreased sharply and her "healthy" behavior increased.

A clinical experiment was then performed to prove the causal link between her behavior and the responses generated in her family. After the 14th day, the therapist instructed the family members to return to providing the patient with attention and solicitude for her complaints. Within three days, she was once again showing a high level of depressive behavior, albeit not as high as initially. When the focus of the family's attentiveness was finally moved back to her coping skills and away from her miserableness, she quickly improved. One year after termination, she was continuing to function well without depressive symptoms. (Liberman & Raskin, 1971, p. 521)

Other behavioral techniques applied in the treatment of depression include training in progressive goal attainment, decision making, self-reinforcement, social skills, and of course such old standbys as relaxation. In one study, in fact, relaxation training proved to be as effective as cognitive-behavioral therapy for depressed adolescents, with both treatments surpassing in outcomes the waiting-list control condition (Reynolds & Coats, 1986).

Of course, in any overall treatment program, it is important to deal with unusual stressors in a patient's life, because an unfavorable life situation may lead to a recurrence of the depression and may necessitate longer treatment. This point was well made in recent studies that extended to the mood disorders the well-established finding that relapse in schizophrenia is correlated with certain noxious elements in family life (Hooley, 1986; Hooley, Orley, & Teasdale, 1986). Spouse behavior that can be interpreted by a former patient as criticism seems especially likely to produce depression relapse (Hooley & Teasdale, 1989). Some type of couples or family intervention, described in Chapter 18, might be required in these situations.

Even without formal therapy, as we have noted, the great majority of manic and depressed patients recover from a given episode within less than a year. With modern methods of treatment, the general outlook has become increasingly favorable—so much so that most hospitalized patients can now be discharged within 60 days. Although relapses may occur in some instances, these can now often be prevented by maintenance therapy.

At the same time, the mortality rate for depressed patients appears to be about twice as high as that for the general population because of the higher incidence of suicide (Leonard, 1974; Zung & Green, 1974). Manic patients also have a high risk of death, due to such circumstances as accidents (with or without alcohol as a contributing factor), neglect of proper health precautions, or physical exhaustion (Coryell & Winokur, 1982). Thus, although the development of effective drugs and other new approaches to therapy have brought greatly improved outcomes for patients with mood disorders, the need clearly remains for still more effective treatment methods, both immediate and long-term. Also, a strong need remains to study the factors that put people at high risk for depressive disorders and to apply relevant findings to early intervention and prevention.

SUICIDE

The risk of **suicide**—taking one's own life—is a significant factor in all depressive states. Though it is obvious that people on occasion commit suicide for other reasons, the vast majority of those who complete the act do so during or in the recovery phase of a depressive episode. Paradoxically, the act often occurs at a point when an individual appears to be emerging from the deepest phase of a depressive attack. The risk of suicide is about 1 percent during the year in which a depressive episode occurs, and it raises to 15 percent over the lifetime of an individual who has recurrent episodes (Klerman, 1982). When compared to rates for other possible causes of death—especially in younger age groups—these are substantial figures.

At the present time, suicide ranks among the first ten causes of death in most Western countries. In the United States, estimates show that more than 200,000 people attempt suicide each year and that over 5 million Americans have made suicide attempts at some time in their lives. Official figures show that some 26,000 successful suicides occur each year, meaning that about every 20 minutes someone in the United States commits suicide (Statistical Abstracts of the United States, 1984). Indeed, the problem may be much more serious than these figures suggest, because many self-inflicted deaths are attributed in official records to other "more respectable" causes. Most experts agree that the number of actual suicides is at least two and possibly several times higher than the number officially reported (Wekstein, 1979).

Statistics, however accurate, cannot begin to convey the tragedy of suicide in human terms. As we will see, probably the great majority of people who commit suicide are actually quite ambivalent about taking their own lives. This irreversible choice is often made when they are alone and in a state of severe psychological distress, unable to see their problems objectively or to evaluate alternative courses of action. Thus a basic humanitarian problem in suicide is the seemingly senseless death of an individual who may be ambivalent about living or who does not really want to die. A second tragic concern arises from the long-lasting distress among those left behind that may result from such action. As Shneidman (1969) has put it, "The person who commits suicide puts his psychological skeleton in the survivor's emotional closet . . ." (p. 22). The aptness of this characterization is poignantly confirmed in "survivors'" descriptions of their experiences, as recently investigated by Lukas and H. Seiden (1990). *HIGHLIGHT 11.4* describes some additional insights provided by this work.

In the discussion that follows, we will focus on various aspects of the incidence and clinical picture in suicide, on factors that appear to be of causal significance, on degrees of intent and ways of communicating it, and on issues of treatment and prevention.

The Clinical Picture and Causal Pattern

Because the clinical picture and etiology of suicide are so closely interrelated, it is useful to consider these topics under one general heading. This approach will lead us to address the following questions: Who commits suicide? What are the motives for taking one's own life? What general sociocultural variables appear to be relevant to an understanding of suicide?

Who Commits Suicide? In the United States, the peak age for suicide attempts is between 24 and 44. Historically, three times as many men as women commit suicide, but more women make suicide attempts. Most attempts occur in the context of interpersonal discord or other severe life stress. For females, the most commonly used method is drug ingestion, usually barbiturates; males tend to use methods more likely to be lethal, particularly gunshot, which is probably the main reason that successful suicides are higher among men. Evidence suggests, however, that this long-established pattern may be changing. Data from various Western countries, including the United States, indicate that the incidence of completed suicide has been increasing at a faster rate for women than for men in recent years. Also, more widows than widowers complete the act (Suter, 1976), although this fact seems due mainly to the disproportionate prevalence of widowhood. The precise reasons for these trends are unknown but are doubtless related to the rapid sociocultural changes, including those relating to sex roles, that are now an inescapable part of our lives.

Another perplexing trend is that rates of completed suicide among teenagers and even children seem to be increasing at an alarming pace (Fremouw, de Perczel, & Ellis, 1990; Peck, Farberow, & Litman, 1985; Pfeffer, 1981; Wells & Stuart, 1981). One recent estimate (Spirito et al., 1989) puts the rate of attempted suicide among high school students at between 8 and 9 percent; between 5 and 40 percent of these are believed to be "repeaters." The trend is by no means limited to youngsters from deprived or problematic backgrounds, although they do account for a sizable percentage of the statistics (Miller, Chiles, & Barnes, 1982); suicide rates for children from affluent circumstances also are on the increase. Youthful suicides are especially likely to follow an "epidemic" pattern, wherein particular communities are rocked by a series of self-destruction episodes within a brief time period. Several years ago, for example, seven students attending the same high school in suburban Omaha made suicide attempts in rapid succession, and three of them succeeded (*Time,* February 24, 1986).

Thus while the overall national rate has increased slightly but consistently in recent years, disproportionate increases have occurred among females and among younger members of the population. The greatest increase has been among 15 to 24 year olds; the rate for this age group has essen-

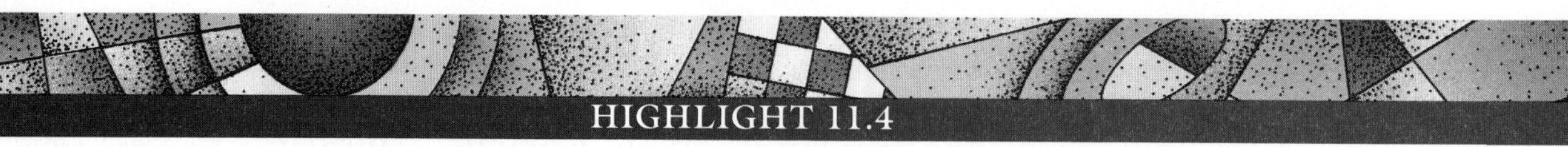

HIGHLIGHT 11.4

"Adjusting" to Suicide: Relationship Trauma Without Closure

Christopher Lukas, himself a childhood suicide survivor, and Henry Seiden (1990), a psychologist, have recently published a sensitive and informed book on suicide survivorship, much of it the product of a survey conducted among people who have endured the experience. The comments that follow are based largely on their findings.

Most of us, fortunately, will never have to cope with the suicide of someone with whom we have shared significant portions of our lives. The involuntary death of a loved one—a parent, a child, a sibling, a spouse, a close friend—through accident or illness often leaves in its wake substantial scars that may never entirely recede. In these cases, however, we are normally spared the additional agony of unanswered and unanswerable questions about the essential cause of the loss and about any role we may have had in bringing it about. For the survivor of a relationship that ends in suicide, questions such as these usually present themselves with a searing, inescapable, and lasting prominence. They can have no final resolution because the one person in the best position to provide answers has deliberately and permanently departed. The first, last, and most central of these unanswered questions for the typical survivor is, why?

Seemingly irresolvable crises are not unique to the situation of the suicide survivor. Everyone's life has its share of them, and every human culture seems to have evolved its own ways of dealing with them. Usually, if not invariably, these coping mechanisms involve substantial communal sharing of the burden, sometimes in formal rituals of one sort or another (such as funerals), but probably more often in less formal exchanges of emotional or material support, information, advice, and counsel from relatives and friends. The professional counselor—shaman, clergy, lawyer, physician, psychotherapist, or similar figure—occupies something of a middle ground here.

The significantly different thing about suicide as an irresolvable crisis, at least in our culture, is its unacceptability as a topic of reference. Not uncommonly, for example, there is no funeral for the suicide. A survivor, deliberately or not, finds himself or herself complying with the general expectation that the act of self-destruction is not to be openly acknowledged, not even within the immediate family. The typical suicide survivor is thus deprived of the healing properties of sharing by virtue of this conspiracy of silence. He or she must face alone the terrible, wrenching, and ultimately impenetrable question, why? According to the data gathered by Lukas and Seiden, few if any survivors emerge psychologically undamaged from this experience, and only the fortunate are able to conquer fully the psychotoxic residue and move on with their lives unimpeded.

Lukas and Seiden use a "bargain" analogy to analyze the differing coping strategies used by survivors to deal with their special dilemma. These bargains have the function of protecting a survivor from the devastating feelings that would otherwise emerge, but they

tially tripled since the mid-1950s, far exceeding its increase as a proportion of the total population (Hendin, 1985). Data from the San Diego Suicide Study suggest that at least some of the increase may be associated with drug abuse (Fowler, Rich, & Young, 1986; Rich, Young, & Fowler, 1986). Suicide ranks as the third most common cause of death for 15 to 24 year olds (the first two are accidents and homicide, respectively; Frederick, 1985).

Most of us feel there is something especially tragic when a young person—physically healthy and having seemingly unlimited potential—undertakes an irreversible, self-destructive action. In fact a sense of hopelessness, strongly correlated with suicide attempts among adults (Beck, Brown, & Steer, 1989; Holden, Medonca, & Serin, 1989), does not appear to be a particularly significant issue in adolescent suicide (Cole, 1989). The motivation to "escape from self" (Baumeister, 1990), on the other hand, possibly has special relevance for this age range; it is discussed further in a later section.

Many college students seem peculiarly vulnerable to the development of suicidal motivations, especially those attending the larger institutions. The rate seems to be higher in large universities than in community colleges and small liberal arts colleges (Peck & Schrut, 1971). The combined stressors of academic demands, social interaction

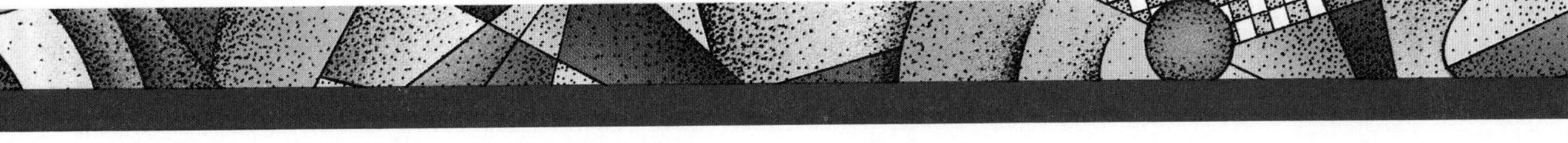

usually also have a hidden "cost" in requiring self-injurious behavior. Some of the more typical of such bargains are as follows:

1. *The long goodbye.* Because survivors often have not had the opportunity to say "good-bye," some become caught up in an unending mourning process in an effort to achieve this type of closure to a relationship. Although severe psychic pain may thereby be avoided, this type of bargain also involves a sort of perpetual moratorium on moving forward with one's life.

2. *Scapegoating.* Here a survivor identifies one or more other people as responsible for the suicide's death, displacing onto them the rage he or she feels toward the actual perpetrator of the act. The hidden cost is that the survivor is prevented from coming to terms with the fact of self-destruction and its meaning.

3. *Guilt as punishment.* Instead of choosing an external scapegoat, some survivors take on to themselves the burden of responsibility for the death; they initiate an interminable self-blame and remain thereafter deep in grief and self-acknowledged guilt.

4. *Cutting off.* Some survivors handle their disruptive emotions by putting a psychological stranglehold on all feelings, turning themselves into emotionless and minimally involved processors of the tasks of living. In one form of this bargain, a survivor loses all tolerance for pleasant experience or joy, turning his or her life, and that of significant others, into a bleak and colorless sequence of emotionally neutral events.

5. *Physical problems.* Here a survivor somatizes the unfinished emotional business of the suicide and becomes preoccupied with various real or imagined illnesses to a crippling degree.

6. *Running.* Some survivors react by involving themselves in endless moves and life changes—in locale, employment, spouses, other relationships, and so on—as a way of distracting themselves from the questions and intensely painful feelings brought about by the suicide. This "running," of course, solves nothing.

7. *Suicide.* Here the bargain—perhaps the saddest of all—is, "Because you died, I'll die." The rage that has no other acceptable target is, finally, turned against the self.

Is there a way out for a survivor? Lukas and Seiden say yes. It is not an easy one, however, not one that accepts the false security of a "bargain." Apparently, no effective substitute exists for facing, working through, and then putting aside the brutal truth of a loved one's suicide, and one's own reactions to it. Fortunately, help is available for doing so, to which these authors provide detailed directions.

problems, and career choices—perhaps interacting with challenges to their basic values—evidently make it impossible for such students to continue making the adjustive compromises their life situations demand. Some 10,000 college students in the United States attempt suicide each year, and over 1,000 of them succeed. For an overview of warning signs for student suicide, see *HIGHLIGHT 11.5*

The greatest incidence of suicidal behavior among college students occurs at the beginning and the end of a school quarter or semester. Echoing the general trend, approximately three times as many female as male students attempt suicide, but more males than females succeed. More than half of those who attempt suicide take pills, about one-third cut themselves, and the remainder—mostly males—use other and more deadly methods, such as hanging, gunshot, or jumping from high places (Klagsbrun, 1976; Ryle, 1969).

Other high-risk groups include depressed people; the elderly (white); alcoholics; separated or divorced people; individuals living alone; migrants; people from socially disorganized areas; members of some Native American tribes (see *HIGHLIGHT 11.6*); and certain professionals, such as physicians, dentists, lawyers, and psychologists (Wekstein, 1979). As might be expected, suicide rates are higher than normal among former mental patients

HIGHLIGHT 11.5

Warning Signs for Student Suicide

A change in a student's mood and behavior is a significant warning of possible suicide. Characteristically, the student becomes depressed and withdrawn, undergoes a marked decline in self-esteem, and shows deterioration in personal hygiene. These signs are accompanied by a profound loss of interest in studies. Often he or she stops attending classes and stays at home most of the day. Usually, the student's distress is communicated to at least one other person, often in the form of a veiled suicide warning. A significant number of students who attempt suicide leave suicide notes.

When college students attempt suicide, one of the first explanations to occur to those around them is that they may have been doing poorly in school. As a group, however, they are superior students, and though they tend to expect a great deal of themselves in terms of academic achievement and to exhibit scholastic anxieties, their grades, academic competition, and pressure over examinations are not regarded as significant precipitating stressors. Also, though many lose interest in their studies prior to the onset of suicidal behavior and thus receive worse grades, the loss of interest appears to be associated with depression and withdrawal caused by other problems. Moreover, when academic failure does appear to trigger suicidal behavior—in a minority of cases—the actual cause of the behavior is generally considered to be loss of self-esteem and failure to live up to parental expectations, rather than the academic failure itself.

For most suicidal students, both male and female, the major precipitating stressor appears to be either the failure to establish, or the loss of, a close interpersonal relationship. Often the breakup of a romance is the key precipitating factor. It has also been noted that significantly more suicide attempts and suicides are made by students from families that have experienced separation, divorce, or the death of a parent. A particularly important precipitating factor among college males appears to be the existence of a close emotional involvement with a parent that is threatened when the student becomes involved with another person in college and tries to break this "parental knot."

Although most colleges and universities have mental health facilities to assist distressed students, few suicidal students seek professional help. Thus it is of vital importance for those around a suicidal student to notice the warning signs and try to obtain assistance.

Sources drawn on for this description include Hendin (1975), Miller (1975), Murray (1973), Nelson (1971), Pausnau and Russell (1975), Peck and Schrut (1971), Shneidman, Parker, and Funkhouser (1970), and Stanley and Barter (1970).

(Black, Warrack, & Winokur, 1985), and as much as 18 times higher among females who had been diagnosed as schizophrenic (Allebeck & Wistedt, 1986). Both female physicians and female psychologists commit suicide at a rate about three times that of women in the general population; male physicians have a suicide rate about twice that of men in the general population (Ross, 1974; Schaar, 1974; Wekstein, 1979). Finally, those who attempt suicide tend to have traits of submissiveness and high arousability (Mehrabian & Weinstein, 1985). *HIGHLIGHT 11.7* provides more information on people at high risk for suicidal behavior. Summing up, R. Seiden (1974) has called suicide "the number one cause of unnecessary, premature, and stigmatizing death" in the United States.

Other Psychosocial Factors Associated with Suicide Events, circumstances, and mental states found to be related to the onset of depression are also generally linked to suicidal behavior. Thus, in addition to the sense of hopelessness already mentioned, we find that current stressors (Slater & Depue, 1981), depressed *and* angry feelings (Weissman, Fox, & Klerman, 1973), interpersonal crises of various sorts (Paykel, Prusoff, & Myers, 1975), failure and consequent self-devaluation (Wekstein, 1979), inner conflicts (Menninger, 1938), and the loss of a sense of meaning (Farberow, Shneidman, & Leonard, 1963) all can produce, independently or in combination, a mental state that looks to suicide as a possible way out. Should a person also happen to be drinking excessively at the time (or

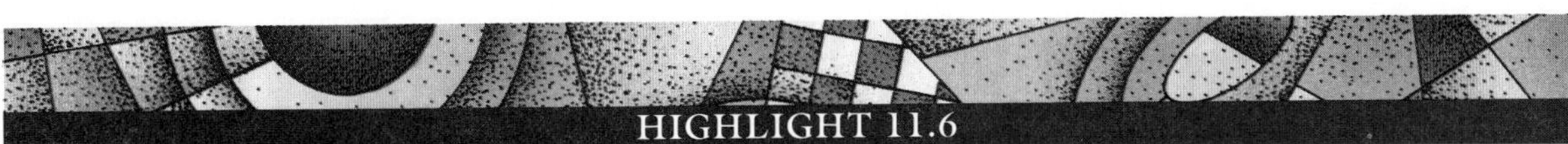

HIGHLIGHT 11.6

Native American Tragedy: The Young Men of Wind River

Between August and October of 1985, nine young men, ages 14 to 25, of the Shoshone tribe at Wind River, Wyoming, killed themselves, all by hanging. This devastating rash of self-destruction is some 24 times in excess of the already-established high rate of suicide among Native American males in this age range. What happened at the Wind River reservation? Apart from obvious elements of suggestion and imitation, we may never completely know. The young men themselves left essentially no clues, and no evidence could be found of a suicide pact among them.

A plausible explanation is that Wind River was host to a lethal concentration of the same problems that beset many Native American societies and that impact especially on their young males: marginal status in the larger American society; a dearth of discernible opportunities to "break out" of a stark and bleak existence; rampant unemployment; erosion of ambition in the face of bureaucratically administered "welfare"; and searing boredom, from which available escapes are largely limited to watching television and getting drunk. To these problems can be added, we surmise, the cruel realization of how far this fall has been for the descendants of the proud warriors who once ruled the continent.

As of the date of the news report from which this *HIGHLIGHT* was adapted (*Time,* October 21, 1985), the wave of suicides had apparently subsided. Of interest and possibly of considerable importance, tribal elders fashioned an intervention program emphasizing tribal history, tradition, and the revival of certain healing rituals to which the young were invited and to which they came in large numbers. If a resurgence of cultural identity and pride can halt an epidemic of suicide, can it also give impetus to an attack on the root causes of tribal despair? We hope so.

using drugs with similar effects), the danger of successful suicide is markedly increased (Murphy & Wetzel, 1990).

The following, a composite profile of the "average" physician suicide, shows how a number of the above factors can lead a person to suicide:

> *Statistically, he is a 48-year-old doctor graduated at or near the top of his high-prestige medical school class, now practicing a peripheral specialty associated with chronic problems, where satisfactions are difficult and laggard. Because he is active, aggressive, ambitious, competitive, compulsive, enthusiastic and individualistic, he is apt to be frustrated easily in his need for achievement and recognition, and in meeting his goals. Unable to tolerate delay in gratification, he may prescribe large amounts of anesthetics or psychoactive drugs in his practice. Add a nonlethal annoying physical illness, mood swings, personal problems with drugs and alcohol—itself a reflection of suicide proneness—in one who may feel a lack of restraints by society, and one who has a likely enough combination to induce significant anxiety and depression, symptoms which not only may require psychiatric treatment, but which also often hamper a worthwhile relationship with a psychiatrist. Self-seeking and self-indulgent, versatile and resourceful, lacking control, he may often resort to hasty, impulsive or immature behavior—possibly suicide. (Ross, 1975, pp. 16–17)*

The specific factors leading a person to suicide may take many forms. For example, one middle-aged man developed profound feelings of guilt after being promoted to the presidency of the bank for which he worked; shortly after his promotion, he fatally slit his throat. Such "success suicides" are undoubtedly related to those occasional depressive

HIGHLIGHT 11.7

A "Lethality Scale" for the Assessment of Suicide Potential

In assessing "suicide potentiality," or the probability that a person might carry out a threat of suicide, the Los Angeles Suicide Prevention Center uses a "lethality scale" consisting of ten categories:

1. *Age and sex.* The potentiality is greater if an individual is male rather than female, and is over 50 years of age. (The probability of suicide is also increasing for young adults aged 15 to 24.)

2. *Symptoms.* The potentiality is greater if an individual manifests such symptoms as sleep disturbances, depression, feelings of hopelessness, or alcoholism.

3. *Stress.* The potentiality is greater if an individual is under stress from the loss of a loved one through death or divorce, the loss of employment, increased responsibilities, or serious illness.

4. *Acute versus chronic aspects.* The immediate potentiality is greater when there is a sudden onset of specific symptoms. The long-term potentiality is greater when there is a recurrent outbreak of similar symptoms, or a recent increase in long-standing maladaptive traits.

5. *Suicidal plan.* The potentiality is greater in proportion to the lethality of a person's proposed method and the organizational clarity and detail of the plan.

6. *Resources.* The potentiality is greater if a person has no family or friends, or if they are unwilling to help.

7. *Prior suicidal behavior.* The potentiality is greater if an individual has made one or more prior attempts or has a history of repeated threats and depression.

8. *Medical status.* The potentiality is greater when an individual has a chronic, debilitating illness or has had many unsuccessful experiences with physicians.

9. *Communication aspects.* The potentiality is greater if communication between an individual and his or her relatives has been broken off and they reject efforts by the individual or others to reestablish communication.

10. *Reaction of significant others.* Potentiality is greater if a significant other, such as a husband or wife, evidences a defensive, rejecting, punishing attitude and denies that the individual needs help.

The final suicide potentiality rating is a composite score based on weighing each of the ten individual items.

Another interesting approach to the assessment of suicide potentiality involves the use of computers and actuarial methods to predict the risk not only of suicide but also of assaultive and other dangerous behaviors (Griest et al., 1974). Clinicians find this information helpful in making decisions regarding the amount of control needed or the amount of freedom that they can safely allow.

Material concerning the lethality scale is based on information supplied by the Los Angeles Suicide Prevention Center.

episodes that seem to be precipitated by positive life events. More often, suicide is associated with negative events, such as severe financial reverses, loss of social status, imprisonment, or similar situations.

Historically, researchers have proposed several overarching theoretical rationales for seriously suicidal behavior, behavior that has as its unadulterated intent the immediate termination of one's own life. As a group, these theories tend to be rather abstract, even impersonal, and therefore to miss something in depicting the emotional charge of the suicidal act. The essential element here, it seems to us, is that a presuicidal individual intends—even if only at the moment of taking fatal action—to put an end to conscious experience, permanently and without recourse. The conceivable states of mind that might lead to such a decision are limited in number and one suspects have in common the quality of intolerability, of desperate need for certain and irrevocable escape. Oblivion thus becomes a positive goal. A recent theoretical analysis of suicide offered by Baumeister (1990) captures this notion of escape from intolerable experience. Baumeister conceives suicide as basically an escape from self, or at least self-awareness. In this effort a person achieves a "cognitive deconstruction," which entails both irrationality and disinhibition, such that drastic action becomes acceptable.

General Sociocultural Factors Suicide rates vary considerably from one society to another. Hungary, with an annual incidence of 44.9 per 100,000, has the world's highest rate. Other Western countries with high rates—20 per 100,000 or higher—include Czechoslovakia, Finland, Austria, Sweden, Denmark, and the (former) Federal Republic of Germany. The United States has a rate of approximately 11.9 per 100,000, which is roughly comparable to that of Canada. Countries with low rates (less than 9 per 100,000) include Greece, Italy, Israel, Spain, and Portugal (World Health Organization, 1982). Among certain groups, such as the aborigines of the western Australian desert, the suicide rate drops to zero—possibly as a result of a strong, culturally determined fear of death (Kidson & Jones, 1968).

Religious taboos concerning suicide and the attitudes of a society toward death are apparently important determinants of suicide rates. Both Catholicism and Muhammadanism strongly condemn suicide, and suicide rates in Catholic and Islamic countries are correspondingly low. In fact most societies have developed strong sanctions against suicide, and many still regard it as a crime as well as a sin.

Japan is one of the few major societies in which suicide has been socially approved under certain circumstances—for example, in response to conditions that bring disgrace to an individual or group. During World War II, many Japanese villagers were reported to have committed mass suicide when faced with imminent capture by Allied forces. There were also reports of group suicide by Japanese military personnel under threat of defeat. In the case of the kamikaze, Japanese pilots who deliberately crashed their explosives-laden planes into American warships during the war's final stages, self-destruction was a way of demonstrating complete personal commitment to the national purpose. It is estimated that 1000 young Japanese pilots destroyed themselves in this exercise of patriotic zeal. Despite the extraordinary effectiveness of this type of attack, one can hardly imagine its being ordered by an American commander, or such an order being obeyed by American pilots.

Societal norms cannot wholly explain differences in suicide rates, however, for the incidence of suicide often varies significantly among societies with similar cultures and also among different subgroups within given societies. For example, it is difficult to account for the marked differences in suicide rates between Sweden and the United States, and we have noted differences in our own society with respect to sex, occupation, and age. In fact the Scandinavian countries, sharing as they do a relatively common ethnic background, cultural pattern, and overall high rates of suicide, pose the puzzling problem of Norway. Here the suicide rate has remained stable and relatively low by world standards for the past century (Retterstøl, 1975)—thus exploding the myth that the high level of social welfare programs in Scandinavia is responsible for encouraging suicide by removing the challenge, and hope, of "making one's own way."

In a pioneering study of sociocultural factors in suicide, the French sociologist Emile Durkheim (1897) attempted to relate differences in suicide rates to differences in group cohesiveness. Analyzing records of suicides in different countries and for different historical periods, Durkheim concluded that the greatest deterrent to committing suicide in times of personal stress is a sense of involvement and identity with other people. More recent studies, including an exceptionally well-designed one by Slater and Depue (1981), tend to confirm this idea.

Durkheim's views also appear relevant to understanding the higher incidence of suicide among subgroups in our society who are subjected to conditions of uncertainty and social disorganization in the absence of strong group ties. In a study sponsored by the National Institute of Mental Health, Hall et al. (1970) found that low-income people from large urban areas have an especially high rate of suicidal gestures and attempts. Similarly, suicide rates have been found to be higher than average among people who are "downwardly mobile" (or who fear they may become so) and among groups undergoing severe social pressures. For example, in 1932 at the height of the Great Depression in the United States, the suicide rate increased from less than 10 to 17.4 per 100,000; during the early years of the severe recession of the mid- and late 1970s, the suicide rate increased to above 12 per 100,000 (NIMH, 1976; Wekstein, 1979). Following the same pattern, we could point to the environmental pressures that appear to contribute to the high rate of suicide among black youth in our society, or to the marked increase in suicide among Eskimo teenagers in Alaska, who find themselves trapped in a sort of no-man's-land between their past culture and assimilation into the "White world" (Parkin, 1974).

Suicidal Ambivalence

From the standpoint of intent or motivation, suicide appears to be one method of obtaining relief from an aversive life situation. However, because most people undergoing severe stress do not commit suicide—for example, only a small number of people who are depressed or who develop terminal cancer take their own lives—the question arises as to why an individual uses this method of coping rather than another. This is not an easy question to answer; it involves consideration not only of stress, but also of other aspects of an individual's psychological state at the time of a suicide attempt.

Degree of Intent The ambivalence that typically accompanies thoughts of suicide finds classic expression in Hamlet's famous soliloquy:

To be, or not to be: that is the question:
Whether 'tis nobler in the mind to suffer
The slings and arrows of outrageous fortune,
Or to take arms against a sea of troubles,
And by opposing end them? To die: to sleep;
No more; and by a sleep to say we end
The heart-ache and the thousand natural shocks
That flesh is heir to, 'tis a consummation
Devoutly to be wish'd. To die, to sleep;
To sleep: perchance to dream: ay, there's the rub;
For in that sleep of death what dreams may come
When we have shuffled off this mortal coil,
Must give us pause. . . .
(Hamlet, Act III, Scene i)

Recognizing that the vast majority of people who contemplate suicide do not in fact kill themselves, some investigators have focused on analyzing the degree of intent associated with suicidal behavior. Thus Farberow and Litman (1970)—echoing Hamlet—have classified suicidal behavior into three categories: "to be," "not to be," and "to be or not to be."

The "to be" group involves individuals who do not really wish to die, but instead want to communicate a dramatic message to others concerning their distress and contemplation of suicide. Their suicide attempts involve minimal drug ingestion, minor wrist-slashing, and similar nonlethal methods. They usually arrange matters so that intervention by others is almost inevitable, although sometimes things go awry. This group is estimated to make up about two-thirds of the total suicidal population. As we have seen, a large—although decreasing—proportion of those who make unsuccessful attempts are women. It seems probable that traditional sex-role socialization of females predisposes many women to feel helpless and to fantasize being rescued—and thus to communicate in this mode (Suter, 1976).

In contrast, the "not to be" group includes people who seemingly are intent on dying. They give little or no warning of their intent to kill themselves, and they usually arrange the suicidal situation so that intervention is impossible. Although these people use a variety of different methods for killing themselves, they generally rely on the more violent and certain means, such as shooting themselves or jumping from high places. Investigators have estimated that this group makes up only about 3 to 5 percent of the suicidal population. Successful preventive intervention with this group is at best a doubtful goal, even when such a person is protectively incarcerated. In an interesting experiment, a pseudosuicidal "patient" (actually one of the investigators) gained admission to a mental hospital ward on "suicidal status." Though he was supposedly being carefully watched, he discovered multiple opportunities to do himself in (Reynolds & Farberow, 1976).

The "to be or not to be" group constitutes about 30 percent of the suicidal population. It is comprised of people who are ambivalent about dying and tend to leave the question of death to chance, or, as they commonly view it, to fate. Although loss of a love object, strained interpersonal relationships, financial problems, or feelings of meaninglessness may be present, this type of person still entertains some hope of working things out. The methods used for the suicide attempt are often dangerous but moderately slow acting, such as drug ingestion or cutting oneself severely on nonvital parts of the body, thus allowing for the possibility of intervention. The feeling during such attempts can be summed up as, "If I die the conflict is settled, but if I am rescued that is what is meant to be." Often the people in this group lead stormy, stress-filled lives and make repeated suicide attempts.

After an unsuccessful attempt, a marked reduction in emotional turmoil usually occurs. This reduction is not stable, however, and in a subsequent trial by fate, the verdict may well be death. In a follow-up study of 886 people who had made suicide attempts, Rosen (1970) classified them as serious (21 percent) or nonserious (79 percent). During the year following the attempts, the rate of successful suicide was twice as high among the group whose earlier attempts had been classified as serious.

Farberow and Litman's classification is largely descriptive and has little practical value in terms of predicting suicidal behavior. As we indicated, however, it does seem possible to infer the degree of intent from the lethality of the method used—a conclusion strongly supported by the more recent findings of Beck, Beck, and Kovacs (1975). The concept of intent is also a useful reminder that most people who contemplate suicide retain at least some urge to live. Their hold on life, however tenuous, provides the key to successful suicide prevention (Fremouw, de Perczel, & Ellis, 1990).

Communication of Suicidal Intent Research has clearly disproved the tragic belief that those who threaten to take their lives seldom do so. In fact such people represent a high-risk group in comparison with the general population. In a cross-cultural study, Rudestam (1971) conducted extensive interviews with close friends or relatives of 50 consecutive suicides in Stockholm and Los Angeles and found that at least 60 percent of the victims in both cities had made "direct" verbal threats of their intent. An additional 20 percent had made "indirect" threats.

In a similar study involving suicide deaths in Vienna and Los Angeles, Farberow and Simon (1975) found substantial differences between the two cities. In Los Angeles, 72 percent had made direct references to intent, versus only 27 percent in Vienna; the corresponding figures for indirect references were 25 percent and 2 percent. It thus appears that cultural factors determine to some extent the likelihood that suicidal intent will be "signaled" to others.

Indirect threats typically include references to being better off dead, discussions of suicide methods and burial, statements such as "If I see you again . . . ," and dire predictions about the future.

Whether direct or indirect, communication of suicidal intent usually represents a cry for help. The person is trying to express distress and ambivalence about suicide; the statements are both warnings and calls for help. Unfortunately, the message is often not received or is received with skepticism and denial. The latter pattern is particularly apt to occur when a suicidal person has given repeated warnings but has not made an actual suicide attempt. As a consequence, the recipients of the message may state that they did not think it would happen, or that they thought it might happen but only if the person became much more depressed. In this area, "crying wolf" needs to be taken seriously.

As several investigators have pointed out, many people who are contemplating suicide feel that living may be preferable if they can obtain the understanding and support of their family and friends. Failing to receive it after a suicidal threat, they go on to actual suicide.

Suicide Notes Several investigators have analyzed suicide notes in an effort to understand better the motives and feelings of people who take their own lives. In a pioneering study of 742 suicides, Tuckman, Kleiner, and Lavell (1959) found that 24 percent left notes, usually addressed to relatives or friends. The notes were either mailed, found on the deceased, or located near the suicide scene. With few exceptions, the notes were coherent and legible. In terms of emotional content, the suicide notes were categorized into those showing positive, negative, neutral, and mixed affect. Of course, some notes showed combinations of these affective components. *HIGHLIGHT 11.8* provides examples of notes showing differing types of emotional content.

Shneidman and Farberow (1957), in another pioneering study, approached the question of suicide notes by comparing 33 notes written by actual suicides with 33 composed by matched subjects who were asked to simulate a presuicidal state. The principal difference between the actual and the fictitious notes was that the actual ones had a greater number of thought units of a "neutral" quality. Evidently, only a genuine writer tends to deal concretely with the idea of actually being gone; thus he or she incorporates much more material of an instructional and admonishing sort to survivors. The genuine writers, however, also expressed more intense feelings of self-blame, hatred, demand, and vengeance.

In another study, Cohen and Fiedler (1974) compared 220 cases of completed suicides who left notes with 813 cases of nonnote suicides. In contrast to the findings of Tuckman et al.—who reported no differences with respect to such variables as sex, race, and marital status—these investigators found that 26 percent of female suicides left notes as contrasted with 19 percent of males. They also found that 40 percent of the separated or divorced females in their sample left notes as contrasted with approximately 31 percent of single females, 25 percent of married females, and 16 percent of widows. Whites left notes almost three times as often as nonwhites. In terms of content, the use of emotional categories corresponded to those reported by Tuckman and his associates—with positive, neutral, mixed, and negative content being used in that order of frequency. In the study by Farberow and Simon (1975) noted earlier, 46 percent of the Los Angeles residents who committed suicide had left notes, but only 18 percent of the Viennese had done so. It appears that the wish to communicate with survivors after the fact varies considerably with a host of demographic and cultural variables.

An understanding of the reasons for or motives underlying note writing (or its absence) could possibly help make the bases of these variations

HIGHLIGHT 11.8

Types of Suicide Notes

The Tuckman et al. (1959) study classified suicide notes by types of emotional content. A sampling of these various types appears in the following excerpts.

Positive Emotional Content

"Please forgive me and please forget me. I'll always love you. All I have was yours. No one ever did more for me than you, oh please pray for me please." (Tuckman et al., 1959, p. 60)

Negative (Hostile) Emotional Content

"I hate you and all of your family and I hope you never have a peace of mind. I hope I haunt this house as long as you live here and I wish you all the bad luck in the world." (Tuckman et al., 1959, p. 60)

Neutral Emotional Content

"To Whom It May Concern,

"I, Mary Smith, being of sound mind, do this day make my last will as follows—I bequeath my rings, Diamond and Black Opal to my daughter-in-law, Doris Jones and any other of my personal belongings she might wish. What money I might have in my savings account goes to my dear father, as he won't have me to help him. To my husband, Ed Smith, I leave my furniture and car.

"I would like to be buried as close to the grave of John Jones as possible." (Darbonne, 1969, p. 50)

Mixed Emotional Content

Dear Daddy,

Please don't grieve for me or feel that you did something wrong, you didn't. I'll leave this life loving you and remembering the world's greatest father.

I'm sorry to cause you more heartache but the reason I can't live anymore is because I'm afraid. Afraid of facing my life alone without love. No one ever knew how alone I am. No one ever stood by me when I needed help. No one brushed away the tears I cried for "help" and no one heard. I love you Daddy, Jeanne

clearer. On this point, Cohen and Fiedler (1974) concluded,

Many note writers seem to be motivated to influence the responses of survivors. The desire to be remembered positively by a survivor may account for the large number of statements expressing positive affect. By statements of love and concern, a note writer may try to reassure both the survivor and himself of the worth of their relationship and his own worth as a person. (pp. 93–94)

These investigators, however, as well as Schneidman (1973), expressed disappointment that suicide notes—written by people on the brink of life's greatest mystery—failed to contain any great insights or special messages for the rest of us. As Cohen and Fiedler (1974) expressed it,

The large quantity of references to the concrete, mundane features of everyday life is not congruent with the romantic conception of suicide as a grand, dramatic gesture preceded and accompanied by a corresponding state of the psyche into which the suicide note should serve as a kind of window. Perhaps all the drama takes place before the action is decided or it is anticipated in the act itself. Whatever role the dramatic elements may play, the large number of references to the commonplace squares best with the conception of suicide notes as communications tailored to the needs of both the suicide and his survivors as these are perceived by the suicide under existing circumstances. (pp. 94–95)

Suicide Prevention

The prevention of suicide is extremely difficult. One complicating factor is that most people who are depressed and contemplating suicide do not realize that their thinking is restricted and irrational and that they are in need of assistance. Less than one-third voluntarily seek psychological help; others are brought to the attention of mental health personnel by family members or friends who are concerned because the person appears depressed or has made suicide threats. The majority, however, do not receive the assistance they desperately need. As we have seen, however, most people who attempt suicide do not really want to die and give prior warning of their intentions; if an individual's cry for help can be heard in time, it is often possible to intervene successfully.

Currently, the main thrust of preventive efforts is on crisis intervention. Efforts are gradually being extended, however, to the broader tasks of alleviating long-term stressful conditions known to be associated with suicidal behavior and trying to better understand and cope with the suicide problem in high-risk groups (Fremouw, de Perczel, & Ellis, 1990).

Crisis Intervention The primary objective of crisis intervention is to help an individual cope with an immediate life crisis. If a serious suicide attempt has been made, the first step involves emergency medical treatment. Typically, such treatment is given through the usual channels—the emergency rooms of general hospitals or clinics. It appears, however, that only about 10 percent of suicide attempts are considered of sufficient severity to warrant intensive medical care; the great majority of people who attempt suicide, after initial treatment, are referred to inpatient or outpatient mental health facilities (Kirstein et al., 1975; Paykel et al., 1974).

When people contemplating suicide are willing to discuss their problems with someone at a suicide prevention center, it is often possible to avert an actual suicide attempt. Here the primary objective is to help these individuals regain their ability to cope with their immediate problems—and to do so as quickly as possible. Emphasis is usually placed on (a) maintaining contact with a person over a short period of time—usually one to six contacts; (b) helping the person realize that acute distress is impairing his or her ability to assess the situation accurately and to choose among possible alternatives; (c) helping the person see that other ways of dealing with the problem are available and preferable to suicide; (d) taking a highly directive and supportive role—for example, fostering a dependent relationship and giving specific suggestions to the person about what to do and what not to do; and (e) helping the person see that the present distress and emotional turmoil will not be endless. When feasible, counselors may elicit the understanding and emotional support of family members or friends; and, of course, they may make frequent use of relevant community agencies. Admittedly, however, these are stopgap measures and do not constitute complete therapy.

In terms of long-range outcomes, people who have made previous suicide attempts are more likely to kill themselves than those who have not, although only about 10 percent of people who unsuccessfully attempt suicide kill themselves at a later time (Seiden, 1974; Wekstein, 1979; World Health Organization, 1974). As Seiden expressed it, the suicidal crisis "is not a lifetime characteristic of most suicide attempters. It is rather an acute situation, often a matter of only minutes or hours at the most" (p. 2). Because the suicide rate for previous attempters is so much higher than that for the population in general, however, it is apparent that those who have attempted suicide remain a relatively high-risk group.

Farberow (1974) has pointed out that it is important to distinguish between (a) individuals who have demonstrated relatively stable adjustment but have been overwhelmed by some acute stress—about 35 to 40 percent of people coming to the attention of hospitals and suicide prevention centers; and (b) individuals who have been tenuously adjusted for some time and in whom the current suicidal crisis represents an intensification of ongoing problems—about 60 to 65 percent of suicidal cases. For individuals in the first group, crisis intervention is usually sufficient to help them cope with the immediate stress and regain their equilibrium. For individuals in the second group, crisis intervention may also be sufficient to help them deal with the present problem, but with their life-style of "staggering from one crisis to another,"

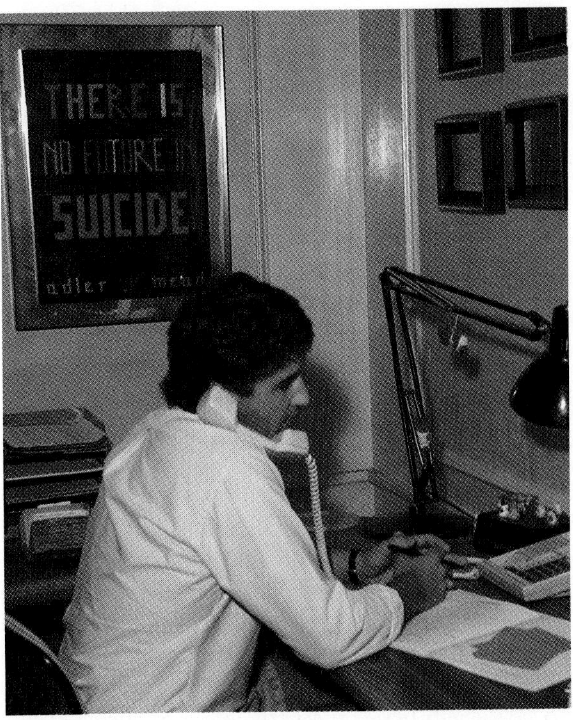

In recent years, the availability of competent assistance at times of suicidal crisis has been expanded through the establishment of suicide prevention centers. These centers are geared toward crisis intervention—usually via 24-hour-a-day availability of telephone contact.

they are likely to require more comprehensive therapy.

During recent years, the availability of competent assistance at times of suicidal crisis has been expanded through the establishment of suicide prevention centers. At present, there are more than 200 such centers in the United States. These centers are geared primarily toward crisis intervention—usually via the 24-hour-a-day availability of telephone contact. Some centers, however, offer long-term therapy programs, and they can refer suicidal people to other community agencies and organizations for special types of assistance. Such suicide prevention centers are staffed by a variety of personnel: psychologists, psychiatrists, social workers, clergy, and trained volunteers. Although initially some doubt existed about the wisdom of using nonprofessionals in the important first-contact role, experience has shown that the empathic concern and peer-type relationships provided by caring volunteers can be highly effective in helping an individual through a suicidal crisis. A guide used by suicide prevention center personnel in gauging the seriousness of suicide threats is provided in *HIGHLIGHT 11.7* on page 416.

It is difficult to evaluate the long-range impact of emergency aid provided by suicide prevention centers, but such facilities seem to have the potential, at least, for significantly reducing suicide rates. The Suicide Prevention Center of Los Angeles has reported that, in comparison with an estimated suicide rate of 6 percent among people judged to be high risks for suicide, the rate has been slightly less than 2 percent among approximately 8000 high-risk people who used their services (Farberow & Litman, 1970).

One difficult problem with which suicide prevention centers must deal is that the majority of people who are seen do not follow up their initial contact by seeking additional help from the center or other treatment agencies. In a follow-up of 53 people who committed suicide after contact with the Cleveland Suicide Prevention Center, Sawyer, Sudak, and Hall (1972) reported that none had recontacted the center just prior to death. They also found that "the interval between the time of last contact with the Center and the time of death ranged from 30 minutes to 32 months with a median interval of 4 months" (p. 232). Since this report was issued, suicide prevention centers have made systematic attempts to expand their services to help them better meet the needs of clients. Thus many centers have introduced long-range after-care or maintenance-therapy programs.

Focus on High-Risk Groups and Other Measures Many investigators have emphasized the need for broadly based preventive programs aimed at alleviating the life problems of people who, on the basis of statistics, fall into high-risk groups with respect to suicide. Few such programs have actually been initiated, but one approach has been to involve older males—a high-risk group—in social and interpersonal roles that help others. These roles may lessen their frequent feelings of isolation and meaninglessness. Among this group, such feelings often stem from forced retirement, financial problems, the death of loved ones, impaired physical health, and feeling unwanted.

Another innovative approach to dealing with people who are contemplating suicide—and who in this sense represent a high-risk group—was originated by a group of volunteers called the Samaritans, begun in England in 1953 by Reverend Chad Varah. The service extended by the Samaritans is simply that of "befriending." Befrienders offer support to a suicidal person with no strings attached. They are available to listen and help in whatever way needed, expecting nothing in return—not even gratitude. Since their founding, the Samaritans have spread throughout the British Commonwealth and to many other parts of the world, and preliminary findings concerning their effectiveness in suicide prevention seem promising (Farberow, 1974, 1975; Wekstein, 1979).

Other measures to broaden the scope of suicide prevention programs include (a) the use of psychological autopsies (psychological profiles of individuals who have committed suicide); (b) the assessment of high-risk groups' environments, often including their work environments; and (c) the training of clergy, nurses, police, teachers, and other professional personnel who come in contact with many people in their communities. An important aspect of such training is to be alert for suicidal threats. For example, a parishioner might clasp the hand of a minister after church services and intensely say, "Pray for me." Because such a request is quite normal, a minister who is not alert to suicidal cries for help might reply with a simple, "Yes, I will" and turn to the next person in line—only to receive the news a few days later that the parishioner has committed suicide.

Ethical Issues in Suicide Prevention Most of us respect the preservation of human life as a worthwhile value. Thus suicide is generally considered not only tragic but "wrong." Efforts to prevent suicide, however, also involve ethical problems. If

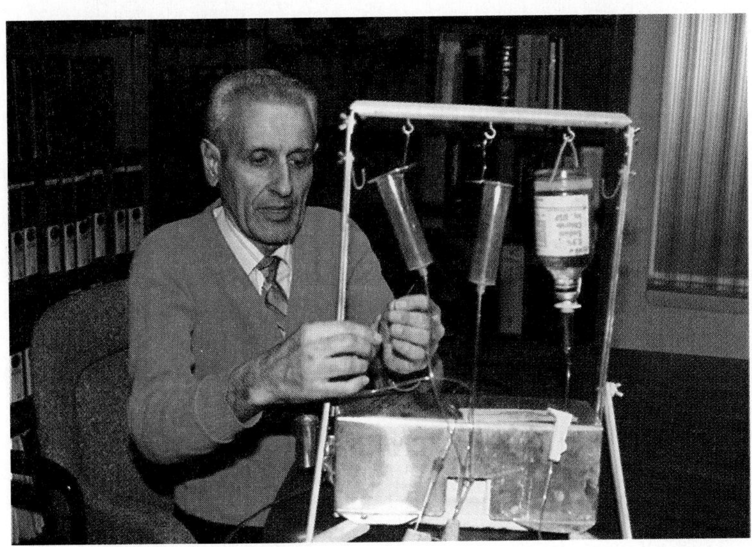

The question of a "right to suicide" is an ethical issue with no easy answers. The issue becomes further clouded in the case of a terminal illness, when a caretaker is faced with the responsibility of a doomed person. One such recent case was that of Janet Adkins, an Alzheimer's patient in the early stages of the disease who decided to take her own life before she became too incapacitated to be able to act for herself. She enlisted the help of Dr. Jack Kevorkian, who had invented a so-called suicide machine, shown here, whereby Ms. Adkins initiated her own suicide through a fatal injection. Though the issue of aiding and abetting a suicide was raised, Dr. Kevorkian was not charged with any crime. The notion of a "suicide machine" further complicates the issue of the right to suicide, and even some who would defend suicide as a reasonable choice under some circumstances feel that such a machine should be illegal.

individuals wish to take their own lives, what obligation—or right—do others have to interfere? This question has been taken seriously by Thomas Szasz (1976), whose view of the problem is captured in the following:

In regarding the desire to live as a legitimate human aspiration, but not the desire to die, the suicidologist stands Patrick Henry's famous exclamation . . . on its head. In effect, he says, "Give him commitment, give him electroshock, give him lobotomy, give him life-long slavery, but do not let him choose death!" By so radically illegitimizing another person's (not his own!) wish to die, the suicide preventor redefines the aspiration of the other as not an aspiration at all. (p. 177)

Needless to say, Szasz's ideas are controversial.

Certainly a persuasive case can be made for the right of people afflicted with a terminal illness, who suffer chronic and debilitating pain, to shorten their agony. But what about the rights of suicidal people who are not terminally ill and who have dependent children, parents, a spouse, or other loved ones who will be adversely affected, perhaps permanently (Lukas & H. Seiden, 1990), by their death? Here a person's "right to suicide," reduced to such nonabstract terms, is not immediately obvious. The right to suicide is even less clear in the case of those who are ambivalent about taking their lives and who might, through intervention, regain their perspective and see alternative ways of dealing with their distress. Still, who has the right to *prevent* another's self-destruction?

Possibly, as has been pointed out by Nelson (1984), the early suicidologists erred in focusing on suicide "prevention." Nelson suggests suicide "intervention" as both a more appropriate term and as descriptive of a more ethically defensible professional approach to suicidal behavior. Suicide intervention, according to this perspective, embodies a more neutral moral stance to suicide than does prevention—it means interceding without the implication of preventing the act—and, in given circumstances, may even hold out the possibility of facilitating the suicidal person's objective.

Here, however, we should reemphasize that the great majority of people who attempt suicide either do not really want to die or are ambivalent about taking their lives; and even for the minority who do wish to die, the desire is often a transient one. With improvement in a person's life situation and a lifting of depression, the suicidal crisis is likely to pass and not recur. As Murphy (1973) has expressed it, "The 'right' to suicide is a 'right' desired only temporarily" (p. 472).

The dilemma becomes intense indeed when prevention requires that an individual be hospitalized involuntarily; when personal items, such as belts and sharp objects, are taken away; and when calming medication is more or less forcibly administered. Sometimes considerable restriction is needed to calm the individual. Not uncommonly, particularly in these litigious times, the responsible clinician feels trapped between threats of legal action on either side of the issue. Undue restriction might lead to a civil rights suit, whereas failure to employ all available safeguards could, in the case of the patient's injury or death, lead to a potentially ruinous malpractice claim initiated by the patient's family (Fremouw, de Perczel, & Ellis, 1990).

Currently, it appears that most practitioners resolve this dilemma by taking the most cautious and conservative course. Thus many patients are hospitalized with insufficient clinical justification. Even where the decision to hospitalize is made on good grounds, however, preventive efforts may be fruitless. For example, in a study of hospitalized people who were persistently suicidal, Watkins, Gilbert, and Bass (1969) reported that "almost one-third used methods from which we cannot isolate them—seven head ramming, two asphyxia by aspiration of paper, one asphyxia by food, and three by exsanguination by tearing their blood vessels with their fingers" (p. 1593). Here again, however, as in the case of terminal illness and suffering, we are talking about a distinct minority of suicide cases.

Admittedly, the preceding considerations do not resolve the issue of a person's basic right to suicide. As in the case of most complex ethical issues, no simple answer is apparent. Unless and until sufficient evidence confirms this alleged right —and society agrees on the conditions under which it may appropriately be exercised—it thus seems the wiser course to encourage existing suicide prevention (intervention) programs and to foster research into suicidal behavior with the hope of reducing the toll in human life and misery taken each year by suicide in our society.

UNRESOLVED ISSUES on Mood Disorders and Suicide

Despite tremendous advances in recent years, especially but not exclusively at the biological level, the phenomena of human depression continue to challenge us with many enigmas. Biological advances have in fact contributed to one of the foremost of these enigmas in giving rise to persistent suggestions that human depression is not, in a strict sense, "human" at all. It is, according to this view, merely an impersonal breakdown of the "machinery" of the brain; an affected patient is, as it were, a nonparticipant in the process and has no responsibility for either the emergence of the problem or its alleviation. The title, and the substance, of an influential book by psychiatrist Nancy Andreasen (1984), *The Broken Brain,* is as good a statement as any of this currently popular position in some segments of psychiatry. It predicts a biological treatment revolution "in the 1980s and 1990s," one whose beginnings even at this advanced date we cannot discern. The argument advanced in Andreasen's book contains the seeds of a ***reductio ad absurdum*** in which, for example, a pill might be prescribed for the "disease" of mourning one's recently deceased child. The human and philosophical implications of the more extremely reductionistic versions of this thesis are, in our judgment, cause for serious concern. Even at a purely pragmatic level, however, this radical view of modern psychiatry's mission has, as we have seen, largely failed to deliver on its inflated promises. Perhaps the time has come for greater restraint among those believing that aberrations of human behavior and personality are reducible to physical malfunctions in the brain that can be set right by tinkering with its parts.

Moving to another but not wholly unrelated matter, serious problems continue in the current taxonomy and nomenclature of the mood disorders. Although there is realistic hope of eventually identifying and isolating a unitary subset of disorders in the bipolar-cyclothymia domain, the remainder of the diagnostic system relating to mood disorders remains in disarray. This situation means that treatment choices are still all too often a matter of "let's see if *this* works." To be sure, many of the impediments to progress in this area relate to its inherent complexities. Others, however, can be traced to researchers' rigidity and prejudices, of which the survival of "endogenous" depression as a concept is, we suspect, an example. As earlier suggested, we think there may be merit in considering depression as analogous to fever, in which case the fine differentiation of subvarieties is a largely pointless exercise, especially where it detracts from a search for the underlying causes of what may be a global and qualitatively uniform (but quantitatively variable) manifestation of psychic distress.

Finally, the vexing ethical problems of whether and to what extent one should intervene in cases of threatened suicide have now been complicated by no less vexing legal ones. As in other areas of professional practice, clinical judgment is no longer the exclusive consideration in intervention decisions. The ramifications of clinical decisions spread widely to matters that were formerly remote or irrelevant, such as the cost of malpractice insurance or the estimated likelihood that a patient or his or her family will sue if the opportunity presents itself. Because this is a societal problem, the solutions—if any—will have to be societal ones.

SUMMARY

Mood disorders (formerly called affective disorders) are those in which extreme variations in mood—either low or high—are the predominant feature. We all experience such variations at mild to moderate levels in the natural course of life. In some instances, however, the extremity of a person's mood in either direction is causally related to behavior that most would consider maladaptive. This chapter describes the official categories of disorder associated with such maladaptive mood variations.

The large majority of these disorders involve some type of mental depression, in which an individual experiences, at the mildest levels, self-depreciation, excessive dependency, and a sense that outcomes are independent of his or her coping efforts. As these problems deepen into disorder, all of these characteristics are intensified, and a person may become preoccupied with feelings of guilt and worthlessness. Often in such cases, basic biological functioning seems to be altered—for example, the sleep pattern may be dramatically altered or the person may become uninterested in food or eating. In the hypomanic or manic variants (for example, in cyclothymia or bipolar disorders in which the current episode is one of being excessively "high"), essentially the opposite pattern exists. Depressive syndromes, however, are much more common than manic ones, and they appear to be much more diffuse and heterogeneous in nature than those in which manic or hypomanic episodes appear in a person's history. In the latter instance, the person is considered to have a (bipolar) predisposition to react in both depressive and manic ways.

Except for certain syndromes that seem secondary to organic brain impairment, the mood disorders are divided into major and nonmajor categories. The major mood disorders are those of major depression and bipolar disorder. Far more common are a variety of depressive (or, less often, hypomanic) conditions that are typically less severe in intensity, including dysthymia, cyclothymia, and adjustment disorder with depressed mood. In general, the efficacy of biologically-based treatments, such as drugs or ECT, is limited to the more severe or major disorders. In the milder forms of mood disorder, psychosocial treatments, of which an increasing variety are available, seem equally or more effective. Combination treatment approaches have shown great promise and may become the treatment of choice for current episodes; considerable evidence suggests that long-term resistance to recurrent depression is best conferred by specialized forms of psychosocial treatment.

Suicide is a constant danger with depressive syndromes of any type or severity. Accordingly, an assessment of suicide risk is essential in the proper management of depressive disorders. A small minority of suicides appears unavoidable—chiefly those of the deliberate "not to be" type. A substantial amount of suicidal behavior (for example, taking slow-acting drugs where the likelihood of discovery is high) is motivated more by a desire for indirect interpersonal communication than by a wish to die. Somewhere between these extremes is a large group of people who are desperately ambivalent about killing themselves and who initiate dangerous actions that they may or may not carry to completion, depending on momentary events and impulses. Most suicide prevention efforts are normally and properly focused on this ambivalent group. Of course, a reasonable and ethical argument can be made that, in certain circumstances, efforts to deter suicide are philosophically questionable.

Key Terms

mood disorders (p. 381)
psychotic behavior (psychosis) (p. 382)
mood-congruent thinking (p. 382)
mania (p. 382)
depression (p. 382)
major depression (p. 382)
bipolar disorder (p. 382)
hypomania (p. 386)
cyclothymia (p. 386)
dysthymia (p. 387)
adjustment disorder with depressed mood (p. 388)
unipolar disorder (p. 391)
schizoaffective disorder (p. 396)
suicide (p. 410)

Chapter 12

The Schizophrenias and Delusional Disorders

Le Voyageur Français, *Le Pays des Météores* (1902–1905). The French Traveler's real name, and most of the details of his life, remain undiscovered. He is thought to have been a professional artist or decorator who was institutionalized at Villejuif, France, for schizophrenia. He painted rather conventional scenes, and then "signed" them in the corner with an intricate pattern composed of abstract masses of color. The painting here shows the extremely bizarre effect resulting from the clash of painting and "signature."

As we saw in Chapter 11, the mood disorders chiefly involve a disturbance of affect. To the extent that disruptions of perceptual, cognitive, and information-processing mechanisms (such as delusions and hallucinations) occur in the mood disorders, they seem secondary to the more primary mood dysfunction. By and large, the opposite is true in schizophrenic and delusional disorders, where disruption of thought processes is primary, and where often no obvious relationship exists between mood and thinking. This observation, however, does not provide a reliable basis for distinguishing these supposedly separate psychopathological entities. As we have already noted in connection with so-called schizoaffective disorders, many cases fall between the cracks.

With the schizophrenias, we move into a realm of behavioral disorder that represents in many ways the ultimate in psychological breakdown. These disorders include some of the most extreme behaviors to be found in human behavior, and they involve virtually all of the psychopathological processes encountered thus far in this text, plus something more. What that "something more" may be, as we will see, is not readily grasped or defined, but its full expression is clearly within the psychotic range; a schizophrenic individual's whole personality is involved, and there is a more or less sharp break with reality as most of us conceive it.

By and large, schizophrenic people display most of the broad characteristics seen in other types of psychopathology. Identifiable stressors usually precede the onset of their disorders. There is evidence of a genetically transmitted diathesis and, in many cases, a psychosocially disturbed family background. A significant subgroup of these patients have demonstrable neurological anomalies. Usually, people diagnosed as schizophrenic engage in a relatively transparent use of ego-defense mechanisms, and anxiety and panic are common accompaniments of the disorder. Often they are bothered with psychogenic physical ailments of one sort or another, particularly in the early or acute phases of the disturbance. They often show pronounced personality or character deviations prior to breakdown. Finally, they are capable of extremes in mood that are easily the equal of anything seen in the major mood disorders.

Paranoid (delusional) conditions have traditionally been seen as separate processes from those of the schizophrenias, although clinical observers have long noted a tendency for them to occur together; thus we have the classical schizophrenia subtype known as *paranoid schizophrenia.* Contemporary investigators (Brennan & Hemsley, 1984; Magaro, 1981; Meissner, 1981) have confirmed the traditional view, concluding that schizophrenic and paranoid processes are quite distinct. Paranoid forms of thinking sometimes accompany other types of disorder, such as mood, and they may also appear by themselves as relatively uncomplicated delusional states, as will be seen in the latter part of this chapter.

THE SCHIZOPHRENIAS

The schizophrenias are a group of psychotic disorders characterized mainly by gross distortions of reality; withdrawal from social interaction; and disorganization and fragmentation of perception, thought, and emotion. We will focus here on the adult forms of such mental derangements. Similar childhood syndromes will be discussed in Chapter 14. Though the clinical picture may vary widely in people diagnosed as schizophrenic, the disorganization of experience that typifies schizophrenic episodes during the psychotic phase is well illustrated in the following composite description:

Suspicious and frightened, the victim fears he can trust neither his own senses, nor the motives of other people . . . his skin prickles, his head seems to hum, and "voices" annoy him. Unpleasant odors choke him, his food may have no taste. Bright and colorful visions ranging from brilliant butterflies to dismembered bodies pass before his eyes. Ice clinking in a nearby pitcher seems to be a diabolic device bent on his destruction.

When someone talks to him, he hears only disconnected words. These words may touch off an old memory or a strange dream. His attention wanders from his inner thoughts to the grotesque way the speaker's mouth moves, or the loud scrape his chair makes against the floor. He cannot understand what the person is trying to tell him, nor why.

When he tries to speak, his own words sound foreign to him. Broken phrases tumble out over and over again, and somewhat fail to express how frightened and worried he is. (Yolles, 1967, p. 42)

Schizophrenic disorders were at one time attributed to a type of "mental deterioration" beginning early in life. In 1860 the Belgian psychiatrist Morel described the case of a 13-year-old boy who had formerly been the most brilliant pupil in his school but who, over a period of time, lost interest in his studies, became increasingly withdrawn, seclusive, and taciturn, and appeared to have forgotten everything he had learned. He talked frequently of killing his father, and evidenced a kind of inactivity that bordered on stupidity. Morel thought the boy's intellectual, moral, and physical functions had deteriorated as a result of hereditary causes and hence were irrecoverable. He used the term *demence precoce* (mental deterioration at an early age) to describe the condition and to distinguish it from disorders of old age.

The Latin form of this term—*dementia praecox*—was subsequently adopted by the German psychiatrist Emil Kraepelin to refer to a group of conditions that all seemed to have the feature of mental deterioration beginning early in life. Actually, however, the term is somewhat misleading, because the problems usually become apparent not during childhood but during adolescence or early adulthood. In addition, there is no conclusive evidence of permanent mental deterioration in the natural course of most of the disorders subsumed by the term. It appears that both Morel and Kraepelin mistook as a manifestation of progressive brain disease the gradual deterioration of psychosocial functioning that was in fact a result of lengthy incarceration in the bleak and demoralizing mental institutions of the time.

It remained for a Swiss psychiatrist, Eugen Bleuler, to introduce in 1911 a more acceptable descriptive term for this general class of disorders. He used *schizophrenia* (split mind) because he thought the condition was characterized primarily by disorganization of thought processes, a lack of coherence between thought and emotion, and an inward orientation away (split off) from reality. The "splitting" thus does not imply multiple personalities, an entirely different form of disorder discussed in Chapter 6, but a splitting within the intellect, between the intellect and emotion, and between the intellect and external reality.

It is by no means clear that schizophrenia is a unitary process, however. The existence of a single diagnostic label—in this case, *schizophrenia*—does not by itself establish similarity of underlying organization in each case of schizophrenia, any more than does a medical diagnosis of high blood pressure, which can be due to many different underlying conditions. Thus many clinicians today believe that there may be several schizophrenias, quite apart from the classic subtypes such as paranoid and catatonic, with different causal patterns and outcomes (Bellak, 1979). As we will see, there is empirical support for this pluralist view. Interestingly, the title of Bleuler's (1911/1950) masterful treatise on the subject refers to "the Group of Schizophrenias."

Schizophrenic disorders seem to occur in virtually all societies, from the aborigines of the western Australian desert to the remote interior jungles of Malaysia to the most technologically advanced societies. In the United States, the estimated incidence of schizophrenia is slightly under 1 percent of the population. The six-month prevalence rate for schizophrenia (that is, the proportion of people considered to be schizophrenic at any time during a prior six-month period) in the United States at present is estimated to be 0.9 percent of those 18 or older—or about 1.5 million affected people (Locke & Regier, 1985). In recent years schizophrenia has been the primary diagnosis for nearly 40 percent of all admissions to state and county mental hospitals, far outstripping all other diagnostic categories; it has been the second most frequent primary diagnosis (the first being either mood or alcohol-related disorders) for every other type of inpatient psychiatric care, including private hospitals (Manderscheid et al., 1985). During calendar year 1986, approximately 900,000 people received hospital or clinic services in the United States for a primary diagnosis of schizophrenia (Rosenstein, Milazzo-Sayre, & Manderscheid, 1989). Because schizophrenic individuals often require prolonged or repeated hospitalization, they usually constitute about half the patient population for all available mental hospital beds in this country (President's Commission on Mental Health, 1978).

Although schizophrenic disorders sometimes occur during childhood or old age, about three-fourths of all first admissions are between the ages of 15 and 45, with a median age of just over 30. The incidence rate is about the same for males and females. Because of their complexity, their high rate of incidence (especially during the most productive years of life), and their tendency to recur or become chronic, the schizophrenias are considered the most serious of all mental disorders, as well as among the most baffling.

■ A Case Study

We depart somewhat from our usual format in discussing the clinical syndromes to present first a unique and uniquely well-documented case study involving the schizophrenic syndrome. We hope this approach will help you more readily understand the many facets of schizophrenia. The case involves a family of six—two biological parents and their four monozygotic, quadruplet daughters—in which all four daughters became schizophrenic prior to age 25. Some appreciation of just how remarkable this circumstance is can be derived from the combined improbability of viable quadruplicate births, identical heredity, and perfect concordance for schizophrenia; a fairly liberal estimate is that it would occur once in every 1.5 *billion* births. We are indebted for the thorough knowledge we have of this unfortunate family to David Rosenthal (1963) and his colleagues, working under the auspices of the National Institute of Mental Health. For obvious reasons, certain specific but nonessential data, such as names and dates, have been omitted or falsified in the report, and we will honor that consideration in our synopsis. Should you be tempted to jump to the conclusion that these are obviously cases of genetically determined disorder, we counsel keeping an open mind on this point.

Background and Early Years Some time in the early 1930s, quadruplet girls were born to Mr. and Mrs. Henry Genain, the product of a marriage occasioned by Mr. Genain's threatening to kill the reluctant Mrs. Genain unless she consented to the marriage. Except for their low birth weights, ranging from Nora's 4 lb, 8 oz, to Hester's 3 lb, the girls appeared to be reasonably normal babies, albeit "premature." Hester had to be fitted with a truss (an abdominal compression device) because of a bilateral hernia but was nevertheless discharged from the hospital with her sisters as basically healthy some six weeks after the birth. These were the only children the Genains ever had.

The most pervasive, if not necessarily the most formative, feature of the girls' early life was their fame. From birth, they received a great deal of attention from the media and the public. Early on, in fact, their parents started charging admission (25 cents) to members of the public to visit the home and view the babies, an enterprise that ended when the parents became concerned about the possibility of kidnapping or the transmission of some disease to the children. In subsequent years the children were encouraged in dancing and singing as a team, and they performed often at various functions and at school assemblies. Partly as a result of their "celebrity" status, the girls tended to stick closely together for mutual protection; they even rebuffed children their own age, with the result that they became social isolates. They were encouraged in this social isolation by their parents, who shared strong anxieties about the dangers of "the outside world."

Notwithstanding their genetic identity and physical similarity, the girls were sharply differentiated by their parents virtually from birth. In fact they were treated as though they were two sets of twins—a superior and talented set consisting of Nora and Myra, and an inferior, problematic set consisting of Iris and Hester. Hester—the "runt of the litter"—was regarded from an early age as oversexed. (Possibly because of irritation from her truss, Hester began to masturbate regularly by the age of three, a habit she continued for many years to the considerable dismay of her parents.) Complying with parental attributions, the girls did in fact pair up for purposes of mutual support and intimacy; when threatened from the outside, however, they became a true foursome.

Mr. Genain held a minor political office for more than 20 years, having been pushed into running by his wife. His job was not very demanding, and he spent most of his time drinking and expressing his various fears and obsessions to his family. Prominent among these were fears that break-ins would occur at the home unless he patrolled the premises constantly with a loaded gun, and, especially as the girls developed into adolescence, that they would get into sexual trouble or be raped unless he watched over them with total dedication.

He imposed almost unbelievable restrictions and surveillance on the girls until the time of their breakdowns. Beginning at an early age and persisting through early adulthood, Mr. Genain insisted on being present when his daughters dressed and undressed. He even insisted on watching them change their sanitary pads during menstruation. He was himself sexually promiscuous around town and was reported to have sexually molested at least two of his daughters; quite possibly Myra, who distanced herself from him with singular persistence, was the only one of the girls to escape his attentions in this regard.

Mr. Genain's preoccupation with sexuality, while extreme and almost preemptive of anything else, was at least matched by that of his wife. Mrs. Genain managed to see sexuality and sexual threats in the most innocuous circumstances and yet was curiously impervious to certain real sexual activity occurring practically before her eyes. When the girls complained to her about Mr. Genain's sexual attentions, she dismissed these happenings with the rationale that Mr. Genain was merely testing their virtue; if they objected to his advances, then clearly all was well. Not that she saw Mr. Genain as a paragon of virtue; on the contrary, she recited his many faults of breeding and grossness to anyone who would listen. Nevertheless, she stuck by him to the end (a typically alcoholic end) and largely confirmed and supported his bizarre constructions of reality. Hester, the chronic masturbator, was a particular thorn in her side—all the more so when she discovered that, at about age 12, Hester had apparently seduced Iris into the practice of mutual masturbation, which Iris found pleasing. Apparently unable to think of any more appropriate response to this dilemma, the parents—on the questionable advice of a physician—forced the two girls to submit to clitoral circumcisions, a measure whose drastic quality was exceeded only by its ineffectiveness in altering the offending behavior. In general, however, Mrs. Genain enjoyed the status accorded her as the mother of quadruplets, and she remained unfailingly and overwhelmingly involved in the girls' lives. Most of her affection was reserved for the "good" quads, Nora and Myra.

Adolescence, Young Adulthood, and Breakdown Except for their extreme social isolation, the girls had a relatively uneventful junior high school experience. They were regarded by their teachers as conforming, hard-working, and "nice," except for some competition among them in respect to grades and adult approval. Hester clearly lagged behind the others, and Iris could not quite keep up with the remaining two in academic performance. Essentially the same pattern continued into high school. In the summer preceding the girls' senior year, Hester, whose behavior had become somewhat peculiar and who was apparently suffering from some type of psychophysiologic gastrointestinal distress, finally became disturbed to the point that her parents could hardly manage her. She was temperamental, often did not seem to know what she was doing, destroyed household furnishings, tore both her own and her sisters' clothing, and on one occasion struck Nora with such force as to render her unconscious. Hester had just turned 18; she never thereafter regained a full measure of effective mental functioning.

The other three girls completed their senior year of high school, engaging in a kind of conspiracy of silence regarding the missing Hester, who remained at home. Outwardly they appeared to be normal adolescents, although they were not permitted to have boyfriends and continued to have various physical difficulties, including menstrual irregularities and persistent enuresis (bed-wetting). Following graduation, they obtained employment as office workers. They continued to be spied on by their suspicious father, however, lest they become involved in sexual liaisons. They were not permitted to date. Of the three, Myra maintained the most independence, defying her father's edict that she not go out at night to meetings and the like.

None of the three young women was comfortable in the world of work, feeling inadequate to the responsibilities heaped on them by allegedly insensitive bosses. Nora was the first to evidence unusual "nervousness," and at age 20 began to have a series of vague physical complaints. She eventually quit her job and took to her bed at home, gradually becoming more disturbed. She stood on her knees and elbows until they became irritated and bled, began to walk and talk in her sleep, and moaned and groaned a great deal, especially at mealtime. Her behavior continued to deteriorate until, at age 22, she underwent her first of several hospital admissions with the diagnosis of schizophrenia. In the meantime, Iris had likewise become increasingly disturbed, also resigning from her job. She was troubled by "spastic colon," vomiting, insomnia, and the belief that people were paying her undue attention. In fact it was later learned that Mr. Genain was at the time greatly attentive to her whereabouts and activities and may have been molesting her. Within several months after Nora's first admission, Iris "just went to pieces." She screamed, was markedly agitated, complained of hearing voices and of people fighting, and drooled at meals, being unable to swallow anything but liquids. She, too, was hospitalized toward the end of her twenty-second year for the first of many times. The diagnosis was schizophrenia.

Myra did not break down until age 24. The onset was similar to that of her sisters: vomiting, panic, insomnia, and waking up at night screaming. Myra resisted hospitalization at this time and, in fact, was not hospitalized until the entire family was shortly thereafter moved to the Clinical Center of the National Institute of Mental Health (NIMH). There, as a unit, they underwent the lengthy and detailed study of which this history is one product. On arrival, Myra was autistic, disordered in thought, and impaired in judgment and reality testing. She was diagnosed as schizophrenic.

It may be significant that in the cases of Nora, Iris, and Myra, deterioration began shortly after an incident in which a man had made rather insistent "improper advances." In paradoxical but characteristic fashion, both parents had minimized the significance of these incidents when the girls complained.

Course and Outcome By the time they arrived at the Clinical Center at age 24, Nora had undergone three separate hospital admissions and Iris five. Hester had somehow escaped hospitalization, although she was often bizarre and psychotic at home. With all four of the daughters simultaneously disturbed in varying degrees, the home atmosphere had become truly chaotic.

Once at the NIMH, the sisters were offered varied forms of treatment and care, including the new antipsychotic medications that had recently become available. They remained at the NIMH for three years. At the end of their stay, Myra was the only one capable of attaining a sustainable discharge. The other three sisters were transferred to a state hospital. Mr. Genain had died of liver disease in the interim.

It is important to note that, though the earliest symptoms of the quads were similar in certain respects, the courses and outcomes of their disorders differed markedly and, to some extent, in ways that could have been predicted. The most serious and deteriorated of the classical types of schizophrenia is the ***disorganized type*** (formerly called ***hebephrenic***). In the various diagnoses assigned to them in the course of their hospitalizations, Nora and Myra were never so diagnosed, although Nora was sometimes regarded as having "hebephrenic features." By contrast, Iris and Hester moved through the "milder" ***catatonic*** and ***undifferentiated types*** into the disorganized type. The quads' outcomes show a corresponding pattern. At the time of Rosenthal's 1963 report, Myra was working steadily, married, and doing well. Nora was making a marginal adjustment outside of the hospital. Iris was still fluctuating between periods of severe disturbance and relative lucidity in which she could manage brief

In 1981, the Genains performed a rendition of "Alice Blue Gown" at a birthday party held in their honor at the National Institute of Mental Health.

stays outside of the hospital. Hester remained continuously hospitalized in a condition of severe psychosis and was considered essentially a "hopeless case."

It is a tribute to the scientific diligence of the NIMH staff and to David Rosenthal, who has maintained both a human and a scientific interest in this unfortunate family, that we had a follow-up report some 20 years after the original one (DeLisi et al., 1984; Mirsky et al., 1984; Sargent, 1982a). In general, the relative adjustment of the sisters, then in their 50s, remained in 1982 as it was in the 1960s. Myra continued to do well and had two children in the interim. The other three women were living at home with their mother, with Nora continuing to show a higher level of functioning than Iris or Hester. All of the quads were on continuous medication, and even the beleaguered Hester appeared to have overcome to an extent her originally dismal prognosis. It is of considerable interest that newer techniques of neurological assessment showed that Nora had impairments of the central nervous system similar to those of Hester, and yet her outcome seemed far better than that of Hester or even Iris. It is possible that the original pairing of Iris with Hester was inappropriate (at least in the limited sense implied here) and quite destructive of Iris' subsequent psychosocial development. In any event, we see that the quads, despite their identical heredity, array themselves along a considerable range of the possible outcomes associated with schizophrenic breakdown.

Interpretive Comment We have here, then, four genetically identical women, all of whom have experienced schizophrenic disorders. The disorders, however, have been different in severity, chronicity, and eventual outcome. Obviously these differences must be ascribed to differences in the environments the quads experienced, including their intrauterine environments, which presumably contributed to their modest variations detectable at birth. Clearly Hester, in relative parental disfavor from the beginning, faced the harshest environmental conditions, followed closely by her "twin," Iris. The outcome for these women has been grim. Myra was the most favored youngster and clearly the one who experienced the least objectionable parental attention, partly owing to a greater independence and assertiveness than her sisters displayed. Nora was a close second in this respect but had the misfortune of being her incestuous father's "favorite"; in recent tests, she also proved to have a compromised central nervous system (specifically, an imbalance of metabolic rates in different brain areas) comparable to that of Hester. Though Nora has not done as well as Myra, she has emerged as clearly superior in functioning to the other two sisters. We see here the enormous power of environmental forces in determining personal destiny.

But let us look again. We have four genetically identical individuals, all of whom became schizophrenic within a period of six years—three of them within a period of some two years. Is this not a compelling case for genetic determination? An independent genealogical history suggests that the quads' father may have harbored some pathogenic genes, which could have been passed on to his daughters. On the other hand, we must ask what might have happened to these girls in the absence of any special genetic impediments. As Rosenthal (1963) points out, their parents failed spectacularly in the most elementary tasks of parenthood. Can we imagine that the Genain sisters would have been reasonably well-adjusted had they possessed no defective genes? This scenario seems rather unlikely.

In the final analysis, a plausible conclusion is that both heredity and environment, operating in some complex and at present mysterious interaction, contributed to the Genain sisters' vulnerabilities. In this instance, unfortunately, it is difficult to make even an estimate of the relative magnitude of the two influences. In some other instances of schizophrenic disorder, one can make a shrewd guess—based on genetic history, developmental experience, and the like—about the relative contribution from each of these two broad sources of behavioral variation. As we have seen, however, and as we will see repeatedly again in this chapter, the central fact always is the interaction between the two. We will refer to the Genains from time to time in the pages that follow.

The Clinical Picture in Schizophrenia

Sometimes schizophrenic disorders develop slowly and insidiously. In such cases the early clinical picture may be dominated by seclusiveness, gradual lack of interest in the surrounding world, excessive daydreaming, blunting of affect (diminished emotional responsivity), and mildly inappropriate responses, such as peculiar grimacing or ineptitude in appreciating social proprieties. This symptom pattern has traditionally been referred to as **process schizophrenia**—that is, it develops gradually over a period of time, not in response to obvious discrete stressors, and tends to be long-lasting. The outcome for process schizophrenia is considered generally unfavorable, doubtless partly because the need for treatment is usually not recognized until the behavior pattern has become firmly entrenched. **Poor**

premorbid (preexisting the occurrence of actual disorder) or **chronic schizophrenia** are alternative terms referring to this pattern.

In other instances, the onset of schizophrenic symptoms is quite sudden and dramatic and is marked by intense emotional turmoil and a nightmarish sense of confusion. This pattern, which usually is associated with identifiable precipitating stressors, is referred to as **reactive schizophrenia** (alternatively, **good premorbid** or **acute schizophrenia**). Here the symptoms often clear up in a matter of weeks, though in some cases an acute episode is the prelude to a more chronic pattern.

Today, particularly in the psychiatric literature, the terms **negative-symptom schizophrenia** and **positive-symptom schizophrenia** are being used to refer to the symptom patterns themselves and appear to overlap considerably with the older *process* and *reactive* designations, respectively (Andreasen, 1985). By *negative symptoms* is meant an absence or deficit of behaviors normally present in a person's repertoire, such as affective expression or reactivity to the environment; these symptoms are typically more "subtle." *Positive symptoms,* by contrast, are those in which something has been *added* to a normal repertoire of behavior and experience, such as marked emotional turmoil, motor agitation, delusional interpretation of events, or hallucinations.

Of the Genain quadruplets, Hester—who never seemed quite as well off mentally as her sisters and who seemed to move in imperceptible steps toward increasing deterioration—would be considered a more process (or poor premorbid, or negative-symptom) type. By contrast, Myra, the least disturbed before her breakdown, the last to succumb, and the one whose symptoms, while dramatic, were most circumscribed in time, would be considered a more reactive (good premorbid, positive-symptom) case. Although the experience of the Genains fits this classic dichotomy as it is conceived, there are some serious problems with this conception, as indicated in what follows.

It is sometimes held that antipsychotic medication affects only positive symptoms. This appears to be an erroneous clinical observation, however, since it has been known for many years that negative symptoms, such as social withdrawal, may also respond to these medications (NIMH Psychopharmacology Service Center Collaborative Study Group, 1964). This finding was reconfirmed by Kay & Singh (1989) in a rigorously designed recent study. Another widespread belief is that positive schizophrenia has a better long-term prognosis than negative schizophrenia, but the 36-month follow-up of their patients by Kay and Singh surprisingly indicated the opposite to be the case.

There thus seems to be some confusion concerning the meaning, if any, of this dichotomy. In fact, it is in all likelihood *not* a dichotomy. With rare exception, the available research evidence indicates that the distinctions mentioned in the preceding paragraphs should really be viewed as continua. In regard to positive- versus negative-symptom patterns, instances of schizophrenic disorder can be seen as distributing themselves in the familiar bell-shaped curve, with relatively few falling at either the negative- or positive-symptom extremes and most falling somewhere in the middle. We thus expect a large percentage of schizophrenic patients to display both positive and negative symptoms, as seems in fact to be the case (Guelfi, Faustman, & Csernansky, 1989). Everything considered, therefore, we have considerable doubt that the distinction now designated by the positive/negative rubric is a valid or useful one. Similar reservations have recently been expressed by Andreasen et al. (1990) following a more comprehensive review of the evidence.

Another distinction commonly made by researchers is that between *paranoid* and *nonparanoid symptom patterns* in schizophrenia. In the paranoid pattern, delusions, particularly persecutory or grandiose ones, are a dominant feature; in the nonparanoid forms, delusions, if present at all, tend to be rare, fleeting, and of inconsistent content. Evidence is building that important differences exist between those who exhibit a predominant paranoid symptom pattern and those who exhibit few, or no, or inconsistent paranoid symptoms.

In general, paranoid schizophrenic individuals tend to be more reactive than process in type and to have more benign courses and outcomes (Ritzler, 1981); they are less likely to show the striking kinds of cognitive or attentional deficits seen in other forms of the disorder (Rabin, Doneson, & Jentons, 1979). They may also be genetically less vulnerable to schizophrenia than nonparanoid types (Kendler & Davis, 1981). It has been found, however, that a substantial number of people originally diagnosed as having paranoid forms of schizophrenic disorder are later diagnosed as having nonparanoid ones (Kendler & Tsuang, 1981). Also, there appears to be a small subgroup of paranoid schizophrenic people whose disorders are extremely intractable and chronic. It is of interest to note that all of the Genain sisters exhibited exclusively nonparanoid symptoms during the active phases of their disorders.

Whether positive, negative, paranoid, or nonparanoid in the general sense of these terms, schizophrenia encompasses many specific symptoms that vary greatly over time in an individual's life and from one individual to another. The basic experience in schizophrenia, however, seems to be disorganization in perception, thought, and emotion. The DSM-III-R specifies in concrete terms a list of criteria for the diagnosis, reproduced in *HIGHLIGHT 12.1.* What follows is a more elaborated version of those criteria.

Disorganization of a Previous Level of Functioning Disorganization of functioning is perhaps the closest we can come to an accepted cardinal sign of schizophrenic breakdown; it distinguishes the schizophrenias from various developmental anomalies, such as infantile autism, in which the person has never attained a degree of integrated behavioral functioning consistent with his or her age. The impairment always occurs in areas of routine daily functioning, such as work, social relations, and self-care, such that observers note that the person is not himself or herself any more.

Disturbance of Language and Communication First described at length by Bleuler (1911/1950) and often referred to as *formal thought disorder,* communication disturbance, too, is usually considered a prime indicator of a schizophrenic disorder. Basically, an affected individual fails to conform to the semantic and syntactic rules governing verbal communication in the known language—but this failure is *not* attributable to low intelligence, poor education, or cultural deprivation. Meehl (1962) aptly referred to the process as one of "cognitive slippage"; others have referred to it as "derailment" or "loosening" of associations. However labeled, the phenomenon is readily recognized by experienced clinicians: the patient *seems* to be using words in combinations that sound communicative, but in the final analysis, the listener becomes aware of understanding little or nothing of what has been said. Meehl cited as an example the statement, "I'm growing my father's hair"; see *HIGHLIGHT 12.2* for additional examples.

Disturbance of Thought Content Disturbances in the content of thought typically involve certain standard types of delusion. Prominent among these are the false beliefs that one's thoughts, feelings, or actions are being controlled by external agents; that one's private thoughts are being broadcast indiscriminately to others; that thoughts are being inserted into one's brain by alien forces; that some mysterious agency has robbed one of one's thoughts; or that some innocuous, impersonal environmental event has an intended personal meaning, often termed an "idea of reference." Other absurd convictions, including delusions of grotesque bodily changes, are regularly observed.

Disruption of Perception Major perceptual disruption often accompanies the criteria already indicated. An apparent breakdown in perceptual filtering is frequently observed wherein the patient seems unable to sort out and properly dispose of the great mass of sensory information to which all of us are exposed in most waking moments. As a result, everything "gets through," overwhelming the meager resources the person has for appropriate information processing. This point is well-illustrated in the following statements of schizophrenic people:

"I feel like I'm too alert . . . everything seems to come pouring in at once . . . I can't seem to keep anything out. . . ."

"My nerves seem supersensitive . . . objects seem brighter . . . noises are louder . . . my feelings are so intense . . . things seem so vivid and they come at me like a flood from a broken dam."

"It seems like nothing ever stops. Thoughts just keep coming in and racing round in my head . . . and getting broken up . . . sort of into pieces of thoughts and images . . . like tearing up a picture. And everything is out of control . . . I can't seem to stop it."

It is estimated that approximately 50 percent of patients diagnosed as schizophrenic experience this breakdown of perceptual selectivity during the onset of their disorders (Freedman & Chapman, 1973).

Other even more dramatic perceptual phenomena include hallucinations—perceptions for which there are no discernible external stimuli. Hallucinations in the schizophrenias are normally auditory, although they can also be visual and even olfactory. The typical hallucination is one in which a voice (or voices) keeps up a running commentary on the individual's behaviors or thoughts.

Inappropriate Emotion The schizophrenic syndromes are often said to include an element of clearly inappropriate emotion, or affect. In the more severe or chronic cases, the picture is usually one of apparent *anhedonia* (inability to experience joy or pleasure) and emotional shallowness, or "blunting" (lack of intensity or clear definition). On casual observation, the person may appear virtually emotionless, so that even the most compelling and dramatic events produce at most an intellectual recognition of what is happening. In other instances, particularly in the acute phases, the person may show strong affect, but the emotion clashes

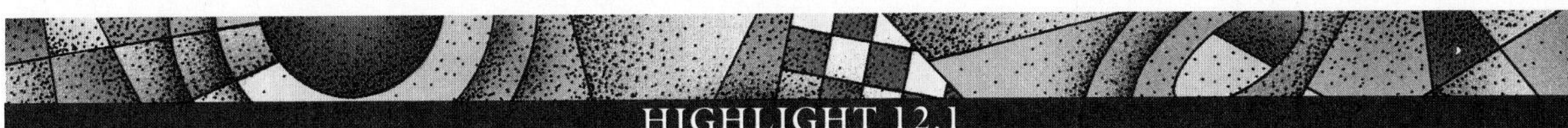

HIGHLIGHT 12.1

DSM-III-R Diagnostic Criteria for Schizophrenia

A. Presence of characteristic psychotic symptoms in the active phase: either (1), (2), or (3) for at least one week (unless the symptoms are successfully treated):

(1) two of the following:
(a) delusions
(b) prominent hallucinations (throughout the day for several days or several times a week for several weeks, each hallucinatory episode not being limited to a few brief moments)
(c) incoherence or marked loosening of associations
(d) catatonic behavior
(e) flat or grossly inappropriate affect

(2) bizarre delusions (i.e., involving a phenomenon that the person's culture would regard as totally implausible, e.g., thought broadcasting, being controlled by a dead person)

(3) prominent hallucinations [as defined in (1) (b) above] of a voice with content having no apparent relation to depression or elation, or a voice keeping up a running commentary on the person's behavior or thoughts, or two or more voices conversing with each other.

B. During the course of the disturbance, functioning in such areas as work, social relations, and self-care is markedly below the highest level achieved before onset of the disturbance (or, when onset is in childhood or adolescence, failure to achieve expected level of social development).

C. Schizoaffective Disorder and Mood Disorder with Psychotic Features have been ruled out, i.e., if a Major Depression or Manic Syndrome has ever been present during an active phase of the disturbance, the total duration of all episodes of a mood syndrome has been brief relative to the total duration of the active and residual phases of the disturbance.

D. Continuous signs of the disturbance for at least six months. The six-month period must include an active phase (of at least one week, or less if symptoms have been successfully treated) during which there were psychotic symptoms characteristic of Schizophrenia (symptoms in A), with or without a prodromal phase, as defined below.

Prodromal phase: A clear deterioration in functioning before the active phase of the disturbance that is not due to a disturbance in mood or to a Psychoactive Substance Use Disorder and that involves at least two of the symptoms listed below.

Residual phase: Following the active phase of the disturbance, persistence of at least two of the symptoms listed below, these not being due to a disturbance in mood or to a Psychoactive Substance Use Disorder.

Prodromal or Residual Symptoms

(1) marked social isolation or withdrawal
(2) marked impairment in role functioning as wage earner, student, or homemaker
(3) markedly peculiar behavior (e.g., collecting garbage, talking to self in public, hoarding food)
(4) marked impairment in personal hygiene or grooming
(5) blunted or inappropriate affect
(6) digressive, vague, overelaborate, or circumstantial speech, or poverty of speech, or poverty of content of speech
(7) odd beliefs or magical thinking, influencing behavior and inconsistent with cultural norms, e.g., superstitiousness, belief in clairvoyance, telepathy, "sixth sense," "others can feel my feelings," overvalued ideas, ideas of reference
(8) unusual perceptual experiences, e.g., recurrent illusions, sensing the presence of a force or person not actually present
(9) marked lack of initiative, interests, or energy

E. It cannot be established that an organic factor initiated and maintained the disturbance.

F. If there is a history of Autistic Disorder, the additional diagnosis of Schizophrenia is made only if prominent delusions or hallucinations are also present.

American Psychiatric Association (1987).

HIGHLIGHT 12.2

Schizophrenic Writings

The personality decompensation in psychotic reactions is frequently manifested in the content and form of patients' letters and other spontaneous writings. These examples clearly reveal the "loosening" and deviations of thought, the distortion of affect, and the lowered contact with reality so common among schizophrenic individuals. The postcard is a reproduction of a card sent by a paranoid schizophrenic man.

The handwritten excerpts are from a letter written by an 18-year-old woman, also diagnosed as paranoid schizophrenic. As is apparent from the first and last parts of the letter, shown here, the handwriting is of two quite different types, suggestive of the writer's emotional conflict and personality disorganization. Lewinson (1940) included this letter in her study of handwriting characteristics of different types of psychotic patients. Among such patients generally, she found that handwriting typically showed abnormal rhythmic disturbances, with rigidity or extreme irregularity in height, breadth, or depth.

To: The football department and its members present and future
The University of New Mexico, Albuquerque, N. M.

I depend on correct, honest supplementation of this card by telepathy as a thing which will make clear the meaning of this card. There exists a Playing of The Great Things, the correct, the constructive, world or universe politics, out-in-the-open telepathy, etc. According to the Great Things this playing is the most feasible thing of all; but it is held from newspaper advertising and correct, honest public world recognition, its next step, by telepathic forces (it seems), physical dangers, and lack of money. Over 10,000 cards and letters on this subject have been sent to prominent groups and persons all over the world. Correct, honest contact with the honest, out-in-the-open world. This line of thought, talk, etc. rule. The plain and frank. Strangers. The Great Things and opposites idea. References: In the telepathic world the correct playings. Please save this card for a history record since it is rare and important for history.

"Dear Dad, 15.) – Oct 9
...... Please come to see me immediately It's very urgent that I see you as quickly as possible

Just now my insides are rotting with each meal I have to eat with very disagreeable old hags

* * * * * * * * *

But it's a matter of life or death & if I don't get any response from you as yet I haven't I swear by that Bible I jump in front of a car that's now in need of fun & am Goddam it Come up as soon as possible Here are the Fatal Day & the one Red Letter day, is the one that I'll do it on when released Last Chance! Danger

Oct 9, 10, 11, 12, 13 14 15 16

be a corpse on 16th of the month when I'm out Goodbye forever

In Memoriam
Helen Dead Oct. 16. 36

Helen R

with the situation or with the content of his or her thoughts. For example, such a person may laugh uproariously on receiving news of a parent's death. Characteristically, affective "blunting" extends to matters of taste, discretion, and social sensibility—so that, for example, the patient may masturbate in public, seemingly oblivious to other people.

Confused Sense of Self A schizophrenic person often is perplexed about his or her identity (including gender identity) and, in addition, frequently is confused about the boundaries separating the self from the rest of the world. The latter confusion is often associated with frightening "cosmic" or "oceanic" feelings of being somehow intimately tied up with universal powers, including the deity. It appears to be related to ideas of external control and similar delusions.

Disrupted Volition Goal-directed activity is almost universally disrupted in schizophrenic individuals, whether due to an intentional flouting of external expectations or to an inability to carry through a course of action. For example, the person may be unable to maintain minimum standards of personal hygiene.

Detached Relationship to the External World Ties to the external world are almost by definition loosened in the schizophrenic disorders, and in extreme instances, the withdrawal may be nearly total. This detachment is usually accompanied by the elaboration of an inner world in which the person develops illogical and fantastic ideational constructions having little or no relationship to reality as perceived by others. Since the days of Bleuler, this process has generally been referred to as *autism.*

Disturbed Motor Behavior Various peculiarities of movement are sometimes observed in the schizophrenias; indeed, this is the chief and defining characteristic of catatonic schizophrenia, of which more will be said later. These motor disturbances range from an excited sort of hyperactivity to a marked decrease in all movement or an apparent clumsiness. Also included here are various forms of rigid posturing, mutism, ritualistic mannerisms, and bizarre grimacing.

Problems in Defining Schizophrenic Behavior

In an effort to provide for a clear-cut diagnosis of schizophrenia and to sharply distinguish it from mood or other disorders, DSM-III and DSM-III-R criteria are far more exact and explicit than those in earlier DSM editions. Recalling our discussion of these matters in Chapter 1, such an approach almost necessarily enhances diagnostic *reliability* (that is, the agreement on what diagnosis should be assigned). Whether or not it does the same for *validity* (the conceptual and predictive meaningfulness of the diagnosis) depends on the adequacy with which the category, so defined, reflects some natural organization of the behaviors defining the category. Put another way, validity depends on the level of arbitrariness with which the purported entity is defined. Like Goldstein (1983) in a historical review of the *concept* of schizophrenia in light of the then-current DSM-III criteria, we find ourselves unconvinced that DSM-III and the similar DSM-III-R diagnoses of schizophrenia have substantially improved validity.

Persistent problems in the differentiation of mood and schizophrenic disorders, touched on in our Chapter 11 description of schizoaffective disorder, provide an instructive example. A number of factors are involved here. Though DSM-III-R clearly distinguishes, by means of exclusionary language, between mood disorders and schizophrenic disorders, whether these are two discrete and mutually exclusive entities is still open for debate (Lehmann, 1985; Noll, Davis, & DeLeon-Jones, 1985; Wing & Bebbington, 1985). DSM-III and its revision resolved this debate by fiat. One clear result is that the numbers of people considered schizophrenic and mood disordered have changed drastically.

In one study, Winters, Weintraub, and Neale (1981) had 68 DSM-II-diagnosed schizophrenic patients rediagnosed according to DSM-III criteria; only 35 survived the cut, the remainder—nearly half—being allocated mostly to the mood disorders. Comparable findings have been reported by Harrow, Carone, and Westermeyer (1985), whose 111 DSM-II diagnosed schizophrenic patients were reduced to 45 on rediagnosis. Taking such results seriously entails the rather disconcerting conclusion that diagnosed schizophrenic people of the 1980s and 1990s are a *different population* from schizophrenic people of the 1970s. Among many problems, these diagnostic differences call into question the current value of research in "schizophrenia" that began prior to the adoption of DSM-III in 1980—many thousands of studies purporting to teach us important things about the disorder. The drastic change in defining criteria would be defensible, and even laudable, had it been based on dramatic new knowledge refining our understanding of some natural order in this realm of psychopathology. It was not.

Other problems with the current diagnostic criteria for schizophrenia, discussed in detail by Carson and Sanislow (1992), deserve brief mention. A serious one is that they represent a hodgepodge of previously suggested indicators of the presumed entity. You may wish to assess the magnitude of this difficulty by trying to use these criteria (chiefly those included under *A;* see *HIGHLIGHT 12.1* on page 435) to construct a mental image of the typical schizophrenic person; we suspect that you will encounter unusual frustration in such an exercise. Additionally, the prominent role assigned to hallucinations (especially "voices") in the criteria for schizophrenia involves a basic problem of reliability of observation, since the only possible observer of such private phenomena is the hallucinator, and no other signs are available to corroborate their occurrence. This is an observer, moreover, whose credibility is suspect, if only because he or she hears disembodied voices talking to him or her. We do not raise this puzzle lightly or facetiously: observational consensus, forever unattainable in this context, is the bedrock of scientific understanding.

It should be stated clearly that in taking this critical stand we are not championing or advocating a return to the relatively vague DSM-II definition of schizophrenia; an unreliable category cannot be a *valid* one. But the enhanced reliability of the DSM-III (and DSM-III-R) definition (see, for example, Robins & Helzer, 1986) does not in itself speak to the issue of validity, and we are entitled to a degree of skepticism about a construct that can so radically change in meaning from one edition of the DSM to another. In addition, as we have seen, a close examination of the DSM-III-R criteria for the diagnosis of schizophrenia provides little reassurance that, in the inevitable trade-off between reliability and validity, the latter has not been sacrificed.

In an unusually direct attempt to assess one aspect of validity—namely, the prediction of short-term case outcome—the DSM-III diagnostic criteria for schizophrenia did relatively well in competition with six alternative approaches to diagnosing the disorder; however, all of them did poorly in an absolute sense. That is, they were notably inadequate in predicting the clinical status of patients a mere 6 to 25 months following their intake diagnoses (Endicott et al., 1986). For example, the DSM-III predicted an "overall outcome" measure at a correlational level of +.12, and a measure of "unusual thoughts or perceptual experiences" at +.18. We know of no other data bearing on validity that seriously challenge this rather dismal performance.

The most radical approach to the problem of defining schizophrenia has been advanced by Sarbin and Mancuso (1980; Sarbin, in press), who suggested, as had Laing (1969) earlier, that there is in fact no such thing as schizophrenia—that the idea is a mythical construction not differing in logical substance from the concept of the unicorn. These authors consider "schizophrenia" to be essentially a "moral verdict" imposed on certain people engaging in unacceptable or unintelligible behavior, rather than a legitimate medical diagnosis. Their argument, admittedly startling, cannot be summarily dismissed when considered thoughtfully and dispassionately. They point out that attributing certain behaviors to a disease entity called schizophrenia does not establish the existence of that entity in the absence of independent, confirmatory evidence, of which little in fact exists, as we will see.

Not even Sarbin and Mancuso deny the existence of the *behaviors* under consideration here, nor do they deny that certain of these behaviors, although not obviously similar to one another, tend to occur together. Such behavior patterns may be analogous to the "syndromes" of symptoms that occur together in various physical (medical) disorders whose underlying causes may not be completely understood—as, for instance, in kidney dysfunctions of undetermined origin. As earlier noted, this is precisely the way in which Bellak (1979) approaches the perplexing problem of defining schizophrenia. He sees the behaviors that we conventionally associate with "schizophrenia" as the "final common pathway" of severe adaptive breakdown, whatever the source of that breakdown. While acknowledging that such issues are far from settled, we think the preponderance of evidence—especially the routine findings of marked heterogeneity among people acquiring the diagnosis—is on Bellak's side. The implication is that some unknown number of relatively distinct pathological processes currently masquerade under the common rubric "schizophrenia." Under this hypothesis, then, it should be possible eventually to disaggregate this overburdened class into its separate and distinct entities. So far, however, little progress has been made on this front.

In any case, it will be clear that the clinical picture in what is called schizophrenia often includes bizarre elements that may be unintelligible to either an affected individual or to external observers. An individual may show peculiarities of movement, gesture, and expression; act out inappropriate sexual and other fantasies; or simply sit apathetically staring into space. We will elaborate on these and other behavioral anomalies in describing the various diagnostic subtypes of schizophrenia.

Clearly not all of the symptoms of schizophrenia occur in every case. In fact, 80 years after the appearance of Bleuler's defining monograph, research has still not revealed a constant, single, universally accepted "sign" of the presence of schizophrenia. Thus the symptom picture may differ markedly from one schizophrenic person to another. Also, the symptom picture may change greatly over time within the same person. Most schizophrenic people "fade in and out of reality" as a function of their own inner state and environmental situation. They might be in "good contact" one day and evidence delusions and hallucinations the next. Likewise, an acute schizophrenic (or *schizophreniform*) reaction may clear up fairly rapidly and never return, or it may progress uninterruptedly to a chronic condition depending on the person and his or her situation.

Subtypes of Schizophrenia

Recent editions of the DSM have listed five subtypes of schizophrenia, which are summarized in the *HIGHLIGHT 12.3*. We will focus on four of these in our present discussion: *undifferentiated, catatonic, disorganized,* and *paranoid*. Of these, the undifferentiated and paranoid types are the most common today.

Undifferentiated Type As the term implies, the diagnosis of **schizophrenia, undifferentiated type** is something of a "wastebasket" category. An individual so diagnosed meets the usual criteria for being schizophrenic—including (in varying combinations) delusions, hallucinations, disordered thoughts, and bizarre behaviors—but does not clearly fit into one of the other types because of a mixed symptom picture. People in the acute, early phases of a schizophrenic breakdown frequently exhibit undifferentiated symptoms, as do those who are in transitional phases from one to another of the standard types, which in fact happens rather often. Each of the Genain sisters was given an undifferentiated diagnosis at least once, and all but Myra received such a diagnosis on several different occasions.

Probably most instances of acute, reactive schizophrenic breakdown occurring for the first time appear undifferentiated in type. However, current diagnostic criteria (that is, DSM-III-R) preclude the diagnosis of schizophrenia and require that of *schizophreniform disorder* (see p. 446) unless there have been signs of the disorder for at least six months, by which time a stable pattern may develop, consistent with a more definite indication of type. Some schizophrenic patients, on the other hand, remain undifferentiated over long time periods. The case of Rick Wheeler is illustrative of the latter course.

Rick Wheeler, 26 years old, neatly groomed, and friendly and cheerful in disposition, was removed from an airplane by airport police because he was creating a disturbance—from his own account probably because he was "on another dimension." On arrest, he was oriented to the extent of knowing where he was, his name, and the current date, but his report of these facts was embedded in a peculiar and circumstantial context involving science fiction themes. Investigation revealed he had been discharged from a nearby state mental hospital three days earlier. He was brought to another hospital by police.

On admission, physical examination and laboratory studies were normal, but Rick claimed he was Jesus Christ and that he could move mountains. His speech was extremely difficult to follow because of incoherence and derailment. For example, he explained his wish to leave the city "because things happen here I don't approve of. I approve of other things but I don't approve of the other things. And believe me it's worse for them in the end." He complained that the Devil wanted to kill him and that his food contained "ground-up corpses." He was born, he claimed, from his father's sexual organs.

Background investigation revealed that Rick's difficulties began, after a successful academic start, in elementary school: "I could comprehend but I couldn't store . . . it's like looking at something but being unable to take it in." He thereafter maintained a D average until he dropped out halfway through his junior year of high school. He had never held a full-time job, and his social adjustment had always been poor. He showed no interest in women until he married, at age 19, a patient he'd met during one of the earliest of some 20 of his hospitalizations, beginning at age 16. A daughter was born from this match, but Rick had lost track of both her and his wife; he had shown no further interest in women. Rick himself was the eldest of five children; there was no known mental disorder in any of his first-degree relatives (that is, siblings and parents).

Unable to maintain employment, Rick had been supported mainly on federal disability welfare—and by virtue of patienthood in public hospitals. His hospital admissions and discharges showed a substantial correlation with his varying financial status; that is, he tended to be released from the hospital around the first of the month, when his welfare check was due, and to be readmitted (or alternatively sent to jail) follow-

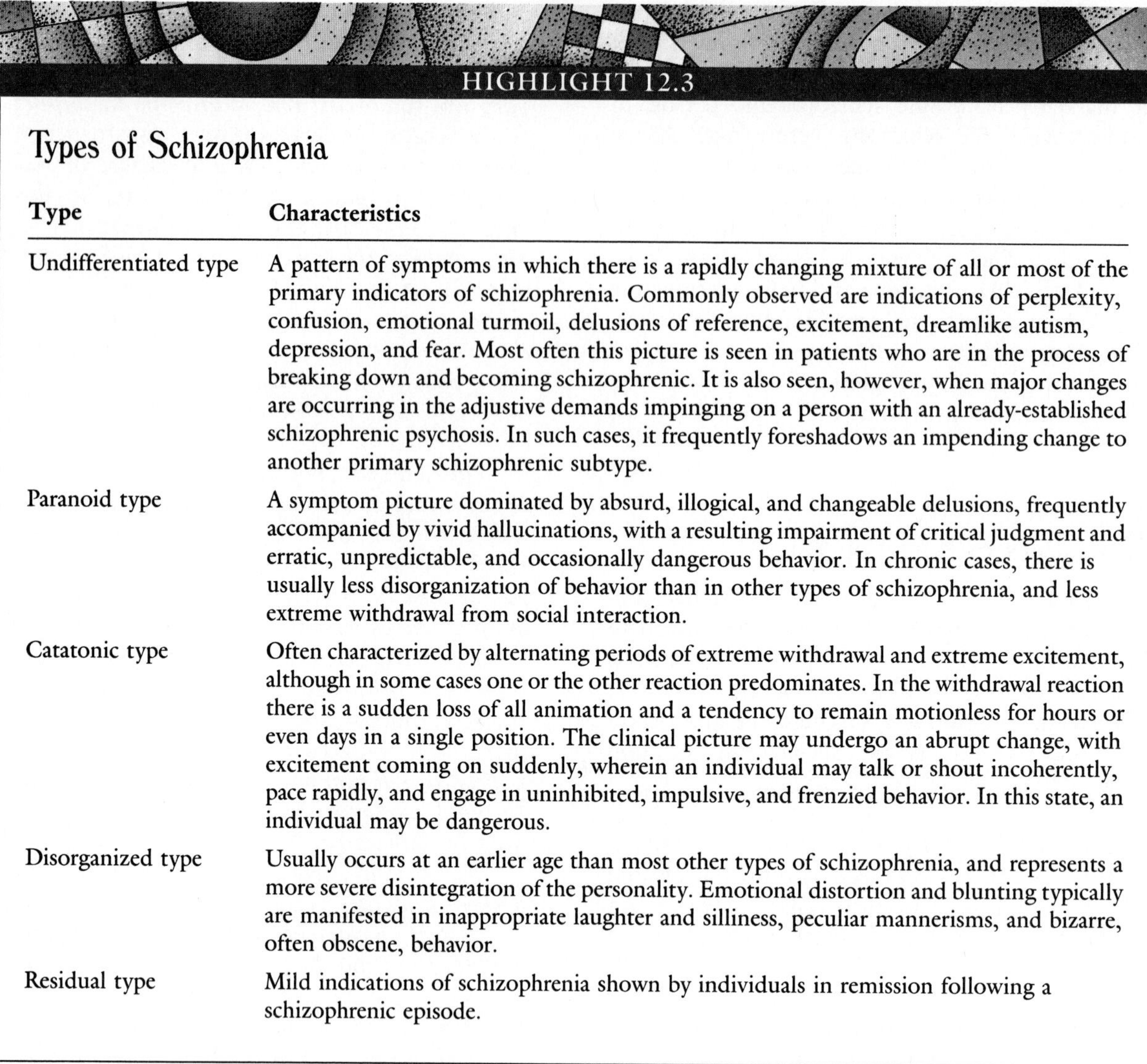

HIGHLIGHT 12.3

Types of Schizophrenia

Type	Characteristics
Undifferentiated type	A pattern of symptoms in which there is a rapidly changing mixture of all or most of the primary indicators of schizophrenia. Commonly observed are indications of perplexity, confusion, emotional turmoil, delusions of reference, excitement, dreamlike autism, depression, and fear. Most often this picture is seen in patients who are in the process of breaking down and becoming schizophrenic. It is also seen, however, when major changes are occurring in the adjustive demands impinging on a person with an already-established schizophrenic psychosis. In such cases, it frequently foreshadows an impending change to another primary schizophrenic subtype.
Paranoid type	A symptom picture dominated by absurd, illogical, and changeable delusions, frequently accompanied by vivid hallucinations, with a resulting impairment of critical judgment and erratic, unpredictable, and occasionally dangerous behavior. In chronic cases, there is usually less disorganization of behavior than in other types of schizophrenia, and less extreme withdrawal from social interaction.
Catatonic type	Often characterized by alternating periods of extreme withdrawal and extreme excitement, although in some cases one or the other reaction predominates. In the withdrawal reaction there is a sudden loss of all animation and a tendency to remain motionless for hours or even days in a single position. The clinical picture may undergo an abrupt change, with excitement coming on suddenly, wherein an individual may talk or shout incoherently, pace rapidly, and engage in uninhibited, impulsive, and frenzied behavior. In this state, an individual may be dangerous.
Disorganized type	Usually occurs at an earlier age than most other types of schizophrenia, and represents a more severe disintegration of the personality. Emotional distortion and blunting typically are manifested in inappropriate laughter and silliness, peculiar mannerisms, and bizarre, often obscene, behavior.
Residual type	Mild indications of schizophrenia shown by individuals in remission following a schizophrenic episode.

ing some public altercation after his money had run out. Numerous attempts to commit Rick to the hospital indefinitely on an involuntary basis had failed because he was able to appear competent at court appearances. He had, however, been declared incompetent to receive his own checks, and various relatives had stepped forward to handle his finances. Now they are afraid to do so because Rick set his grandmother's house afire, having concluded (erroneously, as it turned out) that she was withholding some of his money. He had also threatened others and had been arrested several times for carrying concealed weapons.

In the latest hospitalization, two different antipsychotic medications were tried over a period of five weeks with no discernible improvement. Rick still claimed supernatural powers and special connections with several national governments; was still refusing food because of its contamination with ground corpses; and was still threatening bodily harm to people he found uncooperative. A further attempt was made to commit him and to place his affairs under legal guardianship. As Rick had rather boastfully predicted, this attempt failed because of his lucid defense of himself, and the court dismissed the action. He was discharged to a protected boarding house but disappeared four days later. (Adapted from Spitzer et al., 1983, pp. 153–155)

Fortunately, most patients who show this type of chaotic, undifferentiated pattern do not have the early and slowly developing, insidious onset seen in Rick's case. On the contrary, the breakdown erupts suddenly out of the context of a seemingly unre-

This painting was made by a male patient diagnosed as suffering from undifferentiated schizophrenia. Over a period of about nine years, he did hundreds of paintings in which the tops of the heads of males were always missing, though the females were complete. Although the therapist tried several maneuvers to get him to paint a man's head, the patient never did.

markable life history, usually following some obvious psychic trauma. As we have seen, the initial diagnosis in such cases is schizophreniform disorder, and the episode usually clears up in a matter of weeks or, at most, months. Recurrent episodes, however, are not uncommon in schizophreniform disorder, especially in the absence of vigorous follow-up treatment, leading to the diagnosis of schizophrenia. Such a pattern was seen in Myra Genain's breakdown, and she required several years of psychotherapy to ensure a lasting recovery. In some few instances, treatment efforts are unsuccessful, and the mixed symptoms of the early undifferentiated disorder slide into a more chronic phase, typically developing into the more specific symptoms of other types.

Catatonic Type Though catatonic reactions often appear with dramatic suddenness, usually a patient has shown a background of eccentric behavior, often accompanied by some degree of withdrawal from reality. Though at one time common in Europe and North America, catatonic reactions have become less frequent in recent years.

The central feature of **schizophrenia, catatonic type** is the pronounced motor symptoms, either of an excited or a stuporous type, which sometimes make for difficulty in differentiating this condition from a psychotic mood disorder. As in the case of the Genains, all of whom had early diagnoses of catatonia, the clinical picture is often an early manifestation of a disorder that will become chronic and intractable unless the underlying process is somehow arrested.

Some catatonic patients alternate between periods of extreme stupor and extreme excitement, sometimes quite violent, but in most cases one reaction or the other is predominant. In a study of 250 people diagnosed as suffering from catatonic schizophrenia, Morrison (1973) found that 110 were predominantly withdrawn, 67 were predominantly excited, and 73 were considered "mixed." No significant differences were found between these groups with regard to age, sex, or education.

During a catatonic stupor, a person loses all animation and tends to remain motionless in a rigid, unchanging position—mute and staring into space—sometimes maintaining the same position for hours or even days, until the hands and feet become blue and swollen because of immobility. One patient felt that he had to hold his hand out flat because the forces of "good" and "evil" were waging a "war of the worlds" on his hand, and if he moved it, he might tilt the precarious balance in favor of the evil forces. Surprisingly, despite their seeming withdrawal and apparent lack of attention to their surroundings while in this condition, catatonic individuals may later relate in detail events that were going on around them.

Some of these patients are highly suggestible and will automatically obey commands or imitate the actions of others (*echopraxia*) or mimic their phrases (*echolalia*). If a patient's arm is raised to an awkward and uncomfortable position, he or she may keep it in that position for minutes or even hours. Ordinarily, patients in a catatonic stupor resist stubbornly any effort to change their position and may become mute, resist all attempts at feeding, and refuse to comply with even the slightest request. They pay no attention to bowel or bladder control and may drool. Their facial expression is typically vacant, and their skin appears waxy. Threats and painful stimuli have no effect, and they have to be dressed and washed.

Suddenly and without external provocation or warning, catatonic patients may pass from states of extreme stupor to great excitement, during which they seem to be under great "pressure of activity" and may become violent. They may talk or shout excitedly and incoherently, pace rapidly back and forth, openly indulge in sexual activities such as masturbation, attempt self-mutilation or even suicide, or impulsively attack and try to kill others. The suddenness and extreme frenzy of these attacks make such patients dangerous to both themselves and others. These excited states may last a few hours, days, or even weeks, if potent medication to sedate such patients is not administered. The following case illustrates some of the symptoms typical of catatonic reactions.

Todd Phillips, a 16-year-old high school student, was referred to a psychiatric hospital by his family physician. His family had been very upset by his increasingly strange behavior over the preceding eight months. They had consulted their family physician, who treated him with small doses of antipsychotic medication, without any improvement.

Although Todd has had many problems since he was a small child, there was a distinct change about eight months ago. He began spending more and more time in his room and seemed uninterested in doing many of his usual activities. His grades dropped. He started stuttering. He used to weigh about 215 pounds, but began to eat less, and lost 35 pounds. For no reason, he started drinking large quantities of water.

More recently, there was a change for the worse. A few months ago he began taking Tai Chi lessons and often stood for long periods in karatelike positions, oblivious to what was going on around him. He stopped doing his homework. He took an inordinately long time to get dressed, eat his meals, or bathe. Before getting dressed in the morning he would go through an elaborate ritual of arranging his clothes on the bed before putting them on. When his parents asked him a question, he repeated the question over and over and did not seem to hear or understand what was said.

At school he received demerits for the first time for being late to class. His family began to lose patience with him when he eventually refused to go to school. When his father tried to get him out of bed in the morning, he lay motionless, sometimes having wet the bed during the night. It was at this point that his parents, in desperation, consulted their family physician.

When first seen in the hospital, Todd was a disheveled looking, somewhat obese adolescent, standing motionless in the center of the room with his head flexed forward and his hands at his sides. He appeared perplexed, but was correctly oriented to time and place. He was able to do simple calculations, and his recent and remote memory were intact. He answered questions slowly and in a peculiar manner. An example of his speech follows:

Q: Why did you come to the hospital?

A: Why did I come? Why did I come to the hospital? I came to the hospital because of crazy things with my hands. Sometimes my hands jump up like that . . . wait a minute . . . I guess it's happening. . . . Well, yes, see it's been happening (making robotlike gestures with his hands).

Q: What thoughts go through your head?

A: What thoughts go through my head? What thoughts go through my head? Well, I think about things . . . like . . . yes, well . . . I think thoughts . . . I have thoughts. I think thoughts.

Q: What thoughts?

A: What thoughts? What kinds of thoughts? I think thoughts.

Q: Do you hear voices?

A: Do I hear voices? I hear voices. People talk. Do I hear voices? No. . . . People talk. I hear voices. I hear voices when people talk.

Q: Are you sick?

A: Am I sick? No I'm not sick . . . these fidgeting habits, these fidgeting habits. I have habits. I have fidgeting habits.

Throughout the examination he made repetitive chewing and biting motions. Occasionally, when questioned, he would smile enigmatically. He seemed unresponsive to much of what was going on around him. His infrequent movements were slow and jerky, and he often assumed the karatelike postures that his parents described, in which he would remain frozen. If the examiner placed the patient's hands in an awkward position the patient remained frozen in that position for several minutes. (Spitzer et al., 1983, pp. 139–140)

Although the matter is far from settled, some clinicians interpret a catatonic patient's immobility as a way of coping with the reduced filtering ability and increased vulnerability to stimulation: it seems to provide a feeling of some control over external sources of stimulation, though not necessarily over inner ones. Freeman has cited the explanation advanced by one patient: "I did not want to move, because if I did everything changed around me and upset me horribly so I remained still to hold onto a sense of permanence" (1960, p. 932).

Disorganized Type Compared to the other subtypes of schizophrenia, **schizophrenia, disorganized type** usually occurs at an earlier age and represents a more severe disintegration of the personality. Fortunately, it is considerably less common than the other forms. In pre-DSM-III classifications, this type was called *hebephrenic schizophrenia.*

Typically, an affected individual has a history of oddness, overscrupulousness about trivial things, and preoccupation with religious and philosophical issues. Frequently, he or she broods over the dire results of masturbation or minor infractions of social conventions. While schoolmates are enjoying normal play and social activities, this person gradually becomes more seclusive and more preoccupied with fantasies.

As the disorder progresses, the individual becomes emotionally indifferent and infantile. A silly smile and inappropriate, shallow laughter after little or no provocation are common symptoms. If asked the reason for his or her laughter, the patient may state that he or she does not know or may volunteer some wholly irrelevant and unsatisfactory explanation. Speech becomes incoherent and may include considerable baby talk, childish giggling, a repetitious use of similar-sounding words, and a derailing of associated thoughts that may give a punlike quality to speech. In some instances, speech becomes completely incoherent, a "word salad."

Hallucinations, particularly auditory ones, are common. The voices heard by these patients may accuse them of immoral practices, "pour filth" into their minds, and call them vile names. Delusions are usually of a sexual, religious, hypochondriacal, or persecutory nature, and they are typically changeable, unsystematized, and fantastic. For example, one woman insisted not only that she was being followed by enemies but that she had already been killed a number of times. Another claimed that a long tube extended from the Kremlin directly to her uterus, through which she was being invaded by Russians.

In occasional cases, individuals become hostile and aggressive. They may exhibit peculiar mannerisms and other bizarre forms of behavior. These behaviors may take the form of word salad; facial grimaces; talking and gesturing to themselves; sudden, inexplicable laughter and weeping; and in some cases an abnormal interest in urine and feces, which they may smear on walls and even on themselves. Obscene behavior and the absence of any modesty or sense of shame are characteristic. Although they may exhibit outbursts of anger and temper tantrums in connection with fantasies, they are indifferent to real-life situations, no matter how horrifying or gruesome the latter may be. The clinical picture in disorganized schizophrenia is exemplified in the following interview:

The patient was a divorcée, 32 years of age, who had come to the hospital with bizarre delusions, hallucinations, and severe personality disintegration. She had a record of alcoholism, promiscuity, and possible incestuous relations with a brother. The following conversation shows typical hebephrenic responses to questioning.

Doctor: *How do you feel today?*

Patient: *Fine.*

Doctor: *When did you come here?*

Patient: *1416, you remember, doctor (silly giggle).*

Doctor: *Do you know why you are here?*

Patient: *Well, in 1951 I changed into two men. President Truman was judge at my trial. I was convicted and hung (silly giggle). My brother and I were given back our normal bodies 5 years ago. I am a policewoman. I keep a dictaphone concealed on my person.*

Doctor: *Can you tell me the name of this place?*

Patient: *I have not been a drinker for 16 years. I am taking a mental rest after a "carter" assignment or "quill." You know, a "penwrap." I had contracts with Warner Brothers Studios and Eugene broke phonograph records but Mike protested. I have been with the police department for 35 years. I am made of flesh and blood—see doctor (pulling up her dress).*

Doctor: *Are you married?*

Patient: *No. I am not attracted to men (silly giggle). I have a companionship arrangement with my brother. I am a "looner" . . . a bachelor.*

The prognosis is poor if a person develops disorganized schizophrenia. As we have seen, Iris and Hester, the least functional of the Genain sisters, were also the only sisters to have been definitely diagnosed as hebephrenic, or disorganized, during the course of their disorders. To at least some extent, the disorganized variety of schizophrenia may be regarded as the "last stop" on a downward-coursing path of process schizophrenic psychosis. At this point, no form of treatment intervention yet discovered has a marked likelihood of effecting more than a modest recovery.

Paranoid Type Formerly about one half of all schizophrenic first admissions to hospitals were diagnosed as **schizophrenia, paranoid type.** In recent years, however, the incidence of the paranoid type has shown a substantial decrease, while the undifferentiated type has shown a marked increase. The reasons for these changes are unknown.

Frequently, paranoid-type people show histories of increasing suspiciousness and of severe difficulties in interpersonal relationships. The eventual

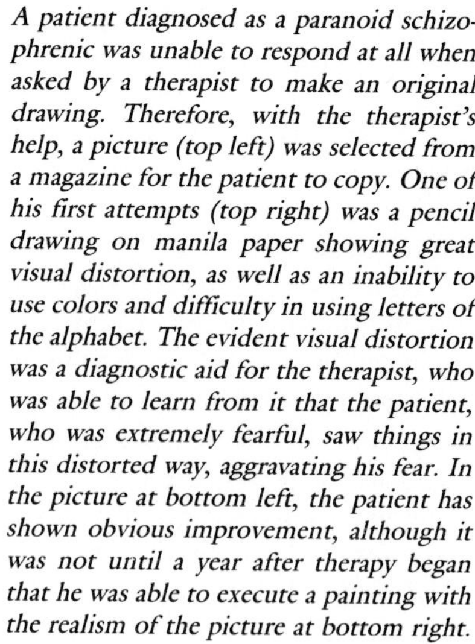

A patient diagnosed as a paranoid schizophrenic was unable to respond at all when asked by a therapist to make an original drawing. Therefore, with the therapist's help, a picture (top left) was selected from a magazine for the patient to copy. One of his first attempts (top right) was a pencil drawing on manila paper showing great visual distortion, as well as an inability to use colors and difficulty in using letters of the alphabet. The evident visual distortion was a diagnostic aid for the therapist, who was able to learn from it that the patient, who was extremely fearful, saw things in this distorted way, aggravating his fear. In the picture at bottom left, the patient has shown obvious improvement, although it was not until a year after therapy began that he was able to execute a painting with the realism of the picture at bottom right.

symptom picture is dominated by absurd, illogical, and often changing delusions. Persecutory delusions are the most frequent and may involve a wide range of ideas and plots. An individual may become highly suspicious of relatives or associates and may complain of being watched, followed, poisoned, talked about, or influenced by various tormenting devices rigged up by "enemies."

In addition to persecutory themes, themes of grandeur are also common in paranoid-type delusions. Individuals with such delusions may, for example, claim to be the world's greatest economist or philosopher, or some prominent person of the past, such as Napoleon, the Virgin Mary, or even Jesus Christ. Rokeach (1964), in fact, has described a bizarre circumstance in which three Christs resided at the same hospital. These delusions are frequently accompanied by vivid auditory, visual, and other hallucinations. Patients may hear singing, or God speaking, or the voices of their enemies, or they may see angels or feel damaging rays piercing their bodies at various points.

An individual's thinking and behavior become centered around the themes of persecution, grandeur, or both in a pathological "paranoid construction" that—for all its distortion of reality—provides a sense of identity and importance perhaps not otherwise attainable. There thus tends to be a higher level of adaptive coping and of cognitive integrative skills in a paranoid-type schizophrenic person than in other schizophrenic individuals. This relative preservation of intact cognitive functioning is undoubtedly one of the important bases for the paranoid-nonparanoid distinction noted earlier and increasingly employed by both clinicians and researchers.

Despite this seeming "advantage" that paranoid-type schizophrenic individuals enjoy, such people are far from easy to deal with. The weaving of delusions and hallucinations into a paranoid construction results in a loss of critical judgment and in erratic, unpredictable behavior. In response to a command from a "voice," such an individual may break furniture or commit other violent acts. Occasionally, paranoid schizophrenic patients can be dangerous, as when they attack people they are convinced have been persecuting them or otherwise causing harm. Somewhat paradoxically, such problems are exacerbated by the fact that such people show less bizarre behavior and less extreme withdrawal from the outside world than individuals with other types of schizophrenia; as a consequence, they are likely *not* to be confined in protective environments.

The following conversation is between a clinician and a man diagnosed as chronic paranoid schizophrenic. The case illustrates well the illogical, delusional symptom picture, together with continued attention to misinterpreted external data, that these individuals experience.

Doctor: *What's your name?*
Patient: *Who are you?*
Doctor: *I'm a doctor. Who are you?*
Patient: *I can't tell you who I am.*
Doctor: *Why can't you tell me?*
Patient: *You wouldn't believe me.*
Doctor: *What are you doing here?*
Patient: *Well, I've been sent here to thwart the Russians. I'm the only one in the world who knows how to deal with them. They got their spies all around here though to get me, but I'm smarter than any of them.*
Doctor: *What are you going to do to thwart the Russians?*
Patient: *I'm organizing.*
Doctor: *Whom are you going to organize?*
Patient: *Everybody. I'm the only man in the world who can do that, but they're trying to get me. But I'm going to use my atomic bomb media to blow them up.*
Doctor: *You must be a terribly important person then.*
Patient: *Well, of course.*
Doctor: *What do you call yourself?*
Patient: *You used to know me as Franklin D. Roosevelt.*
Doctor: *Isn't he dead?*
Patient: *Sure he's dead, but I'm alive.*
Doctor: *But you're Franklin D. Roosevelt?*
Patient: *His spirit. He, God, and I figured this out. And now I'm going to make a race of healthy people. My agents are lining them up. Say, who are you?*
Doctor: *I'm a doctor here.*
Patient: *You don't look like a doctor. You look like a Russian to me.*
Doctor: *How can you tell a Russian from one of your agents?*
Patient: *I read eyes. I get all my signs from eyes. I look into your eyes and get all my signs from them.*
Doctor: *Do you sometimes hear voices telling you someone is a Russian?*
Patient: *No, I just look into eyes. I got a mirror here to look into my own eyes. I know everything that's going on. I can tell by the color, by the way it's shaped.*
Doctor: *Did you have any trouble with people before you came here?*
Patient: *Well, only the Russians. They were trying to surround me in my neighborhood. One day they tried to drop a bomb on me from the fire escape.*
Doctor: *How could you tell it was a bomb?*
Patient: *I just knew.*

Although it is true, as we have seen, that many paranoid schizophrenic individuals have histories of gradual onset and long-lasting difficulties in interpersonal relationships and productive functioning, it is also true that few of them show the true process pattern of schizophrenia (Ritzler, 1981). Sometimes, indeed, onset is quite rapid and occurs in individuals with entirely adequate, even distinguished, pasts. In fact, one of the most famous cases of paranoid schizophrenia involved a high-ranking German judge, Dr. Daniel Paul Schreber, who described his disorder at length in memoirs published after his partial recovery. Freud used these memoirs in developing his now largely discredited theory that paranoid thinking is due to repressed homosexuality.

Schreber's disorder began with the idea that he was to be transformed into a woman by some sort of conspiracy, and, once the transformation was accomplished, he was to be delivered over to a certain man for the purpose of sexual abuse. During the course of the disorder, the idea of conspiracy came gradually to be replaced by the idea that his "emasculation" and subsequent impregnation were inspired by a divine plan involving world redemption. In fact, he would be impregnated by divine rays so that a new race of humans might be created.

Schreber also felt that he was being persecuted by certain people, among them his former physician, and he heaped verbal abuse on these enemies. In turn, he heard voices that mocked him and jeered at him. At various times, he became convinced that he was dying of strange illnesses, such as "softening of the brain" and "the plague." At another point, he believed he was dead and his body, which was being handled by others in all sorts of revolting ways, was decomposing. He was tormented so much by such thoughts that he in fact attempted suicide on several occasions and demanded of the hospital staff that they provide him with the cyanide he was sure they were intending for him anyway. He felt he was "the plaything of the devils." As his thoughts turned more toward religion in the later phases of the disorder, he claimed to see "miraculous apparitions" and to hear "holy music." (Adapted from Spitzer et al., 1981)

In this case, we see clearly the deterioration from a previous level of functioning, the bizarre ideas, and the hallucinatory experiences so characteristic of schizophrenia generally. The paranoid type diagnosis is appropriate because of the prominent delusions of both persecution (being conspired against) and grandiosity (being selected by God to be impregnated and start a new race). Dr. Schreber regained sufficient control to secure his release from the hospital some nine years after the onset of his disorder; at the time, however, he was still considered delusional.

Other Schizophrenic Patterns The remaining subcategories of schizophrenia contained in DSM-III-R, although not necessarily under the schizophrenia rubric, deserve mention. **Schizophrenia, residual type,** which is the fifth officially recognized type of schizophrenia, is a category used for people regarded as having recovered from schizophrenia but still manifesting some signs of their past disorder.

As was noted in the preceding chapter, the term **schizoaffective disorder** (manic or depressive or mixed) is applied to individuals who show features of both schizophrenia and severe affective disorder. In the DSM-III-R classification, this disorder is not listed as a formal category of schizophrenic disorder but rather under *psychotic disorders not elsewhere classified.*

Also included in the latter category is **schizophreniform disorder,** a category reserved for schizophrenia-like psychoses of less than six months' duration. It may include any of the symptoms described in the preceding sections, but is probably most often seen in an undifferentiated form. At the present time, all new cases of schizophrenia first receive a diagnosis of schizophreniform disorder. Because of the possibility of an early and lasting remission in a first episode of schizophrenic breakdown, prognosis for schizophreniform disorder is better than for established forms of schizophrenia, and it appears likely that by keeping it out of the formal category of schizophrenic disorder, the potentially harmful effects of labeling may be minimized.

Biological Factors in Schizophrenia

Despite extensive research, the causal factors underlying the schizophrenias remain unclear. Primary responsibility has been attributed variously to (a) biological factors, including heredity and various biochemical, neurophysiological, and neuroanatomical processes; (b) psychosocial factors, including early psychic trauma, pathogenic interpersonal and family patterns, faulty learning, difficulties in social roles, and decompensation under excessive stress; and (c) sociocultural factors, especially as influences on the types and incidence of schizophrenic reactions. These three sets of factors are not mutually exclusive, of course, and it seems likely that each is involved in at least some cases. We will first discuss biological factors in the following sections.

Heredity In view of the disproportionate incidence of schizophrenia in the family backgrounds of *index* schizophrenic patients (that is, the diagnosed group of people who provide the starting point for inquiry), genetic factors appear to play an important causal role in some instances of the disorder. Though the evidence seems persuasive, it remains circumstantial in that it is (a) entirely correlational in nature, and (b) extremely difficult to disentangle from possibly detrimental environmental factors. Much of this research is based on demonstrations of concordance rates among schizophrenic people and their close relatives. Let us examine some of these areas of research.

Twin studies. The general strategy of twin studies was discussed in Chapter 4 and more specifically in relation to mood disorders in Chapter 11. As in the mood disorders, schizophrenia concordance rates for *identical* twins are routinely found to be significantly higher than those for *fraternal* twins or ordinary siblings. But again, it is difficult to separate hereditary from environmental influences using this method. Excellent technical critiques of perhaps the best of the twin data relating to schizophrenia come to essentially the same conclusion (Wagener & Cromwell, 1984).

Although the incidence of schizophrenia among twins is no greater than for the general population, study after study has shown a higher *concordance* for schizophrenia among identical (monozygotic) twins over people related in any other way, including fraternal (dizygotic) twins. Depending on a variety of factors, the degree of this inflation varies substantially from one study to another and tends to be inversely correlated with the methodological rigor of the study—that is, the more rigorous the methodology, the lower the concordance rate.

The results of two of the more methodologically rigorous twin studies in schizophrenia provide an interesting comparison. One of them, by Cohen et al. (1972), used a large but selected sample consisting of veterans of the American armed forces. Because the armed forces screen their "applicants," it may be assumed that individuals with obvious mental health problems were screened out, resulting in a relatively low incidence of mental disorder, including schizophrenia, among their dischargees. If absolute incidence is low, concordance figures will be correspondingly low. This assumption indeed seems to have been confirmed. In the study, the schizophrenia concordance rate was 23.5 percent for identical twins and 5.3 percent for fraternal twins, both figures being unusually low.

Using a sample more nearly representative of the general population, Gottesman and Shields (1972) arrived at overall schizophrenia concordance rates of 42 percent and 9 percent for identical and fraternal twins, respectively. The Gottesman and Shields figures are close to the medians for recent studies in this area and may be regarded as good estimates of the "true" values.

If schizophrenia were exclusively a genetic disorder, the concordance rate for identical twins would, of course, be 100 percent. In fact, however, there appear to be more *discordant* than *concordant* pairs, notwithstanding the remarkable example of the Genain sisters. On the other hand, some concordance clearly exists. What this means is that a person may have an enhanced risk of schizophrenia if his or her twin is schizophrenic. In other words, twin studies show us that *predisposition* for the disorder is associated with genetic variables. It does not prove a *genetic* transmission of predisposition, however, because common environmental factors cannot be ruled out; as earlier noted, the environments, both prenatal and postnatal, of identical twins must inevitably be more similar on average than the environments of individuals sharing any other type of relationship. Moreover, because somewhat over half of the identical twins of schizophrenic patients do not develop the disorder, it means that there is a good chance the environment will be sufficiently benign to protect even an individual with a substantial predisposition, whatever its source.

A good example of the hazards of too readily accepting twin concordance data as necessarily addressing the question of genetic transmission of a schizophrenic diathesis is unexpectedly provided in studies of identical twins who are *discordant* for the diagnosis of schizophrenia. These are sets of twins in which one member of the pair meets diagnostic criteria for schizophrenia but the other does not and is in fact described as "normal." We will look at two such studies here.

The first study, an unaccountably neglected work by Pollin and Stabenau (1968; Pollin, Stabenau, & Tupin, 1965), involved a nationwide sample of 15 sets of twins who were studied thoroughly, along with their families. The essential results implicated some sort of prenatal biological compromise of the twin who was to become schizophrenic, one that began with a lower birth weight and continued in the form of a failure to match the "normal" twin in rate of progression through the various childhood developmental mileposts. As adults, the schizophrenic twins also showed a significantly greater number of "soft" neurological signs (such as reflex abnormalities), thus confirming the general picture of subtle biological deficit relative to the "normal" twins. These deficits were not, however, so subtle during childhood as to escape the notice of parents, who responded with differential parenting behavior in dealing with the "weak" versus the "strong" twin, apparently producing corresponding differences in emerging personality characteristics; the preschizophrenic twin was invariably described as more "submissive" than the other twin in each of the pairs, thus adding a potential psychosocial impediment to the extant biological one.

The companion study (Suddath et al., 1990) is much more recent and has received considerable notice in the popular media. Also involving 15 pairs of identical twins discordant for schizophrenia, the technique of *magnetic resonance imaging* (MRI) was used to examine the structural properties of the subjects' brains. The results, in brief, showed enlarged cerebral ventricles and reduction in size of a structure called the anterior hippocampus (both of these together indicating reduced brain mass) in the twins who had become schizophrenic. The anomaly cannot be ascribed directly to a genetic origin. The authors also correctly point out that the results do not in themselves permit a ruling out of causal factors that may have been *consequent* to the development of schizophrenia, such as long-term use of antipsychotic medication. As we will see, however, independent evidence suggests that brain abnormalities of the type seen here may make a causal contribution in some instances of schizophrenia.

In terms of hereditary factors in schizophrenia, the essential point made by these studies is that genetic identity does not guarantee biological identity. That is, differential prenatal (or postnatal) environmental factors can have significant biological effects apparently predictive for schizophrenia in cases where heredity is held constant. If this conclusion is accepted, however, it implies that some part of the concordance for schizophrenia in monozygotic twins is in all probability *not* genetically based, because intrauterine pathogenic influences are, overall, more likely to be shared by monozygotic than by dizygotic twins. We know, for example, that a majority of monozygotic twins share the same chorion tissue of the maternal placenta, whereas dizygotic twins never do.

The upshot, it seems to us, is that we can never be sure what, if anything, the classic twin studies of schizophrenia—of which there have been many going back many years—tell us about an alleged genetic contribution to the etiology of this form of disorder.

A seemingly much "cleaner" investigative strategy employing twins was pioneered by Fischer (1971, 1973). Reasoning that genetic influence, if present, would show up in the *offspring* of the nonschizophrenic twins of discordant pairs, she found exactly that outcome in a search of official records in Denmark. Gottesman and Bertelson (1989), in a follow-up of Fischer's subjects, have reported an age-corrected schizophrenia incidence rate (that is, a rate taking into account predicted breakdowns for subjects not yet beyond the age of risk) of 17.4 percent for the offspring of the nonschizophrenic monozygotic twins. This rate, which far exceeds normal expectancy, was not significantly different from that for offspring of the schizophrenic members of discordant pairs, or from that for offspring of schizophrenic dizygotic twins. Assuming that exposure to schizophrenic aunts and uncles would have, at most, limited etiologic significance, these results give impressive support to the genetic hypothesis. They also, as the authors note, indicate that the implicated predisposition may remain "unexpressed" (as in the nonschizophrenic twins of discordant pairs) unless "released" by unknown environmental factors.

Adoption studies. Several studies have attempted to overcome the shortcomings of the twin method in achieving a true and unassailable separation of hereditary from environmental influences by using what is called the ***adoption strategy.*** In this strategy, concordance rates of schizophrenia are compared for the biological and the adoptive relatives of individuals who have been adopted out of their biological families at an early age (preferably at birth) and have subsequently become schizophrenic. If rates of schizophrenia are greater among the patients' biological than adoptive relatives, a hereditary influence is strongly suggested; the reverse pattern would of course argue for environmental causation.

Heston (1966) was apparently the first to use one of several variants of this basic method. In a follow-up study of 47 people who had been born to schizophrenic mothers in a state mental hospital and placed with relatives or in foster homes shortly after birth, Heston found that 16.6 percent of these subjects were later diagnosed as schizophrenic. In contrast, none of the 50 control subjects selected from among residents of the same foster homes—whose mothers were not schizophrenic—later became schizophrenic. In addition to the greater probability of being labeled schizophrenic, Heston found that the offspring of schizophrenic mothers were more likely to be diagnosed as mentally retarded, neurotic, and psychopathic (that is, antisocial). They also had been involved more frequently in criminal activities and had spent more time in penal institutions.

Thus Heston concluded that children born to schizophrenic mothers, even when reared without contact with them, were more likely not only to become schizophrenic but also to suffer a wide spectrum of other difficulties. The diffuseness of these effects on offspring is actually something of an embarrassment for a theory that emphasizes a specific genetic risk for schizophrenia, and it invites speculation that variables other than the psychiatric diagnostic status of the mothers may have come into play. Conceivably, for example, the postnatal experience of these adoptees was in fact not independent of the psychiatric status of their mothers. Additionally, we now know that schizophrenic women, for some unknown reason, as a group have unusual difficulty bearing children, with consequent risk to the latter of subtle but possibly lasting nervous system impairment (Jacobsen & Kinney, 1980;

McNeil & Kaij, 1978). As we will see, such impairment, which is not genetically mediated, would in itself probably enhance the risk for schizophrenia, and possibly other diagnoses as well.

Independent of Heston's work, a large scale and multifaceted adoption study was undertaken in Denmark under the aegis of American investigators working in collaboration with Danish professionals (Kety, 1987; Kety et al., 1968, 1978; Rosenthal et al., 1968; Wender et al., 1974). The well-publicized results of these studies, purporting to establish the case for a genetic contribution to schizophrenia, have had an enormous impact on the field. They will not be reviewed here because their adequate discussion would consume too much space. A recent review of these studies, however, reveals serious shortcomings that preclude any unqualified judgment on the genetic transmission of schizophrenia (Carson & Sanislow, 1992). For example, an impressive incidence of schizophrenia among biological relatives of schizophrenic adoptees is on close examination limited to second-degree relatives (half-siblings, having 25 percent gene sharing) and disappears when only first-degree relatives (parents and full siblings, having 50 percent gene sharing) are considered (see also Benjamin, 1976). These results defy explanation in terms of any genetic transmission process of which we have knowledge, and in fact tend to disconfirm such an hypothesis.

The problems associated with a critical component of the Danish adoption studies were resolved by an independent reanalysis of its data—including the rediagnosis of all cases using DSM-III criteria and the use of other more advanced techniques to improve precision—conducted by Kendler and Gruenberg (1984). These investigators found convincing evidence of a modest genetic contribution to a certain class of disorders having schizophrenic-like features. They include, in addition to schizophrenia, schizotypal and paranoid personality disorders; the three together are said to constitute a "schizophrenia spectrum," a group of disorders believed to share a common, genetically determined diathesis. Thus, as Heston's early work had suggested, the vulnerability conveyed by genetic influences appears here not to be specific for schizophrenia per se but to involve a broader range of compromised functioning.

Regrettably, as now seems clear in retrospect, the Danish adoption studies did not include independent assessments of the child-rearing adequacy of the adoptive families into which index (those who became schizophrenic) and control (those who did not) youngsters had been placed. It remained for Tienari and his colleagues (Tienari et al., 1985, 1987) to remedy this oversight. Their study, still in progress, involves a follow-up of the adopted-away children of all women in Finland hospitalized for schizophrenia, beginning in 1960. Of the 271 index (children whose mothers were schizophrenic) and control (comparable children whose mothers were normal) adoptees evaluated as of the latest (1987) available report, there were *no* instances of "psychosis" among either index (n=51) or control (n=53) children who were raised in families independently considered "healthy." Of the adoptees raised in families considered moderately or severely disturbed, 9 of 73 index children and 2 of 94 controls had become psychotic. *HIGHLIGHT 12.4* tabulates the results of this study in greater detail. Supporting earlier work, these results show a moderate effect that might be considered genetic in origin—the differential breakdown rates of index versus control adoptees independent of family context. The magnitude of that effect, however, is actually exceeded by one associated with the variable of relative family disorganization which will be discussed more fully in a later section.

Parent-child studies. Another line of research has focused on the incidence of schizophrenia among children reared by their schizophrenic parents. Rieder (1973) found a wide spectrum of psychopathology reported among the adult offspring of schizophrenic parents, ranging from schizophrenia to psychopathic personality disorders. The offspring of schizophrenic parents also showed a high incidence of psychological maladjustment as children—estimated at 20 percent—with two types being prominent: a withdrawn schizoid type and a hyperactive, antisocial, delinquent type. Thus Rieder concluded that the offspring of schizophrenic parents differ in important ways from the offspring of nonschizophrenic parents; such a study cannot of course address the question of hereditary versus environmental influence.

In the same vein, Kringlen (1978) showed that 28 percent of children born to parents who had both been diagnosed schizophrenic at some point in their adult lives were classifiable as psychotic or borderline psychotic; 20 percent of these children had developed clinical schizophrenia. Twenty-eight percent of the children of such unions, however, were diagnosed as entirely normal. That is, more than one quarter of these children escaped any form of psychopathology despite a presumably heavy genetic risk *and* the mental health hazards of being reared by two parents who were either psychotic or destined to become so. Evidently, having two schizophrenic (or preschizophrenic) parents increases the risk of poor mental health—but it need not always have ill effects.

HIGHLIGHT 12.4

Psychiatric Status of Adopted-Away Offspring of Schizophrenic (Index) and Normal (Control) Mothers as a Function of the Quality of Their Adoptive Families

The following table includes the numbers of index (n=124) and control (n=147) adoptees in each of four diagnostic groupings arrayed according to the degree of disturbance of the adoptive families. Note that in the "healthy" adoptive family context the "at-risk" and control adoptees are equally free of serious disorder, with no instances of psychosis in either group. The presumed vulnerability of the index adoptees becomes manifest only as the adoptive family dysfunction increases. A statistical model applied to these data shows a significant interaction between index and control status and level of family dysfunction.

Clinical Ratings of Adoptive Families

Offspring Diagnoses	**Healthy**		**Moderately Disturbed**		**Severely Disturbed**		**TOTAL**
	Index	Control	Index	Control	Index	Control	
No diagnosis	41	42	11	26	6	15	141
Neurotic	8	10	10	18	14	15	75
Personality disorder	2	1	5	7	18	11	44
Psychotic	0	0	3	0	6	2	11
TOTAL	51	53	29	51	44	43	271

From Tienari et al. (1987), p. 442.

Studies of high-risk children. The research strategy of long-term monitoring of children known to be at high risk for schizophrenia (by virtue of having been born to a schizophrenic parent) is basically intended to identify the environmental factors that cause breakdown (or resistance to it) in predisposed people. As we have seen in Chapter 4, this strategy, pioneered by Mednick and Schulsinger (1968) and followed up by numerous additional research projects (for reviews see Garmezy, 1978a, 1978b; Neale & Oltmanns, 1980; Rieder, 1979; Watt et al., 1984), has thus far not paid off very well in terms of isolating specific environmental factors. In saying this, however, we must acknowledge both the enormous difficulties that attend long-term and complicated projects of this sort and our own admiration for those who undertake them.

The difficulties are nowhere better illustrated than in the first (and so far only) summary report of the Israeli-NIMH High-Risk Study (see *Schizophrenia Bulletin,* Vol. 11, No. 1, 1985). This project, begun in 1967 and surviving a war and much turmoil in its aftermath, compared the outcomes of an index group of high-risk Israeli youngsters who remained in towns with their biological families to those brought up in the surrogate-parent settlement communities known as ***kibbutzim,*** relative to closely matched control groups of low-risk youngsters. "High risk" was defined as having a schizophrenic mother.

Many behavioral differences were found between index and control children, almost always favoring the controls; few were found for the cross-cutting variable of kibbutz versus normal rearing. Especially impressive was a high frequency of soft neurological signs observed in index children in two separate examinations five years apart. On the critical measure of psychopathological outcome at 15 years following project initiation (the average subject age was 25), rearing context proved apparently significant, although only in index cases and in an unexpected direction. Considering only schizophrenia and schizophrenia "spectrum" diagnoses, 9 of 46 index cases and 0 of 44 control cases had become disordered; 6 of the 9 casualties had been kibbutz-reared and hence to a considerable degree isolated from exposure to a psychotic parent. These trends are, if anything, strengthened when other diagnoses are included. Mirsky et al. (1985), who report these data, speculate that kibbutz living tends to evoke symptoms (although only in predisposed people) because it precludes privacy and "escape."

It may be noted in passing that, once again in this study, the children considered at risk on grounds that were at least implicitly genetic (their mothers being schizophrenic) were discovered as a group to be mildly neurologically compromised in childhood. We can by no means be certain that such compromise, which might itself be a causal factor in schizophrenic outcomes, was mediated by the inheritance of deficient genes—especially in view of the known obstetrical difficulties schizophrenic women tend to have in bearing children.

Although the available results of high-risk studies have generally proven difficult to interpret, they have added abundantly to the observation that having a schizophrenic parent is a good predictor of psychological disorder, including schizophrenia. Despite the complication of birthing difficulties just noted, it seems likely (although unproven) that some of this predictability comes about as a result of the genetic transmission of vulnerability to schizophrenia.

However, one additional problem with a genetic interpretation of such studies is that a child having a psychotic parent, or one whose parent is frequently missing because of required hospitalizations, is not quite comparable in environmental and experiential terms to the otherwise matched youngster whose parents are psychologically well-adjusted. In fact, parental separation seems to be the critical variable in accounting for the parent-to-child effect in many cases (Mednick et al., 1978).

Summing up, the question of genetic transmissibility of a predisposition to schizophrenia is not as easily answered as it may appear to be when first posed. Unfortunately, there is a tendency—even among professionals who should know better—to answer the question resoundingly in the affirmative. We think a more circumspect approach is appropriate, although we incline to the view that some genetic influence probably makes certain individuals vulnerable to schizophrenia. Many independent sources of information—though all of them may be imperfect and incomplete on an individual basis—when taken together point to a relatively strong case for genetic contribution. The data indicate that no such contribution is sufficient in itself to produce schizophrenia, and they provide no basis for concluding that such a contribution is a *necessary* condition for a schizophrenic outcome; indeed, most people who develop schizophrenia probably have no close relatives who are also known to have had the disorder.

We believe, too, that the classic methods of investigation in this field have been exhausted and that nothing definitive is likely to be confirmed by further use of these essentially pedigree-based techniques. It is frequently said that the next major advances in this area will likely come from molecular biology, from genetic linkage studies and gene mapping. As was earlier noted in discussing the mood disorders, however, the productive use of these techniques depends on precise diagnostic criteria that yield highly homogeneous patient groups (Carson & Sanislow, 1992). As we have seen, we are a long way from meeting this requirement in the area of schizophrenia.

Biochemical Factors Research into the possibility of biochemical abnormalities in schizophrenic patients was given a boost in the 1950s when a connection was made between schizophrenic-like symptoms and the fact that the presence of some chemical agents in the bloodstream, even in minute amounts, can produce profound mental changes (Huxley, 1954). Lysergic acid diethylamide (LSD) and mescaline, for example, can lead to a temporary disorganization of thought processes and a variety of psychotic-like symptoms that have been referred to as "model psychoses." Such findings encouraged investigators to look for an *endogenous hallucinogen*—a chemical synthesized within the body, perhaps under stressful conditions—that might account for the hallucinations and disorganization of thought and affect in schizophrenia and other psychotic disorders. The states produced by the ingestion of these chemicals, however, only superficially resemble true psychotic disorders, and researchers have in any event not been able to find a good candidate for the natural hallucinogen role envisaged in this conception.

Instead, if schizophrenia turns out to be in part biochemically caused, it seems likely that it will involve some form of deficit in the quantitative regulation, or balance, of chemicals that occur naturally in the nervous system. At present, as in the case of the more severe mood disorders, the most widely accepted hypothesis is that a biochemical disturbance of synaptic transmission occurs in one or more important neural pathways in the brain. The most attractive of the specific ideas in this area has been the "dopamine hypothesis" of schizophrenia (Sacher et al., 1978; Snyder, 1978). *Dopamine* is a catecholamine neurotransmitter like norepinephrine, of which it is in fact a chemical precursor. It appears to be the main neurotransmitter for perhaps a half-dozen identified brain pathways.

According to the **dopamine hypothesis,** schizophrenia is the product of an excess of dopamine activity at certain synaptic sites. Variants of this view include hypotheses that a schizophrenic person has too many postsynaptic dopamine receptors or that these receptors have for some reason become supersensitive. The most important evidence for the hypothesis is that the effectiveness of the various established antipsychotic drugs, called *neuroleptics,* is highly correlated with the extent to which they block dopamine action at the receptor. Correlation does not, of course, establish a causal relationship, and in recent years the dopamine hypothesis has proven inadequate as a general formulation of etiology (Carlsson, 1988). Dopamine-blocking drugs, for instance, are therapeutically *nonspecific* for schizophrenia (that is, they are also used effectively to treat psychotic symptoms associated with various other disordered states, such as organic mental disorders, some manias, and even drug-induced "bad trips"). Additionally, the receptor-blocking effect is accomplished too quickly (within hours) to be consistent with the clinical picture of a gradual improvement (often over several weeks) following initiation of drug therapy in schizophrenia. In other words, if excess dopamine activity were the cause of schizophrenia, these drugs would have curative effects almost immediately; they do not. Moreover, their therapeutic activity is dependent on reducing dopaminergic activity to *abnormally* low levels. In light of these and other observations, Davis (1978) has suggested that some other (unspecified) factor causes schizophrenia, the symptoms of which are then amplified by dopaminergic neural transmission.

More recent research has provided no serious challenge to this view, although it has shown the dopaminergic systems within the brain to be far more complicated than was originally thought. For example, we now know that more than one type of dopamine receptor site exists on the dendrites of postsynaptic neurons, and that these are involved in differing biochemical processes. The dopamine hypothesis has also been dealt a serious blow by the emergence and recent authorization for routine use of the new antipsychotic drug *clozapine.* The side effects of this drug (which for some patients include a potentially fatal suppression of immune function) have a profile that is very different from that of the dopamine blockers, suggesting that its antipsychotic mode of action significantly differs from that of the neuroleptics. Clozapine has a potent antipsychotic effect for approximately 30 percent of those schizophrenic patients showing little or no response to standard neuroleptic medication (Kane et al., 1988), thus indicating a rather limited range of application.

The demise of the dopamine hypothesis in its etiologic aspect has been a serious disappointment, particularly for those researchers and clinicians sincerely believing that the answer to the schizophrenia puzzle must lie in the domain of biochemistry. To be sure, other biochemical theories of schizophrenia have been, and doubtless will continue to be, advanced, but to date no other such theory appears anywhere near as promising as had the dopamine theory in its prime. Ultimately, it seems extremely likely that a complete understanding of the biochemistry of schizophrenic disorders will have to include a sense of how other influences, including psychological ones, may interact with whatever biochemical aberrations are discovered regularly to accompany schizophrenic behavior.

Neurophysiological Factors A good deal of research has focused on the role of neurophysiological disturbances in schizophrenia. These disturbances are thought to include an imbalance in excitatory and inhibitory processes and inappropriate autonomic arousal. We would expect such disordered physiology to disrupt the normal attentional and information-processing capabilities of an organism, and there seems to be a growing consensus that disturbances of this type underlie and are basic to the cognitive and perceptual distortions characteristic of individuals diagnosed as schizophrenic.

Consistently, schizophrenic people are found to be deficient in their ability to track visually a moving target (Levy et al., 1983), a deficiency attributed to a disorder of nonvoluntary attention. Some evidence even suggests that the close relatives of schizophrenics share this deficit (Kuechenmeister et al., 1977). Earlier work in this area has been well reviewed by Neale and Oltmanns (1980), and follow-up studies have continued to establish the reliability of the phenomenon (Holzman et al., 1988; Iacono, Tuason, & Johnson, 1981; Latham, et al., 1981). It appears that this visual tracking disability may be but one aspect of a more general performance deficit, widely shared among individuals diagnosed as schizophrenic, in the processing of sensory information (Woods, Kinney, & Yurgelun-Todd, 1986). Many researchers (e.g., George & Neufeld, 1985; Neale & Oltmanns, 1980) believe that a deeper and more fine-grained

In card-sort tests, such as the one shown here, in which subjects must sort cards in different ways to test abstract thought, many schizophrenic individuals fail, leading researchers to speculate that schizophrenic people are deficient in the ability to activate the prefrontal cortex, the brain region thought to be associated with abstract thought.

analysis of such deficits might enhance our understanding of hallucinations and other of the more gross and dramatic phenomena of schizophrenia.

Some findings that may well be related at a basic level indicate that individuals who are merely "at risk" for schizophrenia often experience difficulties in maintaining attention, in processing information, and in certain other indicators of cognitive functioning prior to schizophrenic breakdown (Buchsbaum et al., 1978; Erlenmeyer-Kimling & Cornblatt, 1978; J. Marcus et al., 1985b; Mednick, 1978; Silberman & Tassone, 1985; Spring & Zubin, 1978). Neurologic abnormalities, such as reflex hyperactivity, have also been found in the close relatives of schizophrenic individuals (Kinney, Woods, & Yurgelun-Todd, 1986). As yet, however, the role of these abnormalities in the development of schizophrenia is not clear. Conceivably, they only add another measure of compromised functioning in the adjustment struggles of those who, overburdened with many life problems, may eventually succumb to psychosis.

Considerable evidence suggests that schizophrenic people process information in a way that is both abnormal and relatively specific to schizophrenic disorders. In addition to the visual tracking difficulties already noted, reliable findings show a schizophreniform deficit in visual masking tasks (Balogh & Merritt, 1987) and attentional processes involved in reaction time (e.g., Rosenbaum, Shore, & Chapin, 1988). Magaro (1980, 1981) conceives these people as being unable to match the sensory data they receive with the preexisting schematic patterns normally used to interpret or decode such data; a schizophrenic person, according to this view, accomplishes the task "automatically," unguided by preestablished cognitive processes. Applying this general approach, Magaro has been able to integrate and make sense of a multitude of findings showing that schizophrenic people perform deficiently on cognitive tasks. Whether or not Magaro is right remains to be seen.

Deficient performance on cognitive tasks is as well-documented as any finding extant on this group of people (Rabin, Doneson, & Jentons, 1979). However, as Sarbin and Mancuso (1980) have pointed out, such findings are virtually guaranteed in advance by the process of designating certain people to be schizophrenic. Moreover, a distressing number of the studies showing schizophrenic performance "deficits" readily conceived as neurophysiological in origin are as readily conceived in the far more simple terms of psychologically-based motivation and attention shortcomings. What if substantial numbers of these patients just don't care? This question is not facetious nor frivolous.

Abnormal neurophysiological processes in schizophrenia could be genetic in origin, but they could also be the product of faulty early conditioning or of biological deviations caused by other factors. For example, problems of this sort could as likely arise from mechanical difficulties in the birth process as from genetic predestination. The frequency of obstetrical complications in the histories of people who later become schizophrenic is, as already noted, markedly above that of the general population. Such observations have led to a resurgence of interest in an old question—that of the *anatomical* intactness of the schizophrenic brain—to which we now turn.

Neuroanatomical Factors Decisive research on the structural properties of the brain in given clinical groups, particularly among living subjects, was hampered by numerous difficulties until the development of modern computer-dependent technologies, such as computerized axial tomography (CAT) and magnetic resonance imaging (MRI). The use of these techniques in the study of schizophrenic people's brains has developed at an accelerating pace in recent years, with interesting results.

We have now accumulated a substantial amount of evidence indicating that in some cases of schizophrenia, particularly among those of chronic course, there is an abnormal enlargement of the brain's ventricles—the hollow areas filled with cerebrospinal fluid lying deep within the core (Andreasen et al., 1982a, 1982b; Boronow et al., 1985; Goetz & Van Kammen, 1986; Golden et al., 1982; Pearlson et al., 1989). In fact the same anomaly is sometimes found in the "normal" family members of schizophrenic patients (DeLisi et al., 1986) and in the high-risk offspring of schizophrenic mothers. In the latter instance, it appears to be associated with low birth weight and the possibility of fetal damage from some unknown agent, possibly infectious (Lyon et al., 1989; Silverton et al., 1985). Because the brain normally occupies fully the rigid enclosure of the skull, enlarged ventricles imply a decrement in brain tissue mass—that is, some type of atrophy or degeneration. Such decrements have in fact been reported by Andreasen et al. (1986), Pearlson et al. (1989), and others using the recently developed MRI technique, and by Bernhardt, Meertz, and Schonfeldt-Bausch (1985) and Brown et al. (1986) in postmortem studies of the brains of individuals who had been schizophrenic.

The findings of an organic brain anomaly associated with some cases of schizophrenia—largely limited to those in the process, chronic, or negative symptom ranges—is of enormous potential significance for at least these types of schizophrenia. There remains, however, the troubling possibility that at least some of this brain tissue loss is due to long-term use of antipsychotic medication, a possibility rendered more ominous by findings that implicate antianxiety drugs of the benzodiazepine class (such as Valium and Librium) in similar brain degeneration (Lader & Petursson, 1984; Schmauss & Krieg, 1987). Examination of the brain volume of schizophrenic people who have never taken therapeutic drugs—a rare class indeed—would be required to reassure us on this question, and some preliminary findings have already appeared to provide that reassurance (e.g., Weinberger et al., 1982).

Assuming that these basic observations of an organic brain anomaly are confirmed, which appears likely, the discovery is important not only in its own right but also because it invites integration with certain other exciting research initiatives of recent years. In particular, this discovery relates to research on impaired neuropsychological test performances of schizophrenic people (Levin & Yurgelun-Todd, 1989) and to the already-noted subtle neurologic impairments of some children who are at risk for schizophrenia. Though some data suggest a connection between these early neurologic anomalies and ventricular enlargement in adult schizophrenics (Cannon, Mednick, & Parnas; 1989; Silverton et al., 1985), the case has not yet definitely been made.

It certainly cannot be ruled out that these subtle indicators of neurologic compromise in children at risk may be the early manifestations of some sort of progressively debilitating neurological process, possibly even a slowly degenerative one. We should also note the evidence that *some* individuals diagnosed as having a schizotypal personality pattern show behavioral deficit (such as poor perceptual-motor coordination or aberrant reaction-time performance) suggestive of neurological impairment (Rosenbaum, Shore, & Chapin, 1988; Siever, 1985). The relationship of schizotypal disorder (as presently defined) to schizophrenia, however, is less clear than it was once thought to be; that is, schizotypal disorder may not be predictive of schizophrenia (Gunderson & Siever, 1985).

Researchers have noted an overrepresentation in the late winter and early spring months of births of individuals who later become schizophrenic, estimated to be about an 8 percent deviation from norms (DeLisi, Crow, & Hirsch, 1986). This peculiar observation has given rise to a variety of hypotheses involving what has come to be called "the season of birth effect" in the epigenesis of schizophrenia. It now seems, however, that the observation is in all probability an artifact. Assuming that the whole construct of being at risk is a valid one, at-risk people born at an earlier time will have incidence rates in excess of those born at a later time over a considerable range of the at-risk period, simply because they will have been at risk longer. Aggregated data will therefore show a preponderance of births of schizophrenic people to have occurred in earlier rather than later months of the year. The fact that the season of birth effect is observed only among younger schizophrenic people is thus readily explained: few at-risk people remain in an older population.

Mark Lewis (1989a, 1989b, 1990; Lewis & Griffin, 1981), to whom we are indebted for this impressive analysis, and who has demonstrated that dying shows a similar month-of-birth distribution, likens the effect to the time function associated with the burning out of light bulbs; light bulbs become "at risk" when they are placed in electrical circuits, and in general those placed in earliest will be among the first to burn out.

At this point, it is likely that some of you will be committed to a biological *primary cause* interpretation of schizophrenia. Others, including many whose original bias was psychogenic, will be uncertain and perhaps confused. We suspect that few will remain entirely unimpressed with the biological case. We have treated this section in some detail because of our observation that many students tend to come to premature conclusions on either side of the biogenic-psychogenic controversy. We hope we have demonstrated that biological considerations in the etiology of schizophrenia cannot reasonably be dismissed in summary fashion. Nevertheless, comparably tantalizing data exist relating to psychosocial and sociocultural factors, as indeed has already been intimated. When we have a complete theory of the origins of schizophrenic breakdown, it will of necessity encompass biological as well as psychosocial and sociocultural factors. In the meantime, it is reasonable to take the view that *anything* that reduces the adaptive capacity of a person, including varied biological factors, may result in an increased probability of schizophrenic breakdown at some point in the life cycle.

Psychosocial Factors in Schizophrenia

Many behavioral scientists hold views that contrast sharply with those in which schizophrenia is held to be caused primarily by biological factors. Here schizophrenic individuals are seen as persons who escape from an unbearable world and seemingly unsolvable conflicts by altering their inner representations of reality. Although biological factors may contribute to and complicate the clinical picture, the origins of the disorder are held to be primarily psychosocial.

Unfortunately, research on psychosocial factors in the development of schizophrenia has been sparse in recent years, especially when compared with the huge research investment in biological correlates. This is the chief reason for the somewhat dated character of the research on which we will have to depend in the following discussion. Partly the problem seems due to normal cyclical variations in research focus, but it also doubtless reflects differences in the speed of technological advances in the two domains. Currently the field of neurobiology is in the throes of a technical revolution of astounding proportions, and there have been considerable—although sometimes grossly exaggerated—advances in our understanding of biological factors involved in psychopathology, notably including schizophrenia. By contrast, progress on the psychosocial front, lacking in comparable "high tech" investigative tools, has been slow and halting. Something of a self-fulfilling prophecy operates here, however. Funding agencies, notably the National Institute of Mental Health, provide miniscule funding to investigate psychosocial variables, presumably on the grounds of probable limited payoff; they thus ensure precisely that outcome.

Though some might question the validity of research conducted some 20 to 30 years ago, the nature of human behavior is, after all, quite enduring. Unless some critical variable has changed in the interim, we can assume that studies that were empirically sound then are still so today. Though we can hope for more research efforts on possible psychosocial causation, the older studies are as close as we can come to understanding psychosocial factors as they might contribute to schizophrenic outcomes.

In this section, we will deal with the psychosocial patterns that appear particularly relevant to the development of schizophrenia: (a) early psychic trauma and increased vulnerability; (b) pathogenic parent-child and family interactions; (c) faulty learning and coping; (d) social role problems; and (e) excessive stress and decompensation.

Early Psychic Trauma and Increased Vulnerability One of the more unsettling and tragic things we have learned in recent years, mostly through searching investigation of background experience in disorders other than schizophrenia, is the widespread occurrence of various forms of child abuse—as, for example, in multiple personality disorder (Chapter 6). Although we know of no convincing evidence that links the occurrence of such overt abuse to the emergence of schizophrenic behavior, it would not be entirely surprising to discover in future research that childhood abuse, particularly in its more subtle forms, is a contributory background factor in some instances of this type of disorder. In this connection, Karl Menninger has provided a vivid picture of the defenses—and special vulnerabilities—of adolescents and young adults who have suffered deep hurts and have as a result come to view the world as a dangerous and hostile place:

Children injured in this way are apt to develop certain defenses. They cover up, as the slang expression puts it. They deny the injury which they have experienced or the pain which they are suffering. They erect a facade or front, "All's well with me," they seem to say. "I am one of the fellows; I am just like everybody else. I am a normal person." And indeed they act like normal persons, as much as they can. . . . Often they are noticeable only for a certain reticence, shyness, perhaps slight eccentricity. Just as often, they are not conspicuous at all. . . .

What is underneath that front? . . . There is intense conflict and tension and anxiety and strong feelings of bitterness, resentment and hate toward those very people with whom the external relationships may be so perfectly normal. "I hate them! They don't treat me right. They will never love me and I will never love them. I hate them and I could kill them all! But I must not let them know all this. I must cover it up, because they might read my thoughts and then they wouldn't like me and wouldn't be nice to me."

All this is covered up as long as possible. . . . For the chief problem in the person who is going to develop what we call schizophrenia is, "How can I control the bitterness and hatred I feel because of the unendurable sorrow and disappointment that life has brought to me?" . . .

. . . the regimen under which they live has much to do with their successful adaptation. Given certain new stresses, the facade may break down and the underlying bitterness and conflict may break through. (1948, pp. 101–104)

Instead of withdrawing, children who have been traumatized may try to relate aggressively to other people, as we saw in the development of problematic peer relations in Chapter 4. Such children are highly vulnerable to hurt, however, and their existence is usually an anxious one. Often their lives are a series of crises, precipitated by minor setbacks and hurts that they magnify out of all proportion (Arieti, 1974; Dodge & Feldman, 1990). In other instances, a child manifests a pattern of somewhat disorganized paranoid thinking, often coupled with rebellious behavior involving pathological lying, episodes of unbridled aggression, and various types of delinquent behavior.

Although most children who undergo early psychic trauma show residual effects in later life, most do not become schizophrenic. Conversely, it is a virtual certainty that not all schizophrenic patients have undergone such traumatic childhood experiences; indeed, it is not uncommon to discover schizophrenic individuals having excessively overprotected backgrounds. Thus early psychic trauma appears to be, at most, only one among many interactional factors that may contribute to schizophrenia. A good example here is provided in the longitudinal follow-up of Danish "at-risk" children and control-group children of normal parents who had also been institutionalized for one reason or another. The trauma of early childhood institutionalization appears to have had markedly deleterious effects on the psychological adjustment of *only* the "at-risk" children and not the normal ("low-risk") control cases (Parnas, Teasdale, & Schulsinger, 1985). Anthony (1978) has even suggested that early traumatic experiences may be less important than the overall context in which they occur:

The "headline" experiences—the attacks, the paranoid accusations, the incestuous approaches, the brutalities—seem easier for the child to endure than the constant confusions, mystifications, inconsistencies, and other seemingly minor problems of everyday living. It is not abnormality itself that proves so disturbing but the oscillations between normality and abnormality, and the wider these are, the more difficult it is for the child to sustain. (p. 481)

The absence of solid evidence pinpointing specific types of psychic insult or trauma differentiating the backgrounds of schizophrenic from nonschizophrenic people (e.g., Schofield & Balian, 1959) has prompted Meehl (1978, 1989) to suggest that emotionally significant events do not themselves launch a person on the path to schizophrenia; rather the particular patterns and sequences in which the events occur help bring on the disorder. A person who is to become schizophrenic has the "bad luck" to experience emotionally charged events in a temporal network that is, for the particular individual, pathogenic. If Meehl is right, the research task of discovering particular early life events that increase vulnerability to schizophrenia becomes formidable indeed, and perhaps even impossible.

The situation looks somewhat more hopeful when, as Anthony (1978) has recommended, we look at overall contextual features of an individual's development, as we do in the following section.

Pathogenic Parent-Child and Family Interactions Studies of interactions in families having schizophrenic offspring have focused on such factors as (a) "schizophrenogenic" parents; (b) destructive marital interactions; (c) faulty communication; and (d) the undermining of personal authenticity. We should note that the focus of research has shifted in recent years from parent-child to total family interactions. Before we proceed, however, let us take a moment to gain some perspective on this sensitive topic.

In the early years of attention to family variables in schizophrenia, parents were routinely and uniquely assumed to have *caused* their children's disorders through hostility, deliberate rejection, or gross parental ineptitude. Many professionals engaged in high levels of blaming behavior, and their feedback to parents was often angry and insensitive, if not frankly brutal. We hope that nothing in the following discussion appears to condone such attitudes. Both authors know from experience that parenting is at best an inscrutable and hazardous responsibility, a veritable minefield, different for every child and none coming with a map. Most of the parents we have known, whether or not they experienced the "bad luck" of schizophrenia in a child, have done the best that could reasonably be expected, within the limits of their own situations, to foster their children's happiness and success. A few have been incredibly cruel and abusive, although as already noted there is no definitive evidence that such a pattern is especially associated with schizophrenic outcomes. Apart from the fact that it does not help and may indeed worsen matters, blame could only be based on an oversimplified notion of how people become schizophrenic.

"Schizophrenogenic" mothers and fathers. Many studies have been made of the parents of individuals who have developed schizophrenia—particularly the mothers of male patients. Termed **schizophrenogenic,** these mothers have typically been characterized as rejecting, domineering, cold, overprotective, and impervious to the feelings and needs of others (e.g., Fromm-Reichmann, 1948). While verbally such a mother may seem accepting, basically she is said to reject her child. At the same time, she depends on the child rather than the father for her emotional satisfactions and feelings of completeness as a woman. Perhaps for this reason, she tends to dominate, possessively overprotect, and smother the child—encouraging dependence on her.

Muddying the waters, the maternal characteristics attributed to the schizophrenogenic mother have also been alleged to be causally involved in many other types of offspring outcome—such as male homosexuality—so much so that the concept of the schizophrenogenic mother had been largely abandoned by the 1970s. It may have made a partial comeback, however, in the results of a well-designed retrospective study by Roff and Knight (1981). These researchers examined clinic records prepared many years prior to the subjects' schizophrenic breakdowns, thus eliminating the possibility of observer bias reactively affecting the results. They found that a mothering style involving the just-described characteristics did show up as a significant factor in the backgrounds of adult male schizophrenics experiencing unfavorable (that is, relatively chronic) outcomes. While these are impressive findings, they are also correlational in nature and so do not permit unqualified inferences about the etiologic significance of the schizophrenogenic mothering style. Still, we can say that the causal hypothesis remains somewhat tenable, albeit perhaps not specific for schizophrenia.

Often combined with this mothering pattern, observers have noted, are rigid, moralistic attitudes toward sex that cause such a mother to react with horror to any evidence of sexual impulses on her child's part. In many instances the mother is overtly seductive in physical contacts with her son, thus augmenting his sexual conflicts. In general, the mother-son relationship in schizophrenia appears to foster immaturity and anxiety in the youth—depriving him of a clear-cut sense of his own identity, distorting his views of himself and his world, and causing him to suffer from pervasive feelings of inadequacy and helplessness.

Nor are the daughters of such mothers likely to fare very well. In this connection, we refer your attention to the description of Mrs. Genain given at the beginning of this chapter.

Although mothers have been singled out for most of the attention in this area, fathers have not gone entirely unscathed. Roff and Knight (1981) also found that the mother-son relationship just described can be especially damaging if the father is passive and uninvolved in his relationship to his son. This finding is consistent with what has already been observed and reported about fathers and schizophrenia. Available studies (e.g., Lidz, Fleck, & Cornelison, 1965) have typically described a somewhat inadequate, indifferent, or passive father who appears detached and humorless—a father who rivals the mother in his insensitivity to others' feelings and needs. Often, too, he appears to be rejecting toward his son and seductive toward his daughter. At the same time, he is often highly contemptuous and derogatory toward his wife, thus making it clear that his daughter is more important to him. This treatment of the wife tends to force her into competition with her daughter, and it devalues her as a model for her daughter's development as a woman. In fact, the daughter may come to despise herself for any resemblance to her mother. Against this background, the daughter often moves into adolescence feeling an incestuous attachment to her father, which creates severe inner conflict and may eventually prove terrifying to her. The problems of the Genain sisters in attempting to cope with their seriously disturbed father, discussed earlier, are relevant here.

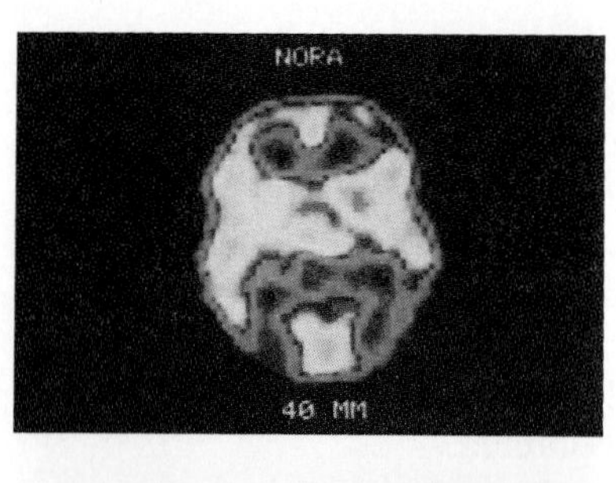

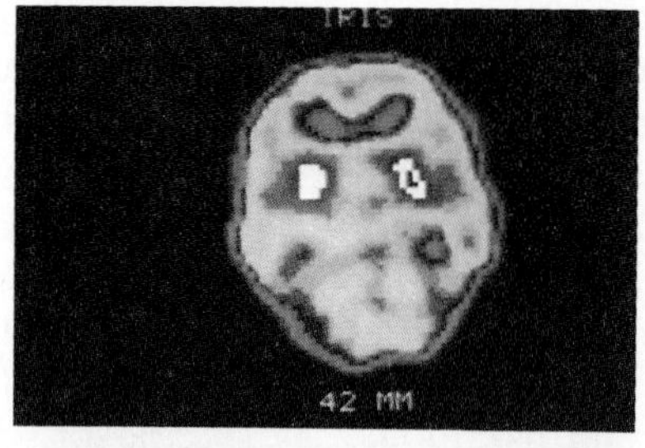

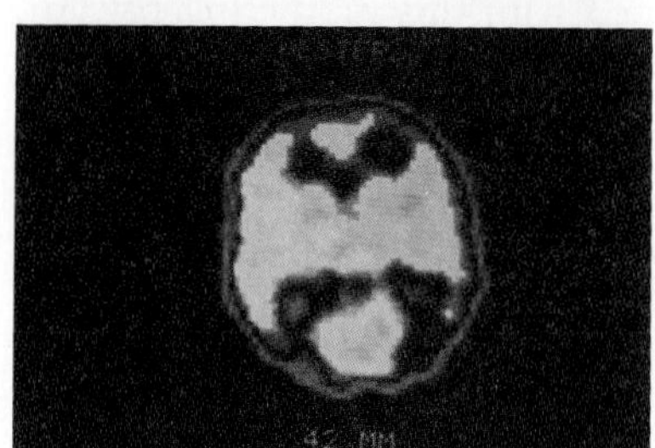

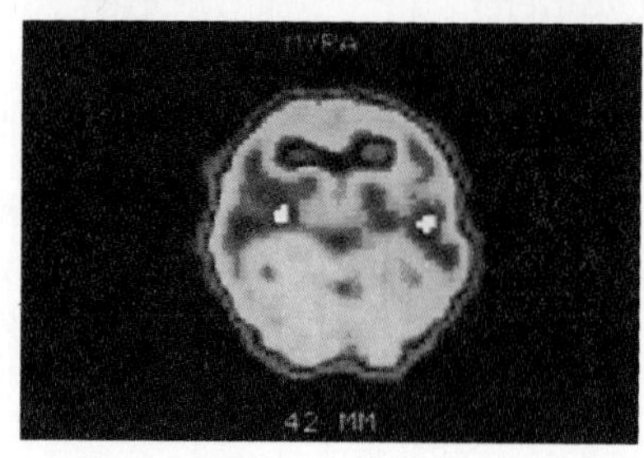

PET scans of the Genain quadruplets suggest a possible psychosocial impact resulting from the early matching of two pairs of co-twins. The scans indicate comparatively more severe brain impairment for Hester and Nora. The large areas of blue and yellow show that their brains consume lower levels of glucose, one indicator of lessened brain activity. The orange spots on the scans of Iris and Myra suggest more normal energy usage. Yet it is Iris, originally "matched" with Hester, who has had the poorer clinical outcome than either Nora or Myra.

As might be expected, studies have shown a high incidence of various emotional disturbances on the part of both mothers and fathers of schizophrenics. Kaufman et al. (1960) reported that both the mothers and fathers of 80 schizophrenic children and adolescents studied were emotionally disturbed: the mothers almost uniformly used psychotic-like defense patterns, and the fathers likewise used seriously maladaptive coping patterns. Other studies concerned with the mental health status of schizophrenics' parents, reviewed by Hirsch and Leff (1975), came to basically similar conclusions.

As was indicated in Chapter 4, however, we cannot reasonably assume that disturbance always passes from parent to offspring: it can work in the other direction as well. Aside from the original source of psychopathology, it appears that once it begins, the members of a family may stimulate each other to increased displays of pathological behavior. For example, studies by Mishler and Waxler (1968) and Liem (1974) both contain unequivocal evidence that parents' attempts to deal with the disturbed behavior of schizophrenic sons and daughters had pathological effects on their own behavior and communication patterns. In fact, the bidirectionality of effects may be the single most important thing we have learned from studying the families of schizophrenic people (Carson, 1984).

Destructive marital interactions. Of particular interest here is the work of Lidz and his associates, which continued over some two decades. In an initial study of 14 families with schizophrenic offspring, Lidz et al. (1965) failed to find a single family that was reasonably well integrated. Eight of the 14 couples lived in a state of severe chronic discord in which continuation of the marriage was constantly threatened—a condition the investigators called **marital schism.** Typical of this relationship was the chronic undermining of the worth of one marital partner by the other, which made it clear to the children that the parents did not respect or value each other. Each parent expressed fear that a child would resemble the other parent; a child's resemblance to one parent was a source of concern and rejection by the other parent.

The other six couples in this study had achieved a state of equilibrium in which the continuation of the marriage was not constantly threatened but in which the relationship was maintained at the expense of a basic distortion in family relationships; in these cases, family members entered into a "collusion" in which the maladaptive behavior of one or more family members was accepted as normal. This pattern was referred to as **marital skew.** The Genain family, for example, would be considered severely skewed because it was organized chiefly around the bizarre actions and ideas of Mr. Genain. Lidz (1978) proposed that a major effect of such severe family disturbance is the encouragement of "egocentric cognitive regression" in youngsters subjected to it, giving rise eventually to the distinctive cognitive derangements characteristic of the schizophrenic state. In these and other cases regarding parental influences, of course, both biological and psychological influences are likely to be involved. Interestingly, the Roff and Knight (1981) study found both types of marital interaction patterns described by Lidz and his colleagues to be predictive of later poor outcomes for schizophrenic offspring. An especially strong effect showed up for loss of a parent before age seven, and, as might be expected, many such losses were due to parental separation or divorce occasioned by marital disharmony.

Often, schizophrenic people have psychologically healthy siblings who were raised with them in the same families. How have these siblings escaped the presumed pathology of the family context? The answer appears to be that the subculture of a family is not constant, that every child raised within a family experiences a family pattern that is to a considerable extent distinctive for him or her. Stabenau and Pollin (1968; Stabenau et al., 1965), taking a direct approach to this issue, studied families in which siblings were discordant for schizophrenia and for juvenile delinquency. They found that 17 of their 19 "psychopathology siblings" (9 of 10 for schizophrenic siblings alone), as compared to only 2 of 29 controls, had encountered periods of maximum family crisis during their early childhoods. These crises, which were identified by the families themselves, included financial disasters, major parental strife, and depressive episodes in one or another parent, among other things.

Faulty communication. Bateson (1959, 1960) was one of the first investigators to emphasize the conflicting and confusing nature of communications among members of schizophrenic families. He used the term **double-bind communication** to describe one such pattern. In this pattern the parent presents to the child ideas, feelings, and demands that are mutually incompatible. For example, a mother may be verbally loving and accepting but emotionally anxious and rejecting; or she may complain about her son's lack of affection but freeze up or punish him when he approaches her affectionately. The mother subtly but effectively prohibits comment on such paradoxes, and the father is too weak and ineffectual to intervene. In essence, such a son is continually placed in situations where he cannot win. He becomes increasingly anxious; presumably, such disorganized and contradictory communications in the family come to be reflected in his own thinking.

Singer and Wynne (1963, 1965a, 1965b) linked the thought disorders in schizophrenia to two styles of thinking and communication in the family —*amorphous* and *fragmented.* The amorphous pattern is characterized by a failure in differentiation; here, attention toward feelings, objects, or people is loosely organized, vague, and drifting. Fragmented thinking involves greater differentiation but lowered integration, with erratic and disruptive shifts in communication. Feinsilver (1970) found supporting evidence for such amorphous and fragmented thinking in the impaired ability of schizophrenic family members to describe essential attributes of common household objects to each other. Bannister (1971) found that schizophrenic thinking tends to be even more "loose" and disordered when an individual is dealing with people and interpersonal relationships than when dealing with objects.

In their later work, Singer and Wynne (Singer, Wynne, & Toohey, 1978; Wynne, Toohey, & Doane, 1979) referred generally to "communication deviance" (or "transactional style deviance") as being at the heart of the purported negative effects parents have on their preschizophrenic children. Following up on this work, Goldstein and colleagues (Doane et al., 1981; Goldstein, 1985; Goldstein et al., 1978; Lewis et al., 1981), in a longitudinal study employing a variant of the "high-risk" strategy (that is, subjects who had been psychological clinic patients, but *not* schizophrenic, as adolescents were followed into adulthood), confirmed such an effect. Specifically, they found that high parental communication deviance, measured during their children's adolescence, did indeed predict the occurrence of adult schizophrenic spectrum disorders among these offspring. An atmosphere of negative affect appears to increase the likelihood of such outcomes. Even if interpreted cautiously, such findings, recently reviewed by Goldstein and Strachan (1987), show promise in enhancing our understanding of the origins of schizophrenia.

Undermining personal authenticity. Philosopher Martin Buber (1957) pointed out that a confirmation of authenticity is essential to normal interpersonal relationships.

In human society at all its levels, persons confirm one another in a practical way, to some extent or other, in their personal qualities and capacities, and a society may be termed human in the measure to which its members confirm one another. . . . (p. 101)

Such confirmation apparently is often denied a person who later becomes schizophrenic. Several investigators (e.g., Wynne et al., 1958) have noted that the members of schizophrenic families consistently disqualify one or more members' statements and actions. In one family, for example, the father strongly approved of whatever the younger son did while he was to an equal extent disapproving of the older son's behavior. Thus the brothers might make similar statements about some matter, and the father would agree with one and find some basis for disqualifying or discrediting the other. Similarly, at

Christmas time, the younger son's present to his father was praised and appreciated, while that of the older son was criticized and found disappointing. The mother and younger sister went along with this differential treatment. Later, at the age of 27, the older son was hospitalized and diagnosed as a paranoid schizophrenic.

Such contradictory and disconfirming communications subtly and persistently mutilate the self-concepts of one or more of the family members, usually that of a particular child, as in the preceding example. The ultimate of this mutilation process occurs when

. . . no matter how [a person] feels or how he acts, no matter what meaning he gives his situation, his feelings are denuded of validity, his acts are stripped of their motives, intentions, and consequences, the situation is robbed of its meaning for him, so that he is totally mystified and alienated. (Laing & Esterson, 1964, pp. 135–136)

In the general context of faulty parent-child and family interactions, we may note that Lidz (1968, 1973) has characterized the parents of schizophrenic individuals as "deficient tutors": they create a family milieu inappropriate for training a child in the cognitive abilities essential for categorizing experience, thinking coherently, and communicating meaningfully. Coupled with feelings of inadequacy and other damage to the child's emerging self-concept, this may help explain the later cognitive distortions, communication failures, difficulties in interpersonal relationships, and identity confusions that commonly occur in schizophrenia.

Nevertheless, most of the children from families with persistently pathogenic characteristics do not become schizophrenic. Thus pathogenic family interactions that undermine personal authenticity cannot be the sole cause of schizophrenia.

Faulty Learning and Coping It appears that faulty learning typically plays a key role in schizophrenia, as it does in most other forms of maladaptive behavior. From early traumatic experiences—both within the family and in the outer world—a child may learn conditioned fears and vulnerabilities that lead to perceiving the world as a dangerous and hostile place. Perhaps of even greater importance is faulty learning on a cognitive level, resulting from irrationalities in social interaction, attempts to meet inappropriate or impossible expectations and demands, and observations of pathological models.

Deficient self-structure. Faulty learning in terms of deficient self-structure is typically reflected in (a) grossly inaccurate assumptions concerning reality, possibility, and value; (b) a confused sense of self-identity coupled with basic feelings of inadequacy, insecurity, and self-devaluation; (c) personal immaturity, often reflected in overdependence on others and overemphasis on being a "good boy" or a "good girl"; and (d) a lack of needed competencies coupled with ineffective coping patterns. These characteristics appear capable of paving the way for schizophrenic and other seriously maladaptive behaviors. If we consider the developmental problems of the Genain sisters in this light, we can see how difficult it must have been for them, as members of a tightly knit and socially isolated foursome, to gain the understandings and skills they needed.

The results of such faulty learning are often seen in such individuals' attempts to deal with inner impulses and establish satisfying interpersonal relationships. In the sexual sphere, schizophrenic individuals' problems are often complicated by rigidly moralistic attitudes toward sexual behavior. At the same time, they usually have had few, if any, meaningful sexual relationships. As a consequence, their sexual fantasies—like those of young adolescents—may be somewhat chaotic and encompass a wide range of sexual objects and behaviors. Such fantasies often lead to severe inner conflicts and to self-devaluation. Similarly, the hostility they may feel toward people important to them is apt to be particularly difficult for such "good" individuals to handle; they tend to view such hostility as both immoral and dangerous and do not know how to express it in socially acceptable ways. At the same time, they may be completely upset at being the object of hostility from those on whom they feel dependent.

This lack of competencies in dealing with sexual and hostile fantasies and impulses, combined with a general deficiency in social skills, usually leads to disappointment, hurt, and devaluation in intimate interpersonal relationships. As we will see, the stresses that commonly precipitate schizophrenic episodes typically center around the difficulties in such relationships. The inability of such individuals to establish and maintain satisfying interpersonal relationships does not void their needs for acceptance, approval, and love; it only reduces their chances for meeting these needs.

The exaggerated use of ego-defense mechanisms. Feeling inadequate and devalued and lacking an adequate frame of reference and needed competencies, such individuals, not surprisingly, learn to rely excessively on ego-defense mechanisms rather than on task-oriented coping patterns. These defense mechanisms often include psychophysiologic elements that have substantial secondary gain by "excusing" a person's withdrawal and nonperformance, particularly in early stages of the disorder. This was apparently the case with the Genain sisters, though somatic symptoms conceivably may also express an underlying biological defect. In any case, the development of a schizophrenic process does not preclude neurotic forms of coping.

The exaggerated use of many ego-defense mechanisms is common. Emotional insulation protects these individuals from the hurt of disappointment and frustration. Regression enables them to lower their level of aspiration and accept a position of dependence. Projection helps them maintain feelings of adequacy and worth by placing the blame for their failures on others and attributing their own unacceptable desires to someone else. Wish-fulfilling fantasies give them some compensation for their frustration and self-devaluation.

In particular, the excessive use of such defense mechanisms as projection and fantasy appears likely to predispose an individual to delusions and hallucinations, which not only represent the breakdown of organized perception and thought processes, but also—as part of a schizophrenic reorganization of reality—may have marked defensive value. Delusions of grandeur and persecution enable these individuals to project the blame for their own inadmissible thoughts and behaviors; hallucinations—such as voices that "pour filth into their minds" or keep them informed of what their "enemies" are up to—may serve a comparable defensive purpose. Delusions of grandeur and omnipotence may grow out of simple wishful thinking and enable them to counteract feelings of inferiority and inadequacy. Hallucinations, such as conversations in which they hear the voice of God confer great power on them and assign them the mission of saving the world, may likewise have comparable defensive value.

In acute schizophrenic episodes, the initial picture is somewhat different, as we have seen, and is dominated by massive disorganization of thought, with panic at the loss of control over thoughts and feelings and desperate attempts to understand the terrifying experience. As yet the individual has not developed defenses to cope with the situation, but no one can continue indefinitely in this state of panic and confusion. Either the acute schizophrenic episode clears up eventually, or various extreme defenses, such as the ones mentioned earlier, are likely to develop.

Although extreme ego-defense mechanisms are commonly observed in schizophrenic patients, it is often unclear to what extent they are a causal factor, as opposed to a reaction to the frightening experience of disorganization. Here it may be emphasized that a schizophrenic breakdown often appears to represent a total defensive strategy. In essence, the individual seems to withdraw from the real world and evolve a defensive strategy that makes it possible to distort and "reshape" aversive experiences so that they can be assimilated without further self-devaluation. Even though this defensive system may be illogical and far from satisfactory, it relieves much of the inner tension and anxiety and protects the individual from complete psychological disintegration.

Social Role Problems Social role behavior has been tied into the development and course of schizophrenic reactions in several different ways. A factor emphasized by Cameron and Margaret (1949, 1951) in their intensive studies of schizophrenic patients was the failure of such individuals to learn appropriate role-taking behavior. Inflexible in their own role behavior and uncomprehending of the role behavior of others, they do not know how to interact appropriately with other people.

Laing (1967, 1969, 1971), has carried this view of role behavior a step further, to seeing a schizophrenic person's creation of his or her own social role as protection from destructive social expectations and demands. Describing the so-called normal world as a place where all of us are "bemused and crazed creatures, strangers to our true selves, to one another, and to the spiritual and material world" (1967, p. 56), Laing maintains that a split arises between the false outer self and the true inner self. When the split reaches a point where it can no longer be tolerated, the result is a psychotic breakdown, which usually takes the form of schizophrenia. In this view, the "madness" labeled schizophrenia represents an individual's attempts to recover a sense of wholeness as a human being.

In essence, according to Laing, such an individual dons the "mask of insanity" as a social role and a barricade. Behind this "false self" and often turbulent facade, however, the real person—the "true inner self"—remains. In this hidden inner world, despite the outward role of madness, the schizophrenic individual's hopes and aspirations may remain intact. Accordingly, Laing thinks treatment

Joseph Rogers was diagnosed as a schizophrenic but later recovered and became chairman of the National Mental Health Consumers' Association. Until recent times the prognosis for schizophrenia was generally considered extremely unfavorable. The introduction of antipsychotic-drug therapy for schizophrenia in the 1950s has done much to relieve symptoms and to get schizophrenic individuals out of hospitals, but the long-range outlook for fully restoring personality and coherent thought is often still limited.

should focus less on removing "symptoms" than on finding a path to this remote and often inaccessible sanctuary and assisting the individual to regain wholeness as a person.

In any event, we do know that the occurrence of schizophrenic symptoms may depend to a considerable extent on the context in which an individual is being observed (Levy, 1976; Ritchie, 1975; Shimkunas, 1972). Such symptoms may come and go or be otherwise modified, depending on what demands are currently being placed on the patient. For example, a demand for intimate exchange appears to exacerbate schizophrenic symptoms. We also know that a certain subset of mental patients diagnosed as schizophrenic have demonstrated considerable skill in controlling both the diagnoses they receive and the likelihood of their discharge from the hospital (Braginsky, Braginsky, & Ring, 1969; Drake & Wallach, 1979). In some ways, these are deeply disconcerting findings that mock much of the research reported. They suggest the need for investigator caution in selecting "schizophrenic" patients for research—if only to weed out from studies those who are feigning their symptoms.

A related issue is the possibly fraudulent use of the insanity defense by people accused of serious crimes. Though this defense is infrequently employed, it tends to arise in dramatic cases in which the felonious act seems senseless, that is, unintelligible, to the average person. We can never be ultimately certain that such a plea is valid, or even that it has a viable meaning (Szasz, 1963). This is a problem with which our society will eventually have to come to grips.

Excessive Life Stress and Decompensation

Brown (1972) found a marked increase in the severity of life stress during the ten-week period prior to an actual schizophrenic breakdown. Problems typically centered around difficulties in intimate personal relationships. Similarly, Schwartz and Myers (1977) found interpersonal stressors to be significantly more common among schizophrenic people than among members of a matched control group. As yet, however, we have not come up with a truly adequate classification of the types of stressors that are likely to precipitate a schizophrenic episode (Dohrenwend & Egri, 1981). Forgus and DeWolfe (1974) found that schizophrenic patients seemed to have been defeated by their whole life situation and by difficulties in close personal relationships.

We do know that relapse into schizophrenia following remission is often associated with a certain type of negative communication, called **expressed emotion (EE),** directed at the patient by family members (Hooley, 1985; Miklowitz, Goldstein, & Falloon, 1983; Vaughn & Leff, 1976, 1981). Originally observed in Great Britain, the effect has also been demonstrated in the United States (Hooley, 1985; Vaughn et al., 1984). Two components appear critical in the pathogenic effects of EE: emotional overinvolvement with the patient, and excessive criticalness. Significantly, EE tends to be associated with familial communication deviance as previously described (Doane et al., 1985; Goldstein, 1985; Miklowitz et al., 1986). Parker, Johnston, and Hayward (1988) pointed out that EE is most likely to occur where a former patient is highly disturbed, a circumstance that might itself prompt rehospitalization. The force of this criticism is mitigated by findings that EE *predicts* schizophrenia prior to its initial onset (Goldstein, 1985). Finally, early results from intervention attempts to reduce EE and associated behaviors in family members have been most encouraging in terms of relapse prevention (Falloon et al., 1985; Hogarty et al., 1986).

As we noted, the course of decompensation (disorganization of thought and personality) in reactive (positive-symptom) schizophrenia tends to be sudden, while that in process (negative-symptom) schizophrenia tends to be gradual. The actual degree of decompensation may vary markedly, depending on the severity of stress and the makeup of the individual. The course of recovery or recompensation may also be relatively rapid or slow. Similarly, the degree of recovery may be complete, even leading to a better-adjusted person than before; it may be partial but sufficient for adequate adjustment; or it may be nonexistent, with the individual eventually receiving a diagnosis of chronic schizophrenia.

Sociocultural Factors in Schizophrenia

While disorders of thought and emotion are common to schizophrenia the world over, cultural factors may influence the type, the symptom content, and even the incidence of schizophrenic disorders in different societies. For example, one of the more puzzling findings is that first admission rates for schizophrenia are very high for Irish Catholics in the Republic of Ireland (southern Ireland), especially in the western regions (Torrey et al., 1984), but not among Irish Catholics residing elsewhere (Murphy, 1978). One possibility is that different diagnostic criteria are used in the Republic of Ireland. This does not seem to be a wholly satisfactory explanation, however, because there are many areas around the world in which the incidence of schizophrenia has been clearly shown to be exceptionally high or exceptionally low when compared to the worldwide incidence rate of just under 1 percent. It appears that certain cultures, like certain families, are schizophrenogenic; conversely, others seem to protect their members from the ravages of the disorder, at least to a degree.

Systematic differences in the content and form of a schizophrenic disorder between cultures and even subcultures were documented by Carothers (1953, 1959) in his studies of different African groups. Carothers found the disorganized type of schizophrenia (known at that time as *hebephrenic schizophrenia*) to be most common among African tribal groups in remote areas. He attributed this finding to a lack of well-developed ego-defense mechanisms among the members of these groups, thus making a complete disorganization of personality more likely when schizophrenia did occur. Similarly, Field (1960) described the initial schizophrenic breakdown among natives in rural Ghana as typically involving a state of panic. In this case it was observed that when individuals were brought quickly to a shrine for treatment, they usually calmed down and in a few days appeared recovered. When there was considerable delay before reaching the shrine, however, individuals often developed classic disorganized disorders.

In another study of schizophrenia among the aborigines of West Malaysia, Kinzie and Bolton (1973) found the acute type to be by far the most common manifestation; they also noted that symptom content often "had an obvious cultural overlay, for example, seeing a 'river ghost' or 'men-like spirits' or talking to one's 'soul' " (p. 773). However, the clinical picture seems to be changing as rural Africans and other people from developing nations are increasingly exposed to modern technology and social change (Copeland, 1968; Kinzie & Bolton, 1973; Torrey, 1973, 1979).

An important consideration in cross-cultural studies is that opinions concerning what is "normal" by professionals from another culture may not always correspond with the opinions held by members of the community in question. For example, in describing the schizophrenic disorders of members of the Hawaii-Japanese community, professional observers emphasized seclusiveness and shallow, blunted emotionality. Community members, on the other hand, were impressed by evidence of uncontrolled emotionality and distrust, behaviors that are strongly counter to the community's values (Katz et al., 1978).

Focusing on sociocultural factors within our own society, Murphy (1968) summarized the abundant evidence that the incidence of schizophrenia in the United States is inversely related to socioeconomic status: the lower the status, the higher the incidence of schizophrenia. Although the data on this point are not as clear as Murphy and others have indicated (Sanua, 1969), his conclusion would probably be accepted by most investigators. Interestingly, a reverse effect seems to exist in India; there, the upper classes (castes) experience higher rates of schizophrenia than the lower classes (Torrey, 1979).

In a sophisticated review of the evidence relating social class and the incidence of schizophrenia, Kohn (1973) suggested that the conditions of lower-class existence impair an individual's ability to deal resourcefully with varied life stressors. The correlation is decidedly imperfect, however, for we know that some lower-class people emerge from their backgrounds with superabundant resourcefulness. We should also emphasize that alleged ethnic differences in the incidence and clinical pictures of schizophrenia—for example, between African Americans, Hispanics, and Anglo-Americans—disappear when social class, education, and related socioeconomic conditions are equated.

In concluding our review of the causal factors in schizophrenia, it may be pointed out that research on the causation of human behavior is, as Shakow (1969) expressed it, "fiendishly complex," even with normal subjects.

> *Research with disturbed human beings is even more so, particularly with those with whom it is difficult to communicate, among them schizophrenics. The marked range of schizophrenia, the marked variance within the range and within the individual, the variety of shapes that the psychosis takes, and both the excessive and compensatory behaviors that characterize it, all reflect this special complexity. Recent years have seen the complication further enhanced by the use of a great variety of therapeutic devices, such as drugs, that alter both the physiological and psychological nature of the organism. Research with schizophrenics, therefore, calls for awareness not only of the factors creating variance in normal human beings, but also of the many additional sources of variance this form of psychosis introduces. (Shakow, 1969, p. 618)*

Or as Bannister (1971) has pointed out, "We will eventually have to develop a theory of what makes all people march before we can say very much about why some people march to a different drummer" (p. 84).

In general, however, it appears that there is no one clinical entity or causal sequence in schizophrenia. Rather we seem to be dealing with several types of psychologically maladaptive processes resulting from an interaction of biological, psychosocial, and sociocultural factors; the role of these factors undoubtedly varies according to the given case and clinical picture. Often the interaction appears to involve a vicious spiral, in which life stress triggers metabolic changes that impair the functioning of a perhaps already compromised central nervous system, the latter, in turn, intensifying anxiety and panic as an individual realizes he or she is losing control. The spiral continues until more permanent reconstitutive patterns are established, treatment is undertaken, or the disorder has run its course. In severe instances, the "course" may be as long as 40 years or more. It is important to note that, although full recovery is rare after such a lengthy period of disorder, it does sometimes occur (M. Bleuler, 1978).

Treatments and Outcomes

Until recent times, the prognosis for schizophrenia was generally considered extremely unfavorable. Under the routine custodial treatment of large, institutionalized mental hospital settings, an approach that had persisted for a century prior to the 1950s, the rate of discharge approximated only 30 percent.

For most schizophrenic individuals, the outlook today is not nearly so bleak. Improvement in this situation came with dramatic suddenness when the phenothiazine class of drugs—then referred to as "major tranquilizers"—were introduced in the mid-1950s. *Pharmacotherapy* (treatment by drugs), especially when combined with other modern treatment methods, permits the majority of cases to be treated in outpatient clinics; a schizophrenic individual who enters a mental hospital or clinic as an inpatient for the first time has an 80 to 90 percent chance of being discharged within a matter of weeks or, at most, months. The rate of readmission, however, is still extremely high, although exact figures are difficult to calculate because the "careers" of individual patients are not readily tracked (Weinstein, 1983).

Overall, about one-third of schizophrenic patients recover, which means technically that they

Tom is a schizophrenic individual who is undergoing drug therapy. The contrast between Tom unmedicated (left) and medicated (right) is dramatic, underscoring the effectiveness of antipsychotic drugs in reducing symptoms of schizophrenia.

HIGHLIGHT 12.5

Conditions Associated with Favorable Outcomes in the Treatment of Schizophrenia

The following conditions often indicate a favorable outcome for a schizophrenic patient:

1. Reactive rather than process schizophrenia, in which the time from onset of full-blown symptoms is six months or less.
2. Clear-cut precipitating stressors.
3. Adequate heterosexual adjustment prior to the schizophrenic episode.
4. Good social and work adjustment prior to the schizophrenic episode.
5. Minimal incidence of schizophrenia and other pathological conditions in family background.
6. Involvement of depression or other schizoaffective pattern.
7. Favorable life situation to return to and adequate aftercare in the community.

In general, the opposite of the preceding conditions—including poor premorbid adjustment, slow onset, and relatives with schizophrenia—are indicative of an unfavorable prognosis.

We should note that in a five-year follow-up study of 61 schizophrenic individuals in the United States, Hawk, Carpenter, and Strauss (1975) failed to find any differences in long-range outcomes between acute and other subtypes of schizophrenia. (Data could be obtained on only 61 out of the original sample of 131 cases.) The study was part of an International Pilot Study of Schizophrenia (IPSS) designed to include transcultural data on over 1200 patients in 9 countries—Columbia, Czechoslovakia, Denmark, India, Nigeria, Taiwan, the U.S.S.R., the United Kingdom, and the United States.

remain symptom-free for five years; only some 10 percent now show the classical pattern of inexorable deterioration and permanent, profound disability. The remainder of people experiencing a first schizophrenic episode—some 60 percent of the total—show varying degrees of personality impoverishment and episodic psychotic behavior. Obviously, this is the group on whom our major treatment efforts should initially be concentrated, but evidence shows that in recent years this group, within our own society, has in fact been seriously neglected—as seen in the common "revolving door" pattern of endless cycles of discharge and brief rehospitalization for medication adjustment. Outcome ratios appear less favorable where the onset of symptoms occurs at an early point in the life cycle (Bender, 1973; Gross & Huber, 1973; Morrison, 1974; Roff, 1974). For an overview of conditions that suggest a favorable prognosis in schizophrenia, see *HIGHLIGHT 12.5*.

As we have done with respect to other disorders, we will postpone until later chapters a detailed discussion of the various kinds of treatment employed for schizophrenia. Here we note merely that, contrary to widespread belief, such treatment is—or should be—by no means limited to biological forms of intervention. It is our belief, in fact, that the pharmacologic approach has been grossly oversold. Consider in this regard the remarks of the distinguished Harvard social psychologist Roger Brown, who attended a meeting of Schizophrenics Anonymous in order to familiarize himself with the problems of these people:

> *[The group leader] began with an optimistic testimony about how things were going with him, designed in part to buck up the others. Some of them also spoke hopefully; others were silent and stared at the floor throughout. I gradually felt hope draining out of the group as they began to talk of their inability to hold jobs, of living on welfare, of finding themselves overwhelmed by simple demands. Nothing bizarre was said or done; there was rather a pervasive sense of inadequacy, of lives in which each day was a dreadful trial. Doughnuts and coffee were served, and then each one, still alone, trailed off into the Cambridge night.*
>
> *What I saw a little of at that meeting of Schizophrenics Anonymous is simply that there is something about schizophrenia that the antipsychotic drugs do not cure or even always remit on a long-term basis. (Brown & Herrnstein, 1975, p. 641)*

Unfortunately, Brown's assessment of the antipsychotic drugs is in our judgment painfully accurate; it may even be excessively generous. The devastating social deficits Brown describes are extremely common accompaniments of schizophrenic disorders and may indeed be far more disabling in their disruptive effects than an occasional eruption of psychotic symptoms. There is no evidence that long-term rates of *social* recovery from schizophrenia have been affected by the availability of these drugs (see, for example, Harding et al., 1987a, 1987b). Nor is it easy to see how drugs of any kind could be expected to provide these patients with the wherewithal, in terms of a social competence that many lacked before becoming actively schizophrenic, to lead reasonably successful and independent lives. We include in this assessment clozapine (Clozaril), mentioned earlier, the first of what will probably turn out to be a new generation of antipsychotics. It seems obvious to us that we are going to have to look elsewhere for a "cure" to this type of problem; the idea of finding a chemical that might do this job for us is, we think, unrealistic.

The tendency to think of the treatment of schizophrenia as being exclusively a matter of biological intervention has obscured some real progress that had been made in psychosocial approaches before this trend gained the force it now commands. In the large scale meta-analysis (see Chapter 18) of therapeutic outcomes conducted by Smith, Glass, and Miller (1980), the "average effect size" for all psychosocial treatments for schizophrenia was +0.68, a respectable figure; by contrast, the average effect size for drugs-alone treatment of schizophrenia was +0.51. Because the training, competence, and experience of the person or persons conducting the treatment are far less critical in drug than in psychosocial approaches (the active ingredients of the drug are the same no matter who writes the prescription), we suspect these figures *underestimate* the potential advantages of psychosocial forms of intervention. In any event, the combination drugs-plus-psychosocial intervention average effect size was as an impressive +.80, which suggests that systematic psychosocial treatment should always be part of the treatment offered in schizophrenia. Our experience suggests that at this time such treatment is actually rare.

Several forms of exclusively psychosocial intervention in schizophrenia have documented high rates of success. These interventions include a therapeutic community-based program having minimal professional oversight (Fairweather et al., 1969; Fairweather, 1980), a rigorous token economy program for chronic state hospital patients (Paul & Lentz, 1977), and specialized individual psychotherapy provided by therapists highly experienced with this group (Karon & Vandenbos, 1981).

DELUSIONAL (PARANOID) DISORDER

The term **paranoia** has been in use a long time. The ancient Greeks and Romans used it to refer more or less indiscriminately to any mental disorder. Our present, more limited use of the term stems from the work of Kraepelin, who reserved it for cases showing delusions and impaired contact with reality but without the severe personality disorganization characteristic of schizophrenia.

Currently two main types of psychoses are included under the DSM-III-R headings relating to (nonschizophrenic) paranoid disorders: **delusional disorder,** formerly called *paranoia* and *paranoid disorder,* and **induced psychotic disorder,** formerly *shared paranoid disorder,* in which two or more people develop persistent, interlocking delusional ideas. The latter of these conditions, historically known as *folie à deux,* is described briefly in *HIGHLIGHT 12.6.* Brief episodes of otherwise uncomplicated delusional thinking have been shifted in DSM-III-R to the "wastebasket" category *psychotic disorders not elsewhere classified.* Our focus in this section will be on delusional disorder. As will become apparent, there is a lack of recent literature on this disorder, and we will thus be forced to focus on a number of early but seemingly definitive studies. Because these earlier studies used the traditional terminology *paranoia* and *paranoid disorder,* we will use those terms and the newer *delusional disorder* classification interchangeably.

DSM-III-R requires that diagnoses of delusional disorder be specified by type, based on the predominant theme of the delusions present. These types are as follows:

- *Persecutory type.* The predominant delusional theme is that one (or someone to whom one is closely related) is being subjected to some kind of malevolent treatment. Legal actions of one sort or another are often instituted to redress the alleged injustice.
- *Jealous type.* The predominant theme is that one's sexual partner is being unfaithful.
- *Erotomanic type.* The predominant theme is that some other person of higher status, frequently someone of considerable prominence, is in love with one and wants to start a sexual liaison.
- *Somatic type.* The predominent theme is an unshakable belief in having some physical

HIGHLIGHT 12.6

Folie à Deux

A relatively neglected phenomenon in the functional psychoses is that of *folie à deux*—a form of psychological "contagion" in which one person copies and incorporates into his or her own personality structure the delusions and other psychotic patterns of another person. Familial relationships between individuals in 103 cases studied by Gralnick (1942) fell within one of the following four categories:

sister	⇄	sister	40 cases
husband	⇄	wife	28 cases
mother	⇄	child	24 cases
brother	⇄	brother	11 cases

Among the explanatory factors—all environmental—emphasized by Gralnick were (a) length of association, (b) dominance-submission, (c) type of familial relationship, and (d) prepsychotic personality. The high incidence in the husband-wife category is particularly striking because common heredity plays no part as an etiological factor in these cases.

In another study, Soni and Rockley (1974) reported on 8 cases of folie à deux seen at a European hospital. Their findings supported those of Gralnick and emphasized the role of pathological prepsychotic characteristics, such as increased suggestability and submissive roles, as well as the type of relationship in explaining why these patients acquired their partner's delusions.

illness or disorder, often bizarre in nature, or in having some abnormality of appearance.

- *Grandiose type.* The predominant theme is that one is a person of extraordinary status, power, ability, talent, beauty, and so on.
- *Other.* This diagnosis is used when no single theme predominates.

Of these types, the persecutory is by far the most common, and our discussion will focus on this form of the disorder.

Although the formal diagnosis of delusional disorder is rare in clinic and mental hospital populations, this observation provides a somewhat misleading picture of its actual occurrence. Many exploited inventors, fanatical reformers, self-styled prophets, morbidly jealous spouses, persecuted teachers, business executives, or other professionals fall into this category. Unless they become a serious nuisance, these individuals are usually able to maintain themselves in the community and do not recognize their paranoid condition nor seek help to alleviate it.

In some instances, however, they are potentially dangerous, and in virtually all instances they are inveterate "injustice-detectors," inclined to undertake retributive actions of one sort or another.

The Clinical Picture in Delusional Disorder

A paranoid, or delusional, individual feels singled out and taken advantage of, mistreated, plotted against, stolen from, spied on, ignored, or otherwise mistreated by "enemies." The delusional system usually centers around one major theme, such as financial matters, a job, an invention, an unfaithful spouse, or another life affair. For example, a woman who is failing on the job may insist that her fellow workers and superiors have it in for her because they are jealous of her great ability and efficiency. As a result, she may quit her job and go to work elsewhere, only to find friction developing again and her new job in jeopardy. Now she may become convinced that the first company has written to her present employer and has turned everyone against her so that she has not been given a fair chance. With time, more and more of the environment is integrated into her delusional system as each additional experience is misconstrued and interpreted in the light of her delusional ideas. See *HIGHLIGHT 12.7* for a list of characteristics typical of paranoid thinking.

Although the evidence that paranoid people advance to justify their claims may be tenuous and inconclusive, they are unwilling to accept any other

HIGHLIGHT 12.7

Sequence of Events in a Paranoid Mode of Thinking

A number of investigators have concluded that the most useful perspective from which to view paranoia is in terms of a *mode of thinking*. The sequence of events that appears to characterize this mode of thinking may be summarized as follows:

1. *Suspiciousness*—the individual mistrusts the motives of others, fears he or she will be taken advantage of, and is constantly on the alert.
2. *Protective thinking*—the individual selectively perceives the actions of others to confirm suspicions and blames others for his or her failures.
3. *Hostility*—the individual responds to alleged injustices and mistreatment with anger and hostility and becomes increasingly suspicious.
4. *Paranoid Illumination*—the moment when everything "falls into place"; the individual finally understands the strange feelings and events being experienced.
5. *Delusions*—the individual has delusions of influence and persecution that may be based on "some grain of truth," presented in a logical and convincing way; often, the later development of delusions of grandeur.

Over time, a paranoid individual may incorporate additional life areas, people, and events into the delusional system, creating a "pseudo-community" whose purpose is to carry out some action against him or her. Paranoid individuals who respond in this manner may come to feel that all the attention they are receiving from others is indicative of their unique abilities and importance, thus paving the way for delusions of grandeur.

Based in part on Meissner (1978) and Swanson, Bohnert, and Smith (1970).

possible explanation and are impervious to reason. A husband may be convinced of his spouse's unfaithfulness because on two separate occasions when he answered the phone the party at the other end hung up. Argument and logic are futile. In fact, any questioning of his delusions only convinces him that his interrogator has sold out to his enemies. The following case illustrates the sometimes tragic results of paranoid delusions:

Milner cited the case of a paranoid man, aged 33, who murdered his wife by battering her head with a hammer. Prior to the murder, he had become convinced that his wife was suffering from some strange disease and that she had purposely infected him because she wished him to die. He believed that this disease was due to a "cancer-consumption" germ. He attributed his conclusion in part to his wife's alleged sexual perversion and also gave the following reasons for his belief:

1. His wife had insured him for a small sum immediately after marriage.

2. A young man who had been friendly with his wife before their marriage died suddenly.

3. A child who had lived in the same house as his wife's parents suffered from fits. (He also believed that his wife's parents were suffering from the same disease.)

4. For several months before the crime his food had had a queer taste, and for a few weeks before the crime he had suffered from a pain in the chest and an unpleasant taste in the mouth. (1949, p. 130)

Although ideas of persecution predominate, many paranoid individuals develop delusions of grandeur in which they endow themselves with superior or unique abilities. Such "exalted" ideas usually center around messianic missions, political or social reforms, or remarkable inventions. Paranoid people who are religious may consider themselves appointed by God to save the world and may spend most of their time "preaching" and "crusading." Threats of fire and brimstone, burning in hell, and similar persuasive devices are liberally employed. Many paranoid people become attached to extremist political movements and are tireless and fanatical crusaders, although they often do their cause more harm than good by their self-righteousness and their condemnation of others.

Some paranoid individuals develop remarkable inventions that they have endless trouble in patenting or selling. Gradually they become convinced that a plot is afoot to steal their invention, or that enemies of the United States are working against them to prevent the country from receiving the benefits of their remarkable talents. Hoffman cited the case of an individual who went to Washington to get presidential assistance in obtaining a patent for a flame thrower that, he claimed, could destroy all the enemies of the United States. He would patiently explain who he was: "There's God who is Number 1, and Jesus Christ who is Number 2, and me, I am Number 3" (1943, p. 574).

Aside from the delusional system, such an individual may appear perfectly normal in conversation, emotionality, and conduct. Hallucinations and the other obvious signs of psychopathology are rarely found. This normal appearance, together with the logical and coherent way in which the delusional ideas are presented, may make the individual most convincing. The following case is typical:

In one case an engineer developed detailed plans for eliminating the fog in San Francisco and other large cities by means of a system of reflectors that would heat the air by solar radiation and cause the fog to lift. The company for which he worked examined the plans and found them unsound. This rejection upset him greatly and he resigned his position, stating that the other engineers in the company were not qualified to pass judgment on any complex and advanced engineering projects like his. Instead of attempting to obtain other employment, he then devoted full time trying to find some other engineering firm that would have the vision and technical proficiency to see the great potential of his idea. He would present his plans convincingly but become highly suspicious and hostile when questions concerning their feasibility were raised. Eventually, he became convinced that there was a conspiracy among a large number of engineering firms to steal his plans and use them for their own profit. He reported his suspicions to the police, threatening to do something about the situation himself unless they took action. As a consequence, he was hospitalized for observation and diagnosed as suffering from paranoia.

The diagnosis of delusional disorder may be rendered difficult at times because of the unclarity of the term ***delusion.*** It is not always possible to determine the truth or falsity of an idea, and some ideas that are patently false are held with sincerity and conviction by many people. For this reason, formal definitions of "delusion" (as in DSM-III-R) usually specify that an idea must be held as preposterous by the majority of a person's own community. As the example of Columbus's fifteenth-century belief that the earth was round shows, however, this qualification does not always solve the problem. These and other difficulties surrounding the notion of delusional thinking have received a thorough airing recently in a book edited by Oltmanns and Maher (1988). A number of the chapters in this work, incidentally, suggest that delusional thinking is not so different from normal thinking as we would perhaps like to think. The problem also remains, of course, of differentiating delusional disorder from paranoid personality disorder (Chapter 8), which also involves a judgment call as to whether or not clearly eccentric and convoluted thinking merits the designation "delusional."

A patient's delusional system is apt to be particularly convincing if one accepts the basic premise or premises on which it is based. For example, where the delusional system develops around some actual injustice, it may be difficult to distinguish between fact and fancy. As a result, the individual's family and friends, as well as well-meaning public officials, may be convinced of the truth of the claims. However, the individual's inability to see the facts in any other light, typical lack of evidence for far-reaching conclusions, and hostile, suspicious, and uncommunicative attitude when the delusional ideas are questioned usually provide clues that something is wrong.

The following case history is a classic description of a mild paranoia. It reveals the development of a logically patterned delusional system and the pertinent selection of environmental evidence that involves more and more individuals in the supposed conspiracy. Despite this woman's delusional system, however, she was not severely out of touch with reality; many nonhospitalized cases in the community reveal similar symptomatology to a more serious degree.

The patient was a 31-year-old nurse who was commissioned a second lieutenant in the Army Nurse Corps shortly after the beginning of World War II. From the start she found it difficult to adjust to fellow nurses and to enlisted men under her supervision, the difficulty apparently arising from her overzealousness in carrying out ward regulations in the minutest detail. In any event, "No one could get along with her." After some two years of service, she was transferred to a new assignment.

. . . Initially she made an excellent impression, but soon showed herself to be a perfectionist, a hypercritical and domineering personality who insisted on the immediate, precise, exact and detailed execution of orders. Within a 14-week period she was transferred on three separate occasions from post to post, and at each new post her manner and her attitude, despite her precise and meticulous efficiency, constituted a virtual demand that nurses, wardmen, patients, and medical officers conform to her exceedingly rigid ideas about the management of ward and even departmental routines. . . .

During the course of her last assignment, she received every possible help. She requested additional responsibility and was, therefore, assigned, as charge nurse, to the Eye, Ear, Nose, and Throat Clinic. Within a week she lodged a complaint with the commanding officer of the hospital, accusing the enlisted men of conspiring against her, the nurses of lying about her, and the officer in charge of lack of cooperation. She was, therefore, transferred to one of the wards, where she expected wardmen, nurses and patients to execute her orders on the instant, in minute and exact detail, and where she violently berated them because of their inability to do so. A week later, the responsible medical officer requested that she be relieved from duty there. Instead, she discussed the problem with the chief nurse and promised to correct her attitude. Within four days, the patients as a group suggested her removal. Two weeks later, the ward officer repeated his request. She was, therefore, given a five-day leave, and during her absence all ward personnel were contacted in an attempt to help her adjust when she returned to duty.

During this period she became convinced that she was being persecuted. She grew tense and despondent, kept rigidly to herself, was unable to sleep in a room with a ticking clock, and frequently burst into tears. As she herself said, "Some of the nurses deliberately went out of their way to annoy and criticize me. They wanted to make me trouble. That's why I was so upset." On three separate occasions, she requested the appointment of a Board of Officers to investigate these alleged discriminatory acts. Finally she demanded that a Board of Officers be convened to determine her efficiency as a nurse. Instead, she was ordered to report to our hospital for psychiatric observation.

On admission, few details of her military history were known. She seemed alert and cooperative, was well oriented in all three spheres [time, place, person], and was thought to be in complete contact. Extreme care, however, was necessary when addressing her. Even fellow patients would warn newcomers to the ward. "Be careful what you say when she's around. She won't mean it, but she'll twist your statements without changing your words, and give them some meaning you never intended." In addition, she was bitter about the unfair treatment she had received in the Army, wished to reform the Medical Department and the Army Nursing Corps, and indignantly repudiated the existence of any condition that could justify placing her under NP [neuropsychiatric] observation. . . .

The diagnosis of "paranoia, true type" was made, and she was returned to the United States, one month after admission to the hospital, a rigid and overzealous individual whose inelasticity had antagonized her associates and aroused severe emotional strain within herself, firmly convinced that she was being persecuted because of the necessary and badly needed work which she had much too efficiently performed. . . . She was received in the States as a patient in the very hospital to whose psychiatric section she had previously, for so brief a period of time, been assigned as ward nurse. (Rosen & Kiene, 1946, pp. 330–333)

Paranoid individuals are not always as dangerous as we have been led to believe by popular fiction and drama, but the chance always exists that they will decide to take matters into their own hands and deal with their enemies in the only way that seems effective. In one instance, a paranoid school principal became convinced that the school board was discriminating against him and shot and killed most of the board members. In another case, a paranoid man shot and killed a group of seven people he thought had been following him. The number of husbands and wives who have been killed or injured by suspicious, paranoid mates is undoubtedly large. As Swanson, Bohnert, and Smith (1970) have pointed out, such murderous violence is commonly associated with jealousy and the loss of self-esteem; the spouse feels that he or she has been deceived, taken advantage of, and humiliated. Paranoid people may also get involved in violent and subversive activities and in political assassinations.

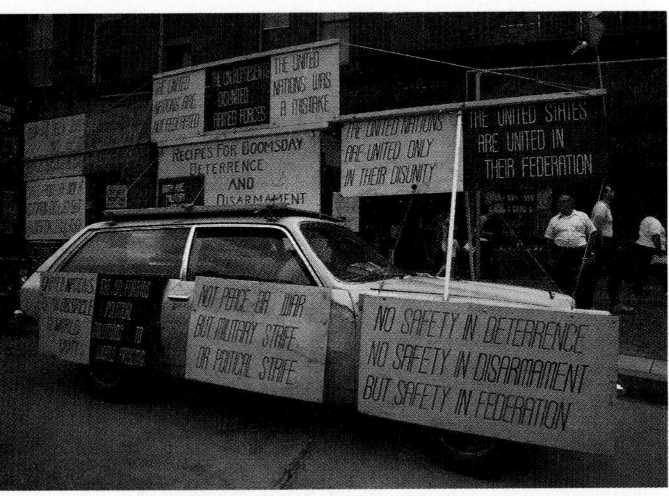

The insistent way the owner of this car has chosen to broadcast his or her ideas and the ideas themselves, which are hostile, suspicious, and a distortion of factual evidence, indicate delusional thinking.

Causal Factors in Delusional Disorder

Most of us on various occasions may wonder if we are not jinxed, when it seems as if everything we do goes wrong and the cards seem to be stacked against us. If we are generally somewhat suspicious and disposed to blame others for our difficulties, we may feel that most people are selfish and ruthless and that honest people, no matter what their abilities, do not have a fair chance. As a result, we may feel abused and become somewhat bitter and cynical. Many people go through life feeling underrated and frustrated, brooding over fancied and real injustices. Meissner (1978) regards such attitudes as a normal and essential phase of personality development, a necessary component in the achievement of personal identity and autonomy. Most people, according to this view, are able to grow beyond this phase, where a central feature is the need for an enemy. Some few are not, however, in which case they chronically entertain paranoid explanations of their problems.

As we have seen, recent thinking in this area has tended to view schizophrenic and paranoid processes as independent of one another, although sometimes occurring together in the same individual, in which case paranoid schizophrenia is the outcome (Magaro, 1980, 1981; Meissner, 1981). According to Magaro, schizophrenic and paranoid cognitions are of a different order and are related to two different stages of information processing. Whereas schizophrenia is seen as a disorder of *perception,* paranoia is regarded as a disorder of *conception.* A paranoid individual, in fact, is said to *overconceptualize* his or her experience to the point of relative inattention to the actual data that are perceived. For example, a (nonparanoid) schizophrenic individual might perceive his or her thoughts as inspired by external sources; a paranoid individual might carry this one step farther and conclude that this experience is due to a systematic plot by his or her "enemies" to harass and punish him or her. As a result, meanings may be imposed on incoming information that have no or at most a minimal relationship to what has happened, at least as far as issues of great personal significance are concerned.

We have already noted that individuals with paranoid schizophrenia tend not to show the extensive cognitive disorganization seen in other forms of schizophrenia. We should also note that biological factors have rarely been implicated in the paranoid disorders, as they have been in schizophrenia—although we must acknowledge that little work has been done in this area. Most observers believe that psychosocial factors are sufficient to account for the development of most of the paranoid disorders.

It may also be noted that the maintenance of a severely paranoid "fix" on the world does indeed require drastic derangements of a person's basic cognitive equipment, although it does not require that such equipment be subject to virtual functional annihilation. If an individual were unable to function on a day-by-day basis, paranoia would be impossible as an effective coping strategy.

Faulty Learning and Development Most paranoid individuals seem as children to have been aloof, suspicious, seclusive, secretive, stubborn, and resentful of punishment. When crossed, they became sullen and morose. Rarely do paranoid individuals show a history of normal play with other children or good socialization in terms of warm, affectionate relationships (Sarvis, 1962; Schwartz, 1963; Swanson et al., 1970).

Often such an individual's family background appears to have been authoritarian and excessively dominating, suppressive, and critical; frequently, some family members have practiced "mind reading" the thoughts of other family members. Such a family is often permeated with an air of superiority that is a cover-up for an underlying lack of self-acceptance and feelings of inferiority, creating for a child, in turn, the necessity of proving superiority. Inevitably, the family background of such individuals colors their feelings about people in general and their way of reacting to others. Inadequate socialization is likely to keep them from understanding others' motives and points of view and to lead them to suspicious misinterpretations of unintentional slights. Also, they tend to enter into social relationships with a hostile, dominating attitude that drives others away. Their inevitable social failures then further undermine their self-esteem and lead to deeper social isolation and mistrust.

In later personality development, these early trends merge into a picture of self-important, rigid, arrogant individuals. Such people long to dominate others and readily maintain their unrealistic self-picture by projecting the blame for difficulties onto others and seeking in others the weaknesses they cannot acknowledge in themselves. They are highly suspicious of the motives of other people and quick to sense insult or mistreatment. Such individuals lack a sense of humor—which is not surprising, since they view life as a deadly serious struggle—and are incapable of seeing things from any viewpoint but their own. Typically, they categorize people and ideas into "good" and "bad" and have difficulty in conceiving of something as having both good and bad qualities or shades of gray. Their goals and expectations are unrealistically high, and they refuse to make concessions in meeting life's problems by accepting more moderate goals. They expect to be praised and appreciated for even minor achievements, and when such praise is not forthcoming, they sulk and withdraw from normal contacts.

Many paranoid individuals' problems can be seen as problems of selfhood. A paranoid person may seem unable to achieve distance from deeply internalized struggles involving issues of aggression, victimization, power, weakness, and humiliation. Although such individuals may have broad interests and appear normal in general behavior, they are usually unable to relate closely to other people; they appear inaccessible, are overly aggressive, and maintain a somewhat superior air. Meissner (1978) views these personality traits largely as manifestations of a desperate attempt to maintain autonomy and a related fear of submission to the will of others, as though submission would constitute nothing less than total personality annihilation.

Failure and Inferiority The lives of paranoid individuals are replete with failures in critical life situations—social, occupational, and marital—stemming from their rigidity, their unrealistic goals, and their inability to get along with other people. Such failures jeopardize their view of themselves as being adequate, significant, and important and also expose their easily wounded pride to what they interpret as the rejection, scorn, and ridicule of others.

These failures are made more difficult to cope with by paranoid individuals' utter inability to understand the causes. Why should their efforts to improve the efficiency of the company—which people approve in principle—lead to such negative reactions from others? Why should people dislike them when they are striving so hard to do the best possible job down to the very last detail? Unable to see themselves or the situation objectively, they simply cannot understand how they tend to alienate others and why they are rebuffed and rejected.

Although such people's feelings of inferiority are masked behind an air of superiority and self-importance, many aspects of their behavior give them away. Clues in profusion are found in their continual craving for praise and recognition, their hypersensitivity to criticism, their exact and formal adherence to socially approved behavior, and their overzealous performance of minute tasks.

In essence, then, a paranoid individual is confronted with experiences of failure that in effect say, "People don't like you," "Something is wrong with you," or "You are inferior." He or she is incapable, however, of dealing with the problem in a task-oriented way, instead tending to intensify the existing defenses, becoming more rigid, opinionated, and prone to blame others. This defensive pattern is a protection against having to face unbearable feelings of inferiority and worthlessness. In this connection, Meissner (1978) reports the case of a young man who was sexually seduced by his drunken mother. He lived in terror that his "sin" would be discovered, and in the process developed an elaborate paranoid system of thought.

Elaboration of Defenses and the "Pseudocommunity" A rigid, self-important, humorless, and suspicious individual such as we have described becomes understandably unpopular with other people—in effect, an aversive stimulus. Thus, as Lemert (1962) has noted, a paranoid person frequently becomes in fact a target of actual discrimination and mistreatment. Ever alert to injustices, both imagined and real, such an individual finds abundant "proof" of persecution.

In this context, Grunebaum and Perlman (1973) have pointed to the naïveté of a "preparanoid" person in assessing the interpersonal world—in terms of who can be trusted and who cannot—as a fertile source of hurtful interactions. As they express it, "The ability to trust others realistically requires that the individual be able to tolerate minor and major violations of trust that are part of normal human relationships." (p. 32). The preparanoid individual is unprepared for the "facts of life," however, tending to both trust and mistrust inappropriately and to overreact when others are perceived, accurately or not, as betraying the trust.

Where delusional disorder develops, it usually does so gradually, as mounting failures and seeming betrayals force these individuals to an elaboration of their defensive structures. To avoid self-devaluation, they search for "logical" reasons for their lack of success. Why were they denied a much-deserved promotion? Why was it given to someone less experienced and obviously far less qualified? They become more vigilant, begin to scrutinize the environment, search for hidden meanings, and ask leading questions. They ponder like a detective over the "clues" they pick up, trying to fit them into some sort of meaningful picture.

Gradually the picture begins to crystallize—a process commonly referred to as "paranoid illumination." It becomes apparent that they are being singled out for some obscure reason, that other people are working against them, that they are being interfered with. In essence, they protect themselves against the intolerable assumption, "There is something wrong with me," with the projective defense, "They are doing something to me." They have failed not because of any inferiority or lack on their part, but because others are working against them. They are on the side of good and the progress of humankind, while their enemies are allied with the forces of evil. With this as their fundamental defensive premise, they proceed to distort and falsify the facts to fit it and gradually develop a logical, fixed, delusional system. Cameron (1959) has referred to this process as the building up of a paranoid "pseudo-community" in which an individual organizes surrounding people (both real and imaginary) into a structured group whose purpose is to carry out some action against him or her.

The role of highly selective information processing in the development of these delusional systems should be emphasized. Once these individuals begin to suspect that others are working against them, they start carefully noting the slightest signs pointing in the direction of their suspicions and ignore all evidence to the contrary (Swanson et al., 1970).

With this frame of reference, it is quite easy, in our highly competitive, somewhat ruthless world, for paranoid individuals to find ample evidence that others are working against them. This attitude itself leads to a vicious circle, for their suspiciousness, distrust, and criticism of others drive their friends and well-wishers away and keep them in continual friction with other people, generating new incidents for them to magnify. Often people do in fact have to conspire behind their backs in order to keep peace and cope with their eccentricities.

One additional factor often mentioned in connection with the development of delusional disorder is that of sexual maladjustment. Like schizophrenic patients, most paranoid individuals reveal sexual difficulties, typically centering around serious problems in interpersonal relationships in general, compounded by overwhelming feelings of inadequacy and inferiority.

Many early schizophrenic and paranoid patients make allusions to being "queer" or "gay," or to the thought that other people think they are. On investigation, it turns out that they typically have never engaged in homosexual behavior and show no indication of wishing to do so. It may be that they have finally hit on an "explanation" for the feeling of being so different from others, and for the slights and contempt they believe are emanating from others. An explanation of this sort may be better than no explanation at all as far as a troubled person is concerned. In brief, however, while underlying sexual conflicts, both heterosexual and homosexual, may be involved in the clinical picture, they do not appear to be of primary significance.

Treatments and Outcomes

In the early stages of delusional disorder, treatment with individual or group psychotherapy (or a combination of both) may prove effective, particularly if an individual voluntarily seeks professional assistance. Behavior therapy appears to show particular promise; for example, paranoid thinking may be altered by a combination of aversive conditioning, removal of the factors in a person's life that are reinforcing the maladaptive behavior, and development of more effective coping patterns.

Once a delusional system is well established, however, treatment is extremely difficult. It is usually impossible to communicate with such individuals in a rational way concerning their problems. In addition, they are not prone to seek treatment, but are more likely to seek justice for all the wrong done to them. Nor is hospitalization likely to help, for they are likely to see it as a form of punishment. They are apt to regard themselves as superior to other patients and will often complain that their families and the hospital staff have had them "put away" for no valid reason. Seeing nothing wrong with themselves, they refuse to cooperate or participate in treatment.

Eventually, however, they may realize that their failure to curb their actions and ideas will result in prolonged hospitalization. As a result, they may make a pretext of renouncing their delusions, admitting that they did hold such ideas but claiming that they now realize the ideas are absurd and are giving them up. After their release, they are often more reserved in expressing their ideas and in annoying other people, but they are far from recovered. Thus the prognosis for complete recovery from paranoia has traditionally been unfavorable.

UNRESOLVED ISSUES on Schizophrenia

The unresolved issues concerning schizophrenia are so manifold that a truly adequate accounting of them would require the better part of an additional chapter. We will point up, therefore, only a few selected problems of the many we encounter in this realm of psychopathology. Issues of treatment, in particular, will be postponed to Chapters 17 and 18.

A major hurdle confronts us at the outset in trying to come to grips with the nature of this purported disorder. More than in any other recognized category of disorder, this one's conceptual boundaries are both murky and shifting. While we now have, in DSM-III and its revision, a set of defining criteria that when properly applied will permit us to say who is and who is not schizophrenic with a high degree of reliability, we remain to an extraordinary extent uncertain of the information contained in any such act of inclusion or exclusion. That is, it remains unusually difficult for most of us to arrive at a coherent picture of what schizophrenia is, one that goes beyond, so to speak, the defining criteria themselves. Considered in this light, the loss of some 50 percent of the category's members in moving from DSM-II to DSM-III is disconcerting. This is a *substantive,* not merely cosmetic, change. If the change is not the product of important conceptual advances (for which there seems little evidence), then to what may it be ascribed? Is this perhaps an example wherein considerations of enhanced reliability have pushed those pertaining to validity too far into the background? By all accounts, DSM-IV is to be installed in 1993 (Frances, Widiger, & Pincus, 1989). It is unreasonable to hope for a substantially improved set of diagnostic criteria for schizophrenia by that time; the extensive research effort that would be needed has not, as of this writing, even so much as begun (Carson, 1991).

In the meantime, we do not have a better definition to offer. Rather, we suspect that changing the definitional criteria for "schizophrenia" without having solid research data to support the change will never produce a satisfactory solution, and it is unclear that such data can be produced in the absence of fundamental redirections of approach. What is needed is some sort of paradigm shift that enables us to view the pertinent behavioral phenomena in a new and more productive light. We feel reasonably certain that any such major conceptual advance will entail not one but many "schizophrenias." That is, it is likely that the class of people who merit this diagnosis is a heterogeneous one in terms of the nature, development, and sources of their aberrant behavior. An important implication is that there may be no single "core" condition. Another implication is that efforts at differentiation of basic subgroups should have a high research priority. Beyond that, the crystal ball is notably hazy.

Assuming eventual solution of the taxonomic problem, major difficulties will likely remain in respect to the observational, scientific, and philosophical status of certain of the major "symptoms" of schizophrenia, in particular hallucinations. In the assessment of such phenomena, we are wholly dependent on a patient's report of them because, unlike reports of most subjective symptoms in medical illness, we typically have no way of independently corroborating their presence or meaning within a network of more objective signs. While the typical schizophrenic patient would not likely be the observer we would choose to make critical appraisals of these subjective and often highly unusual phenomena, if only because of suspected psychosis, he or she is quite literally the only observer we have, the unique experiencer of essentially experiential data. It seems unwise to make such reports the centerpiece of the observational base we use in attempting to diagnose and understand the schizophrenias. Hopefully, we can find better ones more subject to direct public scrutiny.

Most of what we know about the schizophrenias points to the conclusion that their etiologies are extremely complex, involving myriad factors at many levels of organization from the molecular biological to the sociocultural (Carson & Sanislow, 1992). Few if any individual investigators are intellectually prepared to deal with more than limited portions of this matrix, suggesting a need for widespread, intensive collaboration among many different kinds of scientists in seeking solutions to what Gottesman and Shields (1982) have aptly termed the "epigenetic puzzle" of the schizophrenias. In fact such "teamwork" is extremely rare among researchers in this field. Most do not venture beyond their own scientific niche and may know or care little about what is going on in other niches. This sort of "tunnel vision" (Carson, in press-b) imparts to the whole enterprise a curious and insulated compartmentalization that discourages communication and integrative theory construction, and hence progress on the kind of broad front that appears needed. We may have reached the point where we can no longer afford the luxury of isolated research camps.

Finally, the delusional disorders are associated often enough with acts of violence that they confront us once again with difficult questions relating to jurisprudence, civil rights, and appropriate measures, if any, of containment and intervention. As in the case of suicide discussed in the previous chapter, the professional mental health community needs direction from the larger society on what level of homicidal (or other violent) risk is tolerable in light of the uncertainty in forcasting individual patients' behavior. It is *not,* in our judgment, realistic to anticipate that such uncertainty can be substantially eliminated at any time in the foreseeable future.

SUMMARY

The schizophrenic disorders especially, and the delusional (paranoid) disorders often associated with them, represent the major challenge facing the mental health professions—partly because virtually all of the psychopathological processes previously described come together in these classes of disorder.

One extraordinary case—that of the Genain quadruplets—sheds light on the sources and the complexity of schizophrenic disorders. All four of the Genain sisters became schizophrenic prior to the age of 25. After carefully tracking the progress of the Genains through the years, researchers have concluded that both biological and psychosocial factors contributed to their vulnerability to schizophrenia.

The schizophrenias are characterized by a loss in level of previous functioning, disturbances of communication, bizarre delusions and hallucinations, aberrations of perception and affect, and, in some instances, peculiarities of motor behavior. The last symptom is associated with the catatonic type of the disorder.

Other types of schizophrenia include undifferentiated (mixed symptoms not fitting into other categories or moving rapidly among them), disorganized (incoherent, silly, or inappropriate affect and behavior), and paranoid (persistent ideas or hallucinations regarding persecution or grandiosity, or other themes). Given these variations as well as other anomalies, some have questioned whether such a "thing" as schizophrenia exists. The credence of such questions is enhanced by the changing and somewhat arbitrary nature of the diagnostic criteria for schizophrenia.

Hardly anybody questions the existence of a cluster of behaviors, called schizophrenic, that are unintelligible to the average person. Such behaviors have been correlated with biological, psychosocial, and sociocultural variables. As yet, however, none of these broad sources of behavioral variation has been definitely established as *the* etiologic factor in schizophrenia. Several leads in each area are quite promising. The evidence suggests that the traditional pessimism with respect to understanding the sources of schizophrenic behavior and its therapeutic amelioration is to a large extent unjustified, although single approaches—as in the current emphasis on biology and drug treatment—seem to be hampering our efforts to move forward. In the area of treatment, the neglect of psychosocial approaches is inconsistent with their record of achievement.

The delusional (paranoid) disorders, in which schizophrenic disorganization seems not to be a significant factor, form a subgroup of psychoses that are even less well understood than the others. A paranoid individual harbors ideas of persecution, grandiosity, both, or more rarely of other patently false content. The person, however, is entirely functional—including, often, highly organized cognitive functioning—in areas that do not impinge on the delusional thought-structure (the paranoid construction) in which the person is centrally involved. These people can often function at a marginal level in society. Some of them, however, become dangerous, exposing problems at the interface between mental health professionals and society at large that continue unresolved. Treatment of chronically paranoid individuals is currently difficult, at best.

Key Terms

the schizophrenias (p. 428)
process schizophrenia (poor premorbid or chronic schizophrenia) (p. 432)
reactive schizophrenia (good premorbid or acute schizophrenia) (p. 433)
negative-symptom schizophrenia (p. 433)
positive-symptom schizophrenia (p. 433)
schizophrenia, undifferentiated type (p. 439)
schizophrenia, catatonic type (p. 441)
schizophrenia, disorganized type (p. 442)
schizophrenia, paranoid type (p. 443)
schizophrenia, residual type (p. 446)
schizoaffective disorder (p. 446)
schizophreniform disorder (p. 446)
dopamine hypothesis (p. 452)
schizophrenogenic (p. 457)
marital schism (p. 458)
marital skew (p. 458)
double-bind communication (p. 459)
expressed emotion (EE) (p. 462)
paranoia (p. 466)
delusional disorder (p. 466)
induced psychotic disorder (p. 466)

Chapter 13

Organic Mental Disorders

Franz Karl Bühler, *Untitled.* Bühler (1868–?), by trade a metalsmith, lost his job as a teacher in a trade school because of his erratic behavior. He was institutionalized in 1898 because of hallucinations and paranoia. He soon withdrew into an autistic existence that is reflected in his drawings and writings.

In contrast to most kinds of abnormal behavior, certain problems arise partly as a consequence of structural damage to the brain tissue. Such damage typically involves loss of nerve cells and can impair the brain's normal physiological functioning. As the brain is the organ of behavior, damage to it may disrupt effective thought, feeling, and action. The relationship of deficits associated with brain damage to abnormal behavior as we have defined it is complicated and often unclear. Accordingly, it seems wise at this point to digress slightly from the main task of clinical description to get a better understanding of brain damage and brain dysfunction. The next section provides this orientation.

BRAIN DAMAGE AND ABNORMAL BEHAVIOR

When structural defects in the brain occur before birth or at an early age, mental retardation may result, its severity depending to a large extent on the magnitude of the defect. In mental retardation, an individual fails to develop an optimal level of the various skills that underlie adequate and independent coping with environmental demands. Most mentally retarded people do not suffer from gross brain damage, but virtually all those individuals who can be described as *severely* retarded have some form of demonstrable organic pathology. The problem of mental retardation will be discussed in Chapter 14. Other people who sustain prenatal or perinatal (that is, during birth) brain damage may experience normal mental development in most aspects of behavior, but suffer from specific cognitive or motor deficits, such as dyslexia (Chapter 14) or spasticity (excessive muscle contraction that impairs motor performance).

Sometimes the intact brain sustains damage after it has completed all or most of its biological development. A wide variety of injuries, diseases, and toxic substances may result in the functional impairment or death of neurons (neural cells) or their connections, which may lead to obvious deficits in psychological functioning. In some instances such damage is associated with behavior that is not only impaired in various ways but also highly aberrant—even psychotic. People who sustain serious brain damage after they have mastered the basic tasks of life are in a very different situation from those who start life with a deficit of this kind. When brain injury occurs in an older child or adult, there is a *loss* in established functioning, and this loss—this deprivation of already-acquired and customary skills—can be painfully obvious to the victim, adding a psychological burden to the organic one. In other cases the impairment may extend to the capacity for realistic self-appraisal, leaving these patients relatively unaware of their losses and thus poorly motivated for rehabilitation. Many victims may also have to cope with the idea of little improvement, or worse, with a prognosis involving inexorable, progressive decline. The psychological impact in such cases can be devastating.

Brain Impairment and Adult Mental Disorder

In this chapter we will discuss those disorders that occur when the normal adolescent or adult brain has suffered significant organic impairment or damage. In the DSM system of classification these are called **organic mental disorders,** although neuroscientists usually refer to them as **neuropsychological disorders** or *neuropsychological conditions.* They may involve only limited behavioral deficits or a wide range of psychopathology, depending on (a) the nature, location, and extent of neural damage; (b) the premorbid (predisorder) personality of the individual; (c) the individual's total life situation; and (d) the amount of time passed since the first appearance of the condition. Although the degree of mental impairment is usually directly related to the extent of damage, in some cases involving relatively severe brain damage mental change is astonishingly slight; in other cases of apparently mild and limited damage there may be profoundly altered functioning.

As we shall see, some behavioral reactions to brain impairment, such as anxiety or depression, are clinically indistinguishable from disorders in which we have no reason to suspect organic brain involvement. This raises some rather subtle and complicated questions we will have to engage as we proceed. In general, however, we may suspect organic pathology as a contributing factor in a disorder when (a) the psychopathologic symptoms are especially severe, (b) they are accompanied by notable memory or other cognitive deficits, and (c) few other grounds exist for explaining the symptoms (Strayhorn, 1982). More specific suspect symptoms include prolonged catatonia or other movement disorders, anorexia, and a first psychotic episode or notable personality change occurring after age 50 (Weinberger, 1984).

We reiterate here the important distinction, introduced in Chapter 3, between neurological disease or impairment and the aberrant mental and behavioral processes that constitute psychopathological symptoms. It is mere historical accident that some "mental" aspects of organic brain disease, such as personality change, became assigned to the medical specialty of psychiatry, whereas the "physical" ones, such as motor coordination disorders and certain cognitive disorders, often seen in association with physical deficits, became the purview of neurology. The fundamental disorders we are dealing with in this chapter are *always* in the strictest sense neurological ones, although they may have psychological elaborations associated with them.

Some "mental" symptoms in organic mental disorders are therefore the more or less direct product of the physical interruption of the established neural pathways along which the brain's messages travel. The bases of these symptoms are relatively well understood, and the symptoms themselves have relatively constant features among individuals sustaining comparable types of brain insult in terms of location and extent. For example, with mild to moderate *diffuse* (widespread) damage, such as might occur with moderate oxygen deprivation or the ingestion of toxic substances, attentional and self-monitoring impairments are quite common. An individual, for example, may complain of memory problems due to an inability to sustain focused retrieval efforts, while showing an intact ability to store new information. Severe diffuse damage results in *dementia,* described later.

In contrast to diffuse damage, *focal brain lesions* are circumscribed areas of abnormal change in brain structure, such as might occur with traumatic injury to a part of the head. With progressive brain disease, such as Alzheimer's disease or expanding brain tumors, one may see a gradual spreading over more and more focal sites, leading to permanent damage that is both diffuse and severe. Some consequences of organic brain disorders that have mainly focal origins but commonly appear in the context of progressively diffuse damage are as follows:

1. *Impairment of memory*—the individual has notable trouble remembering recent events and less trouble remembering events of the remote past, with a tendency in some patients to confabulate; that is, to "invent" memories to fill in gaps. In severe instances no new experience can be retained for more than a few minutes. It either fails entirely to be stored in long-term memory or is stored in a

way that provides no means for it to be readily retrieved at a later time.

2. *Impairment of orientation*—the individual is unable to locate himself or herself accurately, especially in time but also in space or in relation to the personal identities of self or others.

3. *Impairment of learning, comprehension, and judgment*—the individual displays ideation tending to be concrete and impoverished and is unable to think on higher conceptual levels or to plan with foresight.

4. *Impairment of emotional control or modulation*—the individual manifests emotional overreactivity and easy arousal to laughter, tears, rage, and other extreme emotions.

5. *Apathy or emotional blunting*—the individual shows little emotion, especially where deterioration is advanced.

6. *Impairment in the initiation of behavior*—the individual lacks "self-starting" capability and may have to be repeatedly reminded about what to do next, even where the behavior involved remains well within the person's range of competence.

7. *Impairment of controls over matters of propriety and ethical conduct*—the individual may manifest a marked lowering of personal standards in appearance, personal hygiene, sexuality, language, and so on.

8. *Impairment of receptive and expressive language*—the individual may be unable to comprehend written or spoken language, or may be unable to communicate thoughts orally or in writing.

Most individuals who have a neuropsychological disorder *do not* develop psychopathological symptoms, such as panic disorder or delusions, although many will show at least mild deficits in cognitive processing and self-regulation. The psychopathological symptoms that do sometimes accompany brain impairment are less predictable than those listed and more likely to show individual nuances consistent with the prior personality and the total psychological situation confronting a patient. We consider it important to maintain a sharp distinction between neurological and psychopathological types of "mental" symptoms.

This chapter is concerned with people who have both neurological disease and psychopathological disorder. Though the distinction between these differing types of disorders is reasonably clear in the abstract, it becomes murky in many cases as psychopathology and neuropathology can become inextricably enmeshed with one another. We emphasize that it is erroneous to assume that a behavioral disorder, for example, a serious depression accompanying deficits produced by neuropsychological insult, is necessarily and completely explained by reference to the patient's brain damage; it might better be explained in terms of the considerable psychological challenge presented by the patient's awareness of dramatically lessened competence.

The more variable effects of significant neurological impairment on individuals are explained by the fact that an individual is a functional unit and reacts as such to all stressors, whether they are organic or psychological. A well-integrated personality can usually withstand brain damage or any other stress better than a rigid, immature, or otherwise psychologically handicapped one—except where brain damage is so severe or its location so critical as to destroy the integrity of the personality. Similarly, an individual who has a favorable life situation is likely to have a better prognosis than one who does not. Because the brain is the center for the integration of behavior, however, there are limits to the amount of brain damage an individual can tolerate or compensate for without exhibiting behavior that is decidedly "abnormal."

Hardware and Software

We generally believe it is somewhat hazardous to employ computer analogies in discussions of the brain and mental processes. However, such an analogy seems almost irresistibly appropriate in perhaps shedding additional light in the context of the present discussion of the relationship of brain impairment to behavioral abnormalities. Because the possibilities of such analogizing—for example, about differing kinds of "memory"—are both tantalizing and virtually limitless, we will strictly confine ourselves to only the most elementary and relevant points of contact.

When computers fail to behave adaptively in terms of what we want and expect them to do for us, our troubleshooting speculations normally begin with two possibilities: (a) a "hardware" problem—perhaps a "sticky" chip, a deficient power supply, or a defective resistor or capacitator; or (b) a "software" problem, such as having an inadequate program for the task at hand or a "bug" in the program we load into a machine that is in perfect working

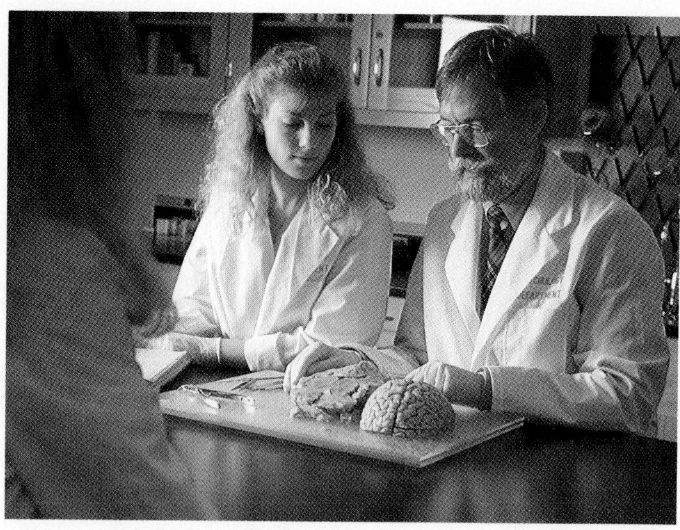

We may consider the intact human brain to be a highly programmable system of "hardware," and psychosocial experience to be functionally equivalent to "software." Organic mental disorders have hardware defects as their primary cause —there is a breakdown in one or several of the brain's components. The symptoms of such a breakdown show up in changes such as memory defects, impaired orientation, impaired learning, impaired language, impaired emotional control, and similar problems.

order. (The third alternative of a flawless machine and a flawless program that are incompatible has interesting possibilities as a model for certain abnormalities of behavior, but we will ignore this alternative here.) Note that the software programs we load into computers have an essentially symbolic, informational status that is prior to and independent of the physical characteristics of the machine itself, although the physical state of the machine is systematically transformed by the act of "loading" a program into it. The software information in a loaded machine *could,* in principle and with great difficulty, be completely and errorlessly reconstructed from a detailed description of the physical state of the machine. The two cannot for that reason be considered identical entities, however, nor is it reasonable to hold that the state of the machine is in any sense more "basic" than the information loaded into it, whose construction will usually in fact have preceded that of the machine.

We may thus consider the intact human brain to be a highly programmable system of "hardware," and psychosocial experience in both its developmental and current aspects to be functionally equivalent to "software." Such an analogy has widespread implications throughout the domain of abnormal psychology—as for example in posing a problem for exclusively biological interpretations of the "functional" (nonorganic) psychoses—but we will focus on so-called organic mental disorders. Using our analogy, these disorders, by definition, have hardware defects as their primary cause. In other words, in such situations the brain cannot perform the physical operations called for in its "design" by virtue of a breakdown in one or another (or several) of its components. The *direct* "symptoms" of such a breakdown should be both limited in extent and, within reason, predictable from a knowledge of how these components "work." In fact they should be similar in general character to the symptoms, such as memory defects, listed in the preceding section.

A breakdown in the brain's hardware will necessarily have pervasive effects on the processing of software. Indeed, in the case of extensive hardware damage, much or perhaps most previously loaded information may be lost because the structural components in which it had been encoded are no longer operative; new information for the same reason fails to be adequately loaded. Such a condition is known clinically as ***dementia.*** With less extensive hardware damage we see effects that depend to a considerable extent on the particular characteristics of the software that constitutes the record of an individual's life experience, parts of which will be unique. We thus expect to see more variation in the "mental" symptoms manifested.

To use a somewhat trivial but obvious example, the delusion that one is Napoleon, rather common in the nineteenth century, would not have been seen in an eighteenth-century Alzheimer's or general paretic (syphilitic brain diseased) patient because the real Napoleon's more illustrious adventures had not yet occurred. Such symptoms are at most only *indirect* manifestations of organic hardware breakdown; their content is obviously a product of life experience, and they sometimes occur in the absence of any demonstrable hardware breakdown at all—in which case we must consider the possibility that they are due entirely to serious flaws in the individual's personality, or "software."

It is obvious that people vary a great deal in the adequacy, complexity, and resourcefulness of the software programs and "subroutines" their experiences have provided. Indeed, as we will see in Chapter 14, such variations are to a certain extent what IQ tests attempt to measure. It is equally obvious that few if any people have deployable programs ready to manage the contingency of *losing* basic competencies and skills that at an earlier time may well have become so automatized that their flawless performance required no deliberate attention or effort. Coping more or less adequately with such a disastrous turn of events thus seems to put a premium on the adaptive flexibility of a person's already extant software library. Failure to cope adequately, on the other hand, places an enormous additional load of stress and frustration on an already limited system, one that may be further compromised by newly acquired hardware defects. Such a "system," we suggest, is likely to develop indirect, secondary psychopathological symptoms, such as the delusional assumption of a new and more impressive personal identity.

Bearing in mind these fundamental and somewhat perplexing issues concerning relationships between the brain, mental events, and behavior, we move now to a consideration of the related clinical syndromes.

CLINICAL FEATURES OF ORGANIC MENTAL DISORDERS

The regenerative capacities of the central nervous system are limited. Cell bodies and neural pathways in the brain do not have the power of regeneration, which means that their destruction is permanent. Some functions lost as a result of brain damage may be relearned, however, typically at a compromised and less efficient level, or an individual may develop techniques to compensate for what is missing. The degree of improvement from disabilities following an irreversible brain lesion may be relatively complete or limited, and it may proceed rapidly or slowly. Because there are limits to both the plasticity and compensatory capacities of the brain, however, brain damage leads to more or less extensive permanent diminishment or loss of function over a wide range of physical and psychological abilities. In general, the greater the amount of tissue damage, the greater the impairment of function.

The damage's location may also play a significant role in determining a patient's ultimate neuropsychological status. The mammalian brain is highly specialized, each part—each cell in fact—making a unique contribution to the functional whole of an organism's activity (see *HIGHLIGHT 13.1*). Thus the two hemispheres, while interacting intimately at many levels, are involved in somewhat different types of mental processing. For example, functions that are dependent on serial processing of familiar information, such as language, take place mostly in the left hemisphere for nearly everyone. The right hemisphere is generally specialized for configurational or *gestalt* processing, which is best suited for grasping overall meanings in novel situations, reasoning on a nonverbal, intuitive level, and appreciation of spatial relations. Even within hemispheres, the various lobes and areas within lobes mediate somewhat specialized functions.

Although none of these relationships between brain location and behavior can be considered constant or universal, it is possible to make certain broad generalizations about the likely effects of damage to particular parts of the brain. Damage to the frontal areas, for example, is associated with either of two contrasting clinical pictures: (a) passivity, apathy, and an inability to give up a given stream of associations or initiate a new one (perseverative thought); or (b) impulsiveness, distractibility, and insufficient ethical restraint (Crockett, Clark, & Klonoff, 1981). Damage to specific areas of the right parietal lobe may produce distortions of body image, while certain aspects of language function can be impaired as a result of significant damage to the left parietal.

Damage to identified structures within the temporal lobes disrupts an early stage of memory storage, such that extensive bilateral temporal damage can produce a syndrome in which remote memory remains relatively intact but nothing new can be effectively stored for later retrieval. Damage to other structures within the temporal lobes is associated with disturbances of eating, sexuality, and the emotions, probably by way of disrupting the functioning of the adjacent limbic lobe. The latter is a deeper center that mediates these "primitive" functions in extensive interaction with frontal lobe structures. Occipital damage produces a variety of visual impairments and visual association deficits, the nature of the deficit depending on the particular site of the lesion; for example, a person may be unable to recognize familiar faces or to correctly visualize and understand symbolic stimuli (Filskov, Grimm, & Lewis, 1981). Unfortunately, many types of brain disease are general and diffuse in their destructive effects, thereby causing multiple and widespread interruptions of the brain's circuitry.

Traditionally, the organic mental disorders have been classified by disease entity or recognizable disorder, such as Huntington's chorea, general paresis, and so on. As we have seen, however, these are basically physical or neurological disorders that may have various kinds of associated psychopathology. In the DSM-III-R, physical disorders are coded on Axis III, and associated "mental" conditions on Axes I and II (psychiatric and personality disorders). Thus with the single (and as far as we can determine unaccountable) exception of the senile and presenile dementias such as Alzheimer's disease, the traditional organic mental disorders no longer appear as Axis I psychiatric categories. In-

HIGHLIGHT 13.1

Implications of Brain Damage

It is difficult to predict the effects of focal injuries to the brain. Because there is some localization of function (as indicated in this drawing of the right cerebral hemisphere), damage to a particular area may cause impairment of the behavioral functioning mediated by the site of the damage. For example, a significant lesion of the occipital lobe is likely to result in some impairment of vision or visual perception. However, the awesome complexity of the brain's organization ensures that virtually all behavior is in fact the product of neuronal activity in many parts of the brain, some in all probability quite distant from the site of primary mediation. A lesion in one of the frontal lobes, for example, might influence neuronal activity at a site in the subcortical limbic system, thus producing some type of emotional dysregulation for the person affected. The upshot is that brain-behavior relationships are never as simple as graphic brain localization charts (such as this one) make them appear to be.

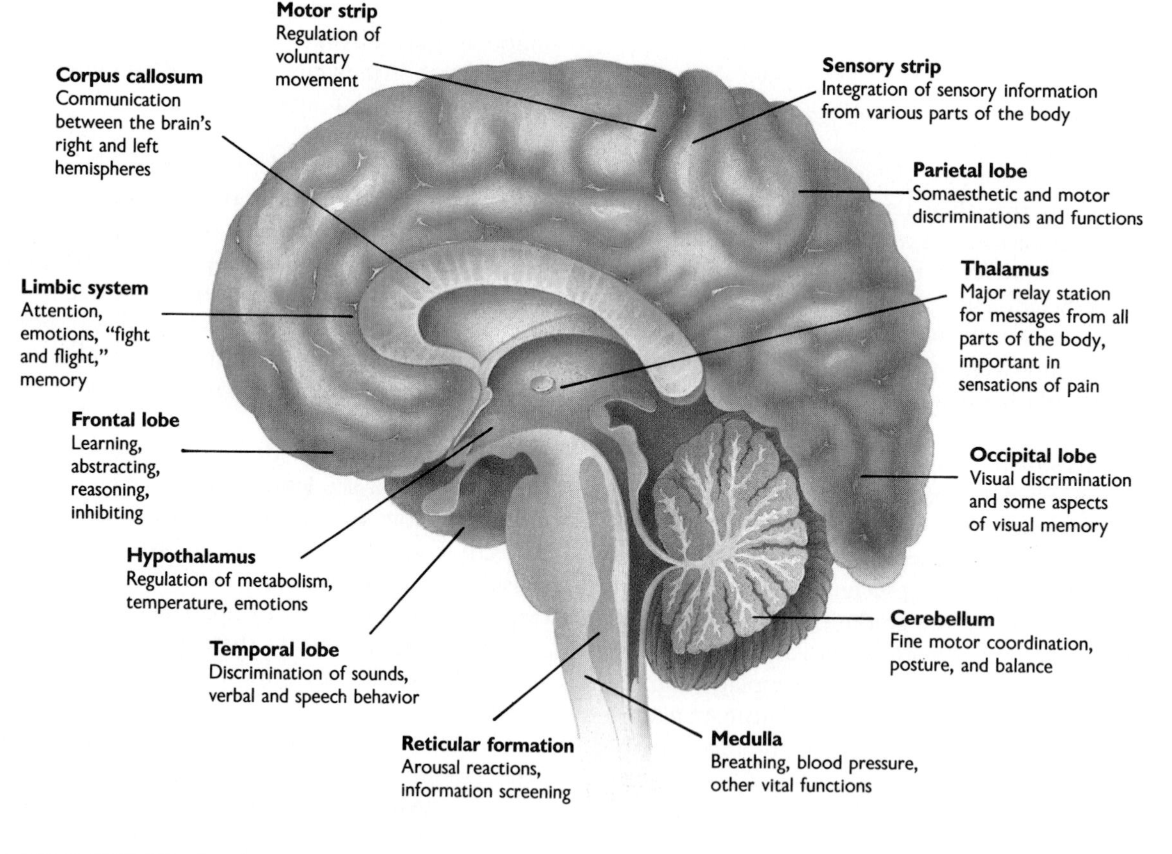

stead, only particular clusters of symptoms presumptively based on brain damage and often seen in the various organic mental disorders are listed on Axis I. In our discussion, we will first describe these clusters of symptoms and then go on to describe the clinical picture, causal factors, and treatment approaches for four of the more common types of disorder associated with brain damage.

Organic Symptom Syndromes

A **syndrome** is a group of symptoms that tend to cluster together. The organic symptom syndromes include many symptoms similar to those that occur in the schizophrenias and the mood disorders, but in these syndromes the symptoms are *assumed* to reflect underlying brain pathology. The specific

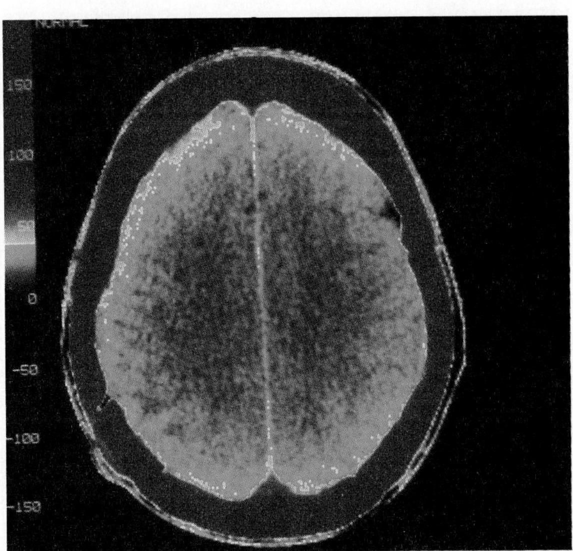

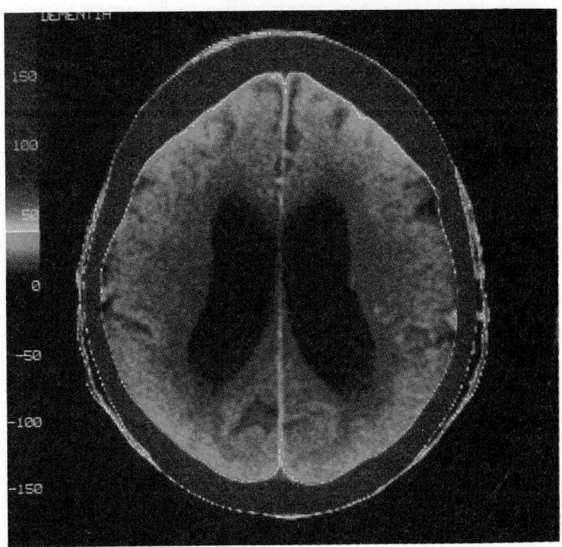

Dramatic differences show up in these CAT scans of a normal brain (left) and the brain of a person afflicted with probable Alzheimer's dementia (right). The dark blue areas in both hemispheres of the diseased brain indicate an enlargement of the ventricles (the large, hollow spaces deep within the brain) due to the degeneration of the brain tissue.

brain pathology may vary; it may be due to some type of brain disease or as a result of the withdrawal of a chemical substance on which a person has become physiologically dependent. The most recently discovered etiological factor is infection with the HIV Type 1 (AIDS) virus, which, as we will see, leads in many cases to brain damage, sometimes of massive degree (Grant & Heaton, 1990). For our purposes, we will group these symptom syndromes into four categories: (a) delirium and dementia; (b) amnestic syndrome and hallucinosis; (c) organic delusional, mood, and anxiety syndromes; and (d) organic personality syndrome.

We should note that more than one syndrome may be present at a time in a given patient and that syndromes and patterns of syndromes may change over a particular disorder's course of development. As already noted, certain syndromes mimic at the behavioral level the types of disorders we have described in previous chapters. Although we suspect these often are basically the same types of (primarily psychogenic) disorders as those discussed earlier, clinicians need always to remain alert to the possibility of organic brain impairment having a *direct* causal role in the symptoms observed. Failure to do so could obviously result in serious diagnostic errors (Geschwind, 1975; Malamud, 1975; Weinberger, 1984).

Delirium and Dementia The syndrome called **delirium** is characterized by a relatively rapid onset of widespread disorganization of the higher mental processes; it is caused by a generalized disturbance in brain metabolism. Information-processing capacities are more or less severely impaired, affecting such basic functions as attention, perception, memory, and thinking. Frequently, the syndrom includes abnormal psychomotor activity, such as wild thrashing about, and disturbance of the sleep cycle. Delirium reflects a breakdown in the functional integrity of the brain; in this respect, it may be seen as only one step above coma and, in fact, it may lead to coma. A delirious person is essentially unable to carry out purposeful mental activity of any kind; current experience appears to make no contact with the individual's previously acquired store of knowledge.

Delirious states tend to be acute conditions that rarely last more than a week, terminating in recovery or, less often, in death due to the underlying pathophysiologic state. They may result from several conditions, such as the following: head injury, toxic or metabolic disturbances, oxygen deprivation, insufficient delivery of blood to brain tissues, or precipitous withdrawal from alcohol or other drugs in an addicted person.

Dementia, already mentioned, has as its essential feature a progressive deterioration of brain functioning occurring after the completion of brain maturation (after, that is, about 15 years of age). Early in the course of the disease, an individual is alert and fairly well attuned to events in the environment. Episodic (memory for events), but not necessarily semantic (language and concept), mem-

HIGHLIGHT 13.2

Dementia in 417 Patients Fully Evaluated for Dementia

Diagnosis	Number	Percent
Alzheimer's disease or dementia of unknown cause	199	47.7
Alcoholic dementia	42	10.0
Multi-infarct dementia	39	9.4
Normal pressure hydrocephalus	25	6.0
Intracranial masses [tumors]	20	4.8
Huntington's chorea	12	2.9
Drug toxicity	10	2.4
Posttraumatic	7	1.7
Other identified dementing diseases[a]	28	6.7
Pseudodementias[b]	28	6.7
Dementia uncertain	7	1.7

[a]Including epilepsy, subarachnoid hemorrhage, encephalitis, amyotropic lateral sclerosis, Parkinson's disease, hyperthyroidism, syphilis, liver disease, and cerebral anoxia episode, all less than 1 percent incidence.
[b]Including depression (16), schizophrenia (5), mania (2), "hysteria" (1), and not demented (4).
Based on Wells (1979).

ory functioning is typically affected in the early stages, especially memory for recent events. Additionally, these patients display increasingly marked deficits in abstract thinking, the acquisition of new knowledge or skills, visuospatial comprehension, motor control, problem solving, and judgment. Personality deterioration and loss of "drive" accompany these other deficits.

Normally, dementia is also accompanied by an impairment in emotional control and in moral and ethical sensibilities. It may be progressive or static; occasionally it is even reversible. Its course depends to a large extent on the nature of the etiology.

Etiologic factors in dementia are many and varied. They include degenerative processes that affect some individuals—usually, but not always, older individuals. Repeated cerebrovascular accidents (strokes); certain infectious diseases, such as syphilis, meningitis, and HIV-1; intracranial tumors and abscesses; certain dietary deficiencies; severe or repeated head injury; anoxia; and the ingestion or inhalation of toxic substances have all been implicated in the etiology of dementias. As *HIGHLIGHT 13.2* makes clear, the most common cause of dementia is degenerative brain disease, particularly of the variety typified by Alzheimer's disease.

The Amnestic Syndrome and Hallucinosis

The essential feature of the **amnestic syndrome** is a striking deficit in the ability to recall ongoing events more than a few minutes after they have taken place. Immediate memory and, to a lesser extent, memory for events that occurred before the disorder's development remain largely intact, as does memory for words and concepts. An amnestic individual, then, is constrained to live for the most part only in the present or the remote past; the recent past is for most practical purposes unavailable. We should add here that the question of whether the recent past is unavailable in some absolute sense is subject to differing interpretations. Some evidence suggests that these individuals may recognize or even recollect events of the recent past if given sufficient cues, which would indicate that the information has been stored. Thus the difficulty may be in the *retrieval* mechanism (Hirst, 1982; Warrington & Weiskrantz, 1973).

In contrast to the dementia syndrome, overall cognitive functioning in the amnestic syndrome remains relatively intact. Theoretically, the disorder involves chiefly the relationship between the short-term and long-term memory systems; the contents of the former, always limited in scope and ephemeral in duration, are not stored in the latter in a way that permits ready accessibility or retrieval (Hirst, 1982).

In the most common forms of amnestic syndrome, those associated with alcohol or barbiturate addiction, the disorder may be irreversible. A wide range of other pathogenic factors may produce the amnestic syndrome. In these cases, depending on the nature and extent of damage to the affected neural structures and on the treatment undertaken, the syndrome may in time abate wholly, in part, or not at all.

The syndrome of **hallucinosis** has as its essential feature the persistent occurrence of hallucinations in the presence of known or suspected brain involvement; the term is not used where hallucinations are part of a more pervasive mental disorder such as schizophrenia. These false perceptions arise in a state of full wakefulness, when a person is alert and otherwise well oriented. The hallucinations most often involve the sense of hearing but may affect any sense; for example, visual hallucinations typically accompany psychedelic drug intoxication.

The course of the syndrome varies with the underlying pathology but rarely exceeds one month, assuming discontinuance of the causative agent. As in the case of the amnestic syndrome, the most common etiologic factor is severe or longstanding alcohol abuse.

Organic Delusional, Mood, and Anxiety Syndromes In the **organic delusional syndrome,** false beliefs or belief systems arise in a setting of known or suspected brain damage and are considered a principal clinical manifestation of this damage. These delusions vary in content depending to some extent on the particular organic etiology. For example, a distinctly paranoid and suspicous delusional system is commonly seen with longstanding abuse of amphetamine drugs, whereas grandiose and expansive delusions are more characteristic of advanced syphilis (general paresis). In addition to infectious processes and the abuse of certain drugs, etiological factors in the organic delusional syndrome include head injury and intracranial tumors.

The **organic mood syndrome,** as the term implies, refers to manic or depressive states caused by the impairment of cerebral function. While the organic delusional syndrome may clinically mimic some forms of schizophrenic disorder, the organic mood syndrome closely resembles the symptoms seen in either depressive or manic mood disorders. Severe depressive syndromes, whether or not associated with organic pathology, may on superficial examination appear as dementias, in which case the term *pseudodementia* is applied. The reaction may be minimal or severe, and the course of the disorder varies widely, depending on the nature of the organic pathology. Etiological factors include cerebrovascular accidents (strokes), Parkinson's disease, head injury, withdrawal of certain drugs, intracranial tumors or tumors of the hormone-secreting organs, and excessive use of steroids (adrenocortical hormones) or certain other medications. Of course, an awareness of lost function or a hopeless outlook might itself make a person depressed; in such instances the diagnosis of "organic" mood disorder may be at best a guess.

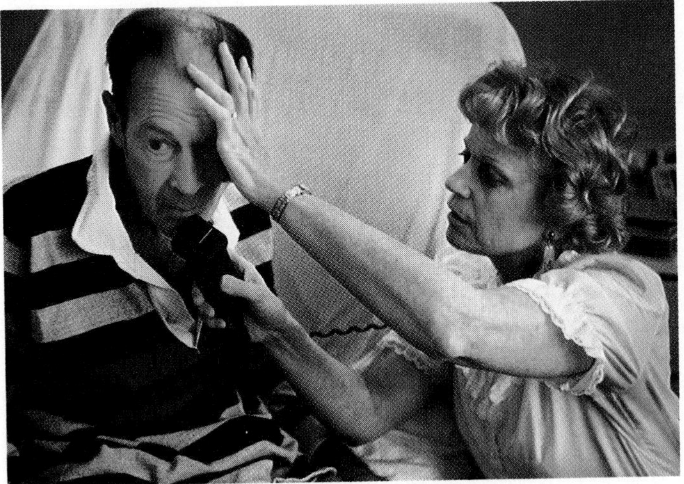

This man has Parkinson's disease, which may be associated with organic mood syndrome, a cluster of symptoms that closely resembles those seen in either depressive or manic mood disorders.

New to the DSM-III-R is the diagnosis **organic anxiety syndrome.** In this syndrome the clinical manifestation of anxiety is thought somehow to be the direct outcome of brain impairment. Although this disorder has to date received scant research attention, we suspect again that as a practical matter it often proves difficult to differentiate from the anxiety reaction a person would be expected to have on discovering impaired ability to perform in various ways.

Organic Personality Syndrome The essential feature of the **organic personality syndrome** is a change in an individual's general personality style or traits following brain damage. Normally the change is in a socially negative direction; it may include impaired social judgment, lessened control of emotions and impulses, diminished concern about the consequences of one's behavior, and an inability to sustain goal-directed activity.

Many different etiologies are associated with the organic personality syndrome, and the course of the disorder depends on its etiology. Occasionally, as when it is induced by medication, it may be transitory. Often, however, it is the first sign of an impending deterioration, as when a kindly and gentle old man makes sexual advances toward a child or when a conservative executive suddenly begins to engage in unwise financial dealings. Some evidence indicates that a common feature in the organic personality syndrome may be damage to the frontal lobes (Blumer & Benson, 1975; Crockett, Clark, & Klonoff, 1981; Hecaen & Albert, 1975; Sherwin & Geschwind, 1978).

All of the organic symptom syndromes may appear singly or in combination in the various types of disorders associated with brain pathology. They are used as Axis I diagnoses where the assumed underlying organic brain impairment is either unknown or is coded as an additional diagnosis on Axis III (medical conditions)—already-noted exceptions being certain degenerative dementias included as separate Axis I disorders. In general, disorders involving the syndromes of delirium, dementia, amnesia, hallucinosis, or delusional thinking may be regarded as roughly equivalent to a psychotic level of functioning. Delirium is nearly always acute and short-lived, whereas disorders that have prominent elements of dementia, amnestic syndrome, or organic personality syndrome usually prove chronic—that is, they normally involve irreversible changes in the brain's anatomy.

The DSM-III-R classification lists about 50 different forms of mental disorder in which organic disturbance is present; many of these are related to drug use and involve only temporary physiological disruption (see Chapter 9). The disorders we will discuss in the rest of this section are longer-term disorders in which major, often permanent, brain pathology occurs but in which an individual's emotional, motivational, and behavioral reactions to the loss of function also play an important role. Indeed, as was earlier suggested, it is often impossible to distinguish between maladaptive behavior that is directly caused by neurological dysfunction and that which is basically part of an individual's psychological reaction to the deficits and disabilities experienced (Fabrega, 1981; Geschwind, 1975).

The four types of organic mental disorder we will discuss in greater detail are HIV-1 infection of the brain, disorders involving brain tumors, disorders involving traumatic head injury, and dementia of the Alzheimer type. Multi-infarct dementia will be addressed, chiefly as a contrast to Alzheimer's disease.

Organic Mental Disorder with HIV-1 Infection

Our discussion of mental disorders associated with the AIDS virus will necessarily be rather brief because the disorder is a newly recognized one. As we saw in Chapter 7, the devastating effects on the immune system produced by infection with the HIV Type 1 virus renders its victims "opportunistically" susceptible to a wide variety of other infectious agents. When organic brain syndromes were first observed among AIDS patients early in the last decade, it was assumed they were due to secondary infections of this sort or to the brain tumors also associated with immune system incompetence. Then, in 1983, Snider and colleagues published the first systematic evidence that the presence of the HIV-1 virus (or a mutant form of it) could itself result in the destruction of brain cells. Since then, two differing forms of such central nervous system pathology have been identified: aseptic meningitis (nonbacterial inflammation of the meninges), and the **AIDS dementia complex (ADC),** a more generalized degeneration of brain tissue. We will here focus on the AIDS dementia complex (ADC).

The neuropathology of ADC involves various changes in the brain, among them generalized atrophy, edema, inflammatory cells, and patches of demyelination (loss of the myelin sheath surrounding nerve fibers), as described by various investigators (Gabuzda & Hirsch, 1987; Gray, Gherardi, & Scaravilli, 1988; Price et al. 1988a). No brain area may be spared, but the damage appears concentrated in the central white matter, the matter surrounding the ventricles, and the gray matter at *subcortical* levels.

Clinical features, which tend to appear as a late phase of HIV infection (although often before the full development of AIDS itself), usually begin with psychomotor slowing, diminished concentration, mild memory difficulties, and perhaps slight motor clumsiness. Progression is typically rapid after this point, with clear-cut dementia appearing in many cases within one year, although considerably longer periods have been reported. The later phases of ADC can be quite grim and include behavioral regression, confusion, psychotic thinking, apathy, and marked withdrawal, leading before death to an incontinent, bedridden state (Navia, Jordan, & Price, 1986; Price et al., 1988a, 1988b).

As many as 80 percent of patients with full-blown AIDS have neuropathological findings at autopsy (Petito, 1988). Thirty-eight percent of 121 living AIDS patients studied by Navia et al. (1986) met DSM criteria for dementia. Patients with

AIDS-related complex (ARC), a pre-AIDS manifestation of HIV infection involving minor infections, various nonspecific symptoms (such as unexplained fever), and blood cell count abnormalities, may also experience cognitive difficulty, although it may be too subtle to be readily detected on clinical observation alone. In one study (Grant et al., 1987), 54 percent of ARC patients demonstrated definite impairment on a neuropsychological test battery. Other studies, reviewed by Grant and Heaton (1990), have shown inconsistent evidence of neuropsychological compromise in pre-ARC people who are merely seropositive for HIV-1. The evidence is thus compelling that infection with this virus poses a substantial threat to the functional integrity of the brain, quite apart from its other frightening characteristics. As of this writing, it is not known what protects the minority of AIDS patients who show no central nervous system involvement during the entire course of their illnesses.

The question of treatment for ADC is of course intimately tied to that involving control or eradication of the HIV-1 infection itself. To date, it is impossible to feel confident about our prospects because of the enormous and unprecedented challenges presented by the complex structure and life cycle of this viral entity (McCutchan, 1990). Thus preventing the infection is the only certain defensive strategy, a circumstance not unlike the problem posed by syphilis, another sexually transmitted and potentially dementing disease, in an earlier era. See *HIGHLIGHT 13.3* for a case description of brain involvement in the latter disorder. In general, humankind has not done well in controlling the spread of sexually transmitted diseases through cautious sexual behavior.

Disorders Involving Brain Tumors

In the writings of Felix Plater (1536–1614), we find the following rather remarkable account of "A Case of Stupor due to a Tumour in the Brain, Circular like a Gland":

> *Caspar Bone Curtius, a noble knight, began to show signs of mental alienation which continued through a period of two years until at last he became quite stupefied, did not act rationally, did not take food unless forced to do so, nor did he go to bed unless compelled, at a table he just lay on his arms and went to sleep, he did not speak when questioned even when admonished, and if he did it was useless. Pituita dropped from his nose copiously and frequently: this condition continued for about six months, and finally he died. . . . At the postmortem when the skull was opened and the lobes of the brain separated, a remarkable globular tumor was found on the upper surface of the Corpus Callosum, resembling a gland fleshly, hard and funguslike, about the size of a medium sized apple, invested with its own membranes and having its own veins, lying free and without any connection with the brain itself. . . . This tumour, by its mass, produced pressure on the brain and its vessels, which caused stupor, torpor, and finally death. Some doctors who had seen this case earlier attributed it to sorcery, others just to the humors, but by opening the skull we made clear the abstruse and hidden cause. (1664)*

A tumor is a *neoplasm,* or new growth, involving an abnormal proliferation of cells. Such growths are most apt to occur in the breast, the uterus, the prostate, the lungs, or the intestinal tract, although they are sometimes found in the central nervous system. In adults, brain tumors occur with the greatest frequency between the ages of 40 and 60.

Some brain tumors are malignant; they invade and destroy the brain tissue in which they arise. Others are benign; they are not destructive except by reason of the pressure they exert. Because the skull is a bony, unyielding container, a relatively small tumor in the brain may cause marked pressure and thus interfere seriously with normal brain functioning. Unlike their benign counterparts, malignant brain tumors usually originate in malignancies in other organs, typically the lungs; the cancer cells are transported to the brain by a process known as *metastasis.*

The Clinical Picture in Disorders Involving Brain Tumors The clinical picture that develops in cases of brain tumor is extremely varied and its determined largely by (a) the location, size, and rapidity of a tumor's growth; and (b) the personality and stress tolerance of an affected individual. Brain tumors may lead to any or all of the recognized organic symptom syndromes discussed earlier.

A brain tumor itself may result in both localized and general symptoms. Damage to a particular part of the brain may result in localized disturbances of sensory or motor functions. General symptoms appear when the tumor becomes large enough to

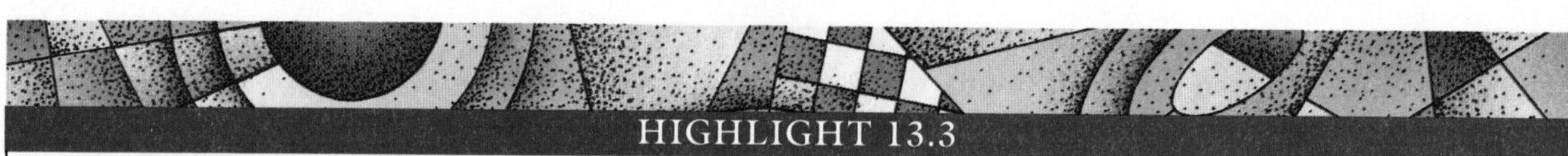

Case Portrayal of General Paresis

General paresis is one of several forms of central nervous system invasion by the organism responsible for syphilitic infection, the spirochete *Treponema pallidum.* The mode of transmission is virtually always sexual. As we saw in Chapter 2, general paresis occupies an important place in the history of the mental health disciplines. Despite the availability of medical resources for total cure in its early stages, syphilis is still a significant medical problem. Unless properly treated, it eventually disables and then kills its victims.

The general paretic form of advanced syphilis is usually a late-stage development of the untreated infection, often making its appearance 10 to 15 years after primary infection and sometimes as many as 40 years later. For unknown reasons it develops in only 5 to 10 percent of those infected, and the large majority of these victims are men. The spirochete, which is present in the brains of affected people, somehow causes widespread and progressive destruction of cerebral tissue, eventuating in the familiar sequence of increasingly severe physical debility and dementia, vegetative delirium, coma, and death. The typical course duration after the initial appearance of symptoms is two to three years.

Although in many preterminal cases the mental symptoms are limited to the always-present dementia, other types of features—such as depression—may be displayed. A dramatic and frequent pattern in general paresis is expansive euphoria, in which a person manifests claims of great power, wealth, physical and sexual prowess, and so on, and also displays the emotional reactions of delight and pride consistent with these claims. The following case shows a fairly typical expansive pattern.

C. W. flew planes from the United States to North Africa. His route began in Florida, passed through Natal, Ascension Island, and terminated in Dakar. His earlier health record was excellent, save for some "difficulty" in his early twenties. Now, at 38, he was strong, well liked, and an expert pilot in the ferry command. He had completed a dozen or more trips.

As he flew his plane eastward on his last journey, C. W. was unusually happy, "It's a great world," he sang. "My rich aunt in Oklahoma is going to leave me $30,000,000."

During the periods of relief by his copilot, he talked loudly and became chummy with other members of the crew. As a matter of fact, he offered to loan the navigator $50,000. Landing safely in Dakar, his high spirits continued. Then his friends found him buying several "diamonds" from an Arab street merchant, spending most of his cash for this purpose.

"Boy," he exclaimed, "I got a swell bargain! Six diamonds for $100 cash now and $100 more on my next trip! I sure fooled that Arab; he's never going to collect the rest from me."

"How do you know the diamonds are genuine?" he was asked.

"I tested them," he boasted, "I struck one with a hammer and it proved hard; diamonds are hard."

Upon the return journey, C. W. continued the story of his expected wealth and the sum grew with the distance of travel.

"It's $40,000,000 I am getting and I expect to share some of it with you guys," he announced. When his copilot received this astounding information with doubt and anxiety, C. W. could not understand it. When the copilot asked him to rest, he assured him that his body was perfect, that he didn't need rest. Then he added that he could fly the plane without gas, which he tried to prove by doing some fancy maneuvers in the sky.

"Funny," he said later, "no one seemed to believe me. Even when I offered them a million each they weren't happy, but looked at each other in such a puzzled way. It made me laugh, how they begged me to rest and how worried they looked when I refused. I was the boss and I showed them."

When the plane landed in Brazil by a miracle, C. W. was examined by a physician, forced into another plane and brought to Florida. Upon examination he was talkative, eyes gleaming, exuberant with statements of wealth and power. "I am now one of the richest men in the world," he said. "I'll give you $5,000,000 to start a hospital. My eyes are jewels, diamonds, emeralds." (Fetterman, 1949, pp. 267–268) result in greatly increased intracranial pressure. Common early symptoms are persistent headaches, vomiting, memory impairment, listlessness, depression, convulsive seizures, and "choked disk"—a retinal anomaly characterized by swelling of the optic nerve caused when cerebrospinal fluid is forced into it by intracranial pressure.

As a tumor progresses and the intracranial pressure increases, there may be clouding of consciousness, disorientation for time and place, carelessness in personal habits, irritability, sensorimotor losses, hallucinations, apathy, and a general or specific impairment of intellectual functions. Terminal stages are usually similar to other types of severe brain damage; the patient is reduced to a vegetative stupor and eventually dies.

Some idea of the relative frequency of symptoms in brain tumor cases may be gleaned from an early study by Levin (1949), who analyzed 22 cases admitted to the Boston Psychopathic Hospital. These patients ranged in age from 22 to 65 years, the majority falling between the ages of 40 and 60 years. The study included 11 males and 11 females. Prior to hospitalization the range of symptoms shown by these patients included the following:

Memory impairment or confusion	13 cases
Depression	9 cases
Seizures	8 cases
Headaches	8 cases
Complaints of visual impairment	6 cases
Drowsiness	6 cases
Irritability	6 cases
Indifference	5 cases
Restlessness	4 cases
Generalized weakness	4 cases
Loss of sense of responsibility	3 cases
Paranoid ideas	2 cases
Tendency to be combative	2 cases
Euphoria	2 cases
Aphasia (communication disorder)	2 cases

The interval between the onset of the symptoms and hospitalization varied from 1 week to 6 years, with an average interval of 17 months. In most cases, symptoms were evident 6 months or more prior to admission to the hospital. In this connection, however, it has been pointed out that minor personality changes and depression often serve to mask the more definitive symptoms of a brain tumor—with the result that accurate diagnosis and appropriate treatment are often delayed (Schwab, 1970).

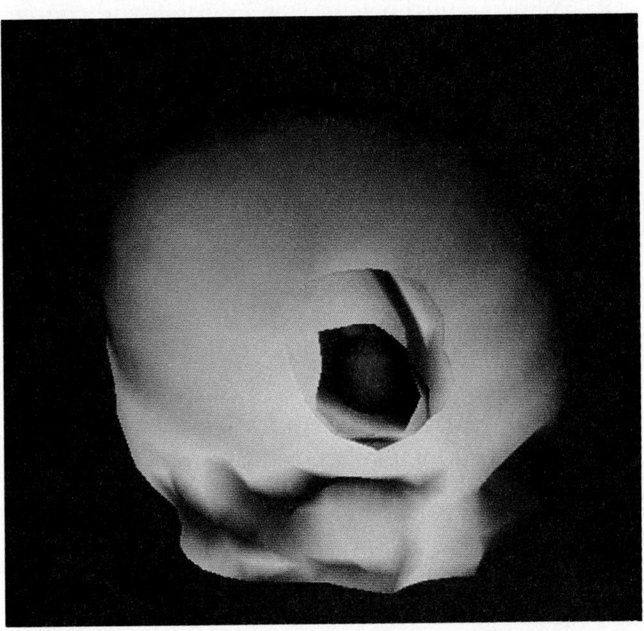

Early detection of brain tumors is critical, and a number of new methods for detection have been developed in recent years. In this computer-generated image based on the CAT scan of a man who collapsed while gambling in Las Vegas, a tumor (vividly red) is visible. In this three-dimensional view, looking through the forehead, the skull's surface is shown as white and the brain's as yellow. Fortunately, surgeons were able to remove the tumor and the man recovered.

Patients' emotional reactions to the organic damage and to the resulting cognitive and other types of impairment vary. Initially, they may be overly irritable and mildly depressed. As their disorder progresses, however, those having some insight into the seriousness of their condition may become severely depressed, anxious, and apprehensive. Patients who have less insight into their condition may be relatively unaware of their failing functions. Those with lesions pressing on certain parts of the brain may actually become expansive and euphoric. These latter patients seem unconcerned about their illness and may joke and laugh, sometimes in a most unrestrained and hilarious manner. The intensity of these reactions seems the result of organic damage to the inhibitory control system; they may be most evident in advanced stages when considerable brain damage or intracranial pressure exists.

Tumors directly producing psychological complications usually involve the frontal, temporal, or parietal lobes. Frontal-lobe tumors often produce subtle peculiarities, such as an inability to concentrate, personal carelessness, loss of inhibitions, and absent-mindedness that later becomes a memory defect. An individual may become silly and prone to punning and general jocularity. In an analysis of 90 patients with frontal-lobe tumors, Dobrokhotova (1968) found three common forms of emotional disorder: (a) the absence of spontaneity; (b) disinhibition and lability of affect—often with euphoria; and (c) forced emotions, which were abruptly expressed and terminated.

Although personality change is so common in brain tumor cases that it is often attributed directly to the activity of a tumor, it must be understood that such symptoms are neither inevitable nor necessarily the result of the tumor alone. As we have noted, adjustive reactions are typically a function of both the stress situation (including biological, psychosocial, and sociocultural stressors) and the personal maturity, stability, and level of stress tolerance of the individual. As brain deterioration advances, however, personality contributions to the patient's general behavior diminish and finally disappear.

Treatments and Outcomes Treatment of brain tumors is primarily a medical matter and thus is outside the scope of our present discussion. We should note, however, that the degree of improvement achieved in such cases depends both on the size and location of the growth and on the amount of brain tissue that must unavoidably be damaged in excising or neutralizing the tumor. In some cases, full function seems to return, while in others, a residue of symptoms remains, such as partial paralysis and a reduction in cognitive abilities. Where tumors are well-advanced and require extensive surgery, the mortality rate is high. German (1959) found that about 40 percent of all brain tumors were potentially curable, about 20 percent were capable of being arrested for periods of 5 years or more, and the remainder were fatal within a short period of time. Since then, newer methods of detecting and determining the precise location of brain tumors, together with more advanced treatment procedures, have resulted in a marked improvement in outcomes (Peterson, 1978).

Disorders Involving Head Injury

Since ancient times, traumatic brain injuries have provided a rich source of material for speculation about mental functions. Hippocrates pointed out that injuries to the head could cause sensory and motor disorders, and Galen included head injuries among the major causes of mental disorders.

Head injuries occur frequently, particularly as a result of falls, blows, and accidents. It has been estimated that well over a million people in the United States suffer head injuries each year in automobile and industrial accidents; a sizable number of cases are the result of bullets or other objects actually penetrating the cranium. Significant brain damage is sustained in some 300,000 of these instances (Chance, 1986). Relatively few people with head injuries find their way into mental hospitals because many head injuries do not involve appreciable damage to the brain, and even where they do psychopathological complications are often not observed.

The Clinical Picture in Disorders with Head Injuries Head injuries usually give rise to immediate acute reactions, the severity of which depends on the degree and type of injury. These acute reactions may then clear up entirely or develop into chronic disorders.

Perhaps the most famous historical case is the celebrated American crowbar case reported by Dr. J. M. Harlow in 1868. Because it is of both historical and descriptive significance, it merits our including a few details:

The accident occurred in Cavendish, Vt., on the line of the Rutland and Burlington Railroad, at that time being built, on the 13th of September, 1848, and was occasioned by the premature explosions of a blast, when this iron, known to blasters as a tamping iron, and which I now show you, was shot through the face and head.

The subject of it was Phineas P. Gage, a perfectly healthy, strong and active young man, twenty-five years of age . . . Gage was foreman of a gang of men employed in excavating rock, for the road way. . . .

The missile entered by its pointed end, the left side of the face, immediately anterior to the angle of the lower jaw, and passing obliquely upwards, and obliquely backwards, emerged in the median line, at the back part of the frontal bone, near the coronal suture. . . . The iron which thus traversed the head, is round and rendered comparatively smooth by use, and is three feet seven inches in length, one and one fourth inches in its largest diameter, and weighs thirteen and one fourth pounds. . . .

The patient was thrown upon his back by the explosion, and gave a few convulsive motions of the extremities, but spoke in a few minutes. His men (with whom he was a great favorite) took him in their arms and carried him to the road, only a few rods distant, and put him into an ox cart, in which he rode, supported in a sitting posture, fully three quarters of a mile to his hotel. He got out of the cart himself, with a little assistance from his men, and an hour afterwards (with what I could aid him by taking hold of his left arm) walked up a long flight of stairs, and got upon the bed in the room where he was dressed. He seemed perfectly conscious, but was becoming exhausted from the hemorrhage, which by this time, was quite profuse, the blood pouring from the lacerated sinus in the top of his head, and also finding its way into the stomach, which ejected it as often as every fifteen or twenty minutes. He bore his sufferings with firmness, and directed my attention to the hole in his cheek, saying, "the iron entered there and passed through my head." (1868, pp. 330–332)

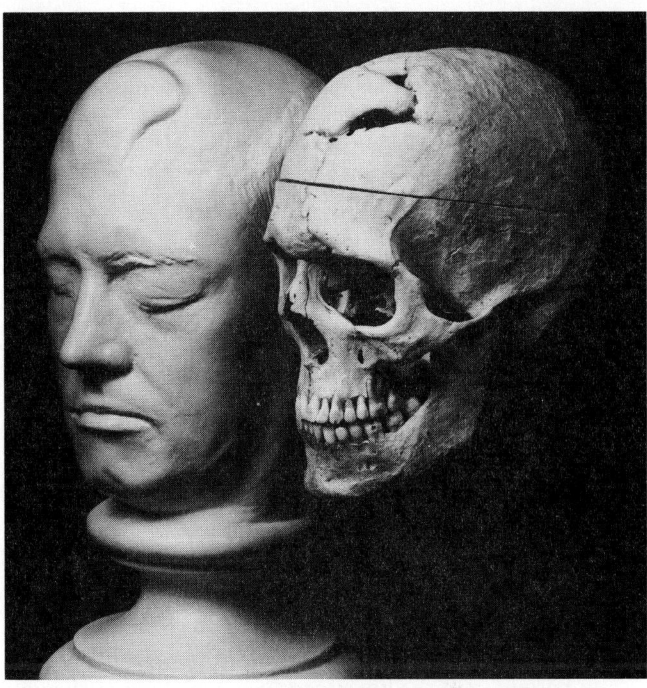

A cast of the head and the actual skull of Phineas Gage. Note the places in the skull pierced by the iron rod.

Some time later Dr. Harlow made the following report:

His physical health is good, and I am inclined to say that he has recovered. Has no pain in head, but says it has a queer feeling which he is not able to describe. Applied for his situation as foreman, but is undecided whether to work or travel. His contractors, who regarded him as the most efficient and capable foreman in their employ previous to his injury considered the change in his mind so marked that they could not give him his place again. The equilibrium or balance, so to speak, between his intellectual faculties and animal propensities, seems to have been destroyed. He is fitful, irreverent, indulging at times in the grossest profanity (which was not previously his custom), manifesting but little deference for his fellows, impatient of restraint or advice when it conflicts with his desires, at times pertinaciously obstinate, yet capricious and vacillating, devising many plans of future operations, which are no sooner arranged than they are abandoned in turn for others . . . his mind is radically changed, so decidedly that his friends and acquaintances said he was "no longer Gage." (1868, pp. 339–340)

It is evident from the above account that Gage acquired an organic personality syndrome from his encounter with the errant crowbar. This relatively dramatic syndrome, however, is not a particularly common sequel to head injury.

Fortunately, the brain is an extraordinarily well-protected organ; but even so, a hard blow on the head may result in a skull fracture in which portions of bone press on or are driven into the brain tissue. Even without a fracture, the force of the blow may result in small, pinpoint hemorrhages throughout the brain or in the rupturing of larger blood vessels in the brain.

A person rendered unconscious by a head injury usually passes through stages of stupor and confusion on the way to recovering clear consciousness. This recovery of consciousness may be complete in the course of minutes, or it may take hours or days. In rare cases an individual may live for extended periods of time without regaining consciousness. In such cases the prognosis for substantial improvement is poor. In some instances, significant cognitive or personality alterations following injury are observed even where a person experiences no loss of consciousness.

Specific symptoms, of course, depend largely on the nature of an injury. Normally, if a head injury is sufficiently severe to result in unconsciousness, the person experiences *retrograde amnesia,* or inability to recall events immediately preceding the injury. Apparently, such trauma interferes with the brain's capacity to consolidate into long-term storage the events that were being mentally processed at the time of the trauma.

Following a severe cerebral injury, a person's pulse, temperature, blood pressure, and important aspects of brain metabolism are all affected, and survival may be uncertain. The duration of the coma is generally related to the severity of the injury. If the patient survives, coma may be followed by delirium, in which acute excitement is manifested, with disorientation, hallucinations, and generally agitated, restless, and confused activity. Often the patient talks incessantly in a disconnected fashion, with no insight into the disturbed condition. Gradually the confusion clears up and the individual regains contact with reality. Again, the severity and duration of residual symptoms depends primarily on the nature and extent of the cerebral damage, the premorbid personality of the patient, and the life situation to which he or she will return. Even where an injury seems relatively mild with good return of function, recent research using highly refined and comprehensive neuropsychological assessments often demonstrates various types of subtle residual impairment.

Some degree of bleeding, or *intracerebral hemorrhage,* can occur with head injuries. In severe injuries, there may be gross bleeding or hemorrhaging at the site of the damage. Enough blood may accumulate within the rigid confines of the skull that disruptive pressure is exerted on neighboring regions of the brain; a common form of this problem is the *subdural hematoma,* which, if not relieved by aspiration of the excess blood, may endanger vital brain functions or produce permanent neuronal damage. When the hemorrhaging involves small spots of bleeding—often microscopic sleeves of red cells encircling tiny blood vessels—the condition is referred to as *petechial hemorrhages.* Some evidence shows tiny, scattered petechial hemorrhages in most brain injuries, but in fatal cases they are usually multiple or generalized throughout the brain. Brain swelling, or *cerebral edema,* occurs in many cases of severe damage, increasing the risk of significant mental impairment or death unless promptly treated.

Professional boxers are likely to suffer such petechial hemorrhaging from repeated blows to the head; they may develop a form of encephalopathy (characterized by an area or areas of permanently damaged brain tissue) from the accumulated damage of such injuries. Consequently, some former boxers suffer from impaired memory, slurred speech, inability to concentrate, involuntary movements, and other symptoms—a condition popularly referred to as being punch-drunk. Johnson (1969) found abnormal electroencephalograms in 10 of 17 retired boxers; Earl (1966) noted that two former welterweight champions suffered so much brain damage in their professional fights that they were confined in mental institutions before they reached the age of 30.

With one-time head injuries, resulting syndromes are usually limited to delirium and perhaps some features of the dementia, amnestic, and hallucinosis syndromes—all on a temporary basis. Where a trauma results in the permanent loss of neural tissue, however, all these syndromes may occur in their full-blown and irreversible forms; in addition to a variety of physical impairments and disabilities, the person may also experience personality disturbance, including delusional syndromes and serious depressive mood disorder.

Treatments and Outcomes Treatment for brain damage due to head injury is primarily a medical matter. Prompt treatment may prevent further injury or damage—for example, when pooled blood under pressure must be removed from the skull. In severe cases, immediate medical treatment may have to be supplemented by a long-range program of reeducation and rehabilitation.

Although many head trauma patients show few residual effects from their injury, particularly if they have experienced only a brief loss of consciousness, other patients sustain definite and long-lasting impairment. Common aftereffects of moderate brain injury are chronic headaches, anxiety, irritability, dizziness, easy fatigability, and impaired memory and concentration. Where the brain damage is extensive, a patient's general intellectual level may be markedly reduced, especially if he or she has suffered severe temporal- or parietal-lobe lesions. In addition, various specific neurological and psychological defects may follow localized brain damage, as we have seen. Some 2 to 4 percent of head-injury cases develop posttraumatic epilepsy, usually within two years of the head injury but sometimes much later.

In a minority of brain-injury cases, personality changes occur, such as those described in the historic case of Phineas Gage. Other kinds of personality changes include passivity, loss of drive and spontaneity, agitation, anxiety, depression, and paranoid suspiciousness. Like cognitive changes, the kinds of personality changes that emerge in severely damaged people will depend, in large measure, on the site and extent of their injury.

The great majority of people suffering from mild concussions improve to a near normal status

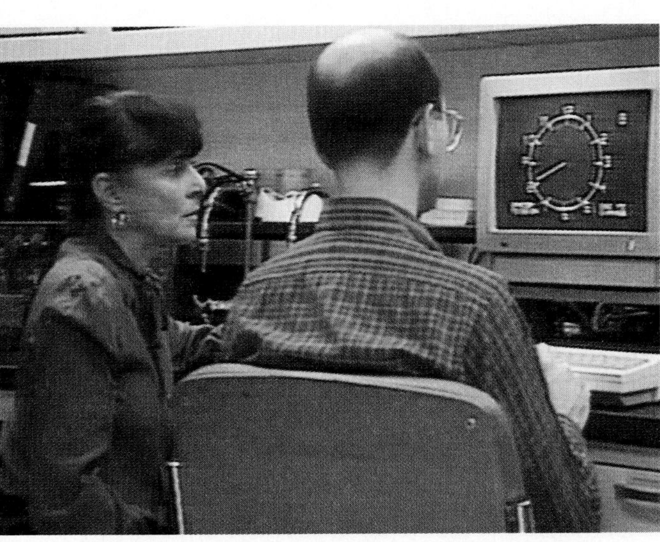

This man has suffered head trauma and his therapist is using a computer as a part of his treatment. Although many head-trauma patients show few residual effects from their injury, other patients sustain definite and long-lasting impairment.

within a short time. With moderate brain injuries, it takes longer for patients to reach their maximum level of improvement, and many suffer from headaches and other symptoms for prolonged periods. A few develop chronic, incapacitating symptoms.

In severe brain-injury cases, the prognosis is less favorable (Jennett et al., 1976). Many of these patients have to adjust to lower levels of occupational and social functioning, while others are so impaired intellectually that they require continuing supervision and, sometimes, institutionalization. Even in cases where considerable amounts of brain tissue have been destroyed, however, a minority of these patients are able to become socially independent. In many cases there is improvement with time, due largely to reeducation and to intact brain areas taking over new functions.

In general, the following factors indicate a favorable prognosis in cases of head injury: (a) a short period of unconsciousness or posttraumatic amnesia; (b) no focal brain lesion; (c) a well-integrated preinjury personality; (d) motivation to recover or make the most of residual capacities; (e) a favorable life situation to which to return; and (f) an appropriate program of retraining (Brooks, 1974; Diller & Gordon, 1981). The last factor, crucial for the future functioning of some individuals, is unfortunately far from generally available (Chance, 1986). Even where such treatment centers are conveniently located, they may be too expensive for many families to take advantage of them.

Other factors may also have a direct bearing on the outcomes of brain injuries. As we mentioned earlier, the results of brain damage in infancy differ from those in adolescence and adulthood, although in both instances the results may range from death to any number of neurological disorders, including epilepsy and mental retardation. Moreover, the outlook for individuals who are also victims of alcoholism, drug dependence, or other organic conditions may be unfavorable. Alcoholics, in particular, are prone to head injuries and other accidents and do not have good improvement records. Severe emotional conflicts sometimes appear to predispose an individual to accidents and also may delay recovery. Although malingering is thought to be rare in brain-injury cases, the hope of receiving monetary compensation—for example, from an insurance settlement—may influence individuals to exaggerate and maintain symptoms.

Dementia of the Alzheimer Type

It is a commonplace observation that the organs of the body deteriorate with aging, a process, biologists tell us, that begins virtually at birth. The cause or causes of this deterioration, however, remain largely obscure; science has not yet solved the riddle of aging. Of course, the brain—truly the master organ—is not spared in the generalized aging process. As time goes on, it too wears out, or degenerates. Mental disorders that sometimes accompany this brain degeneration and occur in old age are traditionally called **senile dementias.** Unfortunately, a number of rare conditions result in degenerative changes in brain tissue earlier in life. Disorders associated with such earlier degeneration of the brain are known as **presenile dementias.**

Not only is the age of onset different in the presenile dementias, but they are also distinguished from the senile dementias by their different behavioral manifestations and tissue alterations (see *HIGHLIGHT 13.4*). One important exception is **Alzheimer's disease,** which is a typical and common senile disorder but which can, in certain individuals, occur well before old age. Alzheimer's disease is a characteristic dementia syndrome having an insidious onset and a usually slow but progressively deteriorating course terminating in death. The formal psychiatric diagnosis, *primary degenerative dementia of the Alzheimer type (DAT),* is normally given when all other potential causes of dementia are ruled out by case history, physical examination, and laboratory tests. The parallel medical diagnosis, *Alzheimer's disease,* is coded on Axis III (medical conditions) of the DSM-III-R, although as of this writing it is in fact usually not possible to establish definitely the presence of the distinctive Alzheimer

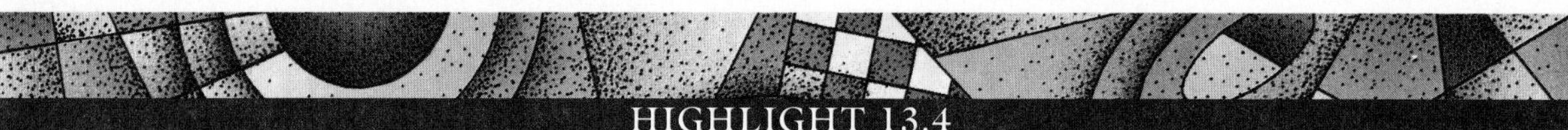

HIGHLIGHT 13.4

Presenile Dementias

In addition to early-occurring Alzheimer's disease, two other forms of presenile dementia occur with sufficient frequency to deserve mention: Pick's disease and Huntington's chorea.

Pick's Disease

Even rarer than early-onset Alzheimer's disease, Pick's disease (first described by Arnold Pick of Prague in 1892) is a degenerative disorder of the brain, usually having its onset in people between the ages of 45 and 50. Its cause is unknown. Women are apparently more subject to Pick's disease than men, at a ratio of about three to two. Onset is slow and insidious, involving difficulty in thinking, slight memory defects, easy fatigability, and, often, character changes with a lowering of many social inhibitions. At first there is a circumscribed atrophy of the frontal and temporal lobes; as the atrophy becomes more severe, the mental deterioration becomes progressively greater and includes apathy and disorientation as well as the impairment of judgment and other intellectual functions. The disease usually runs a fatal course within two to seven years.

Huntington's Chorea

Huntington's chorea is a genetically determined (autosomal dominant) degenerative disorder of the central nervous system. It was first described by the American neurologist George Huntington in 1872. With an incidence rate of about 5 cases per 100,000 people, the disease usually occurs in individuals between 30 and 50 years of age. Behavior deterioration often becomes apparent several years before there are any detectable neurological manifestations (Lyle & Gottesman, 1977). The disease itself is characterized by a chronic, progressive chorea (involuntary and irregular twitching, jerking movements) with mental deterioration leading to dementia and death within 10 to 20 years. Although Huntington's chorea cannot be cured or even arrested at the present time, it can be prevented, at least in theory, by genetic counseling, because its occurrence is a function of known genetic laws.

neuropathology (described later) in living patients. Brain imaging techniques, such as that of magnetic resonance imaging (MRI), may provide supportive evidence in showing enlarged ventricles or widening in the folds (sulci) of the cerebral cortex, indicative of brain atrophy. Nevertheless, the use of antemortem criteria for the diagnosis of dementia of the Alzheimer type (DAT) is somewhat imprecise (Carlsson, 1986) and may result in an overdiagnosis of the disorder as high as 30 percent (Hartford, 1986). DAT takes its name from Alois Alzheimer, a German neuropsychiatrist, who first described it in 1860.

When we try to envisage a "typical" Alzheimer patient—and most of us have had contact with such people—we imagine a person of advanced age. This picture is in fact true only in the statistical sense. Unfortunately, for some, DAT is a presenile dementia that begins in their 40s or 50s; in such cases the progress of the disease and its associated dementia is typically rapid. For example, in one study of early-onset DAT (Heyman et al., 1987) the five-year cumulative mortality rate was 2.5 times the expected rate, with the *younger* of these patients contributing disproportionately to the excess in deaths. Considerable evidence suggests a substantial genetic contribution in early-onset DAT (Davies, 1986). These cases, occurring at the height of careers and in periods of maximum productivity and family responsibilities, portray the tragedy of Alzheimer's disease in an especially stark light.

In fact no way exists to portray the ravages of this disorder in other than an alarming fashion, even if we restrict attention to the more typical instance of onset after age 65. Survival to at least that point is becoming increasingly routine, and after the first decade of the twenty-first century, the first members of the enormous post–World War II baby boom generation will enter the age range of maximum risk. If we have not solved the problem of curing or preventing DAT by that time or shortly thereafter, the social and economic consequences will clearly be devastating (Fisher & Carstensen, 1990).

Nor is there any real assurance, despite our rapidly advancing knowledge about the disorder, that a solution will be found. Just as people do not die of old age per se but rather of failing organs, there is no cure or preventive measure for the aging of living organisms. Some investigators, for example, Selkoe (1986), suggest that Alzheimer's "disease" is merely the product of the aging process as manifested in a particular organ, the brain. Early onset is early brain aging, probably for the most part genetically determined. Prevention or cure, according to this view, would therefore approximate in its unlikelihood the discovery of the Fountain of Youth. Somewhat reassuringly, other researchers, Comfort (1984) and Glenner (1986), for example, reject this notion and hold that DAT is a specific disease process, hence in principle both preventable and curable. The final answer to this fascinating and important debate is nowhere in sight.

Whether or not we face an apocalyptic future in respect to overwhelming numbers of demented elderly people, the magnitude of the problem of DAT—often seriously underestimated—is even now straining societal and family resources, both economic and emotional. As shown in the table of *HIGHLIGHT 13.2*, the disorder accounts for nearly 50 percent of all cases of dementia of whatever cause. The ratio is doubtless considerably higher for people in older age ranges. It is estimated that one of every six people in the United States over age 65 is clinically demented, and one of every ten people in this age range suffers from DAT (Evans et al., 1989). By age 85 the prevalence rate of DAT is nearly 50 percent (Fisher & Carstensen, 1990). This figure translates to over one million victims in this country alone, and the number is increasing rapidly with the advancing average age of the population (Light & Lebowitz, 1989). Some 30 to 40 percent of nursing home residents are DAT patients (Kolata, 1981a). Some of these patients reside in mental hospitals or other types of institutional settings. The majority live in the community, typically with family members (Gurland & Cross, 1982), a circumstance that is often extremely stressful for caregivers (Brane, 1986; Fisher & Carstensen, 1990; Jenkins, Parham, & Jenkins, 1985; Mobily & Hoeft, 1985).

The Clinical Picture in Dementia of the Alzheimer Type As already noted, the onset of Alzheimer's disease in older people is usually gradual, involving slow mental deterioration. In some cases a physical ailment or some other stressful event is a dividing point, but usually an individual passes into a demented state almost imperceptibly, so that it is impossible to date the onset of the disorder precisely. The clinical picture may vary markedly from one person to another, depending on the nature and extent of brain degeneration, the premorbid personality of the individual, the particular stressors that have been or are in operation, and the degree of environmental support.

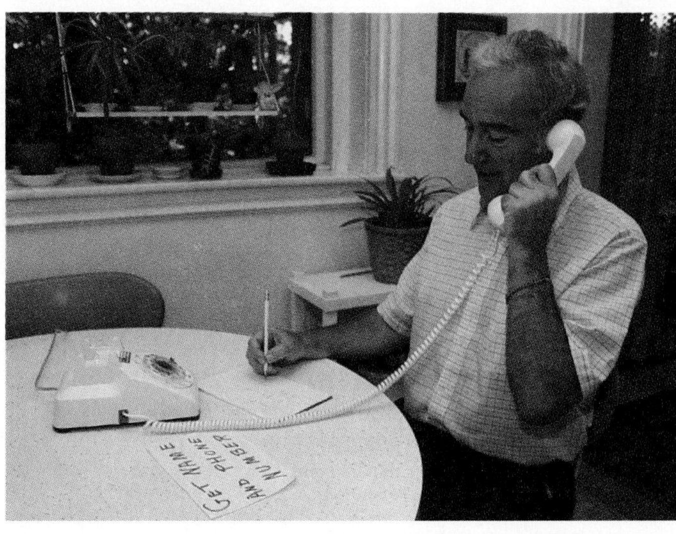

Written reminders can help Alzheimer's victims lead relatively normal lives. In the early stages, they can remember how to do things once they are reminded to do them. Later on, they may lose the ability to do even simple tasks.

Symptoms often begin with an individual's gradual withdrawal from active engagement with life. There is a narrowing of social and other interests, a lessening of mental alertness and adaptability, and a lowering of tolerance to new ideas and changes in routine. Often thoughts and activities become self-centered and childlike, including a preoccupation with the bodily functions of eating, digestion, and excretion. As these changes—typical in a lesser degree of many older people—become more severe, additional symptoms, such as impaired memory for recent events, "empty" speech (in which grammar and syntax remain intact but vague expressions replace meaningful nouns and verbs), messiness, impaired judgment, agitation, and periods of confusion, make their appearance. Specific symptoms may vary considerably from patient to patient and from day to day for the same patient; thus the clinical picture is by no means uniform until the terminal stages, when the patient is reduced to a vegetative level. There is also, of course, individual variation in the rapidity of the disorder's progression. In rare instances the symptoms may reverse and partial function may return, but in true DAT this reversal will prove temporary.

The end stages of Alzheimer's disease involve a depressingly similar pattern of reduction to a vegetative existence and ultimate death from some disease that overwhelms a person's limited defensive resources. Prior to this point, there is, as noted, some distinctiveness in patient behavior. Allowing for inevitable overlapping and individual changes in pattern as DAT develops, a given victim is likely to show one of the several dominant behavioral manifestations described in the following paragraphs.

Approximately half of all DAT patients display a course of *simple deterioration.* That is, they gradually lose various mental capacities, typically beginning with memory for recent events and progressing to disorientation, poor judgment, neglect of personal hygiene, and loss of contact with reality to an extent precluding independent functioning as adults. Distinctly psychopathological symptoms (such as delusions), if they occur at all, are likely to be transitory and inconsistent over time. The following case—involving an engineer who had retired some seven years prior to his hospitalization—is typical of simple deterioration resulting from DAT:

During the past five years, he had shown a progressive loss of interest in his surroundings and during the last year had become increasingly "childish." His wife and eldest son had brought him to the hospital because they felt they could no longer care for him in their home, particularly because of the grandchildren. They stated that he had become careless in his eating and other personal habits and was restless and prone to wandering about at night. He could not seem to remember anything that had happened during the day but was garrulous concerning events of his childhood and middle years.

After admission to the hospital, the patient seemed to deteriorate rapidly. He could rarely remember what had happened a few minutes before, although his memory for remote events of his childhood remained good. When he was visited by his wife and children, he mistook them for old friends, nor could he recall anything about the visit a few minutes after they had departed. The following brief conversation with the patient, which took place after he had been in the hospital for nine months and about three months before his death, shows his disorientation for time and person:

Doctor: *How are you today, Mr.________?*

Patient: *Oh . . . hello (looks at doctor in rather puzzled way as if trying to make out who he is).*

Doctor: *Do you know where you are now?*

Patient: *Why yes . . . I am at home. I must paint the house this summer. It has needed painting for a long time but it seems like I just keep putting it off.*

Doctor: *Can you tell me the day today?*

Patient: *Isn't today Sunday . . . why, yes, the children are coming over for dinner today. We always have dinner for the whole family on Sunday. My wife was here just a minute ago but I guess she has gone back into the kitchen.*

In a less frequent but not uncommon manifestation of Alzheimer's disease, a person develops a *decidedly paranoid orientation* to the environment, becoming markedly suspicious and often convinced that others are engaged in various injurious plots and schemes. Uncooperativeness and verbal abuse are common accompaniments (Brink, 1983), making the task of caregiving significantly more stressful. In the early phases of this reaction pattern, the cognitive deficits characteristic of Alzheimer's disease (memory loss, disorientation) may not be prominent, perhaps enabling the individual to be quite observant and even logical in building the "case" for others' nefarious activities. Though themes of malevolent victimization predominate in this form of the disorder, also common is the so-called jealousy delusion in which the person persistently accuses his or her partner or spouse—who is often of advanced age and physically debilitated—of being sexually unfaithful. Family members may be the perpetrators of various foul deeds, such as poisoning the patient's food or plotting to steal the patient's funds. Fortunately, punitive retribution in the form of physical attacks on the "evildoers" are rare, but a combative pattern does occasionally occur, enormously complicating the patient's management. The following case is fairly typical of the paranoid reaction type:

A woman of 74 had been referred to a hospital after the death of her husband because she had become uncooperative and was convinced that her relatives were trying to steal the insurance money her husband had left her. In the hospital, she complained that the other patients had joined together against her and were trying to steal her belongings. She frequently refused to eat, on the grounds that the food tasted funny and had probably been poisoned. She grew increasingly irritable and disoriented for time and person. She avidly scanned magazines in the ward reading room but could not remember anything she had looked at. The following conversation reveals some of her symptoms:

Doctor: *Do you find that magazine interesting?*

Patient: *Why do you care? Can't you see I'm busy?*

Doctor: *Would you mind telling me something about what you are reading?*

Patient: *It's none of your business . . . I am reading about my relatives. They want me to die so that they can steal my money.*

Doctor: *Do you have any evidence of this?*

Patient: *Yes, plenty. They poison my food and they have turned the other women against me. They are all out to get my money. They even stole my sweater.*

Doctor: *Can you tell me what you had for breakfast?*

Patient: *. . . (Pause) I didn't eat breakfast . . . it was poisoned and I refused to eat it. They are all against me.*

Paranoid orientations tend to develop in individuals who have been sensitive and suspicious. Existing personality tendencies are apparently intensified by degenerative brain changes and the stress accompanying advancing age.

Other patterns seen in Alzheimer patients are comparatively infrequent. Some patients are confused but amiable, usually showing marked memory impairment and a tendency to engage in seemingly pointless activities, such as hoarding useless objects or repetitively performing household tasks in a ritualized manner. Other patients become severely agitated, with or without an accompanying "hand-wringing" depression. Depressed Alzheimer patients tend to develop extremely morbid preoccupations and delusions, such as hypochondriacal ideas about having various horrible diseases, often seen as just deserts for past sins. Suicide is a possibility in such cases should a patient be physically capable of carrying out the act.

In some cases, especially those with early onset, the disease progress is unusually rapid and a patient moves quickly into a state of incoherence verging on delirium. This mental clouding is frequently accompanied by marked agitation and unpredictable combativeness, severely trying the resources of caregivers. As we have seen, all Alzheimer patients who survive long enough eventually enter a stage of continuous delirium.

With appropriate treatment, which may include medication and the maintenance of a calm, reassuring, and unprovocative social milieu, many people with Alzheimer's disease show some symptom alleviation. In general, however, deterioration continues its downward course over a period of months or years. Eventually, patients become oblivious of their surroundings, bedridden, and reduced to vegetative existences. Resistance to disease is lowered, and death usually results from pneumonia or some other infection.

Causal Factors in Dementia of the Alzheimer Type The fundamental, invariant neuropathology of the Alzheimer brain has been known for some time. It has three elements: (a) the widespread appearance of "senile plaques," small areas of dark-colored matter that are in part the debris of damaged nerve terminals; (b) the tangling of the normally regular patterning of neurofibrils (strandlike protein filaments) within neuronal cell bodies; and (c) the abnormal appearance of small holes in neuronal tissue, called granulovacuoles, which derive from cell degeneration. Observation of these changes requires microscopic examination of brain tissue specimens, which is why unequivocal confirmation of the diagnosis can usually be accomplished only after a patient has died.

When sufficiently numerous, these microscopic alterations of the brain's substance lead to generalized brain atrophy, which, as already noted, may be visualized by imaging techniques. Unfortunately from the diagnostic standpoint, such atrophy may occur with other conditions as well. A more promising observation concerns the neurotransmitter acetylcholine, which is known to be important in the mediation of memory. While there is widespread destruction of neurons in DAT, evidence suggests that the most severely and perhaps earliest affected are a cluster of cell bodies located in the basal forebrain and involved in the release of acetylcholine (Coyle, Price, & DeLong, 1983; Whitehouse, et al., 1982). This observation and related ones (e.g., Wester et al., 1988) have given rise to the ***acetylcholine (ACh) depletion theory*** of DAT etiology. Although the evidence is still not conclusive (Perry, 1988), the theory does integrate an impressive array of research data, including the production of a temporary DAT-like syndrome in normal subjects given ACh-blocking drugs (Kopelman, 1986).

If we make the reasonable assumption that ACh depletion plays at least *some* role in the production of DAT symptoms, there is still the question of what place it occupies in the presumed causal chain. What, for example, causes the degeneration of ACh-releasing cells? No shortage of hypotheses purport to answer such questions, but many have proven to have serious flaws, and none has so far gained a dominating level of acceptance. For example, some investigators (e.g., Crapper McLachlan, 1986) have been impressed with the abnormal amounts of aluminum, known to have neurotoxic effects, found in the brains of some DAT patients. Others, however, have argued cogently that these abnormal accumulations of aluminum are

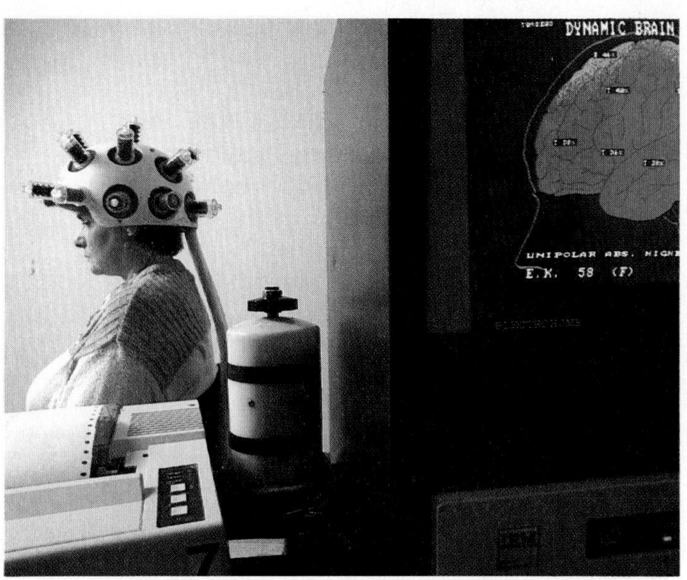

An electrode headset picks up signals from the brain of a 58-year-old woman, and a computer turns them into the brain map on the screen. Brain-mapping can detect the depletion of acetylcholine, which is thought to play a role in the production of Alzheimer's symptoms.

an effect, not a cause, of DAT brain degeneration (e.g., Alfrey, 1986; Wisniewski, Moretz, & Iqbal, 1986).

Some investigators have taken the more direct approach of trying to discover the sources of the primary DAT lesions such as neurofibrillary tangles and senile plaques. The search has yielded a considerable amount of information concerning, in particular, the composition of the latter. As stated earlier, these plaques contain cell debris, but their cores consist of a waxy amyloid protein substance, designated A4, that also occurs in abnormal abundance in other parts of DAT patients' brains (see, for example, Gajdusek, 1986; Hardy et al., 1986; Kang et al., 1987). This finding appears to be extremely important in leading to an understanding of DAT pathogenesis, and it also suggests an approach to the development of a much-needed diagnostic test of high sensitivity and selectivity for DAT that could be used with living patients. Though there have been no dramatic breakthroughs in these areas yet, the evidence suggests that their emergence is imminent.

We have already mentioned that early-onset DAT, in common with numerous other instances of early-onset disease, seems to have a significant genetic component in its etiology. In one particularly interesting study involving early onset, Nee (reported in Sargent, 1982b) traced the disease back eight generations in one family that immigrated to this continent in 1837. Of 531 family members, 53 were identified as suffering from the disease, even though those who lived to 65 without symptoms were considered free of it. Collateral findings of this NIMH project showed that the mean interval between the onset of symptoms and death was 6 years (although in one case it was 24) and that the age at onset ranged between 44 and 64 years.

In fact, widespread evidence, none of it conclusive (Bird, 1986; Henderson, 1986; Reisberg, 1984), shows that a general vulnerability to the development of DAT may be inherited (Breitner, 1986; Davies, 1986). Much of this evidence points to a genetic connection with Down syndrome (see Chapter 14), which is due to a trisomy involving chromosome 21. Most Down syndrome individuals who survive beyond age 35 develop a DAT-like dementia (Bauer & Shea, 1986), with comparable neuropathological changes (Schapiro & Rapoport, 1987). Anomalies of chromosome 21 have also been implicated in DAT (e.g., Van Broeckhoven et al., 1987). Barnes (1987) reported evidence that the *same regions* of chromosome 21 are involved in both Down syndrome and DAT, and that one of the genes in this region produces the A4 amyloid protein that figures so prominently in the neuropathology of DAT. Finally, Hardy et al. (as reported by Marx, 1991) have recently identified a gene mutation on chromosome 21 in a DAT-prone family, one that could be implicated in the release of A4. The case for a connection between DAT and Down syndrome is thus quite strong. Beyond that, we may be on the verge of precisely identifying the genetic basis of one form of early-onset DAT.

One must still be cautious, however, about the general contribution of genetic variables to the pathogenesis of DAT, especially of the late-onset variety. While there is some evidence of genetic influence even for onsets as late as ages 80 to 90 (Mohs et al., 1987; Sturt, 1986), nongenetic variables are clearly involved in the etiology of DAT (Henderson, 1986). Indeed, both Nee et al. (1987) and Renvoize et al. (1986) described monozygotic twins discordant for DAT, a circumstance that can only be explained by some sort of critical environmental variation. A pedigree involving substantial incidence of apparent DAT does not therefore justify undue concern about risk. Unfortunately, we have essentially no reliable information about environmental risk factors; most hypotheses advanced in this area involve environmental toxins, including a (to us) somewhat fanciful theory suggesting entry through the nose (Roberts, 1986).

In considering the activity level and rate of progress in understanding DAT that we have briefly outlined, you may find reason to be impressed. We think it appropriate to echo that sentiment. Although there are still many loose ends to be tied together, and some that may remain resistant to our best efforts, the progress of the last decade in coming to grips with DAT has been nothing less than astonishing. These investigations are truly science of the highest order effectively directed at a human problem of enormous and increasing scope.

Treatments and Outcomes There is to date no known treatment for DAT—medical, psychosocial, retraining-based, or rehabilitative, including attempts at replenishing brain ACh—that produces a sustained reversal or interruption of the deteriorating course. Until some means of accomplishing such an effect appears, we will have to content ourselves with palliative measures that diminish patient *and* caregiver distress and relieve as far as possible those complications of the disorder, such as combativeness, that increase the difficulties of management.

Concerning the latter objectives, Fisher and Carstensen (1990) recently reviewed the considerable literature on behavioral approaches used to control several of the more common problematic behaviors that are associated with DAT (and with other dementing disorders as well), such as wandering off, incontinence, inappropriate sexual behavior, and inadequate self-care skills. Because behavioral approaches need not be dependent on complex cognitive and communicational abilities, which are apt to be lacking in these patients, they may be particularly appropriate for therapeutic intervention with this group. In general, reports of results are at least moderately encouraging in terms of reducing unnecessary frustration and embarrassment for the patient and hassle for the caregiver.

Medication may be of some help for patients who experience difficulty in modulating their emotions and impulses. Some depressed DAT patients respond reasonably well to antidepressant or stimulant medication. Where medications are used, however, dosages must be carefully monitored because unanticipated effects are common and because the frequently debilitated state of these patients makes them susceptible to an exaggerated response.

Any comprehensive approach to therapeutic intervention must consider the extremely difficult situation of caregivers. They are, as a group, at extraordinarily high risk for depression (Cohen & Eisdorfer, 1988). They tend to consume high quantities of psychotropic medication themselves and to report numerous stress symptoms (George, 1984). Because the basic problem usually seems in fact to be one of high and sustained stress, we would anticipate that any measures found successful in the reduction and management of stress and the enhancement of coping resources could be effectively used to ease caregivers' burdens. The available research literature on this problem confirms our assumption (Costa, Whitfield, & Stewart, 1989). Group support programs, for example, may produce measurable reductions in experienced stress and depression (e.g., Glosser & Wexler, 1985; Kahan et al., 1985).

Whether or not, or at what point, to institutionalize a DAT patient whose requirements for care threaten to engulf his or her spouse or other family members can be a vexing and emotional decision. It can also be one with significant financial implications because, on average, nursing home care is about twice as costly as home care (Hu, Huang, & Cartwright, 1986). As we have seen, most DAT patients are cared for at home, mostly for emotional reasons, such as continuing love, loyalty, and a sense of obligation for remembered good times with the now-stricken parent or partner. In one sense at least, the home care decision is a justifiable one; the move to an institution, particularly one lacking in social stimulation and support, may result in an abrupt worsening of symptoms and sometimes a markedly enhanced rate of deterioration—demonstrating once again the power of psychosocial influences even in this instance of widespread brain destruction. On the other hand, the emergence of marked confusion, gross and argumentative demeanor, stuporous depression, inappropriate sexual behavior, and disorientation for time, place, and person, not to mention possible combative violence, can put an intolerable strain on

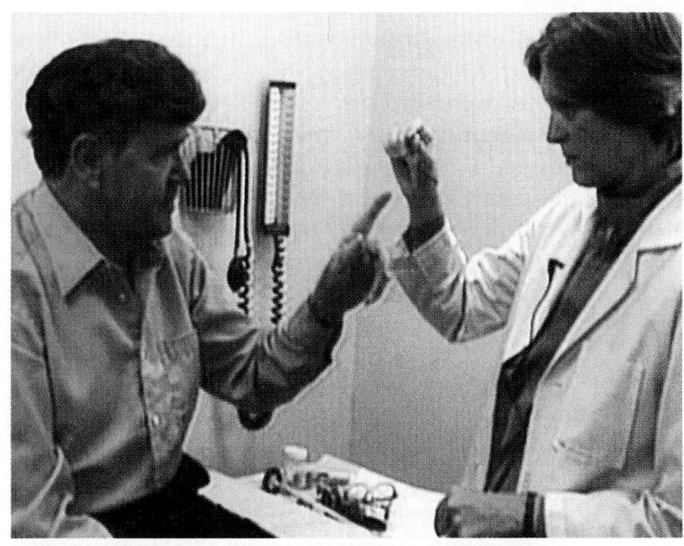

This Alzheimer's patient is being asked to identify keys held by a therapist. There is no known treatment for DAT that can reverse or interrupt the deteriorating course, although certain interventions have proven moderately helpful in controlling problematic behaviors and emotions.

caregivers to the point of psychological collapse. Because in all likelihood such conditions will *not* improve over time but in fact will worsen, wisdom dictates an early rather than a late removal to an institution, which in any event is where most DAT patients will have to spend their final weeks or months.

A Note on Multi-Infarct Dementia

Multi-infarct dementia (MID), frequently confused with DAT because of its somewhat similar clinical picture and its increasing incidence and prevalence rates with advancing age, is actually an entirely different disease in terms of its underlying neuropathology. In this disorder, a series of cerebral infarcts—interruptions of the blood supply to parts of the brain because of arterial disease, commonly known as *strokes*—cumulatively destroy neurons over expanding brain regions. The affected regions become soft and may degenerate over time, leaving only cavities. The progressive loss of cells leads to brain atrophy and behavioral impairments that ultimately mimic those of DAT. The decline, however, is less smooth in course because of (a) the discrete character of infarct events and the processes they initiate, and (b) variations over time in the volume of blood delivered by a seriously clogged artery, producing variations in the functional adequacy of cells that have not yet succumbed to oxygen deprivation. Multi-infarct dementia is far less common than DAT, accounting for only some 10 percent of dementia cases. MID has a much shorter average course because of a patient's vulnerability to sudden death from a large infarct or one that affects vital centers. Occasionally, an unfortunate patient will be discovered to have *both* DAT and MID.

The medical treatment of MID, while hazardous and complicated, offers slightly more hope at this time than that of DAT. Unlike DAT, the basic problem of cerebral arteriosclerosis can be medically managed to some extent, perhaps decreasing the likelihood of further strokes.

The psychological and behavioral aspects of the dementia caused by DAT and MID are similar in many respects, and any management measure found useful in one is likely to be applicable in the other. Likewise, the maintenance of any gains achieved cannot be taken for granted because of the generally progressive nature of the underlying brain pathology. The daunting problems facing caregivers are also very much the same in the two conditions, indicating the appropriateness of support groups, stress reduction techniques, and the like.

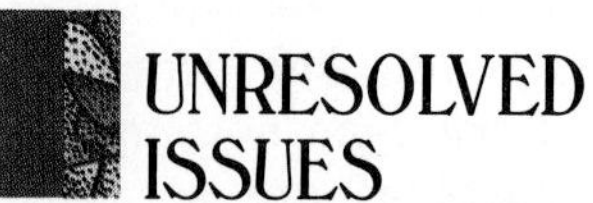

UNRESOLVED ISSUES on Organic Mental Disorders

There remains a great deal of unnecessary confusion concerning the definition and conceptualization of "organic mental disorders." Indeed, the term itself, taken as sincerely intended to be representative of actual clinical entities (as opposed to a mere nominal label for conditions that include both aberrant psychological phenomena and demonstrable brain impairment), poses certain baffling semantic and philosophical questions. One of the authors uses it as a ploy to enliven flagging conversations among colleagues by asking, "What does it *really* mean?"; or if that doesn't work by assertively declaring it to be an oxymoron, which almost always gets *something* going. More seriously, our efforts to differentiate between neurological "mental" symptoms and psychopathological ones, and our introduction of the computer hardware/software analogy early in the chapter, were inspired by an awareness of how difficult it must be for thoughtful students to find their way in the morass of imprecision and unstated assumption that confronts us in regard to this class of disorder. We hope we have not added to your confusion in engaging these issues, nor do we believe our efforts have entirely resolved them—not even for ourselves.

Regarding the dementias associated with aging, notably DAT and MID, our society is in something of a race with time, the stakes being sobering in magnitude. As we have learned how to prevent premature death, including that of infants, the proportion of our citizens living to advanced age has increased and continues to increase to unprecedented levels. This demographic trend carries with it a probably inescapable increase in the proportion of individuals at risk for spending some part of their lives in a demented condition. Indeed, a huge segment of the population is already reeling from the catastrophic monetary and emotional costs of providing adequate care for aging family members who, otherwise reasonably healthy, have lost the mental wherewithal to maintain themselves independently. In the absence of dramatic advances in the prevention of these disorders, no relief is in sight. On the contrary, as was noted, the age group that will put maximum strain on "the system," the baby boomers who were born in the years following World War II, are already among us, moving inexorably toward their generation's maximum-risk period. The impact will be both huge and sustained, the last of this bulging cohort *entering* the risk period (at age 65) in approximately the year 2030.

Clearly then, we must learn how to prevent or effectively arrest these degenerative brain diseases—especially DAT, in terms of numbers affected and life expectancy after onset—within the next two decades or we will face staggering problems of resource development and allocation. Fortunately, as we have seen, a considerable research effort with a record of solid accomplishment is already underway in recognition of the growing problem of dementia. Unfortunately, the ultimate success of the effort is by no means guaranteed within any predictable time frame. Given this uncertainty, we would feel a lot more comfortable about the problem if we detected signs of minimal preparation and contingency planning among government officials, particularly at the federal level. We do not.

SUMMARY

The organic mental disorders are those in which mental symptoms of a neurologic or psychopathologic sort (such as cognitive deterioration and delusions, respectively) are presumed to appear as a result of interference with the functioning of the brain's "hardware," typically involving the destruction of brain tissue. Many of the organic disorders are in some primary sense physical diseases and are accordingly coded on Axis III of DSM-III-R. Exceptions are the senile and presenile dementias (such as Alzheimer's disease); these disorders are accorded Axis I status. The current DSM recognizes certain *organic brain syndromes* that form a basis for an Axis I psychiatric diagnosis where the precise organic etiology is unknown or is implied in an accompanying Axis III disease; they are delirium, dementia, amnestic syndrome, hallucinosis, organic delusional syndrome, organic mood syndrome, organic anxiety syndrome, and organic personality syndrome. These syndromes are conceived as the primary behavioral indicators for organic brain disease. Some of them mimic disorders in which no gross brain pathology can be demonstrated, which may present problems in diagnosis.

Organic mental disorders may be acute and transitory; in this case, brain functioning is only temporarily compromised. Chronic organic mental disorders, on which we have focused, involve the permanent loss of neural cells. Psychosocial interventions are often helpful in minimizing psychopathologic reactions in the chronically disordered, although these people will remain neurologically disabled.

The primary causes of brain tissue destruction are many and varied; common ones include certain infectious diseases (such as the HIV virus), brain tumors, physical trauma, degenerative processes (as in Alzheimer's disease), and cerebrovascular arteriosclerosis, often manifested as multi-infarct dementia. The correlation between neurologic brain impairment and psychiatric disorder, however, is not an especially strong one: some people who have severe damage develop no severe mental symptoms, while others with slight damage have extreme reactions. Although such inconsistencies are not completely understood, it appears that an individual's premorbid personality and life situation are also important in determining his or her reactions to brain damage.

Elderly people are at particular risk for the development of chronic organic mental disorders, especially those related to brain degeneration caused by Alzheimer's disease. As at younger ages, the reaction to brain damage is determined by many nonbiological factors. With disproportionate increases in the numbers of elderly people in the population, and the upcoming wave of baby boomers who will become at risk beginning early in the twenty-first century, we face staggering social, emotional, and economic problems unless some way can be found to prevent or effectively treat Alzheimer's disease.

Key Terms

organic mental disorders (p. 478)
neuropsychological disorders (p. 478)
syndrome (p. 482)
delirium (p. 483)
dementia (p. 483)
amnestic syndrome (p. 484)
hallucinosis (p. 485)
organic delusional syndrome (p. 485)
organic mood syndrome (p. 485)
organic anxiety syndrome (p. 485)
organic personality syndrome (p. 485)
AIDS dementia complex (ADC) (p. 486)
AIDS-related complex (ARC) (p. 487)
senile dementias (p. 493)
presenile dementias (p. 493)
Alzheimer's disease (p. 493)
multi-infarct dementia (MID) (p. 500)

Chapter 14

Mental Retardation and Developmental Disorders

Simone Marye, *Personnage, Chien, et Oiseaux.* Marye (1890–1961) had a successful, if rather conventional, career as a sculptress in the 1920s. Her popularity did not last long, however, and she was dogged by poverty, poor health, and loneliness throughout her last 30 years. She was institutionalized at age 67 with the diagnosis of Alzheimer's disease. Marye drew this strangely proportioned, childlike design while hospitalized; by this time, she was almost totally out of touch with reality, retaining little but a professed devotion to Buddhism.

We begin here a two-chapter sequence on behavior disorders that usually make their first appearance in infancy, childhood, or adolescence. The present chapter focuses on developmental disorders, those childhood disorders that—like adult personality disorders—are currently coded on Axis II of the DSM-III-R. The following chapter (15) will discuss other common disorders of the early years that are considered Axis I disorders.

Various aspects of the distinction just noted have been and remain somewhat controversial, as we will see, and in fact the distinction itself is definitionally somewhat awkward and unclear. A **developmental disorder** can be defined as a problem that is somehow rooted in deviations in the developmental process itself, thus disrupting the acquisition of skills and adaptive behavior and often interfering with the transition to well-functioning adulthood. In general, neurological defects or dysfunctions are tacitly assumed to underlie these developmental anomalies (Kessler, 1988). However, with rare exceptions, such as organically based mental retardation, this assumption is also an issue of sometimes intense controversy.

In fact the entire matter of the classification of disorders appearing in childhood is controversial (Carson, 1990a). We will discuss this issue further in Chapter 15, by which point you will have gained a better appreciation of the problems needing attention. For now, we will concentrate on describing some particular types of early appearing disorders that are considered "developmental" and therefore Axis II in nature. These include mental retardation, the "pervasive developmental disorder" known as early infantile autism, and certain "specific developmental disorders" that involve persistent but circumscribed skill deficits, especially of an academic sort. We begin with mental retardation.

MENTAL RETARDATION

The American Association on Mental Deficiency (AAMD) has defined **mental retardation** as "significantly subaverage general intellectual functioning existing concurrently with deficits in adaptive behavior, and manifested during the developmental period" (AAMD, 1973, p. 11). Mental retardation is thus defined in terms of *level of behavioral performance*. The definition says nothing about causal factors—which may be primarily biological, psychosocial, sociocultural, or a combination of these.

The American Psychiatric Association has adopted the same definitional approach for its latest classification, DSM-III-R, listing mental retardation as an Axis II developmental disorder beginning before the age of 18. By definition, any functional equivalent of mental retardation that has its onset after age 17 must be considered a dementia rather than mental retardation. The distinction is an important one, because, as was pointed out in the previous chapter, the psychological situation of an individual who acquires a pronounced impairment of intellectual functioning after attaining maturity is vastly different from that of an individual whose intellectual resources were subnormal throughout all or most of his or her development. Some of the more important differences will become apparent in what follows.

Mental retardation is considered to be a specific disorder, but it may occur in combination with other disorders. In fact other psychiatric disorders, especially psychoses (Jacobson, 1990), occur at a markedly higher rate among retarded individuals than in the general population.

Mental retardation occurs among children throughout the world. In its most severe forms, it is a source of great hardship to parents as well as an economic and social burden on a community. The incidence of mental retardation in the United States is estimated to be about seven million people (see *HIGHLIGHT 14.1*). This figure is based on a cutoff point of about IQ 70, which is the cutoff point used by the AAMD. Most states have laws providing that individuals with IQs below 70 who show socially incompetent or disapproved behavior can be classified as mentally retarded and committed to an institution.

The incidence of mental retardation seems to increase markedly at ages 5 to 6, to peak at age 15, and to drop off sharply after that. For the most part, these changes in incidence reflect changes in life demands. During early childhood, individuals with only a mild degree of intellectual impairment, who constitute the vast majority of the mentally retarded, often appear to be relatively normal. Their subaverage intellectual functioning becomes apparent only when difficulties with schoolwork lead to a diagnostic evaluation. When adequate facilities are available for their education, children in this group can usually master essential school skills and achieve a satisfactory level of socially adaptive behavior (see *HIGHLIGHT 14.2*). Following the school years, they usually make a more or less acceptable adjustment in the community and thus lose the identity of being mentally retarded.

Levels of Mental Retardation

It is important to remind ourselves once again that any classification system in the behavioral field will have strong features of both arbitrariness and pragmatism. In mental retardation, attempts to define varying levels of impairment have tended to rely increasingly on measurement—largely by means of standardized intelligence (IQ) tests (Robinson & Robinson, 1976). In the previously quoted AAMD definition, for example, the phrase "significantly subnormal general intellectual functioning" translates directly and officially into an IQ test score that is more than two standard deviations below the population mean. That mean, which represents the average test performance for children of a given age, is 100. The standard deviation of most IQ tests is about 15 points, and approximately two-thirds of the population score between plus and minus one standard deviation unit from the mean, that is, between 85 and 115. Thus a score of two standard deviations below the mean would be an IQ of approximately 70. About 2.5 percent of the population score in this range.

It is not improper to define mental retardation in this way, provided we keep in mind the implications of the definition. The original IQ tests were devised for the explicit purpose of predicting academic achievement among schoolchildren. Other IQ tests developed later were also validated largely on school performance and on the basis of how well they could predict scores on the original tests. Generally, then, what IQ tests measure is an individual's likely level of success in dealing with conventional academic materials, and in fact they do this very well when properly utilized. Thus when we speak of varying *levels* of mental retardation, we are to a great extent speaking of levels of ability to succeed at schoolwork.

Of course, this reliance on IQ scores is tempered somewhat by the other main part of the definition—the presence of concurrent "deficits in adaptive behavior." That is, the diagnosis of mental retardation is reserved for individuals who achieve low IQ test scores *and* demonstrate adaptational deficiencies, particularly in the areas of personal independence and social responsibility. The same dual criteria are involved in the officially recognized "levels" of retardation, although the IQ score often tends in practice to be the dominant consideration. This emphasis on the IQ score is reasonable at the lower end of the scale, because an individual with an

HIGHLIGHT 14.1

The Incidence of Mental Retardation in the United States

Level of Retardation	Approximate Incidence
Mild (IQ 50–70)	6,332,100
Moderate and severe (IQ 20–49)	420,000
Profound (IQ 0–19)	105,000

Adapted from Robinson and Robinson (1976, p. 37).

IQ of 50 or below will inevitably exhibit gross deficiencies in overall adaptive behavior as well. At the higher ranges of "retarded" IQ scores, however, behavioral adaptiveness and IQ score seem to be at least partially independent of one another.

Both the American Association on Mental Deficiency and the American Psychiatric Association classifications recognized four levels of retarded mental development, as follows:

1. *Mild mental retardation (IQ 52–67).* As shown in *HIGHLIGHT 14.1*, mildly retarded individuals constitute by far the largest number of those labeled mentally retarded. People in this group are considered ***educable***, and their intellectual levels as adults are comparable with those of average 8- to 11-year-old children. Statements such as the latter, however, should not be taken too literally. A mildly retarded adult with a "mental age" of, say, 10 (that is, intelligence test performance is at the level of the average 10-year-old) may not in fact be comparable to the normal 10-year-old in information-processing ability (Weiss, Weisz, & Bromfield, 1986)—although some investigators (e.g., Hore & Tryon, 1989) dispute the notion of a basic difference in purely intellectual functioning.

In any event, the social adjustment of such people often approximates that of adolescents, although they tend to lack normal adolescents' imagination, inventiveness, and judgment. Ordinarily, they do not show signs of brain pathology or other physical anomalies, but often they require some measure of supervision because of their limited abilities to foresee the consequences of their actions. In fact, individuals at a somewhat higher, "borderline" IQ level (68–84) may also need special services to maximize their potentials (Zetlin & Murtaugh, 1990). With early diagnosis, parental assistance, and special educational programs, the great majority of borderline and mildly retarded individuals can adjust socially, master simple academic and occupational skills, and become self-supporting citizens (Schalock, Harper, & Carver, 1981).

2. *Moderate mental retardation (IQ 36–51).* Moderately retarded individuals are likely to fall in the educational category of ***trainable***, which means that they are presumed able to master certain routine skills, such as cooking or minor janitorial work, if provided specialized instruction in these activities. In adult life, individuals classified as moderately retarded attain intellectual levels similar to those of average 4- to 7-year-old children. Although some can be taught to read and write a little and may manage to achieve a fair command of spoken lan-

Mildly retarded individuals constitute the largest number of those labeled mentally retarded. With help, a great majority of these individuals can adjust socially, master simple academic and occupational skills, and become self-supporting citizens.

HIGHLIGHT 14.2

Difficulties of Mentally Retarded People in Learning Basic Academic Skills

The basic learning processes of most mentally retarded children—aside from a minority with serious neurological defects—are not essentially different from those of normal children. Retarded children, however, learn at a slower rate than normal children and are less capable of mastering abstractions and complex concepts. These limitations are especially apparent in learning language and other skills requiring a high level of ability with symbols. The problems that retarded children typically encounter in learning basic academic skills may be summarized as follows:

1. *Difficulty in focusing attention.* Studies have shown that such children's poor learning is often due to the fact that their attention is focused on irrelevant aspects of learning situations. Once they know what stimulus dimensions are important—for example, attending to form because each letter's shape is important in learning the alphabet—they may quickly master appropriate discrimination skills and show marked improvement in performance and learning.

2. *Deficiency in past learning.* Most formal learning requires prior learning. For example, a child who has not learned basic verbal, conceptual, and problem-solving skills will fall farther behind when he or she begins schooling. Thus a number of programs have been established to help disadvantaged children of preschool age develop basic skills requisite for learning in school.

3. *Expectancy of failure—a self-fulfilling prophecy.* Because of having experienced more failure in learning attempts than other children, a mentally retarded child tends to begin tasks with a greater expectancy of failure and to engage in avoidance behavior as well. Often such children feel that forces beyond their control determine the outcome of their actions. Thus, if they succeed in a task, they may not perceive their success as due to their own efforts or abilities. They become passive, lose their initiative, and begin to rely too much on others. To counteract this tendency, learning experiences must be programmed into manageable components that can yield continuing experiences of success.

Special education classes should thus be directed at helping mentally retarded children discriminate relevant from irrelevant stimuli in learning and problem-solving situations; they should associate new learning with the children's present information, needs, and life situations; and they should structure learning tasks in a sequence of steps that can be readily mastered by the retarded and so provide experiences of success. Such measures, of course, are useful in all educational settings, but are particularly important in training mentally retarded children.

Based on Bijou (1966), Hagan and Huntsman (1971), Hyatt and Rolnick (1974), Karnes et al. (1970), Macmillan and Keogh (1971), Tarver and Hallahan (1974), and Robinson and Robinson (1976).

guage, their rate of learning is relatively slow, and their level of conceptualizing extremely limited. Physically, they usually appear clumsy and ungainly, and they suffer from bodily deformities and poor motor coordination. Some of these children are hostile and aggressive; more typically they present an affable and somewhat vacuous personality picture. In general, with early diagnosis, parental help, and adequate opportunities for training, most moderately retarded individuals can achieve partial independence in daily self-care, acceptable behavior, and economic usefulness in a family or other sheltered environment. Whether they require institutionalization usually depends on their general level of adaptive behavior and the nature of their home situation.

3. *Severe mental retardation (IQ 20–35).* Severely retarded individuals are sometimes referred to as ***dependent retarded.*** Among these individuals, motor and speech development are severely retarded, and sensory defects and motor handicaps are common. They can develop limited levels of personal hygiene and self-help skills, which somewhat lessen their dependence, but they are always dependent on others for care, thus usually requiring institutionali-

zation. However, many profit to some extent from training and can perform simple occupational tasks under supervision.

4. *Profound Mental Retardation (IQ under 20).* The term ***life support retarded*** is sometimes used to refer to profoundly retarded individuals. Most of these people are severely deficient in adaptive behavior and unable to master any but the simplest tasks. Useful speech, if it develops at all, is rudimentary. Severe physical deformities, central nervous system pathology, and retarded growth are typical; convulsive seizures, mutism, deafness, and other physical anomalies are also common. These individuals must remain in custodial care all their lives. They tend, however, to have poor health and low resistance to disease and thus a short life expectancy.

Severe and profound cases of mental retardation can usually be readily diagnosed in infancy because of the presence of obvious physical malformations, grossly delayed habit training, and other obvious symptoms of abnormality. Although these individuals show a marked impairment of overall intellectual functioning, they may have considerably more ability in some areas than in others.

Indeed, in occasional cases, moderately retarded people may show an extraordinarily high level of skill in some specific aspect of behavior that does not depend on abstract reasoning; the French term ***idiot savant*** (learned idiot) is sometimes used to refer to these individuals. Thus, one seriously retarded individual was able to remember the serial number on every dollar bill he was shown or had ever seen; another was able to tell the day of the week of a given date in any year, without resorting to paper and pencil or even to making other numerical calculations. In other exceptional cases, a retarded person may show considerable talent in art or music. Viscott (1970) provided a detailed case study of a "musical idiot savant"; Hill (1975) cited the case of a mildly retarded individual with an IQ of 54 who could play 11 different musical instruments by ear and possessed outstanding skill in calculating dates. Similarly, Morishima (1975) cited the case of a famous Japanese painter whose assessed IQ was 47. Such unusual abilities among the retarded are rare, however.

Contrary to common understanding, the distribution of IQ scores in the United States does not precisely fit "normal curve" expectations, especially at the lower IQ ranges. These ranges tend to show a frequency bulge, with about 200,000 more cases than are expected (Robinson & Robinson, 1976). This finding suggests the operation of an intruding factor that tends to inflate beyond normal-curve expectancy the numbers of cases at lower IQ ranges —probably the presence of major genetic abnormalities, brain injuries, or both that are not characteristic of mild retardation. The next section addresses these factors.

Organic Factors in Mental Retardation

Some instances of mental retardation—something on the order of 25 percent of the cases—occur with known organic brain pathology. In these cases, retardation is virtually always at least moderate, and it is often severe. Profound retardation, fortunately rare, always includes obvious organic impairment. Organically caused retardation is in essential respects similar to dementia as described in Chapter 13, except for a different history of prior functioning. In fact, in the past, a young person with organically caused retardation was referred to as ***amented,*** as distinct from a ***demented*** person.

In this section we will consider five biological conditions that may lead to mental retardation, noting some of the possible interrelations between them. Then we will review some of the major clinical types of mental retardation associated with these organic causes.

Genetic-Chromosomal Factors Mental retardation tends to run in families. This tendency is particularly true of mild retardation. Poverty and sociocultural deprivation, however, also tend to run in families, and with early and continued exposure to such conditions, even the inheritance of average intellectual potential may not prevent subaverage intellectual functioning.

As we noted in Chapter 4, genetic and chromosomal factors play a much clearer role in the etiology of relatively rare types of mental retardation, such as Down syndrome or a condition known as ***Fragile X,*** a constriction or breaking off of the end portion of the long arm of the X sex chromosome. In such conditions specific chromosomal defects are responsible for metabolic alterations that adversely affect the brain's development. Genetic defects leading to metabolic alterations may, of course, involve many other developmental anomalies besides mental retardation. In general, the mental retardation most often associated with known genetic-chromosomal defects, that of Down syndrome, is moderate to severe in degree.

Infections and Toxic Agents Mental retardation may be associated with a wide range of conditions due to infection. If a pregnant woman has syphilis or gets German measles, her child may suffer brain damage. Brain damage may also result from infections occurring after birth, such as viral encephalitis.

A number of toxic agents, such as carbon monoxide and lead, may cause brain damage during fetal development or after birth. In some instances, immunological agents, such as antitetanus serum or typhoid vaccine, may lead to brain damage. Similarly, certain drugs, including an excess of alcohol, taken by a pregnant woman may lead to congenital malformations; an overdose of drugs administered to an infant may result in toxicity and brain damage. In rare cases, brain damage results from incompatibility in blood types between mother and fetus—conditions known as Rh, or ABO, system incompatibility. Fortunately, early diagnosis and blood transfusions can now minimize the effects of such incompatibility.

Prematurity and Trauma (Physical Injury)

Follow-up studies of children born prematurely and weighing less than about 5 pounds at birth have revealed a high incidence of neurological disorders and often mental retardation. In fact, small premature babies are many times more likely to be mentally retarded than normal-size infants (MacDonald, 1964).

Physical injury at birth can also result in retardation. Isaacson (1970) has estimated that in 1 birth out of 1000 brain damage occurs that will prevent the child from reaching the intelligence level of an average 12-year-old. Although the fetus is normally well protected by its fluid-filled bag during gestation, and its skull appears designed to resist delivery stressors, accidents do happen during delivery and after birth. Difficulties in labor due to malposition of the fetus or other complications may irreparably damage the infant's brain. Bleeding within the brain is probably the most common result of such birth trauma. *Hypoxia*—lack of sufficient oxygen to the brain stemming from delayed breathing or other causes—is another type of birth trauma that may damage the brain. Hypoxia may also occur after birth as a result of cardiac arrest associated with operations, heart attacks, near drownings, or severe electrical shocks.

Ionizing Radiation In recent years a good deal of scientific attention has been focused on the damaging effects of ionizing radiation on sex cells and other bodily cells and tissues. Radiation may act directly on the fertilized ovum or may produce gene mutations in the sex cells of either or both parents, which, in turn, may lead to defective offspring.

Sources of harmful radiation were once limited primarily to high-energy X rays used for diagnosis and therapy, but the list has grown to include nuclear weapons testing and leakages at nuclear power plants, among others.

Malnutrition and Other Biological Factors

As we noted in Chapter 4, deficiencies in protein and other essential nutrients during early development can result in irreversible physical and mental damage. Protein deficiencies in a mother's diet during pregnancy, as well as in a baby's diet after birth, have been pinpointed as particularly potent causes of lowered intelligence.

A limited number of cases of mental retardation are also associated with other biological agents, such as brain tumors, that either damage the brain tissue directly or lead to increased cranial pressure and concomitant brain damage. In some instances of mental retardation—particularly of the severe and profound types—the causes are uncertain or unknown, although extensive brain pathology is evident.

Organic Retardation Syndromes

Mental retardation stemming primarily from biological causes can be classified into several recognizable clinical types, of which four will be discussed here. *HIGHLIGHT 14.3* presents information on several other well-known forms.

Down Syndrome First described by Langdon Down in 1866, **Down syndrome** is the most common of the clinical conditions associated with moderate and severe mental retardation. About 1 in every 600 babies born in the United States is diagnosed as having Down syndrome, a condition that "has life-long implications for physical appearance, intellectual achievement and general functioning" (Golden & Davis, 1974, p. 7). The availability of *amniocentesis* with elective abortion should the fetus prove chromosomally defective, while helpful for individual families, appears not to have affected substantially the overall incidence of the disorder. Because of demographic shifts, the majority of Down syndrome infants in recent decades were born to mothers under 35 years of age, not a group for whom amniocentesis is routinely recommended (Evans & Hamerton, 1985).

A number of physical features are often found among children with Down syndrome, but few of these children have all of the characteristics commonly thought of as typifying this group. In such children, the eyes appear almond-shaped, and the skin of the eyelids tends to be abnormally thick. The face and nose are often flat and broad, as is the back

HIGHLIGHT 14.3

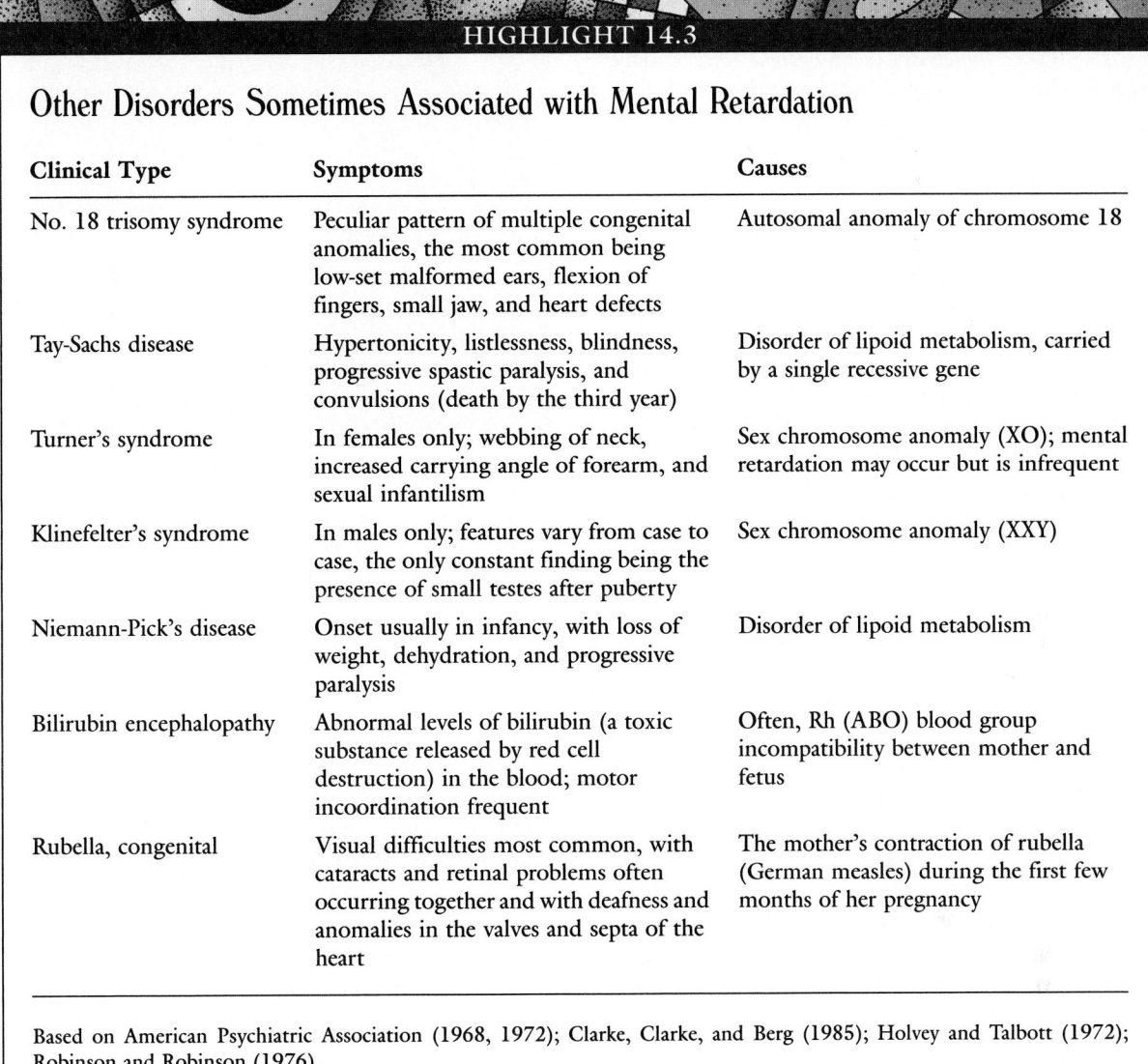

Other Disorders Sometimes Associated with Mental Retardation

Clinical Type	Symptoms	Causes
No. 18 trisomy syndrome	Peculiar pattern of multiple congenital anomalies, the most common being low-set malformed ears, flexion of fingers, small jaw, and heart defects	Autosomal anomaly of chromosome 18
Tay-Sachs disease	Hypertonicity, listlessness, blindness, progressive spastic paralysis, and convulsions (death by the third year)	Disorder of lipoid metabolism, carried by a single recessive gene
Turner's syndrome	In females only; webbing of neck, increased carrying angle of forearm, and sexual infantilism	Sex chromosome anomaly (XO); mental retardation may occur but is infrequent
Klinefelter's syndrome	In males only; features vary from case to case, the only constant finding being the presence of small testes after puberty	Sex chromosome anomaly (XXY)
Niemann-Pick's disease	Onset usually in infancy, with loss of weight, dehydration, and progressive paralysis	Disorder of lipoid metabolism
Bilirubin encephalopathy	Abnormal levels of bilirubin (a toxic substance released by red cell destruction) in the blood; motor incoordination frequent	Often, Rh (ABO) blood group incompatibility between mother and fetus
Rubella, congenital	Visual difficulties most common, with cataracts and retinal problems often occurring together and with deafness and anomalies in the valves and septa of the heart	The mother's contraction of rubella (German measles) during the first few months of her pregnancy

Based on American Psychiatric Association (1968, 1972); Clarke, Clarke, and Berg (1985); Holvey and Talbott (1972); Robinson and Robinson (1976).

of the head. The tongue, which seems too large for the mouth, may show deep fissures. The iris of the eye is frequently speckled. The neck is often short and broad, as are the hands, which tend to have creases across the palms. The fingers are stubby, and the little finger is often more noticeably curved than the other fingers. Although facial surgery is sometimes tried to correct the more stigmatizing features, its success is often limited (Dodd & Leahy, 1989; Katz & Kravetz, 1989).

Well over 50 percent of people with Down syndrome have cataracts, which are not congenital but tend to make their appearance when a child is about 7 or 8 (Falls, 1970). These cataracts aid in diagnosis, but fortunately they rarely become serious enough to warrant surgery. Interestingly, there appears to be little, if any, correlation between the number of physical symptoms and the degree of mental retardation in individuals with Down syndrome.

Death rates for children with Down syndrome have decreased dramatically in the past half century. In 1919, the life expectancy at birth for such children was about nine years; most of the deaths were due to gross physical anomalies, and a large proportion occurred in the first year. Today, thanks to antibiotics, surgical correction of lethal anatomical defects, and better general medical care, many more of these children are living to adulthood (Smith & Berg, 1976). In fact, overall, the mortality rate for this group is only 6 percent higher than that for the general population, though this figure remains higher in the early years and for those who live beyond 40 (Forseman & Akesson, 1965). At present, the average life expectancy for Down syndrome children at birth is about 16 years; by age 1, it increases to about 22 years (Smith & Berg, 1976).

The terms *mongolism* or *mongoloid* were widely used in the past because the almond-shaped eyes were thought to give Down syndrome children facial features similar to those of the Mongolian race. At times, the term *mongolian idiot* was also used. These terms are no longer acceptable, however, because they contain negative racial connotations. In addition, the term "idiot" is inappropriate both in itself and because most afflicted children show only moderate mental retardation.

Despite their limitations, children suffering from Down syndrome are usually able to learn self-help skills, acceptable social behavior, and routine manual skills that enable them to be of assistance in a family or institutional setting. The traditional view has been that Down syndrome youngsters are unusually placid and affectionate. Research has questioned the validity of this generalization. These children may indeed be very tractable, but probably in no greater proportion than normal youngsters; they may also be equally (or more) difficult in various areas (Bridges & Cicchetti, 1982). In general, the adequacy of a child's social relationships is positively correlated with both IQ level and a supportive home environment (Sloper et al., 1990).

Research has also suggested that the intellectual defect in Down syndrome may not be consistent across various abilities. Down syndrome children tend to remain relatively unimpaired in their appreciation of spatial relationships and in visual-motor coordination; they show their greatest deficits in verbal and language-related skills (Mahoney, Glover, & Finger, 1981; Silverstein et al., 1982). Inasmuch as spatial functions are known to be partially localized in the right cerebral hemisphere, and language-related functions in the left cerebral hemisphere, some investigators speculate that the syndrome is especially crippling to the left hemisphere.

Traditionally, the cause of Down syndrome was assumed to be faulty heredity. A number of early studies demonstrated, however, that more than a single case of Down syndrome in a family was unlikely, occurring in less than 1 family in 100 of those already affected. As a consequence of this finding, investigators turned to the study of metabolic factors and concluded that Down syndrome was probably due to some sort of glandular imbalance. Then, in 1959, the French scientists Lejeune, Turpin, and Gauthier found 47 chromosomes, instead of the usual 46, in several Down syndrome cases. A trisomy of chromosome 21 (an error of zygosis in which chromosome 21 is represented in triplicate rather than the normal pair) has now been identified as a characteristic of Down syndrome children, being present in at least 94 percent of cases meeting strict Down syndrome criteria. As was noted in Chapter 13 (see page 498), it is possibly significant that this is the same chromosome that has been implicated in recent research on Alzheimer's disease, especially in light of the fact that surviving victims of Down syndrome are at extremely high risk for Alzheimer's as they get into and beyond their late 30s (Bauer & Shea, 1986; Reid, 1985).

Today many more Down syndrome children than in the past are living to adulthood and are able to learn self-help, social, and manual skills. It is not unusual for Down syndrome children to be mainstreamed to some extent with unimpaired children, such as this girl in a ballet class. Down syndrome children tend to remain relatively unimpaired in their appreciation of spatial relationships and visual-motor coordination; they show their greatest deficits in verbal and language-related skills.

Researchers have long believed that the "extra" chromosome in Down syndrome is in some way contributed by the mother. In 1973, however, it was learned that in certain instances it is in fact contributed by the father (Sasaki & Hara, 1973; Uchida, 1973). The reason for the trisomy of chromosome 21 is not clear, but the anomaly seems definitely related to parental age at conception.

It has been known for many years that the incidence of Down syndrome increases in regular fashion with the age of the mother. A woman in her 20s has about 1 chance in 2000 of conceiving a Down syndrome baby, whereas the risk for a woman in her 40s is 1 in 50 (Holvey & Talbot, 1972). As in the case of all birth defects, the risk of having a Down syndrome baby is high for young mothers whose reproductive systems have not yet fully matured. The advanced maternal age correlation led naturally to the inference that an older woman's capacity to produce a chromosomally normal fetus was somehow impaired by the aging process. This observed effect obscured for many years a possible male contribution; older men tend, of course, to have older women partners.

More recent research has strongly indicated that the father's age at conception is also implicated in the occurrence of Down syndrome, particularly at higher ages (Hook, 1980; Stene et al., 1981). In one study involving 1279 cases of Down syndrome in Japan, Matsunaga and associates (1978) demonstrated an overall increase in incidence with advancing paternal age when maternal age was controlled. The risk for fathers aged 55 years and over was more than twice that for fathers in their early 20s. Curiously, these investigators noted that, in their sample, fathers in their early 40s had a lower risk factor than slightly younger as well as older men.

Thus it seems that advancing age in either parent increases the risk of the trisomy 21 anomaly, although the maternal age effect is the larger one. As yet we do not understand how aging produces this effect. A reasonable guess is that aging is related to cumulative exposure to varied environmental hazards, such as radiation, that might have adverse effects on the processes involved in zygote formation or development.

Whatever the cause of the chromosomal anomaly, the end result is the growth-process distortion characteristic of this syndrome. There is no known effective treatment. When parents have had a child with Down syndrome, they are usually quite concerned about having further children. In such cases, genetic counseling may provide some indication of the risk—which may be quite small—of abnormality in additional children. In recent years, amniocentesis, when used, has made it possible to diagnose most cases of Down's syndrome in utero, thus permitting parents to make a rational (although usually not easy) choice concerning termination of the pregnancy if the fetus is abnormal.

Phenylketonuria (PKU) A rare metabolic disorder, **phenylketonuria (PKU)** occurs in about 1 in 20,000 births. Retarded individuals in institutions who suffer from PKU number about 1 in 100 (Holmes et al., 1972; Schild, 1972).

In PKU, a baby appears normal at birth but lacks a liver enzyme needed to break down phenylalanine, an amino acid found in many foods. The genetic error manifests itself in pathology only when significant quantities of phenylalanine are ingested, something that is virtually certain to occur if the child's condition remains undiagnosed. If the condition is undetected, the amount of phenylalanine in the blood increases and eventually produces brain damage.

The disorder usually becomes apparent between 6 and 12 months after birth, although such symptoms as vomiting, a peculiar odor, infantile eczema, and seizures may occur during the early weeks of life. Often the first symptoms noticed are signs of mental retardation, which may be moderate to severe depending on the degree to which the disease has progressed. Motor incoordination and other neurological manifestations relating to the severity of brain damage are also common, and often the eyes, skin, and hair of untreated PKU patients are very pale.

PKU was identified in 1934 when a Norwegian mother sought to learn the reason for her child's mental retardation and peculiar musty odor. She consulted with many physicians to no avail until Dr. Asbjorn Folling found phenylpyruvic acid in the child's urine and concluded that the child had a disorder of phenylalanine metabolism (Centerwall & Centerwall, 1961).

Most older PKU patients show severe to profound mental retardation, with the median IQ of untreated phenylketonuric adults being about 20. Curiously, however, a number of PKU individuals have PKU relatives with less severely affected intelligence. In addition, Perry (1970) reported the cases of two untreated PKU patients with superior intelligence. These findings have made PKU something of an enigma. It results from a liver enzyme deficiency involving one or more recessive genes, and 1 person in 70 is thought to be a carrier. There may be varying degrees of PKU, however, or another genetic factor may lessen the destructive potential of the enzyme defect (Burns, 1972).

The early detection of PKU by examining urine for the presence of phenylpyruvic acid is now routine in developed countries, and dietary treatment (such as the elimination of phenyalanine-containing foods) and related procedures can be used to prevent the disorder. With early detection and treatment—preferably before an infant is 6 months old—the deterioration process can usually be arrested so that levels of intellectual functioning may range from borderline to normal. A few children suffer mental retardation despite restricted phenylalanine intake and other measures, however.

For a baby to inherit PKU, it appears that both parents must carry the recessive genes. Thus when one child in a family is discovered to have PKU, it is important that other children in the family be screened as well.

Cretinism (Thyroid Deficiency) Resulting from endocrine imbalance, **cretinism** produces a dramatic illustration of mental retardation. In this condition, the thyroid either has failed to develop properly or has undergone degeneration or injury; in either case, an infant suffers from a deficiency in thyroid secretion. Brain damage resulting from this insufficiency is most marked when the deficiency occurs during the prenatal and early postnatal periods of rapid growth.

In the valleys of central Switzerland and in other geographical areas where iodine is deficient in the soil (and therefore in the food grown in it), cretinism was once a common affliction. In such areas, infants often were born with defective thyroid glands that remained undeveloped or atrophied. Because in such areas cretinism was observed to run in families, it was thought to be a hereditary disorder. In 1891, however, Dr. George Murray published his discovery that the injection of thyroid gland extract was beneficial in cases of **myxedema**—a disorder resulting from thyroid deficiency in adult life and characterized by mental dullness. This discovery, in turn, led to the treatment of cretinism with thyroid gland extract and to the realization that this condition, too, was the result of thyroid deficiency.

Although most cases of cretinism result from lack of iodine in the diet, thyroid deficiency may also occur as a result of birth injuries (involving bleeding into the thyroid) or of infectious diseases such as measles, whooping cough, or diphtheria. Less frequently, it may be a result of a genetically determined enzyme defect. The resulting clinical picture depends on the age at which the thyroid deficiency occurs as well as on the degree and duration of the deficiency.

Typical descriptions of individuals with cretinism involve severe thyroid deficiency from an early age, often even before birth. Such an individual has a dwarflike, thick-set body and short, stubby extremities. Height is usually just a little over three feet, the shortness accentuated by slightly bent legs and a curvature of the spine. The individual walks with a shuffling gait that is easily recognizable and has a large head with abundant black, wiry hair. Thick eyelids give the person a sleepy appearance, and the skin is dry, thickened, and cold to the touch. Other pronounced physical symptoms include a broad, flat nose, large and floppy ears, a protruding abdomen, and a failure to mature sexually. The sufferer reveals a bland personality and sluggish thought processes. Most individuals with cretinism fall within the moderate and severe categories of mental retardation, depending on the extent of brain damage. In cases with less pronounced physical signs of cretinism, the degree of mental retardation is usually less severe.

Early treatment of cretinism with thyroid gland extract is considered essential; infants not treated until after the first year of life may have permanently impaired intelligence. In long-standing cases, thyroid treatment may have some ameliorating effects, but the damage to an individual's nervous system and general physical development is beyond repair.

Public health measures on both the national and international levels have concentrated on the use of iodized salt and the early detection and correction of thyroid deficiency. As a result, severe cases of cretinism have become practically nonexistent in the United States and in most, but not all, other countries.

Cranial Anomalies Mental retardation is associated with a number of conditions that involve relatively gross alterations in head size and shape and for which the causal factors have not been definitely established (Wortis, 1973). In **macrocephaly** (large-headedness), for example, there is an increase in the size and weight of the brain, an enlargement of the skull, visual impairment, convulsions, and other neurological symptoms, resulting from the abnormal growth of glia cells that form the supporting structure for brain tissue. Other cranial anomalies include *microcephaly* and *hydrocephalus,* which we will discuss in more detail.

Microcephaly. The term **microcephaly** means "small-headedness." It refers to a type of mental retardation resulting from impaired development of the brain and a consequent failure of the cranium to attain normal size. In an early study of postmortem examinations of microcephalic individual's brains, Greenfield and Wolfson (1935) reported that practically all cases examined showed development to have been arrested at the fourth or fifth month of fetal life. Fortunately, this condition is extremely rare.

The most obvious characteristic of microcephaly is the small head, the circumference of which rarely exceeds 17 inches, as compared with the normal size of approximately 22 inches. Penrose (1963) also described microcephalic youngsters as being invariably short in stature but having relatively normal musculature and sex organs. Beyond these characteristics, they differ considerably from one another in appearance, although there is a tendency for the skull to be cone-shaped, with a receding chin and forehead. Microcephalic children fall within the moderate, severe, and profound categories of mental retardation, but the majority show little language development and are extremely limited in mental capacity.

Microcephaly may result from a wide range of factors that impair brain development, including intrauterine infections and pelvic irradiation during the mother's early months of pregnancy (Koch, 1967). Miller (1970) noted a number of cases of microcephaly in Hiroshima and Nagasaki that apparently resulted from the atomic bomb explosions during World War II. The role of genetic factors is not as yet clear. Treatment is ineffective once faulty development has occurred; at present, preventive measures focus on the avoidance of infection and radiation during pregnancy.

Hydrocephalus. **Hydrocephalus** is a relatively rare condition in which the accumulation of an abnormal amount of cerebrospinal fluid within the cranium causes damage to the brain tissues and enlargement of the skull.

In congenital cases of hydrocephalus, the head is either already enlarged at birth or begins to enlarge soon thereafter, presumably as a result of a disturbance in the formation, absorption, or circulation of the cerebrospinal fluid (Wortis, 1973). The disorder can also develop in infancy or early childhood, following the development of a brain tumor, subdural hematoma, meningitis, or other such conditions. In these cases the condition appears to result from a blockage of the cerebrospinal pathways and an accumulation of fluid in certain brain areas.

The clinical picture in hydrocephalus depends on the extent of neural damage, which, in turn, depends on the age at onset and the duration and severity of the disorder. In chronic cases, the chief symptom is the gradual enlargement of the upper part of the head out of all proportion to the face and the rest of the body. While the expansion of the skull helps minimize destructive pressure on the brain, serious brain damage occurs nonetheless. This damage leads to intellectual impairment and such other effects as convulsions and impairment or loss of sight and hearing. The degree of intellectual impairment varies, being severe or profound in advanced cases.

A good deal of attention has been directed to the surgical treatment of hydrocephalus. With early diagnosis and treatment, this condition can usually be arrested before severe brain damage has occurred (Geisz & Steinhausen, 1974).

Mental Retardation and Sociocultural Deprivation

Investigators formerly believed that all mental retardation was the result of faulty genes or of other causes of brain impairment. In recent years, however, it has become apparent that adverse sociocultural conditions, particularly those involving a deprivation of normal environmental stimulation, may play a primary role in the etiology of mental retardation.

Two subtypes of mental retardation fall in this general category: (a) mental retardation associated with extreme sensory and social deprivation, such as prolonged isolation during the developmental years, as may have happened in the case of the wild boy of Aveyron, discussed in *HIGHLIGHT 14.4*; and (b) **cultural-familial retardation,** in which a child is not subjected to extreme isolation but rather suffers from an inferior quality of interaction with the cultural environment and with other people. Because such sociocultural impoverishment may be associated with genetic deficiency in some cases, a child born to a family in such circumstances may be doubly jeopardized. In any event, it has proven all but impossible to assess adequately the differential influences of nature and nurture in these cases. The field is rife with controversy.

Because the great majority of all retarded individuals are of the cultural-familial type, our discussion will focus on this form of retardation.

Consider the following table depicting the average IQs of 586 Milwaukee children in differing age ranges. The children were separated according to whether or not the IQs of their mothers, all of whom dwelt in slum areas under deprived circumstances, fell below 80.

Note that the two groups of children did not differ in IQ at ages 1 through 2 and that both scored within the normal range. The children whose moth-

TABLE 14.1 Average IQs of 586 Milwaukee Children

Maternal IQ	Age of Children in Months						
	13–35	36–59	60–83	84–107	108–131	132–167	168+
80+ (n=48)	95	93	90	94	87.5	94	90
<80 (n=40)	95	76	84	80	75	70	67.5

(Garber, 1988. Constructed from Figure 2–1, p. 23.)

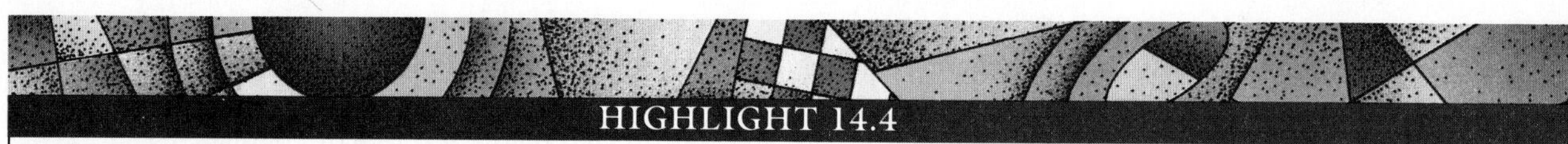

HIGHLIGHT 14.4

The "Wild Boy of Aveyron"

In 1800, long before the development of psychotherapy, Jean-Marc Itard attempted to inculcate normal human abilities in a "wild boy" who had been captured by peasants in the forests of Aveyron, France. The boy, who appeared to be between 10 and 12 years old, had been exhibited in a cage for about a year by his captors when Itard rescued him. By examining scars on the boy's body and by observing his personal habits, Itard concluded that he had been abandoned at the age of 2 or 3.

At first Victor (as Itard named the boy) seemed more animal than human. He was oblivious to other human beings, could not talk, and howled and ate off the ground on all fours like an animal. He evidenced unusual sensory reactions; for example, he did not react if a pistol was fired next to his ear, but he could hear the crack of a nut or the crackling of underbrush at a great distance. No adverse reaction seemed to result from his going unclothed even in freezing weather. In fact, Victor had velvety skin, despite his years of exposure.

Victor exhibited animal-like behavior in many ways. He had an obstinate habit of smelling any object that was given to him—even objects we consider void of smell. He knew nothing of love and perceived other human beings only as obstacles—in other words, he was like the wild animals he had known in the forest. Victor was typically indifferent and uncomplaining but, occasionally, he showed a kind of frantic rage and became dangerous to those around him. If he had any sense of self-identity, it was apparently more that of an animal than a human.

Philippe Pinel, Itard's instructor, diagnosed Victor's condition as congenital idiocy—concluding that the boy was incapable of profiting from training. Itard, however, although only 25 years old and inexperienced in comparison with Pinel, disagreed; in his view, Victor's savage behavior was the result of early and lengthy isolation from other humans. He believed that human contact and intensive training would enable the boy to become a normal person, and, ignoring Pinel's advice, he began his attempt to civilize "the wild boy of Aveyron."

No procedures had yet been formulated that Itard could use in treating Victor; thus he developed a program based on principles that included the following: (a) without contact with its own kind, a human infant—unlike a lower animal—cannot develop normally; (b) the instinct to imitate is the learning force by which our senses are educated, and this instinct is strongest in early childhood and decreases with age; and (c) in all human beings, from the

Based on Itard (1799; tr. Humphrey & Humphrey, 1932) and Silberstein and Irwin (1962).

ers had IQs of 80 or above continued to manifest average IQs in the normal range through age 14. However, children of mothers of IQ less than 80 showed, on average, a progressive (and, after age 5, nonreversing) decline with advancing age that approached the upper limits of the mental retardation range by age 14. Such a progressive loss is not easy to reconcile with a hereditary interpretation; it suggests, rather, the cumulative effects of a deficient environment, one well indexed by the mothers' IQ levels.

Garber (1988) in fact contends that the effect is due to the inadequacy of low IQ mothers in stimulating intellectual growth. Specifically, he maintains that the mothering person is normally responsible for creating the "microenvironment" determining a child's rate of cognitive development, and that a low maternal IQ—which is associated with verbal and other skill deficits—tends to foster an environment that is deficient in its provision of cognitively enriching experience. Although this conclusion is consistent with most available evidence, it would be tragic to convert such evidence to an assignment of blame against these overburdened and sometimes overwhelmed women. They need compassion and help, not blame, and when they get this help, the IQs of their children may be dramatically elevated (Garber, 1988; Ramey & Haskins, 1981).

Whatever the specific etiology, children whose retardation is cultural-familial in origin are usually only mildly retarded; however, they make up the majority of people labeled as mentally retarded. These children show no identifiable brain pathology and are usually not diagnosed as mentally retard-

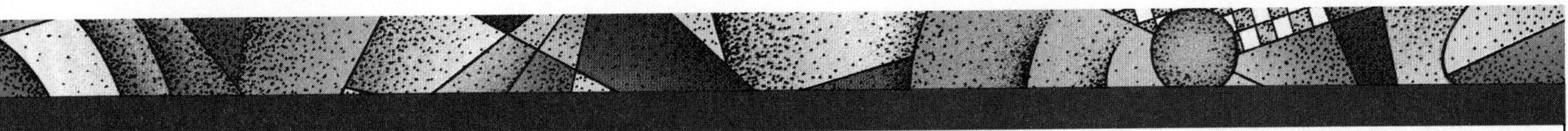

most isolated to the most educated, a constant relationship exists between needs and ideas—the greater the needs, the greater the development of mental capacities to meet them.

In attempting to train Victor, Itard developed methods that have had considerable impact on the subsequent treatment of children with serious learning disabilities. Instructional materials were provided to broaden Victor's discrimination skills in touch, smell, and other sensory modalities, appropriate to his environment; language training was begun through the association of words with the objects Victor wanted; and modeling and imitation were used to reinforce Victor's learning of desired social behaviors.

Initial results were indeed promising. Victor learned to speak a number of words and could write in chalk to express his wants. He also developed affectionate feelings toward his governess.

In June 1801, Itard reported to the Academy of Science in Paris on the rapid progress in the first nine months of training. In November 1806, however, he could only report that despite significant advances in several areas, Victor had not been made "normal" in the sense of becoming a self-directing and socially adjusted person. Being brought into the proximity of girls, for example, only upset the boy, leaving him restless and depressed, and Itard had to abandon his hope for a normal sexual response as a means of fostering Victor's motivation and socialization.

After devoting five and a half years to the task, Itard gave up the attempt to train "the wild boy of Aveyron." As for Victor, he lived to be 40, but never progressed appreciably beyond the achievements of that first year.

The story of Victor is of absorbing interest to both laypeople and scientists. A motion picture that portrays Itard's work with Victor—*The Wild Child*—was produced by François Truffaut. In scientific circles, the lack of conclusive answers will keep psychologists and others puzzling over the question of whether Victor was a congenital mental retardate, a brain-damaged individual, a psychotic, or simply a person who had been so deprived of human contact during early critical periods of development that the damage he had sustained could never be completely remedied.

ed until they enter school and have serious difficulties in their studies. As a large number of investigators have pointed out, most of these children come from economically deprived, unstable, and often disrupted family backgrounds characterized by a lack of intellectual stimulation, an inferior quality of interaction with others, and general environmental deprivation (e.g., Birns & Bridger, 1977; Braginsky & Braginsky, 1974; Feuerstein, 1977).

They are raised in homes with absent fathers and with physically or emotionally unavailable mothers. During infancy they are not exposed to the same quality and quantity of tactile and kinesthetic stimulations as other children. Often they are left unattended in a crib or on the floor of the dwelling. Although there are noises, odors, and colors in the environment, the stimuli are not as organized as those found in middle-class and upper-class environments. For example, the number of words they hear is limited, with sentences brief and most commands carrying a negative connotation. (Tarjan & Eisenberg, 1972, p. 16)

Since a child's current level of intellectual functioning is based largely on previous learning—and since schoolwork requires complex skills, such as being able to control one's attention, follow instructions, and recognize the meaning of a considerable range of words—these children are at a disadvantage from the beginning because they have not had an opportunity to learn requisite background skills or to be motivated toward learning.

Thus with each succeeding year, unless remedial measures are undertaken, they tend to fall farther behind in school performance. They also fall farther behind in relative ratings on intelligence tests, which, as we have seen, are measures of ability for schoolwork. A report by the American Psychological Association (1970) noted the following:

Mental retardation is primarily a psychosocial and psychoeducational problem—a deficit in adaptation to the demands and expectations of society evidenced by the individual's relative difficulty in learning, problem solving, adapting to new situations, and abstract thinking. (p. 267)

This statement was not intended to minimize the possible role of adverse biological factors, including genetic deficiencies, in the total causal pattern. Certainly many of these children reveal histories of prematurity, inadequate diets, and little or no medical care. In the great majority of cases of cultural-familial mental retardation, however, no neurological or physical dysfunction has been demonstrated. Thus, efforts to understand mild mental retardation have focused increasingly on the role of environmental factors in impeding intellectual growth. The likelihood that many of these factors will prove preventable or reversible has given rise to new but as yet still largely unrealized hopes for effective, widespread intervention, as will be seen.

The Problem of Assessment

Because mental retardation is defined in terms of both intellectual (academic) and social competence, it is essential to assess both of these characteristics before labeling a person as mentally retarded.

Unfortunately, neither of the preceding tasks is easy. Errors in IQ assessment can stem from a variety of sources, including (a) errors in administering tests; (b) the personal characteristics of a child, such as a language problem or lack of motivation to do well on tests; and (c) limitations in the tests themselves. The latter point has been succinctly stated by Wortis (1972):

An IQ score, at best, can indicate where an individual stands in intellectual performance compared to others. What others? His nation? His social class? His ethnic group? No intelligence test that has ever been devised can surmount all of these complicating considerations and claim universal validity. (p. 22)

Wortis's point has been widely accepted and echoed by other observers.

Although the assessment of social competence may seem less complicated, especially if it is based on clinical observations and ratings, it is subject to many of the same errors as the measurement of intelligence. The criteria used by the person or persons doing the assessing are of particular importance. For example, if children are well-adapted socially to life in an urban ghetto but not to the demands of a formal school setting, should they be evaluated as having a high, intermediate, or low level of social competence? Competence for what? Again, Wortis's conclusions concerning the assessment of intelligence appear to apply.

To label a child as mentally retarded—as significantly subaverage in intellectual and adaptive capability—is an act likely to have profound effects on both the child's self-concept and the reactions of others, and thus on his or her entire future life. Most immediately, it may lead to institutionalization or to poor upbringing by discouraged, demoralized parents (Richardson, Koller, & Katz, 1985). Over the long term, such a label may become a self-fulfilling prophecy fueled by the tendency to behave in ways consistent with one's self-concept and with others' expectations. Obviously it is a label that has profound ethical and social implications and should never be affixed to anyone without the most careful and considered judgment.

Treatments, Outcomes, and Prevention

A number of programs have demonstrated that significant changes in adaptive capacity are possible through special education and other rehabilitative measures. The degree of change that can be expected is related, of course, to an individual's particular situation and level of mental retardation.

Treatment Facilities and Methods One problem that often inflicts great anxiety on the parents of a mentally retarded child is whether or not to put their child in an institution. In general, the children who are institutionalized fall into two groups: (a) those who, in infancy and childhood, manifest severe mental retardation and associated physical impairment, and who enter an institution at an early age; and (b) those who have no physical impairments but show mild mental retardation and a failure to adjust socially in adolescence, eventually being institutionalized chiefly because of delinquency or other problem behavior. In these cases, social incompetence is the main factor in the decision. The families of those in the first group come from all socioeconomic levels, whereas a significantly higher percentage of the families of those in the second group come from lower educational and occupational strata.

Studies suggest that, in general, mentally retarded children are likely to show better emotional and mental development in a favorable home situation than in an institution (Golden & Davis, 1974). Thus, institutionalization is not generally recommended where a child is making a reasonably satisfactory adjustment at home and in school. Such a conclusion, however, must be tempered with the observation that most institutions for the retarded are decidedly substandard. In a classic study, Skeels (1966) demonstrated that an extraordinarily rich institutional environment can produce dramatic and lasting improvements in both IQ (an average gain of 28 points) and general adaptability among children originally diagnosed as mildly retarded.

The effect of being institutionalized in adolescence depends heavily, of course, on an institution's facilities as well as on individual factors. For the many retarded teenagers who do not have families in a position to take care of them, community-oriented residential care seems particularly promising (Alexander, Huganir, & Zigler, 1985; Landesman-Dwyer, 1981; Seidl, 1974; Thacher, 1978).

Fortunately, as we have seen, most retarded individuals do not need to be institutionalized. For those who do, however, state institutions for the mentally retarded are often desperately overcrowded and woefully inadequate in terms of the quality of care and special education programs offered (Robinson & Robinson, 1976; Tarjan et al., 1973). In 1970 the President's Committee on Mental Retardation reported that in many instances such facilities were no better than prisoner-of-war camps. Since then, some facilities have been greatly improved, but most lack the necessary funds and personnel to provide high-quality enhancement programs. Moreover, most private facilities—which are often, but not always, superior to public ones—are beyond the financial means of even the average family. With rare exceptions, they are hopelessly out of reach of the socioeconomic group most in need of them.

For the mentally retarded who do not require institutionalization, educational and training facilities have also been inadequate. In 1970 an estimated two million mentally retarded people who could have used job training and become self-supporting members of their communities were not getting this training (President's Committee on Mental Retardation, 1970). Although conditions may have since improved somewhat, it still appears that the majority of mentally retarded people in the United States are never reached by services appropriate to their specific needs (Tyor & Bell, 1984).

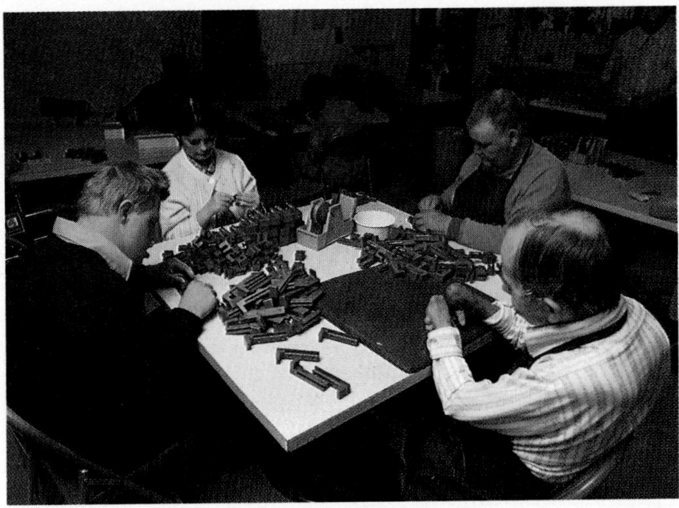

In many more cases than had once been thought possible, institutionalized individuals have been able to get along in the community with adequate preparation and help, such as training in vocational and social skills. In the last 20 years there has been a rapid increase in alternate forms of care for the mentally retarded, and new techniques, materials, and specially trained teachers are producing encouraging results.

This neglect is especially tragic in view of what we now know about helping these individuals. For example, classes for the mildly retarded, which usually emphasize reading and other basic school subjects, budgeting and money matters, and the development of occupational skills, have succeeded in helping many people become independent, productive community members.

Classes for the moderately and severely retarded usually have more limited objectives, but they emphasize the development of self-care and other skills that enable individuals to function adequately and to be of assistance in either a family or institutional setting. Just mastering toilet training and learning to eat and dress properly may mean the difference between remaining at home and being placed elsewhere.

In many more cases than had once been thought possible, institutionalized individuals have been able to get along in the community with adequate preparation and help. For example, Clark, Kivitz, and Rosen (1969) reported on a special project undertaken at the Elwyn Institute in Pennsylvania.

The goal of this program was the successful discharge to independent living in the community of the institutionalized mentally retarded. The entire staff was oriented toward rehabilitation; emphasis was placed on the development of practical vocational skills; special programs provided remedial teaching and the learning of socialization skills; and counseling and assessment assured the individualization of training to meet each person's needs. As a result of this program, many mentally retarded persons who had been institutionalized for from 2 to 49 years were discharged and obtained skilled or semiskilled jobs in the community while coping successfully with everyday problems. Some married and had families; none had to be readmitted to the institutions. (p. 82)

Today about 70 percent of the approximately 150,000 individuals still in institutions for the retarded are severely or profoundly retarded. Even many of these individuals are being helped to be partly self-supporting in community programs (Brown, 1977; Landesman-Dwyer, 1981; Robinson & Robinson, 1976; Rodman & Collins, 1974; Sullivan & Batareh, 1973; Thacher, 1978; Zucker & Altman, 1973). These developments reflect both the new optimism that has come to prevail and also, in many instances, new laws and judicial decisions favorable to the rights of retarded individuals and their families. A notable example is Public Law 94-142, passed by Congress in 1975. This statute, termed the Education for All Handicapped Children Act, asserts the right of mentally retarded people to be educated at public expense in "the least restrictive environment" possible.

During the 1970s, there was a rapid increase in alternate forms of care for the mentally retarded (Tyor & Bell, 1984). These include, but are not limited to, the use of decentralized regional facilities for short-term evaluation and training; small private hospitals specializing in rehabilitative techniques; group homes or "halfway houses" integrated into the local community; nursing homes for the elderly retarded; the placement of severely retarded children in more "enriched" foster-home environments; and varied forms of support to the family for own-home care.

Many of these varied programs are still too new to permit comprehensive evaluation of their long-range effectiveness with different groups of retarded people and differing levels of retardation. At the least, however, it is clear that they provide a much expanded flexibility in considering the needs of any given retarded individual at any particular point in his or her development and rehabilitation (Clarke, Clarke, & Berg, 1985; Robinson & Robinson, 1976). Unfortunately, these gains tend to be distributed in a spotty and inconsistent manner throughout the nation. In addition, many programs still overuse potent medications such as neuroleptics (antipsychotics), whose therapeutic purpose in this area, apart from chemical straight-jacketing, is obscure (Breuning & Poling, 1982). In one study of this problem among a random sample of *noninstitutionalized* mentally retarded people, no fewer than 58 percent of them were found to be taking prescribed drugs of this sort (Davis, Cullari, & Breuning, 1982). In light of the sometimes serious side effects of these drugs, such prescribing verges, in our view, on medical malpractice.

Although much remains to be learned about the most effective educational and training procedures to use with the mentally retarded—particularly the moderate and severe types—new techniques, materials, and specially trained teachers have produced encouraging results. For example, computer-assisted instruction has been introduced in Canadian programs for the retarded and has been found to be more efficient as well as less expensive than traditional tutor-guided instruction (Brebner, Hallworth, & Brown, 1977; Hallworth, 1977). New uses for the computer in this field are developing at a rapid rate (Lovett, 1985). Operant conditioning methods are being used increasingly to teach a wide variety of skills (Kiernan, 1985). Specifically targeted independence training in various everyday functions shows great promise (Matson, 1981). A technique for teaching improved thinking skills, developed by Reuven Feuerstein in Israel, has been extensively evaluated and produces substantial, though not spectacular, improvements in cognitive functioning (e.g., Arbitman-Smith, Haywood, & Bransford, 1984).

Typically, educational and training procedures involve mapping out target areas of improvement, such as personal grooming, social behavior, basic academic skills, and simple occupational skills (for retarded adults). Within each area, specific skills are divided into simple components that can be learned and reinforced before more complex behaviors are required. Target areas are not selected arbitrarily, of course, but realistically reflect the requirements of an individual's life situation and his or her level of competence. Training that builds on step-by-step progression and is guided by such realistic considerations can bring retarded individuals repeated experiences of success and lead to substantial progress even by those previously regarded as uneducable.

For more mildly retarded youngsters, the question of what schooling is best is likely to vex both parents and school officials. For many years, organized parents' groups have fought an uphill battle to ensure the availability of special education classes for retarded children in the public schools, having learned that isolation from peers tends to compound the problem. Too often, however, success in getting a retarded child into a public school has meant that the child is treated as very special indeed and—along with other retarded students—becomes isolated *within* the school.

We have now learned that this type of "special" education may have serious limitations in terms of a child's social and educational development, and that many such children fare better by attending regular classes for at least much of the day. Of course, this type of approach—called **mainstreaming**—does require careful planning, a high level of teacher skill, and facilitative teacher attitudes (Birns & Bridger, 1977; Borg & Ascione, 1982; Budoff, 1977; Hanrahan et al., 1990).

Indeed, a great deal of research in recent years has led to the conclusion that mainstreaming is not the hoped-for panacea (Gottlieb, 1981). In terms of administration, such programs are difficult to launch and to maintain (Lieberman, 1982); their success (or lack of it) seems to depend largely on such change-resistant influences as teacher attitudes and overall classroom climate (Haywood, Meyers, & Switsky, 1982; Miller, 1989). Moreover, any educational gains may come at the expense of deficits in self-esteem suffered by handicapped children as they interact intensively with more cognitively advantaged peers (Haywood, Meyers, & Switsky, 1982). Gresham (1982) argues that such dangers may be decreased or eliminated if retarded children are given social skills training prior to their entry into a mainstream classroom. Recently, a variant of mainstreaming called the Parallel Alternate Curriculum program, which emphasizes specialized instruction in a regular classroom setting, has shown much promise. Even here, however, much attention must be given to teaching-staff development (Chandler, 1985; Smith & Smith, 1985).

A reasonable conclusion at this time is that school systems should not attempt mainstreaming without a great deal of advance planning and preparation. In other words, mere window-dressing to achieve an appearance of progressive educational practice is not enough; the system's leadership must be thoroughly committed to overcoming deeply entrenched attitudes and procedures within the education bureaucracy to ensure the success of the effort.

The mainstreaming of mildly retarded children into regular classes for much of the day requires careful planning and a high level of teacher skill and facilitative teacher attitudes.

New Frontiers in Prevention The problem of preventing mental retardation involves the need to control a wide range of biological and sociocultural conditions. Inevitably, it is a problem concerned with human development in general.

Until recently, the most hopeful preventive approaches have been through routine health measures for pregnant women and their newborns and the use of diagnostic measures to ensure the early detection and, if possible, correction of aberrant biological processes. In recent years, however, two new frontiers have opened up. The first involves work in genetics that has revealed the role of certain genetic defects in faulty development, as in Tay-Sachs disease. Investigators have devised tests to identify parents who have these faulty genes, thus making it possible to provide them with genetic counseling. Over 200 clinics now exist in the United States where such counseling is available.

The second frontier in prevention involves the alleviation of sociocultural conditions that deprive children of the stimulation, motivation, and opportunities necessary for normal learning and the full development of mental capacities. In this connection, Keniston (1977) said,

It is time to match the strong American tradition of healing individual parents and children with equal efforts to change the factors that make those parents and children need healing. To put it another way, it is time for Americans to start holding the social and economic institutions of our society just as accountable for their influence on family life as we traditionally have held parents. (p. 6)

Birns and Bridger (1977), in basic agreement, emphasized that social reforms will need to include a revamping of the educational system to serve better the varying needs of all children. This "new horizon" was well delineated by President John F. Kennedy:

Studies have demonstrated that large numbers of children in urban and rural slums, including preschool children, lack the stimulus necessary for proper development in their intelligence. Even when there is no organic impairment, prolonged neglect and a lack of stimulus and opportunity for learning can result in the failure of young minds to develop. Other studies have shown that, if proper opportunities for learning are provided early enough, many of these deprived children can and will learn and achieve as much as children from more favored neighborhoods. The self-perpetuating intellectual blight should not be allowed to continue. (1963, p. 286)

President Kennedy's report directed the attention of the nation to the tragic and costly problem of mental retardation. It was not until 1970, however—when the President's Committee on Mental Retardation, the American Psychological Association, and other concerned organizations stressed the necessity for a "broad spectrum" approach—that real impetus was given to implementing essential measures for the prevention of mental retardation. This broad spectrum approach focused on three ways of providing a more supportive sociocultural setting to prevent children from being harmed by adverse environmental conditions:

1. *Application of existing knowledge.* The first phase of this approach involved the provision of more adequate medical and general health care for mother and baby prior to, during, and after pregnancy—particularly for the socially disadvantaged and other high-risk groups.

2. *Community services.* Next, the approach focused on the provision of community-centered facilities that would provide a coordinated range of diagnostic, health, education, employment, rehabilitation, and related services. This phase of the program included the training of needed personnel.

A particularly important development in this area has involved efforts to reach high-risk children early with the intensive cognitive stimulation believed to underlie the sound development of mental ability. Project Head Start is a well-known example operating at the local community level, one whose effectiveness is difficult to measure and remains somewhat controversial (Gamble & Zigler, 1989). At the national level, a similar intention has been manifested in specialized television programming for children, such as "Sesame Street" and "Reading Rainbow." Rigorous assessment of the effectiveness of such efforts has never been completed, but they do appear to have positive effects on many children. Somewhat ironically, the children who seem to benefit most from these efforts are the children least in need of them—the children of relatively affluent families in which education is strongly valued and in which the parents are likely to encourage their children to watch enriching television programming.

Also somewhat sobering is the possibility that the educational performance of Head Start children increases primarily because of temporarily enhanced motivation rather than higher rates of cognitive development (Zigler et al., 1982). Where the environment continues to be debilitative over time, the gain for many youngsters exposed to short-term enrichment programs may be lost (Garber, 1988; Gray & Ramsey, 1982). Obviously, much remains to be learned and done in the area of maintaining early gains. Where notable and sustainable gains have been unequivocally demonstrated, as in the relatively lavish program described by Skeels (1966), the initial financial investment may be so great as to strain community resources—thus attracting the kind of short-sighted political opposition commonly directed at expensive "social" programs. The irony is that the money is spent anyway, usually at compounded rates of increase, on such things as ADC (welfare-based aid to dependent children), chronic institutionalization, correctional facilities, and the "war on drugs."

3. *Research.* Finally, emphasis was placed on the facilitation and acceleration of research on all phases of the problem: causality, educational procedures, social effects on the family, psychological effects on the individual, and the changing role and functions of state and community agencies.

Unfortunately, the federal initiatives begun by the Kennedy administration have eroded over the years. Demands on the federal budget for programs

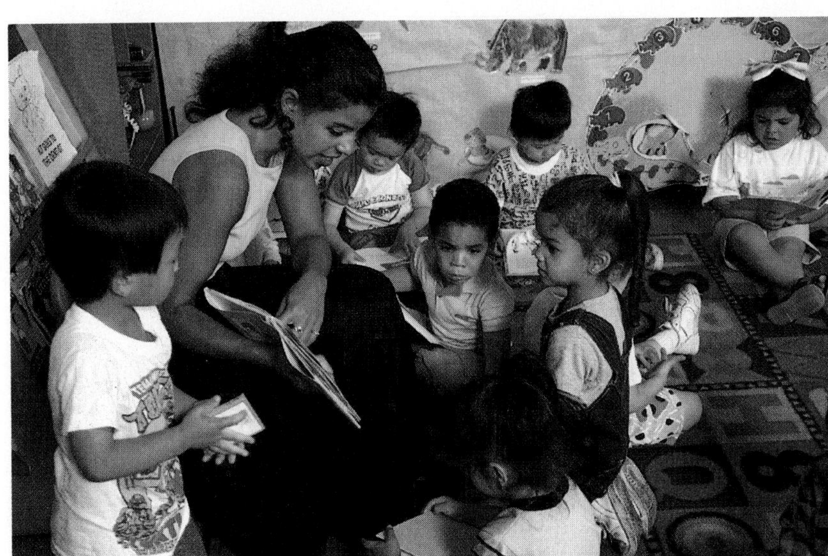

Project Head Start is a well-known example of a community-centered effort to reach high-risk children with the intensive cognitive stimulation that is thought to be necessary for the sound development of mental ability.

seen as having greater national priority have increased, and the funds committed for helping the retarded have suffered devaluation through inflation. Beginning with the Nixon administration of the early 1970s, there were serious cutbacks in training and research in all of the mental health disciplines. The trend has become worse since that time as the national debt has increased to unprecedented levels and as many states have likewise experienced severe fiscal problems. As a result, we have not been able to capitalize fully on our increased understanding of how to reverse or prevent the deficits experienced by mentally retarded youngsters and adults.

PERVASIVE DEVELOPMENTAL DISORDER: AUTISM

The DSM-III-R category involving pervasive developmental disorders includes several severe psychological disorders marked by serious distortions in psychological functioning. These problems cover a wide range of behaviors, including deficits in language, perceptual, and motor development; defective reality testing; and an inability to function in social situations. The term **pervasive developmental disorder** was new with DSM-III, although the disorders included under this category have a long history under the names *symbiotic psychosis in children* and *early infantile autism.* The term *pervasive developmental disorders* was chosen over other possibilities because it focuses on the severe and extensive developmental deficits present in children with these disorders (Gillberg, 1990). We will focus here on the pervasive developmental disorder that has received the greatest amount of attention from researchers—**autistic disorder**—whose central feature is a profound and unyielding imperviousness, or unresponsiveness, to the human environment. The following case illustrates some of the behaviors that may be seen in an autistic child:

The boy is five years old. When spoken to, he turns his head away. Sometimes he mumbles unintelligibly. He is neither toilet trained nor able to feed himself. He actively resists being touched. He dislikes sounds. He cannot relate to others and avoids looking anyone in the eye. He often engages in routine manipulative activities, such as dropping an object, picking it up, and dropping it again. While seated, he often rocks back and forth in a rhythmic motion for hours. Any change in routine is highly upsetting to him. He is in a school for severely disturbed children at UCLA. His diagnosis is childhood autism.

Autism in infancy and childhood was first described by Kanner (1943). It afflicts some 80,000 American children—about 4 children in 10,000—and occurs about four or five times more frequently among boys than girls (Schreibman & Koegel, 1975; Ritvo, Freeman, Pingree, et al., 1989; Steffenburg and Gillberg, 1986; Werry, 1979). It is usually identified before a child is 30 months of age (Rutter, 1978) and often is suspected in the early weeks of life. Autistic children come from all socioeconomic levels, ethnic backgrounds, and family patterns. It was once believed that autism was more prevalent among families in upper socioeconomic levels; however, this finding may have been due to the particular sampling methods used in earlier studies (Wing, 1980). The recent epidemiological survey by Ritvo et al. (1989) has supported the view that autism is not associated with parental education, occupation, racial origin, or religion.

The Clinical Picture in Autistic Disorder

Autistic children form a heterogeneous population, with varying degrees of impairments and capabilities. In this section we will discuss some of the behaviors that may be evident in autism. A cardinal and typical sign is that a child seems apart or aloof from others, even in the earliest stages of life. Mothers often remember such babies as never being "cuddly," never reaching out when being picked up, never smiling or looking at them while being fed, and never appearing to notice the comings and goings of other people. Typically, autistic children do not show any need for affection or contact with anyone, usually not even seeming to know or care who their parents are.

The absence or severely restricted use of speech is characteristic of autistic children. If speech is present, it is almost never used to communicate except in the most rudimentary fashion, as by saying "yes" in answer to a question or by the use of **echolalia** (parrotlike repetition of a few words). Although the echoing of parents' verbal behavior is found to a small degree in normal children as they experiment with their ability to produce articulate speech, persistent echolalia is found in about 75 percent of autistic children (Prizant, 1983). Some research has focused on trying to understand if echolalia in autistic children is functional. Prizant and Duchan (1981) analyzed echolalic verbalizations—previously believed to be meaningless—according to tone, latency, and other speech characteristics. They concluded that, far from being meaningless, these verbalizations could aid clinicians or researchers in understanding the communicative and cognitive functioning of autistic children. Nevertheless, these utterances remain highly cryptic and are, of course, an inadequate substitute for true language functioning.

On the basis of their intensive study of 53 autistic children, Clancy and McBride (1969) suggested that the usual picture of an autistic child as lacking in language ability and being wholly withdrawn is probably oversimplified. They found that at least some autistic children do comprehend language, even though they may not use it to express themselves. These investigators pointed to the occasional normal commencement of language development, followed by its disappearance as the autistic process becomes manifest. Perhaps even more significantly, they found evidence that the autistic children they studied were very much aware of—and actively involved with—their environments:

Autistic children actively seek to arrange the environment on their terms, and so as to exclude certain elements, e.g., intervention from other people and variety in any aspect of routine. (p. 243)

Often autistic children show an active aversion to auditory stimuli, crying even at the sound of a parent's voice. The pattern is not always consistent, however; autistic children "may at one moment be severely agitated or panicked by a very soft sound and at another time be totally oblivious to loud noise" (Ritvo & Ornitz, 1970, p. 6).

Self-stimulation is characteristic of these children, usually taking the form of such repetitive movements as head banging, spinning, and rocking, which may continue by the hour. Other bizarre as well as repetitive behavior is typical. Such behavior is well described by Gajzago and Prior (1974) in the case of a young autistic boy:

A was described as a screaming, severely disturbed child who ran around in circles making high-pitched sounds for hours. He also liked to sit in boxes, under mats, and [under] blankets. He habitually piled up all furniture and bedding in the center of the room. At times he was thought deaf—though he also showed extreme fear of loud noises. He refused all food except in a bottle, refused to wear clothes, chewed stones and paper, whirled himself, and spun objects. . . . He played repetitively with the same toys for months, lining things in rows, collected objects such as bottle tops, and insisted on having two of everything, one in each hand. He became extremely upset if interrupted and if the order or arrangement of things were altered. (p. 264)

In contrast to the behavior just described, some autistic children are skilled at fitting objects together. Thus their performance on puzzles or form boards may be average or above. Even in the manipulation of objects, however, difficulty with meaning is apparent. For example, when pictures are to be arranged in an order that tells a story, autistic children show a marked deficiency in performance.

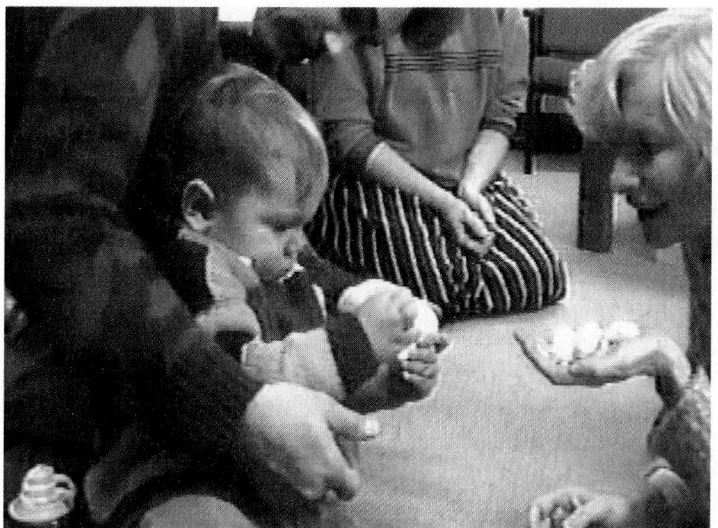

Callum, at left, is thought to have autism, and Ryan, at right, is a normal child. Autism may be difficult to diagnose early, but some of the symptoms are apparent in these video sequences of Callum and Ryan. Autistic children are deficient in two-way communication and social interaction. Callum attends to the shaving cream, but only to the shaving cream, and is oblivious to his father's presence; Ryan, on the other hand, is also delighted with the shaving cream but brings everyone else around him into his play. He is skilled at communication even without words. Callum seemingly doesn't know how things happen or how to make them happen again. For him, each experience is a separate event, with no connection to anything or anyone else. The inability of a young child like Callum to interact with his parents in all the subtle ways that most babies do can result in a socially deficient individual.

Although some have regarded autistic children as potentially of normal intelligence, this view has been challenged by a number of investigators who consider many if not most of these children to be mentally retarded (Goodman, 1972). Prior and Wherry (1986) reported that about three-fourths of autistic children were mentally retarded. Some autistic children, however, show markedly discrepant abilities, such as astounding memory capabilities, as Dustin Hoffman depicted in the award-winning motion picture *Rain Man*. In this context, Goodman described the case of an "autistic-savant" who showed unusual ability at an early age in calendar calculating (rapidly determining the day of any calendar date in history) as well as in other areas, such as naming the capitals of most states and countries. Nevertheless, his language development was severely retarded, and he showed the indifference to others and related symptoms characteristic of autistic children.

Much has been learned recently about the cognitive deficits of autistic children (Wenar, 1990). When compared with other groups of children on cognitive or intellectual tasks, autistic children often show impairment (James & Barry, 1981; Ritvo & Freeman, 1978; Schopler, 1983). Boucher (1981), for example, found autistic children significantly impaired on memory tasks when compared with both normal and retarded children. Whether this cognitive impairment is the result of actual organic brain damage or of motivational deficits has not been established. Koegel and Mentis (1985) have raised the possibility that the deficits result from motivational differences; they found that autistic children can learn and perform tasks at a higher level if motivation for a task is found and appropriate reinforcement is provided.

Many autistic children become preoccupied with and form strong attachments to unusual objects, such as rocks, light switches, film negatives, or keys. In some instances the object is so large or bizarre that merely carrying it around interferes with other activities. When their preoccupation with the object is disturbed—for example, by its removal or by attempts to substitute something in its place—or when anything familiar in their environment is altered even slightly, they may have a violent temper tantrum or a crying spell that continues until the familiar situation is restored. Thus autistic children are often said to be "obsessed with the maintenance of sameness." Furthermore, autistic children have been referred to as "negativistic" because they seemingly do not comply with requests. However, a study by Volkmar, Hoder, and

Cohen (1985) found that, under the carefully structured and reinforcing conditions in a clinic setting, autistic children were not negativistic and generally complied with requests made by staff.

In summary, autistic children typically show difficulties in relationships to other people, in perceptual-cognitive functioning, in language development, and in the development of a sense of identity (L. K. Wing, 1976). They also engage in bizarre and repetitive activities, demonstrate a fascination with unusual objects, and show an obsessive need to maintain environmental sameness. This is indeed a heavy set of handicaps.

Because the clinical picture in autism tends to blend almost imperceptibly with that in schizophrenia, a differential diagnosis is often difficult to make. The chief distinguishing feature appears to be the age of onset, with autism becoming evident very early and schizophrenia appearing more gradually and much later—typically not until adolescence or early adulthood—after several years of apparently normal development. As Bettelheim (1969) has put it, "While the schizophrenic child withdraws from the world, the autistic child fails to ever enter it" (p. 21).

Causal Factors in Autism

No brain pathology has been delineated in infant or childhood autism. Because it does not, in general, appear to run in families, it cannot be attributed directly to a hereditary defect. In a review of the genetic factors in autism and childhood schizophrenia, Smalley (1991) found no evidence for a genetic basis of autism. In a series of papers reviewing various types of evidence relating to both organic deficit and genetic factors in autism, Sanua (1986a, 1986b, 1987) concluded that no such contributions to the disorder have been unequivocally demonstrated. He points out, correctly in our judgment, that many investigators and commentators in this field have made uninformed and apparently biased assumptions about the true quality of the evidence tending to show an etiologic role for genetic or organic brain anomalies. On critical appraisal, the evidence is in fact quite weak.

The possibility remains, however, that defective genes or damage from radiation or other conditions during prenatal development may play a role in the etiologic picture. It seems likely at this point that the disorder we call autism involves both multiple kinds of deficit (Goodman, 1989) and multiple etiologic pathways (Gillberg, 1990). Thus we should perhaps not expect to find large risk factors accounting for autistic outcomes, nor even exceptional levels of consistency from one study to another where differing samples of autistic youngsters have been evaluated. For example, although Goldfine et al. (1985) failed to find the Fragile X chromosomal abnormality in a carefully selected group of 37 autistic children, such an anomaly could still make an etiologic contribution in given instances of the disorder (Bolton et al., 1989). Even subtler constitutional defects cannot of course be ruled out. In fact, most investigators believe that autism begins with some type of inborn defect that impairs an infant's perceptual-cognitive functioning—the ability to process incoming stimulation and to relate to the world. In support of possible genetic factors in autism (perhaps a familial subtype of the disorder), Ritvo et al. (1989) found that 9.7 percent of the affected families had more than one autistic offspring.

In his early studies of childhood autism, Kanner (1943) concluded that an innate disorder in a child is exacerbated by a cold and unresponsive mother, the first factor resulting in social withdrawal and the second tending to maintain this isolation. Most investigators, however, have failed to find the parents of autistic children to be "emotional refrigerators" (Schreibman & Koegel, 1975; Wolff & Morris, 1971). In a well-controlled study, McAdoo and De Myer (1978) found that the personality characteristics of parents of autistic children were not significantly different from those of parents of other types of disturbed children. They also discovered that the mothers of both autistic and disturbed children had significantly fewer psychological problems than did mothers who were being seen as patients in mental health settings.

As Harlow (1969) somewhat wryly pointed out, it is often extremely difficult to pinpoint cause and effect in studying relationships between mother and child:

Possibly . . . some children are rendered autistic by maternal neglect and insufficiency, but it is even more likely that many more mothers are rendered autistic because of an inborn inability of their infants to respond affectionately to them in any semblance of an adequate manner. (p. 29)

Tinbergen (1974) viewed autism as the result of an approach-avoidance conflict in which a child's natural tendency to explore and relate to the world is overbalanced by aversive experiences and fear. According to this view, instead of venturing forth into the world, such children withdraw into a world they create for themselves. This withdrawal, however, is not as haphazard or disorderly as it may seem; rather, it involves systematic avoidance of particular stimuli and events, including people. Some studies also indicate that metabolic processes in the brain are involved in autism (Rumsey et al., 1985).

Clearly, much remains to be learned about the etiology of childhood autism. It appears most reasonable to suppose, however, that this disorder normally begins with an inborn defect or defects in brain functioning, regardless of what other causal factors may subsequently become involved.

Treatments and Outcomes

Medical treatment of autistic children has often been tried but has not proven effective (Rutter, 1985). The drug most often used in the treatment of autism is Haloperidol, but the data on its effectiveness do not warrant use unless a child's behavior is unmanageable by other means (Sloman, 1991). We will thus direct our attention to a variety of psychological procedures that have been more successful in treating autistic children.

Bettelheim (1967, 1969, 1974), at the Orthogenic School of the University of Chicago, reported some success in treating autistic children with a program of warm, loving acceptance accompanied by reinforcement procedures, as can be seen in the case of Joey described in *HIGHLIGHT 14.5.* Similarly, Marchant and her associates (1974) in England have reported improvement using a method for introducing "graded change" into the environment of autistic children, thus tending to shift their behavior gradually from self-defeating to growth-oriented activities.

Another approach to treating autistic children is called **structural therapy.** In this approach the environment is structured to provide spontaneous physical and verbal stimulation in a playful and gamelike manner. The goal of this approach is to increase the amount and variety of stimuli for these children, gradually making them more aware of themselves and more related to their environment. The results of structural therapy have been encouraging, with 12 of 21 cases considered improved enough to be able to return home after the three-year treatment program (Ward, 1978). In another study involving social skills training, the majority of the treated children showed definite improvements in their peer relationships (Williams, 1989).

In an extensive study of autistic children who were mentally retarded, socially unresponsive, and behaviorally disturbed, Bartak and his colleagues at the Maudsley Hospital in England obtained significant results with educational procedures. Children who were assigned to a structured treatment unit focusing on formal schooling showed greater progress than those placed in units stressing play therapy, either free or structured (Bartak & Rutter, 1973; Russell, 1975). As a result of this work, Bartak (1978) suggested a "qualified optimism" for the educational progress of autistic children. The best predictor of a positive outcome in the treatment of autism, according to Bartak and Rutter (1976), is intelligence.

Behavior therapy in an institutional setting has been used successfully in the elimination of self-injurious behavior, the mastery of the fundamentals of social behavior, and the development of some language skills (Lovaas, 1977; Lovaas, Schaeffer, & Simmons, 1974; Williams, Koegel, & Egel, 1981). Lovaas (1987) reported highly positive results from a long-term experimental treatment program of autistic children. Of the treated children, 47 percent achieved normal intellectual functioning and another 40 percent attained the mildly retarded level. In comparison, only 2 percent of the untreated, control children achieved normal functioning and 45 percent attained mildly retarded functioning. These remarkable results did, however, require a considerable staffing effort, with well-qualified therapists working 40 hours per week for two years. Interestingly, studies on the effectiveness of behavior therapy with institutionalized children have found that children who were discharged to their parents continued to improve, whereas those who remained in an institution tended to lose much of what they had gained (Lovaas, 1977; Schreibman & Koegel, 1975).

Wesley is moderately to severely autistic and, because he could not communicate in any meaningful way, was thought to be retarded. When introduced to an electronic keyboard that displays typed messages, however, Wesley began, over a period of time, to type coherent messages to his mother and others, without ever having been taught to read or write. This remarkable feat raises questions about the role of mental retardation in autism: Are autistic individuals lacking in intelligence or are they simply unable to communicate in understandable ways?

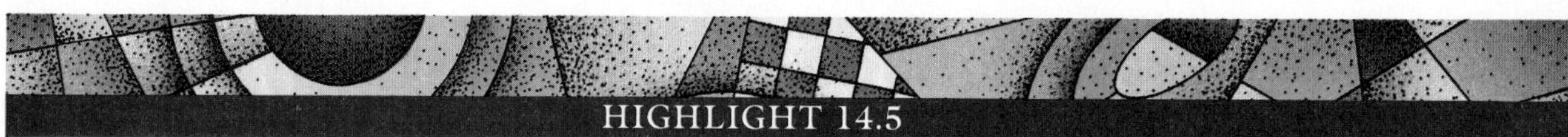

HIGHLIGHT 14.5

Joey: A "Mechanical Boy"

These four pictures were drawn by Joey, an autistic boy who entered the Sonia Shankman Orthogenic School of the University of Chicago at the age of 9. His unusual case history has been reported by Bettelheim (1959).

Joey presumably denied his own emotions because they were unbearably painful. Apparently not daring to be human in a world that he felt had rejected him, Joey withdrew into a world of fantasy and perceived himself as a machine that "functioned as if by remote control." This idea is brought out in drawing 1—a self-portrait in which Joey depicts himself as an electrical robot. Bettelheim interpreted this portrait as symbolizing Joey's rejection of human feelings.

So elaborately constructed and acted out was Joey's mechanical character that "entering the dining room, for example, he would string an imaginary wire from his 'energy source'—an imaginary electrical outlet—to the table. There he 'insulated' himself with paper napkins and finally plugged himself in. Only then could Joey eat, for he firmly believed that the 'current' ran his ingestive apparatus" (p. 117).

Joey's performance was convincing—so much so that others found themselves responding to him as a mechanical boy rather than as a human being: ". . . one had to look twice to be sure there was neither wire nor outlet nor plug. Children and members of our staff . . . avoided stepping on the 'wires' for fear of interrupting what seemed the source of his very life." When his machinery was idle, Joey "would sit so quietly that he would disappear from the focus of the most conscientious observation. Yet in the next moment he might be 'working' and the center of our captivated attention" (p. 117).

In his report on Joey, Bettelheim alluded to the painfully slow process by which Joey was eventually able to establish true relations with other human beings. Three of the drawings depict part of the process. In the earliest of the three (drawing 2), Joey portrays himself "as an electrical 'papoose,' completely enclosed, suspended in empty space and operated by wire-

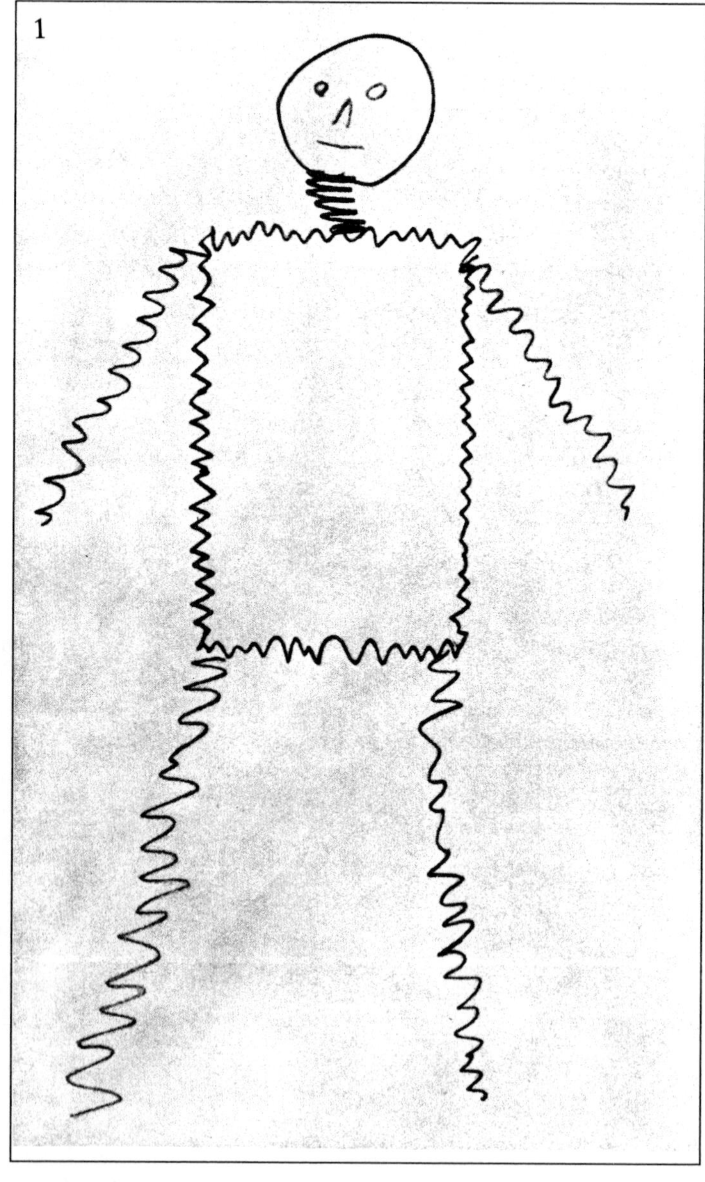

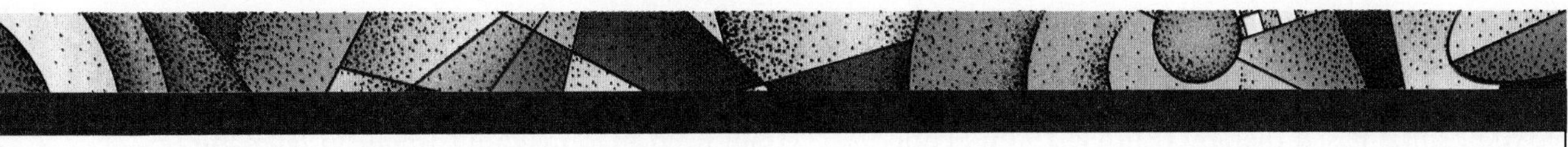

less signals." In the next one (drawing 3), he apparently demonstrates increasing self-esteem, for although he is still operated by wireless signals, he is much larger in stature. In the final drawing (drawing 4), Joey depicts "the machine which controls him," but in this one, unlike the previous drawings, "he has acquired hands with which he can manipulate his immediate environment" (p. 119).

When Joey was 12—three years after he had entered the school—". . . he made a float for our Memorial Day parade. It carried the slogan: 'Feelings are more important than anything under the sun.' Feelings, Joey had learned, are what make for humanity; their absence, for a mechanical existence. With this knowledge Joey entered the human condition" (p. 127).

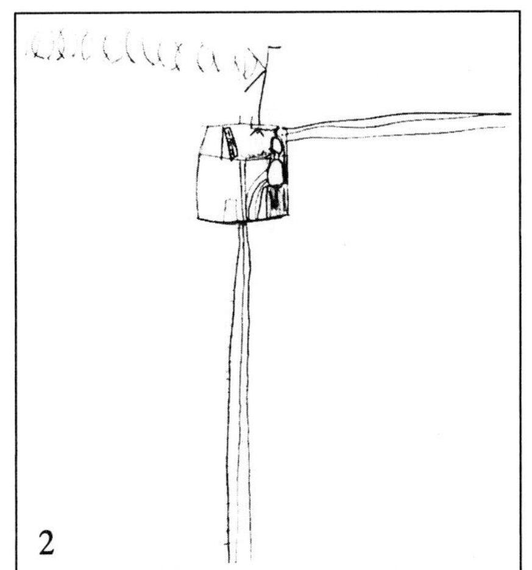
2

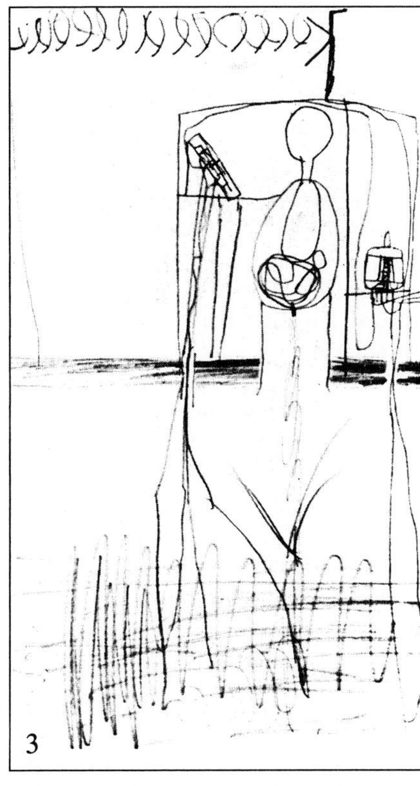
3

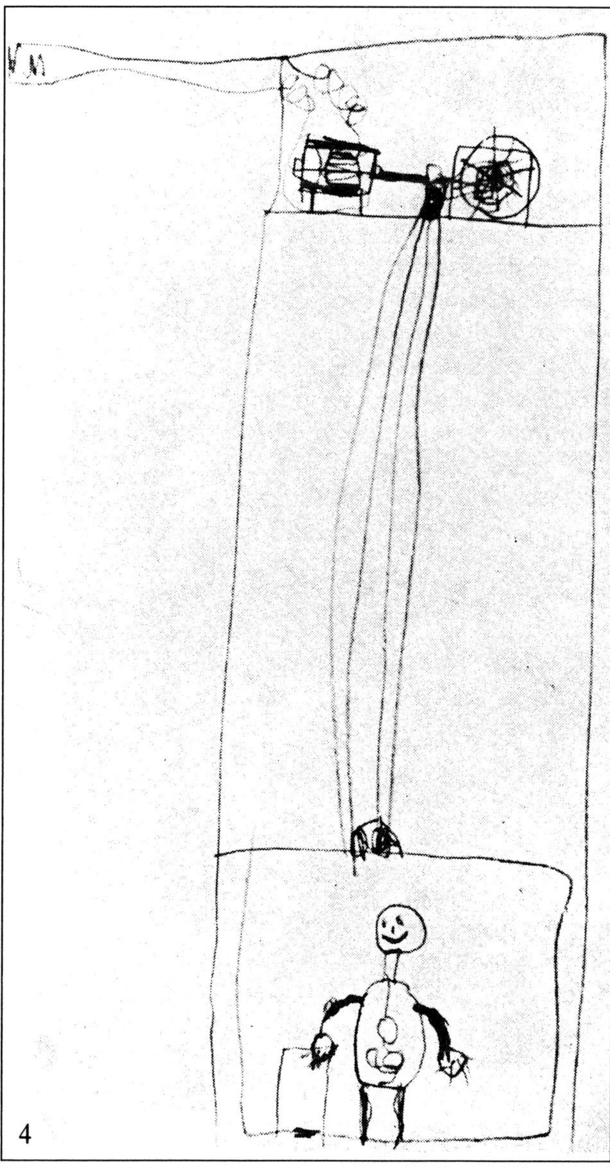
4

Some of the most impressive results with autistic children have been obtained in projects that involve parents, with treatment in the home preferable to hospital-based therapy (Rutter, 1985; Schopler, Mesibov, & Baker, 1982). Treatment "contracts" with parents specify the desired behavior changes in their child and spell out the explicit techniques for bringing about these changes. Such contracting acknowledges the value of the parents as potential change agents—in contrast with the previously held belief that the parents were somehow to blame for their child's disorder (Schopler, 1978). Perhaps the most favorable results are those of Schreibman and Koegel (1975), who reported successful outcomes in the treatment of 10 of 16 autistic children. These investigators relied heavily on the use of parents as therapists to reinforce normal behavior in their children. They concluded that autism is potentially a "defeatable horror."

It is too early to evaluate the long-term effectiveness of these newer treatment methods or the degree of improvement they actually bring about. The prognosis for autistic children, particularly for children showing symptoms before the age of 2, is poor (Hoshino et al., 1980). Traditionally, the long-term results of autism treatments have been unfavorable. A great deal of attention has been given recently to high-functioning autistic children (children who meet the criteria for autism yet develop functional speech). Ritvo et al. (1988) studied 11 parents whom they believed met diagnostic criteria for autism (they were identified through having had children who were autistic). These individuals had been able to make modest adjustments to life, hold down jobs, and get married. The outcome in autism is often problematic, however. Clarke et al. (1989) followed up five high-functioning autistic children and found that four of them later developed symptoms of psychosis.

One important factor limiting treatment success is the problems autistic children experience in generalizing behavior outside the treatment context (Handleman, Gill, & Alessandri, 1988). Children with severe developmental disabilities do not transfer skills across situations very well. Consequently, learned behavior in one situation does not appear to help them meet challenges in others. This important component needs to be addressed if training or treatment programs are to be successful. Even with intensive long-term care in a clinical facility, where gratifying improvements may be brought about in specific behaviors, children are a long way from becoming "normal." Gillberg and Schaumann (1981) have noted that some autistic children make substantial improvement during childhood, only to deteriorate, showing symptom aggravation, at the onset of puberty. Less than one-fourth of the autistic children who receive treatment appear to attain even marginal adjustment in later life.

SPECIFIC DEVELOPMENTAL DISORDERS: LEARNING DISABILITIES

In contrast to pervasive developmental disorders such as autism, **specific developmental disorders** have a circumscribed character and may occur in children who are otherwise normal or even gifted in their overall functioning. The inadequate development may be manifested in academic, language, speech, or motor skills areas, and it is not due to any demonstrable physical or neurological defect. The diagnosis is restricted to those cases in which there is clear impairment in school performance or (if the person is not a student) in daily living activities, not due to mental retardation or a pervasive developmental disorder. By implication, skill deficits due to attention-deficit hyperactivity disorder, described in Chapter 15, are coded under that diagnosis. This coding presents another diagnostic dilemma because some investigators hold that an attentional deficit is basic to many learning disorders. In any event, we will focus in this section on specific developmental disorders involving academic skills, also known as **specific learning disabilities,** or—in DSM-III-R terms—academic skills disorders. Children with these disorders are more generally said to be **learning disabled (LD).** Significantly more boys than girls are diagnosed as learning disabled, but proportional estimates of this gender discrepancy have varied widely from study to study.

The Clinical Picture in Learning Disabilities

LD children are identified as such because of a disparity between their expected academic achievement level and their actual academic performance in one or more of the traditional school subjects, such as math, spelling, writing, or reading. (Reading problems are commonly known as **dyslexia.**) Typically, these children have full-scale IQs, family backgrounds, and exposure to cultural norms and symbols that are consistent with at least average achievement in school. They do not have obvious crippling emotional problems, nor do they seem to be lacking in motivation, cooperativeness, or eagerness to please their teachers and parents—at least not at the outset of their formal education. Nevertheless, they fail, often abysmally and usually with a stubborn, puzzling persistence. Why? As we will see, satisfactory answers are hard to come by.

Frustration for teachers, school officials, parents, professional helpers, and perhaps most notably for the victims themselves (although the last may go unnoticed in the general turmoil) is virtually guaranteed in this scenario, and it is likely to complicate efforts to find a solution. Wenar (1990) poignantly depicts the problem:

You are a child clinical psychologist. It has been a rough day. The climax was a phone call to the principal of Wykwyre Junior High School. It is the kind of suburban school in which children from two-swimming-pool families do not speak to children from one-swimming-pool families. The call had been about Jon Hastings, a 16-year-old with a long history of school failures. The intelligence test showed him to be bright enough to do college work, and yet he is only in the eighth grade. He is articulate, has a talent for making miniature rockets and speedboats, and a real flair for drawing cartoons. Yet the written word is Jon's nemesis. He reads laboriously one word at a time, while his writing is even more painfully slow. Because of repeated failures and because he is now a social misfit with peers, he has begun cutting up in class and talking back to the teacher.

You had phoned the principal to suggest ways of bypassing Jon's reading disability. Since he is sufficiently bright to absorb most of the lecture material, could he be given oral examinations every now and then? If he were taught to type, could he type instead of writing his examinations? Would the principal consider introducing special classes for all the learning-disabled children?

The principal was suave and ingratiating and a compendium of the resistances you have run up against in the past. He "understood your concern" but asked that you "look at the situation from my point of view." The school had "tried everything possible to no avail," "the boy is incorrigible," "you can't help a child unless the child wants help," and finally—you could feel this one coming, since you had heard it so often—"I can't give one student a favor without giving a favor to all of them. I'd have half the mothers in my office next day demanding something extra to pull their child's grades up." You had always doubted the validity of this "special-favor" objection but had never found an effective way of countering it. Stalling for time you asked if you could come in and talk with the principal. He was most gracious. He would be happy to tell you about the school and have a student show you around—which was not at all what you had in mind.

A few years back an insightful but poorly educated mother had remarked, "When I get frustrations I come here and bring them to you. When you get frustrations, where do you put them?" The question comes back at times like these. (p. 197)

It is unfortunately the case that LD, despite its having been recognized as a distinct and rather common type of disorder for more than 30 years, and despite its having generated a voluminous research literature, still fails to be accorded the status it deserves in many school jurisdictions. Instead, as in the preceding example, the familiar diversion of blaming the victim and of attributing the affected child's problems to various character deficiencies is still routinely employed by many classroom teachers and school administrators, whether in public or private settings. Where lockstep uniformity is the rule, as it is in most public and many "alternative" educational systems, a youngster who learns academic skills slowly or in a different way is treated as a troublesome pariah, as a threat to the prevailing theory of education. The consequences of these encounters between LD children and rigidly doctrinaire or regimented school systems can be disastrous to a child's self-esteem and general psychological well-being, and research indicates that these effects do not necessarily dissipate after secondary schooling ends (Bruck, 1987; Cato & Rice, 1982; Saracoglu, Minden, & Wilchesky, 1989). Thus even where LD difficulties are no longer a significant impediment, an individual may bear the scars of many painful school-related episodes into maturity and beyond.

Causal Factors in Learning Disabilities

Probably the most generally held view of the cause of specific learning disabilities is that they are the products of subtle central nervous system disorders. In particular, these disabilities are thought to result from some sort of immaturity, defect, or dysregulation limited to those brain areas supposedly mediating, for normal children, the behaviors that LD children cannot efficiently acquire. A few years back the term *minimal brain dysfunction (MBD)* was in

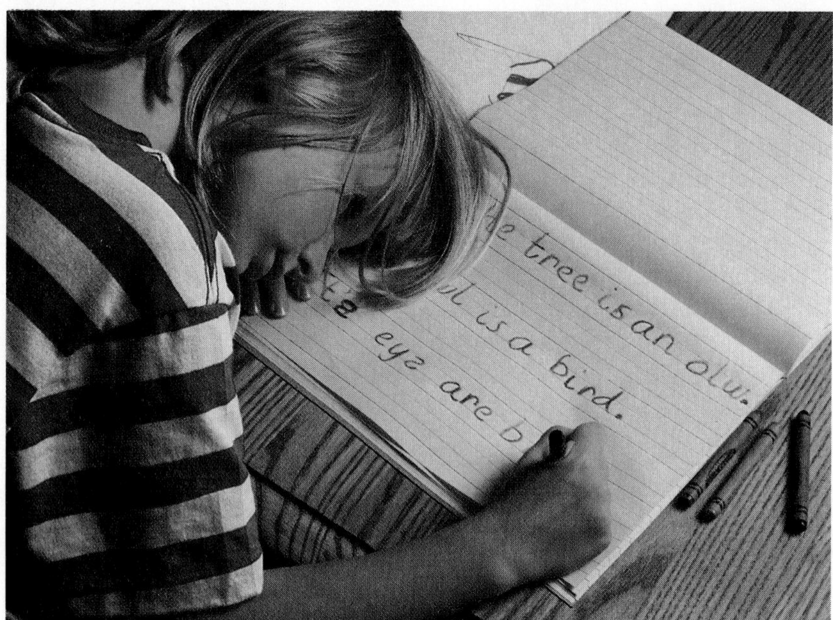

Dyslexia is a learning disability that interferes with the ability to read and write. This dyslexic student is transposing letters and writing other letters backward. Learning-disabled children, frustrated by their academic failures, may become social failures as well. If undiagnosed, these children may be seen by school authorities as troublesome and intractable, thus compounding their problems and further damaging their self-esteem. The long-term academic, social, and personal adjustment for those who grew up with undiagnosed dyslexia is generally discouraging, but there are important exceptions.

popular use to refer to such presumed organic malfunction—until it was generally recognized that nobody had the slightest idea what the term really meant. While some LD children show definite or highly suggestive evidence of brain disease, such as cerebral palsy, epilepsy, or a history of severe head trauma (e.g., Yule & Rutter, 1985), the large majority do not. In others, there may be subtle indications, "soft signs," of neurological compromise, but again such findings are by no means routine. Overall, no convincing evidence shows a specific dysfunction of the central nervous system among LD children generally (Schwartz & Johnson, 1985). The search for such factors has lessened in recent years, possibly because investigators have become discouraged by the meager available findings.

A variant of the central nervous system dysfunction hypothesis proposes some type of defect or imbalance in the brain's normal laterality—that is, in the tendency for specific functions to be localized to a large extent in either the right or the left side of the brain. Studies in this area, mainly concerned with dyslexia, have failed to produce a consistent or coherent set of findings (Kessler, 1988). They have also been plagued with many methodological shortcomings (Hynd & Semrud-Clikeman, 1989).

By this point you are unlikely to be surprised that some investigators believe the various forms of LD, or vulnerability to develop them, may be genetically transmitted. This issue seems not to have been studied with the same intensity or methodologic rigor as in other disorders. Two family pedigree studies, those of Hallgren (1950) and Finucci et al. (1976), showed evidence of familial concordance for "reading disorders" (dyslexia), and Owen (1978) cites a twin study in which monozygosity was associated with 100 percent concordance for reading disorders. As we have seen in other contexts, the methods employed here do not permit a true separation of hereditary from environmental influences, but the magnitude of the concordances reported in all three studies is fairly impressive. The hypothesis of a genetic contribution to at least the dyslexic form of LD therefore remains tenable.

Summing up, biological or organic hypotheses concerning the etiology of LD, though widely held, tend to be rather vague on mechanisms and do not have an exceptionally strong record of evidence supporting them. They continue to have a sort of intuitive appeal that is at least as great as alternative psychosocial theories of causation.

Psychosocially based hypotheses about the origins of LD generally derive from psychodynamic, learning, or cognitive perspectives, or a combination of them. To date, none of them has sufficient empirical support to warrant extended discussion. The apparent complexity of the psychological processes involved in LD (see, for example, Ceci & Baker, 1987) evidently makes it difficult to do rigorous and definitive studies on potential causal factors. Thus the research that is available, most of it again directed to the problem of dyslexia, tends to be riddled with problems of subject selection, inappropriate controls, and other serious methodological flaws (Vellutino, 1987).

Despite what appears to be a multitude of seemingly differing factors involved in LD, there may yet be some common elements. This is the position taken by Worden (1986), who argues that we should study what is characteristic in the approaches taken by good learners to be able to identify the areas of significant weakness from which LD children suffer. He offers the following list as a beginning in this direction:

1. What *memory strategies* are used by normal or good learners, and in what manner do these differ from those employed by LD children?

2. How do normal or good learners *monitor* their ongoing performances? For example, how do good learners use performance information to gauge where they are being successful and where not, and to introduce corrective action as needed?

3. What *metastrategy information* is used by good learners and not by LD children? For example, do LD children understand the advantage of having a strategy at all, as in dealing with the time constraints of many school tasks?

4. What *motivates* good learners, and how does this differ from the motivation of poor learners? Is a learner's orientation one of seeking success or of avoiding failure? To what is success or failure attributed: oneself, task difficulty, chance, or some other factor?

Worden's approach to analyzing the complex issues involved in academic skill acquisition strikes us as a potentially useful beginning. However, even precise information on the manner in which LD children's learning approaches differ from those of normal children would still leave us with unanswered questions about the sources of these differences. Nevertheless, pursuit of this idea might produce a set of rational, fine-tuned strategies for intervening to correct LD children's inefficient modes of learning. We are not aware of any follow-up studies along this line.

Treatments and Outcomes

Because we obviously do not as yet have a confident grasp on what is "wrong" with the average LD child, we have not been too successful in treating these children. While many informal and single-case reports claim success for various treatment approaches, there are few well-designed and well-executed outcome studies on specific treatments for LD problems. Focusing on reading disorders, where most of the effort appears to have been concentrated, Gittelman's (1983) review contains little evidence of impressive results. Moreover, any short-term gains that are made tend in many cases to diminish or even disappear over time (Yule & Rutter, 1985).

We have only limited data on the long-term, adult adjustments of people who grew up with the academic and social problems LD entails. Two recent studies of college students having LD (Gregg & Hoy, 1989; Saracoglu, Minden, & Wilchesky, 1989) suggested that as a group they continue to have problems—academic, personal, and social—into the postsecondary education years. Cato and Rice (1982) extracted from the available literature a lengthy list of somewhat discouraging problems experienced by the typical LD adult. These include—in addition to expected difficulties with self-confidence—continuing problems with deficits in the ordinary skills, such as math, that these people originally encountered as children. The authors did note, however, that there are considerable individual differences in these outcomes, thus reminding us that some adults with LD are able to manage very well.

UNRESOLVED ISSUES on Cultural-Familial Retardation

The problem of cultural-familial mental retardation continues to be a baffling and frustrating one—complicated in no small measure by sensitive issues of race relations and imputed ethnic differences in native abilities. No scientifically respectable evidence in fact suggests that the quality of brain tissue is in any degree correlated with race or ethnicity. A great deal of evidence, on the other hand, shows that different ethnic groups, on average, vary considerably in performance on standardized tests designed to predict academic achievement. Unfortunately, we have long been encouraged to regard such tests as more or less directly measuring "intelligence," which they do not—unless one is willing to accept school grades as the primary defining element of that construct. IQ tests are and have always been validated primarily on their ability to predict school performance.

Schools may reasonably be viewed as having the principal function of transmitting a culture's approved products from earlier to later generations; approved products are those deemed valuable by a cultural elite. So-called intelligence tests, then, are designed to measure the facility with which a child may be expected to acquire and adequately process what the school offers in this respect. It does not seem farfetched to suggest that a child's performance in school will be determined to a considerable extent by the amount of prior and continuing extracurricular exposure he or she has to the products of the dominant culture that the school almost necessarily represents. Indeed, we have a fair amount of empirical evidence showing that this is so. We also have a fair amount of empirical evidence, only a fraction of it reviewed here, suggesting that a person's IQ ("intelligence" quotient) rises significantly with enhanced exposure to these cultural products. It is therefore more than a mere possibility that what IQ tests mostly measure is prior exposure to approved cultural products. Considered from this perspective, the notion of a "culture-free" IQ test that would also do well at predicting school grades is a practical impossibility.

The fact that African Americans in the United States are to a marked degree disproportionately represented among those labeled "retarded" is clearly related to the prominence of the IQ measure in the definition of retardation. African Americans have a persistent 15-point deficit, on average, relative to whites on this type of test. However interpreted—whether in terms of "test bias" or in terms of a "real" difference (and from the preceding argument we suggest that these are the same things)—one implication seems clear. Namely, African Americans *as a group* are seriously disadvantaged in engagements with the standard educational system. Relative success in such engagements, as already noted, is mostly what IQ tests are designed to predict, and for the most part they do so effectively. If, as is often said (we have our own small doubts), conventional academic success leads to such happiness and riches as are attainable in our larger culture, then enormously disproportionate numbers of African Americans will continue to be excluded from the good life unless some remedy can be found and put in place.

As we have seen, serious and broad-based efforts to find a remedy to this problem were begun in the 1960s, Project Head Start being a notable example. Much was learned in the programs that were launched during that era, one of the most important lessons being that genuine and sustained advance was costly and difficult. For example, we learned that the gains in academic skill acquired in an enriched preschool experience, as in Head Start, were not lasting without a more general environmental enrichment. However, subsequent changes in national priorities and in the political atmosphere, particularly at the federal level, precluded a vigorous follow-up of these initiatives. We have not regained momentum in this area, nor does it appear likely, as of this writing, that we soon will. If progress in laying to rest the cold war and in the achievement of "the new world order" were happily to continue, however, sufficient funds and energies might be liberated to contemplate seriously a new *national* order, one in which all of our children might truly be granted equal opportunity. It is a cruel deception, in our judgment, to suggest that they have it now.

SUMMARY

Developmental disorders are those disorders of the early years that are rooted in the developmental process. They are thought to be due to defects or delays in normal development itself, thus manifesting themselves in failures to attain expected levels of mastery, competence, or skill in various areas. Investigators commonly assume that some defect or developmental retardation exists at the organic (brain) level in regard to these disorders, although often without sound empirical support. This chapter is concerned with mental retardation, the pervasive developmental disorder of autism, and specific developmental disorders involving learning disabilities, all of which are coded as DSM-III-R Axis II disorders of childhood.

Certain cases of mental retardation, approximately 25 percent of the total incidence, are related to gross structural defects in the brain. They are distinguished from organic brain syndromes by age-related criteria; that is, the structural defects are either congenital or are acquired before the brain has completed its development. An affected individual is prevented from acquiring certain forms of knowledge and cognitive skills and thus is considered *amented* as opposed to *demented.* In these cases, retardation is likely to be severe or profound and to be accompanied by obvious physical anomalies of one sort or another. Down syndrome and phenylketonuria (PKU) are examples of this type of disorder.

The large majority—some 75 percent—of mental retardation cases are unrelated to obvious physical defects and are considered cultural-familial in origin, a term that acknowledges our inability to disentangle genetic and environmental influences in the disorder. Caution is warranted in applying the label "mentally retarded" because of our heavy reliance on IQ test scores in its definition. The IQ test is—and always has been—a measure of *academic* skill, not of ability to survive and perhaps even prosper in other areas of life. A variety of evidence points to the conclusion that cultural-familial retardation may be treatable and even preventable, provided we can find the means of providing the necessary cognitive stimulation to socially and economically deprived children.

Some of the most severe and inexplicable childhood disorders are the pervasive developmental disorders, the most prominent example of which is infantile autism. In these disorders, extreme maladaptive behavior occurs during the early years and prevents affected children from developing psychologically. Autistic children, for example, seem to remain aloof from others, never responding to or seemingly not caring about what goes on around them. Many never learn to speak. These disorders likely have a biological basis, although definite proof of such a basis has proven elusive. Neither medical nor psychological treatment has been notably successful in fully normalizing the behavior of autistic children, but newer instructional and behavior-modification techniques have sometimes scored significant gains in improving their ability to function. In general, the long-term prognosis in autism appears discouraging.

Specific developmental disorders are those in which failure of mastery is limited to circumscribed areas, chiefly involving academic skills such as reading; general cognitive ability may be normal or superior. Affected children are commonly described as learning disabled (LD). Here again some localized defect in brain development is usually considered the primary cause, although independent corroboration of an organic cause is the exception rather than the rule. These disorders create great turmoil and frustration in victims, their families, schools, and professional helpers. Various remedies, most involving training regimens of one sort or another, are tried and apparently are sometimes successful. However, solid outcome research in the area of intervention techniques is seriously lacking. The long-term prognosis for LD, overall, is not encouraging.

Key Terms

developmental disorder (p. 503)
mental retardation (p. 503)
Down syndrome (p. 508)
phenylketonuria (PKU) (p. 511)
cretinism (p. 512)
myxedema (p. 512)
macrocephaly (p. 512)
microcephaly (p. 512)
hydrocephalus (p. 513)
cultural-familial retardation (p. 513)
mainstreaming (p. 519)
pervasive developmental disorder (p. 521)
autistic disorder (p. 521)
echolalia (p. 522)
structural therapy (p. 525)
specific developmental disorders (p. 528)
specific learning disabilities (p. 528)
learning disabled (LD) (p. 528)
dyslexia (p. 528)

Chapter 15

Behavior Disorders of Childhood and Adolescence

Aloïs Wey, *Maisons* (1977). Wey (1894–?) attended for a short time a primary school where he developed an interest in art and drawing. At the age of 14, Wey quit school and entered upon a difficult life complicated by bouts with alcoholism and by exacting toil, first as a helper in his father's roofing business, later as a master roofer, a factory worker, an electrician, a miner, and a cook. At the age of 80, in retirement and living in a rest home, Wey resumed drawing. Many of his works take as their subjects exotic architectural structures, quite often resembling the architecture of foreign countries (though Wey's travels in other lands were, in fact, quite limited).

During the nineteenth century, little account was taken of the special characteristics of psychopathology in children; maladaptive patterns that are considered relatively specific to childhood, such as hyperactivity, received virtually no attention at all. Since the turn of the twentieth century, with the advent of the mental health movement and the availability of child guidance facilities, marked strides have been made in assessing, treating, and understanding the maladaptive behavior patterns of children and youth. This progress has, however, lagged behind efforts to deal with adult psychopathology. In fact, as we will see, early efforts at classifying problems of childhood were simply extensions of adult-oriented diagnostic systems.

These early conceptualizations seemed to reflect a prevailing view of children as "miniature adults" and failed to take into account special problems, such as those associated with the developmental changes that normally take place in a child or adolescent. Only recently have we come to realize that we cannot fully understand childhood disorders without taking into account these developmental processes; in fact, the field is often referred to as **developmental psychopathology.** Today, even though great progress has been made in providing treatment for disturbed children, our facilities are woefully inadequate in relation to the magnitude of the task, and the majority of problem children do not receive psychological attention (Links, Boyle, & Offord, 1989). The numbers of children affected by psychological problems are considerable. For example, the Office of Technology Assessment (OTA, 1986) places the percentage of American children with psychological disorders at 12 to 15 percent. In a cross-cultural study, Wunsch-Hitzig, Gould, and Dohrenwend (1980) found the incidence of childhood maladjustment to be similar for the United States (11.8 percent) and for Great Britain (13.2 percent). In both countries, maladjustment among boys significantly exceeded that among girls. In a more recent survey of psychological disorder in children, Anderson et al. (1987) found that an overall prevalence of 17.6 percent of 11-year-old children had one or more disorders. Boys were diagnosed more frequently than girls at 1.7 to 1. The most prevalent disorders were attention-deficit hyperactivity disorder and separation anxiety disorders.

In the first section of this chapter we will note some general characteristics of maladaptive behavior in children as compared with adult disorders. Next we will examine the issues surrounding the diagnostic classification of children's disorders. Then we will look at a number of important disorders of childhood and adolescence. In the final section we will give detailed consideration to some of the special factors involved in both the treatment and prevention of children's problems.

MALADAPTIVE BEHAVIOR IN DIFFERENT LIFE PERIODS

Because personality differentiation, developmental tasks, and typical stressors differ for childhood, adolescence, and adulthood, we would expect to find some differences in maladaptive behavior in these different periods. The special characteristics of childhood disorders are discussed here.

Varying Clinical Pictures

The clinical picture in childhood disorders tends to be different from those of other life periods. Although some disorders, such as attention-deficit hyperactivity disorder, are primarily problems of childhood, even the disorders that occur at all life periods reflect the developmental level of the individual experiencing them. For example, the suicidal impulses commonly found in adolescent and adult depression are fairly rare in childhood depression (Kovacs & Beck, 1977). In childhood schizophrenia, although there is the characteristic schizophrenic withdrawal and inability to relate to others, delusions and hallucinations are less common; when they do occur, they are more transient and less well systematized (Elkind & Weiner, 1978). In fact, some of the emotional disturbances of childhood may be relatively short-lived, undifferentiated, and changeable compared with those of later life periods (Lewis et al., 1988). It should be kept in mind, however, that some childhood disorders severely affect future development. Kuperman, Black, and Burns (1988) reported that individuals who had been hospitalized as child psychiatric patients (between the ages of 5 and 17) showed excess mortality in unnatural deaths (about twice the rate of the general population) when followed up from 4 to 15 years later. Suicide accounted for the majority of these deaths, and the suicide rate was significantly greater than in the general population.

Special Vulnerabilities of Young Children

Young children do not have as clear-cut a view of themselves and their world as they will have at a later age. They have less self-understanding and have not yet developed a stable sense of identity and an adequate frame of reference regarding reality, possibility, and value. Immediately perceived threats are tempered less by considerations of the past or future and thus tend to be seen as disproportionately important. As a result, children often have more difficulty in coping with stressful events than do adults.

Children's limited perspectives, as might be expected, lead them to use childlike concepts to explain what is happening. For example, in the comparatively rare case of child suicide, a child may be trying to rejoin a dead parent, sibling, or pet. For young children, suicide—or violence against another person—may be undertaken without any real understanding that death is final.

Children also are more dependent on other people than are adults. Though in some ways this dependency serves as a buffer against other dangers, it also makes them highly vulnerable to experiences of rejection, disappointment, and failure. On the other hand, although their inexperience and lack of self-sufficiency make them easily upset by problems that seem minor to the average adult, children typically recover more quickly from their hurts.

It's easy to spot the one child in this group who seems especially vulnerable to the stress of classroom competition. While others have their hands raised or otherwise look alert, her head is down and her demeanor is withdrawn. Children's inexperience and lack of self-sufficiency make them easily upset by problems that may seem minor to the average adult, and they often have more difficulty in coping with stressful events than they will have when they are older.

Moreover, it is important to view a child's behavior in reference to normal childhood development. One cannot understand or consider as "abnormal" a child's behavior without considering whether the behavior in question is appropriate for the child's age. Behavior such as temper tantrums or eating inedible objects might be viewed as symptoms of abnormal behavior at age 10 but not at age 2. Despite these somewhat distinctive characteristics of childhood disturbances, there is no sharp line of demarcation between the maladaptive behavior patterns of childhood and those of adolescence, nor between those of adolescence and those of adulthood. Thus, although our focus in this chapter will be on the behavior disorders of children and adolescents, we will find some inevitable overlapping with those of later life periods. In this context, it is useful to emphasize the basic continuity of an individual's behavior over time as he or she attempts to cope with the problems of living.

THE CLASSIFICATION OF CHILDHOOD AND ADOLESCENT DISORDERS

Diagnosis of the psychological disorders of childhood has traditionally been a rather confused practice, and until recently no formal, specific system was available for classifying the emotional problems of children and adolescents. Kraepelin's (1883) classic textbook on the classification of mental disorders did not include childhood disorders. Not until 1952, when the first formal psychiatric nomenclature (DSM-I) was published, was a classification system for childhood disorders made available. The DSM-I system, however, was quite limited and included only two childhood emotional disorders: ***childhood schizophrenia*** and ***adjustment reaction of childhood.*** Although several additional categories were added to the 1968 revision (DSM-II), a growing concern remained, both among clinicians attempting to diagnose and treat childhood problems and among researchers attempting to broaden our understanding of childhood psychopathology, that the then-current ways of viewing psychological disorders in children and adolescents were inappropriate and inaccurate.

Several reasons can be found for the early inadequacies of these diagnostic systems. First, the greatest problem stemmed from the fact that the same classification system that had been developed for adult problems was used for childhood problems. No allowance was made for the special considerations that enter into childhood conditions, such as an often mixed symptom pattern. Second, the early systems ignored the fact that in childhood disorders, environmental factors play an important part in the expression of symptoms; that is, symptom manifestations are highly influenced by a family's acceptance or rejection of the behavior. For example, either extreme tolerance of deviant behavior or total rejection and neglect could lead a child to accept his or her extreme behavior as "normal." Third, the symptoms were often incorporated without regard to a child's developmental level. In other words, the troubling behaviors might simply be behaviors a child will grow out of in time.

Over the years, discontent with the classification system for childhood behavior problems has led to considerable rethinking, discussion, and empirical investigation of the issues related to diagnosis. You may recall that in Chapter 1 we discussed various methods of classification. In the classification of childhood disorders, two of these methods —the categorical and the dimensional—have both been prominent. The first approach, a ***categorical strategy,*** is typically used by clinicians and has evolved from previous diagnostic classification systems. DSM-III-R is an example of a categorical strategy. In this strategy, a clinician—or, in the case of DSM-III-R, a group of clinicians—arrives at a descriptive class or category by examining, through clinical study, the behaviors that appear to define that class of children. For example, the similar behaviors that appear in children who are judged to fit the diagnostic class ***attention-deficit hyperactivity disorder*** are used as the defining criteria of that class.

The second approach—which is rarely used by clinicians but which is favored by many empirical researchers in psychopathology—is a ***dimensional strategy.*** This approach involves the application of sophisticated statistical methods to provide clear behavior clusters or "dimensions" for the widely observed symptoms manifested by children. A researcher gathers his or her symptomatic information through teachers', parents', or clinicians' observations or through a child's *presenting symptoms*—that is, the behaviors characteristic of the clinical picture at the time the child is first seen by professional personnel. The researcher then allows the statistical method—for example, factor analysis—to determine the various behavior dimensions evidenced by an individual child. For example, the Child Behavior Checklist (CBCL) is the most widely researched and used dimensional strategy for assessing childhood behavior problems. Achenbach (1985) and his colleagues (Achenbach & Edelbrock, 1983: Achenbach & McConaughy, 1985; Achenbach & Weisz,

1975) rated the symptoms of problem children based on two broad dimensions: *internalizing* and *externalizing,* which describe the differing tendencies to deal with problems through internal processes or through external actions against the environment. Thus symptoms on the internalizing dimension might include depression, social withdrawal, and anxiety, while symptoms on the externalizing dimension might include hyperactivity, aggression, and delinquent behavior.

Both systems are based on observation of an individual's behavior, and both result in classifying the person according to the presence or absence of symptoms. There are marked differences between the systems, however. The categorical approach generally requires the presence of relatively few symptoms to arrive at a diagnosis. The dimensional approach, on the other hand, usually requires the presence of a number of related symptoms before a case is included on a dimension. As a result, a categorical system will tend to have many categories defined by few, sometimes quite rare, behaviors, while dimensional approaches typically involve a small number of general classes covering numerous related behaviors.

Broadly, the categorical approach follows the disease model of psychopathology and attempts to organize or classify the aberrant behavior observed in problem children into meaningful classes of mental diseases to provide useful prognoses and treatments. The dimensional approach is based on the idea that these behaviors are continuous and are found even among many "normals"; it attempts to provide an objective classification scheme for assessing the relative frequency of these behavioral problems in an individual or group. It is possible to see benefits and problems in both these approaches to classification. Because this textbook focuses on the clinical manifestation of disorders, including infrequent symptoms that would be minimized in a dimensional approach, we will, for practical purposes, follow the DSM-III-R classification system of childhood and adolescent disorders. Keep in mind, however, that the approach taken here is only one possible way of viewing disorders.

DISORDERS OF CHILDHOOD

In this section we will discuss several disorders of childhood with a focus on describing the clinical picture of each syndrome, surveying the possible causal factors, and outlining treatment approaches that have proved effective. A broader discussion of treatment methods can be found in Chapters 17 and 18.

The disorders that will be covered are attention-deficit hyperactivity disorder, conduct disorder (including juvenile delinquency), anxiety disorders of childhood, depressive disorders, and several other special symptom disorders. These disorders are less stable than most of the abnormal behavior patterns discussed in earlier chapters and also perhaps more amenable to treatment. If treatment is not received, childhood developmental problems sometimes merge almost imperceptibly into more serious and chronic disorders as the child passes into adulthood, or they manifest themselves later as different disorders (Gelfand, Jenson, & Drew, 1988).

Attention-Deficit Hyperactivity Disorder

The **attention-deficit hyperactivity disorder (ADHD),** often referred to as **hyperactivity,** is characterized by difficulties that interfere with effective task-oriented behavior in children—particularly impulsivity, excessive motor activity, and an inability to attend. The presenting symptoms in attention-deficit hyperactivity disorder are relatively common among children seen at child guidance centers. In fact, hyperactive children are the most frequent psychological referrals to mental health and pediatric facilities, and it is estimated that between 3 and 5 percent of elementary-school-aged children manifest the symptoms (Ross & Pelham, 1981). Attention-deficit hyperactivity disorder is the most frequent disorder among preadolescent boys, with a 6.7 percent prevalence (Anderson et al., 1987). The disorder, which is six to nine times more prevalent among boys (DSM-III-R, 1987), occurs with the greatest frequency before age 8 and tends to become less frequent and with briefer episodes thereafter. As we will see, some residual effects, such as attention difficulties, may persist into adolescence or the adult years. Few well-controlled, prospective, longitudinal studies have focused on hyperactivity, so most of our understanding is based on clinical reports.

The Clinical Picture in Attention-Deficit Hyperactivity Disorder As the term implies, attention-deficit hyperactive children show excessive or exaggerated muscular activity—for example, aimless or haphazard running or fidgeting. Difficulty in sustaining attention is another central feature of the disorder. Hyperactive children are highly distractible and do not follow instructions or respond to demands placed on them. Impulsive behavior and a low frustration tolerance are also characteristic.

Hyperactive children do not typically show deficits in intelligence, but they tend to talk incessantly and to be socially uninhibited and immature. Barkley and Cunningham (1979) reported that hyperactive children usually have great difficulties in getting along with their parents, usually because they do not obey rules. King and Young (1981) found that hyperactive children are viewed negatively by their peers. In general, however, hyperactive children do not appear to be anxious, although their overactivity, restlessness, and distractibility are often interpreted as indications of anxiety. Usually they do poorly in school, commonly showing specific learning disabilities, such as difficulties in reading or in learning other basic school subjects. Hyperactive children also pose behavior problems in the elementary grades. The following case, involving an eight-year-old girl, reveals a typical clinical picture:

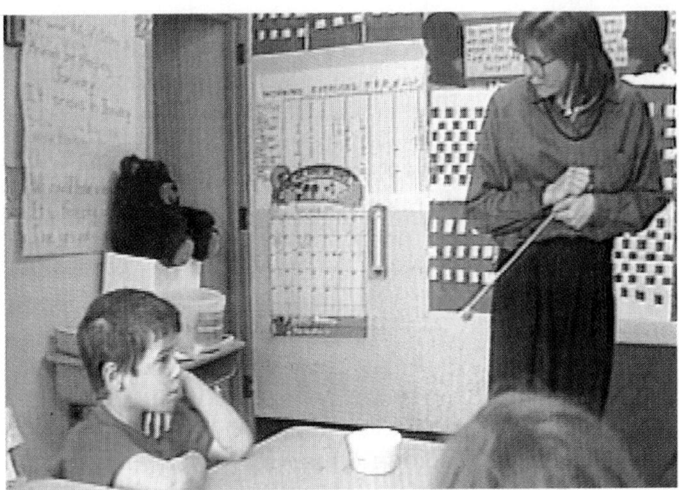

The special education teacher shown here works with children who have behavioral problems, such as attention-deficit hyperactivity disorder. Unrecognized and left untreated, a child with ADHD runs the risk of a multitude of problems with schoolwork, teachers, and other students. In her classroom, this teacher constantly reminds her students about behaviors they are working on, and reinforces positive behaviors with poker chips that may be cashed in for treats, toys, or privileges.

The subject was referred to a community clinic because of overactive, inattentive, and disruptive behavior. She was a problem to her teacher and to other students because of her hyperactivity and her uninhibited behavior. She would impulsively hit other children, knock things off their desks, erase material on the blackboard, and damage books and other school property. She seemed to be in perpetual motion —talking, moving about, and darting from one area of the classroom to another. She demanded an inordinate amount of attention from her parents and her teacher, and she was intensely jealous of other children, including her own brother and sister. Despite her hyperactive behavior, inferior school performance, and other problems, she was considerably above average in intelligence. Nevertheless, she felt "stupid" and had a seriously devaluated self-image. Neurological tests revealed no significant organic brain disorder.

In spite of the frequency with which the diagnosis is made, there is some disagreement about whether a "hyperactive syndrome" really exists. Quay (1979) argued that the research data on objective symptom classification did not support the existence of the hyperactive disorder separate from conduct disorders. This view has received some support from the research literature. In one study, Prinz, Connor, and Wilson (1981) found that hyperactive and aggressive behaviors were often confused with one another and were in fact highly related rather than distinct disorders. In another study, Sanson (1980) found virtually no difference between hyperactivity and conduct disorders and concluded that hyperactivity, as a diagnostic category, appeared to have little meaning with respect to etiology or treatment.

Ross and Pelham (1981) concluded that before substantial progress could be made in the understanding of hyperactivity as a diagnostic category, the criteria for defining the disorder would need to be refined. This process would need to include the development of clear normative data on children's behavior, which would make it possible to determine where a hyperactive child actually deviates from normal development. Meanwhile, the symptoms described earlier remain the usual basis for a diagnosis of hyperactivity.

Causal Factors in Attention-Deficit Hyperactivity Disorder The lack of clarity in diagnosing hyperactivity makes it difficult for researchess to evaluate the possibility that underlying biological conditions might cause the disorder. Rapoport and Ferguson (1981) reviewed the research on possible biological causes for hyperactivity; they found that the correlations between biological data and hyperactivity were weak and that there was no compelling evidence for a biological basis.

One viewpoint (Feingold, 1977) that received a great deal of public attention suggested that hyperactivity in children may be produced by dietary factors—particularly food coloring. Feingold even proposed a dietary treatment for hyperactive children; however, the food-additive theory of hyperactivity has generally been discredited (Mattes & Gittelman, 1981; Stare, Whelan, & Sheridan, 1980). A current variation of the food additive theory was recently published by Marshall (1989). This researcher reviewed the evidence for allergic reactions to certain additives or dyes in foods and concluded that evidence warrants further research into the possibility that allergic reactions could stimulate the nervous system, resulting in hyperactivity in some children. Firm conclusions as to the potential biological basis for ADHD must await further research.

The search for psychological causes of hyperactivity has had similarly inconclusive results. Investigators have not clearly established any psychological causes for the disorder, although they have emphasized both temperament and learning factors. Some evidence shows that the home environment is influential in the development of the disorder (Paternite & Loney, 1980). One study suggested that family pathology, particularly parental personality problems, leads to hyperactivity in children. Morrison (1980) found that many parents of hyperactive children had psychological problems; for example, a large number of them were found to have clinical diagnoses of personality disorder or hysteria. Currently, ADHD is considered to have multiple causes and effects (Campbell & Wherry, 1986).

Treatments and Outcomes Although the hyperactive syndrome was first described more than 100 years ago, disagreement remains over the most effective methods of treatment, especially regarding the use of drugs to calm a hyperactive child. As with other problem behaviors, variations in treatment procedures may be required to meet the needs of individual hyperactive children.

Interestingly—although some data contradict the findings (Lou, Heinriken, & Bruhn, 1984)—research has shown that cerebral stimulants, such as amphetamines, have a quieting effect on hyperactive children—just the opposite of what we would expect from their effects on adults (Green & Warshauer, 1981). In addition, research has shown that amphetamines have similar calming effects on nonhyperactive children (Zahn, Rapoport, & Thompson, 1980). Such medication decreases hyperactive children's overactivity and distractibility and at the same time increases their attention and ability to concentrate. As a result they are often able to function much better at school (Henker & Whalen, 1989). In fact, many hyperactive children who have not been acceptable in regular classes can function and progress in a relatively normal manner when they use such drugs. The medication does not appear to affect their intelligence, but rather seems to help them use their basic capacities more effectively (NIMH, 1971). Although the drugs do not "cure" hyperactivity, they have reduced the behavioral symptoms in about half to two-thirds of the cases in which medication appears warranted.

While the short-term pharmacologic effect of stimulants on the symptoms of hyperactive children is apparently well established, their long-term effects are not well-known (Weiss, 1981). Some concern has been expressed about the effects of the drugs, particularly when used in heavy dosages over time. Safer and Allen (1973) concluded from a longitudinal study of 63 hyperactive children—49 of whom were on medication and 14 of whom were used as controls—that Ritalin, the most commonly used drug, can suppress normal growth in height and weight. In a carefully controlled study, however, Beck and colleagues (1975) failed to find such effects. Nevertheless, the use of such drugs should be carefully monitored to avoid harmful side effects and addiction. Some questions that have been raised concerning the use of these drugs are discussed in *HIGHLIGHT 15.1*. The use of drug therapy with children will be taken up again in Chapter 17.

Another effective approach to treating hyperactive children involves behavior therapy techniques featuring positive reinforcement and the structuring of learning materials and tasks in a way that minimizes error and maximizes immediate feedback and success. The use of behavioral treatment methods (see Chapter 18) for hyperactivity has reportedly been quite successful, at least for short-term gains. Robinson, Newby, and Ganzell (1981), using a token economy system, were able to increase the number of completed school tasks for hyperactive children up to the average number of tasks completed by other children in the school. In another approach, Dunn and Howell (1982) successfully used relaxation training to reduce hyperactivity in a group of boys.

Several investigators have reported that impulsive behavior in children can be successfully modified by the use of cognitive-behavioral techniques in which rewards for desired behavior are combined with training in the use of verbal self-instructions (Kendall, 1981; Meichenbaum, 1977; Meichenbaum & Goodman, 1971). The focus of cognitive-behavioral treatment is to help hyperactive children learn to shift attention less frequently and to behave reflectively rather than impulsively. The following case, reported by Kendall and Finch (1976), shows some aspects of cognitive-behavioral treatment:

HIGHLIGHT 15.1

Drug Therapy with Children

A number of important questions have been raised concerning the increasing use of drugs in the treatment of certain behavior disorders of children. The principal questions include:

1. *Who is being selected for treatment?* Few investigators question the usefulness of amphetamines or related drugs for treating many cases of hyperactivity, but many question the adequacy of the assessment procedures used in identifying children who actually need medication. For example, a clear-cut distinction is not always made between children who appear to need drug therapy because of hyperactivity and children whose inattention and restlessness may be the result of hunger, crowded classrooms, irrelevant curriculum content, or anxiety and depression stemming from a pathogenic home situation.

2. *Are drugs sometimes being used simply to "keep peace in the classroom"?* Those who raise this question point to the possibility that children who manifest bewilderment, anger, restlessness, or lethargy at school may only be showing a normal reaction to educational procedures that fail to spark their interest or meet their needs. These investigators maintain that to label such children as "sick"—as evidencing hyperactivity or some other behavior disorder—and to treat them through medication is to sidestep the difficult and expensive alternative of providing better educational programs. Possibly such an approach also reinforces the notion—all too prevalent in our culture—that if things are not going well, all a person has to do is take some type of drug.

3. *Do the drugs have harmful side effects?* Even in the small dosages usually prescribed for children, drugs sometimes have undesirable side effects. Symptoms including decreased appetite, dizziness, headaches, and insomnia have been reported in some cases to accompany the use of stimulants, such as methylphenidate-hydrochloride (Ritalin); recently these drugs have been implicated in suspected growth retardation. Minor tranquilizers also may have adverse side effects, including lethargy. Even with drugs that seem to produce minimal side effects, the possibility of adverse long-range effects resulting from sustained usage during early growth and development is still being assessed.

The consensus among investigators seems to be that drug therapy for children should be used with extreme caution, and only with those children for whom other alternatives simply do not work, such as a hyperactive child who cannot control his or her behavior without drug therapy. It is also important that drug therapy be undertaken only with the informed consent of the parent, as well as the child if he or she is old enough, and that the child not be given the sole responsibility for taking the medication—a procedure that can lead to drug abuse. At the same time, there is a need to avoid exaggerated public attitudes against the use of drug therapy for children who genuinely need it. Finally, children who do benefit from drug therapy also need other therapeutic measures for dealing with coexisting problems, such as learning deficiencies and psychological, interpersonal, and family difficulties.

Based on Beck et al. (1975), Cole (1975), Eisenberg (1971), Hayes, Panitch, and Barker (1975), Martin and Zaug (1975), Whalen and Henker (1976), and Winsberg et al. (1975).

A nine-year-old boy was referred to a psychiatric facility because of problems at school. The teacher had described him as hyperactive, impulsive, and oversensitive to criticism. After only a month in fourth grade, he had been demoted to third grade because of his inability to adjust.

During the initial interview, the child was constantly moving about. He climbed into and out of chairs, talked rapidly about many topics, and changed the direction and purpose of his behavior without apparent reason. Test data also suggested overactivity and impulsivity to be the central problems.

Therapy sessions started with the therapist working on a maze and talking aloud as he thought through each step he was performing—defining the problem, indicating the focus of his attention and the approach he was using, and including coping statements (after making an intentional error) such as, "I should have gone slower and thought and been more careful." After the therapist finished the maze, the boy worked it, instructing himself aloud in the same way.

Several other mazes were solved in this way, except that the self-instructions were whispered. Then, the use of self-instructions for target behaviors was rehearsed. For example, to learn not to switch topics during a conversation, the boy practiced the following self-instructions: "What should I remember? I'm to finish talking about what I start to talk about. O.K. I should think before I talk and remember not to switch. If I complete what I'm talking about before I start another topic, I get to keep my dimes. I can look at this card [cue] to remind me" (p. 854).

The boy was given several coins, one of which was subject to forfeit each time he switched to some other topic in the middle of what he was saying. Whatever he had left at the end of the session he could keep.

It was hoped that this verbal rehearsal and reinforcement for success would help the boy develop control over his own behavior, and, in fact, it did. The boy's in-therapy behavior became less hyperactive, his test performance improved, and the teacher noted improvements in the classroom.

From the above case, it appears that one way to deal with the problems associated with hyperactivity is to teach children to stop and think before undertaking a behavior so that they can then guide their own performance by deliberate self-instruction. The extent to which such gains made in cognitive-behavioral therapy generalize to other settings, such as the home and play situations, must be further researched.

The continued use of psychological therapy with medication in a total treatment program has reportedly shown good success. Pelham and associates (1980) found that the combination of behavioral intervention and psychostimulant medication was more effective than either treatment alone in modifying the behavior of hyperactive children. Satterfield, Satterfield, and Cantwell (1981) reported that individualized treatment of various types in conjunction with the use of medication resulted in favorable treatment outcomes in a three-year follow-up.

It should be kept in mind, however, that even though behavioral interventions and medication have reportedly enjoyed short-term successes, there has been insufficient critical evaluation of the long-term effects of either treatment method (O'Leary, 1980). One follow-up study of the drug treatment of 75 children over a 10- to 12-year period reported that young adults who had been hyperactive children had less education than control subjects and had a history of more auto accidents and more geographical moves. The authors found, however, that only a minority of the formerly hyperactive subjects continued their antisocial behavior into adulthood or developed severe psychopathology (Weiss et al., 1979). Glow (1981) cautioned against drug treatment for hyperactivity on grounds that, while it may curb the symptoms, it does not cure the disorder. Similarly, Glow claimed that behavioral interventions require a great deal of effort, are not free from hazard, and have not been demonstrated to have long-range effects.

It is clear from an evaluation of the literature on the treatment of hyperactivity that, in addition to a general disagreement about the nature of hyperactivity, an equal degree of controversy exists about the most effective treatment approach.

Even without treatment, hyperactive behavior tends to diminish by the time children reach their middle teens. Research has demonstrated, however, that many hyperactive children go on to have other psychological problems in their late teens and early adulthood. Hechtman, Weiss, and Perlman (1980), for example, found that hyperactive children had significantly more problems than control subjects when they reached young adulthood. The hyperactive subjects had poor social skills and low self-esteem as young adults. This group also may have a higher-than-average incidence of delinquency and other maladaptive behavior during adolescence and beyond (Solomon, 1972). A recent, longitudinal study of ADHD was conducted by Gittleman et al. (1985). These investigators evaluated and followed up a group of 101 boys aged 6 through 12 who showed hyperactivity, contrasting their later adjustment, at 16 to 23 years of age, with a control sample of 100 nonhyperactive boys. They found that the majority of the boys who had been diagnosed as hyperactive showed diminished symptom patterns in later adolescence and early adulthood. However, the full attention deficit disorder persisted in 31 percent of the hyperactive boys, while only 3 percent of the control sample showed hyperactive symptoms at follow-up. The authors also found that the hyperactive boys showed a greater likelihood of developing psychiatric problems than the control boys. Their "most striking finding is the degree to which the syndrome consisting of impulsivity, inattention, and hyperactivity persisted" (p. 943), and boys in which the hyperactivity persisted had a greater likelihood of developing conduct disorders. Hyperactive boys who did not receive a DSM-III-R diagnosis at follow-up showed no differences from the control boys (Mannuzza et al., 1988).

Conduct Disorders

The next group of disorders emphasizes a child's or an adolescent's relationship to social norms and rules of conduct. In **conduct disorders,** aggressive or antisocial behavior is the focus. With these disorders, it is important to distinguish between persistent antisocial acts, in which the rights of others are violated, and the less serious pranks often carried out by "normal" children and adolescents. We should point out, too, that conduct disorders involve misdeeds that may or may not be against the law; *juvenile delinquency*—to be discussed in the next section—is the legal term used to refer to violations of the law committed by minors.

The behavior to be described in the following sections may appear to be similar to the early stages in the development of personality disorders, discussed in Chapter 8. Indeed, the personality characteristics and causal considerations are much the same. It is difficult, if not impossible, to distinguish among a conduct disorder, a "predelinquent" pattern of behavior, and the early stages in the development of an antisocial personality. Behaviorally, the patterns are alike and may simply represent three ways of describing or accounting for the same behavior. Many adult antisocial personalities, as children, showed the aggressive behavior and rule violations that often are labeled conduct disorders, and many came into contact with the authorities as a result of this delinquent behavior. Fortunately, not all children who are described as having conduct disorders or who engage in delinquent behavior grow up to become antisocial personalities or commit themselves to lives of crime. As we will see, although these disorders of conduct are quite serious and rather complex to treat, there are effective ways of working with disordered individuals to help them become accepted and productive members of society.

The Clinical Picture in Conduct Disorders

The essential symptomatic behavior in the conduct disorders involves a persistent, repetitive violation of rules and a disregard for the rights of others. Stewart and associates (1980) found conduct-disordered children to be characterized by fighting, disobedience, destructiveness, meanness, and precocious sexual behavior. Behar and Stewart (1982) reported that conduct disorder began at a much earlier age than other disorders of childhood (excluding autism and organic syndromes). Approximately 9 percent of males and 2 percent of females have conduct disorder problems (DSM-III-R, 1987). The following case is typical of children with conduct disorder and illustrates many of the features commonly found:

Craig, an 8-year-old boy, had already established himself as a social outcast by the time he entered first grade. Previously, he had been expelled from kindergarten two times in two years for being unmanageable. His mother brought him to a mental health center at the insistence of the school when she attempted to enroll him in the first grade. Within the first week of school, Craig's quarrelsome and defiant behavior had tried the special education teacher, who was reputedly "excellent" with problem children like him, to the point where she recommended his suspension from school. His classmates likewise were completely unsympathetic to Craig, whom they viewed as a bully. At even the slightest sign of movement on his part, the other children would tell the teacher that Craig was "being bad again."

At home, Craig was uncontrollable. His mother and six other children lived with his domineering grandmother. Craig's mother was ineffective at disciplining or managing her children. She worked long hours as a domestic maid and "did not feel like hassling with those kids" when she got home. Her present husband, the father of the three youngest children (including Craig), had deserted the family.

In general, children who are seen as conduct disordered manifest such characteristics as overt or covert hostility, disobedience, physical and verbal aggressiveness, quarrelsomeness, vengefulness, and destructiveness. Lying, solitary stealing, and temper tantrums are common. Such children tend to be sexually uninhibited and inclined toward sexual aggressiveness. Some may engage in firesetting (see *HIGHLIGHT 15.2*), vandalism, and even homicidal acts.

HIGHLIGHT 15.2

Fire Setting: An Extreme Conduct Disorder?

Fire setting in children is a potentially dangerous and difficult to understand problem. Estimates of the prevalence of fire setting by children have been as high as 8 percent of all recorded fires (Fire Statistics UK, 1980). Fire setting is more common among boys by about five to one. What motivates children to set fires? Early studies (Lewis & Yarnel, 1951) concluded that fire setters are typically of low intelligence and from disrupted homes. Early clinical theorists placed the cause of fire setting in personality development and considered the problem to co-occur with problems of sexual maladjustment and enuresis (Hellman & Blackmun, 1966; Schmid, 1914). A number of investigators (Jacobson, 1985a; Kuhnley, Hendron, & Quinlan, 1982) report a strong association between fire setting and the presence of conduct disorders. Recent studies, however, report more diagnostic heterogeneity and do not find a consistent association with conduct disorder (Jacobson, 1985b; Kolko, Kazdin, & Meyer, 1985).

Even though the general diagnosis may vary among fire setters, several problems appear to be consistently observed in the children who set fires. They tend to be extremely aggressive and fight a great deal, and they tend to have psychosocial disturbances and poor social skills. It should be noted, however, that the great majority of conduct-disordered, aggressive, and socially unskilled children do not engage in fire setting. Why some disturbed children do is not clearly known.

In DSM-III-R, the broad category *conduct disorder* contains three subtypes. These subtypes are as follows:

- *Group type.* The conduct problems occur in group activity with peers.
- *Solitary aggressive type.* The youngster engages in aggressive behavior against both adults and peers.
- *Undifferentiated type.* Features of both the group type and the solitary aggressive type are present.

Causal Factors in Conduct Disorders Investigators seem generally to agree that the family setting of a conduct-disordered child is typically characterized by ineffective parenting, rejection, harsh and inconsistent discipline, and often parental neglect (Patterson, DeBarsyshe, & Ramsey, 1989). Frequently, the parents have an unstable marital relationship, are emotionally disturbed or sociopathic, and do not provide the child with consistent guidance, acceptance, or affection. Family discord, such as the conflict and disharmony accompanying divorce (Chess & Thomas, 1984), is instrumental in the development of conduct disorders. In a disproportionate number of cases, the child lives in a home broken by divorce or separation, may have a stepparent, or may have had a series of stepparents. Regardless of whether a home is broken or not, a child in a conflict-charged home feels overtly rejected. Rutter and Quinton (1984), for example, concluded that family discord and hostility were "the chief mediating variables" in the association between disturbed parents and disturbed children, particularly with regard to the development of conduct disorders in children and adolescents.

Treatments and Outcomes Therapy for a conduct-disordered child is likely to be ineffective unless some means can be found for modifying the child's environment. This task is difficult when the parents are maladjusted and in conflict with each other. Often an overburdened parent who is separated or divorced and working simply does not have the time or inclination to learn and practice a more adequate parental role. In some cases, the circumstances may call for a child to be removed from the home and placed in a foster home or institution, with the expectation of a later return to the home if intervening therapy with the parents appears to justify it.

Unfortunately, children who are removed to new environments often interpret this removal as further rejection—not only by their parents but by society as well. Unless the changed environment offers a warm, kindly, and accepting—yet consistent and firm—setting, such children are likely to make little progress. Even then, treatment may have

Family discord and hostility have been found to play a role in the development of conduct disorders, but removing a child from the home may be interpreted by the child as further rejection. One program that attempts to involve both parents and children is the Oregon Social Learning Center's foster care program. A child in this program lives with specially trained foster parents for up to six months, and during this time the natural parents meet with a therapist once a week (as shown here) to learn better parenting skills. Through individual and family therapy, the program tries to develop a family pattern that is stable, accepting, consistent, and affectionate.

only a temporary effect. Faretra (1981) followed up 66 aggressive and disturbed adolescents who had been admitted to an inpatient unit. She found that antisocial and criminal behavior persisted into adulthood with a lessening of psychiatric involvement. The most antisocial children were from homes with histories of antisocial problems, one-parent homes, or minority or deprived environments. Zeitlin (1986) studied psychiatric patients who were treated as both children and adults, finding that many conduct-disordered children go on to have personality disorders as adults. Rutter (1988) concluded that "most (but not all) forms of adult personality disorder (and not just the antisocial or sociopathic variety) have been preceded by conduct disorders in children" (p. 490).

Aggressiveness at an early age has been found to be related to adult criminal behavior. Stattin and Magnusson (1989) conducted a study of 1027 boys and girls between late childhood and early adolescence using teacher ratings made at ages 10 and 13. An evaluation of the recorded behavior problems of the boys through age 26 found that high ratings of childhood aggressiveness were characteristic of subjects who later committed violent crimes and damage to public property. The relationship between early aggressiveness and later crime was not associated for girls.

By and large, our society tends to take a punitive, rather than rehabilitative, attitude toward an antisocial, aggressive youth. Thus, the emphasis is on punishment and on "teaching the child a lesson." Such "treatment," however, appears to intensify rather than correct the behavior. Where treatment is unsuccessful, the end product is likely to be an antisocial personality with aggressive behavior. Several studies have shown the long-range negative consequences of unchecked aggressiveness. In one longitudinal study of antisocial, aggressive behavior in childhood, Robins (1970) evaluated aggressive behavior in young adolescent boys and then followed them up in later adolescence and young adulthood. Early aggressive behavior was found to be highly predictive of sociopathic actions in later adolescence and adulthood; similar findings have been reported by Wolkind (1974).

The advent of behavior therapy techniques has, however, made the outlook brighter for children who manifest conduct disorders. Teaching control techniques to the parents of such children is particularly important, so that they function as therapists in reinforcing desirable behavior and modifying the environmental conditions that have been reinforcing maladaptive behavior. The changes brought about when they consistently accept and reward their child's positive behavior and stop focusing attention on the negative behavior may finally change their perception of and feelings toward the child, leading to the basic acceptance that the child has so badly needed.

Though effective techniques for behavioral management can be taught to parents (Fleishman, 1981), often they have difficulty carrying out treatment plans. If this is the case, other techniques, such as family therapy or parental counseling, can be employed to ensure that the parent or person responsible for the child's discipline is sufficiently assertive to follow through on the program. Shoemaker and Paulson (1976) described a program of assertiveness training for mothers in which women who had children with aggressive behavior problems were taught more effective skills in self-expression and verbal discipline. Ratings of their children's behavior showed improvement following the assertiveness training.

Delinquent Behavior

In this section we will examine one of the most troublesome and extensive problems in childhood and adolescence: delinquent behavior. This behavior includes such acts as destruction of property, violence against other people, and various behaviors contrary to the needs and rights of others and in violation of society's laws. As noted earlier, the term

juvenile delinquency is a legal one; it refers to illegal acts committed by individuals under the age of 16, 17, or 18 (depending on state law). Children under 8 who commit such acts are not considered delinquents, because it is assumed that they are too immature to understand the significance and consequences of their actions. Delinquency is generally regarded as calling for some punishment or corrective action.

The Incidence and Severity of Delinquent Acts The actual incidence of juvenile delinquency is difficult to determine because many delinquent acts are not reported. Of the two million young people who go through the juvenile courts each year in the United States, about half are there for actions, such as running away, that are not considered crimes for adults. These actions are referred to as status offenses (see *HIGHLIGHT 15.3*). In 1988, arrests of people under 18 years of age accounted for 28 percent of all crime (Uniform Crime Reports, 1989). Juveniles accounted for over 1 out of every 3 arrests for robbery, 1 out of 3 arrests for crimes against property, 1 out of 6 arrests for rape, and 1 out of 11 arrests for murder. Although most of the juvenile crime was committed by males, the rate has also risen for females. About 1 teenager out of every 15 in the nation was arrested. Well over half of the juveniles who are arrested each year have prior police records (Uniform Crime Reports, 1989). Female delinquents are commonly apprehended for drug usage, sexual offenses, running away from home, and "incorrigibility," but crimes against property, such as stealing, have markedly increased among this group. Male delinquents are commonly arrested for drug usage and crimes against property; to a lesser extent, they are arrested for armed robbery, aggravated assault, and other crimes against people.

Fear of violent juvenile crime has created in many people the idea that juvenile criminals as a group are uncontrollable and antisocial personalities. The extent of dangerous and violent behavior among delinquents has been questioned, however. Dinitz and Conrad (1980) reported that, of a sample of 811 juveniles arrested for violent crimes, only about 2 percent had been involved in repeated aggressive or violent acts; even the acts of this 2 percent were mostly "clumsy and inadvertent" (p. 145).

In general, it is assumed that both the incidence and the severity of delinquent behavior are disproportionately high for slum and lower-class youth. This view has been supported by findings of the President's Commission on Law Enforcement and Administration of Justice (1967) as well as by later reports (Zimring, 1979). Other investigators, however, have found no evidence that delinquency is predominately a lower-class phenomenon. In a study of 433 teenagers who had committed almost 2500 delinquent acts, Haney and Gold (1973) reported "no strong relationship between social status and delinquent behavior" (p. 52). Similar findings have been described by Krohn et al. (1980). It may also be noted that the delinquency rate for socially disadvantaged youths appears about equal for whites and nonwhites (Uniform Crime Reports, 1989). In summary, although much juvenile crime is committed by lower class youth, some problems have been noted in all social strata (Elliott, Dunford, & Huizinga, 1987).

Causal Factors in Delinquency Various conditions, singly and in combination, may be involved in the development of delinquent behavior. In general, however, several key variables seem to play a part: personal pathology, pathogenic family patterns, undesirable peer relationships, general sociocultural factors, and special stress.

Personal pathology. A number of investigators have attempted to "type" delinquents in terms of pervasive patterns and sources of personal pathology.

1. *Genetic determinants.* Although the research on genetic determinants of antisocial behavior is far from conclusive, some evidence indicates possible hereditary contributions to criminality. Schulsinger (1980) identified 57 sociopathic adoptees from psychiatric and police files in Denmark and matched them with 57 nonsociopathic control adoptees on the basis of age, sex, social class, geographic region, and age at adoption. He found that natural parents of the adopted sociopaths, particularly fathers, were more likely to have sociopathic characteristics than the natural parents of the controls. Because these natural parents had little contact with their offspring, thus reducing the possibility of environmental influence, the results are interpreted as reflecting the possibility of some genetic transmission of a predisposition to antisocial behavior.

2. *Brain damage and mental retardation.* In a distinct minority of delinquency cases—an estimated 1 percent or less—brain pathology results in lowered inhibitory controls and a tendency toward episodes of violent behavior (Caputo & Mandell, 1970). Such youths are often hyperactive, impulsive, emotionally unstable, and unable to inhibit themselves when strongly stimulated. Fortunately,

HIGHLIGHT 15.3

Problems That Lead Children to Run Away

Of serious concern in the United States is the problem of youngsters who run away from home—an estimated one million or more each year. Although the average age is about 15, an increasing number are in the 11- to 14-year-old age bracket. Many of these runaways are from the suburbs, and at least half are girls. The following case illustrates this problem:

Joan, an attractive girl who looked older than her 12 years, came to the attention of juvenile authorities when her parents reported her as a runaway. Twice before she had run away from home, but no report had been filed. In the first instance, she had gone to the home of a girlfriend and returned two days later; in the second, she had hitchhiked to another city with an older boy and returned home about a week later. Investigation revealed that the girl was having difficulty in school and was living in a family situation torn by bickering and dissension. In explaining why she ran away from home, she stated simply that she "just couldn't take it anymore—all that quarreling and criticism, and no one really cared anyway."

Why do children and adolescents run away? English (1973) concluded that reasons for running away from home tend to fall into three categories: (a) getting out of a destructive family situation, as in the case of a girl who runs away to avoid sexual advances by her father or stepfather; (b) running away in an effort to better the family situation; and (c) having a secret, unsharable problem, such as, for girls, being pregnant.

In a study of runaway girls, Homer (1974) distinguished between "run from's," who had usually fought with their parents and run away because they were unable to resolve the situation or their anger, and "run to's," who were seeking something outside the home. The "run to's" were typically seeking pleasure—sex, drugs, liquor, escape from school, or a peer group with similar interests. Usually they stayed with friends or at other "peer-established" facilities. The "run from's" usually ran away from home only once, while the "run to's" were more likely to be repetitive runaways.

An increasing number of children are "run from's" who are trying to get away from intolerable home situations. In many instances, for economic or other reasons, they are actually encouraged to leave—and their parents do not want them back. Most do not feel that they can return to their parents but instead want a foster home where they will be treated well and respected.

The majority of runaways are not reported. Of those who are, about 90 percent or more are located by law enforcement officers and, when feasible, returned home. Beginning in 1974, a toll-free hotline was established that informs runaways where the nearest temporary shelter is located and enables them to send messages to their parents if they wish.[1] Treatment for runaways is similar to that for individuals who manifest other emotional problems during childhood and adolescence. Often family therapy is an essential part of the treatment program. In some instances—as in those involving parental abuse, unconcern, or lack of cooperation—juvenile authorities may place a child in a foster home. Parents, however, are by no means always the primary reason for their child's running away, and a "what-have-we-done-wrong" attitude may lead to unnecessary feelings of guilt.

[1]One of the toll-free numbers is 1-800-621-4000. This hotline does not operate in either Alaska or Hawaii.

their inner controls appear to improve during later adolescence and young adulthood. The actual role intellectual factors, particularly learning disabilities, play in causing juvenile delinquency is still being debated. In a recent review of the evidence, Lombardo and Lombardo (1991) concluded that there is no empirical evidence linking learning disabilities with delinquency.

3. *Psychological disorders.* A small percentage of delinquent acts appear to be directly associated with behavior disorders, such as hyperactivity. In some cases, delinquent acts take the form of a behavior such as "peeping" or stealing things that are not needed. This behavior often seems related to deviant sexual gratification in overinhibited adolescents who have been indoctrinated in the belief that masturbation and other overt forms of sexual release are evil and sinful. Often such individuals fight their inner impulses before committing a delinquent act and then feel guilty afterward.

Delinquent acts associated with psychotic behavior often involve a pattern of prolonged emotional hurt and turmoil, culminating, after long frustration, in an outburst of violent behavior (Bandura, 1973). In the case of psychologically disturbed delinquents, the delinquent act is a byproduct of severe personality maladjustment rather than a reflection of antisocial attitudes.

4. *Antisocial traits.* A sizable number of habitual delinquents appear to share the traits typical of antisocial personalities—they are impulsive, defiant, resentful, devoid of feelings of remorse or guilt, incapable of establishing and maintaining close interpersonal ties, and seemingly unable to profit from experience. Because they lack needed reality and ethical controls, they often engage in seemingly senseless acts that are not planned but occur on the spur of the moment. They may steal a small sum of money they do not need, or they may steal a car, drive it a few blocks, and abandon it. In some instances, they engage in impulsive acts of violence that are not committed for personal gain but rather reflect underlying resentment and hostility toward the world. In essence, these individuals are "unsocialized."

Although research has focused primarily on male delinquents, several investigators have also emphasized the high incidence of antisocial personalities among females in state correctional institutions (Cloninger & Guze, 1970; Konopka, 1964, 1967).

5. *Drug abuse.* A sizable number of delinquent acts—particularly theft, prostitution, and assault—are directly associated with alcohol or drug use. Most adolescents who abuse hard drugs, such as heroin, are forced to steal to maintain their habit, which can be very expensive. In the case of female addicts, theft may be combined with or replaced by prostitution as a means of obtaining money.

Pathogenic family patterns. In evaluating the role of pathogenic family patterns in delinquency, it should be emphasized that a given pattern is only one of many interacting factors. Of the various patterns that have been emphasized in the research on juvenile delinquency, the following appear to be the most important:

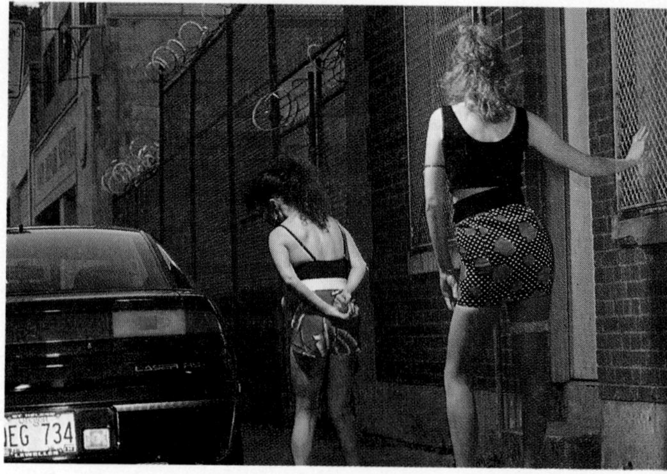

Teen prostitution is often directly associated with alcohol or drug use. For female addicts, prostitution is a means of obtaining money.

1. *Broken homes.* The term "broken home" is a catchall to describe the absence of one or both parents due to a variety of conditions, including desertion, separation, death, or imprisonment. Several investigators have pointed to the high incidence of broken homes and multiple or missing parental figures in the backgrounds of delinquent youths (Lefkowitz et al., 1977). In general, delinquency appears to be much more common among youths coming from homes broken by parental separation or divorce than from homes broken by the death of a parent, suggesting that parental conflict may be a key element in causing delinquency.

As we have seen, however, the effects of broken homes vary greatly. Even when the disruption is due to parental separation or divorce, children in such families may be less adversely affected than children raised in homes torn by parental conflict and dissension. Homes may be "broken" at different times and under varying circumstances; thus these disruptions have differing influences, depending on the individual involved ane his or her total life situation. Consequently, the effects of a given family pattern can be assessed adequately only in relation to an individual's total situation.

2. *Parental rejection and faulty discipline.* In many cases, one or both parents reject a child. When the father is the rejecting parent, it is difficult for a boy to identify with him and use him as a model for his own development. In an early study of 26 aggressively delinquent boys, Bandura and Walters (1963) delineated a pattern in which rejection by the father was combined with inconsistent handling of the boy by both parents. To complicate the pathogenic picture, the father typically used physically punitive methods of discipline, thus modeling aggressive behavior and augmenting the hostility that the boy already felt toward him. The end result of such a pattern was a hostile, defiant, inadequately socialized youth who lacked normal inner controls and tended to act out his aggressive impulses in antisocial behavior.

The detrimental effects of parental rejection and inconsistent discipline are by no means attributable only to fathers. Researchers have found that such behavior by either parent is associated with aggression, lying, stealing, running away from home, and a wide range of other difficulties (Langner et al., 1974; Lefkowitz et al., 1977; Pemberton & Benady, 1973). Often, too, inconsistent discipline may involve more complex family interactions, as when a mother imposes severe restrictions on a youth's behavior and then leaves "policing" to a timid or uncaring father who fails to follow through. In general, parental supervision has been found to be inversely related to delinquency—higher rates of delinquency are found in families that provide less supervision for their children (Morton & Ewald, 1987).

3. *Antisocial parental models.* Several investigators have found a high incidence of antisocial traits in the parents of delinquents—particularly but not exclusively in the father (Bandura, 1973; Glueck & Glueck, 1969). These traits included alcoholism, brutality, antisocial attitudes, failure to provide, frequent unnecessary absences from home, and other characteristics that made the father an inadequate and unacceptable model. Elkind (1967), for example, cited the case of a

father who encouraged his 17-year-old son to drink, frequent prostitutes, and generally "raise hell." This particular father was awakened late one night by the police who had caught his son in a raid on a so-called "massage" parlor. The father's reaction was, "Why aren't you guys out catching crooks?" This same father would boast to his coworkers that his son was "all boy" and "a chip off the old block." (p. 313)

Sociopathic fathers—and mothers—may contribute in various ways to the delinquent behavior of girls as well. Covert encouragement of sexual promiscuity is fairly common, and in some instances there is actual incest with the daughter. In a study of 30 delinquent girls, Scharfman and Clark (1967) found evidence of serious psychopathology in one or both parents of 22 of the girls, including three cases of incest and many other types of early sexual experience. These investigators also reported a high incidence of broken homes (only 11 of the 30 girls lived with both parents) and harsh, irrational, and inconsistent discipline:

Any form of consistent discipline or rational setting of limits was unknown to the girls in their homes. Rather, there was an almost regular pattern of indifference to the activities or whereabouts of these girls, often with the mother overtly or indirectly suggesting delinquent behavior by her own actions. This would alternate with unpredictable, irrational, and violent punishment." (p. 443)

4. *Limited parental relationships outside the family.* Some research suggests that the parents' interpersonal relationships outside the family may contribute to their children's behavioral problems (Griest & Wells, 1983). Wahler (1980) found that the children's oppositional behavior was inversely related to the amount of friendly contacts that parents had outside the home. Wahler et al. (1981) reported that mothers who are isolated or who have negative community interactions are less likely to "track" or control their children's behavior in the community than parents who have friendly relationships outside the family.

Undesirable peer relationships. Delinquency tends to be a shared experience. In their study of delinquents in the Flint, Michigan, area, Haney and Gold (1973) found that about two-thirds of delinquent acts were committed in association with one or two other people, and most of the remainder involved three or four other people. Usually the offender and the companion or companions were of the same sex. Interestingly, girls were more likely than boys to have a constant friend or companion in delinquency. The role of gang membership in delinquency is discussed in the next section.

General sociocultural factors. Broad social conditions may also tend to produce or support delinquency. Interrelated factors that appear to be of key importance include alienation and rebellion, social rejection, and the psychological support afforded by membership in a delinquent gang.

1. *Alienation and rebellion.* Feelings of alienation and rebellion are common to many teenagers from all socioeconomic levels. Alienated teenagers may outwardly submit passively to their elders' demands, or they may openly disobey parental and other adult authority and create no end of problems for themselves and their families. In either event, alienation from family and from the broader society exposes them to becoming captives of their peers, to whom they may turn for guidance and approval. Thus they are vulnerable to pressures to identify with and join peer groups that engage in the use of illegal drugs or other behavior considered delinquent.

2. *The "social rejects."* Our society has become increasingly aware of young people who lack the motivation or ability to do well in school and who drop out as soon as they can (Schwartz & Johnson, 1985). With increasing automation and the demand for occupational skills—whether in the trades or in managerial or professional fields—there are few jobs for which they can qualify. Augmenting this group of youngsters are students who graduate from high school but whose training does not qualify them for available occupational opportunities.

Whether these young people come from upper-, middle-, or lower-income homes, and whether they drop out or continue through high school, they have one crucial problem in common—they discover that they are not needed in our society. They are victims of social progress—"social rejects." While some are able to obtain training in specific job areas, others appear unable to find or hold jobs, and still others drift aimlessly from one unsatisfactory job to another.

3. *Delinquent gang cultures.* With gangs, we are dealing not so much with personal psychopathology as with organized group pathology involving rebellion against the norms of society. As Jenkins (1969) has expressed it:

> *The socialized delinquent represents not a failure of socialization but a limitation of loyalty to a more or less predatory peer group. The basic capacity for social relations has been achieved. What is lacking is an effective integration with the larger society as a contributing member. (p. 73)*

Although the problem of delinquent gangs is most prevalent in lower socioeconomic areas, it is by no means restricted to them. Fusther, delinquent gangs are not a male province—in recent years, females have also formed gangs. Nor does the problem of juvenile delinquent gangs occur only in particular racial, ethnic, or social groups. It is pervasive, most particularly in inner-city areas. Though there are many reasons for joining delinquent gangs—including fear of personal injury from gang members if one does not join—most members appear to feel inadequate in and rejected by the larger society.

Gang membership gives members a sense of belonging and a means of gaining some measure of status and approval. It may also represent a means of committing robberies and other illegal acts for financial gain—acts that an individual could not successfully perform alone (Feldman & Weisfeld, 1973).

We should emphasize that the majority of delinquents do not belong to delinquent gangs, though gang membership may be increasing because young people appear to be joining groups for protection. Not all delinquent gangs are highly organized, cohesive groups. Recently, however, there seems to be an increase in both the organization and cohesiveness of delinquent gangs and in the violence of their activities.

Dealing with Delinquency If they have adequate facilities and personnel, juvenile institutions and training schools can be of great help to youths who need to be removed from aversive environments. These institutions can give youths a chance to learn about themselves and their world, to further their education and develop needed skills, and to find purpose and meaning in their lives. In such settings, youths may have the opportunity to receive psychological counseling and group therapy. In these situations it is of key importance that peer group pressures be channeled in the direction of resocialization, rather than toward repetitive delinquent behavior. Behavior therapy techniques—based on the assumption that delinquent behavior is learned, maintained, and changed according to the same principles as other learned behavior—have shown marked promise in the rehabilitation of juvenile offenders who require institutionalization. Counseling with parents and related environmental changes are generally of vital importance in a total rehabilitation program.

Probation is widely used with juvenile offenders and may be granted either in lieu of or after a period of institutionalization. Many delinquents can be guided into constructive behavior without being removed from their family or community.

The recidivism rate for delinquents—the most commonly used measure for assessing rehabilitation programs—depends heavily on the type of offenders being dealt with and on the particular facility or

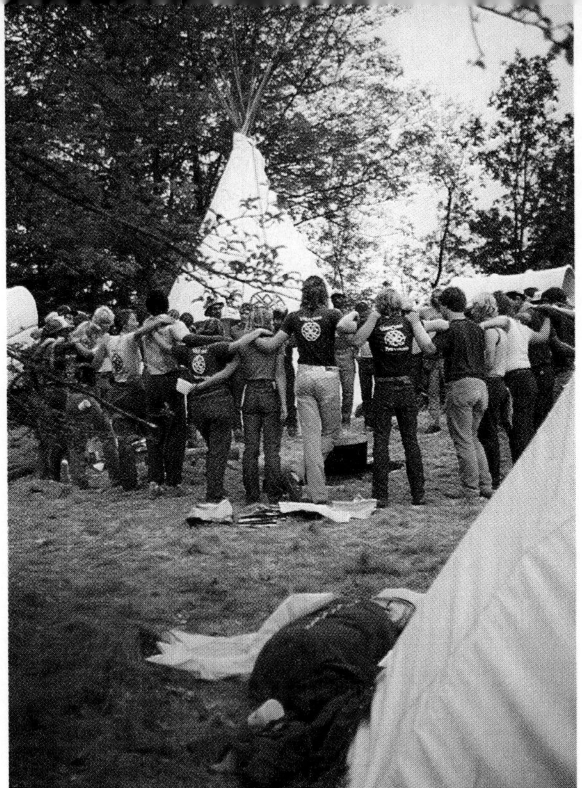

Institutionalizing troubled youths may only aggravate behavior problems. Vision Quest is a social rehabilitative program for troubled teens that offers an alternative to institutionalization by providing positive group experiences with the goal of resocialization.

procedures used. The overall recidivism rate for delinquents sent to training schools has been estimated to be high (Uniform Crime Reports, 1989). Because many crimes are committed by juveniles who have been recently released from custody or who were not incarcerated after being arrested, a number of state officials have become advocates of stiffer penalties for some types of juvenile crime. Individuals who commit crimes of violence or armed assault, or who have a long history of arrests, are often being given harsher penalties than they once would have been (Fersch, 1980).

Institutionalization seems particularly questionable in the case of juvenile status offenders, those youths whose offenses involve acts (such as running away from home or engaging in sexual relations) that would not be considered criminal if committed by an adult. In such instances, institutionalization may aggravate behavior problems rather than correct them. Mixing status offenders with delinquents or adults who have committed violent and antisocial offenses may simply provide them with an unfortunate education in how to become seriously delinquent.

On the other hand, failure to institutionalize youths who have committed serious offenses, such as robbery, assault, and murder, may be a disservice to both the delinquents and the public. In a provocative review of the limitations of programs aimed at reducing juvenile crime by psychological therapies, Clarke (1985) maintained that past efforts aimed at alterations of personality "dispositions" have fallen well short of success. He described a long history of psychological treatment programs in England aimed at promoting better psychological adjustment in convicted delinquents, thereby reducing recidivism and theoretically preventing juvenile crime. All these efforts to remediate delinquents through medical and psychological means had similar and generally disappointing results. Consequently, in Britain delinquency is viewed as a "rational" act and one that should be dealt with through environmental means rather than through psychological treatment. Situational measures that are aimed at eliminating the "opportunity for crime" are viewed as more effective at reducing crime among juveniles than attempts to "treat" individual delinquents. Such measures include

> *flat fare and "no change" systems on public transport, cheque guarantee cards, the control of alcohol sales at football matches, supervision of children's play on public housing estates, vandal-resistant materials and design, defensible space architecture, improved lighting, closed circuit television surveillance, the routine screening of airline passengers and baggage, and the employment of doormen in offices, caretakers in blocks of flats and more shop assistants. (p. 517)*

These environmental modifications are coupled with the continued use of incarceration to suppress involvement with delinquency among individuals who persist in committing criminal acts.

Anxiety Disorders of Childhood and Adolescence

In modern society, no one is totally insulated from anxiety-producing events or situations. Most children are vulnerable to fears and uncertainties as a part of growing up, and most children encounter many normal developmental steps and environmental demands that challenge their adaptation skills.

Children with anxiety disorders appear to share the following characteristics: oversensitivity, unrealistic fears, shyness and timidity, pervasive feelings of inadequacy, sleep disturbances, and fear of school. Children diagnosed as suffering from an anxiety disorder typically attempt to cope with their fears by becoming overly dependent on others for support and help. Symptoms of anxiety disorder are apparently quite common in the general population. Kashani and Orvaschel (1988) reported that

8.7 percent of their community-based school sample clearly met DSM-III-R criteria for an anxiety diagnosis based on a diagnostic interview.

In the DSM-III-R, anxiety disorders of childhood and adolescence are covered in two subclassifications: *separation anxiety disorder* and *overanxious disorder.* Both syndromes are more common among boys than among girls. We will briefly describe the clinical picture of each of these syndromes, then deal with causal factors and treatment considerations.

Separation Anxiety Disorder Children who have **separation anxiety disorder** are characterized by unrealistic fears, oversensitivity, self-consciousness, nightmares, and chronic anxiety. These children lack self-confidence, are apprehensive in new situations, and tend to be immature for their age. Such children often are described by their parents as shy, sensitive, nervous, submissive, easily discouraged, worried, and frequently moved to tears. Typically, they are overly dependent, particularly on their parents. The essential feature of this disorder's clinical picture involves excessive anxiety about separation from major attachment figures, such as mother, and from familiar home surroundings. In most cases a clear psychosocial stressor can be identified, such as the death of a relative or a pet. The following case illustrates the clinical picture in this disorder:

Johnny was a highly sensitive six-year-old boy who suffered from numerous fears, nightmares, and chronic anxiety. He was terrified of being separated from his mother, even for a brief period. When his mother tried to enroll him in kindergarten, he became so upset when she left the room that the principal arranged for her to remain in the classroom. After two weeks, however, this arrangement had to be discontinued, and Johnny had to be withdrawn from kindergarten because his mother could not leave him even for a few minutes. Later, when his mother attempted to enroll him in the first grade, Johnny manifested the same intense anxiety and unwillingness to be separated from her. At the suggestion of the school counselor, Johnny's mother brought him to a community clinic for assistance with the problem. The therapist who initially saw Johnny and his mother was wearing a white clinic jacket, which led to a severe panic reaction on Johnny's part. His mother had to hold him to keep him from running away, and he did not settle down until the therapist removed his jacket. Johnny's mother explained that "he is terrified of doctors, and it is almost impossible to get him to a physician even when he is sick."

When children with separation anxiety disorder are actually separated from their significant others, they typically become preoccupied with morbid fears, such as the worry that their parents are going to become ill or die. They cling helplessly to attachment figures, have difficulty sleeping, and become intensely demanding.

Overanxious Disorder Children with **overanxious disorder** are characterized by excessive worry and persistent fear; however, their fears are usually not specific and are not due to a recent stressful event. Such a child appears generally anxious and may worry a great deal about future events. He or she is preoccupied with trivial problems. His or her anxiety may also be expressed in somatic ways—stomach distress, shortness of breath, dizziness, headaches, and the like (see *HIGHLIGHT 15.4*). Sleeping problems, especially difficulty in falling asleep, are common. Many children showing overanxious disorder appear to have personality characteristics such as perfectionistic ideas and obsessional self-doubt. The disorder is illustrated in the following case:

Cindy, an overweight eleven-year-old girl, was taken to the emergency room following an "attack" of dizziness, faintness, and shortness of breath. She believed she was having a heart attack because of the discomfort she was experiencing in her chest. Cindy had a long history of health problems and concerns and was a frequent visitor to doctors. She had missed, on the average, three days of school a week since school had begun four months before.

Cindy was viewed by her mother as a "very good girl" but "sickly." Cindy was good about helping around the house and with her two younger sisters. She seemed conscientious and concerned about doing things right but seemed to lack self-confidence. She always checked out things with her mother, sometimes several times. She was particularly concerned about safety and would, for example, ask her mother frequently if the kitchen stove was turned off correctly.

Cindy would become extremely fearful at times, often for no external reason. For example, on one clear summer day a few months before,

HIGHLIGHT 15.4

Do Children Develop Psychologically Based Somatic Disorders?

The idea that children may develop somatic symptoms to avoid unpleasant tasks, such as schoolwork, or interpersonal conflict, such as parental discord, is well rooted in clinical observation. The extent to which somatization comprises a distinct disorder in children is not as well understood.

A study by Ernst, Routh, and Harper (1984) established the likelihood of the occurrence of somatization disorder in children. They studied a group of children with functional somatic complaints. They reported that the symptom patterns shown by these children differed from those of children with known organic-medical conditions in terms of duration of illness, body systems affected, and susceptibility to additional symptoms over time.

In an effort to evaluate the possibility of parental influence on the development of somatization disorders in children, Routh and Ernst (1984) employed a clinical-diagnostic interview to evaluate mothers of children with organic physical disease and children with likely somatization disorder. They found that a significantly higher percentage of children with functional abdominal pain had relatives with psychopathology, such as alcoholism, antisocial personality disorder, and somatization disorder. Moreover, they found that 10 of the 20 children with somatization disorder had 1 or more relatives with somatization disorders, while only 1 child with organic disorder had a relative with a somatization disorder. This study raises the possibility that somatization disorders, or the development and expression of functional pain, is influenced by parental personality or psychopathology.

she had become panicked over the possibility that a tornado might strike and had insisted that her family take shelter for several hours in the basement.

Causal Factors in Anxiety Disorders A number of causal factors have been emphasized in explanations of the childhood anxiety disorders. The more important of them appear to be the following:

1. An unusual constitutional sensitivity, an easy conditionability by aversive stimuli, and a buildup and generalization of "surplus fear reactions."

2. The undermining of feelings of adequacy and security by early illnesses, accidents, or losses that involved pain and discomfort. The traumatic effect of such experiences is often due partly to such children finding themselves in unfamiliar situations, as during hospitalization. The traumatic nature of certain life changes, such as moving away from friends and into a new situation, can have an intensely negative effect on a child's adjustment. Kashani and associates (1981a) found that the most common recent life event for children receiving psychiatric care was moving to a new school district.

3. The "modeling" effect of an overanxious and protective parent who sensitizes a child to the dangers and threats of the outside world. Often the parent's overprotectiveness communicates a lack of confidence in the child's ability to cope, thus reinforcing the child's feelings of inadequacy.

4. The failure of an indifferent or detached parent to provide adequate guidance for a child's development. Although the child is not necessarily rejected, neither is he or she adequately supported in mastering essential competencies and in gaining a positive self-concept. Repeated experiences of failure, stemming from poor learning skills, may lead to subsequent patterns of anxiety or withdrawal in the face of "threatening" situations.

Sometimes children are made to feel that they must earn their parents' love and respect through outstanding achievement, especially in school. Such children tend to be overcritical of themselves and to feel intensely anxious and devaluated when they perceive themselves as failing. These children are perfectionists who may actually do well but are left with a feeling of failure because they are sure they should have done better.

The various causal factors we have been discussing in relation to childhood anxiety disorders can obviously occur in differing degrees and combinations. All of them, however, are consistent with the view that these disorders essentially result from maladaptive learning.

Treatments and Outcomes The anxiety disorders of childhood may continue into adolescence and young adulthood—first leading to maladaptive avoidance behavior and later to increasingly idiosyncratic thinking and behavior. Typically, however, this is not the case. As affected children grow and have wider interactions in school and in peer-group activities, they are likely to benefit from such corrective experiences as making friends and succeeding at given tasks. Teachers have become more and more aware of the needs of both overanxious and shy, withdrawn children—and of ways to help them—and thus they are often able to ensure successful experiences for such children and to foster constructive interpersonal relationships.

Behavior therapy procedures, used in structured group experiences within educational settings, can often help speed up and ensure favorable outcomes. Such procedures include assertiveness training, help with mastering essential competencies, and desensitization. This last procedure may be limited in its application to young children, however, for a number of reasons, including the inability of young children to relax while imagining emotionally charged stimuli (Hatzenbuehler & Schroeder, 1978). With children, desensitization procedures must be explicitly tailored to a particular problem, and in vivo methods (using graded real-life situations) may be more effective than the use of imagined situations. For example, Montenegro (1968) described the successful treatment of a six-year-old boy, Romeo, who showed pathological anxiety when he was separated from his mother. The treatment included the following procedures:

1. Exposure of the child to a graded series of situations involving the actual fear-arousing stimulus—that is, separation from the mother for increasingly longer intervals.

2. Use of food during these separations as an anxiety inhibitor—which might involve taking the child to the hospital cafeteria for something to eat.

3. Instruction of the parents on how to reduce the child's excessive dependence on the mother—for example, through letting him learn to do things for himself.

After ten consecutive sessions, Romeo's separation anxiety was reduced to the point that he could stay home with a competent babysitter for an hour and then for increasingly longer periods. During the summer, he was enrolled in a vacation church school, which he enjoyed; when the new semester began at public school, he entered the first grade and made an adequate adjustment. It should be emphasized that the cooperation of the parents—particularly the mother—was a key factor in the treatment. For a look at two other therapies that are often successful with children experiencing anxiety, see *HIGHLIGHT 15.5*

Amanda has separation anxiety disorder and has been in therapy for three years. Amanda's anxiety over being separated from her mother was severe and interfered with going to school, restaurants, movies, friends' houses, and all manner of situations that are common to a child of her age. Her therapist sees both Amanda and her mother in family therapy and also treats Amanda using exposure therapy, which involves a step-by-step process of encouraging the child to confront the situations that create anxiety for her. Amanda is improving and is now able to enjoy activities such as sleepovers at friends' houses.

Childhood Depression

Clinicians working with children in mental health settings have long noted a pattern of symptoms that seemed indicative of depression. Spitz (1946) first described the problem, which he called *anaclitic depression,* as a behavior pattern, similar to adult depression, that occurred in children experiencing prolonged separation from their mothers. This specific childhood depression syndrome included slowed development and such symptomatic behavior as weepiness, sadness, immobility, and apathy.

The Clinical Picture in Childhood Depression Childhood depression has been recognized as a diagnostic problem by a number of investigators (Herzog & Rathbun, 1982; Kashani et al., 1981b; Ryan et al., 1987). It includes behaviors such as withdrawal, crying, avoidance of eye contact, physical complaints, poor appetite, and even aggressive behavior. Moreover, Kovacs (1989) recently noted that there is "compelling evidence from a variety of sources that affective disorders among children and adolescents are more persistent than hitherto thought" (p. 209). Some clinicians have reported that depressive disorders in children are quite commonplace (Costello, 1980). Estimates of the frequency of depressive symptoms in children have ranged from 13 percent (Kashani et al., 1982) to 23 percent (Kashani, Venzke, & Millar, 1981). Lefkowitz and Tesiny (1985), in a large scale study of "normal" children in an elementary school system, found the overall prevalence rate of depression symptoms to be 5.2 percent. Rutter, Izard, and Read (1986) reported that depressive disorders show an increase in incidence over the age span. A marked rise in depression symptoms occurs during teenage years (Fleming, Offord, & Boyle, 1989).

Some investigators have questioned the existence of a separate syndrome of childhood depression (Lefkowitz & Burton, 1978; Schulterbrandt & Raskin, 1977). For one thing, the symptoms listed as central to the syndrome are common in many normal children (MacFarlane, Allen, & Honzik, 1954; Werry & Quay, 1971). Another argument against a special depressive disorder for children is that cross-cultural studies of depression have not supported the idea of a childhood depression (Marsella, 1980). One investigator, Makita (1973), noted that out of 3000 cases of disturbed children in Japan, not one was diagnosed with childhood depression.

Currently, childhood depression is classified using the mood disorder categories in the DSM-III-R adult diagnostic system. This use of adult diagnostic depressive categories with children is considered to be appropriate by many. Lobovits and Handel (1985), for example, found that DSM-III adult diagnostic categories could reliably be used with children. They reported a depression prevalence rate of 35 percent for boys and 31 percent for girls who were being seen for various school-related problems in an outpatient clinic. Lobovits and Handel conclude that the use of DSM-III adult criteria with children "offers a useful starting point for untangling the confusion surrounding the diagnosis and prevalence rate of childhood disorder" (p. 52).

The advisory committee of the American Psychiatric Association chose not to incorporate a special diagnostic disorder for childhood depression in DSM-III-R. Instead, it recommends the use of adult-oriented diagnoses of depression, even though a number of people were lobbying for a special class of depression within the childhood disorders section. It appears that further research will be needed to document more clearly the "uniqueness" in childhood depression before a separate diagnostic category will be devised.

Causal Factors in Childhood Depression

The causal factors described in the childhood anxiety disorders are pertinent to the depressive disorders as well. Maladaptive learning appears to be central in childhood depressive disorders. Children who are exposed to negative parental behavior or negative emotional states may develop depressed affect themselves.

One important area of recent research is focusing on the mother-child interaction in the transmission of depressed affect. Specifically, investigators have been evaluating the possibility that mothers who are depressed, through their interactions with their infants, transfer their low mood to them. Depression among mothers is not uncommon, and can result from several sources. Of course, many women who are clinically depressed have children. Some women, however, become depressed during pregnancy or following the delivery of their child. Several investigators have reported that marital distress, delivery complications, and difficulties with the infant are associated with depression in the mothers (Campbell et al., 1990; Sameroff, Seifer, & Zax, 1982).

Extensive research supports the view that the patterns of mother-infant behavior are critical to the development of attachment in a child (Egeland & Farber, 1984). Negative (depressed) affect and constricted mood on the part of a mother, manifested in unresponsive facial expressions and irritable behavior, can produce similar responses in her infant (Cohn & Tronick, 1983; Tronick & Cohn, 1989). Cohn and Campbell (in press) have shown that "infants respond in specific and characteristic ways to depressed maternal affect, and that these effects carry over to situations in which mothers no longer behave in a depressed way."

Cohn and his colleagues (Cohn & Tronick, 1983; Cohn & Campbell, in press) have shown that when mothers interact with their depressed infants the children respond by turning away from them. Even nondepressed mothers, when trained to simulate a constricted-depressed interaction with their child, produce similar infant coping responses. Moreover, these infant coping responses persist even after the mother has stopped interacting with a "depressive" interaction style (Cohn & Tronick, 1983).

The extent to which an infant's negative response to a mother's depressed, constricted mood results in later childhood depression has not been

HIGHLIGHT 15.5

Family Therapy and Play Therapy with Children

For a number of reasons, therapeutic intervention with children experiencing psychological problems is often a more complicated process than providing psychotherapy for adults. First, the source of a child's problem and the means for changing are often not within the child's power but instead are imbedded in the context of complex family interaction patterns. To remedy the child's problems, it is often necessary to alter those pathological family interaction patterns that produce or maintain the child's behavior. Second, even if the child's problems are viewed as primary and in need of specific therapeutic intervention, he or she may not be motivated for therapy or sufficiently verbal to gain understanding through psychotherapeutic methods that work with adults. Consequently, effective psychological treatment with children may involve using more indirect methods, such as treating an entire family in *family therapy* or providing individual psychological therapy for children in a less intrusive and more familiar way—through the activity of play in *play therapy.* We will examine these two approaches in more detail.

Family therapy. An important means of treating psychological problems in disturbed children is through family therapy. Several family therapy approaches have been developed (Bowen, 1978; Fisch, Weakland, & Segal, 1982; Minuchin, 1974; Patterson, 1971). These approaches differ in some important ways, for example, in terms of how the family is defined (whether to include extended family members, such as grandparents, cousins, and so on); what the treatment process will focus on (for example, whether communications between the family members or the "aberrant behavior" of the problem family members is the focus); what procedures are used in the treatment process (for example, analyzing and interpreting hidden messages in the family communications or focusing on altering the reward and punishment contingencies through behavioral assessment and reinforcement). Regardless of their differences, all family therapies view a child's problems, at least in part, as an outgrowth of pathological interaction patterns within his or her family, and they attempt to bring about positive change in the family members through analysis and modification of the deviant family patterns.

How effective is family therapy at improving disruptive family relationships and promoting a more positive atmosphere for children? This is, of course, a difficult question to answer through research because treatment processes and outcomes are often difficult to measure. Nevertheless, Hazelrigg, Cooper, and Borduin (1987), after comparing the research to date on family therapy, concluded that family therapy had positive effects when contrasted with no-treatment control samples or with alternative treatment approaches, such as individual therapy. Research has shown that negative interaction patterns can be effectively changed by family therapy (Johnson & Maloney, 1979). Moreover, a number of studies have also shown that positive changes in a child's behavior can be brought about more effectively with family therapy than with alternative treatment methods (Christensen et al., 1980).

Play therapy. As a treatment technique, play therapy emerged out of efforts to apply psychodynamic therapy to children. A number of factors limit the application of tra-

fully determined. This research is highly suggestive, however, and may eventually lead to a fuller understanding of the possible link between a mother's mood and her child's behavior.

Treatments and Outcomes The psychological treatment of depressed children and adolescents generally follows the intervention strategies used with children suffering anxiety-based disorders. An important facet of psychological therapy with children involves providing a supportive emotional environment for them to learn more adaptive coping strategies and effective emotional expression. Older children and adolescents can often benefit from a positive therapeutic relationship in which they can discuss their feelings openly. Younger children or those with lower verbal skills may benefit from play therapy when they can, through play activities, experience a more full, positive range of emotions.

In many respects, the treatment of childhood depression has followed the treatment interven-

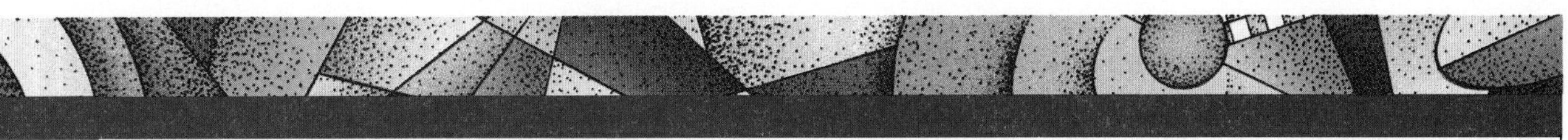

ditional psychodynamic therapy methods to children. Children do not voluntarily seek treatment and their motivation for self-change is different than for many troubled adults. They tend to be oriented to the present and lack the capability for insight and self-scrutiny that psychodynamic therapy requires. Their perceptions of their therapist differ from those of adult patients, and they may have an unrealistic view that the therapist can magically change their environment (Wenar, 1990).

Through their play, children often express their feelings, fears, and emotions in a direct and uncensored fashion, providing a clinician with a considerable means of understanding a child's problems and feelings. The activity of play has become a valuable source of obtaining personality and problem information about children. Psychodynamic techniques have been adapted for children by using play activity (in lieu of free association, used with adults) to enable a therapist to infer emotional conflicts, inappropriate affects, and excessive emotions a child might be experiencing. Play therapy sessions are usually centered around doll or puppet play to give a child a vehicle for expressing feelings. Other activities, particularly construction with different materials, such as play dough, crayons, and paper, are also used to encourage free expression.

In a play therapy session, the therapist usually needs to provide some structure or to guide play activities so that pertinent feelings and emotions are allowed to be expressed. This might mean that the therapist asks direct questions of the child during the play session, such as: "Is the doll happy now?" or "What makes the doll cry?"

In addition to using play activity as a means of understanding a troubled child's problems, it also provides a medium for bringing about change in the child's behavior. A central process in play therapy is that the therapist, through interpretation, providing emotional support, and clarification of feelings (often by labeling them for the child), provides the child with a corrective emotional experience. That is, the therapist provides the child with an accepting and trusting relationship that promotes healthier personality and relationship development. The play therapy situation enables the child to reexpesience conflict or problems in the safety of the therapy room, thereby providing a chance to conquer fears, to acclimate to necessary life changes, or to gain a feeling of security to replace the anxiety and uncertainty that had troubled him or her.

How effective is play therapy in reducing a child's problems and promoting better adjustment? When compared with adult treatment studies, play therapy compares quite favorably. Casey and Berman (1985) conducted a careful study of treatment research with children and concluded that such treatment "appears to match the efficacy of psychotherapy with adults" (p. 395). Play therapy was found to be as effective as other types of treatment, such as behavior therapy.

tions found successful with adults experiencing depression, with both psychological approaches and medications receiving prominence. Moreau (1990), for example, recommended that a combination of individual psychotherapy and tricyclic medication be used in the treatment of childhood depression to provide both a mood elevation and the opportunity for the child to discuss his or her feelings.

An important aspect in the treatment of depression in young people is the necessity of a suicide appraisal, as illustrated by the following case:

Jack was admitted to a child psychiatric hospital unit after he attempted to stab himself in the stomach with a medium sized kitchen knife. The suicide attempt was foiled by his mother, who pulled the knife away from her son. This suicide attempt occurred immediately after Jack had an argument with his father. Jack felt that his "father hates me" and that "I would be better off dead." A variety of factors made Jack vulnerable to suicidal tendencies. Jack grew up in an atmos-

phere in which there was intense disagreement between his parents. His father drank heavily and when drunk would physically assault his mother. Jack's mother was chronically depressed and often said that "life is not worth living." However, she loved her son and felt that because he needed her, she must continue to work and manage the home. Jack has a serious learning disability, and he struggled to maintain his school grades. He had a private tutor who helped him overcome his sad feelings and shame. Often, when teased by his classmates, he thought about ending his life. (Pfeffer, 1985, pp. 218–219)

Depressed mood has come to be viewed as an important risk factor in suicide among children and adolescents (Posener, Le Haye, & Cheifetz, 1989; Rubenstein et al., 1989; Slap et al., 1989; Velez & Cohen, 1987). In fact, over 5000 American adolescents kill themselves each year (Youth Suicide in the United States, 1986), and suicide has tripled for individuals between the ages of 15 and 24 during the 1980s (Blumenthal, 1990).

Other Symptom Disorders

The behavior disorders we will deal with in this section—elimination disorders (enuresis and encopresis), sleepwalking, and tics—typically involve a single outstanding symptom rather than a pervasive maladaptive pattern.

Functional Enuresis The term **enuresis** refers to the habitual involuntary discharge of urine, usually at night, after the age of expected continence (age 5). In DSM-III-R, *functional enuresis* refers to bed-wetting that is not organically caused. Children who have *primary functional enuresis* have never been continent; children who have *secondary functional enuresis* have been continent for at least a year, but have regressed.

Enuresis may vary in frequency, from nightly occurrence to occasional instances when an individual is under considerable stress or is unduly tired. The actual incidence of enuresis is unknown, but it has been estimated that some four to five million children and adolescents in the United States suffer from the inconvenience and embarrassment of this disorder (Turner & Taylor, 1974). Estimates of the prevalence of enuresis reported in DSM-III-R are 7 percent for boys and 3 percent for girls at age 5; 3 percent for boys and 2 percent for girls at age 10; and 1 percent for boys and almost nonexistent for girls at age 18. Research has shown that there are clear sex differences in enuresis as well as age differences. In a recent epidemiological study of enuresis in Holland, Verhulst et al. (1985) determined that between the ages of 5 and 8, the percentages of enuresis problems for boys is about two to three times that for girls. The percentages for boys also diminish at a slower rate; the decline for girls between ages 4 and 6 is about 71 percent, while the declioe for boys is only 16 percent. The authors recommend that the age criteria for boys' enuresis be extended to age 8 because it is at about age 9 that approximately the same percentage of boys as girls reach "dryness," that is, wetting the bed less than once a month.

Although enuresis may result from a variety of organic conditions, such as disturbed cerebral control of the bladder (Kaada & Retvedt, 1981), most investigators have pointed to a number of other possible causal factors: (a) faulty learning, resulting in the failure to acquire a needed adaptive response—that is, inhibition of reflex bladder emptying; (b) personal immaturity, associated with or stemming from emotional problems; and (c) disturbed family interactions, particularly those that lead to sustained anxiety, hostility, or both. In some instances, a child may regress to bed-wetting when a new baby enters the family and becomes the center of attention. Children also may resort to bed-wetting when they feel hostile toward their parents and want to get even, realizing that such behavior is annoying and upsetting to adults. In adolescence and adulthood, enuresis is often associated with other psychological problems. Research evidence supports a multiplicity of possible causes for enuresis, with many cases being explained by either environmental factors or maturational lags (Christie, 1981).

Conditioning procedures have proven effective in the treatment of enuresis (Doleys, 1979). Maurer and Maurer (1938) introduced a procedure in which a child may sleep on a pad that is wired to a battery-operated bell. At the first few drops of urine, the bell is set off, thus awakening the child. Through conditioning, the child comes to associate bladder tension with awakening. Fortunately, with or without treatment, the incidence of enuresis tends to decrease significantly with age. Nevertheless, many experts believe that enuresis should be treated in childhood because no way currently exists to identify which children will remain enuretic into adulthood.

Functional Encopresis The term **encopresis** describes children who have not learned appropriate toileting for bowel movements after age 4. This condition is less common than enuresis. However, about 2.3 percent of 8-year-old boys and 0.7 percent of 8-year-old girls are encopretic (Bellman, 1966). The following list of characteristics was provided by Levine (1976) from a study of 102 cases of encopretic children:

- The average age was 7, with a range from ages 4 to 13.
- About one-third of encopretic children were also enuretic.
- A large sex difference was found, with about six times more boys than girls in the sample.
- Many of the children soiled their clothing when they were under stress. A common time was in the late afternoon after school. Few children actually had this problem at school.
- Most of the children reported that they did not know when they needed to have a bowel movement.

Many encopretic children suffer from constipation; thus an important element in the diagnosis of the disorder involves a physical examination to determine whether physiological factors are contributing to the disorder. The treatment of encopresis usually involves both medical and psychological aspects. Levine and Bakow (1975) found that, of the encopretic children they studied who were treated by medical and behavioral procedures, more than half were cured—that is, no additional incidents occurred within six months following treatment. An additional 25 percent were improved.

Sleepwalking (Somnambulism) Though the onset of **sleepwalking disorder** is usually between the ages of 6 and 12, the disorder is classified broadly under sleep disorders in DSM-III-R rather than under disorders of infancy, childhood, and adolescence. The symptoms of sleepwalking disorder involve repeated episodes in which a person leaves his or her bed and walks around without being conscious of the experience or remembering it later.

Statistics are meager, but it is estimated that 1 to 6 percent of children experience regular or periodic sleepwalking episodes. Children subject to this problem usually go to sleep in a normal manner but arise during the second or third hour of sleep. They may walk to another room of the house or even outside, and they may engage in complex activities. Finally they return to bed and in the morning remember nothing that has taken place.

While moving about, sleepwalkers' eyes are partially or fully open; they avoid obstacles, listen when spoken to, and ordinarily respond to commands, such as to return to bed. Shaking them will usually awaken sleepwalkers, and they will be surprised and perplexed at finding themselves in an unexpected place. Sleepwalking episodes usually last from 15 to 30 minutes. The risk of injury during sleepwalking is illustrated by the following case study:

14-year-old Donald Elliot got up from his bunk in his sleep, looked in the refrigerator, then, still asleep, walked out the back door. It would have been just another sleepwalking episode except that Donald was in a camper-pickup truck traveling 50 miles an hour on the San Diego freeway. Miraculously, he escaped with cuts and bruises. But his experience, and that of many other sleepwalkers, disproves one of the myths about somnambulism: that people who walk in their sleep don't hurt themselves. (Taves, 1969, p. 41)

The causes of sleepwalking are not fully understood. Kales and associates (1966) have shown that sleepwalking takes place during NREM (non–rapid eye movement) sleep, but its relationship to dreaming remains unclear. In general, it appears that sleepwalking is related to some anxiety-arousing situation that has just occurred or is expected to occur in the near future.

Little attention has been given to the treatment of sleepwalking. Clement (1970), however, has reported on the treatment of a 7-year-old boy through behavior therapy, as described in *HIGHLIGHT 15.6*. Nagaraja (1974) has reported the successful treatment of an 8-year-old boy and a 9-year-old girl with a combination of tranquilizers and psychotherapy. Nevertheless, a good deal of additional research is needed before we can determine the most effective treatment procedures for sleepwalking.

Tics A **tic** is a persistent, intermittent muscle twitch or spasm, usually limited to a localized muscle group. The term is used broadly to include blinking the eye, twitching the mouth, licking the lips, shrugging the shoulders, twisting the neck, clearing the throat, blowing the nose, and grimacing, among other actions. Tics occur most frequently between the ages of 6 and 14 (Schowalter, 1980). In some instances, as in clearing the throat, an individual may be aware of the tic when it occurs; but usually he or she performs the act habitually and does not notice it. In fact, many individuals do not even realize they have a tic unless someone brings it to their attention. The psychological impact tics can

HIGHLIGHT 15.6

The Treatment of Sleepwalking Utilizing Conditioning Procedures

Bobby, a 7-year-old boy, walked in his sleep an average of four times a week. His mother kept a record indicating that Bobby's sleepwalking episodes were associated with nightmares, perspiring, and talking in his sleep. During the actual sleepwalking, Bobby usually was glassy-eyed and unsteady on his feet. On one occasion, he started out the front door. The sleepwalking had commenced about six weeks before the boy was brought for therapy. Usually an episode would begin about 45 to 90 minutes after he had gone to bed.

During treatment, the therapist learned that just before each sleepwalking episode Bobby usually had a nightmare about being chased by "a big black bug." In his dream, Bobby thought "the bug would eat off his legs if it caught him" (Clement, 1970, p. 23). Bobby's sleepwalking episodes usually showed the following sequence: after his nightmare began, he perspired freely, moaned and talked in his sleep, tossed and turned, and finally got up and walked through the house. He did not remember the sleepwalking episode when he awoke the next morning.

Assessment data revealed no neurological or other medical problems and indicated that Bobby was of normal intelligence. He was, however, found to be "a very anxious, guilt-ridden little boy who avoided performing assertive and aggressive behaviors appropriate to his age and sex" (p. 23). Assertiveness training and related measures were used but were not effective. The therapist then focused treatment on having Bobby's mother awaken the boy each time he showed signs of an impending episode. After washing Bobby's face with cold water and making sure he was fully awake, the mother would return him to bed, where he was "to hit and tear up a picture of the big black bug." (At the start of the treatment program, Bobby had made up several of these drawings.)

Eventually, the nightmare was associated with awakening, and Bobby learned to wake up on most occasions when he was having a bad dream. Clement considered the basic behavior therapy model in this case to follow that used in the conditioning treatment for enuresis, where a waking response is elicited by an intense stimulus just as urination is beginning and becomes associated with, and eventually prevents, nocturnal bed-wetting.

have on an adolescent is exemplified in the following case:

An adolescent who had wanted very much to be a teacher told the school counselor that he was thinking of giving up his plans. When asked the reason, he explained that several friends had told him that he had a persistent twitching of the mouth muscles when he answered questions in class. He had been unaware of this muscle twitch and even after being told about it could not tell when it took place. However, he became acutely self-conscious and was reluctant to answer questions or enter into class discussions. As a result, his general level of tension increased, and so did the frequency of the tic, which now became apparent even when he was talking to his friends. Thus a vicious circle had been established. Fortunately, it proved amenable to treatment by conditioning and assertiveness training.

An extreme tic disorder involving multiple motor and vocal patterns is **Tourette's syndrome.** This disorder typically involves uncontrollable head movements with accompanying sounds, such as grunts, clicks, yelps, sniffs, or words. About one-third of individuals with Tourette's syndrome manifest *coprolalia,* which is a complex vocal tic involving the uttering of obscenities. The average age of onset for Tourette's syndrome is age 7, and most cases have an onset before age 14. The disorder is about three times more frequent among males. Although the exact cause of Tourette's syndrome is undetermined, some evidence suggests an organic basis for the syndrome.

Most tics, however, do not have an organic basis but usually stem from psychological causes, such as self-consciousness or tension in social situations. As in the case of the adolescent boy previously described, an individual's awareness of the tic often increases the tension—and the tic. Tics have been successfully treated by means of drugs, psychotherapy, and conditioning techniques. Ollendick

(1981) reported success in treating tics by using behavioral techniques of self-monitoring and overcorrection.

PLANNING BETTER PROGRAMS TO HELP CHILDREN AND YOUTH

In our discussion of several problems of childhood and adolescence, we have noted the wide range of treatment procedures available, as well as the marked differences in outcomes. In concluding the chapter, we will discuss certain special factors associated with the treatment of children, the problem of child abuse, and the new emphasis on child advocacy and the rights of children, which involves a social commitment to provide conditions conducive to their optimal development.

Special Factors Associated with Treatment for Children

A number of special factors must be considered in relation to treatment for children.

1. *The child's inability to seek assistance.* The great majority of emotionally disturbed children who need assistance are not in a position to ask for it themselves or to transport themselves to and from child guidance clinics. Thus, unlike an adult or an adolescent, who usually can seek help during crisis periods, a child is dependent, primarily on his or her parents. Adults should realize when a child needs professional help and take the initiative in obtaining it. Sometimes, however, adults neglect this responsibility. Plotkin (1981) pointed out:

Parents have traditionally had the right to consent to health services for their children. In situations where the interest of the parents and children differ the rule has had unfortunate consequences and has left treatment professionals in a quandary. (p. 121)

The law identifies four areas in which treatment without parental consent is permitted: (a) in the case of mature minors (those considered to be capable of making decisions about themselves); (b) in the case of emancipated minors (those living independently—away from their parents); (c) in emergency situations; and (d) in situations in which a court orders treatment. Many children, of course, come to the attention of treatment agencies as a consequence of school referrals, delinquent acts, or parental abuse.

2. *The double deprivation of children from pathogenic homes.* Many families provide an undesirable environment for their growing children. In fact, studies have shown that up to a fourth of American children may be living in inadequate homes (Joint Commission on the Mental Health of Children, 1968; Office of Technology Assessment, 1986). Child care, however, is traditionally the responsibility of parents, and local and state agencies intervene only in extreme cases—usually those involving physical abuse. This means that children growing up in pathogenic homes are at a double disadvantage. Not only are they deprived from the standpoint of environmental influence on their personality development, but they also lack parents who will perceive their need for help and actively seek and participate in treatment programs.

3. *The need for treatment of the parents as well as the child.* Because most of the behavior disorders specific to childhood appear to grow out of pathogenic family interactions, it is usually essential for the parents, as well as their child, to receive treatment. In some instances, in fact, the treatment program may focus on the parents entirely, as in the case of child abuse.

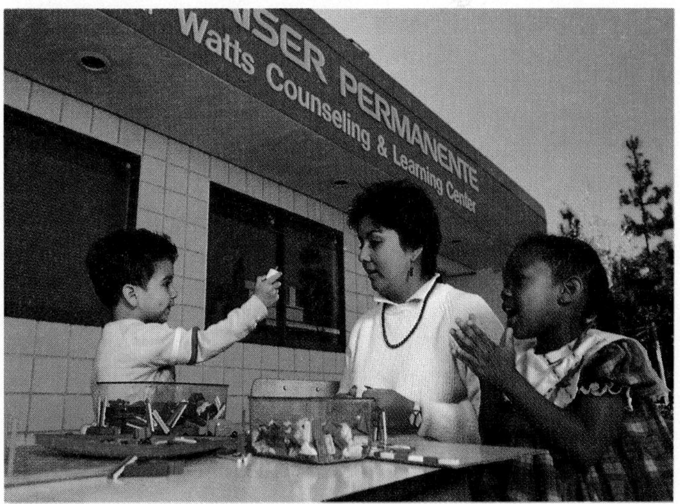

It is important that adults realize when a child needs professional help and take the initiative in obtaining it. For some parents, however, the effort involved in finding appropriate help, not to mention the economic factors of paying for treatment and of taking time away from work to take their child to therapy sessions, are very real deterrents to seeking help.

Increasingly, then, the treatment of children has come to mean family therapy, in which one or both parents, along with the child and siblings, may participate in all phases of the program. For working parents, however, and for parents who basically reject the affected child, such treatment may be difficult to arrange, especially in the case of poorer families who lack transportation and money. Thus, both parental and economic factors help determine which emotionally disturbed children will receive assistance.

4. *The possibility of using parents as change agents.* A recent trend, as we have seen, has been to teach parents to be change agents. In essence, the parents are trained in techniques that enable them to help their child. Typically, such training focuses on helping the parents understand the child's behavior disorder and learn to reinforce adaptive behavior while withholding reinforcement for undesirable behavior. Encouraging results have been obtained with parents who care about their children and want to help (Arnold, 1978; Atkeson & Forehand, 1978; Forehand et al., 1981; Johnson & Katz, 1973; Lexow & Aronson, 1975; Mash et al., 1976; O'Dell, 1974).

5. *The problem of placing the child outside the family.* Most communities have juvenile facilities that, day or night, will provide protective care and custody for young victims of unfit homes, abandonment, abuse, neglect, and related conditions. Depending on the home situation and the special needs of the child, he or she will later either be returned to his or her parents or placed elsewhere. In the latter instance, four types of facilities are commonly relied on: foster homes, private institutions for the care of children, county or state institutions, or the homes of relatives. At any one time, over half a million children are living in foster-care facilities.

The quality of a child's new home, of course, is a crucial determinant of whether the child's problems will be alleviated or made worse. Although efforts are made to screen the placement facilities and maintain contact with the situation through follow-up visits, there have been too many reported cases of mistreatment. Perhaps the most dramatic example of unintended harm from the placement of children in foster homes was the large number of children who were forced to commit suicide by the Reverend Jim Jones in the 1978 Jonestown murder-suicide. Jones was a cult leader who persuaded his followers to leave the United States to live in a jungle compound in Jonestown, Guyana. He received large amounts of money for the foster children in his care.

In cases of child abuse, child abandonment, or a serious childhood behavior problem that parents cannot control, it has often been assumed that the only feasible action was to take the child out of the home and find a temporary substitute. With such a child's own home so obviously inadequate, the hope has been that a more stable outside placement would be better. But when children are taken from their own homes and placed in an impersonal institution (which promptly tries to change them) or in a series of foster homes (where they obviously do not really belong), they are likely to feel rejected by their own parents, unwanted by their new caretakers, rootless, constantly insecure—and lonely and bitter.

Accordingly, the trend today is toward *permanent planning.* First, every effort is made to hold a family together and to give the parents the support and guidance they need for adequate childrearing. If this is impossible, then efforts are made to free the child legally for adoption and to find an adoptive home as soon as possible. This, of course, means that the public agencies need specially trained staffs with reasonable caseloads and access to resources that they and their clients may need.

6. *The importance of intervening early, before problems become acute.* Over the last 20 years, a primary concern of many researchers and clinicians has been to identify and provide early help for children who are at special risk. Rather than wait until these children develop acute psychological problems that may require therapy or major changes in living arrangements, psychologists are attempting to identify conditions in such children's lives that seem likely to bring about or maintain behavior problems and, where such conditions exist, to intervene before a child's development has been seriously distorted. An example of this approach is provided in the work of Wallerstein and Kelly (1980):

These researchers identified children who were at risk for psychological disturbance as a result of their parents going through a divorce. Each of the 66 participating families was seen by a clinician, and the children were seen separately for several sessions. The goals of the counseling sessions were to provide the children with a means of expressing their worries and frustrations and to strengthen their resources for dealing with them.

In addition to the counseling sessions, there were several follow-up sessions after the divorce to examine the psychological changes in the children and the changes in the family structure over time. The interventions were judged to be successful in lowering the tension levels in the family situations and in enhancing the children's adjustment to their new living arrangements.

Such early intervention has the double goal of reducing the stressors in a child's life and strengthening the child's coping mechanisms. If successful, it can effectively reduce the number and intensity of later problems, thus averting much grief for both the individuals concerned and the broader society. It is apparent that children's needs can be met only if adequate preventive and treatment facilities for children exist and are available to the children who need assistance. In the next section, we will look at the specific issue of child abuse, which is of growing concern to researchers and practitioners who want to know what causes it and how it can be prevented. In our final section, we will look at the leadership that government agencies have been providing in spotlighting the special needs of children and youth, and we will also discuss our society's responsibility to meet those needs.

Child Abuse

Child abuse is a growing concern in the United States. A Department of Health and Human Services Report (House of Representatives, 1990) indicated that the numbers of children reported as abused and neglected rose 64 percent from 1980 to 1988, for an astounding total of 2.2 million cases of childhood maltreatment reported in 1988.

In child abuse cases, 20 to 40 percent of the children have been seriously injured. Although children and adolescents of all ages are physically abused, the most frequent cases involve children under 3 years of age. Some evidence suggests that boys are more often abused than girls. It is usually clear that many children brought to the attention of legal agencies for abuse have been abused before (Kempe & Kempe, 1979; President's Commission on Mental Health, 1978).

In a survey of family violence, Gelles (1978) reported that violence well beyond ordinary physical punishment is a widespread phenomenon in parent-child relationships. Milder forms of punishment, Gelles found, were common among respondents; for example, 71 percent of parents reported having slapped or spanked their children, 46 percent reported pushing and shoving incidents, and around 10 percent reported having thrown something at their children. Gelles extrapolated estimates of serious violence from his survey to the general population and concluded that 46 percent of American children had suffered serious abuse, such as being kicked, bitten, or punched by parents.

The seriousness of the child abuse problem in our society was not realized until the 1960s, when researchers began to report case after case like the following two:

The mother of a 29-month-old boy claimed he was a behavior problem, beat him with a stick and screwdriver handle, dropped him on the floor, beat his head on the wall or threw him against it, choked him to force his mouth open to eat, and burned him on the face and hands. After she had severely beaten him, the mother found the child dead.

Because her 2½-year-old daughter did not respond readily enough to toilet training the mother became indignant and in a fit of temper over the child's inability to control a bowel movement gave her an enema with near scalding water. To save the child's life a doctor was forced to perform a colostomy. (Earl, 1965)

Many abused children show impaired cognitive ability and memory when compared with control children (Friedrich, Einbender, & Luecke, 1983). In addition, abused children are likely to show problems in social adjustment and are particularly likely to feel that the outcomes of events are determined by external factors beyond their own control (Barahal, Waterman, & Martin, 1981). They are also more likely to experience depressive symptoms (Kazdin et al., 1985). Abused children are dramatically less likely to assume personal responsibility, and they generally demonstrate less interpersonal sensitivity than control children. Abused children also tend to show more self-destructive behavior than nonabused control subjects (Green, 1978).

When the abuse involves a sexual component, such as incest or rape, the long-range consequences can be very marked. Harter, Alexander, and Neimeyer (1988) found that victims of sexual abuse often suffered interpersonal adjustment difficulties for years following the incident. Jackson and colleagues (1990) found that women who had experienced intrafamily sexual abuse had significantly poorer social adjustment, especially in dating relationships. The women also reported significantly lower sexual satisfaction, more sexual dysfunctions, and lower self-esteem than control women.

The role of sexual abuse in the experience of psychological problems has recently been the subject of several longitudinal studies. A number of investigators have followed up sexually abused children to study the long-term effects of abuse on a victim's behavior. A large percentage of sexually abused children experience intense psychological symptoms following the incident (for example, 74 percent reported by Bentovim, Boston, & Van Elburg, 1987). At follow-up, however, the improvement often seems dramatic. Gomes-Schwartz, Horowitz, and Cardarelli (1990) found that 55 percent of victims had substantially improved at follow-up 18 months later, particularly in terms of sleeping problems, fears of uhe offender, and anxiety. However, 28 percent of the victims showed worsening behavior, such as family conflict and inappropriate attention seeking. Similarly, several other studies have reported substantial improvement of sexually abused victims at follow-up (Bentovim et al., 1987; Conte, Berliner, & Schuerman, 1986).

Although many children experience improvement in the months following the incident, some victims do not actually show problems until buried memories begin to surface during later psychological treatment for other reasons (Courtois & Sprei, 1988). In a recent study of psychiatric outpatients being treated at a university hospital, Jacobson (1989) reported that 68 percent of the women studied had experienced major sexual assault.

Several investigators have conceptualized the residual symptoms of sexual abuse as a type of posttraumatic stress disorder (PTSD) because the symptoms experienced are similar; for example, nightmares, flashbacks, sleep problems, and feelings of estrangement (Donaldson & Gardner, 1985; Frederick, 1986). However, other investigators (e.g., Finkelhor, 1990) object to this explanation on grounds that viewing these symptoms as an example of PTSD will "lead us to miss some of [the] most serious effects" of the sexual abuse experience such as prolonged depression or anxiety (p. 329).

Causal Factors in Child Abuse Since the 1960s, a great deal of research has been aimed at finding out which parents abuse their children and why, in the hope that ultimately these parents can be stopped, or better yet, prevented, from abusing their children. We now know that parents who physically abuse their children tend to be young, with the majority under 30. In most reported cases, they come from the lower socioeconomic levels (Egeland & Erickson, 1990). An important common factor among families with abusing parents is a higher-than-average degree of frustration; many stressors are present in their lives, including marital discord, high unemployment, and alcohol abuse (Egeland, Cicchetti, & Taraldson, 1976). Many incidents of physical abuse occur as parental reactions to a child's misbehavior in areas such as fighting, sexual behavior, aggression, and so on (Herrenkohl, Herrenkohl, & Egolf, 1983). Although no clear and consistent personality pattern emerges as typical of child-abusing parents, they seem to show a higher-than-average rate of psychological disturbance (Serrano et al., 1979). Some evidence from personality testing shows that they tend to be aggressive, nonconforming, selfish, and lacking in appropriate impulse control (Lund, 1975).

Knowledge about causal factors in child abuse is limited and incomplete because most studies have involved retrospective analyses of cases identified through legal agencies. However, one study (Egeland & Brunnquell, 1979) identified 275 families in a population generally at risk for child abuse *before* the birth of a child. From this group, the investigators then identified the 25 mothers at highest risk for child abuse and the 25 mothers most likely not to be child abusers. These two groups have now been followed over several years. Eight of the highest-risk mothers have actually abused their children; none of the other group has done so. There are many striking differences between the two groups. The mothers in the group identified as at lowest risk tend to be older, to show more understanding of the psychological complexity of their children, to have better caretaking skills, and to show more positive feeling for their children. The other mothers, in general, live more chaotic lives. Over twice as many are single (74 percent as compared with 32 percent). They are also more involved in disrupted relationships, physical fights, and heavy drinking in the immediate family. A recent study found that antisocial personality features were common among the women in the sample (Egeland et al., 1990). Another study by Egeland and his colleagues showed a clear intergenerational pattern of child abuse; that is, 70 percent of the mothers who were identified as having been abused as children also mistreated their children (Egeland, Jacobvitz, & Papatola, 1987).

The Prevention of Child Abuse Practitioners and child protection agencies have begun an extensive effort to reduce the amount and impact of child abuse. Their efforts include the following:

- Community education programs have been developed to increase public awareness of the problem. Television advertisements have been especially effective here.
- Child protection teams have been organized by many state and county welfare departments to investigate and intervene in reported cases of child abuse.
- Teams of mental health specialists in many community mental health centers are working to evaluate and provide psychological treatment for!both abused children and their parents.
- Parent support groups, often made up of former child abusers, are forming that can offer abusing parents or those at risk for child abuse alternative ways of behaving toward their children.
- Many communities are making it a legal requirement for physicians and other professionals to report cases of child abuse that come to their attention.

Research designed to enable early intervention with parents identified as likely to abuse their children has been promising. Wolfe and colleagues (1988) identified women who were at high risk for maltreatment of their children. They randomly assigned mothers to either a treatment or control group. The treatment consisted of behaviorally oriented parent training which provided child management skills; instruction in child care; modeling; rehearsal instructions to give clear, concise demands; and the use of "time out" as a punishment. The study showed that this early parent intervention reduced the risk for child abuse among the mothers provided the treatment. Through such efforts on many levels it is hoped that children will be spared abuse and that abusive or potentially abusive parents will be helped to be more effective and nurturant.

Unfortunately, child abuse all too frequently produces maladaptive social behavior in its victims. The treatment of abused children needs to address the problems of social adjustment, depression, and poor interpersonal skills that these children exhibit. An interesting treatment approach to reducing the negative consequences of child abuse is the use of peers to help modify abused children's tendency to withdraw and their poor social skills. Fantuzzo and colleagues (1988) trained peer confederates to make play overtures to abused children. They found that peer-initiated efforts were more effective at increasing the social!interaction of withdrawn children than adult-initiaued treatment efforts. Further work on rehabilitative efforts is needed to assist these unfortunate children in overcoming the psychologically disabling effects of being abused.

Community education programs to increase public awareness of the problem of child abuse are but one of the current efforts to reduce the amount and impact of child abuse.

Child Advocacy Programs

Today there are nearly 68 million people under age 18 in the United States (Spencer, 1989). This figure indicates that a massive social commitment is needed not only to provide adequate treatment facilities for children with problems but also to ensure the physical and social conditions that will foster the optimal development of all children.

Unfortunately, however, both treatment and preventive programs in our society have been—and remain—inadequate. In 1970 the National Institute of Mental Health pointed out that fewer than 1 percent of the disturbed children in our society were receiving any kind of treatment, and less than half of those children were getting adequaue help. In the same year, in its final report, *Crisis in Child Mental Health: Challenge for the 1970s,* the Joint Commission on the Mental Health of Children (1970) referred to our lack of commitment to our children and youth as a "national tragedy." The commission's report concluded:

Either we permit a fifth of the nation's children to go down the drain—with all that this implies for public disorder and intolerable inhumanity—or we decide, once and for all, that the needs of children have first priority on the nation's resources. (p. 408)

Unfortunately, eight years later, the President's Commission on Mental Health (1978) was still calling attention to the fact that children and adolescents were not receiving mental health services commensurate with their needs. The commission's report recommended again that greater efforts and financial resources be expended to serve the mental health needs of children and youth. It appears, however- that the needed financial support and redirected program focuses have not materialized in the years since the report was issued.

One approach to meeting mental health needs, known as **advocacy,** has been prominent in recent years. Advocacy attempts to help children or others receive services that they need but often are unable to obtain for themselves. In some cases, advocacy seeks to better conditions for underserved populations by changing the system (Biklen, 1976; Meyers & Parsons, 1987; Roberts & Peterson, 1984).

Twice in recent years the federal government has established a National Center for Child Advocacy to coordinate the many kinds of work for children's welfare performed by different government agencies. Both times the new agency proved ineffective and was given up after a year or so. Currently, the physical welfare of children is the responsibility of the Children's Bureau of the Labor Department, and the mental health needs of children are the responsibility of the Alcoholism, Drug Abuse, and Mental Health Administration of the Public Health Service. Delinquents are dealt with by the Justice Department. This fragmentation in children's services means that different agencies serve different needs; no government agency is charged with considering the whole child and planning comprehensively for children who need help.

Outside the federal government, until recently, advocacy efforts for children have been supported largely by legal and special-interest citizens' groups, such as the Children's Defense Fund, a public-interest organization based in Washington, D.C. Mental health professionals have typically not been involved. Today, however, there is greater interdisciplinary involvement in attempts to provide effective advocacy programs for children (Hermalin & Morell, 1986).

Unfortunately, although such programs have made important local gains toward bettering conditions for mentally disabled children, a great deal of confusion, inconsistency, and uncertainty still exists in the advocacy movement as a whole (Biklen, 1976; Levine & Perkins, 1987). In addition, the mood at both federal and state levels has for some time been to cut back on funds for social services.

In her presidential address to the Society of Pediatric Psychology, Magrab (1982) warned that economic cutbacks in child-oriented programs and the fragmented nature of existing programs represent a challenge "to the very survival" of psychological services to children. She encouraged mental health and health care professionals working in child advocacy not to become disheartened with the recent and continuing erosion of services but to exert a unified commitment to broadening advocacy programs by using community resources and by working with parents. Clearly, there is a great threat to existing children's programs and the coming years will require substantial effort on the part of professionals, parent groups, and enlightened elected officials to maintain past gains and to expand services to other needed areas. Tuma (1989), in a more recent examination of the problem, called for a better integration of scattered services to provide more effective help to the over 63 million children and adolescents in need of attention.

Clearly, the challenge issued in 1970 by the Joint Commission on the Mental Health of Children has not been adequately answered. Some important beginning steps, however, have been taken in the work toward child advocacy, the new efforts to identify and help high-risk children, and the present push toward permanent planning for

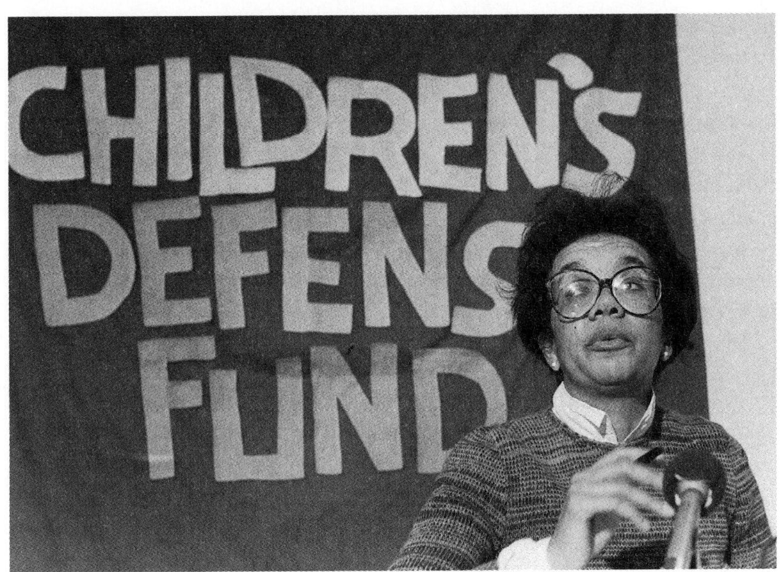

Marion Wright Edelman, leader of the Children's Defense Fund, a child-advocacy public-interest organization based in Washington, D.C.

children formerly sent to institutions or foster homes. If the direction and momentum of these efforts can be maintained and if sufficient financial support for them can be procured, the psychological environment for children could substantially improve.

UNRESOLVED ISSUES on Parental Pathology and Childhood Disorders

A great deal of research effort is being devoted to the question of whether parents' emotional problems are associated with the development of behavior problems in children and adolescents. Research has shown that parents who have children being seen in clinics for emotional problems tend to have more psychological problems than people in general. Furthermore, some recent research has suggested that parents of specific groups of severely disturbed children, such as conduct-disordered children, showed more deviant personality characteristics than parents of attention-deficit hyperactive children (Lahey et al., 1989). The question as to whether specific emotional problems among parents are associated with specific pathology in children and adolescents has not been clearly determined.

Are parents who are experiencing emotional problems transmitting their problems to their children in some way? The evidence seems to be clear that children of disturbed parents are more vulnerable to developing psychological problems themselves than children of parents without emotional problems. For example, children of parents who were clinically depressed have been found to show a reduced level of psychological functioning and an increased preponderance of psychological disorders, including major depression, substance abuse, or internalization problems (Laroche et al., 1987; Weissman et al., 1987; Gotlib & Colby, 1987). Other emotional disorders in parents have also been found to be associated with emotional problems in children. Turner, Beidel, and Costello (1987) reported that children of parents diagnosed with an anxiety disorder showed more fears and more mood disturbance than children of control (community) parents. Dumas, Gibson, and Albin (1989) found that parental pathology was related to more conduct disorders in children.

The actual mechanisms for the transmission of pathology from parent to child remain unclear. Hammen et al. (1987), however, caution that it is not specific diagnoses among parents that result in specific disorders in children, but it is the stress and symptoms that parents experience that influence the child's behavior. Some research suggests that the mechanisms for instilling behavior problems in children are to be found in learning processes. For example, Gelfand and Teti (1990) concluded that maternal depression was associated with undesirable parenting practices, such as unresponsiveness, inattention, intrusiveness, inept discipline, and negative perceptions of children. Other researchers have pointed to family problems that create unfavorable emotional states; for example, tensions evolving from such incidents as parental divorce (Kornberg & Caplan, 1980) may produce psychological problems and achievement problems (Bisnaire, Firestone, & Rynard, 1990) in youngsters.

Although emotionally upsetting events, such as divorce, have been traced to childhood pathology, relationships between these and specific childhood psychopathology have not been clearly determined. Recent evidence suggests that it is not divorce per se that produces disorder in a child—it is parental pathology. Lahey and colleagues (1988) found that parental divorce alone did not account for increased conduct disorder among boys. Rather, antisocial personality characteristics among parents were associated with conduct problems, suggesting that parental identification may be involved. Other researchers have attributed some types of psychopathology in children to genetic factors (Rosenthal et al., 1975).

One extensive effort to understand the relationships between parental pathology and problems in children has been the Rochester longitudinal risk study (Sameroff et al., 1987). These investigators have followed up a sample of chronically ill schizophrenic women and their offspring to determine what, if any, impact their psychological problems and other possible risk factors (such as socioeconomic status, race, and family size) have on the development of behavior problems in their children. The women were initially assessed during their pregnancy and followed periodically since then. Their children have been evaluated over several periods since their birth. Sameroff et al. found that specific maternal diagnoses had the least impact on the development of behavior problems in the children. They reported that both socioeconomic status and the severity of the mother's illness had a greater impact on the child's developing problems. Children with multiple risk factors had much worse outcomes than children with fewer risk factors. The Rochester Adaptive Behavior Inventory (RABI) was used to obtain objective ratings of social-emotional competence on the children at the 4-year follow-up. The risk variables studied were chronicity of illness, anxiety, parental education and occupation, parental perspectives, interaction skill, minority status, family support, family size, and the presence of stressful life events. The graph in *HIGHLIGHT 15.7* shows that multiple risk factors are associated with low social and emotional competence ratings in children. The investigators also reported that although children of schizophrenic mothers are indeed at high risk for developing emotional problems, so too were children of severely ill mothers and those from poor and minority backgrounds.

Whether the transmission of psychopathology from parent to child is due to faulty learning processes, genetic transmission, or some combination of these and other factors, it seems clear that at least some childhood and adolescent disorders are related to parental psychopathology. The precise mechanism or mechanisms for the transmission itself remains for future research to untangle.

SUMMARY

Traditionally, diagnosing behavior problems of children and adolescents has been a rather confused practice, in part because children have sometimes been viewed as "miniature" adults. It was not until the second half of the twentieth century that a diagnostic classification system focused clearly on the special problems of children.

Two broad approaches to the classification of childhood and adolescent behavior problems have been undertaken: a categorical approach, reflected most extensively in the DSM-III-R, and a dimensional approach. Both classification approaches involve organized classes of symptoms that are based on observations of behavior. In the categorical approach, symptoms of behavior problems are grouped together as syndromes based on clinical observations. In the dimensional approach, a broad range of symptoms and observations on cases are submitted to multivariate statistical techniques; the symptoms that group together make up the diagnostic classes referred to as "dimensions."

In this chapter, the DSM-III-R classification system is followed in order to provide clinical descriptions of a wide range of childhood behavior problems. Attention-deficit hyperactivity disorder is one of the more frequent behavior problems of childhood. In this disorder, the child shows impulsive, overactive behavior that interferes with his or her ability to accomplish tasks. There is some controversy over the explicit criteria used to distinguish hyperactive children from "normal" children or from children who exhibit other behavior disorders, such as conduct disorders. This lack of clarity in defining hyperactivity increases the difficulty of determining causal factors for the disorder. The major approaches to treating hyperactive children

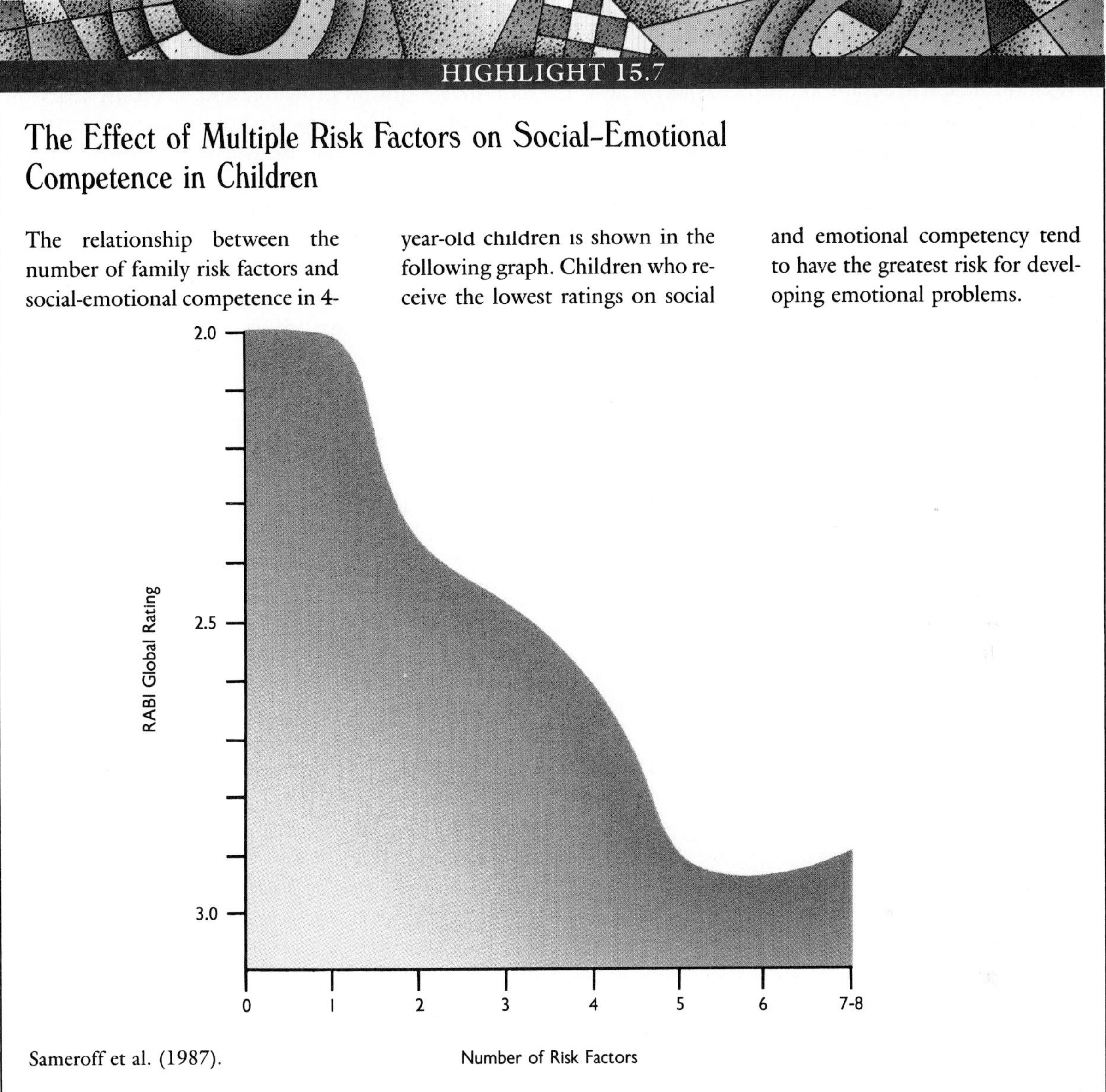

HIGHLIGHT 15.7

The Effect of Multiple Risk Factors on Social-Emotional Competence in Children

The relationship between the number of family risk factors and social-emotional competence in 4-year-old children is shown in the following graph. Children who receive the lowest ratings on social and emotional competency tend to have the greatest risk for developing emotional problems.

Sameroff et al. (1987).

have been medication and behavior therapy. Using medications, such as amphetamines, with children is somewhat controversial. Behavior therapy, particularly cognitive-behavioral methods, has shown a great deal of promise in modifying the behavior of hyperactive children.

Another common behavior problem among children is that of conduct disorder. In this disorder, a child engages in persistent aggressive or antisocial acts. In cases where the child's misdeeds involve illegal activities, the terms *delinquent* or *juvenile delinquent* may be applied. A number of potential causes of conduct disorder or delinquent behavior have been determined, ranging from biological factors to personal pathology to social conditions. Treatment of conduct disorders and delinquent behavior is often frustrating and difficult; treatment is likely to be ineffective unless some means can be found for modifying a child's environment.

Another group of disorders, the childhood anxiety disorders, are quite different from the conduct disorders. Children who suffer from these disorders typically do not cause difficulty for others through their aggressive conduct. Rather they are fearful, shy, withdrawn, insecure, and have difficulty adapting to outside demands. The anxiety disorders may be characterized by extreme anxiety, withdrawal, or avoidance behavior. A likely cause for these disorders is early family relationships that generate anxiety and prevent the child from developing more adaptive coping skills. Behavior therapy approaches—such as assertiveness training and desensitization—may be helpful in treating this kind of disorder.

Several other disorders of childhood involve behavior problems centering around a single outstanding symptom rather than pervasive maladaptive patterns. The symptoms may involve enuresis, encopresis, sleepwalking, or tics. In these disorders, treatment is generally more successful than in the other disorders just described.

A number of potential causal factors were considered for the disorders of childhood and adolescence. Although genetic predisposition appears to be important in several disorders, parental psychopathology, family disruption, and stressful circumstances, such as parental death or desertion and child abuse, can have an important causal influence. Recent research has underscored the importance of multiple risk factors in the development of psychopathology.

There are special problems, and special opportunities, involved in treating childhood disorders. The need for preventive and treatment programs for children is always growing, and in recent years the concept of child advocacy has become a reality in some states. Child abuse is a serious problem that has and continues to foster both research and clinical efforts into finding causes and devising preventive measures and treatment. Unfortunately, financial and other resources necessary for such services are not always readily available, and the future of programs for improving psychological environments for children remains uncertain.

Key Terms

developmental psychopathology (p. 535)
attention-deficit hyperactivity disorder (ADHD) (p. 538)
hyperactivity (p. 538)
conduct disorders (p. 543)
juvenile delinquency (p. 546)
separation anxiety disorder (p. 552)
overanxious disorder (p. 552)
enuresis (p. 558)
encopresis (p. 558)
sleepwalking disorder (p. 559)
tic (p. 559)
Tourette's syndrome (p. 560)
advocacy (p. 566)

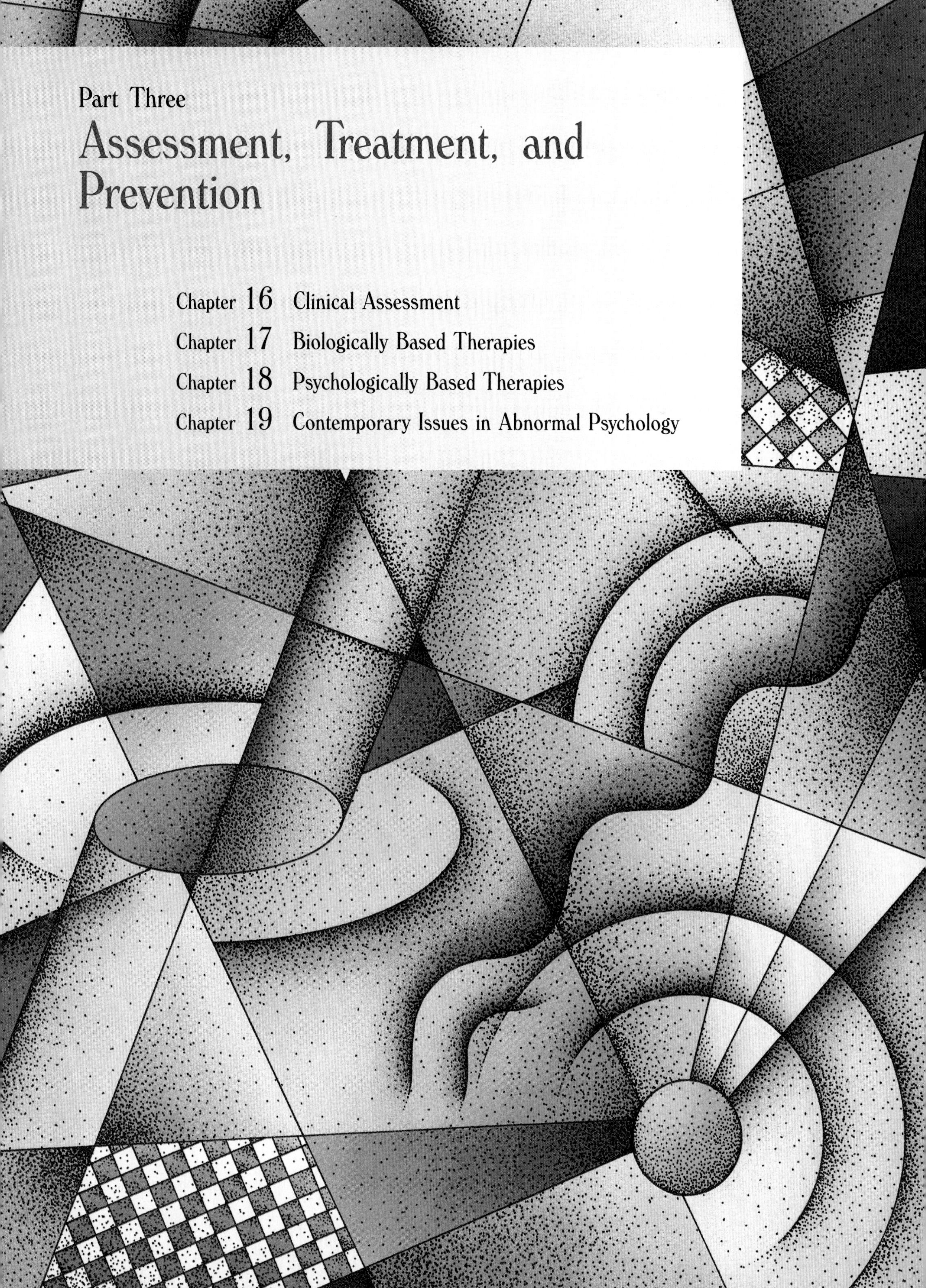

Part Three

Assessment, Treatment, and Prevention

Chapter 16
Clinical Assessment

Robert "Scottie" Wilson, *The City Among Flowers.* Wilson (1890–?) grew up in a poor family in Glasgow, Scotland. An itinerant merchant by trade, he traveled extensively, making his home at various times in Scotland, London, and Canada. In his early forties, while living in Toronto, Wilson suddenly began to make complex sketches in ink on various surfaces. His stylized self-portraits and symbolic designs reveal Wilson's originality and inward-looking vision.

A patient's "presenting complaint" to a clinician always initiates a process of ***assessment,*** whereby the clinician attempts to understand the nature and extent of the problem for which help is being sought. At times this process of inquiry is extremely convoluted and challenging, reminiscent of a Sherlock Holmes exercise in inductive and deductive logic. On other occasions assessment is a relatively straightforward matter in which the clinician may, with a high probability of being correct, come to a rapid conclusion about the basis for the complaint and the proper disposition of the case. Pediatricians whose practices tend to be confined to a local clientele, for example, quickly discern what childhood infections are "going around" at a given time. A child who is brought to the office with complaints that mimic the characteristic symptom profile for a then-common infection will likely be found to have that disease. Even so, the conscientious pediatrician will usually want to confirm the initial diagnostic impression with lab studies that identify, as far as possible, the infectious organism involved before initiating specifically targeted treatment.

Such confirming of diagnostic impressions is thus a matter of good practice even in the most routine clinical situations. For the mental health practitioner, few if any clinical situations are as routine as our pediatric example, and adequate techniques for confirming initial impressions may prove far more elusive. With rare exception, the precisely quantified "lab work" essential to much medical assessment is irrelevant in this domain. Psychological disorders do not as a rule have identifying biological characteristics. Furthermore, they are always interlaced with the personalities of the individuals suffering them and usually with the entire surrounding social fabric. Every instance is to that extent unique and is likely to be the product of a complex organization of contributing factors, many of which may not be apparent on brief or cursory examination, or sometimes even after many months of intense scrutiny in the course of psychotherapy. As this last statement implies, psychological assessment or diagnosis can actually be an ongoing process that proceeds apace with, rather than only preceding, treatment efforts.

In addition, as we have seen in earlier chapters, even where a specific *diagnosis* may be confidently determined it will normally clarify little of direct clinical significance beyond summarizing in descriptive terms the behavioral observations that the clinician has been able to make. It will not reveal, as do most diagnoses of medical conditions, the underlying pathologic processes producing the phenomena (for example, fever) that are observed. For these reasons the assessment process in the domain of mental disorders is usually more difficult, more uncertain, and more protracted than in the case of physical diseases. In the opinions of most mental health practitioners, however, it is no less critically important. No rational, specific treatment plan may be instituted in the absence of at least some general notion of what problems need to be addressed, and ongoing treatment decisions are typically made on the basis of the accumulating evidence pertaining to increasingly refined assessment hypotheses as treatment proceeds.

We will focus in this chapter on assessment procedures especially appropriate to the initial phase of the clinical process, where an attempt is made to circumscribe and identify the main dimensions of a client's problem or problems and to predict the likely course of events under various exigencies. Although a responsible and competent clinician will engage in assessment throughout the course of any treatment undertaken, it is at this initial stage where some of the most crucial decisions have to be made—such as what if any treatment approach is to be offered, whether or not the problem will require hospitalization, to what extent family members will need to be included as co-clients, and so on. Sometimes decisions such as these must be made within a constrained time frame, including emergency conditions, and without recourse to critical information that would probably (but not necessarily) become available with unlimited client contact in a more leisurely clinical context. As will be seen, various special psychological measurement instruments are frequently employed to maximize assessment efficiency in this type of pretreatment examination process.

A variant of this pretreatment type of assessment is the use of psychological assessment instruments in *screening* candidates for various roles and occupations. Here the effort is basically one of identifying individuals who appear to be psychologically unfit (or, alternatively, highly suited) for the particular type of assignment or work sought. For example, a police recruit who appears to have uncertain control of anger and aggressive impulses may need to be counseled about possibly adopting another occupational goal, or about seeking therapy to remedy a lack of control that could be dangerous in an occupation involving both great stress and constant access to lethal weapons.

A less obvious but equally important function of pretreatment assessment is that of establishing baselines for various psychological functions in order to measure with relative precision the effects produced by any treatment offered. In some treatment contexts, criteria based on these measurements are established as part of the treatment plan, such that the therapy is considered successful and is terminated only when client performance meets these predetermined criteria. Also, as will be seen in Chapters 17 and 18, comparison of posttreatment with pretreatment assessment results is an essential feature of many research projects specifically designed to evaluate the efficacy of various therapies for different types of disorder.

In this chapter, we will review some of the more commonly used assessment procedures and show how the data obtained can be integrated into a coherent clinical picture for use in making decisions about referral and treatment. Our survey will include a discussion of neuropsychological assessment, the clinical interview, behavioral observation, and personality assessment through the use of projective and objective psychological tests.

Let us look first at what, exactly, a clinician is trying to learn during psychological assessment of a client.

THE INFORMATION SOUGHT IN ASSESSMENT

What does a clinician need to know? First, of course, *the problem must be identified.* Is it a situational problem precipitated by some environmental stressor, a manifestation of a more pervasive and long-term disorder, or is it perhaps some combination of the two? Is there any evidence of recent deterioration in cognitive functioning? What is the duration of the current complaint and how is the individual dealing with the problem? What if any prior help has been sought? Are there indications of self-defeating behavior and personality deterioration, or is the individual using available personal and environmental resources in a good effort to cope? How pervasively has the problem affected the person's performance of important social roles? Does the individual's symptomatic behavior fit any of the diagnostic patterns in the current edition of the DSM?

As we have seen, there has been a trend against overdependence on diagnostic labeling because of its intrinsic limitations and the potential damage that labels can do in setting up self-fulfilling prophecies for the individual, blinding members of the therapeutic staff to other relevant behavior on the individual's part. On the other hand, it is often important to have an adequate classification of the presenting problem for a number of reasons. In many cases, a formal diagnosis is necessary before insurance claims can be filed. Clinically, knowledge of an individual's type of disorder can help in planning and managing the most appropriate treatment procedures. Administratively, it is essential to know the range of diagnostic problems that are represented among the patient or client population and for which treatment facilities need to be available. If the majority of patients at a facility have been diagnosed as having personality disorders, for example, then the staffing, physical environment, and treatment facilities should be arranged accordingly. Thus, the nature of the difficulty needs to be understood as clearly as possible, including a categorization if appropriate.

For most clinical purposes, a formal diagnostic classification per se is much less important than having *a basic understanding of the individual's history, intellectual functioning, personality characteristics, and environmental pressures and resources.* That is, an adequate assessment includes much more than the diagnostic label. For example, it should include an objective description of the individual's behavior. How does the individual characteristically respond to other people? Are there *excesses* in behavior, such as eating or drinking too much? Are there notable *deficits,* as, for example, in social skills? How *appropriate* is the individual's behavior? Is the individual manifesting behavior that would be acceptable in some contexts but is often displayed where it is plainly unresponsive to the situation or to reasonable social expectations? Excesses, deficits, and appropriateness are key dimensions to be noted if the clinician is to understand the particular disorder that has brought the individual to the clinic or hospital.

In addition, assessment needs to include *a description of any relevant long-term personality characteristics.* Has the individual typically responded in deviant ways to particular kinds of situations, for example, ones requiring submission to legitimate authority? Do there seem to be personality traits or behavior patterns that predispose the individual to behave in maladaptive ways across a broad range of circumstances? Does the person tend to become enmeshed with others to the point of losing his or her identity, or is he or she so self-contained that intimate exchange is routinely aborted? Is the person able to accept help from others? Is the person capable of genuine affection, or of accepting appropriate responsibility for others' welfare? Such questions are necessarily at the heart of many assessment efforts.

It is also important to assess *the social context in which the individual operates.* What kinds of environmental demands are typically placed on the individual, and what supports or special stressors exist in the individual's life situation? For example, being the primary caretaker for a spouse suffering from Alzheimer's disease is sufficiently challenging that relatively few can manage the task without significant psychological impairment, especially where outside supports are lacking. As we have seen, the DSM-III-R classification includes guidelines for rating both the severity of the stressors in an individual's current environment and the level of an individual's overall adjustment in meeting the demands of a complex social environment.

The diverse and often conflicting bits of information about the individual's personality traits, behavior patterns, environmental demands, and so on must then be integrated into a consistent and meaningful picture. Some clinicians refer to this picture as a **dynamic formulation,** because it not only describes the current situation but includes hypotheses about what is driving the person to behave in maladaptive ways. At this point in the assessment, the clinician should have a plausible explanation, for example, for why a normally passive and mild-mannered man suddenly flew into a rage and started breaking up furniture; or why the breakup of a relationship with a clearly unsuitable partner should initiate a stubbornly persistent major depression.

The formulation should *allow the clinician to develop hypotheses about the client's future behavior* as well. What is the likelihood of improvement or deterioration if the individual's problems are left untreated? Which behaviors should be the initial focus of change, and what treatment methods are likely to be most efficient in producing this change? How much change might reasonably be expected from a particular type of treatment?

Where feasible, decisions about treatment are made collaboratively with the consent and approval of the individual. In cases of severe disorder, however, they may have to be made without the patient's participation or in rare instances even without consulting responsible kin. As has already been indicated, a knowledge of the patient's strengths and resources is important; in short, what qualities does the patient bring to the treatment program that can enhance the prognosis?

VARYING TYPES OF ASSESSMENT DATA

Because a wide range of factors can play important roles in causing and maintaining maladaptive behavior, assessment may involve the coordinated use of physical, psychological, and environmental assessment procedures. As we have indicated, however, the nature and comprehensiveness of clinical assessments vary depending on the problem and the treatment agency's facilities. Assessment by phone in a suicide prevention center, for example, is quite different from assessment aimed at determining whether a particular hospitalized patient is sufficiently intelligent, verbal, and psychologically minded to be likely to profit significantly from individual psychotherapy.

Furthermore, exactly how a clinician goes about the assessment process often depends on his or her basic orientation. For example, a biologically oriented clinician, typically a psychiatrist or other medical practitioner, will likely focus on biological assessment methods aimed at determining any underlying organic malfunctioning that may be causing the maladaptive behavior. A psychoanalytically oriented clinician will likely use unstructured personality assessment techniques, such as the Rorschach inkblots or the Thematic Apperception Test (TAT), to identify latent intrapsychic conflicts. A behaviorally oriented clinician, in an effort to determine the functional relationships between environmental events or reinforcements and the abnormal behavior, will rely on such techniques as behavioral observation and systematic self-monitoring to identify maladaptive learned patterns; for a cognitively oriented behaviorist, the focus would shift to the dysfunctional thoughts supposedly mediating those patterns. A humanistically oriented clinician might use interview techniques to uncover blocked or distorted personal growth, and an interpersonally oriented clinician will use such techniques as personal confrontations to pinpoint difficulties in interpersonal relationships.

The preceding examples represent general trends and are in no way meant to imply that clinicians of a particular orientation limit themselves to a particular assessment method or that each assessment technique is limited to a particular theoretical orientation. Such trends are instead a matter of emphasis and point up the fact that certain types of assessments are more conducive than others to uncovering particular causal factors, or for eliciting information about symptomatic behavior central to understanding and treating the disorder within a given conceptual framework.

In what follows, we will discuss the way in which both physical and psychosocial data are collected. Then we will examine an actual psychological study that has drawn on a variety of assessment data.

ASSESSMENT OF THE PHYSICAL ORGANISM

In some situations or with certain psychological problems, a medical evaluation is necessary to rule out physical abnormalities that may be contributing to the problem. The medical evaluation may include both general physical and special examinations aimed at assessing the structural (anatomical) and functional (physiological) integrity of the brain as a behaviorally significant physical system.

The General Physical Examination

A physical examination consists of the kinds of procedures most of us have experienced in getting a "medical checkup." Typically, a medical history is obtained and the major systems of the body are checked. This part of the assessment procedure is of obvious import for disorders that focus on physical problems, such as psychogenically induced disease, and somatoform, addictive, and organic brain syndromes. In addition, a variety of nonobvious, systemic organic conditions, including various hormonal irregularities, can produce in some individuals behavioral symptoms that closely mimic those of certain mental disorders usually considered to have predominantly psychosocial origins. A case in point is the problem of male erectile dysfunction. A diagnostic error in this type of situation could prove costly; hence, in equivocal cases most clinicians insist on a medical clearance before initiating psychosocially based interventions.

The Neurological Examination

Because brain pathology is involved in some mental disorders, a specialized neurological examination is frequently given in addition to the general medical examination. This may involve getting an **electroencephalogram (EEG)** to assess brain-wave patterns in awake and sleeping states. An EEG is a graphic record of the brain's electrical activity. It is obtained noninvasively by placing electrodes on the scalp and by amplifying the minute brain-wave impulses from various brain areas; these amplified impulses drive oscillating pens whose deviations are traced on fanfold paper moving at a constant speed. Much is known about the normal pattern of these impulses in waking and sleeping states and under various conditions of sensory stimulation. Significant divergences from the normal pattern can thus reflect abnormalities of brain function, such as might be caused by a brain tumor or other lesion. Where EEGs reveal such **dysrythmias** in the brain's electrical activity, other specialized techniques may then be used in an attempt to arrive at a more precise diagnosis of the nature and extent of the problem.

Radiological technology, such as **computerized axial tomography,** known in brief as the **CAT scan,** is one of these specialized techniques. Through the use of X rays, a CAT scan reveals images of parts of the brain that might be diseased. This procedure has revolutionized neurological study in recent years by providing rapid access, without surgery, to accurate information about the localization and extent of anomalies in the brain's structural characteristics. The procedure involves the use of computer analysis applied to X-ray beams across sections of a patient's brain to produce images that a neurologist can then interpret.

A newer scanning technique is **positron emission tomography,** the **PET scan.** Though a CAT scan is limited to distinguishing anatomical features, such as the shape of a particular internal structure, a PET scan allows for an appraisal of how an organ is functioning by measuring metabolic processes. The PET scan provides metabolic portraits through tracking natural compounds, like glucose, as they are metabolized by the brain or other organs. By revealing areas of differential metabolic activity, the PET scan enables a medical specialist to obtain more clear-cut diagnoses of brain pathology by, for example, pinpointing sites responsible for epileptic seizures, trauma from head damage or stroke, and brain tumors. Thus the PET scan may be able to reveal problems that are not immediately apparent anatomically. Moreover, the use of PET scans in research on brain pathology occurring in abnormal conditions, such as schizophrenia, depression, and alcoholism, has the potential of leading to important discoveries about the organic processes underlying these disorders, thus providing clues to more effective treatment. To date, unfortunately, progress on this front has not, in our judgment, proven very illuminating.

The newest of these internal scanning techniques is **nuclear magnetic resonance imaging (MRI).** Like a CAT scan, this procedure allows visualization of the anatomical features of internal organs, including the brain. Unlike a CAT scan, protracted x-radiation of the site of interest is not required, and yet the images achieved are often of decidedly higher quality in terms of resolution and clarity. Essentially, MRI involves the precise measurement of variations in magnetic fields that are caused by the varying amounts of water (hydrogen) content of various organs and parts of organs. In this manner the anatomical structure of a "cut" at any given plane through an organ, say the brain, can be computed and graphically depicted with astonishing structural differentiation and clarity.

In fact, MRI technology will likely render obsolete the CAT scan, which was considered at the cutting edge of medical technology only a few years ago. MRI thus makes possible, by noninvasive means, visualization of all but the most minute

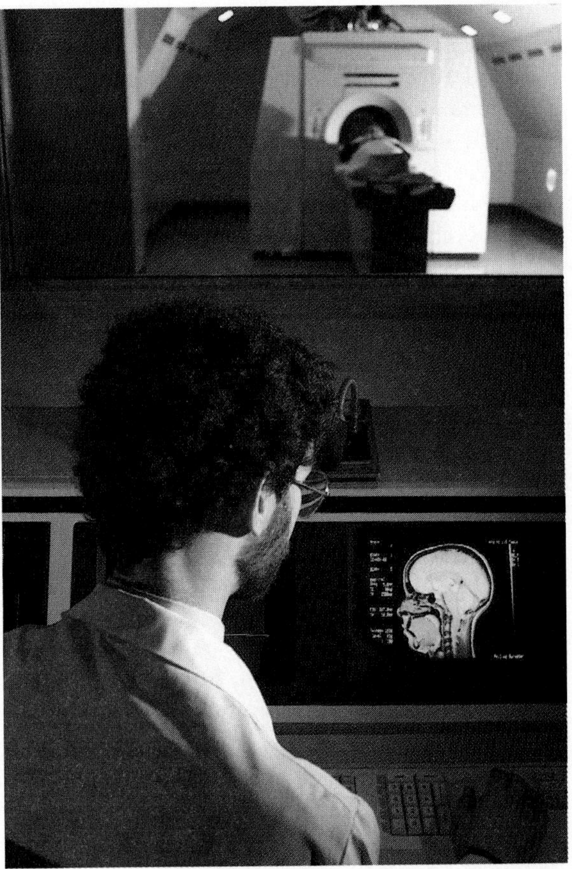

Nuclear magnetic resonance imaging (MRI) allows visualization of the anatomical features of the brain without protracted x-radiation, as in CAT scans. In MRI an anatomical structure can be computed and graphically depicted with astonishing differentiation and clarity.

abnormalities of brain structure. It has been particularly useful in confirming degenerative brain processes, as manifested, for example, in enlarged cerebrospinal fluid spaces within the brain. Again here, MRI studies have considerable potential to illuminate the contribution of brain anomalies to "nonorganic" psychoses, such as schizophrenia, and some progress in this area has in fact been made, as noted in Chapter 12. No genuine "breakthroughs," however, are as yet on the horizon.

The Neuropsychological Examination

The techniques so far described are fairly accurate in identifying abnormalities in the brain's physical properties. Usually, although by no means always, such abnormalities are accompanied by gross impairments in behavior and varied psychological deficits, although the particular nature of the latter may not be accurately predicted even after precisely localizing these physical abnormalities. Also, behavioral and psychological impairments due to organic brain abnormalities may become manifest before any organic brain lesion is detectable by scanning or other means. Needed in these instances are reliable techniques for precisely measuring any alteration in behavioral or psychological functioning that has occurred in consequence of the organic brain pathology. This need is met by a growing cadre of clinical psychologists specializing in the field of **neuropsychological assessment,** which involves the use of an expanding array of testing devices to measure a person's cognitive, perceptual, and motor performance as aids in determining the extent and location of brain damage.

In many instances of known or suspected organic brain involvement, a clinical neuropsychologist will administer a test battery to a patient. The purpose of such testing is to describe the behavioral functioning of the individual in terms of brain-behavior relationships. By means of a battery of tests, the individual's performance on various standardized tasks, particularly perceptual-motor ones, can give valuable clues about that person's cognitive and intellectual impairment following brain damage (Boll, 1978; Filskov & Locklear, 1982; Heaton & Pendleton, 1981). Such testing can even provide clues as to the probable location of the brain damage, though PET scans, MRIs, and other physical tests are still more effective in determining the exact location of the injury.

Many neuropsychologists prefer to select a highly individualized array of tests to administer, depending on a patient's case history and other available information. Others opt for a battery consisting of a standard set of tests that have been preselected so as to sample in a systematic and comprehensive manner a broad range of psychological competencies known to be adversely affected by various types of brain insult. The use of a constant set of tests has many research and clinical advantages, although it may compromise flexibility. One such standard battery, widely used, is the Halstead-Reitan, whose components are described in *HIGHLIGHT 16.1*

Typically taking about six hours to administer, the Halstead-Reitan can be a problem in some clinical settings where time and funding is limited. Understandably, examinee fatigue may also be a limiting factor, particularly where a patient is in a debilitated condition. In the last decade, the Luria-Nebraska battery (Golden, 1978), which takes only about two-and-a-half hours to administer, has been receiving much attention as an alternative to the Halstead-Reitan. Both these batteries, as well as others of similar purpose and construction, provide their information without the risks attendant to more invasive neurological examination procedures (Filskov & Goldstein, 1974). Still, however, the Halstead-Reitan battery continues to grow in use because it yields a great deal of useful information —more than the Luria-Nebraska—about an individual's cognitive and motor processes (Boll, 1980; Filskov & Locklear, 1982; Hartlage, Asken, & Hornsby, 1987).

In summary, the medical and neuropsychological sciences are developing many new procedures to assess brain functioning and behavioral manifestations of organic disorder. Medical procedures to assess organic brain damage include EEGs, and CAT, PET, and MRI scans. The new technology holds a great deal of promise for detecting and evaluating organic brain dysfunction and for providing increased understanding of brain functioning through graphic mapping of the brain. Neuropsychological testing provides a clinician with important behavioral information on how organic brain damage is affecting an individual's present functioning.

PSYCHOSOCIAL ASSESSMENT

Psychosocial assessment attempts to provide a realistic picture of an individual in interaction with the environment. This picture includes relevant information concerning the individual's personality makeup and present level of functioning, as well as information about the stressors and resources in his

HIGHLIGHT 16.1

Neuropsychological Examinations: Determining Brain-Behavior Relationships

The Halstead-Reitan battery is a neuropsychological examination composed of several tests and variables from which an "index of impairment" can be computed (Boll, 1978, 1980). In addition, it provides specific information about a subject's functioning in several skill areas. Though it typically takes four to six hours to complete and requires substantial administrative time, it is being used increasingly in neurological evaluations because it yields a great deal of useful information about an individual's cognitive and motor processes (Filskov & Boll, 1986; Filskov & Goldstein, 1974; Filskov & Locklear, 1982). Moreover, the Halstead-Reitan battery provides valid information without the risk of injury or death that is so great with more invasive procedures. The Halstead-Reitan battery for adults is made up of the following tests:

1. *The Halstead Category Test* measures a subject's ability to learn and remember material and can provide clues as to his or her judgment and impulsivity. The subject is presented with a stimulus (on a screen) that suggests a number between one and four. The subject presses a button indicating which number is "correct." A correct choice is followed by the sound of a pleasant doorbell and an incorrect choice by a loud buzzer. The person is required to determine from the pattern of buzzers and bells what the underlying principle of the correct choice is.

2. *The Tactual Performance Test* measures a subject's motor speed, response to the unfamiliar, and ability to learn and use tactile and kinesthetic cues. The test consists of a board that has spaces for ten blocks of varied shapes. The subject is blindfolded (never actually seeing the board) and asked to place the blocks into the correct grooves in the board. Later, the subject is asked to draw the blocks and the board from tactile memory.

3. *The Rhythm Test* is an auditory perception task used to measure attention and sustained concentration. It is a subtest of Seashore's Test of musical talent and includes 30 pairs of rhythmic beats that are presented on a tape recorder. On this test, a subject is required to determine if the pairs are the same or different.

4. *The Speech Sounds Perception Test* is a test to determine if an individual can identify spoken words. Nonsense words are presented on a tape recorder, and the subject is asked to identify the presented word from a list of four printed words. This task measures the subject's concentration, attention, and comprehension.

5. *The Finger Oscillation Task* measures the speed at which an individual can, with the index finger, depress a lever. Several trials are given with each hand.

In addition to the Halstead-Reitan battery, other tests, referred to as *allied procedures,* may be used in a neuropsychology laboratory. For example, Boll (1980) recommends the use of the modified Halstead-Wepman Aphasia Screening Test for obtaining information about a subject's language ability and about his or her abilities to identify numbers and body parts, to follow directions, to spell, and to pantomime simple actions.

or her life situation. For example, early in the process, clinicians may act like puzzle solvers, absorbing as much information about the client as possible—present feelings, attitudes, memories, demographic facts, and so on—and trying to fit the pieces together into a meaningful pattern. They typically formulate hypotheses and discard or confirm them as they proceed. Starting usually with a global technique, such as a clinical interview, clinicians may later select more specific assessment tasks or tests. The following are some of the psychosocial procedures that may be used.

Assessment Interviews

An assessment interview, often considered the central element of the assessment process, usually involves a face-to-face interaction conducted in such a way that a clinician obtains information about various aspects of a patient's situation, behavior, and personality makeup. The interview may vary from a simple set of questions or prompts, as in the *mental status exam* used chiefly by psychiatrists and other physicians, to a more extended and detailed format. It may be relatively "free-wheeling" in character, with an interviewer making moment-to-moment selections about his or her next probe based on responses to prior ones, or it may be more tightly controlled and structured so as to ensure that a particular set of questions and probes is introduced. In the latter case, the interviewer may choose from a number of highly structured, standardized interview formats whose reliability has been established in prior research. As used here, *reliability* means simply that two interviewers assessing the same client will generate highly similar conclusions about the client, a type of consensus that research shows can by no means be taken for granted.

Although we know of few clinicians who express enthusiasm for the more controlled and structured type of assessment interview, the research data are clear in showing it to yield far more reliable results, in general, than the more flexible format. This appears to be an instance of a widespread overconfidence among clinicians in the accuracy of their own methods and judgments (Garb, 1989; Kleinmuntz, 1990). On the other hand, every rule has its exceptions, and we have seen brilliantly conducted assessment interviews where each probe was fashioned on the spur of the moment. The upshot seems to be that in most instances an assessor would be wise to conduct an interview that is carefully structured in terms of goals, comprehensive symptom review, other content to be explored, and the type of relationship the interviewer attempts to establish with the subject. Such an approach is likely to minimize error over the long course, although we acknowledge that a more creative and spontaneous interview format may be more productive in particular clinical situations.

The reliability of the assessment interview may also be enhanced by the use of rating scales that help focus inquiry and quantify the interview data. For example, a subject may be rated on a three-, five-, or seven-point scale with respect to self-esteem, anxiety, and various other characteristics. Such a structured and preselected format is particularly effective in giving a comprehensive impression or "profile" of the subject and his or her life situation, and in revealing specific problems or crises—such as marital difficulties, drug dependence, or suicidal fantasies—that may require immediate therapeutic intervention (Matarazzo, 1983).

As already suggested, clinical interviews are subject to error and have been criticized as an unreliable source of information on which to base important clinical decisions. Evidence of this unreliability includes the fact that, on the basis of the interview data they elicit for a particular patient, different clinicians have often arrived at different formal diagnoses. It is chiefly for this reason, in fact, that recent versions of the DSM (that is, III and III-R) have emphasized an "operational" assessment approach, one that specifies observable criteria for diagnosis and provides specific guidelines for making diagnostic judgments. A clinician who is seeking to render a formal diagnosis is thus essentially forced to incorporate at least minimal structure into the interview or risk coming up empty-handed in regard to eliciting data essential to such a diagnosis. "Winging it" has thus become a somewhat maladaptive strategy in this type of assessment process. Although the available data on the improved reliability of psychiatric diagnoses have shown the operational approach to have decided advantages, there has also doubtless been some cost in reducing interviewer flexibility and in encouraging undue preoccupation with observable "signs" at the expense of overall understanding of patient functioning (Simons, 1987).

As was suggested in Chapter 1, the developments just described can be characterized as favoring the removal of the diagnostician, as a subjective judge, from the diagnostic process; to the degree possible, diagnosis is rendered "automatic." But if a human judge is unnecessary—perhaps even a troublesome source of error—then why not take the extra step of computerizing the diagnostic process? Computers, after all, are superb at remembering and following explicitly stated rules for decision making. Where clinically feasible, they can even be used on-line to ask the same sorts of questions, and elicit the same sorts of answers, as would a human interviewer; that is, a patient can be "interviewed" by a computer terminal or console.

In fact, efforts of this sort have already been developed to a relatively advanced stage (Erdman, Klein, & Greist, 1985). Computer programs with highly sophisticated branching subroutines are available to "tailor-make" a diagnostic interview for a patient. Stein (1987), for example, designed a program called the Computerized Diagnostic Interview for Children that can conduct a standard psychiatric interview. Several more specific clinical assessment tasks have been adapted for computer administration. For example, Fowler et al. (1987) have designed a Clinical Problem Checklist that can provide a therapist with an overview of a client's presenting symptoms. Allen and Skinner (1987) have designed a computer program that takes down a client's alcohol- and drug-abuse history, and Giannetti (1987) has a computer program that records a client's social history. All these are fairly easy-to-administer programs that can provide a clinician with a wealth of reliable data that can be useful during the assessment process.

Despite the considerable progress made in reducing subjective factors by computerizing or otherwise making various aspects of the assessment process relatively automatic, it is important to understand that excessive reliance on such techniques can also introduce error. The complexity of human behavior is bound to produce many exceptions to any "rule." In the final analysis, therefore, there is probably no adequate substitute for expert clinical judgment (Carson, 1990b). Where such judgment is available as a backstop, these techniques can substantially improve assessment efficiency while minimizing the risks of mindless decision making.

The Clinical Observation of Behavior

Direct observation of an individual's characteristic behavior has long been considered important for adequate psychosocial assessment. The main purpose of direct observation is to find out more about the person's psychological makeup and level of functioning through the objective description of appearance and behavior in various contexts. Though such observations would ideally occur within the individual's natural environment, they are typically confined to clinic or hospital settings. For example, a brief description is usually made of a subject's behavior on hospital admission, and more detailed observations are made periodically on the ward. These descriptions include concise notations of relevant information about the subject's personal hygiene, emotional behavior, delusions or hallucinations, anxiety, sexual behavior, aggressive or suicidal tendencies, and so on.

In addition to making their own observations, many clinicians enlist their patients' help in this endeavor by providing instruction in self-observation and objective reporting of behavior, thoughts, and feeling states as they occur in various natural settings. Such **self-monitoring** can be a valuable aid in determining the kinds of situations, possibly previously unrecognized, in which maladaptive behavior is likely to be evoked, and numerous studies also show it to have therapeutic benefits in its own right. Alternatively, a patient may be asked to fill out a more or less formal *self-report* or a checklist concerning problematic reactions experienced in various situations. Numerous such instruments have been published in the professional literature and are commercially available to clinicians. These approaches recognize that individuals are excellent sources of information about themselves. Assuming that the right questions are asked and that people are willing to disclose information about themselves, the results can have a crucial bearing on treatment planning—for example, by providing essential information for structuring a behavioral treatment intervention.

As in the case of interviews, the use of **rating scales** in clinical observation and in self-reports helps not only to organize information but also to encourage reliability and objectivity. That is, the formal structure of a scale is likely to keep unwarranted observer inferences to a minimum. Rating scales commonly used are those that enable a rater to indicate not only the presence or absence of a trait or behavior but also its prominence. The following is an example of such a rating-scale item; the observer would check the most appropriate alternative.

Sexual behavior:

_____ 1. Sexually assaultive: aggressively approaches males or females with sexual intent.

_____ 2. Sexually soliciting: exposes genitals with sexual intent, makes overt sexual advances to other patients or staff, masturbates openly.

_____ 3. No overt sexual behavior: not preoccupied with discussion or sexual matters.

_____ 4. Avoids sex topics: made uneasy by discussion of sex, becomes disturbed if approached sexually by others.

_____ 5. Excessive prudishness about sex: considers sex filthy, condemns sexual behavior in others, becomes panic-stricken if approached sexually.

Obviously, these sorts of observations may be made not only to fill in the original picture but also to check on the course or outcome of treatment procedures.

One of the rating scales most widely used for recording observations in clinical practice and in psychiatric research is the *Brief Psychiatric Rating Scale (BPRS)*. The BPRS provides a structured and quantifiable format for rating clinical symptoms, such as somatic concern, anxiety, emotional withdrawal, guilt feelings, hostility, suspiciousness, and unusual thought patterns. It contains 18 scales that are scored from ratings made by a clinician following an interview with a patient. The distinct patterns of behavior reflected in the BPRS ratings enable clinicians to make a standardized comparison of their patients' symptoms with the behavior of other psychiatric patients (Overall & Hollister,

1982). The BPRS has been found to be an extremely useful instrument in clinical research, especially for the purpose of assigning patients to treatment groups on the basis of similarity in symptoms. A similar but more specifically targeted instrument, the *Hamilton Rating Scale for Depression (HRSD),* has become almost the standard in this respect for selecting clinically depressed research subjects, and also for assessing the response of such subjects to various treatment interventions.

Observations made in clinical settings by trained observers can provide behavioral data useful in ongoing clinical management. Paul and his colleagues (Lichy, 1982; Mariotto, 1979; Paul, 1982; Paul & Lentz, 1977; Rich, Paul, & Mariotto, 1988), for example, have developed a comprehensive behavioral assessment program that they have implemented experimentally in a number of hospitals. The program includes evaluating the behavior of chronic patients and monitoring the activities of staff members working with them. Through the use of observational rating systems, they have been able to measure staff behavior in the daily management of patients and ongoing patient behavior on the ward. The behavioral ratings can be used to pinpoint specific behaviors to be changed on the part of members of either group.

Recently, a good deal of attention has focused on observing a subject's behavior in his or her natural surroundings. For example, children who have been showing behavior problems may be observed at school, in their peer groups, and in their homes. Here the purpose is to obtain a sampling of their behavior in ordinary situations to understand the problems they are facing, the coping patterns they are using, and the environmental conditions that may be reinforcing their maladaptive behavior.

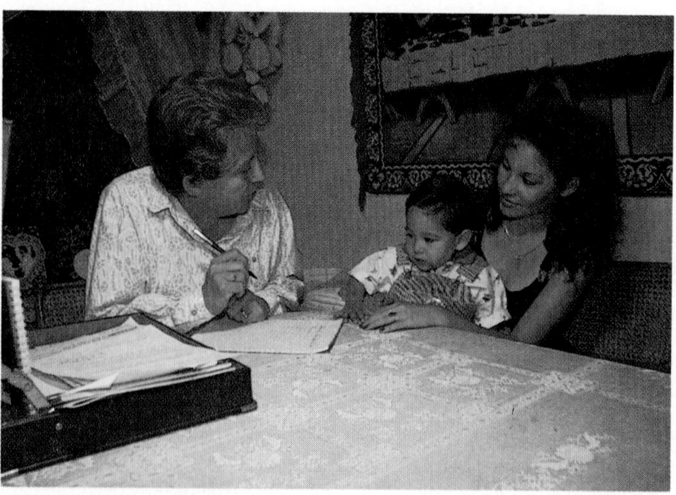

It can be helpful to both a practitioner and a client to observe and assess the client's behavior in an everyday setting, such as his or her home, where there is the opportunity to talk with family members and to discern the stressors and resources in the client's life situation.

The procedures described above focus on a subjects overt behavior, omitting the often equally important consideration of concurrent mental events—that is, the individual's own ongoing thoughts. In an attempt to get a sampling of naturally occurring thoughts, psychologists are experimenting with having individuals carry small electronic beepers that produce a signal, such as a soft tone, at unexpected intervals. At each signal, these individuals are to write down or electronically record whatever thoughts the signal interrupted. These "thought reports" can then be analyzed in various ways, and can be used for some kinds of personality assessment and diagnosis as well as for monitoring progress in psychological therapy.

In situations where it is not feasible to observe a subject's behavior in everyday settings—as when he or she is institutionalized—an entire family may be asked to meet together in the clinic or hospital where their interactions and difficulties can be observed and studied. In other cases, a social worker may obtain relevant data by visiting a subject's home, talking with family members and others who are important to the subject, and observing the stressors and resources in the subject's life situation. In addition to providing important assessment data, this procedure incorporates the "observers" into the therapy program, thereby enhancing the therapy.

Where the object of study is a child, Jones, Reid, and Patterson (1975) have developed a method for coding and quantifying the observations of the child's behavior at school and at home. Concrete instances of behavior and interaction can be observed, recorded, and coded, either by trained observers or by the parents themselves. This method provides the clinician with information about the stimuli that are controlling the child's interactions, which in turn makes it possible for the clinician to evaluate the quality of the child's interactions and to identify the situations that result in behavior problems.

In still other situations where observation in a natural setting is not possible, a clinician may construct or contrive observational opportunities that can provide information about an individual's response to particular circumstances. For example, an individual who has a phobia for snakes might be placed in a situation where snakelike objects and pictures are presented.

An often-used procedure that enables a clinician to observe a client's behavior directly is **role playing.** The client is instructed to play a part—for example, someone standing up for his or her rights. Role playing a situation like this not only can provide assessment information for the clinician but also can serve as a vehicle for new learning for the client.

Extending the use of observational data a bit further, a clinician may analyze situations with which a subject is likely to be confronted in the future. For example, a patient with little education and a history of chronic unemployment might improve sufficiently to leave an institution but be little better off than before, an unfortunately common occurrence, unless treatment has included training in job skills. Thus, knowledge of a troubled individual's life situation not only helps in understanding present maladaptive behavior, but is often essential for planning a treatment program that will enable him or her to meet future challenges in more adaptive ways.

Psychological Tests

Interviews and behavioral observation are relatively *direct* attempts to determine an individual's beliefs, attitudes, and problems. Psychological tests, on the other hand, are a more *indirect* means of assessing psychological characteristics. Scientifically developed psychological tests (as opposed to the recreational ones sometimes appearing in newspapers and magazines) are standardized sets of procedures or tasks for obtaining samples of behavior; a subject's responses to the standardized stimuli are compared with those of other people having comparable demographic characteristics, usually through established test norms or test score distributions. From these comparisons, a clinician can then draw inferences about the extent to which the person's individual psychological qualities differ from those of a reference group, typically a psychologically normal one. Among the characteristics these tests can ascertain are coping patterns, motive patterns, personality characteristics, role behaviors, values, levels of depression or anxiety and intellectual functioning. Impressive advances in the technology of test development have in fact made it possible to develop instruments of acceptable reliability and validity to measure almost any conceivable psychological characteristic in which people vary.

Though more precise and often more reliable than interviews or less standardized observational techniques, psychological tests are far from perfect tools. Often, if not always, their value depends on the competence of the clinician who interprets their outcomes (Carson, 1990b). In general, they are useful diagnostic tools for psychologists in much the same way that blood tests, X-ray films, or MRI scans are useful to physicians competent in interpreting the outputs from those procedures. In all these cases, pathology may be revealed in people who appear on the surface to be quite normal, or a general impression of "something wrong" can be checked against more precise information.

Two general categories of psychological tests for use in clinical practice are *intelligence tests* and *personality tests*. We discuss each in the following sections.

Intelligence Tests A clinician can choose from a wide range of intelligence tests. The Wechsler Intelligence Scale for Children-Revised (WISC-R) and the current revision of the prototypal Stanford-Binet Intelligence Scale are widely used in clinical settings for measuring the intellectual abilities of children. Probably the most commonly used test for measuring adult intelligence is the Wechsler Adult Intelligence Scale-Revised (WAIS-R). It includes both verbal and performance material and consists of 11 subtests. A brief description of two of the subtests—one verbal and one performance—will serve to illustrate the type of functions the WAIS-R measures:

General information (verbal). This subtest consists of questions designed to tap the individual's range of information on material that is ordinarily encountered. For example, the individual is asked to do such things as tell how many weeks there are in a year, name the colors of the American flag, and tell who Martin Luther King was.

Picture completion (performance). This subtest consists of 20 cards showing pictures, each with a part missing. The task for the subject is to indicate what is missing. This test is designed to measure the individual's ability to discriminate between essential and nonessential elements in a situation. (Wechsler, 1981)

An analysis of scores on the various subtests reveals an individual's present level of intellectual functioning. In addition, the subject's behavior in the test situation may reveal much relevant information. For example, he or she may be apprehensive about not doing well, may vacillate in responses, may seek continual reassurance from the clinician, or may be so disturbed that concentration on the tasks presented is difficult. These observed behaviors may tell the clinician as much as the actual test scores.

Individually administered intelligence tests—such as the WISC-R, WAIS-R, and the Stanford-

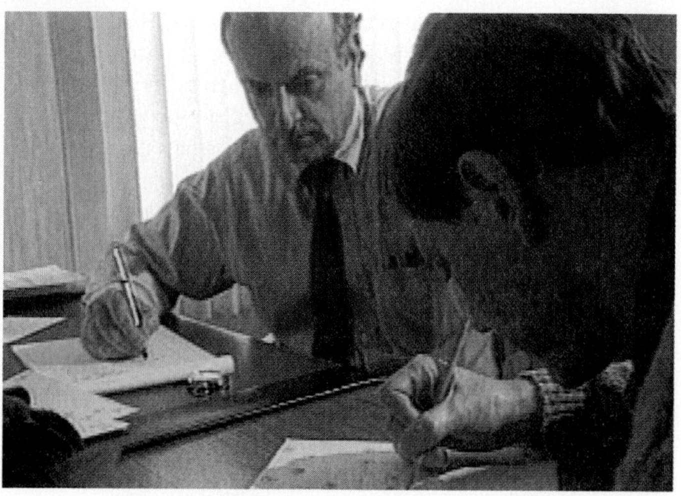

Here a psychologist administers part of the WAIS-R, an intelligence test that provides information about how well an individual performs on a variety of cognitive challenges. An individually administered test such as this can require considerable time—often two to three hours—to give, score, and interpret; as such, it is appropriate to use these types of tests primarily when intelligence testing is considered critical to the diagnosis.

Binet—typically require two to three hours to administer, score, and interpret. In many clinical situations, there is not sufficient time or funding to use these tests in every assessment situation. In cases where intellectual impairment or organic brain damage is suspected to be central to a patient's problem, intelligence testing may be the most crucial diagnostic procedure to include in the test battery. Yet in many clinical settings and for many clinical cases, gaining a thorough understanding of a client's problems and initiating a treatment program do not require knowing the kind of detailed information about intellectual functioning these instruments provide. In these cases, intelligence testing would not be recommended.

Personality Tests There are a great many tests designed to measure personal characteristics other than intellectual facility. It is customary to group these personality tests into *projective* and *objective* tests.

Projective tests. **Projective tests** are unstructured in that they rely on various ambiguous stimuli, such as inkblots or pictures, rather than explicit verbal questions, and subjects' responses are not constrained by a preselected format of the "true," "false," or "cannot say" variety. Through their interpretations of these ambiguous materials, individuals reveal a good deal about their personal preoccupations, conflicts, motives, coping techniques, and other personality characteristics. An assumption underlying the use of projective techniques is that in trying to make sense out of vague, unstructured stimuli, individuals "project" their own problems, motives, and wishes into the situation, inasmuch as they have little else on which to rely in formulating their responses to these materials. Such responses are akin to the childhood pastime of detecting familiar scenes in cloud formations, with the important exception that the stimuli are in this case fixed and largely the same for all subjects. It is the latter circumstance that permits determination of the normative range of responses to the test materials, which in turn can be used to identify objectively deviant responding. Thus projective tests are aimed at discovering the ways in which an individual's past learning and self-structure may lead him or her to organize and perceive ambiguous information from the environment. Prominent among the several projective tests in common use are the Rorschach Test, the Thematic Apperception Test (TAT), and sentence-completion tests.

The **Rorschach Test** is named after the Swiss psychiatrist Hermann Rorschach, who initiated experimental use of inkblots in personality assessment in 1911. The test uses ten inkblot pictures to which a subject responds in succession after being instructed somewhat as follows (Klopfer & Davidson, 1962):

People may see many different things in these inkblot pictures; now tell me what you see, what it makes you think of, what it means to you.

The following excerpts are taken from the responses of a subject to one of the actual blots:

"This looks like two men with genital organs exposed. They have had a terrible fight and blood has splashed up against the wall. They have knives or sharp instruments in their hands and have just cut up a body. They have already taken out the lungs and other organs. The body is dismembered . . . nothing remains but a shell . . . the pelvic region. They were fighting as to who will complete the final dismemberment . . . like two vultures swooping down. . . ."

The extremely gory, violent content of this response was not very common for the particular blot, nor for any other blot in the series. While no responsible examiner would base conclusions on a single instance, such content was consistent with other data from this subject, who was diagnosed as an antisocial personality with strong hostility.

For several reasons, use of the Rorschach test has decreased over the past 20 years (Polyson, Peterson, & Marshall, 1986). Although methods of administering the test vary, some approaches can take several hours and hence must compete for time with other essential clinical services. Furthermore, the results of the Rorschach can be unreliable because of the subjective nature of test data interpretations and thus the high premium placed on the somewhat esoteric skills required of an examiner. In addition, the types of clinical treatments used in the majority of today's mental health facilities generally require more specific behavioral descriptions rather than descriptions of deep-seated personality dynamics, such as those that typically result from Rorschach Test interpretation.

The Rorschach has been criticized, to some extent unfairly, as an instrument with low or negligible validity. In fact, like the stethoscope in medicine, the validity of the "instrument" depends on who is using it (Carson, 1990b). In the hands of a skilled interpreter, the Rorschach has been shown to be quite useful in uncovering certain psychodynamic issues, such as the impact of unconscious motivations on current perceptions of others. Furthermore, there have been attempts to move beyond the original discursive and free-wheeling approaches and to objectify Rorschach interpretations by clearly specifying test variables and empirically exploring their relationship to external criteria, such as clinical diagnosis (Viglione & Exner, 1983). These efforts, indeed, typify and affirm the historic scientist-practitioner tradition of the clinical psychology profession.

The Rorschach, although generally touted as an open-ended, subjective instrument aimed at studying an individual's personality as a uniquely organized system ("idiographically"), has recently been adapted for computer interpretation. Exner (1987) has developed a computer-based interpretation system for the Rorschach that, after scored responses are input, provides scoring summaries and a listing of likely personality descriptions and references about an individual's adjustment. The Exner Comprehensive Rorschach System (an example of which can be found in the case study of Esteban in *HIGHLIGHT 16.3* on page 596) may answer the criticism that Rorschach interpretation is unreliable because the computer output provides a reliable and invariant set of descriptors for any given set of Rorschach scores. Assuming that clinicians agree on the scoring of particular responses, the computer outputs, that is, the interpretations, will be the same.

The **Thematic Apperception Test (TAT)** was introduced in 1935 by its coauthors, Morgan and Murray of the Harvard Psychological Clinic. It uses a series of simple pictures, some highly representational and others quite "abstract," about which a subject is instructed to make up stories. The content of the pictures, much of it depicting people in various contexts, is highly ambiguous as to actions and motives, so that subjects tend to project their own conflicts and worries into it (Bellak, 1975).

Several scoring and interpretation systems have been developed to focus on different aspects of a subject's stories, such as expressions of needs (Atkinson, 1958; Winter, 1973), the individual's perception of reality (Arnold, 1962), and the individual's fantasies (Klinger, 1979). Generally these systems are cumbersome and time-consuming, and little evidence shows that they make a clinically significant contribution. Hence, most often a clinician simply makes a qualitative and subjective determination of how the story content reflects an individual's underlying traits, motives, and preoccupations. Such interpretations often depend as much on "art" as on "science," and there is much room for error in such an informal procedure.

An example of the way an individual's problems may be reflected in TAT stories is shown in the following story based on Card 1 (a picture of a boy staring at a violin on a table in front of him). The client, David, was a 15-year-old male who had been referred to the clinic by his parents because of their concern about his withdrawal behavior and his poor work at school.

David was generally cooperative during the testing although he remained rather unemotional and unenthusiastic throughout. When he was given Card 1 of the TAT, he paused for over a minute, carefully scrutinizing the card.

"I think this is a . . . uh . . . machine gun . . . yeah, it's a machine gun. The guy is staring at it. Maybe he got it for his birthday or stole it or something." (Pause. The examiner reminded him that he was to make up a story about the picture.)

"OK. This boy, I'll call him Karl, found this machine gun . . . a Browning automatic rifle . . . in his garage. He kept it in his room for protection. One day he decided to take it to school to quiet down the jocks that lord it over everyone. When he walked into the locker hall, he cut loose on the top jock, Amos, and wasted him. Nobody bothered him after that because they knew he kept the BAR in his locker."

It was inferred from this story that David was experiencing a high level of frustration and anger in his life. The extent of this anger was reflected in his perception of the violin in the picture as a machine gun—a potential instrument of violence. The clinician concluded that David was feeling threatened not only by people at school but even in his own home where he needed "protection." This example shows how stories based on TAT cards may provide a clinician with information about an individual's conflicts and worries, as well as clues as to how the individual is handling these problems.

The TAT has been criticized on several grounds in recent years. There is a "dated" quality to the test stimuli: the pictures, developed in the 1930s, appear quaint to many contemporary subjects who have difficulty identifying with the characters in the pictures. Subjects will often preface their stories with, "This is something from a movie I saw on the Late Show." Additionally, the TAT can require a great deal of time to administer and interpret. Interpretation of responses to the TAT is generally subjective and limits the reliability and validity of the test. Again, however, we must note that some examiners, notably among those who have accumulated vast experience in the instrument's use, are capable of astonishingly accurate interpretations with TAT stories. Typically, they have difficulty in teaching these skills to others. On reflection, such an observation should not be unduly surprising, but it does point up the essentially "artistic" element involved at this skill level.

Another projective procedure that has proven useful in personality assessment is the **sentence-completion test.** There are a number of such tests designed for children, adolescents, and adults. Such tests consist of the beginnings of sentences that a subject is asked to complete, as in these examples:

1. I wish ______________________
2. My mother ______________________
3. Sex ______________________
4. I hate ______________________
5. People ______________________

Sentence-completion tests are somewhat more structured than the Rorschach and most other projective tests. They help examiners pinpoint important clues to an individual's problems, attitudes, and symptoms through the content of his or her responses. Interpretation of the item responses, however, is generally subjective and unreliable. Despite the fact that the test stimuli (the sentence stems) are standard, interpretation is usually done in an ad hoc manner and without benefit of norms.

In sum, projective tests have an important place in many clinical settings, particularly those that attempt to obtain a comprehensive picture of an individual's psychodynamic functioning and have the necessary trained staff to conduct extensive individual psychological evaluations. The great strengths of projective techniques—their unstructured nature and their focus on the unique aspects of personality—are at the same time their weaknesses because they make interpretation subjective, unreliable, and difficult to validate. Moreover, projective tests typically require a great deal of time to administer and advanced skill to interpret—both scarce quantities in many clinical settings.

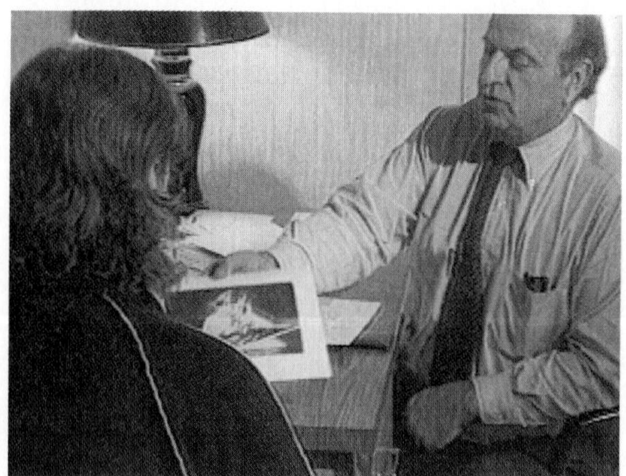

The Thematic Apperception Test, or TAT, asks a patient to make up stories based on a series of drawings. Here a psychologist administers the TAT to John, a psychiatric patient. Like other psychological tests, the TAT's purpose is to give a greater in-depth view of an individual. The interpreter is trained to assess personality characteristics based on the individual's responses.

Objective tests. **Objective tests** are structured—that is, they typically use questionnaires, self-inventories, or rating scales in which questions or items are carefully phrased and alternative responses are specified as choices. They therefore involve a far more controlled format than projective devices and thus are more amenable to objectively based quantification. One virtue of such quantification is that of precision, which in turn enhances the reliability of test outcomes.

One of the major structured inventories for personality assessment is the **Minnesota Multiphasic Personality Inventory (MMPI).** We focus on it here because in many ways it is the prototype and the standard of this class of instruments. By gaining an understanding of "how it works," you should acquire considerable sophistication about more general issues in psychological measurement.

Several years in development, the MMPI was introduced for general use in 1943 by Hathaway and McKinley; it is today the most widely used personality test for both clinical assessment and psychopathologic research in the United States (Lubin et al., 1984, 1985). Moreover, translated versions of the inventory are widely used internationally. In all, the MMPI has been translated into more than 115 languages, and it is used in over 46 countries (Butcher, 1984).

The inventory, a kind of self-report technique, consists of 550 items covering topics ranging from physical condition and psychological states to moral and social attitudes. Normally, subjects are encouraged to answer all 550 items either *true* or *false*. Some sample items follow:

I sometimes keep on at a thing until others lose their patience with me. *T F*

Bad words, often terrible words, come into my mind and I cannot get rid of them. *T F*

I often feel as if things were not real. *T F*

Someone has it in for me. *T F*

(Hathaway & McKinley, 1951, p. 28)

The pool of items for the MMPI was originally administered to a large group of normal individuals (affectionately called the "Minnesota normals") and several quite homogeneous groups of patients having particular psychiatric diagnoses. Answers to all the items were then item-analyzed to see which ones differentiated the various groups. On the basis of the findings, ten clinical scales were constructed, each consisting of the items that were answered by one of the patient groups in the direction opposite to the predominant response of the normal group. This rather ingenious method of scorable item selection, known as *empirical keying,* was original to the MMPI and doubtless accounts for much of the instrument's power. Note that it involves no subjective prejudgment about the "meaning" of a true or false answer to any item; that meaning resides entirely in whether or not the answer is the same as that deviantly given by patients of varying diagnoses. Most examiners do not even review the actual responses made because doing so encourages speculative hypotheses that have a distressingly high likelihood of being wrong. Should an examinee's *pattern* of true/false responses closely approximate that of a particular pathological group, it is a reasonable inference that he or she shares other psychiatrically significant characteristics with that group—and may in fact "psychologically" be a *member* of that group.

Each of these ten "clinical" scales, then, measures tendencies to respond in psychologically deviant ways. Raw scores on these scales are compared with the corresponding scores of the normal population, many of whom did (and do) answer a few items in the critical direction, and the results are plotted on the standard MMPI profile form. By drawing a line connecting the scores for the different scales, a clinician can construct a profile that shows how far from normal a patient's performance is on each of the scales. The *Schizophrenia scale,* for example (and to reiterate the basic strategy), is made up of the items that schizophrenic patients consistently answered in a way that differentiated them from normal individuals. People who score high (relative to norms) on this scale, though not necessarily schizophrenic, often show propensities typical of the schizophrenic population. For example, high scorers on this scale may be socially inept, withdrawn, and have peculiar thought processes; they may have diminished contact with reality and in severe cases may have delusions and hallucinations.

The MMPI also includes four validity scales to detect whether a patient has answered the questions in a straightforward, honest manner. Extreme endorsement of the items on any of these scales may invalidate the test, while lesser endorsements frequently contribute important interpretive insights. In addition to the validity scales and the ten clinical scales, hundreds of "special" scales have been devised, four of which have become so widely used for both clinical and research purposes that they are now listed on the MMPI profile form. There is in principle no limit to the number of additional scales that *could* be generated from the MMPI item pool and available item norms. All the scales listed on the standard original MMPI profile form are given in *HIGHLIGHT 16.2.*

Clinically, the MMPI is used in several ways to evaluate a patient's personality characteristics and clinical problems. Perhaps the most typical use of the MMPI is as a *diagnostic standard.* That is, the individual's profile pattern is compared with profiles of known patient groups. If the profile fits a particular group, then the diagnostic information that has been collected on typical patients in this group can be used as a broad *descriptive diagnosis* of likely behavior, symptoms, and so on, for the patient under study. Another approach to MMPI interpretation, *content interpretation,* is used to supplement the empirical correlates provided in the just-described approach. Here, a clinician focuses on the objective content themes, although not usually individual items, in a person's response to the inventory; such content groups in the MMPI item pool have been identified and can be scaled in the same manner as already described. For example, if an individual endorses an unusually large number of items about fears, a clinician might well conclude that the individual is preoccupied with fear, or

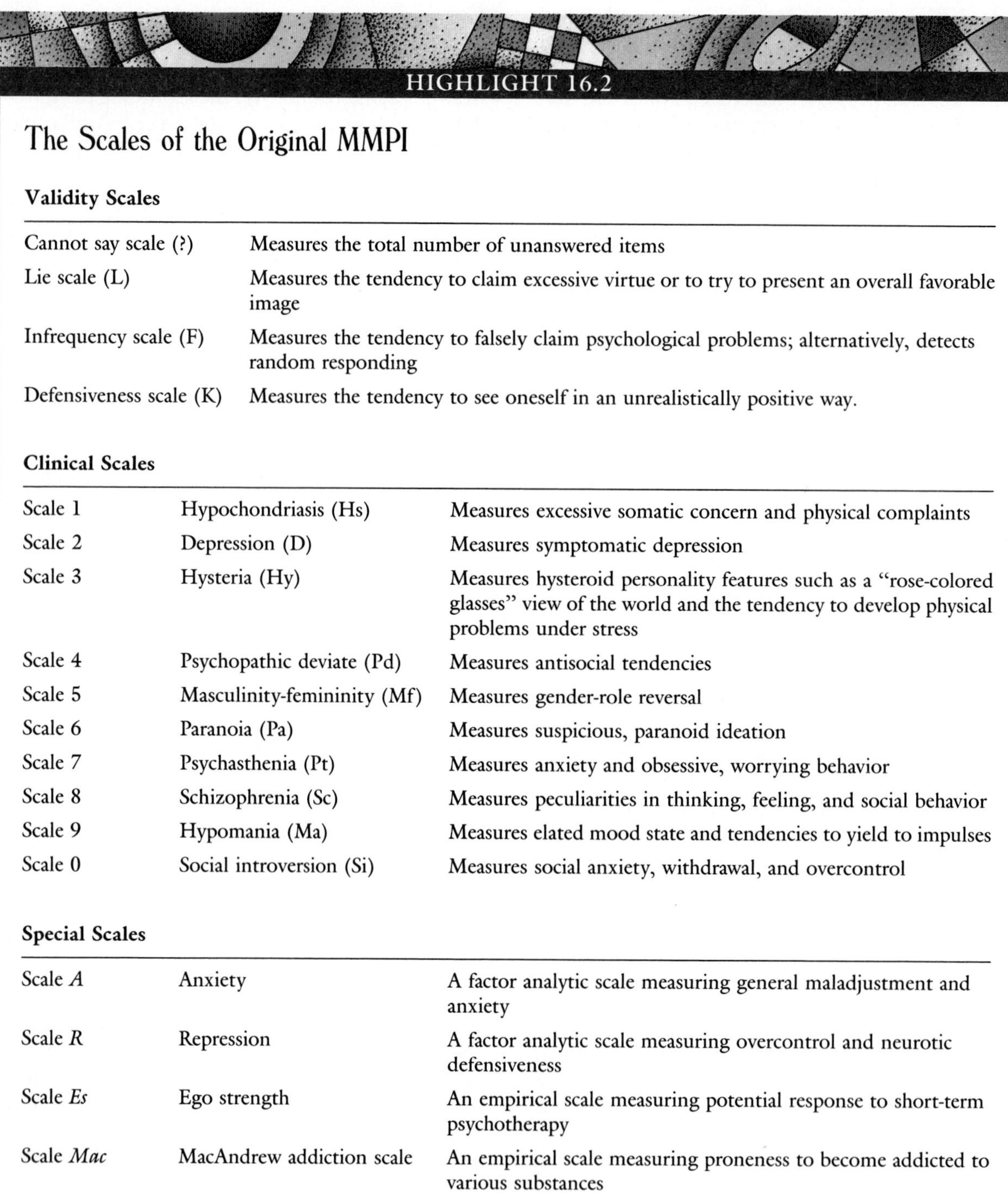

HIGHLIGHT 16.2

The Scales of the Original MMPI

Validity Scales

Cannot say scale (?)	Measures the total number of unanswered items
Lie scale (L)	Measures the tendency to claim excessive virtue or to try to present an overall favorable image
Infrequency scale (F)	Measures the tendency to falsely claim psychological problems; alternatively, detects random responding
Defensiveness scale (K)	Measures the tendency to see oneself in an unrealistically positive way.

Clinical Scales

Scale 1	Hypochondriasis (Hs)	Measures excessive somatic concern and physical complaints
Scale 2	Depression (D)	Measures symptomatic depression
Scale 3	Hysteria (Hy)	Measures hysteroid personality features such as a "rose-colored glasses" view of the world and the tendency to develop physical problems under stress
Scale 4	Psychopathic deviate (Pd)	Measures antisocial tendencies
Scale 5	Masculinity-femininity (Mf)	Measures gender-role reversal
Scale 6	Paranoia (Pa)	Measures suspicious, paranoid ideation
Scale 7	Psychasthenia (Pt)	Measures anxiety and obsessive, worrying behavior
Scale 8	Schizophrenia (Sc)	Measures peculiarities in thinking, feeling, and social behavior
Scale 9	Hypomania (Ma)	Measures elated mood state and tendencies to yield to impulses
Scale 0	Social introversion (Si)	Measures social anxiety, withdrawal, and overcontrol

Special Scales

Scale *A*	Anxiety	A factor analytic scale measuring general maladjustment and anxiety
Scale *R*	Repression	A factor analytic scale measuring overcontrol and neurotic defensiveness
Scale *Es*	Ego strength	An empirical scale measuring potential response to short-term psychotherapy
Scale *Mac*	MacAndrew addiction scale	An empirical scale measuring proneness to become addicted to various substances

minimally that this is a message the individual wishes for some reason to convey to the clinician.

In spite of its extensive use, the MMPI has not been without its critics. Many psychodynamically oriented clinicians feel that the MMPI (like other structured, objective tests) is superficial and does not adequately reflect the complexities of an individual taking the test. Some behaviorally oriented critics, on the other hand, criticize the MMPI, and in fact the entire genre of personality tests, as being too oriented toward measuring unobservable "mentalistic" constructs, such as traits.

A more specific criticism had been leveled at the datedness of the MMPI, including in particular its anachronistic norms and item pool. The original MMPI had been in use since the early 1940s, and even though much of the MMPI interpretive research is much more recent, the item pool and the basic scaling of raw response data had remained unchanged. In response to these criticisms, the publisher of the MMPI contracted to underwrite a revision of the instrument. This revised MMPI, designated MMPI-2 (Butcher et al., 1989), became available for general professional use in mid-1989. Perhaps inevitably, in light of the distinction of its forebear and the strong loyalties this instrument has engendered among clinicians over many years, the introduction of MMPI-2 has not been greeted with unanimous enthusiasm, despite what most acknowledge to be its psychometrically improved character. We will attempt here to outline the changes that have been made and to address briefly some misunderstandings that have arisen concerning MMPI-2.

The most important changes introduced with MMPI-2 were directed at overcoming the deficiencies already noted—namely (a) the outmoded idioms and sometimes prejudicial language of some of the items in the pool, and (b) the outdated and demographically unrepresentative character of the normal standardization sample, most of whose members came from 1930s-vintage rural Minnesota. A third major alteration, too technical for detailed discussion here, involves the scaling method used to convert raw scale scores to standardized ones having common parameters (that is, means and standard deviations).

Changes made in the original MMPI item pool can be summarized as follows:

- The original item pool was edited and modernized to eliminate expressions that were out of date (about 14 percent of the items required alteration).
- Additional items were written to address additional problem areas, such as treatment compliance, Type A behavior, suicide, and personality problems.
- Two separate item pools were established: an adult form and an adolescent form, designated MMPI-A.

The new adult normative sample for MMPI-2—2600 subjects randomly sampled from eight communities across the United States—is considerably more representative of the American population than was that for the original MMPI. Efforts were made to include representative groups from different racial and ethnic backgrounds, age groups, and social classes. Concern has been expressed that the education level of this standardization sample—averaging 14.7 years of schooling—exceeds that of the general U.S. population, which in fact it does by about two years. Available data indicate, however, that the education level of the people who will be examined with the MMPI-2 more closely approximates that of the new than of the original standardization group. In any event, there is no reason to believe that MMPI results are markedly or pervasively affected by modest variations in the educational levels of subjects. Being able to read and comprehend the items (which are at about a sixth-grade level) has of course always been a requirement of MMPI administration.

The adolescent form of the MMPI (MMPI-A) was standardized on 815 girls and 805 boys who were students in public and private schools in seven regions of the United States. Designed for use with youngsters aged 14 through 17, it contains a number of new scales. Its basic clinical scales, as in the case of MMPI-2, are the same as for the original MMPI.

The MMPI-2 has been validated in several clinical studies to date (Butcher & Graham, 1989). The clinical scales, which have been retained in their original form apart from minimal item deletion or rewording, seem, as expected, to measure the same properties of personality organization and functioning as they always have. A comparable stability of meaning is observed for the (also essentially unchanged) standard validity scales, which have been reinforced with three additional scales to detect tendencies to respond untruthfully to some items. The essential psychometric comparability of the main scales of the two adult versions has been empirically demonstrated by Ben-Porath and Butcher (1989). The basic MMPI-2 profile form is reproduced in *HIGHLIGHT 16.3* (page 596), in the case study of Esteban.

Overall, then, the authors of MMPI-2 have retained the central elements of the original instrument, but have added a number of features and refinements to it, including provision for systematic "content" profile analysis. As was their intent, the scales of MMPI-2 correlate highly with those of the original MMPI. Some interpretive adjustments need to be made, however, in respect to *relative* scale elevations because the new normative base may have altered slightly the meaning to be assigned to interscale relationships. Experience with the new version to date indicates that practitioners are able, with little change in their interpretive approaches, to use it in the same manner as they were accustomed to using the original instrument. Recent research (Graham et al., in press) has shown that the two versions produce different results in approximately 1 percent of cases, and that where such discrepancies occur the MMPI-2 profile is typically more valid. Meanwhile, ongoing clinical research with MMPI-2 will doubtless teach us how to get the most out of the instrument, as it did with the original.

Another kind of objective self-report personality inventory uses the statistical procedure of **factor analysis,** a method for reducing a large array of intercorrelated measures to the minimum number of "factors" necessary to account for the observed overlap or associations among them. Because their scales are a product of such a refinement process, tests of this type are considered to measure purportedly basic and relatively independent personality traits. The goal is to measure one trait at a time with maximum precision and selectivity; a personality profile can then be drawn showing the degree to which several such methodologically rarefied traits are characteristic of an individual, as well as the overall pattern of the traits. McCrae and Costa (1986) have in fact recommended the adoption for clinical use of a factor-derived profile consisting of five purportedly "basic" trait dimensions: Introversion-Extraversion, Friendly Compliance-Hostile Noncompliance, Conscientiousness, Neuroticism, and Openness to Experience.

Self-report inventories, such as the MMPI, have a number of advantages over other types of personality tests. They are cost-effective, highly reliable, and objective; they also can be scored and interpreted, or if desired even administered, by computer. A number of general criticisms, however, have been leveled against the use of self-report inventories. As we have seen, some clinicians consider them to be too mechanistic to accurately portray the complexity of human beings and their problems. Also, because these tests require an individual to read, comprehend, and answer verbal material, patients who are illiterate or confused will not be able to take the test. Furthermore, the individual's cooperation is required in self-report inventories, and it is possible that the subject may distort his or her answers to create a particular impression. The validity scales of the MMPI and MMPI-2 are a direct attempt to deal with this last criticism.

Computer Interpretation of Objective Personality Tests Scientifically constructed objective personality inventories, because of their scoring formats and emphasis on test validation, lend themselves particularly well to computer scoring and interpretation. The earliest practical applications of computer technology to test scoring and interpretation involved the MMPI. Over 30 years ago, psychologists at the Mayo Clinic programmed a computer to score and interpret clinical profiles. A number of other highly sophisticated MMPI and MMPI-2 interpretation systems have subsequently been developed (Butcher, 1979; Fowler, 1987).

Computer-based MMPI interpretation systems typically employ, insofar as possible, demonstrably powerful **actuarial procedures.** In such systems, descriptions of the actual behavior or other systematically established characteristics of numerous individuals with particular patterns of test scores have been stored in the computer. Whenever an individual turns up with one of these test score patterns, the appropriate description is printed out in the computer's evaluation. Such descriptions have been written and stored for a number of different test score patterns, most of them based on MMPI scores.

The accumulation of precise actuarial data for an instrument like the MMPI is difficult, time-consuming, and expensive. A large part of this problem is due to the complexity of the instrument itself, because the potential number of significantly different MMPI profile patterns is legion. The result is that the profiles of many subjects to whom the test is administered do not "fit" the criterial specifications of profile types for which adequate actuarial data are available. Problems of actuarial data acquisition also arise at the other end, the events or states of affair to be detected or predicted by the instrument. Many conditions that are of vital clinical importance are relatively rare in occurrence (for example, suicide) or are psychologically complex (for example, possible psychogenic components in a patient's physical illness), thus making it difficult to accumulate a sufficient number of cases to serve as an adequate actuarial data base. In these situations, then, the interpretive program writer is forced to fall back on general clinical lore and wisdom to formulate clinical descriptions appropriate to the types of profiles actually obtained. Hence, the best programs are written by expert clinicians who, in addition, have long experience with the particular instrument *and* keep up with its continuously developing research base (Carson, 1990b).

Examples of computer-generated descriptions appear in the evaluations reprinted in *HIGHLIGHT 16.3* (page 596). Sometimes the different paragraphs generated by the computer will have elements that seem inconsistent. These inconsistencies result from the fact that different parts of an individual's test pattern call up different paragraphs from the computer. The computer simply prints out blindly what has been found to be typical for individuals making similar scores on the various clinical scales. The computer cannot *integrate* the descriptions it picks up, however. At this point the human element comes in: in the clinical use of computers, it is *always* essential that a trained professional further interpret and monitor the assessment data (American Psychological Association, 1986).

Computerized personality assessment is no longer a novelty, but an important, dependable adjunct to clinical assessment. Computerized psychological evaluations are a quick and efficient means of providing a clinician with needed information early in the decision-making process. Some lingering controversies surrounding computerized psychological assessment are discussed in the Unresolved Issues section at the end of this chapter.

The Use of Psychological Tests in Personnel Screening

Many people who are experiencing personal problems or extreme psychological distress are able to function well enough in their job to get by. Some occupations, however, including those of airline flight crews, police officers, fire fighters, air-traffic controllers, nuclear power plant workers, and certain military specialties require a consistently higher level of psychological performance or greater emotional stability than others; these jobs allow for less personal variation in performance. Emotional problems in such employees can be extremely dangerous to other employees and to society as a whole. For example, an individual who holds a key position in a nuclear power plant control room and who is experiencing symptoms of severe depression can have his or her ability to function significantly impaired, possibly resulting in a failure to recognize problems requiring prompt and decisive counteraction.

The potential impact that mistakes in some occupations can have on the lives and safety of others makes the selection of employees and the monitoring of their mental health particularly critical. The psychological disorders that prompted a small group of Los Angeles police officers to repeatedly strike with their nightsticks a prone and helpless motorist in March of 1991, as recorded on videotape, is not simply an internal police matter; it is also a significant issue of concern for all of us. The potential for job failure or for becoming psychologically maladjusted under stress is so great for individuals in some high-stress occupations that measures need to be taken in the preemployment hiring process to evaluate applicants for emotional adjustment and to determine their capability of performing the job.

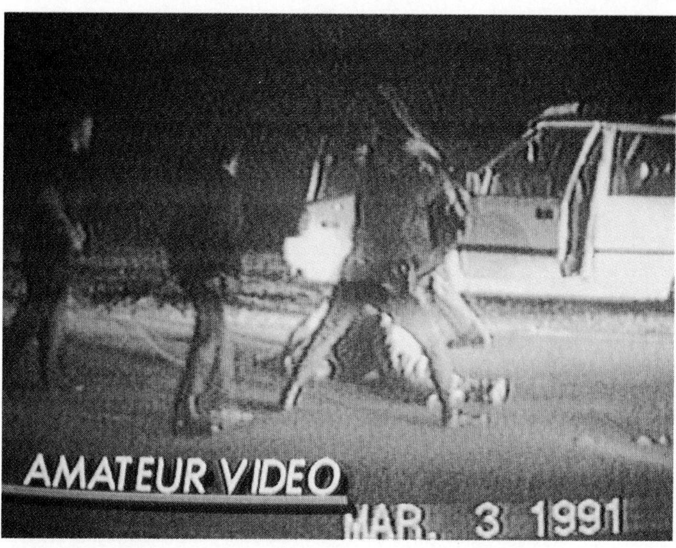

The emotional problems of employees in sensitive or high-stress occupations have potentially dangerous consequences for the lives and safety of others. For example, a small group of Los Angeles police officers physically abused a prone and helpless motorist in March of 1991, as recorded on videotape. Personnel screening for applicants' emotional stability can be an effective tool for determining a person's ability to perform a high-stress job.

Psychological Screening of Emotional Problems The use of personality tests in personnel screening has a long tradition. In fact, the first formal use of a standardized personality scale, the *Woodworth Personal Data Sheet,* was implemented to screen out World War I draftees who were psychologically unfit for military service (Woodworth, 1920). Today, psychological tests are widely used for personnel screening in occupations that require a high degree of emotional stability or great public trust. A recent controversial extension of this work is the attempt by some private corporations to assess potential employees for "honesty."

An important distinction needs to be made between *personnel selection* and *personnel screening* or, phrased differently, between "screening in" versus "screening out" job candidates. In situations where certain personality characteristics are desired for a particular job, a psychologist would choose instruments that directly assess those qualities, such as the 16 PF or the California Psychological Inventory, which measure "normal" range personality characteristics, such as dominance or sociability.

Personnel screening for emotional stability, on the other hand, requires a somewhat different set of assumptions. An important assumption is that personality or emotional problems, such as poor reality contact, impulsivity, or low self-esteem, would adversely impact on the way in which an individual would function in a critical job. In this situation, a psychologist could choose an instrument to assess the presence of psychopathology or maladjustment, such as the MMPI, to detect personality problems or symptoms that would affect personal or interpersonal functioning. To extend an earlier example, in police officer selection, an applicant with an MMPI profile pattern reflecting tendencies toward extreme aggressiveness, making hasty generalizations about others, and impulsivity would be eliminated from consideration or would undergo further evaluation to determine if these personality factors had resulted in negative job behaviors in the past.

Issues in Personality Test Job Screening Before implementing a psychological assessment program of preemployment screening, an ethically responsible psychologist needs to consider a number of issues to determine both the relevance and appropriateness of the procedures to be used. The following questions need to be addressed:

1. *How should the preemployment test be used or how much weight should be given to a particular test in preemployment decisions?* Psychological tests should not be the sole means of determining whether a person should be hired. Instruments like the MMPI should be used in conjunction with evaluations based on an employment interview, a background check, evaluation of previous work record, and so on. Psychological tests provide useful hypotheses concerning an individual's adjustment, but they have not been developed to be or validated as the sole criteria of employment decisions.

2. *Is the use of a psychological test an unwarranted invasion of privacy?* Undeniably, many (and perhaps in a certain sense all) psychological tests, especially clinical tests like the MMPI, invade an individual's privacy by asking many personal questions concerning symptoms, attitudes, and life-styles. Concerns over invasion of privacy have long been expressed and the question of the appropriateness of these tests in employment selection has been the subject of congressional hearings (see Brayfield et al., 1965). Subsequently, the appropriateness of personality testing in employment decisions has been tested in court (*McKenna* v. *Fargo,* 1978), where their use in screening for some occupations was found to be appropriate. Therefore, the question becomes one of determining whether a particular test used in personnel screening is a warranted invasion of privacy—that is, determining whether the particular placement decisions being made are consistent with the greater interests of society. For some occupations, such decisions are deemed justifiable; it is considered within the criterion of "public good" that individuals being placed in positions of high responsibility are emotionally stable according to our best information available.

3. *Are the procedures fair to all candidates, including members of ethnic minorities?* The question of the fairness of psychological tests in personnel screening is an important one. In order for a psychological test to be considered appropriate (both ethically and legally) for use in personnel selection situations, it must be demonstrated that the test does not unfairly portray or discriminate against ethnic minorities. This question needs to be addressed for each psychological test or personnel procedure used. The psychological tests being used must have a demonstrated validity for the particular test application. In the case of the MMPI, which is the most widely used clinical test in personnel screening, minority group performance has been widely studied (Butcher, 1979; Dahlstrom, Lachar, & Dahlstrom, 1986; King, Carroll, & Fuller, 1977; Wennerholm & Lopez-Roig, 1983). Assuming that an individual can read the items (for example, his or her reading level is sufficient or the appropriate language version, such as Spanish, is administered), the MMPI does not portray or discriminate against various ethnic minority subjects in an unfair manner. Given the more representative normative sample for MMPI-2, it is even less likely than its predecessor to present a problem in this respect.

A Psychological Case Study: Esteban

In this section, we will illustrate psychological assessment through an extensive diagnostic case study of a young man who presented a complicated clinical picture that was substantially clarified through psychological and neuropsychological assessment. This is an unusual case in several respects: the young man's problems were quite severe and involved both psychological and organic elements; the case involved cross-cultural considerations—the young man was from South America and assessment was done in both English and Spanish (the latter only as necessary); and a number of psychological specialists participated in the assessment study, including a neuropsychologist, a behaviorally oriented clinical psychologist, a Hispanic clinical psychologist, and a psychiatrist.

Esteban, a 21-year-old student from Colombia, South America, had been enrolled in an English language program at a small college in the United States. He had become disruptive in school, evidencing loud, obnoxious behavior in class and quarreling with his roommates (whom he accused of stealing his wallet). After a period of time during which his behavior did not improve, he was expelled from the program. The director of the program indicated that he felt Esteban needed psychological help for his problems, which included not only the behavioral problems but also, reportedly, severe headaches and confused thinking. The director added that Esteban would be considered for readmission only if he showed significant improvement in therapy.

On hearing of his expulsion, Esteban's parents, who were well-to-do international banking entrepreneurs, flew in from South America and arranged for a complete physical examination for him at a well-known medical center in New York. After an extensive medical and neurological examination to determine the source of his headaches and confusion, Esteban was diagnosed as having some "diffuse" brain impairment, but he was found to be otherwise in good health. His parents then sought a further, more definitive neurological examination. The neurologist at the second hospital recommended a psychological and neuropsychological examination because he suspected that Esteban's mild neurological condition would not account for his extreme psychological and behavioral symptoms. He referred the family to a psychologist for assessment and treatment. Because Esteban was experiencing a number of pressing situational problems —for example, his behavior problems continued, he appeared anxious to find a new English program, and, as we will see, he had some hard issues to face about his career aspirations to become a physician —the psychologist decided to begin with therapy immediately, concurrent with the additional assessment evaluation.

Interviews and Behavior Observations Esteban was seen in the initial session with his parents. The interview was conducted in English with some translation into Spanish (mostly by Esteban) because the parents knew little English. Throughout the session, Esteban was disorganized and distractible. He had difficulty keeping to the topic being discussed and periodically interrupted his own conversation with seemingly random impulses to show the interviewer papers, books, pamphlets, and the like from his knapsack. He talked incessantly, often loudly. He was not at all defensive about his problems but talked freely about his symptoms and attitudes. His behavior resembled that of a hyperactive child—he was excitable, impulsive, and immature. He did not appear to be psychotic; he reported no hallucinations or delusions and was in contact with reality. He related well with the interviewer, seemed to enjoy the session, and expressed an interest in having additional sessions.

During subsequent interviews, Esteban expressed frequent physical complaints, such as headaches, tension, and sleeping problems. He reported that he had a great deal of difficulty concentrating on his studies. He could not study because he always found other things to do—particularly talking about religion. He was seemingly outgoing and sociable and had no difficulty initiating conversations with other people. He tended, however, to say socially inappropriate things or become frustrated and lose his temper easily. For example, during one family interview, he became enraged and kicked his mother.

Family History Esteban's father was a Spanish-Colombian banker in his mid-sixties. He was well-dressed, somewhat passive, though visibly quite warm toward his son. He had had his share of difficulties in recent years; severe business problems coupled with two heart attacks had brought on a depressive episode that had left him ineffective in dealing with his business. His wife and her brother, an attorney from Madrid, had had to straighten out the business problems. She reported that her husband had had several depressive episodes in the past and that Esteban's moods resembled her husband's in his earlier years.

Esteban's mother was a tense, worried, and somewhat hypochondriacal woman who appeared to be rather domineering. Prior to the first and second interviews, she handed the therapist, in secret, written "explanations" of her son's problems. Her own history revealed that she was unhappy in her marriage and that she lived only for her children, on whom she doted.

Esteban's brother, Juan, was an engineering student at an American university and apparently was doing well academically and socially. He was one year older than Esteban.

Esteban's childhood had been marked with problems. His mother reported that although he had been a good baby—noting that he had been pretty and happy as a small child—he had changed after age 2½. At about that time, he had fallen on his head and was unconscious for a while; he was not hospitalized. Beginning in the preschool years, he exhibited behavioral problems, including temper tantrums, negativism, and an inability to get along with peers. These problems continued when he began school. He frequently refused to go to school, had periods of aggressive behavior, and appeared in general to be "hyperactive." It appeared that he was probably overprotected and "infantilized" by his mother.

Esteban was quite close to his brother Juan, with whom he reported having had extensive homosexual relations when they were growing up. The "darkest day" in Esteban's life was reportedly when Juan broke off the homosexual relationship with him at age 16 and told him to "go and find men." Although he later carried on a platonic relationship with a woman in Colombia, it was never a serious one. Esteban had strong homosexual urges of which he was consciously aware and attempted to control through a growing preoccupation with religion.

Esteban had been in psychotherapy on several occasions since he was 11 years old. After he graduated from high school, he attended law school in Colombia for a quarter, but dropped out because he "wanted to become a doctor instead." (In Colombia, professional schools are combined with college.) He left school, according to his parents' report, because he could not adapt. He worked for a time in the family business but had difficulty getting along with other employees and was encouraged to try other work. When that failed, his parents sent him to the United States to study English, rationalizing that Colombia was not as good an environment for him as the United States.

Intelligence Testing Esteban underwent psychological testing to evaluate further the possibility of neurological deficits and to determine if he had the intellectual capabilities to proceed with a demanding academic career. He scored in the borderline to average range of intelligence on the WAIS-R (English version) and on the WAIS (Spanish version). He was particularly deficient in tasks involving practical judgment, common sense, concentration, visual-motor coordination, and concept formation. In addition, on memory tests, he showed a below average memory ability, such as a poor immediate recall of ideas from paragraphs read aloud (in both English and Spanish). Under most circumstances, individuals showing similar intellectual or neurological deficits are able to live comfortable, fulfilling lives in careers whose formal intellectual demands are relatively modest. It was clear from the test data and Esteban's behavior during testing that his stated career aspirations—seemingly nurtured by his parents—exceeded his abilities and might well be a factor in much of his frustration.

Personality Testing Esteban was given both the Rorschach Test and the MMPI. Both tests have been used extensively with Hispanic subjects. The Rorschach is believed by some to be particularly well-suited for cases like Esteban's because the test stimuli are relatively unstructured and not culture-bound. Esteban's performance on the Rorschach revealed tension, anxiety, and a preoccupation with morbid topics. He appeared to be overly concerned about his health, prone to depression, indecisive and yet at other times impulsive and careless. His responses were often immature and he showed a strong and persistent ambivalence toward females. In some responses, he viewed females in highly aggressive ways—often a fusion of sexual and aggressive images was evident. In general, he demonstrated aloofness and an inability to relate well to other people. Although his Rorschach responses suggested that he could view the world in conventional ways and was probably not psychotic, at times he had difficulty controlling his impulses. Esteban's Rorschach protocol was computer analyzed using the Exner Comprehensive Rorschach System.

Esteban took the original version of the MMPI in both English and Spanish. His MMPI profile was virtually identical in both languages. It has been converted to MMPI-2 format and is reproduced in *HIGHLIGHT 16.3* (page 596) along with the original and the MMPI-2-based computer interpretations of his test scores.

Summary of the Psychological Assessment Esteban showed mild neurological deficits on neuropsychological testing and a borderline to average level of intellectual ability. He clearly did not have the academic ability to pursue a demanding medical career. Difficult or demanding intellectual tasks placed a great deal of stress on him and resulted in a high degree of frustration. Furthermore, his poor memory made learning complex material very difficult.

The MMPI interpretation indicated that Esteban's disorganized behavior and symptomatic patterns reflected a serious psychological disorder. Although he was not currently psychotic, both his past behavior and his test performance suggested that he was functioning marginally and that he showed the potential for personality deterioration in some situations.

Esteban's most salient psychological problems concerned his tendency to become frustrated and his ready loss of impulse control. He was volatile and became upset easily. Additionally, it appeared that Esteban's relative isolation during his early years (due in part to his overprotective mother) did not prepare him to function adequately in many social situations. Another important problem area for Esteban was in psychosexual adjustment. The psychological test results and his personal history clearly indicated a gender-identity confusion.

Within the parameters of DSM-III-R, Esteban would receive an Axis I diagnosis of *organic personality syndrome* and an Axis II diagnosis of *borderline personality disorder.* Furthermore, it was recommended that he undertake social-skills training and that—rather than a career in medicine—he be encouraged to pursue occupational goals more in keeping with his abilities. Psychotropic medication (Lithium and Mellaril) were prescribed for his emotional control problems.

A Follow-up Note Esteban was seen in psychological therapy twice a week and was kept on medication. He was also seen in a social-skills training program for ten sessions. Through the help of his therapist, he was admitted to a less-demanding English program, which seemed more appropriate for his abilities.

For the first six months, Esteban made considerable progress, especially after his behavior became somewhat stabilized, largely, it appeared, as a result of the medications. He became less impulsive and more in control of his anger. He successfully completed the English classes in which he was enrolled. During this period, he lived with his mother, who had taken up a temporary residence near the college. She then returned to Colombia, and Esteban moved into an apartment with a roommate, with whom, however, he had increasing difficulty.

Several weeks after his mother left, Esteban quit going to therapy and quit taking his medication. He began to frequent local gay bars, at first out of curiosity but later to seek male lovers. At the same time, his preoccupation with religion increased and he moved into a house near campus that was operated by a fundamentalist religious cult. His parents, quite concerned by his overt homosexual behavior (which he described in detail over the phone, adding the suggestion that they visit the gay bar with him), returned to the United States. Realizing that they could not stay permanently to supervise Esteban, they then sought a residential treatment program that would provide him with a more structured living arrangement. All assessment and therapy records were forwarded to those in charge of the residential program.

THE INTEGRATION OF ASSESSMENT DATA

As assessment data are collected, their significance must be interpreted so that they can be integrated into a coherent working model for use in planning or changing treatment. Clinicians in individual private practice normally assume this often arduous task on their own.

In a clinic or hospital setting, assessment data are usually evaluated in a staff conference attended by members of an interdisciplinary team (perhaps a clinical psychologist, a psychiatrist, a social worker, and other mental health personnel) who are concerned with the decisions to be made regarding treatment. By putting together all the information they have gathered, they can see whether the findings complement each other and form a definitive clinical picture or whether gaps or discrepancies exist that necessitate further investigation.

At the time of an original assessment, integration of all the data may lead to agreement on a tentative diagnostic classification for a patient—such as *paranoid schizophrenia.* In any case, the findings of each member of the team, as well as the recommendations for treatment, are entered in the case record, so that it will always be possible to check back and see why a certain course of therapy was undertaken, how accurate the clinical assessment was, and how valid the treatment decision turned out to be.

New assessment data collected during the course of therapy provide feedback on its effective-

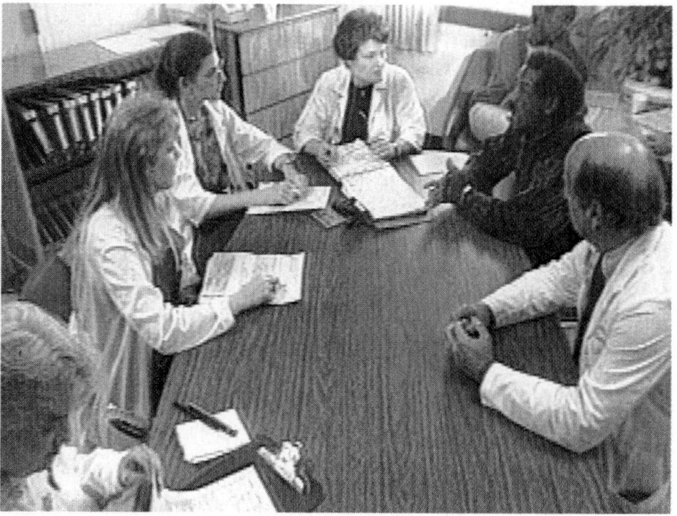

In a clinic or hospital setting, assessment data are usually evaluated in a staff conference attended by members of an interdisciplinary team, including, for example, a clinical psychologist, a psychiatrist, a social worker, and a psychiatric nurse. Sharing findings may lead to a diagnostic classification for a patient and a course of treatment. Staff decisions can have far-reaching consequences for patients; as such, it is important that clinicians be aware of the limitations of assessment.

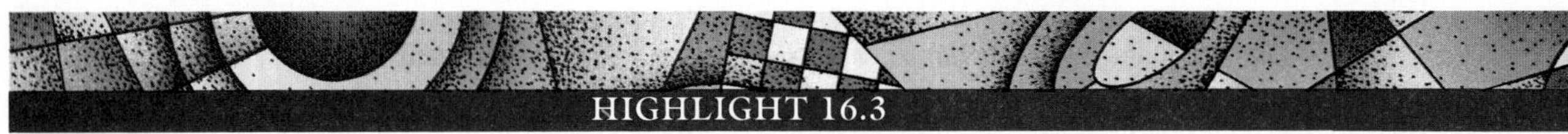

HIGHLIGHT 16.3

Esteban's Rescored MMPI-2 Profile and His Original and MMPI-2 Computer-based Reports

Esteban was originally tested with the original MMPI. His responses from that testing were converted to the MMPI-2 format by J. N. Butcher. The computer-based reports for both editions of the test are provided below.

On the facing page is the converted MMPI-2 profile chart compiled for Esteban. The validity scales are shown in the column at left (the column in which the word MALE appears). The clinical scales are to the right. The special scales are not included in this version of the profile. (*HIGHLIGHT 16.2* on page 588 describes each of these scales.) Based on the scores originally obtained and those you see displayed in the chart, a computer produced the narrative descriptions given below. On pages 598–599 are hypotheses about the psychological functioning of Esteban from a computer-generated report of his Rorschach protocol performed by the Exner Comprehensive Rorschach System.

Computer-based Report: The Original MMPI

Profile validity. This MMPI profile should be interpreted with caution. There is some possibility that the clinical report is an exaggerated picture of the client's present situation and problems. He is presenting an unusual number of psychological symptoms. This extreme response set could result from poor reading ability, confusion, disorientation, stress, or a need to seek attention for his problems.

His test-taking attitudes should be evaluated for the possibility that he has produced an invalid profile. He may be showing a lack of cooperation with the testing or he may be "malingering" by attempting to present a false claim of mental illness. Determining the sources of his confusion, whether conscious distortion or personality deterioration, is important since immediate attention may be required. Clinical patients with this profile are often confused, distractible, and show memory problems. Evidence of delusions and thought disorder may be present. He may be showing a high degree of distress and personality deterioration.

Symptomatic pattern. He is presenting with a mixed pattern of psychological symptoms. This profile shows a pattern of chronic depression and alienation. The client tends to feel quite withdrawn, tense, and anxious. He is having problems concentrating, feels agitated, and is functioning at a very low level of psychological efficiency. He feels apathetic and indifferent and like a passive participant in life. He also feels that he has little energy left over from mere survival to expend on any pleasure in life.

He may be showing signs of serious psychopathology—delusions, problems in thinking, and inappropriate affect. His longstanding lack of achievement and his work behavior have caused him many problems, and he may have serious plans for suicide.

He experiences some conflicts concerning his sex-role identity, appearing somewhat passive and effeminate in his orientation toward life. He may appear somewhat insecure in the masculine role, and he may be uncomfortable in relationships with women. His interests, in general, are more characteristic of women than of men. He tends to be quite passive and submissive in interpersonal relationships, and he tends to make concessions in an effort to avoid confrontation. In addition, he may have low heterosexual drive.

His response content indicates that he is preoccupied with feeling guilty and unworthy, and feels that he deserves to be punished for wrongs he has committed. He feels regretful and unhappy about life, complains about having no zest for life, and seems plagued by anxiety and worry about the future. According to his response content, there is strong possibility that he has seriously contemplated suicide. A careful evaluation of this possibility is suggested. He views his physical health as failing and reports numerous somatic concerns. He feels that life is no longer worthwhile and that he is losing control of his thought processes. He reports in his response content that he is high-strung and believes that he feels things more, or more intensely, than others do. He feels

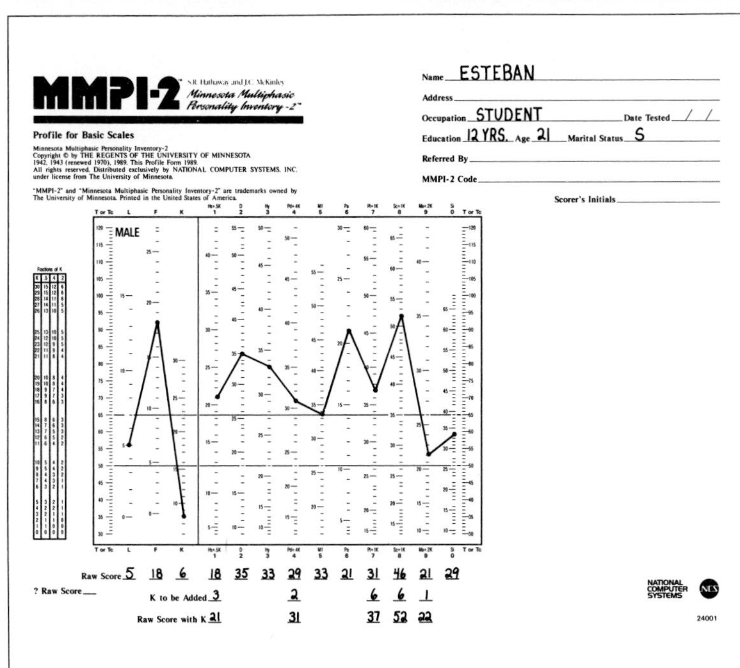

MMPI-2™ S.R. Hathaway and J.C. McKinley
Minnesota Multiphasic Personality Inventory-2™

Profile for Basic Scales

Minnesota Multiphasic Personality Inventory-2
Copyright © by THE REGENTS OF THE UNIVERSITY OF MINNESOTA 1942, 1943 (renewed 1970), 1989. This Profile Form 1989. All rights reserved. Distributed exclusively by NATIONAL COMPUTER SYSTEMS, INC. under license from The University of Minnesota.

"MMPI-2" and "Minnesota Multiphasic Personality Inventory-2" are trademarks owned by The University of Minnesota. Printed in the United States of America.

Name ESTEBAN
Address
Occupation STUDENT Date Tested / /
Education 12 YRS. Age 21 Marital Status S
Referred By
MMPI-2 Code
Scorer's Initials

MALE

	L	F	K	Hs+.5K 1	D 2	Hy 3	Pd+.4K 4	Mf 5	Pa 6	Pt+1K 7	Sc+1K 8	Ma+.2K 9	Si 0
Raw Score	5	18	6	18	35	33	29	33	21	31	46	21	29
K to be Added				3			2			6	6	1	
Raw Score with K				21			31			37	52	22	

? Raw Score ___

NATIONAL COMPUTER SYSTEMS
24001

lonely and misunderstood at times. The content of his responses indicates that he feels as though he is losing his mind, and that he does not understand things going on around him. The items he endorsed included content suggesting that his thinking is confused and bizarre. He feels that others do not understand him and are trying to control him. He is also tending toward withdrawal into a world of fantasy.

Interpersonal relations. He has great problems with alienation and social relationships. He feels vulnerable to interpersonal hurt, lacks trust, and may never form close satisfying relationships. He feels very insecure in relationships and may be preoccupied with guilt and self-defeating behavior.

He appears somewhat shy, with some social concerns and inhibitions. He is a bit hypersensitive about what others think of him and is occasionally concerned over his relationship with others. He appears to be somewhat overcontrolled and submissive in personal relationships and social situations, and may have some difficulty expressing his feelings toward others.

The content of the client's MMPI responses suggests the following additional information concerning his interpersonal relations. He views his home situation as unpleasant and lacking in love and understanding. He feels like leaving home to escape a quarrelsome, critical situation, and to be free of family domination.

Behavioral Stability. Individuals with this profile type often lead stormy, chaotic lives and never seem to develop satisfying relationships.

Diagnostic Considerations. Individuals with this profile tend to have features of both an affective disorder and a thought disorder. In addition, there seems to be a long-standing pattern of maladjustment that is characteristic of people with severe personality disorders. He is likely to be diagnosed as having a Schizophrenic or Major Affective Disorder.

The content of his responses to the MMPI items suggests symptoms (convulsions, paralysis, clumsiness, and double vision) that are associated with neurological disorder. Vague pain symptoms, nausea, etc., that are found in neurotic conditions are also present, however. Further neurological evaluation would be needed to make a clear differentiation.

Treatment Considerations. Multiple-problem life situations and difficulties forming interpersonal relationships make patients with this profile type poor candidates for relationship-based psychotherapy. Their basic lack of trust and withdrawal would also make psychotherapy difficult. Some outpatients with this profile type seem to benefit from minimal contact treatment, such as brief periodic visits with a directive, supportive therapist. Many need psychotropic medication to control their bizarre thinking or to elevate their mood.

Computer-based Report: The MMPI-2

Profile validity. This MMPI-2 profile should be interpreted with caution. There is some possibility that the clinical report is an exaggerated picture of his present situ-

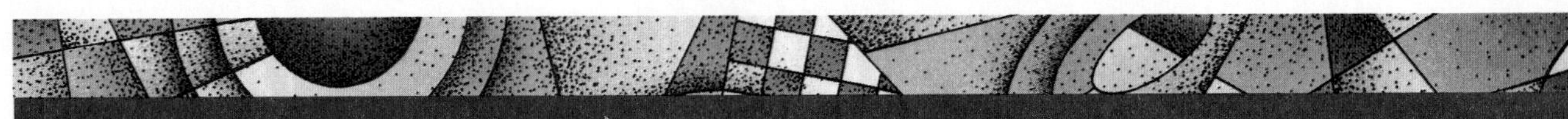

SUBJECT NAME:ESTEBAN.MMPI AGE:21 SEX:M RACE:W MS:Sin ED:14

SEMANTIC INTERPRETATION OF THE RORSCHACH
PROTOCOL UTILIZING THE COMPREHENSIVE SYSTEM
(COPYRIGHT 1976, 1985 BY JOHN E. EXNER, JR.)

THE FOLLOWING COMPUTER-BASED INTERPRETATION IS DERIVED ** EXCLUSIVELY ** FROM THE STRUCTURAL DATA OF THE RECORD AND DOES NOT INCLUDE CONSIDERATION OF THE SEQUENCE OF SCORES OR THE VERBAL MATERIAL. IT IS INTENDED AS A GUIDE FROM WHICH THE INTERPRETER OF THE TOTAL PROTOCOL CAN PROCEED TO STUDY AND REFINE THE HYPOTHESES GENERATED FROM THESE ACTUARIAL FINDINGS.

* * * * *

1. THE RECORD APPEARS TO BE VALID AND INTERPRETIVELY USEFUL.
2. THIS IS THE TYPE OF PERSON WHO IS PRONE TO TRY TO OVERSIMPLIFY STIMULI IN ORDER TO MAKE THE WORLD LESS THREATENING AND/OR DEMANDING. THIS BASIC COPING STYLE TENDS TO BE PERVASIVE WHEN NEW SITUATIONS AND/OR STRESSES OCCUR. WHEN DONE TO EXCESS, AS APPEARS TO BE THE CASE HERE, THE SUBJECT IS LIKELY TO EXPERIENCE FREQUENT SOCIAL DIFFICULTIES BECAUSE THE STYLE PROMOTES A NEGLECT OF THE DEMANDS AND/OR EXPECTATIONS OF THE ENVIRONMENT.
3. THIS SUBJECT USUALLY HAS ENOUGH RESOURCE ACCESSABLE TO PARTICIPATE MEANINGFULLY IN THE FORMULATION AND DIRECTION OF RESPONSES. TOLERANCE FOR STRESS IS LIKE THAT OF MOST PEOPLE, THAT IS, CONTROLS USUALLY WILL NOT FALTER UNLESS THE STRESS IS UNEXPECTED AND INTENSE OR PROLONGED UNREASONABLY.
4. THERE IS EVIDENCE INDICATING THE PRESENCE OF CONSIDERABLE SUBJECTIVELY FELT DISTRESS.
5. THIS SUBJECT TENDS TO INTERNALIZE FEELINGS MUCH MORE THAN IS CUSTOMARY AND THIS OFTEN RESULTS IN SUBSTANTIAL DISCOMFORT THAT CAN TAKE THE FORM OF TENSION AND/OR ANXIETY.
6. THIS IS THE TYPE OF PERSON WHO PREFERS TO DELAY MAKING RESPONSES IN COPING SITUATIONS UNTIL TIME HAS BEEN ALLOWED TO CONSIDER RESPONSE POSSIBILITIES AND THEIR POTENTIAL CONSEQUENCES. SUCH PEOPLE LIKE TO KEEP THEIR EMOTIONS ASIDE UNDER THESE CONDITIONS.
7. THIS PERSON TENDS TO USE DELIBERATE THINKING MORE FOR THE PURPOSE OF CREATING FANTASY THROUGH WHICH TO IGNORE THE WORLD THAN TO CONFRONT PROBLEMS DIRECTLY. THIS IS A SERIOUS PROBLEM BECAUSE THE BASIC COPING STYLE IS BEING USED MORE FOR FLIGHT THAN TO ADAPT TO THE EXTERNAL WORLD.
8. THIS TYPE OF PERSON IS NOT VERY FLEXIBLE IN THINKING, VALUES, OR ATTITUDES. IN EFFECT, PEOPLE SUCH AS THIS HAVE SOME DIFFICULTY IN SHIFTING PERSPECTIVES OR VIEWPOINTS.

SUBJECT NAME:ESTEBAN.MMPI AGE:21 SEX:M RACE:W MS:Sin ED:14

PAGE -2-

9. THERE IS A STRONG POSSIBILITY THAT THIS IS A PERSON WHO PREFERS TO AVOID INITIATING BEHAVIORS, AND INSTEAD, TENDS TOWARDS A MORE PASSIVE ROLE IN PROBLEM SOLVING AND INTERPERSONAL RELATIONSHIPS.
10. THIS SUBJECT DOES NOT MODULATE EMOTIONAL DISPLAYS AS MUCH AS MOST ADULTS AND, BECAUSE OF THIS, IS PRONE TO BECOME VERY INFLUENCED BY FEELINGS IN MOST THINKING, DECISIONS, AND BEHAVIORS.
11. THIS IS A PERSON WHO IS VERY ATTRACTED TO BEING AROUND EMOTIONAL STIMULI. THIS MAY POSE A SIGNIFICANT PROBLEM IN ADAPTATION BECAUSE OF PROBLEMS IN CONTROL. THAT IS, THE MORE EMOTIONAL STIMULI BEING PROCESSED, THE GREATER THE DEMAND FOR EMOTIONAL EXCHANGE. IF THAT EXCHANGE IS NOT WELL CONTROLLED, PROBLEMS CAN EASILY OCCUR.
12. THIS IS AN INDIVIDUAL WHO DOES NOT EXPERIENCE NEEDS FOR CLOSENESS IN WAYS THAT ARE COMMON TO MOST PEOPLE. AS A RESULT, THEY ARE TYPICALLY LESS COMFORTABLE IN INTERPERSONAL SITUATIONS, HAVE SOME DIFFICULTIES IN CREATING AND SUSTAINING DEEP RELATIONSHIPS, ARE MORE CONCERNED WITH ISSUES OF PERSONAL SPACE, AND MAY APPEAR MUCH MORE GUARDED AND/OR DISTANT TO OTHERS.
13. THIS SUBJECT HAS AS MUCH INTEREST IN OTHERS AS DO MOST ADULTS AND CHILDREN. HOWEVER, THE SUBJECT DOES NOT APPEAR TO HAVE A VERY REALISTIC UNDERSTANDING OF PEOPLE. INSTEAD, CONCEPTIONS OF OTHERS TEND TO BE DERIVED MORE FROM IMAGINATION THAN FROM REAL EXPERIENCE.
14. THIS SUBJECT APPEARS TO HAVE AN UNUSUAL BODY PREOCCUPATION.
15. THIS SUBJECT APPEARS TO HAVE A MARKED SEXUAL PREOCCUPATION.
16. THIS SUBJECT IS VERY PRONE TO INTERPRET STIMULUS CUES IN A UNIQUE AND OVERPERSONALIZED MANNER. PEOPLE SUCH AS THIS OFTEN VIEW THEIR WORLD WITH THEIR OWN SPECIAL SET OF BIASES AND ARE LESS CONCERNED WITH BEING CONVENTIONAL AND/OR ACCEPTABLE TO OTHERS.
17. IN SPITE OF THE ABOVE MENTIONED TENDENCY TO MISINTERPRET OR OVERPERSONALIZE THE INTERPRETATION OF STIMULUS CUES, THE SUBJECT DOES TEND TO RESPOND IN CONVENTIONAL WAYS TO SITUATIONS IN WHICH CONVENTIONAL OR EXPECTED RESPONSES ARE OBVIOUS AND EASILY IDENTIFIED.
18. MUCH OF THE COGNITIVE ACTIVITY OF THIS SUBJECT IS LESS SOPHISTICATED OR LESS MATURE THAN IS EXPECTED. THIS MAY BE A FUNCTION OF A DEVELOPMENTAL LAG, DISORGANIZATION, OR MAY SIMPLY REFLECT A RELUCTANCE TO COMMIT RESOURCES TO A TASK.
19. THIS SUBJECT TENDS TO SCAN A STIMULUS FIELD HASTILY AND NOT METHODICALLY. THESE KINDS OF PEOPLE OFTEN COME TO DECISIONS PREMATURELY AND ERRONEOUSLY SIMPLY BECAUSE THEY HAVE NOT PROCESSED ALL AVAILABLE INFORMATION ADEQUATELY. THIS SHOULD NOT BE CONFUSED WITH

ation. He presented an unusual number of psychological problems and symptoms. His test-taking attitudes should be evaluated to determine if his response pattern is a valid approach to the testing. This extreme response set could result from poor reading ability, confusion, disorientation, stress, or a need to seek attention for his problems. Clinical patients with this profile are often confused, distractible, and show memory problems. Evidence of delusions and thought disorder may be present.

Symptomatic pattern. His MMPI-2 profile reflects a high degree of psychological distress at this time. The client is presenting with a mixed pattern of psychological symptoms. He appears to be tense, apathetic, and withdrawn, and is experiencing some personality deterioration. He seems to be quite confused and disorganized, and probably secretly broods about unusual beliefs and suspicions. Autistic behavior and inappropriate affect are characteristic features of individuals with this profile. Some evidence of an active psychotic process is apparent. He may have delusions and occult preoccupations, and may feel that others are against him because of his beliefs. In interviews, he is likely to be vague, circumstantial, and tangential, and may be quite preoccupied with abstract ideas.

He is having problems concentrating, feels agitated, and is functioning at a very low level of psychological efficiency. He feels apathetic, indifferent, and like a passive participant in life. He also feels that he has little energy left over from mere survival to expend on any pleasure in life. He may be showing signs of serious psychopathology such as delusions, problems in thinking, and inappropriate affect. His long-standing lack of achievement and his work behavior have caused him many problems.

Many individuals with this profile consider committing suicide and he may actually have serious plans for self-destruction.

He experiences some conflicts concerning his sex-role identity, appearing somewhat passive and effeminate in his orientation toward life. He may appear somewhat insecure in the masculine role and may be uncomfortable in his relationships with women.

His response content indicates that he is preoccupied with feeling guilty and unworthy, and feels that he deserves to be punished for wrongs he has commit-

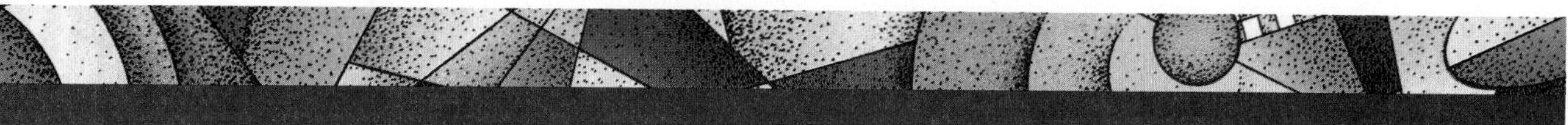

```
SUBJECT NAME:ESTEBAN.MMPI                AGE:21  SEX:M  RACE:W  MS:Sin  ED:14

   PAGE -3-

===============================================================================
    IMPULSIVENESS ALTHOUGH SOME DECISIONS AND BEHAVIORS THAT RESULT MAY
    HAVE THAT FEATURE.  IT IS A CONSEQUENCE OF NEGLECT IN SCANNING AND
    ORGANIZING TACTICS WHICH MAY BE THE PRODUCT OF A PERCEPTUAL DEFICIT,
    PSYCHOLOGICAL HABITS DEVELOPED EARLY IN LIFE, OR CAN BE A FUNCTION OF
    COGNITIVE DISARRAY PROVOKED BY NEUROLOGICALLY RELATED OR
    PSYCHPATHOLOGICAL PROBLEMS. IT SHOULD ALSO BE NOTED FOR THIS SUBJECT
    THAT THE COMPOSITE OF HASTY SCANNING OF STIMULUS FIELDS PLUS LIMITED
    EMOTIONAL CONTROLS IS ONE IMPORTANT FACTOR THAT LEADS TO IMPULSIVE
    LIKE BEHAVIORS.

20. THIS PERSON USUALLY SEEKS AN ECONOMICAL APPROACH TO PROBLEM SOLVING OR
    COPING BY FOCUSING MORE ON THE EASILY MANAGED ASPECTS OF A SITUATION
    AND TENDING TO NEGLECT BROADER ISSUES THAT MAY BE PRESENT.  THIS IS
    TYPICAL OF MANY PEOPLE AND CAN BE AN ASSET.  HOWEVER, IT CAN ALSO
    BECOME A LIABILITY IN MORE COMPLEX AND DEMANDING SITUATIONS THAT
    REQUIRE HIGHER LEVELS OF MOTIVATION AND EFFORT TO ACHIEVE EFFECTIVE
    RESULTS.

21. THIS PERSON IS SOMEWHAT CONSERVATIVE IN SETTING GOALS.  USUALLY PEOPLE
    LIKE THIS WANT TO COMMIT THEMSELVES ONLY TO OBJECTIVES WHICH OFFER A
    SIGNIFICANT PROBABILITY OF SUCCESS.

22. THIS PERSON TENDS TO USE INTELLECTUALIZATION AS A BASIC TACTIC TO
    CONTEND WITH EMOTIONAL THREATS AND STRESSES. PEOPLE LIKE THIS ARE
    OFTEN VERY RESISTIVE DURING EARLY PHASES OF INTERVENTION AS THIS
    TENDENCY TOWARD DENIAL CAUSES THEM TO AVOID ANY AFFECTIVE
    CONFRONTATIONS.

                        * * *  END OF REPORT  * * *

===============================================================================
(c)1976, 1985 by John E. Exner, Jr.
```

ted. He feels regretful and unhappy about life, complains about having no zest for life, and seems plagued by anxiety and worry about the future. According to his response content there is a strong possibility that he has contemplated suicide. A careful evaluation of this possibility is suggested. He views his physical health as failing and reports numerous somatic complaints. He feels that life is no longer worthwhile and that he is losing control of his thought processes. He reports in his response content that he feels things more, or more intensely, than others do.

Interpersonal relations. Disturbed interpersonal relationships are characteristic of individuals with this profile type. He feels vulnerable to interpersonal hurt, lacks trust, and may never form close, satisfying interpersonal ties. He feels very insecure in relationships and may be preoccupied with guilt and self-defeating behavior. Many individuals with this profile are so self-preoccupied and unskilled in sex-role behavior that they never develop rewarding heterosexual relationships. Some never marry.

Behavioral Stability. Individuals with this profile type often lead chronically stormy, chaotic lives.

Diagnostic Considerations. The most likely diagnosis for individuals with this MMPI-2 profile type is Schizophrenia, possibly Paranoid type, or Paranoid Disorder. Similar clients tend to also have features of an affective disorder. In addition, there seems to be a long-standing pattern of maladjustment that is characteristic of people with severe personality disorders.

Because this behavioral pattern may also be associated with Organic Brain Syndrome or Substance-Induced Organic Mental Disorder, these possibilities should be evaluated.

Treatment Considerations. Individuals with this profile may be experiencing considerable personality deterioration, which may require hospitalization if they are considered dangerous to themselves or others.

Psychotropic medication may reduce their thinking disturbance and mood disorder. Outpatient treatment may be complicated by their regressed or disorganized behavior. Multiple-problem life situations and difficulties forming interpersonal relationships make patients with this profile poor candidates for relationship-based psychotherapy. Day treatment programs or other such structured settings may be helpful in providing a stabilizing treatment environment. Long-term adjustment is a problem. Frequent, brief "management" therapy contacts may be helpful in structuring his activities. Insight-oriented or relationship therapies tend not to be helpful for individuals with these severe problems and may actually exacerbate the symptoms. He probably would have difficulty establishing a trusting working relationship with a therapist.

ness and serve as a basis for making needed modifications in an ongoing treatment program. As we have noted, clinical assessment data are also commonly used in evaluating the final outcome of therapy and in comparing the effectiveness of different therapeutic and preventive approaches. Summers (1979), among others, has pointed out the importance of assessing a patient's level of functioning prior to hospital discharge. Too often, individuals who cannot function well outside a mental hospital are released into the community with little or no provision for continuing mental health care.

The decisions made on the basis of assessment data may have far-reaching implications for the people under study. A staff decision may determine whether a depressed person will be hospitalized or remain with his or her family; whether divorce will be accepted as a solution to an unhappy marriage or a further attempt will be made to salvage the relationship; or whether an accused person will be declared competent to stand trial. Thus a valid decision, based on accurate assessment data, is of far more than theoretical importance. Because of the impact that assessment can have on the lives of others, it is important that those involved keep in mind factors that may limit the accuracy of assessment. Some of these factors are noted in *HIGHLIGHT 16.4*

UNRESOLVED ISSUES on the Use of Computerized Assessment

Perhaps the most dramatic innovation in clinical assessment during the last 25 years has been the increasing sophistication and use of computers in individual assessment. As we have seen, computers are used in assessment both to gather information directly from an individual and to put together and evaluate all the information that has been gathered previously through interviews, tests, and other assessment procedures. By comparing the incoming information with data previously stored in its memory banks, a computer can perform a wide range of assessment tasks. It can supply a probable diagnosis, indicate the likelihood of certain kinds of behavior, suggest the most appropriate form of treatment, predict the outcome, and print out a summary report concerning the subject. In many of these functions, a computer is actually superior to an individual clinician because it is more efficient and accurate in recalling stored material.

With the increased efficiency and reliability accompanying the use of computers in clinical practice, one might expect a near unanimous welcoming of computers into the clinic. This is not the case, however. There is controversy over computerized assessment and a reluctance on the part of some practitioners to use computer-based tests in their practice. We will discuss these general issues in turn.

Concerns have been raised by some psychologists that the widespread use of computer-based assessment procedures is not sufficiently supported by pertinent research (Matarazzo, 1986). In addition, some believe that unvalidated measures have been "oversold" to the point that external professional sanctions or even laws might be required to ensure compliance with standards of good practice (Lanyon, 1984; Matarazzo, 1986). Matarazzo, particularly, feels that reliance on present-day computer-based assessment procedures is problematic because it will result in an increase in the cost of health care—with the ready availability of such procedures, clinicians will be tempted to "overtest."

In a rejoinder to Matarazzo's critique, Fowler and Butcher (1986) questioned Matarazzo's position that there are such serious problems with computerized psychological assessment that external controls or legislation are required. Although acknowledging that some largely unvalidated software programs and weak test measures are commercially available, and that practitioners need to exercise care in using computer-based tests, they considered the substantial progress in computer-based psychological testing over the past 25 years to justify further development. According to Fowler and Butcher, many of the problems addressed by Matarazzo have already been resolved and are reflected in the APA guidelines for computer-based assessment (American Psychological Association, 1986). Matarazzo's concern that professionals would "overtest" and increase health care costs was considered by Fowler and Butcher to be overstated. Research has shown that the use of computers in psychological testing can actually *reduce* the cost of services. Available surveys in fact point to an overall lessening of psychodiagnostic testing recently among clinicians (Moreland & Dahlstrom, 1983).

Another of Matarazzo's concerns, in which he called for viewing computerized psychological reports as tools rather than ends in themselves, is an important but not a new concern. The recommended policy for computerized tests, that they be considered as working hypotheses and not as final recommendations, has been a policy since the earli-

HIGHLIGHT 16.4

The Limitations of Psychosocial Assessment

Despite the need for assessment to understand an individual's problems and to plan appropriate treatment, the assessment process has several limitations and possible risks. These are summarized in what follows:

1. *Cultural bias of the instrument or the clinician.* There is the possibility that psychological tests may not elicit valid information from a patient from a minority group (Gynther, 1979), or a clinician from one sociocultural background may have trouble assessing objectively the behavior of an individual from another background, such as a Southeast Asian refugee. It is important to assure, as Dahlstrom, Lachar, and Dahlstrom (1986) have done with the MMPI, that the instrument can be confidently used with individuals from minority group backgrounds.

2. *Theoretical orientation of the clinician.* Assessment is inevitably influenced by a clinician's assumptions, perceptions, and theoretical orientation. For example, a psychoanalyst and a behaviorist might assess the same behaviors quite differently. If the differing assessments should lead to treatment recommendations of significantly differing efficacy for a client's problems, these biases could have serious repercussions.

3. *Overemphasis on internal traits.* Many clinicians overemphasize personality traits as the cause of patients' problems without due attention to the possible role of stressors or other circumstances in their life situations. An undue focus on a patient's personality, which may be encouraged by some assessment techniques, can divert attention from potentially critical environmental factors.

4. *Insufficient validation.* Many psychological assessment procedures have not been sufficiently validated. For example, unlike many of the personality scales, widely used procedures for behavioral observation and behavioral self-report have not been subjected to strict psychometric validation. The tendency on the part of clinicians to accept the results of these procedures at face value has recently been giving way to a broader recognition of the need for more explicit validation.

5. *Inaccurate data or premature evaluation.* There is always the possibility that some assessment data—and any diagnostic label or treatment based on them—may be inaccurate. For example, some risk is always involved in making predictions for an individual on the basis of group data or averages; while "schizophrenic" symptoms normatively imply a difficult treatment course, some people having them recover quickly even without treatment and never experience another episode. Inaccurate data or premature conclusions not only may lead to a misunderstanding of a patient's problem but may close off attempts to get further information, with possibly grave consequences for the patient.

est days of computer assessment and is a central assumption of the American Psychological Association's (1986) most recent guidelines on computer-based assessment. Practitioners should not employ computer-based interpretations as the ultimate criterion. The final responsibility in a diagnostic study rests with a human clinician—it is she or he who must decide the relevance and utility to the particular case of the various (and, as we have seen, sometimes contradictory) elements of a computer narrative printout.

The second issue raised here is the reluctance of some clinicians to use computer-based test interpretations in spite of their demonstrated utility and low cost. Even though many clinics and independent practitioners acquire microcomputers for record-keeping and billing purposes, a minority actually incorporate computer-based clinical assessment procedures into their practice. Possible reasons for the underutilization of computer-based assessment procedures include the following:

- Practitioners trained prior to the microcomputer age, like many in other types of work, may have hesitancy about "newfangled gadgets" and do not feel comfortable with or "have time" to become acquainted with them.

- Many practitioners limit their practice to psychological treatment and do not do extensive pretreatment assessments of their cases. Many also have little interest in, or time for, the systematic evaluation of treatment efficacy that periodic formal assessments would facilitate.
- To some clinicians the impersonal and mechanized look of the booklets and answer sheets common to much computerized assessment is contrary to the image and style of warm and personal engagement they hope to convey to clients.
- Some clinicians view computer-based assessment as a threat to their own functioning. Some are concerned, as suggested in Matarazzo's (1986) critique, that computer-assessment specialists seek to replace human diagnostic functioning with automated reports. Others are concerned that unqualified practitioners may gain access to such reports and "set up shop" as competitors.

Some of these concerns are not unlike those expressed by many craftspersons or production personnel in industry when computers and robots come to the workplace. Are human practitioners in danger of being replaced by computers? Not at all. Computers in psychological assessment have intrinsic limitations consigning them to an accessory role in the process; they would not be useful, in fact quite the contrary, if employed as the sole means of evaluation. It is the clinician who must assume the major organizing role and accept the responsibility for an assessment. An unqualified person wholly dependent on computerized reports for carrying on a practice would quickly be identified as incompetent by discerning referral sources, and probably by most self-referred clients; a thriving practice would not be a likely outcome. On the other hand, judicious use of computerized assessment can free up much time for doing those things that can *only* be accomplished by the personal application of high levels of clinical skill and wisdom (Carson, 1990b).

SUMMARY

Clinical assessment is one of the most important and complex activities facing mental health professionals. The extent to which a person's problems are understood and appropriately treated depend, largely, on the adequacy of the psychological assessment. The goals of psychological assessment include identifying and describing the individual's symptoms; determining the chronicity and severity of the problem; evaluating the potential causal factors in the person's background; and exploring the individual's personal resources, which might be assets in his or her treatment program.

Interdisciplinary sources of assessment data include both physical evaluation methods and psychosocial assessment techniques. Because many psychological problems have physical components, either as underlying causal factors or as symptom patterns, it is often important to include a medical examination in the psychological assessment. In cases where organic brain damage is suspected, it is important to have neurological tests—such as an EEG or a CAT, PET, or MRI scan—to aid in determining the site and extent of organic brain disorder. In addition, it may be important to have the person take a battery of neuropsychological tests to determine if or in what manner the underlying brain disorder is affecting his or her mental and behavioral capabilities.

Psychosocial assessment methods are techniques for gathering relevant psychological information for clinical decisions about patients. The most widely used and most flexible psychosocial assessment methods are the clinical interview and behavior observation. These methods provide a wealth of clinical information. They may be subject, however, to extraneous influences that make them somewhat unreliable, and structured interview formats and objective behavior rating scales have been developed to improve their reliability.

Whereas interviews and behavior observations attempt to assess an individual's beliefs, attitudes, and symptoms directly, psychological tests attempt to measure these aspects of personality indirectly. Psychological tests include standardized stimuli for collecting behavior samples that can be compared with other individuals through test norms. Two different personality testing approaches have been developed: (a) projective tests, such as the Rorschach, in which unstructured stimuli are presented to a subject, who then "projects" meaning or structure on to the stimulus, thereby revealing "hidden" motives, feelings, and so on; and (b) objective tests, or personality inventories, in which a subject is required to read and respond to itemized statements or questions. Objective personality tests provide a cost-effective means of collecting a great deal of personality information rapidly. The MMPI, the most widely used and validated objective personality inventory, and MMPI-2, its recently revised offspring, provide a number of clinically relevant scales for describing abnormal behavior.

Possibly the most dramatic recent innovation in clinical assessment involves the widespread use of computers in the administration, scoring, and interpretation of psychological tests. It is now possible to obtain immediate interpretation of psychological test results, either through a direct computer interactive approach or through modem to a mainframe computer that interprets tests. In the past few years, rapid developments have been taking place in the computer assessment area. It is conceivable that, within the next few years, most clinical assessments will involve computers in some capacity, either for administration, scoring, and interpretation or for completing an entire test battery. Of course, mental health professionals will still play a major role in determining the appropriateness and adequacy of the computer's diagnostic output.

Key Terms

dynamic formulation (p. 575)
electroencephalogram (EEG) (p. 576)
dysrythmias (p. 577)
computerized axial tomography (CAT scan) (p. 577)
positron emission tomography (PET scan) (p. 577)
nuclear magnetic resonance imaging (MRI) (p. 577)
neuropsychological assessment (p. 578)
self-monitoring (p. 581)
rating scales (p. 581)
role playing (p. 582)
projective tests (p. 584)
Rorschach Test (p. 584)
Thematic Apperception Test (TAT) (p. 585)
sentence-completion test (p. 586)
objective tests (p. 586)
Minnesota Multiphasic Personality Inventory (MMPI) (p. 586)
factor analysis (p. 590)
actuarial procedures (p. 590)

Chapter 17

Biologically Based Therapies

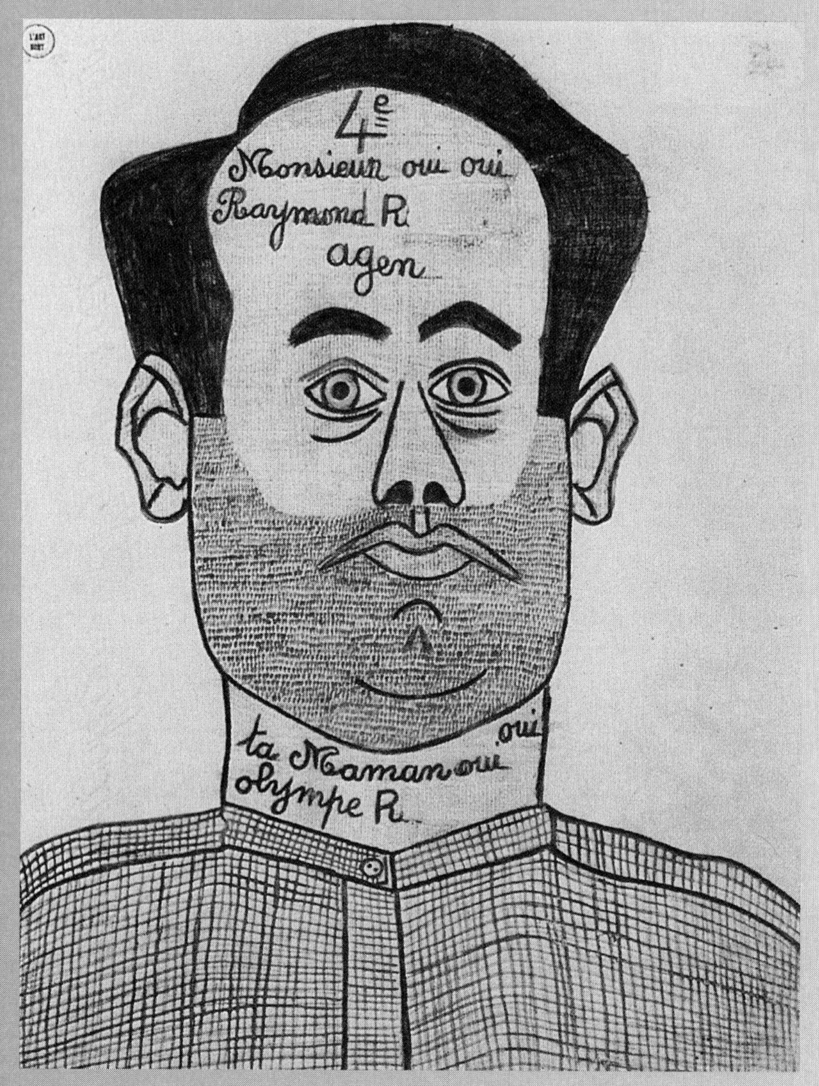

Raymond Oui, *Monsieur Oui Oui* (1948?). Having always suffered from severe psychological impairment, Raymond Oui (b. 1915?) was admitted to a psychiatric institution in Lot-et-Garonne, France, in about 1948. During ordinary conversation, Oui continually interjects the word *oui*. He also includes the word repeatedly in his artwork.

Therapy is directed toward modifying maladaptive behavior and fostering adaptive behavior. The concept of therapy is not new. Throughout recorded history, human beings have tried to help each other with life's problems—including mental disorders—in both informal and formal ways. In Chapter 2 we noted the wide range of procedures that have, throughout history, been advocated for helping the mentally disturbed—from exorcism to incarceration and torture, from understanding and kindness to the most extreme cruelty.

Today both biological and psychological procedures are used in attempts to help individuals overcome psychopathology. In this chapter we will focus on biological methods that have evolved for the treatment of mental disorders, such as the schizophrenias, mood disorders, and disorders in which severe anxiety is central. In the next chapter we will focus on psychological approaches.

EARLY ATTEMPTS AT BIOLOGICAL INTERVENTION

The idea that a disordered mind might be set straight by treatment directed at the body goes back, as we have seen, to ancient times. Beginning with those early "medicine men" who trephined skulls, through to Hippocrates and Kraepelin, and on to modern psychiatrists, there have always been those who believed that, ultimately, the cure of mental aberration would be through alteration of an organism's biological state. Today we still have no reliable knowledge of point-to-point correspondence between certain behaviors and particular events in the brain at cellular or subcellular levels. Nonetheless, the dictum "no twisted thought without a twisted molecule," while philosophically and scientifically naive in certain respects, has been deeply internalized by many workers in the mental health field. For them, it is but a small step to conclude that the search for treatment methods should concentrate on finding effective means of rearranging or reconstituting aberrant molecules—of changing the presumed physical substrate of abnormal mentality.

The history of psychiatry reflects interesting, though by today's standards often extreme and primitive, methods of treating mental illness by altering bodily processes. Some have been widely used in several periods of history. For example, ridding the body of unwanted substances by purging (with laxatives and emetics) was a typical treatment in ancient Rome, during the medieval period, and during the eighteenth century (Agnew, 1985). In fact, purging was so widespread during some periods, particularly the eighteenth century, that it was considered a common practice in medicine and among people in general. Other seemingly more barbaric techniques, such as bleeding, have been widely used as treatments of the mentally disordered just as they have been used for a broad range of physical diseases. The use of bleeding was apparently consistent and acceptable to the views of medical science in the eighteenth century. Interestingly, many medical procedures were derived from or paralleled research and development in other sciences. For example, after the discovery of electricity, many efforts to use electrical stimulation to alter mental states ensued. Early electrical devices were used to stimulate patients' nerves, muscles, and organs as a treatment for a variety of illnesses. The rationale behind early somatic efforts to "treat" mental patients was often unclear, although frightening patients out of their madness or punishing the demons within may have been as much a reason as was any belief that an individual's bodily processes were being restored.

In general, as more has been learned in the various subfields of medicine, treatment measures have become more benign and less risky. As researchers come to understand scientifically the nature of a disorder, they typically are then able to develop biological treatments that are more precisely designed to meet the specific problem. The specificity of these new treatments typically means that they have fewer potentially damaging side effects.

The human brain and mind have yielded their secrets grudgingly. As a result, relative to other medical subdisciplines, psychiatry has had a slow and often uncertain development. It should not be surprising, therefore, to find that it has contributed its own array of dubious treatment techniques in the comparatively short history of its recognition as a medical subspecialty. In fact, by 1917, with the discovery of Wagner-Jauregg that general paresis, or neurosyphilis, could be curbed by intentionally infecting a patient with malaria (the consequent fevers were lethal to the spirochete), the stage was set for the development of extraordinarily bold and often hazardous ventures in the treatment arena. Wagner-Jauregg later received the Nobel Prize for this discovery. We will look now at two treatments that emerged during this period: the convulsive therapies and psychosurgery.

Coma and Convulsive Therapies

Insulin coma therapy, rarely used today, was initially used as a treatment for morphine withdrawal. It was introduced by Sakel in 1932 as a physiologi-

Some of the stranger instruments used for the treatment of the mentally ill in the eighteenth and nineteenth centuries are shown here: at left, glass cups and scarificators—which make cuts in the skin—that were used for bleeding patients; at right, an electrostatic generator that was used to shock patients.

cal treatment for schizophrenia. The technique involves administration of increasing amounts of insulin (a hormone that regulates sugar metabolism in the body) on a daily basis until a patient goes into "shock"—actually a hypoglycemic coma caused by an acute deficiency of glucose (sugar) in the blood. Coma-inducing doses of insulin are administered daily thereafter until the patient has experienced approximately 50 comas, each an hour or more in duration. The comas are terminated by administering glucose. This treatment causes profound biological and physiological stress, especially to the cardiovascular and nervous systems. The patient must be closely monitored both during and after the comatose state because of a variety of medical complications that may ensue, including some that are fatal.

The results of insulin coma therapy have been generally disappointing. Where patients have shown improvement, it has been difficult to determine whether it was due to the experience of the comas or to some other feature associated with the treatment, such as the markedly increased attention of the medical staff. Moreover, patients who do show some improvement tend to be those who would improve readily under other treatment regimens as well; severe, chronic schizophrenic patients remain for the most part unimproved. Finally, the relapse rate for those who improve has been high. With such a record—and in the face of marked medical risks—it is hardly surprising that the use of insulin coma as a therapeutic method has largely disappeared (Kalinowski & Hippius, 1969).

Shortly after the discovery of electricity, electrical stimulation came to be used in the treatment of mental disorders. As early as 1849 the physician Bucknill, working with asylum patients, used galvanic electrical stimulation and potassium oxide to successfully treat patients with melancholia (Beveridge & Renvoize, 1988). During the latter part of the nineteenth century, the therapeutic use of electrical stimulation was fairly widespread. Toward the end of the century, however, great concern over its safety resulted in a diminished use of electricity for treatment.

The potential value of electrostimulation therapy was reconsidered after the Hungarian physician Von Meduna speculated—erroneously, as it turned out—that schizophrenia rarely occurred in individuals with epilepsy. This observation led to the inference that schizophrenia and epilepsy were somehow incompatible, and that thus one might be able to cure schizophrenia by inducing convulsions. Various methods of convulsion induction, including Metrazol, which produced violent convulsions, were attempted. In 1938 two Italian physicians, Cerletti and Bini, after visiting a slaughterhouse and seeing animals rendered unconscious by electric shock, tried the simplest method of all—that of passing an electric current through a patient's head. The method, which became known as **electroconvulsive therapy (ECT),** is much more widely used today than insulin therapy, mostly because of its effectiveness in alleviating depressive episodes. There are two types of ECT—*bilateral* and *unilateral.* The latter is a more recent introduction and is considered, by some, less intrusive. We will review both here.

Despite modest variations in the placement of electrodes and the introduction of safeguards, the standard form of *bilateral ECT* (involving both hemispheres of the brain) remains basically as Cerletti and Bini developed it: an electric current of approximately 150 volts is passed from one side of a patient's head to the other for up to about one and one-half seconds. The patient immediately loses consciousness and undergoes a marked tonic (extensor) seizure of the muscles, followed by a lengthy series of clonic (contractile) ones of lesser amplitude. Typically, sedative and muscle-relaxant premedication is used to prevent violent contractions. In the days before such medication was available, the initial seizure was sometimes so violent as to fracture vertebrae, one of several potential complications of this therapy.

After awakening several minutes later, the patient has amnesia for the period immediately preceding the therapy, and is usually somewhat confused for the next hour or so. With repeated treatments, usually administered three times weekly, the patient gradually becomes disoriented, a state that clears after termination of the treatments. Memory impairment, however, can remain for months (Squire, Slater, & Chase, 1975), or, in some instances, even years (Breggin, 1979).

Normally, a treatment series consists of less than a dozen sessions, although in times past there was widespread overuse of the technique as a means of controlling excited or violent behavior. Today one can still find chronic patients in the "back wards" of mental hospitals whose treatment history includes the inducement of literally hundreds of seizures. The damage created by these excesses is difficult to estimate in precise terms, but it could well be substantial (Breggin, 1979; Palmer, 1981). It is possible that each electroconvulsive treatment administered to a person destroys a varying number of central nervous system neurons.

At present, the use of ECT is still considered controversial. Some support its use as the only effective way of dealing with some severely depressed and suicidal patients. Others within the profession deplore the lack of objective appraisals of this treatment. These contrary views would have been more easy to dismiss in the 1940s, because little else of proven efficacy was then available. Today it is more difficult to defend the widespread use of the technique because effective alternative approaches—such as antidepressant medication—are abundant. These issues have been discussed at length by Breggin (1979) in a comprehensive review of available evidence concerning the potentially damaging effects of ECT.

Although Breggin's treatise has been criticized for its somewhat biased language and style (e.g., Weiner, 1982), there exists no wholly effective counterargument to his expert review of the evidence. For example, demonstrable brain damage has been found in animals sacrificed immediately after ECT treatment. In short, while there is little doubt about the effectiveness of ECT in alleviating certain disorders—chiefly within the psychotic depressive range (although Breggin disputed even this conclusion)—a cautious appraisal of the technique requires that it be considered potentially brain damaging. The appropriate use of the treatment, therefore, should be preceded by a careful assessment of its potential costs and benefits in light of the circumstances attending a particular case. Unfortunately, Breggin noted that such a review is not necessarily routine; this is especially the case, at present, in private psychiatric hospitals, where ECT is often used.

Responding to these sorts of concerns, the citizens of Berkeley, California, in November 1982, voted overwhelmingly to ban the use of ECT treatment within that city (*Science News,* November 13, 1982), an action that was later judicially overturned. Though the wisdom of holding public elections on such issues may be seriously questioned, the event demonstrates increased citizen awareness and concern about the treatment mental patients receive.

In 1985 the National Institute of Mental Health sponsored a Consensus Development Conference on electroconvulsive therapy to evaluate the issues surrounding the use of ECT (NIMH, 1985a). A panel of experts in psychiatry, psychology, neurology, psychopharmacology, epidemiology, and law, along with several laypersons, considered evidence as to (a) the effectiveness of ECT for patients with various disorders; (b) the risks of ECT; (c) the indications for administration of ECT; and (d) the best ways to implement ECT with patients.

The panel recognized a number of potential risks associated with the use of ECT, including such medical problems as limb fractures, circulatory insufficiency, tooth damage, and skin burns. With the present techniques used, however, these risks have been virtually eliminated. Mortality following ECT, a significant problem in the early days of the treatment, has also been significantly reduced to about 2.9 deaths per 10,000 patients. The injury and mortality rates are considered comparable to other somatic treatments, such as barbiturate anesthetics. The panel reached a number of conclusions as to which disorders responded best to ECT. They agreed that the effect of ECT was well established for some types of depression, particularly delusional depression and "endogenous" depression. They also concluded that ECT can be effectively used with some types of manic disorders, particularly acute mania. On the other hand, they found that ECT was not particularly effective with some depressions, such as dysthymic disorder. Although ECT is sometimes used with certain types of schizophrenia, the evidence for effectiveness is not convincing.

Scott (1989) reviewed the literature and found that many depressed patients do not respond to ECT. When therapeutic benefits do result from the use of ECT, they sometimes prove to be short-lived, with a patient relapsing into the previous disorder. The NIMH consensus panel concluded that relapse rates following ECT were high unless the treatment was followed by maintenance doses of antidepressant medication. As has been true with some other techniques, the mechanism by which therapeutic effects are brought about has never been adequately explained. Some researchers believe that the therapeutic effect is mediated by induced changes in the biochemistry of brain synapses (Fink, 1979; Fink et al., 1974).

Despite all the questions and controversy, the therapeutic efficacy of ECT, at least for some depressions and acute mania, is well established in the research literature (Abrams, 1988; Fink, 1979; Scovern & Kilman, 1980) and in personal testimonials from those who have been helped by it (Endler, 1990). The comparatively low mortality rate among depressive individuals, a group considered to be at high risk for early mortality, has been attributed to ECT (Avery & Winoker, 1976; Martin et al., 1985).

A dramatic example of the unprecedented early success of ECT that sometimes occurred following its introduction is provided in the autobiographical account of Lenore McCall (1947), who suffered a severe depressive disorder in her middle years.

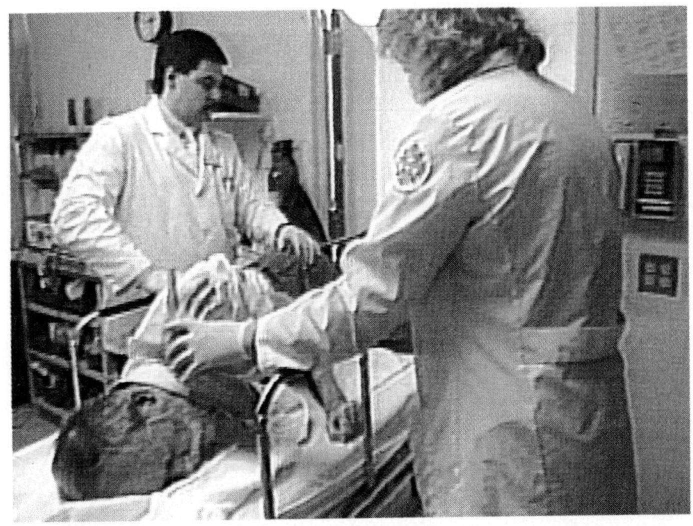

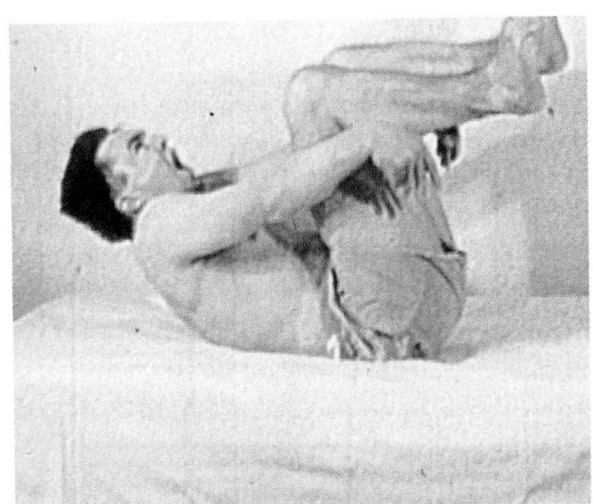

A patient administered electroconvulsive therapy (ECT) today (left) is given sedative and muscle-relaxant premedication to prevent violent contractions. In the days before such medication was available (right), the initial seizure was sometimes so violent as to fracture vertebrae.

Ms. McCall, a well-educated woman of affluent circumstances and the mother of three children, noticed a feeling of persistent fatigue as the first sign of her impending descent into depression. Too fearful to seek help, she at first attempted to fight off her increasingly profound apathy by engaging in excessive activity, a defensive strategy that accomplished little but the depletion of her remaining strength and emotional reserves.

In due course, she noticed that her mental processes seemed to be deteriorating—her memory appeared impaired and she could concentrate only with great difficulty. Emotionally, she felt an enormous loneliness, bleakness of experience, and increasingly intense fear about what was happening to her mind. She came to view her past small errors of commission and omission as the most heinous of crimes and increasingly withdrew from contact with her husband and children. Eventually, at her husband's and her physician's insistence, she was hospitalized despite her own vigorous resistance. She felt betrayed, and shortly thereafter attempted suicide by shattering a drinking glass and ingesting its fragments; to her great disappointment, she survived.

Ms. McCall thereafter spent nearly four years continuously in two separate mental hospitals, during which time she deteriorated further. She was silent and withdrawn, behaved in a mechanical fashion, lost an alarming amount of weight, and underwent a seemingly premature aging process. She felt that she emitted an offensive odor. At this time, ECT was introduced into the therapeutic procedures in use at her hospital.

A series of ECT treatments was given to Ms. McCall over about a three-month period. Then, one day, she woke up in the morning with a totally changed outlook: "I sat up suddenly, my heart pounding. I looked around the room and a sweep of wonder surged over me. God in heaven, I'm well. I'm myself. . . ." After a brief period of convalescence, she went home to her husband and children to try to pick up the threads of their painfully severed lives. She did so, and then wrote the engrossing and informative book from which this history is taken.

Some years ago, a modification in the standard method of administering ECT was introduced. Instead of placing the electrodes on each side of the head in the temple region, thereby causing a transverse flow of current through both cerebral hemispheres, the new procedure involves limiting current flow through only one side of the brain, typically the nondominant (right, for most people) side. This procedure is called *unilateral ECT,* and strong evidence shows that it lessens distressing side effects (such as memory impairment) without decreasing therapeutic effectiveness (Daniel & Crovitz, 1983b; Squire, 1977; Squire & Slater, 1978). Unfortunately, it has been estimated that some 75 percent of psychiatrists who employ ECT still use the original bilateral method exclusively (American Psychiatric Association, 1978; NIMH, 1985b). Though this trend may now be changing in favor of unilateral ECT, we must await further data for confirmation. Evidence also suggests that the use of a lower-energy, pulsating electrical stimulus may produce less mental impairment than the standard treatment (Daniel & Crovitz, 1983a). The extent of this modification's effective use is not known, however.

Psychosurgery

Brain surgery used in the treatment of functional or central nervous system disorders is called **psychosurgery.** In 1935 in Portugal, Moniz introduced a psychosurgical procedure in which the frontal lobes of the brain were severed from the deeper centers underlying them. This technique eventually evolved into an operation known as **prefrontal lobotomy.** This operation stands as a dubious tribute to the levels to which professionals have sometimes been driven in their search for effective treatments for the psychoses. In retrospect, it seems somewhat surprising that this procedure—which results in permanent brain damage to the patient—won for its originator the Nobel Prize in Medicine for the year 1949.

In the two decades between 1935 and 1955 (after which the new antipsychotic drugs became widely available), tens of thousands of mental patients in this country and abroad were subjected to prefrontal lobotomy and related neurosurgical procedures. In fact, in some settings, as many as 50 patients were treated in a single day (Freeman, 1959). As is often the case with newly developed techniques of therapy, initial reports of results tended to be enthusiastic, downplaying complications (including a 1 to 4 percent death rate) and undesirable side effects. It was eventually recognized, however, that the "side effects" of psychosurgery could be very undesirable indeed. In some instances they included a permanent inability to inhibit impulses; in others, an unnatural "tranquility," with undesirable shallowness or absence of feeling. By 1951 the Soviet Union had banned all such operations; though rarely performed, they are still permitted by law in the United States and in many other countries. See *HIGHLIGHT 17.1* for an illustration of the sometimes tragic outcome of lobotomy.

The advent of the major antipsychotic drugs caused an immediate decrease in the widespread use of psychosurgical procedures. Such operations are extremely rare today and are used only as a last resort for the intractable psychoses, severely and chronically debilitating obsessive-compulsive disorders, and occasionally for the control of severe pain in cases of terminal illness.

On the rare occasion when it is employed today, psychosurgery is unquestionably a much more circumspect procedure than in the heyday of lobotomies. Today the permanent damage to the brain has been substantially minimized and thus fewer detrimental side effects follow. The surgical technique involves the selective destruction of minute areas; for example, in the "cingulotomy" procedure—which seems to relieve the subjective experience of pain, including "psychic" pain—a small bundle of nerve fibers connecting the frontal lobes with a deeper structure known as the limbic system is interrupted with virtually pinpoint precision.

Despite these advances, continuing concern has been voiced about such operations, and in the mid-1970s the Congress of the United States called a special national commission to evaluate their effects. The report of that commission indicated some surprisingly beneficial effects that had been achieved with modern psychosurgery—for example, the alleviation of chronic depression—but it also warned that such benefits were often achieved at the expense of the loss of certain cognitive capacities. The commission recommended that cautious exploration of these techniques be continued with selected patients (Culliton, 1976).

The debate about psychosurgery has recently received a thorough airing in two fascinating books by Elliot Valenstein (1980; 1986). Valenstein scrutinized the procedures of psychosurgery—and by implication other "brain-disabling" therapies—in relation to the psychiatric, ethical, legal, and social issues they necessarily raise. In the 1986 book, entitled *Great and Desperate Cures,* Valenstein examined the historical basis of psychosurgery and explained how an unproven and potentially life-threatening treatment could emerge in a field devoted to scientific explanation and become an accepted treatment method with little empirical justification. Factors underlying this premature and "desperate" acceptance of psychosurgery included psychiatry's need to "gain respectability" as a medical science by having an organic-surgical treatment method; the professional rivalry between psychia-

HIGHLIGHT 17.1

The Accomplishments and Subsequent Tragedy of Rosemary Kennedy

One of the tragic victims of the zeal to perform prefrontal lobotomies to alleviate behavior problems was Rosemary Kennedy, the sister of President John F. Kennedy and Senators Robert and Edward Kennedy. Rosemary was the third child of Joseph and Rose Kennedy, born during the height of the flu epidemic of 1918. She was a beautiful baby, with a sweet temperament, but as she grew, her mother became more and more concerned about her developmental delays compared to her brothers and sisters. When the family finally concluded that Rosemary likely was retarded since birth from unknown causes, the best experts in the country at the time could offer no guidance: "We went from doctor to doctor. . . . From all, we heard the same answer: 'I'm sorry, but we can do nothing.' For my husband and me it was nerve-racking and incomprehensible" (Goodwin, 1988, p. 416).

Rose Kennedy and the family rebelled against the suggestion that Rosemary be institutionalized. Instead, she was kept at home with the benefit of a special governess and many private tutors. She participated fully in the Kennedy's family activities, and she made considerable progress. Doris Kearns Goodwin (1988), a biographer of the Fitzgerald and Kennedy families, described an arithmetic paper that the 9-year-old Rosemary completed on February 21, 1927. She correctly answered several multiplication (428 times 32) and division (3924 divided by 6) problems. By the age of 18 years, Rosemary had obtained a fifth-grade level in English and remained at the fourth-grade level in math that she had obtained by age 9.

Because of the considerable stigma associated with mental retardation at the time, Rosemary's parents kept her condition hidden from those outside the family, a major task given the scrutiny of the family by the press. Although her parents and siblings were always nearby to protect her, Rosemary developed the social skills needed to be presented successfully as a debutante and later to the King and Queen of England at Buckingham Palace. The British press complimented Rose Kennedy for her beautiful daughters, never even noticing Rosemary's mental retardation.

Unfortunately, Rosemary's behavior deteriorated around the beginning of World War II when the family returned to the United States from England, where Joseph Kennedy had been ambassador. There are several possible explanations for this deterioration, including her increasing frustration about not being able to do all the things her siblings were able to do and having to leave the school in England where she had felt successful. The 21-year-old Rosemary became quite violent and frequently ran away from home or her convent school. There was considerable concern for her safety, and Joseph Kennedy—without Rose's knowledge—turned to the medical experts of the time, searching for a solution.

These experts convinced Joe that the miracle treatment lay in prefrontal lobotomy. Rosemary Kennedy became one of the thousands submitted to that "desperate" cure. In Rosemary's case, the surgery was a tragic failure—all her previous accomplishments were wiped out, leaving little of her former personality and adaptive ability intact:

"They knew right away that it wasn't successful. You could see by looking at her that something was wrong, for her head was tilted and her capacity to speak was almost entirely gone. There was no question now that she could no longer take care of herself and that the only answer was an institution." (Ann Gargan King, a cousin, as reported by Goodwin, 1988, p. 744)

try, neurology, and neurosurgery; and the need to provide a cost-effective treatment and maintain control over mental hospitals.

Valenstein (1980) further discussed important ethical and philosophical issues underlying the use of psychosurgery. For example, what meaning can be assigned to the concept of *informed consent* if a patient is so disabled that this radical form of intervention is seriously considered? When, if ever, is it justifiable to employ surgical means to alter human personality? It appears we are finally reaching a level of public awareness and surveillance that will make it increasingly unlikely for these extreme measures to be employed without due considera-

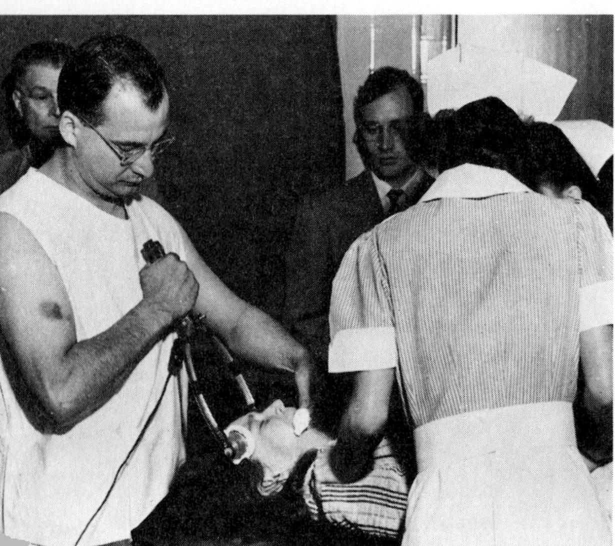

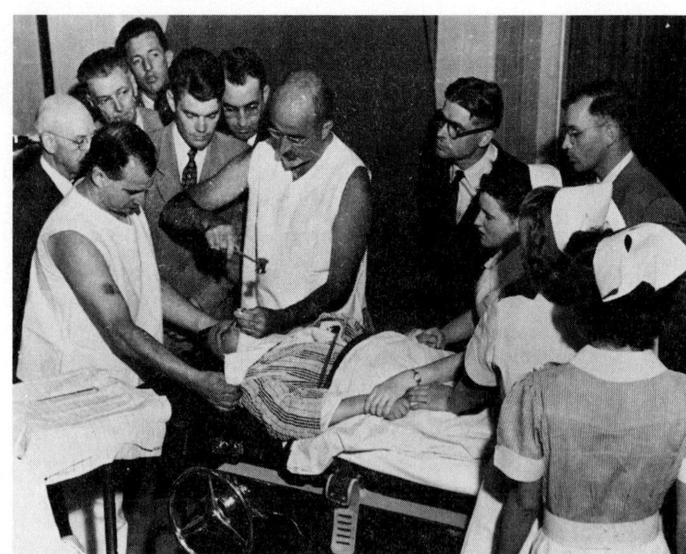

Shown here is a demonstration of a transorbital lobotomy, which was used extensively in this country from the 1940s until the late 1950s. First, a doctor administers ECT to anesthetize the patient (left). Immediately following ECT, another doctor performs the actual lobotomy (right). It is estimated that tens of thousands of patients were subjected to such procedures, resulting in permanent brain damage (which was, after all, the actual intent of the procedure) and sometimes death.

tion—in a context of full disclosure—of the risks as well as the benefits potentially entailed.

THE EMERGENCE OF PHARMACOLOGICAL METHODS OF TREATMENT

A long-term goal of medicine has been to discover drugs that can effectively combat the ravages of mental disorder. This goal, one of the pursuits of **pharmacology,** the science of drugs, has until fairly recently remained elusive. Early efforts in this direction were limited largely to a search for chemical compounds or drugs that would have soothing, calming, or sleep-inducing effects. Such drugs, if they could be found, would make it easier to manage distraught, excited, and sometimes violent patients. Little thought was given to the possibility that the status and course of the disorder itself might actually be brought under control by appropriate medication; the focus was on rendering a patient's overt behavior more manageable and thereby making restraints, such as straitjackets, unnecessary.

As the field of psychopharmacology developed, many such compounds were introduced and tried in the mental hospital setting. Almost without exception, however, those that produced the desired calming effects proved to have serious shortcomings. At effective dosage levels, they often produced severe drowsiness if not outright sleep, and many of them were dangerously addicting. On the whole, little real progress was made in this field until the mid-1950s, at which point, as we will see, a genuine revolution in the treatment of the more severe disorders occurred. This breakthrough was followed shortly by the discovery of drugs helpful in the treatment of the less severe anxiety-based disorders, and eventually by recognition of the therapeutic benefits of antidepressants and lithium salts for the mood disorders.

Types of Drugs Used in Therapy

In this section we will trace the discovery of the four types of chemical agents now commonly used in therapy for mental disorders—antipsychotic drugs, antidepressant drugs, antianxiety drugs (minor tranquilizers), and lithium. These drugs are sometimes referred to as *psychotropic drugs,* in that their main effect is on an individual's mental life. As we examine drugs used in therapy, it is important to remember that individuals differ in how rapidly they metabolize drugs—that is, in how quickly their bodies break down the drugs once ingested.

What this means is that individuals differ, too, in what dosage of a drug they may need to experience the desired therapeutic effect. Determining correct dosage is a critical factor of drug therapy because too much or too little of a drug can be ineffective and (in the case of too much) even life-threatening, depending on the individual.

Antipsychotic Drugs The **antipsychotic drugs** as a group are sometimes called *major tranquilizers,* but this term is somewhat misleading. They are used with the major disorders, such as the schizophrenias, but they do more than tranquilize. Though they do indeed produce a calming effect on many patients, their unique quality is that of somehow alleviating or reducing the intensity of psychotic symptoms, such as delusions and hallucinations. In some cases, in fact, a patient who is already excessively "tranquil" (for example, withdrawn or immobile) becomes active and responsive to the environment under treatment by these drugs. In contrast, the antianxiety drugs, to be described shortly, are effective in reducing tension without in any way affecting psychotic symptoms.

Although the benefits of the antipsychotic drugs have often been exaggerated, it is difficult to convey the truly enormous influence they have had in altering the environment of the typical mental hospital. One of the authors, as part of his training, worked several months in the maximum security ward of one such hospital just before the introduction of this type of medication in 1955. The ward patients fulfilled the common stereotypes of individuals "gone mad." Bizarreness, nudity, wild screaming, and an ever-present threat of violence pervaded the atmosphere. Fearfulness and a near-total preoccupation with the maintenance of control characterized the staff's attitude. Such an attitude was not unrealistic in terms of the frequency of serious physical assaults by patients, but it was hardly conducive to the development or maintenance of an effective therapeutic program.

Then, quite suddenly—within a period of perhaps a month—all of this dramatically changed. The patients began receiving antipsychotic medication. The ward became a place in which one could get to know one's patients on a personal level and perhaps even initiate programs of "milieu therapy," a form of psychosocial therapy in which the entire facility is regarded as a therapeutic community, and the emphasis is on developing a meaningful and constructive environment in which the patients participate in the regulation of their own activities. Promising reports of changes in hospital environments began to appear in the professional literature. A new era in hospital treatment had arrived, aided enormously and in many instances actually made possible by the development of these extraordinary drugs.

The beginnings of this development were quite commonplace. For centuries, the root of the plant *rauwolfia* (snakeroot) had been used in India for the treatment of mental disorders. In 1943 the *Indian Medical Gazette* reported improvements in manic reactions, schizophrenia, and other types of psychopathology following the use of *reserpine,* a drug derived from rauwolfia. Reserpine was first used in the United States in the early 1950s, after it was found to have a "calming" effect on mental patients (Kline, 1954). Early enthusiasm for the drug was tempered, however, by the finding that it also might produce low blood pressure, nasal congestion, and, perhaps most seriously, severe depression. Reanalysis of this latter finding suggested that the danger of serious depression was mainly for patients with a prior history of depression (Mendels & Frazer, 1974). Reserpine is now used mainly for the control of hypertension.

Meanwhile, the first of the phenothiazine family of drugs, *chlorpromazine* (Thorazine), was being synthesized in the early 1950s by one of the major pharmaceutical houses. It was first marketed at about the same time that reserpine was introduced, and it quickly proved to have virtually the same benefits but fewer undesirable side effects. It soon became the treatment of choice for schizophrenia.

The remarkable early successes reported with chlorpromazine led quickly to a bandwagon effect among other pharmaceutical companies, who began to manufacture and market their own variants of the basic phenothiazine compound. Some of the best known variants are trifluoperazine (Stelazine), promazine (Sparine), prochlorperazine (Compazine), thioridazine (Mellaril), perphenazine (Trilafon), and fluphenazine (Prolixin). Currently, too, there are at least six classes of nonphenothiazine antipsychotic drugs available in the United States (Carson, 1984), of which the best known is haloperidol (Haldol). This diversity becomes less bewildering when it is remembered that virtually all of the antipsychotics accomplish a common biochemical effect, namely the blocking of dopamine receptors, as was noted in Chapter 12.

With persistent use or at high dosage, however, all of these preparations have varying degrees of troublesome side effects, such as dryness of the mouth and throat, muscular stiffness, jaundice, and a Parkinson-like syndrome involving tremors of the extremities and immobility of the facial muscles. Which side effects develop appears to depend on the particular compound used in relation to the particular vulnerabilities of the treated patient. Many of

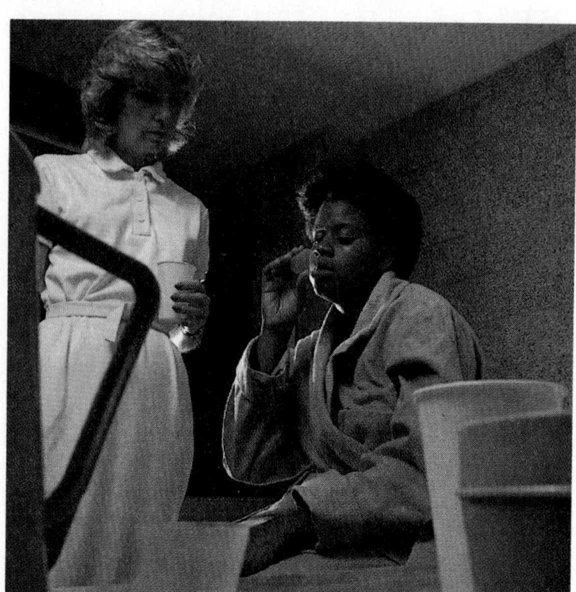

The introduction of antipsychotic drugs in hospital treatment of the mentally ill was a major breakthrough in altering the environment of the typical mental hospital.

these side effects are temporary and may be relieved by substituting another drug of the same class, by switching to a different class of drug, or by reducing the dosage. We should also note that some schizophrenic individuals, particularly those with negative symptoms or chronic schizophrenia, do not respond to antipsychotic drug therapy and may indeed be made worse by it (Buckley, 1982).

For certain patients, a particularly troublesome side effect of long-term antipsychotic drug treatment is the development of a disfiguring disturbance of motor control, particularly of the facial muscles, known as **tardive dyskinesia.** Symptoms of tardive dyskinesia, which often seem to disappear when a patient is asleep, are both dramatic to an observer and disabling to the patient. The symptoms involve involuntary movements of the tongue, lips, jaw, and extremities. An individual with tardive dyskinesia may show involuntary limb movement and usually shows characteristic chewing movements, lip smacking, and sucking of the mouth. There is some indication that the more severe the facial and other symptoms of tardive dyskinesia, the more severe the cognitive deficit (DeWolfe, Ryan, & Wolf, 1988). The disturbance is believed to be due to an imbalance in dopamine and acetylcholine activity in the brain, secondary to alterations in receptor sensitivity by antipsychotics and other drugs commonly used in combination to control their side effects. Side effects of tardive dyskinesia can occur months to years after the antipsychotic drug treatment is initiated and after the treatment has been stopped or the drug reduced in dosage.

Tardive dyskinesia has increased in recent years due to the extensive use of antipsychotic medication with severely schizophrenic individuals (Kane & Smith, 1982), although the manifestation of the disturbance appears to fluctuate in patients over time (Bergen et al., 1989). The use of antipsychotic medications in treatment is usually discontinued if a patient shows symptoms of tardive dyskinesia. Although there are medications that control the symptoms of tardive dyskinesia, drug therapy is generally not recommended (AMA, 1986). In some cases where the patient continues to display psychotic symptoms, the use of antipsychotic medication treatment may be resumed; however, discontinuation of the treatment is recommended if any symptoms of tardive dyskinesia reappear. To reduce the chances of this disturbance during the drug treatment of chronic schizophrenics, clinicians are more frequently using what is called "target dosing" (Rosen, 1986), which entails administering a drug when symptoms appear or are likely to appear rather than giving continuous dosages, as commonly practiced in the past.

A recent trend in the treatment of schizophrenia involves the application of lower doses of standard drugs to reduce negative side effects. Hogarty et al. (1988) have shown that low-dose-treated schizophrenics actually showed more improvement than normal-dose-treated patients in terms of many observable behaviors. Moreover, relapse rates were found to be comparable to patients treated with higher doses.

The range of effects achieved by the antipsychotic drugs may be illustrated by two brief case histories of patients who served as subjects in a clinical research project designed to evaluate differing treatment approaches to the schizophrenias (Grinspoon, Ewalt, & Shader, 1972).

Ms. W. was a 19-year-old, white, married woman who was admitted to the treatment unit as a result of gradually increasing agitation and hallucinations over a three-month period. Her symptoms had markedly intensified during the four days prior to admission, partly as a result of a homosexual seduction she had undergone while under the influence of marijuana. She had had a deprived childhood, but had managed to function reasonably well until breakdown.

At the outset of her hospitalization, Ms. W. continued to have auditory and visual hallucinations and appeared frightened, angry, and con-

fused. She believed that she had a unique relationship with God or the devil. Her thought content displayed loosening of associations, and her affect was inappropriate to this content. Her condition continued to deteriorate for more than two weeks, at which point medication was begun.

Ms. W. was assigned to a treatment group in which the patients were receiving thioridazine (Mellaril). She responded dramatically during the first week of treatment. Her behavior became, for the most part, quiet and appropriate, and she made some attempts at socialization. She continued to improve, but by the fourth week of treatment began to show signs of mild depression. Her medication was increased, and she resumed her favorable course. By the sixth week she was dealing with various reality issues in her life in a reasonably effective manner, and by the ninth week she was spending considerable time at home, returning to the hospital in a pleasant and cheerful mood. She was discharged exactly 100 days after her admission, being then completely free of symptoms.

Mr. S., the eldest of three sons in a fairly religious Jewish family, was admitted to the hospital after developing marked paranoid ideation and hallucinations during his first weeks of college. He had looked forward to going to college, an elite New England school, but his insecurity once on campus caused him to become unduly boastful about his prowess with drinking and women. He stayed up late at night to engage in "bull sessions" and neglected his studies and other responsibilities. Within ten days he panicked about his ability to keep up and tried frantically to rearrange his course schedule and his life, to no avail.

His sense of incompetence was transformed over time into the idea that others—including all the students in his dormitory—were against him, and that fellow male students were perhaps flirting homosexually with him. By the time of his referral to the college infirmary, he was convinced that the college was a fraud he would have to expose, that the CIA was plotting against him, and that someone was going to kill him. He heard voices and smelled strange odors. He also showed a marked loosening of associations and flat, inappropriate affect. At the time of his transfer to the hospital, he was diagnosed as an acute paranoid schizophrenic.

Mr. S. was assigned to a treatment group receiving haloperidol (Haldol). His initial response to treatment was rapid and favorable, but observers noted that his behavior remained immature. Then suddenly during the fifth week of treatment, he became tense, negativistic, and hostile. Thereafter, he gradually became less defiant and angry, and he responded well to a day-care program prescribed by his therapist, although he was nervous and apprehensive about being outside the hospital. He was discharged as improved ten weeks after the initiation of his drug therapy.

Three months later Mr. S. was readmitted to the hospital. Although he had done well at first, he had begun to deteriorate concurrently with his doctor-monitored withdrawal from haloperidol. His behavior showed increasing signs of a lack of effective control. He began to set random fires and was described by the investigators as "sociopathic." Two days after his readmission, he signed himself out of the hospital "against medical advice." His parents immediately arranged for his confinement in another hospital, and the investigators subsequently lost contact with him.

Recent research with treatment-resistant schizophrenics has focused on possible alternative drugs. One such compound that differs from the phenothiazines, Clozapine (a dibenzodiazepine), has produced promising results. Kane et al. (1988) studied the therapeutic effects of clozapine with a large group of treatment-resistant schizophrenics and found the treatment effects modestly encouraging. Thirty percent of the treatment-resistant patients improved under the regimen and no negative side effects were noted. Further research on the side effects of this drug is indicated, however, because some studies have found that many patients taking the drug develop an immune deficiency that is life-threatening and that has resulted in the death of several patients. Even though this medication has been heralded as the most effective treatment for schizophrenia, it appears that few patients will actually receive its benefits. A 30 percent response rate is not a panacea. Also, the potentially lethal characteristic of the drug prompted the drug company to develop and market a highly structured blood-monitoring system along with the medication to guard against its misuse. Unfortunately, the cost of the drug in combination with this monitoring system makes the treatment expensive and drastically limits its availability for most patients needing the drug (Winslow, 1990).

Antidepressant Drugs The **antidepressant drugs** made their appearance shortly after the introduction of reserpine and chlorpromazine. There are two basic classes of these compounds: the monoamine oxidase (MAO) inhibitors and the tricyclics. Many variants of the latter class, including some that are not, strictly speaking, "tricyclic" in their chemical formulation, have appeared in the past few years. Although they differ considerably in their chemical makeup, it is currently believed that they accomplish a common biochemical result—namely, that of increasing the concentrations of the neurotransmitters serotonin and norepinephrine at pertinent synaptic sites in the brain (Berger, 1978; see *HIGHLIGHT 3.1* on p. 61). In fact, there has been speculation that measurably different types of depression may correlate with differing functional levels of these and possibly other neurotransmitters, and that it may be possible to discover how to use antidepressant drugs in a selective manner, depending on which neurotransmitter systems they maximally affect (Akiskal, 1979; Maugh, 1981).

Unfortunately, the *etiological* significance of these ideas is complicated by problems similar to those relating excess dopamine activity to schizophrenia. For example, the effect of these drugs on neurotransmitter synaptic concentrations occurs promptly, whereas the *clinical* effects of the drugs on modifying depressive affect and behavior are often agonizingly delayed. Hence it seems unlikely that depressive phenomena are directly and uniquely caused by the neurotransmitter anomalies purportedly corrected by these substances.

Of the two main classes of antidepressants, the tricyclics and their variants are by far the more often used. This is largely because the MAO inhibitors are more toxic and require troublesome dietary restrictions; in addition, they are widely believed to have less potent therapeutic effects. Nevertheless, some patients who do not respond favorably to tricyclics will subsequently do well on an MAO inhibitor. A minority of severely depressed patients respond to neither type of antidepressant compound, in which case alternative modes of intervention, such as electroconvulsive therapy, may be tried. Commonly used tricyclics are imipramine (Tofranil), amitriptyline (Elavil), and nortriptyline (Aventyl). MAO inhibitors include isocarboxazid (Marplan), phenelzine (Nardil), and tranylcypromine (Parnate).

Antidepressant drugs, particularly tricyclics, continue to be developed, tested, and marketed at a high rate. Among the more recent entrants to the field are amoxapine (Asendin), maprotiline (Ludiomil), and trazodone (Desyrel). Amoxapine is a tricyclic related to certain of the antipsychotic drugs and thus may prove to have a special role in the treatment of schizoaffective disorder. Maprotiline and trazodone are technically not tricyclics at all, but rather tetracyclics; the chemical addition of an extra benzene ring is in each case claimed to reduce problematic side effects. Trazodone, in particular, appeared on introduction to be a very promising drug (Moore, 1982). One study reported, however, that permanent impotence can result from extensive use (Lansky & Selzer, 1984).

A "second generation" antidepressant, chemically unrelated to other antidepressant medications, that has become the preferred antidepressant drug in the 1990s, is *fluoxetine,* better known by the trade name *Prozac.* This drug acts to inhibit the reuptake of serotonin and norepinephrine, thus increasing their availability. Prozac is thought to be a relatively "safe" drug in that it is not considered physiologically addicting and is not found to be fatal in overdose. Clinical trials with fluoxetine have reported that patients tend to improve after about three weeks of treatment with the drug. Several adverse side effects of Prozac have been reported, particularly nausea, nervousness, and insomnia (Cole & Bodkin, 1990; Tacke, 1990). In addition, after a few weeks on the drug, some patients have experienced increased blood pressure levels and others have reported suicidal urges and agitation (Cole & Bodkin, 1990; Papp & Gorman, 1990). Notably, some depressed patients who had not previously been suicidal have reported suicidal thoughts.

Pharmacological treatment for depression often produces dramatic results. Improvement in response to antidepressant medication is in sharp contrast to the effects of antipsychotic medications, which apparently only suppress schizophrenic symptoms. This statement, however, must be tempered with the observation that individuals suffering from severe depression, unlike people with schizophrenia, often respond to any treatment or even no treatment at all.

Over the past ten years, a great deal of research has been undertaken to determine how drugs operate to alleviate depression (McNeal & Cimbolic, 1986), and which treatment or combination of treatments is appropriate for patients who are depressed (Hollon & Beck, 1986). To date, however, little progress has been made in identifying patient characteristics or other clinical factors that relate to success by a given treatment method. In one nationwide study on psychological and pharmacological treatment for depression, Keller et al. (1986) found that there were no consistent patient characteristics related to whether a person received psychotherapy or medications for depression.

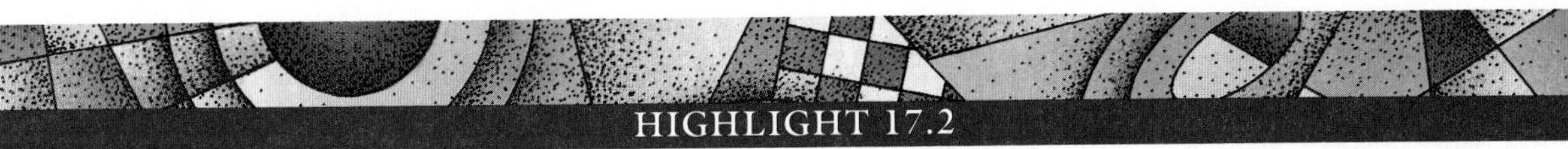

HIGHLIGHT 17.2

Chemically Induced Sleep: Is It Worth the Risks?

Prescriptions for the benzodiazepine class of antianxiety drugs currently exceed 70 million per year in the United States. Of these, a huge proportion are written for the ostensible purpose of enabling people to sleep better at night. The most common benzodiazepine prescribed specifically for this purpose is flurazepam (Dalmane). Some 8 million individuals use this general class of drug sometime during any one year, and up to 2 million people take these pills nightly for more than two months at a time. It is prescribed for many patients hospitalized for physical disease.

Reacting to this overuse, the Institute of Medicine (IOM) of the National Academy of Sciences issued a report outlining the hazards of this remedy for sleeping difficulties—difficulties that in any case they found to be severely overestimated on a routine basis by the people allegedly suffering from them. Noting that the barbiturates justly deserve their reputation as dangerous drugs, the IOM report indicated that the benzodiazepines may be just as risky, and in some cases more so. For example, flurazepam, while not quite as addicting as the barbiturates, remains in the body in the form of metabolites far longer than do the barbiturates, resulting in a buildup of toxic substances in the body that may reach a critical level within a week of regular ingestion. Although flurazepam overdose is usually not in itself lethal, it may interact with other drugs, such as alcohol, to produce lethal effects. Because of these readily misunderstood characteristics, the IOM concluded that, overall, flurazepam does not diminish the number of deaths attributable to sleeping pill medication, relative to earlier types of "hypnotic" drugs, such as the barbiturates.

A particularly worrisome aspect of this problem is the fact that a certain amount of benign "insomnia" naturally accompanies advancing age. Nevertheless, elderly people receive some 39 percent of all sleeping pill prescriptions. For these individuals there is a real danger that the side effects of these drugs, such as daytime lethargy and clouding of consciousness, may be considered indicators of senile deterioration by family members and even by professional caretakers.

Considering the risks involved in taking these drugs, it seems appropriate to keep in mind an observation of one of the IOM members: losing some sleep now and then is *not* a life-threatening problem (Smith, 1979).

Overall, the use of antidepressant medication in the treatment of depressive episodes has shown considerable short-term effectiveness in spite of our lack of specific understanding of how it works and with what type of patient particular treatments are best suited.

Antianxiety Drugs If it is true, as some have observed, that ours is the age of anxiety, it is certainly no less true that ours is also the age of the search for anxiety reducers. At the present time, literally millions of physician-prescribed pills alleged to contain anxiety- and tension-relieving substances are consumed daily by the American public. In addition, Americans employ manifold alternative methods to reduce their anxiety—ranging from biofeedback to the practice of ancient Eastern religious rituals—that promise to relieve "uptight" feelings. The nonprescription drug market, which includes alcoholic beverages, marijuana, and decidedly more problematic substances, has had an unprecedented growth rate since the 1960s—much of it presumably due to the same widespread wish to be somehow relieved of hassle.

Besides the *barbiturates* (see Chapter 9), which are seldom used in treatment today because they have high addictive potential and a low margin of dosage safety, two additional classes of prescription **antianxiety drugs** (minor tranquilizers) have gained widespread acceptance in recent years. One of these, the propanediols (mostly meprobamate compounds), seems to operate mainly through the reduction of muscular tension, which in turn is experienced by a patient as calming and emotionally soothing. Meprobamate drugs are marketed under the trade names Miltown and Equanil.

The other class of antianxiety drugs is the *benzodiazepines,* whose use as sleeping pills is discussed in *HIGHLIGHT 17.2.* Up until recently, their use in this country was increasing at an alarming rate; however, thanks to effective public warnings about the addictive potential of these drugs, this trend is now leveling off. Under this rubric are included chlordiazepoxide (Librium), diazepam (Valium), oxazepam (Serax), clorazepate (Tranxene), flurazepam (Dalmane), and alprazolam (Xanax). In experimental studies on animals, the most striking effect of these drugs has been the recurrence of behavior previously inhibited by conditioned fears, without serious impairment in overall behavioral efficiency. Benzodiazepines, in other words, somehow selectively diminish generalized fear (or anxiety) yet leave adaptive behaviors largely intact. They are thus far superior to many other types of anxiety-reducing chemicals, which tend to produce widespread negative effects on adaptive functioning.

Nevertheless, all of the antianxiety drugs have a basically sedative effect on an organism, and many patients treated with them complain of drowsiness and lethargy. This has been a particular problem among schoolchildren treated with these drugs. We must also emphasize that all of these drugs have the potential of inducing dependence when used unwisely or in excess (Bassuk, Schoonover, & Gelenberg, 1983; Levenson, 1981).

Anxiety drugs' range of application is quite broad. They are used in all manner of conditions in which tension and anxiety may be significant components, including anxiety-based and psychophysiologic disorders. They are also used as supplementary treatment in certain neurological disorders to control such symptoms as convulsive seizures, but they have little place in the treatment of the psychoses. They are now the most widely prescribed of all the drugs available to physicians, a fact that has caused concern among some leaders in the medical and psychiatric fields.

Continuing research on benzodiazepines and related compounds is turning up promising leads that will almost certainly result in important future advances in the treatment of anxiety and other conditions. It is now known that the benzodiazepines produce their effects by chemically binding to specific receptors at neuronal synapses, blocking normal transmission; this finding suggests that these receptors are implicated in mediating the experience of anxiety. Additionally, because these compounds also have sedative, muscle relaxant, and anticonvulsive properties, it might be possible to differentiate specific receptors for each, and to discover variant compounds that will selectively bind to them. In fact, researchers at one of the larger pharmaceutical companies have already discovered a chemical that appears to counteract anxiety and convulsions without being a muscle relaxant or sedative. Work in this area has important implications for our basic understanding of brain processes, in addition to its obvious clinical import.

Lithium for the Bipolar Mood Disorders

Lithium is the lightest of the metals. Its simple salts, such as lithium carbonate, were discovered—as early as 1949 by J. Cade in Australia—to be effective in treating manic disorders. Some 20 years passed before this treatment was introduced in the United States. This delay may have been, in part, for two reasons. First, if not used at the proper dosage, lithium can be toxic, causing numerous side effects, such as delirium, convulsions, and even death. At the same time, if lithium is to have any notable therapeutic effect, it must be used in quantities within the range of potential dangerousness, which varies among different individuals. Thus, at the outset of lithium treatment, a patient's blood levels of lithium must be monitored carefully in relation to observable behavioral effects so that the minimum effective dosage can be established. For each individual, there is a relatively narrow range of effectiveness for the drug. Too little of the drug and the therapeutic effect will be negligible; too much of the drug and the effect could be lethal.

A second possible reason for the delay in widespread lithium usage in the United States may have been the simple fact that researchers were skeptical that it was the lithium itself that was producing the beneficial results; the lithium compounds used in treatment are simple inorganic salts that have no known physiological function (Berger, 1978). Lithium, then, is a somewhat peculiar drug.

Its curious qualities notwithstanding, there can be no doubt at this point concerning lithium's remarkable effectiveness in promptly resolving about 70 to 80 percent of clearly defined manic states, particularly cases in which other psychiatric disorders are not also present (Black et al., 1988). In addition, as we saw in Chapter 11, lithium is sometimes successful in relieving depressions, although possibly only in those patients who are subject to both manic and depressive episodes—that is, who are bipolar in type (Bassuk, Schoonover, & Gelenberg, 1983; Berger, 1978; Segal, Yager, & Sullivan, 1976). More recent research, however, suggests that there may be a subclass of unipolar depressive patients who benefit from lithium treatment (Coppen, Metcalfe, & Wood, 1982).

The drug has been a boon, especially to those people who heretofore have experienced repeated bouts with mania, depression, or both throughout their adult lives. For many, these cycles can now be

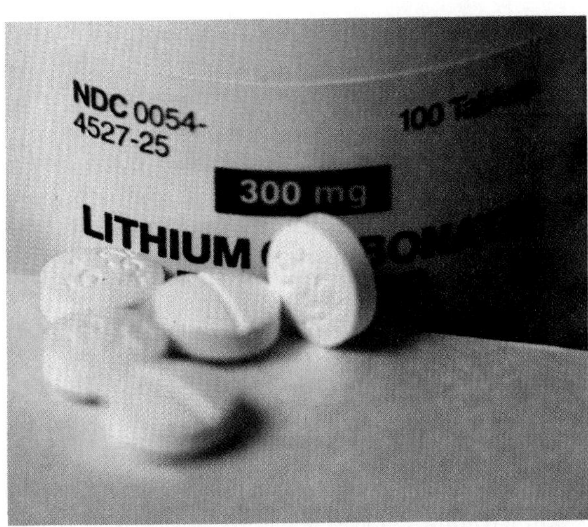

Lithium treatment requires careful monitoring of the dosage—too much can be lethal and too little is ineffective. There is no doubt, however, that the drug has been a boon to those people who have experienced repeated bouts with mania, depression, or both throughout their adult lives.

modulated or even prevented by regular maintenance doses of lithium—for example, by taking a single tablet each morning and evening. Psychiatry may thus have achieved its first essentially preventive treatment method—although, for some patients maintained on the drug for lengthy periods, there may be serious complications, including kidney damage (Bassuk, Schoonover, & Gelenberg, 1983) and memory and motor speed problems (Shaw et al., 1987). There is also some recent evidence that the prevention of further attacks of mania by lithium maintenance treatment may be less reliable than was once thought. In one study, 40 percent of such patients relapsed within 1.7 years following hospital discharge (Harrow et al., 1990).

One of Cade's (1949) own cases will serve well as an illustration of the effects of lithium treatment:

Mr. W. B. was a 51-year-old man who had been in a state of chronic manic excitement for five years. So obnoxious and destructive was his behavior that he had long been regarded as the most difficult patient on his ward in the hospital.

He was started on treatment with a lithium compound, and within three weeks his behavior had improved to the point that transfer to the convalescent ward was deemed appropriate. He remained in the hospital for another two months, during which his behavior continued to be essentially normal. Prior to discharge, he was switched to another form of lithium salts because the one he had been taking had caused stomach upset.

He was soon back at his job and living a happy and productive life. In fact, he felt so well that, contrary to instructions, he stopped taking his lithium. Thereafter he steadily became more irritable and erratic; some six months following his discharge, he had to cease work. In another five weeks he was back at the hospital in an acute manic state.

Lithium therapy was immediately reestablished, with prompt positive results. In another month Mr. W. B. was pronounced ready to return to home and work, provided he would continue taking a prescribed dosage of lithium.

The biochemical basis of lithium's therapeutic effect is unknown. One well-received hypothesis is that it achieves its effect by limiting the availability of norepinephrine and serotonin, which function as neurotransmitters or modulators at certain synapses in the brain. This effect is opposite that of antidepressant drugs and presumably reduces an individual's ability to process the amount of input typical during a manic state. Of course, this still leaves unexplained the fact that lithium can also alleviate some depressions. An alternative hypothesis is that lithium, being a mineral salt, may have an effect on electrolyte balances, which may also alter the properties of neurotransmission within the brain. So far, however, this connection remains largely speculative. Clearly, the riddle of exactly what occurs will be solved only by more and better research.

Recently another drug has been used, with considerable success to treat bipolar disorders. The drug *carbamazepine* (Tegretol), used extensively as an anticonvulsant agent to control grand mal seizures, has been found effective in controlling rapidly cycling mood and reducing aggressivity in bipolar disorders (Ballenger, 1988). Its use has been somewhat disappointing for the treatment of acute mania (Lusznat, Murphy, & Nunn, 1988), which suggests that carbamazepine's usefulness may be more as a prophylactic. Carbamazepine has been associated with significant side effects, especially neurotoxic problems, such as an awkward gait, increased reflexes, and ataxia (Birkhimer, Curtis, & Jann, 1985). As such, careful monitoring of carbamezipine treatment, as with lithium use, is required.

Drug Therapy for Children

Our discussion of the use of drugs in treating maladaptive behavior would be incomplete without some reiteration of their role in the management of childhood disturbances and disorders. We have already addressed this matter to some extent in Chapter 15. Although our society has often been too quick to label as deviant (and thus to "treat") various annoying or inconvenient behaviors in which children sometimes indulge, it is nevertheless true that *some* children do evidence more or less serious behavior disorders. It is also true that some of them may be helped by the judicious use of medication.

Antianxiety, antipsychotic, and antidepressant medications have all been used effectively with children who are, respectively, excessively anxious or "nervous," psychotic, or depressed. Considerable caution must be exercised in the use of these powerful drugs with children, however, to be certain that dosage levels are within tolerable limits for a small and as yet biologically immature organism. Not only are excessive blood levels of these drugs physically dangerous, but in some instances they may produce paradoxical reversal effects—that is, a child's problem may become more severe (Bassuk, Schoonover, & Gelenberg, 1983).

We have already mentioned the apparently widespread problem of excessively tranquilized elementary school pupils. Though the diagnostic terms *hyperactivity, hyperkinesis,* and *specific learning disability* have been used somewhat haphazardly in recent years, there appears to be a subset of highly distractable youngsters of normal but unevenly developed cognitive ability who benefit dramatically, and paradoxically, from drugs that stimulate the central nervous system. As we saw in Chapter 15, the most widely used of these stimulants are the amphetamines; a closely related compound known as methylphenidate (Ritalin) is also used. Recently, Whalen et al. (1989) found that hyperactive children treated with Ritalin were viewed more positively by other children. In certain instances, these drugs promptly terminate hyperactivity, which typically results in an increased attention span and an ability to do schoolwork (Sprague, Barnes, & Werry, 1970; Weiss & Hechtman, 1979; Wender, Reimherr, & Wood, 1981). Normally, a child thus helped is kept on the drug until he or she reaches adolescence, when hyperactivity tends to diminish by an as yet unknown natural process (Bassuk, Schoonover, & Gelenberg, 1983).

The danger, of course, is that restless, overactive children will be summarily diagnosed as "hyperkinetic" or "hyperactive" and treated with drugs *whether or not the problem is essentially a physical one.* If such is the case, the option to use less extreme but potentially effective psychological approaches in treating these children may be forgotten (see Chapter 15).

A Biopsychosocial Perspective on Pharmacological Therapy

Modern psychopharmacology has brought a reduction in the severity and chronicity of many types of psychopathology, particularly the psychoses. It has helped many individuals who would otherwise require hospitalization to function in their family and community settings; it has led to the earlier discharge of those who do require hospitalization and to the greater effectiveness of aftercare programs; and it has made restraints and locked wards largely obsolete. All in all, pharmacological therapy not only has outmoded more drastic forms of treatment but has led to a much more favorable hospital climate for patients and staff alike (see *HIGHLIGHT 17.3* for a summary of the drugs used in psychopharmacological therapy).

Nevertheless, a number of complications and limitations arise in the use of psychotropic drugs. Aside from possible undesirable side effects, the problem of matching drug and dosage to the needs of a given individual is often a difficult one, and it is sometimes necessary to change medication in the course of treatment. In addition, the use of medications in isolation from other treatment methods is usually inappropriate and ineffective because drugs themselves do not cure disorders. As many investigators have pointed out, drugs tend to alleviate symptoms by inducing biochemical changes rather than bring an individual to grips with personal or situational factors that may be reinforcing maladaptive behaviors. Although the reduction in anxiety, disturbed thinking, and other symptoms may tempt therapists to regard a patient as "recovered," it seems important to include psychotherapy in the total program if such gains are to be maintained or improved on.

On the other hand, the failure to incorporate medication into a psychotherapeutic treatment program can lead to serious problems. A recent court case, *Osherhoff* v. *Chestnut Lodge,* raised a number of issues concerning the importance of clinical diagnosis, the effectiveness of medication, and appropriate treatment intervention (Klerman, 1990). Osherhoff, a physician, was severely depressed and functioning so ineffectively that his family hospitalized him at Chestnut Lodge, an exclusively psychoanalytic treatment facility. He was treated with intensive psychoanalytic treatment, without medication, four times a week. After several months, his family became concerned over his lack of progress; he had lost 40 pounds, was experiencing severe sleep disturbance, had marked psychomotor agitation to the point that his pacing caused his feet to become swollen and blistered. The family sought a reevaluation of his case. The staff, in a case conference, decided to continue the treatment program that had been initiated. Dr. Osherhoff's condition worsened and his family had him discharged and admitted into another facility where he was treated with a combination of phenothiazines and tricyclic antidepressants. He improved markedly and was discharged in three months. Later he filed a suit claiming that Chestnut Lodge had not administered the proper treatment—drug therapy—which had caused him to lose a year of employment in his medical practice. Preliminary court arbitration indicated an initial award of damages to Dr. Osherhoff; however, the case was settled out of court before a final judgment was rendered. A number of complicated issues were involved in the case, but the finding that therapists may be liable for failing to provide medication to patients is an important and potentially disruptive new development in the field.

Thus the combination of chemical and psychological forms of therapy is fast becoming the major thrust of current research and treatment for severe psychopathology (Kahn, 1990). This integrative approach involves the use of psychotropic medication and psychosocial approaches, such as behavior therapy or psychoanalysis (Carpenter & Keith, 1986). It has been shown to be valuable with both adults (Liberman & Evans, 1985; Rosen, 1986) and children (Sprague & Brown, 1981). The combined therapeutic approach appears to be especially useful with treatment-resistant disorders in which major mental disorders and persistent personality disorders are involved. Marcus and Bradley (1990), for example, found this approach to be effective in about two-thirds of such treatment-resistant cases. The most effective uses of drugs in the treatment of psychological disorders involve drug administrations that are embedded in the context of other treatment approaches; for example, the use of antidepressant medication along with cognitive-behavioral treatment for depression (Hollon & Beck, 1986). Overall, there is much reason to be optimistic about the combined use of drugs and psychosocial approaches, especially in the more severe disorders, such as schizophrenia (Smith, Glass, & Miller, 1980), and the major mood disorders (Beckham & Leber, 1985a; Klerman & Schechter, 1982).

UNRESOLVED ISSUES on Drug Treatment and Psychiatry's Future

For about a quarter-century following World War II, the medical specialty of psychiatry—its leadership, its professional and research literature, and its residency training programs—was dominated by Freudian and other related psychodynamic viewpoints. (Alternative psychosocial approaches were still largely undiscovered at the time.) The rejection of all things "organic," "biological," and (narrowly) "medical," although not universal in the discipline, was widespread. In some centers, even the emergence of the new psychotropic drugs was greeted with decided ambivalence, sometimes with contempt and scorn, and occasionally with assertions that they were useless or worse. This was an extreme position, so much so that it contained the seeds of its own demise.

The professional tables began to turn as increasingly sophisticated research demonstrated old-line psychodynamic treatment approaches to be relatively ineffective and the newer drug treatments to have considerable, sometimes even astonishing, benefits. Concurrently, some newer psychosocial approaches, notably the behaviorally based therapies, began also to show extraordinary promise. For the most part, however, these latter therapies were developed outside of the purview of psychiatry—chiefly within the increasingly surgent discipline of clinical psychology. Few psychiatrists had the background training necessary for understanding or contributing to the development of these newer and noninvasive psychosocial approaches. The parallel but unfortunately insular developments of these two trends—drug treatment (in psychiatry) on the one hand and newer psychosocial treatments (in psychology) on the other—made interdisciplinary conflict and competition almost inevitable.

We do not intend to suggest that this competition was the only source of the "remedicalization"

HIGHLIGHT 17.3

Frequently Used Drugs in the Treatment of Mental and Behavioral Disorders

Class	Generic Name	Trade Name	Used to Treat	Effects
Antipsychotic				
(a) phenothiazines	chlorpromazine thioridazine promazine trifluoperazine prochlorperazine perphenazine fluphenazine triflupromazine	Thorazine Mellaril Sparine Stelazine Compazine Trilafon Prolixin Temaril	Psychotic (especially schizophrenia) symptoms, such as extreme agitation, delusions, and hallucinations; aggressive or violent behavior	Somewhat variable in achieving intended purpose of suppression of psychotic symptoms. Side effects, such as dry mouth, are often uncomfortable. In long-term use may produce motor disturbances, such as Parkinsonism and tardive dyskinesia.
(b) butyrophenone	haloperidol	Haldol		
(c) thioxanthenes	thiothixine chlorprothixene	Navane Taractan		
(d) dibenzodiazepine	clozapine	Clozaril		
Antidepressant				
(a) tricyclics	imipramine amitriptyline nortriptyline protriptyline doxepin trimipramine maleate	Tofranil Elavil Aventyl Vivactil Sinequan Surmontil	Relatively severe depressive symptoms, especially of psychotic severity and unipolar in type	Somewhat variable in alleviating depressive symptoms, and noticeable effects may be delayed up to three weeks. Multiple side effects—some of them dangerous. Use of MAO inhibitors requires dietary restrictions.
(b) monoamine oxidase (MAO) inhibitors	isocarboxazid phenelzine tranylcypromine	Marplan Nardil Parnate		
(c) norepinephrine/ serotonin reuptake inhibitor	fluoxetine	Prozac	Depressive symptoms	Fluoxetine is effective in reducing depressive symptoms. Effects take about 3 weeks. Safety is considered high; overdose unlikely. Side effect profile is favorable, though some nausea, insomnia, and even suicidal tendencies have been reported.
Antimanic (biopolar)	lithium carbonate	Eskalith Lithane Lithonate Lithotabs Phi-Lithium	Manic episodes and some severe depressions, particularly recurrent ones or those alternating with mania	Usually effective in resolving manic episodes, but highly variable in effects on depression, probably because the latter is a less homogeneous

Class	Generic Name	Trade Name	Used to Treat	Effects
				grouping. Multiple side effects unless carefully monitored; high toxicity potential.
	carbamazepine	Tegretol	Manic episodes	Highly effective in treating bipolar disorders (especially acute mania); treatment of depression is less effective. Neurotoxic side effects have been noted, including unsteady gait, tremor, ataxia, and increased restlessness.
Antianxiety (minor tranquilizers) (a) propanediols (b) benzodiazepines	meprobamate diazepam chlordiazepoxide flurazepam oxazepam clorazepate alprazolam prazepam	Equanil Miltown Valium Librium Dalmane Serax Tranxene Xanax Centrax	Nonpsychotic personality problems in which anxiety and tension are prominent features; also used as anticonvulsants and as sleep-inducers (especially flurazepam)	Somewhat variable in achieving intended purpose of tension reduction. Side effects include drowsiness and lethargy. Dependence and toxicity are dangers.
Stimulant	dextroamphetamine amphetamine methylphenidate	Dexedrine Benzedrine Ritalin	Hyperactivity, distractability, specific learning disabilities, and, occasionally, extreme hypoactivity	Rather unpredictable. When maximally effective, can enable otherwise uneducable children to attend regular schools. Side effects often troublesome, including recently discovered retardation of growth.

Based on data from Goodman, et al. (1985); Tacke (1989).

of psychiatry in recent years. Many other pressures —the political and economic climates, the disappointing levels of new trainees for psychiatry, and so on—were building on the discipline during the period under consideration (roughly the early 1970s to present), prompting one distinguished psychiatrist, early on, to refer to "the death of psychiatry" (Torrey, 1974). This concern has been echoed more recently by many others (e.g., Dietz, 1977; Lehmann, 1986; Talbott, 1985b).

The upshot was to cause psychiatry as both a profession and a scientific discipline to veer even more sharply toward what has been called the "neo-Kraepelinian" revolution (Andreasen, 1984), whose fundamental tenet is the reductionistic one that most of the more significant disorders of behavior we see are in fact disorders (organic diseases) of the brain. Many leading psychiatrists see most behavior disorders, in other words, as *medical* conditions requiring *medical* treatments, by (of course) *medical* doctors. This trend excludes nonmedical practitioners, who in the interim have become numerous and politically powerful in their own right. The downside of this position, for psychiatry, is the fact that nonpsychiatric physicians can and do provide a great deal of such treatment themselves, which is yet another source of anxiety about the profession's survival. If any medical doctor can prescribe psychoactive drugs, and if psychiatrists know little about psychosocial treatment, what is the essential function of psychiatry?

It is unfortunate that this sort of "turf" warfare has driven a deep wedge between the biological and psychosocial camps. We also regret what has clearly become an excessive reliance on drugs in attempts to solve human problems. At least equally distressing, however, is the deleterious effect these tactics have had on the rational search for improved treatment programs. We refer here to the large-scale campaign seemingly led by the biological forces in psychiatry (in conjunction with pharmaceutical companies) to convince the public that biological treatment, chiefly drugs, is exclusively the treatment of choice for nearly the entire realm of abnormal behavior. No objective reading of the evidence, of which there is a great deal (much of it reported in this text), supports such a conclusion. The inevitable long-range consequence, in our judgment, will be a failure of psychiatry, once again, to deliver on its promissory note of a better life for all, this time through chemistry.

When the pendulum once again swings back (which it undoubtedly will) toward a general recognition of the importance of psychosocial and sociocultural factors in the management and treatment of mental disorders, including the most severe ones, we hope that it will not again overcorrect and encourage neglect of the biological route of intervention. We also hope that psychiatry will survive its period of peril; we will need good, solidly trained psychiatrists to bridge the biopsychosocial gap and to make discriminating use of drug therapy in the more limited arena in which we expect it will have a vital role.

SUMMARY

Except for the development of electroconvulsive therapy (ECT) beginning in 1938, the biological approach to the treatment of mental disorders, at least on this continent and in Europe, had made little headway until about 1955. Indeed, some of the early biological treatments, such as insulin coma therapy and lobotomy, probably did more harm than good, as did many early medical treatments for purely physical diseases.

The mode of therapeutic action of ECT, which continues to be widely used, is not yet understood. There is little doubt, however, of its efficacy for certain patients, especially those suffering from severe depression. Appropriate premedication together with other modifications in technique (for example, unilateral placement of electrodes) have made this treatment relatively safe and, for the most part, have checked the serious or long-term side effects. Nevertheless, controversy about this method of treatment persists, and there is evidence that it can produce permanent brain damage. Obviously, ECT should be used with caution and circumspection, and preferably only after less dramatic methods have been tried and have failed.

The antipsychotic compound chlorpromazine (Thorazine) became widely available in the mid-1950s. It was followed shortly by numerous other related (that is, phenothiazine class) and nonrelated antipsychotic drugs of proven effectiveness in diminishing psychotic (especially schizophrenic) symptoms. Thus was initiated a true revolution in the treatment of severe mental disorders—one that, among other things, permanently altered the environment and the function of mental hospitals. Within a short period, too, the antidepressant medications became available to help patients with severe depressions, making it possible in many instances to avoid the use of ECT. Finally, in the late 1960s (after an unaccountable delay in its introduction in this country), the antimanic drug lithium was recognized as having major therapeutic significance. With the availability of these three types of drugs, the major psychoses—for the first time in history—now came to be seen as generally and effectively treatable.

Meanwhile, antianxiety drugs (mild tranquilizers) had been developed that circumvented many of the problems of the barbiturates used earlier in combating excessive tension and anxiety. This development extended the benefit of effective drug treatment to many people who were struggling with neurotic problems or with high-stress life circumstances. The meprobamates (for example, Equanil) were the first of these new antianxiety drugs but were largely superseded by the more potent benzodiazepines (such as Valium) for general use.

New biological treatments for mental disorders will doubtless continue to be proposed, but, as in the case of psychosurgery, many will prove undeserving of a high degree of confidence. A measure of caution is recommended concerning claims made by the proponents of newly introduced therapies.

Finally, the admittedly impressive gains in biological treatment methods may cause us to lose sight of important psychological processes that may be intrinsic to any mental disorder. In fact, some evidence shows that combinations of biologically and psychologically based approaches may be more successful than either alone, at least with some of the more severe disorders.

Key Terms

insulin coma therapy (p. 606)
electroconvulsive therapy (ECT) (p. 607)
psychosurgery (p. 610)
prefrontal lobotomy (p. 610)
pharmacology (p. 612)
antipsychotic drugs (p. 613)
tardive dyskinesia (p. 614)
antidepressant drugs (p. 616)
antianxiety drugs (p. 617)

Chapter 18

Psychologically Based Therapies

Adolf Wölfli, *Saint Adolf Portant des Lunettes, Entre les Deux Villes Geantes Niess et Mia.* Wölfli (1864–1930), born in Bern, Switzerland, was abandoned by his father in early childhood and at the age of 8 was removed from the care of his mother—occurrences that marked the beginning of violent, erratic behaviors that finally culminated in schizophrenic breakdown. In his paintings, Wölfli typically returns to an idealized childhood, in which as "Saint Adolf," a child divinity, he journeys through the universe, often accompanied by assorted gods and goddesses.

Most of us have experienced a time or situation when we were dramatically helped by "talking things over" with a relative or friend. Or perhaps we made a drastic change in our life-style after a particular event led to new understanding. As the noted psychoanalyst Franz Alexander (1946) pointed out long ago, formal psychotherapy as practiced by a mental health professional shares many aspects in common with this type of familiar experience. Most therapists, like all good listeners, rely on a common repertoire of receptiveness, warmth, empathy, and a nonjudgmental approach to the problems their clients present. Most, however, also introduce into the relationship certain psychological interventions that are designed to promote new understandings, behaviors, or both on the client's part. The fact that these interventions are deliberately planned and guided by certain theoretical preconceptions (of the kind discussed in Chapter 3) is what distinguishes professional **psychotherapy,** the treatment of mental disorders by psychological methods, from more informal helping relationships. As we will see, it is the varying nature of these theoretical preconceptions that largely distinguishes a given type of psychotherapy from the others available.

Psychotherapy is based on the assumption that, even in cases where physical pathology is present, an individual's perceptions, evaluations, expectations, and coping strategies also play a role in the development of the disorder and will probably need to be changed if maximum benefit is to be realized. The belief that individuals with psychological problems can change—can learn more adaptive ways of perceiving, evaluating, and behaving—is the conviction underlying all psychotherapy. The goal of psychotherapy, then, is to make this belief a reality.

To achieve this goal, a psychotherapist may attempt to (a) change maladaptive behavior patterns; (b) minimize or eliminate environmental conditions that may be causing or maintaining such behavior; (c) improve interpersonal and other competencies; (d) resolve handicapping or disabling conflicts among motives; (e) modify individuals' cognitions, their dysfunctional beliefs about themselves and their world; (f) reduce or remove discomforting or disabling emotional reactions; and (g) foster a clear-cut sense of self-identity. All these strategies can open pathways to a more meaningful and fulfilling existence.

Achieving these changes is by no means easy. Sometimes an individual's distorted view of the world and unhealthy self-concept are the end products of faulty parent-child relationships reinforced by many years of life experiences. In other instances, inadequate occupational, marital, or social adjustment requires major changes in a person's life situation, in addition to psychotherapy. Magnifying such difficulties is the fact that it is often easier to hold to one's present problematic but familiar course than to risk change and the unpredictability it entails. It would be too much to expect that a psychotherapist, even a highly skilled and experienced one, could in a short time undo an individual's entire past history and prepare him or her to cope with a difficult life situation in a fully adequate manner. Psychotherapists can offer no magical transformations of either selfhood or the realities in which people live their lives. Nevertheless, a well-formulated and -executed plan of psychotherapy holds promise in even the most severe of the mental disorders, and indeed for certain of them may provide the only realistic hope for significant and lasting change.

It has been estimated that several hundred "therapeutic approaches" exist, ranging from psychoanalysis to Zen meditation. Indeed, the last few decades have witnessed a stream of "new therapies" —each winning avid proponents and followers for a time. The faddism in the popular literature on self-change might give the casual reader the idea that the entire field of psychotherapy is in constant flux. In reality, the professional field of psychotherapy has shown both considerable stability over time and coherence around a few basic orientations, albeit ones that vary appreciably in the "visions" they embody of the world and of human nature (Andrews, 1989a). This chapter will explore the most widely used and accepted of these formal psychological treatment approaches.

AN OVERVIEW OF PSYCHOLOGICAL TREATMENT

Before we turn our attention to the specific psychological intervention techniques, we will attempt to gain perspective by considering more closely the individuals involved in therapy and their relationship.

Who Receives Psychotherapy?

People who receive psychotherapy vary widely in their problems and their motivations to solve them. Perhaps the most obvious candidates for psychological treatment are individuals experiencing sudden and highly stressful situations, people who feel so overwhelmed by the crisis conditions in which they find themselves that they cannot manage on their own. These individuals typically feel quite vulnerable and tend to be open to psychological treatment because they are motivated to alter their present intolerable mental states. They often respond well to short-term, directive, crisis-oriented treatment (to be discussed in Chapter 19). In such situations, clients may gain considerably, in a brief time, from the outside perspective provided by their therapist.

Some individuals enter psychological therapy somewhat as a surprise to themselves. Perhaps they had consulted a physician for their headache or stomach pain, only to be told that there was nothing physically wrong with them. Such individuals, referred to a therapist, may at first resist the idea that their physical symptoms are emotionally based, especially if the referring physician has been brusque or unclear as to the rationale for his or her judgment. The resistant attitudes often encountered following this type of referral underscore the fact that motivation to enter treatment differs widely among psychotherapy clients. Reluctant clients may come from many sources—for example, an alcoholic whose spouse threatens "either therapy or divorce," or a suspected felon whose attorney advises that things will go better at trial if it can be announced that the suspect has "entered therapy." A substantial number of angry parents bring their children to therapists with demands that their "uncontrollable" behavior, viewed as independent of the family context, be "fixed."

Many people entering therapy have experienced long-term psychological distress and have had lengthy histories of maladjustment. They may have been experiencing interpersonal problems for some time or may have felt susceptible to low moods that are difficult for them to dispel. Chronic unhappiness and inability to feel confident and secure may finally prompt them to seek outside help. These individuals seek psychological assistance out of dissatisfaction and despair. They may enter treatment with a high degree of motivation but, as therapy proceeds, their persistent patterns of maladaptive behavior may become resistant forces with which a therapist must contend. For example, a narcissistic client who anticipates therapist praise and admiration may become disenchanted and hostile when these are not forthcoming.

A number of people who enter therapy have problems that would be considered relatively normal. That is, they appear to have achieved success, have financial stability, have generally accepting and loving families, and have accomplished many of their life goals. They enter therapy not out of personal despair or impossible interpersonal involvements, but out of a sense that they have not lived up to their own expectations and realized their own potential. These individuals, partly because their problems are more manageable than the problems of others, may make substantial gains in personal growth. Much of these therapeutic gains can be attributed to their high degree of motivation and personal resources. Individuals who seem to have the best prognosis for personality change, according to repeated research outcomes, have been described in terms of the so-called YAVIS pattern (Schofield, 1964)—they are Young, Attractive, Verbal, Intelligent, and Successful. Ironically, those who tend to do best in psychotherapy are those who seem objectively to need it least.

Psychotherapy, however, is not just for individuals who have clearly defined problems, high levels of motivation, and an ability to gain ready insight into their behavior. Psychotherapeutic interventions have been applied to a wide variety of chronic problems. Even a severely disturbed psychotic client may profit from a therapeutic relationship that takes into account his or her level of functioning and maintains therapeutic subgoals that are within the client's present capabilities. Contrary to common understanding (and to frequently biased media reports), the success record for psychological treatment in major psychoses, such as schizophrenia, is very respectable (Carson & Sanislow, 1992).

It should be clear from this brief description of individuals in psychological therapy that there is indeed no "typical" client, nor, as we will see, is there a "model" therapy. No currently extant form of therapy is applicable to all types of clients, and it appears that all of the standard therapies can document success with some types of individuals. Most authorities agree that client variables, such as the extent of the problem and client motivation, are exceedingly important to the outcome of therapy (Bergin & Lambert, 1978; Garfield, 1986; Rounsaville, Weissman, & Prusoff, 1981). As we will see, the various therapies have relatively greater success when a therapist takes the characteristics of a particular client into account in determining the treatment of choice.

In psychological therapy, there is no "typical" client, nor is there a "model" therapy. Client variables, such as the extent of the problem and client motivation, are important to the outcome of therapy, and the therapist who takes these factors into account in determining treatment will likely have greater success.

Who Provides Psychotherapeutic Services?

Members of many different professions have traditionally provided advice and counsel to individuals in emotional distress. Physicians have, in addition to their role of providing care for their clients' physical problems, often become trusted advisers in emotional matters as well. In past eras, before the advent of large health maintenance organizations and highly differentiated medical specialists, the family physicians was called on for virtually all health questions. Even today, the medical practitioner—although he or she may have little psychological background and limited time to spend with individual clients—may be asked to give consultation in psychological matters. Most physicians are trained to recognize psychological problems that are beyond their expertise and to refer individuals to psychological specialists.

Another professional group that deals extensively with people's emotional problems is the clergy. Members of the clergy are usually in intimate contact with the emotional needs and problems of their congregations. A minister, priest, or rabbi may be the first professional to encounter an individual experiencing emotional crisis. Some clergy actively acquire counseling training and supervised experience in dealing with psychological problems and go on to obtain mental health professional credentials, including pastoral counseling degrees.

HIGHLIGHT 18.1

Personnel in Psychotherapy

Professional

Clinical psychologist. Ph.D. in psychology with both research and clinical skill specialization. One-year internship in a psychiatric hospital or mental health center. *Or,* Psy.D. in psychology (a professional degree with more clinical than research specialization) plus one-year internship in a psychiatric hospital or mental health center.

Counseling psychologist. Ph.D. in psychology plus internship in a marital- or student-counseling setting; normally, a counseling psychologist deals with adjustment problems not involving mental disorder.

School psychologist. Ideally a person having doctoral training in child-clinical psychology, with additional training and experience in academic and learning problems. At present, many school systems lack the resources to maintain an adequate school psychology program.

Psychiatrist. M.D. degree with residency training (usually three years) in a psychiatric hospital or mental health facility.

Psychoanalyst. M.D. or Ph.D. degree plus intensive training in the theory and practice of psychoanalysis.

Psychiatric social worker. B.A., M.S.W., or Ph.D. degree with specialized clinical training in mental health settings.

Psychiatric nurse. R.N. degree plus specialized training in the care and treatment of psychiatric clients. Nurses can attain M.A. and Ph.D. degrees in psychiatric nursing.

Occupational therapist. B.S. in occupational therapy plus internship training with physically or psychologically handicapped individuals, helping them make the most of their resources.

Pastoral counselor. Ministerial background plus training in psychology. Internship in mental health facility as a chaplain.

Paraprofessional

Community mental health worker. Capable person with limited professional training who works under professional direction (especially crisis intervention).

Alcohol- or drug-abuse counselor. Limited professional training but trained in the evaluation and management of alcohol- and drug-addicted people.

In both mental health clinics and hospitals, personnel from several fields may function as an interdisciplinary team—for example, a psychiatrist, a clinical psychologist, a social worker, a psychiatric nurse, and an occupational therapist may work together.

Most limit their counseling to religious matters and spiritual support and do not attempt to provide psychotherapy. Rather, they are trained to recognize problems that require professional management and refer troubled individuals to mental health specialists.

Beyond physicians and clergy, the professionals of primary interest to us in this context are those formally trained to identify and treat mental disorders. The three types of mental health professionals found most often in mental health settings are clinical psychologists, psychiatrists, and psychiatric social workers (see *HIGHLIGHT 18.1*). The **clinical psychologist** typically has training at the undergraduate level in psychology and has a Ph.D. or Psy.D. degree in clinical psychology, with specialization in personality theory, abnormal psychology, psychological assessment, and psychotherapy. Most clinical psychologists receive broad clinical experience in assessment and psychotherapy in addition to their mental health research training. The **psychiatrist** is an M.D. who has had further training—minimally a three-year residency—in dealing with clients in a mental health setting. The medical training of psychiatrists qualifies them for administering somatic therapies, such as electroconvulsive therapy and psychotropic medication. In addition, during residency, psychiatric residents receive supervision in psychotherapy. **Psychiatric social workers** are usually trained in social science at the bachelor's level and may hold an M.A. or Ph.D. from a school of social work. Their graduate training usually involves courses in family evaluation, psychotherapy, and supervised field experiences.

In any given therapy program, a wide range of medical, psychological, and social work procedures may be used. Such procedures range from the use of drugs to individual or group psychotherapy and to home, school, or job visits aimed at modifying adverse conditions in a client's life. Often the latter—as in helping a teacher become more understanding and supportive of a child client's needs—is as important as treatment directed toward modifying the client's personality makeup, behavior, or both.

This willingness to use a variety of procedures is reflected in the frequent use of a *team approach* to assessment and treatment, particularly in institutional settings. This approach involves the coordinated efforts of medical, psychological, social work, and other mental health personnel working together as the needs of each case warrant. Also of key importance is the current practice of providing treatment facilities in the community. Instead of considering maladjustment as an individual's private misery, which in the past often required confinement in a distant mental hospital, this approach integrates family and community resources in the treatment.

The Therapeutic Relationship

The therapeutic relationship is formed out of what both a careseeker and a caregiver bring to the therapeutic situation. The client's major contribution is his or her motivation. The humanistic tenet—that all humans are at base far more like each other than different and possess an inner drive toward mental and physical health—makes effective psychotherapy possible. Just as physical medicine, properly used, essentially frees and cooperates with the body's own healing mechanisms, an important ally for a psychotherapist is an individual's own drive toward wholeness and toward the development of unrealized potentialities. Although this inner drive is often obscured in severely disturbed clients, the majority of anxious and confused people are sufficiently discouraged with their situation to be eager to cooperate in any program that holds hope for improvement.

Motivation to change is probably the most crucial element in determining the success or failure of psychotherapy, and a wise therapist is, of course, appropriately cautious about accepting therapeutic responsibility where client motivation may be suspect. Not all prospective clients, regardless of an objective need for treatment, are ready at the time of referral to undertake seriously the often uncomfortable experiences that effective therapy entails. Even the motivation of self-referred clients may dissipate in the face of the painful confrontations good therapy may require.

Almost as important is a client's *expectation* of receiving help. This expectancy is often sufficient in itself to bring about some improvement (Frank, 1978). Just as a placebo pill often lessens pain for an individual who believes it will do so, an individual who expects to be helped by psychotherapy is likely to be helped, almost regardless of the particular methods used by a therapist. The downside of this fact is that a therapist who appears inept, bumbling, or unconfident may compromise potential benefits even where the treatment plan is entirely appropriate for the presenting problem. Those in the helping professions are usually the first to admit that their "art" is inexact and dependent on what a client and therapist bring to the experience of treatment.

To the art of therapy, a therapist brings a variety of professional skills and methods intended to help individuals see themselves and their situations more objectively—that is, to gain a different perspective. Insight and new perspective, however, are only a start and not usually enough alone to bring about the necessary changes in behavior. Besides helping an individual toward a new perspective, most therapy situations also provide a protected setting in which he or she is helped to practice new ways of feeling and acting, gradually developing both the courage and the ability to take responsibility for acting in more effective and satisfying ways.

To bring about such changes, an effective psychotherapist must interact with a client in a such a manner as to discourage old and dysfunctional behavior patterns and induce new and more functional ones in their place. Because differing clients will present varying challenges in this regard, the therapist must be sufficiently flexible to deploy a variety of interactive styles. For example, a therapist who inadvertently but unfailingly takes charge in finding solutions for clients' problems will have considerable difficulty in working with people presenting serious difficulties in the area of inhibited autonomy, as in dependent personality disorder. To at least some extent, effective therapy depends on a good match between client and therapist (Talley, Strupp, & Morey, 1990). Hence, a therapist's own personality is necessarily a factor of some importance in determining therapeutic outcomes, quite aside from his or her background and training or the particular formal treatment plan adopted (Lambert, 1989).

Despite general agreement among psychotherapists on these aspects of the client-therapist relationship, professionals can and do differ in their diagnoses and treatments of psychological disorders. This statement should not be too surprising, of course.

Even in the treatment of physical disorders, we sometimes find that physicians disagree. In psychopathology, such disagreements are even more often the case. The differing viewpoints on human motivation and behavior outlined in Chapter 3 lead, as might be expected, to quite different diagnoses of what "the problem" is and how an individual should be helped to overcome it. The next section provides a brief perspective on the several types of therapy available and on how they are able to coexist and complement one another, despite their evident differences.

A Perspective on Therapeutic Pluralism

Gaining an overall mastery of the sometimes bewildering array of available therapeutic techniques is difficult at best. One way to do so is to reduce the domain to four general types or classes of therapy interventions according to the principal client subsystem targeted for therapeutic attention: affect, behavior, cognition, or environment (ABCE). The ABCE framework (a graphic of which is in *HIGHLIGHT 18.2*) is our own attempt to summarize this complex domain; we hope it will be of value to you by providing a convenient orienting framework.

According to this scheme, biological therapies, reviewed in the preceding chapter, would mainly be considered Type A therapies because they are by and large directed toward altering a client's affects, or emotions, including anxiety. Operant conditioning therapies, on the other hand, would practically always be of Type B because of their focus on bringing about direct changes in maladaptive behavior through the manipulation of reinforcement contingencies.

As we will see, and indeed as might be anticipated, not all therapies fit neatly into one or another of the types; usually, however, a *dominant* therapeutic target is discernible that makes such classification feasible, although not necessarily exhaustive in terms of subsidiary therapeutic strategies used. Of course, such a classification scheme becomes irrelevant for truly comprehensive programs of therapy, such as the so-called multimodal, but these seem (unfortunately, we think) still the exception rather than the rule in clinical practice. Although most therapists describe themselves as "eclectic" in orientation, most in fact strongly favor particular approaches, and some (e.g., Patterson, 1989) doubt even the possibility of "integration." We will point out in the following sections what seem to be the dominant type memberships (either A, B, C, or E) of the several types of psychotherapy to be described.

Before proceeding, one other aspect of *HIGHLIGHT 18.2* deserves mention—namely, its form as a *continuous loop* having neither beginning nor end. We think this form reflects the reality of the relationships among (a) the client, conceived as a system of integrated cognitions and affects; (b) his or her abnormal behavioral output, assumed to be a product of (a); and (c) the reactions of the individual's environment and surroundings to that output, in turn "feeding back" to the person's cognition and affect system some information that, in the typical instance, tends to confirm the "contents" of the system. This aspect of our model is neither idiosyncratic nor new, and explicit developments of certain of its facets now commonly appear in contemporary professional literature (e.g., Andrews, 1989b; Safran, 1990a, 1990b).

The model has two important and related implications for therapy. First, the question of *causal primacy,* of how it (the abnormal behavior) all got started, is not in this context especially relevant; once in operation, the loop, theoretically, is self-sustaining. Second, it should be possible to effect a positive overall outcome by fostering adaptive change in *any* pertinent component of the loop, whether cognitions, affects, overt behaviors, or even the reacting environment. That is, effective therapy, reduced to its most basic operations, consists of interrupting this pathology-sustaining loop. In our view then, most competing types of therapy can realistically claim their share of successes (Smith, Glass, & Miller, 1980) *precisely because* they normally induce adaptive change in one or another of these critical system components, thereby (perhaps in a sense unwittingly) positively affecting the whole (see, for example, Stiles et al., 1986).

Maintaining this overview as a backdrop, we now will consider several forms of psychotherapy that have evolved over the century since Sigmund Freud's first such effort. In fact, we will begin with that tradition.

PSYCHODYNAMIC THERAPY

Psychodynamic therapy is a psychological treatment approach that focuses on individual personality dynamics from a psychoanalytic perspective. Also called *psychoanalytically oriented therapy* or *psychoanalysis* (see Chapter 3), the therapists who practice it are often referred to as *psychoanalysts* or, simply, *analysts.* As developed by Freud and his immediate followers, psychoanalytic therapy is an intensive, long-term procedure for uncovering repressed

HIGHLIGHT 18.2

Classes of Therapeutic Strategies According to the Primary Target for Change

The following figure depicts in schematic fashion the situation of a typical psychotherapy client, who is conceived here as a conglomerate of mutually influencing cognitions and affects. A principal output of this conglomerate system is overt behavior, some of which is maladaptive or abnormal. The impact of this abnormal behavior on the environment (chiefly the social or interpersonal environment) generates information-laden reactions that are in turn registered by the client's cognitive-affect system. (The reverse direction arrow from behavior to client acknowledges the scattered evidence that this type of influence also occurs.) In the case of persisting behavioral abnormality, we assume that much of the information gleaned from the reacting environment is such as to "confirm," or at least not disconfirm, client cognitions and affects; were it otherwise, we would anticipate a restructuring of the system and, typically, a reasonably prompt termination of the abnormal behavior. Therapy is thus a matter of interrupting the self-sustaining loop supporting the behavioral abnormality. Seen in this light, therapy might conceivably be effective by inducing positive change in *any one* of the component nodes of the loop. Differing types of therapy, here organized into Types A (affect), B (behavior), C (cognitions), and E (environment), do in fact tend to focus efforts at therapeutic change on one or another of these nodes, as further described in the text.

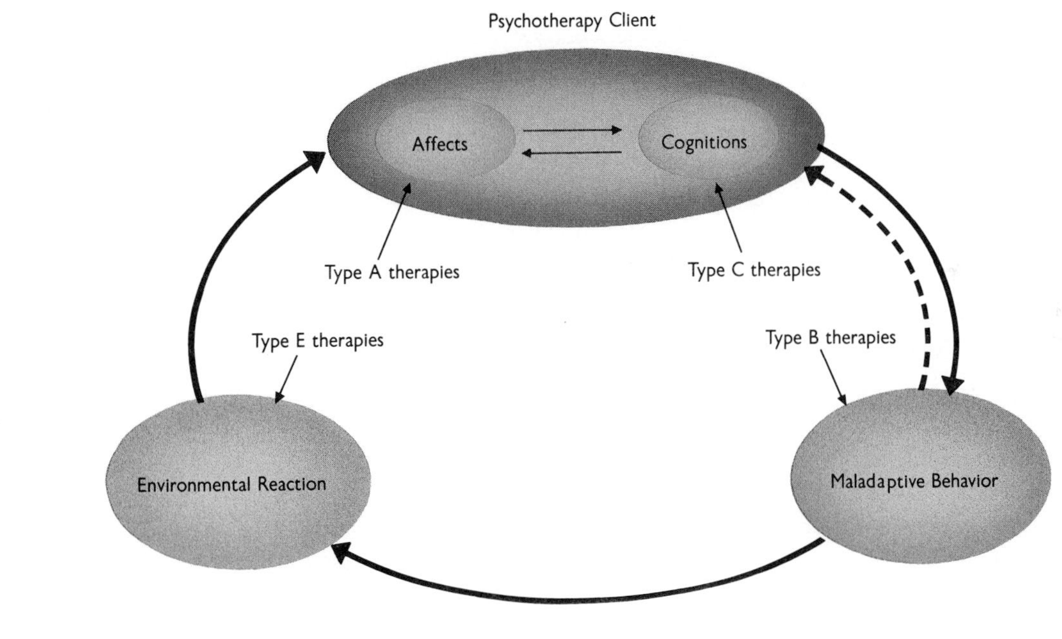

memories, thoughts, fears, and conflicts—presumably stemming from problems in early psychosexual development—and helping individuals come to terms with them in the light of adult reality. It is thought that gaining insight into such repressed material frees individuals from the need to keep squandering their energies on repression and other defense mechanisms. Instead, they can bring their personality resources to bear on consciously resolving the anxieties that prompted the repression in the first place. Freed from this load of threatening material and from the effort of keeping it out of consciousness, they can turn their energies to better personality integration and more effective living.

Other psychodynamic treatment approaches do not rigidly adhere to orthodox Freudian theory yet are, in part, based on psychoanalytic concepts. We will examine first Freud's original treatment methods, in part because of their historical significance and enormous influence; then we will look briefly at some of the contemporary modifications of psychoanalytic therapy.

The Use of Hypnosis in Therapy

Hypnosis was known among the ancient Egyptians and other early peoples, but its modern use in psychotherapy dates only from the time of Mesmer, as we saw in Chapter 3. Since that time, there have been periodic fluctuations in the popularity of hypnosis in psychotherapy, and differing viewpoints have arisen concerning the exact nature of hypnotic phenomena. In general, hypnosis may be defined as an altered state of consciousness involving extreme suggestibility. Hypnotic induction procedures are designed to bring about a heightened state of selective attention in which a subject "tunes out" irrelevant stimuli and concentrates solely on the hypnotist's suggestions. The induction of hypnosis and its therapeutic uses are briefly outlined here.

1. *Induction of hypnosis.* Hypnosis may be induced by a variety of techniques, most of which involve the following factors: (a) enlisting a subject's cooperation and allaying any fears of hypnosis; (b) having the subject assume a comfortable position and relax completely; (c) narrowing and focusing the subject's attention, perhaps by having him or her gaze on some bright object; and (d) directing the subject's activities by means of suggestions. The latter often involves establishing the assumption that normal bodily reactions have in fact come about at the direction of the hypnotist. For example, a subject may be directed to gaze upward toward an object and then be told, "your eyelids are starting to feel heavy." This is a normal reaction to the strain of looking upward, but the subject thinks it is caused by the hypnotist; thus the way is paved to accept further suggestions.

2. *Recall of buried memories.* Traumatic experiences that have been repressed from consciousness may be recovered under hypnosis. This technique was used in treating combat-exhaustion cases during World War II. Under hypnosis, an amnesic soldier could relive his battle experience, thus discharging the emotional tensions associated with it and permitting the experience to be assimilated into his self-structure. Civilian reactions involving amnesia may be similarly handled.

3. *Age regression.* Closely related to memory recall is hypnotic age regression. A hypnotized woman, for example, may be told that she is now a 6-year-old child again and will subsequently act, talk, and think much as she did at the age of 6. Regression to the age just preceding the onset of phobias often brings to light the traumatic experiences that precipitated them. Here again, reliving the traumatic experience may desensitize a subject to it. Age regression *below* the point at which an individual acquired verbally mediated memory

Freudian Psychoanalysis

Psychoanalysis is a system of therapy that evolved over a period of years during Freud's long career. It is not an easy system of therapy to describe, and the problem is complicated by the fact that most people have some more or less inaccurate conceptions of it based on cartoons and other forms of caricature. The best way to begin our discussion is to describe the four basic techniques of this form of therapy: free association, analysis of dreams, analysis of resistance, and analysis of transference. Then we will note some of the most important changes that have taken place in psychoanalytic therapy since Freud's time.

Free Association As we saw in Chapter 3, Freud used hypnosis in his early work to free repressed thoughts from his clients' unconscious (see *HIGHLIGHT 18.3*). Later, he stopped using hypnosis in favor of a more direct method of gaining access to an individual's hidden thoughts and fears—**free association.**

The basic rule of free association is that an individual must say whatever comes into his or her mind, regardless of how personal, painful, or seemingly irrelevant it may be. Usually a client sits comfortably in a chair or lies in a relaxed position on a couch and gives a running account of all the thoughts, feelings, and desires that come to mind as one idea leads to another. The therapist usually takes a position behind the client so as not to in any way distract or disrupt the free flow of associations.

Although such a running account of whatever comes into one's head may seem random, Freud did not view it as such; rather, he believed that associations are determined like other events. As we have

is not possible. Contrary to what some claim, age regression to "past lives" is also not possible.

4. *Dream induction.* Dreams can be induced through hypnosis, although some investigators consider hypnotic dreams to more nearly resemble fantasies than nocturnal dreams. In any event, hypnotic dreams may be used to explore intrapsychic conflicts along the lines of dream analysis worked out by Freud. Perhaps the particular value of such dreams is that a therapist can suggest the theme about which the hypnotic dream should center, using it much like a projective technique in exploring an individual's inner conflicts.

5. *Posthypnotic suggestion.* One of the hypnotic phenomena most widely used in psychotherapy is posthypnotic suggestion. In this technique, a therapist makes suggestions to a subject during the hypnotic state for behavior to be carried out later in the waking state, with the subject remaining unaware of the source of the behavior. For example, a subject may be told that he or she will no longer have a desire to smoke upon coming out of the hypnotic state. Although such suggestions do carry over into the waking state, their duration is usually short. That is, the individual may again experience a desire to smoke in a few hours or a few days. This time factor can be partially compensated for, however, by regular reinforcement of the posthypnotic suggestion in booster sessions.

Some investigators attribute the altered state of consciousness in hypnosis to the subject's strong motivation to meet the demand characteristics of the situation. Barber (1969) has shown that many of the behaviors induced under hypnosis can be replicated in nonhypnotized subjects simply by giving instructions which they are strongly motivated to follow. The preponderance of research evidence, however, indicates that behavior induced in hypnotized subjects does differ significantly from that evidenced during simulated hypnosis or role enactment (Diamond, 1974; Fromm & Shor, 1972; Hilgard, 1973, 1974; Miller & Springer, 1974; Nace, Orne, & Hammer, 1974). For example, a number of investigators have offered dramatic evidence that the pain response can be brought almost completely under hypnotic control in many subjects, permitting a degree of pain reduction well beyond that produced in nonhypnotized subjects.

Such drugs as sodium pentothal can be used to produce phenomena similar to those manifested in a hypnotic trance. This form of biological therapy is referred to as *narcoanalysis* or *narcosynthesis.* Sodium pentothal has been used to treat severe cases of combat exhaustion involving amnesia.

seen, he also thought that the conscious represents a relatively small part of the mind, while the preconscious and unconscious are the much larger portions. The purpose of free association is to explore thoroughly the contents of the preconscious, that part of mind considered subject to conscious attention but largely ignored. The preconscious contents, it is thought, contain derivatives of repressed unconscious material, which if properly "interpreted" can lead to an uncovering of the latter. Analytic interpretation involves a therapist's tying together a client's often disconnected ideas, beliefs, actions, and so forth into a meaningful explanation to help the client gain insight into the relationship between his or her maladaptive behavior and the repressed (unconscious) events and fantasies that drive it.

Analysis of Dreams Another important, related procedure for uncovering unconscious material is dream analysis. When a person is asleep, repressive defenses are lowered and forbidden desires and feelings may find an outlet in dreams. For this reason, dreams have been referred to as the "royal road to the unconscious." Some motives, however, are so unacceptable to an individual that even in dreams they are not revealed openly but are expressed in disguised or symbolic form. Thus a dream has two kinds of content: **manifest content,** which is the dream as it appears to the dreamer, and **latent content,** composed of the actual motives that are seeking expression but are so painful or unacceptable that they are disguised.

It is a therapist's task to uncover these disguised meanings by studying the images that appear in the manifest content of a client's dream and his or her preconscious associations to them. For example, a client's dream of being engulfed in a tidal wave may be interpreted by a therapist as indicating that the client feels in danger of being overwhelmed by inadequately repressed fears and hostilities.

Analysis of Resistance During the process of free association or of associating to dreams, an individual may evidence **resistance**—an unwillingness or inability to talk about certain thoughts, motives, or experiences (Strean, 1985). For example, a client may be talking about an important childhood experience and then suddenly switch topics, perhaps stating that "It really isn't that important," or that "It is too absurd to discuss." Resistance may also be evidenced by the client's giving a too-glib interpretation of some association, or coming late to an appointment, or even "forgetting" an appointment altogether. Because resistance prevents painful and threatening material from entering awareness, its sources must be sought if an individual is to face the problem and learn to deal with it in a realistic manner.

Analysis of Transference As client and therapist interact, the relationship between them may become complex and emotionally involved. Often people carry over and apply to their therapist attitudes and feelings that they had in their relations with a parent or other person close to them in the past, a process known as **transference.** Thus clients may react to their analyst as they did to that earlier person and feel the same hostility and rejection that they felt long ago.

By recognizing the transference relationship, a therapist may provide an individual with insight as to the inappropriateness of his or her reactions in the present context, and may also introduce a corrective emotional experience by behaving in a manner, classically an extraordinarily passive and "impersonal" one, that is distinctly inconsistent with the attitudes and feelings that have been falsely attributed. In this manner it may be possible for the individual to work through the conflict in feelings about the real parent or perhaps to overcome feelings of hostility and self-devaluation that stemmed from the earlier parental rejection. In essence, the pathogenic effects of an undesirable early relationship are counteracted by working through a similar emotional conflict in a therapeutic setting. Because a person's reliving of a pathogenic past relationship in a sense recreates the neurosis in real life, this experience is often referred to as a *transference neurosis.*

It is not possible here to consider at length the complexities of transference relationships, but it may be stressed that a client's attitudes toward his or her therapist usually do not follow such simple patterns as our example suggests. Often the client is ambivalent—distrusting the therapist and feeling hostile toward him or her as a symbol of authority, but at the same time seeking acceptance and love. In addition, the problems of transference are by no means confined to the client, for the therapist may also have a mixture of feelings toward the client. This phenomenon is known as **counter-transference** and must be recognized and handled properly by the therapist in question. For this reason, it is considered important that therapists have a thorough understanding of their own motives, conflicts, and "weak spots"; in fact, all psychoanalysts themselves undergo psychoanalysis before they begin independent practice. The resolution of the transference neurosis is said to be the key element in effecting a psychoanalytic "cure." Such resolution can only occur if an analyst successfully avoids the pitfalls of counter-transference. That is, the analyst must focus on control of the "environmental" (i.e., his or her own) reaction to a client's behavior. Accordingly, we consider psychoanalytically oriented therapy to be primarily Type E in character.

Psychodynamic Therapy Since Freud

Although some psychoanalysts still adhere to standard long-term psychoanalysis—which may take years—most analysts have worked out modifications in procedure designed to shorten the time and expense required. Mann (1973), for example, described what he refers to as "time-limited" psychotherapy. This approach, which focuses on providing symptom relief, follows psychodynamic methods but is confined to a 12-session treatment course. Probably the most extensive program of short-term psychodynamic therapy, and one which involves a strong research/evaluation component, is that of Strupp and his colleagues (Strupp, 1981; Strupp & Binder, 1984). This therapy, known as *time-limited dynamic psychotherapy,* goes beyond the symptom relief of Mann's program; it aims for lasting modification of an individual's personality by applying modified psychodynamic principles in therapy that lasts for 25 to 30 sessions. The modifications introduced here have a substantial *interpersonal* focus, in keeping with a clear trend of contemporary psychodynamic thinking.

The interpersonal focus of much modern psychodynamic therapy, sometimes called *object-relations therapy* (Cashdan, 1988), has roots in England as well as the United States. (As was seen in Chapter

3, a major American figure in this development was Harry Stack Sullivan.) Most generally these procedures make central and build on one of Freud's most brilliant insights—that is, that a person's current relationship to the social environment is determined significantly by precedents laid down in his or her earliest relationships with significant others. While the classical analysts have tended to see these precedents as played out mainly under the special circumstances of transference in psychoanalytic treatment, interpersonal therapists hold that these precedents are in fact *always* operative in a person's relationship to all others, not just to his or her therapist.

Often these precedents, schemas about what people are like and what one may expect from them, are not only erroneous in terms of present circumstances but also quite destructive in their effects on current interpersonal functioning. Sometimes they lead to repeating the same mistakes and the same poor choices in relationships time and time again, and to the maintenance of highly dysfunctional self-fulfilling prophecies (Carson, 1982). Interpersonal and object-relations therapists tend to ignore the sorts of libidinal drives and psychic structures Freudians emphasize and tend to focus their efforts on correcting their clients' distorted views of the interpersonal environment. In this respect the approach is indistinguishable from certain aspects of cognitive therapy, although interpersonalists tend more to use their own relationship to clients as the laboratory for the latter's acquisition of new and more functional cognitive schemas.

An important variant of interpersonally based psychotherapy, Interpersonal Psychotherapy (IPT) for depression, has been developed in recent years by a group of therapist-researchers from Harvard and Yale Universities. It was featured prominently in a national study comparing various treatments for depression (see *HIGHLIGHT 18.8*, page 665).

Other differences in contemporary psychodynamic treatment have also evolved. For example, today's analytic therapists tend to place more emphasis on current ego functioning and see the ego as a developing and controlling agent in an individual's life, not merely an uncertain regulator of uncompromising drives. Thus an individual is seen as more capable of being in control and less dominated by early repressed sexuality than in traditional analysis. Although childhood events are still viewed as important formative experiences, most modern analysts also place more emphasis on clients' current life situations and less on their childhood experiences. Many of the more important of these contemporary situations are, of course, ones involving other people, thus making for a certain rapprochement with other trends already noted.

Evaluation of Psychodynamic Therapy

Despite such modifications, psychodynamic therapy is still commonly criticized for being relatively time-consuming and expensive; for being based on a questionable, stultified, and cultlike theory of human nature; for neglecting a client's immediate problems in the search for unconscious conflicts in the remote past; and for inadequate proof of general effectiveness. Concerning the last of these, we actually have relatively little solid research data on the efficacy of the newer variants of psychodynamic therapy, as these tend to blend with other approaches and are difficult to disentangle from them; there is certainly no good basis for believing them to be *less* effective than other approaches.

The criticisms noted above have been mostly directed at classical psychoanalysis, and in our judgment are merited to a degree. With a few notable exceptions, analysts have been less than enthusiastic to subject their treatment outcomes to rigorous scrutiny, and when they have (see, e.g., Smith, Glass, & Miller, 1980; Wallerstein, 1989) the results have not been especially impressive, at least when considered in relation to the usually optimistic goals and considerable investments involved. Because it expects an individual to achieve insight and major personality change, psychoanalysis is also limited in its applicability. For example, it appears best suited for people who are average or above in intelligence and economically well off, and who do not suffer from severe psychopathology. In the present era of concern for "cost-effectiveness" and "accountability" in the mental therapy field, classical psychoanalysis appears increasingly to be a therapy for the elite.

Nevertheless, many individuals do feel that they have profited from psychoanalytic therapy—particularly in terms of greater self-understanding, relief from inner conflict and anxiety, and improved interpersonal relationships. Psychoanalytically oriented psychotherapy remains the treatment of choice for many individuals who are seeking extensive self-evaluation or insight into themselves. Even many behavior therapists, when they seek treatment for themselves, select this approach over behavioral methods (Gochman, Allgood, & Geer, 1982), which surely says *something* about the value they place on it.

BEHAVIOR THERAPY

Although the use of conditioning techniques in therapy has a long history, it was not until the 1960s that **behavior therapy,** the use (as originally formulated) of therapeutic procedures based on the principles of respondent and operant conditioning, really came into its own. The major reason for the long delay was the dominant position of psychoanalysis in the field. In recent years, however, the therapeutic potentialities of behavior therapy techniques have been strikingly demonstrated in dealing with a wide variety of maladaptive behaviors, and literally thousands of research publications have dealt with the systematic application of behavior-change principles to modify maladaptive behavior.

In the behavioristic perspective, as we saw in Chapter 3, a maladjusted person (unless suffering from brain pathology) is seen as differing from other people only in (a) having failed to acquire competencies needed for coping with the problems of living, (b) having learned faulty reactions or coping patterns that are being maintained by some kind of reinforcement, or (c) both. Thus a behavior therapist specifies in advance the precise maladaptive behaviors to be modified and the adaptive behaviors to be achieved, as well as the specific learning principles or procedures to be used.

Instead of exploring past traumatic events or inner conflicts to bring about personality change, behavior therapists attempt to modify behavior directly by extinguishing or counter-conditioning maladaptive reactions, such as anxiety, or by manipulating environmental contingencies—that is, by the use of reward, suspension of reward, or, occasionally, punishment to shape overt actions. Indeed, for the strict behaviorist, "personality" does not exist except in the form of a collection of modifiable habits. Behavior therapy techniques seem especially effective in altering maladaptive behavior when a reinforcement is administered contiguous with a desired response, and when a person knows what is expected and why the reinforcement is given. The ultimate goal, of course, is not only to achieve the desired responses but to bring them under the control and self-monitoring of the individual.

We have cited many examples of the application of behavior therapy in earlier chapters. In this section, we will elaborate briefly on the key techniques of behavior therapy.

Extinction

Because learned behavior patterns tend to weaken and disappear over time if they are not reinforced, often the simplest way to eliminate a maladaptive pattern is to remove the reinforcement for it. This is especially true in situations where maladaptive behavior has been reinforced unknowingly by others, an extremely common occurrence.

Billy, a 6-year-old first grader, was brought to a psychological clinic by his parents because he "hated school" and his teacher had told them that his showing-off behavior was disrupting the class and making him unpopular. It became apparent in observing Billy and his parents during the initial interview that both his mother and father were noncritical and approving of everything he did. After further assessment, a three-phase program of therapy was undertaken: (a) the parents were helped to discriminate between showing-off behavior and appropriate behavior on Billy's part; (b) the parents were instructed to show a loss of interest and attention when Billy engaged in showing-off behavior while continuing to show their approval of appropriate behavior; and (c) Billy's teacher was instructed to ignore Billy, insofar as it was feasible, when he engaged in showing-off behavior, and to devote her attention at those times to children who were behaving more appropriately.

Although Billy's showing-off behavior in class increased during the first few days of this behavior therapy program, it diminished markedly thereafter when it was no longer reinforced by his parents and teacher. As his maladaptive behavior diminished, he was better accepted by his classmates, which, in turn, helped reinforce more appropriate behavior patterns and changed his negative attitude toward school.

Billy's therapy, thus, was basically of the Type B sort (direct modification of abnormal behavior), as mediated by a Type E strategy—changing the environmental reaction (of his parents and teacher) to the behavior.

Two techniques that rely on the principle of extinction are *implosive therapy* and *flooding.* Both focus on extinguishing the conditioned avoidance of anxiety-arousing stimuli and can thus be used to treat anxiety disorders. Accordingly, they are primarily Type A therapies in focusing on the modification of affect. The techniques are roughly similar, except that implosive therapy involves having a client *imagine* anxiety-arousing situations, usually with much coaching and dramaturgical hype provided by a therapist; flooding, on the other hand, involves inducing a client to undergo repeated exposures to his or her *real-life* anxiety-arousing situations.

In **implosion,** clients are asked to imagine and relive aversive scenes associated with their anxiety. However, instead of trying to banish anxiety from the treatment sessions, as in the older technique of *systematic desensitization,* a therapist deliberately attempts to elicit a massive "implosion" of anxiety. This is somewhat reminiscent of psychodynamic approaches because it often deals with past trauma and with an internal conceptualization of anxiety, though most traditional analysts would doubtless strongly disapprove of the procedure. With repeated exposure in a "safe" setting, the stimulus loses its power to elicit anxiety and the neurotic avoidance behavior is extinguished. Hypnosis or drugs may be used to enhance suggestibility under implosive therapy.

In a report of an actual case, Stampfl (1975) described a young woman who could not swim and was terrified of water—particularly of sinking under the water. Although she knew it was irrational, she was so terrified of water "that she wore a life preserver when she took a bath" (p. 66). She was instructed by the therapist to imagine in minute detail taking a bath without a life preserver in a "bottomless" tub, and slipping under the water. Initially, the client showed intense anxiety, and the scene was repeated over and over. In addition, she was given a "homework" assignment in which she was asked to imagine herself drowning. Eventually, after imagining the worst and finding that nothing happened, her anxiety diminished. After the fourteenth therapy session, she was able to take baths without feelings of anxiety; the maladaptive behavior had been effectively extinguished. Implosion techniques are sometimes referred to as *in vitro* desensitization.

Flooding, or *in vivo* procedures, which involve placing an individual in a real-life situation as opposed to a therapeutic setting, may be used with individuals who do not imagine scenes realistically. For example, a client with a phobia of heights may be taken to the top of a tall building or bridge. This is another means of exposing the client to the anxiety-eliciting stimulus and demonstrating that the feared consequences do not occur. In a study of clients with agoraphobia (fear of open spaces), Emmelkamp and Wessels (1975) concluded that prolonged exposure *in vivo* plainly proved superior to simple reliance on the imagination, and in the past few years the flooding procedure seems to have gained a definite ascendancy over that of implosion (Barlow, 1988).

Flooding is a technique that involves placing an individual in a real-life, anxiety-arousing situation with the goal of extinguishing the conditioned avoidance of an anxiety-provoking stimulus. For example, a client with a fear of heights may be taken to the top of a tall building to demonstrate that the feared consequences do not occur.

Reports on the effectiveness of implosive therapy and flooding have generally been favorable, and they may be considered the treatments of choice for simple phobias (Foa & Kozak, 1985). Some investigators, however, have reported unfavorable as well as favorable results (Emmelkamp & Wessels, 1975; Mealiea, 1967; Wolpe, 1969b). These mixed results appear to be particularly true of flooding *in vivo.* For example, Emmelkamp and Wessels (1975) found that flooding *in vivo* was terrifying for some clients. In one case, the agoraphobic client "hid in a cellar out of fear of being sent into the street for 90 minutes by the therapist" (p. 14). On the other hand, the flooding procedure can be made relatively bearable without diminished effectiveness for even a severely fearful client by increasing therapist support and active guidance during exposure, as was recently demonstrated by Williams and Zane

(1989) in a study also involving the treatment of agoraphobia.

In general, it appears that while many clients respond favorably to implosion or flooding, some do not respond, and a few suffer an exacerbation of their phobias. This finding suggests a need for caution in the use of these techniques, particularly because they involve experiences that may be highly traumatic.

A modified form of flooding that involves repeated exposure to the somatic cues—"false alarms" (Barlow, 1988)—usually preceding panic (for example, heart palpitations), rather than to traumatizing situations themselves, may provide a key to circumventing undesirable reactions to exposure treatment. Accumulating evidence shows that it is these sorts of cues that in fact trigger full-blown anxiety attacks, and Barlow and associates (e.g., Barlow et al., 1989) have developed effective procedures for extinguishing this type of chain reaction, for example, by teaching clients to self-induce their false alarm symptoms repeatedly. In a recent important study in which the exposure to anticipatory cues procedure was a centerpiece in a treatment package for panic disorder, effectiveness was demonstrated to be far superior to drug treatment with alprazolam (Xanax), a benzodiazepine compound touted as having strong antipanic properties (Klosko et al., 1990).

Systematic Desensitization

The process of extinction can be applied to behavior that is positively reinforced or negatively reinforced. Of the two, behavior that is *negatively* reinforced—reinforced by the successful *avoidance* of a painful situation—is harder to deal with. Because an individual with negatively reinforced maladaptive behavior becomes anxious and withdraws at the first sign of the painful situation, he or she never gets a chance to find out whether the expected aversive consequences do in fact come about. In addition, the avoidance is anxiety-reducing and hence is itself reinforced.

One technique that has proven especially useful in extinguishing negatively reinforced behavior involves eliciting an antagonistic or competing response. Because it is difficult if not impossible to feel both pleasant and anxious at the same time, the method of **systematic desensitization** is aimed at teaching an individual to relax or behave in some other way that is inconsistent with anxiety while in the presence (real or imagined) of the anxiety-producing stimulus. The term *systematic* refers to the carefully graduated manner in which the person is exposed to the feared stimulus, the procedural opposite of implosion and flooding. It should be pointed out that systematic desensitization is not used *exclusively* to deal with avoidance behaviors brought about by negative reinforcement—that is, by successfully avoiding aversive experience. It can be used for other kinds of behavioral problems as well. In general, however, it is a Type A therapeutic procedure aimed at anxiety reduction.

The prototype of this approach is the classic experiment of Jones (1924), in which she successfully eliminated a small boy's conditioned fears of a white rabbit and other furry animals. First she brought the rabbit just inside the door at the far end of the room while the boy, Peter, was eating. On successive days, the rabbit was gradually brought closer until Peter could pat it with one hand while eating with the other.

Wolpe (1958; Rachman & Hodgson, 1980) elaborated on the procedure developed by Jones and devised the term *systematic desensitization* to refer to it. On the assumption that most anxiety-based patterns are, fundamentally, conditioned responses, Wolpe worked out a way to train a client to remain calm and relaxed in situations that formerly produced anxiety. Wolpe's approach is elegant in its simplicity, and his method is equally straightforward.

Because more direct techniques of guided exposure, such as implosion and flooding, appear in recent years to have supplanted systematic desensitization to a large extent, our description of the latter procedure can be brief. A client is first taught to induce a state of relaxation, typically by progressive concentration on the relaxing of various muscle groups. Meanwhile, in collaboration with the therapist, an "anxiety hierarchy" is constructed consisting of imagined scenes graded as to their capacity to elicit anxiety. For example, were the problem one of disabling sexual anxiety, a low-anxiety scene might be a candlelight dinner with the prospective partner, while a high-anxiety scene might be imagining the penis actually entering the vagina.

Following these preliminaries, active therapy sessions consist of repeatedly imagining the scenes in the hierarchy under conditions of deep relaxation, beginning with the minimum anxiety items and gradually working toward those rated in the more extreme ranges. A session is terminated at any point where the client reports experiencing significant anxiety, the next session resuming at a lower point in the hierarchy. Treatment continues until all items in the hierarchy can be tolerated without notable discomfort, by which point the client's real-life difficulties will typically have shown substantial improvement. The usual duration of a

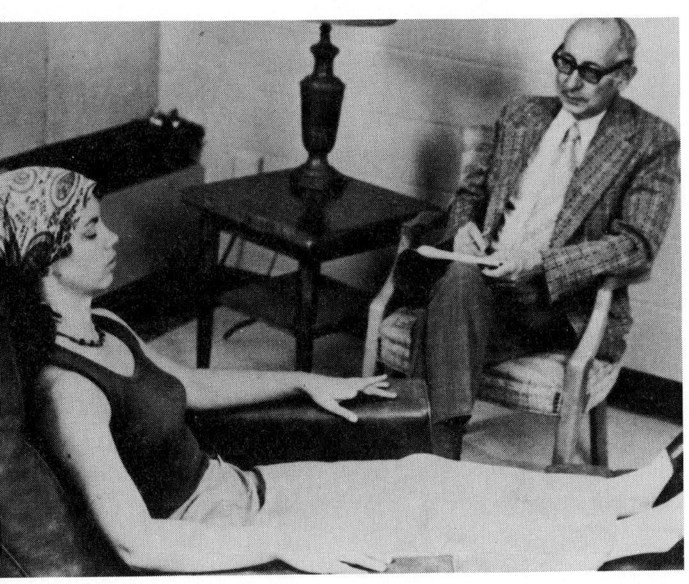

Joseph Wolpe is shown here conducting systematic desensitization therapy to reduce a client's anxiety. The client, in a relaxed state, is told to imagine the weakest anxiety on her list of anxiety-producing stimuli. If she feels anxious, she is instructed to stop imagining and relax again.

desensitization session is about 30 minutes, and the sessions are often given two to three times per week. The overall therapy program may, of course, take a number of weeks or even months. Kennedy and Kimura (1974) have shown, however, that even clients who have progressed only 25 to 50 percent of the way through their anxiety hierarchy show significant therapeutic gains, as evidenced by a marked reduction in specific avoidance behaviors when compared with their pretreatment levels.

Several variants of systematic desensitization have been devised. One variation involves the use of a tape recorder to enable a client to carry out the desensitization process at home. Another utilizes group desensitization procedures—as in "marathon" desensitization groups, in which the entire program is compressed into a few days of intensive treatment. One of the present authors routinely employs hypnosis to induce relaxation (the standard relaxation training can be quite tedious) and to achieve vividness in the imagining of hierarchy scenes. Perhaps the most important variation is *in vivo* desensitization, which is essentially similar to flooding but typically involves graduated exposure to the feared situations after a state of relaxation has been attained.

You will probably have concluded by this point that the truly essential element in the behavioral treatment of anxiety is repeated *exposure* of a client to the stimuli, even if only imaginarily, that elicit the fear response, regardless of the methods employed in achieving that end. Despite some continued wrangling among proponents of one or another specific procedure, that conclusion appears to be fair and accurate. Where a therapist has a choice—that is, depending on client cooperation and tolerance—*in vivo* procedures seem to have an edge in efficiency and possibly in ultimate efficacy over those employing imagery as the mode of confrontation. Overall, the outcome record for exposure treatments is impressive (Emmelkamp, 1986).

Aversion Therapy

Aversion therapy involves modifying undesirable behavior by the old-fashioned method of punishment. Punishment may involve either the removal of desired reinforcers or the use of aversive stimuli, but the basic idea is to reduce the "temptation value" of stimuli that elicit undesirable behavior. The most commonly used aversive stimulus is electric shock, although drugs may also be used. As we will see, however, punishment is rarely employed as the sole method of treatment.

Apparently the first formal use of aversion therapy was made by Kantorovich (1930), who administered electric shocks to alcoholics in association with the sight, smell, and taste of alcohol, an early version of the Antabuse drug treatment in use today. Since that time, aversion therapy has been used in the treatment of a wide range of maladaptive behaviors, including smoking, drinking, overeating, drug dependence, gambling, sexual variants, and bizarre psychotic behavior. As normally employed, it is a Type B therapeutic procedure. Because we have described the use of aversion therapy in the course of our discussion of abnormal behavior patterns, we will restrict ourselves here to a review of a few brief examples and principles.

Lovaas (1977) found punishment by electric shock to be effective in extreme cases of severely disturbed autistic children. In one case, a 7-year-old autistic boy, diagnosed as severely retarded, had to be kept in restraints 24 hours a day because he would continually beat his head with his fists or bang it against the walls of his crib, inflicting serious injuries. Though it may seem paradoxical to employ punishment to reduce the frequency of self-destructive behavior, electric shock following this behavior was nevertheless effective, bringing about complete inhibition of the maladaptive behavior pattern in a relatively short time (Bucher & Lovaas, 1967).

The use of electric shock as an aversive stimulus, however, has generally diminished in recent years because of the ethical and "image" problems involved in its use and because the new behaviors induced by it do not automatically generalize to other settings (Harris & Ersner-Hershfield, 1978). Also, less dangerous and more effective procedures have been found. The method of choice today is probably differential reinforcement of other responses (DOR), in which behaviors incompatible with the undesired behavior are positively reinforced. For example, for a child who indulges in antisocial, destructive behavior, positive reinforcement might be used for every sign of constructive play. At the same time, any reinforcement that has been maintaining maladaptive behavior is removed. Lovaas and his colleagues, who reported the successful use of electric shock with autistic children, have themselves recommended the use of nonpunitive treatment for self-injurious behavior (Russo, Carr, & Lovaas, 1980).

Aversion therapy is primarily a way—often a very effective one—of stopping maladaptive responses for a period of time. With this interruption, an opportunity exists for substituting new behavior or for changing a life-style by encouraging more adaptive alternative patterns that will prove reinforcing in themselves. This point is particularly important because otherwise a client may simply refrain from maladaptive responses in "unsafe" therapy situations, where such behavior leads to immediate aversive results, but keep making them in "safe" real-life situations, where there is no fear of immediate discomfort. Also, there is little likelihood that a previously gratifying but maladaptive behavior pattern will be permanently relinquished unless alternative forms of gratification are learned during the aversion therapy. A therapist who believes it possible to "take away" something without "giving something back" is likely to be disappointed. This is an important point in regard to the treatment of addictions and paraphilias, one often not appreciated in otherwise well-designed treatment programs.

Modeling

As Bandura (1977b) has pointed out,

Learning would be exceedingly laborious, not to mention hazardous, if people had to rely solely on the effects of their own actions to inform them what to do. Fortunately, most human behavior is learned observationally through modeling: from observing others one forms an idea of how new behaviors are performed, and on later occasions this coded information serves as a guide for action. Because people can learn from example what to do, at least in approximate form, before performing any behavior, they are spared needless error. (p. 22)

Although reinforcement of modeled behavior can influence whether an observer-learner attends to a model's actions and strengthens the response imitated, observational learning does not seem to require extrinsic reinforcement. Rather, according to Bandura, reinforcement functions as a facilitative condition to learning. Anticipation of a reinforcement may also make an individual more likely to perform a behavior.

As the name implies, **modeling** involves the learning of skills through imitating another person, such as a parent or therapist who perform the behavior; as such, it is a Type B procedure. A client may be exposed to behaviors or roles in peers or therapists and encouraged to imitate the desired new behaviors. For example, modeling may be used to promote the learning of simple skills, such as self-feeding in a profoundly mentally retarded child, or more complex ones, such as being more effective in social situations for a shy, withdrawn adolescent.

As we have noted, modeling and imitation are used in various forms of behavior therapy. Bandura (1964) found that live modeling of fearlessness combined with instruction and guided participation is the most effective desensitization treatment, resulting in the elimination of snake phobias in over 90 percent of the cases treated.

Systematic Use of Reinforcement

Systematic programs involving the use of reinforcement to elicit and maintain effective behavior (Type B therapy) have achieved notable success, particularly in institutional settings. Response shaping, token economies, and behavioral contracting are among the most widely used of such techniques.

Response Shaping Positive reinforcement is often used in **response shaping;** that is, in establishing by gradual approximation a response that is not initially in an individual's behavior repertoire. This technique has been used extensively in working with children's behavior problems. The following case reported by Wolf, Risley, and Mees (1964) is illustrative:

A 3-year-old autistic boy lacked nominal verbal and social behavior. He did not eat properly, engaged in self-destructive behavior, such as banging his head and scratching his face, and manifested ungovernable tantrums. He had recently had a cataract operation, and required glasses for the development of normal vision. He refused to wear his glasses, however, and broke pair after pair.

The technique of shaping was decided on to counteract the problem with his glasses. Initially, the boy was trained to expect a bit of candy or fruit at the sound of a toy noisemaker. Then training was begun with empty eyeglass frames. First the boy was reinforced with the candy or fruit for picking them up, then for holding them, then for carrying them around, then for bringing the frames closer to the eyes, and then for putting the empty frames on his head at any angle. Through successive approximations, the boy finally learned to wear his glasses up to twelve hours a day.

Token Economies Approval and other intangible reinforcers may be ineffective in behavior therapy programs, especially those dealing with severely maladaptive behavior. In such instances, appropriate behaviors maybe rewarded with tangible reinforcers in the form of tokens that can later be exchanged for desired objects or privileges (Kazdin, 1980). In working with hospitalized schizophrenic clients, for example, Ayllon and Azrin (1968) found that using the commissary, listening to records, and going to movies were considered highly desirable activities by most clients. Consequently, these activities were chosen as reinforcers for socially appropriate behavior. To participate in any of them, a client had to earn a number of tokens by demonstrating appropriate ward behavior. In Chapter 19, we will describe another token economy program, an extraordinarily successful one, with chronic hospitalized clients who had been considered resistant to treatment (Paul, 1982; Paul & Lentz, 1977).

Token economies have been used to establish adaptive behaviors ranging from elementary responses, such as eating and making one's bed, to the daily performance of responsible hospital jobs. In the latter instance, the token economy resembles the outside world where an individual is paid for his or her work in tokens (money) that can later be exchanged for desired objects and activities. The use of tokens as reinforcers for appropriate behavior has a number of distinct advantages: (a) the number of tokens earned depends directly on the amount of desirable behavior shown; (b) tokens, like money in the outside world, may be made a general medium of currency in terms of what they will "purchase"; hence they are not readily subject to satiation and tend to maintain their incentive value; (c) tokens can reduce the delay that often occurs between appropriate performance and reinforcement; (d) the number of tokens earned and the way in which they are "spent" are largely up to the client; and (e) tokens tend to bridge the gap between the institutional environment and the demands and system of payment that will be encountered in the outside world.

The ultimate goal in token economies, as in other programs of extrinsic reinforcement, is not only to achieve desired responses but to bring such responses to a level where their adaptive consequences will be reinforcing in their own right—thus enabling natural rather than artificial rewards to maintain the desired behavior. For example, extrinsic reinforcers may be used initially to help children overcome reading difficulties, but once a child becomes proficient in reading, this skill will presumably provide intrinsic reinforcement as the child comes to enjoy reading for its own sake.

Although their effectiveness has been clearly demonstrated with chronic schizophrenic clients, mentally retarded residents in institutional settings, and children, the use of token economies has declined in recent years. In part, this decline is a result of budget-inspired reductions in trained hospital treatment staffs, which are required for the effective management of such programs. Ironically, the corollary excessive reliance on medication, which in our judgment has little likelihood of enhancing independent living skills, is probably far more expensive in the long run. Token economies are also poorly understood by lay persons, many of whom see them as inhumane or crassly manipulative. If these people are "sick," so the thought goes, they should have medicine and not be expected to "perform" for simple amenities. Unfortunately, such thinking makes for chronic social disability.

Behavioral Contracting A technique called **behavioral contracting** is used in some types of psychotherapy and behavior therapy to identify and agree on the behaviors that are to be changed and to maximize the probability that these changes will occur and be maintained (Nelson & Mowry, 1976). By definition, a contract is an agreement between two or more parties—such as a therapist and a client, a parent and a teenager, or a husband and a wife—that governs the nature of an exchange. The agreement, often in writing, specifies a client's obligations to change as well as the responsibilities

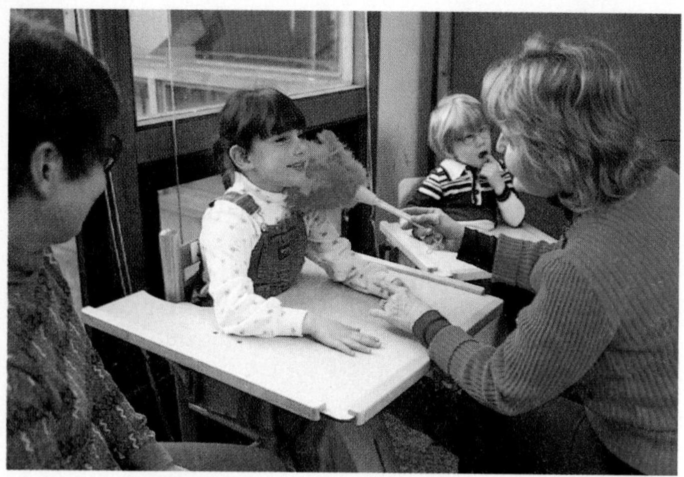

Positive reinforcement is an effective technique for managing behavior problems, with food or other treats or privileges often used as reinforcers. This autistic child is being reinforced for some positive behavior by being stroked with a feather tickler.

of the other party to provide something the client wants in return, such as tangible rewards, privileges, or therapeutic attention. Behavior therapists frequently make behavioral contracting an explicit focus of treatment, thus helping establish the treatment as a joint enterprise for which both parties have responsibility.

Behavioral contracting can facilitate therapy in several ways: (a) the structuring of the treatment relationship can be explicitly stated, giving the client a clear idea of each person's role in the treatment; (b) the actual responsibilities of the client are outlined and a system of rewards is built in for changed behavior; (c) the limitations of the treatment, in terms of the length and focus of the sessions, are specified; (d) by agreement, some behaviors (for example, the client's sexual orientation) may be eliminated from the treatment focus, thereby establishing the "appropriate content" of the treatment sessions; (e) clear treatment goals can be defined; and (f) criteria for determining success or failure in achieving these goals can be built in to the program.

Sometimes a contract is negotiated between a disruptive child and a teacher, according to which the child will maintain or receive certain privileges as long as he or she behaves in accordance with the contract. Usually the school principal is also a party to such a contract to ensure the enforcement of certain conditions that the teacher may not be in a position to enforce, such as removing the child from the classroom for engaging in certain types of misbehavior.

Assertiveness Therapy

Assertiveness therapy or training has been used as an alternative to relaxation in the desensitization procedure and as a means of developing more effective coping techniques. It appears particularly useful in helping individuals who have difficulties in interpersonal interactions because of anxiety responses that may prevent them from speaking up, claiming their rights, or even from showing appropriate affection. Such inhibition may lead to continual inner turmoil, particularly if an individual feels strongly about a situation. Assertiveness therapy may also be indicated in cases where individuals consistently allow others to take advantage of them or maneuver them into uncomfortable situations.

Assertiveness is viewed as the open and appropriate expression of thoughts and feelings, with due regard to the rights of others. Assertiveness training programs typically follow stages in which the desired assertive behaviors are first practiced in a therapy setting. Then, guided by the therapist, the individual is encouraged to practice the new, more appropriately assertive behaviors in real-life situations. Often attention is focused on developing more effective interpersonal skills. For example, a client may learn to ask the other person such questions as "Is anything wrong? You don't seem to be your usual self today." Such questions put the focus on the other person without suggesting an aggressive or hostile intent on the part of the speaker. Each act of intentional assertion is believed to inhibit the anxiety associated with the situation and therefore to weaken the maladaptive anxiety-response pattern. At the same time, it tends to foster more adaptive interpersonal behaviors. Assertiveness therapy is a Type B procedure.

Although assertiveness therapy is a highly useful procedure in certain types of situations, it does have limitations. For example, Wolpe (1969b) has pointed out that it is largely irrelevant for phobias involving nonpersonal stimuli. It may also be of little use in some types of interpersonal situations; for instance, if an individual has in fact been rejected by someone, assertive behavior may tend to aggravate rather than resolve the problem. However, in interpersonal situations where maladaptive anxiety can be traced to lack of self-assertiveness, this type of therapy appears particularly effective.

Biofeedback Treatment

For many years it was generally believed that voluntary control over physiological processes, such as heart rate, galvanic skin response, and blood pressure, was not possible. In the early 1960s, however, this view began to change. A number of investigators, aided by the development of sensitive electronic instruments that could accurately measure physiological responses, demonstrated that many of the processes formerly thought to be "involuntary" were modifiable by learning procedures—operant learning and classical conditioning. Kimmel (1974) demonstrated, for example, that the galvanic skin response could be conditioned by operant learning techniques.

The importance of the autonomic nervous system in the development of abnormal behavior has long been recognized. For example, autonomic arousal is an important factor in anxiety states. Thus many researchers have applied techniques developed in the autonomic conditioning studies in an attempt to modify the internal environment of troubled individuals to bring about more adaptive behavior—for instance, to modify heart rates in clients with irregular heartbeats (Weiss & Engel, 1971), to treat stuttering by feeding back information on the electric potential of muscles in the speech apparatus (Lanyon, Barrington, & Newman, 1976), and to reduce lower-back pain (Wolf, Nacht, & Kelly, 1982) and chronic headaches (Blanchard et al., 1983).

This treatment approach—in which a person is taught to influence his or her own physiological processes—is referred to as **biofeedback.** Several steps are typical in the process of biofeedback treatment: (a) monitoring the physiological response that is to be modified (perhaps blood pressure or skin temperature); (b) converting the information to a visual or auditory signal; and (c) providing a means of prompt feedback—indicating to a subject as rapidly as possible when the desired change is taking place (Blanchard & Epstein, 1978). Given this feedback, the subject may then seek to reduce his or her emotionality, as by lowering the skin temperature. For the most part, biofeedback is oriented to reducing the reactivity of some organ system innervated by the autonomic nervous system—specifically, a physiological component of the anxiety response. Hence we consider biofeedback to be principally a Type A therapy.

Biofeedback treatment is a popular treatment approach that requires the investment of capital to purchase complicated equipment and, in larger centers, a cadre of semiprofessional biofeedback technicians to perform the treatment. Whether its effectiveness justifies this expense is not an easily answered question. Although there is general agreement that many physiological processes can be regulated to some extent by learning, the application of biofeedback procedures to alter abnormal behavior has produced equivocal results. Demonstrations of clinical biofeedback applications abound, but carefully controlled research has not sufficiently supported earlier impressions of clinically significant improvement.

Blanchard and Young (1973, 1974) pointed out that the effects of biofeedback procedures are generally small and often do not generalize to situations outside the laboratory, where the biofeedback devices are not present. Two well-controlled studies have failed to show a treatment effect for biofeedback with migraine clients (Kewman & Roberts, 1979) and Raynaud's disease clients (Gugliemi, 1979). In addition, biofeedback has not been shown to be any more effective than relaxation training, leading to the suggestion that biofeedback may simply be a more elaborate (and usually more costly) means of teaching clients relaxation (Blanchard & Epstein, 1978; Blanchard et al., 1980; Tarler-Benliolo, 1978). As with almost any treatment procedure, however, a small percentage of clients may show an unusually good response with biofeedback.

Evaluation of Behavior Therapy

As compared with psychoanalytic and other psychotherapies, behavior therapy appears to have three distinct advantages. First, the treatment approach is precise. The target behaviors to be modified are specified, the methods to be used are clearly delineated, and the results can be readily evaluated (Marks, 1982). Second, the use of explicit learning principles is a sound basis for effective interventions as a result of their demonstrated scientific validity (Kazdin & Wilson, 1978). Third, the economy of time and costs is quite good. Not surprisingly, then, the overall outcomes achieved with behavior therapy compare favorably with those of other approaches (Smith, Glass, & Miller, 1980). Behavior therapy usually achieves results in a short period of time because it is generally directed to specific symptoms, leading to faster relief of an individual's distress and to lower financial costs. In addition, more people can be treated by a given therapist.

As with other approaches, the range of effectiveness of behavior therapy is not unlimited, and it works better with certain kinds of problems than with others. Generally speaking, the more pervasive and vaguely defined the client problem, the less likely is behavior therapy to be useful. For example, it appears to be only rarely employed to treat Axis II personality disorders, where specific symptoms are rare. On the other hand, behavioral techniques are the backbone of modern approaches to treating sexual dysfunctions, as discussed in Chapter 10. The meta-analysis of therapeutic outcomes confirms the expectation that behavior therapy has a particular place in the treatment of "neurotic" disorders, particularly where anxiety is a manifest feature, and therefore where the powerful Type A exposure techniques of behavior therapy can be brought to bear (Andrews & Harvey, 1981; Smith, Glass, & Miller, 1980). Smith et al.'s (1980) analysis in fact reveals the less expected finding of a relatively good outcome record with the psychoses. Thus, although behavior therapy is not a cureall, it has earned in a relatively brief period a highly respected place among the available psychosocial treatment approaches.

COGNITIVE-BEHAVIORAL THERAPY

Early behavior therapists focused on observable behavior. They regarded the inner thoughts of their clients at best as not really part of the causal chain, and in their zeal to be objective they focused on the relationship between observable behaviors and observable reinforcing conditions. Thus they were often viewed as mechanistic technicians who simply manipulated their subjects without considering them as people. More recently, however, a number of behavior therapists have reappraised the importance of "private events"—thoughts, perceptions, evaluations, and self-statements—seeing them as processes that mediate the effects of objective stimulus conditions and thus help determine behavior (Borkovec, 1985; Mahoney & Arnkoff, 1978).

Homme (1965), a student of Skinner, began this exodus from strict behaviorism in a paper arguing that these private events were behaviors that could be objectively analyzed. He proposed, as had Dollard and Miller (1950) earlier, that thoughts be regarded as emitted internal events comparable to emitted external behaviors, and that a technology be developed for modifying thoughts by using the same learning principles that were proving so effective in changing outer behavior. These internal, private events he called *coverants,* considering them to be operants of the mind. Following Homme's "coverant behaviorism," many investigators began to apply conditioning principles to covert events, such as thoughts and assumptions.

Cognitive-behavioral therapy, as the term suggests, stems from both cognitive psychology, with its emphasis on the effects of thoughts on behavior, and behaviorism, with its rigorous methodology and performance-oriented focus. At the present time, there is no single method of operation in cognitive-behavioral therapy: numerous methods are being developed with varying foci. Two main themes seem to characterize them all, however: (a) the conviction that cognitive processes influence both motivation and behavior, and (b) the use of behavior-change techniques in a pragmatic (hypothesis-testing) manner. That is, the therapy sessions are analogous to experiments in which a therapist and a client apply learning principles to alter the client's cognitions, continuously evaluating the effects that the changes in cognitions have on both thoughts and outer behavior.

The exact nature of the relationship between thought and behavior, a venerable problem whose philosophical roots go back to the distant past, is far from clear even today. Can it be, for example, that thoughts, by some accounts ephemeral and imma-

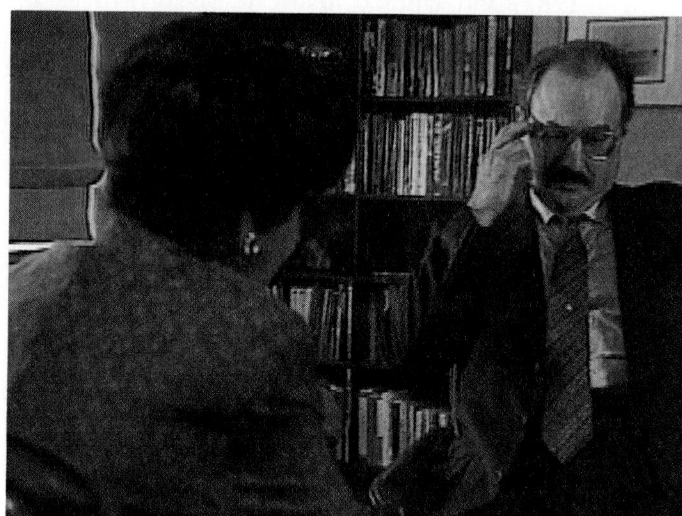

Here an actor using a case history of a real person (for purposes of telecourse instruction) plays Tom, seeking help from a professional psychotherapist because he is having serious problems at work dealing with his boss. The therapist uses a cognitive-behavioral model in working with Tom. She views his complaints as stemming from faulty thinking and attempts to help Tom develop new thought patterns that will lead to more productive behavior. The therapist and Tom role-play new behavior and new ways of communicating that will help Tom cope with his boss and blame himself less when there are problems. With a more realistic picture of his situation, Tom will be able to realize that he is not a failure because his supervisor devalues his work and that he may have to change jobs to be appreciated.

terial in nature, *cause* behavior? Any serious discussion of such an issue would take us far afield indeed, but it is important to understand that the intellectual status of cognitive therapy fuels some controversy. Beck (Beck & Weishaar, 1989), an important leader in the field, acknowledges that disordered cognitions are not a *cause* of abnormal behavior, but rather are an intrinsic (yet alterable) *element* of such behavior. If the critical cognitive components of the behavior can be changed, according to this view, then the behavior will change. Because altering cognitions is central in these therapies, we consider them to be Type C approaches. In our discussion, we will focus on three approaches to cognitive-behavioral therapy: the rational-emotive therapy of Ellis, the cognitive therapy of Beck, and the stress-inoculation training illustrated by the work of Meichenbaum.

Rational-Emotive Therapy (RET)

One of the earliest behaviorally oriented cognitive therapies was the **rational-emotive therapy (RET)** of Ellis (1958, 1973, 1975, 1989). RET attempts to change a client's basic maladaptive thought processes, on which maladaptive emotional responses and thus behavior are presumed to depend. In its infancy, RET was viewed skeptically by many professionals who doubted its effectiveness, but it has now become one of the most widely used therapeutic approaches (Ellis, 1989).

Ellis posited that a well-functioning individual behaves rationally and in tune with empirical reality. For Ellis, thoughts do have causal primacy in behavior, notably *emotional* behavior. Unfortunately, many of us have learned unrealistic beliefs and perfectionistic values that cause us to expect too much of ourselves, leading us to behave irrationally and then to feel unnecessarily that we are worthless failures. For example, a person may continually think, "I should be able to win everyone's love and approval" or "I should be thoroughly adequate and competent in everything I do." Such unrealistic assumptions and self-demands inevitably lead to ineffective and self-defeating behavior in the real world, which reacts accordingly, and then to the recognition of failure and the emotional response of self-devaluation. This emotional response is thus the necessary consequence not of "reality," but of an individual's faulty expectations, interpretations, and self-demands.

As a more specific example, consider a man who has an intense emotional reaction of despair with deep feelings of worthlessness, unlovability, and self-devaluation when he is jilted by his fiancée. With a stronger self-concept and a more realistic picture of both himself and his fiancée, as well as of their actual relationship, his emotional reaction might have been one of relief. It is his interpretation of the situation and of himself, rather than the objective situation, that has led to his intense emotional reaction.

Ellis (1970) believed that one or more of the following core irrational beliefs are at the root of most psychological maladjustment:

- One should be loved by everyone for everything one does.
- Certain acts are awful or wicked, and people who perform them should be severely punished.
- It is horrible when things are not the way we would like them to be.
- Human misery is produced by external causes, or outside people, or events, rather than by the view that one takes of these conditions.
- If something may be dangerous or fearsome, one should be terribly upset about it.
- It is better to avoid life problems if possible than to face them.
- One needs something stronger or more powerful than oneself to rely on.
- One should be thoroughly competent, intelligent, and achieving in all respects.
- Because something once affected one's life, it will indefinitely affect it.
- One must have certain and perfect self-control.
- Happiness can be achieved by inertia and inaction.
- We have virtually no control over our emotions and cannot help having certain feelings.

Irrationality can, however, be viewed in different ways. Arnkoff and Glass (1982) cautioned against an overly simplistic view of irrational behavior as the mere holding of irrational beliefs. Rather, they contended that irrationality may also involve faulty thought processes reflecting a "closed-mindedness" that is more resistant to change than Ellis's view suggests.

The task of rational-emotive therapy is to restructure an individual's belief system and self-evaluation, especially with respect to the irrational "shoulds," "oughts," and "musts" that are preventing a more positive sense of self-worth and a creative, emotionally satisfying, and fulfilling life. Several methods are used.

One method is to *dispute* a person's false beliefs through rational confrontation. For example, a therapist dealing with the jilted young man previously discussed might ask, "Why should your fiancée's changing her mind mean that *you* are worthless?" Here the therapist would teach the client to identify and dispute the beliefs that were producing the negative emotional consequences.

A rational-emotive therapist also uses behaviorally oriented techniques to bring about changed thoughts and behaviors. Sometimes, for example, homework assignments are given to encourage clients to have new experiences and break negative chains of behavior. For example, clients might be instructed to reward themselves by an external reinforcer, such as a food treat, after working 15 minutes at disputing their beliefs. Another method of self-reinforcement might be through covert statements such as "You are doing a really good job."

In some ways, rational-emotive therapy can be viewed as a *humanistic* therapy (to be discussed in a later section) because it takes a clear stand on personal worth and human values. Rational-emotive therapy aims at increasing an individual's feelings of self-worth and clearing the way for self-actualization by removing the false beliefs that have been stumbling blocks to personal growth.

Cognitive-Behavioral Therapy for Depression

Beck's cognitive-behavioral therapy was developed for the treatment of depression (Beck et al., 1979; Hollon & Beck, 1978) and was later extended to anxiety disorders and phobias (Beck, 1985; Beck & Emery, 1985). One basic assumption underlying this approach is that problems like depression result from clients' illogical thinking about themselves, the world they live in, and the future. These illogical ideas are maintained even in the face of contradictory evidence because the individuals typically engage in self-defeating and self-fulfilling behaviors in which they (a) *selectively perceive* the world as harmful while ignoring evidence to the contrary; (b) *overgeneralize* on the basis of limited examples—for example, seeing themselves as totally worthless because they were laid off at work; (c) *magnify* the significance of undesirable events—for example, seeing the job loss as the end of the world for them; and (d) *engage in absolutistic thinking*—for example, exaggerating the importance of someone's mildly critical comment and perceiving it as proof of their instant descent from goodness to worthlessness.

In Beck's cognitive-behavioral therapy, however, clients are not persuaded to change their beliefs by debate and persuasion as in rational-emotive therapy; rather, they are encouraged to gather information about themselves through unbiased experiments that allow them to discomfirm their false beliefs. Together, a therapist and an individual identify the individual's assumptions, beliefs, and expectations and formulate them as hypotheses to be tested. They then design ways in which the individual can check out these hypotheses in the world. These behavior-disconfirmation experiments are planned to give the individual successful experiences, thereby interrupting the destructive loop previously described. They are arranged according to difficulty, so that the least difficult tasks will be accomplished successfully before the more difficult ones are attempted (see *HIGHLIGHT 18.4*).

Sometimes a client and a therapist schedule the client's daily activities on an hour-by-hour basis. Such activity scheduling is an important part of therapy with depressed individuals because by reducing such clients' inactivity, it interrupts their tendencies to ruminate about themselves. An important part of the arrangement is the scheduling of pleasurable events because many depressed clients have lost the capacity for gaining pleasure from their own activities. Both the scheduled pleasurable activities and the rewarding experiences from carrying out the behavioral experiments tend to increase an individual's satisfaction and positive mood.

Besides planning the behavioral assignments, evaluating the results in subsequent sessions, and planning further disconfirmation experiments, such therapy sessions include several other cognitive foci. For example, an individual is encouraged to discover underlying assumptions and "automatic thoughts" that may be leading to self-defeating tendencies. With this background, the individual is taught to self-monitor his or her thought content and to keep challenging its validity.

Stress-Inoculation Therapy

A third cognitive-behavioral approach to treatment is **stress-inoculation therapy**—a type of self-instructional training focused on altering self-statements that an individual is routinely making in order to restructure his or her characteristic approach to stress-producing situations (Meichenbaum & Cameron, 1982). Like other cognitive-behavioral therapies, stress-inoculation therapy as-

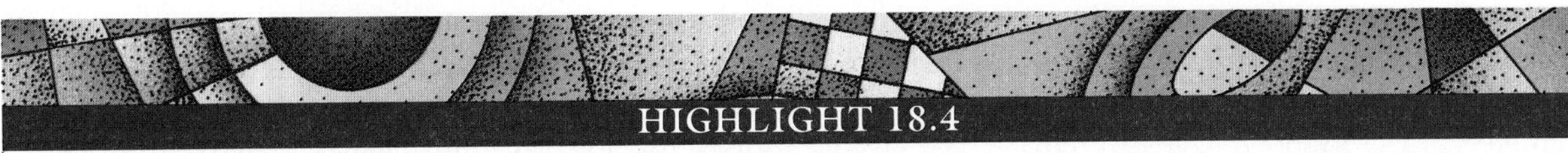

Cognitive-Behavioral Therapy for a Case of Depression

Rush, Khatami, and Beck (1975) have reported several cases of successful treatment using cognitive clarification and behavioral assignments for clients with recurring chronic depression. The following case illustrates their approach:

A 53-year-old white male engineer's initial depressive episode 15 years ago necessitated several months' absence from work. Following medication and psychotherapy, he was asymptomatic up to four years ago. At that time, sadness, pessimism, loss of appetite and weight, and heavy use of alcohol returned.

Two years later, he was hospitalized for six weeks and treated with lithium and imipramine. He had three subsequent hospitalizations with adequate trials of several different tricyclics. During his last hospitalization, two weeks prior to initiating cognitive-behavioral therapy, he was treated with 10 sessions of ECT. His symptoms were only partially relieved with these various treatments.

When the client started cognitive-behavioral therapy, he showed moderate psychomotor retardation. He was anxious, sad, tearful, and pessimistic. He was self-depreciating and self-reproachful without any interest in life. He reported decreased appetite, early morning awakening, lack of sexual interest, and worries about his physical health. Initially he was treated with weekly sessions for 3 months, then biweekly for 2 months. Treatment, terminated after 5 months, consisted of 20 sessions. He was evaluated 12 months after the conclusion of therapy.

Therapist and client set an initial goal of his becoming physically active (i.e., doing more things no matter how small or trivial). The client and his wife kept a separate list of his activities. The list included raking leaves, having dinner, and assisting his wife in apartment sales, etc. His cognitive distortions were identified by comparing his assessment of each activity with that of his wife. Alternative ways of interpreting his experiences were then considered.

In comparing his wife's resume of his past experiences, he became aware that he had (1) undervalued his past by failing to mention many previous accomplishments, (2) regarded himself as far more responsible for his "failures" than she did, and (3) concluded that he was worthless since he had not succeeded in attaining certain goals in the past. When the two accounts were contrasted he could discern many of his cognitive distortions. In subsequent sessions, his wife continued to serve as an "objectifier."

In midtherapy, the client compiled a list of new attitudes that he had acquired since initiating therapy.

These included:

(1) I am starting at a lower level of functioning at my job, but it will improve if I persist.

(2) I know that once I get going in the morning, everything will run all right for the rest of the day.

(3) I can't achieve everything at once.

(4) I have my periods of ups and downs, but in the long run I feel better.

(5) My expectations from my job and life should be scaled down to a realistic level.

(6) Giving in to avoidance never helps and only leads to further avoidance.

He was instructed to re-read this list daily for several weeks even though he already knew the content. The log was continued, and subsequent assumptions reflected in the log were compared to the assumptions listed above.

As the client became gradually less depressed, he returned to his job for the first time in 2 years. He undertook new activities (e.g., camping, going out of town) as he continued his log. (pp. 400–401)

The focus of the therapy was on encouraging the client to restructure his thought content—to reduce the negative self-judgments and to evaluate his actual achievements more realistically. Making and reviewing the list of new attitudes gave the client more perspective on his life situation, which resulted in an improved mood, less self-blame, and more willingness to risk alternative behavior.

sumes that an individual's problems result from maladaptive beliefs that are leading to negative emotional states and maladaptive behavior, familiar elements in the loop we have posited.

Stress-inoculation therapy usually involves three stages. In the initial phase, *cognitive preparation,* client and therapist together explore the client's beliefs and attitudes about the problem situation and the self-statements to which they are leading. The focus is on how the individual's self-talk can influence later performance and behavior. Together, the therapist and the client agree on new self-statements that would be more adaptive. Then the second phase of the stress inoculation, *skill acquisition and rehearsal,* is begun. In this phase, more adaptive self-statements are learned and practiced. For example, an individual undergoing stress-inoculation therapy for coping with the "feeling of being overwhelmed" would rehearse self-statements such as,

When fear comes, just pause.
Keep the focus on the present; what is it you have to do?
Label your fear from 0 to 10 and watch it change.
You should expect your fear to rise.
Don't try to eliminate fear totally; just keep it manageable.
You can convince yourself to do it. You can reason fear away.
It will be over shortly.
It's not the worst thing that can happen.
Just think about something else.
Do something that will prevent you from thinking about fear.
Describe what is around you. That way you won't think about worrying. (Meichenbaum, 1974, p. 16)

The third phase of stress-inoculation therapy, *application and practice,* involves applying the new coping strategies in actual situations. This practice is graduated in such a way that an individual is placed in easier situations first and is only gradually introduced to more stressful situations as he or she feels confident of mastering them.

Stress-inoculation therapy has been successfully used with a number of clinical problems, especially anxiety (Meichenbaum, 1975), pain (Turk, 1974), and Type A behavior (Jenni & Wollersheim, 1979). This approach is particularly suited to increasing the adaptive capabilities of individuals who have shown a vulnerability to developing problems in certain stressful situations. In addition to its value as a therapeutic technique for identified problems, stress-inoculation therapy may be a viable method for preventing behavior disorders. Although the preventive value of this and other cognitive-behavioral therapy procedures has not been demonstrated by empirical study, many believe that the incidence of maladjustment might be reduced if more individuals' general coping skills were improved (Meichenbaum & Jaremko, 1983).

Evaluation of Cognitive-Behavioral Therapy

A review of research evaluating cognitive-behavioral treatment methods suggests that these approaches to intervention are extremely effective in alleviating some behavioral problems (e.g., Hollon & Beck, 1986). Several empirical studies have compared cognitive-behavioral methods with other treatment approaches. Data from these evaluation studies—on Beck's cognitive-behavioral therapy for individuals experiencing depression (see the reviews by Hollon & Garber, 1990; and Robinson, Berman, & Neimeyer, 1990); on rational-emotive therapy (Lipsky, Kassinove, & Miller, 1980; Smith, Glass, & Miller, 1980); and on stress-inoculation procedures (Denicola & Sandler, 1980; Holcomb, 1979; Klepac et al., 1981)—indicate that cognitive-behavioral methods are strongly associated with positive treatment outcomes.

In the case of depression, in fact, considerable evidence, reviewed in Chapter 11, suggests that cognitive-behavioral therapy is superior to drug treatment in all but the most severe cases (and perhaps even in these cases; see *HIGHLIGHT 18.8,* page 665, and our later discussion on The Evaluation of Success in Psychotherapy). In a study by Simons et al. (1986), for example, relapse in the posttreatment year was less likely if a client had been treated with cognitive therapy, *whether or not* there was also treatment with antidepressant drugs.

The combining of cognitive and behavior therapy approaches in practice is growing rapidly. In the next few years, we can expect to see many more studies evaluating the effectiveness of cognitive-behavioral methods as approaches to therapeutic change. There remains disagreement about whether some approaches are "truly" behavioral or "truly" cognitive, and whether or how cognitive change can bring about lasting behavior change (e.g., Hollon, DeRubeis, & Evans, 1987). In light of the present ferment in the field, we anticipate that the cognitive-behavioral viewpoint will undergo a great deal of further theoretical development in the foreseeable future.

HUMANISTIC-EXPERIENTIAL THERAPIES

The **humanistic-experiential therapies** have emerged as significant treatment approaches during the last four decades. To a large extent, they developed in reaction to the psychodynamic and behavioristic perspectives, which many feel do not accurately take into account either the existential problems or the full potentialities of human beings. In a society dominated by self-interest, mechanization, computerization, mass deception, and "mindless" bureaucracy, proponents of the humanistic-experiential therapies see psychopathology as stemming in many cases from problems of alienation, depersonalization, loneliness, and a failure to find meaning and genuine fulfillment. Problems of this sort, it is held, are not likely to be solved either by delving into forgotten memories or by correcting specific responses.

The humanistic-experiential therapies follow some variant of the general humanistic and existential perspectives spelled out in Chapter 3. They are based on the assumption that we have both the freedom and the responsibility to control our own behavior—that we can reflect on our problems, make choices, and take positive action. Whereas some behavior therapists see themselves as "behavior engineers," responsible for changing specific behaviors *they* deem problematic by appropriate modifications in an individual's environment, humanistic-experiential therapists feel that a client must take most of the responsibility for the directions and success of therapy, with a therapist merely serving as counselor, guide, and facilitator. These therapies may be carried out with individual clients or with groups of clients (see *HIGHLIGHT 18.5*). Although differing among themselves in details, the central focus of humanistic-experiential therapies is always that of expanding a client's "awareness"; accordingly, we consider them Type C (cognition-oriented) approaches.

Client-centered Therapy

The **client-centered (person-centered) therapy** of Carl Rogers (1951, 1961, 1966) actually antedated the strong movement toward behavior therapy that began in the 1950s and the "humanistic revolution" of the 1960s. It was developed in the 1940s as a truly innovative alternative to psychoanalysis, the only major psychotherapy of the time.

Rogers rejected both Freud's view of the primacy of irrational instinct and of the therapist's role as prober, interpreter, and director of the therapeutic process. Instead, believing in the natural power of an organism to heal itself, he saw psychotherapy as a process of removing the constraints and hobbling restrictions that often prevent this process from operating. These constraints, he believed, grow out of unrealistic demands that people tend to place on themselves when they believe they should not have certain kinds of feelings, such as hostility. By denying that they do in fact have such feelings, they become unaware of their actual "gut" reactions. As they lose touch with their own genuine experience, the result is lowered integration, impaired personal relationships, and various forms of maladjustment.

The primary objective of Rogerian therapy is to resolve this incongruence—to help clients become able to accept and *be* themselves. To this end, client-centered therapists establish a psychological climate in which clients can feel unconditionally accepted, understood, and valued as people. In this climate they can begin to feel free for perhaps the first time to explore their real feelings and thoughts and to accept hates and angers and "ugly feelings" as parts of themselves. As their self-concept becomes more congruent with their actual experiencing, they become more self-accepting and more open to new experience and new perspectives; in short, they become better-integrated people.

In client-centered therapy, also called *nondirective therapy,* it is not the therapist's task to direct the course of therapy. Thus a therapist does not give answers or interpret what a client says or probe for unconscious conflicts or even steer the client onto certain topics. Rather he or she simply listens attentively and acceptingly to what the client wants to talk about, interrupting only to restate in other words what the client is saying. Such restatements, without any judgment or interpretation by the therapist, help the client clarify further the feelings and ideas that he or she is exploring—really to look at them and acknowledge them. The following excerpt from a counselor's second interview with a young woman will serve to illustrate these techniques of reflection and clarification:

Alice: *I was thinking about this business of standards. I somehow developed a sort of a knack, I guess, of—well—habit—of trying to make people feel at ease around me, or to make things go along smoothly. . . .*

Counselor: *In other words, what you did*

HIGHLIGHT 18.5

Group Therapy

The treatment of clients in groups first received impetus in the military during World War II, when psychotherapists were in short supply. Group therapy was found to be effective in dealing with a variety of problems, and it rapidly became an important therapeutic approach in civilian life. In fact, all the major systematic approaches to psychotherapy that we have discussed—psychoanalysis, behavior therapy, and so on—have been applied in group as well as individual settings.

Group therapy has traditionally involved a relatively small group of clients in a clinic or hospital setting, using a variety of procedures depending on the age, needs, and potentialities of the clients and the orientation of the therapists. The degree of structure and of client participation in the group process varies in different types of groups.

Most often, groups are informal, and many follow the format of encounter groups. Occasionally, however, more or less formal lectures and visual materials are presented to clients as a group. For example, a group of alcoholic clients may be shown a film depicting the detrimental effects of excessive drinking on the human body, with a group discussion afterward. Although this approach by itself has not proven effective in combating alcoholism, it is often a useful adjunct to other forms of group therapy.

An interesting form of group therapy is psychodrama, based on role-playing techniques. A client, assisted by staff members or other clients, is encouraged to act out problem situations in a theater-like setting. This technique frees the individual to express anxieties and hostilities or relive traumatic experiences in a situation that simulates real life but is more sheltered. The goal is to help the client achieve emotional catharsis, increased understanding, and improved interpersonal competencies. This form of therapy, developed initially by Moreno (1959), has proved beneficial for the clients who make up the "audience" as well as for those who participate on the "stage" (Sundberg & Tyler, 1962; Yablonsky, 1975).

Group therapy may also be almost completely unstructured, as in activity groups where children with emotional problems are allowed to act out their aggressions in the safety and control of the group setting.

was always in the direction of trying to keep things smooth and to make other people feel better and to smooth the situation.

Alice: *Yes. I think that's what it was. Now the reason why I did it probably was—I mean, not that I was a good little Samaritan going around making other people happy, but that was probably the role that felt easiest for me to play. I'd been doing it around home so much. I just didn't stand up for my own convictions, until I don't know whether I have any convictions to stand up for.*

Counselor: *You feel that for a long time you've been playing the role of kind of smoothing out the frictions or differences or what not. . . .*

Alice: *M-hm.*

Counselor: *Rather than having any opinion or reaction of your own in the situation. Is that it?*

Alice: *That's it. Or that I haven't been really honestly being myself, or actually knowing what my real self is, and that I've been just playing a sort of a false role. Whatever role no one else was playing, and that needed to be played at the time, I'd try to fill it in. (Rogers, 1951, pp. 152–153)*

In a survey of trends in psychotherapy and counseling, Rogers was rated one of the most influential psychotherapists among clinical practitioners (Smith, 1982). In addition to his influence in clinical settings, Rogers was a pioneer in attempting to carry out empirical research on psychotherapy. Using recordings of therapy sessions, he was able to make objective analyses later of what was said, of the client-counselor relationships, and of many aspects of the ongoing processes in these therapy sessions. He was also able to compare a client's behavior and attitudes at different stages of therapy. These comparisons revealed a typical sequence that clients tended to go through. Early sessions were dominated by negative feelings and discouragement. Then, after a time, tentative statements of hope and greater self-acceptance began to appear. Eventually, positive feelings, a reaching out toward others, greater self-confidence, and interest in future plans appeared. This characteristic sequence gave support to Rogers's hypothesis that, once freed to do so, individuals have the capacity to lead themselves to psychological health.

Pure client-centered psychotherapy, as originally practiced, is rarely used today. It did, however, open the way for a variety of humanistically oriented therapies in which the focus is a client's present conscious problems and in which it is assumed that the client is the primary actor in the curative process, with the therapist essentially being just the facilitator. The newer humanistic therapies thus accept Rogers's concept of an active self, capable of sound value choices; they also emphasize the importance of a high degree of empathy, genuine warmth, and unconditional positive regard on the part of a therapist. They differ from original client-centered therapy in having found various shortcuts by which the therapist, going beyond simple reflection and clarification, can hasten and help focus the client's search for wholeness. Such a therapist might, for example, directly confront a client's deceitful mode of self-presentation. It is still the client's search and the client's insights that are seen as central in therapy, however.

Existential Therapy

Several important concepts underlie **existential psychotherapy.** The existentialist perspective emphasizes the importance of the human situation as experienced by an individual. Existentialists are deeply concerned about the predicament of humankind, the breakdown of traditional faith, the alienation and depersonalization of individuals in contemporary society, and the lack of meaning in individuals' lives. They see individuals, however, as having a high degree of freedom and thus as capable both of doing something about their predicament and of being responsible for doing the best they can. The unique ability of human beings to be aware of their mortality and to reflect on and question their existence confronts them with the responsibility for *being*—for deciding what kind of person to become within the constraint of a single lifetime, for establishing their own values, and for actualizing their potentialities.

The application of existential thought to understanding human problems and to helping individuals alter their lives has been recognized over the years by several psychological theorists, including Binswanger (1942) and May, Angel, and Ellenberger (1958). Binswanger, a psychoanalyst, applied the existential frame of reference to his psychoanalytic work and developed a method he referred to as *Daseinanalyse,* or existential analysis. May et al. followed later with what has become a classic work detailing existential analysis. Existential analysts do not limit themselves to an investigation of conscious and subconscious states, as do traditional analysts; rather, they attempt to assist an individual to reconstruct his or her inner world by focusing on the surrounding external reality. Most existential therapists do not strictly follow the methods of *Daseinanalyse,* but nevertheless accept an existential framework to challenge a client to experience his or her human feelings.

Existential therapists do not follow any rigidly prescribed procedures, but emphasize the uniqueness of each individual and his or her "way of being in the world." They stress the importance of being aware of one's own existence—challenging an individual directly with questions concerning the meaning and purpose of existence—and of the therapeutic encounter—the complex relationship established between two interacting human beings in the therapeutic situation as they both try to be open and "authentic." In contrast to both psychoanalysis and behavior therapy, existential therapy calls for therapists to share themselves—their feelings, their values, and their own existence.

Besides being authentic themselves, it is the task of existential therapists to keep a client responding authentically to the present reality (Havens, 1974; May, 1969). For example, if a client says, "I hate you just like I hated my father," a therapist might respond by saying, "I am not your father, I am me, and you have to deal with me as Dr. S., not as your father." The focus is on the here and now—on what an individual is choosing to do, and therefore to be, at this moment. This sense of immediacy, of the urgency of experience, is the touchstone of existential therapy and sets the stage for the individual to clarify and choose between alternative ways of being.

With what types of clients and which clinical problems does existential therapy work best? Like classical psychoanalytic therapy, existential psychotherapy is probably for the few. It is directed primarily toward intelligent and verbal individuals who appear to be having existential crises. The existential treatment approach is believed to work best with individuals who have anxiety-based disorders or personality disorders rather than psychoses. The following case illustrates the type of problem situation that would lend itself to treatment in the existential framework:

A 42-year-old business executive seeks therapy because he feels that life has lost its meaning—he no longer feels that family matters are important to him (his wife is busy starting her career and his only child recently got married and moved to Alaska). Additionally, his work, at which he has had extraordinary success—earning him both financial security and respect—no longer holds meaning for him. He views his days as "wasted and worthless"—he feels both "bored and panicked"—and he goes through the motions of the business day feeling "numb," as though he isn't even there. At times, he feels fearful and overwhelmed with a sense of dread that this is all that life has left for him.

Gestalt Therapy

The term *gestalt* means "whole," and gestalt therapy emphasizes the unity of mind and body—placing strong emphasis on the need to integrate thought, feeling, and action. **Gestalt therapy** was developed by Frederick (Fritz) Perls (1967, 1969) as a means of teaching clients to recognize the bodily processes and emotional modalities they had been blocking off from awareness. The main goal of gestalt therapy is to increase an individual's self-awareness and self-acceptance.

Although gestalt therapy is commonly used in a group setting, the emphasis is on one individual at a time with whom a therapist works intensively, attempting to help identify aspects of the individual's self or world that are not being acknowledged in awareness. The individual may be asked to act out fantasies concerning feelings and conflicts, or to "be" one part of a conflict while sitting in one chair and then switch chairs to take the part of the "adversary." Often the therapist or other group members will ask questions like, "What are you aware of in your body now?" or "What does it feel like in your gut when you think of that?"

In Perls's approach to therapy, a good deal of emphasis is also placed on dreams:

. . . all the different parts of the dream are fragments of our personalities. Since our aim is to make every one of us a wholesome person, which means a unified person, without conflicts, what we have to do is put the different fragments of the dream together. We have to re-own these projected, fragmented parts of our personality, and re-own the hidden potential that appears in the dream. (1967, p. 67)

In the following dialogue, taken from the transcript of a "dreamwork seminar," Perls (Fritz) helps a young woman (Linda) discover the meaning of her dream:

Linda: *I dreamed that I watch . . . a lake . . . drying up, and there is a small island in the middle of the lake, and a circle of . . . porpoises—they're like porpoises except that they can stand up, so they're like porpoises that are like people, and they're in a circle, sort of like a religious ceremony, and it's very sad—I feel very sad because they can breathe, they are sort of dancing around the circle, but the water, their element, is drying up. So it's like a dying—like watching a race of people, or a race of creatures, dying. And they are mostly females, but a few of them have a small male organ, so there are a few males there, but they won't live long enough to reproduce, and their element is drying up. And there is one that is sitting over here near me and I'm talking to this porpoise and he has prickles on his tummy, sort of like a porcupine, and they don't seem to be a part of him. And I think that there's one good point about the water drying up, I think—well, at least at the bottom, when all the water dries up, there will probably be some sort of treasure there, because at the bottom of the lake there should be things that have fallen in, like coins or something, but I look carefully and all that I can find is an old license plate. . . . That's the dream.*

Fritz: *Will you please play the license plate?*

L: *I am an old license plate, thrown in the bottom of a lake. I have no use because I'm no value—although I'm not rusted—I'm outdated, so I can't be used as a license plate . . . and I'm just thrown on the rubbish heap. That's what I did with a license plate, I threw it on a rubbish heap.*

F: *Well, how do you feel about this?*

L: *(quietly) I don't like it. I don't like being a license plate—useless.*

F: *Could you talk about this? That was such a long dream until you come to find the license plate, I'm sure this must be of great importance.*

L: *(sighs) Useless. Outdated. . . . The use of a license plate is to allow—give a car permission *to go . . . and I can't give anyone permission to do anything because I'm outdated. . . . In California, they just paste a little—you buy a sticker —and stick it on the car on the old license plate (faint attempt at humor). So maybe someone could put me on their car and stick this sticker on me, I don't know . . .*

F: *Okay, now play the lake.*

L: *I'm a lake . . . I'm drying up, and disappearing, soaking into the earth . . . (with a touch of surprise) dying. . . . But when I soak into the earth, I become a part of the earth—so maybe I water the surrounding area, so . . . even in the lake, even in my bed, flowers can grow (sighs). . . . New life can grow . . . from me (cries) . . .*

F: *You get the existential message?*

L: *Yes. (sadly, but with conviction) I can paint—I can create—I can create beauty. I can no longer reproduce. I'm like the porpoise . . . but I . . . I'm . . . I . . . keep wanting to say I'm food . . . I . . . as water becomes . . . I water the earth, and give life-growing things, the water—they need both the earth and water, and the . . . and the air and the sun, but as the water from the lake, I can play a part in something, and producing—feeding.*

F: *You see the contrast: On the surface, you find something, some artifact—the license plate, the artificial you—but then when you go deeper, you find the apparent death of the lake is actually fertility . . .*

L: *And I don't need a license plate, or a permission, a license in order to . . .*

F: *(gently) Nature doesn't need a license plate to grow. You don't have to be useless, if you are organismically creative, which means if you are involved.*

L: *And I don't need permission to be creative . . . Thank you. (Perls, 1969, pp. 81–82)*

In gestalt therapy sessions, the focus is on the more obvious elements of a person's behavior. Such sessions are often called "gestalt awareness training" because the therapeutic results of the experience stem from the process of becoming more aware of one's total self and environment. The technique of working through unresolved conflicts is called "taking care of unfinished business." We all go through life, according to Perls, with unfinished or unresolved traumas and conflicts. We carry the excess baggage of these unfinished situations into new relationships and tend to reenact them in our relations with other people. If we are able to complete our past unfinished business, we then have less psychological tension to cope with and can be more realistically aware of ourselves and our world.

Expressing themselves in front of the group, perhaps taking the part of first one and then another fragment of a scene, and denied the use of their usual techniques for avoiding self-awareness, individuals are brought to an "impasse," at which point they must confront their feelings and conflicts. According to Perls, "In the safe emergency of the therapeutic situation, the neurotic discovers that the world does not fall to pieces if he or she gets angry, sexy, joyous, mournful" (1967, p. 331). Thus individuals find that they can, after all, get beyond impasses on their own.

Evaluation of the Humanistic-Experiential Therapies

The humanistic-experiential therapies have been criticized for their lack of highly systematized models of human behavior and its specific aberrations, their lack of agreed-upon therapeutic procedures, and their vagueness about what is supposed to happen between client and therapist. These very features, however, are seen by many proponents of this general approach as contributing to its strength and vitality. Systematized theories can reduce individuals to abstractions, which can diminish their perceived worth and deny their uniqueness as individuals. Because people are so different, we should expect that different techniques are appropriate for different cases. Rigorous research on the outcomes produced by the humanistic-existential therapies is rare, but some has been carried out on the gestalt variety. This technique has a respectable, though unspectacular, record (Smith, Glass, & Miller, 1980).

In any event, many of the humanistic-experiential concepts—the uniqueness of each individual, the satisfaction that comes from developing and using one's potentials, the importance of the search for meaning and fulfillment, and the human power for choice and self-direction—have had a major impact on our contemporary views of both human nature and psychotherapy.

THERAPY FOR INTERPERSONAL RELATIONSHIPS

In Chapter 3, we noted the interpersonal perspective's emphasis on the role of faulty communications, interactions, and relationships in maladaptive behavior. This viewpoint has had an important impact on approaches to therapy—particularly, as we have seen, on contemporary psychodynamic therapy, but also to a considerable extent on the behavioristic and humanistic-existential therapies. For example, in behavior therapy we have seen a notable rise in concern with the client-therapist relationship and a growing emphasis on modifying social reinforcements that may be maintaining maladaptive responses; in humanistic-existential therapies we have seen the focus on such problems as lack of acceptance, relatedness, and love in an individual's life.

Although the interpersonal perspective is increasingly seen as essential to fully understanding many types of "individual" disorder, numerous problems brought to practitioners are explictly relationship problems. That is, the presenting complaint is not so much one of dissatisfaction with self or one's own behavior as one of inability to achieve satisfactory accords with people who are close enough that one's relationship with them could not readily be given up. A common example is marital distress. The maladaptive behavior is in these instances shared among the members of the relationship; it is, to use the contemporary term, "systemic" (Gurman, Kniskern, & Pinsof, 1986). Such problems require therapeutic techniques that focus on relationships as much as or more than on individuals. As was seen in Chapter 10, many problems presenting as individual sexual dysfunctions turn out to be systemic in character. In this section, we will explore the growing fields of couples and family therapy as examples of this type of multiple-client intervention. In general, these therapies, when placed (as they often are) in the context of helping *individuals* to change, focus on altering the *reactions* of the interpersonal environment to the behavior of each of the involved people. To this extent, they may be considered chiefly Type E approaches.

It is important to note that couples and family therapies can be and are conducted from any of the perspectives discussed in this chapter and in Chapter 3. Thus behavioral marital therapy, often utilizing a contracting approach, is one of several widely available variations on the theme.

Couples Counseling (Marital Therapy)

The large numbers of couples seeking assistance with relationship problems have made couples counseling a growing field of therapy. Typically the partners are seen together, and therapy focuses on clarifying and improving their interactions and relationships. Therapy for only one of the partners has proved less effective for resolving such problems (Gurman & Kniskern, 1978), although it is common at the start of couples therapy for each partner secretly to harbor the wish that only the other will have to do the changing. It is almost always necessary, however, that *both* partners alter their reactions to the other.

Couples counseling, or **marital therapy,** includes a wide range of concepts and procedures. Most therapists emphasize mutual need gratification, social role expectations, communication patterns, and similar interpersonal factors. Not surprisingly, happily married couples tend to differ from unhappily married couples in that they remain good friends, talk more to each other, keep channels of communication open, make more use of nonverbal communication, and show more sensitivity to each other's feelings and needs. For example, in a study comparing distressed versus nondistressed couples, Margolin and Wampold (1981) found that nondistressed couples showed more problem-solving behavior than distressed couples, a result found often in studies of this sort. The extremely common scenario, "He never talks to me, he withdraws" versus "All she does is bitch and complain, so who needs to talk," is one whose resolution obviously calls for considerable problem-solving skill, not to mention a degree of maturity and patience in employing it. Not all people who decide to share their lives are at the time abundantly equipped in these respects.

Faulty role expectations often play havoc with marital adjustment. For example, Paul (1971) cited the case of a couple who came for marital therapy when the 39-year-old husband was about to divorce his wife to marry a much younger woman. During therapy, he broke into sobs of grief as he recalled the death of his Aunt Anna, who had always accepted him as he was and created an atmosphere of peace and contentment. In reviewing this incident, the husband realized that his girlfriend represented his lifelong search for another Aunt Anna. This led to a reconciliation with his wife, who was now more understanding of his needs, feelings, and role expectations and thus altered her behavior toward her husband accordingly.

One of the difficulties in couples therapy is the intense emotional involvement of the partners, which makes it difficult for them to perceive and accept the realities of their relationship. Often wives can see clearly what is "wrong" with their husbands but not what attitudes and behaviors of their own are contributing to the relationship, while husbands tend to have remarkable "insight" into their wives' flaws but not their own. To help correct this problem, videotape recordings have been used increas-

Here two actors using case histories of real people (for purposes of telecourse instruction) role-play a couple in marital therapy. In this session, they argue about the fact that Wanda did not make pork chops for Harry the way he likes them made. The therapist must assume that this disagreement reflects a hidden agenda and try to get at the real issues. A couple in distress may have faulty expectations of their spouse's role in the marriage, may be too emotionally involved to see the realities of the relationship, and may be unskilled at communicating needs and feelings as well as expressing affection and approval. The therapist must focus not only on the relationship, but on the partners' personal limitations, which may be affecting how they react to each other.

ingly to recapture crucial moments of intense interaction between the partners. By watching playbacks of these tapes after immediate tensions have diminished, the partners can gain a fuller awareness of the nature of their interactions. Thus a husband may realize for the first time that he tries to dominate rather than listen to his wife and consider her needs and expectations, or a wife may realize that she is continually undermining her husband's feelings of worth and esteem. The following statement was made by a young wife after viewing a videotape playback of the couple's first therapy session:

"See! There it is—loud and clear! As usual you didn't let me express my feelings or opinions, you just interrupted me with your own. You're always telling me what I think without asking me what I think. And I can see what I have been doing in response—withdrawing into silence. I feel like, what's the use of talking."

This insight was shared with the husband, and the couple was able to work out a much more satisfactory marital relationship within a few months.

Other relatively new and innovative approaches to couples therapy include training the partners to use Rogerian nondirective techniques in listening to each other and helping each other clarify and verbalize their feelings and reactions. A mutual readiness to really listen and try to understand what the other one is experiencing—and an acceptance of whatever comes out in this process—can be both therapeutic for the individuals and productive of a more open and honest relationship in the future.

Eisler et al. (1974) used an interesting combination of videotape playbacks and assertiveness therapy, as illustrated in the following instance:

In one case, a 45-year-old high school teacher was responding passively and ineffectively to his highly critical wife at the beginning of therapy. By watching videotapes of their interactions, they both received feedback on their roles in the interactions. The husband received assertiveness training and practiced being more assertive, continuing to watch videotapes of the gradually changing interactions between him and his wife.

In contrast to the videotapes made at the beginning of therapy, those made at the end showed such positive results as improved communication, more expressions of affection and approval, and a marked increase in the amount of smiling during their interactions. Both spouses stated that their posttreatment marital adjustment seemed more satisfying.

Behavior therapy has also been used to bring about desired changes in marital relationships. Here the spouses are taught to reinforce instances of desired behavior while withdrawing reinforcement for undesired behavior (see *HIGHLIGHT 18.6*). In a recent study comparing behavioral with insight-oriented psychodynamic marital therapy, neither proved superior to the other, but both significantly outperformed a waiting-list control condition (Snyder & Wills, 1989).

How effective in general are marital therapies at resolving marital crises and promoting more effective marriages or intimate partnerships? One study involved a five-year follow-up of 320 former marital therapy clients and compared their divorce rates with those of the general population (Cookerly, 1980). In cases in which both partners underwent therapy together, 56.4 percent had remained married for the five-year period; in cases in which other types of therapy were used, 29 percent had remained married. All forms of therapy were associ-

HIGHLIGHT 18.6

Structured Behavior Therapy for Couples

Margolin, Christensen, and Weiss (1975) developed a brief, highly structured form of couples therapy organized around six topics, or modules. The sequence takes about ten weeks.

1. *Pinpointing contingencies.* In an intensive period, the partners' problem behaviors and the conditions maintaining them are identified.

2. *Training in communication skills.* Several techniques to improve communication, such as paraphrasing and reflecting the partners' feelings, are taught through modeling by the therapist, behavioral rehearsal, and video feedback.

3. *Training in conflict resolution.* Partners view videotapes of other couples illustrating good and bad ways to deal with conflicts. Sometimes a poor method, such as sidetracking or name-calling, is followed by a constructive approach.

4. *Formation of utility matrices.* Here the partners identify rewards and penalties that they can use in contracts with each other about what they will and will not do.

5. *Negotiating and "contingency contracting."* This is one of the most important phases. Practicing their new communication skills, the couple negotiates agreements on behavioral contracts that will provide a more rewarding and less punishing relationship for both of them.

6. *Termination and maintenance.* Once the agreements go into effect, the therapist helps promptly with any problems that arise to ensure that the learned skills are being practiced and the improved relationship maintained. In fact, throughout the course of the therapy sequence, evening phone contacts supplement the laboratory sessions for obtaining information on the partners' interactions, problems, and use of new skills. Treatment is ended gradually as the spouses assume their new roles.

Follow-up is an important part of this therapy. The therapist may make weekly telephone contacts for the first weeks following termination. Booster sessions may be scheduled after termination, if they are needed.

This form of behavioral marital therapy has been shown to be one of the most effective approaches to improving marriage relationships (Gurman, Kniskern, & Pinsof, 1986; Jacobson & Martin, 1976). Moreover, its relatively well-structured modules can be precisely applied and taught readily to beginning therapists. The relatively specific interventions also lend themselves to empirical verification more easily than other, nonbehavioral methods; thus research into marital therapy, a previously neglected area, may now be encouraged.

ated with significantly better results in resolving marital crises and keeping marriages together than was the use of no therapy at all. This conclusion is also supported in Gurman, Kniskern, and Pinsof's (1986) more recent review of numerous outcome studies. Finally, couples therapy has been successfully used as an adjunct in the treatment of individual problems, such as depression, agoraphobia, and alcohol abuse (Jacobson, Holtzworth-Monroe, & Schmaling, 1989).

Of course, a motivational factor in outcome assessments of this sort makes interpretation somewhat difficult. People strongly motivated to stay in their relationships are more likely to give couples therapy a serious try than their less motivated counterparts. Such motivation may itself, irrespective of therapy, make for partnership longevity or, perhaps, tolerance of partner abnormality. On the other hand, as we have seen, strong motivation is a key element in the likely success of *any* psychological therapy, so the research on outcomes of couples therapy has a certain face validity even acknowledging some unclarity about the role of motivational variations.

Family Therapy

Therapy for a family group overlaps with marital therapy but has somewhat different roots. Whereas marital therapy developed in response to the large number of clients who came for assistance with marital problems, family therapy began with the finding that many people who had shown marked improvement in individual therapy—often in institutional settings—had a relapse on their return home. It soon became apparent that many of these people came from disturbed family settings that required modification if they were to maintain their gains. A pioneer in the field of family therapy has described the problem as follows:

Psychopathology in the individual is a product of the way he deals with his intimate relations, the way they deal with him, and the way other family members involve him in their relations with each other. Further, the appearance of symptomatic behavior in an individual is necessary for the continued function of a particular family system. Therefore, changes in the individual can occur only if the family system changes. . . . (Haley, 1962, p. 70)

This viewpoint led to an important concept in the field of psychotherapy, namely, that the problem or disorder shown by an "identified client" is often only a symptom of a larger family problem. A careful study of the family of a disturbed child, for example, may reveal that the child is merely reflecting the pathology of the family unit. As a result, most family therapists share the view that the family —not simply the designated "client"—must be directly involved in therapy if lasting improvement is to be achieved. This is a conclusion also implied in our pathogenic loop model described earlier. Its application is increasingly seen in attempts to understand relapse after recovery from even severe disorder, as in the work on expressed emotion (EE) in mood disorders and schizophrenia (see Chapters 11 and 12).

Perhaps the most widely used approach to family therapy is the "conjoint family therapy" of Satir (1967). Her emphasis is on improving faulty communications, interactions, and relationships among family members and on fostering a family system that better meets the needs of each member. The following example shows Satir's emphasis on the problem of faulty communication:

Husband: *She never comes up to me and kisses me. I am always the one to make the overtures.*

Therapist: *Is this the way you see yourself behaving with your husband?*

Wife: *Yes, I would say he is the demonstrative one. I didn't know he wanted me to make the overtures.*

Th: *Have you told your wife that you would like this from her—more open demonstration of affection?*

H: *Well, no you'd think she'd know.*

W: *No, how would I know? You always said you didn't like aggressive women.*

H: *I don't, I don't like dominating women.*

W: *Well, I thought you meant women who make the overtures. How am I to know what you want?*

Th: *You'd have a better idea if he had been able to tell you. (Satir, 1967, pp. 72–73)*

Another encouraging approach to resolving family disturbances is called **structural family therapy** (Minuchin, 1974). This approach, based on "systems theory," assumes that a family system itself is more influential than individual personality or intrapsychic conflicts in producing abnormal behavior. It assumes that the family system has contributed to the characteristic behaviors that individual family members have developed; if the family context changes, then the individual members will have altered experiences in the family and will behave differently in accordance with the changed requirements of the new family context. Thus an important goal of structural family therapy is to change the organization of the family in such a way that the family members will behave more positively and supportively toward each other.

Structural family therapy is focused on present interactions and requires an active but not directive approach on the part of a therapist. Initially, the therapist gathers information about the family—a "structural map" of the typical family interaction patterns—by acting like one of the family and participating in the family interactions as an insider. In this way, the therapist discovers whether the family system has rigid or flexible boundaries, who dominates the power structure, who gets blamed when things go wrong, and so on.

Armed with this understanding, the therapist then uses himself or herself as a change medium for altering the interaction among the members. For example, Aponte and Hoffman (1973) reported the successful use of structural family therapy in treating an anorexic 14-year-old girl:

Analyzing the communications in the family, the therapists saw a competitive struggle for the father's attention and observed that the girl, Laura, was able to succeed in this competition and get "cuddly" attention from her father by not eating. To bring the hidden dynamics out into the open, they worked at getting the family members to express their desires more directly— in words instead of through cryptic behavioral messages. In time, Laura became much more able to verbalize her wishes for affection and gave up the unacceptable and dangerous method of not eating.

Similarly, Schwartz, Barrett, and Saba (1983) reported successful treatment of bulimia with structural family therapy. Minuchin et al. (1975) conducted a study in which structural family therapy was used successfully with families in which children had developed psychophysiologic illnesses. Stanton and Todd (1976) also related dramatic improvement rates with its use in several families in which one member was an identified heroin addict.

As with couples problems, maladaptive family relationships have also been successfully overcome by behavioristically oriented therapies. With this type of therapy, Huff (1969) has suggested that the therapist's task is to reduce the aversive value of the family for the identified client as well as that of the client for other family members. "The therapist does this by actively manipulating the *relationship* between members so that the relationship changes to a more positively reinforcing and reciprocal one" (p. 26).

N. Hurwitz (1974) has elaborated on the role of the family therapist as an intermediary whose functions include "interpreter, clarifier, emissary, go-between, messenger, catalyst, mediator, arbitrator, negotiator, and referee" (p. 145). As virtually anyone who has ever done family therapy will testify, these role demands are most exacting and emotionally draining; hence they are commonly shared by cotherapists, one male and one female.

After reviewing family therapy approaches, Gurman and Kniskern (1978) concluded that structural family therapy had had more impressive results than most other experientially- and analytically-oriented approaches they had reviewed. In a more recent update (Gurman, Kniskern, & Pinsof, 1986) that included additional work that had been published in the interim on behavioral approaches, the results have tended to favor behavioral intervention.

In addition, many clinicians working with severely disturbed individuals have concluded that family therapy is effective at reducing family tensions and promoting more adaptive functioning of all family members. As was seen in Chapter 12, the work on reducing family expressed emotion (EE) in preventing schizophrenic relapse looks very promising. However, the relative success of family intervention methods versus individual methods of therapy is an exceedingly difficult area of research. Wellisch and Trock (1980) found, at a three-year follow-up, that the previously superior effects of family therapy for severe disorder had deteriorated; 57 percent of the clients had had to be rehospitalized, as compared with 20 percent of the individual therapy cases. We can only speculate about the reasons for this relatively poor showing for family therapy. If these results suggest anything, it is perhaps that, for chronic problems with a pattern of recurrent exacerbation, the more focused impact of individual psychotherapy may in the long run be more beneficial.

THE INTEGRATION OF THERAPY APPROACHES

Although an integration of psychoanalysis and learning theory was attempted as early as 1950 by Dollard and Miller in their *Personality and Psychotherapy,* the two treatment approaches diverged significantly in the 1960s and 1970s. Recently, a great deal has been written about the possibility of gaining a rapprochement between behavior therapy and other schools of therapy, particularly psychodynamic therapy (Arkowitz & Messer, 1984; Goldfried, Greenberg, & Marmar, 1990; Marmor & Woods, 1980; Wachtel, 1977, 1982). At first, this trend may seem surprising, given the generally competitive atmosphere and the critical struggles that have traditionally existed between psychoanalysts and behavior therapists. Early behaviorists were adamant in their criticism of psychoanalysis as inefficient and mystical. The analysts reacted with strong counterarguments, partly in their own defense but also in keeping with their beliefs that behavioral therapies were superficial and treated only symptoms, while psychoanalytic treatments sought "deeper" and more permanent cures.

Over the years, however, behavioral and psychoanalytic proponents have had time to become accustomed (or perhaps "desensitized") to each other's criticisms. With the wide dissemination and practice of behavioral methods, it has become apparent to some psychodynamically oriented therapists that behavioral methods are quite effective in the treatment of many disorders. Similarly, many behaviorally oriented therapists have concluded that it is not simply the application of a *technique* that brings about change in a client. They acknowledge that "relationship" factors are exceedingly important—even when rigorous behavior modification procedures are being used (Lazarus, 1981, 1985). In addition, research comparing both treatment methods has generally shown that neither approach has been demonstrated consistently to be superior to the other (Sloane et al., 1975), although, overall, there seems to be a small advantage for behavior and cognitive-behavioral methods (Lambert, Shapiro, & Bergin, 1986; Smith, Glass, & Miller, 1980).

Kendall (1982b) has concisely summarized the reasons for the current interest in integrating behavior therapy with other methods. He noted that (a) some behaviorists have concluded that the human organism is multifaceted and that focusing only on "behavior" is not sufficient as a treatment goal; (b) the "less than perfect" success of available therapy methods justifies combining the most successful treatment strategies from all approaches; (c) integrating diverse therapies might inspire a new enthusiasm and promote novel applications of varied treatment methods and perhaps promote new formulations of old problems; and (d) integrating diverse therapy schools would require members of a given school to begin to question the assumptions underlying their treatment approaches and would promote a broad reappraisal from different perspectives. Our own "loop" model is, of course, completely in accord with this perspective.

According to Kendall, however, inherent problems face the integrationist position. First, no common language unites the various therapy schools. Second, it is much easier for a trainee to learn a single therapeutic approach than to learn elements of various approaches. Finally, basic conceptual differences exist that would preclude a fully satisfactory merger between behavior therapy and psychodynamic therapy, such as their different emphases on etiological factors, treatment goals, and tactical methods.

Further examination of therapeutic methods from the vantage point of alternative views may, in time, lead to interestingly amalgamated psychosocial therapies. It does not appear at this point, however, that many of the advocates of the various positions will be able to put aside their long identification with particular schools and easily assimilate alien notions and practices, notwithstanding a common self-description among therapists as "eclectic."

Meanwhile, an equally if not more vexing problem concerns the integration of psychosocial and biological forms of treatment. As shown in earlier chapters, combined treatment of this sort, where it has been tried, has often proved to be more effective than either alone. In this area we confront not only philosophical differences but interdisciplinary political and economic ones as well. Although there is a developing movement among a segment of clinical psychologists, endorsed to a degree by the American Psychological Association, to seek prescription-writing privileges that would permit them to administer psychoactive drugs (strongly opposed by organized medicine and psychiatry), as of this writing the overwhelming majority of nonmedical therapists may not legally do so. Even among clinical psychologists, many are opposed to this trend, mostly out of concern that easy access to drug treatment will corrupt the further and much needed development of even more powerful forms of psychosocial intervention. In our judgment, the latter concern is not specious; too frequently, we have seen the clinical process distorted by an excessively hasty and exclusive recourse to what is usually, at best, palliative medication. Still, judicious combined treatment surely has much to recommend it for certain types of disorder. It will be interesting to see how this issue is played out by the mental health professions over the next decade.

In group therapy, the relationship among the group members is as important as the relationship between client and therapist in individual therapy. In this unique setting, the therapy may be of various therapeutic orientations, with the therapist using a combination of psychoanalytic, behavioral, and other approaches.

THE EVALUATION OF SUCCESS IN PSYCHOTHERAPY

Competition between individual therapies has tended to obscure the actual success of therapy. Four decades ago, Eysenck (1952), a well-known British psychologist, shook the field of psychological intervention by concluding in his review of evidence on treatment outcomes that people who were untreated or simply placed on a waiting list for psychotherapy improved about as much as those who actually received therapy. This pronouncement prompted a flurry of research activity and a thorough reanalysis of the existing data. Reevaluation of therapy-outcome research accomplished prior to Eysenck's review, as well as a great deal done since, has painted a different and more positive picture of the overall effectiveness of psychotherapy (Lambert, Shapiro, & Bergin, 1986). In particular, the development of meta-analysis techniques for evaluating therapeutic outcomes, described in *HIGHLIGHT 18.7,* has had an enormous and positive impact in revitalizing a sense of purpose among evaluation researchers.

Problems of Evaluation

Evaluating the effectiveness of psychological treatment is a difficult enterprise for several reasons. At best, it is an inexact process, dependent on inexact and inevitably somewhat subjective data. For example, attempts at evaluation generally depend on one or more of the following sources of information: (a) a therapist's impression of changes that have occurred, (b) a client's reports of change, (c) reports from the client's family or friends, (d) comparison of pretreatment and posttreatment personality test scores, and (e) measures of change in selected overt behaviors.

Unfortunately, each of these sources has serious limitations. A therapist may not be the best judge of a client's progress, since any therapist is likely to be biased in favor of seeing himself or herself as competent and successful. Furthermore, therapists can inflate improvement averages by consciously or unconsciously encouraging difficult clients to discontinue therapy. The problem of how to manage "dropouts" complicates most therapy outcome studies (for example, are they to be counted as "failures" when in fact they receive little or none of the therapy being evaluated?). It has also been somewhat facetiously remarked that a therapist often thinks a client is getting better because he or she is getting accustomed to the client's symptoms.

A client, also, is an unreliable source concerning the outcomes of therapy. Clients may not only want to think that they are getting better for personal reasons, but they may report that they are being helped in an attempt to please the therapist. In addition, because therapy often requires a considerable investment of time, money, and sometimes emotional distress, the idea that it is useless is a dissonant one. Family and relatives may also be inclined to "see" the improvement they had hoped for, although they often seem to be more realistic than either the therapist or the client in their long-term evaluations.

Outside clinical ratings by an independent observer are sometimes used in psychotherapy outcome research to evaluate the progress of a client; these may be more objective than ratings by those directly involved in the therapy. Another widely used objective measure of client change is performance on psychological tests. A client evaluated in this way takes a battery of tests before and after therapy and the differences in scores are assumed to reflect progress or deterioration. Although such tests may indeed show changes, they are, however, likely to focus on the particular measures in which the therapist or researcher is interested. They are not necessarily valid predictors of how the client will behave in real life, nor can they give any indication of whether the changes that have occurred are likely to be enduring. Of interest here, however, is some strong evidence that the effects of psychotherapy in general, as variously measured, are decidedly not ephemeral or temporary (Nicholson & Berman, 1983).

Changes in selected and specifically denoted behaviors appear to be the safest measures of outcome, especially where the occurrence of these outside of the therapy situation itself is systematically monitored. Such techniques, including client self-monitoring, have been widely and effectively used, especially by behavior therapists. Generalized terms such as *recovery, marked improvement,* and *moderate improvement,* as applied to initially problematic behavior and often used in outcome research, are of course open to considerable differences in interpretation. In addition, even under the best of outcome measurement circumstances there is always the possibility that improvement will be attributed to the particular form of treatment used, when it is in fact a product of other events in a client's life or even of "spontaneous" change.

In spite of these difficulties, however, it is to at least some extent possible to study the effectiveness of various treatment approaches separately—determining what procedures work best with various types of individuals (Kendall & Norton-Ford, 1982; Smith, Glass, & Miller, 1980). In the course of our discussion of abnormal behavior patterns, we have mentioned a number of such studies, most of which have demonstrated positive outcomes from psychotherapy.

In this context, it is relevant to ask what happens to people who do not obtain formal treatment. In view of the many ways that people can help each other, it is not surprising that often considerable improvement occurs without therapeutic intervention. Some forms of psychopathology, such as manic and depressive episodes and some instances of schizophrenia, appear to run a fairly brief course with or without treatment, and there are many other instances in which disturbed people improve over time for reasons that are not apparent.

HIGHLIGHT 18.7

Meta-Analysis in the Evaluation of Therapy Outcomes

Systematic outcome studies on the effects of various forms of psychotherapy for various kinds of disorder have been done for decades, and recently there has been a phenomenal increase in their rate of appearance in the professional literature. Although this is doubtless a healthy sign indicating the vitality of the field and its sense of scientific responsibility, the sheer volume and diversity of the work undertaken and published have made it difficult for researchers and clinicians to answer any specific questions they may have—such as what types of therapy produce the best outcomes for a specific type of disorder, or indeed if any do have measurable benefits. Narrative-based summary reviews of portions of this literature, often containing "box scores" of results from different studies, are published from time to time. These can be helpful but are often limited by the difficulties of comparing studies whose essential characteristics, such as the therapy outcome measures used, vary enormously.

The technique of *meta-analysis* was invented as a means of summarizing the results of large and varied data sets of this sort by recasting them into a standard metric format whose meaning, at least statistically, is immediately apparent. As applied in the case of therapeutic outcomes in psychopathology, the technique is quite straightforward, although so mathematically tedious as to require electronic computation.

In the simplest case, three items of information are needed for every outcome measure used in every study in the analysis. These are the means of the outcome measure or measures for both (a) the treated and (b) the untreated (control) sample of patient-subjects, and (c) the standard deviation for the untreated sample. These three figures are usually reported directly by the original investigator, but even where they are not they are frequently recoverable from data that are reported. The basic statistic known as an *effect size* (ES) is computed from these quantities according to the following formula:

$$\text{ES} = \frac{M_{\text{Therapy}} - M_{\text{Control}}}{SD_{\text{Control}}}$$

where:

M_{Therapy} is the mean score for the psychotherapy group on the outcome measure;

M_{Control} is the mean score for the control group; and

SD_{Control} is the control group standard deviation. (Note: some investigators prefer to use a pooled standard deviation calculated from the scores of both the treated and control groups.)

Readers familiar with elementary statistics will recognize this as a variant of the formula for the *z*-score, one that expresses the deviation of the treatment group's mean from that of the control group in (control group or pooled) standard deviation units. In other words, the ES locates the treated group's mean on a distribution of standard ("*z*") scores whose mean is the mean of the control group for the particular outcome measure being considered; in *z*-score units, that mean would be zero. An ES of, let us say, +1.0 would indicate an outcome for the treated group that is one standard deviation above the mean of the control group on that outcome measure. By assuming that the outcome measure for the untreated group is "normally distributed" (that is, approximates the bell-shaped normal probability curve), we could infer from normal curve statistical properties that the treated group's mean performance or level on this measure is at the eighty-fourth percentile of that of the control group; or, to put it another way, we could say that 84 percent of untreated people fall below the mean level of the treated group.

Notice that the ES statistic gives us a powerful means of reducing all manner of quantified outcome data to the same metric or scale, thus allowing for direct comparisons among them. In particular, we can pool the results of many studies having the same or similar independent variables (such as the nature of treatment, the type of disorder treated, and so on) and dependent variables (the outcomes of treatment) to arrive at an overall ES estimate, usually the mean or average of all the ESs obtained. This is then reported as the *Average Effect Size,* or $\overline{\text{ES}}$, for the particular type of treatment or diagnostic group being considered.

In several instances in this text we have used data from meta-analytic studies to estimate the effectiveness of various therapies with various populations of clients. Particular attention has been given in this regard to the original and massive meta-analytic work on mental disorder therapies undertaken by Smith, Glass, and Miller (1980).

Nevertheless, even if many emotionally disturbed individuals tend to improve over time without psychotherapy, it seems clear that psychotherapy can often accelerate improvement or ensure desired behavior change that might not otherwise occur (Lambert, Shapiro, & Bergin, 1986; Telch, 1981). Most researchers today would agree that psychotherapy is more effective than no treatment. The rate of individuals experiencing significant improvement across studies of therapy outcome, regardless of approach, averages about 80 percent; if there is such a thing as "spontaneous" improvement, a doubtful occurrence, it would not in all likelihood exceed 15 percent. Furthermore, improvement seems a function of the number of therapy sessions undertaken—with the largest gains achieved early (that is, within six months) in the therapeutic relationship (Howard et al., 1986). Very long-term psychotherapy is actually quite rare, but such cases tend to create the impression, even among professionals, that disordered behavior is more intractable than for the most part it actually is. In one study of this problem (Howard et al., 1989), 56 percent of the total therapy sessions offered by a clinic were "consumed" by only 16 percent of the clients.

Nonetheless, the issue of treatment evaluation remains a vital one—both ethically and practically —if psychologists and other mental health personnel are to be justified in intervening in other people's lives. The issue becomes especially vital in light of evidence that some clients are *harmed* in their encounters with psychotherapists (Lambert, Shapiro, & Bergin, 1986; Mays & Franks, 1985; Strupp, Hadley, & Gomes-Schwartz, 1977). This problem of negative effects, which many therapists acknowledge when directly queried (see, e.g., Appendix C, pp. 223–343, of the Strupp et al., 1977, volume for interesting first-person accounts), is addressed further in the Unresolved Issues section.

Finally, we must note some problems in the growing trend for varied psychological treatments to be directly compared, within the same study, with the outcomes of biological treatments, usually drug therapies. Although such studies have frequently reported the "superiority" of one or the other of these therapy types in the treatment of various disorders, we remain skeptical that a truly definitive comparison of the outcomes of the two forms of therapy is ultimately possible. In fact, it is not clear that a completely valid outcome study can be done with psychosocial treatment when the design of the study adheres to established modes of evaluating the efficacy of drugs, as most by custom do. As Stiles and Shaprio (1989) have pointed out in a detailed examination of the issues involved, psychotherapy and drug therapy differ on many dimensions of critical importance in deciding on, and in interpreting, issues both of study design and the outcome measures used.

Take, for example, a therapist himself or herself as a variable, including such attributes as experience in treating the particular disorder, interpersonal skill, familiarity with the subcultural background of a client, faith in the treatment, and perhaps even personal attractiveness or charisma as experienced by the client. We have solid reason, based on available research findings, to believe that such things may be of crucial significance in determining the outcome of any psychosocial treatment effort. Now contrast this with the typical situation for drug treatment. Here, the "active ingredient" of the treatment is pretty much the same no matter who writes the prescription, and a therapist's personal attributes or his or her experience in treating the disorder (with the possible exception of a nonspecific placebo component) are largely irrelevant. With such important differences that vary in uncontrolled (and probably uncontrollable) ways in psychotherapy versus drug comparison studies, it is not easy to see how any *general* and *unequivocal* conclusions regarding differential effectiveness could be made, almost regardless of the quantitative results obtained.

Precisely this sort of difficulty, in fact, attends the NIMH multisite "model" study of the treatment of depression described in *HIGHLIGHT 18.8*, where the preliminary results so far reported show a rather disconcerting effect that might, however, have been predicted from the considerations just discussed. Even during their project-specific pretraining, the psychotherapists recruited for this study showed significantly varying aptitudes (and eventual clinical results) in applying the techniques that were to be used for the interpersonal psychosocial treatment (IPT) aspect of the study (O'Malley et al., 1988). When we turn to the short-term outcomes reported for the main project, we observe that they include significant statistical interactions involving the *sites* at which psychosocial treatment took place (Elkin et al., 1989).

In other words, the psychotherapists at some sites had significantly better immediate outcomes than those at others—even though all were supposedly doing the same types of psychosocial interventions. Although it was not possible to rule out, in preliminary analyses, unexpected but conceivable intersite differences in the characteristics of the patients treated, this seems an unlikely alternative explanation because the site interaction effect was apparent mainly among the most severely disordered patients (Elkin et al., 1989). One way of

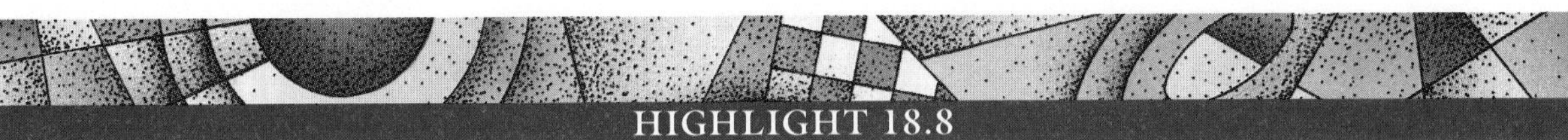

HIGHLIGHT 18.8

Anatomy of a Controlled Field Trial of Therapeutic Outcome

The long-awaited initial results of an NIMH-supported clinical field trial competitively evaluating a cognitive-behavioral therapy (CBT), an interpersonal psychotherapy (IPT), and an antidepressant drug (imipramine) therapy plus clinical management (IMI-CM) in the treatment of unipolar depression became available in late 1989 (Elkin et al., 1989). The design of this study, widely regarded to be state of the art, and its preliminary findings are analyzed here in some detail to give you an appreciation of the choices, the internal logic, and the inference network typically involved in research on therapeutic processes and outcomes in the mental health field.

Subjects. Following prescreening to rule out clearly ineligible patients, 560 purportedly depressed people were seen by a clinical evaluator who used a well-known structured diagnostic interview for establishing a clinical diagnosis. Only patients who met criteria for a current episode of major depressive disorder, and who in addition attained a score of at least 14 on a 17-item version of the Hamilton Rating Scale for Depression (HRSD), were considered eligible for inclusion in the study. The HRSD is a widely used clinician checklist for depressive symptomatology whose validity has been well established. Various exclusion criteria were also applied, chiefly to rule out people having other concurrent mental disorders. Patients who passed this clinical screening were given a complete medical evaluation and then put on a 7- to 14-day waiting and drug-washout period. They were then rescreened by the initial clinical evaluator before final admission to the program. Two hundred fifty people survived the screening procedures and were offered entry into the program as research patient-subjects; 239 actually entered treatment. Of this treated group, only 36 percent had experienced no previous major depressive disorder, and 15 percent had had previous episodes requiring hospitalization. Seventy percent had received some form of previous treatment for depression.

Research sites. Three widely dispersed university psychiatric centers had been chosen as the actual sites in which the clinical trials would be conducted, each recruiting, by the standard means already described, its own group of research subjects. Two of the sites each began with 84 screened subjects, and the third with 82. At each of the sites, patients were assigned at random to one of the three treatments already noted or to a control condition involving administration of a placebo pill plus clinical management (PLA-CM condition). The clinical management component, identical for both imipramine and placebo conditions, involved general encouragement and support, but no specific psychotherapeutic intervention. (The investigators concluded that it was not possible to devise a specifically *psychotherapeutic* control condition.)

Therapists. At each site a different group of experienced therapists (with an overall mean age of 41.5 years and mean experience of 11.4 years) conducted treatment in each of the study conditions, with the exception that the same therapists ("pharmacotherapists") administered either imipramine or placebo, but were blind as to which they were giving in respect to any particular pharmacotherapy-assigned patient-subject. A total of 28 therapists (10 psychologists and 18 psychiatrists) took part. They were given further training in their "specialty" therapies during a training-pilot phase of the study, and they met competence criteria in conducting this therapy prior to assignment to project patient-subjects. Their actual treatment sessions were carried out according to a detailed manual describing the interventions appropriate to the respective specialty therapies, and these sessions were continuously monitored via audiotaping by project staff.

Experimental treatment conditions. All treatments were designed to be 16 weeks in length, but there were 77 early termination cases where the average number of sessions completed was only 6.2. Overall, project patients, of whom there were 162 having at least 15 weeks of treatment, completed an average of 13.0 sessions. Unfortunately, termination evaluations could not be done on 7 of these 162 patients, reducing the number of "completers" to 155. The rates of dropout were not significantly different for the four treatment conditions. The con-

Continued

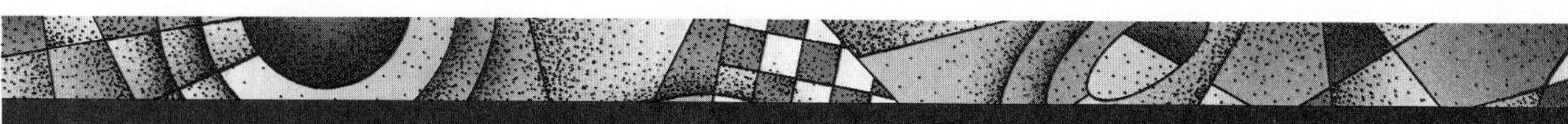

tent of the various therapies is described as follows:

CBT—*Cognitive behavior therapy was conducted as described by Beck and colleagues [see page 648]. . . . The cognitive therapist uses strategies and techniques designed to help depressed patients correct their negative, distorted views about themselves, the world, and the future, and the underlying maladaptive beliefs that give rise to these cognitions.*

IPT—*Interpersonal psychotherapy was conducted as described by Klerman et al. [see page 637]. . . . The IPT therapist seeks to help the patient to identify and better understand his or her interpersonal problems and conflicts and to develop more adaptive ways of relating to others.*

Imipramine-CM—*The pharmacotherapy conditions were [those considered standard]. Medication was administered double blind within the context of a CM [clinical management] session. . . . The average dosage for imipramine hydrochloride completers, averaged over all weeks after the first 2 weeks of treatment, was 185 mg., with 95% of the patients receiving at least 150 mg. . . .*

PLA-CM—*The pill-placebo condition was administered double blind, within the context of a CM session. . . . Although specific psychotherapeutic interventions were proscribed (especially those that might overlap with the two psychotherapies), the CM component approximated a "minimal supportive therapy" condition. (Elkin et al., 1989, p. 973)*

Results. Though therapy outcomes are reported separately for all patients entering treatment (n=239), for those completing at least 3.5 weeks of treatment (n=204), and for those completing at least 15 weeks of treatment (n=155), we will concentrate here on results for this last, full-exposure group.

Principal outcome measures were the Hamilton Rating Scale (HRSD), the Beck Depression Inventory (BDI—a self-administered questionnaire commonly used to measure level of depression), a version of the Hopkins Symptom Checklist (HSCL-90T—a more general questionnaire measuring various symptoms of distress), and the Global Assessment Scale (GAS—a clinician's rating form for general level of functioning). Because all of these measures had been administered pretreatment, it was possible to control for initial levels (none of which varied significantly among the four treatment groups) in analyzing treatment outcomes.

Briefly summarizing a rather complicated set of outcome data, these are the main findings:

1. Compared to their pretreatment scores, all four treatment groups on all four outcome measures showed significant improvement.

2. At treatment end, there was an overall statistically significant variation among the four treatment groups on only the two self-administered outcome measures, the BDI and the HSCL-90T. For the BDI, the highest (most pathological) average score was obtained by the PLA-CM group and the lowest by the IMI-CM group, with the IPT group close on its heels. On the HSCL-90T measure, IMI-CM patients had clearly superior, and PLA-CM patients clearly inferior, outcomes—with the two psychotherapy groups falling between and having virtually identical mean scores.

3. In terms of a predefined level of clinical "recovery" (that is, a score of 6 or less on the HRSD, a score of 9 or less on the BDI, or both) only the HRSD measure showed an overall significant difference among treatment groups. Specifically, IMI-CM, IPT, and CBT patients had HRSD-measured termination recovery rates, respectively, of 57 percent, 55 percent, and 51 percent, which are not significantly different from each other in statistical or probability terms. These contrast with a PLA-CM recovery rate of only 29 percent, marginally significantly different in pair-wise comparison from both IMI-CM and IPT.

4. In secondary analyses, pretreatment HRSD and GAS criteria were separately employed to divide the total patient groups into

viewing the latter finding is that differential psychotherapist efficacy was revealed only in work with more severely disturbed patients—that group of patients for whom antidepressant drug treatment showed its only superiority.

The implication is that some psychotherapists having certain as yet undetermined characteristics might do as well or even better than drugs in working with severe major depressive disorder. If that were the case, the unqualified conclusion that

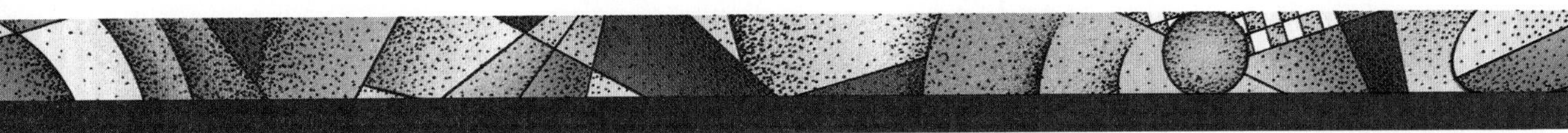

more- and less-severely depressed subgroups. The data were then reanalyzed according to this breakdown. This split resulted in a substantially enhanced differentiation of the outcomes of the treatment groups that was largely limited to the more severely disturbed patients. Both measures of pretreatment severity yielded the same ordinal arrangement of outcome HRSD and GAS scores for these more disturbed patients. The IMI-CM treatment produced the best results, followed in order by the IPT and CBT treatment conditions; PLA-CM came in last. These differences, overall, were statistically significant on the HRSD measure for both the severity criteria; for the GAS severity criterion, they were also significant on the HSCL-90T outcome measure. The general pattern was somewhat different with "recovery" rates as the outcome criterion. Here, the two psychotherapy conditions tended to outperform (but nonsignificantly) IMI-CM and PLA-CM with the less-severely disturbed patients. Among more disturbed patients, IPT and IMI-CM were associated with essentially similar recovery rates, both of them being significantly superior to PLA-CM, with CBT falling in between.

5. Also reported, but not analyzed in detail, was a finding of significant interactions between treatments and sites showing up especially in outcomes for the more disturbed patient subsample. Such patients receiving CBT at one site did extremely well and were comparable on outcome measures to IMI-CM patients. The same was true for IPT patients at another site. These residual findings strike us as quite important conceptually (and possibly practically), and are further discussed in the text.

Discussion. In many ways the most impressive result reported here is the performance of the control condition, PLA-CM. "Recovery" rates of 35 to 40 percent among less-disturbed patients and 15 to 20 percent among the more disturbed for a treatment consisting of pharmacologically inert pills and general support, encouragement, and advice speak to the power of reassurance and suggestion as nonspecific treatment factors presumably inherent in all serious efforts at intervention for major depressive disorder.

Overall, the "active" treatments investigated—antidepressant medication and cognitive-behavioral and interpersonal psychotherapies—all add something to this nonspecific baseline effect. Although the antidepressant drug treatment appeared, on average, to fare somewhat better than the others (although only marginally so than the interpersonal therapy) with those patients having more severe symptoms, outcome differences among the active therapies were in absolute terms rather small. Given the site interaction effects noted, it appears that site (that is, therapist) variation is a more important determinant of outcome in the psychotherapies than drug treatment, which on reflection makes a great deal of sense. A standard dose of imipramine is the same no matter who administers it, whereas this would hardly be true in the case of the two psychotherapies—as the results indeed confirm. The fact that both cognitive and interpersonal psychotherapists at particular sites were as effective as medication in the treatment of the severest cases is a finding of considerable theoretical and practical import.

Finally, it must be emphasized that, as of this writing, we have access only to outcomes measured at the termination of therapy. Other studies, mentioned in Chapter 11, have shown cognitive-behavioral therapy to have superior long-term effects.

drugs work better when a major depression is severe would be unwarranted, or at least potentially misleading. Again, the main point to be made here is that psychotherapy—even psychotherapy bearing a specific label—unlike a particular drug cannot realistically be treated as though it were a uniform and invariant therapeutic input. Plainly, it is not.

Given the few but consistent findings of better *long-term* outcomes with psychosocial, as opposed to drug, treatment of depression (reviewed in Chapter 11), we take it as by no means established that drug therapy is the treatment of choice for severe major depression. The present evidence indicates this to be a valid conclusion only for situations in which maximally competent psychotherapy is unavailable, with the further constraint that it addresses only outcomes measured at treatment end but not in long-term follow-up. "Competence" here, by the way, is probably best assessed by a therapist's outcome record in treating clients of this sort.

Social Values and Psychotherapy

The criticism has been raised—from both inside and outside the mental health professions—that psychotherapy can be viewed as an attempt to get people adjusted to a "sick" society rather than to encourage them to work toward its improvement. As a consequence, psychotherapy has often been considered the guardian of the status quo. This issue is perhaps easier for us to place in perspective by looking at other cultures. For example, there have been frequent allegations that psychiatry was until recently used as a means of political control in the Soviet Union, an abuse that, with *glasnost,* has now been officially acknowledged (see *Schizophrenia Bulletin,* 1990, v. 16, no. 4). It is encouraging to note that these practices had been all but universally condemned by the international mental health community. Although few people make the claim that psychiatry in the Western world is used to gain control over social critics, there is nevertheless the possibility that therapists are, in some ways, placed in the roles of "gatekeepers" of social values. Such charges, of course, bring us back to the question we raised in Chapter 1: What do we mean by *abnormal?* Our answer to that question can only be made in the light of our values.

In a broader perspective, of course, we are concerned with the complex and controversial issue of the role of values in science. Psychotherapy is not, or at least *should* not be, a system of ethics; it is a set of tools to be used at the discretion of a therapist in pursuit of a client's welfare. Thus mental health professionals are confronted with the same kinds of questions that confront scientists in general. Should a physical scientist who helps develop thermonuclear weapons be morally concerned about how they are used? Similarly, should a psychologist or behavioral scientist who develops powerful techniques of behavior control be concerned about how they are used?

Many psychologists and other scientists try to sidestep this issue by insisting that science is value-free—that it is concerned only with gathering "facts," not with how they are applied. Each time therapists decide that one behavior should be eliminated or substituted for another, however, they are making a value choice. The increasing social awareness of today's mental health professionals has brought into sharp focus ethical questions concerning their roles as therapists and value models, as well as their roles as agents for maintaining the status quo or fostering social change. For example, is a therapist to *assume* the depression of a young homemaker-mother who is abused by a drunken husband to be an internally based disorder requiring "treatment"—as once would have been routine—or does the therapist perhaps not have a larger responsibility to look beyond this individual-pathology viewpoint and confront the abnormality implicit in some of our more sacrosanct cultural expectations? Therapy takes place in a context that involves the values of the therapist, the client, and the society in which they live. There are strong pressures on a therapist—from parents, schools, courts, and other social institutions—to help people adjust to "the world as it is." At the same time, there are many counterpressures, particularly from young people who are seeking support in their attempts to become authentic people rather than blind conformists.

The dilemma in which contemporary therapists may find themselves is illustrated by the following case:

A 15-year-old high school sophomore is sent to a therapist because her parents have discovered that she has been having sexual intercourse with her boyfriend. The girl tells the therapist that she thoroughly enjoys such relations and feels no guilt or remorse over her behavior, even though her parents strongly disapprove. In addition, she reports that she is quite aware of the danger of becoming pregnant and is careful to take contraceptive measures.

What is the role of the therapist in such a case? Should the girl be encouraged to conform to her parents' mores and postpone sexual activity until she is older and more mature? Or should the parents be helped to adjust to the pattern of sexual behavior she has chosen? What should be the therapist's goal? As was noted earlier, it is not unusual to find some individuals being referred for psychological treatment because their behavior, not particularly destructive or disturbing, has caused concern among family members who wish the therapist to "fix" them.

It is apparent that there are diametrically opposed ways of dealing with problems in therapy. Society must enforce conformity to certain norms if it is to maintain its organization and survive. But how does one distinguish between norms that are vital for the common good and those that are irrelevant, outmoded, or arbitrarily imposed by thoughtless devotion to a particular subgroup's notion of revealed truth? It is often up to individual therapists to decide what path to take, and this requires value decisions on their part concerning what is best for an individual and for the larger society. Thus a mental health professional is confronted with the problem of "who (or what) controls the controller"; that is, of developing ethical standards and societal safeguards to prevent misuse of the techniques they have developed for modifying individual and group behavior (Lakin, 1991).

UNRESOLVED ISSUES in Psychotherapy

Probably no treatment procedure in general medicine or surgery is without risk in the sense of potentially harmful or even fatal effects on a client. Generally speaking, moreover, the more potent the treatment in terms of potential dramatic benefit, the more risky the procedure. The situation appears to be no different in respect to psychotherapy. As we have noted, the outcomes of psychotherapy do not range, as was once thought, from neutral (no effect) to positive, but rather seem to encompass a significant negative or deteriorative effect. One extreme here is client suicide, although we certainly do not suggest that all such outcomes could be avoided with more skillful psychotherapy. In any event, some client-psychotherapist relationships, approaching perhaps 10 percent in frequency (Lambert, Shapiro, & Bergin, 1986), apparently result in the client's being worse off than if psychotherapy had never been undertaken.

Our judgment about the gravity of this situation would be less severe if it were taken more seriously among professional psychotherapists than our experience suggests, and if we knew more about how to prevent it from happening. Regarding the latter point, we do have some guidelines about factors that should be considered, based in part on reviews of the entire issue in books offered by Mays and Franks (1985) and Strupp, Hadley, and Gomes-Schwartz (1977). By and large, there are few surprises in these works. We know that clients with certain types of disorders that are notoriously difficult to treat (such as borderline personality disorder) are more likely than others to deteriorate in treatment. We have also known for some time that an overly aggressive, intrusive, abruptly defense-challenging therapeutic style can be dangerous to client functioning, particularly where it is unmodulated by therapist warmth and empathy. Similarly, the concurrent occurrence of uncontrollable negative events (such as divorce) in a client's "extra-therapeutic" life can obviously impact negatively on therapeutic progress.

These more obvious therapeutic impasses account for only a portion of the failures. In other instances we find a bewildering network of interactive factors that, operating together and idiosyncratically in an individual case (for example, the "match" of therapist and client characteristics), produce deteriorating outcomes. Our impression, supported by some evidence reviewed by Lambert (1989), is that certain therapists, probably for reasons of personality, just do not do well with certain types of client problems. In light of these intangible factors, we take it as every therapist's responsibility to monitor their work with various types of clients to discover any such deficiencies in therapeutic range, and to refer promptly to other therapists those individuals with whom one may be ill-equipped, for whatever reason, to work.

A special case of therapeutic misadventure is the problem of therapist-client sexual entanglements, typically seduction of a client (or "former" client) by a therapist, which is considered unethical conduct. Given the frequently intense and intimate quality of therapeutic relationships, we should perhaps not be surprised that the issue of sexual attraction arises. What is astonishing is the apparent frequency with which it is manifested in an unethical and unprofessional behavior on the part of therapists—all the more so in light of the fact that virtually all authorities agree that such liaisons are *nearly always* destructive of client functioning in the long run.

A variety of evidence, including anonymous admissions of therapists in various surveys over the years, suggests that this source of client exploitation and likely negative outcome is by no means rare. According to one recent report, (Ethics Committee, American Psychological Association, 1990) 23 of 89 professional ethics cases (26 percent) opened in a recent year involved sexual improprieties. In a recently completed national survey of psychologists (Pope & Vetter, in press), *half* of the respondents reported assessing or treating at least one client who had been sexually intimate with a prior therapist, a total of 958 separate instances; 90 percent of these encounters were judged to have been of harm to the client, with an 11 percent subsequent hospitalization rate and a 14 percent rate of attempted suicide. Most of the victims (87 percent) were female, and three of them were children.

Even these chilling statistics, however, do not do justice to the magnitude of the problem in terms of already vulnerable lives being further undermined, nor do they speak to the difficulties victims often have in seeking redress for their psychic injury. That gap has been partially filled with the publication of a remarkable and courageous book by Bates and Brodsky (1989) that deals informatively with these subjects. In it, Bates renders a compelling account of her own sexual vicitimization by a therapist, one who, incredibly, has given a prominent address on "the problem" before a national professional audience. Her "second victimization," involving painful and humiliating experiences, occurred when she instituted legal means to discourage this man from further violations of professional trust. The book, thoroughly researched, offers little encouragement that an offender in this area can be reliably rehabilitated, and yet it has proven extremely difficult to achieve prevention through delicensing or other professional or legal sanction.

Even allowing for the likelihood of occasional fraudulent or frivolous client complaints in this area—the Pope and Vetter data suggest a frequency of 4 percent—the well-established occurrence of this type of event indicates an appalling level of misconduct, and probable client injury, among people holding themselves out to be "psychotherapists," which incidentally is not in most jurisdictions a legally regulated term. A prospective client seeking therapy needs to be sufficiently wary to spare no effort in determining that the therapist chosen is one of the large majority committed to high ethical and professional standards.

Unfortunately, there are otherwise few guidelines a prospective client can reliably employ in choosing a therapist. Reputation in the community and among professional colleagues and quality of background training and experience are obvious things to consider. We think that a "trial" interview or brief series of them is a good idea as a means of assessing one's "fit" and comfort with a given therapist's style. In the end, however, we do not have the data to predict with even reasonable assurance the outcome or likely benefit of any particular therapist-client relationship. This is a knowledge gap on which research is badly needed.

Finally, we should comment briefly on the seeming disarray of the field of therapy with its many competing variations. One aspect of the competition, already noted, involves a currently intense struggle, fueled by interprofessional rivalries, concerning the place of biological therapies in the mental health field. In this chapter we focus on the several varieties of psychosocial approach. We have already indicated our judgment that probably most of these are "right," at least in the limited sense that they have fashioned intervention techniques having a high probability, when sensitively applied, of helping people overcome their problems. The obvious question, then, is this: Why doesn't the typical therapist employ a multifaceted, multitargeted approach to every client with whom treatment is undertaken, instead of doing his or her "own thing," be it psychoanalysis, behavioral, gestalt, or some other therapy? Wouldn't this approach maximize treatment efficiency? We suspect so, and we have no entirely satisfactory answer to the first part of our query. Ideological commitment has historically been very strong in this field—in large part because virtually nobody had solid research data with which to back their claims. That situation is changing rapidly, but the commitment tends to remain despite the change and despite sincere efforts (e.g., Goldfried, Greenberg, & Marmar, 1990; Goldfried & Safran, 1986) to enhance communication across the many intersecting barriers. As every therapist knows, dysfunctional habits are often hard to break.

SUMMARY

Psychotherapy is aimed at the reduction of abnormal behavior in individuals through psychological means. The goals of psychotherapy include changing maladaptive behavior, minimizing or eliminating stressful environmental conditions, reducing negative affect, improving interpersonal competencies, resolving personal conflicts, modifying an individual's inaccurate assumptions about himself or herself, and fostering a more positive self-image. Although these goals are by no means easy to achieve, psychological treatment methods have been shown to be generally effective in promoting adaptive psychological functioning in many troubled individuals.

Numerous approaches to psychological treatment ("schools of psychotherapy") have been developed to treat individuals with psychological disorders. We have organized these approaches into a scheme that focuses attention on the primary target selected for intervention. Type A therapies are directed at a client's affects or emotions; Type B at client behaviors; Type C at problematic aspects of cognition; and Type E at reactions in a client's environment. It is argued that, because these elements are organized in an unending loop, positive change in any one of them will produce a good therapeutic effect overall.

Nevertheless, this chapter is developed in accord with the traditional breakdown of "schools" of therapy. One of the oldest approaches to psychological treatment, psychoanalysis, or psychodynamic therapy, was originated nearly a century ago by Sigmund Freud. Although complicated systems of psychodynamic treatment have evolved since Freud's time, many features of "orthodox" psychoanalysis today closely resemble Freud's original system. Several other schools of therapy have developed out of the psychoanalytic tradition. These approaches accept some elements of Freudian theory but diverge on key points, such as the length of time to be devoted to therapy or the role of the ego in personality dynamics. By and large, we consider them Type E therapies because of the attention they give to the management of "transference."

A second major approach to psychological intervention is behavior therapy. Originating over 50 years ago, behavior therapy has come to be used extensively in treating clinical problems. Behavior therapy approaches make use of a number of techniques, such as systematic desensitization and biofeedback (which are Type A therapies). Other behavior therapy techniques include aversion therapy, modeling, reinforcement approaches, and assertiveness therapy (all Type B therapies). Recently, behavior therapy methods have been applied to internal processes—that is, thought or cognitions (Type C)—with a great deal of success. Known as cognitive-behavioral therapy, this approach attempts to modify an individual's self-statements to change his or her behavior. Cognitive-behavioral methods have been used for a wide variety of clinical problems—from depression to anger control—and with a range of clinical populations.

Several other psychological treatment methods have been referred to as humanistic-experiential therapies (which we regard as primarily Type C, owing to their focus on "awareness"). One of the earliest of these approaches is the client-centered, or person-centered, therapy of Carl Rogers. This treatment approach, originating in the 1940s, has received broad acceptance and has provided a valuable conceptualization of the client-therapist interaction as well as specific techniques for generating personal change or personal growth in motivated clients.

In addition to individual treatment approaches, some psychological treatment methods are applied in group settings, such as group therapy and marital or family therapy. These approaches typically assume that an individual's problems lie partly in his or her interactions with others. Consequently, the focus of treatment is to change ways of interacting among individuals in the social or family context (a Type E approach).

In recent years an attempt has been made to integrate behavior therapy methods with other psychological treatment approaches, particularly psychodynamic therapy. This effort is a result of the recognition that elements from both approaches can be used to increase our understanding of troubled clients and to bring about desired behavior changes. These integration issues are actually part of a broader problem of therapists largely doing their "own thing," addressed in the chapter's Unresolved Issues section.

Evaluation of the success of psychotherapy in producing desired behavior changes in clients is difficult. Research in psychotherapy, however, has shown that most treatment approaches are more effective than no treatment at all. Beyond the question of evaluating the success of psychotherapy lies other, larger questions involving the ethical dilemmas posed by therapy. Does psychotherapy encourage conformity to the status quo? Should it do this? These constitute some of the difficult moral and social issues that daily confront mental health professionals.

Other unresolved issues include the often perplexing occurrence of negative or deteriorative outcomes in psychotherapy. One likely source of such outcomes, by no means the only or necessarily most common, is sexual misconduct on the part of a therapist.

Key Terms

psychotherapy (p. 627)
clinical psychologist (p. 630)
psychiatrist (p. 630)
psychiatric social workers (p. 630)
psychodynamic therapy (p. 632)
free association (p. 634)
manifest content (p. 635)
latent content (p. 635)
resistance (p. 636)
transference (p. 636)
counter-transference (p. 636)
behavior therapy (p. 638)
implosion (p. 639)
flooding (p. 639)
systematic desensitization (p. 640)
aversion therapy (p. 641)
modeling (p. 642)
response shaping (p. 642)
token economies (p. 643)
behavioral contracting (p. 643)
assertiveness therapy (p. 644)
biofeedback (p. 645)
cognitive-behavioral therapy (p. 646)
rational-emotive therapy (RET) (p. 647)
stress-inoculation therapy (p. 648)
humanistic-experiential therapies (p. 651)
client-centered (person-centered) therapy (p. 651)
existential psychotherapy (p. 653)
gestalt therapy (p. 654)
couples counseling (marital therapy) (p. 656)
structural family therapy (p. 659)

Chapter 19

Contemporary Issues in Abnormal Psychology

Guillaume Pujolle, *Le Provence—Dessin Animé.* Pujolle (1893–?) was born in the Haute-Garonne area in France. A joiner by trade, he was torn by emotional conflicts and was eventually admitted to a hospital in Toulouse. He began to draw in 1935. His pictures have a dreamlike, fluid appearance, composed as they are of a mosaic of broad, undulating strips of color.

Over the years, most efforts toward mental health have been largely restorative, geared toward helping people only after they have already developed serious problems. Prior to the 1960s, mental health professionals typically did not become involved until after an individual had suffered a breakdown; then they often sent such individuals for treatment far away from their home communities, often compounding their distress and disrupting their lives.

Seemingly, a more effective strategy would be to try to catch problems *before* they become severe, or better yet, to establish conditions in which psychological disorders will not occur. Specific causal backgrounds for many mental disorders, however, are not sufficiently understood to enable practitioners to initiate explicit preventive programs. Efforts toward prevention in the mental health field are still based largely on hypotheses about what works rather than on substantial empirical research. Nonetheless, many professionals in the field believe that preventive mental health efforts are worthwhile.

Of course, preventive efforts, like treatment programs, cost money. During periods of economic decline, federal, state, and local governments typically reduce their support for such programs. Unfortunately, programs aimed at prevention, because of their long-range scope and their often indirect focus, are perhaps more difficult to justify because they appear less cost-effective than other programs with more direct and explicit outcome criteria. The irony, of course, is that prevention can be in the long run far less costly (Lorion, 1990).

Where preventive efforts fail and a serious mental health problem develops, today's professionals place more emphasis on the importance of prompt treatment. It is considered preferable, too, that the treatment be in the individual's own community so that clinicians can use available family and other familiar supports and reduce the disruption to the individual's life pattern. If hospitalization becomes necessary, every effort is taken to prevent the disorder from becoming chronic and to return the individual to the community as soon as possible, with whatever aftercare and continued support that may be needed.

In this last chapter, we will examine the kinds of measures that are being taken to prevent maladaptive behavior or limit its seriousness. Our discussion will begin with a review of preventive strategies. Next, we will explore some factors related to the care and hospitalization of individuals with severe psychological problems: commitment, deinstitutionalization, and assessment of dangerousness. Closely related to these factors are the matters of (a) a therapist's duty to warn others if a client threatens violence and (b) the use—and some think abuse—of the insanity defense as a plea in capital crimes. Next, we will briefly survey the scope of organized efforts for mental health both in the United States and throughout the world. Finally, we will conclude the chapter by considering what each of us can do to foster mental health.

PERSPECTIVES ON PREVENTION

In our present discussion we will use the concepts of primary, secondary, and tertiary prevention, which are widely used in public health medicine to describe general strategies of disease prevention. **Primary prevention** is aimed at reducing the possibility of disease and fostering positive health. **Secondary prevention** is typically emergency or crisis intervention, and involves efforts to reduce the impact, duration, or spread of a problem that has already developed—if possible, catching it before it has become serious. **Tertiary prevention** seeks to reduce the long-term consequences of disorders or serious problems. These preventive strategies, although primarily devised for understanding and controlling infectious physical diseases, provide a useful perspective in the mental health field as well.

It is important to note here that this tripartite view of mental health prevention efforts may be creating some problems. Long (1986), for example, feels that the term *prevention* should only be used to refer to *primary* prevention efforts; secondary prevention, such as emergency psychotherapy, and tertiary prevention, such as hospital rehabilitation programs, should be considered, respectively, as *treatment* and *rehabilitation.* Though some may feel that this problem is just a matter of semantics, Long is concerned that it is negatively affecting the funding of primary prevention programs. By being grouped together with treatment and rehabilitative efforts, she argues, primary prevention efforts are not receiving the financial support required to make an impact on reducing mental health problems in society, in large part because the other mental health efforts with which they are grouped seem more urgent and typically get more of the already limited resources. Clearly, funding at all three levels is critical to the future of mental health.

Primary Prevention

In primary prevention, we are concerned with two key tasks: altering conditions that can cause or contribute to mental disorders and establishing conditions that foster positive mental health. In primary prevention, epidemiological studies are particularly important because they help investigators obtain information about the incidence and distribution of various maladaptive behaviors needing prevention efforts (Dohrenwend & Dohrenwend, 1982). These findings can then be used to suggest what preventive efforts might be most appropriate. For example, various epidemiological studies have shown that certain groups of individuals are at high risk for mental disorders, including recently divorced people (Bloom, Asher, & White, 1978), the physically disabled (Freemen, Malkin, & Hastings, 1975), elderly people living alone (Neugarten, 1977) and individuals who have been uprooted from their homes (Westermeyer, Williams, & Nguyen, 1991). Although findings such as these may be the basis for immediate secondary prevention, they may also aid later in primary prevention by telling us what to look for and where to look—in essence by focusing our efforts in the right direction. Primary prevention includes biological, psychosocial, and sociocultural efforts. As Kessler and Albee (1975) have noted, "Everything aimed at improving the human condition, at making life more fulfilling and meaningful, may be considered to be part of primary prevention of mental or emotional disturbance" (p. 557).

Biological Measures Biologically based primary prevention begins with help in family planning and includes both prenatal and postnatal care. A good deal of current emphasis is being placed on guidance in family planning—how many children to have, when to have them in relation to marital and other family conditions, and even whether to have children at all. Such guidance may include genetic counseling, in which tests for diagnosing genetic defects may be administered to potential parents to assess their risk of having children with birth defects that can result in mental disorders.

Breakthroughs in genetic research have also made it possible to detect and often alleviate genetic defects before a baby is born; when in utero treatment is not feasible, such information provides the parents with the choice of having an abortion rather than going on to bear a baby with serious defects. Continued progress in genetic research may make it possible to identify genetic disorders early or even to correct faulty genes, thus providing humankind with fantastic new power to prevent hereditary pathology.

Many of the goals of health psychology can also be viewed as primary prevention. Efforts geared toward improving one's diet, establishing a routine of physical exercise, and overall good health patterns can do much to improve one's physical well-being. To the extent that physical illness always produces some sort of psychological stress that can eventuate in such problems as depression, good health is primary prevention in respect to good mental health.

Parents can be helped to be more effective in their relationships with their children. Diane, shown here with one of her children, is enhancing her parenting skills through the Avance Program *in San Antonio, Texas—a program for low-income Mexican-American families that attempts to prevent child neglect and abuse by helping parents, many of whom were emotionally deprived as children, learn to give appropriate emotional support to their children.*

Psychosocial Measures In regarding normality as optimal development and functioning rather than as the mere absence of pathology, we imply that an individual requires opportunities to learn needed competencies—physical, intellectual, emotional, and social. The first requirement of psychosocial "health" is that an individual develop the skills needed for effective problem solving, for handling emotions constructively, and for establishing satisfying interpersonal relationships; failure to develop these skills places the individual at a serious disadvantage in coping with life problems and at risk for developing mental health problems.

The second requirement for psychosocial health is that an individual acquire an accurate frame of reference on which to build self-identity. We have seen repeatedly that when people's assumptions about themselves or their world are inaccurate, their behavior is likely to be maladaptive. Likewise, an inability to find satisfying values that foster a meaningful and fulfilling life constitutes a fertile source of maladjustment and mental disorders.

Third, psychosocial well-being also requires preparation for the types of problems an individual is likely to encounter during given life stages. For example, pregnancy and childbirth usually have a great deal of emotional significance for both parents and may disturb family equilibrium or exacerbate an already disturbed marital situation. Young people who want to marry and have children must be prepared for the tasks of building a mutually satisfying relationship and helping children develop their potentialities. Similarly, an individual needs to be prepared adequately for other developmental tasks characteristic of given life periods, including retirement and old age.

In recent years, psychosocial measures aimed at ensuring primary prevention have received a great deal of attention. The field of behavioral medicine has had substantial influence here. As we saw in Chapter 7, efforts are being made to change the psychological factors underlying life-style patterns—especially in terms of high-risk habits, such as smoking, excessive drinking, and poor eating, that may be contributing to the development of both physical and psychological problems.

Sociocultural Measures The relationship between an individual and his or her community is a reciprocal one, a fact we sometimes forget in our prizing of individualism. We need autonomy and freedom to be ourselves, but we also need to belong and contribute to a community. Without a supportive community, individual development is stifled. At the same time, without responsible, psychologically healthy individuals, the community will not thrive and, in turn, cannot be supportive. Sociocultural efforts toward primary prevention are focused on making the community as nourishing as possible for the individuals within it.

With our growing realization of the importance of pathological social conditions in producing maladaptive behavior, increased attention must be devoted to creating social conditions that will foster healthy development and functioning in individuals. Efforts to create these conditions are seen in a broad spectrum of social measures ranging from public education and Social Security to economic planning and social legislation directed at ensuring adequate health care for all citizens. Such measures, of course, must take into account the stressors and health problems we are likely to encounter as our rapidly changing society moves into the future.

Primary prevention through social change in the community is difficult. Although the whole psychological climate can ultimately be changed by a social movement, such as the civil rights movement of the 1960s, the payoff of such efforts is generally far in the future and may be difficult or impossible to measure.

An Illustration of Primary Prevention Strategies. Though difficult to formulate and even more difficult to mobilize and carry out, primary prevention efforts can bring about major improvements if successful. We will look in this section at the mobilization of primary prevention resources aimed at curtailing or reducing the problem of teenage alcohol and drug abuse.

Although drug use among most adolescent groups has declined in recent times (Oetting & Beauvais, 1990), teenage drug and alcohol use is still viewed as one of today's most significant psychological and community problems. Mental health professionals and political figures alike have called for a more concerted effort to deal with this enormous social problem. It is clear that traditional health or psychological intervention models, aimed at remediation only *after* a youngster has become addicted to narcotics or alcohol, have not substantially addressed the problem of drug and alcohol abuse among teenagers. Tragically, these traditional treatment approaches are implemented after the child has damaged his or her life through substance use.

Many contemporary researchers and theorists have taken a more proactive position with regard to solving the problems of teenage drug and alcohol use. They have attempted to establish programs that prevent the development of abuse disorders *before* individuals become so involved with drugs or alcohol that their lives are altered to the point that future adjustment becomes difficult, if not impossible. These recent prevention strategies have taken several diverse and hopeful directions, addressing somewhat different aspects of teenagers' lives. We will examine several that show promise and then discuss the limitations to these prevention approaches.

Education programs. Drug and alcohol education programs represent a prevention strategy aimed at providing information about the damaging effects of these substances. Many are school-based and focus on increasing the youngsters' resistance to drugs and alcohol through education. These programs are usually premised on the idea that if children are made aware of the dangers of ingesting dangerous drugs and alcohol, they will choose not to begin using them. Englander-Golden et al. (1986), for example, provided "Say it straight" training to sixth through eighth graders in which they taught them both the dangers of drug and alcohol abuse and how to be assertive enough to resist drugs and alcohol in spite of peer pressure. In a follow-up evaluation, these investigators reported that youngsters who were trained in the program had a lower rate of drug- and alcohol-related suspensions from school than did children who received no training.

Intervention programs for high-risk teens. Intervention programs involve identifying high-risk teenagers and providing special approaches to circumvent their further use of alcohol or potentially dangerous drugs. Programs such as these are often school-based efforts and are not strictly prevention programs; rather, they are treatment programs that provide early intervention for high-risk teens who are vulnerable to drug or alcohol use, in order to reduce the likelihood of their becoming further involved with these substances. Newman et al. (1988–1989) described a procedure for the early identification of young people who are having school-related difficulties because of drug and alcohol use. The developers of this program train school teachers and administrators to effectively identify and manage alcohol- and drug-use problems. Critical to this school intervention is a fair and consistently enforced drug and alcohol policy in the schools.

Parent education and family-based intervention programs. Because parents typically underestimate their own children's drug and alcohol use (Silverman & Silverman, 1987), several programs have been aimed at increasing parent's awareness of the extent of this problem among teens and at teaching them possible ways to deal with drug and alcohol use in the family context. These programs teach parents how to recognize drug- or alcohol-abuse problems so that youngsters can be diverted away from negative and self-destructive behaviors. One such program by Grady, Gersick, and Boratynski (1985) worked with parents whose children were about to become teenagers. They first assessed the parents with regard to their skill in dealing with drug-related issues; then they trained them to understand and respond empathically to youngsters who might be exposed to drugs during their adolescent years. They were then taught to respond to their children's questions and stated concerns and to help them consider alternative, more adaptive behavior.

Other family-oriented programs have been aimed at strengthening the family bonds and providing more positive family relationships to insulate a child from external negative influences. For example, DeMarsh and Kumpfer (1985) developed a program that focused on involving parents or a family in the positive socialization of a child by increasing the communications within the family and enhancing the parents' child-management skills to aid them in appropriate disciplining of their children.

When there is a drug or alcohol problem, assuring family cooperation in the treatment program can be problematic, and many programs have reported low rates of participation. In an effort to increase the participation rate and lower resistance to treatment, Szapocznik et al. (1988) used family-systems therapeutic techniques to reduce the resistance of families to drug treatment. They reported that 77 percent of the families completed the treatment program compared with only 25 percent in a control condition.

Peer group influence programs. Clearly, peers exert a powerful influence on teenagers in every aspect of their lives, including drug and alcohol abuse. Programs designed to help youngsters overcome negative pressures from peers focus on teaching social skills and assertiveness. Of course, peer pressure can be positive as well—in this case, influencing a teen *not* to use drugs or alcohol—and many programs focus on the positive aspects of peer pressure. In fact, Swadi and Zeitlin (1988) advocated the positive use of peer influence because, for teenagers, such influence seems much more powerful than the influence of others, including teachers and even parents.

Programs to increase self-esteem. Programs designed to increase a sense of self-worth attempt to ensure that individuals will be able to fend for themselves more assuredly and not fall into dependent, negative relationships with stronger and more dominant peers. Pentz (1983) designed one such program by providing teenagers with social skills training and the modeling of appropriate behaviors to reduce drug use and other related negative behaviors, such as truancy. In another program, Botvin (1983) relied on cognitive-behavioral intervention techniques to enhance teenagers' feelings of competency in basic life skills and improving their problem-solving skills. This approach was thought to be effective in reducing the impact of tobacco, alcohol, and marijuana use (Botvin, et al., 1990).

Mass media and modeling programs. Most youngsters are bombarded with drug- or alcohol-related stimuli in TV commercials, movies, and other visual blitzes. Airing such TV commercials or programs at times that children may view them serves to glamorize alcohol or drug use by giving youngsters messages such as "Drink Bud" or "Switch to wine coolers" during television programs they view and like. Several recent efforts have been aimed at deglamorizing or counteracting these messages by showing commercials that graphically depict the negative aspects of alcohol and drug use (Coombs, Paulson, & Palley, 1988; Schilling & McAlister, 1990).

The various prevention strategies discussed here are by no means mutually exclusive. Most programs do not rely on a single intervention strategy but actually incorporate one or more of them (Forman & Linney, 1988; Perry & Murray, 1985). For example, Botvin and Tortu (1988) described an extensive five-stage program involving both didactic and peer interaction interventions designed to enhance youngsters' self-esteem and enable them to function effectively in social contexts to resist negative peer influences. In the first component of this program, several sessions are devoted to biofeedback demonstrations of the effects of cigarettes, marijuana, and alcohol on heart rate. In the second component, several sessions are aimed at teaching them how to make effective decisions. In the third component, sessions focus on aiding the youngsters in understanding their self-image and improving their self-esteem. In the

The students shown here are participating in the New Haven Social Development Project, a preventive program designed to teach children the critical thinking skills they need to deal more effectively with stressors and problem solving—skills that will help these children enhance their self-esteem and better handle difficult social situations and pressures.

fourth component, teenagers are taught to deal with anxiety, particularly social anxiety. Finally, the fifth component of the program involves training the teens in both social communication and assertiveness, thus ensuring a more effective peer group interaction.

How successful are primary prevention programs at reducing the overall impact of adolescent drug and alcohol use? It is difficult to say. Some researchers have concluded that drug and alcohol education programs have only limited success (Tobler, 1986). Conducting rigorous research in primary prevention is often problematic because the interventions may be only remotely connected to the behavior being targeted for change. Moreover, it is typically impossible to exert experimental control over all of the relevant variables influencing drug and alcohol use. Clearly, it is difficult to provide a powerful enough intervention to offset the motivation to use or sell drugs many youngsters experience. For many individuals living in abject poverty, the only way they can tolerate or possibly get out of the ghetto is through using or selling drugs. The recent decline in drug use among teenagers does not include minorities living in ghettos, barrios, or American Indian reservations, where drug use continues to grow at record levels (Oetting & Beauvais, 1990).

Some critics of drug and alcohol prevention programs consider the source of drug and alcohol problems in adolescence to be the result of early socialization processes—and not amenable to superficial reeducation efforts occurring so late in a youngster's life. Shedler and Block (1990), in a well-controlled longitudinal study in which subjects were carefully studied from about age 5 to age 18, found clear precursors to frequent drug use in the youngsters' early personality development. They found that teenagers developing drug-abuse patterns in their late teens had clear psychological maladjustment in early childhood, well before they were exposed to drugs; these psychological problems predisposed the adolescents to drug abuse. As such, Shedler and Block considered the "peer-centered" or environmental influence explanations to be flawed and inadequate to explain the behavior. They thus argued that many of the drug education program efforts are inadequate to address the true source of the problem: the personality syndrome that appears to underlie drug abuse.

Unfortunately, many of the recent programs that have been initiated in response to the drug crisis are seen as "too little, too late." The lackluster performance or outright failure of some drug prevention efforts may hinder future research. Because of the lack of clear research findings and an ambiguous demonstration of the effectiveness of prevention programs, it is difficult to convince lawmakers or funding agencies that more extensive financial support for such programs is needed or worth the effort. Policymakers may take such unproductive results as an indication that primary prevention efforts are not effective in reducing the problem behavior being addressed. Thus more substantial, better-designed, and longer-range programs that could be powerful enough to bring about major changes may not be supported.

Secondary Prevention

Secondary prevention emphasizes the early detection and prompt treatment of maladaptive behavior in an individual's family and community setting. In some cases—for example, in a crisis or a disaster—secondary prevention involves immediate and relatively brief intervention to prevent any long-term behavioral consequences. In other cases, secondary prevention is aimed at longer-term consulting and educational services to reduce the consequences of some identified maladaptive behavior or problem. We will look briefly at both types of secondary prevention and then follow with an in-depth examination of secondary prevention efforts after an airplane crash.

Crisis Intervention Crisis intervention has emerged in response to a widespread need for immediate help for individuals and families confronted with especially stressful situations—be they disasters or family situations that have become intolerable (Auerbach & Stolberg, 1986; Butcher & Dunn, 1989; Butcher, Stelmachers, & Maudal, 1983; Gist & Lubin, 1989; Mitchell & Resnik, 1981; Taylor, 1989). Often, people in crisis are in a state of acute turmoil and feel overwhelmed and incapable of dealing with the stress by themselves. They do not have time to wait for the customary initial therapy appointment, nor are they usually in a position to continue therapy over a sustained period of time. They need immediate assistance.

To meet this need, two modes of therapeutic intervention have been developed: (a) short-term crisis therapy involving face-to-face discussion, and (b) the telephone hot line. These forms of crisis intervention are usually handled either by professional mental health personnel or by paraprofessionals—lay people who have been trained for this work.

Short-term crisis therapy. **Short-term crisis therapy,** as the name implies, is of brief duration and focuses on the immediate problem with which an individual or family is having difficulty. Although medical problems may also require emergency treatment, we are concerned here with personal or family problems of an emotional nature. In such crisis situations, a therapist is usually very active, helping to clarify the problem, suggesting plans of action, providing reassurance, and otherwise giving needed information and support. In essence, the therapist tries to provide as much help as the individual or family will accept.

If the problem involves psychological disturbance in one of the family members, emphasis is usually placed on mobilizing the support of other family members. Often this enables the person to avoid hospitalization and a disruption of family life. Crisis intervention may also involve bringing other mental health or medical personnel into the treatment picture. Most individuals and families who come for short-term crisis therapy do not continue in treatment for more than one to six sessions. An example of crisis intervention as a secondary preventive effort is given in *HIGHLIGHT 19.1.*

The telephone hot line. As we noted in Chapter 11, the Los Angeles Suicide Prevention Center opened up a whole new approach to dealing with people undergoing crises—the telephone hot line. Today all major cities in the United States and most smaller ones have developed some form of telephone hot line to help individuals undergoing periods of deep stress. Although the threat of suicide is the most dramatic example, the range of problems that people call about is virtually unlimited—from breaking up with someone to being on a bad drug trip. In addition, there are specific hot lines in various communities for rape victims and for runaways who need assistance.

As with other crisis intervention, a person handling hot-line calls is confronted with the problem of rapidly assessing what is wrong and how bad it is. Even if an accurate assessment is possible and the hot-line therapist does everything within his or her power to help the individual—within the confines imposed by the telephone—a distraught caller may hang up without leaving any name, telephone number, or address. This can be a deeply disturbing experience for the therapist—particularly if, for example, the caller has announced that he or she has just swallowed a lethal dose of sleeping pills. Even in less severe cases, of course, the hot-line therapist may never learn whether the caller's problem has been solved. In other instances, however, the caller may be induced to come in for counseling, making more personal contact possible.

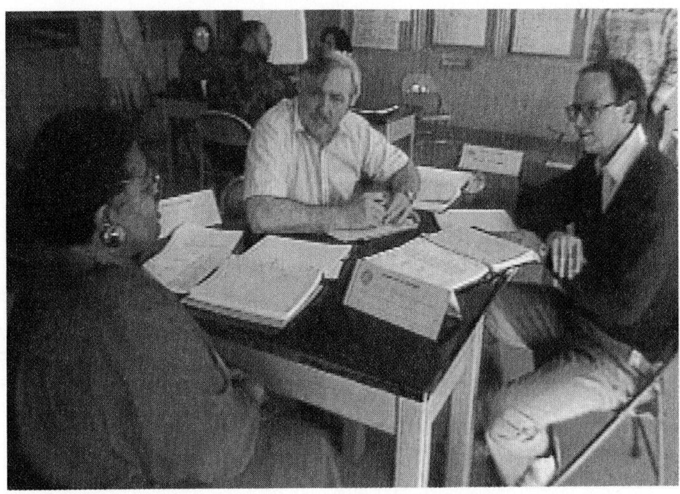

The Jobs Project in Michigan is designed to help recently unemployed workers through the initial stress of unemployment in order to prevent disorders from occurring. For five consecutive mornings, participants attend workshops that enhance both self-esteem and job-hunting skills. Joanna, shown here, is role-playing for a job interview as a factory foreman.

For a therapist, crisis intervention is probably the most discouraging of any treatment approach that we have discussed. The urgency of the intervention and the frequent inability to provide any therapeutic closure or follow-up are probably key factors in this discouragement. Free clinics and crisis centers have reported that their counselors—many of whom are volunteers—tend to burn out after a short period of time. Despite the high frustration level of this work, however, crisis-intervention therapists fill a crucial need in the mental health field, particularly for the young people who make up the majority of their clients. This need is recognized by the many community mental health centers and general hospitals that provide emergency psychological services, either through hot lines or walk-in services. For the thousands of individuals in desperate trouble, an invaluable social support is provided by the fact that there is somewhere they can go for immediate help or someone they can call who will listen to their problems and try to help them. Thus the continuing need for crisis intervention services and telephone hot lines is evident.

Consultation and Education of Intermediaries Often, community mental health professionals, such as psychologists and psychiatrists, are able to reach a larger group of individuals in need of secondary prevention efforts by working through

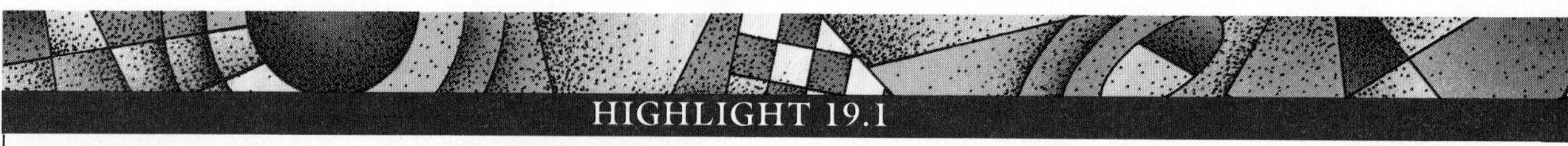

HIGHLIGHT 19.1

Crisis Intervention in Troubled Families

Smith (1938) humorously referred to families as "that dear octopus from whose tentacles we never quite escape, nor, in our innermost hearts, ever quite wish to" (p. 120). Though extremely important to us all, families clearly go awry at times. Family crises involve a disruption in the normal pattern of relationships and aspirations, and such crises produce increased tension in family members by threatening them with unmanageable internal or external forces. Family crises can result from many sources; for example, a family may lose its home through economic emergency, or a family member may die or become severely ill, or one of the family members may become psychotic, or, as in the following case, one of the family members may attempt suicide:

A 17-year-old girl, Leah, was brought into the emergency department of a general hospital by her mother, father, and maternal grandmother. She had walked into her parents' bedroom earlier in the morning and announced that she had swallowed all her mother's pills. The parents had brought their daughter for emergency medical treatment and were enraged when a psychiatrist was called. The history was obtained from mother, since Leah said little, and mother answered every question. During the interview, father paced in and out of the room, repeatedly declaring that he was taking his daughter home. He aggressively asked each person who entered the room "What do you want?" but each time left before a response was possible. Grandmother sat in the room, announcing from time to time, "That girl always makes trouble."

Leah was the oldest of three children. None of them attended school. According to mother, she tutored them at home. Mother also worked outside of the home and complained about how much she had to do. Leah "won't even go to the store alone, so I must accompany her everywhere." Mother said that her husband had told her not to bother with Leah, who would only get married and leave them anyway. But she (mother) had to "bother" because Leah could not go out alone in their neighborhood.

When asked about the suicide attempt, Leah said she would "do it again" if she went home. She wanted to talk to someone about the fights with mother that made her so angry she wanted to die. Mother said it was father's fault. He worked erratically, drank heavily, and made them live in a bad house in a poor neighborhood. They had terrible neighbors who were "nosey" and bothered them.

Since Leah had indicated she still had suicidal intentions and the family conflict continued unabated, hospitalization was recommended. In response, Leah immediately announced she was better and would go home. She said she would not stay in the hospital. Her mother said she could never persuade her to stay and the family gathered itself up to leave (Kress, 1984, p. 419–420).

The family crisis in this case brought to light several difficult problems due, in part, to the psychopathology of the individuals in the family—adjustment problems that threatened the integrity of the family organization. While Leah appeared to be the most disturbed, other family members, particularly the father, seemed to have significant psychological

primary care professionals, such as teachers, social workers, and police personnel (Iscoe, Bloom, & Spielberger, 1977; Levine & Perkins, 1987; Mann, 1978). For such programs, mental health professionals identify a population at risk for the development of psychological disorder and then work with the personnel in community institutions who have frequent contact with members of this population. For example, police officers might be trained to direct individuals involved in domestic quarrels to seek mental health services rather than to settle their differences through violence.

Mental health professionals had originally intended that *consultation and education* (C & E) be included among the services offered by all community mental health centers. This would have meant that the impact of these centers would have been more indirect—helping individuals experiencing

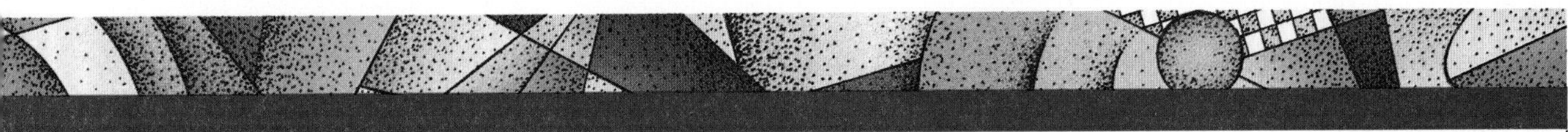

problems that directly affected the family strife as well. The suicide attempt, like many other crises a family is unprepared to resolve, required outside intervention. Not only was an immediate solution needed for the present emergency, but psychological intervention for the longer-term problem of the family's inability to resolve conflict was recommended. However, the closed, almost reclusive, nature of the family suggested that treatment for the individuals involved and for the disturbed family relationships, though needed, was not likely to be accepted at that point. Neither Leah nor her father appeared open to examining their problems or to changing their behavior. Unfortunately, we have no follow-up on the case of Leah. This is often the situation in crisis therapy, where the intervention efforts are limited to what can be accomplished only during the immediate crisis, that is, many such clients never return for more therapy, no matter how adamant the crisis worker's recommendation that they do so.

As is by now obvious, crisis intervention therapy with families is usually different and more limited in scope than family therapy as described in Chapter 18. The goals of family crisis intervention do not involve changing the basic family functioning, as in family therapy, but are usually aimed at returning a disrupted family to precrisis functioning (Umana, Gross, & McConville, 1980). For example, the mental health practitioner's task in the case of Leah involved resolving the immediate emergency and helping ease her life-threatening state of mind while, hopefully, engaging her family in future family or individual treatment to resolve the pressing problems that appeared to have caused the immediate crisis.

Family-oriented crisis intervention is aimed at restoring family equilibrium through resolution of the current situational stressors acting on a family (Auerbach & Stolberg, 1986). It is important for a practitioner to assess clearly the crucial issues underlying the family distress, the family dynamics, and the possible role that individual psychopathology plays in the family relationships. The therapist needs to determine and reinforce those family members who possess strengths that can be enlisted in the change process—that is, to bring about the necessary crisis resolution. The primary role of the therapist in the emergency intervention is to determine how the family resources can be mobilized to solve the immediate problem that prompted the crisis.

The task of resolving individual psychological problems or reorganizing the family structure and dynamics are deferred until after the immediate crisis situation is resolved. If the family can be brought into family or individual therapy later, it will be the task of the therapist to determine what family resources can be engaged to move the family toward the constructive development of more effective problem-solving techniques. In the Leah case, a major goal for later therapy would be determining how the family could be encouraged to become involved in a longer-term solution to their problems. Individual therapy might also be required for some family members to enable them to deal with the ensuing family changes that might occur.

problems by increasing the skill and sensitivity of those who come into contact with them in the community and are in a position to make their lives either more stressful or less so. Currently, however, most community mental health centers provide little such indirect service; only about 4 percent of their total effort is devoted to consultation with and education of primary care professionals. Typically, half or more of this consultation and education involves working with the schools or with other juvenile services; less than a tenth of this effort is spent with police and correctional personnel (NIMH, 1978b).

An Illustration of Secondary Prevention

In many ways, airline disasters are terrifying and unthinkable events. Nevertheless, it is difficult today to deny their reality, considering how many communities have experienced the aftermath of such a disaster. The immediate consequences of an air crash are devastating. Survivors of air crashes typically have traumatic responses to the accident that impair their immediate functioning and place great demands on their psychological adjustment for weeks after the disaster. Family members of air crash victims often experience extensive psychological trauma following the accident; they may need to make extensive changes during their loved one's lengthy recovery period or, more likely, they will need to make major life changes to adjust to their loved one's death. Even various rescue personnel who are caught up in dealing with the aftermath of an airline disaster may suffer from posttraumatic stress disorder.

In many respects the emotional responses of and adjustive demands placed on air crash victims are similar to those of victims of natural disasters, such as hurricanes, floods, and volcanic eruptions (Manglesdorff, 1985). A number of special considerations, however, influence the intensity of the problems seen following airplane crashes: typically airplane crashes are sudden and unexpected; they are usually quite chaotic in terms of their destruction; and air disasters usually occur away from one's familiar settings and with individuals who are strangers. Consequently, the sense of community that characterizes many disasters is lacking. In addition, the impact of an air disaster has a strong emotional *irradiation effect;* that is, it impacts to a greater or lesser degree a larger number of individuals than those immediately affected by the accident itself. Air disasters differ from natural disasters in another important respect—they usually involve considerable blame and anger that can aggravate or intensify the emotional reactions of survivors even months after the crash.

Most airports, particularly those involved in air carrier operations, are required to have a disaster plan that includes fire-rescue and medical evacuation procedures to deal with an airplane crash. Recently, some airport disaster plans have incorporated a psychological support program to provide emergency mental health services to survivors and the family members of crash victims as well as to rescue workers (Butcher, 1980; Butcher & Dunn, 1989). These programs are viewed as secondary prevention efforts in that they are aimed at providing emergency psychological services to prevent the development of psychological disorders or to reduce the severity of such problems if they occur.

Three types of secondary prevention services have been shown to be effective in dealing with the psychological problems related to air disasters: immediate crisis intervention services to crash survivors and surviving family members; crisis telephone hot-line services to provide information and referrals to victims who do not have crisis intervention services available; and postdisaster debriefing sessions for secondary victims, such as rescue personnel, affected by the disaster. We will look at each of these services briefly.

Postdisaster crisis therapy. Timing is critical to crisis intervention, which, when applied in the immediate aftermath of a disaster, can reduce the emotional distress experienced and can result in a more effective future psychological adjustment (Butcher & Hatcher, 1988; Williams, Solomon, & Bartone, 1988). Crisis intervention treatment involves providing a victim with a supportive, understanding crisis intervention specialist to enable the victim to express his or her intense feelings about the incident.

Fewer situations are more intimidating for a mental health professional than to be suddenly cast into a treatment session with grieved individuals—especially those who only recently suffered a sudden loss, such as in a disaster. In these times human beings, regardless of previous level of adjustment, need a great deal more emotional support than traditional mental health roles provide. How do trained crisis counselors help disaster victims manage their emotional distress in the aftermath of a disaster?

Foremost, a crisis counselor *provides objective emotional support.* The mental health professional must maintain an objective perspective when faced with the intense grief and confusion that accompanies tragedy. It is indeed human for individuals working with trauma victims to become affected by the traumatic events as much as others are. Even hardened rescue personnel, such as police officers and fire fighters, may become immediately engrossed in and severely affected by the intense loss in an air disaster. The traditionally distant roles of mental health providers are swept away in situations involving loss through disaster. The crisis worker must strive to maintain a balanced perspective to help those involved in the disaster who will be more intensely affected and will have a more diminished perspective. The mental health professional tries to provide a long-term perspective—to allow victims to see that there is hope of surviving psychologically.

A crisis counselor also *serves as a source of information and a buffer against misinformation* coming from ever-present rumor. Disasters are always followed by periods of confusion, misinformation, and negative emotional states. One important role of the mental health professional in disaster response efforts is to obtain, decipher, and clearly communicate to victims the most accurate picture of the situation obtainable at the moment. The crisis intervention specialist is an information link with the most accurate sources and should maintain an up-to-date picture of the situation. The mental health professional must be knowledgeable about disaster victims' options to provide the information they need for personal decisions.

Finally, a crisis counselor *provides directive, effective suggestions to promote adaptation.* An important facet of the mental health professional's role in dealing with disaster victims is to guide them through the difficult times by providing a perspective on the problems being faced and by offering valuable guidance for alleviating those problems.

Crisis telephone hot-line counseling services. In the aftermath of an air disaster, great confusion prevails. Airplane disasters always involve considerable psychological turmoil and may produce psychological problems among passengers and crew members. Inaccurate information and anxiety-producing doubts can create a tension state that results in demoralization and negative behavior, such as absenteeism from work, excessive drinking, and morale problems. An effective way to deal with this psychological uncertainty and reduce the negative atmosphere following an air disaster is to provide telephone counseling services—an informational hot line of sorts—for all those who feel the need to discuss their concerns, be they airline employees or passenger families. For example, a 24-hour crisis telephone hot-line counseling service was established shortly after the crash of an airliner in Detroit, Michigan, in 1987 in which 156 people died; it continued in operation for four weeks. This service was staffed by qualified psychologists in crisis counseling who provided counseling, information, and referral services.

Postdisaster debriefing sessions. One goal of a disaster response program is to provide aftercare psychological services to passenger-victims, surviving family members, and rescue personnel. Those who appear to function well at the disaster site may experience difficulties after the immediate crisis has subsided and they have returned to family and normal duties. Even hardened disaster workers who are well trained and effective at the site can be affected later by the pressures and problems experienced during the disaster.

The desire to "unwind" in a psychologically safe environment and to share one's experience of the disaster are universal needs of people following a traumatic situation. Debriefing sessions are designed to provide those who might be directly affected by the accident an opportunity to relate their experiences and to express their feelings and concerns about the disaster. Mitchell (1985) and Keating (1987), for example, have explored the use of debriefing sessions in dealing with emergency workers and found this approach to be effective in reducing the emotional reactions of emergency workers to traumatic events.

Immediate crisis intervention, telephone hotline counseling, and debriefing programs have become standard efforts following major disasters to help victims and emergency workers return more quickly and effectively to normal functioning. By reducing the harsh impact of a tragedy, these programs prevent the development of more severe psychological disorders.

Tertiary Prevention

Tertiary prevention involves efforts aimed at reducing the impact of a disorder and restoring an individual to functioning once the mental health problem has been identified. Mental health rehabilitative efforts are important aspects of tertiary prevention and will be discussed in the following sections.

The Mental Hospital as a Therapeutic Community Most of the traditional forms of therapy that we discussed in Chapters 17 and 18 may, of course, be used in a hospital setting to promote tertiary prevention. In addition, in more and more mental hospitals these techniques are being supplemented by efforts to make the hospital environment itself a "therapeutic community" (Gunderson, 1980; Jones, 1953; Paul & Lentz, 1977). That is, all the ongoing activities of the hospital are brought into the total treatment program, and the environment, or *milieu,* is a crucial aspect of the therapy. This approach is thus often referred to as **milieu therapy.**

Three general therapeutic principles guide the milieu approach to treatment:

1. Staff expectations are clearly communicated to patients. Both positive and negative feedback are used to encourage appropriate verbalizations and actions on the part of patients.
2. Patients are encouraged to become involved in all decisions made and all actions taken concerning them. A do-it-yourself attitude prevails.
3. All patients belong to social groups on the ward. The experience of group cohesiveness

gives the patients support and encouragement, and the related process of group pressure helps exert control over their behavior.

In a therapeutic community, as few restraints as possible are placed on the patients' freedom, and the orientation is toward encouraging patients to take responsibility for their behavior and to participate actively in their treatment programs. Open wards permit patients to use the grounds and premises. Self-government programs give patients responsibility for managing their own affairs and those of the ward. All hospital personnel are expected to treat the patients as human beings who merit consideration and courtesy. Research has shown that intensive milieu programs significantly benefit nonchronic patients (Gunderson, 1980).

The interaction among patients—whether in group therapy sessions, social events, or other activities—is planned in such a way as to be of therapeutic benefit. In fact, it is becoming apparent that often the most beneficial aspect of a therapeutic community is the interaction among the patients themselves. Differences in social roles and backgrounds may make empathy between staff and patients difficult, but fellow patients have been there—they have had similar problems and breakdowns and have experienced the anxiety and humiliation of being labeled mentally ill and hospitalized. Thus, constructive relationships frequently develop among patients in a warm, encouraging milieu.

Another highly successful method for helping patients take increased responsibility for their own behavior is the use of **social-learning programs.** These programs use learning principles and techniques, such as token economies, to shape more socially acceptable behavior (Paul, 1979; Paul & Lentz, 1977; Rhoades, 1981).

A persistent concern with hospitalization is that the mental hospital may become a permanent refuge from the world, either because it offers total escape from the demands of everyday living or because it encourages patients to settle into a chronic sick role with a permanent excuse for letting other people take care of them (see *HIGHLIGHT 19.2.)* To keep the focus on returning patients to the community and on preventing a return to the institution, hospital staffs try to establish close ties with patients' families and communities and to maintain a recovery-expectant attitude. Between 70 and 90 percent of patients labeled as psychotic and admitted to mental hospitals can now be discharged within a few weeks, or at most a few months. Current estimates suggest that there are about 2 to 3 million chronically mentally ill individuals in America, of whom about half reside in mental hospitals and the other half live in nursing homes or in the community (Talbott, 1985).

Even where disorders have become chronic, effective treatment methods have been developed. In one of the most extensive and well-controlled studies of chronic hospitalized patients, Paul and Lentz (1977) compared the relative effectiveness of three treatment approaches:

1. *Milieu therapy,* focused on structuring a patient's environment to provide clear communications of expectations, and to get the patient involved in the treatment and participating in the therapeutic community through the group process.
2. *A social-learning treatment program,* organized around learning principles and using a token economy system, with ward staff as reinforcing agents. Undesirable behavior was not reinforced.
3. *Traditional mental hospital treatments,* including pharmacotherapy, occupational therapy, recreational therapy, activity therapy, and individual or group therapy. No systematic application of milieu therapy or the social-learning program was given to this group.

The treatment project covered a period of six years, with an initial phase of staff training, patient assessment, and baseline recording; a treatment phase; an aftercare phase; and a long (year and a half) follow-up. The changes targeted included resocialization, the learning of new roles, and the reduction or elimination of bizarre behavior. There were 28 chronic schizophrenic patients in each treatment group, matched for age, sex, socioeconomic level, symptoms, and duration of hospitalization.

The results of the study were impressive. Both milieu therapy and the social-learning program produced significant improvement in overall functioning and resulted in more successful hospital releases than the traditional hospital care. The behaviorally based social learning program, however, was clearly superior to the more diffuse program of milieu therapy, as evidenced by the fact that over 90 percent of the released patients from the social-learning program remained continuously in the community as compared with 70 percent of the released patients who had had milieu therapy. The figure for the traditional treatment program was less than 50 percent.

Aftercare Programs Even where hospitalization has successfully modified maladaptive behavior and a patient has learned needed occupational and

HIGHLIGHT 19.2

The Hospitalization Syndrome

Although individuals differ markedly in their response to hospitalization, some who reside in large mental hospitals over long periods of time tend to adopt a passive role, losing the self-confidence and motivation required for reentering the outside world. In fact, a sizable number of chronic patients become adept at manipulating their symptoms and making themselves appear "sicker" than they are to avoid the possibility of discharge from the sheltered hospital environment. This pattern is not ordinarily considered to be the result of hospitalization alone, but rather is attributed to an interaction between the patient and the hospital milieu. The following are some of the steps that have been delineated in the development of this hospitalization syndrome or, as it is also called, ***social breakdown syndrome:***

1. *Deficiency in self-concept.* A precondition for the development of the social breakdown syndrome is the presence of severe self-devaluation and inner confusion concerning social roles and responsibilities.

2. *Social labeling.* During an acute crisis period in the person's life, he or she has probably been labeled psychotic and perhaps even dangerous, has been sent involuntarily to a mental hospital, and has been legally certified as incompetent and lacking in self-control.

3. *Induction into the "sick" role.* Admission procedures, diagnostic labeling, and treatment by staff members and other patients all too often initiate the individual into the role of a "sick" person—helpless, passive, and requiring care and external control.

4. *Atrophy of work and social skills.* In institutions that serve primarily as "storage bins" for the emotionally disturbed, basic work and social skills may atrophy through disuse. During prolonged hospitalization, technological changes in the outside world may contribute to the obsolescence of the individual's work skills.

5. *Development of the chronic sick role.* Eventually the confused and devaluated patient becomes a full member of the sick community in which passive dependence and "crazy" behavior are not only common, but expected.

The staffs of large mental hospitals today are more aware of the pitfalls of chronicity than in the past, and they are introducing various corrective procedures for remotivation and resocialization as well as stressing a recovery-expectant attitude.

interpersonal skills, readjustment in the community following release may still be difficult. Many studies have shown that in the past up to 45 percent of schizophrenic patients have been readmitted within the first year after their discharge. This is where tertiary prevention can play a major role, especially in terms of providing former clients and patients with supportive services that will help them toward long-term psychological well-being.

Today, aftercare programs are helping smooth the transition from institutional to community life and are markedly reducing the number of relapses. Glasscote (1978) found that only 16 percent of patients who received adequate aftercare were readmitted within the first six months as compared with 37 percent for patients not receiving aftercare. By the end of 5 years, more of both groups had been readmitted, but 47 percent of the aftercare group were still in the community, as compared with only 30 percent of the group who had not received aftercare.

Aftercare is the responsibility of community mental health facilities and personnel, the community as a whole, and, of course, the person's family. Its goal is to ensure that released patients will be helped to make an adequate readjustment and return to full participation in their home and community with a minimum of delay and difficulty.

Sometimes aftercare includes a "halfway" period in which a released patient has a gradual return to the outside world in what were formerly termed ***halfway houses.*** Community-based treatment programs, now referred to as ***aftercare programs,*** are live-in facilities that serve as a home base for former patients as they make the transition back to adequate functioning in the community. Typically, community-based facilities are run not by profes-

In addition to providing prompt and intense inpatient therapy for patients who need it, tertiary prevention also involves provisions for aftercare, such as this halfway house, to smooth the transition from institutional to community life.

sional mental health personnel but by the residents themselves.

There is even some evidence that community-based living is preferable to hospital confinement for patients who are still actively psychotic. In a pilot program with a group of seriously disturbed mental patients, Fairweather and his colleagues (1969) demonstrated that these patients could function in the community, living in a patient-run facility. Initially, a member of the research staff coordinated the daily operations of the "lodge," but he was shortly replaced by a layperson. The patients were given full responsibility for operating the lodge, for regulating each other's behavior, for earning money, and for purchasing and preparing food.

Forty months after their discharge, a comparison was made of these former patients and a comparable group of 75 patients who had been discharged at the same time but had not had the lodge experience. Whereas most members of the lodge facility were able to hold income-producing jobs, to manage their daily lives, and to adjust in the outside world, the majority of those who had not had the community group-living experience were unable to adjust to life on the outside and required rehospitalization.

Day hospital facilities in community mental health centers may also be used as alternatives to hospitalization. For example, Penk, Charles, and Van Hoose (1978) showed that partial hospitalization in a day treatment setting resulted in as much improvement (at a lower cost) as full inpatient psychiatric treatment in a group of patients they studied.

Similar community-based treatment facilities have been established for alcoholics, drug addicts, and other people attempting to make an adjustment into the community after institutionalization. Such facilities may be said to be specialized in the sense that all residents share similar backgrounds and problems, and this seems to contribute to the facilities' effectiveness.

One of the chief problems of community-based treatment facilities is that of gaining the acceptance and support of community residents. As Dennes (1974) pointed out in the early years of the growth of community-based treatment, this requires educational and other social measures directed toward increasing community understanding, acceptance, and tolerance of troubled people who may differ somewhat from community norms. The viability of such an approach, however, is demonstrated in the example of Geel, Belgium—"the town that cares"—which we discussed in Chapter 2 (Aring, 1975a).

CONTROVERSIAL ISSUES AND THE MENTALLY ILL

A number of important issues arise related to the legal status of the mentally ill. These issues comprise the subject matter of a field referred to as **forensic psychology,** or **forensic psychiatry,** and they center around the rights of mental patients and the rights of members of society to be protected from disturbed individuals. For a survey of some of the legal rights that have been gained for the mentally ill over the years, see *HIGHLIGHT 19.3.*

The issues we will cover in this section are those that have been the center of controversy for many years. We will first review the procedures involved in involuntarily committing disturbed and dangerous individuals to psychiatric institutions. Next, we

HIGHLIGHT 19.3

Patient Advocacy: Important Court Decisions in Establishing Patient Rights

Several important court decisions in recent years have helped establish certain basic rights for individuals suffering from mental disorders.

Right to treatment. In 1972, a U.S. District Court in Alabama made a landmark decision in the case of *Wyatt* v. *Stickney*. The ruling held that a mentally ill or mentally retarded individual had a right to receive treatment. Since the decision, the State of Alabama has increased its budget for the treatment of mental health and mental retardation by 300 percent.

Freedom from custodial confinement. In 1975, the U.S. Supreme Court upheld the principle that patients have a right to freedom from custodial confinement if they are not dangerous to themselves or others and if they can safely survive outside of custody. In the *Donaldson* v. *O'Connor* decision, the defendants were required to pay Donaldson $10,000 for having kept him in custody without providing treatment.

Right to compensation for work. In 1973, a U.S. District Court ruled in the case of *Souder* v. *Brennan* (the secretary of labor) that a patient in a nonfederal mental institution who performed work must be paid according to the Fair Labor Standards Act. Although a 1978 Supreme Court ruling nullified the part of the lower court's decision dealing with state hospitals, the ruling still applied to mentally ill and mentally retarded patients in private facilities.

Right to legal counsel at commitment hearings. The State Supreme Court in Wisconsin decided in 1976, in the case of *Memmel* v. *Mundy*, that an individual had the right to legal counsel during the commitment process.

Right to live in a community. In 1974, the U.S. District Court decided, in the case of *Staff* v. *Miller*, that released state mental hospital patients had a right to live in "adult homes" in the community.

Right to refuse treatment. Several court decisions have provided rulings and some states have enacted legislation permitting patients to refuse certain treatments, such as electroconvulsive therapy and psychosurgery.

Right to less restrictive treatment. In 1975, a U.S. District Court issued a landmark decision in the case of *Dixon* v. *Weinberger*. The ruling establishes the right of individuals to receive treatment in less restrictive facilities than mental institutions.

The need for confinement must be shown by clear, convincing evidence. In 1979, the Supreme Court ruled, in the case of *Addington* v. *Texas*, that a person's need to be kept in an institution must be based on demonstrable evidence.

Based on Bernard (1979), National Association for Mental Health (1979), and Mental Health Law Project (1987).

will turn to the assessment of dangerousness in disturbed individuals; we will also discuss a related issue, which has become of key concern to psychotherapists—the court decision that psychotherapists have a duty to warn potential victims of any threatened violence by their patients. In addition, we will examine the controversial insanity defense for capital crimes as well as the issue of deinstitutionalization, or what some have called the premature "dumping" of mental patients into the community. Finally, in the Unresolved Issues section we will discuss the possibility that contemporary society promotes a trend toward the "criminalization of the mentally ill," that is, incarcerating mentally ill individuals for crimes they commit rather than treating them for the psychological problems that underlie their crimes.

The Commitment Process

Individuals with psychological problems or behaviors that are so extreme and severe as to pose a threat to themselves or others may require protective confinement. Those who commit crimes, whether or not they have a psychological disorder, are dealt with primarily through the judicial system—police arrest, court trial, and, if convicted, possible confinement in a penal institution. Individuals who are judged to be potentially dangerous because of their psychological state may, after civil commitment procedures, be confined in a mental institution.

The steps in the commitment process vary slightly depending on the state law,[1] the available community mental health resources, and the nature of the problem—for example, commitment procedures for a mentally retarded individual will be different from those for a person with an alcohol-abuse problem. A distinction should be made here between voluntary hospitalization and involuntary commitment. In most cases, individuals are placed in mental institutions without court order; that is, they accept voluntary commitment or hospitalization. In these cases, they can, with sufficient notice, leave the hospital if they wish. In cases where an individual is believed to be dangerous or unable to provide for his or her own care, the need for involuntary commitment may arise.

Being mentally ill is not sufficient grounds for placing an individual in a mental institution against his or her will. Although procedures vary somewhat from state to state, several conditions beyond mental illness usually must be met before formal commitment can occur (Schwitzgebel & Schwitzgebel, 1980). In brief, the person must be judged to be

- dangerous to himself or herself;
- incapable of providing for his or her basic physical needs;
- unable to make responsible decisions about hospitalization; and
- in need of treatment or care in a hospital.

Typically, filing a petition for a commitment hearing is the first step in the process of committing an individual involuntarily. This petition is usually filed by a concerned person, such as a relative, physician, or mental health professional. When a petition is filed, a judge appoints two examiners to evaluate the "proposed patient." In Minnesota, for example, one examiner must be a physician (not necessarily a psychiatrist); the other can be a psychiatrist or a psychologist. The patient is asked to voluntarily appear for psychiatric examination prior to the commitment hearing. The hearing must be held within 14 days, which can be extended for 30 more days if good cause for the extension can be shown. The law requires that the court-appointed examiners interview the patient before the hearing.

If an individual is committed to a mental hospital for treatment, the hospital must report to the court within 60 days as to whether the person needs to be confined even longer. If no report is given by the hospital, the patient must be set free. If the hospital indicates that the individual needs further treatment, then the commitment period becomes indeterminate, subject to periodic reevaluations.

Because the decision to commit an individual is based on the judgments of others about the individual's capabilities and his or her potential for dangerous behavior, the civil commitment process leaves open the possibility of the unwarranted violation of a person's civil rights. As a consequence, most states have stringent safeguards in the procedures to assure that any individual who is the subject of a petition for commitment is granted due process, including rights to formal hearings with representation by legal counsel. If there is not time to get a court order for commitment or if there is imminent danger, however, the law allows emergency hospitalization without a formal commitment hearing. In such cases, a physician must sign a statement saying that an imminent danger exists. The patient can then be picked up (usually by the police) and detained under a "hold order," usually not to exceed 72 hours, unless a petition for commitment is filed within that period.

Involuntary commitment in a psychiatric facility is, in large part, contingent on a determination that an individual is dangerous and needs to be confined out of a need to protect himself or herself or society. We will now turn to the important question of evaluating patients in terms of their potential dangerousness.

The Assessment of "Dangerousness"

As we have seen, though the majority of psychiatric patients are not considered dangerous and need no special safety precautions, a minority of individuals are violent and require close supervision—perhaps confinement until their "dangerousness" is no longer a problem. Few psychiatric patients are assaultive at or prior to their admission to psychiatric facilities. Rates of assaultiveness vary from setting to setting, though in all reported studies the number of assaultive patients is relatively low. Tardiff (1984), for example, reported that 10 percent of patients admitted to private psychiatric hospitals were considered to be assaultive at the time of admission. Tardiff and Sweillam (1982) found that 7 percent of chronic patients residing in state hospitals were assaultive, and Tardiff and Koenigsberg (1985) found that only 3 percent of outpatients at two psychiatric clinics had been assaultive toward others. The possibility that an individual is

[1] The examples of the legal procedures for commitment cited in this section are based on Minnesota state law.

dangerous or likely to commit violent acts is, indeed, one of the primary reasons why some individuals are committed to mental institutions—to protect themselves from harm and society from unwanted violence. Rubin (1972) pointed out that approximately 50,000 people a year are kept in preventive confinement, such as maximum security hospitals, and over 400,000 inmates are kept in maximum security prisons because they are believed to be dangerous to society. McNeil and Binder (1986) reviewed the rates of violence preceding psychiatric hospitalization in one psychiatric facility for the ten-year period 1973 through 1983. They found that while the rate of violence among patients did not increase significantly, the use of "dangerousness" as grounds for civil commitment did.

The determination that a patient is potentially dangerous is a difficult one to make (Litwack & Schlesinger, 1987). A 43-year-old homeless Cuban refugee, for example, who had only a few days earlier undergone a psychiatric evaluation and been released, stabbed two tourists to death on the Staten Island ferry because "God told him to kill" (*Time*, July 21, 1986). Obviously, determining potential dangerousness is a crucial judgment for mental health professionals to make—not only from a therapeutic standpoint, to assure that the most appropriate treatment is conducted, but also from a legal point of view, as we will see later. A clinician has a clear responsibility in attempting to protect the public from potential violence from the uncontrolled behavior of dangerous patients. A dramatic incident of a failure to assess the extent of a patient's dangerousness was reported by Gorin (1980, 1982) on the television news program "60 Minutes":

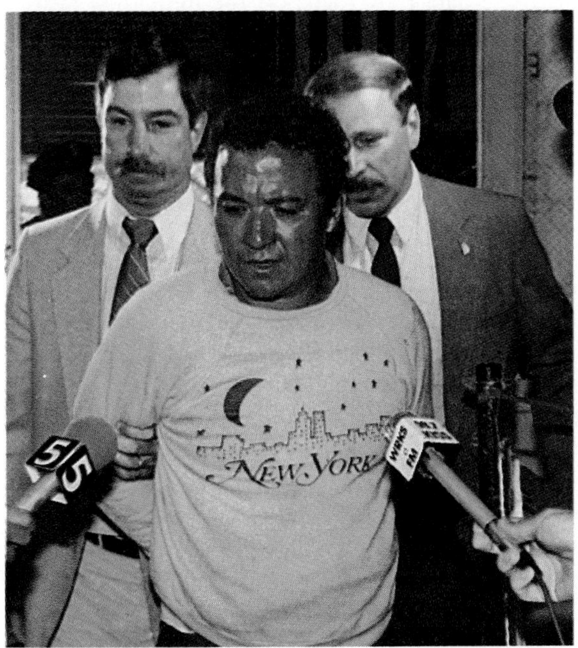

Juan Gonzalez stabbed and killed two people and injured nine others on the Staten Island Ferry. A few days before the incident, Gonzalez had undergone psychiatric evaluation after making wild death threats on the street. Though doctors concluded that he had a psychotic paranoid disorder, Gonzalez was released after two days because there was not enough space at the facility and he could not be involuntarily committed to a mental institution.

In December, 1979, Mrs. Eva B. was brutally stabbed to death by her former husband while a police dispatcher listened to her terrified screams over the telephone. Only hours before the stabbing incident occurred, Mr. B., who had attacked Mrs. B. eight times in the past, had been judged by two staff psychiatrists not to be dangerous. He had then been released, as part of his treatment, on a temporary pass from the Pilgrim State Hospital in New York. The hospital staff had released Mr. B. from confinement at this time despite the fact that both the judge and the prosecuting attorney who had been involved in his trial (for attempting to kill his wife) had independently written the New York State Department of Mental Health recommending that Mr. B. be held in the strictest confinement because of his persistent threats against Mrs. B. (Indeed, on two previous occasions, Mr. B. had escaped from the hospital and attempted to kill her.) The judge and attorney had also recommended that Mrs. B. should be warned if Mr. B. was released. Ironically, six hours after she had been murdered, a telegram from the hospital was delivered to Mrs. B.'s home warning her that her husband had not returned from his pass.

Looking beyond what appears to be some failure to follow through on the court's recommendations, this case illustrates a number of difficult yet critical dilemmas involved in trying to identify or predict dangerousness in psychiatric patients:

- First, it emphasizes the fact that some individuals are capable of uncontrolled violent behavior and hence are potentially dangerous if left unsupervised in the community.
- It also reflects the dilemma faced by mental health professionals who, attempting to rehabilitate disturbed patients by gradually easing them back into society, must exhibit some degree of trust in these individuals.
- Finally, and critically, it illustrates the fact that it is very difficult—for professionals

and laypersons alike—to accurately appraise "dangerousness" in some individuals.

Attempts to Predict "Dangerousness" It is usually an easy matter to determine, after the fact, that an individual has committed a violent act or acts and has demonstrated "dangerous behavior." The difficulty comes when one attempts to determine, in advance, if the individual is going to commit a particular violent act. Assessing a general state of "dangerousness" is not the same thing as predicting whether a violent act will occur.

How well do mental health professionals do in predicting "dangerousness"? The definition of what is "dangerous" is itself unclear. It depends, in large part, on who is asked. Some individuals have a limited or restrictive definition of what behaviors are dangerous and are willing to tolerate more aggressive behavior than others who view a broader range of behaviors as potentially dangerous. There is greater consensus about the dangerousness of extreme behaviors, such as murder, rape, and assault, for example. From the standpoint of society, these kinds of behaviors are condemned as dangerous and viewed as requiring restraint.

Violent acts are particularly difficult to predict because they are apparently determined as much by situational circumstances as they are by an individual's personality traits or violent predispositions. It is, of course, impossible to predict what environmental circumstances are going to occur or if particular circumstances will provoke or instigate aggression on the part of the person. At the individual level, one obvious risk factor is a history of violence (Noble & Rodger, 1989). Some types of patients, particularly schizophrenic and manic individuals (Binder & McNiel, 1988) or patients with well-entrenched delusions (de Pauw & Szulecka, 1988), are more likely to commit violent acts.

Mental health professionals typically err on the conservative side when assessing "violence proneness" in a patient; that is, they overpredict violence. They consider some individuals more dangerous than they actually are and, in general, predict a greater percentage of clients to be dangerous, requiring protective confinement, than actually become involved in violent acts (Megargee, 1970; Monahan, 1981). Gordon (1977) pointed out that the mental health professional's tendency to overpredict dangerousness places him or her in a "no-lose" situation: if the person commits a violent act, he or she can say, "I told you so," and if the patient does not commit a violent act, it's because the patient is locked up—"It is just lucky that no one has triggered this person's dangerousness yet" (p. 234).

Methods for Assessing Potential for "Dangerousness" Evaluating an individual's potential for committing violent acts is difficult because only part of the equation is available for study:

predisposing personality
+ environmental instigation
= aggressive act

As we have noted, psychologists and psychiatrists usually do not know enough about the environmental circumstances the individual will encounter to evaluate what the instigation to aggression will be. Predictions of dangerousness focus, then, primarily on aspects of the individual's personality. The two major sources of personality information are data from personality tests and the individual's previous history. Personality testing can reveal whether the individual shows personality traits of hostility, aggressiveness, impulsiveness, poor judgment, and so on. Nevertheless, many individuals with such characteristics never act on them. Still, as noted, practitioners tend to overpredict the likelihood of aggressive acts. The use of previous history—such as having committed prior aggression, having verbalized threats of aggression, having an available means of committing violence (such as possession of a gun), and so on—are useful predictors (Monahan, 1981). Like personality testing, however, these data only focus on the individual factors and do not account for the situational forces that impinge on the person.

The prediction of violence is even more difficult in the case of an overcontrolled person who does not have a history of aggressive behavior. Megargee (1970) studied extensively the "overcontrolled hostile" person who is the epitome of well-controlled behavior but who, on one occasion, loses control and kills another person. Examples of this type of murder are dramatic: the high school honor student, reportedly civic-minded and fond of helping sick and old people, who is arrested for torturing and killing a 3-year-old girl in his neighborhood; or the mild, passive father of four who loses his temper over being cheated by a car dealer and beats the man to death with a tire iron. These examples illustrate the most difficult type of aggressive behavior to predict—the sudden, violent, impulsive act of a seemingly well-controlled and "normal" individual.

A general pessimism has prevailed in recent years about our ability to predict dangerousness. Several studies in violence prediction, however, have attempted to improve prediction by identifying individuals at risk for violence. Using demographic data on family background, history of violence, friendships, and substance use, Klassen and

O'Connor (1988) were able to identify 76 percent of the people who later became violent. They concluded that predictive assessments could be improved even more so if the context in which violence occurs is taken into consideration.

The Duty to Warn: Implications of the Tarasoff Decision What should a therapist do on learning that one of his or her patients is planning to harm another person? Can the therapist violate the confidence of the therapy and take action to prevent the patient from committing the act? In many states, the therapist not only can violate the confidentiality but is required by law to do so—that is, to warn the endangered person of the threat against him or her. The duty-to-warn doctrine was given a great deal of impetus in a California court ruling in the case of *Tarasoff* v. *The Regents of the University of California et al.* (Cal. Reptr. 14, 551 P., 2d 334, 1976). In this case, Prosenjit Poddar was being seen in outpatient psychotherapy by a psychologist at the university mental health facility. During the treatment, Mr. Poddar indicated that he intended to kill his former girlfriend, Tatiana Tarasoff, when she returned from vacation. The psychologist, concerned about the threat, discussed the case with his supervisors, and they agreed that Mr. Poddar was dangerous and should be committed for further observation and treatment. They informed the campus police, who picked up Mr. Poddar for questioning. The police judged Mr. Poddar to be rational and released him after he promised to leave Ms. Tarasoff alone. Mr. Poddar terminated treatment with the psychologist. About two months later, he killed Ms. Tarasoff. Her parents later sued the University of California and its staff involved in the case for their failure to hospitalize Mr. Poddar and their failure to warn Ms. Tarasoff about the threat to her life.

The court did not find the defendants liable for failing to hospitalize Mr. Poddar; it did, however, find them liable for their failure to warn the victim. In a later analysis of the case, Knapp (1980) said that the court

> *ruled that difficulty in determining dangerousness does not exempt a psychotherapist from attempting to protect others when a determination of dangerousness exists. The court acknowledged that confidentiality was important to the psychotherapeutic relationship but stated that the protective privilege ends where the public peril begins. (p. 610)*

The duty-to-warn ruling in the Tarasoff case, while spelling out a therapist's responsibility in situations where there has been an explicit threat on another's life, left other areas of application unclear. For example, does this ruling apply in cases where a patient threatens to commit suicide? Or when the object of violence is not clearly named, such as when global threats are made? Or would the duty-to-warn ruling hold up in other states?

Knapp and Vandecreek (1982) pointed out in a follow-up review that subsequent court decisions have not extended the duty to protect to suicidal cases. Furthermore, if a patient does not specifically name an intended victim, then the duty-to-warn ruling does not apply. Regarding the application of the Tarasoff precedent in other states, four out of five of those states having related court cases have upheld the Tarasoff decision and required a duty to warn. Interestingly, a Maryland Court decision (*Shaw* v. *Glickman,* 415 A. 2d. 625, MD. Ct. Spec. App. 1980) found that, in Maryland, laws pertaining to privileged communications did not allow a therapist to warn a potential victim—even if a death threat was involved. Thus a psychotherapist must be aware of state laws and judicial precedents in addition to making a determination of potential dangerousness on the part of a patient. The final form of the duty-to-warn doctrine has not fully evolved in the courts; future court decisions will, no doubt, further define a practitioner's responsibility. In the meantime, clinicians are encouraged to follow closely the guidelines for staged responses to such threats and to carefully document and substantiate their decisions for actions taken (Gross et al., 1987).

In response to the ambiguities concerning the actual application of the duty-to-warn doctrine in clinical settings, Appelbaum (1985) discussed practical problems that clinicians face in dealing with this obligation. He pointed out that the most detrimental mistake that clinicians make in applying this legal obligation is to neglect the "basic principles of clinical care when a legal issue arises." A clinician should not lose track of the need to help an individual making a threat while fulfilling the obligation to warn the endangered person.

The Insanity Defense

In recent years, the use of **the insanity defense**—"innocent by reason of insanity"—in capital crime trials has been surrounded by considerable controversy, largely resulting from concerns that criminals may use this plea to avoid criminal responsibility. Actually, the insanity defense has been used in less than 2 percent of cases over time (Fersch, 1980). Studies have confirmed the fact, however, that individuals acquitted of crimes by reason of insanity spend less time, on the whole, in a psychiatric hospital than individuals who are actually convicted of crimes spend in prison (Kahn & Raifman, 1981; Pasewark, Pantle, & Steadman, 1982).

Although historically the insanity defense has been used infrequently, its use has apparently increased over the past 25 years as the definition of "insanity" has been broadened in the courts. Moreover, much of the controversy over the insanity defense has arisen because it has been used in many highly visible trials. For example, following the assassination attempt on President Reagan and the subsequent ruling that the alleged assassin (John Hinckley) was "insane" at the time, there was a great public outcry over the misuse of the insanity defense. Judging from the media coverage, many people apparently doubt the veracity of the insanity defense, believing instead that it may be contrived to escape justice.

The established precedents defining the insanity defense are as follows:

The use of the insanity defense in highly publicized cases, such as John Hinckley's assassination attempt on President Reagan in 1981, has led to controversy over whether it legitimately protects a mentally ill offender's rights or is a contrivance to avoid criminal responsibility.

1. *The M'Naghten Rule (1843).* Under this ruling, people are believed to be sane unless it can be proved that, at the time of committing the act, they were laboring under such a defect of reason (from a disease of the mind) that they did not know the nature and quality of the act they were doing—or, if they did know they were committing the act, they did not know that what they were doing was wrong.

2. *The irresistible impulse (1887).* A second precedent in the insanity defense is the doctrine of the "irresistible impulse." This view holds that accused individuals might not be responsible for their acts, even if they knew that what they were doing was wrong (according to the M'Naghten Rule), if they had lost the power to choose between right and wrong. That is, they could not avoid doing the act in question because they were compelled beyond their will to commit the act (Fersch, 1980).

3. *The Durham Rule.* In 1954, Judge David Bazelon, in a decision of the United States Court of Appeals, broadened the insanity defense further. Bazelon did not believe that the previous precedents allowed for a sufficient application of established scientific knowledge of mental illness and proposed a test that would be based on this knowledge. Under this rule, the accused is "not criminally responsible if his or her unlawful act was the product of mental disease or mental defect." As we have seen, with the expansion of the diagnostic classification of mental disorder, a broad range of behaviors can be defined as mental disease or defect. Which mental diseases serve to excuse a defendant from criminal responsibility? Generally, under M'Naghten, psychotic disorders were the basis of the insanity defense; but under the Durham Rule, other conditions (such as personality disorder or dissociative disorder) might also apply. How, then, is guilt or innocence determined? Many authorities believe that the Durham Rule has broadened the insanity defense in such a way as to require of the courts an impossible task—to determine guilt or innocence by reason of insanity on the basis of psychiatric testimony. In many cases, this has involved conflicting testimony because both the prosecution and the defense have "their" psychiatric witnesses who are in complete disagreement (Fersch, 1980; Marvit, 1981).

4. *Diminished capacity.* An additional insanity test has been proposed by the New York State Department of Mental Hygiene (1978): "Evidence of abnormal mental condition would be admissible to affect the degree of crime for which an accused could be convicted. Specifically, those offenses requiring intent or knowledge could be reduced to lesser included offenses requiring only reckless or criminal neglect." In this insanity defense, the accused would not be declared innocent by reason of insanity, but would be found guilty of a lesser charge, such as criminal negligence instead of murder.

The controversy over the insanity defense has led to much discussion about its reform by professionals in both the mental health and legal fields (Clark, 1987; Simon & Aaronson, 1988). Some individuals would like to do away with the insanity defense altogether, while others would prefer a modification of the defense to allow criminal responsibility to be established before an individual's sanity is considered in a case. Several states have revised the insanity defense to "guilty but mentally ill." In these cases, a defendant may be sentenced but placed in a treatment facility rather than in a prison. This two-part judgment serves to prevent the type of situation where an individual commits a murder, is found not guilty by reason of insanity, is turned over to a mental health facility, is found to be rational and in no further need of treatment by the hospital staff, and is released to the community after only two months of confinement. Under the two-part decision, such an individual would ultimately remain in the custody of the correctional department. Marvit (1981) suggested that this approach might "realistically balance the interest of the mentally ill offender's rights and the community's need to control criminal behavior" (p. 23).

Deinstitutionalization

As we learned in Chapter 2, asylums or mental hospitals were originally viewed as the most humane settings for dealing with chronic patients. The people who founded the institutions and the society that supported them saw these facilities as havens for retarded or disturbed individuals who could not survive in the world on their own. Ironically, though, as hospitals became overcrowded and hospital staffs overworked, patient care deteriorated. Mental hospitals, founded out of a concern for human welfare, came to be viewed as horrid places where humane care was more a philosophy than a practical reality. Bassuk and Gerson (1978) noted that

> *the reform movement, having seen its original objectives apparently accomplished, had ceased to be a significant influence. By early in this century the network of state mental hospitals, once the proud tribute to an era of reform, had largely turned into a bureaucratic morass within which patients were interned, often neglected and sometimes abused. (p. 47)*

Beginning in the 1960s, widespread disenchantment grew with the large, state mental hospitals designed to treat chronic psychiatric patients. Many authorities concluded that these institutions served primarily as "warehouses" for the insane and that they dehumanized individuals rather than helped them resolve their problems and return to society. Mental hospital reformers saw the movement as an opportunity to rid society of an unwelcome evil; hospital administrators and staff members initially viewed this movement as a way of lowering the hospital population to manageable numbers; and state governments viewed the movement with favor because it allowed legislatures (ever concerned about budgets) to reduce state spending. Many reformers recommended that some state mental hospitals be permanently closed and their residents returned either to more humane facilities or to their families and community (Bachrach, 1976). In fact, in a number of cases, the courts decided to close some hospitals.

Paralleling these recommendations was the effort, on the part of many concerned people, to develop expanded community resources to provide chronic patients with continued psychiatric care in their local community. Supporters of this effort believed then—and now—that society should be able to integrate these individuals back into the community and treat patients with the least restrictive alternative. This movement, referred to as **deinstitutionalization,** has become a focus of controversy in the mental health field today. Some authorities consider the emptying of the mental hospitals to be a positive expression of society's desire to confer freedom on previously confined individuals, while others speak of the "abandonment" of chronic patients to a cruel and harsh existence.

There has indeed been a significant reduction in hospital populations: from over 524,878 in 1970 to around 267,638 in 1986 (U.S. Department of Health, 1989). A number of factors have interacted to alter the pattern of mental hospital admissions and discharges over the past 20 years. As has been noted in previous chapters, the introduction of the antipsychotic drugs made it possible for many patients who would formerly have required confinement to be released into the community. The availability of these drugs led many to believe (falsely) that all mental health problems could be managed with medication. In addition, the changing treatment philosophy and the desire to eliminate mental institutions was accompanied by the belief that society wanted and could financially afford to provide better community-based care for chronic patients outside of large mental hospitals.

In theory, the movement to close the mental hospitals seemed workable. Many community-based mental health centers would be opened and would provide continuing care to the residents of hospitals after discharge. Residents would be given welfare funds (supposedly costing the government less than it takes to maintain large mental hospitals) and would be administered medication to keep them stabilized until they could obtain continuing care. Many patients would be discharged to home and family, while others would be placed in smaller, homelike board-and-care facilities or nursing homes.

Many unforeseen problems arose, however. Many residents of mental institutions had no families or homes to go to; board-and-care facilities were often substandard; the community mental health centers were ill-prepared to provide needed services for chronic patients, particularly on an outpatient basis; many patients had not been carefully selected for discharge and were not ready for community living; and many of those who were discharged were not followed up sufficiently or with enough regularity to ensure their successful adaptation outside the hospital. Indeed, countless individuals were discharged to fates that were far more dehumanizing than the conditions in any of the hospitals (Westermeyer, 1987). The following case illustrates the situation:

Dave B., age 49, had been hospitalized for 25 years in a state mental hospital. When the hospital was scheduled for phaseout, many of the patients, particularly those who were regressed or aggressive, were transferred to another state hospital. Dave was a borderline mentally retarded man who had periodic episodes of psychosis. At the time of hospital closing, however, he was not hallucinating and was "reasonably intact." Dave was considered to be one of the "less disturbed" residents because his psychotic behavior was less pronounced and he presented no dangerous problems.

He was discharged to a board-and-care facility (actually an old hotel whose clientele consisted mostly of former inpatients). At first, Dave seemed to fit in well at the facility; mostly he sat in his room or in the outside hallway, and he caused no trouble for the caretakers. Two weeks after he arrived, he wandered off the hotel grounds and was missing for several days. The police eventually found him living in the city dump. He had apparently quit taking his medication and when he was discovered he was regressed and catatonic. He was readmitted to a state hospital.

Concern over the increasing number of vagrants in New York City prompted the *New York Post* to conclude in an article on psychiatric hospitals that "warehousing" of mental patients no longer took place in state institutions but in "New York streets, transport terminals, flophouses, and shelters for the homeless" (May 10, 1982). The increase in "bag ladies" in major cities was attributed to the premature or inappropriate discharging of patients from psychiatric hospitals. The *Post* article reported that the New York state hospitals, which once had held 93,000 patients, in 1982 held only 21,000. It was estimated that 40 percent of the street crime in New York City could be attributed to former psychiatric patients released from hospitals. This situation is, unfortunately, quite common, as Westermeyer (1982a) noted:

> *Patients are returned to the community, armed with drugs to control their illness. The worst aspects of their illnesses may be under control. But many of the patients are not ready to function in society. They need a gradual reintroduction—facilities where someone else can see that they take their drugs, see their psychiatrists, get food, clothing and shelter. Such care is too often more than families can provide and such services are not generally available in a community. As a result, the numbers of bag ladies and men, vagrants and mentally disabled people, living in lonely hotels and dangerous streets, have burgeoned. (p. 2)*

The extent of problems created by deinstitutionalization is not fully known. The ambiguity

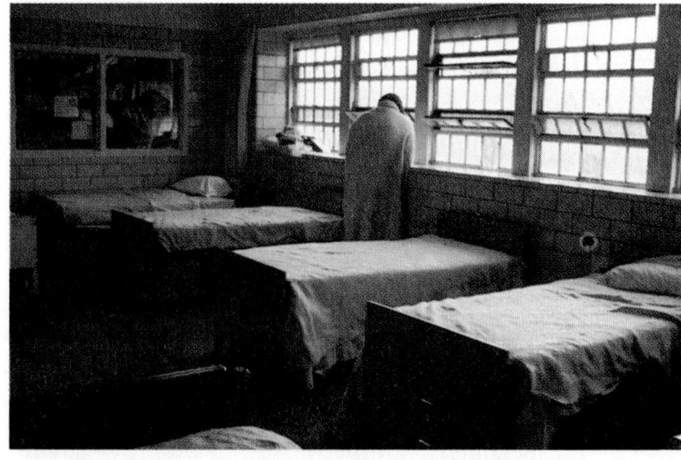

The extent of problems created by deinstitutionalization is not fully known, but some evidence suggests that the emptying of mental hospitals has contributed to the number of homeless people. Deinstitutionalization is not likely to be successful unless continuing care is available and adequate in the community, and unless it allows for readmission to the hospital for short periods if necessary.

comes, in part, from the scarcity of rigorous follow-up data on patients who have been discharged from mental hospitals. There have not been a sufficient number of adequate research studies in this area. Moreover, the research investigations have tended to be difficult to conduct because the patients are transient and are hard to keep track of over time.

Many individuals, once discharged from state hospitals, do join the ranks of what contemporary writers have called "the homeless" and become vulnerable to victimization (French, 1987). Certainly not all homeless people are former mental patients, but evidence suggests that deinstitutionalization has contributed to the number of homeless people (Jones, 1983; Lamb, 1984). Researchers have also demonstrated that a greater percentage of homeless people have significant psychopathology, as reflected in higher rates of hospitalization and felony convictions, than people who have homes. Fischer and colleagues (1986) conducted an epidemiological study of a random sample of homeless people (94 percent men) from four missions in the Baltimore area. These homeless people were interviewed when they came to the transient housing for a room for the night. They were administered the instruments used in the NIMH epidemiological survey (see Regier et al., 1984), the General Health Questionnaire, and the Diagnostic Interview Schedule; their responses were compared with a control sample of subjects from the Baltimore Catchment Area Study of the NIMH study. The results of the study confirmed expectations that homeless people would manifest poorer psychological adjustment: 33 percent of the homeless people had been hospitalized for psychiatric problems while only 5 percent of the control sample had been hospitalized; 58 percent had been arrested versus 24 percent of the control sample; 16 percent had had felony convictions versus 5 percent of controls; and about 35 percent had General Health Questionnaire scores in the impaired-functioning range, which was about three times the number of control subjects. More recently, Rossi (1990) estimated that 33 percent of homeless individuals suffer from chronic mental disorder and about 33 percent have severe addiction problems.

In spite of the problems just described, some data on patient discharge and outcome status support the deinstitutionalization process. Braun et al. (1981), for example, concluded:

The most satisfactory studies allow the qualified conclusion that selected patients managed outside the hospital in experimental programs do no worse and by some criteria have psychiatric outcomes superior to those of hospitalized control patients. (p. 747)

These same researchers, however, also concluded that deinstitutionalization is likely to be unsuccessful in continuing care in the community is not available or if it is inadequate.

After Deinstitutionalization Goering and colleagues (1984) found serious deficiencies in discharge planning and aftercare services. They followed up 505 discharged patients over a two-year period and found that psychological symptoms and distress levels were high. The high readmission rates of these patients (32 to 38 percent within six months and 56 to 67 percent in two years) was considered to result, in part, from the lack of community resources to facilitate the patients' reentry into society.

One of the most significant problems in the maintenance of discharged patients outside of hospitals involves preventing an individual from developing what has been referred to as the "chronic social breakdown syndrome" (Archer & Gruenberg, 1982). This pattern of maladaptive behavior involves the individual's failing to maintain his or her self-care and social functioning skills at the level he or she attained prior to discharge from the hospital. Although maintenance on psychoactive drugs can help such individuals to cope, it is important that assistance be provided to help maintain or attain an adequate social adjustment. This assistance or continuing care in the community can provide a patient with needed structure while he or she is learning new responsibilities and roles that are required in the new living situation.

Some successful programs designed to reintegrate chronic patients into the community were described by Bachrach (1980). All these programs, despite their differences, are based on the following principles:

- *Targeting of chronic patients.* The most successful model programs are targeted toward patients who have been persistently and chronically ill.
- *Linkage with other services.* The most successful programs incorporate "full-spectrum" planning, including treatment and social services.
- *Functional integrity.* Successful programs generally provide for their patients a full range of services that are usually associated with institutional care.

- *Individually tailored treatment.* Treatment programs should allow for social work case management and crisis-intervention services on a 24-hour basis, if needed.
- *Cultural- or ethnic-group relevance.* Successful programs include a consideration of the ethnic or racial characteristics of the population served.
- *Specifically trained staff.* Successful programs employ staff members who are apprised of the problems of chronic mental patients living in community settings.
- *Hospital liaison.* Because some patients may require readmission to a hospital for brief periods, successful modern programs maintain a relationship with a local hospital and coordinate readmissions, if necessary.
- *Internal evaluation.* Successful programs usually maintain an ongoing self-review program to monitor their functioning on a continuous basis.

Successful community care, according to Bachrach, involves the prospect of readmission to a hospital for short periods if necessary. The importance of short-term hospitalization has been noted by other investigators as well (Archer & Gruenberg, 1982). The underlying premise here is that each day that a patient can spend in the real world is better than none. If short-term rehospitalization is necessary to provide the patient with real-world experiences, then it is a valuable treatment approach. Furthermore, the availability of short-term readmission to a hospital can limit the feeling of abandonment that some mental patients may have when they are released into the community. As such, this general pattern of hospital readmission is prevalent today.

The ease with which former mental patients readjust to living in the real world depends, in large part, on the character of the residential surroundings and the social milieu they encounter in their return to the community (Sommers, 1988). To improve the readjustment of former mental patients to society, a new case-management approach has been initiated over the past few years. This novel approach involves assigning a patient to a case manager, usually not a mental health professional, who attempts to improve the quality of the patient's life and reduce readmissions to the hospital by serving as a link or go-between for the patient and the services available in the community. The effectiveness of this approach was recently studied by Franklin et al. (1987). They explored the efficiency and effectiveness of case management by following up a group of patients being served by this approach and comparing them to a group of similarly discharged patients who had community services available but were not case-managed. Unfortunately, the results at 12-month follow-up showed that the case-management approach was no more effective at reducing readmissions to hospitals than the no-case-management condition. Moreover, the patients in the case-management group did not report an improved quality of life. The only difference between the two conditions was that the case-management approach was less cost-effective.

The various approaches that have been implemented to circumvent patient failures to readjust to the community have not been particularly successful at reducing hospital readmissions and at further reducing the census in state hospitals. Nevertheless, advocates for deinstitutionalization continue to maintain that this is the most desirable approach to treating the chronically mental ill. The controversy over deinstitutionalization is likely to continue over the next few years, with advocates on both sides of

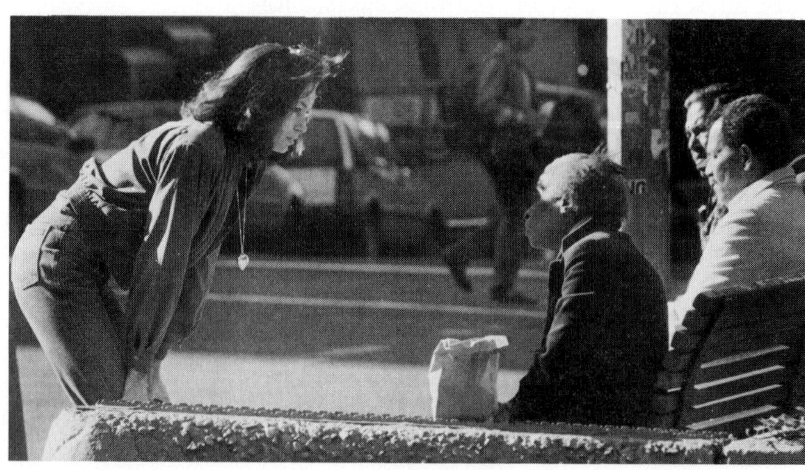

Project Reachout in New York City tries to help mentally ill street people. The workers try to get confused, scared, and disoriented people into the office (they usually gain their trust by giving them food), where they can be helped in many ways, from simply getting a cup of coffee or a shower to obtaining a room and psychiatric care.

the issue laying claim to the correctness of their views until more definitive research is conducted.

It is of interest to note one recent trend in mental health care—privatization. The mental health system appears to be undergoing considerable evolution in recent years, due in large part to changes in funding for mental health care. More and more emotionally disturbed individuals are being admitted to large private institutions. This phenomenon, referred to as the "privatization" of the mental health system (Dorwart et al., 1989), has developed because funding for public treatment facilities has waned and private insurance companies are willing to cover the cost of inpatient mental health services. Several large private hospital corporations have filled the treatment void left by the mental hospital closings and are providing inpatient psychiatric care for a growing number of patients.

Another related development in the care of chronic mental patients is the growth and expansion of private nursing home facilities. Since the deinstitutionalization movement spurred the discharge of psychiatric patients into the community, alternative care facilities have expanded to fill the need for continued care (Morlock, 1989). This expansion of facilities has been made possible through financial incentives provided by Medicare to fund treatment. Nursing homes have become the largest single setting to care for the chronic mentally ill. Mentally ill individuals (a total of 668,000 are currently in nursing homes) make up over 51 percent of the nursing home population at present (Goldman, Feder, & Scanlon, 1986).

ORGANIZED EFFORTS FOR MENTAL HEALTH

Public awareness of the magnitude and severity of our contemporary mental health problem and the interest of government, professional, and lay organizations have prompted programs directed at better understanding, more effective treatment, and long-range prevention. Efforts to improve mental health are apparent not only in our society, but also in many other countries; and international as well as national and local organizations and approaches are involved.

U.S. Efforts for Mental Health

In the United States, the primary responsibility for dealing with mental disorders fell initially to state and local agencies. During World War II, however, the extent of mental disorders in the United States was brought to public attention when a large number of young men—two out of every seven recruits—were rejected for military service for psychiatric reasons. This discovery led to a variety of organized measures for coping with the nation's mental health problem.

The Government and Mental Health In 1946, aware of the need for more research, training, and services in the field of mental health, Congress passed its first comprehensive mental health bill, the National Mental Health Act, which laid the basis for the federal government's programs in the 1950s and 1960s.

The 1946 bill provided for the establishment of a National Institute of Mental Health (NIMH) in or near Washington, D.C., to serve as a central research and training center and as headquarters for the administration of a grant-in-aid program. The grant-in-aid feature was designed to foster research and training elsewhere in the nation and to help state and local communities expand and improve their own mental health services. New powers were conferred on the NIMH in 1956, when Congress, under Title V of the Health Amendments Act, authorized the institute to provide "mental health project grants" for experimental studies, pilot projects, surveys, and general research having to do with the understanding, assessment, treatment, and aftercare of mental disorders.

As a result of organizational changes since then, the NIMH is now one of the three institutes under the Alcoholism, Drug Abuse, and Mental Health Administration, a division of the Public Health Service. The NIMH (a) conducts and supports research on the biological, psychosocial, and sociocultural aspects of mental disorders; (b) supports the training of professional and paraprofessional personnel in the mental health field; (c) assists communities in planning, establishing, and maintaining more effective mental health programs; and (d) provides information on mental health to the public and to the scientific community. Its two companion institutes—the National Institute on Alcohol Abuse and Alcoholism (NIAAA) and the National Institute on Drug Abuse (NIDA)—perform comparable functions in their respective fields (Office of the Federal Registry, 1982).

Although the federal government provides leadership and financial aid, the states and localities actually plan and run most NIMH programs. In addition, the states establish, maintain, and supervise their own mental hospitals and clinics. A number of states have also pioneered, through their legislation, in the development of community mental health centers; rehabilitation services in the community for former patients; and facilities for dealing with alcoholism, drug abuse, and other special mental health problems. In the 1980s, federal support for mental health programs diminished considerably. Most state and local governments, which were expected to assume much of the support of mental health activities, have not been able to fund programs and facilities at 1960s and 1970s levels. As a result, many programs devoted to mental health training, research, and service have been greatly reduced or even abandoned. As to the future, there is widespread uncertainty about continued financial support for mental health activities.

Professional Organizations and Mental Health A number of professional organizations exist in the mental health field. Some of the most influential of these are listed in *HIGHLIGHT 19.4*.

One of the most important functions of these organizations is to set and maintain high professional and ethical standards within their special areas. This function may include (a) establishing and reviewing training qualifications for professional and paraprofessional personnel; (b) setting standards and procedures for the accreditation of undergraduate and graduate training programs; (c) setting standards for the accreditation of clinics, hospitals, or other service operations and carrying out inspections to see that the standards are followed; and (d) investigating reported cases of unethical or unprofessional conduct and taking disciplinary action when necessary.

A second key function of these professional organizations involves communication and information exchange within their areas via meetings, symposia, workshops, refresher courses, the publication of professional and scientific journals, and related activities. In addition, all such organizations sponsor programs of public education as a means of advancing the interests of their professions, drawing attention to mental health needs, and attracting students to careers in their areas.

A third key function of professional organizations, one that is receiving increasing attention, is the application of insights and methods to contemporary social problems, for example, in lobbying national and local government agencies to provide more services for homeless people. Composed as they are of qualified personnel, professional mental health organizations are in a unique position to serve as consultants on mental health problems and programs not only on the national level but also on the state and local levels.

The Role of Voluntary Mental Health Organizations and Agencies Although professional mental health personnel and organizations can give expert technical advice in regard to mental health needs and programs, real progress in helping plan and implement these programs must come from an informed and concerned citizenry. In fact, it has been repeatedly stated that it has been nonprofessionals who have blazed the trails in the mental health field.

Prominent among the many voluntary mental health agencies is the National Association for Mental Health (NAMH). This organization was founded in 1950 by the merger of the National Committee for Mental Hygiene, the National Mental Health Foundation, and the Psychiatric Foundation; it was further expanded in 1962 by merging with the National Organization for Mentally Ill Children. Through its national governing body and some 1000 local affiliates, the NAMH works for the improvement of services in community clinics and mental hospitals; it helps recruit, train, and place volunteers for service in treatment and aftercare programs; and it works for enlightened mental health legislation and for the provision of needed facilities and personnel. It also carries on special educational programs aimed at fostering positive mental health and helping people understand mental disorders.

In addition, the National Association for Mental Health has been actively involved in many court decisions affecting patient rights (NAMH, 1979). In several cases the NAMH has sponsored litigation or served as amicus curiae (friend of the court) in efforts to establish the rights of mental patients to treatment, to freedom from custodial confinement, to freedom to live in the community, and to protection of their confidentiality.

With a program and organization similar to that of the NAMH, the National Association for Retarded Citizens (NARC) works to reduce the incidence of mental retardation, to seek community and residential treatment centers and services for the retarded, and to carry on a program of education aimed at better public understanding of retarded individuals and greater support for legislation on their behalf. The NARC also fosters scientific research into mental retardation, the recruitment and training of volunteer workers, and programs of community action.

These and other voluntary health organizations, such as Alcoholics Anonymous, need the backing of a wide constituency of knowledgeable and involved citizens in order to succeed.

Mental Health Resources in Private Industry Personal problems—such as marital distress or other family problems, alcohol or drug abuse, financial difficulties, or job-related stress—can adversely affect employee morale and performance. Psychological difficulties among employees may result in numerous types of problems, such as absenteeism, accident proneness, poor productivity, and high job turnover. Many corporations have long recognized this fact, and yet it has been a relatively recent phenomenon to see them act on this knowledge. Today many companies have expanded their "obligations" to employees to include numerous psychological services. Often referred to as employee-assistance programs, these are the means through which corporations can actively provide mental health services to employees and their family members.

One corporation that has pioneered in the development of employee-assistance programs is Control Data Corporation of Minneapolis, Minnesota. Following the implementation of a successful alcoholism treatment program in 1974, Control Data's management founded its employee-assistance program, the Employee Advisory Resource (known as EAR). This program was initiated to assist employees and their family members in solving personal or job-related problems. The program—modeled after the telephone hot-line programs—provides a 24-hour telephone counseling service staffed by approximately 40 EAR counselors. In addition, a counselor is on duty at all times in the event that an employee wishes a personal consultation. All counselors have been trained to identify problems and to refer troubled employees to internal counseling resources or to community agencies. Callers may remain anonymous and the contact is completely confidential. The service is provided at no cost to employees.

Control Data's EAR program has proven to be of help to many employees. During the first five years of operation, over 19,000 employee contacts were recorded. The number of counseling contacts has increased to about 5,000 a year at present. Though individuals seek help for a range of problems, the majority of contacts are for legal difficulties, financial problems, alcoholism, and marital stress.

The EAR program provides a number of employee services in addition to personal counseling and referral. These include employee education, providing information on the prevention of future problems, employee relations consultation, and employee input into policy-making decisions. The success of the EAR program is reflected in the fact that since 1976 Control Data has assisted numerous other companies in setting up similar employee-assistance programs.

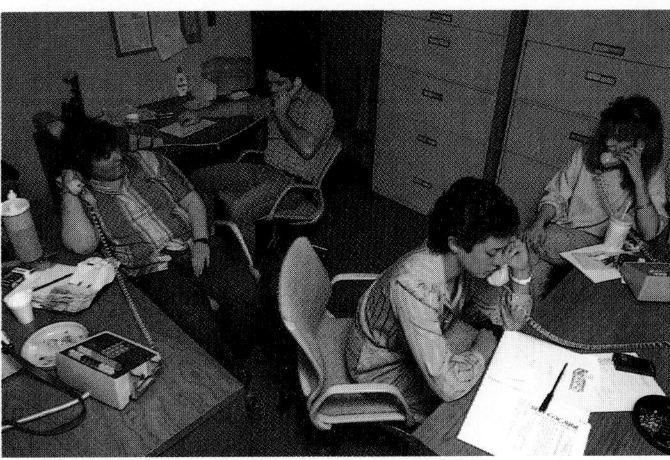

Employee assistance programs are a relatively recent phenomenon that recognizes the link between psychological difficulties and job problems. Corporations are increasingly providing personal counseling and referral programs for employees having legal, financial, marital, and substance-abuse problems. Shown here is one such employee program that provides drug-rehabilitation telephone counseling.

International Efforts for Mental Health

Mental health is a major problem not only in the United States but in the rest of the world as well. Indeed, many of the unfavorable conditions in this country with regard to the causes and treatment of mental disorders are greatly magnified in poorer countries and countries with repressive governments. According to the World Health Organization (WHO, 1978a), 40 million people in the world suffer from severe mental illness; more than 80 million suffer from alcohol and drug addiction, mental retardation, and organic brain disorders; and another 80 million suffer from other mental disorders, such as the neuroses. The severity of the world mental health problem is shown in WHO's estimates that mental disorders affect more than 200 million people worldwide.

It was the knowledge of this great problem that served to bring about the formation of several international organizations at the end of World War

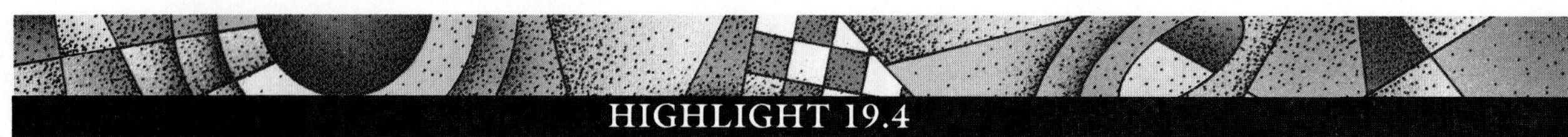

HIGHLIGHT 19.4

Professional Organizations Concerned with Mental Health

American Psychological Association (APA). An association of professionally trained psychologists. Its purpose is to advance psychology as a science, as a profession, and as a means of promoting human welfare. It has over 30 divisions concerned with various special areas within psychology, and it establishes and monitors standards for the training and practice of psychologists in mental health work.

American Psychological Society (APS). An association of academically oriented psychologists whose purpose is to advance psychology as a science and as a means of promoting human welfare.

American Psychiatric Association (APA). An association of physicians with training in psychiatry. Its purpose is to further the study of the nature, treatment, and prevention of mental disorders; to help set, improve, and maintain standards of practice and service in mental hospitals, clinics, general hospital psychiatric units, and institutions for the mentally retarded; to further psychiatric research and education; and to foster enlightened views with regard to the social and legal aspects of psychopathology and the role of psychiatry in fostering human welfare.

American Medical Association (AMA). An association of physicians who are members of constituent state medical associations. In addition to its myriad other functions, it is concerned with mental disorder as a general health problem and with fostering research, education, and legislation to advance comprehensive health efforts in the United States.

American Psychoanalytic Association (APA). An association of analytically trained psychiatrists. It sets standards for the training of psychoanalysts.

Association for Advancement of Behavior Therapy (AABT). An association of behaviorally oriented psychologists interested in promoting the research and application of behavioral techniques in the treatment of mental disorders.

American Sociological Association (ASA). An association of sociologists, social scientists, and other professional people interested in research, teaching, and applications of sociology. Its sections on social psychology, medical sociology, and criminology have special pertinence to mental health.

National Association of Social Workers (NASW). An association of professionally trained social workers, organized to promote the quality and effectiveness of social work and to foster mental health. It establishes and monitors standards for training and practice, encourages research, and interprets the role of social work in the community.

American Nurses Association (ANA). An association of registered nurses concerned with high standards of professional practice. Two of its clinical committee groups (one on psychiatric nursing practice and one on maternal and child health nursing) have special mental health concerns.

American Occupational Therapy Association (AOTA). A society of registered occupational therapists administering medically supervised activities to physically or mentally ill people. It maintains standards of education and train-

II. We will briefly discuss here the World Health Organization and the World Federation for Mental Health.

The World Health Organization (WHO)

The World Health Organization defines health as not simply the absence of disease, but as a positive state of physical, mental, and social well-being. From the first, it has been keenly aware of the close interrelationships between physical, psychosocial, and sociocultural factors—such as the influence of rapid change and social disruption on both physical and mental health; the impossibility of major progress toward mental health in societies where a large proportion of the population suffer from malnutrition, parasites, and disease; and the frequent psychological and cultural barriers to successful programs in family planning and public health.

Formed after World War II as part of the UN system, WHO's earliest focus was on physical diseases; through its efforts dramatic progress has been made toward the conquest of ancient scourges like

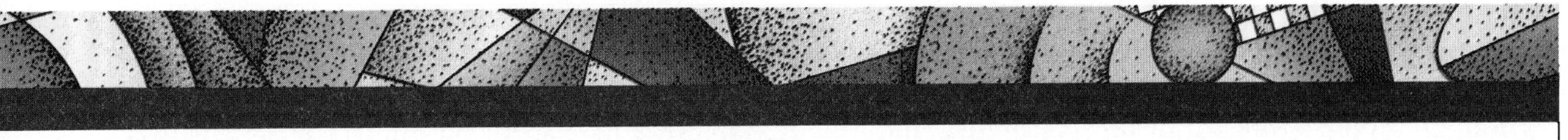

ing, makes surveys and recommendations on request, and works with its state associations in the preparation and certification of occupational therapy volunteer assistants.

National Rehabilitation Association (NRA). An association of physicians, counselors, therapists, and others (including organizations) concerned with the rehabilitation of the physically and mentally handicapped. It reviews existing services and makes recommendations for improved rehabilitation programs.

American Orthopsychiatric Association (AOA). An organization of psychiatrists, psychologists, social workers, sociologists, and members of other disciplines working in a collaborative approach to the study and treatment of human behavior, primarily in clinical settings. Its focus is on the problems of children. The AOA encourages research and is directly concerned with fostering human welfare.

National Council for Family Relations (NCFR). Composed primarily of and directed toward practitioners serving couples and families through counseling, therapy, education, and community service. The NCFR fosters research and the application of its findings to practice.

American Association on Mental Deficiency (AAMD). An interdisciplinary association of physicians, educators, administrators, social workers, psychologists, psychiatrists, and others interested in assisting the mentally retarded. It works with the American Psychiatric Association in setting standards for hospitals and schools for the mentally retarded.

Council for Exceptional Children (CEC). Made up largely of professional workers in fields dealing with mentally retarded, physically handicapped, and emotionally disturbed children. It fosters research and its applications, education, and social legislation relating to exceptional children.

American Association for the Advancement of Science (AAAS). Composed of scientists from many disciplines. Its objectives include furthering the work and mutual cooperation of scientists, improving the effectiveness of science and its contribution to human welfare, and increasing understanding and appreciation of the importance and promise of scientific methods in human progress.

Society for Research in Child Development (SRCD). An association of psychologists whose aim is to study normal processes of child development. Members are concerned with issues related to improving the welfare of children as well as with encouraging scientific research on developmental processes.

Most of these organizations sponsor national conventions, workshops, symposia, and public educational programs, and many publish journals in their respective areas. They are also concerned with broad social problems as well as with the special problems in their professional areas.

smallpox and malaria. Over the years, mental health, too, became an increasing concern among the member countries. In response, WHO's present program now integrates mental health concerns with the broad problems of overall health and socioeconomic development that must be faced by member countries (WHO, 1978a). For example, WHO's program includes strategies to both prevent and control mental disorders. Furthermore, it includes efforts to ensure healthy psychosocial development, to protect traditional cultural values and family relationships in the face of rapid industrialization, and to foster community participation in public health programs.

WHO has headquarters in Geneva and regional offices for Africa, the Americas, Southeast Asia, Europe, the Eastern Mediterranean, and the Western Pacific. Hence its activities extend into areas with diverse physical environments, types of social organization, and mental health facilities. It enters a country only on invitation, helping identify the basic health needs of each country and working with the local authorities to plan and carry out the most useful and appropriate programs. Where possible, it strives to make its services available over a period of several years to ensure continuity and success for the programs that are undertaken.

Another important contribution of WHO has been its International Classification of Diseases, which enables clinicians and researchers in different countries to use a uniform set of diagnostic categories (WHO, 1978b). The American Psychiatric Association's DSM-IV classification is being coordinated with the WHO classification (ICD-10).

The World Federation for Mental Health

The World Federation for Mental Health was established in 1948 as an international congress of nongovernmental organizations and individuals concerned with mental health. Its purpose is to promote cooperation at the international level between governmental and nongovernmental mental health agencies, and its membership now extends to more than 50 countries. The federation has been granted consultative status by WHO and it assists the UN agencies by collecting information on mental health conditions all over the world.

We have now seen something of the maze of local, national, and international measures that are being undertaken in the mental health field. We can expect these efforts to continue. Furthermore, we can expect to see more and more mental health problems unraveled to reveal discoverable causes and to respond to treatment and prevention by scientific means. The 1990s have already witnessed an amazing openness and a diminishing of previously impassable borders. Along with this increased interchange of ideas and cooperation, we expect to see a broader interchange of mental health collaboration. Reductions in international tensions and a greater international cooperation in the sciences and health planning will likely promote more sharing of information and views on mental health.

CHALLENGES FOR THE FUTURE

We have a long way to go before our dreams of a better world are realized. Many question whether the United States or any other technologically advanced nation can achieve mental health for the majority of its citizens in our time. Racism, poverty, the uprooting of third world populations, and other social problems that contribute to mental disorder sometimes seem insurmountable.

Events in the rest of the world affect us also, both directly and indirectly. Worldwide economic instability and shortages and the possibility of the destruction of our planet's life support system breed widespread anxiety about the future. The vast resources we have spent on military programs over the past 45 years to protect against perceived threats have absorbed funds and energy that otherwise might have been turned to meeting human and social needs here and elsewhere in the world. The limited resources we are now willing to apply to solving mental health problems prevent the solution of major problems resulting from cocaine abuse, homelessness, broken families, and squalid living conditions for many families.

The Need for Planning

It seems imperative that more effective planning be done at community, national, and international levels if mental health problems are going to be reduced or eliminated. Many challenges must be met if we are to create a better world for ourselves and future generations. Without slackening our efforts to meet needs at home, we will probably find it increasingly essential to participate more broadly in international measures toward reducing group tensions and promoting mental health and a better world for people everywhere. At the same time, we can expect that measures undertaken to reduce international conflict and improve the general condition of humankind will make their contribution to our own nation's social progress and mental health. Both kinds of measures will require understanding and moral commitment from concerned citizens.

The Individual's Contribution

Each man can make a difference,
and each man should try.
John F. Kennedy

The history of abnormal psychology provides clear examples of individuals whose efforts were instrumental in changing thinking about problems. Recall that Pinel took off the chains, Dorothea Dix initiated an incredible movement to improve the conditions of asylums, and Clifford Beers inspired the modern mental health movement with his autobiographical account of his own experience with mental illness. Who may lead the next revolution in mental health is anyone's guess. What is clear is that a great deal can be accomplished by individual effort.

When students become aware of the tremendous scope of the mental health problem both nationally and internationally and the woefully inadequate facilities for coping with it, they often ask, "What can I do?" This is not an idle question, for much of the progress that has been achieved in the treatment of mental disorders has resulted from the work of concerned citizens. Thus it seems appropriate to suggest a few of the lines of action interested students can profitably take.

Many opportunities in mental health work are open to trained personnel, both professional and paraprofessional. Social work, clinical psychology, psychiatry, and other mental health occupations are rewarding in terms of personal fulfillment. In addition, many occupations, ranging from law enforcement to teaching and the ministry, can and do play key roles in the mental health and well-being of many people. Training in all these fields usually offers individuals opportunities to work in community clinics and related facilities, to gain experience in understanding the needs and problems of people in distress, and to become familiar with community resources.

Citizens can find many ways to be of direct service if they are familiar with national and international resources and programs, and if they invest the effort necessary to learn about their community's special needs and problems. Whatever their roles in life—student, teacher, police officer, lawyer, homemaker, business executive, or trade unionist—their interests are directly at stake. For although the mental health of a nation may be manifested in many ways—in its purposes, courage, moral responsibility, scientific and cultural achievements, and quality of daily life—its health and resources derive ultimately from the individuals within it. In a participatory democracy, it is they who plan and implement the nation's goals.

Besides accepting some measure of responsibility for the mental health of others through the quality of one's own interpersonal relationships, there are several other constructive courses of action open to each citizen, including (a) serving as a volunteer in a mental hospital, community mental health center, or service organization; (b) supporting realistic measures for ensuring comprehensive health services for all age groups; and (c) working toward improved public education, responsible government, the alleviation of group prejudice, and the establishment of a more sane and harmonious world.

All of us are concerned with mental health for personal as well as altruistic reasons, for we want to overcome the harassing problems of contemporary living and find our share of happiness in a meaningful and fulfilling life. To do so, we may sometimes need the courage to admit that our problems are too much for us. When existence seems futile or the going becomes too difficult, it may help to remind ourselves of the following basic facts, which have been emphasized throughout this text:

In Austin, Texas, the Austin Groups for the Elderly (AGE) represents a broad-based preventive effort of more than 15 agencies that provide activities and services to the elderly, thus promoting better mental health either directly or indirectly. Shown here is one of the programs available—Elderhaven, a unique day-care center for elderly adults.

- From time to time, each of us has serious difficulties in coping with the problems of living.
- During such crisis periods, we may need psychological and related assistance.
- Such difficulties are not a disgrace; they can happen to anyone if the stress is sufficiently severe.
- The early detection and correction of maladaptive behavior is of great importance in preventing the development of more severe or chronic conditions.
- Preventive measures—primary, secondary, and tertiary—are the most effective long-range approach to the solution of both individual and group mental health problems.

Recognizing these facts is essential because statistics show that almost all of us will at some time in our lives have to deal with severely maladaptive behavior or mental disorder either in ourselves or in someone close to us. Our interdependence and the loss to us all, individually and collectively, when any one of us fails to achieve his or her potential are eloquently expressed in the famous lines of John Donne (1624):

No man is an island, entire of itself; every man is a piece of the continent, a part of the main. If a clod be washed away by the sea, Europe is less, as well as if a promontory were, as well as if a manor of thy friends or of thine own were: any man's death diminishes me, because I am involved in mankind, and therefore never send to know for whom the bell tolls; it tolls for thee.

UNRESOLVED ISSUES on the Mentally Disordered in the Prison System

Teplin (1990a) reported that the rates of schizophrenia, major depression, and mania were two to three times higher in jails than in the general population. These findings reaffirm the view that many individuals with severe mental disorders are in jails or prisons in the United States rather than in mental health facilities. The incarceration of mentally disabled individuals in prison or jail may result from people being mentally disordered when they commit crimes or, once incarcerated for a crime, becoming mentally disordered in reaction to the imprisonment.

Some investigators have recently argued that the greater prevalence of severe mental disorders in prison inmates than in the general population supports the view that jails, rather than mental hospitals, have become the repository for the chronically mentally disordered. This scenario is thought to be the result of numerous inpatients being released from psychiatric hospitals and being left to fend for themselves. Failing to function in the community, they resort to committing crimes, which results in their eventual imprisonment. This view has been referred to as the *criminalization hypothesis.* Some authorities believe that prisons have also become the dumping grounds for individuals with other problems, such as drug abuse, or for homeless people in winter, when living on the streets becomes difficult (Adler, 1987; Pogrebin & Poole, 1987; Shenson, Dubler, & Michaels, 1990).

Can the fact that there are many psychologically disturbed individuals in prison support the criminalization hypothesis? This view would be more tenable if, for example, the prisons became more filled with former psychiatric patients after deinstitutionalization became fashionable. Teplin (1990a) pointed out, however, that there appears *not* to have been a substantial increase of the mentally disordered in jails over previous estimates of similar studies, which have traditionally been higher than the population at large (Bolton, 1976). That is, the census of mentally disordered individuals in prison appears to have been relatively constant over the years, albeit higher than the general population. Thus the problem is not new and it is not simply a result of deinstitutionalization and the shifting of people from psychiatric facilities to prisons.

Whatever the source, the problem nevertheless exists. Many individuals whose primary problem is mental illness, rather than or in addition to criminality, are institutionalized in facilities where understanding and treatment of mental health problems are sorely lacking. In an extensive study of 486 admissions to Philadelphia prisons using a battery of psychological tests, Guy and colleagues (1985) reported that 34 percent of the inmates were identified as having substantial psychological problems and 11 percent were deemed as in clear need of psychiatric hospitalization.

Mental health resources, however, have traditionally not been available or only minimally available in correctional facilities. It appears that our society has taken the view, at least as far as our past actions reflect, that prisons are places of retention rather than treatment or rehabilitation. Teplin's study (1990b) confirmed this view—when the mentally disordered are incarcerated, few receive attention for their psychological problems. She found that, while somatic illnesses were discovered 91.7 percent of the time for individuals experiencing problems, mental health problems were detected in less than 33 percent of the severely mentally disordered detainees. Symptoms of depression among detainees were frequently overlooked, being detected in only 7.1 percent of the cases. This is a particularly tragic oversight in correctional programs because suicide is the second most frequent cause of death among jail detainees—a total of 39 percent of all inmate deaths (U.S. Justice Department, 1987). Teplin (1990b) found that, of those detainees meeting criteria for severe mental disorder, only about 33 percent were provided treatment within a week of detention. She concluded that "once arrested, treatment is unlikely to be forthcoming. Clearly, society must provide liaison between the criminal justice and mental health systems, as well as improve screening techniques to ensure that mentally disordered detainees receive needed treatment" (p. 236).

Whether these mentally disordered inmates are incarcerated as a result of their disorders or whether their severe psychological disorders resulted from their imprisonment is not important. What is more pertinent is that their problems be recognized and treated. Clearly, many people in prison are suffering from severe psychological disorders and need more attention for their problems than they currently receive.

SUMMARY

Increasingly today, professionals are trying not only to cure mental health problems but also to prevent them, or at least reduce their effects. Prevention can be viewed as focusing on three levels. Primary prevention is aimed at reducing the possibility of disorder and fostering positive mental health efforts. Secondary prevention attempts to reduce the impact or duration of a problem that has already occurred. Tertiary prevention attempts to reduce the long-term consequences of having had a disorder.

In recent years, several legal issues concerning the treatment of mental patients have surfaced. The commitment process and procedures for committing individuals for inpatient care have been reconsidered. Being "mentally ill" is not considered sufficient grounds for commitment. There must be, in addition, evidence that the individual is either dangerous to himself or herself or represents a danger to society. It is not an easy matter, even for trained professionals, to determine in advance if an individual is "dangerous" and likely to cause harm to others. Nevertheless, professionals must, at times, make such judgments. Recent court rulings have found professionals liable when patients they were treating caused harm to others. The Tarasoff decision held that a therapist has a duty to warn potential victims if his or her patient has threatened to kill them.

Another important issue of forensic psychology involves the insanity plea for capital crimes. Many mental health and legal professionals, journalists, and laypersons have questioned the present use of the insanity defense. The original legal precedent, the M'Naghten Rule, held that, at the time of committing the act, the accused must have been laboring under such a defect of reason as to not know the nature and quality of the act or to not know that what he or she was doing was wrong. The more recent broadening of the insanity plea, under the Durham Rule, has placed more credibility on scientific knowledge in that the accused is not "criminally responsible if his or her unlawful act was the produce of mental disease or mental defect." This broadening of the insanity plea has led to its use in more and more cases, and decisions often involve conflicting psychiatric testimony. Many people have been questioning the appropriateness of the insanity plea, and some experts are recommending changes in it, asking that an accused individual's guilt or innocence be established separately from a determination of sanity.

There has been a great deal of legal controversy recently over the release of patients from mental hospitals, called deinstitutionalization, and the failure to provide adequate follow-up of these patients in the community. In their zeal to close large psychiatric institutions, many administrators underestimated the amount of care that would be needed after discharge, and overestimated communities' abilities to deal with patients with chronic problems. The result was that some chronic patients were placed in circumstances that required more adaptive abilities than they possessed. Recent work in the area of aftercare for former mental patients has provided clearer guidelines for discharge and therapeutic follow-up.

A large number of organizations are concerned and involved with establishing organized efforts for mental health. Several government agencies have mental health as their primary mission. For example, federal agencies such as the National Institute of Mental Health (NIMH), the National Institute on Drug Abuse (NIDA), and the National Institute on Alcohol Abuse and Alcoholism (NIAAA) are devoted to promoting varied research, training, and service. State and county government agencies may focus their efforts on the delivery of mental health services to residents on an inpatient or outpatient basis.

Mental health programming in the United States is also the concern of several professional and mental health organizations, many corporations, and a number of voluntary mental health organizations. In addition, international organization, such as the World Health Organization (WHO) and the World Federation for Mental Health, have contributed to mental health programs worldwide.

Key Terms

primary prevention (p. 674)
secondary prevention (p. 674)
tertiary prevention (p. 674)
short-term crisis therapy (p. 679)
milieu therapy (p. 683)
social-learning programs (p. 684)
forensic psychology (forensic psychiatry) (p. 686)
the insanity defense (p. 691)
deinstitutionalization (p. 693)

Glossary

Many of the key terms that appear in the glossary appear in boldface when first introduced in the text discussion. A number of other terms commonly encountered in this or other psychology texts are also included; you are encouraged to make use of this glossary both as a general reference tool and as a study aid for the course in abnormal psychology.

Abnormal behavior. Maladaptive behavior deterimental to an individual and/or a group.

Abnormal psychology. Field of psychology concerned with the study, assessment, treatment, and prevention of abnormal behavior.

Abstinence. Refraining altogether from the use of a particular addictive substance.

Accommodation. Cognitive process whereby new information causes a reorganization of previously existing cognitive maps or structures.

Activation (arousal). Energy mobilization required for an organism to pursue its goals and meet its needs.

Actuarial approach. Application of probability statistics to human behavior, as in insurance.

Actuarial interpretation. Application of interpretations developed from a reference group with test scores similar to those of a subject to evaluate the subject's test performance.

Acute (disorder). Term used to describe a disorder of sudden onset and relatively short duration, usually with intense symptoms.

Acute alcoholic hallucinosis. State of alcoholic intoxication characterized by hallucinations.

Acute posttraumatic stress disorder. Disorder in which symptoms develop within six months of extremely traumatic experience instead of entering recovery stage.

Acute schizophrenia. See **Reactive schizophrenia.**

Addictive behavior. Behavior based on the pathological need for a substance or activity; it may involve the abuse of substances, such as alcohol or cocaine, or the excessive ingestion of high-caloric food, resulting in extreme obesity.

Adjustive behavior. Behavior by which an individual attempts to deal with stress and meet his or her needs, including efforts to maintain harmonious relationships with the environment.

Adjustment. Outcome of an individual's efforts to deal with stress and meet his or her needs.

Adjustment disorders. Category of disorders in which an individual has difficulty adjusting to a common stressor.

Adjustment disorder with depressed mood. Moderately severe mood disorder behaviorally identical to dysthymic disorder or depressed phase of cyclothymic disorder but having an identifiable, though not severe, psychosocial stressor occurring within three months prior to the onset of depression.

Adrenal cortex. Outer layer of the adrenal glands; secretes the adrenal steroids and other hormones.

Adrenal glands. Endocrine glands located at the upper end of the kidneys; consist of inner adrenal medulla and outer adrenal cortex.

Adrenaline. Hormone secreted by the adrenal medulla during strong emotion; causes such bodily changes as an increase in blood sugar and a rise in blood pressure. Also called *epinephrine.*

Advocacy. Approach to meeting mental health needs in which advocates, often an interested group of volunteers, attempt to help children or others receive services that they need but often are unable to obtain for themselves.

Advocacy programs. Programs aimed at helping people in underserved populations to obtain aid with which to improve their situations.

Affect. Experience of emotion or feeling.

Aftercare. Follow-up therapy after release from a hospital.

Aggression. Behavior aimed at hurting or destroying someone or something.

Agitation. Marked restlessness and psychomotor excitement.

Agoraphobia. Morbid fear of large, open places.

AIDS-dementia complex (ADC). Generalized degeneration of brain tissue as a result of HIV-1 infection.

AIDS-related complex (ARC). Pre-AIDS manifestation of HIV infection involving minor infections, various nonspecific symptoms (such as unexplained fever), and blood cell count abnormalities.

Alarm and mobilization reaction. First state of the general adaptation syndrome, characterized by the mobilization of defenses to cope with a stressful situation.

Alcoholic. Individual with serious drinking problems, whose drinking impairs life adjustment in terms of health, personal relationships, and/or occupational functioning.

Alcoholic deterioration. Personality deterioration, including impaired judgment, associated with alcoholism.

Alcoholic intoxication. State reached when alcohol content of blood is 0.1 percent or above.

Alcoholism. Dependence on alcohol to the extent that it seriously interferes with life adjustment.

Algophobia. Irrational fear of pain.

Alienation. Lack or loss of relationships to others.

Alpha waves. Brain waves having a frequency of 8 to 12 cycles per second and accompanied by a state of wakeful relaxation.

Alzheimer's disease. Most common form of senile disorder; in some cases, Alzheimer's disease may occur well before old age.

Amnesia. Total or partial loss of memory.

Amnestic syndrome. Inability to remember events more than a few minutes after they have occurred coupled with the ability to recall the recent and remote past.

Amniocentesis. Technique that involves drawing fluid from the amniotic sac of a pregnant woman so that the sloughed-off fetal cells can be examined for chromosomal irregularities, including that of Down syndrome.

Amphetamine. One type of drug that produces a psychologically stimulating and energizing effect.

Analgesia. Insensitivity to pain without loss of consciousness.

Analogue studies. Studies in which a researcher attempts to simulate the conditions under investigation.

Anal stage. In psychoanalytic theory, stage of psychosexual development in which behavior is presumably focused on anal pleasure and activities.

Analytic psychology. School or system of psychology developed by Carl Jung.

Androgen. Hormone associated with the development and maintenance of male characteristics.

Androgyny. Theoretically, psychologically ideal combination of masculine and feminine traits.

Anesthesia. Loss or impairment of sensitivity (usually to touch but often applied to sensitivity to pain and other senses as well).

Anhedonia. Inability to experience pleasure or joy; believed by some to be a basic characteristic of schizophrenic individuals.

Anorexia nervosa. Loss or severe diminishment of appetite, apparently of psychogenic origin.

Anoxia. Lack of sufficient oxygen.

Antabuse. Drug used in the treatment of alcoholism.

Anterograde amnesia. Loss of memory for events *following* trauma or shock.

Antianxiety drugs. Drugs that are used primarily for alleviating anxiety.

Antibody. Circulating blood substance coded for detection of and binding to a particular antigen.

Antidepressant drugs. Drugs that are used primarily to elevate mood and relieve depression.

Antigen. Substance detected as "foreign" by the body's immune defenses, giving rise to the immune reaction.

Antipsychotic drugs. Group of drugs, sometimes called *major tranquilizers,* that produce a calming effect on many patients as well as alleviate or reduce the intensity of psychotic symptoms, such as delusions and hallucinations.

Antisocial personality disorder. Personality disorder involving a marked lack of ethical or moral development; also commonly referred to as *psychopathic* or *sociopathic personality.*

Anxiety. Generalized feelings of fear and apprehension.

Anxiety attack. Acute episode of intense anxiety.

Anxiety disorder. DSM-III-R category characterized by chronic anxiety and apprehension. Includes generalized anxiety disorder, panic disorder, obsessive-compulsive disorder, posttraumatic disorder, and phobic disorder.

Anxiety hierarchy. Ranking of anxiety-eliciting situations utilized in systematic desensitization therapy.

Anxiety-response pattern. Model of the genesis of anxiety as involving biological, psychological, and environmental events that become a self-sustaining feedback system.

Aphasia. Loss or impairment of ability to communicate and understand language symbols—involving loss of power of expression by speech, writing, or signs, or loss of ability to comprehend written or spoken language—resulting from brain injury or disease.

Aphonia. Inability to speak above a whisper; a conversion disorder.

Approach-avoidance conflict. Type of stress situation involving both positive and negative features.

Apraxia. Loss of ability to perform purposeful movements.

Arousal. See **Activation.**

Arteriosclerosis. Degenerative thickening and hardening of the walls of the arteries, occurring usually in old age.

Assertiveness training. Behavior therapy technique for helping individuals become more self-assertive in interpersonal relationships.

Assimilation. Cognitive process whereby new information is fitted into previously existing cognitive maps or structures.

Astasia-abasia. Inability to stand or walk without the legs wobbling about and collapsing, although a person has normal control of legs while sitting or lying down; no associated organic pathology.

Asylums. Institutions established soley for the care of the mentally ill.

Ataxia. Muscular incoordination, particularly of the arms and legs. See also **Locomotor ataxia.**

At risk. Condition of being considered vulnerable to the development of certain abnormal behaviors.

Atrophy. Wasting away or shrinking of a bodily organ, particularly muscle tissue.

Attention-deficit hyperactivity disorder (ADHD). Disorder of childhood characterized by difficulties—e.g., impulsivity, excessive motor activity, and an inability to focus attention for appropriate periods of time—that interfere with effective task-oriented behavior; also known as *hyperactivity.*

Attribution theory. Theory by which causes in the behavior of others are interpreted, based on unseen or unrecognized qualities in ourselves.

Autistic disorder. Pervasive developmental disorder whose central feature is a profound and unyielding unresponsiveness to the human environment. The disorder begins in infancy and is characterized by an inability to relate to the environment, to others, or to form a normal self-concept.

Automated assessment. Psychological test interpretation by electronic computer or some other mechanical means.

Autonomic nervous system. Section of the nervous system that regulates the internal organs; consists primarily of ganglia connected with the brain stem and spinal cord and may be subdivided into the sympathetic and parasympathetic systems.

Autonomic reactivity. Individual's characteristic degree of emotional reactivity to stress.

Autonomy. Self-reliance; the sense of being an individual in one's own right.

Autosome. Any chromosome other than those determining sex.

Aversion therapy. Form of behavior therapy in which punishment or aversive stimulation is used to eliminate undesired responses.

Aversive conditioning. Use of noxious stimuli to suppress unwanted behavior.

Aversive stimulus. Stimulus that elicits psychic or physical pain.

Avoidance conditioning. Form of conditioning in which a subject learns to behave in a certain way in order to avoid an unpleasant stimulus.

Avoidant personality disorder. Personality disorder characterized by hypersensitivity to rejection, limited social relationships, and low self-esteem.

"Bad trip." Unpleasant or traumatic experience while under the influence of a hallucinogenic drug, such as LSD.

Barbiturate. Type of synthetic sedative drug.

Baseline. In behavior therapy, the initial level of responses emitted by an individual.

B-cell. Variety of lymphocyte (white blood cell) capable of producing specific antibodies to an antigen. Principal element of "humoral" immune functioning.

Bedlam. Popular contraction of the name of the early London asylum of St. Mary of Bethlehem.

Behavioral assessment. Technique to determine the functional relationships between an individual's behavior and environmental stimuli.

Behavioral contracting. Positive reinforcement technique using a contract, often between family members, stipulating privileges and responsibilities.

Behavioral medicine. Broad interdisciplinary field concerned with relations between physical health and the psychological aspects of individuals who have, or are at risk for, physical disease.

Behavioral sciences. Various interrelated disciplines, including psychology, sociology, and anthropology, that focus on human behavior.

Behavior control. Shaping and manipulation of behavior by drugs, persuasion, and other techniques.

Behavior disorder. Synonym for psychological problem.

Behaviorism. School of psychology that formerly restricted itself primarily to study of overt behavior.

Behavioristic perspective. Approach to understanding maladaptive behavior that is organized around the role of learning in human behavior.

Behavior modification. Techniques used to change specific behaviors.

Behavior sample. Assessment data that presumably provide an accurate reflection of a subject's typical behavior.

Behavior therapy. Therapeutic procedures based primarily on principles of respondent and operant conditioning.

Benign. Of a mild, self-limiting nature; not malignant.

Beta waves. Brain waves having a frequency of 18 to 30 cycles per second or associated with problem solving and feelings of tension.

Biochemical disorders. Disorders involving disturbances in internal chemical regulation.

Biofeedback. Treatment technique by which individuals are taught to change and control internal bodily processes formerly thought to be involuntary (e.g., blood pressure and skin temperature); involves giving an individual immediate feedback about the bodily changes as they occur.

Biogenic amines. Chemicals that serve as neurotransmitters or modulators.

Biological clocks. The 24-hour rhythmic fluctuations in metabolic processes of plants and animals. See also **Circadian rhythms.**

Biological viewpoint. Approach to mental disorders emphasizing biological causation.

Bipolar disorder. Manic or depressive episode of mood disorder believed to be a manifestation of an underlying condition predisposing an individual to severe mood swings; has largely replaced the term *manic-depressive psychosis.*

Bisexuality. Sexual attraction to both females and males.

Blocking. Involuntary inhibition of recall, ideation, or communication (including sudden stoppage of speech).

Borderline personality disorder. Personality disorder characterized by instability and drastic mood shifts; such individuals are impulsive and at times may appear psychotic.

Brain pathology. Diseased or disordered condition of the brain.

Brainwashing. Extreme form of thought modification and control.

Brain waves. Minute oscillations of electrical potential given off by neurons in the cerebral cortex and measured by the electroencephalograph.

Brief Psychiatric Rating Scale (BPRS). Objective method of rating clinical symptoms that provides scores on eighteen variables (e.g., somatic concern, anxiety, withdrawal, hostility, and bizarre thinking).

Brief psychotherapy. Short-term therapy, usually 8 to 10 sessions, focused on restoring an individual's functioning and offering emotional support.

Bulimia nervosa. Recurring episodes of seemingly uncontrollable binge eating, accompanied by extreme efforts to disgorge.

Caffeine. Chemical compound found in many commonly available drinks and foods and whose negative effects can include intoxication, restlessness, nervousness, excitement, insomnia, muscle twitching, and gastrointestinal complaints.

Cardiovascular. Pertaining to the heart and blood vessels.

Case study. Assessment information on a specific individual.

Castrating. Refers to any source of injury to or deprivation of the genitals, or more broadly, to a threat to the masculinity or femininity of an individual.

Castration anxiety. As postulated by Freud, the anxiety a young boy experiences when he has incestuous cravings for his mother while at the same time viewing his father as a rival and fearing that his father may harm him by removing his penis; this anxiety forces the boy to repress his sexual desire for his mother and his hostility toward his father.

Catalepsy. Condition in which the muscles are waxy and semirigid, tending to maintain the limbs in any position in which they are placed.

Catecholamine. Class of amines sharing a similar chemical structure and involved chiefly in neural transmission.

Categorical approach. Approach to classifying abnormal behavior that assumes that (a) all human behavior can be sharply divided into the categories *normal* and *abnormal,* and (b) there exist discrete, non-overlapping classes or types of abnormal behavior, often referred to as "mental" illnesses or diseases.

Catharsis. Discharge of emotional tension associated with repressed traumatic material, e.g., by "talking it out."

CAT scan. See **Computerized axial tomography.**

Causal pattern. In a cause-and-effect relationship, the situation where more than one causal factor is involved.

Causation. Relationship in which the preceding variable causes the other(s).

Central nervous system (CNS). The brain and spinal cord.

Cerebral arteriosclerosis. Hardening of the arteries in the brain.

Cerebral concussion. Mild head injury that disrupts brain functions.

Cerebral contusion. Brain damage resulting from head injury severe enough to shift brain and compress it against skull.

Cerebral cortex. Surface layers of the cerebrum.

Cerebral hemorrhage. Bleeding into brain tissue from a ruptured blood vessel.

Cerebral laceration. Tearing of brain tissue associated with severe head injury.

Cerebral syphilis. Syphilitic infection of the brain.

Cerebral thrombosis. Formation of a clot or thrombus in the vascular system of the brain.

Cerebrovascular accident (CVA). Blockage or rupture of large blood vessel in brain leading to both focal and generalized impairment of brain function. Also called *stroke.*

Cerebrum. Main part of brain; divided into left and right hemispheres.

Character disorders. See **Personality disorders.**

Character traits. See **Temperament traits.**

Chemotherapy. Use of drugs to treat mental disorders.

Child abuse. Infliction of physical damage on a child by parents or other adults.

Child advocacy. Movement concerned with protecting rights and ensuring well-being of children.

Childhood depression. Mood disorder occurring in children often in a masked form, e.g., as acting-out behavior.

Chlorpromazine. One of the major antipsychotic drugs.

Chorea. Pathological condition characterized by jerky, irregular, involuntary movements. See also **Huntington's chorea.**

Chromosomal anomalies. Inherited defects or vulnerabilities caused by irregularities in chromosomes.

Chromosomes. Chainlike structures within cell nucleus that contain genes.

Chronic (disorder). Term used to describe a disorder that is a relatively permanent maladaptive pattern or condition.

Chronic schizophrenia. See **Process schizophrenia.**

Circadian rhythms. Regular biological cycle of sleep and activity characteristic of each species.

Civil commitment. Procedure whereby an individual certified as mentally disordered can be hospitalized, either voluntarily or against his or her will.

Classical (respondent) conditioning. Basic form of learning in which a previously neutral stimulus comes to elicit a given response.

Claustrophobia. Irrational fear of small enclosed places.

Client-centered (person-centered) psychotherapy. Nondirective approach to psychotherapy developed chiefly by Carl Rogers and based on his personality theory.

Climacteric. Life period associated with the menopause in women and related glandular and bodily changes in men.

Clinical picture. Diagnostic picture formed by observation of patient's behavior or by all available assessment data.

Clinical problem checklist. Computer-administered psychological assessment procedure for surveying the range of psychological problems a patient is experiencing.

Clinical psychologist. Mental health professional with Ph.D. degree or Psy.D. degree in clinical psychology and clinical experience in assessment and psychotherapy.

Clinical psychology. Field of psychology concerned with the understanding, assessment, treatment, and prevention of maladaptive behavior.

Cocaine. Stimulating and pain-reducing psychoactive drug.

Cognition. Act, process, or product of knowing or perceiving.

Cognitive-behavioral therapy. Treatment approach in which behavioral methods or learning principles are applied to thought processes (cognitions).

Cognitive derailment ("slippage"). Tendency for thoughts and associations not to follow one another in logical order; believed to be a basic characteristic of schizophrenic disorders.

Cognitive dissonance. Condition existing when new information is contradictory to one's assumptions.

Cognitive map. Network of assumptions that form an individual's "frame of reference" for interpreting and coping with his or her world.

Cognitive mediation. Thought processes in an individual that occur between the stimulus and the response.

Cognitive processes (cognition). Mental processes, including perception, memory, and reasoning, by which one acquires knowledge, solves problems, and makes plans.

Cognitive restructuring therapy. Cognitive-behavioral therapy that aims to alter an individual's false or maladaptive frame of reference.

Collective unconscious. Term used by Carl Jung to refer to that portion of the unconscious that he considered common to all humanity.

Coma. Profound stupor with unconsciousness.

Community mental health. Application of psychosocial and sociocultural principles to the improvement of given environments.

Community psychology. Use of community resources in dealing with maladaptive behavior; tends to be more concerned with community intervention rather than with personal or individual change.

Complex. Group of emotionally toned attitudes, desires, or memories which are partially or totally repressed.

Compulsion. Irrational and repetitive impulse to perform some act.

Compulsive gambling. See **Pathological gambling.**

Compulsive personality. Personality disorder characterized by excessive concern with rules, order, efficiency, and work.

Computer assessment. Use of computers to obtain or interpret assessment data.

Computer model. Use of computer to simulate psychological functioning.

Computerized axial tomography (CAT scan). Radiological technique used to locate and assess the extent of organic damage without surgery.

Computerized diagnostic interview for children. Computer-administered and scored diagnostic interview that provides a DSM-III-R diagnosis.

Concordance rates. Rates at which a diagnosis or a trait of one person is predictive of the same diagnosis or trait in relatives.

Concussion. See **Cerebral concussion.**

Conditioned reinforcer. Reinforcer that derives its value from basic unconditioned reinforcers.

Conditioning. Simple form of learning involving stimulus and response. See also **Classical conditioning** and **Operant conditioning.**

Conduct disorders. Childhood disorders marked by persistent acts of aggressive or antisocial behavior that may or may not be against the law.

Confabulation. Filling in of memory gaps with false and often irrelevant details.

Confidentiality. Commitment on part of a professional person to keep information he or she obtains from a client confidential.

Conflict. Simultaneous arousal of opposing impulses, desires, or motives.

Congenital. Existing at birth or before birth but not necessarily hereditary.

Congenital defect. Genetic defect or environmental condition occurring prior to birth and causing a child to develop a physical or psychological anomaly.

Conscience. Functioning of an individual's system of moral values in the approval or disapproval of his or her own thoughts and actions. Roughly equivalent to the Freudian concept of superego.

Consciousness. Awareness of inner and/or outer environment.

Constitution. Relatively constant biological makeup of an individual, resulting from the interaction of heredity and environment.

Constitutional liability. Any detrimental characteristic that is either innate or acquired so early and in such strength that it is functionally similar to a genetic characteristic.

Consultation. Community intervention approach that aims at helping individuals at risk for disorder by working indirectly through caretaker institutions (e.g., police and teachers).

Contingency. Relationship, usually causal, between two events in which one is usually followed by the other.

Continuous reinforcement. Reward or reinforcement given regularly after each correct response.

Control group. Group of subjects compared with an experimental group in assessing the effects of independent variables.

Controlled drinking therapy. Behavioral treatment approach aimed at reducing an individual's drinking by self-control methods.

Conversion disorder. Type of somatoform disorder in which symptoms of organic illness appear in the absence of any related organic pathology; previously called *hysteria.*

Convulsion. Pathological, involuntary muscular contractions.

Coping strategies. Efforts used to deal with stress.

Coprolalia. Verbal tic in which an individual utters obscenities aloud.

Coronary heart disease (CHD). Potentially lethal blockage of the arteries supplying blood to the heart muscle, or myocardium.

Corpus callosum. Nerve fibers that connect the two hemispheres of the brain.

Correlation. Relationship of variables to one another suggesting, but not establishing, a causal context.

Corticovisceral control mechanisms. Brain mechanisms that regulate autonomic and other bodily functions.

Counseling psychology. Field of psychology that focuses on helping people with problems pertaining to education, marriage, or occupation.

Counterconditioning. Relearning by using a particular stimulus to establish a new (and generally more adaptive) response.

Counter-transference. Arousal by a client of inappropriate feelings of transference on the part of an analyst during the course of psychoanalytic therapy.

Couples counseling. Treatment for disordered interpersonal relationships involving sessions with both members of the relationship present; also known as *marital therapy.*

Coverants. Internal, private events, such as thoughts and assumptions, to which conditioning principles are applied in cognitive-behavioral therapy.

Covert. Concealed, disguised, not directly observable.

Covert sensitization. Behavioral treatment method for extinguishing undesirable behavior by associating noxious mental images with that behavior.

Cretinism. Condition arising from thyroid deficiency in early life and marked by mental retardation and distinctive physical characteristics.

Criminal responsibility. Legal question of whether an individual should be permitted to use insanity as a defense after having committed some criminal act.

Crisis. Stress situation which approaches or exceeds adaptive capacities of an individual or group.

Crisis intervention. Various methods for rendering therapeutic assistance to an individual or group during a period of crisis.

Criterion group. Group of subjects who exhibit the variable or disorder under study.

Critical period. Period of development during which an

organism most needs certain inputs or is most ready for acquisition of a given response.

Cultural-familial retardation. Mental retardation as a result of an inferior quality of interaction with the cultural environment and with other people, with no evidence of brain pathology.

Cultural lag. Tendency for formal conceptions of reality and "appropriate" behavior within a given culture to change more slowly than the actual thinking and actions of a society's members.

Cultural relativism. Position that one cannot apply universal standards of normality or abnormality to all societies.

Cushing's syndrome. Endocrine disorder resulting from oversecretion of *cortisone* and marked by mood swings, irritability, and other mental symptoms.

Cyclothymia. Mild mood disorder characterized by extreme mood swings of nonpsychotic intensity.

Day hospital. Community-based mental hospital where the patients are treated during the day, returning to their homes at night.

Decompensation. Ego or personality disorganization under excessive stress.

Defense mechanism. See **Ego-defense mechanism.**

Defense-oriented response. Reaction involving one's feelings of adequacy and worth rather than objective handling of the stress situation.

Deficiency motivation. Motivation directed primarily toward maintaining or restoring physiological or psychological equilibrium rather than toward personal growth.

Deinstitutionalization. Movement to provide chronic patients with continued psychiatric care in the local community rather than committing them to institutions.

Delinquency. Antisocial or illegal behavior by a minor.

Delirium. State of mental confusion characterized by clouding of consciousness, disorientation, restlessness, excitement, and often hallucinations.

Delirium tremens. Acute delirium associated with prolonged alcoholism; characterized by intense anxiety, tremors, and hallucinations.

Delusion. Firm belief opposed to reality but maintained in spite of strong evidence to the contrary.

Delusional disorder. Type of psychosis characterized by a systematized delusional system; formerly called *paranoia* and *paranoid disorder*.

Delusional system. Internally coherent, systematized pattern of delusions.

Delusion of persecution. False belief that one is being mistreated or interfered with by one's enemies. Often found in schizophrenia.

Dementia. Severe mental disorder involving impairment of mental ability; not congenital.

Dementia praecox. Older term for schizophrenia.

Demonology. Viewpoint emphasizing supernatural causation of mental disorder, especially "possession" by evil spirits or forces.

Denial of reality. Ego-defense mechanism by means of which an individual protects himself or herself from unpleasant aspects of reality by refusing to acknowledge them.

Dependency. Tendency to rely overly on others.

Dependent personality disorder. Personality disorder marked by lack of self-confidence and feelings of acute panic or discomfort at having to be alone.

Dependent variable. In an experiment, the factor that the hypothesis predicts will change with changes in the independent variable.

Depersonalization. Loss of sense of personal identity, often with a feeling of being something or someone else.

Depersonalization disorder. Dissociative disorder, usually occurring in adolescence, in which individuals lose their sense of self and feel unreal or displaced to a different location.

Depression. Emotional state characterized by extreme sadness, gloomy ruminations, feelings of worthlessness, loss of hope, and often apprehension.

Depressive neurosis (now called *dysthymia*). Depression of intermediate severity with little or no evidence of personality breakdown or loss of contact with reality.

Depressive stupor. Extreme degree of depression characterized by marked psychomotor underactivity.

Desensitization. Therapeutic process by means of which reactions to traumatic experiences are reduced in intensity by repeatedly exposing an individual to them in mild form, either in reality or in fantasy.

Deterrence. Premise that punishment for criminal offenses will deter that criminal and others from future criminal acts.

Detox. Center or facility for receiving and detoxifying alcohol-or drug-intoxicated individuals.

Detoxification. Treatment directed toward ridding the body of alcohol or other drugs.

Developmental disorder. Problem that is rooted in deviations in the development process itself, thus disrupting the acquisition of skills and adaptive behavior and often interfering with the transition to well-functioning adulthood.

Developmental psychopathology. Field of psychology that studies disorders of childhood within the context of developmental processes.

Deviant behavior. Behavior which deviates markedly from the average or norm.

Dexedrine. Amphetamine drug; a stimulant used to curb appetite or elevate mood.

Diagnosis. Determination of the nature and extent of a specific disorder.

Diathesis. Predisposition or vulnerability toward developing a given disorder.

Diathesis-stress model. View of abnormal behavior as the result of stress operating on an individual with a biological, psychosocial, or sociocultural predisposition toward developing a specific disorder.

Differential reinforcement of other behavior (DOR). Behavior modification technique for extinguishing undesirable behavior by reinforcing incompatible behaviors.

Dilantin. Anticonvulsant medication often used in controlling epileptic seizures.

Dimensional approach. Approach to classifying abnormal behavior that assumes that a person's typical behavior is the product of differing strengths or intensities of behavior along several definable dimensions, such as mood, emotional stability, aggressiveness, gender, identity, anxiousness, interpersonal trust, clarity of thinking and communication, social introversion, and so on.

Directive therapy. Type of therapeutic approach in which a therapist supplies direct answers to problems and takes much of the responsibility for the progression of therapy.

Disaster syndrome. Response pattern that appears to characterize the initial and long-lasting reactions of many victims of catastrophes.

Discordant family. Family in which one or both of the parents is not gaining satisfaction from the relationship and one spouse may express frustration and disillusionment in hostile ways, such as nagging, belittling, and purposely doing things to annoy the other person.

Discrimination. Learning to interpret and respond differently to two or more similar stimuli.

Diseases of adaptation. Stomach ulcers and other disease conditions resulting from the stresses of life.

Disintegration. Loss of organization or integration in any organized system.

Disorganization. Severely impaired integration.

Disorientation. Mental confusion with respect to time, place, or person.

Displacement. Ego-defense mechanism in which an emotional attitude or symbolic meaning is transferred from one object or concept to another.

Disrupted family. Family that is incomplete as a result of death, divorce, separation, or some other circumstance.

Dissociation. Separation or "isolation" of mental processes in such a way that they become split off from the main personality or lose their normal thought-affect relationships.

Dissociative disorders. Disorder in which a person avoids stress by dissociating—in essence by escaping—from his or her own personal identity through behavior patterns such as amnesia, fugue, somnambulism, or multiple personality.

Distress. Negative stress.

Disturbed family. Family in which one or both parents behave in grossly eccentric or abnormal ways and may keep the home in constant emotional turmoil.

Dizygotic (fraternal) twins. Twins that develop from two separate eggs.

DNA. Deoxyribonucleic acid, principal component of genes.

Dominant gene. A gene whose hereditary characteristics prevail in the offspring.

Dopamine. Catecholamine neural transmitter substance.

Dopamine hypothesis. Hypothesis that schizophrenia is the product of an excess of dopamine activity at certain synaptic sites.

Double-approach conflict. Type of conflict in which an individual is confronted with choosing between two or more desirable alternatives.

Double-avoidant conflict. Type of conflict in which an individual is confronted with choosing between two or more aversive alternatives.

Double-bind. Situation in which an individual will be disapproved for performing a given act and equally disapproved if he or she does not perform it.

Double-bind communication. Type of faulty communication in which the one person (e.g., a parent) presents to another (e.g., a child) ideas, feelings, and demands that are mutually incompatible.

Down syndrome. Form of mental retardation associated with chromosomal anomalies.

Dramatization. Defense against anxiety in which an individual engages in attention-getting behavior and self-dramatization.

Dream analysis. Psychotherapeutic technique involving the interpretation of a patient's dreams.

Drive. Internal conditions directing an organism toward a specific goal, usually involving biological rather than psychological motives.

Drug abuse. Use of a drug to the extent that it interferes with health and/or occupational or social adjustment.

Drug addiction (dependence). Physiological and/or psychological dependence on a drug.

Drug therapy. See **Chemotherapy** and **Pharmacotherapy.**

DSM-III-R. Current diagnostic manual of the American Psychiatric Association.

Dwarfism. Condition of arrested growth and very short stature.

Dyad. Two-person group.

Dynamic formulation. Integrated evaluation of a client's traits, attitudes, conflicts, and symptoms that attempts to explain his or her problem.

Dysfunction. Impairment or disturbance in the functioning of an organ or in behavior.

Dyslexia. Impairment of the ability to read.

Dyspareunia. Painful coitus in a male or a female.

Dysrhythmias. Abnormal brain-wave patterns.

Dysthymia. Moderately severe mood disorder characterized by extended periods of nonpsychotic depression and brief periods of normal moods. Also called *depressive neurosis.*

Echolalia. Meaningless repetition of words by an individual, usually of whatever has been said to that person.

Echopraxia. Repetition of another person's actions or gestures.

Ecology. Relation or interaction between organisms and their physical environment.

EEG. See **Electroencephalogram.**

Ego. In psychoanalytic theory, the rational subsystem of the personality which mediates between id and superego demands and reality. More generally, an individual's self-concept.

Egocentric. Preoccupied with one's own concerns and relatively insensitive to the concerns of others.

Ego-defense mechanism (reaction). Type of reaction designed to maintain an individual's feelings of adequacy and worth rather than to cope directly with the stress situation; usually unconscious and reality distorting.

Ego-dystonic homosexuality. Category of "mental disorder" in which an individual wishes to change his or her homosexual orientation.

Ego-ideal (self-ideal). Person or "self" an individual thinks he or she could and should be.

Ego involvement. Perception of a situation in terms of its importance to oneself.

Ejaculatory incompetence. Male's inability to ejaculate.

Electra complex. In psychoanalytic theory, an excessive emotional attachment (love) of a daughter for her father.

Electroconvulsive therapy (ECT). Use of electricity to produce convulsions and unconsciousness; also called *electroshock therapy.*

Electroencephalogram (EEG). Graphic record of the brain's electrical activity, obtained by placing electrodes on the scalp and measuring the brain-wave impulses from various brain areas.

Electrotherapy. Methods of therapy which involve the influence of electric current on the central nervous system.

Embolism. Lodgment of a blood clot in a blood vessel too small to permit its passage.

Emotion. Strong feeling accompanied by physiological changes.

Emotional disturbance. Psychological disorder.

Emotional inoculation. Therapeutic procedures designed to prepare people who face stressful situations, such as surgery, by providing such people with adaptive techniques.

Emotional insulation. Ego-defense mechanism in which an individual reduces the tensions of need and anxiety by withdrawing into a shell of passivity.

Empathy. Ability to understand and to some extent share the state of mind of another person.

Encephalitis. Inflammation of the brain.

Encopresis. Disorder defined by having bowel movements in one's clothing after the age of 3.

Encounter. Term applied to the interaction between client and therapist (in existential therapy) or between clients (in encounter-group therapy).

Encounter group. Small group designed to provide an intensive interpersonal experience focusing on feelings and group interactions; used in therapy or to promote personal growth.

Endocrine glands. Ductless glands that secrete hormones directly into the lymph or bloodstream.

Endogenous factors. Factors originating within an organism that affect behavior.

Endorphins. Opium-like substances produced in the brain and pituitary gland in response to stimulation; thought to play a role in an organism's reaction to pain.

Energizer. Drug that has a stimulating effect.

Engram. Hypothesized physiological change in nervous system; thought to be responsible for memory.

Enuresis. Bed-wetting; involuntary discharge of urine.

Environmental psychology. Field of psychology focusing on the effects of an environmental setting on an individual's feelings and behavior.

Enzyme. Catalyst regulating metabolic activities.

Epidemiology. Study of the distribution of physical or mental disorders in a population.

Epilepsy. Group of disorders varying from momentary lapses of consciousness to generalized convulsions.

Epinephrine. Hormone secreted by the adrenal medulla; also called *adrenaline.*

Episodic (disorder). Term to describe a disorder that tends to abate and to recur.

Equilibrium. Steady state; balance.

Erectile insufficiency. Inability of a male to achieve erection.

Erotic. Pertaining to sexual stimulation and gratification.

Escape learning. Conditioned response in which a subject learns to terminate or escape an aversive stimulus.

Essential hypertension. High blood pressure, presumably of a psychological or emotional origin.

Estrogens. Female hormones produced by the ovaries.

Ethnic group. Group of people who are treated as distinctive in terms of culture and group patterns.
Ethnocentrism. Belief that one's own country and race are superior to other countries and races.
Etiology. Causation; the systematic study of the causes of disorders.
Eugenics. Application of methods of selective breeding of human beings with the intent of improving the species.
Euphoria. Exaggerated feeling of well-being and contentment.
Eustress. Positive stress.
Exacerbate. Intensify.
Excitation. Process whereby activity is elicited in a nerve.
Exhaustion and disintegration. Third and final stage in the general adaptation syndrome, in which an organism is no longer able to resist continuing stress; at the biological level may result in death.
Exhibitionism. Public display or exposure of genitals for the conscious or unconscious purpose of sexual excitement and pleasure.
Existential anxiety. Anxiety concerning one's ability to find a satisfying and fulfilling way of life.
Existentialism. View of human beings that emphasizes an individual's responsibility for becoming the kind of person he or she should be.
Existential neurosis. Disorder characterized by feelings of alienation, meaninglessness, and apathy.
Existential psychotherapy. Type of therapy that is based on existential thought and focuses on individual uniqueness and authenticity on the part of both client and therapist.
Exner Comprehensive Rorschach System. Procedure for scoring and objectively interpreting the Rorschach inkblot test.
Exogenous. Originating from or due to external causes.
Exorcism. Religiously inspired treatment procedure designed to drive out evil spirits or forces from a "possessed" person.
Expanded consciousness. Sensation caused by psychedelic drugs or meditation in which an individual feels his or her mind is opened to new types of experience.
Experimental group. Group of subjects used to assess the effects of independent variables.
Experimental method. Rigorous scientific procedure by which hypotheses are tested.
Experimental neurosis. Neurotic behavior produced in animals by inescapable conflicts and other types of stress.
Expressed emotion (EE). Type of negative communication involving excessive criticalness and emotional overinvolvement directed at a patient by family members.
Extinction. Gradual disappearance of a conditioned response when it is no longer reinforced.
Extrapunitive. Characterized by a tendency to evaluate the source of frustrations as external and to direct hostility outward.
Extraversion. Personality type oriented toward the outer world of people and things rather than concepts and intellectual concerns.

Fabrication. Relating imaginary events as if they were true without intent to deceive; confabulation.
Factor analysis. Statistical technique used in identifying and measuring the relative importance of the underlying variables, or factors, which contribute to a complex ability, trait, or form of behavior.
Fading. Technique whereby a stimulus causing some reaction is gradually replaced by a previously neutral stimulus, such that the latter acquires the property of producing the reaction in question.
Familial. Pertaining to characteristics which tend to run in families and have a higher incidence in certain families than in the general population.
Family therapy. Form of interpersonal therapy focusing on relationships within a family.
Fantasy. Daydream; also, an ego-defense mechanism by means of which an individual escapes from the world of reality and gratifies his desires in fantasy achievements.
Faulty genes. Genes containing information that is inimical to healthy development or functioning.
Feedback. Explicit information pertaining to internal physiological processes or to the social consequences of one's overt behavior.
Female sexual arousal disorder. Dysfunction accompanied by complaints of an absence of sexual arousal feelings and of being unresponsive to most or all forms of erotic stimulation.
Fetal alcohol syndrome. Observed pattern in infants of alcoholic mothers in which there is a characteristic facial or limb irregularity, low body weight, and behavioral abnormality.
Fetishism. Maladaptive sexual deviation in which an individual achieves sexual gratification by means of some inanimate object or nonsexual part of the body.
Fetus. Embryo after the sixth week following conception.
Field properties. Characteristics of the environment surrounding a living system.
Fixation. Unreasonable or exaggerated attachment to some person or arresting of emotional development on a childhood or adolescent level.
Fixed-interval schedule. Schedule of reinforcement based on fixed period of time after previous reinforced response.
Fixed-ratio schedule. Schedule of reinforcement based on reinforcement after fixed number of nonreinforced responses.
Flashback. Recurrence of a drug experience, usually in a negative manner, without further ingestion of the drug.
Flooding. Anxiety-eliciting technique involving placing a client in a real-life, anxiety-arousing situation.
Folie à deux. Psychotic interpersonal relationship involving two people; e.g., husband and wife both become psychotic with similar or complementary symptomatology.
Follow-up study. Research procedure in which individuals are studied over a period of time or are recontacted at a later time after initial study.
Forcible rape. Act of violence in which sexual relations are forced on an unwilling partner who is over the age of 18.
Forensic psychology and psychiatry. Branches of psychology and psychiatry dealing with legal problems relating to mental disorders.
Fraternal twins. Dizygotic twins; fertilized by separate germ cells, thus not having same genetic inheritance. May be of the same or opposite sex.
Free association. Psychoanalytic procedure for probing the unconscious in which an individual gives a running account of every thought and feeling.
Free-floating anxiety. Anxiety not referable to any specific situation or cause.
Frigidity. Inability to experience sexual pleasure or orgasm on the part of a female. Now called *inhibited arousal* or *orgasmic dysfunction.*
Frontal lobe. Portion of the brain active in reasoning and other higher thought processes.
Frustration. Thwarting of a need or desire.
Frustration tolerance. See **Stress tolerance.**
Fugue state. Neurotic dissociative disorder; entails loss of memory accompanied by actual physical flight from one's present life situation to a new environment or less threatening former one.
Functional psychoses. Severe mental disorders for which a specific organic pathology has not been demonstrated.
Future shock. Condition brought about when social change proceeds so rapidly that an individual cannot cope with it adequately.

Gambling. Wagering on games or events in which chance largely determines the outcome.
Gay. Synonym for *homosexual.*
Gender identity. Individual's identification as being male or female.

Gender identity disorder (transsexualism). Identification of oneself with members of the opposite sex, as opposed to acceptance of one's anatomical sexual identity.

General adaptation syndrome (GAS). Reaction of an individual to excessive stress; consists of the alarm reaction, the stage of resistance, and exhaustion.

Generalization. Tendency of a response that has been conditioned to one stimulus to become associated with other similar stimuli.

Generalized anxiety disorder. Chronic diffuse anxiety and apprehension, possibly punctuated by acute anxiety attacks, stemming from no specific, identifiable threat.

Generalized reinforcer. Reinforcer, such as money, which may influence a wide range of stimuli and behaviors.

General paresis. Mental disorder associated with syphilis of the brain.

General systems theory. Comprehensive theoretical model embracing all living systems.

Genes. Ultramicroscopic areas of DNA that are responsible for the transmission of hereditary traits.

Genetic code. Means by which DNA controls the sequence and structure of proteins manufactured within each cell and also makes exact duplicates of itself.

Genetic counseling. Counseling prospective parents concerning the probability of their having defective offspring as a result of genetic defects.

Genetic inheritance. Potential for development and behavior determined at conception by egg and sperm cells.

Genetics. Science of heredity.

Genitalia. Organs of reproduction, especially the external organs.

Genital stage. In psychoanalytic theory, the final stage of psychosexual development involving shift from autoeroticism to heterosexual interest.

Genotype. Genetic characteristics inherited by an individual.

Geriatrics. Science of the diseases and treatment of the aged.

Germ cells. Reproductive cells (female ovum and male sperm) which unite to produce a new individual.

Gerontology. Science dealing with the study of old age.

Gestalt psychology. School of psychology which emphasizes patterns rather than elements or connections; taking the view that the whole is more than the sum of its parts.

Gestalt therapy. Type of psychotherapy emphasizing wholeness of the person and integration of thought, feeling, and action.

Gigantism. Abnormally tall stature resulting from hyperfunctioning of the pituitary.

Glucocorticoids. Adrenocortical hormones involved in sugar metabolism but also having widespread effects on injury-repair mechanisms and resistance to disease; they include hydrocortisone, corticosterone, and cortisone.

Gonads. Sex glands.

Good premorbid schizophrenia. See **Reactive schizophrenia.**

Grand mal epilepsy. Type of epilepsy characterized by generalized convulsive seizures.

Grief work. Necessary period of mourning for an individual to assimilate personal loss into the self-structure and view it as an event of the past.

Group therapy. Psychotherapy with two or more individuals at the same time.

Guilt. Feelings of culpability arising from behavior or desires contrary to one's ethical principles. Involves both self-devaluation and apprehension growing out of fears of punishment.

Habit. Any product of learning, whether it is a customary or transitory mode of response.

Habituation. Process whereby an individual's response to the same stimulus lessens with repeated presentations.

Halfway house. Facility which provides aftercare following institutionalization, seeking to ease an individual's adjustment to the community.

Hallucination. Sense perception for which there is no appropriate external stimulus.

Hallucinogens. Drugs or chemicals capable of producing hallucinations.

Hallucinosis. Persistent hallucinations in the presence of known or suspected organic brain pathology.

Halo effect. Tendency when rating a specific trait to be influenced by another trait, such as appearance, or by one's overall impression.

Halstead-Reitan battery. Neuropsychological test aimed at providing information as to a patient's cognitive ability or intellectual impairment.

Hashish. Strongest drug derived from the hemp plant; a relative of marijuana.

Health psychology. Subspecialty within the behavioral-medicine approach that deals with psychology's contributions to diagnosis, treatment, and prevention of behaviorally caused physical illnesses.

Hebephrenic schizophrenia. See **Schizophrenia, disorganized type.**

Hemiplegia. Paralysis of one lateral half of the body.

Hemophobia. Pathological fear of blood. Also called *hematophobia.*

Heredity. Genetic transmission of characteristics from parents to their children.

Hermaphroditism. Anatomical sexual abnormality in which an individual has sex organs of both sexes.

Heroin. Powerful psychoactive substance, chemically derived from morphine, that relieves pain but is even more intense and addictive than morphine.

Heterosexuality. Sexual interest in a member of the opposite sex.

Hierarchy of needs. Concept that needs arrange themselves in a hierarchy in terms of importance or "prepotence," from the most basic biological needs to those psychological needs concerned with self-actualization.

High-risk. Individuals showing great vulnerability to physical or mental disorders.

Histrionic personality disorder. A personality disorder characterized by excitability, emotional instability, and self-dramatization.

Holistic. Systematic approach to science involving the study of the whole or total configuration; the view of human beings as unified psychobiological organisms inextricably immersed in a physical and sociocultural environment.

Homeostasis. Tendency of organisms to maintain conditions making possible a constant level of physiological functioning.

Homosexuality. Sexual preference for a member of one's own sex.

Hormones. Chemicals released by the endocrine glands that regulate development of and activity in various bodily organs.

Hostility. Emotional reaction or drive toward the destruction or damage of an object interpreted as a source of frustration or threat.

Humanistic-existential therapy. Type of psychotherapy emphasizing personal growth and self-direction.

Humanistic perspective. Approach to understanding abnormal behavior that emphasizes growth and self-actualization rather than the curing of diseases or serious disorders.

Human potential movement. Movement concerned with enrichment of experience, increased sensory awareness, and fulfillment of human potentials.

Huntington's chorea. Incurable disease of hereditary origin, which is manifested in jerking, twitching movements and mental deterioration.

Hydrocephalus. Relatively rare condition in which the accumulation of an abnormal amount of cerebrospinal fluid within the cranium causes damage to the brain tissues and enlargement of the skull.

Hydrotherapy. Use of hot or cold baths, ice packs, etc., in treatment.

Hyper-. Prefix meaning *increased* or *excessive.*

Hyperactivity. See **Attention-deficit-hyperactivity disorder.**

Hyperkinetic (hyperactive) reaction. Disorder of childhood characterized by overactivity, restlessness, and distractibility.

Hyperobesity. Extreme overweight; more than 100 pounds over ideal body weight.

Hypertension. High blood pressure.

Hyperventilation. Rapid breathing associated with intense anxiety.

Hypesthesia. Partial loss of sensitivity.

Hypnosis. Trancelike mental state induced in a cooperative subject by suggestion.

Hypnotherapy. Use of hypnosis in psychotherapy.

Hypnotic regression. Process by which a subject is brought to relive, under hypnosis, early forgotten or repressed experiences.

Hypo-. Prefix meaning *decreased* or *insufficient.*

Hypoactive sexual desire disorder. Sexual desire disorder in which either a man or a woman shows little or no sexual drive or interest.

Hypochondriacal delusions. Delusions concerning various horrible disease conditions, such as the belief that one's brain is turning to dust.

Hypochondriasis. Condition dominated by preoccupation with bodily processes and fear of presumed diseases.

Hypomania. Mild form of manic reaction, characterized by moderate psychomotor activity.

Hypothalamus. Key structure at the base of the brain; important in emotion and motivation.

Hypothesis. Statement or proposition, usually based on observation, which is tested in an experiment; may be denied or supported by experimental results but never conclusively proved.

Hypoxia. Insufficient delivery of oxygen to an organ, especially the brain.

Hysteria. Older term used to include conversion disorders; involves the appearance of symptoms of organic illness in the absence of any related organic pathology.

Hysterical disorder. Disorder characterized by involuntary psychogenic dysfunction of motor, sensory, or visceral processes.

ICD-9. See **International Classification of Diseases.**

Id. In psychoanalytic terminology, the reservoir of instinctual drives; the most inaccessible and primitive stratum of the mind.

Identical twins. Monozygotic twins; developed from a single fertilized egg.

Identification. Ego-defense mechanism in which an individual identifies himself or herself with some person or institution, usually of an illustrious nature.

Ideology. System of beliefs.

Idiot. Older term referring to severe and profound degrees of mental retardation (IQ below 25).

Idiot savant. Mentally retarded person who can perform unusual mental feats, usually involving music or manipulation of numbers.

Illusion. Misinterpretation of sensory data; false perception.

Imipramine. Antidepressant medication.

Immaturity. Pattern of childhood maladaptive behaviors suggesting lack of adaptive skills.

Immune reaction. Complex defensive reaction initiated on detection of an antigen invading the body.

Immune system. Intricately organized bodily apparatus involved in the detection and destruction of antigens.

Immunoglobulin. Naturally occurring substance essential in the formation of antibodies.

Implosion. Therapeutic technique in which clients are asked to imagine and relive aversive scenes associated with the anxiety; the assumption here is that, with repeated exposure in a "safe" setting, the aversive stimulus will lose its power to elicit anxiety.

Implosive therapy. Type of behavior therapy in which desensitization is achieved by eliciting, through the imagination, a massive implosion of anxiety.

Impotence. Inability of a male to achieve erection.

Incentive. External inducement to behave in a certain way.

Incest. Sexual relations between close relatives, such as father and daughter or brother and sister.

Incidence. Occurrence rate of a given disorder in a given population.

Independent variable. Factor whose effects are being examined in an experiment; it is manipulated in some way while the other variables are held constant.

Index case. In a genetic study, an individual who evidences the trait in which the investigator is interested. Same as *proband.*

Induced psychotic disorder. Type of psychosis in which two or more people develop persistant interlocking delusional ideas; formerly called *shared paranoid disorder.*

Infantile autism. Disorder manifested at birth and characterized by the inability of a child to relate to others or to form a normal relationship to reality.

Inferiority complex. Strong feelings of inadequacy and insecurity which color an individual's entire adjustive efforts.

Inhibited female orgasm. Dysfunction in which a female experiences difficulty in achieving orgasm, whether manually or through intercourse.

Inhibited male orgasm. Dysfunction in which a male is unable to ejaculate during intercourse (also known as *retarded ejaculation*).

Inhibition. Restraint of impulse or desire.

Innate. Inborn.

Inner controls. Reality, value, and possibility assumptions that serve to inhibit dangerous or undesirable behavior; could also apply to conditioned avoidance reactions.

Inpatient. Hospitalized patient.

Insanity. Legal term for mental disorder, implying lack of responsibility for one's acts and inability to manage one's affairs.

Insanity defense. "Innocent by reason of insanity" plea used as a legal defense in criminal trials.

Insight. Clinically, an individual's understanding of his or her illness or of the motivations underlying a behavior pattern; in general psychology, the sudden grasp or understanding of meaningful relationships in a situation.

Insight therapy. Type of psychotherapy focusing on helping a client achieve greater self-understanding with respect to his or her motives, values, coping patterns, and so on.

Insomnia. Difficulty in sleeping.

Inspectionalism. See **Voyeurism.**

Instinct. Inborn tendency to particular behavior patterns under certain conditions in absence of learning; characteristic of species.

Instrumental (operant) conditioning. Type of conditioning in which a subject is reinforced for making a predetermined response, such as pressing a lever.

Insulin coma therapy. Biological treatment that involves administration of increasing amounts of insulin until a patient goes into "shock"; the treatment is extremely dangerous and rarely used today.

Integrative properties. Tendency of living systems to maintain their organization and functional integrity.

Intellectualization. Ego-defense mechanism by which an individual achieves some measure of insulation from emotional hurt by cutting off or distorting the emotional charge which normally accompanies hurtful situations.

Intelligence. Pertaining to the ability to learn, reason, and adapt.

Intelligence quotient (IQ). Measurement of "intelligence" expressed as a number or position on a scale. Comparable to term *intellectual level.*

Intelligence test. Test used in establishing a subject's level of intellectual capability.

Interdisciplinary (multidisciplinary) approach. Integration of various scientific disciplines in understanding, assessing, treating, and preventing mental disorders.

Intermittent reinforcement. Reinforcement given intermittently rather than after every response.

International Classification of Diseases (ICD-9). System of classification of disorders published by the World Health Organization.

Interpersonal accommodation. Reciprocal process of give and take meant to promote satisfactory interpersonal relationships.

Interpersonal perspective. Approach to understanding abnormal behavior that views much of psychopathology as rooted in maladaptive behavior we have learned while dealing with our interpersonal environments; it thus focuses on our relationships, past and present, with other people.

Intrapsychic conflict. Psychoanalytic concept referring to conflict between the id, ego, and superego.

Introjection. Incorporation of qualities or values of another person or group into one's own ego structure with a tendency to identify with them and to be affected by what happens to them.

Intromission. Insertion of the penis into the vagina or anus.

Intropunitive. Responding to frustration by tending to blame oneself.

Introspection. Observing (and often reporting on) one's inner experiencing.

Introversion. Direction of interest toward one's inner world of experience and toward concepts rather than external events and objects.

Invasion of privacy. Concerns that an individual's right to privacy has been violated.

In vivo. Taking place in a real-life situation as opposed to the therapeutic or laboratory setting.

Ionizing radiation. Form of radiation; major cause of gene mutations.

Isolation. Ego-defense mechanism by means of which contradictory attitudes or feelings that normally accompany particular attitudes are kept apart, thus preventing conflict or hurt.

Jejunal bypass operation. Surgical treatment for extreme obesity that involves disconnecting and bypassing a large portion of the small intestine.

Juvenile delinquency. Legal term used to refer to illegal acts committed by individuals under the age of 16, 17, or 18 (depending on state law).

Juvenile paresis. General paresis in children, usually of congenital origin.

Klinefelter's syndrome. Type of mental retardation associated with sex chromosome anomaly.

Korsakoff's psychosis. Psychosis usually associated with chronic alcoholism and characterized by disorientation, gross memory defects, and confabulation.

Labeling. Assigning an individual to a particular diagnostic category, such as schizophrenia.

Lability. Instability, particularly with regard to affect.

Latency stage. In psychoanalytic theory, a stage of psychosexual development during which sexual motivations recede in importance and a child is preoccupied with developing skills and other activities.

Latent. Inactive or dormant.

Latent content. In psychoanalytic theory, repressed wishes indirectly expressed in the manifest content of dreams.

Latent learning. Learning that becomes evident only after an incentive is introduced.

Law of effect. Principle that responses that have rewarding consequences are strengthened and those that have aversive consequences are weakened or eliminated.

Learning. Modification of behavior as a consequence of experience.

Learning disabled (LD). Term used to describe children who exhibit deficits in academic skills.

Lesbian. Female homosexual.

Lesion. Anatomically localized area of tissue pathology in an organ.

Lethality scale. Criteria used to assess the likelihood of an individual's committing suicide.

Level of aspiration. Standard by which an individual judges success or failure of his or her behavior.

Libido. In general psychoanalytic terminology, the instinctual drives of the id. In a narrow sense, the drive for sexual gratification.

Life crisis. Stress situation that approaches or exceeds an individual's adjustive capacity.

Life history method. Technique of psychological observation in which the development of particular forms of behavior is traced by means of records of a subject's past or present behavior.

Life-style. General pattern of assumptions, motives, cognitive styles, and coping techniques that characterize the behavior of a given individual and give it consistency.

Lobotomy. Drastic form of psychosurgery rarely used at present. It involves cutting the nerve fibers that connect the frontal lobes to the limbic system.

Locomotor ataxia. Muscular incoordination usually resulting from syphilitic damage to the spinal-cord pathways.

Logic-tight compartments. Form of intellectualization in which contradictory desires or attitudes are "sealed off" in separate areas of consciousness.

Lovemap. Pattern of an individual's own erotic attachments and preferences, his or her idealized scenario for the achievement of sexual fulfillment.

LSD (lysergic acid diethylamide). Potent, chemically synthesized hallucinogen that is odorless, colorless, and tasteless and that can produce intoxication with an amount smaller than a grain of salt.

Lunacy. Old term roughly synonymous with ***insanity.***

Lycanthropy. Delusion of being a wolf.

Lymphocyte. Generalized term for white blood cells involved in immune protection.

Lymphokines. Chemical substances produced by T-cells that facilitate the immune reaction.

Macrocephaly. Type of mental retardation characterized by an increase in the size and weight of the brain as a result of abnormal growth of glial cells in the brain.

Macrophage. Literally, "big eater." A white blood cell that destroys antigens by engulfment.

Madness. Nontechnical synonym for severe mental disorder.

Mainstreaming. Placement of mentally retarded children in regular school classrooms to avoid certain negative effects of "special education."

Maintaining cause. Environmental reinforcers or contingencies that tend to maintain maladaptive behavior.

Major depression (unipolar disorder). Severe mood disorder in which only depressive episodes occur.

Major tranquilizers. Antipsychotic drugs, such as the phenothiazines.

Maladaptive (abnormal) behavior. Behavior that is detrimental to the well-being of an individual and/or group.

Maladjustment. More or less enduring failure of adjustment; lack of harmony with self or environment.

Male erectile disorder. Dysfunction in which a male is unable to achieve or maintain an erection sufficient for successful sexual intercourse.

Malingering. Faking illness or disability symptoms consciously.

Malleus Malleficarum. Infamous handbook prepared by two monks dealing with the "diagnosis" and "treatment" of witches and witchcraft.

Mania. Emotional state characterized by intense and unrealistic feelings of excitement and euphoria. Often used as a suffix, ***-mania,*** denoting a compulsive or morbid preoccupation with some impulse or activity; e.g., compulsive stealing is called ***kleptomania.***

Manic-depressive psychoses. Older term denoting a group of psychotic disorders characterized by prolonged periods of excitement and overactivity (mania) or by periods of depression and underactivity (depression) or by alternation of the two.

Manifest content. In psychoanalytic theory, the apparent meaning of a dream; masks the latent content.

Marathon encounter group. Intensive group experience lasting for two or more days with only brief breaks for sleep.

Marijuana. Drug derived from the plant *cannabis indica;* often used in cigarettes called reefers or joints.

Marital schism. Marriage characterized by severe chronic discord that threatens continuation of the marital relationship.

Marital skew. Marriage maintained at the expense of a distorted relationship.

Marital therapy. See **Couples counseling.**

Masked deprivation. Rejection of a child by a mother; does not involve separation.

Masked disorder. "Masking" of underlying depression or other emotional disturbance by delinquent behavior or other patterns seemingly unrelated to the basic disturbance.

Masochism. Sexual variant in which an individual obtains sexual gratification through the infliction of pain.

Mass hysteria. Group outbreak of hysterical reactions.

Masturbation. Self-stimulation of genitals for sexual gratification.

Maternal deprivation. Lack of adequate care and stimulation by the mother or mother surrogate.

Maturation. Process of development and body change resulting from heredity rather than learning.

Medical model. View of disordered behavior as a symptom of a more basic process, rather than a pattern representing faulty learning. Also associated with approaches to disorder that involve medical ideology, procedures, and rituals—such as the "white coat."

Megalomania. Delusions of grandeur.

Melancholia. Subset of major depression marked by several symptoms; formerly, a mental disorder characterized by severe depression.

Meninges. Membranes that envelop the brain and spinal cord.

Mental age (MA). Scale unit indicating level of intelligence in relation to chronological age.

Mental deficiency. Synonym for *mental retardation;* the latter term is now preferred.

Mental disorder. Entire range of abnormal behavior patterns.

Mental hygiene movement. Movement that, as a method of treatment for the mentally ill, focused almost exclusively on the physical well-being of hospitalized mental patients.

Mental illness. Once used synonymously with mental disorder but now ordinarily restricted to psychoses.

Mental retardation. Significantly subaverage general intellectual functioning that includes deficits in adaptive behavior and is obvious during the developmental period.

Mescaline. Hallucinogenic drug derived from the peyote cactus.

Mesmerism. Theories of "animal magnetism" (hypnosis) formulated by Anton Mesmer.

Methadone hydrochloride. Orally administered synthetic narcotic that replaces the craving for heroin and weans an individual from heroin addiction.

Microcephaly. Form of mental retardation characterized by an abnormally small cranium and retarded development of the brain.

Micturate, micturition. Pertaining to urination.

Migraine headache. Intensely painful, recurrent headache that typically involves only one side of the head and is associated with emotional tension and a change in the flow of blood to the brain.

Mild (disorder). Disorder of a low order of severity.

Milieu. Immediate environment, physical or social or both; sometimes used to include the internal state of an organism.

Milieu therapy. General approach to therapy for hospitalized patients that focuses on making the hospital environment itself a part of the treatment program.

Minimal brain dysfunction (MBD). Controversial term referring to various "soft" neurological signs presumably indicative of malfunctioning of the brain.

Minnesota Multiphasic Personality Inventory-2 (MMPI-2). Widely used and empirically validated personality scale.

Minor tranquilizers. Antianxiety drugs, such as the meprobamates and benzodiazepines.

Model. Analogy that helps a scientist order findings and see important relationships among them.

Modeling. Form of learning in which an individual learns by watching someone else (a model) perform a desired response.

Model psychoses. Psychotic-like states produced by various hallucinogenic drugs, such as LSD.

Moderate (disorder). Disorder of an intermediate order of severity.

Modus operandi. Manner or mode of behavior; a criminal's typical pattern of performing crimes.

Mongolism. See **Down syndrome.**

Monozygotic twins. Identical twins, developed from one fertilized egg.

Mood-congruent thinking. Thinking that is consistent with an individual's predominant mood.

Mood disorders. Psychoses and related disturbances characterized by severe disturbances of feeling or affect.

Moral management. Wide-ranging method of treatment for the mentally ill that focuses on a patient's social, individual, and occupational needs.

Moral therapy. Therapy based on provision of kindness, understanding, and favorable environment; prevalent during early part of the nineteenth century.

Morbid. Unhealthy, pathological.

Morita therapy. Treatment of neuroses involving the deprivation of external stimulation and other procedures.

Moron. Term formerly used to refer to mild degrees of mental retardation.

Morphine. Addictive opiate drug.

Motivation. Often used as a synonym for *drive* or *activation;* implies that an organism's actions are partly determined in direction and strength by its own inner nature.

Motivational selectivity. Influence of motives on perception and other cognitive processes.

Motive. Internal condition that directs action toward some goal; term usually used to include both the drive and the goal to which it is directed.

Motive pattern. Relatively consistent cluster of motives centered around particular strivings and goals.

Multi-infarct dementia. Organic disorder in which a series of cerebral infarcts, commonly known as "strokes," destroy brain cells over expanding brain regions, resulting in brain atrophy and behavioral impairments.

Multiple personality disorder. Type of dissociative disorder characterized by the development of two or more relatively independent personality systems in the same individual.

Mutant gene. Gene that has undergone some change in structure.

Mutation. Change in the composition of a gene, usually causing harmful or abnormal characteristics to appear in the offspring.

Mutism. Refusal or inability to speak.

Myxedema. Disorder due to thyroid deficiency in adult life, characterized by mental dullness.

Nancy School, The. Group of physicians in the nineteenth century who accepted the view that hysteria was a sort of self-hypnosis.

Narcissism. Self-love.

Narcissistic personality disorder. Personality disorder characterized by grandiosity, an exaggerated sense of self-importance, arrogance, and exploitation of others.

Narcolepsy. Disorder characterized by transient, compulsive states of sleepiness.

Narcotherapy (narcoanalysis, narcosynthesis). Psychotherapy carried on while a patient is in a sleeplike state of relaxation induced by a drug, such as sodium pentothal.

Narcotic drugs. Drugs, such as morphine, that lead to physiological dependence and increased tolerance.
Natural killer cell. White blood cell that destroys antigens by chemical dissolution.
Need. Biological or psychological condition whose gratification is necessary for the maintenance of homeostasis or for self-actualization.
Negative-symptom schizophrenia. Schizophrenic disorders characterized by an *absence* of normal or desirable behaviors, such as emotional reactivity.
Negativism. Form of aggressive withdrawal that involves refusing to cooperate or obey commands, or doing the exact opposite of what has been requested.
Neologism. New word; commonly coined by people labeled as schizophrenic.
Neonate. Newborn infant.
Neoplasm. Tumor.
Nervous breakdown. Refers broadly to lowered integration and inability to deal adequately with one's life situation.
Neurasthenic neurosis. Term formerly used to refer to a neurotic disorder characterized by complaints of chronic weakness, easy fatigability, and lack of enthusiasm.
Neurodermatitis. Skin eruption frequently accompanied by intense itching and often considered to be psychosomatically caused.
Neurological examination. Examination to determine the presence and extent of organic damage to the nervous system.
Neurology. Field concerned with the study of the brain and nervous system and disorders thereof.
Neuron. Individual nerve cell.
Neurophysiology. Branch of biology concerned with the functioning of nervous tissue and the nervous system.
Neuropsychological assessment. Use of psychological tests that measure a subject's cognitive, perceptual, and motor performance to determine the extent and locus of brain damage.
Neuropsychological disorders. Disorders that occur when there has been significant organic impairment or damage to a normal adolescent or adult brain.
Neurosis. Nonpsychotic emotional disturbance characterized by the exaggerated use of avoidance behavior and defense mechanisms against anxiety.
Neurosyphilis. Syphilis affecting the central nervous system.
Neurotic behavior. Anxiety-driven, exaggerated use of avoidance behaviors and defense mechanisms.
Neurotic nucleus. Basic personality characteristics underlying neurotic disorders.
Neurotic paradox. Failure of neurotic patterns to extinguish despite their self-defeating nature.
Neurotic style. General personality disposition toward inhibiting certain anxiety-causing behaviors; distinguishable from anxiety, somatoform, and dissociative disorders in that neurotic styles do not manifest themselves in specific, disabling neurotic symptoms.
Neurotransmitters. Chemical substances that transmit nerve impulses from one neuron to another.
Nicotine. Addictive akaloid that is the chief active ingredient in tobacco.
Night hospital. Mental hospital in which an individual may receive treatment during all or part of the night while carrying on his or her usual occupation in the daytime.
Nihilistic delusion. Fixed belief that everything is unreal.
Nomadism. Withdrawal reaction in which an individual continually attempts to escape frustration by moving from place to place or job to job.
Nondirective therapy. Approach to psychotherapy in which a therapist refrains from advice or direction of the therapy. See also **Client-centered psychotherapy.**
Norepinephrine. Catecholamine neurotransmitter substance.
Norm. Standard based on the measurement of a large group of people; used for comparing the scores of an individual with those of others in a defined group.
Normal. Conforming to the usual or norm; healthy.
Normal distribution. Tendency for most members of a population to cluster around a central point or average with respect to a given trait, with the rest spreading out to the two extremes.
NREM sleep. Stages of sleep not characterized by the rapid eye movements that accompany dreaming.
Nuclear magnetic resonance imaging (MRI). Internal scanning technique involving measurement of variations in magnetic fields that allows visualization of the anatomical features of internal organs, including the brain.

Objective tests. Structured personality test—such as a questionnaire, self-inventory, or rating scale—used in psychological assessment that allows for more objectively based quantification.
Object-relations. In psychoanalytic theory, a viewpoint that emphasizes interpersonal relationships by focusing on internalized "objects" that can have varying conflicting properties.
Observational method. Systematic technique by which observers are trained to watch and record behavior without bias.
Obsession. Persistent idea or thought that an individual recognizes as irrational but cannot get rid of.
Obsessive-compulsive disorder. Disorder characterized by the persistent intrusion of unwanted desires, thoughts, or actions.
Obsessive-compulsive personality disorder. Personality disorder characterized by excessive concern with conformity and adherence to ethical values.
Occipital lobe. Portion of cerebrum concerned chiefly with visual function.
Occupational therapy. Use of occupational training or activity in psychotherapy.
Oedipus complex. Desire for sexual relations with parent of opposite sex, specifically that of a boy for his mother.
Olfactory hallucinations. Hallucinations involving the sense of smell, as of poison gas.
Operant conditioning. Form of learning in which a particular response is reinforced and becomes more likely to occur.
Operational definition. Defining a concept on the basis of a set of operations that can be observed and measured.
Opium. Narcotic drug that leads to physiological dependence and the building up of tolerance; derivatives are morphine, heroin, paregoric, and codeine.
Oral stage. First stage of psychosexual development in Freudian theory, in which mouth or oral activities are primary source of pleasure.
Organic anxiety syndrome. Disorder in which the clinical manifestation of anxiety is thought somehow to be the direct outcome of brain impairment.
Organic brain syndromes. Mental disorders associated with organic brain pathology.
Organic delusional syndrome. Delusions or false beliefs caused by known or suspected brain damage.
Organic mental disorders. Mental disorders that occur secondary to damage to the normal brain; also referred to as *neuropsychological disorders.*
Organic mood syndrome. Manic or depressive states caused by brain damage.
Organic personality syndrome. Change in an individual's general personality style or traits caused by brain damage.
Organic viewpoint. Concept that all mental disorders have an organic basis. See also **Biological viewpoint.**
Orgasm. Peak sexual tension followed by relaxation.
Outcome research. Studies of effectiveness of treatment.
Outpatient. Ambulatory client who visits a hospital or clinic for examination and treatment, as distinct from a hospitalized client.
Ovaries. Female gonads.
Overanxious disorder. Disorder of childhood characterized by excessive worry and persistent fears unrelated to any specific event; often includes somatic and sleeping problems.

Overcompensation. Type of ego-defense mechanism in which an undesirable trait is covered up by exaggerating a desirable trait.
Overloading. Subjecting an organism to excessive stress, e.g., forcing the organism to handle or "process" an excessive amount of information.
Overprotection. Shielding a child to the extent that he or she becomes too dependent on the parent.
Overt behavior. Activities which can be observed by an outsider.
Ovum. Female gamete or germ cell.

Pain cocktail. Concoction of all the medication a pain patient is taking in a single liquid that can be systematically controlled and reduced in strength.
Panic. Severe personality disorganization involving intense anxiety and usually either paralyzed immobility or blind flight.
Panic disorder. Type of anxiety disorder involving recurring periods of acute panic or anxiety.
Paradigm. Model or pattern; in research, a basic design specifying concepts considered legitimate and procedures to be used in the collection and interpretation of data.
Paranoia. Symptoms of delusions and impaired contact with reality but without the severe personality disorganization characteristic of schizophrenia.
Paranoid personality disorder. Personality disorder characterized by projection (as a defense mechanism), suspiciousness, envy, extreme jealousy, and stubbornness.
Paranoid state. Transient psychotic disorder in which the main element is a delusion, usually persecutory or grandiose in nature.
Paraphasia. Garbled speech.
Paraphilias. Sexual variant in which unusual objects, rituals, or situations are required for full sexual satisfaction to occur.
Paraprofessional. Individual who has been trained in mental health services, but not at the professional level.
Parasympathetic nervous system. Division of the autonomic nervous system that controls most of the basic metabolic functions essential for life.
Paresis. See **General paresis.**
Paresthesia. Exceptional sensations, such as tingling.
Parkinson's disease (paralysis agitans). Progressive disease characterized by a masklike, expressionless face and various neurological symptoms, such as tremors.
Partial reinforcement. Intermittent reinforcement of a response.
Passive-aggressive personality disorder. Personality disorder characterized by passively expressed aggressiveness.
Path analysis. Statistical technique that takes into account how variables are related to one another through time and how they predict one another.
Pathogenic. Pertaining to conditions that lead to pathology.
Pathological gambling. Addictive disorder in which gambling behavior disrupts an individual's life.
Pathological intoxication. Severe cerebral and behavioral disturbance in an individual whose tolerance to alcohol is extremely low.
Pathology. Abnormal physical or mental condition.
PCP. Phencyclidine; developed as a tranquilizer but not marketed because of its unpredictability. Known on the streets as "angel dust," this drug produces stuporous conditions and, at times, prolonged comas or psychoses.
Pederasty. Sexual intercourse between males via the anus.
Pedophilia. Sexual variant in which an adult engages in or desires sexual relations with a child.
Peptic ulcers. Ulcerations of the stomach or upper intestine as a result of an excessive flow of the stomach's acid-containing digestive juices, which eat away the lining of the stomach or duodenum, leaving a craterlike wound.
Perception. Interpretation of sensory input.
Perceptual defense. Process in which threatening stimuli are filtered out and not perceived by an organism.
Perceptual filtering. Processes involved in selective attention to aspects of the great mass of incoming stimuli that continually impinge on an organism.
Performance test. Test in which perceptual-motor rather than verbal content is emphasized.
Peripheral nervous system. Nerve fibers passing between the central nervous system and the sense organs, muscles, and glands.
Perseveration. Persistent continuation of a line of thought or activity once it is under way. Clinically inappropriate repetition.
Personal constructs. According to Kelly, the uniquely individual ways of perceiving other people and events that people use to interpret events around them.
Personality. Unique pattern of traits that characterizes an individual.
Personality (character) disorders. Group of maladaptive behavior syndromes characterized by immature and distorted personality patterns, which result in persistently maladaptive ways of perceiving, thinking about, and relating to the world.
Personality profile. Graphic summary from several tests or subtests of the same test battery or scale that shows the personality configuration of an individual or group of individuals.
Person-centered therapy. See **Client-centered therapy.**
Pervasive developmental disorder. Severe disorder of childhood marked by deficits in language, perceptual, and motor development; defective reality testing; and inability to function in social situations.
Perversion. Deviation from normal.
Petit mal. Relatively mild form of epilepsy involving a temporary partial lapse of consciousness.
PET scan. See **Positron emission tomography.**
Phagocyte. Circulating white blood cell that binds to antigens and partially destroys them by engulfment.
Phallic stage. In psychoanalytic theory, the stage of psychosexual development during which genital exploration and manipulation occur.
Phallic symbol. Any object that resembles the erect male sex organ.
Pharmacology. Science of drugs.
Pharmacotherapy. Treatment by means of drugs.
Phenomenological. Referring to the immediate perceiving and experiencing of an individual.
Phenylketonuria (PKU). Type of mental retardation resulting from a metabolic deficiency.
Phobia. Persistent and disproportionate fear of some specific object or situation that presents little or no actual danger to a person.
Phobic disorder. Type of anxiety disorder characterized by intense fear of an object or situation which an individual consciously realizes poses no real danger.
Physiological dependence. Type of drug dependence involving withdrawal symptoms when drug is discontinued.
Pick's disease. Form of presenile dementia.
Pineal gland. Small gland at the base of the brain which helps regulate the body's biological clock and may also pace sexual development.
Pituitary gland. Endocrine gland associated with many regulatory functions.
Placebo effect. Positive effect experienced after an inactive treatment is administered in such a way that an individual thinks he or she is receiving an active treatment.
Play therapy. Use of play activities in psychotherapy with children.
Pleasure principle. In psychoanalysis, the demand that an instinctual need be immediately gratified, regardless of reality.
Polygenic. Action of many genes together in an additive or interactive fashion.
Poor premorbid schizophrenia. See **Process schizophrenia.**

Positive reinforcer. Reinforcer that increases the probability of recurrence of a given response.

Positive-symptom schizophrenia. Schizophrenic disorders characterized by elements *added* to normal behavior, such as delusions and hallucinations.

Positron emission tomography (PET scan). Scanning technique that measures the level of metabolic activity in particular regions of the body.

Posthypnotic amnesia. Subject's lack of memory for the period during which he or she was hypnotized.

Posthypnotic suggestion. Suggestion given during hypnosis to be carried out by a subject after he or she is brought out of hypnosis.

Postpartum disturbances. Emotional disturbances associated with childbirth.

Posttraumatic disorders. Residual symptoms following a traumatic experience.

Posttraumatic stress disorder (PTSD). Disorder in which a stressor is severe and residual symptoms occur following the traumatic experience and last for at least one month.

Precipitating cause. Particular stress that triggers a disorder.

Predisposing cause. Factor that lowers an individual's stress tolerance and paves the way for the appearance of a disorder.

Predisposition. Likelihood that an individual will develop certain symptoms under given stress conditions.

Prefrontal lobotomy. Surgical procedure used before the advent of antipsychotic drugs in which frontal lobes of the brain were severed from the deeper centers underlying them, resulting in permanent brain damage.

Prejudice. Emotionally toned conception favorable or unfavorable to some person, group, or idea—typically in the absence of sound evidence.

Premature ejaculation. Inability of a male to inhibit ejaculation long enough to satisfy his partner.

Prematurity. Birth of an infant before the end of a normal period of pregnancy.

Premorbid. Existing prior to the onset of mental disorder.

Prenatal. Before birth.

Presenile dementia. Senile brain deterioration occurring at an early age and accompanied by mental disorder.

Pressure. Demand made on an organism.

Prevalence. Term that refers to the rate of active cases of something under study (in this case, a disorder) that can be identified at a given period in time.

Primary cause. Cause without which a disorder would not have occurred.

Primary erectile insufficiency. Dysfunction in which a male has never been able to sustain an erection long enough to have successful intercourse.

Primary orgasmic dysfunction. Inability on the part of a woman to have an orgasm.

Primary prevention. Preventive efforts aimed at establishing conditions designed to prevent the occurrence of mental disorders.

Primary process. Gratification of an instinctual id demand by means of imagery or fantasy; a psychoanalytic concept.

Primary reaction tendencies. Constitutional tendencies apparent in infancy, such as sensitivity and activity level.

Privileged communication. Freedom from the obligation to report to the authorities information concerning legal guilt revealed by a client or patient.

Proband. In a genetic study, the original individual who evidences the trait in which the investigator is interested. Same as *index case.*

Problem checklist. Inventory used in behavioral assessment to determine an individual's fears, moods, and other problems.

Problem drinker. Behavioral term referring to one who has serious problems associated with drinking. Term is currently preferable to *alcoholic.*

Process schizophrenia. Schizophrenic pattern—marked by seclusiveness, gradual lack of interest in the surrounding world, diminished emotional responsivity, and mildly inappropriate responses—that develops gradually and tends to be long-lasting; alternatively known as *poor premorbid schizophrenia* and *chronic schizophrenia.*

Prognosis. Prediction as to the probable course and outcome of a disorder.

Programmed learning. Method of instruction or learning in which a student is guided through the subject matter step-by-step.

Projection. Ego-defense mechanism in which an individual attributes unacceptable desires and impulses to others.

Projective test. Technique using neutral or ambiguous stimuli that a subject is encouraged to interpret and from which the subject's personality characteristics can be analyzed.

Prospective research. Research that focuses, before the fact, on individuals who have a higher-than-average likelihood of becoming psychologically disordered, following them over time.

Prototypal approach. Approach to classifying abnormal behavior that assumes the existence of prototypes of behavior disorders that, rather than being mutually exclusive, may blend into others with which they share many characteristics.

Pseudocommunity. Delusional social environment developed by a paranoid individual.

Pseudomutuality. Relationship among family members that appears to be mutual, understanding, and open, but in fact is not.

Psilocybin. Hallucinogenic drug derived from a mushroom.

Psychedelic drugs. "Mind expanding" drugs, such as LSD, which often result in hallucinations.

Psychiatric nursing. Field of nursing primarily concerned with mental disorders.

Psychiatric social worker. Professional having graduate training in social work with psychiatric specialization, typically involving a master's degree.

Psychiatrist. Medical doctor who specializes in the diagnosis and treatment of mental disorders.

Psychiatry. Field of medicine concerned with understanding, assessing, treating, and preventing mental disorders.

Psychic pain. Synonym for *anxiety.*

Psychic trauma. Stressful psychological experience of a severely traumatic nature.

Psychoactive drugs. Any drug that primarily affects mental functioning.

Psychoactive substance abuse. Pathological use of a substance resulting in potentially hazardous behavior or in continued use despite a persistent social, psychological, occupational, or health problem.

Psychoactive substance dependence. Use of a psychoactive substance to the point that one has a physiological need for it.

Psychoanalysis. Theoretical model and therapeutic approach developed by Freud.

Psychoanalytic perspective. Theory of psychopathology, initially developed by Freud, that emphasizes the inner dynamics of unconscious motives.

Psychodrama. Psychotherapeutic technique in which the acting of various roles is a cardinal part.

Psychodynamic perspective. Term in psychoanalytic theory referring to the psychic forces and processes developed through an individual's childhood experiences and that influence adult thinking and behavior.

Psychodynamic therapy. Treatment focusing on individual personality dynamics from a psychoanalytic perspective.

Psychogenic. Of psychological origin: originating in the psychological functioning of an individual.

Psychogenic amnesia. Amnesia of psychological origin, common in initial reactions to intolerable traumatic experiences.

Psychogenic illness. Psychologically induced or maintained disease.

Psychogenic pain disorder. Neurotic disorder in which pain is the predominant complaint.

Psychological autopsy. Analytical procedure used to determine whether or not death was self-inflicted.

Psychological need. Need emerging out of environmental interactions, e.g., the need for social approval.
Psychological screening. Use of psychological procedures or tests to detect psychological problems among applicants in preemployment evaluations.
Psychological test. Standardized procedure designed to measure a subject's performance on a specified task.
Psychomotor. Involving both psychological and physical activity.
Psychomotor epilepsy. State of disturbed consciousness in which an individual may perform various actions, sometimes of a homicidal nature, for which he or she is later amnesic.
Psychomotor retardation. Slowing down of psychological and motor functions.
Psychoneuroimmunology. Developing new field whose focus is on understanding the psychological influences affecting immune functioning.
Psychopathic personality. See **antisocial personality disorder.**
Psychopathology. Abnormal behavior.
Psychopharmacological drugs. Drugs used in treatment of mental disorders.
Psychophysiologic (psychosomatic) disorders. Physical disorders in which psychological factors play a major causative role.
Psychosexual development. Freudian view of development as involving a succession of stages, each characterized by a dominant mode of achieving libidinal pleasure.
Psychosexual stages of development. According to Freudian theory, there are five stages of psychosexual development, each characterized by a dominant mode of achieving sexual pleasure: the oral stage, the anal stage, the phallic stage, the latency stage, and the genital stage.
Psychosis. See **psychotic behavior.**
Psychosocial deprivation. Lack of needed stimulation and interaction during early life.
Psychosocial viewpoints. Approaches to understanding behavior disorders that emphasize the importance of early experience and an awareness of social influences and psychological processes within an individual.
Psychosomatic disorders. See **Psychophysiologic disorders.**
Psychosurgery. Brain surgery used in the treatment of functional mental disorders or occasionally to relieve pain.
Psychotherapy. Treatment of mental disorders by psychological methods.
Psychotic behavior. Behavior that represents a loss of contact with reality to the extent that delusional beliefs are harbored or bizarre perceptions (hallucinations) are reported. Also called *psychosis.*
Psychotropic drugs. Drugs whose main effects are mental or behavioral in nature.

Q-sort. Personality inventory in which a subject, or a clinician, sorts a number of statements into piles according to their applicability to the subject.

Racism. Prejudice, and discrimination directed toward individuals or groups because of their racial background.
Random sample. Sample drawn in such a way that each member of a population has an equal chance of being selected; hopefully representative of the population from which drawn.
Rape. Act of violence in which sexual relations are forced on another person.
Rapport. Interpersonal relationship characterized by a spirit of cooperation, confidence, and harmony.
Rating scale. Device for evaluating oneself or someone else in regard to specific traits.
Rational-emotive therapy. Form of psychotherapy focusing on cognitive and emotional restructuring to foster adaptive behavior.
Rationalization. Ego-defense mechanism in which an individual thinks up "good" reasons to justify his or her actions.
Reaction formation. Ego-defense mechanism in which an individual's conscious attitudes and overt behavior are opposite to repressed unconscious wishes.
Reactive schizophrenia. Schizophrenia pattern—marked by confusion and intense emotional turmoil—that normally develops suddenly and has identifiable precipitating stressors; alternatively known as *good premorbid schizophrenia* and *acute schizophrenia.*
Reality principle. Awareness of the demands of the environment and adjustment of behavior to meet these demands.
Reality testing. Behavior aimed at testing or exploring the nature of an individual's social and physical environment; often used more specifically to refer to the testing of the limits of permissiveness of social environment.
Reality therapy. Form of therapy based on the assumption that emotional difficulties arise when an individual violates his or her basic sense of right and wrong.
Recessive gene. Gene which is effective only when paired with an identical gene.
Recidivism. Shift back to one's original behavior (often delinquent or criminal) after a period of treatment or rehabilitation.
Reciprocal inhibition. Technique of desensitization used in behavior therapy in which responses antagonistic to anxiety are paired with anxiety-eliciting stimuli.
Recompensation. Increase in integration or inner organization. Opposite of *decompensation.*
Reentry. Return from the openness of an encounter group to the real world, which is presumably less open and honest.
Referral. Sending or recommending an individual and/or family for psychological assessment and/or treatment.
Regression. Ego-defense mechanism in which an individual retreats to the use of less mature responses in attempting to cope with stress and maintain ego integrity.
Rehabilitation. Use of reeducation rather than punishment to overcome behavioral deficits.
Reinforcement. In classical conditioning, the process of following the conditioned stimulus with the unconditioned stimulus; in operant conditioning, the rewarding of desired responses.
Reinforcing cause. Circumstance tending to maintain behavior that is ultimately maladaptive, as in *secondary gain.*
Rejection. Lack of acceptance of another person, usually referring to such treatment of a child by the parents.
Reliability. Degree to which a test or measuring device produces the same result each time it is used to measure the same thing.
Remission. Marked improvement or recovery appearing in the course of a mental illness; may or may not be permanent.
REM sleep. Stage of sleep involving rapid eye movements (REM), associated with dreaming.
Renaud's disease. Potentially serious constriction of the small blood vessels of the extremities, cutting off adequate blood flow to them; sometimes considered psychosomatic.
Representative sample. Small group selected in such a way as to be representative of the larger group from which it is drawn.
Repression. Ego-defense mechanism by means of which dangerous desires and intolerable memories are kept out of consciousness.
Reserpine. One of the early antipsychotic drugs, now largely supplanted by newer drugs.
Resistance. Tendency to maintain symptoms and resist treatment or uncovering of repressed material.
Resistance to extinction. Tendency of a conditioned response to persist despite lack of reinforcement.
Respondent conditioning. See **Classical conditioning.**
Response shaping. Positive reinforcement technique used in therapy to establish a response not initially in an individual's behavioral repertoire.
Reticular activating system (RAS). Fibers going from the reticular formation to higher brain centers and presumably functioning as a general arousal system.
Reticular formation. Neural nuclei and fibers in the brain stem that apparently play an important role in arousing and

alerting an organism and in controlling attention.
Retrograde amnesia. Loss of memory for events during a circumscribed period prior to brain injury or damage.
Retrospective research. Research that looks backward from the present.
Retrospective study. Research approach that attempts to retrace earlier events in the life of a subject.
Rigid control. Coping patterns involving reliance on inner restraints, such as inhibition, suppression, repression, and reaction formation.
Rigidity. Tendency to follow established coping patterns, with failure to see alternatives or extreme difficulty in changing one's established patterns.
Ritalin. Central nervous system stimulant often used to treat hyperactivity in children.
Role distortion. Violation of expected role behavior in an undesirable way.
Role obsolescence. Condition occurring when the ascribed social role of a given individual is no longer of importance to the social group.
Role playing. Form of assessment or psychotherapy in which an individual acts out a social role other than his or her own or tries out a new role.
Rorschach test. Series of inkblots to which a subject responds with associations that come to mind. Analysis of these productions enables a clinician to infer personality characteristics.

Sadism. Sexual variant in which sexual gratification is obtained by the infliction of pain on others.
Sadistic personality disorder. Proposed diagnostic category of personality disorder that is characterized by a pervasive pattern of cruel, demeaning, and aggressive behavior toward other people.
Sample. Group on which measurements are taken; should normally be representative of the population about which an inference is to be made.
Scapegoating. Displacement of aggression onto some object, person, or group other than the source of frustration.
Schedule of reinforcement. Program of rewards for requisite behavior.
Schizoaffective disorder. Disorder in which a person experiences severe but highly episodic disturbances of psychological functioning, such as mood-incongruent delusions and hallucinations.
Schizoid personality disorder. Personality disorder characterized by shyness, oversensitivity, seclusiveness, and eccentricity.
Schizophrenia. Psychosis characterized by the breakdown of integrated personality functioning, withdrawal from reality, emotional blunting and distortion, and disturbances in thought and behavior.
Schizophrenia, catatonic type. Type of schizophrenia in which the central feature is pronounced motor symptoms, either of an excited or stuporous type, which sometimes make it difficult to differentiate this condition from a psychotic mood disorder.
Schizophrenia, disorganized type. Type of schizophrenia that usually begins at an earlier age and represents a more severe disintegration of the personality than in the other types of schizophrenia.
Schizophrenia, paranoid type. Type of schizophrenia in which an individual is increasingly suspicious, has severe difficulties in interpersonal relationships, and experiences absurd, illogical, and often changing delusions.
Schizophrenia, residual type. Diagnostic category used for people regarded as having recovered from schizophrenia but still manifesting some signs of their past disorder.
Schizophrenia, undifferentiated type. Type of schizophrenia in which an individual meets the usual criteria for being schizophrenic—including (in varying combinations) delusions, hallucinations, thought disorder, and bizarre behavior—but does not clearly fit into one of the other types because of a mixed symptom picture.
Schizophreniform disorder. Category of schizophrenic disorder, usually in an undifferentiated form, of less than six months duration.
Schizophrenogenic (parents). Qualities in parents that appear to be associated with the development of schizophrenia in offspring; often applied to rejecting, cold, domineering, overprotective mothers or passive, uninvolved fathers.
Schizotypal personality disorder. Personality disorder in which egocentricity, avoidance of others, and eccentricity of thought and perception are distinguishing traits.
Scotophilia. See **Voyeurism.**
Secondary cause. Factor which contributes to a mental illness but which in and of itself would not have produced it, as distinct from the *primary* cause.
Secondary drives. Motives for approval, achievement, etc., as distinguished from basic biological needs.
Secondary erectile insufficiency. Condition in which a male has been capable of successful intercourse but is currently dysfunctional.
Secondary gain. Indirect benefit from neurotic or other symptoms.
Secondary prevention. Prevention techniques that typically involve emergency or crisis intervention, with efforts focused on reducing the impact, duration, or spread of a problem.
Secondary process. Reality-oriented rational processes of the ego.
Secondary reinforcer. Reinforcement provided by a stimulus that has gained reward value by being associated with a primary reinforcing stimulus.
Sedative. Drug used to reduce tension and induce relaxation and sleep.
Selective vigilance. Tuning of attentional and perceptual processes toward stimuli relevant or central to goal-directed behavior, with decreased sensitivity to stimuli irrelevant or peripheral to this purpose.
Self (ego). Integrating core of a personality that mediates between needs and reality.
Self-acceptance. Being satisfied with one's attributes and qualities while remaining aware of one's limitations.
Self-actualization. Fulfillment of one's potentialities as a human being.
Self-concept. Individual's sense of his or her own identity, worth, capabilities, and limitations.
Self-defeating personality disorder. Proposed diagnostic category of personality disorder, often called masochistic personality disorder, which is characterized by an individual's avoidance of pleasurable experiences and persistent involvement in disappointing relationships.
Self-differentiation. Degree to which an individual achieves a sense of unique identity apart from a group.
Self-direction. Basing one's behavior on inner assumptions rather than external contingencies.
Self-esteem. Feeling of personal worth.
Self-evaluation. Way in which an individual views the self, in terms of worth, adequacy, etc.
Self-ideal (ego-ideal). Person or "self" an individual thinks he or she could and should be.
Self-identity. Individual's delineation and awareness of his or her continuing identity as a person.
Self-instructional training. Cognitive-behavioral method aimed at teaching an individual to alter his or her covert behavior.
Self-monitoring. Observing and recording one's own behavior.
Self-reinforcement. Reward of self for desired or appropriate behavior.
Self-report inventory. Procedure in which a subject is asked to respond to statements in terms of their applicability to him or her.
Self-statements. Implicit "verbalizations" of what a person is experiencing.
Self-system. According to Sullivan's interpersonal theory, a system that protects an individual from anxiety by controlling awareness—the individual simply does not attend to elements of experience that cause anxiety and may even block

out of consciousness especially severe anxiety-arousing experiences.

Self-theory. Personality theory that utilizes the self-concept as the integrating core of personality organization and functioning.

Senile. Pertaining to old age.

Senile dementia. Deteriorative brain changes due to aging.

Sensate focus learning. Training to derive pleasure from touching one's partner and being touched by him or her; used in sexual therapy to enhance sexual feelings and help overcome sexual dysfunction.

Sensitivity training group (T-group). One type of small group designed to provide intensive group experience and foster self-understanding and personal growth.

Sensory awareness. Openness to new ways of experiencing and feeling.

Sensory deprivation. Restriction of sensory stimulation below the level required for normal functioning of the central nervous system.

Sentence-completion test. Form of projective technique utilizing incomplete sentences that a subject is to complete, analysis of which enables a clinician to infer personality dynamics.

Separation anxiety disorder. Childhood disorder characterized by unrealistic fears, oversensitivity, self-consciousness, nightmares, chronic anxiety, and, typically, overdependency.

Separation-individuation. According to Mahler, a developmental phase in which a child gains an internal representation of self as distinct from representations of other objects.

Sequelae. Symptoms remaining as the aftermath of a disorder.

Severe (disorder). Disorder of a high degree of severity.

Sex chromosomes. Pair of chromosomes inherited by an individual that determines sex and certain other characteristics.

Sexual aversion disorder. Sexual desire disorder in which an individual views sexual intercourse as psychologically aversive.

Sexual deviate. Individual who manifests nonconforming sexual behavior, often of a pathological nature.

Sexual dysfunction. Inability or impaired ability to experience or give sexual gratification.

Shaping. Form of instrumental conditioning; at first, all responses resembling the desired one are reinforced, then only the closest approximations, until finally the desired response is attained.

Sheltered workshops. Workshops where mentally retarded or otherwise handicapped individuals can engage in constructive work in the community.

Short-term crisis therapy. Therapy that is of brief duration and that focuses on the immediate problem—personal or family problems of an emotional nature—with which an individual or family is having difficulty.

Siblings. Offspring of the same parents.

Sick role. Protected role provided by society via medical model for individual suffering from severe physical or mental disorder.

Significant others. In interpersonal theory, parents or others on whom an infant is dependent for meeting all physical and psychological needs.

Simple phobia. See **phobia.**

Simple tension headaches. Commonplace headache in which stress leads to contractions of the muscles surrounding the skull; these contractions, in turn, result in vascular constrictions that cause headache pain.

Situational test. Test that measures performance in a simulated life situation.

Sleepwalking disorder. Disorder of childhood that involves repeated episodes in which a child leaves his or her bed and walks around without being conscious of the experience or remembering it later.

Social exchange. Model of interpersonal relationships based on the premise that such relationships are formed for mutual need gratification.

Social introversion. Trait characterized by shy, withdrawn, and inhibited behavior.

Socialization. Process by which a child acquires the values and impulse controls deemed appropriate by his or her culture.

Socialized-aggressive disorder. Pattern of childhood maladaptive behaviors involving social maladaptation, such as stealing, truancy, gang membership.

Social-learning programs. Behavioral treatment techniques using learning principles, especially token economies, to help chronic patients assume more responsibility for their own behavior.

Social norms. Group standards concerning behaviors viewed as acceptable or unacceptable.

Social pathology. Abnormal patterns of social organization, attitudes, or behavior; undesirable social conditions that tend to produce individual pathology.

Social phobia. Fear of one or more situations in which one is exposed to focused scrutiny by others, and the corollary fear that one may do something or act in such a manner as to risk humiliation or embarrassment.

Social role. Behavior expected of an individual occupying given position in group.

"Social" self. Facade an individual displays to others as contrasted with the private self.

Social work. Applied offshoot of sociology concerned with the analysis of social environments and providing services which assist the adjustment of a client in both family and community settings.

Social worker. Person in a mental health field with a master's degree in social work (MSW) plus supervised training in clinical or social service agencies.

Sociocultural viewpoint. Pertaining to broad social conditions that influence the development and/or behavior of individuals and groups.

Socioeconomic status. Position on social and economic scale in community; determined largely by income and occupational level.

Sociogenic. Having its roots in sociocultural conditions.

Sociopathic personality. See **antisocial personality disorder.**

Sociotherapy. Treatment of interpersonal aspects of an individual's life situation.

Sodium pentothal. Barbiturate drug sometimes used in psychotherapy to produce a state of relaxation and suggestibility.

Sodomy. Sexual intercourse via the anus.

Somatic. Pertaining to the body.

Somatic weakness. Special vulnerability of given organ systems to stress.

Somatization disorder. Type of somatoform disorder beginning before age thirty and continuing for many years, characterized by multiple complaints of physical ailments not necessarily involving organic pathology.

Somatoform disorder. Anxiety-based pattern in which an individual complains of bodily symptoms that suggest the presence of a physical problem, but for which no organic basis can be found.

Somatoform pain disorder. Somatoform disorder characterized by the report of severe and lasting pain for which no physical basis is apparent, or the reaction is greatly in excess of what would be expected from the physical pathology.

Somatotype. Physique or build of a person, as assessed by various theories relating temperament to physical characteristics.

Somnambulism. Sleepwalking.

Spasm. Intense, involuntary, usually painful contraction of a muscle or group of muscles.

Spasticity. Marked hypertonicity or continual overcontraction of muscles, causing stiffness, awkwardness, and motor incoordination.

Specific developmental disorders. Disorders of childhood that reflect inadequate development in academic, language, speech, or motor skills that may occur in children who are otherwise normal or even gifted in their overall functioning.

Specific learning disabilities. Developmental disorders involving deficits in specific academic skills.

Sperm. Male gamete or germ cell.

Split-brain research. Research associated with split-brain surgery, which cuts off the transmission of information from one cerebral hemisphere to the other.

Spontaneous recovery (remission). Recovery of a mental patient without treatment or with minimal treatment.

Stage of exhaustion. Third and final stage in the general adaptation syndrome, in which an organism is no longer able to resist continuing stress; may result in death.

Stage of resistance. Second stage of the general adaptation syndrome.

Standardization. Procedure for establishing the expected performance range on a test.

Stanford-Binet. Standardized intelligence test for children.

Startle reaction. Sudden involuntary motor reaction to intense unexpected stimuli; may result from mild stimuli if a person is hypersensitive.

Statutory rape. Sexual intercourse with a minor.

Steady states (homeostasis). Tendency of an organism to maintain conditions making possible a constant level of physiological functioning.

Stereotype. Generalized notion of how people of a given race, religion, or other group will appear, think, feel, or act.

Stereotypy. Persistent and inappropriate repetition of phrases, gestures, or acts.

Stimulants. Drugs that tend to increase feelings of alertness, reduce feelings of fatigue, and enable an individual to stay awake over sustained periods of time.

Stimulus generalization. Spread of a conditioned response to some stimulus similar to, but not identical with, the conditioned stimulus.

Stress. Internal responses caused by the application of a stressor.

Stress-decompensation model. View of abnormal behavior that emphasizes progressive disorganization of behavior under excessive stress.

Stress-inoculation therapy. Type of self-instructional training focused on altering self-statements that an individual is routinely making in order to restructure his or her characteristic approach to stress-producing situations.

Stress interview. Interview of a subject in which stressors are introduced.

Stressor. Any adjustive demand that requires coping behavior on the part of an individual or group.

Stress tolerance (frustration tolerance). Nature, degree, and duration of stress which an individual can tolerate without undergoing serious personality decompensation.

Stroke. See **Cerebrovascular accident.**

Structural family therapy. Treatment of an entire family by analysis of communication between family members.

Structural therapy. Treatment of autistic children in which the environment is structured to provide spontaneous physical and verbal stimulation.

Stupor. Condition of lethargy and unresponsiveness, with partial or complete unconsciousness.

Stuttering. Speech disorder characterized by a blocking or repetition of initial sounds of words.

St. Vitus's dance. Hysterical chorea of common occurrence during the Middle Ages.

Sublimation. Ego-defense mechanism by means of which frustrated sexual energy is partially channeled into substitutive activities.

Substance-abuse disorders. Pathological use of a substance for at least a month, resulting in self-injurious behavior.

Substance-dependence disorders. Severe form of substance-abuse disorder involving physiological dependence on the substance.

Substance-induced organic disorder. Category of disorders based on organic impairment resulting from toxicity or physiologic changes in the brain.

Substance-use disorder. Patterns of maladaptive behavior centered around the regular use of the substance involved.

Substitution. Acceptance of substitute goals or satisfactions in place of those originally sought after or desired.

Successive approximation. See **Shaping.**

Suicide. Taking one's own life.

Suicidology. Study of the causes and prevention of suicide.

Superego. Conscience; ethical or moral dimensions (attitudes) of personality.

Suppression. Conscious forcing of desires or thoughts out of consciousness; conscious inhibition of desires or impulses.

Surrogate. Substitute parent, child, or mate.

Symbol. Image, word, object, or activity that is used to represent something else.

Symbolism. Representation of one idea or object by another.

Sympathetic division. Division of the autonomic nervous system that is active in emergency conditions of extreme cold, violent effort, and emotions.

Symptom. Observable manifestation of a physical or mental disorder.

Syncope. Temporary loss of consciousness resulting from cerebral anoxia.

Syndrome. Group or pattern of symptoms that occur together in a disorder and represent the typical picture of the disorder.

Syphilophobia. Morbid fear of syphilis.

System. Assemblage of interdependent parts, living or nonliving.

Systematic desensitization. Behavior therapy technique for eliminating maladaptive anxiety responses by teaching an individual to relax or behave in some other way that is inconsistent with anxiety while in the presence of the anxiety-producing stimulus.

Tachycardia. Rapid heartbeat.

Tactual hallucinations. Hallucinations involving the sense of touch, such as feeling cockroaches crawling over one's body.

Tarantism. Dancing mania that occurred in Italy and later spread to Germany and the rest of Europe, where it was known as *St. Vitus's dance.*

Tardive dyskinesia. Neurological disorder resulting from excessive use of phenothiazines. The drug side effects can occur months to years after treatment has been initiated or has stopped. The symptoms involve involuntary movements of the tongue, lips, jaw, and extremities. An affected person usually shows characteristic "chewing movements."

Task-oriented response. Realistic rather than ego-defensive approach to stressors.

Tay-Sachs disease. Genetic disorder of lipoid metabolism usually resulting in death by age 3.

T-cell. Generic type of lymphocyte crucial in "cellular" (non-antibody, or "humoral") immune functioning and having several subtypes that support and regulate the entire immune reaction.

Telepathy. Communication from one person to another without use of any known sense organs.

Teleprocessing. Computer-based data processing procedure by which psychological tests are processed, scored, and interpreted through telephone link-up with a central processing center.

Temperament (character) traits. Personality characteristics that are considered to be primarily hereditary or constitutional.

Temporal lobe. Portion of cerebrum located in front of the occipital lobe and separated from frontal and parietal lobes by the fissure of Sylvius.

Tension. Condition arising out of the mobilization of psychobiological resources to meet a threat; physically, involves an increase in muscle tonus and other emergency changes; psychologically, is characterized by feelings of strain, uneasiness, and anxiety.

Tertiary prevention. Preventive techniques focusing on reducing long-term consequences of disorders or problems by means of short-term hospitalization and intensive aftercare when an emotional breakdown has occurred, with aim of returning an individual to his or her family and community setting as soon as possible.

Testes. Male reproductive glands or gonads.

Testosterone. Male sex hormone.

Test reliability. Consistency with which a test measures a given trait on repeated administrations of the test to given subjects.

Test validity. Degree to which a test actually measures what it was designed to measure.

Thematic Apperception Test (TAT). Psychological test composed of a series of pictures based on which a subject makes up a story. Analysis of the story gives a clinician clues about the individual's conflicts, traits, personality dynamics, and so on.

Therapeutic. Pertaining to treatment or healing.

Therapeutic community. Hospital environment used for therapeutic purposes.

Therapy. Treatment; application of various treatment techniques.

Thermistors. Extremely sensitive small thermometers taped to a subject's skin to provide feedback during biofeedback training.

Theta wave. Brain wave having a frequency of only 5 to 7 cycles per second.

Thyroids. Endocrine glands located in the neck that influence body metabolism, rate of physical growth, and development of intelligence.

Thyroxin. Hormone secreted by the thyroid glands.

Tic. Intermittent twitching or jerking, usually of facial muscles.

Token economy. Reinforcement technique often used in hospital or institutional settings in which individuals are rewarded for socially constructive behavior with tokens that can then be exchanged for desired objects or activities.

Tolerance. Physiological condition in which an increased dosage of an addictive drug is needed to obtain effects previously produced by a smaller dose.

Tonic. Pertaining to muscle tension or contraction; muscle tone.

Tourette's syndrome. Extreme tic disorder in which an individual has extensive uncontrollable motor and verbal mannerisms.

Toxic. Poisonous.

Toxic deliria (psychoses). Severe disturbances in cerebral functions resulting from toxins.

Toxicity. Poisonous nature of a substance.

Trait. Characteristic of an individual that can be observed or measured.

Trance. Sleeplike state in which the range of consciousness is limited and voluntary activities are suspended; a deep hypnotic state.

Tranquilizers. Drugs used for antipsychotic purposes and/or reduction of anxiety and tension. See also **Major tranquilizers** and **Minor tranquilizers.**

Transactional analysis. Form of interpersonal therapy based on interaction of "Child," "Adult," and "Parent" ego states.

Transference. Process whereby a client projects attitudes and emotions applicable to another significant person onto the therapist; emphasized in psychoanalytic therapy.

Transsexualism. Identification of oneself with members of the opposite sex, as opposed to acceptance of one's anatomical sexual identity.

Transvestic fetishism. Achievement of sexual arousal and satisfaction by dressing as a member of the opposite sex.

Transvestism. Persistent desire to dress in clothing of the opposite sex, often accompanied by sexual excitement.

Trauma. Severe psychological or physiological stressor.

Traumatic. Pertaining to a wound or injury, or to psychic shock.

Treatment contract. Explicit arrangement between a therapist and a client designed to bring about specific behavioral changes.

Tremor. Repeated fine spastic movement.

Trephining. Early operation to treat abnormal behavior that consisted of chipping away a circular area of the skull until it was cut through, in the hopes of allowing the evil spirit that was causing the disordered behavior to escape.

Trichotillomania. Nervous habit involving the pulling out of hair.

Turner's syndrome. Form of mental retardation associated with sex chromosome anomaly.

Type-A behavior pattern. Complex set of behaviors—involving excessive competitive drive in the absence of well-defined goals, impatience or time urgency, and hostility—that may be observed in certain individuals under appropriately stressful or challenging circumstances.

Unconscious. As used by Freud, psychological material that has been repressed. Also, loss of consciousness; lack of awareness.

Underarousal. Inadequate physiological response to a given stimulus.

Undoing. Ego-defense mechanism by means of which an individual performs activities designed to atone for his or her misdeeds, thereby, in a sense, "undoing" them.

Unipolar disorder. Severe mood disorder in which only depressive episodes occur, as opposed to ***bipolar disorder*** in which both manic and depressive processes are assumed to occur.

Unsocialized disturbance of conduct. Childhood disorder in which a child is disobedient, hostile, and highly aggressive.

Vaginismus. Involuntary muscle spasm at the entrance to the vagina that prevents penetration and sexual intercourse.

Validity. Extent to which a measuring instrument actually measures what it purports to measure.

Variable. Characteristic or property that may assume any one of a set of different qualities or quantities.

Vasomotor. Pertaining to the walls of the blood vessels.

Vegetative. Withdrawn or deteriorated to the point where an individual leads a passive, vegetable-like existence.

Verbal test. Test in which a subject's ability to understand and use words and concepts is important in making the required responses.

Vertigo. Dizziness.

Virilism. Accentuation of masculine secondary sex characteristics, especially in a woman or young boy, caused by hormonal imbalance.

Viscera. Internal organs.

Voyeurism. Achievement of sexual pleasure through clandestine "peeping," usually watching other people disrobe and/or engage in sexual activities. Also known as ***scotophilia*** and ***inspectionalism.***

Vulnerabilities. Factors rendering an individual susceptible to behaving abnormally.

Wechsler Intelligence Scale for Children (WISC). Standardized intelligence scale for children.

Withdrawal. Intellectual, emotional, or physical retreat.

Withdrawal disturbance. Disorder of childhood in which a child becomes aloof and detached from a world he or she sees as dangerous.

Withdrawal symptoms. Wide range of symptoms evidenced by addicts when the drug on which they are physiologically dependent is not available.

Word salad. Jumbled or incoherent use of words by psychotic or disoriented individuals.

X chromosome. Sex-determining chromosome: all female gametes contain X chromosomes, and if the fertilized ovum has also received an X chromosome from its father it will be female.

XYY syndrome. Chromosomal anomaly in males (presence of an extra Y chromosome) possibly related to impulsive behavior.

Y chromosome. Sex-determining chromosome found in half of the total number of male gametes; uniting with X chromosome always provided by female produces a male offspring.

Zygote. Fertilized egg cell formed by the union of male and female gametes.

References

JOURNAL ABBREVIATIONS

Acta Psychiatr. Scandin.—*Acta Psychiatrica Scandinavica*
Amer. J. Med. Sci.—*American Journal of the Medical Sciences*
Amer. J. Ment. Def.—*American Journal of Mental Deficiency*
Amer. J. Ment. Retard—*American Journal of Mental Retardation*
Amer. J. Nurs.—*American Journal of Nursing*
Amer. J. Orthopsychiat.—*American Journal of Orthopsychiatry*
Amer. J. Psychiat.—*American Journal of Psychiatry*
Amer. J. Psychother.—*American Journal of Psychotherapy*
Amer. J. Pub. Hlth.—*American Journal of Public Health*
Amer. Psychol.—*American Psychologist*
Ann. Int. Med.—*Annals of Internal Medicine*
Annu. Rev. Psychol.—*Annual Review of Psychology*
Arch. Gen. Psychiat.—*Archives of General Psychiatry*
Arch. Int. Med.—*Archives of Internal Medicine*
Arch. Sex. Behav.—*Archives of Sexual Behavior*
Behav. Res. Ther.—*Behavior Research and Therapy*
Behav. Ther.—*Behavior Therapy*
Behav. Today—*Behavior Today*
Brit. J. Psychiat.—*British Journal of Psychiatry*
Brit. Med. J.—*British Medical Journal*
Bull. Menninger Clin.—*Bulletin of the Menninger Clinic*
Canad. J. Psychiat.—*Canadian Journal of Psychiatry*
Child Develop.—*Child Development*
Clin. Psychol.—*The Clinical Psychologist*
Clin. Psychol. Rev.—*Clinical Psychology Review*
Cog. Ther. Res.—*Cognitive Therapy and Research*
Comm. Ment. Hlth. J.—*Community Mental Health Journal*
Compr. Psychiat.—*Comprehensive Psychiatry*
Contemp. Psychol.—*Contemporary Psychology*
Crim. Just. Behav.—*Criminal Justice and Behavior*
Develop. Med. Child Neurol.—*Developmental Medicine & Child Neurology*
Develop. Psychol.—*Developmental Psychology*
Dis. Nerv. Sys.—*Diseases of the Nervous System*
Fam. Hlth.—*Family Health*
Hosp. Comm. Psychiat.—*Hospital and Community Psychiatry*
Human Behav.—*Human Behavior*
Human Develop.—*Human Development*
Human Genet.—*Human Genetics*
Integr. Psychiat.—*Integrative Psychiatry*
Inter. J. Addictions—*International Journal of Addictions*
Inter. J. Psychiat.—*International Journal of Psychiatry*
Inter. J. Psychoanal.—*International Journal of Psychoanalysis*
Inter. J. Soc. Psychiat.—*International Journal of Social Psychiatry*
J. Abnorm. Child Psychol.—*Journal of Abnormal Child Psychology*
J. Abnorm. Psychol.—*Journal of Abnormal Psychology*
J. Abnorm. Soc. Psychol.—*Journal of Abnormal and Social Psychology*
JAMA—*Journal of the American Medical Association*
J. Amer. Acad. Child Psychiat.—*Journal of the American Academy of Child Psychiatry*
J. Amer. Geriat. Soc.—*Journal of the American Geriatrics Society*
J. Appl. Beh. Anal.—*Journal of Applied Behavior Analysis*
J. Autism Devel. Dis.—*Journal of Autism and Developmental Disorders*
J. Behav. Assess.—*Journal of Behavioral Assessment*
J. Behav. Med.—*Journal of Behavioral Medicine*
J. Chem. Depen. Treat.—*Journal of Chemical Dependency Treatment*
J. Child Psychol. Psychiat.—*Journal of Child Psychology and Psychiatry*
J. Clin. Psychiat.—*Journal of Clinical Psychiatry*
J. Clin. Psychopharm.—*Journal of Clinical Psychopharmacology*
J. Clin. Psychol.—*Journal of Clinical Psychology*
J. Cons. Clin. Psychol.—*Journal of Consulting and Clinical Psychology*
J. Couns. Psychol.—*Journal of Counseling Psychology*
J. Exper. Psychol.—*Journal of Experimental Psychology*
J. Gen. Psychol.—*Journal of General Psychology*
J. Learn. Dis.—*Journal of Learning Disabilities*
J. Ment. Sci.—*Journal of Mental Science*
J. Nerv. Ment. Dis.—*Journal of Nervous and Mental Diseases*
J. Pediat. Psychol.—*Journal of Pediatric Psychology*
J. Personal.—*Journal of Personality*
J. Pers. Assess.—*Journal of Personality Assessment*
J. Pers. Soc. Psychol.—*Journal of Personality and Social Psychology*
J. Psychosom. Res.—*Journal of Psychosomatic Research*
J. Speech Hear. Dis.—*Journal of Speech and Hearing Disorders*
J. Stud. Alcoh.—*Journal of Studies on Alcohol*
Ment. Hlth. Dig.—*Mental Health Digest*
Monogr. Soc. Res. Child Develop.—*Monographs of the Society for Research in Child Development*
New Engl. J. Med.—*New England Journal of Medicine*
Profess. Psychol.—*Professional Psychology*
Psychiat. Clin. N. Amer.—*Psychiatric Clinics of North America*
Psychiat. News—*Psychiatric News*
Psychiat. Res.—*Psychiatric Research*
Psychol. Bull.—*Psychological Bulletin*
Psychol. Med.—*Psychological Medicine*
Psychol. Rep.—*Psychological Reports*
Psychol. Rev.—*Psychological Review*
Psych. Today—*Psychology Today*
Psychosom. Med.—*Psychosomatic Medicine*
Schizo. Bull.—*Schizophrenia Bulletin*
Scientif. Amer.—*Scientific American*
Sci. News—*Science News*
Soc. Psychiat.—*Social Psychiatry*

Abel, G. G., Blanchard, E. B., Becker, J. V., & Djenderejian, A. (1978). Differentiating sexual aggressives with penile measures. *Crim. Just. Behav., 5,* 315–32.

Abel, G. G., & Rouleau, J.-L. (1990). The nature and extent of sexual assault. In W. L. Marshall, D. R. Laws, & H. E. Barbaree (Eds.), *Handbook of sexual assault* (pp. 9–22). New York: Plenum.

Abraham, H. D., & Wolf, E. (1988). Visual function in past users of LSD: Psychophysical findings. *J. Abnorm. Psychol., 97,* 443–47.

Abrahamson, D. J., Barlow, D. H., & Abrahamson, L. S. (1989). Differential effects of performance demand and distraction on sexually functional and dysfunctional males. *J. Abnorm. Psychol., 98,* 241–47.

Abramowitz, S. I. (1986). Psychosocial outcomes of sex reassignment surgery. *J. Cons. Clin. Psychol., 54,* 183–89.

Abrams, D. B., Emmons, K. M., Niaura, R. S., Goldstein, M. G., & Sherman, C. B. (in press). Tobacco dependence. In P. E. Nathan, J. W. Langenbucher, B. S. McCrady, and W. Frankenstein (Eds.), *The Annual Review of Addictions: Treatment and Research* (Vol. 1).

Abrams, R. (1988). *Electroconvulsive treatment: It apparently works, but how and at what risks are not yet clear.* New York: Oxford University Press.

Abrams, R., & Essman, W. B. (1982). *Electroconvulsive therapy: Biological foundations and clinical applications.* Jamaica, NY: Sp Medical and Scientific Books.

Abramson, L. Y., Seligman, M. E. P., & Teasdale, J. D. (1978). Learned helplessness in humans: Critique and reformulation. *J. Abnorm. Psychol., 87,* 49–74.

Achenbach, T. M. (1985). *Assessment and taxonomy of child and adolescent psychopathology.* Beverly Hills, CA: Sage.

Achenbach, T. M., & Edelbrock, C. S. (1983). *Manual for the child behavior checklist and revised child behavior profile.* Burlington, VT: University of Vermont.

Achenbach, T. M., & McConaughy, S. H. (1985). *Child interview checklist self—report form; Child interview checklist-observation form.* Burlington, VT: University of Vermont.

Achenbach, T. M., & Weisz, J. R. (1975). Impulsivity-reflectivity and cognitive development in preschoolers: A longitudinal analysis of developmental and trait variance. *Develop. Psychol., 11,* 413–14.
Adams, H. E., & Chiodo, J. (1984). Sexual deviations. In H. E. Adams & P. B. Sutker (Eds.), *Comprehensive handbook of psychopathology.* New York: Plenum.
Adams, H. E., & Sturgis, E. T. (1977). Status of behavioral reorientation techniques in the modification of homosexuality: A review. *Psychol. Bull., 841,* 1171–88.
Adams, M. S., & Neel, J. V. (1967). Children of incest. *Pediatrics, 40,* 55–62.
Ader, R., & Cohen, N. (1984). Behavior and the immune system. In W. D. Gentry (Ed.), *Handbook of behavioral medicine* (pp. 117–73). New York: Guilford.
Adler, A. (1943). Neuropsychiatric complications in victims of Boston's Coconut Grove disaster. *JAMA, 123,* 1098–1101.
Adler, F. (1987). Jails as a respository for former mental patients. *International Journal of Offender Therapy and Comparative Criminology, 30,* 225–36.
Agnew, J. (1985). Man's purgative passion. *Amer. J. Psychother., 39*(2), 236–46.
Agras, W. S. (1982). Behavioral medicine in the 1980's: Non-random connections. *J. Cons. Clin. Psychol., 50*(6), 820–40.
Agras, W. S., Schneider, J. A., Arnow, B., Raeburn, S. D., et al. (1989). Cognitive-behavioral and response-prevention treatments for bulimia nervosa. *J. Cons. Clin. Psychol., 57,* 215–21.
Akhtar, S. (1989). Narcissistic personality disorder: Descriptive features and differential diagnosis. *Psychiat. Clin. N. Amer., 12,* 505–30.
Akhtar, S., & Thompson, J. A. (1982). Overview: Narcissistic personality disorder. *Amer. J. Psychiat., 140,* 1013–16.
Akil, H., Watson, S., Sullivan, S., & Barchas, J. D. (1978). Enkephalin-like material in normal human cerebrospinal fluid: Measurement and levels. *Life Sciences, 23,* 121–26.
Akiskal, H. S. (1979). A biobehavioral approach to depression. In R. A. Depue (Ed.), *The psychobiology of depressive disorders: Implications for the effects of stress.* New York: Academic Press.
Akiskal, H. S., & Simmons, R. C. (1985). Chronic and refractory depressions: Evaluation and management. In E. E. Becham & W. R. Leber (Eds.), *Handbook of depression: Treatment, assessment, and research* (pp. 587–605). Homewood, IL: Dorsey Press.
Al-Issa, I. (1982). Does culture make a difference in psychopathology? In I. Al-Issa (Ed.), *Culture and psychopathology.* Baltimore: University Park Press.
Alander, R., & Campbell, T. (1975, Spring). An evaluation of an alcohol and drug recovery program: A case study of the Oldsmobile experience. *Human Resource Management,* 14–18.
Albertson's Inc. vs. Worker's Compensation Board of the State of California, 131, Cal App 3d, 182 Cal Reptr 304, 1982.
Alcohol, Drug Abuse, and Mental Health Administration. (1982). DHHS Pub. No. (ADM) 82-1190. Washington, DC: U.S. Government Printing Office.
Alden, L. (1989). Short-term structured treatment for avoidant personality disorder. *J. Cons. Clin. Psychol., 57,* 756–64.
Alden, L., & Capp, R. (1988). Characteristics predicting social functioning and treatment response in clients impaired by extreme shyness: Age of onset and the public/private shyness distinction. *Canadian Journal of Behavioural Science, 20,* 40–49.
Aldwin, C., & Revenson, T. A. (1986). Vulnerability to economic stress. *American Journal of Community Psychology, 14,* 161–75.
Alexander, A. B. (1977). Chronic asthma. In R. B. Williams, Jr., & W. D. Gentry (Eds.), *Behavioral approaches to medical treatment* (pp. 7–24). Cambridge, MA: Ballinger.
Alexander, B. (1981). Behavioral approaches to the treatment of bronchial asthma. In C. K. Prokop & L. A. Bradley (Eds.), *Medical psychology: Contributions to behavioral medicine.* New York: Academic Press.
Alexander, B. K., & Hadaway, P. F. (1982). Opiate addiction: The case for an adaptive orientation. *Psychol. Bull., 92*(2), 367–81.
Alexander, F. (1946). Individual psychotherapy. *Psychosom. Med., 8,* 110–15.
Alexander, F. (1948). *Fundamentals of psychoanalysis.* New York: Norton.
Alexander, F. (1950). *Psychosomatic medicine.* New York: Norton.
Alexander, K., Huganir, L. S., & Zigler, E. (1985). Effects of different living settings on the performance of mentally retarded individuals. *Amer. J. Ment. Def., 90,* 9–17.
Alfrey, A. C. (1986). Systemic toxicity of aluminum in man. *Neurobiology of Aging, 7,* 543–45.
Allebeck, P., & Wistedt, B. (1986). Mortality in schizophrenia: A ten-year follow-up based on the Stockholm County Inpatient register. *Arch. Gen. Psychiat., 43,* 650–53.
Allen, B., & Skinner, H. (1987). Lifestyle assessment using microcomputers. In J. N. Butcher (Ed.), *Computerized psychological assessment: A practitioner's guide.* New York: Basic Books.
Allerton, W. S. (1970). Psychiatric casualties in Vietnam. *Roche Medical Image and Commentary, 12*(8), 27.
Alterman, A. I. (1988). Patterns of familial alcoholism, alcoholism severity, and psychopathology. *J. Nerv. Ment. Dis., 176,* 167–75.
Alterman, A. I., Searles, J. S., & Hall, J. G. (1989). Failure to find differences in drinking behavior as a function of familial risk for alcoholism: A replication. *J. Cons. Clin. Psychol., 98,* 50–53.
Altshuler, K. Z. (1984). On the question of bisexuality. *Amer. J. Psychother., 38,* 484–93.
Amcoff, S. (1980). The impact of malnutrition on the learning situation. In H. M. Sinclair & G. R. Howat (Eds.), *World nutrition and nutrition education.* New York: Oxford University Press.
Amenson, C. S., & Lewinsohn, P. M. (1981). An investigation into the observed sex difference in prevalence of unipolar depression. *J. Abnorm. Psychol., 90,* 1–13.
American Association on Mental Deficiency (AAMD). (1973). *Manual on terminology and classification in mental retardation* (rev. ed.). H. J. Grossman (Ed.). Special Publication Series No. 2, 11+. Washington, DC.
American Medical Association. (1982, June 30). *The alcoholism report, 10*(17).
American Medical Association. (1986). *Drug evaluation.* 6th Edition. Chicago: Author.
American Medical Association, Department of Mental Health. (1968a). The crutch that cripples: Drug dependence, Part 1. *Today's Health, 46*(9), 11–12, 70–72.
American Psychiatric Association. (1968). *Diagnostic and statistical manual of mental disorders* (2nd ed.). Washington, DC: Author.
American Psychiatric Association. (1972). Classification of mental retardation. Supplement to the *Amer. J. Psychiat., 128*(11), 1–45.
American Psychiatric Association. (1978). Task Force on Electroconvulsive Therapy. *Report: Electroconvulsive therapy.* Washington, DC: Author.
American Psychiatric Association. (1980). *Diagnostic and statistical manual of mental disorders* (3rd ed.). Washington, DC: Author.
American Psychiatric Association. (1987). *Diagnostic and statistical manual of mental disorders* (3rd ed.—rev.). Washington, DC: Author.
American Psychological Association. (1970). Psychology and mental retardation. *Amer. Psychol., 25,* 267–68.
American Psychological Association. (1986). *Guidelines for computer-based tests and interpretations.* Washington, DC: Author.
American Psychological Association. (1990). Ethical principles for psychologists (amended June 2, 1989). *Amer. Psychol., 45,* 390–95.
Anchin, J. C., & Kiesler, D. J. (Eds.). (1982). *Handbook of interpersonal psychotherapy.* New York: Pergamon.
Andersen, B. L. (1983). Primary orgasmic dysfunction: Diagnostic considerations and review of treatment. *Psychol. Bull., 93,* 105–36.
Anderson, J. C., Williams, S., McGee, R., & Silva, P. A. (1987). DSM III disorders in preadolescent children. *Arch. Gen. Psychiat., 44,* 69–80.
Anderson, N. B., & Jackson, J. S. (1987). Race, ethnicity, and health psychology: The example of essential hypertension. In G. C. Stone (Ed.), *Health psychology: A discipline and a profession* (pp. 265–84). Chicago: University of Chicago Press.
Andrasik, F., Blanchard, E. B., Arena, J. G., Teders, S. J., Teevan, R. C., & Rodichok, L. D. (1982). Psychological functioning in headache sufferers. *Psychosom. Med., 44,* 171–82.
Andrasik, F., Holroyd, K. A., & Abell, T. (1979). Prevalence of headache within a college student population: A preliminary analysis. *Headache, 20,* 384–87.
Andreasen, N. C. (1982). Concepts, diagnosis and classification. In E. S. Paykel (Ed.), *Handbook of affective disorders.* New York: Guilford Press.

Andreasen, N. C. (1984). *The broken brain: The biological revolution in psychiatry.* New York: Harper & Row.

Andreasen, N. C. (1985). Positive vs. negative schizophrenia: A critical evaluation. *Schizophrenia, 11,* 380–89.

Andreasen, N. C., Flaum, M., Swayze, V. W., Tyrrell, G., & Arndt, S. (1990). Positive and negative symptoms in schizophrenia: A critical reappraisal. *Arch. Gen. Psychiat., 47,* 615–21.

Andreasen, N. C., Nasrallah, H. A., Dunn, V., Olson, S. C., Grove, W. M. (1986). Structural abnormalities in the frontal system in schizophrenia: A magnetic resonance imaging study. *Arch. Gen. Psychiat. 43,* 136–44.

Andreasen, N. C., Olsen, S. A., Dennert, J. W., & Smith, M. R. (1982a). Ventricular enlargement in schizophrenia: Definition and prevalence. *Amer. J. Psychiat., 139,* 292–96.

Andreasen, N. C., Olsen, S. A., Dennert, J. W., & Smith, M. R. (1982b). Ventricular enlargement in schizophrenia: Relationship to positive and negative symptoms. *Amer. J. Psychiat., 139,* 297–302.

Andrews, G., & Harvey, R. (1981). Does psychotherapy benefit neurotic patients? A reanalysis of the Smith, Glass, and Miller data. *Arch. Gen. Psychiat., 38,* 1203–8.

Andrews, J. D. W. (1989a). Integrating visions of reality: Interpersonal diagnosis and the existential vision. *Amer. Psychol., 44,* 803–17.

Andrews, J. D. W. (1989b). Psychotherapy of depression: A self-confirmation model. *Psychol. Rev., 96,* 576–607.

Angst, J. (1980). Clinical typology of bipolar illness. In R. H. Belmaker & H. M. van Praag (Eds.), *Mania: An evolving concept.* New York: Spectrum.

Anthony, E. J. (1978). Concluding comments on treatment implications. In L. C. Wynne, R. L. Cromwell, & S. Matthysse (Eds.), *The nature of schizophrenia: New approaches to research and treatment* (pp. 481–84). New York: Wiley.

Antoni, M. H., Schneiderman, N., Fletcher, M. A., & Goldstein, D. A. (1990). Psychoneuroimmunology and HIV-1. *J. Cons. Clin. Psychol., 58,* 38–49.

Apfelbaum, B. (1989). Retarded ejaculation: A much-misunderstood syndrome. In S. R. Leiblum & R. C. Rosen (Eds.), *Principles and practice of sex therapy* (2nd ed., pp. 168–206). New York: Guilford.

Apfelberg, B., Sugar, C., & Pfeffer, A. Z. (1944). A psychiatric study of 250 sex offenders. *Amer. J. Psychiat., 100,* 762–70.

Aponte, H., & Hoffman, L. (1973). The open door. A structural approach to a family with an anorectic child. *Family Process, 12,* 144.

Appelbaum, P. S. (1985). Tarasoff and the clinician: Problems in fulfilling the duty to protect. *Amer. J. Psychiat., 142*(4), 425–29.

Arana, G. W., Baldessarini, R. J., & Ornsteen, M. (1985). The dexamethasone suppression test for diagnosis and prognosis in psychiatry: Commentary and review. *Arch. Gen. Psychiat. 42,* 1193–1204.

Arbitman-Smith, R., Haywood, H. C., & Bransford, J. D. (1984). Assessing cognitive change. In P. Brooks, C. M. Sperber, & R. McCauley (Eds.), *Learning and cognition in the mentally retarded* (pp. 433–72). Hillsdale, NJ: Erlbaum.

Archer, J. and Gruenberg, E. (1982). The chronically mentally disabled and "deinstitutionalized." *Annual Review of Public Health, 3,* 445–68.

Archibald, H. C., & Tuddenham, R. D. (1965). Persistent stress reaction after combat. *Arch. Gen Psychiat., 12*(5), 475–81.

Arieti, S. (1974). An overview of schizophrenia from a predominantly psychological approach. *Amer. J. Psychiat., 131*(3), 241–49.

Arieti, S. (1982). Individual psychotherapy. In E. S. Paykel (Ed.), *Handbook of affective disorders.* New York: Guilford Press.

Arieti, S., & Bemporad, J. R. (1980). The psychological organization of depression. *Amer. J. Psychiat., 237,* 1360–65.

Aring, C. D. (1974). The Gheel experience: Eternal spirit of the chainless mind! *JAMA, 230*(7), 998–1001.

Aring, C. D., (1975a). Gheel: The town that cares. *Fam. Hlth., 7*(4), 54–55, 58, 60.

Aring, C. D., (1975b). Science and the citizen. *Scientif. Amer., 232*(1), 48–49; 52–53.

Arkowitz, H., & Messer, S. B. (Eds.) (1984). *Psychoanalytic and behavior therapy. Is integration possible?* New York: Plenum.

Arnkoff, D. B., & Glass, C. R. (1982). Clinical cognitive constructs: Examination, evaluation, and elaboration. In P. C. Kendall (Ed.), *Advances in cognitive-behavioral research and therapy* (Vol. 1, pp. 2–30). New York: Academic Press.

Arnold, L. E. (1978). *Helping parents help their children.* New York: Brunner/Mazel.

Arnold, M. B. (1962). *Story sequence analysis: A new method of measuring motivation and predicting achievement.* New York: Columbia University Press.

Aronoff, B. (1987). *Needs assessments: What have we learned. Experiences from Refugee Assistance Programs in Hawaii.* Paper given at the Refugee Assistance Program: Mental Health Workgroup Meeting, UCLA, February 12–13.

Atkeson, B. M., Calhoun, K. S., Resick, P. A., & Ellis, E. M. (1982). Victims of rape: Repeated assessment of depressive symptoms. *J. Cons. Clin. Psychol., 50,* 96–102.

Atkeson, B. M., & Forehand, R. (1978). Parent behavior training for problem children: An examination of studies using multiple outcome measures. *J. Abnorm. Child Psychol., 6,* 449–60.

Atkinson, J. W. (Ed.). (1958). *Motives in fantasy, action, and society.* Princeton, NJ: Van Nostrand.

Auerbach, S. M., & Stolberg, A. L. (1986). *Crisis intervention with children and families.* New York: Hemisphere Press.

Averill, J. R. (1973). Personal control over aversive stimuli and its relationship to stress. *Psychol. Bull., 80*(4), 286–303.

Avery, D., & Winoker, G. (1976). Mortality in depressed patients treated with electroconvulsive therapy and antidepressants. *Arch. Gen. Psychiat., 33,* 1619–37.

Ayllon, T., & Azrin, N. H. (1968). *The token economy: A motivational system for therapy and rehabilitation.* New York: Appleton-Century-Crofts.

Bachrach, L. L. (1976). *Deinstitutionalization: An analytic review and sociological perspective.* U.S. Department of Health, Education, and Welfare. National Institute of Mental Health, Washington, DC: U.S. Government Printing Office.

Bachrach, L. L. (1980). Overview: Model programs for chronic patients. *Amer. J. Psychiat., 132,* 1023–31.

Bagley, C. (1969). Incest behavior and incest taboo. *Social Problems, 16*(4), 505–19.

Bagley, C. (1973). Occupational class and symptoms of depression. *Social Science and Medicine, 7*(5), 327–40.

Baker, L., & Lyen, K. R. (1982). Anorexia nervosa. In M. Winick (Ed.), *Adolescent nutrition.* New York: Oxford University Press.

Baker, L. A., & Daniels, D. (1990). Nonshared environmental influences and personality differences in adult twins. *J. Pers. Soc. Psychol., 58,* 103–10.

Bales, R. F. (1946). Cultural differences in rates of alcoholism. *Quarterly Journal of Studies in Alcoholism, 6,* 480–99.

Ballenger, J. C. (1988). The clinical use of carbamazepine in affective disorders. *J. Clin. Psychiat., 49,* 13–19.

Balogh, D. W., & Merritt, R. D. (1987). Visual masking and the schizophrenia spectrum: Interfacing clinical and experimental methods. *Schizo. Bull., 13,* 679–98.

Bandura, A. (1964). *Principles of behavior modification.* New York: Holt, Rinehart & Winston.

Bandura, A. (1969). *Principles of behavior modification.* New York: Holt, Rinehart & Winston.

Bandura, A. (1973). *Aggression: A social learning analysis.* Englewood Cliffs, NJ: Prentice-Hall.

Bandura, A. (1974). Behavior theory and the models of man. *Amer. Psychol., 29*(12), 859–69.

Bandura, A. (1977a). Self-efficacy: Toward a unifying theory of behavioral change. *Psychol. Rev., 84*(2), 191–215.

Bandura, A. (1977b). *Social learning theory.* Englewood Cliffs, NJ: Prentice-Hall.

Bandura, A., & Walters, R. H. (1963). *Social learning and personality development.* New York: Holt, Rinehart & Winston.

Bannister, D. (1971). Schizophrenia: Carnival mirror of coherence. *Psych. Today, 4*(8), 66–69, 84.

Bannister, G., Jr. (1975). Cognitive and behavior therapy in a case of compulsive gambling. *Cog. Ther. Res., 1,* 223–27.

Barahal, R. M., Waterman, J., & Martin, H. P. (1981). The social cognitive development of abused children. *J. Cons. Clin. Psychol., 49*(4), 508–16.

Barbaree, H. E. (1990). Stimulus control of sexual arousal: Its role in sexual assault. In W. L. Marshall, D. R. Laws, & H. E. Barbaree (Eds.), *Handbook of sexual assault* (pp. 115–42). New York: Plenum.

Barber, T. X. (1969). *Hypnosis: A scientific approach.* New York: Van Nostrand Reinhold.

Barchas, J., Akil, H., Elliott, G., Holman, R., & Watson, S. (1978, May 26). Behavioral neurochemistry: Neuroregulators and behavioral states. *Science, 200,* 964–73.

Barkley, R. A., & Cunningham, C. E. (1979). The effects of methylphenidate on the mother-child interaction of hyperactive children. *Arch. Gen. Psychiat., 36,* 201–11.

Barlow, D. H. (1974). The treatment of sexual deviation:

Toward a comprehensive behavioral approach. In K. S. Calhoun, H. E. Adams, & K. M. Mitchell (Eds.), *Innovative treatment methods in psychopathology.* New York: Wiley Interscience Series.

Barlow, D. H. (1986). Causes of sexual dysfunction: The role of anxiety and cognitive interference. *J. Cons. Clin. Psychol., 54,* 140–48.

Barlow, D. H. (1988). *Anxiety and its disorders: The nature and treatment of anxiety and panic.* New York: Guilford.

Barlow, D. H., & Abel, G. G. (1976). Sexual deviation. In W. E. Craighead, A. E. Kazdin, & M. J. Mahoney (Eds.), *Behavior modification: Principles, issues, and applications.* Boston: Houghton Mifflin.

Barlow, D. H., & Cerny, J. A. (1988). *Psychological treatment of panic.* New York: Guilford.

Barlow, D. H., Craske, M. G., Cerny, J. A., & Klosko, J. S. (1989). Behavioral treatment of panic disorder. *Behav. Ther., 20,* 261–82.

Barlow, D. H., Vermilyea, J., Blanchard, E. B., Vermilyea, B. B., & Di Nardo, P. A. (1985). The phenomenon of panic. *J. Abnorm. Psychol., 94,* 320–28.

Barlow, D. H., & Waddell, M. T. (1985). Agoraphobia. In D. H. Barlow (Ed.), *Clinical handbook of psychological disorders* (pp. 1–68). New York: Guilford.

Barnes, D. M. (1987). Defect of Alzheimer's is on chromosome 21. *Science, 253,* 846–47.

Barnes, G. E., & Prosen, H. (1985). Parental death and depression. *J. Abnorm. Psychol., 94,* 64–69.

Barry, H., III. (1982). Cultural variations in alcohol abuse. In I. Al-Issa (Ed.), *Culture and psychopathology.* Baltimore: University Park Press.

Bartak, L. (1978). Educational approaches. In M. Rutter & E. Schopler (Eds.), *Autism: A reappraisal of concepts and treatment.* New York: Plenum.

Bartak, L., & Rutter, M. (1973). Special education treatment of autistic children: A comparative study, I. *J. Child Psychol. Psychiat., 14,* 161–79.

Bartak, L., & Rutter, M. (1976). Differences between mentally retarded and normally intelligent autistic children. *Journal of Autism and Childhood Schizophrenia, 6,* 109–20.

Bartone, P. T., Ursano, R. J., Wright, K. M., & Ingraham, L. H. (1989). The impact of air disaster on the health of assistance workers. *J. Nerv. Ment. Dis., 177,* 317–27.

Bassuk, E. L., & Gerson, S. (1978). Deinstitutionalization and mental health services. *Scientif. Amer., 238*(2), 46–53.

Bassuk, E. L., Schoonover, S. C., & Gelenberg, A. J. (1983). *The practitioner's guide to psychiatric drugs* (2nd ed.). New York: Plenum.

Bates, C. M., & Brodsky, A. M. (1989). *Sex in the therapy hour: A case of professional incest.* New York: Guilford.

Bateson, G. (1959). Cultural problems posed by a study of schizophrenic process. In A. Auerback (Ed.), *Schizophrenia: An integrated approach.* New York: Ronald Press.

Bateson, G. (1960). Minimal requirements for a theory of schizophrenia. *Arch. Gen. Psychiat., 2,* 477–91.

Baucom, D. H. (1983). Sex role identity and the decision to regain control among women: A learned helplessness investigation. *J. Pers. Soc. Psychol., 44,* 334–43.

Bauer, A. M., & Shea, T. M. (1986). Alzheimer's disease and Down syndrome: A review and implications for adult services. *Education and Training of the Mentally Retarded, 21,* 144–50.

Baum, A., Gatchel, R. J., & Schaeffer, M. A. (1983). Emotional, behavioral, and physiological effects of chronic stress at Three Mile Island. *J. Cons. Clin. Psychol., 51,* 565–72.

Baumeister, R. F. (1990). Suicide as escape from self. *Psychol. Rev., 97,* 90–113.

Baumrind, D. (1971). Current patterns of parental authority. *Develop. Psychol., 4*(1), 1–103.

Baumrind, D. (1975). *Early socialization and the discipline controversy.* Morristown, NJ: General Learning Press.

Baxter, L. R., Jr., Phelps, M. E., Mazziotta, J. C., Schwartz, J. M., & Gerner, R. H. (1985). Cerebral metabolic rates for glucose in mood disorders: Studies with positron emission tomography and fluorodeoxyglucose F18. *Arch. Gen. Psychiat., 42,* 441–47.

Bayer, R., & Spitzer, R. L. (1985). Neurosis, psychodynamics, and DSM-III: A history of the controversy. *Arch. Gen. Psychiat., 42,* 187–96.

Bazell, R. J. (1973, Feb. 23). Drug abuse: Methadone becomes the solution and the problem. *Science, 179*(4975), 772–75.

Beardslee, W. R., Bemporad, J., Keller, M. B., & Klerman, G. L. (1983). Children of parents with major affective disorder: A review. *Amer. J. Psychiat., 140,* 825–32.

Beck, A. T. (1967). *Depression: Causes and treatment.* Philadelphia: University of Pennsylvania Press.

Beck, A. T. (1985). Theoretical perspectives on clinical anxiety. In A. H. Tuma & J. D. Maser (Eds.), *Anxiety and the anxiety disorders* (pp. 183–98). Hillsdale, NJ: Lawrence Erlbaum Press.

Beck, A. T., Beck, R., & Kovacs, M. (1975). Classification of suicidal behaviors: I. Qualifying intent and medical lethality. *Amer. J. Psychiat., 132*(3), 285–87.

Beck, A. T., Brown, G., & Steer, R. A. (1989). Prediction of eventual suicide in psychiatric inpatients by clinical ratings of hopelessness. *J. Cons. Clin. Psychol., 57,* 309–10.

Beck, A. T., & Emery, G., (with) Greenberg, R. L. (1985). *Anxiety disorders and phobias: A cognitive perspective.* New York: Basic Books.

Beck, A. T., Hollon, S. D., Young, J. E., Bedrosian, R. C., & Budenz, D. (1985). Treatment of depression with cognitive therapy and amitriptyline. *Arch. Gen. Psychiat., 42,* 142–48.

Beck, A. T., Laude, R., & Bohnert, M. (1974). Ideational components of anxiety neurosis. *Arch. Gen. Psychiat., 31*(3), 319–25.

Beck, A. T., Rush, A. J., Shaw, B., & Emery, G. (1979). *Cognitive therapy of depression: A treatment manual.* New York: Guilford Press.

Beck, A. T., & Weishaar, M. (1989). Cognitive therapy. In A. Freeman, K. M. Simon, L. E. Beutler, & H. Arkowitz (Eds.), *Comprehensive handbook of cognitive therapy* (pp. 21–36). New York: Plenum.

Beck, J. G., & Barlow, D. H. (1984). Current conceptualizations of sexual dysfunction: A review and an alternative perspective. *Clin. Psychol. Rev., 4,* 363–78.

Beck, L., Langford, W. S., Mackay, M., & Sum, G. (1975). Childhood chemotherapy and later drug abuse and growth curve: A follow-up study of 30 adolescents. *Amer. J. Psychiat., 132*(4), 436–38.

Becker, J. V., Hunter, J. A., Jr., Stein, R. M., & Kaplan, M. S. (1989). Factors associated with erection in adolescent sex offenders. *Journal of Psychopathology and Behavioral Assessment, 11,* 353–64.

Becker, W. C. (1964). Consequences of different kinds of parental discipline. In M. L. Hoffman & L. W. Hoffman (Eds.), *Review of child development research* (Vol. 1). New York: Russell Sage Foundation.

Beckham, E. E., & Leber, W. R. (1985a). The comparative efficacy of psychotherapy and pharmacotherapy for depression. In E. E. Beckham & W. R. Leber (Eds.), *Handbook of depression: Treatment, assessment, and research* (pp. 316–42). Homewood, IL: Dorsey.

Beckham, E. E., & Leber, W. R. (Eds.). (1985b). *Handbook of depression: Treatment, assessment, and research.* Homewood, IL: Dorsey Press.

Beech, H. R., Burns, L. E., & Sheffield, B. F. (1982). *A behavioral approach to the management of stress.* New York: John Wiley & Sons.

Beers, C. (1970). *A mind that found itself* (rev. ed.) New York: Doubleday.

Behar, D., & Stewart, M. A. (1982). Aggressive conduct disorder of children. *Acta Psychiatr. Scandin., 65*(3), 210–20.

Belgian Consulate. (1990). Washington, DC. Personal communication.

Bell, A. O. (1974). Homosexualities: Their range and character. In J. K. Cole & E. Dienstbier (Eds.), *Nebraska symposium on motivation, 1973* (pp. 1–26). Lincoln, NE: University of Nebraska Press.

Bell, A. P., & Weinberg, M. S. (1978). *Homosexualities: A study of diversity among men and women.* New York: Simon & Schuster.

Bell, A. P., Weinberg, M. S., & Hammersmith, S. K. (1981). *Sexual preference: Its development in men and women.* Bloomington, IN: Indiana University Press.

Bell, E., Jr. (1958). The basis of effective military psychiatry. *Dis. Nerv. Sys., 19,* 283–88.

Bellak, L. (1975). *The Thematic Apperception Test, the Children's Apperception Test, and the Senior Apperception Technique in clinical use* (3rd ed.). New York: Grune & Stratton.

Bellak, L. (1979). Introduction: An idiosyncratic overview. In L. Bellak (Ed.), *Disorders of the schizophrenic syndrome.* New York: Basic Books.

Bellman, M. (1966). Studies on encopresis. *Acta Paediatrica Scandanovica Suppl., 170,* 121.

Belsky, J., & Steinberg, L. D. (1978). The effects of day care: A critical review. *Child Develop., 49,* 929–49.

Bem, D. J. (1972). Self-perception theory. In L. Berkowitz (Ed.), *Advances in experimental social psychology* (Vol. 6). New

York: Academic Press.
Bemis, K. M. (1978). Current approaches to the etiology and treatment of anorexia nervosa. *Psychol. Bull., 85,* 593–617.
Ben-Porath, Y. S., & Butcher, J. N. (1989). The comparability of MMPI and MMPI-2 scales and profiles. *Psychological Assessment: A Journal of Consulting and Clinical Psychology, 1,* 345–47.
Bender, L. (1973). The life course of children with schizophrenia. *Amer. J. Psychiat., 130*(7), 783–86.
Benedict, R. (1934). Anthropology and the abnormal. *J. Gen. Psychol., 10,* 59–82.
Bengelsdorf, I. S. (1970, Mar. 5). Alcohol, morphine addictions believed chemically similar. *Los Angeles Times,* II, 7.
Benjamin, H. (1966). *The transsexual phenomenon.* New York: Julian Press.
Benjamin, L. S. (1974). Structural analysis of social behavior. *Psychol. Rev., 81,* 392–425.
Benjamin, L. S. (1976). A reconsideration of the Kety and associates study of genetic factors in the transmission of schizophrenia. *Amer. J. Psychiat., 133,* 1129–33.
Benjamin, L. S. (1982). Use of structural analysis of social behavior (SASB) to guide intervention in psychotherapy. In J. C. Anchin & D. L. Kiesler (Eds.), *Handbook of interpersonal psychotherapy.* New York: Pergamon.
Benkelfat, C., Murphy, D. L., Zohar, J., Hill, J. L ., Grover, G., & Insel, T. R. (1989). Clomipramine in obsessive-compulsive disorder: Further evidence for a serotonergic mechanism of action. *Arch. Gen. Psychiat., 46,* 23–28.
Bennett, A. E. (1947). Mad doctors. *J. Nerv. Ment. Dis., 106,* 11–18.
Bentler, P. M., & Prince, C. (1969). Personality characteristics of male transvestites. III. *J. Abnorm. Psychol., 74*(2), 140–43.
Bentler, P. M., & Prince, C. (1970). Psychiatric symptomology in transvestites. *J. Clin. Psychol., 26*(4), 434–35.
Bentler, P. M., Shearman, R. W., & Prince, C. (1970). Personality characteristics of male transvestites. *J. Clin. Psychol., 126*(3), 287–91.
Bentovim, A., Boston, P., & Van Elburg, A. (1987). Child sexual abuse—children and families referred to a treatment project and the effects of intervention. *Brit. Med. J., 295,* 1453–57.
Beres, D., & Obers, S. J. (1950). The effects of extreme deprivation in infancy on psychic structure in adolescence. In R. S. Eissler et al. (Eds.), *The psychoanalytic study of the child* (Vol. 5). New York: International Universities Press.
Berg, A. (1954). *The sadist* (O. Illner & G. Godwin, Trans.). New York: Medical Press of New York.
Bergen, J. A., Eyland, E. A., Campbell, J. A., Jenkins, P., Kellehear, K., Richards, A., & Beumont, P.J.V. (1989). The course of tardive dyskinesia in patients on long-term neuroleptics. *Brit. J. Psychiat., 154,* 523–28.
Berger, P. A. (1978). Medical treatment of mental illness. *Science, 200,* 974–81.
Berger, R. J. (1970). Morpheus descending. *Psych. Today, 4*(1), 33–36.
Bergin, A. E., & Lambert, M. J. (1978). The evaluation of therapeutic outcomes. In S. L. Garfield & A. E. Bergin (Eds.), *Handbook of psychotherapy and behavior change* (2nd ed.). New York: Wiley.
Bergler, E. (1947). Analysis of an unusual case of fetishism. *Bull. Menninger Clin. 2,* 67–75.
Bergsma, D. (Ed.). (1974). *Medical genetics today* (National Foundation Series). Baltimore: Johns Hopkins University Press.
Bernard, J. L. (1979). Reply to Siegal. *Amer. Psychol., 34*(3), 280–82.
Bernhardt, B., Meertz, E., & Schonfeldt-Bausch, P. (1985). Basal ganglia and limbic system pathology in schizophrenia: A morphometric study of brain volume and shrinkage. *Arch. Gen. Psychiat., 42,* 784–91.
Bettelheim, B. (1959, Mar.). Joey: A "mechanical boy." *Scientif. Amer., 200,* 116–27.
Bettelheim, B. (1967). *The empty fortress.* New York: Free Press.
Bettelheim, B. (1969). Laurie. *Psych. Today, 2*(12), 24–25, 60.
Bettelheim, B. (1974). *A home for the heart.* New York: Alfred A. Knopf.
Beveridge, A. W., & Renvoize, E. B. (1988). Electricity: A history of its use in the treatment of mental illness in Britain during the second half of the 19th Century. *Brit. J. Psychiat., 153,* 157–62.
Bibring, E. (1953). The mechanism of depression. In P. Greenacre (Ed.), *Affective disorders.* New York: International Universities Press.
Bijou, S. W. (1966). A functional analysis of retarded development. In N. R. Ellis (Ed.), *International review of research in mental retardation* (Vol. 1). New York: Academic Press.
Biklen, D. (1976). Advocacy comes of age. *Exceptional Children, 42,* 308–13.
Billings, A. G., Cronkite, R. C., & Moos, R. H. (1983). Social-environmental factors in unipolar depression: Comparisons of depressed patients and nondepressed controls. *J. Abnorm. Psychol., 92,* 119–33.
Binder, R. L. & McNiel, D. E. (1988). Effects of diagnosis and context of dangerousness. *Amer. J. Psychiat., 145,* 788–92.
Binswanger, L. (1942). *Grundformen und Erkenntnis Menschlichen Daseing.* Zurich: Max Nichans.
Bird, T. D. (1986). Problems and limitations in studying a genetic component of Alzheimer's disease. *Neurobiology of Aging, 7,* 477–78.
Birkhimer, L. J., Curtis, J. L., & Jann, M. W. (1985). Use of carbamazepine in psychiatric disorders. *Clinical Pharmacy, 4,* 425–34.
Birns, B., & Bridger, W. (1977). Cognitive development and social class. In J. Wortis (Ed.), *Mental retardation and developmental disabilities* (Vol. 9, pp. 203–33). New York: Brunner/Mazel.
Bisnaire, L. M., Firestone, P., & Rynard, D. (1990). Factors associated with academic achievement in children following parental separation. *Amer. J. Orthopsychiat., 60,* 67–76.
Black, D. W., Warrack, G., & Winokur, G. (1985). The Iowa Record-Linkage Study: I. Suicides and accidental deaths among psychiatric patients. *Arch. Gen. Psychiat., 42,* 71–75.
Black, D. W., Winoker, G., Bell, S., Nasrallah, A., & Hulbert, J. (1988). Complicated mania: Comorbidity and immediate outcome in the treatment of mania. *Arch. Gen. Psychiat., 45,* 232–36.
Black, D. W., Yates, W., Petty, F., Noyes, R., & Brown, K. (1986). Suicidal behavior in alcoholic males. *Compr. Psychiat., 27*(3), 227–33.
Blackburn, I. M., Bishop, S., Glen, A. I. M., Whalley, L. J., & Christie, J. E. (1981). The efficacy of cognitive therapy in depression: A treatment trial using cognitive therapy and pharmacotherapy, each alone and in combination. *Brit. J. Psychiat., 139,* 181–89.
Blair, C. D., & Lanyon, R. I. (1981). Exhibitionism: Etiology and treatment. *Psychol. Bull., 89,* 439–63.
Blanchard, E. B., & Andrasik, F. (1982). Psychological assessment and treatment of headache: Recent developments and emerging issues. *J. Cons. Clin. Psychol., 50*(6), 859–79.
Blanchard, E. B., Andrasik, F., Ahles, T. A., Teders, S. J., & O'Keefe, D. (1980). Migraine and tension headache: A metaanalytic review. *Behav. Ther., 11,* 613–31.
Blanchard, E. B., Andrasik, F., Neff, D. F., Saunders, N. L., Arena, J. G., Pallmeyer, T. P., Teders, S. J., & Jurish, S. G. (1983). Four process studies in the behavioral treatment of chronic headache. *Behav. Res. Ther., 21,* 209–20.
Blanchard, E. B., Andrasik, F., Neff, D. F., Teders, S. J., Pallmeyer, T. P., Arena, J. G., Jurish, S. E., Saunders, N. L., & Rodichok, L. D. (1983). Sequential comparisons of relaxation training and biofeedback in the treatment of three kinds of chronic headache or, The machines may be necessary some of the time. *Behav. Res. Ther.*
Blanchard, E. B., Appelbaum, K. A., Radnitz, C. L., Michultka, D., Morrill, B., Kirsch, C., Hillhouse, J., Evans, D. D., Guarnieri, P., Attanasio, V., & Andrasik, F. et al. (1990a). Placebo-controlled evaluation of abbreviated progressive muscle relaxation and of relaxation combined with cognitive therapy in the treatment of tension headache. *J. Cons. Clin. Psychol., 58,* 210–15.
Blanchard, E. B., Appelbaum, K. A., Radnitz, C. L. et al. (1990b). A controlled evaluation of thermal biofeedback and thermal biofeedback combined with cognitive therapy in the treatment of vascular headache. *J. Cons. Clin. Psychol., 58,* 216–24.
Blanchard, E. B., & Epstein, L. H. (1978). *A biofeedback primer.* Reading, MA: Addison-Wesley.
Blanchard, E. B., Miller, S. T., Abel G. G., Haynes, M. R., & Wicker, R. (1979). Evaluation of biofeedback in treatment of borderline essential hypertension. *J. Appl. Beh. Anal., 12,* 99–109.
Blanchard, E. B., & Young, L. D. (1973). Self-control of cardiac functioning: A promise as yet unfulfilled. *Psychol. Bull., 79,* 145–63.
Blanchard, E. B., & Young, L. D. (1974). Clinical applications of biofeedback training: A review of evidence. *Arch. Gen. Psychiat., 30,* 573–89.
Blanchard, R., Steiner, B. W., & Clemmensen, L. H. (1985).

Gender dysphoria, gender reorientation, and the clinical management of transsexualism. *J. Cons. Clin. Psychol., 53,* 295–304.

Blashfield, R. K., & Breen, M. J. (1989). Face validity of the DSM III-R personality disorders. *Amer. J. Psychiat., 146,* 1575–79.

Blaszczynski, A., McConaghy, N., & Frankova, A. (1989). Crime, antisocial personality and pathological gambling. *Journal of Gambling Behavior, 5,* 137–52.

Blatt, S. J., D'Afflitti, J. P., & Quinlan, D. M. (1976). Experiences of depression in normal young adults. *J. Abnorm. Psychol., 85,* 383–89.

Blatt, S. J., Quinlan, D. M., Chevron, E. S., McDonald, C., & Zuroff, D. (1982). Dependency and self-criticism: Psychological dimensions of depression. *J. Cons. Clin. Psychol., 50,* 113–24.

Blau, A., Slaff, B., Easton, K., Welkowitz, J., Springarn, J., & Cohen, J. (1963). The psychogenic etiology of premature births. *Psychosom. Med., 25,* 201–11.

Blazer, D., Crowell, B. A., & George, L. K. (1987). Alcohol abuse and dependence in the rural south. *Arch. Gen. Psychiat., 44,* 736–40.

Blazer, D., George, L. K., Landerman, R., Pennybacker, M., & Melville, M. L. (1985). Psychiatric disorders: A rural/urban comparison. *Arch. Gen. Psychiat., 42,* 651–56.

Bleeker, E. (1968). Many asthma attacks psychological. *Sci. News, 93*(17), 406.

Blehar, M. C., & Rosenthal, N. E. (1989). Seasonal affective disorders and phototherapy: Report of a National Institute of Mental Health-sponsored workshop. *Arch. Gen. Psychiat., 46,* 469–74.

Bleuler, E. (1950). *Dementia praecox or the group of schizophrenias.* New York: International Universities Press. (Originally published in 1911.)

Bleuler, M. (1978). The long-term course of schizophrenic psychoses. In L. C. Wynne, R. L. Cromwell, & S. Matthysse (Eds.), *The nature of schizophrenia: New approaches to research and treatment* (pp. 631–36). New York: Wiley.

Bloch, H. S. (1969). Army clinical psychiatry in the combat zone—1967–1968. *Amer. J. Psychiat., 126,* 289.

Bloom, B. L., Asher, S. J., & White, S. W. (1978). Marital disruption as a stressor: A review and analysis. *Psychol. Bull., 85,* 867–94.

Bloom, F. E. (1983). Endogeneous opiods: Histochemistry, neurophysiology, and pharmacology, *Psychiat. Clin. N. Amer., 9,* 365–76.

The Bloomington Sun Current (1986, June 16). TV news anchor tells story of recovery from alcoholism.

Blount, R. L., Dahlquist, L. M., Baer, R. A., & Wuori, D. (1984). A brief, effective method for teaching children to swallow pills. *Behav. Ther., 15,* 381–87.

Blum, R. (1969). *Society and drugs* (Vol. 1). San Francisco: Jossey-Bass.

Blumenthal, S. J. (1990). Youth suicide: Risk factors, assessment, and treatment of adolescent and young adult suicidal patients. *Psychiat. Clin. N. Amer., 13,* 511–56.

Blumer, D., & Benson, D. F. (1975). Personality changes with frontal and temporal lobe lesions. In D. F. Benson & D. Blumer (Eds.), *Psychiatric aspects of neurological disease* (pp. 151–70). New York: Grune & Stratton.

Bockhoven, J. S. (1972). *Moral treatment in community mental health.* New York: Springer.

Boehm, G. (1968). At last—a nonaddicting substitute for morphine? *Today's Health, 46*(4), 69–72.

Bolen, D. W., & Boyd, W. H. (1968). Gambling and the gambler. *Arch. Gen. Psychiatr., 18*(5), 617–30.

Bolen, D. W., Caldwell, A. B., & Boyd, W. H. (1975, June). *Personality traits of pathological gamblers.* Paper presented at the Second Annual Conference on Gambling, Lake Tahoe, NV.

Bolger, N. (1990). Coping as a personality process: A prospective study. *J. Pers. Soc. Psychol., 59,* 525–37.

Boll, T. J. (1978). Diagnosing brain impairment. In B. B. Wolman, (Ed.), *Clinical diagnosis of mental disorders: A handbook.* New York: Plenum.

Boll, T. J. (1980). The Halstead-Reitan neuropsychological battery. In S. B. Filskov & T. J. Boll (Eds.), *Handbook of neurophysiology.* New York: Wiley Interscience Series.

Bolls, R. C., & Fanselow, M. S. (1982). Endorphins and behavior. *Annu. Rev. Psychol., 33,* 87–101.

Bolton, A. (1976). *A study of the need for and availability of mental health services for mentally disordered jail inmates and juveniles in detention facilities.* Boston: Arthur Bolton Associates.

Bolton, P., Rutter, M., Butler, L., & Summers, D. (1989). Females with autism and the fragile X. *J. Autism Devel. Dis., 19,* 473–76.

Booth-Kewley, S., & Friedman, H. S. (1987). Psychological predictors of heart disease: A quantitative review. *Psychol. Bull., 101,* 343–62.

Borg, W. R., & Ascione, F. R. (1982). Classroom management in elementary mainstreaming classrooms. *J. Educ. Psychol., 74,* 84–95.

Borkovec, T. D. (1970). Autonomic reactivity to sensory stimulation in psychopathic, neurotic, and normal juvenile delinquents. *J. Cons. Clin. Psychol., 35,* 217–22.

Borkovec, T. D. (1985). The role of cognitive and somatic cues in anxiety and anxiety disorders: Worry and relation-induced anxiety. In A. H. Tuma & J. D. Maser (Eds.), *Anxiety and the anxiety disorders* (pp. 463–78). Hillsdale, NJ: Lawrence Erlbaum.

Boronow, J., Pickar, D., Ninan, P. T., Roy, A., & Hommer, D. (1985). Atrophy limited to the third ventricle in chronic schizophrenic patients: Report of a controlled series. *Arch. Gen. Psychiat., 42,* 266–71.

Borus, J. F. (1974). Incidence maladjustment in Vietnam returnees. *Arch. Gen. Psychiat., 30*(4), 554–57.

Boskind-White, M., & White, W. C. (1983). *Bulimarexia: The binge-purge cycle.* New York: W. W. Norton.

Boskind-White, M., & White, W. C. (1986). Bulimarexia: A historical-sociocultural perspective. In K. D. Brownell & J. P. Foreyt (Eds.), *Handbook of eating disorders* (pp. 353–66). New York: Basic Books.

Botvin, G. J. (1983). Prevention of adolescent substance abuse through the development of personal and social competence. *National Institute on Drug Abuse Research Monograph Series, 47,* 115–40.

Botvin, G. J., Baker, E., Dusenbury, L., Tortu, S., & Botvin, E. M. (1990). Preventing adolescent drug abuse through a multimodal cognitive-behavioral approach: Results of a 3 year study. *J. Cons. Clin. Psychol., 58,* 437–57.

Botvin, G. J., & Tortu, S. (1988). Preventing substance abuse through life skills training. In R. H. Price, E. L. Cowen, R. P. Lorion, & J. Ramos-McKay (Eds.), *14 ounces of prevention.* Washington, DC: American Psychological Association.

Bouchard, T. J., Lykken, D. T., McGue, M., Segal, N., & Tellegen, A. (1990). Sources of human psychological differences: The Minnesota Study of Twins Reared Apart. *Science, 250,* 223–28.

Boucher, J. (1981). Memory for recent events in autistic children. *J. Autism Devel. Dis., 11*(3), 293–301.

Bourne, P. G. (1970). Military psychiatry and the Vietnam experience. *Amer. J. Psychiat., 127*(4), 481–88.

Bowen, M. (1978). *Family therapy in clinical practice.* New York: Aronson.

Bowlby, J. (1960). Separation anxiety. *Inter. J. Psychoanal., 41,* 89–93.

Bowlby, J. (1973). Separation: Anxiety and anger. *Psychology of attachment and loss series* (Vol. 3). New York: Basic Books.

Boyd, J. H., & Weissman, M. M. (1982). Epidemiology. In E. S. Paykel (Ed.), *Handbook of affective disorders.* New York: Guilford Press.

Boyd, W. H., & Bolen, D. W. (1970). The compulsive gambler and spouse in group psychotherapy. *International Journal of Group Psychotherapy, 20,* 77–90.

Bradley, L. A., & Prokop, C. K. (1981). The relationship between medical psychology and behavioral medicine. In C. K. Prokop & L. A. Bradley (Eds.), *Medical psychology: Contributions to behavioral medicine.* New York: Academic Press.

Bradley, L. A., & Prokop, C. K. (1982). Research methods in contemporary medical psychology. In P. C. Kendall & J. N. Butcher (Eds.), *Handbook of research methods in clinical psychology.* New York: Wiley Interscience.

Braff, D. L., Silverton, L., Sacuzzo, D. P., & Janowsky, D. S. (1981). Impaired speed of visual information processing in marijuana intoxication. *Amer. J. Psychiat., 138*(5), 613–17.

Braginsky, B. M., & Braginsky, D. D. (1974). The mentally retarded: Society's Hansels and Gretels. *Psych. Today, 7*(10), 18, 20–21, 24, 26, 28–30.

Braginsky, B. M., Braginsky, D. D., & Ring, K. (1969). *Methods of madness: The mental hospital as a last resort.* New York: Holt, Rinehart & Winston.

Brandel, S. K. (1980). Refugees: New dimensions to an old problem. *Communique.* Washington, DC: Overseas Development Council.

Brandsma, J. M., Maultsby, M. C., & Welsh, R. J. (1980).

Outpatient treatment of alcoholism: A review and comparative study. Baltimore: University Park Press.

Brane, G. (1986). Normal aging and dementia disorders: Coping and crisis in the family. *Progress in Neuro-Psychopharmacology & Biological Psychiatry, 10,* 287–95.

Brantley, P., & Sutker, P. B. (1984). Antisocial personalities. In P. Sutker & H. Adams (Eds.), *Comprehensive handbook of psychopathology.* New York: Plenum.

Braun, P., Kochansky, G., Shapiro, R., Greenberg, S., Gudeman, J. E., Johnson, S., & Shore, M. (1981). Overview: Deinstitutionalization of psychiatric patients, a critical review of outcome studies. *Amer. J. Psychiat., 138*(6), 736–49.

Brayfield, A. H. et al. (1965). Special Issue: Testing and public policy. *Amer. Psychol., 20,* 857–1005.

Brebner, A., Hallworth, H. J., & Brown, R. I. (1977). Computer-assisted instruction programs and terminals for the mentally retarded. In P. Mittler (Ed.), *Research to practice in mental retardation* (Vol. 2, pp. 421–26). Baltimore: University Park Press.

Brecksville V. A. Medical Center. (1981). *Annual report for 1981: Gambling treatment program.* Cleveland, OH.

Breggin, P. R. (1979). *Electroshock: Its brain-disabling effects.* New York: Springer.

Breier, A., Charney, D. S., & Heninger, G. R. (1984). Major depression in patients with agoraphobia and panic disorder. *Arch. Gen. Psychiat. 41,* 1129–35.

Breitner, J. C. (1986). On methodology and appropriate inference regarding possible genetic factors in typical, late-onset AD. *Neurobiology of Aging, 7,* 476–77.

Brennan, J. H., & Hemsley, D. R. (1984). Illusory correlations in paranoid and nonparanoid schizophrenia. *British Journal of Clinical Psychology, 23,* 225–26.

Brenner, M. H. (1973). *Mental illness and the economy.* Cambridge, MA: Harvard University Press.

Breslau, N. (1990). Does brain dysfunction increase children's vulnerability to environmental stress? *Arch. Gen. Psychiat., 47,* 15–20.

Brett, E. A., Spitzer, R. L., & Williams, J. B. (1988). DSM III-R criteria for posttraumatic stress disorder. *Amer. J. Psychiat., 145,* 1232–36.

Breuning, S. E., & Poling, A. D. (1982). Pharmacotherapy. In J. L. Matson & R. P. Barrett (Eds.), *Psychopathology in the mentally retarded* (pp. 195–251). New York: Grune & Stratton.

Bridges, F. A., & Cicchetti, D. (1982). Mothers' ratings of the temperament characteristics of Down's Syndrome infants. *Develop. Psychol., 18,* 238–44.

Brink, T. L. (1983). Paranoia in Alzheimer's patients: Prevalence and impact on caretakers. *International Journal of Behavioral Geriatrics, 1,* 53–55.

Brom, D., Kleber, R. J., & Defares, P. B. (1989). Brief psychotherapy for posttraumatic stress disorders. *J. Cons. Clin. Psychol., 57,* 607–12.

Brooks, D. N. (1974). Recognition, memory, and head injury. *Journal of Neurology, Neurosurgery, & Psychiatry, 37*(7), 794–801.

Brown, B. (1974). Depression roundup. *Behav. Today, 5*(17), 117.

Brown, G. W. (1972). Life-events and psychiatric illness: Some thoughts on methodology and causality. *J. Psychosom. Res., 16,* 311–20.

Brown, G. W., & Harris, T. (1978). *Social origins of depression.* London: Tavistock Publications.

Brown, J. D., & McGill, K. L. (1989). The cost of good fortune: When positive life events produce negative health consequences. *J. Pers. Soc. Psychol., 57,* 1103–10.

Brown, J. F., & Menninger, K. A. (1940). *Psychodynamics of abnormal behavior.* New York: McGraw-Hill.

Brown, R., Colter, N., Corsellis, J. A. N., Crow, T. J., & Frith, C. D. (1986). Postmortem evidence of structural brain changes in schizophrenia: Differences in brain weight, temporal horn area, and parahippocampal gyrus compared with average data. *Arch. Gen. Psychiat., 43,* 36–42.

Brown, R., & Herrnstein, R. J. (1977). *Psychology.* Boston: Little, Brown.

Brown, R. I. (1977). An integrated program for the mentally handicapped. In P. Mittler (Ed.), *Research to practice in mental retardation* (Vol. 2, pp. 387–88). Baltimore: University Park Press.

Browne, A., & Finkelhor, D. (1986). Impact of child sexual abuse: A review of the research. *Psychol. Bull., 99,* 66–77.

Browne, E. G. (1921). *Arabian Medicine.* New York: Macmillan.

Brozek, J., & Schurch, B. (1984). *Malnutrition and behavior: Critical assessment of key issues.* Lausanne, Switzerland: Nestle Foundation.

Bruch, H. (1973). *Eating disorders: Obesity, anorexia nervosa and the person within.* New York: Basic Books.

Bruch, H. (1988). *Conversations with anorexics.* New York: Basic Books.

Bruch, R. (1986). Anorexia nervosa: The therapeutic task. In K. D. Brownell & J. P. Foreyt (Eds.), *Handbook of eating disorders* (pp. 328–32). New York: Basic Books.

Bruck, M. (1987). Social and emotional adjustments of learning-disabled children. In S. J. Ceci (Ed.), *Handbook of cognitive, social, and neuropsychological aspects of learning disabilities* (Vol. 1, pp. 361–80). Hillsdale, NJ: Erlbaum.

Bry, B. H., McKeon, P., & Pandina, R. J. (1982). The extent of drug use as a function of number of risk factors. *J. Abnorm. Psychol., 91*(4), 273–79.

Buber, M. (1957). Distance and relation. *Psychiatry, 20,* 97–104.

Bucher, B., & Lovaas, O. I. (1967). Use of aversive stimulation in behavior modification. In M. R. Jones (Ed.), *Miami symposium on the prediction of behavior 1967: Aversive stimulation* (pp. 77–145). Coral Gables, FL: University of Miami Press.

Buchsbaum, M. S., Murphy, D. L., Coursey, R. D., Lake, C. R., & Zeigler, M. G. (1978). Platelet monoamine oxidase, plasma dopamine betahydroxylase and attention in a "biochemical high-risk" sample. In L. C. Wynne, R. L. Cromwell, & S. Matthysse (Eds.), *The nature of schizophrenia: New approaches to research and treatment* (pp. 387–96). New York: Wiley.

Buckley, P. (1982). Identifying schizophrenic patients who should not receive medication. *Schizo. Bull., 8,* 429–32.

Buckner, H. T. (1970). The transvestic career path. *Psychiatry, 3*(3), 381–89.

Budoff, M. (1977). The mentally retarded child in the mainstream of the public school: His relation to the school administration, his teachers, and his age-mates. In P. Mittler (Ed.), *Research to practice in mental retardation* (Vol. 2, pp. 307–13). Baltimore: University Park Press.

Bullard, D. M., Glaser, H. H., Heagarty, M. C., & Pivcheck, E. C. (1967). Failure to thrive in the neglected child. *Amer. J. Orthopsychiat., 37,* 680–90.

Bumbalo, J. H., & Young, D. E. (1973). The self-help phenomenon. *Amer. J. Nurs., 73,* 1588–91.

Burgess, A. W., & Holmstrom, L. (1974). Rape trauma syndrome. *Amer. J. Psychiat., 131,* 981–86.

Burgess, A. W., & Holmstrom, L. (1976). Coping behavior of the rape victim. *Amer. J. Psychiat., 133,* 413–18.

Burns, G. W. (1972). *The science of genetics.* New York: Macmillan.

Burnstein, M. H. (1981). Child abandonment: Historical, sociological, and psychological perspectives. *Child Psychiatry and Human Development, 11,* 213–21.

Burros, W. M. (1974). The growing burden of impotence. *Fam. Hlth., 6*(5), 18–21.

Burstein, A. (1985). How common is delayed posttraumatic stress disorder? *Amer. J. Psychiat., 142*(7), 887.

Buss, A., & Plomin, R. (1975). *A temperament theory of personality development.* New York: Wiley.

Buss, A. H. (1966). *Psychopathology.* New York: Wiley.

Butcher, J. N. (1979). Use of the MMPI in industry. In J. N. Butcher (Ed.), *New developments in the use of the MMPI.* Minneapolis: University of Minnesota Press.

Butcher, J. N. (1980, Nov.). The role of crisis intervention in an airport disaster plan. *Aviation, Space and Environmental Medicine,* 1260–62.

Butcher, J. N. (1984). Current developments in MMPI use: An international perspective. In J. N. Butcher & C. D. Spielberger (Eds.), *Advances in personality assessment* (Vol. 4). Hillsdale, NJ: Lawrence Erlbaum Press.

Butcher, J. N., Dahlstrom, W. G., Graham, J. R., Tellegen, A., & Kaemmer, B. (1989). *Minnesota Multiphasic Personality Inventory: MMPI-2: Manual for administration and scoring.* Minneapolis: University of Minnesota Press.

Butcher, J. N., & Dunn, L. (1989). Human responses and treatment needs in airline disasters. In R. Gist and B. Lubin (Eds.), *Psychosocial aspects of disaster.* New York: John Wiley & Sons.

Butcher, J. N., & Graham, J. R. (Eds.), (1989). *Topics in MMPI-2 interpretation.* Minneapolis: MMPI-2 Workshops and Symposia.

Butcher, J. N., & Hatcher, C. (1988). The neglected entity in air disaster planning: Psychological services. *Amer. Psychol., 43,* 724–29.

Butcher, J. N., & Pancheri, P. (1976). *Handbook of international MMPI research.* Minneapolis: University of Minnesota Press.

Butcher, J. N., Stelmachers, Z., & Maudal, G. R. (1983). Crisis intervention and emergency psychotherapy. In I. Weiner (Ed.), *Handbook of clinical methods* (2nd ed.). New York: Wiley.

Byassee, J. E. (1977). Essential hypertension. In R. B. Williams, Jr. & W. D. Gentry (Eds.), *Behavioral approaches to Medical treatment* (pp. 113–37). Cambridge, MA: Ballinger.

Bychowski, G. (1950). On neurotic obesity. *Psychoanalytic Review, 37,* 301–19.

Cade, J. F. J. (1949). Lithium salts in the treatment of psychotic excitement. *Medical Journal of Australia, 36* (part II): 349–52.

Cadoret, R. J., O'Gorman, T. W., Troughton, E., & Heywood, E. (1985). Alcoholism and antisocial personality: Interrelationships and environmental factors. *Arch. Gen. Psychiat., 42,* 161–67.

Cameron, N. (1959). Paranoid conditions and paranoia. In S. Arieti (Ed.), *American handbook of psychiatry.* New York: Basic Books.

Cameron, N., & Margaret, A. (1949). Experimental studies in thinking. I. Scattered speech in the responses of normal subjects to incomplete sentences. *J. Exper. Psychol., 39*(5), 617–27.

Cameron, N., & Margaret, A. (1951). *Behavior pathology.* Boston: Houghton Mifflin.

Campbell, D. (1926). *Arabian medicine and its influence on the Middle Ages.* New York: Dutton.

Campbell, S.B., Cohn, J.F., Ross, S., Elmore, M., & Popper, S. (April, 1990). *Postpartum adaptation and postpartum depression in primiparous women.* International Conference of Infant Studies, Montreal.

Campbell, S. B., & Wherry, J.S. (1986). Attention deficit disorder (hyperactivity). In H. C. Quay (Ed.), *Psychological disorders of childhood* (3rd ed., p. 111–55). New York: Wiley.

Cannon, T. D., Mednick, S. A., & Parnas, J. (1989). Genetic and perinatal determinants of structural brain deficits in schizophrenia. *Arch. Gen. Psychiat., 46,* 883–89.

Cannon, W. B. (1929). *Bodily changes in pain, hunger, fear and rage.* New York: Appleton.

Caputo, D. V., & Mandell, W. (1970). Consequences of low birth weight. *Develop. Psychol., 3*(3), 363–83.

Carlson, G., & Goodwin, F. K. (1973). The stages of mania: A longitudinal analysis of the manic episode. *Arch. Gen. Psychiat., 28*(2), 221–28.

Carlsson, A. (1986). Searching for antemortem markers premature. *Neurobiology of Aging, 7,* 400–401.

Carlsson, A. (1988). The current status of the dopamine hypothesis of schizophrenia. *Neuropsychopharmacology, 1,* 179–86.

Carothers, J. C. (1947). A study of mental derangement in Africans, and an attempt to explain its peculiarities more especially in relation to the African attitude of life. *J. Ment. Sci., 93,* 548–97.

Carothers, J. C. (1951). Frontal lobe function and the African. *J. Ment. Sci., 97,* 12–48.

Carothers, J. C. (1953). The African mind in health and disease. In *A study of ethnopsychiatry.* Geneva: World Health Organization, No. 17.

Carothers, J. C. (1959). Culture, psychiatry, and the written word. *Psychiatry, 22,* 307–20.

Carpenter, W. T., & Keith, S. J. (1986). Integrative treatments in schizophrenia. *Psychiat. Clin. N. Amer., 9,* 153–64.

Carpenter, W. T., & Strauss, J. S. (1979). Diagnostic issues in schizophrenia. In L. Bellak (Ed.), *Disorders of the schizophrenic syndrome.* New York: Basic Books.

Carr, A. T. (1971). Compulsive neurosis: Two psychophysiological studies. *Bulletin of the British Psychological Society, 24,* 256–57.

Carroll, B. J. (1982). The dexamethasone suppression test for melancholia. *Brit. J. Psychiat. 140,* 292–304.

Carruthers, M., (1980). Hazardous occupations and the heart. In C. L. Cooper & R. Payne (Eds.), *Current concerns in occupational stress.* New York: Wiley.

Carson, R. C. (1969). *Interaction concepts of personality.* Chicago: Aldine.

Carson, R. C. (1979). Personality and exchange in developing relationships. In R. L. Burgess & T. L. Huston (Eds.), *Social exchange in developing relationships.* New York: Academic Press.

Carson, R. C. (1982). Self-fulfilling prophecy, maladaptive behavior, and psychotherapy. In J. C. Anchin & D. J. Kiesler (Eds.), *Handbook of interpersonal psychotherapy* (pp. 64–77). New York: Pergamon.

Carson, R. C. (1983). The social-interactional viewpoint. In M. Hersen, A. E. Kazdin, & A. S. Bellack (Eds.), *The clinical psychology handbook* (pp. 143–54). New York: Pergamon.

Carson, R. C. (1984). The schizophrenias. In H. E. Adams & P. B. Sutker (Eds.), *Comprehensive handbook of psychopathology.* New York: Plenum.

Carson, R. C. (1989). Personality. *Annu. Rev. Psychol.* (Vol. 40, pp. 227–48). Palo Alto, CA: Annual Reviews.

Carson, R. C. (1990a). Needed: A new beginning. *Contemp. Psychol., 35,* 11–12.

Carson, R. C. (1990b). Assessment: What role the assessor? *J. Pers. Assess., 54,* 435–45.

Carson, R. C. (1991). Discussion: Dilemmas in the pathway of DSM-IV. *J. Abnorm. Psychol., 100.*

Carson, R. C. (in press-a). The social-interactional viewpoint. In M. Hersen, A. E. Kazdin, & A. S. Bellack (Eds.), *The clinical psychology handbook* (2nd ed.). Elmsford, NY: Pergamon.

Carson, R. C. (in press-b). Discussion: Tunnel vision and schizophrenia. In W. Flack, D. R. Miller, & M. Wiener (Eds.), *What is schizophrenia?* New York: Springer-Verlag.

Carson, R. C., & Sanislow, C. A., III. (1992). The schizophrenias. In H. E. Adams & P. B. Sutker (Eds.), *Comprehensive handbook of psychopathology* (2nd ed.). New York: Plenum.

Carson, T. P., & Adams, H. E. (1981). Affective disorders: Behavioral perspectives. In S. M. Turner, K. S. Calhoun, & H. E. Adams (Eds.), *Handbook of clinical behavior therapy.* New York: Wiley.

Carson, T. P., & Carson, R. C. (1984). The affective disorders. In H. E. Adams & P. B. Sutker (Eds.), *Comprehensive handbook of psychopathology.* New York: Plenum.

Casey, R. J., & Berman, J. S. (1985). The outcome of psychotherapy with children. *Psychol. Bull., 98,* 388–400.

Cashdan, S. (1988). *Object relations therapy:* Using the relationship. New York: Norton.

Castiglioni, A. (1946). *Adventures of the mind.* New York: Knopf.

Cato, C., & Rice, B. D. (1982). *Report from the study group on rehabilitation of clients with specific learning disabilities.* St. Louis: National Institute of Handicapped Research.

Cautela, J. R. (1967). Covert sensitization. *Psychol. Rep., 20,* 459–68.

Cavillin, H. (1966). Incestuous fathers: A clinical report. *Amer. J. Psychiat., 122*(10), 1132–38.

Ceci, S. J., & Baker, J. C. (1987). How shall we conceptualize the language problems of learning-disabled children?, In S. J. Ceci (Ed.), *Handbook of cognitive, social, and neuropsychological aspects of learning disabilities* (Vol. 2, pp. 103–14). Hillsdale, NJ: Erlbaum.

Celentano, D. D., & McQueen, D. V. (1978). Comparison of alcoholism prevalence rates obtained by survey and indirect estimators. *J. Stud. Alcoh., 39,* 420–34.

Centerwall, W. R., & Centerwall, S. A. (1961). Phenylketonuria (Folling's disease): The story of its discovery. *Journal of the History of Medicine, 16,* 292–96.

Chambers, R. E. (1952). Discussion of "Survival factors . . ." *Amer. J. Psychiat., 109,* 247–48.

Chance, P. (1986, Oct.). Life after head injury. *Psych. Today, 20,* 62–69.

Chandler, H. N. (1985). The kids-in-between: Some solutions. *J. Learn. Dis. 18,* 368.

Charney, F. L. (1979). Inpatient treatment programs. In W. H. Reid (Ed.), *The psychopath: A comprehensive study of antisocial disorders and behaviors.* New York: Brunner/Mazel.

Chase, T., The Troops for (1990). *When rabbit howls.* New York: Jove.

Chesno, F. A., & Kilmann, P. R. (1975). Effects of stimulation on sociopathic avoidance learning. *J. Abnorm. Psychol., 84*(2), 144–50.

Chess, S., & Thomas, A. (1984). *Origins and evolution of behavior disorders: From infancy to early adult life.* New York: Brunner/Mazel.

Chess, S., Thomas, A., & Birch, H. G. (1965). *Your child is a person.* New York: Viking.

Chesser, E. (1971). *Strange loves: The human aspects of sexual deviation.* New York: William Morrow.

Cheung, F. M., & Song, W. Z. (1989). A review on the clinical applications of the Chinese MMPI. *Psychological Assessment: A Journal of Consulting and Clinical Psychology, 1,* 230–38.

Christensen, A., Johnson, S., Phillips, S., & Glasgow, R.

(1980). Cost effectiveness in behavioral family therapy. *Behav. Ther., 11,* 208–26.
Christensen, D., & Rosenthal, R. (1982). Gender and nonverbal decoding skill as determinants of interpersonal expectancy effects. *J. Pers. Soc. Psychol., 42,* 75–87.
Christenson, R. M., Walker, J. I., Ross, D. R., & Maultbie, A. A. (1981). Reactivation of traumatic conflicts. *Amer. J. Psychiat., 138,* 984–85.
Christie, B. L. (1981). Childhood enuresis: Current thoughts on causes and cures. *Social Work Health Care, 6*(3), 77–90.
Claeson, L. E., & Malm, U. (1973). Electro-aversion therapy of chronic alcoholism. *Behav. Res. Ther., 11*(4), 663–65.
Clancy, H., & McBride, G. (1969). The autistic process and its treatment. *J. Child Psychol. Psychiat., 10*(4), 233–44.
Clark, C. R. (1987). Specific intent and diminished capacity. In A. Hess and I. Weiner (Eds.), *Handbook of forensic psychology.* New York: John Wiley & Sons.
Clark, D. A., Beck, A. T., & Stewart, B. (1990). Cognitive specificity and positive-negative affectivity: Complementary or contradictory views on anxiety and depression. *J. Abnorm. Psychol., 99,* 148–55.
Clark, G. R., Kivitz, M. S., & Rosen, N. (1969). Program for mentally retarded. *Sci. News, 96,* 82.
Clark, L. A. (1987). The mutual relevance of mainstream and cross-cultural psychology. *J. Cons. Clin. Psychol., 55,* 461–70.
Clarke, A. M., Clarke, A. D. B., & Berg, J. M. (Eds.). (1985). *Mental deficiency: The changing outlook,* (4th ed.). London: Methuen & Co.
Clarke, D. J., Littlejohns, C. S., Corbett, J. A., & Joseph, S. (1989). Pervasive developmental disorders and psychoses in adult life. *Brit. J. Psychiat., 155,* 692–99.
Clarke, R. V. G. (1985). Jack Tizard Memorial Lecture: Delinquency, environment and intervention. *J. Child Psychol. Psychiat., 26*(4), 505–23.
Clayton, P. J. (1982). Bereavement. In E. S. Paykel (Ed.), *Handbook of affective disorders.* New York: Guilford Press.
Clement, P. (1970). Elimination of sleepwalking in a seven-year-old boy. *J. Cons. Clin. Psychol., 34*(1), 22–26.
Cloninger, C. R. (1987). A systematic method for clinical description and classification of personality invariants. *Arch. Gen. Psychiat., 44,* 161–67.
Cloninger, C. R., & Guze, S. (1970). Psychiatric illness and female criminality: The role of sociopathy and hysteria in the antisocial woman. *Amer. J. Psychiat., 127*(3), 303–11.
Cloninger, C. R., Reich, T., Sigvardsson, S., von Knorring, A. L., & Bohman, M. (1986). The effects of changes in alcohol use between generations on the inheritance of alcohol abuse. In *Alcoholism: A medical disorder.* Proceedings of the 76th Annual Meeting of the American Psychopathological Association.
Coates, T. J., Perry, C., Killen, J., & Slinkard, L. A. (1981). Primary prevention of cardiovascular disease in children and adolescents. In C. K. Prokop & L. A. Bradley (Eds.), *Medical psychology: Contributions to behavioral medicine.* New York: Academic Press.
Cochran, S. D., & Hammen, C. L. (1985). Perceptions of stressful life events and depression: A test of attributional models. *J. Pers. Soc. Psychol. 48,* 1562–71.
Cockayne, T. O. (1864–1866). *Leechdoms, wort cunning, and star craft of early England.* London: Longman, Green, Longman, Roberts & Green.
Cockerham, W. (1981). *Sociology of mental disorder.* Englewood Cliffs, NJ: Prentice-Hall.
Cohen, D., & Eisdorfer, C. (1988). Depression in family members caring for a relative with Alzheimer's disease. *J. Amer. Geriat. Soc., 36,* 885–89.
Cohen, D. B. (1974). On the etiology of neurosis. *J. Abnorm. Psychol., 83,* 473–79.
Cohen, J., & Hansel, M. (1956). *Risk and gambling: A study of subjective probability.* New York: Philosophical Library.
Cohen, S. L., & Fiedler, J. E. (1974). Content analysis of multiple messages in suicide notes. *Life-Threatening Behavior, 4*(2), 75–95.
Cohen, S. M., Allen, M. G., Pollin, W., & Hrubec, Z. (1972). Relationship of schizo-affective psychosis to manic depressive psychosis and schizophrenia. *Arch. Gen. Psychiat., 26*(6), 539–46.
Cohn, J. F., & Campbell, S. B. (in press). Influence of maternal depression on infant affect regulation. In D. Cicchetti & S. Toth (Eds.), *Rochester Symposium on Developmental Psychopathology: Vol. 4. A developmental approach to affective disorders.*
Cohn, J.F., & Tronick, E.Z. (1983). Three months infant's reaction to simulated maternal depression. *Child Develop. 54,* 185–93.
Cohn, J.F., & Tronick, E.Z. (1987). Mother-infant interaction: The sequence of dyadic states at 3, 6, and 9 months. *Develop. Psychol., 23,* 68–77.
Coie, J. D. (1990). Toward a theory of peer rejection. In S. R. Asher & J. D. Coie (Eds.), *Peer rejection in childhood* (pp. 365–402). New York: Cambridge University Press.
Coie, J. D., & Dodge, K. A. (1983). Continuity and changes in children's sociometric status: A five-year longitudinal study. *Merrill-Palmer Quarterly, 29,* 261–82.
Coie, J. D., & Kupersmidt, J. B. (1983). A behavioral analysis of emerging social status in boys' groups. *Child Develop., 54,* 1400–16.
Cole, D. A. (1989). Psychopathology of adolescent suicide: Hopelessness, coping beliefs, and depression. *J. Abnorm. Psychol., 98,* 248–55.
Cole, J. O., & Bodkin, J. A. (1990). Antidepressant drug side effects. *J. Clin. Psychiat., 51,* 21–26.
Cole, S. O. (1975). Hyperkinetic children: The use of stimulant drugs evaluated. *Amer. J. Orthopsychiat., 45*(1), 28–37.
Comfort, A. (1984). Alzheimer's disease or Alzheimerism? *Psychiatric Annals, 14,* 130–32.
Conquest, R. (1986). *The harvest of sorrow: Soviet collectivization and the terror-famine.* New York: Oxford University Press.
Conte, H. R., Plutchik, R., Wild, K. V., & Karasu, T. B. (1986). Combined psychotherapy and pharmacotherapy for depression: A systematic analysis of the evidence. *Arch. Gen. Psychiat., 43,* 471–79.
Conte, J., Berliner, L., & Schuerman, J. (1986). *The impact of sexual abuse on children* (Final Report No. MH 37133). Rockville, MD: National Institute of Mental Health.
Cook, E. W., III, Hodes, R. L., & Lang, P. J. (1986). Preparedness and phobia: Effects of stimulus content on human visceral conditioning. *J. Abnorm. Psychol., 95,* 195–207.
Cookerly, J. R. (1980). Does marital therapy do any lasting good? *Journal of Marital and Family Therapy, 6*(4), 393–97.
Coombs, R. H., Paulson, M. J., & Palley, R. (1988). The institutionalization of drug use in America: Hazardous adolescence, challenging parenthood. *J. Chem. Depen. Treat., 1*(2), 9–37.
Cooper, A. J. (1969). A clinical study of "coital anxiety" in male potency disorders. *J. Psychosom. Res., 13*(2), 143–47.
Cooper, J. E., Kendell, R. E., Gurland, B. J., Sharpe, L., Copeland, J. R. M., & Simon, R. (1972). *Psychiatric diagnosis in New York and London.* London: Oxford University Press.
Coopersmith, S. (1967). *The antecedents of self-esteem.* San Francisco: Freeman.
Coovert, D. L., Kinder, B. N., & Thompson, J. K. (1989). The psychosexual aspects of anorexia nervosa and bulimia: A review of the literature. *Clin. Psychol. Rev., 9,* 169–80.
Copeland, J. (1968). Aspects of mental illness in West African students. *Soc. Psychiat., 3*(1), 7–13.
Coppen, A., Metcalfe, M., & Wood, K. (1982). Lithium. In E. S. Paykel (Ed.), *Handbook of affective disorders.* New York: Guilford Press.
Coryell, W., Keller, M., Lavori, P., & Endicott, J. (1990a). Affective syndromes, psychotic features, and prognosis: I. Depression. *Arch. Gen. Psychiat., 47,* 651–57.
Coryell, W., Keller, M., Lavori, P., & Endicott, J. (1990b). Affective syndromes, psychotic features, and prognosis: II. Mania. *Arch. Gen. Psychiat., 47,* 658–62.
Coryell, W., & Winokur, G. (1982). Course and outcome. In E. S. Paykel (Ed.), *Handbook of affective disorders.* New York: Guilford Press.
Cosby, B. (1986). *Fatherhood.* Garden City, NY: Doubleday.
Costa, P. T., Jr., Whitfield, J. R., & Stewart, D. (Eds.). (1989). *Alzheimer's disease: Abstracts of the psychological and behavioral literature.* Washington, DC: American Psychological Association.
Costello, C. G. (1980). Childhood depression: Three basic but questionable assumptions in the Lefkowitz and Burton critique. *Psychol. Bull. 87,* 187–90.
Cotler, S. B. (1971). The use of different behavioral techniques in treating a case of compulsive gambling. *Behav. Ther., 2,* 579–81.
Cotton, N. S. (1979). The familial incidence of alcoholism. *J. Stud. Alcoh., 40,* 89–116.
Courtois, C., & Sprei, J. (1988). Retrospective incest therapy for women. In L.E.A. Walker (Ed.), *Handbook on sexual abuse of children* (pp 270–308). New York: Springer.

Covi, L., Lipman, R. S., Derogatis, L. R., Smith, J. E., III, & Pattison, J. H. (1974). Drugs and group psychotherapy in neurotic depression. *Amer. J. Psychiat., 13*(2), 191–97.

Cowdry, R. W., & Gardner, D. L. (1988). Pharmacotherapy of borderline personality disorder. *Arch. Gen. Psychiat., 45,* 111–19.

Cox, D. J., Freundlich, A., & Meyer, R. G. (1975). Differential effectiveness of electromyographic feedback, verbal relaxation instructions, and medication placebo with tension headaches. *J. Cons. Clin. Psychol., 43,* 892–98.

Cox, W. M., & Klinger, E. (1988). A motivational model of alcohol use. *J. Abnorm. Psychol., 97,* 168–80.

Coyle, J. T., Price, D. L., & DeLong, M. R. (1983). Alzheimer's disease: A disorder of cortical cholinergic innervation. *Science, 219,* 1184–90.

Coyne, J. C. (1976). Depression and the response of others. *J. Abnorm. Psychol., 55*(2), 186–93.

Crapper McLachlan, D. R. (1986). Aluminum and Alzheimer's disease. *Neurobiology of Aging, 7,* 525–32.

Cravioto, J., & de Licardie, E. R. (1975). Environmental and nutritional deprivation in children with learning disabilities. In W. M. Cruickshank & D. P. Hallahan (Eds.), *Perceptual and learning disabilities in children: Vol. 2. Research and theory.* Syracuse, NY: Syracuse University Press.

Creasy, M. R., & Crolla, J. A. (1974, Mar. 23). Prenatal mortality of trisomy 21 (Down's syndrome). *Lancet, 1*(7856), 473–74.

Crisp, A. H., Douglas, J. W. B., Ross, J. M., & Stonehill, E. (1970). Some developmental aspects of disorders of weight. *J. Psychosom. Res., 14,* 313–20.

Crittenden, P. M. (1985). Maltreated infants: Vulnerability and resilience. *J. Child Psychol. Psychiat., 26,* 85–96.

Crockett, D., Clark, C., & Klonoff, H. (1987). Introduction—an overview of neuropsychology. In S. B. Filskov & T. J. Boll (Eds.), *Handbook of clinical neuropsychology.* New York: Wiley.

Crook, T., & Eliot, J. (1980). Parental death during childhood and adult depression: A critical review of the literature. *Psychol. Bull., 87,* 252–59.

Culliton, B. J. (1970, Jan. 24). Pot facing stringent scientific examination. *Sci. News, 97*(4), 102–5.

Culliton, B. J. (1976). Psychosurgery: National Commission issues surprisingly favorable report. *Science, 194,* 299–301.

Cummings, C., Gordon, J. R., & Marlatt, G. A. (1980). Relapse: Prevention and prediction. In W. R. Miller (Ed.), *The addictive behaviors.* New York: Pergamon Press.

Curlee, J. (1969). Alcoholism and the "empty nest." *Bull. Menninger Clin., 33*(3), 165–71.

Custer, R. L. (1982). An overview of compulsive gambling. In P. A. Carone, S. F. Yolies, S. N. Kieffer, & L. W. Krinsky (Eds.), *Addictive disorders update.* New York: Human Sciences.

Dahlstrom, W. G., Lachar, D., & Dahlstrom, L. E. (1986). *MMPI patterns of American minorities.* Minneapolis: University of Minnesota Press.

Dain, N. (1964). *Concepts of insanity in the United States: 1789–1865.* New Brunswick, NJ: Rutgers University Press.

Daniel W. F., & Crovitz, H. F. (1983a). Acute memory impairment following electroconvulsive therapy: 1. Effects of electrical stimulus and number of treatments. *Acta Psychiatr. Scandin., 67,* 1–7.

Daniel, W. F., & Crovitz, H. F. (1983b). Acute memory impairment following electroconvulsive therapy: 2. Effects of electrode placement. *Acta Psychiatr. Scandin., 67,* 57–68.

Danto, B. L. (1990). Stress experienced by robbery victims, hostages, kidnapping victims, and prisoners of war. In J.D. Noshpitz & R. D. Coddington (Eds.), *Stressors and the adjustment disorders.* New York: Wiley Intersciences.

Darbonne, A. R. (1969). Suicide and age: A suicide note analysis. *J. Cons. Clin. Psychol., 33,* 46–50.

Darke, J. L. (1990). Sexual aggression: Achieving power through humiliation. In W. L. Marshall, D. R. Laws, & H. E. Barbaree (Eds.), *Handbook of sexual assault* (pp. 55–72). New York: Plenum.

Davidson, A. D. (1979a, Spring). Coping with stress reactions in rescue workers: A program that worked. *Police Stress.*

Davidson, A. D. (1979b). Personal communication.

Davidson, L. M., & Baum, A. (1986). Chronic stress and posttraumatic stress disorders. *J. Cons. Clin. Psychol., 54,* 303–8.

Davidson, W.S. (1974). Studies of aversive conditioning for alcoholics: A critical review of theory and research methodology. *Psychol. Bull., 81*(9), 571–81.

Davies, P. (1986). The genetics of Alzheimer's disease: A review and discussion of the implications. *Neurobiology of Aging, 7,* 459–66.

Davis, J. M. (1978). Dopamine theory of schizophrenia: A two-factor theory. In L. C. Wynne, R. L. Cromwell, & S. Matthysse (Eds.), *The nature of schizophrenia: New approaches to research and treatment* (pp. 105–15). New York: Wiley.

Davis, V. J., Cullari, S., & Breuning, S. E. (1982). Drug use in community foster homes. In S. E. Breuning & A. D. Poling (Eds.), *Drugs and mental retardation.* Springfield, IL: Thomas.

Davison, G. C. (1976). Homosexuality: The ethical challenge. *J. Cons. Clin. Psychol., 44*(2), 157–62.

Davison, G. C. (1978). Not can but ought: The treatment of homosexuality. *J. Cons. Clin. Psychol., 46*(1), 170–2.

Day, G. (1951, May 12). The psychosomatic approach to pulmonary tuberculosis. *Lancet,* 6663.

de Pauw, K. W., & Szulecka, T. K. (1988). Dangerous delusions: Violence and misidentification syndromes. *Brit. J. Psychiat., 152,* 91–96.

De Young, M. (1982). Innocent seducer and innocently seduced? The role of the child incest victim. *J. Clin. Child Psychol., 11,* 56–60.

DeFazio, V. J., Rustin, S., & Diamond, A. (1975). Symptom development in Vietnam era veterans. *Amer. J. Orthopsychiat., 45*(1), 158–63.

DeFrancis, V. (1969). *Protecting the child victim of sex crimes committed by adults.* Denver: Children's Division, American Humane Association.

DeLisi, L. E., Crow, T. J., & Hirsch, S. R. (1986). The third biannual winter workshops on schizophrenia. *Arch. Gen. Psychiat. 43,* 706–11.

DeLisi, L. E., Goldin, L. R., Hamovit, J. R., Maxwell, E., & Kuritz, D. (1986). A family study of the association of increased ventricular size with schizophrenia. *Arch. Gen. Psychiat., 43,* 148–53.

DeLisi, L. E., Mirsky, A.F., Buchsbaum, M.S., van Kammen, D.P., Berman, K.F., Phelps, B. H., Karoum, F., Ko, G. N., Korpi, E. R., et al. (1984). The Genain quadruplets 25 years later: A diagnostic and biochemical followup. *Psychiat. Res., 13,* 59–76.

DeMarsh, J., & Kumpfer, K. L. (1985). Family-oriented interventions for the prevention of chemical dependency in children and adolescents. Special Issue: Childhood and Chemical Abuse: Prevention and Intervention. *Journal of Children in Contemporary Society, 18*(1–2), 117–51.

Denicola, J., & Sandler, J. (1980). Training abusive parents in child management and self-control skills. *Behav. Ther., 11,* 263–70.

Dennes, B. (1974). Returning madness to an accepting community. *Comm. Ment. Hlth. J., 10*(2), 163–72.

Department of Labor. (1991, Feb.). *Employment and earnings.* Bureau of Labor Statistics. U.S. Government Printing Office.

Depue, R. A., & Monroe, S. M. (1978). The unipolar-bipolar distinction in the depressive disorders. *Psychol. Bull., 85,* 1001–29.

Depue, R. A., & Monroe, S. M. (1986). Conceptualization and measurement of human disorder in life stress research: The problem of chronic disturbance. *Psychol. Bull., 99*(1), 36–51.

Depue, R. A., Slater, J. F., Wolfstetter-Kausch, H., Klein, D., Goplerud, E., & Farr, D. (1981). A behavioral paradigm for identifying persons at risk for bipolar disorder: A conceptual framework. *J. Abnorm. Psychol., 90,* 381–437.

DeRubeis, R. J. (1983, Dec.). *The cognitive-pharmacotherapy project: Study design, outcome, and clinical followup.* Paper presented at American Association of Behavior Therapy. Washington, DC.

Detels, R., English, P., Visscher, B., Kigsley, L., Chmiel, J., Dudley, J., Eldred, L. J., & Ginzburg, H. (1988, June). *Sexual activity, condom use, and HIV-1 seroconversion.* Paper presented at the Fourth International Conference on AIDS, Stockholm, Sweden.

Detera-Wadleigh, S. D., Berrettini, W. H., Goldin, L. R., Boorman, D., Anderson, S., & Gershon, E. S. (1987) Close linkage of c-harvey-ras-1 and the insulin gene to affective disorders is ruled out in three North American pedigrees. *Nature, 325,* 806–8.

Deur, J. I., & Parke, R. D. (1970). Effects of inconsistent punishment on aggression in children. *Develop. Psychol., 2,* 403–11.

DeWolfe, A. S., Ryan, J. J., & Wolf, M. E. (1988). Cognitive sequelae of tardive dyskinesia. *J. Nerv. Ment. Dis., 176,* 270–74.

Diamond, M. C. (1988). *Enriching heredity: The impact of the environment on the anatomy of the brain.* New York: Free Press.

Diamond, M. J. (1974). Modification of hypnotizability: A review: Psychol. Bull., 81(3), 180–98.

Dietz, P. E. (1977). Social discrediting of psychiatry: The protasis of legal disfranchisement. *Amer. J. Psychiat., 134,* 1356–60.

Diller, L., & Gordon, W. A. (1981). Interventions for cognitive deficits in brain-injured adults. *J. Cons. Clin. Psychol., 49,* 822–34.

Dinitz, S., & Conrad, J. P. (1980). The dangerous two percent. In D. Shichor & D. H. Kelly (Eds.), *Critical issues in juvenile delinquency.* Lexington, MA: Lexington Books.

Dixen, J., & Jenkins, J. O. (1981). Incestuous child sexual abuse: A review of treatment strategies. *Clin. Psychol. Rev., 1,* 211–22.

Doane, J. A., Falloon, I. R. H., Goldstein, M. J., & Mintz, J. (1985). Parental affective style and the treatment of schizophrenia: Predicting course of illness and social functioning. *Arch. Gen. Psychiat., 42,* 34–42.

Doane, J., West, K., Goldstein, M. J., Rodnick, E., & Jones, J. (1981). Parental communication deviance and affective style as predictors of subsequent schizophrenia spectrum disorders in vulnerable adolescents. *Arch. Gen. Psychiat., 38,* 679–85.

Dobrokhotova, T. A. (1968). On the pathology of the emotional sphere in tumorous lesion of the frontal lobes of the brain. *Zhurnal Neuropatologii i Psikhiartrii, 68*(3), 418–22.

Dobson, K. S. (1989). A meta-analysis of the efficacy of cognitive therapy for depression. *J. Cons. Clin. Psychol., 57,* 414–19.

Dodd, B., & Leahy, J. (1989). Facial prejudice. *Amer. J. Ment. Retard., 94,* 111.

Dodge, K. A. (1980). Social cognition and children's aggressive behavior. *Child Develop., 51,* 162–70.

Dodge, K. A. (1983). Behavioral antecedents of peer social status. *Child Develop., 54,* 1386–99.

Dodge, K. A., Coie, J. D., & Brakke, N. P. (1982). Behavioral patterns of socially rejected and neglected preadolescents: The roles of social approach and aggression. *J. Abnorm. Child. Psychol. 10,* 389–410.

Dodge, K. A., & Feldman, E. (1990). Issues in social cognition and sociometric status. In S. R. Asher & J. D. Coie (Eds.), *Peer rejection in childhood,* (pp. 119–55). New York: Cambridge University Press.

Dodge, K. A., & Frame, C. L. (1982). Social cognition biases and deficits in aggressive boys. *Child Develop., 53,* 620–35.

Dodge, K. A., Murphy, R. R., & Buchsbaum, K. (1984). The assessment of intention-cue detection skills in children: Implications for developmental psychopathology. *Child Develop., 55,* 163–73.

Dodge, K. A., Newman, J. P. (1981). Biased decision-making processes in aggressive boys. *J. Abnorm. Psychol., 90,* 375–79.

Dohrenwend, B. P., & Dohrenwend, B. S. (1982). Perspectives on the past and future of psychiatric epidemiology: The 1981 Rena Lapouse Lecture. *Amer. J. Pub. Hlth., 72*(1), 1271–79.

Dohrenwend, B. P., Dohrenwend, B. S., Gould, M. S., Link, B., Neugebauer, R., & Wunsch-Hitzig, R. (1980). *Mental illness in the United States: Epidemiological estimates.* New York: Praeger.

Dohrenwend, B. P., & Egri, G. (1981). Recent stressful life events and episodes of schizophrenia. *Schizo. Bull., 7,* 12–23.

Dole, V. P., & Nyswander, M. (1967). The miracle of methadone in the narcotics jungle. *Roche Report, 4*(11), 1–2, 8, 11.

Dole, V. P., Nyswander, M., & Warner, A. (1968). Successful treatment of 750 criminal addicts. *JAMA, 206,* 2709–11.

Doleys, D. M. (1979). Assessment and treatment of childhood enuresis. In R. J. Finch & P. C. Kendall (Eds.), *Clinical treatment and research in child psychopathology.* New York: Spectrum Publications.

Dollard, J., & Miller, N. E. (1950). *Personality and psychotherapy.* New York: McGraw-Hill.

Donaldson, M. A., & Gardner, R. Jr., (1985). Diagnosis and treatment of traumatic stress among women after childhood incest. In C. R. Filley (Ed.), *Trauma and its wake: The study and treatment of post-traumatic stress disorder* (pp. 356–77). Newbury Park, CA: Sage.

Donne, J. (1624). Meditation XVII. *Devotions upon emergent occasions.* London.

Dooley, D., & Catalano, R. (1980). Economic change as a cause of behavioral disorder. *Psychol. Bull. 87,* 450–68.

Dorfman, D. D. (1978). The Cyril Burt question: New findings. *Science, 201,* 1177–86.

Dorwart, R. A., Schlesinger, M., Horgan, C., & Davidson, H. (1989). The privatization of mental health care and directions for mental health services research. In C. A. Taube, D. Mechanic, & A. A. Hohmann (Eds.), *The future of mental health services research* (pp. 139–54). Washington, DC: U. S. Department of Health and Human Services. US Government Printing Office.

Downey, G., & Coyne, J. C. (1990). Children of depressed parents: An integrative review. *Psychol. Bull., 108,* 50–76.

Downing, R. W., & Rickels, K. (1974) Mixed anxiety-depression: Fact or myth? *Arch. Gen. Psychiat., 30*(3), 312–17.

Draguns, J. G. (1979). Culture and personality. In A. J. Marsella, R. Tharp, & T. Cibowrowski (Eds.), *Perspectives in cross-cultural psychology.* New York: Academic Press.

Drake, R. E., & Wallach, M. A. (1979). Will mental patients stay in the community: A social psychological perspective. *J. Cons. Clin. Psychol., 42*(2), 285–94.

Drug Enforcement Administration, Department of Justice. (1979). *Controlled Substance Inventory List.* Washington, DC.

Dumas, J.E., Gibson, J.A., & Albin, J. B. (1989). Behavioral correlates of maternal depressive symptomatology in conduct-disorder children. *J. Cons. Clin. Psychol., 57,* 516–21.

Dunbar, F., (1943). *Psychosomatic diagnosis.* New York: Harper & Row.

Dunbar, P. (1954). *Emotions and bodily changes* (4th ed.). New York: Columbia University Press.

Dunn, F. M., & Howell, R. J. (1982). Relaxation training and its relationship to hyperactivity in boys. *J. Clin. Psychol., 38*(1), 92–100.

Dunner, D. L., & Hall, K. S. (1980). Social adjustment and psychological precipitants in mania. In R. H. Belmaker & H.M. van Praag (Eds.), *Mania: An evolving concept.* New York: Spectrum.

Dura, J. R., & Bornstein, R. A. (1989). Differences between IQ and school achievement in anorexia nervosa. *J. Clin. Psychol., 45,* 433–35.

Durkheim, E. (1951). *Suicide: A study in sociology* (J.A. Spaulding & G. Simpson, Trans., G. Simpson, Ed.). New York: Free Press. (Originally published 1897.)

Earl, H. G. (1965). 10,000 children battered and starved: Hundreds die. *Today's Health, 43*(9), 24–31.

Earl, H. G. (1966). Head injury: The big killer. *Today's Health, 44*(12), 19–21.

Earlywine, M., & Finn, P. R. (1990, March). Personality, drinking habits, and responses to cues for alcohol. Paper presented at the 5th Congress of the International Society for Biomedical Research on Alcoholism and the Research Society on Alcoholism, Toronto, Canada.

East, W. N. (1946). Sexual offenders. *J. Nerv. Ment. Dis., 103,* 626–66.

Edwards, C. C. (1973). What you can do to combat high blood pressure. *Fam. Hlth., 5*(11), 24–26.

Egbert, L., Battit, G., Welch, C., & Bartlett, M. (1964). Reduction of postoperative pain by encouragement and instruction of patients. *New Engl. J. Med., 270,* 825–27.

Egeland vs. City of Minneapolis, 344 N.W. 2nd 597. (1984).

Egeland, B., & Brunnquell, D. (1979). An at-risk approach to the study of child abuse: Some preliminary findings. *J. Amer. Acad. Child Psychiat., 18,* 219–35.

Egeland, B., Cicchetti, D., & Taraldson, B. (1976, Apr. 26). Child abuse: A family affair. *Proceedings of the N. P. Masse Research Seminar on Child Abuse,* 28–52. Paper presented Paris, France.

Egeland, B., & Erickson, M. F. (1990). Rising above the past: Strategies for helping new mothers to break the cycle of abuse and neglect. *Zero to Three, 11,* 29–35.

Egeland, B., Erickson, M., Butcher, J. N., & Ben-Porath, Y. S. (1990). MMPI-2 profiles of women at risk for child abuse. *J. Pers. Assess.*

Egeland, B., & Farber, E.A. (1984). Infant-mother attachment: Factors related to its development and change over time. *Child Develop., 55,* 753–71.

Egeland, B., Jacobvitz, D., & Papatola, K. (1987). Intergenerational continuity of abuse. In R. Gelles & J. Lancaster (Eds.), *Child abuse and neglect: Biosocial aspects* (pp. 255–76). New York: Aldine de Gruyter.

Egeland, J. A., Gerhard, D. S., Pauls, D. L., Sussex, J. N., Kidd, K. K., Allen, C. R., Hostetter, A. M., & Housman, D. E. (1987). Bipolar affective disorders linked to DNA markers on chromosome 11. *Nature, 325,* 783–87.

Egendorf, A. (1986). *Healing from the war.* Boston: Houghton Mifflin.

Ehrhardt, A.A., & Meyer-Bahlburg, H. F. L. (1981). Effects of prenatal sex hormones on gender-related behavior. *Science, 211,* 1312–18.

Eisenberg, L. (1971). Principles of drug therapy in child psychiatry with special reference to stimulant drugs. *Amer. J. Orthopsychiat., 4*(3). 371–79.

Eisenberg, H. M. (1990). Behavioral changes after closed head injury in children. *J. Cons. Clin. Psychol., 58,* 93–98.

Eisler, R. M., Miller, P. M., Hersen, M., & Alford, H. (1974). Effects of assertive training on marital interaction. *Arch. Gen. Psychiat., 30*(5), 643–49.

Eitinger, L. (1964). *Concentration camp survivors in Norway and Israel.* New York: Humanities Press.

Eitinger, L. (1969). Psychosomatic problems in concentration camp survivors. *J. Psychosom. Res., 13,* 183–90.

Eitinger, L. (1973, Sept.). A follow-up study of the Norwegian concentration camp survivors: Mortality and morbidity. *Israel Annals of Psychiatry and Related Disciplines, 11,* 199–210.

Elkin, I., Shea, M. T., Watkins, J. T., Imber, S. D., Sotsky, S. M., Collins, J. F., Glass, D. R., Pilkonis, P. A., Leber, W. R., Docherty, J. P., Fiester, S. J., & Parloff, M. B. (1989). National Institute of Mental Health Treatment of Depression Collaborative Research Program: General effectiveness of treatments. *Arch. Gen. Psychiat., 46,* 971–82.

Elkind, D. (1967). Middle-class delinquency. *Mental Hygiene, 51,* 80–84.

Elkind, D., & Weiner, I. B. (1978). *Development of the child.* New York: Wiley.

Ellinwood, E. H. (1971). Assault and homicide associated with amphetamine abuse. *Amer. J. Psychiat., 127*(9), 90–95.

Elliott, D. S., Dunford, F. W., & Huizinga, D. (1987). The identification and prediction of career offenders utilizing self-reported and official data. In J. D. Burchard & S. N. Burchard (Eds.), *Prevention of delinquent behavior* (pp. 90–121). Newbury Park, CA: Sage.

Elliott, G. (1989). Stress and illness. In S. Cheren (Ed.), *Psychosomatic medicine: Theory, physiology, and practice* (Vol. 1, pp. 45–90). Madison, CT: International Universities Press.

Ellis, A. (1958). Rational psychotherapy. *J. Gen. Psychol., 59,* 35–49.

Ellis, A. (1970). *Reason and emotion in psychotherapy.* New York: Lyle Stuart.

Ellis, A. (1973). Rational-emotive therapy. In R. J. Corsini (Ed.), *Current psychotherapies.* Itasca, IL: Peacock Publishers.

Ellis, A. (1975). Creative job and happiness: The humanistic way. *The Humanist, 35*(1), 11–13.

Ellis, A. (1977). The treatment of a psychopath with rational therapy. In S. J. Morse & R. I. Watson (Eds.), *Psychotherapies: A comparative casebook.* New York: Holt, Rinehart & Winston.

Ellis, A. (1989). The history of cognition in psychotherapy. In A. Freeman, K. M. Simon, L. E. Beutler, & H. Arkowitz (Eds.), *Comprehensive handbook of cognitive therapy* (pp. 5–19). New York: Plenum.

Ellis, E. M., Atkeson, B. M., & Calhoun, K. S. (1982). An examination of differences between multiple- and single-incident victims of sexual assault. *J. Abnorm. Psychol., 91,* 221–24.

Ellison, K. (1977). Personal communication.

Emmelkamp, P. M. G. (1986). Behavior therapy with adults. In S. L. Garfield & A. E. Bergin (Eds.) *Handbook of psychotherapy and behavior change* (3rd ed., pp. 385–442). New York: Wiley.

Emmelkamp, P. M. G., & Wessels, H. (1975). Flooding in imagination vs. flooding in vivo: A comparison with agoraphobics. *Behav. Res. Ther., 13*(1), 7–15.

Endicott, J., Nee, J., Cohen, J., Fleiss, J. L., & Simon, R. (1986). Diagnosis of schizophrenia: Prediction of short-term outcome. *Arch. Gen. Psychiat., 43,* 13–19.

Endicott, N. A. (1989). Psychosocial and behavioral factors in myocardial infarction and sudden cardiac death. In S. Cheren (Ed.), *Psychosomatic Medicine: Theory, physiology, and practice* (Vol. 2, pp. 611–60). Madison, CT: International Universities Press.

Endler, N. (1990). *Holiday of darkness: A psychologist's journey out of his depression* (rev. ed.). Toronto: Wall & Thompson.

Engel, G. L. (1977). The need for a new medical model: A challenge for biomedicine. *Science, 196,* 129–36.

Engelhardt, D. M. (1974). Pharmacologic basis for use of psychotropic drugs: An overview. *New York State Journal of Medicine, 74*(2), 360–66.

Englander-Golden, P., Elconin, J., Miller, K. J., & Schwarzkopf, A. B., (1986). Brief SAY IT STRAIGHT training and follow-up in adolescent substance abuse prevention. *Journal of Primary Prevention, 6*(4), 219–30.

English, C. J. (1973). Leaving home: A typology of runaways. *Society, 10*(5), 22–24.

Epstein, H. (1979). *Children of the holocaust: Conversations with sons and daughters of survivors.* New York: Putnam.

Epstein, S., & Fenz, W. D. (1962). Theory and experiment on the measurement of approach-avoidance conflict. *J. Abnorm. Soc. Psychol., 64*(1), 97–112.

Epstein, S., & Fenz, W. D. (1965). Steepness of approach and avoidance gradients in humans as a function of experience: Theory and experiment. *J. Exper. Psychol., 70*(1), 1–12.

Erdman, H. P., Klein, M., & Greist, J. H. (1985). Direct patient computer interviewing. *J. Cons. Clin. Psychol., 53*(6), 760–73.

Erlenmeyer-Kimling, L., & Cornblatt, B. (1978). Attentional measures in a study of children at high risk for schizophrenia. In L. C. Wynne, R. L. Cromwell, & S. Matthysse (Eds.), *The nature of schizophrenia: New approaches to research and treatment* (pp. 359–65). New York: Wiley.

Ernst, A. R., Routh, D. K., & Harper, D. C. (1984). Abdominal pain in children and symptoms of somatization disorder. *J. Pediat. Psychol., 9*(1), 77–85.

Eron, L. D., Huesmann, L. R., Lefkowitz, M. M., & Walder, L. O. (1974). How Teaming conditions in early childhood—including mass media—relate to aggression in late adolescence. *Amer. J. Orthopsychiat., 44*(3), 412–23.

Eron, L. D., & Peterson, R. A. (1982). Abnormal behavior: Social approaches. In M. R. Rosenzweig & L. W. Porter (Eds.), *Annu. Rev. Psychol. 33,* 231–65.

Esler, M., Julius, S., Zweifler, A., Randall, O., Harburgh, E., Gardiner, H., & DeQuattro, V. (1977). Mild high-renin essential hypertension: Neurogenic human hypertension? *New Engl. J. Med., 296,* 405–11.

Ethics Committee, American Psychological Association. (1990). Report of the Ethics Committee: 1988. *Amer. Psychol., 45,* 873–74.

Evans, D. A., Funkerstein, H., Albert, M. S., Scherr, P. A., Cook, N. R., Chown, M. J., Hebert, L. E., Hennekens, C. H., & Taylor, J. O. (1989). Prevalence of Alzheimer's disease in a community population of older persons. *JAMA, 262,* 2551–56.

Evans, J. A., & Hamerton, J. L. (1985). Chromosomal anomalies. In A. M. Clarke, A. D. B. Clarke, & J. M. Berg (Eds.). *Mental deficiency: The changing outlook* (4th ed., pp. 213–66). London: Methuen.

Exner, J. E. (1987). Computer assistance in Rorschach interpretation. In J. N. Butcher (Ed.) *Computerized psychological assessment: A practitioner's guide.* NY: Basic Books.

Eysenck, H. J. (1952). The effects of psychotherapy: An evaluation. *Journal of Consulting Psychology, 16,* 319–24.

Eysenck, H. J. (1960). *Behaviour therapy and the neuroses.* London: Pergamon Press.

Eysenck, H. J. (1976). The learning theory model of neurosis: A new approach. *Behav. Res. Ther., 14,* 251–67.

Fabrega, H. (1981). Cultural programming of brain-behavior relationships. In J. R. Merikangas (Ed.), *Brain-behavior relationships.* Lexington, MA: D. C. Heath.

Fabrega, H. (1989). Cultural relativism and psychiatric illness. *J. Nerv. Ment. Dis., 177,* 415–24.

Fairweather, G. W. (Ed.) (1980). *The Fairweather Lodge: A twenty-five year retrospective.* San Francisco: Jossey-Bass.

Fairweather, G. W., Sanders, D. H., Maynard, H., & Cressler, D. L. (1969). *Community life for the mentally ill: An alternative to institutional care.* Chicago: Aldine.

Fallon, A. E., & Rozin, P. (1985). Sex differences in perceptions of desirable body shape. *J. Abnorm. Psychol., 94,* 102–5.

Falloon, I. R. H., Boyd, J. L., McGill, C. W., Williamson, M., & Razani, J. (1985). Family management in the prevention of morbidity of schizophrenia: Clinical outcome of a two-year longitudinal study. *Arch. Gen. Psychiat., 42,* 887–96.

Falls, H. F. (1970). Ocular changes in Down's syndrome help in diagnosis. *Roche Report, 7*(16), 5.

Fantuzzo, J. W., Jurecic, L., Stovall, A., Hightower, A. D., Goins, C., & Schachtel, D. (1988). Effects of adult and peer social initiations on the social behavior of withdrawn, maltreated, preschool children. *J. Cons. Clin. Psychol., 56,* 40–47.

Faraone, S. V., Kremen, W. S., & Tsuang, M. T. (1990). Genetic transmission of major affective disorders: Quantitative models and linkage analysis. *Psychol. Bull., 108,* 109–27.

Faraone, S. V., & Tsuang, M. T. (1985). Quantitative models of the genetic transmission of schizophrenia. *Psychol. Bull., 98,* 41–66.

Farberow, N. L. (1974). *Suicide.* Morristown, NJ: General Learning Press.

Farberow, N. L. (1975). Cultural history of suicide. In N. L. Farberow (Ed.), *Suicide in different cultures* (pp. 1–15). Baltimore: University Park Press.

Farberow, N. L., & Litman, R. E. (1970). A comprehensive suicide prevention program. Suicide Prevention Center of Los Angeles, 1958–1969. Unpublished final report DHEW NIMH Grants No. MH 14946 & MH 00128. Los Angeles.

Farberow, N. L., Shneidman, E. S., & Leonard, C. (1963). Suicide among general medical and surgical hospital patients with malignant neoplasms. Veterans Administration, Dept. of Medicine and Surgery. *Medical Bulletin* MB-9, Feb. 25, 1963, 1–11.

Farberow, N. L., & Simon, M. D. (1975). Suicide in Los Angeles and Vienna. In N. L. Farberow (Ed.), *Suicide in different cultures* (pp. 185–204). Baltimore: University Park Press.

Faretra, G. (1981). A profile of aggression from adolescence to adulthood: An 18-year follow-up of psychiatrically disturbed and violent adolescents. *Amer. J. Orthopsychiat., 51,* 439–53.

Farina, A., Burns, G. L., Austad, C., Bugglin, C., & Fischer, E. H. (1986). The role of physical attractiveness in the readjustment of discharged psychiatric patients. *J. Abnorm. Psychol., 95,* 139–43.

Faris, R. E. L., & Dunham, H. W. (1939). *Mental disorders in urban areas.* Chicago: University of Chicago Press. (Reprinted, 1965.)

Farley, F. H., & Farley, S. V. (1972). Stimulus seeking motivation and delinquent motivation among institutionalized delinquent girls. *J. Cons. Clin. Psychol., 39,* 94–97.

Feingold, B. F. (1977). Behavioral disturbances linked to the ingestion of food additives. *Delaware Medical Journal, 49,* 89–94.

Feinsilver, D. (1970). Communication in families of schizophrenic patients. *Arch. Gen. Psychiat., 22*(2), 143–48.

Feldman, R., & Weisfeld, G. (1973). An interdisciplinary study of crime. *Crime and Delinquency. 19*(2), 150–62.

Fenna, D. et. al. (1971). Ethanol metabolism in various racial groups. *Canadian Medical Association Journal, 105,* 472–75.

Fenz, W. D. (1971). Heart rate responses to a stressor: A comparison between primary and secondary psychopaths and normal controls. *Journal of Experimental Research in Personality, 5*(1), 7–13.

Fersch, E. A., Jr., (1980). *Psychology and psychiatry in courts and corrections.* New York: Wiley.

Ferster, C. B. (1973). A functional analysis of depression. *Amer. Psychol., 28*(10), 857–70.

Fetterman, J. L. (1949). *Practical lessons in psychiatry.* Springfield, IL: Charles C. Thomas.

Feuerstein, R. (1977). Mediated learning experience: A theoretical basis for cognitive modifiability during adolescence. In P. Mittler (Ed.), *Research to practice in mental retardation* (Vol. 2, pp. 105–16). Baltimore: University Park Press.

Field, M. J. (1960). *Search for security: An ethnopsychiatric study of rural Ghana.* Evanston, IL: Northwestern University Press.

Filskov, S. B., & Boll, T. J. (1986). *Handbook of clinical neuropsychology* (2nd ed.). New York: Wiley.

Filskov, S. B., & Goldstein, S. G. (1974). Diagnostic validity of the Halstead-Reitan Neuropsychology battery., *J. Cons. Clin. Psychol., 42,* 383–88.

Filskov, S. B., Grimm, B. H., & Lewis, J. A. (1981). Brain-behavior relationships. In S. B. Filskov & T. J. Boll (Eds.), *Handbook of clinical neuropsychology.* New York: Wiley.

Filskov, S. B., & Locklear, E. (1982). A multidimensional perspective on clinical neuropsychology research. In P. C. Kendall & J. M. Butcher (Eds.), *Handbook of research methods in clinical psychology.* New York: Wiley.

Fine, M. A., & Sansone, R. A. (1990). Dilemmas in the management of suicidal behavior in individuals with borderline disorder. *Amer. J. Psychother., 44,* 160–71.

Fine, R. (1979). *A history of psychoanalysis.* New York: Columbia University Press.

Fink, M. (1979). *Convulsive therapy: Theory and practice.* New York: Raven Press.

Fink, M., Kety, S., McGaugh, I., & Williams, T. A. (Eds.). (1974). *Psychobiology of convulsive therapy.* New York: Wiley.

Finkelhor, D. (1990). Early and long term effects of child sexual abuse: An update. *Professional Psychology: Research and Practice, 21,* 325–30.

Finn, P. R. (1990, March). Dysfunction in stimulus-response modulation in men at high risk for alcoholism. Paper presented at a symposium on the *Genetics of Alcoholism: Recent Advances.* Satellite Symposium of the Annual Meeting of the Research Society on Alcoholism, Montreal, Canada.

Finn, P. R., & Pihl, R.O. (1987). Men at high risk for alcoholism: The effect of alcohol on cardiovascular response to unavoidable shock. *J. Abnorm. Psychol., 96,* 230–36.

Finn, P. R., Zeitouni, N., & Pihl, R. (1990). Effects of alcohol on psychophysiological hyperactivity to nonaversive and aversive stimuli in men at high risk for alcoholism. *J. Abnorm. Psychol., 99,* 79–85.

Finucci, J. M., Guthrie, T., Childs, A. L., Abbey, H., & Childs, B. (1976). The genetics of specific reading disability. *Annals of Human Genetics, 40,* 1–23.

Fire Statistics U.K. (1980). London: Home Office.

Fisch, R., Weakland, J. H., & Segal, L. (1982). *The tactics of change: Doing therapy briefly.* San Francisco: Jossey-Bass.

Fischer, M. (1971). Psychoses in the offspring of schizophrenic monozygotic twins and their normal co-twins. *Brit. J. Psychiat., 118,* 43–52.

Fischer, M. (1973). Genetic and environmental factors in schizophrenia: A study of schizophrenic twins and their families. *Acta Psychiatr. Scandin.,* Suppl. No. 238.

Fischer, P. J., Shapiro, S., Breakey, W. R., Anthony, J. C., & Kramer, M. (1986). Mental health and social characteristics of the homeless: A survey of mission users. *Amer. J. Pub. Hlth. 76*(5), 519–24.

Fischl, M. A., Dickinson, G. M., Scott, G. B., Klimas, N., Fletcher, M. A., & Parks, W. (1987). Evaluation of heterosexual partners, children, and household contacts of adults with AIDS. *JAMA, 257,* 640–44.

Fischman, J. (1987, Feb.). Type A on trial. *Psych. Today, 21,* 42–50.

Fischman, M. W., & Schuster, C. R. (1982). Cocaine self-administration in humans. *Federal Proc. 41,* 241–46.

Fish, B. (1975). Biologic antecedents of psychosis in children. In D. X. Freedman (Ed.), *Biology of the major psychoses.* New York: Raven.

Fisher, J. E., & Carstensen, L. L. (1990). Behavior management for the dementias. *Clin. Psychol. Rev., 10,* 611–30.

Fisher, K. (1986). DSM-III-R protest: Critics say psychiatry has been stonewalling. *Monitor, 17*(7), 4–6.

Fleishman, M. J. (1981). A replication of Patterson's "Intervention for boys with conduct problems." *J. Cons. Clin. Psychol., 49*(3), 342–51.

Fleming, J. E., Offord, D. R., & Boyle, M. H. (1989). Prevalence of childhood and adolescent depression in the community: Ontario Health Study. *Brit. J. Psychiat., 155,* 647–54.

Foa, E. B., & Kozak, M. J. (1985). Treatment of anxiety disorders: Implications for psychopathology. In A. H. Tuma & J. D. Maser (Eds.), *Anxiety and the anxiety disorders* (pp. 421–52). Hillsdale, NJ: Lawrence Erlbaum and Associates.

Foa, E. B., Steketee, G., & Young, M. C. (1984). Agoraphobia: Phenomenological aspects, associated characteristics, and theoretical considerations. *Clin. Psychol. Rev., 4,* 431–57.

Fontana, A. F., & Dowds, B. N. (1975). Assessing treatment outcomes. *J. Nerv. Ment. Dis., 161,* 221–30.

Forehand, R., Rogers, T., McMahon, R. J., Wells, K. C., & Griest, D. L. (1981). Teaching parents to modify child behavior problems: An examination of some follow-up data. *J. Pediat. Psychol., 6*(3), 313–32.

Foreyt, J. P. (1986). Treating the diseases of the 1980s: Eating disorders. *Contemp. Psychol., 31,* 658–60.

Forgac, G. E., & Michaels, E. J. (1982). Personality characteristics of two types of male exhibitionists. *J. Abnorm. Psychol., 91,* 287–93.

Forgus, R. H., & DeWolfe, A. S. (1974). Coding of cognitive input in delusional patients. *J. Abnorm. Psychol., 83*(3), 278–84.

Forman, S. G., & Linney, J. A. (1988). School-based prevention of adolescent substance abuse: Programs, implementation and future directions. *School Psychology Review, 17*(4), 550–58.

Forseman, H., & Akesson, H. O. (1965). Mortality in patients with Down's syndrome. *Journal of Mental Deficiency Research, 9,* 146–61.

Fowler, R. C., Rich, C. L., & Young, D. (1986). San Diego suicide study: Substance abuse in young cases. *Arch. Gen. Psychiat., 43,* 962–65.

Fowler, R. D. (1987). Developing a computer based test interpretation system. In J. N. Butcher (Ed.), *Computerized psychological assessment: A practitioner's guide.* New York: Basic Books.

Fowler, R. D., & Butcher, J. N. (1986). Critique of Matarazzo's view of computerized testing: All sigma and no meaning. *Amer. Psychol., 41,* 94–96.

Fowler, R. D., Finkelstein, A., Penk, W., Bell, W., & Itzig, B.

(1987). An automated problem-rating interview: The DPRI. In J. N. Butcher (Ed.), *Computerized psychological assessment: A practitioner's guide.* New York: Basic Books.
Fox, R. E. (1976). Family therapy. In I. Weiner (Ed.), *Clinical methods in psychology.* New York: Wiley.
Frances, A. (1980). The DSM-III personality disorders section: A commentary. *Amer. J. Psychiat., 137*(9), 1050–54.
Frances, A. J., Widiger, T. A., & Pincus, A. (1989). The development of DSM-IV. *Arch. Gen. Psychiat., 46,* 373–75.
Frank, J. D. (1978). *Persuasion and Healing* (2nd ed.). Baltimore: Johns Hopkins University Press.
Franklin, J. L., Solovitz, B., Mason, M., Clemons, J. R., & Miller, G. E. (1987). An evaluation of case management. *Amer. J. Pub. Hlth., 77*(6), 674–78.
Frederick, C. J. (1985). An introduction and overview of youth suicide. In M. L. Peck, N. L. Farberow, & R. E. Litman (Eds.), *Youth Suicide* (pp. 1–16). New York: Springer.
Frederick, C. J. (1986). Post-traumatic stress disorder and child-molestation. In A. Burgess & C. Hartman (Eds.), *Sexual exploitation of parents by health professionals* (pp. 133–42). New York: Praeger.
Free, M. L., & Oei, T. P. S. (1989). Biological and psychological processes in the treatment and maintenance of depression. *Clin. Psychol. Rev., 9,* 653–88.
Freedman, A. M., Kaplan, H. I., & Sadock, B. J. (1976). *Modern synopsis of comprehensive textbook of psychiatry* (2nd ed.). Baltimore: Williams & Wilkins.
Freedman, B., & Chapman, L. J. (1973). Early subjective experience in schizophrenic episodes. *J. Abnorm. Psychol., 82*(1), 46–54.
Freedman, M. (1975). Homosexuals may be healthier than straights. *Psych. Today, 8*(10), 28–32.
Freeman, R. D., Malkin, S. F., & Hastings, J. O. (1975). Psychosocial problems of deaf children and their families: A comparative study. *American Annals of the Deaf, 120,* 391–405.
Freeman, T. (1960). On the psychopathology of schizophrenia. *J. Ment. Sci., 106,* 925–37.
Freeman, W. (1959). Psychosurgery. In S. Arieti (Ed.), *American handbook of psychiatry* (Vol. 2, pp. 1521–40). New York: Basic Books.
Fremouw, W. J., de Perczel, M., & Ellis, T. E. (1990). *Suicide risk: Assessment and response guidelines.* Elmsford, NY: Pergamon.
French, L. (1987, Nov.–Dec.). Victimization of the mentally ill: An unintended consequence of deinstitutionalization. *Social Work,* 502–5.
Freud, A. (1946). *Ego and the mechanisms of defense.* New York: International Universities Press.
Friedman, H. S., & Booth-Kewley, S. (1987a). Personality, Type A behavior, and coronary heart disease: The role of emotional expression. *J. Pers. Soc. Psychol., 53,* 783–92.
Friedman, H. S., & Booth-Kewley, S. (1987b). The "disease-prone" personality: A meta-analytic view of the construct. *Amer. Psychol., 42,* 539–55.
Friedman, J. H., (1974). Woman's role in male impotence. *Medical Aspects of Human Sexuality, 8*(6), 8–23.
Friedman, M., Manwaring, J. H., Rosenman, R. H., Donlon, G., & Ortega, P. (1973). Instantaneous and sudden death: Clinical and pathological differentiation in coronary artery disease. *JAMA, 225,* 1319–28.
Friedman, M., & Rosenman, R. H. (1959). Association of specific overt behavior pattern with blood and cardiovascular findings. *JAMA, 169,* 1286.
Friedman, M., & Ulmer, D. (1984). *Treating Type A behavior and your heart.* New York: Knopf.
Friedman, P., & Linn, L. (1957). Some psychiatric notes on the Andrea Doria disaster. *Amer. J. Psychiat., 114,* 426–32.
Friedman, R., & Iwai, J. (1976). Genetic predisposition and stress-induced hypertension. *Science, 193,* 161–92.
Friedrich, W., Einbender, A. J., & Luecke, W. J. (1983). Cognitive and behavioral characteristics of physically abused children. *J. Cons. Clin. Psychol., 51*(2), 313–14.
Fromm, E., & Shor, R. E. (1972). *Hypnosis: Research developments and perspectives.* Chicago: Aldine.
Fromm-Reichmann, F. (1948). Notes on the development of treatment of schizophrenics by psychoanalytic psychotherapy. *Psychiatry, 11,* 263–73.
Fry, P. S. (1984). Development of a geriatric scale of hopelessness: Implications for counseling and intervention with the depressed elderly. *J. Couns. Psychol. 31,* 322–31.
Fuller, A. K., & Blashfield, R. K. (1989). Masochistic personality disorder, a prototype analysis of diagnosis and sex bias. *J. Nerv. Ment. Dis., 177,* 168–72.
Fulmer, R. H., & Lapidus, L. B. (1980). A study of professed reasons for beginning and continuing heroin use. *Inter. J. Addictions, 15,* 631–45.
Furby, L., Weinrott, M. R., & Blackshaw, L. (1989). Sex offender recidivism: A review. *Psychol. Bull., 105,* 3–30.
Furlong, W. B. (1971). How "speed" kills athletic careers. *Today's Health, 49*(2), 30–33, 62, 64, 66.

Gabuzda, D. H., & Hirsch, M. S. (1987). Neurologic manifestations of infection with human immunodeficiency virus: Clinical features and pathogenesis. *Ann. Int. Med., 107,* 383–91.
Gager, N., & Schurr, C., (1976). *Sexual assault: Confronting rape in America.* New York: Grosset & Dunlap.
Gajdusek, D. C. (1986). On the uniform source of amyloid in plaques, tangles, and vascular deposits. *Neurobiology of Aging, 7,* 453–54.
Gajzago, C., & Prior, M. (1974). Two cases of "recovery" in Kanner syndrome. *Arch. Gen. Psychiat., 31*(2), 264–68.
Gamble, T. J., & Zigler, E. (1989). The head start synthesis project: A critique. *Journal of Applied Developmental Psychology, 10,* 267–74.
Ganju, V., & Quan, H. (1987). Mental health service needs of refugees in Texas. Paper given at the *Refugee Assistance Program: Mental Health Workgroup Meeting,* UCLA, February 12–13.
Garb, H. N. (1989). Clinical judgment, clinical training, and professional experience. *Psychol. Bull., 105,* 387–96.
Garb, J. R., & Stunkard, A. J. (1974). Effectiveness of a self-help group in obesity control: A further assessment. *Arch. Int. Med., 134,* 716–20.
Garber, H. L. (1988). *The Milwaukee Project: Preventing mental retardation in children at risk.* Washington, DC: American Association on Mental Retardation.
Garfield, S. L. (1986). Research on client variables in psychotherapy. In S. L. Garfield & A. E. Bergin (Eds.), *Handbook of psychotherapy and behavior change* (3rd ed., pp. 213–56). New York: Wiley.
Garmezy, N. (1978a). Current status of other high-risk research programs. In L. C. Wynne, R. L. Cromwell, & S. Matthysse (Eds.), *The nature of schizophrenia: New approaches to research and treatment.* New York: Wiley.
Garmezy, N. (1978b). Observations of high-risk research and premorbid development in schizophrenia. In L. C. Wynne, R. L. Cromwell, & S. Matthysse (Eds.), *The nature of schizophrenia: New approaches to research and treatment.* New York: Wiley.
Garner, D. M. (1986). Cognitive-behavioral therapy for eating disorders. *Clin. Psychol., 39*(2), 36–39.
Garner, D. M. (1986). Cognitive therapy for anorexia nervosa. In K. D. Brownwell & J. P. Foreyt (Eds.), *Handbook of eating disorders* (pp. 301–27). New York: Basic Books.
Gartner, A., & Riessman, F. (1974). Is there a new work ethic? *Amer. J. Orthopsychiat., 44*(4), 563–67.
Gawin, F. H., & Kleber, H. D. (1986). Abstinence symptomatology and psychiatric diagnosis in cocaine abusers. *Arch. Gen. Psychiat., 43,* 107–13.
Gebhard, P. H. (1965). Situational factors affecting human sexual behavior. In F. Beach (Ed.), *Sex and behavior.* New York: Wiley.
Gebhard, P. H., Gagnon, J. H., Pomeroy, W. B., & Christenson, C. V. (1965). *Sex offenders: An analysis of types.* New York: Harper & Row.
Geiser, D. S. (1989). Psychosocial influences on human immunity. *Clin. Psychol. Rev., 9,* 689–715.
Geisz, D., & Steinhausen, H. (1974). On the "psychological development of children with hydrocephalus." (German) *Praxis der Kinderpsychologie und Kinderpsychiatrie, 23*(4), 113–18.
Gelfand, D. M., Jenson, W. R., & Drew, C. J. (1988). *Understanding child behavior disorders* (2nd ed.). New York: Holt, Rinehart & Winston.
Gelfand, D. M., & Teti, D. M. (1990). The effects of maternal depression on children. *Clin. Psychol. Rev., 10,* 329–53.
Gelles, R. J. (1978). Violence toward children in the United States. *Amer. J. Orthopsychiat., 48,* 580–90.
Gentry, W. D. (1984a). Behavioral medicine: A new research paradigm. In W. D. Gentry (Ed.), *Handbook of behavioral medicine* (pp. 1–12). New York: Guilford Press.
Gentry, W. D. (Ed.). (1984b). *Handbook of behavioral medicine.* New York: Guilford.
Gentry, W. D., Chesney, A. P., Gary, H. G., Hall, R. P., &

Harburg, E. (1982). Habitual anger-coping styles: I. Effect of mean blood pressure and risk for essential hypertension. *Psychosom. Med., 44,* 195–202.

George, L., & Neufeld, R. W. J. (1985). Cognition and symptomatology in schizophrenia. *Schizo. Bull., 11,* 264–85.

George, L. K. (1984). The burden of caregiving. *Center Reports of Advances in Research.* Durham, NC: Duke University Center for the Study of Aging and Human Development.

German, W. J. (1959). Initial symptomatology in brain turners. *Connecticut Medicine, 23,* 636–37.

Geschwind, N. (1975). The borderland of neurology and psychiatry: Some common misconceptions. In D. F. Benson & D. Blumer (Eds.), *Psychiatric aspects of neurological disease* (pp. 1–9). New York: Grune & Stratton.

Giannetti, R. A. (1987). The GOLPH Psychosocial History: Response contingent data acquisition and reporting. In J. N. Butcher (Ed.), *Computerized psychological assessment: A practitioners guide.* New York: Basic Books.

Gilbert, J. G., & Lombardi, D. N. (1967). Personality characteristics of young male narcotic addicts. *J. Couns. Psychol., 31,* 536–38.

Gillberg, C., & Schaumann, H. (1981). Infantile autism and puberty. *J. Autism Develop. Dis., 11*(4), 365–71.

Gillberg, C. U. (1990). Autism and pervasive developmental disorders. *Journal of Child Psychology & Psychiatry & Allied Disciplines, 31,* 99–119.

Ginsberg, G. L., Frosch, W. A., & Shapiro, T. (1972). The new impotence. *Arch. Gen. Psychiat., 26*(3), 218–20.

Gist, R., & Lubin, B. (Eds.) (1989). *Psychosocial aspects of disaster.* New York: Wiley.

Gittelman, R. (1983). Treatment of reading disorders. In M. Rutter (Ed.), *Developmental neuropsychiatry* (pp. 520–39). New York: Guilford.

Gittelman, R., Mannuzza, S., Shenker, R., & Bonagura, N. (1985). Hyperactive boys almost grown up. *Arch. Gen. Psychiat., 42,* 937–47.

Glaser, R., Kiecolt-Glaser, J. K., Speicher, C. E., & Holliday, J. E. (1985). Stress, loneliness, and changes in herpes virus latency. *J. Behav. Med., 8,* 249–60.

Glaser, R., Rice, J., Sheridan, J., Fertel, R., Stout, J., Speicher, C., Pinsky, R., Kotur, M., Post, A., Beck, M., & Kiecolt-Glaser, J. (1987). Stress-related immune suppression: Health implications. *Brain, Behavior, and Immunity, 1,* 7–20.

Glaser, R., Rice, J., Speicher, C. E., Stout, J. C., & Kiecolt-Glaser, J. K. (in press). Stress depresses interferon production by lymphocytes and natural killer cell activity in humans. *Behavioral Neuroscience.*

Glasner, P. D., & Kaslow, R. A. (1990). The epidemiology of human immunodeficiency virus infection. *J. Cons. Clin. Psychol., 58,* 13–21.

Glasscote, R. (1978). What programs work and what programs do not work for chronic mental patients? In J. A. Talbott (Ed.), *The chronic mental patient: Problems, solutions and recommendations for a public policy.* Washington, DC: American Psychiatric Association.

Glenner, G. C. (1986). Marching backwards into the future. *Neurobiology of Aging, 7,* 439–41.

Gleser, G., & Sacks, M. (1973). Ego defenses and reaction to stress: A validation study of the Defense Mechanisms Inventory. *J. Cons. Clin. Psychol., 40*(2), 181–87.

Glosser, G., & Wexler, D. (1985). Participants' evaluation of education/support groups for families of patients with Alzheimer's disease and other dementias. *Gerontologist, 25,* 232–36.

Glow, R. A. (1981). Treatment alternatives for hyperactive children—a comment on "problem children" and stimulant drug therapy. *Australian Journal of Psychiatry, 15*(2), 123–28.

Glueck, S., & Glueck, E. (1968). *Non-delinquents in perspective.* Cambridge, MA: Harvard University Press.

Glueck, S., & Glueck, E. T. (1969). Delinquency prediction method reported highly accurate. *Roche Reports, 6*(15), 3.

Gochman, S. I., Allgood, B. A., & Geer, C. R. (1982). A look at today's behavior therapists. *Profess. Psychol., 13*(5), 605–9.

Goering, P., Wasylenki, D., Lancee, W., & Freeman, S. J. (1984). From hospital to community: Six month and two-year outcomes for 505 patients. *J. Nerv. Ment. Dis., 17*(11), 667–73.

Goetz, K. L., & Van Kammen, D. P. (1986). Computerized axial tomography scans and subtypes of schizophrenia: A review of the literature. *J. Nerv. Ment. Dis., 174,* 31–41.

Gold, E. R. (1986). Long-term effects of sexual victimization in childhood: An attributional approach. *J. Cons. Clin. Psychol., 54,* 471–75.

Gold, M. S., & Rea, W. S. (1983). The role of endorphins in opiate addiction, withdrawal, and recovery. *Psychiat. Clin. N. Amer., 6,* 489–520.

Goldberg, J., True, W. R., Eisen, S. A., & Henderson, W. G. (1990). A twin study of the effects of the Vietnam War on posttraumatic stress disorder. *JAMA, 263,* 1227–32.

Goldberg, S., Schultz, C., Schultz, P., et al. (1986). Borderline and schizotypal personality disorders treated with low-dose thiothixene vs. placebo. *Arch. Gen. Psychiat., 43,* 680–86.

Golden, C. J. (1978). *Diagnosis and rehabilitation in clinical neuropsychology.* Springfield, IL: Charles C. Thomas.

Golden, C. J., Graber, B., Blose, I., Berg, P., Coffman, J., & Bloch, S. (1981). Differences in brain densities between chronic alcoholic and normal control patients. *Science, 211*(30), 508–10.

Golden, C. J., MacInnes, W. D., Ariel R. N., Ruedrich, S. L., Chu C-C., Coffman, J. A., Graber, B., & Bloch, S. (1982). Cross-validation of the ability of the Luria-Nebraska Neuropsychological Battery to differentiate chronic schizophrenics with and without ventricular enlargement. *J. Cons. Clin. Psychol., 50,* 87–95.

Golden, D. A., & Davis, J. G. (1974). Counseling parents after the birth of an infant with Down's syndrome. *Children Today, 3*(2), 7–11.

Goldfried, M. R. (1980). Toward the delineation of therapeutic change principles. *Amer. Psychol., 35,* 991–99.

Goldfried, M. R., Greenberg, L. S., & Marmar, C. (1990). Individual psychotherapy: Process and outcome. *Annu. Rev. Psychol.* (Vol. 41, pp. 659–88). Palo Alto, CA: Annual Reviews, Inc.

Goldfried, M. R., Linehan, M. M., & Smith, J. L. (1978). Reduction of test anxiety through cognitive restructuring. *J. Cons. Clin. Psychol., 46*(1), 32–39.

Goldfried, M. R., & Merbaum, M. (Eds.). (1973). *Behavior change through self control.* New York: Holt, Rinehart & Winston.

Goldfried, M. R., & Safran, J. D. (1986). Future directions in psychotherapy integration. In J. C. Norcross (Ed.), *Handbook of eclectic psychotherapy* (pp. 463–83). New York: Brunner/Mazel.

Goldman, H.H., Feder, J., & Scanlon, W. (1986). Chronic mental patients in nursing homes: Reexamining data from the national nursing home survey. *Hosp. Comm. Psychiat., 37,* 269–72.

Goldman, M. S., Williams, D. L., & Klisz, D. K. (1983). Recoverability of psychological functioning following alcohol abuse: Prolonged spatial-visual dysfunction in older alcoholics. *J. Cons. Clin. Psychol., 51*(3), 370–78.

Goldsmith, W., & Cretekos, C. (1969). Unhappy odysseys: Psychiatric hospitalization among Vietnam returnees. *Amer. J. Psychiat., 20,* 78–83.

Goldstein, A., et al. (1974, Mar. 4). Researchers isolate opiate receptor. *Behav. Today, 5*(9), 1.

Goldstein, M. J. (1985). Family factors that antedate the onset of schizophrenia and related disorders: The results of a fifteen year prospective longitudinal study. *Acta Psychiatr. Scandin.* (Suppl. No. 319), *71,* 7–18.

Goldstein, M. J., Rodnick, E. H., Jones, J. E., McPherson, S. R., & West, K. L. (1978). Family precursors of schizophrenia spectrum disorders. In L. C. Wynne, R. L. Cromwell, & S. Matthysse (Eds.), *The nature of schizophrenia: New approaches to research and treatment.* New York: Wiley Medical.

Goldstein, M. J., & Strachan, A. M. (1987). The family and schizophrenia. In T. Jacob (Ed.), *Family interaction and psychopathology: Theories, methods, and findings* (pp. 481–508). New York: Plenum.

Goldstein, W. N. (1983). DSM-III and the diagnosis of schizophrenia. *Amer. J. Psychother., 37,* 168–81.

Gomberg, E. S. (1989). Suicide rates among women with alcohol problems. *Amer. J. Pub. Hlth., 79,* 1363–65.

Gomes-Schwartz, B., Horowitz, J., & Cardarelli, A. (1990). *Child sexual abuse: The initial effects.* Newbury Park, CA: Sage.

Gonzales, L. R., Lewinsohn, P. M., & Clarke, G. N. (1985). Longitudinal follow-up of unipolar depressives: An investigation of predictors of relapse. *J. Cons. Clin. Psychol., 53,* 461–69.

Goodman, J. (1972). A case study of an "autistic-savant": Mental function in the psychotic child with markedly discrepant abilities. *J. Child Psychol. Psychiat., 13*(4), 267–78.

Goodman, R. (1989). Infantile autism: A syndrome of multiple primary deficits? *J. Autism Devel. Dis., 19,* 409–24.

Goodman, R. A., Mercy, J. A., Loya, F., Rosenberg, M.,

Smith, J. C., Allen, N. H., Vargas, L., & Kolts, R. (1986). Alcohol use and interpersonal violence: Alcohol detected in homicide victims. *Amer. J. Pub. Hlth., 76*(2), 144–49.

Goodwin, D. K. (1988). *The Fitzgeralds and the Kennedys: An American saga.* New York: St. Martin's Press.

Goodwin, D. W., Schulsinger, F., Hermansen, L., Guze, S. B., & Winokur, G. (1973). Alcohol problems in adoptees raised apart from alcoholic biological parents. *Arch. Gen. Psychiat., 28*(2), 238–43.

Goodwin, D. W., Schulsinger, F., Moller, N., Hermansen, L., Winokur, G., & Guze, S. B. (1974). Drinking problems in adopted and nonadopted sons of alcoholics. *Arch. Gen. Psychiat., 31*(2), 164–69.

Goplerud, E., & Depue, R. A. (1985). Behavioral response to naturally occurring stress in cyclothymia and dysthymia. *J. Abnorm. Psychol., 94,* 128–39.

Gordon, R. (1977). A critique of the evaluation of Patuxent Institution, with particular attention to the issues of dangerousness and recidivism. *Bulletin of the American Academy of Psychiatry and the Law, 5,* 210–55.

Gorenstein, E. E. (1982). Frontal lobe functions in psychopaths. *J. Abnorm. Psychol., 91,* 368–79.

Gorenstein, E. E. (1987). Cognitive-perceptual deficit in an alcoholism spectrum disorder. *J. Stud. Alcoh., 48,* 310–18.

Gorin, N. (1980). Looking out for Mrs. Berwid. *Sixty Minutes.* (Narrated by Morley Safer.) New York: CBS Television News.

Gorin, N. (1982). It didn't have to happen. *Sixty Minutes.* (Narrated by Morley Safer.) New York: CBS Television News.

Gorman, J. M., Battista, D., Goetz, R. R., Dillon, D. J., Liebowitz, M. R., Fyer, A. J., Kahn, J. P., Sandberg, D., & Klein, D. F. (1989). A comparison of sodium bicarbonate and sodium lactate infusion in the induction of panic attacks. *Arch. Gen. Psychiat., 46,* 145–50.

Gorton, G., & Akhtar, S. (1990). The literature on personality disorders, 1985–1988: Trends, issues, and controversies. *Hosp. Comm. Psychiat., 41,* 39–51.

Gosslin, C. C., & Eysenck, S. B. G. (1980). The transvestite "double image": A preliminary report. *Personality and Individual Differences, 1,* 172–73.

Gotlib, I. H., & Colby, C. A. (1987). *Treatment of depression: An interpersonal systems approach.* New York: Pergamon.

Gottesman, I. I., & Bertelson, A. (1989). Confirming unexpressed genotypes for schizophrenia: Risks in the offspring of Fischer's Danish identical and fraternal discordant twins. *Arch. Gen. Psychiat., 46,* 867–72.

Gottesman, I. I., & Shields, J. (1972). *Schizophrenia and genetics.* New York: Academic Press.

Gottesman, I. I., & Shields, J. (1982). *Schizophrenia: The epigenetic puzzle.* Cambridge, UK: Cambridge University Press.

Gottheil, E., Thornton, C. C., Skoloda, T. E., & Alterman, A. I. (1982). Follow-up of abstinent and non-abstinent alcoholics. *Amer. J. Psychiat., 139*(5), 560–65.

Gottlieb, J. (1981). Mainstreaming: Fulfilling the promise? *Amer. J. Ment. Def., 86,* 115–26.

Gottschalk, L. A., Haer, J. L., & Bates, D. E. (1972). Effect of sensory overload on psychological state: Changes in social alienation—personal disorganization and cognitive-intellectual impairment. *Arch. Gen. Psychiat., 27*(4), 451–56.

Grady, K., Gersick, K.E., & Boratynski, M. (1985). Preparing parents for teenagers: A step in the prevention of adolescent substance abuse. *Family Relations Journal of Applied Family and Child Studies, 34*(4), 541–49.

Graham, J. R. (1978a). *MMPI characteristics of alcoholics, drug abusers and pathological gamblers.* Paper presented at the 13th Annual Symposium on Recent Developments in the Use of the MMPI. Puebla, Mexico, March, 1978.

Graham, J. R. (1978b). The Minnesota Multiphasic Personality Inventory. In B. B. Wolman (Ed.), *Clinical diagnosis of mental disorders: A handbook.* New York: Plenum.

Graham, J. R., Timbrook, R., Ben-Porath, Y. S., & Butcher, J. N. (in press). Code-type congruence between MMPI and MMPI-2: Separting fact from artifact. *J. Pers. Assess.*

Gralnick, A. (1942). Folie a deux—The psychosis of association: A review of 103 cases and the entire English literature, with case presentations. *Psychiatric Quarterly, 14,* 230–63.

Grand, T. P., et al. (1984). Association among alcoholism, drug abuse, and antisocial personality: A Review of the literature. *Psych. Rep., 55,* 455–74.

Grant, I., Atkinson, J. H., Hesselink, J. R., Kennedy, C. J., Richman, D. D., Spector, S. A., & McCutchan, J. A. (1987). Evidence for early central nervous system involvement in the acquired immunodeficiency syndrome (AIDS) and other human immunodeficiency virus (HIV) infections. *Ann. Int. Med., 107,* 828–36.

Grant, I., & Heaton, R. K. (1990). Human immunodeficiency virus-Type 1 (HIV-1) and the brain. *J. Cons. Clin. Psychol., 58,* 22–30.

Grant, L., Sweetland, H. L., Yager, J., & Gerst, M. (1981). Quality of life events in relation to psychiatric symptoms. *Arch. Gen. Psychiat., 38*(3), 335–39.

Grant, V. W. (1953). A case study of fetishism. *J. Abnorm. Soc. Psychol., 48,* 142–49.

Gray, W. W., & Ramsey, B. K. (1982). The early training project: A life-span view. *Human Develop., 25,* 48–57.

Gray, F., Gherardi, R., & Scaravilli, F. (1988). The neuropathology of the acquired immune deficiency syndrome (AIDS). *Brain, 111,* 245–66.

Green, A. (1978). Self-destructive behavior in battered children. *Amer. J. Psychiat., 135,* 579–82.

Green, L., & Warshauer, D. (1981). Note on the "paradoxical" effect of stimulant drugs on hyperactivity with reference to the rate-dependency effect. *J. Nerv. Ment. Dis., 169*(3), 196–98.

Green, R. (1974). *Sexual identity conflict in children and adults.* New York: Basic Books.

Green, R. (1985). Gender identity in childhood and later sexual orientation: Follow-up of 78 males. *Amer. J. Psychiat., 142,* 339–41.

Greenacre, P. (1945). Conscience in the psychopath. *Amer. J. Orthopsychiat., 15,* 495–509.

Greene, M. H., & Dupont, R. L. (1974). Heroin addiction trends. *Amer. J. Psychiat., 131*(5), 545–50.

Greenfield, J. C., & Wolfson, J. M. (1935). Microcephalia vera. *Archives of Neurology and Psychiatry, 33,* 1296–1316.

Greer, S. (1964). Study of parental loss in neurotics and sociopaths. *Arch. Gen. Psychiat., 11*(2), 177–80.

Gregory, I., & Rosen, E. (1965). *Abnormal psychology.* Philadelphia: W. B. Saunders.

Gregg, C., & Hoy, C. (1989). Coherence: The comprehension and production abilities of college writers who are normally achieving, learning disabled, and underprepared. *J. Learn. Dis., 22,* 370–72.

Gresham, F. M. (1982). Misguided mainstreaming: The case for social skills training with handicapped children. *Exceptional Children, 48,* 422–33.

Griest, D. L., & Wells, K. C. (1983). Behavioral family therapy with conduct disorders in children. *Behav. Ther., 14,* 37–53.

Griest, J. H., Gustafson, D. H., Stauss, F. F., Rowse, G. L., Laughren, T. P., & Chiles, J. A. (1974). Suicide risk prediction: A new approach. *Life-Threatening Behavior, 4*(4), 212–23.

Grinker, R. R. (1969). An essay on schizophrenia and science. *Arch. Gen. Psychiat., 20,* 1–24.

Grinspoon, L., Ewalt, J. R., & Shader, R. I. (1972). *Schizophrenia: Pharmacotherapy and psychotherapy.* Baltimore: Williams & Wilkins.

Grob, C. S. (1985). Female exhibitionism. *J. Nerv. Ment. Dis., 173,* 253–56.

Gross, B. H., Southard, M. J., Lamb, H. R., & Weinberger, L. (1987). Assessing dangerousness and responding appropriately: Hedland expands the clinician's liability established by Tarasoff. *J. Clin. Psychiat., 48,* 9–12.

Gross, G., & Huber, G. (1973). Zur prognose der schizophenier. *Psychiatria Clinica, 6*(1), 1–16.

Groth, A. N., Burgess, A. W., & Holmstrom, L. L. (1977). Rape: Power, anger, and sexuality. *Amer. J. Psychiat., 134,* 1239–43.

Grunebaum, H., & Perlman, M. S. (1973). Paranoia and naivete. *Arch. Gen. Psychiat., 28*(1), 30–32.

Guelfi, G. P., Faustman, W. O., & Csernansky, J. G. (1989). Independence of positive and negative symptoms in a population of schizophrenic patients. *J. Nerv. Ment. Dis., 177,* 285–90.

Guerra, F. (1971). *The pre-Columbian mind.* New York: Seminar Press.

Gugliemi, R. S. (1979). *A double-blind study of the effectiveness of skin temperature biofeedback as a treatment for Raynaud's disease.* Unpublished doctoral dissertation, University of Minnesota.

Gunderson, J. G. (1980). A reevaluation of milieu therapy for nonchronic schizophrenic patients. *Schizo. Bull., 6*(1), 64–69.

Gunderson, J. G., & Siever, L. J. (1985). Relatedness of schizotypal to schizophrenic disorders. *Schizo. Bull., 11,* 532–37.

Gunderson, J. G., & Singer, M. T. (1986). Defining borderline patients: An overview. In M. H. Stone (Ed.), *Essential papers on* *borderline disorders* (pp. 453–74). New York: New York University Press.

Gurland, B. J., & Cross, P. S. (1982). Epidemiology of psychopathology in old age. In L. F. Jarvik & G. W. Small (Eds.), *Psychiat. Clin. N. Amer.* Philadelphia: Saunders.

Gurman, A. S., & Kniskern, D. P. (1978). Research on marital and family therapy: Progress, perspective and prospect. In S. L. Garfield & A. E. Bergin (Eds.), *Handbook of psychotherapy and behavior change.* New York: Wiley.

Gurman, A. S., Kniskern, D. P., & Pinsof, W. M. (1986). Research on marital and family therapies. In S. L. Garfield & A. E. Bergin (Eds.), *Handbook of psychotherapy and behavior change* (pp. 565–626). New York: Wiley.

Gurtman, M. B. (1986). Depression and the response of others: Reevaluating the reevaluation. *J. Abnorm. Psychol., 95,* 99–101.

Guy, E., Platt, J. J., Zwerling, I., & Bullock, S. (1985). Mental health status of prisoners in an urban jail. *Crim. Just. Behav., 12,* 29–53.

Gynther, M. D. (1979). Ethnicity and personality. In J. N. Butcher (Ed.), *New directions in MMPI research.* Minneapolis: University of Minnesota Press.

Hafner, R. J. (1984). Predicting the effects on husbands of behavior therapy for wives' agoraphobia. *Behav. Res. Ther., 22,* 227–42.

Hagan, J. W., & Huntsman, N. J. (1971). Selective attention in mental retardation. *Develop. Psychol., 5*(1), 151–60.

Halberstam, M. (1972). Can you make yourself sick? A doctor's report on psychosomatic illness. *Today's Health, 50*(12), 24–29.

Haley, J. (1959). The family of the schizophrenic: A model system. *J. Nerv. Ment. Dis., 129,* 357–74.

Haley, J. (1962). Whither family therapy. *Family Process, 1,* 69–100.

Haley, S. A. (1978). Treatment implications of post-combat stress response syndromes for mental health professionals. In C. R. Figley (Ed.), *Stress disorders among Vietnam veterans.* New York: Brunner/Mazel.

Hall, J. C., Bliss, M., Smith, K., & Bradley, A. (1970, July 1). Suicide gestures, attempts found high among poor. *Psychiat. News,* p. 20.

Hallgren, B. (1950). Specific dyslexia ("congenital word-blindness"). *Acta Psychiatrica Neurologica Scandinavica,* Suppl., *65,* 1–287.

Hallworth, H. J. (1977). Computer-assisted instruction for the mentally retarded. In P. Milder (Ed.), *Research to practice in mental retardation* (Vol. 2, pp. 419–20). Baltimore: University Park Press.

Halmi, K. A., Falk, J. R., & Schwartz, E. (1981). Binge-eating and vomiting: A survey of a college population. *Psychol. Med., 11,* 697–706.

Hammen, C., Adrian, C., Gordon, D., Burge, D., Jaenicke, C., & Hiroto, D. (1987). Children of depressed mothers: Maternal strain and symptom predictors of dysfunction. *J. Abnorm. Psychol., 96,* 190–98.

Hammen, C., Ellicott, A., Gitlin, M., & Jamison, K. R. (1989). Sociotropy/autonomy and vulnerability to specific life events in patients with unipolar depression and bipolar disorders. *J. Abnorm. Psychol., 98,* 154–60.

Hammen, C., Marks, T., Mayol, A., & DeMayo, R. (1985). Depressive self-schemas, life stress, and vulnerability to depression. *J. Abnorm. Psychol., 94,* 308–19.

Hammen, C. L., & Peters, S. D. (1977). Differential responses to male and female depressive reactions. *J. Cons. Clin. Psychol., 45,* 994–1001.

Hammen, C. L., & Peters, S. D. (1978). Interpersonal consequences of depression: Responses to men and women enacting a depressed role. *J. Abnorm. Psychol., 87*(3), 322–32.

Handleman, J. S., Gill, M. J., & Alessandri, M. (1988). Generalization by severely developmentally disabled children: Issues, advances, and future directions. *The Behavior Therapist, 11,* 221–23.

Hanerton, J. L., Canning, N., Ray, M., & Smith, S. (1975). A cytogenetic survey of 14,069 newborn infants: Incidence of chromosome abnormalities. *Clinical Genetics, 8,* 223–43.

Haney, B., & Gold, M. (1973). The juvenile delinquent nobody knows. *Psychol. Today, 7*(4), 48–52, 55.

Hanrahan, J., Goodman, W., & Rapagna, S. (1990). Preparing mentally retarded students for mainstreaming: Priorities of regular class and special school teachers. *Amer. J. Ment. Retard., 94,* 470–74.

Hanson, D. R., Gottesman, I. I., & Meehl, P. E. (1977). Generic theories and the validation of psychiatric diagnoses: Implications for the study of children of schizophrenics. *J. Abnorm. Psychol., 86*(6), 575–88.

Harburgh, E., Erfurt, J. C., Hauenstein, L. S., Chape, C., Schull, W. J., & Schork, M. A. (1973). Socioecological stress, suppressed hostility, skin color, and black-white male blood pressure: Detroit. *Psychosom. Med., 35,* 276–96.

Harder, D. W., Strauss, J. S., Greenwald, D. F., Kokes, R. F., et al. (1989). Life events and psychopathology severity: Comparisons between psychiatric inpatients and outpatients. *J. Clin. Psychol., 45,* 202–9.

Harding, C. M., Brooks, G. W., Ashikaga, T., Strauss, J. S., & Breier, A. (1987a). The Vermont longitudinal study of persons with severe mental illness, I: Methodology, study sample, and overall status 32 years later. *Amer. J. Psychiat., 144,* 718–26.

Harding, C. M., Brooks, G. W., Ashikaga, T., Strauss, J. S., & Breier, A. (1987b). The Vermont longitudinal study of persons with severe mental illness, II: Long-term outcome of subjects who retrospectively met DSM-III criteria for schizophrenia. *Amer. J. Psychiat., 144,* 727–35.

Harding, W. M., Zinberg, N. E., Stelmack, S. M., & Barry, M. (1980). Formerly-addicted-noncontrolled opiate users. *Inter. J. Addictions, 15,* 47–60.

Hardy, J. A., Mann, D. M., Wester, P., & Winblad, B. (1986). An integrative hypothesis concerning the pathogenesis and progression of Alzheimer's disease. *Neurobiology of Aging, 7,* 489–502.

Hare, R. D. (1968). Psychopathy, autonomic functioning and the orienting response. *J. Abnorm. Psychol., 73,* (Monograph Suppl. 3, part 2), 1–24.

Hare, R. D. (1970). *Psychopathy: Theory and research.* New York: Wiley.

Hare, R. D. (1984). Performance of psychopaths on cognitive tasks related to frontal lobe function. *J. Abnorm. Psychol., 93*(2), 133–40.

Hare, R. D., McPherson, L.M., & Forth, A. E. (1988). Male psychopaths and their criminal careers. *J. Cons. Clin. Psychol., 56,* 710–14.

Harlow, H. (1969). A brief look at autistic children. *Psychiatry and Social Science Review, 3*(1), 27–29.

Harlow, J. M. (1868). Recovery from the passage of an iron bar through the head. *Publication of the Massachusetts Medical Society, 2,* 327.

Harris, S. L., & Ersner-Hershfield, R. (1978). Behavioral suppression of seriously disruptive behavior in psychotic and retarded patients: A review of punishment and its alternatives. *Psychol. Bull., 85,* 1352–75.

Harrow, M., Carone, B. J., & Westermeyer, J. F. (1985). The course of psychosis in early phases of schizophrenia. *Amer. J. Psychiat., 142,* 702–7.

Harrow, M., Goldberg, J. F., Grossman, L. S., & Meltzer, H. Y. (1990). Outcome in manic disorders: A naturalistic follow-up study. *Arch. Gen. Psychiat., 47,* 665–71.

Harter, S., Alexander, P.C., & Neimeyer, R. A. (1988). Long term effects of incestuous child abuse in college women: Social adjustment, social cognition, and family characteristics. *J. Cons. Clin. Psychol., 56,* 5–8.

Hartford, J. T. (1986). A review of antemortem markers of Alzheimer's disease. *Neurobiology of Aging, 7,* 401–2.

Hartlage, L., Asken, M., & Hornsby, J. (1987). *Essentials of neuropsychological assessment.* New York: Springer.

Hartmann, E. (1968). Longitudinal studies of sleep and dream patterns in manic-depressive patients. *Arch. Gen. Psychiat., 19,* 312–29.

Hartmann, E., Milofsky, E., Vaillant, G., Oldfield, M., & Falke, R. (1984). Vulnerability to schizophrenia: Predormation. *Arch. Gen. Psychiat., 41,* 1050–56.

Hartup, W. W. (1983). Peer relations. In P. H. Mussen (Ed.), *Handbook of child psychology* (Vol. 4, pp. 274–385). New York: Wiley.

Hathaway, S. R., & McKinley, J. C. (1951). *The Minnesota multiphasic personality inventory* (rev. ed.). New York: Psychological Corporation.

Hatzenbuehler, L. C., & Schroeder, H. E. (1978). Desensitization procedures in the treatment of childhood disorders. *Psychol. Bull., 85,* 831–44.

Havens, L. L. (1974). The existential use of the self. *Amer. J. Psychiat., 131*(1), 1–10.

Hawk, A. B., Carpenter, W. T., & Strauss, J. S. (1975). Diagnostic criteria and five-year outcome in schizophrenia. *Arch. Gen. Psychiat., 32*(3), 343–47.

Hayes, T. A., Panitch, M. L., & Barker, E. (1975). Imipramine dosage in children: A comment on "Imipramine and electrocardiographic abnormalities in hyperactive children." *Amer. J. Psychiat., 132*(5), 546–47.

Haynes, S. G., Feinleib, M., & Kannel, W. B. (1980). The relationship of psychosocial factors to coronary heart disease in the Framingham study: III. Eight-year incidence of coronary heart disease. *American Journal of Epidemiology, 111,* 37–58.

Haywood, H. C., Meyers, C. E., & Switsky, H. N. (1982). Mental retardation. In M. R. Rosenzweig & L. W. Porter (Eds.), *Annu. Rev. Psychol., 33.*

Hazelrigg, M., Cooper, H., & Borduin, C. (1987). Evaluating the effectiveness of family therapies: An integrative review and analysis. *Psychol. Bull., 101,* 428–42.

Hazlett, B. (1971, Mar. 2). Two who played with death—and lost the game. *Los Angeles Times,* II, 1, 5.

Hearn, M. D., Murray, D. M., & Luepker, R. V. (1989). Hostility, coronary heart disease, and total mortality: A 33-year follow-up study of university students. *J. Behav. Med., 12,* 105–21.

Heaton, R. K., & Pendleton, M. G. (1981). Use of neuropsychological tests to predict adult patient's everyday functioning. *J. Cons. Clin. Psychol., 49*(6), 807–21.

Heaver, W. L. (1943). A study of forty male psychopathic personalities before, during and after hospitalization. *Amer. J. Psychiat., 100,* 342–46.

Hecaen, H., & Albert, M. L. (1975). Disorders of mental functioning related to frontal lobe pathology. In D. F. Benson & D. Blumer (Eds.), *Psychiatric aspects of neurological disease* (pp. 137–49). New York: Grune & Stratton.

Hechtman, L., Weiss, G., & Perlman, T. (1980). Hyperactives as young adults: Self-esteem and social skills. *Canad. J. Psychiat., 25*(6), 478–83.

Heckler, M. M. (1983). Fifth special report to the U.S. Congress on Alcohol and Health. U.S. Department of Health and Human Services (NIAAA). Washington, DC: U.S. Government Printing Office.

Hefez, A. (1985). The role of the press and the medical community in the epidemic of "mysterious gas poisoning" in the Jordan West Bank. *Amer. J. Psychiat., 142,* 833–37.

Heider, F. (1958). *The psychology of interpersonal relations.* New York: Wiley.

Heiman, J. R., & Grafton-Becker, V. (1989). Orgasmic disorders in women. In S. R. Leiblum & R. C. Rosen (Eds.), *Principles and practice of sex therapy* (2nd ed. pp. 51–88). New York: Guilford.

Hekimian, L. J., & Gershon, S. (1968). Characteristics of drug abusers admitted to a psychiatric hospital. *JAMA, 205*(3), 125–30.

Heller, K., Sher, K. J., & Benson, C. S. (1982). Problems associated with risk of overprediction in studies of offspring of alcoholics: Implications for prevention. *Clin. Psychol. Rev., 2,* 183–200.

Hellman, D. S., & Blackmun, N. (1966). Enuresis, firesetting, and cruelty to animals: a triad predictive of adult crime. *Amer. J. Psychiat., 122,* 1431–35.

Henderson, V. W. (1986). Non-genetic factors in Alzheimer's disease pathogenesis. *Neurobiology of Aging, 7,* 585–87.

Hendin, H. (1975). Student suicide: Death as a life-style. *J. Nerv. Ment. Dis., 160*(3), 204–19.

Hendin, H. (1985). Suicide among the young: Psychodynamics and demography. In M. L. Peck, N. L. Farberow, & R. E. Litman (Eds.), *Youth suicide* (pp. 19–38). New York: Springer.

Henker, B. & Whalen, C. K. (1989). Hyperactivity and attention deficits. *Amer. Psychol., 44,* 216–23.

Herd, J. A. (1984). Cardiovascular disease and hypertension. In W. D. Gentry (Ed.), *Handbook of behavioral medicine* (pp. 222–81). New York: Guilford.

Hermalin, J., & Morell, J. A. (Eds.). (1986). *Prevention planning in mental health.* Beverly Hills, CA: Sage.

Herman, J. L. (1981). *Father-daughter incest.* Cambridge, MA: Harvard University Press.

Herman, J. L. (1986). Histories of violence in an outpatient population: An exploratory study. *Amer. J. Orthopsychiat., 56*(1), 137–41.

Herman, J. L. (1990). Sex offenders: A feminist perspective. In W. L. Marshall, D. R. Laws, & H. E. Barbaree (Eds.), *Handbook of sexual assault* (pp. 177–94). New York: Plenum.

Herrenkohl, R. C., Herrenkohl, E. C., & Egolf, B. P. (1983). Circumstances surrounding the occurrence of child maltreatment. *J. Cons. Clin. Psychol., 51*(3), 424–31.

Herzog, D. B., & Rathbun, J. M. (1982). Childhood depression: Developmental considerations. *American Journal of Disorders in Children, 136*(2), 15–20.

Heston, L. (1966). Psychiatric disorders in foster home reared children of schizophrenic mothers. *Brit. J. Psychiat., 112,* 819–25.

Hetherington, E. M. (1973). Girls without fathers. *Psych. Today, 6*(9), 47, 49–52.

Hetherington, E. M., Cox, M., & Cox, R. (1978, May). *Family interaction and the social, emotional and cognitive development of children following divorce.* Symposium on the family: Setting priorities, Institute for Pediatric Service, Johnson & Johnson Baby Food Company. Washington, DC.

Heyman, A., Wilkinson, W. E., Hurwitz, B. J., Helms, M. J., et al. (1987). Early-onset Alzheimer's disease: Clinical predictors of institutionalization and death. *Neurology, 37,* 980–84.

Hilgard, E. R. (1973). The domain of hypnosis: With some comments on alternative paradigms. *Amer. Psychol., 28*(11), 972–82.

Hilgard, E. R. (1974). Weapon against pain: Hypnosis is no mirage. *Psych. Today, 8*(6), 120–22, 126, 128.

Hill, A. L. (1975). Investigation of calendar calculating by an idiot savant. *Amer. J. Psychiat., 132*(5), 557–59.

Hine, F. R. (1971). *Introduction to psychodynamics: A conflict-adaptational approach.* Durham, NC: Duke University Press.

Hine, F. R., Carson, R. C., Maddox, G. L., Thompson, R. J., & Williams, R. B. (1983). *Introduction to behavioral science in medicine.* New York: Springer-Verlag.

Hine, F. R., Pfeiffer, E., Maddox, G. L., Hein, P. L., & Friedel, R. O. (1972). *Behavioral science: A selective view.* Boston: Little, Brown.

Hintzman, D. L. (1990). Human learning and memory: Connections and dissociations. *Ann. Rev. Psychol., 41.* Palo Alto, CA: Annual Reviews, Inc.

Hiroto, D. S., & Seligman, M. E. P. (1975). Generality of learned helplessness in man. *J. Pers. Soc. Psychol., 31*(2), 311–27.

Hirsch, S. R., & Leff, J. P. (1975). *Abnormalities in parents of schizophrenics.* London: Oxford University Press.

Hirschfeld, R. M. A., Klerman, G. L., Andreasen, N. C., Clayton, P. J., & Keller, M. B. (1985). Situational major depressive disorder. *Arch. Gen. Psychiat., 42,* 1109–14.

Hirschfeld, R. M. A., Klerman, G. L., Lavori, P., Keller, M. B., Griffith, P., & Coryell, W. (1989). Premorbid personality assessments of first onset of major depression. *Arch. Gen. Psychiat., 46,* 345–50.

Hirst, W. (1982). The amnesic syndrome: Descriptions and explanations. *Psychol. Bull., 91,* 435–60.

Hoberman, H. M., & Lewinsohn, P. M. (1985). The behavioral treatment of depression. In E. E. Beckham, & W. R. Leber (Eds.), *Handbook of depression: Treatment, assessment, and research* (pp. 39–81). Homewood, IL: Dorsey Press.

Hodgson, R. J., & Rachman, S. (1972). The effects of contamination and washing in obsessional patients. *Behav. Res. Ther., 10*(2), 111–17.

Hodkinson, S., Sherrington, R., Gurling, H., Marchbanks, R., Reeders, S., Mallet, J., McInnis, M., Petursson, H., & Brynjolfsson, J. (1987). Molecular evidence for heterogeneity in manic depression. *Nature, 325,* 805–6.

Hoffman, A. (1971). LSD discoverer disputes "chance" factor in finding. *Psychiat. News, 6*(8), 23–26.

Hoffman, J. L. (1943). Psychotic visitors to government offices in the national capital. *Amer. J. Psychiat., 99,* 571–75.

Hogarty, G. E., Anderson, C. M., Reiss, D. J., Kornblith, S. J., & Greenwald, D. P. (1986). Family psychoeducation, social skills training, and maintenance chemotherapy in the aftercare treatment of schizophrenia: 1. One-year effects of a controlled study. *Arch. Gen. Psychiat., 43,* 633–42.

Hogarty, G. E., McEvoy, J.P., Munetz, M., DiBarry, L., Bartone, P., Cather, R., Cooley, S. J., Ulrich, R. F., Carter, M., & Madonia, M.J. (1988). Dose of Fluphanazine, familial expressed emotion, and outcome in schizophrenia. *Arch. Gen. Psychiat., 45,* 797–805.

Hokanson, J. E., & Burgess, M. (1962). The effects of three types of aggression on vascular process. *J. Abnorm. Soc. Psychol., 64,* 446–49.

Hokanson, J. E., Rubert, M. P., Welker, R. A., Hollander, G. R., et al. (1989). Interpersonal concomitants and antecedents of depression among college students. *J. Abnorm. Psychol., 98,* 209–17.

Hokanson, J. E., Sacco, W. P., Blumberg, S. R., & Landrum, G. C. (1980). Interpersonal behavior of depressed individuals in a mixed-motive game. *J. Abnorm. Psychol., 89,* 320–33.

Holcomb, W. (1979). *Coping with severe stress: A clinical application of stress-inoculation therapy.* Unpublished doctoral dissertation, University of Missouri-Columbia.

Holden, R. R., Medonca, J. D., & Serin, R. C. (1989). Suicide, hopelessness, and social desirability: A test of an interactive model. *J. Cons. Clin. Psychol., 57,* 500–4.

Hollander, E., Liebowitz, M. R., Gorman, J. M., Cohen, B., Fyer, A., & Klein, D. F. (1989). Cortisol and sodium lactate-induced panic. *Arch. Gen. Psychiat., 46,* 135–40.

Hollon, S., & Beck, A. T. (1978). Psychotherapy and drug therapy: Comparisons and combinations. In S. L. Garfield & A. E. Bergin (Eds.), *Handbook of psychotherapy and behavior change* (pp. 437–90). New York: Wiley.

Hollon, S., & Beck, A. T. (1986). Research on cognitive therapies. In S. L. Garfield & A. E. Bergin (Eds.), *Handbook of psychotherapy and behavior change* (3rd ed., pp. 443–82). New York: Wiley.

Hollon, S. D., DeRubeis, R. J., & Evans, M. D. (1987). Causal mediation of change in treatment for depression: Discriminating between nonspecificity and noncausality. *Psychol. Bull., 102,* 139–49.

Hollon, S. D., & Garber, J. (1990). Cognitive therapy for depression: A social cognitive perspective. *Personality and Social Psychology Bulletin, 16,* 58–73.

Hollt, V., Dum, J., Blasig, J., Schubert, J. P., & Herz, A. (1975). Comparison of in vivo and in vitro parameters of opiate receptor binding in naive and tolerant dependent rodents. *Life Sciences, 16,* 1823–28.

Holmes, L. B., Moser, H. W., Halldorsson, S., Mack, C., Pant, S., & Matzilevich, B. (1972). *Mental retardation: An atlas of diseases with associated physical abnormalities.* New York: Macmillan.

Holmes, T. H., & Rahe, R. H. (1967). The social readjustment rating scale. *J. Psychosom. Res., 11*(2), 213–18.

Holmes, T. S., & Holmes, T. H. (1970). Short-term intrusions into the life style routine. *J. Psychosom. Res., 14*(2), 121–32.

Holmstrom, L., & Burgess, A. W. (1975). Assessing trauma in the rape victim. *Amer. J. Nurs., 75,* 1288.

Holroyd, K. A., & Andrasik, F. (1978). Coping and the self-control of chronic tension headache. *J. Cons. Clin. Psychol., 46,* 1036–45.

Holroyd, K. A., Andrasik, F., & Westbrook, T. (1977). Cognitive control of tension headache. *Cog. Ther. Res., 1,* 121–33.

Holvey, D. N., & Talbott, J. H. (Eds.). (1972). *The Merck manual of diagnosis and therapy* (12th ed.). Rahway, NJ: Merck, Sharp, & Dohme Research Laboratories.

Holzman, P. S., Kringlen, E., Matthysse, S., Flanagan, S. D., Lipton, R. B., Cramer, G., Levin, S., Lange, K., & Levy, D. L. (1988). A single dominant gene can account for eye tracking dysfunctions and schizophrenia in offspring of discordant twins. *Arch. Gen. Psychiat., 45,* 641–47.

Homans, G. C. (1961). *Social behavior: Its elementary forms.* New York: Harcourt Brace Jovanovich.

Homer, L. E. (1974). The anatomy of a runaway. *Human Behav., 3*(4), 37.

Homme, L. E. (1965). Perspectives in psychology: Control of coverants, the operants of the mind (Vol. 24). *Psychological Record, 15,* 501–11.

Hook, E. B. (1980). Genetic counseling dilemmas: Down's syndrome, paternal age, and recurrence risk after remarriage. *American Journal of Medical Genetics, 5,* 145–51.

Hooker, E. (1957). The adjustment of the male overt homosexual. *Journal of Projective Techniques, 21,* 18–31.

Hooker, E. (1962). The homosexual community. In *Proceedings of the XIV International Congress of Applied Psychology* (Vol. II). *Personality research.* Copenhagen: Munksgaard.

Hooley, J. M. (1985). Expressed emotion: A review of the critical literature. *Clin. Psychol. Rev., 5,* 119–39.

Hooley, J. M. (1986). Expressed emotion and depression: Interactions between patients and high- versus low-expressed-emotion spouses. *J. Abnorm. Psychol., 95,* 237–46.

Hooley, J. M., Orley, J., & Teasdale, J. D. (1986). Levels of expressed emotion and relapse in depressed patients. *Brit. J. Psychiat., 148,* 642–47.

Hooley, J. M., & Teasdale, J. D. (1989). Predictors of relapse in unipolar depressives: Expressed emotion, marital distress, and perceived criticism. *J. Abnorm. Psychol., 98,* 229–35.

Hore, A. P., & Tryon, W. W. (1989). Study of the similar structure hypothesis with mentally retarded adults and nonretarded children of comparable mental age. *Amer. J. Ment. Retard., 94,* 182–88.

Horowitz, M., Marmar, C., Krupnick, J., Wilner, N., & Kaltreider, N. (1984). *Personality styles and brief psychotherapy.* New York: Basic Books.

Horowitz, M. J. (1969a). Flashbacks: Recurrent intrusive images after the use of LSD. *Amer. J. Psychiat., 126*(4), 147–51.

Horowitz, M. J. (1969b). Psychic trauma. *Amer. Gen. Psychiat., 20,* 552–59.

Horowitz, M. J., & Solomon, G. F. (1978). Delayed stress response syndromes in Vietnam veterans. In C. R. Figley (Ed.), *Stress disorders among Vietnam veterans: Theory, research, and treatment.* New York: Brunner/Mazel.

Horowitz, M. J., Wilner, N., & Alvarez, W. (1979). Impact of Events Scale: A measure of subjective stress. *Psychosom. Med., 41,* 209–18.

Horton, D. (1943). The functions of alcohol in primitive societies: A cross-cultural study. *Quarterly Journal of Studies in Alcoholism, 4,* 199–320.

Horton, P. C., Louy, J. W., & Coppolillo, H. P. (1974). Personality disorder and transitional relatedness. *Arch. Gen. Psychiat., 30*(5), 618–22.

Hoshino, Y., et al. (1980). Early symptoms of autism in children and their diagnostic significance, *Japanese Journal of Child and Adolescent Psychiatry, 21*(5), 284–99.

House of Representatives. (1990). No place to call home: Discarded children in America. A report of the Select Committee on Children, Youth, and Families. Washington, DC: U. S. Government Printing Office.

Householder, J., Hatcher, R., Burns, W., & Chasnoff, I. (1982). Infants born to narcotic addicted mothers. *Psychol. Bull., 92*(2), 453–68.

Howard, K. I., Davidson, C.V., O'Mahoney, M.T., & Orlinsky, D. E. (1989). Patterns of psychotherapy utilization. *Amer. J. Psychiat., 146,* 775–78.

Howard, K. I., Kopta, S. M., Krause, M. S., & Orlinsky, D. E. (1986). The dose-effect relationship in psychotherapy. *Amer. Psychol., 41,* 159–64.

Howes, M. J., & Hokanson, J. E. (1979). Conversational and social responses to depressive interpersonal behavior. *J. Abnorm. Psychol., 88,* 625–34.

Howes, M. J., Hokanson, J. E., & Loewenstein, D. A. (1985). Induction of depressive affect after prolonged exposure to a mildly depressed individual. *J. Pers. Soc. Psychol., 49,* 1110–13.

Hsu, L. K. G. (1989). The gender gap in eating disorders: Why are the eating disorders more common among women? *Clin. Psychol. Rev., 9,* 393–407.

Hu, T. -W., Huang, L. -F., & Cartwright, W. (1986). Evaluation of the costs of caring for the senile demented elderly: A pilot study. *Gerontologist, 26,* 158–63.

Huff, F. W. (1969). A learning theory approach to family therapy. *The Family Coordinator, 18*(1), 22–26.

Hughes, J. R., Higgins, S. T., & Hatsukami, D. K. (1990). Effects of abstinence from tobacco: A critical review. In L. T. Kozlowski, H. Annis, & H. D. Cappell, et al. (Eds.), *Recent advances in alcohol and drug problems* (Vol. 10, pp. 317–97).

Hughes, P. L., Wells, L. A., Cunningham, C. J., & Ilstrup, D. M. (1986). Treating bulimia with desipramine: A double-blind, placebo-controlled study. *Arch. Gen. Psychiat., 43,* 182–86.

Humphrey, L. L. (1989). Observed family interactions among subtypes of eating disorders using Structural Analysis of Social Behavior. *J. Cons. Clin. Psychol., 57,* 206–14.

Hunter, E. J. (1976). The prisoner of war: Coping with the stress of isolation. In R. H. Moos (Ed.), *Human adaptation: Coping with life crises.* Lexington MA: D.C. Heath.

Hunter, E. J. (1978). The Vietnam POW veteran: Immediate and long-term effects. In C. R. Figley (Ed.), *Stress disorders among Vietnam veterans.* New York: Brunner/Mazel.

Hunter, E. J. (1981). *Wartime stress: Family adjustment to loss* (USIU Report No. TR-USIU-81-07). San Diego, CA: United States International University.

Hurley, J. R. (1965). Parental acceptance-rejection and children's intelligence. *Merrill-Palmer Quarterly, 11*(1), 19–32.

Hurwitz, N. (1974). The family therapist as intermediary. *The Family Coordinator, 23*(2), 145–58.

Hurwitz, T. D. (1974). Electroconvulsive therapy: A review. *Compr. Psychiat., 15*(4), 303–14.

Huxley, A. (1954). *The doors of perception.* New York: Harper & Row.

Huxley, A. (1965). Human potentialities. In R. E. Farson (Ed.),

Science and human affairs. Palo Alto, CA: Science and Behavior Books.

Hyatt, R., & Rolnick, N. (Eds.). (1974). *Teaching the mentally handicapped child.* New York: Behavioral Publications.

Hymel, S., & Rubin, K. H. (1985). Children with peer relationships and social skills problems: Conceptual, methodological, and developmental issues. *Annals of child development* (Vol. 2). Greenwich, CT: JAI Press.

Hynd, G. W., & Semrud-Clikeman, M. (1989). Dyslexia and brain morphology. *Psychol. Bull., 106,* 447–82.

Iacono, W. G., Tuason, V. B., & Johnson, R. A. (1981). Dissociation of smooth-pursuit and saccadic eye tracking in remitted schizophrenics: An ocular reaction time task that schizophrenics perform well. *Arch. Gen. Psychiat., 38,* 991–96.

Ikemi, Y., Ago, Y., Nakagawa, S., Mori S., Takahashi, N., Suematsu, H., Sugita, M., & Matsubara, H. (1974). Psychosomatic mechanism under social changes in Japan. *J. Psychosom. Res., 18*(1), 15–24.

Imber, S. D., Glanz, L. M., Elkin, I., Sotsky, S. M., & Boyer, J. L. (1986). Ethical issues in psychotherapy research: Problems in a collaborative clinical trials study. *Amer. Psychol., 41,* 137–46.

Ironside, R., & Batchelor, I. R. C. (1945). The ocular manifestations of hysteria in relation to flying. *British Journal of Ophthalmology, 29,* 88–98.

Isaacson, R. L. (1970). When brains are damaged. *Psych. Today, 3*(4), 38–42.

Iscoe, I., Bloom, B. L., & Spielberger, C. D. (Eds.). (1977). *Community psychology in transition.* Washington, DC: Hemisphere.

Itard, J. (1932). *The wild boy of Aveyron* (G. Humphrey & M. Humphrey, Trans.). New York: Century. (Original work published in Paris, 1799).

Jackson, J. L., Calhoun, K., Amick, A. E., Maddever, H. M., & Habif, V. (1990). Young adult women who experienced childhood intrafamilial sexual abuse: Subsequent adjustment. *Arch. Sex. Behav., 19,* 211–21.

Jaco, E. G. (1960). *The social epidemiology of mental disorders.* New York: Russell Sage Foundation.

Jacobsen, B., & Kinney, D. K. (1980). Perinatal complications in adopted and nonadopted schizophrenics and their controls. *Acta Psychiatr. Scandin.* (Suppl. No. 285), *61,* 337–46.

Jacobson, A. (1989). Physical and sexual assault histories among psychiatric outpatients. *Amer. J. Psychiat., 146,* 755–58.

Jacobson, J. W. (1990). Do some mental disorders occur less frequently among persons with mental retardation? *Amer. J. Ment. Retard., 94,* 596–602.

Jacobson, N. S., Holtzworth-Monroe, A., & Schmaling, K. B. (1989). Marital therapy and spouse involvement in the treatment of depression, agoraphobia, and alcoholism. *J. Cons. Clin. Psychol., 57,* 5–10.

Jacobson, N. S., & Martin, B. (1976). Behavioral marriage therapy: Current status. *Psychol. Bull., 83,* 540–56.

Jacobson, R. R. (1985a). Child firesetters: A clinical investigation. *J. Child Psychol. Psychiat., 26*(5), 759–68.

Jacobson, R. R. (1985b). The subclassification of child firesetters. *J. Child Psychol. Psychiat., 26*(5), 769–75.

James, A. L., & Barry, R. J. (1981). General maturational lag as an essential correlate of early onset psychosis. *J. Autism Devel. Dis., 11*(3), 271–83.

James, S. P., Wehr, T. A., Sack, D. A., Parry, B. L., & Rosenthal, N. E. (1985). Treatment of seasonal affective disorder with light in the evening. *Brit. J. Psychiat., 147,* 424–28.

Janis, I. L. (1958). *Psychological stress: Psychoanalytic and behavioral studies of surgical patients.* New York: Wiley.

Janis, I. L., & Leventhal H. (1965). Psychological aspects of physical illness and hospital care. In B. B. Wolman (Ed.), *Handbook of clinical psychology* (pp. 1360–77). New York: McGraw-Hill.

Janis, I. L., Mahl, G. F., Kagan, J., & Holt, R. R. (1969). *From personality: Dynamics, development, and assessment.* New York: Harcourt Brace Jovanovich.

Janowsky, D. S., El-Yousef, M. K., & Davis, J. M. (1974). Interpersonal maneuvers of manic patients. *Amer. J. Psychiat., 131*(3), 250–55.

Janowsky, D. S., Leff, M., & Epstein, R. (1970). Playing the manic game. *Arch. Gen. Psychiat., 22,* 252–61.

Jarvik, M. E. (1967). The psychopharmacological revolution. *Psych. Today, 1*(1), 51–58.

Jeffrey, R. W., Wing, R. R., & Stunkard, A. J. (1978). Behavioral treatment of obesity: The state of the art, 1978. *Behav. Ther., 9,* 189–99.

Jemmott, J. B., III, & Locke, S. E. (1984). Psychosocial factors, immunologic mediation, and human susceptibility to infectious diseases: How much do we know? *Psychol. Bull., 95,* 78–108.

Jenkins, C. D., Zyzansky, S. J., & Rosenman, R. H. (1971). Progress toward validation of a computer-scored test for the Type A coronary-prone behavior pattern. *Psychosom. Med., 33,* 193–202.

Jenkins, C. D., Zyzanski, S. J., & Rosenman, R. H. (1976). Risk of new myocardial infarction in middle-age men with manifest coronary heart disease. *Circulation, 53,* 342–47.

Jenkins, R. L. (1968). The varieties of children's behavioral problems and family dynamics. *Amer. J. Psychiat., 124*(10), 134–39.

Jenkins, R. L. (1969). Classification of behavior problems of children. *Amer. J. Psychiat., 125*(8), 68–75.

Jenkins, T. S., Parham, I. A., & Jenkins, L. R. (1985). Alzheimer's disease: Caregivers' perceptions of burden. *Journal of Applied Gerontology, 4,* 40–57.

Jennet, B., et al. (1976). Predicting outcome in individual patients after severe head injury. *Lancet, 1,* 1031.

Jenni, M. A., & Wollersheim, J. P. (1979). Cognitive therapy, stress-management training and the type A behavior pattern. *Cog. Ther. Res., 3*(1), 61–73.

Johnson, C. A., & Katz, R. C. (1973). Using parents as change agents for their children: A review. *J. Child Psychol. Psychiat., 14*(3), 181–200.

Johnson, J. (1969). The EEG in the traumatic encephalography of boxers. *Psychiatrica Clinica, 2*(4), 204–11.

Johnson, T., & Maloney, H. (1979). Effects of short-term family therapy on patterns of verbal interchange in disturbed families. *Family Therapy, 4,* 207–13.

Joint Commission on the Mental Health of Children. (1968). Position statement: Statement of the American Orthopsychiatric Association on the work of the Joint Commission on the Mental Health of Children. *Amer. J. Orthopsychiat., 38*(3), 402–9.

Joint Commission on the Mental Health of Children. (1970). *Crisis in child mental health: Challenge for the 1970's.* New York: Harper & Row.

Jones, E. E. (1990). *Interpersonal perception.* New York: W. H. Freeman.

Jones, E. E., Farina, A., Hastorf, A. H., Markus, H., & Miller, D. T. (1984). *Social stigma: The psychology of marked relationships.* New York: W. H. Freeman.

Jones, K. L., & Smith, B. W. (1975). The fetal alcohol syndrome. *Teratology, 12,* 1–10.

Jones, K. L., Smith, B. W., & Hansen, J. W. (1976). Fetal alcohol syndrome: A clinical delineation. *Annals of the New York Academy of Science, 273,* 130–37.

Jones, M. (1953). *The therapeutic community.* New York: Basic Books.

Jones, M. C. (1924). A laboratory study of fear: The case of Peter. *Pedagogical Seminary, 31,* 308–15.

Jones, R. (1984). *The pharmacology of cocaine.* National Institute on Drug Abuse Research Monograph Series 50. Washington, DC: National Institute on Drug Abuse.

Jones, R. A. (1977). *Self-fulfilling prophecies: Social, psychological, and physiological effects of expectancies.* Hillsdale, NJ: Erlbaum Associates.

Jones, R. E. (1983). Street people and psychiatry: an introduction. *Hosp. Comm. Psychiat., 34,* 807–11.

Jones, R. R., Reid, J. B., & Patterson, G. R. (1975). Naturalistic observation in clinical assessment. In P. M. Reynolds (Ed.), *Advances in psychological assessment* (Vol. 3). San Francisco: Jossey-Bass.

Jordan, H.A., & Levitz, L. S. (1975). Behavior modification in a self-help group. *Journal of the American Dietetic Association, 62,* 27–29.

Kaada, B., & Retvedt, A. (1981). Enuresis and hyperventilation response in the EEG. *Develop. Med. Child Neurol., 23*(5), 591–99.

Kagan, J. (1973). In B. Pratt (Ed.), Kagan counters Freud, Piaget theories on early childhood deprivation effects. *APA Monitor, 4*(2), 1–7.

Kagan, J., Kearsley, R. B., & Zelazo, P. R. (1976, February). *The effects of infant day-care on psychological development.* Symposium on the effect of early experience on child development, American Association for the Advancement of Science. Boston.

Kagan, J., Reznick, J.S., & Snidman, N. (1988). Biological bases of childhood shyness. *Science, 240,* 167–171.

Kagan, J., Reznick, R. J., Clarke, C., Snidman, N., & Garcia-Coll, C. (1984). Behavioral inhibition and the unfamiliar. *Child Develop., 55,* 2212–25.

Kahan, J., Kemp, B., Staples, F. R., & Brummel-Smith, K. (1985). Decreasing the burden in families caring for a relative with a dementing illness: A controlled study. *J. Amer. Geriat. Soc., 33,* 664–70.

Kahana, B., Harel, Z., & Kahana, E. (1988). Predictors of psychological well-being among survivors of the Holocaust. In J. P. Wilson, Z. Harel, & B. Kahana (Eds.), *Human adaptation to extreme stress: From the Holocaust to Vietnam* (pp. 171–92). New York: Plenum Press.

Kahn, D. (1990). The dichotomy of drugs and psychotherapy. *Psychiat. Clin. N. Amer., 13,* 197–207.

Kahn, M. W., & Raifman, L. (1981). Hospitalization versus imprisonment and the insanity plea. *Crim. Just. Behav., 8*(4), 483–90.

Kahn, R. L. (1969). Stress: from 9 to 5. *Psych. Today, 3*(4), 34–38.

Kaiser Foundation Health Plan, Inc. (1970). *Planning for Health.* Summer, 1–2.

Kales, A., Paulson, M. J., Jacobson, A., & Kales, J. (1966). Somnambulism: Psychophysiological correlates. *Arch. Gen. Psychiat., 14*(6), 595–604.

Kalin, N. H., Risch, S. C., Janowsky, D. S., & Murphy, D. L. (1981). Use of the dexamethasone suppression test in clinical psychiatry. *J. Clin. Psychopharm., 1,* 64–69.

Kalinowski, L. B., & Hippius, H. (1969). *Pharmacological, convulsive and other somatic treatments in psychiatry.* New York: Grune & Stratton.

Kallmann, F. J. (1958). The use of genetics in psychiatry. *J. Ment. Sci., 104,* 542–49.

Kandel, D. B., Davies, M., Karus, D., & Yamaguchi, K. (1986). The consequences in young adulthood of adolescent drug involvement. *Arch. Gen. Psychiat., 43,* 746–54.

Kandel, E., Mednick, S. A., Kirkegaard-Sorensen, L., Hutchings, B., Knop, J., Rosenberg, R., & Schulsinger, F. (1988). IQ as a protective factor for subjects at high risk for antisocial behavior. *J. Cons. Clin. Psychol., 56,* 224–26.

Kane, J., Honigfeld, G., Singer, J., & Meltzer, H. (1988). Clozapine for the treatment-resistant schizophrenic. *Arch. Gen. Psychiat., 45,* 789–96.

Kane, J., Honigfeld, G., Singer, J., Meltzer, H., & Clozapine Collaborative Study Group. (1988). Clozapine for the treatment-resistant schizophrenic: A double-blind comparison with chlorpromazine. *Arch. Gen. Psychiat., 45,* 789–96.

Kane, J. M., & Smith, J. M. (1982). Tardive dyskinesia: Prevalence and risk factors, 1959–79. *Arch. Gen. Psychiat., 39,* 473–81.

Kang, J., Lemaire, H.-G., Unterbeck, A., Salbaum, J. M., et al. (1987). The precursor of Alzheimer's disease amyloid A4 protein resembles a cell surface receptor. *Nature, 325,* 733–36.

Kanin, E. J. (1985). Date rapists: Differential sexual socialization and relative deprivation. *Arch. Sex. Behav., 14,* 219–31.

Kanner, L., (1943). Autistic disturbances of effective content. *Nervous Child, 2,* 217–40.

Kantorovich, F. (1930). An attempt at associative reflex therapy in alcoholism. *Psychological Abstracts,* 4282.

Kaplan, H. S. (1974). *The new sex therapy.* New York: Brunner/Mazel.

Kaplan, H. S. (1975). *The illustrated manual of sex therapy.* New York: Quadrangle/The New York Times Book Company.

Kaplan, H. S. (1987). *The illustrated manual of sex therapy* (2nd ed.). New York: Brunner/Mazel.

Kaplun, D., & Reich, R. (1976). The murdered child and his killers. *Amer. J. Psychiat., 133*(7), 809–13.

Karnes, M. B., Teska, J. A., & Hodgins, A. S. (1970). The effects of four programs of classroom intervention on the intellectual and language development of 4-year-old disadvantaged children. *Amer. J. Orthopsychiat., 40,* 58–76.

Karnesh, L. J. (with collaboration of Zucker, E. M.). (1945). *Handbook of psychiatry.* St. Louis: C. V. Mosby

Karno, M., Golding, J. M., Sorenson, S. B., & Burnam, M. A. (1988). The epidemiology of obsessive-compulsive disorder in five US communities. *Arch. Gen. Psychiat., 45,* 1094–99.

Karon, B. P., & Vandenbos, G. R. (1981) *Psychotherapy of schizophrenia: Treatment of choice.* New York: Jason Aronson.

Kashani, J. H., Cantwell, D. P., Shekim, W. O., & Reid, J. C. (1982). Major depressive disorder in children admitted to an inpatient community mental health center. *Amer. J. Psychiat., 139*(6), 671–72.

Kashani, J. H., Hodges, K. K., Simonds, J. F., & Hilderbrand, E. (1981a). Life events and hospitalization in children: A comparison with a general population. *Brit. J. Psychiat., 139,* 221–25.

Kashani, J. H., Husain, A., Shekim, W. O., Hodges, K. K., Cytryn, L., McKnew, D. H. (1981b). Current perspectives on childhood depression: An overview. *Amer. J. Psychiat., 138*(2), 143–53.

Kashani, J. H., & Orvaschel, H. (1988). Anxiety disorders in mid-adolescence: A community sample. *Amer. J. Psychiat., 145,* 960–64.

Kashani, J. H., Venzke, R., & Millar, E. A. (1981). Depression in children admitted to hospital for orthopaedic procedures. *Brit. J. Psychiat., 138,* 21–25.

Kasper, S., Wehr, T. A., Bartko, J. J., Gaist, P. A., & Rosenthal, N. E. (1989). Epidemiological findings of seasonal changes in mood and behavior. *Arch. Gen. Psychiat., 46,* 823–33.

Kass, F., Spitzer, R. L., Williams, J. B., & Widiger, T. (1989). Self-defeating personality disorder and DSM III-R: Development of diagnostic criteria. *Amer. J. Psychiat., 146,* 1022–26.

Katon, W., Egan, K., & Miller, D. (1985). Chronic pain: Lifetime psychiatric diagnoses and family history. *Amer. J. Psychiat. 142,* 1156–60.

Katz, M. M., Sanborn, K. O., Lowery, H. A., & Ching, J. (1978). Ethnic studies in Hawaii: On psychopathology and social deviance. In L. C. Wynne, R. L. Cromwell, & S. Matthysse (Eds.), *The nature of schizophrenia: New approaches to research and treatment* (pp. 572–85). New York: Wiley.

Katz, S., & Kravetz, S. (1989). Facial plastic surgery for persons with Down syndrome: Research findings and their professional and social implications. *Amer. J. Ment. Retard., 94,* 101–10.

Kaufman, I., Frank, T., Heims, L., Herrick, J., Reiser, D., & Willer, L. (1960). Treatment implications of a new classification of parents of schizophrenic children. *Amer. J. Psychiat., 116,* 920–24.

Kaufmann, W. (1973). *Without guilt and justice: From decidophobia to autonomy.* New York: Peter H. Wyden.

Kay, S. R., & Singh, M. M. (1989). The positive-negative distinction in drug-free schizophrenic patients. *Arch. Gen. Psychiat., 46,* 711–18.

Kazdin, A. E. (1980). *Behavior modification in applied settings* (2nd ed.). Homewood, IL: Dorsey.

Kazdin, A. E., Moser, J., Colbus, D. & Bell, R. (1985). Depressive symptoms among physically abused and psychiatrically disturbed children. *J. Cons. Clin. Psychol., 94*(3), 298–307.

Kazdin, A. E., & Wilson, G. T. (1978). *Evaluation of behavior therapy: Issues, evidence and research strategies.* Cambridge, MA: Ballinger.

Keating, J.P. (1987, Aug.). *An overview of research on human response during disasters: Major fires, earthquakes, tornadoes, and airplane accidents since 1980.* Paper presented at the American Psychological Association, New York.

Keefe, F. J., & Williams, D. A. (1989). New directions in pain assessment and treatment. *Clin. Psychol. Rev., 9,* 549–68.

Keller, M. B., & Shapiro, R. W. (1982). "Double Depression": Superimposition of acute depressive episodes on chronic depressive disorders. *Amer. J. Psychiat., 139,* 438–42.

Keller, M. B., et al. (1983). "Double Depression": Two-year follow-up. *Amer. J. Psychiat., 140,* 689–94.

Kellner, R. (1985). Functional somatic symptoms and hypochondriasis: A survey of empirical studies. *Arch. Gen. Psychiat., 42,* 821–33.

Kelly, J. A., St. Lawrence, J. S., Brasfield, T. L., Lemke, A., Amidei, T., Roffman, R. E., Hood, H. V., Smith, J. E., Kilgore, H., & McNeill, C., Jr. (1990). Psychological factors that predict AIDS high-risk versus AIDS precautionary behavior. *J. Cons. Clin. Psychol., 58,* 117–20.

Kempe, R., & Kempe, H. (1979). *Child Abuse.* London: Fontana/Open Books.

Kendall, P. C. (1981). Cognitive-behavioral interventions with children. In B. Lahey & A. E. Kazdin (Eds.), *Advances in clinical child psychology* (Vol. 4). New York: Plenum.

Kendall, P. C. (1982a). Cognitive processes and procedures in behavior therapy. In C. M. Franks, G. T. Wilson, P. C. Kendall, & K. D. Brownell, (Eds.), *Annual Review of Behavior Therapy* (Vol. 8). New York: Guilford Press.

Kendall, P. C. (1982b). Integration: Behavior therapy and other schools of thought. *Behav. Ther., 13,* 559–71.

Kendall, P. C., & Braswell, L. (1985). *Cognitive behavioral therapy for impulsive children.* New York: Guilford Press.

Kendall, P. C., & Finch, A. J. (1976). A cognitive-behavioral treatment for impulse control: A case study. *J. Cons. Clin. Psychol., 44,* 852–57.

Kendall, P. C., & Norton-Ford, J. D. (1982). Therapy outcome research methods. In P. C. Kendall & J. N. Butcher (Eds.), *Handbook of research methods in clinical psychology.* New York: Wiley.

Kendler, K. S., & Davis, K. L. (1981). The genetics and biochemistry of paranoid schizophrenia and other paranoid psychoses. *Schizo. Bull., 7,* 689–709.

Kendler, K. S., & Gruenberg, A. M. (1982). Genetic relationship between paranoid personality disorder and the "schizophrenic" spectrum disorders. *Amer. J. Psychiat., 139*(9), 1185–86.

Kendler, K. S., & Gruenberg, A. M. (1984). An independent analysis of the Danish adoption study of schizophrenia: VI. The relationship between psychiatric disorders as defined by DSM-III in the relatives and adoptees. *Arch. Gen. Psychiat., 41,* 555–64.

Kendler, K. S., & Tsuang, M. T. (1981). Nosology of paranoid schizophrenia and other paranoid psychoses. *Schizo. Bull., 7,* 594–610.

Keniston, K. (1977, Nov. 28). Meeting the needs of children: I, The necessity of politics. *Christianity and Crisis.*

Kennedy, J. F. (1963). Message from the President of the United States relative to mental illness and mental retardation. *Amer. Psychol., 18,* 280–89.

Kennedy, T. D., & Kimura, H. K. (1974). Transfer, behavioral improvement, and anxiety reduction in systematic desensitization. *J. Cons. Clin. Psychol., 42*(5), 720–28.

Kernberg, O. F. (1984). *Severe personality disorders.* New Haven, CT: Yale University Press.

Kernberg, O. F. (1989). An ego-psychology-object relations theory of the structure and treatment of pathologic narcissism. *Psychiat. Clin. N. Amer., 10,* 723–31.

Kessler, J. W. (1988). *Psychopathology of childhood* (2nd ed.). Englewood Cliffs, NJ: Prentice Hall.

Kessler, M., & Albee, G.W. (1975). Primary prevention. *Annu. Rev. Psychol., 26,* 557–91.

Kety, S. S. (1987). The significance of genetic factors in the etiology of schizophrenia. *Journal of Psychiatric Research, 21,* 423–29.

Kety, S. S., Rosenthal, D., Wender, P. H., & Schulsinger, F. (1968). The types and prevalence of mental illness in the biological and adoptive families of adopted schizophrenics. In D. Rosenthal & S. S. Kety (Eds.), *The transmission of schizophrenia.* Elmsford, NY: Pergamon.

Kety, S. S., Rosenthal, D., Wender, P. H., Schulsinger, F., & Jacobsen, B. (1975). Mental illness in the biological and adoptive families of adopted individuals who have become schizophrenics: A preliminary report based on psychiatric interviews. In R. Fieve, P. Rosenthal, & H. Brill (Eds.), *Genetic research in psychiatry.* Baltimore: Johns Hopkins University Press.

Kety, S. S., Rosenthal, D., Wender, P. H., Schulsinger, F., & Jacobsen, B. (1978). The biologic and adoptive families of adopted individuals who became schizophrenic: Prevalence of mental illness and other characteristics. In L. C. Wynne, R. L. Cromwell, & S. Matthyse (Eds.), *The nature of schizophrenia: New approaches to research and treatment* (pp. 25–37). New York: Wiley.

Kewman, D., & Roberts, A. H. (1979). Skin temperature biofeedback and migraine headaches. Paper presented at the *Annual Conference of the Biofeedback Society of America,* San Diego.

Keys, A., Brozek, J., Henschel, A., Mickelson, O., & Taylor, H. L. (1950). *The biology of human starvation.* Minneapolis: University of Minnesota Press.

Khantzian, E. J., & Treece, C. (1985). DSM-III psychiatric diagnosis of narcotic addicts: Recent findings. *Arch. Gen. Psychiat., 42*(11), 1067–71.

Kidd, K. K., & Morton, L. A. (1989). The genetics of psychosomatic disorders. In S. Cheren (Ed.), *Psychosomatic medicine: Theory, physiology, and practice* (Vol. 1, pp. 385–424). Madison, CT: International Universities Press.

Kidson, M., & Jones, I. (1968). Psychiatric disorders among aborigines of the Australian Western Desert. *Arch. Gen. Psychiat., 19,* 413–22.

Kidson, M. A. (1973). Personality and hypertension. *J. Psychosom. Res., 17*(1), 35–41.

Kiecolt-Glaser, J., & Glaser, R. (1988). Psychological influences in immunity: Implications for AIDS. *Amer. Psychol., 43,* 892–98.

Kiernan, C. (1985). Behaviour modification. In A. M. Clarke, A. D. B. Clarke, & J. M. Berg (Eds.), *Mental deficiency: The changing outlook* (4th ed., pp. 465–511). London: Methuen.

Kiersch, T. A. (1962). Amnesia: A clinical study of ninety-eight cases. *Amer. J. Psychiat., 119,* 57–60.

Kiesler, C. A. (1983). Social psychologic issues in studying consumer satisfaction with behavior therapy. *Behav. Ther., 14,* 226–36.

Kiev, A. (1972). *Transcultural psychiatry.* New York: Free Press.

Kilpatrick, D. G., Sutker, P. B., Roitch, J. C., & Miller, W. C. (1976). Personality correlates of polydrug users. *Psychol. Rep., 38,* 311–17.

Kimmel, H. D. (1974). Instrumental conditioning of autonomically mediated responses. *Amer. Psychol., 29,* 325–35.

King, C. A., & Young, R. D. (1981). Peer popularity and peer communication patterns: Hyperactivity versus active but normal boys. *J. Abnorm. Child Psychol., 9*(4), 464–82.

King, H. F., Carroll, J. L., & Fuller, G. B. (1977). Comparison of nonpsychiatric blacks and whites on the MMPI. *J. Clin. Psychol., 33,* 725–28.

Kingsley, R. G., & Wilson, G. T. (1977). Behavior therapy for obesity: A comparative investigation of long-term efficacy. *J. Cons. Clin. Psychol., 45,* 288–98.

Kinney, D. K., Woods, B. T., & Yurgelun-Todd, D. (1986). Neurologic abnormalities in schizophrenic patients and their families: II. Neurologic and psychiatric findings in relatives. *Arch. Gen. Psychiat., 43,* 665–68.

Kinsey, A. C., Pomeroy, W. B., & Martin, C. E. (1948). *Sexual behavior in the human male.* Philadelphia: W. B. Saunders.

Kinsey, A. C., Pomeroy, W. B., & Martin, C. E. (1953). *Sexual behavior in the human female.* Philadelphia: W. B. Saunders.

Kinzie, J. D., & Bolton, J. M. (1973). Psychiatry with the aborigines of West Malaysia. *Amer. J. Psychiat., 130*(7), 769–73.

Kirmayer, L. J. (1991). The place of culture in psychiatric nosology: Taijin Kyofusho and DSM III-R. *J. Nerv. Ment. Dis., 179,* 19–28.

Kirsch, E. S. (1974). Narcotics overdosage. *Hospital Medicine, 10,* 8–10, 12, 17–24.

Kirstein, L., Prusoff, B., Weissman, M., & Dressler, D. M. (1975). Utilization review of treatment for suicide attempters. *Amer. J. Psychiat., 132*(1), 22–27.

Klagsbrun, F. (1976). *Too young to die: Youth and suicide.* Boston: Houghton Mifflin.

Klassen, D., & O'Connor, W. A. (1988). A prospective study of predictors of violence in adult male mental health admissions. *Law and Human Behavior, 12,* 143–58.

Klein, D. N., & Depue, R. A. (1984). Continued impairment in persons at risk for bipolar affective disorder: Results of a 19-month follow-up study. *J. Abnorm. Psychol., 93,* 345–47.

Klein, D. N., & Depue, R. A. (1985). Obsessional personality traits and risk for bipolar affective disorder: An offspring study. *J. Abnorm. Psychol., 94,* 291–397.

Klein, D. N., Depue, R. A., & Slater, J. F. (1985). Cyclothymia in the adolescent offspring of parents with bipolar affective disorder. *J. Abnorm. Psychol., 94,* 115–27.

Klein, D. N., Depue, R. A., & Slater, J. F. (1986). Inventory identification of cyclothymia: IX. Validations in offspring of bipolar I patients. *Arch. Gen. Psychiat., 43,* 441–45.

Kleinman, A. (1986). *Social origins of distress and disease: Depression, neurasthenia and pain in modern China.* New Haven, CT: Yale University Press.

Kleinman, A., & Good, B. (1985). *Culture and depression.* Berkeley, CA: University of California Press.

Kleinman, P. H., Miller, A. B., Millman, R. B., Woody, G. E., Todd, T., Kemp, J., & Lipton, D. S. (1990). Psychopathology among cocaine abusers entering treatment. *J. Nerv. Ment. Dis., 178,* 442–47.

Kleinmuntz, B. (1990). Why we still use our heads instead of formulas: Toward an integrative approach. *Psychol. Bull., 107,* 296–310.

Klepac, R. K., Hauge, G., Dowling, J., & McDonald, M. (1981). Direct and generalized effects of three components of stress-inoculation for increased pain tolerance. *Behav. Ther., 12,* 417–24.

Klerman, G. L. (1982). Practical issues in the treatment of depression and mania. In E. S. Paykel (Ed.), *Handbook of affective disorders.* New York: Guilford Press.

Klerman, G. L. (1990). The psychiatric patient's right to effective treatment: Implications of Osheroff v. Chestnut Lodge. *Amer. J. Psychiat., 147,* 409–18.

Klerman, G. L., & Schechter, G. (1982). Drugs and psychotherapy. In E. S. Paykel (Ed.), *Handbook of affective disorders.* New York: Guilford Press.

Klerman, G. L., Weissman, M. M., Rounsaville, B. J., & Chevron, E. S. (1984). *Interpersonal psychotherapy of depression.* New York: Basic.

Kline, N. S. (1954). Use of *Rauwolfia serpentina* in neuropsychiatric conditions. *Annals of the New York Academy of Science, 54,* 107–32.

Klinger, E. (1979). Modes of normal conscious flow. In K. S. Pope & J. L. Singer (Eds.), *The stream of consciousness: Scientific investigations into the flow of human experience.* New York: Plenum.

Klopfer, B., & Davidson, H. (1962). *The Rorschach technique: An introductory manual.* New York: Harcourt Brace Jovanovich.

Klosko, J. S., Barlow, D. H., Tassinari, R., & Cerny, J. A. (1990). A comparison of alprazolam and behavior therapy in the treatment of panic disorder. *J. Cons. Clin. Psychol., 58,* 77–84.

Knapp, P. H. (1989). Psychosomatic aspects of bronchial asthma: A review. In S. Cheren (Ed.), *Psychosomatic medicine: Theory, physiology, and practice* (Vol. 2, pp. 503–64). Madison, CT: International Universities Press.

Knapp, S. (1980). A primer on malpractice for psychologists. *Profess. Psychol., 11*(4), 606–12.

Knapp, S., & Vandecreek, L. (1982). Tarasoff: Five years later. *Profess. Psychol., 13*(4), 511–16.

Knight, R. A., Carter, D. L., & Prentky, R. A. (1989). A system for the classification of child molesters: Reliability and application. *Journal of Interpersonal Violence, 4,* 3–23.

Knight, R. A., & Prentky, R. A. (1990). Classifying sexual offenders: The development and corroboration of taxonomic models. In W. L. Marshall, D. R. Laws, & H. E. Barbaree (Eds.), *Handbook of sexual assault* (pp. 23–52). New York: Plenum.

Knittle, J. L., Timmers, K. I., & Katz, D. P. (1982). Adolescent obesity. In M. Winick (Ed.), *Adolescent nutrition.* New York: Oxford University Press.

Knowles, J. H. (1977). Editorial. *Science, 198,* 1103–4.

Kobasa, S. C. (1979). Stressful life events, personality, and health: An inquiry into hardiness. *J. Pers. Soc. Psychol., 37*(1), 1–11.

Kobasa, S. C. O. (1985). Personality and health: Specifying and strengthening the conceptual fill. In P. Shaver (Ed.), *Self situations and social behavior* (pp. 291–311). Beverly Hills, CA: Sage.

Koch, R. (1967). The multidisciplinary approach to mental retardation. In A. A. Baumeister (Ed.), *Mental retardation: Appraisal, education, and rehabilitation.* Chicago: Aldine.

Koegel, R. L., & Mentis, M. (1985). Motivation in childhood autism: Can they or won't they? *J. Child Psychol. Psychiat., 26*(2), 185–91.

Kog, E., & Vandereycken, W. (1985). Family characteristics of anorexia nervosa and bulimia: A review of the research literature. *Clin. Psychol. Rev., 5,* 159–80.

Kohn, M. L. (1973). Social class and schizophrenia: A critical review and a reformulation. *Schizo. Bull., 7,* 60–79.

Kohut, H., & Wolff, E. (1978). The disorders of the self and their treatment: An outline. *Inter. J. Psychoanal., 59,* 413–26.

Kolata, G. B. (1981a). Clues to the cause of senile dementia: Patients with Alzheimer's disease seem to be deficient in a brain neurotransmitter. *Science, 211,* 1032–33.

Kolata, G. B. (1981b). Fetal alcohol advisory debated. *Science, 214,* 642–46.

Kolko, J. D., Kazdin, A. E., & Meyer, E. C. (1985). Aggression and psychopathology in childhood firesetters: Parent and child reports. *J. Cons. Clin. Psychol., 53*(3), 377–85.

Konopka, G. (1964). Adolescent delinquent girls. *Children, 11*(1), 21–26.

Konopka, G. (1967). Rehabilitation of the delinquent girl. *Adolescence, 2*(5), 69–82.

Kopelman, M. D. (1986). The cholinergic neurotransmitter system in human memory and dementia: A review. *Quarterly Journal of Experimental Psychology: Human Experimental Psychology, 38,* 535–73.

Koranyi, E. K. (1989). Physiology of stress reviewed. In S. Cheren (Ed.), *Psychosomatic medicine: Theory, physiology, and practice* (Vol. 1, pp. 241–78). Madison, CT: International Universities Press.

Kornberg, M. S., & Caplan, G. (1980). Risk factors and preventive intervention in child psychopathology: A review. *Journal of Prevention, 1,* 71–133.

Koscheyev, V. S. (October, 1990). Psychological functioning of Chernobyl workers in the period after the nuclear accident. Invited address. University of Minnesota.

Koss, M. P. (1983). The scope of rape: Implications for the clinical treatment of victims. *Clin. Psychol., 36,* 88–91.

Koss, M. P., & Dinero, T. E. (1989). Discriminant analysis of risk factors for sexual victimization among a national sample of college women. *J. Cons. Clin. Psychol., 57,* 242–50.

Koss, M. P., Gidycz, C., & Wisniewski, N. (1987). The scope of rape: Incidence and prevalence of sexual aggression in a national sample of higher education students. *J. Cons. Clin. Psychol., 55,* 162–70.

Koss, M. P., & Oros, C. J. (1982). Sexual experiences survey: A research instrument investigating sexual aggression and victimization. *J. Cons. Clin. Psychol., 50,* 455–57.

Kosten, T. R. (1989). Pharmacotherapeutic interventions for cocaine abuse. Matching patients to treatments. *J. Nerv. Ment. Dis., 177,* 379–89.

Kosten, T. R., & Rounsaville, B.J. (1986). Psychopathology in opoid addicts. *Psychiat. Clin. N. Amer., 9,* 515–32.

Kosten, T. R., Rounsaville, B.J., & Kleber, H. D. (1988). Antecedents and consequences of cocaine abuse among opioid addicts. A 2.5 year follow-up. *J. Nerv. Ment. Dis., 176,* 176–81.

Kovacs, M. (1989). Affective disorders in children and adolescents. *Amer. Psychol., 44,* 209–15.

Kovacs, M., & Beck, A. T. (1977). An empirical clinical approach towards a definition of childhood depression. In J. G. Schulterbrand & A. Raskin (Eds.), *Depression in children: Diagnosis, treatment and conceptual models.* New York: Raven Press.

Kovacs, M., Gatsonis, C., Paulauskas, S. L., & Richards, C. (1989). Depressive disorders in childhood: IV. A longitudinal study of comorbidity with and risk for anxiety disorders. *Arch. Gen. Psychiat., 46,* 776–82.

Kraepelin, E. (1883). *Compendium der psychiatrie.* Leipzig: Abel.

Krafft-Ebing, R. V. (1950). *Psychopathica sexualis.* New York: Pioneer Publications.

Kraines, S. H. (1948). *The therapy of the neuroses and psychoses* (3rd ed.). Philadelphia: Lea & Febiger.

Kramlinger, K. G., & Post, R. M. (1989). The addition of lithium to carbamezine: Antidepressant efficacy in treatment-resistant depression. *Arch. Gen. Psychiat., 46,* 794–800.

Krantz, D. S., & Glass, D. C. (1984). Personality, behavior patterns, and physical illness: Conceptual and methodological issues. In W. D. Gentry (Ed.), *Handbook of behavioral medicine* (pp. 38–86). New York: Guilford.

Krech, D. (1966). *Environment, heredity, brain, and intelligence.* Paper presented to the Southwestern Psychological Association, Arlington, TX.

Krech, D., Rosenzweig, M. R., & Bennett, E. L. (1962). Relations between brain chemistry and problem-solving among rats raised in enriched and impoverished environments. *Journal of Comparative and Physiological Psychology, 55,* 801–7.

Kress, H. W. (1984). Role of family and networks in emergency psychotherapy. Chapter in E. L. Bassuk & A. Birk (Eds.), *Emergency Psychiatry.* New York: Plenum Press.

Kringlen, E. (1978). Adult offspring of two psychotic parents, with special reference to schizophrenia. In L. C. Wynne, R. L. Cromwell, & S. Matthysse (Eds.), *The nature of schizophrenia: New approaches to research and treatment* (pp. 9–24). New York: Wiley.

Krohn, M. D., Akers, R. L., Radosevich, M. J., & Lanza-Kaduce, L. (1980). Social status and deviance. *Criminology, 18*(3), 303–18.

Kroll, J., & Bachrach, B. (1984). Sin and mental illness in the Middle Ages. *Psychol. Med., 14,* 507–14.

Krystal, H. (1968). *Massive psychic trauma.* New York: International Universities Press.

Kuechenmeister, C. A., Linton, P. H., Mueller, T. V., & White, H. B. (1977). Eye tracking in relation to age, sex, and illness. *Arch. Gen. Psychiat., 34,* 578–79.

Kuhn, T. S. (1962). *The structure of scientific revolutions.* Chicago: University of Chicago Press.

Kuhnley, E. J., Hendron, R. L., & Quinlin D. M. (1982). Firesetting by children. *J. Amer. Acad. Child Psychiat., 21,* 560–63.

Kuperman, S., Black, D. W., & Burns, T.L. (1988). Excess mortality among formerly hospitalized child psychiatric patients. *Arch. Gen. Psychiat., 45,* 277–82.

Kupersmidt, J. B., Coie, J. D., & Dodge, K. A. (1990). The role of poor peer relationships in the development of disorder. In S. R. Asher & J. D. Coie (Eds.), *Peer rejection in childhood* (pp. 274–308). New York: Cambridge University Press.

Kurdeck, L. A., Blisk, D., & Siesky, A.E. (1981). Correlates of children's long-term adjustment to their parents' divorce. *Develop. Psychol., 17,* 565–79.

Kurland, H. D. (1967). Extreme obesity: A psychophysiological disorder. *Psychosomatics, 8,* 108–11.

Kushner, M. (1968). The operant control of intractable sneezing. In C. D. Spielberger (Ed.), *Contributions to general psychology: Selected readings for introductory psychology.* New York: Ronald Press.

Ladd, G. W. (1983). Social networks of popular, average, and rejected children in school settings. *Merrill-Palmer Quarterly, 29,* 283–308.

Lader, M. H., & Petursson, H. (1984). Computed axial brain tomography in long-term benzodiazepine users. *Psychol. Med., 14,* 203–6.

Lahey, B. B., Hartdagen, S. E., Frick, P.J., McBurnett, K., Connor, R., & Hynd, G. W. (1988). Conduct disorder: Parsing the confounded relation to parental divorce and antisocial personality. *J. Abnorm. Psychol., 97,* 334–37.

Lahey, B. B., Russo, M.F., Walker, J. L., & Piacentini, J.C. (1989). Personality characteristics of the mothers of children with disruptive behavior disorders. *J. Cons. Clin. Psychol., 57,* 512–15.

Laing, R. D. (1967, Feb. 3). Schizophrenic split. *Time, 56.*

Laing, R. D. (1969). *The divided self.* New York: Pantheon.

Laing, R. D. (1971). Quoted in J. S. Gordon, *Who is mad? Who is sane? R. D. Laing: In search of a new psychiatry. Atlantic, 227*(1), 50–66.

Laing, R. D., & Esterson, A. (1964). *Sanity, madness, and the family.* London: Tavistock.

Lakin, M. (1991). *Coping with ethical dilemmas in psychotherapy.* Elmsford, NY: Pergamon.

Lamb, H. R. (1984). Deinstitutionalization and the homeless mentally ill. *Hosp. Comm. Psychiat., 35,* 899–907.

Lambert, M. J. (1989). The individual therapist's contribution to psychotherapy process and outcome. *Clin. Psychol. Rev., 9,* 469–85.

Lambert, M. J., Shapiro, D. A., & Bergin, A. E. (1986). The effectiveness of psychotherapy. In S. L. Garfield & A. E. Bergin (Eds.), *Handbook of psychotherapy and behavior change* (3rd ed., pp. 157–212). New York: Wiley.

Lamson, B. (1980). *Sexual arousal of heterosexual, homosexual, and bisexual women.* Unpublished master's thesis, University of Georgia.

Landesman-Dwyer, S. (1981). Living in the community. *Amer. J. Ment. Def., 86,* 223–34.

Lando, H. (in press). Formal quit smoking treatments. In C. T. Orleans and J. Slade (Eds.), *Nicotine addiction: Principles & management.*

Lang, A. R., & Kidorf, M. (1990). Problem drinking: Cognitive behavioral strategies for self control. In M. E. Thase, B. A. Edelstein, & M. Hersen (Eds.), *Handbook of outpatient treatment of adults* (pp. 413–42). New York: Plenum.

Lang, A. R., & Marlatt, G. A. (1983). Problem drinking: A social learning perspective. In R. J. Gatchel, A. Baum, & J. E. Singer, (Eds.), *Handbook of psychology and health* (Vol. 1, pp. 121–69). Hillsdale, NJ: Lawrence Erlbaum Associates.

Lang, P. (1970). Autonomic control. *Psych. Today, 4*(5), 37–41.

Langevin, R., Handy, L., Day, D., & Russon, A. (1985). Are incestuous fathers pedophilic, aggressive, and alcoholic? In R. Langevin (Ed.), *Erotic preference, gender identity, and aggression* (pp. 161–80). Hillsdale, NJ: Erlbaum.

Langner, T. S., Gerṣten, J. C., Greene, E. L., Eisenberg, J. G., Herson, J. H., & McCarthy, E. D. (1974). Treatment of psychological disorders among urban children. *J. Cons. Clin. Psychol. 42*(2), 70–79.

Lansky, M. R., & Selzer, J. (1984). Priapism associated with trazodone therapy: Case report. *J. Clin. Psychiat., 45,* 232–33.

Lanyon, R. (1984). Personality assessment. *Annu. Rev. Psychol. 35,* 689–701.

Lanyon, R. I. (1986). Theory and treatment in child molestation. *J. Cons. Clin. Psychol., 54,* 176–82.

Lanyon, R. I., Barrington, C. C., & Newman, A. C. (1976). Modification of stuttering through EMG biofeedback: A preliminary study. *Behav. Ther., 7,* 96–103.

Laroche, C., Sheiner, R., Lester, E., Benierakis, C., Marrache, M., Engelsmann, F., & Cheifetz, P. (1987). Children of parents with manic-depressive illness: A follow-up study. *Canad. J. Psychiat., 32,* 563–69.

Latham, C., Holzman, P. S., Manschreck, T. C., & Tole, J. (1981). Optokinetic nystagmus and pursuit eye movements in schizophrenia. *Arch. Gen. Psychiat., 38,* 997–1003.

Laufer, R. S., Brett, E., & Gallops, M. S. (1985). Dimensions of posttraumatic stress disorder among Vietnam veterans. *J. Nerv. Ment. Dis., 173*(9), 538–45.

Laws, D. R., & Marshall, W. L. (1990). A conditioning theory of the etiology and maintenance of deviant sexual preference and behavior. In W. L. Marshall, D. R. Laws, & H. E. Barbaree (Eds.), *Handbook of sexual assault* (pp. 209–30). New York: Plenum.

Lazarus, A. A. (1981). *The practice of multimodal therapy.* New York: McGraw-Hill.

Lazarus, A. A. (Ed.). (1985). *Casebook of multimodal therapy.* New York: Guilford.

Lazarus, A. A. (1989). Dyspareunia: A multimodal psychotherapeutic perspective. In S. R. Leiblum & R. C. Rosen (Eds.), *Principles and practice of sex therapy* (2nd ed., pp. 89–112). New York: Guilford.

Lazarus, A. P. (1968). Learning theory in the treatment of depression. *Behav. Res. Ther., 8,* 83–89.

Leary, T. (1957). *Interpersonal diagnosis.* New York: Ronald.

Lebedev, B. A. (1967). Corticovisceral psychosomatics. *Inter. J. Psychiat., 4*(3), 241–46.

Lebergott, S. (1964). *Manpower in economic growth: The American record since 1800.* New York: McGraw-Hill.

Lebra, W. (Ed.). (1976). Culture-bound syndromes, ethnopsychiatry and alternate therapies. In *Mental health research in Asia and the Pacific* (Vol. 4). Honolulu: University Press of Hawaii.

Lee, J. R., & Goodwin, M. E. (1987). Deinstitutionalization: A new scenario. *Journal of Mental Health Administration, 14,* 40–45.

Leeman, C. P., & Mulvey, C. H. (1974). Brief psychotherapy of the dependent personality: Specific techniques. *Psychonometrics, 25,* 36–42.

Leff, M. J., Roatch, J. F., & Bunney, W. E., Jr. (1970). Environmental factors preceding the onset of severe depressions. *Psychiatry, 33*(3), 298–311.

Lefkowitz, M. M., & Burton, N. (1978). Childhood depression: A critique of the concept. *Psychol. Bull., 85,* 716–26.

Lefkowitz, M. M., Eron, L. D., Walder, L. O., & Huesmann, L. R. (1977). *Growing up to be violent: A longitudinal study of the development of aggression.* New York: Pergamon Press.

Lefkowitz, M. M., Huesmann, L. R., Walder, L. O., & Eron, L. D. (1973). Developing and predicting aggression. *Sci. News, 103*(3), 40.

Lefkowitz, M. M., & Tesiny, E. P. (1985). Depression in children: Prevalence and correlates. *J. Cons. Clin. Psychol., 53,* 647–56.

Lehmann, H. E. (1967). Psychiatric disorders not in standard nomenclature. In A. M. Freedman, H. I. Kaplan, & H. S. Kaplan (Eds.), *Comprehensive textbook of psychiatry.* Baltimore: Williams & Wilkins.

Lehmann, H. E. (1986). The future of psychiatry: Progress-mutation or self-destruct. *Canad. J. Psychiat., 31,* 362–67.

Lehmann, L. (1985). The relationship of depression to other DSM-III Axis I disorders. In E. E. Beckham & W. R. Leber (Eds.), *Handbook of depression: Treatment, assessment, and research* (pp. 669–99). Homewood, IL: Dorsey Press.

Leiblum, S. R., & Pervin, L. A. (1980). *Principles and practice of sex therapy.* New York: Guilford Press.

Leiblum, S. R., Pervin, L. A., & Campbell, E. H. (1989). The treatment of vaginismus: Success and failure. In S. R. Leiblum & R. C. Rosen (Eds.), *Principles and practice of sex therapy* (2nd ed., pp. 113–40). New York: Guilford.

Leiblum, S. R., & Rosen, R. C. (Eds.) (1989a). *Principles and practice of sex therapy,* 2nd ed. New York: Guilford.

Leiblum, S. R., & Rosen, R. C. (1989b). Introduction: Sex therapy in the age of AIDS. In S. R. Leiblum & R. C. Rosen (Eds.), *Principles and practice of sex therapy,* (2nd ed., pp. 1–18). New York: Guilford.

Leiderman, P. H., & Leiderman, G. F. (1974). Affective and cognitive consequences of polymatric infant care in the East African highlands. In A. Pick (Ed.), *Minnesota symposium on child development* (Vol. 8). Minneapolis: University of Minnesota Press.

Lelliott, P., Marks, I., McNamee, G., & Tobena, A. (1989). Onset of panic disorder with agoraphobia. *Arch. Gen. Psychiat., 46,* 1000–1004.

Lemert, E. M. (1962). Paranoia and the dynamics of exclusion. *Sociometry, 25,* 2–25.

Leon, G. (1976). Current directions in the treatment of obesity. *Psychol. Bull., 83,* 557–78.

Leon, G. L. (1983). *Treating eating disorders: Obesity, anorexia nervosa and bulimia.* Lexington, MA: Lewis.

Leon, G. L., Butcher, J. N., Kleinman, M., Goldberg, A., Almagor, M. (1981). Survivors of the holocaust and their children: Current status and adjustment. *J. Pers. Soc. Psychol., 41*(3), 503–16.

Leon, G. R., & Chamberlain, K. (1973). Emotional arousal, eating patterns, and body image as differential factors associated with varying success in maintaining a weight loss. *J. Cons. Clin. Psychol., 40,* 474–80.

Leon, G. R., Eckert, E. D., Teed, D., & Buckwald, H. (1978). Changes in body image and other psychological factors after intestinal bypass surgery for massive obesity. *J. Behav. Med., 2,* 39–59.

Leon, G. R., & Roth, L. (1977). Obesity: Psychological causes, correlations and speculations. *Psychol. Bull., 84,* 117–39.

Leonard, C. V. (1974). Depression and suicidality. *J. Cons. Clin. Psychol., 42*(1), 98–104.

Levenson, A. J. (1981). *Basic psychopharmacology.* New York: Springer.

Levenson, R.W., Sher, K. J., Grossman, L. M., Newman, J., & Newlin, D. B. (1980). Alcohol and stress response dampening: Pharmacological effects, expectancy and tension reduction. *J. Abnorm. Psychol., 89*(4), 528–38.

Levin, S. (1949). Brain tumors in mental hospital patients. *Amer. J. Psychiat., 105,* 897–900.

Levin, S., & Yurgelun-Todd, D. (1989). Contributions of clinical neuropsychology to the study of schizophrenia. *J. Abnorm. Psychol., 98,* 341–56.

Levine, M., & Perkins, D. V. (1987). *Principles of community psychology: Perspectives and applications.* New York: Oxford University Press.

Levine, M. D. (1976). Children with encopresis: A descriptive analysis. *Pediatrics, 56,* 412.

Levine, M. D., & Bakow, H. (1975). Children with encopresis: A study of treatment outcomes. *Pediatrics, 58,* 845.

Levine, S., & Koenig, J. (Eds.). (1980). *Why men rape: Interviews with convicted rapists.* Toronto: Macmillan.

Levitan, H. (1989). Onset situation in three psychosomatic illnesses. In S. Cheren (Ed.), *Psychosomatic medicine: Theory, physiology, and practice* (Vol 1., pp. 119–34). Madison, CT: International Universities Press.

Levitt, L. P. (1974, Apr. 1). *Illinois State Plan for the Prevention, Treatment, and Control of Alcohol Abuse and Alcoholism (Vol. 1): Objectives—Plan of Action—Basic Data.* Department of Mental Health and Developmental Disabilities, State of Illinois.

Levor, R. M., Cohen, M. J., Naliboff, B. D., & McArthur, D. (1986). Psychosocial precursors and correlates of migraine headache. *J. Cons. Clin. Psychol., 54,* 347–53.

Levy, D. L., Yasillo, N. J., Dorcus, E., Shaughnessy, R. Gibbons, R. D., Peterson, J., Janicak, P.G., Gaviria, M., & Davis, J. M. (1983). Relatives of unipolar and bipolar patients have normal pursuit. *Psychiat. Res., 10,* 285–93.

Levy, S. M. (1976). Schizophrenic symptomatology: Reaction or strategy? A study of contextual antecedents. *J. Abnorm. Psychol., 85,* 435–45.

Lewinsohn, P. M. (1974). A behavioral approach to depression. In R. J. Friedman & M. M. Katz (Eds.), *The psychology of depression: Contemporary theory and research.* New York: Halstead Press.

Lewinsohn, P. M., Zeiss, A. M., & Duncan, E. M. (1989). Probability of relapse after recovery from an episode of depression. *J. Abnorm. Psychol., 98,* 107–16.

Lewinson, T. S. (1940). Dynamic disturbances in the handwriting of psychotics; with reference to schizophrenic, paranoid, and manic-depressive psychoses. *Amer. J. Psychiat., 97,* 102–35.

Lewis, C. E., Cloninger, C. R., & Pais, J. (1983). Alcoholism, anti-social personality, and drug use in a criminal population. *Alcohol and Alcoholism, 18,* 53–60.

Lewis, C. E., Robins, L., & Rice, J. (1985). Association of alcoholism with antisocial personality in urban men. *J. Nerv. Ment. Dis., 173*(3), 166–74.

Lewis, J. M., Rodnick, E. H., & Goldstein, M. J. (1981). Intrafamilial interactive behavior, communication deviance, and risk for schizophrenia. *J. Abnorm. Psychol., 90,* 448–57.

Lewis, M. S. (1989a). Age incidence and schizophrenia: Part I. The season of birth controversy. *Schizo. Bull., 15,* 59–73.

Lewis, M. S. (1989b). Age incidence and schizophrenia: Part II. Beyond age incidence. *Schizo. Bull., 15,* 75–80.

Lewis, M. S. (1990). Res ipsa loquitur: The author replies. *Schizo. Bull., 16,* 17–28.

Lewis, M. S., & Griffin, P. A. (1981). An explanation for the season of birth effect in schizophrenia and certain other diseases. *Psychol. Bull., 89,* 589–96.

Lewis, N. D., & Yarnell, H. (1951). Pathological fire setting (pyromania). *Nervous and Mental Disease Monograph,* No. 82.

Lewis, N. D. C. (1941). *A short history of psychiatric achievement.* New York: Norton.

Lewis, R. J., Dlugokinski, E. L., Caputo, L. M., & Griffin, R. B. (1988). Children at risk for emotional disorders: Risk and resource dimensions. *Clin. Psychol. Rev., 8,* 417–40.

Lewis, W. C. (1974). Hysteria: The consultant's dilemma. *Arch. Gen. Psychiat., 30*(2), 145–51.

Lexow, G. A., & Aronson, S. S. (1975). Health advocacy: A need, a concept, a model. *Children Today, 4*(1), 2–6, 36.

Li, T. K., Lumeng, L., McBride, L., & Murphy, J.M. (1987). Rodent lines selected for factors affecting alcohol consumption. *Alcohol and Alcoholism,* Suppl. 1, 91–96.

Liberman, R. P., & Evans, C. C. (1985). Behavioral rehabilitation for chronic mental patients. *J. Clin. Psychopharm., 5,* 8S–14S.

Liberman, R. P., Mueser, K. T., & DeRisi, W. J. (1989). *Social skills training for psychiatric patients.* Elmsford, NY: Pergamon Press.

Liberman, R. P., & Raskin, D. E. (1971). Depression: A behavioral formulation. *Arch. Gen. Psychiat., 24*(6), 515–23.

Lichy, M. H. (1982). Assessment of client functioning in residential settings. In M. Miraba (Ed.), *The chronically mentally ill; Research and services.* New York: SP Medical and Scientific Books.

Lidz, T. (1968). The family, language, and the transmission of schizophrenia. In D. Rosenthal & S. S. Kety (Eds.), *The transmission of schizophrenia* (pp. 175–84). Elmsford, NY: Pergamon Press.

Lidz, T. (1973). *The origin and treatment of schizophrenoid disorders.* New York: Basic Books.

Lidz, T. (1978). Egocentric cognitive regression and the family setting of schizophrenic disorders. In L. C. Wynne, R. L. Cromwell, & S. Matthysse (Eds.), *The nature of schizophrenia: New approaches to research and treatment* (pp. 526–33). New York: Wiley.

Lidz, T., Fleck, S., & Cornelison, A. R. (1965). *Schizophrenia and the family.* New York: International Universities Press.

Lieberman, L. M. (1982). The nightmare of scheduling. *J. Learn. Dis., 15,* 57–58.

Liebowitz, M. R., Fyer, A. J., Gorman, J. M., Dillon, D., Appleby, I. L., Levy, G., Anderson, S., Palij, M., Davies, S. O., & Klein, D. F. (1984). Lactate provocation of panic. *Arch. Gen. Psychiat., 41,* 764–70.

Liebowitz, M. R., Gorman, J. M., Fyer, A. J., Levitt, M., Dillon, D., Levy, P., Appleby, I. L., Anderson, S., Palij, M., Davis, S. O., & Klein, D. F. (1985). Lactate provocation of panic attacks: II. Biochemical and physiological findings. *Arch. Gen. Psychiat., 42,* 709–19.

Liem, J. H. (1974). Effects of verbal communications of parents and children: A comparison of normal and schizophrenic families. *J. Cons. Clin. Psychol., 42,* 438–50.

Liem, J. H. (1980). Family studies of schizophrenia: An update and commentary. *Schizo. Bull., 6,* 429–55.

Lifton, R. J. (1972). The "Gook syndrome" and "numbed warfare," *Saturday Review, 55*(47), 66–72.

Light, E., & Lebowitz, B. D. (1989). Introduction. *Alzheimer's disease treatment and family stress: Directions for research* (pp. vii–viii). Rockville, MD: U.S. Department of Human Services.

Liljefors, I., & Rahe, R. H. (1970). An identical twin study of psychosocial factors in coronary heart disease in Sweden. *Psychosom. Med., 32*(5), 523–42.

Link, B. G., Cullen, F. T., Frank, J., & Wozniak, J.F. (1987). The social rejection of former mental patients: Understanding why labels matter. *American Journal of Sociology, 92,* 1461–1500.

Links, P. S., Boyle, M. H., & Offord, D. R. (1989). The prevalence of emotional disorder in children. *J. Nerv. Ment. Dis., 177,* 85–91.

Lipsky, M. J., Kassinove, H., & Miller, N. J. (1980). Effects of rational-emotive therapy, rational role reversal and rational-emotive imagery on the emotional adjustment of community mental health center patients. *J. Cons. Clin. Psychol., 48,* 366–74.

Lipton, E. L., Steinschneider, A., & Richmond, J. B. (1966). Psychophysiologic disorders in children. In L. W. Hoffman & M. L. Hoffman (Eds.), *Review of child development research* (pp. 169–220). Russell Sage Foundation.

Lisak, D., & Roth, S. (1988). Motivational factors in nonincarcerated sexually aggressive men. *J. Pers. Soc. Psychol., 55,* 795–802.

Lishman, W. A. (1990). Alcohol and the brain. *Brit. J. Psychiat., 156,* 635–44.

Lishman, W. A., Jacobson, R. R., & Acker, C. (1987). Brain damage in alcoholism: Current concepts. *Acta Medica Scandinavica,* (suppl. 717), 5–17.

Litwack, T. R., & Schlesinger, L. B. (1987). Assessing and predicting violence: Research, law, and applications. In A. Hess & I. Weiner (Eds.), *Handbook of forensic psychology.* New York: John Wiley & Sons.

Livesley, W. J., West, M., & Tanney, A. (1985). Historical comment on the DSM III schizoid and avoidant personality disorders. *Amer. J. Psychiat., 142,* 1344–47.

Livingston, J. (1974, Mar.). Compulsive gamblers: A culture of losers. *Psych. Today,* 51–55.

Lloyd, R. W., Jr., & Salzberg, H. C. (1975). Controlled social drinking: An alternative to abstinence as a treatment goal for some alcohol abusers. *Psychol. Bull., 82,* 815–42.

Lobitz, W. C., & Lobitz, G. K. (1978). Clinical assessment in the treatment of sexual dysfunctions. In J. LoPiccolo & L. LoPiccolo (Eds.), *Handbook of sex therapy* (pp. 85–102). New York: Plenum.

Lobovits, D. A., & Handel, P. (1985). Childhood depression: Prevalence using DSM III criteria and validity of parent and child depression scales. *J. Pediat. Psychol., 10*(1), 45–54.

Locke, B. Z., & Regier, D. A. (1985). Prevalence of selected mental disorders. *Mental Health, United States, 1985* (pp. 1–6). Washington, DC: U. S. Government Printing Office.

Lombardo, V.S., & Lombardo, E.F. (1991). The link between learning disabilities and juvenile delinquency: Fact or fiction? *The Correctional Psychologist, 23,* 1–3.

Long, B. (1986). The view from the top: National prevention policy. In M. Kessler and S. E. Goldston (Eds.), *A decade of progress* (pp. 346–62). Hanover, NH: University Press of New England.

LoPiccolo, J. (1978). Direct treatment of sexual dysfunction. In J. LoPiccolo & L. LoPiccolo (Eds.), *Handbook of sex therapy* (pp. 1–17). New York: Plenum.

LoPiccolo, J., & LoPiccolo, L. (Eds). (1978). *Handbook of sex therapy.* New York: Plenum.

LoPiccolo, J., & Stock, W. E. (1986). Treatment of sexual dysfunction. *J. Cons. Clin. Psychol., 54,* 158–67.

Loranger, A. W., Oldham, J. M., & Tulis, E. H. (1982). Familial transmission of DSM-III borderline personality disorder. *Arch. Gen. Psychiat., 39*(7), 795–99.

Lorenz, V. C., & Shuttlesworth, D. E. (1983). The impact of pathological gambling on the spouse of the gambler. *Journal of Community Psychology, 11,* 67–76.

Lorion, R. P. (1990). *Protecting the children: Strategies for optimizing emotional and behavioral development.* New York: Haworth.

Lorr, M., & Klett, C. J. (1968). Cross-cultural comparison of psychotic syndromes. *J. Abnorm. Psychol., 74*(4), 531–43.

Los Angeles Times. (1973, Sept. 30). A transvestite's plea for understanding and tolerance. IV, 7.

Lothstein, L. M. (1982). Sex reassignment surgery: Historical, bioethical, and theoretical issues. *Amer. J. Psychiat., 139,* 417–26.

Lothstein, L. M. (1983). *Female-to-male transsexualism: Historical, ethical, and theoretical issues.* Boston: Routledge & Kegan Paul.

Lou, H. C., Heinriken, L., & Bruhn, P. (1984). Focal cerebral hypoperfusion in children with dysphasia and/or attention deficit disorder. *Archives of Neurology, 14,* 825–29.

Lovaas, O. I. (1977). *The autistic child: Language development through behavior modification.* New York: Holsted Press.

Lovaas, O. I., Schaeffer, B., & Simmons, J. Q. (1974). In O. I. Lovaas & B. D. Bucker (Eds.), *Perspectives in behavior modification with deviant children.* Englewood Cliffs, NJ: Prentice-Hall.

Lovaas, O. I. (1987). Behavioral treatment of normal educational and intellectual functioning in young autistic children. *J. Cons. Clin. Psychol., 44,* 3–9.

Lovett, S. (1985). Microelectronic and computer-based technology. In A. M. Clarke, A. D. B. Clarke, & J. M. Berg (Eds.), *Mental deficiency: The changing outlook* (4th ed., pp. 549–83). London: Methuen.

Lovibond, S. H., & Caddy, G. R. (1970). Discriminated aversive control in the moderation of alcoholics' drinking behavior. *Behav. Ther. 1,* 437–44.

Lubin, B. (1976). Group therapy. In I. Weiner (Ed.), *Clinical methods in psychology.* New York: Wiley.

Lubin, B., Larsen, R. M., & Matarazzo, J. (1984). Patterns of psychological test usage in the United States, 1935–1982. *Amer. Psychol., 39,* 451–54.

Lubin, B., Larsen, R. M., Matarazzo, J. D., & Seever, M. F. (1985). Psychological test usage patterns in five professional settings. *Amer. Psychol., 40,* 857–61.

Lucas, A. R., Duncan J. W., & Piens, V. (1976). The treatment for anorexia nervosa. *Amer. J. Psychiat., 133,* 1034–38.

Lukas, C., & Seiden, H. M. (1990). *Silent grief: Living in the wake of suicide.* New York: Bantam Books.

Lund, S. N. (1975). *Personality and personal history factors of child abusing parents.* Unpublished doctoral dissertation, University of Minnesota.

Lusznat, R. M., Murphy, D. P., & Nunn, C.M. H. (1988). Carbamazepine vs. lithium in the treatment and prophylaxis of mania. *Brit. J. Psychiat., 153,* 198–204.

Lutz, D. J., & Snow, P. A. (1985). Understanding the role of depression in the alcoholic. *Clin. Psychol. Rev., 5,* 535–51.

Lykken, D. T. (1957). A study of anxiety in the sociopathic personality. *J. Abnorm. Soc. Psychol., 55*(1), 6–10.

Lynch, J. J. (1977). *The broken heart.* New York: Basic Books.

Lyon, M., Barr, C. E., Cannon, T. D., Mednick, S. A., & Shore, D. (1989). Fetal neural development and schzophrenia. *Schizo. Bull., 15,* 149–61.

MacDonald, A. D. (1964). Intelligence in children of very low birth weight. *British Journal of Preventive Social Medicine, 18,* 59–75.

MacDonald, M. R., & Kuiper, N. A. (1983). Cognitive-behavioral preparations for surgery: Some theoretical and methodological concerns. *Clin. Psychol. Rev., 3,* 27–39.

MacFarlane, J. W., Allen, L., & Honzik, M. P. (1954). *A developmental study of the behavior problems of normal children between 21 months and 14 years.* Berkeley, CA: University of California Press.

MacLusky, N. J., & Naftolin, F. (1981). Sexual differentiation of the central nervous system. *Science, 211,* 1294–1303.

MacMillan, D. L., & Keogh, B. K. (1971). Normal and retarded children's expectancy for failure. *Develop. Psychol., 4*(3), 343–48.

MacMillan, J., & Kofoed, L. (1984). Sociobiology and antisocial personality: An alternative perspective. *J. Ment. Dis., 172*(12), 701–6.

Maddi, S. R., Bartone, P. T., & Puccetti, M. C. (1987). Stressful events are indeed a factor in physical illness: Reply to Schroeder and Costa. *J. Pers. Soc. Psychol., 52,* 833–43.

Magaro, P. A. (1980) *Cognition in schizophrenia and paranoia.* Hillsdale, NJ: Laurence Erlbaum Associates.

Magaro, P. A. (1981). The paranoid and the schizophrenic: The case for distinct cognitive style. *Schizo. Bull., 7,* 632–61.

Magrab, P. R. (1982). Services for children: Challenge for the 1980's. *J. Pediat. Psychol., 7*(2), 105–10.

Mahler, M. (1976). *On Human symbiosis and the vicissitudes of individuation.* New York: Library of Human Behavior.

Mahoney, G., Glover, A., & Finger, I. (1981). Relationship between language and sensorimotor development of Down's syndrome and nonretarded children. *Amer. J. Ment. Def., 86,* 21–27.

Mahoney, M., & Arnkoff, D. (1978). Cognitive and self-control therapies. In S. Garfield & A. Bergin (Eds.), *Handbook of psychotherapy and behavior change: An empirical analysis.* New York: Wiley.

Mahoney, M. J. (1974). Cognition and behavior modification. Cambridge, MA: Ballinger.

Maida, C. A., Gordon, N. S., & Farberow, N. L. (1989). *The crisis of competence.* New York: Bruner/Mazel.

Maisch, H. (1972). *Incest.* New York: Stein & Day.

Makita, K. (1973). The rarity of "depression" in childhood. *Acta Psychiatrica, 40,* 37–44.

Malamud, N. (1975). Organic brain disease mistaken for psychiatric disorder: A clinicopathologic study. In D. F. Benson & D. Blumer (Eds.), *Psychiatric aspects of neurological disease* (pp. 287–307). New York: Grune & Stratton.

Malamuth, N. M. (1986). Predictors of naturalistic sexual aggression. *J. Pers. Soc. Psychol., 50,* 953–62.

Malatesta, V. J., Sutker, P. B., & Treiber, F. A. (1981).

Sensation seeking and chronic public drunkenness. *J. Cons. Clin. Psychol., 49,* 292–94.

Malinowski, B. (1927). *Sex and repression in savage society.* New York: Humanities.

Manderscheid, R. W., Witkin, M. J., Rosenstein, M. J., Milazzo-Sayre, L. J., Bethel, H. E., & MacAskill, R. L. (1985). In C. A. Taube & S. A. Barrett (Eds.), *Mental Health, United States, 1985.* Washington, DC: National Institute of Mental Health, U.S. Government Printing Office.

Manglesdorff, D. (1985). Lessons learned and forgotten: The need for prevention and mental health interventions in disaster preparedness. *Journal of Community Psychology, 13,* 239–57.

Mann, J. (1973). *Time-dated psychotherapy.* Cambridge, MA: Harvard University Press.

Mann, L. M., Chassin, L., & Sher, K. J. (1987). Alcohol expectancies and risk for alcoholics. *J. Cons. Clin. Psychol., 55,* 411–17.

Mann, P. A. (1978). *Community psychology: Concepts and applications.* New York: The Free Press.

Mannuzza, S., Gittelman, R., Bonagura, N., Konig, P. H., & Shenker, R. (1988). Hyperactive boys almost grown up. *Arch. Gen. Psychiat., 45,* 13–18.

Marchant, R., Howlin, P., Yule, W., & Rutter, M. (1974). Graded change in the treatment of the behavior of autistic children. *J. Child Psychol. Psychiat., 15*(3), 221–27.

Marcus, E. R., & Bradley, S. S. (1990). Combination psychotherapy and psychopharmacotherapy with treatment-resistent inpatients with dual disorder. *Psychiat. Clin. N. Amer., 13,* 209–14.

Marcus, J., Hans, S. L., Lewow, E., Wilkinson, L., & Burack, C. M. (1985). Neurological findings in high-risk children: Childhood assessment and 5-year followup. *Schizo. Bull., 11,* 85–100.

Marcus, J., Hans, S. L., Mednick, S. A., Schulsinger, F., & Michelson, N. (1985). Neurological dysfunctioning in offspring of schizophrenics in Israel and Denmark: A replication analysis. *Arch. Gen. Psychiat., 42,* 753–61.

Margolin, G., Christensen, A., & Weiss, R. L. (1975). Contracts, cognition, and change: A behavioral approach to marriage therapy. *The Counseling Psychologist, 5*(3), 15–26.

Margolin, G., & Wampold, B. E. (1981). Sequential analysis of conflict and accord in distressed and non-distressed marital partners. *J. Cons. Clin. Psychol., 49*(4), 554–67.

Mariotto, M. J. (1979). Observational assessment systems use for basic and applied research. *J. Behav. Assess., 1*(3), 239–50.

Marks, I. (1978). Behavioral psychotherapy of adult neurotics. In S. L. Garfield & A. E. Bergin (Eds.), *Handbook of psychotherapy and behavior change: An empirical analysis.* New York: Wiley.

Marks, I. M. (1982). Toward an empirical clinical science: Behavioral psychotherapy in the 1980's. *Behav. Ther., 13,* 63–81.

Marlatt, G. A. (1985). Cognitive assessment and intervention procedures for relapse prevention. In G. A. Marlatt & J. R. Gordon (Eds.), *Relapse prevention.* New York: Guilford Press.

Marlatt, G. A., & Gordon, J. R. (1980). Determinants of relapse: Implications for the maintenance of behavior change. In P. Davidson & S. Davidson (Eds.), *Behavioral medicine: Changing health lifestyles.* New York: Brunner/Mazel.

Marmor, J., & Woods, S. M. (Eds.), (1980). *The interface between psychodynamic and behavior therapies.* New York: Plenum.

Marsella, A. J. (1980). Depressive experience and disorder across cultures. In H. C. Triandis, & J. Draguns (Eds.), *Handbook of cross-cultural psychology* (Vol. 6). Boston: Allyn & Bacon.

Marsella, A. J., Sartorius, N., Jablensky, A., & Fenton, F. R. (1985). Cross-cultural studies of depressive disorders: An overview. In A. Kleinman & B. Good (Eds.), *Culture and depression.* Berkeley, CA: University of California Press.

Marshall, P. (1989). Attention deficit disorder and allergy: A neurochemical model of the relation between the illnesses. *Psychol. Bull., 106,* 434–46.

Marshall, W. L. (1974). A combined treatment approach to the reduction of multiple fetish-related behaviors. *J. Cons. Clin. Psychol., 42*(4), 613–16.

Marshall, W. L., & Barbaree, H. E. (1990). An integrated theory of the etiology of sexual offending. In W. L. Marshall, D. R. Laws, & H. E. Barbaree (Eds.), *Handbook of sexual assault* (pp. 257–69). New York: Plenum.

Marshall, W. L., Laws, D. R., & Barbaree, H. E. (Eds.). (1990a). *Handbook of sexual assault.* New York: Plenum.

Marshall, W. L., Laws, D. R., & Barbaree, H. E. (1990b). Present status and future directions. In W. L. Marshall, D. R. Laws, & H. E. Barbaree (Eds.), *Handbook of sexual assault* (pp. 389–95). New York: Plenum.

Martin, G. I., & Zaug, P. J. (1975). Electrocardiographic monitoring of enuretic children receiving therapeutic doses of imipramine. *Amer. J. Psychiat., 132*(5), 540–42.

Martin, R. L., Cloninger, R., Guze, S. B., & Clayton, P. J. (1985). Mortality in a follow-up of 500 psychiatric outpatients: I. Total mortality. *Arch. Gen. Psychiat., 42,* 47–54.

Marvit, R. C. (1981). Guilty but mentally ill—an old approach to an old problem. *Clin. Psychol., 34*(4), 22–23.

Marx, J. (1991). Mutation identified as possible cause of Alzheimer's disease. *Science, 251,* 876–77.

Mash, E. J., Handy, L. C., & Hamerlynck, L. A. (1976). *Behavior modification approaches to parenting.* New York: Brunner/Mazel.

Maslow, A. H. (1962). *Toward a psychology of being.* New York: Van Nostrand.

Maslow, A. H. (1969). Toward a humanistic biology. *Amer. Psychol., 24*(8), 734–35.

Masserman, J. H. (1961). *Principles of dynamic psychiatry* (2nd ed.). Philadelphia: W. B. Saunders.

Masters, W. H., & Johnson, V. E. (1966). *Human sexual response.* Boston: Little, Brown.

Masters, W. H., & Johnson, V. E. (1970). *Human sexual inadequacy.* Boston: Little, Brown.

Masters, W. H., & Johnson, V. E. (1975). *The pleasure bond: A new look at sexuality and commitment.* Boston: Little, Brown.

Matarazzo, J. D. (1983). The reliability of psychiatric and psychological diagnosis. *Clin. Psychol. Rev., 3,* 103–45.

Matarazzo, J. D. (1986). Computerized clinical psychological test interpretations: Unvalidated plus all mean and no sigma. *Amer. Psychol., 41,* 14–24.

Matson, J. L. (1981). Use of independence training to teach shopping skills to mildly mentally retarded adults. *Amer. J. Ment. Def., 86,* 178–83.

Matsunaga, E., Tonomura, A., Hidetsune, O., & Yasumoto, K. (1978). Reexamination of paternal age effect in Down's syndrome. *Human Genet., 40,* 259–68.

Mattes, J. A., & Gittelman, R., (1981). Effects of artificial food colorings in children with hyperactive symptoms: A critical review and results of a controlled study. *Arch. Gen. Psychiat., 38*(6), 714–18.

Mattick, R. P., Peters, L., & Clarke, J. C. (1989). Exposure and cognitive restructuring for social phobia: A controlled study. *Behav. Ther., 20,* 3–23.

Maugh, T. M. (1981). Biochemical markers identify mental states. *Science, 214,* 39–41.

Maurer, R., Cadoret, R. J., & Cain, C. (1980). Cluster analysis of childhood temperament data on adoptees. *Amer. J. Orthopsychiat., 50,* 522–34.

Maurer, O. H., & Maurer, W. M. (1938). Enuresis: A method for its study and treatment. *Amer. J. Orthopsychiat., 8,* 436–59.

Mavissakalian, M. R., & Perel, J. M. (1989). Imipramine dose-response relationship in panic disorder with agoraphobia. *Arch. Gen. Psychiat., 46,* 127–31.

May, R. (1969). *Love and will.* New York: Norton.

May, R., Angel, E., & Ellenberger, H. S. (Eds.). (1958). *Existence: A new dimension in psychiatry and psychology.* New York: Basic Books.

Mays, D. T., & Franks, C. M. (Eds.). (1985). *Negative outcome in psychotherapy and what to do about it.* New York: Springer.

Mays, J. A. (1974, Jan. 16). High blood pressure, soul food. *Los Angeles Times,* II, 7.

Maziade, M., Caron, C., Cote, R., Boutin, P., & Thivierge, J. (1990). Extreme temperament and diagnosis: A study in a psychiatric sample of consecutive children. *Arch. Gen. Psychiat., 47,* 477–84.

McAdoo, W. G., & DeMyer, M. K. (1978). Personality characteristics of parents. In M. Rutter & E. Schopler (Eds.), *Autism: A reappraisal of concepts and treatment.* New York: Plenum.

McAlister, A., Puska, P., Koskela, K., Pallonen, U., & Maccoby, N. (1980). Mass communication and community organization for public health education. *Amer. Psychol., 35,* 375–79.

McCall, L. (1961). *Between us and the dark* (originally published in 1947). Summary in W. C. Alvarez, *Minds that came back.*

McCann, I. L., Sakheim, D. K., & Abrahamson, D. J. (1988). Trauma and victimization: A model of psychological adaptation. *Counseling Psychologist, 16,* 531–94.

McCarthy, B. W. (1989). Cognitive-behavioral strategies and techniques in the treatment of early ejaculation. In S. R. Leiblum & R. C. Rosen (Eds.), *Principles and practice of sex* *therapy* (2nd ed., pp. 141–67). New York: Guilford.

McClelland, D. C. (1979). Inhibited power motivation and high blood pressure in men. *J. Abnorm. Psychol., 88*(2), 182–90.

McCombie, S. L. (1976). Characteristics of rape victims seen in crisis intervention. *Smith College Studies in Social Work, 46,* 137–58.

McCord, W., & McCord, J. (1964). *The psychopath: An essay on the criminal mind.* New York: Van Nostrand Reinhold.

McCrae, R. R., & Costa, P. T. (1986). Clinical assessment can benefit from recent advances in personality psychology. *Amer. Psychol., 41,* 1001–2.

McCutchan, J. A. (1990). Virology, immunology, and clinical course of HIV infection. *J. Cons. Clin. Psychol., 58,* 5–12.

McEwen, B. S. (1981). Neural gonadal steroid actions. *Science, 211,* 1303–11.

McFall, R. M. (1990). The enhancement of social skills: An information-processing analysis. In W. L. Marshall, D. R. Laws, & H. E. Barbaree (Eds.), *Handbook of sexual assault* (pp. 311–30). New York: Plenum.

McFarlane, A. C. (1986). Posttraumatic morbidity of a disaster: A study of cases presenting for psychiatric treatment. *J. Nerv. Ment. Dis., 174*(1), 4–14.

McFarlane, A. C. (1988). The longitudinal course of posttraumatic morbidity: The range of outcomes and their predictors. *J. Nerv. Ment. Dis., 176,* 30–39.

McGlashan, T. H. (1986). The Chestnut Lodge follow-up study: Long-term outcome of borderline personalities. *Arch. Gen. Psychiat., 43,* 20–30.

McLemore, C. W., & Benjamin, L. S. (1979). Whatever happened to interpersonal diagnosis: A psychological alternative to DSM III. *Amer. Psychol., 34,* 17–34.

McNeal, E. T., & Cimbolic, P. (1986). Antidepressants and biochemical theories of depression. *Psychol. Bull., 99*(3), 361–74.

McNeil, D. E., & Binder, R. L. (1986). Violence, civil commitment, and hospitalization. *J. Nerv. Ment. Dis., 174*(2), 107–11.

McNeil, T. F., & Kaij, L. (1978). Obstetrical factors in the development of schizophrenia: Complications in the births of preschizophrenics and in reproduction by schizophrenic parents. In L. C. Wynne, R. L. Cromwell, & S. Matthysse (Eds.), *The nature of schizophrenia: New approaches to research and treatment.* New York: Wiley.

Mead, M. (1949). *Male and female.* New York: Morrow.

Mealiea, W. L., Jr. (1967). *The comparative effectiveness of systematic desensitization and implosive therapy in the elimination of snake phobia.* Unpublished doctoral dissertation, University of Missouri.

Mechanic, D. (1962). *Students under stress.* New York: Free Press.

Medea, A., & Thompson, K. (1974). *Against rape.* New York: Farrar, Straus & Giroux.

Mednick, S. A. (1978). Berkson's fallacy and high-risk research. In L. C. Wynne, R. L. Cromwell, & S. Matthysse (Eds.), *The nature of schizophrenia: New approaches to research and treatment* (pp. 442–52). New York: Wiley.

Mednick, S. A., & Schulsinger, F. (1968). Some premorbid characteristics related to breakdown in children with schizophrenic mothers. In D. Rosenthal & S. S. Kety (Eds.), *The transmission of schizophrenia* (pp. 267–91). Oxford: Pergamon.

Mednick, S. A., Schulsinger, F., Teasdale, T. W., Schulsinger, H., Venables, P., & Rock, D. (1978). Schizophrenia in high risk children: Sex differences in predisposing factors. In G. Serban (Ed.), *Cognitive defects in the development of mental illness.* New York: Brunner/Mazel.

Mednick, S. A., Schulsinger, H., & Schulsinger, F. (1975). Schizophrenia in children of schizophrenic mothers. In A. Davis (Ed.), *Child personality and psychopathology: Current topics* (Vol. 2). New York: Wiley.

Meehl, P. E. (1962). Schizotaxia, schizotypy, schizophrenia. *Amer. Psychol., 17,* 827–38.

Meehl, P. E. (1978). Theoretical risks and tabular asterisks: Sir Karl, Sir Ronald, and the slow progress of soft psychology. *J. Cons. Clin. Psychol., 46,* 806–34.

Meehl, P. E. (1989). Schizotaxia revisited. *Arch. Gen. Psychiat., 46,* 935–44.

Megargee, E. I. (1966). Undercontrolled and overcontrolled personality types in extreme antisocial aggression. *Psychological Monographs, 80* (Whole No. 611).

Megargee, E. I. (1970). The prediction of violence with psychological tests. In C. D. Spielberger (Ed.), *Current topics in clinical and community psychology* (Vol. 2). New York: Academic Press.

Mehrabian, A., & Weinstein, L. (1985). Temperament characteristics of suicide attempters. *J. Cons. Clin. Psychol., 53,* 544–46.

Meichenbaum, D. (1974). *Cognitive behavior modification.* General Learning Corporation, 16.

Meichenbaum, D. (1975). A self-instructional approach to stress management: A proposal for stress-inoculation training. In C. Spielberger & I. Sarason (Eds.), *Stress and anxiety* (Vol. 2). New York: Wiley.

Meichenbaum, D. (1977). *Cognitive-behavior modification.* New York: Plenum.

Meichenbaum, D., & Cameron, R. (1982). Cognitive behavior therapy. In G. T. Wilson & C. M. Franks (Eds.), *Contemporary behavior therapy: Conceptual and empirical foundations.* New York: Guilford.

Meichenbaum, D., & Cameron, R. (1983). Stress inoculation training: Toward a general paradigm for training coping skills. In D. Meichenbaum & M. E. Jaremko (Eds.), *Stress reduction and prevention* (pp. 115–54). New York: Plenum.

Meichenbaum, D., & Goodman, J. (1971). Training impulsive children to talk to themselves: A means of developing self-control. *J. Abnorm. Psychol., 77,* 115–26.

Meichenbaum, D., & Jaremko, M. E. (1983). *Stress reduction and prevention.* New York: Plenum.

Meiselman, K. C. (1978). *Incest.* San Francisco: Jossey-Bass.

Meissner, W. W. (1978). *The paranoid process.* New York: Jason Aronson.

Meissner, W. W. (1981). The schizophrenic and the paranoid process. *Schizo. Bull., 7,* 611–31.

Melges, F. T., & Bowlby, J. (1969). Types of hopelessness in psychopathological process. *Arch. Gen. Psychiat., 20,* 690–99.

Melville, K. (1973). Changing the family game. *The Sciences, 13,* 17–19.

Mendels, J., & Frazer, A. (1974). Brain biogenic amine depletion and mood. *Arch. Gen. Psychiat., 30,* 447–51.

Mendlewicz, J. (1980). X-linkage of bipolar illness and the question of schizoaffective illness. In R. H. Belmaker & H. M. van Praag (Eds.), *Mania: An evolving concept.* New York: Spectrum.

Mendlewicz, J. (1985). Genetic research in depressive disorders. In E. E. Beckham & W. R. Leber (Eds.), *Handbook of depression: Treatment, assessment and research* (pp. 795–815). Homewood, IL: Dorsey Press.

Menninger, K. (1938). *Man against himself.* New York: Harcourt, Brace.

Menninger, K. (1945). *The human mind* (3rd ed.). New York: Knopf.

Menninger, K. (1948). Diagnosis and treatment of schizophrenia. *Bull. Menninger Clin., 12,* 101–4.

Mental Health Law Project. (October, 1987). Court decisions concerning mentally disabled people confined in institutions. *MHLP Newsletter.* Washington, DC.

Merbaum, M. (1977). Some personality characteristics of soldiers exposed to extreme war stress: A follow-up study of post-hospital adjustment. *J. Clin. Psychol., 33,* 558–62.

Merbaum, M., & Hefez, A. (1976). Some personality characteristics of soldiers exposed to extreme war stress. *J. Cons. Clin. Psychol., 44*(1), 1–6.

Merikangas, K. R., Spence, M. A., & Kupfer, D. J. (1989). Linkage studies of bipolar disorder: Methodologic and analytic issues. *Arch. Gen. Psychiat., 46,* 1137–41.

Meyer, C. B., & Taylor, S. E. (1986). Adjustment to rape. *J. Pers. Soc. Psychol., 50,* 1226–34.

Meyer, R. E., & Mirin, S. M. (1979). *The heroin stimulus: Implications for a theory of addiction.* New York: Plenum.

Meyers, J., & Parsons, R. D. (1987). Prevention planning in the school system. In J. Hermalin & J. A. Morell (Eds.), *Prevention planning in mental health.* Beverly Hills, CA: Sage.

Mezey, G. C., & Taylor, P. J. (1988). Psychological reactions of women who have been raped: A descriptive and comparative study. *Brit. J. Psychiat., 152,* 330–39.

Miklowitz, D. J., Goldstein, M. J., & Falloon, I. R. (1983). Premorbid and symptomatic characteristics of schizophrenics from families with high and low levels of expressed emotion. *J. Abnorm. Psychol. 92,* 359–67.

Miklowitz, D. J., Strachan, A. M., Goldstein, M. J., Doane, J. A., & Snyder, K. S. (1986). Expressed emotion and communication deviance in families of schizophrenics. *J. Abnorm. Psychol., 95,* 60–66.

Milby, J. B. (1988). Methadone maintenance to abstinency: How many make it? *J. Nerv. Ment. Dis., 176,* 409–22.

Miles, C. (1977). Conditions predisposing to suicide: A review. *J. Nerv. Ment. Dis., 164,* 232–46.

Miller, J. P. (1975, Spring). Suicide and adolescence. *Adolescence, 10*(37), 11–24.

Miller, K. A. (1989). Enhancing early childhood mainstreaming through cooperative learning: A brief literature review. *Child Study Journal, 19,* 285–92.

Miller, M. L., Chiles, J. A., & Barnes, V. B. (1982). Suicide attempts within a delinquent population. *J. Cons. Clin. Psychol., 50,* 491–98.

Miller, R. (1970). Does Down's syndrome predispose children to leukemia? *Roche Report, 7*(16), 5.

Miller, R. R., & Springer, A. D. (1974). Implications of recovery from experimental amnesia. *Psychol. Rev., 81*(5), 470–73.

Miller, W. R. (1978). Behavioral treatment of problem drinkers: A comparative outcome study of three controlled drinking therapies. *J. Cons. Clin. Psychol., 46,* 74–86.

Miller, W. R. (1979). Problem drinking and substance abuse: Behavioral perspectives. In N. Krasnegar (Ed.), *Behavioral approaches to analysis and treatment of substance abuse.*

Miller, W. R., & Caddy, G. R. (1977). Abstinence and controlled drinking in the treatment of problem drinking. *J. Stud. Alcoh., 38,* 986–1003.

Miller, W. R., & Hester, R. K. (1986). Inpatient alcoholism treatment: Who benefits? *Amer. Psychol., 41,* 794–805.

Miller, W. R., Leckman, A. L., Tinkcom, M., & Rubenstein, J. (1986). Long-term follow-up of controlled drinking therapies. Paper given at the Ninety-fourth Annual Meeting of the American Psychological Association, Washington, DC.

Miller, W. R., & Muñoz, R. F. (1976). *How to control your drinking.* Englewood Cliffs, NJ: Prentice-Hall.

Millon, T. (1981). *Disorders of personality: DSM III, Axis II.* New York: Wiley.

Millon, T. (1986). On the past and future of the DSM-III: Personal recollections and projections. In T. Millon & G. L. Klerman (Eds.), *Contemporary directions in psychopathology: Toward the DSM-IV* (pp. 29–70). New York: Guilford.

Millon, T. (in press). Classification in psychopathology: Rationale, alternatives, standards. *J. Abnorm. Psychol.*

Milner, K. O. (1949). The environment as a factor in the aetiology of criminal paranoia. *J. Ment. Sci., 95,* 124–32.

Milns, R. D. (1986). Squibb academic lecture: Attitudes towards mental illness in antiquity. *Australian and New Zealand J. of Psychiat., 20,* 454–62.

Mindham, R. H. S. (1982). Tricyclic antidepressants and amine precursors. In E. S. Paykel (Ed.), *Handbook of affective disorders.* New York: Guilford Press.

Minuchin, S. (1974). *Families and family therapy.* Cambridge, MA: Harvard University Press.

Minuchin, S., Baker, L., Rosman, B., Liebman, R., Milman, L., & Todd, T. (1975). A conceptual model pf psychosomatic illness in children. *Arch. Gen. Psychiat., 32,* 1031–38.

Mirsky, A. F., DeLisi, L. E., Buchsbaum, M. S., Quinn, O. W., Schwerdt, P., Siever, L. J., Mann, L., Weingartner, H., Zec, R., et al. (1984). The Genain quadruplets: Psychological studies. *Psychiat. Res., 13,* 77–93.

Mirsky, A. F., Silberman, E. K., Latz, A., & Nagler, S. (1985). Adult outcomes of high-risk children. *Schizo. Bull., 11,* 150–54.

Mischel, W. (1973). Toward a cognitive social learning reconceptualization of personality. *Psychol. Rev., 80*(4), 252–83.

Mishler, E. G., & Waxler, N. E. (1968). *Interaction in families: An experimental study of family processes and schizophrenia.* New York: Wiley.

Mitchell, J. (1985). Healing the helper. In National Institute of Mental Health (Ed.), *Role stressors and supports for emergency workers* (pp. 105–18), DHHS Publication No. ADM 85–1408). Washington, DC: U.S. Government Printing Office.

Mitchell, J. E., Pyle, R. L., Eckert, E. D., Hatsukami, D., Pomeroy, C., & Zimmerman, R. (1990). A comparison study of antidepressants and structured intensive group psychotherapy in the treatment of bulimia nervosa. *Arch. Gen. Psychiat., 47,* 149–57.

Mitchell, J. T., & Resnik, H. L. P. (1981). *Emergency response to crisis.* Bowie, MD: Robert J. Brady.

Mobily, K. E., & Hoeft, T. M. (1985). The family's dilemma: Alzheimer's disease. *Activities, Adaptation, and Aging, 6,* 63–71.

Mohr, D. C., & Beutler, L. E. (1990). Erectile dysfunction: A review of diagnostic and treatment procedures. *Clin. Psychol. Rev., 10,* 123–50.

Mohs, R. C., Breitner, J. C., Siverman, J. M., & Davis, K. L. (1987). Alzheimer's disease: Morbid risk among first-degree relatives approximates 50% by 90 years of age. *Arch. Gen. Psychiat., 44,* 405–8.

Monahan, J. (1981). *Predicting violent behavior: An assessment of clinical techniques.* Beverly Hills, CA: Sage.

Money, J. (1974). Prenatal hormones and postnatal socialization in gender identity differentiation. In J. K. Cole & R. Dienstbier (Eds.), *Nebraska symposium on motivation, 1973* (pp. 221–95). Lincoln, NE: University of Nebraska Press.

Money, J. (1980). *Love and love sickness: The science of sex, gender difference, and pair-bonding.* Baltimore: Johns Hopkins University Press.

Money, J. (1986). *Lovemaps: Clinical concepts of sexual/erotic health and pathology, paraphilia, and gender transposition.* New York: Irvington.

Money, J., & Alexander, D. (1969). Psychosexual development and absence of homosexuality in males with precocious puberty. *J. Nerv. Ment. Dis., 148*(2), 111–23.

Money, J., & Ehrhardt, A. A. (1972). *Man & woman, boy & girl: Differentiation and dimorphism of gender identity.* Baltimore: Johns Hopkins University Press.

Money, J., & Lamacz, M. (1989). *Vandalized lovemaps.* Buffalo, NY: Prometheus.

Monnelly, E. P., Woodruff, R. A., & Robins, L. N. (1974). Manic depressive illness and social achievement in a public hospital sample. *Acta Psychiatr. Scandin., 50,* 318–25.

Monroe, S. M., & Steiner, S. C. (1986). Social support and psychopathology: Interrelations with preexisting disorder, stress, and personality. *J. Abnorm. Psychol., 95,* 29–39.

Montenegro, H. (1968). Severe separation anxiety in two preschool children: Successfully treated by reciprocal inhibition. *J. Child Psychol. Psychiat., 9*(2), 93–103.

Moore, D. F. (Ed.). (1982, Aug.). New antidepressants. *Psychopharmacology Update, 3.* Asheville, NC: Appalachian Hall.

Mora, G. (1967). Paracelsus' psychiatry. *Amer. J. Psychiat., 124,* 803–14.

Moreau, D. L. (1990). Major depression in childhood and adolescence. *Psychiat. Clin. N. Amer., 13,* 355–68.

Moreland, K., & Dahlstrom, W. G. (1983). Professional training with and use of the MMPI. *Profess. Psychol., 14,* 218–23.

Moreno, J. L. (1959). Psychodrama. In S. Arieti et al. (Eds.), *American handbook of psychiatry* (Vol. 2). New York: Basic Books.

Morey, L. C., Skinner, H. A., & Blashfield, R. K. (1984). A typology of alcohol abusers: Correlates and implications. *J. Abnorm. Psychol., 93,* 408–17.

Morishima, A. (1975). His spirit raises the ante for retardates. *Psych. Today, 9*(1), 72–73.

Morlock, L.L. (1989). Recognition and treatment of mental health problems in the general health care sector. In C. A. Taube, D. Mechanic, & A. A. Hohmann (Eds.), *The future of mental health services research* (pp. 39–62). Washington, DC: U.S. Department of Health and Human Services. U.S. Government Printing Office.

Morrison, J. (1980). Adult psychiatric disorders in parents of hyperactive children. *Amer. J. Psychiat., 137*(7), 825–27.

Morrison, J. R. (1973). Catatonia: Retarded and excited types. *Arch. Gen. Psychiat., 28*(1), 39–41.

Morrison, J. R. (1974). Catatonia: Prediction of outcome. *Compr. Psychiat., 15*(4), 317–24.

Morrow, J., & Nolen-Hoeksema, S. (1990). Effects of responses to depression on the remediation of depressive affect. *J. Pers. Soc. Psychol., 58,* 519–27.

Morton, T. L., & Ewald, L. S. (1987). Family-based interventions for crime and delinquency. In E. K. Morris & C. J. Braukmann (Eds.), *Behavioral approaches to crime and delinquency: A handbook of application, research, and concepts* (pp. 271–94). New York: Plenum.

Mott, F. W. (1919). *War neuroses and shell shock.* Oxford: Oxford Medical Publications.

Mucha, T. F., & Reinhardt, R. F. (1970). Conversion reactions in student aviators. *Amer. J. Psychiat., 127,* 493–97.

Munro, J. F., & Duncan, L. J. P. (1972). Fasting in the treatment of obesity. *The Practitioner, 208,* 493–98.

Murphy, G. (1988). Suicide and substance abuse. *Arch. Gen. Psychiat., 45,* 593–94.

Murphy, G. E., Simons, A. D., Wetzel, R. D., & Lustman, P. J. (1984). Cognitive therapy and pharmacotherapy: Singly and together in the treatment of depression. *Arch. Gen. Psychiat., 41,* 33–41.

Murphy, G. E., & Wetzel, R. D. (1990). The lifetime risk of suicide in alcoholism. *Arch. Gen. Psychiat., 47,* 383–92.

Murphy, H. B. (1968). Cultural factors in the genesis of schizophrenia. In D. Rosenthal & S. S. Kety (Eds.), *The transmission of schizophrenia* (pp. 137–52). Elmsford, NY: Pergamon Press.

Murphy, H. B. (1978). Cultural influences on incidence, course, and treatment response. In L. C. Wynne, R. L. Cromwell, & S. Matthysse (Eds.), *The nature of schizophrenia: New approaches to research and treatment* (pp. 586–94). New York: Wiley.

Murphy, H. B. M. (1982). Culture and schizophrenia. In I. Al-Issa (Ed.), *Culture and psychopathology.* Baltimore: University Park Press.

Murphy, J. M. (1976). Psychiatric labeling in cross-cultural perspective. *Science, 191,* (4231), 1019–28.

Murray, D. C. (1973). Suicidal and depressive feelings among college students. *Psychol. Rep., 33*(1), 175–81.

Murray, H. A. (1938). *Exploration in personality.* New York: Oxford University Press.

Murrin, M. R., & Laws, D. R. (1990). The influence of pornography on sex crimes. In W. L. Marshall, R. D. Laws, & H. E. Barbaree (Eds.), *Handbook of sexual assault* (pp. 73–92). New York: Plenum.

Myers, J. K., Weissman, M. M., Tischler, G. L., Holzer, C. E., Leaf, P. J., & Stoltzman, R. (1984). Six-month prevalence of psychiatric disorders in three communities: 1980 to 1982. *Arch. Gen. Psychiat., 41,* 959–67.

Myers, M. B., Templer, D. I., & Brown, R. (1985). Reply to Wieder on rape victims. Vulnerability does not imply responsibility. *J. Cons. Clin. Psychol., 53,* 431.

Nace, E. P., Orne, M. T., & Hammer, A. G. (1974). Posthypnotic amnesia as an active psychic process. *Arch. Gen. Psychiat., 31*(2), 257–60.

Nagaraja, J. (1974). Somnambulism in children: Clinical communication. *Child Psychiatry Quarterly. 7*(1), 18–19.

Napoleon, N., Chassin, L., & Young, R. D. (1980). A replication and extension of "Physical attractiveness and mental illness." *J. Abnorm. Psychol., 89,* 250–53.

Narby, J. (1982). The evolution of attitudes towards mental illness in pre-industrial England. *Orthomolecular Psychiatry, 11,* 103–10.

Nation's Health. (1986, Aug. 5). Prevention of Wernicke-Korsakoff Syndrome.

National Academy of Sciences. (1990, Mar.). Expanded community role, comprehensive treatment programs urged for alcohol problems. *News from the Institute of Medicine.*

National Association for Mental Health. (1979, Mar. 23). Bulletin No. 103.

National Center for Health Statistics. (1982). Washington, DC: U.S. Government Printing Office.

National Institute of Drug Abuse. (1981). *Trend report: January 1978–September 1980.* Data from Client Oriented Data Acquisition Program (CODAP) (Series E, No. 24). Washington, DC: U.S. Department of Health and Human Services.

National Institute of Drug Abuse. (1990). Washington, DC: U.S. Department of Health and Human Services.

National Institute of Mental Health. (1971). Amphetamines approved for children. *Sci. News, 99*(4), 240.

National Institute of Mental Health. (1976, Apr. 20). Rising suicide rate linked to economy. *Los Angeles Times,* VIII, 2, 5.

National Institute of Mental Health. (1978a, Oct.). *Third report on alcohol and health.* Washington, DC: U.S. Government Printing Office.

National Institute of Mental Health. (1978b). *Indirect services* (Statistical Note No. 147). Washington, DC: U.S. Government Printing Office.

National Institute of Mental Health. (1985a). *Electroconvulsive therapy Consensus Development Conference statement.* Bethesda, MD: U.S. Department of Health and Human Services.

National Institute of Mental Health. (1985b). *Mental Health, United States, 1985.* Washington, DC: U.S. Government Printing Office.

Navia, B. A., Jordan, B. D., & Price, R. W. (1986). The AIDS dementia complex: I. Clinical features. *Annals of Neurology, 19,* 517–24.

Neale, J. M., & Oltmanns, T. F. (1980). *Schizophrenia.* New York: Wiley.

Nee, L. F., Eldridge, R., Sunderland, T., Thomas, C. B., et al. (1987). Dementia of the Alzheimer type: Clinical and family study of 22 twin pairs. *Neurology, 37,* 359–63.

Nelson, F. L. (1984). Suicide: Issues of prevention, intervention, and facilitation. *J. Clin. Psychol., 40,* 1328–33.

Nelson, H. (1969, Oct. 6). Study compares drug dangers. *Los Angeles Times,* 1, 3, 25.

Nelson, H. (1971, Jan. 26). County suicide rate up sharply among young. *Los Angeles Times, II,* 1.

Nelson, H. (1973, Mar. 27). High blood pressure found in third of adults in survey. *Los Angeles Times,* II, 1, 3.

Nelson, H. (1974, Apr. 29). How to be successfully fired. *Behav. Today, 5*(17), 118–19.

Nelson, Z. P., & Mowry, D. D. (1976). Contracting in crisis intervention. *Comm. Ment. Hlth. J., 12,* 37–43.

Nemiah, J. C. (1961). The case of Mary S. *Foundations of psychopathology.* Cambridge: Oxford University Press.

Nemiah, J. C. (1967). Obsessive-compulsive reaction. In A. M. Freedman & H. I. Kaplan (Eds.), *Comprehensive text book of psychiatry.* Baltimore: Williams & Wilkins.

Neufeld, R. W. (1990). Coping with stress, coping without stress, and stress with coping: In inter-construct redundencies. *Stress Medicine, 6,* 117–25.

Neugarten, B. L. (1977). Personality and aging. In J. E. Birren & K. W. Schaie (Eds.), *Handbook of the psychology of aging.* New York: Van Nostrand.

New York Post (1982, May 10). City streets now "warehouse" the mentally ill.

New York State Department of Mental Hygiene. (1978). *The insanity defense in New York.* New York: The New York Department of Mental Hygiene.

Newman, B., Selby, J. V., Quesenberry, C. P., King, M., Friedman, G. D., & Fabsitz, R. P. (1990). Nongenetic influences of obesity on other cardiovascular disease risk factors: An analysis of identical twins. *Amer. J. Pub. Hlth., 80,* 675–78.

Newman, L., Henry, P. B., DiRenzo, P., & Stecher, T. (1988–89). Intervention and student assistance: The Pennsylvania model. Special Issue: Practical approaches in treating adolescent chemical dependency: A guide to clinical assessment and intervention. *J. Chem. Depen. Treat., 2*(1), 145–62.

Newman, L. E. & Stoller, R. J. (1974). Nontranssexual men who seek sex reassignment. *Amer. J. Psychiat., 131*(4), 437–41.

Newman, M. G., & Cates, M. S. (1977). *Methadone treatment in narcotic addiction.* New York: Academic Press.

Nicholson, R. A., & Berman, J. S. (1983). Is follow-up necessary in evaluating psychotherapy? *Psychol. Bull., 93,* 261–78.

Niederland, W. G. (1968). Clinical observations of the survivor syndrome. *Inter. J. Psychoanal., 49,* 313–16.

Nietzel, M. T., & Harris, M. J. (1990). Relationship of dependency and achievement/autonomy to depression. *Clin. Psychol. Rev., 10,* 279–97.

NIMH Psychopharmacology Service Center Collaborative Study Group (1964). Phenothiazine treatment in acute schizophrenia: Effectiveness. *Arch. Gen. Psychiat., 10,* 246–61.

Noble, E. P. (Ed.). (1979). Alcohol and health: Technical support document. Third special report to the U.S. Congress (DHEW Publication No. ADM79–832). Washington, DC: U.S. Government Printing Office.

Noble, P., & Rodger, S. (1989). Violence by psychiatric inpatients. *Brit. J. Psychiat., 155,* 384–90.

Nolen-Hoeksma, S. (1987). Sex differences in unipolar depression: Evidence and theory. *Psychol. Bull., 101,* 259–82.

Noles, S. W., Cash, T. F., & Winstead, B. A. (1985). Body image, physical attractiveness, and depression. *J. Cons. Clin. Psychol., 53,* 88–94.

Noll, K. M., Davis, J. M., & DeLeon-Jones, F. (1985). Medication and somatic therapies in the treatment of depression. In E. E. Beckham & W. R. Leber (Eds.), *Handbook of depression: Treatment, assessment, and research* (pp. 220–315). Homewood, IL: Dorsey Press.

Notman, N. T., & Nadelson, C. C. (1976). The rape victim: Psychodynamic considerations. *Amer. J. Psychiat., 133*(4), 408–13.

Novaco, R. W. (1977). Stress inoculation: A cognitive therapy for anger and its application to a case of depression. *J. Cons. Clin. Psychol., 45,* 600–608.

Noyes, R., Jr., Crowe, R. R., Harris, E. L., Hamra, B. J., & McChesney, C. M. (1986). Relationship between panic disorder and agoraphobia: A family study. *Arch. Gen. Psychiat., 43,* 227–32.

Nurnberger, J., Roose, S. P., Dunner, D. S., & Fieve, R. R. (1979). Unipolar mania: A distinct clinical entity? *Amer. J. Psychiat., 136,* 1420–23.

Nurnberger, J. I., & Gershon, E. S. (1982). Genetics. In E. S. Paykel (Ed.), *Handbook of affective disorders.* New York: Guilford Press.

O'Brien, D. (1979, Mar.). Mental anguish: An occupational hazard. *Emergency,* 61–64.

O'Connell, M., Cooper, S., Perry, J. C., & Hoke, L. (1989). The relationship between thought disorder and psychotic symptoms in borderline personality disorder. *J. Nerv. Ment. Dis., 177,* 273–78.

O'Connell, P. (1976, Nov.). Trends in psychological adjustment: Observations made during successive psychiatric follow-up interviews of returned Navy–Marine Corps POWs. In R. Spaulding (Ed.), *Proceedings of the 3rd annual Joint meeting concerning POW/MIA matters* (pp. 16–22). San Diego.

O'Dell, S. (1974). Training parents in behavior modification: A review. *Psychol. Bull., 81*(7), 418–33.

O'Leary, A. (1985). Self-efficacy and health. *Behav. Res. Ther., 23,* 437–51.

O'Leary, K. D. (1980). Pills or skills for hyperactive children. *J. Appl. Beh. Anal., 13*(1), 191–204.

O'Malley, S. S., Foley, S. H., Rounsaville, B. J., Watkins, J. T., Sotsky, S. M., Imber, S. D., & Elkin, I. (1988). Therapist competence and patient outcome in interpersonal psychotherapy of depression. *J. Cons. Clin. Psychol., 56,* 496–501.

O'Neill, M., & Kempler, B. (1969). Approach and avoidance responses of the hysterical personality to sexual stimuli. *J. Abnorm. Psychol., 74,* 300–305.

Oetting, E. R., & Beauvais, F. (1990). Adolescent drug use: Findings of national and local surveys. *J. Cons. Clin. Psychol., 58,* 385–94.

Office of the Federal Registry. (1982). *The United States Government Manual 1982/1983.* National Archives and Records Service. Washington, DC: U.S. Government Printing Office.

Office of Technology Assessment, U.S. Congress. (1986, Dec.) *Children's mental health: Problems and services.* (OTA Publication No. OTA-BP-H-33). Washington, DC: U.S. Government Printing Office.

Offit, A. K. (1981). *Night thoughts: Reflections of a sex therapist.* New York: Congdon & Lattés.

Ogata, S. N., Silk, K. R., Goodrich, S., Lohr, N. E., & Hill, E. M. (1990). Childhood sexual and physical abuse in adult patients with borderline personality. *Amer. J. Psychiat., 147,* 1008–13.

Okura, K. P. (1975). Mobilizing in response to a major disaster. *Community Health Journal, 2*(2), 136–44.

Oldenburg, B., Perkins, R. J., & Andrews, G. (1985). Controlled trial of psychological intervention in myocardial infarction. *J. Cons. Clin. Psychol., 53,* 852–59.

Olds, S. (1970). Say it with a stomach ache. *Today's Health, 48*(11), 41–43, 88.

Ollendick, T. H. (1981). Self-monitoring and self-administered overcorrection.: The modification of nervous tics in children. *Behavior Modification, 5*(1), 75–84.

Oltmanns, T. F., & Maher, B. A. (Eds.). (1988). *Delusional beliefs.* New York: Wiley.

Opler, M. K., & Singer, J. L. (1959). Ethnic differences in behavior and psychopathology. *Inter. J. Soc. Psychiat., 2,* 11–23.

Orford, J. (1985). *Excessive appetites: A psychological view of addiction.* New York: John Wiley & Sons.

Orlofsky, J. L., & O'Heron, C. A. (1987). Stereotypic and nonstereotypic sex role trait and behavior orientations: Implications for personal adjustment. *J. Pers. Soc. Psychol., 52,* 1034–42.

Orne, M. T., Dinges, D. F., & Orne, E. C. (1984). On the differential diagnosis of multiple personality in the forensic context. *International Journal of Clinical and Experimental Hypnosis, 32,* 118–69.

Oros, C. J., & Koss, M. P. (1978, Aug.). *Women as rape victims.* Paper presented at the American Psychological Association Annual Meeting, Toronto.

Osler, W. (1892). Lectures on angina pectoris and allied states. New York: Appleton-Century-Crofts.

Ost, L-G, & Hugdahl, K. (1981). Acquisition of phobias and anxiety response patterns in clinical patients. *Behav. Res. Ther., 19,* 439–47.

Ostfeld, A. M., & D'Atri, D. A. (1977). Rapid sociocultural change and high blood pressure. In S. Kasl & F. Reichsman (Eds.), *Advances in psychosomatic medicine: Vol. 9, Epidemiologic studies in psychosomatic medicine* (pp. 20–37). Basel, Switzerland, S. Karger.

Overall, J. E., & Hollister, L. E. (1982). Decision rules for phenomenological classification of psychiatric patients. *J. Cons. Clin. Psychol., 50*(4), 535–45.

Overholser, J. C., & Beck, S. (1986). Multimethod assessment of rapists, child molesters, and 3 control groups on behavioral and psychological measures. *J. Cons. Clin. Psychol., 54,* 682–87.

Owen, F. W. (1978). Dyslexia—genetic aspects. In A. L. Benton & D. Pearl (Eds.), *Dyslexia: In appraisal of current knowledge.* (pp. 267–84). New York: Oxford University Press.

Owens, T. H. (1984). Personality traits of female psychotherapy patients with a history of incest. *J. Pers. Assess., 48,* 606–8.

Palmer, R. L. (Ed.). (1981). *Electroconvulsive therapy: An appraisal.* New York: Oxford University Press.

Papp, L., & Gorman, J. M. (1990). Suicidal preoccupation during fluoxetine treatment. *Amer. J. Psychiat., 147,* 1380.

Parker, G., Johnston, P., & Hayward, L. (1988). Parental "expressed emotion" as a predictor of schizophrenic relapse. *Arch. Gen. Psychiat., 45,* 806–13.

Parkes, C. M., Benjamin, B., & Fitzgerald, R. G. (1969). Broken heart: A statistical study of increased mortality among widowers. *Brit. Med. J., 1,* 740–43.

Parkin, M. (1974). Suicide and culture in Fairbanks: A comparison of three cultural groups in a small city of interior Alaska. *Psychiatry, 37*(1), 60–67.

Parnas, J., Teasdale, T. W., & Schulsinger, H. (1985). Institutional rearing and diagnostic outcome in children of schizophrenic mothers. *Arch. Gen. Psychiat., 42,* 762–69.

Pasewark, R. A., Pantle, M. L., & Steadman, H. J. (1982). Detention and rearrest rates of persons found not guilty by reason of insanity and convicted felons. *Amer. J. Psychiat., 139*(7), 892–97.

Paternite, C. E., & Loney, J. (1980). Childhood hyperkinesis: Relationships between symptomatology and home environment. In C. K. Whelan & B. Henker (Eds.), *Hyperactive children: The social ecology of identification and treatment.* New York: Academic Press.

Paterson, R. J., & Neufeld, R. W. (1987). Clear danger: Situational determinants of the appraisal of threat. *Psychol. Bull., 101,* 404–16.

Patterson, C. H. (1989). Eclecticism in psychotherapy: Is integration possible? *Psychotherapy, 26,* 157–61.

Patterson, G. (1971). *Families: Applications of social learning to family life.* Champaign, IL: Research Press.

Patterson, G. R. (1979). Treatment for children with conduct problems: A review of outcome studies. In S. Feshbach & A. Fraczek (Eds.), *Aggression and behavior change: Biological and social processes.* New York: Praeger.

Patterson, G. R., DeBarsyshe, B. D., & Ramsey, E. (1989). A developmental perspective on antisocial behavior. *Amer. Psychol., 44,* 329–35.

Paul, G. L. (1979). New assessment systems for residential treatment, management, research and evaluation: A symposium. *J. Behav. Assess., 1*(3), 181–84.

Paul, G. L. (1982). The development of a "transportable" system of behavioral assessment for chronic patients. Invited address. University of Minnesota, Minneapolis.

Paul, G. L., & Lentz, R. J. (1977). *Psychosocial treatment of chronic mental patients: Milieu versus social-learning programs.* Cambridge, MA: Harvard University Press.

Paul, N. (1971, May 31). The family as patient. *Time,* 60.

Pauly, I. B. (1968). The current status of the change of sex operation. *J. Nerv. Ment. Dis., 147*(5), 460–71.

Pausnau, R. O., & Russell, A. T. (1975). Psychiatric resident suicide. An analysis of five cases. *Amer. J. Psychiat., 132*(4), 402–6.

Paykel, E. S. (1973). Life events and acute depression. In J. P. Scott & E. C. Senay (Eds.), *Separation and depression,* (pp. 215–36.). Washington, DC: American Association for the Advancement of Science.

Paykel, E. S. (Ed.). (1982a). *Handbook of affective disorders.* New York: Guilford Press.

Paykel, E. S. (1982b). Life events and early environment. In E. S. Paykel (Ed.), *Handbook of affective disorders.* New York: Guilford Press.

Paykel, E. S., Hallowell, C., Dressler, D. M., Shapiro, D. L., & Weissman, M. M. (1974). Treatment of suicide attempters. *Arch. Gen. Psychiat., 31*(4), 487–91.

Paykel, E. S., Prusoff, B. A., & Myers, J. K. (1975). Suicide attempts and recent life events. *Arch. Gen. Psychiat., 32*(3), 327–33.

Payne, R. L. (1975). Recent life changes and the reporting of psychological states. *J. Psychosom. Res., 19*(1), 99–103.

Pearlson, G. D., Kim, W. S., Kubos, K. L., Moberg, P. J., Jayaram, G., Bascom, M. J., Chase, G. A., Goldfinger, A. G., & Tune, L. E. (1989). Ventricle-brain ratio, computed tomographic density, and brain area in 50 schizophrenics. *Arch. Gen. Psychiat., 46,* 690–97.

Peck, M. A., & Schrut, A. (1971). Suicidal behavior among college students. *HSMHA Health Reports, 86*(2), 149–56.

Peck, M. L., Farberow, N. L., & Litman, R. E. (Eds.). (1985). *Youth suicide.* New York: Springer.

Pelham, W. E., Schnedler, R. W., Bologna, N. C., & Contreras, J. A. (1980). Behavioral and stimulant treatment of hyperactive children. A therapy study with methylphenidate probes in a within subject design. *J. Appl. Beh. Anal., 13*(2), 221–36.

Pemberton, D. A., & Benady, D. R. (1973). Consciously rejected children. *Brit. J. Psychiat., 123*(576), 575–78.

Penk, W. E., Charles, H. L., & Van Hoose, T. A. (1978). Comparative effectiveness of day hospital and inpatient psychiatric treatment. *J. Cons. Clin. Psychol., 46,* 94–101.

Penna, M. W. (1986). Classification of personality disorders. In J. R. Lion (Ed.), *Personality disorders: Diagnosis and management,* (pp. 10–31). Malabar, FL: Robert F. Kreiger Publishing.

Penrose, L. S. (1963). *Biology of mental defect* (3rd ed.). New York: Grune & Stratton.

Pentz, M. A. (1983). Prevention of adolescent substance abuse through social skill development. *National Institute on Drug Abuse Research Monograph Series, 47,* 195–232.

Perlberg, M. (1979, Apr.). Adapted from Trauma at Tenerife: The psychic aftershocks of a jet disaster. *Human Behav.,* 49–50.

Perls, F. S. (1967). Group vs. individual therapy. *ETC: A review of general semantics, 34,* 306–12.

Perls, F. S. (1969). *Gestalt therapy verbatim.* Lafayette, CA: Real People Press.

Perris, C. (1979). Recent perspectives in the genetics of affective disorders. In J. Mendlewicz & B. Shopsin (Eds.), *Genetic aspects of affective illness.* New York: SP Medical & Scientific Books.

Perris, C. (1982). The distinction between bipolar and unipolar affective disorders. In E. S. Paykel (Ed.), *Handbook of affective disorders.* New York: Guilford Press.

Perry, C. L., & Murray, D. M. (1985). The prevention of adolescent drug abuse: Implications from etiological, developmental, behavioral, and environmental models. *Journal of Primary Prevention, 6*(1), 31–52.

Perry, E. (1988). Acetylcholine and Alzheimer's disease. *Brit. J. Psychiat., 152,* 737–40.

Perry, T. (1970). The enigma of PKU. *The Sciences, 10*(8), 12–16.

Pert, C. B., & Snyder, S. H. (1973, Mar. 9). Opiate receptor: Demonstration in nervous tissue. *Science, 179*(4077), 1011–14.

Pervin, L. A. (1978). *Current controversies and issues in personality.* New York: Wiley.

Peters, J. J. (1976). Children who are victims of sexual assault and the psychology of offenders. *Amer. J. Psychother., 30,* 398–421.

Peterson, C., & Seligman, M. E. P. (1987). Explanatory style and illness. *J.Personal., 55,* 237–265.

Peterson, C., Villanova, P., & Raps, C. S. (1985). Depression and attributions: Factors responsible for inconsistent results in the published literature. *J. Abnorm. Psychol., 94,* 165–68.

Peterson, G. C. (1978). Organic brain syndrome: Differential diagnosis and investigative procedures. *Psychiat. Clin. N. Amer., 1,* 21–36.

Petito, C. K. (1988). Review of central nervous system pathology in human immunodeficiency virus infection. *Annals of Neurology, Suppl., 23,* 54–57.

Pfeffer, C. R. (1981). The family system of suicidal children. *Amer. J. Psychother., 35,* 330–41.

Pfeffer, C. R. (1981). Self-destructive behavior in children and adolescents, *Psychiat. Clin. N. Amer., 8,* 215–26.

Phifer, J. F., & Murrell, S. A. (1986). Etiologic factors in the onset of depressive symptoms in older adults. *J. Abnorm. Psychol., 95,* 282–91.

Pithers, W. D. (1990). Relapse prevention with sexual aggressors: A method for maintaining therapeutic gain and enhancing external supervision. In W. L. Marshall, D. R. Laws, & H. E. Barbaree (Eds.), *Handbook of sexual assault* (pp. 343–62). New York: Plenum.

Pitt, B. (1982). Depression and childbirth. In E. S. Paykel (Ed.), *Handbook of affective disorders.* New York: Guilford Press.

Plater, F. (1664). *Praxeos medical Tomi tres.* (Basil 1656), *Histories and Observations.* London: Culpeper and Cole.

Plato, (n.d.). *The laws* (Vol. 5). (G. Burges, Trans.). London: George Bell & Sons.

Pliner, P. L., & Cappell, H. D. (1974). Modification of affective consequences of alcohol: A comparison of social and solitary drinking. *J. Abnorm. Psychol., 83*(4), 418–25.

Plotkin, R. (1981). When rights collide: Parents, children and consent to treatment. *J. Pediat. Psychol., 6*(2), 121–30.

Plummer, K. J. (1980). Self-help groups for sexual minorities: The case of the pedophile. In D. J. West (Ed.), *Sexual offenders in the criminal justice system* (pp. 72–90). Cambridge, UK: Cambridge University Press.

Pogrebin, M. R., & Poole, E. D. (1987). Deinstitutionalization and increased arrest rates among the mentally disordered. *Journal of Psychiatry & Law,* Spring, 117–27.

Pogue-Guile, M. F., & Rose, R. J. (1985). Developmental genetic studies of adult personality. *Develop. Psychol., 21*(3), 547–57.

Poland, B. J., & Lowry, R. B. (1974). The use of spontaneous abortuses and stillbirths in genetic counseling. *American Journal of Obstetrics and Gynecology, 118,* 322–26.

Polich, J. M., Armor, D. J., & Braiker, H. B. (1981). *The course of alcoholism: Four years after treatment.* New York: Wiley Interscience.

Pollack, J. H. (1968). Five frequent mistakes of parents. *Today's Health, 46*(5), 14–15, 26–29.

Pollack, J. M. (1979). Obsessive-compulsive personality: A review. *Psychol. Bull. 86*(2), 225–41.

Pollard, C. A., Pollard, H. J., & Corn, K. J. (1989). Panic onset and major events in the lives of agoraphobics: A test of contiguity. *J. Abnorm. Psychol., 98,* 318–21.

Pollin, W., Allen, M. G., Hoffer, A., Stabenau, J. R., & Hrubec, Z. (1969). Psychopathology in 15,909 pairs of veteran twins. *Amer. J. Psychiat., 126,* 597–609.

Pollin, W., & Stabenau, J. R. (1968). Biological, psychological and historical differences in a series of monozygotic twins discordant for schizophrenia. In D. Rosenthal & S. S. Kety (Eds.), *The transmission of schizophrenia.* New York: Pergammon. Pp. 317-332.

Pollin, W., Stabenau, J. & Tupin, J. (1965). Family studies with identical twins discordant for schizophrenia. *Psychiatry, 28,* 60–78.

Polner, M. (1968). Vietnam War stories. *Transaction, 6*(1), 8–20.

Polvan, N. (1969). Historical aspects of mental ills in Middle East discussed. *Roche Reports, 6*(12), 3.

Polyson, J., Peterson, R., & Marshall, C. (1986). MMPI and Rorschach: Three decades of research. *Profess. Psychol. 17*(5), 476–78.

Pope, K. S., & Vetter, V. A. (in press). Prior therapist-patient sexual involvement among patients seen by psychologists. *Psychotherapy.*

Posener, J. A., Le Haye, A., & Cheifetz, P. N. (1989). Suicide notes in adolescence. *Canad. J. Psychiat., 34,* 171–76.

Post, R. M. (1975). Cocaine psychoses: A continuum model. *Amer. J. Psychiat., 132*(3), 225–31.

Poznanski, E., & Zrull, J. P. (1970). Childhood depression. *Arch. Gen. Psychiat., 23*(1), 8–15.

Poznanski, E. O. (1973). Children with excessive fears. *Amer. J. Orthopsychiat., 43*(3), 428–38.

President's Commission on Law Enforcement and Adminstration of Justice. (1967). Katzenbach, N. D. (Chairman), *The challenge of crime in a free society.* Washington, DC: U.S. Government Printing Office.

President's Commission on Mental Health. (1978). *Report to the President.* Washington, DC: U.S. Government Printing Office.

President's Committee on Mental Retardation. (1970). The *decisive decade.* Washington, DC: U.S. Government Printing Office.

Price, R. W., Brew, B., Sidtis, J., Rosenblum, M., Scheck, A. C., & Cleary, P. (1988a). The brain in AIDS: Central nervous system HIV-1 infection and the AIDS dementia complex. *Science, 239,* 586–92.

Price, R. W., Sidtis, J., & Rosenblum, M. (1988b). The AIDS dementia complex: Some current questions. *Annals of Neurology,* Suppl., *23,* 27–33.

Pringle, M. L. K. (1965). *Deprivation and education.* New York: Humanities Press.

Prinz, R. J., Connor, P. A., & Wilson, C. C. (1981). Hyperactive and aggressive behaviors in childhood: Intertwined dimensions. *J. Abnorm. Child Psychol., 9*(2), 191–202.

Prior, M., & Wherry, J. S. (1986). Autism, schizophrenia, and allied disorders. In H. C. Quay and J. S. Wherry (Eds.), *Psychopathological disorders of childhood* (3rd ed., pp. 156–210). New York: Wiley.

Prizant, B. M. (1983). Language acquisition and communicative behavior in autism: Toward an understanding of the "whole" of it. *J. Speech Hear. Dis., 46,* 241–49.

Prizant, B. M., & Duchan, J. F. (1981). The functions of

immediate echolalia in autistic children. *J. Speech Hear. Dis., 465*(3), 241–49.
Project DAWN Drug Enforcement Agency (1988). Drug Abuse Warning Newtwork: Project DAWN.
Provence, S., & Lipton, R. C. (1962). *Infants in institutions.* New York: International Universities Press.
Prusoff, B., & Klerman, G. L. (1974). Differentiating depressed from anxious neurotic outpatients. *Arch. Gen. Psychiat., 30*(3), 302–9.
Puig-Antich, J., Goetz, D., Davies, M., Kaplan, T., Davies, S., Ostrow, L., Asnis, L., Twomey, J., Iyengar, S., & Ryan, N. D. (1989). A controlled family history study of prepubertal major depressive disorder. *Arch. Gen. Psychiat., 46,* 406–18.
Puig-Antich, J., Lukens, D., Davies, M., Goetz, D., & Brennan-Quattrock, J. (1985). Psychosocial functioning in prepubertal major depressive disorders: I. Interpersonal relationships during the depressive episode. *Arch. Gen. Psychiat., 42,* 500–57.
Puska, P. (1983, Feb./Mar.). Television can save lives. *World Health.* Geneva, Switzerland: Magazine of the World Health Organization, 8–11.
Puska, P., Tuomíehto, J., Salonen, J., Neittaanmäki, L., Maki, J., Virtamo, J., Nissinen, A., Koskela, K., & Takalo, T. (1979). Changes in coronary risk factors during a comprehensive five-year community programme to control cardiovascular diseases (North Karelia Project). *Brit. Med. J., 2,* 1173–78.
Putallaz, M., & Gottman, J. M. (1983). Social relationship problems in children: An approach to intervention. In B. B. Lahey & A. E. Kazdin (Eds.), *Advances in clinical child psychology* (Vol. 6). New York: Plenum.
Putnam, F. W., Guroff, J. J., Silberman, E. K., Barban, L., & Post, R. M. (1986). The clinical phenomenology of multiple personality disorder: Review of 100 recent cases. *J. Clin . Psychiat., 47,* 285–93.
Pynoos, R. S., Frederick, C., Nader, K., Arroyo, W., Steinberg, A., Eth, S., Nunez, F., & Fairbanks, L. (1987). Life threat and posttraumatic stress in school-age children. *Arch. Gen. Psychiat., 44,* 1057–63.

Quay, H. C. (1965). Psychopathic personality as pathological stimulation seeking. *Amer. J. Psychiat., 122*(2), 180–83.
Quay, H. C. (1979). Classification. In H. C. Quay & J. S. Wherry (Eds.), *Psychopathological disorders of childhood.* New York: Wiley.
Quinsey, V. L., Chaplin, T. C., & Upfold, D. (1984). Sexual arousal to nonsexual violence and sadomasochistic themes among rapists and non-sex offenders. *J. Cons. Clin. Psychol., 52,* 651–57.

Rabin, A. I., Doneson, S. L., & Jentons, R. L. (1979). Studies of psychological functions in schizophrenia. In L. Bellak (Ed.), *The schizophrenic syndrome.* New York: Basic Books.
Rabkin, J. (1972). Public attitudes about mental illness: A review of the literature. *Schizo. Bull., 10,* 9–33.
Rachman, J. G., & Hodgson, R. (1980). *Obsessions and compulsions.* Englewood Cliffs, NJ: Prentice-Hall.
Rachman, S. J. (1978). *Fear and courage.* San Francisco, CA: Freeman.
Rado, S. (1956). *Psychoanalysis and behavior.* New York: Grune & Stratton.
Ragland, D. R., & Brand, R. J. (1988). Type A behavior and mortality from coronary heart disease. *New Engl. J. Med., 318,* 65–69.
Rahe, R. H. (1974). Life changes and subsequent illness reports. In K. E. Gunderson & R. H. Rahe (Eds.), *Life stress and illness.* Springfield, IL: Thomas.
Rahe, R. H., & Arthur, R. J. (1978). Life changes and illness studies: Past history and future directions. *Journal of Human Stress, 4,* 3–15.
Ramey, C. T., & Haskins, R. (1981). The causes and treatment of school failure: Insights from the Carolina Abecedarian Project. In M. J. Begab, H. C. Haywood, & H. L. Garber (Eds.), *Psychosocial influences in retarded performance,* Vol. II. Baltimore: University Park Press.
Rao, A. V. (1970). A study of depression as prevalent in South India. *Transcultural Psychiat. Research Review, 7,* 116–20.
Rapaport, K., & Burkhart, B. R. (1984). Personality and attitudinal characteristics of sexually coercive college males. *J. Abnorm. Psychol., 93,* 216–21.
Rapoport, J. L., & Ferguson, H. B. (1981). Biological validiation of the hyperkinetic syndrome. *Dev. Med. Child Neurol., 23*(5), 667–82.
Reed, S. D., Katkin, E. S., & Goldband, S. (1986). Biofeedback and behavioral medicine. In F. H. Kanfer & A. P. Goldstein (Eds.), *Helping people change: A textbook of methods* (3rd ed.). Elmsford, NY: Pergamon.
Rees, T. P. (1957). Back to moral treatment and community care. *J. Ment. Sci., 103,* 303–13. In H. B. Adams "Mental illness" or interpersonal behavior? *Amer. Psychologist,* 1964, 19, 191–97.
Regier, D. A., Boyd, J. H., Burke, J. D., Rae, D. S., Myers, J. K., Kramer, M., Robins, L. N., George, L. K., Karno, M., & Locke, B. Z. (1988). One-month prevalence of mental disorders in the United States. *Arch. Gen. Psychiat., 45,* 877–986.
Regier, D. A., Myers, J. K., Kramer, M., Robins, L. N., Blazer, D. G., Hough, R. L., Eaton, W. W., & Locke, B. Z. (1984). The NIMH epidemiologic catchment area program. *Arch. Gen. Psychiat., 41,* 934–48.
Reice, S. (1974). Editorial. *Fam. Hlth., 6*(4), 4.
Reich, J. (1989). Validity of criteria for DSM III self-defeating personality disorder. *Psychiat. Res., 30,* 145–53.
Reich, J., Yates, W., Nduaguba, M. (1989). Prevalence of DSM III personality disorders in the community. *Social Psychiatry and Psychiatric Epidemiology, 24,* 12–16.
Reid, A. H. (1985). Psychiatric disorders. In A. M. Clarke, A. B. D. Clarke, & J. M. Berg (Eds.), *Mental deficiency: The changing outlook,* (4th ed., pp. 291–325). London: Methuen.
Reisberg, B. (1984). "Is Alzheimer's disease inherited? A methodologic review": Commentary. *Integr. Psychiat., 2,* 171–73.
Rentzel, L. (1972). *When all the laughter died in sorrow.* New York: Saturday Review Press.
Renvoize, E. B., Mindham, R. H., Stewart, M., McDonald, R., et al. (1986). Identical twins discordant for presenile dementia of the Alzheimer type. *Brit. J. Psychiat., 149,* 509–12.
Retterstøl, N. (1975). Suicide in Norway. In N. L. Farberow (Ed.), *Suicide in different cultures* (pp. 77–94). Baltimore: University Park Press.
Revitch, E., & Weiss, R. G. (1962). The pedophiliac offender. *Dis. Nerv. Sys., 23,* 73–78.
Reynolds, D. K., & Farberow, N. L. (1976). *Suicide: Inside and out.* Berkeley, CA: University of California Press.
Reynolds, W. M., & Coats, K. I. (1986). A comparison of cognitive-behavioral therapy and relaxation training for the treatment of depression in adolescents. *J. Cons. Clin. Psychol., 54,* 653–60.
Rhoades, L. J. (1981). *Treating and assessing the chronically mentally ill: The pioneering research of Gordon L. Paul.* U.S. Department of Health and Human Services. Public Health Service. (Library of Congress Catalog #81–600097). Washington, DC: U.S. Government Printing Office.
Ribble, M. A. (1944). Infantile experience in relation to personality development. In J. McV. Hunt (Ed.), *Personality and the behavior disorders* (Vol. 2, pp. 621–51). New York: Ronald.
Ribble, M. A. (1945). Anxiety in infants and its disorganizing effects. In N. D. C. Lewis & B. L. Pacella (Eds.), *Modern trends in child psychiatry.* New York: International Universities Press.
Rice, R. D. (1977). Neurophysiological development in premature infants following stimulation. *Develop. Psychol., 13,* 69–76.
Rich, B. E., Paul, G. L., & Mariotto, M. J. (1988). Judgmental relativism as a validity threat to standardized psychiatric relating scales. *Journal of Psychopathology and Behavioral Assessment, 10,* 241–57.
Rich, C. L., Fowler, R. C., Fogarty, L. A., & Young, D. (1988). San Diego suicide study: III. Relationships between diagnoses and stressors. *Arch. Gen. Psychiat., 45,* 589–92.
Rich, C. L., Young, D., & Fowler, R. C. (1986). San Diego suicide study: I. Young vs. old subjects. *Arch. Gen. Psychiat., 43,* 577–82.
Richardson, S. A., Koller, H., & Katz, M. (1985). Relationship of upbringing to later behavior disturbance of mildly mentally retarded young people. *Amer. J. Ment. Def., 90,* 18.
Rieder, R. O. (1973). The offspring of schizophrenic parents: A review. *J. Nerv. Ment. Dis., 157*(3), 179–90.
Rieder, R. O. (1979). Children at risk. In L. Bellak (Ed.), *The schizophrenic syndrome.* New York: Basic Books.

Rimm, D. C., & Lefebvre, R. C. (1981). Phobic disorders. In S. M. Turner, K. S. Calhoun, & H. E. Adams (Eds.), *Handbook of clinical behavior therapy.* New York: Wiley.

Rinear, E. E. (1988). Psychosocial aspects of parental response patterns to the death of a child by homicide. *Journal of Traumatic Stress, 1,* 305–22.

Ritchie, J. C., Carroll, B. J., Olton, P. R., Shively, V., & Feinberg, M. (1985). Plasma cortisol determination for the dexamethasone suppression test: Comparison of competitive protein-binding and commercial radioimmunoassay methods. *Arch. Gen. Psych., 42,* 493–97.

Ritchie, P. L. (1975). *The effect of the interviewer's presentation on some schizophrenic symptomatology.* Unpublished doctoral dissertation, Duke University.

Ritvo, E., Brothers, A. M., Freeman, B. J., & Pingree, J. C. (1988). Eleven possibly autistic parents. *J. Autism Devel. Dis., 18,* 139–43.

Ritvo, E., & Ornitz, E. (1970). A new look at childhood autism points to CNS disease. *Roche Report, 7*(18), 6–8.

Ritvo, E. R., & Freeman, B. J. (1978). Current research on the syndrome of autism. *J. Amer. Acad. Child Psychiat., 17,* 565–75.

Ritvo, E. R., Freeman, B. J., Pingree, C., Mason-Brothers, A., Jorde, L., Jenson, W. R., McMahon, W. M., Peterson, P. B., Mo, A., & Ritvo, A. (1989). The UCLA-University of Utah epidemiologic survey of autism: Prevalence. *Amer. J. Psychiat., 146,* 194–99.

Ritzler, B. A. (1981). Paranoia-prognosis and treatment: A review. *Schizo. Bull., 7,* 710–28.

Roberts, E. (1986). Alzheimer's disease may begin in the nose and may be caused by aluminosilicates. *Neurobiology of Aging, 7,* 561–67.

Roberts, M. C., & Peterson, L. (1984). *Prevention of problems in childhood.* New York: Wiley Interscience.

Robins, L. N. (1970). The adult development of the antisocial child. *Seminars in Psychiatry, 2*(4), 420–34.

Robins, L. N., & Helzer, J. E. (1986). Diagnosis and clinical assessment: The current state of psychiatric diagnosis. In M. R. Rosenzweig & L. W. Porter (Eds.), *Annu. Rev. Psychol.,* (Vol. 37, pp. 409–32). Palo Alto, CA: Annual Reviews.

Robins, L. N., Helzer, J. E., Weissman, M. M., Orvaschel, H., Gruenberg, E., Burke, J. D., & Regier, D. (1984). Lifetime prevalence of specific psychiatric disorders in three sites. *Arch. Gen. Psych., 41,* 949–58.

Robinson, L. A., Berman, J. S., & Neimeyer, R. A. (1990). Psychotherapy for the treatment of depression: A comprehensive review of controlled outcome research. *Psychol. Bull., 108,* 30–49.

Robinson, N. M., & Robinson, H. B. (1976). *The mentally retarded child* (2nd ed.). New York: McGraw-Hill.

Robinson, P. W., Newby, T. J., & Ganzell, S. L. (1981). A token system for a class of underachieving, hyperactive children, *J. Appl. Beh. Anal., 14*(3), 307–15.

Robinson, S., & Winick, H. Z. (1973). Severe psychotic disturbances following crash diet weight loss. *Arch. Gen. Psychiat., 29*(4), 559–62.

Rodin, J. (1974, Apr.). *Obesity and external responsiveness.* Paper presented at the meeting of the Eastern Psychological Association, Philadelphia.

Rodman, D. H., & Collins, M. J. (1974). A community residence program: An alternative to institutional living for the mentally retarded. *Training School Bulletin, 71*(1), 41–48.

Roff, J. D. (1974). Adolescent schizophrenia: Variables related to differences in long-term adult outcome. *J. Cons. Clin. Psychol., 42*(2), 180–83.

Roff, J. D., & Knight R. (1981). Family characteristics, childhood symptoms, and adult outcome in schizophrenia. *J. Abnorm. Psychol., 90,* 510–20.

Roff, J. D., & Wirt, R. D. (1984). Childhood social adjustment, adolescent status, and young adult mental health. *Amer. J. Orthopsychiat., 54,* 595–602.

Roff, M. (1960). Relations between certain preservice factors and psychoneurosis during military duty. *Armed Forces Medical Journal, 11,* 152–60.

Roff, M. (1963). Childhood social interactions and young adult psychosis. *J. Clin. Psychol., 19,* 152–57.

Rogers, C. R. (1951). *Client-centered therapy.* Boston: Houghton Mifflin.

Rogers, C. R. (1959). A theory of therapy personality, and interpersonal relationships as developed in the client-centered framework. In S. Koch (Ed.), *Psychology: A study of a science,* (Vol. 3, pp. 184–256). New York: McGraw-Hill.

Rogers, C. R. (1961). *On becoming a person: A client's view of psychotherapy.* Boston: Houghton Mifflin.

Rogers, C. R. (1966). Client-centered therapy. In S. Arieti et al. (Eds.), *American handbook of psychiatry* (Vol. 3). New York: Basic Books.

Rogers, M. P. (1989). The interaction between brain behavior and immunity. In S. Cheren (Ed.), *Psychosomatic Medicine: Theory, physiology, and practice,* (Vol. 1, pp. 279–330). Madison, CT: International Universities Press.

Rokeach, M. (1964). *The three Christs of Ypsilanti.* New York: Knopf.

Rolfs, R. T., Goldberg, M., & Sharrar, R. G. (1990). Risk factors for syphillis: Cocaine use and prostitution. *Amer. J. Pub. Hlth., 80,* 853–57.

Rolider, A., & Houten, R. V. (1985). Suppressing tantrum behavior in public places through the use of delayed punishment mediated by audio recordings. *Behav. Ther., 16,* 181–94.

Ronningstam, E. & Gunderson, J. (1989). Descriptive studies on narcissistic personality disorder. *Psychiat. Clin. N. Amer., 12,* 585–601.

Rooth, G. (1974). Exhibitionists around the world. *Human Behav., 3*(5), 61.

Rorvik, D. M. (1970, Apr. 7). Do drugs lead to violence? *Look,* 58–61.

Rosen, A. J. (1986). Schizophrenic and affective disorders: Rationale for a biopsychosocial treatment odel. *Integr. Psychiat., 4,* 173–85.

Rosen, D. H. (1970). The serious suicide attempt: Epidemiological and follow-up study of 886 patients. *Amer. J. Psychiat., 127*(6), 64–70.

Rosen, H., & Kiene, H. E. (1946). Paranoia and paranoiac reaction types. *Dis. Nerv. Sys., 7,* 330–37.

Rosen, R. C., & Leiblum, S. R. (1989). Assessment and treatment of desire disorders. In S. R. Leiblum & R. C. Rosen (Eds.), *Principles and practice of sex therapy,* (2nd ed., pp. 19–50). New York: Guilford.

Rosenbaum, G., Shore, D. L., & Chapin, K. (1988). Attention deficit and schizotypy: Marker versus symptom variables. *J. Abnorm. Psychol., 97,* 41–47.

Rosenblatt, A. (1984). Concepts of the asylum in the care of the mentally ill. *Hosp. Comm. Psychiat., 35,* 244–50.

Rosenman, R. H. (1978). The interview method of assessment of the coronary-prone behavior pattern. In T. P. Dembroski, S. M. Weiss, J. L. Shields, S. G. Haynes, & M. Feinleib (Eds.), *Coronary-prone behavior.* New York: Springer-Verlag.

Rosenman, R. H., Brand, R. J., Jenkins, C. D., Friedman, M., & Straus, R. (1975). Coronary heart disease in the Western Collaborative Group Study: Final follow-up experience of 8 ½ years. *JAMA, 233,* 872–77.

Rosenstein, M. J., Milazzo-Sayre, L. J., & Manderscheid, R. W. (1989). Care of persons with schizophrenia: A statistical profile. *Schizo. Bull., 15,* 45–58.

Rosenthal, D. (Ed.). (1963). *The Genain quadruplets.* New York: Basic Books.

Rosenthal, D., Wender, P. H., Kety, S. S., Schulsinger, F., Welner, J., & Ostergaard, L. (1968). Schizophrenics' offspring reared in adoptive homes. In D. Rosenthal & S. S. Kety (Eds.), *The transmission of schizophrenia* (pp. 377–92). New York: Pergamon.

Rosenthal, D., Wender, P. H., Kety, S. S., Schulsinger, F., Welner, J., & Reider, R. O. (1975). Parent-child relationships and psychopathological disorder in the child. *Arch. Gen. Psychiat., 32,* 466–76.

Rosenthal, N. E., Carpenter, C. J., James, S. P., Parry, B. L., Rogers, S. L. B., & Wehr, T. A. (1986). Seasonal affective disorder in children and adolescents. *Amer. J. Psychiat., 143,* 356–58.

Rosenthal, N. E., Sack, D. A., Gillin, J. C., Lewry, A. J., Goodwin, F. K., Davenport, Y., Mueller, P. S., Newsome, D. A., & Wehr, T. A. (1984). Seasonal affective disorder: A description of the syndrome and preliminary findings with light therapy. *Arch. Gen. Psychiat., 41,* 72–80.

Rosenzweig, M. R., Krech, D., Bennett, E. L., & Diamond, M. C. (1968). Modifying brain chemistry and anatomy by enrichment or impoverishment of experience. In G. Newton & S. Levine (Eds.), *Early experience and behavior.* Springfield, IL: Charles C. Thomas.

Ross, A. O., & Pelham, W. E. (1981). Child psychopathology. *Annu. Rev. Psychol., 32,* 243–78.

Ross, C. A. (1989). *Multiple personality disorder: Diagnosis, clinical features, and treatment.* New York: Wiley.

Ross, C. A., Norton, G. R., & Wozney, K. (1989). Multiple personality disorder: An analysis of 236 cases. *Canad. J. Psychiat., 34,* 413–18.

Ross, M. (1974). This doctor will self-destruct. . . . *Human Behav., 3*(2), 54.

Ross, M. (1975). Suicide among physicians. *Tufts Medical Alumni Bulletin, 34,* (3).

Rossi, P. H. (1990). The old homeless and the new homelessness in historical perspective. *Amer. Psychol., 45,* 954–59.

Rosten, R. A. (1961). Some personality characteristics of compulsive gamblers. Unpublished dissertation, UCLA.

Roth, M., & Mountjoy, C. Q. (1982). The distinction between anxiety states and depressive disorders. In E. S. Paykel (Ed.), *Handbook of affective disorders.* New York: Guilford Press.

Roth, S., & Cohen, L. J. (1986). Approach, avoidance, and coping with stress. *Amer. Psychol., 41,* 813–19.

Roth, S., & Lebowitz, L. (1988). The experience of sexual trauma. *Journal of Traumatic Stress, 1,* 79–107.

Rothbart, M. K. (1981). Measurement of temperament in infancy. *Child Develop., 52,* 569–78.

Rotter, J. I., Jones, J. Q., Samloff, I. M., Richardson, C. T., Gursky, J. M., Walsh, J. H., & Rimoin, D. L. (1979). Duodenal-ulcer disease associated with elevated serum pepsinogen I: An inherited autosomal dominant disease. *New Engl. J. Med., 300,* 63–66.

Rounsaville, B. J., Dolinsky, Z. S., Babor, T. F., & Meyer, R. E. (1987). Psychopathology as a predictor of treatment outcome in alcoholics. *Arch. Gen. Psychiat., 44,* 505–13.

Rounsaville, B. J., Kosten, T. R., Weissman, M. M., & Kleber, H. D. (1986). A 2.5 year follow-up of short-term interpersonal psychotherapy in methadone-maintained opiate addicts. *Compr. Psychiat., 27*(3), 201–10.

Rounsaville, B. J., Weissman, M. M., & Prusoff, B. A. (1981). Psychotherapy with depressed outpatients: Patient and process variables as predictors of outcome. *Amer. J. Psychiat., 138,* 67–74.

Routh, D. K., & Ernst, A. R. (1984). Somalization disorder in relatives of children and adolescents with functional abdominal pain. *J. Pediat. Psychol., 9*(4), 427–37.

Rovner, S. (1990, Nov.). Dramatic overlap of addiction, mental illness. *Washington Post Health,* 14–15.

Roy, A. (1985). Early parental separation and adult depression. *Arch. Gen. Psychiat.,* 42, 987–91.

Rubenstein, J. L., Heeren, T., Houseman, D., Rubin, C., & Stechler, G. (1989). Suicidal behavior in "normal" adolescents: Risk and protective factors. *Amer. J. Orthopsychiat., 59,* 59–71.

Rubin, B. (1972). Prediction of dangerousness in mentally ill criminals. *Arch. Gen. Psychiat., 25,* 392–407.

Rubin, R. T., Reinisch, J. M., & Haskett, R. F. (1981). Postnatal gonadal steroid effects on human behavior. *Science, 211,* 1318–24.

Rudestam, K. E. (1971). Stockholm and Los Angeles: A cross-cultural study of the communication of suicidal intent. *J. Cons. Clin. Psychol., 36,*(1), 82–90.

Rumsey, J. M., Duara, R., Grady, C., Rapoport, J., Margolin, R. A., Rapoport, S. I., & Cutler, N. R. (1985). Brain metabolism in autism. *Arch. Gen. Psychiat., 42,* 48–55.

Runcie, J., & Thompson, T. J. (1970), Prolonged starvation—A dangerous procedure? *Brit. Med. J., 3,* 432–35.

Rush, A. J., Beck, A. T., Kovacs, M., & Hollon, S. (1977). The comparative efficacy of cognitive therapy and imipramine in the treatment of depressed out-patients. *Cog. Ther. Res., 1*(1), 17–37.

Rush, A. J., Beck, A. T., Kovacs, M., Weissenburger, J., & Hollon, S. D. (1982). Comparison of the effects of cognitive therapy and pharmacotherapy on hopelessness and self-concept. *Amer. J. Psychiat., 139,* 862–66.

Rush, A. J., Khatami, M., & Beck, A. T. (1975). Cognitive and behavior therapy in chronic depression. *Behav. Ther., 6,* 398–404.

Russell, S. (1975). The development and training of autistic children in separate training centres and in centres for retarded children. *Special Publication No. 6.* Victoria: Mental Health Authority.

Russo, D. C., Carr, E. G., & Lovaas, O. I. (1980). Self-injury in pediatric populations. In J. Ferguson & C. R. Taylor (Eds.), *Comprehensive handbook of behavioral medicine. Vol. 3: Extended applications and issues.* Holliswood, NY: Spectrum Publications.

Rutter, M. (1971). Parent-child separation: Psychological effects on the children. *J. Child Psychol. Psychiat., 12,* 233–60.

Rutter, M. (1972). Maternal deprivation reconsidered. *J. Psychosom. Res., 16*(4), 241–50.

Rutter, M. (1978). Diagnosis and definition. In M. Ruter & E. Schopler (Eds.), *Autism: A reappraisal of concepts and treatment.* New York: Plenum.

Rutter, M. (1979). Maternal deprivations. 1972–1978: New findings, new concepts, new approachs. *Child Develop., 50,* 283–305.

Rutter, M. (1985). The treatment of autistic children. *Journal of Child Psychiatry, 26*(2), 193–214.

Rutter, M. (1988). Epidemiological approaches to developmental psychopathology. *Arch. Gen. Psychiat., 45,* 486–500.

Rutter, M., Izard, C., & Read, P. (Eds.) (1986). *Depression in young people: Developmental perspectives.* New York: Guilford Press.

Rutter, M., & Quinton, D. (1984). Parental psychiatric disorder: Effects on children. *Psychol. Med., 14,* 853–80.

Rutter, M., Tizard, J., & Whitmore, K. (1970). *Education, health and behavior: Psyhologicl and medical study of childhood development.* New York: Wiley.

Ryan, N. D., Puig-Antich, J., Ambrosini, P., Rabinovich, H., Robinson, D., Nelson, B., Iyengar, S. & Twomey, J. (1987). The clinical picture of major depression in children and adolescents. *Arch. Gen. Psychiat., 44,* 854–61.

Ryle, A. (1969). *Student Casualties.* London: Penguin.

Sachar, E. J., Gruen, P. H., Altman, N., Langer, G., & Halpern, F. S. (1978). Neuroendocrine studies of brain dopamine blockade in humans. In L. C. Wynne, R. L. Cromwell, & S. Matthysse (Eds.), *The nature of schizophrenia: New approaches to research and treatment,* (pp. 95–104.). New York: Wiley.

Sack, R. L., Lewry, A. J., White, D. M., Singer, C. M., Fireman, M. J., & Vandiver, R. (1990). Morning vs. evening light treatment for winter depression: Evidence that the therapeutic effects of light are mediated by circadian phase shifts. *Arch. Gen. Psychiat., 47,* 343–51.

Sack, R. L., & Miller, W. (1975). Masochism: A clinical and theoretical overview. *Psychiatry, 38*(3), 244–57.

Safer, D. J., & Allen, R. P. (1973). Stimulant drugs said to suppress height, weight. *Psychiat. News, 8*(9), 9.

Safran, J. D. (1990a). Towards a refinement of cognitive therapy in light of interpersonal theory: I. Theory. *Clin. Psychol. Rev., 10,* 87–105.

Safran, J. D. (1990b). Towards a refinement of cognitive therapy in light of interpersonal theory: II. Practice. *Clin. Psychol. Rev., 10,* 107–21.

Salkovskis, P. M., & Westbrook, D. (1989). Cognitive-behavioral treatment of depressed inpatients. *Behav. Res. Ther., 27,* 149–60.

Salter, A. (1949). *Condition reflex therapy.* New York: Creative Age Press.

Salzman, L. (1968). Obsessions and phobias. *Inter. J. Psychiat., 6,* 451–68.

Sameroff, A., Seifer, R., & Zax, M. (1982). Early development of children at risk for emotional disorders. *Monographs of the Society for Research in Child Development, 47,* (7 No. 199).

Sameroff, A., Seifer, R., Zax, M., & Barocas, R. (1987). Early indicators of developmental risk: Rochester longitudinal study. *Schizo. Bull., 13,* 383–94.

Sanderson, W. C., Rapee, R. M., & Barlow, D. H. (1989). The influence of an illusion of control on panic attacks induced via inhalation of 5.5%-carbon dioxide-enriched air. *Arch. Gen. Psychiat., 46,* 157–62.

Sandhu, H. S., & Cohen, L. M. (1989). Endocrine disorders. In S. Cheren (Ed.), *Psychosomatic Medicine: Theory, physiology, and practice,* (Vol. 2, pp. 661–706). Madison, CT: International Universities Press.

Sanson, A. V. (1980). Classification of hyperactive symptoms. *Medical Journal of Australia, 1*(8), 375–76.

Santiago, J. M., McCall-Perez, F., Gorcey, M., & Beigel, A. (1985). Long-term psychological effects of rape in 35 rape victims. *Amer. J. Psychiat., 142,* 1338–40.

Sanua, V. (1986a). The organic etiology of infantile autism: A critical review of the literature. *International Journal of Neuroscience, 30,* 195–225.

Sanua, V. (1986b). A comparative study of opinions of U.S.A. and European professionals on the etiology of infantile autism. *Inter. J. Soc. Psychiat., 32,* 16–30.

Sanua, V. D. (1969). Sociocultural aspects. In L. Bellak & L. Loeb (Eds.), *The schizophrenic syndrome.* New York: Grune & Stratton.

Sanua, V. D. (1987). Standing against an established ideology: Infantile autism, a case in point. *Clin. Psychol., 4,* 96–10.

Sapolsky, R. M. (1989). Hypercortisolism among socially subordinate wild baboons originates at the CNS level. *Arch. Gen. Psychiat., 46,* 1047–51.

Saracoglu, B., Minden, H., & Wilchesky, M. (1989). The adjustment of students with learning disabilities to university and its relationship to self-esteem and self-efficacy. *J. Learn. Dis., 22,* 590–92.

Sarbin, T. R., (in press). The social construction of schizophrenia. In W. Flack, D. R. Miller, & M. Wiener (Eds.), *What is schizophrenia.* New York: Springer-Verlag.

Sarbin, T. R., & Juhasz, J. B. (1967). The historical background of the concept of hallucination. *Journal of the History of the Behavioral Sciences, 3,* 339–58.

Sarbin, T. R., & Mancuso, J. C. (1970). Failure of a moral enterprise: Attitudes of the public toward mental illness. *J. Cons. Clin. Psychol., 35,* 159–73.

Sarbin, T. R., & Mancuso, J. C. (1980). *Schizophrenia: Medical diagnosis or moral verdict.* New York: Pergamon.

Sargeant, J. K., Bruce, M. L., Florio, L. P., & Weissman, M. M. (1990). Factors associated with 1-year outcome of major depression in the community. *Arch. Gen. Psychiat., 47,* 519–26.

Sargent, M. (1982a, Jul. 16). Schizophrenic quads not identically ill, studies show. *ADAMHA News, 8*(13), 4–5.

Sargent, M. (1982b, Dec. 3), Researcher traces Alzheimer's disease eight generations back in one family. *ADAMHA News, 8*(23), 3.

Sarvis, M. A. (1962). Paranoid reactions: Perceptual distortion as an etiological agent. *Arch. Gen. Psychiat., 6,* 157–62.

Sasaki, M., & Hara, Y. (1973). Paternal origin of the extra chromosome in Down's syndrome. *Lancet, 2*(7840), 1257–58.

Satir, V. (1967). *Conjoint family therapy* (rev. ed.). Palo Alto, CA: Science and Behavior Books.

Satterfield, J. H., Satterfield, B. T., & Cantwell, D. P. (1981). Three year multimodal treatment study of 100 hyperactive boys. *Journal of Pediatrics, 98,*(4), 650–55.

Savasir, I., & Erol, N. (1990). The Turkish MMPI: Translation, standardization, and validation. In J. N. Butcher & C. D. Spielberger (Eds.), *Advances in personality assessment,* (Vol. 8). Hillsdale, NJ: Lawrence Erlbaum Press.

Sawyer, J. B., Sudak, H. S., & Hall, S. R. (1972, Winter). A follow-up study of 53 suicides known to a suicide prevention center. *Life-Threatening Behavior, 2*(4), 227–38.

Scalf-McIver, L., & Thompson, K. J. (1989). Family correlates of bulimic characteristics in college females. *J. Clin. Psychol., 45,* 467–72.

Scarr, S. (1984). *Mother care, other care.* New York: Basic Books.

Schaar, K. (1974). Suicide rate high among women psychologists. *APA Monitor, 5*(7), 1, 10.

Schaefer, J. M. (1977, Aug. 30). Firewater myths revisited: Towards a second generation of ethanol metabolism studies. Paper presented at Cross-cultural Approaches to Alcoholism. Physiological variation: Invited Symposium. NATO Conference, Bergen, Norway.

Schaefer, J. M. (1978). Alcohol metabolism reactions among the Reddis of South India. *Alcoholism: Clinical and experimental research, 2*(1), 61–69.

Schalock, R. L., Harper, R. S., & Carver, G. (1981). Independent living placement: Five years later. *Amer. J. Ment. Def., 86,* 170–77.

Schapiro, M. B., & Rapoport, S. I. (1987). "Pathological similarities between Alzheimer's disease and Down's syndrome: Is there a genetic link?": Commentary. *Integr. Psychiat., 5,* 167–69.

Scharfman, M., & Clark, R. W. (1967). Delinquent adolescent girls: Residential treatment in a municipal hospital setting. *Arch. Gen. Psychiat., 17*(4), 441–47.

Scheff, T. J. (1984). *Being mentally ill: A sociological theory* (2nd ed.). New York: Aldine.

Scheier, M. F., & Carver, C. S. (1987). Dispositional optimism and physical well-being: The influence of generalized outcome expectancies on health. *J. Personal., 55,* 169–210.

Schild, S. (1972). Parents of children with PKU. *Children Today, 1*(4), 20–22.

Schilling, R. F., & McAlister, A. L. (1990). Preventing drug use in adolescents through media interventions. *J. Cons. Clin. Psychol., 58,* 416–24.

Schleifer, S. J., Keller, S. E., & Stein, M. (1985). Central nervous system mechanisms and immunity: Implications for tumor responses. In S. M. Levy, *Behavior and cancer,* (pp. 120–33). San Francisco: Jossey-Bass.

Schleifer, S. J., Keller, S. E., Bond, R. M., Cohen, J., & Stein, M., (1989). Major depressive disorder and immunity: Role of age, sex, severity, and hospitalization. *Arch. Gen. Psychiat., 46,* 81–87.

Schmauk, F. J. (1970). Punishment, arousal, and avoidance learning in sociopaths. *J. Abnorm. Psychol., 76*(3), 325–35.

Schmauss, C., & Krieg, J. C. (1987). Enlargement of cerebrospinal fluid spaces in benzodiazepine abusers. *Psychol. Med., 17,* 869–73.

Schmid, H. (1914). Zur Psychologie der Brandstifter. *Psychologische Abhandlungen, Band, 1,* 80–179.

Schneider, S. (1978). Attitudes toward death in adolescent offspring of holocaust survivors. *Amer. J. Orthopsychiat., 13,* 575–83.

Schneidman, E. S. (1973). Suicide notes reconsidered. *Psychiatry, 36,* 379–94.

Schoeneman, T. J. (1984). The mentally ill witch in textbooks of abnormal psychology: Current status and implications of a fallacy. *Profess. Psychol., 15*(3), 299–314.

Schofield, W. (1964). *Psychotherapy: The purchase of friendship.* Englewood Cliffs, NJ: Prentice-Hall.

Schofield, W., & Balian, L. (1959). A comparative study of the personal histories of schizophrenic and nonpsychiatric patients. *J. Abnorm. Soc. Psychol., 59,* 216–25.

Schopler, E. (1978). Changing parental involvement in behavioral treatment. In M. Rutter & Schopler (Eds.), *Autism: A reappraisal of concepts and treatment.* New York: Plenum Press.

Schopler, E. (1983). New developments in the definition and diagnosis of autism. In B. B. Lahey & A. E. Kazdin (Eds.), *Advances in clinical child psychology* (Vol. 6, pp. 93–127). New York: Plenum Press.

Schopler, E., Mesibov, G., & Baker, A. (1982). Evaluation of treatment for autistic children and their parents. *J. Amer. Acad. Child Psychiat., 21,* 262–67.

Schowalter, J. E. (1980). Tics. *Pediatrics in Review, 2,* 55–57.

Schreiber, F. R. (1973). *Sybil.* New York: Warner Paperback.

Schreibman, L., & Koegel, R. L. (1975). Autism: A defeatable horror. *Psych. Today, 8*(10), 61–67.

Schuckit, M. A., & Gould, R. O. (1988). A simultaneous evaluation of multiple markers of ethanol/placebo challenges in sons of alcoholics and controls. *Arch. Gen. Psychiat., 45,* 211–16.

Schulsinger, F. (1980). Biological psychopathology. *Annu. Rev. Psychol., 31,* 583–606.

Schulsinger, F., Knop, J., Goodwin, D. W., Teasdale, T. W., & Mikkelsen, U. (1986). A prospective study of young men at high risk for alcoholism. *Arch. Gen. Psychiat., 43,* 755–60.

Schulterbrandt, J. D., & Raskin, A. (Eds.). (1977). *Depression in children: Diagnosis, treatment and conceptual models.* New York: Raven Press.

Schwab, J. J. (1970). Comprehensive medicine and the concurrence of physical and mental illness. *Psychosomatics, 11*(6), 591–95.

Schwartz, C. C., & Myers, J. K. (1977). Life events and schizophrenia: I. Comparison of schizophrenics with a community sample. *Arch. Gen. Psychiat., 34,* 1238–41.

Schwartz, D. A. (1963). A review of the "paranoid" concept. *Arch. Gen. Psychiat., 8,* 349–61.

Schwartz, G. E. (1978). Psychobiological foundations of psychotherapy and behavior change. In S. L. Garfield & A. E. Bergin (Eds.), *Handbook of psychotherapy and behavior change* (2nd ed., pp. 63–99). New York: Wiley.

Schwartz, G. E. (1989). Disregulation theory and disease: Toward a general model for psychosomatic medicine. In S. Cheren (Ed.), *Psychosomatic medicine: Theory, physiology, and practice,* (Vol. 1, pp. 91–118). Madison, CT: International Universities Press.

Schwartz, J. L., (1987). *Review and evaluation of smoking cessation methods: The United States and Canada 1978–1985.* US Department of Health and Human Services, NIH Publication No. 87–2940.

Schwartz, R. C., Barrett, M. J., & Saba, G. (1983, Oct.). *Family therapy for bulimia.* Paper presented at American Association for Marriage and Family Therapy, Washington, DC.

Schwartz, S., & Johnson, J. H. (1985). *Psychopathology of childhood: A clinical-experimental approach,* (2nd ed.). New York: Pergamon.

Schwartzman, J. (1974). The individual, incest, and exogamy. *Psychiatry, 37,* 171–80.

Schwitzgebel, R. L., & Schwitzgebel, R. K. (1980). *Law and psychological practice.* New York: Wiley.

Scott, A. I. F. (1989). Which depressed patients will respond to electroconvulsive therapy? The search for biological predictors of recovery. *Brit. J. Psychiat., 154,* 8–17.

Scovern, A. W., & Kilmann, P. R. (1980). Status of electronconvulsive therapy: A review of the outcome literature. *Psychol. Bull., 87,* 260–303.

Searles, J. S. (1988). The role of genetics in the pathogenesis of alcoholism. *J. Abnorm. Psychol., 97,* 153–67.

Sears, R. R. (1961). Relation of early socialization experiences to aggression in middle childhood. *J. Abnorm. Soc. Psychol., 63,* 466–92.

Sears, R. R., Maccoby, E. E., & Levin, H. (1957). *Patterns of child rearing.* New York: Harper & Row.

Sedvall, G., Farde, L., Persson, A., & Wiesel, F. A. (1986). Imaging of neurotransmitter receptors in the living human brain. *Arch. Gen. Psychiat., 43,* 995–1005.

Segal, D. S., Yager, J., & Sullivan, J. L. (1976). *Foundations of biochemical psychiatry.* Boston: Butterworth.

Segal, S. (1978). Attitudes toward the mentally ill: A review. *Social Work, 23,* 211–17.

Segal, Z. V., & Marshall, W. M. (1985). Heterosexual social skills in a population of rapists and child molesters. *J. Cons. Clin. Psychol., 53,* 55–63.

Segal, Z. V., & Stermac, L. E. (1990). The role of cognition in sexual assault. In W. L. Marshall, D. R. Laws, & H. E. Barbaree (Eds.), *Handbook of sexual assault* (pp. 161–75). New York: Plenum.

Seiden, R. H. (1974). Suicide: preventable death. *Public Affairs Report, 15*(4), 1–5.

Seidl, F. W. (1974). Community oriented residential care: The state of the art. *Child Care Quarterly, 3*(3), 150–63.

Seixas, F. A. & Cadoret, R. (1974, Apr. 15). What is the alcoholic man? *New York Academy of Sciences, 223,* 13–14.

Seligman, M. E. P. (1973). Fall into hopelessness. *Psych.Today, 7*(1), 43–47, 48.

Seligman, M. E. P. (1975). *Helplessness: On depression, development, and death.* San Francisco: W. H. Freeman.

Seligman, M. E. P., & Hager, M. (Eds.). (1972). *Biological boundaries of learning.* New York: Appleton-Century-Crofts.

Selkin, J. (1975). Rape. *Psych. Today, 8*(8), 70–72.

Selkin, J., & Loya, F. (1979). Issues in the psychological autopsy of controversial public figures. *Profess. Psychol., 10*(1), 87–93.

Selkoe, D. J. (1986). Altered structural protein in plaques and tangles: What do they tell us about the biology of Alzheimer's disease? *Neurobiology of Aging, 7,* 425–32.

Selling, L. S. (1943). *Men against madness.* New York: Garden City Books.

Selye, H. (1956). *The stress of life.* New York: McGraw-Hill.

Selye, H. (1976a). *Stress in health and disease.* Woburn, MA: Butterworth.

Selye, H. (1976b). *The stress of life* (2nd ed.). New York: McGraw-Hill.

Senay, E. C., & Redlich, F. C. (1968). Cultural and social factors in neuroses and psychosomatic illnesses. *Soc. Psychiat., 3*(3), 89–97.

Sergovich, F., Valentine, G. H., Chen, A. T., Kinch, R., & Smout, M. (1969). Chromosomal aberrations in 2159 consecutive newborn babies, *New Engl. J. Med., 280*(16), 851–54.

Serrano, A. C., Zuelzer, M. B., Howe, D. D., & Reposa, R. E. (1979). Ecology of abusive and nonabusive families, *J. Amer. Acad. Child Psychiat., 18,* 167–75.

Sgroi, S. M. (1977). Sexual molestation of children: The last frontier in child abuse. In S. Chess & A. Thomas (Eds.), *Annual progress in child psychiatry and child development: 1976.* New York: Brunner/Mazel.

Shakow, D. (1969). On doing research in schizophrenia. *Arch. Gen. Psychiat., 20*(6), 618–42.

Shanfield, S. B., & Swain, B. J. (1984). Death of adult children in traffic accidents. *J. Nerv. Ment. Dis., 172*(9), 533–38.

Shapiro, A. K., & Morris, L. A. (1978). The placebo effect in medical and psychological therapies. In S. L. Garfield & A. E. Bergin (Eds.), *Handbook of psychotherapy and behavior change* (2nd ed., pp. 369–410). New York: Wiley.

Shapiro, D. (1965). *Neurotic styles.* New York: Basic Books.

Shapiro, S. (1968). Maturation of the neuroendocrine response to stress in the rat. In G. Newton & S. Levine (Eds.), *Early experience and behavior.* Springfield, IL: Charles S. Thomas.

Shatan, C. F. (1978). Stress disorders among Vietnam veterans: The emotional content of combat continues. In C. R. Figley (Ed.), *Stress disorders among Vietnam veterans: Theory, research and treatment.* New York: Brunner/Mazel.

Shaw, E. D., Stokes, P. E., Mann, J. J., & Manevitz, A. Z. A. (1987). Effects of lithium carbonate on the memory and motor speed of bipolar outpatients. *J. Abnorm. Psychol., 96,* 64–69.

Shaw, J. A. (1990). Stress engendered by military action on military and civilian populations. In J. D. Noshpitz & R. D. Coddington (Eds.), *Stressors and the adjustment disorders.* New York: Wiley Intersciences.

Shedler, J. & Block, J. (1990). Adolescent drug use and psychological health: A longitudinal inquiry. *Amer. Psychol., 45,* 612–30.

Sheldon, W. H. (with the collaboration of C. W. Dupertuis & E. McDermott). (1954). *Atlas of men.* New York: Harper & Row.

Shenson, D., Dubler, N., & Michaels, D. (1990). Jails and prisons: The new asylums? *Amer. J. Pub. Hlth., 80,* 655–56.

Sherrod, B. (1968). *Dallas Times Herald* (n.d.). Quoted in D. Bolen & W. H. Boyd, Gambling and the gambler. *Arch. Gen. Psychiat., 18*(5), 617–30.

Sherwin, I., & Geschwind, N. (1978). Neural substrates of behavior. In A. M. Nicholi (Ed.), *The Harvard guide to modern psychiatry* (pp. 59–80). Cambridge, MA: Harvard University Press.

Shimkunas, A. M. (1972). Demand for intimate self-disclosure and pathological verbalizations in schizophrenia. *J. Abnorm. Psychol., 80,* 197–205.

Shneidman, E. S. (1969). Fifty-eight years. In E. S. Shneidman (Ed.), *On the nature of suicide* (pp. 1–30). San Francisco: Jossey-Bass.

Shneidman, E. S., & Farberow, N. L. (Eds.). (1957). *Clues to suicide.* New York: McGraw-Hill.

Shneidman, E. S., Parker, E., & Funkhouser, G. R. (1970). You and death. *Psych. Today, 4*(3), 67–72.

Shoemaker, M. E., & Paulson, T. L. (1976). Group assertion training for mothers: A family intervention strategy. In E. J. Mash, L. C. Handy, & L. A. Hamerlynck (Eds.), *Behavior modification approaches to parenting.* New York: Brunner/Mazel.

Shore, J. H., Tatum, E. L., & Vollmer, W. M., (1986). Evaluation of mental health effects of disaster. *Amer. J. Pub. Hlth., 76*(Suppl.), 76–83.

Shore, J. H., Vollmer, W. M., & Tatum, E. L. (1989). Community patterns of posttraumatic stress disorders. *J. Nerv. Ment. Dis., 177,* 681–85.

Shrout, P. E., Link, B. G., Dohrenwend, B. P., Skodol, A. E., Stueve, A., & Mirotznik, J. (1989). Characterizing life events as risk factors for depression: The role of fateful loss events. *J. Abnorm. Psychol., 89,* 460–67.

Siegel, J. M., & Kuykendall, D. H. (1990). Loss, widowhood, and psychological distress among the elderly. *J. Cons. Clin. Psychol. 58,* 519–24.

Siegel, R. K. (1984). Hostage hallucinations: Visual imagery induced by isolation and life-threatening stress. *J. Nerv. Ment. Dis., 172*(5), 264–72.

Siever, L. J. (1985). Biological markers in schizotypal personality disorder. *Schizo. Bull. 11,* 564–75.

Siever, L. J. (1986). Schizoid and schizotypal personality disorders. In J. R. Lion (Ed.), *Personality disorders: Diagnosis and management. (pp. 32–64).* Malabar, Fl.: Robert F. Kreiger Publishing.

Sigal J. J., Silver, D., Rakoff, V., & Ellin, B. (1973, Apr.). Some second-generation effects of survival of the Nazi persecution. *Amer. J. Orthopsychiat., 43*(3), 320–27.

Sigerist, H. E. (1943). *Civilization and disease.* Ithaca, NY: Cornell University Press.

Silberman, E. K., & Tassone, E. P. (1985). The Israeli high-risk study: Statistical overview and discussion. *Schizo. Bull. 11,* 138–45.

Silberstein, R. M., & Irwin, H. (1962). Jean-Marc-Gaspard Itard and the savage of Aveyron: An unsolved diagnostic problem in child psychiatry. *J. Amer. Acad. Child Psychiat., 1*(2), 314–22.

Silverman, W. H., & Silverman, M. M. (1987). Comparison of key informants, parents, and teenagers for planning adolescent substance abuse prevention programs. *Psychology of Addictive Behaviors, 1*(1), 30–37.

Silverstein, A. B., Legutki, G., Friedman, S. L., & Takayama, D. L. (1982). Performance of Down's syndrome individuals on the Stanford-Binet Intelligence Scale. *Amer. J. Ment. Def., 86,* 548–5.

Silverton, L., Finello, K. M., Schulsinger, F., & Mednick, S. A. (1985). Low birth weight and ventricular enlargement in a high-risk sample. *J. Abnorm. Psychol., 94,* 405–9

Simon, R. J., & Aaronson, D. E. (1988). *The insanity defense: A critical assessment of law and policy in the post-Hinckley era.* New York: Praeger.

Simon, W. (1975). Male sexuality: The secret of satisfaction. *Today's Health, 53*(4), 32–34, 50–52.

Simons, A. D., Murphy, G. E., Levine, J. L., & Wetzel, R. D. (1986). Cognitive therapy and pharmacotherapy for depression: Sustained improvement over one year. *Arch. Gen. Psychiat., 43,* 43–48.

Simons, R. C. (1987). Applicability of the DSM-III to psychiatric education. In G. L. Tischler (Ed.), *Diagnosis and classification in psychiatry: A critical appraisal of DSM-III* (pp. 510–29). New York: Cambridge University Press.

Simons, R. C., & Hughes, C. C. (Eds). (1985). *The culture bound syndromes.* Boston: Reidel.

Singer, J., & Singer, I. (1978). Types of female orgasm. In J. LoPiccolo & L. LoPiccolo (Eds.), *Handbook of sex therapy* (pp. 175–86). New York: Plenum Press.

Singer, J. E. (1980). Traditions of stress research: Integrative comments. In I. G. Sarason & C. D. Spielberger (Eds.), *Stress and anxiety* (Vol. 7, pp. 3–10). Washington, DC: Hemisphere.

Singer, M., & Wynne, L. C. (1963). Differentiating characteristics of the parents of childhood schizophrenics, childhood neurotics and young adult schizophrenics. *Amer. J. Psychiat., 120,* 234–43.

Singer, M., & Wynne, L. C. (1965a). Thought disorder and family relations of schizophrenics. III. Methodology using projective techniques. *Arch. Gen. Psychiat., 12,* 182–200.

Singer, M., & Wynne, L. C. (1965b). Thought disorder and family relations of schizophrenics. IV. Results and implications. *Arch. Gen. Psychiat., 12,* 201-12.

Singer, M. T., Wynne, L. C., & Toohey, M. L. (1978). Communication disorders and the families of schizophrenics. In L. C. Wynne, R. L. Cromwell, & S. Matthysse (Eds.), *The nature of schizophrenia: New approaches to research and treatment* (pp. 499–511). New York: Wiley.

Skeels, H. M. (1966). Adult status of children with contrasting early life experiences: A follow-up study. *Monographs of the Society for Research in Child Development* (Serial No. 105), *31.*

Skinner, B. F. (1948). *Walden two.* New York: Macmillan.

Skinner, B. F. (1971). *Beyond freedom and dignity.* New York: Knopf.

Skinner, B. F. (1974). *About behaviorism.* New York: Knopf.

Skinner, B. F. (1990). Can psychology be a science of mind? *Amer. Psychol. 45,* 1206–10.

Skolnick, A. S. (1986). *The psychology of human development.* Harcourt Brace Jovanovich.

Slap, G. B., Vorters, D. F., Chaudhuri, S., & Centor, R. (1989). Risk factors for attempted suicide during adolescence. *Pediatrics, 84,* 762–72.

Slater, E., with the assistance of J. Shields. (1953). Psychotic and neurotic illness in twins. Special Report Series No. 278. Medical Research Council (Great Britain).

Slater, E. T. O. (1944). Genetics in psychiatry. *J. Ment. Sci., 90,* 17–35.

Slater, J., & Depue, R. A. (1981). The contribution of environmental events and social support to serious suicide attempts in primary depressive disorder. *J. Abnorm. Psychol., 90,* 275–85.

Sloane, R. B., Staples, F. R., Cristol, A. H., Yorkston, N. J., & Whipple, K. (1975). *Psychotherapy versus behavior therapy.* Cambridge, MA: Harvard University Press.

Sloman, L. (1991). Use of medication in pervasive developmental disorders. *Psychiat. Clin. N. Amer. 14,* 165–82.

Sloper, P., Turner, S., Knussen, C., & Cunningham, C. C. (1990). Social life of school children with Down's syndrome. *Child: Care, health, and development, 16,* 235–51.

Smalley, S. L. (1991). Genetic influences in autism. *Psychiat. Clin. N. Amer., 14,* 125–39.

Smith, D. (1938). *Dear octopus: A comedy in three acts.* Great Britain: Windmill Press.

Smith, D. (1982). Trends in counseling and psychotherapy. *Amer. Psychol., 37*(7), 802–9.

Smith, G., & Smith, D. (1985). A mainstreaming program that really works. *J. Learn. Dis., 18,* 369–72.

Smith, G. F., & Berg, J. M. (1976). *Down's anomaly.* New York: Churchill Livingstone (Distributed by Longman, Inc.).

Smith, M. L., Glass, G. V., & Miller, T. I. (1980). *The benefits of psychotherapy.* Baltimore: Johns Hopkins University Press.

Smith, R. J. (1978). *The psychopath in society.* New York: Academic Press.

Smith, R. J. (1979). Study finds sleeping pills overprescribed. *Science, 204,* 287–88.

Smith, W. (1989). *A profile of health and disease in America.* New York: Facts on File.

Snider, W. D., Simpson, D. M., Nielsen, S., Gold, J. W., Metroka, C. E., & Posner, J. B. (1983). Neurological complications of acquired immune deficiency syndrome: Analysis of 50 patients. *Annals of Neurology, 14,* 403–18.

Snyder, D. K., & Wills, R. M. (1989). Behavioral versus insight-oriented marital therapy: Effects on individual and interspousal functioning. *J. Cons. Clin. Psychol. 57,* 39–46.

Snyder, M., Tanke, E. D., & Berschied, E. (1977). Social perception and interpersonal behavior. On the self-fulfilling nature of social stereotypes. *J. Pers. Soc. Psychol., 35*(9), 656–66.

Snyder, S. H. (1978). Dopamine and schizophrenia. In L. C. Wynne, R. L. Cromwell & S. Matthysse (Eds.), *The nature of schizophrenia: New approaches to research and treatment* (pp. 87–94). New York: Wiley.

Solomon, J. (1972). Why gamble? A psychological profile of pathology. *The Sciences, 12*(6), 20–21.

Solomon, Z. (1989). Psychological sequelae of war. A 3-year prospective study of Israeli combat stress reaction casualties. *J. Nerv. Ment. Dis., 177,* 342–46.

Sommers, I. (1988). The influence of environmental factors on the community adjustment of the mentally ill. *J. Nerv. Ment. Dis., 176,* 221–26.

Soni, S. D., & Rockley, G. J. (1974). Socio-cultural substrates of folie à deux. *Brit. J. Psychiat., 125*(9), 230–35.

Sonnenberg, S. M. (1988). Victims of violence and post-traumatic stress disorder. *Psychiat. Clin. N. Amer., 11,* 581–90.

Sontag, L. W., Steele, W. G., & Lewis, M. (1969). The fetal and maternal cardiac response to environmental stress. *Human Develop., 12,* 1–9.

Spanos, N. P., Weekes, J. R., & Bertrand, L. D. (1985). Multiple personality: A social psychological perspective. *J. Abnorm. Psychol., 94,* 362–76.

Speed, N., Engdahl, B., Schwartz, J., & Eberly, R. (1989). Posttraumatic stress disorder as a consequence of the POW experience. *J. Nerv. Ment. Dis. 177,* 147–53.

Spence, J. T., & Helmreich, R. L. (1978). *Masculinity and femininity: Their psychological dimensions, correlates, & antecedents.* Austin, TX: University of Texas Press.

Spencer, G. (1989). *Projections of the population of the United States, by age, sex, and race: 1988–2080.* U.S. Department of Commerce, Bureau of Census. U. S. Government Printing Office.

Spielberger, C. D., Johnson, E. H., Russell, S. F., Crane, R. J., & Worden, T. J. (1985). The experience and expression of anger. In M. A. Chesney & R. H. Rosenman (Eds.), *Anger and hostility in cardiovascular and behavioral disorders.* New York: Hemisphere.

Spiess, W. F. J., Geer, J. H., & O'Donohue, W. T. (1984). Premature ejaculation: Investigation of factors in ejaculatory latency. *J. Abnorm. Psychol., 93,* 242–45.

Spirito, A., Brown, L., Overholser, J., & Fritz, G. (1989). Attempted suicide in adolescence: A review and critique of the literature. *Clin. Psychol. Rev. 9,* 335–63.

Spitz, R. A. (1945). Hospitalization: An inquiry into the genesis of psychiatric conditions of early childhood. In R. S. Eissler, A. Freud, H. Hartman, & E. Kris (Eds.), *The psychoanalytic study of the child* (Vol. 1). New York: International Universities Press.

Spitz, R. A. (1946). Anaclitic depression. In *Psychoanalytic study of the child* (Vol. 2). New York: International Universities Press.

Spitzer, R. L., Gibbon, M., Skodol, A. E., Williams, J. B. W. & First, M. B. (1989). *DSM-III-R casebook.* Washington, DC: American Psychiatric Press.

Spitzer, R. L., Skodol, A. E., Gibbon, M., & Williams, J. B. W. (1981). *DSM-III case book.* Washington, DC: American Psychiatric Association.

Spitzer, R. L., Skodol, A. E., Gibbon, M., & Williams, J. B. W. (1983). *Psychopathology: A case book.* New York: McGraw-Hill.

Spitzer, R. L., & Williams, J. B. (1988). Having a dream: A research strategy for DSM-IV. *Arch. Gen. Psychiat., 45,* 871–74.

Sprague, R. L., Barnes, K. R., & Werry, J. S. (1970). Methylphenidate and thioridazine: Learning reaction time, activity, and classroom behavior in disturbed children. *Amer. J. Orthopsychiat., 40,* 615–28.

Sprague, R. L., & Brown, T. (1981). Behavioral pharmacology research with children. In T. Thompson and P. B. Dews (Eds.), *Advances in behavioral pharmacology* (Vol. 3). New York: Academic Press.

Spring, B. J., & Zubin, J. (1978). Attention and

information-processing as indicators of vulnerability to schizophrenic episodes. In L. C. Wynne, R. L. Cromwell & S. Matthysse (Eds.), *The nature of schizophrenia: New approaches to research and treatment* (pp. 366–175). New York: Wiley.

Squire, L. R. (1977). ECT and memory loss. *Amer. J. Psychiat., 134,* 997–1001.

Squire, L. R., & Slater, P. C. (1978). Bilateral and unilateral ECT: Effects on verbal and nonverbal memory. *Amer. J. Psychiat., 135,* 1316–20.

Squire, L. R., Slater, P. C., & Chase, P. M. (1975). Retrograde amnesia: Temporal gradient in very long-term memory following electroconvulsive therapy. *Science, 187,* 77–79.

Stabenau, J., & Pollin, W. (1968). Comparative life history differences of families of schizophrenics, delinquents and "normals." *Amer. J. Psychiat. 124,* 1526–34.

Stabenau, J. R. (1984). Implications of family history of alcoholism, antisocial personality, and sex differences in alcohol dependence. *Amer. J. Psychiat., 141*(10), 1178–82.

Stabenau, J. R., Tupin, J., Werner, M., & Pollin, W. (1965). A comparative study of families of schizophrenics, delinquents, and normals. *Psychiatry, 28,* 45–59.

Stampfl, T. G., (1975). Implosive therapy: Staring down your nightmares. *Psych. Today, 8*(9), 66–68, 72–73.

Stanley, E. J., & Barter, J. T. (1970). Adolescent suicidal behavior. *Amer. J. Orthopsychiat., 40*(1), 87–96.

Stanton, M. D., & Todd, T. C. (1976, June). *Structural family therapy with heroin addicts: Some outcome data.* Paper presented at the Society for Psychotherapy Research. San Diego.

Stare, F. J., Whelan, E. M., & Sheridan, M. (1980). Diet and hyperactivity: Is there a relationship?, *Pediatrics, 6*(4), 521–25.

Stattin, H., & Magnusson, D. (1989). The role of early aggressive behavior in the frequency, seriousness, and types of later crimes. *J. Cons. Clin. Psychol., 57,* 710–18.

Steffenberg, S., & Gillberg, C. (1986). Autism and autistic-like conditions in Swedish rural and urban areas: A population study. *Brit. J. Psychiat. 149,* 81–87.

Stein, J. (1970). *Neurosis in contemporary society: Process and treatment.* Belmont, CA: Brooks/Cole.

Stein, S. (1987). Computer-assisted diagnosis for children and adolescents. In J. N. Butcher (Ed.), *Computerized psychological assessment: A practitioner's guide.* New York: Basic Books.

Steinmann, A., & Fox, D. J. (1974). *The male dilemma: How to survive the sexual revolution.* New York: Jason Aronson.

Steketee, G., & Foa, E. B. (1985). Obsessive-compulsive disorder. In D. H. Barlow (Ed.), *Clinical handbook of psychological disorders.* (pp. 69–144) New York: Guilford.

Stene, J., Stene, E., Stengel-Rutkowski, S., & Murken, J. D. (1981). Paternal age and Down's syndrome, data from prenatal diagnoses (DFG). *Human Genet. 59,* 119–24.

Stephens, R., & Cottrell, E. (1972). A follow-up study of 200 narcotic addicts committed for treatment under the narcotic addiction rehabilitation act. *British Journal of Addiction, 67,* 45–53.

Stephens, R. S., Hokanson, J. E., & Welker, R. (1987). Responses to depressed interpersonal behavior: Mixed reactions in a helping role. *J. Pers. Soc. Psychol., 52,* 1274–82.

Stermac, L. E., Segal, Z. V., & Gillis, R. (1990). Social and cultural factors in sexual assault. In W. L. Marshall, D. R. Laws, & H. E. Barbaree (Eds.), *Handbook of sexual assault* (pp. 143–60). New York: Plenum.

Stern, R. L. (1947). Diary of a war neurosis. *J. Nerv. Ment. Dis., 106,* 583–86.

Stern, R. S., Lisedge, M. S., & Marks, I. M. (1973). Obsessive ruminations: A controlled trial of thought-stopping technique. *Behav. Res. Ther., 11*(4), 659–62.

Stewart, A. L., & Brook, R. H. (1983). Effects of being overweight. *Amer. J. Pub. Hlth., 73*(2), 171–78.

Stewart, J. W., McGrath, P. J., Liebowitz, M. R., Harrison, W., & Quitkin, F. (1985). Treatment outcome validation of DSM-III depressive subtypes: Clinical usefulness in outpatients with mild to moderate depression. *Arch. Gen. Psychiat., 42,* 1148–53.

Stewart, M. A., Deblois, C. S., Meardon, J., & Cummings, C. (1980). Aggressive conduct disorder of children. The clinical picture. *J. Nerv. Ment. Dis., 168*(10), 604–10.

Stewart, S. H., Finn, P. R., & Pihl, R. O. (1990, Mar.). The effects of alcohol on the cardiovascular stress response in men at high risk for alcoholism: A dose response study. Paper presented at the annual meeting of the Canadian Psychological Association, Ottawa.

Stierlin, H. (1973). A family perspective on adolescent runaways. *Men. Hlth. Dig., 5*(10), 1–4.

Stiles, W. B., & Shapiro, D. A., (1989). Abuse of the drug metaphor in psychotherapy process-outcome research. *Clin. Psychol. Rev., 9,* 521–43.

Stiles, W. B., Shapiro, D. A., & Elliott, R. (1986). "Are all psychotherapies equivalent?" *Amer. Psychol., 41,* 165–80.

Stokes, P. E., & Sikes, C. R. (1987). Hypothalamic-pituitary-adrenal axis in affective disorders. In H. Y. Meltzer (Ed.), *Psychopharmacology: A third generation of progress.* (pp. 589–607) New York: Raven Press.

Stoller, R. J. (1974). *Sex and gender (Vol. 1): The development of masculinity and femininity.* New York: Jason Aronson.

Stone, A. A., Cox, D. S., Valdimarsdottir, H., Jandorf, N., & Neale, J. M. (1987). Evidence that secretory IgA antibody is associated with daily mood. *J. Pers. Soc. Psychol. 52,* 988–93.

Stone, G. C., Weiss, S. M., Matarazzo, J. D., Miller, N. E., Rodin, J., Belar, C. D., Follick, M. J., & Singer, J. E. (Eds.), (1987). *Health psychology: A discipline and a profession.* Chicago: University of Chicago Press.

Stone, L. J., & Hokanson, J. E. (1969). Arousal reduction via self-punitive behavior. *J. Pers. Soc. Psychol., 12,* 72–79.

Stone, M. H. (1990). Treatment of borderline patients: A pragmatic approach. *Psychiat. Clin. N. Amer., 13,* 265–82.

Stone, S. (1937). Psychiatry through the ages. *J. Abnorm. Soc. Psychol., 32,* 131–60.

Strack, S., & Coyne, J. C. (1983). Social confirmation of dysphoria: Shared and private reactions to depression. *J. Pers. Soc. Psychol., 44,* 798–806.

Strang, J. P. (1989). Gastrointestinal disorders. In S. Cheren (Ed.), *Psychosomatic medicine: Theory, physiology, and practice* (Vol. 2, pp. 427–502). Madison, CT: International Universities Press.

Strange, R. E., & Brown, D. E., Jr. (1970). Home from the wars. *Amer. J. Psychiat., 127,*(4), 488–92.

Strauss, T. S. (1979). Social and cultural influences on psychopathology. *Annu. Rev. Psychol., 30*(4), 397–415.

Stravynski, A., Lesage, A., Marcouiller, M., & Elie, R. (1989). A test of the therapeutic mechanism in social skills training with avoidant personality disorder. *J. Nerv. Ment. Dis., 177,* 739–44.

Strayer, R., & Ellenhorn, L. (1975). Vietnam veterans: A study exploring adjustment patterns and attitudes. *Journal of Social Issues, 31,* 81–93.

Strayhorn, J. M. (1982). *Foundations of clinical psychiatry.* Chicago: Year Book Medical Publishers.

Strean, H. S. (1985). *Resolving resistances in psychotherapy.* New York: Wiley Interscience.

Streissguth, A. P. (1976). Maternal alcoholism and the outcome of pregnancy: A review of the fetal alcohol syndrome. In M. Greenblatt & M. A. Schuckit (Eds.), *Alcoholism: Problems in women and children.* New York: Grune & Stratton.

Strine, G. (1971, Mar. 30). Compulsive gamblers pursue elusive dollar forever. *Los Angeles Times,* III, 1–6.

Strober, M. (1986). Anorexia nervosa: history and psychological concepts. In K. D. Brownell & J. P. Foreyt (Eds.), *Handbook of eating disorders* (pp. 231–46). New York: Basic.

Stroebe, M. S., & Stroebe, W. (1983). Who suffers more? Sex differences in health risks of the widowed. *Psychol. Bull., 93*(2), 279–301.

Strupp, H. H. (1981). Toward a refinement of time-limited dynamic psychotherapy. In S. H. Budman (Ed.), *Forms of brief therapy.* New York: Guilford Press.

Strupp, H. H., & Binder, J. L. (1984). *Psychotherapy in a new key: A guide to time-limited dynamic psychotherapy.* New York: Basic Books.

Strupp, H. H., Hadley, S. W., & Gomes-Schwartz, B. (1977). *Psychotherapy for better or worse: An analysis of the problem of negative effects.* New York: Jason Aronson.

Stuart, R. B. (1967). Behavioral control of overeating. *Beh. Res. Ther., 5,* 357–65.

Stuart, R. B. (1971a). Behavioral contracting within the families of delinquents. *Journal of Behavior Therapy and Experimental Psychiatry, 2,* 1–11.

Stuart, R. B. (1971b). A three-dimensional program for the treatment of obesity. *Beh. Res. Ther., 9,* 177–86.

Stunkard, A., D'Aquili, E., Fox, S., & Filion, R. D. L. (1972). Influence of social class on obesity and thinness in children. *JAMA, 221,* 579–84.

Sturgis, E. T., & Adams, H. E. (1978). The right to treatment: Issues in the treatment of homosexuality. *J. Cons. Clin. Psychol., 46*(1), 165–69.

Sturgis, E. T., & Meyer, V. (1981). Obsessive-compulsive disorders. In S. M. Turner, K. S. Calhoun, & H. E. Adams (Eds.), *Handbook of clinical behavior therapy.* New York: Wiley.

Sturt, E. (1986). Application of survival analysis to the inception of dementia. *Psychol. Med., 16,* 583–93.

Su, C. V., Lin, S., Wang, Y. T., Li, C. H. Hung, L. H., Lin, C. S., & Lin, B. C. (1978). Effects of B-endorphin on narcotic abstinence syndrome in man. *Taiwan I Hoven Hui Tsa Chih, 77,* 133–41.

Suddath, R. L., Christison, G. W., Torrey, E. F., Casanova, M. F., & Weinberger, D. R. (1990). Anatomical abnormalities in the brains of monozygotic twins discordant for schizophrenia. *New Engl. J. Med., 322,* 789–94.

Sue, D., & Sue, S., (1987). Cultural factors in the clinical assessment of Asian Americans. *J. Cons. Clin. Psychol., 55,* 479–87.

Sulkunen, P. (1976). Drinking patterns and the level of alcohol consumption: An international overview. In R. I. Gibbons et al. (Eds.), *Research advances in alcohol and drug problems* (Vol. 3). New York: Wiley.

Sullivan, H. S. (1953). In H. S. Perry & M. L. Gawel (Eds.), *The interpersonal theory of psychiatry.* New York: Norton.

Sullivan, H. S. (1956). *Clinical studies in psychiatry.* New York: Norton.

Sullivan, J. P., & Batareh, G. J. (1973). Educational therapy with the severely retarded. *The Training School Bulletin, 70*(1), 5–9.

Summers, F. (1979). Characteristics of new patient admissions to aftercare. *Hosp. Comm. Psychiat., 30*(3), 199–202.

Summit, R., & Kryso, J. (1978). Sexual abuse of children: A clinical spectrum. *Amer. J. Orthopsychiat., 48,* 237–51.

Sundberg, N. D., & Tyler, L. E. (1962). *Clinical psychology.* New York: Appleton-Century-Crofts.

Surwit, R. S., Shapiro, D., & Good, M. L. (1978). Comparison of cardiovascular biofeedback, neuromuscular biofeedback, and meditation in the treatment of borderline essential hypertension. *J. Cons. Clin. Psychol., 46,* 252–53.

Suter, B. (1976). Suicide and women. In B. B. Wolman & H. H. Krauss (Eds.), *Between survival and suicide* (pp. 129–61). New York: Gardner.

Sutker, P. B., Archer, R. P., & Kilpatrick, D. G. (1979). Sociopathy and antisocial behavior: Theory and treatment. In S. M. Turner, K. S. Calhoun, & H. E. Adams (Eds.), *Handbook of clinical behavior therapy.* New York: Wiley.

Sutker, P. B., Galina, H., & West, J. A. (1990). Trauma-induced weight loss and cognitive deficits among former prisoners of war. *J. Cons. Clin. Psychol., 58,* 323–328.

Svanum, S., & Schladenhauffen, J. (1986). Lifetime and recent alcohol consumption among male alcoholics. *J. Nerv. Ment. Dis., 174*(4), 214–20.

Svrakic, D. M. (1990). The functional dynamics of the narcissistic personality. *Amer. J. Psychother., 44,* 189–203.

Swadi, H., & Zeitlin, H. (1988). Peer influence and adolescent substance abuse: A promising side? *Brit. J. Addiction, 83*(2), 153–57.

Swanson, D. W. (1968). Adult sexual abuse of children: The man and circumstances. *Dis. Nerv. Sys., 29*(10), 677–83.

Swanson, D. W., Bohnert, P. J., & Smith, J. A. (1970). *The paranoid.* Boston: Little, Brown.

Swedo, S. E., Rapoport, J. L., Leonard, H., Lenane, M., & Cheslow, D. (1989). Obsessive-compulsive disorder in children and adolescents: Clinical phenomenology of 70 consecutive cases. *Arch. Gen. Psychiat., 46,* 335–41.

Swenson, C. R., & Wood, M. J. (1990). Issues involved in combining drugs with psychotherapy for the borderline patient. *Psychiat. Clin. N. Amer. 13,* 297–306.

Switzer, E. (1974). Female sexuality. *Fam. Hlth., 6*(3), 34–36, 38.

Symonds, M. (1976). The rape victim. Psychological patterns of response. *American Journal of Psychoanalysis, 36*(1), 27–34.

Szapocznik, J., Perez-Vidal, A., Brickman, A. L., Foote, F. H., Santisteban, D., Hervis, O., & Kurtines, W. M. (1988). Engaging adolescent drug abusers and their families in treatment: A strategic structural systems approach. *J. Cons. Clin. Psychol., 56,* 552–57.

Szasz, T. S. (1961). *The myth of mental illness.* New York: Harper & Row.

Szasz, T. S. (1963). *Law, liberty, and psychiatry.* New York: Macmillan.

Szasz, T. S. (1970). *The manufacture of madness.* New York: Harper & Row.

Szasz, T. S. (1976). The ethics of suicide. In B. B. Wolman & H. H. Krauss (Eds.), *Between survival and suicide* (pp. 163–85). New York: Gardner.

Szmukler, G. I., & Russell, G. F. M. (1986). Outcome and prognosis of anorexia nervosa. In K. D. Brownell & J. P. Foreyt (Eds.), *Handbook of eating disorders* (pp. 283–300). New York: Basic.

Tacke, U. (1990). Fluoxetine: An alternative to the tricyclics in the treatment of major depression. *Amer. J. Med. Sci., 298,* 126–29.

Talbott, J. A. (1985a). Community care for the chronically mentally ill. *Psychiat. Clin. N. Amer., 8,* 437–48.

Talbott, J. A. (1985b, Apr 19.) Psychiatrists must unify to survive. *Psychiat. News,* 14.

Talley, P. F., Strupp, H. H., & Morey, L. C. (1990). Matchmaking in psychotherapy: Patient-therapist dimensions and their impact on outcome. *J. Cons. Clin. Psychol., 58,* 182–88.

Tardiff, K. (1984). Characteristics of assaultive patients in private psychiatric hospitals. *Amer. J. Psychiat., 141,* 1232–35.

Tardiff, K., & Koenigsberg, H. W. (1985). Assaultive behavior among psychiatric outpatients. *Amer. J. Psychiat., 142*(8), 960–63.

Tardiff, K., & Sweillam, A. (1982). Assaultive behavior among chronic inpatients. *Amer. J. Psychiat., 139,* 212–15.

Tarjan, G., & Eisenberg, L. (1972). Some thought on the classification of mental retardation in the United States of America. *Amer. J. Psychiat.,* Suppl., *128*(11), 14–18.

Tarjan, G., Wright, S. W., Eyman, R. K., & Keeran, C. V. (1973). Natural history of mental retardation: Some aspects of epidemiology. *Amer. J. Ment. Def., 77*(4), 369–79.

Tarler-Beniolo, L. (1978). The role of relaxation in biofeedback training: A critical review of the literature. *Psychol. Bull., 85*(4), 727–55.

Tarter, R. E. (1988). Are there inherited behavioral traits that predispose to substance abuse? *J. Cons. Clin. Psychol., 56,* 189–196.

Tarver, S. G., & Hallahan, D. P. (1974). Attention deficits in children with teaming disabilities: A review. *J. Learn. Dis., 7*(9), 560–69.

Tasto, D. L., & Hinkle, J. E. (1973). Muscle relaxation treatment for tension headaches. *Beh. Res. Ther., 11,* 347–50.

Tavel, M. E. (1962). A new look at an old syndrome: Delirium tremens. *Arch. Int. Med., 109,* 129–34.

Taves, I. (1969). Is there a sleepwalker in the house? *Today's Health, 47*(5), 41, 76.

Taylor, A. J. W. (1989). *Disasters and disaster stress.* New York: AMS Press.

Telch, M. J. (1981). The present status of outcome studies: A reply to Frank. *J. Cons. Clin. Psychol., 49*(3), 472–75.

Teplin, L.A. (1990a). The prevalence of severe mental disorder among male urban jail detainees: A comparison with the epidemiologic catchment area program. *Amer. J. Pub. Hlth., 80,* 663–69.

Teplin, L. A. (1990b). Detecting disorder: The treatment of mental illness among jail detainees. *J. Cons. Clin. Psychol., 58,* 233–36.

Thacher, M. (1978, Apr.). First steps for the retarded. *Human Behav.*

Thase, M. E., Frank, E., & Kupfer, D. J. (1985). Biological processes in major depression. In E. E. Beckham & W. R. Leber (Eds.), *Handbook of depression: Treatment, assessment, and research* (pp. 816–913). Homewood, IL: Dorsey Press.

Theodor, L. H., & Mandelcorn, M. S. (1973). Hysterical blindness: A case report and study using a modern psychophysical technique. *J. Abnorm. Psychol., 82*(3), 552–53.

Thibaut, J. W., & Kelley, H. H. (1959). *The social psychology of groups.* New York: Wiley.

Thomas, A., & Chess, S. (1977). *Temperament and development.* New York: Brunner/Mazel.

Thomas, A., Chess, S., & Birch, H. G. (1968). *Temperament and behavior disorders in children.* New York: New York University Press.

Thompson, J. C. (1982). The role of surgery in peptic ulcer. *New Engl. J. Med., 307,* 550–51.

Thompson, N. L., Jr., & McCandless, B. R., & Strickland, B. R. (1971). Personal adjustment of male and female homosexuals and heterosexuals. *J. Abnorm. Psychol., 78*(2), 237–40.

Tiefer, L., & Melman, A. (1989). Comprehensive evaluation of erectile dysfunction and medical treatments. In S. R. Leiblum & R. C. Rosen (Eds.), *Principles and practice of sex therapy* (2nd ed., pp. 207–36). New York: Guilford.

Tien, A. Y., & Anthony, J. C. (1990). Epidemiological analysis of alcohol and drug use as risk factors for psychotic experiences. *J. Nerv. Ment. Dis., 178,* 473–80.

Tienari, P., Lahti, I., Sorri, A., Naarala, M., Moring, J., Wahlberg, K.–E., & Wynne, L. C. (1987). The Finnish adoptive family study of schizophrenia. *Journal of Psychiatric Research, 21,* 437–45.

Tienari, P., Sorri, A., Lahti, I., Naarala, M., Wahlberg, K.–E., Pohjola, J., & Moring, J. (1985). Interaction of genetic and psychosocial factors in schizophrenia. *Acta Psychiatr. Scandin.* (Suppl. No. 319), *71,* 19–30.

Time. (1966, June 17). From shocks to stop sneezes, p. 72.

Time. (1974, Apr. 22). Alcoholism: New victims, new treatment. *103*(16), pp. 75–81.

Time. (1981, May 4). Stomping and whomping galore, pp. 73–74.

Time. (1983, Apr. 18). Ailing schoolgirls. *121*(16), p. 52.

Tinbergen, N. (1974). Ethology and stress disease. *Science, 185*(4145), 20–27.

Tizard, B., & Rees, J. (1975). The effect of early institutional rearing on the behavior problems and affectional relationships of four-year-old children. *J. Child Psychol. Psychiat., 16*(1), 61–73.

Tobler, N. S. (1986). Meta-analysis of 143 adolescent drug prevention programs: Quantitative outcome results of program participation compared to a control or comparison group. *Journal of Drug Issues, 16,* 537–68.

Toffler, A. (1970). *Future shock.* New York: Random House.

Tollison, C. D., & Adams, H. E. (1979). *Sexual disorders.* New York: Gardner Press.

Tollison, C. D., Adams, H. E., & Tollison, J. W. (1979). Cognitive and physiological measurement of sexual arousal in homosexual, bisexual, and heterosexual males. *J. Behav. Assess., 1,* 305–14.

Tomarken, A. J., Mineka, S., & Cook, M. (1989). Fear-relevant selective associations and covariation bias. *J. Abnorm. Psychol., 98,* 381–94.

Torrey, E. F. (1973). Is schizophrenia universal? An open question. *Schizo. Bull., 7,* 53–59.

Torrey, E. F. (1974). *The death of psychiatry.* New York: Penguin Books.

Torrey, E. F. (1979). Epidemiology. In L. Bellak (Ed.), *Disorders of the schizophrenic syndrome.* New York: Basic Books.

Torrey, E. F., et al. (1984). Endemic psychosis in western Ireland. *Amer. J. Psychiat., 141,* 966–70.

Tripp, C. A. (1975). *The homosexual matrix.* New York: McGraw-Hill.

Tronick, E. Z., & Cohn, J. F. (1989). Infant-mother face-to-face interaction: Age and gender differences in coordination and miscoordination. *Child Develop., 59,* 85–92.

Trull, T. J., Widiger, T. A., & Frances, A. (1987). Covariation of criteria sets for avoidant, schizoid, and dependent personality disorders. *Amer. J. Psychiat., 144,* 767–71.

Tseng, W. S. (1973). The development of psychiatric concepts in traditional Chinese medicine. *Arch. Gen. Psychiat., 29*(4), 569–75.

Tuckman, J., Kleiner, R., & Lavell, M. (1959). Emotional content of suicide notes. *Amer. J. Psychiat. 116,* 59–63.

Tuma, J. (1989). Mental health services for children: The state of the art. *Amer. Psychol., 44,* 188–99.

Turk, D. (1974). *Cognitive control of pain: A skills training approach.* Unpublished manuscript, University of Waterloo, Ontario, Canada.

Turner, R. K., & Taylor, P. D. (1974). Conditioning treatment of nocturnal enuresis in adults: Preliminary findings. *Behav. Res. Ther., 12,* 41–52.

Turner, S. M., Beidel, D. C., & Costello, A. (1987). Psychopathology in the offspring of anxiety disorder patients. *J. Cons. Clin. Psychol., 55,* 229–35.

Turner, S. M., Beidel, D. C., & Nathan, R. S. (1985). Biological factors in obsessive-compulsive disorders. *Psychol. Bull.* 97, 430–50.

Tyor, P. L., & Bell, L. V. (1984). *Caring for the retarded in America: A history.* Westport, CT: Greenwood Press.

Tyrer, P. (1988). What's wrong with DSM III personality disorders? *Journal of Personality Disorders, 2,* 281–91.

U.S. Committee for Refugees. (1990). *Refugee Reports,* Vol. XI, No. 12. Washington, DC.

U.S. Department of Health and Human Services. (1988). *The Health Consequences of Smoking: Nicotine addiction.* Public Health Service, Office on Smoking and Health, Maryland.

U.S. Department of Health and Human Services. (1989). *Health United States 1988.* National Center for Health Statistics, Washington, DC: U.S. Government Printing Office.

U.S. Department of Health and Human Services. (1989). *Reducing the Consequences of Smoking: 25 years of Progress.* Public Health Service, Office on Smoking and Health, Maryland.

U.S. Department of Health, Education, and Welfare. (1974). *Alcohol and health.* Morris E. Chafetz, Chairman of the Task Force. Washington, DC: U.S. Government Printing Office.

U.S. Department of Health, Education and Welfare. (1978). *The alcoholism report: The authoritative newsletter for professionals.* Washington, DC: U.S. Government Printing Office, 7(3), 2.

U.S. Department of Justice. (1987). *Jail inmates 1986.* Bureau of Justice Statistics, Washington, DC: U.S. Government Printing Office.

Uchida, I. A. (1973). Paternal origin of the extra chromosome in Down's syndrome. *Lancet, 2*(7840), 1258.

Uhde, T. W., Bierer, L. M., & Post, R. M. (1985). Caffeine-induced escape from dexamethasone suppression. *Arch. Gen. Psychiat., 42,* 737.

Uhlenhuth, E. (1973, Feb. 7). Free therapy said to be helpful to Chicago train wreck victim. *Psychiat. News, 8*(3), 1, 27.

Ullmann, L. P., & Krasner, L. (1975). *Psychological approach to abnormal behavior* (2nd ed.). Englewood Cliffs, NJ: Prentice–Hall.

Umana, R. F., Gross, S. J., & McConville, M. T. (1980). *Crisis in the family.* New York: Gardner Press.

Uniform Crime Reports. (1989). *Federal Bureau of Investigation, U. S. Department of Justice.* U. S. Government Printing Office.

United Press International. (1982, Oct. 24). "Tylenol hysteria" hits 200 at football game. *Chicago Tribune,* Sec. 1, p. 4.

Ursano, R.J., Boydstun, J. A., & Wheatley, R. D., (1981). Psychiatric illness in U.S. Air Force Vietnam prisoners of war: A five-year follow-up. *Amer. J. Psychiat. 138*(3), 310–14.

Vaillant, G. E. (1975). Sociopathy as a human process: A viewpoint. *Arch. Gen. Psychiat., 32*(2), 178–83.

Vaillant, G. E., & Schnurr, P. (1988). What is a case? *Arch. Gen. Psychiat., 45,* 313–19.

Valenstein, E. S. (Ed.). (1980). *The psychosurgery debate: Scientific, legal, and ethical perspectives.* San Francisco: W. H. Freeman.

Valenstein, E. S. (1986). *Great and desperate cures.* New York: Basic Books.

Vallacher, R. R., Wegner, D. M., & Hoine, H. (1980). A postscript on application. In D. Megner & R. R. Vallacher (Eds.), *The sell in social psychology.* New York: Oxford University Press.

Van Broeckhoven, C., Genthe, A. M., Vandenberghe, A., Horsthemke, B. et al. (1987). Failure of familial Alzheimer's disease to segregate with the A4-amyloid gene in several European families. *Nature, 329,* 153–55.

VandenBos, G. R. (1986). Psychotherapy research: A special issue. *Amer. Psychol., 41,* 111–12.

Vandereycken, W. (1982). Paradoxical strategies in a blocked sex therapy. *Amer. J. Psychother., 36,* 103–8.

Vasiljeva, O. A., Kornetov, N. A., Zhankov, A. I., & Reshetnikov, V. I. (1989). Immune function in psychogenic depression. *Amer. J. Psychiat., 146,* 284–85.

Vaughn, C. E., & Leff, J. P. (1976). The influence of family and social factors on the course of psychiatric illness: A comparison of schizophrenic and depressed neurotic patients. *Brit. J. Psychiat., 129,* 125–37.

Vaughn, C.E., Snyder, K. S., Jones, S., Freeman, W. B., & Falloon, I. R. H. (9184). Family factors in schizophrenic relapse: Replication in California of British research on expressed emotion. *Arch. Gen. Psychiat., 41,* 1169–77.

Vega, W. A., & Rumbaut, R. G. (1991). Reasons of the heart: Ethnic minorities and mental health. *Annual Review of Sociology, 17.*

Velez, C. N. & Cohen, P. (1987). Suicidal behavior and ideation in a community sample of children: Maternal and youth reports. *Journal of the American Academia of Child and Adolescent Psychiatry, 27,* 349–56.

Vellutino, F. R. (1987). Linguistic and cognitive correlates of learning disability: Review of three reviews. In S. J. Ceci (Ed.), *Handbook of cognitive, social and neuropsychological aspects of learning disabilities* (Vol. 1, pp. 317–35). Hillsdale, NJ: Erlbaum.

Verhulst, J. H., Van Der Lee, J. H., Akkerhuis, G. W., Sanders-Woudstra, J. A. R., Timmer, F. C., & Donkhorst, I. D. (1985). The prevalence of nocturnal enuresis: Do

DSM–III criteria need to be changed: A brief research report. *J. Child Psychol. Psychiat., 26*(6), 983–93.

Viglione, D. J., & Exner, J. E. (1983). Current research on the Comprehensive Rorschach System. In J. N. Butcher & C. D. Spielberger (Eds.), *Advances in personality assessment* (Vol. 4). New York: Lawrence Erlbaum and Associates.

Viney, W., & Bartsch, K. (1984). Dorthea Lynde Dix: Positive or negative influence on the development of treatment for the mentally ill. *Social Science Journal, 21,* 71–82.

Viscott, D. S. (1970). A musical idiot savant. *Psychiatry, 33*(4), 494–515.

Volkmar, F. R., Hoder, E. L., & Cohen, D. J. (1985). Compliance, "negativism," and the effects of treatment structure in autism: A naturalistic behavioral study. *J. Child Psychol. Psychiat., 26*(6), 865–77.

Wachtel, P. L. (1977). *Psychoanalysis and behavior therapy: Toward an integration.* New York: Basic Books.

Wachtel, P. L. (1982). What can dynamic therapies contribute to behavior therapy? *Behav. Ther., 13,* 594–609.

Wadden, T. A., Luborsky, L., Greer, S., & Crits-Christopher, P. (1985). The behavioral treatment of essential hypertension: An update and comparison with pharamacological treatment. *Clin. Psychol. Rev., 4,* 403–29.

Wagener, D. K., & Cromwell, R. L. (1984). Schizophrenia: A right and just war. (Review of *Schizophrenia: The epigenetic puzzle,* by I. I. Gottesman & J. Shields.) *Contemp. Psychol., 29,* 110–15.

Wagner, G. (1981). Methods for differential diagnosis of psychogenic and organic erectile failure. In G. Wagner, & R. Green (Eds.), *Impotence: Physiological, psychological, surgical diagnosis and treatment.* New York: Plenum.

Wagner, G., & Green, R. (Eds.). (1981). *Impotence: Physiological, psychological, surgical diagnosis and treatment.* New York: Plenum.

Wahler, R. G. (1980). The insular mother: Her problems in parent-child treatment. *J. Appl. Beh. Anal., 13,* 207–19.

Wahler, R. G., Hughey, J. B., & Gordon, J. S. (1981). Chronic patterns of mother-child coercion: Some differences between insular and noninsular families. *Analysis and Intervention in Developmental Disorders, 1,* 145–56.

Walinder, J. (1968). Transsexualism: Definition, prevalence, and sex distribution. *Acta Psychiatr. Scandin., 203,* 255–58.

Wallerstein, J. S. (1984). Children of divorce: Preliminary report of a ten-year follow-up of young children. *Amer. J. Orthopsychiat., 54,* 444–58.

Wallerstein, J. S., & Kelly, J. B. (1980). Surviving the breakup: How children and parents cope with divorce. New York: Basic Books.

Wallerstein, R. S. (1989). The psychotherapy research project of the Menninger Foundation: An overview. *J. Cons. Clin. Psychol., 57,* 195–205.

Walsh, T. B. (1980). The endocrinology of anorexia nervosa. *Psychiat. Clin. N. Amer., 3*(2), 299–312.

Ward, A. J. (1978). Early childhood autism and structural therapy: Outcome after 3 years. *J. Cons. Clin. Psychol., 46,* 586–87.

Warnes, H. (1973). The traumatic syndrome. *Ment. Hlth. Dig., 5*(3), 33–34.

Warrington, E. K., & Weiskrantz, L. (1973). An analysis of short-term and long-term memory defects in man. In J. A. Deutsch (Ed.), *The psychological basis of memory.* New York: Academic Press.

Watkins, C., Gilbert, J. E., & Bass, W. (1969). The persistent suicidal patient. *Amer. J. Psychiat., 125,* 1590–93.

Watson, S., & Akil, H. (1979). Endorphins: Clinical issues. In R. Pickens & L. Heston (Eds.), *Psychiatric factors in drug abuse.* New York: Grune & Stratton.

Watt, N. F., Anthony, E. J., Wynne, L. C., & Rolf, J. E. (Eds.). (1984). *Children at risk for schizophrenia: A longitudinal perspective.* Cambridge: Cambridge University Press.

Weary, G., & Mirels, H. L. (1982). *Integrations of clinical and social psychology.* New York: Oxford University Press.

Wechsler, D. (1981). *Manual for the Wechsler Adult Intelligence Scale.* New York: Psychological Corporation.

Wehr, T. A., & Rosenthal, N. E. (1989). Seasonality and affective illness. *Amer. J. Psychiat., 146,* 829–39.

Wehr, T. A., Jacobsen, F. M., Sack, D. A., Arendt, J., Tamarkin, L., & Rosenthal, N. E. (1986). Phototherapy of seasonal affective disorder. *Arch. Gen. Psychiat., 43,* 870–75.

Weinberg, M., & Williams, C. J. (1974). *Male homosexuals: Their problems and adaptations in three societies.* New York: Oxford University Press.

Weinberger, D. R. (1984). Brain disease and psychiatric illness: When should a psychiatrist order a CAT scan? *Amer. J. Psychiat., 141,* 1521–27.

Weinberger, D. R., DeLisi, L. E., Perman, G. P., Targum, S., & Wyatt, R. J. (1982). Computed tomography in schizophreniform disorder and other acute psychiatric disorders. *Arch. Gen. Psychiat., 39,* 778–83.

Weiner, H. (1977). *Psychobiology and human disease.* New York: Elsevier.

Weiner, H., & Fawzy, F. I. (1989). An integrative model of health, disease, and illness. In S. Cheren (Ed.), *Psychosomatic medicine: Theory, physiology, and practice* (Vol. 1, pp. 9–44). Madison, CT: International Universities Press.

Weiner, H. F., Thaler, M., Reiser, M. F., & Mirsky, I. A. (1957). Etiology of duodenal ulcer: I. Relation of specific psychological characteristics to rate of gastric secretion (Serum pepsenogen). *Psychosom. Med., 19,* 1–10.

Weiner, R. (1982). Another look at an old controversy. *Contemporary Psychiatry, 1,* 61–62.

Weinstein, A. S. (1983). The mythical readmissions explosion. *Amer. J. Psychiat., 140*(3), 332–35.

Weintraub, M., & Frankel, J. (1977). Sex differences in parent-infant interaction during free play, departure, and separation. *Child Develop., 48,* 1240–48.

Weisenberg, M. (1977). Pain and pain control. *Psychol. Bull., 84,* 1008–44.

Weiss, B., Weisz, J. R., & Bromfield, R. (1986). Performance of retarded and nonretarded persons on information-processing tasks: Further tests of the similar structure hypothesis. *Psychol. Bull., 100,* 157–75.

Weiss, G. (1981). Controversial issues of the pharmacotherapy of the hyperactive child. *Canad. J. Psychiat., 26*(6), 385–92.

Weiss, G., & Hechtman, L. (1979). The hyperactive child syndrome. *Science, 205,* 1348–54.

Weiss, G., Hechtman, L., Perlman, T., Hopkins, J., & Wener, A. (1979). Hyperactives as young adults: A controlled prospective ten-year follow-up of 75 children. *Arch. Gen. Psychiat., 36,* 675–81.

Weiss, J. M. (1974). Cited in Depressing situations. *Sci. News, 105*(14), 224.

Weiss, J. M. (1984). Behavioral and psychological influences on gastrointestinal pathology: Experimental techniques and findings. In W. D. Gentry (Ed.), *Handbook of behavioral medicine,* (pp. 174–221). New York: Guilford.

Weiss, S. M., Herd, J. A., & Fox. B. H. (1981). *Perspectives on behavioral medicine.* New York: Academic Press.

Weiss, T., & Engel, B. T. (1971). Operant conditioning of heart rate in patients with premature ventricular contractions. *Psychosom. Med., 33,* 301–21.

Weissman, M. M., Fox, K., & Klerman, G. L. (1973). Hostility and depression associated with suicide attempts. *Amer. J. Psychiat., 130*(4), 450–55.

Weissman, M. M., Gammon, D., John, K., Merikangas, K. R., Warner, V., Prusoff, B. A., & Sholomskas, D. (1987). Children of depressed parents. *Arch. Gen. Psychiat., 44,* 847–53.

Weissman, M. M., Leckman, J. F., Merikangas, K. R., Gammon, G. D., & Prusoff, B. A. (1984). Depression and anxiety disorders in parents and children: Results from the Yale family study. *Arch. Gen. Psychiat., 41,* 845–52.

Weissman, M. M., Pottenger, M., Kleber, H., Ruben, H. L., Williams, D., & Thompson, D. (1977). Symptom pattern in primary and secondary depression. *Arch. Gen. Psychiat., 34,* 854–62.

Wekstein, L. (1979). *Handbook of suicidology: Principles, problems, and practice.* New York: Brunner/Mazel.

Wellisch, D. K., & Trock, G. K., (1980). A three-year follow-up of family therapy. *International Journal of Family Therapy, 2*(3), 169–75.

Wells, C. E. (1979). Diagnosis of dementia. *Psychosomatics, 20,* 517–22.

Wells, C. F., & Stuart, I. R. (Eds.). (1981). *Self-destructive behavior in children and adolescents.* New York: Van Nostrand Reinhold.

Wenar, C. (1990). *Developmental psychopathology: From infancy through adolescence* (2nd ed.). New York: McGraw-Hill.

Wender, P. H., Kety, S. S., Rosenthal, D., Schulsinger, F., & Ortmann, J. (1986). Psychiatric disorders in the biological and adoptive families of adopted individuals with affective disorders. *Arch. Gen. Psychiat., 43,* 923–29.

Wender, P. H., Reimherr, F. W., & Wood, D. R. (1981). Attention deficit disorder (minimal brain dysfunction) in adults. *Arch. Gen. Psychiat., 38,* 449–56.

Wender, P. H., Rosenthal, D., Kety, S. S., Schulsinger, F., & Weiner, J. (1974). Cross-fostering: A research strategy for clarifying the role of genetic and experimential factors in the etiology of schizophrenia. *Arch. Gen. Psychiat., 30*(1), 121–28.

Wennerholm, M., & Lopez-Roig, L. (1983). Use of the MMPI with executives in Puerto Rico. Paper given at the *Eighth Annual Conference on Personality Assessment,* Copenhagen, Denmark.

Werry, J. S. (1979). The childhood psychosis. In H. C. Quay & J. S. Werry (Eds.), *Psychopathological disorders of childhood.* New York: Wiley.

Werry, J. S., & Quay, H. C. (1971). The prevalence of behavior symptoms in younger elementary school children. *Amer. J. Orthopsychiat., 41,* 136–43.

Wertham, F. (1949). *The show of violence.* New York: Doubleday.

West, J. (1976). *The woman said yes: Encounters with life and death.* New York: Harcourt Brace Jovanovich.

Wester, P., Eriksson, S., Forsell, A., Puu, G., & Adolfsson, R. (1988). Monoamine metabolite concentrations and cholinesterase activities in cerebrospinal fluid of progressive dementia patients: Relation to clinical parameters. *Acta Neurologica Scandinavica, 77,* 12–21.

Westermeyer, J. (1982a). Bag ladies in isolated cultures, too. *Behav. Today, 13*(21), 1–2.

Westermeyer, J. (1982b). *Poppies, pipes and people: Opium and its use in Laos.* Berkeley, CA: University of California Press.

Westermeyer, J., (1987). Public health and chronic mental illness. *Amer. J. Pub. Hlth., 77*(6), 667–68.

Westermeyer, J., Neider, J., & Callies, A. (1989). Psychosocial adjustment of Hmong refugees during their first decade in the United States. A longitudinal study. *J. Nerv. Ment. Dis., 177,* 132–39.

Westermeyer, J., Williams, C. L., & Nguyen, N. (Eds.). (1991). *Mental health and social adjustment: A guide to clinical and prevention services.* Washington, DC: U. S. Government Printing Office.

Whalen, C. K., & Henker, B. (1976). Psychostimulants and children: A review and analysis. *Psychol. Bull., 83,* 1113–30.

Whalen, C. K., Henker, B., Buhrmester, D., Hinshaw, S. P., Huber, A., & Laski, K. (1989). Does stimulant medication improve the peer status of hyperactive children? *J. Cons. Clin. Psychol., 57,* 545–49.

Whiffen, V. E., & Gotlib, I. H. (1989). Infants of postpartum depressed mothers: Temperament and cognitive status. *J. Abnorm. Psychol., 98,* 274–79.

White, A. D. (1986). *A history of the warfare of science with theology in Christendom.* New York: Appleton.

Whitehead, W. E., Winget, C., Fedoravicius, A. S., Wooley, S., & Blackwell, B. (1982). Learned illness behavior in patients with irritable bowel syndrome and peptic ulcers. *Digestive Diseases and Sciences, 27,* 202–08.

Whitehouse, P. J., et al. (1982). Alzheimer's disease and senile dementia: Loss of neurons in the basal forebrain. *Science, 215,* 1237–39.

Widiger, T. A., & Frances, A. (1985). Axis II personality disorders: Diagnostic and treatment issues. *Hosp. Comm. Psychiat., 36,* 619–27.

Widiger, T. A., Frances, A., & Trull, T. J. (1987). A psychometric analysis of social-interpersonal and cognitive-perceptual items for the schizotypal personality disorder. *Arch. Gen. Psychiat., 44,* 741–45.

Widiger, T. A., Frances, A., Warner, L., & Bloom, C. (1986). Diagnostic criteria for the Borderline and Schizotypal Personality Disorders. *J. Abnorm. Psychol., 95*(1), 43–51.

Widom, C. S. (1977). A methodology for studying noninstitutionalized psychopaths. *J. Cons. Clin. Psychol., 45,* 674–83.

Wiggins, J. S. (1982). Circumplex models of interpersonal behavior in clinical psychology. In P. C. Kendall & J. N. Butcher (Eds.), *Handbook of research methods in clinical psychology.* New York: Wiley Interscience.

Wilbur, R. S. (1973, June 2). In S. Auerbach (Ed.), POWs found to be much sicker than they looked upon release. *Los Angeles Times,* Part I, p. 4.

Williams, C. L., & Westermeyer, J. (1986). *Refugee mental health in resettlement countries.* New York: Hemisphere Press.

Williams, C. L., Solomon, S. D., & Bartone, P. (1988). Primary prevention in aircraft disasters: Integrating research and practice. *Amer. Psychol., 43,* 724–39.

Williams, J. A., Koegel, R. L., & Egel, A. L. (1981). Response-reinforcer relationships and improved learning in autistic children. *J. Appl. Beh. Anal., 14*(1), 53–60.

Williams, L. M., & Finkelhor, D., (1990). The characteristics of incestuous fathers: A review of recent studies. In W. L. Marshall, D. R. Laws, & H. E. Barbaree (Eds.), *Handbook of sexual assault* (pp. 231–56). New York: Plenum.

Williams, R. B., Jr. (1977). Headache. In R. B. Williams, Jr. & W. D. Gentry (Eds.), *Behavioral approaches to medical treatment* (pp. 41–53). Cambridge, MA: Ballinger.

Williams, R. B., Jr., Barefoot, J. C., & Shekelle, R. B. (1985). The health consequences of hostility. In Chesney, M. A., Goldston, S. E., & Rosenman, R. H. (Eds.), *Anger, hostility, and behavioral medicine* (pp. 173–85). New York: Hemisphere/McGraw-Hill.

Williams, R. B., Jr., & Gentry, W. D. (Eds.), (1977). *Behavioral approaches to medical treatment.* Cambridge, MA: Ballinger.

Williams, R. B., Jr., Haney, T. L., Lee, K. L., Kong, V., & Blumenthal, J. A. (1980). Type A behavior, hostility, and coronary atherosclerosis. *Psychosom. Med., 42,* 529–38.

Williams, S. L., Turner, S. M., & Peer, D. F. (1985). Guided mastery and performance desensitization treatments for severe acrophobia. *J. Cons. Clin. Psychol., 53,* 237–47.

Williams, S. L., & Zane, G. (1989). Guided mastery and stimulus exposure treatments for severe performance anxiety in agoraphobics. *Behav. Res. Ther., 27,* 237–45.

Williams, T. I. (1989). A social skills group for autistic children. *J. Autism Devel. Dis., 19,* 143–55.

Wing, J. K., & Bebbington, P. (1985). Epidemiology of depression. In E. E. Beckham & W. R. Leber (Eds.), *Handbook of depression: treatment, assessment, and research* (pp. 765–94). Homewood, IL: Dorsey Press.

Wing, L. (1980). Childhood autism and social class: A question of selection. *Brit. J. Psychiat., 137,* 410–17.

Wing, L. K., (1976). Diagnosis, clinical description and prognosis. In L. Wing (Ed.), *Early childhood autism.* London: Pergamon Press.

Wing, S., & Manton, K. G. (1983). The contribution of hypertension to mortality in the U.S.: 1968, 1977. *Amer. J. Pub. Hlth., 73*(2), 140–44.

Winick, M. (Ed.). (1976). *Malnutrition and brain development.* New York: Oxford University Press.

Winick, M., & Rosso, P. (1973). Effects of malnutrition on brain development. *Biology of Brain Dysfunction, 1,* 301–17.

Winokur, G. (1985). The validity of neurotic-reactive depression: New data and reappraisal. *Arch. Gen. Psychiat., 42,* 1116–22.

Winokur, G., Clayton, P. J., & Reich, T. (1969). *Manic depressive illness.* St. Louis: Mosby.

Winokur, G., & Pitts, F. N. (1964). Affective disorder: Is reactive depression an entity? *J. Nerv. Ment. Dis., 138,* 541–47.

Winsberg, B. G., Goldstein, S., Yepes, L. E., & Perel, J. M. (1975). Imipramine and electrocardiographic abnormalities in hyperactive children. *Amer. J. Psychiat., 132*(5), 542–45.

Winslow, R. (1990, May 14). Sandoz Corps Clozaril treats schizophrenia but can kill patients. *Wall Street Journal,* p. 1.

Winter, D. G. (1973). *The power motive.* New York: Free Press.

Winters, K. C., Weintraub, S., & Neale, J. M. (1981). Validity of MMPI code types in identifying DSM-III schizophrenics, unipolars, and bipolars. *J. Cons. Clin. Psychol., 49,* 486–87.

Wisniewski, H. M., Moretz, R. C., & Igbal, K. (1986). No evidence for aluminum in etiology and pathogenesis of Alzheimer's disease. *Neurobiology of Aging, 7,* 532–35.

Witzig, J. S. (1968). The group treatment of male exhibitionists. *Amer. J. Psychiat. 125,* 75–81.

Wolf, M., Risley, T., & Mees, H. (1964). Application of operant conditioning procedures to the behavior problems of an autistic child. *Behav. Res. Ther., 1,* 305–12.

Wolf, S. L., Nacht, M., & Kelly, J. L. (1982). EMG feedback training during dynamic movement for low back pain patients. *Behav. Ther., 13,* 395–406.

Wolfe, D. A. (1985). Child-abusive parents: An empirical review and analysis. *Psychol. Bull., 97,* 462–82.

Wolfe, D. A., Edwards, B., Manion, I., & Koverola, C. (1988). Early intervention for parents at risk of child abuse and neglect: A preliminary investigation. *J. Cons. Clin. Psychol., 56,* 34–39.

Wolfe, V. V., Gentile, C., & Wolfe, D. A. (1989). The impact of sexual abuse on children: A PTSD formulation. *Behav. Ther., 20,* 215–28.

Wolff, H. G. (1950). Life stress and cardiovascular disorders. *Circulation, 1,* 187–203.

Wolff, H. G. (1960). Stressors as a cause of disease in man. In J. M. Tanner (Ed.), *Stress and psychiatric disorder.* London: Oxford University Press.

Wolff, P. H. (1972). Ethnic differences in alcohol sensitivity. *Science, 175,* 449–50.

Wolff, W. M., & Morris, L. A. (1971). Intellectual personality characteristics of parents of autistic children. *J. Abnorm. Psychol., 77*(2), 155–61.

Wolkind, S. N. (1974). The components of "affectionless psychopathy" in institutionalized children. *J. Child Psychol. Psychiat., 15*(3), 215–20.

Wolpe, J. (1958). *Psychotherapy by reciprocal inhibition.* Stanford, CA: Stanford University Press.

Wolpe, J. (1969a). For phobia: A hair of the hound. *Psych. Today, 3*(1), 34–37.

Wolpe, J. (1969b). *The practice of behavior therapy.* New York: Pergamon.

Wood, C. (1986). The hostile heart. *Psych. Today, 20,* 10–12.

Wood, W., Rhodes, N., & Whelan, M. (1989). Sex differences in positive well-being: A consideration of emotional style and marital status. *Psychol. Bull., 106,* 249–64.

Woodruff, R. A., Guze, S. B., Clayton, P. J., & Carr, D. (1973). Alcoholism and depression. *Arch. Gen. Psychiat., 28*(1), 97–100.

Woods, B. T., Kinney, D. K., & Yurgelun-Todd, D. (1986). Neurologic abnormalities in schizophrenic patients and their families: I. Comparison of schizophrenic, bipolar, and substance abuse patients and normal controls. *Arch. Gen. Psychiat., 43,* 657–63.

Woods, S. W., Charney, D. S., Goodman, W. K., & Heninger, G. R. (1987). Carbon dioxide-induced anxiety: Behavioral, physiologic, and biochemical effects of 5% CO2 in panic disorder patients and 5 and 7.5% CO2 in healthy subjects. *Arch. Gen. Psychiat., 44,* 365–75.

Woodworth, R. S. (1920). *The Personal Data Sheet.* Chicago, IL: Stoelting Press.

Woody, G. E., McLellan, A. T., Luborsky, L., & O'Brien, C. P. (1985). Sociopathy and psychotherapy outcome. *Arch. Gen. Psychiat., 42,* 1081–86.

Worden, P. E. (1986). Prose comprehension and recall in disabled learners. In S. J. Ceci (Ed.), *Handbook of cognitive, social and neuropsychological aspects of learning disabilities,* (Vol. 1, pp. 241–62). Hillsdale, NJ: Erlbaum.

World Health Organization. (1974, Oct. 25). In W. Tuohy, World health agency zeroes in on suicide. *Los Angeles Times,* VI, 1-3.

World Health Organization. (1975). *Schizophrenia: A multinational study.* Geneva: Author.

World Health Organization. (1978a, Apr.). *Report of the director-general.* Geneva: Author.

World Health Organization. (1978b). *Mental disorders: Glossary and guide to their classification in accordance with the ninth revision of the International Classification of Diseases.* Geneva: Author.

World Health Organization. (1979). *International classification of diseases,* (9th ed.) (ICD-9). Geneva: Author.

World Health Organization. (1982). *EURO reports and studies.* Geneva: Author.

Worthington, E. R. (1978). Demographic and pre-service variables as predictors of post-military adjustment. In C. R. Figley (Ed.), *Stress disorders among Vietnam veterans.* New York: Brunner/Mazel.

Wortis, J. (1972). Comments on the ICD classification of mental retardation. *Amer. J. Psychiat., Suppl., 128*(11), 21–24.

Wortis, J. (Ed.). (1973). *Mental retardation and developmental disabilities: An annual review* (Vol. 5). New York: Brunner/Mazel.

Wortman, C. B., & Silver, R. C. (1989). The myths of coping with loss. *J. Cons. Clin. Psychol., 57,* 349–57.

Wright, L., Schaefer, A. B., & Solomons, G. (1979). *Encyclopedia of pediatric psychology.* Baltimore: University Park Press.

Wunsch-Hitzig, R. Gould, M. S., & Dohrenwend, B. P. (1980). Hypotheses about the prevalence of clinical maladjustment in children in the United States. In S. Salzinger, J. Antrobus, & J. Glick (Eds.), *The ecosystem of the "sick" child: Implications for classification and intervention for disturbed and mentally retarded children.* New York: Academic Press.

Wynne, L. C., Ryckoff, I. M., Day, J., & Hirsh, S. I. (1958). Pseudomutuality in the family relations of schizophrenics. *Psychiatry, 21,* 205–20.

Wynne, L. C., Toohey, M. L., & Doane, J. (1979). Family studies. In L. Bellak (Ed.), The *schizophrenic syndrome.* New York: Basic Books.

Yablonsky, L. (1975). Psychodrama lives. *Human Behav., 4,* 24–29.

Yager, J., Grant, I., & Bolus, R. (1984). Interaction of life events and symptoms in psychiatric patient and nonpatient married couples. *J. Nerv. Ment. Dis., 171*(1), 21–25.

Yap, P. M. (1951). Mental diseases peculiar to certain cultures: A survey of comparative psychiatry. *J. Ment. Sci., 97*(3), 313.

Yates, A. (1981). Narcissistic traits in certain abused children. *Amer. J. Orthopsychiat., 51,* 55–62.

Yates, E. P., Barbaree, H. E., & Marshall, W. L. (1984). Anger and deviant sexual arousal. *Behav. Ther., 15,* 287–94.

Yolles, S. F. (1967, Apr.). Quote from "Unraveling the mystery of schizophrenia." *Today's Health.*

Youth Suicide in the United States, 1970–1980. (1986). Centers for disease control. Atlanta, GA.

Yule, W., & Rutter, M. (1985). Reading and other learning difficulties. In M. Rutter & L. Hersov (Eds.), *Child and adolescent psychiatry: Modern approaches* (2nd ed., pp. 444–64). Oxford, UK: Blackwell.

Zahn, T. P., Rapoport, J. L., & Thompson, C. L. (1980). Autonomic and behavioral effects of dextroamphetamine and placebo in normal and hyperactive boys. *J. Abnorm. Child Psychol., 8*(2), 145–60.

Zeitlin, H. (1986). *The natural history of psychiatric disorder in childhood.* New York: Oxford University Press.

Zetlin, A., & Murtaugh, M. (1990). Whatever happened to those with borderline IQs? *Amer. J. Ment. Retard., 94,* 463–69.

Zigler, E., Abelson, W. D., Trickett, P. K., & Seitz, V. (1982). Is an intervention program necessary in order to improve economically disadvantaged children's IQ scores? *Child Develop., 53,* 340–48.

Zilberg, N. J., Weiss, D. S., & Horowitz, M. (1982). Impact of events scale: A cross validation study and some empirical evidence supporting a conceptual model of stress response syndromes. *J. Cons. Clin. Psychol., 50*(3), 407–14.

Zilbergeld, B., & Evans, M. (1980, Jan.). The inadequacy of Masters and Johnson. *Psych. Today,* 29–43.

Zilbergeld, B., & Kilmann, P. R. (1984). The scope and effectiveness of sex therapy. *Psychotherapy, 21,* 319–26.

Zilboorg, G., & Henry, G. W. (1941). *A history of medical psychology.* New York: Norton.

Zimbardo, P. G., Haney, C., Banks, W. C., & Jaffe, D. (1975). The psychology of imprisonment. Privation, power and pathology. In D. Rosenhan & P. London (Eds.), *Theory and research in abnormal psychology* (2nd ed., pp. 270–87). New York: Holt, Rinehart & Winston.

Zimmerman, M. (1983). Methodological issues in the assessment of life events: A review of issues and research. *Clin. Psychol. Rev., 3,* 339–70.

Zimmerman, M., Coryell, W., & Pfohl, B. (1986). The validity of the dexamethasone suppression test as a marker for endogenous depression. *Arch. Gen. Psychiat., 43,* 347–55.

Zimring, F. (1979). *American Youth Violence.* Chicago: University of Chicago Press.

Zinberg, N. E. (1980). The social setting as a control mechanism in intoxicant use. In D. J. Lettieri, M. Sayers, & H. W. Pearson (Eds.), *Theories on drug abuse: Selected contemporary perspectives.* Rockville, MD: National Institute on Drug Abuse.

Zis, A. P., & Goodwin, F. K. (1982). The amine hypothesis. In E. S. Paykel (Ed.), *Handbook of affective disorders.* New York: Guilford Press.

Zola, I. K. (1966). Culture and symptoms—An analysis of patients' presenting complaints. *American Sociological Review, 31,* 615–30.

Zucker, S. H., & Altman, R. (1973). An on-the-job training program for adolescent trainable retardates. *The School Bulletin, 70*(2), 106–10.

Zuckerman, M. (1972). *Manual and research report for the Sensation Seeking Scale (SSS).* Newark, DE: University of Delaware.

Zuckerman, M. (1978). Sensation seeking and psychopathy. In R. D. Hare and D. Schalling (Eds.), *Psychopathic behavior: Approaches to research.* New York: Wiley.

Zung, W. W. K. (1969). A cross-cultural survey of symptoms in depression. *Amer. J. Psychiat., 126*(1), 116–21.

Zung, W. W. K., & Green, R. L., Jr. (1974). Seasonal variations of suicide and depression. *Arch. Gen. Psychiat., 30*(1), 89–91.

Zwelling, S. S. (1985). *Quest for a cure.* Williamsburg, VA: The Colonial Williamsburg Foundation.

Acknowledgments

Photo Credits

Unless otherwise acknowledged, all photographs are the property of ScottForesman.

Front cover: (t) Hill Gallery, Birmingham, Michigan; **(c)** Collection de l'Art Brut, Lausanne; **(b)** Collection de la'Art Brut, Lausanne; **Back cover and spine:** Collection de l'Art Brut, Lausanne.

Chapter 1: 2, v Collection de l'Art Brut, Lausanne; **3** Dan McCoy/Rainbow; **5(t)** The Tate Gallery, London; **5(b)** Film Stills Archieve/The Museum of Modern Art, New York; **7** Rick Smolan; **8** Courtesy American Heritage Publishing; **9** Will & Deni McIntyre/Photo Researchers; **12** Bob Adelman; **15(t)** AP/Wide World; **15(b)** Bob Daemmrich/The Image Works; **16** Brad Bower/Picture Group; **18** M. Siluk/The Image Works; **20** Robert Brenner/Photo Edit; **22** Hank Morgan/Rainbow; **25** Dan McCoy/Rainbow. **Chapter 2: 28** Collection de l'Art Brut, Lausanne; **30** The Granger Collection, New York; **32** The Granger Collection, New York; **33** The Granger Collection, New York; **34** The Granger Collection, New York; **36(t)** *Removal of the Stone of Folly* by Brueghel/Giraudon/Art Resource, NY; **36 (b)** The Granger Collection, New York; **37** Sven Nackstrand/Gamma-Liaison; **38** The Granger Collection, New York; **39** The Bettmann Archive; **40(t)** Historical Pictures Service, Chicago; **40(b)** Mary Evans Picture Library; **42** The Trustees of Sir John Soane's Museum; **43** Ets J. E. Bulloz; **44** The Granger Collection, New York; **45(all)** Historical Pictures Service, Chicago; **46** Courtesy of the Psychiatric Museum, Saint Joseph Hospital; **47** Historical Pictures Service, Chicago; **48** Brown Brothers; **50** The Bettmann Archive. **Chapter 3: 54** The Prinzhorn Collection, University of Heidelberg; **57** Historical Pictures Service, Chicago; **59** Bouchard's Univ. of Minn. study/*Time* Magazine; **63** Painting/Wellcome Institute for the History of Medicine; **64** The Bettmann Archive; **65(l)** UPI/Bettmann; **65(r)** Culver Pictures; **66** Courtesy, Clark University Archives; **67** Laura Dwight/Peter Arnold, Inc.; **70(l)** UPI/Bettmann; **70(r)** Courtesy Dr. Margaret S. Mahler; **71** The Bettmann Archive; **72(l)** UPI/Bettmann; **72(c)** The Granger Collection, New York; **72(r)** Courtesy of Dr. B. F. Skinner; **76** Courtesy of John Dollard; **77(l)** Courtesy of Neal Miller; **77(c)** Photograph by Ralph Norman, courtesy of Brendan Mahler; **77(r)** Dr. Albert Bandura; **80(l)** The Bettmann Archive; **80(c)** Harvard University News Office; **80(r)** The Bettmann Archive; **81(tl)** The Bettmann Archive; **81(tr)** Hugh L. Wilkerson; **81(b)** Peter Frank/Tony Stone Worldwide; **82(l)** AP/Wide World; **82(c)** New York University; **82(r)** Association for the Advancement of Psychoanalysis of the Karen Horney Psychoanalytic Institute and Center, New York; **83(l)** Jon Erikson; **83(r)** William Alanson White Psychiatric Foundation, Washington, D.C.; **84** Henley & Savage/Tony Stone Worldwide; **85** Tom Campbell/Tony Stone Worldwide; **88** Institute for Intercultural Studies Inc., photo by Theodore Schwartz. **Chapter 4: 94** Hill Gallery, Birmingham, Michigan; **97** The Image Works; **98** Robert Brenner/Photo Edit; **100** D. W. Fawcett/Photo Researchers; **105** Myrleen Ferguson/Photo Edit; **106** Charles Gupton/Stock Boston; **109(all)** Patrick Ward/Discover Publications/Family Media; **110** Wallace Kirkland/*Life* Magazine Time Warner Inc.; **111(t)** Anthony Suau/Black Star; **112** AP/Wide World; **115** AP/Wide World; **116** George Goodwin/The Picture Cube; **117** Tony Freeman/Photo Edit; **120** Carol Palmer/The Picture Cube; **121** Abigail Heyman; **123** Robert Brenner/Photo Edit; **124** Mike Mazzaschi/Stock Boston; **128** Elizabeth Zuckerman/Photo Edit; **129** Don Smetzer/Tony Stone Worldwide; **131** Liane Enkelis/Stock Boston; **132** Michael O'Brien. **Chapter 5: 138** Collection de l'Art Brut, Lausanne; **140(l)** Jean-Claude LeJeune; **140(r)** Baldev/Sygma; **141** The Image Works; **144** Richard G. Shaw; **146** NYT Pictures; **148** R. Maiman/Sygma; **153** Ellis Herwig/The Picture Cube; **154** Michael Grecco/Stock Boston; **157** AP/Wide World; **160** R. Maiman/Sygma; **163** Rhoda Sidney/Photo Edit; **164** United States Coast Guard; **167** Larry Burrows/*Life* Magazine Time Warner Inc.; **170** Ira Wyman/Sygma; **172** U.S. Army Photo; **175** Ledru/Sygma; **176** Charles Crowell/Black Star. **Chapter 6: 180** Collection de l'Art Brut, Lausanne; **180** David C. Bitters/The Picture Cube; **184** Alvin H. Perlmutter Inc.; **186(l)** Rick Friedman/Black Star; **186(r)** The Image Works; **193** Alan Carey/The Image Works; **199** Custom Medical Stock Photo. All Rights Reserved; **201** The National Archives; **207** Susan Greenwood/Gamma-Liaison; **212** Carolyn Brown; **216** McCarten/Photo Edit; **222** Dr. Albert Bandura. **Chapter 7: 228** Collection de l'Art Brut, Lausanne; **231** Robert Frerck/Odyssey Productions, Chicago; **233** Jim Olive/Peter Arnold, Inc.; **235** Lennart Nilsson/Boehringer Ingelheim Zentrale GmbH; **238** David Lissy/The Picture Cube; **240** Robert Frerck/Odyssey Productions, Chicago; **241** Lou Lainey/Discover Publications/Family Media; **244** William Thompson/The Picture Cube; **248** Katrina Thomas/Photo Researchers; **250** Michael Philip Manheim/Picturesque formerly Southern Light; **257** Alvin H. Perlmutter Inc.; **258** Dan McCoy/Rainbow; **259** John Chiasson/Gamma-Liaison. **Chapter 8: 262, vi** Collection de l'Art Brut, Lausanne; **264** Michael Patrick/Picture Group; **266** Richard Hutchings/Photo Researchers; **270** Sandy Herring/The Picture Cube; **272** AP/Wide World; **273** Alvin H. Perlmutter Inc.; **275** Ari Mintz/*New York Newsday;* **279** Alvin H. Perlmutter Inc.; **282** Louis Fernandez/Black Star; **283** UPI/Bettmann; **287** J. Ross Baughman/Visions. **Chapter 9: 294, vii** Collection de l'Art Brut, Lausanne; **297** Paul Conklin/Photo Edit; **299** Alvin H. Perlmutter Inc.; **303** Mike Zerby/*Star Tribune;* **304** Jerry Waxhter/Focus On Sports; **307** Bob Daemmrich/Tony Stone Worldwide; **310(all)** Courtesy of Mrs. Francis M. Erdmann; **312** Leif Skoogfoors/Woodfin Camp & Associates; **318** D&I MacDonald/The Picture Cube; **325** Pamela Price/Picture Group; **327** Larry Milvehill/Photo Researchers; **332** Michael Abramson/Woodfin Camp & Associates; **335** Focus On Sports. **Chapter 10: 340** Collection de l'Art Brut, Lausanne; **342** Ellis Herwig/The Picture Cube; **347** Joel Gordon Photography; **349** Jim Wilson/Woodfin Camp & Associates; **350** Alvin H. Perlmutter Inc.; **354** Tony Korady/Sygma; **356** Peter Yates/Picture Group; **361** Caccavo; **363** Mary Ellen Mark; **366** U.S. Department of Health and Human Services; **369** Bob Mahoney; **373** Ethan Hoffman; **374** Ronald Sheridan/Ancient Art and Architecture Collection; **376** Laima Druskis/Photo Researchers. **Chapter 11: 380** Henrich Anton Muller/Collection de l'Art Brut, Lausanne; **384** Tim Ribar/StockSouth; **385** Rob Nelson/Stock Boston; **387** Robert McElroy/Woodfin Camp & Associates; **390** Erik Feinblatt/Sygma; **393** Alvin H. Perlmutter Inc.; **398(l)** Kevin Horan/Picture Group/With permission of Constance Weil; **398(c)** Kevin Horan/Picture Group; **398(r)** David R. Frazier Photolibrary; **400** From M. E. Phelps, J. C. Mazziotta. Positron Emission Tomograph: "Human Brain Function and Biochemistry," *Science 228:* 799–809, 1985; **406** Alvin H. Perlmutter Inc.; **409** Sudhir/SIPA-Press; **415** Mike McClure; **421** Mary Kate Denny/Photo Edit; **423** Blake Discher/Sygma. **Chapter 12: 426** Collection de l'Art Brut, Lausanne; **431** NIMH; **441** Al Vercoutere, Malibu, Calif.; **444** Al Vercoutere, Malibu, Calif.; **453** Burt Glinn/Magnum Photos; **458** NIMH; **462** Dick Bell/Insight Magazine; **464** Alvin H. Perlmutter Inc.; **471** Ellis Herwig/The Picture Cube. **Chapter 13: 476, viii** The Prinzhorn Collection, University of Heidelberg; **480** Kindra Clineff/The Picture Cube; **483** Dan McCoy/Rainbow; **485** Lynn Johnson/Black Star; **489** Howard Sochurek; **491** Warren Anatomical Museum, Harvard University Medical School; **493** Alvin H. Perlmutter Inc.; **495** Ira Wyman/Sygma; **498** Philip-Lorca di-Corcia; **499** Alvin H. Perlmutter Inc. **Chapter 14: 502** Collection de l'Art Brut, Lausanne; **505** Lawrence Migdale/Stock Boston; **510** Elaine Rebman/Photo Researchers; **517** Will McIntyre/Photo Researchers; **519** Richard Hutchings/Science Source/Photo Researchers; **523** Alvin H. Perlmutter Inc.; **525** Alvin H. Perlmutter Inc.; **526–27** Courtesy of Dr. Bruno Bettelheim; **530** Will & Deni McIntyre/Photo Researchers. **Chapter 15: 534** Collection de l'Art Brut, Lausanne; **536** Tony Freeman/Photo Edit; **539** Alvin H. Perlmutter Inc.; **545** Alvin H. Perlmutter Inc.; **548** John Maher/Stock Boston; **551** E. Williamson/The Picture Cube; **554** Alvin H. Perlmutter Inc.; **561** Michael Grecco/Stock Boston; **565** M. Siluk/The Image Works; **567** AP/Wide World. **Chapter 16: 572** Collection de l'Art Brut, Lausanne; **577** Hank Morgan/Rainbow; **582** Tony Freeman/Photo Edit; **584** Alvin H. Perlmutter Inc.; **586** Alvin H. Perlmutter Inc.; **591** John Mantel/SIPA-Press; **595** Alvin H. Perlmutter Inc. **Chapter 17: 604** Collection de l'Art Brut, Lausanne; **606(l)** Courtesy of Eastern State Hospital; **606(r)** Courtesy of Bakken Library of Electricity in Life; **609(all)** Alvin H. Perlmutter Inc.; **612(all)** UPI/Bettmann; **614** Louis Fernandez/Black Star; **619** Tony Freeman/Photo Edit. **Chapter 18: 626** Adolf Wolfi/Collection de l'Art Brut, Lausanne; **629** Andy Lewis/Photo Researchers; **639** Jacques Chenet/Woodfin Camp & Associates; **657** Alvin H. Perlmutter Inc.; **661** Alvin H. Perlmutter Inc. **Chapter 19: 672**

Collection de l'Art Brut, Lausanne; **675** Alvin H. Perlmutter Inc.; **677** Alvin H. Perlmutter Inc.; **679** Alvin H. Perlmutter Inc.; **686** Christopher Morris/Black Star; **689** AP/Wide World; **691** Courtesy of Dr. Joseph Wolpe; **692** Trippett/SIPA-Press; **694** Alan Carey/The Image Works; **694** Eeric A. Roth/The Picture Cube; **696** Alvin H. Perlmutter Inc.; **696** Keith Meyers/NYT Pictures; **699** D. Goldberg/Sygma; **703** Alvin H. Perlmutter Inc.

Literary, Figure, and Table Credits

12, 13: Reprinted with permission from the *Diagnostic and statistical manual of mental disorders,* 3rd ed. revised. Copyright © 1987 American Psychiatric Association. **124:** Haley, J. The family of the schizophrenic: A model system. *Journal of Nervous and Mental Disease,* 1959, 129, 357–74. **142:** Figure 4, "Changes in anxiety over time," from Niall Bolger, "Coping as a personality process: A prospective study," in *Journal of Personality and Social Psychology* 1990, 59(3),531. Copyright 1990 by the American Psychological Association. Reprinted by permission. **150:** Figure 1.3, "Selye's General Adaptation Syndrome," from *Stress* by Tom Cox. Copyright © 1978 by Tom Cox. Reprinted by permission of Macmillan, London and Basingstoke. **153:** Janis, I. L., Mahl, G. F., Kagan, J., & Holt, R. R. From *Personality: Dynamics, development and assessment.* Published by Harcourt Brace Jovanovich, Inc., 1969. Reprinted by permission. **166:** Stern, R. L. Diary of a war neurosis. *Journal of Nervous and Mental Disease,* 1947, 106, 583–86. Published by the Williams & Wilkins Co. Copyright 1947 and reprinted by permission of The Smith Ely Jelliffe Trust. **169:** Archibald, H. C., & Tuddenham, R. D. Persistent stress reaction after combat. *ARCH. GEN. PSYCHIAT.,* 1965, 12(5), 475–81. **170:** Shatan, C. F. Stress disorders among Vietnam veterans: The emotional content of combat continues. From *Stress disorders among Vietnam veterans: Theory, research and treatment,* edited by Charles R. Figley, Ph.D. Copyright © 1978 by Charles R. Figley. Reprinted by permission of Brunner/Mazel, Publishers. **171:** From "Reactivation of traumatic conflicts" by Randall M. Christenson, John Ingram Walker, Donald R. Ross, and Allan A. Maltric from *American Journal of Psychiatry,* 1981, Vol. 138:7, pp. 984–85. Copyright © 1981, the American Psychiatric Association. **174–75:** From Stephen M. Sonnenberg, M.D., "Victims of violence and post-traumatic stress disorder" in *The Psychiatric Clinics of North America,* Vol. 11, No. 4, December 1988, Case Study No. 1. Copyright 1988 W. B. Saunders Company. Reprinted by permission. **184–85, 213–14, 439–40:** Excerpts from "Anxious Anne," "Paralyzed," and "Another dimension" from *Psychopathology: A case book* by Robert L. Spitzer et al. Copyright © 1983 by McGraw-Hill, Inc. Reprinted by permission. **195:** From *Anxiety disorders and phobias: A cognitive perspective,* by Aaron T. Beck and Gary Emery with Ruth Greenberg. Copyright © 1985 by Aaron T. Beck, M.D. and Gary Emery, Ph.D. Reprinted by permission of Basic Books, Inc., Publishers. **198:** Reprinted with permission from the *Diagnostic and statistical manual of mental disorders,* 3rd. ed. revised. Copyright © 1987 American Psychiatric Association. **200:** Menninger, K. A. *The human mind* (3rd ed.). New York: Knopf, 1945. From pages 139–40 in *The human mind,* by Karl Menninger. Copyright 1930, 1937, 1945, and renewed 1958, 1965 by Karl Menninger. Reprinted by permission of Alfred A. Knopf, Inc. **206:** From Ross A. Colin, M.D., *Multiple personality disorder: Diagnosis, clinical features and treatment.* Copyright © 1989 by John Wiley & Sons, Inc. Reprinted by permission. **207–208:** Spitzer, R. L., Sdodol, A. E., Gibbon, M. and Williams, J. B. W., *DSM-III-R case book.* Washington, D.C.: American Psychiatric Association, 1989. Reprinted with permission. **209–10:** From *Sybil* by Flora Rheta Schreiber. Copyright © 1973 by Flora Rheta Schreiber. Published by Warner Paperback Library, 1974. Reprinted by permission. **236:** Adapted with permission of Macmillan Publishing Company from *Principles of immunology,* 2nd edition by Rose, Milgram and Van Oss. Copyright © 1979 by Macmillan Publishing Company. **241:** Robert A. Wallace, *Biology: The world of life,* 4th ed., pp. 372–73. Copyright © 1981, 1987 Scott, Foresman and Company. **243:** From *American Journal of Epidemiology,* Vol. III, No. 1, Jan. 1980 by Haynes, Feinleib and Kannel. Reprinted by permission of *The American Journal of Epidemiology,* The Johns Hopkins University School of Hygiene and Public Health. **244:** Nemiah, J. C. The case of Mary S., from *Foundations of psychopathology.* Copyright © 1961 by Oxford University Press, Inc. Reprinted by permission. **246–47:** Reproduced from *Bulimarexia: The binge/purge cycle* by Marlene Boskind-White, Ph.D., and William C. White, Jr., Ph.D., by permission of W. W. Norton & Company, Inc. Copyright © 1987 by Marlene Boskind-White and William C. White, Jr. **258:** From *Treating eating disorders* by Gloria Leon. Copyright © 1983 The Lewis Publishing Company. Reprinted by permission. **265:** Reprinted with permission from the *Diagnostic and statistical manual of mental disorders,* 3rd ed., revised. Copyright © 1987 American Psychiatric Association. **267–68:** Spitzer, R. L., Skodol, A. E., Gibbon, M. and Williams, J. B. W., *DSM-III case book.* Washington, D.C.: American Psychiatric Association, 1981. Reprinted by permission. **270:** Spitzer, R. L., Skodol, A. E., Gibbon, M. and Williams, J. B. W., *DSM-III case book.* Washington, D.C.: American Psychiatric Association, 1981. Reprinted by permission. **271–72:** Spitzer, R. L., Skodol, A. E., Gibbon, M. and Williams, J. B. W., *DSM-III case book.* Washington, D.C.: American Psychiatric Association, 1981. Reprinted by permission. **273–74:** Spitzer, R. L., Skodol, A. E., Gibbon, M. and Williams, J. B. W., *DSM-III case book.* Washington, D.C.: American Psychiatric Association, 1981. Reprinted by permission. **284–85:** Excerpt from *Psychopathy: Theory and research* by Robert D. Hare. Copyright © 1970 by John Wiley & Sons, Inc. Reprinted by permission. **300:** "Alcohol levels in the blood," from *TIME,* April 22, 1974. Copyright © 1974 Time, Inc. All rights reserved. Reprinted by permission. **308:** From "TV news anchor tells story of recovery from alcoholism," by Frances Burns in *Bloomington Sun Current,* June 16, 1986, p. 7A. Reprinted by permission. **325:** From "Crack" in *TIME,* June 2, 1986 by Jacob V. Lamar, Jr., p. 18. Copyright © 1986 Time, Inc. All rights reserved. Reprinted by permission from *TIME.* **353:** Adaptation of "Bob, Mae and Susan: Story of a new life," by Eric Black and Jacqui Banaszynski, from *Minneapolis Tribune,* May, 1983, pp. 1A, 4A–6A. Reprinted by permission of Minneapolis Star and Tribune Company. **357:** Stoller, R. J. *Sex and gender (Vol. 1): The development of masculinity and femininity.* Published by Jason Aronson, New York. Copyright © 1968, 1974, by Robert J. Stoller. Reprinted by permission of the author. **371:** *Why men rape* by Sylvia Levine and Joseph Koenig © 1980, International Cinemedia Centre Ltd., Toronto. Based on the film of the same name produced by the National Film Board of Canada. **371:** From Juliet L. Darke, "Sexual aggression: Achieving power through humiliation," by W. L. Marshall et al., in *Handbook of sexual assault* (Plenum Press, 1990), p. 64. Reprinted with permission from Plenum Publishing Corporation. **386–87:** Spitzer, R. L., Skodol, A. E., Gibbon, M. and Williams, J. B. W., *DSM-III case book.* Washington, D.C.: American Psychiatric Association, 1981. Reprinted by permission. **387–88:** Spitzer, R. L., Skodol, A. E., Gibbon, M. and Williams, J. B. W., *DSM-III case book.* Washington, D.C.: American Psychiatric Association, 1981. Reprinted by permission. **395:** From "The stages of mania: A longitudinal analysis of the manic episode," by G. Carlson and F. K. Goodwin, from *Archives of General Psychiatry,* February 1973, Vol. 28, No. 2, 221–28. Copyright © 1973 American Medical Association. Reprinted by permission. **396:** Spitzer, R. L., Skodol, A. E., Gibbon, M. and Williams, J. B. W., *DSM-III-R case book.* Washington, D.C.: American Psychiatric Association, 1989. Reprinted by permission. **402:** Leff, M. J., Roatch, J. F. and Bunney, W. E., Jr. Environmental factors preceding the onset of severe depressions. *Psychiatry,* 1970, 33(3), 298–311. **409–10:** Liberman, R. P., & Raskin, D. E. Depression: A behavioral formulation. Reprinted from *Archives of General Psychiatry,* June 1971, 24(6), 515–23. Copyright © 1971, American Medical Association. **420:** Tuckman, J., Kleiner, R. and Lavell, M. Emotional content of suicide notes. Reprinted from *The American Journal of Psychiatry,* Vol. 1, pp. 59–63, 1959. Copyright © 1959, the American Psychiatric Association. **420:** Darbonne, A. R. Suicide and age: A suicide note analysis. *J. CONS. CLIN. PSYCHOL.,* 1969, 33, 46–50. **435:** Reprinted with permission from the *Diagnostic and statistical manual of mental disorders,* 3rd. ed., revised. Copyright © 1987 American Psychiatric Association. **436:** Lewinson, T. S. Dynamic disturbances in the handwriting of psychotics; with reference to schizophrenic, paranoid, and manic-depressive psychoses. Reprinted from *The American Journal of Psychiatry,* 1940, 97, 102–35. **442:** From *Psychopathology: A case book* by Robert L. Spitzer, et al. Copyright © 1983 by McGraw-Hill, Inc. Reprinted by permission. **445–46:** Spitzer, R. L., Skodol, A. E., Gibbon, M. and Williams, J. B. W., *DSM-III case book.* Washington, D.C.: American Psychiatric Association. Reprinted by permission. **450:** Reprinted with permission from *Journal of Psychiatric Research,* 21(1), Pekka Tienari et al., "The Finnish adoptive family study of schizophrenia." Copyright 1987, Pergamon Press plc. **469–70:** Rosen, H. and Kiene, H. E. Paranoia and paranoiac reaction types. *Diseases of the nervous system,* 1946, 7, 330–37. Reprinted by permission of Physicians Postgraduate Press. **484:** From "Diagnosis of dementia" by Charles E. Wells, in *Psychosomatics,* August 1979, 20(8). Copyright © 1979 The Academy of Psychosomatic Medicine. Reprinted by permission. **488:** Fetterman, J. L. *Practical lessons in psychiatry.* Courtesy of Charles C. Thomas, Publisher, Springfield, Illinois. **526:** Bettelheim, B. "Joey: A 'Mechanical Boy'," *Scientific American,* 1959, 200, 116–27. From "Joey: A 'Mechanical Boy'" by Bruno Bettelheim. Copyright © March 1959 by Scientific American, Inc. All rights reserved. **529:** From Charles Wenar, *Developmental psychopathology: From infancy through adolescence,* 2nd ed. (McGraw-Hill, 1990), p. 197. Reproduced with permission of McGraw-Hill, Inc. **541–42:** Kendall, P. C. and Finch, A. J. A cognitive-behavioral treatment for impulse control: A case study. *Journal of Consulting and Clinical Psychology,* 1976, 44, 852–57. **557–58:** Reprinted from Cynthia R. Pfeffer, "Self-destructive behavior in children and adolescents," in *The Psychiatric Clinics of North America,* Vol. 8, No. 2, June 1985, pp. 218–19. Copyright 1985 W. B. Saunders Company. Reprinted by permission. **569:** Figure 1, from Arnold Sameroff, Ronald Seiler et al.,

"Early indicators of developmental risk: Rochester longitudinal study," in *Schizophrenia Bulletin,* 13: 383–94, 1987. Reprinted with permission from American Psychiatric Association. **598–99:** "Semantic interpretation of the Rorschach protocol utilizing the comprehensive system," by John E. Exner, Jr. Copyright © 1985, 1976 by John E. Exner, Jr. Reprinted by permission. **609:** McCall, L. *Between us and the dark* (originally published in 1947). Summary in W. C. Alvarez, *Minds that came back,* 1961. Reprinted by permission of Gladys A. Muirhead, executor. **614–15:** Grinspoon, L., Ewalt, J. R. and Shader, R. I. *Schizophrenia: Pharmacotherapy and psychotherapy.* Copyright © 1972, The Williams and Wilkins Company, Baltimore. Reprinted by permission. **619:** Cade, J. F. J. Lithium salts in the treatment of psychotic excitement. *Medical Journal of Australia,* 36 (part II): 349–52, 1949. Reprinted by permission. **642–43:** Wolf, M., Risley, T. and Mees, H. "Application of operant conditioning procedures to the behavior problems of an autistic child." *Behavior Research and Therapy,* 1964, *1,* 305–12. **649:** Rush, A. J., Khatami, M. and Beck, A. T. Cognitive and behavior therapy in chronic depression. *Behavior Therapy,* 1975, *6,* 398–404. Copyright © 1975 by Academic Press, Inc. Reprinted by permission. **651–52:** Rogers, C. R. *Client-centered therapy* (Boston: Houghton-Mifflin, 1951). Reprinted by permission of Houghton Mifflin Company and Constable & Company Ltd. **654–55:** Perls, F. S. *Gestalt therapy verbatim* (Lafayette, Calif.: Real People Press, 1969). Reprinted by permission. **694:** From "Psychiatrist-anthropologist: Bag ladies in isolated cultures, too" by Joseph Westermeyer in *Behavior Today* Newsletter, 13(21), May 31, 1982. Reprinted by permission of Atcom, Inc., 2315 Broadway, New York, NY 10024.

Name Index

Subject Index

About the Artwork in This Book

In 1945, Jean Dubuffet began collecting "Art Brut," a term he used to describe art created by people who live outside the cultural mainstream—mental patients, spiritualists, innocents, maladjusted individuals, loners, and those who exist at the fringes of society. Dubuffet wanted to exhibit an art in which "creation shines in its pure state, free of all the compromises which alter the mechanisms in professionals' productions." The collection that resulted—now housed in the Château de Beaulieu in Lausanne, Switzerland—provides an extraordinary glimpse into the inner lives and private visions of cultural outsiders and confirms Dubuffet's sense of the profound talents that often lie within those who are, for one reason or another, considered to be abnormal. We are grateful to the museum in Lausanne for allowing us to use selected works from the collection on our cover and as part of the interior design of the text.

We are also grateful to the proprietors of the Prinzhorn Collection of the Art of the Mentally Ill at the University of Heidelberg for allowing us to reprint several works from that collection, which contains some 6000 works or objects that were created by 516 patients, almost all of whom were chronically ill and many of whom had been institutionalized for most of their lives. Finally, we would like to thank the Carl Hammer Gallery and the Phyllis Kind Gallery for sharing with us works by distinctly American artists who, for one reason or another, were or are outside the cultural mainstream.

At the beginning of each chapter, we display a work by one of the artists, along with a capsule biography and a few words identifying and describing the work. Some of the artists are known to have suffered from specific disorders described in the text; however, in only a few instances will the artist discussed correspond to the subject of the given chapter. The creators of these artworks, like the rest of us, exist along a continuum of human behavior and for the most part cannot readily be categorized or pigeonholed.

About the Cover

Adolf Wolfi, *Saint Adolf Portant des Lunettes, Entre les Deux Villes Geantes Niess et Mia.* For biographical information, see Chapter 18.

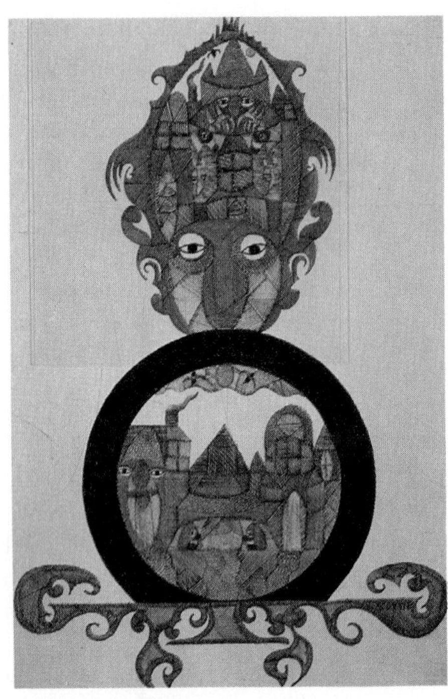

Scottie Wilson, *Thinking About Houses* (detail). For biographical information, see Chapter 16.

Eddie Arning, *Untitled.* For biographical information, see Chapter 4.

Alois Wey, *Maisons* (detail). For biographical information, see Chapter 15.

DSM-III-R Classification

DSM-III-R MULTIAXIAL SYSTEM IN BRIEF

Axis I Clinical Syndromes
Axis II Developmental Disorders/ Personality Disorders
Axis III Physical Disorders and Conditions
Axis IV Severity of Psychosocial Stressors
Axis V Global Assessment of Functioning

Reproduced here are Axes I and II of DSM-III-R. The Axis II categories are set off in boxes; all other categories are Axis I. Axes III, IV, and V are discussed on text pages 10–13.

■ DISORDERS USUALLY FIRST EVIDENT IN INFANCY, CHILDHOOD, OR ADOLESCENCE

AXIS II
DEVELOPMENTAL DISORDERS

Mental Retardation
Mild mental retardation
Moderate mental retardation
Severe mental retardation
Profound mental retardation
Unspecified mental retardation

Pervasive Developmental Disorders
Autistic disorder
Specify if childhood onset
Pervasive developmental disorder NOS

Specific Developmental Disorders
Academic skills disorders
Developmental arithmetic disorder
Developmental expressive writing disorder
Developmental reading disorder
Language and speech disorders
Developmental articulation disorder
Developmental expressive language disorder
Developmental receptive language disorder
Motor skills disorder
Developmental coordination disorder
Specific developmental disorder NOS

Other Developmental Disorders
Developmental disorder NOS

Disruptive Behavior Disorders
Attention-deficit hyperactivity disorder
Conduct disorder,
group type
solitary aggressive type
undifferentiated type
Oppositional defiant disorder

Anxiety Disorders of Childhood or Adolescence
Separation anxiety disorder
Avoidant disorder of childhood or adolescence
Overanxious disorder

Eating Disorders
Anorexia nervosa
Bulimia nervosa
Pica
Rumination disorder of infancy
Eating disorder NOS

From the *Diagnostic and statistical manual of mental disorders (Third Edition-Revised).* Washington, D.C.: American Psychiatric Association, 1987. Reprinted by permission.

Gender Identity Disorders
Gender identity disorder of childhood
Transsexualism
Specify sexual history: asexual, homosexual, heterosexual, unspecified
Gender identity disorder of adolescence or adulthood, nontranssexual type
Specify sexual history: asexual, homosexual, heterosexual, unspecified
Gender identity disorder NOS

Tic Disorders
Tourette's disorder
Chronic motor or vocal tic disorder
Transient tic disorder
Specify: single episode or recurrent
Tic disorder NOS

Elimination Disorders
Functional encopresis
Specify: primary or secondary type
Functional enuresis
Specify: primary or secondary type
Specify: nocturnal only, diurnal only, nocturnal and diurnal

Speech Disorders Not Elsewhere Classified
Cluttering
Stuttering

Other Disorders of Infancy, Childhood, or Adolescence
Elective mutism
Identity disorder
Reactive attachment disorder of infancy or early childhood
Stereotypy/habit disorder
Undifferentiated attention-deficit disorder

■ ORGANIC MENTAL DISORDERS

Dementias Arising in the Senium and Presenium
Primary degenerative dementia of the Alzheimer type, senile onset,
with delirium
with delusions
with depression
uncomplicated
(Note: code Alzheimer's disease on Axis III)

Code following as with delirium, with delusions, with depression, uncomplicated
Primary degenerative dementia of the Alzheimer type, presenile onset, ________
Note: code Alzheimer's disease on Axis III)
Multi-infarct dementia, ________
Senile dementia NOS
Specify etiology on Axis III if known
Presenile dementia NOS
Specify etiology on Axis III if known (e.g., Pick's disease, Jakob-Creutzfeldt disease)

Psychoactive Substance-Induced Organic Mental Disorders
Alcohol
intoxication
idiosyncratic intoxication
Uncomplicated alcohol withdrawal
withdrawal delirium hallucinosis
amnestic disorder
Dementia associated with alcoholism
Amphetamine or similarly acting sympathomimetic
intoxication
withdrawal
delirium
delusional disorder
Caffeine
intoxication
Cannabis
intoxication
delusional disorder
Cocaine
intoxication
withdrawal
delirium
delusional disorder
Hallucinogen
hallucinosis
delusional disorder
mood disorder
Posthallucinogen perception disorder
Inhalant
intoxication
Nicotine
withdrawal
Opioid
intoxication
withdrawal
Phencyclidine (PCP) or similarly acting arylcyclohexylamine
intoxication
delirium
delusional disorder
mood disorder
organic mental disorder NOS
Sedative, hypnotic, or anxiolytic
intoxication
Uncomplicated sedative, hypnotic, or anxiolytic withdrawal
withdrawal delirium
amnestic disorder
Other or unspecified psychoactive substance
intoxication
withdrawal
delirium
dementia
amnestic disorder
delusional disorder
hallucinosis
mood disorder
anxiety disorder
personality disorder
organic mental disorder NOS

Organic Mental Disorders associated with Axis III physical disorders or conditions, or whose etiology is unknown.
Delirium
Dementia
Amnestic disorder
Organic delusional disorder
Organic hallucinosis
Organic mood disorder
Specify: manic, depressed, mixed
Organic anxiety disorder
Organic personality disorder
Specify if explosive type
Organic mental disorder NOS

■ PSYCHOACTIVE SUBSTANCE USE DISORDERS

Alcohol
dependence
abuse
Amphetamine or similarly acting sympathomimetic
dependence
abuse
Cannabis
dependence
abuse
Cocaine
dependence
abuse
Hallucinogen
dependence
abuse
Inhalant
dependence
abuse
Nicotine
dependence
Opioid
dependence
abuse
Phencyclidine (PCP) or similarly acting arylcyclohexylamine
dependence
abuse
Sedative, hypnotic, or anxiolytic
dependence
abuse

The New Tibetan-English Dictionary of Modern Tibetan

Melvyn C. Goldstein
Editor

T. N. Shelling and J. T. Surkhang
Assistant Editors

WITH THE HELP OF
Pierre Robillard

UNIVERSITY OF CALIFORNIA PRESS
Berkeley • Los Angeles • London

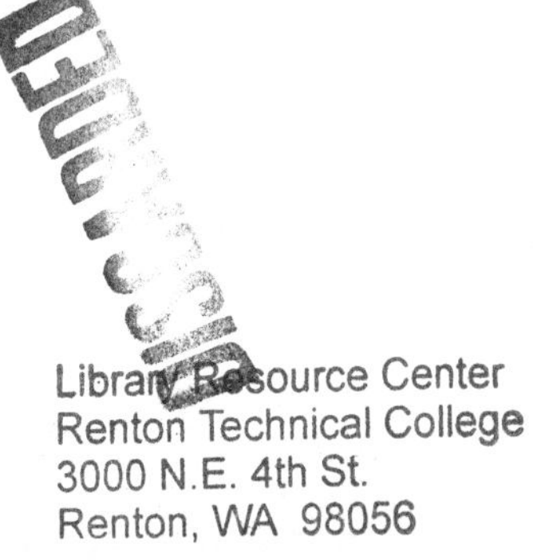

University of California Press
Berkeley and Los Angeles, California

University of California Press, Ltd.
London, England

Library of Congress Cataloging-in-Publication Data

The new Tibetan-English dictionary of modern Tibetan / Melvyn C. Goldstein, editor;
T. N. Shelling and J. T. Surkhang, assistant editors ; with the help of Pierre Robillard.
p. cm.
ISBN 0-520-20437-9 (alk. paper)
1. Tibetan language—Dictionaries—English. I. Goldstein, Melvyn C. II. Shelling, T. N.
III. Surkhang, J. T.

PL3637.E5 N48 2001
495′.4321—dc21 00-047521

Printed in the United States of America

08 07 06 05 04 03 02 01
10 9 8 7 6 5 4 3 2 1

The paper used in this publication meets the minimum requirements
of ANSI/NISO Z39.48-1992 (R 1997) (*Permanence of Paper*). ♾

Contents

Acknowledgments and Preface

The opening of Tibetan areas in China to the outside world and the development of numerous Tibetan communities in exile have brought Western students and researchers face-to-face with an enormous mass of Modern Tibetan official and unofficial written materials. This dictionary has been prepared to assist Westerners to read those materials. Compilation of the dictionary was made possible by grants from the International Research and Studies Program of the Department of Education (PO17A30010) and the National Endowment for the Humanities (RT-21671-95), and I am grateful for their support of this project. I am also very grateful to Tashi Tsering and Ben Jiao for their careful and thoughtful assistance in defining lexical entries, to Pierre Robillard for his unstinting advice and assistance in creating and fine-tuning the Tibetan and linguistic fonts and for converting the entire dictionary into camera-ready copy. And last but certainly not least, I also want to offer thanks to Jan McDonald for her help in proofreading the final camera-ready copy and the many graduate and undergraduate students at Case Western Reserve University who worked on this project.

This dictionary of modern Tibetan contains a wide range of lexical items used in political, social, economic, literary and scientific discourse. It includes the tens of thousands of new words that have been coined or have come into use since the incorporation of Tibet into the People's Republic of China in 1951, as well as new terminology used in the Tibetan exile communities in South Asia. It also contains the core lexical terminology that is used in everyday life and standard modern writing, together with a large corpus of proverbs and sayings that appear frequently in contemporary literary materials.

In addition, the dictionary includes lexical items characteristic of the specialized genre called གཞུང་ཡིག་ or "government language." This genre was used by Tibetan government officials in all government documents, edicts and reports until the uprising in Tibet in 1959. Since large numbers of these materials have been preserved in Tibet's archives and will likely someday become available for research, it was decided to include terms characteristic of this specialized genre of modern Tibetan in the current dictionary.

The items included in this dictionary derive from many sources. First, the terms contained in Goldstein's previous dictionary (*Tibetan-English Dictionary of Modern Tibetan*, 1978) were edited and revised when appropriate. The second source of entries derives from a large corpus of modern literary materials that were read to discover new terms and to check and revise terms from the previous dictionary. Tens of thousands of additional lexical items were selected from these textual (and conversational) sources. And although it is impossible to mention every source from which a word was found, in general these included newspapers, novels, short stories, histories, political articles/reports and textbooks.

The main newspapers and magazines consulted were: བོད་མིའི་རང་དབང་, ཡར་རྒྱས་གོང་འཕེལ་, ཤེས་བྱ་, དམངས་གཙོ་, མི་དམངས་བརྙན་པར་, ལྷ་སའི་ཉིན་རེ་ཚགས་པར་, ལྷ་སའི་དགོང་དྲོའི་ཚགས་པར་, ཀྲུང་གོའི་བོད་ལྗོངས་, བོད་ཀྱི་རྩོམ་རིག་སྒྱུ་རྩལ་, མི་རིགས་བརྙན་པར་, ལྷོ་ཁའི་རྩོམ་རིག་སྒྱུ་རྩལ་, སྤང་རྒྱན་མེ་ཏོག.

The main novels, folktales and histories that were utilized were: གཙུག་གཡུ་, ཆུ་ངོགས་གཏམ་རྒྱུད་; དབུལ་པོའི་ཁྱིམ་ཚང་གི་སྐྱིད་སྡུག, རོ་སྒྲུང་, མི་ཚེའི་སྐྱིད་སྡུག, མི་ཚེའི་བྱུང་བ་བརྗོད་པ་, བཀྲས་ཟུར་ཚང་གི་གཏམ་རྒྱུད་, ལྕང་ནག་ཁྲོད་ཀྱི་བུ་མོད་, སྲིད་ཆོད་དང་ཕྲུ་གུའི་ཕ་མ་, རང་གི་ལོ་རྒྱུས་ལྷད་མེད་རང་བྱུང་ཟངས་, གསར་བརྗེའི་དྲན་པོ་, སྒྲུང་ཐུང་བདམས་བསྒྲིགས་, སྒྲུང་གཏམ་གསར་རྩོམ་གྱི་ཤེས་བྱ་མུན་སེལ་སྒྲོན་མེ, མི་ཚེའི་ཐ་ཚུབས་འཁྱུགས་པོ་, and the nineteen volumes of the series བོད་ཀྱི་ལོ་རྒྱུས་རིག་གནས་དཔྱད་གཞིའི་རྒྱུ་ཆ་བདམས་བསྒྲིགས་.

In addition to these materials, a variety of dictionaries, glossaries and word lists have also been consulted:

From CHINA

དགེ་བཤེས་ཆོས་ཀྱི་གྲགས་. བརྡ་དག་མིང་ཚིག་གསལ་བ་བཞུགས་. China, 1957.

དག་ཡིག་མ་ནོར་ལམ་བཟང་. China, 1958.

དག་ཡིག་གསར་བསྒྲིགས་. China, 1979.

རྒྱ་བོད་མིང་མཛོད་. China, 1979.
བོད་རྒྱ་ཤན་སྦྱར་གྱི་ལྷ་སའི་ཁ་སྐད་ཚིག་མཛོད་. China, 1983.
ཀྲང་དབྱི་སུན་ (Ed.). རྒྱ་བོད་ཚིག་མཛོད་ཆེན་མོ་, China, 1985.
དཔེ་ཆོས་རྣ་བའི་བདུད་རྩི་. China, 1986.
ཧའོ་ལྷུན་ཞིན་ and ཧྲོའུ་ཚུན་ཆེ་ (eds.). བོད་རྒྱ་ཤན་སྦྱར་གྱི་ཤེས་བྱའི་རྣམ་གྲངས་ཀུན་བཏུས་ཚིག་མཛོད་. China, 1987.
བཀྲ་ཤིས་ཚེ་རིང་. དབྱིན་བོད་རྒྱ་གསུམ་ཤན་སྦྱར་གྱི་ཚིག་མཛོད་. China, 1988.
བྱ་ཚིག་ཚིག་མཛོད་. China, 1989.
རྒྱ་བོད་ཤན་སྦྱར་གྱི་ལས་ཁུངས་དང་ཁ་ལས་བྱ་ལས་སྤྱི་ཚན་གྱི་མིང་. China, 1989.
རྒྱ་བོད་ཁྲིམས་ལུགས་མིང་མཛོད་. China, 1990.
སློབ་གྲྭ་འབྲིང་ཆུང་གི་རྒྱུན་མཁོ་དག་ཡིག་ཕྱོགས་བསྒྲིགས་. China, 1990.
རྒྱ་བོད་ཤན་སྦྱར་ཚིག་མཛོད་. China, 1991.
བོད་རྒྱ་ཤན་སྦྱར་གྱི་དངུལ་རྩའི་ཚིག་མཛོད་. China, 1991.
སྐྱེ་དངོས་རིག་པའི་རྒྱ་བོད་ཐ་སྙད་ཤན་སྦྱར་. China, 1992.
སངས་རྒྱས་ཆོས་གཞུང་གི་ཚིག་མཛོད་. China, 1992.
བོད་རྒྱ་ནང་དོན་རིག་པའི་ཚིག་མཛོད་. China, 1993.
ཞི་སའི་ཚིག་མཛོད་རབ་གསལ་མེ་ལོང་. China, 1993.
ནང་རིག་པའི་ཚིག་མཛོད་. China, 1994.
བོད་རྒྱ་དབྱིན་སྐད་ཀྱི་དངོས་ལུགས་རིག་པའི་ཚིག་མཛོད་. China, 1994.
བཀྲས་སྐྱིད་. བོད་དབྱིན་རྒྱ་གསུམ་ཤན་སྦྱར་ཚིག་མཛོད་. China, 1994.
སློབ་མའི་རྒྱུན་མཁོ་མངོན་བརྗོད་ལག་དེབ་. China, 1994.
བོད་རྒྱ་དབྱིན་སྐད་ཀྱི་རྫས་འགྱུར་རིག་པའི་ཚིག་མཛོད་. China, 1994.
བོད་རྒྱ་དབྱིན་སྐད་ཀྱི་གྲངས་རིག་ཚིག་མཛོད་. China, 1994.
དགའ་བའི་རྡོ་རྗེས་. འཁྲུངས་དཔེ་དྲི་མེད་ཤེལ་གྱི་མེ་ལོང་. China, 1995.
བོད་རྒྱ་ལ་གསུམ་གྱི་བོད་སྨན་མིང་མཛོད་. China, 1998.
From INDIA
S.C.Das. Tibetan-English Dictionary. India, 1902.
C.A. Bell. English-Tibetan Colloquial Dictionary. India, 1905.
དུས་གསུམ་རིའུ་མིག་སོམ་ཉིའི་དྲ་གཅོད་པའི་རལ་གྲི་བཞུགས་སོ་. India, 1964.
L.S. Dagyab. བོད་བརྡའ་ཚིག་མཛོད་. India, 1966.
Acharya Sengye T. Naga and Tsepak Rigzin. བོད་དབྱིན་ཤན་སྦྱར་གྱི་ཚིག་ཚོགས་དང་གདམ་དཔེ་. India, 1994.
Pasang Yonden Arya. Dictionary of Tibetan Materia Medica. India: Motilal Banarsidass Publishers, 1998.
མཁར་སྟོད་རྡོ་རྗེ་དབང་ཕྱུག་. དུས་གསུམ་རིའུ་མིག་བྲ་མིའི་དགོངས་གཏེར་. India, nd.
OTHER
B.V. Semechov. Russian-Tibetan Dictionary. Russia, 1963.
E. Richter. German-Tibetan Dictionary. Germany, 1966.
S.H.Buck. Tibetan-English Dictionary. U.S.A., 1969.
H.A. Jaschke. Tibetan-English Dictionary. England, 1881.

The sources for the genre of "government Tibetan" (གཞུང་ཡིག་) were mainly original handwritten documents. Most of these were made available by the Library of Tibetan Works and Studies in Dharamsala, and I am indebted to its former Director Mr. Gyatso Tsering and his staff for allowing us to peruse these to extract གཞུང་ཡིག་ terms. Other documents were found in published collections of documents and in my own private collection.

Finally, although we tried to make this work comprehensive in its inclusion of modern lexical items, terms from the Buddhist philosophical and ritual genre were considered beyond the scope of this dictionary and generally were not included.

Pronunciation

Consonants

g - similar to g in gone
k - similar to k in keep
gy - similar to gu in regulate
ky - similar to cu in cute
ñ - similar to ny in canyon
ŋ - similar to nga in sing-a-long
n - similar to n in name
m - similar to m in man
l - similar to l in let
lh - this is made something like an l with a heavy puff of aspiration said simultaneously
p - similar to p in pet
b - similar to b in bet
j - similar to j in jet
c - similar to ch in champ
dz - similar to ddz in adds up
ts - similar to ts in Patsy
s - similar to s in sit
t - similar to t in tip
d- similar to d in dip
h - similar to h in hip
sh- similar to sh in ship
tr - similar to tr in triumph
dr - similar to dr in drill
r - similar to r in rip
w - similar to w in wet
y - similar to y in yet

Vowels

a - similar to a in pa
u -similar to o in to
o - similar to o in so
ə - similar to a in alone
ɛ - similar to the e in prey
e- similar to e in bet but with the teeth almost closed
ɔ - similar to a in all
ü - similar to the ü in the German füllen
ö - similar to eu in the French seul

Tone markings

Tibetan has three major tones: high, low and falling (high falling and low falling). High tone is indicated by a line over the vowel, low tone by a line under the vowel and falling by a diagonal line over a vowel: dā (high short), dāà (high falling), da̱ (low short), da̱à (low falling). The length of vowels is also phonemic in Tibetan and long vowels are indicated by the vowel written twice, for example, dāā (high long), da̱a̱ (low long). When vowels have no markings, it indicates a tone slightly lower than the preceding high vowel, e.g., mə̄ə̄mi, or slightly higher than the preceding low vowel, qa̱baa.

Using the Dictionary

The order of dictionary entries is main entry, pronunciation in parenthesis, meaning or meanings, and illustrations of usage. For example:

ཁ་དཀྲིས (kə̄drii̖) scarf ¶ ངས་ཁ་དཀྲིས་གསུམ་ཉོས་པ་ཡིན་ I bought three scarves.

A number of special conventions are employed in this dictionary that require comment.

Verbs

Core verbs are single morphemes like བྱེད་ ("to do"). They are either active or involuntary/inactive (similar to transitive and intransitive), and typically undergo declension in accordance with tense. For example, the verb "to do" has four stems: present = བྱེད་, past = བྱས་, future = བྱ་; imperative = བྱོས་.

Dictionary entries will indicate whether a verb is active or involuntary by means of the abbreviations "va." for verb active and "vi." for verb inactive/ involuntary. If the verb has multiple stems, the main entry is cited in the present tense stem followed by its other stems. For example, the four stem verb "to do" will be cited as follows:

བྱེད་: p. བྱས་; f. བྱ་; imp. བྱོས་ (ce̲è) va. to do, to work

However, many verbs have less than four stems and some have only one stem. A one stem verb will be listed as follows:

ན་ (na̲) vi. to be sick/ ill

To facilitate looking up the verb stems one encounters in written materials all stems will be listed separately, e.g., the past tense stem of the verb "to do" (བྱས་), is not only listed in the main entry བྱེད་, but is also listed as a separate entry:

བྱས་ (cɛ̲ɛ̀) p. of བྱེད་

Derived Verbs and Gerundial Nominals

Tibetan has a category of derived verbs and gerundial nominals that require more complicated presentation conventions.

Derived verbs consist of a nominal word or compound such as the noun "work" (ལས་ཀ་) and a verb that verbalizes the nominal, e.g., the verbalizing verb བྱེད་ ("to do"). Thus, where English has a separate verb "to work," Tibetan conveys this verbal notion by a nominal (ལས་ཀ་ work, job) + a verbalizer (བྱེད་ to do), i.e., ལས་ཀ་བྱེད་ means "to do work" or "to work." In a similar fashion, the verbal notion "sing" is conveyed by the nominal "song" (གཞས་) together with another common verbalizing verb, གཏོང་ ("to send"), so that གཞས་གཏོང་ literally means "to send a song" but really means "to sing." The four main verbalizing verbs in Tibetan are: བྱེད་ ("to do"), གཏོང་ ("to send"), རྒྱག་ ("to throw/do"), and ཤོད་ ("to say"). The parallel honorific verbalizers are གནང་/མཛད་ ("to do), སྐྱོན་ ("to throw, to do), གསུང་ ("to say"), ཞུ་ (" to say).

Verbalized nominal phrases are listed in the dictionary with the noun or noun compound as the main entry. For example, the above mentioned examples will be presented as follows:

ལས་ཀ་ (lɛ̲ɛ̀ga) work, job; va.—བྱེད་.

གཞས་ (shɛ̲ɛ̀) song; va.—གཏོང་.

ང་ལོག་ (ŋo̲loò) revolt, uprising; va.—རྒྱག་.

Note that an em-dash (—) is placed before the verbalizing verb as a substitute for the main entry. Thus, va.—གཏོང་ really means va. གཞས་གཏོང་. In some cases where more than one verbalizing verb can be used, the verbalizing verbs are listed in sequence, e.g., ཀ་གྲངས་ (gādraŋ) indexing alphabetically; va.—རྒྱག; —བཟོ་; —འགོད་ to number/

index alphabetically.

In order to conserve space, verbalized nominal phrases normally will not include the English gloss of the verbal meaning (e.g., "to work," "to sing," and "to revolt") because we feel the user will be able to derive these. However, in cases where we decided deriving the verbal meaning is not obvious, the verbal meaning was included. Two examples of this are the nouns མི་མདའ་ (gun) and གནམ་གྲུ་ (airplane):

མི་མདའ་ (m̲enda) gun; va.—རྒྱག་ to shoot a gun.

གནམ་གྲུ་ (nəmdru); airplane; va.—གཏོང་ to fly an airplane.

Another genre of derived verbals consist of verbalizing verbs such as བྱེད་ or གཏོང་ used with nominal compounds that themselves are a combination of two verbs. For example, the term "liberation" or consists of the verb "བཅིངས་" to bind" plus the verb འགྲོལ་ "to release." When placed together, these convey the meaning "liberation" and enter into other nominal compounds such as "liberation movement" (བཅིངས་འགྲོལ་ལས་འགུལ་). This nominal compound in turn is verbalized to convey the verbal notion "to liberate" by adding the common verbalizing verb གཏོང་.

Such compounds will be listed in the dictionary in the same manner as the simple nominals cited above, e.g.: བཅིངས་འགྲོལ་ (jīŋdröö) liberation; va.—གཏོང་.
Once again note that the gloss "to liberate" is not cited.

Verbal nouns

Verbal nouns are verbs which in the gerundial or present participle form function as a noun in the sense that they name an action or state of being. Examples of these in English are: *Running* is good exercise. *Eating* fatty foods is bad. *Being* happy is important.

Tibetan has a class of noun-verb (and verb-verb) compounds that can be read depending on context either as verbs or verbal nouns. For example, the term ཁ་སྒྱུར་ can be read as a verbal phrase meaning "to turn around," the ཁ་ being a noun ("mouth") and སྒྱུར་ being a verb ("to change"). However, these two syllables can also be used together as a verbal noun meaning "turning around" or "changing direction." When used in this sense as a verbal noun, the compound can in turn be verbalized by adding the verbalizer གཏོང་. Thus, ཁ་སྒྱུར་བ་རེད་ and ཁ་སྒྱུར་གཏོང་བ་རེད་ both mean "turned around." Such constructions will be listed with the verbal noun as the head word, e.g.,

ཁ་སྒྱུར་ (kāgyur) turning around, changing direction; va. ཁ་སྒྱུར་; —གཏོང་
The second listing of ཁ་སྒྱུར་ after the va. indicates that ཁ་སྒྱུར་ also functions as a verb by itself.

Illustrative materials in dictionary entries

Many dictionary entries include examples of usage. These are always preceded by the symbol ¶ as in the following example:
ཀ་གྲངས་ (gādraŋ) numbering/ indexing alphabetically; va.—རྒྱག་; —བཟོ་; —འགོད་ to number/ index alphabetically ¶ ཁོས་སྒམ་ཚང་མ་ཀ་གྲངས་གཞི་བཟུང་བཀོད་པ་རེད་ He numbered all the boxes alphabetically.
Note that the verb used in this example (བཀོད་) is the past tense stem of the verb འགོད་ whose present tense is the one listed in the main entry. Some illustrative materials such as this were constructed by the editors, but most derive from examples encountered in the literature. In the case of terms from the government language genre (shungyik), the original sentences/clauses were generally used, even though they are difficult.

Grammatical Introduction

Introduction

A number of the characteristics of the Tibetan language make compiling and using a Tibetan dictionary difficult. Tibetan, unlike Indo-European languages, does not indicate where "words" begin and end. Consequently, instead of the reader encountering a string of clearly delimited words, a string of syllables (separated by dots called ཚེག་) is ecountered. The reader, therefore, must decide how to group the syllables into word units and thus what combinations of syllables to look up in the dictionary. For example, in the sentence བོད་དམག་མི་གཟུགས་པོ་ཆེན་པོ་འདུག ("Tibetan soldiers are tall."), the eight syllables comprise the following five words: བོད་ ("Tibet"), དམག་མི་ ("soldier"), གཟུགས་པོ་ ("body"), ཆེན་པོ་ ("tall") and འདུག ("are").

Disaggregating Tibetan's syllables into discrete word units, however, is difficult because most syllables in Tibetan possess independent meaning, and strings of syllables can be read in different ways depending on context.

For example, just as the English word "soldier" is disyllabic, so too is the Tibetan word for "soldier" (དམག་མི་). However, while neither of the two English syllables has an independent meaning both of the Tibetan syllables do. The syllable དམག་ means "war" and མི་ means "person" or "not." Both Tibetan syllables, moreover, occur in other constructions, and even when side-by-side may not be linked together semantically. For example, in the sentence བོད་དམག་མི་བྲོས་ཀ་མེད་ཕྱིན་པ་རེད་ ("The Tibetan army had no choice but to flee"), although the syllable དམག་ is immediately adjacent to མི་, it is linked semantically to བོད་ ("Tibet") not to མི་. In this sentence, མི་ conveys its second meaning of "not" and modifies བྲོས་ ("flee") so that མི་བྲོས་ཀ་མེད་ means "no choice but to flee." Thus, the breakdown into word units in this sentence is not བོད་ (Tibet), དམག་མི་ ("soldier) and བྲོས་ ("flee"), but rather བོད་དམག་ ("Tibetan army") and མི་བྲོས་.

Moreover, because it is easy for Tibetans to combine syllables in new ways for style or to convey new concepts, there is constant flux in lexical terminology, even for relatively basic ideas. All languages change, of course, but in Tibetan the extent of "flux" is far greater than in English. Consequently, although we have tried to include all frequently occurring word units such as དམག་མི་ and བོད་དམག་, the reader will certainly encounter combinations that are not listed. In such cases, each individual syllable should be looked up and an attempt made to infer the compound meaning from its parts. To facilitate this process, an overview of the main principles of word formation in Tibetan is presented below.

Word Formation

1. Nominal compounds

Nominal compounds consist of two or four syllables each of which is a nonderived noun.

1.1 Synonymic compounds

Synonymic compounds consist of two syllables that are synonyms. The overall meaning of the compound word is identical to the meaning of each of the component parts. For example, སྟོབས་ཤུགས་ ("power, strength") is composed of two syllables: སྟོབས་ ("power, strength") and ཤུགས་ ("power, strength").

(a) སྟོབས་ཀྱིས་ས་མང་པོ་བཟུང་བ་རེད་ (They) seized many areas by force.

(b) ཤུགས་ཀྱིས་ས་མང་པོ་བཟུང་བ་རེད་ (They) seized many areas by force.

(c) སྟོབས་ཤུགས་ཀྱིས་ས་མང་པོ་བཟུང་བ་རེད་ (They) seized many areas by force.

Other common synonymic compounds are: གྲངས་འབོར་ ("quality," "number," "amount") and དུས་སྐབས་ ("time," "period").

1.2 Premodifying compounds

In premodifying constructions the first syllable modifies the second. Thus, in the word "hospital" (སྨན་ཁང་), the first syllable སྨན་ ("medicine") describes what kind of ཁང་(པ་) ("house," "dwelling") it is. Some other common examples of this are: གནམ་གྲུ་ sky-boat: airplane and དམག་མི་ war-person: soldier.

1.3 Conjunctive compounds

Like premodifying compounds, conjunctive compounds have component syllables with different meanings, but here the relationship between them is not modification but one of conjunction or an abstract notion deriving from both. For example, བཟོ་ཞིང་ consists of the first syllable of the word བཟོ་པ་ ("workers") and the first syllable of the word ཞིང་པ་ ("farmer") and means "workers and farmers." Similarly, ཕ་མ་ is composed of ཕ་ ("father") and མ་ ("mother") and as a compound can mean either "father and mother" or "parents."

(a) བཟོ་པ་དང་ཞིང་པ་མང་པོས་ཚོགས་འདུ་ཚོགས་པ་རེད་ Many workers and farmers held a meeting.

(b) བཟོ་ཞིང་མང་པོས་ཚོགས་འདུ་ཚོགས་པ་རེད་ Same as (a).

2. Adjectival compounds

Adjectival compounds are compounds in which at least one of the syllables is an adjective and neither is a verb.

2.1 Adjectival polar compounds

In adjectival polar compounds the two component syllables have opposite meanings but the overall meaning of the compound is either conjunctive or an abstract notion deriving from both. For example:

ཆེ་ཆུང་ big-small; size — རིང་ཐུང་ long-short; length/ distance
ཚ་གྲང་ hot-cold; temperature — བཟང་ངན་ good-bad; quality
སྐམ་རློན་ dry-wet; dampness — མཐོ་དམའ་ high-low; height

2.2 Adjectival postmodifying compounds

Adjectival postmodifying compounds consist of a noun in the first syllable slot and the first syllable of the basic adjective form in the second. The adjective modifies the noun, and the resulting compound is a new noun. The main difference between this construction and that of normal adjectival modification is that only the first syllable of the adjective is used. For example, ཚོགས་ཆེན་ ("big meeting, general assembly, plenary session") consists of the noun ཚོགས་ ("meeting") and the first syllable of the adjective ཆེན་པོ་ ("big").

3. Verbal compounds

Verbal compounds consist of noun/adjective-verb and verb-verb combinations. All such compounds become nominals that then can be used with verbalizers such as བྱེད་ or རྒྱག to make verbal constructions.

3.1 Premodifying compounds: Adj.-Vb.

The first syllable of verbal premodifying compounds (an adjective stem) describes or modifies the second. For example, ལེགས་རྟོགས་ ("good/thorough understanding") consists of ལེགས་ ("good") and རྟོགས་ ("to understand"). Other common examples are:

གསར་བརྗེ་ new-change; revolution — དགའ་བསུ་ happy-receive; welcome
གསལ་སྟོན་ clear-show; demonstration — གསར་བཟོ་ new-make; new product

3.2 Synonymic compounds: Vb.-Vb.

When the meanings of both syllables in a verb-verb combination are the same, the original meaning of each does not change but a verbal noun is created. For example, འགྲོ་སྐྱོད་ ("go" "go") means ("going"), as in the following sentence:

ལྷ་སར་ཕྱི་རྒྱལ་གྱི་མི་རིགས་འགྲོ་སྐྱོད་བཀག་སྡོམ་བྱས་པ་རེད་

[They] prohibited foreign nationals from going to Lhasa.

By adding a verbalizer this verbal noun is transformed back into a verbal construction.

ལྷ་སར་ཕྱི་རྒྱལ་གྱི་མི་རིགས་འགྲོ་སྐྱོད་བྱས་པ་རེད་

Foreign nationals went to Lhasa.

3.3 Summation compounds: Vb.-Vb.

Summation compounds are composed of syllables each of which has a different meaning wherein the overall meaning of the new compound is the summation of the two independent ones. For example, བཅོས་སྒྱུར་ "reform" is composed of བཅོས་ ("to correct") and སྒྱུར་ ("to change"). Like the preceding compounds, these summation compounds function as nominals and take standard verbalizers. For example:

སྲིད་གཞུང་གསར་པས་ས་ཞིང་བཅོས་སྒྱུར་བྱས་པ་རེད་

The new government did land reforms.

A confusing factor in verb compounds is that sometimes the present tense of a verb is used and sometimes the past tense is used (for the same lexical item). Thus བཅོས་སྒྱུར་ is also commonly written བཅོས་བསྒྱུར་ using the past tense stem of the verb "to change." To assist users to deal with this problem we have tried to include the different versions of compounds, e.g., in this case both བཅོས་སྒྱུར་ and བཅོས་བསྒྱུར་ are listed as separate entries.

3.4 Polar compounds: Vb.-Vb.

Polar compounds consist of verbs with opposite meanings. The overall meaning is usually the abstract idea derived from the two syllables, although it may also be simply conjunctive with each syllable retaining its independent meaning. For example, འགྲོ་སྡོད་ breaks down into "going" and "staying" and together usually means either "movement" or "going and staying." For example:

ད་ལྟ་འགྲོ་སྡོད་གཏན་གཏན་མེད་ It is not certain now whether (I) will go or stay.

3.5 Premodifying compounds: Vb.-N.

In these premodifying compounds the first syllable is a verb and modifies the second syllable. For example, སྡོད་ཁང་ ("live-house; residence").

3.6 Premodifying compounds: N.-Vb.

In these premodifying compounds the first syllable is a noun and modifies the second syllable that is a verb. For example, དཔྱིད་འདེབས་ ("spring planting") breaks down into the first syllable དཔྱིད་ ("spring") (from དཔྱིད་ཀ་) and the verb འདེབས་ ("to plant/ sow"). The first syllable tells us what kind of planting it was—a spring planting. This nominal compound can then be verbalized by the addition of a verbalizing verb. For example, ཞིང་པ་ཚོས་དཔྱིད་འདེབས་བྱེད་ཀྱི་ཡོད་པ་རེད་ ("The farmers are doing spring planting.")

3.7 Sequential compounds: Vb.-Vb.

In sequential compound constructions the first verb takes the past stem (if it has more than one stem) and the second either the past or nonpast. The overall meaning consists of the action of the second verb acting on that of the first. For example, in བཅིངས་བཀྲོལ་ the first syllable means "to bind" and the second "to release, "with the overall meaning of" to release or untie that which was bound." This compound is used to express the modern concept of "liberation." Sequential compounds are usually idiomatic in the sense that the meaning is not readily derivable from the constituent elements. Like other compounds, they are usually verbalized by one of the standard verbalizing terms such as གཏོང་ or བྱེད་.

4. Quadrisyllabic compounds

Quadrisyllabic compounds consist of two disyllabic compounds. The relationship between these two disyllabic units is that of premodification (i.e., the first disyllabic compound modifies the second). When a quadrisyllabic compound is encountered each of the two disyllabic subunits should be analyzed separately before the overall meaning is determined. For example, in རྒྱ་བོད་ས་མཚམས་ ("Sino-Tibetan border"), the first disyllabic unit is a conjunctive compound and means "China/Tibet." The second element is a premodifying compound meaning "border" (literally, place-space between). Thus, the first disyllabic unit modifies the second explaining what kind of a border it was.

5. Active and involuntary verbs

Tibetan active verbs express action done by an actor (subject) and are noted in the dictionary by the abbreviation "va." Involuntary verbs express unintentional/ non-purposive action or states and are noted in the dictionary by the abbreviation "vi." The difference between active and involuntary verbs hinges on the dichotomy of intentional/unintentional action. The English sentence "He slept" illustrates this. Tibetan has two separate verbs meaning "to sleep." One of these, གཉིད་ཉལ་, is active (va.) and connotes sleep resulting from the intentional act of going to sleep. The other གཉིད་ཁུག་ is involuntary (vi.) and connotes unintentional sleep, i.e., falling asleep without wanting or trying to do so. Another example of this difference is the notion "to boil." Tibetan has two separate verbs to convey the active (va.) and involuntary (vi.) notions of boiling:

ཆུ་བསྐོལ་བཞག་ (He, she) boiled the water. (va.)

ཆུ་འཁོལ་བཞག་ The water has boiled. (vi.)

Thus, the presence of vi. before a verb such as "change" will indicate that it means "to be" or "get changed," as distinguished from the va. form which means "to actively change or modify."

Active verbs may have as many as four stems and involuntary verbs may have as many as three stems (they have no imperative stem). Examples of active verbs are seen in the following table:

	Past	Present	Future	Imperative
1-stem	འཁྱེར་	འཁྱེར་	འཁྱེར་	འཁྱེར་
2-stem	ཉོ་	ཉོ་	ཉོས་	ཉོས་
3-stem	བབ་	འབབ་	འབབ་	བོབ་
4-stem	བཀླགས་	ཀློག་	བཀླག་	ཀློགས་

All verb main entries are listed in their present tense form, although all tenses are included immediately following the main entry. For example:

ཀློག་: p. བཀླགས་; f. བཀླག་ ; imp. ཀློགས་ (lɔ̄ɔ̀) va. to read.

6. Verb Honorifics

Almost all active and involuntary verbs have honorific forms. These are either a separate stem, e.g., ཉོ་ "to buy" (non-honorific) and གཟིགས་ "to buy" (honorific), or the non-honorific past stem is made honorific by adding a honorific verb like གནང་ "to do" (h.). For example, ཁོས་བཟོས་པ་རེད་ "He made it" becomes ཁོང་གིས་བཟོས་གནང་བ་རེད་ "He (h.) made (h.) it." When verbs have honorific and non-honorific stems both will be listed in the dictionary.

Abbreviations

abbr.	abbreviation
adj.	adjective
arc.	archaic term
bh.	Bhutanese language
CCP.	Chinese Communist Party
ch.	Chinese (language)
ch.eng.	Chinese and English language
ch.tib.	Chinese and Tibetan language
dat.-loc.	dative-locative case
eng.	English language
eng.tib.	English and Tibetan language
f.	future tense
gen.	genitive case
h.	hororific
hind.	Hindi language
id.	idiom
imp.	imperative tense
inst.	instrumental case
KMT.	Koumintang (party)
Lit.	literally
mong.	Mongolian language
neg.	negative particle
p.	past tense
poet.	poetic metaphor
pres.	present tense
PRC	People's Republic of China
rus.	Russian
sb.	somebody
skt.	Sanskrit
skt.tib.	Sanskrit and Tibetan
sm.	same as
sm.*	same as (but indicates this is a non-standard spelling)
sth.	something
shung.	the genre of government Tibetan
tib.	Tibetan language
tib.ch.	Tibetan and Chinese language
tib.hind.	Tibetan and Hindi languge
tt.	traditional Tibetan society
usu.	usually
va.	active verb
vi.	involuntary/inactive verb
—	signifies the main lexical entry
¶	signifies the start of an example

ཀ

ཀ་ (gā) 1. the letter ཀ (used in alphabetical ordering). 2. conjunctive ("together") particle for numbers ¶གཉིས་ཀ་ The two together. ¶གསུམ་ཀ་ The three together (all three). 3. abbr. of ཀ་བ་. 4. (vb. + —) infinitivizing particle ¶ཁོ་ལས་ཀ་བྱེད་ཀ་ཕྱིན་པ་རེད་ He went to do work. 5. the party "A" of two or more parties (e.g., to an agreement). 6. the beginning ¶ཀ་ནས་དག་པ་ Pure from the beginning.

ཀ་ཀ་ (gāga) 1. magpie. 2. magpie's croaking. 3. sheep's knuckle bone.

ཀ་ཀ་ནི་ལ་ (gāga ni̲la) a type of sapphire used in Tibetan medicine.

ཀ་ཀ་རང་ (gāgaraŋ) cucumber.

ཀ་ཀ་རུ་ (gāgaru) crab.

ཀ་ཀུ་བྷ་ཡ་ (gāgu bhāya) skt. a type of tree.

ཀ་ཀོ་ལ་ (gāgola) 1. amomion tsao-ko (used in Tibetan medicine). 2. a crow.

ཀ་ཀོར་ (gāgɔr) sm. ཀ་རེ་ཀོ་རེ་.

ཀ་ཀོར་སླེང་རྙོག (gāgɔr lēŋñog) delaying and making complications/ problems/ difficulties.

ཀ་ཀོར་ནར་འགྱང་ (gāgɔrna̲rgyaŋ) sm. ཀ་ཀོར་ཞག་འགྱང་.

ཀ་ཀོར་ཞག་འགྱང་ (gāgɔr sha̲ggyaŋ) dilly dallying, delaying; va.—བྱེད་.

ཀ་ཀོར་ཞག་འགྱངས་ (gāgɔr sha̲gyaŋ) sm. ཀ་ཀོར་ཞག་འགྱང་.

ཀ་ཀྭ་ (gāga) sm. ཀ་ཀ་.

ཀ་ཀྱག (gāgyaà) sm. ཀ་བཀྱག.

ཀ་བཀོལ་མ་ (gāgöma) sm. ཀ་ཁོལ་མ་.

ཀ་བཀྱག (gāgyaà) the support (usu. a stone) put at the base of a pillar.

ཀ་སྐེད་ (gāgeè) the middle part of a pillar.

ཀ་སྐྱོར་ (gāgyɔɔ) a wooden support/ brace for a pillar.

ཀ་ཁ་ (gā kā) the alphabet; the consonants of the alphabet; va.—སྒྲིག to arrange alphabetically.

ཀ་ཁ་པ་ (gāgawa) a beginning student, a student beginning to study the alphabet.

ཀ་ཁའི་དཔེ་ཆ་ (gāgee bēja) sm. ཀ་དཔེ་.

ཀ་ཁའི་ཐོ་ (gāgee tō) an alphabetical list or index.

ཀ་ཁོངས་ (gāgoŋ) belonging to the category ཀ་ (as in an alphabetical list).

ཀ་ཁོལ་མ་ (gāgöma) name of a historical work supposedly written by king Songtsen gampo (it is also known as བཀའ་ཆེམས་ཀ་ཁོལ་མ་).

ཀ་ཁྱི་ (gɔ̄gyi) a small, rectangular piece of wood used as a support in a grist mill.

ཀ་གྲངས་ (gādraŋ) numbering/ indexing that is done alphabetically; va.—རྒྱག; —བཟོ་; —འགོད་ ¶སྒམ་ཚང་མ་ཀ་གྲངས་གཞི་བཟུང་བཀོད་པ་རེད་ All the boxes were numbered alphabetically.

ཀ་འགོ་ (gāŋgo) 1. head/ top of a pillar. 2. upper part of the Tibetan letter ཀ་. 3. the iron ring used on the wooden axle of a grist mill.

ཀ་རྒྱག (gāgaà) tent pole.

ཀ་རྒྱན་ (gāgyɛn) brocade hung on temple and monastery pillars as decoration.

ཀ་རྒྱུག (gɔ̄rgyuù) 1. tent pole. 2. a stick/ staff used by monastic disciplinary officials.

ཀ་སྒྲིག་དང་གདུང་སྒྲིག (gādrig ta̲ŋ du̲ŋdrig) 1. arranging beams and pillars when building a house; va.—བྱེད་. 2. drawing the design for pillars and beams (on the ground) before building a house; va.—བྱེད.

ཀ་སྒྲོག (gādrɔɔ̀) the call of a crow.

ཀ་སྒྲོམ་ (gādrom) wooden pole used to prop up/ support/ brace a pillar.

ཀ་ཅ་ (gāja) 1. a general name for wealth/ property/ possessions/ goods. 2. utensils, implements, appliances.

ཀ་ཅན་ (gājɛn) 1. a house/ room with a pillar. 2. anything having the letter ཀ་.

ཀ་ཅན་བཞི་ (gājɛn shi̲) sm. ཀ་ཆེན་བཞི་.

ཀ་ཅི་ (gɔ̄ji) white cotton, Benares muslin cloth.

ཀ་ཅི་སྔོན་ཤོག་མ་ (gāji go̲ŋshōŋma) a kind of fine cotton cloth.

ཀ་ཅོག་ཞང་གསུམ་ (gājoò sha̲ŋsum) abbr. the three famous early translators of Indian Buddhist texts.

ཀ་གཅིག (gɔ̄jiì) sm. ཀ་གཅིག་མ་.

ཀ་གཅིག་སྒོ་གཅིག་མ་ (gɔ̄jiì go̲jimɔ) a small or poor house [Lit. one pillar, one door].

ཀ་གཅིག་ལྷམ་གང་མ་ (gɔ̄ji jāmgaŋma) a room the size of one pillar plus a slight additional space due to another ལྷམ་ (roughly a room the size of 1.5 pillars).

ཀ་གཅིག་མ་ (gɔ̄jimɔ) a room with one pillar.

ཀ་ཅྱི་ (gɔ̄ji) sm. ཀ་ཅི་.

ཀ་ཆ་ (gāja) sm. ཀ་ཅ་.

ཀ་ཆུག (gā jūù) arc. sm. དེ་ལྟར་.

ཀ་ཆེན་བཞི་ (gājen shi̲) the four disciples of Marpa (and the Kargyu sect) [Lit. the four great pillars].

ཀ་འཇའ་ལ་ (gānja la̲) a mountain pass in the ཏེ་རྟོར་ དཀར་མཛེས་ prefecture in Sichuan province.

ཀ་ཏ་ (gāda) abbr. of ཀ་ལ་ཀ་ཏར་.

ཀ་ཏ་ཀ་ (gādaga) ch. clarificant.

ཀ་ཏ་པུར་ (gādabur) camphor.

ཀ་ཏ་མན་ཌུ་ (gāda mǝ̲ndu) Kathmandu.

ཀ་ཏ་རུ་ (gādaru) skt. a form, chart, table.

ཀ་ཏན་ (gādɛn) a kind of cotton cloth.

ཀ་ཏོ་ར་ (gādora) a large basin.

ཀ་ཏོར་ (gādɔr) an expended cartridge/ shell.

ཀ་གཏུགས་ (gǝduù) 1. vi. to exhaust the means of doing sth., to reach the end of one's limits ¶ངས་ཀ་གཏུགས་ནས་ཀུ་མ་ཀུ་དགོས་བྱུང་ I reached the end of my limits so I had to steal. 2. sm. ཀ་མེད་.

ཀ་རྟགས་རྡོ་གཙུགས་ (gādaà do̲dzuù) boundary stone/ tablet.

ཀ་ཏེན་ (gāden) sm. ཀ་སྐྱོར་.

ཀ་རྟེགས་ (gādeg) sm. ཀ་བཀྱག.

ཀ་བསྟར་ (gādar) lining up/ organizing/ arranging in alphabetical order; va.—སྒྲིག to line up/ organize/ arrange in alphabetical order ¶དམག་སྒར་ཀ་བསྟར་སྒྲིག་བཀོད་པ་ནི་ As for the regiments that were organized alphabetically.

ཀ་བསྟོད་ (gādöö) a verse that praises sb. using the poetic style in which each line begins with a letter of the Tibetan alphabet in alphabetical order.

ཀ་ཐ་མན་གྲུ་ (gāda mǝ̲ndru) sm. ཀ་ཏ་མན་ཌུ་.

ཀ་ཐོ་ (gādo) an alphabetically arranged list or register.

ཀ་ཐོག (gādɔɔ̀) sm. ཀ་ཐོག་དགོན་.

ཀ་ཐོག་དགོན་ (gādɔɔ gö̲n) a monastery in ཏེ་རྟོར་ དཀར་མཛེས་ prefecture in Sichuan Province.

ཀ་ཐོག་གདུང་བཞག (gātɔɔ̀ du̲ŋshaà) reliable, steady and truthful [Lit. to put a beam on a pillar].

ཀ་འཐུམ་ (gǝndum) shung. cover of a pillar.

ཀ་དག (gādaà) 1. the void. 2. pure/ clean/ perfect from the beginning.

ཀ་དང་སྐུ་སྲུང་ (gādaŋ gūsuŋ) shung. sm. ཀ་དང་དམག་སྒར་.

ཀ་དང་དམག་སྒར་ (gādaŋ māāgar) shung. the "Gadang" or Bodyguard Regiment in tt.

ཀ་དང་མདའ་དཔོན་ (gādaŋ dɛ̲bön) shung. the commander/ general of the ཀ་དང་ Regiment.

ཀ་དམ་པ་ (gādamba) skt. 1. a kind of tree. 2. a water bird.

ཀ་དར་ (gādar) traditional ceremonial scarf that is hung on pillars at celebrations/ auspicious events.

ཀ་གདན་ (gādɛn) sm. ཀ་བཀྱག.

ཀ་གདུང་ (gāduŋ) beam and pillar.

ཀ་རྟོ་ (gādo) 1. sm. ཀ་བཀྱག. 2. sm. ཀ་རྟོར་.

ཀ་རྟོ་སྟོབས་ལྡན་ (gādo dōbdɛn) having a good/ strong political support or base [Lit. a powerful support/ brace].

ཀ་རྟོར་ (gādɔr) 1. abbr. Kalimpong and Darjeeling. 2. an expended cartridge/ shell.

ཀ་སྡེ་ (gāde) the first series of four letters in the Tibetan alphabet (ཀ་ཁ་ག་ང་).

ཀ་ན་ (gāna) Ghana.

ཀ་ནས་ (gānɛɛ̀) from the start/ beginning.

ཀ་གནམ་ (gānam) a district in Kongpo.

ཀ་པ་ (gāba) the first in a series of things listed alphabetically.

ཀ་པ་རུ་ (gābaru) alabaster.

ཀ་པ་ལ་ (gābala) sm. ཀ་པཱ་ལ་.

ཀ་པཱ་ལ་ (gābala) skull.

ཀ་པཱ་ལ་མཐུག་པོ་ (gābala tūgbo) sm. ཀ་ལི་མཐུག་པོ་.

ཀ་པཱ་ལ་མེད་པ་ (gābala me̱eba) sm. ཀ་ལི་མེད་པ་.

ཀ་པཱ་ལ་ཚ་པོ་ (gābala tsābo) sm. ཀ་ལི་ཚ་པོ་.

ཀ་པཱ་ལ་བསིར་པོ་ (gābala si̱rbu) sm. ཀ་ལི་བསིར་པོ་.

ཀ་པཱ་ལི་ (gābali) sm. ཀ་པཱ་ལ་.

ཀ་པི་(ཏ་) (gābitə) 1. glue. 2. resin, tar, pitch.

ཀ་པུར་ (gābur) Kabul.

ཀ་པེད་ (gābeè) sm. ཀ་བེད་.

ཀ་དཔེ་ (gābe) 1. copybook, a book to practice lessons. 2. elementary primer.

ཀ་ཕན་ (gābɛn) silk or brocade that is used to cover/ decorate pillars.

ཀ་ཕིབས་ (gābib) an extended canopy or veranda of a house/ roof under which people sit.

ཀ་ཕུར་ (gābur) a peg/ stake for tying animals.

ཀ་ཕོར་ (gābɔɔ) a part of a water mill.

ཀ་ཕྲེང་ (gādreŋ) sm. ཀ་ལི་ཕྲེང་བསྒྲིགས་.

ཀ་འཕན་ (gāmbɛn) sm. ཀ་རྒྱན་.

ཀ་བ་ (gāwa) pillar; va.—འཛུགས་ to erect a pillar.

ཀ་བ་སྦྲུལ་མགོ་ཅན་ (gāwa drūngojɛn) sm. ཀ་བ་བུམ་པ་ཅན་.

ཀ་བ་བུམ་པ་ཅན་ (gāwa bu̱mbajɛn) name of a pillar in the Tsuglhakang (in front of the Buddha's statue in the Jokhang).

ཀ་བ་ལི་ (gāwali) 1. a receptacle for a religious text. 2. sm. ཀ་པཱ་ལ་.

ཀ་བ་ཤིང་ལོ་ཅན་ (gāwa shi̱ŋlojɛn) name of a pillar in the Tsuglhakang.

ཀ་བ་སེང་མགོ་ཅན་ (gāwa sēŋgojɛn) name of a pillar in the Tsuglhakang.

ཀ་བར་འཛག་མའི་ལྷན་པ་ (gābar ja̱amɛɛ lhēmba) giving or doing things that are useless, e.g., giving money to sb. who is already very rich [Lit. to patch a pillar with a strand from a broom].

ཀ་བེ་གོ་བེ་ (gābe gōbe) stiff, not flexible (e.g., a dry hide).

ཀ་བར་ (gābar) sm. ཀ་དབྲག.

ཀ་བེད་ (gābeè) name of a fruit.

ཀ་བློན་སྦུག (gālönbuù) Kalimpong.

ཀ་དབྱིབས་ཅན་ (gəyibjɛn) pillar shaped.

ཀ་དབྲག (gābraà) 1. gap, space; va.—འཇོག་ to leave a gap/ space; vi.—ལུས་ to have a space/ gap be left ། ལས་བྱེད་པ་གསར་རྙིང་དབར་ལས་ཀ་ཀ་དབྲག་ལུས་བཞག There was a gap in the work (in doing the work) between the old and the new officials. 2. missing/ skipping sth.; va.—འཇོག་ to miss/ skip a turn; vi.—ལུས་ to accidentally make sb. miss or skip a turn ། མི་དེ་ལ་ཐོབ་སྐལ་མ་སྤྲད་པར་ཀ་དབྲག་བཞག་བཞག (They) skipped giving that person his share.

ཀ་སྦུག (gəbuù) abbr. ཀ་ལོན་སྦུག.

ཀ་མ་རུ་ (gāmaru) marble.

ཀ་མ་ལ་ (gāmala) lotus (blue).

ཀ་མང་མ་ (gāmaŋma) a house or room with many pillars, a large house or room.

ཀ་མད་ (gāmɛɛ̀) the Tibetan alphabet (the sequence of letters) ། ཀ་མད་སུམ་ཅུ་ The thirty letters of the Tibetan alphabet.

ཀ་མི་སི་ (gāmisi) hind. shirt.

ཀ་མིག (gəmiì) 1. pillars ། ཁང་པ་ཀ་མིག་གསུམ་ A three pillar house. 2. the letters of the Tibetan alphabet ། ཀ་མིག་སུམ་ཅུ་ The thirty letters of the Tibetan alphabet. 3. a hole in a pillar.

ཀ་མེད་ (gāmeè) (neg. + vb. + —) no choice but to do the verbal action ། ཁོས་མ་བྱས་ན་ང་མ་འགྲོ་ཀ་མེད་རེད་ If he doesn't do it, I have no choice but to go.

ཀ་རྨ་ (gārma) 1. sm. ཀར་མ་པ་. 2. person's name.

ཀ་རྩེ་ (gādze) top of a pillar.

ཀ་རྫོམ་ (gādzom) sm. ཀ་བཤད་.

ཀ་གཞུ་ (gəshu) piece of wood used below the main beam on top of a pillar.

ཀ་གཞུ་རྩིས་འཁྲིང་ (gəshu dzīidreŋ) abacus.

ཀ་བཞི་གདུང་བརྒྱད་ (gəshi du̱ŋgyɛɛ̀) a good room or house [Lit. four pillars and eight beams].

ཀ་ཟླུམ་གྱི་དབྱིབས་ (gədumgi yi̱b) cylindrical shape.

ཀ་གཟའ་ཐེབས་ (gəsa tēb) vi. to have a pillar suddenly collapse [Lit. the pillar had a stroke].

ཀ་གཟའ་ཕོག (gəsa pɔ̀ɔ̀) sm. ཀ་གཟའ་ཐེབས་.

ཀ་གཟུགས་ (gəsug) pillar shaped.

ཀ་གཟོང་ (gāsoŋ) chisel used to roughen the surface of millstones.

ཀ་ཡང་ཙེ་ (gā ya̱ŋdze) superb, the best.

ཀ་ཡེ་ (gāye) a call used to hail sb.

ཀ་ར་ (gāra) 1. sweets, candy. 2. sugar. 3. tent pole.

ཀ་ར་ཀུ་ཤུ་ (gāra gūshu) Chinese pear leafed crab apple.

ཀ་ར་དཀར་པོ་ (gāra gāābo) refined white sugar.

ཀ་ར་ཅི་ (gāraji) Karachi.

ཀ་ར་ཆི་ (gāraji) sm. ཀ་ར་ཅི་.

ཀ་ར་དོག་དོག (gāra dɔ̄gdɔɔ̀) sm.* ཀ་ར་རྡོག་རྡོག.

ཀ་ར་དུ་ཚང་ཀུང་སི་ (gāra tu̱jaŋ gūŋsi) sugar, tobacco and liquor company.

ཀ་ར་རྡོག་རྡོག (gāra dɔ̱gdɔɔ̀) rock sugar.

ཀ་ར་སྨུག་པོ་ (gāra mūgbo) sm. ཀར་སྨུག.

ཀ་ར་བཟོ་ཁང་ (gāra so̱gaŋ) factory/ plant/ workshop that makes sugar or candy.

ཀ་ར་བཟོ་གྲྭ་ (gāra so̱dra) sugar refinery.

ཀ་ར་ཤིང་ (gārashiŋ) sugar cane.

ཀ་ར་ཧ་རི་ (gāra hāri) sm. བུ་རམ་.

ཀ་རག (gāāraà) lime, whitewash; va.—གཏོང་ to whitewash a wall/ building.

ཀ་རས་ (gāārɛɛ̀) a kind of cotton cloth.

ཀ་རིང་ (gāriŋ) long pillar.

ཀ་རུ་ (gəru) 1. sm. དཀར་པོ་. 2. a stake, wedge.

ཀ་རུ་པིན་ད་ (gərubinda) ch. vanilla.

ཀ་རེ་ (gāre) sm. ག་རེ་.

ཀ་རེ་ཀོ་རེ་ (gāre gōre) 1. dillydallying, dawdling, lingering, procrastinating; va.—བྱེད་ ། ཁོས་ཀ་རེ་ཀོ་རེ་བྱས་ནས་དུས་ཐོག་ཏུ་སླེབས་ཐུབ་མ་སོང་ Because of his dillydallying, he wasn't able to arrive on time. 2. (for speech) beating around the bush, not getting to the point directly; va.—ཤོད་ ། ཁོས་དྲང་པོ་མ་བཤད་པར་ཀ་རེ་ཀོ་རེ་བྱས་ནས་སྐོར་ཀྱི་འདུག He is beating around the bush not telling the truth.

ཀ་ལ་ (gāla) hind. 1. the end of a pipe from which water runs. 2. a water outlet or tap.

ཀ་ལ་ཀ་ཏ་ (gāla gāda) sm. ཀ་ལ་ཀ་ཏར་.

ཀ་ལ་ཀ་ཏར་ (gāla gādar) Calcutta.

ཀ་ལ་མདོང་མོ་ (gāla do̱ŋmo) hind.tib. underground water pipe.

ཀ་ལ་པིང་ཀ་ (gāla bi̱ŋgə) name of a legendary bird.

ཀ་ལ་བིང་ཀ་ (gāla bi̱ŋgə) sm. ཀ་ལ་པིང་ཀ་.

ཀ་ལ་ཤ་ (gālasha) pitcher, jar, glass.

ཀ་ལག (gālaà) sm. དཀར་རག.

ཀ་ལི་ (gəli; gəbli) human skull.

ཀ་ལི་ཀ་ཏར་ (gəli gādar) sm. ཀ་ལ་ཀ་ཏར་.

ཀ་ལི་ཀ་ (gəliga) the seed of a white flower used in religious rites.

ཀ་ལི་མཐུག་པོ་ (gəli tūgbo) 1. sb. stubborn, sb. who

insists on his own views/ ideas. 2. sb. who is dull/ not smart/ not clever.

ཀ་ལི་ཕྲེང་བསྒྲིགས་ (gəli trēŋdrig) a poem in which each line begins with a letter of the Tibetan alphabet in alphabetical order.

ཀ་ལི་མེད་པ་ (gəli me̱èba) 1. cowardly, not brave, timid. 2. sb. who is dull/ not smart/ not clever.

ཀ་ལི་ཚ་པོ་ (gəli tsābo) sm. ཀ་ལི་མཐུག་པོ་.

ཀ་ལི་ཤོར་ (gəli shɔ̄ɔ̄) sm. ཏ་ལ་ཤོར་.

ཀ་ལི་བསེར་པོ་ (gāli sīrbu) clever, alert, intelligent.

ཀ་ལིང་ཀ་ (gəliŋga) name of a bird.

ཀ་ལིང་སྒོ་བཞི་ (gəliŋ go̱shi) name of an old stupa that used to be in Lhasa.

ཀ་ལོན་སྤུག (gālönbuù) Kalimpong.

ཀ་ཤ་ (gāsha) 1. a type of white mushroom. 2. a kind of weed/ grass growing in marshy areas.

ཀ་ཤི་ (gāshi) Benares.

ཀ་ཤི་ཀ་ (gəshiga) a fine cotton cloth made in Benares.

ཀ་ཤི་མིར་ (gāshimir) Kashmir.

ཀ་ཤུ་ཀ་ (gəshuga) skt. a stone that is used to rub pieces of gold to determine the quality of gold.

ཀ་ཤུབས་ (gəshub) cloth used to decorate/ encase pillars in a monastery or temple. 2. a case for a cup.

ཀ་ཤོད་ (gāpshöö) name of an aristocratic family (Kapshoba).

ཀ་བཤད་ (gābshɛɛ̀) sm. ཀ་ལི་ཕྲེང་བསྒྲིགས་.

ཀག (gāà) 1. arc. sudden ། གཉིད་ཀག་གིས་བསད་པ་རེད་ (He) woke up suddenly. 2. sm. ཧག.

ཀང་ཀ་ (gāŋga) skt. a vulture type bird whose head is black and back is white.

ཀང་ཀའི་མཆུ་ (gāŋgɛju) skt.tib. a kind of pliers used in traditional Tibetan medicine.

ཀང་ཀོའི་ (gāŋguo) the Congo.

ཀང་ཀོའི་པའུ་ (gāŋguo bū) Brazzaville.

ཀང་ཀོའི་ལི་ (gāŋguoli̱) Leopoldville.

ཀང་ངེ་ཀོང་ངེ་ (gāŋŋe gōŋŋe) uneven/ bumpy/ undulating (for roads and terrain).

ཀང་ཆིན་ (gəŋjin) ch. piano.

ཀང་ཏྲ་ (gāŋdra) hind. fork (for eating).

ཀང་པ་ལིང་ (gāmbaliŋ) hind. blanket.

ཀང་ར་ (gāŋra) hind. cucumber.

ཀང་ལིང་ (gəŋliŋ) ch. program.

ཀང་ལོར་ (gāŋlor) ch.tib. Hong Kong dollar.

ཀང་ཨའོ་ (gāŋao) ch. abbr. of Hong Kong and Macao.

ཀད་ཀྱིས་ (gɛ̀ɛgi) gradually, slowly.

ཀན་ (gɛ̄n) 1. the other side ། ཆུ་ཕར་ཀན་ན་ On the other side of the river. 2. middle finger used in reading pulses in Tibetan medicine. 3. ch. name of the pulse (vein) on the wrist that Tibetan doctors feel with their middle finger.

ཀན་ཀྲང་ (gɛ̄ndraŋ) ch. sm. ཀན་ཁྲང་.

ཀན་ཁྲང་ (gɛ̄ndraŋ) ch. wooden (dough) roller/ rolling pin.

ཀན་ཁྲང་ཁྱེར་ནས་མེ་ལ་ཕུ་བརྒྱབ་ (gɛ̄ndraŋ kyērnɛ me̱la pū gyə̱b) ch.tib. useless work/ action [Lit. carrying a wooden rolling pin while blowing on a fire].

ཀན་དུར་ (gɛ̄ndur) ch. somersault; va.—སློག to somersault.

ཀན་མ་ (gɛ̄nma) sm. ཀན་, 2 and 3.

ཀན་ཙ་ (gɛ̄ndza) ch.tib. sm. ཀན་, 3.

ཀན་ཚལ་ (gɛ̄ndzɛɛ) ch.tib. dried vegetables.

ཀན་མཛུབ་མོ་ (gɛ̄n dzu̱bmo) ch.tib. sm. ཀན་, 2.

ཀན་འཕོག (gɛ̄nwɔɔ̀) ch.tib. sm. ཀན་ཙ་.

ཀན་ཡིའུ་ (gɛ̄nyiu) ch. glycerine.

ཀན་གཡས་འཕོག (gɛ̄nyɛwɔɔ̀) ch.tib. the vein/ pulse taken with the middle finger on the right wrist.

ཀན་གཡོན་འཕོག (gɛ̄nyönwɔɔ̀) ch.tib. the vein/ pulse taken with the middle finger on the left wrist.

ཀན་སུའུ་ (gɛ̄nsu) Gansu Province.

ཀན་ལྷོ་ (gɛ̄nlho) southern Gansu Province.

ཀན་ལྷོ་བོད་རིགས་རང་སྐྱོང་ཁུལ་ (gɛ̄nlho pörig ra̱ŋgyoŋküü) Tibetan Autonomous District in South Gansu.

ཀབ་ (gəb) a kind of gem.

ཀབ་ཀོབ་ (gəbgob) sm. ཀ་བེ་ཀོབ་བེ་.

ཀབ་ཅར་ (gābjar) eng. cultured (pearl).

ཀབ་ཚེ་པ་ (gəbdzeba) a period of great famine (in a past eons).

ཀབ་ལི་ (gəbli) skull.

ཀབ་ལི་མཐུག་པོ་ (gəbli tūgbo) sm. ཀ་ལི་མཐུག་པོ་.

ཀབ་ལི་མེད་པ་ (gəbli me̱èba) sm. ཀ་ལི་མེད་པ་.

ཀབ་ལི་ཚ་པོ་ (gəbli tsāābo) sm. ཀ་ལི་མཐུག་པོ་.

ཀབ་ལི་བསེར་པོ་ (gəbli sīību) sm. ཀ་ལི་བསེར་པོ་.

ཀབ་ཤ་ (gəbsha) a kind of Indian style leather shoe.

ཀམ་ཀམ་ (gāmgam) abbr. of ཀམ་མི་ཀུམ་མི་.

ཀམ་ཀུམ་ (gāmgum) abbr. of ཀམ་མི་ཀུམ་མི་.

ཀམ་པ་ (gāmba) skt. the first Tibetan month.

ཀམ་པ་ནི་ (gāmbani) eng. a company, an enterprise.

ཀམ་པ་ལི་ (gāmbali) hind. blanket.

ཀམ་བྷོགས་ཡ་ (gāmbhogya) Cambodia.

ཀམ་མི་ཀུམ་མི་ (gāmmi gūmmi) 1. wrinkled (for cloth). 2. decrepit (usu. used for an old person unable to get up or walk well).

ཀམ་མེ་ཀེམ་མེ་ (gāmme gēmme) a person whose eyes involuntarily blink a lot.

ཀམ་ཚང་ (gāmdzaŋ) a Karmapa monastery.

ཀའན་སུའུ་ (gānsu) sm. ཀན་སུའུ་.

ཀའི་ལིང་ས་དཀར་ (gɛ̄liŋ sāgar) ch.tib. kaolinite.

ཀའུ་ཀ་རི་ (gāwu gāri) a type of tree.

ཀའུ་ཡ་ཁྲི་ (gāwu ya̱dre) ch. a type of sewing used on collars.

ཀའི་མའི་ལེན་ (gēmelen) ch. calcium magnesium.

ཀའོ་ཡ་ཀོའི་ (gōyago) ch. a pressure cooker.

ཀའོ་ལི་ (gōli) ch. type of edible plant.

ཀའོ་ལིའང་ (gōliaŋ) ch. sorghum.

ཀར་ (gār) 1. sm. གདིང་. 2. pain.

ཀར་ཀོར་ (gārgor) abbr. ཀ་རེ་ཀོ་རེ་.

ཀར་ཀོར་ཁྲལ་སེལ་ (gārgor trɛ̄sɛɛ) working in a manner that is not serious/ diligent, working carelessly; va.—བྱེད་.

ཀར་སྐྱིན་ (gārgyin) loan.

ཀར་བརྒྱུད་ (gārgyü̱ü) abbr. of ཀརྨ་བཀའ་བརྒྱུད་.

ཀར་ཆག (gārcaà) sm. དཀར་ཆག.

ཀར་མ་ (gārma) 1. a person's name. 2. abbr. ཀར་མ་པ་.

ཀར་མ་པ་ (gārmapa) 1. a subsect of the Kagyu sect. 2. a member of the Karma Kagyu subsect.

ཀར་སྣང་གི་རྩིས་ (gārñaŋgi dzīi) shung. weather forecasting done through astrological methods.

ཀར་སྦུག (gārmug) brown sugar, molasses.

ཀར་ཡོལ་ (gāryöö) sm. དཀར་ཡོལ་.

ཀར་ལུགས་ (gārluù) the religious system of the ཀརྨ་བཀའ་བརྒྱུད་.

ཀར་ཤུབས་ (gārshup) covering for a cup.

ཀར་ས་ (gārsa) brick tea.

ཀས་ (gārsa) sm. ཀར་ས་.

ཀརྨ་ (gārma) sm. ཀར་མ་.

ཀརྨ་བཀའ་བརྒྱུད་ (gārma gārgyü̱ü) sm. ཀར་མ་པ་, 1.

ཀརྨ་པ་ (gārmapa) sm. ཀར་མ་པ་.

ཀཱ་ཀ་རུ་ (gāgaru) skt. crab.

ཀཱ་ཀོ་ལ་ (gāgola) skt. 1. name of a legendary bird resembling a large raven. 2. name of a kind of poison.

ཀཱ་ཡ་ (gāya) skt. body.

ཀཱ་རི་ཀ་ (gāriga) skt. a poem written in stanzas.

ཀཱ་ལི་ (gāli) skt. consonants in the Tibetan alphabet.

ཀི་ (gī) 1. sm. ཀི་སྒྲ་. 2. filler particle used as second syllable in words, e.g. ཡ་ཀི་.

ཀི་ཀི་ (gīgi) a yell to get sb.'s attention (like "hey").

ཀི་ཀི་བསོ་བསོ་ (gīgi sōso) a yell when doing an incense offering to the gods.

ཀི་ཀུ་ (gīgu) sm. ཀི་གུ.

ཀི་ཀོང་ (gīguŋ) a kind of wild garlic.

ཀི་གུ (gīgu) the vowel "i".

ཀི་རྒྱག (gī gyaà) sm. ཀི་སྒྲ་རྒྱག.

ཀི་སྒྲ་ (gīdra) a yell/ scream (usu. used when

engaging in battle); va.—རྒྱག; —སྒྲོག.

ཀི་དིར་ (gīdir) sm. ཀི་ལྡིར་.

ཀི་འདེབས་ (gī de̲b) sm. ཀི་སྒྲ་རྒྱག.

ཀི་ལྡིར་ (gīdir) a shrill or piercing sound.

ཀི་ལྡིར་ཤུབ་ལྡིར་ (gīdir shūbdir) a shrill or piercing sound, yelling and shouting; va.—བྱེད་.

ཀི་ཙི་ (gīdzi) tickling; va.—གསོག to tickle; vi.—ཟ་ to get tickled.

ཀི་ཙི་ཚ་པོ་ (gīdzi tsābo) ticklish.

ཀི་ཝིན་དལ་ (gīwindɛ) eng. quintal (100 kg.).

ཀི་ར་ཧོ་ར་ (gīra hōra) yelling and shouting; va.—བྱེད་.

ཀི་རིང་ (gīriŋ) a long ཀི་སྒྲ་.

ཀི་ལ་ཀི་ལན་ (gīlə gīlɛn) revenge, retribution, doing tit for tat; va.— སྤྲོད་; — རྒྱག.

ཀི་ལོ་ (gīlu) eng. kilogram.

ཀི་ལོ་མི་ཏ་ (gīlo mi̲drə) eng. kilometer.

ཀི་ཧི་ཧི་ (gī hīhi) a cry/ shout made when attacking an enemy.

ཀིང་ཀ་ར་ (gīŋgara) messenger.

ཀིང་ཀང་ (gīŋgaŋ) ch. sm. རྡོ་རྗེ་.

ཀིང་ཤུ་ཀ་ (gīŋshugə) sm. ཀེང་ཤུ་ཀ་.

ཀིའུ་ (gīwu) 1. garlic. 2. a shout made to draw the attention of sb. at a distance.

ཀིར་ (gīr) sm. བསྐུར་.

ཀིལ་ (gīl) sm. ག་ལེ་.

ཀུ་ཀུ་བུ་ཤི་ (gūgubushi) a type of bird.

ཀུ་སྒྲ་ (gūdrə) meaningless yelling, noisy talk.

ཀུ་ཅོ་ (gūjo) noise, yelling, clamor, hullabaloo; va.—སྒྲོག; —འདོན་.

ཀུ་ཅོ་ཅ་ཅོ་ (gūjo jājo) sm. ཀུ་ཅོ་.

ཀུ་ཅོ་དི་རི་ (gūjo di̲ri) sm. ཀུ་ཅོ་.

ཀུ་ཐུག (gūduù) sm. ཐབས་ཟད་.

ཀུ་དམ་ (gūdam) a container made from a gourd.

ཀུ་དིང་ངེ་ (gūdiŋŋe) sm. ཀུ་ཅོ་.

ཀུ་དི་རི་ (gūdiri) sm. ཀུ་ཅོ་.

ཀུ་དིར་ (gūdir) sm. ཀུ་ཅོ་.

ཀུ་དིར་བཞད་སྒྲ་ (gūdir she̲dra) yelling and making fun of/ ridiculing.

ཀུ་དོག (gūdɔɔ̀) 1. narrow, tight ¶ ལམ་ཁ་ཀུ་དོག A narrow road. 2. arc. deficiency, shortage.

ཀུ་པ་ (gūbə) Cuba.

ཀུ་བ་ (gūwə) ch. sm. ཀྭ་.

ཀུ་བ་ལ་ (gūwala) sm. ཀུ་མུད་.

ཀུ་མུ་ད་ (gūmuda) sm. ཀུ་མུད་.

ཀུ་མུད་ (gūmüù) water lily.

ཀུ་མུད་ཕན་ (gūmüùpɛ̄n) poet. moonlight.

ཀུ་ཙེ་ (gūdze) ch. a food carrying container (tiffin) that has stacked layers.

ཀུ་ཙེ་ལྔ་བརྩེགས་ (gūdze ŋādzeg) food carrying container (tiffin) that has five stacked layers.

ཀུ་ཡངས་ (gūyaŋ) sm. གུ་ཡངས་.

ཀུ་ཡངས་དོག (gū ya̲ŋdɔɔ̀) sm. གུ་ཡངས་དོག.

ཀུ་རུ་ (gūru) 1. a wooden X shaped cross put on the mouth of a calf to stop it from suckling; va.—རྒྱག. 2. an X shaped spindle for spinning wool. 3. sm. ཀུ་རུ་ཁ་. 4. va.—རྒྱག to block or thwart sb.'s aim/ goal/ source of income/ plan ¶ མི་དེའི་ལས་ཀ་འཕྲོག་ནས་ཁ་ལ་ཀུ་རུ་བརྒྱབ་སོང་. (He) thwarted that person by stealing his job.

ཀུ་རུ་ཁ་ (gāruka) 1. any kind of "X" shaped cross; va.—རྒྱག to make an "X," to make sth. in the shape of an "X."

ཀུ་རུ་ཁ་རྟགས་ (gāru kādaà) 1. the symbol "X." 2. sm. ཀུ་རུ་, 2.

ཀུ་རུ་པིན་ད་ (gəru bīndə) a type of grass.

ཀུ་རུ་ཟམ་པ་ (gəru sa̲mba) colloquial name of a bridge in southeast Lhasa.

ཀུ་རུ་ཡོག་ག (gəru yɔ̲ɔ̀ga) an X shaped wooden spindle used in spinning.

ཀུ་རུམ་ (gūrum) 1. giving in, capitulating, accepting defeat, surrendering (in battle, games, sports, arguments); va.—ཞུ་ to give in/ capitulate/ surrender/ accept defeat ¶ རྩེད་མོའི་འགྲན་སྡུར་ནང་ཁོ་པས་ཀུ་རུམ་ཞུས་སོང་ He accepted defeat in the sports contest. 2. being afraid/ scared.

ཀུ་རེ་ (gūre) kidding around, joking; va.—བྱེད་; —ཞུ་ to kid, to joke; vi.—ཐལ་ to have a joke be carried too far (and the person gets angry) ¶ ངས་ཁྱེད་རང་ལ་ཀུ་རེ་ཞུས་པ་ལས་དོན་དངོས་དེ་ལྟར་མིན་ I was just kidding. I didn't mean it.

ཀུ་རེ་གཏམ་མཚར་ (gūre dāmdzar) talk that is interesting and humorous.

ཀུ་ལ་གངས་རི་ (gūlə kə̲ŋri) Mt. Kula Kangri (in Bhutan).

ཀུ་ལི་ (gūli) hind. porter, coolie.

ཀུ་ཤ་ (gūshə) a kind of reedlike grass that is considered auspicious in religion and is commonly used as a broom in lay society.

ཀུ་ཤུ་ (gūshu) apple; va.—འཐོག to pick an apple.

ཀུ་ཧྲང་ (gūhraŋ) 1. goat. 2. wild ass.

ཀུག (gūg) sm. ཀུག་ཀུག.

ཀུག་ཀུག (gūgguù) 1. sound of the cuckoo bird. 2. the cuckoo bird. 3. གུག་གུག.

ཀུང་ཀྲང་ (gūŋdraŋ) ch. section chief/ foreman (in a workshop or on a building site).

ཀུང་ཁང་ (gūŋgaŋ) ch.tib. postal station in tt. transportation/ communications system.

ཀུང་ཁྲི་ (gūŋdre) ch. meter (the distance unit).

ཀུང་ཁྲིང་ཧྲི་ (gūŋdreŋhre) ch. engineer.

ཀུང་ཅིན་ (gūŋjin) ch. kilogram.

ཀུང་ཆིང་ (gūŋciŋ) ch. hectare.

ཀུང་ཏང་ (gūŋdaŋ) ch. the Labor Party.

ཀུང་དུང་ཀང་ལིང་ (gūŋduŋ gəŋliŋ) ch. the "common programme" promulgated in 1949 as a precursor to the Chinese constitution [in Tib. སྤྱི་མཉམ་རྩ་འཛིན་].

ཀུང་ཙེ་རིལ་བའི་ཇ་རིལ་ (gūŋdze re̲wei jə̲rii) a type of round brick tea that comes from Yunnan.

ཀུང་ཟི་ (gūŋsi) ch. sm. ཀུང་སི་.

ཀུང་ལི་ (gūŋle) ch. millimeter.

ཀུང་ལི་ (gūŋli) ch. kilometer.

ཀུང་སི་ (gūŋsi) ch. company, firm, corporation ¶ ཨར་ལས་ཀུང་སི་ Construction company.

ཀུང་ཧྲུ་ (gūŋhru) ch. government office.

ཀུང་ཧྲེ་ (gūŋhre) ch. commune.

ཀུང་ཧྲེང་ (gūŋhreŋ) ch. liter.

ཀུན་ (gün) all, every, entire ¶ དེ་མི་ཀུན་གྱིས་ཤེས་ཀྱི་ཡོད་པ་རེད་ All people know that.

ཀུན་དཀྱིལ་ (güngyii) amidst all, in the center of a group.

ཀུན་དཀྲིས་ (gündriì) a type of delusion that sometimes comes when meditating.

ཀུན་བཀྲམ་ (gündram) disseminating, diffusing, broadcasting.

ཀུན་སྐྱབས་ (güngyəb) sb. in whom everyone places their hope for protection, the savior/ refuge of all sentient beings, epithet of the Buddha and bodhisattvas.

ཀུན་སྐྱབས་གླིང་ (güngyəbliŋ) a garden in Shigatse that belongs to the Panchen Lama.

ཀུན་སྐྱེ་ (güngye) able to grow everywhere.

ཀུན་སྐྱོ་ (güngyo) sadness/ regret everywhere, widespread sadness/ regret.

ཀུན་བཀོས་ (güngüù) poet. a well.

ཀུན་ཁྱབ་ (güngyəb) 1. widespread, universal, all-pervasive; vi.—ཏུ་འགྲོ་ to become widespread/ universal ¶ དམངས་གཙོ་ནི་འཛམ་གླིང་ཀུན་ཁྱབ་ཀྱི་ལམ་ལུགས་ཤིག་ཏུ་གྱུར་ཡོད་ Democracy has become widespread throughout the world. 2. an epithet of the Buddha.

ཀུན་ཁྱབ་གློག་འཕྲིན་ཁང་ (güngyəb lɔ̲gdringaŋ) sm. ཀུན་ཁྱབ་རླུང་འཕྲིན་ཁང་.

ཀུན་ཁྱབ་ཏུ་ (güngyəbtu) in all areas, universally, everywhere, widespread ¶ དམངས་གཙོ་ནི་འཛམ་གླིང་ཀུན་ཁྱབ་ཏུ་གྱུར་ཡོད་ Democracy has become widespread throughout the world.

ཀུན་ཁྱབ་བདེན་དོན་ (güngyəb de̲dön) universal truth.

ཀུན་ཁྱབ་ནད་ཡམས་ (güngyəb ne̲yam) widespread epidemic.

ཀུན་ཁྱབ་དཔེ་དེབ་ (gũngyəb bēdep) popular edition, a book that has become widespread.

ཀུན་ཁྱབ་རྩ་ཚིག་ (gũngyəb dzədzii) shung. a proclamation/ edict disseminated everywhere.

ཀུན་ཁྱབ་རང་བཞིན་ (gũngyəb rəŋshin) universal nature, universality ། མ་ལེ་རིང་ལུགས་ཀྱི་ཀུན་ཁྱབ་རང་བཞིན་དེ་མི་རྣམས་ཤེས་སུ་འཇུག་དགོས་ We have to make everyone know the universal nature of Marxist-Leninism.

ཀུན་ཁྱབ་རླུང་འཕྲིན་ (gũngyəb lūŋdrin) radio broadcasting.

ཀུན་ཁྱབ་རླུང་འཕྲིན་ཁང་ (gũngyəb lūŋdringãŋ) radio broadcasting station.

ཀུན་ཁྱབ་རླུང་འཕྲིན་ལས་ཁུངས་ (gũngyəb lūŋdrin lɛ̀ɛ̀guŋ) radio station, broadcasting station.

ཀུན་ཁྱབ་སློབ་གསོ་ (gũngyəb lōbso) a teaching/ type of education that is widespread or universal.

ཀུན་མཁས་ (gũnkɛɛ̀) expert in all.

ཀུན་མཁྱེན་ (gũnkyen) 1. omniscient, all-knowing. 2. an epithet of the Buddha and bodhisattvas.

ཀུན་མཁྱེན་ཀུན་ཐུབ་ (gũnkyen gũndub) knowing all and able to do all.

ཀུན་མཁྱེན་ཀུན་གཟིགས་ (gũnkyen gũnsii) 1. omniscient and all-seeing. 2. an epithet of the Buddha and bodhisattvas.

ཀུན་མཁྱེན་ཉིད་ (gũnkyen ñii) omniscience, knowledge of all.

ཀུན་མཁྱེན་ཡེ་ཤེས་ (gũnkyen yeshɛɛ̀) all-knowing/ omniscient wisdom.

ཀུན་གྱི་མིག་ལར་འདོམས་པ་ (gũngi miglar domba) setting an example for everybody ། མི་ངན་ལ་ཀུན་གྱི་མིག་ལར་འདོམས་པའི་ཁྲིམས་གཅོད་གཏོང་དགོས་ We must punish evil persons to set an example for everybody.

ཀུན་གྱིས་བཀུར་བ་ (gũngii gũrwa) sb. everyone respects.

ཀུན་གྱིས་ཤེས་གསལ་ (gũngii shēsɛɛ) common knowledge, known by everybody.

ཀུན་གྲུབ་ (gũndrub) 1. vi. to accomplish all/ everything. 2. poet. autumn.

ཀུན་དགའ་ (gũŋgə) 1. popular, liked by all. 2. a person's name.

ཀུན་དགའ་ཅན་ (gũŋgəjɛn) happy, joyous.

ཀུན་དགའ་མཉམ་སྒྲོ་ (gũnga ñamdro) everyone being happy and joyful.

ཀུན་དགའ་དོན་འགྲུབ་ (gũnga töndrub) (slang) money ། ཀུན་དགའ་དོན་འགྲུབ་མེད་ན་ཚར་བ་རེད་ If (you) don't have money (you) are finished. [Lit. that which achieves all one's happiness].

ཀུན་དགའ་ལྡན་ (gũŋgədɛn) sm. ཀུན་དགའ་ཅན་.

ཀུན་དགའ་བོ་ (gũŋgawo) Ananda, one of the disciples of the Buddha.

ཀུན་དགའ་མཚོ་ (gũŋgatso) Lake Kokonor.

ཀུན་དགའ་བཟང་པོ་ (gũnga saŋbo) name of the lama who founded the Ngor sect (1382-1456).

ཀུན་དགའ་ར་བ་ (gũnga rawa) 1. temple or shrine in a monastery. 2. debating grove in a monastery. 3. garden, park. 4. library in a monastery.

ཀུན་དགའ་ར་བ་པ་ (gũnga rawaba) 1. a monk studying in the debating grove. 2. sb. who looks after a ཀུན་དགའ་ར་བ་.

ཀུན་དགའ་རྭ་བ་ (gũnga rawa) sm. ཀུན་དགའ་ར་བ་.

ཀུན་དགའ་རྭ་བ་པ་ (gũnga rawaba) sm. ཀུན་དགའ་ར་བ་པ་.

ཀུན་དགའི་དཔྱིད་དུ་འགྱུར་ (gũngɛ jìidu gyur) shung. vi. to become joyful/ happy ། ལུགས་གཉིས་བུ་བའི་འཇུག་ཕྱོགས་མ་འཆོལ་བས་སྐྱེ་བོ་ཀུན་དགའི་དཔྱིད་དུ་གྱུར་ Because (they) chose the right path on both spiritual and temporal matters, all the people became happy.

ཀུན་དགའི་ར་བ་ (gũngɛ rawa) sm. ཀུན་དགའ་ར་བ་.

ཀུན་དགའི་རོས་ཚིམ་ (gũngɛ röödzim) shung. vi. to be happy and content ། སྲོག་བྲལ་སྲོག་གི་དབང་པོ་སླར་ཐོབ་པ་ལྟར་གདོང་ཅན་པ་མཐའ་དག་ཡིད་ཀུན་དགའི་རོས་ཚིམ་པར་གྱུར་ཏོ་ All the Tibetans became happy and content as if they died and came to life again.

ཀུན་འགེངས་ (gũngeŋ) poet. sky.

ཀུན་འགྲུབ་ (gũndrub) sm. ཀུན་གྲུབ་.

ཀུན་འགྲོ་ (gũndro) 1. all-pervasive. 2. poet. sky.

ཀུན་ཆུབ་ (gũnjub) sm. ཤེས་རབ་.

ཀུན་མཉམ་ (gũñam) equal in all ways.

ཀུན་སྙོམ་ (gũñom) all even.

ཀུན་ཏུ་ (gũndu) 1. everywhere, in all places ། ཡུལ་ཀུན་ཏུ་དར་བའི་ལམ་ལུགས་ A custom that has spread everywhere. 2. all the time, always ། དུས་ཀུན་ཏུ་གནས་གཅིག་ཏུ་བསྡད་པས་ Because (they) lived in one place all the time. 3. (— + vb.) completely, very, extremely ། ཀུན་ཏུ་ལེགས་ Completely good.

ཀུན་ཏུ་སྐྱོ་ (gũndu gyō) sm. ཀུན་སྐྱོ་.

ཀུན་ཏུ་ཁྱབ་ (gũndu kyəb) sm. ཀུན་ཁྱབ་.

ཀུན་ཏུ་འཇུག་ (gũndu jug) 1. va. to have many applications/ uses ། འདི་ཀུན་ཏུ་འཇུག་པའི་འཕྲུལ་འཁོར་གྱི་ལྷུ་ལག་ཅིག་རེད་ This is a machine part that has many applications. 2. one of the noble truths—suffering.

ཀུན་ཏུ་རྟོག་ (gũndu dɔ̄ɔ̀) 1. va. to investigate/ consider thoroughly. 2. sm. རྣམ་པར་རྟོག་པ་.

ཀུན་ཏུ་བཟང་པོ་ (gũndu saŋbo) 1. completely good. 2. epithet for Buddha and bodhisattvas.

ཀུན་ཏི་ (gũnte) name of the mother of the five Pandava brothers.

ཀུན་བཏུས་ (gũndüü) abbr. ཀུན་ལས་བཏུས་.

ཀུན་རྟོག་ (gũndɔɔ̀) abbr. ཀུན་ཏུ་རྟོག.

ཀུན་ཐམས་ཅད་ (gũn tāmjɛɛ̀) all.

ཀུན་ཐུབ་ (gũndub) 1. able to do anything/ everything, almighty, omnipotent ། ཀུན་ཐུབ་ཀྱི་སྟོབས་ཤུགས་ Power that is capable of doing anything. 2. universal, all-purpose, all-around ། ཀུན་ཐུབ་ལུས་རྩལ་པ་ An all-round athlete. 3. epithet for the Buddha.

ཀུན་ཐུབ་འཁོར་སྐྱོགས་ (gũndub kōrdeg) all-purpose/ universal machine tool or lathe.

ཀུན་ཐུབ་འདྲུད་འཐེན་འཁོར་ལོ་ (gũndub dründen kɔ̄ɔ̄lo) all-purpose tractor.

ཀུན་ཐུབ་འདྲུད་འཐེན་འཕྲུལ་འཁོར་ (gũndub dründen trüügɔɔ) sm. ཀུན་ཐུབ་འདྲུད་འཐེན་འཁོར་ལོ་.

ཀུན་ཐུབ་ལུས་རྩལ་པ་ (gũndub lüdzɛba) all-around athlete.

ཀུན་མཐོང་ (gũndoŋ) nh. of ཀུན་གཟིགས་.

ཀུན་དང་ཀུན་མོས་ (gũndɛɛ̀ gũnmöö) person who is admired and respected by all.

ཀུན་དོང་ (gũndoŋ) onion, leek.

ཀུན་དོན་ (gũndün) public welfare, public interest, interest of all ། ཀུན་དོན་ལ་མི་ཚང་མས་སེམས་ཁུར་བྱ་དགོས་ All people should be concerned with public welfare.

ཀུན་བདག་ (gũndaà) lord of the universe, lord of all.

ཀུན་བདེ་ (gũnde) all happy.

ཀུན་བདེ་གླིང་ (gũndeliŋ) 1. Kundeling Labrang/ monastery (in Lhasa). 2. the Kundeling Rinpoche (one of the Hutukthu incarnations who served as regent of Tibet and who was head of Kundeling monastery).

ཀུན་བདེ་གླིང་རྟ་ཚག་ (gũndeliŋ dādzaà) sm. ཀུན་བདེ་གླིང་.

ཀུན་བདེན་ (gũnden) all true.

ཀུན་དྲིལ་ན་ (gũn driinə) sm. སྤྱིར་བསྡོམས་.

ཀུན་འདྲེན་ (gũndren) the Buddha.

ཀུན་ལྡན་ (gũndɛn) poet. Iron-Mouse year.

ཀུན་ལྡན་འཐེན་ཤུགས་ (gũndɛn tēnshuù) the ability to attract everything.

ཀུན་ནས་ (gũnnɛɛ̀) 1. from all, in all ། ཀུན་ནས་ལེགས་པ་ Good in all ways. 2. from everywhere ། ས་གནས་ཀུན་ནས་ཡོང་བའི་འཐུས་མི་ The delegates who came from all localities. 3. by all/ everyone ། མི་སེར་ཀུན་ནས་ངོ་ལོག་བརྒྱབ་སོང་ All the subjects revolted.

ཀུན་ནས་གྲགས་པ་ (gũnnɛɛ̀ tragba) known by all, famous.

ཀུན་ནུས་ (gũnnüü) sm. ཀུན་ཐུབ་.

ཀུན་པོ་ (gũmbo) all.

ཀུན་སྤྱོད་ (gũnjüü) 1. conduct, behavior (refers to behavior, thoughts, personality) ¶ བུ་མོ་དེ་ཀུན་སྤྱོད་བཟང་པོ་ཡོད་པ་རེད་ That girl is well behaved. 2. moral/ ethical (conduct) ¶ ཀུན་སྤྱོད་ཀྱི་སློབ་གསོ་ Moral education. 3. widely used, widespread ¶ ཀུན་སྤྱོད་ཐོན་རྫས་ A widely used product. 4. all purpose.

ཀུན་སྤྱོད་ཀྱི་བློ་སྦྱོང་ (gũnjüügi lõjoŋ) moral cultivation/ practice.

ཀུན་སྤྱོད་ཀྱི་སློབ་གསོ་ (gũnjüügi lõbso) moral training/ education.

ཀུན་སྤྱོད་སྐོར་གྱི་ལྟ་ཚུལ་ (gũnjüü gɔ̃ɔrgi dādzüü) moral ideas/ views.

ཀུན་སྤྱོད་ཀྱི་འདུ་ཤེས་ (gũnjüügi du̲sheè) moral concept.

ཀུན་སྤྱོད་ཀྱི་གནད་དོན་ (gũnjüügi nɛ̃ɛdön) a moral/ life-style problem (term used during the Cultural Revoution for people who committed moral lapses such as adultery).

ཀུན་སྤྱོད་ངན་འགྱུར་ (gũnjüü ŋ̲engyur) declining moral conduct ¶ ཕྲུ་གུ་དེ་ཀུན་སྤྱོད་ངན་འགྱུར་བྱུང་བཞག The child's moral conduct has declined.

ཀུན་སྤྱོད་ཆ་ཚུལ་ (gũnjüü cādzüü) moral way of dressing.

ཀུན་སྤྱོད་ཉམས་ཉེས་ (gũnjüü ñamñeè) moral crisis.

ཀུན་སྤྱོད་ཐ་སྙད་ (gũnjüügi tãñeè) words that are broadly/ widely used in language.

ཀུན་སྤྱོད་དག་བཅོས་ (gũnjüü ta̲gjöö) sm. ཀུན་སྤྱོད་དག་ཐེར་.

ཀུན་སྤྱོད་དག་ཐེར་ (gũnjüü ta̲gdee) rectification/ improvement of moral behavior, the method of criticism and self-criticism to cleanse thinking and improve moral behavior; va.—བྱེད་ ¶ ཀུན་སྤྱོད་དག་ཐེར་གྱི་ལས་འགུལ་ Rectification campaign.

ཀུན་སྤྱོད་དར་སྤེལ་ (gũnjüü ta̲gsöö) the spreading of moral conduct/ morality.

ཀུན་སྤྱོད་འཕྲུལ་ཆས་ (gũnjüü trũüjɛɛ̀) a universal/ all-purpose machine.

ཀུན་སྤྱོད་སློབ་གསོ་ (gũnjüü lõbso) education or guidance in morals/ ethics.

ཀུན་སྤྱོད་གསུམ་དང་སྤྱོད་ཚུལ་ལྔ་ (gũnjüüsum da̲ŋ jöödzüü ŋ̲ā) the three behaviors and five conducts: the three behaviors are subjectivism, bureaucracy and sectarianism; the five conducts are: bureaucratic airs, lethargy, extravagance, arrogance and coquettishness.

ཀུན་སྤྱོད་བསམ་བློ་ (gũnjüü sãmlo) behaving and thinking ¶ ཁོའི་ཀུན་སྤྱོད་བསམ་བློ་འཁྱེར་སྟངས་ཡག་པོ་ཡོད་པ་རེད་ His way of behaving and thinking are good.

ཀུན་ཕན་ (gũnbɛn) beneficial to all, all purposeful ¶ ཀུན་ཕན་གྱི་བསམ་བློ་བཟང་པོ་ Good thoughts benefiting all.

ཀུན་ཕན་རིང་ལུགས་ (gũnbɛn ri̲nluù) humanitarianism [Lit. the system of benefiting everyone].

ཀུན་འགྲོད་སྒྲིག་སྲོལ་ (gũndröö dri̲gsüü) a general/ universal rule, a rule that is suitable everywhere.

ཀུན་བྱམས་ (gũnjam) universal love/ kindness.

ཀུན་མིང་ (gũnmiŋ) demonstrative pronoun.

ཀུན་རྨོངས་ (gũnmoŋ) complete ignorance/ stupidity.

ཀུན་འཛིན་མ་ (gũn dzi̲nmə) poet. earth, world.

ཀུན་འཛོམས་ (gũndzom) all collected together, aggregated ¶ ཡོན་ཏན་ཀུན་འཛོམས་ཀྱི་མཁས་པ་ A scholar who has (collected together) all kinds of knowledge.

ཀུན་འཛོམས་གློག་འཕྲུལ་བཟོ་གྲྭ་ (gũndzom lõgdrü so̲dra) general/ multipurpose electrical machinery plant.

ཀུན་འཛོམས་འཆར་འགོད་ཁའུ་ (gũndzom cārgöö kɔ̄wu) general planning office.

ཀུན་འཛོམས་ཚོང་ཁང་ (gũndzom tsõŋgaŋ) general store.

ཀུན་འཛོམས་ལས་སྣོན་བཟོ་གྲྭ་ (gũndzom le̲nön so̲dra) general/ multipurpose processing factory.

ཀུན་འཛོམས་སློབ་གྲྭ་ཆེན་མོ་ (gũndzom lābdra cẽmmo) university.

ཀུན་རྫོགས་ (gũndzɔɔ̀) 1. completely exhausted. 2. all/ everything complete.

ཀུན་གཞི་ (gũnshi) character, nature ¶ མི་དེ་ཀུན་གཞི་ལེགས་པོ་ཡོད་པ་རེད་ That person has a good character.

ཀུན་གཞི་དུལ་བ་ (gũnshi tü̲ü̲wə) calm/ gentle nature ¶ ཀུན་གཞི་དུལ་བས་མི་རྣམས་ཤུགས་ཀྱིས་འཁོར་ Because of the gentle nature (of that person), people are naturally drawn to him.

ཀུན་གཞིའི་རྣམ་ཤེས་ (gũnshi nāmsheè) sm. ཀུན་གཞི་.

ཀུན་གཟིགས་ (gũnsii) "all seeing"—an honorific title used for the Panchen Lamas. 2. poetic name for the Buddha.

ཀུན་བཟང་ (gũnsaŋ) 1. all-good. 2. person's name. 3. poetic name for the Buddha.

ཀུན་བཟོད་ (gũnsöö) 1. earth. 2. all-tolerant, able to bear all.

ཀུན་ཡོད་འཐེན་ཤུགས་ (gũnyüü tẽnshuù) gravity.

ཀུན་ར་ (gũnra) abbr. ཀུན་དགའ་ར་བ་.

ཀུན་རིག (gũnrig) all-seeing, all-knowing.

ཀུན་ལ་ (gũnla) sm. ཀུན་དུ་.

ཀུན་ལམ་འདོམས་པ་ (gũnlam do̲mba) shung. (a punishment) that sets an example for all ¶ ཁྲིམས་ཀྱི་ར་བར་ཆུག་པའི་བདའ་འདེད་ཡན་སོང་མེད་པ་ཀུན་ལམ་འདོམས་པ་ཞིག་ཐུགས་རྗེ་ཆེ་བ་དང་ (We) request the (goverment) to set an example (through punishment) so all people will be law-abiding.

ཀུན་ལས་ (gũnlɛɛ̀) sm. ཀུན་ནས་.

ཀུན་ལས་བཏུས་ (gũnlɛɛ̀ dǖǜ) vi. to collect/ put everything together into one ¶ ཤེས་བྱ་ཀུན་ལས་བཏུས་ Collecting all knowledge.

ཀུན་ལེགས་ (gũnleg) sm. ཀུན་བཟང་, 1.

ཀུན་ཤེས་ (gũnsheè) 1. well-known, known by all. 2. knowing all.

ཀུན་ཤེས་གཅིག་ཐུབ་ (gũnsheè jĩgduù) knowing a lot about many things but not any one in depth.

ཀུན་ཤེས་ཡོངས་གྲགས་ (gũnsheè yo̲ŋdraà) sm. ཀུན་ཤེས་ཡོངས་གསལ་.

ཀུན་ཤེས་ཡོངས་གསལ་ (gũnsheè yo̲ŋsɛɛ) 1. well-known, known by all, completely clear to all. 2. popular.

ཀུན་བཤད་གཅིག་མཐུན་ (gũnshɛɛ̀ jĩgdün) with one voice, with unanimous agreement.

ཀུན་སྲིད་ཀུན་དར་ (gũnsiì gũndar) widespread, widely known everywhere.

ཀུན་སྲོལ་ (gũnsöö) shung. a custom that is widely/ generally used ¶ གསར་རྙིང་རྫོང་སྐབས་ཐེམ་བཞིར་བྱེད་པ་རྒྱ་ཁྱབ་ཀུན་སྲོལ་ལ་ As it has been a custom to check each household when the incumbent hands over a dzong to the new dzongpon.

ཀུན་སློང་ (gũnloŋ) morals, motives ¶ ཀུན་སློང་ངན་པ་ Bad morals ¶ ཁྱེད་ཀྱི་ཀུན་སློང་ཡག་པོ་འདི་འདྲ་ཡོད་པ་ངའི་བསམ་ཡུལ་ལས་འདས་སོང་ It was beyond my expectation that your morals were so good.

ཀུན་སློང་གི་སྤྱོད་ལམ་ (gũnloŋgi jöölam) moral behavior, morality, motives.

ཀུན་སློང་འཁྱེར་སྟངས་ (gũnloŋ keēdaŋ) morals, motives, motivation ¶ ཁོའི་ཀུན་སློང་འཁྱེར་སྟངས་ནི་རང་རྒྱལ་གཞན་ཕམ་རེད་ His motivation is selfish.

ཀུན་སློང་རང་རྒྱལ་གཞན་ཕམ་ (gũnloŋ ra̲ŋgyɛɛ she̲mbam) selfish motives [Lit. motives—oneself winning, others losing].

ཀུན་སློང་རང་རྒྱལ་གཞན་འཕུང་ (gũnloŋ ra̲ŋgyɛɛ she̲mbuŋ) sm. ཀུན་སློང་རང་རྒྱལ་གཞན་ཕམ་.

ཀུན་གསལ་ (gũnsɛɛ) 1. completely clear, completely understood/ known. 2. name of the official newspaper of the Government of Bhutan (Kuensel). 3. poet. sun.

ཀུན་གསལ་གསར་ཤོག (gũnsɛɛ sārshɔɔ̀) sm. ཀུན་གསལ་, 2.

ཀུན་གསོ་སྨན་རིལ་ (gũnso mẽnrii) a pill that cures all,

a panacea.

ཀུམ་ (gūm) 1. va. to sit/ sleep in a contracted position, to sit/ sleep in the fetal position ¶ཁྱེད་རང་ཀུམ་བྱས་མ་སྡོད་ Don't sit with your hands and feet contracted (bent or crouched over).

ཀུམ་ཀུམ་ (gūmgum) sm. ཀུམ་.

ཀུམ་དིང་ (gūmdiŋ) sm. ཀུ་དིང་.

ཀུམ་པོ་ (gūmbu) 1. a position in which the limbs are contracted, a crouching position ¶ཁོ་ཀུམ་པོར་ཉལ་བརྡད་བཞག He slept with his limbs contracted (in the fetal position). 2. zigzag, crooked. 3. sb. who feels inferior, self-abasing.

ཀུའང་དུང་ (gūaŋduŋ) Guangdong Province.

ཀུའན་པོའོ་ (gūambo) ch. broadcasting.

ཀུའན་པོའོ་དཔའན་སྲའི་ (gūambo dāndei) ch. sm. ཀུའན་པོའོ་བབ་ཚུགས་.

ཀུའན་པོའོ་དྲ་བ་ (gūanbo drawa) ch.tib. radio/ broadcasting network.

ཀུའན་པོའོ་བབ་ཚུགས་ (gūanbo pəpdzuù) ch.tib. radio/ broadcasting station.

ཀུའི་ (gūi) ch. sm. ཀུའི་.

ཀུའི་གྲེའོ་ (gūi drēwo) ch. sm. ཀུས་གྲོའུ་.

ཀུའུ་ལྕགས་ (gūwu jāà) ch.tib. cobalt.

ཀུའུ་པ་ (gūbə) Cuba.

ཀུའུ་ཙི་ (gūwudzi) ch. sm. ཀུ་ཙེ་.

ཀུའི་ (gūwe) ch. silicon.

ཀུའི་ཕེ་གློག་ནད་ (gūwefe lɔ̄ɔnɛɛ̀) ch.tib. silicosis.

ཀུའི་ཧྭ་ (gūwehwa) ch. sweet-scented osmanthus.

ཀུར་རྟགས་ (gūrdaà) the symbol X; va.—རྒྱག to make the mark X (e.g., in lieu of a signature).

ཀུས་གྲོའུ་ (gūdro) Guizhou Province.

ཀེ་ཀ་ (gēga) magpie.

ཀེ་ལྕགས་ (gējaà) ch.tib. chromium.

ཀེ་ཆུ་ (gēju) a river in Kham.

ཀེ་ཏུ་ (gēdu) skt. 1. sm. རྒྱལ་མཚན་. 2. meteor.

ཀེ་གཏེར་ (gēder) ch.tib. chromium mine.

ཀེ་སྤྲུལ་ (gēdrūü) abbr. Ketsang Lama.

ཀེ་ཛི་ (gēdzi) a kind of garlic.

ཀེ་ར་ (gēēra) hind. banana.

ཀེ་ར་ལ་ (gērala) Kerala Province (India).

ཀེ་རེ་ (gēre) erect, upright; va.—ལངས་ to stand or sit erect ¶འཁྱག་རི་ནགས་ཚལ་ལྟར་ཀེ་རེར་ལངས་བསྡད་ཡོད་ The ice mountains were standing erect like a forest.

ཀེ་རེམ་ (gērem) hind. carom (a game); va.—རྒྱག.

ཀེ་རོམ་ (gērom) sm. ཀེ་རེམ་.

ཀེ་ལ་ (gēla) sm. ཀེ་ར་.

ཀེ་ལ་ཤ་ (gēlasha) poet. snow mountain.

ཀེ་ལ་ཤའི་རྒྱལ་པོ་ (gēlase gyɛɛbo) Mt. Kailash.

ཀེག (gēg) sm. སྐེག.

ཀེག་འཕྲང་ (gēgdraŋ) the year when one is exposed to the heightened danger of being harmed (this begins when one is 13 years old, and then reoccurs every 12th year afterwards).

ཀེང་རུས་ (gīŋrüù) skeleton.

ཀེང་ཤུའི་ཤིང་ (gēŋsüshiŋ) sm. རྒྱ་སྐྱེགས་ཤིང་.

ཀེན་དུར་གློག (gēndur lɔ̄ɔ) ch.tib. sm. ཀན་དུར་གློག.

ཀེབ་ (gēb) eng. a cap.

ཀེབ་ཞྭ་ (gēbsha) eng.tib. cap, hat ¶ཀེབ་ཞྭ་ཉི་སྒྲིབ་ཅན་ A cap with a brim to shade the sun.

ཀེབ་ཀ་ན་སྦ་རལ་ (gēb gānabarɛl) Cape Canaveral.

ཀེམ་ཀེམ་ (gēmgem) sm. ཁེམ་ཁེམ་.

ཀེམ་ཀེམ་དུ་ལྷ་ (gēmgem) sm. ཟུམ་པོར་ལྷ་.

ཀེའུ་ (gēwu) ch. a kind of wild garlic.

ཀེའུ་ཙེ་ (gēwudze) ch. sm. ཀེའུ་ཛེ་.

ཀེའུ་ཛེ་ (gēwudze) ch. a kind of necklace.

ཀེའུ་ཚང་ (gēwudzaŋ) cave.

ཀེར་ (gēr) 1. va. to raise, to lift, to point upwards ¶མཛུབ་མོ་ཀེར་ནས་སྐད་ཆ་བཤད་པ་རེད་ He held up his finger and spoke. 2. man, person.

ཀེར་ཀེར་ (gērgēr) upright, erect, straight up; va.—བྱེད་ ¶མགོ་ཀེར་ཀེར་བྱེད་དགོས་ You have to hold your head upright. ¶རང་གཟུགས་པོ་འགུལ་བསྐྱོད་མེད་པར་ཀེར་ཀེར་སྡོད་ Stay still (upright) without moving your body.

ཀེར་ཐིག (gīrdii) a straight line.

ཀེར་མོ་ (gērmo) 1. alone. 2. naked.

ཀེར་རུས་ (gērrüù) sm. ཀེང་རུས་.

ཀེར་རེ་ (gērre) sm. ཀེར་ཀེར་.

ཀེར་ལངས་ (gērlaŋ) standing up, standing erect; va.—བྱེད་.

ཀེར་ལེབ་སྐར་གསུམ་ (gērleb gursum) shung. three types of taxes in tt.—people, land, animals.

ཀོ་ (gɔ̄ɔ) 1. leather. 2. ch. 1/10 liter. 3, abbr. of ཀོ་བ་.

ཀོ་ཀོ་གཡག (gōgo yāà) 1. a hybrid yak. 2. a derogatory term for racially mixed persons (Chinese and Tibetan).

ཀོ་ཀོང་ (gōgoŋ) low-lying.

ཀོ་ཀྲད་ (gɔ̄drɛɛ̀) 1. leather sole (of a Tibetan boot/ shoe). 2. worn out leather sole.

ཀོ་དཀར་ (gɔ̄gar) white leather.

ཀོ་རྒྱལ་ (gɔ̄gyɛɛ) a leather/ hide bag.

ཀོ་སྐུད་ (gɔ̄güü) a strip/ rope/ thread of rawhide.

ཀོ་སྐྱ་ (gɔ̄gyaà) an oar (for a coracle).

ཀོ་སྐྱི་ (gōgyi) sm. སྐོགས་སྐྱི་.

ཀོ་ཁུག (gɔ̄guù) a leather purse/ bag.

ཀོ་ཁུན་ (gɔ̄gün) a kind of flat bread.

ཀོ་ཁྲབ་ (gɔ̄drəb) leather armor.

ཀོ་ཁྲོལ་ (gɔ̄dröö) a sieve made from rawhide.

ཀོ་མཁན་ (gɔ̄ɔgɛn) 1. a person who makes things from leather, leather craftsman. 2. a person who rows a coracle (boat).

ཀོ་སྐྱོང་ལག་མཉེས་ (gōgyoŋ lagñeè) incorrigible, uncorrectable, unmanageable [Lit. kneading stiff leather by hand].

ཀོ་གྲུ་ (gɔ̄dru) 1. a hide boat (coracle). 2. abbr. coracle and boat.

ཀོ་གྲུ་གར་གཏོང་མཉན་པའི་ལག (gɔ̄dru kardoŋ ñɛ̃mbɛ lag) the head/ leader has the power to decide what to do, the one in power makes the decisions [Lit. where to sail the coracle is in the hands of the boatman].

ཀོ་གླ་ (gɔ̄la) fee for use of a coracle.

ཀོ་རྒྱུག (gɔ̄gyuù) long pole for propelling a boat, punt-pole.

ཀོ་རྒྱུན་ (gɔ̄gyün) a thin strip of rawhide.

ཀོ་སྒམ་ (gɔ̄gam) leather suitcase/ trunk/ box.

ཀོ་སྒྲིབ་ (gɔ̄drib) shung. deducting the weight of the skin/ hide in which butter is wrapped ¶མར་ལྷང་འདེགས་ཁལ་༡༢་ཡོད་པ་རེ་རེར་ཀོ་སྒྲིབ་གཞུང་སྲོལ་རེ་ཉ་ག་༡༤་བརྩིས་ From each load of butter which weighs 12 ke, according to goverment tradition (we) have deducted 14 nyaga for the equivalent of the weight of the hide in which the butter is wrapped.

ཀོ་སྒྲོག (gɔ̄drɔɔ̀) rawhide rope/ strap.

ཀོ་སྒྲོམ་ (gɔ̄drom) a hide box (usu. for storing butter or meat), a leather shelf.

ཀོ་སྒྲོལ་ (gɔ̄dröö) shung. crossing a river by coracle ¶ཚ་ཞག་གར་བབས་སུ་རྩྭ་ཆག་སོགས་ཡུལ་ཐང་གླ་རིན་སྤྲོད་ལེན་གྱི་ཀོ་སྒྲོལ་དང་བཅས་མར་ལམ་ཐེངས་གཅིག་སྒྲིག་གཏོང་ངེས་ Wherever they break camp or stay overnight, for one time, (you) must arrange to provide fodder and hay for their horses at local prices and take them across the river by coracle.

ཀོ་བཅར་ (gɔ̄bjaa) sm.* ཀོ་ཕྱུར་.

ཀོ་ལྕག (gɔ̄jaà) a small/ flat leather whip attached to a stick (usu. used to hit the cheeks as punishment); va.—གཞུ་ to strike/ hit with a ཀོ་ལྕག.

ཀོ་ཆས་ (gɔ̄jɛɛ̀) leatherware.

ཀོ་ཆས་བཟོ་མཁན་ (gɔ̄jɛɛ̀ soñɛn) person who makes leather goods.

ཀོ་ཆས་བཟོ་གྲྭ་ (gɔ̄jɛɛ̀ sodra) leather factory.

ཀོ་ཆུ་ (gūju) a standing pool of water.

ཀོ་ཆེན་ (gɔ̄jen) a yak skin.

ཀོ་མཉེད་རྒྱུ་ཆ་ (gɔ̄ñeè gyuja) material to be tanned.

ཀོ་མཉེད་པ་ (gɔ̄ñeèba) person who tans skins, leather tanner.

ཀོ་བརྙན་ཟློས་གར་ (gɔ̄ñɛn dȫögar) shadow play.

ཀོ་བརྙན་ཟློས་གར་ཚོགས་པ་ (gɔ̄ñɛn dȫögar tsōgba) shadow play troupe.

ཀོ་བཏུམས་ (gɔ̄dum) shung. 1. execution by sewing a person inside a skin and throwing him/ her in a river; va.—རྒྱག. 2. tea or butter that has been sewn tightly in a skin case.

ཀོ་དོ་ (gɔ̄do) a type of Tibetan boot with a leather sole.

ཀོ་ཐག (gɔ̄daà) 1. a leather strap/ rope/ thong. 2. a rope used to tie a coracle; va.—རྒྱག.

ཀོ་ཐག་སྐྱེལ་འདྲེན་འཁོར་ལོ་ (gɔ̄daà gyēndren kɔ̄ɔ̄lo) conveyor belt.

ཀོ་ཐག་འཐུས་ཤོར་ (gɔ̄daà tǖǖshɔɔ) letting sb. down; va.—གཏོང་.

ཀོ་ཐག་གློད་ (gɔ̄daà lȫȫ) vi. to be left in the lurch, to be left adrift (to have sth. necessary that had been promised not arrive or be done due to the another's failure), to be let down by sb. ¶ དེ་རིང་ངའི་གྲོགས་པོས་ཀོ་ཐག་གློད་བྱུང་ Today my friend left me in the lurch. [Lit. releasing the coracle's rope].

ཀོ་ཐུམ་ (gɔ̄dum) sm. ཀོ་བཏུམས་.

ཀོ་ཐོག (gɔ̄tɔɔ̀) by/ via coracle.

ཀོ་མཐིལ་ (gɔ̄dil) a leather sole.

ཀོ་འཐུམ་ (gɔ̄ndum) sm. ཀོ་བཏུམས་.

ཀོ་དམ་ (gɔ̄dam) a leather bag for holding Tibetan beer (ཆང་).

ཀོ་དོང་ (gɔ̄doŋ) sm. ཀང་དོང་.

ཀོ་གདན་ (gɔ̄dɛn) a leather mattress.

ཀོ་དར་ (gɔ̄dar) a leather strap for sharpening a razor.

ཀོ་ལྡིང་ (gɔ̄diŋ) a large leather container (usu. to hold oil).

ཀོ་སྡེར་ (gɔ̄der) a leather plate.

ཀོ་སྣོད་སྒམ་ (gɔ̄nögam) a leather box/ vessel.

ཀོ་པ་ (gɔ̄ba) boatman, ferryman (for a coracle).

ཀོ་པི་ (gōbii) sm. ཀོ་པིག.

ཀོ་པིག (gōbii) hind. cauliflower.

ཀོ་དཔོན་ (gɔ̄bön) 1. sm. ཀོ་དཔོན་གཉེར་པ་. 2. a polite term of address for a boatman.

ཀོ་དཔོན་གཉེར་པ་ (gɔ̄bön ñērba) shung. person in charge of coracle.

ཀོ་ལྤགས་ (gɔ̄baà) hide, skin.

ཀོ་ལྤགས་མཁན་ (gɔ̄baàñɛn) sb. who works with leather.

ཀོ་ལྤགས་སྒྲུབ་རྫས་བཟོ་ལས་ཀུང་སི་ (gɔ̄baà drubdzɛɛ̀ solɛɛ̀ gūŋsi) leather products industrial company.

ཀོ་ལྤགས་བཅོས་མ་ (gɔ̄baà jȫöma) synthetic leather.

ཀོ་ལྤགས་བཅོས་མའི་བཟོ་གྲྭ (gɔ̄baà jȫömɛ sodra) synthetic leather factory.

ཀོ་ལྤགས་བཟོ་གྲྭ་ (gɔ̄baà sodra) sm. ཀོ་ལྤགས་བཟོ་གྲྭ་ཁང་.

ཀོ་ལྤགས་བཟོ་གྲྭ་ཁང་ (gɔ̄baà sodrakaŋ) a leather factory.

ཀོ་ཕི་ (gōbi) eng. coffee.

ཀོ་སྦྱིན་ (gɔ̄jin) adhesive/ glue made from leather.

ཀོ་ཕིད་ (gōbii) sm. ཀོ་པིག.

ཀོ་ཕུབ་ (gɔ̄bub) a leather shield.

ཀོ་ཕོར་ (gɔ̄bɔɔ) a leather bowl.

ཀོ་ཕྱར་ (gɔ̄jar) a large flat leather hide used for chopping meat or spreading grain.

ཀོ་འཕྱགས་ (gɔ̄jaà) shung. a tax in tt. paid in skins.

ཀོ་བ་ (gɔ̄ɔ̄) 1. leather; va.—མཉེད་ to tan leather (hides) ¶ ཀོ་བའི་སྟོད་ཐུང་ Leather jacket/ shirt 2. a boat made from hide (a coracle); va.—གཏོང་ to sail a coracle.

ཀོ་བ་ཀྲག (gɔ̄ɔ̄ drāà) sm. ཀོ་བ་བསྲིགས་.

ཀོ་བ་མཁན་ (gɔ̄ɔ̄gɛn) sm. ཀོ་མཁན་.

ཀོ་བ་གཅིག་ནས་དྲས་པའི་རྒྱན་བུ་ (gɔ̄ɔ̄ jīgnɛ trɛbɛ gyumbu) of the same ilk, cut from the same mould [Lit. leather ropes cut from the same hide].

ཀོ་བ་མཉེད་མཁན་ (gɔ̄ɔ̄ ñēèñɛn) a tanner of skins.

ཀོ་བ་མཉེད་མ་ (gɔ̄ɔ̄ ñēèma) a tanned hide.

ཀོ་བ་མཉེད་རྫས་ (gɔ̄ɔ̄ ñēèdzɛɛ̀) things used for tanning hides/ leather.

ཀོ་བ་མཉེད་ལོག་ཐེབས་ (gɔ̄ɔ̄ ñēèlɔɔ̀ tēb) vi. to become hard after being tanned (because the skin wasn't tanned well).

ཀོ་བ་ནག་ཆུང་ (gɔ̄ɔ̄ nagjuŋ) coracle (in Tibetan songs).

ཀོ་བ་འཕྲེད་བཅད་ (gɔ̄ɔ̄ trēèjɛɛ̀) rowing a coracle across a river; va.—གཏོང་.

ཀོ་བ་དམར་ཀོ་ (gɔ̄ɔ̄ mārgɔ) fresh leather/ skin that is still untanned.

ཀོ་བ་དམར་པོ་ (gɔ̄ɔ̄ mārbo) sm. ཀོ་བ་དམར་ཀོ་.

ཀོ་བ་དམར་རོ་ (gɔ̄ɔ̄ māāro) sm. ཀོ་བ་དམར་ཀོ་.

ཀོ་བ་གཞུང་ཀོ་ (gɔ̄ɔ̄ shuŋgɔ) rowing a coracle down a river; va.—གཏོང་.

ཀོ་བ་ལྷོན་པའི་ཞོ་མོ་ (gɔ̄ɔ̄ lōmbɛɛ shamo) sm. ཀོ་ལྷོན་གྱི་ཞོ་མོ་.

ཀོ་བ་སྲིག (gɔ̄ɔ̄ sēg) sm. ཀོ་བསྲིགས་.

ཀོ་བ་ཧྲག་དོ་ (gɔ̄ɔ̄ hrāgdo) sm.* ཀོ་བ་ཧྲང་དོ་.

ཀོ་བ་ཧྲང་དོ་ (gɔ̄ɔ̄ hrāŋdo) an untanned skin that has become hard.

ཀོ་བའི་དངུལ་ཁུག (gōwɛ ŋǖǖguù) leather wallet for money.

ཀོ་བའི་རྡོ་ཁུག (gōwɛ doguù) leather pouch for putting/ holding stones.

ཀོ་བའི་བཟོ་གྲྭ་ཁང་ (gɔ̄wɛɛ sodragaŋ) sm. ཀོ་ལྤགས་བཟོ་གྲྭ་ཁང་.

ཀོ་བའི་ཨུ་ལག (gɔ̄wɛ ulaà) shung. corvee tax requiring the transportation of goods by coracle.

ཀོ་བུགས་ (gɔ̄buù) sm.* ཀོ་བུབས་.

ཀོ་བུབས་ (gɔ̄bup) a whole or uncut skin/ hide.

ཀོ་འབིགས་ (gɔ̄big) sm. ཀོ་འབུགས་.

ཀོ་འབུགས་ (gɔ̄mbuù) an awl used in leatherwork; va.—རྒྱག to make holes in leather with an awl.

ཀོ་འབུབས་ (gɔ̄bub) sm. ཀོ་བུབས་.

ཀོ་འབེ་ (gɔ̄mbe) a piece of leather used under saddles as a kind of saddle blanket.

ཀོ་འབོ་ (gɔ̄mbo) shung. a square leather container the size of a འབོ་ that is used to measure grain.

ཀོ་འབོག (gōmbɔɔ̀) a leather sack for carrying bedding when traveling.

ཀོ་འབོལ་ (gɔ̄mböö) a cushion with a leather covering.

ཀོ་སྦྲེལ་ (gɔ̄ɔ̄dre) two coracles tied together (to create greater stability); va.—གཏོང་ to tie coracles together and sail them.

ཀོ་མོག (gɔ̄mog) a puddle of water.

ཀོ་ཙེ་ (gɔ̄dze) ch. pumpkin seed.

ཀོ་བརྩགས་ (gɔ̄bdzaà) sm. ཀོ་རྩེག.

ཀོ་རྩེག (gɔ̄dzeg) a shoe sole consisting of several layers of leather sewn together.

ཀོ་རྩེག་འཇའ་མ་ (gɔ̄dzeg jaama) a Tibetan women's boot decorated with colored leather.

ཀོ་བརྩེགས་ (gɔ̄dzeg) sm. ཀོ་རྩེག.

ཀོ་ཚགས་ (gɔ̄dzaà) a sieve made from leather.

ཀོ་ཚལ་ (gɔ̄dzɛɛ) sm. ཀོ་རྫས.

ཀོ་རྫས་ (gɔ̄dzɛɛ) leather products, leatherware ¶ ཀོ་རྫལ་བཟོ་གྲྭ་ Leather products factory.

ཀོ་ཞྭ་ (gɔ̄sha) abbr. of ཀོ་ལྷོན་གྱི་ཞྭ་མོ་.

ཀོ་གཞོང་ (gɔ̄shoŋ) a leather basin.

ཀོ་གཟར་ (gɔ̄saa) sm. ཀོ་འབེ་.

ཀོ་གཟིངས་ (gɔ̄siŋ) raft made of leather/ skins.

ཀོ་བཟོ་བ་ (gɔ̄sowa) a leather worker.

ཀོ་བཟོས་ (gɔ̄söö) made from leather.

ཀོ་བཟོས་གྱོན་ཆས་ (gɔ̄söö kōnjɛɛ̀) leather clothing.

ཀོ་བཟོས་དངོས་རྫས་ (gɔ̄söö ŋȫödzɛɛ̀) leather products/ goods.

ཀོ་བཟོས་ཐོན་རྫས་ (gɔ̄söö tōndzɛɛ̀) sm. ཀོ་བཟོས་དངོས་རྫས་.

ཀོ་ཡོལ་ (gɔ̄yöö) ch. adhesive tape (commonly used on face for headaches/ toothaches).

ཀོ་ཡོལ་དཀར་པོ་ (gɔ̄yöö gāābo) medical tape (white).

ཀོ་ཡོལ་ནག་པོ་ (gɔ̄yöö nagbo) electrical tape (black).

ཀོ་རི་ཡ་ (gōriya) Korea.

ཀོ་རུ་ཁ་ (gōruka) sm.* ཀུ་རུ་ཁ་.

ཀོ་རུལ་ (gɔ̄rüü) a rotten hide.

ཀོ་རུལ་རྒྱུན་བུ་མི་ཉན་ (gɔ̄rüü gyṳ̄mbu miñɛn) one cannot utilize people/ things/ materials that are useless or unfit [Lit. rawhide rope cannot be made from a rotten hide].

ཀོ་རེ་ (gɔ̄re) round.

ཀོ་རོ་ (gɔ̄ro) a round leather mould used in casting.

ཀོ་ལོན་གྱི་ཞྭ་མོ་ (gɔ̄löngi shamo) sth. that becomes progressively more constrictive with time, sth. that is comfortable at first and then becomes painful/ terrible [Lit. a hat made of wet leather].

ཀོ་ལ་ (gɔ̄la) a type of insect that infests and ruins leather.

ཀོ་ལུ་བི་ཡ་ (gɔ̄lubiya) Colombia.

ཀོ་ལེབ་སྐེད་རགས་ (gɔ̄leb gēraà) a leather belt (the flat Western style).

ཀོ་ལོག (gɔ̄lɔɔ̀) a coracle capsizing; vi.—ཐེབས་ to capsize (a coracle).

ཀོ་ལོང་ (gɔ̄loŋ) getting angry over a small thing; vi.—ལངས་ to get angry over a small thing.

ཀོ་ལོང་ཆེན་པོ་ (gɔ̄loŋ cēmbo) sm. ཀོ་ལོང་ཚ་པོ་.

ཀོ་ལོང་ཚ་པོ་ (gɔ̄loŋ tsābo) sb. who gets angry over small things.

ཀོ་ལོམ་བོ་ (gɔ̄lombo) Colombo ¶ ཀོ་ལོམ་བོའི་འཆར་གཞི་ The Colombo Plan.

ཀོ་ཤིག (gɔ̄shi) dandruff, flaking skin; vi.—རྒྱག to get dandruff.

ཀོ་ཤེལ་ (gɔ̄shel) synthetic/ plastic glass.

ཀོ་ས་ (gɔ̄ɔ̀sa) place where coracles congregate or are kept (usu. waiting to be hired).

ཀོ་སག (gɔ̄saà) sandpaper (traditional sandpaperlike cloth or strip of leather onto which sand has been glued); va.—རྒྱག to sand.

ཀོ་སེག (gɔ̄seg) sm. ཀོ་སག.

ཀོ་བསེ་ (gɔ̄se) piece of leather whose top side is varnished.

ཀོ་བསྲེགས་ (gɔ̄bdraà) leather that has been heated/ smoked (usu. used for making soles of shoes or boots).

ཀོ་ཧྥི་ (gɔ̄bi) eng. coffee.

ཀོ་ཧྲུག (gɔ̄hrug) leftover small pieces of leather (after making sth.).

ཀོ་ལྷམ་ (gɔ̄lam) leather boot/ shoe (Western style).

ཀོ་ལྷམ་ཡུ་རིང་ (gɔ̄lam yuriŋ) Western style long boot.

ཀོ་ལྷམ་བཟོ་གྲྭ་ (gɔ̄lam sodra) leather boot/ shoe factory.

ཀོག (gɔ̄ɔ̀) 1. wrapper, covering, casing, envelope; va.—རྒྱག to package, to cover/ wrap (as with the casing for butter) ¶ མར་ཀོག The skin casing in which butter is sewn for storage. ¶ ཡི་གེའི་ཀོག་རྒྱག To make an envelope for a letter. 2. a thick and hard skin.

ཀོག་སྐྱི་ (gɔ̄ɔ̀ki) dandruff, flaking skin; vi.—རྒྱག to get dandruff.

ཀོག་གིས་ (gɔ̄ɔ̀gi) arc. suddenly, quickly.

ཀོག་སྡེ་ (gɔ̄gde) sm. ཀོག་གིས་.

ཀོག་པ་ (gɔ̄gba) sm. ཀོག.

ཀོག་མན་ (gɔ̄ɔ̀mɛn) ch. noodles.

ཀོག་རྫེ་ (gɔ̄gdze) trap, snare.

ཀོག་ཚེ་ (gɔ̄gdze) sm. ཀོག་རྫེ་.

ཀོག་ཤི་ (gɔ̄gshi) sm. ཀོག་སྐྱི་.

ཀོང་ (gɔ̄ŋ) 1. sm. ཀོང་ཀོང་. 2. abbr. ཀོང་པོ་; ཀོང་བུ་.

ཀོང་ཀན་ (gɔ̄ŋgɛn) ch. tangerine.

ཀོང་ཀོ་ (gɔ̄ŋgo) Congo.

ཀོང་ཀོང་ (gɔ̄ŋgoŋ) 1. concave, indented; vi.—ཆགས་ to become concave. 2. rut/ groove/ hole on a road.

ཀོང་ཀྲུ་ (gɔ̄ŋdru) Guangzhou.

ཀོང་ཀྲུའུ་ (gɔ̄ŋdruu) sm. ཀོང་ཀྲུ་.

ཀོང་སྐྲ་ (gɔ̄ŋdra) Kongpo's traditional hair style; va.—རྒྱག.

ཀོང་ཅོ་ (gɔ̄ŋjo) ch. the Chinese wife of King Srongtsen Gampo.

ཀོང་ཆས་ (gɔ̄ŋjɛɛ̀) the style of dress used in Kongpo.

ཀོང་ཛོ་ (gɔ̄ŋjo) ch. 1. sm. ཀོང་ཅོ་. 2. Guangzhou.

ཀོང་ཏའོ་ (gɔ̄ŋdao) Hiroshima.

ཀོང་ཏུང་ (gɔ̄ŋduŋ) Guangdong Province.

ཀོང་སྟོང་ (gɔ̄ŋdoŋ) sm. ཀོང་དོང་.

ཀོང་དོང་ (gɔ̄ŋdoŋ) a hole.

ཀོང་དྲེལ་ (gɔ̄ŋdree) a small mule from Kongpo.

ཀོང་རྣ་ (gɔ̄ŋna) shung. an earring worn on the right ear with the ceremonial dress called རྒྱ་ལུ་ཆས་.

ཀོང་རྣ་པན་དོག (gɔ̄ŋna bɛ̄ndɔɔ̀) shung. the left and right earring worn with the ceremonial dress called རྒྱ་ལུ་ཆས་.

ཀོང་སྣམ་ (gɔ̄ŋnam) woolen cloth made in Kongpo.

ཀོང་པར་ (gɔ̄ŋbar) intaglio engraving/ printing.

ཀོང་པོ་ (gɔ̄ŋbo) Kongpo—a region in southeastern Tibet.

ཀོང་པོ་རྒྱ་མདའ་ (gɔ̄ŋbo gyamda) a district (and the major town) in Kongpo.

ཀོང་པོ་ཉང་ཆུ་ཁ་ (gɔ̄ŋbo ñaŋcuga) a river in Kongpo.

ཀོང་པོ་བ་ (gɔ̄ŋpowa) a person from Kongpo.

ཀོང་པོ་པར་ལ་ (gɔ̄ŋbo parla) the pass between the Lhasa and Kongpo.

ཀོང་པོ་བུ་ཆུ་ (gɔ̄ŋbo pucu) name of a temple in Kongpo.

ཀོང་པོའི་མེ་ཏོག་ལུག་མིག (gɔ̄ŋbö medog lugmig) a medicinal herb from Kongpo.

ཀོང་པོའི་ལོ་གསར་ (gɔ̄ŋbö losar) the New Year's celebration in Kongpo (held in 10th lunar month).

ཀོང་སྤྲེལ་ (gɔ̄ŋdree) a type of monkey found in Kongpo.

ཀོང་ཕྱུར་ (gɔ̄ŋcur) square dried cheese from Kongpo.

ཀོང་ཕྲུག (gɔ̄ŋdruù) a young person from Kongpo.

ཀོང་བུ་ (gūŋbu) small bowl/ cup used as a butter lamp.

ཀོང་འབྲས་ (gɔ̄ŋdrɛɛ̀) rice from Kongpo.

ཀོང་མོ་ (gɔ̄ŋmo) 1. a female from Kongpo. 2. a concave depression.

ཀོང་བཙུན་དེ་མོ་ (gɔ̄ŋdzün temo) the protective deity of Kongpo who is one of the 12 protective deities of Tibet.

ཀོང་ཙི་ (gɔ̄ŋdzi) ch. photon.

ཀོང་འཛིན་འུལ་མི་ (gɔ̄ŋdzin üümi) shung. a corvee tax wherein people had to work setting out and taking in butter lamps (e.g., during the Ganden ŋamjö festival in Lhasa).

ཀོང་ཞི་གྲོང་རིགས་རང་སྐྱོང་ལྗོངས་ (gɔ̄ŋshi drɔ̄ŋrig raŋgyoŋjoŋ) Guangxi Zhong (Chuang) Nationality Autonomous Region.

ཀོང་ཞྭ་ (gɔ̄ŋsha) style of hat from Kongpo.

ཀོང་ཡུལ་ (gɔ̄ŋyüü) the Kongpo region.

ཀོང་རོང་ (gɔ̄ŋroŋ) sm. གཡང་རོང་.

ཀོང་རིས་ཚོགས་པ་ (gɔ̄ŋreè tsɔ̄gba) Congress Party (in India).

ཀོང་ཤུར་ (gɔ̄ŋshur) hollow depression.

ཀོང་ཤིས་ (gɔ̄ŋshiì) ch. Guangxi.

ཀོང་ཤེལ་ (gɔ̄ŋshee) a concave lens.

ཀོང་ས་ (gɔ̄ŋsə) an area that is lower than those around it, an area with a depression, a concave area.

ཀོང་སྲས་ (gɔ̄ŋsɛɛ̀) a pampered son of a wealthy/ influential family.

ཀོང་ལྷམ་ (gɔ̄ŋlham) boots in the Kongpo style.

ཀོན་ཏའོ་ (gɔ̄ndao) Guam.

ཀོབ་ཀྲག (gɔ̄bdraà) sm. ཀོ་བསྲེགས་.

ཀོབ་རྒྱག (gɔ̄b gyaà) va. to engage in lesbian sexual acts.

ཀོབ་ལ་ (gɔ̄bla) sm. ཀོ་ལ་.

ཀོབ་ཤ་ (gɔ̄bsha) a type of Tibetan stew made with pieces of meat and bread.

ཀོའང་ཏུང་ (gɔ̄ŋduŋ) Guangdong Province.

ཀོའང་ཤིས་ (gɔ̄ŋshiì) ch. sm. ཀོང་ཤིས་.

ཀོའི་པེག (gɔ̄biì) hind. cauliflower.

ཀོའི་མན་ (gɔ̄mɛn) ch. Chinese noodles.

ཀོའི་རྩེ་ (gɔ̄dze) ch. pumpkin seed, melon seed,

sunflower seed.

ཀོར་ (gɔ̄ɔ) eng. coat.

ཀོར་ཀོར་ (gɔ̄ɔgɔɔ) round.

ཀོར་སུ་ཊྲ་ (gɔ̄rsudra) eng. an english style suit.

ཀོར་ཕྲུ་པོ་ལོ་ (gɔ̄rfu pōlo) eng. 1. golf. 2. golf ball.

ཀོལ་མ་ (gōōma) sm. བསྐོལ་མ་.

ཀོས་ཀོ་ (gōōgo) chin bone.

ཀོས་སྐོ་ (gōōgo) ཀོས་ཀོ་.

ཀོས་ཐག (gōdaà) arc. poor, humble.

ཀོས་སྙུང་ (gōñuŋ) a thin/ pointy chin.

ཀྭ་ (gwā) ch. melon, gourd, cucumber.

ཀྭ་ཙེ་ (gwādze) 1. ch. sunflower seed, pumpkin seed, melon seed. 2. ch. Chinese vest.

ཀྭ་ཡེ་ (gāye) sm. ཀྭ་.

ཀྭའི་ (gāyi) sm. ཀྭ་.

ཀྭའུ་ (gwā) sm. ཀྭ་.

ཀྭའོ་ལིའང་ (gwāliŋ) ch. sorghum.

ཀྱ་ཀྱུ་ (gyāgyu) curving, meandering, twisting ། ཀྱ་ཀྱུའི་ཆུ་ལུང་ A meandering river running through a valley.

ཀྱ་རེ་ཀྱོ་རེ་ (gyāre gyōre) stumbling, walking unsteadily (usu. babies, drunks); vi.—བྱེད་.

ཀྱག (gyāà) sm. བཀྱག.

ཀྱག་ཀྱག (gyāggyaà) kidding, joking; va.—བྱེད་; —ཞུ་ to kid around, to joke.

ཀྱག་ཀྱོག (gyāggyɔ̀ɔ) 1. crooked, zigzag, winding, circuitous ། ལམ་ཁ་དེ་ཀྱག་ཀྱོག་རེད་ That road is winding. 2. difficulties, ups and downs ། མདུན་ལམ་འདི་འོད་ཟེར་ལྡན་པ་དང་ད་ལྟའི་འགྲོ་ལམ་ནི་ཀྱག་ཀྱོག་རེད་ The future road is glorious; the current road has difficulties and will have ups and downs.

ཀྱག་གེ་ཀྱོག་གེ་ (gyāge gyōgge) sm. ཀྱག་ཀྱོག.

ཀྱག་རྫུན་ (gyāgdzün) sm. སྐྱག་རྫུན་.

ཀྱག་བཤད་ཀྱོག་བཤད་ (gyāgshɛɛ̀ gyōgshɛɛ̀) beating around the bush (in speech); va.—བྱེད་.

ཀྱང་ (kāŋ) 1. also, too (used after final ག,ད,བ,ས་) [ཡང་ is used after ན] ། ཁྱེད་ཀྱང་ཡོང་དགོས་རེད་ You also have to come. 2. even ། ཁོས་ཚིག་གཅིག་ཀྱང་བཤད་མ་སོང་ He didn't say even a word. 3. (vb. + —) although, even though, but ། ངས་དྲང་པོ་བཤད་ཀྱང་ཡིད་ཆེས་ཀྱི་མ་རེད་ Although I told the truth, (they) will not believe it. ། ང་མོ་ལ་དགའ་པོ་ཡོད་ཀྱང་མོས་ང་ལ་ཙ་བ་ནས་དགའ་གི་མི་འདུག I like her but she doesn't like me at all. 4. (interrogative + —) whoever, whatever, wherever ། སུས་བཤད་ཀྱང་མོས་ཉན་གྱི་མ་རེད་ She won't listen whoever speaks. ། ཁྱོད་ལ་གང་དགོས་ཀྱང་ང་ལ་གསུང་རོགས་གནང་ Whatever you need please tell me.

ཀྱང་ཀྱོང་ (gyāŋgyoŋ) 1. sm. ཁོང་ཁོང་. 2. terrain in which hills and depressions alternate. 3. sth. wrinkled or having furrows.

ཀྱང་ངེ་ཀྱོང་ངེ་ (gyāŋŋe gyōŋŋe) sm. ཀྱང་ཀྱོང་.

ཀྱང་རུང་ (gyāŋruŋ) sm. ཀྱང་, 3.

ཀྱམ་ཀྱམ་པ་ (gyāmgyāmba) a walk/ stroll.

ཀྱམ་པ་ (gyāmba) arc. leftover.

ཀྱམ་མེ་ (gyāmme) glittering (light) ། མཆོད་མེའི་འོད་ཀྱམ་མེར་བསྡད་འདུག A glittering butter lamp was sitting there.

ཀྱམས་མེ་ (gyāmme) sm.* ཀྱམ་མེ་.

ཀྱར་ཀྱར་ (gyārgyaa) even, level, flat; equal.

ཀྱར་ཀྱོར་ (gyārgyɔr) abbr. ཀྱ་རེ་ཀྱོ་རེ་.

ཀྱར་པོ་ (gyārbo) sm. ཀྱར་ཀྱར་.

ཀྱལ་ཀ་ (gyɛ̄ɛ̄ga) sm. ཀ་རེ་.

ཀྱལ་ཀྱིལ་རེ་ (gyēgyere) shung. few, little.

ཀྱལ་ཀྱིལ་རེ་རྙིང་ (gyēgye reñiŋ) sm. ཀྱལ་ཀྱིལ་རེ་.

ཀྱལ་ཀྱོལ་ (gyēlgyöl) a stumbling walk (usu. the walk of a sick/ weak person).

ཀྱལ་གཏམ་ (gyēldam) 1. meaningless talk; va.—ཤོད་ to talk meaninglessly. 2. joking talk; va.—ཤོད་ to joke, to jest.

ཀྱལ་པ་ (gyēlba) 1. a joke, a jest; va.—བྱེད་; —ཤོད་; —མཛད་ to jest, to joke. 2. meaningless talk; va.—བྱེད་; — ཤོད་; —མཛད་ to talk meaninglessly, to talk nonsense.

ཀྱེས་ (gyɛɛ̀) a disrespectful term of address.

ཀྱི་ (gyi) 1. of (genitive particle used after final ད, བ, ས) ། མི་དམངས་ཀྱི་བསམ་ཚུལ་ The opinion of the people. ། ཁྱོད་ཀྱི་ཕྱག་དེབ་ Your book. 2. particle used in present and future verb complements ། ཁོས་འདི་ཤེས་ཀྱི་འདུག He knows this. ། ཁོ་ལས་ཀ་བྱེད་ཀྱི་རེད་ He will work.

ཀྱི་ལྕེ་ (gyīje) large-leaved gentian (gentiana macrophylla) (used in Tibetan medicine).

ཀྱི་ལི་ལི་ (gyīlili) turning/ twirling/ spinning/ swirling around in a circular motion; va.—སྐོར་ to turn/ twist/ spin/ swirl in a circular motion ། ཉི་གདུགས་ཀྱི་ལི་ལི་བསྐོར་བ་རེད་ (He) twirled the umbrella around.

ཀྱི་བསེར་ (gyīser) sm. ཀྱིང་བསེར་.

ཀྱི་ཧུད་ (gyīhüü) a cry of lamentation, e.g., "alas," "oh my"; va.—འདོན་ to issue such a cry.

ཀྱིག་རྩེ་ (gyīgdze) unfired brick.

ཀྱིང་ཁབ་ (gyīŋgəb) a kind of brocade made in India that is commonly used as the hemming of villagers' collars.

ཀྱིང་བསེར་ (gyīŋser) a strong/ cold wind.

ཀྱིན་ (gyīn) present (continuing) tense particle ། ང་ལས་ཀ་བྱེད་ཀྱིན་ཡོད་ I am working (at present).

ཀྱིར་ཀྱིར་ (gyīrgyir) the sound of birds chirping.

ཀྱིལ་ལི་ (gyīīle) coiled up; vi.—འཁྱིལ་ to be coiled up ། སྦྲུལ་དེ་ཀྱིལ་ལི་ར་འཁྱིལ་ནས་བསྡད་བཞག The snake was sitting there coiled up.

ཀྱིལ་ལེ་ཉོན་ (gyīīle ñon) va. to listen well.

ཀྱིས་ (gyīi) 1. by (instrumental particle used after final ད,བ,ས) ། བཀྲ་ཤིས་ཀྱིས་དེབ་གཅིག་ཉོས་སོང་ Tashi bought a book. (A book was bought by Tashi). 2. because of ། སློབ་གྲྭའི་ཡིག་ཚད་ཀྱིས་ཡོང་ཐུབ་མ་སོང་ Because of the school examination, (they) were unable to come.

ཀྱུ་ (gyū) used as second syllable of words to indicate sth. is curved.

ཀྱུ་ཁུ་ (gyūgu) a piece of wood or metal placed between two larger pieces (of wood or metal) to make them stable.

ཀྱུ་མ་ (gyūmə) turquoise.

ཀྱུ་རུ་ར་ (gyūrurə) a medicinal herb.

ཀྱུ་རུ་རུ་ (gyūruru) chirping sound of birds and animals.

ཀྱུག་ཀྱུག (gyūggyug) shinny, glittering ། འོད་ཀྱུག་ཀྱུག A glittering light.

ཀྱུང་བུ་ (gyūŋbu) arc. hammer.

ཀྱུར་ཀྱུར་ (gyūrgyur) sm. ཀྱུ་རུ་རུ་.

ཀྱེ་ (gyē) 1. an interjection: "oh" ། ཀྱེ་རྒྱལ་པོ་ཆེན་པོ་ Oh, great king. 2. hey!

ཀྱེ་ཀྱེ་ (gyēgye) sm. ཀྱེ་.

ཀྱེ་མ་ (gyēma) a cry of lamentation: "oh my."

ཀྱེ་མ་ཀྱི་ཧུད་ (gyēma gyēhüü) sm. ཀྱེ་མ་.

ཀྱེ་མ་ཧུད་ (gyēmahüü) sm. ཀྱེ་མ་.

ཀྱེ་མ་ཧོ་ (gyēmaho) an exclamation of wonder/ marvel—"wow."

ཀྱེ་མའོ་ (gyēmao) sm. ཀྱེ་མ་.

ཀྱེ་རེ་ (gyēre) sm.* ཀེ་རེ་.

ཀྱེ་ཧུད་ (gyēhüü) sm. ཀྱེ་མ་ཀྱི་ཧུད་.

ཀྱེ་ཧོ་ (gyēho) sm. ཀྱེ་མ་ཧོ་.

ཀྱོ་བ་ (gyōwa) a hook.

ཀྱོག (gyɔ̄ɔ) vi. to be crooked/ twisting/ not straight ། ཐིག་དེ་ཀྱོག་བཞག The line is crooked.

ཀྱོག་ཀྱོག (gyōggyɔ̀ɔ) 1. crooked, twisted, bent, zigzag, winding; va.—བཟོ་ to make crooked/ twisting, to bend; va.—བྱེད་ to twist/ turn; to zigzag ། ལམ་ཁ་ཀྱོག་ཀྱོག A winding road. ། སྨྱུག་མ་དེ་ཀྱོག་ཀྱོག་བཟོས་བཞག (They) bent the bamboo. ། རྩིག་པ་ཀྱོག་ཀྱོག་བརྒྱབ་བཞག (They) built the wall crooked. 2. (with བསམ་བློ་) deceptive, untruthful, deceitful ། མི་འདི་རྒྱུན་དུ་བསམ་བློ་ཀྱོག་ཀྱོག་གཏོང་མཁན་ཞིག་ཡིན་ཙང་གཞན་གྱིས་ཡིད་ཆེས་བྱེད་ཀྱི་མེད་པ་རེད་ Because he is sb. who is always untruthful, others do not trust him.

ཀྱོག་སྐོར་ (gyɔ̄ɔ̄gɔɔ) not straight/ direct, a detour.

ཀྱོག་གེ་པ་ (gyɔ̄ggewa) sm. ཀྱོག་ཀྱོག.

ཀྱོག་ཐིག (gyɔ̄gtig) a crooked line.

ཀྱོག་པ་ (gyɔ̄ba) sm. ཀྱོག་ཀྱོག.

ཀྱོག་པོ་ (gyɔ̄gbo) sm. ཀྱོག་ཀྱོག.

ཀྱོག་ལམ་ (gyɔ̄glam) a winding/ twisting road.

ཀྱོག་ཤད་ (gyɔ̄gshɛɛ̀) a type of ཤད་ used at the start of a sentence.

ཀྱོག་ཤིང་ (gyɔ̄shiŋ) a crooked tree.

ཀྱོག་བཤད་ (gyɔ̄gshɛɛ̀) deceitful/ devious/ untrue speech; va.—བྱེད་.

ཀྱོང་ (gyōŋ) 1. sm. ཀྱོང་ས་. 2. hard. 3. obstinate, stubborn.

ཀྱོང་ཀྱོང་ (gyōŋgyoŋ) sm. ཀྱོང་ས་.

ཀྱོང་ཁ་ (gyōŋga) sm. ཀྱོང་ས་.

ཀྱོང་པོ་ (gyōŋbo) sm. ཀྱོང་ས་.

ཀྱོང་བུ་ (gyōŋbu) 1. a small spoonlike instrument used in Tibetan medicine. 2. an instrument used in weeding. 3. sm. ཀྱོང་ས་.

ཀྱོང་མོ་ (gyōŋmo) sm. ཀྱོང་ས་.

ཀྱོང་ས་ (gyōŋsa) a concave depression in the ground, an area that has sunk below its surroundings, a low-lying area.

ཀྱོམ་ཀྱོམ་ (gyōmgyom) shaking a liquid in a container to stir it just before serving; va.—བྱེད་ ¶ ཁོས་བོད་ཇ་དེ་ཀྱོམ་ཀྱོམ་ཁ་ཤས་བྱས་ནས་ཕོར་པའི་ནང་བླུགས་སོང་ He shook the Tibetan tea (in its teapot) a few times and poured it into the cup.

ཀྲ་ཀའོ་ (drāgao) ch. fried cake.

ཀྲ་དན་ (drādɛn) ch. bomb; va.—དབྱུག to throw/ drop a bomb.

ཀྲ་དན་གཡུག་བྱེད་གནམ་གྲུ་ (drādɛn yūgjeè nāmdru) ch.tib. bomber (airplane).

ཀྲ་ཡེ་ (drāye) eng. a necktie; va.—རྒྱག to put on/ tie a necktie.

ཀྲག (drāà) sm.* བཀྲག.

ཀྲག་ཀྲག (drāgdraà) 1. luxuriant looking; vi.—ཆགས་ to become luxuriant. 2. hard, stiff (for paper and materials). 3. of good character/ morals/ behavior.

ཀྲག་ཟན་ (drāgsɛn) ch. sesame seed cake.

ཀྲང་ (drāŋ) ch. director, leader, chief, head. ¶ ཅུས་ཀྲང་ Director of a bureau.

ཀྲང་ཀྲང་ (drāŋdraŋ) alley, lane.

ཀྲང་ཀྲོང་ (drāŋdroŋ) abbr. ཀྲང་ངེ་ཀྲོང་ངེ་.

ཀྲང་གོ་ཧྭ་ (drāŋgohua) Zhang Guohua, the commander of the Chinese forces in Tibet in the 1950's.

ཀྲང་ངེ་ (drāŋe) abbr. ཀྲང་ངེ་ཀྲོང་ངེ་.

ཀྲང་ངེ་ཀྲོང་ངེ་ (drāŋŋe drōŋŋe) upright, erect, straight ¶ གཟུགས་པོ་ཀྲང་ངེ་ཀྲོང་ངེ་བྱས་ནས་བསྡད་འདུག (He) is sitting erect.

ཀྲང་ངེ་བ་ (drāŋewa) sm. ཀྲང་ངེ་ཀྲོང་ངེ་.

ཀྲང་ཅིན་ཝུའུ་ (drāŋjiŋwu) Zhang Jingwu, the Central Committee's representative in Lhasa during the 1950's.

ཀྲང་ཉ་ (drāŋña) ch. octopus.

ཀྲང་དའི་པེའོ་ (drāŋdebeo) ch. Representative Zhang (Zhang Jingwu).

ཀྲང་ད་རན་ (drāŋdarɛn) 1. name of a Manchu amban. 2. a flower named after the amban who brought the seeds to Tibet.

ཀྲང་པན་ (drāŋbɛn) ch. sm.* ཏམ་པན་.

ཀྲང་མན་ (drāŋmɛn) ch. silk wadding used in bedding, clothes, etc.

ཀྲང་མའོ་ཙེ་ (drāŋmaodze) ch. a type of black Chinese skullcap (often with tassel).

ཀྲང་མེན་ (drāŋmen) sm. ཀྲང་མན་.

ཀྲང་གཞོན་ (drāŋshön) ch.tib. vice head/ leader/ director/ chief.

ཀྲང་ལ་རྒྱུགས་ (drāŋla gyu̱ù) vi. to become leggy and hard (for vegetables, this conveys that they are not good to eat) ¶ པད་ཚལ་ཀྲང་ལ་བརྒྱུགས་བཞག The cabbage has become leggy and hard.

ཀྲང་སི་ལིང་ (drāŋsiliŋ) ch. Commander Zhang (Zhang Guohua).

ཀྲད་ (drɛɛ̀) a strip of thin leather used for making bow strings.

ཀྲད་ཀོར་ (drɛɛgɔɔ) a thick ring worn by men on the thumb (originally used for shooting arrows, later decorative).

ཀྲད་ཀྲད་ (drɛdɛɛ̀) 1. comparing; va.—གཏོང་. 2. competing; va.—གཏོང་.

ཀྲད་འཁོར་ (drɛɛgɔɔ) sm. ཀྲད་ཀོར་.

ཀྲད་རྒྱུན་ (drɛgyün) leather thread.

ཀྲད་པ་ (drɛba) leather sole for boots/ shoes.

ཀྲན་ཀྲང་ (drɛndraŋ) ch. stationmaster.

ཀྲན་མ་ (drɛnma) sm.* སྲན་མ་.

ཀྲབ་ (drəb) sm.* སྲབ་.

ཀྲབ་ཀྲབ་ (drəbdrəb) tremors, trembling; vi.—བྱེད་ ¶ ཁྱི་འདི་ཤི་ཁྲབས་བྱེད་སྐབས་ལག་པ་ཀྲབ་ཀྲབ་བྱས་སོང་ When the dog was about to die his forelegs trembled.

ཀྲབ་ཀྲོབ་ (drəbdrōb) abbr. ཀྲབ་བེ་ཀྲོ་བེ་.

ཀྲབ་པོ་ (drəbo) sm.* སྲབ་པོ་.

ཀྲབ་བེ་ཀྲོ་བེ་ (drəbe drōbe) 1. deceitful, cunning, tricky (for persons). 2. a style of dancing.

ཀྲབ་ཙམ་ཀྲབ་ཙམ་ (drəbdzam drəbdzam) 1. sm. ཀྲབ་ཀྲབ་. 2. (for eyes) blinking, opening and closing quickly; va.—བྱེད་ ¶ རྨས་དམག་དེ་ཤི་ཁར་མིག་ཀྲབ་ཙམ་ཀྲབ་ཙམ་བྱེད་ཀྱི་འདུག The wounded soldier was blinking quickly just before he died.

ཀྲམ་ (drām) ch. cabbage.

ཀྲམ་སྐྱུར་ (drāmgyur) ch.tib. sauerkraut.

ཀྲའུ་ཙུང་ལི་ (drāo tsūŋli) ch. Premier Zhou (Enlai).

ཀྲའུ་ཨེན་ལེ་ (drā ēnle) Zhou Enlai.

ཀྲའོ་ཙི་དབྱང་ (drāo tsīyaŋ) Zhao Ziyang.

ཀྲི་ཀ་སི་ (drīgasi) eng. sm. ཀྲི་ཀི་ཀྲི་.

ཀྲི་ཀི་ཀྲི་ (drīgidri) eng. 1. postal stamp. 2. ticket.

ཀྲི་ཁ་ (drīgə) 1. a small magpielike bird. 2. sm. ཀྲི་ག.

ཀྲི་ག (drīgə) 1. epicanthus. 2. the rim of a bowl. 3. a fence around a well.

ཀྲི་ཅ་ཀོ་ (drījago) Chicago.

ཀྲི་ཕུའུ་ (drībuu) ch. branch (of an organization) ¶ དང་གི་ཀྲི་ཕུའུ Branch party office.

ཀྲི་ཕུའུ་ཧྲུའུ་ཅི་ (drībuu hrūji) ch. branch secretary.

ཀྲི་མིང་ཏི་ (drīmiŋdi) ch. colony, colonial.

ཀྲི་མིང་ཏི་ཕྱེད་ཙམ་ (drīmiŋdi chētsam) ch.tib. semicolonial.

ཀྲི་མིང་ཏི་རིང་ལུགས་ (drīmiŋdi ri̱ŋluù) ch.tib. colonialism.

ཀྲི་ཙེ་དུལ་ཐུན་ (drēdzi dü̱drɛn) ch.tib. sm. ཀྲི་ཙེ་.

ཀྲི་ལི་ (drīli) Chile.

ཀྲི་སི་ (drīsi) eng. ticket.

ཀྲི་སིང་ (drīsin) eng. station.

ཀྲི་ཧྲུའུ་ (drīhru) abbr. of ཀྲི་ཕུའུ་ཧྲུའུ་ཅི་.

ཀྲིག་ཀྲིག (drīgdriì) 1. promptly, on time ¶ ཚགས་ཤོག་ཞོགས་ལྟར་ཀྲིག་ཀྲིག་འབྱོར་གྱི་ཡོད་ The newspaper arrives on time every morning. 2. (སོ་ + སྒྲ་ + —) chattering teeth; vi.—བྱེད་; —སྒྲོག ¶ ཁོང་འཁྱགས་ནས་སོ་སྒྲ་ཀྲིག་ཀྲིག་དུ་སྒྲོག་གི་འདུག He got cold and his teeth are chattering. 3. (མིག + —) staring intently/ intensely to scare or intimidate ¶ དམག་མིས་བཙོན་པར་མིག་ཀྲིག་ཀྲིག་ལྟ་གི་འདུག The soldiers were staring intently at the prisoners. 4. (མེ་མདའ་ + —) holding a gun firmly at attention ¶ སྲུང་དམག་རྣམས་ལག་དུ་མེ་མདའ་ཀྲིག་ཀྲིག་དུ་བཟུང་ནས་ལངས་འདུག The bodyguards stood at attention holding guns in their hands.

ཀྲིག་ཅར་ (drīgjar) 1. decided on as a policy/ rule ¶ གཞུང་དོན་ཕྱོགས་ཐོན་སྐབས་ཉིན་རེ་ལ་མ་དོད་སྒོར་ལྔ་རེ་ཀྲིག་ཅར་གནང་གི་རེད་ On official government trips the rule is to give a traveling allowance of five dollars a day. ¶ ཆུ་ཚོད་དགུ་པར་ཡོང་རྒྱུ་ཀྲིག་ཅར་བཟོས་སོང་ (They) decided (that people should) come at nine o'clock. 2. sm. ཀྲིག་ཀྲིག.

ཀྲིག་ཅར་བྱེད་སྒོ་ (drīgjar cego) customary/ daily/ regular/ routine duties.

ཀྲིག་ཆགས་ (drīgcaà) sm. ཀྲིག་ཅར་.

ཀྲིག་ཕུ་ (drīgfu) ch. uniform.

ཀྲིན་ཀན་ (drīngɛn) eng. stun gun.

ཀྲིན་ནད་ (drinnɛ̀) ch.tib. colic.
ཀྲིན་ལུང་ (drinluŋ) ch. steamer for food.
ཀྲུ་ཀྲུ་ (drūdru) a bird similar to a pigeon.
ཀྲུ་མ་ཀྲུའུ་ (drūmadru) eng. tomato.
ཀྲུ་མ་ཀྲུའུ་སྐྱོ་མ་ (drūmadru gyōma) eng. tib. catsup.
ཀྲུ་ཞི་ (drūshi) ch. sm. ཀྲུའུ་ཞི་.
ཀྲུག་ར་ (drūgra) hind. small piece, remnant, end of sth. ¶ ཐ་མག་གི་ཀྲུག་ར་ Cigarette butt/ end.
ཀྲུགས་ (drūù) arc. sm. འཁྲུག.
ཀྲུང་ (drūŋ) ch. 1. central. 2. abbr. of ཀྲུང་གོ་ and ཀྲུང་དབྱང་.
ཀྲུང་ཀྲུང་ (drūŋdruŋ) sm.* ཁྲུང་ཁྲུང་.
ཀྲུང་ཀྲོན་ (drūŋdrön) ch. specialized middle school, special or technical school, polytechnic school.
ཀྲུང་ཁུ་ (drūŋgu) sm. ཀྲུམ་ཁུ་.
ཀྲུང་གུང་ (drūŋguŋ) ch. abbr. Chinese Communist Party (CCP).
ཀྲུང་གུང་ཀྲུང་དབྱང་ (drūŋduŋ drūŋyaŋ) Central Committee of the CCP.
ཀྲུང་གུང་ཀྲུང་དབྱང་ཆབ་སྲིད་ཅུས་ (drūŋguŋ drūŋyaŋ cə̄psiì jüù) ch.tib. Political Bureau (Politburo) of the Central Committee of the CCP.
ཀྲུང་གུང་བོད་ལས་དོན་ཨུ་ཡོན་ལྷན་ཁང་ (drūŋguŋ pö̱ö lɛ̱̀dön üyün lhɛ̄ngaŋ) ch.tib. the Tibet Work Commission of the CCP (the main Chinese administrative office in Tibet in the 1950s).
ཀྲུང་གོ་ (drūŋgo) ch. China.
ཀྲུང་གོ་གུང་ཁྲན་ཏང་ (drūŋgo ku̱ŋdrɛndaŋ) ch. the Communist Party of China (CCP).
ཀྲུང་གོ་གུང་ཁྲན་ཏང་གི་ཀྲུང་དབྱང་ཨུ་ཡོན་ལྷན་ཁང་ (drūŋgo ku̱ŋdrɛndaŋgi drūŋyaŋ üy¨n lhɛ̄ngaŋ) ch.tib. the Central Committee of the Communist Party of China.
ཀྲུང་གོ་གུང་ཁྲན་རིང་ལུགས་ན་གཞོན་ཚོགས་པ་ (drūŋgo ku̱ŋdrɛn ri̱ŋluù na̱shön tsōgba) ch.tib. the Communist Youth League of China.
ཀྲུང་གོ་གུང་ཁྲན་རིང་ལུགས་གཞོན་ནུ་ཚོགས་པ་ (drūŋgo ku̱ŋdrɛn ri̱ŋluù shö̱nnu tsōgba) ch.tib. the Communist Youth League of China.
ཀྲུང་གོ་གོ་མིན་ཏང་གསར་བརྗེ་ཨུ་ཡོན་ལྷན་ཁང་ (drūŋgo go̱mindaŋ sārje üyün lhɛ̄ngaŋ) the Revolutionary Committee of the Guomindang of China.
ཀྲུང་གོ་རྒྱུས་ཡོད་མཁན་ (drūŋgo gyūyööñɛn) ch.tib. China-hands, experts on China.
ཀྲུང་གོ་གཅིག་གི་སྲིད་ཇུས་ (drūŋgo ji̱ggi siìjüù) ch.tib. "One China Policy."
ཀྲུང་གོ་གཉིས་ཀྱི་སྲིད་ཇུས་ (drūŋgo ñiìgi siìjüù) ch.tib. "Two China Policy."
ཀྲུང་གོ་བ་ (drūŋgowa) ch.tib. a Chinese.
ཀྲུང་གོ་བོད་ལྗོངས་རྒྱལ་སྤྱིའི་ལུས་རྩལ་ཡུལ་སྐོར་ཀུང་སི་ (drūŋgo bo̱njoŋ gyɛ̱ɛjii lü̱ü dzɛɛ yü̱ügɔɔ gūŋsi) ch.tib. Tibet International Sports and tourism Corporation of China.
ཀྲུང་གོ་མི་དམངས་ (drūŋgo mi̱maŋ) ch.tib. Chinese people.
ཀྲུང་གོ་མི་དམངས་དངུལ་ཁང་ (drūŋgo mi̱maŋ nüügaŋ) People's Bank of China.
ཀྲུང་གོ་མི་དམངས་གསར་བརྗེའི་དམག་དོན་དངོས་མང་བཤམས་སྟོན་ཁང་ (drūŋgo mi̱maŋ sārjee māgdön ŋöömaŋ shāmdöngaŋ) ch.tib. Chinese People's Revolutionary Army Museum.
ཀྲུང་གོ་དམངས་གཙོ་ཡར་སྐྱོལ་ལྷན་ཚོགས་ (drūŋgo māŋdzo ya̱rgül lhɛ̄ndzo) ch.tib. the China Association for Promoting Democracy.
ཀྲུང་གོ་དམངས་གཙོའི་རྒྱལ་འཛུགས་ལྷན་ཚོགས་ (drūŋgo māŋdzö gyɛ̱ɛdzug lhɛ̄ndzo) ch.tib. China Democratic National Construction Association.
ཀྲུང་གོ་ཚན་རིག་ཁང་ (drūŋgo tsɛ̄nriìgaŋ) ch.tib. the Chinese Academy of Sciences.
ཀྲུང་གོ་ཞིང་བཟོ་དམངས་གཙོ་ཏང་ (drūŋgo shi̱ŋso māŋdzo dāŋ) ch.tib. China Peasants' and Workers' Democratic Party.
ཀྲུང་གོ་བཟོ་ཞིང་དམར་དམག་ (drūŋgo so̱shiŋ mārmaà) the Chinese Workers' and Peasants' Red Army (1928—1937).
ཀྲུང་གོ་རི་འཛེགས་མཐུན་ཚོགས་ (drūŋgo ri̱dzeg tũndzɔɔ̀) Chinese Mountainering Association.
ཀྲུང་གོ་གསར་སྤེལ་ཁང་ (drūŋgo sārbelgaŋ) China News Service.
ཀྲུང་གོའི་གུང་ཁྲན་ཏང་ (drūŋgü ku̱ŋdrɛndaŋ) ch. sm. ཀྲུང་གོ་གུང་ཁྲན་ཏང་.
ཀྲུང་གོའི་གུང་ཁྲན་ཏང་ཀྲུང་དབྱང་ཨུ་ཡོན་ལྷན་ཁང་ (drūŋgü ku̱ŋdrɛndaŋ drūŋyaŋ üyün lhɛ̄ngaŋ) ch.tib. Central Committee of the CCP.
ཀྲུང་གོའི་གུང་ཁྲན་རིང་ལུགས་ཀྱི་གཞོན་ནུ་ཚོགས་པ་ (drūŋgü ku̱ŋdrɛn ri̱ŋluùgi shü̱nu tshōgba) ch.tib. Communist Youth League of China.
ཀྲུང་གོའི་གོ་མིན་ཏང་ (drūŋgü go̱mindaŋ) ch. the Guomindang Party of China.
ཀྲུང་གོའི་གོ་མིན་ཏང་གསར་བརྗེ་ཨུ་ཡོན་ལྷན་ཁང་ (drūŋgü go̱mindaŋ sārjee üyün lhɛ̄ngaŋ) ch.tib. the Revolutionary Committee of the Guomindang Party of China.
ཀྲུང་གོའི་རྒྱལ་ཁོངས་ (drūŋgü gyɛ̱ɛkoŋ) ch.tib. belonging to China, part of China's territory ¶ ནང་སོག་ནི་ཀྲུང་གོའི་རྒྱལ་ཁོངས་རེད་ Inner Mongolia is part of China's territory.
ཀྲུང་གོའི་རྒྱལ་སྤྱིའི་ཡུལ་སྐོར་ལས་དོན་ཁང་ (drūŋgü gyɛ̱ɛjii yü̱ügɔɔ lɛ̱̀döngaŋ) Chinese International Travel Service.
ཀྲུང་གོའི་ནང་བསྟན་མཐུན་ཚོགས་ (drūŋgü na̱ŋdɛn thũntsɔɔ̀) ch.tib. Chinese-Buddhist Association.
ཀྲུང་གོའི་སྤྱི་ཚོགས་ (drūŋgü jītsoò) ch.tib. Chinese society.
ཀྲུང་གོའི་སྤྱི་ཚོགས་ཚན་རིག་ཁང་ (drūŋgü jītsoò tsɛ̄nrigaŋ) ch.tib. the Chinese Academy of Social Sciences.
ཀྲུང་གོའི་སྲྭ་མི་ (drūŋgü drə̄mi) Peking Man, Sinanthropus Pekinensis.
ཀྲུང་གོའི་བོད་ལྗོངས་ (drūŋgü bo̱njoŋ) China's Tibet (magazine published in Beijing).
ཀྲུང་གོའི་མི་དམངས་བཅིངས་བཀྲོལ་དམག་ (drūŋgü mi̱maŋ jiŋdrüü māà) ch.tib. the People's Liberation Army of China.
ཀྲུང་གོའི་མི་དམངས་ཆབ་སྲིད་གྲོས་མོལ་ཚོགས་འདུ་ (drūŋgü mi̱maŋ cə̄bsi trö̱möö tsōndu) ch.tib. Chinese People's Political Consultative Conference.
ཀྲུང་གོའི་མི་དམངས་དང་ལྷངས་དམག་ (drūŋgü mi̱maŋ ta̱nlaŋ māà) ch.tib. Chinese People's Volunteer army.
ཀྲུང་གོའི་དམངས་གཙོའི་རྒྱལ་འཛུགས་ལྷན་ཚོགས་ (drūŋgü māŋdzöö gyɛ̱ɛdzuù lhɛ̄ntsɔɔ̀) ch.tib. Democratic National Construction Association of China.
ཀྲུང་གོའི་དམངས་གཙོའི་མནའ་མཐུན་ (drūŋgü māŋdzöö nə̄tün) ch.tib. Democratic League of China.
ཀྲུང་གོའི་དམངས་གཙོའི་རིང་ལུགས་གསར་པའི་གཞོན་ནུ་ཚོགས་པ་ (drūŋgü māŋdzöö ri̱ŋluù sāābɛɛ shü̱nu tsōgba) ch.tib. New Democratic Youth League of China.
ཀྲུང་གོའི་ཚན་རིག་ཁང་ (drūŋgü tsɛ̄nriìgaŋ) ch.tib. Chinese Academy of Sciences.
ཀྲུང་གོའི་ཞིང་བཟོ་དམངས་གཙོའི་ཏང་ (drūŋgü shi̱ŋso māŋdzöö dāŋ) ch.tib. Chinese Peasants' and Workers' Democratic Party.
ཀྲུང་གོའི་གཞོན་ནུའི་ཚགས་པར་ (drūŋgü shü̱nu tsāgbaa) ch.tib. Youth Newspaper of China.
ཀྲུང་གོའི་གཞོན་ནུའི་ཡུལ་སྐོར་ལས་དོན་ཁང་ (drūŋgü shü̱nü yü̱ügɔɔ lɛ̱̀döngaŋ) ch.tib. China Youth Travel Service.
ཀྲུང་གོའི་ཡ་ཧྥེ་མཐུན་སྒྲིལ་ཨུ་ཡོན་ལྷན་ཁང་ (drūŋgü ya̱fe tündrii üyün lhɛ̄ngaŋ) ch.tib. Chinese Committee for Afro-Asian Solidarity.
ཀྲུང་གོའི་རི་མོ་ (drūŋgü re̱mo) ch.tib. Chinese (traditional) painting.
ཀྲུང་གོའི་ལོ་ཆུང་ཚགས་པར་ (drūŋgü lo̱juŋ tsāgbaa) ch.tib. the Children's Newspaper of China.
ཀྲུང་གོའི་སྲོལ་རྒྱུན་རི་མོ་ (drūŋgü sööḡyün re̱mo) ch.tib. Chinese traditional painting.
ཀྲུང་གོ་རང་ངོ་རྒྱལ་བྱེད་པའི་གླུ་གཞས་མཉམ་གདོང་ (drūŋgɔɔ

ŋo̲göö ce̲èbɛɛ lüshɛɛ̀ ñämdoŋ chēmbo) ch.tib. the big anti-China chorus.

ཀྲུང་ཅང་ (drūŋjaŋ) ch. lieutenant general (in British and U.S. Army), air marshal (in British Air Force), vice admiral (in British and U.S. Navy).

ཀྲུང་ཅང་གཙང་པོ་ (drūŋjaŋ tsāŋbo) Pearl River.

ཀྲུང་ཅི་ཆང་ (drūŋ jījaŋ) ch. heavy machine gun.

ཀྲུང་དུང་ (drūŋduŋ) ch. the Middle East.

ཀྲུང་དེ་ (drūŋde) ch. abbr. China and Germany.

ཀྲུང་ཐང་ (drūŋtaŋ) ch. 1. central scroll (hung in the middle of the wall of the main room). 2. a form of address for a Grand Secretary in the Ming and Qing Dynasties.

ཀྲུང་ཕྱི་ཟུང་འབྲེལ་ནད་བརྟག་ཁང་ (drūŋji su̲ŋdre ne̲daàgaŋ) a clinic practicing both traditional Chinese and allopathic Western medicine.

ཀྲུང་དབན་ (drūŋwen) a medium size porcelain bowl.

ཀྲུང་དབྱང་ (drūŋyaŋ) ch. 1. central, center. 2. central government, central authorities. 3. central committee (of CCP).

ཀྲུང་དབྱང་གི་གཅིག་སྡུད་དབང་ཆ་ (drūŋyaŋgi jīgdüù wāŋca) ch.tib. centralized authority of the central government.

ཀྲུང་དབྱང་དངུལ་ཁང་ (drūŋyaŋ ŋüükaŋ) 1. Central Bank of China. 2. Goumindang State Bank (started in 1928).

ཀྲུང་དབྱང་ཇུས་ (drūŋyaŋjüü) ch. bureau of the government.

ཀྲུང་དབྱང་ཆབ་སྲིད་ཇུས་ (drūŋyaŋ cəbsiì jüù) ch.tib. the Politburo, the Political Bureau of the Central Committee of the Chinese Communist Party.

ཀྲུང་དབྱང་ཆབ་སྲིད་གྲོས་ཚོགས་ (drūŋyaŋ cəbsiì tro̲ödzɔɔ̀) ch.tib. the Central Political Consultative Conference.

ཀྲུང་དབྱང་ཐད་གཏོགས་ལས་ཁུངས་ (drūŋyaŋ tɛ̄doò lɛ̲ɛ̀guŋ) ch.tib. departments directly under the central government.

ཀྲུང་དབྱང་འཐབ་ཕྱོགས་གཅིག་གྱུར་པུའུ་ (drūŋyaŋ təbjɔɔ̀ jīggyur bū) ch.tib. the United Work Department of the Central Committee of the Chinese Communist Party.

ཀྲུང་དབྱང་དྲིལ་བསྒྲགས་པུའུ་ (drūŋyaŋ tri̲idraà bū) tib.ch. Propaganda Department of the Central Committee of the Chinese Communist Party.

ཀྲུང་དབྱང་བློ་འདོན་པའི་ཨུ་ཡོན་ལྷན་ཁང་ (drūŋyaŋ lō do̲mbe üyün lhɛ̄ngaŋ) ch.tib. Central Advisory Commission (of the Central Committee of the Chinese Communist Party).

ཀྲུང་དབྱང་མི་དམངས་ཀུན་ཁྱབ་རླུང་འཕྲིན་ལས་ཁུངས་ (drūŋyaŋ mi̲maŋ gūngyəb lūŋdrin lɛ̲ɛ̀guŋ) ch.tib. Central People's Broadcasting Office.

ཀྲུང་དབྱང་མི་དམངས་སྲིད་གཞུང་ (drūŋyaŋ mi̲maŋ sīshuŋ) ch.tib. People's Government of China.

ཀྲུང་དབྱང་མི་རིགས་སློབ་གྲྭ་ཆེན་པོ་ (drūŋyaŋ mi̲riì lābdra chēmbo) ch.tib. Central Institute for Nationalities (also called the National Minorities Institute).

ཀྲུང་དབྱང་དམག་དོན་ཨུ་ཡོན་ལྷན་ཁང་ (drūŋyaŋ māgdön üyüün lhɛ̄ngaŋ) ch.tib. the Military Committee of the Central Committee of the Chinese Communist Party/ Central Military Commission.

ཀྲུང་དབྱང་དམག་ཨུ་ (drūŋyaŋ māg ū) ch.tib. sm. ཀྲུང་དབྱང་དམག་དོན་ཨུ་ཡོན་ལྷན་ཁང་.

ཀྲུང་དབྱང་ཡན་ལག་ཇུས་ (drūŋyaŋ ye̲nlaà jüù) ch.tib. branch office of the Central Committee (of CCP).

ཀྲུང་དབྱང་རིག་གནས་གསར་བརྗེ་ཚོགས་ཆུང་ (drūŋyaŋ ri̲gnɛɛ̀ sārjēē) ch.tib. the central cultural revolution committee (started by Mao that came to be dominated by Jiang Qing and was a major power during the Chinese Cultural Revolution).

ཀྲུང་དབྱང་སྲིད་གཞུང་ (drūŋyaŋ sīishuŋ) ch.tib. central government.

ཀྲུང་དབྱང་གསང་འཕྲིན་ཇུས་ (drūŋyaŋ sāŋdrin jüù) ch.tib. Central Intelligence Agency (U.S.A.).

ཀྲུང་དབྱང་ཨུ་ཡོན་ (drūŋyaŋ üyün) a member of the Central Committee (of CCP).

ཀྲུང་དབྱང་ཨུ་ཡོན་ལྷན་ཁང་ (drūŋyaŋ üyün lhɛ̄ngaŋ) Central Committee (of the CCP).

ཀྲུང་དབྱང་ཨུ་ཡོན་ལྷན་ཁང་ཚང་འཛོམས་གྲོས་ཚོགས་ (drūŋyaŋ üyün lhɛ̄ngaŋ tsāŋdzom tro̲dzɔɔ̀) ch.tib. plenary session of the meeting of the party Central Committee.

ཀྲུང་དབྱངས་ (drūŋyaŋ) ch. sm. ཀྲུང་དབྱང་.

ཀྲུང་དབྱི་སྨན་པ་ (drūŋyi mɛ̄mba) ch.tib. a doctor trained in traditional Chinese medicine.

ཀྲུང་དབྱི་ཡོན་ (drūŋyiyön) sm. ཀྲུང་དབྱི་ཡོའན.

ཀྲུང་དབྱི་ཡོའན་ (drūŋyi yo̲an) ch. House of Representatives, Congress (in the U.S.A., Japan, Australia, etc.), Chamber of Deputies (in Italy, Mexico, Chile, etc.).

ཀྲུང་དབྱི་ཡོའན་གྲོས་ཚོགས་ (drūŋyi yo̲an tro̲dzɔɔ̀) ch.tib. sm. ཀྲུང་དབྱི་ཡོའན་.

ཀྲུང་དབྱིན་ (drūŋyin) ch.eng. abbr. China and Britain.

ཀྲུང་འབར་ (drūŋbar) ch.eng. abbr. China and Burma.

ཀྲུང་མེ་ (drūŋme) ch. abbr. China and the United States.

ཀྲུང་སྨན་ (drūŋmen) ch.tib. Chinese traditional medicine.

ཀྲུང་སྨན་ཁའོ་ (drūŋmenkəwu) ch.tib. department of traditional Chinese medicine (in a hospital).

ཀྲུང་སྨན་སྡེ་ཁག (drūŋmen de̲gaà) ch.tib. department of traditional Chinese medicine (in a university).

ཀྲུང་སྨན་ནད་ཁང་ (drūŋmen ne̲gaŋ) ch.tib. ward where Chinese (traditional) medicine is practiced.

ཀྲུང་སྨན་ནད་བརྟག་ཁང་ (drūŋmen ne̲daàkaŋ) ch.tib. clinic of traditional Chinese medicine.

ཀྲུང་སྨན་ཚོང་ཁང་ (drūŋmen tsōŋgaŋ) ch.tib. pharmacy selling traditional Chinese medicines.

ཀྲུང་སྨན་ཞིབ་འཇུག་ཁང་ (drūŋmen shi̲mjuùgaŋ) ch.tib. Academy of Traditional Chinese medicine, Institute of Chinese traditional medicine.

ཀྲུང་སྨན་བཟོ་གྲྭ་ (drūŋmen so̲dra) ch.tib. Chinese medicine factory.

ཀྲུང་སྨན་སློབ་གྲྭ་ (drūŋmen lābdra) ch.tib. School of Traditional Chinese Medicine.

ཀྲུང་ཙི་ (drūŋdzi) ch. neutron.

ཀྲུང་ཙི་རྡུལ་ཕྲན་ (drūŋdzi du̲drɛn) ch.tib. sm. ཀྲུང་ཙི་.

ཀྲུང་ཙེ་ (drūŋdze) ch. sm. ཀྲུང་ཙི་.

ཀྲུང་ཝེ་ (drūŋwe) ch. first lieutenant (in U.S. Army, and Air force), lieutenant junior grade (in U.S. Navy), lieutenant (in British Army), sublieutenant (in British Navy).

ཀྲུང་ཝེའུ་ (drūŋwe) ch. sm. ཀྲུང་ཝེ་.

ཀྲུང་ཝེའུ་ (drūŋwe) ch. sm. ཀྲུང་ཝེ་.

ཀྲུང་ཤའོ་ (drūŋshao) ch. lieutenant colonel (in U.S. Air Force and in the British and U.S. armies), Commander (in the British and U.S. navies), Wing Commander (in the British Air Force).

ཀྲུང་ཤི་ (drūŋshi) ch. Chinese and Western ¶ ཀྲུང་ཤི་གཉིས་ཀྱི་ཐབས་ལ་བརྟེན་ནས་སྨན་བཅོས་བྱེད་ཀྱི་ཡོད་ (They) treat illness based on both traditional Chinese and Western medicine.

ཀྲུང་ཡའོ་སྨན་རིགས་ (drūŋyao mɛ̄nriì) ch.tib. traditional Chinese medicine.

ཀྲུང་ཡིས་ (druŋyiì) ch. traditional Chinese medicine.

ཀྲུང་ཡིས་སྨན་པ་ (druŋyiì mɛ̄mba) ch.tib. doctor of traditional Chinese medicine.

ཀྲུང་ཡོ་ (drūŋyo) ch. abbr. China and Vietnam, Sino-Vietnamese.

ཀྲུང་ཡོན་ས་ཁུལ་ (drūŋyön səgüü) ch.tib. the central plains of China (comprising the middle and lower reaches of the Yellow River).

ཀྲུང་གཡང་ (drūŋyaŋ) ch. sm. ཀྲུང་དབྱང་.

ཀྲུང་རི་ (drūŋri) ch. abbr. China and Japan.

ཀྲུང་རི་འཐབ་འཁྲུག (drūŋri təbdruù) ch.tib. Sino-Japanese War (1894-95).

ཀྲུང་སུའུ་ (drūŋsu) ch. abbr. China and the Soviet Union, Sino-Soviet.

ཀྲུང་ཧིན་ (drūŋhin) ch. abbr. China and India, Sino-Indian.

ཀྲུང་ཧིན་མཐའ་མཚམས་ཞིང་འཁྲུག (drūŋhin tāndzam s<u>i</u>ŋdruù) ch.tib. China-India border disturbance (war) of 1962.

ཀྲུང་ཧྭ་ (drūŋha) ch. China.

ཀྲུང་ཧྭ་རྒྱལ་ཡོངས་ (drūŋha gy<u>ɛ</u>yoŋ) ch.tib. all of China, China-wide.

ཀྲུང་ཧྭ་རྒྱལ་ཡོངས་སྤྱི་ཁྱབ་བཟོ་ཚོགས་ (drūŋha gy<u>ɛ</u>yoŋ jīgyəp s<u>o</u>dzoò) ch.tib. All-China Federation of Trade Unions.

ཀྲུང་ཧྭ་རྒྱལ་ཡོངས་བུད་མེད་མཉམ་འབྲེལ་ལྷན་ཚོགས་ (drūŋha gy<u>ɛ</u>yoŋ p<u>ü</u>meè ñāmdree lhɛ̄ndzoò) ch.tib. All-China Women's Federation.

ཀྲུང་ཧྭ་རྒྱལ་ཡོངས་གཞོན་ནུ་མཉམ་འབྲེལ་ལྷན་ཚོགས་ (drūŋha gy<u>ɛ</u>yoŋ sh<u>ö</u>nnu ñāmdree lhɛ̄ndzoò) ch.tib. All-China Federation of Youth.

ཀྲུང་ཧྭ་རྒྱལ་ཡོངས་སློབ་གྲྭ་བའི་མཉམ་འབྲེལ་ལྷན་ཚོགས་ (drūŋha gy<u>ɛ</u>yoŋ lōbdrawe ñāmdree lhɛ̄ndzoò) All-China Students' Federation.

ཀྲུང་ཧྭ་མི་དམངས་སྤྱི་མཐུན་རྒྱལ་ཁབ་ (drūŋha m<u>i</u>maŋ jīdün gy<u>ɛɛ</u>gəb) ch.tib. the People's Republic of China.

ཀྲུང་ཧྭ་མི་རིགས་ (drūŋha m<u>i</u>riì) ch.tib. the nationalities of China, the Chinese nation.

ཀྲུང་ཧྭ་མི་སེར་རྒྱལ་ཁབ་ (drūŋha m<u>i</u>se gy<u>ɛɛ</u>gəb) ch.tib. Republic of China (1912-1949).

ཀྲུང་ཧྭ་དམངས་རྒྱལ་ (drūŋha māŋgyɛɛ̀) ch.tib. the Guomindang government.

ཀྲུང་ཧྭ་དམངས་གཙོ་མནའ་འབྲེལ་ (drūŋha māŋdzo nādree) ch.tib. the China Democratic Alliance.

ཀྲུང་ཧྭེ་ (drūŋhe) sm. ཀྲུང་ཧྲེ་.

ཀྲུང་ཧྲན་གྱོན་ཆས་ (drūŋhren k<u>ö</u>njɛɛ̀) ch.tib. Chinese tunic suit.

ཀྲུང་ཧྲན་ཆ་ལུགས་ (drūŋhren cəlug) ch.tib. sm. ཀྲུང་ཧྲན་གྱོན་ཆས་.

ཀྲུང་ཧྲན་ལྭ་བ་ (drūŋhren lāwa) ch.tib. sm. ཀྲུང་ཧྲན་གྱོན་ཆས་.

ཀྲུང་ཧྲི་ (drūŋhri) ch. sergeant (in British and U.S. Army/ Air Force), petty officer (in U.S. and British navies).

ཀྲུང་ཨ་ (drūŋ ā) ch. abbr. 1. China and United States, Sino-American. 2. China and Albania.

ཀྲུང་ཨུ་ (drūŋ ū) ch. abbr. Central Committee (of CCP).

ཀྲུང་ཨུ་ཚང་འཛོམས་གྲོས་ཚོགས་ (drūŋ ū tsāŋdzom tr<u>ö</u>tsɔɔ̀) ch.tib. plenary session of the Central Committee (of CCP).

ཀྲུངས་ (drūŋ) sm. སྲས་.

ཀྲུངས་ཐུག (drūŋdug) sm. སྲུས་ཐུག.

ཀྲུབ་གཟན་ (drūbsɛn) sm. སྲུབ་གཟན་.

ཀྲུམ་ (drūm) meat (h.) ¶ ཀྲུམ་ཁུ་ Meat broth/ soup.

ཀྲུམ་ཁོག (drūmgɔɔ) h. of ཤ་ཁོག.

ཀྲུམ་ཐུག (drūmtuù) meat soup/ stew (h.).

ཀྲུམ་དོད་ (drūmdöö̀) a money substitute for an obligation to provide meat (h.).

ཀྲུམ་མདའ་ (drūmda) pistol.

ཀྲུམ་རིགས་ (drūmrig) kinds/ types of meat (h.).

ཀྲུམས་ (drūm) sm. ཀྲུམ་.

ཀྲུའང་ (drūaŋ) ch. Zhuang (a nationality in China).

ཀྲུའན་ཅའ་ (drūanja) ch. specialist, expert.

ཀྲུའུ་ཞི་ (drūshi) ch. chairman; va.— བྱེད་; —གནང་ to act as chairman.

ཀྲུའུ་ཞི་བཞུགས་སྟེགས་ (drūshi sh<u>u</u>gdeg) ch.tib. rostrum, platform (at meetings/ conventions).

ཀྲུའུ་ཞི་གཞོན་པ་ (drūshi sh<u>ö</u>mba) ch.tib. vice chairman.

ཀྲུའུ་ཞིའི་སྟེགས་བུ་ (drūshi tēgbu) sm. ཀྲུའུ་ཞི་བཞུགས་སྟེགས་.

ཀྲུའུ་ཞིའི་སྟོན་ (drūshi tȫn) ch. sm. ཀྲུའུ་ཞིའི་ཚོགས་པ་.

ཀྲུའུ་ཞིའི་ཚོགས་པ་ (drūshi tsɔ̄gba) 1. presidium. 2. people seated on the rostrum/ platform at meetings.

ཀྲུའུ་རིན་ (drūrin) ch. sm. ཀྲུའུ་རེན་.

ཀྲུའུ་རེན་ (drūren) ch. director, head, chief, president.

ཀྲུའུ་རེན་གཞོན་པ་ (drūren sh<u>ö</u>mba) ch.tib. vice ཀྲུའུ་རེན་.

ཀྲུའུ་ལའི་ (drūlai) Chu Lai (S. Vietnam).

ཀྲུའུ་ལོའོའི་དུས་རབས་ (drūluo t<u>ü</u>rəb) ch.tib. Jurassic Period.

ཀྲེ་ (drē) ch. sm. ཀྲེས་ཀྲེས་.

ཀྲེ་ཅང་ (drējaŋ) Zhejiang Province.

ཀྲེ་ལྕགས་ (drējaà) hasp, lock; va.—རྒྱག; —གཡོགས་.

ཀྲེ་ནག (drēnaà) 1. the soot that collects on the bottom of a pot. 2. soot used on face by dobdo monks (as decoration to enhance fierceness).

ཀྲེ་ཙི་ (drēdzi) ch. proton.

ཀྲེ་སི་ (drēse) eng. 1. postal stamp. 2. ticket.

ཀྲེང་གྷ་རིལ་ (drēŋgari) eng.hind. tank.

ཀྲེང་དང་ (drēŋdaŋ) ch. political party.

ཀྲེང་ལོང་ (drēŋloŋ) ch. a food steamer.

ཀྲེང་ཨུ་ (drēŋu) ch. political commissar (of a People's Liberation Army unit).

ཀྲེང་ཨུད་ (drēŋüǜ) ch. sm. ཀྲེང་ཨུ་.

ཀྲེན་ (drēn) ch. an administrative unit within a city.

ཀྲེན་ཀྲང་ (drɛ̄ndraŋ) ch. chief administrator/ head of a ཀྲེན་.

ཀྲེན་སྡོང་ (drēndoŋ) ch.tib. hazel tree.

ཀྲེན་ཤིང་ (drēnshiŋ) ch.tib. sm. ཀྲེན་སྡོང་.

ཀྲེབ་འཁོར་ (drēbgɔɔ) eng.tib. tape recorder ¶ ཀྲེབ་འཁོར་ནས་ཕབས་ Transcribing from a tape recorder.

ཀྲེས་ཀྲེས་ (drēèdreè) mixing; va.—གཏོང་ to mix.

ཀྲོ་ (drō) sm.* སྲོ་.

ཀྲོ་ཀ་ (drōga) sm.* སྲོག་ཀ་.

ཀྲོ་མ་ཀྲོ་ (drōmadro) eng. tomato.

ཀྲོ་མར་ (drōmar) sm.* སྲོ་མར་.

ཀྲོ་ཤད་ (drōsheè) sm.* སྲོ་ཤད་.

ཀྲོག་ཀྲོག (drɔ̄gdrɔɔ̀) 1. showing off; va.—བྱེད་. 2. a banging noise; va.—གཏོང་ to bang (usu. on a door).

ཀྲོག་ཀྲོག་ཚ་པོ་ (drōgdroò tsābo) a show-off, show-offish.

ཀྲོག་ཁྱོ་ (drɔ̄ggyo) Tokyo.

ཀྲོག་མཁྲགས་པོ་ (drɔ̄ɔ̀ trāgo) sm.* སྲོག་མཁྲེག་ཤ་པོ་.

ཀྲོག་མཁྲེགས་པོ་ (drɔ̄ɔ̀ trāgo) sm. ཀྲོག་མཁྲགས་པོ་.

ཀྲོག་མེད་པ་ (drɔ̄ɔ̀ m<u>e</u>èba) fragile, not durable.

ཀྲོང་ (drōŋ) ch. the "dealer" in mahjong (the one who throws the dice).

ཀྲོང་ཀྲོང་ (drōŋdroŋ) 1. sm. ཀྲོང་ངེར་. 2. (with རྣ་ཅོག་) listening carefully ¶ རྣ་ཅོག་ཀྲོང་ཀྲོང་བྱས་ནས་ཉན་ He was listening carefully. ¶ ང་ལ་ལས་ཀ་ཡག་པོ་ཞིག་རག་རྒྱུ་རྣ་ཅོག་ཀྲོང་ཀྲོང་བྱས་ནས་བསྡད་ཡོད་ I am listening carefully so that I can get a good job. [Lit. ears erect].

ཀྲོང་ངེར་ (drōŋer) upright, erect, straight up; va.—སྡོད་,—གནས་ to sit upright/ erect; va.—ལང་ to stand upright/ erect ¶ སྒོ་སྲུང་བ་དེ་ཀྲོང་ངེར་ལངས་འདུག The guard was standing erect.

ཀྲོང་ཅ་ (drōŋja) ch. armor, armored.

ཀྲོང་ཅ་འཁོར་ལོ་ (drōŋja kɔ̄ɔ̄lo) ch.tib. an armored vehicle.

ཀྲོང་ཅ་དམག (drōŋja māà) ch.tib. armored soldiers/ troops.

ཀྲོང་ཅ་དམག་དཔུང་ (drōŋja məgbuŋ) ch.tib. sm. ཀྲོང་ཅ་དམག.

ཀྲོང་སྡོད་ (drōŋdöö̀) 1. staying or standing upright; va.—བྱེད་. 2. standing at attention; va.—བྱེད་.

ཀྲོང་ཙེ་ (drōŋdze) ch. name of a stroke in written Chinese.

ཀྲོང་ཡོན་ (drōŋyon) ch. "Number One Scholar" (a title conferred on the person who was first in the national imperial examination in traditional China).

ཀྲོང་རིགས་ (drōŋriì) ch.tib. the Zhuang nationality.

ཀྲོངས་ (drōŋ) sm.* བཀྲོངས་.

ཀྲོད་ (drȫò) sm.* སྲོད་.

ཀྲོན་ (drō̃n) eng. a ton.

ཀྲོན་ཀྲོན་ (dröndrön) 1. hanging. 2. vacillating, wavering.

ཀྲོན་ཅ་ (drōnja) ch. specialist, expert.

ཀྲོན་ཆུས་ (drōnjöö) ch. prefecture, administrative region ། གཞིས་རྩེ་ཀྲོན་ཆུས་ Shigatse Prefecture.

ཀྲོན་ཡོན་ (drōnyön) ch. abbr. of ཀྲོན་ཡོན་ཀུང་ཧྲུའུ་.

ཀྲོན་ཡོན་ཀུང་ཧྲུའུ་ (drōnyön gūŋhru) ch. prefectural commissioner's office.

ཀྲོན་ཡོན་གཞུང་སྐྱབ་ལས་ཁུངས་ (drōnyön gūŋhru) ch.tib. sm. ཀྲོན་ཡོན་ཀུང་ཧྲུའུ་.

ཀྲོན་ཧྲུའུ་ (drōnhru) abbr. party secretary of a prefecture.

ཀྲོབ་ (drōb) 1. eng. tub, bathtub. 2. a snap (fastener); va.—རྒྱག to fasten a snap; va.—འགྲོལ་ to untie/ undo/ unhook/ unfasten a snap.

ཀྲོམ་ (drōm) a big grain container woven from twigs.

ཀྲོམ་མདའ་ (drōmda) pistol.

ཀྲོམས་ (drōm) sm.* ཁྲོམས་.

ཀྲོའུ་ (drōu) ch. region, state, county ། ཡ་ཀྲོའུ་གི་རྒྱལ་ཁབ་ The countries of Asia (the Asian region).

ཀྲོའུ་ཀང་ (drōu drāŋ) ch. administrative head of a ཀྲོའུ་.

ཀྲོའུ་རྒྱལ་རབས་ (drōu gyɛ̱rəb) ch.tib. Chou dynasty (1100-221 B.C.).

ཀྲོའུ་ཨན་ལའི་ (drōu ēnlai) Zhao Enlai.

ཀྲོའོ་ལུང་ (drāolūŋ) ch.tib. methane gas.

ཀླ་ཀློ་ (lālo) barbarian, savage.

ཀླ་ཀློའི་ཆོས་ལུགས་ (lālö cũũluù) primitive religion, religion of barbarians/ savages.

ཀླག་ (lāà) 1. sm.* བཀླག. 2. thick wool cloth.

ཀླག་ཅོར་ (lāgjor) clamor, noise.

ཀླགས་ (lāà) arc. superior, better.

ཀླགས་པ་ (lāgba) sm. ཀླགས་.

ཀླད་ (lɛ̄ɛ̀) 1. over/ above the head ། ཁོས་རལ་གྲི་འདི་ཀླད་ལ་བསྐོར་སོང་ He swung the sword over his head. 2. abbr. of ཀླད་པ་.

ཀླད་ཀོར་ (lɛ̄ɛ̀gɔɔ) zero.

ཀླད་དཀྲུག (lɛ̄ɛ̀drug) abbr. ཀླད་པ་དཀྲུག་དཀྲུག.

ཀླད་སྐོགས་ (lɛ̄ɛ̀gɔɔ̀) skull.

ཀླད་སྐྱི་ (lɛ̄ɛ̀gyii) meninges.

ཀླད་སྐྱིའི་ཚ་ཚད་ (lɛ̄ɛ̀gyii tsādzɛɛ̀) cerebro-spinal meningitis.

ཀླད་སྐྱིའི་ཤ་སྐྲན་ (lɛ̄ɛ̀gyii shādrɛn) brain tumor.

ཀླད་སྐྱོན་ (lɛ̄ɛ̀gyön) a disease of the brain.

ཀླད་སྐྲན་ (lɛ̄ɛ̀drɛn) brain tumor, brain cancer.

ཀླད་ཁུ་ (lɛ̄ɛ̀gu) brain fluid.

ཀླད་ཁོག (lɛ̄ɛ̀gɔɔ̀) cranial cavity.

ཀླད་ཁྱིམ་ (lɛ̄ɛ̀gyim) the place where the brain sits/ rests.

ཀླད་ཁྲག (lɛ̄ɛ̀draà) blood in the brain; vi.—རྒྱས་; —འཐོན་; —ཤོར་ to have a brain/ cerebral hemorrhage.

ཀླད་ཁྲག་འཁྱོམ་ (lɛ̄ɛ̀trāà kyōm) vi. to be dazed because of a blow on the head, to have brain damage as a result of striking one's head against sth.

ཀླད་ཁྲག་རྒྱས་ནད་ (lɛ̄ɛ̀draà gyɛ̱nɛɛ̀) a brain hemorrhage.

ཀླད་ཁྲག་ཉམས་ (lɛ̄ɛ̀draà ña̱m) cerebral anemia.

ཀླད་ཁྲག་ཉམས་ནད་ (lɛ̄ɛ̀draà ña̱mnɛɛ̀) cerebral anemia.

ཀླད་ཁྲག་ཉམས་པ་ (lɛ̄ɛ̀draà ña̱mba) cerebral anemia.

ཀླད་ཁྲག་འདྲེ་ (lɛ̄ɛ̀draà drɛ̱) vi. to get an illness or have an accident which causes the brain and cerebral blood to mix.

ཀླད་མཁྲེགས་ (lɛ̄ɛ̀dreg) sm. ཀླད་པ་མཁྲེགས་པོ་.

ཀླད་འཁྱོམ་ཐེབས་ (lɛ̄ɛ̀kyom tēè) sm. ཀླད་ཁྲག་འཁྱོམ་.

ཀླད་གྱེན་མིན་བུ་ (lɛ̄ɛ̀gyen mĩmbu) pineal body.

ཀླད་འགེམས་ཀྱི་དུང་ཏེག (lɛ̄ŋgemgi du̱ŋdeg) striking a telling/ stunning blow, defeating tellingly; va.—གཏོང་ ། དགྲ་བོར་ཀླད་འགེམས་ཀྱི་དུང་ཏེག་བཏང་བ་རེད་ (They) inflicted a severe defeat on the enemy. [Lit. hit the brain a stunning/ powerful blow].

ཀླད་རྒྱ་ (lɛ̄ɛ̀gya) cerebral membrane.

ཀླད་རྒྱའི་ཁྲག་ལུད་ (lɛ̄ɛ̀gyee drəglüü) apoplexy.

ཀླད་རྒྱའི་གཉན་ཚད་ (lɛ̄ɛ̀gyee ñɛ̄ndzɛɛ̀) sm. ཀླད་རྒྱའི་ཚ་ནད་.

ཀླད་རྒྱའི་ཚ་ནད་ (lɛ̄ɛ̀gyɛɛ tsānɛɛ̀) cerebral meningitis.

ཀླད་རྒྱས་ (lɛ̄ɛ̀gyɛɛ̀) 1. meninges. 2. a disease involving enlargement of the brain.

ཀླད་རྒྱུངས་སྐྱི་མོ་ (lɛ̄ɛ̀gyuŋ gyĩmu) cerebral membrane.

ཀླད་རྒྱུངས་སྐྱི་མོ་གཉན་ཚད་ (lɛ̄ɛ̀gyuŋ gyĩmu ñɛ̄ntsɛɛ̀) cerebrospinal meningitis.

ཀླད་སྒོ་ (lɛ̄ɛ̀go) fontanel.

ཀླད་ཆུ་ (lɛ̄ɛ̀ju) cerebrospinal fluid.

ཀླད་ཆུང་ (lɛ̄ɛ̀juŋ) 1. cerebellum. 2. a person with little or no imagination, a person with limited mental capacity.

ཀླད་ཆེན་ (lɛ̄ɛ̀jen) cerebrum.

ཀླད་ཆེན་སྐྱི་རིམ་ (lɛ̄ɛ̀jen gyĩrim) cerebral cortex.

ཀླད་ཆེན་གྱི་དབང་རྩ་ (lɛ̄ɛ̀jengi wāŋdza) cerebral nerve.

ཀླད་ཆེན་གྱི་ཚ་ནད་ (lɛ̄ɛ̀jengi tsānɛɛ̀) cerebritis.

ཀླད་ལྗང་ (lɛ̄ɛ̀jaŋ) abbr. ཀླད་པ་ལྗང་ཁུ་.

ཀླད་རྙིང་མཁྲེགས་པོ་ (lɛ̄ɛ̀ñiŋ trēgbo) sm. ཀླད་རྙིང་འཁྲེགས་བཟུང་.

ཀླད་རྙིང་མཁྲེགས་བཟུང་ (lɛ̄ɛ̀ñiŋ trēgsuŋ) extremely conservative, a hardline conservative; va.—བྱེད་.

ཀླད་ལྟག་རུས་པ་ (lɛ̄ɛ̀daà ru̱bə) back of the skull.

ཀླད་དུ་བཀར་ (lɛ̄ɛ̀du gār) sm. ཀླས་ལ་བཀར་.

ཀླད་དོན་ (lɛ̄ɛ̀dön) the first/ beginning section of a book, the introduction of a book.

ཀླད་འདར་ (lɛ̄ɛ̀dar) cowardly.

ཀླད་ནད་ (lɛ̄ɛ̀nɛɛ̀) brain disease.

ཀླད་ནས་ཕྱར་ (lɛ̄ɛ̀nɛɛ̀ cār) va. to hold (a sword) high above one's head.

ཀླད་པ་ (lɛ̄ɛ̀ba) brain; va.—དཀྲུག to use one's brain.

ཀླད་པ་དཀྲུག (lɛ̄ɛ̀ba drūù) va. to brainwash.

ཀླད་པ་དཀྲུག་དཀྲུག (lɛ̄ɛ̀ba drūgdruù) using one's brain, innovating; va.—གཏོང་.

ཀླད་པ་སྐྱེན་པོ་ (lɛ̄ɛ̀ba gyēnbo) sm. ཀླད་པ་བསིར་པོ་.

ཀླད་པ་འཁྱོམ་ (lɛ̄ɛ̀ba kyōm) sm. ཀླད་ཁྲག་འཁྱོམ་.

ཀླད་པ་མགྱོགས་པོ་ (lɛ̄ɛ̀ba gyo̱bo) sm. ཀླད་པ་བསིར་པོ་.

ཀླད་པ་འགུལ་ (lɛ̄ɛ̀ba gu̱ü) va. to use one's brains, to innovate.

ཀླད་པ་འགེམས་ (lɛ̄ɛ̀ba ge̱m) sm. ཀླད་འགེམས་.

ཀླད་པ་སྒྱུར་ (lɛ̄ɛ̀ba gyu̱r) va. to brainwash.

ཀླད་པ་ལྗང་ཁུ་ (lɛ̄ɛ̀ba jə̱ŋgu) a conservative, a very traditional person.

ཀླད་པ་མདུན་མ་ (lɛ̄ɛ̀ba du̱nmə) the front of the brain.

ཀླད་པ་མེད་པ་ (lɛ̄ɛ̀ba me̱ɛba) sm. ཀླད་མེད་.

ཀླད་པ་དམར་པོ་ (lɛ̄ɛ̀ba māābo) 1. sb. who is pro-communist. 2. bald.

ཀླད་པ་ཡོད་པ་ (lɛ̄ɛ̀ba yo̱öba) sm. མགོ་འཚོས་པོ་.

ཀླད་པ་སྤྲབ་པོ་ (lɛ̄ɛ̀ba drəbu) person who is easily swayed or follows what others say, changeable, fickle.

ཀླད་པ་གསལ་པོ་ (lɛ̄ɛ̀ba sɛ̄ɛbo) clearheaded, sb. who keeps a cool head.

ཀླད་པ་བསིར་པོ་ (lɛ̄ɛ̀ba sĩrbu) sb. who understands and thinks quickly.

ཀླད་པའི་སྐྱི་དཀར་ (lɛ̄ɛ̀bɛ gyĩgar) sm. ཀླད་རྒྱ་.

ཀླད་པའི་ཁྱིམ་ཆུ་ (lɛ̄ɛ̀bɛ kyĩmju) hyrdocephaly, hydrocephalus.

ཀླད་པའི་ཁྲག་རྩའི་ནད་ (lɛ̄ɛ̀bɛ trāgdzɛ nɛ̱ɛ̀) cerebrovascular disease.

ཀླད་པའི་ངལ་རྩོལ་ (lɛ̄ɛ̀bɛ ŋɛ̱ɛ̱dzö) brainwork, mental work; va.—བྱེད་.

ཀླད་པའི་གཉན་ཚད་ (lɛ̄ɛ̀bɛ ñɛ̄ndzɛɛ̀) encephalitis, cerebritis.

ཀླད་པའི་ནུས་པ་ (lɛ̄ɛ̀bɛ nu̱ũba) brain power, mental energy.

ཀླད་པའི་ཕྱི་ནད་ (lɛ̄ɛ̀bɛ cĩnɛɛ̀) neurosurgical illnesses ། ཀླད་པའི་ཕྱི་ནད་ཚན་ཁག Department of neurosurgery.

ཀླད་པའི་དབང་རྩ་ (lɛ̄ɛ̀bɛ wāŋdza) cranial nerve.

ཀླད་པའི་ཚ་ནད་ (lɛ̄ɛ̀bɛ tsānɛɛ̀) encephalitis.

ཀླད་པའི་ལས་རྩོལ་ (lɛ̄ɛ̀bɛ lɛ̱ɛ̱dzö) sm. ཀླད་པའི་ངལ་རྩོལ་.

ཀླད་པོ་ཆེ་ (lɛ̄ɛ̀boje) sb. who thinks on a grand scale ༈ མི་ཀླད་པོ་ཆེ་ཡིས་ལས་དོན་ཆེན་པོ་སྒྲུབ་ཐུབ་ A person who thinks on a grand scale can accomplish big tasks.

ཀླད་དཔྱད་གློག་རླབས་ (lɛ̄ɛ̀jɛɛ̀ lɔ̄glɘb) sm. ཀླད་སྤྱད་གློག་རླབས་.

ཀླད་སྤྱད་གློག་རིས་ (lɛ̄ɛ̀jɛɛ̀ lɔ̄grii̇) electroencephalogram (EEG).

ཀླད་སྤྱད་གློག་རླབས་ (lɛ̄ɛ̀jɛɛ̀ lōglɘb) brain wave.

ཀླད་སྦྲི་ (lɛ̄ɛ̀dri) sm. ཀླད་རྒྱ་.

ཀླད་ཕོར་ (lɛ̄ɛ̀bɔɔ) a cup made from a human skull.

ཀླད་བྱི་ (lɛ̄ɛ̀ji) bald.

ཀླད་མ་ (lɛ̄ɛ̀ma) 1. at first, in the beginning ༈ དུས་ཀྱི་ཀླད་མ་ In the beginning (time). 2. above, before.

ཀླད་མེད་ (lɛ̄ɛ̀meè) 1. encephalitis. 2. foolish, stupid, shallow, not profound ༈ མི་དེ་ཀླད་མེད་རེད་ That person is stupid.

ཀླད་མེད་བྱབ་ཆུང་ (lɛ̄ɛ̀meè cɘ̄bjuŋ) sm. ཀླད་མེད་, 2.

ཀླད་དམར་ (lɛ̄ɛ̀maa) bald.

ཀླད་རྩ་ (lɛ̄ɛ̀dza) cranial nerves.

ཀླད་རྩ་འགགས་ནད་ (lɛ̄ɛ̀dza gɛ̱nɛɛ̀) a cerebral stroke.

ཀླད་རྩལ་ (lɛ̄ɛ̀dzɛɛ) a thoughtful person, a person who is mentally adroit.

ཀླད་རྩལ་ཆེན་པོ་ (lɛ̄ɛ̀dza cēmbo) sm. ཀླད་རྩལ་.

ཀླད་ཚད་ (lɛ̄ɛ̀dzɛɛ̀) inflammation of the brain, encephalitis.

ཀླད་ཚད་ཁ་པ་ (lɛ̄ɛ̀dzɛɛ̀ kāba) encephalitis B.

ཀླད་མཚོ་འཁྱོམས་པ་ (lɛ̄ɛ̀tso kyōmba) cerebral concussion.

ཀླད་ཞབས་འཕྱང་གཟུགས་ (lɛ̄ɛ̀shɘb cāŋsuù) hypophysis cerebri.

ཀླད་ཞོ་ (lɛ̄ɛ̀sho) 1. brain. 2. grey matter (of brain).

ཀླད་གཞུངས་ (lɛ̄ɛ̀shuŋ) sm. རྒྱུངས་པ་.

ཀླད་ཟམ་ (lɛ̄ɛ̀sam) mesencephalon.

ཀླད་གཟེར་ (lɛ̄ser) a brain disease/ stroke; vi.—རྒྱག.

ཀླད་ཡུ་འཁོར་ (lɛ̄yu kɔ̄ɔ) vi. to be/ get dizzy.

ཀླད་རིད་གློག་གཟིགས་ (lɛ̄ɛ̀rii̇ lɔ̄gsii̇) electroencephalogram ༈ ཀླད་རིད་གློག་གཟིགས་ཁང་ Room where electroencephalograms are done.

ཀླད་རིད་གློག་གཟིགས་ཁང་ (lɛ̄ɛ̀rii̇ lɔ̄gsii̇) electroencephalogram room.

ཀླད་རིས་གློག་གཟིགས་ཁང་ (lɛ̄ɛ̀rii̇ lɔ̄gsii̇) sm. ཀླད་རིད་གློག་གཟིགས་.

ཀླད་རུས་ (lɛ̄ɛ̀rüü̇) skull.

ཀླད་ལ་བཀར་ (lɛ̄ɛ̀la gār) sm. ཀླས་ལ་བཀར་.

ཀླད་ཤུན་ (lɛ̄ɛ̀shün) brain membrane.

ཀླད་ཤུབས་ (lɛ̄ɛ̀shub) sm. ཀླད་ཤུན་.

ཀླད་སྲིན་ནད་ (lɛ̄ɛ̄sinnɛɛ̀) a brain disease.

ཀླན་ (lɛ̄n) 1. va. to answer, to respond. 2. va. to revenge.

ཀླན་ཀ་ (lēnga) 1. blaming, finding fault; va.—འཚོལ་ to search out other's faults; va.—བྱེད་ to find fault with others ༈ ཁྱོད་ཀྱིས་ཉེས་མེད་ཀྱི་མི་ལ་ཀླན་ཀ་འཚོལ་བའི་རྒྱུ་མཚན་གང་ཡིན་ Why are you looking to find fault with sb. who has done nothing wrong? 2. dispute, controversy, argument ༈ ས་ཆ་དེ་སུ་ལ་བདག་མིན་སྐོར་ཀླན་ཀ་ཞིག་བྱུང་བ་རེད་ There was a dispute over who owned that land.

ཀླན་ཀ་ཡོང་གཞི་ (lēnga yo̱ŋshi) the cause of a dispute/ argument.

ཀླབ་ (lɘ̄b) arc. thick woolen (woven) cloth.

ཀླམ་པ་ (lām) arc. sm. ཀླབ་.

ཀླལ་ (lām) sm. བསྒྲིང་.

ཀླས་ (lɛ̄ɛ̀) arc. the residence of a king's female servants/ consorts.

ཀླས་པ་ (lɛ̄ɛ̀) sm. མཐའ་ཡས་པ་.

ཀླས་ལ་བཀར་ (lɛ̄ɛ̀la gār) 1. va. to put all one's efforts into finishing or completing sth., to strive tirelessly/ incessantly to complete sth. ༈ ཚིག་མཛོད་ཀྱི་ལས་ཀ་དེ་ཀླས་ལ་བཀར་ནས་མཇུག་སྒྲིལ་དགོས་ (We) must strive to complete the dictionary project. ༈ ཀླས་ལ་བཀར་ནས་ལས་འགན་སྒྲུབ་པ་བྱས་པ་ཡིན་ I exerted great effort in order to complete my task. 2. va. to ask for sth. in an extremely insisting way, to insist on doing sth., to pressure/ force sth. ༈ ངའི་གྲོགས་པོས་ཀླས་ལ་བཀར་ནས་དངུལ་གཡར་དགོས་ཟེར་གྱི་འདུག My friend is insisting that I lend him money.

ཀླུ་ (lū) serpentine deity (nāga in Sanskrit) (a kind of spirit being that is believed to reside underground and is easily angered).

ཀླུ་ཁང་ (lūkaŋ) 1. a place or temple where nāgas live. 2. name of an aristocratic family. 3. the nāga temple on the island behind the Potala Palace in Lhasa.

ཀླུ་ཁང་གཞིས་ཀ་ (lūkaŋ sẖiigɘ) an estate belonging to the ཀླུ་ཁང་ family.

ཀླུ་འགུག (lū gu̱ù) va. to call/ summon a new bride's nāga to her new residence.

ཀླུ་རྒྱལ་ (lūgyɛɛ) king of nāgas.

ཀླུ་སྒུག (lūguù) a place in Lhasa.

ཀླུ་སྒུག་སྒར་སྒྲིག (lūguù ga̱rdrig) shung. a ceremony that occurs after Monlam in Lhasa when soldiers parade in ancient uniforms.

ཀླུ་སྒུག་ན་སྡེ་ (lūguù na̱de) a place on the south side of Lhasa.

ཀླུ་སྒྲུབ (lūdrub) a Buddhist deity (Nagārjuna).

ཀླུ་གཉན་ (lūñɛn) 1. abbr. of two kinds of bad spirits/ demons: ཀླུ་ and གཉན་. 2. a kind of powerful and harmful ཀླུ་.

ཀླུ་གཏོར་ (lūdɔr) a torma offering to a nāga.

ཀླུ་ཐིབས་ (lūtib) celebration when nāgas are propitiated.

ཀླུ་ཐེབས་ (lūteb) sm. ཀླུ་ཐིབས་.

ཀླུ་ཐོར་ (lūdɔr) pimples thought to be caused by a nāga; vi.—སྐྱེ་; —ཐོན་ to break out in pimples.

ཀླུ་དུག (lūduù) harm caused by a nāga.

ཀླུ་བདུད་ (lūdüü̇) an evil/ harmful nāga.

ཀླུ་བདུད་རྡོ་རྗེ་ (lūdüü̇ dɔje) a traditional Tibetan medicine used for diseases caused by a nāga (codonopsis pilosula).

ཀླུ་ནད་ (lūnɛɛ̀) skin diseases (such as boils/ sores) thought to be caused by nāga.

ཀླུ་གནོད་ (lūnöö̇) harm caused by a nāga.

ཀླུ་ཕྲུག (lūdruù) nāga children.

ཀླུ་འབུམ་ (lūmbum) 1. a Bonpo text. 2. a residence unit (khamtsen) in Drepung monastery.

ཀླུ་མོ་ (lūmu) a female ཀླུ་.

ཀླུ་དམག (lūmaà) nāga soldiers/ army.

ཀླུ་བཙན་ (lūdzɛn) abbr. of two kinds of bad spirits/ demons: ཀླུ་ and བཙན་.

ཀླུ་སིལ་མ་ (lū sīimɘ) prickly heat, rashes.

ཀླུ་བསངས་ (lūsaŋ) an incense offering to a nāga; va.—གཏོང་.

ཀླུང་ (lūŋ) 1. river/ stream in a valley (usu. preceded by ཆུ་) ༈ ཆུ་ཀླུང་ཆེན་པོའི་ཁ་ར་ On the bank of a big river. 2. a valley ༈ རི་ཀླུང་རྩི་ཤིང་མེ་ཏོག་གིས་ཁེངས་པའི་ཡུལ་ A country where the mountains and the valleys are full of trees and flowers.

ཀླུང་ཁང་ (lūŋgaŋ) a house built in a valley.

ཀླུང་རྒྱ་ (lūŋgya) shung. a law/ edict prohibiting sth. in a valley or area (e.g. hunting); va.—སྡོམ་.

ཀླུང་རྒྱུན་ (lūŋgyün) the current/ flow of a river.

ཀླུང་སྒོག (lūŋgɔg) a kind of garlic that grows in valleys (allium fasciculation rendle).

ཀླུང་ལྕང་ (lūŋjaŋ) salix babylonica.

ཀླུང་ཆུ་ (lūŋcu) a stream/ river in a valley.

ཀླུང་རྟ་ (lūŋdɘ) luck, fortune; vi.—ཆག་; —ཉམས་ to have or get bad luck/ bad fortune, to have one's luck deteriorate ༈ ཉེ་སྐབས་ངའི་ཀླུང་རྟ་དམའ་པོ་རེད་ My luck is bad (low) these days.

ཀླུང་ཐང་ (lūŋdaŋ) a plain, a valley.

ཀླུང་པ་ (lūŋbɘ) a person living in a valley.

ཀླུང་ཕྱུགས་ (lūŋcuù) cattle kept in valleys or lowlands.

ཀླུང་འབབ་ (lūŋbab) a river flowing from the

highlands to a valley.

ཀླུང་མ་ (lūŋmə) sm. ཀླུང་, 1.

ཀླུང་ཙྭ་ (lūŋdza) a kind of reed that grows in a river valley.

ཀླུང་གཞུང་ (lūŋshuŋ) a river valley ¶ སྐྱིད་ཆུ་ཀླུང་གཞུང་ The Kyichu River valley.

ཀླུང་རགས་ (lūŋraà) a dam on a valley river.

ཀླུང་ཤ་ (lūŋsha) a type of mushroom found around river valleys.

ཀླུང་ཤོ་ (lūŋsho) rumex sp. (used in Tibetan medicine.

ཀླུང་ཤོད་ (lūŋshüǜ) 1. a low-lying area, the lower part of an area. 2. name of a palace of Reting Rinpoche.

ཀླུངས་ (lūŋ) 1. sm. ཀླུང་. 2. name of a place.

ཀླུད་བགོང་ (lǖgoŋ) sm.* ཀླུད་འགོང་.

ཀླུབ་: p. ཀླུབས་; f. ཀླུབ་; imp. ཀླུབས་ (lūb) 1. va. to wear, to get dressed, to put on. 2. name of an early clan/ lineage.

ཀླུབས་ (lūb) p. and imp. of ཀླུབ་.

ཀླུའི་ཕོ་བྲང་ (lǖü pōdraŋ) 1. a palace of a ཀླུ་. 2. a high quality/ excellent house ¶ ཁོས་ཀླུའི་ཕོ་བྲང་ནང་བཞིན་བརྒྱབས་བཞག (He) has built an excellent house (a house like a ཀླུ་ palace).

ཀླེས་ (lɛ̄ɛ̀) coat hanger, clothes rack.

ཀློ་ (lō) 1. sm. གློ་. 2. abbr. of ཀློ་པ་.

ཀློ་པ་ (lōba) 1. uncivilized person, savage, barbarian. 2. a nationality located in southeast Tibet and what is now Arunachal Pradesh in India.

ཀློ་རྫོང་ (lōdzoŋ) the Tibetan officials sent to the ཀློ་པ་ people to deliver a message and gifts and induce them to take a vow not to harm Buddhist pilgrims passing through their area.

ཀློ་ཡུལ་ (lōyüü) an area in southeastern Tibet inhabited by ཀློ་པ་.

ཀློ་ཤོག (lōshog) sm.* གློ་ཤོག.

ཀློག: p. (བ)ཀླགས་; f. (བ)ཀླག; imp. ཀློགས་ (lɔ̄ɔ̀) va. to read ¶ ཁོ་དེབ་ཀློག་གི་འདུག He is reading a book.

ཀློག་ཀླག (lɔ̄glaà) sm. ཀློག.

ཀློག་སྐྱ་ (lɔ̄ggya) a place in Tsang.

ཀློག་ཁྲིད་ (lɔ̄gdrìì) leading a class in reading aloud; va.—རྒྱག.

ཀློག་མཁྱེན་ (lɔ̄ggyen) a literate person.

ཀློག་གི་སློབ་དཔོན་ (lɔ̄gi lōbbön) a person who teaches reading.

ཀློག་གྲྭ་ (lɔ̄gdra) a school/ class where reading is taught.

ཀློག་རྒྱུག (lɔ̄ggyuù) pointer used by teachers when going over lessons on blackboards.

ཀློག་རྟགས་ (lɔ̄gdaà) a highlighting mark (e.g., underlining) on a word or phrase to indicate special attention when reading; va.—བྱེད་.

ཀློག་དར་ (lɔ̄gdaa) sm. ཀློག་དེབ་.

ཀློག་དེབ་ (lɔ̄gdeb) a reader, a primer, a textbook for reading.

ཀློག་བདེ་པོ་ (lɔ̄ɔ̀ de̱bo) 1. able to read fluently. 2. easy to read.

ཀློག་འདོན་ (lɔ̄ŋdön) reading/ reciting aloud; va.—བྱེད་.

ཀློག་པ་པོ་ (lɔ̄gbabo) a reader.

ཀློག་པའི་སློབ་དཔོན་ (lōgbɛ lōbbön) sm. ཀློག་གི་སློབ་དཔོན་.

ཀློག་སྦྱོང་ (lōgjoŋ) practicing reading.

ཀློག་བཟང་པོ་ (lɔ̄ɔ̀ sa̱ŋbo) people who read quickly and well.

ཀློག་ར་ (lɔ̄gra) a grove or walled-in area where reading is taught.

ཀློག་ཤུ་ (lɔ̄gshu) dandruff.

ཀློག་ཤེས་ (lɔ̄gsheè) sm. ཀློག་མཁྱེན་.

ཀློག་སློབ་ (lɔ̄glob) a student learning to read.

ཀློགས་ (lɔ̄ɔ̀) imp. of ཀློག.

ཀློགས་མ་ (lɔ̄gma) shung. female official.

ཀློང་ (lōŋ) 1. middle, center ¶ ནམ་མཁའི་ཀློང་ལ་ In the center of the sky. 2. realm, scope, area ¶ ཆོས་ཀྱི་ཀློང་ The realm of religion. 3. one of the three groups into which the Nyingmapa's doctrinal system is divided.

ཀློང་དཀྱིལ་ (lōŋgyii) sm. ཀློང་, 1.

ཀློང་འཁོར་ (lōŋgɔɔ) whirlpool, vortex, eddy.

ཀློང་འཁྱིལ་ (lōŋgyii) 1. halo. 2. sm. ཀློང་འཁོར་.

ཀློང་གྱུར་ (lōŋgyur) sm. ཀློང་དུ་འགྱུར་.

ཀློང་འགྱུར་ (lōŋgyur) sm. ཀློང་དུ་འགྱུར་.

ཀློང་ཆེན་ (lōŋjen) profound knowledge/ wisdom.

ཀློང་དུ་འགྱུར་ (lōŋdu gyu̱r) vi. to come to know ¶ ཁོང་ནི་ཤེས་བྱ་ཐམས་ཅད་ཀློང་དུ་འགྱུར་བ་ཞིག་རེད་ He is sb. who has come to know all knowledge.

ཀློང་སྡེ་ (lōŋde) the ཀློང་ subdivision of the Nyingma teachings.

ཀློང་བརྡོལ་ (lōŋ dö̱ö̱) vi. to pour/ gush out.

ཀློང་ཡང་ (པོ་) (lōŋyaŋ) 1. vast/ extensive in thought or in physical area. 2. even tempered. 3. sb. who is broad-minded and understands the big picture.

ཀློང་ཡངས་ (པོ་) (lōŋyaŋ) sm. ཀློང་ཡང་.

ཀློན་ (lȭn) sm.* གློན་.

དཀག (gāà) vi. to congeal/ coagulate ¶ མཆོད་ཀོང་ནང་མར་ཁུ་དཀག་འདུག The melted butter coagulated in the butter lamp.

དཀག་མཚམས་ (gāgdzam) the temperature at which a liquid congeals.

དཀན་ (gɛ̄n) 1. the roof of the mouth, the palate. 2. sm. ཀྱེན་.

དཀན་གཉེར་ (gɛ̄nñer) the undulation on the roof of mouth (hard palate).

དཀའ་ (gā) difficult, hard ¶ ཤེས་རྟོགས་དཀའ་སྟབས་ Because it is difficult to understand.

དཀའ་དཀའ་ (gāga) sm. དཀའ་ངལ་.

དཀའ་ཁག (gā kāà) difficult, hard.

དཀའ་ཁལ་ (gāgɛɛ) shung. net weight, the weight of sth. without the wrapping.

དཀའ་ཁྲ་ (gādra) a white kite with a red or black tail.

དཀའ་ཁྲི་ཁྱད་བསད་ (gādri kyɛ̄sɛɛ̀) overcoming many difficulties/ hardships [Lit. getting rid of 10,000 difficulties].

དཀའ་ཁྲི་སྡུག་སྟོང་ (gādri du̱gdoŋ) many hardships and much suffering [Lit. 10,000 difficulties and 1,000 sufferings].

དཀའ་འགག (gāŋgaà) a difficulty, a difficult point/ juncture ¶ དཀའ་འགག་དེ་ནས་བརྒལ་ན་ལས་སླ་པོ་རེད་ If that difficulty is overcome, it will be easy.

དཀའ་འགྲེལ་ (gāndree) explanation or commentary on a difficult point/ issue/ question; va.—རྒྱག.

དཀའ་སྒྲུབ་ (gədrub) achieving sth. by hard work/ striving/ perseverance; va.—བྱེད་ ¶ ང་ཚོའི་དམིགས་ཡུལ་འགྲུབ་ཆེད་དཀའ་སྒྲུབ་བྱེད་དགོས་ We must work hard in order to achieve all our goals.

དཀའ་སྒྲུབ་མཁས་སྒྲུབ་ (gədrub kɛ̄ɛ̄drub) succeeding by working hard and skillfully; va.—བྱེད་.

དཀའ་སྒྲུབ་དངོས་སྒྲུབ་ (gədrub ŋȫȫdrub) being successful by working hard; va.—བྱེད་.

དཀའ་སྒྲུབ་ནན་སྒྲུབ་ (gədrub ne̱ndrub) working hard and carefully; va.—བྱེད་.

དཀའ་ངལ་ (gāŋɛɛ) 1. difficulty, hardship; vi.—འཕྲད་ to meet with difficulty/ hardship; vi.—མྱོང་ to experience difficulties/ hardship; va.—རྒྱག; —སྤྱོད་ to work hard, to undergo difficulties (in doing sth.); va.—བཟོ་ to cause trouble/ hardship; va.—སེལ་ to remove or eliminate hardships/ difficulties ¶ མི་རིགས་ཀྱི་དཀའ་ངལ་སེལ་ཐབས་བྱེད་བཞིན་ཡོད་པ་རེད་ (They) are trying to solve the difficulties of the nationalities. ¶ ཁོང་དཀའ་ངལ་བརྒྱབས་ནས་ཕྱུག་པོ་ཆགས་པ་རེད་ He worked hard (undergoing hardship) and became rich. ¶ ཁོ་ཚོས་བྲོས་བྱོལ་དུ་ཡོང་དུས་དཀའ་ངལ་ཆེན་པོ་སྤྱད་ཡོད་ When they came seeking refuge they underwent a lot of hardships.

དཀའ་ངལ་ཁྱད་གསོད་ (gāŋɛɛ kyɛ̄ɛ̄söö̀) ignoring hardships/ difficulties; va.—བྱེད་ ¶ རང་གི་དཀའ་

ངལ་ཁྱད་གསོད་ཀྱིས་ནད་གཡོག་ལ་དང་བླངས་ཞུས་པ་རེད་ Ignoring their own hardship, (they) volunteered to act as nurses.

དཀའ་ངལ་ཁྱད་བསད་ (gāŋεε kyε̄ε̄sεὲ) sm. དཀའ་ངལ་ཁྱད་གསོད་.

དཀའ་ངལ་གདོང་ལེན་ (gāŋεε dōŋlen) facing/ confronting difficulties or hardship; va.—བྱེད་.

དཀའ་ངལ་སྤྱད་ (gāŋεε jε̄ὲ) p. of དཀའ་ངལ་སྤྱོད་.

དཀའ་ངལ་སྤྱོད་ (gāŋεε jöö) see དཀའ་ངལ་.

དཀའ་ངལ་བཟོ་ (gāŋεε so) see དཀའ་ངལ་.

དཀའ་ངལ་བཟོད་ (gāŋεε söö) vi. to tolerate difficulties ¶ ཁོང་ནི་དཀའ་ངལ་བཟོད་ཐུབ་མཁན་ཞིག་རེད་ He is a person who is able to tolerate difficulties.

དཀའ་ངལ་སེལ་ (gāŋεε sēē) see དཀའ་ངལ་.

དཀའ་བཅུ་ (gāju) a lower level geshe degree given by Tashilhunpo monastery.

དཀའ་ཆེན་ (gājen) a high geshe degree given by Tashilhunpo monastery (equivalent to Lharamba).

དཀའ་ཉེན་ (gāñen) 1. sm. དཀའ་ངལ་. 2. abbr. difficulties and danger.

དཀའ་རྙོག (gāñɔɔ̀) difficulties, troubles, problems ¶ ཡུལ་ནང་གི་དཀའ་རྙོག Troubles within the region. ¶ དཀའ་རྙོག་ཆེད་བཟོས་ Intentionally causing troubles/ problems/ difficulties.

དཀའ་བསྟུན་གནོད་སྐྱེལ་ (gādün nōngyel) harming sb. when they are down/ in trouble/ weak/ undergoing hardship; va.—བྱེད་ ¶ མི་དེས་རང་ཉིད་ཀྱི་གྲོགས་པོའི་ཁང་པར་མེ་ཤོར་སྐབས་དཀའ་བསྟུན་གནོད་སྐྱེལ་བྱས་པ་རེད་ That person harmed his friend when his house burned down.

དཀའ་ཐག་ཆོད་ (gā tāgjöö) 1. extremely difficult. 2. extremely tired out.

དཀའ་ཐལ་ཆེ་བ་ (gātεε cēwa) extremely tired ¶ ཁོང་དཀའ་ཐལ་ཆེ་བའི་རྐྱེན་གྱིས་ན་ཚ་ཕོག་པ་རེད་ Because he got extremely tired, he got sick.

དཀའ་ཐུབ་ (gādub) 1. working hard, enduring or tolerating suffering/ hardship; asceticism; va.—སྤྱོད་ to tolerate or bear suffering/ hardship, to practice asceticism ¶ དཀའ་ཐུབ་སྤྱད་ན་ཕྱུག་པོ་ཆགས་ཀྱི་རེད་ If you work hard and endure hardship you will become rich.

དཀའ་ཐུབ་ཀྱི་སྤྱོད་པ་ (gāduùgi jööba) activities that involve hardship/ difficulties.

དཀའ་ཐུབ་ཆེན་པོ་ (gādup cēmbo) one who is able to tolerate/ endure great hardship.

དཀའ་ཐུབ་ཉིན་འདུད་ (gādup ñimbüü) it is hard to pass the time of day.

དཀའ་ཐུབ་ནགས་ཚལ་ (gādup nagdzεε) 1. a grove/ forest where ascetics practice. 2. a peaceful or isolated grove/ forest.

དཀའ་ཐུབ་པ་ (gādubə) an ascetic.

དཀའ་འཐབ་ (gədəb) 1. a hard fought battle/ struggle/ fight, a fight in which one undergoes difficulties; va.—བྱེད་ ¶ ང་ཚོའི་དམག་མིས་དགྲ་བོ་དང་དཀའ་འཐབ་བྱས་པ་རེད་ Our soldiers fought a hard fought battle with the enemy. 2. combatting hardship to achieve sth.; va.—བྱེད་ ¶ ཟམ་པ་ཆེན་པོ་འདི་རྒྱག་སྐབས་བཟོ་པ་ཚོས་དཀའ་འཐབ་མང་པོ་བྱས་པ་རེད་ When the big bridge was built, the workers combatted many hardships.

དཀའ་དུབ་ (gədup) sm.དཀའ་ངལ་.

དཀའ་མདོ་ (gāndo) arc. sm. ཀ་མདོ་.

དཀའ་འདོར་ཡང་ལེན་ (gādɔɔ yaŋlen) sm. དཀའ་གཡོལ་སླ་འཚང་.

དཀའ་ལྡན་ (gāndεn) 1. whitish tint added to other colors. 2. pale blue.

དཀའ་སྡུག (gədug; gəduù) sm. དཀའ་ངལ་.

དཀའ་སྡུག་བཟོད་བསྲན་ (gədug söösεn) tolerating difficulties and suffering; va.—བྱེད་.

དཀའ་གནད་ (gānεὲ) sth. important that is difficult, a tough problem/ issue; va.—སེལ་ to solve an important problem or difficulty.

དཀའ་གནས་ (gānεὲ) difficult situation, a place where there is a difficulty/ problem.

དཀའ་སྣང་ (gānaŋ) abbr. of དཀའ་ལས་ཁག་སྣང་.

དཀའ་པོ་ (gāābo) sm. ངལ་ཐུབ་.

དཀའ་སྤྱད་ (gājεὲ) undergoing/ enduring hardship and difficulties; va.—བྱེད་.

དཀའ་སྤྱད་གཉེར་སྐྱོང་ (gājεὲ ñērgyoŋ) sm. དཀའ་སྤྱད་དོན་གཉེར་.

དཀའ་སྤྱད་སྙིང་རུས་ (gājεὲ ñiŋrüü) working hard and persevering/ enduring, doing difficult things diligently; va.—བྱེད.

དཀའ་སྤྱད་དོན་གཉེར་ (gājεὲ tönñer) working hard/ perservering to manage/ oversee sth.; va.—བྱེད་ ¶ སློབ་ཕྲུག་དེས་དཀའ་སྤྱད་དོན་གཉེར་བྱས་སྐབས་ཡིག་ཚད་ཡག་པོ་ལོན་པ་རེད་ Because the student worked (studied) hard, (he) did well on the exam.

དཀའ་སྤྱད་སྡུག་འཁུར་ (gājεὲ duggur) sm. དཀའ་སྡུག་བཟོད་བསྲན་.

དཀའ་སྤྱད་སྡུག་གདགས་ (gājεὲ dugdaà) sm. དཀའ་སྡུག་བཟོད་བསྲན་.

དཀའ་སྤྱད་ནན་ཏན་ (gājεὲ nεndεn) sm. དཀའ་སྤྱད་སྙིང་རུས་.

དཀའ་སྤྱད་བབ་ཆགས་ (gājεὲ pəbjaà) living simply while working hard, living the simple life; va.—བྱེད་.

དཀའ་སྤྱད་འབད་བརྩོན་ (gājεὲ bεεdzön) working hard and enduring difficulties.

དཀའ་སྤྱད་འབད་འཐབ་ (gājεὲ bεεtəb) sm. དཀའ་སྤྱད་འབད་བརྩོན་.

དཀའ་སྤྱད་སྦྱོང་བདར་ (gājεὲ joŋdar) practicing/ training hard; va.—བྱེད་.

དཀའ་སྤྱད་བརྩོན་ཞིབ་ (gājεὲ dzönshib) working hard/ undergoing hardship while doing a thorough investigation; va.—བྱེད་.

དཀའ་སྤྱད་ཤེས་ཐོབ་ (gājεὲ shēèdob) working hard and becoming knowledgeable.

དཀའ་བ་ (gāwa) 1. difficult, hard ¶ ལས་ཀ་འདི་བྱེད་དཀའ་བ་ཞིག་འདུག This is a task that is difficult to do. 2. difficulty, hardship; va.—སྤྱོད་ to do sth. that requires undergoing hardship/ difficulty ¶ ཁོ་ཚོས་ཡུལ་གྱི་རང་བཙན་གྱི་དོན་ལ་དཀའ་བ་མང་པོ་སྤྱད་པ་རེད་ They went through many hardships for (their) country's freedom.

དཀའ་བ་སྔོན་སྤྱོད་སྐྱིད་པ་རྗེས་སྤྱོད་ (gāwa ŋönjöö gyiibə jeèjöö) one first has to work hard and endure difficulties so that later one can enjoy happiness.

དཀའ་བ་གཅོད་ཐེངས་གཅིག་ལ་གནན་བདེ་འགྲུབ་ (gāwa jöödēŋ jiglə dēnde drub) one has to undergo hardship once to achieve permanent happiness.

དཀའ་བའི་དུས་སུ་གྲོགས་པོ་བཟང་ངན་རྟོགས་ འདམ་རྫབ་ནང་དུ་རྟ་ཕོའི་ཤེད་ཤུགས་ཤེས་ (gāwa tüüsu trɔgbo saŋŋεn dōg damdzəb naŋdu dābö shε̄ε̄shuù shēè) hard times show what sb. is made of [Lit. one knows whether a friend is good or bad during difficult times; one knows the strength of a horse when it is in a muddy swamp].

དཀའ་བའི་བྲག་དང་མ་ཐུག་ན་ བདེ་བའི་སྤང་ལ་སླེབས་མི་ཐུབ་ (gāwε tragdaŋ mətuùna dewε bāŋla lēbmi tüù) one must work hard and undergo difficulties to get sth. good [Lit. unless one climbs the difficult rocks, one will not reach the pleasant meadow].

དཀའ་བྱུང་ (gājung) experiencing difficulty/ hardship.

དཀའ་སྦྱོང་ (gājoŋ) 1. rigorous training/ study, undergoing great hardship in training; va.—བྱེད་ ¶ ཁོ་ཚོས་དམག་རྒྱག་གྲ་སྒྲིག་གི་ཆེད་དུ་དཀའ་སྦྱོང་བྱེད་ཀྱི་ཡོད་པ་རེད་ They are undergoing rigorous training in order to prepare for war. 2. hardship, difficulty ¶ དཀའ་སྦྱོང་ཆེ་བའི་དུས་སྐབས་ནས་ཐར་བ་རེད་ (They) overcame a time of great difficulty.

དཀའ་སྦྱོང་ཅི་ཆེ་ (gājoŋ jīce) shung. suffering extreme hardship ¶ དཔལ་འབྱོར་ལོལ་པའི་གྲོལ་བ་དང་དཔུང་འཐབ་བྱེད་པའི་ནང་དཀའ་སྦྱོང་ཅི་ཆེ་བྱུང་བ་རེད་

They suffered extreme hardship in the battle against the invader.

དཀའ་མེད་ (gāmeè) sm. ཀ་མེད་.

དཀའ་མོ་ (gāmo) difficult, hard ༎ འདི་ཡིད་ཆེས་དཀའ་མོ་རེད་ This is hard to believe.

དཀའ་སྙོང་སྡུག་སྙོང་ (gāñoŋ du̱gñoŋ) experiencing hardship and suffering, full of suffering and misery.

དཀའ་ཚད་ (gādzɛɛ̀) the degree of difficulty/ hardship.

དཀའ་ཚེགས་ (gādzeg) sm. དཀའ་ངལ་.

དཀའ་བཞི་པ་ (gə shi̱bə) a type of geshe lower than a Lharamba.

དཀའ་བཟོད་ (gāsöö) tolerating/ enduring/ bearing difficulty or hardship; vi.—བྱེད་.

དཀའ་བཟོད་ངལ་རྩོལ་ (gāsöö ŋɛɛdzöö) ability to bear/ tolerate/ endure hardship and work hard; va.—བྱེད་.

དཀའ་གཡོལ་སླ་འཚང་ (gāyöö lādzaŋ) avoiding difficulties and taking the easy way; va.—བྱེད་.

དཀའ་རུག (gərug) arc. a helper, a colleague.

དཀའ་ལས་ (gālɛɛ̀) 1. toil, hard work; va.—རྒྱག to work hard, to toil ༎ འདིའི་དོན་ལ་ཁོ་ཚོས་དཀའ་ལས་ཆེན་པོ་བརྒྱབས་པ་རེད་ They worked very hard for this purpose. 2. vi.—ཁ་; —ཁག to get tired ༎ ངལ་གསོ་མེད་པར་ཡུན་རིང་ལས་ཀ་བྱས་ཙང་དཀའ་ལས་ཁ་པ་རེད་ (They) got tired because they worked for a long time without rest. 3. difficulty, problems, hardship; va.—བཟོ་ to create hardships/ difficulties ༎ ད་རེས་ཀྱི་ས་གཡོས་དེས་དཀའ་ལས་ཆེན་པོ་བཟོས་བྱུང་ The earthquake caused great difficulty.

དཀའ་ལས་སྐྱ་བས་བརྒྱབ་ ལོངས་སྤྱོད་གཟར་བུས་བཏང་ (gālɛɛ̀ gyāwɛ gyə̱b lo̱ŋjöö sa̱rbüü dāŋ) reaping the fruit of the hard work done by another [Lit. the སྐྱ་པ་ (stirring spoon) does the hard work, the གཟར་བུ་ (serving) spoon enjoys (the fruits)].

དཀའ་ལས་ཁག་སྣང་ (gālɛɛ̀ kāgnaŋ) visibly showing signs that one is undergoing difficulty or hardship or is tired (usu. for work, school); va.—བྱེད་.

དཀའ་ལས་ཁག་པོ་ (gālɛɛ̀ kāgbo) difficult, hard, tiring ༎ ལས་ཀ་འདི་དེ་ཙམ་དཀའ་ལས་ཁག་པོ་མི་འདུག This work is not that difficult.

དཀའ་ལས་རྒྱག་རོགས་ (gālɛɛ̀ gya̱roò) sb. who works hard together with another; va.—བྱེད་ ༎ བཟོ་གྲྭ་དེའི་ནང་ཁོང་ནི་ངའི་དཀའ་ལས་རྒྱག་རོགས་གཙོ་བོ་དེ་ཡིན་ In this factory, he is the main one who works hard with me.

དཀའ་ལས་བརྒྱབ་པའི་དཀའ་ཆང་དང་ མཛོ་བོ་བསད་པའི་སྡིག་གླ་ (gālɛɛ̀ gyəbbɛ gāchaŋ ta̱ŋ dzo̱bo sɛɛ̀bɛ di̱gla) one should get what one deserves [Lit. beer for working hard, a sin wage for slaughtering a dzo].

དཀའ་ལས་རང་གིས་བརྒྱབ་ལོངས་སྤྱོད་མི་ཡིས་བཏང་ (gālɛɛ̀ ra̱ŋgi gyə̱b lo̱ŋjöö mi̱yii dāŋ) sm. དཀའ་ལས་སྐྱ་བས་བརྒྱབ་ ལོངས་སྤྱོད་གཟར་བུས་བཏང་.

དཀའ་སེ་བ་ (gāsewa) a little bit difficult/ hard.

དཀའ་སེལ་ (gāsee) abbr. of དཀའ་ངལ་སེལ་.

དཀར་ (gār) 1. white ༎ མི་རིགས་དཀར་ནག The black and white races. 2. dairy products. 3. abbr. of དཀར་ཡོལ་.

དཀར་ཀྲིང་ (gədriŋ) the white of an egg.

དཀར་དཀར་ (gārgar) sm. དཀར་རྐྱང་.

དཀར་རྐྱང་ (gārgyaŋ) completely white, snow-white.

དཀར་སྐྱ་ (gārgya) whitish.

དཀར་སྐྱིན་ (gərgyin) h. of སྐྱིན་.

དཀར་སྐྱོང་ (gārgyoŋ) vegetarian diet/ food; va.—བྱེད་ to eat (only) vegetarian food ༎ དེ་རིང་དཀར་སྐྱོང་རེད་ Today is vegetarian food (day).

དཀར་ཁང་ (gārgaŋ) a light/ bright house.

དཀར་ཁུང་ (gərgun) 1. skylight. 2. window.

དཀར་ཁྱུག་ཁྱུག (gār kyūggyuù) whitish (usu. used to describe flashing light).

དཀར་ཁྲ་ (gārtra) 1. a colored pattern on a white background. 2. a design with a lot of white squares intermixed with other colors.

དཀར་ཁྲ་མན་ (gārtramɛn) a kind of གཟི་.

དཀར་ཁྲ་མེན་ (gārtramɛn) sm. དཀར་ཁྲ་མན་.

དཀར་ཁྲི་ནག་སྟོང་ (gərtrii̱ na̱gdoŋ) a wealthy nomad owning many animals [Lit. 10,000 sheep, 1,000 yak].

དཀར་ཁྲིགས་ (gārdrig) sm. དཀར་འཁྲིགས་.

དཀར་ཁྲོམ་མེ་ (gār trōmme) sm. དཀར་ཅེམ་ཅེམ་.

དཀར་ཁྲོམ་མེ་བ་ (gār trōmewa) sm. དཀར་ཅེམ་ཅེམ་.

དཀར་མཁས་འགྲོ་ལམ་ (gārkɛɛ̀ dro̱lam) the path of being merely expert (an expression used in the late 1950's for intellectuals who were neglecting politics and trying to be merely experts).

དཀར་འཁྱིལ་ལི་བ་ (gār ki̱lewa) a white, shiny, roundish light.

དཀར་འཁྱོངས་ (gār kyōŋ) sm. དཀར་སྐྱོང་.

དཀར་འཁྲིགས་ (gərdrig) 1. white. 2. bright. 3. shining, sparkling.

དཀར་གོང་ (gārgoŋ cēma) 1. quartz. 2. white porcelain.

དཀར་གོང་ཆུ་ཚོད་ (gārgoŋ cūdzöö) quartz clock/ watch.

དཀར་གོང་ཕྱེ་མ་ (gārgoŋ) quartz sand.

དཀར་གྲིབ་ (gərdrib) cataracts.

དཀར་འགྱེད་ (gārgyee) diary products such as butter given as alms to monks.

དཀར་རྒྱན་ (gārgyɛn) floral decorations made with butter on torma (གཏོར་མ་); va.—རྒྱག.

དཀར་རྒྱག (gārgyaà) sm. དཀར་རྟགས་རྒྱག.

དཀར་རྒྱུ་ (gərgyu) large intestine.

དཀར་སྒམ་ (gārgam) a box/ cabinet for storing cups or china.

དཀར་བརྒྱུད་པ་ (gərgyübə) 1. the Kargyu sect of Tibetan Buddhism. 2. an adherent of the Kargyu sect.

དཀར་ཆ་ (gārja) light, bright (usu. used to describe a room).

དཀར་ཆ་དོད་པོ་ (gārja tö̱öbo) well-lit, light/ bright.

དཀར་ཆག (gārjaà) table of contents, index, catalogue.

དཀར་ཆག་ཤོག་བྱང་ (gārjaà shōgjaŋ) card catalogue.

དཀར་ཅབ་ཅབ་ (gār cəbjəb) whitish.

དཀར་ཅལ་ (gārjɛɛ) sm. རྡོ་གཅལ་.

དཀར་ཆས་ (gājɛɛ̀) white dress/ robe worn by lay tantric practitioners (སྔགས་པ་).

དཀར་ཅིལ་ལི་ (gār cii̱le) sm. སྐྱ་ཅིལ་ལི་.

དཀར་ཅུ་ (gərju) general name for dairy products.

དཀར་ཅུང་ཞོ་ནུ་ (gərjuŋ sho̱nu) fritillaria thunbergii (used in Tibetan medicine).

དཀར་ཅུང་བརྟན་སྐར་ (gərjuŋ dɛ̄ngar) white dwarf star.

དཀར་ཅེམ་ཅེམ་ (gār cēmjem) glittering/ sparkling white.

དཀར་ཆེམ་མེ་བ་ (gār chēmmewa) sm. དཀར་ཅེམ་ཅེམ་.

དཀར་ཆོས་ (gārjöö) a meritorious/ virtuous deed; va.—བྱེད་ ༎ ཁོང་དཀར་ཆོས་བྱེད་མཁན་ཞིག་རེད་ He is sb. who does virtuous deeds.

དཀར་མཆོད་དམར་མཆོད་ (gārjöö mārjöö) dairy and animal/ human sacrifice offerings to gods.

དཀར་ཇག (gārjag) white bandits (derogatory name for the Guomindang and the White Army of Russia).

དཀར་འཇམ་ (gānjam) 1. a soft white cloth/ material. 2. tranquil, peaceful ༎ དེང་སང་ལྷ་ས་དཀར་འཇམ་དུ་གནས་ཡོད་པ་རེད་ These days Lhasa is peaceful.

དཀར་ཉེ་ (gārñe) shung. a close friend ༎ སྐུ་ཞབས་ཕུར་བུ་ནས་ཆོས་ཡོན་དཀར་ཉེའི་ལར་དགོངས་ཁྱིམ་རྒྱལ་གནམ་འཆར་མི་འབྱུང་བའི་བཀའ་གསལ་ཇི་སྙིད་གནང་བ་ Purbu, on a account of being a close friend and also being in the relationship of priest and patron, gave advice so that the dispute should be settled within the family and not be exposed outside.

དཀར་གཉེར་ (gārñe) wrinkles on the face.

དཀར་རྟགས་ (gārdaà) 1. an auspicious white mark/

handprint put on houses (usu. the kitchen) just before the New Year (usu. before the 29th of the 12th month); va.—རྒྱག. 2. sm. ཡས་བཟང་.

དཀར་སྟོན་ (gārdön) a vegetarian food banquet or dinner.

དཀར་ཐག (gārtag) the strings of musical instruments.

དཀར་ཐིག (gārtig) 1. white decorative lines drawn with lime on the ground in front of a house and in the kitchen on special occasions; va.—འཐེན་ to draw such lines. 2. white lines drawn on the ground to indicate not to do sth., e.g., not to urinate there.

དཀར་ཐིགས་ (gārdig) a drop of melted butter dropped into a burning butter lamp as an offering; va.—རྒྱག.

དཀར་ཐེབས་སེམས་ཅན་ (gārdeb sēmjɛn) shung. an animal given to a monastery for the purpose of using its milk to make butter.

དཀར་དོན་ (gārdön) sm. དཀར་འདོན་.

དཀར་དུས་ (gərdüü) the time of the year when milk is plentiful.

དཀར་དྲོ་ (gārdro) the skim layer that forms on the top of boiled milk.

དཀར་མདངས་ (gārdaŋ) white in color, whitish hue.

དཀར་མདངས་དམར་གསལ་ (gārdaŋ māāsɛɛ) pale complexion with reddish cheeks.

དཀར་མདོག (gārdog) white color.

དཀར་འདོན་ (gāndön) exonerating, deciding sb. is innocent after an investigation; va.—བྱེད་ ¶ རིག་གནས་གསར་བརྗེའི་རྗེས་སུ་ལས་བྱེད་པ་མང་པོ་དཀར་འདོན་བྱས་པ་རེད་ After the Cultural Revolution, many officials were exonerated.

དཀར་ལྡན་ (gārdɛn) white.

དཀར་སྡུད་པ་ (gərdüübə) shung. 1. a collector of diary product taxes (butter and cheese). 2. a collector of donations/ contributions in dairy products.

དཀར་སྡེར་ (gāāder) porcelain saucer/ plate/ dish.

དཀར་ནག (gārnaà) 1. black and white. 2. right and wrong, true or false. 3. sheep and yak/ cattle ¶ ཕྱུགས་རིགས་དཀར་ནག Livestock including sheep and yak/ cattle.

དཀར་ནག་ཁྲ་བསྲེས་ (gārnaà trədüü) good and bad mixed together, having good and bad qualities [Lit. black, white and colored combined].

དཀར་ནག་ཁྲ་གསུམ་ (gārnaà trāsum) 1. white, black and colored. 2. sb. who is not dependable/ consistent, e.g., sb. who is sometimes friendly and is sometimes unfriendly ¶ མི་དེ་གདོང་དཀར་ནག་ཁྲ་གསུམ་སྟོན་མཁན་ཞིག་ཡིན་ཙང་མི་ཚོས་ཡིད་ཆེས་བྱེད་ཀྱི་མེད་པ་རེད་ Because he is not dependable people do not believe him. 3. an early legal code describing three punishments: the worst, middle and least bad.

དཀར་ནག་གོ་ལྡོག (gārnaà kondɔɔ̀) doing sth. untrue/ unjust/ criminal, mistaking right from wrong; va.—བྱེད་ ¶ དཀར་ནག་གོ་ལྡོག་གི་ལས་ཀ་བྱས་སྐབས་བཙོན་ཁང་ལ་ལོ་བཅུ་སྡོད་དགོས་བྱུང་བ་རེད་ Because (he) did sth. criminal he was imprisoned for ten years.

དཀར་ནག་འཇུག་ལྡོག (gārnaà jundɔɔ̀) doing what is right ¶ དཀར་ནག་འཇུག་ལྡོག་མ་ནོར་བ་བྱ་དགོས་ (One) must act in accordance with what is right without error.

དཀར་ནག་བདེན་རྫུན་ (gārnaà dendzün) what is false and what is true, what is right and what is wrong ¶ ད་རེས་ཁྲིམས་ཁང་ནས་དཀར་ནག་བདེན་རྫུན་གྱི་དབྱེ་བ་ཡག་པོ་ཕྱེ་སོང་ This time the court determined well what is false and what is true.

དཀར་ནག་ཕྱིན་ཅི་ལོག (gārnaà cīnjilɔɔ̀) sm. དཀར་ནག་གོ་ལྡོག.

དཀར་ནག་དབྱེ་འབྱེད་ (gārna yenjɛɛ̀) sm. དཀར་ནག་ཤན་འབྱེད་.

དཀར་ནག་རྩིས་ཁྲ་ (gārnaà dzīdra) shung. an enumeration/ accounting of the number of livestock.

དཀར་ནག་མཚམས་ (gārnaà tsām) an acupuncture point between the breasts.

དཀར་ནག་ཤན་འབྱེད་ (gārnaà shēnjɛɛ̀) distinguishing between right and wrong or true and false ¶ ད་རེས་ཁ་མཆུ་དེ་དཀར་ནག་ཤན་འབྱེད་ཡག་པོ་བྱུང་སོང་ This time the dispute was settled well with a clear distinction made between right and wrong.

དཀར་སྣང་ (gārnaŋ) 1. a feeling/ vision of white light. 2. a feeling of love.

དཀར་པོ་ (gāābo) 1. white. 2. good, kind, sincere ¶ ཁོང་སེམས་དཀར་པོ་རེད་ He is a good person. 3. facial powder (makeup); va.—འབྱུག to powder one's face.

དཀར་པོ་དཀར་རྒྱང་ (gāābo gārgyaŋ) completely white.

དཀར་པོ་གྱེན་དེད་དང་ནག་པོ་ཐུར་དེད་ (gāābo gyenteè taŋ nagbo türteè) promoting right/ truth and putting down wrong/ untruth [Lit. pursuing the white uphill and pursuing the black downhill].

དཀར་པོ་དངུལ་ (gāābo ŋǖǖ) poet. silver.

དཀར་པོ་རྣམ་གསུམ་ (gāābo nāmsum) shung. the three founders of the Sakya sect.

དཀར་པོ་སྤལ་རྒྱབ་ (gāābo bɛɛgyab) a mineral used in making Tibetan medicines.

དཀར་པོ་དམར་པོ་ (gāābo māābo) cosmetics, facial makeup; va.—འབྱུག to wear/ put on makeup or cosmetics.

དཀར་པོའི་འཇིགས་སྐྲག (gāābö jigdraà) 1. the white terror—the time in 1927 when the Guomindang Party turned on the Communist Party. 2. any major attack on the communists by their enemies internationally.

དཀར་པོའི་འཇིགས་ཁུལ་ (gāābö jiggüü) the white terror area (the area controlled by the Guomindang Party where the White Terror occurred).

དཀར་པོའི་ལས་ (gāābö lɛɛ) good/ meritorious deeds.

དཀར་པོའི་ལས་འབྲས་ (gāābö lɛndreè) the good karmic consequence of meritorious deeds ¶ དཀར་པོའི་ལས་འབྲས་ལ་བརྟེན་ནས་ཚེ་འདིར་ཁོང་ཕྱུག་པོ་ཆགས་པ་རེད་ Because of the effect of good karma, he became rich in this life.

དཀར་པོའི་ས་ཁུལ་ (gāābö sɔgüü) the area controlled by the Guomindang Party [Lit. the white area].

དཀར་པོའི་སོ་སྟོན་ དམར་པོའི་ལྕེ་སྟོན་ (gāābö sō dön mārbö jē dön) requesting sth. with a smiling and respectful demeanor [Lit. show white teeth, show red tongue].

དཀར་སྤུའི་ཐོན་འབྲས་ (gārbü tōmdrɛɛ̀) shung. dairy products and animal fiber/ skin products, i.e., the products produced by nomads.

དཀར་སྤྱད་ (gārjɛɛ̀) equipment/ tools used in dairy production work.

དཀར་སླང་ (gārdraŋ) a beggar who begs for dairy products.

དཀར་སྒྲིན་ (gərdrin) the white of an egg.

དཀར་སྒྲོ་ (gārdro) shung. a type of fried cookie that is stacked up ceremonially on special occasions.

དཀར་སྒྲོ་ལྔ་བརྩེགས་ (gārdro ŋādzeg) shung. a type of fried cooky that is stacked into five layers (on special occasions).

དཀར་ཕེབས་ (gəbii) porch, balcony, veranda.

དཀར་ཕུད་ (gərbüü) dairy offerings to a deity; va.—འབུལ་ to make a dairy offering to a deity.

དཀར་ཕྱེ་ (gārce) abbr. of དཀར་རག་ཕྱེ་མ་.

དཀར་ཕྱོགས་ (gārcɔɔ̀) 1. religious work, religious activities. 2. the period from the 1st to the 15th of the Tibetan lunar month.

དཀར་ཕྱོགས་ཀྱི་གྲལ་ཚེས་དགེ་བར་ (gārcɔɔ̀gi trɛɛdze gewar) shung. an auspicious day between the 1st and the 15th day of the lunar month ¶ དཀར་ཕྱོགས་ཀྱི་གྲལ་ཚེས་དགེ་བར་ཁྲི་འདོན་མཛད་སྒོ་བསྐྱང་རྒྱུ་ཐག་གཅོད་འཁེལ་བ་ It was decided to hold the inauguration on an auspicious day between the 1st and the 15th day of the month.

དཀར་བ་ (gārwa) sm. དཀའ་བ་.

དཀར་བོང་བོང་ (gār boŋboŋ) a heap of sth. white (e.g., snow).

དཀར་བྱུག (gər jug) 1. va. to whitewash the exterior of a house. 2. va. to put melted butter on torma offerings.

དཀར་བྱུག་པ་ (gərjugbə) a person who whitewashes houses.

དཀར་བྱེད་ (gārjɛɛ̀) bleach, bleaching.

དཀར་མི་ (gərmi) 1. a person who has taken an oath. 2. a close friend.

དཀར་མིན་ (gərmin) 1. not white, dark; gloomy, somber. 2. a sin, a sinful act.

དཀར་མིན་ཅན་ (gərminjen) 1. dark, gloomy, somber. 2. sinful.

དཀར་མེ་ (gārme) a votive butter lamp.

དཀར་མེ་བསྔོ་ཞུ་ (gārme ŋoshu) the offering (money, butter, etc.) given by friends and neighbors for the purpose of lighting butter lamps on behalf of the deceased (the day before the corpse is taken from home to the sky burial site).

དཀར་མོ་གྲི་འགག (gārmo drengaà) a sheep disease in which the throat gets blocked.

དཀར་དམག (gārmaà) the White Army (in Russia).

དཀར་དམར་ (gārmaa) abbr. of དཀར་པོ་ and དམར་པོ་.

དཀར་དམར་ཤལ་ (gārmārshɛ) sm. དཀར་ཤལ་དམར་ཤལ་.

དཀར་གཙང་ (gārdzaŋ) completely white.

དཀར་རྩི་ (gərdzi) 1. white paint; va.—གཏོང་. 2. lime powder.

དཀར་རྩིས་ (gərdzii) astrology.

དཀར་རྩིས་པ་ (gərdziibə) 1. astrologist. 2. person in charge of the cups and dishes during parties.

དཀར་རྩེར་ (gārdzer) 1. extremely white. 2. extremely beautiful.

དཀར་བརྩེགས་ (gārdzeg) felt pads put under saddles.

དཀར་ཚོགས་ (gārtsoò) shung. relatives and friends.

དཀར་ཚོར་འབྲེལ་བ་ (gārtsor dreewa) shung. friendly relations ¶ བོད་གོར་གཉིས་ཀྱང་རྒྱལ་མཆོག་ལྔ་པ་ཆེན་པོའི་དུས་ནས་དཀར་ཚོར་འབྲེལ་བ་ཡིན་འདུག Since the 5th Dalai Lama, Nepalese and Tibetans have had friendly relations.

དཀར་མཛེས་ (gāndzeè) Ganze (a town and prefecture in Sichuan).

དཀར་མཛེས་བོད་རིགས་རང་སྐྱོང་ཁུལ་ (gāndzeè pöriì raŋgyong kǖǖ) Ganze Tibetan Nationality Autonomous Area.

དཀར་མཛོད་ (gārdzöö) warehouse.

དཀར་འཛིན་ (gəndzin) poet. breasts.

དཀར་ཞོད་ (gārshöö) milk.

དཀར་ཟལ་ (gārsɛl) an animal with mixed colors.

དཀར་ཟལ་དམར་ཟལ་ (gārsɛɛ mārsɛɛ) sm. དཀར་ཟིལ་དམར་ཟིལ་.

དཀར་ཟས་ (gārsɛɛ̀) dairy foods.

དཀར་ཟས་ལས་ཀ་ (gārsɛɛ̀ lɛ̀ɛga) dairy production work.

དཀར་ཟིལ་དམར་ཟིལ་ (gārsil mārsii) colorful, filled with color.

དཀར་ཟླ་ (gānda) 1. moon. 2. the 5th month of the Tibetan calendar.

དཀར་ཟླུམ་ (gāndum) white and round/ protruding.

དཀར་བཟོ་ (gārso) making oneself look good/ handsome/ attractive; va.—འདོན་ to make oneself look handsome/ attractive ¶ མོ་དཀར་བཟོ་བཏོན་ནས་སླེབས་འདུག She made herself look attractive and came.

དཀར་བཟོ་དོད་པོ་ (gārso töbo) good looking, handsome, attractive ¶ ཁྱེད་རང་གི་བུ་དཀར་བཟོ་དོད་པོ་ཤི་དྲག་འདུག Your son is very good looking.

དཀར་བཟོ་ཕྱེ་མ་ (gārso cēma) bleaching powder.

དཀར་བཟོ་རྫས་ (gārsodzɛɛ̀) bleaching agent, decolorant.

དཀར་བཟོ་གཤེར་ཁུ་ (gārso shērgu) bleaching liquid.

དཀར་འོད་ (gāröö) white light.

དཀར་ཡ་ (gārya) 1. tin, stannum.

དཀར་ཡིག (gəryii) letters made with white stones on the side of mountains.

དཀར་ཡོལ་ (gāāyöö) 1. porcelain ¶ དཀར་ཡོལ་གྱི་བུམ་པ་ A porcelain vase. 2. porcelain cup/ bowl ¶ དཀར་ཡོལ་གཉིས་ཉོས་པ་ཡིན་ (I) bought two porcelain cups. 3. a cloth fence/ curtain placed around sth. (e.g., an area on the street inside of which beer is sold).

དཀར་ཡོལ་དཀར་སངས་ (gāāyöö gārsaŋ) a completely white porcelain cup.

དཀར་ཡོལ་བཀྱོག་དཀར་ (gāāyöö gyōggar) a porcelain serving bowl.

དཀར་ཡོལ་ཁ་དཀྲུམ་ (gāāyöö kādrum) sm.* དཀར་ཡོལ་ཁ་ཆག.

དཀར་ཡོལ་ཁ་གྲུམ་ (gāāyöö kādrum) sm. དཀར་ཡོལ་ཁ་ཆག.

དཀར་ཡོལ་ཁ་ཆག (gāāyöö kājaà) a cup with a chipped lip.

དཀར་ཡོལ་གྱི་ཅ་ལག (gāāyöögi jālaà) chinaware, porcelainware.

དཀར་ཡོལ་ཇ་དཀར་ (gāāyöö jagar) a porcelain tea cup.

དཀར་ཡོལ་རྙིང་མ་ (gāāyöö ñiŋmə) an antique porcelain bowl/ cup.

དཀར་ཡོལ་ད་པན་ (gāāyöö tabɛn) ch.tib. a very large porcelain bowl.

དཀར་ཡོལ་མདོག་གོག (gāāyöö dəggɔɔ̀) an inferior type of porcelain.

དཀར་ཡོལ་དོ་རྩི་ (gāāyöö dodzi) a varnish used on porcelain.

དཀར་ཡོལ་ཕོ་དཀར་ (gāāyöö pōgar) a porcelain cup used by males.

དཀར་ཡོལ་འབྲུག་རིས་ཅན་ (gāāyöö drugrijɛn) a porcelain bowl with a dragon design.

དཀར་ཡོལ་འབྲུག་རིས་མ་ (gāāyöö drugrima) sm. དཀར་ཡོལ་འབྲུག་རིས་ཅན་.

དཀར་ཡོལ་མོ་དཀར་ (gāāyöö mogar) a woman's porcelain cup (usu. a cup smaller than that used by males and often having a handle).

དཀར་ཡོལ་ཚལ་དཀར་ (gāāyöö tsɛ̄ɛ̄gar) a porcelain bowl for vegetables.

དཀར་ཡོལ་འཛུགས་དཀར་ (gāāyöö dzuggar) the first bowl of food served.

དཀར་ཡོལ་ཡུ་རིང་ (gāāyöö yuriŋ) a cup with a stem.

དཀར་ཡོལ་གསབ་དཀར་ (gāāyöö səbgar) a bowl used to pour a second serving into sb.'s bowl.

དཀར་གཡའ་ (gārya) a white varnish used on copperware; va.—གཏོང་.

དཀར་གཡེང་ (gāryeŋ) shung. distinguishing between good and evil.

དཀར་རག (gāraà) whitewash used on the outside of buildings; va.—གཏོང་; —འབྱུག་; —བཤོས་; —གསོལ་ to whitewash buildings/ walls.

དཀར་རག་དུས་རབས་ (gāraà tüürəb) Cretaceous period.

དཀར་རག་ས་རིམ་ (gāraà sərim) Cretaceous stratigraphic layer/ level.

དཀར་རག་ཕྱེ་མ་ (gāraà cēmə) powdered lime/ whitewash.

དཀར་རིགས་ (gārig) dairy products.

དཀར་རིལ་ (gārii) white and round.

དཀར་རུ་ (gārru) 1. white. 2. a herd of sheep.

དཀར་ལམ་མེ་ (gār lamme) completely white.

དཀར་ལས་ (gārlɛɛ̀) 1. dairy production work, dairy industry. 2. abbr. དཀར་པོའི་ལས་.

དཀར་ལས་པ་ (gārlɛɛ̀ba) a worker in the dairy industry.

དཀར་ལོང་ (gārloŋ) blindness caused by cataracts.

དཀར་ཤ་ (gāsha) 1. a white mushroom. 2. a kind of barley.

དཀར་ཤལ་དམར་ཤལ་ (gārshɛ mārshɛ) shung. a kind of ornament worn by ལྷ་ལྕམ་ on dresses in tt.

དཀར་ཤས་ (gārshɛɛ̀) whitish color.

དཀར་ཤུབས་ (gārshub) a container for holding or keeping porcelain cups/ bowls.

དཀར་ཤེད་ (gārshe) shung. leasing female animals in exchange for a specified amount of dairy products such as butter and/or cheese; va.—གཏོང་.

དཀར་བཤད་ནག་བཤད་ (gārsheὲ nagshεὲ) saying sth. carelessly/ thoughtlessly.

དཀར་བཤལ་ (gārshεε) diarrhea/ dysentery characterized by white mucous in the stool.

དཀར་ས་ (gārsa) 1. white/ light colored earth or soil. 2. shung. getting cleared of charges, coming out innocent in an investigation; vi.—(ར་) ཐོན་ ¶ ཁོས་རང་ཉེས་ངོས་ལེན་བྱས་པས་གཡོག་པོ་རྣམས་དཀར་སར་ཐོན་ Because he confessed his mistake the servants were cleared of the charges.

དཀར་ས་ནག་འདེད་ (gārsa naŋdeè) sm. དཀར་ནག་ཤན་འབྱེད་.

དཀར་སངས་ (gārsaŋ) completely white.

དཀར་སེམས་ནག་སྒྲིབ་ (gārsem nəgdrib) pure/ good thoughts or values being spoiled or corrupted.

དཀར་སེམས་ནག་བསྒྲིབ་ (gārsem nəgdrib) sm. དཀར་སེམས་ནག་སྒྲིབ་.

དཀར་སེར་ (gārser) a color that is a mixture of white and yellow, a pale yellow color.

དཀར་སྲན་ (gārsεn) a type of white bean.

དཀར་སླེལ་ (gārleè) a whitish basket (carried on the back) that is made of wood from which the bark has been peeled.

དཀར་སློང་ (gārloŋ) 1. begging for dairy products; va.—རྒྱག. 2. va. to go begging for dairy products.

དཀར་གསལ་ (gārsεε) white and light/ bright, light and airy ¶ ཁང་པ་དེ་དཀར་གསལ་ཡག་པོ་འདུག That house is nice and light and airy.

དཀར་གསལ་ཀུ་ཡངས་ (gārsεε kuyaŋ) light and spacious, light and roomy.

དཀར་གསལ་དོད་པོ་ (gārsεε tööbo) light and airy for houses/ rooms.

དཀར་གསལ་ཟླ་བ་ (gārsεε dawa) the bright clear moon.

དཀར་གསུམ་ (gār sūm) the three (dairy products): milk, butter and yogurt.

དཀར་གསུམ་མངར་གསུམ་ (gārsum ŋārsum) the three dairy products (དཀར་གསུམ་) and the three sweets: (rock sugar, brown sugar/ molasses and honey).

དཀར་གསུར་ (gārsur) dairy products used for གསུར་.

དཀར་བསོད་ (gārsöö) the custom of monks (and lamas) going to nomad areas to beg for dairy products or to do rituals/ prayers, or both.

དཀུ་ (gū) 1. uterus, womb. 2. hip bone. 3. stomach. 4. vi. to smell. 5. vi. to fall. 6. arc. vi. to be leftover.

དཀུ་ལྟོ་ (gūdo) stomach, abdomen.

དཀུ་ནད་ (gūnεὲ) a disease of the kidney.

དཀོག་ཉུལ་ (gūgñul) arc. sm. ཕྱོག་ཉུལ་.

དཀོན་ (gōn) abbr. of དཀོན་པོ་.

དཀོན་ཅོག (gūnjoò) sm. དཀོན་མཆོག.

དཀོན་མཆོག (gūnjoò) 1. sth. precious [Lit. the rarest and the best]. 2. sm. དཀོན་མཆོག་གསུམ.

དཀོན་མཆོག་ཀུན་འདུས་ (gūnjoò gündüü) root guru.

དཀོན་མཆོག་གི་ཐུགས་རྗེས་ (gūnjoògi tūjeè) by the grace of the three precious jewels (Buddha, monks and dharma) ¶ དཀོན་མཆོག་གི་ཐུགས་རྗེས་ང་རང་གཟུགས་པོ་བདེ་པོ་བྱུང་སོང་ By the grace of the three precious jewels I have been healthy.

དཀོན་མཆོག་གིས་མཁྱེན་ (gūnjoògi kyēn) an exclamation/ prayer: "may the three precious jewels [དཀོན་མཆོག་གསུམ] help" ¶ ཡིག་ཚད་ཡག་པོ་ཡོང་བ་ཞོག་དཀོན་མཆོག་མཁྱེན་ May the three precious jewels help make the exam go well.

དཀོན་མཆོག་གིས་གཟིགས་ (gūnjoògi sii) sm. དཀོན་མཆོག་གིས་མཁྱེན་.

དཀོན་མཆོག་དཔང་བཙུགས་ (gūnjoò bāŋdzuù) swearing by the three precious jewels ¶ དཀོན་མཆོག་དཔང་བཙུགས་ངས་སྐྱག་རྫུན་ཤོད་ཀྱི་མིན་ I swear by the three precious jewels I am not lying.

དཀོན་མཆོག་ཕོ་བྲང་ (gūnjoò pōdraŋ) a temple.

དཀོན་མཆོག་ཚད་བཙུགས་ (gūnjoò tsεὲdzuù) sm. དཀོན་མཆོག་དཔང་བཙུགས་.

དཀོན་མཆོག་བཞི་ (gūnjoò shi) the three precious jewels and one's root guru.

དཀོན་མཆོག་བཞི་པ་ (gūnjoò shibə) the fourth precious jewel: one's root guru.

དཀོན་མཆོག་གསུམ་ (gūnjoò sūm) the three jewels or precious things: the Buddha, the dharma and the clergy.

དཀོན་གཉེར་ (gōnñer) a monk in charge of taking care of a temple.

དཀོན་དུས་ (gūndüü) scarce season.

དཀོན་ནོར་ (gūnnɔɔ) things that are scarce/ rare.

དཀོན་པ་ (gōmba) sm. དཀོན་པོ་.

དཀོན་པའི་ལྕགས་རིགས་ (gōnbε jāgrii) precious or rare metals.

དཀོན་པོ་ (gōmbo) rare, scarce ¶ གོ་སྐབས་འདི་འདྲ་དཀོན་པོ་རེད་ An opportunity like this is rare. ¶ དེང་སང་ཤ་དཀོན་པོ་འདུག Meat is scarce these days.

དཀོན་དཔང་ (gōmbaŋ) abbr. of དཀོན་མཆོག་དཔང་བཙུགས་.

དཀོན་བུ་ (gūmbu) a small container.

དཀོན་མོ་ (gōnmo) sm. དཀོན་པོ་.

དཀོན་མོད་ (gūnmöö) sm. དཀོན་ལོས་.

དཀོན་ཟོག (gōnsɔɔ) scarce commodities/ merchandise/ goods.

དཀོན་ཟོག་སྡེབ་བསགས་ (gōnsɔɔ debsaà) stockpiling/ hoarding scarce goods.

དཀོན་ལོས་ (gōnlöö) the degree of scarcity ¶ དེང་སང་ལྷ་སར་མར་དཀོན་ལོས་ག་འདྲ་འདུག How scarce is butter these days in Lhasa?

དཀོར་ (gōr) 1. wealth or property given out of religious belief. 2. property, wealth (in general).

དཀོར་སྐྱིད་ (gōrgyeè) manager or person in charge of property/ wealth in a monastery.

དཀོར་ཁང་ (gōrgaŋ) sm. དཀོར་མཛོད་.

དཀོར་གྱིས་འཚིག (gōrgi tsii) vi. to be corrupted by wealth (for monks—e.g., a monk lives off of alms but doesn't act as a proper monk) [Lit. to be burned by wealth generated from religion].

དཀོར་གྱིས་འཚིགས་ (gōrgi tsii) sm. ཀོར་གྱིས་འཚིག.

དཀོར་དངོས་ (gōŋöö) sm. དཀོར་.

དཀོར་གཉེར་ (gōñer) sm. དཀོར་སྐྱིད་.

དཀོར་བདག (gōdaà) property owner.

དཀོར་མདུང་རང་འདེབས་ (gōduŋ randeb) an ancient magical spear that attacks people by itself.

དཀོར་འདྲུབ་པ་ (gōdrubbə) storekeeper, storeman.

དཀོར་ནོར་ (gōnɔɔ) sm. དཀོར་.

དཀོར་པ་ (gōba) sm. དཀོར་སྐྱིད་.

དཀོར་བླ་ (gōla) sm. དཀོར་སྐྱིད་.

དཀོར་ཚིག (gōdzii) sm. དཀོར་གྱིས་ཚིག.

དཀོར་མཛོད་ (gōrdzöö) a treasury/ storehouse for valuables.

དཀོར་ཟ་ (gōr sa) 1. va. to take/ use religious alms or offerings. 2. to live off (for monks/ nuns) religious gifts/ offerings but not genuinely do religious work.

དཀོར་ཟ་དཀོར་ཁུངས་ (gōrsa gōrguŋ) 1. in tt. a place or region where a monk/ lama has the exclusive authority to do rites and receive alms. 2. the source of offerings for monks/ lamas.

དཀོར་ཟས་དཀོར་ཆུ་ (gōrsεε kōrju) food and drinks obtained from alms/ offerings.

དཀོར་ཟུག (gōr sug) sm. དཀོར་ཚིག.

དཀོར་སྲུང་ (gōrsuŋ) 1. person who watches/ protects/ defends wealth. 2. a protective deity that protects wealth.

དཀོལ་པ་ (gööba) sb. who suffers pain.

དཀོས་ཐག་པ་ (göödagba) arc. a poor, suffering person.

དཀྱིལ་ (gyii) 1. middle, center ¶ ལྕོག་ཙེ་འདིའི་དཀྱིལ་ལ་མེ་ཏོག་གི་བུམ་པ་གཅིག་འདུག There is a flower vase in the middle of the table. 2. among, in the midst of ¶ མི་དེ་ཚོའི་དཀྱིལ་ལ་ Among those people.

དཀྱིལ་ཀྱོང་ (gyīigyoŋ) a depression.

དཀྱིལ་ཀྲུང་ (gyīidruŋ) sm. སྐྱིལ་ཀྲུང་.

དཀྱིལ་ཀླད་ (gyīilɛɛ̀) the midbrain.

དཀྱིལ་དཀྱིལ་རྒྱང་ (gyii gyīgyaŋ) right in the middle.

དཀྱིལ་དཀྲུངས་ (gyīidruŋ) sitting cross-legged; va.— བསྡད་ to sit cross-legged.

དཀྱིལ་ཁང་ (gyīigaŋ) 1. a middle room. 2. a college in Tashilhunpo monastery.

དཀྱིལ་ཁུལ་ (gyīigüü) 1. middle area/ region. 2. the interior of a country.

དཀྱིལ་ཁྲོ་ (gyīdro) the pot (usu. made from ཁྲོ་) that is made for the middle opening of a traditional Tibetan hearth/ stove with several openings.

དཀྱིལ་ཁྲོམ་ (gyīidrom) a display of goods set out in the middle of the marketplace.

དཀྱིལ་འཁོར་ (gyīŋgɔɔ) 1. circle, sphere. 2. a mandala; va.—བཞེངས་ i. va. to build/ construct a mandala. ii. va. to be lost in thought (thinking intently about sth.), to be oblivious to what is going on around one.

དཀྱིལ་འཁོར་སྒང་ (gyīŋgɔɔ ga̱ŋ) cemetery, place for doing sky burial.

དཀྱིལ་གུ་ (gyīigu) 1. wooden nail. 2. wooden shoetree.

དཀྱིལ་རྒྱུད་ (gyīigyüü) the middle part/ section/ area of sth.

དཀྱིལ་སྒོ་ (gyīigo) the main door, the door one encounters after entering a courtyard.

དཀྱིལ་རྟ་ (gyīida) the center horse of a team pulling a cart.

དཀྱིལ་ཐང་ (gyīidaŋ) shung. a thanka that is hung midway between other thankas.

དཀྱིལ་ཐད་ (gyīidɛɛ̀) in the middle, halfway along ¶ ཁྲོམ་གྱི་དཀྱིལ་ཐད་ལ་ In the middle of the market.

དཀྱིལ་ཐིག (gyīidii) the middle line used when beginning a thanka painting.

དཀྱིལ་དྲེལ་ (gyīidre) the middle mule in a mule team.

དཀྱིལ་གདུག་དཀར་པོ་ (gyīidug gāābo) shung. the white umbrella that comes in the middle line of the ཚོགས་མཆོད་སེར་སྦྲེང་.

དཀྱིལ་གདུང་ (gyīiduŋ) the center/ middle beam.

དཀྱིལ་ནས་ (gyīinɛɛ̀) from the middle, from among ¶ སློབ་གྲྭ་མང་པོའི་དཀྱིལ་ནས་ From among many schools.

དཀྱིལ་སྣོད་ (gyīinöö̀) the pot/ vessel that is made for the middle opening of a traditional Tibetan hearth/ stove with several openings.

དཀྱིལ་ཕྱོགས་ (gyīijɔɔ̀) the middle part/ section of sth.

དཀྱིལ་མ་ (gyīmə) middle, center.

དཀྱིལ་ཚོམས་ (gyīdzom) middle/ center hall or room.

དཀྱིལ་མཛུབ (gyīndzuù) middle finger.

དཀྱིལ་མཛུབ་ (gyīndzub) sm. དཀྱིལ་མཛུབ.

དཀྱིལ་མཛུབ་གང་ (gyīndzub ka̱ŋ) a measure equal to the distance between the thumb and middle finger outstretched.

དཀྱིལ་མཛེས་ (gyīndzeè) shung. China ¶ དཀྱིལ་མཛེས་མི་དམངས་སྤྱི་མཐུན་རྒྱལ་ཁབ་ The People's Republic of China.

དཀྱིལ་གཞུང་ (gyīishuŋ) sm. དཀྱིལ་མ་.

དཀྱིལ་ཟངས་ (gyīisaŋ) a copper pot that is made for the middle hole/ opening in a traditional Tibetan stove or hearth that has several openings.

དཀྱིལ་གཤགས་ (gyīishaà) sth. split into two, sth. split down the middle.

དཀྱིལ་སྲུང་རྒྱག་མཁན་ (gyīisuŋ gya̱ñɛn) center guard (in soccer).

དཀྱུ་: p. and imp. དཀྱུས་, f. དཀྱུ་ (gyū) va. to run, to gallop.

དཀྱུ་རྟ་ (gyūdə) race horse.

དཀྱུ་པོ་ (gyūbo) 1. jockey. 2. runner in a race.

དཀྱུ་བ་པོ་ (gyūwabo) sm. དཀྱུ་པོ་.

དཀྱུ་བོ་ (gyūbo) curved.

དཀྱུ་ས་ (gyūsə) race track.

དཀྱུས་ (gyǖü) 1. length ¶ སྤང་ལེབ་དཀྱུས་ལ་སྨི་གཉིས་དང་འཕྲེད་ལ་སྨི་ཕྱེད་ཙམ་ A plank two meters in length and half a meter in width. 2. abbr. of དཀྱུས་མ་.

དཀྱུས་དཀར་ (gyǖügar) an ordinary/ common cup or bowl.

དཀྱུས་ཁྲོམ་ (gyǖüdrom) displaying goods on blankets or tables in the market rather than having a store (connotes lower status); va.— འདོན་ to display goods for sale in this way.

དཀྱུས་གཅིག (gyǖüjig) in one line.

དཀྱུས་ལྕོག (gyǖüjoò) ordinary or plain Tibetan table.

དཀྱུས་ཆང་ (gyǖnjaŋ) ordinary quality Tibetan beer, i.e., beer made from the second addition of water to the fermented barley grain.

དཀྱུས་ཆས་ (gyǖüjɛɛ̀) regular/ plain/ ordinary/ everyday clothes.

དཀྱུས་ཇ་ (gyǖüja) regular/ plain/ ordinary/ everyday tea.

དཀྱུས་བཏགས་ (gyǖüdaà) ordinary/ common quality ceremonial scarf.

དཀྱུས་ཐག (gyǖüdaà) distance in length, the length of sth.

དཀྱུས་བུར་ (gyǖübur) ordinary/ common quality brown sugar.

དཀྱུས་འབོལ་ (gyǖmböö) an ordinary/ common cushion.

དཀྱུས་འབྲས་ (gyǖndrɛɛ̀) ordinary/ common rice.

དཀྱུས་འབྲུ་ (gyǖndru) ordinary/ common grain.

དཀྱུས་མ་ (gyǖüma) 1. ordinary/ common in rank. 2. the lowest lay officials (7th rank) ¶ གཞུང་གི་ལས་བྱེད་དཀྱུས་མ་ཞིག A common (low rank) government official.

དཀྱུས་མའི་སློབ་དེབ་ (gyǖümɛ lōbdeb) an ordinary text book.

དཀྱུས་མའི་སློབ་གསོ་ (gyǖümɛ lōbso) ordinary/ common education.

དཀྱུས་མོ་ (gyǖümo) arc. quick, rapid.

དཀྱུས་ཚད་ (gyǖütsɛɛ̀) sm. དཀྱུས་, 1.

དཀྱུས་ཞེང་ (gyǖüsheŋ) width.

དཀྱུས་བཞིན་ (gyǖüshin) usually, as usual; daily.

དཀྱུས་རིང་ (gyǖüriŋ) long (in length).

དཀྱུས་རིང་གྲུ་བཞི་ (gyǖüriŋ dru̱bshi) long and rectangular.

དཀྱུས་ཤོག (gyǖüshoō) ordinary quality paper.

དཀྱུས་སུ་ (gyǖüsu) 1. sm. དཀྱུས་. 2. warp (in weaving).

དཀྱེར་ལ་ (gyērla) shung. alms, donations.

དཀྱེལ་ (gyēē) extent, size.

དཀྱེལ་ཆེ་ (gyēē cēwa) 1. (with ཡངས་) broad-minded, tolerant ¶ འགོ་ཁྲིད་དེ་ཁོང་ཡངས་དཀྱེལ་ཆེ་བ་ཞིག་ཡོད་པ་རེད་ The leader is sb. who is broad-minded. 2. spacious, broad (in expanse).

དཀྱེལ་པོ་ཆེ་ (gyēboce) 1. sm. དཀྱེལ་ཆེ་བ་. 2. the world, the universe.

དཀྱེལ་ཡངས་པ་ (gyēēyaŋba) broad-minded, tolerant.

དཀྱོར་འཛིན་ (gyōrjin) sm. སྐྱོར་འཛིན་.

དཀྲི་: p. དཀྲིས་; f. དཀྲི་; imp. དཀྲིས་ (drī) 1. va. to wrap around, to wind up, to bind/ tie/ bandage ¶ ཁོས་རས་དེ་མོའི་རྐང་པར་དཀྲིས་པ་རེད་ He tied the piece of cloth around her leg. 2. sm. འཁྲིད་. 3. (with འགན་ or similar nouns) va. to charge with/ give responsibilities ¶ ལས་ཁངས་ཀྱི་འགོ་ཁྲིད་ཀྱིས་གཤམ་རིམ་ལ་ལས་ཀའི་འགན་དཀྲིས་པ་རེད་ The head of the office gave work responsibilities to the lower officials.

དཀྲི་ག (drīgə) sm. དཀྲི་ག་ཉིས་བརྩེགས་.

དཀྲི་ག་ཉིས་བརྩེགས་ (drīgə ñīdzeg) epicanthic fold.

དཀྲི་དམ་ (drīdam) shung. a seal put on tt. government official letters.

དཀྲི་ཕང་ (drībaŋ) a spindle for spinning thread.

དཀྲི་ཤིང་ (drīshiŋ) a piece of cylindrical wood used

to wind thread that has been spun.

དཀྲིག: p. and imp. དཀྲིགས་; f. དཀྲིག (drīi) vi. to be covered/ encased with, to be full of ¶ རི་ལུང་སྨུག་པས་དཀྲིགས་འདུག The mountains and valleys were covered with fog.

དཀྲིག་ཙར་ (drīgjaa) sm. ཀྲིག་ཙར་.

དཀྲིགས་ (drīg; drīi) p. and imp. of དཀྲིག.

དཀྲིལ་ལི་ (drīile) 1. complete, whole. 2. clear, obvious.

དཀྲིས་ (drīi) 1. p. and imp. of དཀྲི་. 2. marks on the horns of older animals. 3. in conjunction with other words it conveys tying/ binding ¶ སྐེད་དཀྲིས་ Tied around waist.

དཀྲིས་དམ་ (drīdam) shung. things wrapped or tied up and then implanted with a seal where it is fastened so it cannot be opened without breaking the seal; va.—རྒྱག.

དཀྲིས་མ་ (drīmə) anything bound or tied up or wrapped.

དཀྲིས་རས་ (drīrεὲ) a cloth for wrapping things.

དཀྲུག: p. and imp. དཀྲུགས་; f. དཀྲུག (drūù) 1. va. to stir, to shake ¶ ཁོས་ཐུག་པ་དེ་དཀྲུགས་སོང་ He stirred the stew. 2. va. to agitate, to stir up, to disturb, to cause havoc ¶ རྐུན་ཇག་དེ་ཚོས་ཡུལ་གྱི་བདེ་འཇགས་དཀྲུག་གི་འདུག The bandits and robbers are disturbing the area. 3. va. to lathe ¶ ཁོ་ཚོས་ཤིང་གི་དངོས་ཆས་སྣ་མང་དཀྲུག་ཐུབ་ཀྱི་ཡོད་པ་རེད་ They are able to lathe many kinds of wooden things.

དཀྲུག་དཀྲུག (drūgdruù) sm. དཀྲུག; va.—གཏོང་; —བྱེད་.

དཀྲུག་རྒྱུན་ (drūggyen) the cause of incitement/ provocation.

དཀྲུག་འཁོར་ (drūgɔɔ) a lathe, a milling machine.

དཀྲུག་གྲི་ (drūgdri) the knife/ blade used in a lathe or milling machine.

དཀྲུག་རྒྱག་བཟོ་པ་ (drūggyəb sobə) sm. དཀྲུག་པ་.

དཀྲུག་སྡེགས་ (drūgdeè) sm. དཀྲུག་འཁོར་.

དཀྲུག་བདར་འབྲུལ་འཁོར་ (drūgdaa drūūgɔɔ) planing machine.

དཀྲུག་སྣོད་ (drūgnöö) a vessel used for shaking or mixing things.

དཀྲུག་པ་ (drūgbə) a lathe operator.

དཀྲུག་སྤྱད་ (drūgjεὲ) equipment for lathing.

དཀྲུག་མདའ་ (drūŋda) stirring implements.

དཀྲུག་ཚག (drūgdzaà) 1. a soup prepared with ground meat. 2. the first beer drunk in the morning.

དཀྲུག་འཛིང་ (drūgdziŋ) tangled (for thread, yarn), messed up.

དཀྲུག་གཞོག་འཁོར་སྡེགས་ (drūgshɔ̀ɔ kɔ̄rdeg) sm. དཀྲུག་འཁོར་.

དཀྲུག་གཞོག་ལས་གྲྭ་ (drūgshɔ̀ɔ lεὲdra) milling and slotting shop/ plant.

དཀྲུག་ཟིང་ (drūgsiŋ) sm. དཀྲུག་ཤིང་.

དཀྲུག་ལས་ (drūglεὲ) milling work, lathe work; va.—བཟོ་ to mill/ lathe.

དཀྲུག་ལས་བཟོ་པ་ (drūglεὲ sobə) sm. དཀྲུག་པ་.

དཀྲུག་ལས་བཟོ་རིགས་ (drūglεὲ sorii) industrial work involving milling or lathing.

དཀྲུག་ཤིང་ (drūgshiŋ) 1. instigation, incitement, provocation; creating divisiveness/ dissension; va.—རྒྱག; —བྱེད་ ¶ མོས་དཀྲུག་ཤིང་བརྒྱབ་ནས་ཁོ་ཚོ་མ་མཐུན་པ་བཟོས་པ་རེད་ She instigated and made them unfriendly towards each other. 2. wood used in lathing.

དཀྲུག་ཤིང་དབྱེན་སྦྱོར་ (drūgshiŋ yēnjɔɔ) sm. དཀྲུག་ཤིང་, 1.

དཀྲུག་གསོར་ (drūgsɔɔ) 1. a drill used in lathe work. 2. a planing tool.

དཀྲུགས་ (drūù) p. and imp. of དཀྲུག.

དཀྲུགས་སྡེགས་ (drūgdeè) sm. དཀྲུག་སྡེགས་.

དཀྲུགས་ཡིག (drūgyii) words in which the prefixes and suffixes are mixed up.

དཀྲུགས་ཤིང་ (drūgshiŋ) sm. དཀྲུག་ཤིང་.

དཀྲུམ་ (drūm) meat (h.).

དཀྲུམ་: p. དཀྲུམས་; f. དཀྲུམ་; imp. ཀྲུམས་ (drūm) va. to break.

དཀྲུམ་ཁུ་ (drūmgu) 1. meat broth/ soup. 2. broth of any food.

དཀྲུམ་ཁོག (drūmgɔ̀ɔ) carcass of an animal that was killed for food.

དཀྲུམ་དོད་ (drūmdüü) shung. money paid as a substitute for an obligation to provide meat.

དཀྲུམ་མདའ་ (drūndə) pistol, revolver.

དཀྲུམ་ཕག (drūmbaà) pork.

དཀྲུམས་ (drūm) p. of དཀྲུམ་.

དཀྲེ་ (drē) the tip/ foreskin of the penis.

དཀྲེ་སྐོར་ (drēgɔɔ) a machine that spins thread.

དཀྲོག: p. དཀྲོགས་; f. དཀྲོག་; imp. དཀྲོགས་ (drɔ̄ɔ̀) 1. va. to churn ¶ མར་དཀྲོག་དུས When churning butter. 2. va. to scare away/ frighten (usu. birds or other animals) ¶ ཞིང་གཞི་ནང་གི་བྱིའུ་དཀྲོགས་པ་རེད་ (They) scared away the birds on the fields.

དཀྲོག་དཀྲོག (drōgdroò) showing off, boasting, acting as a braggart; va.—བྱེད་.

དཀྲོག་རྒྱུན་ (drɔ̄ggyen) the cause of a disturbance/ quarrel/ agitation; va.—སློང་ to cause or instigate a disturbance/ quarrel (usu. by lies and slander).

དཀྲོག་གཏམ་ (drɔ̄gdam) inflammatory talk/ rumors (that are false), talk that causes quarrels or dissension, calumny, slander; va.—བཟོ་; —ཤོད་ to cause/ incite trouble by rumors or talk.

དཀྲོག་གཏམ་དཀྲུག་ཤིང་ (drɔ̄gdam drūgshiŋ) sm. དཀྲོག་གཏམ་.

དཀྲོག་གཏམ་གོ་ཐོས་ (drɔ̄gdam kodöö) དཀྲོག་གཏམ་ that has spread or become widespread.

དཀྲོག་སློང་ (drōgloŋ) shung. picking/ provoking a quarrel or dispute (usu. by telling lies and falsehoods); va.—བྱེད་ ¶ མི་ངན་དོན་མ་གོ་འགའ་ཞིག་ནས་དོན་མེད་དཀྲོག་སློང་བྱེད་སྲིད་པས་ Some bad people who do not understand the issue may provoke quarrels for no reason.

དཀྲོག་བརྡ་ (drɔ̄ŋda) causing a disturbance; va.—སློང to cause/ incite a disturbance ¶ དཀྲོག་གཏམ་དེས་ཡུལ་འདིའི་ནང་དཀྲོག་བརྡ་བསླངས་འདུག The rumors caused a disturbance in that place.

དཀྲོགས་ (drɔ̄ɔ̀) p. and imp. of དཀྲོག.

དཀྲོགས་མདའ་ (drɔ̄ŋda) 1. shooting a rifle to scare sth. away (e.g., into the air); va.—རྒྱག ¶ ཛམ་སློན་བྱེད་སྐབས་ཉེན་རྟོག་པས་དཀྲོགས་མདའ་བརྒྱབ་པ་རེད་ The police fired in the air during the demonstration. 2. sm. དཀྲོག་བརྡ་.

དཀྲོགས་མ་ (drɔ̄ŋma) sth. that has been churned ¶ ཇ་དཀྲོགས་མ་ Churned butter tea.

དཀྲོང་བསྐྱེད་ (drɔ̄ŋgyeè) a stage in meditation in which one suddenly visualizes oneself as the deity.

དཀྲོང་སྟེ་ (drɔ̄ŋde) 1. suddenly. 2. sitting or standing upright/ straight.

དཀྲོངས་ (drōŋ) sm.* བཀྲོངས་.

དཀྲོལ་ (drȫȫ) 1. va. (རོལ་མོ་ + —) to play music using a striker (e.g., a bell or lute). 2. va. to ring a bell. 3. sm.* བཀྲོལ་. 4. engraving, carving; va.—བྱེད་.

དཀྲོལ་ཚགས་ (drȫȫdzaà) relief carving/ molding.

དཀྲོས་ (drȫȫ) sm. དཀྲོལ་.

དཀྲོས་མ་ (drȫȫma) sm. དཀྲོལ་མ་.

བཀག (gāà) p. of འགོག.

བཀག་བཀའ་ (gāgga) a law/ order that proscribes or prohibits.

བཀག་སྐོར་མེད་པ་ (gāggɔɔ meèba) without problems/ hindrances/ obstructions/ delays ¶ འགྲུལ་པ་རྣམས་འགག་སྒོ་ནས་བཀག་སྐོར་མེད་པར་བཏང་འདུག (They) sent the travelers through customs without problems.

བཀག་བསྐྱིལ་ (gɔ̄ggyii) detaining, keeping in custody, holding back, halting; va.—བྱེད་ ¶ ཁོ་ལྷ་སར་བཀུག་དེ་དོན་མེད་རྒྱུན་རིང་བར་བཀག་བསྐྱིལ་བྱས་པ་རེད་ (They) summoned him to Lhasa and for no reason detained him there for a long time.

བཀག་བསྐྱིལ་ཁང་ (gɔ̄ggyigaŋ) detention house/

center.

བཀག་བསྐྱིལ་ཁེ་སྒྲུག (gəggyii kēguù) hoarding for profit, profiteering.

བཀག་བསྐྱིལ་འཁེལ་ (gāggyii kēl) vi. to be placed in confinement/ detention ། འཐུས་མི་རྣམས་ལ་ལག་ཁྱེར་མེད་སྐབས་གནམ་ཐང་དུ་བཀག་སྐྱིལ་འཁེལ་འདུག The delegates were detained at the airport because they didn't have visas.

བཀག་ཁྲིམས་ (gāgdrim) a ban/ prohibition; va.—གློད་ to lift a ban/ prohibition; va.—གནོན་ to impose a ban/ prohibition.

བཀག་འགོག (gāngɔɔ̀) preventing, blocking, obstructing, stopping, halting, restricting, prohibiting, jamming a radio transmission; va.—བྱེད ། འཐབ་དམག་གི་ལས་འགུལ་བཀག་འགོག་བྱེད་དགོས་ (We) must stop the guerrilla campaign. ། གཞུང་ནས་ལྟ་སྐོར་བ་རྒྱ་གར་ནང་འགྲོ་རྒྱུ་བཀག་འགོག་བྱེད་ཀྱི་ཡོད་པ་རེད་ The government is stopping tourists from going into India.

བཀག་འགོག་བྱེད་མཁན་དངོས་པོ་ (gāngɔɔ̀ cēñɛn ŋööbo) things that cause an obstacle/ barrier.

བཀག་འགོག་མེད་པ་ (gāngɔɔ̀ mēèba) no impediment, no obstacle, without hindrance.

བཀག་འགོག་བཙན་པོ་ (gāngɔɔ̀ dzɛ̄mbo) a strict restriction ། ཡུལ་ནང་ཚོང་འགྲུལ་བཀག་འགོག་བཙན་པོ་བྱས་སོང་ There were very strict restrictions placed on merchants and travelers in that area.

བཀག་རྒལ་ (gāggɛɛ) overcoming/ passing over obstacles.

བཀག་རྒལ་བང་རྩལ་འགྲན་བསྡུར་ (gāggɛɛ paŋdzɛɛ drendur) obstacle race; steeplechase va.—བྱེད.

བཀག་རྒལ་བང་རྩེད་ (gāggɛɛ paŋdzɛɛ) sm. བཀག་རྒལ་བང་རྩལ་འགྲན་བསྡུར་.

བཀག་རྒོལ་ (gāggöö) an attack to block an enemy force; va.—བྱེད་.

བཀག་རྒྱ་ (gāggya) ban, prohibition, proscription, restriction; va.—གློད་ to remove a ban/ prohibition/ proscription/ restriction.

བཀག་རྒྱ་དང་འགལ་ (gāggya taŋ gɛɛ) vi. to break or violate a prohibition/ ban/ restriction.

བཀག་རྒྱའི་བཀའ་ (gāggyɛ gā) an order prohibiting/ restraining/ banning sth.

བཀག་རྒྱའི་དངོས་རྫས་ (gāggyɛ ŋöödzɛɛ̀) contraband goods, banned/ prohibited materials.

བཀག་རྒྱའི་ས་ཁུལ་ (gāggyɛ sōgüü) an area that is restricted or prohibited.

བཀག་བརྒལ་ (gāggyɛ) sm. བཀག་རྒལ་.

བཀག་སྒོ་ (gāggo) 1. sluice gate. 2. valve ། བཀག་སྒོ་བཟོ་གྲྭ་ Valve factory.

བཀག་སྐོར་ (gāggɔr) hindering, blocking, impeding, retarding; va.—རྒྱག.

བཀག་དངོས་ (gāŋŋöö) abbr. བཀག་རྒྱའི་དངོས་རྫས་.

བཀག་བཅོམ་ (gāgjom) stealing by blocking/ cutting off (e.g., setting up a roadblock and then robbing people); va.—རྒྱག.

བཀག་ཆ་ (gāgja) obstacle, barrier, prohibition, ban, restriction; va.—བྱེད་.

བཀག་ཉར་ (gāgñar) sm. བཀག་བསྐྱིལ་.

བཀག་ཉར་བཟང་བཙོན་ (gāgñar saŋdzön) a type of detention similar to house arrest.

བཀག་ཉར་ཧམ་ཚོང་ (gāgñar hāmdzoŋ) financial speculation, hoarding for later sale, profiteering; va.—རྒྱག.

བཀག་གདོང་ (gāgdoŋ) closing and opening (e.g., a faucet).

བཀག་གདོང་མཆུ་ཏོ་ (gāgdoŋ cūdo) a faucet/ tap.

བཀག་གདོང་མེ་ཤུགས་འཕུར་མདའ་ (gāgdoŋ meshug phūnda) retro-rocket.

བཀག་འདོམས་ (gāgdom) prohibition, ban, restriction; va.—བྱེད་ to prohibit/ ban/ restrict; va.—གློད་ to lift a prohibition/ ban/ restriction ། དེང་སང་བོད་ལ་མ་ཇང་བཀག་འདོམས་བྱེད་ཀྱི་མེད་པ་རེད་ These days they are not banning mahjong in Tibet.

བཀག་རྡོ་ (gāgdo) an obstacle, stumbling block ། སྤྱི་ཚོགས་རིང་ལུགས་གཞུང་ལམ་ཐོག་གི་བཀག་རྡོ་ཚང་མ་མེད་པ་བཟོས་པ་རེད་ All the stumbling blocks on the path to socialism have been eliminated. [Lit. a stone that is an obstacle].

བཀག་སྡོམ་ (gāgdom) sm. བཀག་འདོམས་.

བཀག་སྡོམ་དངོས་རྫས་ (gāgdom ŋöödzɛɛ̀) contraband goods, banned/ prohibited/ illegal materials.

བཀག་སྡོམ་ཉེས་གཅོད་ (gādom ñēèjöö) sm. བཀག་སྡོམ་ཉེས་ཆད་.

བཀག་སྡོམ་ཉེས་ཆད་ (gādom ñēèjɛɛ̀) a punishment that bans sb. from doing sth. or restricts their movement; va.—གཏོང་ ། ལས་མི་རུ་ཁག་གི་མི་ཁ་ཤས་ལ་གཟའ་ཉི་མར་ཕྱིར་འགྲོ་མི་ཚོག་པའི་བཀག་སྡོམ་ཉེས་ཆད་བཏང་འདུག Some people in the labor camp were punished by not being allowed to go outside on Sunday.

བཀག་སྡོམ་དང་འགལ་ (gāgdom taŋ gɛɛ) violating or breaking a ban/ prohibition/ restriction.

བཀག་སྡོམ་ས་ཁུལ་ (gādom sōgüü) a restricted/ prohibited area.

བཀག་སྡོམ་ས་མཚམས་ (gāgdom sāndzam) a blockade line.

བཀག་བསྡོམས་ (gāgdom) sm. བཀག་སྡོམ་.

བཀག་བྱ་ཐོགས་ལྷུང་མེད་པ་ (gāgja cōglhuŋ mēèba) shung. a ban/ restriction/ prohibition that is implemented fairly and impartially.

བཀག་མེད་འཕྲལ་གཏོང་ (gāgmeè trɛɛ̄doŋ) shung. va. to perform a corvee tax immediately without delays ། ལམ་ཐོག་ཉེ་ཁུལ་རྣམས་བཀག་མེད་འཕྲལ་གཏོང་དགོས་རྒྱུ་ All those who are along the route must do the corvee tax immediately without causing delays.

བཀག་བཙིར་ (gāgdzir) controlling, suppressing, disciplining; va.—བྱེད་.

བཀག་རྩྭ་ (gāgdza) shung. a pasture set aside for hay making (i.e., animals are banned from grazing on the pasture before the hay is cut) ། བཀག་རྩྭར་ར་ལུག་བཏང་བྱུང་ཞེ་སྐོར་ Regarding the reports saying that sheep and goats had grazed on the pasture that was banned from animals.

བཀག་ཡིག (gāgyig) sm. སྒོ་ཐིལ་.

བཀག་ཤིང་ (gāgshiŋ) 1. a stick used to block sth.; va.—བརྒལ་; —འགོམ་ to overcome, to go through or over a barrier. 2. hurdles in racing events; va.—བརྒལ་ to jump over hurdles (in a race).

བཀག་བཤེར་ (gāgsher) stopping and inspecting/ checking; va.—བྱེད་.

བཀག་བཤེར་དམ་བསྒྲགས་ (gāgsher damdraà) stopping and inspecting/ checking (e.g., at a border checkpost).

བཀག་ས་ (gāgsa) sm. བཀག་སྡོམ་ས་ཁུལ་.

བཀང་ (gāŋ) p. of འགེངས་.

བཀང་འཇུག (gāŋjuù) sm. བཀར་འཇུག.

བཀད་ (gɛɛ̀) p. of འགད་.

བཀད་དང་པོ་ (gɛɛ̀ taŋbo) for the first time.

བཀད་ས་ (gɛɛ̄sa) 1. kitchen. 2. a meeting/ gathering place.

བཀན་ (gēn.) va. 1. to push against, to lean against, to get leverage against ། རྐང་པ་རྡོ་ལ་བཀན་ནས་ཐག་པ་འཐེན་གྱི་འདུག Pushing against the rock with his foot (for leverage), (he) is pulling on the rope. 2. va. to brace oneself, to hold onto sth. ། རྒན་ཁོག་དེས་ལག་པ་རྩིག་པར་བཀན་ནས་ཡར་ལངས་སོང་ That old person braced himself against the wall and rose up. 3. va. to not accept ། ལས་འགན་འདི་བཀན་ན་འོས་པོ་མི་འདུག It is inappropriate if you don't accept this responsibility.

བཀན་གཟོང་ཀ་མ་ (gēnsoŋ kama) a blacksmith's hammer.

བཀན་ཤར་ (gēnshar) sm. བཀན་གཟོང་ཀ་མ་.

བཀན་ཤིང་ (gēnshiŋ) a stick used to hold up/ prop up/ brace up sth.

བཀབ་ (gōb) p. of འགེབས་.

བཀབ་བཀབ་སྦུབ་སྦུབ་ (gōbgōb sūbsub) hiding/ concealing sth.; va.—བྱེད་ ། ཚོང་ཁྲལ་སྦྱད་མཁན་ཡོང་

སྐབས་ཚོང་པ་དེས་ཁེ་བཟང་བཀབ་བཀབ་སྦས་སྦས་བྱས་པ་རེད་ When the tax collector came, the trader concealed his profits.

བཀབ་བདེགས་མ་ཁྱབ་པ་མེད་པ་ (gābdeg məkyəbə meèba) shung. boundless benevolence ¶ གནམ་ས་ཆེ་བ་བཀབ་བདེགས་མ་ཁྱབ་པ་མེད་ཅིང་བར་ནང་ཡོད་པའི་དངོས་པོ་སྣ་ཚོགས་བདེ་བ་ All things in the universe owe their well being to the boundless benevolence of heaven and earth.

བཀབ་སྦྱར་ (gābjar) hind. a hinge.

བཀའ་ (gā) 1. an order, command (h.); va.—གཏོང་; —འབེབས་; —བབས་; —གནང་ to order, to give a command ¶ འདི་ནི་གུང་ཁྲན་ཏང་གི་བཀའ་རེད་ This is an order from the communist party. ¶ ནག་ཅན་དེ་འཛིན་བཟུང་བྱེད་རྒྱུ་བཀའ་ཕབ་སོང་ (They) issued orders to arrest the criminal. 2. direct teachings of the Buddha. 3. va.—གནང་ to say, to tell (h.) ¶ དེ་འདྲ་བྱེད་རྒྱུའི་འཆར་གཞི་མེད་ཅེས་བཀའ་གནང་སོང་ (He) said, "We have no plans to do such things." 4. shung. abbr. for བཀའ་བློན་ and བཀའ་ཤག ¶ བཀའ་མདའ་ Council Minister and General.

བཀའ་བཀོད་ (gāgöö) 1. an order, command, direction, instruction; va. བཀའ་བཀོད་; —བྱེད་; —གཏོང་ to order, command, direct, instruct; va.—ཉན་ to obey an order ¶ གཞུང་གི་ཐད་ཀའི་བཀའ་བཀོད་འོག Under the direct order of the government.

བཀའ་བཀོད་ཁང་ (gāgöögaŋ) headquarters, command center.

བཀའ་བཀོད་ཉན་ (gāgöö ñɛ̄n) see བཀའ་བཀོད་.

བཀའ་བཀོད་པུའུ་ (gāgöö bū) tib.ch. sm. བཀག་བཀོད་ཁང་.

བཀའ་བསྐྱོན་ (gābgyön) scolding, reprimanding (h.); va. བཀའ་བསྐྱོན་; —གནང་; —གསུང་. to scold, to reprimand (h.); vi.—ཐོབ; —འཁེལ་ to get scolded, to be reprimanded ¶ དགེ་རྒན་གྱིས་སློབ་ཕྲུག་བར་ཉིན་ལྟར་བཀའ་བསྐྱོན་གནང་གི་ཡོད་པ་རེད་ The teacher scolds the students every day. ¶ སློབ་སྦྱོང་ཡག་པོ་མ་བྱས་ན་དགེ་རྒན་གྱིས་བཀའ་བསྐྱོན་ཐོག་གི་རེད་ If you do not study well, you will receive a scolding from the teacher.

བཀའ་བཀྲམ་ (gā drām) va. to circulate/ distribute an order.

བཀའ་བསྒྲོལ་ (gādröö) p. of བཀའ་འགྲོལ་.

བཀའ་སྐུལ་ (gā gǖü) va. to appeal for sth. (h.).

བཀའ་སྐོར་ (gāgɔɔ) shung. asking the appropriate higher authorities (h.); va.—བྱེད་; —ཞུ་ ¶ གོང་རིམ་ལ་བཀའ་སྐོར་མེད་པར་གང་སྙིང་བྱེད་མི་ཆོག Without asking the appropriate superior authorities, one is not allowed to do whatever one wants.

བཀའ་ཁོན་ (gāgön) hatred.

བཀའ་ཁོལ་ (gāgöö) sm. བཀའ་འཁོལ་.

བཀའ་ཁྱབ་ (gəgyəp) shung. a general order/ edict/ proclamation (h.); va.—གནང་; —མཛད་ ¶ གནད་དོན་འདི་སྐོར་གཞུང་ནས་བཀའ་ཁྱབ་མཛད་ཤག་ལ་ I am sure the government will give an order regarding this issue.

བཀའ་ཁྱབ་ཞིབ་གསལ་ (gəgyəp shipsɛɛ) shung. an explicit or formal order/ edict/ proclamation/ decree.

བཀའ་ཁྲ་ (gādra) shung. verdict ¶ བླ་དཔོན་གོང་མས་བཀའ་ཁྲ་ཕེབས་བཞིན་པར་ད་ཆ་སྐལ་ཐོབ་སྤྲོད་ལེན་མ་བདེ་ཞིང་ Since the superiors are in the process of issuing a verdict, it is not appropriate for us to give and accept the dowry.

བཀའ་ཁྲ་གཏན་ཚིགས་ (gādra dēndzii) shung. land tenure document.

བཀའ་ཁྲིད་ (gādrii) lecturing, teaching, instructing; va.—གནང་ to lecture/ teach/ instruct; va.—ཞུ་ to ask for advice.

བཀའ་ཁྲིམས་ (gādrim) a law, an edict (h.); va.—གནང་; —གཏོང་ to issue a law/ edict; to prosecute, to bring before the law; vi.—འགལ་ to break the law.

བཀའ་ཁྲིམས་སྐེ་ཐོག་ཏུ་གཏོང་ (gādrim gētɔgdu dōŋ) shung. 1. va. to execute, to behead ¶ གལ་སྲིད་གོང་དོན་དང་འགལ་ཆར་འགྲོ་རིགས་ཤར་ཚེ་བཀའ་ཁྲིམས་སྐེ་ཐོག་ཏུ་གཏོང་རྒྱུ་ Whoever violates the things mentioned above will be executed. 2. va. to punish in accordance with the law.

བཀའ་ཁྲིམས་ཉི་མ་གུང་འཆར་ (gādrim ñimə kuŋjar) shung. the law (that is like a sun shining in the midst of the sky) ¶ བཀའ་ཁྲིམས་ཉི་མ་གུང་འཆར་ཞུགས་རྗེ་ཆེ་བ་ (We) request (the goverment) to issue a law that is like a sun shining in the midst of the sky.

བཀའ་ཁྲིམས་གདུགས་དཀར་བཙན་པོ་ (gādrim duggar dzēmbo) shung. the law (that is like a white umbrella) ¶ གནམ་བསྐོས་གོང་མའི་བཀའ་ཁྲིམས་གདུགས་དཀར་བཙན་པོས་བསིལ་ལྡན་གྱི་ལྗོངས་འདིར་ཁྱབ་དེ་ The law of the Emperor who reigns by the mandate of Heaven, that is like a white umbrella covering all over Tibet.

བཀའ་ཁྲིམས་བརྡལ་བཤིག (gādrim dɛɛshig) shung. breaking/ violating the law; va.—བྱེད་ ¶ བཀའ་ཁྲིམས་བརྡལ་བཤིག་བྱེད་མཁན་རེ་ཟུང་ལ་ཆད་པ་གཅོད་དགོས་ Those few who violate the law should be punished.

བཀའ་ཁྲིམས་ཚོད་ལོང་ (gādrim tsöölɔŋ) shung. sm. ཁྲིམས་ས་ཚོད་ལོན་.

བཀའ་ཁྲིམས་ཚོད་ལོན་ (gādrim tsöölön) shung. disregarding the law (conveys that sb. doesn't care about the law since he knows what the punishment will be and isn't afraid of it) ¶ བཀའ་ཁྲིམས་ཚོད་ལོན་གྱི་བྱ་སྤྱོད་དེ་རིགས་འཕྲལ་དུ་མཚམས་འཛུག་བྱ་དགོས་ You must immediately stop all acts which disregard the law.

བཀའ་ཁྲིམས་གསེར་གྱི་གཉའ་ཤིང་ (gədrim sērgi ñāshing) shung. the law (that is like a golden yoke).

བཀའ་གྲོལ་ཞུ་སྒྲུབ་ཚོགས་ཆུང་ (gədröö shudröö tsōgjuŋ) Committee on Authorization.

བཀའ་འཁོར་ (gākɔɔ) 1. servant. 2. sm. བཀའ་. 3. shung. vi. to receive an answer from a superior ¶ གནད་དོན་འདིའི་སྐོར་ད་ལྟ་གོང་རིམ་གྱི་བཀའ་འཁོར་མ་བྱུང་ Regarding this matter, (I) didn't receive any answer from the superiors (those above).

བཀའ་འཁོལ་ (gāgöö) 1. sb. who accepts an order, a servant. 2. an important order.

བཀའ་འཁྲིའི་འབབ་འབུལ་ (gədrii bambüü) shung. punishment/ payment for violating a legal verdict ¶ ཁྲ་དོན་ལས་འགལ་ཆར་འགྲོ་རིགས་སྤུ་ཙམ་ཞུས་སྲིད་ཚེ་ཁྲིམས་ཞབས་རིན་པོ་ཆེའི་མདུན་སར་བཀའ་འཁྲིའི་འབབ་འབུལ་གཙང་སྤྲུ་ཐོག Anyone who violates the verdict in the slightest should go before the judge and pay a fine.

བཀའ་འགྲོལ་ (gādröö) shung. permission, approval, consent (h.); vi. བཀའ་འགྲོལ་; —ཐོབ་; —བྱུང་ to get permission, approval, consent; va.—སྤྲོད་; —གནང་ to give permission/ consent/ approval ¶ ཁོས་དེ་བྱེད་ཆོག་པའི་བཀའ་འགྲོལ་ཐོབ་པ་རེད་ (He) got permission to do that. ¶ ཁོང་ལ་ཚོང་རྒྱག་ཆོག་པའི་བཀའ་འགྲོལ་སྤྲད་པ་ཡིན་ (I) gave him permission to do trading. ¶ ཁོང་གིས་ཚོང་རྒྱག་ཆོག་པའི་བཀའ་འགྲོལ་གནང་བྱུང་ He gave me permission to trade.

བཀའ་གུང་ (gākuŋ) shung. abbr. བཀའ་བློན་ and གུང་ (a rank in tt.) ¶ བཀའ་གུང་ཕུན་ཁང་ Punkang, the Council Minister and Gung.

བཀའ་གུང་བློན་ (gā gunlön) shung. 1. name of the office of Council of Ministers established in 1720-21. 2. council ministers ¶ དཔལ་ལྡན་ས་སྐྱོང་མི་དབང་བཀའ་དགུང་བློན་ In the presence of the glorious, powerful Council Ministers.

བཀའ་གྱེན་ལོག་ཞུ་ (gā gyenlɔg shu) shung. va. to reject/ oppose/ struggle against orders from above.

བཀའ་གྲོལ་ (gādröö) shung. sm. བཀའ་འགྲོལ་.

བཀའ་གྲོས་ (gādröö) 1. discussion, talk, conference (h.); va.—གནང་ to discuss, to hold a conference/ talk; —ཞུ་; —འདྲི་ to ask for, to request ¶ གནད་དོན་འདི་སྐོར་འབྲེལ་ཡོད་ལས་ཁངས་ལ་བཀའ་གྲོས་ཞུས་

ཡོད་ I have discussed this matter with the related offices. 2. arc. to offer suggestions/ ideas to the king or ruler.

བཀའ་གྲོས་ཆེན་པོ་དྲུག (gādröö cēmbo truù) the six great consultations (of King Songtsen Gambo about the governing of the country).

བཀའ་གྲོས་གསུང་གླིང་ (gādröö) sm. བཀའ་གྲོས་.

བཀའ་གླེགས་ (gāleg) 1. a letter, correspondence. 2. a religious text/ book.

བཀའ་དགོངས་ (gāgoŋ) shung. an order ¶ གོང་ས་མཆོག་གི་བཀའ་དགོངས་བཞིན་ In accordance with the order of the Dalai Lama.

བཀའ་དགོངས་འགལ་རིགས་ (gāgoŋ g̲ɛɛrig) shung. anything that violates an order ¶ གལ་སྲིད་བཀའ་དགོངས་འགལ་རིགས་གླིང་ངན་སྦྲང་སྒྲ་ཙམ་ཞུས་རིགས་ཤར་ཚེ་ If there is the slightest violation of the order.

བཀའ་དགོན་ (gāgön) shung. abbr. a monastery of the Kagyu sect.

བཀའ་བགྲོས་ (gādröö) sm. བཀའ་གྲོས་.

བཀའ་མགྲོན་ (gāndrön) shung. an aide in the office of the Kashag.

བཀའ་འགག (gā ga̲à) shung. abbr. of བཀའ་ཤག་འགག.

བཀའ་འགུགས་ (gəguù) shung. a summoning order; va. བཀའ་འགུགས་; —བྱེད་; —གནང་ ¶ ལས་ཁུངས་ནས་བཀའ་འགུགས་གནང་བར་ཕྱིན་ རང་མི་བཅར་བ་གང་རེད་ Why didn't you come when the office summoned you?

བཀའ་འགོ་ (gāŋgo) abbr. of བཀའ་ཤག་འགོ་མཆན་.

བཀའ་འགོ་དམ་དམར་ (gāŋgo ta̲mmar) shung. decision or order by the Dalai Lama or the Regent written on the top of a document/ report/ petition submitted to him through the Kashag (includes the red seal used by these two only).

བཀའ་འགྱངས་ (gāŋgyaŋ) a delay, a postponement (h.); va.—གནང་ to (give permission) to delay/ postpone sth.; va.—ཞུ་ to ask for a delay/ postponement ¶ ཁོང་གིས་ངའི་བུ་ལོན་བཀའ་འགྱངས་གནང་བ་རེད་ He postponed (the payment of) my debt.

བཀའ་འགྱུར་ (gāngyur) Kanjur (the canonical texts consisting of the teachings and precepts of the Buddha).

བཀའ་འགྱུར་ལ་ཤོག་ལྷན་ (gāngyurla shōglhɛn) an unnecessary correction/ addition [Lit. a patch on the Kanjur].

བཀའ་འགྱུར་ (gā gyu̲r) sm.* བཀའ་སྒྱུར་.

བཀའ་འགྲེལ་ (gāndree) commentary on the Buddha's teaching (usu. refers to written commentaries); va.—རྒྱག.

བཀའ་འགྲོལ་ (gāndröö) sm. བཀའ་འགྲེལ་.

བཀའ་འགྲོས་ཆེན་མོ་དྲུག (gādröö cēmmo tru̲ù) the six great political programs laid down by king Songtsen Gampo.

བཀའ་རྒྱ་ (gāgya) shung. a government edict/ order; va.—འགྲེམ་; —གཏོང་ to proclaim/ issue an edict or order.

བཀའ་རྒྱ་གནང་རྟེན་ (gāgya nāŋden) shung. a government edict and gift ¶ ད་ལམ་བཀའ་རྒྱ་གནང་རྟེན་དང་བཅས་ཉམས་མེད་སྤྱི་སོན་ཕྱུང་དོན་ Concerning the government edict and gift I recieved this time.

བཀའ་རྒྱ་མ་ (gāgya̲ma) shung. a confidential/ secret document (usu. affixed with a seal) ¶ རྩེ་ཡིག་ཚང་དུ་ཡིག་རིགས་བཀའ་རྒྱ་མ་ཁག་ཅིག་ཡོད་པ་རེད་ There are some sealed documents in the Yigtsang Office in the Potala Palace.

བཀའ་རྒྱ་རིན་པོ་ཆེ་ (gāgya ri̲mboje) shung. the precious order (refers to an order issued by the Kashag) ¶ ད་ལམ་བཀའ་རྒྱ་རིན་པོ་ཆེའི་ཕྱི་ཞིབས་དགོངས་དོན་ As for the content of the precious order of the Kashag that we have received (this is usu. followed by the writer's response).

བཀའ་སྒུག (gāguù) shung. va. to wait for an order ¶ གོང་གི་བཀའ་སྒུག་ནས་དམག་རྒྱག་དགོས་ (You) have to wait for the order from above to go to war.

བཀའ་སྒོ་: p. **བཀའ་བསྒོས་**; f. **བཀའ་བསྒོ་**; imp. **བཀའ་སྒོས་** (gāgo) shung. 1. va. to order, to command ¶ དམག་མི་ཚོ་མདུན་ཚང་བྱེད་རྒྱུ་བཀའ་བསྒོས་པ་རེད་ (They) ordered the soldiers to advance.

བཀའ་སྒོས་ (gā gö̲ö) imp. of བཀའ་བསྒོ་.

བཀའ་སྒྱུར་ (gəgyur) shung. 1. the transmission of an order of a superior such as the Dalai Lama, Panchen Lama, Regent or the Kashag (informing sb. of their decision); va. བཀའ་སྒྱུར་; va.—གནང་ to pass down such an order ¶ མགྲོན་གཉེར་ཆེན་མོས་ལས་ཚན་བསྐོ་གཞག་སྐོར་གྱི་བཀའ་སྒྱུར་གནང་བ་རེད་ The Lord Chamberlain passed down the order (of the Dalai Lama) concerning the appointment of officials. 2. scolding; va.—གཏོང་ ¶ དགེ་རྒན་གྱིས་སློབ་ཕྲུག་ལ་བཀའ་སྒྱུར་བཏང་བ་རེད་ The teacher scolded the students. 3. direct giving of an order/ instructions ¶ བཀའ་བློན་ཁྲི་པས་བློན་ལམ་གྱི་ཞལ་ངོར་བཀའ་སྒྱུར་བཏང་བ་རེད་ The senior Minister gave instructions to the བློན་ལམ་ཞལ་ངོ་.

བཀའ་སྒྱུར་དཔོན་ (gōgyurbön) shung. the official who passes down the orders of a superior.

བཀའ་སྒྲུབ་ (gədrub) following or carrying out orders; va. བཀའ་སྒྲུབ་; —བྱེད་; —གནང་; —ཞུ་ to follow or carry out orders ¶ ལས་ཁུངས་ཀྱི་འགོ་ཁྲིད་ཚོའི་བཀའ་སྒྲུབ་དགོས་པ་རེད་ (We) must carry out the order of the office leaders.

བཀའ་སྒྲུབས་ (gā dru̲b) imp. of བཀའ་སྒྲུབ་.

བཀའ་སྒྲོག (gādrɔɔ) shung. announcing/ proclaiming an order; va. བཀའ་སྒྲོག; —བྱེད་ to announce or proclaim an order ¶ ལས་ཁུངས་ཀྱི་བཀའ་སྒྲོག་དགོས་པ་རེད་ (We) must announce the office's order.

བཀའ་སྒྲོགས་ (gā drɔɔ) imp. of བཀའ་སྒྲོག.

བཀའ་བརྒྱུད་ (gəgyüü) 1. oral transmission. 2. sm. བཀའ་བརྒྱུད་པ་.

བཀའ་བརྒྱུད་པ་ (gəgyübə) 1. the Kagyu sect. 2. a follower of the Kagyu sect.

བཀའ་བསྒོ་ (gā g̲o) 1. f. of བཀའ་སྒོ་. 2. an order/ command by a lama exorcising a ghost, demon, etc. va.; —བྱེད་; —གནང་ ¶ བླ་མས་ནད་པར་བཀའ་བསྒོ་གནང་བ་རེད་ The lama exorcised the demon from the sick person. 3. sm. བཀའ་སྒོ་.

བཀའ་བསྒོས་ (gā gö̲ö) p. of བཀའ་སྒོ་.

བཀའ་བསྒྱུར་ (gəgyuu) sm. བཀའ་སྒྱུར་.

བཀའ་བསྒྲག (gā dra̲à) f. of བཀའ་སྒྲོག.

བཀའ་བསྒྲགས་ (gā dra̲à) p. of བཀའ་སྒྲོག.

བཀའ་བསྒྲུབ་ (gā dru̲b) f. of བཀའ་སྒྲུབ་.

བཀའ་བསྒྲུབས་ (gā dru̲b) p. of བཀའ་སྒྲུབ་.

བཀའ་ངོ་མ་ལོག (gā ŋ̲oma dɔɔ) h. of ངོ་མ་ལོག.

བཀའ་མངགས་ (gāŋaà) placing an order for sth., reserving sth. (h.); va.—གནང་; —ཞུ་ ¶ ཁོང་གིས་ཚོང་ཁང་དེ་ནས་ན་བཟའ་ཞིག་བཀའ་མངགས་གནང་སོང་ He ordered clothing from that shop. ¶ ཁོང་གིས་ང་ལ་འདི་བཟོ་དགོས་པའི་བཀའ་མངགས་གནང་བྱུང་ He placed an order with me to make this.

བཀའ་གཅོག (gā jöò) va. to disobey or go against an order/ teaching, to break an order ¶ ཁོས་བླ་མའི་བཀའ་བཅག་པ་རེད་ He didn't follow the order of the (his) lama.

བཀའ་བཅག (gā jāà) p. of. བཀའ་གཅོག.

བཀའ་བཅད་ (gājɛɛ̀) sm. བཀའ་དཔྱད་.

བཀའ་བཅོས་ (gājöö) correcting, editing (h.); va.—ཞུ་ to ask/ submit for corrections; va.—སྙན་; —གནང་ to edit, to correct.

བཀའ་ཆག (gācaà) shung. an exemption/ reduction from a tax.

བཀའ་ཆད་ (gācɛɛ̀) shung. fine, punishment, penalty; va.—གནང་.

བཀའ་ཆེན་ (gājen) a monastic degree (awarded at Tashilhunpo monastery).

བཀའ་ཆེམས་ (gājem) h. of ཁ་ཆེམས་.

བཀའ་ཆོས་ (gājöö) a sermon, a religious teaching (h.); va.—གནང་.

བཀའ་མཆན་ (gājɛn) shung. a notational comment/ footnote in a book or on a document.

བཀའ་མཆིད་ (gājii) sm. བཀའ་མོལ་.

བཀའ་ཉན་ (gā ñɛn) 1. va. to listen to an order/ instructions ¶ཁ་པར་ཐོག་ནས་འགོ་ཁྲིད་ཀྱི་བཀའ་ཉན་པ་རེད་ (He) listened to the boss's order over the phone. 2. shung. an obedient servant/ subject (one who listens to the orders) ¶བཀའ་ཉན་གྱི་འབངས་འཁོར་རྣམས་ལ་བཀའ་བསྒོ་བ་ To give orders to obedient subjects. ¶བཀའ་ཉན་གྱི་སྲུང་མར་འཕྲིན་བཅོལ་ཞུ་བ་ To ask protection from protective deities who fulfill one's requests.

བཀའ་ཉེས་ (gāñeè) shung. judicial punishment (h.); va.—གཏོང་གནང་; —གནང་ to punish; vi.—གཟེད་ to receive punishment.

བཀའ་ཉེས་ཡན་པོར་མ་སོང་བ་ (gāñeè yɛmbor masoŋwa) shung. punishing severely without mercy, punishing mercilessly ¶མི་ངན་ཡུལ་གྱི་གཤེད་མར་བཀའ་ཉེས་ཡན་པོར་མ་སོང་བ་ཅི་ནས་ཡོང་བ་ (We) request (the government) to punish severely those malevolent persons.

བཀའ་གཉན་པོ་ (gā ñɛmbo) 1. fierce, strict, vindictive ¶སྲུང་མ་འདི་བཀའ་གཉན་པོ་ཡིན་པས་གཟབ་གཟབ་བྱེད་དགོས་ Because that protective deity is fierce, you should be careful (not to do sth. that will irritate him). ¶རྒྱལ་པོ་དེ་བཀའ་གཉན་པོ་ཡིན་ཙང་བཀའ་གསུང་ཅི་སྒྲུབ་ཞུ་དགོས་པ་རེད་ Because the king is very strict, one has to obey what he says. 2. short-tempered, quick to get angry.

བཀའ་གཉན་བཙན་པོ་ (gāñɛn dzɛ̄mbo) sm. བཀའ་གཉན་པོ་.

བཀའ་ཏར་ (gātar) ch. telegram.

བཀའ་གཏན་ (gādɛn) shung. a land tenure/ land ownership document.

བཀའ་གཏན་ཚིགས་ (gādra dēndzii) sm. བཀའ་གཏན་.

བཀའ་གཏན་ལག་འཁྱེར་ (gādɛn laggyee) credentials (for government officials); va.—འབུལ་ to present one's credentials.

བཀའ་གཏོགས་ (gā dōg) 1. va. to obey orders. 2. a protective deity. 3. shung. a subject ¶བཀའ་གཏོགས་རྣམས་ལ་ To all my subjects.

བཀའ་གཏོགས་པ་ (gādogba) a subject ¶བཀའ་གཏོགས་པ་རྣམས་དགེ་བཅུའི་ཁྲིམས་ཀྱིས་བསྐྱངས་པ་རེད་ The subjects were governed according to the ten virtuous laws.

བཀའ་གཏོང་ (gā dōŋ) shung. va. to issue a decree/ order ¶དམག་མི་རྣམས་འཕྲལ་དུ་ཐོན་དགོས་པའི་བཀའ་བཏང་བ་རེད་ (He) ordered that the soldiers leave immediately.

བཀའ་བཏགས་ (gā dāà) shung. to declare/ proclaim an order ¶རྒྱལ་ཁམས་ཁྱོན་དུ་དམག་སྐུལ་གྱི་བཀའ་བཏགས་པ་རེད་ An order for recruiting soldiers was declared all over the country.

བཀའ་རྟགས་ (gādaà) shung. 1. a seal. 2. a document that has the seal of the government affixed.

བཀའ་རྟེན་ (gāden) shung. a gift.

བཀའ་ལྟར་ (gādar) according to an order.

བཀའ་བསྟན་ (gādɛn) abbr. of བཀའ་འགྱུར་ and བསྟན་འགྱུར་.

བཀའ་བསྟན་འགྱུར་ (gā dɛ̄ngyur) abbr. of བཀའ་འགྱུར་ and བསྟན་འགྱུར་.

བཀའ་བསྟན་ལྷ་ཁང་ (gādɛn lhāgan) a temple containing the main Tibetan religious texts—the Kangyur and Tengyur.

བཀའ་བསྟུན་ (gā dũn) shung. adherence/ adhering to an order; va.—ཞུ་ to adhere to an order ¶བླ་བྲང་ནས་ཞུ་སྔོའི་སྒོར་སྟར་རྒྱུན་བཞིན་ཞེས་ཕེབས་གཤིས་བཀའ་བསྟུན་ཞུ་མ་ཐུབ་པ་ Because the Labrang said that we should continue doing as before, therefore we were not able to adhere to the order.

བཀའ་ཐང་ (gādaŋ) biography, testament, the writings of a deceased author.

བཀའ་ཐམ་ (gādam) 1. a seal; va.—ཕབ་; —རྒྱག to affix a seal. 2. shung. the seal of the Kashag ¶ལམ་ཡིག་བཀའ་ཐམ་འབྱར་མ་མིག་སྟོན་བྱུང་དོན་ He showed me the travel document which has the Kashag's seal (that gives permission to receive corvee services when traveling).

བཀའ་ཐམ་ཞུ་འབེབས་ (gādam shumbeb) shung. requesting a Kashag document/ decision (with its seal affixed).

བཀའ་ཐོ་ (gādo) shung. a decision/ settlement ¶གོང་མའི་བཀའ་ཐོ་ཡིས་བཙད་པའི་འཚོ་ཐེབས་ཀྱི་ཡོང་སྒོ་ Income from the trust which was created by the Emperor's decision.

བཀའ་ཐོག་གོད་བཞིན་འབེབ་ (gādɔ̀ɔ gööshin beb) va. to give a very shocking order.

བཀའ་ཐོབ་ (gā tōb) vi. to receive orders, to be or get briefed about orders/ instructions.

བཀའ་རྟགས་མདའ་མོ་ (gādaà damo) shung. an arrow that symbolizes an order from above.

བཀའ་དམ་ (gādam) shung. sm. བཀའ་ཐམ་.

བཀའ་དར་ (gādar) a banner on which an order is written.

བཀའ་དོན་ (gādön) shung. the instructions/ content of an order or edict ¶ཁོང་གི་བཀའ་དོན་བཞིན་ According to the content of his order.

བཀའ་དོན་ཐོད་བཅིངས་ (gādön tööjiŋ) shung. sm. བཀའ་གསུང་ཅི་སྒྲུབ་.

བཀའ་དྲང་གསུང་དག (gādraŋ sūŋdag) orders that are good/ just/ correct.

བཀའ་དྲི་ (gəndri) sm. བཀའ་འདྲི་.

བཀའ་དྲིན་ (gədrin) gratitude; va.—གསོབ་ to repay kindness, to show gratitude ¶ཕ་མའི་བཀའ་དྲིན་གསོབ་དགོས་ One must repay the kindness of one's parents.

བཀའ་དྲིན་བསྐྱངས་སུ་འཇུག (gədrin gyāŋsu juù) shung. va. to make people grateful (by good acts) ¶ཆབ་འབངས་རྣམས་ལ་བཀའ་དྲིན་བསྐྱངས་སུ་འཇུག་པའི་མཛད་འཕྲིན་མཐའ་ཡས་པ་ To carry out acts so that (the people) will be grateful.

བཀའ་དྲིན་ཅན་ (gədrinjen) grateful, gratitude ¶ཕ་མ་བཀའ་དྲིན་ཅན་གྱི་ཞབས་ཕྱི་ཞུ་དགོས་ One must serve one's parents to whom one is grateful.

བཀའ་དྲིན་ཆེ་ (gədrin cē) 1. thanks, thank you. 2. (vb. + —) conveys thanks or being grateful for a verbal action ¶རིན་པོ་ཆེ་ང་ཚོའི་སྡོད་གནས་སུ་ཆིབས་བསྒྱུར་བཀའ་དྲིན་ཆེ་སོང་ We were grateful to Rimpoche for coming to our home. 3. va.—ཞུ་ va. to convey thanks, to express gratitude ¶ཁྱེད་ཚོ་ཚང་མར་བཀའ་དྲིན་ཆེ་ཞུ་གི་ཡོད་ (I) thank you all.

བཀའ་དྲིན་ཆེན་པོ་ (gədrin cēmbo) gratitude, thanks, appreciation ¶ཁྱེད་རང་ང་ལ་བཀྲིན་ཆེན་པོ་ཡིན་ I am grateful to you.

བཀའ་དྲིན་རྗེས་དྲན་ (gədrin jedrɛn) remembering or commemorating sb.'s kindness; va.—ཞུ་ to remember/ commemorate a kindness, to be grateful ¶ང་ཚོའི་རྒན་ལགས་ཀྱི་བཀའ་དྲིན་རྗེས་དྲན་དུ་ In remembrance of the kindness of our teacher ¶ཕ་མའི་བཀའ་དྲིན་རྗེས་དྲན་ཞུ་གི་ཡིན་ I will remember the kindness of my parents.

བཀའ་དྲིན་སྙིང་བཅངས་ (gədrin ñīŋjaŋ) holding gratitude in one's heart for sb.'s kindness, holding sb.'s kindness in one's heart; va.—བྱེད; —ཞུ་.

བཀའ་དྲིན་དྲན་ (gədrin trɛn) vi. to remember/ keep in mind a kindness or favor ¶ཕ་མའི་བཀའ་དྲིན་དྲན་ནས་སློབ་སྦྱོང་ཧུར་བརྩོན་བྱེད་ཀྱི་ཡིན་ Keeping in mind the kindness of my parents, I will study hard.

བཀའ་དྲིན་བླ་ན་མ་མཆིས་པ་ (gədrin lāna maciba) shung. sm. བཀའ་དྲིན་མཚུངས་ཟླ་མ་མཆིས་པ་.

བཀའ་དྲིན་མཚུངས་ཟླ་མ་མཆིས་པ་ (gədrin tsūŋda maciba) shung. unequaled gratitude, extremely grateful ¶ཁྲི་པོ་ཅག་ལ་བཀའ་དྲིན་མཚུངས་ཟླ་མ་མཆིས་པ་རྫོང་དཔོན་ཞིང་གཤེགས་དེ་ཉིད་ We are extremely grateful to the late District Commissioner.

བཀའ་དྲིན་གསབ་ (gədrin sāp) sm. བཀའ་དྲིན་གསོབ་.

བཀའ་དྲིན་གསོབ་ (gədrin sōp) va. to repay a favor/ kindness, to show one's gratitude ¶ཕ་མའི་བཀའ་དྲིན་གསོབ་ཆེད་ In order to repay the kindness of my parents.

བཀའ་དྲིན་གསོལ་ (gədrin söö) sm. བཀའ་དྲིན་གསོབ་.

བཀའ་དྲིན་བསམ་ (gādrin sām) sm. བཀའ་དྲིན་རྗེས་དྲན་.

བཀའ་དྲིན་བསམ་ཤེས་ (gādrin sāmsheè) sm. བཀའ་དྲིན་རྗེས་དྲན་.

བཀའ་དྲིས་སྔོན་པོར་ཞུ་ལན་ལྗང་ཁུ་ (gādriì ŋõmbor shulɛn jaŋgu) giving an answer that is unrelated to the question; va.—རྒྱག [Lit. to give a green answer to a blue question].

བཀའ་དྲུང་ (gədruŋ) shung. secretary to the Kashag.

བཀའ་གདམས་ (gādam) the Kadam sect (later absorbed into the Gelug sect).

བཀའ་གདམས་པ་ (gādamba) a follower of the Kadam sect.

བཀའ་གདམས་གསར་མ་ (gādam sārma) the new Kadam (i.e., the Gelug sect).

བཀའ་མདའ (gānda) shung. 1. abbr. of བཀའ་བློན་ and མདའ་དཔོན་. 2. an arrow-shaped banner of authority used in the army in ancient China.

བཀའ་མདའ་རྩིས་གསུམ་ (gān da dzī sūm) shung. abbr. the three (high officials in tt.): བཀའ་བློན་, མདའ་དཔོན་ and རྩིས་དཔོན.

བཀའ་འདོམས་ (gāndom) sm. བཀའ་བཀོད་.

བཀའ་འདྲི་ (gəndri) a question, inquiry (h.); va.—གནང་; —ཞུ་ to ask, to inquire about ༎ཁོང་གིས་ངའི་མིང་བཀའ་དྲི་གནང་བ་རེད་ He asked my name.

བཀའ་འདྲི་བསྐྱངས་འཕེར་ (gəndri gyāŋper) shung. (if you don't trust me) you can ask others ༎ཚང་མའི་མཁྱེན་ཚོད་བཀའ་འདྲི་བསྐྱངས་འཕེར་དང་ This is known by all; you can ask others.

བཀའ་སྡོད་ (gādöò) a protective deity.

བཀའ་བརྡ་ (gāda) shung. a command, an order (usu. military).

བཀའ་བསྡུར་ (gādur) a discussion, discussing (h.); va.—གནང་; —བྱེད་ to discuss ༎ཐག་མ་བཅད་གོང་ལ་ཚོགས་འདུ་ར་བཀའ་བསྡུར་གནང་ན་ཡག་གི་རེད་ Before (we) come to a decision it is better to discuss it in a meeting.

བཀའ་བསྒོམས་ (gādom) shung. a decision, verdict (h.); va.—གནང་ to render or issue a decision or verdict ༎ཁ་མཆུ་འདིའི་བཀའ་བསྒོམས་གཞུང་གིས་གནང་བ་རེད་ The government issued a verdict in the dispute.

བཀའ་ནན་ (gānɛn) shung. criticism (from superiors); vi.—ཕེབས་ to be criticized from above ༎ལས་ཀ་ཡག་པོ་མ་བྱས་ན་གོ་རིམ་གྱི་བཀའ་ནན་ཕེབས་ཀྱི་རེད་ If one doesn't work well he will be criticized from above.

བཀའ་ནན་ལྗི་སྐྱོལ་ (gānɛn jīdzöl) shung. strong/ stern/ strict criticism (from above) ༎ང་ཚོས་ལས་འགན་ཡག་པོ་མ་བསྒྲུབས་ན་གོང་རིམ་ནས་བཀའ་ནན་ལྗི་སྐྱོལ་ཡོང་གི་རེད་ If we do not fulfill our task, we will be criticized severely from above.

བཀའ་ནན་ཆེ་ཕེབས་ (gānɛn cē pēb) shung. to get severely criticized from above ༎ཞུ་བབ་འོས་མིན་ཡིན་ཚུལ་བཀའ་ནན་ཆེ་ཕེབས་ (I was) severely criticized (by the leader) who said that it was inappropriate for me to say that.

བཀའ་ནན་པོ་ (gānɛn) sm. བཀའ་ནན་.

བཀའ་ནན་ཕེབས་གཞི་ (gānɛn pēbshi) shung. cause/ reason/ basis for being criticized severely (from above) ༎གོང་རིམ་གྱི་བཀའ་ནན་ཕེབས་གཞིའི་རིགས་མི་འབྱུང་བ་བྱེད་དགོས་ You have to act so as to not create any reason for being criticized from above.

བཀའ་རྣམ་འབེབས་ (gā nampeb) shung. whenever the order is given ༎གཞུང་སའི་ཞབས་འདེགས་བཀའ་རྣམ་འབེབས་ལ་ཞུས་ཆོག་པ་ (We) will be ready to serve the goverment whenever the order is given.

བཀའ་གནང་ (gā nāŋ) see བཀའ་, 1 and 3.

བཀའ་གནང་མངོན་བསྒྲོད་ (gānaŋ ŋöndöö) shung. complying with an order; va.—བྱེད་; —ཞུ་ ༎སློབ་ཕྲུག་ཚོས་དགེ་རྒན་གྱི་བཀའ་གནང་མངོན་བསྒྲོད་ཞུ་གི་ཡོད་པ་རེད་ The students are complying with the teacher's orders.

བཀའ་གནང་རང་ (gānaraŋ) of course!

བཀའ་པོད་ལྔ་ (gā böò ŋā) the five volumes of the Gelugpa sect's religious dialectics curriculum.

བཀའ་དཔྱད་ (gājɛɛ̀) shung. verdict, decision (in a dispute/ case), settlement (h.); va.—གནང་; —གཏོང་ ༎ཁྲིད་དོན་འདིའི་སྐོར་ཁྲིམས་ཁང་ནས་བཀའ་དཔྱད་བཏང་བ་རེད་ The court issued a verdict concerning this dispute.

བཀའ་སྤྱི་ཕེབས་སུ་ (gāji pēbsu) shung. according to the order that is decreed ༎ད་ལྟ་གོང་ས་མཆོག་ནས་བཀའ་སྤྱི་ཕེབས་སུ་ Now, according to the order of H.H. the Dalai Lama.

བཀའ་སྤྱི་ཁྱུར་ (gāji kūr) sm. བཀའ་གསུང་ཅི་སྒྲུབ་.

བཀའ་སྤྱི་ལྷན་རྒྱས་ (gəji lhēngyɛɛ̀) joint meeting of བཀའ་བློན་ and སྤྱི་འཁྱུས་.

བཀའ་སྤྲིང་བློན་ (gā driŋlön) minister.

བཀའ་ཕབ་ (gā pōb) see བཀའ་, 1.

བཀའ་ཕེབས་ (gā pēb) shung. vi. to receive an order/ instruction ༎ང་རང་ལས་ཁུངས་ནས་བཀའ་ཕེབས་བྱུང་ I received an order from the office.

བཀའ་ཕེབས་སྤྱི་སྨིན་ (gāpeb jīmin) shung. sm. བཀའ་བབས་སྤྱི་སྨིན་.

བཀའ་ཕྱིར་ཕེབས་ (gə cīr pēb) shung. receiving an answer/ reply from above ༎བླ་དཔོན་གོང་མར་སྙན་སྒྲོན་ཡོད་པ་ནས་བཀའ་ཕྱིར་ཕེབས་བྱུང་མཚམས་ Please report this matter to the superior and when you get an answer from above.

བཀའ་འཕྲིན་ (gəndrin) a letter (h.); vi.—ཕེབས་ to receive a letter ༎རྫོང་དཔོན་ནས་ང་ལ་བཀའ་འཕྲིན་ཕེབས་བྱུང་ I received a letter from the District Commissioner.

བཀའ་བབ་ (gā pəp) sm. བཀའ་བབས་.

བཀའ་བབས་ (gā pəp) va. to receive an order.

བཀའ་བབས་ལྗི་པོ་ (gāpəb jīmin) shung. a strict/ severe order ༎བཀའ་བབ་ལྗི་པོ་འདི་རིགས་སྔར་བྱུང་མ་མྱོང་བ་ཞིག་རེད་ Severe orders like this have never been issued before.

བཀའ་བབས་སྤྱི་སྨིན་ (gāpəb jīmin) shung. receiving an order/ request/ response ༎གོང་རིམ་གྱི་བཀའ་བབས་སྤྱི་སྨིན་བྱུང་ I received an order from (my) superiors. ༎གསུང་པའི་ཞུ་དོན་སྐོར་བཀའ་བབས་སྤྱི་སྨིན་བཀའ་དྲིན་གྱི་དཔལ་དུ་ཆེ་ I thank you very much for responding to my request.

བཀའ་བམ་ (gābam) 1. shung. written order issued by a king or emperor. 2. scriptures, religious texts.

བཀའ་བྱང་ (gājaŋ) a board on which an order is written.

བཀའ་བྱང་འགོ་དཔོན་ (gājaŋ gobön) the official who carried the board on which an order is written.

བཀའ་བྲིས་ (gədriì) shung. a written order ༎བླ་དཔོན་གོང་མའི་བཀའ་བྲིས་དགོངས་དོན་ According to the written order from the superiors.

བཀའ་བློ་ (gālo) shung. consulting, deliberating, talking over.

བཀའ་བློན་ (gālön) shung. a Council/ Minister in tt. (one of the heads of the བཀའ་ཤག་) ༎བཀའ་བློན་ང་ཕོད་ Council Minister Ngabö.

བཀའ་བློན་ཁྲི་པ་ (gālön tribə) shung. the senior Council Minister.

བཀའ་བློན་གྱི་གཟིམ་འགག (gālöngi simgaà) aide to a Kashag minister.

བཀའ་བློན་བླ་མ་ (gālön lāma) shung. the Council Minister who is a monk official.

བཀའ་བློན་ཤག་ (gālön shāà) shung. the name of the Council of Ministers begun in the time of the 5th Dalai Lama.

བཀའ་དབང་ (gāwaŋ) 1. minister ༎རྒྱལ་པོས་བཀའ་དབང་ལ་བཀའ་བསྒོས་པ་ The king ordered the minister. 2. religious initiation ༎བླ་མས་བཀའ་དབང་གནང་བ་ The lama gave an initiation.

བཀའ་འབངས་ (gāmbaŋ) shung. subjects (of a ruler) ༎བཀའ་འབངས་ཐམས་ཅད་བདེ་ལ་འགོད་པ་ To bring peace and prosperity to all subjects.

བཀའ་འབངས་མི་སེར་ (gāmbaŋ misee) shung. sm. བཀའ་འབངས་.

བཀའ་འབབ་ (gā bab) shung. sm. བཀའ་འབེབས་.

བཀའ་འབབ་སྤྱི་སྨིན་ (gāmbab jīmin) shung. sm. བཀའ་བབས་སྤྱི་སྨིན་.

བཀའ་འབབ་རིང་ལུགས་ (gāmbəb rinluù) shung. sm. བཀའ་འབེབས་རིང་ལུགས་.

བཀའ་འབེབས་ (gā beb) see བཀའ, 1.

བཀའ་འབེབས་རིང་ལུགས་ (gāmbeb rinluù) authoritarianism, commandism.

བཀའ་འབྲེལ་ (gāndree) shung. in accordance with an order, in connection with an order ¶ ང་བཀའ་འབྲེལ་ལྡི་ལིར་འགྲོ་དགོས་བྱུང་ In accordance with the order I had to go to Delhi.

བཀའ་མ་ (gāma) the actual teachings/ words of the Buddha.

བཀའ་མེད་ (gāmeè) sm. ཀ་མེད་.

བཀའ་མོལ་ (gāmöö) conversation, talking, discussion (h.); va.—གནང་; —ཞུ་; —གསུང་ to converse, to talk, to have a conversation.

བཀའ་མོལ་སྟོན་པོ་ (gāmöö tõmbo) h. of སྐད་ཆ་སྟོན་པོ་.

བཀའ་གཙང་མ་ (gā dzāŋma) shung. 1. an order that is clear ¶ ད་རེས་ལས་ཀ་བཏོད་སྒྲིག་སྐོར་འགོ་ཁྲིད་ཀྱིས་ང་ལ་བཀའ་གཙང་མ་གནང་བྱུང་ The boss gave me clear orders this time regarding what work should be done. 2. pure vows.

བཀའ་གཙིགས་ (gədzig) shung. 1. last testament. 2. an oath, a promise. 3. a letter written by a lama/ chief/ official.

བཀའ་བཙན་ (gā dzēn)sm. བཀའ་བཙན་པོ་.

བཀའ་བཙན་པོ་ (gā dzēmbo) shung. a strict/ severe order; va.—གནང་ ¶ འགོ་རིམ་གྱི་མི་དམངས་ཚོ་ལ་བཀའ་བཙན་པོ་ཞིག་དྲག་གནང་ཡོད་པ་རེད་ The leaders have issued very strict orders to the people below them.

བཀའ་རྩ་ (gādza) shung. an ordinance/ rule/ edict ¶ ཆུ་ཕག་བཀའ་རྩ་ The ordinance of the Water-Pig Year.

བཀའ་རྩ་ཕྱོགས་འགལ་ (gādza cōŋgεε) shung. violating an ordinance/ rule/ edict ¶ གལ་སྲིད་བླ་དཔོན་བཀའ་རྩ་ཕྱོགས་འགལ་གྱི་རྩོལ་མིན་བྱ་སྤྱོད་རིགས་སུ་ཐད་ནས་ཞུས་སྲིད་ཆེ་ If there are any immoral activities that violate the order from above.

བཀའ་རྩི་ (gədzi) sm. བཀའ་བརྩི་.

བཀའ་རྩོམ་ (gādzom) composing, writing, authoring (h.); va.—གནང་.

བཀའ་རྩོམ་གཅེས་བདུས་ (gādzom jēēdüù) sm. བཀའ་རྩོམ་གཅེས་བསྡུས་.

བཀའ་རྩོམ་གཅེས་བསྡུས་ (gādzom jēēdüù) an anthology/ selection of articles.

བཀའ་རྩོམ་གནང་མཁན་ (gādzom nāññεn) a composer, an author (h.).

བཀའ་རྩོམ་ཕྱག་བསྐྲར་མ་ (gādzom cāgdarma) handwritten letters or writings.

བཀའ་སྩོལ་ (gādzöl) sm. བཀའ་གནང་.

བཀའ་བརྩད་ (gādzεὲ) 1. looking or searching for sth. (h.); va.—གནང་ ¶ ཁོང་ལྷ་སར་ཕེབས་འཕྲལ་ཁོང་གི་སྐུ་མཆེད་བཀའ་བརྩད་གནང་གི་ཡོད་པ་རེད་ After arriving in Lhasa he immediately started looking for his relatives. 2. looking into/ investigating sth. or sb. ¶ ལས་ཁུངས་ནས་གནད་དོན་དེའི་སྐོར་བཀའ་བརྩད་གནང་གི་འདུག The office is looking into that matter.

བཀའ་བརྩི་ (gədzi) shung. obeying/ heeding an order or command (h.); va. བཀའ་བརྩི་; —གནང་; —ཞུ་ to obey/ heed ¶ གོང་རིམ་གྱི་བཀའ་བརྩི་ཞུ་དགོས་རེད་ (You) must obey the orders of your superiors.

བཀའ་བརྩི་ཁྲིམས་འཁུར་ (gədzi trīmgur) shung. law-abiding, lawful; va.—གནང་; —ཞུ་.

བཀའ་བསྩལ་ (gā dzεε) p. of བཀའ་སྩོལ་.

བཀའ་ཚ་ནན་ (gā tsānεn) sm. བཀའ་ནན་.

བཀའ་ཚ་པོ་ (gā tsābo) shung. a severe/ harsh order ¶ དཔོན་པོས་བཀའ་ཚ་པོ་གནང་བ་རེད་ The lord gave a severe order.

བཀའ་ཚབ་ (gədzəp) shung. acting Council Minister in tt.

བཀའ་ཚིགས་ (gədzig) sm. བཀའ་གཙིགས་.

བཀའ་ཚོགས་ (gādzɔɔ̀) a letter, a reply, correspondence.

བཀའ་མཚོན་མདའ་མོ་ (gādzog damo) sm. བཀའ་མདའ་.

བཀའ་ཞིབ་ (gəshib) shung. 1. investigating (h.); va.—གནང་ to investigate ¶ གྱོད་དོན་འདི་སྐོར་དེང་སང་བཀའ་ཞིབ་གནང་བཞིན་པ་རེད་ These days the court is investigating this case. 2. an investigation committee.

བཀའ་ཞུ་དམ་འབེབས་ (gəshu tambeb) shung. requesting an official land tenure document from the government; va.—བྱེད་ ¶ སྒེར་པ་ཁག་ཤས་ཀྱིས་རང་ཉིད་ཀྱི་གཞིས་ཀར་བཀའ་ཞུ་དམ་འབེབས་བྱེད་ཀྱི་རེད་ Some aristocrats asked (the government) for land tenure document to confirm their estates.

བཀའ་གཞིས་ (gāshii) shung. an estate held by a Council Minister as a perk of holding office (in tt.).

བཀའ་བཞིན་སྒྲུབ་ (gāshin drub) va. to fulfill a policy/ order/ decree.

བཀའ་བཞེས་ (gāsheè) sm. ཞལ་བཞེས་.

བཀའ་བཞེས་བཟང་པོ་ (gāsheè sanbo) shung. to receive a positive answer/ acknowledgement ¶ ད་ལའི་བླ་མའི་ཡང་སྲིད་རིན་པོ་ཆེའི་མཆོག་སྤྲུལ་དུ་ངོས་འཛིན་ཞུས་འཐུས་ཡོང་འགྲོ་ཞེས་བཀའ་བཞེས་བཟང་པོ་ཐོབ་པ་ We have received a positive acknowledgement that (this child) can be recognized as the reincarnation of the Dalai Lama.

བཀའ་བཞེས་བཟང་ཐོབ་ (gāsheè saŋdob) sm. བཀའ་བཞེས་བཟང་པོ་.

བཀའ་ཟུར་ (gəsur) shung. a former or ex-Kashag (Council) Minister (in tt.).

བཀའ་བཟང་འགོ་མཆན་རིན་པོ་ཆེ་ (gāsaŋ gocεn rimboce) shung. sm. འགོ་མཆན་.

བཀའ་བཟང་སྤྱི་སྨིན་ (gāsaŋ jīmin) sm. བཀའ་བབས་སྤྱི་སྨིན་.

བཀའ་འོག་ཏུ་བསྡུ་ (gā wɔgdu du) va. to put under sb.'s control.

བཀའ་ཡི་ཁྲིམས་ཡིག་ཆེན་པོ་དྲུག (gəyiì trīmluù cēmbo truù) the six great laws of King Songtsen Gambo.

བཀའ་ཡིག (gəyii) shung. a written order or command usu. issued by the Dalai Lama ¶ ལྷ་གོང་ས་སྐྱབས་མགོན་ཆེན་པོའི་བཀའ་ཡིག་གྱི་ཕེབས་དགོངས་དོན་ According to the letter I received from H.H. the Dalai Lama.

བཀའ་ཡིག་རྒྱ་མ་ (gəyiì gyama) shung. a seal-bearing written order/ letter/ command usu. from the Dalai Lama ¶ ད་ལམ་བཀའ་ཡིག་རྒྱ་མ་གྱི་ཕེབས་དགོངས་དོན་ In accordance with the content of the seal-bearing letter I received from H.H. the Dalai Lama.

བཀའ་ཡིག་སྤྱི་ཕེབས་ (gəyiì jīpeb) shung. receiving an order/ command/ letter usu. issued by the Dalai Lama ¶ ལྷ་གོང་ས་སྐྱབས་མགོན་ཆེན་པོའི་བཀའ་ཡིག་སྤྱི་ཕེབས་དགོངས་དོན་ In accordance with the order I received from H.H. the Dalai Lama.

བཀའ་ཡིས་བསྐོད་ (gəyiì göò) va. to order, to give an order.

བཀའ་ཡུལ་གཉན་པོ་ (gəyüü ñēmbo) 1. easy to anger and quick to punish ¶ དཔོན་པོ་འདི་བཀའ་ཡུལ་གཉན་པོ་ཡིན་པར་བརྟེན་ཁྱེད་རང་གཟབ་གཟབ་བྱ་དགོས་ The lord is easy to anger and quick to punish so you should be careful. 2. risky ¶ གཞུང་དོན་བཀའ་ཡུལ་གཉན་པོ་ཡིན་པར་བརྟེན་ཁྱེད་རང་གཟབ་གཟབ་བྱ་དགོས་ Because this government business is risky you should be careful.

བཀའ་ཡོ་གལ་འཆོས་པ་ (gāyo kεεjööba) sm. བཀའ་སྙན་.

བཀའ་རམས་པ་ (gā ramba) a type of geshe.

བཀའ་རུག (gərug) shung. colleague in a job/ office/ position.

བཀའ་ལ་འཁྲི་པ་ (gāla tribə) shung. obedience ¶ སངས་རྒྱས་རྒྱ་མཚོ་ཟུར་པ་སྡོད་མ་ལས་ཐུགས་བསམ་དང་

བཀའ་ལ་འཁྲི་བ་སོགས་གང་ཅེ་ནས་སྐལ་ཤས་མཐོ་བ་དགོས་ཚུལ་ Because Sangye Gyatso was much more obedient, etc. than the former incumbents, (he) deserves more shares.

བཀའ་ལ་ཉན་ (gāla ñɛn) va. to obey/ heed ¶ ཕྲུ་གུ་དེ་ཕ་མའི་བཀའ་ལ་ཉན་ཚང་སློབ་སྦྱོང་ཡག་པོ་ཡོད་པ་རེད་ Because that boy obeys his parents he is good at his studies.

བཀའ་ལ་བདགས་ (gāla dāà) va. to give sb. the authority to issue orders.

བཀའ་ལ་རྫི་ (gāla dzī) sm. བཀའ་ལ་ཉན་.

བཀའ་ལ་བརྫི་ (gāla dzī) sm. བཀའ་ལ་རྫི་.

བཀའ་ལན་ (gālɛn) 1. an answer, a reply (h.); va.—སྩོན་; —གནང་ to reply, to answer ¶ ཕྱག་བྲིས་འདི་ལ་བཀའ་ལན་ལམ་སེང་གནང་རོགས་གནང་ Please reply to this letter at once. 2. a message (h.) ¶ ཁྱེད་རང་གི་བཀའ་ལན་འབྱོར་མ་བྱུང་ I did not receive your message.

བཀའ་ལན་སྔོན་པོ་ལ་ཞུ་ལན་ལྗང་ཁུ་ (gālɛn ŋōmbola shulen jəŋgu) an inappropriate/ rude response [Lit. a green response to a blue message].

བཀའ་ལན་ལྷུག་རྗེན་ (gālɛn lhūgjen) a frank/ open response.

བཀའ་ལམ་རིན་པོ་ཆེ་ (gālam rimboce) shung. sm. ལམ་ཡིག.

བཀའ་ལས་འགོངས་ (gālɛɛ̀ goŋ) va. to disobey an order.

བཀའ་ལུང་ (gāluŋ) 1. prophecy, prediction (h.); va.—གནང་; va.—སྩོན་ to prophecize, to make a prophecy ¶ ཆོས་སྐྱོང་གིས་བོད་དོན་སྐོར་བཀའ་ལུང་བསྟན་པ་རེད་ The oracle made a prophecy about Tibet. 2. shung. order/ edict of the emperor ¶ བཀའ་ལུང་གཉན་པོ་རི་གཟར་གྱི་ཐང་རྡོ་ལྟ་བུར་གྱིན་ལོག་ཞུ་ནུས་བྱུང་བ་ Not daring to go against the strict edict that is unstoppable like a boulder rolling down from a mountain.

བཀའ་ལོག (gā lɔg) 1. va. to disobey an order. 2. va. to go against one's oath.

བཀའ་ལོག་གླེང་འགེལ་ (gā lɔɔ̀ lēŋ gɛɛ) imposing wrong orders/ instructions (refers to the Cultural Revolution).

བཀའ་ལོག་པ་ (gā lɔgba) monks or nuns who have lost their vow of celibacy.

བཀའ་ཤག (gāshaà) shung. the Council of Ministers (Kashag) in the tt.

བཀའ་ཤག་འགག (gāshaà gaà) shung. the secretariat of the Kashag ¶ བཀའ་ཤག་འགག་ཏུ་འབྱོར་ཞུ་ཞུ་དགོས་ One must inform the Kashag secretariat of one's arrival (back in Lhasa). ¶ རྒྱལ་ཁབ་ཏུ་འབྱོར་བསྟུན་ངེས་ལམ་འདི་ཡང་བཀའ་ཤག་འགག་བརྒྱུད་ཕྱིར་འབུལ་ཡོང་བ་བྱེད་ As soon as you arrive in Lhasa, you must return this travel document (that permitted requisition of corvee labor).

བཀའ་ཤག་མགྲོན་གཉེར་ (gāshaà drönñer) shung. the title of the government official who served as aide to the Kashag in tt.

བཀའ་ཤག་འགོ་མཆན་ (gāshaà gocɛn) shung. a decision or order by the Kashag that is written on the top of a document/ report/ petition that has been submitted to it for its deliberation ¶ བཀའ་ཤག་འགོ་འཆན་གྱི་དགོངས་དོན་ཁལ་དགུ་བཅག་པ་ལག་བྱུང་འབྲུ་ཁལ་༡༠༠བྱུང་འདུག In accordance with the order of the Kashag (we) reduced 9 ke and received 100 ke of barley.

བཀའ་ཤག་སྡིང་ཤོད་ (gāshaà dēŋshöö) shung. the two subordinate offices in the Kashag—བཀའ་ཤོད་ and བཀའ་སྡིང་. The བཀའ་སྡིང་ office consisted of the བཀའ་མགྲོན་ and བཀའ་དྲུང་ while the བཀའ་ཤོད་ consisted of three secretaries of the 7th rank who were under the བཀའ་དྲུང་.

བཀའ་ཤག་དྲུང་མགྲོན་ཁང་ (gāshaà druŋdrön kāŋ) shung. the office of the Kashag's བཀའ་མགྲོན་ and བཀའ་དྲུང་.

བཀའ་ཤག་མདོ་སྦུག (gāshaà dobuù) shung. the inner office in the Kashag where the Council Ministers stay and outer office where the Kashag's aides stay.

བཀའ་ཤག་དྲུང་ཡིག་ཆུང་བ་ (gāshaà truŋyig cūŋwa) shung. the position of junior secretary in the Kashag.

བཀའ་ཤག་དྲུང་ཡིག་ཆེ་བ་ (gāshaà truŋyig cēwa) shung. the position of senior secretary in the Kashag.

བཀའ་ཤག་ལ་ཞུ་སྙན་ (gāshaàla pūñɛn) shung. a report to the Kashag ¶ ད་ལམ་བཀའ་ཤག་ལ་ཞུ་སྙན་ངེས་འབྱོར་བྱུང་དོན་ As we received in your report to the Kashag.

བཀའ་ཤག་ཤོད་པ་ (gāshaà shōba) the secretaries of the seventh rank who are under the Kashag's བཀའ་དྲུང་ ¶ བཀའ་ཤག་ཤོད་པ་ནས་རྟ་ཁལ་ཐོབ་འཛིན་ཞུས་པ་ We got from the བཀའ་ཤག་ཤོད་ a certificate of authorization for levying corvee taxes.

བཀའ་ཤག་སྲིད་གཞུང་ (gāshaà sīshuŋ) the traditional Tibetan government [Lit. the Kashag government—this term came into prominent use after 1951].

བཀའ་ཤགས་ (gāshaà) shung. a confrontation in court.

བཀའ་ཤེད་ (gāsheè) sm. བཀའ་བགོད་.

བཀའ་ཤོག (gāshɔɔ̀) shung. 1. an official order/ edict/ document ¶ ད་ལམ་བཀའ་ཤོག་དམ་འབྱར་ངེས་བསྐྱངས་སོང་དོན་བཞིན་དེ་དོན་སྒྲུང་དོར་ལེ་མེད་དགོས་རྒྱུ་ In accordance with the official order/ edict with an affixed seal that we sent, you should implement it without making mistakes. 2. a written communiqué/ statement/ notice; va.—སྤེལ་ to issue a communiqué/ statement/ notice ¶ ཟུང་འབྲེལ་བཀའ་ཤོག A joint communiqué.

བཀའ་ཤོག་ཐམ་ལྡན་ (gāshɔɔ̀ tāmdɛn) shung. a written order/ edict/ notice that has been affixed with an official seal.

བཀཤོག (gāshɔɔ̀) shung. abbr. of བཀའ་ཤོག.

བཀའ་ཤོད་ (gāshöö) abbr. of བཀའ་ཤག་ཤོད་པ་.

བཀའ་སམ་ (gāsam) h. of སམ་བྲ་.

བཀའ་སྲུང་ (gāsuŋ) protective deity, guardian deity.

བཀའ་སློབ་ (gālob) advice, teaching (h.); va.—བསྩལ་; —སྩོན་; —གནང་ to give advice, to teach; va.—ཞུ་ to seek/ ask for advice ¶ ངའི་ལས་ཀའི་ཐད་ཁོང་གིས་བཀའ་སློབ་གནང་གི་ཡོད་ He gives me advice about my work. ¶ ལས་ཀ་འདིའི་སྐོར་ཁོང་ལ་བཀའ་སློབ་ཞུས་པ་ཡིན་ I sought advice from him about this job.

བཀའ་སློབ་བསྒྱུར་བསྒྲིགས་ (gālob gyārdrig) edited teachings/ advice.

བཀའ་སློབ་གྱི་སྒྲོལ་དང་བསྟུན་ (gālob jīdzöö taŋdün) shung. in accordance with your advice ¶ བཀའ་སློབ་གྱི་སྒྲོལ་དང་བསྟུན་ནས་ཞུ་སྒོ་འགྲུས་ཚང་ལེ་མེད་ཡོང་བ་ཞུ་རྒྱུ་ In accordance with your advice, (we) will try our best to accomplish our tasks.

བཀའ་སློབ་འཕྲལ་མྱུར་ཞལ་གསལ་ (gālob trɛ̄ɛ̄ñur shɛɛsɛl) shung. asking to give advice as soon as possible ¶ བླ་དཔོན་གོང་རིམ་ནས་བཀའ་སློབ་འཕྲལ་མྱུར་ཞལ་གསལ་གྱི་སྒྲོལ་ཡོང་བ་ We request the higher authorities to advise us as soon as possible.

བཀའ་གསལ་ (gāsɛɛ) an answer, a reply (h.); va.—གནང་ to answer, to reply; vi.—ཕེབས་ to receive an answer/ reply; va.—ཡོང་བ་ཞུ་; —གནང་རོགས་གནང་ to request an answer/ reply ¶ སྙན་ཞུ་འདིའི་སྐོར་ད་ལྟ་གོང་རིམ་གྱི་བཀའ་གསལ་ཕེབས་མ་བྱུང་ The higher authorities have not replied to the petition.

བཀའ་གསུང་ (gāsuŋ) an order (h.).

བཀའ་གསུང་ཅི་སྒྲུབ་ (gāsuŋ jīdrub) putting into practice or complying with whatever is ordered from above; va.—བྱེད་; —ཞུ་ ¶ སློབ་གྲྭ་བ་ཆོས་དགེ་རྒན་གྱི་བཀའ་གསུང་ཅི་སྒྲུབ་ཞུ་གི་ཡོད་པ་རེད་ The students are complying with whatever the teacher orders.

བཀའ་གསུང་དང་ལེན་ (gāsuŋ taŋlen) sm. བཀའ་གསུང་ཅི་སྒྲུབ་.

བཀའ་གསེད་ (gāseè) shung. advice and explanation ¶ འཁྲུང་རྩོལ་གནམ་འཆར་མི་འབྱུང་བའི་བཀའ་གསེད་ཇེ་སྙེད་རིམ་ཕེབས་བྱུང་བར་ In order not to have the dispute get exposed, (we) received advice many times.

བཀའ་བསླད་མ་ (gā lɛ̄ɛ̀ma) false teachings of the Buddha.

བཀའི་ཇ་བོ་ཆེ་ (gɛ̄ɛ ŋāwoce) shung. a grand/ illustrious/ great order ¶ བཀའི་ཇ་བོ་ཆེ་རྒྱལ་ཁམས་ཡོངས་སུ་བསྒྲགས་པ་ The illustrious order was declared all over the country. [Lit. an order (like) a large drum].

བཀའི་ཅོད་པན་ (gɛ̄ɛ jȫòbɛn) shung. བཀའ་གསུང་ཅི་སྒྲུབ་.

བཀའི་རྗེས་སུ་འབྲངས་ (gɛ̄ɛ j̲eèsu dra̲ŋ) shung. to follow/ obey a superior's command ¶ བླ་དཔོན་གོང་མའི་བཀའི་རྗེས་སུ་འབྲངས་ནས་འགན་བབ་ཞུ་སྒོ་ལེ་མེད་ཞུ་རྒྱུ་ (I) will follow the order of the higher authorities and accomplish my task.

བཀའི་མདུན་བློན་ (gɛ̄ɛ dü̲nlön) shung. top minister(s) ¶ བཀའི་མདུན་བློན་རྣམས་ནས་ཆབ་འབངས་ཀྱི་བདེ་ཐབས་ལ་བགྲོས་པ་ The ministers discussed the matter regarding the prosperity of the people. [Lit. a minister who sits at the side of the king].

བཀའི་སྒྲིང་བློན་ (gɛ̄ɛ drīŋlön) shung. minister.

བཀའི་ཕྱིང་སང་ (gɛ̄ɛ cīŋsaŋ) shung. ch.tib. minister ¶ བཀའི་ཕྱིང་སང་རྣམས་ཆབ་སྲིད་ཀྱི་དོན་ཆེན་ལ་ལེགས་པར་བགྲོས་ནས་རྒྱལ་པོར་སྙན་སེང་ཞུས་ The ministers discussed the political matters thoroughly and reported to the king.

བཀའི་འཕྲིན་ལས་ཀྱི་གཙོ་བོ་ (gɛ̄ɛ trīnlɛɛ̀gi dzōwo) shung. the ministers (of the Emperor) ¶ གོང་མ་བདག་པོ་ཆེན་པོའི་བཀའི་འཕྲིན་ལམ་ཀྱི་གཙོ་བོ་ The ministers of the great Emperor.

བཀའི་དབྱིངས་ས་ (gɛ̄ɛ yīŋsa) sm. བཀའི་ཕྱིང་སང་.

བཀའི་ལུས་ (gɛ̄ɛ lüù) the main texts of the Buddhist teachings.

བཀར་ (gār) 1. p. of དཀར་. 2. va. to corner, to question forcefully ¶ ཁྲིམས་ཁང་ནས་ཉེས་ཅན་དེ་བཀར་བ་རེད་ The court questioned the criminal forcefully. ¶ ཁྱི་རྩིག་ཁུག་ལ་བཀར་ན་ཁ་ལོག་རྒྱུག If you corner a dog, it will turn on you. ¶ གསར་འགྱུར་འགོད་མཁན་གྱིས་སྲིད་འཛིན་ལ་གསང་བའི་ཡིག་ཆའི་སྐོར་དྲིབ་བཏོན་ནས་བཀར་བ་རེད་ The reporter cornered the president through questions about the secret document.

བཀར་སྐྱིན་ (gārgyin) shung. things used to reimburse/ replace items taken from storage or from a storehouse; va.—འཇུག to replenish/ replace sth. taken from a storehouse ¶ བཀར་ཁང་དུ་བཀར་སྐྱིན་འབྲུ་ཁལ་༡༠༠་བཙུག་པ་རེད་ (They) replaced 100 khal of grain in the storeroom.

བཀར་ཁང་ (gārgaŋ) shung. storeroom, storehouse, warehouse, granary ¶ གཞུང་འབབ་རྣམས་འབྲུ་དངུལ་བཀར་འཇུག་པ་ནམ་ཕེབས་ལ་ཤེལ་དཀར་བཀར་ཁོངས་རང་དུ་སྒྲུབ་འབུལ་ཞུ་རྒྱུ་ Whenever the officials in charge of storing grain come, we will transport and pay the grain and money to the Shelkar storehouse.

བཀར་རྒྱ་ (gārgya) shung. a seal used to secure a storehouse/ granary so that it can not be opened without authorization; va.—རྒྱག; —ཕབ་ to seal a granary in this way.

བཀར་རྒྱ་བ་ (gārgyawa) shung. the keeper/ overseer of a storehouse or granary.

བཀར་དངུལ་ (gārŋüü) shung. silver or coins that are stored in a storehouse.

བཀར་བཙུག (gārjuù) p. of བཀར་འཇུག.

བཀར་བཙུག་རྒྱུ་ཆས་ (gārjuù gyu̲jɛɛ̀) goods/ property kept in a storehouse.

བཀར་བཙུག་རྒྱུ་ནོར་ (gārjuù gyu̲nor) sm. བཀར་བཙུག་རྒྱུ་ཆས་.

བཀར་འཇུག (gə̄njuù) storing sth. in a storehouse/ warehouse; va. བཀར་འཇུག; —རྒྱག; —བྱེད་ ¶ འདི་ལོ་ལོ་ལེགས་བྱུང་ཙང་འབྲུ་རིགས་འབོར་ཆེན་བཀར་འཇུག་བརྒྱབ་པ་རེད་ The harvest was good this year (so) they stored a large amount of grain in the storeroom.

བཀར་འཛོག (gānjɔɔ̀) putting/ leaving sth. aside, putting sth. into storage; va.—བྱེད་ ¶ གུང་སེང་དུ་ཕྱིན་པའི་སློབ་གྲྭ་བ་དེའི་ཅ་ལག་རྣམས་བཀར་འཛོག་བྱས་ཡོད་པ་རེད་ The student who went on vacation has left his things in storage.

བཀར་བདགས་ (gārdaà) 1. cornering sb. when questioning/ interrogating; va.—གཏོང་. 2. keeping in mind, not forgetting 3. subduing spirits and transforming them into protective deities.

བཀར་སྙིང་ (gārdeŋ) shung. from the grain kept in storage, from the storehouse ¶ སོ་ལས་བཅུ་བོགས་བཀར་སྙིང་ནས་ From the grain stored through the 10% tax collected by the agriculture department.

བཀར་ཐམ་ (gārdam) shung. the seal placed on the door of a storehouse/ storeroom.

བཀར་ཐམ་འབྱར་མ་ (gārtam ja̲rma) shung. the seal of a storehouse/ storeroom ¶ ཞལ་བཤུས་བཀར་ཐམ་འབྱར་མ་སྣ་རྩེ་བཅུ་བརྒྱད་ཡིག་ཁོངས་སུ་ཡོད་པ་ A copy with the seal of the storeroom affixed was kept with the documents of Nangkartse District.

བཀར་འབོ་དམ་འབྱར་ (gāmbo ta̲mjar) shung. an official grain measuring container (affixed with a seal) that was equal to one khal (kept in granaries).

བཀར་འབྲུ་ (gāndru) shung. stored grain, reserve grain.

བཀར་འབྲུ་འདོན་སྤྲོད་དོ་དམ་ (gāndru tö̲ndröò to̲dam) shung. the person in charge of delivering stored/ reserve grain.

བཀར་རྩིས་ (gə̄rrdziì) shung. 1. the list of items taken in and released from a storehouse. 2. an accounting of items in a granary/ storehouse; va.—རྒྱག ¶ བཀར་ཁང་རྣམས་བཀར་རྩིས་གཞིར་བཟུང་རྫོང་གསར་རྙིང་དབར་རྩིས་སྤྲོད་འགན་གཙང་དགོས་རྒྱུ་ The storerooms should be handed over by the incumbent Dzongpon in accordance with the accounts of the storeroom.

བཀར་མཛོད་ (gāndzöò) sm. བཀར་ཁང་.

བཀར་བཟོ་འདོན་ (gārso dö̲n) va. to make oneself look/ appear good ¶ ཕོ་གསར་དེ་བཀར་བཟོ་བཏོན་ནས་སླེབས་བྱུང་ The young person made himself look good and came.

བཀར་བཟོ་དོད་པོ་ (gārso tö̲òbo) sm. དཀར་བཟོ་དོད་པོ་.

བཀར་ཡོང་ (gāryoŋ) shung. grain collection/ storage and revenue collection/ collectors ¶ རྫོང་རྩིས་གཞིས་རྩིས་བཀར་ཡོང་གི་རྩིས་སོགས་ནས་ཐོན་པའི་ར་འཕྲོད་ཆད་རིགས་བླ་ཕྱག་ཏུ་སྒྲུབ་རྒྱུ་ The deficits from the accounts of the districts, estates, storehouses and the revenue collectors should be paid to the Lachag Treasury.

བཀལ་ (gɛ̄ɛ) 1. p. of འགེལ་. 2. p. and f. of འཁལ་/ འཁེལ་.

བཀལ་ཐགས་ (gɛ̄ɛ̄daà) abbr. spinning and weaving.

བཀས་ (gɛ̄ɛ̀) 1. sm. བཀའ་ཡིས་. 2. p. of འགས་.

བཀས་བཀོད་རྒྱུད་འཛིན་ (gɛ̄ɛ̀göò gyü̲ndzin) feudal ¶ བཀས་བཀོད་རྒྱུད་འཛིན་གྱི་ཞིང་བྲན་ལམ་ལུགས་ The feudal serf system.

བཀས་བཀོད་རྒྱུད་འཛིན་གྱི་ཁྱད་དབང་ (gɛ̄ɛ̀göò gyü̲ndzingi kyɛ̄waŋ) feudal privilege, feudal special rights.

བཀས་བཀོད་རྒྱུད་འཛིན་གྱི་མངའ་བདག (gɛ̄ɛ̀göò gyü̲ndzingi ŋādaà) feudal lord.

བཀས་བཀོད་རྒྱུད་འཛིན་གྱི་མངའ་གཞིས་ (gɛ̄ɛ̀göò gyü̲ndzingi ŋə̄shiì) feudal estate.

བཀས་བཀོད་རྒྱུད་འཛིན་གྱི་བཅད་བཟུང་ (gɛ̄ɛ̀göò gyü̲ndzingi jɛ̄ɛ̀suŋ) feudal separatism.

བཀས་བཀོད་རྒྱུད་འཛིན་གྱི་སྤྱི་ཚོགས་ (gɛ̄ɛ̀göò gyü̲ndzingi jīdzoò) feudal society.

བཀས་བཀོད་རྒྱུད་འཛིན་གྱི་དམག་དཔོན་ (gɛ̄ɛ̀göò gyü̲ndzingi māgbön) feudal warlord.

བཀས་བཀོད་རྒྱུད་འཛིན་གྱི་རྨོངས་དད་ (gɛ̄ɛ̀göò gyü̲ndzingi mōŋdeè) feudal superstition.

བཀས་བཀོད་རྒྱུད་འཛིན་གྱི་ཞིང་བདག (gɛ̄ɛ̀göò gyü̲ndzingi shi̲ŋdaà) feudal landlord.

བཀས་བཀོད་རྒྱུད་འཛིན་གྱི་ཞིང་བྲན་བདག་པོ་ (gɛ̄ɛ̀göö gyü̲ndzingi shi̲ŋdrɛn da̲go) feudal serf owner.

བཀས་བཀོད་རྒྱུད་འཛིན་གྱི་ཞིང་བྲན་ལམ་ལུགས་ (gɛ̄ɛ̀göö gyü̲ndzingi shi̲ŋdrɛn la̲mluù) the system of feudal serfdom.

བཀས་བཀོད་རྒྱུད་འཛིན་གྱི་རིམ་ཡོད་ལམ་ལུགས་ (gɛ̄ɛ̀göö gyü̲ndzingi ri̲myüü la̲mluù) the system of feudal classes/ strata.

བཀས་བཀོད་རྒྱུད་འཛིན་གྱི་བཤུ་གཞོག (gɛ̄ɛ̀göö gyü̲ndzingi shūshoò) feudal exploitation.

བཀས་བཀོད་རྒྱུད་འཛིན་ཕྱེད་ཙམ་ (gɛ̄ɛ̀göö gyü̲ndzin cēèdzam) semifeudal.

བཀས་བཀོད་རྒྱུད་འཛིན་རིང་ལུགས་ (gɛ̄ɛ̀göö gyü̲ndzin ri̲ŋluù) feudalism.

བཀས་སྐུལ་ (gɛ̄ɛ̀ gǖü) va. to give an order (by a superior).

བཀས་བསྐོ་ (gɛ̄ɛ̀ gō) va. to appoint by order of the king/ ruler/ chief.

བཀས་མངགས་ (gɛ̄ɛ̀ŋaà) shung. ordering sth. or sb. (to be sent) ¶ གོང་མའི་བཀས་མངགས་པའི་ཨམ་བན་བོད་དུ་འབྱོར་ The Amban who was ordered by the Emperor has arrived in Tibet.

བཀས་མངགས་པའི་ཨམ་བན་ (gɛ̄ɛ̀ŋagbe āmban) shung. an imperial commissioner, a commissioner ordered somewhere (by the Emperor) of China.

བཀས་གཅོད་ (gɛ̄ɛ̀ jöö) 1. va. to decide by a superior's order/ command. 2. to decide by law.

བཀས་བཅད་ (gɛ̄ɛ̀ jɛ̄ɛ̀) p. of བཀས་གཅོད་.

བཀས་མ་བཟོ་གསུམ་ (gɛ̄ɛ̀ ma̲ so̲sum) abbr. the three: feudalism, capitalism, and revisionism.

བཀས་གསར་གཅོད་ (gɛ̄ɛ̀sar jöö) sm. བཀས་གཅོད་.

བཀུ་: p. བཀུས་; f. བཀུ་; imp. བཀུས་ (gū) va. to brew/ boil a long time to concentrate or to extract the juice or essence of sth. ¶ སྤོ་སྨན་མ་བཏང་གོང་ཡུན་རིང་བཀུ་དགོས་པ་རེད་ Before using the herbal medicine, one has to brew it a long time.

བཀུག (gūù) 1. p. of འགུགས་. 2. sm. གདངས་.

བཀུམས་ (gūm) p. of འགུམས་.

བཀུམས་ཕྱག (gūmjaà) prostration done by bending at waist rather than by stretching on the ground.

བཀུར་ (gūr) va. to show respect/ esteem/ honor ¶ ཁོང་གིས་བླ་མ་གོང་དུ་བཀུར་བ་རེད་ He respected lamas.

བཀུར་སྐྱོང་ (gūrgyoŋ) shung. respecting and governing ¶ དཔོན་འབངས་བཀུར་སྐྱོང་སོགས་ཆོས་དང་སྲིད་ཀྱི་འཇུག་ལྡོག་མ་འཆོལ་བ་ For the lord to govern/ administer and the subject to obey and respect the lord and with respect to both religious and secular affairs (both parties) should do the right thing.

བཀུར་སྟི་ (gūrdi) respect, esteem, honor; va.—བྱེད་; —ཞུ་ to respect, to pay homage, to show esteem.

བཀུར་འདེབས་ (gūr de̲b) va. to slander, to malign.

བཀུར་བའི་ཆོ་ལོ་འཛའ་ས་ཐམ་ཀ་ (gūrwe cōlo ja̲sa tāmga) shung. a title and seal given out of respect or honor for sb. (as a king, etc.).

བཀུར་ཚིག (gūrdzii) words of respect/ honor/ reverence; praise.

བཀུར་བཟོས་ (gūrsöö) respecting and praising; va.—བྱེད་ ¶ ཤེས་ཡོན་ཅན་ལ་བཀུར་བཟོས་བྱེད་དགོས་ One should respect and praise intellectuals.

བཀུརའི་ (gūrwɛ) shung. abbr. of བཀུར་བའི་.

བཀུར་འོས་ (gūrwüü) worthy of respect or esteem, honored ¶ བཀུར་འོས་ཀྱི་གཉེན་བཤེས་ Esteemed relatives.

བཀུས་ (gūü) p. and imp. of བཀུ་.

བཀོག (gɔ̄ɔ̀) 1. va. to rip out, to pluck out/ uproot/ root out/ detach from ¶ ཡིག་བསྐྱུར་རྩིག་པ་ནས་བཀོག་སྟེ་བཀའ་ཤག་ལ་སྤྲད་སོང་ (They) ripped the poster from the wall and gave it to the Kashag. 2. p. of འགོག.

བཀོང་ (gōŋ) 1. va. to frighten/ scare ¶ བཙན་འཛུལ་པ་བཀོང་སྟེ་ཕྱིར་འཐེན་རྒྱག་དགོས་བྱུང་བ་རེད་ (They) scared the invaders who had to withdraw. 2. sm.* སྐོང་.

བཀོད་ (göö) 1. p. of འགོད་. 2. va. to create, to bring about, to cause ¶ སྲིད་ཇུས་གསར་པ་དེས་མི་སེར་བདེ་ལ་བཀོད་པ་རེད་ The new policy brought happiness to the subjects.

བཀོད་ཁྱབ་ (göögyəp) shung. spreading/ giving/ distributing a command or order or instruction; va.—བྱེད་; —གཏོང་; —སྤེལ་ to give or distribute a command/ order/ direction/ instruction ¶ མི་སེར་ལ་བཀོད་ཁྱབ་གསལ་པོ་བྱེད་དགོས་ One must give orders clearly to the subjects. ¶ རྩ་ཚིག་རིན་པོ་ཆེའི་དགོངས་དོན་རྣམས་ས་གནས་སྤྱི་དམངས་མི་སེར་རྣམས་ལ་བཀོད་ཁྱབ་འཐུས་ནན་དགོས་རྒྱུ་ In accordance with the contents of the proclamation, you should give clear orders to the subjects.

བཀོད་ཁྱབ་པ་ (göögyəbə) director, commander (the one who does བཀོད་ཁྱབ་).

བཀོད་རྒྱ་ (göögya) a written order/ command; va.—གཏོང་.

བཀོད་སྒྲིག (göödrii) deploying, disposing; organizing, arranging, planning, adjusting; va.—བྱེད་ ¶ ཏང་གིས་ཡང་དག་བཀོད་སྒྲིག་འོག Under the perfect organization of the party. ¶ སྐུ་མཐུད་དགོན་པར་སྡོད་མཁན་གྲྭ་པ་སུམ་བརྒྱ་བཅུ་གཉིས་ལ་འཚོ་བ་བཀོད་སྒྲིག་བྱས་པ་མ་ཟད་ Not only did (they) organize the livelihood for 312 monks who wished to remain living in the monastery.

བཀོད་སྒྲིག་པ་ (göödrigbə) an organizer, a planner.

བཀོད་སྒྲིག་བྱེད་སྟངས་ (göödrig ce̲daŋ) sm. བཀོད་སྒྲིག་བྱེད་ཚུལ་.

བཀོད་སྒྲིག་བྱེད་ཚུལ་ (göödrig ce̲dzüü) manner or method of arranging/ planning.

བཀོད་མངགས་ (gööŋaà) organizing, arranging; va.—བྱེད་ ¶ འགོ་ཁྲིད་ལས་བྱེད་པ་གུང་གསེང་དུ་མ་འགྲོ་གོང་གཤམ་འོག་ལ་ལས་དོན་བཀོད་མངགས་ཡག་པོ་བྱས་སོང་ Before the leader went on vacation, he organized the work tasks for his subordinates well.

བཀོད་མངགས་འཛུགས་སྒྲིག (gööŋaà dzu̲gdrii) organizing, deploying, disposing, arranging, adjusting and establishing; va.—བྱེད་ ¶ ལས་འགུལ་བཀོད་མངགས་འཛུགས་སྒྲིག་བྱ་རྒྱུའི་སྐོར་ Concerning the organizing and establishing of a political campaign.

བཀོད་བཅོས་ (gööjöö) giving guidance, directing and rearranging, reorganizing.

བཀོད་འཆུན་ (gööjün) sb. whose order others will obey ¶ བཀོད་འཆུན་གྱི་འགོ་ཁྲིད་ཅིག་དགོས་ (We) need a leader that others will obey.

བཀོད་ཇུས་ (gūüjüü) direction, guidance, supervision; va.—གཏོང་ ¶ ལས་དོན་གྱིས་ཞིང་པ་རྣམས་ལ་བཀོད་ཇུས་གཏོང་གི་འདུག The foreman is supervising the farmers.

བཀོད་འཇོག (gönjɔɔ̀) placement, deploying, assigning, arranging and organizing ¶ ལས་བྱེད་རྣམས་ལ་ལས་ཀ་འདྲ་མིན་བཀོད་འཇོག་བྱས་པ་རེད་ All the cadre were assigned different tasks.

བཀོད་དོག་དོག (göö dōgdoò) clean and neat, clean and orderly ¶ ཕྲུ་གུ་རྣམས་ལ་གྱོན་ཆས་བཀོད་དོག་དོག་གཡོགས་བཞག The children were dressed cleanly and neatly. ¶ ནང་གི་ཨ་མས་ཁང་པ་བཀོད་དོག་དོགབཟོས་བཞག The mother of the house made the house clean and orderly.

བཀོད་གཏོང་ (göö dōŋ) abbr. of བཀོད་པ་གཏོང་.

བཀོད་གཏོང་པ་ (gödoŋwa) a person who gives directions/ instructions.

བཀོད་སྟོན་ (göödōn) supervising, directing, instructing; va.—བྱེད་ ¶ ལས་གྲྭ་དཔུ་ཆེན་གྱི་བཀོད་སྟོན་འོག་ལས་ཀ་བྱེད་པ་ Working under the supervision and direction of the engineer.

བཀོད་འཐབ་པ་ (göndabba) abbr. of commander and common soldier.

བཀོད་འདོམས་ (göndom) command, direction, order; va.—བྱེད་ ¶ བཀོད་འདོམས་ལ་ཉན་འཇོག་བྱེད་ཀྱི་ཡོད་ (I am) obeying orders.

བཀོད་འདོམས་ཁང་ (göndomgaŋ) headquarters,

commander's office, command post.

བཀོད་འདོམས་ཆེ་གྲས་ (gõndom cēdreɛ̀) high level administrators/ commanders.

བཀོད་འདོམས་པ་ (gõndomba) commander, administrator, person in charge.

བཀོད་འདོམས་སྤུའུ་ (gõndombu.) tib.ch. sm. བཀོད་འདོམས་ཁང་.

བཀོད་འདོམས་དབྱུག་པ་ (gõndom yūgbə) 1. staff indicating authority. 2. baton used by commanding officers.

བཀོད་འདོམས་དམག་གྲུ་ (gõndom māgdru) naval commander's ship, fleet command ship.

བཀོད་འདོམས་དམག་དཔོན་ (gõdom māgbön) commanding officer, commander.

བཀོད་འདོམས་རིམ་པ་སོང་བ་ (gõndom r̲imba sōŋwa) shung. a series of commands/ orders that were given before and after ། ལས་ཁུངས་འདི་ནས་བཀོད་འདོམས་རིམ་པ་སོང་བར་བཀའ་བརྩི་དང་ལེན་མི་བྱེད་པ་ (They) did not adhere to the series of orders given by this office.

བཀོད་ལྷན་ (gõndɛn) 1. the 11th month in the Tibetan calendar. 2. the constellation Sagittarius.

བཀོད་པ་ (gõba) 1. instruction, direction, order, command; va.—ཤོད; —གནང་; —འདོན་ to instruct, to direct, to order ། ཁོས་དམག་མིར་བཀོད་པ་བཏང་བ་རེད་ He instructed the soldiers. 2. va.—ཤོད་ to be punished/ scolded/ rebuked ། བཀའ་ལ་མ་ཉན་ན་བཀོད་པ་ཤོད་དགོས་བྱས་ཡོང་ང་ If (one) doesn't obey the order then (one) may be punished. 3. vi.—འགྲོ་ to have an order obeyed ། དེང་སང་སློབ་གྲྭ་བ་ཚོར་དགེ་རྒན་གྱི་བཀོད་པ་འགྲོ་གི་མི་འདུག These days the teachers don't have their orders obeyed by the students. 4. design, plan; va.—གཏོང་ to design, to make a plan ། ཁང་པ་འདི་བཀོད་པ་ཡག་པོ་འདུག The design of this house is good.

བཀོད་པ་འགྲོ་པོ་ (gõba dr̲obo) obedient ། བོད་ཀྱི་མི་སེར་བཀོད་པ་འགྲོ་པོ་ཡོད་པ་རེད་ The citizens of Tibet are obedient.

བཀོད་པ་ཐོན་པོ་ (gõba tõmbo) well-designed, well-planned (usu. for buildings and houses).

བཀོད་པ་མཐུན་པོ་ (gõba tũmbo) sm. བཀོད་པ་ཐོན་པོ་.

བཀོད་པ་དོད་པོ་ (gõba d̲öbo) sm. བཀོད་ལེགས་.

བཀོད་པ་གཙང་མ་ (gõba dzāŋma) sm. བཀོད་པ་ཐོན་པོ་.

བཀོད་པ་མཛེས་པོ་ (gõba dz̲ebo) well-designed decorated/ furnished/ arranged house ། ཁང་པ་འདིའི་འཛིན་ཆས་བཀོད་པ་མཛེས་པོ་འདུག The furniture in this house is well arranged.

བཀོད་པས་འཆུན་ (gõõbɛ cũn) va. to obey or listen to orders/ instructions ། པ་མའི་བཀོད་པས་འཆུན་གྱི་མེད་པ་རེད་ (The child) doesn't listen to his parents.

བཀོད་བྱུས་ (gũũjüü) sm.བཀོད་ཇུས་.

བཀོད་འབྲེལ་ (gõndree) shung. an order, a command ། ས་གནས་རྫོང་གི་བཀོད་འབྲེལ་ཁྲལ་རིགས་སྒྲུབ་རྒྱུགས་ཞུ་སྒྲོ་ལེ་མེད་དགོས་རྒྱུ་ In accordance with the order of the District commissioner, you should do/ pay the corvee taxes without delay.

བཀོད་མ་ (gõõma) a spring/ water that shoots up ། བཀོད་མའི་ཆུ་ Spring water.

བཀོད་གཙང་ (gõõdzaŋ) abbr. བཀོད་པ་གཙང་མ་.

བཀོད་འཛུགས་ (gõndzuù) establishing, founding; va.—བྱེད་ ། ཡུལ་དམག་ནི་རྫོང་ནས་ཐད་ཀར་བཀོད་འཛུགས་བྱས་པ་ཞིག་རེད་ The militia was directly established by the district.

བཀོད་ཡིག (gõyii) shung. an order written in a letter (or sent in a letter) ། གོང་རིམ་གྱི་བཀོད་ཡིག་འབྱོར་མ་ཐག As soon as they received the letter containing their superior's order.

བཀོད་ལུགས་ (gũũluù) the manner or method of arranging/ planning/ ordering/ designing.

བཀོད་ལུང་ (gõõluŋ) shung. orders and instructions ། གཡོག་བསྟན་འཛིན་ནས་ངོ་མའི་བཀོད་ལུང་དང་མ་འབྲེལ་བར་དགའ་མིན་རང་མཚམས་ཏ་ལྕག་འཕར་གཏོང་བགྱིས་པར་ཉེས་པ་སྲང་༣་སྒྲུབས་ Servant Tenzin shall be fined 3 srangs for whipping people on his own without orders and instructions from his master.

བཀོད་ལུང་འགྲོ་མིན་རིགས་ (gõõluŋ dr̲omin r̲ig) shung. people who do not observe discipline or obey rules ། གལ་སྲིད་ཆབ་འབངས་ཀྱི་ཁྲོད་དུ་བཀོད་ལུང་འགྲོ་མིན་རིགས་ཡོད་ཚེ་རྒྱལ་ཁྲིམས་བཙན་པོས་ཆ་ར་གཅོད་རྒྱུ་ If anyone among the masses does not observe the rules they shall be punished according to government law.

བཀོད་ལེགས་ (gõõleg) well-planned, nicely arranged/ designed.

བཀོད་ལེགས་སྤུས་དག (gõõleg bũũdag) well-designed and good in quality.

བཀོད་བཤད་ (gõõ shɛ̃ɛ̀) shung. ordering, instructing ། དགེ་བཤད་སྡིག་དཀྲོལ་གྱི་བཀོད་བཤད་བགྱིས་པ་ (He) gave instructions explaining the pros and cons of doing good deeds and bad deeds.

བཀོད་གསལ་ (gõõsɛɛ) according to what is stated or written ། གསར་ཤོག་དེའི་ནང་བཀོད་གསལ་ལ་ According to what was stated in the newspaper.

བཀོན་ (gõn) 1. sm. སྐོན་. 2. arc. va. to hate.

བཀོན་པུ་ (gõmbu) a small basket.

བཀོལ་ (gõõ) 1. va. to make someone work ། མི་དེ་ཚོ་བྲན་གཡོག་ཏུ་བཀོལ་ཆེད་ For the purpose of making those people work as slaves. 2. va. to set aside, to keep apart ། མི་དེ་མང་ཚོགས་ཀྱི་དཀྱིལ་ནས་ཟུར་དུ་བཀོལ་བ་རེད་ That man was kept apart from the people. 3. p. and f. of འཁོལ་.

བཀོལ་བཀོད་རིག་པ་ (gõõgöö r̲igbə) operations research.

བཀོལ་མཁས་འཛོག་ཤེས་ (gõõkɛɛ j̲ogsheɛ̀) an efficient person.

བཀོལ་མངག (gõõŋaà) appointing to a position, designating to do a job/ task.

བཀོལ་སྙིགས་ (gõõñii) waste material, useless/ cast-off things.

བཀོལ་བདེ་ (gõõde) easy to use ། བཀོལ་བདེའི་ཡོ་ཆས་ Easy to use utensils.

བཀོལ་བདེ་པོ་ (gõõ d̲ebo) sm. བཀོལ་བདེ་.

བཀོལ་སྤྱོད་ (gõõjöö) making sb. or sth. work, using or utilizing sth.; va.—བྱེད་; —གཏོང་ ། འཕྲུལ་འཁོར་འདི་ཚོར་ལག་རྩལ་བ་མེད་ན་བཀོལ་སྤྱོད་བྱེད་ཐུབ་ཀྱི་མ་རེད་ These machines cannot be used unless there are technicians. ། ལག་རྩལ་མི་སྣ་བཀོལ་སྤྱོད་བྱེད་ཆེད་ For the purpose of utilizing technicians.

བཀོལ་སྤྱོད་དུད་འགྲོ་དང་མཚུངས་པ་ (gõõjöö d̲ündro t̲aŋ tsūŋbə) shung. to be treated/ worked like an animal ། ཆབ་འབངས་རྣམས་ལ་བཀོལ་སྤྱོད་དུད་འགྲོ་དང་མཚུངས་པ་ The subjects were treated like animals.

བཀོལ་སྤྱོད་ལག་རྩལ་ (gõõjöö l̲agdzɛɛ) working/ operating skill.

བཀོལ་སྤྱོད་ལུགས་སྲོལ་ (gõõjöö l̲ugsüü) working/ operating regulations.

བཀོལ་ཕྱུགས་ (gõõjuù) draft animals, beasts of burden.

བཀོལ་བེད་ (gõõbeè) shung. using for work ། ས་ཞིང་ཐ་རེངས་སུ་སོང་བ་བཀོལ་བེད་ལེགས་པར་སྤྱོད་དགོས་རྒྱུ་ One should make good use of those fields not being cultivated.

བཀོལ་ཚད་ (gõõdzeɛ̀) rate of use ། ཕྱུགས་རིགས་བཀོལ་ཚད་རན་པོ་ཞིག་བྱ་དགོས་ The rate of use of animals should be moderate/ appropriate.

བཀོལ་ཟོག (gõõsɔɔ̀) sm. བཀོལ་ཕྱུགས་.

བཀྱག (gyāà) f. of འགྱོགས་.

བཀྱག་དཀར་ (gyāàgaa) a porcelain serving bowl.

བཀྱགས་ (gyāà) p. of འགྱོགས་.

བཀྱལ་བ་ (gyɛ̄ɛ̄wa) meaningless/ idle talk.

བཀྱིག (gyīg) f. of འཁྱིག.

བཀྱིག་ཐག (gyīgdaà) a rope for tying.

བཀྱིག་རྡུང་ (gyīgduŋ) tying and beating; va.—གཏོང་.

བཀྱིགས་ (gyīì) p. of འཁྱིག.

བཀྱེ་ (gyē) f. of འགྱེད་.

བཀྱེ་ཚོགས་ཞུ་ (gyējoò sh̲u) shung. va. to ask the Dalai Lama for permission to serve the special fried cookies at the New Year's Ceremony (by the Lord Chamberlain).

བཀྱེ་ལམ་ (gyēlam) shung. a way to send sth.

བཀྱེད་ (gyēè) va. to bend backwards.

བཀྱེས་ (gyēè) p. of འཀྱེད་.

བཀྱོན་ (gyōn) 1. h. of གཤེ་. 2. see བཀའ་བཀྱོན་.

བཀྱོན་འདྲི་ (gyūndri) questioning/ interrogating harshly; va.—བྱེད་.

བཀྱོན་འབེབས་ (gyōnbeb) scolding/ rebuking; va.—བྱེད་.

བཀྲ་ (drā) abbr. of བཀྲ་བ་.

བཀྲ་བ་ (drāwa) multicolored, variegated; beautiful, lovely; bright ¶ ལང་ཚོ་ནམ་པར་བཀྲ་བ་ The beauty of youth. ¶ ཁ་དོག་ནམ་པར་བཀྲ་བ་ Multicolored.

བཀྲ་ལྷལ་ལྷལ་ (drā wɛɛwɛ) bright, clear ¶ གློག་འོད་བཀྲ་ལྷལ་ལྷལ་དུ་འཆར་བ་རེད་ The electric light shone brightly.

བཀྲ་མ་ཤིས་ (drā mashii) sm. བཀྲ་མ་ཤིས་པ་.

བཀྲ་མ་ཤིས་པ་ (drā mashiiba) unfortunate, unlucky, bad luck.

བཀྲ་ལ་ཤིས་པ་ (drāla shiibə) auspicious, lucky ¶ བཀྲ་ལ་ཤིས་པའི་ཉིན་མོ་ An auspicious day.

བཀྲ་ལམ་འཆར་ (drālam cār) vi. to shine brightly.

བཀྲ་ལམ་མེ་ (drā lamme) radiant, brilliant, brightly shining.

བཀྲ་ཤིས་ (drəshii) 1. abbr. of བཀྲ་ལ་ཤིས་པ་. 2. persons' name.

བཀྲ་ཤིས་ཀྱི་རྫ་ (drəshiigi dzā) the medicinal herb glossy ganoderma.

བཀྲ་ཤིས་ཁང་གསར་ (drəshii kāŋsar) shung. official in Drepung appointed by the traditional Tibetan government to oversee the daily morning tea that the government provided the monks.

བཀྲ་ཤིས་ཁྲ་རིང་ (drəshii trāriŋ) colorful brocade banners hanging from ropes attached to poles that are placed on roofs of houses on special occasions; va.—འགྲེམས་ to display such brocade banners.

བཀྲ་ཤིས་འཁྱིལ་ (drəshiigyii) a monastery in Amdo.

བཀྲ་ཤིས་དགུ་ཚོགས་ (drəshii gudzii) a type of Tibetan herbal medicine.

བཀྲ་ཤིས་སྒང་ (drəshiigaŋ) a place in Western Tibet.

བཀྲ་ཤིས་སྒོ་མང་ (drəshii gomaŋ) a monastery in Gansu province.

བཀྲ་ཤིས་སྒོར་མོ་ (drəshii gormo) type of Tibetan fried cookie.

བཀྲ་ཤིས་ལྟ་ལྟས་ (drəshii ŋādɛɛ) sign of good luck, a good omen.

བཀྲ་ཤིས་ཆོས་རྫོང་ (drəšii chōdzoŋ) a place in Bhutan.

བཀྲ་ཤིས་ཉིས་བརྩེགས་ (drəshii ñiidzag) sm.* བཀྲ་ཤིས་ཉིས་བརྩེགས་.

བཀྲ་ཤིས་ཉིས་བརྩེགས་ (drəshii ñiidzeg) double good luck.

བཀྲ་ཤིས་གཏམ་བཟང་ (drəshii dāmsaŋ) good news.

བཀྲ་ཤིས་རྟགས་བརྒྱད་ (drəshii dāggyɛɛ) the eight auspicious Buddhist symbols.

བཀྲ་ཤིས་ཐེམ་པ་ཡར་འཛེགས་ (drəshii tēmba yardzeg) shung. rapidly advancing in one's career, achieving success after success.

བཀྲ་ཤིས་བདེ་ལེགས་ (drəshii delee) 1. congratulations, greetings; va.—ཞུ་ to congratulate, to give one's best wishes ¶ བསོད་ནམས་ལ་བཀྲ་ཤིས་བདེ་ལེགས་ཞུ་རྒྱུ་ཡིན་ (I) will congratulate Sonam. 2. an expression of greetings.

བཀྲ་ཤིས་བདེ་ལེགས་ཕུན་སུམ་ཚོགས་ (drəshii delee phūnsum tsɔɔ) a traditional Tibetan New Year's greeting.

བཀྲ་ཤིས་པའི་ལས་དོན་ (drā shiibe lɛɛdön) a happy affair, an occasion for joy; a wedding.

བཀྲ་ཤིས་འཁྲིན་བཟང་ (drəshii trīnsaŋ) sm. བཀྲ་ཤིས་གཏམ་བཟང་.

བཀྲ་ཤིས་བླ་མ་ (drəshii lāma) the Panchen Lama.

བཀྲ་ཤིས་མེ་ཏོག (drəshii medog) good luck flower.

བཀྲ་ཤིས་རྫས་བརྒྱད་ (drəshii dzɛɛgyɛɛ) the eight auspicious things.

བཀྲ་ཤིས་ཟླ་བ་ (drəshii dawa) a month in the Tibetan calendar when there are no added or subtracted days.

བཀྲ་ཤིས་རེ་ཁ་ (drəshii rega) shung. auspicious designs/ signs ¶ བཀྲ་ཤིས་རེ་ཁས་བརྩན་པའི་ལྷ་རིག་སྤྱོད་ན་རིང་བ་སྣན་ཞལ་དུ་ཕུལ་བ་ (They) offered a long ceremonial scarf which was decorated (woven) with auspicious signs.

བཀྲ་ཤིས་ལུགས་ལེགས་ (drəshii lugleg) auspicious ¶ འབྲུང་སའི་ནིན་འགྲིལ་བཀྲ་ཤིས་ལུགས་ལེགས་བྱུང་སོང་ The marriage ceremony went auspiciously.

བཀྲ་ཤིས་ལེགས་སྐྱེས་ (drəshii leggyeè) a congratulatory present/ gift.

བཀྲ་ཤིས་ལོ་ལེགས་ (drəshii loleg) a year with a bumper harvest.

བཀྲ་ཤིས་ཤོག (drəshii shōò) "may we have good fortune" (used in prayers).

བཀྲ་ཤིས་ལྷུན་པོ་ (drəshii lhūmbu) Tashilhunpo Monastery in Shigatse (the seat of Panchen Lamas).

བཀྲག (drāà) sm. བཀྲག་མདངས་.

བཀྲག་ཆེན་པོ་ (drāà cēmbo) sm. བཀྲག་མདངས་.

བཀྲག་མདངས་ (drāndaŋ) glittering, brilliant, dazzling, splendid ¶ སྐར་མ་ནམས་དོ་དགོང་བཀྲག་མདངས་ཆེན་པོ་འདུག The stars are very dazzling tonight.

བཀྲག་མདངས་གཟི་བརྗིད་ (drāgdaŋ sijii) sm. བཀྲག་མདངས་.

བཀྲག་མེད་པ་ (drāgmeèba) dull, lackluster; boring, tedious ¶ བཀྲག་མེད་པའི་ཕྲ་ཚོམ་ Dull-looking jewelry.

བཀྲག་རྩི་ (drəgdzi) paint, enamel, varnish, lacquer; va.—གཏོང་.

བཀྲག་རྩི་རྗེན་པ་ (drəgdzi jemba) raw lacquer.

བཀྲག་རྩི་དམར་པོ་ (drəgdzi mārbo) red lacquer, red paint.

བཀྲག་རྩི་མཚལ་ཀ་ (drəgdzi tsɛɛga) a bright red lacquer.

བཀྲག་རྩི་ཤིང་ (drəgdzi shiŋ) a tree that is used for making lacquer (tung oil tree).

བཀྲག་རྩིའི་རི་མོ་ (drəgdzii rimo) oil painting.

བཀྲག་རས་ (drāgrɛɛ) oil cloth.

བཀྲག་ཤོག (drāgshɔɔ) oil paper.

བཀྲག་ལྷག་གེ་བ་ (drāg lhāgewa) sm. བཀྲག་ཆེན་པོ་.

བཀྲབ་: p. **བཀྲབས་**; f. **བཀྲབ་**; imp. **བཀྲོབས་** (drəp) va. to choose, to select ¶ སོན་བཟང་བཀྲབས་ཆེད་ In order to select good seed.

བཀྲབས་ (drəp) p. of བཀྲབ་.

བཀྲམ་ (drām) p. of འགྲེམས་.

བཀྲམ་དངོས་ཤེལ་སྒྲོམ་ (drāmŋöö shēēdrön) glass showcase.

བཀྲམ་སྟོན་ (drāmdön) an exhibit, exhibition; va.—བྱེད་.

བཀྲམ་སྟོན་ཁང་ (drāmdönkāŋ) exhibition hall.

བཀྲམ་བཞག་ཁང་ (drāmshakaŋ) sm. བཀྲམ་སྟོན་ཁང་.

བཀྲམས་འཚོང་ (drāmtsoŋ) displaying/ exhibiting for sale.

བཀྲམས་འཚོང་ཚོགས་འདུ་ (drāmtsoŋ tsōndu) meeting where things are exhibited for sale.

བཀྲལ་ (drɛɛ) 1. va. to impose (usu. a corvee tax). 2. p. of འགྲེལ་.

བཀྲས་བདགས་ (trɛɛdaà) a special kind of Chinese brocade originally brought into Tibet by Tashilhunpo.

བཀྲས་བླ་ (drɛɛla) shung. abbr. Tashilhunpo Labrang.

བཀྲས་བླ་ནང་སྒང་ (drɛɛla naŋgaŋ) shung. the main administrative office of the Tashilhunpo Labrang (i.e., the Panchen Lama's government [ནང་མ་སྒང་]).

བཀྲས་ལྷུན་ (drɛɛlhun) shung. abbr. of Tashilhunpo.

བཀྲི་ (drī) sm. འཁྲིད་.

བཀྲིན་ (gādrin) abbr. of བཀའ་དྲིན་.

བཀྲིན་ཅན་ (gādrinjɛn) having gratitude ¶ བཀྲིན་ཅན་གྱི་ཡབ་ The father for whom (one) has gratitude.

བཀྲིས་ (drīì) p. of ཀྲི་.

བཀྲིས་ (drəshiì) abbr. of བཀྲ་ཤིས་.

བཀྲིས་སྒང་ (drəshiì ga̲ŋ) a place in Bhutan.

བཀྲིས་ཆོས་རྫོང་ (drəshiì chȫdzoŋ) a place in Bhutan.

བཀྲུ་ (drū) f. of འཁྲུད་.

བཀྲུ་འཇམ་ (drūnjam) sm. བཀྲུ་སྨན་.

བཀྲུ་དག (drūdaà) clearing doubts/ suspicions by swearing or making an oath; va. བཀྲུ་དག; —བྱེད་.

བཀྲུ་སྨན་ (drūmɛn) laxative.

བཀྲུ་ཤལ་ (drūshɛɛ) washing and rinsing; va.—བྱེད་.

བཀྲུས་ (drū̄ù) p. of འཁྲུད་.

བཀྲུས་ཀྱིས་མ་དག (drū̄ùgi ma̲daà) real, beyond doubt, indisputable, irrefutable.

བཀྲུས་ཆག (drū̄ùjaà) shung. a tax concession based on a sworn oath that one doesn't have enough grain.

བཀྲུས་འཕྱིད་མ་དག (drū̄ùci ma̲daà) sm. བཀྲུས་ཀྱིས་མ་དག.

བཀྲེན་ (drēn) abbr. of བཀྲེན་པོ་.

བཀྲེན་རྒྱལ་ (drēngyɛɛ) abbr. of བཀྲེན་པོ་.

བཀྲེན་ངར་ཅན་ (drēnŋəbjɛn) sm. བཀྲེན་ངམ་.

བཀྲེན་ངམ་ (drēnŋam) 1. miserly, stingy, avaricious. 2. poor, destitute.

བཀྲེན་པོ་ (drēmbo) 1. miserly, stingy, avaricious ¶ ཁོ་ལག་པ་བཀྲེན་པོ་ཞེ་དྲག་འདུག He's very stingy. 2. poor, destitute ¶ འཚོ་བ་བཀྲེན་པོ་ཞིག་སྐྱེལ་གྱི་ཡོད་པ་རེད་ (They) are living in a destitute manner (with a poor livelihood).

བཀྲེས་ (drēè) 1. vi. to feel hunger, to be hungry (h.) ¶ ཁོང་གསོལ་ཁྲོད་བཀྲེས་འདུག He is hungry. 2. hunger.

བཀྲེས་སྐོམ་ (drēègom) hunger and thirst.

བཀྲེས་སྐོམ་ལྟོགས་ཤི་ (drēgom dōgshi) dying of hunger and thirst; vi.— ཐེབས་ to die of hunger and thirst; va.—གཏོང་ to cause to die of hunger and thirst.

བཀྲེས་ང་བ་ (drēèŋawa) hunger.

བཀྲེས་ངར་ (drēèŋəb) sm. བཀྲེས་ངམ་.

བཀྲེས་ངམ་ (drēèŋəm) greedy, avaricious.

བཀྲེས་ངམ་ཅན་ (drēŋamjɛn) 1. a beggar 2. greedy, avaricious.

བཀྲེས་ཐུབ་ (drēŋəb) sm. བཀྲེས་ངམ་.

བཀྲེས་ལྟོགས་ (drēdɔɔ̀) hunger.

བཀྲེས་ལྟོགས་ཅན་ (drēdogjɛn) hungry.

བཀྲེས་སྣང་ (drēnaŋ) sign/ appearance of feeling hungry; va.—བྱེད་ to show signs of feeling hunger/ hungry ¶ དེ་རིང་ཁོང་གསོལ་ཁྲོད་བཀྲེས་སྣང་བྱེད་ཀྱི་འདུག Today he is showing signs of feeling hungry.

བཀྲོངས་ (drōŋ) p. of དཀྲོང་.

བཀྲོབས་ (drōb) imp. of བཀྲབ་.

བཀྲོལ་ (drȫȫ) p. of འཁྲོལ་.

བཀྲོལ་བཤད་ (drȫȫshɛɛ̀) sm. འགྲེལ་བཤད་.

བགླག (lāà) f. of གློག.

བགླགས་ (lāà) p. of གློག.

བགླུབས་ (lūb) p. of གླུབ་.

ཀ་ (gā) irrigation canal (for fields); va.—འཁྲིད་ to irrigate via a canal.

ཀ་མགོ (gāngo) the start/ upper part of an irrigation canal.

ཀ་འགོ (gāngo) sm. ཀ་མགོ་.

ཀ་གཅིག་གི་ཆུ་མིག (gājiggi cūmiì) having the same origin [Lit. spring water (coming through) one canal].

ཀ་གཅེས་ཞིང་གཅེས་ (gājeè shi̲ŋjeè) shung. taking care of the irrigation canal and the fields ¶ ཀ་གཅེས་ཞིང་གཅེས་ཀྱིས་ཀ་ལས་འུལ་མི་ཆུ་འཁོར་གྱི་དགེ་བོད་ལ་བརྟེན་གསུམ་གཉིས་སྟེང་བྱང་པ་དང་ གསུམ་གཅིག་ཁང་གསར་ས་ནས་འུལ་མི་གོ་ཐང་གཏོང་རྒྱུ་ In order to take care of the irrigation canal and fields, Tengchangpa will sent two thirds of the irrigation corvee workers and Kangsar will send one third of them.

ཀ་ཆུ་ (gəcu) water in an irrigation canal.

ཀ་མཇུག (gəŋjuù) the end/ lower part of an irrigation canal.

ཀ་དེབ་ (gādeb) shung. a book listing the order that fields are to be irrigated ¶ ཀ་དེབ་ནང་གསལ་ཞིང་ཆུ་གཏོང་དགོས་པ་ One must irrigate the fields according to the clear instructions of the irrigation book.

ཀ་འབོལ་ (gāmböö) the first time a field is irrigated.

ཀ་མོ་ཆེ་ (gāmoje) the main irrigation canal.

ཀ་ཙམ་(རྩེང་) (gādzam) shung. in a twinkling.

ཀ་ཞིང་ (gəshiŋ) an irrigated field.

ཀ་རིགས་འདེབས་ལྡོག (gərig de̲bdɔɔ̀) shung. irrigation and plowing ¶ ཀ་རིགས་འདེབས་ལྡོག རྩྭ་ཆུ་ཤིང་གསུམ་གྱི་དགེ་བོད་འདྲ་སྙོམས་སུ་གཙོད་ཅིང་ The use of water for irrigation and plowing, for grass, and for trees, should be done in a equal manner.

ཀ་ལན་ (gālɛn) the second irrigation on a field.

ཀ་སྲུང་པ་ (gā sūŋba) person who looks after irrigation canals.

ཀང་ (gāŋ) 1. abbr. of ཀང་པ་. 2. a unit for sth. long and cylindrical, e.g., a cigarette, a match, a strand of hair ¶ ཐ་མག་ཀང་གཉིས་ Two cigarettes. 3. main, basic; mainly, basically ¶ ལས་འགན་གྱི་ཀང་དེ་འགོ་འཁྲིད་ལ་འཁྲིས་པ་རེད་ The main responsibility for the work fell on the leaders. ¶ སློབ་གསོ་ཀང་རེད་ Education is the main one. 4. shung. a land unit in tt. for which one full tax unit had to be paid ¶ དམག་ཀང་གཅིག One military ཀང་ (the field from which a soldier has to be provided as a tax). 5. the tightness of a weave ¶ རས་འདི་ཀང་ཡག་པོ་མི་འདུག This cloth is not woven tightly.

ཀང་གོར་ (gāŋgɔɔ) bangles worn on the feet.

ཀང་ཀྱོག (gāŋgyɔɔ̀) lame.

ཀང་ཀྲབ་ (gāŋdrəb) a foot pedal on a loom.

ཀང་དཀྲིས་ (gəŋdriì) cloth used to wrap feet.

ཀང་བཀུག (gəŋguù) (intentionally) tripping; va.—རྒྱག.

ཀང་བཀྱག (gāŋgyaà) a stepping-stone (e.g., across a stream).

ཀང་སྐུམ་ལག་སྐུམ་ (gāŋgum la̲ggum) pulling in/ drawing back one's hands and feet when hiding.

ཀང་རྐྱང་འདུར་སྒྲུབ་ (gāŋgyaŋ du̲rdrub) shung. calculating land taxes in a manner in which one འདོན་ is taxed at the rate of two ཀང་.

ཀང་སྐས་ (gāŋgɛɛ̀) a tree "ladder" made by inserting pegs in a tree trunk as steps for climbing.

ཀང་སྐོར་རྒྱག (gāŋgɔɔ ga̲à) sm. ཀང་གཡུག་རྒྱག.

ཀང་སྐོར་འབྲུ་རྡུང་འཕྲུལ་འཁོར་ (gāŋgɔɔ dru̲duŋ trū̄ügɔɔ) pedal-driven thresher.

ཀང་བརྐྱང་ལག་བརྐྱངས་ (gāŋgyaŋ la̲ggyaŋ) stretching hands and feet sideways; va.—བྱེད་.

ཀང་བསྐྱོད་ (gāŋgyȫȍ) going on foot, walking; va.—བྱེད་.

ཀང་ཁུམ་ལག་ཁུམ་ (gāŋkum la̲ggum) sm. ཀང་འཁུམ་ལག་འཁུམ་.

ཀང་ཁོབ་ལག་ཁོབ་ (gāŋkob la̲gkob) sm. ཀང་ཁོབ་ལག་ཁོབ་.

ཀང་ཁྲ་ (gāŋdra) fork (the eating utensil).

ཀང་ཁྲི་ (gəŋdri) sm. ཀང་སྟེགས་.

ཀང་འཁུམ་ལག་འཁུམ་ (gāŋkum la̲gkum) 1. cowardly, overcautious, timid ¶ ཁྱེད་རང་ཀང་འཁུམ་ལག་འཁུམ་བྱས་ནས་མ་བསྡད་པར་བློ་རྒྱ་ཆེན་པོས་ལས་ཀ་བྱེད་དགོས་ You shouldn't be overly cautious. You should go ahead boldly. 2. pulling in/ contracting feet and hands [Lit. shrinking/ contracting of legs, shrinking/ contracting of hands].

ཀང་འཁོབ་ལག་འཁོབ་ (gāŋgob la̲ggob) awkward, clumsy.

ཀང་འཁོར་ (gāŋgɔɔ) bicycle; va.—བཞོན་; —གཏོང་ to ride a bicycle.

ཀང་འཁོར་འཁོར་གསུམ་མ་ (gāŋgɔɔ kɔ̄rsum) tricycle.

ཀང་འཁོར་བཞོན་རྩལ་ (gāŋgɔɔ shö̲ndzɛɛ) trick cycling.

རྐང་འཁོར་བཟོ་གྲྭ (gāŋgɔɔ so̱dra) bicycle factory.

རྐང་འཁྱོག (gāŋgyɔɔ̀) sm. རྐང་ཀྱོག.

རྐང་འཁྱོགས་ (gāŋgyɔɔ̀) sm. རྐང་ཀྱོག.

རྐང་འཁྱོར་ (gāŋgyɔɔ) va. to stamp one's feet.

རྐང་འཁྲབ་ (gāŋdrəb) dancing; va.—བྱེད་.

རྐང་འཁྲབ་ལག་འཁྲབ་ (gāŋdrəb la̱gdrəb) 1. doing one's utmost ¶ ངས་རྐང་འཁྲབ་ལག་འཁྲབ་ཀྱིས་ལས་ཀ་བཙལ་ཀྱང་རྙེད་མ་བྱུང་ I did my utmost to look for work but didn't find any. 2. flailing around in pain; —བྱེད་. 3. jumping/ dancing with joy; —བྱེད་ [Lit. dancing with hands, dancing with legs].

རྐང་འཁྲབ་ལག་གཡོབ་ (gāŋtrəb la̱gyob) doing too many things at one time [Lit. feet dancing, hand waving].

རྐང་ག་རིལ་ (gāngəri) tib.hind. sm. རྐང་སྣ་རི་.

རྐང་གིས་ཡན་ལག་འཁྲིད་ (gāŋgi ye̱nlaà trii̖) a guiding principle, a principle that leads and directs other secondary ones.

རྐང་གོས་ (gāngöö̀) 1. trousers, pants. 2. footwear.

རྐང་གྱོག (gāngyɔɔ̀) sm. རྐང་ཀྱོག.

རྐང་གྱོལ་པོ་ (gāŋ gyö̱ö̱bo) sm. རྐང་ཀྱོག.

རྐང་གྲ་འགྲིགས་པོ་ (gāŋdra drigbu) marching in formation; va.—བྱེད་ ¶ དམག་མི་རྣམས་རྐང་གྲ་འགྲིགས་པོ་བྱས་ནས་ཐོན་ཕྱིན་པ་རེད་ The soldiers departed marching in formation.

རྐང་གྲངས་ (gāŋdraŋ) shung. the number of རྐང་ (the land unit).

རྐང་གྲུམ་གྱི་ནད་ (gāŋdrumgi nɛ̱ɛ̀) gout.

རྐང་གླ་ (gāŋla) fee paid to sb. to deliver sth.

རྐང་གླིང་ (gəŋliŋ) "musical" instrument made from human thigh bone (used in religious rites).

རྐང་བགྲོད་ (gāŋdröö̀) going on foot; va.—བྱེད་ ¶ ལྷ་ས་བར་རྐང་བགྲོད་བྱས་ནས་ཕྱིན་པ་ཡིན་ (I) went to Lhasa on foot.

རྐང་མགོ (gāngo) the area from the ankle to the tip of the toes.

རྐང་མགོའི་རུས་པ་ (gāŋgö rü̱übə) bone from ankle to the tip of toes.

རྐང་མགྱོགས་ (gāŋgyɔɔ̀) swift, fast, fleet-footed.

རྐང་འགུགས་ (gāŋguù) tripping; va.—རྒྱག.

རྐང་འགྲུལ་ (gāndrüü) going/ traveling on foot; va.—རྒྱག.

རྐང་འགྲོ་ (gāndro) 1. going on foot/ in person. 2. shung. taking/ delivering things on foot (e.g., a porter, messenger) ¶ ངས་ལས་ཁུངས་ནང་ལ་རྐང་འགྲོའི་ལས་ཀ་བྱེད་ཀྱི་ཡོད་ I do delivering work (by walking) in the office. 3. a corvee tax involving the sending of people for work.

རྐང་འགྲོ་བོགས་སྐྱུར་ (gāŋdro bɔggyur) shung. leasing one's corvee tax obligation by leasing land and the tax obligation.

རྐང་འགྲོ་ལག་འདོན་ (gāŋdro la̱gdön) shung. 1. two types of taxes: those taxes that involve sending corvee people and animals to work and those that involve sending goods-in-kind or money. 2. helping by going and doing sth. and providing things; va.—བྱེད་ ¶ རྐང་འགྲོ་ལག་འདོན་གཉིས་ཀའི་རོགས་རམ་བྱས་པ་རེད་ (They) helped by going in person and providing things.

རྐང་འགྲོའི་ཁྲལ་ཨུལ་ (gāŋdrö trɛ̄ɛwüü) shung. sm. རྐང་འགྲོ་, 2.

རྐང་འགྲོས་ (gāŋdröö̀) 1. sm. རྐང་བགྲོད་. 2. the manner of walking.

རྐང་འགྲོས་ལག་འགྲོས་ (gāŋdröö̀ la̱ŋdröö̀) going/ crawling on hands and feet.

རྐང་རྒྱན་ (gāŋgyɛn) a foot ornament.

རྐང་རྒྱུ་ (gəŋgyu) sm. རྐང་འགྲུལ་.

རྐང་སྣ་རི་ (gāngari) bicycle.

རྐང་སྣ་རིལ་ (gāngari) sm. རྐང་སྣ་རི་.

རྐང་སྣ་རིའི་ར་ཅོ་ (gāŋgarii ra̱jo) bicycle handlebars.

རྐང་སྒྲ་ (gāŋdra) the sound of footsteps.

རྐང་སྒྲོག་ལག་སྒྲོག་ (gāŋdrɔɔ̀ la̱gdrɔɔ̀) sm. རྐང་སྒྲོག་ལག་ལྕགས་.

རྐང་སྒྲོག་ལག་ལྕགས་ (gāŋdrɔɔ̀ la̱gjaà) leg-irons/ fetters and handcuffs; va.—རྒྱག to put sb. in leg and hand irons/ shackles/ fetters.

རྐང་སྒྲོག་ལག་བསྡམ་ (gāŋdrɔɔ̀ la̱gdam) sm. རྐང་སྒྲོག་ལག་ལྕགས་.

རྐང་བརྒྱ་པ་ (gāŋgyaba) sm. རྐང་བརྒྱ་མ་.

རྐང་བརྒྱ་མ་ (gāŋgyəma) centipede.

རྐང་བརྒྱ་ལག་བརྒྱ་ (gāŋgya laggya) sm. རྐང་བརྒྱ་མ་.

རྐང་ངར་ (gāŋŋar) shin bone.

རྐང་ངོས་ཀྱི་རུས་པ་ (gāŋŋöögi rü̱üba) metatarsal bones.

རྐང་དངུལ་ (gəŋüü) share, stock (in a company, enterprise, etc.).

རྐང་དངུལ་འཛིན་ཤོག (gāŋŋüü dzi̱nyii̖) share/ stock certificate.

རྐང་དངུལ་འཛིན་ལོར་ (gāŋŋüü dzi̱nlɔr) sm. རྐང་དངུལ་འཛིན་ཤོག.

རྐང་གཅིག་གི་ལྷས་མ་དང་ལག་གཅིག་གི་ཁྲོག་པ་ (gāŋjiggi lhɛ̄ma ta̱ŋ lāgjiggi dɔgba) sth. impossible to be accomplished by only one side [Lit. a braid with one strand, clapping with one hand].

རྐང་གཅིག་རང་གཅིག (gāŋjig ra̱njig) only one piece of sth.

རྐང་ལྕགས་ (gāŋjaà) leg-irons, leg shackles/ fetters; va.—རྒྱག to shackle with leg irons.

རྐང་ལྕགས་ལག་ལྕགས་ (gāŋjaà la̱gjaà) handcuffs and leg irons, hand and foot shackles; va.—རྒྱག.

རྐང་ཆག་ལག་གྲུམ་ (gāŋcaà la̱gdrum) broken hands and feet, crippled in hands and feet.

རྐང་ཆག་ལག་བུག (gāŋjaà la̱gbuù) sm. རྐང་ལྕགས་ལག་གྲུམ་.

རྐང་ཆེན་ (gāŋjen) shung. a large taxpayer family with many fields.

རྐང་འཇབ་ལག་འཇབ་ (gāŋjəb la̱njəb) hiding; va.—བྱེད་.

རྐང་འཇོག་པང་ལེབ་ (gāŋjɔɔ̀ bāŋleb) footstool, footrest.

རྐང་རྗེན་ (gāŋjen) barefeet.

རྐང་རྗེན་མ་ (gāānjema) barefeet.

རྐང་རྗེན་སྨན་པ་ (gāŋjen mɛ̄mba) sm. རྐང་རྗེན་ཨེམ་ཆི་.

རྐང་རྗེན་ཨེམ་ཆི་ (gāŋjen ə̄mci) barefoot doctor (name used at one time in PRC for people who worked as part-time peasants and part-time health providers).

རྐང་རྗེས་ (gāŋjeè) footprint.

རྐང་རྗེས་ལག་བསུབ་ (gāŋjeè lə̱gsub) shung. having sth. positive wiped away by a negative act, wiping away one's prior reputation; va.—བྱེད་ [Lit. wiping out a footprint with one's hand].

རྐང་རྗེས་ལག་བསུབས་ (gāŋjeè lə̱gsub) sm. རྐང་རྗེས་ལག་བསུབ་.

རྐང་ཉ་ (gāŋña) calf (of leg).

རྐང་གཉིས་ (gāŋñii̖) person, human being ¶ རྐང་གཉིས་གཙོ་བོ་ The principal human (epithet of the Buddha). [Lit. two feet].

རྐང་གཉིས་མཆོག (gāŋñii̖ cɔ̄ɔ̀) the Buddha.

རྐང་གཉིས་ཐིག་སྒྱུད་ (gāŋñii̖ ti̱gjɛɛ̀) surveying instrument.

རྐང་གཉིས་མི་བརྒྱ་ (gāŋñii̖ mi̱gya) all of the people.

རྐང་མཉམ་ (gāŋñam) verses that have the same number of words.

རྐང་གཏད་ (gāŋdɛɛ̀) on purpose ¶ ཁོང་གིས་རྐང་གཏད་བྱས་པ་ཞིག་མ་རེད་ He didn't do it on purpose.

རྐང་རྟགས་རྡོ་གཙུགས་ (gāŋdaà do̱dzug) 1. setting up markers to delimit a རྐང་ unit of land. 2. demarcating a border/ boundary.

རྐང་རྟེན་ (gāŋden) sm. རྐང་སྟེགས་.

རྐང་རྟེན་རྡོ་ (gāŋden do̱) stepping-stone (in a stream).

རྐང་སྟབས་ (gāŋdəb) sm. གོམ་སྟབས་.

རྐང་སྟེགས་ (gāŋdeg) footstool, footrest ¶ རྐང་སྟེགས་ཞིག་གི་སྟེང་ལ་ལངས་ན་སྙོབ་ཀྱི་འདུག If (I) stand on a footstool (I) reach it.

རྐང་སྟེང་ལུས་བཏེགས་ (gāndeŋ lü̱deg) self-supporting, standing on one's own feet ¶ ཐོག་མར་རྐང་སྟེང་ལུས་བཏེགས་ཐུབ་པ་ཞིག་བྱ་དགོས་ First of all, (we) have to be able to stand on (our) own two feet [Lit. support one's body on one's feet].

ཀང་སྟོང་ (gāŋdoŋ) getting no result after going to ask sb. a favor.

ཀང་ཐང་ (gāŋdaŋ) on foot.

ཀང་ཐང་འགྲོ་ས་ (gāŋdaŋ drosa) footway.

ཀང་ཐང་བདེ་བགྲོད་ (gāŋdaŋ dedröö̀) walking leisurely.

ཀང་ཐང་པ་ (gāŋdaŋba) walker, hiker, pedestrian.

ཀང་ཐང་བ་ (gāŋdaŋwa) sm. ཀང་ཐང་པ་.

ཀང་ཐང་མ་ (gāŋdaŋma) walker, hiker, pedestrian.

ཀང་ཐང་མར་འགྲོ་ (gāŋdaŋ maa dro) va. to go on foot.

ཀང་ཐང་ལ་འགྲོ་ (gāŋdaŋla dro) sm. ཀང་ཐང་མར་འགྲོ་.

ཀང་ཐོ་ (gāŋdo) 1. kicking; va.—གཞུ་ to kick ¶ ང་ལ་རྟས་ཀང་ཐོ་བཞུས་བྱུང་ The horse kicked me. 2. shung. a tax list of ཀང.

ཀང་ཐོགས་ལག་ཐོགས་ (gāŋdɔɔ̀ lagdɔɔ̀) being in the way, being a hindrance.

ཀང་ཐོང་ (gāŋtoŋ) man-drawn plow.

ཀང་མཐིལ་ (gəŋdii) sole of foot.

ཀང་མཐིལ་ཀྱོང་མེད་ (gəŋtii gyōŋmeè) sm. ཀང་པ་སྦོ་ལེབ་.

ཀང་མཐིལ་ལ་ཉི་མ་མ་ཤར་བར་དུ་ (gəŋdiilə ñimə masharbardu) sth. that is impossible, sth. that will never happen [Lit. until the sun shines on the sole of the foot].

ཀང་འཐིང་ (gāŋdeŋ) sm. ཀང་ཀྱོག.

ཀང་འཐིང་ལག་སྐྱོལ་ (gāŋdeŋ läggyöö) sm. ཀང་ཞ་ལག་འཐེན་.

ཀང་འཐིང་ལག་ཞ་ (gāŋdeŋ lagsha) sm. ཀང་ཞ་ལག་འཐིང་.

ཀང་དུང་ (gəŋduŋ) sm. ཀང་གླིང་.

ཀང་དུམ་ (gəŋdum) legless, sb. who has lost his leg(s).

ཀང་དུམ་པ་ (gəŋdumba) legless, paraplegic.

ཀང་དུམ་ལག་དུམ་ (gəŋdum lagdum) legless and armless, paraplegic.

ཀང་དྲིན་ (gāŋdren) sm. ཀང་པ་འཐེན་.

ཀང་གདན་ (gāŋdɛn) door mat.

ཀང་གདུང་ (gāŋduŋ) tibia bone.

ཀང་གདུབ་ (gəŋdup) foot bangle/ bracelet.

ཀང་གདོས་ (gāŋdöö̀) sm. ཀང་ལྷུགས་.

ཀང་བདེ་ (gāŋde) working dexterously/ agilely and diligently; va.—བྱེད་.

ཀང་འདེགས་ (gāŋdeè) sm. ཀང་རྟེན་རྡོ་.

ཀང་འདོན་ (gāŋdön) shung. two kinds of land measurement units: ཀང་ and འདོན་ (one འདོན་ = 2 ཀང་).

ཀང་འདྲེད་ (gāŋdreè) slipping; vi.—ཤོར་ to slip ¶ ང་འཁྱགས་པའི་སྟེང་ཀང་འདྲེད་ཤོར་ནས་རིལ་བྱུང་ (I) slipped on the ice and fell.

ཀང་འདྲེན་ (gāŋdren) sm. ཀང་པ་འཐེན.

ཀང་རྡུང་ལག་རྡུང་ (gəŋduŋ lagduŋ) beating with hands and feet; va.—བྱེད་.

ཀང་རྡུམ་ (gəŋdum) sm. ཀང་དུམ་.

ཀང་རྡུམ་ལག་རྡུམ་ (gəŋdum) sm. ཀང་དུམ་ལག་དུམ་.

ཀང་རྡོག (gāŋdɔɔ̀) leather sole (of shoe/ boot).

ཀང་བརྡ་ལག་བརྡ་ (gāŋda lagda) signaling with hands and feet, sending a sign with hands and feet; va.—བྱེད་.

ཀང་བརྡབ་ (gāŋ dəb) 1. vi. to bang one's leg against sth. 2. va. to bang/ stomp one's feet on the ground.

ཀང་བརྡབ་ལག་བརྡབ་ (gāŋdab lagdab) stomping one's feet and hands; va.—བྱེད་ ¶ ཀང་བརྡབ་ལག་བརྡབ་བྱེད་བཞིན་པར་གཤེ་གཤེ་བཏང་བ་རེད་ (He) scolded (them) stomping (his) feet and hands (in anger).

ཀང་བརྡབ་ལག་ཕུར་ (gāŋdab lagbur) sm. ཀང་བརྡབ་ལག་བརྡབ་.

ཀང་བརྡེག (gāŋdeè) kicking; va.—གཞུ་ to kick ¶ ཀུན་མ་དེ་བཟུང་ནས་མི་ཚང་མས་ཀང་བརྡེག་བཞུས་པ་རེད་ After they caught the thief, everyone kicked him.

ཀང་ནད་ལ་མགོ་སྨན་ (gāŋnɛɛ̀la gomɛn) doing sth. that isn't useful, doing the wrong or inappropriate thing [Lit. giving head medicine for a sick foot].

ཀང་ནས་མེད་ (gāŋnɛɛ̀ meè) there definitely does not exist, completely/ definitely/ absolutely without ¶ མི་སེར་རྣམས་ལ་བདེ་བའི་གོ་སྐབས་ཀང་ནས་མེད་པ་རེད་ The subjects have absolutely no chance for happiness.

ཀང་གནོན་ཐོང་གཤོལ་ (gāŋnön thōŋshöö) sm. ཀང་ཐོང་.

ཀང་གནོན་ཤུར་མདའ་ (gāŋnön shūnda) a type of arrow shot by placing the foot/ feet on the bow.

ཀང་སྣམ་ (gāŋnam) trousers.

ཀང་སྣམ་ཁ་ཐིག (gāŋnam kədiì) the string belt that ties pants at the waist.

ཀང་སྣམ་གྱི་འདོམས་ (gāŋnamgi dom) sm. ཀང་སྣམ་ཁ་ཐིག.

ཀང་སྣེ་རྡོ་ཐོགས་ (gāŋne dodɔɔ̀) unable to achieve one's objective because of an obstacle [Lit. stumble on a piece of rock].

ཀང་བསྣོལ་ (gāŋnöö̀) crossing one's leg when sitting (considered disrespectful); va.—བྱེད་.

ཀང་པ་ (gāŋba) foot, leg.

ཀང་པ་འཁྱོག (gāŋba kyɔ̄ɔ̀) vi. to limp, to walk with a limp.

ཀང་པ་གུག་གུག (gāŋba guùguù) bowlegged.

ཀང་པ་བགྲད་བགྲད་ (gāŋba drɛɛ̀drɛɛ̀) 1. a wide/ squat foot. 2. standing with legs spread apart; va.—བྱེད་.

ཀང་པ་གོད་པ་ (gāŋba göö̀ba) sb. who wanders/ roams around a lot.

ཀང་པ་གཅིག་ལ་ཚེར་མ་བརྒྱ་ (gāŋba jīglə tsērma gya) having many problems/ difficulties [Lit. a hundred thorns in one foot].

ཀང་པ་འཇིམ་བཟོས་ཅན་གྱི་མི་ཆེན་ (gāŋba jimsüùjɛngi mijen) sb. who is big but is not really strong or powerful, a "paper tiger" [Lit. a giant with feet of clay].

ཀང་པ་ཉིས་འཛུགས་ (gāŋba ñīìdzug) doing two things at once, laying down roots in two places; va.—བྱེད་ ¶ བུ་མོ་དེས་ས་གནས་མི་འདྲ་གཉིས་ལ་ཁྱོ་ག་རེ་བཙལ་ནས་ཀང་པ་ཉིས་འཛུགས་བྱས་ཡོད་པ་རེད་ That girl has laid down roots in two places at once by having a man in two different locations [Lit. to put down/ plant two feet].

ཀང་པ་གཉིས་སྦྲོས་ནས་འགྲོ་བའི་བྱེད་ཕྱོགས་ (gāŋbañīì bö̀önɛɛ̀ drowɛɛ cejɔɔ̀) "two legs policy," i.e., doing several alternative things at the same time, diversifying ¶ བཟོ་ལས་དང་ཞིང་ལས་གཉིས་ཀ་གཉེར་བ་དེ་ཀང་པ་གཉིས་སྦྲོས་ནས་འགྲོ་བའི་སྲིད་བྱུས་ཤིག་རེད་ Managing (both) industry and agriculture is (an example) of the "two legs policy".

ཀང་པ་མཉམ་པ་ (gāŋba ñamba) sm. ཀང་མཉམ་.

ཀང་པ་བརྟན་པོ་ (gāŋba dɛ̄mbo) safe/ firm footing, firm foundation; vi.—ཚུགས་ to be on a sound/ firm footing, to be on a firm foundation ¶ ལོ་ཁ་ཤས་ནས་ང་ཚོའི་ཁེ་ལས་ཀང་པ་བརྟན་པོ་ཚུགས་ཐུབ་པའི་རེ་བ་ཡོད་ We hope that our enterprise will be on firm footing in a few years.

ཀང་པ་འཐེན་ (gāŋba tēn) 1. va. to pull/ stretch the foot. 2. va. to disgrace, to make a spectacle of oneself, to lose face ¶ རང་གི་ཁྱིམ་ཚང་གི་ཀང་པ་འཐེན་མི་རུང་ One should not disgrace one's family.

ཀང་པ་བརྡབ་ (gāŋba dəb) 1. vi. to bang one's leg against sth. 2. va. to stomp one's foot.

ཀང་པ་ན་ན་ (gāŋba nana) va. to go somewhere (looking/ searching) until one is tired (until one's feet hurt) ¶ ངས་ཀང་ན་ན་ཕྱིན་ཀྱང་ཅ་ལག་དེ་རྙེད་མ་བྱུང་ I went (searched) everywhere until I was tired but didn't find the thing.

ཀང་པ་ཕར་བརྐྱངས་ ཉི་མ་ཚུར་བསྲོས་ (gāŋba pāā gyāŋ ñimə tsūū sȫö̀) relaxing, lazing around [Lit. stretching one's legs and basking in the sun].

ཀང་པ་སྦོ་ལེབ་ (gāŋba boleb) sm. ཀང་པ་ལེབ་ལེབ་.

ཀང་པ་ཚུགས་ས་ (gāŋba tsūgsa) sm. ཀང་པ་འཛུགས་ས་.

ཀང་པ་འཛུགས་ས་ (gāŋba dzugsə) a foothold [Lit. a place to put one's foot].

ཀང་པ་རྫུས་མ་ (gāŋba dzü̲ü̲mə) artificial leg.

ཀང་པ་ཞ་བོ་ (gāŋba sha̲wo) sm. ཀང་པ་ཞ་རིལ་.

ཀང་པ་ཞ་རིལ་ (gāŋba shə̲rii) club foot.

ཀང་པ་ཡང་པོ་ (gāŋba ya̲ŋbo) light-footed, fast.

ཀང་པ་ལེབ་ལེབ་ (gāŋba le̲blee̍) flat feet, flat-footed.

ཀང་པ་ཤོར་ (gāŋba shɔ̄ɔ) vi. to slip.

ཀང་པའི་དཀྱུང་མོ་ (gāŋbɛ gu̲ŋmo) middle toe.

ཀང་པའི་རྐལ་པ་ (gāŋbɛ gɛ̲ɛba) the back of the foot.

ཀང་པའི་ངར་གདུང་ (gāŋbɛ ŋa̲rduŋ) shin.

ཀང་པའི་ཉ་རིལ་ (gāŋbɛ ñə̲rii) calf.

ཀང་པའི་རྟིང་ག (gāŋbɛ di̲ŋgə) heel.

ཀང་པའི་མཐེ་བོང་ (gāŋbɛ tēboŋ) the big toe.

ཀང་པའི་སྦོ་ (gāŋbɛ bo̲) instep.

ཀང་པའི་རྩ་ (gāŋbɛ dzā) veins of the feet.

ཀང་པའི་ཚིགས་ (gāŋbɛ tsīi) leg joint.

ཀང་པའི་ཚིགས་རྡོག (gāŋbɛ tsīgdog) ankle bone.

ཀང་པའི་མཛུ་གུ་ (gāŋbɛ dzu̲gu) sm. ཀང་པའི་མཛུབ་གུ་.

ཀང་པའི་མཛུག་གུ་ (gāŋbɛ dzu̲gu) sm. ཀང་པའི་མཛུབ་གུ་.

ཀང་པའི་མཛུབ་གུ་ (gāŋbɛ dzu̲gu) toes.

ཀང་པའི་མཛུབ་ཆུང་ (gāŋbɛ dzu̲bcuŋ) smallest toe.

ཀང་པའི་མཛུབ་རུས་ (gāŋbɛ dzu̲brüü) toe bones.

ཀང་པའི་རི་མོ་ (gāŋbɛ ri̲mo) lines on the sole of the feet (like the lines on the palm of hands).

ཀང་པའི་སེན་མོ་ (gāŋbɛ sēnmo) toe nails.

ཀང་པའི་སྲིན་ལག (gāŋbɛ sīnlaà) the fourth toe (the one next to the small toe).

ཀང་པས་ལུས་མི་འགྱོག (gāŋbɛ lü̲ü̲ mi̲gyoò) unable to support/ stand on one's own feet, becoming or being dependent [Lit. the leg is unable to support the body].

ཀང་པས་ས་མ་རེག་ལ་སྤྱི་བོས་གནམ་རྟོལ་ (gāŋbɛ sāmaregla jīwöö nāmdöö) overly optimistic, trying to achieve sth. that is impossible, trying to obtain a high post without resources [Lit. the foot doesn't reach the ground, the crown of the head punches a hole in the sky].

ཀང་འཕྲ་ (gāŋdra) kicking; va.—རྒྱག.

ཀང་བའི་གུང་ལོ་ (gāŋwɛ gu̲nlo) the second toe.

ཀང་བའི་རྟིང་ག (gāŋwɛ di̲ŋgə) the heel.

ཀང་བའི་མཐེ་བོ་ (gāŋwɛ tēbo) the big toe.

ཀང་བའི་མཐེའུ་ (gāŋwɛ tēwu) the little toe.

ཀང་བའི་ཕྱི་རྟིང་ (gāŋwɛ di̲ŋgə) the heel.

ཀང་བའི་སྲིན་ལག (gāŋwɛ sīnlaà) the fourth toe.

ཀང་བོལ་ (gāŋböö) back of the foot.

ཀང་བྱེད་ (gāŋ ce̲è) va. to be the backbone/ mainstay/ core/ nucleus/ spine.

ཀང་བྱེད་མཁན་ (gāŋ ce̲ŋgɛn) those who are the backbone or mainstay, leaders ¶ ལས་འགུལ་དེའི་ཀང་བྱེད་མཁན་ཁ་ཤས་འཛིན་བཟུང་བྱས་པ་རེད་ Some people who were the backbone of the movement were arrested.

ཀང་བྱེད་སྒྲུབ་ཆ་ (gāŋje tru̲bja) a main or important part/ element/ constituent ¶ ཁང་པ་འདིའི་ཀང་བྱེད་སྒྲུབ་ཆ་ལྕགས་དང་ཨར་འདམ་རེད་ The main elements in the house are iron and cement.

ཀང་བྲོ་ (gāŋdro) a dance, dancing.

ཀང་བྲོ་གླུ་གར་ (gāŋdro lūgar) singing and dancing; va.—འཁྲབ་; —གཏོང་.

ཀང་བྲོ་གླུ་གཞས་ (gāŋdro lūshɛɛ̀) sm. ཀང་བྲོ་གླུ་གར་.

ཀང་འབམ་ (gāŋbam) elephantiasis.

ཀང་འབབ་ལེན་ (gāŋba le̲n) va. to take a major responsibility/ major role ¶ ཁོང་གིས་ལས་ཀ་ཀང་འབབ་བླངས་ནས་བྱས་བཞག He has taken a major responsibility in that work.

ཀང་འབོར་ (gāŋbɔr) shung. the amount of land (in ཀང་ units) ¶ ཁྲལ་འདེབ་གསར་རྙིང་སོ་སོའི་ཀང་འབོར་ཁྲལ་རྟེན་བསྡོམ་དཀྲི་ (They) made some adjustments on the amount of ཀང་ of the old and new taxpayers.

ཀང་མང་ (gāŋmaŋ) poet. crab, insect with many legs.

ཀང་མང་ལག་མང་ (gāŋmaŋ la̲gmaŋ) crowded, bustling [Lit. many hands and many feet].

ཀང་མར་ (gāŋmaa) marrow (of bone).

ཀང་དམག (gāŋmaà) 1. infantry. 2. infantryman.

ཀང་བཙུགས་ (gāŋdzuù) on purpose, deliberately, intentionally ¶ ཡི་གེ་དེ་ཀང་བཙུགས་ནས་བཏང་བ་རེད་ (He) sent the letter intentionally.

ཀང་རྩ་ (gāŋdza) 1. capital (monetary). 2. leg veins. 3. shoes.

ཀང་རྩེ་ (gāŋdze) tip of the toes.

ཀང་རྩེད་སྤོ་ལོ་ (gāŋdzeè bōlo) 1. soccer; va.—རྒྱག. 2. soccer ball.

ཀང་ཚ་ (gāŋdza) a county in the Haibei Autonomous Prefecture in Qinghai.

ཀང་ཚད་དངུལ་འཛིན་ (gāŋdzɛɛ̀ ŋü̲ndzin) stock certificate, certificate of shares (in a company).

ཀང་ཚིགས་ (gəŋdzii) ankle; va.—འཆུས་ to twist one's ankle.

ཀང་ཚུགས་ (gāŋ tsūù) vi. to be or get started ¶ བཟོ་གྲྭ་དེའི་ལས་ཀ་ཀང་ཚུགས་བཞག The factory has started to work.

ཀང་ཚེགས་ (gāŋdzeg) weary/ tired legs ¶ དེ་རིང་ཉིན་གང་གོམ་པ་བརྒྱབ་ནས་ཀང་ཚེགས་ཆེན་པོ་བྱུང་ Today (I) walked the whole day so my feet are tired.

ཀང་འཚབ་ལག་འཚབ་ (gāŋdzəb la̲gdzəb) in a frantic rush.

ཀང་མཛུབ་ (gəŋdzub) toe.

ཀང་མཛུབ་རུས་པ་ (gāŋdzub rü̲bə) toe bone.

ཀང་མཛེར་ (gəŋdzer) corns on toes.

ཀང་འཛིན་ (gəŋdzin) 1. sm. ཀང་བྱེད་. 2. specialized field/ profession, specialized subject ¶ རིགས་གཅིག་ཀང་འཛིན་གྱི་བཟོ་པ་ A specialized worker.

ཀང་འཛིན་འགོ་ཁྲིད་ (gəŋdzin gu̲drii) key members of the leadership ¶ རྒྱལ་ཁབ་ཀྱི་གལ་ཆེའི་གནད་དོན་རྣམས་ཀང་འཛིན་འགོ་ཁྲིད་ཚོས་ཐག་གཅོད་ཀྱི་ཡོད་པ་རེད་ The key members of the leadership decide the nation's important issues.

ཀང་འཛིན་པ་ (gəŋdzimbə) the main person ¶ ཁོང་ཁྱེད་རང་གི་ཞིབ་འཇུག་ལས་ཀའི་ཀང་འཛིན་པ་རེད་ He is the main person (doing) your research.

ཀང་འཛིན་བྱེད་མཁན་ (gəŋdzin ce̲ñɛn) 1. sm. ཀང་འཛིན་པ་. 2. specialist, expert.

ཀང་འཛིན་ཡུལ་དམག (gəŋdzin yü̲ü̲maà) the principal militia.

ཀང་འཛིན་སློབ་གྲྭ་ (gəŋdzin lāpdra) technical school, vocational school.

ཀང་འཛུགས་ (gāŋ dzu̲ù) va. to start/ begin. 2. va. to make/ establish as the main.

ཀང་འཛུགས་སྐྱེ་ (gāŋdzuù gyē) vi. to have a breech birth.

ཀང་འཛུགས་མཁན་ (gāŋdzuùñɛn) the main one's making/ doing/ establishing sth. ¶ བཟོ་གྲྭ་འདིའི་ལས་ཀའི་ཀང་འཛུགས་མཁན་བཟོ་པ་བགྲེས་སོང་རྣམས་རེད་ The older workers are the main one's doing the factory work.

ཀང་བརྫུས་དང་ལག་བརྫུས་ (gāŋdzüü ta̲ŋ lə̲gdzüü) artificial limbs (arms and feet).

ཀང་ཞ་བ་ (gāŋshawa) sm. ཀང་རིལ་.

ཀང་ཞ་ལག་འཐེན་ (gāŋsha la̲gden) 1. quadriplegic, sb. with hands and arms not functional. 2. shung. making excuses; va.—བྱེད་ ¶ རང་འཁྲིའི་ཁྲལ་རིགས་སྒྲུབ་རྒྱུགས་ཞུ་སྒོ་ཀང་ཞ་ལག་འཐེན་དུ་མ་སོང་བ་དགོས་རྒྱུ་ One should not make excuses regarding performing corvee tax duties.

ཀང་གཞི་ (gəŋshi) foundation, base ¶ ལས་ཀའི་ཀང་གཞི་ Foundation of the work.

ཀང་གཞུ་ལག་གཞུ་ (gāŋshu la̲gshu) unrestrained behavior [Lit. strike with hand, strike with feet].

ཀང་བཞག (gāŋshaà) thigh.

ཀང་བཞི་ (gəŋshi) quadruped.

ཀང་བཞིའི་རྒྱལ་པོ་ (gəŋshii gyɛ̲ɛbo) lion.

ཀང་ཟམ་ (gāŋsam) small bridge, footbridge.

ཀང་ཟོམ་ (gāŋsom) Tibetan style woolen boot.

ཀང་འོག་གི་རྡེའུ་དཔྲལ་བར་འཕར་ (gāŋɔɔgi di̲u drɛ̄ɛwar pār) 1. a meteoric rise. 2. getting abused/ attacked by those beneath or subservient to you [Lit. a stone under the foot hits the forehead].

ཀང་འོག་རྡེའུ་ (ཀང་འོག་གི་རྡེའུ་) sb. who is looked down on with scorn/ contempt/ disdain [Lit. a pebble underfoot].

ཀང་ཡག་པོ་ (gāŋ yagbo) sturdy.

ཀང་ཡུ་ (gāŋyu) stalk/ stem of a plant.

ཀང་ཡོན་ (gāŋyön) sm. ཀང་འཁྱོག.

ཀང་གཡུག (gāŋyuù) incomplete control over movement of the leg (e.g., due to a stroke); vi.—རྒྱག ¶ བུ་མོ་དེའི་ཀང་པ་ཡ་གཅིག་ལ་གྲིབ་ཕོག་ནས་ཀང་གཡུག་བརྒྱབ་ནས་འགྲོ་གི་འདུག The girl, having had a stroke in one leg, walks having incomplete control over one leg.

ཀང་རིང་ (gāŋriŋ) a long leg.

ཀང་རིལ་ (gāŋrii) foot binding (the traditional Chinese custom for women); va.—བྱེད་ ¶ རྒྱ་མོ་ཀང་རིལ་ A Chinese woman with bound feet.

ཀང་དྲིལ་ (gāŋrüü) foot odor.

ཀང་རུས་ (gāŋrüù) foot bone.

ཀང་བརླག (gāŋ lāà) vi. to be bankrupt/ broke, to lose one's capital ¶ ད་རེས་ཚོང་ཉེས་བྱུང་ནས་ངའི་མ་རྩའི་ཀང་བརླགས་སོང་ This time business was bad so (I) lost my capital (went bankrupt).

ཀང་ལག (gāŋlaà) feet and hands, limbs. va.—གཅོད་ to cut off sb.'s limbs.

ཀང་ལག་ཀྲབ་ཀྲབ་ (gāŋlaà drābdrəb) feet and arms shaking (involuntarily).

ཀང་ལག་འགྱུས་པ་ (gāŋlaà gyüübə) the fifth week of fetal development in Tibetan medicine (i.e., the time when the arms and the legs are formed).

ཀང་ལག་བརྟེན་ཤིང་ (gāŋlaà dēnshiŋ) crutches.

ཀང་ལག་བདེ་པོ་ (gāŋlaà debo) physically adroit (with hands and feet).

ཀང་ལག་བཟོས་མ་ (gāŋlaà dzüüma) artificial limbs.

ཀང་ལག་བཞི་ (gāŋlaà shi) limbs, the four hands and feet.

ཀང་ལམ་ (gāŋlam) footpath.

ཀང་ལེན་ (gāŋ len) sm. ཀང་འཛིན་.

ཀང་ལེབ་ (gāŋleb) crushing, flattening (by feet); vi.—འཐེབ་ ¶ འབུ་དེ་ཀང་ལེབ་ཐེབས་བཞག That insect was crushed underfoot.

ཀང་ལོགས་ (gāŋlɔɔ) surface of the legs.

ཀང་ལོང་ (gāŋlɔŋ) ankle.

ཀང་ཤིང་ (gāŋshiŋ) 1. wooden shackles/ cangue (for feet); va.—རྒྱག to attach wooden shackles on feet. 2. a pedal on a spinning lathe.

ཀང་ཤུ་ (gāŋshu) 1. a sore on the foot. 2. beriberi.

ཀང་ཤུབས་ (gāŋshub) stockings, socks.

ཀང་སུག (gāŋsuù) sm. ཀང་ཤུབས་.

ཀང་སོར་ (gāŋsor) toe.

ཀང་གསུམ་ (gāŋsum) three-legged; tripod.

ཀང་གསུམ་འཁོར་ལོ་ (gāŋsum kɔ̄ɔlo) tricycle.

ཀང་གསུམ་སྡིགས་བུ་ (gāŋsum dēgbu) tripod.

ཀང་ལྷམ་ (gāŋlham) 1. shoe. 2. pants, trousers.

ཀན་ (gɛ̄n) palate (of mouth).

ཀན་སྒྲ་ (gɛ̄ndra) 1. palatal sound. 2. a clicking sound made by the tongue and palate; va.—གཏོང་ (usu. the sound used to stop a horse).

ཀན་རྙིལ་ (gɛ̄nñii) gum (of the mouth).

ཀན་འདེབས་ (gɛ̄ndeb) 1. touching the palate with one's tongue; va.—བྱེད་. 2. the chewing of food on the gums by a toothless person; va.—བྱེད་.

ཀན་དེབ་ (gɛ̄ndeb) sm. ཀན་འདེབས་.

ཀན་ན་པོ་བྱེད་ (gɛ̄n nabo cee) va. to make/ treat sth. seriously in a negative way.

ཀན་ནད་ (gɛ̄nnɛɛ̀) disease of the palate.

ཀན་ཕུག (gɛ̄nbuù) soft palate.

ཀན་དབུས་ (gɛ̄nwüü) the center of the palate.

ཀན་འབྲུམ་ (gɛ̄ndrum) a pimple/ blister on the palate.

ཀན་མར་ (gɛ̄nmar) soft butter that is stuck on the palate of newly born babies (including colts) for the purpose for stimulating the sucking response.

ཀན་སྨིན་ (gɛ̄nmen) sm. ཀན་འབྲུམ་.

ཀན་སྨིན་གཟུགས་ཅན་ (gɛ̄nmen sugjɛn) tonsil.

ཀན་རལ་ (gɛ̄nrɛɛ) cleft palate.

ཀན་རུས་ (gɛ̄nrüü) upper jaw bone.

ཀན་ལ་སྤུ་སྐྱེ་ (gɛ̄nla bū gyē) sth. bad coming/ occurring ¶ མི་གཞན་གྱི་རྒྱུ་ནོར་བཟས་དུས་ན་རང་གི་ཀན་ལ་སྤུ་སྐྱེ་གི་རེད་ If you take another's possessions sth. bad will come to you. [Lit. hair growing on the palate].

ཀུ་: p. བརྐུས་; f. བརྐུ་; imp. རྐུས་ (gū) va. to steal ¶ གཞན་ནོར་བརྐུས་ན་ཁྲིམས་གཅོད་ཕོག་གི་རེད་ If you steal another's wealth, you will be punished by the courts.

ཀུ་ཁྱེར་ (gūgyer) sm. ཀུ་འཁྱེར་.

ཀུ་འཁྱེར་ (gūgyer) stealing; va.—བྱེད་.

ཀུ་ཇག་ཁྲམ་གསུམ་ (gū jaà trām sūm) abbr. the three: thief, bandit, swindler.

ཀུ་འཇལ་ (gūnjɛɛ) shung. fine/ punishment for theft ¶ ཀུ་མ་བརྐུས་ན་དངོས་པོའི་བདག་པོར་ཀུ་འཇལ་སྤྲོད་དགོས་པ་རེད་ If you steal you will have to pay a fine to the owner of the property.

ཀུ་འཕྲོག (gūndrɔɔ) looting, plundering, robbing; va.—བྱེད་.

ཀུ་བ་བཅུ་ (gūwa jū) ten ways/ methods of stealing.

ཀུ་བས་ལོངས་སྤྱོད་ཕོངས་ (gūwɛɛ loŋjöö pōŋ) stealing will lead to poverty.

ཀུ་བྱེད་ (gū cee) sm. ཀུ་མ་ཀུ་.

ཀུ་མ་ (gūma) thief; va.—རྒྱག; —ཀུ་ to steal; vi.—ཤོར་ to get stolen.

ཀུ་མ་གཅིག་ལ་ཉེས་པ་བརྒྱ་ (gūmajigla ñeeba gya) punishing/ blaming many for the theft of one [Lit. one thief, one hundred punishments].

ཀུ་མ་ནང་ལ་བཞག སྒོ་ལྕགས་ཕྱི་ལ་རྒྱག (gūma naŋla shaà gojaà cīlə gyaà) worrying about external threats when the problem is internal [Lit. leave the thief inside the house, lock the door from the outside].

ཀུ་མ་ཚ་པོ་ (gūma tsābo) an incorrigible/ recidivist thief.

ཀུ་མར་ལྷ་མེད་ (gūma lhāmeè) having bad luck ¶ ཀུ་མར་ལྷ་མེད་ཅེར་བ་ལྟར་ངང་དུ་འཛུལ་བ་དང་ཁོས་ཀུན་མ་བརྐུས་པ་གཉིས་དུས་མཚུངས་སོང་ Like the saying, "thieves don't have any gods," I entered the house just as he was stealing [Lit. thieves don't have any gods (to help them)].

ཀུ་བཙུགས་ (gū dzüù) va. to frame sb. for theft, to fabricate a charge of theft against sb.

ཀུ་ཚོང་ (gūdzoŋ) sm. ཀུ་འཚོང་.

ཀུ་འཚོང་ (gūdzoŋ) selling stolen goods; va.—རྒྱག.

ཀུ་རྫས་ (gūdzɛɛ̀) loot, stolen goods.

ཀུ་ལེན་ (gū len) va. to steal.

ཀུ་ཤས་ (gūshɛɛ̀) share of loot/ booty/ stolen goods.

ཀུ་ཤོར་ (gū shɔ̄ɔ) vi. to be/ get stolen or robbed ¶ ང་ཕྱིར་འགྲོ་ཤུལ་ལ་ནང་དུ་ཀུ་ཤོར་བཞག While I went outside, my house got robbed.

ཀུ་བཤུས་ (gūshüü) plagiarism, illegal copying ¶ ཀུ་བཤུས་རྩོམ་རིགས་ A plagiarized article/ book.

ཀུ་སེམས་ (gūsem) thoughts of stealing.

ཀུ་སེམས་ལ་ཉེ་རིང་མེད་ (gūsemla ñeriŋ meè) a thief makes no difference between those distant and close to him [Lit. there is no difference between near and far when one has thoughts of stealing].

ཀུན་ (gūn) abbr. ཀུན་མ་.

ཀུན་སྐད་ (gūngɛɛ̀) talk or rumors about thieves/ robberies ¶ དེང་སང་ཀུན་སྐད་མང་པོ་འདུག These days there is much talk about robberies.

ཀུན་ཁག་གཞན་གཡོགས་ (gūnkaà shenyɔɔ) blaming/ accusing another for one's own theft.

ཀུན་འགོག (gūngɔɔ) preventing theft; va.—བྱེད་ ¶ གུང་སེང་དུ་འགྲོ་རེང་ནང་དུ་ཀུན་འགོག་གི་ལས་ཀ་ཡག་པོ་བྱེད་དགོས་ When one goes on vacation, one should take good measures to prevent robbery.

ཀུན་རྒྱབ་རྫུན་བསྣོན་ (gūngyəb dzünnön) sm. ཀུན་རྒྱབ་རྫུན་ལངས་.

ཀུན་རྒྱབ་རྫུན་ལངས་ (gūngyəb dzünlaŋ) a thief/ criminal assisted or supported by lies ¶ ཁྲིམས་ཁང་ནང་དུ་ཀུན་རྒྱབ་རྫུན་ལངས་བྱས་ཙང་སྒྲོད་གཞི་ཐག་གཅོད་དྲང་པོ་ཡོང་གི་མེད་པ་རེད་ In court, people were in cahoots and lied to support the thief so it was difficult to settle the case honestly. [Lit a liar supporting a thief].

ཀུན་བཅོམ་ (gũ̄njom) sm. ཀུ་འཕྲོག.

ཀུན་ཇག (gũ̄njaà) abbr. of ཀུན་མ་ཇག་པ་.

ཀུན་ཉེས་གྱོད་གཞི་ (gũ̄ñeè gyö̱ö̀shi) a case about stealing.

ཀུན་ཐོ་ (gũ̄nto) a list of stolen goods.

ཀུན་དོང་ (gũ̄ndoŋ) hiding place for stolen goods/ loot.

ཀུན་ནོར་ (gũ̄nnɔɔ) sm. ཀུན་རྫས་.

ཀུན་པོ་ (gũ̄mbo) sm. ཀུན་མ་.

ཀུན་པོ་གནོང་གིས་འདྲོག (gũ̄mbo nōŋgi drɔ̱ɔ̀) va. to have a guilty conscience about stealing.

ཀུན་དཔོན་ (gũ̄nbön) the chief/ head of a group of thieves.

ཀུན་བུ (gũ̄mbu) sm. ཀུན་མ་.

ཀུན་བྱི་ (gũ̄nji) abbr. thief and adulterer.

ཀུན་མ་ (gũ̄nma) thief, robber; va.—ཀུ་; —རྒྱག to steal, to rob; vi.—ཤོར་ to get robbed.

ཀུན་མ་ཇག (gūmajag) sb. who is partly a thief and partly a bandit.

ཀུན་མ་ནང་ལ་བཞག སྒོ་ལུགས་ཕྱི་ལ་རྒྱག (gũ̄nma na̱ŋla sha̱à go̱jaà cīlə gya̱à) sm. ཀུ་མ་ནང་ལ་བཞག་སྒོ་ལུགས་ཕྱི་ལ་རྒྱག.

ཀུན་མ་གཡག་ལ་བཞོན་ གཡག་མགོས་རྟ་རྒྱུགས་གཏོང་ (gūma yāàla shö̱n yāŋgö̀ö dəgyuù dōŋ) doing bad things in excess or without restraint [Lit. the thief rides a yak and runs like a horse].

ཀུན་མ་ལ་དཔའ་དར་ སྤྱང་ཀི་ལ་ཚེ་ཐར་ (gūmala bādar jəŋgila tsētar) rewarding or showing unwarranted favoritism to an evil person ¶ རྫོང་དཔོན་ནས་མི་ངན་དེ་ར་གཟིགས་བསྐྱངས་ཆེན་པོ་གནང་བ་དེ་ཀུན་མར་དཔའ་དར་དང་། སྤྱང་ཀི་ལ་ཚེ་ཐར་བཏང་བ་རེད་ The District Commissioner's favoritism to that evil person is like "awarding the thief and setting the wolf free." [Lit. award the thief for bravery and set the wolf free].

ཀུན་མ་ལ་ལྷ་མེད་ (gūmala lhāmeè) thieves always get discovered [Lit. deities do not support thieves].

ཀུན་མ་ཤོར་ (gūma shɔ̄ɔ̄) see ཀུན་མ་.

ཀུན་མས་འཁྲིད་པའི་བ་ (gumɛɛ̀ trīìbɛ pa̱) being forced to do sth. by another ¶ གྱོད་དོན་འདིའི་ནང་བུ་མོ་དེ་ཀུན་མས་འཁྲིད་པའི་བ་ཡིན་པ་ལས་ནག་ཉེས་གང་ཡང་མེད་འདུག In this law case, that woman, other than being forced by another (to do sth.) has committed no crime. [Lit. a cow led by a thief].

ཀུན་མོ་ (gũ̄nmo) female thief.

ཀུན་ཚང་ (gũ̄ndzaŋ) thieves' den, hideout; va.—བྱེད་ to make a den/ hideout for thieves.

ཀུན་རྫས་ (gũ̄ntsɛɛ̀) sm. ཀུ་རྫས་.

ཀུན་རོགས་ (gũ̄nroò) an accomplice to a thief; va.—བྱེད་.

ཀུན་སྲུང་ (gũ̄nsuŋ) guard, watchman; va.—བྱེད་.

ཀུབ་ (gūb) 1. anus, ass. 2. bottom, end, rear ¶ སྣོད་ཆས་ཀྱི་ཀུབ་བརྡོལ་བཞག The bottom of the container has burst.

ཀུབ་ཀྱག (gūbgyaà) 1. chair; va.—བྱེད་ to sit on a chair. 2. sofa.

ཀུབ་ཀྱག་གི་ཤུབས་ (gūbgyaàgi shūb) couch or sofa cover.

ཀུབ་ཀྱག་ཉེམ་འབོལ་ (gūbgyaà ne̱mböö) a soft chair.

ཀུབ་ཀྱག་མ་ཀྲ་ (gūpkaà ma̱dra) camp stool, folding stool.

ཀུབ་ཀྱི་ཨི་ཁུང་ (gūbgi īguŋ) anus, anal opening.

ཀུབ་བཀྱག (gūbgyaà) sm. ཀུབ་ཀྱག.

ཀུབ་ཀུབ་ (gūbgub) at the very end (of) ¶ ཁོང་བསྡོད་ས་ཀུབ་ཀུབ་དེ་ར་འདུག His seat is right at the end.

ཀུབ་གྲལ་ (gūbtrɛɛ) a row (of seats/ people); va.—སྒྲིག to arrange seats/ rows side by side.

ཀུབ་འགག (gūb ga̱à) vi. to have sth. get blocked up ¶ ཁྲུས་གཞོང་གི་ཀུབ་འགག་བཞག The bottom (drain) of the washing basin has gotten blocked up.

ཀུབ་ཆག (gūb cāà) vi. to lose money/ capital ¶ ད་རེས་ཚོང་གི་ཀུབ་ཆག་སོང་ This time (he) lost some of his capital in trading.

ཀུབ་ལྡིད་པོ་ (gūb ji̱ìbo) lethargic, lazy, sb. who doesn't volunteer to do things.

ཀུབ་རྡོལ་ (gūb dȫȫ) va. to expose, to uncover ¶ ལྐོག་ཚོང་གི་ཀུབ་བརྡོལ་བ་རེད་ (They) exposed the smuggling business.

ཀུབ་སྡེགས་ (gūbdeg) sm. ཀུབ་ཀྱག.

ཀུབ་སྡེགས་འཁོར་ལོ་ (gūbdeg kɔ̄ɔ̄lo) wheel chair.

ཀུབ་སྡེགས་ཐོབ་ (gūbdeg tōb) vi. to obtain a seat (in an organization), to be seated ¶ རྒྱ་དམར་ནག་གཉིས་སུ་ལ་རྒྱལ་ཚོགས་ནང་ཀུབ་སྡེགས་ཐོབ་མིན་དེ་ The question of whether Red China or Nationalist China will be seated in the UN.

ཀུབ་དྲུད་ (gūbdrüǜ) moving by dragging oneself while sitting (on one's behind); va. ཀུབ་དྲུད་; —རྒྱག.

ཀུབ་འདེགས་ (gūbdeg) sm. ཀུབ་སྡེགས་.

ཀུབ་རྡིབ་ (gūb di̱b) sm. ཀུབ་ཆག.

ཀུབ་ལྡག (gūb da̱à) va. to flatter ¶ མི་དེས་རྟག་པར་འགོ་ཁྲིད་ཀྱི་ཀུབ་ལྡག་གི་ཡོད་པ་རེད་ He always flatters the boss. [Lit. to lick the ass].

ཀུབ་ལྡག་མཁན་ (gūb da̱àñɛn) flatterer.

ཀུབ་སྡོད་ (gūbdöö̀) the last/ lowest one in a line or on an exam.

ཀུབ་སྡོད་སྣང་མ་ (gūbdöö̀ ga̱ŋma) second to last.

ཀུབ་སྡུལ་ (gūbdöö) sm. ཀུབ་སྡོད་.

ཀུབ་བརྡབས་ (gūb də̱b) vi. 1. to fall on one's buttock. 2. vi. to fail to get an expected position or job, to get stymied ¶ ལས་ཀ་གསར་པ་ཞིག་རག་ཐབས་བྱས་ཀྱང་ཀུབ་བརྡབས་བྱུང་ Even though he used various means to get the job, he failed.

ཀུབ་བརྡོལ་ (gūb dö̱ö̱) 1. vi. to fall out (the bottom), to burst open ¶ ཁོག་ཕྱིར་གྱི་ཀུབ་བརྡོལ་ནས་ཇ་ཚང་མ་བོར་སོང་ The bottom of the pot burst and all the tea spilled. 2. vi. to be/ get exposed ¶ ཁོའི་རྫུན་གཏམ་ཀུབ་བརྡོལ་བ་རེད་ His lies were exposed. 3. a container with a hole in the bottom ¶ ཁོག་ཕྱིར་ཀུབ་བརྡོལ་ A tea pot with a hole in the bottom.

ཀུབ་ཕྱགས་སློག (gūbbaà lɔ̄ɔ̀) va. to raise up the lower part of one's dress/ robe and show one's ass (to demonstrate disrespect).

ཀུབ་ནས་རྩིས་ (gūbnɛ dzī) va. to count backwards.

ཀུབ་ཕོངས་ (gūbboŋ) sm. ཀུབ་ཙོས་.

ཀུབ་འཕག (gūmbaà) bucking (by a horse, mule, yak); va.—རྒྱག.

ཀུབ་འཕྱིས་ (gūbjiì) 1. toilet paper. 2. va. to wipe one's ass (e.g., with toilet paper).

ཀུབ་དབྱུག (gūb yūù) 1. va. to prostitute oneself. 2. va. to sway one's buttock while walking.

ཀུབ་འབུ་ (gūmbu) worms in excrement.

ཀུབ་སྦྲེལ་ (gūbdrel) a bad/ conspirational relationship, criminal/ evildoers in cahoots; va.—བྱེད་ ¶ མི་དེས་མི་ངན་དང་ཀུབ་སྦྲེལ་བྱས་པ་རེད་ That man was in cahoots with evil men.

ཀུབ་མ་འཚིག་ན་སྐུད་པ་གློད་ (gūb ma̱tsiìnə gũ̄ùbə lȫö̀) a hail (challenge) used in kite flying which means if you are not afraid, send up your kite for competition.

ཀུབ་ཙོས་ (gūbdzüǜ) buttocks, buttock cheeks.

ཀུབ་ཚོས་ (gūbdzöö̀) sm. ཀུབ་ཙོས་.

ཀུབ་མཚང་རྡོལ་ (gūbdzaŋ dȫȫ) sm. ཀུབ་རྡོལ་.

ཀུབ་འཚག (gūbdzag) 1. sm. ཀུབ་འཕག. 2. va.—ཤོར་ to be infatuated with sb. because of their beauty or good looks ¶ མཛེས་སྡུག་ལྡན་པའི་གཞོན་ནུ་མ་འདི་མཐོང་སྐབས་ང་རང་ཀུབ་འཚག་ཤོར་བྱུང་ When I saw the beautiful girl, I became infatuated with her. 3. vi.—ཤོར་ to be extremely scared ¶ དགེ་རྒན་གྱིས་གཤེ་གཤེ་དྲག་པོ་བཏང་བས་ཀུབ་འཚག་ཤོར་བྱུང་ Because the teacher scolded (me) very harshly, (I) became very scared.

ཀུབ་འཚིག (gūbdziì) sm. ཀུ་རུམ་ཞུ་.

ཀུབ་ཡང་པོ་ (gūb ya̱ŋbo) alert and active.

ཀུབ་གཡོག (gūbyɔɔ̀) servant, lackey, follower; va.—རྒྱུག to act as a servant/ lackey/ follower.

ཀུབ་ལ་འཁྲིས་ (gūbla trīì) vi. to be left in the lurch (usu. sb. a middleman helped to get a loan doesn't repay and the middleman is left with responsibility for the loan).

ཀུབ་ལུག (gūb lu̱ù) 1. vi. to have the rectum come out from the anus (due to illness) 2. sm. ཀུབ་བརྡོལ་.

ཀུབ་ཤིག་རྒྱག (gūbshiì gya̱à) va. to move to one side while sitting.

ཀུབ་བཤིགས་ (gūbshiì) crowded in (side by side, usu. for animals in pens); vi.—རྒྱག to be crowded in.

ཀུབ་སུལ་ (gūbsüù) 1. the folds in the back of Tibetan men's dresses; va.—སྡུད་ to make the folds in the back of Tibetan men's dresses when tying it with a belt. 2. skin folds around the anal opening.

ཀུབ་སླ་པོ་ (gūb lābo) promiscuous (for women).

ཀུས་ (gũù) imp. of ཀུ་.

ཀེ་བ་ (gēwa) thin, lean, emaciated.

ཀེད་ (gēè) abbr. for ཀེད་པ་.

ཀེད་དཀྲིས་ (gēdriì) an outer waist covering that women wear for extra warmth.

ཀེད་སྐབས་ (gēgəp) sm. ཀེད་པ་.

ཀེད་སྐབས་ཕྱིད་པ་ (gēgəb cēēba) having a thin waist (for females).

ཀེད་སྐབས་ཕྲ་བ་ (gēègəb trāwa) sm. སྐེད་སྐབས་ཕྲ་བ་.

ཀེད་རྒྱན་ (gēègyen) belt.

ཀེད་ང་ (gēèŋa) a waist drum ¶ ཀེད་ང་རུ་ཁག A waist drum unit/ team/ troupe.

ཀེད་མཉམ་ (gēèñam) isosceles ¶ ཀེད་མཉམ་ཟུར་གསུམ་ Isosceles triangle.

ཀེད་ན་ (gēèna) in the middle/ center ¶ བྲག་རིའི་ཀེད་ན་ In the middle of the rocky mountain.

ཀེད་ནད་ (gēènɛɛ̀) 1. menstruation. 2. kidney disease.

ཀེད་པ་ (gēèba) 1. waist. 2. the middle/ center ¶ ཀེད་པ་ནས་བཅག་པ་རེད་ (They) broke it from the middle. 3. menstruation; vi.—བབ་ to menstruate; vi.—ཆད་ to stop/ cease menstruating ¶ བོད་ལ་བུ་མོ་རང་ལོ་བཅོ་ལྔ་ཙམ་ནས་ཀེད་པ་རྒྱག་འགོ་ཚུགས་ཀྱི་རེད་ Girls start menstruating at about fifteen years of age in Tibet.

ཀེད་ཕྲ་མ་ (gēè trāma) beautiful (for women) [Lit. thin/ slender waist].

ཀེད་ཚིགས་ (gēèdziì) lumbar vertebra.

ཀེད་མཚམས་ (gēndzam) the point at which the vertebrae joins the waist.

ཀེད་མཚུངས་ (gēètsuŋ) sm. ཀེད་མཉམ་.

ཀེད་རགས་ (gēèraà) belt, sash.

ཀོ་: p. (བ) ཀོས་; f. བཀོ་; imp. ཀོས་ (gō) 1. va. to dig out ¶ ཁྲོན་པ་བཀོས་པ་རེད་ (They) dug a well. 2. va. to carve (usu. wood or stone) ¶ དངོས་ཆས་དེ་ཚོའི་ཐོག་ཡི་གེ་མང་པོ་བཀོས་འདུག (They) carved many letters on the objects.

ཀོ་ཆུ་ (gūju) well water.

ཀོ་འདོན་ (gōndön) digging, mining, excavating; va.—བྱེད་ ¶ ཁྲོན་པ་འབྲུ་སྐབས་ས་ཀོ་འདོན་བྱ་དགོས་པ་རེད་ When digging a well, one must excavate much soil.

ཀོ་འདྲུ་ (gōndru) sm. ཀོ་, 1.

ཀོ་འདྲུ་འཕྲུལ་འཁོར་ (gōndru trũũgɔɔ) excavating machine, bulldozer.

ཀོ་སྤྱད་ (gōjɛɛ̀) 1. carving tools. 2. excavating/ digging tools.

ཀོ་བྱེད་ (gōjeè) 1. digging tools such as shovel. 2. animals that dig holes such as rats.

ཀོ་འབྲི་ (gūndri) carving an inscription; va.—བྱེད་.

ཀོ་མ་ (gōma) 1. hoe; va.—རྒྱག to hoe; to weed a field with a hoe.

ཀོ་མ་པ་ (gōmaba) a person who works with a hoe.

ཀོ་མའི་མཆུ་འདྲུ་ (gōmɛ cūndru) a Tibetan surgical tool for extracting broken bones.

ཀོ་མོ་ (gōmo) a well.

ཀོ་འཚོལ་ (gōndzöö) excavating in search of sth.; va.—བྱེད་.

ཀོ་བཟོ་ (gō so̱) sm. ཀོ་, 2.

ཀོང་དཀར་ (gōŋgar) sm. ཀོང་པ་.

ཀོང་པ་ (gōŋba) a skin disease characterized by itching (tinea).

ཀོང་པོ་ (gōŋbo) sm. ཀོང་བུ་.

ཀོན་པ་ (gōnba) a net used as a trap/ snare.

ཀོན་བུ་ (gūnbu) sm. ཀོན་པ་.

ཀོམ་ཚུགས་ (gōmdzug) resting the chin on one's hand (or on a stick); va.—རྒྱག.

ཀོས་ (gõò) p. and imp. of ཀོ་.

ཀོས་མཁན་ (gõõñɛn) a carver.

ཀོས་རྒྱག་མཁན་ (gõò gya̱ñɛn) a carver.

ཀོས་མ་ (gõòma) sth. carved, sth. that has carving.

ཀོས་ཤིང་ (gũũshiŋ) 1. wood for carving. 2. carved wood.

ཀྱ (gyā) 1. a single strand (of a thread, rope, etc.); va.—རྒྱག to twist/ weave two pieces of rope or string together to make thicker. 2. poet. bridge.

ཀྱ་འཐབ་ (gyā tōb) 1. sm. ཀྱ་རྒྱག. 2. conspiring/ being in cahoots; va.—བྱེད་.

ཀྱ་པ་ (gyāba) sm. སྐྱ་མི་.

ཀྱ་བ་ (gyāwa) sm. སྐྱ་བ་.

ཀྱ་བར་ (gyāwar) a plumb string that is stretched horizontally so that walls, etc., will be built level; va.—འཐེན་ to pull a plumb line taut.

ཀྱ་མ་ (gyāma) sm. སྐྱ་མ་.

ཀྱ་མི་ (gyāmi) sm. སྐྱ་མི་.

ཀྱ་རགས་ (gyāraà) a band of horsemen.

ཀྱང་ (gyāŋ) 1. Tibetan wild ass. 2. (vb. + — + vb.) to do without question/ hesitation ¶ མ་འགྲིགས་པ་འདུག་ན་གསུང་ཀྱང་གནང་རོགས་གནང་ If there is anything wrong, please say so right away (without hesitation). 3. (adj. + —) only, entirely, completely ¶ ཁོ་ལ་གྱོན་པ་གསར་ཀྱང་ཉོས་པ་རེད་ (They) bought him a completely new outfit.

ཀྱང་དཀར་ (gyāŋgar) light brown (for horses).

ཀྱང་ཀྱང་ (gyāŋgyaŋ) 1. solely, singly, only, purely ¶ ཚོས་གཞི་སྔོན་པོ་ཀྱང་ཀྱང་གི་དཔེ་རིས་ A design of only blue. 2. light brown (for horses).

ཀྱང་ཀྱོང་ (gyāŋgyoŋ) abbr. of ཀྱང་ངེ་ཀྱོང་ངེ་.

ཀྱང་སྐྱས་ (gyāŋgyɛɛ̀) single plank ladder.

ཀྱང་སྐྱུམ་ (gyāŋgum) sm.* བཀྱངས་སྐྱུམ་.

ཀྱང་ཁ་དཀར་ལ་ཇོ་བརྒྱབ་ན་ ལས་སོ་ཅན་གྱི་བསྟན་པར་གནོད་ (gyāŋka gārla ŋōgyəbna yɛ̱ɛ̀sojɛngi de̱mbar nöö) sm. སྤྲལ་པ་རྨ་ཅན་.

ཀྱང་ཁ་ལོ་སྒྱུར་ན་ཞོན་རྟ་དང་ འབྲོང་ཁ་ལོ་སྒྱུར་ན་སྣ་ལོ་བྱེད་འདོད་པ་ (gyāŋ kālo gyu̱rna sho̱n dā ta̱ŋ dro̱ŋ kālo gyu̱rna nālo ce̱èndööba) desiring to train/ convert sb. who is spoiled or undisciplined into sb. who is disciplined/ useful/ under control [Lit. wishing to tame a wild ass into a riding horse and a wild yak into a riding yak].

ཀྱང་ཁག (gyāŋkuù) odd and even.

ཀྱང་ཁྲ་ (gyāŋdra) zebra.

ཀྱང་འཁྱེར་གཞན་འགྲུབ་དམིགས་མེད་ (gyāŋkyer she̱ndrub mi̱gmeè) shung. a single person without the means to repay a loan ¶ གཞུང་སྒེར་ཆོས་གསུམ་འབུ་དང་དལ་བུན་བཏང་རིགས་ལ་ཆོས་སྡེ་རང་ནས་ཀྱང་འཁྱེར་གཞན་འགྲུབ་དམིགས་མེད་རིགས་ལ་ཆག་ཡང་ཕྱུན་བུ་གནང་རྒྱ་བགྱིས་ཏེ་ Regarding the loans given to the subjects of the goverment, aristocrats and monasteries, the Chode monastery shall give some exemptions to single individuals who do not have the means to repay the loans.

ཀྱང་གོས་ (gyāŋgöò) clothing without lining, thin clothes.

ཀྱང་གླུ་ (gyāŋlu) solo (song).

ཀྱང་འགྲོའི་ལམ་ཐིག (gyāŋdröö ləmdiì) a one-way street.

ཀྱང་རྒྱག (gyāŋgyaà) singles (in games such as tennis).

ཀྱང་ངེ་ཀྱོང་ངེ་ (gyāŋŋe gyōŋŋe) 1. an uneven surface (with depressions, holes, etc.). 2. sm. གྱང་ངེ་གྱོང་ངེ་.

ཀྱང་ཐག (gyāŋtaà) a long rope.

ཀྱང་སྟར་ (gyāŋtar) a single line/ row.

ཀྱང་ཐང་ (gyāŋdaŋ) a wide or flat ground/ field, a

plain, grassland area.

རྐྱང་ཐང་ན་ཁ་ (gyāŋdaŋ naga) name of a grassy plain between the Potala and Drepung monastery.

རྐྱང་ཐང་ན་ཁའི་སྒང་ལ་རྟ་ལས་བོང་བུ་མགྱོགས་པ་ བོང་བུ་མགྱོགས་པ་མ་རེད་ སྒལ་རྨ་ཚ་བ་རེད་ (gyāŋtaŋ nagɛ gaŋla dāle puŋgu gyɔ̀ɔgaà puŋbu gyɔgba gɛɛ mā tsāwa reè) sth. or sb. being forced or compelled to go or do sth. fast [Lit. the donkey is running faster on the grassy plain between the Potala and Drepung monastery because he has a sore on his back].

རྐྱང་འདེད་ (gyāŋdeè) focusing/ concentrating on one thing or subject; va.—བྱེད་ ¶ ལས་དོན་སྣེ་གཅིག་གི་ཐོག་ལ་རྐྱང་འདེད་བྱེད་དགོས་ One must focus only on one aspect of the project.

རྐྱང་འདེབས་ (gyāŋdeb) one-crop farming, monoculture.

རྐྱང་དྲང་ (gyāŋdaŋ) horizontal bar (in gymnastics).

རྐྱང་རྡེལ་ (gyāŋdee) shung. preliminary or simple calculation in the traditional Tibetan system of arithmetic calculation.

རྐྱང་ལྟབ་ (gyāŋdab) folded once, folded into one layer.

རྐྱང་ནག (gyāŋnag) dark brown (for horses).

རྐྱང་པ་ (gyāŋba) 1. single, alone ¶ ཁོ་ནང་ལ་རྐྱང་པ་རེད་ He is alone at home. 2. only, of one kind ¶ ཚོང་ཁང་འདིའི་ནང་རྩེད་ཆས་རྐྱང་པ་འཚོང་གི་ཡོད་པ་རེད་ In this store only toys are sold. 3. pure, genuine. ¶ གསེར་རྐྱང་པ་ Pure/ genuine gold. 4. (with ཁེ་བཟང་) net (profit). 5. a letter with suffix or prefixes.

རྐྱང་པའི་གྲངས་ཀ་ (gyāŋpɛ traŋga) a whole number (in math).

རྐྱང་པོ་ (gyāŋbo) light brown (for horses).

རྐྱང་འཕར་ (gyāŋpar) net increase ¶ མོ་ཊའི་ཐོན་སྐྱེད་རྐྱང་འཕར་ The net increase in car production.

རྐྱང་འཕུར་ (gyāŋbur) solo flight; va.—གཏོང་.

རྐྱང་འཕུལ་ (gyāŋbüü) words in Tibetan language that do not have vowels and super and subfixed letters but do have prefixes and the suffix འ་ (e.g., དགའ་).

རྐྱང་འཕེལ་ (gyāŋpel) sm. རྐྱང་འཕར་.

རྐྱང་མ་ (gyāŋma) 1. sm. རྐྱང་པ་. 2. the name of a vein in Tibetan medicine.

རྐྱང་མོ་ (gyāŋmo) 1. a light brown mare. 2. a female wild ass.

རྐྱང་དམར་ (gyāŋmar) purplish red.

རྐྱང་ཚད་ (gyāŋzɛɛ̀) purity (in science).

རྐྱང་གཞིས་ (gyāŋshɛɛ̀) sm. རྐྱང་ཟླ་.

རྐྱང་ཟླ་ (gyāŋda) 1. alone, by oneself. 2. nighttime.

རྐྱང་ལོ་ (gyāŋlo) a single leaf.

རྐྱང་ཤད་ (gyāŋshɛɛ̀) a single ཤད་.

རྐྱང་སེར་ (gyāŋser) a horse of yellowish brown color.

རྐྱང་ལྷོ་ལ་ཤི་ཡང་ མགོ་བྱང་ལ་གཏད་ཡོང་ (gyāŋ lhōla shīyaŋ go caŋla dɛ̄ɛ̀yoŋ) one always thinks of one's home whatever predicament one finds oneself in [Lit. although the wild ass dies in the south, his head will face the north].

རྐྱན་ (gyɛ̄n) jar, pot.

རྐྱན་བུ་ (gyɛ̄mbu) sm. རྐྱན་.

རྐྱལ་: p. and f. རྐྱལ་; imp. རྐྱོལ་ (gyɛ̄ɛ̄) va. to swim.

རྐྱལ་ (gyɛ̄ɛ̄) swimming; va.—རྒྱག ¶ ང་རྐྱལ་རྒྱག་ཤེས་ཀྱི་མེད་ I don't know how to swim.

རྐྱལ་ཀ (gyɛ̄ɛ̄ga) 1. empty talk. 2. mocking talk.

རྐྱལ་གོག (gyɛ̄ɛ̄gɔɔ̀) a skin or leather bag/ pouch.

རྐྱལ་གོག་ཆེན་པོའི་ཞབས་ར་ (gyɛ̄ɛ̄gɔɔ̀ cēmbö shabra) even though sb. has suffered a heavy financial loss, he still has some means [Lit. the bottom of a large leather pouch].

རྐྱལ་གོག་མཐིལ་དོལ་ (gyɛ̄ɛ̄gɔɔ̀ tīldöö) becoming bankrupt, having no means/ resources left [Lit. a leather pouch with a hole in the bottom].

རྐྱལ་འགྲོད (gyēndröö̀) crossing/ traversing by swimming; va.—རྒྱག.

རྐྱལ་རྒྱག་ས་ (gyɛ̄ɛ̄gyasa) swimming pool, swimming area.

རྐྱལ་མཆོང་ (gyɛ̄ɛ̄joŋ) diving (into the water); va.—རྒྱག.

རྐྱལ་མཆོང་རྫིང་བུ་ (gyɛ̄ɛ̄joŋ dziŋbu) diving pool (i.e., a swimming pool in which diving can be done).

རྐྱལ་སྟོང་ (gyɛ̄ɛ̄doŋ) nice looking on the outside but without substance [Lit. an empty leather pouch].

རྐྱལ་པ་སྟོང་པ་དཀྲུགས་ཀྱང་དོན་རྒྱུ་གང་ཡང་མེད་པ་ (gyɛ̄ɛ̄ba dōŋba drūggyu töŋgyu kaŋyaŋmeè) no result after extensive discussions [Lit. nothing comes out after shaking an empty pouch].

རྐྱལ་པ་ (gyɛ̄ɛ̄wa) a skin or leather bag/ pouch.

རྐྱལ་པ་ཆུ་ཐུབ་ (gyɛ̄ɛ̄wa cūdub) a type of Tibetan herbal medicine used to stimulate urination.

རྐྱལ་བུ་ (gyɛ̄ɛ̄bu) a small leather pouch.

རྐྱལ་རྩལ་ (gyɛ̄ɛ̄dzɛɛ) swimming skill.

རྐྱལ་རྩེ་ (gyɛ̄ɛ̄dze) swimming, playing in the water.

རྐྱལ་རྩེད་ (gyɛ̄ɛ̄dzeè) water sports, swimming competition.

རྐྱལ་རྩེད་རྫིང་བུ་ (gyɛ̄ɛ̄dzeè dziŋbu) swimming pool.

རྐྱལ་རྫིང་ (gyɛ̄ɛ̄dziŋ) abbr. of རྐྱལ་རྩེད་རྫིང་བུ.

རྐྱལ་ས་ (gyɛ̄ɛ̄sa) swimming pool/ area.

རྐྱེན་ (gyēn) 1. (vb. + —) because ¶ ཀྲོལ་འཛིང་ཤུགས་ཆེ་བྱས་རྐྱེན་དམག་མི་སྟོང་ཕྲག་མང་པོར་བསད་རྨས་བྱུང་ཡོད་པ་རེད་ Because (they) fought fiercely, many thousands of soldiers were killed or wounded. 2. the cause of sth. ¶ ནང་འཁྲུག་ལངས་རྐྱེན་ནི་ As for the cause of the civil war erupting. 3. see རྐྱེན་བྱེད་.

རྐྱེན་ཁ་ལེན་ཁ་ (gyēnga lenga) unfortunate, prone to accidents/ misfortunes.

རྐྱེན་གང་ལ་ཐུག་རུང་ (gyēn kaŋla tūùruŋ) whatever circumstances/ situations one encounters.

རྐྱེན་གོད་ (gyēngöö) abbr. of རྐྱེན་གོད་ཆགས་.

རྐྱེན་གོད་ཆགས་ (gyēn gööcaà) accident, catastrophe, misfortune ¶ མི་ཚང་འདི་ལ་རྐྱེན་གོད་ཆགས་ཆེན་པོ་བྱུང་སོང་ This family has had great misfortune.

རྐྱེན་གྱིས་ (gyēngi) sm. རྐྱེན་, 1.

རྐྱེན་ངན་ (gyēnŋɛn) misfortune, accident, disaster, sad event/ circumstance/ incident ¶ ཆུ་ལོག་གི་རྐྱེན་ངན་བྱུང་བའི་ས་གནས་ཁག་ལ་སྐྱོབ་གསོའི་རོགས་རམ་བྱས་པ་རེད་ (They) gave relief (aid) to the regions that experienced flood disasters.

རྐྱེན་ངན་གོད་ཆགས་ (gyēnŋɛn gööcaà) sm. རྐྱེན་ངན་.

རྐྱེན་ངན་གྲོགས་ཤར་ (gyēŋɛn trogshar) a bad/ negative/ malevolent/ harmful event that leads to sth. good or positive ¶ ལུང་པའི་ནང་ཆུ་ལོག་བྱུང་རྐྱེན་སྲིད་གཞུང་ནས་ཁང་པ་གསར་པ་བརྒྱབ་པ་དེ་རྐྱེན་ངན་གྲོགས་ཤར་རེད་ཟེར་ཆོག་གི་རེད་ The government's building of the new houses because the area had a flood can be called "a bad event leading to sth. good."

རྐྱེན་ངན་ཐོག་བབས་ (gyēŋɛn tɔ̄ɔbab) sudden misfortune [Lit. misfortune falling like lightening].

རྐྱེན་ངན་སྡུག་ཁུར་ (gyēŋɛn duggur) bearing or enduring hardship/ misfortunes.

རྐྱེན་ངན་བར་ཆད་ (gyēŋɛn parjɛɛ̀) sm. རྐྱེན་ངན་.

རྐྱེན་ངན་ཡོ་ལངས་ (gyēŋɛn yolaŋ) sm. རྐྱེན་ངན་.

རྐྱེན་ངན་རུ་འཛིང་ (gēnŋɛn rudziŋ) one disaster/ misfortune leading to another.

རྐྱེན་ཆག (gyēnjaà) sm. རྐྱེན་གོད་ཆགས་.

རྐྱེན་ཆག་སྣ་འདོམས་ (gyēncaà nēndom) a convergence of misfortunes/ disasters.

རྐྱེན་ཆགས་ (gyēnjaà) sm. རྐྱེན་ཆག.

རྐྱེན་སྙེད་ (gyēn ñeè) sm. རྐྱེན་འཕྲད་.

རྐྱེན་བསྡུན་འཕྲོག་བཅོམ་ (gyēndün trōgjom) robbing/ stealing/ looting at the time of a misfortune; va.—བྱེད་ ¶ མི་ཚང་དེ་ར་མེ་ཤོར་སྐབས་མི་ངན་གྱིས་རྐྱེན་བསྡུན་འཕྲོག་བཅོམ་བྱས་པ་རེད་ When that family had a fire, bad people looted (their house).

རྐྱེན་ཐུབ་ (gyēn tūb) able to withstand/ face/ confront/ tolerate hardship ¶ ལས་ཀའི་རྐྱེན་ཐུབ་པ་ལ་སྙིང་རུས་ཆེ་དགོས་ One has to persevere greatly and tolerate the hardships of work.

རྐྱེན་ཐེག (gyēn tēg) sm. རྐྱེན་ཐུབ་.

རྐྱེན་ཐེབས་ (gyēndeb) interference.

རྐྱེན་འདས་ (gyēndɛɛ̀) dying of unnatural causes (e.g., in an accident); vi.—བྱུང་ to die of unnatural causes ¶ ངའི་གྲོགས་པོ་གློ་བུར་རྐྱེན་འདས་བྱུང་བ་རེད་ My friend suddenly died of an unnatural cause.

རྐྱེན་ནད་མི་ཐེག་པ་ (gyēnnɛɛ̀ mi̱degbə) shung. unable to tolerate/ endure ¶ ཆབ་འབངས་རྣམས་བརྡབ་གསིག་མནར་གཅོད་ཀྱི་རྐྱེན་ནད་མ་ཐེག་པར་བླ་དཔོན་གོང་མར་སྙན་ཞུ་ཕུལ་བ་ The subjects were unable to tolerate the brutal oppression and made a petition to the higher authorities.

རྐྱེན་པས་ (gyēmbɛɛ̀) sm. རྐྱེན་གྱིས་.

རྐྱེན་འཕྲད་ (gyēndrɛɛ̀) vi. to be caused by sth., to encounter sth. that causes another action (could be either good or bad) ¶ མི་དེ་ལ་རྐྱེན་ཞིག་འཕྲད་ནས་ལུང་པ་འདིར་སླེབས་པ་རེད་ That person came to this region as a result of an encounter.

རྐྱེན་བྱེད་ (gyēn cɛ̱ɛ̀) va. to cause ¶ མི་མང་པོ་ཤི་པ་དེ་ཆུ་ལོག་གིས་རྐྱེན་བྱས་པ་རེད་ The flood caused many deaths. ¶ ནད་རིམས་ཀྱིས་རྐྱེན་བྱས་ནས་མི་མང་པོ་ཤི་པ་རེད་ Because of the epidemic, many people died.

རྐྱེན་དབང་ (gyēnwaŋ) shung. due to a cause/ reason ¶ རྐྱེན་དབང་གིས་སྔར་ཡང་ཞིབ་དེབ་ཕྱིར་བསྡུ་བར་མ་དོར་ལུས་འདུག Due to certain reasons, (they) had to take back the book containing the list of the population, the number of fields, and the taxes to be collected.

རྐྱེན་འབབ་ (gyēmbəb) in accordance with the time/ circumstances ¶ རྐྱེན་འབབ་ཀྱི་དགོས་མཁོའི་ཡོ་ཆས་ཚང་མ་འཛོམས་འདུག They have all the necessities needed in these circumstances.

རྐྱེན་མ་བྱུང་གོང་ལ་ཟློག་པ་ (gyēn ma̱juŋ go̱ŋla dɔ̱gba) preparing for a rainy day (for a problem before it occurs).

རྐྱེན་མེད་ (gyēnmeè) without cause, for no reason, motiveless ¶ འགོ་འཁྲིད་དེ་རྐྱེན་མེད་ཀྱིས་ང་ལ་ཁོང་ཁྲོ་ལངས་སོང་ The boss got angry at me for no reason.

རྐྱེན་སྨན་ (gyēnmɛn) 1. a type of Tibetan herbal medicine. 2. a medicine to help determine the cause of an illness.

རྐྱེན་རྩ་ (gyēndza) reason, cause ¶ གནད་དོན་དེའི་རྐྱེན་རྩ་ The cause of that problem/ issue.

རྐྱེན་རྩ་ཆུང་ཟློག (gyēndza cūŋdɔ̱ɔ̀) sm. རྐྱེན་མ་བྱུང་གོང་ལ་ཟློག.

རྐྱེན་རྩི་ (gyēndzi) sm. རྐྱེན་སྨན་.

རྐྱེན་ཟློག (gyēn dɔ̱ɔ̀) overcoming an obstacle/ impediment; va. རྐྱེན་ཟློག; —བྱེད་ ¶ རྐྱེན་ཟློག་གི་ཞབས་བརྟན་བྱས་སོང་ (They) did a religious rite for overcoming obstacles.

རྐྱེན་བཟང་པོ་ (gyēn sa̱ŋbo) a fortunate/ happy/ lucky event; vi.—འཕྲད་ to get or meet a fortunate/ happy/ auspicious event ¶ ང་ལ་རྐྱེན་བཟང་པོ་འཕྲད་ནས་སློབ་གྲྭ་ཆེན་མོར་འགྲོ་ཐུབ་བྱུང་ A fortunate thing happened to me and I was able to go to college.

རྐྱེན་རིས་ (gyēnrii̇̀) sm. ཆ་རྐྱེན་.

རྐྱེན་ལང་དོན་འཕྲད་ (gyēnlaŋ tö̱ndrɛɛ̀) sm. རྐྱེན་ཕྲད་.

རྐྱེན་ལམ་ (gyēnlam) killing, va.—དུ་. གཏོང་ to kill ¶ འགྲུལ་པ་དེ་ཇག་པས་རྐྱེན་ལམ་དུ་བཏང་བ་རེད་ The bandit killed the traveler.

རྐྱེན་ལམ་ལ་འགྲོ་ (gyēnlamla dro̱) vi. to be killed ¶ མཚན་མོ་ནགས་གསེབ་ཏུ་ཕྱིན་ན་རྐྱེན་ལམ་དུ་འགྲོ་རྒྱུའི་ཉེན་ཁ་ཡོད་ If one goes in the forest at night there is danger of being killed.

རྐྱེན་སེལ་ (gyēnsel) sm. རྐྱེན་ཟློག.

རྐྱེན་སློང་ (gyēn lōŋ) va. to instigate or cause trouble.

རྐྱེན་སློང་རྩོད་སྦྱོར་ (gyēnloŋ dzō̄òjɔr) instigating/ causing trouble, picking or causing a quarrel.

རྐྱོང་: p. བརྐྱངས་; f. བརྐྱང་; imp. རྐྱོངས་ (kōŋ) 1. va. to stretch, to extend ¶ བྱ་རྒོད་རྣམས་གཤོག་པ་བརྐྱངས་ནས་ལྡིང་སྐོར་རྒྱག་བཞིན་འདུག The vultures stretched their wings and are hovering in a circle. 2. va. to raise one's hand to vote ¶ འཐུས་མི་ཚོས་ལག་པ་བརྐྱངས་ནས་འགོ་ཁྲིད་བདམས་པ་རེད་ The representatives raised their hands (in a vote) and selected the leader.

རྐྱོང་རིང་ (gyōŋriŋ) a long traditional Tibetan folding mattress.

རྐྱོང་གདན་ (gyōŋdɛn) a traditional Tibetan folding mattress.

རྐྱོང་ཤད་ (gyōŋsheè) stretching one's arms (e.g., to loosen up or when one wakes); va.—བྱེད་ ¶ ཁོང་ལས་ཀ་དཀའ་ལས་ཁག་པོ་བྱུང་ཙང་རྐྱོང་ཤད་ཡང་སེ་བྱེད་ཀྱི་འདུག Because the work is difficult, (he) often stretches.

རྐྱོང་ཤུགས་ (gyōŋshuù) tensile force/ strength.

རྐྱོངས་ (gyōŋ) imp. of རྐྱོང་.

རྐྱོལ་ (gyō̄ō) imp. of རྐྱལ་.

སྐག་སྐོགས་ (gāggɔɔ̀) remote, out-of-the-way, boondocks.

སྐུག (gūg) sm. སྐུགས་.

སྐུགས་ (gūg) abbr. of སྐུགས་པ་.

སྐུགས་ཀྱི་ (gūggye) stupid, foolish.

སྐུགས་རྐྱལ་ (gūggyee) sm. སྐུགས་ཚོད་ཚོད་.

སྐུགས་གར་ (gūggar) pantomime dance; va.—འཁྲབ་ to perform a pantomime dance.

སྐུགས་དགོད་ (gūggöò) laughing foolishly.

སྐུགས་རྟགས་ (gūgdaà) stupid, stupidly; va.—བྱེད་; —སྟོན་ to act stupidly, to act foolishly ¶ མི་དེས་ཚོགས་འདུའི་ཐོག་ལ་སྐུགས་རྟགས་བསྟན་ཙང་ཚང་མ་གད་མོ་ཤོར་བ་རེད་ Everyone laughed because the person acted stupidly at the meeting.

སྐུགས་རྟགས་ཚ་པོ་ (gūgdaà tsābo) 1. a stupid person. 2. a person who is stubborn in a stupid way.

སྐུགས་འཐོམ་འཐོམ་ (gūg tōmdom) stupidly, foolishly.

སྐུགས་ལྡིབ་ (gūgdip) 1. mute. 2. stuttering.

སྐུགས་བརྡ་ (gūgda) nonverbal gesture/ signal, sign language; va.—བྱེད་.

སྐུགས་བརྡ་ཟློས་གར་ (gūgda dö̱ògar) pantomime play/ show/ performance.

སྐུགས་པ་ (gūgbə) 1. a person who is mute/ dumb. 2. stupid, idiotic ¶ འདི་ནི་སྐུགས་པའི་ལས་ཀ་ཞིག་རང་རེད་ This is really an idiotic act. ¶ མི་འདི་སྐུགས་པ་རང་རེད་ He is really an idiot.

སྐུགས་པ་ཀླད་སྟོང་ (gūgbə lɛ̄ɛ̀doŋ) stupid, idiotic.

སྐུགས་པ་སྐུགས་རྐྱང་ (gūgbə gūggyaŋ) totally/ completely/ stupid or idiotic.

སྐུགས་པ་སྤྱང་མདོག (gūgbə jāŋdoò) sb. who is stupid trying to act clever/ smart.

སྐུགས་པས་ཚྭ་བཟས་པ་ལྟར་ (gūgbɛ tsā sɛ̱ɛ̀bə dār) having a feeling but not being able to express/ explain it [Lit. like a mute who ate salt].

སྐུགས་པ་ཨུ་བཙུགས་ (gūgbə ūdzuù) stupidly stubborn/ bullheaded/ obstinate, insisting in a way that is stupid; va.—བྱེད་; —རྒྱག ¶ སྐུགས་པ་ཨུ་བཙུགས་བྱས་ན་ལས་དོན་ལེགས་པར་བསྒྲུབ་མི་ཐུབ་ If (one) is stupidly stubborn (one) cannot complete the work well.

སྐུགས་པའི་སྤྱང་སྤྱོད་ (gūgbɛ jāŋjöò) a stupid person trying to be clever ¶ སྐུགས་པའི་སྤྱང་སྤྱོད་བྱས་ན་མངོན་གསལ་གཞན་ལས་དོད་པ་ A fool trying to act clever is more conspicuous than others.

སྐུགས་པས་ལྷ་མཐོང་ (gūgbɛ lhā tōŋ) being amazed/ stunned/ shocked ¶ སྐད་ཆ་དེ་གོ་མ་ཐག་ཁོ་སྐུགས་པས་ལྷ་མཐོང་བ་ནང་བཞིན་བསྡད་སོང་ As soon as (he) heard that he sat stunned [Lit. an idiot seeing a god].

སྐུགས་བུ་ (gūgbu) sm. སྐུགས་ལྡིབ་.

སྐུགས་རྩུལ་ (gūgdzüü) sm. སྐུགས་རྫུ་ (but takes the verb སྟོན་).

སྐུགས་ཚོད་ཚོད་ (gūg tsō̄òdzöò) not very clever, simpleminded, stupid.

སྐུགས་རྫུ་ (gūgdzu) pretending to be stupid; va.—འདེབས་ to pretend to be stupid ¶ མི་དེས་སྐུགས་རྫུ་བཏབས་ནས་ཉེས་ཆད་འཁེལ་མ་དགོས་པ་བྱུང་བ་རེད་ That person didn't have to pay the fine because he pretended to be stupid.

སྐུགས་བཟོས་སྲིད་ཇུས་ (gūgsöò sīìjüù) the policy of

leaving sb. (or some group) backwards.

ལྐུགས་ལོར་ (gūglor) stupid ། མི་འདི་ལྐུགས་ལོར་ཞིག་འདུག This man is stupid.

ལྐུགས་སེ་ (gūgse) rather stupid ། མི་འདི་ལྐུགས་སེ་ཡོད་པ་རེད་ This person is rather stupid.

ལྐོ་མོག (gōmog) a puddle, a hole into which water has puddled ། ལྐོ་མོག་གི་ཆུ་འཐུང་མི་ཉན་ Water from a puddle is not fit to drink.

ལྐོག (gɔ̄ɔ) in secret, covertly, clandestinely, furtively ། ལས་འགུལ་འདི་ཐོག་མར་ལྐོག་ལ་སྒྲིགས་འཛུགས་བྱས་པ་རེད་ The movement at first was organized in secret.

ལྐོག་བཀྲོང་ (gɔ̄gdroŋ) sm. ལྐོག་གསོད་.

ལྐོག་ལྐོག (gɔ̄ggɔɔ̀) sm. ལྐོག.

ལྐོག་ལྐོག་སུད་སུད་ (gɔ̄ggɔɔ̀ sūùsüù) sm. ལྐོག.

ལྐོག་ཁ་གཏོང་ (gɔ̄ɔga dōŋ) va. to talk behind sb.'s back.

ལྐོག་ཁྲོམ་ (gɔ̄gdrom) black market.

ལྐོག་གི་འཚལ་མོ་ (gɔ̄gi cɛ̄ɛmo) prostitute.

ལྐོག་གད་ (gɔ̄ggɛɛ̀) laughing/ snickering secretly; va.—དགོད་ to laugh secretly, to snicker; vi.—ཤོར་ to involuntarily laugh/ snicker secretly.

ལྐོག་གན་ (gɔ̄ggɛn) secret agreement/ deal.

ལྐོག་གྱུར་ (gɔ̄ggyuu) 1. secret, covert, hidden, clandestine ། ལས་ཀ་འདི་ལྐོག་གྱུར་རེད་ This work is secret. 2. occult, mysterious, enigmatic.

ལྐོག་གྱུར་གྱི་རིག་པ་ (gɔ̄ggyuugi rigpə) mysticism, occultism; Taoism.

ལྐོག་གྱུར་རིང་ལུགས་ (gɔ̄ggyuu riŋluù) mysticism, occultism.

ལྐོག་གྱུར་ཨང་རྟགས་ (gɔ̄ggyuu āŋdaà) secret code.

ལྐོག་གྲོས་ (gɔ̄gdröö) plot, machination; va.—བྱེད་ ། སྲིད་གཞུང་ལ་ངོ་ལོག་རྒྱག་རྒྱུའི་ལྐོག་གྲོས་བྱས་ཡོད་པ་རེད་ They plotted to rebel against the government.

ལྐོག་གླུ་ (gɔ̄glu) singing in a low voice so others can't hear; va.—གཏོང་.

ལྐོག་བགྲོད་ (gɔ̄gdröö) traveling in secrecy; va.—བྱེད་.

ལྐོག་རྒལ་ (gɔ̄ggɛl) sm. ལྐོག་བརྒལ་.

ལྐོག་རྒོལ་ (gɔ̄ɔgöö) surprise/ secret attack; va.—བྱེད་ ། འཐབ་དམག་ཚོས་ལྐོག་རྒོལ་བྱས་པ་རེད་ The guerrillas launched a surprise attack.

ལྐོག་བརྒལ་ (gɔ̄ggɛl) 1. crossing (a river, stream, etc.) secretly or illegally; va.—བྱེད་. 2. running a blockade.

ལྐོག་ངན་ (gɔ̄gŋɛn) bribe or gift given as graft; va.—སྤྲོད་; —སྡེར་ to give a bribe; va.—ལེན་; —ཟ་ to accept a bribe ། ལག་འཁྱེར་རག་པའི་ཆེད་དུ་ལས་བྱེད་པར་ལྐོག་ངན་སྤྲད་འདུག In order to get the permit (he) gave a bribe to the official.

ལྐོག་ངན་སྡེར་བྱིན་ (gɔ̄gŋɛn dērjin) bribing, giving graft.

ལྐོག་བཅོམ་ (gɔ̄gjom) ambushing to rob/ steal, raiding to rob/ steal; va.—བྱེད་.

ལྐོག་ཆད་ (gɔ̄gcɛɛ̀) secret/ clandestine agreement; va.—བྱེད་ ། བྲོས་བྱོལ་འགྲོ་རྒྱུའི་ལྐོག་ཆད་བྱས་སོང་ (They) secretly agreed to run away.

ལྐོག་ཆོས་ (gɔ̄gcöö) secret religious teaching given to only selected disciples.

ལྐོག་འཚལ་མ་ (gɔ̄g cɛ̄ɛma) prostitute.

ལྐོག་ཇུས (gɔ̄gjüü) covert plot, secret plan; va.—འདིང་ (ས་); —བྱེད་; —གཞོམ་ to plot, to plan secretly ། ཁོ་ཚོས་ངོ་ལོག་རྒྱག་རྒྱུའི་ལྐོག་ཇུས་བཏིངས་པ་རེད་ They secretly planned to rebel.

ལྐོག་འཛབ་ (gɔ̄gjəb) guerrilla warfare; va.—བྱེད་; —རྒྱག.

ལྐོག་འཛབ་དགྲ་རྒྱག (gɔ̄gjəb dragyaà) sm. ལྐོག་འཛབ་.

ལྐོག་བརྗེ་ (gɔ̄gjə) surreptitiously substituting/ changing.

ལྐོག་ཉན་ (gɔ̄gñɛn) secretly listening/ eavesdropping; va.—རྒྱག; —བྱེད་.

ལྐོག་ཉན་ཡོ་བྱད་ (gɔ̄gñɛn yobcɛɛ̀) instrument used for eavesdropping.

ལྐོག་ཉར་ (gɔ̄gñaa) sth. kept secretly/ hidden; va.—བྱེད་ ། ལྐོག་ཉར་རྒྱུ་ནོར་ Hidden wealth.

ལྐོག་ཉར་ཧམ་ཚོང་ (gɔ̄gñaa hāmtsoŋ) hoarding and then selling at a profit, profiteering; va.—བྱེད་.

ལྐོག་ཉོ་ (gɔ̄gño) buying in secrecy; va.—རྒྱག.

ལྐོག་ཏུ་ (gɔ̄gdu) secretly, in secret ། ཁོ་ཚོ་ལྐོག་ཏུ་བྲོས་ཐོན་པ་རེད་ They secretly fled.

ལྐོག་ཏུ་འགྱུར་ (gɔ̄gdu gyur) vi. to be or become secret/ hidden/ covert ། ལས་དོན་འདི་ལྐོག་ཏུ་གྱུར་བ་ཞིག་མ་རེད་ This work is not one that became secret.

ལྐོག་གཏམ་ (gɔ̄gdam) secret/ hidden talks; va.—ཤོད་ to talk secretly ། གྲོགས་པོ་གཉིས་བར་ལྐོག་གཏམ་ཤོད་ཀྱི་ཡོད་པ་རེད་ The two friends are having secret talks.

ལྐོག་གཏོང་ (gɔ̄gdoŋ) sm. ལྐོག་འདྲེན་.

ལྐོག་ལྟ་ (gɔ̄gda) spying, peeping; secretly looking at or observing; va.—བྱེད་.

ལྐོག་ལྟའི་རྒྱང་ཤེལ་ (gɔ̄gdɛ gyāŋshee) periscope.

ལྐོག་བལྟས་ཚོད་དཔག (gɔ̄gdɛ tsōōbaà) spying (on sth. or sb.) to get information on or an estimate of sb.'s capabilities ། བཀོད་འདོམས་པས་དགྲ་བོའི་སྟོབས་ཤུགས་ཇི་ཡོད་ལ་ལྐོག་བལྟས་ཚོད་དཔག་བྱས་པ་རེད་ The commander spied to get a better idea of the enemy's strength.

ལྐོག་ཐབས་ (gɔ̄gdəp) secret or covert schemes/ means/ methods ། ཁོང་ཚོས་ལྐོག་ཐབས་ལ་བརྟེན་ནས་དགྲ་བོའི་འཆར་གཞི་ཤེས་ཐུབ་པ་བྱུང་བ་རེད་ They were able to know the enemy's plan by covert means.

ལྐོག་མཐུན་ (gɔ̄gdün) secretly partial to/ friendly with, secret friendship/ alliance; va.—བྱེད་ ། རྒྱ་དམར་དང་ལག་འབྲེལ་ལྐོག་མཐུན་བྱས་སོང་ (He) secretly made friendly relations with the Chinese Communists.

ལྐོག་མཐོང་རྒྱང་ཤེལ་ (gɔ̄gdoŋ gyāŋshee) sm. ལྐོག་ལྟའི་རྒྱང་ཤེལ་.

ལྐོག་འཐབ་ (gɔ̄gdəp) fighting secretly/ behind the scenes, using underhanded means.

ལྐོག་དོན་ (gɔ̄gdön) secret matter/ issue/ affair ། ཏང་མི་ལ་ཡི་གེ་གཏོང་རྒྱུ་དེ་ལྐོག་དོན་ཞིག་རེད་ Sending letters to party members is a secret matter.

ལྐོག་མདའ་ (gɔ̄ŋda) an arrow or gun shot from a hidden location, shooting arrows from a hidden location, sniping; an attack by a hidden enemy; va.—རྒྱག; —འཕེན་.

ལྐོག་མདའ་ལྐོག་སྒྱོགས་ (gɔ̄ŋgda gɔ̄ggyɔɔ̀) sm. ལྐོག་མདའ་.

ལྐོག་མདའ་བརྒྱབ་ནས་མི་ལ་གནོད་ཚེ་གཏོང་ (gɔ̄ŋda gyəbnɛ milə nōōtsɛ dōŋ) va. to slander sb. behind his/ her back, to stab sb. in the back, to injure sb. by underhanded means [Lit. harm sb. by shooting an arrow from hiding].

ལྐོག་མདུད་ (gɔ̄ŋdüü) Adam's apple.

ལྐོག་འདུན་ (gɔ̄ŋdün) secret talks/ discussions; va.—བྱེད་ ། བློན་པོ་ཚོས་རྒྱལ་པོ་དགོང་རྒྱུའི་ལྐོག་འདུན་བྱས་པ་རེད་ The ministers talked secretly about killing the king.

ལྐོག་འདྲེན་ (gɔ̄ŋdren) smuggling; va.—བྱེད་ ། ངོ་ལོག་པ་ཚོས་མེ་མདའ་མང་པོ་ལྐོག་འདྲེན་བྱས་པ་རེད་ The rebels smuggled a lot of guns.

ལྐོག་རྡུང་ (gɔ̄gduŋ) beating/ hitting in secret; va.—གཏོང་ ། དམག་ནོད་ཉེས་ཅན་ལྐོག་རྡུང་བཏང་སོང་ (They) secretly beat the war criminals.

ལྐོག་སྡེབ་ཏུ་འགྲོ་ (gɔ̄gdebdu dro) va. to elope.

ལྐོག་སྡོད་ (gɔ̄gdöö) staying in a place secretly; va.—བྱེད་.

ལྐོག་བརྡ་ (gɔ̄gda) secret code/ signal; va.—གཏོང་.

ལྐོག་ན་མོ་ (gɔ̄ɔ namo) sm. ལྐོག་གྱུར་.

ལྐོག་ནས་སྐྱོན་འདོགས་ (gɔ̄gneè gyōndɔɔ̀) sm. ལྐོག་གནོད་.

ལྐོག་ནས་ལྕུགས་ཀྱུ་མ་ (gɔ̄gnɛɛ̀ jəggyumə) barley with awns that are shaped like a hook.

ལྐོག་ནོར་ (gɔ̄gnɔr) hidden or secret wealth/ property.

ལྐོག་གནས་ (gɔ̄gnɛɛ̀) larynx, throat.

ལྐོག་གནོད་ (gɔ̄gnöö) secretly harming/ injuring, sabotaging; va.—སྐྱེལ་ to secretly harm/ injure, to sabotage ། མི་དེས་རང་གི་གྲོགས་པོར་ལྐོག་གནོད་བསྐྱལ་བ་རེད་ That person secretly harmed his friend.

ལྐོག་ཕྲ་ (gōgdra) sowing/ creating dissension, inciting; va.—རྒྱག ། མི་དེས་ཚོགས་པ་ནང་ཁུལ་དུ་ལྐོག་ཕྲ་རྒྱག་གི་ཡོད་པ་རེད་ That person is secretly creating dissension in the party.

ལྐོག་འཕེལ་གནས་ཚུལ་ (gōgpel nɛ̄ɛ̄tsüü) undercurrents.

ལྐོག་འཕྱང་ (gōgjaŋ) the flabby skin that hangs from the neck of cows and oxen.

ལྐོག་བྲོས་ (gōgdröö) secretly fleeing; va.—བྱེད་ ། ཁོས་བཙོན་ཁང་ནས་ལྐོག་བྲོས་བྱས་པ་རེད་ He secretly fled from jail.

ལྐོག་དབེན་ (gōgben) remote/ isolated place.

ལྐོག་འབྲེལ་ (gōŋdree) secret/ covert relations, conspiracy; va.—བྱེད་ ། རྒྱལ་ཁབ་དེ་གཉིས་དབར་ལྐོག་འབྲེལ་ཡོད་པ་རེད་ These two countries have secret relations.

ལྐོག་འབོམ་ (gōgbom) tib.eng. booby trap [Lit. secret bomb].

ལྐོག་སྦྱོར་ (gōgjɔɔ) secret/ illicit sexual relations.

ལྐོག་མ་ (gōgma) chin.

ལྐོག་མེན་ (gōgmen) sm. ལྐོག་མེན་དངོས་གཟུགས་.

ལྐོག་མེན་དངོས་གཟུགས་ (gōgmen ŋōōsug) tonsils.

ལྐོག་སྨད་ (gōgmɛɛ̀) sm. ལྐོག་ཁ་གདོང་.

ལྐོག་རྩ་ (gōgdza) veins under the chin (in Tibetan medicine).

ལྐོག་རྫིས་ (gōgdzii) secretly plotting/ conspiring; va.—རྒྱག.

ལྐོག་ཚོང་ (gōgtsoŋ) black marketeering, smuggling; va.—རྒྱག.

ལྐོག་མཚང་རྗེན་འབྱིན་ (gōgtsaŋ jenjin) revealing, exposing, unmasking; va.—བྱེད་ ། ཁོང་གིས་གསང་བའི་ཚོགས་པ་དེའི་གནས་ཚུལ་ཚང་མ་ལྐོག་མཚང་རྗེན་འབྱིན་བྱས་པ་རེད་ He revealed everything about the secret group.

ལྐོག་མཚོན་ (gōgdzön) hidden weapon, concealed weapon.

ལྐོག་འཛིང་ (gōŋdziŋ) fighting secretly ། དམག་མི་གཉིས་པོ་ལྐོག་འཛིང་བྱས་པ་རེད་ The two soldiers fought secretly.

ལྐོག་འཛུལ་ (gōŋdzüü) secretly entering/ slipping into, secretly infiltrating; va.—བྱེད་ ། བོད་ནང་སོ་པ་གཉིས་ལྐོག་འཛུལ་བྱས་པ་རེད་ The two spies secretly entered Tibet.

ལྐོག་ཞུ་ (gōgshu) secret report; va.— བྱེད་.

ལྐོག་ཟ་ (gōgsa) embezzling; va.—བྱེད་ ། སྲིད་གཞུང་གི་ནང་དུ་ལྐོག་ཟའི་གནས་ཚུལ་མང་པོ་འདུག There is much embezzling in the government.

ལྐོག་ཟ་ཀུ་ཁྱེར་ (gōgsa gūkyer) embezzling, engaging in corruption.

ལྐོག་ཟ་ཁོག་རུལ་ (gōgsa kɔ̄grüü) embezzling and corruption ། སྲིད་གཞུང་གི་ནང་དུ་ལྐོག་ཟ་ཁོག་རུལ་གྱི་གནས་ཚུལ་མང་པོ་འདུག There is much embezzling and corruption in the government.

ལྐོག་ཟ་ཆུད་ཟོས་ (gōgsa cūsöö) embezzling and wasting.

ལྐོག་ཟ་བྱེད་མཁན་ (gōgsa ceñɛn) a person who embezzles.

ལྐོག་ཟ་གཡོ་ཟོལ་ (gōgsala yosöö) fraudulent practices, malpractice, embezzlement.

ལྐོག་ཟ་ལ་ངོ་རྒོལ་ (gōgsala ŋogöö) opposing corruption/ embezzlement (This was one of the "three antis" campaign of 1951-1952).

ལྐོག་ཟན་ (gōgsɛn) corruption, embezzlement; va.—ཟ་ to embezzle, to engage in corruption.

ལྐོག་ཟོས་ཀུ་རྒྱག་ (gōgsöö gūgyaà) embezzling and robbing/ stealing ། དེང་སྐབས་བཟོ་གྲྭའི་ནང་ལྐོག་ཟོས་ཀུ་རྒྱག་གི་གནས་ཚུལ་མང་པོ་ཐོན་སོང་ These days many incidents of embezzlement and robbery have occurred in the factory.

ལྐོག་ཟོས་ཉེས་ཅན་ (gōgsöö ñeèjɛn) an embezzler.

ལྐོག་བཟས་ (gōgsɛɛ̀) eating secretly/ on the sly.

ལྐོག་གཡོ་ (gōgyo) sm. ལྐོག་གསོམ་.

ལྐོག་གཡོ་ངན་ཇུས་ (gōgyo ŋənjüü) secretly plotting/ conspiring.

ལྐོག་གཡོས་དོན་སྒྱུར་ (gōgyöö töngyur) secretly changing/ altering the meaning, using subterfuge to change the meaning.

ལྐོག་ལབ་ (gōgləb) slandering, defaming, saying bad things behind sb.'s back; va.—རྒྱག ། མིའི་རྒྱབ་ཏུ་ལྐོག་ལབ་རྒྱག་པ་ལས་གདོང་གདུགས་ནས་སྐྱོན་བརྗོད་བྱེད་པ་དགའ་ It is better to criticize a person to his face than secretly talk behind his back.

ལྐོག་ལས་ (gōglɛɛ̀) secret activity/ work, working without others knowing; va.—བྱེད་ ། མི་དེས་ལྐོག་ལས་བྱས་ནས་དངུལ་མང་པོ་བཟོས་འདུག That man made a lot of money doing work without others knowing.

ལྐོག་ཤལ་ (gōgshɛɛ) sm. ལྐོག་འཕྱང་.

ལྐོག་གསོམ་ (gōgshom) secretly conspiring, secretly plotting; va.—བྱེད་ to plot, conspire; va.—འཆང་ to secretly hold a plot/ deceptive scheme ། དམག་འཁྲུག་གསར་པ་སློང་རྒྱུའི་ལྐོག་གསོམ་བྱས་པ་རེད་ They secretly conspired to incite a new war.

ལྐོག་གསོམ་པ་ (gōgshomba) conspirator, secret plotter.

ལྐོག་བཤད་ (gōgshɛɛ̀) sm. ལྐོག་ལབ་.

ལྐོག་བཤེར་ (gōgsher) secret search/ investigation; va.—རྒྱག ། ནག་ཚོང་རྒྱག་མཁན་གྱི་ཁང་པ་ལྐོག་བཤེར་བྱས་པ་རེད་ (They) secretly searched the smuggler's house.

ལྐོག་གསོག་ (gōgsɔɔ̀) 1. crop of a bird, the cheek pouch of a monkey, etc. 2. secretly accumulating/ storing up; va.—རྒྱག ། གྲྭ་པ་དེས་རྒྱུ་ནོར་མང་པོ་ལྐོག་གསོག་བརྒྱབ་འདུག That monk secretly accumulated a lot of wealth.

ལྐོག་གསོད་ (gōgsöö) secretly murdering/ assassinating; va.—གཏོང་ ། རྒྱལ་ཁབ་ཀྱི་སྲིད་འཛིན་ལྐོག་གསོད་བྱས་པ་རེད་ (They) assassinated the president of the country.

ལྐོག་བསུབ་ (gōgsub) shung. hiding sth. secretly; va.—བྱེད་.

སྐ་ཅིག (gājii) sm. སྐད་ཅིག.

སྐ་པ་ (gāwa) 1. thick (for fluids) ། འབྲས་ཐུག་སྐ་པ་ A thick rice broth. 2. strong (usu. for tea, coffee). 3. name of an ancient Tibetan lineage.

སྐ་རགས་ (gāraà) sm. སྐེད་རགས་.

སྐ་ལ་ (gāla) sm.* སྐལ་བ་.

སྐ་སླ་ (gā lā) 1. strong and weak (regarding tea, coffee, etc.). 2. thick and watery/ thin (regarding broths, stews, soups) ། ཐུག་པ་འདི་སྐ་སླ་རན་པོ་བྱུང་བཞག The broth came out not too thick and not too thin (just right).

སྐག (gāg) 1. an inauspicious year astrologically when one is most open to personal misfortune or danger (occurs once every twelve years in one's animal birth year). 2. a type of red color.

སྐག་བསྐུས་པ་ལྟར་ (gāggüü dār) blushing out of shame/ embarrassment [Lit. like applying red color].

སྐག་འགོ (gāŋgo) the beginning of a སྐག year.

སྐག་སྔ་བསུ་ (gā ŋāsu) the year before a སྐག year.

སྐག་ཐོག (gāgtɔɔ̀) during the year of one's སྐག.

སྐག་ཕྱི་བསུ་ (gāg cīsu) the year after a སྐག year.

སྐག་རྩིས་ (gəgdzii) the astrological system of calculating སྐག years.

སྐག་གཞུག (gāgshuù) the latter part of a སྐག year.

སྐག་ཡོལ་ (gāgyöö) vi. to have a སྐག year finish.

སྐག་ལ་སླེབས་ (gāgla lēè) vi. to have a སྐག year arrive/ begin.

སྐང་ར་ (gāŋra) sm. འཁང་ར་.

སྐད་ (gɛɛ̀) 1. voice, sound, noise; va.—རྒྱག to shout/ scream, to make noise ། སྐད་མ་རྒྱག Don't shout. ། བྱ་འདིས་སྐད་ཁྱད་མཚར་ཞིག་རྒྱག་གི་འདུག This bird is making strange noises. 2. language; va.—རྒྱག to speak a language ། ཁོ་བོད་སྐད་རྒྱག་ཐུབ་ཀྱི་འདུག་གས་ Is he able to speak Tibetan? 3. (vb. + —) it is said, it is said to be ། ཁོ་ལ་དངུལ་མང་པོ་ཡོད་སྐད་འདུག It is said that he has a lot of money.

སྐད་ཀྱི་འགྲོ་ལུགས་ (gɛ̄ɛ̀gi droluù) structure or grammar of speech/ language.

སྐད་ཀྱི་སྒྲ་གདངས་ (gɛ̄ɛ̀gi dradaŋ) 1. intonation/ tone of speech. 2. phonetics.

སྐད་ཀྱི་ང་རོ་ (gɛ̄ɛ̀gi ŋaro) sm. སྐད་ཀྱི་སྒྲ་གདངས་.

སྐད་ཀྱི་གདངས་ (gɛ̄ɛ̀gi daŋ) sm. སྐད་ཀྱི་སྒྲ་གདངས་.

སྐད་ཀྱི་རིག་པ་ (gɛ̄ɛ̀gi rigbə) linguistics.

སྐད་སྐུར་ (gɛ̄ɛ̀ gūr) sm. ལན་སྐུར.

སྐད་སྐྱེལ་འཕྲུལ་འཁོར་ (gɛ̄ɛ̀gyee drüū̃gɔɔ) transmitter (machine).

སྐད་སྐྱོ་པོ་ (gɛ̄ɛ̀ gyōbo) 1. a weak voice ༎ ནད་པ་དེས་སྐད་སྐྱོ་པོ་ཞིག་རྒྱག་གི་འདུག The sick person speaks with a weak voice. 2. a sound of poor quality ༎ སྒྲ་སྙན་འདི་སྐད་སྐྱོ་པོ་འདུག The lute has a poor sound. 3. speaking in a sad tone. ༎ སྤྲང་པོ་དེས་སྐད་སྐྱོ་པོ་ཞིག་བརྒྱབ་ནས་སློང་གི་འདུག The beggar is asking for alms with a sad tone in his voice.

སྐད་ཁུངས་རིག་པ་ (gɛ̄ɛ̀kuŋ rigbə) the study of the etymology (of words).

སྐད་ཁོངས་ (gɛ̄ɛ̀koŋ) language stock/ family ༎ འབར་བོད་སྐད་ཁོངས་ Tibeto-Burman language family.

སྐད་འཁོར་ (gɛ̄ɛ̀kɔɔ) tape recorder; va.—གཏོང་.

སྐད་གྲགས་ (gɛ̄ɛ̀draà) fame, repute, reputation; vi.—ཆོད་ to become famous/ well-known (for good or bad); vi.—བྱེད་ to be famous/ well-known; vi.—འཛགས་ to lose fame; va.—བཞག to make oneself famous as a result of doing sth. ༎ ཁོང་གིས་དེབ་དེ་བཏོན་ཙང་རྒྱལ་ཁབ་ནང་དུ་སྐད་གྲགས་ཆོད་བཞག Because he published that book he became famous in the country. ༎ འཛམ་གླིང་ཐོག་དམག་འཁྲུག་ཡོང་རྒྱུའི་སྐད་གྲགས་ཆེན་པོ་བྱེད་ཀྱི་འདུག It is becoming well known in the world that a war is coming. ༎ གློག་བརྙན་འཁྲབ་མཁན་དེའི་སྐད་གྲགས་དེང་སང་འཛགས་བཞག These days the fame of that movie star has declined. ༎ རྐང་རྩེད་སྡེ་ཚན་འདི་རུ་ཁག་གིས་འགྲན་སྡུར་ནང་སྐད་གྲགས་བཞག་འདུག The soccer team made itself famous in the competition.

སྐད་གྲགས་ཅན་ (gɛ̄ɛ̀draàjɛn) famous, well-known.

སྐད་གྲགས་ཆེན་པོ་ (gɛ̄ɛ̀draà cēmbo) famous, well-known.

སྐད་གྲགས་ཡོད་པ་ (gɛ̄ɛ̀draà yöba) sm. སྐད་གྲགས་ཅན་.

སྐད་འགག (gɛ̄ɛ̀ gaà) vi. to become hoarse.

སྐད་འགག་དོ་ (gɛ̄ɛ̀ gagdo) hoarse (voice).

སྐད་འགགས་ (gɛ̄ɛ̀ gaà) p. of སྐད་འགག.

སྐད་འགྲོ་ (gɛ̄ngo) voice, sound.

སྐད་འགྲོ་མཐོ་པོ་ (gɛ̄ngo tōbo) loud (talk/ voice), high-pitched voice.

སྐད་འགྲོ་གནོན་ (gɛ̄ngo nǒn) va. to control one's voice (so as not to let it show anger or other emotions) ༎ ཁོང་གི་སེམས་གཞིང་ལ་ཁོང་ཁྲོ་ཡོད་ཀྱང་སྐད་འགྲོ་མནན་ནས་སྐད་ཆ་བཤད་པ་རེད་ Although he felt angry inside, he spoke controlling his voice.

སྐད་འགྲོ་དམའ་པོ་ (gɛ̄ngo māābo) low voice/ talk, low-pitched voice.

སྐད་འགྱུར་ (gɛ̄ɛ̀ gyur) vi. to have one's voice change ༎ ཕྲུ་གུ་དེ་ལོ་བཅོ་ལྔ་ལ་སླེབས་སྐབས་སྐད་འགྱུར་སོང་ When the boy reached fifteen his voice changed.

སྐད་རྒྱག (gɛ̄ɛ̀ gyaà) see སྐད་, 1.

སྐད་རྒྱུད་ (gɛ̄ɛ̀gyüù) sm. སྐད་ཁོངས་.

སྐད་བརྒྱབ་ (gɛ̄ɛ̀ gyəb) p. of སྐད་རྒྱག.

སྐད་སྒོ་དམའ་པོ་ (gɛ̄ɛ̀go maabo) sm. སྐད་འགྲོ་དམའ་པོ་.

སྐད་སྒྱུར་ (gɛ̄ɛ̀gyur) 1. interpreter, translator (of speech). 2. va. སྐད་སྒྱུར་; —བྱེད་ to translate ༎ གཏམ་བཤད་དེའི་སྐད་བསྒྱུར་བ་རེད་ (They) translated that speech.

སྐད་སྒྱུར་མཁན་ (gɛ̄ɛ̀gyurñɛn) translator, interpreter.

སྐད་སྒྱུར་སྒྲ་སྐྱེལ་འཕྲུལ་ཆས་ (gɛ̄ɛ̀gyur drakee drüū̃jɛɛ̀) earphones (used in simultaneous translation).

སྐད་སྒྲ་ (gɛ̄ɛ̀dra) sound, noise ༎ བྱ་བྱིའུ་དང་ཆུའི་སྐད་སྒྲ་ The sound of birds and water.

སྐད་སྒྲ་བདེ་སྦྱོད་ (gɛ̄ɛ̀dra dadröö) sm. སྐད་ཡིག་བདེ་སྦྱོད་.

སྐད་སྒྲོག་འཕྲུལ་ཆས་ (gɛ̄ɛ̀drɔɔ̀ trüū̃jɛɛ̀) radio transmitter/ receiver.

སྐད་བསྒྱུར་ (gɛ̄ɛ̀gyur) sm. སྐད་སྒྱུར་.

སྐད་ངན་ (gɛ̄ɛ̀ŋɛn) 1. a cry of anguish, scream of pain; vi.—ཤོར་ to scream/ cry out in anguish ༎ ཁོང་ལག་པ་ཆག་ཙང་སྐད་ངན་ཤོར་སོང He cried out in pain because he broke his arm. 2. va.—རྒྱག to cry out/ complain in anguish or suffering ༎ མི་སེར་གྱི་འཚོ་བ་སྐྱོ་པོ་ཡིན་ཙང་སྐད་ངན་རྒྱག་མཁན་མང་པོ་འདུག Because the people's livelihood is poor, many people were complaining of their suffering.

སྐད་ངན་རྗེས་བཞག (gɛ̄ɛ̀ŋɛn jeèshaà) leaving behind a bad reputation/ name; va.—བྱེད་ ༎ མི་དེས་རྒྱལ་ཁབ་བཙོངས་པའི་སྐད་ངན་རྗེས་བཞག་བྱས་ནས་ཤི་བ་རེད་ He sold out his country and died leaving behind a bad reputation.

སྐད་ངན་རླུང་འཕྱིར་ (gɛ̄ɛ̀ŋɛn lūŋgyer) a bad reputation/ scandal spreads like the wind, bad news spreads fast ༎ ས་གཡོས་ཀྱི་གནས་ཚུལ་དེ་སྐད་ངན་རླུང་འཕྱིར་གྱིས་གང་ས་གང་དུ་ཁྱབ་འདུག The news of the earthquake has spread everywhere like the wind.

སྐད་ངོ་ (gɛ̄ɛ̀ŋo) voice; vi.—ཆོད་ to recognize sb.'s voice ༎ ཁ་པར་ཐོག་ནས་སྐད་ངོ་མ་ཆོད་ན་ལན་མ་རྒྱབས་ If you don't recognize (his) voice on the phone, do not answer.

སྐད་ཅིག (gɛ̄ɛ̀jig) a moment, an instant, at once, in a flash ༎ སྐད་ཅིག་གཅིག་ལ་གློག་ཚང་མ་ཤི་སོང་ The electricity went out all at once. ༎ བདེ་བའི་གནས་སྐབས་སྐད་ཅིག་ཙམ་མེད་པ་རེད་ They didn't have even a moment of pleasure.

སྐད་ཅིག་སྐད་ཅིག (gɛ̄ɛ̀jig gɛ̄ɛ̀jig) sm. སྐད་ཅིག.

སྐད་ཅིག་ཆ་མེད་ (gɛ̄ɛ̀jig cāmeè) sm. སྐད་ཅིག.

སྐད་ཅིག་ཉིད་ (gɛ̄ɛ̀jigñii) in a moment/ instant/ flash ༎ གཟུགས་བརྙན་དེ་སྐད་ཅིག་ཉིད་ལ་ཡལ་བ་རེད་ The image disappeared in a flash.

སྐད་ཅིག་མ་ (gɛ̄ɛ̀jigmə) sm. སྐད་ཅིག.

སྐད་ཅིག་མ་གཅིག (gɛ̄ɛ̀jigmə) a moment/ instant, instantaneously.

སྐད་ཅིག་ཙམ་ (gɛ̄ɛ̀jigdzam) as much as an instant, even an instant ༎ བདེ་བའི་གནས་སྐབས་སྐད་ཅིག་ཙམ་མེད་པ་རེད་ They didn't have even a moment of pleasure.

སྐད་ཅོར་ (gɛ̄ɛ̀jɔɔ) uproar, racket, din, tumult; va.—རྒྱག; —སྒྲོག ༎ སློབ་ཁང་ནང་སློབ་ཕྲུག་ཚོས་སྐད་ཅོར་རྒྱག་གི་འདུག The students are creating a racket in the class room.

སྐད་ཅོར་ཝུར་ཅོར་ (gɛ̄ɛ̀jɔɔ wurjɔɔ) sm. སྐད་ཅོར་.

སྐད་གཅོམ་ (gɛ̄ɛ̀jom) discussion, talk, parley; va.—བྱེད་ ༎ མི་ཚང་མས་སྐད་གཅོམ་ལེགས་པར་བྱས་འདུག Everyone had a good discussion.

སྐད་ཆ་ (gɛ̄ja) 1. conversation, talk, discussion; va.—ཤོད་ to talk, to speak; va.—བྱེད་ to discuss/ consult/ negotiate; va.—འགྲེམས་ to spread/ disseminate word/ talk of sth. ༎ ཚོགས་འདུའི་ཐོག་སྐད་ཆ་ཤོད་མི་ཆོག One is not permitted to speak during the meeting. ༎ རྩོད་རྙོག་དེ་ཞི་འགྲིག་ཡོང་བར་སྐད་ཆ་བྱེད་ཀྱི་ཡོད་པ་རེད་ (They) are negotiating to reach a peaceful settlement of the dispute. ༎ ལས་ཁུངས་ནང་ནས་ཡིག་ཆ་ཀ་ཤོར་བྱུང་བའི་སྐོར་ཁོས་སྐད་ཆ་བཀྲམ་འདུག He spread word that documents were stolen from the office.

སྐད་ཆ་སྟོམ་པོ་ (gɛ̄ja gāmbo) empty/ meaningless talk; va.—ཤོད་ ༎ ཁོས་སྐད་ཆ་སྟོམ་པོ་ཤོད་པ་ལས་ལག་ལེན་གཏན་ནས་བསྟར་གྱི་མེད་པ་རེད་ He only does empty talk, he never puts it into practice.

སྐད་ཆ་སྐམ་ (gɛ̄ja gūm) va. to stop talking about sth. (usu. when sb. else comes) ༎ ང་སླེབས་མ་ཐག་ཁོ་ཚོས་སྐད་ཆ་བསྐུམས་སོང་ As soon as I came they stopped talking.

སྐད་ཆ་སྐོར་ (gɛ̄ja gɔ̄ɔ̄) va. to say sth. in a roundabout manner ༎ ང་བོད་ལ་ཡོང་མི་ཆོག་པའི་སྐོར་ཁོང་གིས་སྐད་ཆ་སྐོར་ནས་ཤོད་ཀྱི་འདུག He said I couldn't come to Tibet in a roundabout way.

སྐད་ཆ་སྐྱུག་བྲོ་པོ་ (gɛ̄ja gyūg trobo) nauseating/ unpleasant/ dirty talk; va.—ཤོད་.

སྐད་ཆ་སྐྱོ་པོ་ (gɛ̄ja gyōbo) 1. sad/ sorrowful talk ༎

ཞིང་པ་དེས་རང་གིས་སྡུག་བསྔལ་མྱོང་ཚུལ་གྱི་སྐད་ཆ་སྐྱོ་པོ་ཞིག་བཤད་སོང་ The farmer talked of his sorrowful experience. 2. meaningless/ poor speech or talk ¶ འགོ་ཁྲིད་དེས་ཚོགས་འདུའི་ཐོག་སྐད་ཆ་སྐྱོ་པོ་ཞིག་བཤད་སོང་ The leader gave a poor speech at the meeting.

སྐད་ཆ་གྲམ་ (gɛ̄ja dram) vi. to have word/ talk of sth. spread ¶ ལས་ཁུངས་ནང་ནས་ཡིག་ཆ་རྐུ་ཤོར་བྱུང་བའི་སྐོར་སྐད་ཆ་གྲམ་འདུག Word has spread that documents were stolen from the office.

སྐད་ཆ་རྒྱག (gɛ̄ja gyaà) va. to mediate ¶ ཁ་མཆུའི་ཁ་གཏད་གཉིས་དབར་སྐད་ཆ་རྒྱག་གི་ཡོད་པ་རེད་ (He) is mediating between the two parties in the lawsuit.

སྐད་ཆ་ངར་པོ་ (gɛ̄ja ŋarbo) strong/ forceful language or speech; va.—ཤོད་ to speak in strong/ forceful language or speech.

སྐད་ཆ་ངོ་མ་ (gɛ̄ja ŋoma) true/ real/ correct/ accurate speech or talk.

སྐད་ཆ་རྔོག (gɛ̄ja ŋɔ̄ɔ̀) va. to get a person unsuspectingly to reveal sth. through conversation.

སྐད་ཆ་གཅིག་མཐུན་ (gɛ̄ja jīgdün) 1. the same/ identical talk or speech ¶ ཉེས་ཅན་དེ་གཉིས་ཁྲིམས་ཁང་ནང་སྐད་ཆ་གཅིག་མཐུན་རེད་བཤག The two criminals said identical things in court. 2. common language ¶ བོད་མི་ཚང་མ་སྐད་ཆ་གཅིག་མཐུན་ཡོང་བ་བྱེད་རྒྱུ་དེ་གལ་ཆེན་པོ་ཡིན་ It is important to work towards all Tibetans having a common language.

སྐད་ཆ་ལྗིད་པོ་ (gɛ̄ja jiibu) talk that makes things seem more important than they are; va.—ཤོད་.

སྐད་ཆ་ཉུང་ཉུང་ (gɛ̄ja ñūŋñuŋ) taciturn; va.—ཤོད་ to speak taciturnly.

སྐད་ཆ་སྙན་པོ་ (gɛ̄ja ñɛ̄mbo) 1. interesting/ engaging/ fascinating conversation; va.—ཤོད་. 2. flattery; va.—ཤོད་ ¶ འགོ་འཁྲིད་ལ་སྐད་ཆ་སྙན་པོ་བཤད་པ་རེད་ (He) flattered the leader.

སྐད་ཆ་སྟོང་པོ་ (gɛ̄ja dōŋbo) empty speech/ talk, silly/ useless/ meaningless speech or talk.

སྐད་ཆ་ཐོན་པོ་ (gɛ̄ja tōmbo) fluent in speech, very verbal.

སྐད་ཆ་དུམ་དུམ་ (gɛ̄ja dumdum) 1. pithy talk, talk that is brief and to the point; va.—ཤོད་. 2. a person who speaks in a pithy manner.

སྐད་ཆ་དོན་མེད་ (gɛ̄ja dönmeè) pointless/ meaningless talk.

སྐད་ཆ་དྲིས་ (gɛ̄ja trii) p. of སྐད་ཆ་འདྲི་.

སྐད་ཆ་འདྲ་ཆགས་པོ་ (gɛ̄ja dra cāgbo) 1. sweet talk ¶ མི་དེས་རྟག་པར་སྐད་ཆ་འདྲ་ཆགས་པོ་བཤད་ནས་མི་ལ་མགོ་སྐོར་གཏོང་གི་ཡོད་པ་རེད་ That person deceives people all the time by his sweet talk. 2. tactful way of saying sth., speaking in a way that does not offend ¶ ཁོང་གི་སྐད་ཆ་འདྲ་ཆགས་པོ་ཁོ་ན་བཤད་ནས་མི་ལ་ཕོག་ཐུག་གཏོང་གི་མེད་པ་རེད་ He talks tactfully and so does not offend people.

སྐད་ཆ་འདྲི་ (gɛ̄ja tri) va. to inquire, to ask ¶ ཁོས་ཁྱེད་རང་གི་སྐོར་སྐད་ཆ་འདྲི་གི་འདུག He is asking about you.

སྐད་ཆ་འདྲི་ས་ (gɛ̄ja trisə) 1. sb. one asks for information/ advice ¶ ཁོང་ནི་ངའི་རྒྱུན་གཏན་གྱི་སྐད་ཆ་འདྲི་ས་ཞིག་ཡིན་ He is the person from whom I regularly ask questions/ advice. 2. information/ inquiry office.

སྐད་ཆ་གནག་པོ་ (gɛ̄ja nagbo) talk that causes pain to others, hurtful talk; va.—ཤོད་ ¶ མི་དེ་དོན་དག་ཆུང་ཆུང་ཡིན་ན་ཡང་སྐད་ཆ་གནག་པོ་ཤོད་མཁན་ཞིག་རེད་ Even for petty things, that person is sb. who says hurtful things.

སྐད་ཆ་རྣོ་པོ་ (gɛ̄ja nōbo) harsh/ abrasive speech, sharp/ biting comments; va.—ཤོད་.

སྐད་ཆ་འཕྲོག (gɛ̄ja trɔ̄ɔ̀) sm. ཁ་འཕྲོག.

སྐད་ཆ་བྱེད་ (gɛ̄ja ceè) see སྐད་ཆ་.

སྐད་ཆ་སྦུག་སྦུག (gɛ̄ja bugbuù) speech that is not clear or detailed because the speaker is holding back sth; va.—ཤོད་.

སྐད་ཆ་མ་ཡིན་ (gɛja məbin) false talk, lies; va.—ཤོད་.

སྐད་ཆ་མང་པོ་ (gɛja maŋbo) long-winded, talkative ¶ མི་འདི་སྐད་ཆ་མང་པོ་ཞིག་འདུག This person is long-winded (talks a lot).

སྐད་ཆ་མེད་པ་ (gɛja meèba) there is no problem/ question about sth., there is no need to ask ¶ མི་དེ་བློས་འཁེལ་ཡོས་ལ་སྐད་ཆ་མེད་པ་རེད་ There is no question regarding the trustworthiness of that person.

སྐད་ཆ་དམར་པོ་ (gɛja māābo) abrupt/ insensitive/ rude speech; va.—ཤོད་.

སྐད་ཆ་རྩུབ་པོ་ (gɛ̄ja dzūbu) rough/ harsh words; va.—ཤོད་.

སྐད་ཆ་རྫོར་པོ་ (gɛ̄ja dzɔrbo) dirty talk.

སྐད་ཆ་རྫུན་མ་ (gɛ̄ja dzünmə) lies, falsehoods; va.—ཤོད་.

སྐད་ཆ་གཟེར་པོ་ (gɛ̄ja serbo) sm. སྐད་ཆ་རྣོ་པོ་.

སྐད་ཆ་བཟོ་ (gɛ̄ja so) 1. va. to start a rumor. 2. va. to talk/ discuss.

སྐད་ཆ་ཡོང་ (gɛ̄ja yoŋ) vi. to have a talk later/ in the future.

སྐད་ཆ་གཡོལ་ (gɛ̄ja yöö) va. to avoid talking/ having a talk, to change topics while talking.

སྐད་ཆ་ལ་གནས་ (gɛ̄jala nɛ̄ɛ) vi. to do what one says, to keep one's word ¶ དེ་སྔོན་གྲོས་མོལ་བྱས་པའི་སྐད་ཆ་ལ་གནས་མེད་པ་རེད་ (They) did not keep their word regarding the talks they previously had.

སྐད་ཆ་ལབ་པེ་ལོབ་པེ་ (gɛ̄ja ləbe lobe) wordy, verbose; va.—ཤོད་.

སྐད་ཆ་ཤོད་སྟངས་ (gɛ̄ja shōdaŋ) 1. manner/ way of talking ¶ ཁོ་སྐད་ཆ་ཤོད་སྟངས་ཞེ་དྲག་ཉེས་པོ་འདུག He has a terrible way of talking. ¶ ཁོའི་སྐད་ཆ་ཤོད་སྟངས་ལ་བལྟས་ན་ང་ཚོའི་རོགས་རམ་དགོས་ཀྱི་ཡོད་བཟོ་འདུག From the way he spoke it seems that (he) needs our help 2. tone of voice, accent, intonation.

སྐད་ཆ་ཤོད་ཐལ་ (gɛ̄ja shōtɛɛ) vi. to inadvertently say sth., to have a slip of the tongue ¶ ངས་ཚོགས་འདུའི་ཐོག་སྐད་ཆ་ཤོད་ཐལ་བྱུང་ནས་མི་ལ་ཕོག་ཐུག་ཕྱིན་སོང་ At the conference, I had a slip of the tongue and offended people.

སྐད་ཆ་ཤོད་དབང་ (gɛ̄ja shōwaŋ) freedom of speech ¶ མི་དམངས་ལ་སྐད་ཆ་ཤོད་དབང་མེད་པ་རེད་ The people don't have freedom of speech.

སྐད་ཆ་བཤད་ནས་གང་ཡོང་ (gɛ̄ja shɛ̄ɛnɛ gaŋyöö) excellent, superb, no question about sth. [Lit. why talk about it].

སྐད་ཆ་སོམས་ལ་ཤོད་ ཙམ་པ་ལྡད་ལ་མིད་ (gɛ̄ja sōmla shöö dzāmba dɛ̄ɛla mii) think before acting [Lit. one should think before talking and chew the tsamba before swallowing].

སྐད་ཆ་གསང་པོ་ (gɛ̄ja sāŋbo) speaking without reservation, talking frankly; va.—ཤོད་.

སྐད་ཆའི་སྐད་ཆ་ (gɛ̄jɛ gɛ̄ja) 1. just talk, sth. improbable, sth. out of the question ¶ ཨ་རི་ར་འགྲོ་ཐུབ་རྒྱུ་སྐད་ཆའི་སྐད་ཆ་རེད་ Being able to go to America is just talk. 2. conversation ¶ སྐད་ཆའི་སྐད་ཆའི་ནང་ལ་ང་ཚོ་ཚོང་གི་སྐད་ཆ་བྱུང་ We discussed business in the course of our conversation.

སྐད་ཆའི་གར་ (gɛ̄jɛ dögar) sm. སྐད་ཆའི་ཟློས་གར་.

སྐད་ཆའི་གླེང་གཞི་ (gɛ̄jɛ lēŋshi) the subject or topic of a conversation/ discussion/ talk ¶ སྐད་ཆའི་གླེང་གཞི་སྲིད་དོན་རེད་ The topic of the conversation was politics.

སྐད་ཆའི་ཟློས་གར་ (gɛ̄jɛ döögar) a theatrical play.

སྐད་ཆུང་ཆུང་ (gɛ̄ɛ̀ cūŋjuŋ) low voice.

སྐད་ཆེན་པོ་ (gɛ̄ɛ̀ cēmbo) loud voice, loud noise.

སྐད་ཉན་ (gɛ̄ ñɛn) va. to listen to a voice/ talk/ speech.

སྐད་གཉའ་ (gɛ̄ña) sm. སྐད་ཤུགས་.

སྐད་གཉིས་པ་ (gɛ̄ñiiba) sm. སྐད་གཉིས་སྨྲ་བ་.

སྐད་གཉིས་སྨྲ་བ་ (gɛ̄ñii māwa) translator, sb. who knows two languages.

སྐད་གཉིས་ཤན་སྦྱར་ (gɛ̄ñii shēnjar) a dictionary/ word list in two languages.

སྐད་རྟོལ་རྟོལ་ལྷར་འབོད་ (gɛ̄ ñööñöödar böö) va. to talk in a low and humble voice (like begging).

སྐད་སྙན་ (gɛ̄ñɛn) melodious, pleasant sounding ¶ སྐད་སྙན་གྱི་གཞས་གདངས་ ¶ A melodious song.

སྐད་སྙན་པོ་ (gɛ̄ɛ ñɛ̄mbo) a melodious/ pleasant sound or voice.

སྐད་སྙན་བྱིའུ་ (gɛ̄ñɛn ciwu) nightingale.

སྐད་བརྙན་ (gɛ̄ñɛn) echo.

སྐད་གཏོང་ (gɛ̄ɛ dōŋ) va. 1. to call sb. (to come) ¶ ཁོང་ལས་ཁུངས་ལ་སྐད་བཏང་བ་རེད་ He was called to the office. 2. va. to invite ¶ ཁོང་ཐུགས་སྒྲོར་སྐད་བཏང་བ་རེད་ He was invited to the party.

སྐད་གཏོང་གི་ས་ (gɛ̄ɛdoŋgi sā) the distance from which one can hear sb. calling.

སྐད་གཏོང་བརྡ་རྒྱག་ (gɛ̄ɛdoŋ dagyaà) calling/ inviting people and delivering messages; va.—བྱེད་ ¶ ང་ལས་ཁུངས་ནང་སྐད་གཏོང་བརྡ་རྒྱག་གི་ལས་ཀ་བྱེད་ཀྱི་ཡོད་ My work in the office is delivering messages and calling people.

སྐད་བཏང་ (gɛ̄ɛ dāŋ) p. of སྐད་གཏོང་.

སྐད་མཐུན་པ་ (gɛ̄ɛ tũmbu) 1. speaking the same language, linguistic compatibility ¶ སྐད་མཐུན་པའི་མི་དང་མཉམ་དུ་གཤིབ་བདེ་པོ་ཡོད་ People who speak the same language get along well. 2. singing in the same tone/ pitch.

སྐད་མཐོ་པོ་ (gɛ̄ɛ tōbo) high voice/ tone.

སྐད་དེབ་ (gɛ̄ɛdeb) language primer.

སྐད་དོང་ (gɛ̄ɛdoŋ) microphone.

སྐད་དོད་ (gɛ̄ɛdöö) equivalent word ¶ ཆེད་ལས་མིང་ཚིག་གི་སྐད་དོད་རྙེད་ཁག་པོ་ཡོད་པ་རེད་ It is difficult to find the equivalent of the technical term.

སྐད་དྲག་པོ་ (gɛ̄ɛ dragbo) 1. screaming, yelling; va.—རྒྱག ¶ ན་ཚ་བཏང་ནས་སྐད་དྲག་པོ་རྒྱག་གི་འདུག (He) is screaming with pain. 2. harsh/ stern words or talk ¶ སྐད་དྲག་པོའི་ཐོག་ནས་གཤེ་གཤེ་བཏང་བྱུང་ I got scolded in a harsh manner.

སྐད་གདངས་ (gɛ̄ɛdaŋ) tone (of voice), tune ¶ གཞས་ཀྱི་སྐད་གདངས་ Song's tune. ¶ ལོག་སྤྱོད་པའི་སྐད་གདངས་ The reactionaries' tune.

སྐད་གདོང་གཉིས་བཙན་ (gɛ̄ɛdoŋ ñiidzɛn) angry in expression and speech.

སྐད་འདར་ (gɛ̄ɛdar) quivering/ trembling voice.

སྐད་བརྡའ་ (gɛ̄ɛda) verbal signal/ command/ order, e.g., commands such as " right face;" va.—གཏོང་ to issue a verbal command/ order; vi.—འཕྲོད་ to be able to communicate verbally ¶ ཁོ་ཚོ་ཕན་ཚུན་བར་སྐད་བརྡ་འཕྲོད་མི་ཐུབ་པའི་དཀའ་ངལ་ཡོད་པ་རེད་ They had difficulty communicating with each other.

སྐད་བརྡའ་ (gɛ̄ɛda) sm. སྐད་བརྡ་.

སྐད་པ་ (gɛ̄ɛba) sm. ཟེར་བ་.

སྐད་པར་ (gɛ̄ɛbaa) abbr. of སྐད་པར་འཁོར་ལོ་.

སྐད་པར་ཁབ་ (gɛ̄ɛbar kāb) phonograph needle/ stylus.

སྐད་པར་འཁོར་ལོ་ (gɛ̄ɛbaa kɔ̄ɔlo) phonograph.

སྐད་པར་ཕེན་ཙེ་ (gɛ̄ɛbaa pēndze) tib.ch. phonograph record.

སྐད་པོ་ཆེ་ (gɛ̄ɛboce) famous, well-known.

སྐད་ཕྲ་པོ་ (gɛ̄ɛ drəbu) high-pitched voice.

སྐད་འཕང་ (gɛ̄ŋbaŋ) sm. སྐད་གདངས་.

སྐད་འབོད་ (gɛ̄mböö) 1. shouting loudly (usu. conveys shouting slogans at a demonstration); va.—བྱེད་; —རྒྱག to shout loudly ¶ མི་དམངས་ཚོས་དམངས་གཙོའི་སྐད་འབོད་བྱེད་ཀྱི་འདུག The people are shouting democratic slogans.

སྐད་འབོད་ངུ་འབོད་ (gɛ̄mböö ŋumböö) shouting and wailing; va.—བྱེད་; —རྒྱག.

སྐད་སྦོམ་པོ་ (gɛ̄ɛ bombo) a low pitched/ deep voice.

སྐད་སྦྱར་ (gɛ̄ɛjar) telling, informing, passing on via speech, transmitting, notifying though speech.

སྐད་སྦྱོར་ཁང་ (gɛ̄ɛjɔrgaŋ) dubbing room/ studio.

སྐད་མེད་སྐད་བཟོས་ (gɛ̄ɛmeè gɛ̄ɛsöö) making a fuss out of nothing, talking about sth. one doesn't know about [Lit. without sound, making sound].

སྐད་མེད་གློག་བརྙན་ (gɛ̄ɛmeè lɔ̄ŋñɛn) silent film.

སྐད་དམའ་པོ་ (gɛ̄ɛ māābo) low voice, low tone.

སྐད་ཚ་པོ་ (gɛ̄ɛ tsābo) noisy, loud ¶ ཁང་པ་འདིའི་ནང་ལ་སྡོད་མཁན་ཚོ་སྐད་ཚ་པོ་འདུག The people who live in this house are noisy.

སྐད་འཛེར་ (gɛ̄ɛ dzee) vi. to be/ get hoarse.

སྐད་འཛེར་ཤུགས་ཟད་ (gɛ̄ndzee shūgsɛɛ) completely exhausted; vi.—འགྱུར་ to become completely exhausted ¶ དེ་རིང་ཉིན་གང་སློབ་ཚན་ཁྲིད་ནས་སྐད་འཛེར་ཤུགས་ཟད་དུ་གྱུར་སོང་ Today I taught class all day and (I'm) completely exhausted. [Lit. voice hoarse, strength weakened].

སྐད་ཛིག་པོ་ (gɛ̄ɛ dzigu) rich/ sonorous voice.

སྐད་ཟུར་ཆག (gɛ̄ɛ surjaà) changed pronunciations ¶ ལྷ་སའི་ཁ་སྐད་ནང་སྐད་ཟུར་ཆག་མང་པོ་ཡོད་པ་རེད་ There are many changed pronunciations in spoken Lhasa dialect.

སྐད་ཟུར་ཉམས་ (gɛ̄ɛ surñam) sm. སྐད་ཟུར་ཆག.

སྐད་གཟེང་ (gɛ̄ɛseŋ) sm. སྐད་གསང་.

སྐད་གཟེང་མཐོན་པོ་ (gɛ̄ɛseŋ tõmbo) sm. སྐད་གསང་མཐོན་པོ་.

སྐད་བཟང་པོ་ (gɛ̄ɛ saŋbo) a good voice (for singing, etc.).

སྐད་བཟང་བ་ (gɛ̄ɛ saŋwa) sm. སྐད་བཟང་པོ་.

སྐད་འུར་ (gɛ̄ɛwur) the loud/ thundering noise made by a crowd; vi.—རྒྱག.

སྐད་འུར་སྒྲ་འུར་ (gɛ̄ɛwur drawur) sm. སྐད་འུར་.

སྐད་ཡག་པོ་ (gɛ̄ɛ yagbo) sm. སྐད་བཟང་པོ་.

སྐད་ཡིག (gɛ̄ɛyii) language and literature, speech and writing.

སྐད་ཡིག་ཁྲིད་དཔྱད་ཁང་ (gɛ̄ɛyii trījöögaŋ) language teaching and research room.

སྐད་ཡིག་བརྡ་སྤྲོད་ (gɛ̄ɛyii dadröö) 1. sign language (for the deaf and mute). 2. grammar.

སྐད་ཡིག་རྩོམ་རིག་ཞིབ་འཇུག་ཁང་ (gɛ̄ɛyii dzōmrii shīmjugaŋ) Institute of Language and Literature.

སྐད་ཡིག་ཚན་ཁག (gɛ̄ɛyii tsɛ̄nkaà) language department.

སྐད་ཡིག་མཛུབ་འཁྲིད་ཨུ་ཡོན་ལྷན་ཁང་ (gɛ̄ɛyii dzubdrii ūyün lhɛ̄ngaŋ) see མི་རིགས་སྐད་ཡིག་མཛུབ་འཁྲིད་ཨུ་ཡོན་ལྷན་ཁང་.

སྐད་ཡིག་ལས་དོན་ (gɛ̄ɛyii lɛ̄ɛdön) language administration/ work.

སྐད་ཡོད་གློག་བརྙན་ (gɛ̄ɛyöö lɔ̄ɔñɛn) talking film, sound film.

སྐད་ར་མ་ལུག (gɛ̄ɛ ramalug) mixed speech (e.g., speech mixing several dialects or languages).

སྐད་རིགས་ (gɛ̄ɛrii) languages ¶ སྐད་རིགས་མ་གཅིག་པ་ Different languages.

སྐད་རིགས་བརྟག་དཔྱད་ཁང་ (gɛ̄ɛrii dāgjɛgaŋ) linguistic institute.

སྐད་རིགས་ཡན་ལག (gɛ̄ɛrii yɛnlaà) language branch.

སྐད་རིགས་རིག་པ་ (gɛ̄ɛrii rigbə) linguistics.

སྐད་རིང་ (gɛ̄ɛriŋ) calling from a distance.

སྐད་རིམ་ (gɛ̄ɛrim) word order.

སྐད་ལུགས་ (gɛ̄ɛuù) dialect.

སྐད་ལོག (gɛ̄ɛlɔɔ) sm. སྐད་ཅོར་.

སྐད་ལོག་འུར་ལོག (gɛ̄ɛlɔɔ wurlɔɔ) sm. སྐད་ཅོར་འུར་ལོག.

སྐད་ཤུགས་ (gɛ̄ɛshug) loudness of speech.

སྐད་ཤོར་ (gɛ̄ɛ shɔ̄ɔ) vi. to cry/ scream out of fright or anguish ¶ འཇིགས་སྣང་ཆེ་བའི་གཟུགས་བརྙན་འདི་མཐོང་བ་དང་མོ་སྐད་ཤོར་སོང་ She screamed when she saw the terrifying figure.

སྐད་གསང་མཐོན་པོ་ (gɛ̄ɛsaŋ tõmbo) loudly, loud and clear.

སྐད་གསང་པོ་ (gɛ̄ɛ sāŋbo) clear/ distinct voice.

སྐད་གསར་བཅད་ (gɛ̄ɛ sārjɛɛ) simplifying language/ spelling; va.—བྱེད་ ¶ བོད་ཡིག་འབྲི་ཀློག་བདེ་ཆེད་ལོ་རྒྱུས་ཐོག་སྐད་གསར་བཅད་ཐེངས་གཉིས་བྱེད་ཡོད་པ་རེད་ For the purpose of making it easier to read and write Tibetan, historically the Tibetan language was simplified twice.

སྐད་གསལ་ (gɛ̄ɛsɛl) clear/ distinct voice.

སྐན་ (gɛ̄n) (vb. + རེ་ + —) swearing not to do sth. ¶ ང་བོད་ལ་འགྲོ་རེ་སྐན་ I swore not to go to Tibet.

སྐན་འཛའ་ (gēndza) sm.* སྐས་འཛེགས་.

སྐབས (gə̄p) 1. time, occasion ¶ སྐབས་དེར་ At that time. ¶ དལ་ཡོར་སྡོད་པའི་སྐབས་མེད་ Without leisure time. ¶ སྐབས་དེར་ཁོང་དང་མཇལ་བྱུང་ I met him at that time. 2. opportunity ¶ སྐབས་ཡག་པོ་ཞིག་བྱུང་ན་ If (you) get a good opportunity. 3. (— + number) the place/ number in a sequence ¶ ཚོགས་ཆེན་སྐབས་བརྒྱད་པའི་གྲོས་ཚོགས་བཞི་པ་ The fourth session of the Eighth General Assembly. 4. at the time of, when, during ¶ དམག་འཁྲུག་དེའི་སྐབས་ During that war. ¶ ལྷ་སར་འགྲོ་པའི་སྐབས་ལ་ When going to Lhasa. 5. sm. ཡིབ་.

སྐབས་སྐབས་ (gə̄pgəb) sm. སྐབས་འགར.

སྐབས་སྐབས་ལ་ (gə̄pgəblə) sm. སྐབས་འགར.

སྐབས་འཁེལ་ (gə̄pgee) occurring at the same time as, coinciding with ¶ མོས་ཉོ་བར་ཡོང་དུས་བཙོངས་ཟིན་པ་དང་སྐབས་འཁེལ་སོང་ When she came to buy (they) were sold out. ¶ ཁོ་ཚོ་ཡོང་རྒྱུ་དེ་ལོ་གསར་དང་སྐབས་འཁེལ་གྱི་རེད་ Their coming will coincide with the new year.

སྐབས་གང་འཁེལ་ (gə̄p kaŋgee) 1. anytime. 2. waiting for one's chance.

སྐབས་འགའ་ (gə̄pga) sm. སྐབས་འགར་.

སྐབས་འགར་ (gə̄pgar) sometimes, occasionally ¶ སྐབས་འགར་བོད་ཟས་བཟོ་གི་རེད་ Sometimes (they) make Tibetan food.

སྐབས་འགྲིག (gə̄p drig) vi. to coincidentally happen/ occur ¶ བླ་མ་ཕེབས་པ་དང་སྐབས་འགྲིག་ནས་ཆོས་ཞུས་སོང་ The lama happened to come (coincidental to my being somewhere) and (I) asked for teachings.

སྐབས་སྒྲིག (gə̄p drig) va. to arrange (usu. to meet) ¶ ང་ཚོ་ལྷ་སར་ཐུག་རྒྱུའི་སྐབས་བསྒྲིགས་པ་ཡིན་ We arranged to meet in Lhasa.

སྐབས་ཅིག (gə̄pjig) sm.* སྐབས་ཤིག.

སྐབས་ཅིག་རིང་ (gə̄pjig riŋ) sm. སྐབས་ཅིག.

སྐབས་མཆིས་ (gə̄p cĩi) vi. to have the time/ opportunity/ chance ¶ དགེ་རྒན་ཕེབས་པའི་སྐབས་མཆིས་ཚེ་བཀའ་འདྲི་ཞུ་དགོས་ཡོད་ If I get the opportunity when the teacher comes, I have some questions to ask.

སྐབས་རྗེས་མ་ (gə̄p jeema) (the) next time ¶ སྐབས་རྗེས་མར་ཉིན་མ་མང་ཙམ་སྡོད་ཀྱི་ཡིན་ (I) will stay more days the next time.

སྐབས་རྙེད་ (gə̄p ñēè) va. to find time, to find an opportunity ¶ ཕྱི་རྒྱལ་ལ་འགྲོ་རྒྱུའི་སྐབས་རྙེད་པ་རེད་ (They) found an opportunity to go abroad.

སྐབས་སྟུན་ (gə̄pdün) sm. སྐབས་བསྟུན་.

སྐབས་བསྟུན་ (gə̄pdün) 1. in accordance with time/ situation, fitting or proper with respect to the period or circumstance ¶ བློན་ཆེན་ཇི་དགོས་སྲིད་བློན་གྱིས་སྐབས་བསྟུན་བསྐོ་གཞག་གནང་གི་རེད་ The Prime Minister will appoint as many ministers as the situation requires. ¶ སྐབས་བསྟུན་གྱི་ཚོང་རྒྱག་རྒྱུ་གལ་ཆེན་པོ་རེད་ It is important to do business according to the (market) situation. 2. random ¶ སྐབས་བསྟུན་དཔེ་འདེམ་ Random sampling.

སྐབས་བསྟུན་ཁ་གཉེར་ (gə̄pdün kēñer) managing sth. according to the situation; va.—བྱེད་.

སྐབས་བསྟུན་ཁེ་འཚོལ་ (gə̄pdün kēdzöö) doing sth. opportunistically, seeking profits by taking advantage of the situation/ time.

སྐབས་བསྟུན་གང་བདེ་ (gə̄pdün kaŋde) acting in accordance with the times.

སྐབས་བསྟུན་གྱིས་ (gə̄pdüngi) sm. སྐབས་བསྟུན་.

སྐབས་བསྟུན་འགྱུར་ལྡོག (gə̄pdün gyundɔɔ̀) changing according to circumstances; va.—གཏོང་.

སྐབས་བསྟུན་འགྱུར་ཚད་ (gə̄pdün gyundzɛɛ̀) random variable.

སྐབས་བསྟུན་རྒྱུ་རྐྱེན་ (gə̄pdün gyugyen) random factor.

སྐབས་བསྟུན་ཐག་གཅོད་ (gə̄pdün tāgjöö̀) deciding in accordance with a situation or circumstances; va.—བྱེད་.

སྐབས་བསྟུན་བརྙས་བཅོས་ (gə̄pdün ñɛ̄bjöö̀) taking an opportunity to abuse sb.

སྐབས་བསྟུན་ཐབས་འཚོལ་ (gə̄pdün tābdzüü) seeking solutions/ means in accordance with the situation (rather than with customs, etc.); va.—བྱེད་.

སྐབས་བསྟུན་ནོར་ཚད་ (gə̄pdün nɔdzɛɛ̀) random error.

སྐབས་བསྟུན་དཔེ་འདེམ་ (gə̄pdün bēndem) random sampling.

སྐབས་བསྟུན་འཕོ་འགྱུར་ (gə̄pdün pōgyur) changing in accordance with the circumstances/ time.

སྐབས་བསྟུན་བློ་རྫུས་ (gə̄pdün lōjüü) a policy or strategy that is in accordance with the situation; va.—འདོན་.

སྐབས་བསྟུན་དམར་དཔེ་ (gə̄pdün mārbe) random sampling.

སྐབས་ཐོག (gə̄pdɔɔ̀) at the time, current(ly) ¶ སྐབས་ཐོག་སོ་སོའི་ལས་འགན་བསྒྲུབས་པ་རེད་ Accomplishing (one's) current responsibility.

སྐབས་ཐོག་གི་གནས་ཚུལ་ (gə̄pdɔɔ̀gi nɛ̄ɛdzüü) current situation/ condition, current news/ events.

སྐབས་ཐོབ་ (gə̄ptob) sm. སྐབས་མཆིས་.

སྐབས་དང་བསྟུན་ (gə̄pdaŋdün) sm. སྐབས་བསྟུན་.

སྐབས་དང་པོ་ (gə̄p taŋbo) the first time/ occasion. ¶ སྐབས་དང་པོའི་ཚོགས་འདུ་ The first meeting.

སྐབས་དང་སྦྱོར་ (gə̄pdaŋ jɔɔ) sm. སྐབས་བསྟུན་.

སྐབས་དེར་ (gə̄pdee) at that time, during that period ¶ སྐབས་དེར་ང་ཁྱེད་རང་མཇལ་ཐུབ་མ་སོང་ At that time I was unable to meet you.

སྐབས་དོན་ (gə̄pdön) current events, current affairs, events of a time/ occasion ¶ ཚོགས་འདུའི་ཐོག་སྐབས་དོན་སྙན་ཞུ་ཕུལ་པ་རེད་ Regarding the meeting, (they) made a report of its events.

སྐབས་དོན་དཔྱད་གླེང་ (gə̄pdön jɛ̀ɛleŋ) a commentary/ editorial on current events.

སྐབས་སྡོད་བྱ་རིགས་ (gə̄pdöö̀ cərig) birds in a location temporarily while on their migratory route.

སྐབས་ཕྱི་མ་ (gə̄p cĩmə) sm. སྐབས་རྗེས་མ་.

སྐབས་ཕྱིན་ (gə̄p cĩn) vi. to have gotten an opportunity ¶ ཁོང་ལ་ལས་ཀ་བྱེད་པའི་སྐབས་ཕྱིན་པ་རེད་ He got the opportunity to work.

སྐབས་ཕྱེད་ (gə̄p cēè) 1. va. to create an opportunity ¶ ཁོང་ལ་ལས་ཀ་བྱེད་པའི་སྐབས་ཕྱེད་པ་རེད་ (They) made an opportunity for him to work. 2. thin waist.

སྐབས་འཕྲལ་ (gə̄pdrɛɛ) 1. temporary ¶ ཁོང་གིས་སྐབས་འཕྲལ་གྱི་འཆར་གཞི་ཞིག་བཏིངས་པ་རེད་ He made a temporary plan. 2. immediately, on the spot, right away ¶ ནད་གཞི་ཡོང་ན་སྐབས་འཕྲལ་སྨན་བཅོས་བྱ་དགོས་ If one is sick one should get treatment immediately.

སྐབས་འཕྲལ་གླ་པ་ (gə̄pdrėė lāba) temporary worker.

སྐབས་འཕྲལ་སྲིད་གཞུང་ (gə̄pdrɛɛ sĩishuŋ) provisional/ interim government.

སྐབས་བབ་(ས་) (gə̄pbəb) opportunely, timely, in accord with the current situation; va.—བྱེད་ ¶ སྐབས་བབ་ཐག་གཅོད་ or སྐབས་བབ་སས་གཅོད་ A timely/ opportune/ prompt decision (or a decision in accordance with the current situation).

སྐབས་འབྱེད་ (gə̄p jeè) va. to separate or divide into different periods/ eras/ times ¶ བོད་ཀྱི་ལོ་རྒྱུས་དེ་སྐབས་ཕྱེ་ནས་བྲིས་ཡོད་པ་རེད་ (He) wrote the history of Tibet dividing it into periods. 2. va. to start/ begin a new work ¶ འཛུགས་སྐྲུན་གྱི་ལས་གཞིའི་སྐབས་འབྱེད་པ་རེད་ (They) started a new construction project.

སྐབས་སྦྱར་ (gə̄pjar) 1. sm. སྐབས་བསྟུན་. 2. door hinge.

སྐབས་སྦྱར་དགོས་མཚམས་ (gə̄pjar göndzam) shung. at the time when sth. is needed ¶ འདི་ཕྱོགས་ཞབས་ཞུའི་མི་སྣ་སྐབས་སྦྱར་དགོས་མཚམས་སོ་སོར་བསྐོང་འདུད་བྱ་རྒྱུ་ We will recruit government servants at the time we need them.

སྐབས་སྦྱར་སོ་སོ་ (gə̄pjar sōso) shung. at the time of

sth. ། ས་གནས་སུ་གནས་ཚུལ་སྐབས་སྦྱར་སོ་སོར་སྙན་འབུལ་དགོས་ཀྱི། You should make a report at the time of each event/ incident.

སྐབས་སྦྱོར་ (gāpjɔɔ) sm. སྐབས་བསྟུན་.

སྐབས་མིན་ (gāpmin) 1. irregularly, occasionally. 2. not in time.

སྐབས་མེད་ (gāpmeè) not having an opportunity/ chance ། སློབ་སྦྱོང་བྱེད་པའི་སྐབས་མེད་ Not having the opportunity to study.

སྐབས་མཚམས་ (gāpdzam) stage, sequence, order, phase ། ལས་གཞིའི་སྐབས་མཚམས་སོ་སོར་མི་སྣ་བཀོད་སྒྲིག་གསལ་པོ་བྱེད་དགོས་ At the various stages of the project (one) must clearly assign the proper people.

སྐབས་མཚམས་བབ་སྟུན་ (gāpdzam bābdün) sm. སྐབས་མཚམས་བབས་བསྟུན་.

སྐབས་མཚམས་བབས་བསྟུན་ (gāpdzam bābdün) shung. according to the circumstances/ situation ། གནས་ཚུལ་ཆུང་ཚགས་སྐབས་མཚམས་བབས་བསྟུན་ཐག་གཅོད་བགྱིས་འཐུས་ (You) can settle minor events according to the situation.

སྐབས་འཚམ་པོ་ (gāb tsāmbo) at the right/ opportune moment.

སྐབས་འཚོལ་ (gābdzöö) opportunism, speculation, profiteering; va. སྐབས་འཚོལ་; —བྱེད་ ། མི་དེས་ཚོང་ཟོག་འབེལ་དུས་ཆུར་ཉོས་ནས་སྐབས་འཚོལ་བྱས་ནས་དཀོན་དུས་ཕར་འཚོང་རྒྱུའི་བསམ་བློ་ཡོད་པ་རེད་ That man buys commodities when they are abundant and speculates thinking to sell them when they are scarce.

སྐབས་འཚོལ་མགོ་བདེ་ (gāpdzüü gode) sm. སྐབས་འཚོལ་.

སྐབས་འཚོལ་པ་ (gāpdzüwa) opportunist, speculator, profiteer.

སྐབས་འཚོལ་ཚོང་རྒྱག (gāpdzüü tsōŋ gyaà) va. to engage in speculative or opportunistic business activities.

སྐབས་འཚོལ་གཡོ་འཁྲུལ་ (gāpdzüü yōdrüü) exploitive/ opportunistic deceit.

སྐབས་འཚོལ་རིང་ལུགས་ (gāpdzüü riŋluù) opportunism.

སྐབས་འཚོལ་ལམ་ལུགས་ (gāpdzüü ləmluù) sm. སྐབས་འཚོལ་རིང་ལུགས་.

སྐབས་རིམ་ (gāprim) 1. sequence, order. 2. all the previous individuals in a sequence ། སྐབས་རིམ་བྱུང་གི་མཁན་པོ་རྣམས་ All previous abbots (in a line or sequence of abbots).

སྐབས་རིས་ (gāprii) illustration/ drawing in a book.

སྐབས་རེ་ (gāpre) sm. སྐབས་འགར་.

སྐབས་ཤིག (ལ་) (gāpshiilə) at one time ། སྐབས་ཤིག་ལ་ཁོང་གིས་དགེ་རྒན་བྱས་པ་རེད་ At one time he was a teacher.

སྐབས་ཤིག་རིང་ (gāpshigriŋ) 1. at one time ། སྐབས་ཤིག་རིང་ང་རྒྱ་གར་ལ་ཚོང་རྒྱག་སྡོད་ At one time I did business in India. 2. for the time being ། སྐབས་ཤིག་རིང་ང་ས་གནས་འདི་ལ་སྡོད་རྩིས་ཡོད་ I plan on being here for the time being.

སྐབས་སུ་ (gāpsu) when, at the time of ། ལྷ་སར་འགྲོ་བའི་སྐབས་སུ་ At the time of going to Lhasa.

སྐབས་སུ་བབས་ (gāmsu bəb) sm. སྐབས་བབ.

སྐབས་སེང་ལ་ (gābseŋla) sm. སྐབས་སྐབས་ལ་.

སྐབས་གསུམ་ (gāp sūm) 1. past, present and future. 2. the present, the past and the next life.

སྐམ་ (gām) 1. abbr. of སྐམ་པོ་. 2. milch animals that are dry. 3. name of an ancient Tibetan lineage. 4. beef/ yak meat.

སྐམ་: p. **བསྐམས་**; f. **སྐམ་** (gām) 1. vi. to become dry (for milch animals) ། བ་ཕྱུགས་དེ་གློ་བུར་དུ་བསྐམས་བཞག The cow suddenly went dry. 2. vi. to become thin.

སྐམ་ཀྲོག་གེ་ (gāmdrɔge) sm. སྐམ་ཐག་གེ་.

སྐམ་གྲོང་བ་ (gām drōŋwa) tall and skinny.

སྐམ་བཀྲུས་ (gāmdrüù) p. of སྐམ་འཁྲུད་.

སྐམ་སྐོམ་ (gāmgom) dry/ parched and thirsty.

སྐམ་སྐྱེད་ (gāmgyeè) shung. ten percent interest on a loan ། འདི་ལོའི་སྐམ་སྐྱེད་ཁལ་བཅུ་ This year's ten percent interest is 10 ke (of grain).

སྐམ་སྐྱེས་ (gāmgyeè) terrestrial (creatures).

སྐམ་སྐྱེས་ཅིན་ཚལ་ (gāmgyeè cindzεε) xerophyte celery.

སྐམ་སྐྱོད་དམག་གྲུ་ (gāmgyöö məgdru) amphibious military boat; landing craft.

སྐམ་སྐྲགས་ (gāmdraà) 1. dry; vi.—འཐེབ་ to become dry ། ཆར་པ་ཡུན་རིང་མ་བབས་ཙང་ཞིང་ཁ་སྐམ་སྐྲགས་ཐེབས་བཞག Because it didn't rain for a long time the fields have become dry. 2. a kind of bread made on special ceremonial occasions.

སྐམ་ཁབ་ (gāmbəb) acupuncture needle; va.—རྒྱག to use a needle for acupuncture treatment.

སྐམ་འཁོལ་ (gəmgöö) a type of common cold that causes aches, pains and fever.

སྐམ་འཁྲུད་ (gāmdrüù) dry cleaning; va.—བྱེད་.

སྐམ་གྱོང་ (gāmgyoŋ) dry and hard.

སྐམ་གློ་ (gāmlo) a dry cough; va.—རྒྱག.

སྐམ་གློག (gāmlɔɔ) 1. lightening (without rain). 2. dry cell, battery. 3. gasoline generated electricity (usu. in contrast to hydro-generated electricity).

སྐམ་རྒྱགས་ (gāmgyaà) dry food for use on a trip.

སྐམ་སྒྲིགས་ (gəmdrii) putting sth. together as a test to see how it fits; va.—བྱེད་.

སྐམ་བརྔོས་འབྲས་ (gāmŋöödrε) parched rice (rice popped over dry heat).

སྐམ་ཆག་བཅུ་ཟུར་ (gāmjaà jūsur) government's method of storing grain in tt. whereby an allowance was made for a 10% reduction in the weight and space of the grain due to drying and shrinkage.

སྐམ་ཆས་ (gāmjεὲ) furniture.

སྐམ་ཆུ་གཉིས་འཚོ་ (gəmcu ñīndzo) amphibian, creature that lives on both land and water.

སྐམ་ཆུང་ (gəmjuŋ) a kind of tweezer used by blacksmiths.

སྐམ་ཆེན་ (gāmjen) abbr. of སྐམ་ས་ཆེན་པོ་.

སྐམ་ཇ་རྒྱག (gāmja gyaà) va. to add dry tea leaves to boiling water.

སྐམ་རྙིད་ (gəmñii) semidry ། ཤ་སྐམ་རྙིད་ Semidry meat.

སྐམ་སྨྱུག (gəmñuù) ballpoint pen.

སྐམ་ཐག་གེ་ (gām tāge) in a very dry state ། ཆར་ཆུ་མེད་པར་ཞིང་ཁ་ཚང་མ་སྐམ་ཐག་གེ་བསྡད་འདུག The fields, not receiving rainfall (without water from rainfall), were all very dry.

སྐམ་ཐག་ཆོད་ (gāmdaà cöö) 1. vi. to be completely dry/ dried out ། ཤ་སྐམ་ཐག་ཆོད་བཞག (The) meat is completely dry. 2. vi. to be too dry/ dried out ། ཤ་སྐམ་ཐག་ཆོད་འདུག (The) meat is too dry.

སྐམ་ཐལ་ (gāmtεε) the powdered dirt from sheep pens and the like that is used as manure for fields; va.—རྒྱག to spread such manure on a field.

སྐམ་ཐུན་ (gəmdün) shung. dry gunpowder ། སྐམ་ཐུན་ནོན་ཐུན་གྱི་སྣོད་མི་ཐོད་གཉིས་ Two human skulls used as containers of dry gunpowder.

སྐམ་ཐེར་ (gāmder) bleak, desolate.

སྐམ་ཐོག (gāmdɔɔ) 1. overland, by land. 2. on land ། སྐམ་ཐོག་དམག Land warfare.

སྐམ་ཐོག་སྐྱེལ་འདྲེན་ (gāmdɔɔ gyēndren) transport by land, transport by road.

སྐམ་ཐོག་གྲུ་ཁ་ (gāmdɔɔ drugə) name of a ferry crossing in Derge.

སྐམ་ཐོག་འགྲིམ་འགྲུལ་ (gāmdɔɔ drimdrüü) overland transportation, land travel.

སྐམ་ཐོག་དམག་མི་ (gāmdɔɔ māāmi) troops that fight on land (as opposed to the air force and navy).

སྐམ་དྲས་ (gāmdrεὲ) sm. སྐམ་ཕྲིས་.

སྐམ་རྡུང་ (gəmduŋ) a beating by hand or stick (in which no blood is spilled); va.—གཏོང་.

སྐམ་སྡེབ་ (gāmdeb) a method of gilding.

སྐམ་བད་ (gāmda) clearing one's throat to give a

signal; va.—རྒྱག.

སྐམ་བརྡར་ (gāmdar) dry milling; va.—རྒྱག.

སྐམ་གནོན་ (gāmnöö) the metal trigger that ignites Tibetan matchlocks by depressing the burning wick; va.—འཐེན་ to pull such a trigger.

སྐམ་སྣུམ་ (gəmnum) pincers, pliers, wrench, tongs ¶ ཁོས་གཟེར་དཀར་སྐམ་སྣུམ་གྱིས་འཐེན་སོང་ He pulled the nail out with pliers.

སྐམ་པ་ (gāmba) pincers, pliers, wrench, tongs. 2. trigger of a gun; va.—གནོན་ to squeeze the trigger.

སྐམ་པ་ཡུ་རིང་ (gāmba yuriŋ) wrench (long handle).

སྐམ་པོ་ (gāmbo) 1. dry ¶ ཤ་སྐམ་པོ་ Dried meat. 2. thin, skinny ¶ ཁོ་ཤ་སྐམ་པོ་ཆགས་བཞག He has become thin.

སྐམ་པོ་རྡོས་རྡུངས་རློན་པ་གྲིས་ཆོད་ (gāmbo döö duŋ lōmba trii cöö) one should use an appropriate method [Lit. one should smash dry things with a stone and cut the wet with a knife].

སྐམ་པོ་སོབ་སོབ་ (gāmbo sobsoò) soft and dry.

སྐམ་པོར་བྱེད་ (gāmbor cee) va. to dry.

སྐམ་དཔྱ་བཅུ་ཟུར་ (gāmja jūsur) shung. 10% interest rate on loans.

སྐམ་སྦྱོད་བཟོ་པ་ (gāmjöö sopa) sm. སྐམ་འཛིན་བཟོ་པ་.

སྐམ་ཕོགས་ (gāmpɔɔ̀) wages paid to employees and servants in dry foods like grain (i.e., wages that do not include the provision of tea or beer).

སྐམ་ཕྱིས་ (gāmcii) drying by rubbing; va.—རྒྱག.

སྐམ་བྲིས་ (gəmdrii) 1. charcoal or pencil drawing/ sketch. 2. "dry writing"—writing on a chalk-powdered writing board (without ink); va.—རྒྱག.

སྐམ་འབྲས་ (gāmdrɛɛ̀) dry rice (i.e., rice grown without irrigation).

སྐམ་སྦྱོང་ (gāmjoŋ) 1. rehearsing/ practicing (without full costumes); va.—བྱེད་. 2. military exercise/ maneuver/ practice (without live ammunition); va.—བྱེད་.

སྐམ་མ་ (gāmma) a barren female bovine (that is not producing milk).

སྐམ་དམག (gāmmaà) land forces, army ¶ རྒྱ་ནག་གི་སྐམ་དམག་ནི་འཛམ་གླིང་ཐོག་གྲངས་ཀ་མང་ཤོས་རེད་ China has the largest army in the world.

སྐམ་རྩྭ་ (gāmdza) dried grass.

སྐམ་ཚག (gāmdzaà) 1. skinny, thin, lean. 2. dry pieces of sth.

སྐམ་ཚོགས་ (gāmdzɔɔ̀) monks' prayer assembly (in monasteries) at which tea is not served.

སྐམ་མཚོ་མཁའ་གསུམ་ (gāmtso kāsum) the three: land, sea, and air ¶ སྐམ་མཚོ་མཁའ་གསུམ་གྱི་དམག་དཔུང་ Three branches of the military—land, sea and air forces.

སྐམ་འཛིང་རུ་ཁག (gəmdziŋ rugaà) land troops/ forces.

སྐམ་འཛིན་བཟོ་པ་ (gāmdzin soba) fitter, mechanic.

སྐམ་ཞིང་ (gəmshiŋ) nonirrigated farm land/ fields.

སྐམ་ཞིང་རྙིད་པ་ (gəmshiŋ ñiibə) dried out and withered ¶ མེ་ཏོག་སྐམ་ཞིང་རྙིད་པ་ Dried out and withered flowers.

སྐམ་ཟན་ (gāmsɛn) sm. སྐམ་ཟས་.

སྐམ་ཟམ་ (gāmsam) bridge approach, highway ramp.

སྐམ་ཟས་ (gāmsɛɛ̀) dry/ dried food.

སྐམ་ཟུག (gəmsuù) aches and pain; vi.—རྒྱག.

སྐམ་ཟོག (gāmsɔɔ̀) dry goods.

སྐམ་འོན་ (gām w ön) type of disease that is characterized by deafness.

སྐམ་རིད་ (gəmrii) abbr. of སྐམ་ཞིང་རྙིད་པ་.

སྐམ་རིས་ (gāmrii) pencil sketch, charcoal drawing; va.—རྒྱག.

སྐམ་རུབ་ (gəmrub) dry, withered.

སྐམ་རུལ་ (gəmrüü) 1. dry and rotten. ¶ ཤ་སྐམ་རུས་ Dry meat that has become rotten. 2. skinny/ thin as a result of illness.

སྐམ་རོ་ (gəmro) dry, withered.

སྐམ་རློན་ (gāmlön) 1. the degree of moistness [Lit. wet-dry] ¶ གྱོ་ཞིབ་དེ་སྐམ་རློན་དག་དག་རེད་བཞག The moistness of the dough is just right. 2. uncooked and cooked ¶ ཁ་ལག་སྐམ་རློན་ Wet and dry food. 3. dry and wet/ liquid food ¶ མི་གླ་ཚམས་ལ་སྐམ་རློན་གཉིས་ཀ་སྤྲོད་དགོས་བྱུང་སོང་ (He) had to give the hired hands both dry food and drinks (wet food).

སྐམ་རློན་གཉིས་ཀར་འཚོ་ཐུབ་པའི་སྲོག་ཆགས་ (gāmlön ñiigar tsōtubɛ sɔ̄gjaà) amphibious animals.

སྐམ་ལམ་ (gāmlam) a land route.

སྐམ་ལུ་ (gəmlu) a dry cough; vi.—རྒྱག.

སྐམ་ལུག་ཤ་ལས་སྒྲོན་བཟོ་གྲྭ་ (gəmluùsha lɛɛ̀nön sodra) beef/yak and mutton processing plant.

སྐམ་ལུག་ཤའི་ཚོང་ཁང་ (gəmluùshɛ tsōŋgaŋ) beef/yak and mutton meat shop.

སྐམ་ཤ་ (gāmsha) 1. dried meat. 2. beef/ yak meat.

སྐམ་ཤས་ (gāmshɛɛ̀) the degree of the dryness (and heat) ¶ ས་ཆ་འདི་སྐམ་ཤས་ཆེན་པོ་འདུག This place is very dry and hot.

སྐམ་གཤེར་ (gāmsher) dry and damp/ humid.

སྐམ་བཤད་ (gāmshɛɛ̀) empty talk/ speech; va.—བྱེད་ ¶ ཁོས་སྐད་ཆ་སྐམ་བཤད་ཁོ་ན་བྱེད་པ་ལས་ལག་ལེན་བསྟར་གྱི་མེད་པ་རེད་ His talk is empty talk; he doesn't put (what he says) into practice.

སྐམ་ས་ (gāmsa) land (as opposed to sea).

སྐམ་ས་ཆེན་པོ་ (gāmsa cēmbo) mainland ¶ རྒྱ་ནག་སྐམ་ས་ཆེན་པོ་ Mainland China.

སྐམ་ས་སྡིགས་བསགས་ (gāmsa ñigsaà) continental deposit.

སྐམ་སང་ (gāmsaŋ) sm. སྐམ་སངས་.

སྐམ་སངས་ (gāmsaŋ) completely dry ¶ ཤ་འདི་སྐམ་སངས་རེད་འདུག This meat is completely dry.

སྐམ་སའི་རང་བཞིན་གྱི་གནམ་གཤིས་ (gāmsɛɛ rəŋshingi nəmshii) continental climate.

སྐམ་སའི་སྲོག་ཆགས་ (gāmsɛ sōgjaà) terrestrial animals.

སྐམ་སར་སྐྱོད་ (gāmsar gyöö) va. to go ashore, to land (at), to disembark ¶ མཚོ་དམག་རྣམས་སྐམ་སར་བསྐྱོད་པ་རེད་ The marine corps landed.

སྐམ་སར་ཐོན་སྐྱོད་དཔུང་སྡེ་ (gāmsaa tōngyöö puŋde) expeditionary force.

སྐམ་སར་ཐོན་སྐྱོད་དམག་གྲུ་ (gāmsaa tōngyöö məgdru) landing craft (military).

སྐམ་སར་འཐབ་མཁན་མཚོ་དམག (gāmsaa təbñɛn tsōmaà) marines, marine corps.

སྐམ་སོག (gāmsɔɔ̀) a type of inferior tsampa in which the barley is roasted without first being wet/ soaked.

སྐམ་སོབ་ (gāmsob) dry and soft.

སྐམ་སོས་ (gāmsöö) a technique of drying meat during the winter when the temperature is very cold (so the dried meat remains soft) ¶ དེ་རིང་གནམ་གྲང་མོ་ཡོད་ཙང་ཤ་སྐམ་སོས་གཏོང་དགོས་ (We) have to dry the meat today because the weather is cold.

སྐམ་སྲེག (gāmseg) sm. སྐམ་སྐྲགས་.

སྐམ་སྲོ་ (gāmso) tempering, firing (as with pottery); va.—གཏོང་.

སྐམ་གསེང་ (gāmseŋ) sm. སྐམ་སོབ་.

སྐམ་གསེད་ (gāmseè) sm. སྐམ་གསེས་.

སྐམ་གསེས་ (gāmseè) drying sth. in the sun; va.—གཏོང་.

སྐམ་གསོལ་ (gāmsöö) a ritual offering to a god that involves burning incense; va.—གཏོང་.

སྐམས་ (gām) sm.* སྐམ་, 2.

སྐར་ (gār) abbr. of སྐར་མ་.

སྐར་སྐྱེད་ (gārgyeè) abbr. of ཟླ་སྐར་སྐར་སྐྱེད་.

སྐར་སྐྱོད་ (gārgyöö) 1. firefly. 2. interplanetary [Lit. going to the stars].

སྐར་སྐྱོད་མེ་ཤུགས་འཕུར་མདའ་ (gārgyöö mishuù pūndə) interplanetary rocket.

སྐར་ཁུང་ (gərguŋ) 1. skylight. 2. window.

སྐར་ཁོངས་ (gārgoŋ) constellation (of stars).

སྐར་མཁན་ (gārgɛn) astrologer, astronomer.

སྐར་གྲངས་ (gārdraŋ) points, grades, score, work points (as used in calculating income during the commune period in the PRC); va.—འགོད་ to score or record points; va.—སྡུར་ (བསྡུར་) to evaluate work points ¶ ཞིང་པ་མང་ཆེ་བས་ལས་ཀའི་སྐར་གྲངས་འགོད་ཤེས་པ་རེད་ Most farmers knew how to write (record) (their) work points. ¶ སྐར་གྲངས་ཀྱི་རིན་ཐང་ The cash/ monetary value of a work point. ¶ ལུས་རྩལ་འགྲན་བསྡུར་གྱི་སྐར་གྲངས་བསྡོམས་འབོར་མཐོ་ཤོས་ The highest total score in the sport event.

སྐར་གྲངས་བརྒྱའི་འགོད་ཐབས་ (gārdraŋ gyε̱ε̱ gö̱ö̀dəb) centigrade system.

སྐར་གྲངས་གཙོ་བཟུང་ (gārdraŋ dzōsuŋ) putting grades in command, making attaining high grades on exams the most important thing (considered a negative value in PRC during Mao's era).

སྐར་བྲལ་ (gārdrεε) the whole set of stars out at night; vi.—སྒྲིག to have the whole set/ constellation of stars be out visible in the sky; vi.—ཞིག to have the whole set/ constellation of stars vanish from the sky (from sight).

སྐར་ངན་མཇུག་རིང་ (gārŋεn ju̱griŋ) sm. སྐར་མ་དུ་བ་མཇུག་རིང་.

སྐར་ལྔ་ (gārŋa) five སྐར་མ་, five stars.

སྐར་ལྔ་དང་ལྡན་པ་ (gārŋadaŋ dε̱mba) five star (as in hotel).

སྐར་ལྔའི་རྒྱལ་དར་ (gārŋεε gyε̱ε̱dar) sm. སྐར་ལྔའི་དར་དམར་.

སྐར་ལྔའི་དར་དམར་ (gārŋεε tha̱rmaa) the ("five-starred") national flag of the PRC.

སྐར་ལྕགས་ (gārjaà) meteoric iron.

སྐར་ཆ་ (gārja) a second (of time).

སྐར་ཆ་སྟོན་མདའ་ (gārja dõnda) the second hand of a watch.

སྐར་ཆའི་ཆུ་ཚོད་ (gārjε cūdzöö̀) stop watch.

སྐར་ཆའི་དུས་ཚོད་འཁོར་ལོ་ (gārjε tü̱dzöö̀ kɔ̄ɔ̄lo) sm. སྐར་ཆའི་ཆུ་ཚོད་.

སྐར་ཆུ་ (gərju) water obtained before the stars have disappeared from the sky (used for medicinal purposes).

སྐར་ཆེན་ (gārjen) Venus.

སྐར་རྟགས་ (gārdaà) asterisk.

སྐར་རྩིས་ (gārdεὲ) 1. astrology; va.—རྩི་ to divine/ do astrology by the stars. 2. astronomy.

སྐར་རྩིས་མཁན་ (gārdεὲñεn) 1. astrologer. 2. astronomer.

སྐར་མདའ་ (gānda) meteor, shooting star.

སྐར་མདའ་འཁྱུག་པ་ལྟར་ (gānda kyūgbə dār) very fast, quick ¶ དམག་དོན་སྐམ་སྦྱོང་སྐབས་མེ་ཤུགས་ཕུར་མདའ་མང་པོ་སྐར་མདའ་འཁྱུག་པ་ལྟར་འཕེན་གྱི་འདུག During the military maneuver they were firing many missiles very quickly. [Lit. like a shooting star].

སྐར་མདའ་སྒྱུལ་ཞིབ་རྟ་དམག (gānda ñu̱lshib dāmaà) a reconnaissance cavalry that travels very fast (like a shooting star).

སྐར་མདའི་ཁྱུ་ཚོ་ (gāndε kyūdzo) meteor shower.

སྐར་མདའི་ལྕགས་རྡོག (gāndε jāgdog) 1. meteor. 2. an iron cannon ball that is shot like a meteor.

སྐར་མདའི་ཕུང་པོ་ (gāndε pūŋbo) sm. སྐར་རྡོ་.

སྐར་མདའི་ཚོམ་བུ་ (gāndε tsōmbu) sm. སྐར་རྡོ་.

སྐར་རྡོ་ (gārdo) meteorite, aerolite.

སྐར་རྡོའི་ཆར་པ་ (gārdö cārba) meteorite shower.

སྐར་གནས་འཕོ་འགྱུར་ (gārnεὲ pōgyur) the changing position of the stars.

སྐར་དཔྱད་ (gārjεὲ) sm. སྐར་རྩིས་.

སྐར་དཔྱད་པ་ (gārjεba) sm. སྐར་རྩིས་པ་.

སྐར་སྤྲིན་ (gārdrin) 1. nebula. 2. abbr. stars and clouds.

སྐར་སྤྲིན་ཚོམ་པོ་ (gārdrin tsōmbo) cluster of nebulae.

སྐར་ཕྱེད་བརྒྱད་ (gār cēègyεὲ) shung. 3/4 of a ཞོ་ (7.5 སྐར་མ་).

སྐར་ཕྱེད་གསུམ་ (gār cēèsum) shung. a quarter of a ཞོ་ (2.5 སྐར་མ་).

སྐར་འབྲུ་ (gāndru) grain paid to workers according to the number of days they work (or the number of work points they have accumulated).

སྐར་མ་ (gārma) 1. star ¶ སྐར་མ་རྣམས་དོ་དགོང་བཀྲག་མདངས་ཆེན་པོ་འདུག The stars are very bright tonight. 2. the lowest denomination of Tibetan currency (a unit = 1/100 of a སྲང་ and 1/10 of a ཞོ་). 3. a minute (of time) ¶ ཆུ་ཚོད་གཉིས་དང་སྐར་མ་བཅུ་ Two hours and ten minutes. 4. a work-point (the basic unit of work calculation in communes). 5. 1/10th of a ཤུ་.

སྐར་མ་ཀུན་བཟང་ (gārma gũnsaŋ) a village located east of Lhasa.

སྐར་མ་སྐར་ཆེན་ཞིག་གིས་ སྐར་ཆུང་གཡང་ལ་དབྱུགས་སོང་ (gārma gārcenshig gi gārcuŋ yāŋlə yūùsoŋ) a stronger person/ group defeats a weaker one. [Lit. the large star throws the small star into the chasm].

སྐར་མ་མཁན་ (gārmagεn) astrologer.

སྐར་མ་དངོས་གཞི་ (gārma ŋȫö̀shi) a day determined by an astrologer as auspicious for making offerings on behalf of the deceased.

སྐར་མ་ཆ་སྡོད་ (gārma cādöö̀) double star.

སྐར་མ་བརྟན་པ་ (gārma tε̄mba) Polaris, the pole star, the north star.

སྐར་མ་འཐགས་སོ་ (gārma tāgso) Vega.

སྐར་མ་འཐེན་པ་ (gārma tēmba) Sirius.

སྐར་མ་དུ་བ་འཇུག་རིང་ (gārma du̱wa ju̱griŋ) comet.

སྐར་མ་དོལ་པ་ (gārma dö̱ö̱ba) sm. སྐར་མ་རི་ཁྱི་.

སྐར་མ་གནམ་རྒྱལ་ (gārma nāmgyεε) Uranus.

སྐར་མ་སྤུན་བདུན་ (gārma bũndün) the Big Dipper constellation.

སྐར་མ་ཕར་བསྐྱལ་ ཉི་མ་ཚུར་བསུ་ (gārma pārgyεὲ ñi̱mə tsūr sū) working extremely long hours, working day and night [Lit. to see the stars off and welcome the sun].

སྐར་མ་སྨིན་བདུན་ (gārma mīndün) the Big Dipper constellation.

སྐར་མ་ཚོམ་ཚོམ་ (gārma tsōmdzom) a group/ constellation of stars.

སྐར་མ་མཚོ་རྒྱལ་ (gārma tsōgyεε) Neptune.

སྐར་མ་ཞོ་བརླགས་ (gārma sho̱laà) pound foolish penny wise, trying to save a little only to lose a lot [Lit. for a སྐར་མ་, losing a ཞོ་].

སྐར་མ་རི་ཁྱི་ (gārma ri̱ji) the bathing festival in Lhasa (the time when a particular star is visible in the sky during the 7th month of the Tibetan calendar).

སྐར་མ་རི་བྱི་ (gārma ri̱ji) sm. སྐར་མ་རི་ཁྱི་.

སྐར་མ་རི་ཤི་ (gārma ri̱shi) sm. སྐར་མ་རི་ཁྱི་.

སྐར་མ་ཤར་གླིང་ཀ་ (gārma shārliŋgə) a park in the east of Lhasa.

སྐར་མ་གསར་པ་ (gārma sāāba) a nova, a new star.

སྐར་མ་ཨ་བརྟན་ (gārma āden) sm. སྐར་མ་བརྟན་པ་.

སྐར་མའི་ཁ་གསབ་ (gārmε kāsəb) extra work points given by the commune to officials and workers when they travel on commune business.

སྐར་མའི་གོ་ལ་ (gārmε ko̱la) celestial/ heavenly body.

སྐར་མའི་གོས་དང་ཟླ་བའི་ཞྭ་མོ་གྱོན་ (gārmε gö̱ö̀taŋ da̱wε sha̱mo kö̱n) working or traveling at night [Lit. wearing stars as clothes and the moon as a hat].

སྐར་མའི་འགྲོས་ (gārmε trö̱ö̀) the four ways that stars travel in tt. astrology.

སྐར་མའི་མདའ་ཁབ་ (gārmε da̱gəb) minute hand (on watch).

སྐར་མའི་མ་ལག (gārmε ma̱laà) the planetary/ star system.

སྐར་མའི་འོད་ (gārmε wö̱ö̀) starlight.

སྐར་མས་ཞྭ་བྱེད་ བ་མོས་ལྷམ་བྱེད་ (gārmε sha̱ceè pa̱mö lhāmjeè) working or traveling at night [Lit. wearing stars as hat and frost as shoes].

སྐར་མེད་ཀུབ་སྐྱོག (gārmeὲ gūbgyoò) bragging or showing off though poor [Lit. not even having a penny (སྐར་མ་) but walking with a swagger].

སྐར་དམར་ (gārmar) red star.

སྐར་རྩིས་ (gərdzii̇) astrology.

སྐར་རྩིས་ཁང་ (gərdziiḡaŋ) sm. སྐར་རྩིས་ཞིབ་བལྟ་ཁང་.

སྐར་རྩིས་རྒྱང་ཤེལ་ (gərdzii̇ gya̱ŋshel) astronomical telescope.

སྐར་རྩིས་པ་ (gāmdzibə) astrologer.

སྐར་རྩིས་དཔྱད་སྟེགས་ (gəmdzii̇ jɛ̄ɛ̀deg) sm. སྐར་རྩིས་ཞིབ་ལྟ་ཁང་.

སྐར་རྩིས་ཞིབ་ལྟ་ཁང་ (gəmdzii̇ shi̱bdəkaŋ) observatory, planetarium.

སྐར་རྩིས་ལས་ཁྲངས་ (gəmdzii̇ shi̱bdəgaŋ) observatory, planetarium.

སྐར་ཚད་ (gārdzɛɛ̀) measures, measurements.

སྐར་ཚོགས་ (gārdzɔɔ̀) a cluster of stars.

སྐར་ཚོགས་ལྟར་བཀྲམ་པ་ (gārdzɔɔ̀dar drāmba) scattered all over like starts in the sky.

སྐར་ཚོགས་ནང་གི་ཟླ་བ་ (gārdzɔɔ̀ na̱ŋgi da̱wa) the best of the best, creme de la creme [Lit. the moon in the cluster of stars].

སྐར་ཚོམ་ (gārdzom) a constellation of stars.

སྐར་འཛིན་ (gərdzin) doing sth. or going somewhere prior to the actual day planned since the actual day is astrologically inauspicious; va.—བྱེད་.

སྐར་གཟུགས་ (gərsug) celestial body.

སྐར་འོད་ (gārwöö̀) 1. the light/ rays of a star, starlight. 2. firefly, lightening bug.

སྐར་གསལ་ (gārsɛɛ) sm. སྐར་ཁུང་.

སྐར་ལྷུང་སྤྲིན་འཐོར་ (gārlhuŋ drīndɔɔ) scattering everywhere ¶ དམག་སར་གློ་བུར་དུ་བྱེ་མའི་ཐལ་རླུང་བརྒྱབ་ནས་དམག་མི་རྣམས་སྐར་ལྷུང་སྤྲིན་འཐོར་ལྟ་བུར་གྱུར་བ་རེད་ When the dust storm suddenly came to the battlefield the soldiers were scattered everywhere [Lit. stars fall and clouds scattered].

སྐལ་ (gɛ̄l) abbr. of སྐལ་བ་.

སྐལ་གྲངས་ (gɛ̄ɛ̄draŋ) sm. སྐལ་ཆ་.

སྐལ་འགྲོ་ (gɛ̄ndro) shung. the shares to be given/ distributed ¶ སྐལ་འགྲོའི་ཐད་བླ་སྤྲུལ་ལས་ཁྲིར་འཕར་ As for the shares to be given, the incumbent reincarnated Lamas should be given extra shares.

སྐལ་ངན་ (gɛ̄ɛ̄ŋɛn) negative/ unmeritorious karma ¶ སྐལ་ངན་གྱིས་རྐྱེན་པས་དབུལ་པོ་ཆགས་པ་རེད་ Because of his unmeritorious karma, (he) became poor. 2. unlucky, unfortunate.

སྐལ་ངན་མ་ (gɛ̄ɛ̄ŋɛnma) a woman with negative/ unmeritorious karma.

སྐལ་དངུལ་ (gɛ̄ɛ̄ŋüü) a share (of money) ¶ མི་སོ་སོའི་སྐལ་དངུལ་སྤྲད་པ་རེད་ (They) gave each person his share of the money.

སྐལ་ཆ་ (gɛ̄ɛ̄ja) a share, an allotment.

སྐལ་ཆད་ (gɛ̄ɛ̄jɛɛ̀) 1. vi. to be missing one's share. 2. unlucky, unfortunate.

སྐལ་མཉམ་ (gɛ̄ɛ̄ñam) sm. སྐལ་བ་མཉམ་པ་.

སྐལ་ཐོ་ (gɛ̄ɛ̄do) 1. the list which contains the dowry items for the bride (or inmarrying groom); va.—རྒྱག; —འགོད to make a list which contains the amount of dowry. 2. a list containing the items in each share when a family separates/ splits; va.—རྒྱག; —འགོད་.

སྐལ་ཐོབ་ (gɛ̄ɛ̄dob) sm. སྐལ་ཆ་.

སྐལ་ཐོབ་འཚེམ་མེད་སྤྲེལ་ (gɛ̄ɛ̄dob tsēmmeè gyēē) shung. va. to give shares without any part missing ¶ གྲྭ་ཚང་གི་སྐལ་ཐོབ་འཚེམ་མེད་སྤྲེལ་དགོས་ The shares to the monastic colleges should be given without any part missing.

སྐལ་དོད་ (gɛ̄ɛ̄döö̀) share (usu. used for the share given to a bride or bridegroom).

སྐལ་ལྡན་ (gɛ̄ndɛn) 1. meritorious karma, having accumulated good merit (can also connote pious) ¶ བླ་མ་དེར་སྐལ་ལྡན་གྱི་སློབ་མ་མང་པོ་ཡོད་པ་རེད་ That lama has many meritorious followers. 2. fortunate, lucky.

སྐལ་ལྡན་དང་བ་འདྲེན་ངེས་ (gēndɛn ta̱ŋ pa̱ndren ŋe̱ɛ̀) shung. pleasing and meritorious ¶ སྐྱེས་བུ་དམ་པ་དེས་སྐལ་ལྡན་དང་བ་འདྲེན་ངེས་ཀྱི་གསུང་ཆོས་རྒྱས་པར་གནང་བ་ The great lama gave a teaching that was pleasing and meritorious to the disciples.

སྐལ་ལྡན་ཤིང་རྟ་ (gɛ̄ndɛn shīŋda) poet. the River Ganges.

སྐལ་བསྡུས་ཀུང་སི་ (gɛ̄ɛ̄düǜ gūŋsi) joint-stock company.

སྐལ་སྤམ་མཐོ་བ་ (gɛ̄ɛ̄bam tōwa) shung. a greater share.

སྐལ་འཕར་ (gɛ̄mbar) an extra share ¶ དགོན་པའི་དབུ་མཛད་ལ་སྐལ་འཕར་གསུམ་ཡོད་པ་རེད་ ¶ The chant leader in a monastery is given three extra shares of alms.

སྐལ་བ་ (gɛ̄ɛ̄wa) 1. share, portion, inheritance ¶ ཁོའི་ས་ཞིང་གི་སྐལ་བ་བཙོངས་བ་རེད་ (He) sold his share of the land. ¶ སྡུག་པོ་འདི་འདྲ་མཐོང་དགོས་པ་ང་ཚོའི་ཚེ་སྔོན་ལས་ཀྱི་སྐལ་བ་རེད་ It is due to the inheritance of our previous life's karma that we have to see such suffering. 2. fate, fortune ¶ སྐལ་བ་བཟང་པོ་ Good fortune.

སྐལ་བ་ངན་ (gɛ̄waŋɛn) unlucky, unfortunate.

སྐལ་བ་ཅན་ (gɛ̄wajɛn) lucky, fortunate.

སྐལ་བ་གཅོད་ (gɛ̄ɛ̄wa jöö̀) va. to not give sb. a share, to cut off sb.'s share ¶ གྲྭ་པ་དེ་ཚོགས་ལ་མ་ཡོང་བར་བརྟེན་འགྱེད་ཀྱི་སྐལ་བ་བཅད་པ་རེད་ Because the monk failed to attend the prayer ceremony they did not give him his share of alms.

སྐལ་བ་ཆེ་ (gɛ̄waje) fortunate, lucky.

སྐལ་བ་ཆད་ (gɛ̄wa cɛ̄ɛ̀) 1. vi. to get or become unfortunate/ unlucky. 2. vi. to not get a share, to not give sb. a share.

སྐལ་བ་མཉམ་པ་ (gɛ̄wa ñāmba) 1. an equal share/ portion. 2. equal luck/ fortune.

སྐལ་བ་དང་ལྡན་པ་ (gɛ̄ɛ̄wa ta̱ŋ dɛ̱mba) sm. སྐལ་ལྡན་.

སྐལ་བ་མེད་པ་ (gɛ̄ɛ̄wa me̱èba) 1. having bad/ negative/ unmeritorious karma ¶ སྐལ་བ་མེད་པའི་མི་དེ་ཕྱུག་པོ་ཆགས་ཐབས་མེད་ There is no way that that person who has an accumulation of bad karma can become rich. 2. unfortunate, unlucky.

སྐལ་བ་བཟང་པོ་ (gɛ̄ɛ̄wa sa̱ŋbo) 1. meritious, having accumulated good/ positive/ meritorious karma. 2. good fortune/ good luck due to good karma. ¶ དེ་རིང་ང་ཚོ་ཏཱ་ལའི་བླ་མ་མཇལ་ནི་སྐལ་བ་བཟང་པོ་བྱུང་ Today we had the good fortune (due to our good karma) to have met the Dalai Lama.

སྐལ་འབུ་ (gɛ̄mbu) a type of insect.

སྐལ་མེད་ (gɛ̄ɛ̄meè) abbr. སྐལ་བ་མེད་པ་.

སྐལ་མེད་མ་ (gɛ̄ɛ̄meèma) an unmeritorious woman, a woman with an accumulation of bad karma.

སྐལ་རྫོང་ (gɛ̄ɛ̄dzoŋ) dowry, a share (of sth.).

སྐལ་ཞིང་ (gɛ̄ɛ̄shin) a share/ inheritance/ allotment of land.

སྐལ་གཞུང་ (gɛ̄ɛ̄shuŋ) shung. a list of shares ¶ སྐྱ་གཉེར་གྱི་སྐལ་ཐོབ་སོགས་སྐལ་གཞུང་ཁྲངས་ཐུབ་ཉར་དགོས་ཀྱུ་ (You) should keep a list of shares for such things as the caretaker's share.

སྐལ་བཟང་ (gɛ̄ɛ̄saŋ) abbr. of སྐལ་བ་བཟང་པོ་. 2. person's name.

སྐལ་བཟང་མེ་ཏོག (gɛ̄ɛ̄saŋ me̱doò) a type of chrysanthemum.

སྐལ་བཟང་སེམས་ཅན་ (gɛ̄ɛ̄saŋ sēmjɛn) humans with accumulations of good/ positive/ meritorious karma.

སྐལ་བཟང་བསིལ་གཡབ་ (gɛ̄ɛ̄saŋ sīiyəb) type of Tibetan hat.

སྐལ་རིན་ (gɛ̄ɛ̄riŋ) price or value of a share.

སྐལ་ལ་ (gɛ̄ɛ̄la) sm.* སྐལ་བ་.

སྐལ་ལེན་ (gɛ̄ɛ̄len) the right of some monks to receive a share of alms even though they do not attend the prayer session at which the alms are distributed.

སྐས་ (gɛ̄ɛ̀) sm. སྐས་ཀ་.

སྐས་ཀ་ (gɛ̄ɛ̀ga) ladder, stairs; rungs of a ladder, steps on stairs ¶ སྐས་ཀ་གཅིག One rung of a ladder.

སྐས་སྐོར་ཁྲ་མ་ (gɛ̄ɛ̀gɔr trāma) handrail, banister.

སྐས་སྐོར་ (gɛ̄ɛ̀gyɔr) ladder or stair handrail, banister.

སྐས་སྐོར་རྒྱུག་ཁྲ་ (gɛ̄ɛ̀gyɔr gyu̱gdra) balustrade.

སྐས་ཁུང་ (gɛ̄ɛ̀guŋ) an opening on the roof where a ladder is placed.

སྐས་འགོ་ (gɛ̄ŋgo) top of the stairs/ ladder.

སྐས་འགོ་ལ་མ་མཇལ་ན་ཡང་སྐས་མཇུག་ལ་མཇལ་ཡོང་ (gɛ̄ŋgo ma̱njɛɛna ya̱ŋ gɛ̄njugla jɛ̱ɛyoŋ) if you do not help sb. now later you will want help from them and they will not give it [Lit. if we do not meet at the top of the ladder we will meet at the bottom of the ladder].

སྐས་འགྲམ་ (gɛ̄ŋdram) handle, railing, banister (on the sides of a ladder or staircase).

སྐས་སྐམ་ (gɛ̄ɛ̀gam) steps, staircase.

སྐས་སྒོ་ (gɛ̄ɛ̀go) door at the front of a staircase.

སྐས་སྒོར་ (gɛ̄ɛ̀gɔɔ) winding staircase, spiral staircase.

སྐས་མཇུག (gɛ̄ŋjug) the bottom of a staircase/ ladder.

སྐས་འཛུ་ (gɛ̄nju) railing/ banister on stairs or ladder.

སྐས་རྟེང་ (gɛ̄ɛ̀diŋ) base/ foot of a ladder or stairs.

སྐས་ཐེམ་ (gɛ̄ɛ̀dem) sm. སྐས་གདང་.

སྐས་ཐེམ་རིམ་འཛེག (gɛ̄ɛ̀tem ri̱mdzeè) gradually working one's way up a hierarchy; va.—བྱེད་ ¶ ལས་བྱེད་པ་དེ་སྐས་ཐེམ་རིམ་འཛེག་བྱས་ནས་འགོ་ཁྲིད་ལ་སླེབས་པ་རེད་ That official worked his way up gradually to become the leader. [Lit. climb a ladder step by step].

སྐས་མཐིལ་ (gɛ̄ɛ̀dii) sm. སྐས་གདང་.

སྐས་གདང་ (gɛ̄ɛ̀daŋ) step/ rung of a ladder.

སྐས་གདང་མས་འཛེག (gɛ̄ɛ̀daŋ me̱ndzeɛ̀) sm. སྐས་ཐེམ་རིམ་འཛེག.

སྐས་དབྱིབས་ (gɛ̄ɛ̀yip) 1. shape of a ladder, a shape similar to a ladder. 2. trapezoid, trapezium.

སྐས་འཛེག (gɛ̄ntseè) sm. སྐས་ཀ་.

སྐས་འཛེག་མ་འཛེགས་པར་ཐོག་ཁར་སླེབས་པ་ (gɛ̄ntseè ma̱dzegbar tɔ̄ɔ̀gaa lēēba) getting promoted suddenly/ quickly, getting promoted to a higher position without going through intermediate steps [Lit. arriving on the roof without climbing a ladder].

སྐས་ཞིང་ (gɛ̄ɛ̀shiŋ) terraced fields.

སྐས་རིང་ (gɛ̄ɛ̀riŋ) long ladder.

སྐས་རིམ་ (gɛ̄ɛ̀rim) 1. sm. སྐས་གདང་. 2. abbr. of སྐས་ཐེམ་རིམ་འཛེག.

སྐས་རིམ་ཅན་གྱི་ཞིང་ཁ་ (gɛ̄ɛ̀rimjɛngi shi̱ŋgə) sm. སྐས་ཞིང་.

སྐས་རུ་ (gɛ̄ɛ̀ru) sm. སྐས་འགྲམ་.

སྐས་ལ་འཛེག (gɛ̄ɛ̀la dze̱g) va. to climb a ladder.

སྐས་ལེབ་ (gɛ̄ɛ̀leb) a ladder rung that is flat.

སྐས་ཤིང་ (gɛ̄ɛ̀shiŋ) ladder.

སྐས་ཤུར་ (gɛ̄ɛ̀shur) sliding down a banister/ railing; va.—སློད་ to slide down a banister/ railing.

སྐས་གཤམ་ (gɛ̄ɛ̀sham) sm. སྐས་རྟེང་.

སྐས་བཤད་ (gɛ̄ɛ̀shɛɛ̀) auspicious sayings said as a bride goes up the stairs of her new home for the first time; va.—རྒྱག.

སྐས་གསུམ་སྦྲེལ་ (gɛ̄ɛ̀sum dre̱l) system of having three joined staircases with the middle one used only by the Emperor (in China) or the Dalai Lama (in Tibet).

སྐས་ཧྲིལ་ (gɛ̄ɛ̀hrii) a ladder that uses rounded rather than flat rungs.

སྐུ་ (gū) 1. body (h.). 2. statue, icon, image (h.). 3. particle used to make nonhonorific terms honorific ¶ སྐུ་ཁྲག Blood (h.).

སྐུ་དཀར་ (gūgar) whitewash (h.); va.—གསོལ་ to whitewash.

སྐུ་ཀྱི་ (gūgyi) sm.* སྐུ་མཁྱེན་.

སྐུ་ཀྱི་ཨོ་ཀོ་ (gūgyi ōgɔɔ̀) sm. སྐུ་ཀྱི་.

སྐུ་དཀྱིལ་གསལ་དྭངས་ (gūgyi sɛ̄ɛ̄daŋ) good health (h.) ¶ ཁྱེད་རང་སྐུ་དཀྱིལ་གསལ་དྭངས་ཡིན་ནམ་ Are you in good health?

སྐུ་སྐེད་ (gūkeè) waist (h.).

སྐུ་རྐྱང་ (gūgyaŋ) alone (h.); va.—ཕེབས་ to go/ come alone ¶ ཁོང་སྐུ་རྐྱང་ལ་ཕེབས་པ་རེད་ He came alone.

སྐུ་སྐལ་ (gūgɛɛ) h. of སྐལ་.

སྐུ་སྐྱེ་ (gūgye) a rebirth of an incarnate lama (h.); va.—བཞེས་; —ཕེབས་ to be reborn as an incarnate lama, to incarnate into a human form (for lamas). ¶ མི་ཚང་འདིའི་ནང་ལ་བླ་མའི་སྐུ་སྐྱེ་ཞིག་ཕེབས་པ་རེད་ A lama was incarnated (born) in this family.

སྐུ་སྐྱེ་མ་ (gū gyēma) female (h.) ¶ དེ་རིང་སྐུ་སྐྱེ་མ་མང་པོ་ཕེབས་འདུག Today a lot of women came.

སྐུ་སྐྱིད་ (gūgyeè) h. of འཚར་ལོང་.

སྐུ་སྐྱེས་ (gūgyeè) a present, gift (h.).

སྐུ་ཁེ་ (gūge) h. of ཁེ་བཟང་.

སྐུ་ཁབ་ (gūgəb) 1. injection. (h.); va.—སྐྱོན་; —སྒྲོན to give an injection. 2. needle (h.).

སྐུ་ཁམས་ (gūgəm) body health, physical well-being ¶ རྣམ་པ་ཚོ་སྐུ་ཁམས་བདེ་པོ་ཡིན་པས་ Are you all well?

སྐུ་ཁམས་བདེ་པོ་ (gūgəm de̱bo) good health, well-being.

སྐུ་ཁམས་མ་འཚོ་ (gūgəm ma̱ndzo) sm. སྐུ་ཆེ་མ་ཟིན་.

སྐུ་ཁམས་བཟང་ (gūgəm sa̱ŋ) a common greeting equivalent to "How are you?"

སྐུ་ཁམས་བཟང་པོ་ (gūgəm sa̱nbo) sm. སྐུ་ཁམས་བདེ་པོ་.

སྐུ་ཁོག (gūgɔɔ̀) sm. སྐུ་རྟེན་.

སྐུ་ཁྲག (gūdraà) 1. h. of ཁྲག. 2. menstruation (h.); vi.—སྐྱོན་ to menstruate; —ཆད་ to stop menstruating.

སྐུ་ཁྲུས་ (gūdrüù) sprinkling statues or deities with water as a symbolic cleansing; va.—གསོལ་. 2. h. of ཁྲུས་.

སྐུ་མཁར་ (gūgar) h. of མཁར་.

སྐུ་མཁར་མ་རུ་ (gūkārmaru) a place north of Lhasa where Srongtsen Gampo is said to have retreated to study the Tibetan written language.

སྐུ་མཁྱེན་ (gūgyen) please (h.) ¶ སྐུ་མཁྱེན་ང་ལ་རོགས་རམ་གནང་རོགས་གནང་ Please help me.

སྐུ་འཁོར་ (gūgɔɔ) 1. retinue (h.) ¶ འབྲུག་རྒྱལ་སྐུ་འཁོར་ The King of Bhutan and his retinue. 2. family member, relative (h.) ¶ ཁོ་ཚོའི་སྐུ་འཁོར་ཁ་ཤས་བོད་ལ་ཡོད་པ་རེད་ Some of their relatives are in Tibet.

སྐུ་འཁོར་དཔོན་རིགས་ (gūgɔɔ bǖnrii) retinue of an official or lama.

སྐུ་འཁྱུག (gūngyaà) h. of འཁྱུག.

སྐུ་འཁྲུག (gūndruù) fighting (verbal or physical) (h.); va.—སྒྲོན་; to fight; vi.—ཤོར་ to get into a fight, to have a fight occur.

སྐུ་འཁྲུགས་ (gū drüù) vi. to feel physically low/ not well ¶ ཁོང་སྐུ་འཁྲུགས་པའི་རྐྱེན་གྱིས་ཕྱག་ལས་ལ་ཕེབས་ཐུབ་མ་སོང་ He was unable to come to work because he was not feeling well.

སྐུ་འཁྲུངས་ (gū drüŋ) vi. to be born (h.).

སྐུ་གམ་ (gūgəm) in/ at the presence of (h.) ¶ བློན་པོ་དེ་དུས་རྒྱུན་དུ་རྒྱལ་པོའི་སྐུ་གམ་ལ་བཅར་མཁན་ཞིག་རེད་ That minister is one who always is in the presence of the king.

སྐུ་གེགས་ (gūgeg) misfortune, disaster (h.) ¶ ལོ་འདིའི་ནང་ཁོང་ལ་སྐུ་གེགས་ཆེན་པོ་བྱུང་སོང་ This year he has had great misfortune.

སྐུ་གོང་མ་ (gū ko̱ŋma) the previous one (h.) ¶ རྒྱལ་བ་སྐུ་གོང་མ་ The previous Dalai Lama.

སྐུ་གྱོང་ (gūgyoŋ) loss (monetary) (h.); vi.—ཕོག to get a loss ¶ བར་ལམ་གྱི་ཚོང་འཁོར་ནང་ཁོང་ལ་སྐུ་གྱོང་ཆེན་པོ་ཕོག་བཞག Recently his business took a great loss.

སྐུ་གྲིབ་ (gūdrib) contamination, pollution (h.); vi.—ཕོག to get/ become contaminated ¶ སྤྲུལ་སྐུ་དེ་རང་སྐུ་གྲིབ་ཕོག་ནས་ཞལ་དིག་དིག་ཆགས་འདུག The tulku is stuttering because he became polluted.

སྐུ་གྲོངས་ (gū dro̱ŋ) vi. to die (h.).

སྐུ་བགྲེས་པ་ (gū dre̱ba) the senior, the elder (h.) ¶ ཡོངས་འཛིན་སྐུ་བགྲེས་པ་ The senior tutor (of the

Dalai Lama).

སྐུ་བགྲེས་ཤ་དོད་པོ་ (gū dresha tööbo) looking older than (one's) age (h.).

སྐུ་མགྲོན་ (gūndrön) guest (h.) ¶ ཐུགས་སྟོར་སྐུ་མགྲོན་མང་པོ་ཕེབས་འདུག There were many guests at the party.

སྐུ་མགྲོན་ཁང་ (gūndröngaŋ) guest house.

སྐུ་མགྲོན་སྣེ་ལེན་ཁང་ (gūndrön nelengaŋ) sm. སྐུ་མགྲོན་ཁང་.

སྐུ་མགྲོན་རུ་ཁག (gūndrön rugaà) visiting team/ group/ party ¶ རྒྱ་གར་ནས་ཚོང་དོན་གྱི་སྐུ་མགྲོན་རུ་ཁག་ཅིག་ཕེབས་པ་རེད་ A visiting group of business men came from India.

སྐུ་འགག (gūŋgaà) h. of སྟོད་འགག.

སྐུ་འགྱེད་ (gūngyeè) alms, donations, (h.); va.—འབུལ་ to give a donation/ alms.

སྐུ་འགྲམ་ (gūndram) sm. སྐུ་གམ་.

སྐུ་རྒྱན་ (gūgyen) 1. ornament (h.); va.—མཆོད་ to wear ornaments; —སྐྲོན་ to put ornaments on sb. 2. a lottery (h.); va.—སྒྲོན་ to draw lots ¶ སྐུ་མཆེད་བགྲེས་གཞོན་གཉིས་དབར་ཁང་པ་སུ་ལ་ཐོབ་མིན་སྐུ་རྒྱན་བསྒྲོན་པ་རེད་ The two brothers drew lots to see who would get the house. 3. a bet (h.) ¶ རྟ་རྒྱུགས་ལ་སྐུ་རྒྱན་བཞག་གནང་བ་རེད་ (They) placed bets on horse racing.

སྐུ་རྒྱབ་ (gūgyəb) 1. behind, in back of (h.) ¶ ཕྱག་དེབ་ཁོང་གི་སྐུ་རྒྱབ་ལ་འདུག The book is behind his back. 2. one's back (h.) ¶ ཁོང་གི་སྐུ་རྒྱབ་ཡག་པོ་དྲག་མི་འདུག His back hasn't healed well.

སྐུ་རྒྱུ་ (gūgyu) 1. wealth (h.) ¶ ཁོང་ལ་སྐུ་རྒྱུ་ཆེན་པོ་ཡོད་པ་རེད་ (He) has great wealth. 2. the material from which a statue or icon is made ¶ སྐུ་རྒྱུ་གསེར་ཟངས་ལས་གྲུབ་པའི་སྣང་བརྙན་ Statues and icons made of gilded brass.

སྐུ་རྒྱུ་ཕྱག་རྫས་ (gūgyu cāgdzεὲ) sm. སྐུ་རྒྱུ་.

སྐུ་རྒྱུད་ (gūgyüù) 1. lineage, descent line (h.); va.—འདེད་ to trace (one's) lineage/ descendent line ¶ ཁོང་གི་སྐུ་རྒྱུད་དེད་པ་ཡིན་ན་ཆོས་རྒྱལ་ལ་ཐུག་གི་ཡོད་ If one traces his lineage, he is a descendent of the Dharmaraja Kings. 2. va.—ཁྲིད་ vi. to take after a relative in behavior/ personality/ character ¶ རྒྱལ་སྲས་དེའི་སྤྱོད་ལམ་རྒྱལ་པོའི་སྐུ་རྒྱུད་ཁྲིད་བཞག The prince has taken after his father the king in his behavior.

སྐུ་སྒེར་ (gūgee) private (h.) ¶ སྐུ་སྒེར་དྲུང་ཆེ་ Private secretary.

སྐུ་སྒེར་བླ་བྲང་ (gūgee lābraŋ) the labrang of the regent.

སྐུ་སྒེར་ཡིག་ཚང་ (gūgee yigdzaŋ) 1. private secretariat (usu. of the Dalai Lama). 2. the private office of the Dalai Lama.

སྐུ་ངང་འཐེན་ (gūŋaŋ tēn) 1. delaying/ postponing (h.); va.—གནང་ ¶ གནས་སྐོར་ལ་ཕེབས་རྒྱུ་ཉིན་ཤས་སྐུ་ངང་འཐེན་གནང་བ་རེད་ (He) postponed his pilgrimage for a few days. 2. beseeching an oracle/ medium not to go out of his trance; va.—གནང་.

སྐུ་ངང་ཙམ་ (gūŋaŋdzam) sm. སྐུ་ངང་འཐེན་, 1.

སྐུ་ངལ་ (gūŋεε) hardship, difficulty (h.); va.—སྒྲོན་ to experience/ underdo difficulties or hardships, to work hard (undergoing difficulties/ hardships) ¶ ཁོང་སྐུ་ངལ་ཆེན་པོ་བྱུང་བཞག He experienced a lot of hardship. ¶ ཁོང་གིས་སྐུ་ངལ་བསྒྲོན་པའི་འབྲས་བུ་ The result of his working hard undergoing difficulties.

སྐུ་ངལ་གནང་ (gūŋεε nāŋ) va. to rest, to relax (h.) ¶ ཁོང་སློབ་གྲྭ་ནས་ཕེབས་ནས་སྐུ་ངལ་གནང་ནས་བཞུགས་བཞག He is relaxing after coming back from school.

སྐུ་ངལ་གསོ་ (gūŋεε sō) sm. སྐུ་ངལ་གནང་.

སྐུ་ངལ་གསོས་ (gūŋεε söò) p. of སྐུ་ངལ་གསོ་.

སྐུ་ངོ་ (gōŋöò) 1. title of address for lay (aristocratic) government officials. 2. aristocrat.

སྐུ་ངོ་མཁྱེན་ (gōŋöò kyēn) shung. please O lord, please honorable sir.

སྐུ་ངོ་གནམ་བདག (gōŋöò nāmdaà) shung. title of an emperor's who abdicates in favor of his son.

སྐུ་ངོ་མ་ (gū ŋoma) he himself, in person (h.) ¶ ཁོང་སྐུ་ངོ་མ་ལས་སར་ཕེབས་པ་རེད་ He came to the work site in person.

སྐུ་དངོས་ (gūŋüù) sm. སྐུ་ངོ་མ་.

སྐུ་བཅར་ (gūjaa) personal attendant, servant, retinue (h.); va.—ཞུ་ to call on or pay a visit to sb. higher in rank or status.

སྐུ་བཅར་མཁན་པོ་ (gūjaa kēmbo) shung. sm. སྤྱི་ཁྱབ་མཁན་པོ་.

སྐུ་ཆག (gūjaà) sm. སྐུ་གེགས་.

སྐུ་ཆམ་ (gūjam) h. of ཆམ་ཆམ་.

སྐུ་ཆས་ (gūjεὲ) h. of ཅ་ལག.

སྐུ་ཆིངས་ (gūjiŋ) ch. (waist) belt.

སྐུ་ཆེན་པོ་ (gū cēmbo) 1. a large statue. 2. a great person.

སྐུ་ཚོས་ (gūjöò) 1. h. of ཚོས་. 2. sm. ཚོས་གོས་.

སྐུ་མཆེད་ (gōmceè) relative (h.).

སྐུ་མཆོད་ (gūcöò) ceremonial observance commemorating the death of a religious figure.

སྐུ་འཆམ་ (gūnjam) h. of འཆམ་པ་.

སྐུ་རྗེས་ (gūjüù) h. of རྗེས་.

སྐུ་མཇལ་ (gūnjεε) interview, audience (h.); va.—ཞུ་ to get an interview/ audience; to ask for an interview/ audience.

སྐུ་འཇུག (gūnjuù) h. of འོག་འཇུག.

སྐུ་རྗེས (gūjeè) the imprint of a body miraculously left on rocks (by lamas/ saints).

སྐུ་ཉམས་ (gūñəm) dignity, elegance, sophistication (h.); va.—གནང་; —སྟོན་ to act dignified/ elegant/ sophisticated.

སྐུ་ཉིད་ (gūñiì) you (h.) ¶ སྐུ་ཉིད་ཕེབས་པའི་རྗེས་སུ་ After you left.

སྐུ་ཉེ་ (gūñe) relative, kinsman (h.).

སྐུ་ཉེ་སྐུ་འཁོར་ (gūñe gūgɔɔ) sm. སྐུ་ཉེ་འཁོར་བཅས་.

སྐུ་ཉེ་འཁོར་བཅས་ (gūñe kɔ̄rjεὲ) 1. retinue, attendants (h.). 2. relatives (h.).

སྐུ་ཉེ་ལྟོས་བཅས་ (gūñe döòjεὲ) sm. སྐུ་ཉེ་འཁོར་བཅས་.

སྐུ་གཉེར་ (gūñer) steward/ caretaker of a monastery, temple or chapel room in a monastery.

སྐུ་གཉེར་བླ་བྲང་ (gūñer lābraŋ) shung. the labrang of the Regent.

སྐུ་མཉེ་ (gūñe) 1. arc. fire. 2. sm. བཞུགས་གདན་.

སྐུ་མཉེལ་ (gū ñēē) vi. to get tired/ exhausted (h.) ¶ ཁོང་ཕྱག་ལས་གནང་ཙང་སྐུ་མཉེལ་བ་རེད་ He got tired because he worked.

སྐུ་མཉེལ་པོ་ (gū ñēēbo) 1. tired, exhausted (h.). 2. difficult, hard (h.) ¶ ཡིག་ཚད་སྐུ་མཉེལ་པོ་བྱུང་མ་སོང་ངམ་ Was the test difficult?

སྐུ་སྙེ་ (gūñe) cushion for supporting one's back.

སྐུ་སྙེས་ (gū ñēè) sm. སྐུ་སྙེ་.

སྐུ་བརྙན་ (gūñεn) statue, image (h.).

སྐུ་རྟེན་ (gūden) 1. the medium/ oracle of a deity (the person through whose body the deity speaks) ¶ གནས་ཆུང་སྐུ་རྟེན་ The medium of Nechung. 2. a statue.

སྐུ་ལྟབ་ (gūdəb) folding, folded (h.); va.—སྒྲོན་ to fold.

སྐུ་ལྟེམ་ (gū dēm) vi. to be ill, to get sick (h.) ¶ ཁོང་དེང་སང་སྐུ་ལྟེམ་གྱི་ཡོད་པ་འདྲ་ (I) think he is feeling sick these days.

སྐུ་སྟོད་ (gōdöò) 1. one's back (h.) ¶ ཁོང་སྐུ་སྟོད་སྣུང་གི་འདུག His back is hurting. 2. the upper part of the body (h.) ¶ སྐུ་བརྙན་དེའི་སྐུ་སྟོད་བཞེངས་ཚར་མ་སོང་ The upper half of the statue isn't finished yet. 3. shirt, blouse, coat, garment for the upper body (h.) ¶ ཁོང་གིས་སྐུ་སྟོད་གསར་པ་ཞིག་གཟིགས་པ་རེད་ He bought a new shirt.

སྐུ་སྟོབས་ཆེན་པོ་ (gūdob cēmbo) stout, husky, well-built (h.).

སྐུ་སྟོབས་ཞན་པོ་ (gūdob shεmbo) small in stature, weak or ill-looking, skinny, scrawny (h.).

སྐུ་བལྟམས་ (gū dām) sm. སྐུ་འཁྲུང་.

སྐུ་བསྟོད་ (gūdöò) 1. h. of བསྟོད་བསྔགས་. 2. praise of a lama or deity.

སྐུ་ཐང་ (gūdaŋ) thanka (h.); va.—བཞེངས་ to make/ paint a thanka.

སྐུ་ཐང་མཉེལ་ (gūdaŋ ñēē) vi. to be tired (h.).

སྐུ་ཐང་མཉེལ་པོ་ (gūtaŋ ñēēbo) sm. སྐུ་མཉེལ་པོ་.

སྐུ་ཐིམ་ (gū tīm) vi. to die (h.) ¶ སྐུ་ཐིམ་པའི་རྗེས་སུ་ After (he) died.

སྐུ་ཐོག་ (gūdoò) lifetime, generation (h.) ¶ སྐུ་མདུན་སྐུ་ཐོག་འདིའི་རིང་ During the lifetime of this Dalai Lama.

སྐུ་ཐོག་གོང་མ་ (gūdoò goŋma) 1. the former/ previous generation (h.). 2. previous incarnations in an incarnation line or lineage of kings, rulers.

སྐུ་ཐོག་རྗེས་མ་ (gūdoò jeèma) the succeeding/ next generation (h.).

སྐུ་ཐོག་ན་རིམ་ (gūdoò narim) sm. སྐུ་ཐོག་རིམ་པ་.

སྐུ་ཐོག་རིམ་པ་ (gūdoò rimbə) a series of holders of a position spanning several generations, e.g. a lineage of kings or incarnations ¶ རྒྱལ་དབང་སྐུ་ཐོག་རིམ་པའི་དུས་ནས་ལམ་ལུགས་དེ་དར་བ་རེད་ This custom flourished during the time of the successive Dalai Lamas.

སྐུ་ཐོག་རིམ་བྱུང་ (gūoò rimjuŋ) h. of སྐྱེ་བ་རིམ་བརྒྱུད་.

སྐུ་དྭངས་ (gū taŋ) vi. to recover from an illness (h.)

སྐུ་དུས་ (gūdüü) time (h.) ¶ སྟོན་པའི་སྐུ་དུས་སུ་ During the Buddha's time.

སྐུ་དོན་ (gūdön) purpose, reason (h.) ¶ ཁྱེད་འདིར་ཕེབས་པའི་སྐུ་དོན་ག་རེ་ཡིན་ For what purpose did you come here?

སྐུ་དྲག་ (gūdraà) noble, aristocrat; nobility, aristocracy.

སྐུ་དྲིན་ (gūdrin) sm. བཀའ་དྲིན་.

སྐུ་དྲུང་ (gūdruŋ) presence, vicinity (h.) ¶ ཁོང་རྒྱལ་པོའི་སྐུ་དྲུང་ལ་སྡོད་མཁན་ཞིག་རེད་ He is a person who stays in the presence of the king.

སྐུ་དྲུང་དུ་ (gūdruŋdu) 1. in the presence of (h.) 2. a standardized form of address used in letter headings ¶ སྐུ་ཞབས་བཀྲ་ཤིས་ལགས་ཀྱི་སྐུ་དྲུང་དུ་ Dear Mr. Tashi [Lit. to the presence of Tashi].

སྐུ་དྲུང་པ་ (gū druŋbə) a personal attendant, sb. who serves in the presence of a superior (h.).

སྐུ་གདུང་ (gūduŋ) corpse, remains (h.) ¶ ཆོས་རྒྱལ་གྱི་སྐུ་གདུང་ The remains of the Dharmaraja (religious king).

སྐུ་གདུང་ཞུགས་འབུལ་ (gūduŋ shuŋbüü) cremation, cremating (h.); va.—ཞུ་ to cremate (h.).

སྐུ་མདུན་ (gündün) 1. in front of (h.) ¶ གསོལ་ཇ་ཁོང་གི་སྐུ་མདུན་ལ་བཞག་པ་རེད་ (They) put the tea in front of him. 2. in the presence of (usu. refers to the Dalai Lama and other high-ranking lamas) (h.).

སྐུ་མདུན་པ་ (gū dümbə) shung. personal attendants ¶ བཞུགས་ཁྲིའི་མཐར་གམ་བཅར་སྐུ་མདུན་པ་ཆེན་པོ་རྣམས་ནས་མཎྜལ་རྟེན་གསུམ་སོགས་ཐོགས་པ་ The attendants were holding a mandala beside the throne.

སྐུ་མདོག (gūdɔɔ̀) color (usu. of deities).

སྐུ་འདད་ (gū dεὲ) h. of འདད་.

སྐུ་འདར་ (gū dar) 1. va. to shiver (h.); 2. vi.—སྐྱོན་ to involuntarily shiver (h.) ¶ ཁོང་སྐུ་བསིལ་ནས་སྐུ་འདར་སྐྱོན་གྱི་འདུག He got cold and is shivering.

སྐུ་འདས་ (gū dεὲ) vi. to die (h.) ¶ བླ་མ་སྐུ་འདས་ནས་ཡང་སྲིད་ཚད་གཙོད་ཞུས་པ་རེད་ After the lama died (they) searched for his reincarnation.

སྐུ་འདྲ་ (gūndrə) sm. སྐུ་བརྙན་.

སྐུ་ལྡིར་ (gūder) clay statue.

སྐུ་སྡིག (gūdig) h. of སྡིག་པ་.

སྐུ་བརྡབ་ (gūdəb) falling (h.); vi.—ཟག; —གནང་ to fall ¶ སྲས་ཆུང་དེ་སྐུ་བརྡབ་ཟག་བཞག The young boy has fallen.

སྐུ་བརྡབ་ (gūdəb) falling (h.); vi.—ཟག; —གནང་ to fall ¶ སྲས་ཆུང་དེ་སྐུ་བརྡབ་ཟག་བཞག The young boy has fallen.

སྐུ་ན་བགྲེས་པོ་ (gūnə dreèbo) old, aged (h.).

སྐུ་ན་ཕྲ་བ་ (gūnə trāwa) young (h.) ¶ སྐུ་ན་ཕྲ་བའི་སྐབས་སུ་སློབ་སྦྱོང་གནང་དགོས་ (You) should study when (you) are young.

སྐུ་ན་སྨིན་པ་ (gūnə mīmba) sm. སྐུ་ན་བགྲེས་པོ་.

སྐུ་རྣག (gūnag) h. of རྣག.

སྐུ་པང་ (gūbaŋ) 1. h. of པང་པ་. 2. h. of པང་ཁེབས་.

སྐུ་པར་ (gūbaa) photograph, portrait (h.); va.—སྒྲོན་ to photograph (if that which is photographed is honorific) ¶ ཁོང་གི་བླ་མར་སྐུ་པར་བསྒྲོན་པ་རེད་ He took a photograph of the lama. va.—སྐྱོན་ to photograph (if that which is photographed is nonhonorific but the photographer is honorific) ¶ ཁོང་གི་ཁང་པ་དེར་སྐུ་པར་བསྐྱོན་སོང་ He took a picture of the house.

སྐུ་པར་བྲིས་མ་ (gūbaa driimə) a portrait (drawn or painted) (h.).

སྐུ་པུར་ (gūbur) sm. སྐུ་ཕུང་.

སྐུ་དཔངས་ (gūbaŋ) the height (of a statue).

སྐུ་དཔར་ (gūbar) sm. སྐུ་པར.

སྐུ་དཔུང་ (gūbuŋ) h. of དཔུང་པ་.

སྐུ་སྤུར་ (gūbur) sm. སྐུ་ཕུང་.

སྐུ་ཕུང་ (gūbuŋ) dead body, corpse (h.) ¶ ངའི་ཕ་མ་དམ་པའི་སྐུ་ཕུང་ The dead bodies of my late parents.

སྐུ་ཕུང་མཇལ་སྟོན་ (gūbuŋ jεεmön) type of funeral ceremony where the body is placed in view or is left lying in state.

སྐུ་ཕུང་གདན་ཞུ་ (gūbuŋ dḛnshu) funeral ceremony (h.).

སྐུ་ཕོག་ (gū pɔɔ̀) harming one's health (h.).

སྐུ་ཕྱག་ (gūjaà) prostration (h.); va.—གནང་; —འབུལ་ to prostrate.

སྐུ་ཕྱྭ་ (gūja) life's fortune or luck ¶ སྐུ་ཕྱྭ་ཤིན་ཏུ་འཚུབ་པ་ Having very bad fortune in one's life.

སྐུ་ཕྱྭ་མཛད་འཕྲིན་ (gūja dzεndrin) abbr. of སྐུ་ཕྱྭ་ and མཛད་འཕྲིན་.

སྐུ་ཕྲེང་ (gūndreŋ) 1. lineage/ line of reincarnations ¶ རྒྱལ་བའི་སྐུ་ཕྲེང་ The reincarnation line of the Dalai Lamas. 2. a lama/ incarnation in a line of incarnations ¶ ཏཱ་ལའི་བླ་མ་སྐུ་ཕྲེང་ལྔ་པའི་དུས་ At the time of the 5th. Dalai Lama.

སྐུ་ཕྲེང་རིམ་བརྒྱུད་ (gūtreŋ rimgyüü) h. of སྐྱེ་བ་རིམ་བརྒྱུད་.

སྐུ་འཕྲེང་ (gūndreŋ) sm. སྐུ་ཕྲེང་.

སྐུ་བག (gūbaà) bride or bridegroom. (h.); va.—བཞེས་ to take a bride or bridegroom.

སྐུ་བད་རྒྱས་ (gūbεὲ gyεὲ) vi. to be drunk (h.) ¶ ཐུགས་སྒྲོར་ཕེབས་ནས་སྐུ་བད་རྒྱས་བཞག (He) went to the party and got drunk.

སྐུ་བེམ་ (gūbem) cloak (h.).

སྐུ་བེར་ (gūber) sm. སྐུ་བེམ་.

སྐུ་བོན་ (gūbön) Bon priests (who used to serve as attendants to the early kings of Tibet).

སྐུ་བྱུག (gūjuù) rubbing sth. on the body (h.); va.—སྐྱོན་.

སྐུ་བྲང་ (gūdraŋ) h. of བྲང་ཁོག.

སྐུ་དབང་ (gūwaŋ) power, authority (h.); va.—གནང་ to exercise power/ authority ¶ ཁོང་ལ་སྐུ་དབང་ཡོད་པ་མ་རེད་ He has no power. ¶ ཁོང་གི་གཟིམས་ཤག་ནང་སྐུ་དབང་ཆེན་པོ་ཞི་དྲག་གནང་གི་ཡོད་པ་རེད་ He exercises great power in his home.

སྐུ་དབང་ཆེན་པོ་ (gūwaŋ cēmbo) bossy, authoritative, autocratic (h.).

སྐུ་དབྱིབས་ (gūyib) statue-like shape/ body (h.) ¶ སྐུ་དབྱིབས་ཤིན་ཏུ་ལེགས་པ་ A beautiful statue-like shape.

སྐུ་འབག (gūmbaà) 1. statue (h.). 2. mask (h.).

སྐུ་འབུམ་ (gūmbum) 1. Kumbum Monastery (in Amdo). 2. a stupa that contains many clay religious tablets. 3. a hundred thousand statues.

སྐུ་འབུམ་བྱམས་པ་གླིང་ (gūmbum cāmbaliŋ) sm. སྐུ་འབུམ་, 1.

སྐུ་འབུར་མ་ (gū burma) relief images of the Buddha and Buddhist deities (carved on rocks, etc.).

སྐུ་རྨ་ (gūma) h. of རྨ་.

སྐུ་སྨད་ (gūmεὲ) the lower part of the body (h.).

སྐུ་བཙོག (gūdzɔɔ̀) dirt, pollution (h.); vi.—ཤོར་ to

get/ be dirty; to get/ be polluted ༡ ཁོང་ལ་མཁའ་རླུང་ངན་པའི་སྐུ་བཙོག་ཕོག་ནས་སྤྱན་སྣང་བ་རེད་ ༡ He got polluted by the air and this caused his eyes to hurt.

སྐུ་རྩ་ (gūdza) vein (h.); va.—གཟིགས་ to feel a pulse to ascertain health.

སྐུ་རྩལ་ (gūdzɛɛ) h. of རྩལ་ལག.

སྐུ་རྩེ་ (gōdze) sm. སྐུ་རྩེད་.

སྐུ་རྩེད་ (gōdzeè)1. games, playing around (h.); va.—གནང་ to play games. 2. kidding, joking (h.); va.—ཞུས་; —གནང་; —གསུང་ to kid around, to joke ༡ ཁོང་གིས་ང་ལ་སྐུ་རྩེད་གནང་ནས་རྒྱ་གར་ལ་འགྲོ་གི་ཡིན་གསུང་གི་འདུག He joked and said that he was going to India.

སྐུ་རྩེར་ (gūdzee) arguing, argument (h.); va.—སྐྱོན་ to argue; vi.—ཕོར་ to have an argument occur/ breakout ༡ དགེ་རྒན་ཕན་ཚུན་སྐུ་རྩེར་སྐྱོན་གྱི་འདུག The teachers are arguing among themselves. ༡ ཡབ་ཡུམ་གཉིས་བར་སྐུ་རྩེར་ཕོར་བཞག Argument broke out between the father and the mother.

སྐུ་ཚ་ (gūdzə) 1. niece, nephew (h.) 2. relatives of high personages (e.g., the Dalai Lama) ༡ རྒྱལ་བའི་སྐུ་ཚ་ The relatives of the Dalai Lama.

སྐུ་ཚགས་ (gūdzaà) traditional Tibetan fleece-lined dress (h.).

སྐུ་ཚད་ (gūdzɛɛ) 1. size ༡ འདུ་སྐུ་དེ་སྐུ་ཚད་ཆེན་པོ་བཞེངས་བཞག (They) have built a large statue. ༡ སྲས་ཆུང་དེ་སྐུ་ཚད་ཆེན་པོ་བཞེངས་བཞག The small child has grown a lot in size. 2. fever ༡ ཁོང་སྐུ་ཚད་ཆེན་པོ་རྒྱས་བཞག He got a high fever.

སྐུ་ཚབ་ (gūdzəb) representative, deputy, delegate.

སྐུ་ཚབ་གྲོས་ཚོགས་ (gūdzəb drȫödzɔ̀) meeting or conference of representative/ delegates.

སྐུ་ཚབ་དོན་གཅོད་པ་ (gūdzəb tö̱njööba) representative, delegate, emissary.

སྐུ་ཚབ་ཚོགས་ཆེན་ (gūdzəb tsɔ̄gjen) congress/ conference/ meeting of representatives or delegates.

སྐུ་ཚབ་ཚོགས་པ་ (gūdzəb tsɔ̄gba) delegation, mission ༡ ཏང་སྲིད་སྐུ་ཚབ་ཚོགས་པ་ The delegation from the party and the government.

སྐུ་ཚབ་ལྷན་ཚོགས་ (gūdzəb lhɛ̄ndzɔɔ̀) sm. སྐུ་ཚབ་གྲོས་ཚོགས་.

སྐུ་ཚར་ (gūdzar) sm. སྐུ་ཚགས་.

སྐུ་ཚིགས་ (gūdziì) h. of བདུན་ཚིགས་.

སྐུ་ཚེ་ (gūdze) life, span of life (h.); vi.—རྫོགས་; —འདས to die ༡ སྐུ་ཚེ་རིང་པོ་ Long life.

སྐུ་ཚེ་བསྐལ་བརྒྱ་ལ་བརྟན་པར་ཤོག (gūdze kɛ̄ɛ̄gyala dɛ̄mbar shōō) Long Live! [Lit. may your life remain for 100 eons].

སྐུ་ཚེ་ཁྲི་ཕྲག་(དུ)བརྟན་པ་ཤོག (gūdze tri̱draà (du) dɛ̄mbar shōō) Long live! [Lit. may your life remain for 10,000 (years)].

སྐུ་ཚེ་མ་ཟིན་ (gūdze ma̱ si̱n) vi. to die early, to not live one's full life.

སྐུ་ཚེ་མཛད་འཕྲིན་ (gūdze dzɛ̱ɛ̀drin) the deeds/ work of one's life.

སྐུ་ཚེ་ཞབས་པད་བརྟན་པར་ཤོག (gūdze shə̱bbɛɛ̀ dɛ̄mbar shōō) sm. སྐུ་ཚེ་ཁྲི་ཕྲག་(དུ་)བརྟན་པ་ཤོག.

སྐུ་ཚེ་རིང་ (gū tsēriŋ) 1. please (h.). 2. sm. སྐུ་ཚེ་རིང་པོ་.

སྐུ་ཚེ་རིང་པོ་ (gūdze ri̱ŋbu) long life (h.) ༡ སྐུ་ཚེ་རིང་པོ་ཡོང་བ་ཤོག May (you) live long.

སྐུ་ཚེ་ཧྲིལ་པོ་ (gūdze hrīību) entire life, whole life (h.) ༡ སྐུ་ཚེ་ཧྲིལ་པོ་མི་དམངས་ཀྱི་ཞབས་འདེགས་ཞུས་གནང་བ་རེད་ He served the people his entire life.

སྐུ་ཚེའི་སྟོད་ (gūdzee dōō) sm. སྐུ་ཚེའི་སྟོད་ཆ་.

སྐུ་ཚེའི་སྟོད་ཆ་ (gūdzee dōōja) early part of one's life (h.) ༡ སྐུ་ཚེའི་སྟོད་ཆ་ལ་སྐུ་ངལ་མང་པོ་བྱུང་ཡོད་པ་རེད་ He suffered greatly during the early part of his life.

སྐུ་ཚེའི་འདུ་བྱེད་སྟོང་ (gūdzee du̱jeè dōŋ) sm. སྐུ་ཚེའི་འཕེན་པ་རྫོགས་.

སྐུ་ཚེའི་འཕེན་པ་རྫོགས་ (gūdzee pɛ̄mba dzɔ̱ɔ̀) vi. to pass away, to die (h.).

སྐུ་ཚེའི་སྨད་སྨད་ (gūdzee mɛ̄ɛ̀mɛɛ̀) sm. སྐུ་ཚེའི་སྨད་ཆ་.

སྐུ་ཚེའི་སྨད་ཆ་ (gūdzee mɛ̄ɛ̀ja) the latter part of one's life.

སྐུ་ཚེའི་རིང་ (gūtsee ri̱ŋ) during a lifetime ༡ ཁོང་གི་སྐུ་ཚེའི་རིང་ལ་སྐུ་ལས་ཞི་དྲག་བསྐྱོན་པ་རེད་ He worked extremely hard during his life time.

སྐུ་ཚོང་ (gūdzoŋ) h. of ཚོང་.

སྐུ་མཚམས་ (gūndzam) in retreat (meditation) (h.); va.—གནང་; —ལ་བཞུགས་ to stay in retreat.

སྐུ་མཚལ་ (gūndzɛɛ) 1. blood (h.). 2. menstrual blood, menstruation; vi.—སྐྱོན to menstruate; —ཆད་ to stop menstruating.

སྐུ་ཞང་ (gūshaŋ) maternal uncle (h.).

སྐུ་ཞབས་ (gūshəb) shung. 1. an honorific term used before names that conveys a semantic range including "his/ your excellency," "the honorable," "Mr." ༡ སྐུ་ཞབས་རྡོ་རྗེ་ལགས་ཕེབས་སྐབས་ When the honorable Dorje comes. 2. term of address for monks.

སྐུ་ཞབས་སུ་ (gūshəbsu) shung. sm. སྐུ་དྲུང་དུ་.

སྐུ་ཞིང་ལ་ཕེབས་ (gūshiŋlə phēē) shung. vi. to die (h.) ༡ བླ་མ་སྐུ་ཞིང་ལ་ཕེབས་པའི་རྗེས་སུ་ After the death of the lama.

སྐུ་གཤོགས་ (gūshoò) sm. སྐུ་ཞབས་.

སྐུ་གཞོན་ (gūshön) 1. the junior, the younger. 2. vice (h.) ༡ རྒྱ་གར་སྲིད་འཛིན་སྐུ་གཞོན་ The Vice President of India.

སྐུ་བཞེངས་ (gū she̱ŋ) va. to make a statue (h.).

སྐུ་བཞེངས་གནང་ (gūsheŋ nāŋ) va. to get up, to rise, to stand up (h.).

སྐུ་ཟིལ་ཆེ་ (gū si̱lje) magnificent, glorious, majestic (h.).

སྐུ་ཟླ་ (gūndə) spouse (h.).

སྐུ་ཟླུམ་ (gūndam) h. of ཟླ་གམ་.

སྐུ་གཟན་ (gūsɛn) monk's upper robe (h.).

སྐུ་གཟིམས་ (gūsim) sleep (h.); vi.—གནང་ to sleep.

སྐུ་གཟུགས་ (gūsuù) the body (h.); va.—བསིལ་ to bathe, to shower (h.) 2. statue (h.).

སྐུ་གཟུགས་བདེ་པོ་ (gūsuù de̱bo) in good health, well (h.) ༡ ཁྱེད་རང་སྐུ་གཟུགས་བདེ་པོ་ཡིན་པས་ Are you well?

སྐུ་གཟུགས་ལ་ཐུགས་ཙག་གནང་ (gūsuùlə tūùjaà nāŋ) look after yourself, take good care of yourself ༡ རྒྱ་ནག་ལ་ཕེབས་དུས་སྐུ་གཟུགས་ལ་ཐུགས་ཙག་གནང་ When you go to China take good care of yourself.

སྐུ་ཡལ་ (gū yɛ̱ɛ̱) vi. to go out of trance (h.) ༡ ཆོས་སྐྱོང་སྐུ་ཡལ་བ་རེད་ The oracle went out of trance.

སྐུ་ཡི་ཟིལ་བརྗིད་ (gūyi si̱lgyeè) looking vigorous and majestic/ regal/ imposing.

སྐུ་ཡོན་ (gūyün) h. 1. education, knowledge (h.); va.—གསན་བཞེས་(གནང་) to receive education (h.) ༡ ཁོང་གིས་སྐུ་ཡོན་གསན་བཞེས་ཚང་མ་རྒྱ་གར་ལ་གནང་ཡོད་པ་རེད་ He received all (his) education in India. 2. wages for monks (h.).

སྐུ་ཡོན་ཆེན་པོ་ (gūyün cēmbo) knowledgeable, learned, educated well (h.).

སྐུ་ཡོན་གསན་སྦྱོང་ (gūyün sɛ̄njoŋ) education, study, training.

སྐུ་གཡང་ཞུ་ (gūyaŋ shu̱) a polite phrase conveying: "I'm sorry I've caused you a lot of trouble/ bother," or "I'm sorry that I've inconvenienced you" ༡ དེ་རིང་ང་ཁྱེད་རང་གི་རྩ་ལ་སླེབས་ནས་སྐུ་གཡང་ཞི་དྲག་ཞུས་སོང་ I'm sorry my coming to you today has caused you a lot of trouble.

སྐུ་ར་ (gūrə) intoxication (h.); vi.—བབ་ to be or get drunk/ intoxicated.

སྐུ་ར་དྭངས་ (gūrə ta̱ŋ) vi. to sober up, to become sober (h.).

སྐུ་རགས་ (gūraà) h. of སྐེ་རགས་.

སྐུ་རིང་ (gūriŋ) a lifetime (h.) ༡ མཁན་པོ་དེའི་སྐུ་རིང་ལ་ During the lifetime of that abbot.

སྐུ་རིམ་ (gūrim) sm. ཞབས་བརྟན་.

སྐུ་རུ་ (gūru) shung. abbr. of སྐུ་སྲུང་དུ་དཔོན་.

སྐུ་རུས་ (gūrüù) 1. bones, skeleton (h.). 2. lineage.

སྐུ་ལུང་ (gūluŋ) h. of ལུང་.

སྐུ་ལུང་ཅོད་པན་ (gūluŋ jõòbɛn) shung. prayer flag.

སྐུ་ལུང་དར་འཛུགས་ (gūluŋ tardzuù) h. of ལུང་དར་འཛུགས་.

སྐུ་ལ་དར་ (gūla dar) arc. སྐུ་ལ་སྡོ་.

སྐུ་ལ་སྡོ་ (gūla do) arc. va. to endanger someone's life.

སྐུ་ལང་ (gūlaŋ) h. of སྐུག་ལང་.

སྐུ་ལས་ (gūlɛɛ̀) 1. h. of དཀའ་ལས་; va.—སྐྱོན་. 2. h. of ལས་.

སྐུ་ལས་ཁག་པོ་ (gūlɛɛ̀ kāgo) hardship, difficulty; hard, difficult (h.) ¶ ཁོང་རིག་གནས་གསར་བརྗེའི་སྐབས་སྐུ་ལས་ཁག་པོ་བྱུང་བ་རེད་ He experienced difficulties at the time of the Cultural Revolution.

སྐུ་ལུས་ (gūlüù) sm. སྐུ་གཟུགས་.

སྐུ་ཤ་ (gūsha) human flesh (h.).

སྐུ་ཤ་སྐམ་པོ་ (gūsha gāmbo) thin, skinny (h.).

སྐུ་ཤ་རྒྱགས་པ་ (gūsha gyagba) fat (h.).

སྐུ་ཤ་འབྱོར་པོ་ (gūsha jɔɔbo) sm. སྐུ་ཤ་རྒྱགས་པ་.

སྐུ་ཤུགས་ (gūshuù) h. of ཤུགས་.

སྐུ་ཤེད་ (gūsheè) sm. སྐུ་ཤུགས་.

སྐུ་གཤེགས་ (gūsheg) 1. deceased, the late (h.) ¶ སྐུ་གཤེགས་སྲིད་བློན་དེ་ The late Prime Minister. 2. vi. to die, to pass away (h.).

སྐུ་གཤེགས་པ་ (gūshegba) sm. སྐུ་གཤེགས་.

སྐུ་གཤེགས་དཔའ་བོ་ (gūsheg bāwo) a courageous martyr (h.).

སྐུ་གཤེགས་མྱ་ངན་ (gūsheg ñaŋɛn) mourning the dead (h.); va.—ཞུ་ to mourn the dead.

སྐུ་གཤེན་ (gūshen) Bon tutor to ancient kings.

སྐུ་སྲིང་ (gūsiŋ) younger sister of high status people (h.).

སྐུ་སྲུང་ (gūsuŋ) 1. security guard, bodyguard. 2. va. to protect/ shield/ safeguard. ¶ དམག་མི་ཚོས་བླ་མའི་སྐུ་བསྲུངས་པ་རེད་ The soldiers protected the life of the lama.

སྐུ་སྲུང་ཁྲུའུ་ (gūsuŋ trūwu) tib.ch. security/ guard office.

སྐུ་སྲུང་སྟོང་དཔོན་ (gūsuŋ dōŋbön) shung. a commander of 1,000 troops of the སྐུ་སྲུང་ regiment.

སྐུ་སྲུང་མདའ་དཔོན་ (gūsuŋ dɛɛbön) shung. the general in command of the སྐུ་སྲུང་ regiment (the Dalai Lama's Bodyguard Regiment).

སྐུ་སྲུང་དམག (མི་) (gūsuŋ māɔmi) shung. 1. the bodyguard regiment. 2. soldiers in the bodyguard regiment.

སྐུ་སྲུང་དམག་དཔུང་ (gūsuŋ māgbuŋ) the bodyguard regiment.

སྐུ་སྲུང་རུ་དཔོན་ (gūsuŋ rubön) shung. captains in the bodyguard regiment [there are two རུ་དཔོན་ who are immediately subordinate to the སྐུ་སྲུང་མདའ་དཔོན་].

སྐུ་སྲོག (gūsoò) h. of སྲོག.

སྐུ་གསུང་ཐུགས་ (gūsuŋ tūù) body, speech and mind (h.).

སྐུ་གསུང་ཐུགས་རྟེན་ (gūsuŋ tūden) the three representations of the Buddha: statues (his body), scriptures (his speech), stupa (his mind).

སྐུ་གསུམ་ (gūsum) the three bodies of the Buddha: truth body, the enjoyment body, and the emanation body.

སྐུ་གསེང་ (gūseŋ) time off, spare time (h.) ¶ སྐུ་གསེང་དུ་གླིང་ཀར་ཕེབས་པ་རེད་ During (their) spare time (they) went to the park.

སྐུ་གསོབ་ (gūsob) a stuffed effigy of a deity.

སྐུ་གསོལ་ཞུ་ (gūsöö shu) va. to ask the medium of a deity to go into trance.

སྐུ་བསིལ་ (gū sii) vi. to be cold (h.) ¶ ཁྱེད་རང་མདང་དགོང་སྐུ་བསིལ་མ་བྱུང་ངས་ Weren't you cold last night?

སྐུ་བསིལ་པོ་ (gū siibu) cool, cold (h.) ¶ དགུན་ཁ་བོད་ལ་སྐུ་བསིལ་པོ་ཞེ་དྲག་ཡོད་པ་རེད་ It is very cold in Tibet in winter.

སྐུ་བསོད་ (gūsöò) h. of བསོད་ནམས་.

སྐུ་ལྷ་ (gūlha) a local protective deity.

སྐུ་ལྷོད་ལྷོད་ (gū lhõlöò) h. of ལྷོད་ལྷོད་.

སྐུག :p. བསྐུགས་; f. བསྐུག; imp. སྐུགས་ (gūù) va. to bet/ wager ¶ ཁོང་གིས་རྒྱན་ཆེན་བསྐུགས་པ་རེད་ He made a big wager.

སྐུགས་ (gūù) 1. imp. of སྐུག. 2. stake, bet, wager ¶ མཁར་དབང་སྐུགས་སུ་འཛུགས་རྒྱུ་ To wager all one's possessions.

སྐུགས་འཇོག (gūŋjoò) a game of chance played with dice and a bowl.

སྐུང་ :p. བསྐུངས་; f. བསྐུང་; imp. སྐུངས་ (gūŋ) va. to conceal, to hide ¶ ཁོས་གསེར་རྣམས་ས་འོག་དུ་བསྐུངས་སོང་ He hid the gold under the ground.

སྐུང་འཕྲང་ (gūŋdraŋ) a narrow passage along the face of a mountain overlooking a ravine/ river.

སྐུང་ཟྭ་ (gūŋsa) the inner/ inside lock of a traditional Tibetan door.

སྐུང་ས་ (gūŋsə) sm. སྐུང་འཕྲང་.

སྐུངས་ (gūŋ) imp. of སྐུང་.

སྐུད་ (gũù) thread, wire, string, yarn ¶ སྲིང་སྐུད་ Cotton yarn. ¶ གློག་སྐུད་ Electrical wire.

སྐུད་: p. བསྐུས་; f. བསྐུ་; imp. སྐུས་ (gũù) va. to apply, to put on ¶ རྨ་ལ་སྨན་བསྐུས་པ་རེད་ (He) applied medicine on the sore.

སྐུད་བསྒྲིལ་འཁོར་ལོ་ (gũùdrii kɔ̄ɔlo) winding/ spinning machine (for thread).

སྐུད་རྩན་ (gũùjün) a ball/ bunch of thread.

སྐུད་སྙིགས་ (gũùñii) waste yarn/ thread.

སྐུད་བདུམས་ལྕུགས་སྐུད་ (gũùdum jāggüù) cotton-covered wire.

སྐུད་འཐེན་ཟམ་འཛུགས་ (gũùden samdzug) helping establish a relationship with sb. [Lit. making thread, putting up a bridge].

སྐུད་འཐེན་བཟོ་གྲྭ་ (gũùden sodra) wire/ thread (making) factory.

སྐུད་འདྲིལ་རྩེད་འཁོར་ (gũndrii dzēègɔɔ) a yo-yo; va.—རྩེ་ to play with a yo-yo.

སྐུད་སྡོམ་ (gũùdom) a roll of thread.

སྐུད་ནག (gũùnaà) wrong (political) line/ position ¶ དང་ལ་ངོ་རྒོལ་བྱེད་ཡས་ཀྱི་སྐུད་ནག་དམར་རྗེན་དུ་བཏོན་པ་རེད་ They exposed the wrong line of the opposing party. [Lit. the black line].

སྐུད་སྣེ་ (gũùne) end of a thread. ¶ སྐུད་པ་འཛིངས་པ་དེའི་སྐུད་སྣེ་རྙེད་བྱུང་ (I) found the end of the tangled threads.

སྐུད་སྣེ་ཁབ་ཁྲིད་ (gũùnə kābdrii) easily led by others [Lit. the end of the thread led by the needle].

སྐུད་པ་ (gũba; gūba) thread; va.—རྨིལ; —འཁིལ་; va.—སྲིམ་ to spin/ make thread; va.—བརྒྱུས་; —རྒྱུད་ to thread a needle ¶ ཁབ་དང་སྐུད་པ་ Needle and thread.

སྐུད་པ་རྐྱང་མ་ (gũùba gyāŋma) a single strand/ thread.

སྐུད་པ་སྐམ་ཁང་ (gũùba gāmkaŋ) drying room (for thread/ yarn).

སྐུད་པ་གྲུ་གུ་ (gũùba drugu) a ball of thread.

སྐུད་པ་གློད་ (gũùba lõò) 1. va. to let go of a kite's string. 2. va. to spend a lot of money on sth.

སྐུད་པ་སྒ་རིམ་ (gũùba gərim) sm. སྐུད་པ་སྒ་རིལ་.

སྐུད་པ་སྒ་རིལ་ (gũùba gərii) tib.hind. a spool for thread.

སྐུད་པ་སྒོའི་ལི་ (gũùba gɔɔli) tib.hind. spool for thread.

སྐུད་པ་བརྒྱུས་ (gũùba gyüù) see སྐུད་པ་.

སྐུད་པ་ཉིས་སྲིམས་ (gũùba ñiidrim) two-ply thread.

སྐུད་པ་ཉིས་གཤིབ་ (gũùba ñiishib) sm. སྐུད་པ་ཉིས་སྲིམས་.

སྐུད་པ་དྲུ་གུ་ (gũùba tugu) sm. སྐུད་པ་གྲུ་གུ་.

སྐུད་པ་ལྡོག (gũùba dɔɔ̀) va. to roll thread or string onto sth. such as a stick.

སྐུད་པའི་དོག་པ་ (gũùbe togba) thread or string rolled into a coil (the material is coiled between the hand and the elbow).

སྐུད་པའི་འབུ་ (gũùbe bu) sm. སྐུད་འབུ་.

སྐུད་པོ་ (gũùbu) brother-in-law.

སྐུད་འཕང་ (gūùbaŋ) spindle.

སྐུད་འབུ་ (gūmbu) silkworm.

སྐུད་མེད་ (gūùmeè) wireless.

སྐུད་མེད་ཀུན་ཁྱབ་ལྷུང་འཕྲིན་ (gūùmeè gūngyəb lūŋdrin) wireless radio broadcast; va.—གཏོང་.

སྐུད་མེད་ཁ་པར་ (gūùmeè kābar) wireless phone, cordless phone, cellular phone; va.—གཏོང་; —རྒྱག.

སྐུད་མེད་གློག་གི་རྒྱང་བསྒྲགས་ས་ཚིགས་ (gūùmeè lɔ̄ɔ̀gi gya̲ŋdraà sədzii) radio broadcasting station.

སྐུད་མེད་གློག་གི་སྒྲིག་ཆས་ (gūùmeè lɔ̄ɔ̀gi dri̲gjɛɛ̀) wireless equipment.

སྐུད་མེད་གློག་གི་དངོས་རྫས་མཁོ་སྒྲོད་ས་ཚིགས་ (gūùmeè lɔ̄ɔ̀gi ŋöödzɛɛ̀ kōdröö sədzīì) radio material supply station.

སྐུད་མེད་གློག་གི་དེན་ཙི་རིག་པ་ (gūùmeè lɔ̄ɔ̀gi dēndzi ri̲gpə) tib.ch. radio/ wireless electronics.

སྐུད་མེད་གློག་ཆས་ (gūùmeè lōgjɛɛ̀) radio equipment.

སྐུད་མེད་གློག་ཆས་ཀུང་སི་ (gūùmeè lōgjɛɛ̀ gūŋsi) radio equipment company.

སྐུད་མེད་གློག་ཆས་བཟོ་གྲྭ་ (gūùmeè lōgjɛɛ̀ so̲dra) radio factory.

སྐུད་མེད་གློག་ཆས་ཞིག་གསོ་ཁང་ (gūùmeè lōgjɛɛ̀ shi̲gsogaŋ) radio repair shop.

སྐུད་མེད་གློག་བརྡ་ (gūùmeè lōgda) wireless transmission/ broadcast; va.—གཏོང་ to transmit/ broadcast; va.—ལེན་ to receive a transmission/ broadcast.

སྐུད་མེད་གློག་འཕྲིན་ (gūùmeè lōŋdrin) wireless telegraph/ telegram.

སྐུད་མེད་གློག་འཕྲིན་ཁང་ (gūùmeè lōŋdrin kāŋ) wireless telegraph station.

སྐུད་མེད་གློག་རླབས་ (gūùmeè lōgləp) radio waves.

སྐུད་མེད་རྒྱང་བསྒྲགས་ལས་ཁུངས་ (gūùmeè gya̲ŋdraà lɛ̲ɛ̀guŋ) radio station, wireless broadcasting station.

སྐུད་མེད་སྦྲགས་ཏར་པ་ (gūùmeè dra̲gdarba) tib.hind. wireless operator.

སྐུད་མོ་ (gūùmu) sister-in-law.

སྐུད་ཡོད་གློག་འཕྲིན་ (gūùyöò lōŋdrin) telegraph that uses wires.

སྐུད་ཡོད་རྒྱང་བསྒྲགས་ (gūùyöò gya̲ŋdraà) PA system, loudspeaker (through wires); va.—གཏོང་.

སྐུད་ཡོད་འཕྲིན་སྐྱེལ་ (gūùyöò drīngyee) telegraph/ telephone communication (through wires).

སྐུད་ཡོད་ལྷུང་འཕྲིན་ (gūùyöò lūŋdrin) sm. སྐུད་ཡོད་རྒྱང་བསྒྲགས་.

སྐུད་རོ་ (gūùro) leftover/ excess/ remnant thread; va.—སྒྲུག to pull out old threads when altering sth.; va.—འདྲིག to cut off excess thread after sewing sth.

སྐུད་ལམ་ (gūùləm) telegraph or telephone line.

སྐུན་པོ་ (gūnbo) 1. small cup, shot glass (for whisky, etc.). 2. bowl, basin.

སྐུན་བུ་ (gūnbu) sm. སྐུན་པོ་.

སྐུམ་: p. བསྐུམས་; f. བསྐུམ་; imp. སྐུམས (gūm) 1. va. to draw back, to pull in/ contract (limbs) ¶ ངས་ལག་པ་བཏང་ཡང་ཁོས་ལག་པ་བསྐུམས་སོང་ I went to shake his hand but he pulled his hand back. 2. va. to withhold/ refrain from ¶ ཁོས་གནད་དོན་འདིའི་ཐོག་ལ་སྐད་ཆ་བསྐུམས་སོང་ He refrained from speaking on this matter.

སྐུམ་ཤུགས་ (gūmshuù) the ability to coil and spring forward, elasticity.

སྐུམས་ (gūm) imp. of སྐུམ་.

སྐུའི་བཀོད་པ་བསྡུས་ (gūū gōòba du̲ù) vi. to die (h.) ¶ བླ་ཆེན་འདིའི་སྐུའི་བཀོད་པ་བསྡུས་པ་རེད་ The high lama died.

སྐུའི་ཐིག་ལེ་ (gūū tīgle) semen, sperm. (h.).

སྐུའི་རྣམ་འགྱུར་ (gūū nəmgyur) body appearance/ demeanor (h.) ¶ རྒྱལ་སྲས་ཀྱི་སྐུའི་རྣམ་འགྱུར་ཤིན་ཏུ་ལེགས་པོ་འདུག The prince's demeanor is extremely good.

སྐུའི་འཕྲིན་ལས་ (gūū drīnlɛɛ̀) deeds, actions (h.) ¶ མཁན་པོ་དེ་ཕྱི་རྒྱལ་ལ་ཕེབས་སྐབས་སྐུའི་འཕྲིན་ལས་རྒྱས་པོ་བྱུང་འདུག When the abbot traveled abroad he achieved a great deal.

སྐུའི་ཚིགས་ (gūūdzii) joints of the body (h.).

སྐུའི་ཚུགས་ (gūūdzuù) shape of a body, physique (h.).

སྐུར་: p. བསྐུར་; f. བསྐུར་; imp. སྐུར་ (gūū) 1. va. to send ¶ ངས་ཁོ་ལ་ཡི་གེ་གཅིག་བསྐུར་བ་ཡིན་ I sent him a letter 2. va. to load ¶ དོ་པོ་འདི་ངའི་རྒྱབ་ལ་བསྐུར་རོགས་གནང་ Please load the pack on my back.

སྐུར་མཁན་ (gūrgɛn) person who takes/ delivers letters or things for other people.

སྐུར་གླ་ (gūrla) fee for sending sth.

སྐུར་འདེབས་ (gūndeb) blaspheming, slandering, maligning; va.—ཉུ་; —བྱེད་.

སྐུར་འདེབས་སྒྲོ་འདོགས་ (gūndeb dro̲ndɔɔ̀) slanderous/ defamatory statements.

སྐུར་བ་ (gūrwə) slandering, blaspheming, defaming; va.—འདེབས་ to slander, blaspheme, defame ¶ བླ་མ་ལ་སྐུར་བ་བཏབས་ན་སྡིག་པ་ཡོད་ It is a sin to speak ill of a lama.

སྐུར་མ་ (gūrmə) 1. parcel (for shipping or sending) ¶ ངའི་སྐུར་མ་ཞིག་རྒྱ་གར་ལ་སྐྱོམ་རོགས་གནང་ (Please) take my parcel to India. 2. present, gift.

སྐུར་ཡིག (gūryii) letter (that is sent).

སྐུར་ཡོན་ (gūryön) sm. སྐུར་གླ་.

སྐུལ་: p. བསྐུལ་; f. བསྐུལ་; imp. སྐུལ་ (gūū) 1. va. to persuade, to motivate, to stimulate ¶ མི་རྣམས་ཆོས་ལ་བསྐུལ་བ་རེད་ (They) persuaded the people to become religious. 2. va. to call to act, to appeal to do ¶ ཁོ་ཚོའི་ལས་འགུལ་ལ་རྒྱབ་སྐྱོར་བྱེད་དགོས་པར་བསྐུལ་བ་རེད་ (They) appealed for support for their movement. 3. va. to make/ compel/ order one to act or work ¶ ཁོས་ང་ལ་ལས་ཀ་སྐུལ་གྱི་འདུག He is making me work. 4. (དྲན་གསོ་ + —) va. to remind, to make sb. remember ¶ སང་ཉིན་ང་ལ་དྲན་གསོ་སྐུལ་རོགས་གནང་ Please remind me tomorrow. 5. (ཁྲེལ་བ་ + —) va. to hurry, to hasten ¶ བསམ་བློ་གཏོང་ལོང་མེད་པའི་ཁྲེལ་བ་སྐུལ་གྱི་འདུག (They) are hurrying (me) so much that (I) hardly get a chance to think. 6. (འཇིགས་སྣང་ + —) va. to threaten/ scare/ frighten ¶ འཛམ་གླིང་ཞི་བདེར་འཇིགས་སྣང་ཚབས་ཆེན་བསྐུལ་བ་རེད་ (They) seriously threatened world peace. ¶ ཕྲུ་གུ་ལ་གདོན་འདྲེའི་སྒྲུང་བཤད་ནས་འཇིགས་སྣང་བསྐུལ་བ་རེད་ (They) frightened the children by telling ghost stories.

སྐུལ་ཁྲིད་ (gūūdrii) leadership, direction; va.—བྱེད་ ¶ ཁོང་གི་སྐུལ་ཁྲིད་འོག Under his direction.

སྐུལ་མཁན་ (gūūñɛn) overseer, supervisor, leader.

སྐུལ་རྒྱུ་ (gūūgyu) hormone, hormonal.

སྐུལ་ངན་ (gūūŋɛn) sm. ངན་སྐུལ་.

སྐུལ་མངགས་ (gūūŋaà) instructing, ordering, directing; va.—བྱེད་ ¶ ལས་ཀ་སྐུལ་མངགས་བྱས་པ་རེད་ (He) ordered (them) to work.

སྐུལ་ལྕག (gūūjaà) sm. སྐུལ་མ་.

སྐུལ་གཏམ་ (gūūdam) directive, order; va.—གཏོང་ ¶ འུལ་ལག་སྐུལ་རྒྱུའི་སྐུལ་གཏམ་བཏང་བ་རེད་ (He) ordered them to do corvee labor.

སྐུལ་ཐེབས་ (gūūdeb) vi. to get stimulated/ encouraged.

སྐུལ་བདེ་ (gūūde) easy to order/ push around ¶ ཁོང་སེམས་ཆུང་ཡིན་ཙང་ཚང་མས་སྐུལ་བདེ་བྱེད་ཀྱི་ཡོད་པ་རེད་ Because he is not assertive everyone pushes him around.

སྐུལ་འདེད་ (gūndeè) strongly urging/ encouraging/ inspiring/ motivating; va.—བྱེད་; —གཏོང་ ¶ སྐུལ་འདེད་ཀྱི་ནུས་ཤུགས་ The power of motivation. ¶ ཚོགས་འདུ་དེ་ཚོགས་ནས་ལས་འགུལ་ལ་སྐུལ་འདེད་བྱུང་བ་རེད་ The meeting was convened and the campaign was strongly urged on.

སྐུལ་འདེབས་ (gūndeb) sm. སྐུལ་ལྕག.

སྐུལ་བརྡ་ (gūūda) summoning/ calling/ appealing; va.—གཏོང་; —བྱེད་ ¶ ལས་ཁུངས་ནང་གཙང་སྦྲའི་སྐུལ་བརྡ་བཏང་བ་རེད་ (They) made a call for cleanliness in offices.

སྐུལ་བརྡ་དང་ལེན་ (gũũda ta̲ŋlen) voluntary acceptance of a summons/ appeal/ call; va.—བྱེད་; —ཞུ་ to respond voluntarily/ willingly to a summons/ appeal/ call.

སྐུལ་སྤེལ་ (gũũbel) motivating and spreading/ disseminating/ increasing; va.—གཏོང་ ¶ རྒྱ་ནག་ནང་གསར་བརྗེའི་ལས་འགུལ་སྐུལ་སྤེལ་བཏང་བ་རེད་ (They) urged and disseminated the revolutionary movement in China.

སྐུལ་སྦྱོད་ (gũũjöö) sm. བཀོལ་སྤྱོད་.

སྐུལ་བེད་གང་མཁས་ (gũũbe ga̲ŋgɛɛ̀) shung. using or working in a most appropriate way ¶ བརྡབ་གསིག་གནོད་འགལ་མེད་པ་བ་ལས་འོ་འཇོ་བཞིན་སྐུལ་བེད་གང་མཁས་དགོས་རྒྱུ་ Instead of causing trouble and harming the subjects (you) should make them work in a most appropriate way, just like milking a cow.

སྐུལ་བྱེད་ (gũũjeè) horsewhip.

སྐུལ་བྱེད་ཚིག་གྲུབ་ (gũũjɛɛ̀ tsīgdrub) imperative sentence.

སྐུལ་མ་ (gũũmə) stimulus, encouragement, inspiration, motivation; va.—བྱེད་; —གཏོང་; —འདེབས་ to stimulate, to encourage, to inspire, to motivate, to move; vi.—ཐེབས་ to get stimulated/ encouraged/ inspired/ motivated/ moved ¶ དེ་ནི་ཡོ་ནན་ལྷོ་ཕྱོགས་ཀྱི་མི་དམངས་ལ་སྐུལ་མ་ཧ་ཅང་ཆེན་པོ་གཏོང་བ་ཞིག་ཡིན་ (That) gave great encouragement to the people of South Vietnam.

སྐུལ་ཚིག (gũũtsiì) abbr. སྐུལ་བྱེད་ཚིག་གྲུབ་.

སྐུལ་གཞུང་ (gũũshuŋ) shung. list of corvee work to be done.

སྐུལ་ཟད་ (gũũsɛɛ̀) wear and tear, wearing out due to use; vi.—འགྲོ་ to wear out ¶ སྟོད་ཐུང་འདི་ཐད་དེ་སྐུལ་ཟད་ཐེབས་བཞག The shirt got completely worn out.

སྐུལ་འོད་ (gũũwöö̀) laser beam/ light.

སྐུལ་འོད་ཆུན་པོ་ (gũũwöö̀ cũmbo) laser beam.

སྐུལ་འོད་བརྡ་གཏོང་ (gũũwöö̀ da̲doŋ) laser communication.

སྐུལ་འོད་ནུས་ཚད་ (gũũwöö̀ nṳṳ̀dzɛɛ̀) laser energy.

སྐུལ་འོད་ཕྲ་མཐོང་དཔྱད་ཆས་ (gũũöö̀ trādoŋ jɛ̄cɛɛ̀) laser microscope.

སྐུལ་འོད་འདར་གཡོ་ཆས་ (gũũöö̀ da̲ryojɛɛ̀) laser oscillator.

སྐུལ་འོད་ཚན་རིག (gũũwöö̀ tsɛ̄nriì) laser science.

སྐུལ་ཡིག (gũũyiì) shung. a written order/ command ¶ ཆང་དང་འདུལ་ཁྲིམས་སྐོར་ཛ་ཛོང་ལྷན་རྒྱས་ནས་སྐུལ་ཡིག་འཐུས་ནན་བསྒྲུལ་བ་ Regarding drinking beer and monk's vows, the dzasa (a tt. official) and the district commissioner issued a stern written order.

སྐུལ་སློང་ (gũũloŋ) mobilization, mobilizing; va.—བྱེད་ ¶ མང་ཚོགས་སྐུལ་སློང་བྱས་ནས་ལག་ཤེས་བཟོ་ལས་སྣ་ཚོགས་ཚ་འཛུགས་བྱས་པ་རེད་ (They) mobilized the masses and organized various handicraft industries. ¶ སྐུལ་སློང་གི་བཀའ་ A mobilization order. ¶ སྐུལ་སློང་ཚོགས་འདུ་ A mobilization meeting.

སྐུས་ (gũù) imp. of སྐུད་.

སྐེ་ (gē) neck, throat.

སྐེ་ཀྱོག་ཀྱོག (gē gyōggyoò) crooked neck.

སྐེ་གྲོང་གྲོང་ (gē drōŋdroŋ) a straight/ erect neck (for humans and animals when they are on the lookout or when they are alert); va.—བལྟ་ to look with a straight/ erect neck.

སྐེ་དཀྲིས་ (gēdriì) scarf.

སྐེ་བཀག (gēgaà) strangling; va.—གཏོང་ ¶ རྒྱལ་སྲས་སྐེ་བཀག་བཏང་ནས་བསད་པ་རེད་ (They) killed the prince by strangling.

སྐེ་ཁྲིར་ནས་ཞགས་པ་ཉོས་ (gē kyērnɛ sha̲gba ñö̲ö̀) sm. སྐེ་ཁྲིར་ཞགས་འཛོད་.

སྐེ་ཁྲིར་ཞགས་ཉོས་ (gēgyer sha̲gñöö̀) sm. སྐེ་ཁྲིར་ཞགས་འཛོད་.

སྐེ་ཁྲིར་ཞགས་འཛོད་ (gēgyer sha̲gdzeè) creating one's own troubles, inviting trouble [Lit. putting one's neck in a noose].

སྐེ་འཁོར་ (gēgɔɔ) 1. collar; va.—འདོགས་ to put on a collar (usu. for dogs). 2. the brocade collars worn by villagers. 3. necklace; va.—འདོགས་ to wear a necklace.

སྐེ་འཁྲིར་ཞགས་ཉོ་ (gēgyer sha̲gño) sm. སྐེ་ཁྲིར་ཞགས་འཛོད་.

སྐེ་གུ་ (gēgu) an ornament worn around the neck that sits on the chest.

སྐེ་འགག (gēŋgaà) throat disease (of animals).

སྐེ་རྒྱན་ (gēgyɛn) 1. necklace; va.—འདོགས་ to wear a necklace. 2. brocade collar worn by villagers.

སྐེ་རྒྱན་གདུ་བུ་ (gēgyɛn du̲bu) necklace.

སྐེ་བརྒྱན་ (gēgyɛn) sm. སྐེ་རྒྱན་.

སྐེ་སྒོ་ (gēgo) vagina; va.—འགོག to use birth control; va.—གཅོད་ to sterilize a woman.

སྐེ་སྐོར་ (gēgɔɔ) sm. སྐེ་འཁོར་.

སྐེ་གཅོད་ (gē jöö̀) va. to behead.

སྐེ་གཅོད་སྡེགས་བུ་ (gējöö̀ dēgbu) the guillotine.

སྐེ་གཅོད་སྣུམ་གཏིག (gējöö̀ nūmdiì) interrogating through torture and threat [Lit. beheading and squeezing the oil (out of a person's body)].

སྐེ་བཅད་ (gē jɛɛ̀) p. of སྐེ་གཅོད་.

སྐེ་བཅད་ན་འོ་མ་ཡིན་ (gējɛɛ̀na o̲ma yi̲n) being innocent [Lit. when the head is cut off it is milk (that comes out instead of blood)].

སྐེ་བཅད་ནས་ཨོག་མར་བྱིལ་བྱིལ་ (gējɛɛ̀nɛ ōgmar ci̲i̲jii) very proud (even in defeat) [Lit. stroking the chin after the neck is cut off].

སྐེ་ཁྲབ་ཞུབས་ (gējib) an armor plate worn around the neck; va.—འདོགས་ to wear armor plate around the neck.

སྐེ་ཆ་ (gēja) sm. སྐེ་རྒྱན་.

སྐེ་ཆས་ (gējɛɛ̀) sm. སྐེ་རྒྱན་.

སྐེ་ཆིངས་ (gējiŋ) necktie; va.—འདོགས་ to wear a necktie.

སྐེ་འཆུས་ (gē cũù) vi. to strain (one's) neck.

སྐེ་མཇིང་ (gējiŋ) front and back of the neck.

སྐེ་སྙིང་སྙིང་ (gē ñeŋñeŋ) stretching one's neck to look at sth.; va.—བྱེད་.

སྐེ་སྟོང་ (gēdoŋ) space below the Adam's apple where the clavicle bones meet.

སྐེ་ཐག (gēdag) a rope that is tied around an animal's neck; va.—རྒྱག; —འདོགས་ to tie a rope around an animal's neck.

སྐེ་ཐག་བསྡམས་ཏེ་དཔྱང་ (gēdaà da̲mde jāŋ) sm. སྐེ་བསྡམས་སྲོག་གཅོད་.

སྐེ་ཐིག (gēdig) sm. སྐེ་ཐག.

སྐེ་དར་ (gēdar) scarf ¶ སྐེ་དར་དམར་པོ་ Red scarf (worn by the Young Pioneers).

སྐེ་འདོགས་ (gēdɔɔ̀) 1. neck ornament for animals. 2. sm. སྐེ་སྡོམ་.

སྐེ་འདོད་ནས་ལྦ་བ་མི་འདོད་ (gē dö̲önɛ ba̲a̲ mi̲döö̀) wanting only the good without its associated problems [Lit. wanting the neck but not the goiter].

སྐེ་སྡེམ་ (gē da̲m) sm. སྐེ་སྡོམ་.

སྐེ་སྡོམ་ (gē do̲m) va. to strangle, to hang.

སྐེ་བསྡམས་ (gē da̲m) p. of སྐེ་སྡོམ་.

སྐེ་བསྡམས་སྲོག་གཅོད་ (gēdam sɔ̄gjöö̀) executing by hanging/ strangling, strangling to death.

སྐེ་ཕྲུག (gēdruù) a bead necklace.

སྐེ་འཕྲུག (gēndrug) sm. སྐེ་ཕྲུག.

སྐེ་ཕྲེང་ (gēdreŋ) sm. སྐེ་འཕྲེང་.

སྐེ་འཕྲེང་ (gēdreŋ) a small necklace.

སྐེ་བལ་ (gēbɛɛ) wool from the neck of sheep.

སྐེ་འབྱར་ (gēnjar) carcass of a sheep with the head still attached. 2. a person with a short neck.

སྐེ་འབྲེག (gē drēè) va. to behead.

སྐེ་འབྲེལ་ (gēndrel) sm. སྐེ་སྦྲེལ་.

སྐེ་ལྦ་ (gēba) goiter, thyroid gland.

སྐེ་སྦྲེལ་ (gēdrel) tying neck to neck; va.—གཏོང་ ¶ ཞིང་ཁ་རྨོ་དུས་གཡག་གཉིས་སྐེ་སྦྲེལ་གཏོང་དགོས་ When plowing (with yaks) one has to tie two yaks neck-to-neck.

སྐེ་མིག་འབེན་འཛུགས་ (gēmig be̲ndzuù) shung. swearing upon one's life ༈ འཁྲུག་འཛིང་གཏན་ནས་མི་ཞུ་བའི་ཕྱི་ཁག་ནང་ཁག་དང་འབྲེལ་སྐེ་མིག་འབེན་བཙུགས་ཀྱིས་དགོངས་དྲངས་ཡོང་བ་ཞུ་རྒྱུ་ We swear upon our lives not to fight again and apologize for our past deeds.

སྐེ་མ་ (gēma) sores around the neck.

སྐེ་སྨིན་ (gēmen) scrofula.

སྐེ་སྨྱུང་སྨྱུང་ (gē ñaŋñaŋ) sm. སྐེ་སྙིང་སྙིང་.

སྐེ་བཙིར་ (gē dzīr) strangling; va.—གཏོང་.

སྐེ་བཙིར་སྲོག་གཅོད་ (gē dzīr sōgjöö) strangling to death (usu. with hands); va.—གཏོང་.

སྐེ་རྩོང་ (gēdzoŋ) 1. sm. སྐེ་ཀྲོང་ཀྲོང་. 2. a skinny person.

སྐེ་ཚིགས་ (gēdzii̇) neck joint; vi.—འཆུས་ to sprain (one's) neck.

སྐེ་ཚེ་ (gēdze) a type of Tibetan herbal medicine.

སྐེ་མཚམས་བར་ (gēndzam) 1. leaving to the last moment; va.—འཇོག to leave until the last moment ༈ ལས་ཀ་སྐེ་མཚམས་བར་འཇོག་རྒྱུ་མེད་ You shouldn't leave doing your work until the last moment. 2. filling sth. up to the brim. ༈ ཨ་རག་ཤེལ་དམ་གྱི་སྐེ་མཚམས་བར་བླུགས་བཞག (They) filled the bottle right up to the brim with liquor.

སྐེ་འཚེར་ཐག་པ་ (gēdzir tāgba) hangman's rope/ noose.

སྐེ་ཡན་ (ཆད་) གྱི་མཛའ་བཤེས་ (gēyɛn (cɛ̄ɛ̀) gi dza̲sheè) superficial/ artificial friendship.

སྐེ་ཡོན་ (gēyön) sm. སྐེ་ཀྱག་ཀྱག.

སྐེ་རགས་ (gēraà) sm. སྐེད་རགས་.

སྐེ་རགས་ལས་སྣེ་འཛར་རིང་བ་ (gēraàlɛ nēdzar ri̲ŋwa) a subordinate out doing or overtaking the master [Lit. the frill/ fringe/ tassel of the belt is longer than the belt itself].

སྐེ་རགས་གསེར་ཁེབ་ (gēraà sērgeb) shung. a type of belt used on ceremonial dresses worn by the ཡ་སོར་ཁྲི་པ་ (the head of those dressed as ancient troops during Monlam).

སྐེ་རས་ (gērɛɛ̀) scarf; va.—དཀྲི་ to wear a scarf.

སྐེ་རིང་ (gēriŋ) a long/ slender neck ༈ སྐེ་རིང་ལྟོ་ཕྱིར་གྱི་བུམ་པ་ A vase with a long, slender neck and a bulging base.

སྐེ་ཤིང་ (gēshiŋ) yoke.

སྐེག (gēg) sm. སྐྱེག.

སྐེག་ཚོས་ (gēgdzöö) cosmetics (such as rouge, powder).

སྐེགས་ (gēg) a type of bird.

སྐེད་ (gēè) 1. abbr. of སྐེད་པ་. 2. just at the time of ༈ ཞིང་འཁྲུགས་ཀྱི་སྐེད་དེར་ Just at the time of the disturbance. 3. abbr. of སྐེད་པ་, 1.

སྐེད་དཀྲིས་ (gēèdrii̇) 1. attached/ fastened to the waist. 2. a cloth/ skin that is wrapped around the waist to provide warmth and support; va.—དཀྲི་.

སྐེད་སྐབས་ (gēēgəb) sm. སྐེད་པ་, 2.

སྐེད་འཁྱོག (gēègyog) 1. crooked waist. 2. the Big Dipper.

སྐེད་གྲི་ (gēèdri) a knife worn on the waist; va.—འདོགས་ to fasten a knife one the waist/ belt.

སྐེད་རྒྱན་ (gēègyɛn) ornament worn on the waist; va.—འདོགས་ to wear a waist ornament.

སྐེད་སྒྲེང་སུག་འཛུགས་ (gēèdreŋ sūgdzuù) trying to regain one's footing, standing up after falling or being knocked down.

སྐེད་ང་ (gēèŋa) a drum that is tied on the waist when played; va.—འདོགས་ to wear/ attach a waist drum.

སྐེད་བཅད་ (gēèjɛɛ̀) 1. cutting from the middle; va.—གཏོང་. 2. crossing a river widthwise.

སྐེད་འཆིང་ (gēèjiŋ) belt; va.—རྒྱག to wear/ put on a belt. 2. hat band.

སྐེད་འཆིང་ཁུག་མ་ (gēèjiŋ kūgmə) purse/ bag tied to the waist or belt.

སྐེད་ཉག (gēñaà) sm. སྐེད་པ་ཉག་ཉག.

སྐེད་ཉག་དོག་བརྡེག (gēñag do̲gdzii̇) kicking sb. when they are down; va.—གཏོང་ [Lit. stomping on sb.'s waist].

སྐེད་གཏུབ་ (gēèdub) splitting/ cutting crosswise; va.—གཏོང་ ༈ པང་ལེབ་དེ་སྐེད་གཏུབ་བཏང་བཞག (They) have cut the plank crosswise.

སྐེད་ད་ (gēèda) sm. སྐེད་པ་.

སྐེད་ནད་ (gēènɛɛ̀) disease/ pain in the waist.

སྐེད་པ་ (gēèba) 1. waist ༈ སྐེད་པ་ཕྲ་པོ་ Thin (slim) waist. 2. the middle ༈ རི་འདིའི་སྐེད་པར་བྲག་ཕུག་ཅིག་ཡོད་པ་རེད་ There is a cave in the middle of the mountain. 3. menstruation, menstruating; va.—རྒྱག; to menstruate; vi.—ཆད་ to stop menstruating.

སྐེད་པ་ཀྱག་ཀྱག (gēèba gyōggyoò) crooked waist.

སྐེད་པ་འཆུས་ (gēèba cūū) vi. to sprain one's back.

སྐེད་པ་ཉག་ཉག (gēèba ña̲gñaà) a hour glass shape.

སྐེད་པ་མཉེན་པོ་ (gēèba ñēmbo) agile, nimble, flexible (waist).

སྐེད་པར་གཟེར་ (gēèbar se̲r) va. to wear sth. in one's waist band/ belt (e.g., a sword or gun).

སྐེད་ཕྲ་མ་ (gēè trāma) poet. a beautiful woman.

སྐེད་ཚིགས་ (gēèdzii̇) waist/ pelvic joints.

སྐེད་མཚམས་ (gēndzam) halfway, middle ༈ ཁྲོན་པའི་སྐེད་མཚམས་ན་ Halfway down the well.

སྐེད་གཟེར་ (gēèser) putting one's hands on one's hips; va.—བྱེད་.

སྐེད་རགས་ (gēraà) belt; va.—འཆིང་ to wear/ tie a belt.

སྐེད་རགས་རྒྱ་མ་ (gēraà gya̲ma) a hand pleated or woven belt.

སྐེད་རགས་ལྷས་མ་ (gēraà lhɛ̄ɛ̀ma) sm. སྐེད་རགས་རྒྱ་མ་.

སྐེད་ལུང་ (gēèluŋ) handle (of sth. like a suitcase).

སྐེད་སོ་ (gēèso) waistline, at the waist.

སྐེམ་: p. བསྐམས་; f. བསྐམ་; imp. སྐོམས་ (gēm) 1. va. to dry ༈ མོས་གོས་ལོག་རྣམས་ཉི་མར་བསྐམས་སོང་ She dried the clothes in the sun. 2. vi. to lose weight, to become thin ༈ ཁོ་ན་ནས་ཞི་དྲག་བསྐམས་འདུག He lost a lot of weight after he got sick.

སྐེམ་སྐམ་ (gēmgam) a dryer (for clothes).

སྐེམ་ནད་ (gēmnɛɛ̀) consumption, tuberculosis.

སྐེམ་པོ་ (gēmbo) sm. སྐམ་པོ་.

སྐེམ་བྱེད་ (gēmjeè) drying, for drying.

སྐེམ་བྱེད་མ་ (gēmjeèma) a kind of malevolent spirit that causes drought.

སྐེམ་རིད་ (gēmrii̇) thin.

སྐེའི་གའུ་ (gēē ka̲wu) a གའུ་ worn around the neck.

སྐེའི་འཕྲེང་བ་ (gēē trēŋwa) sm. སྐེ་ཕྲེང་.

སྐོ་: p. བསྐོས་; f. བསྐོ་; imp. སྐོས་ (gō) va. to appoint, to select ༈ ཁོང་མདའ་དཔོན་བསྐོས་པ་རེད་ (They) appointed him general. 2. vi. to cause ༈ ཚེ་འདིར་དབུལ་པོར་གྱུར་པ་དེ་ཚེ་སྔོན་ལས་ཀྱིས་བསྐོས་པ་རེད་ Being poor in this life is caused by the karma of (my) previous life.

སྐོ་སྐོ་ (gogo) chin.

སྐོ་ཙེ་ (gōdze) an inferior quality tea.

སྐོག (gɔ̄ɔ̀) sm. སྐོགས་, 1.

སྐོགས་ (gɔ̄ɔ̀) 1. shell, bark, peel; va.—བཤུ་ to skin, to peel off. 2. sth. that envelopes or wraps sth. else ༈ ཡིག་སྐོགས་ An envelope.

སྐོགས་སྐྱི་ (gōggyi) dandruff; vi.—ཡོང་; —རྒྱག to have/ get dandruff.

སྐོགས་ཁ་སྦྱར་ (gɔ̄ɔ̀ kā ja̲r) va. to close/ seal an envelope.

སྐོགས་རྒྱག (gɔ̄ɔ̀ gya̲à) va. to put a letter in an envelope.

སྐོགས་ཅན་འབུ་ (gōgjɛn bu̲) beetle.

སྐོགས་ཕྱགས་ (gōgbaà) 1. the residue left on a utensil after sth. has been boiled in it. 2. sm. སྐོགས་, 1. 3. shell of animals.

སྐོགས་བུ་ (gōgbu) sm. སྐོགས་ཤུན་.

སྐོགས་རོ་ (gōgro) leftover scraps of butter in a leather container of butter.

སྐོགས་ཤུན་ (gōgshun) dandruff. 2. sm. སྐོགས་ཕྱགས་, 2 and 3.

སྐོགས་ཤོག (gōgshɔɔ̀) envelope.

སྐོགས་བཤུས་ (gōg shǖū) va. to peel off skin.

སྐོང་: p. བསྐངས་; f. བསྐང་; imp. སྐོངས་ (gōŋ) va. 1. to fulfill, to fill ། མི་དམངས་ཀྱི་རེ་བ་སྐོང་ཆེད་ཁོ་ཚོས་འབད་འཐབ་བྱས་ཡོད་པ་རེད་ (They) struggled to fulfill the hopes of the people. 2. va. to make up a deficiency ། ལོ་འདིའི་སྔོན་རྩིས་ཀྱིས་དངུལ་འབབས་ཆད་པ་དེ་ཁ་བསྐངས་པ་རེད་ (They) made up the deficiency from this year's budget. 3. sm. ཁ་སྐོང་.

སྐོང་: p. བསྐོངས་; f. བསྐོང་; imp. སྐོངས་ (gōŋ) va. to summon, to call up, to convene ། ཚོགས་འདུ་དེར་ས་གནས་མང་པོ་ནས་འཐུས་མི་བསྐོངས་ཡོད་པ་རེད་ (They) have summoned representatives from many regions to that meeting.

སྐོང་འཁྲབ་ (gōŋdrəb) gathering performers from various regions or localities for a joint performance; va.—བྱེད་.

སྐོང་འགུག་ (gōŋguù) sm. བསྐོང་འགུག.

སྐོང་སྒྲིག་ (gōŋdrig) recruiting and dispatching; va.—བྱེད་.

སྐོང་འཐེན་ (gōŋten) recalling a worker/ official from one place or office and transferring him to another; va.—བྱེད་ ། ད་ལོ་ལས་ཁངས་གསར་པ་འགོ་ཚུགས་སྐབས་ལས་ཁུངས་མང་པོ་ནས་ལས་བྱེད་པ་སྐོང་འཐེན་བྱས་པ་རེད་ When the new offices were opened this year, they recalled and transferred officials from many offices.

སྐོང་དུ་དིབ་ (gōŋdu dib) sm. ཀོང་ཀོང་ཆགས.

སྐོང་བསྡུ་ (gōŋdu) recruiting, collecting, enrolling; va.—བྱེད་ ། གྲོང་གསེབ་ནས་དམག་མི་སྐོང་བསྡུ་བྱེད་པ་རེད་ They recruited soldiers from the villages.

སྐོང་འབྲི་ (gōŋdri) filling in forms; va.—བྱེད་.

སྐོང་ཚིག་ (gōŋdzig) the complement (in grammar).

སྐོང་ཚོགས་ (gōŋdzɔ̀ɔ) sm. སྐོང་འཚོག.

སྐོང་འཚོག་ (ས་) (gōŋdzɔ̀ɔ) summoning/ convoking/ convening a meeting; —བྱེད་ ། བོད་ལྗོངས་ཚོགས་འདུ་སྐོང་འཚོག་བྱས་པ་རེད་ (They) convened the Tibetan Assembly.

སྐོང་ཞགས་ (gōŋshaà) fishing net.

སྐོང་བཤེར་ (gōŋsher) summoning/ recruiting and inspecting/ checking out; va.—བྱེད་ ། དམག་མི་གསར་པ་ཁག་ཅིག་སྐོང་བཤེར་བྱས་འདུག They recruited (summoned) a new batch of soldiers and then inspected them.

སྐོང་གསབ་ (gōŋsəb) providing, deploying, outfitting; va.—བྱེད་.

སྐོངས་ (gōŋ) imp. of སྐོང་.

སྐོན་: p. and f. བསྐོན་; imp. སྐོན་ (gōn) 1. va. to dress (sb.), to put clothes (on sb.) ། ཨ་མས་ཕྲུ་གུར་གོས་ལོག་སྐོན་གྱི་འདུག The mother is dressing the child. 2. va. to hang up, to hook on ། ལྕུགས་ཀྱུ་དེ་ཨ་ལོང་ལ་སྐོན་ནས་འཐེན་སྐབས་ When the hook was hung on the ring and pulled. 3. see གོ་སྐོན་སློབ་གསོ་. 4. sm. གོན་.

སྐོན་བུ་ (gōmbu) 1. small cup. 2. a trap, a net; va.—རྒྱག་ to trap. 3. small woven bamboo utensils.

སྐོབས་ (gōb) arc. 1. dilemma, quandary ། ཁོང་ཚོང་ལས་ཀྱི་སྐོབས་སུ་ཚུད་པ་རེད་ He got into a quandary in (his) business. 2. a ditch, pothole.

སྐོམ་: p. སྐོམས་; f. སྐོམ་ (gōm) (usu. ཁ་ + —) vi. to be thirsty ། ང་ཁ་སྐོམ་གྱི་འདུག I am thirsty.

སྐོམ་སྐྱུར་ (gōmgyur) sour drinks that quench thirst.

སྐོམ་ཆང་ (gōmjaŋ) barley beer.

སྐོམ་སྙོགས་ (gōmñeg) thirst, thirsty.

སྐོམ་དད་ (gōmdɛɛ) thirst, thirsty ། སྐོམ་དད་ཆེ་བ་ Great thirst.

སྐོམ་དྲི་ (gōmdri) the smell of a beverage; va.—ཁ་ to smell drinks/ beverages.

སྐོམ་གདུང་ (gōmduŋ) suffering thirst.

སྐོམ་ལྡུད་ (gōm düü) va. to give/ offer a drink ། ཁོང་གིས་ནད་པར་སྐོམ་ལྡུད་པ་རེད་ He gave a drink to the patient.

སྐོམ་པ་ (gōmba) thirst; vi.—སེལ་; —བསངས་ to be/ get quenched (thirst). 2. a thirsty person.

སྐོམ་པ་ཆུ་འདོད་ (gōmba cūndöö) having great desire for sth. [Lit. like a thirsty person craving for water].

སྐོམ་པ་ཆུ་འདོད་འདྲ་ (gōmba cūndöödra) sm. སྐོམ་པ་ཆུ་འདོད་.

སྐོམ་པ་ཆུ་ཡིས་གདུང་འདྲ་ (gōmba cūyii dundra) sm. སྐོམ་པ་ཆུ་འདོད་.

སྐོམ་པས་ཆུ་དང་ལྟོགས་པས་ཟས་འདོད་ (gōmbɛ cūdaŋ dɔ̄gbɛ sɛ̀ɛndöö) sm. སྐོམ་པ་ཆུ་འདོད་.

སྐོམ་པོ་ (gōmbo) thirsty.

སྐོམ་ཤ་ (gōmsha) beef.

སྐོམ་ཤི་ (gōmshi) dying of thirst; vi.—ཐེབས་ to die of thirst.

སྐོམ་གསོས་ (gōmsöö) sth. to quench thirst.

སྐོམས་ (gōm) imp. of སྐེམ་.

སྐོར་: p. and f. བསྐོར་; imp. སྐོར་ (gɔ̄r) 1. va. to turn around, to rotate ། དེ་སྔ་འཁོར་ལོ་དེ་ཚོ་ལག་པས་སྐོར་དགོས་ཀྱི་ཡོད་པ་རེད་ In the old days these wheels had to be turned by hand. 2. va. to surround, to encircle ། མཐའ་ནས་ཤིན་ཏུ་མཐོ་བའི་རི་རྒྱུད་ཀྱིས་བསྐོར་ཡོད་ From the outside it is surrounded by extremely high mountains. 3. va. to make a detour ། ལམ་བཟོ་བྱེད་སྐབས་ལམ་ཁ་བསྐོར་ནས་བསྐྱོད་པ་རེད་ During the road construction (they) had to detour. 4. va. to make a circuit, to make rounds.

སྐོར་ (gɔ̄r) 1. about, concerning, regarding ། ཆིངས་ཡིག་བཞག་པའི་སྐོར་ Concerning the signing of the treaty ། ཆོས་སྲིད་སྐོར་ལ་ About religion and politics. 2. approximately, around, about ། མི་དམངས་བརྒྱ་ཆ་60% སྐོར་གྱིས་ By about 60% of the people. 3. area, region ། མངའ་རིས་སྐོར་གསུམ་ The three regions of མངའ་རིས་. 4. vicinity, proximity, nearby, around ། ཁང་པའི་ཉེ་སྐོར་ལ་མེ་ཏོག་བཏབ་པ་རེད་ (He) planted flowers in the vicinity of the house. 5. the amount/ number of times greater ། འདི་ལོའི་སྟོན་ཐོག་བརྒྱད་སྐོར་བྱུང་བཞག This year's crop yield is eight times the amount (of seed planted). 6. va. to go around the marketplace in search of sth. ། ཅ་ལག་ཁྲོམ་ག་ས་ག་སར་བསྐོར་ཀྱང་རག་མ་བྱུང་ Even though I went around searching all over the marketplace for the goods, I didn't obtain them.

སྐོར་ཀྱུག (gɔ̄rgyoò) 1. crooked, zigzag. ། ལམ་སྐོར་ཀྱུག A crooked road. 2. beating about the bush, not coming to the point, not being straight to the point ། མི་དེས་སྐད་ཆ་སྐོར་ཀྱུག་ཤོད་ཀྱི་འདུག This person beats around the bush when he talks.

སྐོར་སྐད་པ་ (gɔ̄r gèèba) shung. a group of people whose work is to pray loudly while circumambulating the Bakor all night during the Great Prayer Festival (Monlam) in Lhasa.

སྐོར་སྐོར་བྱེད་ (gɔ̄rgɔɔ ceè) va. to go around to many shops looking to find cheaper prices.

སྐོར་སྐྱིལ་ (gɔ̄rgyii) surrounding and blocking/ cutting off/ containing; va.—བྱེད་ ། རང་དམག་གིས་དགྲ་བོའི་དམག་མི་ནགས་གསེབ་ཏུ་སྐོར་སྐྱིལ་བྱས་འདུག Our soldiers surrounded and contained the enemy soldiers in the forest.

སྐོར་སྐྱིལ་འདེམས་སྒམ་ (gɔ̄rgyee demgam) mobile ballot box.

སྐོར་སྐྱོད་ (gɔ̄rgyöö) sm. སྐོར་བསྐྱོད་.

སྐོར་བསྐྱོད་ (gɔ̄rgyöö) moving around from place to place, mobile, circuit ། སྐོར་བསྐྱོད་སྨན་བཅོས་རུ་ཁག A mobile medical unit.

སྐོར་བསྐྱོད་འཁྲབ་སྟོན་ (gɔ̄rgyöö trəbdün) traveling around to perform shows.

སྐོར་བསྐྱོད་འཁྲབ་སྟོན་རུ་ཁག (gɔ̄rgyöö trəbdün rugaà) a mobile unit/ troupe that perform shows.

སྐོར་བསྐྱོད་གློག་བརྙན་སྟོན་མཁན་རུ་ཁག (gɔ̄rköö gɔ̄ɔ̀ñɛn dõŋgɛn rugaà) a traveling unit that shows movies to villagers.

སྐོར་བསྐྱོད་མ་དངུལ་ (gɔ̄rgyöö mənüü) circulating fund.

སྐོར་བསྐྱོད་དམག་འཐབ་ (gɔ̄rgyöö māgdəb) mobile warfare.

སྐོར་བསྐྱོད་སྨན་བཅོས་ (gɔ̄rgyöö mɛ̄njöö) mobile medical service.

སྐོར་བསྐྱོད་སྨན་བཅོས་རུ་ཁག (gɔ̄rgyöö̀ mɛ̄njöö̀ rugaà) mobile medical team.

སྐོར་བསྐྱོད་སོ་པ་ (gɔ̄rgyöö̀ sōba) person on patrol duty.

སྐོར་ཁང་ (gɔ̄rgaŋ) a place/ temple that houses prayer wheels.

སྐོར་མཁན་ (gɔ̄rgɛn) sb. who goes on patrol.

སྐོར་འགོ་ (gɔ̄ŋgo) 1. a chapter or section. 2. a basic number in calculating (in math).

སྐོར་གོལ་ (gɔ̄rgöö) sm. སྐོར་བཅོམ་.

སྐོར་རྒྱག་ཉ་དྲ་ (gɔ̄rgyaà ñadra) purse seine.

སྐོར་རྒྱུག (gɔ̄rgyuù) 1. roaming, running around, going around in circles; va.—བྱེད་ ¶ སྐོར་རྒྱུག་མ་བྱེད་ Don't run around all over the place. 2. beating around the bush.

སྐོར་རྒྱུགས་ (gɔ̄rgyuù) sm. སྐོར་རྒྱུག.

སྐོར་བརྒྱ་གསོག (gɔ̄rgya sɔ̄ɔ̀) va. to circumambulate a religious site a hundred times.

སྐོར་གཅིག (gɔ̄rjig) sm. ཁག་ཅིག.

སྐོར་བཅོམ་ (gɔ̄rjom) encirclement and attack, surrounding and attacking, laying siege to, besieging; va.—བྱེད་.

སྐོར་ལྕག་པ་ (gɔ̄ɔ̄jagba) sm.* སྐོར་འཆག་པ་.

སྐོར་ཆས་ཀང་གཉིས་མ་ (gɔ̄rjɛɛ̀ gāŋñiìmə) sm. ཀང་གཉིས་ཐིག་སྐྱུད་.

སྐོར་ཆུང་ (gɔ̄ɔ̄juŋ) 1. a small circle; vi.—རྒྱག to turn around in a small circle. 2. revolving on one's axis. (e.g., the earth); vi.—རྒྱག.

སྐོར་ཆེན་ (gɔ̄rjen) 1. a large circle; vi.—རྒྱག. 2. (for earth) revolving around the sun; vi.—རྒྱག.

སྐོར་འཆག་པ་ (gɔ̄ɔ̄jagba) shung. a low level worker in Lhasa in tt. who patrolled the streets and delivered messages/ notices for the office of the mayor of Lhasa.

སྐོར་འཆག་དམག (gɔ̄ɔ̄jagmaà) police force.

སྐོར་འཆམ་ (gɔ̄njam) going around to different places; va.—བྱེད་; — + verbs of motion.

སྐོར་གཏམ་ (gɔ̄ɔ̄dam) beating around the bush in speech; va.—ཤོད་; va.—རྒྱག ¶ སྐོར་གཏམ་མ་བཤད་པར་སྐད་ཆ་ཁ་ཐུག་ཤོད་དགོས་ You must talk straight and not beat around the bush.

སྐོར་གཏུག (gɔ̄ɔ̄duù) encirclement; va.—བྱེད་.

སྐོར་གཏོར་ (gɔ̄ɔ̄dɔr) 1. sm. སྐོར་བཅོམ་. 2. breaking an encirclement; va.—བྱེད་ to break through (an encirclement) 2. encircling and annihilating; va.—བྱེད་ to encircle and annihilate.

སྐོར་རྟགས་ (gɔ̄ɔ̄daà) sm. སྐོར་རྟགས་.

སྐོར་ལྟ་ (gɔ̄ɔ̄da) making an inspection.

སྐོར་ཐག (gɔ̄ɔ̄daà) 1. circumference ¶ འཛམ་གླིང་གི་སྐོར་ཐག The circumference of the earth. 2. distance of a detour. ¶ ལམ་ཁ་འདིར་ཕྱིན་ན་སྐོར་ཐག་རིང་པོ་ཞེ་དྲག་ཡོད་པ་རེད་ If (one) takes this road, the distance of the detour is very long.

སྐོར་ཐང་ (gɔ̄rdaŋ) shung. 1. exchange rate ¶ དེང་སང་ཚྭ་དང་འབྲུའི་སྐོར་ཐང་ག་ཚོད་རེད་འདུག་གམ་ These days what is the rate of exchange between salt and barley? 2. sm. སྐོར་, 5.

སྐོར་ཐབ་ (gɔ̄rdəb) open-hearth furnace, Bessemer (converter).

སྐོར་ཐབས་ (gɔ̄ɔ̄dəb) shung. exchanging/ bartering things ¶ བྱང་ཐོད་ཚྭ་ལེན་སྐོར་ཐབས་སོགས་གཤོག་ཆེའི་ཚོང་ཐབས་མེད་པར་ (They) don't have the means to go to the north and trade for salt.

སྐོར་ཐིག (gɔ̄ɔ̄dii) a compass (for drawing circles).

སྐོར་ཐེངས་ (gɔ̄ɔ̄deŋ) number of times sth. or sb. circles/ turns ¶ སའི་གོ་ལས་ལོ་གཅིག་གི་ནང་ཉི་མར་སྐོར་ཐེངས་གཅིག་འཁོར་གྱི་ཡོད་པ་རེད་ The earth circles the sun once a year.

སྐོར་ཐོ་ (gɔ̄rdo) shung. a report of an inspection.

སྐོར་འདེད་བཀག་བཅད་ (gɔ̄ɔ̄deè gāgjɛɛ̀) chasing and cutting off, intercepting, pursuing and surrounding; va.—བྱེད་.

སྐོར་འདྲི་ (gɔ̄ndri) interrogating or questioning in a roundabout manner; va.—བྱེད་.

སྐོར་རྡུང་ (gɔ̄ɔ̄duŋ) an encirclement attack, encircling and attacking ¶ ཇག་པ་རྣམས་ལ་སྙིང་རྗེ་མེད་པའི་སྐོར་རྡུང་བཏང་བ་རེད་ (They) encircled and attacked the bandits in a merciless manner; va.—གཏོང་.

སྐོར་ལྡན་ཀུབ་བཀྱག (gɔ̄rdɛn gūbgya) a chair that swivels on wheels.

སྐོར་ནས་ (gɔ̄ɔ̄nɛɛ̀) 1. from the point of view of, regarding ¶ ཞིང་ལས་ཐོན་སྐྱེད་ཀྱི་སྐོར་ནས་བཤད་ན་ If (one) speaks from the point of view of agricultural production. 2. (— + vb. of motion) to go from/ around sth. ¶ ཁོང་ཞིང་ཁ་དེ་ར་བསྐོར་ནས་ཕེབས་ཀྱི་འདུག He is coming/ going around the field.

སྐོར་སྒྱུད་ (gɔ̄ɔ̄jɛɛ̀) any machine that revolves.

སྐོར་འཕྲོ་ (gɔ̄ndro) diffraction.

སྐོར་བ་ (gɔ̄rwa) 1. a turn, a round, a lap, an orbit, a revolution; a circumambulation; va.—རྒྱག; — to circumambulate, to go around, to make a lap, to orbit, to revolve; vi.—འཁོར་; —རྒྱག to turn around, to rotate, to revolve ¶ ཁོང་གི་ཞོགས་ལྟར་ལྷ་སའི་གྲོང་ཁྱེར་ལ་སྐོར་བ་རེ་རྒྱག་གི་ཡོད་པ་རེད་ He circumambulates Lhasa once every morning. ¶ མིས་བཟོས་སྲུང་སྐར་གྱིས་ས་གཞི་རིལ་མོར་སྐོར་བ་མང་པོ་འཁོར་གྱི་ཡོད་པ་རེད་ The satellite makes many revolutions around the earth. 2. vi. to reach around sth. ¶ ཐག་པ་རིང་པོ་དེས་ཁང་ཆེན་འདིར་སྐོར་བ་འཁོར་གྱི་འདུག The rope (is long enough) to go/ reach around the big house. 3. vi. to turn over (earn back) one's capital in business ¶ ད་རེས་ང་དངུལ་སྐོར་བ་འཁོར་གྱི་མི་འདུག་པས་བུ་ལོན་ཕྲན་བུ་གཡར་དགོས་བྱུང་སོང་ This time, because I didn't earn back my capital, I had to take a small loan.

སྐོར་བ་འཁོར་ (gɔ̄ɔ̄wa kɔ̄ɔ̄) see སྐོར་བ་.

སྐོར་བ་འཁོར་ཚད་ (gɔ̄ɔ̄wa kɔ̄ɔ̄dzɛɛ̀) 1. the turnover rate (of capital). 2. computation/ measurement of how many times a machine turns.

སྐོར་བ་རྒྱག (gɔ̄ɔ̄wa gyaà) see སྐོར་བ་.

སྐོར་བ་ཐེབས་ (gɔ̄ɔ̄wa tēb) vi. to get/ become wrapped around sth. inadvertently ¶ གློག་སྐུད་ཤིང་སྡོང་ལ་སྐོར་བ་ཐེབས་བཞག The electrical wire got wrapped around the tree trunk.

སྐོར་བར་འགྲོ་ (gɔ̄ɔ̄war dro) va. to go around, to circumambulate.

སྐོར་བྱ་དམག་མི་ (gɔ̄rcja mə̄ə̄mi) sm. ཉེན་རྟོགས་པ་.

སྐོར་བྱེད་དམག་མི་ (gɔ̄rjeè mə̄ə̄mi) military patrol.

སྐོར་བྲོ་ (gɔ̄rdro) a Tibetan circle dance; va.—རྒྱག.

སྐོར་དབྱེ་ (gɔ̄ɔ̄ye) 1. a bamboo pan used to separate stones from grains. 2. abbr. of སྐོར་ཞིབ་དབྱེ་འབྱེད་.

སྐོར་སྦྱོང་ (gɔ̄rjoŋ) circumambulating; va.—བྱེད་.

སྐོར་དམག (gɔ̄rmaà) 1. soldiers who lay siege, soldiers who are surrounding sth.; va.—རྒྱག to lay siege. 2. soldiers on patrol.

སྐོར་ཚན་ (gɔ̄ɔ̄dzɛn) group, unit, section, brigade, team.

སྐོར་ཚོ་ (gɔ̄ɔ̄dzo) shung. investigating on the spot; va.—བྱེད་; va.—བགྱིས་ ¶ ད་ལམ་ས་གནས་སུ་སྐོར་ཚོ་བགྱིས་པ་ཡང་ཞིང་མིང་སོགས་ཆོས་སྡེར་བདག་ལུགས་འདི་ཡིན་ཁུངས་སྐྱེལ་དཀའ་གཤིས་ This time when we investigated on the spot, because the names of the fields were (not clear), we found that it was difficult to prove that those fields belong to Chöde Monastery.

སྐོར་ཚོགས་ (gɔ̄ɔ̄dzɔɔ̀) a gang or group of people.

སྐོར་འཚུབ་ (gɔ̄ɔ̄dzub) tornado, cyclone.

སྐོར་འཚོང་ (gɔ̄ɔ̄dzoŋ) door-to-door sales, going around to different places selling; va.—རྒྱག.

སྐོར་ཞིབ་ (gɔ̄ɔ̄shib) an inspection (tour), inspecting; va.—བྱེད་ to inspect, to go on an inspection tour ¶ མི་གསོད་ཉེས་ཅན་སུ་ཡིན་སྐོར་ས་གནས་མང་པོར་སྐོར་ཞིབ་བྱེད་པར་རུ་ཁག་ཁ་ཤས་བཏང་བ་རེད་ (They) sent several teams to investigate who the murderer is.

སྐོར་ཞིབ་པ་ (gɔ̄ɔ̄shibə) an inspector.

སྐོར་ཞིབ་དབྱེ་འབྱེད་ (gɔ̄ɔ̄shib yējeè) inspecting and identifying/ classifying/ distinguishing; va.—བྱེད་ ¶ སྲིད་གཞུང་ནས་ཞིང་གྲོང་གི་གྲལ་རིམ་ལ་སྐོར་ཞིབ་དབྱེ་

འབྱེད་བྱེད་པར་ལས་བྱེད་པ་ཁག་ཅིག་བཏང་བ་རེད་ The government sent a group of cadres to the villages to inspect and classify the people of different classes.

སྐོར་ཞིབ་དམག་གྲུ་ (gōɔ̄shib mɔ̄gdru) cruiser, patrol boat.

སྐོར་ཞིབ་སོ་ལྟ་ (gōɔ̄shib sōda) security patrolling, making rounds on guard duty; va.—བྱེད་.

སྐོར་གཞོག (gōɔ̄shɔɔ̄) 1. lathe; va.—རྒྱག to make sth. on a lathe. 2. lathe worker.

སྐོར་གཟིགས་ (gōɔ̄sii) inspection tour (h.) ¶ དམག་སྤྱིས་དམག་སྒར་ཁག་ལ་སྐོར་གཟིགས་གནང་བ་རེད་ The commander in chief went on an inspection tour of the various regiments.

སྐོར་གཡུག (gōɔ̄yuù) waving in a circular motion/ movement (e.g., the tail of a dog); va.—བྱེད་.

སྐོར་གཡེང་ (gōɔ̄yeŋ) patrolling, inspecting; va.—བྱེད་; —རྒྱག ¶ མཚན་མོའི་སྐོར་གཡེང་ A night patrol.

སྐོར་གཡེང་གྲུ་གཟིངས་ (gōɔ̄yeŋ drudzin) a patrol boat.

སྐོར་གཡེང་ཞིབ་འཇུག (gōɔ̄yeŋ shimjuù) patrolling, going around and investigating/ examining.

སྐོར་ར་ (gōɔ̄ra) sm.* སྐོར་བ་.

སྐོར་ར་ཐེབས་ (gōɔ̄ra tēè) 1. sm. སྐོར་བ་ཐེབས་. 2. vi. to be finished or completed (with regard to work) ¶ འདི་འདྲ་བྱས་ན་དུས་ཚོད་སྐོར་ར་ཐེབས་ཀྱི་མ་རེད་ If (you) act like this (you) will not finish (your work) in time. 3. turnover ¶ ཚོང་ཟོག་རྣམས་གོང་ཁེ་ཙམ་ལ་བཙོངས་ན་སྐོར་ར་ཐེབས་མགྱོགས་ཀྱི་རེད་ If the goods are sold at a slightly cheaper price the turnover will be much quicker.

སྐོར་རུ་ (gōɔ̄ru) a wooden spindle used to spin thread.

སྐོར་རེས་ (gōɔ̄reè) rotating, taking turns, alternating by turn; va.—བྱེད་ ¶ ཁྱིམ་ཚང་དེ་ཚོས་ཕྲུ་གུ་སློབ་གྲྭར་སྐྱེལ་རྒྱུ་སྐོར་རེས་བྱས་པ་རེད་ Those families take turns taking the children to school.

སྐོར་ལམ་ (gōɔ̄lam) 1. the path for circumambulating a holy site, the path a person or object goes around sth. 2. a roundabout way, a detour.

སྐོར་ལིང་ (gōɔ̄liŋ) a flail for threshing grain.

སྐོར་ལོག (gōɔ̄lɔɔ̄) sm. ཕྱི་སྐོར་.

སྐོར་བཤད་ (gōɔ̄shɛɛ̀) speaking in a roundabout manner; va.—བྱེད་.

སྐོར་བཤད་ཟུར་འདྲི་ (gōɔ̄shɛɛ̀ surdri) asking questions indirectly, talking indirectly; va.—བྱེད་.

སྐོར་བཞེར་ (gōɔ̄shee) sm. སྐོར་ཞིབ་.

སྐོར་སྲུང་ (gōɔ̄suŋ) patrolling for security, patrolling to police an area; va.—བྱེད་ to patrol/ police; va.—དུ་འཛུག to leave sb. to patrol on guard.

སྐོར་སྲུང་དཔུང་སྡེ་ (gōɔ̄suŋ būŋde) police force.

སྐོར་སྲུང་དཔུང་དམག (gōɔ̄suŋ būŋmaà) sm. སྐོར་སྲུང་དཔུང་སྡེ་.

སྐོར་སྲུང་སྤྱི་ཁྱབ་ (gōɔ̄suŋ jīgyəp) Chief Inspector of Police.

སྐོར་སྲུང་བ་ (gōɔ̄suŋwə) policeman, guard.

སྐོར་སྲུང་དམག་མི་ (gōɔ̄suŋ mɔ̄ɔ̄mi) sm. སྐོར་སྲུང་དཔུང་སྡེ་.

སྐོལ་: p. and f. **བསྐོལ་**; imp. **སྐོལ་** (gȫȫ) va. to boil ¶ ཆུ་བསྐོལ་ན་ If (you) boil water.

སྐོལ་ཆས་ (gȫȫjɛɛ̀) utensils for boiling/ cooking.

སྐོལ་ལྡན་ (gȫndɛn) thick soup/ stew made from tsamba and barley beer.

སྐོལ་ཟངས་ (gȫȫsaŋ) copper cooking pot.

སྐོས་ (gȫȫ) imp. of སྐོ་.

སྐོས་མལ་ (gȫȫmɛɛ) residence, dwelling.

སྐྱ་ (gyā) 1. economy, living standard ¶ ཡུལ་གྱི་སྐྱ་རྒྱས་པོ་འདུག The economy of the area is good. 2. wall ¶ ཁང་པའི་སྐྱ་ The wall of a house. 3. layman ¶ སེར་སྐྱ་ Monks and layman. ¶ སྐྱ་ཁང་ A layman's house. 4. sm. སྐྱ་བ་. 5. abbr. of སྐྱ་པོ་. 6. sm. སྐྱ་མདའ་.

སྐྱ་: p. **བསྐྱས་**; f. **བསྐྱ་**; imp. **སྐྱོས་** (kā) va. to move (residence) ¶ འབྲོག་པ་བྱང་ལ་བསྐྱས་པ་རེད་ The nomads moved north.

སྐྱ་ཀ་ (gyāga) sm. སྐྱ་ག.

སྐྱ་ཀ་ཁྲ་མོ་ (gyāga trāmo) sm. སྐྱ་ག.

སྐྱ་སྐྱ་ (gyāgya) sm. སྐྱ་བ་, 4.

སྐྱ་ཁོག་ཁོག (gyā kōgɔɔ̄) whitish ¶ ཁོའི་གདོང་སྐྱ་ཁོག་ཁོག་ཆགས་བཞག His face has become whitish.

སྐྱ་ཁྲ་ (gyādra) sparrow hawk.

སྐྱ་ཁྲིག་གེ་བ་ (gyā trēgewa) sth. that is whitish and in a row ¶ མི་རྒན་དེ་སོ་སྐྱ་ཁྲིག་གེ་བ་འདུག The old man has a row of white teeth.

སྐྱ་འཁོག་ས་འཁོགས་ (gyāgɔɔ̄ sāgɔɔ̄) sm. སྐྱ་ཁོག་ཁོག.

སྐྱ་འཁྱིལ་འཁྱིལ་ (gyā kyīīgyi) round and whitish ¶ རི་རྩེར་སྤྲིན་པ་སྐོར་སྐོར་ཞིག་སྐྱ་འཁྱིལ་འཁྱིལ་འཁོར་འདུག A round whitish cloud has formed on top of the mountain.

སྐྱ་འཁྱིལ་ལིའི་ (gyā kyīīlii) sm. སྐྱ་འཁྱིལ་འཁྱིལ་.

སྐྱ་འཁྲུད་རྩི་ཤིང་ (gyāgyüü dzīshiŋ) plants/ vines that climb along a wall.

སྐྱ་ག (gyāga) a magpie.

སྐྱ་ག་དཀར་པོ་ (gyāga) sm. སྐྱ་ག.

སྐྱ་ག་ཁྲ་མོ་ (gyāga trāmo) sm. སྐྱ་ག.

སྐྱ་ག་ཐིག་ཚགས་ (gyāga tīgdzaà) patching the roof of a Tibetan house with earth before the start of the rainy season; va.—བྱེད་.

སྐྱ་གྲིབ་ (gyədrib) cataract; vi.—ཐོག to get a cataract.

སྐྱ་འགེལ་ (gyāgyee) a wall hanging ¶ ཁང་པའི་ནང་ལ་སྐྱ་འགེལ་གྱི་རི་མོ་མང་པོ་འདུག There are many wall hanging paintings in the house.

སྐྱ་འགྲམ་ (gyādram) along/ near the wall.

སྐྱ་འགྲིབ་ (gyədrib) sm. སྐྱ་གྲིབ་.

སྐྱ་རྒྱག (gyā gyaà) sm. སྐྱ་བ་རྒྱག.

སྐྱ་རྒྱལ་ (gyāgyɛɛ) 1. sm. སྐྱ་རྒྱས་. 2. a minister who rebels against the king.

སྐྱ་རྒྱས་ (gyā gyɛ̱ɛ̀) vi. to have a good livelihood/ economy (usu. because of a good harvest) ¶ འདི་ལོ་ཆར་ཆུ་དུས་སུ་བབས་པར་བརྟེན་ཞིང་པའི་ས་ཁུལ་ལ་སྐྱ་རྒྱས་བྱུང་སོང་ This year because of the timely rain in the farm area their (the farmer's) livelihood is good because of a good harvest.

སྐྱ་སྒམ་ (gyāgam) a plain wooden box (without paint or varnish).

སྐྱ་སྒྱུར་བྱེད་ (gyāgyur ce̱è) va. to make a monk give up his celibacy ¶ གཞུང་གིས་གྲྭ་པ་མང་པོ་ཞིག་སྐྱ་སྒྱུར་བྱེད་དུ་བཅུག་ཡོད་ The government made many monks give up their celibacy (made them marry).

སྐྱ་ངོ་ (gyāŋo) economy, livelihood ¶ འདི་ལོ་སྐྱ་ངོ་རྒྱས་པོ་འདུག This year (we) have a good economy (usu. means a good crop).

སྐྱ་སྔོ་ (gyāŋo) sm. སྐྱ་ངོ་.

སྐྱ་ཅན་སྔོ་གདུགས་ (gyājɛɛ̀ ŋōduù) sm. སྐྱ་ཟན་སྔོ་གདུགས་.

སྐྱ་ཆན་སྔོ་དུགས་ (gyāsɛɛ̀ ŋōduù) sm. སྐྱ་ཟན་སྔོ་གདུགས་.

སྐྱ་ཆས་ (gyājɛɛ̀) laymen's clothes; va.—སྐྱས་; —གྱོན་ to wear layman's clothes.

སྐྱ་ཅིལ་ཅིལ་ (gyā cīījii) (for liquids) flowing and whitish ¶ ཆུའི་ཐ་རླབས་སྐྱ་ཅིལ་ཅིལ་ Flowing white waves.

སྐྱ་ཅིལ་ལི་ (gyā cīīli) sm. སྐྱ་ཅིལ་ཅིལ་.

སྐྱ་ཅེམ་ཅེམ་ (gyā cēmjem) twinkling, shining, gleaming, sparkling ¶ སྐར་མ་སྐྱ་ཅེམ་ཅེམ་ Twinkling stars.

སྐྱ་ཆོས་ (gyājöö) a Tibetan religious text written on white paper.

སྐྱ་མཇུག (gyəmjuù) rudder (of a boat); va.—རྒྱག to steer with a rudder.

སྐྱ་ཉིལ་ (gyəñii) 1. zinc. 2. abbr. of སྐྱ་ཉིལ་ལི་བ་.

སྐྱ་ཉིལ་ལི་བ་ (gyə ñīīliwə) a whitish/ muddy/ cloudy substance ¶ རྡོ་ཞོ་སྐྱ་ཉི་ལི་བར་བོར་བཞག The whitish, cloudy whitewash spilled (from the container).

སྐྱ་དིང་དིང་ (gyā dīŋdiŋ) white, whitish ¶ རས་དཀར་པོ་སྐྱ་དིང་དིང་དུ་བཏིངས་བཞག (They) have laid out a white sheet.

སྐྱ་གདོང་ (gyā dōŋ) sm. སྐྱ་མདའ་གདོང་.

སྐྱ་ཕྱིམ་མེ་ (gyā dēmme) whitish (usu. for liquids) ¶ དཀར་ཡོལ་གྱི་ནང་འོ་མ་སྐྱ་ཕྱིམ་མེར་བཀང་བཞག The cup has been filled with (whitish) milk.

སྐྱ་ཐང་རྒྱལ་པོ་ (gyādaŋ gyɛɛbo) sm. སྐྱ་རྒྱས.

སྐྱ་ཐ་ལི་ (gyā tāle) sm. སྐྱ་ཐལ་ལི་.

སྐྱ་ཐལ་ལི་ (gyā tɛ̄le) 1. whitish and dusty-looking ¶ ཆར་པ་མ་བབ་ཙང་ལམ་ཁ་སྐྱ་ཐལ་ལི་བསྡད་བཞག Because it did not rain, the road is looking whitish and dusty. 2. arid/ barren land.

སྐྱ་ཐིག (gyədig) 1. sketch/ draft for a building blueprint or a painting. 2. a class of designs consisting of white spot(s) on a dark background.

སྐྱ་ཐིང་དཀུ་ཐིང་ (gyādiŋ gudiŋ) sm. སྐྱ་ཧྲིང་ཧྲིང་.

སྐྱ་ཐིང་ངེར་ (gyā tĩŋŋee) sm. སྐྱ་ཧྲིང་ཧྲིང་.

སྐྱ་ཐིང་ཐིང་ (gyā tĩŋdiŋ) sm. སྐྱ་ཧྲིང་ཧྲིང་.

སྐྱ་ཐིབ་ཐིབ་ (gyā tĩbdib) whitish (usu. falling snow) ¶ གངས་སྐྱ་ཐིབ་ཐིབ་ལ་འབབ་བཞིན་འདུག The whitish snow is falling.

སྐྱ་ཐུད་ (gyādüü) an inferior quality of ཐུད་.

སྐྱ་ཐུམ་མེ་བ་ (gyā tümmewa) whitish and hazy ¶ སྨུག་པའི་དཀྱིལ་ནས་འགྲོ་ལམ་སྐྱ་ཐུམ་མེ་བ་ཞིག་ལས་མཐོང་གི་མི་འདུག (One) can only see a hazy road amidst the fog.

སྐྱ་ཐེར་ཐེར་ (gyā tēēdee) sm. སྐྱ་ཐལ་ལི་.

སྐྱ་ཐོར་ (gyādɔɔ) sm. ཐྲིབ་འདུར་.

སྐྱ་འཐིབས་འཐིབས་ (gyā tĩbdib) sm. སྐྱ་ཐིབ་ཐིབ་.

སྐྱ་འཐོར་ (gyā dɔ̃ɔ) 1. vi. to have a thread unravel ¶ སྐུད་པ་སྐྱ་འཐོར་ཙང་དབྱུག་བཞག་པ་རེད་ Because the thread unraveled, (they) threw it away. 2. vi. to have a wall collapse/ fall apart ¶ ཆུ་ལོག་གིས་རྐྱེན་པས་ཁང་པའི་སྐྱ་འཐོར་བ་རེད་ Because of the flood, the wall of the house collapsed.

སྐྱ་དར་ (gyā thar) sm. སྐྱ་རྒྱས་.

སྐྱ་མདའ་ (gyāmda) dawn; vi.—གཏོང་; —ཤར་ to be dawn ¶ སྐྱ་མདའ་བཏང་མ་ཐག་ལས་ཀར་འགྲོ་དགོས་པ་རེད་ As soon as it is dawn one must go to work.

སྐྱ་མདོག (gyāndɔɔ) white color, whitish ¶ ཕྱུ་པ་སྐྱ་མདོག A white dress.

སྐྱ་འདོབ་འདོབ་ (gyā dobdob) whitish (for liquids).

སྐྱ་ལྡེབས་ (gyādeb) on the wall ¶ སྐྱ་ལྡེབས་ལ་པར་མང་པོ་སྦྱར་འདུག There are many pictures affixed to the wall.

སྐྱ་ནམ་རྒྱས་པོ་ (gyānam gyɛɛbo) sm. སྐྱ་རྒྱས་.

སྐྱ་ནར་ (gyānar) a type of grass.

སྐྱ་སྤོ་ (gyābo) sm. སྐྱ་.

སྐྱ་ཕག་ཕག (gyā pāgbaà) pale, whitish. ¶ མི་དེ་ན་ཚ་ཕོག་ནས་ངོ་གདོང་སྐྱ་ཕག་ཕག་ཆགས་བཞག That person has been sick and has become pale.

སྐྱ་ཕྱུར་ (gyācur) an inferior quality of white cheese.

སྐྱ་ཕྱུར་ཕྱུར་ (gyā cūrjur) whitish ¶ དུ་བ་སྐྱ་ཕྱུར་ཕྱུར་ Whitish smoke.

སྐྱ་ཕྱིད་ཕོ་ཕྱིད་ (gyājeè ŋōjeè) greying, salt and pepper in color (for hair and beard) ¶ ངའི་སྐྲ་སྐྱ་ཕྱིད་ཕོ་ཕྱིད་ཡིན་ My hair is salt and pepper in color.

སྐྱ་ཕྲོམ་ཕྲོམ་ (gyā trōmdrom) sm. སྐྱ་ཁྲོམ་ཁྲོམ་.

སྐྱ་འཕམ་པོ་ (gyā pāmbo) poor, destitute, impoverished ¶ འདི་ལོ་ཐན་སྐྱོན་གྱིས་རྐྱེན་པས་ལུང་པའི་ནང་སྐྱ་འཕམ་པོ་བྱུང་བཞག This year because of the drought many people have become destitute in the area.

སྐྱ་བ་ (gyā) 1. oar; va.—རྒྱག; —སྐྱོད་ to row or paddle with an oar. 2. wooden stirring spoon for tea and stew. 3. sm. སྐྱ་པོ་.

སྐྱ་བག (gyābaà) 1. iron-grey in color. 2. a thin pancake.

སྐྱ་བབ་ (gyābəb) sm. སྐྱ་བབས་.

སྐྱ་བབས་ (gyābəb) vi. to become a layman again (for monks).

སྐྱ་བུན་ (gyābün) dusty and gloomy.

སྐྱ་པོ་ (gyāwo) 1. white, whitish ¶ གོས་སྐྱ་པོ་ White clothes. 2. shung. a layman ¶ ཁོང་སྐྱ་པོ་ཡིན་ཀྱང་ Even though he is a layman. ¶ དཔོན་སྐྱ་པོ་ Lay officials.

སྐྱ་པོ་སེང་པོ་ (gyāwo sēŋbo) pale and skinny looking.

སྐྱ་བྱིལ་ལི་ (gyā ciile) sm. སྐྱ་ཆིལ་ལི་.

སྐྱ་བྲ་ (gyābra) white buckwheat.

སྐྱ་འབུར་ (gyāmbur) a protruding part of a building.

སྐྱ་འབྲེལ་ (gyāndrɛɛ) (rooms) separated by a wall ¶ ང་གཉིས་ཀྱི་ཉལ་ཁང་སྐྱ་འབྲེལ་རེད་ Our bedrooms are separated by a wall.

སྐྱ་སྦབ་ (gyābəb) 1. swelling, dilation. 2. dropsy.

སྐྱ་སྦྱོར་ (gyājɔr) 1. pure/ good deeds. 2. philanthropic action.

སྐྱ་མ་ (gyāma) a single-ply string/ rope.

སྐྱ་མི་ (gyəmi) a rider, a horseman.

སྐྱ་མིང་ (gyəmiŋ) the name of a monk before he became a monk (i.e. his layman's name).

སྐྱ་མིན་སེར་མིན་ (gyāmin sērmin) neither layman nor monk (a phrase that describes a monk who lives ostensibly as a monk but has a mistress).

སྐྱ་མེ་རེ་ (gyāmere) sm. སྐྱ་ཞིམ་མེ་.

སྐྱ་མོ་བ་ (gyāmowa) sm. མི་སྐྱ་.

སྐྱ་དམག (gyāmaà) an army comprised of civilians (as opposed to monks).

སྐྱ་བཙུན་ (gyādzun) a monk and his original family.

སྐྱ་ཙ་ (gyādza) shung. 1. the original (lay) family of a monk. 2. shung. one's lord ¶ མི་དེ་ཚོའི་སྐྱ་ཙ་འབྲས་སྤུངས་རེད་ The lord of these people is Drepung.

སྐྱ་ཙ་འདོད་གཅིག (gyādza dööjig) shung. a monk/ nun rejoining his original family.

སྐྱ་ཙ་ཕྱི་ལོག (gyādza cīlɔɔ) shung. reverting to one's previous lord (occurs when a monk/ nun leaves the monastic order).

སྐྱ་ཙ་རང་བདག (gyādza randaà) shung. becoming a subject of one's original lord after leaving the monastic order.

སྐྱ་ཙལ་རུ་ཁག (gyādzɛ rugaà) equestrian team.

སྐྱ་ཙི་ (gyədzi) a Tibetan medicine used to treat lung disease.

སྐྱ་རྩིག (gyā dzĩi) va. to build a wall ¶ ཁང་པའི་མཐའ་སྐོར་ལ་ཁོང་ཚོས་རེའི་སྐྱ་བརྩིགས་པ་རེད་ They built a wall around the house.

སྐྱ་རྩྭ་ (gyādza) dried hay/ grass.

སྐྱ་ཚར་ (gyādzar) a traditional Tibetan dress made of sheepskin that does not have an outer (cloth) covering.

སྐྱ་ཚུབ་ཚུབ་ (gyā tsūbdzub) sm. སྐྱ་འཚུབ་འཚུབ་.

སྐྱ་ཚོས་ (gyādzöö) sm. སྐྱ་པོ་, 1.

སྐྱ་འཚུབ་འཚུབ་ (gyā tsūbdzub) whitish.

སྐྱ་རྫས་ (gyādzɛɛ) water vapor, fog, smog.

སྐྱ་ཞྭ་ (gyāsha) 1. a plain white hat/ cap. 2. layman's cap/ hat.

སྐྱ་ཟད་སྔོ་གདུགས་ (gyāsɛɛ ŋōduù) shung. 1. the most difficult time of the year subsistence-wise (i.e., the end of spring when the senescent grass is exhausted and the new grass hasn't appeared yet). 2. a crisis caused by using up what is at hand and not having new ones to replace them ¶ བཟོ་གྲྭའི་བཟོ་པ་རྙིང་པ་རྣམས་གནས་ཡོལ་དུ་སོང་ནས་གཞན་པས་ཚབ་བྱེད་མ་ཐུབ་པའི་སྐྱ་ཟད་སྔོ་གདུགས་ཀྱི་གནས་སུ་གྱུར་འདུག After the old workers retired, the factory did not have new workers to replace them.

སྐྱ་ཟད་སྔོ་དུགས་ (gyāsɛɛ ŋōduù) sm. སྐྱ་ཟད་སྔོ་གདུགས་.

སྐྱ་ཟན་ (gyāsɛn) vegetarian food.

སྐྱ་བཟོ་ (gyāso) the initial/ rudimentary/ embryonic stage of a thing ¶ ཁང་པའི་སྐྱ་བཟོ་ The rudimentary stage of a house (e.g., the frame).

སྐྱ་འོད་ (gyāwöö) rays of dawn, daybreak.

སྐྱ་ཡ་ (gyāya) a single string/ thread.

སྐྱ་ཡོར་ཡོར་ (gyā yɔryɔɔ) large, whitish and swaying in the distance; vi.—བྱེད་ ¶ མཚན་མོ་རྒྱང་རིང་ནས་གུར་ཞིག་སྐྱ་ཡོར་ཡོར་བྱས་པ་མཐོང་བྱུང་ From a distance in the evening I saw a white tent swaying.

སྐྱ་ར་ (gyāra) wall; va.—རྩིག to build a wall.

སྐྱ་རིབ་ (gyərib) cataract; vi.—འཕོག to get a cataract.

སྐྱ་རིམས་ (gyərim) the beginning stage of an epidemic.

སྐྱ་རིས་ (gyəriì) 1. sketch, line drawing; va.—རྒྱག. 2. fresco.

སྐྱ་རེངས་ (gyāreŋ) dawn; vi.—ཤར་; —འཆར་ to become dawn.

སྐྱ་རེངས་སྐར་མ་ (gyāreŋ gāāma) Venus.

སྐྱ་རེངས་ཐ་མ་ (gyāreŋ tāma) the last phase/ stage of dawn just before daybreak.

སྐྱ་རེངས་དང་པོ་ (gyāreŋ tanbo) the first light of dawn.

སྐྱ་རེངས་བར་མ་ (gyāreŋ parma) middle stage of dawn.

སྐྱ་རེངས་གཞོན་ནུ་ (gyāreŋ shönnu) start/ beginning of dawn.

སྐྱ་ལ་ངོ་འབྱར་ (gyāla ŋōjar) associating with bad company; va.—བྱེད་ ། མི་ངན་དང་སྐྱ་ལ་ངོ་འབྱར་བྱས་ན་རང་ཉིད་འཕུང་རྒྱུ་རང་ཡིན་ Associating with bad people will only lead to one's ruin.

སྐྱ་ལམ་ཚོད་ཙམ་ (gyā cöödzam) hardly able to see ། ཁོང་གི་མིག་གཡས་པ་སྐྱ་ལམ་ཚོད་ཙམ་ལས་མི་འདུག His right eye can hardly see (images).

སྐྱ་ལམ་ལམ་ (gyā lamlam) dazzling.

སྐྱ་ལུད་ (gyālüü) an inferior type of manure.

སྐྱ་ལེབ་ (gyāleb) 1. lizard. 2. rudder of a boat. 3. sth. white and flat.

སྐྱ་ལེབ་ལེབ་ཆགས་ (gyālebleb cāà) vi. to be carried away by the wind (for kites when their string is cut or breaks).

སྐྱ་ལོག (gyā lɔ̄ɔ̀) vi. to lose one's celibacy (for monks) ། གྲྭ་པ་དེ་སྐྱ་ལོག་པའི་རྗེས་སུ་ཆང་ས་བརྒྱབ་པ་རེད་ The monk got married after having lost his celibacy.

སྐྱ་ལོག་ངོ་ལོག (gyālɔ̄ɔ ŋōlɔ̄ɔ̀) off-white, greyish.

སྐྱ་ལོང་ལོང་ (gyā loŋloŋ) a wave of sth. white (e.g., clouds) ། ནམ་མཁར་སྤྲིན་པ་སྐྱ་ལོང་ལོང་འཁོར་གྱི་འདུག (There) is a wave of white clouds forming in the sky.

སྐྱ་ཤག་ཤག (gyā shāgshaà) whitish ། བུད་མེད་དེས་ཕྱུ་པ་སྐྱ་ཤག་ཤག་ཅིག་གྱོན་བཞག The woman has on a whitish looking dress.

སྐྱ་ཤར་ (gyāshar) smallpox.

སྐྱ་ཤར་རེ་ (gyā shārre) distinct, clear (and whitish) ། ནགས་ཚལ་གྱི་དཀྱིལ་དུ་ལམ་ཆུང་ཞིག་སྐྱ་ཤར་རེ་མཐོང་གི་འདུག (He) sees a small, clear white path in the middle of the forest.

སྐྱ་ཤར་ཤར་ (gyā shāshaa) sm. སྐྱ་ཤག་ཤག.

སྐྱ་ཤས་ (gyā shɛ̄ɛ̀) sm. དཀར་ཤས་.

སྐྱ་ཤིག་ཤིག (gyā shīgshiì) many, a huge number of sth. whitish ། རྒྱ་དམག་སྐྱ་ཤིག་ཤིག་ཏུ་ཡོང་གི་འདུག Many Chinese soldiers are coming.

སྐྱ་ཤོབ་ཤོབ་ (gyā shōbshoò) sm. སྐྱ་ཤག་ཤག.

སྐྱ་བཤིགས་ (gyā shiì) va. to unravel or take apart sth. woven/ knitted ། ཁོང་གི་འབལ་ལྷན་རྙིང་པ་ཞིག་སྐྱ་བཤིགས་ནས་གསར་པ་ཞིག་བསླས་པ་རེད་ (She) unravel an old sweater and knitted a new one.

སྐྱ་སང་ (gyā saŋ) sm. སྐྱ་སང་ངེ་.

སྐྱ་སང་ངེ་ (gyā sāŋŋe) clean and white, bright, clear ། སྟོད་ཐུང་བཙོག་པ་དེ་བཀྲུས་ནས་སྐྱ་སང་ངེ་ར་དག་སོང་ (I) washed the dirty shirt and it came out clean and white. ། ཁང་མིག་དེ་ར་ཚོན་དཀར་པོ་བཏང་རྗེས་སྐྱ་སང་ངེ་ར་ཕྱིན་སོང་ The room looks bright after painting it white.

སྐྱ་སང་སང་ (gyā sāŋsaŋ) 1. relieved, alleviated, at ease; vi.—བྱེད་ ། ང་ཡིག་ཚད་ལོན་པ་ཤེས་རྗེས་སྐྱ་སང་སང་བྱས་བྱུང་ I was relieved after finding out that I had passed the exam. 2. sm. སྐྱ་སང་ངེ་.

སྐྱ་སར་བབ་ (gyāsar pəb) sm. གྲྭ་པ་ལོག.

སྐྱ་སེང་ངེ་ (gyā sēŋŋe) sm. སྐྱ་སང་ངེ་.

སྐྱ་སེང་སེང་པོ་ (kāseŋ sēŋbo) a color that ranges from light blue to dull grey.

སྐྱ་སེར་ (kāsee) 1. shung. laymen and monks. 2. pale yellow.

སྐྱ་སོབ་སོབ་ (gyā sōbsoò) sm. སྐྱ་ཤག་ཤག.

སྐྱ་སྲབ་(པོ་) (gyā trəbu) indigent, poor ། ན་ལོ་ལུང་པ་དེ་སྐྱ་སྲབ་པོ་ཞིག་ཆགས་འདུག The country has become very poor because there was famine last year.

སྐྱ་གསོབ་ (gyāsob) sm. སྐྱ་སོབ་སོབ་.

སྐྱ་བསང་ (gyāsaŋ) sm. སྐྱ་སང་.

སྐྱ་བསངས་ (gyāsaŋ) sm. སྐྱ་བསང་.

སྐྱ་ཧྲོག་གེ (gyā hrōgge) whitish looking.

སྐྱ་ལྷག (gyālhaà) leftover grain and tsampa.

སྐྱ་ལྷག་གེ་བ་ (gyā lhāgewa) pale and sickly looking, ashen colored ། མི་གདོང་སྐྱ་ལྷག་གེ་བ་དེ་ན་བ་འདི་ཞེ་དྲག་ན་གི་ཡོད་པ་འདྲ་ (I) think the person who is pale and sickly looking is very sick. 2. whitish.

སྐྱ་ལྷག་ལྷག (gyā lhāglhaà) sm. སྐྱ་ལྷག་གེ་བ་.

སྐྱ་ལྷམ་ (gyālham) 1. plain white boots/ shoes. 2. layman's boots/ shoes.

སྐྱ་ལྷེབ་བེ་ (gyā lhēbbe) white and flatish. 2. sm. སྐྱ་ལྷེབ་ལྷེབ་.

སྐྱ་ལྷེབ་ལྷེབ་ (gyā lhēblheb) flapping and whitish.

སྐྱག་ཀྱེ་ (gyāggye) person who farts a lot ། མི་དེ་སྐྱག་ཀྱེ་ཞི་པོ་ཅིག་ཡོད་པ་རེད་ He is a person who farts a lot.

སྐྱག་ཁང་ (gyāggaŋ) toilet, lavatory.

སྐྱག་ཁྲལ་ཚ་པོ་ (gyāgdrɛɛ tsābo) impudent, cheeky, audacious, impertinent ། མི་དེ་འགོ་ཁྲིད་ཀྱི་མདུན་ལ་ཡང་སྐྱག་ཁྲལ་ཚ་པོ་ཡོད་པ་རེད་ That man is impudent even in front of his leader.

སྐྱག་རྐུབ་ (gyāggub) sm. རྐུབ་, 1.

སྐྱག་གཅིན་ (gyāgjin) urine and excrement; urinating and defecating; va.—གཏོང་.

སྐྱག་དོང་ (gyāgdoŋ) hollowed out ground that is used for collecting excrement (to be ultimately utilized as fertilizer).

སྐྱག་དྲི་ (gyəgdri) smell of excrement; vi.—ཁ་ to smell the odor of excrement.

སྐྱག་པ་ (gyāgba) feces, excrement; va.—གཏོང་ to defecate; va.—བཙིར་ to squeeze/ strain when defecating; vi.—ཤོར་ to involuntarily defecate/ pass stool; vi.—སྡོ་ to feel like defecating, to have the urge to defecate.

སྐྱག་པ་ཟོ་ (gyāgba so) slang. eat shit!

སྐྱག་པ་ཤོར་ཤོར་ (gyāgba shɔ̄ɔshɔɔ) 1. working sb. very hard [Lit. until the shit involuntarily comes out]. 2. making or causing sb. to suffer extreme hardship/ difficulty, defeating totally/ completely; va.—བཟོ་ ། ཨ་ཕ་དང་ཚོད་དུ་ཁྱོས་ང་སྐྱག་པ་ཤོར་ཤོར་བཟོས་བྱུང་ He gave me a hard time when he completely defeated me in wrestling.

སྐྱག་པ་རོ་ (gyāgbaro) an expression conveying sth. is very easy or unimportant ། སྐྱག་པ་རོ་ལས་ཀ་འདི་ལ་ད་ལས་རྒྱུ་གང་མེད་ It is nothing. There is nothing amazing about this work (it is very easy).

སྐྱག་འཕྲིན་ (gyəŋdrin) derogatory term for a letter.

སྐྱག་འབུ་ (gyəmbu) worms in feces.

སྐྱག་རྫུན་ (gyəgdzün) a lie; va.—ཤོད་ to tell a lie ། ཕྲུ་གུ་དེས་ཕ་མར་སྐྱག་རྫུན་བཤད་ནས་སློབ་གྲྭར་འགྲོ་གི་ཡོད་ལབ་པ་རེད་ The child lied to his parents and told them that he goes to school.

སྐྱག་རྫུན་སྐྱག་ནག (gyəgdzün gyāgnaà) completely false/ untrue, sb. who is a complete liar ། ཁོས་བཤད་པའི་སྐད་ཆ་འདི་སྐྱག་རྫུན་སྐྱག་ནག་རེད་བཞག What he said is completely false.

སྐྱག་རྫུན་ཚ་པོ་ (gyəgdzün tsābo) sb. who always lies.

སྐྱག་ཟན་ (gyāgsɛn) a derogatory term used for scolding people [Lit. shit eater].

སྐྱག་ཟོམ་ (gyāgsom) wooden bucket for transporting excrement.

སྐྱག་ཡུལ་རྒྱག (gyāgyüü gyaà) va. (derogatory term) to search for sth. bad, to seek to dig up dirt on sb. or sth. [Lit. (dog) searching for shit].

སྐྱག་ལང་ (gyāglaŋ) 1. spoiled behaviorally; va.—གཏོང་ to spoil; vi.—ཤོར་ to get spoiled ། ཕ་མ་གཉིས་ལ་ཕྲུ་གུ་གཅིག་ལས་མེད་ཙང་སྐྱག་ལང་བཏང་བ་རེད་ Because the parents have only one child they have spoiled (him). 2. getting into a habit; vi.—ཤོར་ to get into a habit ། ང་ཐ་མག་འཐེན་རྒྱུ་སྐྱག་ལང་ཤོར་བཞག I have gotten into the habit of smoking cigarettes.

སྐྱག་ལུད་ (gyāglüü) manure.

སྐྱང་ཉུལ་ (gyāŋñüü) sm. སྐྱང་ནུལ་.

སྐྱང་ནུལ་ (gyāŋnüü) arc. plaster, pavement; va.—བྱེད་ to plaster, to pave.

སྐྱབས་ (gyəb) 1. protection, defense; va.—བཙལ་ to ask or seek protection/ defense ༎ རྒྱལ་ཁབ་ཆུང་བ་དེས་རྒྱལ་ཁབ་ཆེ་བར་སྐྱབས་བཅོལ་བ་རེད་ The smaller nation sought protection from the bigger nation. 2. abbr. of སྐྱབས་འཇུག.

སྐྱབས་ཀྱི་སྦྱིན་པ་ (gyəbgi jīmbə) a type of charity that involves giving protection.

སྐྱབས་མགོན་ (gyəmgün) savior, protector ༎ འཇིག་རྟེན་གྱི་སྐྱབས་མགོན་ The savior of the world.

སྐྱབས་མགོན་ཆེན་པོ་ (gyəmgün cēmbo) title of Dalai Lama (and several other high lamas).

སྐྱབས་མགོན་དོན་གྱི་བདག་པོ་ (gyəmgün tö̱ngi ta̱gbo) a title of the Dalai Lama.

སྐྱབས་མགོན་སྦུག (gyəmgün bu̱ù) the Dalai Lama.

སྐྱབས་མགོན་རྩེ་ཤོད་ (gyəmgün dzēshöö) shung. the Dalai Lama and the Regent.

སྐྱབས་མགོན་ཡས་ཕྱིན་ (gyəmgün yɛ̱̀ɛjin) shung. sm. སྐྱབས་མགོན་རྩེ་ཤོད་.

སྐྱབས་མགོན་རིན་པོ་ཆེ་ (gyəmgün ri̱mboce) sm. སྐྱབས་མགོན་ཆེན་པོ་.

སྐྱབས་འགྲོ་ (gyəmdro) a type of religious prayer that seeks refuge in the Buddha, the Dharma and the monks; va.—འདོན་; —སྐོར་ to pray to seek refuge in the Buddha, the dharma and the monks.

སྐྱབས་འགྲོ་བཞི་སྐོར་ (gyəmdro shi̱gɔɔ) the four refuges in the Tibetan Buddhism: the Buddha, the dharma, the monks (sangha) and the lamas.

སྐྱབས་སྒྲིལ་ (gəmdrii) a rolled up ceremonial scarf which generally contains a gift of money (usu. given when seeing a lama or when asking a favor of someone); va.—འབུལ་ to give such a scarf.

སྐྱབས་གཅིག་པུ་ (gyəb jīgbu) the only source of refuge ༎ ཁོང་གིས་བོད་མི་དམངས་ཀྱི་སྐྱབས་གཅིག་པུ་དེ་ཞི་གོང་ས་སྐྱབས་མགོན་ཆེན་པོ་ཡིན་ཟེར་གསུངས་སོང་ He said, "The only source of refuge for Tibetans is the Dalai Lama."

སྐྱབས་བཅའ་ (gyəbjaa) f. of སྐྱབས་འཆའ་.

སྐྱབས་བཅས་ (gyəbjɛ̀ɛ) p. of སྐྱབས་འཆའ་.

སྐྱབས་བཅོལ་ (gyəbjöö) 1. refugee; va. སྐྱབས་བཅོལ་; —ཞུ་ h. to seek refuge/ protection ༎ ཁོ་ཚོས་ཕྱི་རྒྱལ་ལ་སྐྱབས་བཅོལ་ཞུས་པ་རེད་ They sought refuge in foreign countries. ༎ སྐྱབས་བཅོལ་བོད་མིའི་སྡོད་སྒར་ Tibetan refugee camp.

སྐྱབས་བཅོལ་བ་ (gyəbjööba) refugee.

སྐྱབས་བཅོལ་རོགས་རམ་ཚོགས་པ་ (gyəbjöö r̲ɔɔram tsɔ̄gba) refugee aid agency/ organization.

སྐྱབས་མཆོག་ (gyəmcɔɔ) sm. དཀོན་མཆོག་གསུམ་.

སྐྱབས་འཆའ་ (gyəb cāā) sm. སྐྱབས་བཅོལ་ཞུ་.

སྐྱབས་འཚོལ་ (gyəb cöö) sm. སྐྱབས་བཅོལ་ཞུ་.

སྐྱབས་འཇུག་ (gyəmjuù) a request for sth., a favor; va.—ཞུ་ to make a request, to ask a favor; va.—གནང་ to grant/ do a favor/ request ༎ བླ་མར་མཇལ་ཁ་ཞིག་སྐྱབས་འཇུག་ཞུ་གི་ཡོད་པ་རེད་ (He) is requesting an audience with the lama.

སྐྱབས་རྗེ་ (gyəbje) one's root lama ༎ ངས་སྐྱབས་རྗེ་རིན་པོ་ཆེ་སྐུ་མདུན་ནས་ཆོས་ཞུས་པ་ཡིན་ I received teaching from my root lama.

སྐྱབས་རྗེ་ཡོངས་འཛིན་རྣམ་པ་ (gyəbje yo̱ŋdzin nāmba) shung. term for the tutors of the Dalai Lama.

སྐྱབས་རྗེ་ཡོངས་འཛིན་སྐུ་བགྲེས་ (gyəbje yo̱ŋdzin gūdreè) shung. the senior tutor of the Dalai Lama.

སྐྱབས་རྗེ་ཡོངས་འཛིན་སྐུ་གཞོན་ (gyəbje yo̱ŋdzin gūshön) shung. the junior tutor of the Dalai Lama.

སྐྱབས་རྗེ་རིན་པོ་ཆེ་ (gyəbje ri̱mboce) shung. term of address for high lamas.

སྐྱབས་རྟེན་ (kābdeen) a present given when asking for a favor/ help (often analogous to a bribe); va.—འབུལ་; —སྤྲོད་ to give such a present; va.—ལེན་; —ཟ་; —ཞུ་ to accept such a present.

སྐྱབས་སྟོན་ (gyəbdön) va. to teach dharma/ religion.

སྐྱབས་ཐོ་ (gyə̱bdo) letter together with a donation requesting particular prayers be said during the monk's prayer assembly (in a monastery); va.—འབུལ་ to give such a letter.

སྐྱབས་གནས་ (gyəbnɛɛ̀) person or place where help and protection (either material or spiritual) is sought, place of refuge; va.—བཙལ་ to seek refugee ༎ སྐྱབས་གནས་དཀོན་མཆོག་གསུམ་ལ་འཚོལ་དགོས་ One should seek refuge in the three precious jewels.

སྐྱབས་པ་མེད་མགོན་མ་མེད་ (gyəb pāmeè gö̱n ma̱meè) shung. sm. སྐྱབས་མེད་མགོན་མེད་.

སྐྱབས་བྲན་ (gyəbdrɛn) shung. slave ༎ འདི་པའི་ལྷ་སྡེ་མི་སྡེ་སྐྱབས་བྲན་དང་འཛིན་འཁོར་དུ་མ་འཁྱེར་དགོས་བདག་ཏུ་མ་བཟུང་ These monks and commoners are not to be owned as slaves and captives.

སྐྱབས་བྲལ་ (gyəbdrɛɛ) helpless, without protection/ protectors.

སྐྱབས་སྦྱིན་ (gyəbjin) 1. mudras (symbolic gestures of the hands and fingers). 2. va. to help/ protect ༎ ཁོ་ཚོས་མི་སེར་དབུལ་ཕོངས་རྣམས་ལ་སྐྱབས་སྦྱིན་པ་རེད་ They gave protection to the poor subjects. ༎ ཇག་རྐུན་གྱི་གནོད་འཚེ་ལས་སྐྱབས་སྦྱིན་པ་རེད་ They protected the subjects from the harm of bandits and thieves.

སྐྱབས་མེད་མགོན་མེད་ (gyəbmeè gö̱nmeè) without help and protection, helpless ༎ དྭ་ཕྲུག་སྐྱབས་མེད་མགོན་མེད་རྣམས་ལ་ཕྱི་རྒྱལ་གྱི་རོགས་རམ་མང་པོ་ཐོབ་པ་རེད་ The helpless orphans got much aid from foreign countries.

སྐྱབས་མེད་ཟས་སྦྱིན་ (gyəbmeè sɛ̱̀ɛjin) giving food (alms) to the poor; va.—གཏོང་.

སྐྱབས་མེད་བཤེས་བྲལ་ (gyəbmeè shēèdrɛɛ) having no one to depend on or to help oneself.

སྐྱབས་འཛིན་ (gyəmdzin) a bribe offer (given formally in writing) ༎ དཔོན་པོར་སྐྱབས་འཛིན་ཕུལ་ནས་ཁ་མཆུ་ཐོབ་ཐབས་བྱས་པ་རེད་ He tried to win his lawsuit by offering a bribe to the official (in written format).

སྐྱབས་ཞུ་ (gyəbshu) sm. སྐྱབས་འཇུག་ཞུ་.

སྐྱབས་འོས་ (gyəbwöö) 1. worthy of asking for help/ protection ༎ བཙན་བྱོལ་བ་ཚོས་ཕྱི་རྒྱལ་གྱི་སྐྱབས་འོས་རྒྱལ་ཁབ་ཚང་མར་རོགས་རམ་གྱི་འབོད་སྐུལ་ཞུས་པ་རེད་ The refugees appealed for aid to worthy countries. 2. worthy of receiving help/ protection ༎ རྒྱལ་སྤྱིའི་རོགས་རམ་ཚོགས་པ་ཁག་ནས་སྐྱབས་འོས་ཉམ་ཐག་རྣམས་ལ་ཟས་གོས་ཀྱི་རོགས་རམ་བྱས་པ་རེད་ The various international relief agencies gave aid to those poor who are worthy of receiving help by giving them food and clothing.

སྐྱབས་ཡུལ་ (gyəbyüü) sm. སྐྱབས་གནས་.

སྐྱབས་ཡུལ་མཆོད་གནས་ (gyəbyüü cȫnɛɛ̀) place of refuge (e.g., the three jewels); place/ object where religious offerings are made.

སྐྱབས་རེ་འཆའ་ (gyəb re̱ja) sm. རེ་ལྟོས་བྱེད་.

སྐྱབས་སུ་འགྲོ་ (gyəbsu dro̱) va. to seek protection, to take refuge ༎ དཀོན་མཆོག་གསུམ་ལ་སྐྱབས་སུ་འགྲོ་བ་བྱ་དགོས་ One should take refugee in the three jewels.

སྐྱབས་སུ་མཆི་ (gyəbsu chī) sm. སྐྱབས་སུ་འགྲོ་.

སྐྱབས་གསུམ་ (gyəbsum) sm. དཀོན་མཆོག་གསུམ་.

སྐྱབས་གསོལ་སྙན་སྒྲོན་ (gyəbsöö ñēndrön) an appeal.

སྐྱར་ (gyār) sm. བསྐྱར་.

སྐྱར་སྐོར་ (gyārgɔɔ) sm. བསྐྱར་སྐོར་.

སྐྱར་སྐྱེས་ (gyārgyeè) sm. བསྐྱར་སྐྱེས་.

སྐྱར་སྐྱོར་ (gyārgyɔɔ) sm. སྐྱ་རེ་སྐྱོ་རེ་.

སྐྱར་བསྒོ་ (gyārgo) sm. བསྐྱར་བསྒོ་.

སྐྱར་ཁ་མ་ (gyārkama) picric acid.

སྐྱར་གོག (gyārgɔɔ) naked, without clothes.

སྐྱར་གྲོས་ (gyārdröö) sm. བསྐྱར་གྲོས་.

སྐྱར་འགལ་ (gyāngɛɛ) sm. བསྐྱར་འགལ་.

སྐྱར་འགོད་ (gyāngöö) sm. བསྐྱར་འགོད་.
སྐྱར་འགྲེལ་ (gyāndrel) sm. བསྐྱར་འགྲེལ་.
སྐྱར་རྒྱུགས་སྤྲོད་ (gyārgyuù drȫö) va. to take an examination again.
སྐྱར་རྒྱུགས་ལེན་ (gyārgyuù le̲n) va. to give an examination again.
སྐྱར་སྒྲིག (gyārdrig) sm. བསྐྱར་སྒྲིག.
སྐྱར་བཅགས་ (gyārjaà) sm. བསྐྱར་བཅགས་.
སྐྱར་བཅོས་ (gyārjöö) sm. བསྐྱར་བཅོས་.
སྐྱར་ལྕུག (gyārjaà) sm. བསྐྱར་ལྕུག.
སྐྱར་རྩ་ (gyārjcu) sm. བསྐྱར་རྩ་.
སྐྱར་དུ་ (gyārdu) sm. བསྐྱར་དུ་.
སྐྱར་འདེབས་ (gyār de̲b) sm. བསྐྱར་འདེབས.
སྐྱར་པར་ (gyārbar) sm. བསྐྱར་པར་.
སྐྱར་པོ་ (gyārbo) egret.
སྐྱར་དཔྱད་ (gyārjɛɛ̀) sm. སྐྱར་ཞིབ་.
སྐྱར་སྦྱོང་ (gyārjoŋ) sm. བསྐྱར་སྦྱོང་.
སྐྱར་སྦྱོང་སློབ་གཞི་ (gyārjoŋ lōbshi) topic or lesson that has to be relearned/ restudied.
སྐྱར་མ་ (gyārma) again ༈ཁོང་ངའི་ནང་ལ་སྐྱར་མ་སླེབས་བྱུང་ He came to my house again.
སྐྱར་མོ་ (gyārmo) sm. སྐྱར་པོ་.
སྐྱར་མོ་གང་རིང་ (gyārmo gāŋriŋ) egret.
སྐྱར་མོས་ཉ་ལེན་ (gyārmöö ña̲len) carrying out one's work efficiently, skillfully [Lit. egret catching a fish].
སྐྱར་ཞིབ་ (gyārshib) sm. བསྐྱར་ཞིབ་.
སྐྱར་ཟློས་ (gyāndöö) sm. བསྐྱར་ཟློས་.
སྐྱར་བཟོ་ (gyārso) sm. བསྐྱར་བཟོ་.
སྐྱར་ལེབ་ (gyārleb) a type of duck.
སྐྱར་ལོག (gyārlɔɔ̀) sm. བསྐྱར་ལོག.
སྐྱར་གཤོར་ (gyārshɔɔ) sm. བསྐྱར་གཤོར་.
སྐྱར་བཤེར་ (gyārsher) sm. བསྐྱར་བཤེར་.
སྐྱར་གསལ་ (gyārsɛɛ) sm. སྐྱར་གསལ་.
སྐྱར་གསོ་ (gyārso) sm. བསྐྱར་གསོ་.
སྐྱས་ (gyɛɛ̀) nomadic camp/ campsite; va.—སྤོ་ to move/ shift camp ༈འབྲོག་པ་ཚོ་དཔྱིད་ཀ་སྐྱས་མ་སྤོས་གོང་ Before the nomads move (their) camp in the spring.
སྐྱས་ཆེན་འདེགས་ (gyɛɛ̀cen de̲g) 1. va. to relocate/ move completely ༈འབྲོག་པ་རྣམས་སྐྱས་ཆེན་བཏེགས་ནས་རྩྭ་ཁ་བཟང་སར་སྤོས་པ་རེད་ The nomads relocated to a more fertile area. 2. vi. to die.
སྐྱས་བཏེག (gyɛɛ̀ dēg) sm. སྐྱས་སྤོ་.
སྐྱས་འདེབས་རྒྱག (gyɛɛ̀deb gya̲à) sm. སྐྱས་སྤོ་.
སྐྱས་སྤོ་ (gyɛɛ̀ bō) see སྐྱས་.
སྐྱི་ (gyī) abbr. of སྐྱི་མོ་.
སྐྱི་: p. བསྐྱིས་; f. བསྐྱི་; imp. སྐྱིས་ (gyī) 1. va. to borrow ༈ལོ་ཉེས་བྱུང་ཙང་ཞིང་པ་རྣམས་ནས་འབྲུ་དངུལ་མང་པོ་བསྐྱིས་པ་རེད་ Because the farmers had a bad year they had to borrow a lot of money and grain. 2. a Tibetan medicine.
སྐྱི་དཀར་ (gyīgar) the thin layer between the skin and flesh.
སྐྱི་ཁྲུས་ (gyīdrüü) sweat.
སྐྱི་གས་ (gyīgɛɛ̀) a crack/ split in the skin (due to dryness) ༈ཁོང་གི་ལག་པར་སྐྱི་གས་མང་པོ་འདུག He has many skin cracks on his hands.
སྐྱི་གོས་ (gyīgöö) leather clothing.
སྐྱི་སྒྲི་ (gyīdri) 1. scraper for removing the thin underlayer of skin on a hide. 2. a knife used for leather.
སྐྱི་སྒམ་ (gyīgam) a hide covered box.
སྐྱི་དངུལ་ (gyīŋüü) a loan.
སྐྱི་དངོས་ (gyīŋöö) leather goods, leatherware.
སྐྱི་འཇིགས་ (gyī jig) sm. སྐྱི་གཡའ་.
སྐྱི་གཏོང་ (gyī dōŋ) va. to loan, to lend.
སྐྱི་བསྡུམ་ (gyīdum) anything packed/ wrapped in hide; va.—རྒྱག.
སྐྱི་ནག (gyīnaà) outer skin of a hide.
སྐྱི་ནད་སྡེ་ཚན་ (gyīnɛɛ̀ de̲dzɛn) dermatology department.
སྐྱི་པགས་ (gyībaà) skin, hide.
སྐྱི་པགས་ཚ་ནད་ (gyībaà tsānɛɛ̀) skin rash.
སྐྱི་བུང་ (gyībuŋ) sm. སྐྱི་གཡའ་.
སྐྱི་བུད་ (gyībüü) vi. to peel skin.
སྐྱི་མོ་ (gyīmu) outer layer of skin/ hide.
སྐྱི་རྨ་ (gyīma) a sore on skin.
སྐྱི་ཚ་ (gyīdza) heat rash.
སྐྱི་ཚེར་ (gyīdzer) 1. a hangnail. 2. acne.
སྐྱི་ཞྭ་ (gyīsha) leather cap.
སྐྱི་གཡའ་ (gyī yā) vi. to shake/ tremble with fear, to have gooseflesh out of fear ༈ཉ་བར་ཐོས་པ་ཙམ་གྱིས་སྐྱི་གཡའ་བ་གདུག་རྩུབ་ཀྱི་ཁྲིམས་གཅོད་བཏང་བ་རེད་ (They) handed out a cruel and harsh punishment so that just the mention of it causes (one) to tremble with fear.
སྐྱི་རལ་ (gyī rɛ̲ɛ̲) vi. to get ripped/ torn (for hide, skin, etc.).
སྐྱི་ཤ་ (gyīsha) 1. skin and flesh. 2. diaphragm.
སྐྱི་ཤིང་ (gyīshiŋ) 1. wooden stick used for scrapping leather hides. 2. a kind of tree.
སྐྱི་ཤུན་དཀར་པོ་ (gyīshün gāābo) dandruff.
སྐྱི་ཤུས་ལོག (gyīshü lɔ̲ɔ̀) vi. to have skin shed/ come off.
སྐྱི་སེར་ (gyīser) wind, breeze; vi.—རྒྱག to have the wind blow, to be breezy.
སྐྱི་བསེར་ (gyīser) sm. སྐྱི་སེར་.
སྐྱིག་པ་ (gyīgbə) sm. སྐྱིགས་པ་.
སྐྱིགས་བྲ་ (gyīgdrə) sm. སྐྱིགས་བུ་.
སྐྱིགས་པ་ (gyīgbə) sm. སྐྱིགས་བུ་.
སྐྱིགས་བུ་ (gyīgbu) hiccups; vi.—རྒྱག.
སྐྱིང་ཁབ་ (gyīŋgəb) brocade with gold thread.
སྐྱིང་ཁེབ་ (gyīŋgeb) sm. སྐྱིང་ཁབ་.
སྐྱིང་སེར་ (gyīŋser) a kind of eagle.
སྐྱིད་ (gīì) abbr. of སྐྱིད་པོ་.
སྐྱིད་ཀྱིས་རྒྱགས་པ་ (gyīìgi gya̲gba) sm. སྐྱིད་མ་འཁྱོག.
སྐྱིད་ཀྱིས་སྡུག་ཉོས་ (gyīìgi du̲gñöö) as a result of doing all sorts of pleasurable things one causes suffering to oneself [Lit. by happiness buying suffering].
སྐྱིད་སྐྱིད་ (gyīgyiì) 1. happy, joyful. 2. a picnic, party; va.—གཏོང་ ༈སློབ་གྲྭ་གྲོལ་ནས་སྐྱིད་སྐྱིད་གཏོང་བར་ཕྱིན་པ་རེད་ After school (they) went to have a picnic.
སྐྱིད་གྲོང་ (gyīìroŋ) place in SW Tibet.
སྐྱིད་གླིང་ (gyīìliŋ) euphemistic term for an old people's home [Lit. happy grove].
སྐྱིད་གླུ་ (gyīìlu) joyful/ happy song; va.—གཏོང་.
སྐྱིད་གུ་འཛོམས་ (gyīìgu dzo̲m) vi. to have achieved/ accumulated all forms of happiness.
སྐྱིད་འགོ་ཚུགས་ (gyīŋgo tsūù) vi. to start/ begin a good era or happy life/ time ༈དམག་ཐག་ཆོད་ནས་གཞི་ནས་སྐྱིད་འགོ་ཚུགས་པ་རེད་ After the war was over only then did the good era begin.
སྐྱིད་རྒན་ (gyīìgɛn) an old person who has led a happy life.
སྐྱིད་ཅིང་རྒྱགས་པ་ (gyīìjiŋ gya̲gba) happy and bountiful ༈དམངས་གཙོའི་སྤྱི་ཚོགས་ནང་མི་དམངས་རྣམས་འཚོ་བ་སྐྱིད་ཅིང་རྒྱགས་པ་སྐྱེལ་གྱི་ཡོད་པ་རེད་ In a democratic society, the people lead a bountiful and happy livelihood.
སྐྱིད་ཆགས་སྡུག་བྲོལ་ (gyīìcaà du̲gjöl) becoming happy and avoiding suffering.
སྐྱིད་ཆུ་ (kīìcu) the Kyichu River (the Lhasa River).
སྐྱིད་ཆེས་པ་ (gyīì cēèba) sm. སྐྱིད་མ་འཁྱོག.
སྐྱིད་ཆོས་ (gyīìjöö) joy, gladness.
སྐྱིད་ཉམས་དོད་པོ་ (gyīìñam tö̲öbo) happy, cheerful.
སྐྱིད་ཉལ་ (gyīìñɛɛ) resting or lying down in a happy/ contented state; va.—བྱེད་.
སྐྱིད་གཏམ་སྡུག་གཏམ་ (gyīìdam du̲gdam) talking about happiness and suffering (usu. in the past); va.— ཤོད་.
སྐྱིད་སྟོང་ངེ་ (gyīìdöö) sm. སྐྱིད་ཐེང་ངེ་.
སྐྱིད་སྟོད་ (gyīìdöö) the upper regions of the Kyichu River.
སྐྱིད་དར་ (gyīìdar) the spread of happiness ༈སྐྱིད་དར་གྱི་དུས་སུ་ At the time of the spread of happiness.
སྐྱིད་དལ་ (gyīìdɛɛ) joyful/ happy and relaxed.
སྐྱིད་དུ་ཕངས་པ་ (gyīìdu pāŋwa) jealous/ envious

because of another's well being/ happiness.

སྐྱིད་འདོད་ (gyīndöö̀) desire for happiness/ pleasure; va.—བྱེད་ to wish or desire pleasure/ happiness ¶ སྐྱིད་འདོད་མེད་པའི་མི་གཅིག་ཀྱང་མེད་ There isn't a single person who does not have a desire for happiness. ¶ སྐྱིད་འདོད་བྱས་ཀྱང་སྡུག་བསྔལ་ཁོ་ན་བྱུང་ Even though (he) wished for pleasure he only got suffering.

སྐྱིད་འདོད་ཁོག་རུལ་ (gyīìndöö̀ kōgrüü) hedonistic and corrupt; va.—བྱེད་ ¶ སྲིད་གཞུང་ཁོག་རུལ་ཡིན་ཙང་མི་དམངས་ཚོ་ལ་བདེ་སྐྱིད་མེད་པ་རེད་ Because the government is hedonistic and corrupt the people are unhappy.

སྐྱིད་འདོད་འཁུལ་འཆེར་ (gyīndöö̀ g̲ü̲ndzer) desiring pleasure without having to work for it, lazy; va.—བྱེད་.

སྐྱིད་འདོད་ན་རྒས་པོའི་ཆུང་མ་བྱེད (gyīndöna g̲ɛ̲bö cūŋma c̲ḛè) the wife of an old man is happy [Lit. if you want to be happy be the wife of an old man].

སྐྱིད་འདོད་རིང་ལུགས་ (gyīndöö̀ r̲i̲ŋluù) hedonism.

སྐྱིད་འདོད་ལས་གཡོལ་ (gyīìndöö̀ l̲ɛ̲ɛ̀yüü) sm. སྐྱིད་འདོད་འཁུལ་འཆེར་.

སྐྱིད་འདོད་ལས་བསྐུན་ (gyīìndöö̀ l̲ɛ̲ɛ̀sün) sm. སྐྱིད་འདོད་འཁུལ་འཆེར་.

སྐྱིད་འདོད་སོ་གསོད (gyīìndöö̀ sōsöö̀) loving pleasure and comfort.

སྐྱིད་ལྡན་ (gyīìdɛn) auspicious, prosperous, happy.

སྐྱིད་སྡུག (gyīduù) 1. livelihood, living standard/ condition ¶ ཞིང་ལས་ཡར་རྒྱས་བཏང་ནས་སོ་ནམ་པའི་སྐྱིད་སྡུག་ལ་ཕན་ཐོགས་ཆེན་པོ་བྱུང་བ་རེད་ The farmers' livelihood benefited greatly by the improvement of agriculture. [Lit. happiness and misery]. 2. club, association; va.—ཕུད་ to expel from a club/ association ¶ བོད་རིགས་གཞོན་ནུའི་སྐྱིད་སྡུག་གཅིག་གསར་དུ་བཙུགས་པ་རེད་ (They) established a new Tibetan youth club. 3. good and bad things, happiness and misery/ unhappiness; vi.—མྱོང་ to experience the good and bad, to experience the misery and happiness of life; to have experienced life ¶ སྐྱིད་སྡུག་གི་གནས་ཚུལ་སྐོར་ Concerning the happy and unhappy situation.

སྐྱིད་སྡུག་ཁ་བྲལ་ (gyīduù kādrɛɛ) vi. to be/ get separated from either one's family or from a club/ association.

སྐྱིད་སྡུག་གན་ལྡེ་མགོ་སྒྲིལ་ (gyīduù g̲ɛ̲nde g̲o̲drel) sm. སྐྱིད་སྡུག་སྣང་གཤོང་མི་སྙོམ་.

སྐྱིད་སྡུག་བགོད་ (gyīduù g̲ö̲ö̀) va. to divide/ split up a family or a club/ association.

སྐྱིད་སྡུག་སྣང་གཤོང་མི་སྙོམ་ (gyīduù g̲a̲ŋshoŋ m̲i̲ñom) the ups and downs of life, the linkage of the joys and suffering of life.

སྐྱིད་སྡུག་གཅིག་པ་ (gyīduù jīgbə) 1. living together (as a family), being one family; being in the same club/ association; va.—བྱེད་ ¶ གྲོགས་པོ་ཚོ་རྒྱ་གར་ལ་སླེབས་རྗེས་སྐྱིད་སྡུག་གཅིག་པ་བྱས་པ་རེད་ After arriving in India the friends lived together as a family. 2. having the same/ equal livelihood.

སྐྱིད་སྡུག་མཉམ་འཁུར་ (gyīduù ñāmgur) sm. སྐྱིད་སྡུག་མཉམ་མྱོང་, 3.

སྐྱིད་སྡུག་མཉམ་འབྲེལ་ (gyīduù ñāmdre) sm. སྐྱིད་སྡུག་གཅིག་པ་.

སྐྱིད་སྡུག་མཉམ་མྱོང་ (gyīduù ñāmñon) 1. experiencing the joys and sorrows of life. 2. experiencing the same livelihood/ lot. 3. sharing joy and sorrow together.

སྐྱིད་སྡུག་སྙེ་མ་འཕོན་གཅིག (gyīduù ñyema pȭnjig) sm. སྐྱིད་སྡུག་མཉམ་མྱོང་.

སྐྱིད་སྡུག་སྙོམས་མཐར་ (gyīduù ñōmdar) shung. equalizing livelihoods, making livelihoods equal ¶ འདི་ག་ནས་ཀྱང་མངའ་འབངས་སྐྱིད་སྡུག་སྙོམས་མཐར་དང་ From here on (I) will make the livelihood of the people equal.

སྐྱིད་སྡུག་འཐེན་ (gyīduù tēn) va. to withdraw as a member from an association, club, etc.

སྐྱིད་སྡུག་དར་རྒུད་ (gyīduù t̲a̲rgüǜ) sm. སྐྱིད་སྡུག་སྣང་གཤོང་མི་སྙོམ་.

སྐྱིད་སྡུག་དྲི་ (gyīduù tri̲) sm. སྐྱིད་སྡུག་འདྲི་.

སྐྱིད་སྡུག་འདྲི་ (gyīduù dri̲) va. to ask about sb.'s livelihood/ welfare/ living conditions.

སྐྱིད་སྡུག་བློན་པོ་ (gyīduù lȭmbo) Home Minister.

སྐྱིད་སྡུག་མི་སྙོམས་པ་ (gyīduù mi̲ ñōmba) unequal living standard ¶ སྐྱིད་སྡུག་མི་སྙོམས་པའི་རྐྱེན་གྱིས་གསར་བརྗེ་ལངས་པ་རེད་ The revolution started because of the unequal living standards.

སྐྱིད་སྡུག་མི་དང་འཛེར་པ་ཤིང་ (gyīduù mi̲ t̲a̲ŋ dz̲e̲rba shīŋ) inevitability [Lit. joy and sorrow for humans; burls for trees].

སྐྱིད་སྡུག་མྱོང་ཚུལ་ (gyīduù ñ̲o̲ŋtsul) sm. སྐྱིད་སྡུག་མཉམ་མྱོང་.

སྐྱིད་སྡུག་ཚོགས་པ་ (gyīduù tsōgba) sm. སྐྱིད་སྡུག་, 2.

སྐྱིད་སྡུག་བཟང་ངན་ (gyīduù s̲a̲ŋŋɛn) the quality of one's livelihood, standard of living.

སྐྱིད་སྡུག་ཡག་པོ་ (gyīduù y̲a̲gbo) good livelihood/ conditions/ welfare ¶ ཁོ་ཚོ་སྐྱིད་སྡུག་ཡག་པོ་ཡོད་ཙང་ཁང་པ་གསར་པ་ཞིག་ཉོས་པ་རེད་ Because they have a good livelihood, they were able to buy a new house.

སྐྱིད་སྡུག་རེས་མོས་ ལ་ཐུར་མཉམ་འབྲེལ་ (gyīduù r̲e̲möö̀ l̲a̲tuu ñyāmdre) sm. སྐྱིད་སྡུག་སྣང་གཤོང་མི་སྙོམ་.

སྐྱིད་སྡུག་ལ་ཞུགས་ (gyīduùla sh̲u̲ù) va. to join an organization/ association/ club.

སྐྱིད་སྡུག་གསབ་བྱེད་ (gyīduù səbceè) gifts given in return for a gift given on an occasion like a wedding.

སྐྱིད་ན་ཆང་དྲན་ སྡུག་ན་ཆོས་དྲན་ (gyīnə cūdrɛn d̲u̲gna cȭòdrɛn) when people are happy they think of drinking beer, when people are suffering they think of religion.

སྐྱིད་ན་སྐྱིད་མཉམ་དང་སྡུག་ན་སྡུག་མཉམ་ (gyīnə gyīñām t̲a̲ŋ d̲u̲gna d̲u̲gñām) sm. མཉམ་སྐྱིད་མཉམ་སྡུག.

སྐྱིད་ན་མཉམ་སྐྱིད་དང་སྡུག་ན་མཉམ་སྡུག (gyīnə ñāmgyiì t̲a̲ŋ d̲u̲gna ñāmdug) sm. མཉམ་སྐྱིད་མཉམ་སྡུག.

སྐྱིད་ན་རང་ཡུལ་སྐྱིད་པ་ཡིན བྱམས་ན་ཕ་མ་བྱམས་པ་ཡིན་ (gyīnə r̲ə̲ŋyüü gyīìbə yi̲n c̲a̲mna pāma c̲a̲mba yi̲n) one's homeland is the most happy and one's parents are the most kind [Lit. as for happiness, one's homeland is happier; as for kindness, one's parents are kinder].

སྐྱིད་སྣང་ (gyīnaŋ) in a happy/ joyous state; va.—ཤར་ to become happy/ joyous/ glad; va.—བྱེད་ to show a happy appearance.

སྐྱིད་སྣང་གླུས་དྲངས་ (gyīnə lȭùdraŋ) joy brought by singing.

སྐྱིད་སྣང་དོད་པོ་ (gyīnaŋ t̲ö̲ö̲bo) in good spirits, in a happy state; va.—བྱེད་ to be in good spirits, to be in a happy state ¶ ཁོང་དེང་སང་ཚོང་ཡག་པོ་ཡོད་ཙང་སྐྱིད་སྣང་དོད་པོ་བྱེད་ཀྱི་འདུག He is in high spirits because his business is doing well these days.

སྐྱིད་པ་ (kīìbə) happy; happier ¶ ལུས་བདེ་ལ་སེམས་སྐྱིད་པ་ Physically fit and mentally happy ¶ ན་ནིང་ལས་ད་ལོ་སྐྱིད་པ་བྱུང་ (We) were happier this year than last year.

སྐྱིད་པའི་རང་བཞིན་ (gyi̲ì̲bɛ r̲ə̲ŋshin) happiness.

སྐྱིད་པོ་ (gyīìbu) happy, glad, joyful; pleasant, nice, enjoyable; va.—བྱེད, —གཏོང་ to enjoy oneself, to have a good time; va.—བཟོ་ to make sb. happy ¶ ང་ལ་དངུལ་རྙེད་ཙང་སྐྱིད་པོ་ཞེ་དྲག་བྱུང་ I was very happy because I found some money. ¶ ལུང་པ་འདི་སྐྱིད་པོ་འདུག This country is very nice. ¶ ཁོང་ལ་དངུལ་མང་པོ་ཡོད་ཙང་སྐྱིད་པོ་གཏོང་གི་འདུག Because he has a lot of money, he is having a good time. ¶ ཁོང་གིས་ཕ་མ་དགོན་པ་ཁག་ལ་གནས་མཇལ་ཁྲིད་ནས་ཕ་མ་སྐྱིད་པོ་བཟོས་པ་རེད་ He made his parents happy because he took them for a religious visit to monasteries.

སྐྱིད་པོ་གཉིས་བརྩེགས་མེད་པར་སྡུག་པོར་གསུམ་བརྩེགས་ (gyīìbu ñīìdzeg m̲e̲èbar d̲u̲gbor sūmdzeg) great misfortune/ suffering/ unhappiness [Lit. without having double happiness, having triple suffering].

སྐྱིད་པོ་བདེ་མོ་ (gyīìbu demo) sm. སྐྱིད་པོ་.

སྐྱིད་པོ་ལ་སྒུག་ལོང་དང་སྡུག་པོ་ལ་སངས་དུས་ (gyīìbulə guùloŋ daŋ dugbola sāŋtüü) one can wait for happiness, there is a time when suffering will be cleared up.

སྐྱིད་ཕྱོགས་ཀུན་མཐུན་ (gyīìoò gūndün) name of Lungshar's political party (in 1934).

སྐྱིད་ལྡན་ (gyiīlün) abbr. of སྐྱིད་སྡུག་ལྡན་པོ་.

སྐྱིད་འགོལ་ལི་ (gyīìböle) being in a relaxed and happy/ contented state ¶ ཁོང་རྟས་ཡོལ་བྱས་ནས་སྐྱིད་འགོལ་ལིར་བསྡད་འདུག He retired and is living in a relaxed and happy manner.

སྐྱིད་མ་འཁྱོག (gyīì mā kyɔ̄ɔ̀) vi. to do pleasurable things in excess ¶ བཟའ་ཚང་དེ་གཉིས་ལ་དངུལ་ཏ་ཙང་མང་པོ་གློ་བུར་དུ་བྱུང་ཙང་སྐྱིད་མ་འཁྱོགས་པར་ཉིན་ལྟར་ཤོ་ སྣག་བརྒྱབ་པ་རེད་ Because they suddenly got a huge sum of money, the couple sought pleasure excessively and gambled every day.

སྐྱིད་མ་འཁྱོག སྡུག་འཁྱོག (gyīì mā kyɔ̄ɔ̀ dugkyɔɔ̀) (if one) does pleasurable things in excess one must bear the suffering that follows.

སྐྱིད་མེད་སྡུག་ཟད་ (gyīìmeè dugsɛɛ̀) doing things in a disorderly/ rash/ devil-may-care manner (i.e., with no thought of the consequences); va.—བྱེད་ ¶ ཁྱེད་རང་གིས་ལས་ཁུངས་ནང་སྐྱིད་མེད་སྡུག་ཟད་ཀྱི་ལས་ཀ་འདི་འདྲ་བྱས་ན་ལས་ཁུངས་ནས་འབུད་རྒྱུའི་ཉེན་ཁ་ཡོད་པ་ རེད་ If you work in the office in this disorderly manner there is a danger that you may be laid off.

སྐྱིད་ཚལ་ (gyīìtsɛɛ) sm. སྐྱིད་ཚལ་.

སྐྱིད་འཛོམས་ (gyīndzom) 1. a woman's name. 2. combination of all that is pleasurable.

སྐྱིད་བཞག་སྡུག་ཉོ་ (gyīshaà dugño) leaving/ giving up joy and happiness and buying/ taking on suffering ¶ ད་རེས་ཁྱེད་རང་གི་ལས་ཀ་བརྗེས་པ་དེ་སྐྱིད་བཞག་སྡུག་ཉོ་རང་རེད་ Your changing jobs this time is like leaving happiness and buying suffering [Lit. leaving happiness; buying sadness].

སྐྱིད་ཟིང་ངེ་ (gyīì siŋŋe) joyful, happy.

སྐྱིད་ཡུལ་ (gyīìyüü) sm. སྐྱིད་ས་.

སྐྱིད་རོགས་ (gyīrɔɔ̀) friends with whom one shares happy times.

སྐྱིད་ལ་ཁའི་རྩྭ་ལ་མཉམ་ཟ་དང་ སྡུག་སྔོན་མོའི་ཆུ་ལ་མཉམ་འཐུང་ (gyīì lakɛ dzāla ñāmsɛɛ̀daŋ dug ŋō̃nmö cūlə ñə̄mtuŋ) sharing happiness and sorrow together [Lit. happiness— eating (the best) mountain grass together, suffering — drinking blue water together].

སྐྱིད་ལོས་ (gyīìlöö̀) the degree/ extent of happiness, how happy? ¶ ཁྱེད་རང་ཨ་རིར་སྐྱིད་ལོས་འདུག How happy are you in America?

སྐྱིད་ཤང་ (gyīìshaŋ) extremely happy ¶ དེང་སང་ལྟོ་གོས་ཀྱི་སེམས་ཁྲལ་མེད་པར་སྐྱིད་ཤང་རེད་ These days (we) are extremely happy because we don't have to worry about food and clothing.

སྐྱིད་ས་ (gyīìsə) a happy/ pleasant place ¶ ས་ཆ་སྐྱིད་ས་ཞིག་ལ་སྤོ་གི་ཡིན་ (I am) moving to a pleasant place.

སྐྱིད་གསུམ་སྡུག་གསུམ་ (gyīìsum dūgsum) life includes both happiness and suffering ¶ མི་ཚེ་རིང་པོ་སྐྱིད་གསུམ་སྡུག་གསུམ་ཡིན་ དཔྱིད་ཉི་རིང་པོ་གྲང་གསུམ་དྲོ་གསུམ་ཡིན་ A person who lives long faces both happiness and hardship, and the long days of spring have both warm and cold (days) [Lit. three happinesses and three sufferings].

སྐྱིད་ལྷོད་ (gyīìlhöö̀) happy and relaxed.

སྐྱིན་ (gyīn) abbr. of སྐྱིན་པ་.

སྐྱིན་ཁབ་ (gyīngəb) a type of brocade from India.

སྐྱིན་འཁྲི་ཆབ་གསུམ་ (gyīntri cə̄bsum) shung. three kinds of settlements/ punishments for theft: replacement, fine, returning the things stolen.

སྐྱིན་གོར་ (gyīŋgɔɔ) snow frog.

སྐྱིན་ཐང་ (gyīntaŋ) hail storm.

སྐྱིན་ཐང་ཆུ་ (gyīntaŋ cū) flood after a hail storm.

སྐྱིན་ཐང་དུས་ (gyīntaŋ cū) a bad/ lean year, a famine year (due to severe weather).

སྐྱིན་པ་ (gyīmbə) replacement, payment for sth. lost/ damaged, payment for a debt; va.—སྤྲོད་; —འཇལ་; —གཞལ་ to repay/ replace sth.; va.—ལེན་ to collect a debt, to take a repayment; vi.—འཁོད་ to meet one's debt, to be repay/ replace sth. ¶ དངུལ་གཡར་པ་དེའི་སྐྱིན་པ་སྤྲད་པ་རེད་ (He) repaid the money that he borrowed.

སྐྱིན་པ་ཆུ་ཡིན་རུང་སླ་བར་མ་གཏོང་ (gyīmbə cūyinruŋ lāwar madoŋ) repaying in full without shortchanging [Lit. Even if the repayment is water, don't dilute it].

སྐྱིན་པ་ཐོད་གཏུག (gyīmbə tō̃òdug) offsetting, canceling each other out, counteracting.

སྐྱིན་པོ་ (gyīmbo) sm. སྐྱིན་པ་.

སྐྱིན་མི་ (gyīnmi) a debtor.

སྐྱིན་ཚབ་ (gyīntsəp) repayment, replacement, compensation, indemnity, reparation; va.—སྤྲོད་; —གནང་; —འཇལ་ to repay, to replace, to compensate, to pay an indemnity, to make reparations ¶ ངས་ཁྱེད་རང་གི་ཕྱུག་སྨྱུག་ཆག་པའི་སྐྱིན་ཚབ་སྤྲོད་ཀྱི་ཡིན་ I'll replace the pen of yours that (I) broke.

སྐྱིན་རྫས་ (gyīndzüù) a type of inferior brocade.

སྐྱིན་ལུས་ (gyīnlüù) sth. still left to be repaid.

སྐྱིབས་ (gyīb) shelter, cover ¶ བྲག་སྐྱིབས་ Shelter in the rocks. ¶ ཆར་སྐྱིབས་ Shelter from the rain.

སྐྱིམ་ (gyīm) sth. whose outside is covered with paint or lacquer.

སྐྱིམ་ཙེ་ (gyīmdze) scissors.

སྐྱིལ་: p. and f. བསྐྱིལ་; imp. སྐྱིལ་ (gyīl) 1. va. to dam up (for water), to make water puddle, to shut up, to contain, to pen up ¶ རྫིང་དུ་ཆུ་བསྐྱིལ་ནས་ཞིང་ཆུ་བཏང་བ་རེད་ (They) filled the reservoir up with water and irrigated the field. ¶ དུས་སྐབས་ལ་བཀོལ་སྤྱོད་ཀྱིས་བཙན་རྒྱལ་རིང་ལུགས་ཀྱི་སྟོབས་ཤུགས་སྐྱིལ་ཐབས་བྱེད་ཀྱི་ཡོད་པ་རེད་ (They) are using the opportunity to try and contain the power of imperialism. 2. see བསྙེན་སྐྱིལ་.

སྐྱིལ་ཀྲུང་ (gyīdrum) sitting cross-legged; va.—བྱེད་; —སྒྲིག to sit cross-legged.

སྐྱིལ་ཀྲུང་ཕྱེད་པ་ (gyīdrum cēèba) semi-cross-legged (one leg is stretched out over the other leg that is bent).

སྐྱིལ་ཆུ་ (gyīcu) a puddle of water.

སྐྱིལ་ཆུ་ལྷུག་སྣོད་ (gyīcu lūùnöö̀) pot used to hold water.

སྐྱིལ་མོ་ཀྲུང་ (gyīmudruŋ) sm. སྐྱིལ་ཀྲུང་.

སྐྱིས་ (gyīì) imp. of སྐྱི་.

སྐྱུ་གང་ (gyūkaŋ) 1. facial cosmetics. 2. a measurement unit spanning from the middle joint of the thumb to the tip of the thumb. 3. sm. མཐེབ་སྐྱུ་.

སྐྱུ་ཚ་ (gyūtsə) sm. མཐེབ་སྐྱུ་.

སྐྱུ་རུ་ར་ (gyūrurə) hawthorn.

སྐྱུ་རུའི་ཤ་ (gyūrü shā) fruit of the hawthorn tree.

སྐྱུ་རུ་ཤིང་ (gyūrurshiŋ) hawthorn tree.

སྐྱུ་རུམ་ (gyūrum) arc. 1. stew, soup. 2. vegetables.

སྐྱུ་རུམ་མཁན་ (gyūrumgɛn) one who cooks vegetable dishes.

སྐྱུག: p. བསྐྱུགས་; f. བསྐྱུག; imp. སྐྱུགས་ (gyūù) 1. vi. to vomit ¶ དེ་རིང་ཁ་ལག་བཟས་པ་ཚང་མ་བསྐྱུགས་སོང་ I vomited all the food I ate today. 2. va. to pay/ give back ¶ ལས་ཀར་ཉི་མ་མང་པོ་མ་ཕྱིན་ན་ཉེས་ཆད་ལ་དངུལ་སྐྱུག་དགོས་ཡོད་ If you miss many days of work, you have to pay back money as a fine.

སྐྱུག་མདངས་ (gyūgdaŋ) feeling of nausea, nauseous, nauseating; vi.—བྱེད་ to be nauseous ¶ སྐྱེ་དམན་དེ་སྐྱུག་མདངས་བྱེད་ཀྱི་འདུག ཕལ་ཆེར་མཁྲིས་ནད་རྒྱག་གི་ཡོད་པ་རེད་ That woman feels nauseous, perhaps it is morning sickness.

སྐྱུག་ལྡང་ (gyūgdaŋ) sm. སྐྱུག་མདངས་.

སྐྱུག་ལྡད་ (gyūgdɛɛ̀) chewing cud; va.—བྱེད་.

སྐྱུག་ནད་ (gyūgnɛɛ̀) diseases involving vomiting.

སྐྱུག་པ་ (gyūgbə) vomit; va.—སྐྱུག་ to intentionally vomit; vi.—ཤོར་; —སྐྱུག་ to involuntarily vomit ¶ སྐྱེ་དམན་དེ་སྐྱུག་པ་སྐྱུག་གི་ཡོད་པ་རེད་ That woman is vomiting.

སྐྱུག་སློད་ (gyūg drȫȍ) shung. va. to return/ pay back ¶ སྔོན་མ་ཁྲལ་དོད་སྒྲང་དངུལ་དགས་ནས་པར་ཆད་ཡོད་ན་སྐྱུག་སློད་བྱེད་དགོས་ Previously, when (you) took too much money as a substitute for taxes (in kind), if the other side (the givers) have a deficit (paid too much), then you have to return (the excess).

སྐྱུག་བྲོ་ (kūg tro̱) feeling dirty/ nauseated/ disgusted/ revolted; va. སྐྱུག་བྲོ་; —བྱེད་ ¶ བུ་མོ་དེ་ཕྲུ་གུའི་ཆབ་གདན་འཁྲུད་ལས་ལ་སྐྱུག་བྲོ་ནས་བུ་བཙོལ་ཁང་གི་ལས་ཀ་བཞག་པ་རེད་ The girl gave up the nursery job because she felt disgusting washing the children's diapers.

སྐྱུག་བྲོ་དགོས་པའི་རིགས་ (gyūgtro gö̱öbɛrig) things that disgust/ revolt/ nauseate.

སྐྱུག་བྲོ་པོ་ (gyūg tro̱bo) disgusting, revolting, sickening, nauseating; va.—བཟོ་ to make sth. awful/ disgusting/ revolting/ ugly ¶ ཕྲུ་གུ་འདིའི་སྤྱོད་ལམ་སྐྱུག་བྲོ་པོ་འདུག The (boy's) behavior is disgusting. ¶ དབུ་ལོག་བཟོ་ད་སྐྱུག་བྲོ་པོ་བཟོས་བཞག (He) made an ugly dress. 2. dirty (in a sexual sense) ¶ སྐད་ཆ་སྐྱུག་བྲོ་པོ་མ་ཤོད་ Don't talk dirty.

སྐྱུག་བྲོ་བ་ (gyūg tro̱wa) sm. སྐྱུག་བྲོ་པོ་.

སྐྱུག་མེར་ (kōŋmee) nauseating; disgusting; vi.—ལང་; —བྱེད་ to feel nauseous; to feel revolted; va.—སློང་ to make sb. nauseous ¶ ཁ་ལག་ཞག་ཚི་མང་དྲགས་ནས་སྐྱུག་མེར་ལངས་བྱུང་ Because the food was too greasy I got nauseous. ¶ མི་འདིའི་སྤྱོད་པ་སྐྱུག་མེར་ལང་དགོས་པ་ཞིག་འདུག This person's behavior is revolting. ¶ ཁ་ལག་ཟ་སྐབས་ཁོས་གསང་སྤྱོད་སྐོར་སྐད་ཆ་བཤད་ནས་མི་ཚང་མར་སྐྱུག་མེར་བསླངས་པ་རེད་ His talking about the toilet when eating nauseated everyone.

སྐྱུག་སྨན་ (gyūgmɛn) emetic.

སྐྱུག་ལོག (gyūglɔɔ̀) sm. སྐྱུག་མེར་ལང་.

སྐྱུག་ལོང་ལོང་བྱེད་ (gyūg lo̱ŋloŋ ce̱è) sm. སྐྱུག་མེར་ལང་.

སྐྱུག་བཤལ་ (gyūgshɛɛ) cholera.

སྐྱུག་བཤལ་ནད་འབུ་ (gyūshɛɛ nɛ̱nbu) cholera germs.

སྐྱུགས་ (kūù) imp. of སྐྱུག.

སྐྱུང་: p. བསྐྱུངས་; f. བསྐྱུང་; imp. སྐྱུངས་ (kūŋ) 1. va. to reduce/ diminish, to make smaller, to lower ¶ ཕྲུ་གུ་སྐྱེ་འཕྱུར་ཚད་གཞི་བཟོས་ནས་མི་འབོར་བསྐྱུངས་བ་རེད་ They reduced the population by putting limits on births. 2. va. to renounce/ give up (pride, hatred, etc.) ¶ སྒེར་སེམས་བསྐྱུངས་ནས་གཞན་ལ་རོགས་རམ་བྱས་འདུག He gave up thoughts of personal gain and helped others.

སྐྱུང་ཀ་ (gyūŋgə) a type of raven.

སྐྱུང་ཀ་རྗེ་རྐྱོང་ (gyūŋgə dzēgyoŋ) an engraving tool that resembles a raven's beak.

སྐྱུང་པོ་ (gyūŋbo) sm. སྐྱུང་བུ་.

སྐྱུང་བར་བྱེད་ (gyūŋwar ce̱è) sm. སྐྱུང་.

སྐྱུང་བུ་ (gyūŋbu) awl.

སྐྱུངས་ (gyūŋ) imp. of སྐྱུང་.

སྐྱུད་: p. and f. བསྐྱུད་; imp. སྐྱུད་ (kǖù) vi. sm. བརྗེད་.

སྐྱུར་: p. and f. བསྐྱུར་; imp. སྐྱུར་ (gyūr) 1. vi. to become sour/ spoiled/ curdled ¶ ཇ་དེ་བསྐྱུར་འདུག That tea has become spoiled. 2. va. to give up/ abandon/ discard/ throw/ cast away, to repudiate ¶ རང་གི་ནང་མི་དང་རྒྱུ་ནོར་ཚང་མ་བསྐྱུར་དགོས་བྱུང་ (I) had to abandon my family and all my possessions. 3. abbr. of སྐྱུར་པོ་. 4. vi. to have a color fade ¶ རས་དེ་བཀྲུས་ནས་ཚོས་བསྐྱུར་བཞག The cloth faded after washing. 5. foods that taste sour/ acidic ¶ བོད་སྨན་འདི་གཏོང་སྐབས་སྐྱུར་སྤོང་དགོས་པ་རེད་ When taking this Tibetan medicine you have to give up eating acidic foods.

སྐྱུར་ཁ་ (gyūrgə) a piece of cloth that is stitched between two pieces of cloth; va.—གཏོང་.

སྐྱུར་ཁུ་ (gyūrku) a sour/ acidic liquid. 2. whey.

སྐྱུར་འགོག (gyūngɔɔ̀) acid resistance; acid proof.

སྐྱུར་འགོང་ (gyōŋgoŋ) being a nuisance verbally when drunk; va.—ཤོད་ to be a nuisance verbally when drunk.

སྐྱུར་སྐྱུར་ (gyūrgyur) acidification.

སྐྱུར་དངོས་ (gyūrŋöö̀) things that are thrown away.

སྐྱུར་ཆུ་ (gyūrcu) the acidic liquid that one throws up.

སྐྱུར་བསྙལ་ (gyūr ñɛ̄ɛ) setting sth. aside to ferment; va.—རྒྱག ¶ འོ་མ་བསྐོལ་ནས་ཞོ་སྐྱུར་བསྙལ་བརྒྱབ་པ་རེད་ (They) boiled milk and set it aside to ferment into yogurt.

སྐྱུར་རྫས་ (gyūrdum) acidic material.

སྐྱུར་རྡ་ (gyūrdə) sm. སྐྱུར་རྩི་.

སྐྱུར་དད་ (kūrdɛɛ̀) the desire/ need to drink alcohol ¶ མི་འདི་སྐྱུར་དད་ཆེན་པོ་འདུག This man needs to drink a lot of alcohol.

སྐྱུར་དྲི་ (gyūrtri) sour/ rancid smell; vi.—ཁ་ to smell sth. sour/ rancid.

སྐྱུར་འདོད་ (gyūntöö̀) 1. desiring to throw sth. away; va.—བྱེད་ ¶ ཁོས་དབུ་ལོག་རྙིང་པ་རྣམས་སྐྱུར་འདོད་བྱེད་ཀྱི་འདུག He wants to throw away all his old clothes. 2. desiring to give up/ abandon; va.—བྱེད་ ¶ ཁོང་གིས་ཨ་རག་འཐུང་རྒྱུ་སྐྱུར་འདོད་བྱེད་ཀྱི་འདུག He wants to give up drinking.

སྐྱུར་མནམ་ (gyūrnam) tart/ acidic in flavor.

སྐྱུར་པོ་ (gyūrbu) sm. སྐྱུར་མོ་.

སྐྱུར་ཕྱུར་ (gyūcur) sour cheese.

སྐྱུར་བ་ (gyūrwə) comparative form of སྐྱུར་མོ་.

སྐྱུར་བག (gyūrbaà) sour/ rancid smelling.

སྐྱུར་བུལ་ (gyūrbül) acid base ¶ སྐྱུར་བུལ་དོ་མཉམ་ Acid base equilibrium.

སྐྱུར་མ་ (gyūrma) 1. sm. སྐྱུར་རྩི་. 2. abortion.

སྐྱུར་མོ་ (gyūrmu) sour, acidic.

སྐྱུར་མོ་གཅིག་དང་མ་འཕྲད་ན་ མངར་མོ་ཐམས་ཅད་ཅང་ཅང་ཡིན་ (gyūrmojig ta̱ŋ ma̱trɛnna ŋārmo tāmjɛɛ̀ jāŋjaŋ yi̱n) unless one experiences hardship, one cannot appreciate the pleasures of life [Lit. if one does not taste sth. sour, everything sweet is bland/ tasteless].

སྐྱུར་མོ་ཚྭ་ (gyūrmo tsā) alum.

སྐྱུར་རྩ་ལང་ (gyūrdza la̱ŋ) 1. vi. to get sexually excited/ aroused (usu. as a result of drinking alcohol). 2. vi. to get acid reflux.

སྐྱུར་རྩབས་ (gyūrdzəb) sm. སྐྱུར་རྩི་.

སྐྱུར་རྩི་ (gyūrdzi) any kind of fermenting agent, a starter for fermentation.

སྐྱུར་རྩི་ཐེག་ཐུབ་ (gyūrdzi tēgtup) 1. an antifermenting agent. 2. acid proof; acid resisting.

སྐྱུར་རྩིའི་ཤུན་སྔོན་ (gyūrdzii shǖnŋön) a Chinese medicine used for stomach illnesses.

སྐྱུར་ཚད་ (gyūrdzɛɛ̀) (the degree of) acidity.

སྐྱུར་ཚད་ལྟ་བྱེད་ (gyūrdzɛɛ̀ tājee) an instrument for measuring acidity, acidimeter.

སྐྱུར་ཚད་རྩི་ཆས་ (gyūrtsɛɛ̀ dzīcɛɛ̀) pH meter.

སྐྱུར་ཚད་ཡོ་བྱད་ (gyūrdzɛɛ̀ yo̱pjɛɛ̀) sm. སྐྱུར་ཚད་ལྟ་བྱེད་.

སྐྱུར་ཚལ་ (gyūtsɛɛ) pickled/ fermented vegetables.

སྐྱུར་རྫས་ (gyūrdzɛɛ̀) acid, acidic.

སྐྱུར་ཞན་ (gyūrshɛn) weakly acidic.

སྐྱུར་ཞོ་ (gyūrsho) yogurt.

སྐྱུར་ཟས་ (gyūrsɛɛ̀) sour foods.

སྐྱུར་ཟོ་ (gyūrso) a wooden container for yeast.

སྐྱུར་ཤས་ཆུང་རིགས་ (gyūrshɛɛ̀ cūŋrig) sm. སྐྱུར་ཞན་.

སྐྱུར་ཤོར་ (gyūr shɔ̄ɔ) vi. to go sour, to curdle.

སྐྱུར་གཤིས་ (gyūrshii) acid solvent.

སྐྱུས་ (gyǖù) a generation ¶ སྐྱུས་ཐོག་གཅིག་པ་ The same generation.

སྐྱེ་: p. སྐྱེས་; f. སྐྱེ་ (gyē) 1. vi. to grow ¶ ས་ཆ་འདིར་མེ་ཏོག་ཡག་པོ་སྐྱེ་གི་འདུག Flowers grow well in this place. 2. vi. to be born, to give birth, to have a baby ¶ མོ་ལ་བུ་གཅིག་སྐྱེས་པ་རེད་ She gave birth to a boy. 3. (usu. noun + —) vi. to arise, to come forth ¶ སློབ་ཕྲུག་ཚོས་དགེ་རྒན་ལ་སྐྲག་སྣང་བྱེད་ཀྱི་ཡོད་པ་རེད་ The students are afraid of the teacher [Lit.

fear arises].

སྐྱེ་སྐར་ (gyēgar) sm. སྐྱེས་སྐར་.

སྐྱེ་སྐར་བརྡག (gyēgar dā) va. to foretell sb.'s future by calculating the year, month, day and the hour in which a person is born.

སྐྱེ་སྐྲ་ (gyēdra) the head hair a child is born with.

སྐྱེ་ཁ་ (gyēka) vagina, cervix [Lit. mouth from where one gives birth].

སྐྱེ་ཁག (gyēkaà) married couples in the same household/ family.

སྐྱེ་ཁམས་ (gyēkam) physically ། ཕྲུ་གུ་དེ་སྐྱེ་ཁམས་ཀྱི་ཐོག་ནས་ཡག་པོ་ལོང་འདུག That child has physically grown up well.

སྐྱེ་ཁུངས་ (gyēkuŋ) birth status/ origin, class/ class origin ། ངའི་སྐྱེ་ཁུངས་ཞིང་པ་དབུལ་པོ་ཡིན་ My class origin is that of poor peasant. ། སྐྱེ་ཁུངས་གཙང་མ་ Good (clean) class origins ། སྐྱེ་ཁུངས་བཙོག་པ་ Bad (dirty) class origins.

སྐྱེ་ཁུངས་ཁོ་ན་སྨྲ་བ་ (gyēguŋ kōna māwa) the theory of the unique importance of class origin.

སྐྱེ་ཁུངས་ཁོ་ནར་ལྟ་བ་ (gyēguŋ kōnar dāwa) sm. སྐྱེ་ཁུངས་ཁོ་ན་སྨྲ་བ་.

སྐྱེ་གུ་ (gyēgu) sm. སྐྱེ་དགུ་.

སྐྱེ་གྲོགས་ (gyēdrɔɔ̀) midwifery; va.— བྱེད་.

སྐྱེ་གྲོགས་ཁང་ (gyēdrɔɔ̀kaŋ) midwifery/ birthing hospital.

སྐྱེ་གྲོགས་སྨན་པ་ (gyēdrɔɔ̀ mɛ̄mba) midwife.

སྐྱེ་དགུ་ (gyegu) sentient beings, mankind, humanity ། སྐྱེ་དགུའི་བདེ་སྐྱིད་ The happiness of sentient beings.

སྐྱེ་འགག (gyēngaà) things that are impermanent.

སྐྱེ་འགོག (gyēngɔɔ̀) birth control; va.—བྱེད་ to practice birth control ། རྒྱ་ནག་ནང་སྐྱེ་འགོག་གི་སྲིད་ཇུས་ལག་ལེན་བསྟར་བ་རེད་ In China, they put birth control policy into practice.

སྐྱེ་འགོག་སྨན་ (gyēngɔɔ̀ mɛ̄n) birth control medicine, contraceptives.

སྐྱེ་འགོག་སྨན་བཅོས་ (gyēngɔɔ̀ mɛ̄njöö) birth control/ family planning treatment.

སྐྱེ་འགོག་ཨ་ལོང་ (gyēngɔɔ̀ āloŋ) I.U.D. contraceptive (intrauterine device).

སྐྱེ་འགྲོ་ (gyēndro) sm. སྐྱེ་དགུ་.

སྐྱེ་ག་ན་འཆི་ (gyēga nci) birth, old age, sickness, death (the four stages of human beings).

སྐྱེ་གུ་ (gyēgu) abbr. of སྐྱེ་དགུ་.

སྐྱེ་གུ་མདོ་ (gyēgudo) Jyekundo (Yushu): a town and region in southern Qinghai Province.

སྐྱེ་གུ་བོད་རིགས་རང་སྐྱོང་ཁུལ་ (gyēgu pöriì rāŋgyoŋküü) Jyekundo (Yushu) Autonomous area (in Qinghai Province).

སྐྱེ་རྒྱས་ (gyēgyɛɛ̀) poet. man.

སྐྱེ་རྒྱུས་ (gyēgyüü) 1. biography. 2. sm. སྒྲུང་.

སྐྱེ་སྒོ་ (gyēgo) the outlet of the birth canal.

སྐྱེ་ངན་ (gyēŋɛn) the three forms of lower births (according to Buddhism).

སྐྱེ་དངོས་ (gyēŋöö) biology; living things, organic matter.

སྐྱེ་དངོས་ཀྱི་ཁམས་ (gyēŋöögi kām) the world of living things.

སྐྱེ་དངོས་ཀྱི་འགག་བཅོས་ (gyēŋöögi gagjöö) biological control (e.g. of insects); va.—བྱེད་.

སྐྱེ་དངོས་ཀྱི་མཚོན་ཆ་ (gyēŋöögi tsönja) biological weapon.

སྐྱེ་དངོས་ཀྱི་བཟོ་བཀོད་ (gyēŋöögi sogöö) bio-engineering.

སྐྱེ་དངོས་ཀྱི་རིག་པ་ (gyēŋöögi rigbə) biology.

སྐྱེ་དངོས་ཀྱི་རིགས་ (gyēŋöögi rig) species.

སྐྱེ་དངོས་ཁྲིད་དཔྱོད་ཚན་སྒར་ (gyēŋöö triìjöö tsɛ̄ngaà) biology teaching and research group.

སྐྱེ་དངོས་སྡེ་ཁག (gyēŋöö dekaà) department of biology.

སྐྱེ་དངོས་གནས་ལུགས་དོ་མཉམ་ (gyēŋöö nɛ̄ɛ̀lug doñam) ecological/ biological balance.

སྐྱེ་དངོས་ཕྲ་རབ་ (gyēŋöö trərəb) biological microorganism.

སྐྱེ་དངོས་འཕེལ་འགྱུར་གྱི་རིག་པ་ (gyēŋöö pēlgyurgi rigbə) sm. སྐྱེ་དངོས་འཕེལ་འགྱུར་སྨྲ་བ་.

སྐྱེ་དངོས་འཕེལ་འགྱུར་སྨྲ་བ་ (gyēŋöö pēlgyur māwa) evolutionary theory.

སྐྱེ་དངོས་སྨན་སྦྱོར་བཟོ་གྲྭ་ (gyēŋöö mɛ̄ndeb sodra) biopharmaceutical factory.

སྐྱེ་དངོས་རྫས་འགྱུར་ (gyēŋöö dzɛɛ̀gyur) bio-chemistry.

སྐྱེ་དངོས་རྫས་འགྱུར་གྱི་སྨན་རིགས་ (gyēŋöö dzɛɛ̀gyurgi mɛ̄nrig) biochemical medicines.

སྐྱེ་དངོས་རྫས་འགྱུར་ཚོད་ལྟ་བཤེར་ཁང་ (gyēŋöö dzɛɛ̀gyurgi dōgsherkaŋ) biochemistry laboratory.

སྐྱེ་དངོས་ཞིབ་འཇུག་ཁང་ (gyēŋöö shimjukaŋ) biological research institute, institute of biology.

སྐྱེ་དངོས་རིག་པ་ (gyēŋöö rigbə) biology.

སྐྱེ་དངོས་རིག་པའི་མཁས་པ་ (gyēŋöö rigbe kɛɛ̄ba) biologist.

སྐྱེ་དངོས་རིགས་ (gyēŋöö rig) a species.

སྐྱེ་དངོས་རིགས་འགྱུར་ (gyēŋöö riggyur) biological mutation; biological evolution.

སྐྱེ་དངོས་རུལ་ལུད་ (gyēŋöö rüülüü) organic manure.

སྐྱེ་དངོས་ལ་བརྟེན་པའི་བཟོ་བཀོད་ (gyēŋööla dēnbɛ sogöö) sm. སྐྱེ་དངོས་ཀྱི་བཟོ་བཀོད་.

སྐྱེ་གཅོད་གཤག་བཅོས་ཁང་ (gyēcöö shāgjöögaŋ) (birth control) sterilization clinic/ room.

སྐྱེ་མཆེད་ (gyēceè) 1. brother. 2. sm. དབང་པོ་.

སྐྱེ་མཆེད་ལྔགས་པ་ (gyēceè) sm. སྐྱེ་འབྲས་དྭངས་པོ་.

སྐྱེ་འཆི་ (gyē ci) abbr. birth and death.

སྐྱེ་གཉིས་ (gyēñii) twice born (for castes in India such as Brahman).

སྐྱེ་རྡགས་ (gyēdaà) sm. སྐྱེ་བརྡག.

སྐྱེ་སྡོང་ (gyēdoŋ) a kind of tree (sth. like a banana).

སྐྱེ་སྟོབས་ (gyēdop) 1. growth (innate or natural) ། ཁོང་ལ་སྐྱེ་སྟོབས་དང་སྦྱང་སྟོབས་གཉིས་ཀའི་ཡོན་ཏན་ཚང་ཡོད་པ་རེད་ He has both innate and learned knowledge. 2. growing, growth; vi.—རྒྱས་ to grow well/ vigorously ། འདི་ལོའི་སྟོན་ཏོག་སྐྱེ་སྟོབས་བཟང་པོ་འདུག This year's harvest grew well. ། ད་ལོ་སྟོན་ཏོག་རྒྱས་པ་དང་འགྲོག་ལས་སྒོང་འཕེལ་བྱུང་ This year the crops grew well and the animals increased.

སྐྱེ་སྟོབས་ཀྱི་དཔལ་ཡོན་ (gyēdopgi bɛɛ̄yön) (innate) vigor, vitality; vi.—རྒྱས་; —འཕེལ་ to be full of innate vigor/ vitality, to be imbued with vitality, to be full of youthful spirit ། སྐྱེ་སྟོབས་ཀྱི་དཔལ་ཡོན་རྒྱས་པའི་གཞོན་ནུ་ཚོས་ནུས་པ་ཆེན་གྱི་ལས་དོན་སྒྲུབ་ཐུབ་ཀྱི་ཡོད་པ་རེད་ Youths who are imbued with vigor can accomplish great tasks.

སྐྱེ་སྟོབས་ཀྱི་ཡོན་ཏན་ (gyētopgi yöndɛn) natural/ innate intelligence.

སྐྱེ་སྟོབས་ཀྱི་རིག་པ་ (gyēdopgi rigbə) innate intelligence ། སྐྱེ་སྟོབས་ཀྱི་རིག་པ་ཅན་ An innately intelligent person.

སྐྱེ་སྟོབས་ཀྱི་ཤེས་རབ་ (gyēdopgi sērəp) innate/ inherent wisdom.

སྐྱེ་སྟོབས་ཀྱི་ཤེས་རབ་སྨྲ་བ་ (gyēdopgi shērəp māwa) the theory of natural/ innate intelligence.

སྐྱེ་སྟོབས་རྒྱས་པ་ (gyēdop gyɛɛ̄ba) growing vigorously/ well ། སྤྱི་ཚོགས་གསར་པའི་ནང་གཞོན་ནུ་རྣམས་སྐྱེ་སྟོབས་རྒྱས་བཞིན་པ་རེད་ Youth in the new society are growing vigorously (mentally and physically).

སྐྱེ་སྟོབས་ལྡན་པ་ (gyēdop dɛmba) 1. having innate/ inherent gifts/ qualities ། ཕྲུ་གུ་དེ་སྐྱེ་སྟོབས་ལྡན་པ་ཞིག་ཡིན་ཙང་སློབ་སྦྱོང་གང་བྱས་ཀྱང་ལས་སླ་པོ་ཡོད་ Because the child is gifted whatever he studies is easy for him. 2. growth (iso. strong/ powerful/ good growth) ། ཚན་རིག་གི་ཐབས་ཤེས་སྤྱད་པར་བརྟེན་ཞིང་ཁ་རྣམས་སྐྱེ་སྟོབས་ལྡན་པ་ཞིག་ཏུ་གྱུར་བ་རེད་ Because they used scientific methods the growth of the crops have been very good.

སྐྱེ་སྟོབས་དཔལ་ཡོན་ (gyēdop bɛɛ̄yön gyɛɛ̀) sm. སྐྱེ་སྟོབས་ཀྱི་དཔལ་ཡོན་.

སྐྱེ་སྟོབས་འཕེལ་ (gyēdop pēl) see སྐྱེ་སྟོབས་.

སྐྱེ་བརྡག (gyēdaà) a thanka commissioned on behalf

of a person who has died; va.—བཞེངས་ to commission a thanka on behalf of sb. who has died.

སྐྱེ་བརྟག་ཞལ་འདེབས་ (gyēdaà shḏndeb) the offering made on the 49th day after death (to help the deceased attain a good rebirth).

སྐྱེ་ཐོག (gyētog) lifetimes, rebirths ¶ སྐྱེ་ཐོག་མང་པོའི་རྗེས་ལ་ཐར་པ་ཐོབ་པ་རེད་ After many rebirths, (he) obtained liberation (nirvana).

སྐྱེ་ཐོབ་ (gyētob) sm. སྐྱེས་སྟོབས་.

སྐྱེ་དུས་ (gyētüü) birth date, birthday.

སྐྱེ་མདོ་ (gyēndo) abbr. སྐྱེ་ནུ་མདོ་.

སྐྱེ་ལྡན་ (gyēndɛn) 1. organic, living ¶ སྐྱེ་ལྡན་གྱི་དངོས་པོ་ Organic/ living matter. 2. the universe.

སྐྱེ་ལྡན་གྱི་ཁམས་ (gyēndɛngi kām) the organic world.

སྐྱེ་ལྡན་གྱི་དངོས་པོ་ (gyēndɛngi ŋȫōbo) organic matter.

སྐྱེ་ལྡན་གྱི་ཕུང་པོ་ (gyēndɛngi pūŋbu) an organism.

སྐྱེ་ལྡན་གྱི་ལུད་ (gyēndɛngi lüü) organic fertilizer.

སྐྱེ་ལྡན་སྟོབས་ཤུགས་ (gyēndɛn dōbshuù) effective strength ¶ དགྲ་བོའི་སྐྱེ་ལྡན་སྟོབས་ཤུགས་ནི་ As for the enemy's effective strength.

སྐྱེ་ལྡན་འདྲེས་སྦྱོར་ (gyēndɛn drḛɛ̀cɔɔ) organic synthesis.

སྐྱེ་ལྡན་ཕྲ་རབ་ (gyēndɛn trərəp) microorganism, microbe.

སྐྱེ་ལྡན་རྫས་འགྱུར་ (gyēndɛn dzḛɛ̀gyur) organic chemistry.

སྐྱེ་ལྡན་རྫས་འགྱུར་རིག་པ་ (gyēndɛn dzḛɛ̀gyurgi ri̱gbə) sm. སྐྱེ་ལྡན་རྫས་འགྱུར་.

སྐྱེ་ལྡན་རྫས་བཟོ་བཟོ་གྲྭ་ (gyēndɛn dzḛɛ̀so so̱dra) organic chemical factory.

སྐྱེ་ལྡན་རིག་པ་ (gyēndɛn ri̱gbə) sm. སྐྱེ་རིག.

སྐྱེ་ལྡུམ་ (gyēdum) 1. Asiatic plantain. 2. a type of grass.

སྐྱེ་སྡོང་ (gyēdoŋ) tree.

སྐྱེ་གནས་ (gyēnɛɛ) 1. sm. སྐྱེ་ཡུལ་. 2. place from where birth originates; vagina. 3. place from which sth. originates.

སྐྱེ་གནས་རྐན་ཡིན་པའི་སྒྲ་ (gyēnɛɛ̀ gēnyimbɛ dra̱) palatal sound (in linguistics).

སྐྱེ་གནས་མཆུ་ཡིན་པའི་སྒྲ་ (gyēnɛɛ̀ cūyimbɛ dra̱) bilabial sound (in linguistics).

སྐྱེ་གནས་སྣ་ཡིན་པའི་སྒྲ་ (gyēnɛɛ̀ nāyimbɛ dra̱) nasal sound (in linguistics).

སྐྱེ་གནས་མཚུངས་པ་ (gyēnɛɛ̀ tsūŋmə) siblings with the same mother.

སྐྱེ་གནས་བཞི་ (gyēnɛɛ̀ shi̱) four types of birth (1. via an egg, e.g. birds; 2. via a womb, e.g., humans; 3. miraculously, e.g., a lama; 4. via warm substances, e.g., bugs).

སྐྱེ་གནས་སོ་ཡིན་པའི་སྒྲ་ (gyēnɛɛ̀ sō yi̱mbɛ dra̱) dental sound (in linguistics).

སྐྱེ་དཔལ་ (gyēbɛɛ) abbr. of སྐྱེ་སྟོབས་ཀྱི་དཔལ་ཡོན་.

སྐྱེ་སྤྲེལ་ (gyēbel) poet. sexual intercourse.

སྐྱེ་སྤྲུལ་ (gyīdrüü) an incarnation, a reincarnation.

སྐྱེ་ཕྲེང་ (gyēteŋ) sm. སྐྱེ་ཕྲེང་.

སྐྱེ་འཕེལ་ (gyēmbee) growth/ increase by reproduction (e.g., in the number of livestock or people); va.—བྱེད་ to increase (by reproduction/ breeding) ¶ སྒོ་ཕྱུགས་སྐྱེ་འཕེལ་ཆེན་པོ་བྱུང་ཡོད་པ་རེད་ They had a great increase in animal livestock.

སྐྱེ་འཕེལ་གྱི་ནུས་པ་ (gyēmbeegi nṳ̄ṳ̄bə) virility; reproductive growth/ strength.

སྐྱེ་འཕེལ་ཕྲ་ཕུང་ (gyēmbee trəbuŋ) reproductive cell.

སྐྱེ་འཕེལ་དབང་པོ་ (gyēmbee wāŋbo) reproductive organs; genitals.

སྐྱེ་འཕྲེང་ (gyētreŋ) sm. སྐྱེ་ཕྲེང་.

སྐྱེ་འཕྲོ་ཆད་ (gyētro cɛ̄ɛ̀) vi. to have reached the (physiological) end of the period of child bearing for women, to have reached menopause.

སྐྱེ་བ་ (gyēwa) birth ¶ མིའི་སྐྱེ་བ་ Human birth (birth as a human). ¶ སྐྱེ་བ་ཕྱི་མ་ future birth; vi.—ལེན་ to be or get born/ reborn ¶ མིའི་སྐྱེ་བ་བླངས་ཙང་ཆོས་བྱེད་པའི་གོ་སྐབས་བྱུང་བ་རེད་ Because he achieved human rebirth he got the opportunity to practice the dharma.

སྐྱེ་བ་སྔོན་མ་ (gyēwa ŋȫnma) previous birth/ life.

སྐྱེ་བ་མཐུན་པ་ (gyēwa tṻmbə) 1. a person born at the same time (year, month, day) as oneself. 2. having the same parents; of the same clan/ lineage.

སྐྱེ་བ་མཐོང་ (gyēwa dōŋ) vi. to experience great hardship/ difficulty ¶ ད་ལོ་ལུང་པའི་ནང་ས་གཡོས་ཆེན་པོ་བྱུང་ཙང་ང་ཚོ་མི་དམངས་རྣམས་སྐྱེ་བ་མཐོང་བྱུང་ Because there was a great earthquake in the country, we the people experienced great hardship.

སྐྱེ་བ་པོ་ (gyēwabo) sentient being.

སྐྱེ་བ་ཕྱི་མ་ (gyēwa cīmə) the next rebirth/ life.

སྐྱེ་བ་ཕྲ་མོ་ (gyēwa trāmo) 1. insects. 2. a shoot (of a plant). 3. sm. བར་དོ་.

སྐྱེ་བ་འཕོ་ (gyēwa pō) vi. to be reborn ¶ མིའི་སྐྱེ་བ་འཕོས་ནས་དུད་འགྲོར་སྐྱེས་པ་རེད་ (He) was reborn as an animal.

སྐྱེ་བ་མོ་ (gyēwamo) sm. སྐྱེ་བ་དམན་.

སྐྱེ་བ་དམན་ (gyēwa mēn) woman.

སྐྱེ་བ་བཟང་པོ་ (gyēwa sa̱ŋbo) the three higher realms of birth (gods, demigods and humans).

སྐྱེ་བ་རིམ་བརྒྱུད་ (gyēwa ri̱mgyüü) the chain of birth and rebirths.

སྐྱེ་བ་ལེན་ (gyēwa le̱n) see སྐྱེ་བ་.

སྐྱེ་བའི་ལམ་སྒོར་ (gyēwɛ la̱mder) poet. mother.

སྐྱེ་བས་རྒྱས་ (gyēwɛ gyɛ̱ɛ̀) poet. man.

སྐྱེ་བས་མཐོ་ (gyēwɛɛ̀ tō) poet. man.

སྐྱེ་བས་དམན་པ་ ((gyēwɛɛ̀ mēnba) poet. woman.

སྐྱེ་བོ་ (gyēwo) 1. mankind ¶ སྐྱེ་བོ་ཀུན་གྱི་བདེ་དོན་ For the good of mankind. 2. person ¶ སྐྱེ་བོ་འགའ་གླས་ནས་ Having hired several persons.

སྐྱེ་བོ་ཀུན་འཛུག (gyēwo gṻnjuù) poet. brothel.

སྐྱེ་བོ་ངན་པ་ (gyēwo ŋḛmba) a knave, an evil/ mean person.

སྐྱེ་བོ་ཅོད་པན་ (gyēwo jȫōbɛn) poet. hat.

སྐྱེ་བོ་ཆ་ལུགས་ (gyēwo cālug) clothes; ornaments.

སྐྱེ་བོ་ཐ་མལ་བ་ (gyēwo tāmɛɛwa) ordinary lay person.

སྐྱེ་བོ་དམ་པ་ (gyēwo ta̱mba) a good/ righteous person.

སྐྱེ་བོ་ཕལ་བ་ (gyēwo pɛ̄ɛwa) the people, the common folk, the general public.

སྐྱེ་བོའི་ཚོགས་ (gyēwȫ tsōò) gathering of many people ¶ ཁོང་གིས་སྐྱེ་བོའི་ཚོགས་ཀྱི་དཀྱིལ་དུ་གཏམ་བཤད་བྱས་པ་རེད་ He gave a speech amidst a gathering of many people.

སྐྱེ་བོས་བསྐུར་མ་ (gyēwöö gṻümə) madam of a brothel.

སྐྱེ་འབྲས་ (gyēndrɛɛ̀) body, appearance, features, looks ¶ སྐྱེ་འབྲས་དྭངས་པོ་; སྐྱེ་འབྲས་མཚར་པོ་; སྐྱེ་འབྲས་གཙང་མ་ Beautiful, good-looking, attractive.

སྐྱེ་འབྲས་ལེགས་པ་ (gyēndrɛɛ̀ le̱gba) beautiful, good-looking.

སྐྱེ་སྦྱང་ཉོང་གསུམ་གྱི་ཡོན་ཏན་ (gyējaŋ ño̱ŋsumgi yö̱ndɛn) the three types of knowledge: innate, by learning and training, by experience.

སྐྱེ་མ་ (gyēma) woman ¶ སྐྱེ་མའི་ཁྲུས་ཁང་ Woman's shower room.

སྐྱེ་མ་མོ་ (gyēmamo) woman.

སྐྱེ་མེད་ (gyēmeè) inorganic, nonliving.

སྐྱེ་མེད་ཀྱི་རྩ་ (gyēmeègi tsā) sm. སྐྱེ་མེད་རྩ་.

སྐྱེ་མེད་ཁམས་ (gyēmeè kām) the inorganic world.

སྐྱེ་མེད་དངོས་པོ་ (gyēmeè ŋȫōbo) inorganic matter.

སྐྱེ་མེད་དངོས་རྫས་ (gyēmeè ŋȫōdzɛɛ̀) inorganic matter.

སྐྱེ་མེད་འཆི་མེད་ (gyēmeè cīmeè) 1. a tradition of leasing animals among the nomads of Tibet wherein the return payment of butter is fixed regardless of the increase or decrease of the leased animals. 2. policy in China's post 1978 private responsibility system wherein commune land was distributed semipermanently to households and new births don't get additional land while land isn't lost when a household member dies.

སྐྱེ་མེད་བདེ་ཆེན་ (gyēmeè decen) the great joy of nirvana.

སྐྱེ་མེད་འདྲེས་སྦྱོར་དངོས་རྫས་ (gyēmeè dreèjɔɔ ŋöödzɛɛ̀) inorganic compounds.

སྐྱེ་མེད་ཐུག་ཟད་ (gyēmeè tugsɛɛ̀) sm. སྐྱེད་མེད་ཐུག་ཟད་.

སྐྱེ་མེད་བཙན་ས་ (gyēmeè dzɛ̄nsa) nirvana.

སྐྱེ་མེད་ཚྭ་ (gyēmeè tsā) inorganic salts.

སྐྱེ་མེད་རྫས་འགྱུར་ (gyēmeè dzɛɛ̀gyur) inorganic chemistry.

སྐྱེ་མེད་རྫས་འགྱུར་གྱི་རིག་པ་ (gyēmeè dzɛɛ̀gyurgi rigpə) sm. སྐྱེ་མེད་རྫས་འགྱུར་.

སྐྱེ་མེད་ལུད་རྫས་ (gyēmeè lüüdzɛɛ̀) inorganic fertilizer.

སྐྱེ་མེད་ཤི་མེད་ (gyēmeè shīmeè) sm. སྐྱེ་མེད་འཆི་མེད་.

སྐྱེ་དམན་ (gyēmɛn) woman.

སྐྱེ་རྨོངས་ (gyēmoŋ) ignorant people (those who don't know religion).

སྐྱེ་ཚེ་ (gyēdze) 1. sm. སྐྱེ་ཚེ་. 2. sm. སྐྱེ་ཚེས་.

སྐྱེ་ཚེས་ (gyēdzè) birth date.

སྐྱེ་ཚོགས་ (gyēdzoò) growing in a dense clump/ area.

སྐྱེ་འཚར་ (gyētsar) growth ¶ ཕྲུ་གུ་སྐྱེ་འཚར་ཡག་པོ་བྱུང་བཞག The child grew well.

སྐྱེ་འཛིན་ (gyēndzin) poet. vagina.

སྐྱེ་གཞི་རྫས་ཕྲ་ (gyēshi dzɛɛ̀dra) a cell (biological).

སྐྱེ་ཟུག (gyīsuù) labor pain; vi.—རྒྱག to have labor pains.

སྐྱེ་ཟླ་ (gyēda) sm. སྐྱེས་ཟླ་.

སྐྱེ་གཟུགས་ (gyēsug) sm. སྐྱེས་གཟུགས་.

སྐྱེ་གཟུགས་ཚར་པོ་ (gyēsug tsārbo) sm. སྐྱེ་གཟུགས་མཛེས་པོ་.

སྐྱེ་གཟུགས་མཛེས་པོ་ (gyēsug dzeebo) beautiful, good-looking, attractive.

སྐྱེ་གཟེར་ (gyēser) labor pains; vi.—རྒྱག.

སྐྱེ་བཟང་པོ་ (gyē saŋbo) growing well (as of plants), healthy growth ¶ ཞིང་ཁ་འདི་སྟོན་ཏོག་སྐྱེ་བཟང་པོ་འདུག This field has a crop that is growing well.

སྐྱེ་བཟང་བྱེ་ (gyēsaŋ ce) vi. to become bald.

སྐྱེ་ཡུལ་ (gyēyüü) sm. སྐྱེས་ཡུལ་.

སྐྱེ་ཡོད་འཆི་ཡོད་ (gyēyöö cīyöö) a system of leasing animals among the nomads of Tibet where butter is paid in accordance to the increase or decrease of the leased animals.

སྐྱེ་ཡོད་ཤི་ཡོད་ (gyēyöö shīyöö) sm. སྐྱེ་ཡོད་འཆི་ཡོད་.

སྐྱེ་གཡོག (gyēyɔɔ) midwifery, midwife; va.—རྒྱག; —བྱེད་ to act as a midwife.

སྐྱེ་གཡོག་མཁན་ (gyēyɔɔgɛn) sm. སྐྱེ་གཡོག་རྒྱུགས་མཁན་.

སྐྱེ་གཡོག་རྒྱུགས་མཁན་ (gyēyɔɔ gyungɛn) midwife.

སྐྱེ་རབས་ (gyērəb) 1. present life. 2. social standing. 3. chronological generations.

སྐྱེ་རིག (gyērig) physiology.

སྐྱེ་རུས་ (gyērüü) abbr. birth and class/ lineage ¶ སྔོན་ཚོགས་སྡེ་རྙིང་པའི་གཉེན་སྒྲིག་སྐབས་སྐྱེ་རུས་བཟང་ཞན་དེ་གལ་ཆེན་པོར་བརྩི་གི་ཡོད་པ་རེད་ In the old society, great importance was placed on the birth and class of people when marrying.

སྐྱེ་རོགས་ (gyēroò) sm. སྐྱེ་གཡོག་རྒྱུགས་མཁན་.

སྐྱེ་རོགས་ཁང་ (gyēroògaŋ) delivery room.

སྐྱེ་རོགས་མ་ (gyēroòma) sm. སྐྱེ་གཡོག་རྒྱུགས་མཁན་.

སྐྱེ་རོགས་སྨན་པ་ (gyēroò mɛ̄mba) obstetrician.

སྐྱེ་ལམ་ (gyēlam) vagina.

སྐྱེ་ལུགས་ (gyēlug) physiology.

སྐྱེ་ལེན་ (gyēlen) sm. སྐྱེ་གཡོག.

སྐྱེ་ལེན་པ་ (gyēlemba) sm. སྐྱེ་གཡོག་རྒྱུགས་མཁན.

སྐྱེ་ལེན་ས་ཚིགས་ (gyēlen sədzii) delivery/ midwifery station.

སྐྱེ་ཤིང་ (gyēshiŋ) tree.

སྐྱེ་ཤུགས་ (gyēshuù) growth, growing power ¶ ད་ལོ་ཆར་ཆུ་དུས་སུ་བབས་ཙང་མེ་ཏོག་སྐྱེ་ཤུགས་ཆེན་པོ་བྱུང་བ་རེད་ This year because the rain came in time the flowers grew greatly (in abundance).

སྐྱེ་ཤོར་ (gyēshɔɔ) miscarriage; vi.—ཐེབས་ to have a miscarriage.

སྐྱེ་ས་ (gyēsa) 1. sm.* སྐྱེ་ཡུལ་. 2. sm. སྐྱེ་རུས.

སྐྱེ་ས་མཐོ་པོ་ (gyēsa tōbo) high birth, birth into a high class or caste.

སྐྱེ་ས་དམའ་པོ་ (gyēsa maabo) low birth, birth into a low class or caste.

སྐྱེ་ས་རུས་ཁུངས་ (gyēsa rüüguŋ) sm. སྐྱེ་རུས་.

སྐྱེ་སས་ཡར་འཐེན་ སྤྱོད་པས་མར་འཐེན་ (gyēsɛɛ̀ yarten jööbɛɛ̀ marten) sb. of high/ noble birth ruining his status or reputation by bad behavior [Lit. pulled up by birth, pulled down by behavior].

སྐྱེ་སེར་རླུང་ (gyēserluŋ) cool breeze.

སྐྱེ་སྲིང་ (gyēsiŋ) growth.

སྐྱེ་སྲིད་ (gyēsii) reincarnation ¶ ཁོང་བླ་མའི་སྐྱེ་སྲིད་རེད་ He is the reincarnation of a lama.

སྐྱེ་བསུ་ (gyēsu) helping in childbirth; va.—བྱེད་ ¶ ཁོང་ཕྲུ་གུ་སྐྱེ་དུས་ཁོ་རང་གི་ཨ་མས་སྐྱེ་བསུ་བྱས་པ་རེད་. When (she) gave birth, her mother helped in the childbirth.

སྐྱེ་ལྷ་ (gyēlha) deity of the area of one's birth, one's birth deity.

སྐྱེག (gyēg) sm. སྐྱིག.

སྐྱེགས་ (gyēg) sm. སྐྱིག.

སྐྱེངས་ (kēŋ) sm. ཁ་སྐྱེངས་.

སྐྱེངས་སྣབས་ (gyēŋdəb) embarrassed, ashamed ¶ མི་དེའི་རྫུན་ཀུ་བ་བརྡོལ་ཙང་སྐྱེངས་སྣབས་ཀྱིས་ཕྱིར་ཐོན་སོང་ Because the man was exposed as lying he was embarrassed and left.

སྐྱེངས་པ་སྣར་ (gyēŋba dēr) va. to make sb. feel embarrassed/ ashamed.

སྐྱེད་: p. བསྐྱེད་; f. སྐྱེད་ (gyēè) 1. vi. to grow larger/ bigger, to widen, to expand, to increase ¶ ཁོ་ཚོ་ལུང་པ་ཡར་རྒྱས་གཏོང་ལག་ལ་སེམས་ཤུགས་ཆེན་པོ་ཞིག་བསྐྱེད་པ་རེད་ Their enthusiasm for developing the country grew. ¶ ལོ་རེ་ནས་ལོ་རེ་བཞིན་ཞིང་ལས་རྒྱ་ཆེར་སྐྱེད་ཀྱི་ཡོད་པ་རེད་ Agriculture has expanded every year. 2. interest ¶ བུ་ལོན་གྱི་སྐྱེད་ Interest of a loan; va.—རྒྱག to charge interest. 3. sm. བཞེས་. 4. vi. to give birth to, to procreate.

སྐྱེད་ཀ་ (gyēèga) sm. སྐྱེད་ཁ་.

སྐྱེད་བཀག (gyēè gāà) shung. arrangement/ terms for the payment of interest ¶ གན་རྒྱ་ནང་གསལ་བུ་ལོན་ངོ་སྐྱེད་ཐོག་ནས་གསུམ་ཟུར་ཆག་ཡང་གིས་འཁྲོས་ལ་སྐྱེད་བཀག་གིས་ལོ་ངོ་གསུམ་གྱི་ཁོངས་སུ་སྤྲོད་ལེན་དགོས་པ་ཡོད་ One third of the principal and interest of the loan will be reduced and the balance will be interest free and payable within a period of 3 years.

སྐྱེད་བཀག་ལོ་དུས་རྒྱས་དཔྱད་ (gyēègaà lotüü gyɛɛ̀jɛɛ̀) shung. making a fixed period for repayment of interest and principal on a loan.

སྐྱེད་སྒྲུན་ (gyēèdrün) expanding, enlarging; va.—བྱེད་.

སྐྱེད་ཁ་ (kēèga) interest, dividends; va.—ལེན་; —རྒྱག to charge interest; va.—གཏོང་ to lend money with interest; vi.—ཆག to have the interest rate decrease/ decline; va.—གཅོག to decrease/ lessen the interest; va.—འབར་ to have the interest rate increase; va.—ཟ་ to charge interest on sth. lent. ¶ མི་ཚང་དེས་བུ་ལོན་ལ་སྐྱེད་ཁ་ཆེན་པོ་ལེན་གྱི་ཡོད་རེད་ That family charges high interest. ¶ ཁོང་སང་ཉིན་བུ་ལོན་གྱི་སྐྱེད་ཁ་ལེན་པར་འགྲོ་གི་རེད་ Tomorrow he is going to collect the interest on his loan.

སྐྱེད་ཁའི་ཚད་ (gyēgɛɛ tsɛ̄ɛ̀) interest rate.

སྐྱེད་འགྲེམས་ (gyēdrem) shung. giving out loans.

སྐྱེད་གཅིག་མ་ (gyēè jīgmə) simple interest (on loans).

སྐྱེད་བཅོལ་ (gyējöö) bank deposit.

སྐྱེད་ལྕི་ (gyēji) high interest.

སྐྱེད་ཆག (gyēcaà) a reduction in interest; va.—གཏོང་.

སྐྱེད་ཆད་ (gyēcɛɛ̀) a shortage/ deficit in (paying) interest; va.—འཛོག to not pay the interest due on a loan on time ¶ མི་ཚང་དེས་སྐྱེད་ཆད་བཞག་ཙང་ཞིང་ཁ་ཤོར་བ་རེད་ Because that family was short on paying interest on the loan, they lost their field.

སྐྱེད་ཆད་ངོ་སྐྱུར་ (gyēcɛɛ ŋogyur) a shortage/ deficit in interest owed is converted into principal.

སྐྱེད་ཆེ་ (gyēcee) 1. high interest (for loans). 2. growing fast (for children).

སྐྱེད་ཆེའི་བུ་ལོན་ (gyēcee pu̲lün) a high interest loan.

སྐྱེད་གཏོང་བྱེད་ (gyēdoŋ ce̲è) va. to lend with interest.

སྐྱེད་ཐོག་སྐྱེད་བརྩེགས་ (gyētɔɔ gyēdzeg) shung. interest on interest; va.—བྱེད་.

སྐྱེད་ཐོན་ (gyētön) progress, advance, development ¶ ད་ལོ་ཕྲུ་གུ་འདི་སློབ་གྲྭ་དེའི་ནང་སློབ་སྦྱོང་སྐྱེད་ཐོན་ཞིག་བྱུང་མ་སོང་ This year the student did not make much progress in school.

སྐྱེད་སྤགས་ (gyēbaà) interest.

སྐྱེད་སྤེལ་ (gyēbel) sm. སྐྱེད་འཕེལ་.

སྐྱེད་འཕེལ་ (gyēmbee) 1. sm. སྐྱེ་འཕེལ་. 2. profit.

སྐྱེད་བྱེད་ (gyēceè) 1. father ¶ བྱམས་བརྩེ་བཀའ་དྲིན་མཚུངས་མེད་སྐྱེད་བྱེད་མཆོག་གི་ཞབས་དྲུང་དུ་. To my father with love and gratitude (heading of a letter). 2. earth. 3. inventor, creator. 4. tree.

སྐྱེད་བྱེད་མ་ (gyēcema) sm. སྐྱེད་མ་.

སྐྱེད་མ་ (gyēma) mother.

སྐྱེད་མེད་ (gyēmeè) interest free ¶ སྐྱེད་མེད་བུ་ལོན་ An interest free loan.

སྐྱེད་མེད་དངུལ་བུན་ (gyēmeè ŋǖübün) an interest free loan of money.

སྐྱེད་མེད་བུ་ལོན་ (gyēmeè pu̲lön) an interest free loan.

སྐྱེད་མེད་གཡར་དངུལ་ (gyēmeè yārŋüü) sm. སྐྱེད་མེད་དངུལ་བུན་.

སྐྱེད་མོས་ཚལ་ (gyēmöö tsɛ̄ɛ) garden, park, grove.

སྐྱེད་དམན་ (gyīmɛn) sm. སྐྱེ་དམན་.

སྐྱེད་ཚད་ (gyētsɛè) 1. interest rate ¶ སྐྱེད་ཚད་མཐོ་པོ་ High interest rate. 2. degree of increase ¶ མི་འབོར་གྱི་སྐྱེད་ཚད་ The increase rate of the population.

སྐྱེད་ཚལ་ (gyētsɛɛ) abbr. of སྐྱེད་མོས་ཚལ་.

སྐྱེད་ཚལ་ཁྲུའུ་ (gyētsɛɛtrū) tib.ch. department of landscape/ gardening.

སྐྱེད་ཚལ་དོ་དམ་ཁྲུའུ་ (gyētsɛɛ t̲odamtrū) tib.ch. department of landscape/ gardening management.

སྐྱེད་ཚལ་ཅན་དུ་འགྱུར་ (gyētsɛɛjɛ̄ntu gyu̲r) vi. to become changed into a garden or a park ¶ གང་སར་ཤིང་སྡོང་མང་པོ་བཏབས་པས་ཡུལ་ལུང་སྐྱེད་ཚལ་ཅན་དུ་འགྱུར་བ་རེད་ Because they have planted greeneries everywhere, the place has become changed into a garden.

སྐྱེད་ཚལ་ལྗོངས་སྐྱུར་རུ་ཁག (gyētsɛɛ jo̲ŋgyur ru̲gaà) garden care team.

སྐྱེད་ཚལ་དུ་འགྱུར་ (gyētsɛɛtu gyu̲r) sm. སྐྱེ་ཚལ་དུ་འགྱུར་.

སྐྱེད་ཚལ་དོ་དམ་ཁྲུའུ་ (gyētsɛɛ t̲odam trū) tib.ch. landscape administration.

སྐྱེད་བཞེས་གནང་ (gyēsheè nāŋ) va. to take (h.) ¶ གོང་ས་མཆོག་སྐུ་གཞོན་ནུའི་དུས་ནས་ལུགས་གཉིས་ཆོས་སྲིད་ཀྱི་ཐུགས་འགན་སྐྱེད་བཞེས་གནང་བ་རེད་ H.H. the Dalai Lama took responsibility for both religious and secular affairs as a young man.

སྐྱེད་བཟང་ (gyēsaŋ) sm. སྐྱེད་བསངས་.

སྐྱེད་ཡོད་མ་རྩ་ (gyēyö m̲adza) interest generating capital.

སྐྱེད་ར་ (gyēēra) fence around a garden.

སྐྱེད་ལ་སྐྱེད་རྒྱག (gyēla gyē gya̲à) shung. va. to add the interest from a loan onto the principal of that loan when the debtor can't make the interest payment; va.—བྱེད་ ¶ བུ་ལོན་གྱི་སྐྱེད་ཁ་ཆད་ཙང་སྐྱེད་ལ་སྐྱེད་རྒྱག་བྱས་པ་རེད་ Because (they) couldn't make the interest payment they added the interest onto the principal.

སྐྱེད་ཤིང་ (gyēshiŋ) trees, fruit tree.

སྐྱེད་སྲིང་ (gyēsiŋ) bringing up, rearing, raising, nourishing; va.—བྱེད་ ¶ གཞོན་ནུ་དེ་ཚོ་གཞུང་གི་རོགས་རམ་འོག་སྐྱེད་སྲིང་བྱུང་བ་རེད་ Those young people were raised with the help of the government.

སྐྱེད་གསོ་ (gyē sō) va. to raise/ bring up children ¶ སྲིད་གཞུང་ནས་སྐྱབས་བཅོལ་བའི་ཕྲུ་གུ་རྣམས་སྐྱེད་གསོ་བྱེད་ཀྱི་ཡོད་པ་རེད་ The government is bringing up the children of the refugees.

སྐྱེད་བསངས་ (gyēsaŋ) shung. clearing up (paying) the old/ overdue interest on a loan; va.—རྒྱག ¶ གཞུང་བུན་རྙིང་པ་རྣམས་ཀྱི་སྐྱེད་བསངས་བརྒྱབ་པ་རེད་ (They) cleared up the interest (owed) on (their) old government loans.

སྐྱེད་བསྲིང་ (gyēsiŋ) sm. སྐྱེད་སྲིང་.

སྐྱེན་པ་ (gyēmba) sm. སྐྱེན་པོ་.

སྐྱེན་པོ་ (kēmbo) 1. skillful, talented ¶ ལག་པ་སྐྱེན་པོ་ Skillful with hands. 2. easy, easily, fast, rapid, quick ¶ ལུགས་སྲོལ་གསར་པ་དར་སྐྱེན་པོ་བྱུང་བ་རེད་ The new custom caught on easily. ¶ མི་འདི་ཁྲོང་ལངས་སྐྱེན་པོ་ཡོད་རེད་ This person is quick to anger.

སྐྱེན་ཡང་པོ་ (gyēn ya̲ŋbo) sm. སྐྱེན་ཡང་བ་.

སྐྱེན་ཡང་བ་ (gyēn ya̲ŋwa) adroit, skillful, agile, nimble ¶ ལུས་རྩལ་སྐྱེན་ཡང་བ་ Very agile in gymnastics.

སྐྱེམ་ (gyēm) sm. སྐྱེམས་.

སྐྱེམས་ (gyēm) 1. a drink, a beverage (h.); va.—བཞེས་ to drink 2. vi. to get/ be thirsty (h.) ¶ ཁོང་ཞལ་སྐྱེམས་ཙང་སྐྱེམས་ཞིག་ཕུལ་བ་རེད་ They gave him something to quench his thirst because he was thirsty.

སྐྱེམས་ཆང་ (gyēmcaŋ) beer.

སྐྱེམས་ཆུ་ (gyēmcu) water for drinking.

སྐྱེམས་བྲུས་ (gyēmcu) arc. a pot for storing ཆང་.

སྐྱེམས་དངས་ (gyēmtaŋ) a kind of liquor.

སྐྱེམས་ཚུགས་ (gyēmtsuū) a cup for beverages.

སྐྱེམས་ཚུལ་ (gyēmtsul) a drink.

སྐྱེམས་ཛི་ (gyēmje) arc. a small clay pot for ཆང་.

སྐྱེམས་ཤོག (gyēmsoò) a type of high quality traditional Tibetan paper that was made in Kongpo.

སྐྱེམས་གསོལ་ (gyēmsöö) sm. སྐྱེམས་, 1.

སྐྱེར་ཀ་ (gyērga) pale yellow.

སྐྱེར་དཀར་ (gyērgar) 1. pale yellow. 2. berberis jamesiana forrest (Tibetan herbal medicine).

སྐྱེར་སྐྱ་ (gyērgya) sm. སྐྱེར་ཀ་.

སྐྱེར་སྐྱེར་ (gyērgyer) lonely.

སྐྱེར་པ་ (gyērba) a type of plant used for making Tibetan medicines.

སྐྱེར་བའི་བར་ཤུན་ (gyērwɛ pa̲rshün) yellow cypress (a kind of medicine).

སྐྱེར་མ་ (gyērma) acanthaceous indigo.

སྐྱེར་ཚེར་ (gyērma) a type of tree that has thorns.

སྐྱེལ་: p. and f. **བསྐྱལ་**; imp. **སྐྱོལ་** (gyēē) 1. va. to deliver, to carry/ bring/ take ¶ ཁྱིམ་སྡོད་བུད་མེད་ཚོར་དཔེ་དེབ་དང་ཚགས་པར་སྐྱེལ་གྱི་ཡོད་པ་རེད་ (They) deliver books and newspapers to the housewives. 2. va. to see off ¶ ཁོ་ཚོ་ཐོན་སྐབས་གནམ་ཐང་བར་སྐྱེལ་བར་ཕྱིན་པ་རེད་ When they left (they) went to the airport to see them off. 3. va. to pass time, to live one's life ¶ ཁོང་གི་མི་ཚེ་མང་བ་རྒྱ་གར་ལ་བསྐྱལ་བ་རེད་ He lived most of his life in India. ¶ ལས་ཀ་མེད་ཙང་དུས་ཚོད་སྐྱེལ་ཁག་པོ་འདུག Because (I) have no work it is hard to pass the time.

སྐྱེལ་ཁུངས་འཁྱོལ་ (gyēēkuŋ kyȫö) 1. vi. to be able to survive/ subsist ¶ ལས་ཀ་འདིས་འཚོ་སྐྱེལ་ཁུངས་འཁྱོལ་ས་མ་རེད་ I will not be able to survive with this job.

སྐྱེལ་ཁུངས་འཁྱོལ་ཙམ་ (gyēēkuŋ kyȫödzam) just managing to survive/ live/ subsist ¶ གླ་ཕོགས་ཕྲན་བུ་འཕར་ཙང་འཚོ་བ་སྐྱེལ་ཁུངས་འཁྱོལ་ཙམ་བྱུང་ I just managed to survive because I got a slight increase in my wage.

སྐྱེལ་གླ་ (gyēēla) delivery fee; va.—སྤྲོད་ to pay a delivery fee.

སྐྱེལ་སྒྲོལ་ (gyēēdröö) escorting; va.—བྱེད་ ¶ བདེ་སྲུང་མི་སྣ་བཞིས་ཁོ་ཚོ་སྐྱེལ་སྒྲོལ་བྱས་པ་རེད་ Four security men escorted them.

སྐྱེལ་དངོས་ (gyēēŋöö) gift, present.

སྐྱེལ་བཅོལ་ (gyēējöö) 1. entrusting/ leaving sth. or sb., checking sth. like luggage; va.—བྱེད་ ། གནམ་ཐང་དུ་འབྱོར་འཕྲལ་ཅ་ལག་རྣམས་སྐྱེལ་བཅོལ་བྱ་དགོས་ As soon as one arrives at the airport, (one) should check one's luggage. 2. requesting sb. to do a favor and take/ deliver sth. ། ངའི་གྲོགས་པོར་ཕྲུ་གུ་སློབ་གྲྭར་སྐྱེལ་བཅོལ་བྱས་པ་ཡིན་ (I) asked my friend to take (my) child to school.

སྐྱེལ་ཆང་ (gyēēcaŋ) beer/ drinks served at the time of the departure of friends/ guests; va.—འགྱོག; —བྱེད་ to serve beer/drinks [Lit. the seeing-off beer].

སྐྱེལ་གཏོང་ (gyēēdoŋ) sending (a letter, etc.); va.—བྱེད་ ། ཡི་གེ་ཞིག་ཁོང་གི་སྐུ་ཚབ་ལ་སྐྱེལ་གཏོང་བྱས་འདུག (They) sent a letter to his representative.

སྐྱེལ་གཏོང་ཁའོ་ (gyēēdoŋ kāwu) allocation and transport office.

སྐྱེལ་སྟོན་ (gyēēdön) party for sb. who is departing.

སྐྱེལ་ཐུང་ (gyēēduŋ) seeing sb. off (but not going too far from one's home to do so); va.—བྱེད་.

སྐྱེལ་དར་ (gyēēdar) ceremonial white scarf given to people who are leaving/ departing; va.—སྤྲོད་; —གཡོགས་ to put a ceremonial white scarf on people who are departing.

སྐྱེལ་འདེན་ (gyēndɛn) ch. liquid nitrogen.

སྐྱེལ་འདྲེན་ (gyēndren) transportation, shipping; va.—བྱེད་ ། མཚོ་ཐོག་སྐྱེལ་འདྲེན་ Ocean transportation.

སྐྱེལ་འདྲེན་ཀུང་སི་ (gyēndren gūŋsi) tib. ch. transport company.

སྐྱེལ་འདྲེན་བཀག་འགོག (gyēndren gāngɔɔ̀) embargo, va.—བྱེད་.

སྐྱེལ་འདྲེན་གྱི་དྲ་བ་ (gyēndrengi trawa) transport network.

སྐྱེལ་འདྲེན་གྱི་བྱ་བ་ (gyēndrengi cawa) transportation service/ work, transportation.

སྐྱེལ་འདྲེན་གྱི་ལམ་ཐིག (gyēndrengi ləmdiì) transportation line/ route.

སྐྱེལ་འདྲེན་གྲུ་གཟིངས་ (gyēndren trudziŋ) cargo ship.

སྐྱེལ་འདྲེན་འཁྱིག་ཐག (gyēndren gyigdaà) conveyor belt.

སྐྱེལ་འདྲེན་སྒྲིག་གཏོང་ཁའོ་ (gyēndren gyigdoŋ kāwu) tib.ch. transport dispatcher's office.

སྐྱེལ་འདྲེན་མཉམ་ལས་ཁང་ (gyēndren ñāmlɛɛgaŋ) transport/ shipping cooperative.

སྐྱེལ་འདྲེན་ཐག་ལེབ་ (gyēndren tāgleb) conveyer belt.

སྐྱེལ་འདྲེན་ཐོ་དམ་ཇུའུ་ (gyēndren todam jūū) tib.ch. transport administration, transport management bureau.

སྐྱེལ་འདྲེན་དྲ་བ་ (gyēndren trawa) sm. སྐྱེལ་འདྲེན་གྱི་དྲ་བ་.

སྐྱེལ་འདྲེན་གནམ་གྲུ་ (gyēndren nəmdru) transport/ cargo plane.

སྐྱེལ་འདྲེན་མེ་ཤུགས་འཕུར་མདའ་ (gyēndren meshuù pūnda) carrier rocket.

སྐྱེལ་འདྲེན་དམག་གྲུ་ (gyēndren məgdru) military transport plane.

སྐྱེལ་འདྲེན་དམག་དཔུང་ (gyēndren məgbuŋ) transportation branch of the military.

སྐྱེལ་འདྲེན་བཟོ་པ་ (gyēndren soba) transportation worker.

སྐྱེལ་འདྲེན་ཡོ་བྱད་ (gyēndren yocɛɛ̀) transportation equipment.

སྐྱེལ་འདྲེན་ལམ་ཐིག (gyēndren ləmdiì) transportation route line.

སྐྱེལ་འདྲེན་ས་ཚུགས་ (gyēndren sədzuù) transportation station.

སྐྱེལ་བྱེད་འཁྱིག་ཐག (gyēēceè gyigdaà) sm. སྐྱེལ་འདྲེན་འཁྱིག་ཐག.

སྐྱེལ་བྱེད་མེ་ཤུགས་འཕུར་མདའ་ (gyēēceè mishuù pūndə) carrier rocket.

སྐྱེལ་འབྱོར་ (gyēnjɔɔ) delivering/ transporting sth. and (having it) arrive ། ལོ་གསར་གོང་ལྷ་སར་སྐྱེལ་འབྱོར་ཐུབ་པ་དགོས་ཀྱི་འདུག (They) need to have it delivered in Lhasa before New Year's day.

སྐྱེལ་འདྲིལ་འགྲོ་ལམ་ (gyēndree drolam) sm. སྐྱེལ་འདྲེན་གྱི་ལམ་ཐིག.

སྐྱེལ་མ་ (gyēēma) escort; va.—བྱེད་ to escort ། འབྲས་ལྗོངས་བར་གཞུང་གི་སྐྱེལ་མ་མི་གཅིག་ཡོད་ (We) had one government escort up to Sikim.

སྐྱེལ་མི་ (gyēēmi) person who sees sb. off; va.—བྱེད་ to see sb. off.

སྐྱེལ་རྫོང་ (gyēdzoŋ) going away gift/ present.

སྐྱེལ་རེས་ (gyēēreè) 1. giving reciprocally; va.—བྱེད་. 2. the scheduling of a time (e.g., once a week or month) when family members can bring food and clothing to prisoners; va.—བྱེད་.

སྐྱེལ་རོགས་ (gyēērɔɔ̀) 1. escorting; va.—བྱེད་ to escort ། སྐུ་མགྲོན་སྐྱེལ་རོགས་བྱེད་ Escorting the guests. 2. conveying; va.—བྱེད་ ། ལན་སྐྱེལ་རོགས་བྱེད་པ་ To convey a message.

སྐྱེལ་བསུ་ (gyēēsu) welcoming/ receiving and sending off; va.—བྱེད་ ། འགྲུལ་པ་སྐྱེལ་བསུ་བྱེད་མཁན་གྱི་མི་སྣ་ The people who welcome and see off travelers.

སྐྱེས་ (gyēè) 1. p. of སྐྱེ. 2. present, gift ། སྐྱེས་སྐར་གྱི་སྐྱེས་ A birthday present. 3. (name of place/ area + —) born in that area ། བོད་སྐྱེས་ Born in Tibet. 4. people ། སྐྱེས་པོ་མོ་ཐམས་ཅད་ All people, male and female.

སྐྱེས་ཀྱི་མཆོག (gyēègi cɔɔ̀) precious/ valuable gift.

སྐྱེས་སྐར་ (gyēègar) birthday, date of birth; va.—བརྟག to examine/ investigate astrologically a person's birthday/ birth star.

སྐྱེས་སྐར་ཤོག་བྱང་ (gyēègar shɔgjaŋ) birthday card.

སྐྱེས་ཁ་མོ་བསྒྱུར་ (gyēèga mogyur) a woman taking charge (of a household) because of an incompetent man.

སྐྱེས་རྒྱལ་དམན་ (gyēègyemɛn) abbr. man and woman.

སྐྱེས་དངོས་ (gyēèŋöö̀) living things.

སྐྱེས་དངོས་རྫས་འགྱུར་རིག་པ་ (gyēèŋöö̀ dzɛgyur rigbə) biochemistry.

སྐྱེས་དངོས་རིག་པ་ (gyēèŋöö̀ rigbə) biology.

སྐྱེས་དངོས་རིག་པའི་མཁས་པ་ (gyēèŋöö̀ rigbee kɛ̄ɛba) biologist.

སྐྱེས་ཆེན་ (དམ་པ་) (gyēècen) 1. a holy person (usu. refers to a lama). 2. large gift/ present.

སྐྱེས་མཆོག (gyēcɔɔ̀) sm. སྐྱེས་ཆེན་.

སྐྱེས་རྗེས་ཁྲག་ཤོར་ (gyēējeè trāgshɔɔ) postpartum hemorrhaging/ bleeding.

སྐྱེས་སྟོབས་ (gyēèdɔb) sm. སྐྱེ་སྟོབས་.

སྐྱེས་སྟོབས་ཀྱི་ཡོན་ཏན་ (gyēèdobgi yöndɛn) natural/ innate intelligence.

སྐྱེས་སྟོབས་ཀྱི་རིག་པ་ (gyēèdobgi rigbə) སྐྱེ་སྟོབས་ཀྱི་རིག་པ་.

སྐྱེས་སྟོབས་ཀྱི་ཤེས་རབ་ (gyēèdobgi shērəb) sm. སྐྱེ་སྟོབས་ཀྱི་རིག་པ་.

སྐྱེས་སྟོབས་ཀྱི་ཤེས་རབ་སྨྲ་བ་ (gyēèdobgi shērəb māwa) sm. སྐྱེ་སྟོབས་ཀྱི་ཤེས་རབ་སྨྲ་བ་.

སྐྱེས་སྟོབས་དམའ་པོ་ (gyēèdob māābo) low natural/ innate intelligence ། མི་དེ་སྐྱེས་སྟོབས་དམའ་པོ་ཡིན་པས་ཡོན་ཏན་ཤེས་ཁག་པོ་འདུག Because the person is of low intelligence it is hard for him to gain knowledge.

སྐྱེས་ཐོབ་ (gyēèdob) sm. སྐྱེས་སྟོབས་.

སྐྱེས་ཐོབ་ཀྱི་ཤེས་རབ་ (gyēèdobgi shēèrəb) natural genius.

སྐྱེས་ཐོབ་མི་དབང་ (gyēèdob miwaŋ) inalienable rights, rights that one is born with ། གདམ་བརྗོད་ཀྱི་རང་དབང་ནི་སྐྱེ་བོ་ཚང་མའི་སྐྱེས་ཐོབ་མི་དབང་ཡིན་ Freedom of speech is an inalienable right of all people.

སྐྱེས་ཐོབ་རང་བཞིན་ (gyēèdob rəŋshin) inherent, inborn, innate.

སྐྱེས་ཐོབ་ཤེས་རབ་ (gyēèdob shērəb) sm. སྐྱེ་སྟོབས་ཤེས་རབ་.

སྐྱེས་མཐའ་འཆི་ (gyēèdaa cī) death follows birth ། སྐྱེས་མཐའ་འཆི་ནི་འཇིག་རྟེན་གྱི་ཆོས་ཉིད་ཅིག་ཡིན་ It is a universal law of samsara that death follows birth.

སྐྱེས་དྲིན་ལས་གསོས་དྲིན་ཆེ་ (gyēèdrinlɛ sōödrin cē) one should be more grateful to the one who rears you than the one who gave birth to you.

སྐྱེས་བདག (gyēèdag) poet. iron sheep year.

སྐྱེས་ལྡན་ (gyēèdɛn) human beings.

སྐྱེས་ནག (gyēènag) a lay person.

སྐྱེས་ནོར་ (gyēènɔr) betrothal gifts from the groom to the bride's family.

སྐྱེས་པ་ (gyēba) man, male.

སྐྱེས་པ་ཁྱོ་ག (gyēba kyōga) sm. སྐྱེས་པ་.

སྐྱེས་པ་འགྱུར་ (gyēèba gyur) vi. to have one's sex changed.

སྐྱེས་པ་སྒྱུར་ (gyēèba gyūr) va. to change one's sex.

སྐྱེས་པ་ནང་ཁུལ་གྱི་འཁྲིག་སྤྱོད་ (gyēèba naŋgügi trīgjüü) homosexual relations.

སྐྱེས་པ་པོ་ (gyēèba pō) male.

སྐྱེས་པ་པོ་ལུས་ (gyēèba pōlüü) male body/ form.

སྐྱེས་པའི་གནས་སྐབས་ལྔ་ (gyēèbɛ nɛ̄ɛ̀gəb ŋā) the five stages of life: child, youth, adulthood, middle age and old age.

སྐྱེས་པའི་འབྲས་བུ་ཕྱུང་ (gyēèbɛ drɛ̄ɛ̀bu cūŋ) sm. ཉུག་རུམ་.

སྐྱེས་སྦོར་ (gyēèbor) measurement tool.

སྐྱེས་བོ་ (gyēèbo) sm. སྐྱེས་པ་.

སྐྱེས་ཕྲན་ (gyēètrɛn) 1. youth. 2. prime of adulthood. 3. a small present/ gift. 4. microorganism.

སྐྱེས་ཕྲན་ཚོད་ལྟ་ཁང་ (gyēèdrɛn dzöödagaŋ) microorganism laboratory.

སྐྱེས་བུ་ (gyēèbu) person, human being.

སྐྱེས་བུ་དམ་པ་ (gyēèbu tamba) sm. སྐྱེས་ཆེན་, 1.

སྐྱེས་བུ་ཟོག་པོ་ (gyēèbu sogbo) hypocritical, hypocrite.

སྐྱེས་བུ་རབ་ (gyēèbu rəb) sm. སྙིང་སྟོབས་.

སྐྱེས་བྱེད་ (gyēèjɛɛ̀) sm.* སྐྱེད་བྱེད་.

སྐྱེས་སྦྱང (ས་) (gyēèjaŋ) abbr. knowledge that is both innately acquired and learned ། ཁོང་ལ་སྐྱེས་སྦྱངས་གཉིས་ཀྱི་ཡོན་ཏན་ཡོད་པ་རེད་ He has both innately acquired and learned knowledge.

སྐྱེས་མ་ (gyēèma) poet. 1. woman. 2. bride.

སྐྱེས་མ་ཐག (gyēèmadaà) newborn, just born, new shoots (of a plant) ། སྐྱེས་མ་ཐག་པའི་བྱིས་པ་ A newborn baby.

སྐྱེས་མའི་གུང་སེང་ (gyēèmɛɛ kuŋsaŋ) maternity leave; va.—ལེན་ to take maternity leave; va.—གཏོང་ to give maternity leave.

སྐྱེས་མའི་མཉམ་འབྲེལ་ལྷན་ཚོགས་ (gyēèmɛɛ ñamdree lhɛ̄ndzɔɔ̀) women's federation.

སྐྱེས་མའི་ཚ་ནད་ (gyēèmɛɛ tsānɛɛ̀) puerperal fever.

སྐྱེས་མེད་ལས་བྱེད་སློབ་གྲྭ་ (gyēèmeè lɛ̄ɛ̀jeè lōbdra) school for female cadre.

སྐྱེས་མེད་ཤི་མེད་ (gyēèmeè shīmeè) sm. སྐྱེ་མེད་འཆི་མེད་.

སྐྱེས་དམན་ (gyēèmɛn) sm. སྐྱེ་དམན་.

སྐྱེས་ཚེས་ (gyēdzeè) birthday, day of birth.

སྐྱེས་རྫོང་ (gyēdzoŋ) manor, estate.

སྐྱེས་ཟླ་ (gyēnda) 1. a person's birth month. 2. vi.—ཤར་ to have the month in which a baby is due to be born begin. 3. a month of maternity leave.

སྐྱེས་གཟུགས་ (gyēèsug) physical appearance/ looks ། སྐྱེས་གཟུགས་མཛེས་པོ་ A beautiful appearance.

སྐྱེས་བཟང་ (gyēèsaŋ) beautiful, handsome.

སྐྱེས་ཡུལ་ (gyēèyüü) birthplace ། ངའི་སྐྱེས་ཡུལ་ལྷ་ས་ཡིན་ Lhasa is my birthplace.

སྐྱེས་རབས་ (gyēèrəb) history of a series of previous lives (usu. the Jataka stories of the Buddha's previous lives).

སྐྱེས་རབས་རྣམ་ཐར་ (gyēèrəb nāmtar) sm. སྐྱེས་རབས་.

སྐྱེས་ལ་སྐྱེས་ལན་ (gyēèla gyēèlen) returning a gift with a gift.

སྐྱེས་ལན་ (gyēèlen) a return gift/ present.

སྐྱེས་ལོ་གཅིག་པ་ (gyēèlo jīgbə) people born in the same year.

སྐྱེས་ཤོར་ (gyēèshɔɔ) a miscarriage; vi.—ཐེབས་ to have/ get a miscarriage.

སྐྱེས་ས་ (kēèsa) place of birth.

སྐྱེས་སུ་སྐུར་ (kēèsu gūü) va. to send as a present ། ཤིན་ཏུ་མཛེས་པའི་བུམ་པ་ཞིག་སྐྱེས་སུ་བསྐུར་པ་རེད་ (They) sent a beautiful vase as a present.

སྐྱེས་བསུ་ (gyēèsu) delivering a child, practicing midwifery; va.—བྱེད་.

སྐྱེས་ལྷ་ (gyēèlha) sm. སྐྱེ་ལྷ་.

སྐྱོ་ (gyō) abbr. of སྐྱོ་པོ་.

སྐྱོ་བཀག (gyōgaà) a paste (mixture of glue and wood dust) used to fill holes/ cracks in wood furniture, etc.; va.—རྒྱག.

སྐྱོ་སྐད་ (gyōgɛɛ̀) sm. སྐྱོ་ངག.

སྐྱོ་གར་ (gyōgar) tragedy, sad or melancholy drama.

སྐྱོ་གླུ་ (gyōlu) sad/ melancholy song; va.—གཏོང་.

སྐྱོ་གྲོགས་ (gyōdrɔɔ̀) sm. སྐྱོ་རོགས་.

སྐྱོ་ངག (gyōŋaà) crying in anguish/ sorrow; va.—འདོན་ to cry in anguish/ sorrow ། ལུང་པའི་ནང་ནད་མུག་ཆབས་ཆིག་བྱུང་སྐབས་མི་དམངས་རྣམས་སྐྱོ་ངག་འདོན་གྱི་འདུག Because of the great famine and epidemic in that land the people are crying in anguish.

སྐྱོ་ངད་ (gyōŋɛɛ̀) sm. སྐྱོ་སྣང་.

སྐྱོ་ངེས་ (gyōŋeè) regretting, repenting.

སྐྱོ་ངམ་ (gyōŋam) solemn and stirring.

སྐྱོ་ངོགས་ (gyōŋɔɔ̀) sm. སྐྱོ་སློགས་.

སྐྱོ་སློགས་ (gyōŋɔɔ̀) 1. reviving, renewing, raising; va.—བྱེད་; —བྱས་ ། རྩོད་གཞི་རྙིང་པ་སྐྱོ་སློགས་བྱས་པ་རེད་ (He) again raised an old dispute. 2. lawsuit, dispute.

སྐྱོ་ཆད་དེ་བ་ (gyōjɛɛ̀ tewa) being fed up with sth. or sb., being in an anguished/ gloomy/ sad state of mind ། ལས་ཀའི་ནང་རྙོག་དྲ་མང་པོ་བྱུང་ཙང་ཡིད་སྐྱོ་ཆད་དེ་བ་ཞིག་བྱུང་ I was fed up because there were so many problems at work. ། བཟའ་ཟླ་ཁ་བྲལ་བྱུང་ཙང་སེམས་པ་སྐྱོ་ཆད་དེ་བ་ཞིག་བྱུང་ Because of my separation from my wife I was in a sad state of mind.

སྐྱོ་ཉམས་ཤར་ (gyōñam shāā) sm. སྡུག་ཉམས་ཤར་.

སྐྱོ་དིང་ངེ་བ་ (gyō dīŋŋewa) sm. སྐྱོ་ཆད་དེ་བ་.

སྐྱོ་གདམ་ (gyōdam) memorial speech.

སྐྱོ་ཐང་ (gyōdaŋ) 1. sm. སྐྱོ་འདུར་. 2. a paste made from glue and yellow earth that is used in relief frescos.

སྐྱོ་དར་ (gyōdar) prayer flags erected in cemeteries.

སྐྱོ་གདུང་ (gyōduŋ) sadness.

སྐྱོ་གདོང་ (gyōdoŋ) sad looking face, sad expression.

སྐྱོ་མདངས་ (gyōdaŋ) sad expression.

སྐྱོ་མདོག (gō dɔɔ̀) shabby/ poor/ miserable looking.

སྐྱོ་འདུར་ (gōmdur) a paste-like broth.

སྐྱོ་ལྡུར་ (gyōdur) sm. སྐྱོ་འདུར་.

སྐྱོ་གནས་ (gyōnɛɛ̀) sad or sorrowful news/ situation/ story.

སྐྱོ་སྣང་ (gyōnaŋ) a sad feeling, a feeling of depression/ pessimism; vi.—སྐྱེ་ to feel sad/ depressed/ pessimistic; vi.—སེལ་; va.—སངས་ to overcome or remove sadness/ depression/ pessimism.

སྐྱོ་སྣང་ཡིད་ཆད་ (gyōnaŋ yijɛɛ̀) sad and despondent/ depressed.

སྐྱོ་སྣང་རིང་ལུགས་ (gyōnaŋ riŋluù) pessimism.

སྐྱོ་སྣོན་ (gyōnön) sm. གྲན་གསབ་.

སྐྱོ་པོ་ (gyōbo) 1. sad ། ལོ་རྒྱུས་འདི་སྐྱོ་པོ་འདུག This story is sad. 2. poor ། གནས་སྟངས་སྐྱོ་པོ་དེ་ནས་ From that poor condition. 3. weak ། ཁོང་གི་གཟུགས་པོ་སྐྱོ་པོ་འདུག His physical condition (health) is weak.

སྐྱོ་བ་ (gyōwa) sorrow, sadness, grief; vi.—སྐྱེ་ to feel or become sad/ sorry.

སྐྱོ་བའི་ཟློས་གར་ (gyōwɛɛ dögaa) a tragedy (drama), a sad play.

སྐྱོ་དབྱངས་ (gyōyaŋ) a sad tune.

སྐྱོ་འབུར་ (gyōmbur) a type of Tibetan painting where the paint is raised as in relief carving.

སྐྱོ་བྲན་ (gyōdrɛn) servant, serf.

སྐྱོ་སྦྱར་ (gyōjar) paste, glue; va.—གཏོང་.

སྐྱོ་མ་ (gyōma) 1. a thick, paste-like mixture; va.—

ལྡག to eat [Lit. lick] such a paste mixture. 2. causing a dispute between people by spreading rumors; va.—བྱེད་; —གཡོ་ to cause trouble between people.

སྐྱོ་མ་མངར་མོ་ (gyōma ŋārmo) jam, jelly.

སྐྱོ་མ་སྔ་སྦྱོར་ (gyōma ŋājɔr) the person who first files a lawsuit.

སྐྱོ་མ་སྔ་བཙན་ (gyōma ŋādzɛn) the person who first files a lawsuit has an advantage.

སྐྱོ་མ་འཛུམ་ (gyō ma̲ dzu̲m) partly sad and partly smiling.

སྐྱོ་མོ་ (kōma) sm. སྐྱོ་མ་.

སྐྱོ་མོ་ལུང་ (gyōmaluŋ) an area in the west of Lhasa.

སྐྱོ་མོ་ལུང་པ་ (gyōmoluŋŋɔ) 1. a person from སྐྱོ་མོ་ལུང་. 2. name of an opera troupe in Lhasa.

སྐྱོ་ཚ་ (gyōdza) 1. broth, gruel. 2. a vegetable dish.

སྐྱོ་ར་ (gyōra) a low wall around a house.

སྐྱོ་རིད་ (gyōrii̖) sad looking and thin.

སྐྱོ་རོགས་ (gyōrɔ̄ɔ) 1. a person who consoles sb. in grief; va.—བྱེད་ ། སེམས་པ་སྐྱོ་བའི་སྐབས་སེམས་གསོ་གཏོང་མཁན་གྱི་སྐྱོ་རོགས་ཤིག་དགོས་ཀྱི་འདུག When one is sad, one needs a person to console one. 2. a person who shares suffering with another ། ཁོང་ང་ཚོ་བཙོན་ཁང་ནང་གི་སྐྱོ་རོགས་རེད་ He is sb. who shared his suffering with us in prison.

སྐྱོ་རླུང་སྡུག་ཆར་ (gyōluŋ du̲gjar) bad event/ occurrence [Lit. sad wind, bad rain].

སྐྱོ་ལོག (gyōlɔ̀ɔ) sm. གཉེན་ལོག.

སྐྱོ་ཤས་ (gyōshɛ̀ɛ) sm. སྐྱོ་བ་.

སྐྱོ་ཤུག (gyōshuù) sm. སྐྱོ་བ་.

སྐྱོ་བཤད་ (gyōshɛ̀ɛ) va. to express/ say/ vent one's grievances or one's sadness.

སྐྱོ་སངས་ (gyōsaŋ) sth. to relieve one's sadness, to divert oneself from sadness/ worries ། དེ་རིང་ཁོང་གླིང་ཀར་སྐྱོ་སངས་ལ་ཕྱིན་པ་རེད་ Today he went on a picnic to relieve his sadness.

སྐྱོ་སངས་གནས་ (gyōsaŋ nɛ̄ɛ) holiday resort/ park/ garden.

སྐྱོ་སུན་ (gyōsün) sad, unhappy.

སྐྱོ་གསོས་ (gyōsöö) sm. སྐྱིད་གསོ་.

སྐྱོ་བསང་ (gyōsaŋ) sm. སྐྱོ་སངས་.

སྐྱོ་ལྷང་ལྷང་ (gyō lhāŋlhaŋ) feeling of grief/ sorrow/ sadness.

སྐྱོག (gyɔ̄ɔ) 1. va. to turn, to rotate. 2. va. to step/ move aside.

སྐྱོག་ཙམ་བྱེད་ (gyɔ̄gdzam ce̲è) va. to step/ move aside a little.

སྐྱོགས་ (gyɔ̄ɔ) large ladle.

སྐྱོགས་ལྤྲ་འབུ་ (gyōg dōbu) 1. snail. 2. a person who is slow/ obtuse.

སྐྱོགས་ནག (gyōgnag) iron ladle.

སྐྱོགས་ཤར་ (gyɔ̄ɔshar) churning tea/ soup with a ladle; va.—གཏོང་.

སྐྱོང་: p. བསྐྱངས་; f. བསྐྱང་; imp. སྐྱོང་ (gyōŋ) 1. va. to protect, to take care of, to look after ། མ་ཡིས་དྲིན་དང་བྱམས་པས་རང་གི་ཕྲུ་གུ་བསྐྱངས་པ་བཞིན་ Like a mother taking care of (her) children through love and kindness. 2. va. to rule, to govern ། རྒྱལ་ཚབ་དེས་ཆབ་སྲིད་ལོ་ཉི་ཤུ་བསྐྱངས་ཡོད་པ་རེད་ The Regent has ruled the government for twenty years. 3. a verb used after other verbs to indicate politeness ("please") ། བཀའ་གསལ་གནང་སྐྱོང་ Please reply (h.). 4. va. to manage, to run ། བཟོ་གྲྭ་སྐྱོང་རྒྱུ་ Managing a factory.

སྐྱོང་གྲོགས་ (gyōŋdroò) 1. helping to rule or manage; va.—བྱེད་. 2. sb. who helps to rule or manage/ run.

སྐྱོང་འཐར་བྱེད་ (gyōŋdar ce̲è) sm. སྐྱོང་, 1. and 4.

སྐྱོང་བྲན་ (gyōŋdrɛn) shung. a support, a supporter ། ངེད་ཀྱིས་ཀྱང་བསྟན་པའི་སྐྱོང་བྲན་ལེགས་པར་བྱེད་འདོད་པ་དང་ I also wish to be a good supporter of the dharma.

སྐྱོང་མ་ (gyōŋma) 1. guardian, supporter. 2. mother.

སྐྱོང་འོག (gyōŋwɔ̀ɔ) under the protection/ rule ། རྒྱ་གར་གྱི་སྐྱོང་འོག Under the protection of India.

སྐྱོང་གསོ་ (gyōŋso) nurturing, fostering.

སྐྱོངས་ (gyōŋ) imp. of ཀྱོགས་.

སྐྱོད་: p. བསྐྱོད་; f. སྐྱོད་ (gyöö) 1. va. to go ། ཁོ་ལྷ་སར་བསྐྱོད་འདུག He has gone to Lhasa. 2. vi. to be carried off (by wind, etc.) ། ཤིང་ལོ་སྐམ་པོ་རླུང་གིས་བསྐྱོད་པ་ཆུ་ལ་ལྷུངས་པ་རེད་ A dry leaf carried by the wind fell in the water. 3. (place + —) bound for somewhere ། བོད་སྐྱོད་ Tibet bound.

སྐྱོད་འཁོད་བྱེད་ (gyöögöö ce̲è) va. to go somewhere and reside there.

སྐྱོད་འགྲུལ་ལག་ཁྱེར་ (gyöödüü la̲ggyer) a traveling permit.

སྐྱོད་སའི་འཁོར་ལམ་ (gyöösɛ kɔ̄ɔlam) moving orbit.

སྐྱོན་ (gyön) 1. fault, defect, damage; vi.—ཤོར་; —ཐེབས་ to get damaged/ injured; va.—གཏོང་; —རྒྱག; —བྱེད་ to cause damage/ harm ། འཕྲུལ་འཁོར་འདིར་སྐྱོན་འདུག This machine has a defect. ། སྐྱེལ་འདྲེན་སྐབས་འཕྲུལ་འཁོར་དེ་སྐྱོན་ཤོར་བ་རེད་ During transportation, this machine got damaged. ། སོ་པས་འཕྲུལ་འཁོར་ལ་སྐྱོན་གཏོང་བར་ཡོང་བ་རེད་ The spies came to damage the machines. ། ཁོང་དགོངས་པ་ཞུས་པ་དེས་ལས་ཀར་སྐྱོན་ཆེན་པོ་བརྒྱབ་པ་རེད་ His resigning harmed the work a lot. 2. (adj. + —) too much or too little of the adjective ། ལས་ཀ་ཉུང་ལ་མི་མང་སྐྱོན་འདུག There are too many people for the few jobs.

སྐྱོན་: p. བསྐྱོན་; f. སྐྱོན་ (gyön) h. of རྒྱག.

སྐྱོན་ཀུན་སེལ་ཡོན་ཏན་ཀུན་ལྡན་ (gyöngünsēl yo̲ndɛn gündɛn) removing all faults and having all knowledge (i.e., a Buddha).

སྐྱོན་དགྲིས་ (gyön drii̖) va. to blame ། ངས་ནོར་འཁྲུལ་གྱི་ལས་ཀ་བྱས་ནས་གཞན་ལ་སྐྱོན་དགྲིས་པ་ཡིན་ I made an error on the job and blamed sb. else.

སྐྱོན་སྐྱེ་ (gyöngye) faulty, damaged, broken ། ཁོང་གིས་མེ་མདའ་སྐྱོན་སྐྱེ་ཞིག་ཉོས་བཞག He bought a faulty gun.

སྐྱོན་སྐྱོབ་ (gyöngyob) covering up for sb.; va.—བྱེད་ ། ལས་ཁུངས་ཀྱི་སྒྲིག་ཁྲིམས་རྒྱབ་འགལ་བྱེད་མཁན་ལ་སྐྱོན་སྐྱོབ་བྱེད་རྒྱུ་མེད་ (One) should not cover up for sb. who breaks office regulations.

སྐྱོན་གནོད་ (gyöngöö) damage, harm ། ལུང་པ་དེ་ལ་འདི་ལོ་ཐན་པའི་སྐྱོན་གནོད་ཆེན་པོ་བྱུང་བཞག This year's drought caused great damage in that place.

སྐྱོན་བགྲང་ (gyön dra̲ŋ) sm. སྐྱོན་བརྗོད་བྱེད་.

སྐྱོན་འགེབས་ (gyöngeb) covering up/ concealing/ disguising one's fault or error; va.—བྱེད་.

སྐྱོན་འགེབས་མཛེས་འཚོས་ (gyöngeb dze̲njöö) covering up, concealing, disguising a fault or error so that it looks attractive; va.—བྱེད་ ། མི་ངན་གྱིས་སྐྱོན་འགེབས་མཛེས་འཚོས་ཇི་ལྟར་བྱས་ཀྱང་སྔ་ཕྱིར་མ་ལྟོས་པར་གདོང་རིས་ངོ་མ་ཐོན་ངེས་ཡིན་ No matter how an evil person tries to conceal his faults, sooner or later he is sure to reveal his true self.

སྐྱོན་འགེལ་ (gyöngee) sm. སྐྱོན་དགྲིས་.

སྐྱོན་སྒྲོག་གདུག་བཤེར་ (gyöndrɔ̄ɔ dūgsher) accusing sb. by specifying his wrongdoings; va.—བྱེད་ ། ཁྲིམས་ཁང་ལ་ཉེས་ཅན་གྱི་སྐྱོན་སྒྲོག་གདུག་བཤེར་བྱས་པ་རེད་ (He) exposed the criminal and openly specified his wrongdoings in court.

སྐྱོན་རྔོག (gyön ŋɔ̄ɔ) va. to dig up or uncover faults/ mistakes/ shortcomings ། མི་དེས་རྟག་པར་གཞན་གྱི་སྐྱོན་རྔོག་གི་ཡོད་པ་རེད་ That person digs up other people's faults all the time.

སྐྱོན་ཅན་ (gyönjɛn) faulty, defective, damaged ། དཀར་ཡོལ་སྐྱོན་ཅན་ A damaged cup/ bowl. ། ཆབ་སྲིད་ཀྱི་བསམ་བློ་སྐྱོན་ཅན་ Defective political thoughts.

སྐྱོན་བཅོས་ (gyönjöö) 1. correcting, rectifying; va.—བྱེད་ ། ཡིག་ཆ་འདི་ལ་སྐྱོན་བཅོས་ཤིག་གནང་རོགས་གནང་ Please correct this document.

སྐྱོན་ཆ་ (gyönja) fault, defect, shortcoming ། མི་འདི་ལ་སྐྱོན་ཆ་མང་པོ་ཡོད་པ་རེད་ This person has a lot of faults.

སྐྱོན་ཆག (gyönjaà) damage, harm ། ས་གཡོས་དེས་སྐྱོན་ཆག་ཆེན་པོ་བཟོས་བཞག The earthquake caused great damage.

སྐྱོན་འཇུ་ (gyõn j<u>u</u>) va. to hold onto and pursue sb.'s mistakes/ faults ¶ མི་དེས་ཚོགས་འདུའི་ཐོག་གཞན་གྱི་སྐྱོན་འཇུས་ནས་དྲི་བ་མང་པོ་འདོན་གྱི་ཡོད་པ་རེད་ That person pursued other's mistakes at the meeting and put forth many questions (to them).

སྐྱོན་བརྗོད་ (gyõnjöò) criticism; va.—སྐྱོན་བརྗོད་; —བྱེད་ ¶ ཨ་རིའི་སྲིད་ཇུས་ལ་སྐྱོན་བརྗོད་པ་རེད་ (They) criticized U.S. policy.

སྐྱོན་བརྗོད་འགོག་གནོན་ (gyõnjöò g<u>ɔ</u>gnön) suppressing/ muzzling criticism.

སྐྱོན་བརྗོད་དང་རང་སྐྱོན་རང་བརྗོད་ (gyõnjöòt<u>a</u>ŋ r<u>a</u>ŋgyön r<u>a</u>ŋjöò) criticism and self-criticism.

སྐྱོན་གཏོང་ (gyõn dõŋ) va. to cause damage ¶ ཕྲུ་གུ་འདིས་ཆུ་ཚོད་ལ་སྐྱོན་བཏང་བཞག The child has damaged the watch.

སྐྱོན་གཏོང་ཤོར་ (gyõndoŋ shɔ̃ɔ) vi. to have an injury/ damage occur ¶ མཚོན་ཆ་ལ་སྐྱོན་གཏོང་ཤོར་ན་ If a weapon gets damaged.

སྐྱོན་བདགས་ (gyõndaà) p. of སྐྱོན་འདོགས་.

སྐྱོན་བདགས་ཚོག་ཚོག (gyõndaà cõjoò) quick/ ready to criticize ¶ མི་དེ་ཚོགས་འདུའི་ཐོག་གཞན་ལ་སྐྱོན་བདགས་ཚོག་ཚོག་ཡོད་པ་རེད་ At the meeting that person was quick to criticize others.

སྐྱོན་བདོན་ (gyõn dõn) p. of སྐྱོན་འདོན་.

སྐྱོན་ཏོག (gyõndɔ̀ɔ) supervision, inspection, surveillance, watching over; va.—བྱེད་.

སྐྱོན་ཐོ་ (gyõndo) marking demerits, recording faults; va.—འགོད་ to mark down a demerit, to record a fault.

སྐྱོན་དུ་བསྒྲང་ (gyõndu dr<u>a</u>ŋ) sm. སྐྱོན་བསྲང་.

སྐྱོན་དུ་ལྟ་ (gyõntu dā) sm. སྐྱོན་དུ་འཛིན་.

སྐྱོན་དུ་འཛིན་ (gyõndu dz<u>i</u>n) va. to regard or consider sth. as a fault/ flaw/ error ¶ འགོ་འཁྲིད་དེས་གཞམ་རིམ་ལས་བྱེད་པས་ལས་ཀ་ག་རེ་བྱས་ཀྱང་སྐྱོན་དུ་འཛིན་གྱི་ཡོད་པ་རེད་ That leader regards whatever work the lower officials do as flawed.

སྐྱོན་འདོགས་ (gyõndɔ̀ɔ) finding faults, raising faults; va. སྐྱོན་འདོགས་; —བྱེད་ ¶ འགོ་ཁྲིད་ཀྱིས་ལས་བྱེད་པ་དེ་ལ་སྐྱོན་འདོགས་བྱས་ཏེ་ལས་ཁུངས་ནས་ཕུད་པ་རེད་ The leader raised faults regarding the official and fired him.

སྐྱོན་འདོན་ (gyõn d<u>õ</u>n) sm. སྐྱོན་བརྗོད་.

སྐྱོན་ལྡན་ (gyõndɛn) sm. སྐྱོན་ཅན་.

སྐྱོན་གནོད་ (gyõnnöò) damage, destruction; va.—གཏོང་ ¶ དམག་འཁྲུག་དེས་མི་དམངས་ལ་སྐྱོན་གནོད་ཆེན་པོ་བཏང་བ་རེད་ That war caused great destruction to the people.

སྐྱོན་དཔྱོད་ (gyõnjöò) investigating faults or damages; va.—བྱེད་ ¶ ཁྲིམས་གསར་པ་དེ་ལ་སྐྱོན་དཔྱོད་བྱས་པ་རེད་ They investigated the new law to determine its faults.

སྐྱོན་སྤང་དགེ་སྒྲུབ (gyõnbaŋ g<u>e</u>drup) give up faults/ mistakes and take up what is right and just; va.—བྱེད་.

སྐྱོན་སྤངས་ (gyõnbaŋ) p. of སྐྱོན་སྤོང་.

སྐྱོན་སྤང་གསར་སྒྱུར་ (gyõnbaŋ sãngyur) starting with a clean slate, a new man [Lit. renounce faults, make new].

སྐྱོན་སྤོང་ (gyõn bõŋ) va. to renounce or give up one's mistakes/ faults/ defects/ shortcomings ¶ མི་དེས་ཆང་རག་འཐུང་བའི་སྐྱོན་སྤངས་པ་རེད་ That person gave up the fault of drinking alcohol.

སྐྱོན་སྤོང་དགེ་སྒྲུབ (gyõnbaŋ g<u>e</u>drub) sm. སྐྱོན་སྤང་དགེ་སྒྲུབ.

སྐྱོན་ཕབ (gyõn pə̄b) sm. སྐྱོན་འཛུགས་.

སྐྱོན་བྱེད་ (gyõn c<u>e</u>è) see སྐྱོན་.

སྐྱོན་བྲལ་ (gyõndrɛɛ) without fault/ damage ¶ སྐྱོན་བྲལ་མི་ནི་ཡོད་མ་ཡིན་ There is no person without faults. ¶ འཕྲུལ་ཆས་དེ་སྐྱོན་བྲལ་རེད་ That machine has no faults (is in perfect condition).

སྐྱོན་བྲལ་ལེགས་འཛོམས་ (gyõndrɛɛ l<u>e</u>gdzom) complete, everything good [Lit. without faults, amassing virtue].

སྐྱོན་བྲུས་ (gyõndrüù) sm. སྐྱོན་ཐོག.

སྐྱོན་སྦེད་ (gyõn b<u>e</u>è) va. to hide errors or mistakes.

སྐྱོན་མ་ (gyõnma) sm. སྐྱོན་ཅན་.

སྐྱོན་མེད་ (gyõnmeè) sm. སྐྱོན་བྲལ་.

སྐྱོན་མེད་སྐྱོན་འཚོལ་ (gyõnmeè gyõndzöò) seeking faults where there are none; va.—བྱེད་.

སྐྱོན་མེད་སྐྱོན་འཛུགས་ (gyõnmeè gyõndzuù) blaming (a person) although he is not at fault; va.—བྱེད་.

སྐྱོན་མེད་ཐང་འབབ (gyõnmeè tãŋbəb) safe landing (of a plane).

སྐྱོན་བཙལ་ (gyõn dzɛ̃ɛ) p. of སྐྱོན་འཚོལ་.

སྐྱོན་བཙུགས་ (gyõn dzũù) p. of སྐྱོན་འཛུགས་.

སྐྱོན་ཚིག (gyõndzii) words conveying faults/ flaws/ defects, criticism; va.—འདོན་ to criticize.

སྐྱོན་མཚང་ (gyõndzaŋ) fault, flaw, defect; va.—འབྲུ་; —རྟོལ་ to dig up or expose faults/ flaws/ defects.

སྐྱོན་འཚོལ་ (gyõndzöò) finding fault with, seeking faults/ shortcomings; va. སྐྱོན་འཚོལ་; —བྱེད་ to find faults/ shortcomings.

སྐྱོན་འཚོལ་འཕྲུལ་ཆས་ (gyõndzöò trũũjɛ̀ɛ) lie detector machine.

སྐྱོན་འཛིན་ (gyũn dz<u>i</u>n) 1. va. to keep other's faults/ defects in mind ¶ ཁོས་མི་གཞན་གྱི་སྐྱོན་བཟུང་ནས་ཚོགས་འདུའི་ཐོག་སྐྱོན་རྗོད་དུ་རྩིས་བྱེད་ཀྱི་ཡོད་པ་རེད་ He is keeping in mind the faults of the others and is planning to bring them out at the meeting. 2. sm. སྐྱོན་དུ་འཛིན་.

སྐྱོན་འཛུགས་ (gyõndzuù) accusing, blaming, criticizing; va. སྐྱོན་འཛུགས་; —བྱེད་ ¶ མི་དེ་ཚོར་གཞུང་དངུལ་ཕྱིག་ཟོས་བྱས་པའི་སྐྱོན་འཛུགས་བྱས་པ་རེད་ (They) accused those people of stealing government money.

སྐྱོན་ཞིབ (gyõnshib) checking up or examining for defects/ faults; va.—བྱེད་ ¶ བཟོ་པ་དེ་ཚོས་འཕྲུལ་འཁོར་ལ་སྐྱོན་ཞིབ་བྱེད་ཀྱི་ཡོད་པ་རེད་ The mechanics check the machines for defects.

སྐྱོན་གཞི་ (gyõnshi) the root or base of a flaw/ defect/ fault ¶ ཨ་རག་འཐུང་རྒྱུ་མང་དྲགས་པ་དེ་ཁོང་གི་སྤྱོད་ལམ་གྱི་སྐྱོན་གཞི་གཙོ་བོ་ཡིན་ The basic flaw in his character is his drinking too much.

སྐྱོན་ཟློག (gyõntɔ̀ɔ) preventing or blocking damage/ harm from occurring, saving a bad situation; va. སྐྱོན་ཟློག; —བྱེད་ ¶ ཆུ་རགས་གསར་པ་བརྒྱབ་པ་དེས་ཆུ་ལོག་གི་སྐྱོན་ཟློག་ཐུབ་པ་བྱུང་བ་རེད་ By building the new dam (they) were able to prevent damage.

སྐྱོན་བཟོ་ (gyõn s<u>o</u>) vi. to cause damage/ destruction ¶ ས་གཡོམ་དེས་ལུང་པའི་ནང་ཆབས་ཆེ་བའི་སྐྱོན་བཟོས་བཞག The earthquake has caused great destruction in the land.

སྐྱོན་ཡོན་ (gyõnyön) faults and good points, merit and demerit; va.—བརྗོད་ to explicate the faults and good points ¶ རིག་རྩལ་སྒྲོར་གྱི་སྐྱོན་ཡོན་ The merits and demerits of art and literature (art criticism).

སྐྱོན་ཡོན་བརྗོད་མཁན་ (gyõnyön j<u>öö</u>ñɛn) critics.

སྐྱོན་ཡོན་གསལ་ཡིག (gyõnyön sɛ̃ɛyii) letter of appraisal, letter of criticism.

སྐྱོན་ཤེས་ (gyõnsheè) 1. a knowledgeable/ learned person. 2. arc. doctor.

སྐྱོན་ཤོར་ (gyõn shɔ̃ɔ) see སྐྱོན་.

སྐྱོན་ཤོར་འགན་སྲུང་ (gyõnshɔɔ g<u>e</u>nsuŋ) damage insurance.

སྐྱོན་སེང་ (gyõnseŋ) sm. སྐྱོན་སེལ་.

སྐྱོན་སེལ་ (gyõnsee) repairing, correcting, removing (of faults/ damages/ mistakes) va. སྐྱོན་སེལ་; —བྱེད་ to repair/ remove/ correct faults or damage or mistakes; va.—ཞུ་ to point out/ show a mistake ¶ ལས་ཀའི་ནང་སྐྱོན་ཆ་བྱུང་རིགས་སྐྱོན་སེལ་བྱེད་དགོས་ One should correct the mistakes that occur during work.

སྐྱོན་བསལ་ (gyõn sɛ̄ɛ) p. of སྐྱོན་སེལ་.

སྐྱོན་བསྲང་ (gyõnsaŋ) rectifying or correcting or pointing out sb.'s mistakes/ errors/ faults; va.—བྱེད་ ¶ གྲོགས་པོ་ཉེ་འདོད་ན་ཕན་ཚུན་སྐྱོན་བསྲངས་བྱ་དགོས་པ་རེད་ If (people) desire to be close friends they have to correct each other's mistakes.

སྐྱོབ་: p. **བསྐྱབས་**; f. **བསྐྱབ་**; imp. **སྐྱོབས་** (gyɔ̄b) va. to defend/ protect/ support, to rescue/ save ¶ སྨན་བཅོས་ཀྱི་རོགས་རམ་དེས་མི་མང་པོའི་སྲོག་བསྐྱབས་ཐུབ་པ་རེད་ Because of the medical aid (they) were able to save the lives of many people.

སྐྱོབ་མཁན་ (gyōbgɛn) protector, rescuer, savior.

སྐྱོབ་འཁོར་ (gyōbkɔɔ) ambulance.

སྐྱོབ་གྲུ་ (gyōbdru) lifeboat.

སྐྱོབ་དངུལ་ (gyōbŋüü) relief money/ funds.

སྐྱོབ་སྟོན་ (gyōbdön) protector, rescuer.

སྐྱོབ་ཐབས་ (gyōbdəb) means of helping/ saving/ rescuing; va.—བྱེད་ to do sth. to save/ rescue ¶ སྨན་པས་སྐྱོབ་ཐབས་ཇི་ལྟར་བྱས་ཀྱང་ Even though the doctor tried to save the patient by all means.

སྐྱོབ་ཐབས་མེད་པ་ (gyōbdəb me̱èba) incurable, hopeless, helpless ¶ ཁོང་ལ་སྐྱོབ་ཐབས་མེད་པའི་ནད་གཞི་ཞིག་ཡོད་པ་རེད་ He has a sickness that is incurable. ¶ སྐྱོབ་ཐབས་མེད་པའི་གནས་ཚུལ་ A hopeless situation.

སྐྱོབ་དམག་ (gyōbmaà) relief troops.

སྐྱོབ་རལ་ (gyōbrɛɛ) dirty, soiled (usu. from food, e.g. coagulated tsampa paste on the lip of a cup) ¶ དཀར་ཡོལ་འདི་ལ་སྐྱོབ་རལ་འདུག There is dirt on this cup.

སྐྱོབ་རལ་ཡོག་ཡོག་ (gyōbrɛɛ yo̱gyɔɔ̀) sm. སྐྱོབ་རལ་.

སྐྱོབ་རོགས་ (gyōbrɔɔ̀) 1. aiding/ supporting/ providing relief; va.—བྱེད་ ¶ འགོ་ཁྲིད་དེས་མི་དམངས་རྣམས་སྡུག་བསྔལ་ལས་སྐྱོབ་རོགས་བྱེད་ཀྱི་ཡོད་པ་རེད་ This leader is helping overcome the suffering of the people. 2. protecting, defending; va.—བྱེད་ ¶ ཇག་རྐུན་གྱི་ཉེན་ཁ་ལས་སྐྱོབ་རོགས་བྱས་པ་རེད་ (They) protected the people from bandits and thieves.

སྐྱོབ་སྲུང་ (gyōbsuŋ) sm. སྐྱོབ་རོགས་, 2.

སྐྱོབ་སྲུང་འཁོར་ལོ་ (gyōbsuŋ kɔ̄ɔlo) ambulance.

སྐྱོབ་གསོ་ (gyōbso) relief, aid ¶ སྐྱོབ་གསོ་ཚོགས་པ་ Relief/ aid organization.

སྐྱོབས་ (gyōb) imp. of སྐྱོབ་.

སྐྱོབས་འོག་ (gyōbwɔɔ̀) protected (usu. in an environmental sense) ¶ སྐྱོབས་འོག་འདབ་ཆགས་ Protected birds.

སྐྱོམ་: p. **བསྐྱོམས་**; f. **བསྐྱོམ་**; imp. **སྐྱོམ་** (gyōm) va. to shake, to stir up (liquids) ¶ རི་བསྒུལ་མཚོ་སྐྱོམ་ To move mountains and shake the oceans.

སྐྱོམ་སྐྱོམ་ (gyōmgyom) shaking/ stirring a teapot in a circular motion to re-emulsify the butter with the tea just before pouring it into a cup; va.—བྱེད་; —གཏོང་.

སྐྱོམ་རླབས་ (gyōmləb) blast/ shock wave.

སྐྱོམ་ཤུགས་ (gyōmshuù) sm. སྐྱོམ་རླབས་.

སྐྱོམས་ (gyōm) imp. of སྐྱོམ་.

སྐྱོར་: p. **བསྐྱོར་**; f. **བསྐྱོར་**; imp. **སྐྱོར་** (gyɔ̄ɔ) 1. va. to recite (from memory) ¶ གྲྭ་པ་ཚོས་རྟག་པར་དཔེ་ཆ་སྐྱོར་གྱི་འདུག The monks always recite the books from memory. 2. va. to support, prop/ brace up/ reinforce/ bolster ¶ བོད་སྐྱོར་དངོས་རྫས་ Things (to) support Tibet. ¶ ནད་པ་དེ་མི་གཞན་གྱིས་སྐྱོར་མ་དགོས་པར་འགྲོ་ཐུབ་ཀྱི་འདུག That sick person was able to go around without the support of others. 3. va. to serve second/ additional helpings (of food) ¶ སྐུ་མགྲོན་རྣམས་ལ་བཞེས་ཐུག་ཡང་ཡང་བསྐྱོར་བ་རེད་ (They) frequently served the guests additional helpings of noodles. 4. (vb. + —) to do the verbal action again ¶ བཀའ་མོལ་དེ་གསུང་སྐྱོར་གནང་རོགས་གནང་ (Please) repeat what you were saying again.

སྐྱོར་དཀར་ (gyɔ̄ɔgar) the bowl containing the second/ additional helping of noodles (and from which the noodles are poured into the empty first bowl) ¶ བཞེས་ཐུག་སྐྱོར་དཀར་ཁ་ཕས་ཁྱེར་ཤོག Brings some second helpings of noodles.

སྐྱོར་སྐྱོར་ (gyɔ̄ɔgyɔɔ) fence/ divider/ screen around sth.; va.—འཐེན་ to put up a screen around sth. ¶ ཁོང་ཚོ་གླིང་ཁའི་ནང་སྐྱོར་སྐྱོར་འཐེན་ནས་བསྡད་འདུག They are in the park (picnicking) surrounded by a screen.

སྐྱོར་གྲྭ་ (gyɔ̄ɔdra) place where monks recite in unison the lessons they have memorized.

སྐྱོར་རྒྱག་ (gyɔ̄ɔ gya̱à) sm. སྐྱོར་, 2.

སྐྱོར་དངུལ་ (gyɔ̄ɔŋüü) money to help alleviate a problem.

སྐྱོར་འདོན་ (gyɔ̄ɔdön) reciting texts/ scriptures from memory; va.—བྱེད་.

སྐྱོར་འདྲེན་ (gyɔ̄ɔ gya̱à) supporting sb. with the hand; va.—བྱེད་.

སྐྱོར་དཔོན་ (gyɔ̄rbön) a monk who oversees the སྐྱོར་གྲྭ་ and the monk's recitations.

སྐྱོར་འབྱར་ (gyɔ̄ɔjar) mixing/ aerating tea with a ladle; va.—གཏོང་.

སྐྱོར་འཛིན་ (gyɔ̄njin) sm. གཡོ་སྐྱ་.

སྐྱོར་སྦྱངས་ (gyɔ̄ɔjaŋ) reciting a text/ scripture from memory; va.—བྱེད་ ¶ གྲྭ་པ་ཚོས་དཔེ་ཆ་སྐྱོར་སྦྱངས་བྱེད་ཀྱི་འདུག The monks are reciting texts from memory.

སྐྱོར་མོ་ལུང་ (gyɔ̄rmoluŋ) sm. སྐྱོ་མོ་ལུང་.

སྐྱོར་མོ་ལུང་པ་ (gyɔ̄rmo luŋba) sm. སྐྱོ་མོ་ལུང་པ་.

སྐྱོར་ཚིག་ (gyɔ̄rdzii) 1. text/ prayers/ lessons that are to be recited. 2. words that are repeated (in writing or speech) ¶ མི་དེའི་སྐད་ཆའི་ནང་སྐྱོར་ཚིག་མང་པོ་འདུག That man repeats many things when he talks.

སྐྱོར་ཡ་ (gyɔ̄rya) sb. who supports/ helps/ props up another ¶ སློབ་ཕྲུག་ཚོ་སློབ་སྦྱོང་བྱེད་སྐབས་ལ་སྐྱོར་ཡ་ལེགས་པོ་ཞིག་དགོས་ The students need sb. good to help them in their studies.

སྐྱོར་ཤིང་ (gyɔ̄rshiŋ) a piece of wood used to support/ prop up sth. ¶ ཁང་པ་རྙིང་པ་དེ་ར་སྐྱོར་ཤིང་མང་པོ་བརྒྱབ་འདུག There are many pieces of wood propping up the old house.

སྐྱོལ་ (gyɔ̄l) 1. imp. of སྐྱེལ་. 2. arc. va. to spin thread.

སྐྱོས་ (gyɔ̄ɔ̀) imp. of སྐྱོ་.

སྐྱོས་མ་ (gyɔ̄ɔ̀ma) present, gift.

སྐྲ་ (drā) hair (on head); va.—འབྲེག་ to cut hair, to get a haircut.

སྐྲ་ཀ་ (drāga) sm.* སྐྲ་ཀ་.

སྐྲ་དཀར་ (drāgaa) white/ grey hair.

སྐྲ་དཀར་ཅན་ (drāgaajɛn) white or grey haired person.

སྐྲ་དཀར་གདོང་དམར་ (drāgaa do̱ŋmar) old but healthy looking [Lit. white hair, red face].

སྐྲ་དཀར་མ་ (drāgaama) "The White-Haired Girl" (a revolutionary play).

སྐྲ་དཀར་སང་སང་ (drāgaa sāŋsaŋ) completely white hair.

སྐྲ་དཀར་སོ་ཆག (drāgaa sōjaà) old [Lit. white hair and broken teeth].

སྐྲ་བཀྱིགས་ (drāgyig) sm. སྐྲ་འཁྱིག.

སྐྲ་རྐང་ (drāgaŋ) strand of hair.

སྐྲ་རྐང་གཅིག་གིས་པ་བོང་དཔྱང་བ་ (drāgaŋ jĭggi pa̱boŋ jāŋwa) being in great danger [Lit. a boulder hanging by a single strand of hair].

སྐྲ་སྐུད་ (drɔ̄güü) sm. སྐྲ་འཆིང་.

སྐྲ་སྐོར་ (drāgɔɔ) braided hair that is wrapped around the head; va.—རྒྱག.

སྐྲ་བསྐྱིངས་ (drāgyiŋ) women's hair with gems braided into it.

སྐྲ་ཁང་ (drāgaŋ) barbershop.

སྐྲ་ཁྱིམ་ (drɔ̄kyim) sm. དཔྱལ་པ་.

སྐྲ་ཁྲུས་རྫས་ (drā trǚǜdzɛɛ̀) hair shampoo.

སྐྲ་མཁན་ (drāgɛn) barber.

སྐྲ་འཁྱིག (drāgyig) ornament used by women to connect the ends of two braids.

སྐྲ་གའུ་ (drā ka̱wu) gold box ornament worn on the head of officials of the 4th rank and above in tt.

སྐྲ་གྲངས་ (drātraŋ) sm. སྐྲ་གྲངས་ཆུ་གཉེར་.

སྐྲ་གྲངས་ཆུ་གཉེར་ (drādraŋ cũñer) countless, innumerable ¶ མི་དམངས་ཀྱིས་མྱོང་བའི་སྡུག་བསྔལ་ནི་སྐྲ་གྲངས་ཆུ་གཉེར་ནང་བཞིན་རེད་ The sufferings that the people went through are innumerable [Lit.

the amount of hair on the head; the ripples in the water].

སྐྲ་གྲི་ (drədri) razor; va.—རྒྱག to shave one's head hair with a razor.

སྐྲ་གླ་ (drāla) haircut fee.

སྐྲ་གློད་ (drālöö) wearing one's hair hanging down loosely.

སྐྲ་རྒས་རྒྱག (drāgyeɛɛ̀ gyaà) vi. to look old or weak because of not having one's hair cut for a long time.

སྐྲ་རྒྱན་ (drāgyen) head/ hair ornament.

སྐྲ་སྐྲེ་ཅན་ (drā drejɛn) thin haired, slightly bald.

སྐྲ་བཅད་ལུས་བསྒྱུར་ (drājɛɛ̀ lüügyur) shung. becoming a monk [Lit cutting the hair, transforming the body].

སྐྲ་བཅིངས་ (drəjiŋ) sm. སྐྲ་ཆིངས་.

སྐྲ་ལྕུག (drājoò) 1. a type of hat worn in the Tibetan opera. 2. sm. ཞྭ་ལྕུག.

སྐྲ་ཆིངས་ (drəc'jiŋ) hair ribbon.

སྐྲ་འཆིང་ (drəciŋ) hair ribbon.

སྐྲ་བརྙན་ (drāñɛɛn) wig, toupee.

སྐྲ་རྡིང་ (drādiŋ) sm. སྐྲ་རྩེ་.

སྐྲ་མཐུག་པོ་ (drā tūgbu) thick hair.

སྐྲ་མཐུད་ (drādüü) sm. ལན་ཚེ་.

སྐྲ་འདག་རྫས་ (drā tagdzɛɛ̀) hair shampoo.

སྐྲ་འདབས་ (drəndəb) the end/ tip of hair.

སྐྲ་སྣུམ་ (drənum) hair oil; va.—བྱུག to put/ apply oil on hair.

སྐྲ་པིང་ (drəbiŋ) tib.eng. hair pin, bobby pin, hair clip; va.—རྒྱག.

སྐྲ་པིན་ (drəbin) sm. སྐྲ་པིང་.

སྐྲ་ཕུད་ (drəbüü) the tuft of hair that is left on the shaved head of a boy becoming a monk so that it can be cut during the monk initiation ceremony; va.—འབུལ་; —ཞེན་.

སྐྲ་ཕོན་ (drābön) 1. hair tied in a bun on the head. 2. a bunch of hair.

སྐྲ་ཕྲེང་ (drādreŋ) sm. ལན་བུ་.

སྐྲ་འཕྱིངས་ (drāciŋ) vi. to have hair get/ be tangled, to have unkempt hair.

སྐྲ་བུད་ (drā büü) vi. to get bald, to lose one's hair.

སྐྲ་བུད་ནད་ (drā büünɛɛ̀) a disease that causes loss of hair.

སྐྲ་བྱི་ (drā ci) vi. to lose one's hair, to have one's hair fall out.

སྐྲ་བྱི་སོ་བུད་ (drəji sōbüü) old and decrepit [Lit. hair falling out, losing teeth].

སྐྲ་བྱུག་སྣུམ་ (drā cūnum) sm. སྐྲ་སྣུམ་.

སྐྲ་བྲེགས་ (drā treg) p. of སྐྲ་འབྲེག.

སྐྲ་འབལ་ (drā bɛɛ) va. to rub one's hair with one's fingers.

སྐྲ་འབྲེག (drā treg) sm. སྐྲ་བཞར་.

སྐྲ་འབྲེག་མཁན་ (drā tregñɛn) sm. སྐྲ་མཁན་.

སྐྲ་བད་མགོ་ (drā bɛɛ̀go) bangs (type of hair style).

སྐྲ་བད་བད་ (drā bɛɛ̀bɛɛ̀) a hair style where hair length is up to about the ears.

སྐྲ་བད་ལིང་ (drā bɛliŋ) sm. སྐྲ་བད་མགོ་.

སྐྲ་བྷང་ཀ་ལི་ (drā baŋgali) tib. hind. Western-style hair (for men).

སྐྲ་སྦྲིལ་ (drādree) sm. སྐྲ་འཁྲིག.

སྐྲ་མེད་སྤྱི་ཐེར་ (drāmeè jīter) baldness.

སྐྲ་རྩ་ (drādza) hair roots.

སྐྲ་རྩ་མཐུག་པོ་ (drādza tūgbu) thick hair.

སྐྲ་རྩུབ་པོ་ (drā dzūbu) coarse hair.

སྐྲ་རྩ་གཟིངས་ (drādza siŋ) vi. to have hair stand on end (due to anger/ fear) ¶ ཁོང་དྲག་པོ་ལངས་ནས་སྐྲ་རྩ་གཟིངས་པ་རེད་ His hair stood on end when he got extremely angry.

སྐྲ་རྩེ་ (drādze) the end of a strand of hair.

སྐྲ་རྩེས་བླངས་པའི་ཆུ་ཐིགས་ (drādzeè lāŋbɛ cūdig) very small, minute [Lit. a drop of water taken by the end of a strand of hair].

སྐྲ་ཚབ་ (drədzəb) sm. སྐྲ་བརྙན་.

སྐྲ་ཚར་ (drādzar) ribbon woven into braided hair; va.—རྒྱག to weave a ribbon in one's braids.

སྐྲ་ཚོགས་ (drādzɔɔ̀) volume/ amount of hair ¶ སྐྲ་ཚོགས་མཐུག་པོ་ Thick hair.

སྐྲ་ཚོགས་མཐུག་པོ་ (drātsɔɔ̀ tūgbu) thick hair.

སྐྲ་ཚོམ་ (drādzom) sm. སྐྲ་ཕོན་, 1.

སྐྲ་མཚམས་ (drəndzam) hair part; va.—འབྱེད་ to part the hair.

སྐྲ་འཛིངས་ (drā dziŋ) vi. to be tangled/ disheveled (for head hair).

སྐྲ་འཛིངས་གོས་རུལ་ (drəndziŋ kööhrüü) poor like a beggar [Lit. disheveled (hair) and tattered clothes].

སྐྲ་འཛིན་ (drəndzin) shung. the money paid for permission to wear two braids during the Great Prayer Festival in Lhasa.

སྐྲ་རྫུས་ (drədzüü) sm. སྐྲ་བརྙན་.

སྐྲ་རྫོགས་མཐུག་པོ་ (drədzɔɔ̀ tūgbu) sm. སྐྲ་ཚོགས་མཐུག་པོ་.

སྐྲ་བརྫུས་ (drəbdzüü) sm. སྐྲ་བརྙན་.

སྐྲ་ཞགས་ (drāshaà) 1. women's long braid. 2. poet. women's hair.

སྐྲ་གཞར་ (drā shaa) 1. va. to shave the head. 2. va. to give a haircut, to cut hair.

སྐྲ་གཞར་ཁང་ (drāshagaŋ) barber shop.

སྐྲ་གཞར་ཡོ་བྱད་བཟོ་གྲྭ་ (drāshaa yobjɛɛ̀ sodra) haircutting implements/ equipment factory.

སྐྲ་གཞུག (drəbshuù) hair ribbon/ tassel.

སྐྲ་བཞར་ (drā shaa) p. of སྐྲ་གཞར་.

སྐྲ་བཞར་ཁང་ (drābshagaŋ) barbershop.

སྐྲ་བཞར་པ་ (drābsharwa) barber.

སྐྲ་བཞར་ར་ (drābshara) sm. སྐྲ་བཞར་པ་.

སྐྲ་ཟིང་ཟིང་ (drā siŋsiŋ) unkempt/ untidy hair.

སྐྲ་ཟིང་སོ་བུད་ (drāsiŋ sōbüü) sm. སྐྲ་བྱི་སོ་བུད་.

སྐྲ་གཟིངས་པ་ (drāseŋba) fluffy-haired.

སྐྲ་གཟེར་ (drāsee) sm. སྐྲ་པིང་.

སྐྲ་བཟང་ (drāsaŋ) 1. a man's name. 2. good hair. 3. a Tibetan herbal medicine.

སྐྲ་བཟང་ཟིལ་པ་ (drāsaŋ silwa) corydalis conspera maxim (used in in Tibetan medicine).

སྐྲ་བཟེད་ (drāseè) the cloth/ apron a barber puts around a customer's neck.

སྐྲ་བཟོ་ (drā so) 1. va. to do/ make up one's hair ¶ མོ་སྐྲ་བཟོ་བར་ཕྱིན་སོང་ She went to have her hair made up. 2. hair style.

སྐྲ་རིལ་ (drəril) sm. སྐྲ་ཕོན་, 1.

སྐྲ་ལས་ཁང་ (drālɛgaŋ) barber shop, beauty parlor.

སྐྲ་ལི་བ་ (drāliwə) curly hair.

སྐྲ་ལོ་ (drālo) hair.

སྐྲ་ཤད་ (drāshɛɛ̀) 1. comb; va. སྐྲ་ཤད་; —རྒྱག to comb. 2. a strand of hair.

སྐྲ་ཤུབས་ (drəshub) 1. tassel tied at the end of braided hair. 2. hair net.

སྐྲ་གཤོར་པོ་ (drā shōrbo) coarse hair.

སྐྲ་སིལ་བུ་ (drā siìbu) unbraided hair.

སྐྲ་སུ་རུ་ (drā sūru) sm. སྐྲ་སུ་ལུ་.

སྐྲ་སུ་ལུ་ (drā sūlu) curly hair.

སྐྲ་སེ་ (drāse) salt and pepper hair.

སྐྲ་སེང་ (drāseŋ) space between hair.

སྐྲ་སེང་སེང་ (drā sēŋseŋ) thin hair.

སྐྲ་བསླས་མ་ (drā lɛɛ̀ma) braided hair.

སྐྲ་ལྷ་ (drā lhā) va. to pleat/ braid hair.

སྐྲ་ལྷས་ (drālhɛɛ̀) p. of སྐྲ་ལྷ་.

སྐྲ་ལྷས་མ་ (drā lhɛɛ̀ma) braided hair.

སྐྲ་ལྷུང་ནད་ (drā lhūŋnɛɛ̀) a disease causing baldness.

སྐྲག (drāà) vi. to be scared/ afraid ¶ དཀའ་ཚེགས་ལ་མི་སྐྲག་པར་ Not being afraid of hardship.

སྐྲག་དོགས་ (drāgdɔɔ̀) fear and doubt/ suspicion; va.—བྱེད་ to fear and have doubts/ suspicions.

སྐྲག་འདར་ (drāgdar) shaking with fear; va.—རྒྱག.

སྐྲག་སྣང་ (drānaŋ) fear, fright; vi.—བྱེད་ to fear, to be frightened, to be scared; va.—བསྐུལ་; —སློང་ to scare, to frighten sb. ¶ དམག་མི་རྣམས་ནི་སྐྲག་སྣང་གང་ཡང་མེད་པ་རེད་ The soldiers have no fear at all. ¶ དགེ་རྒན་གྱིས་སློབ་ཕྲུག་ལ་སྐྲག་སྣང་བསྐུལ་བ་རེད་ The teacher scared the students. ¶ སློབ་ཕྲུག་ཚོས་དགེ་རྒན་ལ་སྐྲག་སྣང་བྱེད་ཀྱི་ཡོད་པ་རེད་ The students are afraid of the teacher.

སྐྲག་པ་ཤིང་ (drāgbashiŋ) Chinese hawthorn.

སྐྲག་མ་དངངས་ (drāg ma̱ ŋāŋ) both afraid and shocked.

སྐྲག་མ་འདར་ (drāg ma̱ da̱r) both afraid and shaking, shaking with fear.

སྐྲག་མེད་མ་ (drāgmeèma) a fearless woman.

སྐྲག་ཤོར་ (drāgshɔɔ) sm. སྐྲར་མ.

སྐྲག་སེམས་ (drāgsem) fear; vi.—སྐྱེ་ to be/ get afraid ¶ གདོན་འདྲེ་མཐོང་མ་ཐག་སྐྲག་སེམས་སྐྱེས་པ་རེད་ As soon as he saw the ghost he got scared.

སྐྲག་སློང་ (drāgloŋ) threatening, frightening, intimidating; va.—བྱེད་.

སྐྲང་: p. **སྐྲངས་**; f. **སྐྲང་** (drāŋ) vi. to swell up ¶ ཁོའི་ལག་པ་སྐྲངས་བཞག His hand swelled up.

སྐྲང་པོ་ (drāŋbo) a swelling ¶ སྨན་བཏང་ནས་སྐྲང་པོ་འཇོམས་བཞག He took the medicine and the swelling receded.

སྐྲང་འཇོམས་ (drāŋjom) treating/ overcoming swelling of the body.

སྐྲང་འབུར་ (drāŋbur) an abscess, pimple.

སྐྲང་སྦོས་ (drāŋböö) sm. སྐྲང་འབུར་.

སྐྲངས་ (drāŋ) p. of སྐྲང་.

སྐྲངས་པོ་ (drāŋbo) sm.* སྐྲང་པོ་.

སྐྲངས་སྦོས་ (drāŋböö) sm.* སྐྲང་སྦོས་.

སྐྲན་ (drɛ̄n) 1. tumor. 2. cancerous growth.

སྐྲན་ཆགས་ (drɛ̄n cāà) 1. to become tumorous. 2. vi. to become enemies.

སྐྲན་ནད་ (drɛ̄nnɛɛ̀) sm. སྐྲན་.

སྐྲན་ནད་སྡེ་ཚན་ (drɛ̄nnɛɛ̀ de̱dzɛn) cancer department, department dealing with turmors.

སྐྲན་རོ་ནག་པོ་ (drɛ̄nro na̱gbo) tumor of the womb.

སྐྲན་གསང་ (drɛ̄nsaŋ) a point below the chest where moxabustion is done.

སྐྲབ་: p. **སྐྲབས་** or **བསྐྲབས་** (drāp) arc. 1. sm. འཁྲབ་. 2. va. to knock/ bang. 3. va. to stamp on/ trample.

སྐྲའི་དོ་ཀེར་ (drɛ̄ɛ to̱ger) sm. སྐྲ་ཡོན་, 1.

སྐྲའི་ལན་བུ་ (drɛ̄ɛ lɛ̱mbu) hair plaits/ braids.

སྐྲའི་ལྷས་མ་ (drɛ̄ɛ lhɛ̄ɛma) sm. སྐྲའི་ལན་བུ་.

སྐྲི་ (drī) arc. sm. གདོང་.

སྐྲུ་: p. **བསྐྲུས་**; f. **བསྐྲུ་**; imp. **སྐྲུས་** (drū) 1. va. to beg (usu. food, money). 2. arc. to deceive. 3. arc. va. to cut into pieces.

སྐྲུ་མ་ (drūmə) beggar.

སྐྲུག (drūù) sm. དཀྲུག, 3.

སྐྲུན་: p. and f. **བསྐྲུན་**; imp. **སྐྲུན་** (drūn) 1. va. to make, to construct, to produce ¶ ལག་རྩལ་པ་དེ་ཚོས་གསེར་ལས་སྐུ་འདྲ་མང་པོ་བསྐྲུན་ཡོད་པ་རེད་ Those artisans produced many statues from gold. 2. va. to publish (books) ¶ དཔེ་དེབ་དེ་ཚོ་མི་རིགས་དཔེ་སྐྲུན་ཁང་ནས་བསྐྲུན་པ་རེད་ The Minority Language Press published those books.

སྐྲུམ་ (drūm) meat (h.).

སྐྲུས་ (drūù) imp. of སྐྲུ་.

སྐྲོག: p. **བསྐྲོགས་**; f. **བསྐྲོག**; imp. **སྐྲོགས་** (drɔ̄ɔ) 1. va. to beat/ play a damaru drum (by turning the wrist so the two strikers hit). 2. va. to churn/ stir with a rod/ plunger.

སྐྲོག་ཀ་ (drōga) a lump of fresh butter.

སྐྲོགས་ (drɔ̄ɔ) imp. of སྐྲོག.

སྐྲོང་ས་ (drōŋsa) a town in Bhutan.

སྐྲོད་: p. and f. **བསྐྲད་**; imp. **སྐྲོད་** (dröö) va. to expel, to drive/ kick out ¶ ཁོ་ཚོས་བཙན་འཛུལ་པ་ཚང་མ་རྒྱལ་ཁབ་ནས་སྐྲོད་འདོད་བྱེད་ཀྱི་ཡོད་རེད་ The want to kick all the invaders out of (their) country.

བརྐམ་: p. and f. **བརྐམ་** (gām) vi. to desire/ want/ lust after ¶ རྒྱུ་ནོར་ལ་བརྐམ་པ་ནི་ As for desiring wealth.

བརྐམ་ཆགས་ (gāmjaà) 1. desire, lust. 2. stinginess.

བརྐམ་སེད་ (gāmseè) sm. བརྐམ་ཆགས་.

བརྐུ་ (gū) f. of རྐུ་.

བརྐུན་ (gūn) arc. sm. རྐུ་.

བརྐུས་ (gūù) p. of རྐུ་.

བརྐུས་འཕྲོར་ (gūùgyer) theft, robbery, plunder; va.—བྱེད་.

བརྐུས་དངུལ་ (gūùŋüü) stolen money.

བརྐུས་དངོས་ (gūùŋöö) sm. བརྐུས་ནོར་.

བརྐུས་འཇལ་ (gūnjɛɛ) fine/ penalty for stealing.

བརྐུས་ནོར་ (gūùnɔɔ) stolen goods, loot, plunder.

བརྐུས་ཚོང་ (gūùdzoŋ) selling stolen goods.

བརྐུས་རྫས་ (gūùdzɛɛ̀) sm. བརྐུས་ནོར་.

བརྐུས་ཟོག (gūùsoò) sm. བརྐུས་ནོར་.

བརྐུས་བཟུང་ (gūùsuŋ) seizure of property by dishonest/ illegal means; —བྱེད་.

བརྐུས་ལེན་ (gūùlen) sm. བརྐུས་འཕྲོར་.

བརྐུས་བཤུས་ (gūùshüü) plagiarism; va.—བྱེད་.

བརྐོ་ (gō) f. of རྐོ་.

བརྐོ་བཞེངས་ (gōsheŋ) erecting a statue/ carving; va.—བྱེད་ ¶ དཔའ་བོའི་གཟུགས་བརྙན་བརྐོ་བཞེངས་བྱས་སོང་ (He) erected a statue of the hero.

བརྐོས་ (göö) p. of རྐོ་.

བརྐོས་དཀྲོལ་ (gööröö) carving; va.—རྒྱག ¶ ལྕོག་རྩེ་ལ་བརྐོས་དཀྲོལ་བརྒྱབ་འདུག (He) did carving on the table.

བརྐོས་ཆུ་ (gööju) well water.

བརྐོས་པར་ (gööbar) a carved wooden mould for stamping religious prayers/ mantras.

བརྐོས་བྱང་ (gööjaŋ) wood/ metal on which Tibetan letters are carved.

བརྐོས་མ་ (gööma) sth. carved ¶ ཀ་བ་བརྐོས་མ་ A carved pillar.

བརྐོས་ཡིག (gööyiì) carved letters.

བརྐོས་རིས་ (göörii) a design that is carved.

བརྐོས་ཤུལ་ (gööshüü) remains/ trace of sth. that has been dug up ¶ ས་བརྐོས་ཤུལ་ལ་ཆུ་འཁྱིལ་བཞག Water has puddled in the place in the ground that was dug up.

བརྐྱང་ (gyāŋ) f. of རྐྱོང་.

བརྐྱང་སྐུམ་ (gyāŋgum) sm. བརྐྱངས་སྐུམ་.

བརྐྱང་ནུལ་ (gyōŋnüü) arc. sm. ཞ་ལ་.

བརྐྱངས་ (gyāŋ) : p. of རྐྱོང་.

བརྐྱངས་སྐུམ་ (gyāŋgum) 1. stretching and bending/ contracting ¶ མོ་ཊ་ཆུང་དྲགས་ནས་རྐང་པ་བརྐྱངས་སྐུམ་བྱེད་ས་མི་འདུག Because the car is so small it is hard to stretch/ bend one's legs. 2. flexible, not rigid and fixed ¶ གྲོས་མོལ་བྱེད་སྐབས་སྐད་ཆ་བརྐྱངས་སྐུམ་བྱེད་ས་ཡོད་པ་གོ་དགོས་ When negotiating one must be flexible.

བརྐྱངས་སྐུམ་བྱེད་ས་ཡོད་པ་ (gyāŋgum ce̱sa yö̱öba) see བརྐྱངས་བསྐུམ་.

བརྐྱངས་ཁྲུ་ (gyāŋdru) a measurement equal to the span from the elbow to the tip of the middle finger.

བརྐྱངས་མཐིད་ (gyāŋgyiì) a measurement equal to the span from the tip of the little finger to the tip of the outstretched thumb.

བརྐྱངས་ཉལ་ (gyāŋñɛɛ) sleeping with outstretched arms and legs; va.— བྱེད་.

བརྐྱངས་འདོམ་ (gyāŋdom) a measurement equal to the span from the tip of the fingers of one outstretched arm to the tip of the other; va.—འཇལ་ to measure using this measurement ¶ བརྐྱངས་འདོམ་གང་ One བརྐྱངས་འདོམ་.

བརྐྱངས་ན་མདའ་ཉིན་ བཀུག་ན་གཞུ་ཉིན་ (gyāŋna da̱ñɛn gūgna shu̱ñɛn) sb. who is flexible and can adopt according to the circumstances [Lit. if stretched it can be used as an arrow, if bent used as a bow].

བརྐྱངས་ཕྱག (gyāŋjaà) a form of prostration in which the body is extended flat on the ground; va.—འཚལ་ to do a བརྐྱངས་ཕྱག.

བརྐྱངས་ཙམ་སྐུམ་ཙམ་ (gyāŋdzam gūmdzam) 1. stretching and pulling in hands or legs; va.—བྱེད་. 2. talking/ confessing about sth. and suddenly stopping; va.—བྱེད་.

བརྐྱངས་ཆར་པའི་ཁུ་ཚུར་དེ་ཚུར་བསྐུམ་ཐབས་མ་བྱུང་བ (gyāŋ tsārwɛ kūdzurde tsūr gūmdəb ma̱juŋwa) one can not withdraw/ undo what was already done [Lit. the fist that has been stretched out (to hit), can not be withdrawn].

བརྐྱངས་ཤད་ (gyāŋshɛ̀ɛ) stretching (usu. after waking up from sleep); va.—བྱེད་.

བརྐྱངས་སོར་ལྔ་ (gyāŋsor ŋā) a measurement equal to the span from the knuckle of thumb held under the first finger to the knuckle of pinkie; va.—འཇལ་ to measure using this measurement.

བརྐྱལ་ (gyɛ̄ɛ̀) p. of རྐྱལ་.

བསྐ་བ་ (gāwa) bitter in taste, astringent ¶ རོ་བསྐ་བ་ Bitter taste. 2. thick (for broth, soup).

བསྐང་ (gāŋ) f. of སྐང་ and སྐོང་.

བསྐང་བསྐུལ་ (gāŋgüü) shung. sm. བསྐང་གསོ་.

བསྐང་གཏོར་ (gāŋdɔɔ) torma used in བསྐང་གསོ་ ritual; va.—འབུལ་ to do a བསྐང་གསོ་ ritual.

བསྐང་འཕར་ (gāŋbar) shung. an additional བསྐང་གསོ་ ritual.

བསྐང་རྫས་ (gāŋdzɛɛ̀) materials used in a བསྐང་གསོ་ ritual.

བསྐང་བཤགས་ (gāŋshaà) offering one' s repentance as a part of བསྐང་གསོ་ ritual.

བསྐང་གསོ་ (gāŋso) a ritual to propitiate a protective deity; va.—གཏོང་.

བསྐངས་ (gāŋ) p. of སྐང་ and སྐོང་.

བསྐམ་ (gām) f. of སྐེམ་.

བསྐམས་ (gām) p. of སྐེམ་.

བསྐལ་དུས་བཟང་པོ་ (gɛ̄ɛdüü saŋbo) sm. སྐལ་བཟང་.

བསྐལ་དུས་བཟང་པོའི་ཇ་ཆང་ ནམ་དུས་ངན་པའི་ཁྲལ་ལ་འགྱུར་ (gɛ̄ɛdüü saŋbö cacaŋ namdüü ŋɛmbɛ trɛ̄ɛla gyur) the giving of a voluntary gift is converted into an obligation [Lit. the tea and beer of good times becomes the tax of bad times].

བསྐལ་པ་ (gɛ̄ɛba) era, period, eon.

བསྐལ་པ་ངན་པ་ (gɛ̄ɛba ŋɛmba) a Buddhist period when there were no Buddhas, a bad era/ period.

བསྐལ་པ་གཉིས་ (gɛ̄ɛbañiì) the two periods: the period when there were Buddhas and the period when there were no Buddhas.

བསྐལ་པ་ཐོག་མ་ (gɛ̄ɛba tɔ̄ɔma) sm. བསྐལ་པ་དང་པོ་.

བསྐལ་པ་དང་པོ་ (gɛ̄ɛba taŋbo) the era when the universe first started, the first era.

བསྐལ་པ་བཟང་པོ་ (gɛ̄ɛba saŋbo) a Buddhist periods when there were Buddhas, a good era.

བསྐལ་པ་བཟང་རབ་ (gɛ̄ɛba saŋrəb) sm. བསྐལ་པ་བཟང་པོ་.

བསྐལ་པ་ཡ་ཐོག (gɛ̄ɛba yadɔɔ̀) a Buddhist period when people lived ten thousand years and didn't have to plant crops to subsist.

བསྐལ་པའི་མཐའ་ (gɛ̄ɛbɛ tā) 1. endless. 2. the final eon/ era/ period.

བསྐལ་པ་ཡ་ཐོག (gɛ̄ɛwa yatog) primeval time.

བསྐལ་བཟང་ (gɛ̄ɛsaŋ) abbr. བསྐལ་པ་བཟང་པོ་.

བསྐལ་བཟང་རྒྱ་མཚོ་ (gɛ̄ɛsaŋ gyadzo) name of the 7th Dalai Lama.

བསྐུ་ (gū) f. of སྐུད་.

བསྐུ་མཉེ་ (gūñe) massage, massaging; va.—བྱེད་.

བསྐུག (gūù) f. of སྐུག.

བསྐུགས་ (gūù) p. of སྐུག.

བསྐུང་ (gūŋ) f. of སྐུང་.

བསྐུངས་ (gūŋ) p. of སྐུང་.

བསྐུངས་ཡིག (gūŋyiì) an abbreviated word.

བསྐུམ་ཁྲུ་ (gūmtru) sm. བསྐུམས་ཁྲུ་.

བསྐུམས་ (gūm) p. of སྐུམ་.

བསྐུམས་ཁྲུ་ (gūmdru) a measurement equal to the span from the knuckles of the clenched fist to the elbow.

བསྐུམས་མཁྱིད་ (gūmgyi) a measurement equal to the span from the knuckle of the little finger (in a clenched fist) to the tip of the outstretched thumb.

བསྐུམས་འདོམ་ (gūmdom) a measurement equal to the span from the tip of one outstretched arm to the other.

བསྐུམས་ཕྱག (gūmjaà) prostrating on knees and hands without fully extending one's body.

བསྐུམས་སོར་ལྔ་ (gūmsor ŋā) a measurement equal to the span from the knuckle of the little finger of a clenched fist to the knuckle of the thumb with the tip of the thumb touching the outside of the first finger.

བསྐུར་ (gūr) p. and f. of སྐུར་.

བསྐུར་བཙོལ་ཀུང་སི་ (gūrjöö gūŋsi) tib.ch. shipping company.

བསྐུར་དངུལ་ (gūrŋüü) money that was sent/ mailed to sb.

བསྐུར་ཡིག (gūryiì) letter, correspondence; va.—གཏོང་.

བསྐུར་གསོམ་ (gūrshom) preparing/ getting sth. ready to send; va.—བྱེད་ ¶ གྲོགས་པོར་ལག་རྟགས་བསྐུར་གསོམ་བྱེད་ཀྱི་ཡོད་པ་རེད་ (He) is preparing to send a present to his friend.

བསྐུལ་ (gūū) p. of སྐུལ་.

བསྐུལ་བསྐྱོད་འཁོར་ལོ་ (gūūgyüü kɔ̄ɔlo) sm. སྐུལ་བསྐྱོད་འཁོར་ལོ་.

བསྐུལ་ཁྲིད་ (gūūdrii) sm. སྐུལ་ཁྲིད་.

བསྐུལ་མཁན་ (gūūñɛn) sm. སྐུལ་མཁན་.

བསྐུལ་ངན་ (gūūŋɛn) sm. སྐུལ་ངན་.

བསྐུལ་སྟོབས་ (gūūdob) sm. སྐུལ་སྟོབས་.

བསྐུལ་འདེད་ (kūndeè) sm. སྐུལ་འདེད་.

བསྐུལ་འདེབས་ (gūndeb) sm. སྐུལ་འདེབས་.

བསྐུལ་བརྡ་ (gūūdə) sm. སྐུལ་བརྡ་.

བསྐུལ་སྤེལ་ (gūūbee) sm. སྐུལ་སྤེལ་.

བསྐུལ་བ་ (gūūwa) sm. སྐུལ་བ་.

བསྐུལ་མ་ (gūūmə) sm. སྐུལ་མ་.

བསྐུལ་ཚིག (gūūdzii) sm. སྐུལ་ཚིག.

བསྐུལ་ཟེར་ (gūūsɛɛ̀) sm. སྐུལ་ཟེར་.

བསྐུལ་སློང་ (gūūloŋ) sm. སྐུལ་སློང་.

བསྐུས་ (gūū) p. of སྐུད་.

བསྐོ་ (gō) f. of སྐོ་.

བསྐོ་མངག་ (ས) (gōŋaà) making an appointment (to a post/ job/ position) and giving instructions; va.—བྱེད་; —གནང་ ¶ ཁོང་ལ་ལས་དོན་གསར་པ་བསྐོ་མངགས་བྱས་པ་རེད་ (They) appointed him to a new position (and gave him instructions as to its duties).

བསྐོ་འཐེན་ (gōden) appointment and dismissal ¶ ལས་ཁངས་དེ་ར་ལས་བྱེད་བསྐོ་འཐེན་གྱི་དབང་ཆ་ཡོད་པ་རེད་ That office has power over appointments and dismissals.

བསྐོ་འཐེན་མིང་ཐོ་ (gōten miŋto) shung. list of appointments and dismissals.

བསྐོ་བསྡུལ་ (gōdzɛɛ) sm. བསྐོ་གཞག་གནང་.

བསྐོ་འཛུགས་ (gūndzuù) appointing and establishing; va.—བྱེད་.

བསྐོ་རྫོངས་ (gōdzoŋ) shung. appointing and dispatching; va.—བྱེད་; —གནང་ ¶ སྲིད་གཞུང་ནས་ལས་བྱེད་གསར་པ་མང་པོ་ལས་གནས་སོ་སོར་བསྐོ་རྫོངས་གནང་བ་རེད་ The government appointed and dispatched many new officials to different posts.

བསྐོ་གཞག (gōshaà) appointing (to a position or office); va.—བྱེད་; va.—གནང་ ¶ ཁོང་ལ་ལས་ཚན་གསར་པ་བསྐོ་གཞག་གནང་བ་རེད་ (They) appointed him to a new position.

བསྐོང་ (gōŋ) f. of སྐོང་.

བསྐོང་འགུགས་ (gōŋguù) summoning or calling sb.; va.—བྱེད་ ¶ ལས་ཁུངས་ཀྱིས་ལས་བྱེད་པ་དེ་བསྐོང་འགུགས་བྱས་པ་རེད་ The office summoned the cadre.

བསྐོང་གཏོང་ (gōŋdoŋ) summoning/ recalling and sending; va.—བྱེད་ ¶ དེང་སང་ལས་ཁུངས་ནང་ལས་བྱེད་པ་བསྐོང་གཏོང་གི་ལས་བྲེལ་ཆེན་པོ་འདུག These days the office is very busy summoning and sending officials.

བསྐོང་བསྡུ་ (gōŋdüü) recruiting, enrolling; va.—བྱེད་ ¶ མཐོ་སློབ་ནས་སློབ་ཕྲུག་གསར་པ་ཁག་ཅིག་བསྐོང་བསྡུ་བྱས་པ་རེད་ The university enrolled a batch of new students.

བསྐོང་འཚོགས་ (gōŋdzoò) convening/ summoning people or groups to a meeting ¶ སྲིད་གཞུང་ནས་རྒྱལ་ཡོངས་ཚོགས་འདུ་བསྐོང་འཚོགས་བྱས་པ་རེད་ The government asked the National Assembly to

convene a meeting.
བསྐོངས་ (gōŋ) p. of སྐོང་.
བསྐོན་ (gõn) p. and f. of སྐོན་.
བསྐོར་ (gɔ̄ɔ̄) p. and f. of སྐོར་.
བསྐོར་སྐྱིལ་ (gɔ̄rgyil) surrounding, besieging; va.—བྱེད་ ¶ དམག་འཁྲུག་ནང་དགྲ་བོས་གྲོང་ཁྱེར་དེ་བསྐོར་སྐྱིལ་བྱས་པ་རེད་ During the battle the enemy surrounded the city.
བསྐོར་བསྐྱོད་ (gɔ̄rgyöö̀) sm. སྐོར་བསྐྱོད་.
བསྐོར་བསྐྱོད་དམག་འཐབ་ (gɔ̄rgyöö̀ māgdəb) sm. སྐོར་བསྐྱོད་དམག་འཐབ་.
བསྐོར་བསྐྱོད་སྨན་ཁང་ (gɔ̄rgyöö̀ mɛ̄ngaŋ) traveling medical clinic.
བསྐོར་བསྐྱོད་སྨན་བཅོས་ (gɔ̄rgyöö̀ mɛ̄njöö̀) sm. སྐོར་བསྐྱོད་སྨན་བཅོས་.
བསྐོར་བཅོམ་ (gɔ̄rjom) sm. སྐོར་བཅོམ་.
བསྐོར་འཆག (gɔ̄ɔ̄jaà) sm. སྐོར་འཆག.
བསྐོར་གཏོར་ (gɔ̄rdɔr) sm. སྐོར་གཏོར་.
བསྐོར་ཐེངས་ (gɔ̄rdeŋ) sm. སྐོར་ཐེངས་.
བསྐོར་ཐོ་ (gɔ̄rdo) shung. notes of an inspection tour.; va.—རྒྱག; —འགོད་ to write notes when inspecting/ investigating sth.
བསྐོར་འདྲི་ (gɔ̄ndri) sm. སྐོར་འདྲི་.
བསྐོར་རྡུང་ (gɔ̄ɔ̄duŋ) sm. སྐོར་རྡུང་.
བསྐོར་སྡེམ་ (gɔ̄ɔ̄dem) sm. བསྐོར་སྐྱིལ་.
བསྐོར་གནས་ (gɔ̄ɔ̄nɛɛ̀) sm. སྐོར་གནས་.
བསྐོར་ཕྱག (gɔ̄ɔ̄ca) a style/ manner of greeting sb. of higher status (paying one's respects) by taking off one's hat and swinging one's hand around in a circular motion to the front of one's body; va.—ཞུ་.
བསྐོར་བ་ (gōwaa; gōra) sm. སྐོར་བ་.
བསྐོར་བྱ་བ་ (gɔ̄rcawa) shung. policeman in tt.
བསྐོར་ཞིབ་ (gɔ̄rship) sm. སྐོར་ཞིབ་.
བསྐོར་གཡེང་ (gɔ̄ryeŋ) sm. སྐོར་གཡེང་.
བསྐོར་ར་ (gɔ̄rra) sm. སྐོར་ར་.
བསྐོར་རེས་ (gɔ̄rreè) sm. སྐོར་རེས་.
བསྐོར་ལམ་ (gɔ̄rlam) sm. སྐོར་ལམ་.
བསྐོར་ལོག (gɔ̄rlɔɔ̀) sm. སྐོར་ལོག.
བསྐོར་བཤད་ (gɔ̄rshɛɛ̀) sm. སྐོར་བཤད་.
བསྐོར་བཤེར་ (gɔ̄rsher) sm. སྐོར་བཤེར་.
བསྐོར་སྲུང་ (gɔ̄ɔ̄suŋ) sm. སྐོར་སྲུང་.
བསྐོར་སྲུང་དཔུང་སྡེ་ (gɔ̄ɔ̄suŋ būŋde) sm. སྐོར་སྲུང་དཔུང་སྡེ་.
བསྐོལ་ (gȫö) p. and f. of སྐོལ་.
བསྐོལ་གྲང་ (gȫödraŋ) boiled water that has cooled off.
བསྐོལ་ལྡན་ (gõndɛn) a broth eaten on the first day of New Year containing chang, tsamba and cheese.
བསྐོལ་ཕྱུགས་ (gȫöjug) animals used for work (e.g., dzo, yak, mules, etc.).
བསྐོལ་མ་ (gȫöma) sm. ཀོལ་མ་.
བསྐོས་ (gȫö̀) p. of སྐོ་.
བསྐོས་ཐང་ (gȫö̀daŋ) sm. ལས་སྐལ་.
བསྐོས་བཞག (gȫö̀shaà) sm. ལས་དབང་.
བསྐྱ་ (gyā) f. of སྐྱ་.
བསྐྱང་ (gyāŋ) 1. f. of སྐྱོང་. 2. va. to act, to do (h.) ¶ ཚོགས་འདུ་དེའི་སར་སྲིད་འཛིན་མཆོག་ནས་གསུང་བཤད་བསྐྱང་རྒྱུ་ཡིན་པ་རེད་ The president is going to speak at that meeting.
བསྐྱང་བྱ་ (gyāŋja) those who are protected, those who are subjects of another ¶ བསྐྱང་བྱའི་རྒྱལ་ཁབ་ A protectorate (country/ state).
བསྐྱངས་ (gyāŋ) p. of སྐྱོང་.
བསྐྱད ' (gyɛ̄ɛ̀) arc. 1. va. to compete/ challenge. 2. va. to kill.
བསྐྱད 'དུ་མེད་པ་ (gyɛ̄ɛ̀tu me̱èba) arc. immeasurable.
བསྐྱབ་ (gyə̄p) f. of སྐྱོབ་.
བསྐྱབས་ (gyə̄b) p. of སྐྱོབ་.
བསྐྱམ་ (gyām) f. of སྐྱོམ་.
བསྐྱམས་ (gyām) p. of སྐྱོམ་.
བསྐྱར་ (gyār) 1. p. and f. of སྐྱོར་. 2. (— + vb. + བྱེད་) to repeat/ redo the verbal act ¶ གནས་ཚུལ་དེ་ཚོ་ཚོགས་འདུར་བསྐྱར་བཤད་བྱས་པ་རེད་ The news was retold at the meeting.
བསྐྱར་སྐྱེ་ (gyārgye) giving birth again (usu. after a woman thought she was finished reproducing); va.—རྒྱག.
བསྐྱར་སྐོར་ (gyārgɔɔ) repeating; va.—རྒྱག ¶ ཡིག་ཚད་ཡག་པོ་མ་ལོན་ཙང་འཛིན་གྲྭ་ལྔ་པར་སྐྱར་སྐོར་རྒྱག་དགོས་བྱུང་བ་རེད་ (He) had to repeat the fifth grade again because (he) did not do well in the test.
བསྐྱར་སྐྱོར་ (gyārgyɔɔ) sm. སྐྱ་རེ་སྐྱོ་རེ་.
བསྐྱར་བསྐོས་ (gyārgöö̀) reinstatement or restoration to a post/ position.
བསྐྱར་སྐྱེས་ (gyārgyeè) vi. to be born again, to regenerate.
བསྐྱར་བསྐྲུན་ (gyərdrün) rebuilding, reconstruction; va.—བྱེད་.
བསྐྱར་ཁ་མ་ (gyārgama) picric acid.
བསྐྱར་གྲངས་ (gyārdraŋ) plurality, plural number (in math).
བསྐྱར་གྲོས་ (gyārdröö̀) rediscussion, talking over sth. again; va.—བྱེད་.
བསྐྱར་བགོ་ (gyārgöö̀) redividing; va.—བྱེད་.
བསྐྱར་འགལ་ (gyāngɛɛ) repeating an offense/ violation/ error, breaking the law again; va.—བྱེད་ ¶ ཉེས་ཅན་དེ་ཁྲིམས་དང་སྐྱར་འགལ་བྱུང་ཙང་ཡང་བསྐྱར་འཛིན་བཟུང་བྱས་པ་རེད་ The criminal broke the law again and was apprehended.
བསྐྱར་འགོད་ (gyāŋgöö̀) reproduction, restatement, republication, reprinting; va.—བྱེད་ ¶ གནས་ཚུལ་དེ་ས་གནས་ཚགས་པར་ཁག་བསྐྱར་འགོད་བྱས་ཡོད་པ་རེད་ (They) have reprinted the news in the regional papers.
བསྐྱར་འགྲེལ་ (gyāndrel) repeating/ saying/ explaining again; va.—བྱེད་.
བསྐྱར་སྒྲིག (gyārdrig) rearranging, reorganizing, readjusting, reassembling; va.—བྱེད་ ¶ འགོ་ཁྲིད་གསར་པ་དེ་འབྱོར་ནས་ལས་ཁུངས་སྐྱར་སྒྲིག་བྱས་པ་རེད་ After the new head of the office arrived (he) reorganized the office. ¶ ཁོ་ཚོའི་ནང་གི་འཛིན་ཆས་ཚང་མ་སྐྱར་སྒྲིག་བྱས་པ་རེད་ They rearranged all the furniture in the house.
བསྐྱར་བསྒྲགས་ (gyārdrag) restatement, reannouncement; va.—བྱེད་.
བསྐྱར་བསྒྲིགས་ (gyərdrig) sm. སྐྱར་སྒྲིག.
བསྐྱར་གཅོད་དབང་ཆ་ (gyārjöö̀ wāŋja) the right to bring up sth. to be decided again; e.g., in a court of appeals.
བསྐྱར་བཅགས་ (gyārjaà) remembering, recalling, recollecting; va.—བྱེད་.
བསྐྱར་བཅོས་ (gyārjöö̀) altering/ modifying again, remodeling, revision; va.—བྱེད་; —ཞུ་ ¶ ཁོང་ཚོའི་འཆར་གཞིར་ཚོགས་འདུ་ནས་ བསྐྱར་བཅོས་བྱས་ཡོད་པ་རེད་ The meeting modified their plan again.
བསྐྱར་ལྕག (gyārjaà) urging again; va.; va.—བྱེད་; —ཞུ་.
བསྐྱར་ཆགས་ཤུན་ཐིགས་ (gyārjaà shü̱ndig) recrystallization.
བསྐྱར་ཆུ་ (gyārju) irrigating again; va.—གཏོང་.
བསྐྱར་འཇོག (gyārjɔɔ̀) replaying; va.—གཏོང་.
བསྐྱར་ཉེས་ (gyārñeè) sm. བསྐྱར་འགལ་.
བསྐྱར་གཏོང་ (gyārdoŋ) sending again; va.—བྱེད་.
བསྐྱར་དུ་ (gyārdu) again, once more ¶ ཁོང་ལ་བསྐྱར་དུ་བཀའ་མོལ་ཞུ་གི་ཡིན་ (We) are going to talk to him again.
བསྐྱར་འདེབས་ (gyār de̱b) 1. va. to replant, to resow ¶ ཞིང་ཁར་ཐན་སྐྱོན་བྱུང་ཙང་ལོ་ཏོག་སྐྱར་འདེབས་བྱེད་དགོས་བྱུང་བ་རེད་ Because there was drought (they) had to replant the field. ¶ སྐྱར་འདེབས་ས་ཁྱོན་ The size of the area that was (or will be) replanted. 2. double cropping. 3. reprinting.
བསྐྱར་འདེམས་ (gyārdem) reelection, reselection; va.—བྱེད་.
བསྐྱར་ལྡབ་ (gyāndəb) over and over, repeatedly ¶ ཁོང་གིས་སྐད་ཆ་ཤོད་སྐབས་བསྐྱར་ལྡབ་བྱེད་ཀྱི་འདུག (He) repeats himself over and over when he talks.
བསྐྱར་བསྡུར་ (gyərdur) sm. བསྐྱར་ཞིབ་.
བསྐྱར་སྣོན་ (gyārnön) supplementary, additional;

va.—བྱེད་.

བསྐྱར་པར་ (gyārbaa) republication, reprinting; va.—རྒྱག; —འདེབས་.

བསྐྱར་དཔར་ (gyārbar) sm. བསྐྱར་པར་.

བསྐྱར་སྒྲིལ་ (gyārbel) redoing; va.—བྱེད་.

བསྐྱར་བའི་སྒྲ་ (gyārwɛ dra) the form of the adverb "even/ also" that occurs after different finals.

བསྐྱར་སྦྱོང་ (gyārjoŋ) studying/ practicing again, homework; va.—བྱེད་.

བསྐྱར་སྦྱོང་གི་ས་བོན་ (gyārjoŋgi sābön) sm. བསྐྱར་སྦྱོང་སློབ་གཞི་.

བསྐྱར་སྦྱོང་སློབ་གཞི་ (gyārjoŋ lōbshi) an exercise/ problem (in a course).

བསྐྱར་མ་ (gyārma) again ¶ ཚོང་པ་དེ་བསྐྱར་མ་སླེབས་བྱུང་ The trader came again.

བསྐྱར་བཙས་ (gyārdzɛɛ̀) 1. giving a new life to sb. (used when sb. saves the life of another and thus gives him/ her the equivalent of a new birth). 2. regeneration.

བསྐྱར་ཚད་ (gyārdzɛɛ̀) frequency of occurrence.

བསྐྱར་ཚིག (gyārdziì) a repetitive word.

བསྐྱར་འཛུགས་ (gyəndzuù) reconstruction, reestablishment, reconstitution; va.—བྱེད་ ¶ དམག་འཁྲུག་གི་རྗེས་སུ་སློབ་གྲྭ་མང་པོ་བསྐྱར་འཛུགས་བྱས་པ་རེད་ After the war (they) had to reconstruct many schools.

བསྐྱར་ཞིབ་ (gyārshib) reviewing, rechecking, reinvestigating, reexamining; va.—བྱེད་ ¶ གྱོད་དོན་འདི་ལ་ཁྲིམས་ཁང་གོང་མས་སྐྱར་ཞིབ་བྱས་པ་རེད་ This case was reinvestigated by the high court.

བསྐྱར་ཞུགས་ (gyərshuù) rejoining, going back to; va.—བྱེད་ ¶ ཁོས་ལོ་ཤས་ལས་ཀ་ནས་སློབ་གྲྭར་བསྐྱར་ཞུགས་བྱས་པ་རེད་ He worked for a few years and went back to school.

བསྐྱར་ཟློས་ (gyāndöö) 1. redoing, doing sth. again; va.—རྒྱག ¶ ལས་རིམ་དང་པོར་ཞིབ་ཚགས་མ་བྱུང་ཙང་ལས་ཀ་སྐྱར་ཟློས་རྒྱག་དགོས་བྱུང་བ་རེད་ Because the first stage of the work was not done well they had to redo it. 2. repeating sth. ¶ ཁྱེད་ཀྱི་སྐད་ཆ་དེ་བསྐྱར་ཟློས་བྱེད་རོགས་ Please repeat what you said.

བསྐྱར་ཟློས་ཡང་ཟློས་ (gyāndöö yaŋdöö) repeating or redoing again and again.

བསྐྱར་བཟོ་ (gyārso) 1. reproducing, remanufacturing, remaking, rebuilding; va.—བྱེད་ ¶ འཁྱིགས་འཁོར་བསྐྱར་བཟོ་བྱེད་པའི་བཟོ་གྲྭ་ A factory for reprocessing rubber tires. 2. revising, restoring, rebuilding, remaking; va.—བྱེད་ ¶ དཔྱ་ཁྲལ་བསྡུ་རྒྱའི་ཚད་གཞི་བསྐྱར་བཟོ་བྱས་པ་རེད་ (They) revised the rate of taxation. ¶ ཁོང་གིས་ཁང་པ་རྙིང་པ་དེ་སྐྱར་བཟོ་བྱས་པ་རེད་ He rebuilt that old house.

བསྐྱར་བཟོའི་དངོས་རྫས་ (gyārsoö ŋödzɛɛ̀) sm. བསྐྱར་བཟོས་དངོས་རྫས་.

བསྐྱར་བཟོས་ (gyārsöö) sm. བསྐྱར་བཟོ་.

བསྐྱར་བཟོས་འཁྱིག (gyārsöö gyig) reprocessed rubber.

བསྐྱར་བཟོས་དངོས་རྫས་ (gyārsöö ŋödzɛɛ̀) reprocessed/ recycled articles, remade/ remanufactured articles.

བསྐྱར་བཟློས་ (gyārdöö) sm. བསྐྱར་ཟློས་.

བསྐྱར་ལོག (gyārlɔɔ̀) 1. returning back again; va.—བྱེད་ ¶ མི་མང་པོ་ཞིག་རང་ཡུལ་དུ་བསྐྱར་ལོག་བྱས་པ་རེད་ Many people returned back to their home. 2. making a comeback, reviving; va.—རྒྱག ¶ དམངས་གཙོ་ཏང་དེ་ཡང་སྐྱར་སྲིད་སྟེགས་ཐོག་བསྐྱར་ལོག་བརྒྱབ་པ་རེད་ The democratic party made a comeback in the political arena. ¶ ལུགས་སྲོལ་རྙིང་པ་བསྐྱར་ལོག་རྒྱག་རྩིས་བྱེད་ཀྱི་ཡོད་པ་རེད་ They were planning to revive/ bring back the old custom. 3. relapsing, reoccurring ¶ ཚ་བའི་ས་ཁུལ་དུ་སླེབས་རྗེས་ནད་གཞི་རྙིང་པ་སྐྱར་ལོག་བརྒྱབ་པ་རེད་ After coming to a place where the climate is hot he had a relapse from his old illness.

སྐྱར་གཞོར་ (gyārshɔɔ) shung. measuring again ¶ སྐྱར་གཞོར་བྱས་གོང་འབོར་ཐོག་ནས་དུའི་ཁལ་༡༠ཆག་པ་ After measuring the (grain) again, (they found) that it had decreased by ten ཁལ་.

བསྐྱར་བཤད་ (gyārshɛɛ̀) sm. བསྐྱར་བསྒྲགས་.

བསྐྱར་བཤེར་ (gyārsher) rechecking, reexamining.

བསྐྱར་གསལ་ (gyārsɛɛ) reiterating, reaffirming, reclarifying; va.—བྱེད་.

བསྐྱར་གསོ་ (gyārso) recovering, restoring, renovating, restituting; va.—བྱེད་ ¶ ལྷ་ཁང་དེ་མགྱོགས་མྱུར་བསྐྱར་གསོ་བྱེད་དགོས་ (We) have to renovate the temple quickly. ¶ རང་བཙན་གཙང་མ་བསྐྱར་གསོ་བྱེད་དགོས་ (We) must restore complete independence. ¶ ལམ་ལུགས་རྙིང་པ་མང་པོ་བསྐྱར་གསོ་བྱས་པ་རེད་ (They) revived many old customs.

བསྐྱར་ལྷོང་ (gyārlhoŋ) sm. བསྐྱར་གསོ་.

བསྐྱལ་ (gyɛɛ) p. of སྐྱེལ་.

བསྐྱལ་མགོ་རིལ་ (gyɛɛgori) derogatory term used for sb. who always loses things.

བསྐྱུས་ (gyɛɛ̀) p. of སྐྱུ་.

བསྐྱི་ (gyī) f. of སྐྱི་.

བསྐྱིག (ས་) (gyīg) sm. འཁྱིག.

བསྐྱིལ་ (gyiì) p. and f. of སྐྱིལ་.

བསྐྱིས་ (gyiì) p. of བསྐྱི་.

བསྐྱུང་ (gyūŋ) f. of སྐྱུང་.

བསྐྱུངས་ (gyūŋ) p. of སྐྱུང་.

བསྐྱུད་ (gyüù) p. of སྐྱུད་.

བསྐྱུར་ (gyūr) p. and f. of སྐྱུར་.

བསྐྱུར་འཇོག (gyūnjoò) leaving/ abandoning/ setting aside; va.—བྱེད་ ¶ ལས་ཀ་སྐབས་འཕྲལ་སོ་སོར་བྱེད་དགོས་པ་ལས་རང་བཞིན་བསྐྱུར་འཇོག་བྱེད་རྒྱུ་མེད་ You shouldn't casually abandon your work; you should do it on time.

བསྐྱེང་ (gyēŋ) sm. བསྐྱིང་.

བསྐྱེད་ (gyēè) p. of སྐྱེད་.

བསྐྱེད་བསྐྲུན་ (gyēdrün) expansion, extension, growing wider, bigger; va.—བྱེད་ ¶ ལོ་ལྔ་པོ་དེའི་ནང་མཉམ་འབྲེལ་ཁེ་ལས་དེ་ཚོ་བསྐྱེད་བསྐྲུན་བྱས་ཡོད་པ་རེད་ During those five years (they) expanded the cooperative enterprise.

བསྐྱེད་བསྲིངས་ (gyēsiŋ) sm. བསྐྱེད་སྲིང་.

བསྐྱོད་ (gyöö) p. of སྐྱོད་.

བསྐྱོད་འཁོད་བྱེད་ (gyōgöö cḛè) va. to go and stay (somewhere) ¶ འབྲོག་པའི་ས་ཁུལ་ལ་བསྐྱོད་འཁོད་བྱས་སོང་ (He) went to nomad country and stayed there.

བསྐྱོད་པ་ཡང་བ་ (gyōba yaŋwa) sb. who likes to travel.

བསྐྱོན་ (gyōn) p. and f. of སྐྱོན་.

བསྐྱོར་ (gyōr) p. and f. of སྐྱོར་.

བསྐྲད་ (drɛɛ̀) p. and f. of སྐྲོད་.

བསྐྲུན་ (drūn) p. and f. of སྐྲུན་.

བསྐྲུས་ (drūù) p. of སྐྲུ་.

ཁ་ (kā) 1. the second letter of the alphabet, the second item in an alphabetical list. 2. mouth ¶ཁོའི་ཁ་ཆུང་ཆུང་རེད་ His mouth is small. 3. an opening (usu. for a jar, pot, etc.) ¶སྣོད་ཆས་ཁ་ཆེན་པོ་ཞིག་དགོས་ I need a container with a large opening. ¶རྨ་ཁ་ The opening of a wound. 4. bank, shore ¶མཚོའི་ཁ་ལ་མི་ཞིག་འདུག There is a man on the shore of the lake. 5. surface ¶སྣུམ་ཚང་མ་ཆུ་ཁ་ལ་འཁྱིལ་བཞག All the oil has puddled on the surface of the water. 6. a measuring unit for cloth and similar materials equaling one square of the width of the material ¶རས་ཁ་དོ་ཉོས་པ་ཡིན་ I bought two squares of cotton cloth. 7. direction; vi.—ཕྱོགས; —བསྒྲིག to face in a direction ¶ཁང་པ་དེ་ཁ་ཤར་ལ་བསྒྲིགས་བཞག The house faces east. ¶ཁ་ནུབ་དུ་ཕྱོགས་ནས་ Facing towards the west. 8. appearance ¶མོ་ཊ་འདི་ཉོས་ནས་ལོ་མང་པོ་ཕྱིན་ཀྱང་ད་དུང་ཁ་གསར་མདོག་ཁ་པོ་འདུག Even though this car was bought many years ago, it still looks new. 9. vi. to involuntarily experience/ feel sth. ¶ང་དཀའ་ལས་ཁ་བྱུང་ I got tired. ¶དྲི་མ་ཁ་ To smell (a fragrance/ odor). ¶དྲོ་བ་ཁ་ To taste. 10. talk, speech ¶ཕ་མའི་ཁ་ལ་ཉན་དགོས་ One should listen to one's parents. 11. a mouthful ¶འབྲས་ཁ་གང་བཟས་པ་ཡིན་ (I) ate a mouthful of rice. 12. (vb. + — + dat.-loc.) on the verge of, just as was about to happen ¶ཁོ་འགྲོ་ཁར་ཡི་གེ་འབྱོར་སོང་ He received a letter just as he was about to leave. 13. the age (of an animal, mainly cattle and horses) ¶རྟ་ཁ་རྒན་ An old horse. ¶རྟ་ཁ་ཆུང་ A colt. 14. (— + འགྲིག) vi. to come to an agreement. 15. (— + འཆམས་) sm. ཁ་འགྲིག.

ཁ་གོང་གོང་ (kāgoŋgoŋ) sth. with a flat/ concave looking mouth.

ཁ་ཀྱོག (kāgyɔ̀ɔ) 1. a crooked mouth/ lips, a mouth askew. 2. vi. to have one's mouth get/ become crooked ¶གྲིབ་སྐྱོན་གྱིས་རྐྱེན་པས་ཁ་ཀྱོག་བཞག His mouth has become crooked because of a stroke.

ཁ་ཀྱོག་ཀྱོག (kā gyōgyɔ̀ɔ) sm. ཁ་ཀྱོག.

ཁ་ཀྱོག་མིག་ཀྱོག (kāgyɔ̀ɔ miggyɔ̀ɔ) crooked mouth and eyes ¶ཁོང་གི་གདོང་པ་རྨས་ནས་ཁ་ཀྱོག་མིག་ཀྱོག་ཆགས་བཞག His face was injured and his mouth and eyes have become crooked.

ཁ་གྲབ་ (kā drə̄b) va. to smack one's lips together.

ཁ་གྲེ་ (kādre) sm.* ཁ་སྒྲེ་.

ཁ་ལྷོ་ (kālo) a person who lives in the upper part of ལྷོ་ཡུལ་ in the Tibet Autonomous Region.

ཁ་དཀར་ (kāgaa) 1. white mouth ¶རྐྱང་ཁ་དཀར་ A white-mouthed wild ass. 2. sm. ཁ་དཀར་ངོ་དཀར་.

ཁ་དཀར་རྐྱང་ (kā gārgyaŋ) 1. completely white, pure white ¶གོས་ཆེ་འདི་ཁ་དཀར་རྐྱང་རེད་ This silk is completely white. 2. a white-mouthed wild ass.

ཁ་དཀར་རྐྱང་ལ་ཁ་ལོ་བསྒྱུར་ འབྲི་སེར་འབྲོང་ལ་སྣ་ལོ་བསྒྱུར་ (kāgar gyāŋla kālo dǖǖ dre̱ser dro̱ŋla na̱lo dǖǖ) overcoming/ subduing stubborn and hardheaded people [Lit. taming the white-mouthed wild ass, taming the yellow-faced wild yak].

ཁ་དཀར་ཁོག་ནག (kāgaa kɔ̄gnaà) deceitful, treacherous, sb. who says nice things but is really evil inside; va.—བྱེད་ to be deceitful, to be treacherous ¶ཁ་དཀར་ཁོག་ནག་མ་བྱེད་ Don't be deceitful. [Lit. mouth white, inside black].

ཁ་དཀར་ངོ་དཀར་ (kāgaa ŋo̱gaa) in broad daylight ¶ཇི་མ་ཁ་དཀར་ངོ་དཀར་ལ་རྐུན་མ་སླེབས་སོང་ A thief came in broad daylight. [Lit. mouth white, face white].

ཁ་དཀར་གདོང་ནག (kāgaa dīŋnaà) sm. ཁ་དཀར་ཁོག་ནག.

ཁ་དཀར་པོ་ (kā gārbo) 1. good luck, lucky ¶གཡོག་པོ་དེ་ཁ་དཀར་པོ་བྱུང་ ཁོ་སླེབས་ནས་ང་ཚོ་ཚོང་ལམ་འགྲོ་ཆེན་པོ་བྱུང་སོང་ The servant brought luck. After he came we had good fortune in trading. 2. white ¶རས་ཆོས་གཞི་ཁ་དཀར་པོ་ A white piece of cloth.

ཁ་དཀྲི་ (kəndrii̇) sm.* ཁག་དཀྲི་.

ཁ་དཀྲིས (kədrii̇) scarf.

ཁ་བཀག (kā gāà) 1. va. to stop, to block, to obstruct ¶གཞུང་གི་ཚོང་ཁང་བཙུགས་པ་དེས་བར་ཁེ་ཟ་མཁན་རྣམས་ཀྱིས་ཁེ་བཟང་ཟ་རྒྱུའི་ཁ་བཀག་པ་རེད་ The establishing of government stores stopped middlemen from making profit. ¶བར་དཔང་ལ་ལྐོག་ཟན་སྤྲད་ནས་ར་སྤྲོད་གཏོང་རྒྱུའི་ཁ་བཀག་པ་རེད་ (They) bribed the witness to stop them from giving proof. 2. va. to stop sth. that is moving, e.g., applying brakes on a vehicle or reining in a horse ¶མོ་ཊ་ཏོག་ཙམ་ཁ་བཀག་རོགས་ Please stop the car for a moment. 3. va. to seal an opening, to make an opening airtight ¶ཤེལ་དམ་ཁ་བཀག་པ་ཡིན་ (I) sealed the bottle. 4. p. of ཁ་འགོག (but also used in all tenses on its own).

ཁ་བཀལ་ (kā gɛ̄ɛ) sm.* ཁག་བཀལ་.

ཁ་བཀུག (kā gūù) 1. with respect to riding animals, refusing to obey the rider, usu. by pulling its head against the reins; va. ཁ་བཀུག; —རྒྱག ¶རྟ་འདི་ཁ་བཀུག་བརྒྱབ་ཙང་རྟ་པ་གཞན་དང་མཉམ་དུ་འགྲོ་མ་ཐུབ་པ་རེད་ The horse pulled at the reins and refused to obey the rider so (the rider) wasn't able to go along with the other riders. 2. va. ཁ་བཀུག; —བྱེད་ to fold over an edge of a garment or piece of material to sew a hem ¶ཅག་དར་གྱི་ཁ་བཀུག་པ་རེད་ (He) folded the edge of the sheet to make a hem (and sewed it). 3. va. to expose sth. to darken the color of a dye ¶སྣམ་བུ་རྩྭ་ཐང་ལ་སྣམ་བུ་ཁ་བཀུག་པ་རེད་ (He) left the wool fabric on the grass so that the color (dye) would darken.

ཁ་བཀོད་ (kāgöö̀) instructions, orders (oral); va.—བྱེད་; —གཏོང་.

ཁ་བཀོད་མཛུབ་ཁྲིད་ (kāgöö̀ dzu̱btrii̇) verbal orders and directions/ instructions ¶ཕྲུ་གུ་འདིས་ཕ་མའི་ཁ་བཀོད་མཛུབ་ཁྲིད་ལ་ཉན་གྱི་མི་འདུག The child doesn't listen to his parents' orders and instructions.

ཁ་བརྒྱག (kāgyaà) a flat stone that is the takeoff point at the end of the runway that dobdo monks use in their jumping competition.

ཁ་བརྒྱག་བརྒྱག (kā gyāggyag) raising one's head (with pride), holding one's head high (literally and figuratively); va.—བྱེད་ ¶གསར་བརྗེ་ཡངས་ཅང་དབུལ་པོ་ཚོ་ཁ་བརྒྱག་བརྒྱག་བྱེད་ཐུབ་པ་བྱུང་སོང་ Because of the revolution, the poor were able to raise up their heads with pride.

ཁ་བཀྲམ་ (kā drām) va. to disperse/ spread out/ scatter ¶ང་ཚོས་ཁ་བཀྲམ་ནས་ཁོ་འཚོལ་བར་ཕྱིན་པ་ཡིན་ We spread out and went to search for him.

ཁ་བཀྲམ་ནས་བདག་གཉེར་ (kā drāmnɛɛ̀ da̱gñer) decentralized management.

ཁ་བཀྲམ་དམག་འཐབ་ (kādram māgdəb) a method/ strategy of warfare in which forces are dispersed and then do battle.

ཁ་བཀྲལ་ (kā drɛ̄ɛ) separating into piles/ groups/ sections, etc.; va. ཁ་བཀྲལ; —བྱེད་ ¶དམག་མི་ཚོ་ཁ་བཀྲལ་ནས་ཕྱིན་པ་རེད་ The soldiers separated (into groups) and went.

ཁ་བཀྲེན་ (kā drɛ̄n) va. to be thrifty with regard to one's food expenses.

ཁ་རྐྱང་ (kāgyaŋ) 1. alone ¶ཁོ་ཁ་རྐྱང་ཕྱིན་པ་རེད་ He went alone. 2. completely, entirely, only ¶ཤོག་དངུལ་ཁ་རྐྱང་སྤྲད་བྱུང་ (He) gave (me) only paper money.

ཁ་སྐུགས་ (kā gūg) sm. ཁ་སྐུགས་པ་.

ཁ་སྐུགས་པ་ (kā gūgpə) mute, dumb.

ཁ་སྐད་ (kāgɛɛ̀) spoken/ colloquial language ¶ཨ་

རིའི་སློབ་ཕྲུག་དེས་བོད་པའི་ཁ་སྐད་ཡག་པོ་ཤེས་ཀྱི་འདུག The American student knows spoken Tibetan well.

ཁ་སྐད་ཀྱི་འགྲོ་སྟངས་ (kāgɛ̀ɛgi dro̱daŋ) the colloquial/ spoken style of speech ¶ ཡིག་སྐད་དང་ཁ་སྐད་ཀྱི་འགྲོ་སྟངས་ཁག་ཁག་རེད་ The written and spoken language styles are different.

ཁ་སྐད་ཁ་རྒྱུན་ (kāgɛɛ̀ kāgyaŋ) completely colloquial language ¶ ཁོས་བོད་སྐད་ཁ་སྐད་ཁ་རྒྱུན་རྐྱང་ཀྱི་འདུག He speaks completely colloquial Tibetan.

ཁ་སྐམ་པ་ (kāgamba) sm. བསོད་སྙམས་པ་.

ཁ་སྐུད་ (kāgüü) a string used for tying the mouth of sacks/ bags.

ཁ་སྐོང་ (kāgoŋ) 1. sth. that makes up a shortage or deficit; va.—བྱེད་; —སྐོང་ to make up a shortage/ deficit/ to add on, to supplement ¶ ལམ་གྲོན་གྱི་དངུལ་འབབ་སྒོར་མོ་བརྒྱ་ཐམ་པ་ཆད་པ་དེ་གཞུང་ནས་ཁ་སྐོང་བྱས་པ་རེད་ The government made up the 100 dollar deficit in travel expenses.

ཁ་སྐོང་དག་བཅོས་ (kāgoŋ ta̱gjöö) adding on to/ supplementing/ amending and correcting; va.—བྱེད་ ¶ དགེ་རྒན་གྱིས་སློབ་ཕྲུག་དེའི་རྩོམ་ཡིག་ལ་ཁ་སྐོང་དག་བཅོས་བྱས་འདུག The teacher has corrected and added to that student's paper (to make it complete).

ཁ་སྐོམ་ (kā gōm) 1. vi. to be thirsty ¶ ལུས་རྩལ་བྱས་པའི་རྗེས་སུ་ཁ་སྐོམ་པ་རེད་ (They) were thirsty after exercising. 2. a drink.

ཁ་སྐོམ་ལྕེ་སྐམ་ (kāgom jēgam) work or activity that is very hard or difficult [Lit. mouth thirsty, tongue dry].

ཁ་སྐོམ་ནས་ཁྲོན་པ་འདྲུ་ (kā gōmnɛ trōmba dru̱) doing something too late, exhibiting a lack of foresight [Lit. digging a well after becoming thirsty].

ཁ་སྐོམས་ (kāgom) sm. ཁ་སྐོམ་.

ཁ་སྐོར་ (kāgɔɔ) 1. circumference, perimeter ¶ དཀར་ཡོལ་འདིར་ཁ་སྐོར་ལ་ཀུང་ཕིང་བཅུ་ཡོད་པ་རེད་ The circumference of this cup is 10 centimeters. 2. va. to shop around for the best price, to collect estimates, to ask many individuals and compare answers ¶ ངས་མོ་ཊ་ཁ་སྐོར་བར་ཕྱིན་པ་ཡིན་ I went to shop around for a car. 3. va. to turn around, to change direction ¶ མོ་ཊ་ཁ་སྐོར་ནས་ལོག་ཕྱིན་པ་རེད་ (He) turned the car around and returned. 4. va. to discuss sth. in turns so everyone has a chance to talk ¶ གནད་དོན་འདི་གལ་ཆེན་པོ་ཡིན་ཙང་མི་ཚང་མས་ཁ་སྐོར་གྲོས་སྡུར་བྱ་དགོས་ This issue is very important so everyone has to take turns discussing this. 5. va. to trick a dog by taking it somewhere and leaving it there.

ཁ་སྐྱ་ (kāgya) white mouth (for animals).

ཁ་སྐྱུར་ (kā gyūr) 1. vi. to get a sour taste in one's mouth ¶ ཇ་མངར་མོ་བཏུངས་དྲགས་ནས་ཁ་སྐྱུར་བཞག Having drunk too much sweet tea (I) got a sour taste in (my) mouth. 2. the gradations in shading/ color that are used in Tibetan style painting; va.—གཏོང་.

ཁ་སྐྱུར་པོན་ (kāgyurbön) Chinese olive tree.

ཁ་སྐྱུར་བ་ (kāgyurwa) sour (in taste) ¶ ཆུ་ར་ཆུ་ར་འདི་ཁ་སྐྱུར་བ་ཞིག་འདུག This rhubarb tastes sour.

ཁ་སྐྱེངས་ (kā gyēŋ; kā gyāŋ) vi. to feel embarrassed, to feel ashamed ¶ མི་ངན་དེའི་རྫུན་ཀུབ་བརྗོད་ཙང་ཁ་སྐྱེངས་ནས་ལོག་ཕྱིན་སོང་ The evil person was exposed and left feeling ashamed.

ཁ་སྐྱེངས་པོ་ (kā gyēŋbo) embarrassed, ashamed ¶ ཚོགས་འདུར་ཕྱིས་དྲགས་ཙང་ཁ་སྐྱེངས་པོ་བྱུང་ Because (I) arrived late for the meeting, I was embarrassed.

ཁ་སྐྱེངས་ཁྲོ་ལངས་ (kāgyaŋ drōlaŋ) 1. embarrassed and (simultaneously) angry ¶ ཀང་རྩེད་སྤོ་ལོའི་འགྲན་བསྡུར་ཕམ་ཙང་ཁོ་ཁ་སྐྱེངས་ཁྲོ་ལངས་བྱུང་བ་རེད་ He got embarrassed and angry because (they) lost the soccer match. 2. vi. to get embarrassed and angry ¶ ཀང་རྩེད་སྤོ་ལོའི་འགྲན་བསྡུར་ཕམ་ཙང་ཁོ་ཁ་སྐྱེངས་ཁྲོ་ལངས་པ་རེད་ He got embarrassed and angry because (they) lost the soccer match.

ཁ་སྐྱེངས་བག་འཛེར་ (kāgyeŋ pa̱gdzer) sm. ཁ་སྐྱེངས་.

ཁ་སྐྱེལ་ (kā gyēē) va. to kiss ¶ གཞོན་ནུ་དེས་གྲོགས་མོར་ཁ་བསྐྱལ་པ་རེད་ The young man kissed his girlfriend.

ཁ་སྐྱོང་ (kāgyɔŋ) supporting, assisting, helping sb. (especially with regard to livelihood); va.—བྱེད་ ¶ སྲིད་གཞུང་ནས་དྭ་ཕྲུག་རྣམས་ལ་ཁ་སྐྱོང་བྱེད་ཀྱི་ཡོད་པ་རེད་ The government is assisting in the orphans (with respect to livelihood).

ཁ་སྐྱོར་ (kāgyɔɔ) 1. raising the edge of a container or vessel so that its contents will not spill over; va. ཁ་སྐྱོར་; —གཏོང་ ¶ ཆར་པ་ཞེ་དྲག་གཏོང་གི་ཡོད་ཙང་ཆུ་རྫིང་ལ་ཁ་སྐྱོར་གཏོང་གི་འདུག They are raising the walls of the dam (to prevent flooding) because it is raining so much. 2. holding one's hand(s) near the mouth when calling people or whispering; va.—བྱེད་. 3. sm. འགྲམ་སྐྱོར་.

ཁ་བསྐངས་ (kā gāŋ) p. of ཁ་སྐོང་.

ཁ་བསྐངས་ཟུར་རྒྱན་ (kāgaŋ su̱rgyɛn) a note/ letter/ attachment/ agreement that is secondary to a main item, e.g., a codicil.

ཁ་བསྐོར་ (kā gɔ̄ɔ) p. of ཁ་སྐོར་.

ཁ་བསྐྱོགས་ (kā gyɔ̄g) 1. va. to turn around, to change direction ¶ ལམ་ནོར་བྱུང་ཙང་མོ་ཊའི་ཁ་བསྐྱོགས་པ་རེད་ Because (he) went on the wrong road (he) turned the car around (changed direction). 2. va. to change the subject (in a conversation) ¶ ཟིང་འཁྲུག་སྐོར་བཤད་ཚར་ནས་གྲོས་གཞིའི་ཁ་བསྐྱོགས་པ་རེད་ After (they) finished talking about the disturbances (they) changed the subject of the discussion.

ཁ་ཁ་ (kāga) separate, apart; va.—བྱེད་ to keep apart, to separate/ split up (a family or a marriage), to divorce ¶ འདི་གཉིས་ཁ་ཁ་བཞག་དགོས་རེད་ You have to keep these two apart. ¶ བཟའ་ཚང་གཉིས་ཁ་ཁ་བྱས་པ་རེད་ The couple divorced. ¶ བུ་ཆེན་པ་ཚང་གཉིས་ཁ་ཁ་བྱས་པ་རེད་ The oldest son split off from his father's household.

ཁ་ཁ་རོག་བསྡད་ན་ཁ་མཆུ་ཉུང་ (kā kāro dɛ̱ɛ̀na kəmju ñu̱ŋ) if one is not careful about what one says one will get involved in disputes [Lit. if you keep quiet there will be fewer lawsuits/ law cases].

ཁ་ཁ་ལ་ (kā gāla) sm. ཁ་ཁར་.

ཁ་ཁ་སོ་སོ་ (kāga sōso) separate, apart; va.—འགྲོ་ to each go his own way/ separately ¶ ཁོ་གཉིས་ཁ་ཁ་སོ་སོ་བསྡད་པ་རེད་ The two of them lived separately.

ཁ་ཁག་ (kāgaà) sm. ཁ་ཁ་.

ཁ་ཁག་སོ་སོ་ (kāka sōso) sm. ཁ་ཁ་སོ་སོ་.

ཁ་ཁར་ (kāgaa) 1. stealthily, secretly, on the sly ¶ ཁོས་མེ་མདའ་ཁ་ཁར་བཙོངས་བ་རེད་ He sold the gun secretly. 2. quietly, silently, without speaking or talking aloud ¶ ཁོས་འདོན་པ་ཁ་ཁར་བསྐོར་པ་རེད་ He said his prayers silently.

ཁ་ཁར་སྡོད་ (kāgaà döö) Shut up!, Be quiet! ¶ དགེ་རྒན་གྱིས་སློབ་ཕྲུག་ཚོར་ཁ་ཁར་སྡོད་ཅེས་ལབ་པ་རེད་ The teacher told the pupils, "Be quiet."

ཁ་ཁར་བཞུགས་ (kāgaa shu̱ù) h. of ཁ་ཁར་སྡོད་.

ཁ་ཁུ་ (kəgu) 1. (usu. used with neg.) saying/ telling/ informing about sth. ¶ ཕྲུ་གུ་དེས་པ་མར་ཁ་ཁུ་མེད་པར་ཕྱིར་བསྐྱོད་འདུག That child went out without telling (his) parents. 2. news, information ¶ དེང་སང་བོད་ནང་གི་གནས་ཚུལ་སྐོར་ཁ་ཁུ་གཞི་མི་འདུག These days there is no news of Tibet.

ཁ་ཁུ་སིམ་པོ་ (kəgu sīmbu) quiet, silent, peaceful, tranquil (people and places), taciturn (for people) ¶ མི་འདི་རྒྱུན་དུ་ཁ་ཁུ་སིམ་པོ་ཞིག་རེད་ This person is always very quiet. ¶ ཁོང་ཁ་ཁུ་སིམ་པོའི་ལུང་པ་ཞིག་ལ་བསྡད་ཡོད་པ་རེད་ He lives in a quiet place.

ཁ་ཁུག་ (kə kūù) vi. to taste old/ rancid (usu. of meat) ¶ ཤ་འདི་ཁ་ཁུག་ཤག The meat has become rancid.

ཁ་ཁུག་སིམ་པོ་ (kəgu sīmbu) sm. ཁ་ཁུ་སིམ་པོ་.

ཁ་ཁུངས་ (kəguŋ) a person or place where sb.'s need can be met; va.—བྱེད་ to do sth. to meet sb.'s needs ༈ བྱེད་རང་ལ་ངས་ལས་ཀ་ཞིག་ཁ་ཁུངས་བྱེད་ཀྱི་ཡིན་ I'll look around for a person or place where your need for a job can be met. ༈ ཅ་ལག་འདི་ཚོ་འཚོང་ས་ཞིག་ངས་ཁ་ཁུངས་བྱེད་ཀྱི་ཡིན་ I'll look around for a place (or person) to sell (your) goods.

ཁ་ཁེངས་ (kākeŋ) an animal with all its teeth (i.e., a fully grown/ adult animal).

ཁ་ཁེབས་ (kākeb) lid, cover.

ཁ་ཁོག་གཅིག་པ་ (kāgɔɔ̀ jīgbə) saying what one feels/ thinks [Lit. mouth and inside same].

ཁ་ཁོག་པ་འདྲེས་ཤིང་ བློ་རྒྱུ་མ་འདྲེས་པ་ (kā kōgba drēēshiŋ lō gyuma drēēba) sm. ཁ་ཁོག་པས་མ་གསང་ བློ་རྒྱུ་མས་མ་བསྐུམས་.

ཁ་ཁོག་པས་མ་གསང་ བློ་རྒྱུ་མས་མ་བསྐུམས་ (kā kōgbɛ masāŋ lō gyumɛ magūm) speaking frankly [Lit. not keeping secrets in the body, not hiding sth. in the intestines].

ཁ་ཁོག་མི་མཚུངས་པ་ (kāgɔɔ̀ mitsuŋwə) a person who does not say what he thinks.

ཁ་ཁོག་མི་འཛིན་པ་ (kāgɔɔ̀ midzimbə) sm. ཁ་ཁོག་གཅིག་པ་.

ཁ་ཁོག་མེད་པ་ (kāgɔɔ̀ meeba) sm. ཁ་ཁོག་གཅིག་པ་.

ཁ་ཁོང་ལྟོ་བཅུད་དུ་སོང་ (kāgoŋ dōjüüdu sōŋ) vi. to be/ get embezzled ༈ རྒྱལ་ཁབ་ཀྱི་རྒྱུ་ནོར་དེ་མི་སྒེར་ཞིག་གིས་ཁ་ཁོང་ལྟོ་བཅུད་དུ་སོང་བ་རེད་ The country's wealth was embezzled by an individual.

ཁ་ཁོབ་ (kāgɔb) va. to cover the mouth.

ཁ་ཁོར་ (kāgɔr) near, nearby ༈ ཁང་པའི་ཁ་ཁོར་དུ་ཤིང་སྡོང་བཙུགས་སོང་ (They) planted a tree near the house.

ཁ་ཁྱག་ (kɛ̄ɛ̄gyaà) guarantor, cosigner ༈ བུ་ལོན་ལེན་པར་ཁ་ཁྱག་ཅིག་དགོས་ To get a loan (you) need a guarantor.

ཁ་ཁྱུད་ (kāgyüü) the rim of a vessel/ container/ etc.

ཁ་ཁྱེར་ (kāgyee) 1. the edge of a table/ desk/ etc. 2. sm. ཁ་ལ་འཁྱེར་. 3. a stand (for putting things on).

ཁ་ཁྱེར་ནས་རྡོ་ཉོ་བ་ (kākyernɛ doñowa) causing trouble for oneself because of one's own actions or speech [Lit. bringing the mouth to buy a stone].

ཁ་ཁྲག་ (kātraà) bleeding from the mouth; vi.—ཐོན་ to bleed from the mouth.

ཁ་ཁྲག་སྣ་ཁྲག་ (kātraà nātraà) beaten badly/ severely [Lit. bloody mouth, bloody nose].

ཁ་ཁྲམ་ (kā trām) 1. a lie, an untruth, a fabrication; va.—བཤད་ ༈ ཁ་ཁྲམ་གཡོ་གཏམ་ལ་མ་ཉན་ Don't listen to lies and deceitful talk. 2. a liar.

ཁ་ཁྲལ་ (kā trɛ̄ɛ̄) 1. the beginning curriculum in monastic education. 2. sth. one must say, sth. one has no choice but to say, an obligatory statement/ talk/ speech ༈ ཏང་ལ་བསྟོད་ར་གཏོང་རྒྱུ་དེ་ལས་བྱེད་པ་ཚོའི་ཁ་ཁྲལ་རེད་ It is obligatory for cadre to praise the party.

ཁ་ཁྲས་ཁྲས་ (kā trɛ̄ɛtrɛ) smiling; va.—བྱེད་ to smile.

ཁ་ཁྲིམས་ (kātrim) sth. that people are prohibited/ forbidden from talking about; va.—སྡོམ་ to prohibit/ forbid people from talking about sth.

ཁ་ཁྲིམས་ཚ་ཁྲིམས་ (kātrim tsātrim) a nomad custom prohibiting the use of bad language on trading or salt collecting trips and requiring the use of a set of special terms that substitute for everyday names).

ཁ་ཁྲེ་ (kātre) ch. truck, lorry.

ཁ་མཁས་ཁོག་སྟོང་ (kākɛɛ kōgdoŋ) a loquacious but shallow person, a glib talker without real substance, sb. who is superficially clever ༈ ཁ་མཁས་ཁོག་སྟོང་གི་མིས་ལས་ཀ་གང་ཡང་བྱས་མི་འདུག The loquacious but shallow person did not do any work (well).

ཁ་མཁས་མགོ་སྐོར་ (kākɛɛ gogɔɔ) tricking/ swindling by verbal means, cheating through glibness.

ཁ་མཁས་ལྕེ་བདེ་ (kākɛɛ jēde) sm. ཁ་མཁས་པོ་.

ཁ་མཁས་སྟོང་བཤད་ (kākɛè dōŋshɛɛ̀) eloquent speech devoid of meaning/ content.

ཁ་མཁས་འདྲ་ཆགས་ (kāgɛɛ dracaà) nice sounding/ pleasing/ eloquent talk and good-looking or elegant (depending on context this can also have a negative connotation conveying insincerity or flattery to superiors); va.—ཤོད་.

ཁ་མཁས་པོ་ (kā kɛ̄ɛ̄bo) verbal, skilled in verbal communication ༈ འགོ་ཁྲིད་ལ་ཁ་མཁས་པོ་བྱས་ན་ལས་དོན་འགྲུབ་བདེ་པོ་ཡོད་ One can achieve one's work easily by speaking skillful to the leaders (depending on context this can also convey insincerity/ flattery to superiors).

ཁ་མཁས་ཚིག་འཇམ་ (kākɛɛ tsīŋjam) gentle speech or advice.

ཁ་མཁས་ཚིག་སྙན་ (kākɛɛ tsīgñɛn) sm. ཁ་མཁས་འདྲ་ཆགས་.

ཁ་འཁུར་ (kā kūr) sm. ཁ་ལ་འཁྱེར་.

ཁ་འཁུར་ངན་ཤེད་ (kākur ŋenshɛè) using sb. else's power to bully/ oppress/ suppress.

ཁ་འཁེབས་ (kā kēb) vi. to cover/ meet expenses ༈ འགྲོ་སོང་ཁ་འཁེབས་མ་སོང་ (They) didn't meet their expenses.

ཁ་འཁོགས་འཁོགས་ མིད་ཐག་སྐམ་སྐམ་ (kā kɔ̄ɔ̀gɔɔ̀ mitaà gāggām) to talk a lot [Lit. mouth aged, throat dry].

ཁ་འཁོན་ཚིག་འཁོན་ (kākön tsīgkön) quarreling/ disagreeing verbally.

ཁ་འཁོར་ (kākɔɔ) 1. vi. to have expenditures be balanced by income, to have one's investment returned ༈ ད་ལོའི་འགྲོ་སོང་ཁ་འཁོར་གྱི་འདུག This year expenditures are balanced by income. 2. vi. to change one's view/ position ༈ ཁོའི་བསམ་བློ་ཏང་གི་ལྟ་བའི་ཕྱོགས་ལ་ཁ་འཁོར་བཞག His thinking has come around to the party's viewpoint. 3. sm. ཁ་འཁོར་མ་.

ཁ་འཁོར་གྱི་ཚད་ (kākɔɔgi tsēè) circumference.

ཁ་འཁོར་པོ་ (kā kōrbo) expenditures balanced by income.

ཁ་འཁོར་མ་ (kā kōrma) a bride who leaves her husband and returns to her natal home.

ཁ་འཁོལ་ (kā kȫȫ) vi. to salivate, to have one's mouth water in anticipation (usu. for food or drink) ༈ ལུག་ཤ་ཟ་འདོད་ཀྱིས་ཁ་འཁོལ་བྱུང་ The desire to eat mutton made (my) mouth water.

ཁ་འཁྱག (kā kyāg) sm. ཁ་འཁྱགས་.

ཁ་འཁྱགས་ (kākyag) sarcastic comments/ talk.

ཁ་འཁྱགས་འཁྱགས་ (kā kyāggyaà) proud in a positive sense, holding one's head high with pride ༈ ཁོང་གི་ཕྲུ་གུ་ཡིག་ཚད་ཡག་པོ་བྱུང་ཙང་ཁོང་རང་ཁ་འཁྱགས་འཁྱགས་བྱེད་ཐུབ་པ་བྱུང་བ་རེད་. Because his son did well on the exam, he was able to hold his head high with pride.

ཁ་འཁྱགས་ངོ་འཁྱགས་ (kākyag ŋogyaà) angry/ unpleasant words and a bad/ angry facial expression; va.—བྱེད་.

ཁ་འཁྱར་ (kā kyār) sm. ཁ་ཀྱར་.

ཁ་འཁྱིག (kā gyīg) va. to tie the mouth shut as a means of slaughtering sheep and goats by suffocation.

ཁ་འཁྱེར་ (kā kyēr) sm. ཁ་ལ་འཁྱེར་.

ཁ་འཁྲུག (kātruù) sm. ཁ་རྩོད་.

ཁ་འཁྲུད་ལག་འཁྲུད་ (kātrüü lagtrüü) washing face and hands.

ཁ་འཁྲུད་ལག་བཤལ་ (kātrüü lagshɛɛ) sm. ཁ་འཁྲུད་ལག་འཁྲུད་.

ཁ་འགྲིགས་ (kādrɔɔ̀) deciding/ agreeing spontaneously (by several people); va.—བྱེད་ ༈ ང་གཉིས་ཁ་འགྲིགས་བྱས་རྒྱ་གར་ལ་ཕྱིན་པ་ཡིན་ We decided on the spot and went to India.

ཁ་གང་ (kāgaŋ) 1. a mouthful ༈ ཆུ་ཁ་གང་གནང་རོགས་ Please give me a mouthful of water. 2. one square of material ༈ ང་ལ་རས་ཁ་གང་དགོས་ I need one square of material. 3. a traditional Tibetan monetary unit equal to 1/4 of a ཞོ་. 4. a paltry amount, a pittance ༈ ཁ་གང་སྐར་མའི་དོན་ལ་དཀའ་

ལས་འདི་འདྲ་བརྒྱབ་ན་དོན་དག་མི་འདུག It makes no sense to work this hard for such a paltry amount. 5. sm. ཁ་ཁེངས་.

ཁ་གང་བ་ (kā kaŋwa) 1. full to the brim ¶ དཀར་ཡོལ་ནང་ཇ་ཁ་གང་བ་བླུགས་བཞག The cup was filled to the brim with tea. 2. sm. ཁ་ཚང་, 2.

ཁ་གང་དབྱིབས་ (kāgaŋ yīb) square in shape.

ཁ་གང་མ་ (kāgaŋma) square (for rugs or fabrics) ¶ ཁ་གདན་ཁ་གང་མ་ A type of Tibetan rug that is square.

ཁ་གང་ལིང་ཚ་ (kāgaŋ liŋdza) square matrix.

ཁ་གབ་ (kāgəp) lid, cover; va.—རྒྱག to cover with a lid.

ཁ་གོང་ (kāgoŋ) snowball.

ཁ་གོན་ (kāgön) 1. outer garment, jacket, overcoat. 2. shung. outer red coat worn by lay officials above the 5th rank in tt.

ཁ་གོར་ (kāgɔɔ) a muzzle ¶ ཁྱི་ལ་ཁ་གོར་གཡོགས་པ་རེད་ (He) put a muzzle on the dog.

ཁ་གོས་ (kāgöö) sm. ཁ་གོན་, 1.

ཁ་གྱར་ (kā gyar) vi. to go astray, to become separated (from a group or herd) ¶ ལུག་མང་པོ་ཁ་གྱར་ནས་བརླག་པ་རེད་ Many sheep got separated from the herd and were lost.

ཁ་གྱུ་ (kāgyu) sm. ཁ་རྩུར་ཕྱོགས་.

ཁ་གྱེན་དུ་ (kā gyɛntu) upwards ¶ མེ་ཐུར་ལ་འབར་ནས་གྱེན་དུ་རྒྱུགས་འགྲོ་གི་འདུག The fire ignited at the bottom and is moving upwards.

ཁ་གྱེན་ཕྱོགས་ (kā gyɛncɔɔ̀) facing upwards.

ཁ་གྱེས་ (kā gyɛ̀ɛ) p. of ཁ་འགྱེས་.

ཁ་གྱེས་ཟུར་འཛུགས་ (kāgyɛè surdzug) separating from one unit and setting up a branch/ side unit; va.—བྱེད་.

ཁ་གྱེས་རིང་ལུགས་ (kāgyɛè riŋluù) separationism, separatism.

ཁ་གྱོང་པོ་ (kā kyoŋbo) 1. verbally formidable/ aggressive, able to hold one's own verbally; va.—བྱེད་ ¶ ཚོགས་འདུའི་སར་ལ་འདྲི་ལན་ཁ་གྱོང་པོ་བྱས་ནས་བརྒྱབས་སོང་ (He) was able to answer questions formidably at the meeting. 2. headstrong (for horses) ¶ རྟ་དེ་ཁ་གྱོང་པོ་ཞི་དྲག་འདུག That horse is very headstrong. 3. a person who is particular/ finicky about what he eats.

ཁ་གྱོང་ཚིག་བརྡུངས་ (kāgyoŋ tsīiduŋ) harsh/ aggressive talk.

ཁ་གྱོན་ (kā kyon) sm. ཁ་གོན་.

ཁ་གྲགས་ (kā traà) vi. to emit a sound/ noise, to utter a word ¶ ཕྲུ་གུ་བརྟེམས་དེ་ཁ་གྲགས་ཡས་མི་འདུག The child was shocked and didn't utter a sound. ¶ མི་དེ་ང་ལ་ཁ་གྲག་གི་མི་འདུག That person doesn't say a word to me.

ཁ་གྲངས་ (kādraŋ) number, quantity, amount ¶ ཁ་གྲངས་ཆིག་སྟོང་ཉིས་བརྒྱ་ An amount (equal to) twelve hundred. ¶ ཁ་གྲངས་མང་པོ་ A large number (of sth.).

ཁ་གྲམ་ (kā tram) vi. to be/ get scattered/ separated ¶ གཡག་ཁ་གྲམ་པ་དེ་ཚོ་རྩྭ་ཟ་གི་འདུག The yaks that got scattered are grazing.

ཁ་གྲུ་ (kədru) 1. the left and right corner of the mouth. 2. the inside corner or angle of a box. 3. the size of an area.

ཁ་གྲོག་ཕྱིས་ཕུད་ (kādrɔɔ̀ jēèpüù) losing/ blowing an opportunity, spoiling one's chance for sth. good to come by a misdeed in speech or action ¶ མི་དེ་ལ་ལས་ཀ་ཡག་པོ་ཞིག་ཐོབ་ཀྱང་ཁོ་པས་སློབ་གྲྭའི་གནས་ཚད་སྐོར་རྫུན་བཤད་ཙང་ཁ་གྲོག་ཕྱིས་ཕུད་ཀྱིས་ལས་ཀ་ཤོར་བ་རེད་ Although he got a good job, because he lied about his educational level, he blew the opportunity and lost the job.

ཁ་གྲོགས་ (kādrɔɔ̀) false friend ¶ དཀའ་ངལ་ཡོད་པའི་སྐབས་ལ་ཕན་མ་ཐོགས་པའི་གྲོགས་པོ་དེ་ཁ་གྲོགས་རང་རེད་ Friends who are of no help when times are hard are really false friends.

ཁ་གྲོས་ (kādröö) sm. གྲོས་སྡུར་.

ཁ་བླ་ (kābla) fee for sth. rented.

ཁ་བླགས་ཁེལ་ (kā lāà kēē) vi. to be able to verbally defeat or cope with sb. ¶ རྩོད་པ་རྒྱག་དུས་མི་འདི་སུས་ཀྱང་ཁ་བླགས་ཁེལ་གྱི་མ་རེད་ No one can defeat this person in debating.

ཁ་གླལ་ (kā lɛ̀ɛ) vi. to yawn.

ཁ་གླིང་ (kāliŋ) the two tribes (Ling and the Muslims) in the Gesar epic.

ཁ་གློང་ (kā lōŋ) va. to tantalize/ tease/ torment.

ཁ་གློད་ (kā lȫȫ) va. to go back to eating normally after following a diet for some time.

ཁ་དགབ་ (kāgab) va. to cover, to hide.

ཁ་དགའ་ངོ་དགའ་ (kāgaa ŋogaa) 1. pretending to like sb.; va.—བྱེད་ ¶ ཁོས་འགོ་འཁྲིད་ལ་ཁ་དགའ་ངོ་དགའ་བྱེད་ཀྱི་ཡོད་པ་རེད་ He pretends to like the leader. 2. showing/ exhibiting a pleasant demeanor (depending on context this can have negative or positive connotation) ¶ མི་གཞན་གྱིས་རང་ལ་རེ་འདུན་བཏོན་ན་ཁ་དགའ་ངོ་དགའི་ཐོག་ནས་ལན་རྒྱག་དགོས་པ་རེད་ If sb. asks you to do them a favor, you should answer in a pleasant manner.

ཁ་དགའ་ངོ་བསྟོད་ (kāgaa ŋodöö) sm. ཁ་དགའ་ངོ་དགའ་, 1.

ཁ་དགའ་ངོ་སྲུང་ (kāgaa ŋosuŋ) sm. ཁ་དགའ་ངོ་དགའ་, 1.

ཁ་དགའ་རྩེ་མཚར་ (kāga dzēdzar) sb. who enjoys telling jokes.

ཁ་དྲག་སྣ་དྲག་གསོག (kādra nādra sɔ̄ɔ̀) va. to hurt a person verbally.

ཁ་བཀག (kā gāà) vi. to be or get blocked/ obstructed.

ཁ་བགྱིད་ (kāgyiì) sm. ཁ་གཏོང་.

ཁ་བགྲད་བགྲད་ (kā trɛ̀ɛdrɛɛ̀) showing one's teeth to express anger or displeasure, barring one's fangs; va.—བྱེད་.

ཁ་བགྲད་མཆེ་གཙིགས་ (kādrɛɛ̀ cēdzig) exhibiting anger by showing one's teeth/ barring one's fangs in anger; va.—བྱེད་ [Lit. showing teeth and showing canines].

ཁ་བགྲད་མིག་བགྲད་ (kādrɛɛ̀ migdrɛɛ̀) expressing anger by showing one's teeth and looking harshly; va.—བྱེད་.

ཁ་འགགས་ (kā gaà) 1. vi. to be rendered speechless ¶ ཁོང་ཁྲོས་ཆེན་པས་ཁ་འགགས་ནས་སྐད་ཆ་ཤོད་ཐུབ་མ་སོང་ He was rendered speechless because of his anger. 2. vi. to get blocked up ¶ ས་འོག་ཆུ་འགྲོའི་ཁ་འགག་བཞག The underground water pipeline got blocked.

ཁ་འགལ་ཚིག་འགལ་ (kāgɛɛ tsīggɛɛ) inconsistency between an earlier and a later speech/ comment.

ཁ་འགུལ་ (kā güü) 1. va. to eat (slang) ¶ ཁོ་ད་ལྟ་ཁ་འགུལ་བཞིན་འདུག He is eating now. 2. va. to speak/ tell.

ཁ་འགུལ་ལུས་འགུལ་ (kāgüü lüügüü) acting upon one's words; va.—བྱེད་ [Lit. move the mouth, move the body].

ཁ་འགོ་བ་ (kā gowa) foreman, overseer, person in charge.

ཁ་འགོག (kā gɔɔ̀) see ཁ་བཀག.

ཁ་འགྱུར་ (kāgyur) 1. technique used in Tibetan painting of blending/ shading one color into a second color; va.—གཏོང་. 2. sm. ཁ་འགལ་ཚིག་འགལ་.

ཁ་འགྱེད་ (kāgyeè) vi. to have side shoots/ suckers grow from the main root/ stem.

ཁ་འགྱེས་ (kāgyeè) vi. to separate/ split/ divide ¶ ང་ཚོ་གནམ་གྲུ་ཐང་ནས་ཁ་གྱེས་པ་ཡིན་ We separated at the airport.

ཁ་འགྲིག (kā drig) vi. to agree, to come to an agreement ¶ བཟོ་པ་ཚོ་ཁ་འགྲིགས་ནས་ལས་མཚམས་བཞག་པ་རེད་ The workers came to an agreement and went on strike. 2. vi. to fit together well/ tightly ¶ ལྕུགས་མདོང་གཉིས་ཁ་ཡག་པོ་འགྲིགས་བཞག The two pipes fit together well. 3. vi. to be unable to open one's mouth ¶ གྲིབ་སྣོན་ཕོག་ནས་ཁ་འགྲིགས་བཞག He had a stroke and was unable to open his mouth.

ཁ་འགྲིག་པོ་ (kā drigbo) 1. united, unified ། ཁོ་ཚོ་ཁ་འགྲིག་པོ་ཡོད་ཙང་ལས་ཀ་ཡག་པོ་བྱེད་ཐུབ་པ་རེད་ Because they were united, they were able to work well. 2. well-fitted ། ཏ་ཡང་དོའི་ཁེབས་གཙོད་ཁ་ཁ་འགྲིགས་པོ་འདུག The lid of the pot fits well.

ཁ་འགྲིག་སེར་མེད་ (kā drig sērmeè) a perfect fit—two pieces fitting together perfectly without a gap/ space between them.

ཁ་འགྲིག་སོ་འགྲིག (kādrig sōdrig) balanced, equalized (e.g., assets and liabilities); va.—བྱེད་; vi.—དུ་འགྱུར་ ། མི་ཚང་དེའི་མཁར་རྫེ་དབང་ཐང་དང་བུ་ལོན་གཉིས་ཁ་འགྲིག་སོ་འགྲིག་དུ་གྱུར་སོང་ That household's possessions and debts have become balanced.

ཁ་འགྲིལ་ (kā drii) 1. vi. to be in accord/ agreement ། དོན་ཚན་འདིའི་སྐོར་ལ་མི་དམངས་ཁ་འགྲིལ་བ་རེད་ The people were in accord regarding this matter. 2. hem lining.

ཁ་འགྲིལ་ཉིས་འགྲོམ་ (kāndrii ñiidroma) double hem lining on Tibetan brocade collars.

ཁ་འགྲིལ་པོ་ (kā driibu) in accord/ agreement ། དོན་ཚན་འདིའི་སྐོར་ལ་མི་དམངས་ཁ་འགྲིལ་པོ་ཡོད་པ་རེད་ The people are in accord regarding this matter.

ཁ་འགྲེམ་: p. **ཁ་བཀྲམས་**; f. **ཁ་དཀྲམ་** (kā drem) 1. va. to separate/ divide up ། དམག་མི་རྣམས་ཁ་བཀྲམས་ནས་དགྲ་བོ་གཏོར་བ་རེད་ The soldiers separated (from one unit into smaller units) and destroyed the enemy. 2. va. to distribute/ communicate sth. ། གོང་རིམ་གྱི་སྲིད་ཇུས་དེ་གཤམ་འོག་ཏུ་ཁ་འགྲེམས་སྤྲངས་ཡག་པོ་བྱུང་མེད་པ་རེད Communicated the policy of the higher authorities to those below was not done well.

ཁ་རྒན་ (kāgɛn) old, elderly (for animals).

ཁ་རྒས་ (kā gɛɛ̀) vi. to become old (for animals) ། སེམས་ཅན་འདི་ཁ་རྒས་ནས་བསད་པ་རེད་ After this animal became old (he) killed it.

ཁ་རྒས་པོ་ (kā gɛɛ̀bo) sm. ཁ་རྒན་.

ཁ་རྒོད་(པོ་) (kā göōbo) 1. talking big ། མི་འདི་འཛིན་ཐང་མེད་པར་ཁ་རྒོད་པོ་འདུག This man talks big but is not capable. 2. sm. ཁ་སྒྱོང་པོ་.

ཁ་རྒོད་གདིང་རྒོད་ (kāgö dĩŋgö) courageous/ brave (in words and thought) ། མི་དམངས་ཀྱིས་སྲིད་གཞུང་དེ་ར་ཁ་རྒོད་གདིང་རྒོད་ཀྱིས་ངོ་རྒོལ་བྱས་པ་རེད་ The people opposed that government courageously in both words and thoughts.

ཁ་རྒྱ་ (kāgya) extent, area ། བོད་ལ་མི་འབོར་ཆེན་པོ་མེད་ན་ཡང་ས་ཁ་རྒྱ་ཆེན་པོ་རེད་ Although the population of Tibet is small, it is huge (in area).

ཁ་རྒྱ་བོད་གསུམ་ (kāgya pöōsum) the three: Hui, Han and Tibetans.

ཁ་རྒྱག (kā gyaà) 1. va. to close (a lid/ cover) ། སྒམ་དེ་ཁ་རྒྱག་དགོས་ The box needs to be closed. 2. va. to measure material/ fabrics in squares. 3. va. to put one's mouth on a cup or utensil ། ཁོས་ངའི་དཀར་ཡོལ་ལ་ཁ་བརྒྱབ་ཙང་ངས་ཇ་མ་བཏུངས་ He put his mouth on my cup so I didn't drink the tea (there is a notion of pollution implied).

ཁ་རྒྱགས་པ་ (kā gyagba) 1. talking big, exaggerating (in speech). 2. cheeky, sassy, impertinent ། མི་འདི་ཁ་རྒྱགས་པ་འདུག This man is impertinent.

ཁ་རྒྱགས་པོ་ (kā gyagpo) sm. ཁ་རྒྱགས་པ་.

ཁ་རྒྱགས་མིག་མ་རྒྱགས་ (kā gyaà mĩg magyaà) eating even though one is full [Lit. the mouth is full but not the eyes].

ཁ་རྒྱན་ (kāgyɛn) gold or silver decoration put on the mouth/ lip of a wooden bowl; va.—རྒྱག; —གཏོང་.

ཁ་རྒྱབ་གོན་པ་ (kāgyəb kömba) clothing.

ཁ་རྒྱབ་གཉིས་མེད་ (kāgyəb ñiimeè) poor (without clothes or food).

ཁ་རྒྱལ་ (kāgyɛɛ) 1. va. to win a debate or argument. 2. pride.

ཁ་རྒྱུ་དྲོ་རྒྱུ་ (kāgyu trogyu) (+ neg.) 1. (regarding food) tasteless ། ཁ་ལག་ཁ་རྒྱུ་དྲོ་རྒྱུ་མེད་པ་ Food that is tasteless. 2. meaningless, perfunctory (regarding speech) ། ཁོའི་སྐད་ཆ་ལ་ཁ་རྒྱུ་དྲོ་རྒྱུ་མི་འདུག. His talk is meaningless. 3. incapable, stupid (regarding people) ། མི་དེ་ཁ་རྒྱུ་དྲོ་རྒྱུ་མེད་པ་གཅིག་རེད་ That person is not capable. 4. (regarding trade and business) profitless, without any return ། ངས་མ་རྩ་བཞག་ནས་དེ་ལ་ཁ་རྒྱུ་དྲོ་རྒྱུ་བྱུང་མ་སོང་ I obtained no profit on my capital.

ཁ་རྒྱུ་དབང་ཐང་ (kāgyu wāŋdaŋ) all one's possessions ། ཁོའི་ཁ་རྒྱུ་དབང་ཐང་ནི་ཉལ་ཆས་རུལ་པོ་ཞིག་ལས་མེད་པ་རེད་ As for all his possessions, there was only tattered bedding.

ཁ་རྒྱུ་གཤིན་པོ་ (kāgyu shĩmbu) 1. gentle, gently ། ཁ་རྒྱུ་གཤིན་པོའི་ཐོག་ནས་མི་ལ་སྐད་ཆ་ཤོད་དགོས་རེད་ You should talk in a gentle manner when speaking with people. 2. obedient ། ཕྲུ་གུ་དེ་ལ་ལས་ཀ་ག་རེ་བསྐུལ་ན་ཡང་ཁ་རྒྱུ་གཤིན་པོ་ཡོད་ Whatever work one gives to that child, he obeys (is obedient).

ཁ་རྒྱུག (kāgyuù) following what others say; va.—བྱེད་ ། མི་དེ་རྟག་དུས་ཡིན་ན་ཡང་མི་གཞན་གྱི་ཁ་རྒྱུག་བྱེད་ཀྱི་ཡོད་པ་རེད་ That person always follows what others say.

ཁ་རྒྱུག་རྫོམ་ (kāgyu dzōm) oral sayings.

ཁ་རྒྱུགས་ (kāgyuù) 1. oral examination; va.—ལེན་ to give an oral examination; va.—སྤྲོད་ to take an oral examination ། ང་དེ་རིང་ཁ་རྒྱུགས་སྤྲོད་ཀྱི་ཡིན་ I will take an oral examination today. 2. sm. ཁ་རྒྱུག.

ཁ་རྒྱུགས་པོ་ (kā gyugbo) 1. flowing smoothly/ freely from an opening ། སྨྱུ་གུ་འདི་ཁ་རྒྱུགས་པོ་ཞི་དྲག་འདུག The pen writes well (a pen from which ink flows easily from the nib). 2. sth. selling well ། ཅ་ལག་འདི་ཁ་རྒྱུགས་པོ་ཡོད་པ་རེད་ This commodity sells well.

ཁ་རྒྱུད་ (kāgyüü) by word of mouth, via oral transmission ། ཁ་རྒྱུད་ཀྱི་གཏམ་དཔེ་ A story transmitted by word of mouth.

ཁ་རྒྱུན་ (kāgyün) oral tradition, folk saying, common usage ། ཁ་རྒྱུན་ནས་བྱུས་ན་ According to oral tradition ། བཤད་སྟོལ་འདི་མི་རྣམས་ཀྱི་ཁ་རྒྱུན་དུ་ཆགས་འདུག This way of speaking has become common usage.

ཁ་རྒྱུན་གྱི་རྩོམ་རིག (kāgyüngi dzōmrig) oral literature; vi.—དུ་འགྱུར་; —དུ་ཆགས་ to become a part of oral tradition, to become generally known/ used ། སྐད་ཆ་འདི་ཁ་རྒྱུན་དུ་གྱུར་བ་རེད་ This speech (language) has become a part of oral tradition.

ཁ་སྒུར་ (kā gur) bending the head (in the sense of a riding animal refusing to obey the rider by bending down its head and pulling against the reins); va.—རྒྱག.

ཁ་སྒོ་ (kāgo) 1. talk, speech ། ཁ་སྒོ་ཡངས་པོ་ Fluent speech. 2. mouth ། ཁ་སྒོ་ཕྱེ་ནས་ཨེམ་ཆི་སོ་ལ་བརྟག་དཔྱད་བྱས་པ་རེད་ (He) opened his mouth and the doctor examined his teeth. 3. face ། ཁ་སྒོ་མཛེས་པོ་ A beautiful face. ། ཁ་སྒོ་ལེགས་པོ་ A beautiful face.

ཁ་སྒོ་མོ་ (kā gomo) sm. ཁ་སྒོ་, 2.

ཁ་སྒོ་མོ་རྒྱུད་ཀྱི་གཞི་མ་ (kā gomo gyöögi shimə) be careful what you say because it is the source of disputes [Lit. the mouth is the source of disputes].

ཁ་སྒོར་ (kāgɔɔ) a round leather patch that is sewn around the hole of a pouch.

ཁ་སྒྱུར་ (kāgyur) 1. turning around, changing direction (e.g., for vehicles); va. ཁ་སྒྱུར་; —བྱེད་; —གཏོང་ ། ཁོས་མོ་ཊ་ཁ་བསྒྱུར་བ་རེད་ He turned the car around. 2. va. to change a color (usu. by mixing a different color paint into it). 3. va. to change the topic (in speech).

ཁ་སྒྱུར་འཁོར་ལོ་ (kāgyur kɔ̄ɔlo) steering wheel.

ཁ་སྒྱུར་མཇུག་གཤོག (kāgyur jugshog) rudder.

ཁ་སྒྲིལ་ (kā drii) va. to unify, to agree (to do) ། ཁོ་ཚོ་ཁ་སྒྲིལ་ནས་ལས་ཀ་བྱས་པ་རེད་ They united and did the work. 2. using a piece of material to make a hem on another piece of material; va.—གཏོང ། ཁོས་སྟོད་ཐུང་ལྭང་ཁ་ཞིག་ལ་ཁ་སྒྲིལ་དམར་པོ་བཏང་འདུག

He made a hem with a piece of red material on the green shirt.

ཁ་སྒྲིལ་པོ་ (kā driibu) unified, dissentless ། ཁོ་ཚོ་ཁ་སྒྲིལ་པོ་བྱས་ནས་ལས་ཀ་བྱས་པ་རེད་ They worked in unity.

ཁ་སྒྲོག (kādrɔɔ̀) 1. the string that ties the mouth of a bag/ pouch/ sack closed; va.—རྒྱག to tie a bag, pouch, sack shut; va.—བཤིག; —འགྲོལ་ to untie the string that closes a bag/ pouch/ sack shut. 2. sm. ཁ་རས་.

ཁ་སྒྲོབ་ (kādrob) bragging, boasting; va.—ཤོད་ to boast/ brag.

ཁ་སྒྲོབ་ཚ་པོ་ (kādrob tsāābo) braggart, boastful ། མི་ཁ་སྒྲོབ་ཚ་པོ་འདི་དངོས་གནས་འཇོན་ཐང་གང་ཡང་མི་འདུག The boastful man actually has no ability.

ཁ་སྒྲོམ་ (kādrom) sm. ཁ་སྒྲོབ་.

ཁ་བརྒྱ་ (kāgya) talking a lot, gossiping ། ཁ་བརྒྱ་བཤད་པ་ལས་དོན་གཅིག་སྒྲུབ་ན་དགའ་ It is better to get one thing accomplished than do a lot of talking [Lit. 100 mouths].

ཁ་བརྒྱ་གཅིག་མཐུན་ (kāgya jīgtün) speaking with one voice, unanimous agreement [Lit. 100 mouths in agreement].

ཁ་བརྒྱ་ལྕེ་སྟོང་ (kāgya jēdoŋ) conveys sth. that cannot be finished or completely enumerated [Lit. 100 mouths and 1,000 tongues]; vi.—སྤྲུལ་ to magically get one hundred mouths and one thousand tongues ། ཁོ་ཚོའི་ནོར་འཁྲུལ་ཁ་བརྒྱ་ལྕེ་སྟོང་དུ་སྤྲུལ་ན་ཡང་བཤད་ཚར་གྱི་མ་རེད་ Even if one magically gets one hundred mouths and one thousand tongues, one can not finish talking about their mistakes.

ཁ་བརྒྱ་ཚིག་གཅིག (kāgya tsīgjig) sm. ཁ་བརྒྱ་གཅིག་མཐུན་.

ཁ་བརྒྱབ་ (kā gyəb) p. of ཁ་རྒྱག.

ཁ་བརྒྱུད་ (kā gyüü) 1. va. to say/ tell sth. on behalf of another (person or office) ། ངས་མི་གཞན་ཞིག་གི་ཁ་བརྒྱུད་ནས་འགོ་ཁྲིད་ལ་རེ་འདུན་བཏིན་པ་ཡིན་ I made a request to the boss through sb. else. 2. a custom that is no longer done but has become part of oral folklore.

ཁ་བསྒོ་ (kāgo) giving advice, giving a verbal order; va.—བྱེད་.

ཁ་བསྒོ་སྐྱེས་འབྲས་ (kāgo gyēndrɛɛ̀) sm. ཁ་བསྒོ་.

ཁ་བསྒོས་ (kā göö) va. to give advice, to give a verbal order.

ཁ་ངན་ (kāŋɛɛn) nasty/ mean/ hurtful/ insulting language or speech; va.—ཤོད་; —བརྗོད་.

ཁ་ངན་ཁོག་ངན་ (kāŋɛn dāmŋɛn) evil/ bad in speech and mind.

ཁ་ངན་གདམ་ངན་ (kāŋɛn dāmŋɛn) evil in speech, bad or nasty speech/ talk.

ཁ་ངན་གདམ་བཙོག (kāŋɛn dāmdzɔɔ̀) insulting and dirty speech/ words/ language; va.—ཤོད་; —བརྗོད་ to use insulting/ mean/ crude/ hurtful words or language.

ཁ་ངན་པོ་ (kā ŋɛmbo) sb. who uses insulting/ bad/ nasty/ mean/ hurtful/ disparaging language; va.—ཤོད་; —བརྗོད་ to use insulting/ mean/ crude/ hurtful words or language ། སློབ་སྦྱོང་ཡག་པོ་ཡོད་ཀྱང་ཁ་ངན་པོ་འདུག Although (he) is well educated (he) uses crude/ insulting language.

ཁ་ངན་དམའ་འབེབས་ (kāŋɛn māmbeb) speech or talk that disparages/ demeans/ insults.

ཁ་ངན་ཚིག་ངན་ (kāŋɛn tsīgŋɛn) bad/ abusive/ nasty/ disparaging speech or talk.

ཁ་ངལ་ (kāŋɛl) vi. to be tired from talking ། ཁ་ལ་མི་ཉན་མཁན་ལ་བསླབ་བྱ་བརྒྱབ་ན་ཁ་ངལ་རོགས་རེད་ If you give advice to sb. who doesn't listen you will just get tired from talking [i.e. waste your time].

ཁ་ངལ་ལྕེ་ལྐུག (kāŋɛɛ jēgug) talking a lot with no result, shouting oneself hoarse [Lit. mouth tired, tongue stupid].

ཁ་ངུ་ (kāŋu) crying ། ཁ་ངུ་དང་མ་བྲལ་བ་ Crying all the time.

ཁ་ངོ་ (kāŋo) face ། ཁ་ངོ་ཁྲུས་ Wash (your) face! ། ཁ་ངོ་དྭངས་མ་ A beautiful (face).

ཁ་ངོ་ལྟ་ (kāŋo dā) va. to help sb. for the sake of a friend ། ཁོ་ལ་རོགས་བྱས་པ་ནི་གྲོགས་པོའི་ཁ་ངོ་བལྟས་པ་ཡིན་ I helped him because of my friendship (with someone else).

ཁ་ངོ་ལྡོག (kā ŋodɔɔ̀) va. to renege/ go back on one's promise.

ཁ་ངོམ་ (kā ŋom) sm. ཁ་ངོམས་.

ཁ་ངོམས་ (kā ŋom) vi. to have one's thirst quenched ། ཆུ་བཏུངས་ནས་ཁ་ངོམས་བྱུང་ (My) thirst was quenched after I drank the water.

ཁ་ངོམས་གྲོད་འགྲངས་ (kāŋom trōndraŋ) sm. ཁ་ངོམས་གྲོད་རྒྱགས་.

ཁ་ངོམས་གྲོད་རྒྱགས་ (kāŋom trōōgyaà) satiated, satisfied [Lit. thirst quenched, stomach full].

ཁ་ངོར་ལྟ་ (kāŋɔr dā) sm. ཁ་ངོ་ལྟ་.

ཁ་དངོམ་ (kāŋom) sm. ཁ་སྒྲོབ་.

ཁ་མངག (kāŋaà) ordering/ reserving/ sth. verbally, asking sb. to do sth.; va.—བྱེད་ ། ཁོས་རྒྱ་གར་ནས་སྨན་སྣ་ཁ་མངག་བྱས་པ་རེད་ He ordered spices from India [i.e. asked sb. to bring or have a store send the spices].

ཁ་མངར་ (kāŋaa) sm. ཁ་མངར་མོ་.

ཁ་མངར་མོ་ (kā ŋāāmo) 1. sweet. 2. saying things a person wants to hear but having no intention of really doing them [usu. by a superior with regard to a request], saying sth. that will please sb. even though it isn't true or one isn't planning to do it; va.—ཤོད་ ། མི་དེ་རྟག་པར་ཁ་མངར་མོ་ཤོད་པ་ལས་དོན་དག་ངོ་མ་གཏན་ནས་སྤྲོད་ཀྱི་མ་རེད་ That person always says what people want to hear but never does (gives) what is needed.

ཁ་མངལ་ (kāŋɛl) a sickness or symptom wherein the patient loses the sense of taste.

ཁ་སྔ་བ་ (kā ŋāwa) speaking up or asking for sth. before sb. else; va.—བྱེད་ ། ཁོ་ཁ་སྔ་བ་ཡིན་ཙང་ཁང་པ་དེ་ཁོ་ལ་ཐོབ་པ་རེད་ He got the house because he spoke up for it first.

ཁ་སྔོག (kā ŋɔɔ̀) 1. va. to look or rummage through sth. (conveys searching for sth.) ། ཉེན་རྟོག་པས་སྒམ་འདི་ཁ་བསྔོགས་པ་རེད་ The police rummaged through the box. 2. sm. སྐད་ཆ་སྔོག.

ཁ་སྔོག་མཐིལ་འཚོལ་ (kāŋɔɔ̀ tiltsöö) getting to the bottom of sth. by asking questions/ interrogating; va.—བྱེད་ ། མི་གསོད་གྱོད་དོན་དེའི་སྐོར་མི་མང་པོའི་ཁ་སྔོག་མཐིལ་འཚོལ་བྱས་པ་རེད་ (They) got to the bottom of the murder case by questioning many people.

ཁ་སྔོན་ (kā ŋön) some time ago ། ཁ་སྔོན་འབྱོར་པའི་ཡི་གེ་ A letter that was received some time ago.

ཁ་བསྔལ་ (kā ŋɛ̄ɛ) vi. to get tired from talking ། སྐད་ཆ་བཤད་དྲགས་པས་ཁ་བསྔལ་བྱུང་བ་རེད་ (He) was tired from talking too much.

ཁ་བསྔོགས་ (kā ŋɔɔ̀) p. of ཁ་སྔོག.

ཁ་ཅལ་ཅལ་ (kā jɛɛ̄jɛɛ̀) indistinct/ unclear speech or enunciation ། ཁོ་ཁ་ཅལ་ཅལ་རེད་ He is someone whose speech is indistinct.

ཁ་ཅིག (kā jīg) some, a few ། དགེ་རྒན་ཁ་ཅིག་ཡག་པོ་འདུག Some of the teachers are good.

ཁ་ཅེ་མིའོ་ (kāje mio) ch. BCG vaccine.

ཁ་ཅོལ་ (kājöö) 1. idle or small talk. 2. meaningless/ nonsensical talk ། ཁ་ཅོལ་མང་པོ་བཤད་པ་རེད་ (He) spoke a lot of nonsense.

ཁ་གཅང་པོ་ (kā jāŋbo) eloquent, skillful (in speaking) ། ཁོང་ཁ་གཅང་པོ་ཡོད་ཙང་ཚང་མས་ཁོང་གི་སྐད་ཆ་ཉན་འདོད་བྱེད་ཀྱི་ཡོད་པ་རེད་ Everyone wants to listen to him talk because he is eloquent.

ཁ་གཅིག (kā jīg) 1. speaking with the same voice, speaking in agreement, saying unanimously. 2. saying one thing.

ཁ་གཅིག་ཁོག་གཉིས་ (kājig kōgñii) insincere/ deceptive talk [Lit. one mouth, two insides].

ཁ་གཅིག་གྲགས་ (kājig drag) speaking unanimously/ in agreement, everyone saying the same thing ། དཔལ་འབྱོར་ཡར་རྒྱས་གཏོང་དགོས་ཞེས་ཚང་མས་ཁ་གཅིག

གྲགས་བྱས་པ་རེད་ Everyone is unanimous about the need to improve the economy.

ཁ་གཅིག་ལྕེ་གཉིས་ (kājig jēñìì) speaking with two tongues, saying different/ contradictory things to different people at different times; va.—བྱེད་ ¶ཁ་གཅིག་ལྕེ་གཉིས་ཀྱི་སྐད་ཆ་མ་ཤོད་ Don't say things to contradict yourself. [Lit. one mouth, two tongues].

ཁ་གཅིག་མཐུན་ (kā jīgdün) sm. ཁ་གཅིག་གྲགས་.

ཁ་གཅུ་ (kā jū) 1. va. to turn/ twist around, to change direction, to veer ¶ཁོས་ཕྲུ་གུ་མཐོང་པ་དང་མོ་ཊ་ཁ་གཅུས་པ་རེད་ He turned the car as soon as he saw the child. 2. va. to win/ take away sb.'s sweetheart ¶ཁོས་ངའི་གྲོགས་མོ་ཁ་གཅུས་སོང་ He took away my girlfriend.

ཁ་གཅུས་ (kā jüü) p. of ཁ་གཅུ་.

ཁ་གཅུས་སྣ་གཅུས་ (kājüü nājüü) shaking one's head left and right in disagreement, expressing "no" by shaking one's head; va.—བྱེད་.

ཁ་གཅོད་ (kāpjöö) cover, cap, lid; va.—རྒྱག to cover, to put on a cap ¶མོས་ཤེལ་དམ་ལ་ཁ་གཅོད་རྒྱག་གི་རེད་ She will put a cap on the bottle.

ཁ་གཅོད་མཉེན་ཤིང་ (kāpjöö ñēnshiŋ) a cork lid/ stopper (for a bottle).

ཁ་བཅགས་བཅགས་ (kā jāgjaà) chewing, munching; va.—བྱེད་ ¶ཁ་ལག་ཟ་དུས་ཁ་བཅགས་བཅགས་ཡག་པོ་བྱེད་དགོས་ (One) needs to chew food well when eating.

ཁ་བཅུད་ (kājüü) plaster (in medical treatment).

ཁ་བཅུས་ (kā jüü) 1. p. of ཁ་འཆུ་. 2. sm. ཁ་གཅུས་.

ཁ་བཅོལ་ (kājöö) leaving a verbal message (verbal); va.—བྱེད་.

ཁ་བཅོལ་ངག་བཅོལ་ (kājöö ŋagjöö) leaving a verbal message; va.—བྱེད་. 2. asking sb. verbally to do sth.; va.—བྱེད་.

ཁ་ལྕགས་ (kājaà) bit (in mouth of horse).

ཁ་ལྕེ་རྡོ་ (kā jēdo) unclear/ indistinct speech ¶ཁ་ལྕེ་རྡོའི་སྐད་ཆ་ Talk that is unclear.

ཁ་ལྕེ་རྟུལ་པོ་ (kāje dǖübo) awkward, clumsy when speaking.

ཁ་ལྕེ་བདེ་པོ་ (kāje debo) sm. ཁ་བདེ་པོ་.

ཁ་ཆ་ (kāja) verbal message; va.—གཏོང་; va.—སྐུར་ to give/ send a verbal message ¶ནང་མི་བདེ་པོ་ཡིན་པའི་ཁ་ཆ་བསྐུར་བཞག I received a message that my family members were well.

ཁ་ཆག (kājaà) broken/ chipped edge ¶དཀར་ཡོལ་ཁ་ཆག་ནང་ལ་ཇ་མ་འཐུངས་ Don't drink tea from a chipped cup.

ཁ་ཆག་སྣ་རལ་ (kājaà nārεε) harm, injury, misfortune ¶མི་ཚང་པ་གིར་ཁ་ཆག་སྣ་རལ་མང་པོ་བྱུང་པ་རེད་ That family has had much misfortune. [Lit. broken mouth, torn nose].

ཁ་ཆད་ (kājεὲ) 1. an oral agreement/ promise/ contract; va.—བྱེད་; —འཇོག; —བསྒོ་ to make or agree to an oral agreement/ promise/ contract ¶ཁང་གླ་སྒོར་མོ་བརྒྱ་སྤྲོད་རྒྱུའི་ཁ་ཆད་བྱས་པ་རེད་ (He) agreed to pay 100 dollars rent. va.—ལ་བརྩི་; —ལ་བརྩི་འཇོག་བྱེད་; —ལ་གནས་ to keep one's word/ promise, to abide by one's agreement ¶མི་འདི་ཁ་ཆད་ལ་གནས་མཁན་ཞིག་རེད་ This is a man who keeps his word. va.—དོར་ to break an agreement/ promise ¶མི་དེས་ལས་ཀ་བྱ་རྒྱུའི་ཁ་ཆད་དོར་ནས་ལུང་པ་གཞན་དག་ལ་ཕྱིན་པ་རེད་ That person broke his agreement to do the work and went to another region. vi.—ལ་མ་གནས་; —ཤོར་ to have an agreement/ promise be broken ¶ཁ་ཆད་ཤོར་ཙང་ཁྲིམས་ཁང་ལ་ཐུག་པ་རེད་ Since the agreement was broken, (we) had to go to court. 2. an appointment, engagement, date; va.—བྱེད་; —འཇོག; —བསྒོ་ to make an appointment/ engagement/ date ¶ཐུག་འཕྲད་བྱེད་རྒྱུའི་ཁ་ཆད་བྱས་པ་རེད་ (They) made an appointment to meet.

ཁ་ཆད་འགྱུར་མེད་ (kājεὲ gyurmeè) a promise that will not be changed.

ཁ་ཆད་རྒྱབ་སྐྱུར་ (kājεὲ gyəbgyur) going back/ reneging on a agreement or promise; va.—བྱེད་.

ཁ་ཆད་བསྒོ་ (kājεὲ go) see ཁ་ཆད་.

ཁ་ཆད་གཅིག་ཐོག (kājεὲ jīgdɔɔ̀) an unwavering or unanimous agreement/ decision.

ཁ་ཆད་དོར་ (kājεὲ dɔɔ) see ཁ་ཆད་.

ཁ་ཆད་བུ་ལོན་ (kājεὲ pulön) sth. that has been promised must be kept/ fulfilled (usu. debts) [Lit. promise, debt].

ཁ་ཆད་མེད་པ་ (kājεὲ meèba) unconditional ¶ཁ་ཆད་མེད་པའི་མགོ་བདགས་ཞུས་པ་རེད (They) surrendered unconditionally.

ཁ་ཆད་ལ་གནས་ (kājεὲla nεὲ) see ཁ་ཆད་.

ཁ་ཆད་ལ་བརྩི་འཇོག (kājεὲla dzīnjoò) see ཁ་ཆད་.

ཁ་ཆད་ལག་བསྟར་ (kājεὲ lagdar) putting an agreement into practice; va.—བྱེད་ ¶སྲིད་བྱུས་དེ་ཁ་ཆད་ལག་བསྟར་བྱས་མ་སོང་ That policy was not put into practice.

ཁ་ཆད་ཤོར་ (kājεὲ shɔ̄ɔ) see ཁ་ཆད་.

ཁ་ཆར་ (kājar) snow and rain.

ཁ་ཆར་བུ་ཡུག (kājar puyuù) blizzard, storm with snow and rain mixed.

ཁ་ཆིངས་ (kāciŋ) sm. ཁ་སྒྲོག.

ཁ་ཆུ་ (kāju) spit, spittle; vi.—འཛར་; —གཏོང་; —སྒྲོང་; —ཤོར་; —ལྷུང་ to drool/ dribble ¶ཕྲུ་གུ་ཁ་ཆུ་འཛར་མཁན་འདིའི་ཁ་འཕྱིས་པ་རེད་ (She) wiped the mouth of the child that was drooling. vi.—འཁོར་ to have one's mouth water, to salivate ¶ཁོས་ཁ་ལག་བཟས་པ་མཐོང་ནས་ཁ་ལ་ཁ་ཆུ་འཁོར་བྱུང་ When I saw him eat, my mouth watered.

ཁ་ཆུ་འཛར་འཛར་ (kāju dzardzar) drooling spit/ spittle.

ཁ་ཆུང་ (kācuŋ) sm. ཁ་ཆུང་ཆུང་.

ཁ་ཆུང་ཆུང་ (kā cūnjun) 1. small mouth. 2. young (for animals). 3. small caliber (for guns). 4. a vessel/ vase/ jar with a small opening or mouth.

ཁ་ཆེ་ (kāce) 1. Muslim, Islam ¶ཁ་ཆེའི་ཆོས་ལུགས་ Islamic religion. ¶ཁ་ཆེའི་དམག་མི་ Muslim troops. 2. a Kashmiri.

ཁ་ཆེ་གུར་ཀུམ་ (kāce gurgum) sm. ཁ་ཆེ་ཤ་སྐམ་.

ཁ་ཆེ་གུར་གུམ་ (kāce gurgum) sm. ཁ་ཆེ་ཤ་སྐམ་.

ཁ་ཆེ་གླིང་ཁ་ (kāce līŋgə) name of a park in Lhasa [Lit. Muslim park].

ཁ་ཆེ་དབང་ཐང་ (kāce wāŋdaŋ) sm. ཁ་རྒྱ་དབང་ཐང་.

ཁ་ཆེ་ཡང་སྣ་ཁུང་འོག་རེད་ (kāceyaŋ nəguŋwɔɔ̀ reè) being under sb's control [Lit. even though the mouth is big, it is under the nose].

ཁ་ཆེ་རུང་སྣའི་འོག་རེད་ (kāceruŋ nεε wɔɔ̀ reè) sm. ཁ་ཆེ་ཡང་སྣ་ཁུང་འོག་རེད་.

ཁ་ཆེ་ཤ་ཀ་མ་ (kāce shāgama) sm. ཁ་ཆེ་ཤ་སྐམ་.

ཁ་ཆེ་ཤ་ཁ་མ་ (kāce shāgama) sm. ཁ་ཆེ་ཤ་སྐམ་.

ཁ་ཆེ་ཤ་སྐམ་ (kāce shāgam) saffron.

ཁ་ཆེ་ཤ་ཁ་མ་ (kāce shāgama) sm. ཁ་ཆེ་ཤ་སྐམ་.

ཁ་ཆེམས་ (kācem) last testament, will; va.—འཇོག to leave/ make a will or last testament ¶ཕ་མའི་ཁ་ཆེམས་བཞིན་དུ་བུ་ཕྲུག་ཚོས་རྒྱུ་ནོར་ཚང་མ་བགོ་བཤའ་བརྒྱབ་པ་རེད་ The children divided all the wealth according to the will left by their parents.

ཁ་ཆེམས་རླུང་བསྐུར་ (kācem lūŋgur) disregarding/ ignoring sb.'s will or last testament [Lit. sending a will into the air].

ཁ་ཆེའི་གོས་ཆེན་ (kāje gøjεn) Kashmiri satin/ brocade.

ཁ་ཆེའི་ཆོས་ལུགས་ (kāje cǖluù) Islam, the Muslim religion.

ཁ་ཆེའི་བསྟན་སྲུང་དམག (kāje dεnsuŋ māà) Islamic Jihad.

ཁ་ཆེའི་བསྟན་སྲུང་དམག་དཔུང་ (kāje dεnsuŋ məgbuŋ) Islamic fighters defending the faith, Islamic Jihad forces, mujahedeen.

ཁ་ཆེའི་བསྟན་སྲུང་ཡུལ་དམག་སྒྲིག་འཛུགས་ (kāje dεnsuŋ yüümaà drigdzuù) Islamic Jihad (Palestine).

ཁ་ཆེའི་མཐུན་ཚོགས་ (kāje tǖndzoò) Islamic League.

ཁ་ཆེའི་ལ་ཐོད་ (kājee lεὲdöö) type of turban worn by Muslims.

ཁ་ཚོད་ (kāpjöö) sm. ཁ་གཅོད་.

ཁ་ཆོས་ (kājöö) hypocrite with regard to religion, sb. who talks as if he is religious but really isn't; va.—བྱེད་ ། བྱམས་དང་སྙིང་རྗེ་མ་ལྡན་ན་ཆོས་ལ་དད་པ་ཡོད་ཅེས་པ་ནི་ཁ་ཆོས་རང་རེད་ If one does not have love and compassion, then it is religiously hypocritical to say (you) have faith in the dharma. [Lit. mouth religion].

ཁ་མཆུ་ (kāmju) dispute, altercation, law case, lawsuit; va.—རྒྱག; —འཛུགས་ to dispute, to sue, to file or bring a lawsuit ། ཁོའི་ལྡངས་འཁོར་གྱིས་མོ་བརྫིས་ཙང་མོས་ཁོ་ལ་ཁ་མཆུ་བཙུགས་པ་རེད་ Because his car ran over her, she brought a lawsuit against him. va.—སློང་ to cause a lawsuit/ legal case to be brought against sb. ། ཁོ་དགེ་རྒན་ལ་དགའ་པོ་མེད་ཙང་དགེ་རྒན་དང་སློབ་ཕྲུག་དབར་ཁ་མཆུ་སློང་གི་ཡོད་པ་རེད་ Because he doesn't like the teacher, he caused a lawsuit to be filed between the students and the teacher.

ཁ་མཆུ་དུག་རོ་ (kāmju tugro) having a bitter dispute/ quarrel remain after an attempt to settle it; vi.—ལུས་ ། ཁྲིམས་ཁང་ནས་ཐག་གཅོད་བྱས་པའི་རྗེས་སུ་ཁ་མཆུ་དུག་རོ་ལུས་ཡོད་པ་རེད་ After the court issued a decision, the bitter dispute remained (alive).

ཁ་མཆུ་ནང་འཇགས་ (kāmju nanjaà) resolving a problem internally; va.—བྱེད་.

ཁ་མཆུ་བོགས་མར་ལེན་ (kāmju bɔɔmaa lēn) 1. va. to take on sb.'s lawsuit/ law case and provide them help (sth. like a lawyer in tt.) ། ཁོས་ཁ་མཆུ་བོགས་མར་བླངས་དེ་འཚོ་བ་སྐྱེལ་གྱི་ཡོད་པ་རེད་ He makes his living by taking on the cases of others. [Lit. leasing a law case]. 2. (— + མཁན་) sb. who pries/ interferes in another's conflict.

ཁ་མཆུ་འཛུགས་ (kāmju dzuù) see ཁ་མཆུ་.

ཁ་མཆུ་སློང་ (kāmju lōŋ) see ཁ་མཆུ་.

ཁ་འཆམ་ (kānjam) an agreement; va. ཁ་འཆམ་; va.—བྱེད་ to agree to sth. ། ཁ་འཆམ་དེ་ནི་ན་ནིང་བྱུང་བ་རེད་ That agreement was obtained last year. ། ཆིངས་ཡིག་འཛུགས་རྒྱུར་ཁ་འཆམས་པ་རེད་ (They) agreed to sign a treaty.

ཁ་འཆམ་གྲོས་འགྲིག (kājam trööòdrig) agreeing to sth. discussed or talked about; va.—བྱེད་.

ཁ་འཆམ་པོ་ (kā cāmbo) agreeable, agreement ། ལས་ཀ་དེའི་སྐོར་ཁོ་ཚོ་ཁ་འཆམ་པོ་བྱུང་བཞག They were in agreement about that work.

ཁ་འཆམ་ཟུང་སྦྲེལ་ (kājam sundrel) jointly agreeing, agreeing to do sth. together ། མི་ཚང་གཉིས་པོ་དེས་ཁ་འཆམ་ཟུང་སྦྲེལ་གྱི་ཐོག་ནས་ཟ་ཁང་དེ་གཉེར་བ་རེད་ The two families agreed to manage the restaurant together.

ཁ་འཆམ་ཡིད་མཐུན་ (kājam yiidün) agreeing in speech/ thought/ thinking; va.—བྱེད་ ། བཟོ་པ་ཚོར་ཁང་པ་གསར་པ་རྒྱག་རྒྱུའི་སྐོར་འགོ་ཁྲིད་རྣམས་ཁ་འཆམ་ཡིད་མཐུན་བྱུང་བ་རེད་ The leaders were in agreement regarding building new houses for the workers.

ཁ་འཆམས་ (kā cām) p. of ཁ་འཆམ་.

ཁ་འཆམས་ཕྲུགས་གཅིག (kājam trūgjig) agreeing unanimously ། འཐུས་མི་ཚོ་ཆིངས་ཡིག་འཛུགས་རྒྱུར་ཁ་འཆམས་ཕྲུགས་གཅིག་བྱུང་བ་རེད་ The delegates unanimously agreed to sign the treaty.

ཁ་འཆལ་ (kājɛɛ) babble, meaningless talk; va.—ཤོད་ to babble, to chatter ། རྒན་མོ་འདིས་རྟག་ཏུ་ཁ་འཆལ་ཤོད་ཀྱི་འདུག This old woman always chatters meaninglessly.

ཁ་འཆིང་ (kājiŋ) tying/ sealing sth.; va.—རྒྱག to tie/ seal up.

ཁ་འཆུ་ (kā cū) vi. to turn ། མོ་ཊ་འདི་གཡས་ལ་ཁ་གཙུས་ཀྱང་གཡོན་ལ་ཁ་འཆུ་གི་འདུག Even though (he) turned the car to the right, it is turning to the left.

ཁ་འཆུས་ (kā cüù) p. of ཁ་འཆུ་.

ཁ་འཆོལ་ (kā cöl) sm. ཁ་ཅལ་ཅལ་.

ཁ་འཇམ་ (kānjam) sm. ཁ་འཇམ་པོ་.

ཁ་འཇམ་ཁོག་རྩུབ་ (kānjam kɔ̄gdzub) sm. ཁ་འཇམ་གདིང་(ག)ནག.

ཁ་འཇམ་ཁོག་རྫུལ་ (kānjam kɔ̄gdzub) sm. ཁ་འཇམ་གདིང་(ག)ནག.

ཁ་འཇམ་ཁོང་རྩུབ་ (kānjam kɔ̄gdzub) sm. ཁ་འཇམ་གདིང་(ག)ནག.

ཁ་འཇམ་གདིང་(ག)ནག (kānjam dīŋnaà) saying nice things (speaking gently/ nicely) on the outside but being mean/ nasty/ cruel inside ། མི་འདིའི་གཤིས་ཀ་ཁ་འཇམ་གདིང་ནག་རེད་འདུག The character of this man is that he speaks nicely but is cruel inside.

ཁ་འཇམ་གདིང་རྩུབ་ (kānjam dīŋdzub) sm. ཁ་འཇམ་གདིང་(ག)ནག.

ཁ་འཇམ་པོ་ (kā jambo) gentle in speech, soft-spoken ། ཁ་འཇམ་པོ་བྱས་ནས་སྐད་ཆ་བཤད་པ་རེད་ He spoke in a gentle manner.

ཁ་འཇམ་སྤྲེལ་ལད་ (kājam pēlɛɛ) sycophantic talk/ speech, flattery.

ཁ་འཇམ་ཚིག་སྙན་ (kājam tsīgñɛn) 1. speaking gently and using pleasing words; va.—ཤོད་. 2. sweet-talking.

ཁ་འཇམ་ཞེ་གནག (kājam shenag) sm. ཁ་འཇམ་གདིང་གནག.

ཁ་འཇམ་ཞེ་རྩུབ་ (kājam shedzub) sm. ཁ་འཇམ་གདིང་གནག.

ཁ་འཇལ་ (kā jɛɛ) va. to measure ། རས་དེ་ཚོ་ཁ་འཇལ་རྒྱུ་ཡིན་ (I) still have to measure that cloth.

ཁ་འཛུག (kā juù) va. to interfere/ interrupt/ intervene verbally ། གཞན་གྱིས་སྐད་ཆ་ཤོད་དུས་ཁ་འཛུག་བྱེད་མི་ཉན་ When sb. is speaking you should not interrupt.

ཁ་རྗེ་ (kāje) merit in the religious sense.

ཁ་རྗེ་དབང་ཐང་ (kāje wāŋtaŋ) everything one owns, all one's possessions/ property ། རྒྱ་གར་ལ་ཡོད་པའི་བོད་མི་ཁ་ཤས་ཁ་རྗེ་དབང་ཐང་ཚང་མ་ཤོར་ནས་བོད་ནས་བྲོས་ཡོང་པ་རེད་ Some of the Tibetans in India fled from Tibet after losing everything they owned.

ཁ་རྗེའི་ཁྱུ་མཆོག (kājee kyūjoò) a person who has accumulated a lot of religious merit.

ཁ་རྗེས་སུ་འབྲང་ (kā jeèsu draŋ) va. to follow what sb. says ། མི་དེས་རང་གིས་བསམ་བློ་མ་བཏང་བར་གཞན་གྱི་ཁ་རྗེས་སུ་འབྲང་གི་ཡོད་པ་རེད་ That person doesn't think for himself (but rather) follows what others says.

ཁ་ལྦིད་པོ་ (kā jiibu) not talkative, taciturn ། ཨ་རི་ར་སླེབས་རྗེས་ཁ་ལྦིད་པོ་བྱས་ན་དབྱིན་སྐད་ཤེས་ཀྱི་མ་རེད་ If you come to America and aren't talkative, you won't learn to speak English.

ཁ་ལྗོངས་ (kājoŋ) Tibet.

ཁ་ཉན་ (kāñɛn) sm. ཁ་ཉན་པོ་.

ཁ་ཉན་པོ་ (kā ñɛmbo) obedient, sb. who listens to others ། ཕྲུ་གུ་ཁ་ཉན་པོ་འདི་ལ་དགེ་རྒན་ཚང་མས་དགའ་པོ་བྱེད་ཀྱི་ཡོད་པ་རེད་ The obedient (boy) is liked by all the teachers.

ཁ་ཉན་ཚིག་བཙེ་ (kā ñɛmbo) sm. ཁ་ཉན་པོ་.

ཁ་ཉམས་ཞིབ་དཔྱད་ (kā ñɛmbo) 1. thorough internal investigation ། ཐག་གཅོད་མ་བྱས་གོང་ཁ་ཉམས་ཞིབ་དཔྱད་བྱེད་དགོས་ Before deciding, you have to do a thorough internal investigation. 2. sm. ཁ་ནང་ཞིབ་རྒྱུས་.

ཁ་ཉི་མས་དྲོས་པའི་སྐད་ཆ་ (kā ñimɛ trööbɛ gɛ̃ɛja) useless/ meaningless/ idle talk [Lit. talk when people get their mouth warm in the sunshine].

ཁ་ཉིན་ (kənīn) sm. ཁ་ཉིན་ཀ་.

ཁ་ཉིན་ཀ་ (kɛ̄ ñiŋgə) the day before yesterday.

ཁ་ཉིན་མོ་ (kɛ̄ ñinmo) sm. ཁ་ཉིན་ཀ་.

ཁ་ཉུང་ (kāñuŋ) sm. ཁ་ཉུང་ཉུང་.

ཁ་ཉུང་ཉུང་ (kā ñuñun) 1. a person who does not say much, laconic, quiet [this is considered a good trait] ། ཁོ་ཁ་ཉུང་ཉུང་ཡིན་ཙང་ཚང་མས་དགའ་པོ་བྱེད་ཀྱི་ཡོད་པ་རེད་ Everyone likes him because he does not talk much. 2. a person who does not talk behind other's backs ། ལས་ཁུངས་ནང་ཁ་ཉུང་ཉུང་བྱས་ཙང་ཚང་མ་མ་མཐུན་སྒྲིལ་ཡག་པོ་ཡོད་པ་རེད་ Since (they) do not talk behind each other's back in the office, everyone gets along well.

ཁ་ཉུང་ལག་གཙང་ (kāñuŋ lagdzaŋ) a person who does not say much and is honest (doesn't steal) ༑ མི་འདི་ཁ་ཉུང་ལག་གཙང་ཡིན་ཙང་ལས་ཀ་རག་པ་རེད་ This man got the job because he is quiet and doesn't steal [Lit. taciturn, clean hands].

ཁ་ཉུལ་ (kāñul) collecting/ extracting information by asking questions, collecting intelligence; va.—བྱེད་ ༑ དགྲ་བོས་དམག་ས་འི་གནས་ཚུལ་ཁ་ཉུལ་བྱས་པ་རེད་ The enemy collected information about the situation at the battlefield.

ཁ་ཉེན་ (kāñen) verbal mistake.

ཁ་ཉེར་ (kāñer) making a facial expression showing disapproval; va. ཁ་ཉེར་; —བྱེད་ ༑ ངས་ཁོ་ལ་རེ་བ་བཏོན་པར་ཁོ་པས་ཁ་ཉེར་བྱས་ནས་ཁས་ལེན་བྱེད་ཀྱི་མི་འདུག I made a request (to him) and he made a facial expression of disapproval and isn't approving it.

ཁ་ཉེར་ཉེར་ (kāñerñer) sm. ཁ་ཉེར་.

ཁ་ཉེར་སྣ་ཉེར་བྱེད་ (kāñer nāñer) sm. ཁ་ཉེར་.

ཁ་ཉོག (kāñog) sm. ཁ་ནོག.

ཁ་གཉིས་ (kāñii) two-faced, double-dealing ༑ མི་ཁ་གཉིས་ཅན་གྱི་ཚིག་ལ་ཡིད་ཆེས་དཀའ་པོ་འདུག It is hard to believe the words of a two-faced person.

ཁ་གཉེར་སྣ་གཉེར་ (kāñer nañer) sm. ཁ་ཉེར་.

ཁ་མཉན་ (kāñɛn) sm. ཁ་ཉན་.

ཁ་མཉམ་(པ་) (kā ñām) 1. equal, even. 2. reaching to the brim ༑ ཇ་དཀར་ཡོལ་གྱི་ཁ་མཉམ་པ་ཞིག་བླུགས་པ་རེད་ (He) poured tea up to the brim of the cup.

ཁ་མཉམ་གྲགས་ (kā ñāmdraà) with one voice/ opinion, being of the same viewpoint ༑ གནད་དོན་དེའི་ཐོག་ཁོ་ཚོ་ཁ་མཉམ་གྲགས་རེད་བཞག They have the same viewpoint on that issue.

ཁ་རྙིང་ (kāñiŋ) old, used, worn out (pertaining to things) ༑ གྲུམ་ཁ་རྙིང་ཞིག་ཉོས་པ་ཡིན་ I bought an old rug.

ཁ་རྙིང་པ་ (kā ñiŋbə) sm. ཁ་རྙིང་.

ཁ་རྙོག (kāñog) va. to get into a habit, to get hooked on sth. ༑ ཟ་ཁང་དེའི་ཁ་ལག་ཞིམ་པོ་བྱུང་ཙང་ང་རང་ཁ་རྙོག་ནས་ཟ་ཁང་དེར་ཡང་སེ་འགྲོ་དགོས་བྱུང་ Because I ate at that restaurant and found the food delicious, I got hooked on it and had to go there often. ༑ ཕྲུ་གུར་ལས་ཀ་མེད་པར་དངུལ་བྱུང་ན་ཁ་རྙོག་གི་རེད་ If children are given money without working, they will get into the habit (of expecting this).

ཁ་སྙན་ཁོང་རྫུབ་ (kānɛn kōŋdzub) sm. ཁ་འཇམ་གདིང་གནག.

ཁ་སྙན་པོ་ (kā ñɛ̃mbo) sm. ཁ་མཁས་འདུ་ཆགས་.

ཁ་སྙན་ཚིག་སྙན་ (kāñɛn tsīgñɛn) sm. ཁ་མཁས་འདུ་ཆགས་.

ཁ་སྙིགས་ (kāñig) leftovers (food/ hay) that is fed to animals.

ཁ་སྙོམས་ (kā ñōm) making two or more things the same amount or size, equalizing; va. ཁ་སྙོམས་; —བྱེད་; va.—བཟོ་ ༑ དཀར་ཡོལ་གསུམ་གྱི་ནང་ཇ་ཁ་སྙོམས་བླུགས་པ་རེད་ (They) poured tea into three cups up to the same level.

ཁ་བནུས་བགོ་ (kāñog) sm. བནུས་བགོ་.

ཁ་བནོགས་ (kāñog) sm. ཁ་ནོག.

ཁ་བསྙད་ (kāñɛ̃ɛ̀) blaming/ accusing; va.—འཛུགས་ to blame/ accuse.

ཁ་ད་ (kāda) 1. advice, counsel; va.—བྱེད་ ༑ མོ་ལ་ཁ་ད་ག་ཚོད་བྱས་ནས་ཡང་མ་ཉན་ཉན་ However much advice (he) gave, she didn't listen (to it). 2. arc. va. to hold/ consider precious.

ཁ་ད་བསྐུལ་ལྕག (kāda gũũjaà) advising in a way that encourages/ motivates; va.—བྱེད་ ༑ སློབ་གྲྭ་ཆེན་མོར་འགྲོ་རྒྱུའི་རེ་བ་ཡོད་སྐོར་དགེ་རྒན་གྱི་སློབ་ཕྲུག་ཚོར་ཁ་ད་བསྐུལ་ལྕག་བྱས་པ་རེད་ The teacher advised the students in an encouraging way, telling them that he hopes they will (be able) to go to college.

ཁ་ད་སློབ་སྟོན་ (kāda lōbdön) advising.

ཁ་ད་བསླབ་བྱ་ (kāda lāpja) sm. ཁ་ད་.

ཁ་དས་བློ་ཁུག (kādɛɛ̀ lūguù) persuading through advice; va.—བྱེད་ ༑ ངའི་བུ་འཁྱམས་པོ་དེ་ཁ་དས་བློ་ཁུག་བྱས་ནས་ནང་ལ་ལོག་བྱུང་ Through advice (I) persuaded my wandering son to return home.

ཁ་དིག (kādii) bitter taste; vi.—ཁ་; —རྒྱག to taste bitter ༑ སྨན་འདི་ཁ་དིག་ཞེ་དྲག་ཁ་གི་འདུག This medicine tastes very bitter.

ཁ་དོག (kādɔɔ̀) snack (usu. pastries, cookies, delicacies) ༑ ཨ་མས་ཕྲུ་གུར་ཁ་དོག་ཉོ་ཡས་གི་དངུལ་སྤྲེར་བ་རེད་ The mother gave the children money to buy snacks.

ཁ་དོག་མཉེན་སོབ་ (kādɔɔ̀ ñɛ̃nsob) a type of cookie that is soft/ spongy.

ཁ་དོག་ཙག་ཙིག (kādɔɔ̀ dzɔ̄gdzig) sm. ཁ་ལྡིག.

ཁ་དོན་ (kādön) saying/ reciting/ intoning prayers; va.—བྱེད་ ༑ ཁོང་གིས་མཚན་མོ་ཁ་དོན་བྱེད་ཀྱི་ཡོད་པ་རེད་ He says his prayers at night.

ཁ་གདད་ (kāpdɛɛ̀) 1. rival, opponent, adversary ༑ ང་གཉིས་ཁ་གདད་རེད་ We are opponents. 2. vi.—བྱེད་; —དུ་ལངས་ to become a rival/ opponent/ adversary, to rise up in opposition, to act as a rival/ opponent ༑ མི་དམངས་ཀྱིས་སྲིད་གཞུང་གི་ཁ་གདད་དུ་ལངས་པ་རེད་ The people rose in opposition against the government. 3. va.—གཙོག; —བྱེད་; —འཛིང་ to challenge, to compete against, to oppose ༑ ཁོར་ཁ་གདད་གཙོག་མཁན་མི་འདུག There is no one to challenge him. ༑ དཔུང་དམག་བཙན་འཛུལ་བྱུང་ན་ཁ་གདད་གཙོག་གི་ཡིན་ If troops invade, (we) will oppose them. 4. va. ཁ་གདད་ to face towards, to side with, to be on the side of ༑ ཚོང་ཁང་འདི་ཤར་ལ་ཁ་གདད་འདུག The shop is facing east. ༑ མདུན་ལམ་དུ་ཁ་གདད་ Facing the future. ༑ ཁོས་སོ་སོའི་རྒྱལ་ཁབ་ལ་ཁ་གདད་ནས་ལོག་ཡོང་བ་རེད་ He sided with his country and returned. 5. vi. to be at the start/ beginning of an age or period ༑ ཁོ་ལོ་བཅུ་ལ་ཁ་གདད་པ་རེད་ He is going to be ten years old soon (He reached the point where he will be ten years old).

ཁ་གདད་གྱོང་མཉམ་ (kāpdɛɛ̀ gyoṉñam) two sides refusing to budge on an issue or refusing to yield/ give up a view or position ༑ སྦྲི་ག་འགྲན་མཁན་དེ་གཉིས་ཁ་གདད་གྱོང་མཉམ་ཡིན་ཙང་ཐོབ་ཕམ་བྱུང་མ་སོང་ The two wrestling opponents are equally tough so neither one won.

ཁ་གདད་གྲོང་ཁྱེར་ (kāpdɛɛ̀ troṉgyer) an inland Chinese city attached to a Tibetan city/ county in a relationship in which it helps the Tibetan area alleviate poverty.

ཁ་གདད་རྒྱབ་སྡོད་ (kāpdɛɛ̀ gyəbdröö) rival enemies; va.—བྱེད་ ༑ གྲོགས་པོ་བློ་མཐུན་དེ་གཉིས་གྲོགས་མོ་སྲིག་སྐབས་ཀྱི་ཐོག་ནས་ཁ་གདད་རྒྱབ་སྡོད་ཆགས་འདུག The two good friends both were (romantically) pursuing a girl and became rivals.

ཁ་གདད་ཚོག (kāpdɛɛ̀ cɔ̄ɔ̀) vi. to be able to challenge/ compete/ handle ༑ རྒྱལ་ཁབ་འདི་མི་འབོར་ཉུང་ཉུང་ཡིན་ཙང་མི་འབོར་མང་བའི་རྒྱལ་ཁབ་ཀྱི་ཁ་གདད་ཚོག་གི་མ་རེད་ Because this country has a small population, it can't compete with a country with a large population.

ཁ་གདད་འཇལ་ཐབས་ (kāpdɛɛ̀ je̱etəb) responding to a challenge/ competition, taking counter measures/ counter moves.

ཁ་གདད་དུ་ལངས་ (kāpdɛɛ̀tu lāŋ) see ཁ་གདད་.

ཁ་གདད་དོ་ཟླ་ (kāpdɛɛ̀ do̱nda) sm. ཁ་གདད་.

ཁ་གདད་དོ་ཟླར་ལངས་ (kāpdɛɛ̀ do̱ndar la̱ŋ) sm. ཁ་གདད་དུ་ལངས་.

ཁ་གདད་ཕྱོགས་ (kā dɛ̄cɔɔ̀) 1. the direction sth. or sb. faces (can connote both physical and ideological direction/ orientation); va.—བྱེད་ ༑ ཁང་པ་འདི་ཁ་གདད་ཕྱོགས་ནོར་ཙང་ཉི་མ་དྲོ་པོ་མི་འདུག Because the house faces in the wrong direction, it doesn't get the warm sun. ༑ མི་སོ་སོའི་ཁ་གདད་ཕྱོགས་མ་ནོར་བ་བྱ་རྒྱུ་དེ་གལ་ཆེན་པོ་ཡིན་ It is very important for each person to have the correct ideological orientation. 2. one party/ side ༑ གནད་དོན་དེའི་སྐོར་ཁ་གདད་ཕྱོགས་ནས་ཁས་ལེན་བྱེད་ཀྱི་མི་འདུག Regarding this matter, one of the parties will not agree.

ཁ་གདད་ཞིང་ཆེན་ (kāpdɛɛ̀ shiṉjen) an inland Chinese province attached to a Tibetan prefecture in a relationship in which it helps the Tibetan area alleviate poverty.

ཁ་གདན་ཚིག་གནས་ (kādɛn tsīgnɛɛ̀) sm.* ཁ་དན་ཚིག་གནས་.

ཁ་གདམ་ (kādam) 1. talk, lecture; va.—གཏོང་; —ཤོད་ to give a talk, lecture ¶ཁོས་ཁ་གདམ་སྣན་པོ་ཞིག་བཤད་པ་རེད་ He gave an interesting talk. 2. a customary saying.

ཁ་གདིང་ (kādiŋ) 1. top and bottom; va.—སློག to turn upside down; vi.—ལོག to get turned upside down. 2. what is said and what is felt/ thought ¶ཁ་གདིང་མེད་པར་དྲང་པོ་བཤད་པ་རེད་ (He) told the truth frankly (without differentiating what he felt and what he said).

ཁ་གདིང་གཉིས་མེད་ (kādiŋ ñiimeè) sm. ཁ་ཞེ་གཉིས་མེད་.

ཁ་གདིང་གཉིས་ཡོད་ (kādiŋ ñiiyöö) sm. ཁ་གདིང་མ་མཚུངས་པ་.

ཁ་གདིང་མ་མཚུངས་པ་ (kādiŋ mətsūŋbə) saying one thing while thinking/ feeling another ¶ཁ་གདིང་མ་མཚུངས་པའི་སྐད་ཆ་བཤད་ན་མིས་ཆ་འཇོག་གི་མ་རེད་ If one says one thing while thinking another, people will not trust you. [Lit. mouth and thought not the same].

ཁ་གདིང་མི་མཐུན་པ་ (kādiŋ midünba) sm. ཁ་གདིང་མ་མཚུངས་པ་.

ཁ་གདིང་མེད་པ་ (kādiŋ meèba) sm. ཁ་གདིང་མཚུངས་པ་.

ཁ་གདིང་མཚུངས་པ་ (kādiŋ tsūŋwə) thinking/ feeling the same as what one says, being frank/ candid/ straightforward.

ཁ་གདིང་ལོག (kādiŋ lɔ̀ɔ̀) 1. vi. to be/ get turned upside down by accident ¶ཁོའི་དཀར་ཡོལ་ཁ་གདིང་ལོག་པ་རེད་ His cup got turned upside down. 2. sm. ཁ་གདིང་མ་མཚུངས་པ་.

ཁ་གདིང་སློག (kādiŋ lɔ̄ɔ̄) va. to turn upside down ¶ཁོས་དཀར་ཡོལ་ཁ་གདིང་བསློགས་པ་རེད་ (He) turned the cup upside down.

ཁ་གདུགས་ (kā dūù) 1. va. to put one's mouth on another's mouth ¶ནད་པར་ཁ་གདུགས་ནས་དབུགས་འཐེན་པ་རེད་ The patient was given mouth to mouth resuscitation. 2. va. to bring together (usu. regarding marriage) ¶ཁོ་གཉིས་ཕ་མས་ཁ་གདུགས་པའི་རྗེས་སུ་ཆང་ས་རྒྱབ་པ་རེད་ After the parents brought them together (they) were married. 3. va. to kiss. 4. va. to meet together ¶ཕྱོགས་གཉིས་ཀྱི་དམག་དཔུང་ཁ་གདུགས་འཕྲལ་ཤི་རྨས་མང་པོ་བཟོས་པ་རེད་ As soon as the troops from the two sides met, there were many casualties.

ཁ་གདོགས་ (kā dōg) va. to intervene/ interfere/ meddle.

ཁ་གདོང་ (kā dōŋ) va. to complain, to speak out, to grumble about ¶དེང་སྐབས་རྒྱ་ནག་ལ་མའོ་ལ་ཁ་གདོང་མཁན་མི་མང་པོ་འདུག These days there are many people in China who complain about Mao. 2. va. to talk/ gossip about sb. behind their back.

ཁ་གཏོར་ (kā dɔ̄r) va. to scatter, to disperse ¶བོམ་གཡུགས་ནས་དམག་མི་ཁ་གཏོར་བ་རེད་ They scattered the soldiers by bombing them.

ཁ་གཏོར་དགུ་གཏོར་ (kādɔr gudɔr) scattering completely; va.—གཏོང་ ¶བོམ་གཡུགས་ནས་དམག་མི་ཁ་གཏོར་དགུ་གཏོར་བཏང་བ་རེད་ They scattered the soldiers completely by bombing them.

ཁ་བཏགས་ (kādaà) 1. Tibetan ceremonial scarf; va.—གཏོང་ to give sb. a ceremonial scarf (usu. when asking for a favor) ¶ངས་ཁོང་ལ་ཁ་བཏགས་གཅིག་བཏང་ནས་བུ་ལོན་གཡར་རོགས་གནང་ཞུས་པ་ཡིན་ I gave him a ceremonial scarf and asked for a loan.; va.—གཡོགས་ to put a ceremonial scarf on sb.'s neck, usu. at an occasion such as a wedding or departure. 2. scarf.

ཁ་བཏགས་ (kā dāà) 1. va. to weaken, to impair. 2. va. to kill (in large numbers) ¶ཁྱི་ར་བས་རི་དྭགས་ཁ་བཏགས་པ་རེད་ The hunter killed animals en mass.

ཁ་བཏགས་ཐང་ལེན་ (kādaà tāŋlen) picking up a scarf from the ground while galloping full speed.

ཁ་བཏགས་ནང་མཛོད་ (kādaà naŋdzö) the best quality ཁ་བཏགས་.

ཁ་བཏགས་སྣ་དུག (kādaà nāduù) a derogatory term used for the worst type of ཁ་བཏགས་.

ཁ་བཏགས་ཕྱི་མཛོད་ (kādaà cīndzöö) a kind of Tibetan ཁ་བཏགས་.

ཁ་བཏགས་བར་མཛོད་ (kādaà pandzöö) a middle quality ཁ་བཏགས་.

ཁ་བཏགས་རྣམ་དབང་མ་ (kādaà namwaŋma) a high quality Tibetan ཁ་བཏགས་.

ཁ་བཏགས་ཨ་ཤེ་ (kādaà āshe) a second quality Tibetan ཁ་བཏགས་

ཁ་བཏང་ (kā dāŋ) p. of ཁ་གཏོང་.

ཁ་བཏུམ་ (kā dūm) wrapping, sealing; va. ཁ་བཏུམ; —བྱེད་.

ཁ་བཏུལ་ (kā dūl) breaking in/ taming a horse; va. ཁ་བཏུལ་; —བྱེད་.

ཁ་རྟེན་ (kāden) sm. ཁ་དན་.

ཁ་ལྟ་ (kā dā) 1. va. to follow/ adhere to (a policy, ideology, position, etc.) ¶མི་མང་པོ་ང་ཚོའི་ཕྱོགས་སུ་ཁ་བལྟས་ཏེ་རྒྱ་གར་དུ་ཡོང་འདོད་ཡོད་པ་རེད་ Many people adhere to our position and want to come to India. 2. va. to face a direction, to look towards a direction (can be a real direction or a position or point of view) ¶ངས་ཤར་ཕྱོགས་སུ་ཁ་བལྟས་པ་ཡིན་ I looked to the east.

ཁ་ལྟ་འགྲོགས་བཟང་ (kāda drogsaŋ) a close friend.

ཁ་ལྟ་པོ་ (kā dābo) a good year for breeding animals (i.e., they have increased/ multiplied) ¶ལོ་འདི་ར་ལུག་ཁ་ལྟ་པོ་བྱུང་སོང་ This year was a good year for sheep and goats (i.e., they have multiplied).

ཁ་ལྟ་མིག་ལྟ་ (kāda mida) looking after, caring for; va.—བྱེད་ ¶ངའི་ཕྲུ་གུ་འདི་ལ་ཁྱེད་རང་གིས་ཁ་ལྟ་མིག་ལྟ་ཡག་པོ་གནང་རོགས་གནང་ Would you please look after my child well (implies the child is living with the other person or has moved into his area, e.g., to go to school). [Lit. look at the mouth, look at the eyes].

ཁ་ལྟབ་ (kā dəb) va. to fold sth. such as paper/ clothes ¶ཤོག་བུ་ཁ་ལྟབ་པ་ནི་ As for folding the paper.

ཁ་ལྟས་ (kā dɛɛ̀) foretelling, forecasting; va.—ཤོད་ to foretell, to forecast ¶ཕྱི་ལོ་མུ་གེ་ཆེན་པོ་ཞིག་ཡོང་གི་ཡོད་པའི་སྐོར་ཁ་ལྟས་ངན་པོ་ཞིག་བྱུང་སོང་ There has been a bad forecast stating that next year will bring a big famine.

ཁ་ལྟས་ངན་པ་ (kādaà ŋɛmba) pessimist, pessimistic, fatalistic ¶མི་ཁ་ཤས་ཀྱིས་ག་དུས་ཡིན་ན་ཡང་ཁ་ལྟས་ངན་པ་ཤ་ཏག་ཤོད་ཀྱི་ཡོད་ Some people always speak pessimistically.

ཁ་ལྟིར་ (kādir) a pitcher of chang that costs a ཁ་གང་.

ཁ་སྟན་ (kādɛn) sm. ཁ་གདན་.

ཁ་སྟབས་ (kātəb) ability, capability ¶མི་འདི་ར་ཁ་སྟབས་མི་འདུག This man is not capable.

ཁ་སྟར་ཁ་འདྲ་པོ་ཚུམས་ (kā dārga drabo tsūm) shut up, shut your mouth (term used for scolding or when joking with someone) [Lit. shut your mouth like a walnut].

ཁ་སྟོང་ (kādoŋ) 1. mere words, empty talk (talk without action) ¶ཁ་སྟོང་བཤད་ནས་ཕན་ཐོགས་མེད་ Mere talk is not enough. 2. a lot of talk ¶བཟོ་གྲྭ་འདིའི་ནང་མི་སྟོང་ཁ་སྟོང་ཡོད་པས་འགོ་ཁྲིད་ཀྱིས་གཟབ་གཟབ་བྱེད་དགོས་རེད་ Because there are many workers and much talking in this factory, the leaders have to be careful.

ཁ་སྟོང་ནང་གི་ཚིག་སྟོང་ (kādoŋ naŋgi tsīgdoŋ) 1. talk that is completely meaningless or pointless ¶མི་འདི་ཁ་སྟོང་ནང་གི་ཚིག་སྟོང་རྐང་རྐང་ཤོད་མཁན་ཞིག་ཡིན་ཙང་ཁོ་ལ་འདེམས་ཤོག་ཐོབ་ཀྱི་མ་རེད་ Because this man is sb. whose speech is meaningless, he will not win the election. 2. gossip.

ཁ་སྟོང་པའི་ལྟོ་གཡུག་གཡུག (kādoŋ) sm. ཁ་སྟོང་ནང་གི་ཚིག་སྟོང་.

ཁ་སྟོང་ཚིག་སྟོང་ (kādoŋ) sm. ཁ་སྟོང་ནང་གི་ཚིག་སྟོང་.

ཁ་སྟོང་ལག་སྟོང་ (kādoŋ lagdoŋ) poor, destitute ¶ཁ་

སྐྱོང་ལག་སྟོང་གིས་བཟོ་གྲྭ་འཛུགས་རྒྱུ་ཟེར་བའི་གཏམ་འདི་གོད་བྲོ་བ་ཞིག་རེད། The talk that a destitute (person) wants to set up a factory is laughable. [Lit. empty mouth, empty hand].

ཁ་སྟོན་ (kā dõn) 1. va. to show (one's) face ¶ ཕྲུ་གུ་དེས་ངོ་ཚ་ནས་ཁ་སྟོན་ནུས་ཀྱི་མི་འདུག The child is embarrassed and doesn't dare show (his) face. 2. va. to exhibit/ make a facial expression ¶ ཁོ་ཁོང་ཁྲོ་ཟ་དུས་ཁ་ག་འདྲ་ཞིག་སྟོན་གྱི་འདུག་གམ། When he is angry, what kind of a facial expression does he exhibit.

ཁ་སྟོབས་ (kādob) sm. ཁ་ཤུགས་ཆེན་པོ་.

ཁ་སྟོབས་ ཆེན་པོ་ (kādob cēmbo) sm. ཁ་ཤུགས་ཆེན་པོ་.

ཁ་སྟོར་ (kā dɔ̄r) 1. va. to disperse/ scatter ¶ སློབ་གྲྭ་ཐོན་པའི་གཞོན་ནུ་རྣམས་ཁ་བསྟོར་ནས་ལས་ཁུངས་ཁག་ལ་ལས་བགོས་བརྒྱབ་པ་རེད། Those students that graduated were dispersed and given work in different offices. 2. va. ཁ་སྟོར་; —བཟོ་ to cause to separate/ split up/ disperse ¶ མི་ངན་འདིས་ཟ་ཚང་ཁ་སྟོར་སོང་ The evil person caused the husband and wife to split up.

ཁ་བརྟན་པོ་ (kā dēmbo) sm.* ཁ་བརྟན་ཚིག་བརྟན་.

ཁ་བརྟན་ཚིག་བརྟན་ (kādɛn tsīgdɛn) 1. dependable, reliable ¶ མི་འདིས་སྐད་ཆ་བཤད་པ་རྣམས་ཁ་བརྟན་ཚིག་བརྟན་རེད་འདུག Everything this man said is reliable. 2. tight-lipped, able to keep secrets ¶ གནད་དོན་དེའི་སྐོར་གསང་བ་ཤོར་རྒྱུའི་ཉེན་ཁ་ཡོད་ཙང་མི་ཁ་བརྟན་ཚིག་བརྟན་ཞིག་དགོས་ཀྱི་འདུག Because there is a danger of losing secrecy regarding that important issue, we need a person who is tight-lipped.

ཁ་བལྟ་ (kā dā) sm. ཁ་ལྟ་.

ཁ་བལྟ་མིག་བལྟ་ (kāda mi̱gda) sm. ཁ་ལྟ་མིག་ལྟ་.

ཁ་བལྟས་ (kā dɛ̄ɛ̀) p. of ཁ་ལྟ་.

ཁ་བསྟན་ (kā dɛ̄n) p. of སྟོན་.

ཁ་ཐག་ཤང་པོ་ (kātaà shāŋbo) sm. ཁ་གསངས་པོ་.

ཁ་ཐག་གསང་པོ་ (kātaà sāŋbo) sm. sm. ཁ་གསངས་པོ་.

ཁ་ཐད་ (kādɛɛ̀) sm.* ཁ་གཏད་.

ཁ་ཐབས་ (kādab) sm. ཁ་སྟབས་.

ཁ་ཐམ་ (kə tām) sm. ཁ་འཐམ་.

ཁ་ཐལ་ (kā tɛ̄ɛ) vi. 1. to make a slip of the tongue ¶ ཁོས་ཁ་ཐལ་ནས་བཤད་པ་རེད། He had a slip of the tongue and said it. 2. vi. to run out of control (for horses, mules, etc.) ¶ རྟ་ཁ་ཐལ་ནས་ལམ་ཁར་ཕྲུ་གུ་ཞིག་བརྫིས་སོང་ The horse ran out of control and ran over a child on the road.

ཁ་ཐལ་ཤོར་ (kātɛ shɔ̄ɔ) sm. ཁ་ཐལ་.

ཁ་ཐི་ (kāti) a kind of satin/ brocade.

ཁ་ཐིའི་རིས་ཅན་ (kātii ri̱jɛn) a type of design on satin/ brocade.

ཁ་ཐིག (kātig) sm. ཁ་ལྕོག.

ཁ་ཐིག་ཚང་མིན་ (kādig tsāŋmin) shung. incomplete, sth. missing.

ཁ་ཐིགས་པོ་ (kā tīgbu) phrase conveying: "you said it;" "you can say that again," "what you said hits the spot."

ཁ་ཐུག (kāduù) 1. straight, direct ¶ ལམ་ཁ་འདི་ཁ་ཐུག་རེད། This road is straight. ¶ ཁོ་ནང་ལ་ཁ་ཐུག་ཕྱིན་པ་རེད། He went straight home. ¶ ཁོས་སྐད་ཆ་ཁ་ཐུག་བཤད་པ་རེད། He spoke directly. ¶ ཁོས་ཞྭ་མོ་ཁ་ཐུག་ལ་གྱོན་མ་སོང་ He didn't wear his hat straight. 2. vi. to get married informally, to live together as a couple (to set up household together) ¶ ཁོ་གཉིས་ཁ་ཐུག་ནས་ཕྲུ་གུ་གཉིས་བྱུང་བ་རེད། The two of them began to live together as a couple and had two children. 3. vi. to coincide/ match/ concur, to correspond with ¶ ཁོས་བཤད་པ་དང་ངས་མཐོང་བ་གཉིས་ཁ་ཐུག་གི་མི་འདུག What he says and what I saw don't coincide. 4.—འཁེལ་; —རྒྱག vi. to have sth. occur coincidentally or fortuitously with a primary activity ¶ ཁྲོམ་ལ་འགྲོ་སྐབས་བསོད་ནམས་དང་ཁ་ཐུག་འཁེལ་སོང་ When I was going to the market, I bumped into Sonam (coincidentally met Sonam). 5. directly opposite ¶ སྒོའི་ཁ་ཐུག་གི་ལྕོག་ཙེ་ The table that is opposite the door.

ཁ་ཐུག་ཁ་ཐུག (kəduù kətug) 1. directly, straight. 2. at once, without delays.

ཁ་ཐུག་གདོང་ཐུག (kəduù do̱ŋdug) 1. meeting face-to-face; va.—བྱེད་ ¶ གནད་དོན་འདི་ང་གཉིས་ཁ་ཐུག་གདོང་ཐུག་ཐོག་ནས་ཐག་གཅོད་བྱེད་ཀྱི་ཡིན་ We will settle this matter when we meet face-to-face. 2. meeting unexpectedly.

ཁ་ཐུམ་ (kōtur) gauze mouth mask.

ཁ་ཐུར་ (kədur) spoon.

ཁ་ཐེག (kādeg) sm. ཁག་ཐེག.

ཁ་ཐེག་པ་ (kādegbə) sm. ཁག་ཐེག་པ་.

ཁ་ཐེར་ (kāder) eng. cartel.

ཁ་ཐེར་ཐེར་ (kā tērder) a kind of flat face (with lips that are wide). 2. a type of bowl/ cup characterized by a wide opening.

ཁ་ཐོག (kātɔɔ̀) 1. verbally, orally ¶ ཁ་ཐོག་གི་ལན་ A verbal reply. 2. the upper level or story (of house) ¶ ཁང་པའི་ཁ་ཐོག The top story of a house.

ཁ་ཐོག་གིས་ (kātɔɔ̀gi) sm. ཁ་ཐོག་ནས་.

ཁ་ཐོག་ཏུ་ (kātɔ̄gdu) on top of, on ¶ ལྕོག་ཙེའི་ཁ་ཐོག་ཏུ་དེབ་མང་པོ་འདུག There are many books on (top of) the table.

ཁ་ཐོག་དོན་གནས་ (kātɔɔ̀ tõnnɛɛ̀) adhering to an oral agreement/ promise.

ཁ་ཐོག་ནས་ (kātɔɔ̀nɛ) 1. from on top of ¶ ལྕོག་ཙེའི་ཁ་ཐོག་ནས་དེབ་གཅིག་ཟག་པ་རེད། A book fell from (on top of) the table. 2. verbally, orally ¶ ཁ་ཐོག་ནས་ལན་འཇོར་བྱུང་ (I) received the reply verbally.

ཁ་ཐོག་ལག་བཞག (kātɔɔ̀ la̱gshaà) making good on one's word, doing what one says/ promises, acting in accordance with what one says; va.—བྱེད་ ¶ ཁ་ཐོག་ལག་བཞག་གི་རོགས་རམ་བྱས་པ་རེད། (They) helped (us) as they had promised. ¶ ཁ་ཐོག་ལག་བཞག་བྱས་ཙང་གྲུབ་འབྲས་ཡག་པོ་བྱུང་བ་རེད། Because (he) did what he said (he'd do), the results were good.

ཁ་ཐོག་ལག་བཤད་ (kātɔɔ̀ la̱gshaà) sm. ཁ་ཐོག་ལག་བཞག.

ཁ་ཐོན་ (kā tõn) vi. to mature, to grow up ¶ དེང་སང་ཕྲུ་གུ་རྣམས་ཁ་ཐོན་ཙང་ང་རང་ནུས་ཡོལ་བྱེད་ཆོག་པ་འདུག Because the children have grown up, I can retire.

ཁ་ཐོན་པོ་ (kā tõmbo) verbal, articulate.

ཁ་ཐོར་ (kātɔɔ) scattered, dispersed, separated, disunified, disintegrated; vi. ཁ་ཐོར་; —དུ་འགྱུར་ to become scattered, dispersed, separated, disunified, split up; va.—(དུ་) གཏོང་; —དུ་འཇུག to (cause to) scatter/ disperse/ fragment ¶ ཁ་ཐོར་བའི་དུས་སྐབས་ A time of disunity. ¶ དམག་མི་མང་པོ་ཁ་ཐོར་ཙང་དམག་ཤོར་སོང་ Because many soldiers got scattered, (they) lost the battle. ¶ ངོ་ལོག་པས་རྒྱལ་ཁབ་ཀྱི་སྲིད་དབང་ཁ་ཐོར་དུ་བཏང་བ་རེད། The rebels undermined the political authority of the government.

ཁ་ཐོར་དགུ་ཐོར་ (kātɔɔ gu̱tɔɔ) sm. ཁ་ཐོར་.

ཁ་ཐོར་ཡ་ཐོར་ (kātɔɔ ya̱dɔɔ) sm. ཁ་ཐོར་ཡ་བྲལ་.

ཁ་ཐོར་ཡ་བྲལ་ (kātɔɔ ya̱drɛɛ) scattered, broken-up, separated; vi.—ཆགས་ to become scattered, broken-up, separated; va.—(དུ་) གཏོང་ to scatter/ break up/ separate ¶ ནང་མི་ཚང་མ་ཁ་ཐོར་ཡ་བྲལ་ཆགས་སོང་ All the family members got scattered. ¶ གཞུང་གིས་གུང་ཁྲན་ཚོགས་པ་ཁ་ཐོར་ཡ་བྲལ་བཏང་བ་རེད། The government broke up the communist party.

ཁ་ཐོར་རིང་ལུགས་ (kātɔɔ ri̱ŋluù) the system of extreme decentralization.

ཁ་མཐའ་ (kāta) a stitch on the edge of a Tibetan woolen boot.

ཁ་མཐུན་ (kā tũn) vi. to come to an agreement on sth. ¶ ཁོ་ཚོ་ཁ་མཐུན་ནས་དངུལ་ཁང་འདིར་ཀུན་མ་བརྐུས་པ་རེད། They agreed to rob the bank.

ཁ་མཐུན་ཁོག་འགལ་ (kādũn kɔ̄ŋgɛɛ) overtly agreeing but internally differing/ disagreeing; va.—བྱེད་.

ཁ་མཐུན་གྲོས་བསྡུར་ (kādũn tro̱dur) reaching agreement through consultation/ discussion.

ཁ་མཐུན་ངོས་ལེན་ (kādũn ŋo̱len) acting in collusion to make confessions or statements tally; va.—

བྱེད་.

ཁ་མཐུན་པོ་ (kā tũmbu) friendly, amicable ། སྲིད་ཀྱི་ཐོག་ལ་རྒྱ་ནག་དང་རྒྱ་གར་གཉིས་ཁ་མཐུན་པོ་མི་འདུག Politically, China and India are not friendly. 2. getting along well with, compatible with, of the same view, in agreement; va.—བྱེད་ ། ཁོ་གཉིས་ཁ་མཐུན་པོ་འདུག The two of them get along well. ། མི་ཚང་གི་ནང་མི་ཁ་མཐུན་པོ་བྱེད་དགོས་ Family members should get along well.

ཁ་མཐུན་ཞི་མཐུན་ (kādũn shedün) sm. ཁ་ཞི་གཉིས་མེད་.

ཁ་མཐུན་ལག་སྒྲིལ་ (kādün landree) sm. ངན་པ་ལག་སྒྲིལ་.

ཁ་འཐབ་ (kādəb) 1. income equal to expenses (e.g., in a business); va.—གཏོང་ to do an accounting of income vis-à-vis initial investment; vi.—ཐེབས་ to have an original expenditure being matched by income ། བྱུང་སོང་ཁ་འཐབ་བཏང་ནས་འབྲུ་རིགས་ཁལ་ ༡༠༠ ལྷག་བཞག After doing an accounting (of initial investment and income), we had 100 khal of grain left over. ། བྱུང་སོང་ཁ་འཐབ་ཐེབས་བཞག Our initial output (expenditures) was matched (by the income we received). 2. sm. ཁ་ཚོད་.

ཁ་འཐབ་གཙང་སེལ་ (kātəp dzãŋsel) balancing an account by making up a shortfall/ discrepancy; va.—བྱེད་.

ཁ་འཐབ་རང་དག (kādab raŋdag) sm. ཁ་འཐབ་གཙང་སེལ་.

ཁ་འཐམ་ (kā tãm) 1. vi. to have an illness (like lockjaw) where one's jaw is clenched shut ། ནད་གཞི་དྲག་པ་ཡོང་ཙང་ནད་པོ་དེ་ཁ་འཐམ་པ་རེད་ Due to severe illness, the patient's jaw was closed shut. 2. vi. to be dumb, to be unable to speak.

ཁ་འཐེན་ (kā tēn) va. to pull on a horse's mouth (the reins) to bring it to a stop.

ཁ་འཐོན་པོ་ (kā tõmbo) sm. ཁ་མཐོན་པོ་.

ཁ་འཐོར་ (kā tɔ̃ɔ) sm. ཁ་ཐོར་.

ཁ་འཐོར་དགུ་ཐོར་ (kādɔr gudɔr) sm. ཁ་ཐོར་.

ཁ་འཐོར་ཡ་བྲལ་ (kātɔɔ yatrɛɛ) sm. ཁ་ཐོར་.

ཁ་དག (kā tag) 1. sm. ཁ་འཐབ་. 2. assets balanced by liabilities ། མི་ཚང་དེའི་རྒྱུ་ཅ་ལག་དང་བུ་ལོན་ཁ་དག་ཏུ་སོང་བ་རེད་ That family's possessions have become equal to their debts. 3. arc. vi. to die ། ཡུལ་མི་ཚང་མ་ཁ་དག་ཏུ་གྱུར་པ The whole population in that area died. 4. poverty, poor.

ཁ་དག་ཞབས་རྫོགས་ (kādag shəbdzɔ̃ɔ) annihilating, obliterating; va.—གཏོང་.

ཁ་དང་ (དམག་སྒར་) (kādaŋ (māgar)) the ཁ་དང་ or "Trabchi" Regiment (in tt. army).

ཁ་དང་ཁ་སྤུ་དབྱེ་བ་འབྱེད་དགོས་ (kādaŋ kābu yēwa cegöö) one should differentiate/ sort/ classify clearly ། གཞུང་གི་མ་དངུལ་དང་སྒེར་གྱི་མ་དངུལ་རྣམས་ཁ་དང་ཁ་སྤུ་དབྱེ་བ་འབྱེད་དགོས་ One should differentiate clearly between government and private funds. [Lit. one should differentiate between the mouth and moustache].

ཁ་དང་མེ་ལྕགས་གཙང་ན་བདེ་ (kādaŋ mejaà dzābnə de) practice makes perfect [Lit. the more one uses the flint stone and the mouth, the better].

ཁ་དང་ཞལ་ཐུག (kādaŋ sheeduù) futility with regard to saying sth. [Lit. an ordinary mouth meeting an honorific mouth].

ཁ་དང་ལག་པ་མཉམ་འགྲོགས་ (kādaŋ lagba ñamgyɔɔ) beating and scolding at the same time.

ཁ་དང་ལག་པ་ཐག་ཉེ་ (kādaŋ lagba tāàñeè) one shouldn't take things that do belong to others ། གཞན་གྱིས་བཅོལ་བའི་ཤ་མར་ཁ་དང་ལག་པ་ཐག་ཉེ་བྱེད་རྒྱུ་ཡོད་པ་མ་རེད་ You shouldn't use the meat and butter left by others in your care. [Lit. hand and mouth are close].

ཁ་དན་ (kādɛn) a verbal promise/ oath/ agreement, one's word; va.—བྱེད་; —འཛུགས;—བཟོ་ to make a promise/ oath; va.—གནས་ to keep a promise/ oath ། ཁ་དན་ལ་གནས་དགོས་རེད་ One should keep (one's) promise/ oath; vi.—འགྱུར་ to have a promise/ oath be broken.

ཁ་དན་གན་རྒྱ་ (kādɛn kengya) a written contract regarding an agreement; va.—འཛུགས to make a written contract regarding an agreement.

ཁ་དན་གན་འཛིན་ (kādɛn kendzin) sm. ཁ་དན་འཛིན་ཡིག.

ཁ་དན་རྒྱབ་བསྒྱུར་ (kādɛn gyəbgyuu) violating or breaking a promise/ oath; va.—བྱེད་.

ཁ་དན་རྒྱབ་ཏུ་བསྐྱུར་ (kādɛn gyəbdu kyūr) va. to violate or break a promise/ oath.

ཁ་དན་ཚིག་དན་ (kādɛn tsigdɛn) sm. ཁ་དན་ཚིག་གནས་.

ཁ་དན་ཚིག་གནས་ (kādɛn tsignɛɛ) adhering/ abiding to an agreement or promise; va.—བྱེད་ ། ཁ་དན་ཚིག་གནས་བྱས་མ་བྱུང་ (He) didn't abide by his agreement. ། མི་ཁ་དན་ཚིག་གནས་མི་བྱེད་མཁན་ལ་ཆ་འཇོག་རྒྱུ་ཡོང་མ་རེད་ One cannot rely on a person who does not adhere to his promise.

ཁ་དན་འཛིན་ཡིག (kādɛn dzinyig) 1. a written contract regarding an agreement (usu. for minor issues); va.—འཛུགས to make a written contract regarding an agreement. 2. a warranty/ guarantee.

ཁ་དམ་པོ་ (kā tambo) 1. tight-lipped, able to keep secrets ། མི་འདི་ཁ་དམ་པོ་ཡོད་ཙང་ཚང་མས་བློས་ཁ་གཏོལ་གྱི་ཡོད་པ་རེད་ Because this man is able to keep secrets everyone relies on him. 2. va.—འགོག to seal tightly, to make sth. airtight ། ཤེལ་དམ་འདི་ཁ་དམ་པོ་རྒྱག་དགོས་རེད་ You must seal the bottle tightly.

ཁ་དམ་གསང་ཚུགས་ (kādam sãŋdzuù) sm. ཁ་དམ་པོ་.

ཁ་དར་ (kādar) 1. vi. to spread, to be successful. 2. sm. ཁ་བཏགས་.

ཁ་དལ་པོ་ (kā tɛɛbo) not engaging in useful verbal activities, e.g., prayers or work ། ཁ་དལ་པོར་མ་སྡོད་ མ་ཎི་དྲོངས་ Don't sit idle (verbally). Do mani (prayers).

ཁ་དལ་སྡོད་དལ་ (kātɛɛ jõdɛɛ) idle, not working; va.—བྱེད་ ། ཁ་དལ་སྡོད་དལ་བྱས་ནས་མ་སྡོད་ ལས་ཀ་འཚོལ་བར་རྒྱུགས་ Don't stay idle without working. Look for work.

ཁ་དིག་ལྕེ་སྡྲོག (kādig jēdrog) sm. ཁ་དིག་ལྕེ་དིག.

ཁ་དིག (kādig) sm. ཁ་དིག་དིག.

ཁ་དིག་ལྕེ་དིག (kādig jēdig) impaired in speech (usu. stuttering) ། ཁ་དིག་ལྕེ་དིག་གིས་གདམ་བཤད་ཅི་ལ་ཡོང་ How can sb. with a speech impairment give a lecture.

ཁ་དིག་ལྕེ་རེངས་ (kādig jēreŋ) sm. ཁ་དིག་ལྕེ་དིག.

ཁ་དིག་དིག (kā digdiì) a speech impairment/ defect, stuttering, stammering ། ཁོས་སྐད་ཆ་ཤོད་དུས་ཁ་དིག་དིག་བྱས་ནས་ཤོད་ཀྱི་འདུག He stammers when he speaks.

ཁ་དིག་པ་ (kā digdba) sm. ཁ་དིག་དིག.

ཁ་དུམ་ (kā tum) vi. to agree, to consent ། ལས་ཀ་འདི་བྱ་རྒྱུར་ནང་མི་ཚང་མ་ཁ་དུམ་པ་རེད་ All the family members agreed to do this work.

ཁ་དུལ་པོ་ (kā tüübo) 1. mild and tactful in speech; va.—བྱེད་. 2. gentle (for horses and riding mules).

ཁ་དེབ་ཚད་འཛིན་ (kādeb tsēndzin) an oral story/ tale/ account that has to be depended on since there are no written records.

ཁ་དོག (kādɔɔ) 1. attitude ། ཕྱུག་ནའང་ཁ་དོག་མི་འགྱུར་ Even if (we) are rich, our attitude will not change. 2. color ། ཁ་དོག་དཀར་པོ་ White color. 3. color in the sense of a viewpoint/ philosophy/ system ། ང་ཚོའི་རྒྱལ་ཁབ་འདི་ཁ་དོག་གཏན་ནས་མི་འགྱུར་བ་ཞིག་བྱེད་དགོས་ We must work so that our nation's political color (viewpoint) never changes; vi.—ཡལ་ to have a color/ complexion fade.

ཁ་དོག་སྒྲིག (kādɔɔ drig) va. to arrange/ match colors.

ཁ་དོག་མཆོག (kādɔɔ cɔ̃ɔ) poet. the best woman.

ཁ་དོག་པོ་ (kā togo) 1. cramped, narrow, small (opening) ། ལུང་པ་ཁ་དོག་པོར་ལམ་ཁ་བཟོ་ཁག་པོ་ཡོད་ It is hard to build a road in a narrow valley.

ཁ་དོན་མི་མཚུངས་པ་ (kādön mitsuŋba) actions not

squaring with one's words.

ཁ་དྲ་ (kādra) a muzzle on an animal (usu. horse or mule) to prevent it from eating or drinking.

ཁ་དྲག (kādraà) sm. ཁ་དྲག་པོ་.

ཁ་དྲག་ཅན་ (kā tragjɛn) 1. domineering, bossy. 2. ཁ་དྲག་པོ་.

ཁ་དྲག་དྲག (kā tragdraà) sm. ཁ་དྲག་པོ་.

ཁ་དྲག་པོ་ (kā tragbo) strong/ vehement in speech, a person domineering in speech ། ཁ་དྲག་པོའི་ངང་ནས་མ་ལབ་ Don't speak vehemently.

ཁ་དྲག་དཔུང་ཤུགས་ (kātrag būŋshuù) sm. ཁ་དྲག་དབང་ཤེད་.

ཁ་དྲག་དབང་བཙན་ (kādrag wāŋdzɛn) sm. ཁ་དྲག་དབང་ཤེད་.

ཁ་དྲག་དབང་ཤེད་ཅན་ (kādrag wāŋdzɛn) ཁ་དྲག་དབང་ཤེད་.

ཁ་དྲག་དབང་ཤེད་ (kādrag wāŋsheè) domineering, dictatorial, bossy (of those in power) ། བཀའ་བློན་བཞི་པོའི་ནང་ནས་ཁ་དྲག་དབང་ཤེད་ཅན་དེས་གང་བཤད་པར་ཚང་མས་མོས་མཐུན་བྱེད་ཀྱི་ཡོད་པ་རེད་ Among the four Kalons, whatever the domineering one said, all the others agreed.

ཁ་དྲང་པོ་ (kā draŋbo) truthful, frank.

ཁ་དྲངས་ (kā draŋ) sm. ཁ་འདྲེན་.

ཁ་དྲལ་ (kāra) vi. to be or get demolished/ destroyed/ obliterated ། ས་གཡོས་ཀྱིས་རྐྱེན་པས་ཁང་པ་མང་པོ་ཁ་དྲལ་བྱུང་བ་རེད་ The earthquake caused many houses to be destroyed.

ཁ་དྲི་ (kɔ̄dri) 1. bad breath. 2. the way/ manner of speaking ། སྐད་ཆ་ཤོད་དུས་ཁ་དྲི་འཇམ་པོ་བྱེད་དགོས་ When speaking, one should talk in a gentle manner.

ཁ་དྲོ་ (kādro) abbr. of ཁ་དྲོ་པོ་.

ཁ་དྲོ་པོ་ (kā trobo) 1. lucky, auspicious ། ལུང་པ་འདིར་སྤོས་ནས་ཁ་དྲོ་པོ་བྱུང་ (I've) been lucky since (I) moved to this place. 2. in Kham and Amdo—"goodbye" and "hello."

ཁ་དྲོག (kādrɔɔ̀) 1. fortune, good luck (usu. with regard to obtaining food). 2. temporary good fortune, a windfall.

ཁ་གདངས་ (kā daŋ) 1. va. to open one's mouth. 2. va. to talk/ speak.

ཁ་གདངས་ནས་ཁོག་པ་རིག་རྒྱུ་ (kādaŋnɛ kōgba riggyu) sm. ཁ་གདངས་གློ་མཐོང་.

ཁ་གདངས་གློ་མཐོང་ (kādaŋ lōtoŋ) speaking openly/ frankly ། ཁ་གདངས་གློ་མཐོང་བའི་བསམ་འཆར་བཤད་པ་ཡིན་ (I) gave them a frank suggestion. [Lit. open the mouth, see the lungs].

ཁ་གདངས་མིག་བགྲད་ (kādaŋ mīidrɛɛ̀) astonished, dumfounded ། ཁོའི་སྤྱོད་པས་ཚང་མ་ཁ་གདངས་མིག་བགྲད་བཟོས་པ་རེད་ His behavior astonished everyone.

ཁ་གདངས་མིག་ཅེར་ (kādaŋ mīijer) sm. ཁ་གདངས་མིག་བགྲད་.

ཁ་གདངས་མིག་གདངས་ (kādaŋ mīidaŋ) sm. ཁ་གདངས་མིག་བགྲད་.

ཁ་གདངས་ལག་པ་རྐྱོང་ཡུལ་ (kādaŋ lagba gyōŋyüü) sb. to whom one asks for help when there is difficulty ། རང་དཔོན་ནི་ང་ཚོའི་ཁ་གདངས་ལག་པ་རྐྱོང་ཡུལ་ཞིག་ཡིན་ Our chief is the one we turn to for help. [Lit. the place to which one opens the mouth and holds out the hand].

ཁ་གདན་ (kādɛn) 1. rug, carpet. 2. cloth used on top of Tibetan cushions or mattresses to keep them clean.

ཁ་གདོང་དུ་བཅར་ (kādoŋtu jāā) va. to go before sb., to go to the presence of sb.

ཁ་བདག་མེད་ཚིག་ཚོད་མེད་ (kā dagmeè tsīg tsōōmeè) talking irresponsibly, speaking without thought of the consequences; va.—ཤོད་ ། ཁ་བདག་མེད་ཚིག་ཚོད་མེད་བྱས་ནས་གསང་བ་ཤོར་བ་རེད་ (He) spoke irresponsibly and the secret got out. [Lit. the mouth has no control, the word has no limit].

ཁ་བདར་ (kābdar) chatting, casual idle talk, chit-chat; va.—སྡོད་ to chat ། ལས་ཀའི་བར་སེང་ལ་ཆུ་ཚོད་གཅིག་ཁ་བདར་སྡོད་ནས་བསྡད་པ་ཡིན་ During my work break, I stayed chatting for one hour.

ཁ་བདེ་ (kāde) sm. ཁ་བདེ་པོ་.

ཁ་བདེ་ཁ་གཟེར་ (kāde kāser) sharp-tongued/ cutting in speech; va.—བྱེད་.

ཁ་བདེ་ལྕེ་བདེ་ (kāde jēde) 1. sm. ཁ་བདེ་པོ་. 2. verbally skilled at conning or swindling; va.—ཤོད་; —བྱེད་.

ཁ་བདེ་གནད་འཕིགས་ (kāde nēbig) a person who is articulate and gets right to the heart of the matter (in his speech) ། ཁོང་གིས་ཁ་བདེ་གནད་འཕིགས་ཀྱི་ཐོག་ནས་གཏམ་བཤད་བྱས་སོང་ He gave a lecture that got to the heart of the matter.

ཁ་བདེ་པོ་ (kā debo) verbal, articulate, eloquent ། ཕྲུ་གུ་འདི་ལོ་ལ་དཔགས་པས་ཁ་བདེ་པོ་ཞི་དྲག་འདུག For his age the child is very articulate. ། ཁ་བདེ་པོ་བྱེད་པ་ལས་ལས་ཀ་རྣམ་དག་བྱས་ན་ཡག་གི་རེད་ It is better to work sincerely than to be eloquent.

ཁ་བདེ་ཚིག་རྣོ་ (kāde tsīgno) articulate and incisive/ biting.

ཁ་བདེ་ལག་བདེ་ (kāde lagde) skilled in terms of speech and in terms of doing things.

ཁ་བདེ་ཤོད་མཁས་ (kāde shōōkɛɛ̀) a good speaker, verbal, eloquent, articulate.

ཁ་མདེལ་སྒྲིལ་ (kāndee drɛɛ̀) va. to load a bullet into the barrel of a gun preparatory to firing.

ཁ་མདོག (kāmdɔɔ̀) sm. ཁ་དོག.

ཁ་མདོག་ཉེས་པོ་ (kāmdɔɔ̀ ñeèbo) ugly, unpleasant to look at ། མི་འདི་ཁ་མདོག་ཉེས་པོ་ཞི་དྲག་ཆགས་ཡོད་པ་རེད་ This man has become very unpleasant to look at.

ཁ་མདོག་ལོང་བ་ (kāmdɔɔ̀ lōŋwa) color blind.

ཁ་འདམ་ (kāndam) 1. ginger. 2. mud used to seal beer pots.

ཁ་འདར་ (kāndar) chattering of teeth due to cold; vi.—ཤོར་ to chatter from cold (teeth).

ཁ་འདིག (kādig) sm. ཁ་སྡིག.

ཁ་འདུམ་ (kāndum) meditation; va. ཁ་འདུམ་; —བྱེད་ to mediate ། བླ་མས་མི་ཚང་དེ་གཉིས་ཀྱི་རྩོད་གཞི་ཁ་འདུམ་ཐུབ་པ་བྱུང་བ་རེད་ The lama mediated between the two families.

ཁ་འདེད་ཁུངས་གཏུགས་ (kāndeè kūŋduù) getting to the bottom of sth.

ཁ་འདེབས་ (kāndeb) 1. adding to sth. ། ཇ་གར་པོ་མི་འདུག་པས་ཁ་འདེབས་དོག་ཙམ་རྒྱག་དགོས་ Because the tea is not strong, you should add a bit (more tea). 2. nh. of ཞལ་འདེབས་.

ཁ་འདེབས་རག་ལས་ (kāndeb raglɛɛ̀) shallow ploughing.

ཁ་འདེམས་ (kā dem) the first stage in local elections—the local people selecting candidates through discussion at a meeting.

ཁ་འདོགས་ (kā dɔg) arc. va. to kill (indiscriminately).

ཁ་འདོན་ (kāndön) prayer, praying; va.—བྱེད་ ། གྲྭ་པ་ཚོས་ཉིན་ལྟར་ཁ་འདོན་བྱེད་ཀྱི་ཡོད་པ་རེད་ The monks pray daily.

ཁ་འདོན་དགེ་སྦྱོར་ (kāndön gejɔɔ) praying and doing virtuous acts.

ཁ་འདོན་ཡིད་བརྟག (kāndön yiidaà) intoning prayers and thinking about them; va.—བྱེད་.

ཁ་འདོན་ལག་ལེན་ (kāndön laglen) keeping one's promise, doing what one says; va.—བྱེད་.

ཁ་འདྲི་ (kəndri) 1. getting a measure of sb. through questioning/ talking to them, testing sb. by talking/ questioning; va.—བྱེད་ ། གནས་ཚུལ་དེ་ངས་ཤེས་ཡོད་མེད་ཁོས་ང་ལ་ཁ་འདྲི་བྱེད་ཀྱི་འདུག He is testing me regarding whether or not I know about the event. 2. va. to inquire after sb.'s sickness/ illness ། སྙུན་ཁང་དུ་ནད་པར་ཁ་འདྲི་བྱས་པ་རེད་ (He) asked the patient in the hospital how he was doing.

ཁ་འདྲིས་ཁོག་འདྲིས་ (kəndriì kɔ̄gdriì) extremely close relations/ familiarity, good friends.

ཁ་འདྲེན་ (kəndrin) va. to lead/ guide (usu. for moral/ ethical issues) ། མི་རབས་རྗེས་མ་རྣམས་ལ་

རབས་སྤྱོད་བཟང་གི་ལམ་དུ་ཁ་འདྲེན་རྒྱུ་དེ་གལ་ཆེན་པོ་ཡིན་ Leading the future generation on the road of ethical morality is very important.

ཁ་རྡབ་ (kā dəp) vi. to stumble, to fall.

ཁ་རྡིབ་ (kādib) 1. an avalanche; va.—ཤོར་ to have an avalanche occur ¶ ཁ་རྡིབ་ཤོར་ནས་སེམས་ཅན་མང་པོ་ཤི་བ་རེད་ There was an avalanche and many animals died. 2. a sunken mouth (due to loss of teeth).

ཁ་རྡུང་ (kəpduŋ) verbal abuse, scolding, denouncing, condemning; va.—གཏོང་ to abuse verbally, to scold/ denounce/ condemn; vi.—གཟེད་; vi.—འཁྲིལ་ to get scolded/ yelled at/ criticized/ verbally abused ¶ བཙན་འཛུལ་པར་ཁ་རྡུང་བཏང་ཡོད་པ་རེད་ (They) denounced the invaders. ¶ ཁོང་ཡིག་ཚད་མ་ལོན་ཙང་ཕ་མའི་ཁ་རྡུང་གཟེད་པ་རེད་ Because he did not pass his exam, he got scolded by his parents.

ཁ་རྡུམ་ (kārdum) stubby, squat, short.

ཁ་རྡེའུ་ (kādewu) gravel used as roadbed.

ཁ་ལྡག (kā dag) 1. va. to lick. 2. va. to flatter, to fawn on.

ཁ་ལྡིག་པ་ (kā digbə) sm. ཁ་དིག་དིག.

ཁ་སྡུག་ཆགས་ (kā dugjaà) having a dirty mouth, cursing a lot ¶ གྲོགས་པོ་སྡུག་ཆགས་ཀྱིས་རྐྱེན་པས་ཁོང་གི་ཕྲུ་གུ་ཚོ་ཁ་སྡུག་ཆགས་ཆགས་ཡོད་པ་རེད་ Because of bad friends his children have come to have dirty mouths.

ཁ་སྡུད་ (kā düù) 1. va. to tie the mouth of a bag shut with a string or rope. 2. va. to gather together (people), to assemble.

ཁ་སྡུམ་ (kədum) mediation; va.—བྱེད་; —གཏོང་.

ཁ་སྡུར་ (kədur) 1. talking, chatting; va.—བྱེད་. 2. va. to compete regarding who is more verbal.

ཁ་སྡེབ་དབང་ (kā debwaŋ) the right to talk, the right of speech.

ཁ་སྡོམ་ (kādom) 1. sealing/ closing up sth.; va. ཁ་སྡོམ་; —བྱེད་ ¶ རས་ཁུག་གི་ཁ་སྡོམ་བྱེད་སྐུད་པ་ཞིག་དགོས་ཀྱི་འདུག A string is needed to tie the bag closed. 2. va. to stop, to restrain (speech) ¶ ལས་ཁུངས་ནང་རྐུན་མ་ཤོར་བའི་གནས་ཚུལ་དེ་ཁ་བསྡམས་འདུག (They) have restrained people from talking about the robbery in the office.

ཁ་བརྡ་ (kāpda) 1. signaling with the mouth; va.—བྱེད་. 2. talk, conversation; va.—བྱེད་.

ཁ་བརྡ་ཅན་ (kāpdajɛn) talkative.

ཁ་བརྡ་མིག་བརྡ་ (kāpda migda) signaling with eyes and mouth; va.—བྱེད་; —གཏོང་ to signal with the eyes and mouth.

ཁ་བརྡབ་ལག་བརྡབ་ (kāpdab lagdab) sm. རྐང་བརྡབ་ལག་བརྡབ་.

ཁ་བརྡའི་རྟེན་འབྲེལ་སྒོ་འབྱེད་ (kābdɛ dēmdree gojɛɛ̀) an auspicious saying used during Tibetan New Year.

ཁ་བརྡར་ (kāpdaa) sm. ཁ་བདར་.

ཁ་བརྡུང་ (kəpduŋ) sm. ཁ་རྡུང་.

ཁ་བསྡུ་སྣ་བསྡུ་ (kədu nədu) collecting things from different places and sources and putting them together to do sth.

ཁ་ན་ན་བཤད་ (kā nana shɛ̄ɛ̀) talking a lot, talking until one is blue in the face.

ཁ་ནག་པོ་ (kā nago) 1. dark shade/ color. 2. gloomy, morose, sad ¶ ངའི་གྲོགས་པོར་ཚོང་ཉེས་བྱུང་ཙང་ཁ་ནག་པོ་ཞིག་སྟོན་གྱི་འདུག Because my friend had a business loss, he is showing a sad (long) face. 3. unfriendly ¶ དེང་སྐབས་ངའི་གྲོགས་པོ་འདི་ཁ་ནག་པོ་ཞིག་ཆགས་འདུག Lately my friend has become unfriendly. 4. unlucky, inauspicious ¶ ཁང་པ་འདི་ཁ་ནག་པོ་ཞིག་བྱུང་ ¶ This house has been unlucky. 5. angry (countenance) ¶ དཔོན་པོ་དེས་ཁ་ནག་པོ་བསྟན་ནས་གཡོག་པོར་གཤེ་གཤེ་བཏང་བ་རེད་ The chief showed an angry face and scolded the servant.

ཁ་ནང་ (kānaŋ) 1. yesterday morning. 2. inside the mouth.

ཁ་ནང་གི་རྨ་ ཁ་ནང་དུ་གསོ་ (kānaŋgi mā kānaŋtu sō) 1. resolving a problem internally. 2. sm. ཁ་མཆུ་ནང་འཇགས་.

ཁ་ནང་ལྕེ་རྒྱུས་ (kānaŋ jēgyüù) knowing the internal workings/ politics of sth., knowing the ropes; va.—བྱེད་ to explain or tell the internal workings/ operations of an office ¶ ལས་ཀ་བྱེད་སྟངས་སྐོར་ལས་ཁུངས་ནང་གི་མིས་ཁ་ནང་ལྕེ་རྒྱུས་བྱ་དགོས་པ་རེད་ Concerning how to work, a person in the office has to explain how things are done to the new cadres. [Lit. the tongue knows what's in the mouth].

ཁ་ནང་དུ་ལྟ་བ་ (kānaŋtu dāwa) sm. ཁ་འཁོར་བ་, 2.

ཁ་ནད་ (kānɛɛ̀) mouth disease.

ཁ་ནད་སྡེ་ཚན་ (kānɛɛ̀ dedzɛn) stomatology department.

ཁ་ནར་ཅན་ (kā narjɛn) rectangular.

ཁ་ནས་ (kānɛɛ̀) orally, verbally, by word of mouth; va.—བརྗོད་; —ཤོད་ to tell/ narrate/ explain orally ¶ ཁོས་ཁ་ནས་ལན་བསྐྱལ་བ་རེད་ He delivered the message orally.

ཁ་ནས་གང་ཐོན་ཤོད་ (kānɛɛ̀ kandön shōò) va. to say whatever comes to mind (can have positive or negative connotation) ¶ མི་དྲང་པོ་འདི་ཁ་ནས་གང་ཐོན་ཤོད་ཀྱི་ཡོད་པ་རེད་ The honest man says whatever comes to (his) mind.

ཁ་ནས་གང་བྱུང་ཤོད་ (kānɛɛ̀ kəŋjuŋ shōò) va. to say all sorts of things (negative connotation) ¶ མི་དེས་ཁ་ནས་གང་བྱུང་བཤད་ཙང་འགོ་ཁྲིད་རྣམས་ལ་ཡོག་ཐུག་འགྲོ་གི་ཡོད་པ་རེད་ Because the person said all sorts of things, the bosses are offended.

ཁ་ནས་ཐོན་ལ་མ་ཐོན་ (kānɛɛ̀ tōnla matōn) speaking hesitantly, hemming and hawing ¶ གནད་དོན་དེའི་སྐོར་ཁོང་ལ་དྲི་བ་འདོན་སྐབས་ཁ་ནས་ཐོན་ལ་མ་ཐོན་གྱིས་ལན་བརྒྱབ་སོང་ When he was asked about that issue he responded hesitantly.

ཁ་ནས་འདོན་ཞིང་ཡིད་ལ་བརྟག་པ་ (kānɛɛ̀ tönshiŋ yiìlə dāgba) sm. ཁ་ནས་འདོན་ཡིད་བརྟག.

ཁ་ནས་དཔོད་ (kānɛɛ̀ bōò) va. to dictate (to sb. who is writing it down).

ཁ་ནས་མུ་ཏིག་ཤོར་དོགས་ (kānɛɛ̀ mudig shɔ̄ɔ̄dɔɔ̀) reluctant to share knowledge/ information [Lit. having the suspicion that pearls will fall out of the mouth].

ཁ་ནས་ཚིག་ཤོར་ཡུ་བ་ཐུང་ (kānɛɛ̀ tsīgshɔɔ yuwa tūŋ) a slip of the tongue is hard to recall [Lit. sth. said inadvertently has a short handle].

ཁ་ནས་ལུད་ (kānɛɛ̀ lüù) vi. to spill over from the brim of a cup or bowl, etc. ¶ མེ་ཚ་དྲགས་ནས་ཐུག་པ་ཁ་ནས་ལུད་ཀྱི་འདུག The fire was too hot so the broth spilled over (the brim).

ཁ་ནི་སྡིག་པའི་སྒོ་ཡིན་ (kāni digbɛ goyin) sm. ཁ་སྒོ་མོ་སྒྲོད་ཀྱི་གཞི་ས་.

ཁ་ཉིང་ (kəniŋ) last year ¶ ཁ་ཉིང་ང་ཚོ་བོད་ལ་འགྲོ་ཡག་གི་འཆར་གཞི་བཟོས་པ་རེད་ Last year we made plans to go to Tibet.

ཁ་ནུབ་ (kənub) 1. the night before last ¶ ཁ་ནུབ་དགོང་དག་ང་ཚོ་ཐུགས་སྐྱོར་ཕྱིན་པ་ཡིན་ The night before last we went to a party. 2. see ཁ་.

ཁ་ནུབ་དགོང་དག (kənub gondaà) sm. ཁ་ནུབ་.

ཁ་ནུབ་དགོང་མོ་ (kənub goŋmo) sm. ཁ་ནུབ་.

ཁ་ནེ་ཁོ་ནེ་ (kāne kōne) 1. hesitatingly, stumbling (for speech) ¶ ཁོས་ཁ་ནེ་ཁོ་ནེ་བྱས་ནས་གསར་འགྱུར་བཤད་པ་རེད་ He hesitatingly told the news. ¶ ཁོས་ཁ་ནེ་ཁོ་ནེ་མེད་པར་ངོས་ལེན་ཞུས་ཙང་ཚང་མས་ཡིད་ཆེས་སྐྱེས་པ་རེད་ Because he confessed without stumbling or hesitating, everyone believed him. 2. mistakes, errors ¶ ཁོའི་ལས་ཀའི་ནང་ཁ་ནེ་ཁོ་ནེ་བྱུང་སོང་ There were many mistakes in his work.

ཁ་ནེ་འཁོན་ནེ་ (kāne kōne) 1. sm. ཁ་ནེ་ཁོ་ནེ་.

ཁ་ཉམ་ (kānem) slightly used or old ¶ དུག་ལོག་ཁ་ཉམ་ལ་གོང་ཁེ་པོ་ཡོད་ The price for slightly used clothes is cheap.

ཁ་ནོག (kānog) slightly dirty, not clean.

ཁ་ནོར་ (kā nɔɔ) vi. to misspeak, to say the wrong

thing.

ཁ་གནག་པོ་ (kā nāgbo) malicious/ spiteful/ vengeful in talk.

ཁ་གནམ་ལ་གཏད་ (kā nāmla dɛ̄ɛ̀) va. to put/ place sth. face up.

ཁ་གནོད་ (kānöö) shung. abbr. of ཁ་བའི་གནོད་འཚེ་.

ཁ་གནོན་ (kānön) 1. antidote, sth. that counteracts, a counterforce ¶ ནད་ཀྱི་ཁ་གནོན་ལ་སྨན་དགོས་ (One) needs medicine to counteract sickness. 2. suppressing, oppressing; va. ཁ་གནོན་; —བྱེད་ to suppress/ oppress ¶ གཞུང་གིས་མང་ཚོགས་ལས་འགུལ་གྱི་ཁ་གནོན་བྱས་པ་རེད་ The government suppressed the people's movement. 3. va. to put a hand over someone's mouth to stop them from talking. 4. va. to seal an envelope.

ཁ་མནན་ (kānɛn) p. of ཁ་གནོན་.

ཁ་རྣོ་པོ་ (kā nōbo) sharp-tongued.

ཁ་རྣོ་ཚིག་རྣོ་ (kāno tsīgno) 1. sm. ཁ་རྣོ་པོ་. 2. engaging in a verbal battle or a battle of words.

ཁ་རྣོ་ཚིག་བཙན་ (kāno tsīgdzɛn) sm. ཁ་རྣོ་པོ་.

ཁ་སྣོན་ (kānön) replenishing, making up a shortage, reinforcing, supplementing, a supplement; va.—བྱེད་; —སྤྲོད་; —རྒྱག ¶ དམག་རྒྱག་སྐབས་ཧྲས་མདེལ་ཁ་སྣོན་སྤྲོད་དགོས་བྱུང་སོང་ During the battle (they) had to replenish ammunition.

ཁ་པ་ (kāba) 1. an alphabetically filed box in tt. that is marked ཁ་. 2. skillful in speech, verbal, articulate (has a slightly negative connotation) ¶ མི་འདི་ཁ་པ་ཞེ་པོ་ཞིག་འདུག This man is very verbal. 3. go between person, negotiator between two traders/ merchants.

ཁ་པང་ (kābaŋ) top of a table.

ཁ་པར་ (kābaa) telephone; va.—གཏོང་; —རྒྱག to make a phone call; vi.—སླེབས་ to receive a phone call; va.—ལེན་ to pick up/ answer the phone.

ཁ་པར་སྐུད་ལམ་ (kābaa gṻūləm) telephone wire/ line.

ཁ་པར་གྱི་ཨང་གྲངས་འདྲི་ས་ (kābaagi āŋdraŋ tri̱sə) telephone information (operator/ office).

ཁ་པར་གློག་སྐུད་ (kābaa lōggüü) sm. ཁ་པར་སྐུད་ལམ.

ཁ་པར་རྒྱག་སའི་ཁང་ཆུང་ (kābaa gyasɛ kāŋjuŋ) phone booth.

ཁ་པར་ཅུས་ (kābaa jṻù) tib. ch. telephone exchange/ bureau.

ཁ་པར་འཕྲུལ་འཁོར་ (kābaa trṻūgɔɔ) telephone.

ཁ་པར་འཕྲུལ་ཆས་ (kābaa trṻūjeè) telephone equipment.

ཁ་པར་བ་ (kābaawa) telephone operator.

ཁ་པར་ཚོགས་འདུ་ (kābaa tsōndu) phone conference.

ཁ་པར་འཛུགས་ (kābaa dzu̱ù) va. to install a phone.

ཁ་པར་ལུང་འཕྲིན་ (kābaa lūŋdrin) radiotelephone.

ཁ་པར་ཨང་གྲངས་ (kābaa āŋdraŋ) telephone number.

ཁ་པར་ཨང་གྲངས་འདྲི་ས་ (kābaa āŋdraŋ dri̱sa) sm. ཁ་པར་གྱི་ཨང་གྲངས་འདྲི་ས་.

ཁ་པར་ཨང་གྲངས་འཚོལ་དེབ་ (kābaa āŋdraŋ tsōōdeb) telephone book.

ཁ་པིང་ (kābiŋ) harmonica.

ཁ་པིན་མེ་མདའ་ (kābin me̱nda) eng.tib. carbine rifle.

ཁ་པུར་ (kābur) Kabul.

ཁ་པོ་ (kōbo) 1. (མདོག + —) looks like, seems like ¶ ཁང་པ་འདི་ཡག་མདོག་ཁ་པོ་འདུག This looks like a good house. 2. excessively (for taste) ¶ ཚྭ་ཁ་པོ་ Too salty. 3. bitter, strong (in taste) ¶ ཇ་འདི་ཁ་པོ་འདུག The tea is bitter.

ཁ་པོ་ཆེ་ (kāboce) boastful, show-offish.

ཁ་དཔར་ (kābaa) sm. ཁ་པར་.

ཁ་དཔེ་ (kābe) a saying, proverb.

ཁ་དཔྱ་ (kā jā) making fun of, humiliating; va.—བྱེད་.

ཁ་ལྤགས་ (kābaà) 1. skin around the lips. 2. sm. ཁ་གོན་.

ཁ་ལྤགས་ཁྲས་ཁྲས་ (kābaà) smiling (usu. a forced or fake smile); va.—བྱེད་.

ཁ་སྤམ་ (kābam) a kind of cap worn by བཀའ་ཤག་མགྲོན་གཉེར་ in tt.

ཁ་སྤིང་ (kəpiŋ) sm.* ཁ་སྤྱིན་.

ཁ་སྤུ་ (kəbu) moustache, beard.

ཁ་སྤུ་དབྱེ་འབྱེད་ (kəbu yējeè) shung. va. to separate from ¶ གྲྭ་བཙུན་ཁོངས་མི་ཟ་ཇེ་སྐྱིད་ཡོད་པ་ཁ་སྤུ་དབྱེ་འབྱེད་ཡོད་པ་ (We) request that you separate out the serfs from among the monks.

ཁ་སྤུབ་ (kəbub) face down; va. ཁ་སྤུབ་; —ལོག to put/ turn face down; vi.—ལོག to get turned face down (accidentally) ¶ དཀར་ཡོལ་ཁ་སྤུབ་ལོག་ནས་བཞག་རོགས་གནང་ Please leave the cup face down.

ཁ་སྤུབས་ (kā būb) p. of ཁ་སྤུབ་.

ཁ་སྤོ་ (kā bō) 1. va. to change, to shift, to move ¶ སྨན་པ་འདི་ཕན་པོ་མ་བྱུང་ཙང་གཞན་དག་ཅིག་ལ་ཁ་སྤོས་པ་ཡིན་ Because this doctor wasn't beneficial, (I) changed to another. ¶ དབྱར་ཁའི་རིང་ལས་ཀ་བྱེད་ས་ལྷོ་ཕྱོགས་སུ་ཁ་སྤོ་གི་ཡིན་ I'm going to move south to work during the summer. 2. sm. ཁོང་ཁྲོ་.

ཁ་སྤོས་ (kā bȫö̀) p. of ཁ་སྤོ་.

ཁ་སྦྱིན་ (kājin) a type of Tibetan dry glue (that is wet by the lips).

ཁ་སྤྲད་ (kā drɛ̄ɛ̀) p. of ཁ་སྤྲོད་.

ཁ་སྤྲོད་ (dröö̀) face-to-face, facing; va. ཁ་སྤྲོད་; —བྱེད་ to bring/ put face-to-face ¶ ངའི་ཁང་པ་སྨན་ཁང་དང་ཁ་སྤྲོད་རེད་ My house faces the hospital. ¶ ལྕགས་མདོང་འདི་གཉིས་ཁ་སྤྲད་ནས་མཐུད་པ་རེད་ (He) joined the two pipes (face-to-face) at their opening. ¶ ཁང་པ་རྒྱ་མཚོ་དང་ཁ་སྤྲོད་ཡིན་པ་ཞིག་རྒྱག་གི་ཡིན་ I'm going to build a house facing the sea.

ཁ་སྤྲོད་མ་ (kādröma) sm. ཁ་སྤྲོད་.

ཁ་སྤྲིས་ (kādriì) the cream that forms on the surface when milk or yogurt is boiled.

ཁ་ཕན་ཚིག་ཕན་ (kābɛn tsīgbɛn) helpful/ sincere advice.

ཁ་ཕར་ཕྱོགས་ (kā pāā chɔ̄ɔ̀) va. to turn to the opposite side, to side with the opposition ¶ མི་དེ་དགྲ་བོའི་ཕྱོགས་སུ་ཁ་ཕར་ཕྱོགས་པ་རེད་ ¶ That person sided with the enemy. ¶ མི་དེ་ཁ་ཕར་ཕྱོགས་པའི་གྲས་རེད་ He is in the group/ clique/ segment that is siding with the opposition.

ཁ་ཕར་ལྡོག (kā pār lɔ̄ɔ̀) va. to turn one's head ¶ མཛེས་མ་མཐོང་པ་དང་གར་ཁོས་ཁ་ཕར་བསྒྲིགས་ནས་བལྟས་སོང་ As soon as he saw the beautiful woman he turned his head and looked.

ཁ་ཕེ་ (kābe) eng. 1. coffee. 2. caffeine.

ཁ་ཕེ་ཁོ་ཕེ་ (kābe kōbe) sloppy, untidy, ungraceful ¶ མི་འདི་ལས་ཀ་ཁ་ཕེ་ཁོ་ཕེ་ཞིག་བྱེད་ཀྱི་འདུག This man works sloppily.

ཁ་ཕེན་ (kāben) card.

ཁ་ཕོ་ (kābo) 1. boasting, bragging; va.—བཤོ་; —ཤོད་ to boast/ brag. 2. —འདོན་ sm. སྐད་ཅོར་རྒྱག.

ཁ་ཕོ་ཆེ་ (kāboce) boastful, conceited ¶ ཁ་ཕོ་ཆེ་བའི་མིས་བཤད་པའི་སྐད་ཆ་ར་གཞན་གྱི་ཆ་འཛིན་གི་མ་རེད་ People will disregard the remarks of a boastful person.

ཁ་ཕོ་འུད་སྒྲོག (kābo wö̱ö̀drɔɔ̀) making a great fanfare about sth., hyping sth.

ཁ་ཕོག་སྣ་ཕོག (kābog nābog) doing or saying sth. carelessly so that it unintentionally harms or hurts people; vi.—འགྲོ་; va.—བཟོ་ ¶ ཁོས་ཁ་ཕོག་སྣ་ཕོག་འགྲོ་ཡག་གི་སྐད་ཆ་བཤད་པ་རེད་ He said things that were hurtful to others. ¶ སྐད་ཆ་གང་བྱུང་བཤད་ན་ཁ་ཕོག་སྣ་ཕོག་ཡོང་གི་རེད་ If you say all sorts of things, you will hurt people. [Lit. mouth was hit, nose was hit].

ཁ་ཕོར་ (kābɔɔ) a person's regular eating/ drinking cup or bowl.

ཁ་ཕྱི་ (kāci) an inferior grade scarf.

ཁ་ཕྱིན་ (kā cīn) see ཁ་, 13.

ཁ་ཕྱིར་སྐོར་ (kācii gɔ̄ɔ̄) sm. ཁ་ཕྱིར་ལོག.

ཁ་ཕྱིར་ལྟ་ (kācii dā) sm. ཁ་ཕྱིར་ལོག.

ཁ་ཕྱིར་ལོག (kācii lɔ̄ɔ̀) va. to face or turn backwards, to reverse direction ¶ ཁ་ཕྱིར་བསློགས་ནས་ལྷོ་ཕྱོགས་ལ་བྲོས་བྱིན་པ་རེད་ Turning around, (they) fled to the south.

ཁ་ཕྱིས་ (kācii) 1. napkin. 2. handkerchief. 3. va. to wipe (mouth).

ཁ་ཕྱེ་ (kā cē) vi. and va. to open up, to blossom ¶ མེ་ཏོག་ཞལ་ཁ་ཕྱེ་ཞག The flowers have blossomed. ¶ ངས་སྒམ་འདི་ཁ་ཕྱེ་པ་ཡིན་ I opened the box.

ཁ་ཕྱེད་ (kāpjeè) a monetary unit in tt. (see དངུལ).

ཁ་ཕྱོགས་ (kāpjɔɔ̀) 1. direction ¶ འདི་ནས་ལྷ་ས་ཁ་ཕྱོགས་ག་པར་ཡོད་པ་རེད་ What direction is Lhasa from here? ¶ གསར་བརྗེའི་ཁ་ཕྱོགས་ཡང་དག་པ་ The correct revolutionary direction. va. ཁ་ཕྱོགས་; —སྒྱུར་; —སྐོར་; va.—ལྡོག to change directions, to shift allegiances ¶ བརྡ་ལེན་འཕྲུལ་འཁོར་གྱི་ཁ་ཕྱོགས་སྒྱུར་སྟེ་གནམ་གྲུ་ལ་བལྟ་ཞིབ་བྱས་པ་རེད་ They changed the direction of the radar to investigate the planes. vi.—འགྱུར་ to have the direction change. va.—ལྡོག to do sth. contrary/ opposite, to change directions, to shift allegiances ¶ ཁོས་སྐད་ཆ་ཚང་མ་ཁ་ཕྱོགས་བསློགས་ཏེ་བཤད་པ་རེད་ He said everything in a way that is opposite to normal. 2. sm. འཁོར་ཕྱོགས་.

ཁ་ཕྱོགས་སྐོག་ལྟ་ (kāpjɔɔ̀ gōgda) secretly seeing which way the wind is blowing (on some issue); va.—བྱེད་.

ཁ་ཕྱོགས་བསྐོར་མཚམས་ (kāpjɔɔ̀ gōndzam) a turning point ¶ འཕོ་འགྱུར་གྱི་དུས་སྐབས་སུ་ཁ་ཕྱོགས་སྐོར་མཚམས་ནོར་ན་དོན་དག་འཕྱུག་གི་རེད་ In time of change, if (you) make a wrong decision at a turning point you will miss achieving your goal.

ཁ་ཕྱོགས་འགྱུར་མཚམས་ (kāpjɔɔ̀ gyu̱ndzam) sm. ཁ་ཕྱོགས་སྐོར་མཚམས་.

ཁ་ཕྱོགས་སྒྱུར་ (kāpjɔɔ̀ gyu̱r) see ཁ་ཕྱོགས་.

ཁ་ཕྱོགས་ཆེན་པོ་ (kāpjɔɔ̀ cēmbo) things that make an enormous difference in which direction party/ people/ etc. follow ¶ སྤྱི་ཚོགས་རིང་ལུགས་ཀྱི་ལམ་དུ་འགྲོ་དང་ མ་རྩའི་རིང་ལུགས་ཀྱི་ལམ་དུ་འགྲོ་རྒྱུ་གཉིས་ཁ་ཕྱོགས་ཆེན་པོའི་དོན་ཞིག་རེད་ Going on the socialist or capitalist road is an issue that makes an enormous difference.

ཁ་ཕྱོགས་ལྟ་ཆས་ (kāpjɔɔ̀ dājɛɛ̀) compass.

ཁ་ཕྱོགས་སྟོན་ (kāpjɔɔ̀ dȭn) va. to show/ indicate direction ¶ ལྡོབ་དཔོན་ལྷན་དིའི་དགོངས་པས་རྒྱ་གར་མི་དམངས་ལ་རང་བཙན་གྱི་ཁ་ཕྱོགས་བསྟན་པ་རེད་ Mahatma Gandhi's thoughts showed the direction of freedom to the Indian people.

ཁ་ཕྱོགས་སྟོན་རྟགས་ (kāpjɔɔ̀ dȭndaà) direction signal, sign (usu. on a road).

ཁ་ཕྱོགས་ནོར་ (kāpjɔɔ̀ n̲ɔ̲ɔ̲) vi. to lose one's bearings, to lose direction.

ཁ་ཕྱོགས་འཛོལ་ (kāpjɔɔ̀ dzö̱ö̱) sm. ཁ་ཕྱོགས་ནོར་.

ཁ་ཕྱོགས་བརླག (kābjɔɔ̀ lāà) sm. ཁ་ཕྱོགས་ནོར་.

ཁ་ཕྱོགས་ལོག (kāpjɔɔ̀ l̲ɔ̲ɔ̀) 1. vi. to go in the opposite/ wrong/ contrary direction ¶ ཁ་ཕྱོགས་ལོག་ནས་ཕྱིན་པ་རེད་ (He) went in the wrong direction. 2. vi. to do the opposite (unintentionally), to be contrary, to invert (unintentionally) ¶ ཁོས་སྐད་ཆ་ཤོད་སྟངས་ཁ་ཕྱོགས་ལོག་པ་རེད་ His manner of speaking was opposite (of others).

ཁ་ཕྱོགས་ལྡོག (kāpjɔɔ̀ lɔ̄ɔ̀) 1. va. to go in the opposite/ wrong direction (purposely) ¶ ཁ་ཕྱོགས་བསློགས་ནས་ཕྱིན་པ་རེད་ (He) went in the opposite direction. 2. va. to do the opposite, to act contrary ¶ ལུང་པ་འདི་ཡག་པོ་ཡོད་ཀྱང་ ཁོས་ཁ་ཕྱོགས་བསློགས་ནས་ཡག་པོ་མི་འདུག་ཟེར་བྱུང་ Even though this area is good, he acted contrary and said it was no good.

ཁ་ཕྲད་ཕྲད་ (kā trɛ̄drɛɛ̀) smiling/ happy face and demeanor (often conveys that a person is internally angry but is outwardly smiling).

ཁ་ཕྲལ་ (kā trɛ̄ɛ̄) va. to separate, to split up, to take apart ¶ ཁྱི་འཛིང་ཁ་ཕྲལ་མ་ཐུབ་པ་ལྟར་ Like being unable to separate fighting dogs. ¶ འཕྲུལ་འཁོར་གྱི་ཡན་ལག་ཁ་ཕྲལ་ནས་བཟོ་བཅོས་བརྒྱབ་པ་རེད་ (They) took the machine apart and repaired it.

ཁ་ཕྲལ་(དུ་)གཏོང་ (kātrɛɛtu dōŋ) va. to separate, to split up, to take apart.

ཁ་ཕྲལ་དབང་སྒྱུར་ (kātrɛɛ wāŋgyur) divide and conquer.

ཁ་ཕྲལ་རིང་ལུགས་ (kātrɛɛ ri̱ŋluù) separatism, secessionism, factionalism ¶ ཁ་ཕྲལ་རིང་ལུགས་པ་ A separatist, a secessionist.

ཁ་ཕྲུ་ (kətru) taking a mouthful of water and blowing out a fine stream of water (e.g., when ironing clothes); va.—གཏོར་.

ཁ་ཕྲུམ་ (kədrum) cartilage, gristle.

ཁ་འཕངས་ (kāmbāŋ) blaming, accusing (falsely); va. ཁ་འཕངས་; —འཛོག to blame / accuse; vi.—འཁུར་ to suffer a false accusation.

ཁ་འཕངས་མཐོན་པོ་ (kābāŋ tȭmbo) talking big, showing off, bragging.

ཁ་འཕངས་ གླུང་སྟོན་ (kābaŋ lūŋdön) showing one's anger and blaming sb.

ཁ་འཕངས་ལག་ཕྱིས་ (kābaŋ l̲agcii̱) blaming others; va.—བྱེད་ ¶ རང་གི་སྐྱོན་ཆ་གཞན་ལ་ཁ་འཕངས་ལག་ཕྱིས་བྱས་པ་རེད་ (He) blamed others for his own mistakes.

ཁ་འཕངས་ལག་འཕྱིས་ (kābaŋ l̲agcii̱) sm. ཁ་འཕངས་ལག་ཕྱིས་.

ཁ་འཕེར་པོ་ (kā pērbo) verbal, articulate.

ཁ་འཕྱིད་ (kā cii̱) 1. vi. to suffice, to be enough, to manage ¶ ཁྲོམ་བཙོང་པ་ཡིན་ན་ལྟོ་གོས་ཁ་འཕྱིད་ཙམ་ཡོང་གི་རེད་ If you sell in the market place your livelihood will suffice. ¶ ཁྱེད་རང་གི་འཚོ་བ་ག་འདྲ་འདུག ཨོ་ཙེ་ ཁ་འཕྱིད་ཙམ་འདུག How is your livelihood? So so. (I'm) managing. 2. va. to wipe.

ཁ་འཕྱུག (kā cūù) sm. ཁ་ནོར་.

ཁ་འཕྱུར་ (kā cūr) vi. to be heaped up, to be overflowing ¶ འབྲུ་འབོ་ཁ་འཕྱུར་བ་ཞིག་སྤྲད་པ་རེད་ (They) gave (him) an overflowing 'bo' (a standard volume measure in Tibet) of grain.

ཁ་འཕྲལ་ (kā trɛ̄ɛ̄) sm. ཁ་ཕྲལ་.

ཁ་འཕྲལ་དུ་གཏོང་ (kātrɛtu dōŋ) sm. ཁ་ཕྲལ་དུ་གཏོང་.

ཁ་འཕྲི་ (kətri) a deduction, deducting.

ཁ་འཕྲིད་འཕྲིད་ སྐྱིད་ཞ་ཞ་ (kā trītrii̱ gyi̱i̱ sha̱sha) sm. ཁ་འཕྲེད་འཕྲེད་ སྐྱིད་ཞ་ཞ་.

ཁ་འཕྲིན་ (kāndrin) a verbal message.

ཁ་འཕྲེད་འཕྲེད་ སྐྱིད་ཞ་ཞ་ (kā trēèdreè gyi̱i̱ sha̱sha) servility, subservience, cringing.

ཁ་འཕྲོག (kā trɔ̄ɔ̀) va. to interrupt someone talking.

ཁ་འཕྲོད་པོ་ (kā trōbo) 1. sm. ཁ་ལྟ་པོ་. 2. one's work matching one's words.

ཁ་བ་ (kāwa) 1. snow; vi.—འབབ་ to snow; va.—འགེབས་ to cover with snow ¶ ཁ་བས་བཀབ་པའི་ཞིང་ཁ་ Fields covered with snow. 2. sm. ཁ་. 3. bitter.

ཁ་བ་སྐྱ་ཐུལ་ཐུལ་ (kāwa gyā tū̃ū̃düü) softly falling snow.

ཁ་བ་ཅན་ (kāwajɛn) 1. snowy. 2. Tibet.

ཁ་བ་ཅན་གྱི་ཞིང་ཁམས་ (kāwajɛngi shi̱ŋgam) land of snows (commonly used to mean Tibet).

ཁ་བ་ཆར་ལྡོག (kāwa cāndog) the time during the first Tibetan month when snow changes to rain.

ཁ་བ་ཆུང་ (kāwajuŋ) the 10th month of the Tibetan calendar when the first light snow falls.

ཁ་བ་ཆེ་ (kāwace) the 12th month of the Tibetan calendar when heavy snow starts to fall.

ཁ་བ་བུ་ཡུག (kāwa pu̱yuù) snow storm, blizzard.

ཁ་བ་མཚམས་ཐིག (kāwa tsāmdig) snow line (on a mountain).

ཁ་བ་རི་ (kāwari) sm. ཁ་བ་ཅན་.

ཁ་བ་རི་པ་ (kāwa ri̱bə) 1. a Tibetan. 2. people who live on mountains (where there is snow).

ཁ་བད་ (kābɛɛ̀) 1. a parapet. 2. railing, banister.

ཁ་བབ་ལྗི་པོ་ (kābab ji̱i̱bu) sm. ཁ་བབ་ལྗིད་པོ་.

ཁ་བབ་ལྗིད་པོ་ (kābab ji̱i̱bu) a person who doesn't express what he feels, a person who says little, a person who is closemouthed (opposite of ཁ་གསངས་པོ་) ¶ མི་འདི་ཁ་བབ་ལྗིད་པོ་ཞེ་དྲག་འདུག This man does not talk much at all.

ཁ་བབ་ཙམ་ (kābabdzam) slightly old/ used ¶ ཁོའི་ནང་གི་འཛིན་ཆས་ཁ་བབ་ཙམ་རེད་འདུག The furniture in his house is slightly old.

ཁ་བའི་འདབ་མ་ (kāwɛɛ dəbmə) snow flake.

ཁ་བའི་མེ་ཏོག (kāwɛɛ medog) sm. ཁ་བའི་འདབ་མ་.

ཁ་བའི་ལྷུན་པོ་ (kāwɛɛ lhũnbo) snow mountain.

ཁ་པལ་ (kāpɛɛ) abbr. Muslims and Nepalese.

ཁ་བུ་རམ་ལས་མངར་བ་ ཁོང་ཚེར་མ་ལས་རྩུབ་པ་ (kā buramlɛ ŋārwa kōŋ tsērmalɛ dzūbbə) sm. ཁ་འཇམ་གདིང་གནག.

ཁ་བུབ་ (kəbuù) tripping, stumbling, falling face down; vi.—(དུ་) ལོག; —འགྱེལ་ to trip, to stumble, to fall face down ¶ མི་དེ་ཁ་བུབ་ལོག་ནས་རིལ་སོང་ That man fell face down. 3. va.—སློག to lay sth. face down ¶ སྣོད་ཆས་ཁ་བུབ་བསློགས་བཞག (He) turned the utensil face down.

ཁ་བེ་ཁོ་བེ་ (kəbe kōbe) sm. ཁབ་བེ་ཁོ་བེ་.

ཁ་བོ་ (kāwo) sm. ཁ་མོ་.

ཁ་བྱང་ (kājaŋ) 1. tag, label; va.—འགོད་; —སྦྱོར་ to make a tag/ label. 2. address ¶ ཁྱེད་རང་གི་ཁ་བྱང་ག་རེ་རེད་ What is your address? 3. title (of book, article, etc.). 4. front page of a book or magazine ¶ ཁ་བྱང་རྣམ་འགོད་ Designing the cover (of a book or magazine).

ཁ་བྱང་བ་ (kā caŋwa) nh. of ཞལ་བྱང་བ་.

ཁ་བྱང་མ་ (kā caŋma) verbal/ eloquent (as a result of practice) ¶ རླུང་འཕྲིན་ཕོད་མཁན་དེ་ཁ་བྱང་མ་ཆགས་འདུག The radio broadcaster became eloquent through practice.

ཁ་བྱང་ལག་བྱང་ (kājaŋ lagjaŋ) skilled through practice/ familiarity.

ཁ་བྱམས་ཚིག་འཇམ་ (kājam tsīgjam) gentle/ mild in speech.

ཁ་བྱེ་ (kā ce) 1. vi. to come open, to separate. 2. the first words uttered by an infant.

ཁ་བྱིའུ་ (kā ciu) lark (bird).

ཁ་བྲག (kāpdraà) sm. ཁ་དབྲག.

ཁ་བྲག་ཁུང་ཙམ་གདངས་ (kā drəguŋdzam daŋ) opening one's mouth very wide [Lit. open one's mouth like a cave].

ཁ་བྲང་ (kābraŋ) a nomad satellite herding camp.

ཁ་བྲལ་ (kā drɛɛ) 1. split, separated, parted; vi. ཁ་བྲལ་; —བྱེད་ to become separated, to be parted, to get split up ¶ ལྷ་སའི་ཟིང་འཁྲུག་སྐབས་ནང་མི་ཁ་བྲལ་བ་རེད་ During the time of the disturbances in Lhasa, families got separated. 2. vi. to fall/ come apart ¶ སྟོད་ཐུང་གི་ཚེམ་བུ་ཁ་བྲལ་འདུག The stitching in the shirt has come apart. 3. p. of འབྲལ་.

ཁ་བྲལ་དུ་གཏོང་ (kādrɛtu dōŋ) sm. ཁ་ཕྲལ་དུ་གཏོང་.

ཁ་བྲལ་མི་རུང་བ་ (kādrɛɛ miruŋwə) inseparable, integral ¶ ལུང་པ་འདི་ནི་རང་རེའི་མེས་རྒྱལ་དང་ཁ་བྲལ་མི་རུང་བའི་ཆ་ཤས་ཤིག་རེད་ This country is an integral part of our motherland.

ཁ་བྲལ་རིང་ལུགས་ (kādrɛɛ riŋluù) separatism, secessionism (usu. refers to those who advocate separation or secession from China).

ཁ་བྲལ་རིང་ལུགས་པ་ (kādrɛɛ riŋlugbə) a separatist, a secessionist (usu. a person advocating political separation from China).

ཁ་བྲལ་བསིལ་བུ་ (kādrɛɛ) separated into parts, disintegrated, scattered; va.—གཏོང་.

ཁ་བྲི་ (kā dri) vi. to decrease.

ཁ་བློན་ (kālön) local chief/ lord.

ཁ་དབང་ (kāwaŋ) 1. wealth, fortune, property; vi.—སྟོངས་ to go bankrupt ¶ ཁོའི་ཁ་དབང་ཚང་མ་གཞུང་གིས་གཞུང་བཞེས་བཏང་སོང་ The government confiscated all his wealth. 2. the power/ authority to speak.

ཁ་དབང་ཆེན་པོ་ (kāwaŋ cēmbo) a person who is bossy/ overbearing/ autocratic or dogmatic in speech.

ཁ་དབང་དཔུང་ཤུགས་ (kāwaŋ būŋshuù) having authority and the force to back it up.

ཁ་དབུགས་ (kāwuù) mouth breath.

ཁ་དབྲག (kāraà) 1. bifurcated, forked, V-shaped ¶ ཤིང་ཁ་དབྲག་ཡོད་པ་གཅིག་དགོས་ I need a tree with bifurcating branches. 2. space between, in between ¶ ཆུ་གཉིས་ཀྱི་ཁ་དབྲག་ལ་ལུང་པ་འདི་གནས་ཡོད་པ་རེད་ This country is (situated) between two rivers. 3. a two-pronged traditional Tibetan surgical tool for extracting bullets.

ཁ་དབྲག་ཟོར་ (kāraà sər) people who always speak badly of others.

ཁ་འབབ་ (kā bəb) 1. snowfall ¶ ཁ་འབབ་ཀྱི་དུས་སུ་ At the time of snowfall. 2. vi. to fall on/ upon ¶ སྲོག་ཉེན་ཁ་འབབ་ A life threatening danger falling on sb.

ཁ་འབབ་བཞི་ (kāmbəb shi) the four rivers that flow out from the Mt. Kailash area.

ཁ་འབར་ (kā bar) 1. (with བ་) intense or strong (like a fire) ¶ དགེ་རྒན་གྱིས་གཤེ་གཤེ་ཁ་འབར་བ་ཞིག་བཏང་བྱུང་ The teacher gave me a strong scolding. 2. vi. to become rich suddenly ¶ ཚོང་པ་དེ་གློ་བུར་དུ་ཁ་འབར་བ་རེད་ The trader suddenly became wealthy.

ཁ་འབལ་པོ་ (kā bɛɛbo) a person who talks a lot, a talkative person.

ཁ་འབུག (kā buù) va. to talk.

ཁ་འབུབ་ (kābub) sm.* ཁ་སྦུབ་.

ཁ་འབུར་ (kābur) 1. a carpenter's tool. 2. letting sb. talk/ speak; va.—འཇོག to let sb. talk/ speak.

ཁ་འབུས་ (kā büù) 1. vi. to bloom, to open into a flower ¶ མེ་ཏོག་གི་ཐེའུ་ཁ་འབུས་བཞག The flower bud bloomed. 2. a flower just about to bloom, a bud. 3. child's first vocalization.

ཁ་འབེལ་པོ་ (kā bɛɛbo) 1. abundant, plentiful. 2. talkative, unable to keep things to oneself.

ཁ་འབོག (kābɔɔ̀) a feed bag that is put over an animal's mouth.

ཁ་འབོག་འབོག (kā bɔgbɔg) 1. filled to the top/ brim; va.—བྱེད་. to fill to the brim. 2. a facial shape that has a protruding mouth.

ཁ་འབྱམས་ (kā jam) vi. to get into meaningless/ idle talk.

ཁ་འབྱར་ (kɛ̄njaa) 1. waistcoat, vest, undershirt. 2. vi. to misfire. 3. vi. to have two things stick together.

ཁ་འབྱེད་ (kā ceè) 1. va. to open ¶ ཡིག་སྐོགས་ཁ་འབྱེད་ཡག་ལ་ For opening the envelope.

ཁ་འབྱེད་འཕྲུལ་ཆས་ (kājeè trũũjɛɛ̀) a machine that opens things.

ཁ་འབྲལ་ (kā drɛɛ) see. ཁ་བྲལ་.

ཁ་འབྲས་སྐྱེས་མཚར་ (kāndrɛɛ̀ gyēndzar) good-looking, attractive ¶ བུ་མོ་ཁ་འབྲས་སྐྱེས་མཚར་ལྡན་པ་ An attractive female.

ཁ་འབྲས་གཙང་མ་ (kāndrɛɛ̀ dzāŋma) sm. ཁ་འབྲས་སྐྱེས་མཚར་.

ཁ་འབྲས་མཚར་བ་ (kāndrɛɛ̀ tsārwa) sm. ཁ་འབྲས་སྐྱེས་མཚར་.

ཁ་འབྲིད་ (kā drii) 1. va. to lure/ seduce/ tempt ¶ བྱི་བ་ཟས་ཀྱིས་ཁ་བྲིད་ནས་བཟུང་བ་རེད་ (They) lured the mouse (into a trap) and caught it. 2. va. to reduce/ diminish ¶ འགྲོ་སོང་མང་དྲགས་ནས་ཁ་འབྲིད་དགོས་བྱུང་བ་རེད་ Because the expenses were too high (they) had to reduce them.

ཁ་འབྲུ་ (kā dru) sm. ཁ་ཐོག.

ཁ་རྦད་ (kābɛɛ̀) 1. boastful, conceited; va.—ཤོད་ to boast, to talk conceitedly ¶ ཁ་རྦད་ཁོ་ན་བཤད་ཀྱང་དངོས་སུ་ལག་ལེན་བྱེད་ཀྱི་མེད་པ་རེད་ Though he always boasted, in reality he cannot put what he says into practice. 2. joking, kidding; va.—ཤོད་ to joke, to kid.

ཁ་སྦིར་ (kābir) a tingling/ numbing sensation (in the mouth) ¶ སོའི་སྨན་པས་སོ་རྙིལ་ལ་ཁབ་བརྒྱབས་ནས་ཁོའི་ཁ་སྦིར་པ་རེད་ His mouth became numb after the dentist injected him in his gum.

ཁ་སྦུག་དོག་པོ་ (kəbuù dogo) sm. ཁ་ཞེད་པོ་.

ཁ་སྦུབ་ (kā bub) va. to put face down ¶ དཀར་ཡོལ་ཁ་སྦུབ་ནས་བཞག་འདུག (He) put the cup face down.

ཁ་སྦུབ་དུ་ཉལ་ (kā bubtu ñɛɛ) va. to lie on one's stomach, to lie face down, to put sth. face down ¶ ཁོ་ན་སྐབས་ཁ་སྦུབ་དུ་ཉལ་བ་རེད་ He laid face down when he was sick.

ཁ་སྦོང་ (kāboŋ) sm.* ཁབ་སྦོམ་.

ཁ་སྦྱང་ (kājaŋ) sm. ཁ་བྱང་.

ཁ་སྦྱར་ (kā jār) p. of ཁ་སྦྱོར་.

ཁ་སྦྱར་ཤེལ་དམ་ (kājar shēēdam) an ampoule.

ཁ་སྦྱོང་ (kā joŋ) 1. vi. to get used to a food or drink. 2. va. to practice verbal skills ¶ ཁྱེད་རང་ཡིག་གི་ཀློག་པའི་ཁ་སྦྱོང་དགོས་ You should practice reading (aloud).

ཁ་སྦྱོར་ (kā jɔ̄ɔ) 1. va. to stick together, to seal ¶ ཡིག་སྒྲོགས་ཁ་སྦྱར་ནས་བཏང་པ་ཡིན་ I sealed the envelope and mailed it. 2. va. to have sexual intercourse. 3. va. to kiss ¶ ཁོ་གཉིས་ཁ་སྦྱོར་གྱི་འདུག Those two are kissing. 4. va. to match make regarding marriage.

ཁ་སྦྲང་རྩི་ཁོག་སྣག་ཚ་ (kā drəŋtsi kōg nagdza) sm. ཁ་འཇམ་གདིང་ནག [Lit. mouth honey, inside ink].

ཁ་སྦྲང་རྩི་ཁོག་ཚེར་མ་ (kā drəŋtsi kōg tsērma) sm. ཁ་འཇམ་གདིང་ནག [Lit. mouth honey, inside thorns].

ཁ་སྦྲང་རྩི་ཁོག་རལ་གྲི་ (kā drəŋtsi kōg rεεtri) sm. ཁ་འཇམ་གདིང་ནག [Lit. mouth honey, inside sword].

ཁ་སྦྲང་རྩི་ལས་མངར་བ་དང་ཁོག་སོལ་བ་ལས་ནག་པ་ (kā drəŋtsilε ŋārwa daŋ kōg sōōwalε nagba) sm. ཁ་འཇམ་གདིང་ནག.

ཁ་སྦྲང་རྩི་ལས་མངར་བ་སེམས་ཚེར་མ་ལས་རྩུབ་པ་ (kā drəŋtsilε ŋārwa sēm tsērmalε dzūbə) sm. ཁ་འཇམ་གདིང་ནག [Lit. mouth sweeter than honey, mind rougher than thorns].

ཁ་སྦྲིད་ (kā drii) sm. ཁ་སྦྲིར་.

ཁ་མ་ (kāma) nib/ point of a pen.

ཁ་མ་སྐྱེངས་ (kā ma gyēŋ) vi. to do sth. to save face, to do sth. to counter embarrassment ¶ མི་དེའི་རྫུན་ཀུན་བརྗོལ་ཙང་ཁ་མ་སྐྱེངས་ལ་ཁ་རྩོད་ཤུགས་ཆེན་པོ་བརྒྱབ་པ་རེད་ Because that person's lies were exposed, he tried to save face by arguing forcefully.

ཁ་མ་འགུལ་ ཨོག་མ་འགུལ་ (kā magül ōgma gül) indicating displeasure by gesture rather than words [Lit. not moving the mouth, moving the chin].

ཁ་མ་ཆར་ (kā macar) slush (neither snow nor rain).

ཁ་མ་ཆེ་ (kā mace) do not exaggerate, do not talk big ¶ མས་བུ་ལ་ "བུ་ཆུང་ཁ་མ་ཆེ་" ཞེས་བརྗོད་ She said to her son, "Son, don't exaggerate when you speak."

ཁ་མ་ཐུག་གོང་ནས་སྣ་ཐུག (kā matūù goŋnε nāduù) fighting/ disputing before sth. occurs or in anticipation of sth. [Lit. the noses touch before the mouths meet].

ཁ་མ་དྲོ་ (kā madro) unlucky, inauspicious ¶ ཁ་མ་དྲོ་བའི་གཏམ་བཤད་ན་གཞན་གྱིས་དགའ་པོ་བྱེད་ཀྱི་མ་རེད་ If (you) speak of unlucky things others will not like it.

ཁ་མ་འདྲེས་ན་ཆམ་པ་འགོས་དོགས་མེད་ (kā madreèna cāmba göödɔg meè) if one doesn't have improper relations there will be no doubts about collusion [Lit. if the mouths aren't mixed there is no suspicion about catching a cold].

ཁ་མང་ (kāmaŋ) sm. ཁ་མང་ལྕེ་མང་.

ཁ་མང་གྱོད་ཀྱི་རྩ་བ་ བྱ་མང་བྱུར་གྱི་སྣ་འདྲེན་ (kāmaŋ gyöögi dzāwa camaŋ curgi nādren) too much talking and activities causes trouble and disputes [Lit. talking much is the root of law cases/ disputes, too many activities lead to disasters].

ཁ་མང་ལྕེ་མང་ (kāmaŋ jēmaŋ) 1. talkative (has a pejorative meaning in describing the kind of person who doesn't keep things to himself or says things without really knowing them) ¶ ཁ་མང་ལྕེ་མང་བྱས་པའི་རྐྱེན་གྱིས་སུས་ཀྱང་ཁ་འཛེག་གི་མེད་པ་རེད་ Nobody trusts (him) because he is talkative. 2. a discussion with many opinions.

ཁ་མང་གཏམ་མང་ (kāmaŋ tāmaŋ) sm. ཁ་མང་ལྕེ་མང་.

ཁ་མང་དོང་ལམ་ (kāmaŋ doŋlam) a tunnel with many entrances/ exits.

ཁ་མང་ན་དགྲ་སྡང་ (kāmaŋna dradaŋ) too much talk causes the hatred of enemies.

ཁ་མང་པོ་ (kā maŋbo) sm. ཁ་མང་ལྕེ་མང་.

ཁ་མང་རྫུན་ཤོད་ (kāmaŋ dzünshöö) sb. who talks a lot and lies.

ཁ་མང་ལ་ཚིག་གནན (kāmaŋla tsïgnaà) talkative (person) who uses cruel/ harsh words.

ཁ་མར་རྒྱག (kāmar gyaà) va. to add extra butter to tea that has already been churned.

ཁ་མར་གདད་ (kā maa dεὲ) va. to look down, to look below ¶ རིའི་སྟེང་ནས་ཁ་མར་གདད་པ་རེད་ (He) looked down from the mountain.

ཁ་མར་སློག (kāmaa lɔ̀ɔ) 1. va. to turn away from, to turn in another direction, to turn back ¶ ང་མཐོང་པ་དང་ཁོས་ཁ་མར་བསློགས་ནས་ཕྱིན་སོང་ As soon as he saw me he turned the other way and went. 2. va. to sit facing the door ¶ སྒོ་ལ་ཁ་མར་བསློགས་ནས་བསྡད་པ་རེད་ (They) sat facing the door.

ཁ་མི་ཁ་སྐྱེངས་ (kāmi kāgyeŋ) sm. ཁ་སྐྱེངས་.

ཁ་མི་གསལ་ (kā misεε) indistinct, not clear ¶ ཐོ་འདིར་ཁ་མི་གསལ་བའི་ཅ་ལག་འཚོང་ཡས་མ་རེད་ All the things not (shown) clearly on this list are not for sale.

ཁ་མིག (kā mig) eyes and mouth.

ཁ་མིག་མར་ལྟ་ (kā mig maa dā) following a bad example, learning bad things from others; va.—བྱེད་.

ཁ་མིག་ཡར་ལྟ་ (kā mïg yaa dā) following a good example, learning good things/ habits from others; va.—བྱེད་.

ཁ་མིང་སྣ་མིང་འདོགས་ (kāmiŋ nāmiŋ dɔɔ) sm. མིང་འདོགས་རྒྱག.

ཁ་མིན་རུ་ཚོགས་ (kāmin rudzɔɔ) sm. ཁ་མིན་རུབ་འཛོམས་.

ཁ་མིན་རུབ་འཛོམས་ (kāmin rubdzom) all types/ kinds of people ¶ ཚོགས་པ་དེའི་ནང་ལ་མི་ཚང་མ་ཁ་མིན་རུབ་འཛོམས་རེད་ There are all kinds of people in that meeting (good, bad, etc.).

ཁ་མུར་ (kā mur) sucking/ chewing (usu. by people without teeth); va.—བྱེད་ ¶ རྒན་མོ་དེ་ཤ་ཁ་མུར་བྱེད་བཞིན་འདུག That old woman is sucking meat (implies she has no teeth to chew).

ཁ་མེ་རུང་ (kāmeruŋ) Cameroon.

ཁ་མེད་ (kāmeè) (neg. + vb. + —) no choice but to do the verbal action ¶ ང་མ་འགྲོ་ཁ་མེད་བྱུང་ I had no choice but to go. 2. nothing to say ¶ ཤོད་དགོས་ན་ཁ་མེད་ (He) has nothing to say when there is a need to say something. 3. type of kidney disease.

ཁ་མེད་འདི་མེད་ (kāmeè dimeè) sm. ཁ་མེད་མིག་མེད་.

ཁ་མེད་སྣ་མེད་ (kāmeè nāmeè) sm. ཁ་མེད་མིག་མེད་.

ཁ་མེད་མིག་མེད་ (kāmeè mïgmeè) very many or much, a lot ¶ ཁོ་ཚོས་སྡུག་པོ་ཁ་མེད་མིག་མེད་བཏང་ཙང་མ་བྲོས་ཁ་མེད་བྱུང་བ་རེད་ Because they were mistreated a lot (they) had no choice but to flee.

ཁ་མེད་དམིགས་མེད་ (kāmeè mïgmeè) sm. ཁ་མེད་མིག་མེད་.

ཁ་མོ་ (kāmo) bitter.

ཁ་མོས་ཞེ་མོས་ (kāmöö shemöö) totally/ completely in agreement ¶ ཁོང་གི་དགོངས་འཆར་དེར་ཚང་མ་ཁ་མོས་ཞེ་མོས་བྱུང་ Everyone was in complete agreement with his suggestions. [Lit. mouth agrees, inside agrees].

ཁ་དམར་ (kāmar) 1. astrological prophecy/ prediction; va.—འདོགས་ to prognosticate, to make predictions. 2. arc. guarantor.

ཁ་དམར་ནང་གི་ཚིག་དམར་རེད་ པ་མགར་ལག་གི་ལྕགས་དམར་རེད་ (kāmar naŋgi tsïgmar reè pā gar laggi jāàmar reè) one should keep one's word [Lit. red words come from a red mouth, hot iron comes from a blacksmith's hand].

ཁ་དམར་པ་ (kāmara) 1. baby, infant. 2. a guarantor.

ཁ་སྨ་ལྷོག་པ་ (kā mā lhōgba) an ulcerous disease of the mouth (for animals).

ཁ་སྨད་ (kāmεὲ) insulting speech/ talk; va.—གཏོང་.

ཁ་སྨང་ (kā māŋ) arc. va. to talk/ speak garrulously.

ཁ་སླས་ (kā mɛ̄ɛ̀) speaking ill of people; vi.—ཟུག to be spoken ill of; va.—གཏོང་ to speak ill of ❘ཁོང་ལ་མི་གཞན་གྱིས་ཁ་སླས་གཏོང་གི་ཡོད་པ་རེད་ Other people are speaking ill of him. ❘ཁྱེད་རང་གི་སྐད་ཆ་འདི་ཁ་སླས་ཟུག་རྒྱུའི་སྐད་ཆ་ཞིག་རེད་ Your comment is one that will have people talking ill of you.

ཁ་སླས་གླེང་གཞི་ (kāmɛɛ̀ lēŋshi) speaking ill of and causing a dispute/ quarrel.

ཁ་ཙ་ར་ (kādzara) a person of mixed Nepalese and Tibetan parentage.

ཁ་ཙང་ (kādzaŋ) the day before.

ཁ་ཙམ་ (kādzam) 1. in word only (i.e., not in deed) ❘ཁ་ཙམ་གྱི་ཞབས་འདེགས་ Lip service. 2. as wide as an open mouth ❘མིག་ཁ་ཙམ་གདངས་ (He) opened his eyes as wide as an open mouth.

ཁ་ཙམ་མིན་པ་ (kādzam mi̲mbə) really, truly, not just with words ❘ཁོས་ནད་པ་ཚོར་ཁ་ཙམ་མིན་པའི་ལྟ་སྐྱོང་བྱས་པ་རེད་ He really looked after the sick.

ཁ་ཙམ་ཚིག་ཙམ་ (kādzam tsi̅gdzam) sm. ཁ་ཙམ་, 1.

ཁ་ཙོག་འཇོག (kādzog jɔ̀ɔ̀) va. to let/ leave eat or enjoy sth. ❘སེམས་ཅན་རྣམས་ཞིང་ཁའི་ནང་ལ་ཁ་ཙོག་བཞག (They) let the animals eat in the fields.

ཁ་གཙག (kā dzāà) va. to press/ extract oil from seeds.

ཁ་གཙང་མིན་ (kādzaŋmin) shung. sick (animal).

ཁ་གཙོ་ (kādzo) acting as the spokesman, being the main speaker; va.—བྱེད་ ❘ཚོགས་འདུ་ཐོག་ལ་ཁ་གཙོ་ཤོད་མཁན་ཁོང་རེད་ He is the main speaker at the conference.

ཁ་བཙན་པོ་ (kā dzɛ̄mbo) 1. a person who speaks in a harsh manner. 2. a person who is secretive, sb. who doesn't say much. 3. a tight-fitting lid for a jar or bottle.

ཁ་བཙན་ཞི་འཇམ་ (kādzɛ̄n shenjam) verbally aggressive but mild/ gentle internally.

ཁ་བཙུམས་ (kā dzūm) p. of ཁ་འཛུམ་; 1.

ཁ་བཙོག་པ་ (kā dzōgba) foulmouthed.

ཁ་རྩ་ (kādza) expenses; va.—གཏོང་ to spend money on expenses.

ཁ་རྩང་ (kādzaŋ) sm. ཁ་སང་.

ཁ་རྩའི་ཟས་དང་ལག་རྩའི་དངུལ་ (kādzɛɛ sɛ̄ɛtaŋ lə̲gdzii ŋǖǖ) sth. that is depleted or consumed fast.

ཁ་རྩ་ར་འཁྲིལ་པོ་ (kādzar tri̅ibo) sb. who is obedient, sb. who listens to what he/ she is told.

ཁ་རྩལ་ (kādzɛɛ) verbally eloquent.

ཁ་རྩལ་གདོང་ནག (kādzɛɛ di̅ŋnaà) verbally eloquent but inwardly evil/ nasty/ bad.

ཁ་རྩིས་ (kədzii) oral calculation; va.—རྒྱག.

ཁ་རྩུབ་ཁོག་ཡག (kādzub kōgyag) one who uses harsh words but is kind/ good at heart.

ཁ་རྩུབ་པོ་ (kā dzūbbu) one who uses coarse/ harsh language; va.—བྱེད་ ❘ཁ་རྩུབ་པོ་བྱས་ནས་སྐད་ཆ་བཤད་ན་ If you speak harshly.

ཁ་རྩེད་ (kādzeè) joking verbally; va.—རྩེ་.

ཁ་རྩོད་ (kādzöö) argument, dispute, debate, arguing, disputing, quarreling, debating; va.—བྱེད་; —རྒྱག to debate/ dispute/ quarrel/ argue; vi.—ཤོར་ to get or fall into an argument/ dispute/ quarrel/ debate.

ཁ་རྩོད་མགོ་བོ་ཞག་ཞག་རྒྱག (kādzöö g̲owo sh̲agshaà gy̲aà) va. to dispute/ argue/ quarrel strongly [Lit. disputing/ arguing until one's head is broken].

ཁ་རྩོད་སྣ་རྩོད་ (kādzöö nādzöö) sm. ཁ་རྩོད་ཚིག་རྩོད་.

ཁ་རྩོད་ཚིག་རྩོད་ (kādzöö tsi̅gdzöö) quarreling, arguing, squabbling, bickering ❘ཁོ་གཉིས་གྲོགས་པོ་ཡིན་ན་ཡང་ཁ་རྩོད་ཚིག་རྩོད་ཤོར་བ་རེད་ Although they are friends, they quarreled.

ཁ་ཚ་ (kātsa) sm. ཁ་ཚ་བ་.

ཁ་ཚ་ཁོག་འཇམ་ (kātsa kōgjam) a person who is sharp tongued but not malicious inside.

ཁ་ཚ་དགོས་མཁོ་ (kātsa g̲öökо) essential needs and wants ❘འགྲུལ་རྒྱག་དུས་ཁ་ཚ་དགོས་མཁོ་ཚང་མ་འཁྱེར་དགོས་ When traveling one should take all the essentials.

ཁ་ཚ་དགོས་གལ་ (kātsa g̲öögɛɛ) pressing, vital, urgent ❘ཁ་ཚ་དགོས་གལ་གྱི་དོན་གནད་ A pressing issue.

ཁ་ཚ་དགོས་གདུགས་ (kātsa g̲ööduù) sm. ཁ་ཚ་དགོས་གལ་.

ཁ་ཚ་གདོང་ནག (kātsa di̅ŋnaà) harsh in speech and evil inside; va.—བྱེད་.

ཁ་ཚ་དུས་གདུགས་ (kātsa g̲ööduù) sm. ཁ་ཚ་དགོས་མཁོ་.

ཁ་ཚ་པོ་ (kā tsābo) 1. hot (spicy) ❘ཚལ་འདི་ཁ་ཚ་པོ་འདུག This vegetable dish is hot (spicy). 2. sharp-tongued ❘མི་དེ་ཁ་ཚ་པོ་འདུག That man is sharp-tongued. 3. vital, essential.

ཁ་ཚ་བ་ (kā tsāwa) 1. urgent, acute ❘ཁ་ཚ་བའི་ལས་འགན་ནི་ As for the urgent tasks. ❘དགོས་གནད་ཁ་ཚ་བ་ An urgent need. 2. hot (spicy).

ཁ་ཚ་རྨིག་ཚ་ (kātsa mi̅gtsə) hoof-and-mouth disease.

ཁ་ཚ་ར་ (kādzara) sm. ཁ་ཙ་ར་.

ཁ་ཚག (kātsag) chipped (of bowls, cups).

ཁ་ཚང་ (kātsaŋ) 1. making up a shortage/ deficit; va.—བྱེད. 2. cattle with a full set of adult teeth).

ཁ་ཚད་ (kātsɛɛ̀) 1. caliber (of a gun). 2. sm. ཁ་འཁོར་གྱི་ཚད་. 3. va. to compete in a debate. 4. va.—ལྟ་ to taste to see if the saltiness is right ❘ཇ་ཚྭ་འགྲིག་ས་ཡོད་མེད་ཁ་ཚད་བལྟས་པ་ཡིན་ (I) I tasted to see if the saltiness of the tea was all right.

ཁ་ཚན་ (kātsɛn) 1. amount of snowfall. 2. ferociousness (of a dog).

ཁ་ཚན་ཆེན་པོ་ (kātsɛn cēmbo) sm. ཁ་ཤུགས་ཆེན་པོ་.

ཁ་ཚབ་ (kātsəb) a person speaking on behalf of another, a spokesman; va.—བྱེད་ to speak on behalf of another.

ཁ་ཚར་ (kātsaa) 1. a fringe, a tassel. 2. adding sth. to make it complete; va.—འདེབས་ to add sth. to make complete.

ཁ་ཚས་གདོང་གནག (kātseɛ̀di̅ŋnaà) duplicitous, outwardly smiling but inwardly hostile.

ཁ་ཚིག (kā tsi̅i) 1. talk. 2. vi. to burn one's mouth (from eating sth. hot).

ཁ་ཚིག་གྲུགས་ལོང་མེད་པ་ (kātsig dr̲agloŋ m̲eèba) sm. ཁ་ཚིག་འགྲིལ་ལོང་མེད་པར་.

ཁ་ཚིག་འགྲིལ་ལོང་མེད་པ་ (kātsig dr̲eloŋ m̲eèba) breaking out in an argument the moment talking starts ❘ཁོ་གཉིས་ཁ་ཚིག་འགྲིལ་ལོང་མེད་པར་ཁ་རྩོད་ཤོར་སོང་ These two had an argument the moment they started talking.

ཁ་ཚིག་ལག་བརྡ་ (kādzig l̲agda) waving one's hands about when quarrelling.

ཁ་ཚུགས་པོ་ (kā tsūgbu) a dependable person who can keep secrets; va.—བྱེད་ to act in a reliable/ dependable way with regard to speech.

ཁ་ཚུབ་ (kātsub) a covering/ flap used over a tent smoke hole when it rains or snows; va.—རྒྱག.

ཁ་ཚུབ་དབྱུག་པ་ (kādzub yūgba) the pole used to open and close the tent smoke hole.

ཁ་ཚུམས་ (kā tsūm) imp. of ཁ་བཙུམ་.

ཁ་ཚུར་སྐོར་ (kā tsūū gɔ̄ɔ) va. to turn around (in the opposite direction one is going).

ཁ་ཚུར་བསྐོར་ (kā tsūū gɔ̄ɔ) sm. ཁ་ཚུར་སྐོར་.

ཁ་ཚུར་གཏད་ (kā tsūū dɛ̄ɛ) va. to turn toward (physically and figuratively) ❘ཁོས་རང་ཉིད་ཀྱི་རྒྱལ་ཁབ་ལ་ཁ་ཚུར་གཏད་ནས་ལོག་ཡོང་བ་རེད་ He turned towards his own country and returned.

ཁ་ཚུར་ཕྱོགས་ (kā tsūū cɔ̄ɔ) sm. ཁ་ཚུར་གཏད་.

ཁ་ཚེ་ཚེ་ (kā tsēdze) smile, smiling; va.—བྱེད་.

ཁ་ཚེགས་ (kā tsēdze) sm. ཁ་དྲང་.

ཁ་ཚེར་ཚེར་ (kā tsērtser) sm. ཁ་ཚེ་ཚེ་.

ཁ་ཚོགས་ (kā tsɔ̄ɔ) va. to keep sth. secret ❘གནད་དོན་འདི་ཁ་ཚོགས་དཀའ་པོ་རེད་ It is difficult to keep this matter a secret.

ཁ་ཚོགས་པོ་ (kā tsɔ̄gbo) sb. who keeps secrets well.

ཁ་ཚོང་ (kātsoŋ) a person who shops around but doesn't buy anything; va.—རྒྱག.

ཁ་རྩོད་ (kā dzöö) 1. testing what sb. knows/ thinks; va.—ལེན་. 2. speaking, talking.

ཁ་རྩོད་མཐོ་བ་ (kādzöö tōwa) talking forcefully.

ཁ་ཚོད་ཟིན་པོ་ (kādzöö simbo) sm. ཁ་རྒྱགས་པོ་.

ཁ་ཚོན་ (kādzön) deciding sth. (and saying it); va.—གཅོད་ to decide, to come to conclusion. ¶ བཟོ་པ་ཚོས་ཉིན་དེ་རང་ལ་ལས་མཚམས་འཇོག་རྒྱུ་ཡིན་ཟེར་ཁ་ཚོན་བཅད་པ་རེད་ The workers decided and said they will go on strike that same day. ¶ ཁོ་ཀུན་མ་མ་ཡིན་པ་ངས་ཁ་ཚོན་གཅོད་ཐུབ་ཀྱི་རེད་ I can say definitely that he is not a thief.

ཁ་ཚོན་པ་ (kādzõmba) a person who makes decisions.

ཁ་ཚོས་རྒྱག (kādzöö gyaà) va. to paint in color.

ཁ་མཚམས་ (kāndzam) 1. mouth of a pouch ¶ ཁ་མཚམས་སུ་རྟགས་ཐེལ་བརྒྱབ་སྟེ་ Putting a seal on the mouth of the pouch. 2. a period/ time/ era; va.—འབྱེད་ to separate into periods/ times.

ཁ་མཚར་ཀུ་རེ་ (kātsar gūre) joking, being humorous, pulling sb.'s leg.

ཁ་མཚར་གྱི་གཏམ་ (kātsargi dām) interesting/ humorous stories.

ཁ་མཛུལ་ (kādzul) 1. lips. 2. cheeks.

ཁ་འཚང་ (kā tsāŋ) vi. to choke (on food or drink) ¶ ཁ་ལག་ཟ་རྒྱུ་མགྱོགས་དྲགས་ན་ཁ་འཚང་གི་རེད་ If you eat too fast you will choke. 2. va. to interrupt or impose oneself in a conversation. ¶ མི་གཞན་དག་སྐད་ཆ་ཤོད་སྐབས་ཁ་འཚང་རྒྱུ་མེད་ (One) shouldn't interrupt when sb. is talking.

ཁ་འཚུབ་ (kāndzub) a heavy snowfall, a snowstorm; vi.—རྒྱག ¶ མདང་དགོང་མཚན་གང་ཁ་འཚུབ་བརྒྱབ་སོང་ It snowed heavily all last night.

ཁ་འཚོགས་ (kā tsɔ̀ɔ) 1. va. to gather/ assemble (for discussion) ¶ གནད་དོན་དེ་མི་མང་པོ་ཁ་འཚོགས་ནས་ཐག་བཅད་པ་རེད་ Concerning this issue, many people got together and settled it.

ཁ་ཛར་ (kādzar) 1. fraction or remainder (in math). 2. remnant, odds and ends. 3. sm. ཁ་ཕྲང་.

ཁ་འཛིང་ (kōndziŋ) verbal fighting; va.—རྒྱག; vi.—ཤོར་ ¶ ཁོ་གཉིས་ཁ་འཛིང་རྒྱག་གི་ཡོད་པ་རེད་ The two of them are fighting verbally.

ཁ་འཛིང་ལག་འགྱོགས་ (kōndziŋ laŋgyɔ̀ɔ) sm. ཁ་འཛིང་ལག་གདུག.

ཁ་འཛིང་ལག་གདུག (kōndziŋ lagduù) va.—བྱེད་ to argue verbally and fight physically.

ཁ་འཛིང་ལག་འཛིང་ (kōndziŋ lɔŋdziŋ) sm. ཁ་འཛིང་ལག་གདུག.

ཁ་འཛིན་ (kōndzin) 1. the right of ownership ¶ གཞུང་ནས་གཞིས་ཀ་འདིའི་ཁ་འཛིན་དགོན་པར་གསོལ་རས་གནང་བ་རེད་ The government gave the right of ownership of the estate to the monastery. 2. va.—བྱེད་ to look after ¶ མི་ཚང་གི་པ་ཕས་ཁྱིམ་གྱི་ཁ་འཛིན་བྱེད་ཀྱི་འདུག The father of the house looks after the family. 3. sm. ཕྱོད་ཕྱོགས་. 4. va.—བྱེད་ to side with ¶ ཁོང་ཚོས་རང་གི་མི་རིགས་ཀྱི་ཁ་འཛིན་བྱས་པ་རེད་ They sided with their ethnic group.

ཁ་འཛིན་གཏན་འཇགས་ (kōndzin dɛ̄njaà permanent right of ownership.

ཁ་འཛིན་རོགས་དན་ (kōndzin rɔgdɛn) giving aid/ help/ assistance; va.—བྱེད་ ¶ མི་སེར་ཉམ་ཐག་རྣམས་ལ་ཚོགས་པ་དེས་ཁ་འཛིན་རོགས་དན་གང་ཐུབ་བྱེད་ཀྱི་འདུག That association is giving as much help as possible to the poor.

ཁ་འཛུམ་ (kā dzum) 1. va. to keep one's mouth shut, to keep quiet, to shut up ¶ མི་རྒན་པ་རྣམས་སྐད་ཆ་ཤོད་དུས་ཕྲུ་གུ་ཁྱེད་རྣམས་ཁ་འཛུམ་མི་ཐུབ་པ་གང་ཡིན་ When elders talk, why aren't you kids able to shut up. 2. (with negatives) vi. to have a smile break out ¶ ཁོ་དགའ་ཐག་ཆོད་དེ་ཁ་ཡང་འཛུམ་མི་ཐུབ་པ་ཆགས་པ་རེད་ He was extremely happy and couldn't keep a smile from breaking out on his face.

ཁ་འཛེམ་ (kā dzem) va. to follow a diet/ food regimen (usu. for health reasons) ¶ ཨེམ་ཆིས་ནད་པར་ཁ་འཛེམ་དགོས་ཀྱི་རེད་ལབ་འདུག The doctor told the patient to maintain a diet. ¶ ཁ་མ་འཛེམ་ཙང་ན་ཚ་སྡུག་ཏུ་ཕྱིན་པ་རེད་ Because (he) did not stick to the prescribed diet his illness worsened.

ཁ་འཛོམས་ (kā dzom) meeting, gathering; va. ཁ་འཛོམས་; —བྱེད་.

ཁ་འཛོལ་ (kāndzöö) a verbal mistake; vi.—ཤོར་ to make a verbal mistake.

ཁ་ཇིག་ངོ་ཇིག (kādzig ŋodzig) powerful or fierceful/ intimidating in look and speech, angry in expression and speech; va.—སྟོན་.

ཁ་རྫུན་ (kādzün) lying.

ཁ་རྫུན་ལག་བརྐུས་ (kādzün laggüù) lying and cheating/ stealing.

ཁ་རྫོགས་རྒྱུ་མེད་པ་ (kā dzɔ̀ɔgyu meèba) talkative, loquacious.

ཁ་བརྫེས་ (kā dzɛɛ̀) va. to wind up, to twist an edge.

ཁ་ཝ་ (kāwa) name of an ethnic minority in southwest Yunnan.

ཁ་ཝ་རིགས་ (kāwarig) sm. ཁ་ཝ་.

ཁ་ཝང་ (kāwaŋ) a musical instrument.

ཁ་ཞག (kāshag) 1. floating oil/ grease. 2. vi. to split or crack open ¶ བྲག་ཆེན་པོ་དེ་ཁ་བཞག་པ་རེད་ The big rock cracked open.

ཁ་ཞན་རྒྱབ་ཆད་ (kāshɛn gyəbjɛɛ̀) poor with no one to help/ support/ back one up.

ཁ་ཞན་ཉམ་ཆུང་ (kāshɛn ñəmjuŋ) poor with no supporters/ helpers ¶ མི་སེར་རྣམས་འཚོ་བ་ཁ་ཞན་བརྒྱབ་ཆད་ཀྱིས་རྒྱུན་པས་གཞན་ཡུལ་དུ་མི་སྤོར་ཀ་མེད་བྱུང་བ་རེད་ Because the people were poor and had no backers, they had no choice but to move to another area.

ཁ་ཞན་པ་ (kāshemba) 1. having no authority ¶ སྔར་དུས་སུ་ཁྱིམ་ཚང་ནང་བུད་མེད་རྣམས་ཁ་ཞན་པས་གཞན་གྱིས་བརྩི་བཀུར་བྱེད་ཀྱི་མེད་ In the past, because women had no authority, others did not respect them highly. 2. sm. ཁ་ཞན་རྒྱབ་ཆད་.

ཁ་ཞལ་ (kāshɛɛ) plastered (for walls, etc), paved (for roads).

ཁ་ཤིག (kā shig) vi. to come unfastened/ open.

ཁ་ཤུགས་ (kāshug) sm. ཁ་རྟོག.

ཁ་ཤུན་ (kāshun) oil lamp (cup).

ཁ་ཤེ་ (kāshe) speech and mind.

ཁ་ཤེ་གོ་ལྡོག (kāshe godɔ̀ɔ) sm. ཁ་ཤེ་རྒྱབ་འགལ་.

ཁ་ཤེ་གོ་ལོག (kāshe golɔ̀ɔ) sm. ཁ་ཤེ་རྒྱབ་འགལ་.

ཁ་ཤེ་རྒྱབ་འགལ་ (kāshe gyəbgɛɛ) saying one thing but thinking/ feeling differently.

ཁ་ཤེ་གཉིས་ (kāshe ñìì) speaking differently from what one feels/ thinks, being insincere.

ཁ་ཤེ་གཉིས་མེད་ (kāshe ñììmeè) sincere, forthright, saying what one feels/ thinks ¶ ཁོ་ནི་དམངས་ཀྱི་དོན་དུ་ཁ་ཤེ་གཉིས་མེད་ཀྱི་ལས་ཀ་བྱེད་མཁན་ཞིག་རེད་ He is sb. who is sincerely working for the well-being of the people.

ཁ་ཤེ་མཐུན་པ་ (kāshe tũmbə) sm. ཁ་ཤེ་གཉིས་མེད་.

ཁ་ཤེ་མི་གཅིག (kāshe mijig) sm. ཁ་ཤེ་རྒྱབ་འགལ་.

ཁ་ཤེ་མི་མཚུངས་པ་ (kāshe midzuŋwə) to say one thing but think/ feel another ¶ མི་དེ་ཁ་ཤེ་མི་མཚུངས་པའི་མི་ཞིག་ཡིན་ཙང་ཚང་མས་ཆ་འཇོག་གི་མེད་པ་རེད་ Because he says one thing but really thinks something else, no one relies on him.

ཁ་ཤེ་མེད་པ་ (kāshe meèba) sm. ཁ་ཤེ་གཉིས་མེད་.

ཁ་ཤེ་མཚུངས་པ་ (kāshe tsūŋbə) sm. ཁ་ཤེ་གཉིས་མེད་.

ཁ་ཤེང་ (kāsheŋ) width, breadth (e.g., of a road).

ཁ་ཤེན་ (kāshen) 1. sb. who likes idle talk. 2. sb. who falsely gives the appearance of liking sb.

ཁ་གཤུང་ (kāshuŋ) diameter.

ཁ་གཤེས་ཉིན་ཀ་ (kāsheè ñinga) the day before yesterday.

ཁ་གཤོན་པ་ (kā shõmba) sm. ཁ་ཆུང་བ་.

ཁ་ཟག (kāsaà) pipe (for smoking).

ཁ་ཟས་ (kāsɛɛ̀) 1. foodstuffs, food. 2. fried dough.

ཁ་ཟུག་ལོག (kāsug lɔ̀ɔ) sm. ཁ་དག་.

ཁ་ཟུངས་ (kāsuŋ) 1. the rope used in a trap/ snare. 2. sm. ཁ་རྩམས་.

ཁ་ཟུམ་ (kā sum) vi. to be/ get closed ¶ རྨ་ཁ་ཟུམ་བཞག The cut has closed (healed).

ཁ་ཟུམ་གློག་ལམ་ (kāsum lõglam) closed circuit (television, etc.).

ཁ་ཟུམ་མེ་ཏོག་དུ་ཞི་རྡུལ་རུམ་པ་ (kāsum medogtu sedüü rumbə) cleistogamy.

ཁ་ཟུར་ (kāsur) 1. corner of the mouth. 2. even a word ¶ གནད་དོན་དེའི་སྐོར་ཁ་ཟུར་ཙམ་ཡང་བཤད་མ་སོང་ (He) did not say even a word regarding this matter.

ཁ་ཟེར་ (kā ser) va. to speak ill of others.

ཁ་ཟླ་ (kānda) 1. assisting sb. in an argument/ dispute; va.—བྱེད་ ¶ ཁྲིམས་རྩོད་པས་རྩོད་གཞི་དེའི་ནང་བུད་མེད་དེའི་ཁ་ཟླ་བྱས་སོང་ The lawyer assisted the woman in the law case. 2. keeping sb. company by entertaining/ chatting with them ¶ ངས་མགྲོན་པོ་ཚོའི་ཁ་ཟླ་བྱས་པ་ཡིན་ I kept the guests entertained by chatting with them.

ཁ་གཟན་པོ་ (kā sembo) sm. ཁ་གཟེར་པོ་.

ཁ་གཟར་ (kāsar) spoon.

ཁ་གཟི་ (kəsi) a rake.

ཁ་གཟེ་ (kāse) sm. ཁ་གཟི་.

ཁ་གཟེད་ (kā seè) 1. va. to hold open the mouth (of a bag, etc.) ¶ རས་ཁུག་གི་ཁ་གཟེད་རོགས་ (Please) hold the bag open. 2. cuspidor.

ཁ་གཟེར་ (kāser) sm. ཁ་གཟེར་པོ་.

ཁ་གཟེར་པོ་ (kā serbo) telling it like it is, not mincing words, frank and straightforward in speech ¶ མི་འདི་སྐད་ཆ་ཤོད་དུས་ཁ་གཟེར་པོ་ཞིག་འདུག This man is frank and does not mince words.

ཁ་བཟང་ཚིག་བཟང་ (kāsaŋ tsīgsaŋ) sincere talk/ advice.

ཁ་བཟས་འགབ་བདང་ (kāsεὲ gəbdaŋ) ungrateful; va.—བྱེད་ ¶ སྲིད་གཞུང་ནས་ཁོ་ལ་བཀའ་དྲིན་ཆེན་པོ་གནང་བ་དེ་ཁ་བཟས་འགབ་བདང་བྱས་ནས་ངོ་ལོག་བརྒྱབ་པ་རེད་ The government was kind to him but he was ungrateful and rebelled.

ཁ་བཟས་ལྕེ་ཐིམ་ (kāsεὲ jētim) being bound to reciprocate to sb. as a result of taking or using sth. of his [Lit. eaten by the mouth, sunk into the tongue].

ཁ་བཟོ་སྐྱིན་འདྲས་ (kāpso gyīndrεὲ) sm. ཁ་བཟོ་སྐྱེ་འདྲས་.

ཁ་བཟོ་སྐྱེ་འདྲས་ (kāpso gyēndrεὲ) body and facial looks ¶ བུ་མོ་འདི་ཁ་བཟོ་སྐྱེ་འདྲས་བཟང་པོ་འདུག This girl's body and face are beautiful.

ཁ་བཟོ་དོད་པོ་ (kāpso tööbo) sm. ཁ་བཟོ་འཕེར་པོ་.

ཁ་བཟོ་འཕེར་པོ་ (kāpso pērbo) eloquent, verbal ¶ མི་འདི་ཁ་བཟོ་འཕེར་པོ་ཞིག་འདུག This man is an eloquent speaker.

ཁ་བཟོ་ལེགས་པོ་ (kāpso legbo) beautiful, handsome.

ཁ་འོ་རྒྱལ་རྒྱལ་ (kā wo gyεεgyεε) talking a great deal (until one is tired).

ཁ་འོ་མ་ཁོག་ཚེར་མ་ (kā oma kōg dzērma) sm. ཁ་འཇམ་གཉིང་གནག [Lit. mouth milk, inside thorn].

ཁ་འོ་མ་ལས་དཀར་བ་ཁོག་ཚེར་མ་ལས་རྩུབ་པ་ (kā oma lεὲ gārwa kōg tsērmalε dzūbbə) sm. ཁ་འཇམ་གཉིང་གནག [Lit. mouth whiter than milk, inside rougher than thorns].

ཁ་འོ་མ་ལས་འཇམ་པ་ཁོག་ཚེར་མ་ལས་རྩུབ་པ་ (kā oma lεὲ jamba kōg tsērmalε dzūbbə) sm. ཁ་འཇམ་གཉིང་གནག [Lit. mouth softer than milk, inside rougher than thorns].

ཁ་འོག (kā ɔɔ) 1. under, below, beneath, the bottom ¶ སྔོན་མ་ཨ་རི་དབྱིན་ཇིའི་ཁ་འོག་རེད་འདུག In the past the Americans were under the British. 2. before one's eyes ¶ དེབ་འདི་ཁྱོད་ཀྱི་ཁ་འོག་དེ་གར་འདུག The book is right before your eyes.

ཁ་འོག་ཙམ་ (kāwɔgdzam) a cup or bowl that is filled to just under/ below the rim.

ཁ་ཡ་ (kāya) 1. attentiveness, attention (to another); va.—བྱེད་ to pay attention to, to be attentive to ¶ ཁོས་འདི་འདྲ་བྱས་ན་ཁ་ཡ་བྱེད་རྒྱུ་མི་འདུག If he acts like this, (you) shouldn't pay attention (to him). 2. a match, partner, one of a pair ¶ ལྷམ་འདིའི་ཁ་ཡ་བརླག་པ་རེད་ The other shoe to the pair is lost. 3. keeping sb. company; va.—བྱེད་ ¶ ནད་པ་འདི་ལ་ཁ་ཡ་བྱེད་མཁན་རྟག་ཏུ་ཡོད་རེད་ There is always sb. keeping this sick person company. 4. a response; va.—བྱེད་ ¶ ཁོས་སྐད་ཆ་དྲིས་ཀྱང་ཁ་ཡ་བྱས་མ་སོང་ He questioned (him/ her), but there was no response. 5. —ཚོག to be able to compete/ challenge.

ཁ་ཡ་རྒྱ་ཡ་ (kāya gyāya) lifelong partner/ spouse.

ཁ་ཡ་ངོ་ཡ་ (kāya ŋoya) acting as a host or a liaison person, looking after guests; va.—བྱེད་ ¶ འགྲུལ་པར་ཁ་ཡ་ངོ་ཡ་བྱས་པ་རེད་ (They) hosted the travelers.

ཁ་ཡ་ངོས་ལེན་ (kāya ŋölen) sm. ཁ་ཡ་ངོ་ཡ.

ཁ་ཡ་བྱེད་ (kāya ceè) see ཁ་ཡ་.

ཁ་ཡ་བྱེད་ལ་མི་བྱེད་ (kāya cela miceè) va. to attend or look after sb. halfheartedly.

ཁ་ཡ་མ་ལྡོགས་ (kāya mājog) not having time to pay attention to sth. or sb. ¶ ཁོ་ལས་ཀ་མང་དྲགས་ནས་སྐྱ་མགྲོན་ལ་ཁ་ཡ་མ་ལྡོགས་པ་རེད་ He was unable to pay attention to his guests because he had too much work.

ཁ་ཡག (kāyaà) speaking well/ nicely; va.—བྱེད་.

ཁ་ཡག་ངོ་དགའ་ (kāyaà ŋoyaà) sm. ཁ་ཡག་ངོ་བསྟོད་.

ཁ་ཡག་ངོ་བསྟོད་ (kāyaà ŋodöö) flattery; va.—བྱེད་.

ཁ་ཡག་ཚིག་ཡག (kāyaà tsīgyaà) auspicious/ pleasant/ nice speech or talk.

ཁ་ཡང་ (kāyaŋ) sm. ཁ་ཡང་པོ་.

ཁ་ཡང་པོ་ (kā yaŋbo) 1. not introverted or shy about speaking or asking questions; va.—བྱེད་. 2. talkative, loose-lipped; va.—བྱེད་ ¶ འགོ་ཁྲིད་དེ་ཁ་ཡང་པོ་ཡིན་ཙང་གསང་བ་ཚང་མ་གཞན་ལ་བཤད་པ་རེད་ Because the leader was talkative, he told all the secrets to others.

ཁ་ཡང་སྤྱོད་ཡང་ (kāyaŋ jōyaŋ) easygoing, carefree, undisciplined; va.—བྱེད ¶ ཁ་ཡང་སྤྱོད་ཡང་བྱེད་མཁན་ལ་ཡིད་མ་ཆེས་ Don't trust those who are undisciplined. [Lit. light mouth, light behavior].

ཁ་ཡན་ (kā yen) 1. vi. to have outsiders learn of an inner discussion or internal matter, to let internal matters become known to outsiders. 2. sm. ཁ་ཐོར་.

ཁ་ཡབ་ཡབ་ (kā yəbyəb) not doing carefully or in detail, doing sth. in a slipshod manner ¶ དེ་རིང་མོས་གད་ཕྱིས་ཁ་ཡབ་ཡབ་ཅིག་བྱས་འདུག Today she did a slipshod job sweeping.

ཁ་ཡར་ (kāyaa) 1. straying away ¶ ལུག་ཅིག་ཁྱུ་ནས་ཁ་ཡར་བ་རེད་ A sheep strayed away from the flock. 2. scattered, dispersed ¶ གྲོང་ཚོ་ཁ་ཡར་འགའ་ཤས་ཡོད་པ་རེད་ There are a few scattered villages. 3. sm. འགའ་ཤས་.

ཁ་ཡར་གདང་ (kā yar dεὲ) va. to look upward ¶ ཁ་ཡར་གདང་ནས་རི་ཆེན་པོ་དེ་འཛེགས་པ་རེད་ He looked upward and climbed the big mountain.

ཁ་ཡིག (kəyiì) address, label; va.—རྒྱག to address, to label.

ཁ་ཡིག་རང་འགྲིགས་ (kəyiì randrig) an envelope with an address on it, a self-addressed envelope.

ཁ་ཡུ་ (kā yu) sm. ཁུ་ཡུ་.

ཁ་ཡུག (kəyuù) a signal or sign made by moving the lips or mouth; va.—རྒྱག.

ཁ་ཡེལ་ (kāyel) uncovered (usu. for kettles or pots).

ཁ་ཡོག (kāyog) sm. ཁ་གཡོགས་.

ཁ་ཡོད་ལག་སྡོང་ (kāyog lagdoŋ) sm. ཁ་ཡོད་ལག་མེད་.

ཁ་ཡོད་ལག་མེད་ (kāyöö lagmeè) 1. talking big but having nothing to show for it (all talk no action). 2. saying one has sth. when one really does not.

ཁ་ཡོད་ལག་ཡོད་ (kāyöö lagyöö) doing or following through in practice with what one says, talk in conformity with reality.

ཁ་ཡོད་སེམས་མེད་ (kāyöö sēmmeè) sm. ཁ་བཙན་ཞེ་འཇམ་.

ཁ་ཡོན་ (kāyön) crooked mouth.

ཁ་ཡོལ་ (kāyöl) mouth mask.

ཁ་གཡང་སྒྲོག (kāyaŋ drɔɔ) sm. ཁ་གཡང་འབོད་.

ཁ་གཡང་འབོད་ (kāyaŋ böö) 1. va. to say auspicious words at a wedding party. 2. va. to shout slogans.

ཁ་གཡའ་ (kā yāā) vi. to itch.

ཁ་གཡར་ (kā yāā) va. to use as a pretext/ excuse ། མི་དམངས་བཅིངས་འགྲོལ་གཏོང་རྒྱུར་ཁ་གཡར་ནས་བཙན་འཛུལ་བྱས་པ་རེད་ On the pretext of liberating the people, (they) invaded.

ཁ་གཡར་གཡར་ (kā yāāyaa) sm. ཁ་གཡར་.

ཁ་གཡར་ས་ (kā yāāsa) 1. unjustly accused or blamed ། རང་གིས་ལས་ཀ་དྲང་པོ་བྱས་ན་རྗེས་སུ་ཁ་གཡར་ས་ཡོང་གི་མ་རེད་ If you work honestly, no one can later blame you unjustly. 2. using as a pretext/ excuse ། མོས་ན་ཚ་ཡོད་ཁུལ་ཁ་གཡར་ས་བྱས་ནས་ལས་ཀར་མ་ཡོང་པ་རེད་ Pretending that she was sick, she used that as a pretext to not come to work.

ཁ་གཡལ་ (kā yɛ̄ɛ̄) vi. to yawn.

ཁ་གཡེང་ (kā yēŋ) vi. to be lost in one's thought, to let one's mind wander, to be inattentive.

ཁ་གཡེང་མིག་གཡེང་ (kāyeŋ mīgyeŋ) inattentive, not paying attention; va.—བྱེད་ to be inattentive, to not pay attention ། ཁོས་འཛིན་གྲྭའི་ནང་ཁ་གཡེང་མིག་གཡེང་བྱེད་ཀྱི་འདུག He is not paying attention in class.

ཁ་གཡེངས་ (kā yēŋ) sm. ཁ་གཡེང་.

ཁ་གཡེར་ (kā yēr) sm. ཁ་ཡེར་ཡེར་.

ཁ་གཡོ་ཁོག་སྐྱུང་ (kāye kōgguŋ) hiding one's true feelings.

ཁ་གཡོ་ངོས་ལེན་ (kāyo ŋölen) pretending to agree; va.—བྱེད་.

ཁ་གཡོག (kāyɔɔ̀) 1. spoon. 2. sm. ཁ་གཡོགས་.

ཁ་གཡོག་མཛུབ་འཁྲི་ (kāyɔɔ̀ dzubdri) a responsibility that one can not shun ། ལས་ཀ་འདི་ཁ་གཡོག་མཛུབ་འཁྲིའི་ལས་འགན་ཞིག་རེད་ This work is a responsibility that one cannot shun.

ཁ་གཡོག་ལག་པས་བྱེད་ (kāyɔɔ̀ lagbɛɛ̀ ceè) shung. one should take care of one's belonging ། གཙུག་ལག་ཁང་གི་ཞིག་གསོ་ཁ་གཡོག་ལག་པས་བྱེད་དགོས་གསལ་བཞིན་པར་ The cathedral should be renovated in a manner as if it belongs to oneself. [Lit. one's hand should serve one's mouth].

ཁ་གཡོགས་ (kāyɔɔ̀) wrongly blaming or accusing; va. ཁ་གཡོགས་; —བྱེད་ to blame/ accuse wrongly or unjustly ། ཁོས་ང་ལ་ཁ་གཡོགས་བྱས་བྱུང་ He wrongly blamed me.

ཁ་གཡོགས་བསྙོན་དྲི་ (kāyɔɔ̀ ñōndri) sm. ཁ་གཡོགས་.

ཁ་གཡོན་ (kā yōn) the left side; va.—ལ་སྒྲིག to turn or face left.

ཁ་གཡོལ་ཚིག་གཡོལ་ (kāyöö tsīgyöö) avoiding, evading, hedging, equivocating; va.—བྱེད་ ། ཁོང་གིས་ཚོགས་འདུའི་ཐོག་གསང་བ་གཞན་གྱིས་ཤེས་པར་དོགས་ཏེ་ཁ་གཡོལ་ཚིག་གཡོལ་བྱས་པ་རེད་ Doubting that others would know the secret, he avoided telling it at the meeting.

ཁ་ར་ (kāra) 1. a nose muzzle (usu. two pieces of wood fixed into an "x" shape and placed over an animal's nose and mouth so as to prevent them from nursing); va.—རྒྱག to put such a nose muzzle on an animal. 2. blocking sb. from getting sth.; va.—རྒྱག ། ཁོ་ལ་ལས་ཀ་རག་རྒྱུར་མི་གཞན་གྱིས་ཁ་ར་བརྒྱབ་པ་རེད་ Another person blocked him from getting the job. 3. a feeding trough.

ཁ་ར་ཆི་ (kāraji) Karachi.

ཁ་རག (kāraà) a forked stick.

ཁ་རལ་ (kāra) 1. harelipped. 2. toothless because of old age.

ཁ་རས་ (kārɛɛ̀) a cloth mouth mask (worn for hygiene); va.—རྒྱག to wear such a mask.

ཁ་རི་ཁ་ཐུག (kāri kōduù) 1. direct, pointed, straight to the point ། ཁོང་གིས་སྐད་ཆ་ཁ་རི་ཁ་ཐུག་བཤད་པ་རེད་ He spoke straight to the point. 2. a frank/ straightforward person ། མི་འདི་ཁ་རི་ཁ་ཐུག་ཅིག་འདུག This man is frank.

ཁ་རིས་མ་ (kāriìmə) a design on or just below the rim.

ཁ་རིམས་ (kārim) an infant epidemic-like disease that causes sores in the mouth.

ཁ་རི་ (kāri) a volume measurement equal to about 20 liters.

ཁ་རིས་ (kārii) 1. a design on a seal; va.—རྐོ་ to carve a design on a seal. 2. facial shape.

ཁ་རུ་ངར་པོ་ (kāru ŋarbo) very particular about one's food (likes and dislikes) ། ཕྲུ་གུ་འདི་ཁ་རུ་ངར་པོ་ཡོད་ཙང་ཁ་ལག་བཟོ་ཁག་པོ་འདུག It's hard to cook for this child because he is very particular about his food.

ཁ་རུ་ཛ་ (kārudza) a kind of medicine.

ཁ་རུད་ (kārüù) avalanche; vi.—རྒྱག ། ཁ་རུད་ཆེན་པོ་བརྒྱབ་ཙང་ལམ་ཁ་བཀག་བཞག Because there was a big avalanche the road was blocked.

ཁ་རུབ་ (kārub) ganging up to verbally attack sb.; va.—བྱེད་; —རྒྱག ། མི་ཚོས་ཁོ་ལ་ཁ་རུབ་བརྒྱབ་སོང་ The people attacked him verbally.

ཁ་རུམ་ (kārum) rope tied near the mouth of a horse or mule that is attached to a cart.

ཁ་རུལ་ (kā rüü) 1. va. to be secretly in league or in cahoots with sb. (usu. to do sth. bad) ། ཁོ་གཉིས་ཁ་རུལ་ཙང་མ་ཇོང་ཐོབ་སོང་ They won in mahjong because they were secretly in league. 2. bad breath.

ཁ་རུལ་ནང་བཤང་ (kārüü naŋshaŋ) internal problems should be taken care of internally ། ལས་ཁུངས་ཀྱི་ནང་ཚོད་གླེང་ཁ་རུལ་ནང་བཤང་གིས་ཐག་གཅོད་བྱས་ན་དགའ་ It is better if the office's internal dispute is settled internally. [Lit. (if the) mouth rots, clean out the insides].

ཁ་རེ་སྐྱེང་ (kā re gyēŋ) vi. to be embarrassed/ ashamed.

ཁ་རེ་ཁོ་རེ་ (kāre kōre) untruthful, sly, crafty, cunning.

ཁ་རོ་ (kāro) 1. leftover food from a meal. 2. taste.

ཁ་རོག (kārɔɔ̀) quietly, secretly, stealthily ། བཙོན་ཁང་ནང་ནས་ཁ་རོག་ཏུ་བྲོས་ཕྱིན་པ་རེད་ (They) escaped stealthily from the prison.

ཁ་རོག་སྡོད་ (kārɔɔ̀ döö) 1. va. to keep quiet/ silent ། ཏོག་ཙམ་ཁ་རོག་སྡོད་དང་ ངས་ཁ་པར་ཡག་པོ་གོ་གི་མི་འདུག Keep quiet for a moment. I can't hear (what is being said) on the phone. 2. keeping inactive ། སློབ་སྦྱོང་མ་བྱས་པར་ཁ་རོག་བསྡད་ན་ཡར་རྒྱས་འགྲོ་གི་མ་རེད་ If you stay inactive without studying, you won't improve.

ཁ་རོང་དོག་པོ་ (kāroŋ togbo) a place located in a narrow mountain valley.

ཁ་རླངས་ (kālaŋ) mouth steam/ breath; vi.—ཐོན་ to have steam come from mouth when breathing, to have a window/ glass fog up from breath; va.—གཏོང་ to exhale steam from the mouth when breathing (when it is cold outside); vi.—ཕོག to be poisoned by a snake.

ཁ་བརླང་པོ་ (kā lāŋbo) speaking harshly; va.—བྱེད་ ། ཁ་བརླང་པོ་བྱས་ན་གཞན་ལ་ཕོག་ཐུག་འགྲོ་གི་རེད་ If you speak harshly, you will offend others.

ཁ་ལ་སྐྱེས་པའི་ཁ་སྤུ་མིན་ཀྱང་ལུས་ལ་སྐྱེས་པའི་བ་སྤུ་ (kāla gyēbɛ kābu mingyaŋ lüüla gyēbɛ pəbu) although one is not the main person in some activity, being a part of it is still valuable [Lit. although it is not the mustache, it is a hair follicle].

ཁ་ལ་ཁར་ (kāla kār) a moment before, just as one is about to do sth. ། ང་འགྲོ་ཁ་ལ་ཁར་ཁོ་སླེབས་བྱུང་ He arrived just as I was about to go.

ཁ་ལ་འཁྱེར་ (kāla kēē) va. to do sth. in the name of, to use sb.'s name ། རིག་གནས་གསར་བརྗེ་ཁ་ལ་འཁྱེར་ཏེ་རྙིང་དངོས་རྙིང་པ་རྣམས་རྩ་མེད་བཏང་བ་རེད་ In the name of the Cultural Revolution (they) destroyed the old relics.

ཁ་ལ་རྒྱ་བྱིན་ (kāla gyajin) unable to retaliate verbally [Lit. to put a seal on the mouth].

ཁ་ལ་ཅ་ལེ་བ་ (kāla jālewa) floating (on a liquid).

ཁ་ལ་ཉན་ (kāla ñen) va. to obey, to listen to ། དགེ་རྒན་གྱི་ཁ་ལ་ཉན་དགོས་རེད་ (You) have to listen to the teacher.

ཁ་ལ་ཉན་པོ་ (kāla ñembo) obedient; va.—བྱེད་ to act

obedient ¶ ཁྱི་འདི་ཁ་ལ་ཉན་པོ་ཡོད་ This dog is obedient.

ཁ་ལ་བལྟ་ (kāla dā) va. to follow sb.'s advice/ position/ views, to believe what someone says ¶ མི་མང་གིས་ཁོའི་ཁ་ལ་བལྟས་པ་རེད་ The people followed his views.

ཁ་ལ་ཐེམ་པ་མེད་པ་ (kāla tēmba me̱èba) having no control over one's speech, i.e., being unable to keep a secret.

ཁ་ལ་དཔག་པའི་སོ་དང་མི་ཆུང་ལ་འོས་པའི་ལྷམ་ཆུང་ (kāla bāgbɛ sōtaŋ mi̱cuŋla ö̱òbɛ lhāmcuŋ) suitable, appropriate [Lit. teeth suitable for the mouth and small shoes suitable for a small person].

ཁ་ལ་ཕུད་ན་སྨན་དང་ཁོག་ལ་བཟུང་ན་དུག (kāla pü̃ùnə mɛ̄ndaŋ kɔ̄gla su̱ŋna tu̱ù) one should speak one's mind freely and openly [Lit. speaking frankly is like medicine, holding things inside is like poison].

ཁ་ལ་འཕྱོ་ (kāla cō) vi. to float on the surface (of a liquid).

ཁ་ལ་བྱེད་ (kāla ce̱è) va. to tell sb. to do sth.

ཁ་ལ་མོར་ (kāla mɔ̱ɔ̱) sm. ཁ་ལ་ཁར་.

ཁ་ལ་མཚར་བ་ (kāla tsārwa) beautiful, pretty.

ཁ་ལ་ཞག་འཁྱིལ་ གདིང་ལ་སྙིགས་ཡོད་ (kāla sha̱gkyil dīŋla ñīgyöò) gaining fame and fortune [Lit. grease floating on the top, dregs on the bottom].

ཁ་ལ་ཡུག (kālayug) sm. ཁུག་རྟ་.

ཁ་ལ་ལ་ཚ་ མིག་ལ་བུ་རམ་ (kāla la̱ja mīìlə pu̱rəm) deceptive [Lit. sealing wax to the mouth, candy to the eyes].

ཁ་ལག (kālaà) 1. food, a meal; va.—ཟ་ to eat ¶ ཁ་ལག་བཟས་ནས་ནང་ལ་ལོག་པ་རེད་ He ate and then he returned home. va.—གཏོང་ to give a party (that has food), to invite people for a meal ¶ སང་ཉིན་ཁོའི་ནང་ལ་ཁ་ལག་གཏོང་གི་རེད་ Tomorrow he will give a party at his house.

ཁ་ལག་གཏོང་ (kālaà dōŋ) see ཁ་ལག.

ཁ་ལག་པ་སི་ (kālaà bāse) tib.eng. food ticket, meal pass.

ཁ་ལག་སྤྱོད་གསུམ་ (kālag jȫò sūm) the three: speech, action, and behavior.

ཁ་ལག་ཟ་ (kālaà sa̱) see ཁ་ལག.

ཁ་ལག་བཟོ་ (kālaà so̱) va. to prepare/ make food.

ཁ་ལང་ (kālaŋ) 1. an infant illness in which pimples grow in the mouth. 2. being in the habit of saying sth.; vi.—ཤོར་ to make a verbal utterance (e.g., hum, sing, talk, whistle) out of habit (i.e., without thinking about it) ¶ མི་ཚང་དེ་ར་མི་ཤི་བྱུང་ནའང་ཕྲུ་གུ་དེ་ཁ་ལང་ཤོར་ནས་སི་གླུ་གཏོང་གི་འདུག The child is whistling out of habit even though there is a death in the family.

ཁ་ལད་ (kālɛɛ̀) 1. vi. to get into the habit of using dirty words ¶ ཁ་ལད་ནས་སྤུན་མཆེད་ཡོད་པར་བཙོག་གཏམ་ཤོད་ཤོར་སོང་ (He) got into the habit of saying bad words and accidentally used them in front of his relatives. 2. vi. to eat the wrong type of food.

ཁ་ལན་ (kālen) a verbal message; va.—སྐུར་; —གཏོང་ to send a verbal message; va.—ལྡོག to talk back (to), to answer or argue back ¶ ཁོང་ཐུག་འཕྲད་བྱ་རྒྱུའི་ཁ་ལན་བསྐུར་པ་རེད་ (They) sent a verbal message asking to meet him. ¶ ཕྲུ་གུ་འདི་ཨ་མར་ཁ་ལན་བརྒྱགས་ཅང་ཁོ་ལ་ཉེས་པ་བཏང་པ་རེད་ The child was punished because he talked back to his mother.

ཁ་ལན་ཚིག་རྒྱག (kālen tsīggyaà) talking or answering back sarcastically.

ཁ་ལབ་ (kāləp) talk, conversation; va.—བྱེད་; —གཏོང་; —ཤོད་.

ཁ་ལབ་ཤབ་ཤུབ་ (kāləp shābshub) talking in a whisper or a low voice; va.—གཏོང་.

ཁ་ལས་ (kālɛɛ̀) 1. joking, kidding; va.—ཤོད་ to joke, to kid ¶ ཁ་ལས་བཤད་དྲགས་ན་མི་ལ་ཡོག་ཐུག་འགྲོ་ཉེན་ཡོད་ If you joke too much you might offend people.

ཁ་ལས་ཆེ་ (kālɛɛ̀ce) sm. ཁ་ལས་.

ཁ་ལི་དུག་རྫས་སྦྱིར་སྡོམ་ཚོགས་པ་ (kāli she̱èbɛ tu̱gdzɛɛ̀ ge̱rdom tsōgba) Cali cartel.

ཁ་ལུང་པ་ (kāluŋba) 1. a person who lives in remote places. 2. boasting, bragging.

ཁ་ལུད་ (kālüù) 1. fertilizer (top dressing); va.—རྒྱག ¶ ཞིང་གའི་སྟེང་ལ་ཁ་ལུད་ཐེངས་གཉིས་བརྒྱབ་པ་རེད་ (They) fertilized the field twice. 2. spit; va.—འདོར་; —དབྱུག to spit ¶ ཁ་ལུད་གང་ས་གང་ལ་དབྱུག་མི་ཆོག It is not allowed to spit anywhere. 3. overflowing, boiling over; vi.—རྒྱག ¶ མེ་ཚ་དྲག་ནས་ཐུག་པ་ཁ་ལུད་རྒྱག་གི་འདུག The fire was too hot so the broth is overflowing.

ཁ་ལུས་ཀྱི་མདོག (kālüùgi dɔ̱ɔ̀) facial and body appearance (color).

ཁ་ལེ་ནག་པོ་ (kāle na̱gbo) a kind of stroke that leaves the victim's face distorted.

ཁ་ལེན་ (kālen) 1. look after, taking care of; va.—བྱེད་ ¶ གནས་མོས་ཉིན་ལྟར་འགྲུལ་པ་མང་པོར་ཁ་ལེན་བྱེད་དགོས་ཀྱི་ཡོད་ The (female) innkeeper has to take care of many guests everyday. 2. sharpening a knife on a leather strap; va. ཁ་ལེན་; —རྒྱག ¶ སྐྲ་བཞར་བས་གྲི་ཁ་ལེན་གྱི་འདུག The barber is sharpening the knife. 3. va. to round up livestock, to bring livestock home from grazing. 4. va. to lead an animal.

ཁ་ལེན་ངོ་ལེན་ (kālen ŋo̱len) sm. ཁ་ལེན་, 1.

ཁ་ལེབ་ (kāleb) 1. cover, lid. 2. a type of fish that is flat.

ཁ་ལེབ་པ་ (kā le̱bba) a person with a flatish face/ jaw ¶ མི་འདི་ཁ་ལེབ་པ་རེད་ This man has a flat face.

ཁ་ལོ་ (kālo) 1. piloting, steering, controlling the movement of sth. or sb.; va.—སྒྱུར་ to control, to pilot, to dominate, to manage ¶ ཁོས་གནམ་གྲུའི་ཁ་ལོ་བསྒྱུར་སྐབས་ When he was piloting the plane. ¶ ཚོགས་པས་ཁ་ལོ་སྒྱུར་བའི་འཐུས་མི་ The delegates who were controlled by the association. 2. the leaves of root vegetables. 3. (— + neg.) uncontrollable ¶ མི་འདིའི་ཁ་ལ་ཁ་ལོ་ཡོག་མ་རེད་ (This) person can't control what he says. 4. (with a word conveying wealth) extremely wealthy ¶ མི་ཚང་འདི་རྒྱུ་ལ་ཁ་ལོ་མེད་པ་རེད་ The family is extremely rich.

ཁ་ལོ་སྐོར་ཅས་ (kālo gɔ̄ɔ̄jɛɛ̀) steering wheel.

ཁ་ལོ་འཁོར་མཚམས་ (kālo kɔ̄ndzam) a turning point.

ཁ་ལོ་སྒྱུར་ (kālo gyu̱r) see ཁ་ལོ་.

ཁ་ལོ་སྒྱུར་ཁང (kālo gyu̱rkaŋ) control center.

ཁ་ལོ་སྒྱུར་མཁན་ (kālo gyu̱rñɛn) one with controlling power, ruler ¶ མི་དེ་ཆབ་སྲིད་ཀྱི་ཁ་ལོ་སྒྱུར་མཁན་ཞིག་རེད་ That man is a political ruler.

ཁ་ལོ་སྒྱུར་ཆས་ (kālo gyu̱rjɛɛ̀) steering wheel (for cars, planes, etc.).

ཁ་ལོ་སྒྱུར་དབང་ (kālo gyu̱rwaŋ) domination, hegemony, supremacy, control ¶ རྒྱ་གར་སོགས་རྒྱལ་ཁབ་མང་པོ་དབྱིན་ཇིའི་ཁ་ལོ་སྒྱུར་དབང་འོག་གནས་པ་རེད་ Many countries such as India were under the domination of the English.

ཁ་ལོ་འདི་ལོ་མེད་པ་ (kālo di̱lo me̱èba) sm. ཁ་ལོ་, 3 and 4.

ཁ་ལོ་འདུལ་ (kālo dü̱ü̱) va. to tame animals.

ཁ་ལོ་པ་ (kālowa) sm. ཁ་ལོ་བ་.

ཁ་ལོ་པའི་འཛིན་གྲྭ་ (kālowɛ dzi̱ndra) sm. ཁ་ལོ་བའི་འཛིན་གྲྭ་.

ཁ་ལོ་པའི་སློབ་གྲྭ་ (kālowɛ lābdra) sm. ཁ་ལོ་པའི་འཛིན་གྲྭ་.

ཁ་ལོ་བ་ (kālowa) driver, pilot ¶ རླངས་འཁོར་ཁ་ལོ་བ་གསུམ་ Three automobile drivers.

ཁ་ལོ་བའི་འཛིན་གྲྭ་ (kālowɛ dzi̱ndra) class for teaching driving, driving school.

ཁ་ལོ་བའི་སློབ་གྲྭ་ (kālowɛ lābdra) driving school.

ཁ་ལོ་བ་མེད་པའི་གནམ་གྲུ་ (kālowa me̱èbɛ nāmdru) pilotless plane, robot plane, drone.

ཁ་ལོ་མི་གསོར་ (kālo mi̱sɔr) unable to manage or

cope.

ཁ་ལོག (kālɔ̀ɔ) 1. va. ཁ་ལོག; —རྒྱག to talk back/ answer back (to a superior) ¶ ཁ་ས་དགེ་རྒན་ལ་ཁ་ལོག་བརྒྱབ་བཞག (They) talked back to the teacher yesterday. 2. vi. to become blunt (for knives, tools, etc.) ¶ གྲིབ་གྲི་འདི་ཁ་ལོག་ནས་རྣོ་མི་འདུག This knife has become blunt and is not sharp.

ཁ་ལོག་ངོ་ལོག (kālɔ̀ɔ ŋolɔ̀ɔ) revolting, rebelling; va.—བྱེད་; —རྒྱག.

ཁ་ལོག་ཚིག་ལོག (kālɔ̀ɔ tsīglɔ̀ɔ) sm. ཁ་ལོག, 1.

ཁ་ལོངས་ (kā loŋ) 1. (number + —) enough/ sufficient, adequate (to meet a target, etc.) ¶ གཏན་འཁེབས་གྲངས་ཚད་ཁ་ལོངས་པ་ཡོད་པ་རེད་ There are an adequate number of (workers) to meet the established target. 2. vi. to reach a predetermined amount ¶ ཁང་པའི་རིན་འབབས་ཁ་ལོངས་པའི་དངུལ་གཡར་མཁན་མ་བྱུང་ (I) couldn't get anyone to lend enough money to meet the cost of the house.

ཁ་ལོན་ (kālön) sm. ཁ་ལོངས་.

ཁ་ལོབས་ (kālob) sm. ཟ་ཁ་ལོབས་.

ཁ་ཤ་ (kāsha) 1. type of deer. 2. a white (tanned) skin worn as a dress over the normal skin dress. 3. the flesh around the mouth, the lower cheeks. 4. beak. 5. bird.

ཁ་ཤའི་པགས་པ་ག་ནས་འཐེན་འཐེན་རེད་ (kāshɛ bāgba kənɛɛ̀ tēnten reè) malleable, subject to many interpretations [Lit. a deer's skin can be stretched any place].

ཁ་ཤག་ཤག་པོ་ (kāshag shāgbo) sm. ཁ་གཟེར་པོ་.

ཁ་ཤགས་ (kāshag) sm. ཚིགས་རྒྱག.

ཁ་ཤན་ (kāshɛn) the edge/ rim, the band on a rim.

ཁ་ཤས་ (kāshɛɛ̀) several, a few, some ¶ མི་ཁ་ཤས་ཡོང་བ་རེད་ Several people came.

ཁ་ཤས་ཁ་ཤས་ (kāshɛɛ̀ kāshɛɛ̀) sm. ཁ་ཤས་.

ཁ་ཤིང་ (kəshiŋ) 1. two pieces of wood attached to a bellow. 2. sm. ཁ་ནུ་. 3. shoetree. 4. a decorated piece of wood placed over a door.

ཁ་ཤུ་ (kəshu) whistling; va.—རྒྱག ¶ ཁོ་སྐྱིད་པོ་བྱུང་ན་ཁ་ཤུ་རྒྱག་གི་རེད་ He whistles when he is happy.

ཁ་ཤུགས་ཅན་ (kā shūgjɛn) the dominant speaker in a group ¶ དཔོན་པོ་དེ་ཁ་ཤུགས་ཅན་ཡིན་ཙང་ཁོས་བཤད་པའི་བསམ་འཆར་དེ་ཐལ་ཆེར་གནད་འཁེལ་རྒྱུ་རེད་ Because the leader is the dominant speaker they will most likely agree to his suggestion.

ཁ་ཤུགས་ཆེན་པོ་ (kəshug cēmbo) speaking forcefully/ dominantly.

ཁ་ཤུགས་སུ་གཏོང་ (kəshugsu dōŋ) arc. sm. ཁ་འཐོར་.

ཁ་ཤུར་ (kəshur) carpenter's tool, chisel with a curved tip.

ཁ་ཤེད་ (kāsheè) forceful/ effective speech; va.—ཤོད་ ¶ ལས་བྱེད་པ་དེ་ཚོགས་འདུའི་ཐོག་ཁ་ཤེད་ཆེན་པོ་ཡོད་པ་རེད་ That official spoke forcefully at the meeting.

ཁ་ཤེད་ལྕེ་ཤེད་ (kāsheè jēsheè) sm. ཁ་ཤེད་.

ཁ་ཤོ་ (kāsho) 1. harelip. 2. gap, rift, breach; va.—བཟོ་; —འདོན་ to make a gap/ hole (in a dam, wall, etc.) ¶ རྐུན་མ་དེས་ལྕགས་རི་ལ་ཁ་ཤོ་བརྡོན་པ་རེད་ The thief made a hole in the wall.

ཁ་ཤོག (kā shōg) cover (of a book, magazine).

ཁ་ཤོབ་ (kāpshob) 1. joking, kidding; va.—ཤོད་ to joke, to kid. 2. bragging, boasting.

ཁ་ཤོམ་ (kāshom) boasting, bragging, showing off; va.—ཤོད་.

ཁ་ཤོར་ (kā shɔ̄ɔ) 1. vi. to have a slip of the tongue, to disclose/ reveal sth. accidentally ¶ ཚིག་དེ་ཁ་ཤོར་བ་རེད་ That word slipped out (from my mouth). 2. vi. to have sth. go out of control ¶ མོ་ཊ་ཁ་ཤོར་ནས་གཡང་ལ་ཟགས་པ་རེད་ The car went out of control and fell over the precipice. 3. vi. to discharge accidentally (for guns) ¶ མེ་མདའ་ཁ་ཤོར་ནས་མི་ཞིག་བསད་པ་རེད་ The gun accidentally went off and killed sb.

ཁ་ཤྭ་ (kā shā) 1. marmot. 2. sm. ཁ་ཤོ་.

ཁ་གཤགས་ (kāshag) sm. ཁ་ཤགས་.

ཁ་གཤིབ་གྲོས་སྡུར་ (kāshib trödur) discussing in detail; va.—བྱེད་.

ཁ་གཤིས་ (kā shīī) a person's manner or style of talking ¶ ཁ་གཤིས་འཇམ་པོ་ A gentle manner of speaking.

ཁ་གཤོག: p. ཁ་བཤགས་ (kā shōg) va. to split open ¶ ཤིང་ཁ་བཤགས་པ་རེད་ (They) split the wood.

ཁ་བཤགས་ (kāshaà) 1. p. of ཁ་གཤོག. 2. dividing in half; va.—གཏོང་; —སྒྲོག.

ཁ་བཤད་ (kāshɛɛ̀) 1. talk, speech, conversation ¶ ཁ་བཤད་ཙམ་ལ་ཡིད་ཆེས་བྱ་རྒྱུ་མེད་ One should not trust only talk (i.e., there is a need to see action). 2. sm. བཤད་པ་.

ཁ་བཤད་རྒྱབ་ལྡང་ (kāshɛɛ̀ gyəblaŋ) speaking in support of sb., backing up sb. verbally; va.—བྱེད་.

ཁ་བཤད་ཆུ་བོ་འབབ་འབབ་ (kāshɛɛ̀ cūwo bəbbəb) sb. whose words flow like a stream, an eloquent speaker.

ཁ་བཤད་ཆུའི་ལྦུ་བ་ ལག་ལེན་གསེར་གྱི་ཐིགས་པ་ (kāshɛɛ̀ cūū būwa laglen sērgi tīgbə) action speaks louder than words [Lit. talk is like bubbles on water, action is like golden drops].

ཁ་བཤད་དམ་པོ་ (kāshɛɛ̀ tambo) an introvert, a person who doesn't speak much ¶ ཡོན་ཏན་ཡོད་ཀྱང་ཁ་བཤད་དམ་པོ་བྱུང་ན་ཕན་ཐོགས་མི་འདུག Even though (one) is educated it is useless if one is an introvert.

ཁ་བཤད་དོན་གནས་ (kāshɛɛ̀ tönnɛɛ̀) keeping one's word, doing what one says.

ཁ་བཤད་དཔའ་བོ་ (kāshɛɛ̀ pāwo) sb. who talks big but doesn't follow through.

ཁ་བཤད་དཔེ་སྟོན་ (kāshɛɛ̀ pēdön) instructing/ showing by words and example; va.—བྱེད་.

ཁ་བཤད་ལག་སྒྲུབ་ (kāshɛɛ̀ lagdrub) sm. ཁ་བཤད་ལག་ལེན་.

ཁ་བཤད་ལག་བསྟར་ (kāshɛɛ̀ lagdar) sm. ཁ་བཤད་ལག་ལེན་.

ཁ་བཤད་ལག་དུང་ (kāshɛɛ̀ lagduŋ) scolding and beating at the same time.

ཁ་བཤད་ལག་ལེན་ (kāshɛɛ̀ laglen) doing what one says, deeds matching words, doing what one preaches, keeping one's promise; va.—བྱེད་ ¶ ཁ་བཤད་ལག་ལེན་དུ་བསྟར་མཁན་གྱི་མི་ཞིག་རེད་ He is a person who does what he says.

ཁ་བཤལ་ (kāshɛɛ) rinsing one's mouth; va.—གཏོང་.

ཁ་བཤལ་སྨན་ཆུ་ (kāshɛl mɛ̄ncu) medicine for rinsing one's mouth, mouthwash.

ཁ་བཤིག (kā shīī) va. to unpack/ unwrap, to open up ¶ ཁོས་ནང་ལ་སླེབས་ནས་རྡེ་པོ་ཁ་བཤིག་པ་རེད་ He opened up the package after he got home.

ཁ་བཤུས་ (kā shūū) va. to peel/ skin/ pare/ scrape off.

ཁ་བཤེར་ (kāsher) sm. ངག་གཤེར་.

ཁ་ས་ (kɛ̄ɛ̄sə) 1. yesterday. 2. the surface of the ground/ earth ¶ ཁ་ས་སོབ་སོབ་ Soft earth on the surface.

ཁ་ས་ཁ་ཉིན་ (kɛ̄ɛ̄sa kāñin) lately, recently, a short while ago ¶ ཁ་ས་ཁ་ཉིན་ང་འདིར་བསྡད་མེད་ Recently I was not staying here. [Lit. yesterday and the day before].

ཁ་ས་ཁས་ཉིན་ (kɛ̄ɛ̄sa kɛ̄ñin) sm. ཁ་ས་ཁ་ཉིན་.

ཁ་སང་ (kāsan) 1. some time ago, some days ago ¶ ཁ་སང་ནས་ང་རྒྱ་ནག་ལ་འགྲོ་ཡག་གི་འཆར་གཞི་ཡོད་ I had plans to go to China sometime ago. 2. yesterday.

ཁ་སང་ཁ་ཉིན་ (kāsaŋ kāñin) yesterday or the day before, a few days ago.

ཁ་སང་ཁས་ཉིན་ (kāsaŋ kɛ̄ñin) sm. ཁ་སང་ཁ་ཉིན་.

ཁ་སང་དེ་རིང་ (kāsaŋ teriŋ) lately, recently [Lit. yesterday and today].

ཁ་སངས་ (kāsaŋ) frank, straightforward.

ཁ་སངས་ཟོལ་མེད་ (kāsaŋ sööméè) frank, without reservations.

ཁ་སི་སྤོག (kāsiboò) perfume.

ཁ་སུག (kāsuù) tripping, stumbling, falling forward;

vi.—ལོག ། མི་འདི་ཁ་སུག་ལོག་ནས་རེལ་སོང་ This man stumbled and fell. va.—སློག to (intentionally) trip ། ཕྲུ་གུ་འདིས་རྩེད་མོ་རྩེད་དུས་ཁོའི་གྲོགས་པོ་ཁ་སུག་བསློགས་པ་རེད་ The boy tripped his friend while playing.

ཁ་སུབ་ (kā sūb) 1. va. to pull sb. to the ground face down ། གཅེན་པས་ཆུང་བར་ཁ་སུབ་ནས་ཉེས་སོང་ The older (boy) pulled the younger (one) to the ground by his neck and beat (him). 2. the flap that covers a tent chimney hole. 3. closing tight, closing to make airtight; va.—གཏོང་. 4. va. to erase ། དག་ཆ་ནོར་པ་ཚང་མ་ཁ་སུབ་པ་རེད་ (He) erased all the wrong spellings.

ཁ་སུར་ (kāsur) date (the fruit) ། ཁ་སུར་སྡོང་པོ་ Date tree.

ཁ་སེ་ཐེ་ལུའུ་ (kāsetelu) Castro.

ཁ་སེང་ (kəseŋ) sm. ཁ་སང་.

ཁ་སོ་ (kāso) mouth and teeth.

ཁ་སོ་ན་གྲངས་མེད་པ་ (kāso nadraŋ meèba) very old (for animals).

ཁ་སོ་ཕྱགས་པས་མི་འདུམ་པ་ (kāso bāgbɛ mindumbə) smiling with great joy.

ཁ་སོ་མིག་སོ་ (kāso mīgso) watching, doing surveillance; va.—བྱེད་.

ཁ་སོང་ (kāsoŋ) old animals.

ཁ་སོན་ (kāsön) reseeding, replenishing planting; va.—རྒྱག.

ཁ་སོས་ (kā söö) imp. of ཁ་གསོ་.

ཁ་སོས་རྒྱབ་ཁེབས་ (kāsöö gyəbkeb) having enough to eat and wear.

ཁ་སོས་པོ་ (kā sööbo) one who converses easily or strikes up a conversation easily, a good conversationalist.

ཁ་སོས་སོས་པོ་ (kāsöö sööbo) sm. ཁ་སོས་པོ་.

ཁ་སྲ་པོ་ (kā trābo) 1. an introvert. 2. a headstrong horse/ mule.

ཁ་སྲབ་ (kā trəb) sm. སྲབ་.

ཁ་སྲབ་པོ་ (kā trəbu) thin.

ཁ་སྲི་ (kā sī) reducing/ subtracting the amount of sth.; va.—རྒྱག ། དགོས་དངུལ་གྱི་ཐོག་ནས་འགྲོ་སོང་ཁ་སྲི་བྱས་པའི་ལྷག་མ་གཞུང་ལ་ཕུལ་བ་རེད་ (They) subtracted their expenses from the money (they were given) for expenses and gave the remainder to the government.

ཁ་སྲེ་ (kā sē) va. to eat/ drink from the same cup or bowl that someone else has eaten or drunk from ། རྒྱ་གར་གྱི་རིགས་རྒྱུད་མཐོ་བ་ཚོས་གཞན་དང་ཁ་སྲེ་གྱི་མེད་པ་རེད་ Higher caste Indians do not eat or drink from the same cup or bowl that others have used. [Lit. mixing mouths].

ཁ་སྲོང་ (kā sōŋ) sm. ཁ་གསངས་.

ཁ་སླ་པོ་ (kā lābo) 1. talkative, loose-lipped ། མི་ཁ་སླ་པོ་འདིས་སྐད་ཆ་གང་བྱུང་མང་བྱུང་ཤོད་ཀྱི་འདུག The loose-lipped person is saying all sorts of things. 2. a person who eats indiscriminately, a compulsive eater, a gluttonous person ། ཨེམ་ཆིས་ཁ་འཛེམ་དགོས་ལབ་ན་ཡང་མི་འདི་ཁ་སླ་པོ་ཡིན་ཙང་ལྟོ་འདྲ་མིན་སྣ་ཚོགས་ཟ་གི་འདུག Although the doctor advised him against eating indiscriminately, he eats all kinds of food.

ཁ་སློག (kā lōò) 1. see ཁ་, 6. 2. va. to turn on sb., to talk back to a superior ། ཁྱི་ལ་རྒྱུག་པ་གཞུས་ན་ཚུར་ཁ་སློག་རྒྱག་གི་རེད་ If you hit a dog with a stick, it will turn on you. ། དཔོན་པོས་གཡོག་པོར་གཤེ་གཤེ་ཕྲན་བུ་བཏང་པར་གཡོག་པོས་ཁ་སློག་ཤུགས་ཆེན་པོ་བརྒྱབ་པ་རེད་ The lord scolded the servant a little and the servant talked back strongly to him.

ཁ་སློང་ (kā lōŋ) sm. ཁ་གསབ་.

ཁ་སློབ་ (kālob) (verbal) advice.

ཁ་སློབ་སློ་སློབ་ (kālob lōlob) giving advice.

ཁ་གསག (kāsaà) obsequious flattery; va.—བྱེད་ ། ཁ་གསག་སྐྱུག་བྲོ་དགོས་པའི་ཞིག་བྱས་པ་རེད་ (He) flattered (them) nauseatingly.

ཁ་གསག་ངོ་སྲུང་ (kāsag ŋosuŋ) flattering and doing what sb. likes.

ཁ་གསང་(ས་) (kā sāŋ) va. to speak frankly, to say something without reservation/ hesitation ། ཚོགས་འདུར་ཁ་གསངས་ནས་ལབ་མཁན་ཡོད་པ་མ་རེད་ No one spoke frankly at the meeting.

ཁ་གསང་གདམ་དྲང་ (kāsaŋ dāmdraŋ) speaking straightforwardly/ frankly/ honestly.

ཁ་གསང་གོ་བདེ་ (kāsaŋ kode) it is easier to understand if one is frank/ straightforward.

ཁ་གསང་ན་གོ་བདེ་ ནམ་ལངས་ན་འགྲོ་བདེ་ (kāsaŋna kode namlaŋna drode) it is good to do or say things openly/ frankly [Lit. it is easy to understand if one speaks frankly, it is easy to go if daybreak has occurred].

ཁ་གསང་ན་གོ་བདེ་ ལམ་གསངས་ན་འགྲོ་བདེ་ (kāsaŋna kode lamsaŋna drode) sm. ཁ་གསང་ན་གོ་བདེ་ ནམ་ལངས་ན་འགྲོ་བདེ་. [Lit. it is easy to understand if one speaks frankly, it is easy to go if the road is clear].

ཁ་གསང་ཟོལ་མེད་ (kāsaŋ sömeè) sm. ཁ་གསང་གདམ་དྲང་.

ཁ་གསངས་ (kāsaŋ) sm. ཁ་གསང་.

ཁ་གསངས་པོ་ (kā sāŋbo) outspoken, utterly frank ། མི་འདི་ཁ་གསངས་པོ་ཞི་དྲག་འདུག This man is very outspoken.

ཁ་གསབ་ (kāsəp) that which makes up a shortage/ deficiency (e.g., a subsidy, supplement, compensation), replenishment; va. ཁ་གསབ་; —བྱེད་ to make up a shortage, deficiency, to subsidize, to supplement, to replenish ། ཁ་གསབ་དངུལ་ Monetary subsidy. ། ཁ་གསབ་རོགས་རམ་ Subsidy aid. ། སློབ་གྲྭའི་འགྲོ་སོང་བརྒྱ་ཆ་ལྔ་བཅུ་གཞུང་ནས་ཁ་གསབ་བྱེད་ཀྱི་ཡོད་པ་རེད་ The government subsidizes fifty percent of the school's expenses. 2. sth. additional ། ཡང་སྲིད་དེའི་ངོས་འཛིན་སྐོར་ཁ་གསབ་ཕྲན་བུ་ཞུ་རྒྱུ་ཡིན་ I will tell you some additional things about (how) the incarnation was recognized.

ཁ་གསར་ (kāsar) 1. sth. old that looks new ། དེབ་འདི་ཁ་གསར་རེད་ This book looks new. 2. new.

ཁ་གསར་པ་ (kā sääba) sm. ཁ་གསར་.

ཁ་གསལ་ (kāsɛɛ) clear, distinct, explicit ། ཁོས་བོད་ཀྱི་གནས་སྟངས་ཁ་གསལ་བཤད་པ་རེད་ He gave (told) a clear account of the Tibetan situation. ། ངས་རྩིས་ཐོ་ཁ་གསལ་པོ་བཟོས་ཡོད་ I have made a clear (errorless) accounting. 2. va. to say separately or in detail ། ཡིག་ཆ་འདིའི་ནང་དཔལ་འབྱོར་སྐོར་ཁ་གསལ་འཁོད་མི་འདུག In this document, economics is not written about (covered) separately.

ཁ་གསལ་གོ་བདེ་ (kāsɛɛ gode) clear and easy to understand, simple/ easy to read and understand.

ཁ་གསལ་གོ་སླ་ (kāsɛɛ gola) sm. ཁ་གསལ་གོ་བདེ་.

ཁ་གསལ་གཏིང་གསལ་ (kāsɛɛ dīŋsɛɛ) saying openly and frankly what one thinks and feels.

ཁ་གསལ་དོན་གསལ་ (kāsɛ̄ɛ tönsɛɛ) clear in speech and meaning.

ཁ་གསལ་པོ་ (kā sɛ̄ɛbo) sm. ཁ་གསལ་.

ཁ་གསལ་ཚིག་གསལ་ (kāsɛɛ tsīgsɛɛ) sm. ཁ་གསལ་.

ཁ་གསུབ་ (kā sūp) sm. ཁ་སུབ་.

ཁ་གསེ་ (kā sē) sm. ཁ་གཤོག.

ཁ་གསོ་ (kā sō) taking care of, supporting, feeding, rearing, replenishing; vi. and va.—བྱེད་ ། ཚོང་ལས་འདིས་མི་མང་པོའི་ཁ་གསོ་ཐུབ་ཀྱི་ཡོད་པ་མ་རེད་ This business cannot support many people. ། མཆོད་མེ་ཁ་གསོ་བྱེད་རྗེས་ After adding butter to the butter lamp.

ཁ་གསོ་བྱེད་སྦྱད་ (kāso ceèjɛɛ) sth. done to maintain one's livelihood.

ཁ་གསོས་ (kā söö) sm. ཁ་སྐོན་.

ཁ་བསུམ་ (kāsum) shut up!

ཁ་བསོད་ (kā söö) 1. abbr. a type of inferior Tibetan ceremonial scarf. 2. lucky with respect to getting food to eat ། ང་སླེབས་པ་དང་ཁ་ལག་རྒྱས་པོ་བཟོས་པ་དུས་མཚུངས་པ་དེ་ནི་ངའི་ཁ་བསོད་རང་རེད་བཞག When I arrived they were making an elaborate meal—it is my good luck.

ཁ་བསྲེ་ (kā sɛ) sm. སྲེ་.

ཁ་བསླངས་ (kā lāŋ) p. of ཁ་སློང་.

ཁ་བསླངས་ནས་བཞག (kālaŋnɛ sha̱a̱) 1. va. to leave open ¶ ཅོག་ཙེའི་སྟེང་ལ་དེབ་ཁ་བསླངས་ནས་བཞག་རོགས་ Please leave the book open on the table. 2. va. to leave standing upright ¶ བུམ་པ་བཀྲུས་ནས་ཁ་བསླངས་ནས་བཞག་པ་རེད་ (He) washed the vase and left it standing upright.

ཁ་བསླུས་ (kəplüü) swindling, conning; va.—རྒྱག ¶ ཁོས་ངའི་ཅ་ལག་ཁ་བསླུ་བརྒྱབ་སོང་ He swindled me out of my things.

ཁ་ཧམ་ཆེན་པོ་ (kā hām cēmbo) bold, audacious, daring (verbally).

ཁ་ཧུབ་ (kāhub) a gulp; va.—རྒྱག to gulp ¶ ཆུ་ཁ་ཧུབ་གང་རྒྱག To gulp a (mouthful) of water.

ཁ་ཕེ་ (kāfe) eng. coffee ¶ ཁ་ཕེའི་ཟ་ཁང་ Coffee house.

ཁ་ཕེ་མདོག (kāfe dɔ̄ɔ̄) coffee color.

ཁ་ཧྱབ་ (kāhyəb) sm. ཁ་ཧྱབ་ཧྱབ་.

ཁ་ཧྱབ་ཧྱབ་ (kā hyəbhyəb) superficially, not in depth; va.—བྱེད་ ¶ གཞོན་ནུ་ཚོས་དེང་སང་ལས་ཀ་ཁ་ཧྱབ་ཧྱབ་བྱེད་ཀྱི་ཡོད་པ་རེད་ These days the youth do their work superficially.

ཁ་ཧྲག (kāhraà) sm. ཁེ་རག.

ཁ་ཧྲག་པོ་ (kā hrāgbo) headstrong, stubborn; va.—བྱེད་.

ཁ་ཧྲི་གར་ (kāhrigar) Kashgar.

ཁ་ལྷ་ཁར་ (kā lhāgar) sm. ཁ་ལ་གར་.

ཁ་ལྷ་མོར་ (kā lhāmo) sm. ཁ་ལ་མོར་.

ཁ་ལྷག (kālhaà) surplus, leftover.

ཁ་ལྷག་འཁྲོལ་འཁྱིལ་ (kālhaà trōōkyii) surplus, leftover, extra; va.—འཇོག to leave spare/ extra things; to leave room for future possibilities or unforeseen circumstances ¶ ཐུགས་སྒྲོ་བཏང་བའི་རྒྱུ་ཆ་ཁ་ལྷག་འཁྲོལ་འཁྱིལ་མང་པོ་འདུག There is a lot of leftover materials from the party.

ཁ་ལྷག་འཁྲོལ་འཁྱིལ་ (kālhaà trūūgyee) sm. ཁ་ལྷག་འཁྲོལ་འཁྱིལ་.

ཁག (kāà) 1. a plurality of different kinds of units, sections, parts ¶ འཛམ་གླིང་རྒྱལ་ཁབ་ཆེ་ཁག The bigger nations of the world. ¶ ཚོགས་པ་ཁག་མང་པོ་འདུག There are many different associations. 2. a division, section, group, part, batch ¶ དམག་མི་ཁག་ཅིག་ས་མཚམས་ལ་བཏང་བ་རེད་ (They) sent one division (unit) of soldiers to the border region. 3. blame, fault (with negatives) ¶ ཁོར་ཁག་མི་འདུག He is not to be blamed.

ཁག་དྲི་ (kāà drī) sm. ཁག་འཁྲི་.

ཁག་དྲི་ (kāà drī) 1. vi. to be responsible for sth., to be the cause of sth. ¶ ཁྱེད་རང་གི་རྙོག་དྲ་འདི་ང་ལ་ཁག་དྲི་ཡོང་གཞི་མེད་ There is no basis for my being responsible for your problems. 2. blaming/ accusing (when not valid or true); va.—བྱེད་; —བཞག; —འདོགས་ to blame/ accuse ¶ བསོད་ནམས་ལགས་ལ་ཕྱི་རྒྱལ་སོ་པ་རེད་ཟེར་ཁག་དྲི་བཏགས་པ་རེད་ They accused Sonamla of being a foreign spy. 3. a pretext; va.—འཛིན to use as a pretext ¶ མི་དམངས་ལ་བཅིངས་འགྲོལ་གཏོང་རྒྱུར་ཁག་དྲི་བཞག་ནས་བཙན་འཛུལ་བྱས་པ་རེད་ Under the pretext of liberating the people they invaded the country.

ཁག་དྲི་བསྙོན་འཛུགས་ (kāgdri ñōndzuù) blaming or accusing sb. of wrongdoing.

ཁག་བཀལ་ (kāà gɛ̄ɛ̄) p. of ཁག་འགེལ་.

ཁག་སྐུར་ (kāgur) sm. ཁག་དྲི་བསྙོན་འཛུགས་.

ཁག་ཁག (kāgaà) separate, different; va.—བྱེད་ to separate, to do differently; va.—བཟོ་ to make separate, to separate ¶ བུ་དང་བུ་མོ་ཁག་ཁག་བཟོས་པ་རེད་ (They) separated the boys from the girls. ¶ དོན་དག་འདི་གཉིས་ཁག་ཁག་རེད་ These two meanings are different. ¶ ལས་ཀ་འདི་གཉིས་ཁག་ཁག་བྱས་ནས་བྱེད་དགོས་རེད་ (You) have to do these two jobs separately. 2. divorcing, separating (for couples) ¶ ཆང་ས་བརྒྱབ་པ་དང་ལམ་སང་ཁག་ཁག་བྱས་སོང་ As soon as (they) got married (they) got divorced.

ཁག་ཁག་སོ་སོ་ (kāgaà sōso) separately ¶ ཁོ་ཚོ་ཁག་ཁག་སོ་སོར་ཕྱིན་པ་རེད་ They went separately.

ཁག་ཁྱག (kāàgyaà) sm. ཁག་འཁྱག.

ཁག་ཁྲིད་ (kāà trīi) sm.* ཁག་འཁྲིད་.

ཁག་འཁུར་ (kāà kūr) va. to take the blame ¶ ཁོ་ཚོའི་ནོར་འཁྲུལ་གྱི་ཁག་ངས་འཁུར་ཐུབ་ཀྱི་མ་རེད་ I can't take the blame for their mistake.

ཁག་འཁྱག (kāgyaà) sm. ཁག་ཐེག.

ཁག་འཁྲི་ (kāà trīi) 1. vi. to charge sb. with responsibility, to hold sb. responsible ¶ ལས་འགན་འདི་སྒྲུབ་རྒྱུ་ཁྱེད་རང་ཁག་འཁྲིས་གི་ཡོད་ You are responsible for accomplishing this task. 2. va. to accuse/ blame.

ཁག་འཁྲིས་ (khāà trīi) p. of ཁག་འཁྲི་.

ཁག་བགོད་ (kā gö̱ö̱) dividing into parts/ sections/ units; va. ཁག་བགོད་; —བྱེད་.

ཁག་བགོས་ (kā gö̱ö̱) p. of ཁག་བགོད་.

ཁག་བགོས་དུས་བགོས་ (kāgöö dṳ̄ṳ̄göö) dividing time and people into batches ¶ ཨ་རིའི་ནང་གཞིས་ཆགས་སུ་འགྲོ་མཁན་རྣམས་ཁག་བགོས་དུས་བགོས་ཀྱིས་བཏང་བ་རེད་ People going to America for resettlement were sent in different batches at different times.

ཁག་བགོས་ནས་དབང་སྒྱུར་ (kāàgöönɛ wāŋgyur) divide and conquer; va.—བྱེད་.

ཁག་བགོས་དཔུང་སྐྱོད་ (kāgöö būŋgyöö) advancing to battle separately (in separate units).

ཁག་བགོས་རྩིས་ཐོ་ (kāgöö dzīito) account ledger.

ཁག་བགོས་ལོགས་སྡོད་ (kāgöö lɔ̱gdöö) splitting off and living separately, setting up one's own household; va.—བྱེད་.

ཁག་འགན་འཁུར་ (kāà gɛ̱nkur) vi. to unjustly/ unfairly bear responsibility for sth. ¶ རྙོག་དྲ་འདིའི་སྐོར་ངས་ཁག་འགན་འཁུར་དགོས་བྱུང་སོང་ I unjustly had to bear responsibility for this problem.

ཁག་འགེལ་ (kāà ge̱è) 1. va. to use as a pretext/ excuse ¶ ཁྲོམ་ལ་འགྲོ་རྒྱུ་ཁག་བཀལ་ཏེ་ཆང་ཁང་ལ་ཕྱིན་པ་རེད་ On the pretext of going to the market, (he) went to the tavern. 2. va. to blame ¶ ཁུངས་སྐྱེལ་རྒྱུ་མེད་ཙང་ཁག་བཀལ་ན་འགྲིག་གི་མ་རེད་ Because there is no proof, it is not all right to blame him.

ཁག་འཇོག (kāà jɔ̄ɔ̀) sm. ཁ་འགེལ་.

ཁག་ཏིག (kātii) sm.* ཁ་ཏིག.

ཁག་བཏགས་ (kāà dāà) p. of ཁག་འདོགས་.

ཁག་ཐེག (kāgteg) 1. guarantor, guaranteeing ¶ ཁག་ཐེག་མེད་ན་བུ་ལོན་གཡར་གྱི་མི་འདུག Without a guarantor, one cannot get a loan. 2. va. ཁ་ཐེག; —བྱེད་ to act as guarantor, to provide security or bail ¶ ཁྱེད་རང་གི་བུ་ལོན་འདི་ཁག་ཐེག་པ་འདུག་གས་ Can you act as guarantor.

ཁག་ཐེག་དངུལ་ (kāgteg ŋǖǖ) bail money.

ཁག་ཐེག་པ་ (kāgtegba) guarantor ¶ ཁག་ཐེག་པ་མེད་པར་ཨ་རི་ར་ཡོང་མི་ཆོག No one is allowed to come to the United States without a guarantor.

ཁག་ཐེག་བཙུགས་ནས་གློད་ (kāgteg dzuùnɛ lȫȫ) va. to release on bail.

ཁག་ཐེག་ཚོང་རྟགས་ (kāgteg tsōŋdaà) registered trademark.

ཁག་ཐེག་ཞུ་ཡིག (kāgteg shu̱yii) letter of guarantee, written pledge, warranty.

ཁག་ཐེག་ཡི་གེ་ (kāgteg yigi) sm. ཁག་ཐེག་ཞུ་ཡིག.

ཁག་འདོགས་ (kā dɔ̱ɔ̄) using as a pretext/ excuse; va.—བྱེད་.

ཁག་འདོགས་ས་ (kāà do̱gsa) excuse, pretext ¶ ཁོང་ཚོས་ཁག་འདོགས་ས་མ་རྙེད་ཙང་མི་དེ་ལ་ཉེས་པ་འགེལ་ཐུབ་མེད་པ་རེད་ Because they couldn't find an excuse, they were unable to levy a fine on that person.

ཁག་སྣང་ (kāànaŋ) finding sth. difficult; va.—བྱེད་ ¶ ཁོང་རྒྱ་གར་ལ་འགྲོ་རྒྱུར་ཁག་སྣང་བྱེད་ཀྱི་འདུག He is finding it difficult to go to India.

ཁག་པོ་ (kāgbo) 1. difficult, hard ¶ ཞབས་བྲོ་རྒྱག་སྟངས་འདི་ཙང་ཁག་པོ་ཞིག A very difficult dance step. 2. (vb. + —) difficult to do the verbal action ¶ དབུགས་གཏོང་ཁག་པོ་འདུག It is difficult to breathe. 3. va.—བཟོ་ to make sth. difficult ¶ དཔལ་འབྱོར་ཕན་རྒྱུའི་སྐྱོར་མ་བྱས་ཙང་ང་ཚོའི་འཚོ་བ་ཁག་པོ་བཟོས་པ་རེད་ (They) made our economic well-being difficult because they didn't give us financial aid.

ཁག་ཕར་བཀལ་ཚུར་བཀལ་ (kāà pāā gɛ̄ɛ̄ tsüū gɛ̄ɛ̄) passing the buck, blaming each other; va.—བྱེད་ ¶ གཞམ་རིམ་ལས་བྱེད་པ་ཚོས་ཁག་ཕར་བཀལ་ཚུར་བཀལ་བྱས་ནས་ལས་འགན་ཡག་པོ་སྒྲུབ་ཀྱི་མི་འདུག The subordinate officials were blaming each other and the work wasn't being accomplished well.

ཁག་ཕྱེ་ (kāà cē) p. of ཁག་འབྱེད་.

ཁག་འབྱེད་ (kāg jeè) va. to divide/ separate into parts or components ¶ ཕོ་མོ་ཁག་ཕྱེ་ནས་ Separating the men from the women.

ཁག་འབྱེད་འཕྲུལ་ཆས་ (kāgjeè trüūjɛ̀ɛ̀) a machine that separates things.

ཁག་སྦྱོང་ (kāgjoŋ) sm. ཐུག་སྦྱོང་.

ཁག་མང་ (པོ་) (kāà maŋ) many things/ items/ units/ groups ¶ ཚོང་ཁང་འདིའི་ནང་ལ་ཅ་ལག་ཁག་མང་པོ་འདུག This store has many different items.

ཁག་མི་འདུག (kāà minduù) id. blameless, faultless ¶ དགེ་རྒན་ཡག་པོ་མེད་ཙང་སློབ་ཕྲུག་ཡིག་ཚད་མ་ཐོན་པ་དེ་ཁག་མི་འདུག Because the teacher is bad, the students are not to be blamed for not passing the exam.

ཁག་མེད་ (kāà meè) sm. ཁག་མི་འདུག.

ཁག་འཛུད་ (kāg dzuù) sm. ཁག་དཀྲི་བསྐོན་འཛུགས་.

ཁག་བཞག (kā shaà) sm. ཁག་དཀྲི་.

ཁག་གཟེད་ (kāà sɛ̀ɛ̀) sm. ཁག་འགན་འཁུར་.

ཁག་བཟོ་ (kāà so) abbr. of ཁག་ཁག་བཟོ་.

ཁག་གཡོག (kāà yɔ̄ɔ̀) sm. ཁག་གཡོགས་.

ཁག་གཡོགས་ (kāà yɔ̄ɔ̀) blaming/ accusing (sb. else); va.—བྱེད་ ¶ བདེན་དཔང་མེད་ན་གཞན་ལ་རྐུན་མའི་ཁག་གཡོགས་བྱེད་མི་ཉེན་ If (one) does not have the evidence, (one) shouldn't blame others for stealing.

ཁག་རུབ་ (kāàrub) gathering, assembling, collecting together (from different section/ areas/ etc.); va. ཁག་རུབ་; —བྱེད་.

ཁག་ས་ (kāgsa) difficult/ hard (path) ¶ ལམ་ཁག་ས་ནས་འགྲོ་གི་རེད་ (They) are taking the difficult road.

ཁག་བསྙུན་ (kāsün) shung. trouble and hardship.

ཁང་ (kāŋ) abbr. of ཁང་པ་.

ཁང་ཀླད་ (kāŋlɛ̀ɛ̀) middle of a room/ house.

ཁང་སྐོར་ (kāŋgɔɔ) going around a house/ building; va.—རྒྱག.

ཁང་སྐྲུན་རུ་ཁག (kāŋdrün kāà) building/ housing construction unit.

ཁང་ཁུངས་ (kɔ̄ŋguŋ) part of, belonging to, owned by ¶ གཞུང་གི་ཁང་ཁུངས་ཁང་པ་རྙིང་པ་ཚོ་ The old houses belonging to/ owned by the government.

ཁང་ཁོངས་ (kāŋkoŋ) sm. ཁང་ཁུངས་.

ཁང་ཁྱིམ་ (kāŋkyim) sm. ཁང་པ་.

ཁང་ཁྲལ་ (kāŋtrɛɛ) tax on houses; va.—རྒྱག to levy a tax on houses; va.—རྒྱུགས་ to do corvee labor (to fulfill a tax on people who rent apartments in tt.).

ཁང་འཁྱག (kāŋgyaà) a cold room/ house.

ཁང་འགྲོལ་ (kāŋdröö) extra room, empty house/ room, vacant room.

ཁང་གད་ (kāŋgɛɛ) shung. abbr. of ཁང་གཉེར་ and གད་པ་.

ཁང་གོག་གྱང་རུལ་ (kāŋgɔɔ gyaŋhrüü) a dilapidated/ ruined house or building.

ཁང་གླ་ (kāŋla) rent (for house, apartment); va.—སྤྲོད་; —གཏོང་ to pay rent, to rent out (a house, apartment); va.—སྡུད་ to collect rent ¶ ཟླ་རེ་ཁང་གླ་སྒོར་ལྔ་བརྒྱ་སྤྲོད་ཀྱི་ཡོད་ (I) pay five hundred dollars rent every month. ¶ རྒྱ་གར་ལ་ཡོད་པའི་ཁང་པ་དེ་ཁོས་ཁང་གླར་གཏོང་གི་ཡོད་པ་རེད་ He is renting out the house that he has in India. ¶ ཟླ་རེ་ཁང་གླ་བསྡུས་པ་རེད་ (He) collected rent every month.

ཁང་རྒྱབ་ (kāŋgyəb) back of a house.

ཁང་སྒྲོམ་ (kāŋdrom) 1. compartment, apartment ¶ རེ་ལིའི་ཁང་སྒྲོམ་ A train compartment. 2. house frame.

ཁང་ཅུན་ཟོའི་སྨན་ (kāŋjɛn somɛn) ch.tib. antibiotics.

ཁང་ཆུང་ (kəŋjuŋ) a small room/ house. 2. a branch household, a household that is an offshoot of a larger household.

ཁང་ཆེན་ (kāŋcen) the main household (as opposed to ཁང་ཆུང་).

ཁང་ཆེན་ཆོས་མཛད་ (kāŋcen cōndzɛɛ) the class of monks who are exempt from the monastic work young monks are required to perform because they have made a substantial offering to the monastery.

ཁང་ཆེན་ནས་ (kāŋjenɛɛ) an aristocratic family name.

ཁང་ཆེན་བསོད་ནམས་རྒྱལ་པོ་ (kāŋjenɛɛ sōnam gyɛɛbo) the aristocrat form the Khangchenbnɛ family who headed the Tibetan Cabinet in the early 18th century.

ཁང་ཇུན་སུའུ་ (kāŋjünsu) ch. sm. ཁང་ཅུན་ཟོའི་སྨན་.

ཁང་གཉེར་ (kāŋñer) person in whose charge a house is left, superintendent/ manager of a house or building.

ཁང་རྟགས་ (kāŋdaà) house number.

ཁང་ལྟག (kāŋdaà) sm. ཁང་རྒྱབ་.

ཁང་སྟེང་ (kāŋdeŋ) sm. ཁང་ཐོག.

ཁང་སྟོང་ཀུན་མ་ (kāŋdoŋ gūnma) unnecessarily suspicious [Lit. house empty, (but worried about) a thief].

ཁང་ཐོག (kāŋtɔɔ) roof.

ཁང་ཐོག་ཆུ་འགྲོ་ (kāŋtɔɔ cūndro) a roof drain.

ཁང་ཐོག་ཕུ་ཤུ་ (kāŋtɔɔ būshu) roof railing on Tibetan houses.

ཁང་ཐེབ་ (kāŋteb) a detailed list of items in a house.

ཁང་བདག (kāŋdaà) landlord, house owner ¶ ཁང་བདག་ལ་ཁང་གླ་སྤྲད་པ་ཡིན་ I paid rent to the landlord.

ཁང་རྡིབ་ (kāŋdib) collapsing (for a house); va.—གཏོང་ to cause a house to collapse ¶ ཁོས་ཁང་རྡིབ་བཏང་ནས་མི་མང་པོ་བསད་པ་རེད་ He caused the house to collapse and killed many people; vi.—ཤོར་ to have a house collapse.

ཁང་པ་ (kāŋba) house, home; va.—རྒྱག to build a house.

ཁང་པ་གོག་དོ་ (kāŋba gɔgdo) sm. ཁང་པ་གྱང་གོག.

ཁང་པ་གྱང་གོག (kāŋba gyaŋgɔɔ) dilapidated house ¶ ཁང་པ་གྱང་གོག་དེ་ཚོ་བཤིགས་ནས་གསར་དུ་རྒྱག་གི་ཡོད་པ་རེད་ They are tearing down and rebuilding the dilapidated houses.

ཁང་པ་ཕྱམ་གང་མ་ (kāŋba jām kaŋna) a small narrow room (one half of a one pillar room).

ཁང་པ་ཉམས་གསོ་ (kāŋba ñamso) sm. ཁང་པ་ཞིག་གསོ་.

ཁང་པ་སྦྲབས་བདེ་ (kāŋba dəbde) a prefabricated house.

ཁང་པ་ཐོག་གཅིག་མ་ (kāŋba tɔ̄ɔjigma) one story house.

ཁང་པ་ཐོག་བཤུས་ (kāŋba tɔ̄ɔshüù) stripping off the ceiling of a house; va.—རྒྱག.

ཁང་པ་མདོ་ (kāŋba do) outer house leading into an inner house.

ཁང་པ་མདོ་སྦུག (kāŋba dobug) the front and back room (of a house).

ཁང་པ་ཞིག་གསོ་ (kāŋba shigso) house repair, house maintenance; va.—བྱེད་.

ཁང་པ་ཞིག་གསོ་བཟོ་སྐྲུན་ཀུང་སི་ (kāŋba shigso sodrün gūŋsi) tib.ch. a house maintenance company.

ཁང་པ་གཡར་གཏོང་གི་སྦྱར་ཡིག (kāŋba yārdoŋ jəryig) a bulletin board on which rental properties are listed.

ཁང་པ་ཀློག (kāŋba lɔ̄g) va. to tear down a house or building.

ཁང་པ་གསར་གཏོད་ཀུང་སི་ (kāŋba sārdöò gūŋsi) tib.ch. real estate development agency.

ཁང་པའི་སྦུག (kāŋbɛ buù) inner room of a house. 2. the inside of a house.

ཁང་པའི་རྩིག་རྨང་ (kāŋbɛ dzīgmaŋ) house foundation; va.—འདིངས་ to lay a house's foundation.

ཁང་པའི་རྩེ་ཐོག (kāŋbɛ dzētɔɔ) roof.

ཁང་པའི་ཚོན་རྩི་ (kāŋbɛ tsȭndzi) paint for use on a house; va.—གཏོང་.

ཁང་དཔོན་ (kāŋbön) caretaker of a building/ house; va.—བྱེད་ to work as an official in charge of a house.

ཁང་སྦྲིལ་ (kāŋjii) a one room house/ hut/ cabin.

ཁང་བུ་ (kāŋbu) sm. ཁང་ཆུང་.

ཁང་བྱིའུ་ (kāŋciu) sparrow.

ཁང་བྱིའུ་ཆུང་ཡང་ནང་གྲོལ་ཚང་ཡོད་ (kāŋciu cūŋyaŋ naŋtröö tsāŋyöö) small but complete [Lit. even though the sparrow is small, it has all the internal organs].

ཁང་བྱིལ་ (kāŋcii) sm. ཁང་བྱིའུ་.

ཁང་བྱེའུ་ (kāŋceu) sm. ཁང་བྱིའུ་.

ཁང་མིག་ (kāŋmiì) room (in a house) ¶ ངའི་ནང་ལ་ཁང་མིག་བཞི་ཡོད་ I have four rooms in my house.

ཁང་མིག་སྦུག་མ་ (kāŋmiì bu̱gma) inner room.

ཁང་མོ་ཆེ་ (kāŋmoce) a big house.

ཁང་དམར་ (kāŋmar) a village and district south of Gyantse.

ཁང་རྨང་ (kāŋmaŋ) foundation of a house.

ཁང་རྩ་ (kāŋdza) 1. the foundation of a house. 2. the vicinity around a house/ building.

ཁང་རྩིག་ (kāŋdzig) the wall of a house/ building; va.—རྒྱག་ to build a wall around a house/ building.

ཁང་བརྩེགས་ (kāŋdzeg) a multistoried house/ building.

ཁང་ཚན་ (kāŋdzen) 1. section of a house. 2. dormitory unit in a monastery.

ཁང་ཚེ་ཨེན་ (kāŋdzeen) eng. (a business) concern.

ཁང་མཚེས་ (kāmdzɛɛ̀) neighbor.

ཁང་འཛིན་ (kāŋdzin) 1. title of house ownership. 2. receipt for rent payment.

ཁང་ཞིང་ (kāŋshiŋ) house and fields.

ཁང་གཞི་ (kāŋshi) foundation of a house; va.—འདིངས་ to lay the foundation of a house/ building.

ཁང་ཟུར་ (kāŋsur) corner of a house.

ཁང་བཟང་ (kāŋsaŋ) a good house.

ཁང་བཟོ་ (kāŋso) construction of houses/ buildings; va.—བྱེད་.

ཁང་གཡབ་ (kāŋyab) porch, portico.

ཁང་རུལ་ (kāŋrüü) an old or dilapidated house/ building.

ཁང་རོ་ (kāŋro) a ruined house, the rubble of a house.

ཁང་རོ་སྒྱུང་གོག་ (kāŋro gya̱ŋgɔɔ̀) dilapidated, in ruins (buildings).

ཁང་རོ་ཚྭ་ཁ་ (kāŋro tsāga) name of a salt lake in Shenzha county in Tibet.

ཁང་ཤག་ (kāŋshaà) 1. house. 2. real estate.

ཁང་ཤག་དང་ཁང་ས་དོ་དམ་ཅུའུ་ (kāŋshaà) tib. ch. real estate administration.

ཁང་ཤག་དོ་དམ་ཁྲུའུ་ (kāŋshaà) tib. ch. housing department, real estate office/ department.

ཁང་ཤིས་ (kāŋshiì) the Qing emperor Kangxi.

ཁང་ཤུལ་སྒྱུང་རོ་ (kāŋshü gya̱ŋro) dilapidated, in ruins (buildings).

ཁང་ཤུལ་སྟོང་པ་ (kāŋshü dōŋba) an empty or desolate area with ruined buildings.

ཁང་བཤེར་ (kāŋsher) searching a house; va.—རྒྱག ¶ ཨྱོག་ཚོང་རྒྱག་མཁན་ལ་ཁང་བཤེར་བརྒྱབ་པ་རེད་ (They) searched the house of the smuggler.

ཁང་ས་ (kāŋsa) the land on which a house is built.

ཁང་སྲུང་བ་ (kōŋsuŋa) guard, watchman, caretaker (of a house/ building).

ཁང་གསོལ་ (kāŋsöö) housewarming (party), celebration on the occasion of moving into a new house or on completion of the construction of a new house; va.—གཏོང་.

ཁང་ཧྲུལ་སྒྱུང་གོག (kāŋhrüü gya̱ŋgɔɔ̀) dilapidated, in ruins (buildings).

ཁངས་ (kāŋ) sm.* ཁྱིང་.

ཁངས་འཕྲོས་བླུག (kāŋdröö lūù) sm. ཁྱིངས་འཕྲོས་བྱུག.

ཁད་ (kɛ̄ɛ̀) 1. (vb. + dat.-loc. + —) on the verge of doing the action of the preceeding verb ¶ གནམ་གྲུ་འཕུར་ལ་ཁད་ལ་སྐྱོན་ཤོར་སོང་ When the plane was on the verge of taking off, it broke down. 2. distance. 3. as soon as ¶ ནང་དུ་སླེབས་མ་ཁད་ As soon as I arrived home.

ཁད་ཀྱིས་ (kɛ̄ɛ̀giì) gradually, slowly ¶ ང་ལུང་པ་དེའི་ཕྱོགས་སུ་ཁད་ཀྱིས་བཅར་སྐབས་ When I gradually came closer to that place.

ཁད་ཀྱིས་ཁད་ཀྱིས་ (kɛ̄ɛ̀giì kɛ̄ɛ̀giì) gradually, slowly.

ཁད་འགྱངས་ཁ་ཐོར་ (kɛ̄ɛ̀gyaŋ kātɔr) dispersed/ scattered widely.

ཁད་རྒྱང་ (kɛ̄ɛ̀gyaŋ) long distance ¶ ལུང་པ་དེ་གཉིས་བར་ས་ཁད་རྒྱང་ཡོད་པ་རེད་ There is a long distance between these two places.

ཁད་ཉེ་ (kɛ̄ɛ̀ñe) short distance.

ཁད་མཉམ་ (kɛ̄ɛ̀ñam) the same distance/ height.

ཁད་སྙོམས་ (kɛ̄ɛ̀ñom) sm. ཁད་མཉམ་.

ཁད་དུ་ (kɛ̄ɛ̀tu) sm. ཁད, 3.

ཁད་ཡངས་པ་ (kɛ̄ɛ̀yaŋba) sm. ཁད་ཡངས་པོ་.

ཁད་ཡངས་པོ་ (kɛ̄ɛ̀yaŋbo) spacious, large.

ཁད་རིང་ (kɛ̄ɛ̀riŋ) sm. ཁད་རྒྱང་.

ཁན་ (kɛ̄n) a little, a small part of, a few.

ཁན་ཅར་ (kɛ̄njar) ch. sm. ཁན་སྦྱར་.

ཁན་ནེ་ཁོན་ནེ་ (kɛ̄nne kȭnne) friction, conflict, discord.

ཁན་པ་སློག (kɛ̄mba lɔ̄ɔ̀) va. to pay cash to make up the difference in a barter trade in which one item is more valuable.

ཁན་སྦྱར་ (kɛ̄njar) ch. waistcoat, sleeveless coat, vest.

ཁན་སྦྱར་ཨང་རྟགས་ཅན་ (kɛ̄njar āŋdaàjɛn) a vest with numbers that is used in sports events to identify competitors.

ཁབ་ (kāp) 1. needle; va.—རྒྱག to stick/ poke with a needle, to give an injection ¶ གློག་ཚད་ལྟ་བྱེད་ཡོ་བྱད་ཀྱི་ཁབ་དམར་མོ་ The red needle of an electric meter. 2. palace ¶ རྒྱལ་པོའི་ཁབ་ The king's palace. 3. wife ¶ ཁོང་གིས་བུ་མོ་ཞིག་ཁབ་ཏུ་བླངས་པ་རེད་ He took a girl as his wife.

ཁབ་ཀྱི་རྩེ་མོ་ཙམ་ (kāpgi dzēmo dzām) a very tiny amount, very small [Lit. like a needle tip].

ཁབ་སྐུད་ (kāpgüü) needle and thread ¶ མང་ཚོགས་ཀྱི་ཁབ་སྐུད་ཙམ་ཡང་འཁྱེར་མི་ཆོག Even a needle and thread (the smallest item) may not be taken from the masses.

ཁབ་སྐུད་སྐར་མདའ་འཁྱུག་འཁྱུག (kāpgüù gānda kyūgkyug) doing something very quickly and well [Lit. needle and thread as quick as a shooting star].

ཁབ་སྐུད་ཁུག་མ་ (kāpgüù kūgmə) needle and thread case, sewing kit.

ཁབ་སྐུད་ལྷུག་ཤུབས་ (kāpgüù lūshub) sm. ཁབ་སྐུད་ཁུག་མ་.

ཁབ་སྐྱོན་ (kāb gyö̱n) h. of ཁབ་རྒྱག.

ཁབ་ཁ་ (kāpka) point of a needle.

ཁབ་ཁོབ་ (kāpkob) sm. ཁབ་བེ་ཁོ་བེ་.

ཁབ་གོང་གཟེར་ (kāb go̱nser) 1. keeping sth. in a very safe, secure place; va.—བྱེད་ [Lit. fastening a needle on one's lapel]. 2. shung. sending one's subject to serve another taxpayer/ lord; va.—བྱེད་.

ཁབ་མགོ་ (kābgo) a medical instrument used to check head injuries (in tt.).

ཁབ་མགོ་ཆེ་ (kāpgoce) a pin/ needle with a round head.

ཁབ་རྒྱག (kāp ka̱à) see ཁབ་.

ཁབ་རྒྱག་སྨན་ཆུ་ (kāpgyaà mɛ̄nju) liquid medcine for use in a syringe.

ཁབ་ཆུང་མ་ (kāb cūnma) younger wife.

ཁབ་ཆེན་མ་ (kāb cēmma) older wife.

ཁབ་སྙུང་གང་འགྲོ་ (kābñuŋ ka̱ŋdro) 1. acting according to the situation; va.—བྱེད་. 2. testing to see how far one can go or get away with sth.; va.—བྱེད་ ¶ མི་དེས་ཁབ་སྙུང་གང་འགྲོའི་ཐོག་ནས་ཚོང་གི་ཁེ་བཟང་ཟ་ཐབས་བྱེད་ཀྱི་འདུག He is trying to see how far he can go to make the most profit (e.g., asking for 100% profit, and if that fails, 90% etc.) [Lit. wherever the needle and awl will go].

ཁབ་དུ་ལེན་ (kəbdu len) va. to take as wife.

ཁབ་དུ་ལོངས་ (kəbdu loŋ) imp. of ཁབ་དུ་ལེན་.

ཁབ་དུ་བསུ་ (kəbdu sū) imp. of ཁབ་དུ་ལེན་.

ཁབ་འཐག (kəptaà) knitting; va.—རྒྱག to knit ¶ཁབ་འཐག་བཟོ་གྲྭ་ Knitting factory.

ཁབ་འཐག་དངོས་རྫས་ཚོང་ཁང་ (kəptaà ŋödzɛ tsōŋgaŋ) a knitted goods store.

ཁབ་འཐག་ཐོན་སྐྱེད་མཉམ་ལས་ཁང་ (kəptaà tōngyeè ñāmlɛgaŋ) a knitting cooperative enterprise.

ཁབ་འཐག་བཟོ་གྲྭ་ (kəbdaà sodra) knitting mill/ factory.

ཁབ་དང་མེ་བཙའ་ (kəptə medza) acupuncture and moxibustion; va.—རྒྱག.

ཁབ་དང་སྲིད་འཛིན་ (kəptə sīndzin) taking responsibility as a wife/ female head of household.

ཁབ་སྣོད་ (kəbnöö) needle case.

ཁབ་སྤང་ (kəb bāŋ) va. to renounce family life (marriage) and become a monk.

ཁབ་སྦྲིད་ (kəbdriì) acupuncture induced anaesthesia.

ཁབ་ཕ་པོ་ (kəb pābo) sm.* ཁབ་ཕྲ་པོ་.

ཁབ་ཕྲ་(པོ་) (kəbdra) a thin needle.

ཁབ་བེ་ཁོ་བེ་ (kəbbe kōbe) a clumsy/ awkward person.

ཁབ་སྦོམ་ (kəb bom) a thick needle.

ཁབ་མིག (kəbmiì) eye of a needle; va.—བརྒྱུ་ to thread a needle.

ཁབ་མིག་གཅིག་གི་ལྟ་ཚུལ་ (kəbnug jīggi dātsul) a narrow view, tunnel vision. [Lit. the view from the eye of a needle].

ཁབ་སྨན་ (kəbmɛn) medicine in liquid form used as an injection; va.—འཛུགས་; —རྒྱག to inject, to give an injection.

ཁབ་གཙག (kəbdzaà) needle, lancet; va.—རྒྱག to stick with a needle, to do acupuncture; to tattoo.

ཁབ་གཙག་ཐབས་ (kəb dzāàtəb) method of accupuncture, way to insert accupuncture needle.

ཁབ་གཙང་ (kəbdzaŋ) sm. ཁེ་གཙང་.

ཁབ་བཙའ་ (kəbdzə) acupuncture and moxibustion.

ཁབ་བཙའ་སྨན་བཅོས་ཁང་ (kəbdzə mɛ̄njöögaŋ) acupuncture ward/ clinic.

ཁབ་བཙའི་གསོ་ཐབས་ (kəbdzɛ sōtəp) acupuncture and moxibustion therapy/ treatment.

ཁབ་བཙུགས་གསོ་ཐབས་ (kəbdzuù sōtəp) acupuncture therapy/ treatment.

ཁབ་བཙུན་མ་ (kəb dzūnma) 1. queen. 2. ཁབ་འཛིན་མོ་.

ཁབ་རྩེ་ (kəbdze) point of a needle.

ཁབ་ཚུགས་ (kəbtsuù) the space between stitches.

ཁབ་ཚོར་ (kəbtsor) the pricking sensation when acupuncture is done.

ཁབ་འཚེམས་མངགས་ སྦུད་པ་དབུགས་མངགས་ (kəbdzeg ŋāà pūübə bug) doing the work that one is assigned/ supposed to do [Lit. needle is commissioned for sewing, bellow is commissioned for blowing].

ཁབ་འཛིན་མོ་ (kəb dzinmo) the woman head of a household.

ཁབ་འཛུགས་སྟང་འཛུགས་ (kəbdzuù ñūŋdzuù) imposing one's views on others, making sb. else do what one wants; va.—བྱེད་ [Lit. sticking a needle in, sticking an awl in].

ཁབ་ཟུག་སྟང་འགྲོ་ (kəbsug ñūŋdro) sm. ཉལ་ས་བྱུང་ན་ སྐྲོང་ས་དྲན་ [Lit. sticking an awl after the needle has gone].

ཁབ་ཟུར་ (kəbsur) temporarily, briefly, momentarily ¶ཁབ་ཟུར་གི་ལས་ཀ་ Temporary work.

ཁབ་ཟུར་ཞུན་མར་ཞུ་རྫས་དམ་ཁ་བརྒྱ་ལས་ལྷག་པ་ (kəbsur shūnmar shudzɛɛ̀ tāŋga gyalɛɛ̀ khāgba) sth. that fulfills one's immediate needs is more valuable that sth. that is valuable but doesn't meet present needs [Lit. a temporary oil lamp is more valuable than 100 thankas].

ཁབ་གཟེད་ (kəb seè) vi. to be/ get inoculated, to get an injection ¶ང་ཁབ་གཟེད་པར་འགྲོ་གི་ཡིན་ I am going to get an injection.

ཁབ་གཟེར་ (kəbsee) safety pin, pin.

ཁབ་བཟུང་ (kəbsuŋ) 1. sm. ཁབ་གཟེར་. 2. broach.

ཁབ་ར་ (kəbra) sm.* ཁ་ར་.

ཁབ་རལ་ (kəbrɛɛ) sm. ཁབ་ཤུབས་.

ཁབ་ལད་ (kəblɛɛ̀) sm.* ཁ་ལད་.

ཁབ་ལས་ (kəblɛɛ̀) tailoring work; va.—བྱེད་.

ཁབ་ལེན་ (kəblen) magnet.

ཁབ་ལེན་དཀར་རྫས་ (kəblen gārdzɛɛ̀) magnetic ceramics.

ཁབ་ལེན་འཁོར་གཞོང་ (kəblen kōōshoŋ) magnetic disc.

ཁབ་ལེན་གྱི་རྒྱུན་ (kəblengi gyün) magnetic current.

ཁབ་ལེན་གྱི་ལྟེ་སྙེ་ (kəblengi dēne) magnetic core.

ཁབ་ལེན་གྱི་འཐེན་ཤུགས་ (kəblengi tēnshuù) magnetic force, magnetism.

ཁབ་ལེན་གྱི་མདའ་ (kəblengi da) magnetic needle.

ཁབ་ལེན་གྱི་སྦུ་གུ་ (kəblengi būgu) magnetic tube.

ཁབ་ལེན་གྱི་འོད་འགྱུར་ནུས་པ་ (kəblengi wöögyur nüüba) magnetic optical effect.

ཁབ་ལེན་གྱི་རང་བཞིན་ (kəblengi rəŋshin) magnetic properties.

ཁབ་ལེན་གྱི་ཤུགས་ (kəblengi shūg) magnetic force.

ཁབ་ལེན་རྒྱུ་ཆ་བཟོ་གྲྭ་ (kəblen gyupja sodra) magnetic materials plant/ factory.

ཁབ་ལེན་རྒྱུ་ཚད་ (kəblen gyutsɛɛ̀) magnetic permeability; magnetic permeability rate.

ཁབ་ལེན་གློག་སྒོ་ (kəblen lɔ̄ɔ̀go) magnetic switch.

ཁབ་ལེན་གློག་འཕྲུལ་ (kəblen lɔ̄ɔ̀drüü) magnetoelectric.

ཁབ་ལེན་རྒྱུགས་ཚད་ (kəblen gyugdzɛɛ̀) magnetic flux.

ཁབ་ལེན་རྒྱུན་གྲངས་ (kəblen gyundraŋ) magnetic constant.

ཁབ་ལེན་མགོ་ (kəblen go) magnetic head (of a recorder).

ཁབ་ལེན་འགོག་རྫས་ (kəblen gogdzɛɛ̀) antimagnetic.

ཁབ་ལེན་ང་ར་ལྕགས་ (kəblen ŋarjaà) magnetic steel.

ཁབ་ལེན་རྔ་ (kəblen ŋā) magnetic drum.

ཁབ་ལེན་ཅན་དུ་འགྱུར་ (kəblenjɛntu gyur) vi. to get magnetized.

ཁབ་ལེན་མཉམ་བསྲེས་ལྕགས་རིགས་ (kəblen ñāmseè jəgrig) magnetic alloy.

ཁབ་ལེན་དམ་བི་ (kəblen tambi) magnetic bottle.

ཁབ་ལེན་དུ་འགྱུར་ (kəblentu gyur) vi. to get magnetized.

ཁབ་ལེན་འདྲེན་ཚད་ (kəblen drentsɛɛ̀) sm. ཁབ་ལེན་རྒྱུ་ཚད་.

ཁབ་ལེན་རྡོ་ (kəblen do) magnet, magnetic ore.

ཁབ་ལེན་རྡོའི་རྒྱུག་པ་ (kəblen dö gyugbə) magnetic bar/ stick.

ཁབ་ལེན་ནུས་ཉེན་སྨན་བཅོས་ (kəblen nüüden mɛ̄njöö) magnetic therapy.

ཁབ་ལེན་ནུས་འདེམས་ (kəblen nündem) magnetic separation.

ཁབ་ལེན་ནུས་འདེམས་འཕྲུལ་འཁོར་ (kəblen nündem trüügɔɔ) magnetic separator (machine).

ཁབ་ལེན་སྣང་ཚུལ་ (kəblen nəŋtsul) magnetic phenomenon.

ཁབ་ལེན་སྙེ་མ་ (kəblen nēma) magnetic pole.

ཁབ་ལེན་སྙེ་མོ་ (kəblen nēmo) sm. ཁབ་ལེན་སྙེ་མ་.

ཁབ་ལེན་བར་དངོས་ (kəblen parŋöö) magnetic medium.

ཁབ་ལེན་བར་ཐག (kəblen partag) magnetic moment.

ཁབ་ལེན་ཚ་འགྱུར་ (kəblen tsəngyur) magnetic storm.

ཁབ་ལེན་གཟུགས་ (kəblen sug) magnetic body.

ཁབ་ལེན་གཞོལ་ཟུར་ (kəblen shöösur) magnetic inclination.

ཁབ་ལེན་ཡོན་ཟུར་ (kəblen yönsur) magnetic declination.

ཁབ་ལེན་ར་བ་ (kəblen rawa) magnetic field.

ཁབ་ལེན་ར་བའི་འབུད་ཤུགས་ (kəblen rawɛ büüshug) repulsion of magnetic field.

ཁབ་ལེན་ར་བའི་ནུས་པ་ (kəblen rawɛ nüübə) magnetic field energy, magnetic field effect.

ཁབ་ལེན་ར་བའི་ཤུགས་ཆེ་ཆུང་ (kəblen rawɛ shūg cĭjuŋ) magnetic field intensity.

ཁབ་ལེན་ཤུགས་ (kəblen shūg) magnetic force.

ཁབ་ལེན་ཤུགས་ཐིག (kəblen shūgtig) magnetic line of force.

ཁབ་ལེན་ཤུགས་ཐེབས་ (kəblen shūgteb) magnetic induction.

ཁབ་ལེན་ཤུལ་ལྷག (kəblen shǖǖlhaà) residual magnetism.

ཁབ་ལེན་སོར་གནས་ (kəblen sōrnɛɛ̀) magnetic hysteresis.

ཁབ་ལེན་སྲོག་ཤིང་ (kəblen sōgshiŋ) magnetic axis.

ཁབ་ལོ་ (kəblo) needle of conifer tree.

ཁབ་ལོའི་ནགས་ཚལ་ (kəblö nagtsɛɛ) coniferous forest.

ཁབ་ཤུབས་ (kəbshuù) needle case, needle holder.

ཁབ་ཤུལ་ (kəbshüü) needle mark (left after an injection).

ཁབ་ཤུལ་སྐུད་པས་གང་ནོན་ (kəbshüü gǖübɛ kaŋnön) continuing the work of one's predecessors ¶ ཕ་ཕ་གྲོང་རྗེས་ཕྲུ་གུ་ཚོས་ཁབ་ཤུལ་སྐུད་པས་གང་ནོན་བྱས་པ་ཕའི་ལས་གཞུག་བསྒྲུབ་པ་རེད་ After the father died, the children, like a thread fills the needle hole, continued their father's work. [Lit. thread fills a needle hole].

ཁབ་ས་གདིབ་གདོང་ (kəbsa dĭbdoŋ) destroying or killing sb. so that no one knows it [Lit. sticking a needle into the earth].

ཁབ་སོ་ (kəbso) king's treasury.

ཁབ་སུབ་ (kəbsub) sm. ཆེམ་སུབ་.

ཁབ་སླས་ (kəblɛɛ̀) sm. ཁབ་བསླས་.

ཁབ་གསོག་འབིག་དང་འབིག་གསོག་གྲི་ (kəbsɔɔ̀ big taŋ bigsɔɔ̀ tri) building up little by little [Lit. accumulate needles to make an awl and accumulating awls to make a sword].

ཁབ་བསླས་ (kəblɛɛ̀) knitting, knitted.

ཁབ་བསླས་ཁ་གྱོན་ (kəblɛɛ̀ kāgyön) sm. ཁབ་བསླས་གྱོན་ཆས་.

ཁབ་བསླས་གྱོན་ཆས་ (kəblɛɛ̀ gyönjɛɛ̀) knitted clothes/ apparel, jersey.

ཁབ་བསླས་དངོས་རྫས་ (kəblɛɛ̀ ŋöödzɛɛ̀) knitted goods.

ཁབ་བསླས་བཟོ་གྲྭ་ (kəblɛɛ̀ sodra) knitting factory.

ཁབ་ལྷས་ (kəblhɛɛ̀) sm. ཁབ་བསླས་.

ཁབས་ (kāb) freckles.

ཁབས་གཅོད་ (kābjöö) lid, cover; va.—རྒྱག to cover with a lid.

ཁམ་ (kām) 1. a mouthful ¶ ཁམ་གང་རེ་གང་རེ་བྱས་ནས་བཟས་པ་རེད་ (They) ate it a mouthful at a time. 2. abbr. ཁམ་བུ་.

ཁམ་དཀར་ (kāmgar) 1. ginkgo tree. 2. reddish brown (yak, cow, etc.).

ཁམ་སྐམ་ (kām) dried ཁམ་བུ་.

ཁམ་སྐྱུར་ (kāmgyur) bitter peach.

ཁམ་ཁམ་ (kāmkam) sm. ཁམ་པ་, 1.

ཁམ་ཁུམ་ (kāmkum) abbr. ཁམ་མི་ཁུམ་མི་.

ཁམ་ཁུམ་གཉེར་མ་ (kāmkum ñerma) abbr. ཁམ་མི་ཁུམ་མི་.

ཁམ་ཁྲ་ (kāmdra) reddish brown uneven coloring (for animals).

ཁམ་གང་ (kāmgaŋ) a mouthful.

ཁམ་སྟར་ (kāmdar) abbr. peach and walnut.

ཁམ་མདོག (kāmdɔɔ̀) peach color.

ཁམ་སྡོང་ (kāmdoŋ) peach tree.

ཁམ་ནག (kāmnag) dark brown.

ཁམ་པ་ (kāmba) 1. reddish brown color for animals. 2. sm. ཁམས་པ་.

ཁམ་ཕོར་ (kāmpɔr) clay/ earthenware cup.

ཁམ་འཕྲོ་ (kāmdro) leftover food.

ཁམ་བུ་ (kəmbu) peach (sometimes also used for apricot).

ཁམ་བུ་དབྱང་ཐའོ་ (kəmbu yāŋtawo) ch. 1. carambola tree. 2. fruit from the carambola tree.

ཁམ་བུ་མ་ཆུ་ (kəmbu macu) a river in southern Tibet that flows through Yadong into Bhutan.

ཁམ་བུ་སྒྲི་ཏོའུ་ (kəmbu yāŋtawo) ch. sm. ཁམ་བུ་དབྱང་ཐའོ་.

ཁམ་བུ་རག་ཤ་ (kəmbu ragsha) peach.

ཁམ་བུ་རི་ཁམ་ (kəmbu rigam) a kind of peach that grows wild in the hills.

ཁམ་བུའི་ལྡུམ་ར་ (kəmbü dumra) peach grove/ orchard/ garden.

ཁམ་བུའི་མེ་ཏོག (kəmbü metog) flower of the peach tree.

ཁམ་པོ་ཏྲ་ཡ་ (kāmbotrəyə) Cambodia.

ཁམ་འབྲས་ (kāmdrɛɛ̀) sm. ཁམ་བུ་.

ཁམ་མི་ཁུམ་མི་ (kāmme kūmmi) 1. (with གཉེར་མ་) wrinkles, wrinkled ¶ རྒན་པོའི་གདོང་ལ་གཉེར་མ་ཁམ་མི་ཁུམ་མི་མང་པོ་ཡོད་པ་རེད་ Old people have a lot of wrinkles on their faces. 2. creases on a piece of paper that has been crushed/ folded ¶ ཤོག་བུ་དེ་གཉེར་མ་ཁ་མི་ཁུམ་མི་ཆགས་བཞག་ That paper has become all creased. 3. timid; va.—བྱེད་ to act/ be timid ¶ ཁམ་མི་ཁུམ་མི་མ་བྱེད་ Don't be timid.

ཁམ་མེ་ཁུམ་མེ་ (kāmme kūmme) sm. ཁམ་མི་ཁུམ་མི་.

ཁམ་ཚད་ (kāmdzɛɛ̀) a mouthful of food.

ཁམ་ཚལ་ (kāmdzɛɛ) peach garden/ grove.

ཁམ་ཚིག (kāmdzii) seed/ pit of peach or apricot.

ཁམ་ཚིག་གི་ནང་རྩི་ (kəmdziigi naŋdzi) the kernel of a peach seed.

ཁམ་ཚིག་ནང་སྙིང་ (kəmdziigi naŋñiŋ) sm. ཁམ་ཚིག་གི་ནང་རྩི་.

ཁམ་ཚོད་ (kəmdzöö) sm. ཁམ་ཚད་.

ཁམ་ཟས་ (kāmsɛɛ̀) eating sth. in one mouthful; va.—བྱེད་.

ཁམ་ལེབ་སེར་པོ་ (kāmleb sēēbo) mango.

ཁམ་ཤིང་ (kāmshiŋ) peach tree, apricot tree.

ཁམ་ས་ (kāmsa) reddish-brown earth/ soil.

ཁམ་སེར་(མདོག) (kāmser) yellowish brown (apricot) color.

ཁམས་ (kām) 1. health, physical condition; va.—འདྲི་ to ask about another's health ¶ ཁམས་བཟང་པོ་ Good health. 2. name of a large subcultural region in Eastern Tibet ¶ ཁམས་པ་ An Eastern Tibetan. 3. a domain, territory ¶ རྒྱལ་ཁམས་ Kingdom. 4. an element ¶ ཁམས་དྲུག The six elements. 5. abbr. of ཁམས་དཀར་ and ཁམས་དམར་.

ཁམས་ཀྱི་དྭངས་མ་ (kāmgi taŋma) sperm.

ཁམས་དཀར་ (kāmgaa) sperm; va.—ལེན་ to obtain sperm, va.—འབྱིན་ to ejaculate; vi.—འཛག to have a wet dream.

ཁམས་དཀར་རྒྱུག་སའི་རྩ་ (kāmgaa gyugsɛ dzā) sm. ཁམས་རྒྱུག་སའི་རྩ་.

ཁམས་དཀར་རྒྱུག་རྩ་ (kāmgaa gyugdza) sm. ཁམས་རྒྱུག་སའི་རྩ་.

ཁམས་དཀར་སྔ་འཚོར་ (kāmgaa ŋanjor) vi. to have a premature ejaculation.

ཁམས་དཀར་འདྲེན་སྦུག (kāmgaa drenbuù) sm. ཁམས་དཀར་འདྲེན་སྦུག.

ཁམས་དཀར་འདྲེན་སྦུག་སྡོམ་པ་ (kāmgar drenbug domba) vasoligation.

ཁམས་དཀར་འདྲེན་སྦུབས་ (kāmgar drenbug bub) seminal duct, sperm duct.

ཁམས་དཀར་སྣོད་ (kāmgaa nöö) spermatocyst.

ཁམས་དཀར་འབྱིན་སྦུག (kāmgaa jimbuù) the sperm duct.

ཁམས་སྐད་ (kāmkɛɛ̀) Kham dialect; va.—རྒྱག to speak the Kham dialect.

ཁམས་ཁུལ་ (kāmgüü) the region of Kham (Eastern Tibet).

ཁམས་འཁྲུགས་ (kām trūg) vi. to feel ill/ sick.

ཁམས་གྲི་ (kəmdri) a short knife made in Eastern Tibet.

ཁམས་གླུ་ (kəmlu) a song in the style of the Kham region.

ཁམས་འགྲོ་ཁག་གི་ལས་ཆག (kāmdrokaàgi lɛɛ̀jaà) shung. reducing or canceling taxes for somebody going to Kham on official work.

ཁམས་རྒྱུག་སའི་རྫ་ (kāmgyusɛ dzā) spermatic duct.

ཁམས་ལྔ་ (kām ŋā) the five basic elements.

ཁམས་ཆེན་ (kāmcen) 1. the earth. 2. the empire.

ཁམས་ཉོག (kāmñɔg) sm. ཁམས་རྙོག.

ཁམས་རྙོག (པོ) (kāmñɔg (bo)) tired, run down, not well, ill ¶ མཚན་ལ་གཉིད་ཡག་པོ་མ་ཁུག་ཙང་དེ་རིང་ཁམས་རྙོག་པོ་ཞིག་འདུག Since I didn't sleep well (last night), today I feel tired.

ཁམས་སྙོམས་ (kāmñɔm) good health, well-being.

ཁམས་སྟོད་ (kāmdöö) the upper/ higher part of Kham.

ཁམས་ཐ་མ་ (kām tāma) 1. worst character/ nature. 2. sm. འདོད་ཁམས་.

ཁམས་དྭངས་ (པོ་) (kām taŋbo) 1. clear, distinct ¶ ཆུ་འདི་ཁམས་དྭངས་པོ་འདུག This water is clear. 2. errorless, correct ¶ ངས་རྩིས་ཁྲ་ཁམས་དྭངས་པོ་བཟོས་ཡོད་ I made the accounting clear and correct. 2. good health, well-being.

ཁམས་དྲིས་ (kām trii) p. of ཁམས་འདྲི་.

ཁམས་དྲུག (kām truu) the six elements.

ཁམས་བདེ་ (པོ་) (kāmde (bo)) good health, wellness ¶ ངའི་ནང་མི་ཚང་མ་ཁམས་བདེ་པོ་རེད་ Everyone is well in my family.

ཁམས་བདེ་འདྲི་ (kāmde tri) sm. ཁམས་འདྲི་ཞུ་.

ཁམས་འདྲི་ (kām tri) asking after sb.'s health; va.—ཞུ་ (h.).

ཁམས་ལྡོག (kām dɔ̀ɔ) sm. ཁམས་ལོག.

ཁམས་པ་ (kāmba) a person from Kham.

ཁམས་ནང་ཆེན་དཔོན་ (kām naŋjen bõn) shung. chief of Nangchen in Eastern Tibet.

ཁམས་འཕོ་ (kām pō) 1. vi. to have an ejaculation. 2. vi. to die.

ཁམས་བོད་ (kām pö̀ö) Kham-Tibet ¶ ཁམས་བོད་གཞུང་ལམ་ The Kham-Tibetan highway. ¶ ཁམས་བོད་རླངས་འཁོར་འགྲོ་ལམ་ The Kham-Tibetan motor highway ¶ ཁམས་བོད་ས་མཐོ་ The Kham-Tibetan plateau.

ཁམས་བྲིས་ (kāmdrii) style of painting and writing from Kham.

ཁམས་འབྲས་ (kāmdrɛɛ̀) sm. སྐྱེ་འབྲས་.

ཁམས་མི་ཉག (kām miñaà) a region in Kham.

ཁམས་མོ་ (kāmmo) a female from Kham.

ཁམས་དམར་ (kāmmar) 1. egg, ovum; vi.—གཏོང་ to ovulate. 2. menstrual period.

ཁམས་དམར་གྱི་ཁུངས་ (kāmmargi kūŋ) sm. ཁམས་དམར་འབྱུང་གནས་.

ཁམས་དམར་གྱི་སྣོད་ (kāmmargi nõ̀ö) ovary.

ཁམས་དམར་གྱི་ཕྲ་ཕུང་ (kāmmargi trāpuŋ) egg cell, ovum.

ཁམས་དམར་རྒྱུག་རྫ་ (kāmmar gyugdza) sm. ཁམས་དམར་འདྲེན་སྦུག.

ཁམས་དམར་རྒྱུག་སའི་རྫ་ (kāmmar gyugsɛ dzā) sm. ཁམས་དམར་འདྲེན་སྦུག.

ཁམས་དམར་སྒོ་ང་ (kāmmar goŋa) woman's egg (from ovary).

ཁམས་དམར་འདྲེན་སྦུག (kāmmar drēnbug) oviduct, fallopian tube.

ཁམས་དམར་འདྲེན་སྦུབས་སྡོམ་པ་ (kāmmar drenbub domba) tubal ligation.

ཁམས་དམར་འབྱུང་གནས་ (kāmmar cuŋnɛɛ̀) womb, ovary.

ཁམས་རྙ་བ་ (kām ñawa) sm. ཁམས་རྙོག་པ་.

ཁམས་སྨད་ (kām mɛ̃ɛ) lower part of the Kham region.

ཁམས་གཙང་ (kāmdzaŋ) clean.

ཁམས་གཙང་པོ་ (kām dzāŋbo) clean.

ཁམས་གཙང་མ་ (kām dzāŋma) sm. ཁམས་གཙང་

ཁམས་རྩ་འཁྲུགས་ (kāmdza trūg) vi. to get angry ¶ གནས་ཚུལ་དེ་གོ་ནས་ཁོང་གི་ཁམས་རྩ་འཁྲུགས་པ་རེད་ After he heard the news he got angry.

ཁམས་ཚན་ (kāmdzɛn) a residential dormatory unit within a "college" that contain monks from designated regions ¶ སྒོ་མང་གྲྭ་ཚང་ལ་ཁམས་ཚན་བཅུ་དྲུག་འདུག Gomang College has 16 "khamtsen."

ཁམས་ཚན་དགེ་རྒན་ (kāmdzɛn gegɛn) the monastic official in charge of a ཁམས་ཚན་ unit in a monastery.

ཁམས་མཚོ་ (kāmtso) Kham-Qinghai ¶ ཁམས་མཚོ་རླངས་འཁོར་འགྲོ་ལམ་ the Kham-Qinghai motor highway.

ཁམས་ཞྭ་ (khāmsha) a type of hat used in Kham.

ཁམས་བཞི་ (khām shi) the four elements: earth, water, fire and wind.

ཁམས་བཟང་པོ་ (khām saŋgo) well, healthy ¶ རྒྱ་གར་དུ་སྡོད་སྐབས་གཟུགས་ཁམས་བཟང་པོ་བྱུང་ While staying in India (I) was in good health.

ཁམས་བཟང་ཞལ་འཛུམ་ (kāmsaŋ sheedzum) smiling with good spirits and health.

ཁམས་ཡངས་པོ་ (kām yaŋbo) 1. gay, lighthearted, carefree, easygoing; va.—བྱེད་ ¶ སེམས་ཁམས་ཡང་པོ་བྱ་རྒྱུ་དེ་ལུས་པོར་ཕན་ཐོགས་ཡོད་ Being carefree is essential to the well-being of a person's health. 2. spacious and airy ¶ ཁང་པ་འདི་ཁམས་ཡངས་པོ་འདུག This house is spacious and airy.

ཁམས་ཡངས་པག་ཕེབས་ (kāmyaŋ pagbee) sm. ཁམས་ཡངས་པོ་.

ཁམས་གཡག (kām yāa) a yak from Kham.

ཁམས་རིགས་ (kām rig) a person from Kham, the Khamba ethnic group.

ཁམས་ལོག (kām lɔ̀ɔ) vi. to get sick of sth, to lose one's appetite for sth., to get fed up with sth. ¶ བར་ལམ་ང་ཤ་བཟའ་ཡག་ལ་ཁམས་ལོག་བཞག I have lost the appetite for meat these days.

ཁམས་ལྭ་ (kāmla) a type of woolen material traditionally made in Kham.

ཁམས་གཤིས་དྭངས་པོ་ (kāmshii taŋbo) attractive, good-looking ¶ བུ་དང་བུ་མོ་ཁམས་གཤིས་དྭངས་པོ་འདུག The boys and girls are good-looking.

ཁམས་གཤེར་ (kāmsher) seminal fluid.

ཁམས་སངས་པོ་ (kām sāŋbo) 1. an alert/ sharp/ high-spirited individual ¶ ཕྲུ་གུ་དེ་ཁམས་སངས་པོ་དང་གྲུང་སེར་སེར་ཞིག་འདུག That child is alert and high spirited. 2. well, in good health ¶ ཁྱེད་རང་ཁམས་སངས་པོ་འདུག་གམ་ Are you well?

ཁམས་སོས་ (kām sö̀ö) vi. to recover from an illness, to have one's health restored.

ཁམས་སོས་པོ་ (kām sö̀öbo) 1. well rested ¶ དབྱར་ཁའི་གུང་སེང་རིང་ང་རང་ཁམས་སོས་པོ་ཞིག་བྱུང་ I got a (good) rest during my summer vacation.

ཁམས་སླང་ (kām laŋ) earthenware pot/ frying pan.

ཁམས་སླེའུ་ (kām lēwu) 1. a type of woven blanket from Kham. 2. a woven basket from Kham.

ཁམས་གསུམ་ (kāmsum) the three realms: the realm of desire, the realm form, and the realm of formlessness.

ཁམས་གསུམ་ན་སྤྱོད་པ་ (kāmsumna jö̀öba) sentient beings that dwell in the three realms.

ཁམས་གསུམ་དབང་འདུས་ (kāmsum wāŋdüü) conqueror of the three realms.

ཁམས་གསུམ་ཚོམས་ཆེན་ (kāmsum tsōmgaŋ) the assembly hall above the western entrance to the Jokang.

ཁམས་གསེང་ (kāmseŋ) an outing, passing the time, whiling away time ¶ དེ་རིང་ང་གླིང་ཁའི་ནང་ཁམས་གསེང་ལ་འགྲོ་གི་ཡིན་ Today I am going on an outing to the park.

ཁམས་གསོ་ (kām sō) va. to restore health or physical well-being.

ཁམས་གསོ་ཁང་ (kāmsogaŋ) rest home, sanitarium.

ཁམས་གསོ་གླིང་ (kāmsoliŋ) sm. ཁམས་གསོ་ཁང་.

ཁམས་བསང་ (kām sāŋ) sm. ཁམས་གསེང་.

ཁམས་བསིལ་ (kām sīl) 1. vi. to feel cold. 2. cold air.

ཁམས་བསིལ་ཕྱེ་དཀར་ (kāmsil cēgar) talcum powder.

ཁམས་བསིལ་སྨན་ཕྱེ་ (kāmsil mēnje) sm. ཁམས་བསིལ་ཕྱེ་དཀར་.

ཁའི་ཉིན་ (kēñin) sm. ཁའི་ཉིན་ཀ་.

ཁའི་ཉིན་ཀ་ (kɛ ñiŋgə) the day before yesterday.

ཁའི་དེ་བཞིན་གཤེགས་པས་ལུས་ཀྱི་སྒྲིབ་པ་མི་དག (kɛ̃ɛ teshin shēgbɛ lüügi tribmə mitag) deeds not words are needed (often used to criticize people who recite prayers without thinking about or understanding them) ¶ ཁའི་བདེ་བཞིན་གཤེགས་པས་ལུས་ཀྱི་སྒྲིབ་པ་མི་དག་ཅེར་བ་ལྟར་ཁ་རྐྱང་པ་བཤད་ནས་ལས་ཀ་མ་བྱས་ན་ཕན་ཐོགས་གང་ཡང་མེད་ Like the saying "the mouth's Tatagatha will not cleanse the body's pollution," if you just talk and don't work, it will be of no benefit. [Lit. the mouth's Tatagatha will not cleanse the body's pollution].

ཁའི་མདུན་ (kēdün) right in front of, face-to-face.

ཁའི་སྐྲག་ཆ་ནད་ (kɛ̄ɛ bugja nɛɛ̀) stomatitis.

ཁའི་ཚང་ཐིག (kɛ̄ tsāŋtig) 1. ཁ་གཞུང་. 2. bore, caliber (of a gun).

ཁའི་ཞག་རྒྱབ་ (kɛ̄ɛ shaghyəb) va. to collect the layer of coagulated butter that forms on the top of a cup of Tibetan tea.

ཁའི་གཞིས་ཉིན་ཀ་ (kɛ̄ɛ sheè ñinga) sm. ཁ་གཞིས་ཉིན་ཀ་.

ཁའི་ལོ་ (kēlo) Cairo.

ཁའི་ཧྥིང་ (kɛ̄feŋ) Kaifeng.

ཁའོ་ (kāo) ch. section, department, subdivision of an administrative unit ¶ ཀྲུང་སྨན་ཁའོ་ Department of Chinese medicine.

ཁའོ་ཀྲང་ (kāo drāŋ) ch. head, director of a ཁའོ་.

ཁའོ་ཅིས་ (kāo jìi) ch. accountant, bookkeeper.

ཁའོ་ཆིན་ (kāojin) ch. mouth organ, harmonica.

ཁར་ (kār) 1. (vb. + —) just before, right before ¶ ཉལ་ཁར་སོ་འཁྲུད་རྒྱུ་དེ་གལ་ཆེ་པོ་ཡིན་ It's important to brush (one's) teeth just before going to bed. 2. (vb. + — adj. stem + —) on top of, in addition to ¶ དུད་ཚང་ 280 ལ་གློག་བཞུ་འཛུགས་ཐུབ་པ་བྱུང་ཁར་ On top of being able to put in electric lights for 280 families. 3. as well as ¶ ཁོ་ཆེ་གཟུགས་ཆེ་ཁར་ཤུགས་ཀྱང་ཆེན་པོ་འདུག He is big as well as strong. ¶ ཁོ་སློབ་གྲྭར་འགྲོ་ཁར་བཟོ་གྲྭ་ཁང་འགྲོ་གི་ཡོད་པ་རེད་ He goes to school as well as to the factory. 4. in/ to the mouth.

ཁར་འཁྱེར་ (kār kyēē) sm. ཁ་ལ་འཁྱེར་.

ཁར་སྒོང་ (kāāgoŋ) sm. དཀར་སྒོང་.

ཁར་མངོན་ (kāāŋön) visible, overt ¶ རྒྱ་འཛུལ་གྲུ་གཟིང་དེ་ད་ལྟ་ཆུ་ཁར་མངོན་གྱི་འདུག The submarine now is visible on the water.

ཁར་ཉན་པ་ (kāā ñɛmba) sm. ཁ་ལ་ཉན་པ་.

ཁར་ཉིན་ (kārñin) sm. ཁའི་ཉིན་ཀ་.

ཁར་ཏུམ་ (kārdum) Khartoum.

ཁར་ཐུག (kərtuù) straight, directly; straightforward ¶ ཁར་ཐུག་ལ་ཕྱིན་ན་སླེབས་ཀྱི་རེད་ If you go straight you'll get there. ¶ སྐད་ཆ་ཁར་ཐུག་ལ་བཤད་ན་ཡག་པོ་འདུག If you speak straightforwardly, it will be good.

ཁར་ཕོག་སྣར་ཕོག (kārbɔɔ̀ nārbɔɔ̀) offending, displeasing ¶ ཁོང་གི་ཚོགས་འདུའི་ཐོག་འགོ་ཁྲིད་ལ་ཁར་ཕོག་སྣར་ཕོག་འགྲོ་ཡག་གི་སྐད་ཆ་བཤད་པ་རེད་ He said things at the meeting that offended the leader.

ཁར་རྫང་ (kārdzaŋ) sm. ཁ་སྲང་.

ཁར་རི་ཁར་ཐུག (kəri kātuù) sm. ཁར་ཐུག.

ཁར་སང་ (kārsaŋ) sm. ཁ་སང་.

ཁལ་ (kɛ̄ɛ) 1. basic unit of twenty in some Tibetan/ Bhutanese numerical systems ¶ ཁལ་གཅིག Twenty. ¶ ཁལ་གཉིས་ forty ¶ ཁལ་གཅིག་དང་ཕྱེད་ཀ་ Thirty. ¶ ཁལ་གཉིས་དང་བཅུ་གཉིས་ Fifty two. 2. a standard Tibetan measure of volume equal to about thirty pounds of barley. 3. in contemporary Tibet a land area unit equal to one mu.

ཁལ་ཁ་ (kālka) 1. the Khalkha, the main Mongol ethnic group in (Outer) Mongolia. 2. Urga, the capital of Outer Mongolia (the old name for Ulaanbaator).

ཁལ་ཁ་ཁུ་རལ་ (kālka kūrɛɛ) ch. Urga (the old name for Ulaanbaator).

ཁལ་ཁ་རྗེ་བཙུན་དམ་པ་ (kālka jedzün tamba) the highest incarnation in Mongolia.

ཁལ་ཁ་གཟུགས་ (kālka sug) a kind of official dress in the tt. government that initially came from Mongolia.

ཁལ་གླང་ (kɛ̄ɛlaŋ) a pack ox.

ཁལ་རྒྱབ་ (kɛ̄ɛgyab) a pack animal's load (one ཁལ་རྒྱབ་ is made up of two loads, one on each side of the animal).

ཁལ་སྒ་ (kɛ̄ɛga) pack animal saddle on which loads are tied; va.—རྒྱག to put on a pack saddle.

ཁལ་རྔ་ (kɛ̄ɛŋa) yak tail.

ཁལ་ཇགས་ (kɛ̄ɛjaà) sm. ཁལ་འཛུགས་.

ཁལ་རྗེས་ (kɛ̄ljeè) person who accompanies pack/ transport animals.

ཁལ་རྟ་ (kɛ̄ɛda) a pack horse.

ཁལ་དོ་ (kɛ̄ɛ to) 1. a load for a pack animal; va.—རྒྱག to make a load for a pack animal. 2. two ཁལ་.

ཁལ་དྲེལ་ (kɛ̄ɛtre) a pack mule.

ཁལ་འདེད་ (kɛ̄ɛ teè) va. to drive a train or caravan of pack animals.

ཁལ་འདེད་པ་ (kɛ̄ɛteba) person who drives a pack animal train.

ཁལ་སྡེམ་ (kɛ̄ɛdem) a package of twenty rolls of Tibetan paper tied together.

ཁལ་པ་ (kɛ̄ɛba) people who go with transport animals, e.g., muleteers.

ཁལ་ཕྱུགས་ (kɛ̄ɛjuù) shung. carrying animals, transport animals.

ཁལ་འཛུགས་ (kɛ̄ɛcaà) shung. a form of taxation wherein the government uses private animals as a special tax for transportation; va.—རྒྱག.

ཁལ་བོང་ (kɛ̄ɛboŋ) a pack donkey.

ཁལ་བོང་བུས་ཁྱེར་ རྒྱ་ལམ་སྐེད་པ་ན་ (kɛ̄ɛ puŋbüü kyēr gyalam kēba na) inappropriate complaint [Lit. the donkey carries the load, the road's waist hurts].

ཁལ་མ་ (kɛ̄ɛma) an animal used for carrying or transport, a pack animal.

ཁལ་ཚུགས་ (kɛ̄ɛtsug) shung. one day's journey with loaded pack animals.

ཁལ་རྫ་ (kɛ̄ɛdza) a large earthenware pot that holds one khal of grain and is used for making Tibetan beer.

ཁལ་གཡག (kɛ̄ɛyaà) a pack yak.

ཁལ་ལུག (kɛ̄ɛluù) a pack sheep.

ཁལ་སློག (kɛ̄ɛlɔɔ̀) shung. a person who accompanies the corvee transport animals to the next station and then brings back the animals to the starting station.

ཁས (kɛ̄ɛ̀) verbally, orally, by the mouth [Lit. ཁ་ + inst.].

ཁས་ཁྱག (kɛ̄ɛ̀gyaà) 1. guarantee, surety, bail, bond (for a loan or agreement); va.—བྱེད་ to act as a guarantor, to post bail/ bond; va.—ཞུ་ to act as a guarantor (h.).

ཁས་ཁྱག་དགེ་རྒན་ (kɛ̄ɛ̀gyaà gegɛn) monk guarantor of a new monk.

ཁས་ཁྱག་བྱེད་མཁན་ (kɛ̄ɛ̀gyaà cegɛn) one who acts as a guarantor/ bondsman.

ཁས་ཁྱགས་ (kɛ̄ɛ̀gyaà) sm. ཁས་ཁྱག.

ཁས་འཆེ་ (kɛ̄ɛ̀ cē) va. to agree/ promise to do sth.

ཁས་འཆེ་བ་ (kɛ̄ɛ̀cewa) a person who has made an agreement/ guarantee.

ཁས་བརྗོད་ (kɛ̄ɛ̀jöö) poet. song.

ཁས་ཉིན་ཀ་ (kɛ̄ɛ̀ ñinga) the day before yesterday.

ཁར་ཉིན་ཀར་ (kārñingar) sm. ཁས་ཉིན་ཀ་.

ཁས་ཉིན་མོ་ (kɛ̄ɛ̀ ñinmo) sm. ཁས་ཉིན་ཀ་.

ཁས་ཐེག (kɛ̄ɛ̀ tēg) va. to bear/ take responsibility, to act as a guarantor ¶ མི་དེ་ལ་བུ་ལོན་གཡར་ན་ཁྱེད་རང་གིས་ཁས་ཐེག་པ་འདུག་གམ་ If that person gets a loan, can you be the guarantor.

ཁས་དྲག (kɛ̄ɛ̀trag) persuading, persuasion.

ཁས་བླང་ (kɛ̄ɛ̀ lāŋ) f. of ཁས་ལེན་.

ཁས་བླངས་ (kɛ̄ɛ̀ lāŋ) p. of ཁས་ལེན་.

ཁས་བླངས་རྒྱབ་བསྒྱུར་ (kɛ̄ɛ̀laŋ gyəbgyur) reneging on a promise/ agreement, a breach of faith.

ཁས་བླངས་ཐེབས་གཅོག (kɛ̄ɛ̀laŋ tēbjöö̀) sm. ཁས་བླངས་རྒྱབ་བསྒྱུར་.

ཁས་བླངས་ལག་བསྟར་ (kɛ̄ɛlaŋ lagdar) doing/ implementing what one has promised/ agreed; va.—བྱེད་.

ཁས་བླངས་སོས་ཐེག (kɛ̄ɛlaŋ sȫödeg) guaranteeing, pledging.

ཁས་མི་ལེན་ (kɛ̄ɛ milen) va. to disagree, to not acknowledge/ consent/ confirm ¶ཁོང་གི་ལས་ཀ་དེ་ཁས་མི་ལེན་པའི་རྒྱུ་མཚན་ནི་གླ་ཆ་ཆུང་དྲགས་པ་དེ་རེད་ The reason he did not agree to do the job is because the salary was too low.

ཁས་མི་ལེན་པའི་དབང་ཆ་ (kɛ̄ɛ milenbɛ wāŋja) veto, veto power.

ཁས་མེ་ལྟར་བླངས་ ཐེབས་རྫ་ལྟར་བཅག (kɛ̄ɛ midar lāŋ tēb dzadar jāà) breaking one's promise [Lit. promising like fire, breaking like clay].

ཁས་དམན་ (kɛ̄ɛmɛn) poor.

ཁས་ཞན་པ་ (kɛ̄ɛ shɛmba) sm. ཁ་ཞན་པ་.

ཁས་ཞན་དབང་ཆུང་ (kɛ̄ɛshɛn wāŋjuŋ) sm. ཁ་ཞན་པ་.

ཁས་གཞིས་ཉིན་ (kɛ̄ɛ shɛñin) the day before yesterday and the day before that (two and three days ago).

ཁས་གཞིས་ཉིན་ཀ་ (kɛ̄ɛshɛɛ ñinga) sm. ཁ་གཞིས་ཉིན་ཀ་.

ཁས་ལེན་ (kɛ̄ɛlen) 1. guaranteeing, promising, agreeing; va. ཁས་ལེན་; —བྱེད་ to guarantee, to promise; vi.—ཤོར་ to break a promise ¶ལས་ཀ་འདི་དོ་དགོང་ཚར་བ་ཁས་ལེན་བྱེད་ཀྱི་ཡིན་ I guarantee to finish the work by tonight. 2. acceptance, consent, agreement, recognition; va. ཁས་ལེན་; —བྱེད་ or —ཞུ་ to accept, to agree, to consent to, to own up to, to recognize ¶ཆོས་པ་ཞིག་གིས་གུང་ཁྲན་གྱི་ལྟ་བ་ཇི་ལྟར་ཁས་ལེན་བྱེད་ཐུབ་ཀྱི་རེད་ How can a religious person accept the ideology of communism? ¶ནོར་འཁྲུལ་ཕྱིན་ནས་ཁས་ལེན་གྱི་མེད་པ་རེད་ He absolutely wouldn't own up to his mistakes.

ཁས་ལེན་འགན་ཁུར་ (kɛ̄ɛlen genkur) responsibilities/ duties one has agreed to do; va.—བྱེད་.

ཁས་ལེན་འགལ་ཟླ་ (kɛ̄ɛlen genda) contrary to an agreement or promise; vi.—འགྱུར་; —ཆགས་ to become contrary to an agreement or promise ¶མི་དེས་ཐོག་མར་རོགས་རམ་བྱ་རྒྱུའི་ཁས་ལེན་འགལ་ཟླར་གྱུར་བ་རེད་ That person acted contrary to his initial promise of helping us.

ཁས་ལེན་རྒྱབ་བསྒྱུར་ (kɛ̄ɛlen gyabgyur) sm. ཁས་ལེན་ཆུ་བསྒྱུར་.

ཁས་ལེན་སྒྱུར་བཅོས་ (kɛ̄ɛlen gyurjöö) sm. ཁས་ལེན་བཟོ་བཅོས་.

ཁས་ལེན་ངོས་ལེན་ (kɛ̄len ŋöölen) accepting, recognizing ¶རྒྱ་གཞུང་གིས་ང་ཚོའི་ལམ་ཡིག་ཁས་ལེན་ངོས་ལེན་བྱས་མ་སོང་ The Chinese government did not recognize our passport.

ཁས་ལེན་ཆུ་བསྒྱུར་ (kēlen cūgyur) withdrawing/ reneging on an agreement or promise; va.—བྱེད་.

ཁས་ལེན་དམ་གཙང་ (kēlen tamdzaŋ) an honorable agreement/ promise.

ཁས་ལེན་པ་ (kɛ̄ɛlemba) a volunteer ¶ཁས་ལེན་པ་མི་བརྒྱད་དགྲ་བོའི་དམག་སྒར་ནང་ཕྱིན་པ་རེད་ Eight volunteers went into the enemy camp.

ཁས་ལེན་རྩོད་མེད་ (kɛ̄ɛlen dzōmeè) being in total agreement, accepting without argument; va.—བྱེད་.

ཁས་ལེན་བཟང་ཐོབ་ (kɛ̄ɛlen saŋ tōb) vi. to obtain a favorable promise or assurance ¶ཁོང་གི་ང་ཚོར་རྒྱབ་སྐྱོར་གནང་བའི་ཁས་ལེན་བཟང་ཐོབ་བྱུང་ (We) got an assurance (from him) that he would support us.

ཁས་ལེན་བཟོ་བཅོས་ (kɛ̄ɛlen sobjöö) revising/ amending an agreement or promise; va.—རྒྱག.

ཁས་ལེན་ལག་བསྟར་ (kɛ̄ɛlen lagdar) implementing a guarantee/ promise/ agreement; va.—བྱེད་.

ཁས་ལེན་ཤོར་ (kɛ̄ɛlen shɔ̄ɔ) see ཁས་ལེན་.

ཁས་ལེན་སོས་ཐེག (kɛ̄ɛlen sȫöteg) sm. ཁས་ལེན་.

ཁས་ས་ (kɛ̄ɛsa) sm. ཁ་ས་.

ཁྭ་ (kā) crow, raven.

ཁྭ་སྐད་ (kāgɛɛ) cawing cry of crows and ravens.

ཁྭ་སྐྱག (kāgyaà) sm. ཁྭ་.

ཁྭ་ཏ་ (kāda) sm. ཁྭ་.

ཁྭ་ཏ་འུག་པའི་འཁོན་ (kāda ugbɛ kön) a sworn enemy [Lit. enmity between ravens and owls].

ཁྭ་ཏའི་ཁྱུ་ (kādɛɛ kyū) an undisciplined mob, a disorderly group/ crowd, rabble [Lit. a flock of crows].

ཁྭ་ཏའི་ཁྱུ་ཚོགས་ (kādɛɛ kyūtsog) sm. ཁྭ་ཏའི་ཁྱུ་.

ཁྭ་ཝ་ཊོ་ (kāwato) eng. quark.

ཁྱིའུ་ (kīu) fine part of an animal's coat.

ཁི་ལོ་ཝ་ཊེ་ (kilowate) eng. kilowatt.

ཁིངས་ (kīŋ) sm. འཁིང་.

ཁུ་ (kū) 1. abbr. of ཁུ་བ་. 2. name of an ancient Tibetan tribe.

ཁུ་ཁོག (kūgɔɔ) a large wok used to fry dough.

ཁུ་ཁོག་ལགས་ (kūgɔɔlaà) the person who fries dough in a ཁུ་ཁོག.

ཁུ་ཁྲག (kū trāà) sperm and ovum.

ཁུ་གུ (kūgu) 1. paternal uncle. 2. small bag.

ཁུ་གེ་ (kūge) sm. ཁུ་གུ་, 2.

ཁུ་སྒྱུར་ (kū gyur) sm. ཁུ་འགྱུར་.

ཁུ་འགྱུར་ (kū gyur) vi. to become liquid, to get liquified.

ཁུ་ཐུ་ཆེ་ (kūtuchi) mong. servant.

ཁུ་དིར་དིར་ (kū tirdir) noisy/ boisterous/ uproarious talk and laughter.

ཁུ་གདུས་ (kū düü) va. to brew/ boil/ cook.

ཁུ་འདུས་ (kūndüü) 1. simple, not elaborate, plain ¶མི་ཚེ་སྐྱིལ་སྟངས་རྒྱས་སྤྲོས་མེད་པའི་ཁུ་འདུས་ཤིག་ཡིན་ནའང་ Even though we lead a simple life. 2. managing, maintaining keeping up ¶ཕ་མ་གློ་བུར་དུ་གྲོངས་ཙང་མི་ཚང་ཆེན་པོ་དེ་ཁུ་འདུས་མ་ཐུབ་པ་བྱུང་བ་རེད་ Because the father and mother died suddenly, that big family was unable to manage.

ཁུ་འདུས་པོ་ (kū düübo) sm. ཁུ་འདུས་.

ཁུ་འདེབས་ (kū deb) va. to yell/ shout.

ཁུ་དུལ་ (kū dül) sm. ཁུ་ཁྲག.

ཁུ་སྡུད་ (kū düü) 1. sm. ཁུ་བསྡུ་. 2. va. to pool/ combine money.

ཁུ་བསྡུ་ (kūdu) 1. curtailing, cutting back, reducing, simplifying, streamlining; va.—བྱེད་ ¶ལས་ཁུངས་ཁུ་བསྡུ་བྱེད་དགོས་ (We) must simplify (cut back) the offices. ¶ལས་ཁུངས་དེའི་ལས་བྱེད་པ་ཁུ་བསྡུ་བྱས་པ་རེད་ The staff was reduced. [this has two connotations: a. with regard to a specific office, it means eliminated. b. with regard to officials in general, it means a cut back or curtailment in numbers].

ཁུ་བསྡུ་གྲོན་ཆུང་ (kūdu drönjuŋ) simplifying or curtailing by reducing expenses ¶ཁུ་བསྡུ་གྲོན་ཆུང་གི་སྒོ་ནས་འཆར་གཞི་བསྒྲུབ་ཐུབ་ན་ If (we) can carry out the plan by means of streamlining and reducing expenses.

ཁུ་བསྡུ་གཞུང་ལས་ཁང་ (kūdu shuŋlɛɛgaŋ) simplified/ streamlined administration office.

ཁུ་བསྡུས་ (kū düü) p. of ཁུ་སྡུད་.

ཁུ་ནུ་ (kūnu) 1. abbr. older and younger brother. 2. name of a region in western Tibet.

ཁུ་ནུ་རི་བོ་ (kūnu riwu) Kunlun Mountains.

ཁུ་ནུ་ལ་ (kūnula) sm. ཁུ་ནུ་རི་བོ་.

ཁུ་འཁྲིག (kūdrig) doubt, suspicion; va.—བྱེད་.

ཁུ་བ་ (kōwə) 1. the juice/ liquid of anything ¶ཤིང་འབྲས་ཁུ་བ་ Fruit juice. 2. gravy, broth, soup. 3. sperm.

ཁུ་བ་དཀར་པ་ (kōwə gārwa) 1. milk or any other white liquid/ juice. 2. sperm.

ཁུ་བ་འཆོར་ (kūwə cɔ̄r) vi. to have a wet dream.

ཁུ་བ་ཐར་ (kōwə tār) vi. to cook meat until all the water is absorbed ¶ཁུ་བ་ཐར་བའི་ཤ་བཙོས་པ་དེ་ཞིམ་ཤོས་རེད་ Meat that has been cooked until all the liquid has been absorbed is the tastiest.

ཁུ་བ་དྭངས་མ་ (kōwə tāŋma) sm. ཁུ་བ་.

ཁུ་བ་འབྱིན་པའི་ལྷག་མ་ (kōwō jinbɛ lhāàma) a sexual act that does not involve the vagina, anus or mouth (e.g., the monk's style of intercourse between the thighs).

ཁུ་བ་ཟད་ (kōwə sɛ̱ɛ̀) vi. to run out of sperm, to have one's sperm become exhausted.

ཁུ་བོ་ (kōwō) sm. ཁུ་གུ.

ཁུ་བྱུག (kūyuù) cuckoo (bird).

ཁུ་བྱུག་གྲག་ཟླ་ (kūyuù tra̱nda) the third month of the Tibetan calendar.

ཁུ་བྱུག་མེ་ཏོག (kūyuù me̱dɔ̀ɔ) rhododendron.

ཁུ་བྱུག་རྩི་ཐོག (kūyuù dzīdoò) a type of plan used in traditional Tibetan medicine.

ཁུ་དབོན་ (kūbön) uncle and nephew.

ཁུ་དབྱུག (kūyuù) sm.* ཁུ་བྱུག.

ཁུ་མ་རྩིད་ (kūmadzi) mixture of ཁུ་ལུ་ and རྩིད་པ་.

ཁུ་མག (kūmag) sm. ཁུག་མ་.

ཁུ་མུག (kūmug) sm. ཁུག་མ་.

ཁུ་ཚན་ (kūtsɛn) abbr. uncle and nephew.

ཁུ་ཚུར་ (kūtsur) fist; va.—གཞུ་ to box, to punch; va.—འགྱོགས་ to raise one's fist (and arm) either as a sign of approval or in struggle session when accusing a person; va.—སྡོང་; —འཚང་ to clench one's fist.

ཁུ་ཚུར་དྲག་དེག (kūtsur tra̱gdeg) striking a powerful blow, walloping, hitting or punching hard.

ཁུ་ཚུར་སྣུན་རྩལ་ (kūtsur nūndzɛɛ) boxing (the sport); va.—འགྲན་ to compete in boxing ¶ཁུ་ཚུར་སྣུན་རྩལ་གྱི་འགྲན་སྡུར་ A boxing match.

ཁུ་ཚུར་བྲག་རྒྱབ་ (kūtsur traggyəb) fighting against impossible odds; va.—བྱེད་ [Lit. to hit a rock with one's fists].

ཁུ་ཚུར་གཞུ་རྩལ་ (kūtsur shu̱dzɛɛ) sm. ཁུ་ཚུར་སྣུན་རྩལ་.

ཁུ་ཡིས་འདེབས་ (kūyi de̱b) va. to shout/ yell.

ཁུ་ཡུ་ (kūyu) hornless animals in a species that normally has horns.

ཁུ་ཡུག (kūyuù) sm. ཁུ་བྱུག.

ཁུ་ར་ (kūra) pancake (usu. made from buckwheat).

ཁུ་རུབ་ (kūrub) gathering or collecting together; va.—རྒྱག ¶ཁོ་ཚོས་ཡིག་ཆ་ནམས་ཁུ་རུབ་བྱས་པ་རེད་ They collected the documents together.

ཁུ་རླངས་ (kūlaŋ) steam (usu. from cooking food).

ཁུ་ལུ་ (kūlu) the soft undercoat ("cashmere") of animals, e.g., goat, yaks, antelopes.

ཁུ་ལུ་ཚི་རིང་ (kūlu tsīriŋ) the longer fibers of ཁུ་ལུ་.

ཁུ་ལུམ་ (kūlum) eng. coulomb.

ཁུ་ལུའི་ཕྱིང་པ་ (kūlü ci̱ŋbə) felt made from ཁུ་ལུ་.

ཁུ་ལེ་ (kūle) 1. the piece of wood on which a weighing scale is hung. 2. a wooden bucket.

ཁུ་ལེམ (kūlem) sm. ཁུ་ལུམ་.

ཁུ་ཤ་ (kūshə) meat broth.

ཁུ་སིམ་ (kū sīm) sm. ཁུ་སིམ་པོ་.

ཁུ་སིམ་འཇམ་ཐིང་ (kūsim ja̱mtiŋ) sm. ཁ་ཁུ་སིམ་པོ་.

ཁུ་སིམ་དྲིག་ཟླ་ (kūsīm di̱gdra) a person who gives the appearance of being shy and quiet but is a womanizer.

ཁུ་སིམ་པོ་ (kū sīmbu) quiet, peaceful.

ཁུ་སིམ་དབེན་བཞུགས་ (kūsim wēnshuù) living quietly/ peacefully in a remote place.

ཁུ་སིམ་མེ་ (kū sīmme) sm. ཁུ་སིམ་པོ་.

ཁུ་སིམ་སིམ་ (kū sīmsim) sm. ཁུ་སིམ་པོ་.

ཁུ་སླང་ (kūlaŋ) large frying pan (wok).

ཁུ་གསོག་སྣོད་ (kūsog nȫȫ) spermatocyst.

ཁུག (kūù) 1. corner, nook, remote, out of the way place ¶རི་ཁུག A remote part of a mountain. 2. vi. to come/ get ¶ཁོ་གཉིད་ཁུག་པ་རེད་ He fell asleep (got sleep). 3. vi. to become well/ healthy ¶ཁོང་སྙུན་གཞི་དྲག་སྐྱིད་བྱུང་ནས་ཞལ་རས་ཁུག་བཞག He recovered from his illness and his face looks healthy. 4. abbr. of ཁུག་མ་. 5. vi. to change behavior from bad to good (with སེམས་) ¶ཕྲུ་གུ་འཚུབ་པོ་དེ་དེང་སང་སེམས་ཁུག་བཞག The unruly child has become well behaved these days.

ཁུག་ཀྱོག (kūgyoò) 1. out of the way, remote, boondocks ¶ལུང་པ་ཁུག་ཀྱོག་འདི་འདྲ་ལ་ཚོང་ཡག་པོ་ཡོང་གི་མ་རེད་ Business won't be good in a remote place like this. 2. corner, nook ¶རྩིག་པའི་ཁུག་ཀྱོག་ཏུ་ཡོད་པའི་པར་ The picture in the corner.

ཁུག་ཁུག (kūguù) sm. ཁུག.

ཁུག་ཁུག་ཀྱོག་ཀྱོག (kūgkuù gyɔggyɔɔ) sm. ཁུག་ཀྱོག.

ཁུག་ཁྲ་ (kūdra) an ornament worn on the waist of officials in the tt. government when they wear the རྒྱ་ལུ་ costume.

ཁུག་འཁྱོག (kūggyoò) sm. ཁུག་ཀྱོག.

ཁུག་ཆ་ (kūgja) angle (in geometry).

ཁུག་ཆུང་ (kūjuŋ) a type of traditional medicine.

ཁུག་ད་ (kūgdə) sm. ཁུག་ཏ་.

ཁུག་ཏ་ (kūgdə) swallow (bird).

ཁུག་མདུད་ (kūgdüü) tying a horse's tail in a knot before a race; va.—བྱེད་.

ཁུག་ན་ (kūgna) fog, mist, vapor, miasma.

ཁུག་སྣ་ (kūgna) sm. ཁུག་ན་.

ཁུག་པ་ (kūgbə) mellowed, matured.

ཁུག་བྱི་ (kūgci) kangaroo.

ཁུག་མ་ (kūŋma) bag, purse.

ཁུག་རིགས་ཁུག་ཀྱོག (kūgrii küggyɔɔ) sm. ཁུག་ཀྱོག.

ཁུག་སེང་ (kūŋseŋ) sheltered area ¶རི་ཁུག་སེང་ཞིག་ལ་ངལ་གསོ་བརྒྱབ་པ་ཡིན་ I rested in a sheltered area on the mountain.

ཁུག་ན་ (kūgna) mist.

ཁུག་ཤོ་ (kūgsho) bamboo or wicker basket used to carry children on one's back.

ཁུགས་ (kūù) p. of ཁུག.

ཁུགས་ལྡིང་ (kūgdiŋ) birds flying suddenly when startled/ frightened.

ཁུང་ (kūŋ) hole ¶ཁུང་ཡོད་པའི་ལམ་དུ་ On a road with holes.

ཁུང་ཕུག (kūŋ pūg) p. of ཁུང་འབིགས་.

ཁུང་ཕུའུ་ཙེ་ (kūŋ pūdze) ch. sm. ཁུང་ཙེ་.

ཁུང་བུ་ (kūnbu) small hole, a hollow cavity, tunnel.

ཁུང་བུ་རིམ་གསབ་ (kūŋbu ri̱msəb) cavities/ holes/ tunnels gradually filling up; va.—བྱེད་.

ཁུང་འབིགས་ (kūŋbii) perforating, drilling, punching holes; va. ཁུང་འབིགས་; —བྱེད་ ¶རི་ལ་ཁུང་འབིགས་བྱས་ནས་རི་ལའི་ལྕགས་ལམ་བཟོས་འདུག They drilled a hole in the mountain and made railway tracks.

ཁུང་འབིགས་འཕྲུལ་འཁོར་ (kūŋbii trüügɔɔ) a perforating machine, a machine that drills holes.

ཁུང་འབྲུག (kūŋdrug) ch.tib. a dinosaur.

ཁུང་སྦུབས (kūŋbub) the inside of a hole/ opening.

ཁུང་མིང་ (kūŋmiŋ) Kunming.

ཁུང་མིན་ལྒང་ཞུ་ (kūŋmin ga̱ŋshu) eng.tib. Coleman lantern.

ཁུང་མེན་གྱི་ལུགས་ (kūŋmengi lu̱g) ch.tib. the doctrines of Confucius and Mencius.

ཁུང་ཧྥུ་ཙེ་ (kūŋ fūdze) ch. sm. ཁུང་ཙེ་.

ཁུང་ཙེ་ (kūŋdzi) ch. Confucius.

ཁུང་ཚང་ (kūŋdzaŋ) ch.tib. the family of Confucius.

ཁུང་ཟབ་གསོར་སྙེགས་ (kūŋsəb sōrdeg) deep hole drilling machine.

ཁུང་ཟོང་ (kūŋsoŋ) an awl for making holes in leather.

ཁུང་གསེང་ (kūŋseŋ) hole.

ཁུངས་ (kūŋ) 1. origin, source. 2. (vb. + —) the source of the preceeding verb ¶བཟའ་བཅའ་ཡོང་ཁུངས་བོད་རེད་ The source of obtaining foodstuffs was Tibet. 3. the place to which one originally belongs ¶ལྷ་ས་ནས་ཁུངས་སོ་སོར་བཏང་བ་རེད་ From Lhasa, (they) sent them each to their own place.

ཁུངས་སྐྱེལ་ (kūŋ gyēē) 1. va. to prove ¶ཀུན་མ་ཁོ་མིན་པ་ཁུངས་སྐྱེལ་ཐུབ་པ་རེད་ (They) were able to prove he wasn't a thief. ¶ཁྲིམས་མཐུན་ཁུངས་སྐྱེལ་ཡག To prove the legality (of). 2. proof ¶ཁུངས་སྐྱེལ་གཞན་དང་མཉམ་དུ་ Together with other proof.

ཁུངས་སྐྱེལ་མཁན་ (kūŋ gyēēñɛn) witness, testifier, person who proves sth.

ཁུངས་སྐྱེལ་དངོས་པོ་ (kūŋgyee ŋȫȫbo) an item that proves sth.

ཁུངས་སྐྱེལ་དག་འབུད་ (kūŋgyee ta̱gbüü) accounting for or answering everything, providing convincing evidence to clear an issue, proving everything; va.—བྱེད་.

ཁུངས་སྐྱེལ་དཔེ་མཚོན་ (kūŋgyee bētsön) illustration/

example that proves sth., a case in point; va.—སྟོན་ to give an example that proves or demonstrates sth.

ཁུངས་སྐྱེལ་རྩིས་སྤྲོད་ (kūŋgyee dzīìdröö) handing over proof/ evidence (e.g., about one's expenses at the end of a contract); va.—བྱེད་.

ཁུངས་སྐྱེལ་ར་འཕྲོད་ (kūŋgyee radröö) proof, evidence; va.—བྱེད་.

ཁུངས་སྐྱེལ་ལུང་འདྲེན་ (kūŋgyee luŋdren) quoting from many sources; va.—བྱེད་.

ཁུངས་བསྐྱལ་ (kūŋ kε̄ε̄) p. of ཁུངས་སྐྱེལ་.

ཁུངས་བསྐྱེལ་ (kūŋ gyeē) sm. ཁུངས་སྐྱེལ་.

ཁུངས་འཁྱོལ་ (kūŋ kyöö) vi. to accomplish, to succeed ། འཆར་གཞི་རྙིང་པ་ཁུངས་འཁྱོལ་མ་བྱུང་གོང་གསར་པ་འདི་འགོ་འཛུགས་བྱེད་རྒྱུ་མེད་ (We) shouldn't begin the new project before the old one is accomplished. ། ང་ཨ་མེ་རི་ཀར་ཁུངས་འཁྱོལ་པ་མི་འདུག I couldn't succeed in America.

ཁུངས་སྒྲིག (kūŋdriì) 1. organizing/ arranging a job or work; va. ཁུངས་སྒྲིག; —བྱེད་. 2. replacing, substituting (for sth. lost); va. ཁུངས་སྒྲིག; —བྱེད་ ། ལས་ཁུངས་ཀྱི་ཅ་ལག་མ་ཚང་བ་རྣམས་ཁུངས་སྒྲིག་བྱེད་དགོས་ (One) must replace the items missing from the office.

ཁུངས་གཅིག་ཐ་སྙད་ (kūŋjig tāñεὲ) cognate words.

ཁུངས་ཚོད་ (kūŋtsöö) vi. to know the real situation, to get to the bottom of the story ། གྱོད་གཞི་འདིའི་སྐོར་ཁུངས་ཚོད་པ་ཞིག་བྱ་དགོས་ Regarding this lawsuit, (we) must get to the bottom of it.

ཁུངས་གདན་ (kūŋdεn) reliable, valid, authentic ། ཡིག་ཆ་ཁུངས་གདན་ཡོང་ཆེད་དམ་ཕྱག་རྒྱག་དགོས་ In order to make the document authentic one has to affix a seal on it.

ཁུངས་གདུགས་ (kūŋduù) finding proof/ documentation; va. ཁུངས་གདུགས་; —བྱེད་ ། ཞིབ་འཇུག་བྱེད་སྐབས་ཡིག་ཆ་ལ་ཁུངས་གདུགས་དགོས་ When one does research one must find proof in documents.

ཁུངས་བསྟན་ (kūŋ dε̄n) va. to show the direction, to point sth. out.

ཁུངས་ཐུབ་པོ་ (kūŋ tūbu) 1. durable ། ཨ་རིའི་མོ་ཊ་ཁུངས་ཐུབ་པོ་ཡོད་རེད་ American cars are durable. 2. authentic, valid, reliable, trustworthy ། ཁོ་ཚོར་བཀའ་གནད་ཁུངས་ཐུབ་པོ་ཞིག་ཡོད་རེད་ They have an authentic land tenure document.

ཁུངས་ཐོན་ (kūŋdön) vi. to have proof/ evidence emerge or come out.

ཁུངས་མཐུག་པོ་ (kūŋ tūgbu) sm. ཁུངས་ཐུབ་པོ་.

ཁུངས་འདུས་ (kūŋdüù) shung. combining.

ཁུངས་འཐོར་ (kūŋtɔɔ) things scattered and lost.

ཁུངས་དག (kūŋdaà) 1. reliable, authentic, trustworthy ། རླུང་འཕྲིན་ནས་ཐོས་པའི་གནས་ཚུལ་ད་ཁུངས་དག་རེད་འདུག The news we heard from the radio is reliable. ། རྒྱལ་རབས་ལོ་རྒྱུས་ཁུངས་དག A reliable history. 2. durable.

ཁུངས་དག་པོ་ (kūŋ tagbo) reliable, dependable, trustworthy, authentic.

ཁུངས་དག་སྤུས་གཙང་ (kūŋdag būùdzaŋ) durable/ reliable/ dependable and of good quality.

ཁུངས་དག་བཟོ་ (kūŋdaà so) va. to repay all debts.

ཁུངས་དེད་རྩད་གཅོད་ (kūŋdeè dzε̄ὲjöö) searching to trace the origins of sth.

ཁུངས་དོར་ (kūŋdɔɔ) shung. missing.

ཁུངས་དྲངས་ (kūŋ traŋ) va. to cite evidence/ proof, to account for/ justify with evidence ། རྩོད་པ་རྒྱག་སྐབས་རྒྱུ་མཚན་གྱི་ཁུངས་དྲངས་ནས་བདར་ཤ་གཅོད་དགོས་ When debating (one) must justify (one's) argument with evidence.

ཁུངས་འདེད་ (kūŋ teè) sm. ཁུངས་གདུགས་.

ཁུངས་ལྡན་ (kūŋdεn) sm. ཁུངས་དག.

ཁུངས་ལྡན་ལུང་ཡོད་ (kūŋdεn luŋyöö) a reliable/ true account, an account supported by proof and citations.

ཁུངས་སྣེ་ (kūŋne) clue, hint, indication; va.—འཚོལ་ to search for a clue ། གཞུང་དངོས་རྐུ་འཕྲིར་གྱི་གྱོད་གཞི་དེའི་ཁུངས་སྣེ་ཞིབ་པར་འཚོལ་དགོས་ (One) must look carefully for a clue regarding the government property that was stolen by thieves.

ཁུངས་འཕེར་ (kūŋper) reliable/ authentic proof, verification ། རྩད་བཅད་ནས་དཔང་རྟགས་ཁུངས་འཕེར་བྱུང་ན་ After investigation, if we can get reliable evidence.

ཁུངས་འཕེར་པོ་ (kūŋ pērbo) sm. ཁུངས་འཕེར་.

ཁུངས་མ་ (kūŋma) 1. real, genuine, authentic ། ལོ་རྒྱུས་ཁུངས་མ་ Authentic history. 2. orthodox ། འདུ་ཤེས་ཁུངས་མ་ Orthodox ideas.

ཁུངས་མ་དག (kūŋmadaà) shung. unreliable, undependable.

ཁུངས་མི་གཙང་བའི་རྒྱུ་ནོར་ (kūŋ midzāŋwε gyunor) wealth that was obtained immorally/ unethically.

ཁུངས་མིང་ཡོད་པ་ (kūŋmiŋ yööba) having status.

ཁུངས་མེད་ (kūŋmeè) 1. baseless, unfounded, without substance ། ཁུངས་མེད་སྐྱོན་བརྗོད་ Baseless criticism. 2. senseless, meaningless ། འཆར་གཞི་འདི་ཁུངས་མེད་རེད་ This plan is senseless.

ཁུངས་མེད་མཁྲེགས་བཟུང་ (kūŋmeè trēgsuŋ) hardheaded, stubborn; va.—བྱེད་.

ཁུངས་མེད་ངན་སྐལ་ (kūŋmeè ŋengεε) abbr. of ཁུངས་མེད་ and ངན་ཤེད་སྐལ་རབ་.

ཁུངས་མེད་སྙོན་འཛུགས་ (kūŋmeè ñööndzug) baseless/ unfounded blame or accusation; va.—བྱེད་.

ཁུངས་མེད་གཏམ་གླེང་ (kūŋmeè dāmleŋ) sm. ཁུངས་མེད་གཏམ་འཆལ་.

ཁུངས་མེད་གཏམ་འཆལ་ (kūŋmeè dāmcεε) baseless or unfounded gossip/ talk, slanderous rumors; va.—ཤོད་ to make baseless or unfounded statements, to say slanderous rumors.

ཁུངས་མེད་བློ་བཀོད་ (kūŋmeè lōgöö) senseless/ useless strategy or plan.

ཁུངས་མེད་རྫུན་བཟོ་ (kūŋmeè dzünso) fabricating a case or crime against sb., trumping up a case/ accusation; va.—བྱེད་.

ཁུངས་མེད་ལུགས་མེད་ (kūŋmeè lugmeè) sm. ཁུངས་མེད་.

ཁུངས་མེད་ལུང་མེད་ (kūŋmeè luŋmeè) ཁུངས་མེད་.

ཁུངས་གཙང་ (kūŋdzan) pure, authentic ། བོད་སྐད་ཁུངས་གཙང་ Pure Tibetan language.

ཁུངས་གཙིགས་ (kūŋdzig) sth. that has meaning/ substance/ sense.

ཁུངས་བཙན་ (kūŋdzεn) sm. ཁུངས་དག་པོ་.

ཁུངས་འཚོལ་ (kūŋdzöö) searching for the source/ origin of sth., searching for evidence/ proof; va.—བྱེད་ ། མི་གསོད་ཀྱི་གྱོད་གཞི་དེའི་སྐོར་ཁྲིམས་ཁང་ནས་ཁུངས་འཚོལ་བྱེད་བཞིན་པ་རེད་ Concerning the murder case, the court is searching for evidence (to settle it).

ཁུངས་འཚོལ་ར་སྤྲོད་ (kūŋdzöö radröö) searching for evidence/ documentation that will prove sth.; va.—བྱེད་ ། ཁྲིམས་ཁང་ནས་ཁུངས་འཚོལ་ར་སྤྲོད་ཀྱིས་ཉེས་ཅན་དེ་འཛིན་བཟུང་བྱས་པ་རེད་ The court searched for evidence and proof and then arrested the criminal.

ཁུངས་ཞན་པ་ (kūŋ shεmba) a poor/ unreliable source.

ཁུངས་ཡོད་ལུང་ཡོད་ (kūŋyöö luŋyöö) 1. reliable, authentic, factual, authentic ། ལོ་རྒྱུས་ཁུངས་ཡོད་ལུང་ཡོད་ A factual history. 2. justified, sound, rational ། ཁུངས་ཡོད་ལུང་ཡོད་ཀྱི་ཉེས་ཆད་ A justified punishment.

ཁུངས་ལུང་ (kūŋluŋ) 1. foundation, basis ། དེབ་འདིའི་ཁུངས་ལུང་ཚན་རིག་ལ་གདུགས་ཡོད་ The foundation of this book is science. 2. meaning, substance, sense ། ཁོས་རི་མོ་ཁུངས་ལུང་ཡོད་པ་རྟག་པར་འབྲི་གི་འདུག He always draws pictures with substance. 3. citations, quotations, references; va.—འདྲེན་; —དྲངས་ to cite references, to quote from sources.

ཁུངས་ལུང་དན་དིག (kūŋluŋ dε̄ndig) based on certain/ definite evidence.

ཁུངས་ལུང་མེད་པ་ (kūŋluŋ meèba) sm. ཁུངས་མེད་.

ཁུངས་ལུང་བཙན་པོ་ (kūŋluŋ dzēmbo) sm. ཁུངས་དག.
ཁུངས་ལུང་ཡོད་པ་ (kūŋluŋ yö̱ö̱ba) sm. ཁུངས་ལུང་.
ཁུངས་སུ་སྤྲོད་ (kūŋsu drȫö) va. to give/ deliver to the concerned person/ office/ etc. ¶ ཡི་གེ་རྣམས་ཁུངས་སུ་སྤྲད་པ་ཡིན་ (I) gave the letter to the concerned person.
ཁུངས་སུ་བྱེད་ (kūŋsu ce̱è) va. to use as a source/ reference.
ཁུངས་བསུབ་ (kūŋ sūb) va. to destroy/ wipe out the source of sth.
ཁུད་པ་ (kūba) 1. folds. 2. special gifts. 3. arc. va. to leave aside, to put aside. 4. private.
ཁུན་པ་ (kūmbə) arc. sm. ཅ་ཅོ་.
ཁུན་སྒྲ་ (kūndra) sm. འཁུན་སྒྲ་.
ཁུན་ཅུ་ལི་ (kūnjuli) brocade with crane-like patterns or designs.
ཁུན་མིང་ (kūnmiŋ) Kunming.
ཁུམ་ (kūmba) sm.* འཁུམ་.
ཁུམ་སྐྱེ་ (kūmgye) 1. wrinkled ¶ དྲག་ལོག་ཁུམ་སྐྱེ Wrinkled clothes. 2. timid.
ཁུམ་ཁུམ་ (kūmgum) wrinkled ¶ རས་འདི་གཉེར་མ་ཁུམ་ཁུམ་ཆགས་ཞག The material has become wrinkled.
ཁུམས་ (kūm) sm.* འཁུམ་.
ཁུའི་ཉིང་ (kūñiŋ) eng. quinine.
ཁུར་ (kūū) 1. p. of འཁུར་. 2. see ཁུར་བྱེད་. 3. dandelion.
ཁུར་དཀར་ (kūrgar) white dandelion.
ཁུར་སྐྱུར་ (kūr gūr) 1. va. to make sb. carry a load, to put a load on someone's back ¶ མི་དེའི་སྒལ་པར་ཁུར་བསྐྱུར་འདུག (He) put a load on that person's back. 2. va. to give responsibility ¶ ལས་བྱེད་གཞོན་པ་རྣམས་ལ་ལས་ཀའི་ཁུར་བསྐྱུར་དགོས་ One should give responsibility to young cadres.
ཁུར་ཁོག (kūrkog) a type of cookie/ biscuit that is hollow.
ཁུར་འཁྱེར་ (kūr khēē) sm. ཁུར་ལེན་.
ཁུར་འགྲི་ (kūrdri) duty, obligation, responsibility ¶ ཚང་མས་རང་ལ་ཁུར་འགྲིའི་ལས་འགན་རྣམས་བསྒྲུབ་ན་ If everyone accomplishes the work that each is responsible for.
ཁུར་གླ་ (kūrla) carrying fee for coolies and porters.
ཁུར་འགེལ་ (kūr gee) sm. ཁུར་སྐྱུར་.
ཁུར་སྒྱེ་ (kūrgye) sack or bag for carrying (on one's back).
ཁུར་རྔན་ (kūrŋɛn) a gratuity/ gift/ tip for carrying sth.; va.—སྤྲོད་ to give a gratuity/ payment for carrying sth.
ཁུར་ལྗི་ (kūrji) 1. heavy load. 2. heavy responsibility.
ཁུར་ཆེན་ (kūrcen) sm. ཁུར་ཆེན་པོ་.
ཁུར་ཆེན་པོ་ (kūr cēmbo) 1. a big load. 2. a big responsibility; va.—འཁྱེར་ to take a big/ major responsibility ¶ ཁོང་གིས་ལས་ཁུངས་ནང་ལས་ཀའི་ཁུར་ཆེན་པོ་འཁྱེར་གྱི་འདུག He is taking a major responsibility in the office. 3. very proud/ vain; va.—བྱེད་ ¶ བུ་མོ་དེ་རྣམ་པའི་ཁུར་ཆེན་པོ་བྱེད་ཀྱི་འདུག That girl is being very vain about her looks.
ཁུར་ལྗིད་ (kūrjii) sm. ཁུར་ལྗི་.
ཁུར་ལྗིད་ལྷུར་ལེན་ (kūrjii lhūrlen) taking on a heavy burden/ responsibility; va.—བྱེད་.
ཁུར་མཉམ་ལེན་ (kūrñam le̱n) va. to take responsibility together/ jointly.
ཁུར་ཐག (kūrtaà) rope used to tie a load (on the back); va.—སྡམ་ to tie a load on the back with a rope.
ཁུར་ཐོགས་ (kūrtog) in office, holding a post/ position.
ཁུར་དུ་མ་སོང་རྒྱན་དུ་སོང་ (kūrtu ma̱soŋ gyṳ̄ndu sōŋ) a blessing in disguise ¶ རིག་གནས་གསར་བརྗེའི་སྐབས་མི་དེ་རྒྱལ་ཁོངས་ནས་ཕུད་པ་དེ་ཁོའི་ཁུར་དུ་མ་སོང་བར་རྒྱན་དུ་སོང་བ་རེད་ Being banished from (his) country during the Cultural Revolution was a blessing in disguise.
ཁུར་དུ་ལོང་བ་ (kūŋtu lo̱ŋwa) one load (for one's back) ¶ དེ་རིང་ངས་མེ་ཤིང་ཁུར་དུ་ལོང་པ་ཞིག་བསྒྲུག་ཐུབ་བྱུང་ Today I was able to collect enough firewood for one back load.
ཁུར་དུ་སེམས་པ་ (kūrdu sēmba) shung. considering/ thinking that sth. is a burden.
ཁུར་གདང་ (kūrdaŋ) bamboo or wooden pole used to carry loads on the shoulder.
ཁུར་འདེགས་ (kūrteg) taking/ carrying a load, assuming/ fulfilling a job; va. ཁུར་འདེགས་; —བྱེད་ ¶ འགན་ཚབ་ཆེའི་ལས་འགན་གྱི་ཁུར་འདེགས་ཐུབ་པའི་ལས་བྱེད་པ་ཁག་ཅིག་གསོ་སྐྱོང་བྱ་དགོས་ (We) should develop officials who can fulfill important responsibilities.
ཁུར་འདྲེན་ (kūndre̱n) carrying a load; va. ཁུར་འདྲེན་; —བྱེད་.
ཁུར་ནག (kūrnag) a kind of dandelion.
ཁུར་སྣོན་ (kūrnön) an additional burden.
ཁུར་པ་ (kūrba) porter, coolie.
ཁུར་པོ་ (kūrbo)1. load, burden (mental) ¶ བསམ་བློའི་ཁུར་པོ་ Mental burden. 2. a load (physical) ¶ མེ་ཤིང་ཁུར་པོ་ A load of firewood.
ཁུར་བ་ (kūrwa) sm. ཁུར་ཚོས་.
ཁུར་བབ་ (kūrbəb) sth. that has come to be one's duty.
ཁུར་བོ་ (kūrbor) sm. ཁུར་ཚ་.
ཁུར་བོར་ (kūrbor) va. to put aside, to leave or give up one's job or responsibility ¶ ཁོང་གཟུགས་པོ་བདེ་པོ་མེད་ཙང་ལས་ཀའི་ཁུར་བོར་བ་རེད་ Because he was not well, he gave up his job.
ཁུར་བྱེད་ (kūr ce̱è) 1. va. to take responsibility ¶ ལས་ཁུངས་ཀྱི་འགོ་ཁྲིད་བསྡད་མེད་པའི་སྐབས་ལས་ཀའི་ཁུར་བྱེད་མཁན་མི་འདུག When the head of the office was absent there was no one to take responsibility. 2. va. to act proud/ self-important/ vain/ conceited ¶ མི་དེས་ཡོན་ཏན་གྱི་ཁུར་བྱེད་ཀྱི་འདུག That man is acting conceited about his knowledge.
ཁུར་མང་ (kūrmaŋ) dandelion.
ཁུར་མེད་ (kūrmɛɛ̀) 1. not fulfilling responsibilities or burdens, irresponsible; va.—བྱེད་ ¶ ལས་བྱེད་པ་དེས་ལས་ཀར་ཁུར་མེད་བྱས་ཙང་ལས་ཁུངས་ནས་ཕུད་པ་རེད་ Because that official acted irresponsible he was fined.
ཁུར་མེད་བསྐྱུར་འཛོག (kūrmɛɛ̀ gyūnjog) not doing one's task/ responsibility, abandoning one's obligation; va.—བྱེད་ ¶ ལས་བྱེད་པ་དེས་མི་སེར་ལ་སྐྱོབ་གསོ་བྱ་རྒྱུའི་ལས་ཀ་ཁུར་མེད་བསྐྱུར་འཛོག་བྱས་འདུག That official didn't do the work of giving aid to the people.
ཁུར་མེད་སྣང་ཆུང་ (kūrmeè nāŋjuŋ) sm. ཁུར་མེད་.
ཁུར་མེད་ལྷོད་ཡངས་ (kūrmɛɛ̀) sm. འཁུར་མེད་.
ཁུར་མོང་ (kūrmoŋ) sm. ཁུར་མང་.
ཁུར་ཚ་ (kūrdza) a load, pack; va.—ཁུར་ to carry a load/ pack.
ཁུར་ཚ་བ་ (kūrdzawa) sm. ཁུར་པ་.
ཁུར་ཙ་ (kūrdza) dandelion root.
ཁུར་ཚེ་ (kūrdza) sm. ཁུར་ཚ་.
ཁུར་ཚད་ (kūrdzɛɛ̀) the size of a load.
ཁུར་ཚོད་ (kūrdzöö) a broth made from dandelions.
ཁུར་ཚོས་ (kūrdzüü) cheek.
ཁུར་འཛིན་ (kūndzin) sm. ཁུར་ལེན་.
ཁུར་བཟོད་ (kūrdzöö) sm. ཁུར་འདེགས་.
ཁུར་ལང་ (kūrlaŋ) vi. to be in heat (animals).
ཁུར་ལེན་ (kūr le̱n) va. to take/ bear responsibility ¶ ཁོང་གིས་འབྲོག་སར་འགྲོ་རྒྱུའི་ལས་ཀའི་ཁུར་བླངས་པ་རེད་ He took responsibility for going to nomad country.
ཁུར་ཤིང་ (kūrshiŋ) a Tibetan rucksack.
ཁུར་སེམས་ (kūrsem) sense of responsibility/ duty ¶ ཁོང་གིས་ཁུར་སེམས་ཆེན་པོ་བཅངས་ནས་ལས་འགན་སྒྲུབ་བཞིན་ཡོད་པ་རེད་ He is accomplishing his tasks with a great sense of responsibility.
ཁུར་སེམས་མེད་པ་ (kūrsem me̱èba) irresponsible, indifferent, nonchalant.
ཁུལ་ (kūū) 1. region, area ¶ འབྲས་ཐོན་ཁུལ་ A rice producing area. ¶ ལྷ་སའི་ཁུལ་ Lhasa area. 2. to

pretend (vb. + — +) ¶ དམག་མི་ཚོས་ཕྱིར་འཐེན་བྱེད་ཁུལ་བྱས་ནས་ The soldiers, having pretended to withdraw. 3. sm. ཁུ་ལུ་. 4. (va.+ —) a convention used to convey modesty, (in the sense that rather than the speaker saying "I did something," he/ she uses ཁུལ་ ["to pretend"] to have done something, although in essence it means simply he/ she did it ¶ དེབ་འདི་ངས་རྩོམ་པའི་ཁུལ་རེད་ I wrote this book.

ཁུལ་སྐུད་ (kũgüü) thread made from ཁུ་ལུ་.

ཁུལ་སྒྱེ་ (kũgye) sack/ bag made from ཁུ་ལུ་.

ཁུལ་ཐག (kũdaà) a rope made from ཁུ་ལུ་.

ཁུལ་འཐག་བཟོ་གྲྭ (kũdaà sodra) a factory that weaves ཁུ་ལུ་.

ཁུལ་ཕྱིང་ (kũciŋ) felt made from ཁུ་ལུ་.

ཁུལ་བ་ (kũwaa) sm. ཁུ་ལུ་.

ཁུལ་བལ་ (kũũpɛɛ) 1. sm. ཁུ་ལུ་. 2. abbr. བལ་ and ཁུ་ལུ་.

ཁུལ་རྫིད་ (kũũdzii) abbr. ཁུ་ལུ་ and རྫིད་པ་.

ཁུལ་ཤིས་ (kũũshii) hind. freedom.

ཁུལ་ཤོ་ (kũũsho) swaddling clothes.

ཁུས་སྐད་ (kũgɛɛ̀) crying, wailing; va.—རྒྱག.

ཁུས་འདེབས་ (kũũ deb) sm. ཁུས་སྐད་རྒྱག.

ཁུས་མོ་ (kũũmə) sm. ཁུས་སྐད་.

ཁེ་ (kē) 1. profit ¶ ཁེ་ཆེ་བ་ལས་ཉེན་ཆུང་བ་དགའ་ it is better to take less risk than to go for greater profit. 2. ch. gram.

ཁེ་རྒྱང་ (kēgyaŋ) sm. ཁེར་རྒྱང་.

ཁེ་སྐྱེད་ (kēgyeè) 1. interest ¶ བུ་ལོན་གྱི་ཁེ་སྐྱེད་ Interest on a loan. 2. abbr. profit and interest.

ཁེ་ཁོལ་ (kēgöl) dyed material that has not taken the dye well and has blotches.

ཁེ་ཁྱེ་ (kēgye) benefit; interest/ profit on investment.

ཁེ་གུན་ (kēgün) sm. ཁེ་ཉེན་.

ཁེ་གུན་ཁོངས་འཐུས་ (kēgün kōŋtüü) sm. ཁེ་གྱོང་མཉམ་ཁུར་.

ཁེ་གྱོང་ (kēgyoŋ) profit and loss/ damage/ harm ¶ ཁེ་གྱོང་གཉིས་མེད་ Neither profit nor loss.

ཁེ་གྱོང་ཁ་འཐབ་ (kēgyoŋ kātəb) balancing between profit and loss, breaking even; va.—བྱེད་.

ཁེ་གྱོང་མཉམ་ཁུར་ (kēgyoŋ nyāmgur) being jointly responsible whether profit or loss (occurs); va.—བྱེད་ ¶ ང་ཚོ་མི་ཚང་གཉིས་ཀྱིས་ཁེ་གྱོང་མཉམ་ཁུར་བྱ་རྒྱུའི་ཟ་ཁང་ཞིག་བཙུགས་པ་རེད་ We two families have started a restaurant where we are jointly responsible for profits and losses.

ཁེ་གྱོང་རྩོད་གཞི་ (kēgyoŋ dzöòshi) conflict of interest ¶ བཟོ་གྲྭ་འདི་ང་རང་སྒེར་གྱི་ཡིན་པས་གཞན་སུ་ཞིག་གིས་ཁེ་གྱོང་རྩོད་གཞི་མེད་ This factory is my private property and there is no conflict of interest with anyone else.

ཁེ་གྲགས་ (kēdraà) abbr. wealth and fame, fame and fortune.

ཁེ་གྲགས་གཉིས་མེད་ (kēdraà ñiimeè) neither profit nor fame ¶ ད་རེས་ཁོང་གི་ཁེ་གྲགས་གཉིས་མེད་ཀྱི་ལས་ཀ་བྱས་སོང་ This time he did work that resulted in neither profit nor fame.

ཁེ་གྲགས་དོན་གཉེར་ (kēdraà tönñer) striving to gain both profit and fame; va.—བྱེད་.

ཁེ་གྲགས་འཕྲོག་ལེན་ (kēdraà trōōlen) spending one's energy in pursuit of fame and wealth; va.—བྱེད་.

ཁེ་གྲི་ (kēdri) scissors.

ཁེ་ཀོལ་ (kēgöö) ch. Chinese sorghum.

ཁེ་སྒྲུབ་ (kēdrub) trying to get profit; va.—བྱེད་ ¶ འཚོ་བ་ཡར་རྒྱས་གཏོང་ཆེད་ཚོང་ལས་ལ་བརྟེན་ནས་ཁེ་སྒྲུབ་བྱེད་ཀྱི་ཡོད་ In order to improve our livelihood, (we) are trying to make profit through trade.

ཁེ་ཧམ་ཆེན་པོ་ (kēŋam cēmbo) greedy with regard to taking profit.

ཁེ་ཅན་ (kējɛn) profitable.

ཁེ་ཆུང་ (kējuŋ) little/ small profit.

ཁེ་ཆུང་སྒྲིན་མང་ (kējuŋ drinmaŋ) small profit but fast turnover in sales.

ཁེ་ཆེ་ཉེན་ཆུང་ (kēce ñenjuŋ) large profit/ benefit and low risk/ danger of loss.

ཁེ་ཆེ་བ་ལས་ཉེན་ཆུང་བ་དགའ་ (kē cēwalɛ ñenjuŋ ga) it is better to take less risk than to go for greater profit [Lit. than great profit, low danger/ risk is better].

ཁེ་འཇའ་ (kēnja) ch. a vest.

ཁེ་ཉེན་ (kēñɛn) profit and benefit and danger/ risk/ loss ¶ ཁེ་ཉེན་འདམ་ག་མ་ནོར་བ་བྱ་དགོས་ One should correctly choose in a way that foresees the possibility of profit and loss. ¶ ཁེ་ཉེན་མ་མཐོང་བའི་ལས་ཀ་ Work that does not see (take into account) the benefits and dangers.

ཁེ་ཉེན་གོ་འཛོལ་ (kēñɛn gondzöö) mistaking profit and loss, thinking one will get profit and instead getting a loss.

ཁེ་ཉེན་གོ་ཤེས་ (kēñɛn goshɛɛ̀) knowing the benefits and dangers/ risks; va.—བྱེད་.

ཁེ་ཉེན་གདོང་གཏུག (kēñɛn doŋdug) confronting risks (benefits and risks) regardless of consequence; va.—བྱེད་.

ཁེ་ཉེན་མ་འཛོལ་ (kēñɛn madzöö) va. not making a mistake between profit and dangers ¶ ཁེ་ཉེན་མ་འཛོལ་བའི་སྒོ་ནས་ལས་ཀའི་འཆར་གཞི་བཟོ་དགོས་པ་རེད་ (We) have to make a work plan without making mistakes (as to profit and danger).

ཁེ་ཉེན་འཛོལ་མེད་ (kēñɛn dzöömeè) sm. ཁེ་ཉེན་མ་འཛོལ་.

ཁེ་ཉོ་དཀོན་ཚོང་ (kēño gōndzoŋ) profiteering, speculating; va.—བྱེད་ [Lit. buy cheap, sell scarce].

ཁེ་གཉེར་ (kēñer) 1. a profit making business, a commercial enterprise; va.—བྱེད་ to operate/ manage a business for profit. 2. abbr. of ཁེ་ལས་བདག་གཉེར་.

ཁེ་གཉེར་ཁྱབ་ཁོངས་ (kēñer kyəbgoŋ) business scope.

ཁེ་འདོད་ (kēndöö) the desire for profit.

ཁེ་འདོད་གྲགས་འདོད་ (kēndöö tragdöö) desiring fame and fortune; va.—བྱེད་.

ཁེ་རྡུལ་ཕྲན་ (kē düdren) atomic weight.

ཁེ་ན་ཌ་བོད་དོན་ཚོགས་པ་ (kēnada pöödön tsōgba) Canada Tibet Committee.

ཁེ་ན་ཌའི་རྒྱང་སྲིང་མཉམ་སྒྲིལ་ (kēnada gyaŋsiŋ ñamdree) Canadian Broadcasting Corporation (CBC).

ཁེ་པ་ (kēba) a private person who sells small items for profit, a vendor.

ཁེ་པོ་ (kēbo) cheap, inexpensive ¶ གོང་ཁེ་པོ་ Cheap (in price).

ཁེ་པོ་སྒྲིན་པོ་ (kēbo drimbu) sm. ཁེ་ཆུང་སྒྲིན་མང་.

ཁེ་སྤོགས་ (kēbɔɔ̀) profit, gain.

ཁེ་སྤོགས་ཀྱི་ཚད་ (kēbɔɔ̀gi tsɛɛ̀) rate of profit, degree/ level of profit.

ཁེ་སྤོགས་དངོས་ (kēbɔɔ̀ ŋöö) sm. ཁེ་གཙང་གཙང་.

ཁེ་སྤོགས་ཆེ་ (kēbɔɔ̀ cē) high interest.

ཁེ་སྤོགས་འཐེན་ཉར་གྱི་ཆ་ (kēbɔɔ̀ tēnñargi cā) sm. ཁེ་སྤོགས་འཐེན་ཆ་.

ཁེ་སྤོགས་འཐེན་ཆ་ (kēbɔɔ̀ tēnca) retained profits.

ཁེ་སྤོགས་འདོད་གདུང་ (kēbɔɔ̀ dööduŋ) striving for profit, strong profit motive.

ཁེ་སྤོགས་དམར་རྒྱང་ (kēbɔɔ̀ mārgyaŋ) net profit/ gain.

ཁེ་ཕན་ (kēbɛn) advantage, gain, benefit ¶ མི་དམངས་ཀྱི་ཁེ་ཕན་གྱི་ཆེད་དུ་ For the benefit of the people.

ཁེ་ཕན་མཉམ་ཐོབ་ (kēbɛn ñamtob) receiving equal profit/ benefit.

ཁེ་ཕན་རིང་ལུགས་ (kēbɛn riŋluù) utilitarianism.

ཁེ་ཕན་བསམ་ཤེས་ (kēbɛn sāmsheè) understanding the advantage/ benefit of sth.

ཁེ་ཕམ་ (kēbam) sm. ཁེ་གྱོང་.

ཁེ་བུ་སུ་ (kēbusu) sm. གཙང་གདན་.

ཁེ་བེད་ (kēbeè) sm. ཁེ་ཕན་.

ཁེ་བོ་ (kēbo) cheap, inexpensive.

ཁེ་བོགས་ (kēbɔɔ̀) abbr. of profit and lease fee.

ཁེ་དབང་ (kēwaŋ) rights ¶ འགྲོ་བ་མིའི་ཁེ་དབང་ Human rights.

ཁེ་དབང་ཐོབ་ཐང་ (kēwaŋ tōpdaŋ) rights and prerogatives.

ཁེ་འབབ་ (kēmbəb) 1. amount of profit ། ཁེ་འབབ་ཆེན་པོ་བྱུང་བ་རེད་ (He) made large profit. 2. sm. ཁེ་སྤོགས་.

ཁེ་འབབ་དཔྱ་ཁྲལ་ (kēmbab jātrεε) tax on profits.

ཁེ་འབབ་ཚད་ (kēmbab tsεὲ) rate of profit.

ཁེ་མེད་ (kēmeè) unprofitable, without profit.

ཁེ་མེད་གྱོང་མེད་ (kēmeè gyoŋmeè) no profit and no loss.

ཁེ་མེར་རུཇ་འཛབ་དམག་ཚོགས་པ་ (kēmer ruj jəbmaà tsōgba) Khmer Rouge.

ཁེ་གཙང་ (kēptsaŋ) 1. exclusively, purely, solely ། བོད་ཕྲུག་ཁེ་གཙང་ཡོད་པའི་སློབ་གྲྭ་ A school exclusively for Tibetan children. 2. alone, apart, separate ། ཁོང་ཁང་པ་ཁེ་གཙང་ཞིག་ལ་བསྡད་འདུག He lives alone.

ཁེ་གཙང་གཙང་ (kē dzāŋdzaŋ) net profit ། འགྲོ་སོང་ཚང་མ་ཕུད་པས་ཁེ་གཙང་གཙང་སྒོར་བཅུ་ལས་མི་འདུག After all the expenses are deducted, the net profit is only ten dollars.

ཁེ་ཚོང་ (kēdzoŋ) trade, commerce (usu. retail level); va.—རྒྱག; —བྱེད་ to trade, to engage in commerce, to sell retail.

ཁེ་ཚོང་པ་ (kē tsōŋba) trader, vendor, peddler.

ཁེ་འཚོལ་ (kētsöö) profit seeking; va. ཁེ་འཚོལ་; —བྱེད་ to seek profit.

ཁེ་འཚོལ་བའི་ལྟ་རྒྱལ་ (kē tsöōwεε dədzüü) the point of view of profit seeking; va.—འཛིན་ to hold the point of view of profit seeking.

ཁེ་ཟ་ (kēsa) sm. ཁེ་བཟང་ཟ་.

ཁེ་བཟང་ (kēpsaŋ) profit; va.—ཟ་; —ལོན་ to make or take a profit ། ཚལ་བཙོངས་ནས་ཁེ་བཟང་ལོན་པ་རེད་ (They) made a profit from selling vegetables. vi.—ཐོབ་; —བྱུང་; —ལོན་; —རག to get a profit.

ཁེ་བཟང་ཁོ་ན་དོན་གཉེར་ (kēpsaŋ kōna tönñer) working exclusively for profit; va.—བྱེད་.

ཁེ་བཟང་དང་སྐད་གྲགས་ (kēpsaŋtaŋ gēdraà) profit/ wealth and fame.

ཁེ་བཟང་འཚོལ་ (kēpsaŋ tsöō) sm. ཁེ་འཚོལ་.

ཁེ་བཟང་ཡོད་པ་ (kēpsaŋ yöba) profitable, having profit.

ཁེ་བཟང་ཟ་ (kēpsaŋ sa) see ཁེ་བཟང་.

ཁེ་ར་མ་ (kērama) sm. ཁེ་རུ་མ་ཕ་.

ཁེ་རག (kēraà; kēbara) hay fork, pitchfork.

ཁེ་རུ་མ་ (kēruma) alone ། ཁོ་རང་ཁེ་རུ་མ་ཕྱིན་པ་རེད་ He went alone.

ཁེ་ལ་ (kēla) eng. carat.

ཁེ་ལན་ཊན་ (kēlεnton) Clinton.

ཁེ་ལས་ (kēlεὲ) 1. commerce ། བཟོ་ཚོང་ཁེ་ལས་ Industry and commerce. 2. business enterprise/ venture, factory, mill, profit making business (in contrast to nonprofit) ། དེང་རབས་ཅན་གྱི་ཁེ་ལས་ A modern enterprise.

ཁེ་ལས་ཀུང་སི་ (kēlεὲ gūŋsi) tib.ch. enterprise, corporation, company.

ཁེ་ལས་སྔོན་རྩིས་ཁང་ (kēlεὲ ŋōndzii kāu) tib.ch. budgeting department of a company.

ཁེ་ལས་ཅན་དུ་འགྱུར་ (kēlεὲ jεntu gyur) vi. to commercialize.

ཁེ་ལས་ཆུང་རིགས་ (kēlεὲ cūŋrii) small business/ enterprise.

ཁེ་ལས་དོ་དམ་ (kēlεὲ dodam) sm. ཁེ་ལས་བདག་གཉེར་.

ཁེ་ལས་དོ་དམ་ཨུ་ཡོན་ལྷན་ཁང་ (kēlεὲ dodam üyön lhεngaŋ) enterprise management committee.

ཁེ་ལས་བདག་གཉེར་ (kēlεὲ dagñer) management of an enterprise, business administration.

ཁེ་ལས་བདག་གཉེར་ཁང་ (kēlεὲ dagñer kāwo) tib.ch. department of business management, business administration office.

ཁེ་ལས་བདག་གཉེར་ཨུ་ཡོན་ལྷན་ཁང་ (kēlεὲ dagñer üyön lhengaŋ) committee of business management, business administration committee.

ཁེ་ལས་སྡེ་ཚན་ (kēlεὲ dedzεn) enterprise unit.

ཁེ་ལས་ནོར་དོན་ཁྲུའུ་ (kēlεὲ nordön trū) tib.ch. accounting department of a company.

ཁེ་ལས་པ་ (kēlεὲba) entrepreneur.

ཁེ་ལས་ཚོགས་ཁག (kēlεὲ tsɔ̄ɔgaà) business conglomerate.

ཁེ་ལས་ཡིད་རྟོན་དངུལ་བུན་ཁང་ (kēlεὲ yidön ŋǖübün kəu) tib.ch. credit department of a company.

ཁེ་ལས་རུ་ཚོགས་ (kēlεὲ rutsoò) enterprise group.

ཁེ་ལིམ་པོ་བྲང་ (kēlem podraŋ) Kremlin.

ཁེ་ལོ་ཝ་ཊི་ (kēlo wade) eng. kilowatt.

ཁེ་ལོག་ཚོང་ལོག་ (kēlɔɔ̀ tsōŋlɔɔ̀) exorbitant profit ། ཁེ་ལོག་ཚོང་ལོག་རྒྱག་མཁན་ལ་མི་དམངས་ཀྱིས་དགའ་པོ་བྱེད་ཀྱི་མེད་ The people do not like those who make exorbitant profit.

ཁེ་སླེབས་ཀྱི་ཁྲལ་ (kēlebgi trεε) sm. ཁེ་སླེབས་དཔྱ་ཁྲལ་.

ཁེ་སླེབས་དཔྱ་ཁྲལ་ (kēleb jātrεε) tax on profits.

ཁེ་གསུམ་གཞིས་ཀ་ (kēsum shigə) name of an aristocratic estate in southern Tibet.

ཁེ་ཧན་ (kēhan) mong. khan.

ཁེ་ཧྲན་ནད་ (kēhrεnnεὲ) keshan (beg) disease.

ཁེ་ལྷག (kēlhaà) sm. ཁེ་འཕྲུས་.

ཁེག (kēgba) vi. to be obstructed, to be blocked ། ཆུ་ལོག་ཁེག་ཐུབ་པའི་ཆུ་རགས་ཆེན་པོ་ཞིག་རྒྱག་དགོས་ (We) have to build a big dam that will be able to block floods.

ཁེང་ (kēŋ) arc. slave.

ཁེང་: p. ཁེངས་; f. ཁེང་ (kēŋ) vi. to be full of, to be filled with ། ཁང་མིག་འདི་མིས་ཁེངས་བཞག This room is filled with people. ། དཀར་ཡོལ་ནང་ལ་ཇ་ཁེངས་པ་བླུག་ཡོད་ (I) have poured tea in the cup so that it is full. ། མེ་མདའི་སྐད་སྒྲས་ལུང་པ་ཁེངས་ The sound of gunfire filled the area.

ཁེང་ལོག (kēŋlog) sm. ཁེང་ལོག.

ཁེང་པོ་ (kēŋbo) sm. ཁེང་.

ཁེང་ལོག (kēŋlɔɔ̀) arc. rebellion, uprising, insurrection ། ཁེང་ལོག་ཆེན་པོ་ཞིག་བྱུང་སོང་ A great rebellion occurred.

ཁེངས་ (kēŋ) p. of འཁེངས་.

ཁེངས་སྐྱུང་ (kēŋgyuŋ) modesty, modestly; va.—བྱེད་ ། ལས་བྱེད་པ་རྣམས་ཀྱིས་ཁེངས་སྐྱུང་གི་སྒོ་ནས་ལོ་རྒྱུས་བྲིས་པ་རེད་ The cadres wrote about the events modestly.

ཁེངས་སྐྱུང་ཆེན་པོ་ (kēŋgyuŋ chēmbo) very modest, a person without pride or arrogance or haughtiness.

ཁེངས་སྐྱུང་དྲེགས་སྤོང་ (kēŋgyuŋ tregboŋ) sm. ཁེངས་སྐྱུང་.

ཁེངས་སྐྱུང་བག་ཡོད་ (kēŋgyuŋ pagyöö) modest and upright, principled ། ཁེངས་སྐྱུང་བག་ཡོད་ཀྱིས་འཚོ་བ་སྐྱེལ་གྱི་ཡོད་པ་རེད་ (He) is earning his livelihood in a modest and principled manner.

ཁེངས་སྐྱུང་བབ་ཅགས་ (kēŋgyuŋ pagcaà) sm. ཁེངས་སྐྱུང་བག་ཡོད་.

ཁེངས་སྐྱུངས་ (kēŋgyuŋ) sm. ཁེངས་སྐྱུང་.

ཁེངས་སྐྱུངས་གུས་ཞབས་ (kēŋgyuŋ güüshəb) modest and respectful.

ཁེངས་བསྐྱུངས་ (kēŋgyuŋ) sm. ཁེངས་སྐྱུང་.

ཁེངས་སྒྲ་ (kēŋdra) stereophonic sound.

ཁེངས་ངོམ་གཞན་བརྙས་ (kēŋŋom shεnñεὲ) throwing one's weight around, being overbearing.

ཁེངས་ཆུང་ (kēŋjuŋ) humble, modest ། མི་འདི་ཁེངས་ཆུང་རེད་ This man is humble.

ཁེངས་ཆུང་གཤིས་འཇམ་ (kēŋjuŋ shinjam) humble/ modest and gentle (personality).

ཁེངས་ཆེ་ལུགས་འཁྱལ་ (kēŋce luggεε) sm. ཁེངས་དྲེགས་ལུགས་འཁྱལ་.

ཁེངས་གཏམ་ (kēŋdam) proud/ boastful/ arrogant speech; va.—བཤད་.

ཁེངས་དྲེགས་ (kēŋdreg) conceit, arrogance, haughtiness; va.—བྱེད་ ། ཁོ་ཁེངས་དྲེགས་ཆེ་བས་རང་སྐྱོན་མ་མཐོང་བ་རེད་ Because of his great conceit he didn't see his own faults.

ཁེངས་དྲེགས་ཀྱི་ཧམ་སེམས་ (kēndreggi hāmsem) wild ambition; va.—འཆང་ to have/ hold wild ambitions.

ཁེངས་དྲེགས་ཆེན་པོ་ (kēŋdreg chēmbo) conceited, arrogant, haughty; va.—བྱེད་.

ཁེངས་དྲེགས་རང་བཀུར་ (kēŋdreg rəŋgur) sm. ཁེངས་

དྲེགས་.

ཁེངས་དྲེགས་ལུགས་འགལ་ (kēŋdreg luggɛɛ) conceit/ arrogance that violates custom; va.—བྱེད་.

ཁེངས་ལྡན་མ་ (kēŋdɛnma) a girl in her prime years.

ཁེངས་པ་ (kēŋba) sm. ཁེངས་དྲེགས་.

ཁེངས་པ་སྐྱུང་ (kēŋba gyūŋ) sm. ཁེངས་སྐྱུང་བྱེད་.

ཁེངས་སྒོབས་ (kēŋbob) sm. ཁེངས་དྲེག.

ཁེངས་འཕྱོས་བླུག (kēŋdröö lū) va. to add to a partially empty cup so as to fill it to the top/ brim ། དཀར་ཡོལ་ནང་ཇ་ཁེངས་འཕྱོས་བླུགས་སོང་ (They) added tea to the cup to fill it to the brim.

ཁེངས་ཞུམ་གཉིས་སྤོང་ (kēŋshum ñiiboŋ) renouncing both conceitedness and humbleness.

ཁེངས་རློམ་ (kēŋlom) arrogant, conceited; va.—བྱེད་.

ཁེངས་རློམ་གཞན་བརྙས་ (kēŋlom shɛnñɛɛ̀) arrogant and domineering/ abusive/ bullying; va.—བྱེད་.

ཁེངས་ཟས་ (kēŋsɛɛ̀) cold food.

ཁེངས་སེམས་ (kēŋsem) sm. ཁེངས་དྲེགས་.

ཁེངས་སེམས་མེད་པ་ (kēŋsem meèbə) modest, unassuming, humble.

ཁེངས་སེམས་ཚད་མེད་ (kēŋsem tsɛɛ̀meè) extremely arrogant/ proud/ conceited; va.—བྱེད་.

ཁེད་ (kēè) a riddle.

ཁེན་ (kēn) 1. ch. a type of astrology (one of the eight trigrams). 2. va. to lean on sth. ། ཤིང་སྡོང་ལ་ཁེན་དུས་ When I was leaning on a tree.

ཁེན་ཉི་ཡ་ (kēnñeya) Kenya.

ཁེན་ནམ་ (kēnnam) sm. ཁེན་.

ཁེབ་ (kēb) sm. ཁེབས་, 1.

ཁེབས་ (kēp) 1. vi. to cover sth. ། རས་འདིས་ལྕོག་ཙེ་ཁེབས་ཀྱི་མི་འདུག This piece of cloth doesn't cover the table. 2. va.—རྒྱག to cover, to spread over ། ལྕོག་ཙེའི་སྟེང་ལ་རས་ཀྱིས་ཁེབས་བརྒྱབ་འདུག (They) covered the table with a cloth. 3. vi. to be sufficient ། སློབ་གྲྭ་པ་ཚང་མར་དེབ་ཁེབས་སོང་ངམ་ Were there sufficient books for all the students?

ཁེབས་གཅོད་ (kāpjöö) 1. cover, lid; va.—རྒྱག; —གཡོགས་ to cover with a lid, to put on a cap (as on a bottle). 2. va.—རྒྱག to conceal, hide ། རང་སྐྱོན་ལ་ཁེབས་གཅོད་རྒྱག To conceal one's errors.

ཁེབས་ཆེ་བ་ (kēb cēwa) widespread, spread widely.

ཁེབས་ཐིག (kēbtig) a rope tied to the corner of a lid or cover.

ཁེབས་ལྡན་ (kēbdɛn) covered, having a roof/ cover ། ཁེབས་ལྡན་ར་བ་ A covered corral.

ཁེབས་པ་ (kēbba) covered, veiled.

ཁེབས་འབུབས་ (kēbbub) sm. ཁེབས་གཡོགས་.

ཁེབས་མ་ (kēbma) a covering used on the backs of horses and mules; va.—གཡོགས་ to put on such a covering.

ཁེབས་མེད་ (kēbmeè) open, uncovered. ། ཁེབས་མེད་རྡོ་སོལ་གཏེར་ཁ་ An open coal mine. ། ཁེབས་མེད་འཁོར་ལོ་ A vehicle without a roof (convertible).

ཁེབས་ཡོད་དོས་འཁོར་ (kēbyöö töökɔɔ) a covered truck.

ཁེབས་གཡོགས་ (kēp yɔ̄ɔ̀) see ཁེབས་.

ཁེབས་རས་ (kēprɛɛ) a covering cloth/ sheet.

ཁེབས་རིམ་ (kēbrim) covering layer.

ཁེབས་སངས་ (kēp sāŋ) va. to take off a cover, to remove a covering.

ཁེམ་ (kēm) shovel; va.—རྒྱག.

ཁེམ་ཆས་བཟོ་གྲྭ (kēmjɛɛ̀ sodra) shovel factory.

ཁེམ་བུ་ (kēmbu) spoon, small ladle.

ཁེའི་ཤེར་ཁེའི་ཙི་ (kēr kēdzi) Kirghiz.

ཁེར་རྐྱ་ (kērgya) oneself, on one's own; va.—འཛིན་ to do by oneself; vi.—ལུས་ to be left alone ། ན་གཞོན་དེ་ཁེར་རྐྱ་འཛིན་པའི་བློ་ནུས་ལས་ཀ་བྱེད་ཐུབ་ཀྱི་འདུག That youth is able to work by himself. ། གཞན་དང་མཐུན་སྒྲིལ་ཡག་པོ་མ་བྱས་ན་གྲོགས་མེད་ཁེར་རྐྱང་ལུས་ཀྱི་རེད་ If (you) don't get along with others then you will be alone without any friends.

ཁེར་རྐྱང་ (kērgyaŋ) alone, individual, single, isolated; va.—དུ་འཛུག to isolate, to leave alone/ by oneself ། རང་ཉིད་ཁེར་རྐྱང་གི་རྒྱལ་ཁ་ལེན་ཐབས་བྱེད་མི་རུང་ (One) should not try to get a victory for themselves alone. ། གྲོགས་མེད་ཁེར་རྐྱང་ Isolated without friends.

ཁེར་རྐྱང་ཁེ་གཉེར་ (kērgyaŋ kēñer) an individually run profit making business or commercial operation.

ཁེར་རྐྱང་ཁེ་གཉེར་མཁན་ (kērgyaŋ kēñergɛn) an individual doing businesses for profit.

ཁེར་རྐྱང་ཁེ་ལས་ (kērgyaŋg kēlɛɛ̀) an individually operated business or enterprise.

ཁེར་རྐྱང་གི་ངལ་རྩོལ་པ་ (kērgyaŋgi ŋɛɛdzöwa) individual laborer.

ཁེར་རྐྱང་གི་དཔལ་འབྱོར་ (kērgyaŋgi bēnjɔɔ) individual economy, petty economy (an economy where basic unit is the individual working alone).

ཁེར་རྐྱང་གི་འབྲོག་པ་ (kērgyaŋgi drogba) nomads herding on an individual basis (in contrast to collectively working nomads).

ཁེར་རྐྱང་གི་ཞིང་པ་ (kērgyaŋgi shiŋbə) individual farmer/ peasant (in contrast to farmers working collectively).

ཁེར་རྐྱང་གི་ཞིང་ལས་ (kērgyaŋgi shiŋlɛɛ̀) the system of individual farming.

ཁེར་རྐྱང་གི་ལག་ཤེས་བཟོ་ལས་ (kērgyaŋgi lagshɛɛ̀ solɛɛ̀) the system of individually operated craft industry.

ཁེར་རྐྱང་ངལ་རྩོལ་པ་ (kērgyaŋ ŋɛɛdzöwa) individual laborer.

ཁེར་རྐྱང་དཔལ་འབྱོར་ (kērgyaŋ bēnjɔɔ) sm. ཁེར་རྐྱང་གི་དཔལ་འབྱོར་.

ཁེར་རྐྱང་ཞིང་ལས་ (kērgyaŋ shiŋlɛɛ̀) sm. ཁེར་རྐྱང་ཞིང་ལས་.

ཁེར་རྐྱང་ཡུལ་པོ་ (kērgyaŋ yüübo) isolated, alone.

ཁེར་རྐྱང་རིང་ལུགས་ (kērgyaŋ riŋluù) isolationism.

ཁེར་རྐྱང་ལ་དབང་བའི་ལམ་ལུགས་ (kērgyaŋlə wāŋwɛɛ ləmluù) the system of private property.

ཁེར་རྐྱང་ལུས་ (kērgyaŋ lüü) see ཁེར་རྐྱང་.

ཁེར་སྐྱེས་བུ་བུ་མོའི་དབང་ཡིག (kērgyeè pu pomö wāŋyik) certificate of only child (the agreement of Tibetan cadre to have only one child instead of the two they are permitted).

ཁེར་དགོད་ (kēr göö) laughing by oneself; va.—བྱེད་.

ཁེར་བགྲོད་ (kērdruoò) sm. ཁེར་འགྲོ་.

ཁེར་འགྲོ་ (kēr dro) va. to go alone ། ཁེར་འགྲོ་དམག་འཐབ་ Going off to fight on one's own/ alone.

ཁེར་གོད་ (kērgöò) sm. ཁེར་དགོད་.

ཁེར་ངོམ་བདེན་རློམ་ (kērŋom denlom) sb. who believes he is always right; va.—བྱེད་.

ཁེར་བཅད་ (kērjɛɛ̀) setting/ putting/ keeping aside; va.—བྱེད་ ། རྒན་པོ་གྲོངས་མཁན་དེའི་ཅ་ལག་ཁེར་བཅད་བྱས་ནས་བཞག་འདུག The possessions of the old man who died were set aside.

ཁེར་བཅད་བཟའ་བཅའ་ (kērjɛɛ̀ sabcɛ) a set meal.

ཁེར་ཆགས་གླིང་ཕྲན་ (kērcaà līŋdɛn) an isolated island, an island not part of archipelago.

ཁེར་ཉིན་ (kērñin) sm. ཁ་སང་.

ཁེར་གཉེར་ (kērñer) individual management/ control (of business); va.—བྱེད་ to individually manage/ control ། ཁེར་གཉེར་ཁྱིམ་ཚང་ A family that manages its own farm or enterprise.

ཁེར་གདུགས་ (kērdug) two people fighting alone; va.—བྱེད་.

ཁེར་སྡོད་སྣ་ཉུང་གི་གཤིས་ཀ (kērdöö māñuŋgi shīigə) a hermit-type personality, a loner.

ཁེར་གནས་རིང་ལུགས་ (kērnɛɛ riŋluù) isolationism.

ཁེར་བྲོ་ (kērdro) a solo dance; va.—འཁྲབ་ to perform a solo dance.

ཁེར་འབབ་ (kērbəb) doing sth. alone; va.—བྱེད་.

ཁེར་མ་ (kērma) solitary, alone, only ། རིག་པ་མེད་ན་བརྩོན་འགྲུས་ཁེར་མས་ཤེས་ཡོན་སྦྱོང་མི་ཐུབ་ If one doesn't have intelligence, one can not learn by diligence alone.

ཁེར་གཙང་ (kērdzaŋ) sm. ཁ་གཙང་.

ཁེར་བཀླགས་ (kēndɛɛ̀) reciting sth. alone.

ཁེར་འཛིན་དཔའ་བོ་ (kēndziŋ bāwo) a hero in

individual combat.

ཁེར་ཡ་ (kērya) sm. ཁེར་རྐྱང་.

ཁེར་རེ་མ་ (kērema) sm. ཁེར་རྐྱང་.

ཁེར་ལྷོམ་ (kērlom) arrogant, selfish; va.—བྱེད་.

ཁེར་ལངས་རི་བོ་ (kērlaŋ riwo) a solitary/ isolated mountain.

ཁེར་ལབ་ (kērlab) talking or mumbling to one's self; va.—བྱེད་; —རྒྱག.

ཁེར་ལབ་ཁེར་བཤད་ (kērlab kērshɛɛ̀) sm. ཁེར་ལབ་.

ཁེར་ལས་ (kērlɛɛ̀) sm. ཁེར་གཅིར་.

ཁེར་ལས་དུད་ཚང་ (kērlɛɛ̀ düdzaŋ) a private household (in contrast to one that is part of a collective).

ཁེར་ལུས་ (kēr lüü) alone, isolated, separated, by oneself.

ཁེར་བཤད་བྱེད་ (kērshɛɛ̀ cèè) sm. ཚིག་ལབ་རྒྱག.

ཁེལ་ (kēē) p. of འཁེལ་.

ཁེས་ (kēè) vi. to hit the target/ mark.

ཁེས་ཉིན་ (kēñin) sm. ཁ་ཉིན་.

ཁེས་ཉིན་ཀ་ (kēñinga) sm. ཁ་ཉིན་.

ཁོ་ (kō) he, it ¶ཁོ་ངའི་གྲོགས་པོ་རེད་ He is my friend.

ཁོ་ཀྲང་ (kōdraŋ) ch. sm. ཁའོ་ཀྲང་.

ཁོ་ཁ་དབྱིན་ (kōkayin) eng. cocaine.

ཁོ་ཁོ་ (kōko) eng. cocoa.

ཁོ་ཁོ་ཤི་ལི་ (kōko shila) Koko Hsili Mountains.

ཁོ་ཚོ་ (kōjaà) they ¶ཁོ་ཚོ་ལྷ་ས་ནས་ཡོང་བ་རེད་ They came from Lhasa.

ཁོ་ཅུས་ (kōjüü) ch. the Chinese imperial examination system.

ཁོ་ཆིན་ (kōjin) ch. harmonica.

ཁོ་ཉིད་ (kōñii) he himself.

ཁོ་གཉིས་ (kūñii) those two, the two of them.

ཁོ་ཐག་ (kōdaà) deciding, judging.

ཁོ་ཐག་ཆོད་ (kōdaà cöö) vi. to have lost all hope ¶འདི་ལོ་སྟོན་དག་ཡག་པོ་ཡོང་རྒྱུ་ཁོ་ཐག་ཆོད་སོང་ This year we have lost all hope of having a good harvest.

ཁོ་ཐོ་ (kōto) a leather pouch for gunpowder.

ཁོ་མཐིང་ལྷ་ཁང་ (kōtiŋ lhāgaŋ) name of a monastery in southern Tibet.

ཁོ་ན་ (kōna) purely, solely, only ¶དམག་དོན་ཁོ་ནའི་ལྟ་ཚུལ་ The purely military viewpoint. ¶ཁོང་གི་དབང་ཆ་སྲུང་སྐྱོབ་ཁོ་ནའི་ཆེད་དུ་ For the purpose solely of protecting his own power.

ཁོ་ན་ཉིད་ (kōnañii) sm. ཁོ་ན་.

ཁོ་ནར་ (kōnar) that only, that alone ¶ཁོ་ཚོས་ངལ་རྩོལ་མང་དུ་གཏོང་རྒྱུ་ཁོ་ནར་བསམ་བློ་བཏང་བ་རེད་ They thought only of increasing labor.

ཁོ་ནས་སྲིད་དབང་ (kōnɛɛ̀ siwaŋ) dictatorship.

ཁོ་པ་ (kōba) sm. ཁོ་.

ཁོ་པ་ཚོ་ (kōbatso) sm. ཁོ་ཚོ་.

ཁོ་བོ་ (kōwo) I, myself (masculine) ¶ཁོ་བོ་མགྱོགས་པོ་ཡོང་གི་ཡིན་ I will come soon.

ཁོ་བོ་ཅག་ (kōwojaà) we, us, ourselves ¶ཁོ་བོ་ཅག་སློབ་གྲྭར་ཡོང་གི་ཡིན་ We will come to school.

ཁོ་མོ་ (kōmo) 1. she ¶ཁོ་མོ་གཉིས་ Those two (females). 2. I, myself (feminine) ¶ཁོ་མོའི་བུ་ Her son.

ཁོ་ཙེ་ (kōdze) ch. chopsticks.

ཁོ་ཚག་ (kōdzaà) ch. a food steamer.

ཁོ་ཚོ་ (kōntso) they.

ཁོ་ཤི་ཁར་ (kōshigar) Kashgar.

ཁོ་ཡོན་ (kōyön) ch. office member, member of an administrative section.

ཁོ་ར་ (kōra) that itself ¶ངས་དངོས་གནས་ཁོ་ར་མཐོང་བྱུང་ I really saw that.

ཁོ་ར་ (kōra) wall, fence (that goes around sth.).

ཁོ་ར་ཁོར་སྲུག་ (kōra kōrsug) sm. ཁོ་ར་ཁོར་ཡུག.

ཁོ་ར་ཁོར་ཡུག་ (kōra kōryuù) 1. the environment, surroundings ¶འབྲས་སྤུངས་དགོན་པའི་ཁོ་ར་ཁོར་ཡུག་དུ་ཤིང་སྡུ་མང་པོ་བཏབ་འདུག In the environment around Drepung Monastery they planted many kinds of trees. 2. fence.

ཁོ་རང་ (kōraŋ) he, he himself.

ཁོ་རང་ཚོ་ (kōraŋdzo) they.

ཁོ་རང་རང་ཉིད་ (kōraŋ raŋñii) he himself.

ཁོ་རའི་ (kōrɛɛ) his, his own.

ཁོ་རེ་ (kōre) term of address for males of the same or lower status.

ཁོ་ལག་ (kōlaà) 1. the body, limbs; vi.—རྫོགས་ to be fully developed physically ¶ལུས་ཀྱི་ཁོ་ལག་རྫོགས་ནས་ Having become fully developed physically. 2. width of a river.

ཁོ་ལག་ཡངས་པ་ (kōlaà yaŋba) 1. a vast area. 2. physically strong.

ཁོ་ལུའི་པར་གཞི་ (kōluu bārshi) colophon.

ཁོ་ལོམ་པི་ཡ་ (kōlombiya) Colombia.

ཁོ་ལོམ་པོ་ (kōlombo) Colombo.

ཁོ་ཤེད་ (kōsheè) he said.

ཁོ་ས་ཏ་རི་ཁ་ (kōsa tā riga) Costa Rica.

ཁོ་ཧྥི་ (kōfe) eng. coffee.

ཁོ་ཧྲི་ (kōhri) ch. administrative or technical offices.

ཁོག་ (kɔ̄ɔ̀) 1. sm. ཁོག་པ་, 1. 2. a dressed carcass (with the intestines taken out) ¶ཤ་ཁོག་གསུམ་ Three dressed carcasses. 3. imp. of འགོག.

ཁོག་སྐྱོན་ཞུགས་ (kɔ̄ggyön shuù) sm. ཁོང་སྐྱོན་ཞུགས་.

ཁོག་ཁེབས་ (kɔ̄gkep) pot lid/ cover.

ཁོག་གད་ (kɔ̄ggyɛɛ̀) laughing inwardly when sb. does sth. wrong or inappropriate; vi.—ཤོར་ to involuntarily laugh inwardly ¶སྐྱ་མགྲོན་རིས་གསོལ་སྟོན་སྐབས་སྐད་ཆ་ཁྱད་མཚར་ཞིག་བཤད་ཙང་ང་རང་ཁོག་གད་ཤོར་བྱུང་ At the party, because the guest said sth. weird, I laughed inwardly.

ཁོག་གི་སྙིང་བཞིན་གཅེས་ (kɔ̄ɔ̀gi ñiŋshin jēè) very precious/ dear [Lit. loving/ cherishing like one's own heart].

ཁོག་གྲིམས་ (kɔ̄gdrim) steady, staid.

ཁོག་རྒས་ (kɔ̄ggɛɛ̀) old and weak/ feeble ¶ཁོག་རྒས་ནད་གཅོང་གི་མི་རྒན་ A sick and feeble old man.

ཁོག་རྒྱ་ཆུང་བ་ (kɔ̄ggya cūŋwa) 1. shortsighted ¶ཁོག་རྒྱ་ཆུང་བའི་མིས་ལས་དོན་ཆེན་པོ་བསྒྲུབ་མི་ཐུབ་ A shortsighted person will not be able to accomplish great tasks. 2. withdrawn, not outgoing, timid ¶ཁོག་རྒྱ་ཆུང་བའི་མི་དང་གཤིབ་ཁག་པོ་ཡོད་ It is hard to get along with a withdrawn person.

ཁོག་རྒྱ་ཆེ་བ་ (kɔ̄ggya cēwa) sm. ཁོག་རྒྱ་ཆེན་པོ་.

ཁོག་རྒྱ་ཆེན་པོ་ (kɔ̄ggya cēmbo) 1. patient, tolerant. 2. broad-minded, thinking grandly/ broadly/ big, farsighted.

ཁོག་བརྒྱངས་སེང་སློང་ (kɔ̄ggyaŋ siŋloŋ) instigating/ stirring up trouble, fomenting disturbances; va.—བྱེད་.

ཁོག་གཅོང་ (kɔ̄gjoŋ) chronic internal illness/ disease.

ཁོག་ཆུང་ (kɔ̄gjuŋ) 1. sm. ཁོག་རྒྱ་ཆུང་བ་. 2. a small earthenware pot.

ཁོག་ཆུད་ (kɔ̄gjüü) sm. ཁོག་ཏུ་ཆུད་.

ཁོག་ཏུ་ཆུད་ (kɔ̄gtu cüü) vi. to know/ comprehend/ understand ¶སློབ་ཚན་ཚང་མ་ཁོག་ཏུ་ཆུད་ན་ཡིག་ཚད་གཏོང་རྒྱུར་སྐྲག་མི་དགོས་ If (one) knows all the subjects there should be no fear of taking the exam.

ཁོག་གདམ་ (kɔ̄gdam) talk regarding one's innermost thoughts/ feelings; —ཤོད་ to talk about one's innermost thoughts/ feelings.

ཁོག་རྟེན་ (kɔ̄gden) 1. parasitic [Lit. depending on the inside]. 2. see གཞན་པའི་ཁོག་རྟེན་.

ཁོག་ལྡིར་ (kɔ̄gdir) sm. ཁོག་ལྡིར་.

ཁོག་སྡེགས་ (kɔ̄gdeg) a stand on which a pot is placed.

ཁོག་སྟོང་ (kɔ̄gdoŋ) 1. hollow ¶ཤིང་ཁོག་སྟོང་ཞིག A hollow tree. 2. having an empty stomach, hungry ¶ཁོག་སྟོང་གིས་ལས་ཀ་བྱེད་ཐུབ་ཀྱི་མ་རེད་ A hungry person will not be able to work.

ཁོག་སྟོང་རྒྱ་ཐུག་ (kɔ̄gdoŋ gyəduù) macaroni-type noodle that is hollow.

ཁོག་སྟོང་རང་ཚུགས་མི་ཐུབ་ (kɔ̄gdoŋ rəndzuù mitub) without wealth/ resources a person will not be able to stand on his own two feet [Lit. anything empty (such as a bag) can not stand upright].

ཁོག་སྟོད་ (kɔ̄gdöö) upper part of the body.

ཁོག་སྟོད་ལ་དབུགས་འཚངས་ (kɔ̄gdööla ūgtsaŋ) pneumothorax.

ཁོག་བརྗོད་ (kɔ̄g dȫö) va. to say sth. openly/ clearly.

ཁོག་དུག (kɔ̄gdug) sm. མཐོང་དུག.

ཁོག་དྲང་ (kɔ̄gdraŋ) honest, upright, fair ¶ཁ་གསལ་ཁོག་དྲང་གི་མི་ལ་ཉེ་པོ་བྱེད་དགོས་ One should be close to people that are open and honest.

ཁོག་འདར་ (kɔ̄gdar) shivering inside or internally (due to cold or fear); vi.—ཤོར་ to shiver inside/ internally.

ཁོག་ཕྱིར་ (kɔ̄gdir) earthenware tea kettle/ pot.

ཁོག་སྡུག་འཚང་ (kɔ̄gduù cāŋ) sm. སེམས་ངན་འཚང་.

ཁོག་ན་ཡི་གེ་མེད་ (kɔ̄gna yi̱ge me̱è) unfamiliar/ uninformed about a particular subject or thing.

ཁོག་ན་ཡི་གེ་ཡོད་ (kɔ̄gna yi̱ge yö̱ö) familiar/ knowledgeable about a particular subject or thing.

ཁོག་ནང་ཕྲུ་གུ་ (kɔ̄gnaŋ trūgu) fetus.

ཁོག་ནང་དུ་མེ་འབར་ཡང་ཁ་ནས་དུ་བ་མ་ཐོན་པ་ (kɔ̄gnaŋtu me̱baryaŋ wānɛ tu̱da ma̱tön) sm. སྣ་ཁུང་ནས་དུ་བ་མི་ཐོན་པ་.

ཁོག་ནང་ཞུགས་ (kɔ̄gnaŋ shu̱ù) va. to put bad ideas in sb.'s mind about someone else, to instigate ¶ཨ་མས་པ་ཕའི་ཁོག་ནང་ཞུགས་ནས་ཕྲུ་གུར་གཤེ་གཤེ་བཏང་བ་རེད་ The mother instigated the father, and he scolded the children.

ཁོག་ནད་ (kɔ̄gnɛɛ̀) internal disease/ illness.

ཁོག་ནད་སྨན་བཅོས་སྡེ་ཁག (kɔ̄gnɛɛ̀ mɛ̄njöö̀ de̱khag) internal medicine division.

ཁོག་ནས་ཁས་ལེན་ (kɔ̄gnɛɛ̀ kɛ̄ɛ̀len) tacit consent/ acceptance.

ཁོག་ནས་མེ་འབར་ཡང་སྣ་ཁུང་ནས་དུ་བ་མ་ཐོན་པ་བྱ་དགོས་ (kɔ̄gnɛɛ̀ me̱bar ya̱ŋ nɔ̄guŋnɛ tu̱wə ma̱tön ca̱göö̀) keeping one's anger inside [Lit. even when the belly is on fire, one must not let the smoke out of the nose].

ཁོག་གནོན་ (kɔ̄gnön) pressure in the stomach.

ཁོག་མནའ་ (kɔ̄gna) a sincere promise or oath; va.—སྐྱེལ་ to make a sincere promise or oath.

ཁོག་པ་ (kɔ̄gba) 1. the inside of the trunk of the body ¶སྦལ་པའི་ཁོག་པ་བཤགས་ཏེ་ནང་ཁྲོལ་ལ་བལྟས་པ་རེད་ (They) cut open the frog's body and examined its insides. 2. internal capacity ¶སྣོད་ཆས་འདི་ཁོག་པ་ཆེན་པོ་འདུག This container has a large capacity. 3. tolerant, patient ¶མི་འདི་ཁོག་པ་ཆེན་པོ་འདུག This man is very tolerant. va.—བྱེད་; —འཁྱེར་ to be tolerant, patient. 4. va.—སྐྱོང་ to instigate, to incite ¶ཁོས་སློབ་ཕྲུག་བ་ཚོར་ངོ་རྒོལ་སློར་ལངས་བྱེད་དགོས་ཟེར་ཁོག་པ་བསྐྱངས་པ་རེད He instigated the students to rebel. 5. va.—སྔོག; —འདྲུ་ to ferret out secrets (from a person) by devious means ¶སོ་པ་དེས་ངའི་ཁོག་པ་སྔོག་གི་འདུག The spy is trying to ferret out secrets from me by devious means. 6. va.—འདྲུ་ digging up the insides of sth. (e.g., the trunk of a tree to make a boat). 7. vi.—འགྲིམ་ to have diarrhea.

ཁོག་པ་འཁུར་ (kɔ̄gba kūr) see ཁོག་པ་བྱེད་.

ཁོག་པ་གྲང་མོ་སོང་ (kɔ̄gba tra̱ŋmo sōŋ) vi. to feel extremely sad after hearing some bad news, etc. [Lit. to have one's insides get cold].

ཁོག་པ་འགྲིམ་ (kɔ̄gba dri̱m) sm. ཁོག་པ་, 7.

ཁོག་པ་སྐྱོང་ (kɔ̄gba gyo̱ŋ) see ཁོག་པ་, 4.

ཁོག་པ་བསྐྱང་ (kɔ̄gba gya̱ŋ) f. of ཁོག་པ་སྐྱོང་.

ཁོག་པ་བསྐྱངས་ (kɔ̄gba gya̱ŋ) p. of ཁོག་པ་སྐྱོང་.

ཁོག་པ་སྔོག (kɔ̄gba ŋɔ̄ɔ̀) see ཁོག་པ་.

ཁོག་པ་བསྔོག (kɔ̄gba ŋɔ̄ɔ̀) f. of ཁོག་པ་སྔོག.

ཁོག་པ་བསྔོགས་ (kɔ̄gba ŋɔ̄ɔ̀) p. of ཁོག་པ་སྔོག.

ཁོག་པ་ཅན་ (kɔ̄gbajɛn) tolerant, patient; va.—བྱེད་ to be tolerant, to be patient.

ཁོག་པ་ཆུང་ཆུང་ (kɔ̄gba cu̱jün) 1. intolerant, impatient; va.—བྱེད་ to be intolerant, to be impatient. 2. small capacity (of a container).

ཁོག་པ་ཆེན་པོ་ (kɔ̄gba cēmbo) 1. tolerant, patient; va.—བྱེད་ to be tolerant, to be patient. 2. large capacity (of a container).

ཁོག་པ་ཡངས་པོ་ (kɔ̄gba ya̱ŋbo) 1. sm. ཁོག་རྒྱ་ཆེན་པོ་. 2. carefree.

ཁོག་པ་ལེན་ (kɔ̄gba le̱n) va. to probe/ test indirectly ¶ངས་གནས་ཚུལ་དེའི་སྐོར་ཤེས་ཡོད་མེད་ཁོས་ངའི་ཁོག་པ་ལེན་གྱི་འདུག He is probing to see whether or not I know that information.

ཁོག་པ་ལོན་ (kɔ̄gba lȫn) vi. to have probed/ tested sb.

ཁོག་པ་གཤག (kɔ̄gba shāà) va. to cut open, to dissect, to operate.

ཁོག་པའི་སྙིང་དང་དཔྲལ་བའི་མིག (kɔ̄gbɛ ñi̱ŋdaŋ drɛ̄ɛwɛ mi̱i) sm. ཁོག་གི་སྙིང་བཞིན་གཅེས་ [Lit. the body's heart; the forehead's eye].

ཁོག་པའི་སྙིང་བཞིན་གཅེས་ (kɔ̄gbɛ ñi̱ŋshin jēè) sm. ཁོག་གི་སྙིང་བཞིན་གཅེས་.

ཁོག་པའི་ནང་ལ་ནད་མེད་ན་ གདོང་ལ་དྲིགས་པ་ཆགས་དོན་མེད་ (kɔ̄gbɛ na̱ŋla nɛ̱ɛ̀ me̱èna do̱ŋla tre̱gba cāàdön me̱è) if one is innocent, one should not fear [Lit. if there is no sickness internally, there is no reason for black spots on the face].

ཁོག་པར་འཛུལ་ (kɔ̄gbaa dzu̱ü) sm. ཁོག་ཞུགས་.

ཁོག་པར་ཤོང་ (kɔ̄gbaa shō̄ŋ) vi. to be magnanimous and tolerant ¶རྐྱེན་ངན་ཆེན་པོ་འདི་འདྲ་བྱུང་ཀྱང་ཁོང་གི་ཁོག་པར་ཤོང་གི་ཡོད་པ་རེད་ Even after this great misfortune he is still magnanimous.

ཁོག་སྤུན་ (kɔ̄gbün) the inner yarn in a woven blanket.

ཁོག་ཕེབས་ (kɔ̄gpeb) the entrance of a deity into the body of a medium or shaman; va.—བྱེད་/གནང་.

ཁོག་ཕྲུག (kɔ̄gdrug) a small ཁོག་མ་.

ཁོག་འབུ་ (kɔ̄g bu̱) internal parasite.

ཁོག་འབུབས་ (kɔ̄g bu̱b) 1. va. to set up a tent or umbrella. 2. va. to put things in order or sequence.

ཁོག་སྦུབས་ (kɔ̄gbub) 1. cavity (of abdomen, mouth, tooth). 2. capacity.

ཁོག་མ་ (kɔ̄ɔma) earthenware pot/ vase ¶མེ་ཏོག་ཁོག་མ་ Flower pot.

ཁོག་མེད་ (kɔ̄gmeè) 1. not solid, hollow ¶ཁོག་མེད་སྒྲོགས་མདེལ་ Hollow cannon ball. 2. narrow in width.

ཁོག་སྨད་ (kɔ̄gmɛɛ̀) lower part of the body.

ཁོག་སྨད་དབུགས་འཚངས་ (kɔ̄gmɛɛ̀ ūüdzaŋ) pneumoperitoneum.

ཁོག་སྨད་ཞ་བ་ (kɔ̄gmɛɛ̀ sha̱wa) paralysis of the lower part of the body.

ཁོག་སྨན་ (kɔ̄gmɛn) medicine to be taken internally.

ཁོག་རྩིས་ (kɔ̄gdzii) 1. internal calculation, mental arithmetic, mental estimating/ calculation. 2. an inner plan, a secret motive/ idea; va.—རྒྱག ¶ཁྱེད་རང་ལ་མ་འོངས་པའི་ལས་ཀའི་སྐོར་ཁོག་རྩིས་གང་ཡོད་དམ་ What is your inner plan concerning future work.

ཁོག་རྩིས་ཆུང་ཆུང་ (kɔ̄gdzii cūŋjuŋ) internal thinking/ planning/ calculating on a small scale.

ཁོག་རྫེ་ (kɔ̄gdze) trap/ snare; va.—རྒྱག.

ཁོག་ཚིལ་ (kɔ̄gtsil) internal fat, fat in the body.

ཁོག་ཚ་ལང་ (kɔ̄gdza la̱ŋ) vi. to have a frightening feeling inside the body.

ཁོག་ཚོད་ལེན་ (kɔ̄gdzöö̀ le̱n) sm. ཁོག་པ་ལེན་.

ཁོག་འཛུམ་ (kɔ̄gdzum) smiling inside (but not openly out of modesty) ¶ཕ་མ་གཉིས་ནས་བུ་མོར་མག་པ་ལེན་རྒྱུ་ཡིན་ཞེས་བཤད་སྐབས་བུ་མོ་དེ་ཁོག་འཛུམ་ཤོར་བ་རེད་ When the father and mother said they are getting a bridegroom for their daughter she smiled inside (but did not show it externally).

ཁོག་རྫས་ཅན་ (kɔ̄gdzɛɛ̀jɛn) not hollow, not solid inside.

ཁོག་རྫས་ཡོད་པ་ (kɔ̄gdzɛɛ̀ yö̱ba) sm. ཁོག་རྫས་ཅན་.

ཁོག་ཞུགས་ (kɔ̄gshuù) 1. possessed by a god/ spirit; vi.—བྱེད་ to be possessed by a god/ spirit ¶གྲྭ་པ་དེ་ལ་ལྷ་ཁོག་ཞུགས་ཡང་ས་བྱེད་ཀྱི་ཡོད་པ་རེད་ That monk is often possessed by gods. 2. instigating, inciting, brainwashing, filling one's head with ideas; va.—བྱེད་ ¶མི་ངན་ཁོག་ཞུགས་ཀྱིས་རྒྱུན་པའི་སློབ་ཕྲུག་བ་ཚོས་ཞིང་ཆ་བསླངས་པ་རེད་ The evil person's instigation was the cause of the disturbance in the school.

ཁོག་གཞི་ (kōgshi) 1. body frame ། གྲུ་གཟིངས་ཁོག་གཞིའི་བཟོ་ཁང་ A repair shop for ship bodies. 2. shung. sm. སྐུ་ཁོག.

ཁོག་ཡངས་ (kōgyaŋ) 1. spacious, having a large capacity. 2. patient, tolerant; va.—བྱེད་ ། མི་དེ་ཁོག་ཡངས་ཤིག་ཡིན་ཙང་ལམ་སེང་ཁྲོང་ལང་གི་མེད་པ་རེད་ Because he is patient he doesn't get angry at once. 3. carefree, untroubled, lighthearted ། མི་དེ་ཁོག་ཡངས་ཤིག་ཡིན་ཙང་སྡུག་བསྔལ་ག་འདྲ་ཞིག་བྱུང་ནའང་སྣང་དག་གནོང་གི་མེད་པ་རེད་ Because he is a carefree person, whatever kind of misfortune occurs doesn't bother him.

ཁོག་ཡངས་དཀྱིལ་ཆེ་ (kōgyaŋ gyēce) 1. thinking grandly/ broadly/ big, farsighted, broad-minded; va.—བྱེད་ ། ཁོག་ཡངས་དཀྱིལ་ཆེ་མེད་ན་འཆར་གཞི་ཆེན་པོ་འདིང་མི་ཐུབ་ If one doesn't think broadly one cannot make a big plan. 2. sm. ཁོག་ཡངས་.

ཁོག་ཡངས་པོ་ (kōgyaŋ) sm. ཁོག་ཡངས་, 1.

ཁོག་ཡངས་ཕམ་ཁུར་ (kōgyaŋ pāmkur) accepting defeat with grace/ class.

ཁོག་ཡངས་བྱམས་བརྩེ་ (kōgyaŋ camdze) tolerant and kind/ loving.

ཁོག་རིས་ (kōgrii) a design inside sth., e.g., the rifling inside a gun barrel.

ཁོག་རུལ་ (kōgrüü) 1. decayed, rotten, corrupt; vi.—དུ་འགྱུར་ to become decayed/ rotten/ corrupt ། ཤིང་སྡོང་ཁོག་རུལ་ A tree that is rotten inside. ། གཞུང་ཁོག་རུལ་ཡིན་ཙང་ Because the government is corrupt. 2. malicious, spiteful, mean.

ཁོག་རུལ་ངན་འགྱུར་ (kōgrüü ŋεngyur) corrupt and degenerate/ evil.

ཁོག་རུལ་ནུས་མེད་ (kōgrüü nüümeè) corrupt/ rotten and ineffective.

ཁོག་ལ་ཚུད་ (kōgla tsüü) sm. ཁོག་ལ་ཆུད་.

ཁོག་ལེན་ (kōglen) sm. ཁོག་པ་ལེན་.

ཁོག་ཤིང་ (kōgshiŋ) core of a tree.

ཁོག་སོབ་ (kōgsob) the rotten core (of a tree).

ཁོང་ (kōŋ) 1. he (h.). 2. inside (the body) ། གད་མོ་ཁོང་ནས་ཤོར་པ་རེད་ (He) laughed deeply (from inside).

ཁོང་རྨྱོན་ (kōŋgyön) internal injury; vi.—ཞུགས་ to get/ be injured internally.

ཁོང་ཁྲག (kōŋdro) blood in the body cavity.

ཁོང་ཁྲོ་ (kōŋdro) anger, angry, indignation (h.); vi.—ཟ་; —ལངས་; —བྱེད་. to get angry; vi.—འཇགས་ to have anger to subside; vi.—འབར་ to be/ get very angry [Lit. to burn with anger]; va.—སློང་ to make/ cause anger, to provoke anger; va.—གནོན་ to overcome/ suppress/ control anger ། འོས་པའི་ཁོང་ཁྲོ་ Righteous anger, indignation. ། གཞན་གྱིས་རང་ལ་སེམས་བཟང་གིས་སྐྱོན་བརྗོད་བྱས་པར་ཁོང་ཁྲོ་ཟ་རྒྱུ་མེད་ One shouldn't get angry if sb. offers well intended criticism. ། ཕྲུ་གུ་དེས་ཕ་མར་དགོངས་སེལ་ཞུས་ཙང་ཕ་མའི་ཁོང་ཁྲོ་འཇགས་འདུག Because the child apologized (his) parent's anger subsided. ། སློབ་ཕྲུག་གིས་དགེ་རྒན་ལ་ཁ་ལན་བསློགས་ཙང་དགེ་རྒན་ཁོང་ཁྲོ་འབར་སོང་ Because the student answered back to his teacher, the teacher was extremely angry. ། མི་དེ་ཁོང་ཁྲོ་གནོན་མ་ཐུབ་པར་གཞན་དང་ཁ་ཙོད་ཤོར་གྱི་འདུག That person is unable to control (his) anger and gets into arguments with others.

ཁོང་ཁྲོ་ཞི་འཇགས་ (kōŋdro shijaà) sm. ཁོང་ཁྲོ་ཞི་འཇགས་.

ཁོང་ཁྲོ་བཙོད་སྒོམ་ (kōŋdro sögom) controlling anger; va.—བྱེད་ ། ཁོང་ཁྲོ་བཙོད་སྒོམ་མ་བྱས་ན་རྟག་པར་མི་གཞན་དང་ཁ་ཙོད་ཤོར་གྱི་རེད་ If one doesn't control one's anger one will always get into arguments with others.

ཁོང་ཁྲོས་སྙིང་གས་ (kōŋdröö ñiŋgεὲ) extreme anger; vi.—བྱེད་ [Lit. anger that splits one's heart].

ཁོང་འཁྲིད་ (kōŋtrii) va. to take control from inside.

ཁོང་འཁྲུགས་ (kōŋdruù) sm. ཁོང་ཁྲོ་.

ཁོང་གློད་ (kōŋ lȍȍ) vi. to have peace of mind, to be relaxed/ calm.

ཁོང་སྒྲིལ་ (kōŋdrii) arc. iron chain/ fetters.

ཁོང་ངན་ལག་ཡང་ (kōŋŋεn lagyaŋ) evil/ malicious and quick to get into fights.

ཁོང་གཅོང་ (kōŋjoŋ) sm. ཁོག་གཅོང་.

ཁོང་ཆུད་ (kōŋla) sm. ཁོང་དུ་ཆུད་.

ཁོང་ཉར་བསམ་དོན་ (kōŋñar sāmdön) thoughts one keeps inside/ secret ། ཕྱི་རྒྱལ་དུ་འགྲོ་རྒྱུ་དེ་ངའི་ཁོང་ཉར་བསམ་དོན་ཞིག་ཡིན་ I am keeping secret my going abroad.

ཁོང་གཉིས་ (kōŋñii) those two, the two of them ། ཁོང་གཉིས་སློབ་གྲྭར་མཉམ་དུ་འགྲོ་གི་ཡོད་པ་རེད་ The two of them go to school together.

ཁོང་སྙིང་ (kōŋñiŋ) 1. the heart. 2. the core of a tree, the rings of a tree core.

ཁོང་སྙོམ་ (kōŋñom) arc. lazy, idle.

ཁོང་སྙོམས་པོ་ (kōŋ ñombo) sm. ཁོང་སྙོམས་.

ཁོང་སྟོང་ (kōŋtoŋ) sm. ཁོག་སྟོང་.

ཁོང་དུ་ཆུད་ (kōŋtu cüü) vi. to master, to comprehend thoroughly ། རྩོམ་དྲ་ཆེ་བའི་ལག་རྩལ་མགྱོགས་མྱུར་ཁོང་དུ་ཆུད་པ་རེད་ (They) quickly mastered the complicated technique.

ཁོང་དུ་ཆུད་པ་བྱེད་ (kōŋdu cüüba ce̱e̱) va. to make sb. comprehend/ master thoroughly ། གཞུང་གིས་སོ་ནམ་པ་ཚོར་སོན་གསར་འདེབས་སྟངས་ཀྱི་ལག་རྩལ་ཁོང་དུ་ཆུད་པ་བྱས་པ་རེད་ The government made the farmers learn thoroughly how to plants the new seeds.

ཁོང་ན་ (kōŋna) internally, inwardly ། མོ་ནི་ཕྱི་ངོས་ནས་བལྟས་ན་གཞུང་དྲང་མདོག་ཁ་པོ་ཡོད་ན་ཡང་ཁོང་ན་བསམ་ངན་ཡོད་པ་ཞིག་རེད་ Externally, even though she gives the appearance of being upright, inwardly she had evil thoughts.

ཁོང་ནང་ (kōŋnaŋ) inside the body.

ཁོང་ནད་ (kōŋnεὲ) internal medicine.

ཁོང་ནད་ལྟ་རྟོག་ཁང་ (kōŋnεὲ dādogaŋ) medical observation ward.

ཁོང་ནད་སྡེ་ཚན་ (kōŋnεὲ de̱dzεn) department of internal medicine.

ཁོང་ནད་ཚན་ཁག (kōŋnεὲ tsεngaà) department of internal medicine.

ཁོང་གནག (kōŋnag) cruel, malicious, vindictive.

ཁོང་རྣམ་པ་ (kōnamba) they (h.).

ཁོང་རྣམ་ཚོ་ (kōnandzo) sm. ཁོང་རྣམ་པ་.

ཁོང་པ་ (kōŋpa) 1. interior, inside. 2. they (h.).

ཁོང་པའི་དྲོད་ (kōŋbε trȍȍ) body heat/ temperature.

ཁོང་འབྲས་ (kōŋdrεὲ) a disease in Tibetan medicine roughly equivalent to cancer.

ཁོང་ཚར་ (kōŋtsar) the skin/ fleece of an unborn sheep.

ཁོང་ཚོ་ (khōndzo) they (h.).

ཁོང་འཛིན་ (kōŋ dzi̱n) sm. འཁོན་འཛིན་.

ཁོང་འཛུམ་ (kōŋ dzu̱m) sm. ཁོང་དགོད་.

ཁོང་ཡངས་ (kōŋyaŋ) easygoing, lighthearted, broad-minded, tolerant.

ཁོང་ཡངས་དཀྱིལ་ཆེ་ (kōgyaŋ gyēce) sm. ཁོག་ཡངས་.

ཁོང་ཡངས་པ་ (kōŋyaŋba) sm. ཁོག་ཡངས་.

ཁོང་ཡངས་པོ་ (kōŋyaŋbo) sm. ཁོག་ཡངས་.

ཁོང་ཡུས་ (kōŋyüü) making a big deal out of sth. (verbally); va.—ཤོད་ to make a big deal out of sth. verbally ། ཁོས་ང་ལ་རོགས་རམ་ཕྲན་བུ་བྱས་པར་ཁོང་ཡུས་ཞི་པོ་ཅིག་ཤོད་ཀྱི་འདུག He is making a big deal out of giving me a little help.

ཁོང་རབ་ཡངས་པ་ (kōŋrəb ya̱ŋba) a vast capacity ། ཁོང་རབ་ཡངས་པའི་ཚོགས་ཁང་ A hall possessing a vast capacity.

ཁོང་རུལ་ (kōŋrüü) 1. sm. ཁོག་རུལ་. 2. a traitor within a group.

ཁོང་ལ་ (kōŋla) sm. ཁོང་ན་.

ཁོང་ལག་གདོང་ (kōŋlaà dōŋ) va. to kill an animal by making an incision in the chest and pulling out the artery from the heart with one's hand.

ཁོང་ཤིང་ (kōŋshiŋ) sm. ཁོག་ཤིང་.

ཁོང་སྲུབས་ (kōŋsub) augmenting, supplementing; va.—བྱེད་.

ཁོང་སོབ་ (kōŋsob) sm. ཁོག་སོབ་.

ཁོང་སྲན་ (kōŋsɛn) patient, tolerant; va.—བྱེད་.

ཁོང་སྲིན་ (kōŋsin) internal parasite.

ཁོང་གསེང་ (kōŋseŋ) a gap or space between walls or buildings, a hollow area.

ཁོང་གསེབ་ (kōŋseb) sm. ཁོང་གསེང་.

ཁོངས་ (kōn) under the jurisdiction of, belonging to, part of, among ། གྲོག་མ་ཡོང་མཁན་སྐྱབས་བཅོལ་བའི་ཁོངས་ནས་འཁོགས་མང་པོ་མི་འདུག There were not many old people among the refugees who came first. ། དམར་ཤོག་གི་ཁོངས་ལ་གནམ་གྲུ་ག་ཚོད་ཡོད་པ་རེད་ How many planes do the communists have? ། དབུལ་ཕོངས་ཚོ་འབྱོར་མེད་གྲལ་རིམ་གྱི་ཁོངས་རེད་ The poor belong to the proletarian class.

ཁོངས་རྒྱུད་ (kōŋkǖǖ) system.

ཁོངས་གཏོགས་ (kōŋdɔɔ̀) 1. belonging to or part of sth.; va.—བྱེད་ to agree to belong to sth. or to become part of sth. ། རྒྱལ་ཁབ་ཆུང་ཆུང་དེས་རྒྱལ་ཁབ་ཆེ་བ་ཞིག་གི་ཁོངས་གཏོགས་བྱས་པ་རེད་ That small nation (agreed to) become a part of that large country. 2. classification, categorization; va.—བྱེད་; —བཟོ་ to classify/ categorize/ make part of sth. ། ངའི་ཁྱིམ་ཚང་དབུལ་ཕོངས་གྲལ་རིམ་གྱི་ཁོངས་གཏོགས་སུ་བཙུག་པ་རེད་ (They) classified my family as belonging to the proletarian class. ། སྟོབས་ཆེན་རྒྱལ་ཁབ་ཀྱིས་རྒྱལ་ཁབ་ཆུང་བ་ཁག་ཅིག་རང་ཉིད་ཀྱི་ཁོང་གཏོགས་བཟོས་པ་རེད་ The powerful country made the small nation a part of it. ། ཚོང་པ་མང་ཆེ་བ་འབྱོར་ལྡན་གྲལ་རིམ་གྱི་ཁོང་གཏོགས་བཟོས་པ་རེད་ Most of the traders were made a part of the bourgeoisie class.

ཁོངས་གཏོགས་ཀྱི་འབྲེལ་བ་ (kōŋdɔɔ̀gi dreewa) subordinate relationship.

ཁོངས་གཏོགས་རྒྱལ་ཁབ་ (kōŋdɔɔ̀ gyɛɛgəb) dependent/ satellite country.

ཁོངས་གཏོགས་ས་ཆ་ (kōŋdɔɔ̀ sāca) place one belongs to.

ཁོངས་འདུས་ (kōŋdǖǖ) linked together, joined/ included together ། ཉེས་པ་སྔ་ཕྱི་ཁོངས་འདུས་ཀྱི་ཉེས་ཆད་སྲང་བཅུ་བཏང་བ་རེད་ They fined him 10 sang for the former and later crimes together.

ཁོངས་མི་ (kūŋmi) member, constituent ། ཁོང་ལས་ཁུངས་འདིའི་ཁོངས་མི་རེད་ He is a member of this office.

ཁོངས་མཚམས་ (kōŋtsam) boundary.

ཁོངས་འཛིན་རྒྱལ་ཁབ་ (kōŋdzin gyɛɛgəb) suzerain, colonial state.

ཁོངས་ཞུགས་ (kōŋshuù) member, constituent ། དབྱིན་ཇི་འཛམ་གླིང་རྒྱལ་ཚོགས་ཁོངས་ཞུགས་རྒྱལ་ཁབ་རེད་ England is a member state of the United Nations.

ཁོངས་སུ་གཏོགས་ (kōŋsu dɔɔ̀) vi. to be a part of, to belong to, to be subsumed under ། ལས་ཁུངས་འདི་ཕྱི་སྲིད་ཀྱི་ཁོངས་སུ་གཏོགས་པ་རེད་ This office came under External Affairs. ། མི་རིགས་འདི་སོག་རིགས་ཀྱི་ཁོངས་སུ་གཏོགས་པ་རེད་ This nationality belongs to the Mongoloid race.

ཁོངས་སུ་བདག (kōŋsu daà) sm. ཁོངས་སུ་གཏོགས་.

ཁོངས་སུ་འདུ་ (kōŋsu du) vi. to be included in, to encompass, to be subsumed in ། འགྲོ་སོང་དེ་འདི་ལོའི་སྔོན་རྩིས་ཁོངས་སུ་འདུས་ཡོད་པ་རེད་དམ་ Is that expense included in this year's budget?

ཁོངས་སུ་ཚུད་ (kōŋsu tsǖǖ) sm. ཁོངས་སུ་གཏོགས་.

ཁོད་ (kōō) 1. surface, exterior. 2. imp. of འགོད་.

ཁོད་ཁ་སྙོམ(ས)་ (kōōgañom) sm. ཁོད་སྙོམ་.

ཁོད་བཅའ་ཡུལ་ (kōō jaaazüü) the places where the 36 divisions of land were made during the time of King Songtsen Gambo.

ཁོད་སྙོམ(ས)་ (kōōñom) 1. level, even ། ས་ཆ་ཁོད་སྙོམས་ཐོག On level ground. 2. equal; va. ཁོད་སྙོམ་; —བྱེད་; —བཟོ་ to make level, to equalize ། གཉིས་ཀར་གཟིགས་སྐྱོང་ཁོད་སྙོམ་གནང་བ་རེད་ (They) looked after both equally. ། ཁོང་ཁོང་དེ་ར་ས་བརྒྱངས་ནས་ཁོད་སྙོམས་པ་རེད་ (They) filled the depression with earth and made it level.

ཁོད་སྙོམ་ཁ་གསབ་ (kōōñom kāsəb) adding sth. extra to equalize.

ཁོད་སྙོམ་ནས་བགོད་ (kōōñomnɛ göō) va. to divide equally/ proportionately.

ཁོད་སྙོམ་པོ་ (kōō ñōmbo) even, equal; level.

ཁོད་སྙོམ་བཟོ་བྱེད་འཁྲུལ་འཁོར་ (kōōñom socɛɛ trǖǖkɔɔ) a steamroller.

ཁོད་སྙོམས་ (kōōñom) sm. ཁོད་སྙོམ་.

ཁོད་དཔོན་ (kōōbön) official in charge of the 36 divisions of land made during the time of King Songtsen Gambo.

ཁོད་ར་ (kōōra) the hollow area along the rim of the stone grinding wheel where the ground flour falls.

ཁོད་སོ་དྲུག (kōō sōdruù) the 36 divisions of land made during the time of King Songtsen Gambo.

ཁོན་ (kōn) p. of འཁོན་.

ཁོན་ཁོན་ཐོགས་ཐོགས་མེད་པ་ (kōnkön tōgtɔg meeba) smoothly, without trouble or hindrances (in traveling or work) ། ང་ནང་ལ་ཁོན་ཁོན་ཐོགས་ཐོགས་མེད་པར་ལོག་ཕྱིན་པ་ཡིན་ I went directly home without trouble.

ཁོན་ཁོན་ལེ་ཐོགས་མེད་པ་ (kōnkön letōg meeba) sm. ཁོན་ཁོན་ཐོགས་ཐོགས་མེད་པ་.

ཁོན་བཙུག (kōnjug) sm. འཁོན་བཙུག.

ཁོན་འཛུག (kōnjug) sm. འཁོན་འཛུག.

ཁོན་དུང་ཧྭ་ (kōnduŋhwa) ch. coltsfoot flower (used in herbal medicine).

ཁོན་ཐོགས་མེད་པ་ (kōntɔg meeba) sm. ཁོན་ཁོན་ཐོགས་ཐོགས་མེད་པ་.

ཁོན་འཛིན་ (kōndzin) sm. འཁོན་འཛིན་.

ཁོན་བཟོ་ (kōnyöö) va. to start a dispute/ conflict, to make enemies.

ཁོབ་ (kōb) 1. vi. to become rusty (of skills), to be clumsy/ bungling/ uncoordinated, to lose one's dexterity ། ཡུན་རིང་མ་བརྒྱབ་ཙང་ངའི་བོད་སྐད་འདི་ཁོབ་བཞག I didn't speak Tibetan for a long time so it has become rusty. 2. sm. འཁེབས་.

ཁོབ་དོ་ (kōbdo) 1. old, worn-out, beat up ། མོ་ཊ་འདི་ཁོབ་དོ་ཞི་པོ་ཅིག་འདུག This car is very old (beat up). 2. clumsy ། ཁོ་ཚོ་ལག་གསར་པ་ཡིན་ཙང་ལས་ཀ་བྱེད་ཡས་ཁོབ་དོ་འདུག Because they are novices they work clumsily.

ཁོབ་པོ་ (kōbo) sm. ཁོབ་དོ་.

ཁོབ་ཤ་ཚ་པོ་ (kōbsha tsābo) sm. ཁོབ་དོ་.

ཁོམ་ (kōm) 1. vi. to have free time, to have time to do sth. ། དེ་དགོང་ལྟད་མོར་ཁོམ་གྱི་ཡོད་པས་ Do you have time for (to see) a show tonight? ། དེ་རིང་ཁོམ་མིན་ཟེར་ (He) said, "Today I don't have time." 2. (vb. + —) time to do the preceeding verbal action ། ཁོ་ཚོས་བཀོད་འདོམས་བྱེད་ཁོམ་མ་བྱུང་བ་རེད་ They didn't have time to give orders.

ཁོམ་དུས་ (kōmdǖǖ) free time, spare time ། ཁྱེད་ལ་ཁོམ་དུས་བྱུང་མཚམས་མཇལ་འཕྲད་ཞུ་གི་ཡིན་ When you have spare time I will come to see you.

ཁོམ་པ་ (kōmba) free time, spare time; va.—བྱེད་ to make time ། དེ་རིང་ཤ་ཉོ་རྒྱུ་ཁོམ་པ་ཡོད་པས་ Do you have any time today to buy meat? ། སྨན་པ་འདིས་རྟག་པར་དུས་ཚོད་ཁོམ་པ་བྱས་ནས་ཕྲུ་གུ་ཚོར་ལུས་པོ་བརྟག་དཔྱད་བྱེད་པར་ཡོང་གི་ཡོད་པ་རེད་ The doctor always makes time to come to examine the children.

ཁོམ་པ་མེད་མཁན་ (kōmba mengɛn) a busy person.

ཁོམ་འབོག (kōmbɔɔ̀) a large skin/ leather bag used for putting clothing.

ཁོམ་ལོང་ (kōmloon) sm. ཁོམ་པ་.

ཁོམ་གསེང་ (kōmseŋ) sm. ཁོམ་པ་.

ཁོའི་ (kōō) his, of him (ཁོ་ + gen.) ། དེབ་འདི་ཁོའི་རེད་ This book is his. ། ཁོའི་དེབ་ His book.

ཁོའི་ཙེ་ (kōōdze) ch. chopsticks; va.—རྒྱག to use chopsticks.

ཁོའུ་ཆིན་ (kōjin) ch. harmonica.

ཁོའོ་ (kōwo) ch. section, department.

ཁོའོ་ཀྲང་ (kōwo drāŋ) ch. department/ section chief.

ཁོའོ་པན་ (kōwobɛn) ch. allegro (in music).

ཁོའོ་ཛི་ (kōwodze) sm. ཁོའི་ཙེ་.

ཁོར་ (kɔ̄ɔ̄) to him (ཁོ་ + dat.-loc.).

ཁོར་རྒྱ་ (kɔ̄rka) sm. འཁོར་རྒྱ་.

ཁོར་མོ་ཡུག (kɔ̄rmoyug) constantly, incessantly ¶ ཉིན་མཚན་ཁོར་མོ་ཡུག་ཏུ་ལས་ཀ་བྱས་པ་རེད་ (He) worked constantly day and night.

ཁོར་མོར་ (kɔ̄rmor) 1. continuously, constantly ¶ ལོ་མང་རིང་མི་དམངས་ཚོས་སྡུག་བསྔལ་ཁོར་མོར་མྱངས་པ་རེད་ The people suffered continuously for many years. 2. va.—བསྐོར་ to completely surround ¶ དགྲ་བོས་རང་དམག་གི་མཐའ་ཁོར་མོར་བསྐོར་ཡོད་པ་རེད་ Our army was completely surrounded by the enemy. 3. abbr. of ཁོར་མོ་ཡུག.

ཁོར་ཡུག (kɔ̄ryug) environment, surroundings ¶ ཁོར་ཡུག་ལ་གཙང་བཤེར་རྒྱག་རྒྱུ་ Cleaning up the environment. ¶ ལྷ་ཁང་གི་ཁོར་ཡུག་ལ་མེ་ཏོག་མང་པོས་བསྐོར་ཡོད་ The surroundings of the temple are filled with flowers.

ཁོར་ཡུག་གི་གཙང་སྦྲ་ (kɔ̄ryuggi dzāŋdra) environmental cleanliness.

ཁོར་ཡུག་གཅེས་སྲུང་དང་འབྲེལ་བའི་ཞིབ་འཇུག་ལས་ཁང་ (kɔ̄ryug jēèsuŋdaŋ drēēwɛ shimjuù lɛ̀ɛgaŋ) Earthwatch.

ཁོར་ཡུག་ཆུང་བ་ (kɔ̄ryug cūŋwa) microhabitat.

ཁོར་ཡུག་ཏུ་ (kɔ̄ryugtu) all around, surrounding ¶ གྲོང་ཁྱེར་གྱི་ཁོར་ཡུག་ཏུ་ Surrounding the city.

ཁོར་ཡུག་ཏོག་ཞིབ་ས་ཚིགས་ (kɔ̄ryug dōgshib sətsig) environmental monitoring station.

ཁོར་ཡུག་འཕྲོད་བསྟེན་ (kɔ̄ryug trōōdɛn) environmental health.

ཁོར་ཡུག་འཕྲོད་བསྟེན་དོ་དམ་ས་ཚིགས་ (kɔ̄ryug trōōdɛn) environmental health management station.

ཁོར་ཡུག་གཙང་སྦྲ་ (kɔ̄ryug dzāŋdra) environmental cleanliness; va.—བྱེད་.

ཁོར་ཡུག་བཙོག་སྐྱུར་ (kɔ̄ryug dzōggyur) environmental degradation/ despoilation.

ཁོར་ཡུག་སྲུང་སྐྱོང་ཅུའུ་ (kɔ̄ryug sūŋgyoŋ) environmental protection agency/ bureau.

ཁོར་ཡུག་སྲུང་སྐྱོབ་ (kɔ̄ryug sūŋgyob) environmental protection; va.—བྱེད་.

ཁོར་ཡུག་སྲུང་སྐྱོབ་ཀྱི་ཐེབས་རྩ་ (kɔ̄ryug sūŋgyobgi tēbdza) Environmental Defense Fund.

ཁོར་ཡུག་སྲུང་སྐྱོབ་ལས་ཁང་ (kɔ̄ryug sūŋgyob lɛ̀ɛgaŋ) Environmental Protection Agency (U.S.A.).

ཁོར་སྲུང་ (kɔ̄rsuŋ) abbr. of འཁོར་ཡུག་སྲུང་སྐྱོབ་.

ཁོལ་ (kōō) 1. p. of འཁོལ་. 2. imp. of འགོལ་. 3. setting aside a section/ portion/ fragment ¶ དངུལ་ཁག་གཅིག་ཁོལ་དུ་བཏོན་པ་རེད་ (They) set aside a portion of the money.

ཁོལ་རྒྱལ་ (kōōgyɛɛ) the leather pouch of a bellows.

ཁོལ་ཁོལ་ (kōōköö) 1. dying to do sth.; va.—བྱེད་ ¶ ཆང་འཐུང་སྙིང་འདོད་ནས་ཁ་ཁོལ་ཁོལ་བྱེད་ཀྱི་འདུག (I am) dying to have a drink of chang. 2. chaotic, confused; va.—བྱེད་ to act in a chaotic/ confused way.

ཁོལ་རྒྱུད་ (kōōgyüü) a servant or serf lineage/ descent line.

ཁོལ་མཆུ་ (kōōncu) the mouth (iron pipe) of a bellows.

ཁོལ་དུ་ཕྱུང་ (kōltu cūŋ) va. to set aside, to keep/ place separately ¶ ཅ་ལག་མཁོ་མེད་རྣམས་ཁོལ་དུ་ཕྱུང་པ་རེད་ (They) set aside the unneeded things.

ཁོལ་པ་ (kōōba) boiled.

ཁོལ་པོ་ (kōōbo) male servant.

ཁོལ་ཕྱུང་མཐོང་ཤེས་ (kōōjuŋ tōŋsheè) excerpts.

ཁོལ་བུ་ (kōōbo) 1. bellows. 2. child-servant. 3. section, branch, part.

ཁོལ་བྲན་ (kōōbo) servant, slave.

ཁོལ་མ་ (kōōma) 1. boiled ¶ ཆུ་ཁོལ་མ་ Boiled water. 2. window, skylight.

ཁོལ་མོ་ (kōōmo) 1. bellows. 2. maid-servant.

ཁོལ་མོ་མེ་སྦར་ (kōōmo mebar) instigating, inducing [Lit. lighting a fire with bellows].

ཁོལ་ཤིང་བཟོ་གྲྭ་ (kōlshiŋ sodra) (wood and bamboo) furniture factory.

ཁོས་ (kōō) by him (ཁོ་ + inst.) ¶ ཁོས་བྱས་པ་རེད་ He (by him) did it.

ཁོས་མགོ་ (kōŋgo) the hole (in a Tibetan stove) where the ashes are taken out.

ཁྱ་ཁྱོར་ (kyāgyɔɔ) abbr. of ཁྱ་རེ་ཁྱོ་རེ་.

ཁྱ་གི་ཁྱོ་གི་ (kyāge kyōge) 1. crooked, not in a straight line ¶ གྲོང་ཁྱེར་འདིའི་ལམ་ཀ་ཚང་མ་ཁྱ་གི་ཁྱོ་གི་རེད་ All the roads in this town are crooked. 2. roundabout.

ཁྱ་མ་ (kyāma) fuel.

ཁྱ་རེ་ཁྱོ་རེ་ (kyāre kyōre) unsteady, precarious, wavering, unstable, staggering; not fluent ¶ ཆབ་སྲིད་ཀྱི་གནས་སྟངས་ཁྱ་རེ་ཁྱོ་རེ་ཡིན་སྐབས་ Because the political situation is precarious. ¶ ཡི་གེ་ཁྱ་རེ་ཁྱོར་ཤེས་ཀྱི་འདུག (He) doesn't know how to read fluently.

ཁྱག (kyāà) 1. vi. to endure/ bear/ tolerate ¶ མི་དེ་དཀའ་ངལ་ཆེན་པོ་ཁྱག་ཐུབ་མཁན་ཞིག་ཡིན་ That man can bear much hardship. 2. vi. to be able to carry/ lift ¶ བོང་བུས་ཁལ་ཆེན་པོ་ཁྱག་མི་ཐུབ་ The donkey can't carry that big load.

ཁྱག་ཁྱོག (kyāgkyɔɔ) sm. ཁྱ་གི་ཁྱོ་གི་.

ཁྱག་དེ་ཁ་ལ་ (kyāgde kāla) all of a sudden ¶ ཁྱག་དེ་ཁ་ལ་ལངས་ནས་ཕྱིན་སོང་ (He) got up and left all of a sudden.

ཁྱག་རུམ་ (kyəgrum) sm. འཁྱགས་རུམ་.

ཁྱག་རོམ་ (kyəgrom) sm. འཁྱགས་རོམ་.

ཁྱགས་ (kyāà) sm. འཁྱག.

ཁྱགས་རུམ་ (kyəgrum) sm. འཁྱགས་རུམ་.

ཁྱད་ (kyɛ̀ɛ) 1. difference, distinction ¶ འདི་གཉིས་ལ་ཁྱད་ག་རེ་ཡོད་པ་རེད་ What is the difference between these two? 2. in order to ¶ དཔེ་མཛོད་ཁང་གི་ཉེ་འགྲམ་དུ་སྡོད་ཡག་དེ་དཔེ་དེབ་གཡར་བདེ་བའི་ཁྱད་ཡིན་ The reason for my living near the library is that it is more convenient to borrow books.

ཁྱད་མཁས་ (kyɛ̀ɛgɛɛ) expert, specialist.

ཁྱད་གྲངས་ (kyɛ̀ɛtraŋ) amount of difference expressed by numbers.

ཁྱད་མངག་ (kyɛ̀ɛŋaà) specially assigned ¶ ཁྱད་མངག་སྐུ་ཚབ་ A specially assigned representative.

ཁྱད་ཅན་ (kyɛ̀ɛjɛn) special, distinctive ¶ ཁྱད་ཅན་དམག་དཔུང་ Special troops.

ཁྱད་ཅི་ཡོད་ (kyɛ̀ɛjiyöö) what's the difference? ¶ བུད་མེད་དེ་ར་ཁོས་ཉེས་དུང་ཚབས་ཆེན་འདི་འདྲ་བཏང་བ་ནི་བསད་པ་དང་ཁྱད་ཅི་ཡོད་ When he beat her so badly, what's the difference with killing her.

ཁྱད་ཆེ་ (kyɛ̄ɛce) big/ bigger difference.

ཁྱད་ཆེན་པོ་ (kyɛ̄ɛ cēmbo) sm. ཁྱད་ཆེ་.

ཁྱད་ཆོས་ (kyɛ̀ɛjöö) 1. characteristic, salient feature; va.—སྟོན་ to reveal the salient features or characteristics ¶ ལས་འགུལ་འདིའི་ཁྱད་ཆོས་ག་རེ་ཡོད་པ་རེད་ What are the characteristics of this movement? 2. style ¶ བོད་ཀྱི་ཁྱད་ཆོས་ལྡན་པའི་སྡོད་ཁང་ A residential building in the Tibetan style.

ཁྱད་ཆོས་ཀྱི་ཚིག (kyɛ̀ɛjöögi tsīg) an adjective.

ཁྱད་ཆོས་སྟོན་པའི་ཚིག (kyɛ̀ɛjöö dönbɛ tsīg) sm. ཁྱད་ཆོས་ཀྱི་ཚིག.

ཁྱད་ཆོས་ལྡན་པ་ (kyɛ̀ɛjöö dɛmba) sm. ཁྱད་ཆོས་.

ཁྱད་ཆོས་ཟུར་ལྡན་ (kyɛ̀ɛjöö surdɛn) distinctive.

ཁྱད་བཏོན་ (kyɛ̀ɛdön) special ¶ ཁྱད་བཏོན་བྱ་དགའ་ Special award.

ཁྱད་རྟགས་ (kyɛ̀ɛdaà) sm. ཁྱད་ཆོས་.

ཁྱད་ཐོན་ (kyɛ̀ɛtön) specially produced ¶ ཁྱད་ཐོན་དངོས་རྫས་ Specially produced products.

ཁྱད་ཐོན་པ་ (kyɛ̀ɛtömba) extremely, effective ¶ སྨན་པ་དེས་ནད་པར་ཁྱད་ཐོན་པའི་སྨན་བཅོས་བྱས་འདུག That doctor treated the patient extremely effectively.

ཁྱད་དུ་ (kyɛ̀ɛtu) sm. ཁྱད་པར་དུ་.

ཁྱད་དུ་ཐོན་ (kyɛ̀ɛtu tön) sm. ཁྱད་ཐོན་.

ཁྱད་དུ་འཕགས་པ་ (kyɛ̀ɛtu pāgbə) sm. ཁྱད་འཕགས་.

ཁྱད་དུ་གསོད་ (kyɛ̀ɛtu söö) sm. ཁྱད་གསོད་བྱེད་.

ཁྱད་དུ་བསད་ (kyɛ̀ɛtu sɛ̄ɛ) p. of ཁྱད་དུ་གསོད་.

ཁྱད་དོན་ (kyɛ̀ɛtön) special matter.

ཁྱད་འདོན་ (kyɛ̀ɛdön) sm. ཁྱད་ཐོན་.

ཁྱད་ལྡན་ (kyɛ̀ɛdɛn) special ¶ ཁྱད་ལྡན་བཟོ་རྩལ་བཟོ་གྲྭ་

Special handicrafts factory.

ཁྱད་ནུས་ (kyɛ̄ɛ̀nüù) special characteristic of sth. ¶ རང་བྱུང་ཁམས་ཀྱི་ཁྱད་ནུས་ The special character of the natural environment.

ཁྱད་ནུས་འདོན་སྤེལ་ (kyɛ̄ɛ̀nü tō̱nbel) giving full play to sb.'s special characteristics/knowledge/skills.

ཁྱད་ནོར་ (kyɛ̄ɛ̀nor) special wealth/ goods.

ཁྱད་པར་ (kyɛ̄ɛ̀bar) difference, distinction ¶ བསམ་པའི་ངལ་རྩོལ་དང་ལུས་ཀྱི་ངལ་རྩོལ་བར་གྱི་ཁྱད་པར་རྣམས་ The difference between mental and physical labor.

ཁྱད་པར་བཀོད་ (kyɛ̄ɛ̀bar gṑò) va. to show or expose a difference ¶ ཡིག་ཆ་དེའི་ནང་སྤྱི་ཚོགས་གསར་རྙིང་གི་ཁྱད་པར་གསལ་པོ་བཀོད་འདུག This document shows the difference between the old and new society.

ཁྱད་པར་བཀོད་པ་ (kyɛ̄ɛ̀bar gṑòba) specially designed (house, building, etc.).

ཁྱད་པར་གྱི་རང་བཞིན་ (kyɛ̄ɛ̀bargi rə̱ŋshin) a unique, special or distinguishing trait or characteristic.

ཁྱད་པར་ཅན་ (kyɛ̄ɛ̀barjɛn) special, unusual ¶ དབུ་ལོག་དེའི་བཟོ་དབྱིབས་ཁྱད་པར་ཅན་ཞིག་བཟོས་བཞག (He) has made specially shaped clothes (that are fashionable).

ཁྱད་པར་རྟོགས་ (kyɛ̄ɛ̀bardog) va. to know or understand the difference, to differentiate between things.

ཁྱད་པར་དུ་ (kyɛ̄ɛ̀bartu) particularly, in particular ¶ སྤྱིར་བཏང་གནས་ཚུལ་གསལ་པོ་གསུངས་པས་མ་ཟད། ཁྱད་པར་དུ་བོད་པའི་གནས་ཚུལ་ཞིབ་ཕྲ་གསུངས་སོང་ Not only did he talk about the news in general, in particular he talked in detail about Tibet.

ཁྱད་པར་དུ་འགྲོ་ (kyɛ̄ɛ̀bartu dro̱) va. to advance, to go forward, to go higher and higher.

ཁྱད་པར་བ་ (kyɛ̄ɛ̀barwa) special, different, unique.

ཁྱད་འཕགས་ (kyɛ̄ɛ̀pag) 1. great, extraordinary, magnificent, excellent, superior ¶ གྲུབ་འབྲས་ཁྱད་འཕགས་ཤིག་རེད་ A magnificent accomplishment. ¶ བོད་ཀྱི་ཁྱད་འཕགས་སྟོབས་ཤུགས་འདོན་སྤེལ་བྱེད་ Utilizing Tibet's superior strengths.

ཁྱད་འཕགས་ཀྱི་རང་བཞིན་ (kyɛ̄ɛ̀paggi rə̱ŋshin) an extraordinary/ noteworthy/ superior quality or characteristic, superiority ¶ སྣུམ་གྲོན་ཆུང་བ་སོགས་ནི་སྣང་འཁོར་འདི་རིགས་ཀྱི་ཁྱད་འཕགས་ཀྱི་རང་བཞིན་རེད་ Such things as gas consumption is a superior characteristic of this type of car.

ཁྱད་འཕགས་ཅན་ (kyɛ̄ɛ̀pagjɛn) the best, the greatest, the most supreme/ extraordinary.

ཁྱད་དབང་ (kyɛ̄ɛ̀waŋ) special privilege ¶ གྲུབ་འབྲས་ལ་གཞིགས་ཏེ་ཁྱད་དབང་སྤྲད་པ་རེད་ Special privileges were granted in accordance with (their) accomplishments.

ཁྱད་མི་འདུག (kyɛ̄ɛ̀ mi̱nduù) sm. ཁྱད་མེད་.

ཁྱད་མེད་ (kyɛ̄ɛ̀meè) same, no difference, alike, doesn't matter ¶ ང་ཚོ་དོ་དགོང་ག་པར་ཕྱིན་ནའི་ང་ལ་ཁྱད་མེད་ It makes no difference to me where we go tonight.

ཁྱད་རྩལ་ (kyɛ̄ɛ̀dzɛɛ) special skill.

ཁྱད་མཚར་ (kyɛ̄ntsaa) strange, unusual, weird ¶ ཁོས་སྐད་ཁྱད་མཚར་ཅིག་བརྒྱབ་པ་རེད་ He made a weird noise.

ཁྱད་མཚར་བརྒྱ་དང་ཁྱད་མཚར་སྟོང་ (kyɛ̄ntsar gya̱taŋ kyɛ̄ntsar dōŋ) many weird or strange events/ acts/ happenings.

ཁྱད་མཚར་པོ་ (kyɛ̄n tsāābo) strange, unusual, weird; va.—བྱེད་ to act in a strange way ¶ ཁྱད་མཚར་པོའི་སྣང་བ་ A strange, weird feeling.

ཁྱད་འཛིན་ (kyɛ̄ndzin) discrimination; va.—བྱེད་ to discriminate ¶ མི་རིགས་ཀྱི་ཁྱད་འཛིན་ Ethnic discrimination.

ཁྱད་རྫས་ (kyɛ̄ɛ̀dzɛɛ̀) special product, local speciality (product).

ཁྱད་ཞུགས་ (kyɛ̄ɛ̀ shu̱ù) vi. to be different, to have a difference occur ¶ ཐོན་ཟོག་སྔ་རྗེས་དབར་ཡག་ཉེས་ཁྱད་ཞུགས་བཞག There is a difference between the quality of the old and new products.

ཁྱད་གཞི་ (kyɛ̄ɛ̀shi) the word that an adjective modifies.

ཁྱད་ཡོད་ (kyɛ̄ɛ̀yö̀ö) different, distinctive, characteristic.

ཁྱད་ཡོན་ (kyɛ̄ɛ̀yö̀ö) special knowledge.

ཁྱད་ལས་ (kyɛ̄ɛ̀lɛɛ̀) specialized work/ trade/ occupation ¶ ཁྱད་ལས་སློབ་གྲྭ་ A school that teaches specialized trades/ occupations.

ཁྱད་སེལ་ (kyɛ̄ɛ̀sel) sm.* ཁྱད་གསོད་.

ཁྱད་གསོད་ (kyɛ̄ɛ̀sö̀ö) contempt, disrespect; va.—བྱེད་; — གཏོང་ to look down on, to treat with contempt/ disrespect, to belittle/ scorn ¶ ཁོས་ཚང་མར་ཁྱད་གསོད་བྱས་ཙང་གྲོགས་པོ་གཅིག་ཀྱང་ཡོད་པ་མ་རེད་ Because he treats everyone with contempt, he doesn't have any friends. ¶ དཀའ་ངལ་ཁྱད་གསོད་བྱེད་ཀྱི་ཡོད་པ་རེད་ (They) treat hardship with contempt.

ཁྱད་བསད་ (kyɛ̄ɛ̀sɛɛ̀) sm. ཁྱད་གསོད་.

ཁྱབ་ (kyə̄p) 1. vi. to spread (over an area), to become widespread, to become popular ¶ ཁོང་གི་མཚན་སྙན་རྒྱལ་ཡོངས་ལ་ཁྱབ་པ་རེད་ His fame spread all over the country. 2. (ཡིན་པས་ or ཡོད་པས་+ —) indicates that a statement necessarily follows from a preceding conditional clause ¶ མེ་ཡིན་ན་ཚ་པོ་ཡིན་པས་ཁྱབ་ If its fire, it must be hot. ¶ རྒྱ་མི་ཡིན་ན་དམར་པོ་ཡིན་པས་མ་ཁྱབ་ If he is Chinese, it doesn't necessarily follow he is a communist.

ཁྱབ་ཁུལ་ (kyə̄bküü) the area in which sth. has become distributed/ disseminated/ widespread ¶ ལུང་པ་འདིར་ནད་ཡམས་ཁྱབ་ཁུལ་རྒྱ་ཆེན་པོ་ཡོད་པ་རེད་ In that area, the epidemic is widespread.

ཁྱབ་ཁོངས་ (kyə̄bgoŋ) realm, field, domain, sphere, scope ¶ འདུ་ཤེས་འཛིན་སྟངས་ཀྱི་ཁྱབ་ཁོངས་ The ideological field. ¶ བོད་གཞུང་ཁྱབ་ཁོངས་མི་མང་ People under the Tibetan government's domain. ¶ ཁེ་གཉེར་ཁྱབ་ཁོངས་ Business scope.

ཁྱབ་འགོས་ (kyāmgö̀ö) contamination, infection, contagion; va.—བྱེད་ ¶ ན་ཚ་ཕར་ཚུར་ཁྱབ་འགོས་མི་ཡོང་བའི་ཆེད་ So as not to have the disease infect others.

ཁྱབ་འགྱེད་ (kyə̄mgyeè) radiating. expanding, diffusing; va.—བྱེད་.

ཁྱབ་འགྲེམ་(ས) (kyə̄mdrem) distribution, dissemination; va.—བྱེད་ to distribute, disseminate ¶ སྲིད་གཞུང་གི་ཡིག་ཆ་ཁག་དུས་ཐོག་ཁྱབ་འགྲེམས་བྱ་དགོས་ The government documents must be distributed on time.

ཁྱབ་རྒྱས་ (kyə̄bgyɛɛ̀) widespread, disseminated widely ¶ ད་རེས་གསར་འགྱུར་དེ་ཁྱབ་རྒྱས་ཆེན་པོ་བྱུང་བཞག These days the news has spread widely.

ཁྱབ་བསྒྲགས་ (kyə̄bdraà) 1. notice, announcement, proclamation; va.—བྱེད་ ¶ གཞུང་གི་སྲིད་ཇུས་ཁྱབ་བསྒྲགས་ They announced clearly the government's policy. 2. publicity ¶ ཁྱབ་བསྒྲགས་དབུ་འཛིན་ Publicity chairman.

ཁྱབ་བསྒྲགས་བརྡ་ཡིག (kyə̄bdraà də̱yig) a written notice/ communiqué/ announcement.

ཁྱབ་བསྒྲགས་ཡི་གེ་ (kyə̄bdraà yi̱gi) sm. ཁྱབ་བསྒྲགས་བརྡ་ཡིག.

ཁྱབ་ཆ་ (kyə̄pja) spread, scope, range.

ཁྱབ་ཆུང་ (kyə̄pjun) not widespread, parochial, limited in scope/ spread/ range.

ཁྱབ་ཆེ་ཆུང་ (kyə̄b cījuŋ) the degree/ extent/ scope of spread or dissemination.

ཁྱབ་ཆེ་བ་ (kyə̄p cēwa) widespread, broad in scope/ range ¶ ཐོག་མར་ཁྱབ་ཆེ་བའི་ནད་གཞི་རྣམས་བཅོས་ཐབས་བྱ་དགོས་ First we have to cure the widespread disease.

ཁྱབ་ཆེན་པོ་ (kyə̄b cēmbo) sm. ཁྱབ་ཆེ་བ་.

ཁྱབ་མཆེད་ (kyə̄p cēè) vi. to spread widely.

ཁྱབ་མཆེད་ཆེན་པོ་ (kyə̄mjeè cēmbo) widespread ¶ ནད་ཡམས་ཁྱབ་མཆེད་ཆེན་པོ་བྱུང་བ་རེད་ The epidemic was widespread.

ཁྱབ་འཇུག (kyə̄mjug) the Hindu god Vishnu.

ཁྱབ་གདམ་ (kyə̄pdam) broadcast, notice, statement,

announcement, report; va.—སྒྲོག་; —འདོན་ to issue a statement, announcement, report, notice ༑ ཟུང་འབྲེལ་གྱིས་བཏོན་གནང་བའི་ཁྱབ་གདམས་གཅིག་གི་ནང་ལ་ In a jointly issued statement.

ཁྱབ་གདམས་སྒྲོག་མཁན་ (kyāpdam pēēñɛn) spokesman, publicity man.

ཁྱབ་སྟངས་ (kyābdaŋ) means of spreading widely, the way to make widespread ༑ གསར་འགྱུར་ངན་པ་དེ་ཁྱབ་སྟངས་ག་འདྲ་ཁྱབ་པ་རེད་ By what means did that bad news spread.

ཁྱབ་གདལ་ (kyābdɛɛ) spreading widely/ extensively, widespread, general, universal; va.—གཏོང་; —བྱེད་; —སྒྲོལ་ to make widespread, to disseminate widely; vi.—འགྲོ་ to become widespread, to get widely disseminated ༑ སློབ་ཆུང་སློབ་གསོ་ཁྱབ་གདལ་དུ་བཏང་ཡོད་ (They) have made primary education widespread. ༑ དེང་དུས་ཀྱི་གསོ་རིག་གི་ཤེས་ཡོན་འཛམ་གླིང་ཡོངས་ལ་ཁྱབ་གདལ་དུ་འགྲོ་གི་ཡོད་པ་རེད་ Modern medical knowledge is becoming widespread in the world.

ཁྱབ་འདོམས་བྱེད་པོ་ (kyāmdom cɐ̱èbo) one who is authorized to give orders, district commissioner, manager.

ཁྱབ་འདོམས་ལྷོད་ཡང་ (kyāmdom lhȍȍyaŋ) loose discipline ༑ ཞིང་ཆ་འཁྲུག་ཟིང་ཏོང་གི་སྐྱིག་ལམ་ཁྱབ་འདོམས་ལྷོད་ཡང་བྱུང་བ་རེད་ Because there was an uprising, the district's discipline became loose.

ཁྱབ་སྡོད་ (kyābdȍȍ) popular, widespread; vi. ཁྱབ་སྡོད་; —བྱེད་ to be popular, to be widespread ༑ སྒྲུང་གཏམ་དེ་བོད་ཀྱི་ས་གནས་གང་སར་ཁྱབ་བརྡད་ཡོད་ That story has become widespread in all parts of Tibet.

ཁྱབ་བདལ་ (kyābdɛɛ) sm. ཁྱབ་གདང་.

ཁྱབ་པ་ (kyābbɘ) sm. ཁྱབ་, 2.

ཁྱབ་པར་འཛུག་ (kyābbar ju̱ù) sm. ཁྱབ་, 2.

ཁྱབ་སྤེལ་ (kyāb bēl) sm. ཁྱབ་གདལ་.

ཁྱབ་སྤེལ་ཁང་ (kyābbel kāo) tib.ch. department of publicity/ advertising/ dissemination, popularization.

ཁྱབ་སྤེལ་ཐབས་ལམ་ (kyābbel tāblam) means/ methods/ channels of dissemination or publicity.

ཁྱབ་འཕེལ་ (kyābbee) sm. ཁྱབ་གདང་.

ཁྱབ་རྩལ་དཔེ་རིས་ (kyābdzül bēriì) a map or diagram that depicts a network.

ཁྱབ་ཡུལ་ (kyābyüü) the extent/ range that sth. has been spread or disseminated.

ཁྱབ་ཤུགས་ (kyābshuù) extent of diffusion/ spread ༑ བོད་ནང་རྒྱ་སྐད་ཀྱི་ཁྱབ་ཤུགས་ཇི་ཙམ་ཐེབས་པ་གནས་ཚུལ་འདིའི་ཐོག་ནས་རྟོགས་རྒྱུ་རེད་ The extent of the diffusion of Chinese language in Tibet will be understood from this.

ཁྱམ་ཁྱམ་ (kyāmgyam) roaming about, drifting from place to place, leading a vagrant life.

ཁྱམ་ཁྱོམ་ (kyāmgyom) swaying, shaking, trembling; vi.—བྱེད་ ༑ ས་གཡོས་ཀྱི་རྐྱེན་པས་ཁང་པ་ཁྱམ་ཁྱོམ་བྱས་པ་རེད་ The house shook because of the earthquake.

ཁྱམ་མེ་ཁྱོམ་མེ་ (kyāmme kyōmme) sm. ཁྱམ་ཁྱོམ་.

ཁྱམས་ (kyām) 1. courtyard. 2. corridor.

ཁྱམས་སྟོད་ (kyāmdȍȍ) upper courtyard.

ཁྱམས་སྨད་ (kyāmmɛɛ̀) lower courtyard.

ཁྱམས་ར་ (kyāmra) sm. ཁྱམས་.

ཁྱམས་ར་ཆེན་པོ་ (kyāmra cēmbo) the main courtyard in the Tsuglagang temple.

ཁྱམས་རིང་ (kyāmriŋ) a long covered corridor or walkway.

ཁྱམས་ར་ (kyāmra) sm. ཁྱམས་ར་.

ཁྱམས་ཤ་ (kyāmsha) sm. བར་ཁྱམས་.

ཁྱར་ཁྱོར་ (kyārgyor) staggering; vi.—བྱེད་ ༑ ནད་པ་དེ་ཁྱར་ཁྱོར་བྱས་ནས་འགྲོ་གི་འདུག That patient was staggering (going in a staggering manner).

ཁྱི་ (kyī) dog.

ཁྱི་བཀག (kyī gāà) p. of ཁྱི་འགོག.

ཁྱི་ཀུན་ (kyīgün) a dog that steals.

ཁྱི་སྐད་ (kyīgɛɛ̀) barking; va.—རྒྱག to bark.

ཁྱི་སྐད་ཁྱི་ཟུག (kyīgɛɛ̀ kyīsug) following blindly [Lit. the barking of one dog followed by others].

ཁྱི་སྐྱག (kyīgyaà) dog excrement.

ཁྱི་སྐྱག་ཕག་སྐྱག (kyīgyaà pāggyaà) derogatory term conveying that several actions are of the same negative category, e.g., stealing and lying [Lit. dog and pig shit].

ཁྱི་སྐྱག་ཕུང་པོ་ (kyīgyaà pūŋbo) a derogatory term for a collection of bad things [Lit. a heap of dog shit].

ཁྱི་སྐྲོད་ (kyīdrȍȍ) driving away a dog; va.—གཏོང་.

ཁྱི་ཁང་ (kyīgaŋ) dog house, kennel.

ཁྱི་ཁ་འགོག (kyī kā gɔ̱ɔ̀) sm. ཁྱི་འགོག.

ཁྱི་ཁ་ཝུར་ (kyī kāwur) dogs barking/ howling.

ཁྱི་ཁར་རུས་བཟུང་ (kyīgar ru̱ùsuŋ) not letting go of sth., holding on tenaciously to sth. ༑ ལས་བྱེད་རྙིང་པ་དེ་ཚོས་ལས་གནས་ཁྱི་ཁར་རུས་བཟུང་བྱེད་ཀྱི་ཡོད་པ་རེད་ These old cadres won't let go of their responsibilities. [Lit. a dog holding a bone in its mouth].

ཁྱི་ཀོག་མར་མི་འདྲུག (kyī kɔ̄ɔ̀ maa minduù) 1. one should not tell important matters to evil/ bad people. 2. one shouldn't try to teach sb. who isn't capable or worthy [Lit. one should not put butter in a dog's skin].

ཁྱི་འཁྱར་ (kyīgyar) a stray dog.

ཁྱི་གུ་ (kyīgu) sm. ཁྱི་ཕྲུག.

ཁྱི་གློ་སྤྱང་སྙིང་ (kyīlo jāŋñi) cruel and fierce/ inhuman/ merciless [Lit. a dog's lung and a wolf's heart].

ཁྱི་གློད་ (kyīlȍȍ) sm. མཁྱིད་.

ཁྱི་མགོ་སྡེར་ཐོག (kyī go̱ de̱r tɔ̄ɔ̀) putting an evil/ bad person in a high position [Lit. putting a dog's head on a platter].

ཁྱི་འགོག (kyī gɔ̱ɔ̀) 1. va. to hold one's tied guard dog (when sb. enters one's house so it doesn't bite) ༑ རྒྱལ་སྒོ་མ་འཛུལ་གོང་ཁྱི་བཀག་རོགས་གནང་ཞེར་དགོས་ Before entering the main door (of a house) one must say "hold your dog." 2. va. to prevent/ block/ hold off dogs.

ཁྱི་འགྱེད་ (kyī gye̱è) va. to set a dog loose after sb. ༑ ཀུན་མའི་རྗེས་སུ་ཁྱི་འགྱེད་པ་རེད་ (They) set the dog loose on the thief.

ཁྱི་རྒན་ (kyīgɛn) derogatory explicative similar to "pig" in English [Lit. old dog].

ཁྱི་རྒན་ངར་ཕོག (kyīgɛn ŋōbɔ̄ɔ̀) an old mangy dog.

ཁྱི་རྒན་ནང་འཛིང་ (kyīgɛn na̱ŋdziŋ) fighting among rogues/ evil people [Lit. fighting among old dogs].

ཁྱི་རྒན་གཞོགས་རྒྱག (kyīgɛn sho̱ggyuù) sm. ཁྱི་གཅིག་ཟུག་ན་སྒོ་ཁྱི་ཚང་མ་མཉམ་དུ་ཟུག.

ཁྱི་རྒན་རུས་པར་འཕྲད་ (kyīgɛn ru̱ùbar drɛɛ̄) sm. ཁྱི་ཁར་རུས་བཟུང་.

ཁྱི་རྒྱ་པོ་ (kyī gya̱wo) black dog with yellowish mouth and spots over the eyes.

ཁྱི་རྒྱགས་ན་མི་ཟུག་གུ་ཟུག མི་རྒྱགས་ན་མི་ཤོད་གུ་ཤོད་ (kyīgyaà na̱m mi̱sug gu̱sug mi̱gyaàna mi̱shȍȍ gu̱shȍȍ) when people are well-off they say and do all sorts of irresponsible things [Lit. when dogs' bellies are full they bite everyone, when peoples' bellies are full they say all sorts of rubbish].

ཁྱི་རྒྱགས་ནམ་མཁའི་སྐར་མར་ཟུག (kyīgyaà na̱mkɛ kārmaa ma̱a su̱g) 1. meddling/ interfering for no reason. 2. when one's belly is full one causes trouble for those above [Lit. when the dog is full it barks at the stars].

ཁྱི་སྒྲ་ (kyīdra) the bark of a dog.

ཁྱི་སྒོག (kyīgog) a type of garlic.

ཁྱི་ངན་ (kyīŋɛn) 1. a bad dog. 2. a ferocious dog.

ཁྱི་ངན་སྒོ་ཁར་བཙན་ (kyīŋɛn go̱kar dzēn) aggressive/ threatening behavior based on the power of a backer or supporter [Lit. a bad dog that is fierce at the door].

ཁྱི་ངན་རྡོ་ཕྱིར་འབྲང་ (kyīŋɛn do̱cir dra̱ŋ) cowardly

[Lit. a bad dog follows a stone].

ཁྱི་ངན་ལུང་པ་ཀུ་ཅོས་ཁེངས་ མི་ངན་པས་རུ་སྡེ་འཕུང་ལ་སྦྱོར་ (kyīŋɛn luŋba gūjöö kēŋ miŋɛmbɛ rude pūŋla jɔr) evil people ruin a community [Lit. a bad dog's barking makes noise everywhere, evil people ruin the community].

ཁྱི་ངར་བ་ (kyīŋarwa) a fierce dog.

ཁྱི་རྔོ་ (kīŋo) dog scabies/ mange.

ཁྱི་གཅིག་ཟུག་ན་སྒོ་ཁྱི་ཚང་མ་མཉམ་དུ་ཟུག (kyījig sugna gokyi tsāŋma ñāmtu sug) following the example/ behavior of sb. who does bad things [Lit. one dog barks and all the dogs follow suit].

ཁྱི་ལྗེ་ (kyīje) dog tongue (a derogatory epithet).

ཁྱི་ཉ་ (kyīña) pike (a type of fish).

ཁྱི་ཉར་འཁྲིམ་འཛིན་ (kyīñar trīmdzin) license/ certificate for keeping a dog.

ཁྱི་ཉལ་རྒྱུགས་སློང་ (kyīñɛl gyuglɔɔ̀) picking a fight with sb. who isn't looking for one [Lit. wake a lying dog by hitting it with a stick].

ཁྱི་ཉལ་བའི་མགོ་ལ་རྡོ་འཕངས་ མི་རང་བསྡད་མགོ་ལ་ཁྲིད་བཞག (kyīñɛl gyuglɔɔ̀) picking a fight with sb. who isn't looking for trouble [Lit. throwing a rock on the head of a sleeping dog, putting a lawsuit on the head of a person not doing anything].

ཁྱི་གདོང་ (kyī dōŋ) sm. ཁྱི་འགྱིད་.

ཁྱི་སྐྱག (kyīdug) dog shit.

ཁྱི་ཐག (kyīdag) a rope for tying dogs.

ཁྱི་ཐམ་ (kyītam) sm. ཁྱི་དམ་.

ཁྱི་ཐུ་པོ་ (kyī tūbu) a fierce dog.

ཁྱི་མཐོང་རི་འཁུར་ (kyīdoŋ rikur) even though others look down on you, you carry a great responsibility/ burden ༈ འགོ་ཁྲིད་ཀྱིས་ཁོང་རང་ལ་རྒྱུན་དུ་མཐོང་ཆུང་བྱེད་ཀྱང་ཁོང་གིས་ཁྱི་མཐོང་རི་འཁུར་གྱིས་ལས་འགན་ཆེན་པོ་འཁྱེར་གྱི་འདུག Even though the boss always looks down on him, like the saying, "regarded as dog, carrying a mountain," he is carrying a big responsibility. [Lit. regarded as dog, carrying a mountain].

ཁྱི་དང་གློ་བ་འཕྲད་ (kyīdaŋ lōtrɛ̄ɛ̀) acting hastily without thinking ༈ དགའ་གྲོགས་འཚོལ་སྐབས་གཟབ་ནན་བྱེད་དགོས་པ་ལས་ཁྱི་དང་གློ་བ་འཕྲད་པ་ནང་བཞིན་བྱ་རྒྱུ་མེད་ When searching for a girl (or boy) friend, you should be careful and not act like a dog coming across a lung. [Lit. a dog coming across a lung].

ཁྱི་དང་ཉེ་ན་མ་དང་ཉེ་ (kyīdaŋ ñena mādaŋ ñe) being/ getting close to evil people will cause one trouble [Lit. if one gets close to dogs one is close to getting bitten].

ཁྱི་དང་ཕྲུ་གུ་བུད་མེད་གསུམ་ རྒྱག་འདྲེ་སློང་བའི་གཞི་པོ་ཡིན་ (kyīdaŋ trūgu pūümeè sūm gyamdre lōŋwɛ dēbo yin) dogs, children and women are the main cause of fighting/ disputes.

ཁྱི་དམ་ (kyīdam) shung. a branding iron/ seal that has the word "dog" inscribed on it that is used for branding criminals on their forehead; va.—རྒྱག.

ཁྱི་དུག (kyīduù) rabies; vi.—ཕོག to get/ catch rabies.

ཁྱི་མདུད་ (kyī düü) two dogs getting stuck together after intercourse; vi.—ཐེབས་ to get stuck after having sexual intercourse.

ཁྱི་འདོགས་ (kyī dɔɔ̀) va. to tie up a dog.

ཁྱི་རྡུང་ (kyīduŋ) going out at night to womanize [Lit. hit the dog].

ཁྱི་ལྡོམ་ (kyīdom) stray dog.

ཁྱི་བརྡུངས་ཕག་དྲོས་ (kyī duŋ pāg trö̤ö̤) intimidating people by punishing sb. as an example [Lit. beat the dog, pig flees].

ཁྱི་ནག་སྐྱག་གཟན་ (kyīnag gyāgsɛn) derogatory epithet to reproach sb. [black dog that eats shit].

ཁྱི་སྣ་ (kyīna) a kind of design with curving lines.

ཁྱི་སྣ་ཝ་ཁྲིད་ (kyīna watrii) evil people leading evil people [Lit. fox leading dogs].

ཁྱི་པགས་ཀོ་ཡོལ་ (kyībaà gōyöö) tib.ch. 1. quack medicine. 2. dogskin plaster (used for rheumatism, strains, etc.) [Lit. dog skin, plaster-tape].

ཁྱི་པགས་སྦྱར་སྨན་ (kyībaà jarmɛn) sm. ཁྱི་པགས་ཀོ་ཡོལ་.

ཁྱི་པགས་སྲམ་བརྫུས་ (kyībaà drāmdzüü) tricking or deceiving sb. [Lit. faking a dog skin as an otter skin].

ཁྱི་སྤྱང་ (kyībjaŋ) jackal.

ཁྱི་སྤྱང་ཁ་འདྲིལ་ (kyījaŋ kāndril) sm. ཁྱི་སྤྱང་ངན་འདྲིལ་.

ཁྱི་སྤྱང་ངན་འདྲིལ་ (kyījaŋ ŋɛndree) collusion/ conspiracy/ alliance between evil forces, a pack of rouges/ scoundrels [Lit. alliance of dog and wolf].

ཁྱི་སྤྱང་ཚ་ (kyījaŋdza) sm. ཁྱི་སྤྱང་.

ཁྱི་སྤྱང་ལག་འདྲིལ་ (kyījaŋ laŋdree) sm. ཁྱི་སྤྱང་ངན་འདྲིལ་.

ཁྱི་སྤྱང་ལག་སྒྲིལ་ (kyījaŋ laŋdree) sm. ཁྱི་སྤྱང་ངན་འདྲིལ་.

ཁྱི་སྤྲང་ (kyīdraŋ) dog and beggar.

ཁྱི་ཕུར་ (kyīpur) a stake used to tie dogs.

ཁྱི་ཕྲུག (kyīdruù) puppy.

ཁྱི་བོས་ནས་མར་རྡུང་ (kyī pö̤öñɛ maa duŋ) deceitful, duplicitous [Lit. summon a dog and beat him].

ཁྱི་བྲུ་ (kyīdru) a dog that bites.

ཁྱི་བོད་ (kyībɛɛ̀) sm. ཁྱི་འགྱིད་.

ཁྱི་སྦྲང་ (kyīdraŋ) 1. dog fly. 2. dog flea.

ཁྱི་མི་སྨུགས་ཀ་མེད་ཀུན་མས་སྒོ་རྡུང་ (kyī mimug kāmeè gūmɛ goduŋ) being forced to do sth, having no choice but to do sth. [Lit. the dog had no choice but to bite (since) the thief knocked at the door].

ཁྱི་མིག (kyīmig) a kind of chrysanthemum (used in Tibetan medicine).

ཁྱི་མིག་བཞི་ (kyī migshi) a dog with two yellowish spots above its eyes.

ཁྱི་མོ་ (kyīmu) female dog.

ཁྱི་མོ་ཚང་མ་ (kyīmu tsāŋma) a pregnant dog.

ཁྱི་སྨུགས་ (kyī mūg) 1. va. to bite (by a dog). 2. a dog bite.

ཁྱི་སྨྱོན་ (kyīñon) mad/ rabid dog; vi.—ཐེབས་ to become rabid.

ཁྱི་སྨྱོན་གྱི་ནད་ (kyīñongi nɛɛ̀) rabies.

ཁྱི་སྨྱོན་རིམས་འགོག་སྨན་སོན་ (kyīnön rimgɔɔ̀ mɛnsön) rabies vaccine.

ཁྱི་སྨྱོས་ (kyīñöö) sm. ཁྱི་སྨྱོན་.

ཁྱི་ཙ་སྦྲེལ་ (kyīdza drel) sm. ཁྱི་མདུད་ཐེབས་.

ཁྱི་ཙ་ལང་ (kyīdza laŋ) vi. to come into heat (for dogs).

ཁྱི་ཙིག་ཁུགས་ལ་བཀར་ན་ཁ་ལོག་རྒྱག (kyī dzīgguùla gārna kālog gyaà) people pushed into a corner are dangerous [Lit. if you corner a dog it will turn on you].

ཁྱི་ཚང་ (kyīdzaŋ) sm. ཁྱི་ཁང་.

ཁྱི་འཛིང་ཤོར་ཀྱང་ཁྱི་པགས་མི་རལ་ (kyīdziŋ shɔ̄ɔgyaŋ kyībag mirɛɛ) even though relatives and friends fight they never lose their ties [Lit. though dogs fight they never tear their skin].

ཁྱི་རྫི་ (kyīdzi) dog-keeper, person who looks after dogs.

ཁྱི་གཞོང་ (kyīshoŋ) dog trough (for feeding).

ཁྱི་ཟན་མི་ལྡུད་ (kyīsɛn midɛɛ̀) going to the next lesson/ text before comprehending or understanding the prior ones [Lit. dog swallows tsampa without chewing].

ཁྱི་ཟུག (kyī sug) va. to bark.

ཁྱི་ཟླ་ (kyīnda) the 9th. month of the Tibetan lunar calendar.

ཁྱི་གཟིག (kyīsii) a type of small leopard.

ཁྱི་ཡན་ (kyīyɛn) sm. ཁྱི་འཁྱར་.

ཁྱི་ཡི་ཁ་ནས་བ་སོ་ལེན་པ་དང་འདྲ་བ་ (kyīyi kāne paso lembadaŋ drawa) sm. used to describe sb. from whom it is extremely difficult to get information [Lit. like getting ivory from a dog's mouth].

ཁྱི་ར་ (kyīrə) hunting; va.—རྒྱག.

ཁྱི་ར་རྒྱག་མཁན་ (kyīrə gyagɛn) sm. ཁྱི་ར་བ་.

ཁྱི་ར་བ་ (kyīrəwə) hunter.

ཁྱི་རོ་ (kyīro) dog carcass.

ཁྱི་ལ་སྤགས་ཀྱིས་སྡིགས་ར་ (kyīlə bāàgi digra) thinking one is punishing sb. but having the opposite result [Lit. frightening a dog with tsamba balls].

ཁྱི་ལ་སེང་གེའི་མིང་བཏགས་ (kyīlə sēŋgee miŋ dāà) giving an (inappropriate) name/ title to sb. not worthy of it [Lit. giving a dog the name of lion].

ཁྱི་ལས་ལོད་ (kyīlɛ löö) a bad person ¶ མི་ངན་འདི་ཁྱི་ལས་ལོད་པ་འདུག That bad person is worse than a dog. [Lit. worse than a dog].

ཁྱི་ལུད་བཞིན་དུ་བོར་ (kyīlüü shintu bɔr) va. to discard/ cast off/ throw away as if sth. has no value [Lit. like throwing away dog manure].

ཁྱི་ལོ་ (kyīlo) year of the dog.

ཁྱི་ཤ་ (kyīsha) 1. dog meat. 2. meat for feeding to dogs.

ཁྱི་ཤ་མཐོང་བ་ (kyīsha tōŋwa) sm. ཁྱི་དང་གྲོ་བ་འཕྲད་པ་.

ཁྱི་ཤི་ན་ཕོ་རོག་གི་གྲོག (kyīshinə poroògi trɔ̀ɔ) sb. becoming more valued/ important due to its demise [Lit. if the dog dies the crow benefits].

ཁྱི་ཤི་ས་མ་རྙེད་པ་ལྟ་བུ་ (kyīshisə məñiìbə dābu) not having or finding a place to live/ stay [Lit. dog can not find a place to die].

ཁྱི་ཤིག (kyīshiì) (dog) flea.

ཁྱི་ཤིང་ (kyīshiŋ) a type of herbal medicine.

ཁྱི་ཤོར་ (kyī shɔ̄ɔ) vi. to get loose, to run away (dogs).

ཁྱི་སོ་ (kyīso) dog teeth.

ཁྱི་སློང་ཉ་འཛུ་ (kyīloŋ ñanju) provoking/ harassing/ inciting/ irritating a person will result in their fighting back [Lit. incite a dog and it will bite one's calf].

ཁྱིར་སེང་མིང་བཏགས་ (kyīseŋ miŋdaà) abbr. of ཁྱི་ལ་སེང་གེའི་མིང་བཏགས་.

ཁྱི་གསར་ (kyīsar) a young dog.

ཁྱི་ཨབ་སོག (kyī āpsoò) a type of small Tibetan dog known in the West as "Lhasa Apso."

ཁྱི་ཨ་སོབ་ (kyī āpsoò) sm. ཁྱི་ཨབ་སོག.

ཁྱིགས་ (kyīì) imp. of འཁྱིག.

ཁྱིང་ (kyīŋ) sm.* འཁིང་.

ཁྱིད་ (kyīì) sm. མཁྱིད་.

ཁྱིམ་ (kyīm) house, home, residence ¶ ངའི་ཁྱིམ་ལྷ་སར་ཡོད་ My home is in Lhasa.

ཁྱིམ་སྐོར་འགྲོ་ (kyīmgɔɔ dro) va. to go around from house to house.

ཁྱིམ་སྐྱེས་ (kyīmkeè) native, indigenous, born locally ¶ རྟ་འདི་ང་ཚོའི་ཁྱིམ་སྐྱེས་རེད་ This horse is one that was born here.

ཁྱིམ་སྐྱོང་ (kyīmkoŋ) 1. family/ household head. 2. va. to manage a family/ household ¶ ནང་གི་པ་ཕས་ཁྱིམ་སྐྱོང་གི་ཡོད་པ་རེད་ The father manages the household.

ཁྱིམ་ཁང་ (kyīmgaŋ) sm. ཁྱིམ་ཚང་.

ཁྱིམ་ཁོལ་ (kyīmgöö) household servant.

ཁྱིམ་ཁྲིམས་ (kyīmdrim) family rules/ regulations.

ཁྱིམ་འཁོར་ (kyīmgɔɔ) family/ household members ¶ ཁྱིམ་འཁོར་རྩོད་གླེང་ Family quarrel.

ཁྱིམ་གྱི་འཁོར་ལོ་ (kyīmgi kɔ̄ɔlo) poet. sun's orbit.

ཁྱིམ་གྱི་གོ་ལ་ (kyīmgi gola) sm. ཁྱིམ་གྱི་འཁོར་ལོ་.

ཁྱིམ་གྱི་ངལ་རྩོལ་ (kyīmgi ŋɛɛtsöö) household chores.

ཁྱིམ་གྱི་རྗེ་དཔོན་ (kyīmgi jebön) head of family/ household.

ཁྱིམ་གྱི་དག་ར་ (kyīmgi tagra) courtyard.

ཁྱིམ་གྱི་ཚལ་ (kyīmgi tsɛ̄ɛ) garden of a house.

ཁྱིམ་གྱི་འཚོ་ཐིས་ (kyīmgi tsōtiì) sm. ཁྱིམ་གྱི་སོ་ཚིས་.

ཁྱིམ་གྱི་ཞོར་ལས་ (kyīmgi shɔɔlɛɛ̀) domestic sideline occupation.

ཁྱིམ་གྱི་རིག་པ་ (kyīmgi rigbə) home economics.

ཁྱིམ་གྱི་སོ་ཚིས་ (kyīmgi sōdziì) the livelihood of a household ¶ ཁྱིམ་གྱི་སོ་ཚིས་ཞིང་ལས་ལ་བརྟེན་གྱི་ཡོད་པ་རེད་ The livelihood of that household depends on farming.

ཁྱིམ་གྱི་སློབ་གསོ་ (kyīmgi lōbso) family education.

ཁྱིམ་གྲངས་ (kyīmdraŋ) 1. the number of families/ households. 2. members in a household; vi.—ཤོར་ to have a family/ household disintegrate.

ཁྱིམ་གྲོགས་ (kyīmdrog) neighbor.

ཁྱིམ་གྲོང་ (kyīmdroŋ) village.

ཁྱིམ་བགོ་ (kyīmgo) partitioning/ dividing a family; va.—བྱེད་.

ཁྱིམ་རྒྱུད་ (kyīmgyüù) family (as a continuing unit over time).

ཁྱིམ་རྒྱུད་ཀྱི་སྤྱི་ཚོགས་ (kyīmgyüùgi jītsoò) tribal society, patriarchal society.

ཁྱིམ་རྒྱུད་ཀྱི་ལུགས་སྲོལ་ (kyīmgyüù lugso) sm. ཁྱིམ་རྒྱུད་ལམ་ལུགས་.

ཁྱིམ་རྒྱུད་བགྲང་ (kyīmgyüù draŋ) va. to count the number of generations within a family (lineage).

ཁྱིམ་རྒྱུད་ནོར་བུ་ (kyīmgyüù nɔɔbu) 1. family heirloom. 2. cherished tradition/ heritage.

ཁྱིམ་རྒྱུད་རིང་ལུགས་ (kyīmgyüù riŋluù) tribalism.

ཁྱིམ་རྒྱུད་ལམ་ལུགས་ (kyīmgyüù ləmluù) tribal system.

ཁྱིམ་སྒོ་ (kyīmgo) family, household.

ཁྱིམ་སྒོ་གཞི་མཚུངས་ (kyīmgo shitsuŋ) sm. ཁ་དབང་མཉམ་པ་.

ཁྱིམ་སྔགས་པ་ (kyīm ŋāgba) a layman who does tantric rites.

ཁྱིམ་སྔོག (kyīmŋɔɔ̀) sm. ཁྱིམ་བཤེར་; va.—བྱེད་.

ཁྱིམ་བཅུ་གཉིས་ (kyīm jūŋñiì) the twelve zodiac symbols.

ཁྱིམ་ཆགས་ (kyīm cāg) vi. to settle in a new area, to establish oneself in a locality ¶ བོད་པ་མང་པོ་རྒྱ་གར་ནང་ཁྱིམ་ཆགས་ཡོད་པ་རེད་ Many Tibetans have settled in India.

ཁྱིམ་ཆུང་ (kyīm cūŋ) individual families [Lit. small family].

ཁྱིམ་ཆེན་ (kyīm cēn) the state, the community [Lit. big family].

ཁྱིམ་སྟོང་ (kyīmdoŋ) 1. an empty house. 2. a household that has become extinct ¶ ནད་ཡམས་དེས་རྐྱེན་པས་ཁྱིམ་མང་པོ་སྟོང་བཞག Because of the epidemic, many households became extinct.

ཁྱིམ་སྟོངས་ (kyīm dōŋ) sm. ཁྱིམ་སྟོང་.

ཁྱིམ་བརྟག་པའི་དཔྱད་ (kyīmdagbɛ jɛ̄ɛ̀) looking for auspicious signs to decide where to build a house.

ཁྱིམ་ཐབ་ (kyīdəb) 1. spouse. 2. married couple, husband and wife; va.—སྒྲིག to get married.

ཁྱིམ་ཐབ་མ་ (kyīm tābmə) sm. ཁྱིམ་ཐབ་མོ་.

ཁྱིམ་ཐབ་མོ་ (kyīm tābmo) wife.

ཁྱིམ་འཐོར་ནོར་སྟོང་ (kyīmdɔɔ nöndoŋ) sm. ཁྱིམ་འཐོར་ནོར་བརླག.

ཁྱིམ་འཐོར་ནོར་བརླག (kyīmdɔɔ nɔɔlaà) a family that has disintegrated/ scattered and become bankrupt ¶ ཁྱིམ་འཐོར་ནོར་བརླག་སོགས་སྡུག་པོ་དེ་འདྲ་བྱུང་ཙང་ Because he suffered hardships such as the breakup of his family and bankruptcy.

ཁྱིམ་དར་རྒྱ་འཕེལ་ (kyīmdar gyumbel) building up a family's fortune, a family flourishing.

ཁྱིམ་དར་ཕྱུག་འགྱུར་ (kyīmdar cūggyur) sm. ཁྱིམ་དར་རྒྱ་འཕེལ་.

ཁྱིམ་དུད་ (kyīmdüù) sm. ཁྱིམ་ཚང་.

ཁྱིམ་དོན་ (kyīmtön) household affairs ¶ ཁྱིམ་དོན་གྱི་ངལ་རྩོལ་ Housework.

ཁྱིམ་བདག (kyīmdaà) head of family.

ཁྱིམ་བདག་མ་ (kyīmdagma) sm. ཁྱིམ་བདག་མོ་.

ཁྱིམ་བདག་མོ་ (kyīmdagmo) female head of household, lady of the house.

ཁྱིམ་ལྡན་ (kyīmdɛn) lizard.

ཁྱིམ་སྡོད་བུད་མེད་ (kyīmdüù pööme̍è) housewife, a female who stays at home.

ཁྱིམ་ནོར་ (kyīmnɔr) household property/ wealth.

ཁྱིམ་གནས་ (kyīmnɛɛ̀) 1. a household. 2. poet. bride.

ཁྱིམ་གནས་སྐྱེད་མ་ (kyīmnɛɛ̀ kēma) poet. mother.

ཁྱིམ་པ་ (kyīmbə) 1. householder. 2. layman.

ཁྱིམ་པ་སྐྱ་བོ་ (kyīmbə gyəwu) layman.

ཁྱིམ་པ་མི་ནག (kyīmbə minag) layman.

ཁྱིམ་པ་མོ་ (kyīmbəmo) female household member.

ཁྱིམ་པའི་ཆ་ལུགས་ (kyīmbɛ cālug) lay person's attire/ dress.

ཁྱིམ་དཔོན་ (kyīmbön) 1. king. 2. minister of the treasury/ interior.

ཁྱིམ་སྤངས་ (kyīm bāŋ) va. to become a monk [Lit. to renounce family].

ཁྱིམ་སྤོ་ (kyīm bō) va. to move (for a family/ household) ། མུ་གེ་བྱུང་ཙང་མི་ཚང་མང་པོ་རྫོང་གཞན་ལ་ཁྱིམ་སྤོས་བཞག Because there was famine, many households moved to another district.

ཁྱིམ་སྤྱོད་ (kīmjöö) goods for use at home, household goods ། ཁྱིམ་སྤྱོད་གློག་ཆས་ Electrical appliances for the home.

ཁྱིམ་སྤྱོད་གློག་ཆས་ (kīmjöö lōgjɛɛ̀) Household electrical appliances.

ཁྱིམ་སྤྱོད་ཡོ་ཆས་ (kīmjöö yobjɛɛ̀) household utensils.

ཁྱིམ་ཕུགས་ (kyīm pūg) arc. sm. ཁྱིམ་འབིགས་.

ཁྱིམ་ཕུང་ (kyīm pūŋ) internal quarreling in a family.

ཁྱིམ་ཕུབ་ (kyīm pūb) va. to establish a family/ household, to set up a home.

ཁྱིམ་ཕྱྭ་ (kyīm cā) va. to divine the fortune of a family by feeling the pulse of family members.

ཁྱིམ་བྱ་ (kyīmja) domestic fowl/ poultry.

ཁྱིམ་འབིགས་ (kyī big) va. to break into a home by boring a hole through the wall.

ཁྱིམ་འབྱོར་པ་ (kyīm jorba) wealthy/ rich person.

ཁྱིམ་འབྲེལ་ཐོན་འགན་གཙང་ལེན་ (kyīmdree tōn gɛndzaŋ len) several households jointly having a production related contract.

ཁྱིམ་སྦྱོང་ (kyīmjoŋ) homework; va.—བྱེད་.

ཁྱིམ་མང་ར་བ་ (kyīmmaŋ rawa) a compound or courtyard with many families/ households.

ཁྱིམ་མི་ (kyīmmi) family/ household member, dependent.

ཁྱིམ་མི་ཁ་ཐོར་ (kyīmmi kā tɔ̄ɔ) vi, to break up/ scatter (of a family/ household).

ཁྱིམ་མི་ཁ་གསོ་ (kyīmmi kā sō) va. to take care of/ feed one's family or household.

ཁྱིམ་མི་རྒན་གཞོན་ (kyīmmi gɛnshön) all members of a family (old and young).

ཁྱིམ་མི་མོ་ (kyīmmimo) female family member.

ཁྱིམ་གཙོ་ (kyīmdzo) sm. ཁྱིམ་བདག.

ཁྱིམ་གཙོ་བུད་མེད་ (kyīmdzo pümeè) sm. ཁྱིམ་བདག་མོ་.

ཁྱིམ་བཙུགས་ལས་གཉེར་ (kyīmdzug lɛñer) getting married and starting one's career/ work.

ཁྱིམ་ཚང་ (kyīmdzaŋ) family, household; vi.—ཁྱེས་ to split a family, to cause family fission ། སྤུ་སྤུན་གཉིས་སོ་སོར་མནའ་མ་བླངས་ནས་ཁྱིམ་ཚང་ཁྱེས་ཏེ་ཞིང་ཁ་བགོ་བཤའ་བརྒྱབ་འདུག The two brothers each took brides (got married) and split up the family and divided the fields.

ཁྱིམ་ཚང་གི་འབྱུང་ཁུངས་ (kyīmdzaŋgi cuŋguŋ) social origin (of a family/ household).

ཁྱིམ་ཚང་གི་ལག་ཤེས་ (kyīmdzaŋgi lagsheè) household/ home industries.

ཁྱིམ་ཚང་ཆེན་པོ་ (kyīmdzaŋ cēmo) the motherland, the fatherland.

ཁྱིམ་ཚང་ལོགས་དགར་ (kyīmdzaŋ lɔɔgaa ceè) splitting a family/ household; va.—བྱེད་.

ཁྱིམ་ཚེས་ (kyīm tsiì) sm. ཁྱིམ་གྱི་སོ་ཚེས་.

ཁྱིམ་རྫུགས་ (kyīmdzuù) 1. the wealth/ fortune a family/ household accumulated over time. 2. the foundation of a family's livelihood.

ཁྱིམ་ཚོ་ (kyīmdzo)1. sm. ཁྱིམ་རྫུགས་. 2. vi.—ཐེན་ to be able manage one's own family/ household; va.—འཛིན་ to manage one's family/ household ། ཕྲུ་གུ་རང་ལོ་ ༡༨ ལ་སླེབས་ནས་ཁྱིམ་ཚོ་ཐེན་ཐུབ་པ་རེད་ When the child reached 18 years of age, he was able to manage his own household.

ཁྱིམ་མཚེས་ (kyīmdzeè) neighbor ། མཛའ་མཐུན་ཁྱིམ་མཚེས་རྒྱལ་ཁབ་ Friendly neighboring countries.

ཁྱིམ་མཚེས་ཆགས་སྡང་མེད་ན་ གྲོང་ལ་ཡར་རྒྱས་མི་ཡོང་ (kyīmdzeè cāgdaŋ meèna tronla yargyɛɛ̀ miyoŋ) there will not be progress without competition [Lit. if there is no jealousy between neighbors, there will be no improvement in the village].

ཁྱིམ་མཚེས་རུ་སྐོར་ (kyīmdzeè rugɔɔ) to be surrounded by neighbors and friends; va.—བྱེད་.

ཁྱིམ་འཚོ་ (kyīmdzo) abbr. of ཁྱིམ་གྱི་འཚོ་ཐབས་.

ཁྱིམ་འཛིན་ (kyīm dzin) running/ managing a household/ family; va. ཁྱིམ་འཛིན་; —བྱེད་.

ཁྱིམ་འཛིན་མ་ (kyīmtsinmə) mistress of a house.

ཁྱིམ་འཛུགས་དོད་འཛུགས་ (kīmdzuù döödzug) sm. ཁྱིམ་གཞིས་འཛུགས་སྒྲོན་.

ཁྱིམ་གཞི་ (kyīmshiì) home, homeland.

ཁྱིམ་གཞིས་ (kyīmshiì) household, family; vi.—ཆགས་ to have a household/ family/ home get established, to get settled down; va.—འཛུགས་ to establish a household/ family/ home.

ཁྱིམ་གཞིས་བདག་གཉེར་ (kyīmshiì dagñer) the steward or manager of a household; va.—བྱེད་.

ཁྱིམ་གཞིས་འཛུགས་ (kīmshiì dzuù) to establish a household ། ཁོང་གཉིས་ཆང་ས་བརྒྱབ་ནས་ཁྱིམ་གཞིས་གསར་པ་བཙུགས་པ་རེད་ ། After these two got married, they set up a new household.

ཁྱིམ་གཞིས་འཛུགས་སྒྲོན་ (kyīmshiì dzugdrön) money paid to assist in setting up a household (usu. in a new area), a settling-in allowance.

ཁྱིམ་གཞིས་འཛུགས་དངུལ་ (kyīmshiì dzugŋüü) sm. ཁྱིམ་གཞིས་འཛུགས་སྒྲོན་.

ཁྱིམ་ཟླ་ (kyīmda) wife.

ཁྱིམ་གཡབས་ (kyīmyəb) covered corridor/ veranda.

ཁྱིམ་རབས་བརྒྱུད་སྒྲོད་ (kyīmrəb gyüüdröö) family heirloom.

ཁྱིམ་ལས་ (kyīmlɛɛ̀) housework, household affairs; va.—བྱེད་ to do housework.

ཁྱིམ་ལས་པ་ (kyīmlɛɛ̀ba) one who works in the house, housekeeper.

ཁྱིམ་ལུགས་ (kyīmluù) family custom/ tradition.

ཁྱིམ་ལུད་ (kyīmlüü) manure collected from the toilet or stable of a Tibetan home.

ཁྱིམ་ཤུལ་སྐྱོང་ (kyīmshüü gyōŋ) va. to succeed/ perpetuate one's family.

ཁྱིམ་བཤེར་ (kyīmsher) searching a house; va.—བྱེད་; —གཏོང་ ། ལྐོག་ཚོང་རྒྱག་མཁན་དེ་ལ་ཁྱིམ་ཤེར་བྱས་འདུག They searched the house of the smuggler.

ཁྱིམ་ས་ (kyīmsə) place where your home is.

ཁྱིམ་སོ་བཟུང་ (kyīmso suŋ) 1. va. to keep/ run one's household. 2. va. to get married.

ཁྱིམ་ས་ཚོ་ (kyīmsa tsō) sm. ཁྱིམ་ཚོ་འཛིན་.

ཁྱིམ་སྲིད་ (kīmsiì) sm. ཁྱིམ་རྒྱུད་.

ཁྱིམ་སྲིད་འཛིན་ (kīmsiì dzin) sm. ཁབ་དང་སྲིད་འཛིན་.

ཁྱིམ་སྲུང་ (kīmsuŋ) 1. defending/ protecting one's home; va.—བྱེད་. 2. sb. who protects/ defends a house.

ཁྱིམ་སྲུང་རྒྱལ་སྐྱོབ་ (kyīmsuŋ gyɛɛgyob) defending home and country; va.—བྱེད་.

ཁྱིམ་སྲོལ་ (kyīmsöö) family tradition/ custom.

ཁྱིམ་སློག (kyīmlɔɔ̀) sm. ཁྱིམ་བཤེར་.

ཁྱིམ་གསར་ (kyīmsar) a new household/ family.

ཁྱིམ་གསར་མ་ (kyīmsarma) a new bride.

ཁྱིམ་གསོ་ (kyīm sō) 1. maintaining/ repairing one's house; va.—བྱེད་. 2. earning a livelihood; va. ཁྱིམ་གསོ་; —བྱེད་. 3. domestic.

ཁྱིམ་གསོ་བྱ་རིགས་ (kyīmso charig) sm. ཁྱིམ་བྱ་.

ཁྱིམ་གསོ་སེམས་ཅན་ (kyīmso sēmjɛn) domestic animals.

ཁྱིམ་གསོས་དར་སྲིན་ (kyīmsöö tarsin) silkworms raised by a family/ household.

ཁྱིམ་ལྷ་ (kyīmlha) family deity.

ཁྱིའི་མགོ་ལ་ཟུ་ཙོ་སྐྱེ་ (kyīī gū) sm. ཁྱིའི་རྐུབ་ལ་ཉི་མ་ཤར་.

ཁྱིའི་རྐུབ་ལ་ཉི་མ་ཤར་ (kyīī gūbla ñīmə shār) inconceivable, impossible, never occurred previously [Lit. the sun shinning on a dog's ass].

ཁྱིའི་གློ་དང་སྤྱང་ཀིའི་སྙིང་ (kyīlodaŋ jāŋgii ñīŋ) sm. ཁྱིམ་གློ་སྤྱང་སྙིང་.

ཁྱིའུ་ (kyīu) piece of wood/ peg used to split a log; va.—རྒྱག.

ཁྱིའུ་ཀ་ (kyīuga) tree stump.

ཁྱིལ་ཁྱིལ་ (kyīlgyil) curled up, wound around sth.

ཁྱིལ་གྱིས་སྡོད་ (kyīlgi dö̱ö̱) va. to sit suddenly.

ཁྱིལ་འབུ་ཕྲ་མ་ (kyīmbu trāmo) trichina.

ཁྱིས་སྐྱག་པ་ཟས་པ་བཙོས་མི་ཐུབ་ (kyīi gyāgba sɛ̱ɛ̀wa jö̱ö̀ mi̱dub) evil people can't change their bad ways [Lit. dogs can't change their habit of eating shit].

ཁྱིས་འཙང་ (kyīi cāŋ) va. to bark (dog). ¶ དགོང་མོ་རྟག་པར་ཁྱིས་འཙང་གི་འདུག The dog barks every night.

ཁྱིས་ཟ་ཟ་ཕག་ཉལ་ཉལ་ (kyīi sa̱sa pāg ñɛ̱ɛ̱ñɛɛ) a lazy, gluttonous person [Lit. eat like a dog and sleep like a pig].

ཁྱུ་ (kyū) herd, flock, group; va.—སྐྱོང་ to herd a flock ¶ ལུག་ཁྱུ་གཅིག A herd of sheep.

ཁྱུ་སྐད་ (kyūgɛɛ̀) noises/ sounds made by a herd/ flock of birds or animals; va.—རྒྱག.

ཁྱུ་སྐྱོང་ (kyū kōŋ) see ཁྱུ་.

ཁྱུ་རྒྱན་ (kyūgyɛn) the best among a group of people ¶ ཁོ་ནི་པོ་ཐོད་བརྒྱ་ཡི་ཁྱུ་རྒྱན་ཡིན He is the best among hundred of young able men.

ཁྱུ་སྒྲིག (kyū dri̱g) vi. to be arranged into a herd/ group/ crowd, to form a herd ¶ རྟ་རྒོད་ཁྱུ་བསྒྲིགས་ནས་བྱང་ཐང་ལ་འགྲོ་གི་འདུག The wild horses formed a herd and are going to the Changtang Plain. 2. a large formation (of people) ¶ གཞོན་ནུ་ཚོ་ཁྱུ་བསྒྲིག་ནས་འགྲོ་གི་འདུག The youths formed into a large group and are going.

ཁྱུ་མཆོག (kyūncog) the best in a herd or group, sth. unique ¶ མིའི་ནང་གི་ཁྱུ་མཆོག The best amongst the people.

ཁྱུ་མཆོག་ཁྱད་འཕགས་ (kyūcog kyɛ̄ɛ̀pag) the best of the best.

ཁྱུ་དང་ཁྱུ་བྱེད་ (kyūtə kyū ce̱è) va. to form in herds/ groups/ crowds.

ཁྱུ་འདྲེས་ (kyūndreè) joining/ mixing two herds together; va.—བྱེད་.

ཁྱུ་ལྡན་ (kyūndɛn) weeping willow tree.

ཁྱུ་སྣ་འདྲེན་ (kyū nā dre̱n) va. to lead a herd/ group/ organization.

ཁྱུ་སྣོན་ཉོས་སྒྲུབ་ (kyūnön bǖǜdrub) shung. buying supplementary animals.

ཁྱུ་བ་ (kyūwa) stud yak.

ཁྱུ་བྲལ་ཁྲུང་ཁྲུང་ (kyūdre drūŋdruŋ) isolated, completely alone [Lit. a crane separated from its flock].

ཁྱུ་བྲལ་བྱ་ལོང་ (kyūdre ca̱loŋ) isolated, completely alone [Lit. a goose separated from the flock].

ཁྱུ་མ་ (kyūma) hemp, flax.

ཁྱུ་རྩེད་ (kyū dzēè) dance or games participated in by groups or lines of people.

ཁྱུ་ཚོགས་སྒྲིལ་ (kyūtsog dri̱l) sm. ཁྱུ་དང་ཁྱུ་བྱས་ནས་.

ཁྱུ་བཟུང་ (kyū su̱ŋ) shung. va. to choose/ select one animal from a herd.

ཁྱུ་ཝུར་རྒྱག (kyū wu̱rgya̱à) vi. to stampede (a herd) ¶ འདམ་སེང་ཡོང་མ་ཐག་རི་དྭགས་རྣམས་ཁྱུ་ཝུར་བརྒྱབ་སོང་ As soon as the lion came the animals stampeded.

ཁྱུག (kyūù) 1. Tibetan cursive script. 2. lithe.

ཁྱུག་ཁྱུག (kyūggyuù) darting, going zigzag.

ཁྱུག་པོ་ (kyūgbo) agile, quick, lithe.

ཁྱུག་ཙམ་ (kyūgdzam) briefly, a moment, flashing (for lightening) ¶ མདང་དགོང་ནམ་མཁར་གློག་ཁྱུག་ཙམ་བྱས་པ་རེད་ Last night lightening flashed briefly in the sky. ¶ ཚུར་ལམ་ངས་ཁོའི་སྡོད་སར་ཁྱུག་ཙམ་ཕྱིན་པ་ཡིན་ On the way here I went briefly to his residence.

ཁྱུག་ཡག (kyūgyaà) sm. ཁྱུ་པ་.

ཁྱུག་ཡིག (kyūyig) Tibetan cursive script.

ཁྱུགས་ (kyūù) sm. ཁྱུག.

ཁྱུགས་སེ་ཁྱུག (kyūgsekyūù) twinkling, glimmering.

ཁྱུང་ (kyūŋ) a mythological bird (garuda).

ཁྱུང་དཀར་ (kyūŋgaa) cross between a female yak and a bull.

ཁྱུང་ལྔ་ (kyūŋŋa) a traditional Tibetan medicine.

ཁྱུང་ཆེན་ (kyūŋjen) large mythological bird (garuda).

ཁྱུང་ཆེན་སྒེ་རིང་ (kyūŋjen gēriŋ) sm. ཁྱུང་ཁྱུང་.

ཁྱུང་སྡེར་ (kyūŋder) 1. garuda's talon. 2. a type of herbal medicine.

ཁྱུང་སྡེར་དཀར་པོ་ (kyūŋder gāābo) a type of herbal medicine.

ཁྱུང་པོ་སྟེང་ཆེན་ (kyūŋbo dēŋjen) a place in Kham.

ཁྱུང་འབྲུག (kyūŋ dru̱g) abbr. garuda and dragon.

ཁྱུང་མ་ (kyūŋmə) sm. ཁྱུང་.

ཁྱུང་རམ་ (kyūŋrəm) name of an aristocratic family.

ཁྱུང་རིལ་ (kyūŋril) a type of round basket.

ཁྱུད་ (kyǖǜ) p. of འཁྱུད་.

ཁྱུད་ཁོར་ (kyǖǜgɔɔ) complete, whole ¶ ལོ་གཅིག་ཁྱུད་ཁོར་ལ་སློབ་གྲྭར་བསྐྱོད་པ་རེད་ (I) went to school for one complete year.

ཁྱུད་འཁོར་ (kyǖǜgɔɔ) sm. ཁྱུད་ཁོར་.

ཁྱུད་འཁོར་ལོ་ (kyǖǜkɔ̄ɔ̄lo̱) a complete year, a full year.

ཁྱུད་མོ་ (kyǖǜmo) 1. surrounding, encircling ¶ ཁང་པའི་ཁྱུད་མོ་ Surrounding a house. 2. the distance between two arms outstretched to the tips of the fingers.

ཁྱུའི་གཙོ་བོ་ (kyǖ dzōwo) leader of a herd/ troop/ flock.

ཁྱུར་ཁྱུར་ (kyūrgyur) wriggling, slithering ¶ རྩྭ་ཁྲོད་དུ་སྦྲུལ་ཞིག་ཁྱུར་ཁྱུར་དུ་འགྲོ་བཞིན་འདུག A snake was wriggling in the grass.

ཁྱུར་མིད་ (kyūrmiì) 1. swallowing; va. ཁྱུར་མིད་; —གཏོང་ to swallow ¶ རིལ་བུ་འདི་ཁྱུར་མིད་གཏོང་དགོས་ You have to swallow this pill (whole). 2. annexing, swallowing up; va.—གཏོང་ to swallow up, to annex ¶ འཛམ་གླིང་རིལ་པོ་ཁྱུར་མིད་གཏོང་རྩིས་བྱེད་ཀྱི་འདུག (They) plan to swallow up the whole world.

ཁྱེ་ཆུང་ (kyējuŋ) 1. young boys and girls. 2. arc. small profit.

ཁྱེ་པོ་ (kyēwo) short curved knife typically used by shoemakers.

ཁྱེ་བོགས་མཁན་ (kyēbɔɔ̀ñɛn) a person who lives on interest and/ or rent.

ཁྱེ་མ་ (kyēma) vitiligo (skin disease characterized by white blotches on the skin).

ཁྱེད་ (kyēè) you (h.).

ཁྱེད་ཅག (kyēèjaà) you (pl.) (h.) ¶ ཁྱེད་ཅག་ག་ནས་ཕེབས་པ་ Where did you come from?

ཁྱེད་ཉིད་ (kyēèñiì) you, yourself (h.).

ཁྱེད་ཚོ་ (kyēèdzo) you (pl.) (h.).

ཁྱེད་རང་ (kyēraŋ) you (yourself) (h.) ¶ ཁྱེད་རང་གིས་ང་ལ་བཤད་བྱུང་ You yourself told me.

ཁྱེད་རང་ཚོ་ (kyēraŋdzo) sm. ཁྱེད་ཚོ་.

ཁྱེད་རང་རང་ (kyēraŋ ra̱ŋ) you yourself ¶ ཁྱེད་རང་རང་ཡོང་དགོས་ཟེར་གྱི་འདུག (They) are saying that only you yourself should come.

ཁྱེད་རྣམ་པ་ (kyēènamba) you (pl.) (h.).

ཁྱེད་རྣམ་ཚོ་ (khēè nāndzo) you (pl.) (h.).

ཁྱེབས་ (kēb) sm. ཁེབས་.

ཁྱེམ་ (kyēm) sm. ཁེམ་.

ཁྱེམ་བུ་ (kyēmbu) sm. ཁེམ་བུ་.

ཁྱེའུ་ (kyēwu) 1. children. 2. sm. ཁྱེ་པོ་.

ཁྱེའུ་ཁ་ (kyēwu kā) sm. མི་ཏོག་གི་ཐིའུ་.

ཁྱེའུ་གེལ་པོ་ (kyēwu ge̱ebo) a fat boy.

ཁྱེའུ་ཆུང་ (kyēwu cūŋ) infant, baby.

ཁྱེའུ་ཐོན་ (kyēwu tön) 1. vi. to be born. 2. shoots (of plants and grains).

ཁྱེའུ་མདུང་ (kyēwu du̱ŋ) a type of spear.

ཁྱེའུ་ཚང་ (kyēwutsaŋ) arc. new.

ཁྱེར་ (kyēr) p. of འཁྱེར་.

ཁྱེར་དམན་ (kyērmɛn) poor, in poverty.

ཁྱེར་ཤོག (kyērshoò) bring! ¶ དཀར་ཡོལ་ཞིག་ཁྱེར་ཤོག Bring a cup!

ཁྱེར་སོ་ (kyērso) sm. འཁྱེར་སོ་.

ཁྱེལ་བཞུགས་ (kyēē shu̱ù) va. to sit erect/ upright (h.).

ཁྱེས་ (kyēè) imp. of འཁྱེད་.

ཁྱོ་ (kyō) 1. man ¶ ཁྱོ་རྡོ་རྗེ་ The man Dorje. 2.

husband.

ཁྱོ་ག (kyōga) sm. ཁྱོ་.

ཁྱོ་ག་མེད་པ་ (kyōga me̱èba) unmarried/ single woman.

ཁྱོ་ག་ཟུར་པ་ (kyōga su̱rba) male equivalent of a mistress.

ཁྱོ་གའི་ཕྱུ་པ་ (kyōgɛ cūbə) man's dress.

ཁྱོ་གའི་དབང་ཆ་ (kyōgɛ wāŋca) sm. ཁྱོ་དབང་.

ཁྱོ་རྒྱུད་ (kyōgyüü) patrilineal lineage.

ཁྱོ་གཅིག་ཞུག་གཅིག (kyōjig shūgjig) monogamy.

ཁྱོ་གཅིག་ཞུག་མང་ (kyōjig shūgmaŋ) polygamy.

ཁྱོ་དོ་གསར་སྤེལ་ལས་ཁང་ (kyōdo sērbelgaŋ) Kyodo News Agency.

ཁྱོ་ཐང་ (kyōdaŋ) sm. ཕོ་གསར་.

ཁྱོ་པོ་ (kyōpo) 1. father of the house. 2. bridegroom.

ཁྱོ་བོ་ (kyōwo) 1. man. 2. husband ། གཞོན་ནུ་མ་དེས་རང་གི་ཁྱོ་བོ་ཡོང་རྒྱུར་ཉིན་མཚན་སྒྲིལ་ནས་བསྒུགས་པ་རེད་ That young woman waited all day and night for her husband to come. 3. sm. ཁྱིམ་བདག.

ཁྱོ་བོའི་རྗེས་འབྲང་ནས་སྡོད་པ་ (kyōwɛ je̱èdraŋnɛ dö̱öba) the system of patrilocal residence at marriage (i.e., the bride coming to live in the groom's house).

ཁྱོ་དབང་ (kyōwaŋ) authority of a husband over his wife, man's prerogative.

ཁྱོ་མང་ (kyō ma̱ŋma) whore, prostitute.

ཁྱོ་མང་ཞུག་གཅིག (kyōmaŋ shūgjig) polyandry.

ཁྱོ་མེད་མ་ (kyōmeèma) single/ unmarried woman, widow (a woman without a husband).

ཁྱོ་མོ་ (kyōmo) a married woman.

ཁྱོ་ཡན་ (kyōyɛn) sm. ཁྱོ་ག་ཟུར་པ་.

ཁྱོ་ཤ་ (kyōsha) husband's flesh.

ཁྱོ་ཤུག (kyūshuù) husband and wife, a couple.

ཁྱོ་ཤུག་གི་ཕུ་ནུ་ (kyūshuùgi pūnu) wife's brother, brother-in-law.

ཁྱོ་ཤུག་ཚོང་ཁང་ (kyūshuù tsōŋgaŋ) shop run by a husband and wife, mom-and-pop store.

ཁྱོག (kyɔ̄ɔ̀) p. of འཁྱོག.

ཁྱོག་ཐེབས་མེད་པ་ (kyōgtəb me̱èba) unable to lift or carry sth.

ཁྱོག་པོ་ (kyōgbo) curved, bent.

ཁྱོགས་ (kyɔ̄ɔ̀) sedan chair; stretcher; va.—འཁྱེར་ to carry a sedan chair or stretcher.

ཁྱོགས་ཁྲི་ (kyōgtri) sm. ཁྱོགས་.

ཁྱོགས་ལྡ་ལྡི་ཅན་ (kyōgda dijɛn) sedan chair that is adorned with brocade and silk.

ཁྱོགས་དཔྱངས་ (kyōgjaŋ) sm.* ཁྱོགས་བྱམས་.

ཁྱོགས་སྒྲིལ་ (kyɔ̄gjii) sm. ཁྱོགས་.

ཁྱོགས་བྱམས་ (kyōgjam) palanquin, sedan chair.

ཁྱོགས་གཡོགས་ (kyōgyog) sedan chair cover.

ཁྱོད་ (kyȫȍ) you (h.).

ཁྱོད་ཁ་དང་ངའི་སྣ་བྱས་པ་ཤོད་ (kyȫȍ kādaŋ ŋɛ̱ɛ̱ nā cɛ̱èba shȫȍ) getting into a verbal quarrel.

ཁྱོད་དགའ་ང་སྐྱིད་ (kyȫȍga ŋagyiì) a happy conversation, exchanging pleasantries [Lit. you are good I am happy].

ཁྱོད་རྒྱུས་ང་དང་ང་རྒྱུས་ཁྱོད་ (kyȫȍ gyü̱ü ŋa daŋ ŋa gyü̱ü kyȫȍ) knowing each other [Lit. you know me and I know you].

ཁྱོད་ཅག (kyȫȍjaà) sm. ཁྱོད་ཚོ་.

ཁྱོད་ཅན་ (kyȫȍjɛn) 1. you (pl.). 2. you two.

ཁྱོད་དང་ང་གཅིག (kyȫȍdaŋ ŋa jīg) sm. ཁྱོད་དང་ང་མེད་.

ཁྱོད་དང་ང་མེད་ (kyȫȍdaŋ ŋa me̱è) making no distinction between me and you or yours and mine; very close, inseparable.

ཁྱོད་རྣམས་ (kyȫȍnam) you (pl.).

ཁྱོད་སྒྲིལ་ (kyȫȍdrel) shung. you two people holding the same position.

ཁྱོད་དམར་ཡག་སྟག་གི་ཁ་ཆེན ང་འབྲི་སེར་འགྲོང་གི་གཉའ་ལོས་སྦོམ་ (kyȫȍ mārya's dāàgi kācen ŋa dre̱ser dro̱ŋgi ña̱lȫȍ bo̱m) I can match your strengths [Lit. you, the tiger with a big mouth, I, the yellow-faced wild yak with a thick neck].

ཁྱོད་ཚོ་ (kyȫȍdzo) you (pl.).

ཁྱོད་བཟང་ང་བཟང་ (kyȫȍsaŋ ŋasaŋ) saying only good/ nice things, praising back and forth, not saying faults/ mistake ། སྐྱོན་ཡོད་ན་ཕན་ཚུན་ཐད་ཀར་བརྗོད་དགོས་པ་ལས་ཁྱོད་བཟང་ང་བཟང་ཁོ་ན་ཤོད་མི་རུང་ If there are faults it is not good only to say good things.

ཁྱོད་ར་ (kyȫȍra) you.

ཁྱོད་རང་ (kyȫraŋ) you (yourself).

ཁྱོད་རང་ཚོ་ (kyȫȍraŋdzo) sm. ཁྱོད་རྣམས་.

ཁྱོད་ཤི་ང་གསོན་ (kyȫȍ shī ŋa sȫn) a struggle between incompatibles in which no compromise is possible, a life and death struggle [Lit. you die, I live].

ཁྱོན་ (kyȫn) 1. all, all over ། འཛམ་གླིང་ཁྱོན་ལ་ All over the world. 2. all told, in all ། ཟླ་ ༡ ནས་ཟླ་ ༢ བར་ཁྱོན་ཉི་མ་སུམ་ཅུ་སོ་གཉིས་ From January to February, all told, 32 days.

ཁྱོན་གྲངས་ (kyȫndraŋ) total number ། སློབ་གྲྭ་བའི་ཁྱོན་གྲངས་ ༡༠༠༠ ཙམ་ཡོད་པ་རེད་ The total number of students is about 1000.

ཁྱོན་རྒྱ་ཆེན་པོ་ (kyȫngya chēmbo) sm. ཁྱོན་ཆེན་པོ་.

ཁྱོན་བསྒྲིལ་ (kyȫn dri̱l) vi. to combine/ add together/ merge ། ཁྱོན་བསྒྲིལ་ནས་མཐུན་མི་ ༡༠༠ ཙམ་ཚོགས་འདུར་སླེབས་བཞག Combining altogether, about 100 delegates arrived at the meeting.

ཁྱོན་ངོས་ (kyȫnŋöö) on the surface.

ཁྱོན་ཆས་ (kyȫnjɛ̀ɛ̀) clothing ། ཁྱོན་ཆས་ཁང་ Clothing store.

ཁྱོན་ཆེ་ (kyȫnce) sm. ཁྱོན་ཆེན་པོ་.

ཁྱོན་ཆེན་པོ་ (khȫn chēmbo) extensive, widespread, a lot ། ཆུ་ལོག་དེས་ས་ཞིང་ཁྱོན་ཆེན་པོ་འདེབས་ལས་མ་ཐུབ་པ་བཟོས་པ་རེད་ The flood made extensive agricultural areas uncultivatable. ། ཁྲག་ཁྱོན་ཆེ་ཐོན་པས་དྲན་པ་འཐོར་སོང་ (He) fainted because he lost a lot of blood.

ཁྱོན་སྡོམ་ (kyȫndom) sm. ཁྱོན་བསྡོམས་.

ཁྱོན་བསྡོམས་ (kyȫndom) in all, all together, all told, in total ། འགྲོ་སོང་ཁྱོན་བསྡོམས་སྒོར་ཁྲི་བརྒྱད་ལྷག་བཏང་ཡོད་པ་རེད་ In all, more than 80,000 dollars have been spent (in expenses).

ཁྱོན་ནས་ (kyȫnnɛ̀ɛ̀) (with negatives) never, not at all ། ང་ཁོ་ཚོའི་ནང་ལ་ཁྱོན་ནས་འགྲོ་གི་མེད་ I never go to their home.

ཁྱོན་པོ་ (kyȫnbo) mostly, more than half.

ཁྱོན་འབོར་ (kyȫmbɔɔ) total amount ། འདི་ལོ་ཚོང་ཟོག་ནང་འདྲེན་ཁྱོན་འབོར་ཆེན་པོ་བྱས་འདུག This year we imported a large amount of commodities.

ཁྱོན་ཚད་ (kyȫndzɛɛ) size/ scale of an area ། གྲོང་ཁྱེར་འདིའི་ཁྱོན་ཚད་ག་ཚོད་ཡོད་དམ་ What is the size of this city?

ཁྱོན་གཞི་ནས་ (kyȫnshinɛ) sm. མ་གཞི་ནས་.

ཁྱོན་ཡངས་ (kyȫnyaŋ) sm. ཁྱོན་ཡངས་པོ་.

ཁྱོན་ཡངས་པོ་ (kyȫn ya̱ŋbo) vast, extensive, broad ། བོད་ཀྱི་ལྷོ་ཕྱོགས་སུ་ཞིང་ཁ་ཁྱོན་ཡངས་པོ་ཡོད་པ་རེད་ The farmland in the southern regions of Tibet is vast.

ཁྱོན་ཡོངས་ (kyȫnyoŋ) overall, entire, all over, general, wide, broad ། རྒྱལ་ཁབ་ཁྱོན་ཡོངས་ལ་ཡར་རྒྱས་གཏོང་ཆེད་ In order to make improvements all over the nation (nationwide). ། ཁྱོན་ཡོངས་ཀྱི་ལྟ་རྩལ་ Overall viewpoint. ། ཁྱོན་ཡོངས་ཀྱི་འཕེལ་རྒྱས་ Overall development.

ཁྱོམ་ (kyōm) sm. འཁྱོམ་.

ཁྱོམ་ཁྱོམ་ (kyōmgyom) dizzy, unsteady; vi.—བྱེད་ to be dizzy/ unsteady.

ཁྱོམ་ཤུགས་ (kyōmshuù) the shock wave produced by a blast/ explosion.

ཁྱོར་གང་ (kyōrgaŋ) one handful.

ཁྱོར་འགེལ་ (kyōrgel) sm. འཁྱོར་འགེལ་.

ཁྱོར་ཆུ་ (kyōrju) a cupped hand filled with water.

ཁྱོར་དོ་ (kyōrdo) two cupped handfuls.

ཁྱོར་བ་ (kyōrwa) a cupped handful ། ཆུ་ཁྱོར་བ་གང་ A handful of water.

ཁྱོལ་ (kyȫȍ) p. of འཁྱོལ་.

ཁྱོས་མ་ (kyȫȍma) 1. leftover food. 2. gifts, presents.

ཁྲ་ (trā) 1. sparrow hawk, falcon. 2. stripes ¶ དཀར་པོའི་ཐོག་ཁྲ་ནག་པོ་ཡོད་པའི་སྟོད་ཐུང་གཅིག A white shirt with black stripes. 3. the grain in wood.

ཁྲ་ཀྱག (trāgya) 1. stand for a teacup. 2. saucer (for placing under a cup).

ཁྲ་ཀྱག་ཁེབས་གཙོད་ (trāgya kēbjöö) a set of a teacup (porcelain) stand and lid.

ཁྲ་བཀྱག (trāgya) sm. ཁྲ་ཀྱག.

ཁྲ་ཀྱི་ལི་ (trā gyīli) sparkling, glittering, shinning.

ཁྲ་ཁྲ་ (trātra) 1. variegated, brightly colored, colorful. 2. impure, dishonest (slang) ¶ བླ་མ་ཁྲ་ཁྲ་ An impure Lama.

ཁྲ་ཁྲ་བ་ཁྲ་ (trātra batra) sm. ཁྲ་ཁྲ་.

ཁྲ་ཁྲ་མ་ཁྲ་ (trātra matra) sm. ཁྲ་ཁྲ་.

ཁྲ་ཁྲ་རིག་རིག (trātra rigrig) sm. ཁྲ་ཁྲ་.

ཁྲ་ཁྲོ་ཅན་ (trādrojɛn) quick-tempered, easy to anger ¶ མི་ཁྲ་ཁྲོ་ཅན་དང་གཤིབ་ཁག་པོ་ཡོད་ It is difficult to get along with a quick-tempered person.

ཁྲ་གན་ (trāgɛn) shung. abbr. of ཁྲ་མ་ and གན་རྒྱ་.

ཁྲ་གླག་སྤྱང་གསུམ་ (trālajaŋ sūm) very capable, clever ¶ མི་དེ་ར་ཁྲ་གླག་སྤྱང་གསུམ་ཡོད་པ་རེད་ That person is very capable. [Lit. the three: hawk, eagle and wolf].

ཁྲ་གླིང་ (trəliŋ) window frame.

ཁྲ་གླིང་རུ་བཞི་ (trəliŋ rushi) window frame/ sash.

ཁྲ་གོད་ (trāgöö) a type of large eagle.

ཁྲ་རྒྱ་ (trāgya) trap to catch hawks/ falcons; va.—འཛུགས་ to trap hawks/ falcons.

ཁྲ་རྒྱས་བཟང་པོ་ (trāgyɛɛ saŋbo) handsome and smart/ clever.

ཁྲ་སྒོར་སྒོར་ (trā gɔɔgɔɔ) bright and round (for eyes).

ཁྲ་སྒྲིག་རྡོ་གཅལ་ (trādrig dojɛɛ) a stone floor with square designs.

ཁྲ་ཅེམ་མེ་ (trā jēme) sm. ཁྲ་ཅེམ་ཅེམ་.

ཁྲ་བཅད་ (trājɛ̀ɛ̀) room divider/ screen; va.—རྒྱག to divide a room with a screen/ divider.

ཁྲ་ཅིལ་གུ་ཅིལ་ (trāci guci) sm. ཁྲ་ཁྲ་, 1.

ཁྲ་ཅིལ་ཅིལ་ (trā ciiji) 1. sm. ཁྲ་ཁྲ་. 2. sparkling, glittering (conveys presence of many lights).

ཁྲ་ཅིལ་བི་ཅིལ་ (trəci bici) sm. ཁྲ་ཁྲ་, 1.

ཁྲ་ཅིལ་ལི་བ་ (trā ciilewa) sm. ཁྲ་ཅིལ་ཅིལ་.

ཁྲ་ཆུང་མིག (trā cūŋmig) eyes.

ཁྲ་ཆུང་ལིང་སྒྲིབ་ (trājuŋ liŋdrib) cataract.

ཁྲ་ཆེམ་ཆེམ་ (trā cēmjem) glittering, sparkling.

ཁྲ་ཆོད་ (trājöö) sm. ཁྲ་བཅད་.

ཁྲ་ཆོལ་ (trājöö) mixed colors of barley.

ཁྲ་སྙན་ (trādɛn) multicolored rug.

ཁྲ་ཐ་རེ་ (trādare) 1. colorful and shining. 2. streaming (with tears).

ཁྲ་ཐིག (trādig) spots ¶ གཟིག་གི་ཁྲ་ཐིག The spots of a leopard.

ཁྲ་ཐིང་དགུ་ཐིང་ (trātiŋ gudiŋ) variegated, sparkling, shinning.

ཁྲ་ཐིང་ཐིང་ (trā tiŋdiŋ) sm. ཁྲ་ཐིང་དགུ་ཐིང་.

ཁྲ་དོན་བརྡལ་བཞིག (trādön dɛɛshii) shung. violating the content of a verdict.

ཁྲ་འདྲ་གླ་འདྲ་ (trāndra lāndra) strong and tough [Lit. like hawk, like eagle].

ཁྲ་པ་ (trāba) 1. hunter. 2. embroiderer of Tibetan shoes.

ཁྲ་བེར་ཙམ་ (trā berdzam) slightly drunk; va.—བྱེད་ to be slightly drunk ¶ ང་མདང་དགོང་ཐུགས་སྐྱིད་སར་ཁྲ་བེར་ཙམ་བྱས་བཞག I was slightly drunk at last night's party.

ཁྲ་བོ་ (trābo) sm. ཁྲ་ཁྲ་.

ཁྲ་དཔན་ (trābɛn) ch. tea bowl.

ཁྲ་དཔན་ཁྲ་ཀྱག (trābɛn trāgyaà) ch.tib. tea cup and stand (usu. made of silver or brass).

ཁྲ་འབྲུག་དགོན་པ་ (trādruù gömba) sm. ཁྲ་འབྲུག་ལྷ་ཁང་.

ཁྲ་འབྲུག་ལྷ་ཁང་ (trādruù lhāgaŋ) name of a temple.

ཁྲ་མ་ (trāma) 1. a verdict in a law case; va.—གཏོང་ to issue a verdict (in a law case). 2. framed window; va.—བརྒྱར་ to put up/ hang a window.

ཁྲ་མ་མེས་པོའི་དྲང་ཐིག (trāma meèbö traŋdig) shung. a just verdict like those of the past.

ཁྲ་མའི་སྡེགས་བུ་ (trāmɛ dēgbu) window sill.

ཁྲ་མའི་སྦྱར་རིས་ (trāmɛ jārrii) window decoration, paper stuck on a window as decoration.

ཁྲ་མིག (trāmig) window pane/ square.

ཁྲ་མེན་ (trāmen) a gem used in the preparation of Tibetan medicines.

ཁྲ་མེར་བ་ (trāmerwa) gleaming, sparkling, brilliant, glittering.

ཁྲ་མོ་ (trāmo) multicolored, colorful.

ཁྲ་འཚུབ་འཚུབ་ (trā tsūbdzub) sm. ཁྲ་ལྷེམ་མེར་.

ཁྲ་ཛོམ་ (trādzom) sm. ཁྲ་སྒྲིག.

ཁྲ་ཟིལ་ཟིལ་ (trā siisii) sm. ཁྲ་ཁྲ་, 1.

ཁྲ་བཟུང་དམ་སྒྲིགས་ (trāsuŋ damdrig) shung. being selective and demanding.

ཁྲ་ཡོལ་ (trāyöö) window curtain, drape; va.—རྒྱག to close drapes/ curtains.

ཁྲ་རྭ་ (trāra) animal horn with variegated colors.

ཁྲ་རས་ (trārɛɛ̀) gauze-like material used as window covering; va.—རྒྱག.

ཁྲ་རིལ་རིལ་ (trā riirii) gleaming, sparkling, shining, glittering; wide-eyed ¶ མིག་ཁྲ་རིལ་རིལ་བྱས་ནས་ With gleaming eyes.

ཁྲ་རིས་ (trārii) grain in wood.

ཁྲ་རུ་ (trāru) wooden window frame.

ཁྲ་ལམ་མེ་ (trālamme) sm. ཁྲ་རིལ་རིལ་.

ཁྲ་ལོག (trālɔɔ̀) rejecting a verdict, not accepting a judgement; va.—རྒྱག to reject a verdict ¶ རྫོང་ནས་བཏང་བའི་ཁྲ་མར་ཁྲ་ལོག་བརྒྱབ་ཙང་ཁོ་པ་ལྷ་སར་རྫོང་བདེ་བརྒྱབ་པ་རེད་ He refused to accept the district's verdict, and an order was issued to for him to go to Lhasa.

ཁྲ་ལོག་ལྡང་ཡན་ (trālɔɔ̀ lūŋyɛn) the resurgence of a political group or person that had once been put down; va.—རྒྱག.

ཁྲ་ཤིག་ཤིག (trā shīshi) colorful.

ཁྲ་ཤིང་ (trā shīŋ) zebrawood tree.

ཁྲ་ཤེལ་ (trāshee) window-panel.

ཁྲ་སང་ (trāsaŋ) sm. ཁྲ་རས་.

ཁྲ་སིར་བི་སིར་ (trāsii bisii) sm. ཁྲ་ཁྲ་, 1.

ཁྲ་སློག (trā lɔɔ̀) sm. ཁྲ་ལོག.

ཁྲ་ཧར་ (trāhar) Chahar tribe (of Inner Mongolian).

ཁྲ་ཧྲིག་ཧྲིག (trā hrīghrig) sm. ཁྲ་ཆེམ་ཆེམ་.

ཁྲ་ལྷམ་ལྷམ་ (trā lhāmlham) sm. ཁྲ་ལྷེམ་མེར་.

ཁྲ་ལྷེམ་མེར་ (trā lhēmme) 1. sparkling, glittering. 2. clearly/ vividly (with མིག) ¶ ངའི་མིག་ལམ་དུ་མོའི་གདོང་ཁྲ་ལྷེམ་མེར་འཁོར་བྱུང་ I saw her face vividly in my vision.

ཁྲ་ལྷེམ་ལྷེམ་ (trā lhēmlhem) sm. ཁྲ་ལྷེམ་མེར་.

ཁྲག (trāà) blood; va.—འདོན་ to draw blood, to cause to bleed; va.—རྒྱག; —གཏར་; —བཙག to draw/ let blood, e.g., to donate blood; va.—གཅོད་; —འགག to stop bleeding; vi.—ཐོན་; —ཤོར་ to bleed, to lose blood; vi.—རྒྱག to menstruate.

ཁྲག་བཀག (trāà) see ཁྲག.

ཁྲག་བཀྲ་ (trāà trā) sm. ཁྲག་མདངས་.

ཁྲག་ཀང་ (trāàgaŋ) a type of traditional Tibetan medicine (thalictrum glandulosis-simum).

ཁྲག་སྐེམ་ (trāàgem) a traditional Tibetan medicine used to stop bleeding.

ཁྲག་སྐྱིན་ (trāàgyin) blood-debt, blood vengeance; va.—སྒྲུབ་; —འཇལ་; —ལེན་ to take blood vengeance, to pay back a blood-debt ¶ ཕ་བསད་པའི་ཁྲག་སྐྱིན་དེ་ལེན་དགོས་པའི་དུས་རེད་བསམ་ནས་ Thinking this is the time to take blood vengeance for the killing of his father.

ཁྲག་སྐྱུག (trāà gyūù) vi. to vomit blood.

ཁྲག་སྐྱོ་ (trā gyō) blood plasma.

ཁྲག་སྐྱོ་སྤྲི་དཀར་ (trāgyo trīgar) blood protein.

ཁྲག་སྐྲངས་ (trāàdraŋ) hematoma.

ཁྲག་སྐྲན་ (trāgdrɛn) leukemia (cancer of the blood).

ཁྲག་སྐྲན་ཧྲེམ་པོ་ (trāgdrɛn hrēmbo) cancer of the womb.

ཁྲག་ཁུ་ (trāàku) blood plasma.

ཁྲག་ཁྱིང་ (trāgyiŋ) blood clot.

ཁྲག་ཁྲལ་ (trāàtɛɛ) shung. tax on slaughtering

animals.

ཁྲག་ཁྲིག (trə̄gdriì) 1. 100 billion. 2. an enormous number.

ཁྲག་འཁྲུག (trə̄gdruù) 1. unrest, disorder; disturbance, instability; va.—བྱེད་ to cause or stir up unrest/ disorder ¶ཁོ་ཚོའི་ཚོགས་པའི་ནང་ལ་ཁྲག་འཁྲུག་གི་གནས་ཚུལ་བྱུང་བ་རེད་ Unrest occurred in their organization. 2. scrambled, jumbled, mixed up. 3. unwell. 4. dirty.

ཁྲག་གྲོག་པ་ (trāg drōgba) 1. a Tibetan medicine (lepidium apetalum). 2. sm. ཁྲག་འཁྲུག.

ཁྲག་མཁྲིས་ (trāà trīì) a disease of the gall bladder.

ཁྲག་འཁོན་ (trāàgön) blood feud, blood grudge.

ཁྲག་འཁོར་སའི་དབང་པོ་ (trāà kɔ̄ɔ̄sɛɛ wāŋbo) organs of the circulatory system.

ཁྲག་འཁྱིལ་ (trāàgyil) a pool of blood.

ཁྲག་འཁྲུགས་ (trə̄trug) blood pressure disease.

ཁྲག་གི་སྐྱོ་མ་ (trāàgi gyōma) blood plasma.

ཁྲག་གི་ཁྲུག་གི་ (trə̄gi trūgi) sm. ཁྲག་འཁྲུག.

ཁྲག་གི་གྲུབ་ཆའི་དཔེ་རིས་ (trāàgi drubcɛ bērii) hemogram.

ཁྲག་གི་མངར་ཆ་ (trāàgi ŋārja) blood sugar.

ཁྲག་གི་མདོག་རྫི་ (trāàgi dɔgdzi) hemochrome.

ཁྲག་གི་ཕྲ་ཕུང་ (trāàgi trəbuŋ) blood cell, hemocyte.

ཁྲག་གི་བུ་ལོན་ (trāàgi pulön) sm. ཁྲག་སྐྱིན་.

ཁྲག་གི་བུ་ལོན་ཁྲག་གིས་འཇལ་ (trāàgi pulön trāàgiì jɛɛ) blood vengeance [Lit. repaying a debt of blood with blood].

ཁྲག་གི་ཞིབ་འབུ་ (trāàgi shimbu) blood platelet.

ཁྲག་གི་རིགས་ (trāàgi rig) blood type, blood group.

ཁྲག་གི་སོ་ནད་ (trāàgi nɛɛ̀) gum disease.

ཁྲག་གི་བསླབ་ཆ་ (trāàgi lābja) a powerful lesson, a lesson not easily forgotten [Lit. a bloody lesson].

ཁྲག་གི་ཁྲུག་གི་ (trəgi trūgi) sm. ཁྲག་འཁྲུག.

ཁྲག་གོས་ (trāà kö̀ö) bloody clothes.

ཁྲག་གྲང་སྲོག་ཆགས་ (trāàdraŋ sōgjaà) cold-blooded animal.

ཁྲག་སྒྲོན་ (trāgdrön) shedding one's blood, sacrificing one's own blood/ life (for sth.); va.—གཏོང་ ¶ཁྲག་སྒྲོན་ལ་བརྟེན་ནས་རང་བཙན་ལེན་དགོས་ (We) have to sacrifice our own blood to get independence. 2. spilling blood, bloody ¶ཁྲག་སྒྲོན་དམག་འཐབ་ A bloody war.

ཁྲག་བཀག (trāà gaà) vi. to have the flow of blood stop.

ཁྲག་འགགས་ (trā gaà) sm. ཁྲག་བཀག.

ཁྲག་རྒྱག (trāà gyaà) see ཁྲག.

ཁྲག་རྒྱས་པ་ (trāà gyɛɛ̀ba) hyperemia.

ཁྲག་རྒྱུ་ (trəggyu) blood sausage.

ཁྲག་རྒྱུད་ (trāàgyüù) maternal side, maternal lineage ¶ཁྲག་རྒྱུད་སྤུན་ཉེ་ Maternal relatives. [Lit. blood lineage].

ཁྲག་རྒྱུན་ (trəggyün) blood circulation.

ཁྲག་རྒྱུན་འཁོར་རྒྱུག (trəggyün kɔ̄ɔ̄gyaà) blood circulation.

ཁྲག་རྒྱུན་ཞིབ་བཤེར་ཁང་ (trəggyün shibshergaŋ) blood testing room.

ཁྲག་མངར་ (trāàŋar) blood sugar.

ཁྲག་རྔུལ་ (trāà ŋǖǖ) blood and sweat ¶ཁྲག་རྔུལ་ལ་བརྟེན་ནས་རྒྱལ་ཁབ་འཛུགས་སྐྲུན་བྱས་པ་རེད་ (They) built the country through the blood and sweat (of the people).

ཁྲག་ཅན་ (trāgjɛn) bloody.

ཁྲག་གཅིན་ (trāàjin) 1. blood in the urine. 2. blood and urine.

ཁྲག་གཅོད་ (trāà jö̀ö) va. to stop bleeding ¶ཁྲག་གཅོད་སྨན་ཕྱེ་ A powder that stops bleeding.

ཁྲག་གཅོར་ (trāgjɔɔ) corporal punishment.

ཁྲག་ཆགས་ (trāgcaà) sentient beings.

ཁྲག་ཆད་ (trāà cɛɛ̀) vi. to have bleeding stop.

ཁྲག་ཆུ་ (trəgcu) watery blood.

ཁྲག་འཇིག་ནད་ (trāà jignɛɛ̀) septicemia.

ཁྲག་འཇིབ་ (trā jib) va. to suck blood.

ཁྲག་འཇིབ་ཁོང་སྲིན་ (trāàjib kōŋsin) internal blood sucking parasite.

ཁྲག་འཇིབ་གདོན་འདྲེ་ (trāàjib döndre) bloodsucker.

ཁྲག་འཇིབ་འབུ་ (trāàjib bu) leech, blood sucker, blood fluke.

ཁྲག་འཇིབ་འབུ་ཕྲ་ (trāàjib budra) blood sucking parasite, blood fluke.

ཁྲག་འཇིབ་འབུ་ཕྲའི་ནད་ (trāàjib budrɛ nɛɛ̀) schistosomiasis.

ཁྲག་འཇིབ་སྲིན་འབུ་ (trāàjib sīnbu) sm. ཁྲག་འཇིབ་འབུ་ཕྲ་.

ཁྲག་རྗེས་ (trāàjeè) bloodstain, blood spot.

ཁྲག་ཉམས་ (trāàñam) vi. to be/ get anemic.

ཁྲག་ཉམས་འགོག་བྱེད་སྐྱུར་རྫས་ (trāàñam gɔgjeè gyurdzɛɛ̀) ascorbic acid, vitamin C.

ཁྲག་ཉམས་པའི་ནད་ (trāà ñambɛɛ nɛɛ̀) anemia.

ཁྲག་ཏིག (trāàdig) petechia, ecchymosis, spotting on the skin.

ཁྲག་གཏར་ (trāgdar) see ཁྲག.

ཁྲག་གཏར་བའི་གསོ་བཅོས་ (trāgdarwɛ sōjö̀ö) treatment involving bloodletting.

ཁྲག་བཏུངས་མནའ་བསྐྱལ་ (trāàtuŋ nagyee) sm. ཁྲག་འཐུང་མནའ་སྐྱེལ་.

ཁྲག་བཏོན་ (trāà dön) p. of ཁྲག་འདོན་.

ཁྲག་བཏོན་སྲོག་འདོར་ (trāgdön sɔ̄ɔ̀dɔr) sacrificing one's life (for sth.) [Lit. shedding blood, abandoning life].

ཁྲག་ཐིག (trəgtig) a drop of blood; vi.—རྒྱག to drip blood.

ཁྲག་ཐིག་པགས་ནད་ (trāàtig bāgnɛɛ̀) petechia.

ཁྲག་ཐོན་ (trāà tön) vi. to lose blood, to bleed ¶ཁྲག་ཐོན་ཆེ་ཐོན་པས་དྲན་པ་འཐོར་བ་རེད་ He fainted because he lost a lot of blood.

ཁྲག་ཐོན་གྱོད་གཞི་ (trəgtön gyö̀öshi) murder case.

ཁྲག་ཐོན་ལྷ་བའི་ནད་ (trāàtön lābɛ nɛɛ̀) hemophilia.

ཁྲག་འཐུང་མནའ་སྐྱེལ་ (trāà tūŋ nagyee) blood oath.

ཁྲག་འཐུང་འབུ་ (trāà tūŋ bu) sm. ཁྲག་འཇིབ་འབུ་.

ཁྲག་འཐུང་སྲིན་བུ་ (trāà tūŋ sīmbu) sm. ཁྲག་འཇིབ་འབུ་.

ཁྲག་དང་མིག་ཆུ་ (trāà daŋ migju) blood and tears ¶ཁྲག་དང་མིག་གི་ལོ་རྒྱུས་ A history written in blood and tears. ¶ཁྲག་དང་མིག་ཆུའི་རྩིས་ཁྲ་ A debt of blood and tears.

ཁྲག་དུག (trəgduù) blood poisoning.

ཁྲག་དྭངས་མ་ (trāà daŋma) blood serum.

ཁྲག་དྭངས་མིག་ཆུའི་ཞེ་སྡང་ (trāàdaŋ migjü shedaŋ) extreme hatred, a hatred of blood and tears, a hatred based on extreme suffering.

ཁྲག་དྲི་ (trāà tri) smell of blood; vi.—ཁ་ to smell blood.

ཁྲག་དྲི་དྲོ་བ་ (trəgti drowa) bloody, reeking of blood ¶ཁྲག་དྲི་དྲོ་བའི་དྲག་གནོན་ Bloody suppression.

ཁྲག་དྲི་དྲོ་བའི་དབང་སྒྱུར་ (trəgti drowɛ wəŋgyur) controlling by bloody suppression.

ཁྲག་དྲོན་ (trāgdrön) warm/ fresh blood; va.—འདོན་ to cause bloodshed, to shed blood.

ཁྲག་དྲོན་འཁོལ་བ་ (trāgdrön kȫöwa) burning with righteous indignation [Lit. boiling blood].

ཁྲག་དྲོན་ཅན་ (trāgdrönjɛn) warm-blooded.

ཁྲག་དྲོན་པ་ལྷབས་ (trāgdrön bələb) sm. ཁྲག་དྲོན་འཁོལ་བ་.

ཁྲག་དྲོན་སྲོག་ཆགས་ (trāgdrön sōgjaà) warm-blooded animal.

ཁྲག་གདན་ (trāgdɛn) a mat/ carpet on which a person who has been killed is placed.

ཁྲག་མདངས་ (trāgdaŋ) the color of blood.

ཁྲག་མདུད་ (trāgdüù) thrombosis.

ཁྲག་མདོག (trāgdɔɔ̀) color of blood.

ཁྲག་མདོག་རྒྱུ་ (trāà doggyu) haemochrome.

ཁྲག་འདོན་ (trāà dön) 1. va. to draw blood, to bleed. 2. va. to pay for in blood ¶ཁྲག་བཏོན་ནས་ཐོབ་པའི་ཉམས་མྱོང་ An experience for which we paid in blood.

ཁྲག་འདོན་གྱི་དུས་ཤིང་ (trāàdöngi tüüsiŋ) a bloody disturbance.

ཁྲག་དུལ་ (trāgdüü) blood platelet.

ཁྲག་རྡོག (trāgdog) blood clot.

ཁྲག་རྡོག་རྡོག (trāà dogdoò) blood clot.

ཁྲག་ནང་གི་མངར་ཆ་ (trāgnaŋgi ŋāāja) blood sugar.

ཁྲག་ནད་ (trāānɛὲ) disease of the blood; vi.—ན་; —ཕོག to be sick with a blood disease.

ཁྲག་སྣ་ (trāāna) a drop of blood used in religious rituals.

ཁྲག་པང་ལེབ་ཆུང་ (trāà bāŋleb cūŋ) blood platelet.

ཁྲག་དྲི་ (trāgdrī) cholestorol.

ཁྲག་ཕྱེ་ (trāgce) blood meal.

ཁྲག་ཕྱེད་ (trāgceè) hemodialyser.

ཁྲག་ཕུན་ (trāgbün) sm. ཁྲག་སྦྱིན་.

ཁྲག་བླུག (trāà lūù) va. to give a blood transfusion.

ཁྲག་དབྱིབས་ (trəgyip) 1. blood cell shape. 2. sm. ཁྲག་རིགས་.

ཁྲག་འབབ་ (trā bəb) sm. ཁྲག་ཐོན་.

ཁྲག་འབྱར་ཐེབས་ (trāgjar tēb) 1. vi. to get matted/ stuck/ stained with blood (e.g., the clothing of sb. wounded). 2. vi. to get drenched with blood.

ཁྲག་འབྱིན་ (trāg jin) sm. ཁྲག་འདོན་.

ཁྲག་སྦྱིན་ (trāgjin) donating blood; va. ཁྲག་སྦྱིན་; —གཏོང་ to donate blood.

ཁྲག་སྦྱིན་མཁན་ (trāgjingɛn) blood donor.

ཁྲག་སྦྱོར་ (trāgjɔɔ) bloodshed; va.—བྱེད་ to shed blood ། མི་གསོད་ཁྲག་སྦྱོར་གྱི་གནས་ཚུལ་བྱུང་བ་རེད་ There were incidents of killing and bloodshed.

ཁྲག་མ་དོན་མཛོ་པོ་བཤའ་ཐབས་ (trāà madön dzobo shādəb) trying to do sth. quietly without leaving any trace that you did it [Lit. trying to slaughter a dzo without spilling blood].

ཁྲག་མ་ཆོད་པའི་མོ་ནད་ (trāà macööbɛ monɛὲ) hemorrhaging after child birth or during menstruation.

ཁྲག་མལ་རྒྱ་བཤལ་ (trāàñɛɛ cūshɛɛ) totally/ completely destroying; va.—གཏོང་ [Lit. rinsed with blood].

ཁྲག་དམར་ (trāàmar) 1. bloody. 2. red blood 3. red blood cell.

ཁྲག་དམར་ཀུ་བཤུར་བཤུར་ (trāàmar gū shūrshur) bloody, blood running like water in a canal.

ཁྲག་དམར་དངོས་འབྱར་ (trāàmar ŋönjar) sm. ཁྲག་དམར་ལུས་འབྱར་.

ཁྲག་དམར་ཅིལ་ཅིལ་ (trāàmar cījiī) sm. ཁྲག་དམར་འཛར་འཛར་.

ཁྲག་དམར་དྲི་དཀར་ (trāgmar drīgar) red and white blood cells.

ཁྲག་དམར་ཙ་རེ་བ་ (trāàmar dzārewa) sm. ཁྲག་དམར་འཛར་འཛར་.

ཁྲག་དམར་འཛར་འཛར་ (trāàmar dzardzar) drenched/ dripping with blood, bloody.

ཁྲག་དམར་ལུས་འབྱར་ (trāàmar lünjar) drenched with blood.

ཁྲག་སྨན་ (trāgmɛn) blood tonic.

ཁྲག་གཙག (trāà dzāà) va. to drain or draw blood (as therapy).

ཁྲག་གཙང་ (trāgdzaŋ) blood serum.

ཁྲག་བཙོག (trāgdzog) blood stain.

ཁྲག་རྩ་ (trāgdza) blood vessel; vi.—རྒྱས་ to swell/ vasodilate (blood vessels).

ཁྲག་རྩ་འགག (trāgdza gaà) vi. to have an embolism.

ཁྲག་རྩ་འགག་རྫས་ (trāgdza gagdzɛὲ) embolus.

ཁྲག་རྩ་རྒྱས་ (trāgdza) see ཁྲག་རྩ་.

ཁྲག་རྩ་ཆེ་བ་ (trāgdza cēwa) aorta.

ཁྲག་རྩ་མདུད་ཁེགས་ (trāgdza dükeg) thrombosis.

ཁྲག་རྩ་ཕྲ་མོ་ (trāgdza trāmo) blood capillary.

ཁྲག་རྩ་ཕྲན་བུ་ (trāgdza trɛ̄mbu) sm. ཁྲག་རྩ་ཕྲ་མོ་.

ཁྲག་རྩ་ཡང་ཕྲ་ (trāgdza yaŋdra) sm. ཁྲག་རྩ་ཕྲ་མོ་.

ཁྲག་རྩ་སྲེངས་འགྱུར་ (trāgdza hrēŋgyur) vascular sclerosis.

ཁྲག་རྩ་གསལ་འབྱེད་པར་ལེན་ (trāgdza sɛ̄lceè bārlen) aniography.

ཁྲག་རྩའི་ཚ་ནད་ (trāgdzɛ tsānɛὲ) vasculitis.

ཁྲག་རྫི་དམར་པོ་ (trāgdzi mārbo) haemochrome.

ཁྲག་ཚབས་ (trāgtsəb) diseases relating to irregular menstruation.

ཁྲག་ཚབས་སྐོར་པ་ (trāgtsəb kɔrwa) one of the ten types of ཁྲག་ཚབས་.

ཁྲག་ཚིལ་ (trāgtsil) cholesterol.

ཁྲག་མཚོ་ (trāgtso) bloodbath, a sea of blood ། མི་དམངས་རྣམས་ལོ་བཅུའི་རིང་གི་ནང་འཁྲུག་གི་ཁྲག་མཚོའི་ནང་དུ་བསྙུགས་པ་རེད་ (They) threw the people into the bloodbath of ten years of civil war.

ཁྲག་འཚབ་ (trāàdzəb) avenging a murder.

ཁྲག་མཛོད་ (trāgdzöö) blood bank.

ཁྲག་འཛགས་ (trāà dzaà) vi. to drip blood.

ཁྲག་འཛིང་ (trəgdziŋ) bloody battle/ fight; va.—བྱེད་.

ཁྲག་ཞུན་རྒྱུ་རྫི་ (trəgshun gyudzi) hemolysin.

ཁྲག་བཞུར་ (trāg shur) sm. ཁྲག་འདོན་, 1.

ཁྲག་བཞུར་སྲོག་བསྲོས་ (trāgshur sɔ̄ɔdöö) sm. ཁྲག་བཏོན་སྲོག་འདོར་.

ཁྲག་ཡིག (trāgyig) a letter written in one's own blood (expressing one's determination, last wish, etc.).

ཁྲག་ཡོད་ཤ་ཡོད་ (trāgyöö shāyöö) vivid, true to life (writing style).

ཁྲག་རལ་ཡོད་པ་ (trāgrɛɛ yöba) a person with blood on his hands (sb. who has killed or murdered).

ཁྲག་རིགས་ (trəgrig) blood type, blood group.

ཁྲག་རིལ་ (trəgrii) blood corpuscle, blood cell.

ཁྲག་རིལ་དཀར་པོ་ (trəgrii gāābo) white blood cell, white corpuscle.

ཁྲག་རིལ་དཀར་པོའི་འབྲས་སྐྲན་ (trəgrii gāābö drɛdɛn) leukemia.

ཁྲག་རིལ་དཀར་དམར་ (trəgrii gārmar) red and white blood cells.

ཁྲག་རིལ་ཐིམ་ཚད་ (trəgrii timtsɛὲ) erythrocyte sedimentation rate.

ཁྲག་རིལ་དམར་པོ་ (rəgrii māābo) red blood cell, red corpuscle.

ཁྲག་རུལ་ (trəgrüü) pus (in blood).

ཁྲག་རོ་ (trāgro) clotted blood.

ཁྲག་རྭ་ (trāgra) pilose antler (an antler used as an aphrodisiac that is soft with blood inside).

ཁྲག་རླངས་ (trāglaŋ) steam coming from warm blood (e.g., when an animal is slaughtered and the blood is collected).

ཁྲག་རླུང་ (trāgluŋ) 1. blood pressure. 2. great anger; vi.—ལངས་ to be/get extremely angry.

ཁྲག་རླུང་སྟོད་འཚང་ (trāgluŋ döödzaŋ) 1. name of a type of "wind" disease. 2. great anger.

ཁྲག་ལམ་ (trāglam) blood vessel.

ཁྲག་ལམ་སྲེངས་ནད་ (trāglam hrēŋnɛὲ) sm. ཁྲག་རྩ་སྲེངས་འགྱུར་.

ཁྲག་ལིང་ (trəgliŋ) blood clot.

ཁྲག་ལུ་ (trāà lu) vi. to vomit blood.

ཁྲག་ལུག (trāgluù) sm. ཁྲག་བླུག.

ཁྲག་ལུད་ (trāglüü) blood and spittle/ phlegm.

ཁྲག་ལེན་ཁང་ (trəglenkaŋ) a laboratory or clinic where blood samples are taken/ collected.

ཁྲག་ལོང་ (trāgloŋ) right side of intestines.

ཁྲག་ཤ་ (trāgsha) blood that is coagulated by boiling and then eaten [Lit. blood meat].

ཁྲག་ཤུལ་ (trāgshüü) sm. ཁྲག་རྗེས་.

ཁྲག་ཤེད་ (trāgsheè) blood pressure.

ཁྲག་ཤེད་ཉམས་པ་ (trāgsheè ñamba) low blood pressure.

ཁྲག་ཤེད་མཐོ་པོ་ (trāgsheè tōbo) high blood pressure.

ཁྲག་ཤེད་དཔྱད་ཆས་ (trāgsheè jɛ̄jɛɛ) blood pressure cuff, sphygmomanometer.

ཁྲག་ཤེད་དམའ་པོ་ (trāgsheè māābo) low blood pressure.

ཁྲག་ཤོར་ (trāà shɔ̄ɔ) see ཁྲག.

ཁྲག་ཤོར་ཁྲག་ལེན་ (trāà shɔ̄ɔ trāg len) blood vengeance [Lit. blood spilled, blood taken].

ཁྲག་གཤེར་ (trāgsher) liquid blood.

ཁྲག་གཤེར་འཁོར་སྐྱོད་ (trāgsher kɔ̄ɔgyöö) blood circulation.

ཁྲག་བཤལ་ (trāà shɛ̄ɛ) vi. to have dysentery (with blood).

ཁྲག་བཤིག་རྫས་རྒྱུ་ (trāgshiì dzɛ̄ɛ̀gyu) heparin.

ཁྲག་སྲིན་དུག་མཆེད་ཀྱི་ནད་ (trāàsin tugjɛɛ̀gi nɛὲ) sm. ཁྲག་འཛིག་ནད་.

ཁྲག་གསོག་བཟོ་གྲྭ་ (thrāgso sodra) blood bank.

ཁྲག་རྣག (trāà nāg) blood and pus.

ཁྲང་ (trāŋ) ch. factory.

ཁྲང་ཀྲང་ (trāŋdraŋ) ch. head/ manager of a factory.

ཁྲང་ཀྲང་གི་འགན་ཁུར་ལམ་ལུགས་ (trāŋdraŋgi gɛnkur ləmlug) ch.tib. system of overall responsibility being taken by the factory manager.

ཁྲང་ཆི་ (trāŋci) Nagasaki.

ཁྲང་ཐང་ (trāŋtaŋ) hard, solid, robust.

ཁྲང་ཞི་ (trāŋshi) ch. traditional Chinese opera; va.—འཁྲབ་ to perform Chinese opera.

ཁྲང་ཞི་འཁྲབ་ས་ (trāŋshi trəbsə) ch.tib. theater where Chinese opera is performed.

ཁྲང་ཞི་ཟློས་གར་ (trāŋshi döögar) ch.tib. traditional Chinese opera.

ཁྲང་ཞིའི་སློབ་གྲྭ་ (trāŋsi lōbdra) ch.tib. Chinese opera school.

ཁྲང་ཧྲ་ (trāŋhra) Changsha.

ཁྲང་ཨན་ (trāŋan) Changan.

ཁྲད་ཁྲོད་ (trɛ̄ɛtröö) sm. ཁོང་སེང་.

ཁྲན་ཐོན་ (trɛ̄ntön) cicada's slough (used in Tibetan medicines).

ཁྲབ་ (trəb) armor.

ཁྲབ་མཁན་ (trəbgɛn) people who make armor.

ཁྲབ་གོས་ (trəbgöö) sm. ཁྲབ་.

ཁྲབ་གྱོན་མཚོན་ཐོགས་ (trəbkön tsɔ̄ntɔɔ̀) being a warrior, preparing for war [Lit. wear armor, carry weapon].

ཁྲབ་ཅན་ (trəbjɛn) 1. beetle. 2. anything with a hard, crust-like outer surface.

ཁྲབ་ཕྱིབས་ (trəbjib) the lining inside armor.

ཁྲབ་ཐེངས་ (trəbteŋ) the number of times a show has been performed, the performance number.

ཁྲབ་ལྡན་ (trəpdɛn) armored ¶ཁྲབ་ལྡན་འཁོར་ལོ་ Armored vehicle ¶ཁྲབ་ལྡན་དམག་དཔུང་ Armored troops ¶ཁྲབ་ལྡན་སྐྱེལ་འདྲེན་འཁོར་ལོ་ Armored carrier ¶ཁྲབ་ལྡན་རྟ་དམག Armored cavalry ¶ཁྲབ་ལྡན་དམག Armored force/ troops.

ཁྲབ་སྦྲས་ (trəbdrɛɛ̀) sm. ཁྲབ་ལྡན་.

ཁྲབ་བྱང་ (trəpjaŋ) scales on armor.

ཁྲབ་མ་ (trəpma) 1. soldiers clad in armor. 2. arc. armor.

ཁྲབ་རྨོག (trəpmog) armor and helmet; va.—འགྱོན་ to put on/ wear armor and helmet.

ཁྲབ་རང་བྱོན་ (trəp raŋgyön) an ancient magical armor that comes on the body by itself.

ཁྲབ་ཤོག་ཅན་གྱི་རིགས་ (trəpshɔɔ̀jɛngi rig) lepidopterous insects.

ཁྲམ་ (trām) 1. notch, nick, cut; va.—རྒྱག to cut slits on a corpse to induce vultures to come to eat the flesh (in the traditional Tibetan funeral rite). 2. lying, deceiving; va.—ཤོད་ to tell a lie, to deceive.

ཁྲམ་རྐུན་ (trəmgün) liar and thief.

ཁྲམ་ཁ་ (trāmga) 1. sm. ཁྲམ་. 2. astrological chart. 3. the cross-shape (similar to the Christian cross); va.—རྒྱག to cut a corpse with many crosses to make it easy for the vultures to eat the flesh.

ཁྲམ་ཁྲམ་ (trāmdram) 1. spreading out ¶དངོས་པོ་རྣམས་ཁྲམ་ཁྲམ་དུ་བཀྲམས་བཞག (They) have spread out all (their) things. 2. streaming/ flowing down ¶མཆི་མ་ཁྲམ་ཁྲམ་འདོན་ Tears streaming down.

ཁྲམ་ཁྲུམ་ (trāmdrum) 1. scattered. 2. coarsely ground.

ཁྲམ་ཁྲུས་ (trāmdrüü) broken pieces.

ཁྲམ་ནག (trāmnaà) incorrigible liar, a swindler, con man.

ཁྲམ་པ་ (trāmba) (for people) liar, swindler, con man; (for actions) swindling, cheating, fraudulent practices, malpractice; va.—བྱེད་.

ཁྲམ་པ་མགོ་བདེ་ (trāmba gode) sm. ཁྲམ་པ་.

ཁྲམ་དཔོན་ (trāmbön) head of swindlers/ con men, etc.

ཁྲམ་སྤྱོད་ (trāmjöö) swindling, lying, cheating, conning; va.—འཁྲབ་ to swindle/ lie/ cheat/ con.

ཁྲམ་བམ་ (trāmbam) sm. རྒྱ་གྲམ་.

ཁྲམ་མི་ཁྲུམ་མི་ (trəmmi trümmi) exhausted, tired, fatigued ¶ཉིན་གང་ངལ་རྩོལ་བྱས་ནས་གཟུགས་པོ་ཁྲམ་མི་ཁྲུམ་མི་ཆགས་བཞག Having worked all day, my body has become exhausted.

ཁྲམ་དམག (drāmmaà) an undisciplined/ lawless army, ruffians/ riffraff in the army ¶གྲོང་ཚོ་འདིར་ཁྲམ་དམག་ཁག་གཅིག་སླེབས་ནས་བརྡབ་གསིག་མང་པོ་བཏང་འདུག A lawless army came to this town and did much looting and injuring.

ཁྲམ་ཚོང་ (trāmtsoŋ) swindling, conning; va.—རྒྱག.

ཁྲམ་ཚོན་ (trāmdzön) arc. account book.

ཁྲམ་ཟོལ་ (trāmsöö) sm. ཁྲམ་པ་.

ཁྲམ་གཡོ་ (trāmyo) deceiving, swindling; va.—བྱེད་; —སྒྱུ་.

ཁྲམ་ལ་འདེབས་ (trāmla deb) va. to put up a wooden tablet containing sb.'s name as a form of curse.

ཁྲམ་གཤོམ་ (trāmshom) plotting/ conspiring/ conniving to swindle or con; va.—རྒྱག.

ཁྲམ་གཤོས་ (trāmshöö) scattering, casting out.

ཁྲམ་སེམས (trāmsem) (having thoughts of) lying, swindling, conning; va.—འཆང་ to lie, to swindle, to con.

ཁྲད་དན་ཉིང་ (trādɛnñiŋ) ch. tannic acid.

ཁྲའི་ཡིའུ་ (trɛ̄yiu) ch. diesel oil.

ཁྲའི་ཡིའུ་ཅི་ (trɛ̄yiuji) ch. sm. ཁྲའི་ཡིའུ་ཅི་འཁྲུལ་འཁོར་.

ཁྲའི་ཡིའུ་ཅི་འཁྲུལ་འཁོར་ (trɛ̄yiuji tüügɔɔ) ch.tib. diesel engine.

ཁྲའི་ཡིའུ་ཅི་འཕྲུལ་འཁོར་ (trɛ̄yiuji tüügɔɔ) ch.tib. sm. ཁྲའི་ཡིའུ་ཅི་འཁྲུལ་འཁོར་.

ཁྲའི་ཡིའུ་ནང་འབར་འཁྲུལ་འཁོར་ (trɛ̄yiu naŋbar tüügɔɔ) ch.tib. diesel internal combustion engine.

ཁྲའི་ཡིའུ་སྣུམ་ (trɛ̄yiu nūm) ch.tib. diesel oil.

ཁྲའི་ཡིའུ་འཕྲུལ་འཁོར་ (trɛ̄yiu trüügɔɔ) ch.tib. diesel engine.

ཁྲའི་ཡིའུ་ (trɛ̄yiu) ch. sm. ཁྲའི་ཡིའུ་.

ཁྲའི་ཡིའུ་སྣུམ་ (trɛ̄yiu nūm) ch. sm. ཁྲའི་ཡིའུ་སྣུམ་.

ཁྲའོ་ཞན་ (trāoshɛn) Korea.

ཁྲའོ་ཞན་དམངས་གཙོ་རིང་ལུགས་མི་དམངས་སྤྱི་མཐུན་རྒྱལ་ཁབ་ (trāoshɛn māŋdzö riŋluù mimaŋ jītün gyɛgəb) Korean Democratic People's Republic.

ཁྲའོ་ཞན་ལྷོ་རྒྱུད་ (trāoshɛn lhōgyüù) South Korea.

ཁྲའོ་ཤན་ (trāoshɛn) sm. ཁྲའོ་ཞན་.

ཁྲའོ་ཤིའན་ (trāoshɛn) sm. ཁྲའོ་ཞན་.

ཁྲལ་ (trɛ̄ɛ) tax, custom's duty; va.—སྤྲོད་; —འཇལ་; —རྒྱག; —སྐྱེལ་ to pay taxes; va.—སྡུད་; —ཞིན་ to collect taxes; va.—རྒྱག; —འཁྲི་; —འགེལ་; —སྐྱལ་; —འགོད་ to establish/ levy a tax; va.—འབྲོལ་; —བྲོལ་བྱེད་ to flee to avoid paying taxes; vi.—ཐོག; —འཁེལ་; —འཁྲི་ to get/ be taxed, to carry/ bear a tax load; va.—སྐྱང་; —སྲིད་ to not pay taxes in full, to underpay/ evade taxes; va.—རྒྱུགས་ to perform a corvee labor tax ¶ཞིང་པས་ཁྲལ་ལྕི་པོ་འཇལ་དགོས་པ་རེད་ The farmers have to pay heavy taxes. ¶གཞུང་གིས་མི་སེར་ས་ནས་ཁྲལ་མང་པོ་བསྡུས་བཞག The government is collecting a lot of taxes from the peasants. ¶ད་ལོ་ཁྲལ་གསར་པ་མང་པོ་ཞིག་བཀལ་འདུག This year many new taxes were levied. ¶མི་སེར་གྱི་གཞིས་ཀར་ཉིན་ལྟར་ཁྲལ་རྒྱུགས་དགོས་ཀྱི་ཡོད་པ་རེད་ The peasants have to go to do (corvee) taxes on the estates every day. ¶མི་སེར་མང་པོ་ཞིག་ཁྲལ་རྒྱུགས་མ་ཐུབ་པར་ཡུལ་གཞན་དུ་ཁྲལ་བྲོལ་བྱ་དགོས་བྱུང་འདུག Many peasants were unable to do the corvee taxes and fled to another area to avoid the tax. ¶མི་སེར་འདི་ཚོར་ཁྲལ་ལྕི་པོ་འཁྲི་གི་ཡོད་པ་རེད་ These peasants are carrying a heavy tax (load). ¶ཚོང་པ་དེས་ཚོང་ལས་པོ་མེད་ཙང་གཞུང་གི་ཁྲལ་ཁག་ཅིག་བསྐྱང་བཞག Because that trader had bad sales (he) evaded paying a part of the taxes (he owed) to the government.

ཁྲལ་བཀལ་ (trɛ̄ɛ gɛ̄ɛ) 1. p. of ཁྲལ་འགེལ་. 2. sm. ཁྲལ་འགེལ་.

ཁྲལ་བཀལ་ (trɛ̄ɛ̄drɛɛ) see ཁྲལ་.

ཁྲལ་བཀོད་ (trɛ̄ɛ̄göö̀) p. of ཁྲལ་འགོད་.

ཁྲལ་རྐང་ (trɛ̄ɛ̄gaŋ) shung. a land measurement that was equal to one tax unit.

ཁྲལ་སྐྱུང་ (trɛ̄ɛ̄guŋ) see. ཁྲལ་.

ཁྲལ་སྐྱུང་ཁྲལ་ཆད་ (trɛ̄ɛ̄guŋ trɛ̄ɛ̄jɛɛ̀) evading and underpaying taxes; va.—འཛོག to evade and underpay taxes.

ཁྲལ་སྐྱུལ་ (trɛ̄ɛ̄güü) va. to levy a tax, to make sb. perform corvee labor.

ཁྲལ་སྐྱེལ་ (trɛ̄ɛ gyēē) paying a tax; va. ཁྲལ་སྐྱེལ་; —བྱེད་.

ཁྲལ་ཁུངས་ (trɛ̄ɛ̄guŋ) shung. the feudal lord to whom one owed taxes.

ཁྲལ་ཁུངས་རྒྱབ་བསྐྱུར་ (trɛ̄ɛ̄guŋ gyə̱bgyur) leaving/ fleeing from one's feudal lord or suzerain.

ཁྲལ་ཁོངས་ (trɛ̄ɛ̄goŋ) those who are liable to pay taxes ¶ མི་མང་པོ་ཞིག་ཁྲལ་ཁོངས་སུ་ཚུད་མེད་པ་རེད་ Many people were not included as taxpayers (e.g., were not liable to pay taxes).

ཁྲལ་ཁྲལ་ (trɛ̄ɛ̄tɛɛ) 1. disorderly. 2. the sound made by fingers tapping on sth.

ཁྲལ་ཁྲིམས་ (trɛ̄ɛ̄trim) 1. taxes and the law. 2. tax law.

ཁྲལ་ཁྲིམས་འཁུར་ཞེས་ (trɛ̄ɛ̄trim kūrsheè) abiding by the law and fulfilling taxes; va.—བྱེད་.

ཁྲལ་ཁྲིམས་མཛོད་པོ་ (trɛ̄ɛ̄drim dzɛ̱ɛ̀bo) shung. people in charge of taxes and the law.

ཁྲལ་ཁྲུལ་ (trɛ̄ɛ̄trül) 1. destroyed, scattered. 2. in the dark, at a loss.

ཁྲལ་འཁྲི་ (trɛ̄ɛ trī) sm. ཁྲལ་བཀལ.

ཁྲལ་གྱོང་ (trɛ̄ɛ̄gyoŋ) mistakenly paying a tax.

ཁྲལ་གྲོང་ (trɛ̄ɛ̄droŋ) shung. family that pays taxes.

ཁྲལ་མགོ་གསོས་གསོས་ (trɛ̄ngo sō̄ösöö) sm. ཁྲལ་མངོན་ ལྷ་བཙོས་.

ཁྲལ་འགོད་ (trɛ̄ɛ gö̱ö̀) va. to levy/ establish a tax.

ཁྲལ་རྒྱག (trɛ̄ɛ gya̱à) see ཁྲལ་.

ཁྲལ་རྒྱུག་ཁྲིམས་འཁུར་ (trɛ̄ɛ̄guù trīmgur) shung. doing corvee labor and abiding by the law.

ཁྲལ་སྒོ་ (trɛ̄ɛ̄go) customs station/ barrier, toll booth/ gate.

ཁྲལ་ངན་ (trɛ̄ɛ̄ŋɛn) oppressive tax.

ཁྲལ་ངན་བུན་ངན་ (trɛ̄ɛ̄ñɛn bü̱nŋɛn) oppressive taxes and loans.

ཁྲལ་དངུལ་ (trɛ̄ŋüü) tax money/ revenue.

ཁྲལ་མངོན་སྐལ་རལ་ (trɛ̄ɛ̄ŋön gɛ̱ɛ̱rɛɛ) not working well or diligently (i.e., as if it was a tax).

ཁྲལ་མངོན་ལྷ་བཙོས་ (trɛ̄ɛ̄ŋön lājöö̀) doing quickly/ carelessly/ in a shoddy manner; va.—བྱེད་ [Lit. do superficially as if it was a tax obligation].

ཁྲལ་ཆག (trɛ̄ɛ̄jaà) shung. tax exemption; va.—གཏོང་ to grant a tax exemption; vi. ཁྲལ་ཆག to get a tax exemption.

ཁྲལ་ཆད་ (trɛ̄ɛ̄jɛɛ̀) unpaid/ missing taxes, taxes in arrears; vi. ཁྲལ་ཆད་; —འཛོག to be in arrears for taxes.

ཁྲལ་ཆད་ཁྲལ་སྐྱུང་ (trɛ̄ɛ̄jɛɛ̀ trɛ̄ɛ̄guŋ) evading and underpaying taxes.

ཁྲལ་འཇལ་ (trɛ̄ɛ cɛ̱ɛ̱) see ཁྲལ་.

ཁྲལ་འཇལ་ཁྲིམས་འཁུར་ (tre̱e̱jɛɛ trīmgur) sm. ཁྲལ་ཁྲིམས་འཁུར་ཞེས་.

ཁྲལ་ཉིན་ (trɛ̄ɛ̄ñin) shung. a day spent doing corvee tax work.

ཁྲལ་རྟེན་ (trɛ̄ɛ̄den) shung. the land basis for paying a tax (usu. refers to the land held by serfs/ subjects of lords).

ཁྲལ་རྟེན་བཏབ་ལོ་ (trɛ̄ɛ̄den dəblo) shung. year in which the tax land was planted.

ཁྲལ་དོན་ (trɛ̄ɛ̄dön) tax matters.

ཁྲལ་དོན་ཁང་ (trɛ̄ɛ̄döngaŋ) tax office.

ཁྲལ་དོན་ལས་ཁུངས་ (trɛ̄ēdön lɛ̱ɛ̀guŋ) tax affairs office.

ཁྲལ་འདེད་ (trɛ̄ɛ de̱è) va. to pursue taxpayers to collect taxes owed.

ཁྲལ་སྡུད་ (trɛ̄ɛ dü̱ù) collecting taxes, taxation; va. ཁྲལ་སྡུད་; —བྱེད་ to collect taxes.

ཁྲལ་སྡུད་བཅའ་ཁྲིམས་ (trɛ̄ɛ̄düù jətrim) tax laws.

ཁྲལ་སྡུད་ཞིབ་སྒྲོལ་ (trɛ̄ɛ̄düù shi̱psüü) shung. tax collection regulations/ documents ¶ ཁྲལ་སྡུད་ཞིབ་སྒྲོལ་ནང་འཁོད་ལྟར་ As recorded in the tax collection regulations.

ཁྲལ་སྡུད་ལམ་ལུགས་ (trɛ̄ɛ̄düù lə̱mluù) system of taxation/ tax collection.

ཁྲལ་བརྡ་ (trɛ̄ɛ̄da) a tax notice; va.— གཏོང་.

ཁྲལ་བསྡུ་ (trɛ̄ɛ du̱) f. of ཁྲལ་སྡུད་.

ཁྲལ་བསྡུ་ཁྲིམས་གནོན་ (trɛ̄ɛ̄du trīmnön) shung. collecting taxes and practicing justice/ the law.

ཁྲལ་བསྡུས་ (trɛ̄ɛ dü̱ù) p. of ཁྲལ་སྡུད་.

ཁྲལ་འཐེན་ཞུ་ (trɛ̄ɛ̱den shu̱) shung. to withdraw from paying covee taxes.

ཁྲལ་སྣེ་ (trɛ̄ɛ̄ne) shung. different type of taxes.

ཁྲལ་སྣོན་ (trɛ̄ɛ̄nön) shung. the practice of a lord sending a serf/ subject as a servant to help another of his taxpayer serfs/ subjects; va.—བྱེད་.

ཁྲལ་པ་ (trɛ̄ɛ̄ba) taxpayer serf/ subject, name of a category of serf who held taxable land.

ཁྲལ་པོ་ (trɛ̄ɛ̄bo) see ངག་ལ་ཁྲལ་པོ་.

ཁྲལ་དཔོན་ (trɛ̄ɛ̄bön) shung. officials in charge of tax collection.

ཁྲལ་སྤྲོད་ (trɛ̄ɛ drō̄ö̀) see ཁྲལ་.

ཁྲལ་འཕར་ (trɛ̄par) increased/ additional tax, new tax; va.—སྒྲོར་ to increase a tax, to add a new tax; vi. ཁྲལ་འཕར་ to have a tax increase ¶ འདི་ལོ་དམག་འཁྲུག་བྱུང་ཙང་གཞུང་གིས་ཁྲལ་འཕར་མང་པོ་ཞིག་སྤར་འདུག This year because there was a war, the government added many new taxes. ¶ འདི་ལོ་དམག་འཁྲུག་བྱུང་ཙང་ཁྲལ་མང་པོ་འཕར་བཞག This year because there was a war, many new taxes were levied.

ཁྲལ་བུན་ (trɛ̄ɛ̄bön) taxes and debts/ loans.

ཁྲལ་བོགས་ (trɛ̄ɛ̄bɔɔ̀) taxes and lease/ rent (fee), taxes and rent; va.—སྐྱེལ་; —སྤྲོད་ to pay taxes and rent.

ཁྲལ་འབབ་ (trɛ̄ɛ̄bəp) amount of tax revenue ¶ རྒྱལ་ཡོངས་ཁྲལ་འབབ་བརྒྱ་ཆ་ཉི་ཤུ་ཙམ་དམག་ཐོག་གཏོང་དགོས་ཀྱི་ཡོད་ About 20% of the government's revenue has to be spent on the military.

ཁྲལ་འབབ་འཁྲི་སྒྲུབ་ (trɛ̄nbəb trīdrub) sm. ཁྲལ་འཇལ་.

ཁྲལ་འབབ་ཆག་ཡང་ (trɛ̄nbəb cāà) sm. ཁྲལ་ཆག.

ཁྲལ་འབྱོལ་ (trɛ̄jöl) see ཁྲལ་.

ཁྲལ་སྦེད་ (trɛ̄beè) see ཁྲལ་.

ཁྲལ་མི་ (trɛ̄ɛ̄mi) taxpayer.

ཁྲལ་དམག (trɛ̄ɛ̄maà) shung. military conscription tax, soldiers conscripted through corvee taxes.

ཁྲལ་ཚད་ (trɛ̄ɛ̄tsɛɛ̀) tax rate, level of taxes.

ཁྲལ་འཛིན་ (trɛ̄ndzin) sm. ཁྲལ་མི་.

ཁྲལ་ཞིང་ (trɛ̄́ɛ̄shiŋ) shung. field/ farm for which taxes have to be paid.

ཁྲལ་གཞལ་ (trɛ̄ɛ shɛ̱ɛ̱) f. of ཁྲལ་འཇལ་.

ཁྲལ་ཟླ་ (trɛ̄nda) shung. 1. fellow taxpayer, co-taxpayer, person who shares in fulfilling a tax. 2. people under the same lord.

ཁྲལ་ཟླ་ཁྲལ་གཅེས་ (trɛ̄nda trɛ̄ɛ̄jeè) shung. co-taxpayers taking care of the corvee tax.

ཁྲལ་ཟླ་ཁྲལ་རོགས་ (trɛ̄ɛ̄da trɛ̄ɛ̄roò) sm. ཁྲལ་ཟླ་.

ཁྲལ་ཟླ་ནང་སྦྱོར་ (trɛ̄nda na̱ŋjɔɔ) shung. finding a co-taxpayer from within the unit (estate, etc.).

ཁྲལ་ཨུ་ལག (trɛ̄ɛ wu̱laà) shung. 1. corvee labor taxes; va.—རྒྱུགས་ ¶ སྣེར་ཞིང་གི་ཐོག་དུ་རྟག་པར་ཁྲལ་ཨུ་ལག་རྒྱུགས་མཁན་དེ་ཚོ་ Those who always do corvee labor on aristocratic lords' fields. 2. taxes-in-kind and taxes-in-corvee labor.

ཁྲལ་ཨུལ་ (trɛ̄wüü) sm. ཁྲལ་ཨུ་ལག.

ཁྲལ་ཨུལ་ལམ་ལུགས་ (trɛ̄wüü lə̱mluù) the system of taxation in-kind and in-corvee labor.

ཁྲལ་གཡོག (trɛ̄yoò) servant of a taxpayer.

ཁྲལ་གཡོལ་ (trɛ̄ɛ̄yöö) 1. sm. ཁྲལ་འབྱོལ་. 2. ཁྲལ་སྐྱུང་.

ཁྲལ་གཡོལ་བ་ (trɛ̄ɛ̄yööwa) tax evader, tax dodger.

ཁྲལ་རིགས་ (trɛ̄ɛ̄riì) taxes, kinds of taxes.

ཁྲལ་རིགས་སྒྲུབ་ཁུངས་ (trɛ̄ɛ̄riì dru̱bguŋ) sources from

which taxes are collected.

ཁྲལ་རིགས་སྒྲུབ་རྟེན་ (trɛ̄ɛrii drubden) sm. ཁྲལ་རྟེན་ས་ཞིང་.

ཁྲལ་རིགས་ཆག་ཆུ་ (trɛ̄ɛrii cāgju) tax reduction; va.—གཏོང་; —གཏོང་ to give a tax reduction ¶ གཞུང་གི་ཁྲལ་རིགས་ཆག་ཆུ་གཏོང་དགོས་ The government should give tax reductions.

ཁྲལ་རིགས་འཇའ་མོ་ཆེ་ (trɛ̄ɛrii jaamoje) shung. taxes for the maintenance of postal stations.

ཁྲལ་ལི་ཁྲུལ་ལི་ (trɛ̄li trǖlli) dangling, hanging, drooping ¶ ཤིང་གི་ཡལ་ག་ཁྲལ་ལི་ཁྲུལ་ལི་བྱས་ནས་བསྡད་འདུག The branches are dangling from the tree.

ཁྲལ་ལེན་ (trɛ̄ɛlen) see ཁྲལ་.

ཁྲལ་ལོ་ཕུད་ (trɛ̄ɛlo pṳ̈ü) shung. vi. to exceed the age at which one is eligible for taxes.

ཁྲལ་སེལ་ (trɛ̄ɛsel) sm. ཁྲལ་སེལ་ལྷ་བཙོས་.

ཁྲལ་སེལ་ཅན་ (trɛ̄ɛseejɛn) sm. ཁྲལ་སེལ་.

ཁྲལ་སེལ་ལྷ་བཙོས་ (trɛ̄ɛse lājöö) doing hastily or carelessly, doing superficially, working halfheartedly, doing mediocre work; va.—བྱེད་ ¶ བཟོ་པ་ཚོར་ལྷ་ཆ་ཡག་པོ་མ་སྤྲད་ཙང་ལས་ཀར་ཁྲལ་སེལ་ལྷ་བཙོས་བྱེད་ཀྱི་ཡོད་པ་རེད་ Because the workers were not given good wages, they did their work in a mediocre way.

ཁྲལ་གསར་ (trɛ̄ɛsar) new taxes.

ཁྲལ་གསོག་སྡེབས་སྒྲིག (trɛ̄ɛsoò debdrig) shung. paying accumulated taxes all at once.

ཁྲས་བྱིའུ་འཛིན་པ་ལྟར་ (trɛ̄ɛ ciwu dzimba dār) the strong preying on the weak [Lit. like a hawk catching a bird].

ཁྲི་ (trī) 1. throne ¶ རྒྱལ་པོའི་ཁྲི་ King's throne. 2. ten thousand ¶ ཁྲི་གཉིས་ Twenty thousand.

ཁྲི་ཀང་ (trīgaŋ) leg of a throne.

ཁྲི་སྐུད་ (trīgüü) a thick blue silk thread that is used to hem the edge of the arm opening of a monk's vest.

ཁྲི་སྐོར་ (trīgɔɔ) 1. roughly/ approximately ten thousand. 2. an area/ unit which is populated by ten thousand families.

ཁྲི་ཁྲི་ (trītri) one hundred million.

ཁྲི་ཁྲི་འབུམ་འབུམ་ (trītri bumbum) innumerable, countless.

ཁྲི་སྒྲོགས་ (trīgyɔɔ) 1. sedan chair. 2. cannon.

ཁྲི་སྒྲ་དཔུང་བཙན་ (trīdra būŋdzɛn) the 26th of the early kings of Tibet.

ཁྲི་བརྒྱའི་ཆ་གཅིག (trīgyɛ cājig) one millionth.

ཁྲི་ང་ (trīŋa) a type of drum that sits on a table.

ཁྲི་ལྕོག (trījɔɔ) table put in front of the throne of a lama.

ཁྲི་ཆས་ (trījɛɛ) all parts of a throne (e.g., cushion, back support, etc.).

ཁྲི་ཆེན་ (trījen) title of a high lama.

ཁྲི་མཇལ་ (trīnjɛɛ) an audience with a lama who is not present so the audience is made to the lama's clothes that are draped on his throne; va.—ཞུ་ to make an audience before the clothes of an absent lama [Lit. meet the throne].

ཁྲི་གཉན་ (trīñɛn) sm. ཁྲི་སྙན་.

ཁྲི་གཉན་གཟུགས་བཙན་ (trīñɛn sugdzɛn) the 29th ancient king of Tibet.

ཁྲི་སྙན་ (trīñɛn) goral.

ཁྲི་སྙན་སྔ་ར་ (trīñɛn sāra) sm. ཁྲི་སྙན་.

ཁྲི་སྙན་སྔ་ལེ་ (trīñɛn sāle) sm. ཁྲི་སྙན་.

ཁྲི་སྟན་ (trīdɛn) throne and cushion.

ཁྲི་སྟེགས་ (trīteg) sm. ཁྲི་, 1.

ཁྲི་སྟོང་ (trītoŋ) tens of thousands, very many, a huge amount.

ཁྲི་སྟོན་ (trīdön) sm. ཁྲི་འདོན་.

ཁྲི་ཐུབ་ (trīdub) 1. vanquishing ten thousand enemies. 2. life span of ten thousand years.

ཁྲི་ཐོག་ཁྲི་བརྩེགས་ (trītɔɔ trīdzeg) superfluous, unnecessary, duplicating [Lit. putting one throne on top of another].

ཁྲི་ཐོག་ནས་འབེབས་ (trītɔɔnɛ beb) vi. to be made to step down from the throne ¶ གོང་མ་ཁྲི་ཐོག་ནས་འབེབས་དགོས་བྱུང་སོང་ The emperor had to step down from the throne.

ཁྲི་ཐོག་པ་ (trī thɔ̄gba) incumbent, the one currently at a job, post (usu. of a high ranking official).

ཁྲི་དར་མ་འུ་དུམ་བཙན་ (trīdarma ūdumdzɛn) name of the last in the line of Tibetan kings (Langdarma).

ཁྲི་གདན་ (trīdɛn) mattress/ cushion of a throne.

ཁྲི་གདུགས་ཉི་མ་ (trīduù ñīmə) sun.

ཁྲི་འདོན་ (trīndön) inauguration, installation; va.—ཞུ་; — གནང་; —བྱེད་ to inaugurate, to install (in a position) ¶ རྒྱལ་ཚབ་ཀྱི་ཁྲི་འདོན་སང་ཉིན་རེད་ The regent's inauguration is tomorrow.

ཁྲི་ལྡེ་གཙུག་བརྟན་ (trīde dzūgdzɛn) the 37th ancient Tibetan King.

ཁྲི་ལྡེ་ཡུམ་བརྟན་ (trīde yumdɛn) son of Langdarma's first wife.

ཁྲི་ལྡེ་སྲོང་བཙན་ (trīde sūŋdzɛn) son of king Trisrong Detsen.

ཁྲི་སྡེ་ (trīde) an administrative unit containing 10,000 households.

ཁྲི་གནས་ (trīnɛɛ) throne.

ཁྲི་པ་ (trīpə) 1. the senior among several of the same rank/ position ¶ བཀའ་བློན་ཁྲི་པ་ The senior of the Council Ministers. 2. the head of Ganden Monastery.

ཁྲི་ཕེབས་ (trīpeè) assuming the throne; va.—གནང་ to assume the throne. ¶ ༸གོང་ས་མཆོག་སྐུ་གཞོན་ནུའི་དུས་ནས་ཁྲི་ཕེབས་གནང་བ་རེད་ H.H. the Dalai Lama assumed the throne when he was young.

ཁྲི་ཕེབས་མཛད་སྒོ་ (trīpeè dzɛɛgo) enthronement ceremony.

ཁྲི་ཕྲག (trīdraà) ten thousand(s).

ཁྲི་ཕྲག་སྟོང་ཕྲག (trīdraà dōŋdraà) a huge amount, very many [Lit. ten thousands and thousands].

ཁྲི་ཕྲག་བརྟན་པར་ཤོག (trīdraà dɛ̄mbar šōò) sm. ཁྲི་ལོ་བརྟན་པར་ཤོག.

ཁྲི་འཕང་ (trīpaŋ) height of a throne.

ཁྲི་བྱང་བླ་བྲང་ (trījaŋ lābraŋ) the བླ་བྲང་ of ཁྲི་བྱང་རིན་པོ་ཆེ་.

ཁྲི་སྦྲེལ་མ་ (trī drēma) two thrones joined together.

ཁྲི་མུན་ (trīmün) prison, dungeon.

ཁྲི་མོན་ (trīmön) sm. ཁྲི་མུན་.

ཁྲི་རྨང་ (trīmaŋ) base/ foundation of a throne.

ཁྲི་སྨོན་ (trīmön) name of an aristocratic family.

ཁྲི་ཙ་དར་ (trīdzadar) hind. contractor.

ཁྲི་གཙུག་ལྡེ་བཙན་ (trīdzug dedɛn) The 41st ancient king of Tibet.

ཁྲི་བཙན་ནམ་ (trīdzug nam) the 25th inb the line of ancient kings of Tibet.

ཁྲི་བཙུན་ (trīdzün) the Nepalese wife (queen) of King Srongtsen Gambo.

ཁྲི་རྩེ་འབུམ་བཞེར་གྱི་ཁྲིམས་ (trīdze bumshergi trīm) the first law code of King Srongtsen Gambo.

ཁྲི་ཚོ་ (trītso) ten thousand ¶ ཁྲི་ཚོ་ཉི་ཤུ་ 200,000.

ཁྲི་ཟི་ (trīsi) ch. official post, billet, commision.

ཁྲི་ཟུར་ (trīsuu) 1. an ex/ former ཁྲི་པ་ ¶ བཀའ་བློན་ཁྲི་ཟུར་ The ex བཀའ་བློན་ཁྲི་པ་. 3. one ten thousandth.

ཁྲི་ཡོལ་ (trīyöö) a curtain/ covering put on a throne.

ཁྲི་རལ་ (trīrɛɛ) abbr. of ཁྲི་རལ་པ་ཅན་.

ཁྲི་རལ་པ་ཅན་ (trī rɛɛbajɛn) sm. ཁྲི་གཙུག་ལྡེ་བཙན་.

ཁྲི་རིན་པོ་ཆེ་ (trī rimboce) sm. དགའ་ལྡན་ཁྲི་པ་.

ཁྲི་ལ་བསྐོ་ (trīlə gō) va. to enthrone/ crown, to raise to the throne.

ཁྲི་ལམ་ (trīlam) road/ path for sedan chairs and carriages.

ཁྲི་ལོ་ (trīlo) 1. ten thousand years. 2. years of a reign, number of years on the throne ¶ ཆན་ལུང་ཁྲི་ལོ་ལྔ་བཅུ་ The 50th year of the reign of (the Manchu) Emperor ཆན་ལུང་.

ཁྲི་ལོ་བརྟན་པར་ཤོག (trīlo dɛ̄mbar shōò) long live ¶ འཛམ་གླིང་ཞི་བདེ་ཁྲི་ལོར་བརྟན་པར་ཤོག Long Live World Peace.

ཁྲི་ལོར་བརྟན་པར་ཤོག (trīlor dɛ̄mbar shōò) sm. ཁྲི་ལོ་

བརྟན་པར་ཤོག.

ཁྲི་ཤིང་ (trīshiŋ) sm. འཁྲི་ཤིང་.

ཁྲི་བཤམས་ (trī shām) va. to erect a throne.

ཁྲི་སྲོང་ལྡེ་བཙན་ (trīsoŋ d̲edzɛn) the 38th ancient king of Tibet.

ཁྲི་སྲོང་ལྡེའུ་བཙན་ (trīsoŋ d̲edzɛn) sm. ཁྲི་སྲོང་ལྡེ་བཙན་.

ཁྲི་གསོལ་ (trīsöö) sm. ཁྲི་འདོན་.

ཁྲིག་ཁྲིག (trīgdriì) 1. precisely, punctually; certainly, clearly, surely ¶ ཞོགས་པ་ཆུ་ཚོད་དགུ་པར་ལས་ཁུངས་ཁྲིག་ཁྲིག་འཚོགས་གི་རེད་ The office convenes/ starts/ opens punctually at nine in the morning. 2. arranged, orderly; va.—བྱེད་ to arrange, to order ¶ དཔེ་མཛོད་ཁང་གི་དེབ་ཚང་མ་ཁྲིག་ཁྲིག་བྱས་ནས་བཞག་འདུག All the library books have been arranged in an orderly fashion. 3. mediocre, so-so, questionably ¶ ས་གདན་འདིའི་རྒྱུ་ཆ་ཁྲིག་ཁྲིག་རེད་ The material of this rug is mediocre. ¶ མི་འདི་ཁྲིག་ཁྲིག་ཅིག་འདུག This person is of questionable character.

ཁྲིག་གཅིག (trīgjiì) all together ¶ སློབ་གྲྭ་བ་ཚང་མ་ཁྲིག་གཅིག་ལ་སླེབས་སོང་ All the students came together.

ཁྲིག་སྙོམས་ (trīgñom) sm. ཆ་སྙོམས་.

ཁྲིག་པ་གང་ (trīgbə ka̱ŋ) full, filled to the top/ brim ¶ འབྲས་རྫ་རས་ཁྲིག་པ་གང་བླུགས་བཞག (They) filled the bag to the brim with rice.

ཁྲིགས་ཁྲིགས་ (trīgdrig) sm. ཁྲིག་ཁྲིག.

ཁྲིགས་ཆགས་སུ་ (trīg cāgsu) in sequential order, in line, in order ¶ འཐུས་མིའི་མིང་རྣམས་ཁྲིགས་ཆགས་སུ་བཀོད་འདུག The names of the delegates were put in sequential order.

ཁྲིགས་ཏེ་ (trīgde) all, completely ¶ ལས་ཀ་ཁྲིགས་ཏེ་ཚར་སོང་ (I) finished all my work.

ཁྲིགས་སུ་ཆགས་ (trīgsu cāà) in sequence, in line, in order ¶ གཞུང་ལམ་གཡས་གཡོན་གྱི་ཤིང་སྡར་ཁྲིགས་སུ་ཆགས་པ་དང་ The main road is lined with trees on both its left and the right side.

ཁྲིགས་སེ་ (trīgsi) sm. ཁྲིགས་ཏེ་.

ཁྲིད་ (triì) p. of འཁྲིད་.

ཁྲིད་སྐྱེལ་ (triìgyee) taking or escorting and turning/ handing over; va.—བྱེད་.

ཁྲིད་ཆེན་ (triìjen) an elaborate/ detailed teaching or explanation; va.—རྒྱག; —གནང་.

ཁྲིད་མཇལ་ (triìnjɛɛ) taking a person to introduce them to someone else; va.—བྱེད་; —ཞུ་.

ཁྲིད་ཉན་ (triì ṉ̃ɛn) attending and listening to a class; va.—བྱེད་ to attend and listen to a class; va.—ཆད་ to miss a lesson in a class, to cut a class.

ཁྲིད་སྟོན་ (trīdün) leading, guiding, directing; va.—བྱེད་ ¶ གསར་བརྗེ་ལ་ཁྲིད་སྟོན་བྱེད་ཡས་ཀྱི་དགོངས་པ་ཞིག་རེད་ It is a thought for guiding the revolution.

ཁྲིད་དེབ་ (trīteb) a textbook, a book used to teach.

ཁྲིད་མདའ་ (trīntə) missile ¶ ཁྲིད་མདའ་དཔུང་ཁག Missile forces.

ཁྲིད་ཕྲུག (trīdruù) pupil, student.

ཁྲིད་བྱ་ (trīja) teaching materials.

ཁྲིད་སྦྱོང་ (trījoŋ) receiving teachings and practicing them; va.—བྱེད་.

ཁྲིད་མཚམས་འཇོག (trīndzam j̱ɔɔ̀) va. to stop teaching.

ཁྲིད་གཞི་ (trīshi) 1. mimeographed/ printed/ typed teaching materials. 2. the draft or text of a speech.

ཁྲིད་གཟུགས་ (trīsug) conductivity, conductor (in physics).

ཁྲིད་ཡིག (trīyiì)1. sm. ཁྲིད་དེབ་. 2. a lesson (for use in a class).

ཁྲིད་ཡིག་གི་ས་བཅད་ (trīyiì gi sāpjɛɛ̀) topic/ subject of a lesson.

ཁྲིད་ཡིག་ཟིན་བྲིས་ (trīyiìgi si̱ndriì) 1. notes taken in class. 2. draft of a lesson.

ཁྲིད་བཤད་ (trīshɛɛ̀) sm. འགྲེལ་བཤད་.

ཁྲིན་ཏུའུ་ (trīndu) Chengdu.

ཁྲིམ་འཛིན་ཁྲུའུ་ (trīmdzin trū) tib.ch. judicial office/ bureau.

ཁྲིམ་འཛིན་པུའུ་ (trīmdzin bū) tib.ch. Ministry of Justice.

ཁྲིམས་ (trīm) law, rule; legal verdict/ sentence; va.—གཏོང་; —གཅོད་ to make a law/ rule; to render a verdict/ sentence in a case.

ཁྲིམས་ཀྱི་ཁ་ལོ་བ་ (trīmgi kālowa) magistrate.

ཁྲིམས་ཀྱི་ཁྱབ་ཁོངས་ (trīmgi kyəpgoŋ) domain of the law.

ཁྲིམས་ཀྱི་གྲུབ་མཐའ་ (trīmgi dru̱bda) the legalist school.

ཁྲིམས་ཀྱི་འགྲོ་ལུགས་ (trīmgi dro̱lug) legal system, the way the law is practiced.

ཁྲིམས་ཀྱི་ངོ་བོ་ (trīmgi ŋo̱wo) the nature of the law.

ཁྲིམས་ཀྱི་དྲ་བ་ (trīmgi dra̱wa) sm. ཁྲིམས་རྒྱ་.

ཁྲིམས་ཀྱི་གདུགས་དཀར་ (trīmgi du̱ggar) shung. the law which is like a white umbrella ¶ གཞུང་ས་དགའ་ལྡན་ཕོ་བྲང་གི་ཁྲིམས་ཀྱི་གདུགས་དཀར་བཙན་པོ་བསིལ་ལྡན་ལྗོངས་འདིར་ཡོངས་སུ་ཁྱབ་པ་ The law of the Tibetan goverment covers all over Tibet just like a white umbrella.

ཁྲིམས་ཀྱི་སྨན་པ་ (trīmgi mɛ̄mba) forensic expert, forensic doctor.

ཁྲིམས་ཀྱི་སྨན་དཔྱད་རིག་པ་ (trīmgi mɛ̄njɛɛ̀ ri̱gbə) forensic medicine.

ཁྲིམས་ཀྱི་གཞུང་ལུགས་ (trīmgi shu̱ŋluù) theory of law.

ཁྲིམས་ཀྱི་གཞུང་དཔེ་ (trīmgi shu̱ŋbe) statute book, code of law.

ཁྲིམས་ཀྱི་རིག་པ་ (trīmgi ri̱gbə) the study of law, legal studies.

ཁྲིམས་ཀྱི་ལག་ལེན་པ་ (trīmgi la̱glɛmba) lawyer, barrister.

ཁྲིམས་ཀྱི་སྲོལ་རྒྱུན་ (trīmgi sȫögyün) sm. ཁྲིམས་རྒྱུན་.

ཁྲིམས་ཀྱིས་སྐྱོང་བའི་རྒྱལ་ཁབ་ (trīmgi gyōŋwɛ gye̱e̱gəb) a state that is controlled/ ruled/ governed by law.

ཁྲིམས་བཀུར་ (trīmkur) respecting the law, law-abiding; va.—བྱེད་ ¶ ཁྲིམས་བཀུར་དུད་ཚང་ A law-abiding household.

ཁྲིམས་བཀོད་ (trīmgöö̀) legal.

ཁྲིམས་བཀོད་ཀྱི་ཉིན་ (trīmgöö̀gi ñi̱n) set/ fixed/ established by law.

ཁྲིམས་བཀོད་ཁུངས་གསེང་ (trīmgöö̀ kūŋsan) legal holiday.

ཁྲིམས་བཀོད་ཁོངས་གདོགས་ (trīmgöö̀ kōŋdoò) legal jurisdiction.

ཁྲིམས་བཀོད་གོ་རིམ་ (trīmgöö̀ ko̱rim) legal procedures.

ཁྲིམས་བཀོད་ངལ་གསོའི་ཉིན་མོ་ (trīmgöö̀ ŋɛ̱ɛ̱söö ñi̱nmu) a day that is a legal holiday.

ཁྲིམས་བཀོད་ངོ་ཚབ་ (trīmgöö̀ ŋo̱dzəb) a legal representative.

ཁྲིམས་བཀོད་དངུལ་ལོར་ (trīmgöö̀ ŋǖülor) legal tender.

ཁྲིམས་བཀོད་གཉེན་སྒྲིག་ལོ་ཚད་ (trīmgöö̀ ñēndrig lo̱dzɛɛ̀) legal marriage age.

ཁྲིམས་བཀོད་ལྟ་སྐྱོང་པ་ (trīmgöö̀ dāgyoŋba) legal guardian.

ཁྲིམས་བཀོད་འཐུས་ཚབ་པ་ (trīmgöö̀ tǖüdzəbbə) sm. ཁྲིམས་བཀོད་ངོ་ཚབ་.

ཁྲིམས་བཀོད་དུས་བཅད་ (trīmgöö̀ tü̱üjɛɛ̀) legal time limit.

ཁྲིམས་བཀོད་དུས་ཚོད་ (trīmgöö̀ tü̱üdzöö̀) legal time.

ཁྲིམས་བཀོད་དུས་མཚམས་ (trīmgöö̀ tü̱üdzam) a time/ time span set by law.

ཁྲིམས་བཀོད་བདེན་དཔང་ (trīmgöö̀ de̱mbaŋ) legal evidence.

ཁྲིམས་བཀོད་རྣམ་བཞག (trīmgöö̀ nāmshaà) legal form.

ཁྲིམས་བཀོད་དབང་ཆ་ (trīmgöö̀ wāŋja) legal rights.

ཁྲིམས་བཀོད་མ་དངུལ་ (trīmgöö̀ ma̱ŋüü) legal capital.

ཁྲིམས་བཀོད་མི་གྲངས་ (trīmgöö̀ mi̱draŋ) quorum.

ཁྲིམས་བཀོད་ཚབ་སྒྲུབ་ (trīmgöö̀ tsābdrub) legal representative.

ཁྲིམས་བཀོད་ཚབ་མི་ (trīmgöö̀bɛ tsābmi) legal representative.

ཁྲིམས་བཀོད་ཡུན་ཚད་ (trīmgöö̀ yü̱ntsɛɛ̀) sm. ཁྲིམས་

བཀོད་དུས་མཚམས་.

ཁྲིམས་བཀོད་ལོ་ཚད་ (trīmgöö lodzɛɛ̀) legal age, lawful age.

ཁྲིམས་བཀོད་ཤུལ་འཛིན་ (trīmgöö shūndzin) inheritance law.

ཁྲིམས་ཀུན་ (trīmgün) shung. taking the law into one's own hands.

ཁྲིམས་ཀུན་ལྐོག་བཏུངས་ (trīmgün gōgduŋ) shung. taking the law into one's own hands and using it to abuse others, usurping the law and harming others.

ཁྲིམས་སྐྱོང་ (trīmgyoŋ) governing/ ruling by law; va. ཁྲིམས་སྐྱོང་; —བྱེད་ ༑ གཞུང་གསར་པ་དེས་མི་སེར་རྣམས་ལ་ཁྲིམས་སྐྱོང་བྱས་པ་རེད་ The new government ruled the citizens according to the law.

ཁྲིམས་སྐྱོང་རིས་མེད་ (trīmgyoŋ riīmeè) enforcing the law without bias.

ཁྲིམས་ཁ་ལེན་ (trīmga len) va. to exercise legal authority, to decide a legal case.

ཁྲིམས་ཁང་ (trīmgaŋ) court of law.

ཁྲིམས་ཁང་གི་ཀྲུའུ་ཞི་ཚོགས་པ་ (trīmgaŋgi trūshi tsōgba) tib.ch. court presidium, panel of judges hearing a case.

ཁྲིམས་ཁང་གི་ཡོན་ཀྲང་ (trīmgaŋgi yöndraŋ) tib.ch. president of a court.

ཁྲིམས་ཁང་མཐོ་ཤོས་ (trīmgaŋ tōshöö) highest court of law, supreme court.

ཁྲིམས་ཁོངས་མི་གྲངས་ (trīmgoŋ mitraŋ) quorum.

ཁྲིམས་ཁུར་ (trīmgur) sm. ཁྲིམས་འཁུར་.

ཁྲིམས་འཁུར་ (trīmgur) abiding by the law; va. ཁྲིམས་འཁུར་; va.—བྱེད་ to abide by the law.

ཁྲིམས་འཁུར་མི་དགོས་པའི་དབང་ཆ་ (trīmgur migüùbɛ wāŋja) 1. diplomatic immunity. 2. extraterritoriality.

ཁྲིམས་འཁྱེར་ (trīmkyer) law-abiding; va. ཁྲིམས་འཁྱེར་; va.—བྱེད་ to abide by the law.

ཁྲིམས་གྲི་ (trīmdri) sword used for executing prisoners.

ཁྲིམས་འགལ་ (trīmgɛɛ) illegal, unlawful; va.—བྱེད་ to violate the law.

ཁྲིམས་འགལ་མཁན་ (trīmgɛñen) lawbreaker, criminal.

ཁྲིམས་འགལ་གྱི་ཚོང་པ་ (trīmgɛɛgi tsōŋba) trader who violates the law.

ཁྲིམས་འགལ་འགན་འཛོལ་ (trīmgɛɛ gendzöö) violating/ breaking the law and neglecting one's duties.

ཁྲིམས་འགལ་སྒྲིག་དཀྲུག (trīmgɛɛ drigdrug) lawbreaking, not abiding by the rules/ regulations; va.—རྒྱག.

ཁྲིམས་འགལ་ཅན་ (trīmgɛjɛn) a violator of the law, a criminal.

ཁྲིམས་འགལ་གཅར་རྡུང་ (trīmgɛɛ jārduŋ) brutal torture.

ཁྲིམས་འགལ་བྱ་འགུལ་ (trīmgɛɛ cagüü) illegal activities.

ཁྲིམས་འགལ་བྱ་སྤྱོད་ (trīmgɛɛ cajöö) illegal activities.

ཁྲིམས་འགལ་བཙན་ཤེད་ (trīmgɛɛ dzɛ̄nsheè) illegal oppression/ suppression.

ཁྲིམས་འགལ་ཚབས་ཆེན་ (trīmgɛɛ tsə̄bjen) serious illegal activities.

ཁྲིམས་འགལ་འཛིན་བཟུང་ (trīmgɛɛ dzinsuŋ) illegal arrest.

ཁྲིམས་འགལ་ཞིང་བདག (trīmgɛɛ shiŋdaà) illegal landlord.

ཁྲིམས་འགལ་ལུགས་དཀྲུག (trīmgɛɛ lugdruù) sm. ཁྲིམས་འགལ་སྒྲིག་དཀྲུག.

ཁྲིམས་འགལ་ལུགས་འགལ་ (trīmgɛɛ luggɛɛ) sm. ཁྲིམས་མེད་ལུགས་མེད་.

ཁྲིམས་འགོ་ (trīmgo) legal jurisdiction.

ཁྲིམས་འགོ་ནོན་ (trīmgo nön) vi. to rule/ control by the law.

ཁྲིམས་འགོ་རང་བཙན་ (trīmgo raŋdzɛn) shung. sm. ཁྲིམས་འགོ་རང་བཙན་གྱི་དབང་ཆ་.

ཁྲིམས་འགོ་རང་བཙན་གྱི་དབང་ཆ་ (trīmgo raŋdzɛngi wāŋja) 1. right to punish or exercise legal jurisdiction over one's subjects. 2. extraterritoriality.

ཁྲིམས་རྒྱ་ (trīmgya) judicial/ legal net, the net of justice.

ཁྲིམས་རྒྱུག (trīmgyuù) 1. a staff (stick) used to mete out justice. 2. a staff symbolizing judicial authority.

ཁྲིམས་རྒྱུན་ (trīmgyün) legal customs, traditional laws.

ཁྲིམས་སྒོ་ (trīmgo) court; va.—འགྲོ་ to go/ take to court.

ཁྲིམས་སྒྱུར་ལུགས་སྒྱུར་ (trīmgyur luggyur) changing laws and customs; va.—བྱེད་.

ཁྲིམས་བསྒྲགས་ (trīm drag) va. to declare/ proclaim a law.

ཁྲིམས་ང་ (trīmŋa) an early tradition in Tibet wherein a drum is beaten when a sentence is passed for a criminal; va.—རྡུང་ to beat the drum when passing a sentence.

ཁྲིམས་ངའི་ཁང་པ་ (trīmŋɛ kāŋba) sm. ཁྲིམས་ཁང་.

ཁྲིམས་གཅོད་ (trīmjüü) sentence, verdict; legal punishment; va. ཁྲིམས་གཅོད་; —བྱེད་; —གཏོང་; va.—འཁུར་ to serve a sentence; vi.—ཐོག to get sentenced ༑ ངལ་རྩོལ་གྱི་ཁྲིམས་གཅོད་བྱས་པ་རེད་ (They) were sentenced to hard labor.

ཁྲིམས་གཅོད་རྒྱུ་མཚན་ (trīmjüü gyumdzɛn) reason for a ruling/ sentence/ decision.

ཁྲིམས་གཅོད་ཉེན་རྟོག་རུ་ཁག (trīmjüü ñendog rugaà) police team that handles criminal cases.

ཁྲིམས་གཅོད་པ་ (trīmjüüba) judge.

ཁྲིམས་གཅོད་པུའུ་ (trīmjüü bū) tib.ch. office of judge, magistrate's office.

ཁྲིམས་གཅོད་དཔེ་གཞི་ (trīmjüü bēshi) legal (judicial) precedent.

ཁྲིམས་གཅོད་དབང་ཞ་ (trīmjüü wāŋca) the right to settle/ adjudicate a dispute or crime, jurisdiction.

ཁྲིམས་གཅོད་ཡུལ་ (trīmjüü yüü) 1. sm. ཁྲིམས་ར་. 2. criminal, lawbreaker.

ཁྲིམས་གཅོད་ཡོངས་བསྒྲགས་ (trīmjüü yoŋdraà) a judicial decision known by all.

ཁྲིམས་གཅོད་ལས་མཁན་ (trīmjöö lengɛn) one who executes/ carries out the law.

ཁྲིམས་བཅའ་ (trīm jā) sm. ཁྲིམས་འཆའ་.

ཁྲིམས་བཅད་ (trīm jɛ̄ɛ̀) p. of ཁྲིམ་གཅོད་.

ཁྲིམས་ཆད་ (trīmjɛɛ̀) sm. ཁྲིམས་གཅོད་.

ཁྲིམས་ཆད་ལྕི་གཅོད་ (trīmjɛɛ̀ jījöö) heavy punishment.

ཁྲིམས་ཆད་དང་མི་མཐུན་པའི་ཉེས་རྡུང་ (trīmjɛɛ̀daŋ mitümbɛ ñeduŋ) illegal punishment/ beating/ torture.

ཁྲིམས་ཆད་ཚགས་དམ་ (trīmjɛɛ̀ tsāgdam) brand put on a criminal's face as a symbol of punishment.

ཁྲིམས་ཆད་རང་ལོག (trīmjɛɛ̀ raŋlɔɔ̀) sentencing/ punishing a person who falsely accused another ༑ མི་གཞན་དག་ལ་ནག་མེད་བྱས་པའི་འབྲས་བུར་རང་ཉིད་ལ་ཁྲིམས་ཆད་རང་ལོག་བྱུང་བ་རེད་ The result of unjustly blaming another was to get punished oneself.

ཁྲིམས་ཆས་ (trīmjɛɛ̀) instruments used to inflict legal punishments (such as whips, brands, etc.); va.—སྤྱོད་; —བཀོལ་ to inflict corporal punishiment.

ཁྲིམས་ཆས་གདུག་རྩུབ་ (trīmjɛɛ̀ dūgdzub) cruel punishment.

ཁྲིམས་ཆེན་དྲུག (trīmjɛn truù) the six codes of law (of Srongtsen Gambo)—forbidding murder, theft, lying, adultery, drinking (alcohol) and rebellion.

ཁྲིམས་ཆེན་བདུན་ (trīmjɛn dün) the seven codes of law (of Srongtsen Gambo) —forbidding murder, theft, lying, adultery, drinking (alcohol) rebellion, and digging tombs.

ཁྲིམས་འཆའ་ (trīm cā) va. to enact laws.

ཁྲིམས་འཆལ་ (trīmjɛɛ) shung. lawlessness.

ཁྲིམས་འཇགས་ (trīm jaà) vi. to have laws continue

to exist as when they were issued/ proclaimed.

ཁྲིམས་འཇལ་ (trĩm jɛɛ) va. to measure out or issue a legal judgment/ decision/ verdict/ sentence.

ཁྲིམས་གཉིས་ (trĩmñii) shung. religious and secular laws/ affairs ¶ ཁྲིམས་གཉིས་འཇུག་པའི་སྒྲིག་ཡིག Regulations concerning religious and secular law.

ཁྲིམས་གདམ་ (trĩmdam) 1. legal or court judgment/ decision/ verdict. 2. talk about legal systems/ the law.

ཁྲིམས་གདོང་ (trĩm dōŋ) sm. ཁྲིམས་གཅོད་.

ཁྲིམས་གདོང་ལུང་སྒྱུར་ (trĩmdoŋ luŋgyur) ruling and sentencing.

ཁྲིམས་བཏང་ནས་གསོད་ (trĩmdaŋnɛ sȍȍ) va. to execute as legal punishment.

ཁྲིམས་ཐག (trĩmdaà) verdict, court decision/ sentence; va.—གཅོད་ to decide or settle a court case, to issue a sentence/ verdict ¶ ཁྲིམས་ཐག་ལྗིད་པོ་ A heavy sentence.

ཁྲིམས་ཐལ་ (trĩmtɛɛ) shung. punishment/ penalty that is too severe or harsh.

ཁྲིམས་ཐུ་མོ་ཆེ་ (trĩm tūmoje) a strict law code, a heavy verdict/ sentence.

ཁྲིམས་ཐོག་མར་འགལ་བ་ (trĩm thɔ̀ɔmar gɛɛwa) a first time offender.

ཁྲིམས་ཐོགས་ (trĩm thɔ̀ɔ) sm. ཁྲིམས་འགལ་.

ཁྲིམས་ཐོགས་མཁན་ (trĩm thɔ̀ɔñɛn) sm. ཁྲིམས་འགལ་མཁན་.

ཁྲིམས་མཐུན་ (trĩmdün) legal, legitimate, lawful ¶ ཁྲིམས་མཐུན་ཁུངས་སྐྱེལ་དགོས་ It is necessary to prove it is legal.

ཁྲིམས་མཐུན་འཁུར་ཤེས་ (trĩmdün kūrsheè) shung. law-abiding.

ཁྲིམས་མཐུན་གོ་གནས་ (trĩmdün gonɛɛ̀) legal status.

ཁྲིམས་མཐུན་རྒྱུ་རྐྱེན་ཞུ་ (trĩmdün gyugyen shu) va. to present one's case in court in accordance with the rules.

ཁྲིམས་མཐུན་གཅོད་རྒྱ་ (trĩmdün jȍȍgya) legal written agreement/ verdict/ accord.

ཁྲིམས་མཐུན་འཐབ་རྩོད་ (trĩmdün tәbdzüù) legal/ lawful struggle.

ཁྲིམས་མཐུན་གདན་ཐོབ་ (trĩmdün dendob) legal seat (in assembly, congress, etc.).

ཁྲིམས་མཐུན་ཚ་འཛུགས་ (trĩmdün dzәndzuù) legal/ lawful organization.

ཁྲིམས་དང་བསྟུན་ (trĩmdәdün) in accordance with the law.

ཁྲིམས་དང་མཐུན་པ་ (trĩmdә tũmbә) sm. ཁྲིམས་མཐུན་.

ཁྲིམས་དང་ལྡན་ (trĩmdaŋdɛn) lawful, legal.

ཁྲིམས་དང་མ་མཐུན་པ་ (trĩmdaŋ mәthümbә) sm. ཁྲིམས་དང་མི་མཐུན་པ་.

ཁྲིམས་དང་མི་མཐུན་པ་ (trĩmdә mitümbә) illegal, unlawful.

ཁྲིམས་དང་མི་མཐུན་པའི་ཉེས་ཆད་ (trĩmdaŋ mitümbɛ ñeèjɛɛ̀) illegal punishment.

ཁྲིམས་དང་མི་མཐུན་པའི་ཐོབ་བྱ་ (trĩmdә mitũmbɛ tōbja) illegal gain/ profit.

ཁྲིམས་དང་མི་མཐུན་པའི་སྤྱོད་ཚུལ་ (trĩmdә mitümbɛ jōtsul) sm. ཁྲིམས་དང་མི་མཐུན་པའི་བྱ་སྤྱོ་.

ཁྲིམས་དང་མི་མཐུན་པའི་འཕྲོག་ལེན་ (trĩmdә mitümbɛ trōglen) illegal confiscation, taking things illegally.

ཁྲིམས་དང་མི་མཐུན་པའི་བྱ་སྤྱོད་ (trĩmdә mitümbɛ cajȍȍ) sm. ཁྲིམས་དང་མི་མཐུན་པའི་བྱེད་སྒོ་.

ཁྲིམས་དང་མི་མཐུན་པའི་བྱེད་སྒོ་ (trĩmdә mitümbɛ cego) illegal activities.

ཁྲིམས་དང་མི་མཐུན་པར་ཐེ་ཇུས་ (trĩmdә mitümbar tējȍȍ) illegal interference; va.—བྱེད་.

ཁྲིམས་དང་མི་མཐུན་པར་ཤུག་སྤྲོད་ (trĩmdә mitümbar shūgdrȍȍ) illegal transfer of goods (either by selling or as a gift); va.—བྱེད་.

ཁྲིམས་དམ་པོ་ (trĩm dambo) strict law.

ཁྲིམས་དུང་ (trĩmduŋ) 1. horn blown when a major sentence/ punishment is to be carried out. 2. horn blown to signal start of a court hearing.

ཁྲིམས་དེབ་ (trĩmteb) law book/ documents.

ཁྲིམས་དོན་ (trĩmdön) legal matter, legal affair/ issue.

ཁྲིམས་དོན་མཁས་པ་ (trĩmdön kɛ̃ɛba) legal expert, lawyer.

ཁྲིམས་དོན་གྲོས་གཞི་ (trĩmdön trōshi) sm. ཁྲིམས་གཞི་.

ཁྲིམས་དོན་འགྲོ་ལུགས་ (trĩmdön drolug) legal system ¶ ཁྲིམས་དོན་འགྲོ་ལུགས་ཀི་བློ་འདོན་པ་ Legal consultant/ advisor.

ཁྲིམས་དོན་སྤྱི་ཚོགས་ (trĩmdön jĩdzoò) legislative assembly.

ཁྲིམས་དོན་བློན་ཆེན་ (trĩmdön lõnjen) Minister of Justice.

ཁྲིམས་དོན་ཚན་རིག་ལག་རྩལ་ཞིབ་འཇུག་ཁང་ (trĩmdön tsɛ̃nrig lagdzɛɛ shimjugaŋ) research legal institute.

ཁྲིམས་དོན་ཡིག་རིགས་ (trĩmdön yigrig) legal document, judicial records.

ཁྲིམས་དྲག་པོ་ (trĩm tragbo) harsh/ stern/ heavy law; va.—གདོང་.

ཁྲིམས་དྲང་(པོ་) (trĩmdraŋ) just/ honest law; va.—བྱེད་; —གདོང་.

ཁྲིམས་དྲལ་ (trĩm trɛɛ) destroying the law; va.—བྱེད་.

ཁྲིམས་བདག (trĩmdaà) sm. ཁྲིམས་དཔོན་.

ཁྲིམས་བདག་ཁྲིམས་གཅེས་ (trĩmdaà trĩmjeè) shung. the judge (master of law) should treasure the law.

ཁྲིམས་བདག་རིན་པོ་ཆེ་ (trĩmdaà rimboce) shung. sm. ཁྲིམས་དཔོན་.

ཁྲིམས་འདུམ་ (trĩmdum) arbitration in a dispute/ crime; va.—བྱེད་.

ཁྲིམས་འདུམ་དབང་ཆ་ (trĩmdum wãŋja) the right to arbitration in a dispute/ crime.

ཁྲིམས་འདོམས་ (trĩmdom) exercising/ applying the law; va.—བྱེད་ ¶ རྫོང་གིས་ཁྲིམས་འདོམས་ནན་པོ་མ་བྱུང་བར་བརྟེན་ཁྲིམས་འགལ་གྱི་དོན་རྐྱེན་མང་པོ་ཐོན་འདུག Because the governor didn't apply the law strictly, many illegal incidents occurred.

ཁྲིམས་འདོམས་ཉེས་ཆད་ (trĩmdom ñeèjɛɛ̀) giving punishment, applying/ executing the law; va.—གཏོང་ ¶ ཁྲིམས་འགལ་ཉེས་ཅན་ལ་ཁྲིམས་འདོམས་ཉེས་ཆད་ནན་པོ་གཅོད་དགོས་ One has to give severe punishments to those who violate the law in order to apply the law.

ཁྲིམས་འདོམས་འབྱུག་པ་ (trĩmdom yūgbә) a stick/ staff symbolizing authority to exercise the law.

ཁྲིམས་ལྡན་ (trĩmdɛn) lawful, legal.

ཁྲིམས་སྡོམ་ (trĩm dom) va. to make a law banning sth. ¶ བོད་ནང་ཕྱི་རྒྱལ་གྱི་དངོས་ཟོག་འཚོང་མི་ཆོག་པའི་ཁྲིམས་བསྡམས་བཞག (They) banned the sale of foreign goods in Tibet.

ཁྲིམས་ནུས་ (trĩmnüü) ability to execute the law effectively ¶ ཁྲིམས་དཔོན་དེས་ཁྲིམས་ནུས་ཐོན་པ་ཞིག་བྱུང་མི་འདུག That judge was unable to exercise the law effectively.

ཁྲིམས་ནོན་(པོ་) (trĩmnön) sm. ཁྲིམས་འདོམས་.

ཁྲིམས་གནས་ (trĩmnɛɛ̀) 1. sm. ཁྲིམས་ལ་གནས་. 2. a place where cases are heard and judgments are passed, a court.

ཁྲིམས་གནོན་ (trĩmnön) sm. ཁྲིམས་འདོམས་.

ཁྲིམས་དཔོན་ (trĩmbön) judge, magistrate.

ཁྲིམས་དཔོན་གཙོ་བོ་ (trĩmbön dzōwo) Chief Justice.

ཁྲིམས་དཔོན་ལྷན་ཁང་ (trĩmbön lhɛ̃ngaŋ) the judiciary, justice department.

ཁྲིམས་དཔྱད་སྨན་པ་ (trĩmjɛɛ̀ mɛ̃mba) forensic doctor, forensic expert.

ཁྲིམས་དཔྱོད་ (trĩmjȍȍ) judging or deciding legal questions/ issues; va.—བྱེད་.

ཁྲིམས་ཕོག (trĩm pɔ̀ɔ) vi. to receive punishment/ sentence.

ཁྲིམས་ཕྱིའི་ཉེས་ཆད་ (trĩmcii ñeèjɛè) punishment that is outside the law, torture.

ཁྲིམས་ཕྱེད་འགལ་བ་ (trĩmjeè gɛɛwa) partly breaking the law.

ཁྲིམས་ཕྱེད་ཙམ་སྲུང་བ་ (trĩmjeèdzam sũŋwә) partly

observing the law.

ཁྲིམས་ཕྲན་སུམ་ཅུ་སོ་བརྒྱད་ (trīmtrɛn sūmju sōbgyɛɛ̀) the 36 legal codes and principles of King Srongtsen Gambo.

ཁྲིམས་དབང་ (trīmwaŋ) legal rights, the right/ authority to decide cases.

ཁྲིམས་འབྲེལ་ཁུར་འཁྲི་ (trīmdree kūrdri) legal responsibility.

ཁྲིམས་འབྲེལ་གྱི་དོན་དངོས་ (trīmdreegi tönŋöò) legal matter/ issue.

ཁྲིམས་འབྲེལ་བྱ་སྤྱོད་ (trīmdree cajöò) legal activity, activities connected with the legal system.

ཁྲིམས་སྐྱོར་ (trīmjɔr) bringing/ filing a lawsuit; va. ཁྲིམས་ལ་སྐྱོར་; —བྱེད་ to file/ bring a lawsuit, to take sb. to court ¶ཁོང་གིས་ཚོང་པ་དེ་ར་པ་ལམ་འདི་བརྫུས་མ་ཡིན་ན་ཁྱེད་རང་ཁྲིམས་ལ་སྐྱོར་གྱི་ཡིན་ཞེས་བཤད་འདུག He said to the trader, "If the diamond is fake, I'll take you to court."

ཁྲིམས་སྐྱོར་གྱེན་ལོག (trīmjɔr gyenlɔɔ̀) rejecting a legal appeal/ lawsuit; va.—བྱེད་.

ཁྲིམས་སྐྱོར་སྙན་ཞུ་ (trīmjɔr ñēnshu) a lawsuit, a legal petition.

ཁྲིམས་སྐྱོར་ཞུ་མཁན་ (trīmjɔr shuñɛn) sm. ཞུ་གཏུག་བྱེད་མཁན་.

ཁྲིམས་མི་ (trīmmi) legal person, juridical person.

ཁྲིམས་མེད་ (trīmmeè) lawless; va.—བྱེད་ to act lawless.

ཁྲིམས་མེད་བཙན་ཤེད་ (trīmmeè dzēnshɛɛ̀) illegally forcing/ imposing/ harassing; va.—བྱེད་.

ཁྲིམས་མེད་ལུགས་མེད་ (trīmmeè lugmeè) unrestrained by laws or customs, lawless, savage, wild, ruthless, outrageous; va.—བྱེད་ ¶ཁྲིམས་མེད་ལུགས་མེད་ཀྱི་ཁྲལ་ Outrageous taxes. [Lit. without laws and without customs].

ཁྲིམས་རྨོངས་ (trīmmoŋ) people who are ignorant of the law, legal illiterates.

ཁྲིམས་གཙང་ལུགས་ལེགས་ (trīmdzaŋ lugleg) just and orderly (society, government, etc.).

ཁྲིམས་བཙུན་ (trīmdzün) monks who have taken vows.

ཁྲིམས་རྩ་ (trīmdzə) constitution, code of law.

ཁྲིམས་རྩོད་ (trīmdzöò) arguing or trying a case in court; va.—རྒྱག.

ཁྲིམས་རྩོད་པ་ (trīmdzöòbə) lawyer, attorney.

ཁྲིམས་རྩོད་ཞིབ་འཇུག་པ་ (trīmdzöò shimjuùbə) attorney general.

ཁྲིམས་བརྩི་ (trīimdzi) abiding/ adhering to the law; va. ཁྲིམས་བརྩི་; —བྱེད་; —ཞུ་.

ཁྲིམས་འཛིན་ (trīmdzin) judicial ¶འདི་ནི་ཁྲིམས་འཛིན་གྱི་གནད་དོན་ཞིག་རེད་ This is a judicial question.

ཁྲིམས་འཛིན་ཉེན་རྟོག་པ་ (trīmdzin ñēndogba) court bailiff, judicial police.

ཁྲིམས་འཛིན་པུའུ་ (trīmdzin būwu) tib.ch. Ministry of Justice.

ཁྲིམས་འཛིན་ལས་ཁུངས་ (trīmdzin lɛɛguŋ) judicial organs/ departments/ offices.

ཁྲིམས་འཛུགས་རྒྱལ་པོ་ (trīmdzuù gyɛɛbo) constitutional monarch.

ཁྲིམས་འཛུགས་རྒྱལ་པོའི་ཏང་ (trīmdzuù gyɛɛbö dāŋ) tib.ch. the party of constitutional monarchy.

ཁྲིམས་འཛུགས་རྒྱལ་པོའི་རིང་ལུགས་ (trīmdzuù gyɛɛbö riŋluù) the system of constitutional monarchy.

ཁྲིམས་འཛུགས་རྒྱལ་པོའི་ལམ་ལུགས་ (trīmdzuù gyɛɛbö ləmluù) sm. ཁྲིམས་འཛུགས་རྒྱལ་པོའི་རིང་ལུགས་.

ཁྲིམས་འཛུགས་དམངས་གཙོའི་ཏང་ (trīmdzuù māŋdzö dāŋ) tib.ch. constitutional democratic party.

ཁྲིམས་འཛུགས་ཨུ་ཡོན་ (trīmdzuù ūyün) tib.ch. legislative committee (yuan).

ཁྲིམས་ཞབས་ (trīmshəb) 1. judge, court. 2. the law.

ཁྲིམས་ཞབས་རིན་པོ་ཆེ་ (trīmshəb rimboce) shung. sm. ཁྲིམས་ཞབས་.

ཁྲིམས་ཞིབ་ (trīmshib) investigating a case; va.—གཅོད་ to investigate a case.

ཁྲིམས་གཞི་ (trīmshi) 1. bill ¶འོས་བསྡུའི་ལོ་ཚད་ཀྱི་ཁྲིམས་གཞི་གསར་པ་བཟོ་གི་ཡོད་པ་རེད་ (They) are making a new bill concerning the voting age. 2. legal principle.

ཁྲིམས་གཞིའི་རིག་པ་ (trīmshi rigbə) legal studies, jurisprudence.

ཁྲིམས་གཞུང་ (trīmshuŋ) code of law, the law, statue book.

ཁྲིམས་བཟོ་ (trīmso) making laws, legislating; va. ཁྲིམས་བཟོ་; va.—བྱེད་ ¶ཁྲིམས་བཟོའི་གོ་རིམ་ (trīmsüü gurim) Legislative procedure.

ཁྲིམས་བཟོའི་དུས་ཚོད་ (trīmsö tüüdzüü) legislative session.

ཁྲིམས་བཟོའི་དབང་འཛིན་ (trīmsö wəŋdzin) legislative authority.

ཁྲིམས་བཟོའི་མི་གྲངས་ (trīmsö midraŋ) quorum.

ཁྲིམས་ཡིག (trīmyiì) law, legal code.

ཁྲིམས་ཡིག་ལག་དེབ་ (trīmyiì lagteb) handbook of the law.

ཁྲིམས་ཡོད་ (trīmyüù) legal, lawful.

ཁྲིམས་གཡོལ་ (trīmyüù) avoiding/ escaping punishment ¶མི་དེ་ཁྲིམས་གཡོལ་བྱས་ནས་ཕྱི་རྒྱལ་དུ་བྲིན་པ་རེད་ That person went abroad to avoid punishment.

ཁྲིམས་ར་ (trīmrə) 1. court of law. 2. prison, jail.

ཁྲིམས་རའི་ཟིན་ཐོ་ཡིག (trīmrɛ töyig) court notes.

ཁྲིམས་རིག (trīmrig) legal studies, jurisprudence.

ཁྲིམས་ལ་བཀོད་པའི་ཁོངས་གཏོགས་ (trīmlə gööbɛ kōŋdoò) legal jurisdiction.

ཁྲིམས་ལ་བཀོད་པའི་ཉི་མ་ (trīmlə gööbɛ ñimə) legal date.

ཁྲིམས་ལ་བཀོད་པའི་གོ་རིམ་ (trīmlə gööbɛ gorim) legal procedures.

ཁྲིམས་ལ་བཀོད་པའི་གཉེན་སྒྲིག་ལོ་ཚད་ (trīmlə gööbɛ ñēndrig lodzɛɛ̀) legal marriage age.

ཁྲིམས་ལ་བཀོད་པའི་ལྟ་སྐྱོང་པ་ (trīmlə gööbɛ dāgyoŋba) legal guardian.

ཁྲིམས་ལ་བཀོད་པའི་དུས་ཚད་ (trīmlə gööbɛ tüüdzɛɛ̀) legal time limit.

ཁྲིམས་ལ་བཀོད་པའི་རྣམ་བཞག (trīmlə göö bɛ nāmshaà) legal form.

ཁྲིམས་ལ་བཀོད་པའི་མི་གྲངས་ (trīmlə gööbɛ mitraŋ) quorum.

ཁྲིམས་ལ་བཀོད་པའི་ཚབ་སྒྲུབ་ (trīmlə gööbɛ tsəbdrub) legal representative.

ཁྲིམས་ལ་བཀོད་པའི་ཚབ་མི་ (trīmlə gööbɛ tsəbmi) legal representative.

ཁྲིམས་ལ་བཀོད་པའི་ལོ་ཚད་ (trīmlə gööbɛ lodzɛɛ̀) legal or lawful age.

ཁྲིམས་ལ་བཀོད་པའི་ཤུལ་འཛིན་ (trīmlə gööbɛ shūndzin) legal inheritance.

ཁྲིམས་ལ་བཀོད་པའི་ཤུལ་འཛིན་པ་ (trīmlə gööbɛ shūndzinbə) legal heir.

ཁྲིམས་ལ་གནས་ (trīmlə nɛɛ̀) va. to abide by the law ¶ཁྲིམས་ལ་མ་གནས་པའི་ལས་ཀ་བྱས་ན་ཉེས་ཆད་ཕོག་གི་རེད་ If you act in ways that do not abide by the law you will get punished.

ཁྲིམས་ལུགས་ (trīmluù) legal system, code of law.

ཁྲིམས་ལུགས་ཀྱི་འདུ་ཤེས་ (trīmluùgi tüüsheè) legal sense.

ཁྲིམས་ལུགས་ཀྱི་རྩ་དོན་ (trīmluùgi dzādön) legal issue.

ཁྲིམས་ལུགས་ཀྱི་སློབ་གསོ་ (trīmluùgi lōbso) legal education, teaching about the law.

ཁྲིམས་ལུགས་མཁས་པ་ (trīmluù kɛ̄ɛba) legal expert, lawyer.

ཁྲིམས་ལུགས་ཅན་དུ་འགྱུར་ (trīmluù jēndu gyur) vi. to legalize.

ཁྲིམས་ལུགས་གནོན་འཁུར་ (trīmluù nōngur) shung. execute the law and abide by the law.

ཁྲིམས་ལུགས་སྨན་པ་ (trīmluù mēmba) legal medical expert.

ཁྲིམས་ལུགས་སྨན་པའི་ནད་ལུགས་རིག་པ་ (trīmluù mēmbe nalug rigbə) legal medical pathology.

ཁྲིམས་ལུགས་སྨན་པའི་དུག་རྫས་རིག་པ་ (trīmluù mēmbe tugdzɛɛ̀ rigbə) legal medical toxicology.

ཁྲིམས་ལུགས་སྨན་པའི་ཚན་རིག (trīmluù mēmbe

tsēnrig) forensic science, the science of pathology.

ཁྲིམས་ལུགས་སྨན་པའི་རུས་ནད་རིག་པ་ (trīmluù mēmbe rüünɛɛ̀ rigbə) legal medical osteology.

ཁྲིམས་ལུགས་སྨན་པས་ལས་ཁང་ (trīmluù mēmbe lɛ̀ɛ̀gaŋ) legal medical expert's office.

ཁྲིམས་ལུགས་སྨན་དཔྱད་རིག་པ་ (trīmluù mēmjɛɛ̀ rigbə) forensic research studies, pathology research studies; va.—བྱེད་.

ཁྲིམས་ལུགས་སྨན་དཔྱད་རིག་པ་མཁས་པ་ (trīmluù mēmjɛɛ̀ rigbə kɛ̄ɛ̀ba) forensic pathologist, forensic expert.

ཁྲིམས་ལུགས་སྨན་པས་གཤགས་ནས་ཞིབ་བཤེར་ (trīmluù mēmbɛ shāgnɛ shibsher) autopsy; va.—བྱེད་.

ཁྲིམས་ལུགས་མཚན་ཉིད་རིག་པ་ (trīmluù tsēnñii rigbə) the study of legal philosophy.

ཁྲིམས་ལུགས་རིག་པ་ (trīmluù rigbə) science of law.

ཁྲིམས་ལུགས་རིག་པའི་པོ་ཧྲི་ (trīmluù rigbɛ bōhri) tib.ch. doctor of jurisprudence.

ཁྲིམས་ལུགས་རིག་པའི་གཞི་རྩའི་གཞུང་ལུགས་ (trīmluù rigbɛ shidzɛ shuŋluù) basic theory of law.

ཁྲིམས་ལུགས་ཨུ་ཡོན་ལྷན་ཁང་ (trīmluù ūyön lhēnkaŋ) Commission for Legal Affairs.

ཁྲིམས་ལུང་བཙན་པོའི་རྒྱ་ (trīmluŋ dzēmbö gya) shung. the strict arm of the law.

ཁྲིམས་ཤེས་ཁྲིམས་འགལ་ (trīmsheɛ̀ trīmgɛɛ) knowingly violating the law; va.—བྱེད་.

ཁྲིམས་ཤེས་ཁྲིམས་སྲུང་ (trīmsheɛ̀ trīmgɛɛ) knowing and obeying the law.

ཁྲིམས་བཤིག (trīmshii) sm. ཁྲིམས་དྲལ་.

ཁྲིམས་ས་ (trīmsə) sm. ཁྲིམས་ར་.

ཁྲིམས་ས་གོང་མ་ (trīmsa koŋma) shung. higher level court.

ཁྲིམས་ས་བར་གཅོད་ (trīmsə parjöö) va. to settle out of court improperly/ illegally; va.—བྱེད་ ། ཁྲིམས་ཁང་ནས་ཐག་གཅོད་མ་བྱས་གོང་གཞམ་རིམ་ལས་ཁུངས་ནས་ཁྲིམས་ས་བར་གཅོད་བྱས་མི་ཆོག Before a court settles a case it is not permitted for a lower office to illegally settle it.

ཁྲིམས་ས་ཚོད་ལོངས་ (trīmsə tsöölon) disregarding/ ignoring the law (by evaluating the risk of doing so as low); va.—བྱེད་.

ཁྲིམས་ས་འཚོག (trīmsə tsɔ̄ɔ̀) va. to convene a court hearing.

ཁྲིམས་སའི་འགོ་འཛིན་ (trīmsɛ gondzin) head magistrate, head of a court.

ཁྲིམས་སའི་བརྟག་དཔྱད་ (trīmsɛ tāgjɛɛ̀) court examination.

ཁྲིམས་སའི་ཐོ་ཡིག (trīmsɛ tōyig) court notes.

ཁྲིམས་སའི་རྩོད་བཤེར་ (trīmsɛ dzōsher) court debate.

ཁྲིམས་སར་སྐྱེལ་ (trīmsar gyēē) va. to take to court, to bring to justice, to file/ bring a lawsuit.

ཁྲིམས་སར་འདྲི་གཅོད་ (trīmsɛ tijöö) court hearing, court trial.

ཁྲིམས་སར་སྐྱོར་ (trīmsaa jɔ̀ɔ̀) sm. ཁྲིམས་སར་སྐྱེལ་.

ཁྲིམས་སུ་བཅའ་ (trīmsu jāā) shung. va. to make a law.

ཁྲིམས་སྲིད་ (trīmsii) 1. law and politics/ government. 2. constitutional government.

ཁྲིམས་སྲུང་ (trīmsuŋ) law-abiding, law-respecting; va. ཁྲིམས་སྲུང་; —བྱེད་ to abide by the law, to respect the law ། རྒྱལ་གཅེས་ཁྲིམས་སྲུང་གི་གྲྭ་པ་ Patriotic and law-abiding monks.

ཁྲིམས་སྲུང་བ་ (trīmsuŋwa) policeman, police.

ཁྲིམས་སྲུང་ཙམ་ (trīmsūŋdzam) partly observing the law.

ཁྲིམས་སྲོལ་ (trīmsöö) legal custom, legal system.

ཁྲིམས་སྲོལ་གྱི་གོ་རིམ་ (trīmsöögi gorim) legal procedures.

ཁྲིམས་སྲོལ་དང་སྒྲིག་ལམ་ (trīmsöö taŋ driglam) law and discipline.

ཁྲིམས་སྲོལ་ཕྱོགས་བསྡུས་ (trīmsöö cōgdüü) compilation of laws and regulations.

ཁྲིམས་སྲོལ་ལམ་ལུགས་ (trīmsöö ləmlug) sm. ཁྲིམས་སྲོལ་.

ཁྲིམས་གསལ་གུང་གསེང་ (trīmsɛɛ guŋsaŋ) legal holiday.

ཁྲིམས་གསལ་རྒྱུགས་སྤྲོད་ (trīmsɛɛ gyugdröö) an examination mandated by the law.

ཁྲིམས་གསལ་ཤུལ་འཛིན་ (trīmsuŋba) inheritance laws.

ཁྲིམས་ལྷོད་ (trīmlhöö) lenient laws.

ཁྲིའུ་ (trīwu) small wooden folding chair.

ཁྲིའུ་ཁྱོགས་ (trīwu kyɔ̄ɔ) sedan chair/ palanquin; va.—འཁྱོགས་ to carry a palanquin.

ཁྲིའུ་ཤིང་ (trīwushiŋ) small wooden folding chair.

ཁྲིར་བཞུགས་ (triishuù) reigning ། ཁྲིར་བཞུགས་རྒྱལ་པོ་ Reigning king.

ཁྲིས་ (trīi) a piece of sth.

ཁྲིས་སྐད་ (triigüù) sm. ཁྲི་སྐད་.

ཁྲུ་ (trū) cubit ། ཁྲུ་གང་ One cubit.

ཁྲུ་གང་ཁོར་ཡུག (trūgaŋ kɔ̄ɔyuù) a square cubit.

ཁྲུ་འཇལ་ (trū jɛɛ) va. to measure by cubits.

ཁྲུ་ཐིལ་ (trūūtii) ch. drawer.

ཁྲུ་དོ་ (trūdo) two cubits.

ཁྲུ་མ་ (trūma) sm. ཁྲུ་.

ཁྲུ་ཙེ་ (trūdze) ch. ruler.

ཁྲུ་ལོག (trū lɔ̀ɔ) vi. to get/ be ruined or spoiled ། ཁོ་བོད་ལ་འགྲོ་ཡས་གི་འཆར་གཞི་འདི་ཁྲུ་ལོག་བཞག His plan to go to Tibet got ruined.

ཁྲུ་ལོག་ལོག (trū lɔ̀ɔlɔ̀ɔ) rolling on one's back (for animals); va.—བྱེད་.

ཁྲུ་སློག (trūlɔ̀ɔ) 1. breaking, digging up, turning over soil (usu. before plowing); cultivating; va. ཁྲུ་སློག; —རྒྱག ། ཁྲུ་སློག་བརྒྱབས་ནས་སོན་བཏབས་པ་རེད་ (He) planted seed after turning over the soil. 2. va. to overturn a decision.

ཁྲུག་ཁྲུག (trūgdrug) dangling, hanging down; vi.—བྱེད་ ། ལུག་གི་རྐང་པ་ཆག་ནས་ཁྲུག་ཁྲུག་བྱེད་ཀྱི་འདུག The sheep broke its leg and (the leg) was dangling.

ཁྲུང་ (trūŋwa) alcoholic drinks (h.).

ཁྲུང་རྒྱན་ (trūŋgyen) a pot for serving chang or other alcoholic beverages.

ཁྲུང་ཁྲུང་ (trūŋdruŋ) crane (bird).

ཁྲུང་ཁྲུང་དཀར་སྐྱ་ (trūŋdruŋ gārgyaà) white crane.

ཁྲུང་ཁྲུང་དཀར་ཡང་གཞུག་རྩེ་ནག (trūŋdruŋ gāryaŋ shugdze nag) a long period of good service ends in disrepute [Lit. although the crane is white the tip of its tail is black].

ཁྲུང་ཁྲུང་སྐེ་ནག (trūŋdruŋ gēnaà) black-necked crane.

ཁྲུང་ཁྲུང་ཁ་སྤྲོད་ (trūŋdruŋ kādröö) two cranes facing each other (a design in Chinese and Tibetan art).

ཁྲུང་ཁྲུང་མགོ་དམར་ (trūŋdrun gomaa) red-necked crane.

ཁྲུང་ཁྲུང་བྱང་ལ་འགྲོ་བར་ཕག་པར་རྗེས་དོག་མི་འདུག (trūŋdrun caŋla drowar pāgbar jüdog minduū) sm. རྟ་པོའི་རྗེས་གདོག་གཡག་ལ་མི་འདུག.

ཁྲུང་གིས་བད་ (trūŋgi phɛɛ̀) vi. to get drunk (h.) ། ཁ་སང་ཁྲུང་གིས་བད་བཞག He got drunk yesterday.

ཁྲུང་ཆིང་ (trūŋjiŋ) Chongqing.

ཁྲུང་སྟོན་ (trūŋdön) a party at which ཆང་/ alcohol is served.

ཁྲུང་དག (trūŋda) "bottoms up;" va.—སྐྱོན་ or གནང་ (h.) ། འགོ་ཁྲིད་ནས་གསོལ་སྟོན་ཐོག་གསུང་བཤད་གནང་རྗེས་ཚང་མ་བཞིན་རག་ཁྲུང་དག་གནང་རོགས་གནང་གསུངས་སོང་ After the speech at the banquet, the boss said, "Everyone, bottoms up."

ཁྲུང་ནད་ (trūŋnɛɛ̀) h. of ཆང་ནད་.

ཁྲུང་སྣོད་ (trūŋnöö) vessel/ container for ཆང་.

ཁྲུང་ཕོར་ (trūŋpɔr) bowl for drinking ཆང་.

ཁྲུང་བན་ (trūŋbɛn) container/ vessel for ཆང་.

ཁྲུང་བན་རྟ་མགོ་མ་ (trūŋbɛn dāgoma) a large vessel for Tibetan beer which has a mouth that looks like the head of a horse (it is in the Tsulhagang and is said to have been used by Srongtsen Gambo).

ཁྲུང་མ་ (trūŋma) sm. ཁྲུང་ཞུ་མ་.

ཁྲུང་ཞུ་མ་ (trūŋshumə) woman who serves ཆང་ or alcoholic beverages at parties.

ཁྲུང་ར་བད་ (trūŋra pɛɛ̀) sm. ཁྲུང་གིས་བད་.

ཁྲུང་རིན་ (trūŋrin) h. of ཚང་རིན་.

ཁྲུང་ར་ (trūŋrə) bar, tavern.

ཁྲུང་ས་ (trūŋsə) marriage (h.); va.—སྐྱོན་ to get married ༎ཁོང་གཉིས་ཀྱི་ཁྲུང་ས་ག་དུས་རེད་ When are they getting married?

ཁྲུང་སེར་ (trūŋser) yellow crane.

ཁྲུང་ཧྲེང་དའོ་ (trūŋhreŋdao) Okinawa.

ཁྲུད་ (trǖǜ) 1. p. of འཁྲུད་ and ཁྲུ་. 2. sm. ཁྲུས་.

ཁྲུད་ཁང་ (trǖǜgaŋ) sm. ཁྲུས་ཁང་.

ཁྲུད་མ་ (trǖǜmə) washed ༎དུག་ལོག་ཁྲུད་མ་ Washed clothes.

ཁྲུད་ཤལ་དབྱུ་གུ་ (trǖshεε yūgu) a wooden stick/ club used to beat clothes while washing.

ཁྲུན་ (trǖn) 1. height, altitude. 2. length. 3. controversy, conflict, dispute.

ཁྲུན་ག་པ་ (trǖngaba) ch. propyl alcohol.

ཁྲུན་གཅོད་ (trǖn jöö) sm. ཁྲུན་ཐག་གཅོད་.

ཁྲུན་ཆིའུ་དུས་རབས་ (trǖnciu du̱rab) ch. tib. "the spring and autumn period" (in Chinese history —770-476 BC).

ཁྲུན་ཐག་གཅོད་ (trǖndaà jöö) sm. འཁྲུན་ཐག་གཅོད་.

ཁྲུན་ཐག་ཆོད་ (trǖndaà chöö) sm. འཁྲུན་ཐག་ཆོད་.

ཁྲུན་ཞང་གནོད་འབུ་ (trǖnshaŋ nōmbu) ch. tib. a foul smelling bug.

ཁྲུན་གཞི་ (trǖnshi) cause of a dispute.

ཁྲུན་རིང་ (trǖnriŋ) vertical height/ length.

ཁྲུམ་ཁྲུམ་ (trūmdrum) 1. an appetizing or mouth-watering sound; va.—བྱེད་ 2. bubbling, foaming; vi.—བྱེད་ to bubble, to foam up ༎ཆང་གི་ལྦུ་བ་ཁྲུམ་ཁྲུམ་བྱེད་ཀྱི་འདུག The Tibetan beer is foaming (at the top of the glass).

ཁྲུམས་སྟོད་ཟླ་བ་ (trūmdöö da̱wa) the 8th month in the Tibetan calendar.

ཁྲུམས་ཟླ་ (trūmda) the period between the 16th day of the 7th month and the 15th day of the 8th Tibetan month.

ཁྲུའུ་ (trūū) ch. department, office, bureau.

ཁྲུའུ་ཀྲང་ (trūdraŋ) ch. head/ director/ chief of an office or bureau.

ཁྲུའུ་ཏིའི་ (trūūdi) ch. drawer.

ཁྲུའུ་ཙི་ (trǖǜdzi) ch. silk.

ཁྲུལ་ལེ་ཁྲུལ་ལེ་ (trūle trūle) dangling.

ཁྲུས་ (trǖǜ) washing; va.—རྒྱག ༎ཞོགས་སྔར་ཁྲུས་རྒྱག་དགོས་ You should wash every morning.

ཁྲུས་ཁང་ (trǖǜgaŋ) 1. bathroom, washroom. 2. bath house ༎མི་དམངས་ཁྲུས་ཁང་ Public bathhouse.

ཁྲུས་ཆབ་ (trǖǜjəb) water that has been blessed.

ཁྲུས་ཆལ་ (trǖǜjεε) sm. ཁྲུས་རྫས་.

ཁྲུས་ཆས་ (trǖǜjεὲ) washing utensils such as soap, towel, etc.

ཁྲུས་ཆུ་ (trǖǜju) water used for washing.

ཁྲུས་དར་ (trǖǜdar) a cloth for cleaning holy statues.

ཁྲུས་བདར་ (trǖǜdar) sm. ཁྲུས་དབང་.

ཁྲུས་སྡེར་ (trǖǜder) basin (for holding baptismal water).

ཁྲུས་བུམ་ (trǖǜbum) vessel/ pitcher for religious use.

ཁྲུས་དབང་ (trǖǜwaaŋ) baptism.

ཁྲུས་རྩ་ (trǖǜdza) cogongrass.

ཁྲུས་ཙི་ (trǖǜdzi) soap.

ཁྲུས་རྫས་ (trǖǜdzεὲ) soap for washing clothes (usu. powdered).

ཁྲུས་རྫས་ཕྱེ་མ་ (trǖǜdzεὲ cēma) detergent.

ཁྲུས་རྫིང་ (trǖǜdziŋ) a bathing pool.

ཁྲུས་ཞུགས་ཚོ་ག (trǖǜshug cōga) ritual of baptism; va.—གཏོང་ to perform baptism.

ཁྲུས་གཞོང་ (trǖǜshoŋ) 1. bathtub. 2. wash basin.

ཁྲུས་རས་ (trǖǜrεὲ) washcloth, bath towel.

ཁྲུས་ལ་ཞུགས་ (trǖǜla shu̱ù) va. to bathe.

ཁྲུས་བཤལ་ (trǖǜshεε) washing; rinsing; va.—བྱེད་; —གཏོང་.

ཁྲུས་གསོལ་ (trǖǜsüü) ablution; va. ཁྲུས་གསོལ་; —བྱེད་ to do ablution.

ཁྲེ་ (trē) 1. millet. 2. sm. ཁྲེ་ཙེ་.

ཁྲེ་ཀྲང་ (trēdraŋ) ch. captain.

ཁྲེ་རྒོད་ (trēgöö) wild millet.

ཁྲེ་ཐུག (trēduù) millet porridge/ gruel.

ཁྲེ་ཏོ་ (trēdo) ch. porcelain, china.

ཁྲེ་བོ་ (trēwo) millet.

ཁྲེ་འབྲུ་ (trēndruù) millet.

ཁྲེ་ཙི་གྲུ་ཀྱུག (trēdzi tru̱gyɔɔ̀) ch.tib. a carpenter's right angle ruler.

ཁྲེ་ཙེ་ (trēdze) ch. 1. a ruler. 2. a linear measure equal to 0.32 meters (1 foot).

ཁྲེ་ཙེ་གྲུ་བཞི་ (trēdze dru̱bshi) ch.tib. 1. a right angle ruler. 2. a square ཁྲེ་ཙེ་.

ཁྲེ་ཙེ་སྒྲིལ་མ་ (trēdze dri̱ima) ch.tib. tape measure.

ཁྲེ་ཙེ་ཉ་མགོ་ཅན་ (trēdze tāgojεn) ch.tib. spreading calipers.

ཁྲེ་ཙེ་ལྟེབ་མ་ (trēdze dēbma) ch.tib. folding ruler.

ཁྲེ་གཡིས་འཁྲུལ་འཁོར་ (trēyiì trǖǖgɔɔ) ch.tib. diesel engine.

ཁྲེ་སེར་ (trēser) a type of millet.

ཁྲེགས་ཆོད་ (trēngjöö) a practice of the Dzogchen school ("cutting through").

ཁྲེང་ཀོན་ཀྲུས་ (trēngün jǖǜ) ch. municipal government, city district.

ཁྲེང་ཏུའུ་ (trēŋdu) Chengdu.

ཁྲེང་ཧྥུན་ (trēŋfun) sm. གཞི་ཁུངས་.

ཁྲེད་ཁྲེད་ (trēdre) 1. light ༎རས་ཚོས་གཞི་ནག་ཁྲེད་ཁྲེད་ཅིག་ཉོས་བཞག (He) bought a light black cloth. 2. faint, dim.

ཁྲེད་ཙེ་ (trēdze) ch. sm. ཁྲེ་ཙེ་.

ཁྲེན་ (trēn) arc. mistake, error.

ཁྲེན་པོ་ཏ་ (trēn bōda) Chen Pota.

ཁྲེན་དབྱི་ (trēnyī) Chen Yi.

ཁྲེབ་དོ་ (trēbdo) 1. useless, worthless (for things). 2. sb. who ignores the admonitions of people in authority, sb. who resists doing the required work, study or instructions from above; va.— བྱེད་ ༎འགོ་ཁྲིད་ཀྱིས་སློབ་གསོ་ག་ཚོད་བརྒྱབ་ཀྱང་ཁོས་ཁྲེབ་དོ་བྱས་ནས་ལས་ཀར་འགྲོ་གི་མི་འདུག No matter how much the leader advises him, he ignores this and doesn't go to work.

ཁྲེབ་ཚ་པོ་ (trēb tsābo) sm. ཁྲེབ་དོ་.

ཁྲེབ་འཛོང་ (trēb dzōŋ) va. to not follow the rules/ authority, to be rebellious/ obstinate ༎ཕྲུ་གུ་དེས་སློབ་གྲྭར་མ་ཕྱིན་པར་ཁྲེབ་བཙོངས་ནས་བསྡད་འདུག This student is rebellious and is sitting around not going to school.

ཁྲེམ་གཉེར་ (trēmñer) skin folds; wrinkles (usu. of fat people) ༎ཁྲེམ་གཉེར་གྱི་འཁྱིངས་པའི་མི་རྒན་རྒྱགས་པ་ A wrinkled, fat old man.

ཁྲེམ་མེ་བ་ (trēmmewa) sparkling, shinning, glittering ༎མཚན་མོ་གྲོང་ཁྱེར་གྱི་སྒྲོན་འོད་ཁྲེམ་མེ་བ་ The glittering lights of the city at night.

ཁྲེམས་ (trēm) vi. to get absorbed/ soaked into sth. (e.g. for water to soak into the soil) ༎ཚལ་ཞིང་ནང་དུ་ཆུ་ཁྲེམས་པ་རེད་ Water soaked into the (soil of the) vegetable garden.

ཁྲེལ་ (trēē) 1. modesty, shame ༎ཁྲེལ་དང་ངོ་ཚ་བྲལ་བའི་མི་ A person who is devoid of modesty and shame. 2. va. to deride/ ridicule ༎གཞན་གྱིས་ཁྲེལ་བའི་ལས་ཀ་བྱེད་མི་རུང་ One must not do (things) that others will ridicule.

ཁྲེལ་གད་ (trēēgεὲ) sm. ཁྲེལ་རྒོད་.

ཁྲེལ་གྲགས་མཉམ་འཁུར་ (trēēdraà ñəmgur) shouldering both bad and good together [Lit. shouldering derision and fame together].

ཁྲེལ་དགོད་ (trēēgöö) sm. ཁྲེལ་རྒོད་.

ཁྲེལ་དགོད་ཟུར་ཟ་ (trēēgöö su̱rsə) satire, ridicule; va.—བྱེད་ to satirize, to ridicule.

ཁྲེལ་བགད་ (trēgεὲ) sm. ཁྲེལ་རྒོད་.

ཁྲེལ་རྒོད་ (trēgöö) jeering, ridiculing, making fun of, sarcasm; va.—བྱེད་; —དགོད་ to laugh at sb. in a ridiculing way.

ཁྲེལ་ཅན་ (trēējεn) sm. ཁྲེལ་, 1.

ཁྲེལ་བལྟས་ (trēē dεὲ) va. to look at sth. sarcastically/ deridingly.

ཁྲེལ་དོགས་ (trēēdog) fear that others will make fun

of oneself; vi.—བྱེད་ ¶འབྲོག་པ་འདིས་ལྷ་སར་སྐད་ཆ་ཤོད་སྐབས་མི་གཞན་གྱིས་ཁྲེལ་དོགས་བྱས་ནས་ད་ཅང་གཟབ་གཟབ་བྱེད་ཀྱི་ཡོད་པ་རེད་ When the nomad gave a speech in Lhasa, he was afraid of being made fun of and was very careful.

ཁྲེལ་གདོང་ (trēēdoŋ) a look of embarrassment/ shame; vi.—སྟོན་ to show or manifest a look of embarrassment/ shame ¶མི་མང་པོའི་སར་ཁོང་ལ་འཕྱ་ལད་བརྒྱབ་ཙང་ཁོང་རང་ཁྲེལ་གདོང་སྟོན་བཞིན་པར་ཕྱིར་ཐོན་སོང་ Because he was ridiculed in front of many people, he left with a look of embarrassment on his face.

ཁྲེལ་འདེབས་ (trēndeb) va. to recount/ list/ accuse sb. of faults or mistakes ¶འགོ་ཁྲིད་ཀྱིས་ཁོའི་སྤྱོད་ངན་ལ་ཁྲེལ་འདེབས་པ་རེད་ The boss listed his bad behavior (to his face).

ཁྲེལ་ལྡན་ (trēndɛn) modest, decent.

ཁྲེལ་བག (trēēbag) modest, decent (of people).

ཁྲེལ་བག་གི་ལ་ཉེ་ (trēēbaggi la̱ñe) shung. modest/ decent in character.

ཁྲེལ་བོར་ (trēēbor) sm. ཁྲེལ་མེད་.

ཁྲེལ་བྲལ་ (trēēdrɛɛ) sm. ཁྲེལ་མེད་.

ཁྲེལ་མེད་ (trēēmeè) shameless, immodest, brazen, contemptible.

ཁྲེལ་མེད་ངོ་སྲུང་ (trēēmeè ŋo̱suŋ) shameless subservience, shamelessly restraining from saying sth. another would not like to hear.

ཁྲེལ་མེད་གནང་བྲལ་ (trēēmeè nāŋdrɛɛ) shameless, brazen.

ཁྲེལ་མེད་འུད་སྒྲོག (trēēmeè wu̱droò) sm. ཁྲེལ་མེད་འུད་ཤོབ་.

ཁྲེལ་མེད་འུད་ཤོབ་ (trēēmeè wu̱shob) shameless/ brazen exaggeration or boasting.

ཁྲེལ་མེད་གཡོ་ཐབས་ (trēēmeè yōdab) shameless deceit/ trickery.

ཁྲེལ་མེད་རང་བསྟོད་ (trēēmeè ra̱ŋdöö) shameless self-praise.

ཁྲེལ་མེད་ལུགས་མེད་ (trēēmeè lu̱gmeè) sm. ཁྲེལ་མེད་.

ཁྲེལ་གཞུང་ (trēēshuŋ) sm. ཁྲེལ་, 1.

ཁྲེལ་གཞུང་མེད་པ་ (trēēshuŋ me̱èba) sm. ཁྲེལ་མེད་.

ཁྲེལ་ཟེད་ (trēēsɛè) sm. ཁྲེལ་མེད་.

ཁྲེལ་ཡོད་ (trēēyöö) sm. ཁྲེལ་, 1.

ཁྲེལ་ཤེས་ (trēesheè) sm. ཁྲེལ་ཅན་.

ཁྲེས་ (trēè) 1. reed/ straw mat. 2. arc. all, entire, complete, whole.

ཁྲེས་ཁུར་ (trēègur) sm. ཁྲེས་པོ་.

ཁྲེས་ཁྲེས་སུ་ན་ (trēèdreèsu na̱) vi. to be in agonizing/ extreme pain.

ཁྲེས་པོ་ (trēèbo gya̱à) a bundle, a load; va.—རྒྱག to tie into bundles.

ཁྲོ་ (trō) 1. cast iron. 2. an inferior kind of copper. 3. large cast-iron cauldrons used in monastic kitchens.

ཁྲོ་: p. ཁྲོས་; f. ཁྲོ་; imp. ཁྲོས་ (trō) va. to get angry/ mad ¶ཁོ་དེ་རིང་ང་ར་ཁྲོས་ཤག He got angry at me today.

ཁྲོ་གོང་ (trōgoŋ) butter lamp cast from bronze.

ཁྲོ་དཀར་ (trōgar) white cast iron.

ཁྲོ་རྒྱན་ (trōgyen) cast-iron kettle.

ཁྲོ་སྐད་ (trōgɛè) angry shouting; va.—སྒྲོག to shout angrily.

ཁྲོ་ཁང་ (trōgaŋ) abode of wrathful deities (in a mandala).

ཁྲོ་ཁུལ་ (trōkul) pretending to be angry.

ཁྲོ་ཁོག (trōgɔɔ̀) cast-iron pot/ bowl for cooking.

ཁྲོ་ཁོག་ཆེན་པོ་ (trōgɔɔ̀ cēmbo) the "iron (rice) bowl" — i.e., a permanent job from which one can not be fired.

ཁྲོ་འཁོར་ (trōgɔɔ) a hat worn by officials of the tt. government together with the རྒྱ་ལུ་ costume.

ཁྲོ་འཁྲུགས་ (trō trūù) vi. to be angry/ agitated/ annoyed.

ཁྲོ་རྒྱལ་ (trōgyɛɛ) the head of wrathful deities.

ཁྲོ་ངར་ (trōŋar) ferocious anger.

ཁྲོ་ངམས་ (trōŋam) showing/ expressing/ manifesting one's anger vehemently; va.—སྟོན་ to show/ express/ manifest one's anger vehemently.

ཁྲོ་ལྕགས་ (trōjaà) cast iron.

ཁྲོ་ལྕགས་དཀར་པོ་ (trōjaà gāābo) white cast iron.

ཁྲོ་ལྕགས་ལུགས་མ་ (trōjaà lu̱gma) molded cast iron.

ཁྲོ་ཆུ་ (trōcu) 1. molten cast iron. 2. the sweat that comes when one is angry.

ཁྲོ་འཇོམས་འདོད་སྤང་ (trōnjom dö̤öbaŋ) curbing one's temper and desires, guarding against losing one's temper and repressing one's sexual passion, stopping anger and restraining lust; va.—བྱེད་.

ཁྲོ་ཉམས་ (trōñam) fierce/ angry countenance or look; va.—སྟོན་ to show or manifest a fierce/ angry look.

ཁྲོ་ཉམས་ངམ་བརྗིད་ (trōñam ŋə̱mjiì) an awesome bearing, a commanding presence.

ཁྲོ་གཉེར་ (trōñer) a wrathful expression (usu. for wrathful deities); va.— སྟོན་ to show a wrathful expression.

ཁྲོ་གཉེར་ཅན་ (trōñerjɛn) sm. ཁྲོ་གཉེར་.

ཁྲོ་གདུམ་ (trōdum) wrathful and ferocious, extremely angry ¶ཁྲོ་གདུམ་གྱི་རྣམ་འགྱུར་བསྟན་པ་རེད་ (He) showed an expression of ferocious wrath.

ཁྲོ་གདུམ་པོ་ (trō dūmbu) wrathful and ferocious.

ཁྲོ་སྟར་ (trōdar) cast-iron axe.

ཁྲོ་ཐབ་ (trōdəp) steam boiler, blast furnace ¶ཁྲོ་ཐབ་བཟོ་གྲྭ་ Boiler factory.

ཁྲོ་ཐབ་ཁང་ (trōdəbgaŋ) boiler room.

ཁྲོ་ཐབ་ཆེན་པོ་ (trōdəb cēmbo) big blast furnace.

ཁྲོ་ཐབ་བཟོ་གྲྭ་ (trōtəb so̱dra) boiler factory.

ཁྲོ་གདོང་ (trōdoŋ) angry/ vicious face ¶བཙན་རྒྱལ་མི་སེར་གླིང་ལུགས་ཀྱི་ཁྲོ་གདོང་དམར་རྗེན་དུ་འདོན་དགོས་ We have to expose the vicious face of imperialist colonialism.

ཁྲོ་མདངས་ (trōdaŋ) sm. ཁྲོ་ཉམས་.

ཁྲོ་མདུད་སྡུད་ (trōdüü dü̱ü) vi. to show a very angry countenance.

ཁྲོ་འདར་ (tō da̱r) vi. to shake/ tremble in anger.

ཁྲོ་ལྡན་ (trōndɛn) angry.

ཁྲོ་སྡང་ (trōdaŋ) anger, indignation.

ཁྲོ་ནག (trōnag) black cast iron.

ཁྲོ་སྣོད་ (trōnöö) cast-iron container/ vessel/ kettle.

ཁྲོ་བ་ (trōwaa) anger, wrath, indignation; vi.—བྱེད་; —འགྱུར་ to become angry; vi.—ཞི་ to have anger subside; va.—སྐྱུང་ to reduce/ restrain anger.

ཁྲོ་བ་ཞི་ཐབས་ (trōwa shi̱dəb) ways of cooling down anger.

ཁྲོ་བའི་འགོག་པ་ (trōwɛ gɔ̱gba) a style in Tibetan poetry.

ཁྲོ་བའི་རྒོད་ (trōwɛ gö̤ö) vi. to not pay attention because of anger, to be wild with anger.

ཁྲོ་བའི་མེ་འབར་ (trōwɛ me̱bar) burning with anger.

ཁྲོ་བོ་ (trōwo) wrathful ¶ལྷ་ཁྲོ་བོ་ A wrathful deity.

ཁྲོ་བོའི་རྡོ་རྗེ་ (trōwo do̱rje) a type of vajra.

ཁྲོ་བྲལ་ (trōdrɛɛ) without anger ¶ཁྲོ་བྲལ་སྙིང་རྗེའི་བསམ་ A thought of compassion without anger.

ཁྲོ་མིག (trōmiì) angry look/ glance; va.—བལྟ་ to give an angry look.

ཁྲོ་མོ་ (trōmo) 1. an angry female. 2. wrathful (for female gods).

ཁྲོ་དམག་རྒྱལ་ངེས་ (trōmaà gyɛɛ̱ŋeè) if one goes into battle angry one will certainly be victorious.

ཁྲོ་རྩུགས་སུ་ལྟ་ (trōdzub) sm. ཁྲོ་མིག་ལྟ་.

ཁྲོ་རྩུབ་ (trōdzub) anger; vi.—ལངས་ to be/ get angry.

ཁྲོ་ཞི་ (trō shi̱) vi. to have anger subside.

ཁྲོ་ཟངས་ (trōsan) copper caldron/ pot.

ཁྲོ་རླབས་ (trōləp) great anger/ wrath; vi.—ལངས་ to get/ be very angry.

ཁྲོ་ལ་ (trōla) Trola Pass (in E. Tibet).

ཁྲོ་ལོ་ལོ་ (trō lo̱lo) the sound made by small hand-held drums.

ཁྲོ་སེམས་ (trōsem) anger, rage, fury, angry

thoughts.

ཁྲོག (trɔ̃ɔ̀) vi. to be roasted/ broiled, to be done roasting/ broiling ། ཤ་འདི་ཁྲོག་བཞག The meat is done roasting.

ཁྲོག་ཁྲོག (trɔ̄gdrɔg) the grumbling sound made by the stomach.

ཁྲོག་ཆུང་ (trōgjuŋ) a type of herbal medicine.

ཁྲོག་ཆེན་ (trōgcen) a type of herbal medicine.

ཁྲོག་པོ་ (trōgbo) well roasted, well cooked, well-done.

ཁྲོག་སྨན་ (trōgmɛn) raw/ unprocessed traditional Tibetan medicines.

ཁྲོང་ངེ་བ་ (trōŋŋewa) va. to be standing upright/ erect ། གཟུགས་པོ་ཁྲོང་ངེ་བར་ལངས་འདུག (He) is standing erect.

ཁྲོད་ (trö̃ö̀) in, among ། མི་དམངས་ཀྱི་ཁྲོད་དུ་ Among the people.

ཁྲོན་ (trȫn) 1. a well. 2. ch. Sichuan (abbr. of སི་ཁྲོན).

ཁྲོན་སྐྱོགས་ (trȫngyɔɔ̀) a ladle for drawing water from a well.

ཁྲོན་བརྐོ་གྲུ་གཟིངས་ (trȫngo tru̱dziŋ) a well-drilling ship.

ཁྲོན་བརྐོ་རུ་ཁག (trȫngo rugaà) a well-drilling unit/ team.

ཁྲོན་ཁ་ (trȫnka) a well.

ཁྲོན་ཆུ་ (trȫnju) well water; va.—གཏོང་ to irrigate (with well water).

ཁྲོན་མཆོངས་གཞན་སྐྱོབ་ (trȫnjoŋ she̱ngyob) risking one's life to save another, to save another without regard to the risk to one's life [Lit. jump into the well to save another].

ཁྲོན་སྡིགས་ (trȫndeg) well-drilling derrick.

ཁྲོན་ཐག (trȫndaà) the rope tied to a bucket that is used to draw water from a well.

ཁྲོན་པ་ (trȫnba) well; va.—བརྐོ་; —འདུ་ va.—འབིགས་ to drill/ dig a well; va.—བཤང་ to clean/ drain a well (when it is blocked).

ཁྲོན་པ་མཐིལ་འབྲེལ་མ་ (trȫnba ti̱ldrema) an irrigation system consisting of wells connected by underground channels (used in Xinjiang).

ཁྲོན་བུ་ (trȫmbu) a small well.

ཁྲོན་བོད་ (trȫnbö̀ö) ch.tib. Sichuan-Tibet.

ཁྲོན་འབིགས་ (trȫnbiì) well-drilling; va.—བྱེད་; —བཟོ་ to drill wells.

ཁྲོན་འབིགས་བཟོ་པ་ (trȫnbiì so̱ba) well-driller.

ཁྲོན་འབིགས་རུ་ཁག (trȫnbiì rūgaà) well-drilling group/ team.

ཁྲོན་སྦལ་ (trȫnbɛɛ) well frog.

ཁྲོན་མ་ (trȫnma) 1. coarse. 2. uncouth.

ཁྲོན་དམག (trȫnmaà) ch.tib. Sichuan troops/ army.

ཁྲོན་ཚྭ་ (trȫn tsā) well salt.

ཁྲོན་འཛིན་ (trȫndzin) shung. a permit issued by the Drepung monastery to use wells during the Monlam Chemmo Prayer Festival in Lhasa.

ཁྲོན་ཟོམ་ (trȫnsom) well bucket.

ཁྲོན་ལྷུང་རྡོ་གནོན་ (trȫnlhuŋ do̱nön) kicking sb. when he is down [Lit. piling rocks on sb. who has fallen into a well].

ཁྲོམ་ (trōm) 1. market, bazaar. 2. arc. military. 3. street.

ཁྲོམ་བཀྱག (trōmgyaà) a stand/ table for goods that are displayed in the marketplace.

ཁྲོམ་སྐོར་ (trōmgɔɔ) 1. demonstrating; parading; va.—བྱེད་, to demonstrate, to parade ། བཟོ་པ་ཚོས་གཞུང་ལ་ངོ་རྒོལ་གྱི་ཁྲོམ་སྐོར་བྱས་པ་རེད་ The workers demonstrated against the government. 2. going around shopping; va.—བྱེད་ to go around shopping from place to place in a market/ bazaar.

ཁྲོམ་སྐྱོད་གྲོང་སྐོར་ (trōmgyöö tro̱ŋgɔɔ) making the rounds of streets and alleys (e.g., to shop or to demonstrate); va.—བྱེད་.

ཁྲོམ་བསྐོར་ (trōmgɔɔ) sm. ཁྲོམ་སྐོར་.

ཁྲོམ་བསྐོར་རུ་ཕྲེང་ (trōmgɔɔ ru̱dreŋ) a line of people demonstrating.

ཁྲོམ་ཁ་ (trōmga) sm. ཚོང་འདུས་.

ཁྲོམ་ཁྲོམ་ (trōmdrom) shung. a red tassel worn by horses of officials of the traditional Tibetan government indicating status.

ཁྲོམ་གོང་ (trōmgoŋ) market price.

ཁྲོམ་གྱི་རུ་སྣ་ (trōmgi ru̱na) arc. commander of an army.

ཁྲོམ་གྲགས་ (trōmdraà) sm. ཁྲོམ་བསྒྲགས་.

ཁྲོམ་གྲོལ་ (trōm drö̱ö̱) vi. to be the time at the end of the day when shops close.

ཁྲོམ་བསྒྲགས་ (trōmdraà) well-known in the bazaar, known everywhere, public knowledge; va.—བྱེད་ ། ཁོ་གཉིས་ཀྱི་གནས་ཚུལ་ཁྲོམ་བསྒྲགས་རེད་ The story of those two is known everywhere. ། ཁྲོམ་བསྒྲགས་མེད་པར་རོགས་རམ་བྱས་པ་རེད་ (They) helped without making it public. [Lit. called out in the bazaar].

ཁྲོམ་བསྒྲགས་ཀྱི་གསང་བ་ (trōmdraàgi sāŋwa) an open secret.

ཁྲོམ་བསྒྲགས་ཡི་གེ་ (trōmdraà yi̱gi) open letter, a letter/ proclamation put up (posted) on the street.

ཁྲོམ་ཆས་ (trōmjɛɛ̀) goods set out in a market/ marketplace.

ཁྲོམ་ཆེན་ (trōmjen) the main/ central market place

ཁྲོམ་གདམ་ (tromdam) sm. ལམ་གདམ་.

ཁྲོམ་གདམ་ལམ་ཆ་ (thrōmdam la̱mja) bazaar-talk, talk of the street, common rumors.

ཁྲོམ་བདབ་ (trōm dəb) arc. va. to fight a war. 2. va. to set up a camp.

ཁྲོམ་སྟེགས་ (trōmdeg) a table or stand on which merchandise is displayed.

ཁྲོམ་སྟོན་ (trōmdön) 1. exhibiting/ displaying merchandise in the market, displaying publicly, va.—བྱེད་ ། ཆོས་ལྡན་གྱི་ཞིང་སར་མིའི་མགོ་ལག་ཁྲོམ་སྟོན་བྱེད་པ་དེ་དཔེ་རེད་ཟེར་པ་རེད་ Displaying a person's head and hands (cut off) publicly in a holy place is "something else," he said. 2. exposing sth. publicly (e.g., lies, etc.); va.—བྱེད་ ། ཁོའི་བྱ་ངན་ཚང་མ་ཁྲོམ་སྟོན་བྱས་པ་རེད་ (They) publicly exposed all his bad deeds.

ཁྲོམ་སྟོན་བྱེད་མི་ (trōmdön ce̱mi) shopkeeper, person who displays/ sells goods in the market).

ཁྲོམ་སྟོན་ས་ (trōm dȫnsa) place where a market is held, a marketplace ། ཐོག་མེད་ཁྲོམ་སྟོན་ས་ An open air marketplace.

ཁྲོམ་ཐང་ (trōmdaŋ) 1. marketplace. 2. market price.

ཁྲོམ་ཐོག་ཆོད་ (trōmdaà cö̃ö̀) vi. to get or become famous/ well known ། དེ་རིང་གི་ལུས་རྩལ་འགྲན་སྡུར་ནང་བུ་མོ་དེས་ཁྲོམ་ཐོག་ཆོད་སོང་ That girl became famous in today's athletic competition.

ཁྲོམ་འདུས་ (trōmdüü) marketplace.

ཁྲོམ་འདོན་ (trōm dö̱n) va. to set up a store/ shop in the market.

ཁྲོམ་སྡུད་ (trōm düü) va. to close a store/ shop in the market.

ཁྲོམ་པ་ (trōmba) shopkeeper, vendor, peddler.

ཁྲོམ་པ་བ་ (trōmbəba) sm. ཁྲོམ་པ་.

ཁྲོམ་དཔོན་ (trōmbön) official in charge of a marketplace.

ཁྲོམ་བུ་ (trōmbu) root of the euphorbia (used in Tibetan medicines).

ཁྲོམ་དབང་ (trōmwaŋ) religious initiation given in marketplaces.

ཁྲོམ་སྦྱར་རི་མོ་ (trōmjar ri̱mo) a wall poster; va.—སྦྱར་ to stick up/ post a wall poster.

ཁྲོམ་མེ་ (trōmme) shining, glittering.

ཁྲོམ་དམངས་ཨུ་ཡོན་ལྷན་ཁང་ (trōmmaŋ ūyün lhɛ̄ngaŋ) street committee.

ཁྲོམ་ཚིག (trūmdzii) announcement, proclamation, notice; va.—སྒྲོགས་ to announce, to proclaim, to issue a public notice.

ཁྲོམ་ཚོགས་ (trōmdzɔɔ̀) sm. ཁྲོམ་ཆེན་.

ཁྲོམ་ཚོང་པ་ (trōmdzoŋbə) ཁྲོམ་པ་.

ཁྲོམ་ཚོང་བཤོལ་ (trōmdzoŋ shōō) va. to close shops as a protest or strike.

ཁྲོམ་ཚོལ་ (trōm tsōō) arc. va. to fight a war.

ཁྲོམ་འཛིན་ (trōmdzin) vendor's license.

ཁྲོམ་གཞུང་ (trōmshuŋ) main business section/ area.

ཁྲོམ་གཞུང་ཆེན་པོ་ (trōmshuŋ cēmbo) sm. ཁྲོམ་གཞུང་.

ཁྲོམ་གཞུང་ཚོགས་འདུ་ (trōmshuŋ tsōndu) a street meeting, meeting held in the marketplace.

ཁྲོམ་གཟིགས་ (trōmsiì) going shopping; va.—གནང་ to go shopping (h.).

ཁྲོམ་གཟིགས་ཁང་ (trōmsigaŋ) the name of the main marketplace in the center of Lhasa.

ཁྲོམ་ར་ (trōmra) market, marketplace; vi.—ཚོགས་ to have the market open for the day.

ཁྲོམ་ར་དོ་དམ་ཨུ་ཡོན་ལྷན་ཁང་ (trōmra to̲dam ūyön lhēngaŋ) marketplace management committee.

ཁྲོམ་རའི་དཔལ་འབྱོར་ (trōmrɛ bēnjɔɔ) market economy.

ཁྲོམ་ལམ་ (trōmlam) main business street.

ཁྲོམ་ལམ་བཞི་མདོ་ (trōmlam shi̲do) sm. ལམ་བཞི་མདོ་ཁ་.

ཁྲོམ་ལམ་གསུམ་མདོ་ (trōmlam sūmto) three-way intersection (roads).

ཁྲོམ་ས་ (trōmsa) sm. ཁྲོམ་ར་.

ཁྲོམ་སྲང་ (trōmsaŋ) an alley, a narrow street.

ཁྲོམ་གསེབ་ (trōmseb) around the market ¶ཁྲོམ་གསེབ་ལ་བཟའ་བཅའ་འཚོང་མཁན་མང་པོ་འདུག There are many sellers of food products around the market place.

ཁྲོམས་ (trōm) imp. of འཁྲིམ་.

ཁྲོལ་ (trōō) imp. of འཁྲིལ་.

ཁྲོལ་ཁྲོལ་ (trōōdröö) sm. ཁྲོ་ལོ་ལོ་.

ཁྲོལ་རྒྱག (trōō gya̲à) va. to turn the soil over a second time (when planting).

ཁྲོལ་ཆུང་ (trōōjuŋ) shung. small family.

ཁྲོལ་བུ་ (trōōbu) 1. bits and pieces; va.—ལ་གཏོང་ to break up into bits and pieces. 2. sieve, sifter, strainer.

ཁྲོལ་མ་ (trōōma) sm. ཁྲོལ་ཚགས་.

ཁྲོལ་མོ་ (trōōmo) fragile, brittle.

ཁྲོལ་ཚགས་ (trōōdzaà) sieve, sifter, strainer; va.—རྒྱག to sift, to strain, sieve.

ཁྲོལ་ཚགས་སོན་འདེམས་ (trōōdzaà sōndeb) choosing seed through sifting grains.

ཁྲོས་ (trōò) p. of ཁྲོ་.

ཁྲོས་འཁྲུག་ངམ་པར་འགྱུར་ (trōòdruù ŋāmbar gyu̲r) vi. to get extremely angry.

ཁྲོས་མིག (trōòmiì) an angry look.

ཁྲོས་ཚིག (trōòdziì) angry words; va.—བརྗོད་; —ཤོད་ to say angry words ¶ཁྲོས་ཚིག་ཤོད་རེས་བྱས་པ་རེད་ Angry words were exchanged.

མཁན་ (ñēn) (vb. + —) agentive particle conveying the one who does the verbal action ¶ཁོ་བོད་ལ་འགྲོ་མཁན་རེད་ He is going to Tibet (He is one who is going to Lhasa).

མཁན་དཀར་ (kēngar) a plant used for incense.

མཁན་སྐྱ་ (kēngya) an herbal medicine.

མཁན་མགྲོན་ཆེ་བ་ (kēndrön cēwa) shung. sm. མགྲོན་གཉེར་ཆེན་མོ་.

མཁན་མགྲོན་ལོ་གསུམ་ (kēndrön lo̲sum) shung. abbr. three monk official representatives of the tt. government stationed in Beijing (initially to teach Tibetan to the Qing Emperor's family so that they could read prayer books).

མཁན་སྐར་ (kēngar) shung. abbr. of མཁན་ཆུང་ and སྐར་དཔོན་.

མཁན་བརྒྱུད་ (kēngyüù) 1. transmission of vows taken by monks. 2. the lineage/ line of abbots in a monastery.

མཁན་ཆུང་ (kēnjuŋ) shung. title of a monk official of the 4th. rank in the Tibetan government.

མཁན་ཆུང་སེར་མགོ་ (kēnjuŋ sērgo) yellow wormwood artemisia (used in Tibetan medicine).

མཁན་ཆེ་ (kēnje) shung. sm. མཁན་ཆེན་.

མཁན་ཆེན་ (kēnjen) shung. 1. monk official of the third rank in the tt. government. 2. honorific title used for the abbots of monasteries.

མཁན་ཐོག (kēntoò) shung. the term of an abbot, the duration of an abbot's term of office ¶ང་གཉིས་གྲྭ་པ་བྱེད་དུས་མཁན་ཐོག་གཅིག་པ་རེད་ We two both became monks during the term of office of the same abbot.

མཁན་འཐུས་ (kēn tūù) shung. 1. a representative of an abbot (usu. a representative of one of the abbots of the colleges of Sera, Drepung, and Ganden monasteries). 2. abbr. of abbot and representative.

མཁན་དྲུག (kēndruù) the six heads of craftsmen in ancient Tibet, i.e., the head of blacksmiths, saddle makers, bow makers, arrow makers, armor makers and sculptors.

མཁན་དྲུང་ (kēndruŋ) shung. sm. དྲུང་ཡིག་ཆེན་མོ་.

མཁན་དྲུང་ཏཱ་བླ་མ་ (kēndruŋ dāā lāma) shung. the seniormost མཁན་དྲུང་.

མཁན་དྲུང་སྤྲེལ་པོ་ (kēndruŋ drēēbo) shung. the four main heads (together) of the ཡིག་ཚང་ office of the traditional Tibetan government.

མཁན་འདྲ་ (kēndra) yellow wormwood artemisia (used in Tibetan medicine).

མཁན་ལྡུམ་ (kēndum) sm. མཁན་པ་.

མཁན་སྡེ་ཆེ་ཆུང་ (kēnde cījuŋ) shung. abbr. of མཁན་ཆེ་ and མཁན་ཆུང་.

མཁན་ནག (kēnnag) black artemesia (used in Tibetan medicine).

མཁན་པ་ (kēmba) wormwood artemisia (used in Tibetan medicine).

མཁན་པོ་ (kēmbo) abbot of a monastery.

མཁན་པོ་ནང་མ་ཁང་ (kēmbo na̲ŋmagaŋ) shung. the top administrative office in the Panchen Lama's government.

མཁན་ཕྱག (kēnjaà) abbr. the manager (ཕྱག་མཛོད་) of an abbot.

མཁན་བུ་ (kēn bu̲) disciple of an abbot.

མཁན་རྩིས་ (kēndziì) shung. abbr. མཁན་ཆུང་ and རྩིས་དཔོན་.

མཁན་ཚབ་ (kēndzəb) shung. 1. a temporary/ acting abbot. 2. acting སྤྱི་ཁྱབ་མཁན་པོ་.

མཁན་འཛིན་ (kēndzin) holder of an abbotship, abbot; va.—གནང་.

མཁན་ཟུར་ (kēnsur) an ex-abbot.

མཁན་རབས་ (kēnrab) 1. the line of monks who served as abbots of a monastery.

མཁན་རིམ་ (kēnrim) 1. the line/ lineage of successive abbots. 2. shung. abbr. monk and lay officials of the 4th rank in the traditional Tibetan government (མཁན་ཆུང་ and རིམ་བཞི་).

མཁན་ལས་ (kēnlɛɛ̀) abbr. of མཁན་པོ་ and ལས་སྣེ་.

མཁན་ས་ (kēnsa) monastery.

མཁན་ས་པར་གཅོད་ (kēnsa pa̲rjöö) shung. a lower ranking monk exercising the authority of the abbot.

མཁན་ས་ལས་འཛིན་ (kēnsa le̲ndzin) shung. holding the post of abbot.

མཁན་སེར་ (kēnser) yellow artemisia argyi (used in Tibetan medicine).

མཁན་སློབ་ (kēnlob) a lama and his disciples.

མཁན་སློབ་ཆོས་གསུམ་ (kēnlob cōòsum) the three: Shantiraksita, Padmasambhava and Trisongdetsen.

མཁའ་ (kā) sky.

མཁའ་ཀློང་ (kāloŋ) (middle of the) sky ¶མཁའ་ཀློང་སྤྲིན་པས་ཁེངས་པ་འདུག The sky is filled with clouds.

མཁའ་སྐྱོད་ (kāgyöò) aviation, flight, air travel; va.—བྱེད་ to fly/ travel by air ¶བྱང་ངོས་ལ་ལམ་ཁ་མེད་ཙང་མཁའ་སྐྱོད་བྱས་པ་རེད་ Because there was no road to the north they flew (there).

མཁའ་སྐྱོད་ཀྱི་བྱུར་ཉེས་ (kāgyöògi cu̲rñeè) aviation/ air disaster, plane crash.

མཁའ་སྐྱོད་ཁོལ་མ་ (kāgyöò kōōma) airline

stewardess.

མཁའ་སྐྱོད་ལྡི་གནས་ (kāgyöö dēnɛɛ) airport.

མཁའ་སྐྱོད་གནམ་གཤིས་རིག་པ་ (kāgyöö nəmshii rigbə) aeronautical meteorology.

མཁའ་སྐྱོད་དམག་དཔུང་ (kāgyöö məgbuŋ) air force.

མཁའ་སྐྱོད་ཚོད་ལྟ་ (kāgyöö tsööda) test flight/ flying; va.—བྱེད་.

མཁའ་སྐྱོད་ཡོ་བྱད་ (kāgyöö yojɛɛ) flight equipment, aircraft /flying materials.

མཁའ་སྐྱོད་རུ་ཁག (kāgyöö rugaà) air team, air unit.

མཁའ་སྐྱོད་ས་ཚིགས་ (kāgyöö sədzii) airport.

མཁའ་བསྐྱོད་ (kāgyöö) sm. མཁའ་སྐྱོད་.

མཁའ་ཁོངས་ (kāgoŋ) air space ¶ ཨ་རིའི་མཁའ་ཁོངས་ལ་ In America's air space.

མཁའ་ཁྱབ་ (kāgyəb) all over ¶ མཁའ་ཁྱབ་ཀྱི་སེམས་ཅན་ཐམས་ཅད་ Sentient beings all over the universe.

མཁའ་གྲུ་ (kədru) airplane.

མཁའ་གློག (kālɔɔ) lightening; vi.—འཁྱུགས་ to flash (lightening).

མཁའ་འགྲུལ་ (kəndrüü) aviation, air travel; va.—བྱེད་ to fly/ travel by air.

མཁའ་འགྲུལ་ཀུང་སི་ (kəndrüü gūŋsi) tib.ch. airline company.

མཁའ་འགྲུལ་གྱི་ལྡི་གནས་ (kəndrüügi dēnɛɛ) airport.

མཁའ་འགྲུལ་གྱི་བྱུར་ཉེས་ (kəndrüügi curñeè) airplane disaster/ accident, plane crash.

མཁའ་འགྲུལ་ལྡི་གནས་ (kəndrüü dēnɛɛ) sm. མཁའ་འགྲུལ་གྱི་ལྡི་གནས་.

མཁའ་འགྲུལ་དང་མཚོ་འགྲུལ་གྱི་དབང་ཆ་ (kəndrüüdaŋ tsōndrüügi wāŋja) the right of (free) air and sea travel/ transportation.

མཁའ་འགྲུལ་གནམ་གཤིས་རིག་པ་ (kəndrüü nəmshii rigbə) aeronautical meteorology.

མཁའ་འགྲུལ་བ་སི་ལས་ཁུངས་ (kəndrüü bāse lɛɛguŋ) tib.eng. airline ticket office.

མཁའ་འགྲུལ་སྤྲིང་ཡིག (kəndrüü triŋyii) sm. མཁའ་འགྲུལ་འཕྲིན་ཡིག.

མཁའ་འགྲུལ་འཕྲིན་ཡིག (kəndrüü trinyii) air mail.

མཁའ་འགྲུལ་སྒྲག་གཏོང་ (kəndrüü dragdoŋ) via air mail.

མཁའ་འགྲུལ་ཡོ་བྱད་ (kəndrüü yobjɛɛ) sm. མཁའ་སྐྱོད་ཡོ་བྱད་.

མཁའ་འགྲུལ་རིག་པ་ (kəndrüü rigbə) aeronautics.

མཁའ་འགྲུལ་རུ་ཁག (kəndrüü rugaà) air team, air unit.

མཁའ་འགྲུལ་ལས་ཁུངས་མཚོན་རྟགས་ (kəndrüü lɛɛguŋ tsōndaà) insignia or symbol of an airline.

མཁའ་འགྲུལ་ས་ཚིགས་ (kəndrüü sədzig) air station.

མཁའ་འགྲུལ་སྲུང་སྐྱེལ་ (kəndrüü sūŋgyee) convoying/ escorting planes; va.—བྱེད་ to convoy/ escort planes.

མཁའ་འགྲུལ་སློབ་གྲྭ་ (kəndrüü lōbdra) aviation school/ institute.

མཁའ་འགྲོ་ (kāndro) 1. sm. མཁའ་བསྐྱོད་. 2. མཁའ་འགྲོ་མ་. 3. girl's name.

མཁའ་འགྲོ་འདུ་བའི་དུས་ཚེས་ (kāndro tuwɛ düdzöö) ceremony during the Great Prayer Festival in Lhasa when high officials go to Meru Temple to make an offering of incense (10th day of Tibetan first month).

མཁའ་འགྲོ་མ་ (kāndroma) a kind of female deity, a dakini.

མཁའ་འགྲོ་ལ་ཕུག (kāndro labuù) a Tibetan herbal medicine.

མཁའ་འགྲོ་ལག་རྩལ་ (kāndro lagdzɛɛ) skill in making/ repairing airplanes ¶ མཁའ་འགྲོ་ལག་རྩལ་པ་ Airplane mechanic.

མཁའ་རྒོལ་ (kāgöö) air attack, air raid; va.—བྱེད་.

མཁའ་རྒོལ་ཉེན་བརྡ་ (kāgöö ñenda) air raid siren/ alarm/ warning signal.

མཁའ་ཇག (kājag) air hijacker, air pirate.

མཁའ་མཉམ་ (kāñam) sm. མཁའ་ཁྱབ་.

མཁའ་མཉམ་རྒྱལ་ཞྭ་ (kāñam gyɛɛsha) the Chinese Emperor's crown.

མཁའ་སྙེག (kāñeg) tall, reaching for the sky ¶ མཁའ་སྙེག་གི་ཁང་ཆེན་ཚར་དུ་དངར་བ་ Many skyscrapers lined up to the sky.

མཁའ་ཐོག (kātɔɔ) in or concerning the air/ sky ¶ ཡི་གེ་མཁའ་ཐོག་ནས་བསྐུར་པ་རེད་ (They) sent the letter via air.

མཁའ་ཐོག་སྐུར་བ་ (kātɔɔ gürwa) sm. མཁའ་ཐོག་སྤྲིང་པ་.

མཁའ་ཐོག་སྐྱེལ་འདྲེན་ (kātɔɔ gyēndren) air transportation.

མཁའ་ཐོག་སྐྱེལ་འདྲེན་ཀུང་སི་ (kātɔɔ gyēndren gūŋsi) air transport company.

མཁའ་ཐོག་སྐྱེལ་འདྲེན་ལས་རིགས་ (kātɔɔ gyēndren lɛɛrig) air transportation affairs.

མཁའ་ཐོག་གི་ཞབས་འདེགས་ (kātɔɔgi shamdeg) serving passengers in an airline; va.—ཞུ་.

མཁའ་ཐོག་གི་ཞབས་འདེགས་པ་ (kātɔɔgi shamdegba) aircraft crew, flight crew, stewards and stewardesses.

མཁའ་ཐོག་པར་འདེབས་ (kātɔɔ bārdeb) aerial photography.

མཁའ་ཐོག་སྤྲིང་པ་ (kātɔɔ driŋbə) via airmail (as opposed to sea mail).

མཁའ་ཐོག་འཕྲིན་སྐྱེལ་ (kātɔɔ gyēē) airmail.

མཁའ་ཐོག་ཚད་འཇལ་ (kātɔɔ tsēnjɛɛ) aerial survey; va.—བྱེད་.

མཁའ་མཐོངས་ (kā tōŋ) sm. ནམ་མཁའི་མཐོངས་.

མཁའ་འཐབ་ (kādəp) battle in the air, air combat, a dog fight; va.—བྱེད་.

མཁའ་འདྲེན་ (kāndren) air transportation; va.—བྱེད་.

མཁའ་ལྡིང་ (kādiŋ) garuda.

མཁའ་སྣང་མེ་ཁྱེར་ (kānaŋ megyer) firefly.

མཁའ་སྤྲིང་ཡི་གེ་ (kādriŋ yige) airmail (as opposed to sea mail).

མཁའ་སྤྲིན་ (kādrin) clouds.

མཁའ་འཕྲིན་ (kādrin) airmail.

མཁའ་བབས་མཆོངས་གདུགས་ (kābəb chōŋduù) a parachute; va.—བྱེད་.

མཁའ་དབུགས་ (kāwūù) air.

མཁའ་དབུགས་གནོན་ཅས་བཟོ་གྲྭ་ (kāwuù nōnjɛɛ sodra) air compressor plant/ factory.

མཁའ་དབྱིངས་ (kəyin) sky ¶ མཁའ་དབྱིངས་མཐོན་པོར་ལྡིང་སྐོར་རྒྱག་པ་ནི་ As for circling high in the sky.

མཁའ་དབྱིངས་གོང་མ་ (kəyin goŋma) space ¶ མཁའ་དབྱིངས་གོང་མའི་དུས་རབས་ The space age.

མཁའ་དབྱིངས་བརྟག་ཞིབ་འཁྱུལ་འཁོར་ (kəyin dəgship trüügoo) spy/ sensor satellite.

མཁའ་དབྱིངས་གནམ་རིག (kəyin nəmrig) astronomy.

མཁའ་དབྱིངས་སྙུལ་ཞིབ་གནམ་གྲུ་ (kəyiŋ ñülshib nəmdru) high altitude spy/ reconnaissance plane.

མཁའ་དབྱིངས་རྩད་ཞིབ་ལས་ཁང་ (kəyiŋ dzɛɛship lɛɛgaŋ) space research institute.

མཁའ་དབྱིངས་མཚོན་ཆ་ (kəyin tsōnja) space weapons.

མཁའ་དབྱིངས་རླུང་རྒྱུན་ (kəyiŋ lūŋgyün) upper air flow/ current.

མཁའ་དབྱུགས་ (kəyuù) dropping/ parachuting from a plane (bombs, food, etc.); va.—བྱེད་.

མཁའ་འབབ་ (kāmbəb) parachuting.

མཁའ་འབབ་མཆོངས་གདུགས་ (kāmbəb cōŋduù) parachute, parachuting; va.—བྱེད་.

མཁའ་དམག (kāmaà) air force, air force soldier ¶ མཁའ་དམག་རྟེན་གཞི་ Air force base.

མཁའ་ཟམ་ (kāsam) pedestrian walkway over a highway.

མཁའ་ཟོན་ (kāsön) air defense, civil defense; va.—བྱེད་ to defend against air attack.

མཁའ་ཟོན་གབ་ཁུང་ (kāsön kəbguŋ) sm. མཁའ་ཟོན་གབ་ས་.

མཁའ་ཟོན་གབ་གནས་ (kāsön kəbnɛɛ) sm. མཁའ་ཟོན་གབ་ས་.

མཁའ་ཟོན་གབ་ས་ (kāsön kəbsə) air raid shelter.

མཁའ་ཟོན་ནང་སྦྱོང་ (kāsön nanjoŋ) air defense exercise/ drill; va.—བྱེད་.

མཁའ་ཟོན་འཕུར་མདེལ་ (kāsön pūndee) air defense missile.

མཁའ་ཟོན་དམག (kāsönmaà) air defense forces/

troops.

མཁའ་ཟློན་འོབས་དོང་ (kāsön wo̱bdoŋ) air defense trench; va.—འདུ་ to dig air defense trenches.

མཁའ་ཟློན་ས་འོབས་ (kāsön sāwob) air raid dugout/ trench.

མཁའ་གཡུགས་ (kā yuù) air dropping (weapons, food, etc.); va. མཁའ་གཡུགས་; —བྱེད་.

མཁའ་རླངས་ (kālaŋ) humidity.

མཁའ་རླུང་ (kəluŋ) air, atmosphere.

མཁའ་རླུང་འཁོར་སྐྱོད་ (kəluŋ kɔ̄ɔgyöö) air circulation/ current.

མཁའ་རླུང་འཁོར་མ་ (kəluŋ kɔ̄rma) swirling wind, circulatory air current.

མཁའ་རླུང་གི་རྒྱུ་བ་ (kəluŋgi gyu̱wa) air wake (air flow caused by a moving object such as a plane or car).

མཁའ་རླུང་གི་མཐུག་ཚད་ (kəluŋgi tūgdzɛɛ̀) air density.

མཁའ་རླུང་གི་གནོན་ཤུགས་ཆེ་བའི་ས་ཁུལ་ (kəluŋgi nōnshug cēwɛ səgul) high pressure area.

མཁའ་རླུང་རྒྱུ་ (kəluŋ gyu̱) vi. to flow (for air).

མཁའ་རླུང་ཉུང་བ་ (kəluŋ ñu̱ŋwə) rarefied air/ atmosphere (e.g., at high altitude).

མཁའ་རླུང་སྙོམས་སྒྲིག་ (kəluŋ ñōmdrig) sm. མཁའ་རླུང་སྙོམས་སྒྱུར་.

མཁའ་རླུང་སྙོམས་སྒྱུར་ (kəluŋ ñōmjɔɔ) adjusting air circulation or air temperature, cooling air by air conditioning; va.—བྱེད་.

མཁའ་རླུང་སྙོམས་སྒྱུར་འཁྲུལ་ཆས་ (kəluŋ ñōmjɔɔ trǖüjɛɛ̀) air conditioner.

མཁའ་རླུང་གནོན་བཙིར་ (kəluŋ nǖndzii) compressed air.

མཁའ་རླུང་འབག་བཙོག་ (kəluŋ ba̱gdzɔɔ̀) air pollution.

མཁའ་རླུང་གཙང་མ་ (kəluŋ dzāŋma) fresh air, clean air.

མཁའ་རླུང་བཙིར་གནོན་ (kəluŋ dzīrnün) sm. མཁའ་རླུང་གནོན་བཙིར་.

མཁའ་རླུང་བཙོག་འགྱུར་ (kəluŋ dzōggyur) air pollution.

མཁའ་རླུང་སྦྲབ་པོ་ (kəluŋ drābu) sm. མཁའ་རླུང་ཉུང་བ་.

མཁའ་རླུང་གསར་པ་ (kəluŋ sāāba) fresh air, clean air.

མཁའ་ལམ་ (kālam) 1. air route ། ལྷ་ས་ནས་ལྡི་ལི་བར་མཁའ་ལམ་གསར་པ་བཙུགས་པ་རེད་ (They) opened a new air route between Lhasa and New Delhi. 2. air mail (that is written on envelopes).

མཁའ་ལམ་སྐྱེལ་འདྲེན་ (kālam kēndren) air transportation; va.—བྱེད་.

མཁའ་ལམ་འཁྲིད་ (kālam triì) va. to navigate a plane.

མཁའ་ལམ་འཁྲིད་མཁན་ (kālam triìñɛn) navigator (on planes).

མཁའ་ལམ་གྱི་སྣེ་ཁྲིད་ (kālamgi nədriì) navigation; va.—བྱེད་ to navigate.

མཁའ་ལམ་གྱི་སྣེ་ཁྲིད་པ་ (kālamgi nətribə) navigator.

མཁའ་ལམ་གྱི་སྦྲགས་འཛིན་ (kālamgi tra̱gdzin) air mail stamp.

མཁའ་ལམ་འགྲིམ་འགྲུལ་ (kālam dri̱mdrül) air travel, air traffic.

མཁའ་ལམ་གཏུ་ (kəlam jū) va. to steer a plane.

མཁའ་ལམ་ཚད་བརྟག་རུ་ཁག (kəlam tsɛ̄ɛ̀daà ru̱gaà) aerial surveying team.

མཁའ་བཤེར་གློག་སྒྲོན་ (kāshee lɔ̄gdrön) searchlight (in sky).

མཁའ་སྲུང་ (kəsuŋ) sm. མཁའ་ཟློན་.

མཁའ་གསལ་གློག་བཤུ་ (kāsɛɛ lɔ̄gshu) sm. མཁའ་བཤེར་གློག་སྒྲོན་.

མཁར་ (kār) 1. castle, fort. 2. in the sky (མཁའ་ + dat.-loc.).

མཁར་ཁང་ (kārgaŋ) sm. མཁར་.

མཁར་ཁལ་ (kārgɛɛ) shung. abbr. of མཁར་རུའི་ཁལ་.

མཁར་གོང་ (kārgoŋ) a Tibetan medicine made from minerals.

མཁར་གྱང་ (kārgyaŋ) wall around a fort/ castle.

མཁར་གྲོང་ (kārdroŋ) 1. a walled city. 2. urban and rural.

མཁར་རྒྱ་ (kārgya) a traditional weighing unit (equal to about 4 kilograms). 2. a weighing instrument.

མཁར་སྒོ་ (kārgo) gate in a wall around a fortress or walled city.

མཁར་སྒོའི་ལྕོག་ཁང་ (kārgö jɔ̄ggaŋ) defense tower over a gate in a fort or city's wall.

མཁར་སྒོའི་ཟུར་ལྕོག (kārgö su̱rɔg) the watch tower on either side of a fort or city's gate.

མཁར་སྒོར་མེ་སྐྱོན་ཤོར་ནས་ གནོད་ཚེ་ཉ་ལ་འཁྱེལ་ (kārgɔɔ me̱gyön shɔ̄ɔnɛ nɔ̄ɔtse ña̱la kēē) innocent bystanders in a disturbance getting harmed [Lit. when the gate of the fort wall catches fire, it gets carried to the fish (in the moat)].

མཁར་དངོས་ (kārŋöö) home and belongings ། མཁར་དངོས་གཞུང་བཞེས་གཏོང་བ་ To confiscate one's belongings and house.

མཁར་སྔོན་པོ་ (kār ŋōmbo) Huhhot (capital of Inner Mongolia).

མཁར་རྗེ་ (kārje) 1. sm. རྫོང་དཔོན་. 2. merit, good deeds.

མཁར་ཉག (kārñaà) a unit of weight which is 1/20 of a མཁར་རྒྱ་.

མཁར་དོང་ (kārdoŋ) a walled fort/ castle/ city with a moat.

མཁར་འདེགས་ (kārdeg) sm. མཁར་རྒྱ་.

མཁར་འདབས་ (kārdəb) near the house ། མཁར་འདབས་སུ་མི་ཞིག་སླེབས་འདུག A man has come near the house.

མཁར་རྡོ་ (kārdo) sulfide stone.

མཁར་རྡོ་བླ་མ་ (kārdo lāma) an incarnate lama who was a close advisor to Reting Rimpoche in the 1930s and 40s.

མཁར་སྦིའུ་ (kārbewu) watchtower.

མཁར་བུ་ (kārbu) 1. a small room. 2. a small fort.

མཁར་བྲེ་ (kārdre) a measuring container that is 1/20th of a མཁར་རུ་.

མཁར་དབང་ (kārwaŋ) wealth.

མཁར་དབང་སྒེར་འཛིན་ (kārwaŋ ge̱ndzin) private ownership of property/ wealth.

མཁར་འབོ་ (kārbo) sm. མཁར་རུ་.

མཁར་དམར་པོ་ (kār mārbo) the Red Fort in Delhi.

མཁར་བཙན་ (kārdzɛn) fortress, fort.

མཁར་འཛིན་བདག་མོ་ (kārdzin da̱àmo) sm. ཁྱིམ་བདག་མོ་.

མཁར་རྫོང་ (kārdzoŋ) fortress, fort, citadel.

མཁར་ཞོལ་ (kār shö̱ö̱) the area below or at the foot of a fort or castle.

མཁར་ཟུག (kārsug) sm. མཁའ་སྙེག.

མཁར་ཟུག་ཐོག་ཁང་ (kārsug tɔ̄ɔ̀gaŋ) skyscraper.

མཁར་རུ་ (kəru) abbr. of བསྟན་འཛིན་མཁར་རུ་ (a standard government volume measure that equaled about 27-33 lbs. for barley).

མཁར་རུའི་ཁལ་ (kəru) sm. མཁར་རུ་.

མཁར་རོ་ (kārro) sm. གྲང་རོ་.

མཁར་ལན་ (kārlɛn) arc. repairs, renovations.

མཁར་ལས་ (kārlɛɛ̀) fort/ building construction; va.—བྱེད་.

མཁར་ཤུལ་ལ་རྩ་བསྐྱེས་པར་བྱེད་ (kārshüüla dzāgyēbar ce̱è) to destroy completely without a trace.

མཁར་སྲུང་ (kārsuŋ) a fort/ fortress used for defense or protection; va.—བྱེད་ to defend/ protect using a fort or fortress.

མཁར་སྲུང་ཆུ་འོབས་ (kārsuŋ cūwob) a defensive moat (around a castle/ fort).

མཁར་སྲུང་དམག་ཁུལ་ (kārsuŋ məggüü) a military garrison area ། པེ་ཅིང་མཁར་སྲུང་དམག་ཁུལ་ the Beijing Garrison Command area.

མཁར་གསིལ་ (kārsil) a spear-shaped walking stick carried by དགེ་སློང་ monks.

མཁར་ལྷན་ (kārlhɛn) repairs, renovations to a fort/ castle; va.—བྱེད་.

མཁལ་ (kɛ̄ɛ) abbr. of མཁལ་མ་.

མཁལ་གྲང་ (kēēdraŋ) a kidney disease in Tibetan

medicine characterized by pain in the neck and the lower part of the body.

མཁལ་མགོ་ཡུ་ (kɛ̄ɛ̄ goyu) beetle nut.

མཁལ་འགྲམས་ (kɛ̄ɛ̄dram) one of the eight kidney diseases in Tibetan medicine.

མཁལ་གཅོང་ (kɛ̄ɛ̄joŋ) chronic kidney disease.

མཁལ་མདོག (kɛ̄ndɔg) kidney color.

མཁལ་ནད་ (kɛ̄ɛ̄nɛɛ̀) kidney disease.

མཁལ་ནད་བརྒྱད་ (kɛ̄ɛ̄nɛɛ̀ gyɛɛ̀) the eight types of kidney disease in Tibetan medicine.

མཁལ་ནད་སྨན་བཅོས་ཁང་ (kɛ̄ɛ̄nɛɛ̀ mɛ̄njögaŋ) kidney disease clinic, kidney dialysis center.

མཁལ་ནུས་ (kɛ̄ɛ̄nüü) kidney function, the power of the kidney.

མཁལ་སྣོད་ (kɛ̄ɛ̄nöö) renal pelvis.

མཁལ་ཕོར་ (kɛ̄ɛ̄bor) sm. མཁལ་སྣོད་.

མཁལ་མ་ (kɛ̄ɛ̄ma) kidney.

མཁལ་མ་ཞོ་ཤ་ (kɛ̄ɛ̄ma shosha) a type of bean used in Tibetan medicine for treating kidney disease.

མཁལ་མའི་རྡེའུ་སྐྲན་ (kɛ̄ɛ̄mɛ diudrɛn) kidney stone.

མཁལ་མའི་ནད་ (kɛ̄ɛ̄mɛ nɛɛ̀) sm. མཁལ་ནད་.

མཁལ་མའི་ནུས་པ་ (kɛ̄ɛ̄mɛ nüübə) sm. མཁལ་ནུས་.

མཁལ་རྩ་ (kɛ̄ɛ̄dza) kidney veins.

མཁལ་ཚ་ (kɛ̄ɛ̄tsa) nephritis.

མཁལ་ཚད་ (kɛ̄ɛ̄tsɛɛ̀) urethritis, kidney malady.

མཁལ་ཚིལ་ (kɛ̄ɛ̄tsii) kidney fat.

མཁལ་ཞོ་དཀར་པོ་ (kɛ̄ɛ̄sho gārbo) white hyacinth bean.

མཁལ་རིལ་ (kɛ̄ɛ̄rii) sm. མཁལ་མ་.

མཁས་ (kɛ̀ɛ̀) abbr. of མཁས་པོ་.

མཁས་ཁུར་འཛིན་ (kɛ̀ɛ̀gur dzin) va. to pose/ act as if one is a scholar or expert.

མཁས་མཁས་འཇིགས་འཇིགས་ (kɛ̀ɛ̀gɛɛ̀ jigjig) sm. མཁས་ཁུར་འཛིན་པ་.

མཁས་མཁས་སྙན་སྙན་ (kɛ̀ɛ̀gɛɛ̀ ñɛnñɛn) sm. མཁས་སྙན་.

མཁས་གྲུབ་ (kɛ̀ɛ̀drub) 1. one who has acquired both knowledge and wisdom, an expert. 2. man's name.

མཁས་གུ་ (kɛ̀ɛ̀gu) all the learned people and scholars.

མཁས་སྒྲུབ་ (kɛ̀ɛ̀drub) doing/ achieving sth. through skillful or clever means.

མཁས་བརྒྱ་འགྲན་གླེང་ (kɛ̀ɛ̀gya drɛnlɛŋ) sm. མཁས་བརྒྱ་མཉམ་གླེང་.

མཁས་བརྒྱ་མཉམ་གླེང་ (kɛ̀ɛ̀gya ñāmlɛŋ) let a hundred schools (of thought) contend (the name of the 1957-58 political campaign in China).

མཁས་ངོམ་ (kɛ̀ɛ̀ŋom) showing off one's skills/ abilities/ intellect; va.—བྱེད་.

མཁས་ངོམ་ཞབས་འདྲེན་ (kɛ̀ɛ̀ŋom shamdrɛn) showing off one's skills/ abilities/ intellect but ending up disgracing oneself or others; va.—བྱེད་.

མཁས་ཅན་ (kɛ̀ɛ̀jɛn) expert.

མཁས་གཅིག་རྒྱང་གླེང་ (kɛ̀ɛ̀jig gyāŋlɛŋ) 1. expounding the teachings of only one school (of thought). 2. teaching individually (in contrast to teaching in groups).

མཁས་ཆེན་ (kɛ̀ɛ̀jɛn) expert.

མཁས་མཆོག (kɛ̀ɛ̀joò) 1. a written term of address for a scholar ¶ མཁས་མཆོག་དགེ་འདུན་ཆོས་འཕེལ་གྱི་རྟོགས་བརྗོད་ The biography of the scholar Gendun Chompel. 2. sm. མཁས་པ་.

མཁས་མཉམ་ (kɛ̀ɛ̀ñam) equal in skill/ knowledge; vi.—ཐུག to be equal in skill/ knowledge.

མཁས་སྙན་ (kɛ̀ɛ̀ñɛn) 1. sweet-talk, coaxing, flattery; va.—ཤོད་ to sweet-talk, to flatter, to cajole, to coax. 2. polite, courteous. 3. abbr. of མཁས་པའི་སྙན་གྲགས་.

མཁས་ཐག་ཆོད་ (kɛ̀ɛ̀daà cöö) sm. མཁས་ཐལ་ཤོར་.

མཁས་ཐལ་ཤོར་ (kɛ̀ɛ̀dɛɛ shöö) vi. to fail as a result of trying to be too clever, to outsmart oneself ¶ མོ་ཊ་གཏོང་མཁས་ཅན་དེ་མཁས་ཐལ་ཤོར་ནས་གཡང་ལ་ལྷུང་བཞག The expert driver overdid his driving skill and went over the cliff.

མཁས་དྲག (kɛ̄drag) good and skillful.

མཁས་འདོད་གྲགས་འདོད་ (kɛ̄ndöö tragdöö) wishing to be known as a scholar or an expert.

མཁས་གནས་ (kɛ̀ɛ̀nɛɛ̀) school.

མཁས་པ་ (kɛ̀ɛ̀ba) an expert, a learned/ skilled person, a scholar ¶ རྩོམ་མཁས་པ་ A skilled writer.

མཁས་པ་མཁས་པའི་དྲུང་ན་མཛེས་ (kɛ̀ɛ̀ba kɛ̀ɛ̀bɛ truŋnə dzēè) its better to associate with one's own kind [Lit. a scholar is recognized and appreciated by other scholars].

མཁས་པའི་དགའ་སྟོན་ (kɛ̀ɛ̀bɛ gadön) title of a famous Tibetan history book.

མཁས་པའི་བྱ་བ་གསུམ་ (kɛ̀ɛ̀bɛ cawa sūm) the three areas of skill of a learned person: teaching, debating and writing.

མཁས་པར་འགྱུར་ (kɛ̀ɛ̀bar gyur) vi. to become an expert ¶ ཚད་མ་རིག་པར་མཁས་པར་གྱུར་པ་རེད་ He became an expert on philosophy.

མཁས་པར་ཀློམ་ (kɛ̀ɛ̀bar lōm) sm. མཁས་ཀློམ་.

མཁས་པོ་ (kɛ̀ɛ̀bo) 1. expert, skilled. 2. (vb. + —) expert/ skilled in the preceeding verbal action ¶ བུ་མོ་དེ་ཁ་ལག་བཟོ་མཁས་པོ་འདུག She is an expert cook.

མཁས་པོ་བྱེད་ (kɛ̀ɛ̀bo cèè) va. to act tactfully/ discretely, to act cleverly ¶ མི་དེས་མཁས་པོ་བྱས་ནས་དོན་དག་བསྒྲུབས་སོང་ That man was able to achieve his goals by being tactful and clever.

མཁས་བླུན་མཉམ་གནས་ (kɛ̀ɛ̀lün ñāmnɛɛ̀) wise and foolish together, good and bad together.

མཁས་དབང་ (kɛ̀ɛ̀waŋ) 1. title for a learned person/ scholar ¶ མཁས་དབང་སྐུ་ཞབས་རྡོ་རྗེ་ The learned Mr. Dorje. 2. an authority ¶ ཁོང་བོད་ཀྱི་རིག་གནས་ཀྱི་མཁས་དབང་ཞིག་རེད་ He is an authority on Tibetan culture.

མཁས་དབང་ཆེན་པོ་ (kɛ̀ɛ̀waŋ cēmbo) great scholar/ expert, a renowned authority.

མཁས་དབང་བླུན་པོའི་ཚུལ་ (kɛ̀ɛ̀waŋ lūnbö tsūl) a truly learned person will give the appearance of an ignorant person.

མཁས་མ་ (kɛ̀ɛ̀ma) a learned female.

མཁས་མྱོང་ཅན་ (kɛ̀ɛ̀ñoŋjɛn) experienced and expert.

མཁས་རྩལ་ (kɛ̀ɛ̀dzɛɛ) talent, skill; va.—འདོན་ to show/ manifest one's skill.

མཁས་རྩལ་མངོན་ཐབས་ (kɛ̀ɛ̀dzɛɛ ŋōntəb) trying to show off one's skills or abilities; va.—བྱེད་ ¶ བཟོ་པ་དེས་མི་མང་པོའི་དཀྱིལ་དུ་མཁས་རྩལ་མངོན་ཐབས་བྱེད་ཀྱི་འདུག The worker is trying to show off his skill in front of many people.

མཁས་བརྩོན་བཟང་གསུམ་ (kɛ̀ɛ̀dzün sansum) the three (good characteristics): knowledgeable, hardworking and good-natured/ kind.

མཁས་མཛངས་ (kɛ̄ɛ̀dzaŋ) wise ¶ སྲིད་ཇུས་མཁས་མཛངས་ལྡན་པ་ A wise policy.

མཁས་ཀློམ་ (kɛ̄ɛ̀lom) pretending to be learned ¶ བླུན་པོས་མཁས་ཀློམ་བྱེད་པ་ཀློད་རེ་བྲོ་ It is funny when a stupid person pretends to be knowledgeable.

མཁས་ཀློམ་སྟོང་བཤད་ (kɛ̄ɛ̀lom dōŋshɛɛ̀) pretending to be learned but saying meaningless things; va.—བྱེད་.

མཁས་ཀློམ་བཤད་ཡམས་ (kɛ̀ɛ̀lom shɛ̀ɛ̀yam) sm. མཁས་ཀློམ་སྟོང་བཤད་.

མཁུར་ (kūr) abbr. of མཁུར་ཚོས་.

མཁུར་མགོ་ (kūrgo) upper part of the cheek.

མཁུར་སྒོ་ (kūrgo) sm. མཁུར་ཚོས་.

མཁུར་བ་ (kūrwə) sm. མཁུར་ཚོས་.

མཁུར་ཚོས་ (kūrdzöö) cheeks.

མཁུར་ཚོས་ལ་མཚམས་སྤྲིན་འཁྲིགས (kūrdzöölа tsəmdrin trig) face becoming red [Lit. sunset's clouds on the cheek].

མཁུར་འཛུམ་ (kūrdzum) smiling, va.—བྱེད་ to smile.

མཁུར་རུས་ (kūrrüü) cheek bones.

མཁེ་ཉེན་འདེམས་ཀ་ (kēñen demga) shung. making a choice between what is beneficial and what is dangerous.

མཁེ་ཉེན་བསམ་ཤེས་ (kēñen sāmsheè) shung.

considering what is beneficial and what is dangerous.

མཁེ་གཙང་ (kēdzaŋ) sm.* ཁེ་གཙང་.

མཁོ་ (kō) 1. need, necessity ༈ གློག་མཁོ་ Electric needs. 2. vi. to need, to require ༈ ཡི་གེ་འབྲི་བར་སྨྱུ་གུ་གཅིག་མཁོ་གི་འདུག (You) need a pen to write.

མཁོ་མཁན་ (kōgɛn) need, want ༈ ཅ་ལག་འདི་མཁོ་མཁན་མི་འདུག There is no need for this thing.

མཁོ་གལ་ (kōgɛɛ) need, necessity, requirement ༈ དངོས་པོ་འདི་ང་ལ་མཁོ་གལ་ཆེན་པོ་འདུག I have a great need for this utensil.

མཁོ་དགུ་ (kōgu) sm. མཁོ་རྒུ་.

མཁོ་དགོས་ (kōgöö) sm. མཁོ་གལ་.

མཁོ་རྒུ་ (kōgu) every need, all needs, necessities ༈ ཚོང་ཁང་འདིའི་ནང་མཁོ་རྒུའི་ཡོ་ཆས་ཚང་མ་འཛོམས་པོ་འདུག All necessities are in that shop.

མཁོ་སྒྲུབ་ (kūdrub) buying, acquiring, procuring; va.—བྱེད་ to buy/ acquire/ procure ༈ ལས་ཁུངས་དེས་དགོས་མཁོ་ཚང་མ་མཁོ་སྒྲུབ་བྱེད་ཀྱི་ཡོད་པ་རེད་ That office acquires everything that it needs.

མཁོ་སྒྲུབ་ཀྱི་ལས་ཀ་ (kūdrubgi lɛ̱ɛ̀gə) sm. མཁོ་སྒྲུབ་ལས་དོན་.

མཁོ་སྒྲུབ་པུའུ་ (kūdrub bū) tib.ch. sm. མཁོ་སྒྲུབ་ལས་ཁུངས་.

མཁོ་སྒྲུབ་ཚོང་ཁང་ (kūdrub tsōŋgaŋ) department store, variety store.

མཁོ་སྒྲུབ་ལས་ཁུངས་ (kūdrub lɛ̱ɛ̀guŋ) supply/ procurement/ logistics office, rear-service department.

མཁོ་སྒྲུབ་ལས་དོན་ (kūdrub lɛ̱ɛ̀dön) the work of supplying/ procuring; va.—བྱེད་.

མཁོ་དངོས་ (kōŋöö) necessary goods ༈ མཁོ་དངོས་སྐྱེལ་ལམ་ A supply line for necessary goods.

མཁོ་ཅན་ (kōjɛn) useful, needed ༈ མཁོ་ཅན་གྱི་དངོས་པོ་ Useful goods.

མཁོ་ཆས་ (kōjɛ̀ɛ̀) equipment, gear, needed things ༈ ཕྱོགས་ལ་འགྲོ་དུས་མཁོ་ཆས་ཡག་པོ་འཁྱེར་དགོས་ When (you) go on a trip you have to take good equipment.

མཁོ་ཆས་ཚང་འཛོམས་ (kōjɛ̀ɛ̀ tsāŋdzom) completely equipped, having all the necessary equipment/ gear.

མཁོ་ཆུ་འདྲེན་ཕུད་ (kōcu dö̱nbüü) supplying water and eliminating sewerage.

མཁོ་ཆེན་པོ་ (kō cēmbo) sm. མཁོ་ཆོད་པོ་.

མཁོ་ཆོད་ (kō cȫö) vi. to be useful.

མཁོ་ཆོད་པོ་ (kō cōbo) useful ༈ སྨྱུ་གུ་འདི་མཁོ་ཆོད་པོ་ཞིག་དུག་སྣང་ This pen was very useful.

མཁོ་བདམས་ (kōdüü) selecting what is needed.

མཁོ་བདོན་ (kōdön) sm. མཁོ་འདོན་.

མཁོ་བསྟུན་ (kōdün)) in accordance with what is needed ༈ ད་ལམ་ངས་ལས་ཁུངས་ཀྱི་མཁོ་བསྟུན་དངོས་ཟོག་ཁག་ཅིག་ཉོ་སྒྲུབ་བྱས་ཡོད་ Recently I bought goods in accordance with the needs of the office.

མཁོ་བསྟུན་ཐོབ་སྤྲོད་ (kōdün tōbdröö) "to each according to his need."

མཁོ་མཐེར་ལྷ་ཁང་ (kōder lhāgaŋ) a temple built by king Srongtsen Gambo in southern Tibet.

མཁོ་འདོན་ (köndön) supplies, supplying; va.—བྱེད་ ༈ ང་ལོག་པར་མོ་མཚོན་མཁོ་འདོན་བྱས་པ་རེད་ (They) supplied arms to the rebels.

མཁོ་སྤྱད་ (kōjɛɛ̀) sm. མཁོ་ཆས་.

མཁོ་སྤྲོད་ (kōdröö) sm. མཁོ་འདོན་.

མཁོ་སྤྲོད་ཀྱི་ཚད་མ་ལོངས་ (kōdröögi tsɛ̄ɛ̀ ma̱ lo̱n) vi. to be undersupplied, to have supply fail to meet demand.

མཁོ་སྤྲོད་ཁང་ (kōdröögaŋ) supply station.

མཁོ་སྤྲོད་ཁྲུའུ་ (kōdröö trū) tib.ch. supply office.

མཁོ་སྤྲོད་དགོས་ཚད་ལས་འདས་པ་ (kōdröö gö̱ö̱dzɛɛ̀lɛ dɛ̱ɛ̀) vi. to be oversupplied, to have supply exceed demand.

མཁོ་སྤྲོད་ལམ་ལུགས་ (kōdröö lə̱mluù) supply system.

མཁོ་སྤྲོད་ལས་དོན་ (kōdröö lɛ̱ɛ̀dön) the work of supplying.

མཁོ་སྤྲོད་ས་ཚིགས་ (kōdröö sədzii) sm. མཁོ་སྤྲོད་ཁང་.

མཁོ་ཕན་ (kō pēn) needed and useful ༈ མཁོ་ཕན་ཡོད་རིགས་ All things that are needed and useful.

མཁོ་བྱེད་ (kōjɛɛ̀) sm. མཁོ་ཆས་.

མཁོ་སྦྱོར་ (kōjɔɔ) sm. མཁོ་སྤྲོད་.

མཁོ་མ་བཟོད་ (kō ma̱ sö̱ö) vi. to become useless ༈ མཁོ་མ་བཟོད་པའི་དངོས་པོ་ཚང་མ་དབྱུགས་དགོས་ One must throw away everything that has become useless.

མཁོ་མེད་ (kōmeè) 1. useless, unnecessary. 2. scrap, salvage.

མཁོ་མེད་ཀྱི་རྒྱུ་ཆ་ (kōmeègi gyu̱bjə) useless materials, salvage materials ༈ མཁོ་མེད་ཀྱི་རྒྱུ་ཆ་ཚང་མ་མེར་བསྲེགས་པ་རེད་ (They) burnt all the useless materials.

མཁོ་མེད་ཀྱི་དངོས་རྫས་ (kōmeègi ŋö̱ödzɛɛ̀) sm. མཁོ་མེད་དངོས་རྫས་.

མཁོ་མེད་མཁན་ (kōmeègɛn) useless things.

མཁོ་མེད་ངར་ལྕགས་ (kōmeè ŋ̱arjaà) scrap steel/ metal ༈ མཁོ་མེད་ངར་ལྕགས་བཟོ་གྲྭ་ Scrap metal factory.

མཁོ་མེད་དངོས་རྫས་ (kōmeè ŋ̱ödzɛɛ̀) waste/ scrap salvage materials ༈ མཁོ་མེད་དངོས་རྫས་ཉོ་སྒྲུབ་ཁང་ Scrap/ salvage purchasing department.

མཁོ་མེད་དངོས་རྫས་ཉོ་སྡུད་ས་ཚིགས་ (kōmeè ŋ̱ödzɛɛ̀ ṉ̃odüü sədzig) a station for buying and collecting waste and salvage materials.

མཁོ་མེད་དངོས་རྫས་ཕྱིར་སྡུད་ཀུང་སི་ (kōmeè ŋ̱ödzɛɛ̀ cīrdüü gūŋsi) tib.ch. a waste recycling company.

མཁོ་མེད་རྙིང་རུལ་ (kōmeè ṉ̃ĩŋhrüü) old and useless materials.

མཁོ་མེད་མི་ (kōmeè mi̱) a useless person.

མཁོ་ཚད་ (kōdzɛɛ̀) 1. all/ everything/ whatever that one needs ༈ མཁོ་ཚད་ཉོས་བཞག (They) bought everything that they needed. 2. the amount that one needs, what is needed ༈ བཟོ་གྲྭ་དེར་རྒྱུ་ཆ་མཁོ་ཚད་ཆེན་པོ་འདུག The factory needs a lot of materials.

མཁོ་ཚོང་ (kōdzoŋ) supply and marketing.

མཁོ་ཚོང་ཁྲུའུ་ (kōdzoŋ trū) tib.ch. supply and marketing office/ department.

མཁོ་རྫས་ (kōdzɛɛ̀) sm. མཁོ་ཆས་.

མཁོ་ཡག་ (kōya) sm. མཁོ་གལ་.

མཁོ་བཤུས་ (kōshüü) excerpt, extract; va.—བྱེད་ ༈ དམ་བུ་འདི་མའོ་ཀྱི་དེབ་ཀྱི་ནང་ནས་མཁོ་བཤུས་བྱས་པ་ཞིག་རེད་ This piece (of writing) is an excerpt from Mao's book.

མཁོན་ (kön) shung. abbr. of མཁན་པོ་.

མཁོས་ (kȫö) sm.* འཁོས་ཀ་.

མཁོས་ཀ་ (kȫöga) sm.* འཁོས་ཀ་.

མཁོས་ཁྱབ་ (kȫögyəb) sm. འཁོས་པ་.

མཁོས་ཕབ་ (kȫö pə̄b) vi. to be relaxed, to be at ease, to have peace of mind, to be at home ༈ ཕ་ཡུལ་དང་བྲལ་ཕྱིན་མི་ཡུལ་ག་འདྲ་ཞིག་ཏུ་ཡང་རང་སེམས་མཁོས་ཕབ་ཅིག་ཡོང་ཐབས་མི་འདུག Once (one) is separated from (one's) homeland it is impossible to feel at home anywhere.

མཁོས་ཕེབས་ (kȫö pēb) sm.མཁོས་ཕབ་.

མཁོས་ཞན་ (kȫöshɛn) arc. meaningless, unnecessary.

མཁོས་སུ་ཕབ་ (kȫösu pə̄b) sm. མཁོས་ཕབ་.

མཁོས་སུ་ཕེབས་ (kȫösu pēb) sm. མཁོས་ཕབ་.

མཁྱིད་ (kyi̋i) a measure equal to the length of a hand made into a fist from the tip of the thumb to the end of the pinkie ༈ མཁྱིད་གང་ The span of one མཁྱིད་.

མཁྱུད་ (kyű̋ü) va. to keep sth. secret.

མཁྱུད་སྤྱད་ (kyű̋üjɛɛ̀) sm. དཔེ་མཁྱུད་.

མཁྱེན་ (kyēn) va. 1. to know/ understand (h.) ༈ ཁོང་བོད་སྐད་ཡག་པོ་མཁྱེན་གྱི་ཡོད་པ་རེད་ He knows Tibetan well. 2. "Please" (as a rhetorical) ༈ སྲོག་ལ་བབས་པའི་ཁྲིམས་ཆད་མི་ཐོག་པ་མཁྱེན་ Please don't let me get the death penalty.

མཁྱེན་རྒྱ་ (kyēngya) scope of knowledge.

མཁྱེན་རྒྱ་ཅན་ (kyēngyajɛn) learned, knowledgeable ༈ མཁྱེན་རྒྱ་ཅན་གྱི་སློབ་གསོར་ཞུན་དགོས་ (One) should listen to the teaching of someone who is learned.

མཁྱེན་རྒྱ་ཆེན་པོ་ (kyēngya cēmbo) knowledgeable, learned.

མཁྱེན་ཚོད་ལྟར་ (kyēncöö̀dār) as (you) know (h.) ¶ ཁྱེད་རང་གི་མཁྱེན་ཚོད་ལྟར་ང་བོད་ལ་འགྲོ་གི་ཡིན་ As you know, I am going to Tibet.

མཁྱེན་མཚོད་ལྟར་ (kyēncöö̀dār) sm. མཁྱེན་ཚོད་ལྟར་.

མཁྱེན་མཚོད་ལགས་ན་ (kyēncöö̀lāàna) as (you) know (h.) ¶ རང་སྣང་གང་དྲན་གྱིས་འབོ་ཉག་ཆེ་ཆུང་ངེས་མེད་འདི་ཆར་དམིགས་རྫ་ཚོག་རིན་པོ་ཆེ་དང་ཁྲིམས་འབྲས་ལ་གདུབ་མིན་མཁྱེན་མཚོད་ལགས་ན་ As you are fully aware, making measures and scales according to one's own wish is against the law.

མཁྱེན་རྟོགས་ (kyēndɔɔ̀) knowing, understanding (h.) ¶ གཞོན་ནུ་རྣམས་ནས་མཁྱེན་རྟོགས་ཆེད་ For the purpose (of making) the young come to understand.

མཁྱེན་ལྡན་ (kyēndɛn) learned, knowledgeable, intelligent.

མཁྱེན་ལྡན་མ་ (kyēn dɛnma) a learned/ knowledgeable/ intelligent woman.

མཁྱེན་ནུས་ (kyēnnüù) intellectual power.

མཁྱེན་ནུས་འགྲན་མེད་ (kyēnnüù drɛnmeè) unmatched knowledge, extremely knowledgeable (h.).

མཁྱེན་པ་ (kyēnba) knowledge, understanding ¶ཁོང་མཁྱེན་པ་རྒྱས་པོ་ཡོད་པ་རེད་ He has wide knowledge.

མཁྱེན་པའི་སྟོབས་ (kyēmbɛ dōb) power of intelligence/ knowledge/ understanding ¶མཁྱེན་པའི་སྟོབས་ཀྱིས་ཚན་རིག་གི་ཤེས་ཡོན་ལ་མངའ་བརྙེས་པ་རེད་ (His) power of intelligence enabled him to have a complete grasp of science.

མཁྱེན་དཔྱོད་ (kyēnjöö̀) wisdom, intelligence, knowledge, understanding.

མཁྱེན་དཔྱོད་ཡངས་པ་ (kyēnjöö̀ yaŋba) wide/ broad knowledge.

མཁྱེན་སྤྱན་ (kyēnjɛn) sm. མཁྱེན་དཔྱོད་.

མཁྱེན་སྤྱོད་ (kyēnjöö̀) abbr. knowledge and behavior.

མཁྱེན་འབྱོན་གཉིས་ལྡན་ (kyēnjön ñiidɛn) having both knowledge and capableness.

མཁྱེན་བརྩེ་ (kyēndze) wisdom and compassion.

མཁྱེན་བརྩེ་མཚུངས་མེད་ (kyēndze tsüŋmeè) a phrase used in letter headings for friends and relatives that is somewhat equivalent to the English: "dear" or "dearest."

མཁྱེན་ཚད་ (kyēndzɛɛ̀) a standard or level of knowledge ¶མཁྱེན་ཚད་མཐོ་པོ་ A high level of knowledge.

མཁྱེན་ཚོར་ kyēndzɔɔ) knowing, understanding.

མཁྱེན་གཟིགས་ (kyēnsiì) knowing, comprehending, understanding ¶ཐམས་ཅད་མཁྱེན་གཟིགས་ཆེན་པོ་ The omnipotent (usu. refers to the Dalai Lama).

མཁྱེན་བཟང་ (kyēnsaŋ) sm. མཁྱེན་ཡངས་.

མཁྱེན་ཡངས་ (kyēnyaŋ) learned, knowledgeable.

མཁྱེན་ཡུལ་ (kyēnyüü) sm. མཁྱེན་རྒྱ་.

མཁྱེན་ཡོན་ (kyēnyön) knowledge.

མཁྱེན་ཡོན་ཅན་ (kyēnyönjɛn) sm. མཁྱེན་ཡོན་ལྡན་པ་.

མཁྱེན་ཡོན་ལྡན་པ་ (kyēnyön dɛmba) wise, knowledgeable, learned.

མཁྱེན་རབ་ (kyēnrəb) sm. མཁྱེན་ཡོན་.

མཁྱེན་རླབས་ (kyēnləb) sm. མཁྱེན་ཡོན་.

མཁྱེན་ཤག་རེད་ (kyēnshaàreè) I am sure that you know this.

མཁྱེན་གསལ་ (kyēnsɛɛ) as you know well, as you understand well ¶ཁྱེད་རང་གིས་མཁྱེན་གསལ་ལྟར་ང་བོད་ལ་འགྲོ་གི་ཡིན་ As you know well, I am going to Tibet.

མཁྲགས་པོ་ (trāgbo) sm.* མཁྲེགས་པོ་.

མཁྲང་ཐང་ (trāŋdaŋ) physically well and strong, hale and hearty, healthy.

མཁྲང་པོ་ (trāŋbo) 1. firm, stiff, hard ¶རྒྱུ་པ་མཁྲང་པོ་ A stiff stick. 2. steady, dependable ¶བློ་མཁྲང་པོ་ A steady/ dependable (person).

མཁྲིག་དཀར་ (trīggar) horses and mules that have white patches on the upper part of their heel.

མཁྲིག་མ་ (trīgmə) wrist; ankle.

མཁྲིག་རྩ་ (trīgdza) ulnar artery.

མཁྲིག་རྩ་ནང་མ་ (trīgdza naŋma) arteries on wrist and ankle.

མཁྲིག་རྩ་ཕྱི་མ་ (trīgdza cīmə) radial artery.

མཁྲིག་ཚིགས་ (trītsiì) wrist and ankle joint.

མཁྲིག་རུས་ (trīgrüù) wrist and ankle bone, carpus.

མཁྲིག་རུས་ནང་མ་ (trīgrüù naŋma) ulna (bone of the forearm on the side opposite to the thumb).

མཁྲིག་རུས་ཕྱི་མ་ (trīgrüù cīmə) radius (bone on the forearm on the thumb side).

མཁྲིག་གསང་ (trīgsaŋ) a point where acupuncture is applied.

མཁྲིས་སྐྲན་ (trīidrɛn) gallstone.

མཁྲིས་ཁ་ (trīiku) sm. མཁྲིས་པ་.

མཁྲིས་ཁྲག་ (trīitraà) a blood disease of the gall bladder.

མཁྲིས་གླང་ (trīilaŋ) sm. མཁྲིས་སྣོད་གཉན་ཚད་.

མཁྲིས་ཆེན་བཞི་ (trīicenshi) the four gall bladders (of humans, bears, vultures and fish) that are used in traditional Tibetan medicine.

མཁྲིས་རྡོ་ (trīido) sm. མཁྲིས་སྐྲན་.

མཁྲིས་ནད་ (trīinɛɛ̀) a disease of the gall bladder, jaundice.

མཁྲིས་ནད་ཅན་གྱིས་དུང་དཀར་སེར་པོར་མཐོང་ (trīinɛɛ̀jɛngi duŋgar sērbor tōŋ) inability to see things clearly because of one's biases [Lit. a person with jaundice will see the white conch shell as yellow].

མཁྲིས་སྣོད་ (trīinöö̀) gall bladder.

མཁྲིས་སྣོད་གཉན་ཚད་ (trīinöö̀ ñɛ̄ndzɛɛ̀) cholecystitis (inflammation of the gall bladder).

མཁྲིས་པ་ (trīibə) gall bladder, bile; jaundice; va.—ན་ to have/ get jaundice, to have/ get a disease of the gall bladder.

མཁྲིས་པ་ཁ་ལུད་ (trīibə kəlüù) a type of bile/jaundice disease.

མཁྲིས་པ་ཅན་ (trīibəjɛn) short-tempered, quick to anger.

མཁྲིས་པ་མིག་སེར་ (trīibə migser) the yellowish eyes that accompany jaundice.

མཁྲིས་པའི་ལྗང་གཞིར་ (trīibɛ jaŋser) biliverden.

མཁྲིས་པའི་རྡོ་སྐྲན་ (trīibɛ dotrɛn) gallstone.

མཁྲིས་པའི་སྦུ་གུ་ (trīibɛ) bile duct.

མཁྲིས་པའི་དམར་གཞིར་ (trīibɛ mārsher) bilirubin.

མཁྲིས་བུལ་ (trīibüü) choline.

མཁྲིས་སྦུག་ (trīibuù) bile duct.

མཁྲིས་སྨན་ (trīimɛn) medicine for bilious diseases.

མཁྲིས་ཚད་ (trīidzɛɛ̀) bilious fever.

མཁྲིས་གསང་ (trīisaŋ) a point on the second and the tenth vertebrae that is used in acupuncture.

མཁྲེགས་ (trēg) hard, solid, firm ¶ཤིང་འདི་མཁྲེགས་པོ་འདུག This wood is hard.

མཁྲེགས་མཁྲེགས་ (trēgdreg) sm. མཁྲེགས་.

མཁྲེགས་མགོ་སྨོངས་གླད་ (trēŋgo mōŋlɛɛ̀) stupid and stubborn.

མཁྲེགས་འགྱུར་ (trēŋgyur) a callous, a corn.

མཁྲེགས་རྒོལ་ (drēggöö) stubborn resistance/ opposition; va.—བྱེད་ to stubbornly resist/ oppose.

མཁྲེགས་ཆས་ (drēgjɛɛ̀) hardware.

མཁྲེགས་དོ་ (trēgdo) sm. མཁྲེགས་རྡོ་.

མཁྲེགས་གདན་ (trēgdɛn) a hard seat/ mat.

མཁྲེགས་རྡོ་ (trēgdo) an unreliable/ obstinate/ stubborn person ¶མི་མཁྲེགས་རྡོ་ཡིན་ན་བུ་ལོན་གཏོང་གི་མ་རེད་ (They) won't give out loans to unreliable people.

མཁྲེགས་པོ་ (trāgo) 1. hard, solid, firm ¶ཤིང་འདི་མཁྲེགས་པོ་ཞི་དྲག་འདུག This wood is very hard. 2. stubborn, obstinate ¶ཁོ་མགོ་མཁྲེགས་པོ་འདུག He is an obstinate person.

མཁྲེགས་ཚད་ (trāgdzɛɛ̀) degree of hardness.

མཁྲེགས་ཚིལ་ (trēgdzii) stearin.

མཁྲེགས་བཟུང་ (trēgsuŋ) 1. persisting, maintaining;

va.—བྱེད་ to persist in, to hold onto (strongly) ¶ དྲག་པོའི་སྲིད་ཇུས་མཁྲེགས་བཟུང་བྱས་པ་རེད་ (They) persisted in a militant policy. ¶ ཆབ་མདོ་མཁྲེགས་བཟུང་བྱས་ཀྱང་སླགས་མ་འཁྱིལ་བ་རེད་ Even though they tried to hold on to Chamdo strongly, they were unable to keep it. 2. a person who is stubborn and refuses to admit mistakes and change views ¶ མཁྲེགས་བཟུང་དྲག་གཅོད་ Punishing harshly those who refuse to change their views.

མཁྲེགས་བཟུང་གི་གནས་སུ་གྱུར་ (trēgsuŋgi nɛ̄ɛ̀su gya̱r) vi. to come to a deadlock.

མཁྲེགས་རིལ་རིལ་ (trēg ri̱irii) hard and round.

མཁྲེགས་ཤིང་ (trēgshiŋ) hardwood.

མཁྲེགས་ཤེལ་ (trēgshee) 1. plexiglass. 2. bulletproof glass.

མཁྲེགས་ཤོག (trēgshɔɔ̀) cardboard.

མཁྲེགས་ས་ (trēgsa) cement.

མཁྲེགས་སྲུང་ (trēgsuŋ) holding on to stubbornly; va.—བྱེད་.

མཁྲེགས་བསྲེས་ལྕགས་རིལ་ (trēgseè jāərii) carbon alloy steel.

མཁྲེགས་ལྷུ་ (trēglhu) hardware.

འཁང་: p. **འཁངས་**; f. **འཁང་** (kāŋ) vi. to feel dislike/ anger/ hatred.

འཁང་སྐད་ (kāŋgɛɛ̀) complaining, carping, grumbling, va.—རྒྱག.

འཁང་སྒྲ་ (kāŋdra) sm. འཁང་སྐད་.

འཁང་བ་ (kāŋwa) dislike, anger, hatred.

འཁང་ཚིག (kāŋtsig) sm. འཁང་སྐད་.

འཁང་ར་ (kāŋra) sm. འཁང་བ་.

འཁང་སེམས་ (kāŋsem) sm. འཁང་བ་.

འཁངས་ (kāŋ) p. of འཁང་.

འཁད་ (kɛɛ̀) 1. va. to sit ¶ རྟ་ལ་འཁད་དུས་ When (he was) sitting on the horse. 2. vi. to get stuck entangled/ caught up ¶ ཁོ་རྐང་པ་འཁད་ནས་འགྱེལ་བ་རེད་ His foot got tangled and he fell.

འཁན་པ་ (kɛ̄mba) sm. མཁན་པ་.

འཁམས་ (kām) vi. to become unconscious, to faint ¶ གནས་ཚུལ་ངན་པ་དེ་ཐོས་རྗེས་གློ་བུར་དུ་འཁམས་པ་རེད་ After hearing the bad news he suddenly fainted.

འཁར་རྒྱུག (kārgyuù) walking stick, cane.

འཁར་ང་ (kāŋa) gong; va.—རྡུང་ to beat or sound a gong.

འཁར་ངེའུ་ (kār ŋēwu) a small gong.

འཁར་ཆུ་ (kārju) molten bronze.

འཁར་རྡུང་ལམ་འབྱེད་ (kārduŋ la̱mjeè) exhorting on behalf of sth.; va.—བྱེད་ ¶ དམངས་གཙོའི་ལས་འགུལ་གྱི་ཆེད་དུ་འཁར་རྡུང་ལམ་འབྱེད་བྱེད་ཀྱི་ཡོད་པ་རེད་ They are exhorting on behalf of the democratic campaign. [Lit. beating gongs to clear the way (for a coming person or procession)].

འཁར་སྡེར་ (kārde) a plate/ dish made from brass/ bronze.

འཁར་སྡོད་ (kār dö̱ö̀) vi. to be stuck ¶ རླངས་འཁོར་ཞིག་འདམ་གྱི་དཀྱིལ་ལ་འཁར་བསྡད་བཞག A car is stuck in the mud.

འཁར་ཕོར་ (kārbɔɔ̀) a small bowl made from brass/ bronze.

འཁར་བ་ (kārwa) 1. sm. འཁར་རྒྱུག. 2. a stick ¶ སྨྱུ་འཁར་ A bamboo stick. 3. brass/ bronze.

འཁར་བའི་མེ་ལོང་ (kārwɛ me̱loŋ) a mirror made from brass/ bronze.

འཁར་ཡུག (kāryuù) sm. འཁར་རྒྱུག.

འཁར་དབྱུག (kāryuù) sm. འཁར་རྒྱུག.

འཁར་གཞོང་ (kārshoŋ) a basin made from brass/ bronze.

འཁར་ཟངས་ (kārsaŋ) 1. abbr. brass/ bronze and copper. 2. a large brass/ pot.

འཁར་བཟོ་བ་ (kārsowa) craftsman who works with brass/ bronze.

འཁར་གསིལ་ (kārsii) gelong's staff, mendicant's staff; va.—གསིལ་ to bang the staff on ground when asking for alms.

འཁལ་: p. **བཀལ་**; f. **བཀལ་**; imp. **འཁོལ་** (kɛ̄ɛ) va. to spin ¶ སྐུད་པ་བཀལ་བ་རེད་ (They) spun thread.

འཁལ་མཁན་ (kɛ̄ɛ̄ñɛn) a person who spins thread.

འཁལ་འཁོར་ (kɛ̄ɛ̄gɔɔ) a spinning wheel.

འཁལ་འཁོལ་ (kɛ̄ɛ̄göö) abbr. of འཁལ་ལེ་འཁོལ་ལེ་.

འཁལ་འཐག (kɛ̄ɛ̄daà) spinning and weaving; va.—བྱེད་.

འཁལ་འཐག་ཐོན་ཛས་ (kɛ̄ɛ̄daà tō̃ndzɛɛ̀) textile products.

འཁལ་འཐག་འཕྲུལ་འཁོར་ (kɛ̄ɛ̄daà trū̃ū̃gɔɔ) a textile machine.

འཁལ་འཐག་ཚི་སྣ་ (kɛ̄ɛ̄daà tsīnə) textile fibers.

འཁལ་འཐག་བཟོ་གྲྭ་ (kɛ̄ɛ̄daà so̱dra) a textile mill.

འཁལ་འཐག་ལས་རིགས་ (kɛ̄ɛ̄daà lɛ̱ɛ̀rig) textile industry.

འཁལ་འཕང་ (kɛ̄ɛ̄baŋ) a spindle.

འཁལ་ལེ་འཁོལ་ལེ་ (kɛ̄lle kō̃lle) desiring sth. a lot, itching to get sth. ¶ མ་ཇོང་རྒྱག་འདོད་ཀྱིས་འཁལ་ལེ་འཁོལ་ལེ་བྱས་བྱུང་ (I) was itching to play mahjong.

འཁུ་ (kū) 1. vi. to hate ¶ བཙན་འཛུལ་པ་ལ་འཁུ་བའི་སྐུལ་སློང་བྱེད་ཀྱི་ཡོད་པ་རེད་ They are inciting (them) to hate the invaders. 2. va. to oppose, to turn against ¶ རང་གི་རྒྱལ་ཁབ་ལ་འཁུ་བའི་མི་ངན་འཛིན་བཟུང་བྱེད་ཀྱི་འདུག They are arresting evil people who oppose their own country. 3. arc. stingy, tightfisted. 4. arc. va. to cause to turn back. 5. like, as good as ¶ ལྷ་ཡུལ་གྱི་དཔལ་ལ་འཁྲུ་བའི་ལོངས་སྤྱོད་ Enjoyment that is like the glory of heaven.

འཁུ་ལྡོག (kūdɔɔ̀) dislike, anger, hatred (usu. by a protective deity) ¶ ལྷ་སྲུང་ལ་ཕོག་ཐུག་བཏང་ཙང་འཁུ་ལྡོག་བྱུང་བ་རེད་ Because (he) offended the protective deity, the god became angry.

འཁུ་འཁྲིག (kūndrig) doubt, suspicion ¶ རྐྱེན་ངན་ལ་འཕྲད་ཡོང་བསམས་པའི་འཁུ་འཁྲིག་མེད་པ་ Having no suspicion of pending disaster.

འཁུ་བྱེད་ (kūjeè) conspiring/ plotting against sb.

འཁུ་རུབ་ (kūrub) gathering, collecting; va.—བྱེད་ ¶ འཕོ་འགྱུར་ཇི་བྱུང་གནས་ཚུལ་འཁུ་རུབ་བྱེད་ཆེད་སོ་པ་བཏང་བ་རེད་ Spies were sent to gather information on what changes took place.

འཁུ་སེམས་ (kūsem) sm. འཁུ་བསམ་.

འཁུ་བསམ་ (kūsam) thoughts of hatred/ anger; vi.—འཆང to have/ hold thoughts of hatred/ anger ¶ མི་དེ་ནང་ཆོས་ལ་འཁུ་བསམ་འཆང་མཁན་ཞིག་རེད་ That man is sb. who has thoughts of hatred towards Buddhism.

འཁུགས་ (kūù) sm. ཁུག་པ་.

འཁུན་ (kū̃n) vi. to groan, to moan

འཁུན་སྐད་ (kū̃ngɛɛ̀) sound of groaning/ moaning; vi. and va.—འདོན་; —གྲགས་; —རྒྱག; —འབྱིན་ to groan, to moan ¶ ནང་ནས་འཁུན་སྐད་རྒྱག་པ་ཐོས་ (We) heard groaning sounds from inside.

འཁུན་གོར་ (kū̃ngɔɔ) a type of bread.

འཁུན་སྒྲ་ (kū̃ndrə) sm. འཁུན་སྐད་.

འཁུན་དུར་དུར་ (kū̃n tu̱rdur) moaning, groaning.

འཁུམ་: p. **འཁུམས་**; f. **འཁུམ་** (kūm) vi. 1. to shrink, to shrivel, to get reduced in size ¶ སྟོད་ཐུང་འདི་ཞེ་དྲག་འཁུམས་བཞག The shirt has shrunk a lot. ¶ རང་ས་སེན་རྒྱ་ཙམ་འཁུམ་ཤོར་མི་འཇུང་བ་ Not reducing the size of our country even the size of a finger nail. 2. vi. to be or get curled/ huddled up (in fetal position) due to illness ¶ ནད་གཞིས་རྐྱེན་པས་ཁོང་གི་རྐང་ལག་འཁུམས་བཞག Because of illness, his hand and feet curled up in the fetal position. 3. vi. to cringe in terror/ fear ¶ དམག་ཐེངས་དང་པོ་རྒྱག་པའི་སྐབས་ནས་དགྲ་བོ་འཁུམས་སོང་ From the first battle, the enemy cringed in terror.

འཁུམ་འཁུམ་ (kūmgum) sm. འཁུམས་འཁུམས་.

འཁུམ་འགོག (kūmgɔɔ̀) shrink-proof.

འཁུམ་འདར་ (kūmdar) curling up and shaking (from cold); cringing and shaking (from fear); vi.—བྱེད་; —རྒྱག.

འཁུམ་མེར་སྡོད་ (kūmmer dö̱ö̀) va. to stay or sit cringing/ curling up due to fright or cold.

འཁུམ་ཚུལ་སྟོན་ (kūmdzüü dō̃n) va. to feign that one is cringing with fear.

འཁུམ་ཤོར་ (kūm shɔ̄ɔ) shung. vi. to get reduced in

size, to shrink/ contract ། རང་ས་སེན་རྒྱ་ཙམ་འཁུམ་ཁོར་མི་འཇུག་པ་ Not reducing the size of our country even the size of a finger nail.

འཁུམས་ (kūm) p. of འཁུམ་.

འཁུམས་འཁུམས་ (kūmgum) huddling or curling up due to cold; cringing with fear; va.—བྱེད་; vi.—ཆགས་.

འཁུམས་འཁུམས་ཞུམ་ཞུམ་ (kūmgum shu̲mshum) cringing with fear.

འཁུམས་འཁུམས་སིག་སིག་ (kūmgum si̋gsii̊) crawling, creeping.

འཁུར་: p. ཁུར་; f. འཁུར་; imp. ཁུར་ (kūr) va. 1. to carry, to shoulder, to take (on) ། དེ་བོ་ཁུར་བ་རེད་ He carried a load. ། འགན་འཁུར་གྱི་རེད་ (He) will take responsibility. 2. va. to bear suffering/ misfortune ། གཉའ་གནོན་ལོ་མང་པོ་ཁུར་ནས་ Having suffered oppression for many years.

འཁུར་བསྐྱོད་ཐུབ་པ་ (kūrgyüü tūbə) carrying capacity ། མི་གྲངས་ 240 འཁུར་བསྐྱོད་ཐུབ་པའི་དམག་པོའི་གྲུ་གཟིངས་ A military ship with a carrying capacity of about two hundred and forty persons.

འཁུར་ཁུག་ (kūrguù) handbag.

འཁུར་ཁྱབ་ (kūrgyəb) shung. taking responsibility and giving instructions.

འཁུར་འཁྲི་ (kūrdri) sm. འཁུར་འགན་.

འཁུར་འགན་ (kūrgɛn) responsibility; va.—ལེན་ to take responsibility.

འཁུར་མཉམ་ལེན་ (kūr ñāmlen) taking joint responsibility; va.—བྱེད་ ། རང་བཙན་གྱི་དོན་དུ་ཚང་མས་འཁུར་མཉམ་ལེན་བྱེད་དགོས་ All should take responsibility together for independence.

འཁུར་ཐག་ (kūrdaà) a carrying strap/ rope.

འཁུར་བ་ (kūrwə) 1. cookie, pastry. 2. sm. འཁུར་.

འཁུར་བ་འཕྱོག་འདོད་ཀྱིས་འཁུར་བ་ཤོར་ (kūrwa drɔ̄ŋdöögi kūrwa shɔ̄ɔ) greedy, avaricious [Lit. to lose the cookie that one has because of one's desire for more].

འཁུར་བྱེད་པོ་ (kūr cḙèbo) person in charge.

འཁུར་བླངས་ (kūr lāŋ) p. of འཁུར་ལེན་.

འཁུར་བརྩོན་ (kūrdzün) sm. ཧུར་བརྩོན་.

འཁུར་ར་ (kūrrə) sm. འཁུར་བ་.

འཁུར་ལུང་ (kūrluŋ) the leather strap attached to a tea churn.

འཁུར་ལེན་ (kūr len) sm. འཁུར་འགན་ལེན་.

འཁུར་ཤེད་ (kūrsheè) the strength to carry ། མི་དེ་དོག་ཁྱིས་ཁུར་ཤེད་ཆེན་པོ་འདུག་ That man has the strength to carry heavy loads.

འཁུར་སེམས་ (kūrsem) sm. འཁུར་བསམ་.

འཁུར་བསམ་ (kūrsam) sense of responsibility/ duty ། མི་དེ་ལས་ཀའི་ཐོག་འཁུར་སེམས་ཆེན་པོ་ཡོད་པ་རེད་ That person has a great sense of responsibility.

འཁུར་བསམ་ཅན་ (kūrsamjɛn) a responsible person, sb. who does one's duty or responsibility sincerely.

འཁུར་བསམ་རྣམ་དག་ (kūrsem nāmdaà) devoted to one's work, sincere in doing one's responsibility; va.—བྱེད་ ། ཁོས་འཁུར་བསམ་རྣམ་དག་གི་ཐོག་ནས་ལས་འགན་བསྒྲུབས་པ་རེད་ (He) worked devotedly and accomplished his responsibility.

འཁུལ་ (kǖü) 1. vi. to get subdued/ tamed ། རྟ་རྒོད་བཞོན་པར་འཁུལ་མི་ཐུབ་ A wild horse can't be subdued so as to become a riding horse. 2. vi. to be able to do/ carry.

འཁུས་ (kǖü) va. to hide.

འཁེགས་ (kēg) va. to stop, to refuse.

འཁེང་: p. འཁེངས་; f. འཁེང་ (kēŋ) vi. to freeze/ harden/ coagulate ། མར་ཁུ་འཁེངས་བཞག The melted butter has coagulated.

འཁེང་ཚད་ (kēŋdzɛɛ̀) sm. འཁེངས་ཚད་.

འཁེངས་ (kēŋ) p. of འཁེང་.

འཁེངས་འགྱུར་ (kēŋ gyu̲r) vi. to coagulate.

འཁེངས་འགྱུར་འགོག་རྫས་ (kēŋgyur go̲gdzɛɛ̀) anticoagulant.

འཁེངས་པོའི་རང་བཞིན་ (kēŋbö ro̲ŋshin) the nature of solidification/ coagulation.

འཁེངས་རྩི་ (kēŋdzi) the greasy film that coagulates on the surface of a liquid.

འཁེངས་ཚད་ (kēŋdzɛɛ̀) the point at which a liquid coagulates, the freezing point.

འཁེབ་ (kēb) va. to cover.

འཁེལ་: p. ཁེལ་; f. འཁེལ་; imp. ཁོལ་ (kēē) vi. to fall on, to coincide with ། སྐྱེ་སྐར་བཅུ་པའི་ཚེས་གཉིས་ལ་འཁྲུངས་ཚེས་འཁེལ་བས་ Because (his) birthday fell on the second of October. ། ཚོང་ཟོག་ནང་འདྲེན་བྱེད་ཡས་དེ་དུས་ཐོག་ལ་དག་དག་འཁེལ་བ་རེད་ (His) importing of commodities came at the right time. 2. vi. to get sth. unpleasant ། བཟོ་གྲྭ་དེ་ཁྲུངས་མ་འཁྱིལ་བར་བརྟེན་བཟོ་པ་རྣམས་ལ་གནོད་རྐྱེན་འཁེལ་བ་རེད་ The workers were harmed when the factory failed. 3. va. to spin thread. 4. (སྐབས་ + —) see སྐབས་. 5. to get implicated/ blamed ། ཡ་ལ་འཁེལ་བ་ To be implicated. 6. (གཏན་ + —) vi. to get settled/ decided/ confirmed ། ཐོན་ཚེས་གཏན་འཁེལ་དུས་ When they settled on the departure date. 7. (ཡིད་ + —) trustworthy, reliable.

འཁེལ་འཁོར་ (kēēgɔɔ) sm. འཁལ་འཁོར་.

འཁེལ་འཐག་ (kēēdaà) textiles; va.—བྱེད་ to make textiles, to spin and weave.

འཁེལ་འཐག་ཐོན་རྫས་ (kēēdaà tōndzɛɛ̀) textile goods/ commodities.

འཁེལ་འཐག་ཐོན་ཟོག་ (kēēdaà tōnsɔɔ̀) sm. འཁེལ་འཐག་ཐོན་རྫས་.

འཁེལ་འཐག་འཕྲུལ་འཁོར་ (kēēdaà trǖügoo) weaving/ spinning machine.

འཁེལ་འཐག་འཕྲུལ་ཆས་ (kēēdaà trǖüjɛɛ̀) textile machinery.

འཁེལ་འཐག་བཟོ་གྲྭ་ (kēēdaà so̲dra) textile mill/ factory.

འཁེལ་འཐག་བཟོ་ལས་ (kēēdaà so̲lɛɛ̀) textile industry ། འཁེལ་འཐག་བཟོ་ལས་ཡུའུ་ Textile Industry Ministry.

འཁེལ་འཐག་ལས་རིགས་ (kēēdaà lɛ̲̀ɛrii) textile work.

འཁེལ་ཚད་ (kēēdzɛɛ̀) ply, the number of strands twisted to make yarn.

འཁེལ་ལས་ (kɛ̄ɛlɛɛ̀) spinning work.

འཁེལ་ལས་འཕྲུལ་འཁོར་ (kɛ̄ɛlɛɛ̀ trǖügɔɔ) spinning machine.

འཁེལ་ལས་བཟོ་གྲྭ་ (kɛ̄ɛlɛɛ̀ so̲dra) soinning factory.

འཁོགས་ (kɔ̄ɔ̀) aged, old, decrepit ། མི་རྒན་འཁོགས་ An old man.

འཁོགས་འཁོགས་པོ་ (kɔ̄ɔ̀ kɔ̄ɔ̀bo) a term that is descriptive of the way old people walk.

འཁོད་ (kȫȍ) 1. vi. to be written ། གསར་ཤོག་དེ་ནང་འཁོད་དོན་ལྟར་ According to what was written in that newspaper. 2. vi. to exist, to be situated, to be present ། འདིར་འཁོད་སྐུ་མགྲོན་ཡོངས་ལ་ To all the guests present here. ། ཚོགས་འདུར་འཁོད་པའི་མི་ People present at the meeting ། གནས་ལ་འཁོད་ To settle (in a place). 3. labeled, called ། གནམ་གྲུ་འབི་ལྔ་བཅུ་ལྔ་གཉིས་འཁོད་པ་ The airplane called B-52.

འཁོད་བགོས་ (kȫȍgöö) distribution, allocation; va. འཁོད་བགོས་; — བྱེད་ to distribute, to allocate.

འཁོད་སྙོམ་ (kȫȍñom) sm. འཁོད་སྙོམས་.

འཁོད་སྙོམས་ (kȫȍñom) leveling, evening, equalizing; va.—གཏོང་ to level, to even, to equalize.

འཁོད་སྙོམས་ཁ་གསབ་ (kȫȍñom kāsəb) evening up or equalizing sth. by supplementation.

འཁོད་སྙོམས་པོ་ (kȫȍ ñōmbo) level, even, equal.

འཁོད་སྙོམས་རིང་ལུགས་ (khȫñom ri̲ŋluù) equalism, averageism.

འཁོད་དོན་ (kȫȍdön) phrase indicating that the content of sth. ("what was written") will be cited below ། གསལ་བསྒྲགས་ནང་འཁོད་དོན་ The content of what was in the announcement (follows).

འཁོད་ཚུལ་ (kǖüdzüü) the manner/ way/ circumstances that sth. was written ། གནས་ཚུལ་དེ་ཡིག་ཆའི་ནང་འཁོད་ཚུལ་ག་འདྲ་ཡིན་མིན་ཤེས་མ་བྱུང་ I don't know the manner in which the document was written.

འཁོན་ (kõn) 1. hatred, malice, bad feelings, hostility, anger; va.—འཛུག to cause/ create hostility ¶ གྲོགས་པོ་ངན་པ་དེས་གཅེན་གཅུང་གཉིས་འཁོན་བཙུག་བཞག That bad friend has caused hostility between the elder and younger brothers. 2. vi. to feel hatred/ malice/ hostility ¶ ཁོ་ཚོ་ནང་ཁུལ་འཁོན་བསྡད་ཡོད་པ་རེད་ Hostile feelings exist between them. 3. vi. to get hooked accidentally ¶ དབའ་ལོག་གཟེར་དཀར་ལ་འཁོན་ནས་རལ་སོང་ The clothes got caught on a nail and tore.

འཁོན་སྐྲན་ (kõndrɛn) extreme anger/ hostility; vi.—ཞུགས་ to get extremely angry.

འཁོན་འཁོན་ཐོགས་ཐོགས་ (kõngön tõgdɔɔ) trouble, hindrances, difficulty, problem, obstacle ¶ ལམ་བར་ལ་འཁོན་འཁོན་ཐོགས་ཐོགས་མང་པོ་བྱུང་ཙང་རྗེས་ལུས་ཐེབས་སོང་ (I) came late because (I) encountered many difficulties on the road. ¶ ཁོང་གི་མོ་ཊ་འཁོན་འཁོན་ཐོགས་ཐོགས་མེད་པར་གཏོང་གི་ཡོད་པ་རེད་ He is driving the car without running into problems.

འཁོན་འཁོན་ཐོགས་ཐོགས་མེད་པ་ (kõnkön tõgtog meèba) without hindrances/ obstacles.

འཁོན་འཁྲུག (kõndrug) sm. འཁོན་འཁྲུགས་.

འཁོན་འཁྲུགས་ (kõndrug) anger/ hostility/ hatred and fighting ¶ རྒྱ་དམར་འགོ་ཁྲིད་ནང་ཁུལ་འཁོན་འཁྲུགས་ཇེ་ཆེ་ཡོང་གི་ཡོད་པ་རེད་ There is increasing hatred and fighting among the Red Chinese Leaders.

འཁོན་གྲིབ་ (kõndrib) stroke caused by anger/ hatred.

འཁོན་དགྲ་ (kõndra) hated enemy/ foe.

འཁོན་འགྲས་ (kõndrɛɛ) sm. འཁོན་འཛིན་.

འཁོན་བཙུག (kõncuù) p. of འཁོན་འཛུག.

འཁོན་འཛུག (kõn juù) 1. see འཁོན་, 1.

འཁོན་ཐོགས་ (kõndɔɔ) sm. འཁོན་འཁོན་ཐོགས་ཐོགས་.

འཁོན་ཐོགས་མེད་པ་ (kõndɔg meèba) sm. འཁོན་འཁོན་ཐོགས་ཐོགས་མེད་པ་.

འཁོན་འདུམ་པའི་གཟུ་བ་ (kõndumbɛ suwə) sm. འདུམ་པ་.

འཁོན་སྡང་ (kõndaŋ) sm. འཁོན་འཛིན་.

འཁོན་སྡང་ཞེ་འཛིན་ (kõndaŋ shendzin) sm. འཁོན་འཛིན་ཁོག་བཅང་.

འཁོན་ནད་ (kõnnɛɛ) sm. འཁོན་སྐྲན་.

འཁོན་འབར་ (kõn bar) vi. to get very angry.

འཁོན་མེད་ (kõnmeè) 1. without malice/ hatred/ spite/ hostility. 2. sm. འཁོན་ཐོགས་མེད་པ་.

འཁོན་མེད་ཉི་མ་སྤྲིན་བྲལ་ (kõnmeè ñimə drĩndrɛɛ) disappearance of malice/ hatred/ spite/ hostility (like a cloud makes the sun disappear).

འཁོན་མེད་དབྱེན་མེད་ (kõnmeè yēnmeè) a relationship without malice and hostility.

འཁོན་ཚིག (kũndzii) words of hatred/ anger, hostile words; va.—ཤོད་ to speak words of hatred and hostility/ anger.

འཁོན་འཛིན་ (kõndzin) hatred, enmity; va.—བྱེད་ ¶ གྲལ་རིམ་གྱི་འཁོན་འཛིན་བཅངས་ནས་ Holding class hatred.

འཁོན་འཛིན་ཁོག་བཅང་ (kõndzin kõgjaŋ) holding on to hatred/ enmity, holding a grudge and hating; va.—བྱེད་.

འཁོན་འཛིན་ཆེན་པོ་ (kõndzin cēmbo) bitter and deep-seated hatred, profound hatred ¶ ཁོ་གཉིས་བར་ལ་འཁོན་འཛིན་ཆེན་པོ་ཞིག་ཞུགས་འདུག A bitter and deep seated hatred has arisen between the two of them.

འཁོན་འཛིན་སྡང་སེམས་ (kõndzin daŋsem) sm. འཁོན་འཛིན་.

འཁོན་འཛིན་ཞེ་ནད་ (kõndzin shenɛɛ) sm. འཁོན་འཛིན་ཁོག་བཅང་.

འཁོན་ཞུགས་ (kõn shug) vi. to enter into a state of hatred/ enmity ¶ གྲོགས་པོ་གཉིས་དབར་འཁོན་ཞུགས་བཞག Hatred has arisen between the two friends.

འཁོན་ཞུགས་འཐབ་འཛིང་ (kõnshug tāmdziŋ) struggling/ fighting based on hatred; va.—བྱེད་.

འཁོན་ཟབ་སྡང་ཆེ་ (kõnsəb daŋ cē) sm. འཁོན་འཁྲུས་ཆེན་པོ་.

འཁོན་བཟོད་ (kõnsöö) 1. bearing/ tolerating hatred; va.—བྱེད་.

འཁོན་རེས་ (kõnreè) feuding, hating reciprocally; va.—བྱེད་ to feud/ hate (back and forth).

འཁོན་ལན་ (kõnlɛn) revenge, vengeance, retaliation; va.—སློག་; —སྤྲོད་ to avenge, to retaliate.

འཁོན་ལན་ལྡན་ (kõnlɛn lɛ̃n) see འཁོན་ལན་.

འཁོན་ལན་རིང་ལུགས་ (kõnlɛn riŋluù) retaliationism, revanchism.

འཁོན་ལན་སློག (kõnlɛn lɔ̃ɔ) see འཁོན་.

འཁོན་ལན་སློག་པའི་རིང་ལུགས་ (kõnlɛn lɔ̃gbɛɛ riŋluù) sm. འཁོན་ལན་རིང་ལུགས་.

འཁོན་ལན་བསློགས་ (kõnlɛn lɔ̃ɔ) p. of འཁོན་ལན་སློག.

འཁོན་ཤ་ (kõnsha) revenge; va.—ལེན་.

འཁོན་སེམས་ (kõnsem) sm. འཁོན་འཛིན་.

འཁོན་སློག་ཉེས་འགེལ་ (kõnlɔɔ ñeègee) retaliating and blaming/ accusing.

འཁོན་གསོད་ (kõnsöö) killing out of hatred, premeditated murder.

འཁོབ་ (kõb) sm. ཁོབ་.

འཁོབ་དོ་ (kõbdo) see ཁོབ་དོ་.

འཁོབ་བལ་ (kõbbɛɛ) the coarse wool under the chest of sheep.

འཁོབས་ (kõb) sm. ཁོབ་.

འཁོར་ (kõɔ) 1. vi. to revolve, to rotate, to spin, to go around ¶ རླུང་གཡབ་འཁོར་བ་དང་ལྷག་པ་སིལ་སིལ་ཚོར་བ་རེད་ As soon as the fan spun they felt a cool breeze. 2. vi. (time + —) to have time elapse ¶ ང་ཨ་རི་རུ་སླེབས་ནས་ལོ་གསུམ་འཁོར་སོང་ Three years have elapsed since I arrived in America. ¶ ལོ་བཅུ་འཁོར་བའི་དགའ་སྟོན་བྱེད་ཀྱི་ཡོད་ (We) are celebrating the tenth anniversary. ¶ ངའི་སློབ་གྲྭར་གད་བདར་བྱེད་རེས་ཟླ་བ་གཅིག་ནང་ཚར་གཉིས་ཙམ་འཁོར་གྱི་ཡོད་ At my school my turn to sweep comes about twice a month. 3. vi. to be attracted/ drawn to ¶ མི་རྣམས་མེ་སྤྲོང་མཐའ་ལ་འཁོར་བ་རེད་ The people were drawn to the bonfire. 4. vi. to conceive, to get pregnant ¶ མོ་ལ་ཕྲུ་གུ་འཁོར་ནས་ཟླ་བ་བརྒྱད་སོང་ Its been eight months since she became pregnant. 5. vi. to get (an idea, thought) ¶ ང་བསམ་བློ་ཞིག་འཁོར་བྱུང་ I got an idea. 6. vi. to return ¶ རྒྱ་གར་ནས་ཚུར་འཁོར་ནས་ Having returned from India. 7. retinue, attendant. 8. (— + dat.-loc.) surrounding, around ¶ ཁང་པ་དེའི་མཐའ་འཁོར་ལ་ལྕགས་རི་འདུག There is a wall around that house. 9. a vehicle ¶ རླངས་འཁོར་ Automobile.

འཁོར་བཀག (kõɔgaà) braking (for cars/ motorcycles, etc.); va.—རྒྱག to brake.

འཁོར་སྐར་ (kõɔgaa) satellite (in space) ¶ འཁོར་སྐར་གྱི་བརྙན་འཕྲིན་ Satellite TV.

འཁོར་སྐར་བཟོས་མ་ (kõɔgaa jõõma) man-made satellite.

འཁོར་སྐར་ས་ངོས་ཚུར་སྡུད་ས་ཚིགས་ (kõɔgaa sãŋöö tsũũdüù sɔ̃dzii) a ground station that receives satellite transmissions/ signals.

འཁོར་སྐྱོད་ (kõrgyöö) sm. འཁོར་བསྐྱོད་.

འཁོར་སྐྱོད་ངན་པ་ (kõrgyöö ŋɛmba) vicious circle.

འཁོར་སྐྱོད་ལྟ་འཛལ་ཁང་ (kõrgyöö dãjɛɛgaŋ) a mobile observation/ checking station.

འཁོར་སྐྱོད་དཔེ་མཛོད་ཁང་ (kõrgyöö bēndzögaŋ) a traveling/ mobile library.

འཁོར་སྐྱོད་མ་ལག (kõrgyöö malaà) sm. འཁོར་བསྐྱོད་ཀྱི་རྒྱུད་རིམ་.

འཁོར་སྐྱོད་ཚན་སྒར་ (kõrgyöö tsɛ̃ngɔɔ) a mobile unit/ group.

འཁོར་བསྐྱོད་ (kõrköö) 1. circulation, circulating, revolving around. 2. making a circuit, going around.

འཁོར་བསྐྱོད་ཀྱི་རྒྱུད་རིམ་ (kõrgyöögi gyürim) the circulatory system.

འཁོར་ཁ་ (kõrga) a cycle (day, month, year).

འཁོར་ཁང་ (kõrgaŋ) workshop.

འཁོར་ཁེབས་ (kõrgeb) the cover or convertible hood of a car/ truck; va.—རྒྱག to cover with a hood.

འཁོར་ཁྱམས་ (kɔ̄ɔgyam) courtyard, corridor.
འཁོར་ཁྲི་ (kɔ̄ɔdri) sm. འཁོར་སྟེགས་.
འཁོར་འཁོར་ (kɔ̄ɔgɔr) coming around again and again, revolving, turning in circuits; vi.—བྱེད་ ¶ ངའི་སྙིང་སྡུག་གི་ཞལ་རས་ཡིད་ལ་འཁོར་འཁོར་བྱེད་ཀྱི་འདུག My sweetheart's face comes into my vision again and again.
འཁོར་གྱི་བློན་པོ་ (kɔ̄ɔgi lȭnbo) sm. འཁོར་བློན་.
འཁོར་གྲངས་ (kɔ̄ɔdraŋ) the number of revolutions/ turns/ circuits.
འཁོར་གྲི་ (kɔ̄ɔdri) a lathe or turning tool.
འཁོར་གྲུ་ (kɔ̄ɔdru) any kind of boat with a motor/ engine.
འཁོར་གླ་ (kɔ̄ɔla) fare for any vehicle (e.g., car rental fee).
འཁོར་གླ་གྲུ་གླ་ (kɔ̄ɔla dru̱la) fare for any vehicle or boat.
འཁོར་བགེགས་ (kɔ̄ɔgeg) a road/ traffic accident.
འཁོར་མགྲོན་ (kɔ̄ɔdrön) steward of an aristocrat.
འཁོར་འགུལ་ (kɔ̄ngüü) revolving, turning, swiveling ¶ འཁོར་འགུལ་རྐུབ་སྟེགས་ Swivel chair (or chair on rollers).
འཁོར་འགྲུལ་ (kɔ̄ndrüü) wheeled travel, vehicular travel.
འཁོར་འགྲོ་ (kɔ̄ndro) sm. འཁོར་བསྐྱོད་.
འཁོར་རྒྱ་ (kɔ̄ɔgya) 1. circumference, perimeter ¶ དཀར་ཡོལ་འདིའི་འཁོར་རྒྱ་ཆུང་ཆུང་རེད་ The circumference of the cup is small. 2. area, space ¶ གཞིས་ཀ་འདིར་ས་ཞིང་གི་འཁོལ་རྒྱ་ཆེན་པོ་ཡོད་པ་རེད་ This estate has a large area of (arable) fields.
འཁོར་རྒྱུག (kɔ̄ɔgyuù) turnover (in sales/ business) ¶ ལུང་པ་འདི་ཚ་བ་ཆེན་པོ་ཡིན་ཙང་དབྱར་དུས་ཚོང་གི་འཁོར་རྒྱུག་ཆེན་པོ་མི་འདུག Because this place is very hot, the turnover in sales is small during the summer.
འཁོར་རྒྱུག་བྱེད་ཚད་ (kɔ̄ɔgyuù ce̱dzɛɛ̀) the rate of turnover.
འཁོར་སྒམ་ (kɔ̄ɔgam) sm.* འཁོར་སྒྲོམ་.
འཁོར་སྒུག་ཁང་ (kɔ̄ɔguùgaŋ) waiting room at a bus or train station.
འཁོར་སྒྱུར་ (kɔ̄ɔgyur) sm. འཁོར་ལོས་སྒྱུར་.
འཁོར་སྒྲ་ (kɔ̄ɔdra) the sound/ noise of machines, cars, etc.
འཁོར་སྒྲོམ་བཟོ་གྲྭ་ (kɔ̄rgam so̱dra) railway carriage factory.
འཁོར་སྒྲོལ་ (kɔ̄ɔdröö) railway car/ carriage ¶ འཁོར་སྒྲོམ་ཉི་ཤུ་ཡོད་པའི་མེ་འཁོར་ A train consisting of twenty cars.
འཁོར་བཅས་ (kɔ̄ɔjɛɛ̀) attendants, retinue, dependents ¶ ང་ཚོ་ནང་མི་འཁོར་བཅས་ཚང་མ་གླིང་ཀར་ཕྱིན་པ་ཡིན་ The whole family including the servants went on a picnic. ¶ བློན་པོ་འཁོར་ཆས་ The minister and his retinue.
འཁོར་ཆས་ (kɔ̄ɔjɛɛ̀) tools or equipment used for a car or vehicle.
འཁོར་ཆས་སྒ་ཆས་ (kɔ̄rjɛɛ̀ ga̱jɛɛ̀) harnessing/ tying equipment used on an animal-pulled cart.
འཁོར་ཆུ་ (kɔ̄ɔju) whirlpool.
འཁོར་རྗེས་ (kɔ̄ɔjeè) the track/ imprint of a wheel (on the ground).
འཁོར་ཉེ་དབང་ (kɔ̄ɔñewaŋ) retinue/ attendents of a king or ruler.
འཁོར་གཉིས་ལྕགས་གཉིས་ཀྱི་ཐོང་གཤོལ་ (kɔ̄ɔñiì cəgñiìgi thōŋshöö) a two-pronged plow with two wheels.
འཁོར་གཉིས་མ་ (kɔ̄ɔñimə) sth. with two wheels.
འཁོར་གཏན་ (kɔ̄ɔdɛn) door knob.
འཁོར་རྟགས་ (kɔ̄ɔdaà) license plate, car or truck number.
འཁོར་རྟེན་ (kɔ̄ɔden) axle (of a vehicle) ¶ འཁོར་རྟེན་བཟོ་གྲྭ་ An axle factory.
འཁོར་ལྟེ་ (kɔ̄ɔde) axle.
འཁོར་ལྟེ་ལྕགས་རིལ་ (kɔ̄ɔde jəərii) ball bearing ¶ འཁོར་ལྟེ་ལྕགས་རིལ་བཟོ་གྲྭ Ball bearing factory.
འཁོར་ལྟེ་ལྕགས་རིལ་ཅན་ (kɔ̄ɔde jəgrijen) sm. འཁོར་སྟེགས་ལྕགས་རིལ་ཅན་.
འཁོར་སྟེགས་ (kɔ̄ɔdeg) a lathe, a machine tool ¶ འཁོར་སྟེགས་ཀྱིས་གཏུབ་གཞོག་བྱེད་པ་ Cutting by means of a lathe.
འཁོར་སྟེགས་ལྕགས་རིལ་ཅན་ (kɔ̄ɔdeg jārijɛn) having ball bearings.
འཁོར་སྟེགས་མདེལ་རིལ་མ་ (kɔ̄ɔdeg dɛ̱riimə) sm. འཁོར་སྟེགས་ལྕགས་རིལ་ཅན་.
འཁོར་སྟེགས་རྡུང་སྒྲུན་བཟོ་གྲྭ་ (kɔ̄ɔdeg du̱ŋdrün so̱dra) a machine tool forging factory.
འཁོར་སྟེགས་ཞིག་གསོ་བཟོ་གྲྭ་ (kɔ̄ɔdeg shi̱gso so̱dra) a machine tool maintenance factory.
འཁོར་སྟེགས་བཞུ་ལྡུག་བཟོ་གྲྭ་ (kɔ̄ɔdeg shu̱dug so̱dra) a machine tool casting/ founding factory.
འཁོར་སྟེགས་ལྷུ་ལག་བཟོ་གྲྭ་ (kɔ̄ɔdeg lhūlaà so̱dra) a machine tool parts factory.
འཁོར་སྟེགས་བཟོ་གྲྭ་ (kɔ̄ɔdeg so̱dra) machine tool factory.
འཁོར་བརྟེན་ (kɔ̄ɔden) sm. འཁོར་རྟེན་.
འཁོར་མཐའ་ (kɔ̄ɔda) circumference, perimeter ¶ ལུས་རྩལ་ཐང་གི་འཁོར་མཐའ་ The circumference of a sports playing field.
འཁོར་མཐའ་མེད་པ་ (kɔ̄ɔda me̱èba) 1. that which can never be repaid ¶ བཀའ་དྲིན་འཁོར་མཐའ་མེད་པ་ Gratitude that which can never be repaid. 2. samsara (cycle of life and death in Buddhism).
འཁོར་འཐོམས་ (kɔ̄ndom) vi. to become dazed and giddy.
འཁོར་དུས་ (kɔ̄ɔdüǜ) a turn, a rotation; va.—བཟོ་ ¶ ལས་ཁུངས་ནང་གཙང་སྦྲ་བྱ་རྒྱུའི་རེས་མོས་འཁོར་དུས་ཞིག་བཟོས་ན་ཡག་པོ་འདུག It will be good if we make a rotation (schedule) for cleaning up the office.
འཁོར་དོན་ཁང་ (kɔ̄ɔdöngaŋ) a division of the railway service responsible for the operation and maintenance of trains.
འཁོར་གདུང་ (kɔ̄ɔduŋ) abbr. འཁོར་ལོའི་གདུང་མ་.
འཁོར་མདའ་ (kɔ̄nda) sm. འཁོར་རྟེན་.
འཁོར་མདའ་རྒྱུ་སྣོད་ (kɔ̄nda gyu̱nöò) hub of a wheel.
འཁོར་འདབས་ (kɔ̄ndəb) (— + dat.-loc.) surrounding, near, around ¶ ཁང་པའི་འཁོར་འདབས་ལ་ཤིང་སྣ་མང་པོ་བཏབས་འདུག Many different kinds of trees have been planted around the house.
འཁོར་འདས་ (kɔ̄ndɛɛ̀) abbr. samsara and nirvana.
འཁོར་རྡར་ (kɔ̄ɔdar) emery wheel, grinding wheel ¶ འཁོར་རྡར་བཟོ་གྲྭ་ An emery/ grinding wheel factory.
འཁོར་རྡོ་ (kɔ̄ɔdo) rock placed under a tire to prevent the car from rolling down a hill; va.—རྒྱག.
འཁོར་ནས་འགྲོ་ (kɔ̄ɔnɛ dro̱) vi. to revolve, to turn round.
འཁོར་ནུས་ལྡན་པ་ (kɔ̄ɔnüù dɛ̱mba) powered ¶ རྡུལ་ཕྲ་རབ་ཀྱི་འཁོར་ནུས་ལྡན་པའི་གྲུ་གཟིངས་ Nuclear powered ship.
འཁོར་པོ་ (kɔ̄ɔbo) 1. servant, attendant (male). 2. see ཁ་འཁོར་པོ་. 3. spinning, revolving, turning ¶ རླངས་འཁོར་གྱི་འཁོར་ལོ་འདི་འཁོར་པོ་མི་འདུག The wheel of the car is not spinning well.
འཁོར་དཔོན་ (kɔ̄ɔbön) minister.
འཁོར་ཕྱོགས་ (kɔ̄ɔjɔɔ̀) 1. direction of rotation/ turning/ revolving. 2. tendency, trend, direction ¶ དུས་ཀྱི་འཁོར་ཕྱོགས་ཀྱི་ཟིལ་ཤུགས་འོག་གཞི་ནས་མོས་མཐུན་ཞུས་པ་རེད་ They only agreed because of the popular trend of the times. ¶ དམངས་སེམས་འཁོར་ཕྱོགས་ The inclination of the masses.
འཁོར་ཕྲེང་ (kɔ̄ɔdreŋ) a series or line of cars/ carts/ vehicles ¶ འཁོར་སྒྲོམ་ 20 ཡོད་པའི་འཁོར་ཕྲེང་ A train of twenty cars (compartments).
འཁོར་བ་ (kɔ̄ɔwa) transmigratory existence, the world of samsara.
འཁོར་བ་ཉམས་ལེན་ (kɔ̄ɔwa ña̱mlen) bearing the sufferings of samsara; va.—བྱེད་ to bear the sufferings of samsara.
འཁོར་བ་དོང་སྤྲུགས་ (kɔ̄ɔwa to̱ŋdruù) shung. overcoming all the sufferings of samsara.
འཁོར་བ་པ་ (kɔ̄ɔwaba) sentient beings living in samsara.
འཁོར་བ་འཛིན་ (kɔ̄ɔwa dzi̱n) 1. va. to establish a

family/ household ¶ ཁོང་ལ་མནའ་མ་བླངས་ནས་འཁོར་བ་འཛིན་པ་རེད་ He took a bride and established a family. 2. va. to come back as a human to help all sentient beings (for Bodhisattvas).

འཁོར་བའི་སྐྱོན་ (kɔ̄ɔ̄wɛ gyȫn) defects of samsara: birth, old age, sickness and death.

འཁོར་བའི་ཁྱིམ་ (kɔ̄ɔ̄wɛ kyīm) home of a layperson.

འཁོར་བའི་རྒྱ་མཚོ་ (kɔ̄ɔ̄wɛ gya̲tso) ocean of samsara/ existence.

འཁོར་བའི་ཆོས་ (kɔ̄ɔ̄wɛ cȫȫ) secular philosophy.

འཁོར་བའི་འཐེན་ཐག་ (kɔ̄ɔ̄wɛ tēntaà) the causes that makes it difficult to cut one's ties to samsara.

འཁོར་བའི་ལས་ (kɔ̄ɔ̄wɛ lɛ̲ɛ̀) the work of samsara, behavior in the world of samsara, karmic existence.

འཁོར་བར་དགའ་སྟོན་རྟེན་འབྲེལ་ (kɔ̄ɔ̄waa ga̲dön de̲mdree) commemorative/ anniversary celebration.

འཁོར་བར་ནས་སྤྱད་ (kɔ̄ɔ̄waa nɛ̲ɛ̀jɛɛ̀) using last year's production until the new harvest comes in.

འཁོར་བར་ཞེན་ཆགས་མེད་པ་ (kɔ̄ɔ̄waa she̲ncaà me̲èba) the renunciation of desire and worldly attachments.

འཁོར་བྱང་ (kɔ̄ɔ̄jaŋ) vehicle license plate.

འཁོར་བྱེད་སོ་གྲི་ (kɔ̄ɔ̄jeɛ̀ sōdri) a hobbing cutter.

འཁོར་བློན་ (kɔ̄ɔ̄lȫn) courtier.

འཁོར་འབངས་ (kɔ̄ɔ̄baŋ) retinue, circle of one's family/ friends/ subjects ¶ དཔོན་ཆེན་དེས་འཁོར་འབངས་མང་པོ་ཞིག་ཁྲིད་འདུག The high official has brought a large retinue of people with him. ¶ འཁོར་འབངས་བྱམས་བརྩེས་སྐྱོང་བ་ To treat one's family/ friends/ subjects with compassion.

འཁོར་མ་ (kɔ̄ɔ̄ma) flail.

འཁོར་མོ་ (kɔ̄ɔ̄mo) female servant.

འཁོར་མོ་ཡུག (kɔ̄ɔ̄moyug) all (year) round ¶ ལོ་འཁོར་མོ་ཡུག་ལས་ཀ་བྱས་པ་ཡིན་ (I) worked all year round.

འཁོར་དམག (kɔ̄ɔ̄maà) common soldiers.

འཁོར་རྩིབས་ (kɔ̄ɔ̄dzib) spoke on a wheel.

འཁོར་རྩིས་ (kɔ̄ɔ̄dzii) making a calculation in one's head; va.—རྒྱག.

འཁོར་ཚད་ (kɔ̄ɔ̄dzɛɛ̀) rate of rotation/ revolution/ turn.

འཁོར་ཚོགས་ (kɔ̄ɔ̄dzoò) a meeting of retinue ¶ བློན་ཆེན་འཁོར་ཚོགས་ A meeting of the Prime Minister and his retinue.

འཁོར་འཚེམ་ (kɔ̄ɔ̄dzem) stitches (sown by a sewing machine); va.—རྒྱག.

འཁོར་ཞག (kɔ̄ɔ̄shaà) home-leave; va.—ཞུ་ to request home-leave.

འཁོར་ཞག་གུང་སེང་ (kɔ̄ɔ̄shaà gu̲ŋsaŋ) sm. འཁོར་ཞག.

འཁོར་གཟུགས་ (kɔ̄ɔ̄suù) car/ vehicle body.

འཁོར་གཟུགས་བཟོ་གྲྭ་ (kɔ̄ɔ̄sug so̲dra) automobile/ vehicle body plant.

འཁོར་བཟོས་ཤོག་བུ་ (kɔ̄ɔ̄söö̀ shūgu) machine-made paper.

འཁོར་ གླུམ་ (kɔ̄ndum) mediating between relatives/ friends.

འཁོར་ཡུག (kɔ̄ɔ̄yuù) sm. ཁོར་ཡུག.

འཁོར་ཡུག་སྐྱིད་སྡུག (kɔ̄ɔ̄yuù gyīduù) an environmental association.

འཁོར་ཡུག་སྲུང་སྐྱོབ་ (kɔ̄ɔ̄yuù sūŋgyob) sm. ཁོར་ཡུག་སྲུང་སྐྱོབ་.

འཁོར་ཡུན་ (kɔ̄ɔ̄yün) the cycle of time it takes for sth. to be done or occur ¶ འཛིག་རྟེན་འཕུར་གྲུས་འཛམ་གླིང་ལ་སྐོར་བ་ཐེངས་གཅིག་འཁོར་ཡུན་ནི་ As for the cyclic time it takes for a spaceship to go around the earth.

འཁོར་ཡུན་གྱི་རང་བཞིན་ (kɔ̄ɔ̄yüngi rə̲ŋshin) periodicity, cyclicity (in chemistry) ¶ འཁོར་ཡུན་གནས་ལུགས་ Periodic law (in chemistry/ physics).

འཁོར་ཡུན་རེའུ་མིག (kɔ̄ryün ri̲umig) periodic table/ chart.

འཁོར་གཡག (kɔ̄ɔ̄yaà) bolt, lock.

འཁོར་གཡབ་ (kɔ̄ɔ̄yəb) sm. འཁོར་ཁྲམས་.

འཁོར་གཡོག (kɔ̄ɔ̄yɔɔ̀) servants, entourage, retinue.

འཁོར་རེས་ (kɔ̄ɔ̄reè) by rotation, by turns; va.—བྱེད་ ¶ ལས་ཀ་འདི་འཁོར་རེས་བྱེད་ཀྱི་ཡོད་དམ་ Is this work done by turns?

འཁོར་རོ་རོ་ (kɔ̄ɔ̄ ro̲ro) encircling, circling around ¶ མི་མང་པོ་འཁོར་རོ་རོ་བྲོ་འཁྲབ་བཞིན་འདུག Many people are circling around dancing.

འཁོར་ལངས་ (kɔ̄ɔ̄ la̲ŋ) vi. to be in heat (for animals).

འཁོར་ལམ་ (kɔ̄rlam) motorable road/ highway.

འཁོར་ལས་ (kɔ̄ɔ̄lɛɛ̀) lathe work.

འཁོར་ལོ་ (kɔ̄ɔ̄lo) 1. wheel. 2. vehicle; va.—གཏོང་; —སྐྱུར་ to drive a (wheeled vehicle); va.—འགོག to brake/ stop (a vehicle).

འཁོར་ལོ་རྒྱུགས་ཤུལ་ (kɔ̄ɔ̄lo gyu̲gshüü) wheel tracks/ ruts.

འཁོར་ལོ་སྦྲག (kɔ̄ɔ̄lo drɔ̲ɔ̀) va. to harness an animal to a cart.

འཁོར་ལོ་ཅན་ (kɔ̄rlojɛn) a wheeled vehicle/ implement.

འཁོར་ལོ་གཏོང་ (kɔ̄ɔ̄lo dōŋ) see འཁོར་ལོ་.

འཁོར་ལོ་འཐེན་ (kɔ̄ɔ̄lo) va. to pull a vehicle, cart, carriage.

འཁོར་ལོ་ལྡོག་གཏོང་ (kɔ̄ɔ̄lo dɔ̲gdoŋ) backing up/ reversing a vehicle; va.—རྒྱག.

འཁོར་ལོ་ཕྱིར་སྐོར་ (kɔ̄ɔ̄lo cīīgɔɔ) sm. འཁོར་ལོ་ལྡོག་གཏོང་.

འཁོར་ལོ་ཕྱིར་ཤེག (kɔ̄ɔ̄lo cīrshiì) sm. འཁོར་ལོ་ལྡོག་གཏོང་.

འཁོར་ལོ་བའི་ལག་ཁྱེར་ (kɔ̄ɔ̄lowɛ la̲ggyer) driver's license.

འཁོར་ལོ་བར་བརྗེ་ (kɔ̄ɔ̄lo pa̲rje) changing or transferring vehicles on a trip; va.—བྱེད་.

འཁོར་ལོ་འབབ་ཚུགས་ (kɔ̄ɔ̄lo bə̲bdzuù) bus station/ depot.

འཁོར་ལོ་རྩིབས་བརྒྱད་ (kɔ̄ɔ̄lo dzībgyɛɛ̀) wheel with eight spokes (Buddhist symbol).

འཁོར་ལོ་རྩིབས་སྟོང་ (kɔ̄ɔ̄lo dzībdoŋ) wheel with a thousand spokes (Buddhist symbol).

འཁོར་ལོ་ཚོད་ལྟ་ (kɔ̄ɔ̄lo tsȫȫda) test/ trial of a vehicle; va.—བྱེད་.

འཁོར་ལོ་གཟུར་ (kɔ̄ɔ̄lo su̲r) va. to give/ yield the right of way to another vehicle.

འཁོར་ལོ་རིན་པོ་ཆེ་ (kɔ̄ɔ̄lo ri̲mboje) precious wheel (one of the seven auspicious royal symbols).

འཁོར་ལོ་ས་ཚིགས་ (kɔ̄ɔ̄lo sədzig) a bus or train station.

འཁོར་ལོ་ས་ཚིགས་ཀྱི་དོག་ཁྲིས་ཁང་ (kɔ̄ɔ̄lo sədziggi dɔ̲gdreègaŋ) luggage room at a bus or train station.

འཁོར་ལོ་ས་ཚིགས་ཀྱི་འཛིན་བྱང་འཚོང་ས་ (kɔ̄ɔ̄lo sədziggi dzi̲njaŋ tsɔŋsa) ticket office at a bus or train station.

འཁོར་ལོ་སོ་ཅན་ (kɔ̄ɔ̄lo sōjɛn) gear, cogwheel.

འཁོར་ལོག་རྒྱག (kɔ̄ɔ̄log gya̲à) vi. to be barren (for women).

འཁོར་ལོའི་འགྱིག་ལྤགས་ (kɔ̄ɔ̄lö gyigbaà) rubber tire of a car/ vehicle.

འཁོར་ལོའི་འགྲན་བསྡུར་ (kɔ̄ɔ̄lö dre̲ndur) motor race, vehicle race; va.—བྱེད་.

འཁོར་ལོའི་རྒྱུ་མ་ (kɔ̄ɔ̄lö gyu̲mə) spokes on a wheel.

འཁོར་ལོའི་སྒུག་ཁང་ (kɔ̄ɔ̄lö gu̲ggaŋ) waiting room (in a railway or bus station).

འཁོར་ལོའི་ལྕགས་ཐག་ (kɔ̄ɔ̄lö jāgdaà) tire chains.

འཁོར་ལོའི་ཏིང་ག (kɔ̄ɔ̄lö dīŋgə) lathe on which wooden bowls are made.

འཁོར་ལོའི་ཏིང་ལྕགས་ (kɔ̄ɔ̄lö dīŋjaà) metal instrument used to carve wooden bowls on a lathe.

འཁོར་ལོའི་སྟེགས་ཤུབས་ (kɔ̄ɔ̄lö dēgshub) covering/ sheath on a seat in a vehicle.

འཁོར་ལོའི་གདུང་མ་ (kɔ̄ɔ̄lö du̲ŋma) axle.

འཁོར་ལོའི་འདུག་སྟེགས་ (kɔ̄rlö du̲ŋdeg) seat in a vehicle.

འཁོར་ལོའི་བར་ཐག (kɔ̄ɔlö pardaà) track/ tread on a wheel.

འཁོར་ལོའི་སྣར་འཛུ་ (kɔ̄ɔlö banju) handlebars (of vehicles).

འཁོར་ལོའི་མུ་ཁྱུད་ (kɔ̄ɔlö mugyüù) rim of a wheel.

འཁོར་ལོའི་ཚེམ་བུ་ (kɔ̄ɔlö tsı̄mbu) stitching done by a sewing machine.

འཁོར་ལོའི་རིགས་ (kɔ̄ɔlö rig) (the category) vehicles.

འཁོར་ལོའི་སོ་ (kɔ̄ɔlö sō) teeth of a gear/ cogwheel.

འཁོར་ལོའི་སྲོག་ཤིང་ (kɔ̄ɔlö sōgshiŋ) vehicle axle.

འཁོར་ལོའི་ཨ་མ་ (kɔ̄ɔlö āma) a vehicle engine/ motor.

འཁོར་ལོའི་ཨང་རྟགས་ (kɔ̄ɔlö āŋdaà) license plate or car number.

འཁོར་ལོའི་ཨང་རིམ་ (kɔ̄ɔlö āŋrim) serial number of a vehicle.

འཁོར་ལོས་སྒྱུར་བའི་རྒྱལ་པོ་ (kɔ̄ɔlöö gyurwɛ gyɛɛbo) universal monarch (in Buddhism).

འཁོར་ལོས་རྫི་ (kɔ̄ɔlöö dzī) vi. to be run over (by a vehicle) ¶ ཕྲུ་གུ་དེ་འཁོར་ལོས་བརྫིས་པ་རེད་ The child was run over by a car.

འཁོར་ཤུགས་ (kɔ̄ɔshuù) coupling, impacting (in physics).

འཁོར་ཤུགས་ཐེབས་ས་ (kɔ̄ɔshuù tēbsa) point of impact (in physics).

འཁོར་ཤུལ་ (kɔ̄ɔshüü) sm. འཁོར་ལོ་རྒྱུགས་ཤུལ་.

འཁོར་ཤུལ་ཀོང་ཆུའི་ནང་གི་ཉ་ (kɔ̄ɔshüü gōŋcü naŋgi ña) a hopeless situation [Lit. a fish in a puddle made by a wheel].

འཁོར་ས་ (kɔ̄ɔsa) 1. a meeting/ gathering, an assembling/ rallying place. 2. near, adjacent to. 3. sm. ལྷུགས་རི་.

འཁོར་སུག་ (kɔ̄ɔsug) small wheels attached to suitcases, etc.

འཁོར་སོ་ (kɔ̄ɔso) tooth of a gear/ cogwheel.

འཁོར་སོ་སྒྲིག་སྦྱོར་ (kɔ̄ɔso drigjɔr) cog or gear wheels engaging.

འཁོར་སོ་བར་སྟོང་ (kɔ̄ɔso pardoŋ) neutral gear (on a car's transmission).

འཁོར་སྲུང་ (kɔ̄ɔsuŋ) abbr. of འཁོར་ལུགས་སྲུང་སྐྱོབ་.

འཁོར་གསུམ་ (kɔ̄ɔsum) 1. tricycle. 2. (in Tibetan grammar) the doer, the action and the object. 3. a phrase said when making a point in debating. 4. body, mind and speech. 5. bow and arrow, sword and spear.

འཁོར་གསུམ་རྐང་འཁོར་ (kɔ̄ɔsum gāŋgɔɔ) pedicab, tricycle.

འཁོར་གསོར་ (kɔ̄ɔsɔr) a drill (tool).

འཁོལ་: p. ཁོལ་; f. འཁོལ་ (kōō) vi. to be/ get boiled ¶ ཆུ་ཁོལ་བཞག The water has boiled.

འཁོལ་: p. བཀོལ་; f. བཀོལ་; imp. ཁོལ་ (kōō) va. to make sb. serve/ work.

འཁོལ་འཁོལ་ (kōōgöö) sm. འཕལ་ལི་འཁོལ་ལི་.

འཁོལ་གྲང་ (kōōdraŋ) cold water that has been boiled.

འཁོལ་ཆུ་ (kōōju) boiled water.

འཁོལ་པོ་ (kōōbo) 1. boiled; va.—བྱེད་ ¶ ཆུ་འདི་འཁོལ་པོ་བྱུང་མི་འདུག This water has not boiled well. 2. see སེམས་ཆུ་འཁོལ་པོ་.

འཁོལ་མ་ (kōōma) 1. maid-servant. 2. boiled water.

འཁོལ་ཚད་ (kōōdzɛɛ̀) boiling point.

འཁོལ་གསོས་རྒྱག (kōōsöö gyaà) va. to add cold water to sth. that is cooking.

འཁོས་ཀ་ (kōōga) standard of living, livelihood ¶ འཁོས་ཀ་ཞན་པ་ A low/ inferior standard of living. ¶ འཁོས་ཀར་གཞིགས་པས་ཁྲལ་འདུས་པ་རེད་ They collected taxes on the basis of their livelihood.

འཁོས་ཀ་ཞན་པ་ (kōōga shɛmba) 1. poor, low/ inferior standard of living. 2. incapable.

འཁོས་ཁ་ (kōōga) sm. འཁོས་ཀ་.

འཁོས་འཁྱིལ་ཚུགས་ (kōōgyil tsūù) va. to settlle families.

འཁོས་ལྡོགས་ (kōōjoò) according to one's ability/ capability ¶ རང་ཉིད་ཀྱི་འཁོས་ལྡོགས་ལ་གཞིགས་པས་ལས་ཀ་བྱེད་དགོས་ One should work according to one's ability.

འཁོས་ཆུང་ (kōōjuŋ) sm. མཁོས་ཀ་ཞན་པ་.

འཁོས་བསྟུན་ (kōōdün) according to one's means ¶ ཁོང་གིས་འཁོས་བསྟུན་གྱི་ཞལ་འདེབས་ཕུལ་བ་རེད་ He donated according to his means.

འཁོས་ཐང་དཔག་ཐང་ (kōōtaŋ bāgtaŋ) sm. འཁོས་དཔག.

འཁོས་ཐབས་ (kōndəb) sm. འཁོས་ཀ་.

འཁོས་བདེ་ (kōōde) good livelihood/ standard of living/ means.

འཁོས་དཔག་ (kōōbaà) standard of living, livelihood ¶ ང་རང་འཁོས་དཔག་ལ་གཞིགས་པའི་འཚོ་བ་སྐྱེལ་གྱི་ཡོད་ I am living according to my standard of living.

འཁོས་བབ་ (kōbab) sm. འཁོས་ཀ་.

འཁོས་འབྱོར་ (kōnjɔɔ) sm. འཁོས་ཀ་.

འཁོས་ཞན་ (kōōshɛn) poor livelihood/ standard of living.

འཁྱག: p. འཁྱགས་; f. འཁྱག (kyāà) 1. vi. to be/ get cold ¶ བྱང་ངོས་ལ་འགྲོ་དུས་ང་ཐེངས་མང་པོ་འཁྱགས་བྱུང་ When I went north I was cold many times. 2. vi. to become frozen, to freeze ¶ ཆུ་འཁྱགས་ཐེབས་བཞག The water froze. 3. also used interchangeably with འཁྱགས་ in compounds. 4. (with སེམས་པ་) vi. to be sad, to have a heavy heart [Lit. to have one heart/ mind get cold].

འཁྱག་གླུང་ (kyəgluŋ) sm. འཁྱགས་གླུང་.

འཁྱག་སྒྲང་ (kyāgdraŋ) sm. འཁྱགས་སྒྲོས་.

འཁྱག་འཁྱོག (kyāŋgyog) crooked, zigzag, winding ¶ ལམ་འཁྱག་འཁྱོག A winding road.

འཁྱག་གྲང་ (kyāgdraŋ) sm. འཁྱགས་གྲང་.

འཁྱག་གྲུ་ (kyəgdru) sm. འཁྱགས་གྲུ་.

འཁྱག་རྒྱག (kyāà gyaà) vi. to become frozen, to freeze over ¶ ཆུ་འཁྱག་བརྒྱབ་བཞག The water froze over.

འཁྱག་སྒམ་ (kyāgam) sm. འཁྱགས་སྒམ་.

འཁྱག་སྒོམ་ (kyāggom) sm. འཁྱགས་སྒོམ་.

འཁྱག་ཆུ་གདོང་ (kyəgju dōŋ) sm. འཁྱགས་ཆུ་གདོང་.

འཁྱག་གདོང་ (kyāà dōŋ) sm. འཁྱགས་གདོང་.

འཁྱག་གདོར་གྲུ་གཟིངས་ (kyāgdɔr trudzin) sm. འཁྱགས་གདོར་གྲུ་གཟིངས་.

འཁྱག་གདོར་དུལ་ཕྲན་གྲུ་གཟིངས་ (kyādɔr dütren trudzin) sm. འཁྱགས་གདོར་དུལ་ཕྲན་གྲུ་གཟིངས་.

འཁྱག་ལྡོགས་ (kyāà dōg) sm. འཁྱགས་ལྡོགས་.

འཁྱག་ལྡོགས་སྐྱོམ་གསུམ་ (kyāà dōg gōmsum) sm. འཁྱགས་ལྡོགས་སྐྱོམ་གསུམ་.

འཁྱག་ཐེབས་ (kyāà tēè) sm. འཁྱགས་ཐེབས་.

འཁྱག་ཐོག་སྤོ་ལོ་ (kyāgdɔɔ bōlo) sm. འཁྱགས་ཐོག་པོ་ལོ་.

འཁྱག་དུས་ (kyəgdüü) sm. འཁྱག་དུས་.

འཁྱག་དུས་གོས་དང་ལྡོགས་དུས་ཟས་ (kyāgdüü kōōdaŋ dōgdüü sɛɛ̀) sm. འཁྱགས་དུས་གོས་དང་ལྡོགས་དུས་ཟས་.

འཁྱག་དོང་ (kyāgdoŋ) sm. འཁྱགས་དོང་.

འཁྱག་འདར་ (kyāgdar) sm. འཁྱགས་འདར་.

འཁྱག་ནད་ (kyāgnɛɛ̀) sm. འཁྱགས་ནད་.

འཁྱག་སྣང་ (kyāgnaŋ) sm. འཁྱགས་སྣང་.

འཁྱག་པ་ (kyāgba) sm. འཁྱགས་པ་.

འཁྱག་པ་ལག་མཐིལ་ཙམ་ལ་ཉི་མ་སྤུན་བདུན་ཤར་ (kyāgba lagtiidzamlə ñimə bündün shār) many people engaged on a trivial matter that could be done by a few, overkill [Lit. (for) a palmful of ice, seven suns shining].

འཁྱག་པག (kyāgbaà) sm. འཁྱགས་པ་.

འཁྱག་པོ་ (kyāgbo) sm. འཁྱགས་པོ་.

འཁྱག་ཕད་ (kyāgpɛɛ̀) sm. འཁྱགས་ཕད་.

འཁྱག་བག (kyāgbaā) sm. འཁྱགས་བག.

འཁྱག་འབུར་ (kyāgbur) sm. འཁྱགས་འབུར་.

འཁྱག་འབྱར་ (kyāgjar) sm. འཁྱགས་འབྱར་.

འཁྱགས་འབྲུམ་ (kyəgdrum) sm. འཁྱགས་འབྲུར་.

འཁྱག་སྦོས་ (kyāgböö) sm. འཁྱགས་སྦོས་.

འཁྱག་སྦྲིད་ (khəgdri) sm. འཁྱགས་སྦྲིད་.

འཁྱག་ཚད་ (kyāgdzɛɛ̀) sm. འཁྱགས་ཚད་.

འཁྱག་མཛོད་ (kyāgdzöö) sm. འཁྱགས་མཛོད་.

འཁྱག་བཞུད་དབྱུག་རྩེད་ (kyāgshüü yūgdzeè) hockey.

འཁྱག་བཞུད་དབྱུག་རྩེད་མཐུན་ཚོགས་ (kyāgshüü yūgdzeè tūndzɔɔ) hockey league/ association.

འཁྱག་ཟམ་ (kyāgsam) sm. འཁྱགས་ཟམ་.

འཁྱག་ཟས་ཚོང་ཁང་ (kyāgsɛɛ̀ tsōŋgaŋ) sm. འཁྱགས་ཟས་ཚོང་ཁང་.
འཁྱག་བཟོ་ཁང་ (kyāgsogaŋ) sm. འཁྱག་མཛོད་.
འཁྱག་བཟོ་འཕྲུལ་འཁོར་ (kyāgso) sm. འཁྱགས་བཟོ་འཕྲུལ་འཁོར་.
འཁྱག་ར་ (kyāgra) sm. འཁྱགས་ར་.
འཁྱག་རངས་ (kyāgraŋ) sm. འཁྱགས་རེངས་.
འཁྱག་རལ་ (kyāgrɛɛ) sm. འཁྱགས་རལ་.
འཁྱག་རལ་ཁྲིག་ཁྲིག (kyāgrɛɛ drɔ̄gdrɔ̄g) sm. འཁྱགས་རལ་ཁྲིག་ཁྲིག.
འཁྱག་རི་ (kyə̄gri) sm. འཁྱགས་རི་.
འཁྱག་རིམ་ (kyə̄grim) sm. འཁྱགས་རིམ་.
འཁྱག་རུམ་ (kyə̄grum) sm. འཁྱགས་རུམ་.
འཁྱག་རེངས་ (kyāgreŋ) sm. འཁྱགས་རེངས་.
འཁྱག་རོམ་ (kyāgrom) sm. འཁྱགས་རོམ་.
འཁྱག་ལྷུང་ (kyāgluŋ) sm. འཁྱགས་ལྷུང་.
འཁྱག་ལས་བཟོ་གྲྭ་ (kyāglɛɛ̀ sodra) sm. འཁྱགས་ལས་བཟོ་གྲྭ་.
འཁྱག་ལུམས་ (kyāglum) sm. འཁྱགས་ལུམས་.
འཁྱག་ཤ་ (kyāgsha) sm. འཁྱགས་ཤ་.
འཁྱག་ཤི་ (kyə̄gsi) sm. འཁྱགས་ཤི་.
འཁྱག་ཤུད་ (kyə̄gshüù) sm. འཁྱགས་ཤུད་.
འཁྱག་ཤུར་ (kyə̄gshur) sm. འཁྱག་ཤུར་.
འཁྱག་ཤུར་ཤུར་ (kyāg shūrshur) sm. འཁྱགས་ཤུར་ཤུར་.
འཁྱག་ཤུར་ལྷམ་གོག (kyə̄gshu lhāmgɔ̀ɔ̀) sm. འཁྱགས་ཤུར་ལྷམ་གོག.
འཁྱག་ས་ (kyāgsa) sm. འཁྱགས་ས་.
འཁྱག་ཧྲུག (kyə̄ghruù) sm. འཁྱགས་ཧྲུག.
འཁྱག་ལྷང་ལྷང་ (kyāg lhāŋlhaŋ) sm. འཁྱགས་ཤུར་ཤུར་.
འཁྱགས་ (kyāà) 1. p. of འཁྱག. 2. used in compounds interchangeable with འཁྱག.
འཁྱགས་ཀླུང་ (kyə̄gluŋ) glacier.
འཁྱགས་ཀོ་ཡོ་བྱད་ (kyāggo yobjɛɛ̀) ice pick, implement for breaking ice.
འཁྱགས་བཀོས་མ་ (kyāggöma) ice carving, ice sculpture.
འཁྱགས་སྐྲང་ (kyāgdraŋ) sm. འཁྱགས་སྐྲོས་.
འཁྱགས་གས་ (kyāggɛɛ̀) crack or split because of the cold; vi.—ཐེབས་ to crack/ split because of the cold.
འཁྱགས་གོང་ (kyāggoŋ) frozen; vi.—ཆགས་ to become frozen.
འཁྱགས་གྲང་བཟོ་ (kyāgdraŋ so) va. to make ice.
འཁྱགས་གྲི་ (kyə̄gdri) freezing to death; vi.—ཐེབས་ to freeze to death.
འཁྱགས་གྲུ་ (kyə̄gdru) ice boat that goes on runners/ skies; va.—གཏོང་ to sail an ice boat.
འཁྱགས་གླིང་ (kyə̄gliŋ) 1. iceberg. 2. Iceland.
འཁྱགས་འགོག་ཅུག་རྫས་ (kyāggɔ̀ɔ̀ cugdzɛɛ̀) antifreezing agent.

འཁྱགས་རྒྱག (kyāà gyaà) vi. to be frozen, to freeze ། བོད་ལ་ཤ་ཕྱི་ལ་བཞག་ན་འཁྱགས་རྒྱག་གི་རེད་ In Tibet, if you leave meat outside it will freeze.
འཁྱགས་སྒམ་ (kyāgam) refrigerator, freezer.
འཁྱགས་སྒོང་ (kyāggoŋ) frozen egg.
འཁྱགས་སྒོམ་ (kyāggom) bearing/ tolerating/ enduring the cold; vi.—རྒྱག to bear/ endure/ tolerate the cold ། ཁོང་གིས་ཕྱི་ལོགས་ལ་འཁྱགས་སྒོམ་བརྒྱབ་ནས་བུ་མོ་དེ་སྒུག་བསྡད་བཞག He endured the cold outside while waiting for the girl.
འཁྱགས་ཆུ་ (kyə̄gju) irrigating fields by flooding and letting them freeze over in winter; va.—གཏོང་.
འཁྱགས་གཏོང་ (kyāà dōŋ) va. to freeze ། ཤ་འདི་འཁྱགས་གཏོང་དགོས་ We must freeze this meat.
འཁྱགས་གཏོར་གྲུ་གཟིངས་ (kyāgdɔr trudzin) icebreaker (ship).
འཁྱགས་གཏོར་རྡུལ་ཕྲན་གྲུ་གཟིངས་ (kyāgdɔr dütren trudzin) nuclear icebreaker (ship).
འཁྱགས་ལྟོགས་ (kyāàdɔg) cold and hunger/ hungry.
འཁྱགས་ལྟོགས་སྐོམ་གསུམ་ (kyāà dōg gōm sūm) the three: cold, hunger and thirst ། འཁྱག་ལྟོགས་སྐོམ་གསུམ་གྱི་དཀའ་སྡུག་མྱངས་ (They) experienced the hardship of cold, hunger and thirst.
འཁྱགས་སྟེང་ཤུད་གྲུ་ (kyāgdeŋ shüüdru) ice sled.
འཁྱགས་ཐེབས་ (kyāà tēè) vi. to get frozen.
འཁྱགས་ཐོག་སྤོ་ལོ་ (kyāgtɔɔ̀ bōlo) ice hockey; va.—རྒྱག.
འཁྱགས་དུས་ (kyə̄gdüü) 1. the time when it is cold. 2. poet. winter.
འཁྱགས་དུས་གོས་དང་ལྟོགས་དུས་ཟས་ (kyāgdüü köödaŋ dōgdüü sɛɛ̀) timely assistance/ help [Lit. clothing when cold, food when hungry].
འཁྱགས་དོང་ (kyāgdoŋ) ice cave, ice well.
འཁྱགས་འདར་ (kyāgdar) shivering from cold; vi.—ཤོར་ to shiver from cold.
འཁྱགས་འདྲེད་ (kyāgdreè) slipping on ice; vi.—ཤོར་ to slip on ice.
འཁྱགས་འདྲེད་སྤོ་ལོ་ (kyāgdɔɔ̀ bōlo) sm. འཁྱགས་ཐོག་སྤོ་ལོ་.
འཁྱགས་སྡོང་ (kyāgdoŋ) icicle; vi.—ཆགས་ to have formed into icicles.
འཁྱགས་བསྡམས་ (kyāgdam) vi. to have frozen over, to have closed or sealed because of freezing.
འཁྱགས་ནད་ (kyāgnɛɛ̀) frostbite.
འཁྱགས་སྣང་ (kyāgnaŋ) feeling of (being) cold; vi.—བྱེད་ ། ཁོང་གིས་དབྱར་ལོག་མཐུག་པོ་གྱོན་ནའང་ད་དུང་འཁྱགས་སྣང་བྱེད་ཀྱི་འདུག Even though he wore thick clothes, he still felt cold.
འཁྱགས་པ་ (kyāgbaà) ice; vi.—རྒྱག; —ཐེབས་; —ཆགས་ to become frozen; va.—གཏོང་ to freeze, to make frozen.
འཁྱགས་པ་བྱི་རིལ་ (kyāgba cirii) popsicle, ice cream bar.
འཁྱགས་པ་ཚྭའུ་སྐྱོང་ (kyāba tsūūgyoŋ) glacial acetic acid.
འཁྱགས་པའི་ཕྱི་སྐོགས་ (kyāgbɛ cigɔɔ) ice crust.
འཁྱགས་པའི་བང་རིམ་ (kyāgbɛ baŋrim) a layer of ice.
འཁྱགས་པོ་ (kyāgbo) cold ། དེ་རིང་ང་འཁྱགས་པ་ཞེ་དྲག་བྱུང་ I was very cold today.
འཁྱགས་སྤྲི་ (kyə̄gdri) ice cream.
འཁྱགས་ཕད་ (kyāgbɛɛ) bag for carrying ice.
འཁྱགས་བག (kyāgbaà) 1. sm. འཁྱགས་པ་. 2. sm. འཁྱགས་པ་བྱི་རིལ་.
འཁྱགས་བག་བྱི་རིལ་ (kyāgbaà cerii) sm. འཁྱགས་པ་བྱི་རིལ་.
འཁྱགས་འབུར་ (kyāgbur) goose bumps; vi.—ཐོན་; —སྐྱེ་; —ཟུག to get goose bumps ། ཁོང་འཁྱགས་ནས་གཟུགས་པོར་འཁྱགས་འབུར་དོན་འདུག He got goose bumps because he was cold.
འཁྱགས་འབྱར་ (kyāgjar) frozen (stuck) together; vi.—ཐེབས་ to get frozen together ། འཁྱགས་སྒམ་ནང་ཤ་འཁྱག་འབྱར་ཐེབས་བཞག The meat in the refrigerator got frozen together.
འཁྱགས་འབྲུམ་ (kyə̄gdrum) sm. འཁྱག་འབུར་.
འཁྱགས་སྦོས་ (kyāgböö) frostbite; vi.—ཐེབས་ to be/ get frostbitten.
འཁྱགས་སྦྲིད་ (kyə̄gdrii) anesthesia.
འཁྱགས་སྦྲེབས་ (kyāgdreb) losing one's sense of feeling because of cold, becoming numb because of the cold; vi.—ཤོར་ to lose one's sense of feeling or become numb because of cold.
འཁྱགས་སྦྲེས་ (kyāgdreè) cold and hunger ། འཁྱགས་སྦྲེས་ཀྱི་སྡུག་བསྔལ་མྱངས་པ་ To suffer from cold and hunger.
འཁྱགས་ཚད་ (kyāgdzɛɛ̀) freezing point.
འཁྱགས་མཚོའུ་ (kyə̄gtsewu) small glacial lake.
འཁྱགས་མཛོད་ (kyāgdzöö) cold storage, freezer.
འཁྱགས་མཛོད་ཁང་ (kyāgdzöögaŋ) sm. cold storage warehouse/ plant.
འཁྱགས་ཞིབ་ཟས་མངར་ (kyə̄gshib sɛɛ̀ŋar) a food consisting of ice shavings mixed with syrup.
འཁྱགས་ཞུན་ (kyə̄gshün) melted ice.
འཁྱགས་ཞོ་ (kyāgsho) frozen yogurt.
འཁྱགས་ཟམ་ (kyāgsam) ice bridge.
འཁྱགས་ཟས་ཚོང་ཁང་ (kyāgsɛɛ̀ tsōŋgaŋ) store that sells cold beverages and ice cream.
འཁྱགས་ཟིལ་ (kyə̄gsii) ice crystals.
འཁྱགས་གཟོང་ (kyāgsoŋ) ice chisel.

འཁྱགས་བཟོ་ཁང་ (kyāgsogaŋ) 1. ice making factory/ plant. 2. cold storage room.

འཁྱགས་བཟོ་འཕྲུལ་འཁོར་ (kyāgso trüügɔɔ) 1. a freezer, a refrigerator. 2. ice making machine.

འཁྱགས་ར་ (kyāgra) ice rink.

འཁྱགས་རགས་ (kyāgraà) ice dam/ dike.

འཁྱགས་རངས་ (kyāgraŋ) sm. འཁྱགས་རེངས་.

འཁྱགས་རལ་ (kyāgrɛɛ) icicle.

འཁྱག་རལ་ཁྲོག་ཁྲོག (kyāgrɛɛ drɔ̄gdrɔg) having many icicles, filled with icicles.

འཁྱགས་རི་ (kyəgri) 1. an ice covered peak/ mountain. 2. iceberg.

འཁྱགས་རིམ་ (kyəgrim) an ice layer.

འཁྱགས་རུད་ (kyəgrüü) avalanche.

འཁྱགས་རུམ་ (kyəgrum) 1. ice field, glacier. 2. blocks of ice ། འཁྱགས་རུམ་དུ་བཟའ་བཅའ་བཙུག་ནས་གླིང་ཁར་ཁྱེར་བ་རེད་ (They) put food in blocks of ice and took it on a picnic.

འཁྱགས་རུམ་གྱི་ཆུ་ (kyəgrumgi cū) glacial water.

འཁྱགས་རུམ་གླིང་ཕྲན་ (kyəgrum lĩŋdrɛn) iceberg.

འཁྱགས་རུམ་རྒྱ་མཚོ་བྱང་མ་ (kyəgrum gyatso caŋma) Arctic Ocean.

འཁྱགས་རུམ་གཏོར་བྱེད་གྲུ་གཟིངས་ (kyəgrum dɔ̄rceè trudziìn) icebreaker (ship).

འཁྱགས་རུམ་གཏོར་བཤང་ (kyəgrum dɔ̄rshaŋ) breaking up ice in a river to reduce the danger of ice blockage and flooding.

འཁྱགས་རེངས་ (kyāgreŋ) frozen; vi.—ཐེབས་ to be/ get frozen.

འཁྱགས་རོམ་ (kyāgrum) glacier.

འཁྱགས་རོམ་དུས་རིམ་ (kyāgrom tüürim) glacial epoch, ice age.

འཁྱགས་རོམ་མཚོའུ་ (kyāgrom tsēwu) small glacial lake.

འཁྱགས་རླུང་ (kyəgluŋ) a cold wind.

འཁྱགས་ལས་བཟོ་གྲྭ་ (kyāglɛ̀ɛ sodra) cold storage plant.

འཁྱགས་ལུམས་ (kyāglum) cold compress, ice pack.

འཁྱགས་ཤ་ (kyāgsha) frozen meat.

འཁྱགས་ཤི་ (kyəgshi) freezing to death; vi.—ཐེབས་ to freeze to death.

འཁྱགས་ཤུད་ (kyəgshüü) ice skating; va.—རྒྱོད་; —གཏོང་ to ice skate.

འཁྱགས་ཤུད་འགྲུལ་འཁོར་ (kyəgshüü drüügɔɔ) sleigh, snowmobile.

འཁྱགས་ཤུད་མྱུར་ཚད་འགྲན་བསྡུར་ (kyəgshüü ñurdzɛɛ̀ drɛndur) speed skating race.

འཁྱགས་ཤུད་ར་བ་ (kyəgshüü rawa) ice skating rink.

འཁྱགས་ཤུད་ལུས་རྩལ་ (kyəgshüü lüüdzɛɛ) ice-skating sports.

འཁྱགས་ཤུད་ལྷམ་ (kyəhshüü lhām) ice skates.

འཁྱགས་ཤུར་ (kyəgshuu) skating/ sliding on ice; va.—རྒྱོད་ to skate/ slide on ice; vi.—རྒྱག to feel chilled, to shiver when one has a cold or fever.

འཁྱགས་ཤུར་ཤུར་ (kyāg shūrshur) feeling of coldness (emotional or physical); vi.—བྱེད་ ། དེ་རིང་གི་གནམ་གཤིས་འདིས་འཁྱག་ཤུར་ཤུར་བྱས་བྱུང་ Today the weather made me feel cold.

འཁྱགས་ཤུར་ལྷམ་གོག (kyāgshu lhāmgɔɔ̀) ice skates.

འཁྱགས་གཤིས་རིག་པ་ (kyəgshiì rigbə) glacial geology.

འཁྱགས་ས་ (kyāgsa) frozen earth.

འཁྱགས་སུབས་ (kyəgsub) ice crevice.

འཁྱགས་བསྲན་ཆེན་པོ་ (kyāgdrɛn cēmbo) high tolerance for cold.

འཁྱགས་རྡུག (kyəgruù) ice cubes (ice broken into small pieces).

འཁྱགས་ཧྲུལ་ (kyəghrüü) thin coating of ice on the surface of water.

འཁྱགས་ཧྲེངས་ (kyāghreŋ) sm. འཁྱགས་རེངས་.

འཁྱགས་ལྷམ་ (kyāhlham) snow shoes.

འཁྱགས་ལྷམ་གྱི་སོ་ (kyāglhamgo sō) 1. crampons. 2. the blade of ice skates.

འཁྱམ་ (kyām) sm. འཁྱམས་.

འཁྱམ་ཁྱི་ (kyəmki) sm. འཁྱམས་ཁྱི་.

འཁྱམ་འཁྱམ་པ་ (kyām kyāmba) sm. འཁྱམས་འཁྱམས་པ་.

འཁྱམ་: p. འཁྱམས་; f. འཁྱམ་; imp. འཁྱོམས་ (kyām) va. to loaf, to wander (about), to roam ། ཁོས་ཉིན་ལྟར་ལྷ་སར་འཁྱམ་གྱི་འདུག He roams around Lhasa everyday. ། བཙན་བྱོལ་པ་ལུང་པ་ཤོར་ནས་ཡུལ་གཞན་དུ་འཁྱམ་གྱི་ཡོད་པ་རེད་ The refugees lost their land and are wandering around to other places.

འཁྱམ་འགྲོ་ (kyāmdro) sm.འཁྱམས་འགྲོ་.

འཁྱམ་རྒྱུག (kyəmgyu) sm. འཁྱམས་.

འཁྱམ་ཉུལ་ (kyəmñüü) sm. འཁྱམས་.

འཁྱམ་པོ་ (kyāmbo) sm. འཁྱམས་པོ་.

འཁྱམ་པོ་བསམ་ཤེས་པ་ (kyāmbo sāmshɛ̀ɛba) sm. འཁྱམས་པོ་བསམ་ཤེས་པ་.

འཁྱམ་སྙུལ་ (kyāmñüü) sm. འཁྱམ་ཉུལ་.

འཁྱམས་ (kyām) p. of འཁྱམ་.

འཁྱམས་ཀྱེ་ (kyāmgye) wanderer, loafer.

འཁྱམས་ཀུན་ (kyəmgün) drifter/ wanderer who steals; va.—བྱེད་.

འཁྱམས་སྐད་ (kyāmgɛɛ̀) rumors.

འཁྱམས་སྐྱོད་ (kyāmgyöö) wandering (without any permanent roots), drifting about, roaming; va.—བྱེད་.

འཁྱམས་བསྒྱུར་ (kyāmgyur) abandoning, relinquishing.

འཁྱམས་ཁྱི་ (kyəmgyi) stray dog.

འཁྱམས་འཁྱམས་པ་ (kyām kyāmba) sb. who is always wandering/ loafing/ roaming ། ཕྲུ་གུ་འདི་གང་སར་གང་དུ་འཁྱམས་འཁྱམས་པ་རེད་ This child wanders about everywhere.

འཁྱམས་གྲོགས་ (kyāmdrɔɔ̀) person who accompanies another in wandering/ loafing/ fooling around.

འཁྱམས་འགྲོ་ (kyām dro) sm. འཁྱམ་.

འཁྱམས་རྒོལ་ (kyāmgöö) guerrilla warfare; va.—བྱེད་.

འཁྱམས་རྒོལ་དམག་རུ་ (kyāmgöö məgru) guerrilla unit/ group.

འཁྱམས་གདམ་ (kyāmdam) sm. འཁྱམས་སྐད་.

འཁྱམས་གདུགས་དམག་འཁྲུག (kyəmdug məgdruù) guerrilla war/ warfare.

འཁྱམས་གདུགས་དམག་རུ་ (kyāmdug məgru) guerrilla group/ unit.

འཁྱམས་སྡུད་ཁང་ (kyāmdügaŋ) sm. འཁྱམས་པོ་སྤོ་སྐྱེལ་ས་ཚིགས་.

འཁྱམས་སྡོད་ (kyām döö) va. to live by wandering, roaming (without a permanent home) ། ལྷ་སའི་ཁྲོམ་ལ་འཁྱམས་བསྡད་པའི་དབུལ་པོ་ཚོ་ The poor who live by wandering from place to place in the Lhasa market.

འཁྱམས་བདུང་ (kyəmduŋ) sm. འཁྱམས་རྒོལ་.

འཁྱམས་བསྡད་ (kyām dɛɛ̀) p. of འཁྱམས་སྡོད་.

འཁྱམས་པོ་ (kyāmbo) vagabond, tramp, wander, drifter.

འཁྱམས་པོ་སྤོ་སྐྱེལ་ས་ཚིགས་ (kyāmbo bōgye sādziì) a detention center where illegal or homeless people are kept until being sent home.

འཁྱམས་དམག (kyāmmaà) guerrilla forces/ troops; va.—རྒྱག to wage guerrilla warfare.

འཁྱམས་འོག (kyāmwɔɔ̀) name of a verandah in the Tsuglagang Temple in Lhasa.

འཁྱམས་ཤོད་ (kyāmshöö) va. to go around selling an idea, to go around drumming up support for an idea/ plan.

འཁྱམས་སློང་ (kyāmloŋ) wandering and begging.

འཁྱར་ (kyār) vi. to stray/ wander/ roam ། ཡིག་ཆ་འདི་མི་གཞན་གྱི་ལག་པར་འཁྱར་འདུག The document has strayed into another person's hand.

འཁྱར་འཁྱོར་ (kyārgyōr) sm. འཁྱར་རེ་འཁྱོར་རེ་.

འཁྱར་མདའ་ (kyānda) stray arrow or bullet ། ཁོང་ལ་འཁྱར་མདའ་ཕོག་པ་རེད་ He was struck by a stray bullet/ arrow.

འཁྱར་སྡོད་ (kyārdöö) wandering and living in other places.

འཁྱར་པོ་ (kyārbo) sm. འཁྱམས་པོ་.

འཁྱར་བཞུགས་ (kyārshuù) h. of འཁྱར་སྡོད་.

འཁྱར་རེ་འཁྱོར་རེ་ (kyāre kyōre) staggering; va.—བྱེད་ ། མི་འདི་ར་བཟི་ནས་འཁྱར་རེ་འཁྱོར་རེ་བྱས་ནས་ནང་ལ་ལོག་སོང་ The man got drunk and staggered home. 2. shabby, poor ། གྲྭ་ཆུང་འདིས་དཔེ་ཆ་འཁྱར་རེ་འཁྱོར་རེ་མ་གཏོགས་འཁྱོར་གྱི་མི་འདུག The young monk recited the scriptures in a poor/ shabby manner.

འཁྱལ་ (kyɛ̄ɛ) sm. འཆལ་.

འཁྱལ་ཚིག་ (kyɛ̄ɛdzig) idle/ useless/ meaningless talk.

འཁྱི་ (kyī) sm. འཁྱིར་.

འཁྱིག: p. **བཀྱིགས་**; f. **བཀྱིག**; imp. **ཁྱིགས་** (kyīi) va. to tie, to bind, to fasten ། ཁོའི་ལག་པ་གཉིས་རྒྱབ་ལ་བཀྱིགས་པ་མ་ཚད་ Not only did (they) tie his hands behind his back.

འཁྱིགས་ (kyīi) p. of འཁྱིག.

འཁྱིད་ (kyīi) 1. sm. འཁྱིར་. 2. va. to drag/ pull/ haul.

འཁྱིམ་ (kyīm) sm. འཁྱིམས་.

འཁྱིམས་ (kyīm) 1. arc. vi. to be/ get encircled/ surrounded by ། ཉི་མའི་འོད་ཀྱིས་མཐའ་ནས་འཁྱིམས་ Encircled by rays of sunlight. 2. a halo or crown of light.

འཁྱིར་ (kyīr) vi. to turn around, to rotate, to spin ། མ་ཎི་འདི་ཨག་པོ་འཁྱིར་གྱི་མི་འདུག This praywheel is not spinning around well.

འཁྱིར་སོང་ (kyīrsoŋ) sm. གྲོག་ཟ་འཁྱིར་སོང་

འཁྱིལ་ (khīl) 1. vi. to gather/ accumulate/ collect, to become puddled (for water) ། ས་དམའ་ས་གང་ཡིན་ལ་ཆུ་འཁྱིལ་དེ་སྡོད་པ་ལྟར་ Just as water puddles in all the low lying areas. 2. va. to coil up (snakes, etc.). 3. a type of ཆང་ container.

འཁྱིལ་ཆུ་ (kyīlcu) a (nonmoving) puddle of water, stagnant water.

འཁྱིལ་ཆུ་བཅོས་ (kyīlju jöö) va. to regulate water, to correct/ drain off puddled/ stagnant.

འཁྱིལ་ཆུ་གཏོང་ (kyīlju dōŋ) sm. འཁྱིལ་ཆུ་ཕྱིར་འཕུད་.

འཁྱིལ་ཆུ་ཕྱིར་འཕུད་ (kyīlju cīmbüü) va. to drain a waterlogged area.

འཁྱིལ་ཆུ་འབུད་ཡུར་ (kyīlju büyur) a canal for draining off puddled/ stagnant water.

འཁྱིལ་ཆུ་གཤོ་ (kyīlcu shō) to bail (puddled) water.

འཁྱིལ་ཆུ་གཤོང་ (kyīlju shōŋ) sm. འཁྱིལ་ཆུ་གཤོ་.

འཁྱིལ་ཆུ་བཤང་ཡུར་ (kyīlju shāŋyur) sm. འཁྱིལ་ཆུ་འབུད་ཡུར་.

འཁྱིལ་ཆུའི་གནོད་པ་ (kyīlju nööba) damage due to waterlogging, flood damage.

འཁྱིལ་ལྡང་ (kyīlluŋ) whirlwind, cyclone; vi.—རྒྱག.

འཁྱིལ་ལེ་བ་ (kyīlewa) coiled, twisted ། ཐག་པ་སྒོར་འཁྱིལ་ལེ་བར་བཞག་འདུག The rope was left in a coiled manner.

འཁྱུ་ (kyū) bending, curved, not straight.

འཁྱུག (khūù) 1. lightning; vi.—རྒྱག to be/ get lightning ། ཁ་ས་འཁྱུག་ཞི་དྲག་བརྒྱབ་སོང་ Yesterday there was a lot of lightening. 2. a Tibetan cursive script. 3. darting quickly ། ཆུ་ནང་ཉ་མོ་འཁྱུག་འགྲོ་གི་འདུག The fish darted quickly in the water. 4. see ཡིན་འཁྱུག་འཁྱུག་བྱེད་.

འཁྱུག་འཁྱུག (kyūggyug) sm. འཁྱུག, 3.

འཁྱུག་བསྒྲོད་བྱེད་ (kyūgdröö cee) va. to dart quickly (fishes).

འཁྱུག་གློག་གི་གློག་རྒྱུན་ (kyūglɔɔ̄gi lɔ̄ggyün) electric current from lightening.

འཁྱུག་འགྲོས་ (kyūgdröö) darting (of fishes); va.—བྱེད་.

འཁྱུག་སྒོ་ (kyūggo) camera shutter.

འཁྱུག་སྒྲ་ (kyūgdra) portamento (gliding from one musical pitch or tone to another).

འཁྱུག་ཆེན་ (kyūgjen) the form of cursive script that is the most abbreviated.

འཁྱུག་བདེ་ (kyūgde) agile, flexible (of the body).

འཁྱུག་ཨྱེམ་ (kyūgdem) swaying (of the body, usu. for females) ། འཁྱུག་ཨྱེམ་གྱི་འགྲོ་སྟངས་ Walking in a swaying manner.

འཁྱུག་པོ་ (kyūgbu) 1. commercially successful/ popular, in demand, selling well ། དེང་སང་རྒྱ་གར་གྱི་ཚོང་ཟོག་འཁྱུག་པོ་འདུག These days Indian goods are selling well. ། ཁོ་རྒྱལ་པོའི་སྤྱན་ལ་འཁྱུག་པོ་ཡོད་པ་རེད་ He is looked upon with favor by the King. 2. a cursive script that is highly abbreviated.

འཁྱུག་མ་ཚུགས་ (kyūg matsug) a Tibetan script that is slightly larger than the cursive script.

འཁྱུག་ཙམ་ (kyūgdzəm) a moment, an instant, a short time ། ང་ཕྱིར་འཁྱུག་ཙམ་འགྲོ་གི་ཡིན་ I am going outside for a moment.

འཁྱུག་གཞས་ (kyūgshɛɛ̀) the fast section of a Tibetan song; va.—རྒྱག.

འཁྱུག་འོད་ (kyūgwöö) a flash of light/ lightening; vi.—རྒྱག.

འཁྱུག་ཡིག (kyūùyii) cursive script.

འཁྱུག་རིས་ (kyūgrii) sm. འཁྱུག་ཡིག.

འཁྱུག་ཤེད་ (kyūgsheè) the power/ strength of flexibility ། ན་གཞོན་ཚོའི་བསམ་བློའི་འཁྱུག་ཤེད་ཆེན་པོ་ཡོད་པ་རེད་ Youths have great power of flexibility in their thinking.

འཁྱུགས་ (kyūù) sm. 1. འཁྱུག་ཡིག. 2. p. of འཁྱུག.

འཁྱུགས་ལ་རྩེན་ (kyūgla dzēn) darting quickly (for fishes).

འཁྱུགས་སེ་འཁྱུག (kyūgse kyūg) sm. ཁྱུགས་སེ་ཁྱུག.

འཁྱུད་ (kyūù) 1. va. to hug, to embrace ། མི་དེས་གཞོན་ནུ་མ་ལ་འཁྱུད་པ་རེད་ That man embraced the young woman. 2. va. to shin / climb up a rope or tree ། སྤྲེའུ་ཡིས་ཤིང་སྡོང་གི་ཡལ་ག་ར་འཁྱུད་པ་རེད་ The monkey shinned up the branches of the tree. 3. vi. to climb (for vines, flowers, etc.) ། མེ་ཏོག་ཐག་འཁྱུད་ Climbing (flowers) plants. 4. va. to have sexual intercourse.

འཁྱུད་འཛམ་ (kyūùdam) 1. hugging, embracing; va.—བྱེད་. 2. sexual intercourse; va.—བྱེད་.

འཁྱུད་ནས་སྣང་བའི་མ་ནིང་ (kyūùnɛ daŋwɛ məniŋ) one kind of hermaphrodite.

འཁྱུད་བུ་ (kyūùbu) mistress, lover (female).

འཁྱུད་འདྲིལ་ (kyūndree) sm. འཁྱུད་.

འཁྱུད་སྦྱར་ (kyūùjar) sexual intercourse; va.—བྱེད་.

འཁྱུད་འཛེགས་ (kyūùdzeg) a climbing vine/ plant.

འཁྱུར་ (kyūr) vi. to be finished/ terminated/ completed/ over (usu. for a term of office) ། ཁོང་ད་ལོ་སྲིད་འཛིན་འཁྱུར་གྱི་ཡོད་པ་རེད་ His term of president is over this year.

འཁྱུར་མིད་ (kyūrmii) swallowing whole; va.—གཏོང་ to swallow (whole) ། རིལ་པོ་འདི་འཁྱུར་མིད་གཏོང་དགོས་ (You) must swallow the pill whole (i.e., without chewing it).

འཁྱུར་རིས་ (kyūrrii) a design, a pattern.

འཁྱུས་ (kyūù) va. to flee, to run away.

འཁྱེར་: p. **ཁྱེར་**; f. **འཁྱེར་**; imp. **ཁྱེར་** (kyēr) va. to take, to carry ། སྒམ་འདི་སྐལ་པར་ཁྱེར་བ་རེད་ (He) carried this box on his back.

འཁྱེར་འཁོས་ (kyēnköö) 1. financial condition ། ང་རང་འཁྱེར་འཁོས་ཞན་པོ་ཡིན་པར་བརྟེན་ཚོང་རྒྱག་ཐུབ་ཀྱི་མི་འདུག Because my financial condition is poor, I am unable to do business. 2. va. to mount (a riding animal).

འཁྱེར་འགྲོ་ (kyēē dro) va. to go taking/ carrying sth. ། ཁོས་དེབ་འཁྱེར་ཕྱིན་པ་རེད་ He went taking the book.

འཁྱེར་སྟོན་ (kyēēdön) a parade that displays/ exhibits sth. ། གོ་མཚོན་འཁྱེར་སྟོན་ A parade that displays arms.

འཁྱེར་བདེ་ (kyērde) easy to carry, portable, pocket ། འཁྱེར་བདེའི་ཚིག་མཛོད་ A pocket dictionary.

འཁྱེར་བདེ་ཚིག་མཛོད་ (kyērdē tsiŋdzöö) pocket/ portable dictionary.

འཁྱེར་བདེ་པོ་ (kyēr dēbo) easy to carry/ take.

འཁྱེར་འདམ་ (kyēēdam) silt.

འཁྱེར་ཕྱོགས་ (kyērcoò) viewpoint, attitude, the way one thinks ། མི་སོ་སོའི་བསམ་བློའི་འཁྱེར་ཕྱོགས་ Each individual's point of view.

འཁྱེར་བའི་བྱེ་མ་ (kyērwɛɛ cema) shifting sands.

འཁྱེར་དམན་ (kyērmɛn) poor, destitute ། འཁྱེར་དམན་རྣམས་ལ་རོགས་རམ་བྱེད་དགོས་ One should help the poor.

འཁྱེར་ཞན་ (kyērshɛn) sm. འཁྱེར་དམན་.

འཁྱེར་སོ་ (kyērso) demeanor, bearing, manner, way ¶ གཟུགས་པོ་འཁྱེར་སོ་ Way of carrying oneself. ¶ བསམ་པའི་འཁྱེར་སོ་ Way of thinking.

འཁྱེར་གསོག་བྱེ་འདམ་ (kyēēsɔɔ̀ chetam) sm. འཁྱེར་འདམ་.

འཁྱེར་གསོག་བྱེ་མ་ (kyērsɔɔ̀ cema) sm. འཁྱེར་འདམ་.

འཁྱིལ་ (kyēl) va. to hit/ strike.

འཁྱོག (kyɔ̃ɔ̀) 1. vi. to be able to carry/ lift/ bear (either an object or responsibility) ¶ ཏོན་སུམ་སྟོང་འཁྱོག་པའི་གྲུ་གཟིངས་ A ship able to carry 3,000 tons. ¶ ལས་འགན་འཁྱོག་ཐུབ་པའི་གཞོན་ནུ་ A youth able to carry responsibility. 2. va. to lift ¶ སྣར་མཐིལ་ནང་འཁྱོག་པ་རེད་ (He) lifted it in the palm of his hand. 3. vi. to be twisted/ crooked/ lame/ crippled ¶ ཁོང་ཚིག་བུབ་བརྒྱབ་ནས་རྐང་པ་འཁྱོག་བཞག He twisted his ankle and his foot was lame. ¶ ཁོའི་རྐང་པ་འཁྱོག་བཞག His foot is crooked. 4. a twist, a bend ¶ སྨྱུག་དེ་འཁྱོག་བསྲང་དགོས་རེད་ The bends in the bamboo need to be straightened. 5. see འཁྲུན་བསྟུར་.

འཁྱོག་ཁབ་ (kyɔ̃ggəb) paper clip.

འཁྱོག་ཁྲི་ (kyɔ̃gdri) stretcher, litter.

འཁྱོག་འཁྱོག (kyɔ̃ggyɔɔ̀) crooked ¶ ལམ་ཁ་འཁྱོག་འཁྱོག A crooked road.

འཁྱོག་འཁྱོག་ནར་རིང་ (kyɔ̃ggyɔɔ̀ narriŋ) winding, crooked, twisting ¶ འཁྱོག་འཁྱོག་ནར་རིང་གི་ལམ་ A winding road.

འཁྱོག་གེ་ (kyōgge) sm. འཁྱོག་འཁྱོག.

འཁྱོག་བགྲོད་ (kyōgdrö̀ö̀) 1. moving in a winding manner (e.g., like a snake). 2. detouring, going around sth.; va.—བྱེད་ ¶ ལམ་འཁྱོག་བགྲོད་བྱེད་དགོས་ (One) has to make a detour on the road.

འཁྱོག་ངོས་ (kyōgŋö̀ö̀) curved/ winding surface.

འཁྱོག་བརྗོད་ (kyōgjö̀ö̀) 1. sm. འཁྱོག. 2. a style in Tibetan poetry.

འཁྱོག་གདམ་ (kyōgdam) sm. འཁྱོག་བཤད་.

འཁྱོག་ཐིག (kyōgdiì) curved line.

འཁྱོག་ཐིག་འགུལ་བསྐྱོད་ (kyōgtiì güügyö̀ö̀) curvilinear motion (in physics).

འཁྱོག་ལྡེམ་ (kyōgdem) bending and swaying (usu. for branches of trees).

འཁྱོག་པོ་ (kyōgbo) crooked, curved, zigzag, winding ¶ ཐིག་ཤིང་འདི་འཁྱོག་པོ་རེད་ This ruler is crooked.

འཁྱོག་པོ་ལྡེམ་ལྡེམ་ (kyōgbo demdem) sm. འཁྱོག་ལྡེམ་.

འཁྱོག་པོ་ཡོ་སྲང་ (kyōgbo yosaŋ) correcting sth. that is crooked/ curved/ zigzag.

འཁྱོག་བྲལ་ (kyōgdrɛɛ) sm. འཁྱོག་མེད་.

འཁྱོག་འབྲིལ་ (kyōgdree) twisting, crooked, winding, zigzag ¶ འཁྱོག་འབྲིལ་གྱི་རི་ཚོགས་ A twisting mountain range.

འཁྱོག་མེད་ (kyōgmeè) straight, direct, honest, fair, just [Lit. not twisted].

འཁྱོག་ཚད་ (kyōgtsɛɛ̀) 1. carrying capacity ¶ མོ་ཊ་འདི་འཁྱོག་ཚད་ཆེན་པོ་ཡོད་པ་རེད་ This vehicle has a large carrying capacity. 2. carrying or bringing as much as (one) can ¶ ཁོས་ཤ་འཁྱོག་ཚད་འཁྱེར་ཞག He has brought as much meat as he can.

འཁྱོག་ཚད་ལས་བརྒལ་ (kyōgdzɛɛ̀lɛ gɛɛ) 1. vi. to overload, to overtax, to exceed the carrying capacity. 2. vi. to exceed one's ability, to take on more than one can handle ¶ འཁྱོག་ཚད་ལས་བརྒལ་བའི་ལས་འགན་བླངས་པས་འཆར་གཞི་ཕྱི་ལྡུག་པ་རེད་ Because he took on more than he could handle, the plan fell through.

འཁྱོག་ཚིག (kyōgdzig) a lie, an untruth, speech or writing that misrepresents/ distorts.

འཁྱོག་ཡོན་ (kyōgyön) unjust, untrue ¶ འཁྱོག་ཡོན་གྱི་ཁྲིམས་ An unjust law.

འཁྱོག་རིས་ (kyōgriì) curved lines.

འཁྱོག་བཤད་ (kyōgshɛɛ̀) distorting/ misrepresenting speech; va.—བྱེད་ to distort, to misrepresent, to talk using sophistry ¶ སྤྱི་ཚོགས་རིང་ལུགས་ཀྱི་ངོ་བོ་འཁྱོག་བཤད་བྱས་པ་རེད་ (They) misrepresented the nature of socialism.

འཁྱོག་བཤད་གྲུབ་མཐའ་ (kyōgshɛɛ̀ drubda) school or sect advocating sophistry.

འཁྱོག་བཤད་སྨྲ་བ་ (kyōgshɛɛ̀ māwa) sophistry.

འཁྱོགས་ (kyɔ̃ɔ̀) 1. sm. འཁྱོག. 2. p. of འཁྱོག.

འཁྱོགས་ཁྲི་ (kyōgdri) stretcher, litter.

འཁྱོགས་འདེགས་རུ་ཁག (kyōgdeè rugaà) medic corps, stretcher corps.

འཁྱོགས་དཔྱང་ (kyōgjaŋ) sm. འཁྱོགས་ཁྲི་.

འཁྱོགས་བྱམས་ (kyōgjam) sm. འཁྱོགས་ཁྲི་.

འཁྱོང་: p. **འཁྱོངས་**; f. **འཁྱོང་** (kyōŋ) vi. to be able to see through to the end, to be able to complete sth. ¶ ལས་ཀ་མཐར་འཁྱོངས་མ་སོང་ (They) were unable to complete the work.

འཁྱོངས་ (kyōŋ) p. of འཁྱོང་.

འཁྱོམ་འཁྱོམ་ (kyōmgyom) swaying, tottering (as when dizzy); vi.—བྱེད་.

འཁྱོམ་: p. **འཁྱོམས་**; f. **འཁྱོམ་** (kyōm) 1. vi. to rock, to sway, to roll, to move ¶ ཆར་རླུང་གིས་གྲུ་གཟིངས་འཁྱོམས་པ་རེད་ The wind and rain caused the ship to roll. 2. vi. to get agitated/ stirred up.

འཁྱོམས་ (kyōm) p. of འཁྱོམ་.

འཁྱོར་ (kyōr) vi. to stagger/ totter ¶ ཁོང་ར་བཟི་ཙང་གཟུགས་པོ་འཁྱོར་གྱི་འདུག He got drunk and was tottering.

འཁྱོར་འཁྱོར་ (kyōrgyor) staggering, tottering.

འཁྱོར་འགེལ་ (kyōrgel) shung. imposing or levying a tax for which there is no custom/ precedent; va.—བྱེད་ ¶ ཁྲལ་རིགས་འཁྱོར་འགེལ་ Illegally imposed taxes.

འཁྱོར་འགྲོ་ (kyōrdro) going along in a staggering manner, staggering along; vi.—བྱེད་.

འཁྱོར་ནས་འགྲོ་ (kyōrnɛ dro) va. to stagger along, to go along staggering ¶ ར་བཟི་བ་འདི་འཁྱོར་ནས་འགྲོ་གི་འདུག The person who is drunk is staggering along.

འཁྱོར་པོ་ (kyōrbo) 1. reciting sth. that has been memorized. 2. sm. འཁྱོར་འཁྱོར་.

འཁྱོར་རོ་རོ་ (kyōr roro) staggering.

འཁྱོལ་ (kyö̃ö̀) vi. to reach the end/ destination, to finish ¶ མི་ཁ་ཤས་ལམ་དུ་ཆད་ནས་རྒྱ་གར་དུ་འཁྱོལ་མ་སོང་ Some people got exhausted on the road and could not reach their destination India.

འཁྱོལ་པོ་ (kyö̃ö̀bo) (for meaning or content) well, exact ¶ ཡིག་ཆ་ཚིག་འདི་དོན་དག་འཁྱོལ་པོ་བྱུང་བཞག This word conveys the meaning well/ exactly. 2. (with messages) accurately, entirely ¶ བསོད་ནམས་ལགས་ལན་འཁྱོལ་པོ་ཡོད་པ་མ་རེད་ Sonamla doesn't give messages accurately/ entirely.

འཁྱོས་མ་ (kyö̃ö̀ma) arc. gift, present.

འཁྱོས་ཚིག (kyö̃ö̀dziì) congratulatory speech.

འཁྲ་: p. **འཁྲས་**; f. **འཁྲ་** (trā) 1. vi. to refuse to budge or do sth. ¶ ཕྲུ་གུ་འདིས་ནང་ལ་འཁྲས་བསྡད་ནས་སློབ་གྲྭར་འགྲོ་གི་མི་འདུག The child is refusing to budge from his home and go to school. 2. va. to hide ¶ ཁོས་ནགས་གསེབ་ཏུ་འཁྲས་བཞག He hid in the forest.

འཁྲུ་འཁྲུ་ (trūdru) laundry; va.—རྒྱག; —སྐྱོན་ (h.) to do laundry; va.—སྐེམ་ to dry laundry.

འཁྲ་ས་ (trāsa) arc. 1. sb. or sth. to depend on. 2. a place to prop sth. up against.

འཁྲང་ག (trāŋga) sm. མཁྲང་པོ་.

འཁྲང་བ་ (trāŋwa) sm. མཁྲང་པོ་.

འཁྲད་ (trɛ̃ɛ̀) va. to drive away, to expel.

འཁྲེན་ཆ་ (trēnja) sm. འཁྲིན་ཆ་.

འཁྲབ་ཁང་ (trābgaŋ) a theater.

འཁྲབ་ཁྲི་པ་ (trāp triwə) director of a play or movie.

འཁྲབ་མཁན་ (trābgɛn) actor, performer.

འཁྲབ་མཁན་གཙོ་བོ་ (trābgɛn dzöwo) leading actor, actor playing the main character/ title role.

འཁྲབ་འཁྱེར་ (trābgyer) style of performing.

འཁྲབ་: p. **འཁྲབས་**; f. **འཁྲབ་**; imp. **འཁྲོབས་** (trāp) va. 1. to act, to perform ¶ ཁོང་གིས་གློག་བརྙན་ནང་དཔའ་བོ་ཞིག་འཁྲབས་པ་རེད་ He acted as a hero in the movie. 2. va. to stage a performance, to put on a show ¶ ཁོ་ཚོས་ཟློས་གར་ཞིག་འཁྲབས་པ་རེད་ They put on a show.

འཁྲབ་འགོ་འབྱེད་ (trāpgo je̱è) sm. འཁྲབ་སྒོ་འབྱེད་.

འཁྲབ་འགོ་འཛུགས་ (trāpgo) sm. འཁྲབ་སྒོ་འབྱེད་.

འཁྲབ་སྒོ་འབྱེད་ (trāpgo ce̱è) va. to begin a performance of a play/ show, to raise the opening cutain.

འཁྲབ་སྒུག (trāpguù) waiting to go on stage to perform.

འཁྲབ་ཆས་ (trāpjɛɛ̀) costume; va.—གཡོགས་ to put on/ dress in a costume.

འཁྲབ་ཆས་ཁང་ (trābjɛɛ̀gaŋ) dressing room (in a theatre).

འཁྲབ་ཆས་སྒྲས་ (trāpjɛɛ̀ drɛ̄ɛ̀) va. to dress up in costume.

འཁྲབ་མཇུག་ཐུགས་རྗེ་ཆེ་ (trāmjuù tōjece) va.—ཞུ་ take a curtain call, to thank the audience after a performance.

འཁྲབ་ལྗོངས་ (trābjoŋ) backdrop/ set in a theatre, scenery in a performance.

འཁྲབ་སྟེགས་ (trābdeg) theatrical stage.

འཁྲབ་སྟོན་ (trābdön) a stage performance/ presentation, a show; va.—བྱེད་.

འཁྲབ་པ་པོ་ (trābəbo) sm. འཁྲབ་མཁན་.

འཁྲབ་སྦྱོང་ (trābjoŋ) rehearsal for a play/ show.

འཁྲབ་སྦྱོང་ཁང་ (trābjoŋgaŋ) rehearsal room.

འཁྲབ་མི་ན་ (trābminə) a character in a play/ show.

འཁྲབ་མིང་ (trābmiŋ) stage name (of an actor).

འཁྲབ་རྩལ་ (trābdzɛɛ) quality of acting; va.—འགྲན་ to compete in performing shows.

འཁྲབ་ཚན་ (trābdzɛn) parts of a performance, e.g., an act/ scene; va.—ཞུ་ to announce the start of a scene.

འཁྲབ་ཚབ་བྱེད་མཁན་ (trābdzɛn ce̱èñɛn) understudy, stand-in (actor).

འཁྲབ་ཚིག (trābdzii) actor's lines/ part.

འཁྲབ་ཚུལ་ (trābdzüü) plot (in a play).

འཁྲབ་མཚམས་ཀྱི་རོལ་མོ་ (trābdzamgi rö̱lmo) the music played during a show.

འཁྲབ་གཞུང་ (trābshuŋ) 1. script, screen play; va.—རྩོམ་ to write a play. 2. a play in Tibetan folk opera ¶ ལྷ་མོ་འགྲོ་བ་བཟང་མོའི་འཁྲབ་གཞུང་ནང་ In the folk opera Drowa Sangmo.

འཁྲབ་གཞུང་འཁྲིད་ (trābshuŋ trii) va. to direct a play/ movie.

འཁྲབ་གཞུང་འཁྲིད་མཁན་ (trābshuŋ triiñɛn) director of a play or movie.

འཁྲབ་ཡུལ་སྒྲིག་གཤོམ་ (trābyüü dri̱gshom) stage decoration, stage set.

འཁྲབ་ཡོལ་ (trābyöö) stage curtain; va.—རྒྱག་ to close/ bring down the curtain, to end a show/ play.

འཁྲབ་ར་ (trābrə) theater, stage.

འཁྲབ་རོགས་ (trābroò) costar in a play/ show.

འཁྲབ་ལུགས་ (trābluù) 1. performance skills. 2. a school or style of performing/ acting.

འཁྲབས་ (trāp) p. of འཁྲབ་.

འཁྲལ་འཁྲུལ་ (trɛ̄ɛdrüü) dazed, in a stupor.

འཁྲས་ (trɛ̄ɛ̀) p. of འཁྲ་.

འཁྲི་; p. **འཁྲིས་**; f. **འཁྲི་** (trī) vi. to have a duty/ responsibility fall on sb. ¶ ལས་ཀ་འདི་ཁོ་ཚོར་འཁྲི་གི་རེད་ The responsibility for doing the job will fall on them. ¶ ཁོ་ལ་ཁྲལ་འཁྲི་པ་རེད་ The (responsibility for paying the) tax fell on him.

འཁྲི་ཁུངས་ (trīguŋ) 1. the base/ basis used for paying taxes ¶ ལུང་པ་དེ་ར་བོད་དམག་འཁྲི་ཁུངས་ཁྲལ་ཞིང་ཁག་གཉིས་འདུག In that place, the basis for paying the military tax is two kinds of tax fields. 2. the area of responsibility ¶ ལས་ཀ་འདི་ངའི་འཁྲི་ཁུངས་མ་རེད་ This work is not in the area of my responsibility.

འཁྲི་ཁྲལ་ (trītrɛɛ) a tax one is responsible for paying.

འཁྲི་འཁེལ་ (trī kēē) sm. འཁྲི་.

འཁྲི་འགན་ (trīgɛn) sm. འགན་འཁྲི་.

འཁྲི་སྒྲུབ་ (trīdrub) doing/ fulfilling one's responsibility; va.—བྱེད་ ¶ ཁྲལ་རིགས་ཚང་མ་འཁྲི་སྒྲུབ་བྱས་པ་རེད་ (They) paid all the taxes for which they were responsible.

འཁྲི་ཡི་སྒྲུབ་བྲལ་ (trīji dru̱bdrɛɛ) shung. a heavy responsibility that is impossible to fulfill.

འཁྲི་ཆ་ (trīja) onus, burden, responsibility, duty, task, tax; va.—འགེལ་ to levy a duty/ burdern/ tax/ etc. ¶ ལས་འགན་འདི་ངའི་འཁྲི་ཆ་རེད་ This work is my duty/ responsibility.

འཁྲི་ནད་ (trīnɛɛ̀) morning sickness for (pregnant) women.

འཁྲི་བ་ (trīwa) 1. sm. འཁྲི་. 2. attachment ¶ རང་དོན་གྱི་འཁྲི་བ་སྤངས་པ་ནི་ As for renouncing one's attachments.

འཁྲི་འབབ་ (trīmbəb) the amount of tax one has to pay.

འཁྲི་ཤིང་ (trīshiŋ) 1. a climbing/ creeping plant or vine. 2. cane, rattan ¶ འཁྲི་ཤིང་རྐུབ་བཀྱག A cane chair.

འཁྲི་ས་ (trīsə) 1. things for which a tax has to be paid ¶ ཁོང་གིས་ཕྱི་རྒྱལ་ནས་ཁྲལ་འཁྲི་པའི་ཅ་ལག་མང་པོ་ཁྱེར་བཞག He has brought many things from abroad for which taxes are due. 2. a person one relies/ depends on ¶ ཕྲུ་གུ་འཁྲི་ས་ཕ་མ་རེད་ Children depend on their parents.

འཁྲིག་སྐད་ (trīggɛɛ̀) sm. འཁྲིག་ཚིག.

འཁྲིག་ཆགས་ (trīgjaà) the desire to have sex/ intercourse; vi.—འདོད་ to desire to have sex.

འཁྲིག་འདོད་ (trīgdöö) sm. འཁྲིག་ཆགས་.

འཁྲིག་པ་ (trīgbə) copulation, sexual intercourse; va.—སྤྱོད་ to copulate.

འཁྲིག་པའི་སྐར་ཚོམ་ (trīgbɛ gārdzom) the constellation Gemini.

འཁྲིག་སྤྱོ་ (trīgjo) sm. འཁྲིག་སྤྱོད་.

འཁྲིག་སྤྱོད་ (trīgjöö) copulation, sexual intercourse; va.—བྱེད་.

འཁྲིག་སྤྱོད་རང་དབང་ (trīgjöö ra̱ŋwaŋ) sexual freedom.

འཁྲིག་མ་ (trīgmə) wrist.

འཁྲིག་ཚིག (trīgdzii) obscene talk; va.—ཤོད་ to speak obscenely.

འཁྲིག་སྲེད་ (trīgseè) licentiousness, sexuality.

འཁྲིག་སྲེད་ཅན་ (trīgsejɛn) a licentious person.

འཁྲིགས་ (trīg) vi. to be overcast ¶ ནམ་མཁར་སྤྲིན་པ་འཁྲིགས་བཞག The sky is overcast with clouds.

འཁྲིད་; p. **ཁྲིད་**; f. **འཁྲིད་**; imp. **ཁྲིད་** (trīi) 1. va. to take/ bring (for animate beings), to lead, to guide ¶ ཨ་མས་ཁོ་གཉིས་སྨན་ཁང་ལ་ཁྲིད་པ་རེད་ The mother took the two of them to the hospital. ¶ ཁོས་ཉེན་ཁ་མེད་སར་ཁྲིད་ཕྱིན་པ་རེད་ He took them to a place where there was no danger. ¶ མས་ཕྲུ་གུ་ཚོ་འདིར་ཁྲིད་ཡོང་བ་རེད་ The mother brought the children here. 2. va. to teach ¶ མོས་སློབ་ཕྲུག་ཁྲིད་པ་རེད་ She taught the children.

འཁྲིད་སྐྱེལ་ (trīigyee) extraditing; va.—བྱེད་ to extradite.

འཁྲིད་ཁ་ཞྱིད་པོ་ (trīgə ji̱ibu) animals (such as horses, yaks) that are headstrong/ difficult to control.

འཁྲིད་འཁོར་ (trīigɔɔ) cog wheels.

འཁྲིད་རྒྱུན་ (trīigyün) a tradition of teaching/ learning; vi.—ཆད་ to have a tradition of teaching/ learning become extinct.

འཁྲིད་སྟོན་ (trīidön) teaching, instruction; va. འཁྲིད་སྟོན་; — བྱེད་ to teach, to instruct ¶ དགེ་རྒན་གྱི་ཁྲིད་སྟོན་འོག་སློབ་ཕྲུག་རྣམས་ཡར་རྒྱས་བྱུང་བ་རེད་ Under the teaching of the teacher, the students improved.

འཁྲིད་འཐེན་འཁོར་ལོ་ (trīiden trüügɔɔ) hauling machine.

འཁྲིད་དེབ་ (trīideb) an instruction/ teaching manual.

འཁྲིད་ཇ་ (trīijə) teaching/ educational materials.

འཁྲིད་སྦྱོང་ (trīijoŋ) teaching and practice; va.—བྱེད་ to do training/ teaching and practice.

འཁྲིད་སྦྱོང་འཛིན་གྲྭ་ (trīijoŋ dzi̱ndrə) a class where there is teaching and practice.

འཁྲིད་གཞི་ (trīishi) notes or materials which will be used for teaching a class.

འཁྲིད་ཡིག (trīyii) lecture notes.

འཁྲིམས་ (trīm) sm. འཛེགས་.

འཁྲིལ་ (trīī) vi. to wind/ coil around ། གློག་སྐུད་དེ་ཤིང་སྡོང་ལ་འཁྲིལ་བཞག The electric wire was wound around the tree trunk.

འཁྲིལ་སྒོར་ (trīīgɔɔ) tendril.

འཁྲིལ་འཁོར་ (trīīkɔɔ) twisted/ entangled (for rope or thread); vi.—ཐེབས་ to get entangled/ twisted.

འཁྲིལ་ཐག་འཁོར་ (trīīdaà kɔ̄ɔ̄) 1. vi. to get coiled around sth., to get twisted/ tangled. 2. vi. to be engrossed/ engaged in a lot of things at once ། ད་རེས་ང་ལས་ཀའི་རྙོག་འཛིང་གི་ནང་དུ་འཁྲིལ་ཐག་འཁོར་ནས་བསྡད་ཡོད་ These days I am engaged in complicated work.

འཁྲིལ་ལྡན་རྩི་ཤིང་ (trīndɛn dzīshiŋ) climbing plant.

འཁྲིལ་ལྡེམ་ (trīndem) swaying.

འཁྲིལ་པོ་ (trīību) 1. friendly ། ཕྲུ་གུ་འདི་མི་སུ་ལ་ཡང་འཁྲིལ་པོ་འདུག That child is friendly with everyone. 2. emotionally attached ། ཁྱི་འདི་བདག་པོར་འཁྲིལ་པོ་ཡོད་ The dog is attached to (its) owner.

འཁྲིལ་བག་ཆགས་པ་ (trīībaà cāgba) 1. charming and graceful. 2. suitable, becoming, attractive ། འཁྲིལ་བག་ཆགས་པའི་རྒྱན་གོས་ Clothes and jewelry that are very becoming.

འཁྲིལ་འདྲིལ་ (trīndree) coiled together, entwined, wound around; vi.—བྱེད་.

འཁྲིལ་ཙོར་ (trīīdzor) a tendril.

འཁྲིལ་ཤིང་ (trīshiŋ) a climbing/ coiling/ creeping tree or plant.

འཁྲིས་ (trīī) 1. (— + dat.-loc.) near, close to ། འདིའི་འཁྲིས་ལ་མ་བཞུགས་ Don't sit near this. 2. bank, shore ། ཆུ་འཁྲིས་ River bank. 3. p. of འཁྲི་.

འཁྲིས་སུ་ (trīīsu) near, close, adjacent.

འཁྲུ་: p. འཁྲུས་; f. འཁྲུ་ (trū) 1. (ཁྲོད་ཁོག + —) vi. to have diarrhea/ dysentery ། ཁྲོད་ཁོག་འཁྲུ་གི་འདུག (He) has diarrhea.

འཁྲུ་སྐྱུག (trūgyug) diarrhea/ dysentery and vomiting.

འཁྲུ་ཁང་ (trūgaŋ) bathhouse.

འཁྲུ་ད་ (trūda) a brush for cleaning pots and pans.

འཁྲུ་ནད་ (trūnɛɛ̀) diarrhea, dysentery ། འཁྲུ་ནད་ཨ་མྦི་པ་ Amebic dysentery.

འཁྲུ་བ་ (trūwə) diarrhea; va.—གཅོད་ to stop a diarrhea attack.

འཁྲུ་བག (trūbaà) sm. འཁྲུ་ནད་.

འཁྲུ་སྦྱོང་ (trūjoŋ) doing things to relieve constipation; va.—བྱེད་.

འཁྲུ་སྨན་ (trūmɛn) laxative, purgative; va.—གཏོང་.

འཁྲུ་གཞི་ (trūshi) 1. the cause of diarrhea/ dysentery. 2. sm. འཁྲུ་ནད་.

འཁྲུ་གཞོང་ (trūshoŋ) a basin for washing.

འཁྲུ་ར་ (trūra) a mop.

འཁྲུ་བཤལ་ (trū shɛ̄ɛ̄) vi. to have diarrhea.

འཁྲུ་གསར་ (trūsar) newly cultivated fields.

འཁྲུག་: p. འཁྲུགས་: p. འཁྲུག (trūù) 1. vi. to get into a fight/ quarrel ། རྒྱ་མི་དང་བོད་པ་འཁྲུགས་པ་རེད་ The Chinese and Tibetans got into a fight. 2. vi. to get disturbed/ upset/ stirred up/ shaken up/ mixed up ། ཁོང་ལས་ཀ་ཤོར་བར་བརྟེན་སེམས་འཁྲུགས་བཞག Because he lost his job, he became disturbed. ། ལྷག་པ་བརྒྱབ་པ་ནས་དཔེ་ཆའི་ཤོག་ལྷེ་ཚང་མ་འཁྲུགས་བཞག The wind mixed up all the pages of the book. ། མོ་ཊ་འདིའི་ནང་ཡོང་ནས་ངའི་གཟུགས་པོ་ཞེ་དྲག་འཁྲུགས་བཞག I came by car and my body got all shaken up. 3. vi. to blaze (fire) ། རྒྱབ་ཕྱོགས་མེ་ལྕེབས་རབ་དུ་འཁྲུག Behind, a fire was blazing. 4. vi. to break out/ erupt ། ད་ལོ་དམག་འཁྲུག་བཞག This year war broke out.

འཁྲུག་རྐྱེན་ (trūggyen) incitement, provocation; va.—སློང་; —བཟོ་ to incite/ provoke a fight/ disturbance ། ཡིག་བསྒྲགས་དེས་མང་ཚོགས་ཚང་མ་འཁྲུགས་རྐྱེན་བཟོས་པ་རེད་ That poster incited all the masses to rebel.

འཁྲུག་འཁྱོམ་ (trūggyom) turbulence, upheaval ། དེང་སང་ལུང་པ་འདིའི་ནང་འཁྲུག་འཁྱོམ་ཆེན་པོ་འདུག There is a lot of upheaval in this place these days.

འཁྲུག་གོས་ (trūggöö̀) military outfit (usu. for earlier periods when armor was worn).

འཁྲུག་རྔ་ (trūgŋa) war drum, battle drum.

འཁྲུག་ཆ་ (trūgja) sm. འཁྲུག་ཆ་དོད་པོ་.

འཁྲུག་ཆ་དོད་པོ་ (trūgja tö̱öbo) lively, active ། དེ་རིང་གི་ཁྲོམ་འཁྲུག་ཆ་དོད་པོ་ཞེ་དྲག་འདུག Today's market was very lively [conveys that there was meat, vegetables, etc.].

འཁྲུག་ཆེན་ (trūgjen) large-scale war.

འཁྲུག་ཉམས་ (trūgñam) sm. འཁྲུག་ཆ་དོད་པོ་.

འཁྲུག་ཏུ་འགྲོ་ (trūgdu dro̱) vi. to become lively/ active/ quick (e.g., for dancing or sales).

འཁྲུག་ཐིག (trūgdii) front line, battle front.

འཁྲུག་ཐེག (trūgteg) shock-proof ། འཁྲུག་ཐེག་ལག་འདོགས་ཆུ་ཚོད་ A shock-proof wristwatch.

འཁྲུག་པ་ (trūgbə) quarrel, dispute, fight; va.—རྒྱག to quarrel/ dispute; vi.—ཤོར་ to have a quarrel/ dispute break out; va.—སློང་ to incite a quarrel/ dispute.

འཁྲུག་པ་མགོ་བོ་ཞག་ཞག་རྒྱག (trūgbə go̱wo sha̱gshag gya̱à) sm. ཁ་ཙོད་མགོ་བོ་ཞག་ཞག་རྒྱག.

འཁྲུག་པའི་ས་གཞི་ (trūgbɛ sɔ̄shi) battlefield, battleground.

འཁྲུག་པོ་ (trūgbu) 1. lively, bustling, active; va.—བྱེད་ ། མི་དེ་འཁྲུག་པོ་ཞིག་འདུག That person is very lively. (In slang: He's with it.) ། ལུང་པ་འདི་འཁྲུག་པོ་ཞིག་འདུག This is a bustling place. 2. a promiscuous man or woman ། བུ་མོ་དེ་འཁྲུག་པོ་ཞིག་འདུག This woman is promiscuous. 3. romantic/ sexual activities ། མོ་དང་མདངས་དགོང་ཁྱེད་རང་གཉིས་འཁྲུག་པོ་བྱུང་སོང་ Last night you two were engaged in romantic activities.

འཁྲུག་པོ་མེད་པ་ (trūgu me̱èba) dull, not lively.

འཁྲུག་དཔོན་ (trūgbön) commander.

འཁྲུག་སྦྱོར་ (trūgjɔr) sm. འཁྲུག་རྐྱེན་.

འཁྲུག་མི་ (trūgmi) soldiers, combatants.

འཁྲུག་རྩ་ (trūgdza) the main cause of a fight/ conflict/ disturbance.

འཁྲུག་རྩོད་ (trūgdzüù) 1. conflict, dispute, quarrel, fight; va.—བྱེད་. 2. warfare.

འཁྲུག་མཚམས་ (trūgdzam) cease-fire; va.—འཛོག to make a cease fire.

འཁྲུག་འཛིང་ (trūgdziŋ) sm. འཁྲུག་འཛིངས་.

འཁྲུག་ཞུ་ལང་མདོག་ཁ་པོ་ (trūgshu la̱ndo kābo) sb. who looks like he/ she likes to quarrel/ dispute/ fight.

འཁྲུག་གཞས་ (trūgshɛɛ̀) the fast section of Tibetan songs.

འཁྲུག་གཞི་ (trūgshi) sm. འཁྲུག་རྩ་.

འཁྲུག་ཟིང་ (trūgsiŋ) sm. འཁྲུག་རྩོད་.

འཁྲུག་ལས་ (trūglɛɛ̀) military activities/ work.

འཁྲུག་ལོང་ (trūgloŋ) 1. dispute, argument. 2. battle, warfare.

འཁྲུག་སློང་འདོད་མཁན་ (trūgloŋ dö̱ngɛn) 1. instigator of a quarrel/ dispute. 2. warmonger.

འཁྲུག་སློང་ནག་ཅན་ (trūgloŋ na̱gjɛn) instigator of sth. criminal.

འཁྲུགས་ (trūù) p. of འཁྲུག.

འཁྲུགས་རྒྱག (trūg gya̱à) vi. to shake, to tremble, to quiver. ། མོ་ཊ་འདི་འཁྲུགས་ཞེ་དྲག་རྒྱག་གི་འདུག This car shakes a lot.

འཁྲུགས་སྒྲིག (trūgdrig) war preparations; va.—བྱེད་.

འཁྲུགས་ཆེན་ (trūgjen) battle ། གནམ་དམག་འཁྲུག་ཆེན་ཐེངས་དང་པོ་ The first air battle.

འཁྲུགས་ཆེན་པོ་ (trūg cēmbo) shaking, jolting a lot ། མོ་ཊ་འཁྲུགས་ཆེན་པོ་ཞིག A car that jolts a lot.

འཁྲུགས་ཚད་ (trūgdzɛɛ̀) a type of fever (accompanied by shaking).

འཁྲུགས་འཛིངས་ (trūgdziŋ) 1. disturbance, unrest, chaos, disorder ། ལུང་པ་དེ་ལ་འཁྲུགས་འཛིངས་ཀྱི་གནས་ཚུལ་བྱུང་བཞག There was news of a disturbance in that place. 2. fighting, combat, a battle.

འཁྲུང་: p. འཁྲུངས་; f. འཁྲུང་ (trūŋ) vi. to be born (h.) ¶ བླ་མ་འདི་ད་ལོ་འཁྲུངས་པ་རེད་ ¶ The lama was born this year.

འཁྲུང་བརྟག་ཞལ་འདེབས་ (trūŋdaà shendeb) donations made for the purpose of having a thanka or icon commissioned for the deceased.

འཁྲུང་ལྷ་དབྱར་གསོལ་ (trūŋla yāāso) festival celebrating the birth of the 14th Dalai Lama (making offerings to his "birth lha").

འཁྲུངས་ (trūŋ) p. of འཁྲུང་.

འཁྲུངས་སྐར་ (trūŋgar) birthday (h.); va.—བརྟག to consult a horoscope concerning one's birthdate.

འཁྲུངས་སྐར་གྱི་ཞལ་ཏོག (trūŋgargi sheedoò) birthday cake.

འཁྲུངས་སྐར་གྱི་ལེགས་འབུལ་ (trūŋgargi leŋbüü) birthday present.

འཁྲུངས་སྐར་གྱི་གསོལ་སྟོན་ (trūŋgargi söödön) birthday party/ banquet.

འཁྲུངས་སྐར་ལྗོན་ཤིང་ (trūŋgar jōnshiŋ) Christmas tree.

འཁྲུངས་སྐར་རྟེན་འབྲེལ་ (trūŋgar dēmdrεε) birthday celebration.

འཁྲུངས་སྐར་དུས་ཆེན་ (trūŋgar tüjen) the celebration for the Dalai Lama's birthday.

འཁྲུངས་མཁར་ (trūŋgar) the house in which one was born.

འཁྲུངས་ལྟས་ (trūŋdεὲ) signs appearing when sb. is born.

འཁྲུངས་བརྟག (trūŋdaà) h. of སྐྱེ་བརྟག.

འཁྲུངས་རྩིས་ (trūŋdzeè) sm. འཁྲུངས་སྐར་.

འཁྲུངས་ཞུ་མ་ (trūŋshumə) female servants or hired women who serve wine during festivals/ celebrations.

འཁྲུངས་གཞས་མ་ (trūŋ sheema) hired women who serve wine and sing at festive celebrations.

འཁྲུངས་ཡུལ་ (trūŋyüü) birthplace, native land (h.).

འཁྲུངས་གཡང་ཕུད་གཏོར་ (trūŋyaŋ pūūdɔr) shung. offering of sprinkled chang made by the ཞལ་གཉེར་ at a government ceremony.

འཁྲུངས་གཡོག (trūŋyɔɔ̀) shung. assistants to the འཁྲུངས་ཞུ་མ་ who serve chang to the ཡ་སོར་ (at Monlam).

འཁྲུངས་རབས་ (trūŋrəb) Jataka stories (stories of the Buddha's previous lives as a Bodhisattva) (h.).

འཁྲུངས་གཤེགས་ (trūŋsheg) birth and death ¶ འཁྲུངས་གཤེགས་ཀྱི་ལོ་ཚིགས་ The year of sb.'s birth and death.

འཁྲུངས་ས་ (trūŋsə) 1. sm. ཁྲུངས་ཡུལ་. 2. marriage (h.); va.—སྐྱོན་ to marry.

འཁྲུངས་ལྷ་ (trūŋlha)1. birth god (h.). 2. name of temple in southeast Lhasa where the 14th Dalai Lama's "birth god" is located.

འཁྲུད་: p. བཀྲུས་; f. བཀྲུ་; imp. ཁྲུས་ (trüü) va. to wash.

འཁྲུད་ཁང་ (trüügaŋ) bathing room, washroom.

འཁྲུད་འཁོར་ (trüügɔɔ) washing machine.

འཁྲུད་འཁྲུད་འཐག་འཐག (trüüdrüü tāgdaà) sm. འཁྲུད་འཁྲུད་བཤལ་བཤལ་.

འཁྲུད་འཁྲུད་བཤལ་བཤལ་ (trüüdrüü shεεshεε) washing and cleaning up; va.—བྱེད་ to wash and clean up.

འཁྲུད་གོས་ (trüügöö) clothes worn when bathing.

འཁྲུད་ཆབ་ (trüücəb) water that has been blessed.

འཁྲུད་ཆུ་ (trüücu) washing water.

འཁྲུད་ད་ (trüüda) sm. འཁྲུད་དར་.

འཁྲུད་དར་ (trüüdar) a wooden brush/ stick used to clean pots.

འཁྲུད་དར་པང་ལེབ་ (trüüdar bāŋleb) washing board.

འཁྲུད་བྱེད་ (trüüjee) washing ¶ ཁོས་ཀང་པ་འཁྲུད་བྱེད་ཀྱི་ཆུ་ཚ་པོ་བསྐྱལ་བ་རེད་ He brought hot water for washing (his) feet.

འཁྲུད་རྫས་ (trüüdzεὲ) cleaning materials/ agents (e.g., soap, detergent).

འཁྲུད་རྫིང་ (trüüdziŋ) a pool in a bathhouse.

འཁྲུད་ཤད་འཁོར་ཁང་ (trüüshεὲ kɔ̄rgaŋ) washing and carding workshop (for wool).

འཁྲུན་ (trün) 1. va. to distinguish/ differentiate between things. 2. a conflict, dispute.

འཁྲུན་གཅོད་ (trünjöö) sm. འཁྲུན་ཐག་གཅོད་.

འཁྲུན་ཆོད་ (trüncöö) resolution of a dispute/ conflict ¶ དམག་འཁྲུག་འཁྲུན་ཆོད་བྱུང་རྗེས་ After the resolution of the war.

འཁྲུན་ཐག་གཅོད་ (trūndaà jöö) va. to settle (an issue, controversy, law case, conflict, sport events) ¶ རྒྱལ་ཁབ་གཉིས་ཀྱི་ས་མཚམས་ཀྱི་ཁྲུན་ཐག་གཅོད་པར་བཀའ་མོལ་ཞིག་རྒྱུགས་ཀྱི་ཡོད་པ་རེད་ Discussions are being held to settle the controversy over the boundaries between the two countries.

འཁྲུན་ཐག་ཆོད་ (trūndaà cöö) vi. to have an issue/ controversy/ law case/ conflict/ deal get resolved or settled ¶ བསམ་བློའི་འགལ་བ་འཁྲུན་ཐག་ཆོད་པ་རེད་ The contradictions in (their) thoughts were resolved.

འཁྲུན་རིང་ (trünriŋ) sm. ཁྲུན་རིང་.

འཁྲུལ་ (trüü) 1. vi. to have an illusion, to hallucinate, to falsely or mistakenly see sth. ¶ མིག་འཁྲུལ་ནས་དུ་བ་རླངས་པར་མཐོང་བ་ (He) mistakenly saw the smoke as steam ¶ ནད་པ་འཁྲུལ་ནས་ཁང་པའི་ནང་ལ་ཤིང་སྡོང་མཐོང་བ་རེད་ The patient hallucinated and a saw a tree in the room. 2. sm. འཁྲུལ་བ་.

འཁྲུལ་རྐྱེན་ (trüügyen) negative influence.

འཁྲུལ་སྐྱོན་ (trüügyön) sm. འཁྲུལ་.

འཁྲུལ་འཁོར་ (trüükɔɔ) tricking, deceiving, fooling.

འཁྲུལ་གཏམ་ (trüüdam) fallacious or misleading rumor/ talk; va.—ཤོད་ ¶ འཁྲུལ་གཏམ་ཤོད་པར་བརྟེན་ནས་ཟིང་ཆ་སློང་བ་རེད་ A disturbance was caused by fallacious rumors.

འཁྲུལ་དུ་འཇུག (trüütu jüù) va. to delude; to mislead, to beguile.

འཁྲུལ་སྣང་ (trüünaŋ) illusion, hallucination; vi.—སྐྱེད་ to hallucinate, to have an illusion.

འཁྲུལ་སྣང་གི་ཡུལ་ལྗོངས་ (trüünaŋgi yüüjoŋ) a mirage.

འཁྲུལ་སྣང་བདེན་འཛིན་ (trüünaŋ dendzin) holding illusions as truth.

འཁྲུལ་པ་ (trüüwə) mistake, error.

འཁྲུལ་པ་སྤུ་ཙམ་མེད་པ་ (trüüwə būdzam meeba) absolutely true, authentic, bona fide ¶ ཡང་སྲིད་འདི་ལ་འཁྲུལ་པ་སྤུ་ཙམ་མེད་པ་ There is no question as to the authenticity of this incarnate (lama).

འཁྲུལ་བའི་ཆད་ལྷག (trüüwε cεεlhaà) minor/ inadvertent errors ¶ རྩིས་ཁྲ་འདིའི་ནང་འཁྲུལ་བའི་ཆད་ལྷག་ཕྲན་བུ་བྱུང་འདུག Minor errors were made in this account.

འཁྲུལ་བྲལ་ (trüüdrεε) sm. འཁྲུལ་མེད་.

འཁྲུལ་མིན་ (trüümin) sm. འཁྲུལ་མེད་.

འཁྲུལ་མེད་ (trüümeè) genuine, true ¶ འདི་ཕ་ལམ་འཁྲུལ་མེད་རེད་ This is a genuine diamond.

འཁྲུལ་མེད་ངེས་སྨེད་ (trüümeè ŋeèmeè) sm. འཁྲུལ་མེད་.

འཁྲུལ་གཞི་ (trüüshi) 1. confusing/ unclear with regard to what is true and erroneous or false ¶ གནད་དོན་འདི་གཉིས་བར་འཁྲུལ་གཞི་ཆེན་པོ་འདུག It is difficult to differentiate which is true and false between these two. 2. basis or foundation for mistakes/ errors/ illusions.

འཁྲུལ་བཟོ་ (trüüso) sm. འཁྲུལ་གཞི་.

འཁྲུལ་ལབ་ (trüüləb) delirious/ hallucinatory talk; va.—རྒྱག ¶ ཚ་བའི་རྐྱེན་གྱིས་ནད་པ་དེས་འཁྲུལ་ལབ་རྒྱག་གི་འདུག The fever is causing the sick person to talk deliriously.

འཁྲུལ་ལས་ཆེས་འཁྲུལ་ (trüülε cēè trüü) vi. to make one mistake on top of another.

འཁྲུལ་ཤེས་ (trüüsheè) hallucination, delusion.

འཁྲུལ་སོ་ (trüüso) sm. འཁྲུལ་གཞི་.

འཁྲུས་ (trüü) p. of འཁྲུ་.

འཁྲུས་ལོང་ (trüüloŋ) shung. an iron ring.

འཁྲེགས་པ་ (trēgba) sm. སྤྲ་བ་.

འཁྲེང་ (trēŋ) va. to hate to leave, to be reluctant to

part.

འབྲེང་ཚིག (trēŋtsig) words conveying not wanting to leave/ part.

འབྲེན་ (trēn) arc. vi. to get emotionally attached to ¶ དགའ་རོགས་ལ་སེམས་འབྲེན་པ་རེད་ (He) was emotionally attached to his girlfriend.

འབྲེབ་: p. འབྲེབས་; f. འབྲེབ་ (trēb) vi. to be stubborn/ inflexible/ difficult.

འབྲེབ་ཏོ་ (trēbdo) sm. བྲེབ་ཏོ་.

འབྲེབས་ (trēb) p. of འབྲེབ་.

འབྲོ་ (trɔ̄ɔ̀) vi. to get angry.

འབྲོག་: p. འབྲོགས་; f. འབྲོག (trɔ̄ɔ̀) 1. vi. to twist or dislocate a joint ¶ རྐང་པའི་ཚིག་འབྲོག་པ་རེད་ (He) twisted his leg. 2. vi. to have a grumbling sound coming from the stomach. 3. vi. to be deaf. 4. sm.* དཀྲོག.

འབྲོག་རྐྱེན་ (trɔ̄ɔ̀gyen) sm.* དཀྲོག་རྐྱེན་.

འབྲོག་ལང་ (trɔ̄ɔ̀ la̱ŋ) vi. to get stirred up ¶ མང་ཚོགས་འབྲོགས་ལང་བཞག The masses have been stirred up.

འབྲོགས་ (trɔ̄ɔ̀) p. of འབྲོག.

འབྲོབས་ (trōb) imp. of འབྲབ་.

འབྲོལ་ (trȫȫ) 1. sm. གྲོལ་. 2. vi. to receive permission. ¶ བོད་ལ་འགྲོ་ཡག་གི་དགོངས་པ་འབྲོལ་བ་རེད་ He got permission to go to Tibet. 3. vi. to hear a sound ¶ རོལ་མོའི་སྒྲ་འབྲོལ་བ་ To hear the sound of musical instruments.

འབྲོལ་འཁྱིལ་ (trȫȫgyii) extra, spare, leftover ¶ འབྲུ་རིགས་འབྲོལ་འཁྱིལ་ Leftover grains.

འབྲོལ་ཆ་ (trȫȫja) 1. sm. འབྲོལ་འཁྱིལ་. 2. permission, approval; va.—གནང་ to give/ issue approval or permission (h.).

འབྲོལ་དམ་ (trǖǖdam) shung. document giving permissiom to do sth. that has a seal affixed to it.

འབྲོལ་པོ་ (trȫȫbo) frank, outspoken ¶ མི་དེ་ཁ་གཤིས་འབྲོལ་པོ་འདུག This person is outspoken.

འབྲོལ་འཛིན་ (trǖndzin) a letter or document giving approval to leave, a permit, a license; va.—གཏོང་.

འབྲོལ་ཤིང་ (trǖǖshiŋ) a clapper used to keep time with rhythmic talk.

ག

ག་ (ka̲) 1. the letter *g* (used in alphabetical ordering). 2. (vb.+ —) infinitivizing particle that conveys "to do" the verbal action) ¶ རོགས་རམ་བྱེད་ག་ཡོང་བ་རེད་ (They) came to (do) help. 3. particle used after འགྲིག to convey "it is okay" ¶ དེ་འདྲ་བྱས་ན་འགྲིག་ག If you do that it's okay. 4. particle used at end of clauses to convey "shall I?" ¶ ངས་བྱས་ག Shall I do it? 5. a receding hairline. 6. what, how? ¶ དེ་བྱས་ན་ག་ལ་འགྲིགས་ If you do that how can it be okay?

ག་ཁྲལ་ (ka̲drɛɛ) animal tax; va.—རྒྱག to pay an animal tax ¶ ས་གནས་སོ་སོའི་ལོ་རེའི་ག་ཁྲལ་དུས་ཐོག་ངེས་འབུལ་དགོས་རྒྱུ་ From each locality every year the animal tax had to be given on time.

ག་ག་ཚིལ་ (ka̲gadzil) tickling.

ག་གན་ (ka̲gɛn) mong. title of Mongol emperor.

ག་གའི་ (kə̲gɛɛ) where ¶ ཕོ་ཚོ་ག་གའི་འདུག Where are they? 2. sm. ག་གས་.

ག་གས་ (ka̲ kɛ̲ɛ̀) (— + neg.) nothing at all, anything at all ¶ ང་ཚོས་ག་གས་མ་བྱས་ We didn't do anything at all.

ག་གི་ (kə̲gi) which ¶ ཁྱེད་རང་གི་དེབ་ག་གི་རེད་ Which is your book?

ག་གིར་ (kə̲gir) to which ¶ མི་ག་གིར་དངུལ་སྤྲད་པ་རེད་ To which person did (he) give the money?

ག་གིས་ (kə̲gii) by which ¶ ཁྱི་ག་གིས་ཤ་བཟས་པ་རེད་ Which dog ate the meat?

ག་གེ་མོ་ (ka̲gemo) such and such, some, certain.

ག་གོན་ (ka̲gön) 1. turnip. 2. lead.

ག་འགྲོ་འདི་འགྲོ་མེད་པ་ (ka̲ndro di̲ndro me̲èba) not knowing/ uncertain where to go ¶ ས་ཡོམ་ཆེན་པོ་བྱུང་སྐབས་མི་ཚང་མ་དངངས་སྐྲག་སྐྱེས་ནས་ག་འགྲོ་འདི་འགྲོ་མེད་པ་ཆགས་པ་རེད་ During the great earthquake all the people got scared and became uncertain about where to go.

ག་འགྲོ་མེད་པ་ (ka̲ndro me̲èba) sm. ག་འགྲོ་འདི་འགྲོ་མེད་པ་.

ག་འགྲིག (ka̲ dri̲g) va. to put together/ assemble. 2. sm. ག་རྒྱག.

ག་རྒྱག (ka̲ gya̲à) 1. vi. to have comments/ accounts tally, to have separate statements or enumerations come out the same.

ག་སྒྱུར་ (kə̲gyur) converting, exchanging; va.—གཏོང་.

ག་ཅི་ (kə̲ji) what ¶ འདི་ག་ཅི་མོ་ What is this?

ག་ཅེན་ (ka̲jen) sm.* འགའ་ཆེན་.

ག་ཆག (ka̲jaà) submerging woolen fabrics in a basin of water to make the weave tighter; va.—བྱེད་.

ག་ཆད་ (ka̲ cɛ̄ɛ̀) vi. to be tired of (sth.); to lose one's patience, to be fed up.

ག་གཉིས་ (kə̲ñiì) which two ¶ དེབ་ག་གཉིས་ཁྱེད་རང་གིས་བཀླགས་པ་རེད་ Which two books did you read?

ག་བཏང་གོ་ཆོད་ (ka̲daŋ ko̲jöò) a person who is capable of doing all sorts of things, a handyman.

ག་ཐག (ka̲dag) arc. all.

ག་མཐོ་པོ་ (ka̲ tōbo) sb. with a high forehead/ hairline.

ག་དག (ka̲dag) sm. ག་ཐག.

ག་དང་ (ka̲daŋ) sm. ག་དང་དམག་སྒར་.

ག་དང་དམག་སྒར་ (ka̲daŋ māgar) the "ག" or Shigatse Regiment in the traditional Tibetan army.

ག་དི་གུ་དི་ (kə̲di ku̲di) miscellaneous work ¶ ང་ལས་ཀ་གཙོ་བ་བྱེད་མཁན་མིན། ག་དི་གུ་དི་བྱེད་མཁན་ཡིན་ I am not the main worker; I am sb. who does miscellaneous work.

ག་དུར་ (kə̲dur) bergenia purpuras cens (a plant used in Tibetan medicine).

ག་དུས་ (kə̲düù) when ¶ ཕོ་ག་དུས་འགྲོ་གི་རེད་ When is (he) going?

ག་དུས་ག་པར་ (kə̲düù ka̲baa) when and where ¶ ཕོ་ཚོ་ག་དུས་ག་པར་འབྱོར་གི་ཡོད་མེད་ཤེས་ཀྱི་མི་འདུག (They) do not know when and where they are arriving.

ག་དུས་ཡིན་ནའང་ (kə̲düù yi̲naŋ) whenever, every time, all the time ¶ སློབ་ཕྲུག་འདི་ག་དུས་ཡིན་ནའང་དཔེ་མཛོད་ཁང་ལ་སླེབས་ཀྱི་འདུག The student comes to the library all the time.

ག་དུས་ཡིན་ནའི་ (kə̲düù yi̲nɛɛ) sm. ག་དུས་ཡིན་ནའང་.

ག་དུས་ཡིན་རུང་ (kə̲düù yi̲nruŋ) sm. ག་དུས་ཡིན་ནའང་.

ག་འདྲ་ (ka̲ndra) 1. how ¶ མི་དེ་ཚོ་ལས་ཀ་ག་འདྲ་འདུག་གམ་ How do those people work? 2. what, what sort/ kind of ¶ ཕོས་ལས་ཀ་གང་འདྲ་ཞིག་བྱེད་ཀྱི་ཡོད་པ་རེད་ What kind of work does he do?

ག་འདྲ་བྱས་ (**ནས་** or **སྟེ་**) (ka̲ndra cɛ̲ɛ̀) 1. how, in what way ¶ ཕོས་འདི་ག་འདྲ་བྱས་ནས་བྱས་པ་རེད་ How did he do this? 2. sm. ག་འདྲ་བྱས་ཀྱང་.

ག་འདྲ་བྱས་ཀྱང་ (kə̲ndra chɛ̲gyaŋ) whatever means, however you look at sth. ¶ ག་འདྲ་བྱས་ཀྱང་ང་ཚོ་གནས་ཚུལ་དེ་ཐག་གཅོད་བྱེད་དགོས་ We have to settle this issue using whatever means (we can). ¶ ག་འདྲ་བྱས་ཀྱང་དེང་སྐབས་བོད་ཀྱི་གནས་ཚུལ་དེ་ཡག་པོ་ཞིག་ཡོང་བ་མི་འདུག However you look at it, the present news from Tibet will not be good.

ག་འདྲ་བྱས་ནའི་ (kə̲ndra chɛ̲nɛɛ) sm. ག་འདྲ་བྱས་ཀྱང་.

ག་འདྲ་ཞིག (kə̲ndrashig) what, what sort/ kind of ¶ འཕྲུལ་འཁོར་གསར་པ་འདི་ག་འདྲ་ཞིག་ཡོད་པ་རེད་ What kind of new machine is it?

ག་འདྲས་ (kə̲ndrɛɛ̀) sm. ག་འདྲ་.

ག་འདྲས་ཡིན་ནའི་ (kə̲ndrɛɛ̀ yi̲nnɛɛ) no matter what ¶ ལས་ཀ་ག་འདྲས་ཡིན་ནའི་ང་ལ་ཁྱད་མི་འདུག No matter what the job is, it makes no difference to me.

ག་འདྲས་སེ་ (kə̲ndrɛs) how ¶ ཁྱེད་རང་ག་འདྲས་སེ་ཡོང་བ་རེད་ How did you come?

ག་ན་ (ka̲na) where ¶ ཁོང་ག་ན་བཞུགས་ཡོད་པ་རེད་ Where is he staying?

ག་ནས་ (kə̲nɛɛ̀) 1. from where ¶ མི་འདི་ག་ནས་རེད་ Where is this person from? 2. how, how could (conveys amazement) ¶ དུས་ཚོད་ཐུང་ཐུང་དེའི་ནང་ཁང་པ་དེ་ག་ནས་རྒྱག་ཐུབ་ཀྱི་རེད་ How will they be able to build the house in that short a time?

ག་ནས་ག་ནས་ (kə̲nɛɛ̀ kə̲nɛɛ̀) (exclamation of modesty) No, no. ¶ ཁྱེད་རང་གི་ལས་ཀ་ཡག་པོ་ཞེ་དྲག་འདུག ག་ནས་ག་ནས་ Your work is excellent. (answer) No, no (not at all).

ག་ནས་ག་ཡོང་མེད་པ་ (kə̲nɛ ka̲yoŋ me̲èba) not knowing where sb. came from ¶ ག་ནས་ག་ཡོང་མེད་པའི་མི་གསར་པ་ཞིག་སླེབས་བཞག A new person arrived, from where (we) don't know.

ག་ནས་ནུས་ (kə̲nɛɛ̀ nü̲ù) How can (I) ¶ ངས་ཁྱེད་རང་ལ་འགྲན་ག་ནས་ནུས་ How can I compete with you?

ག་པར་ (ka̲baa) where.

ག་པར་ག་པར་ (ka̲baa ka̲bar) 1. where ¶ རྒྱ་གར་ལ་བོད་མི་ག་པར་ག་པར་གནས་ཡོད་པ་རེད་ Where are the Tibetans living in India? 2. sm. ག་ནས་ག་ནས་.

ག་པར་ལས་མ་བལྟས་ (ka̲barlɛ ma̲dɛɛ̀) disregarding the consequences ¶ ཁོང་གིས་གནས་ཚུལ་ག་པར་ལས་མ་བལྟས་པར་རྒྱ་ནག་ལ་ཕྱིན་པ་རེད་ He disregarded the situation and went to China.

ག་ཕྱི་གོ་ལོག (kə̲ji ko̲loò) sm. གབ་ཕྱི་ལོག.

ག་ཕྱི་ལོག (kə̲jilɔɔ̀) sm. གབ་ཕྱི་ལོག.

ག་བུར་ (kə̲bur) camphor, moth balls.

ག་བུར་དྲིས་ལོ་ (kə̲bur dīìlo) delphinium trichorum (a plant used in Tibetan medicine).

ག་བུར་རིལ་བུ་ (kə̲bur ri̲ibu) moth balls.

ག་བེ་གོ་བེ་ (ka̲be ko̲be) sm. གོག་དོ་.

ག་བྱས་ (ka̲jɛɛ̀) sm. གང་བྱས་.

ག་བྱེད་འདི་བྱེད་མི་ཤེས་པ་ (ka̲jèe di̲jeɛ̀ mi̲shēèba) sm. ག་བྱེད་འདི་བྱེད་མེད་པ་.

ག་བྱེད་འདི་བྱེད་མེད་པ་ (ka̲jèe di̲jeè me̲èba) having a hard time figuring out what or how to deal with an unexpected situation ¶ སྐུ་མགྲོན་མང་པོ་ཞིག་ངའི་

ནང་གློ་བུར་ཕེབས་ཙང་ང་ག་བྱེད་འདི་བྱེད་མེད་པ་ཞིག་བྱུང་ Because many guests suddenly came to my house, I didn't know what to do.

ཀ་བྲ་ (kadra) rubus subornatus focke.

ཀ་འབབ་ (kəmbəb) animal tax.

ཀ་མན་ཀོ་ལོག (kamɛn koləə) sm. ཀ་ཕྱི་ཀོ་ལོག.

ཀ་མིན་འདི་མིན་ (kəmin dimin) at strange/ unusual times ¶ ཁྱེད་རང་དུས་ཚོད་ཀ་མིན་འདི་མིན་ལ་མ་ཕེབས་ Don't come at unusual times.

ཀ་དམའ་པོ་ (ka maabo) sb. whose hairline starts low on his forehead.

ཀ་ཙམ་ (kadzam) sm. ཀ་ཚོད་.

ཀ་ཚད་ (kədzɛɛ) sm. ཀ་ཚོད་.

ཀ་ཚོད་ (kədzöö) how much, how many, how long ¶ ཁོ་ལ་ས་ཞིང་ཀ་ཚོད་ཡོད་པ་རེད་ How much land does he have? ¶ ཁོང་རྒྱ་གར་ལ་ཀ་ཚོད་བཞུགས་པ་རེད་ How long did he stay in India? ¶ ཁོ་ལོ་ཀ་ཚོད་རེད་ How old is he? 2. (— + vb. + ཀྱང་/ཡང་/འང་) no matter how many/ much ¶ དམག་མི་ཀ་ཚོད་བཏང་ཡང་ No matter how many soldiers (they) sent. 3. (— + vb.1 + པ་/བ་ + དེ་ཙམ་ + vb. 2) how much vb. 1, that much vb. 2 ¶ ལས་ཀ་ཀ་ཚོད་བྱས་པ་ཙམ་གླ་ཆ་དེ་ཙམ་ཐོབ་ཀྱི་རེད་ However much (you) work, that much (you) will get in wages.

ཀ་ཚོད་ཉུང་ནའི་ (kədzöö ñuŋne) however few, at least ¶ རྒྱ་གར་ལ་བོད་མི་ཀ་ཚོད་ཉུང་ནའི་ 100,000 ལྷག་ཙམ་ཡོད་རེད་ There are at least 100,000 Tibetans in India.

ཀ་ཚོད་ཐུབ་ཐུབ་ (kədzöö tūbdub) as much as possible.

ཀ་མཚུངས་ (ka tsūŋ) vi. to be balanced ¶ ཁོང་གི་ལས་ཀ་དང་གླ་ཕོགས་ཀ་མཚུངས་ཀྱི་མ་རེད་ His work and salary are not in balance.

ཀ་འཛོལ་ (kandzöö) imbalanced, unbalanced ¶ ཐོན་སྐྱེད་དང་མི་འབོར་ཀ་འཛོལ་དུ་གྱུར་བ་རེད་ Population and production became imbalanced.

ཀ་ཞ་ (kasha) jeering, mocking, making fun of va.—བྱེད་; —སྒྲོག ¶ མི་དེས་ཚོགས་འདུའི་ཐོག་སྐད་ཆ་ཁྱད་མཚར་ཞིག་བཤད་ཙང་ཚང་མས་ཀ་ཞ་བསྒྲགས་པ་རེད་ Because he said weird things at the meeting everyone made fun of him.

ཀ་གཞའ་ (ka sha) sm. ཀ་ཞ་.

ཀ་གཞུང་ (kəshuŋ) shung. a list/ book containing the number of animals households owe as taxes ¶ ཀ་གཞུང་ནང་གསལ་ཁྲལ་འབབ་སྤྲོད་འབུལ་དགོས་རྒྱུ་ One should pay the taxes in accordance with the animal tax list.

ཀ་ཟེར་འདི་ཟེར་ (kasee disee) sm. ཀ་གོད་འདི་གོད་མེད་པ་.

ཀ་ཡིན་འདི་ཡིན་མེད་པ་ (kəyin diyin meēba) 1. nonsense, absurd, ridiculous ¶ མི་དེས་སྐད་ཆ་ཀ་ཡིན་འདི་ཡིན་མེད་པ་ཞིག་བཤད་སོང་ That man talked nonsense. 2. speech where the meaning isn't clear ¶ མི་དེས་རྟག་པར་སྲིད་དོན་གྱི་ལྟ་བའི་སྐོར་སྐད་ཆ་ཀ་ཡིན་འདི་ཡིན་མེད་པ་ཞིག་གཤོད་ཀྱི་ཡོད་པ་རེད་ That person always speaks unclearly concerning his political views.

ཀ་ཡོང་ཅི་ཡོང་ (kayoŋ jīyoŋ) doing one's best; va.—བྱེད་ ¶ ལས་ཀ་ཀ་ཡོང་ཅི་ཡོང་བྱས་ཀྱང་གླ་ཆ་ཆུང་ཆུང་ཞིག་ལས་སྤྲོད་ཀྱི་མི་འདུག Even though (I) did my best at work they paid me a low wage.

ཀ་ཡོང་འདི་ཡོང་མེད་པ་ (kayoŋ diyoŋ meēba) unimaginable, impossible, incredible (in a bad sense), shocking ¶ ལོ་འདིའི་ནང་གནས་ཚུལ་གང་ཡོང་འདི་ཡོང་མེད་པ་དེ་འདྲ་ཡོང་གི་འདུག This year incredible situations are occurring.

ཀ་ར་ (kara) sheep.

ཀ་རུ་ (kəru) sm. ཀ་ན་.

ཀ་རུ་ཡང་ (kəruyaŋ) sm. ཀ་ར་ཡང་.

ཀ་རེ་ (kare) what ¶ ད་ག་རེ་བྱེད་དགོས་རེད་ Now what should (I) do?

ཀ་རེ་ཀ་རེ་ (kare kare) what kind/ sort ¶ ཁྱེད་རང་གི་ལས་ཀ་ཀ་རེ་ཀ་རེ་བྱེད་ཐུབ་ཀྱི་ཡོད་ What kind of work can you do?

ཀ་རེ་བྱས་ནའི་བྱེད་ (kare cɛne ceè) (I) don't care what happens (or what is done) ¶ ཁྱེད་རང་གིས་ཀ་རེ་བྱེད་ནའི་བྱེད་ང་ཞེད་ཀྱི་མི་འདུག (I) don't care what you do. I'm not afraid of you.

ཀ་རེ་ཡིན་ནམ་ (kare yinnaa) why ¶ ཁྱེད་རང་གིས་དངུལ་མང་པོ་སྤྲོད་དགོས་ཡག་དེ་ག་རེ་ཡིན་ནམ་ Why did you have to give (him) so much money?

ཀ་རེ་ཡིན་ནའི་ (kare yinɛ) whatever ¶ ཁོས་ལས་ཀ་ཀ་རེ་ཡིན་ནའི་བྱེད་ཐུབ་ཀྱི་རེད་ He will be able to do whatever work there is.

ཀ་རེ་ཡིན་ནའི་མིན་ནའི་ (kare yinɛ minnɛ) regardless of, no matter what ¶ ཀ་རེ་ཡིན་ནའི་མིན་ནའི་ང་ནི་གློག་བརྙན་ལ་འགྲོ་ཐག་ཆོད་ཡིན་ Regardless of what, I am definitely going to the movie.

ཀ་རེས་ (kareè) by what ¶ ཁྱེད་རང་ལ་ཀ་རེས་བརྒྱབས་པ་རེད་ By what were you hit with?

ཀ་ལ་ (kala) how, how could (conveys amazement/ incredulity) ¶ ངས་ཁྱེད་ལ་འདི་འདྲས་ཀ་ལ་བྱེད་ How could I do a thing like that to you?

ཀ་ལ་འགྲིག (kaladrig) how is it okay.

ཀ་ལ་ཆོག (kala cōò) how can sth. be okay, how could sth. occur/ be ¶ དེ་འདྲས་བྱས་པས་ཀ་ལ་ཆོག How it be okay to do that?

ཀ་ལ་ཐུབ་ (kala tūb) (vb. + —) how is it possible ¶ དེ་ལྟར་མིན་ཚེ་བོད་ངོས་ནས་བཤད་ན་ཀྱང་དབུས་ལ་བརྩི་བཀུར་ཞུ་བ་དེ་ཡོད་ཀ་ལ་ཐུབ་ If it is not like that, how is it possible to say that Tibet respects the central government.

ཀ་ལ་ཕོད་ (kala pöö) how does one dare ¶ གོང་རིམ་ལ་ཁ་ལན་སློག་ཀ་ལ་ཕོད་ How does one dare answer back to one's superiors.

ཀ་ལ་པ་དེར་ (kala pader) wherever there is ¶ དམག་མི་ཡོད་ས་ཀ་ལ་པ་དེར་དམག་བརྒྱབ་པ་རེད་ Wherever there were soldiers staying, (they) attacked (them).

ཀ་ལ་བཙི་ (kala dzi) how can one be harmed ¶ མཚོན་སྲུང་གྱོན་ན་མེ་མདས་ཀ་ལ་བཙི་ If one wears a protective amulet how can a gun harm you.

ཀ་ལ་ཡོད་ (kala yöö) sm. ཀ་ལ་སྲིད་.

ཀ་ལ་རུང་ (kala ruŋ) sm. ཀ་ལ་འགྲིག.

ཀ་ལ་སྲིད་ (kala sii) 1. (neg. + vb. + —) how is it possible not to ¶ དགའ་ཚོར་མི་སྐྱེ་བ་ཀ་ལ་སྲིད་ How is it possible not to be happy.

ཀ་ལེ་ (kəle) slowly, gradually ¶ རྐང་འཁོར་ཀ་ལེ་གཏང་ན་ཉེན་ཁ་མེད་ (If you) ride the bicycle slowly there is no danger.

ཀ་ལེ་ཀ་ལེར་ (kəle kəlee) slowly, gradually ¶ འབད་བརྩོན་བྱས་ན་ཀ་ལེ་ཀ་ལེར་ཤེས་ཀྱི་རེད་ If you work diligently, you will gradually learn it.

ཀ་ལེ་གུ་ལེ་ (kəle gule) doing things slowly and unhurriedly.

ཀ་ལེ་རྒྱུགས་ (kəle gyuù) 1. go slowly. 2. good bye (said by the one staying).

ཀ་ལེ་ཆིབས་བསྒྱུར་གནང་ (kəle cībgyur nāŋ) good-bye (said by the one staying) (h.).

ཀ་ལེ་ཆིབས་བསྒྱུར་གནང་གོག (kəle cībgyur nāŋgəə) sm. ཀ་ལེ་ཆིབས་བསྒྱུར་གནང་.

ཀ་ལེ་ཕེབས་ (kəle pēè) good-bye (said by the one staying) (h.).

ཀ་ལེ་བཞུགས་ (kəle shuù) good-bye (said by the one leaving) (h.).

ཀ་ལེ་བཞུགས་གདན་འཛམས་གོག (kəle shudɛnjaàgə) sm. ཀ་ལེ་བཞུགས་.

ཀ་ལེ་བཞུགས་ཨ་ (kəle shuùa) sm. ཀ་ལེ་བཞུགས་; va.—བྱེད་.

ཀ་ལེར་ལ་ (kaleela) sm. ཀ་ལེ་ཀ་ལེར་.

ཀ་ལོག (kaləə) 1. exaggerating; va.—བྱེད་. 2. heretical or evil ideas/ thoughts.

ཀ་ཤ་ (kasha) a strap worn over one side of the shoulder that goes under the other arm va.—གཡོག to put on such a strap.

ཀ་ཤལ་ (kashɛɛ) a flower/ wreath/ ornament that is worn over one shoulder and under the other arm; va.—གཡོག to put on such an ornament.

ཀ་ཤེད་ (kasheè) a place (conveys a vagueness about which place) ¶ ང་ཡུལ་ཀ་ཤེད་ལ་འགྲོ་གི་ཡིན་ I am going to a place.

ག་ཤེལ་ (kashee) glass bead.

ག་ཤེས་ (kasheè) see ཁ་ཏང་.

ག་ཤོད་འདི་ཤོད་མེད་པ་ (kashöö dishöö meèba) not knowing what to say ། ང་ལ་གྲ་སྒྲིག་མེད་ཙང་ཚོགས་འདུའི་ཐོག་ག་ཤོད་འདི་ཤོད་མེད་པ་ཆགས་སོང་ I wasn't prepared, so I didn't know what to say at the meeting.

ག་ས་ག་ནས་ (kasa kanεὲ) from everywhere, from all over ། གྲོང་ཁྱེར་འདིའི་ནང་གི་མི་མང་ཆེ་བ་ས་ཆ་ག་ས་ག་ནས་ཡོང་པ་རེད་ Most of the people in this city came from all over the country.

ག་ས་ག་ལ་ (kasa kala) everywhere, all over ། གནས་ཚུལ་འདི་ག་ས་ག་ལ་ཁྱབ་པ་རེད་ This news spread everywhere.

ག་ས་གར་ (kasakaa) sm. ག་ས་ག་ལ་.

ག་སེལ་ (kasel) crossing out/ voiding a written agreement after the terms of the contract or loan are completed; va.—གཏོང་; —བྱེད་ ། བུ་ལོན་རྙིང་པ་ཚང་མ་སྤྲད་ནས་གན་རྒྱར་ག་སེལ་བཏང་བ་རེད་ Having paid off all the old loans, (he) voided the contract.

ག་སེལ་རྫིས་དག་ (kasee dzìidaà) shung. to to make up sth. owed so as to complete a contract/ loan/ obligation ། འདེགས་གཏོར་ལྷག་ཆད་ཇི་བྱུང་ལས་འཛིན་སོ་སོས་ག་སེལ་རྫིས་དག་ཞུ་རྒྱུ When doing the weighing, the managers themselves should make up whatever discrepancy occurs (between what is required and what they weigh).

ག་སོང་ག་འདེད་ (kasoŋ kandeè) pursuing everywhere; va.—གཏོང་ ། ཉེས་ཅན་དེ་ག་སོང་ག་འདེད་གཏོང་དགོས་ This criminal should be pursued everywhere.

ག་སོང་འདི་སོང་མེད་པ་ (kasoŋ disoŋ meèba) not knowing where sth. went, unable to trace/ ascertain/ detect where sth. is ། ཁོང་པ་ཡུལ་ནས་ཁ་བྲལ་རྗེས་ག་སོང་འདི་སོང་མེད་པ་ཆགས་སོང་ After he left his home area, (we) have been unable to ascertain his whereabouts.

གག་གེ་གོག་གེ་ (kage koge) a clumsy, awkward person.

གག་གོག (kaggɔ̀ɔ) 1. abbr. of གག་གེ་གོག་གེ. 2. preventing, stopping, holding back, blocking; va.—བྱེད་. 3. meandering, winding, zigzagging.

གག་ཐེབས་ (kag tēb) vi. when cooking rice to have the water be almost absorbed by the rice.

གག་པ་ (kagba) a disease or infection of the tongue.

གགས་གོགས་ (kaggɔ̀ɔ) sm. གག་གོག.

གང་ (kaŋ) 1. what ། དེ་གང་རེད་དམ་ What is that? 2. vi. to be filled up, to be full ། སྣོད་ཆས་དེ་ཆུས་གང་འདུག The pot is full of water. 3. one of sth. that is full or complete ། ཇ་ཕོར་པ་གང་འཐུང་ Drink one cup of tea. 4. (— + adj.) as — as possible ། ཡུལ་གཉིས་དབར་གྱི་མཐུན་སྒྲིལ་གང་ཡག་ཡོད་པ་རེད་ The friendship of the two countries is as good as possible. 5. (— + adj. + adj.) as — as possible ། གང་མང་མང་ As many as possible.

གང་སྐྱོལ་དེ་སྒྲུབ་ (kaŋgüü tedrub) fulfilling whatever task is given; va.—བྱེད་ ། ལོ་མང་པོའི་རིང་ངས་འགོ་ཁྲིད་གིས་ལས་འགན་གང་སྐྱོལ་དེ་སྒྲུབ་བྱས་པ་ཡིན་ For many years I have fulfilled the responsibilities given to me by my leader.

གང་སྐྱོལ་དེ་བྱེད་ (kangüü tejeè) sm. གང་སྐྱོལ་དེ་སྒྲུབ་.

གང་སྐྱིད་པ་ཡུལ་ སུ་བྱམས་པ་མ་ (kangyiì pāyüü sūcam pāma) sm. གར་སྐྱིད་པ་ཡུལ་ སུ་བྱམས་པ་མ་.

གང་མཁས་གང་སྙན་ (kaŋgεὲ kaŋñen) (talking) as pleasantly and interestingly as possible; va.—ཤོད

གང་མཁོ་གང་ལེན་ (kaŋgo kaŋlen) whatever one needs one can take; va.:བྱེད་ ། རང་གི་གྲོགས་པོའི་ས་ནས་ཅ་ལག་གང་མཁོ་གང་ལེན་བྱེད་ཀྱི་ཡོད་ I take whatever I need from my friends.

གང་མཁོ་དེ་སྤྲོད་ (kaŋgo tedröö) giving/ distributing according to need.

གང་ག (kaŋga) all ། མི་འདིས་ང་ཚོའི་ནང་གི་ཅ་ལག་གང་ག་བརྐུས་བཞག This man stole all the belongings in our home.

གང་ག (kaŋga) Ganges River.

གང་ག་ཆུང་ (kaŋga cūŋ) gentiana urnula (a plant used in Tibetan medicine).

གང་གི་ཆ་ནས་ (kaŋgi cānε) sm. གང་ཅིའི་ཐད་ནས་.

གང་གི་ཆེད་དུ་ (kaŋgi cēèdu) sm. གང་གི་ཕྱིར.

གང་གི་ཐད་ནས་ (kaŋgi tε̄εnε) sm. གང་ཅིའི་ཐད་ནས་.

གང་གི་ཐོག་ནས་ (kaŋgi tɔ̄ɔnε) sm. གང་ཅིའི་ཐད་ནས་.

གང་གི་དོན་ལ་ (kaŋgi tönla) sm. གང་གི་ཕྱིར་.

གང་གི་ཕྱིར་ (kaŋgi cīr) for what purpose/ reason, why ། ཁོ་གང་གི་ཕྱིར་འདི་ནས་ཕྱིན་པ་རེད་ For what reason did he go from here?

གང་གི་སླད་དུ་ (kaŋgi lε̄εdu) sm. གང་གི་ཕྱིར་.

གང་གིས་ (kaŋgiì) 1. by what/ which, because of what ། སྨན་གང་གིས་ནད་འདི་ལ་ཕན་གྱི་རེད་ What medicine will be good for this illness? 2. by what, how ། གང་གིས་ཐོན་སྐྱེད་ཆེ་རུ་འགྲོ་ཐུབ་པ་དྲིལ་བསྒྲགས་བྱས་པ་རེད་ (They) publicized how one will be able to increase production. 3. of/ from what ། འདི་གང་གིས་བཟོས་པ་རེད་ What is this made from?

གང་གིས་ཤེ་ན་ (kaŋgiì shēèna) why, if you ask why ། ཁོང་རྒྱ་གར་ལ་སྐྱིད་པོ་བྱུང་མི་འདུག གང་གིས་ཤེ་ན་ ཚ་བའི་གནམ་གཤིས་མ་འཕྲོད་པའི་རྐྱེན་རེད་འདུག If you ask why he was not happy in India, it is because the heat doesn't suit him.

གང་གུས་ཅི་གུས་ (kaŋgüü jīgüü) respecting sb. as much as possible.

གང་གླེང་བར་བྱ་བ་ (kaŋleŋwar cawa) what I want to say is (used at start of articles/ essays to introduce the main section).

གང་དགའ་ (kaŋ ga) whatever makes one happy, to one's heart's content; va.—བྱེད་.

གང་དགའ་གང་སྐྱིད་ (kaŋ ga kaŋ gyiì) as good/ pleasant a time as possible; va.—བྱེད་ to have as good a time as possible ། སློབ་ཕྲུག་ཚོས་གུང་གསེང་སྐབས་གང་དགའ་གང་སྐྱིད་བྱས་སོང་ During their vacation, the students had as good a time as possible.

གང་དགའ་གང་འདོད་ (kaŋ ga kaŋ döö) sm. གང་བདེ་ཅི་འདོད་.

གང་དགའ་ཅི་དགའ་ (kaŋ ga jī ga) 1. sm. གང་དགའ་ཅི་ལེགས་ 2. doing whatever one likes, doing to one's heart's content; va.—བྱེད་ ། མི་སོ་སོས་གང་དགའ་ཅི་དགའ་བྱས་ན་འགྲིགས་ It is okay for everyone to do whatever pleases them.

གང་དགའ་ཅི་བདེ་ (kaŋ ga jī ga) sm. གང་དགའ་ཅི་དགའ་.

གང་དགའ་ཅི་ལེགས་ (kaŋga jīleg) as good/ well as possible ། དེའི་སྐོར་གང་དགའ་ཅི་ལེགས་ཀྱི་གྲོས་བསྡུར་བྱས་པ་རེད་ (We) discussed what will be best regarding this issue.

གང་དགེ་ (kaŋge) what is good/ better ། ཁོང་གིས་གང་དགེའི་དགོངས་འཆར་གནང་སོང་ He gave an opinion as to what is better.

གང་དགོས་ཅི་དགོས་ (kaŋgö jīgöö) whatever one wants ། ཚོང་ཁང་འདིའི་ནང་ལ་ཅ་ལག་གང་དགོས་ཅི་དགོས་ཡོད་པ་རེད་ That store has whatever goods you want.

གང་མགོ་ (kaŋgo) pipe for smoking tobacco.

གང་མགྱོགས་ (kaŋgyɔ̀ɔ) 1. as soon as ། གང་མགྱོགས་ཕེབས་རོགས་གནང་ (Please) come as soon as possible. 2. as fast as ། གང་མགྱོགས་ཕྱིན་པ་རེད་ (He) went as fast as possible.

གང་མགྱོགས་མགྱོགས་ (kaŋ gyɔgyɔ̀ɔ) as fast/ quick as possible ། ང་ཚོས་ཡིག་ཚད་གང་མགྱོགས་མགྱོགས་བཏང་པ་ཡིན་ We did our exam as quick as we could.

གང་མགྱོགས་ཅི་མགྱོགས་ (kaŋgyɔ̀ɔ jīgyɔ̀ɔ) sm. གང་མགྱོགས་མགྱོགས་.

གང་འགབ་ (kaŋgɔ̀b) whatever is good/ best ། ཁོ་ཚོས་གང་འགབ་གྲོས་བསྡུར་བྱས་སོང་ They discussed what is best.

གང་འགབ་ཇི་ལེགས་ (kaŋgɔ̀b jileg) sm. གང་འགབ་.

གང་ངུ་འདི་ངུ་མེད་པ་ (kaŋŋu diŋu meèba) crying a great deal.

གང་སྔ་ (kaŋŋa) sm. གང་སྔ་སྔ་.

གང་སྔ་སྔ་ (kaŋ ŋāŋa) as early as possible ། ཁོ་ཚོ་གནམ་གྲུའི་ཐང་ལ་གང་སྔ་སྔ་ཕྱིན་པ་རེད་ They went to the airport as early as possible.

གང་ཅི་ (kəŋji) all kinds of, every aspect ། ཁོང་གང་ཅིར་ཧུར་བརྩོན་ཆེན་པོ་ཡོད་པ་རེད་ He is diligent in every aspect. ། ཁོ་ཚོར་གང་ཅིའི་རོགས་རམ་ཐོབ་ཡོད་པ་རེད་ They got all kinds of aid.

གང་ཅི་འདོར་མེད་ (kəŋji dɔɔmeè) shung. not overlooking or bypassing anything ། ཆབ་འབངས་རྣམས་ལ་བྱམས་གཟིགས་མཛད་འོས་གང་ཅི་འདོར་མེད་ཡོང་བ་ Regarding the treatment of our subjects, do not overlook anything

གང་ཅིག (kəŋjii) sm. གང་ཞིག.

གང་ཅིའི་ཐད་ནས་ (kəŋjii tɛ̀ɛnɛ) by all means, in all respects ། ལུང་པ་འདི་གང་ཅིའི་ཐད་ནས་མཐུན་རྐྱེན་ཡག་པོ་འདུག In all respects, this country has good resources. ། མོས་གང་ཅིའི་ཐད་ནས་ཕྲུ་གུ་དེ་སློབ་གྲྭར་གཏོང་ཐབས་བྱས་པ་རེད་ She utilized all means to send the child to school.

གང་ཅིའི་ཐོག་ནས་ (kəŋjii tɔ̀ɔnɛ) sm. གང་ཅིའི་ཐད་ནས་.

གང་ཅིའི་ལག་འཛངས་ (kəŋjii laŋdzaŋ) a shortage of all things.

གང་ཅེར་ (kəŋjii) sm. གང་ཅི་.

གང་ལྕོགས་ (kaŋjoò) sm. གང་ལྕོགས་ལྕོགས་.

གང་ལྕོགས་ཅི་ནུས་ (kaŋjoò jīnüü) sm. གང་ལྕོགས་ལྕོགས་.

གང་ལྕོགས་ལྕོགས་ (kaŋ jōgjoò) doing whatever/ as much as one can do ། ངས་ལས་ཀ་གང་ལྕོགས་ལྕོགས་བྱས་ཀྱང་ཚར་མ་སོང་ I did as much as I could but didn't finish (the job).

གང་ཉིད་ (kaŋñii) you (h.) ། གང་ཉིད་སང་ཉིན་ངའི་ནང་ལ་ཕེབས་རོགས་གནང་ Would you please come to my house tomorrow.

གང་མཉེས་ (kaŋñeè) eat/ drink as much as you want, eat/ drink freely (said to guests at a party/ dinner) (h.) ། གསོལ་ཚིགས་གང་མཉེས་གནང་རོགས་གནང་ Please eat as much as you want.

གང་དིག (kəŋdii) arc. getting or having one's own way, doing as one desires/ pleases.

གང་ལྟར་ (kaŋdar) however, anyway, in any case ། ཁྱེད་རང་གིས་རེ་བྱེད་ཀྱི་ཡིན་ཡང་གང་ལྟར་ངར་ཁྱད་མི་འདུག In any case, whatever you do makes no difference to me.

གང་ལྟར་མང་ལྟར་ (kaŋdar maŋdar) sm. གང་ལྟར་.

གང་ལྟར་ཡང་སྙིང་ (kaŋdar yəŋñiŋ) anyway, anyhow.

གང་སྟབས་བདེ་བ་ (kaŋdəb dewa) whatever is more convenient.

གང་ཐད་ (kaŋdɛɛ̀) sm. གང་ཅིའི་ཐད་ནས་.

གང་ཐད་གང་འོས་ (kaŋdɛɛ kaŋwöò) shung. doing everything/ whatever is appropriate.

གང་ཐད་གང་རིགས་ (kaŋdɛɛ kaŋrig) shung. sm. གང་འཐད་གང་འོས་.

གང་ཐད་གཅིག་མཐུན་ (kaŋdɛɛ̀ jīgdün) isotropy (in physics).

གང་ཐད་ནས་ (kaŋdɛɛ̀nɛ) sm. གང་ཅིའི་ཐད་ནས་.

གང་ཐད་ལ་ (kaŋdɛɛ̀la) sm. གང་ཅིའི་ཐད་ནས་.

གང་ཐུབ་ (kaŋdub) sm. གང་ཐུབ་ཅི་ཐུབ་.

གང་ཐུབ་ཀྱིས་ (kaŋdubgi) sm. གང་ཐུབ་ཅི་ཐུབ་.

གང་ཐུབ་ཅི་ཐུབ་ (kaŋdub jīdub) as far as possible, as much as one can; va.—བྱེད་ to work hard for, to do as much as one can ། ང་ཚོས་རོགས་རམ་གང་ཐུབ་ཅི་ཐུབ་བྱས་ཡོད་ We have helped them as much as we can.

གང་ཐུབ་ཐུབ་ (kaŋ tūbdub) sm. གང་ཐུབ་ཅི་ཐུབ་.

གང་ཐེབས་ཅི་ཐེབས་ (kaŋdeb jīdeb) rushing around to get as much as possible; va.—བྱེད་.

གང་ཐོན་ཐོན་ (kaŋ tōndön) whatever comes to mind, whatever comes out; va.—ཤོད་ to say whatever comes to mind. 2. whatever you can spare ། ང་ལ་དངུལ་གང་ཐོན་ཐོན་ཞིག་གཡར་རོགས་ Please lend me whatever money you can spare.

གང་ཐོབ་ཅི་ཐོབ་ (kaŋdob jīdob) as much as one can get.

གང་འཐད་ (kaŋdɛɛ̀) sm. གང་ཐད་.

གང་འཐུང་རྒྱག (kaŋduŋ gyaà) va. to drink only one cup of sth.

གང་དག (kaŋdaà) whatever there is ། ཁང་པ་འདིའི་ནང་གི་དངོས་པོ་གང་དག་ཁྱེད་རང་ལ་བདག་པ་རེད་ Whatever things there are in the house belong to you.

གང་དང་གང་གི་ཐད་ནས་ (kaŋdaŋ kaŋgi tɛ̀ɛnɛ) sm. གང་ཅིའི་ཐད་ནས་.

གང་དང་གང་གི་ཐོག་ནས་ (kaŋdaŋ kaŋgi tɔ̀ɔnɛ) sm. གང་ཅིའི་ཐད་ནས་.

གང་དང་གང་ཞིག (kaŋdaŋ kaŋshig) 1. such and such, so and so ། མི་ཞིག་གིས་ང་ཡུལ་གང་དང་གང་ཞིག་ལ་ཕྱིན་པ་ཡིན་ཟེར་ན་ If a person says, "I have been to such and such a place." 2. (— + རུང་/ཀྱང་) whatever ། མི་ཡུལ་གྱི་བྱས་རྗེས་གང་དང་གང་ཞིག་ཡིན་ཡང་ Whatever human accomplishments there are.

གང་དང་ཅི་ (kaŋdaŋ jī) sm. གང་ཅི་.

གང་དུ་ (kaŋtu) where ། ཁང་པ་དེ་ག་པར་ཡོད་དམ་ Where is that house?

གང་དོ་ (kaŋto) one or two ། ཇ་དཀར་ཡོལ་གང་དོ་བཏུངས་པ་ཡིན་ I drank one or two cups of tea.

གང་དྲག (kaŋdraà) 1. as good/ well as possible, the best one can do ། ངས་ཐབས་ཤེས་གང་དྲག་བྱས་པ་ཡིན་ I tried as best as I could. 2. what to do? ། ངས་རྐྱལ་རྒྱག་མི་ཤེས། ད་གང་དྲག་ཅེས་བཤད་པ་རེད་ (He) said, "I can't swim. Now what to do?" 3. too bad, its a pity ། མི་མིག་མེད་པ་དེ་གང་དྲག That man without eyes, what a pity!

གང་དྲག་ཅི་དྲག (kaŋdraà jīdraà) sm. གང་དྲག.

གང་དྲན་ (kaŋdrɛn shöò) whatever comes to mind, whatever is remembered; va.—ཤོད་ to say what comes to mind or is remembered.

གང་དྲན་གང་ཞུས་ (kaŋdrɛn kaŋshüü) saying whatever comes to mind or one remembers; va.—བྱེད་.

གང་དྲན་དྲན་ཤོད་ (kaŋdrɛn trɛnshöò) sm. གང་དྲན་ཤོད་.

གང་བདེ་ཅི་འདོད་ (kaŋde jīndöò) whatever is convenient, whatever one desires or wants to do; va.—བྱེད་ ། གནད་དོན་འདིའི་སྐོར་ཁྱེད་རང་གི་གང་བདེ་ཅི་འདོད་ཀྱི་ཐག་གཅོད་གནང་ན་འགྲིགས་ Concerning this issue, you can settle it however you wish.

གང་འདོད་ (kaŋdöò) whatever one desires/ wants/ likes; va.—བྱེད་ to do whatever one desires/ want/ likes ། ཁྲིམས་དང་བསྟུན་ན་མ་གཏོགས་གང་འདོད་བྱེད་ཆོག་གི་མ་རེད་ (You) can only act according to the law. You cannot do as you like.

གང་འདོད་གང་བྱས་ (kaŋdö kaŋjɛɛ̀) doing whatever one pleases ། ཁོ་ཕ་མའི་ཁ་ལ་མ་ཉན་པར་གང་འདོད་གང་བྱས་བྱེད་ཀྱི་ཡོད་པ་རེད་ He doesn't obey his parents and does whatever pleases him.

གང་འདོད་ཅི་སྒྲུབ་ (kaŋdö jīdrub) 1. doing whatever one wants ། ང་རྒྱ་གར་ལ་འགྲོ་དུས་ལས་ཀ་གང་འདོད་ཅི་སྒྲུབ་བྱས་པ་ཡིན་ When I went to India, I did whatever work I wanted. 2. acquiring what one wants/ desires ། ངས་བོད་ནས་ཚོང་ཟོག་གང་འདོད་ཅི་སྒྲུབ་བྱས་པ་ཡིན་ I acquired from Tibet whatever merchandise I wanted.

གང་འདོད་འདོད་ (kaŋ dödöò) whatever one desires/ likes/ wishes.

གང་འདོད་དབང་ཤེད་ (kaŋdöò wāŋsheè) autocratic/ tyrannical/ dictatorial rule.

གང་འདྲ་ (kaŋdra) 1. how, like, what, in what way ། ཁོ་ལ་གང་འདྲ་ལབ་དགོས་རེད་ How should I tell him? ། བོད་ལ་གནམ་གཤིས་གང་འདྲ་ཡོད་པ་རེད་ What is the climate in Tibet like? 2. (— + ཞིག) what kind of ། ཁོ་ལ་ལས་ཀ་གང་འདྲ་ཞིག་ཡོད་པ་རེད་ What kind of job does he have? 3. however, whatever means, in all ways ། ཐབས་ཤེས་ག་འདྲ་བྱས་ཀྱང་ལས་ཀ་དེ་བསྒྲུབས་མ་སོང་ Whatever methods I tried, I couldn't succeed in the work.

གང་འདྲ་ཅིག་ཡིན་ནའང་ (kaŋdrajig yinnayaŋ) whatever it is/ may be.

གང་འདྲ་བྱས་དེ་ (kaŋdra cɛ̀ɛde) sm. གང་འདྲ་.

གང་འདྲ་བྱས་ནས་ (kaŋdra cɛ̀ɛnɛ) sm. གང་འདྲ་.

གང་འདྲ་ཤིག (kaŋdrashig) sm. གང་འདྲ་.

གང་འདྲ་ཟེར་ (kaŋdraser) sm. གང་འདྲ་.

གང་འདྲས་ (kəndrɛɛ̀) sm. གང་འདྲ་.

གང་ན་ (kaŋna) sm. ག་ན་.
གང་ན་གང་ཡོད་ (kaŋna kaŋyöö) sm. གང་ན་དེ་ཡོད.
གང་ན་ཅི་ཡོད་ (kaŋna jiyöö) sm. གང་ན་དེ་ཡོད.
གང་ན་དེ་ཡོད་ (kaŋna teyöö) whatever there is, whatever exists ། གནས་ཚུལ་དེ་སྐོར་རང་ལ་གང་ན་དེ་ཡོད་གསུང་དང་ Please say whatever (you think) about that situation.
གང་ན་སུ་ (kaŋnasu) shung. where ever ། སྐྱེ་མཆོག་དམ་པ་ས་ཕྱོགས་གང་ན་སུ་བཞུགས་ The great lamas, where ever they live.
གང་ནས་ (kaŋnεὲ) sm. ག་ནས་.
གང་ནུས་ (kaŋnüü) sm. གང་ཐུབ་.
གང་ནུས་ཅི་ནུས་ (kaŋnüü jinüü) sm. གང་ཐུབ་ཅི་ཐུབ་.
གང་ནུས་དེ་སྒྲུབ་ (kaŋnüü tedrub) from each according to his ability, to each according to his needs.
གང་པོ་ (kaŋbo) whole, complete, all, entire ། མི་ཚེ་གང་པོ་འཕྲོ་བརླག་ཕྱིན་སོང་ (His) entire life was ruined.
གང་ཕན་ཅི་ཕན་ (kaŋpεn jipεn) doing the utmost to help.
གང་བ་ (kaŋwa) full.
གང་བ་མེད་པ་ (kaŋba meèba) incomplete, not full.
གང་བུ་ (kəŋbu) pea pod.
གང་བུ་ཅན་གྱི་ལོ་ཏོག (kəŋbujεngi lodoò) leguminous crop.
གང་བྱས་ (kaŋjεὲ) 1. however, whatever, whichever ། ལས་དོན་གང་བྱས་མི་དམངས་ཀྱི་འདོད་པ་བསྟུན་དགོས་ Whatever the task, (we) have to act according to the wishes of the people. 2. able to do whatever what one wants ། ལས་ཁུངས་འདིའི་ནང་ཁོང་གིས་གང་བྱས་རེད་ In this office he can do whatever he wants.
གང་བྱས་གང་ལྟར་ (kaŋjεὲ kaŋdar) sm. གང་ལྟར་.
གང་བྱས་བྱས་ཡོད་ (kaŋjεὲ cεὲyöö) sm. གང་བྱས་, 2.
གང་བྱས་མ་བྱས་ (kaŋjεὲ majεὲ) sm. གང་ལྟར་.
གང་བྱུང་ (kəŋjuŋ) 1. indiscriminate, reckless, wantonly, in excess, overdoing, being carried away ། ས་གནས་མང་པོར་གང་བྱུང་མེ་འཕེན་བྱས་ཡོད་པ་རེད་ (They) have fired indiscriminately at many places. 2. whatever ། ཁོང་ཚོས་རོགས་རམ་གང་བྱུང་ལེན་གྱི་ཡོད་པ་རེད་ They take whatever help they get.
གང་བྱུང་བ་ (kaŋcuŋwa) whatever (one) gets.
གང་བྱུང་བྱུང་ (kaŋcunjuŋ) sm. གང་བྱུང་.
གང་བྱུང་མང་བྱུང་ (kəŋjuŋ məŋjuŋ) sm. གང་བྱུང་, 1.
གང་བྱུང་རང་དགར་འཇོག (kəŋjuŋ raŋgar jɔɔ̀) va. to let things run their course.
གང་མང་ (kaŋmaŋ) as much/ many as possible ། ང་ཚོར་རོགས་རམ་གང་མང་གནང་རོགས་གནང་ Please give us as much assistance as possible.
གང་མང་མང་ (kaŋ maŋmaŋ) sm. གང་མང་.
གང་མིན་ (kaŋmin) sm. གང་མིན་ཚད་.
གང་མིན་ཚད་ (kaŋ mindzεὲ) 1. (— + adj.) extraordinarily, absolutely, extremely, immeasurably, completely ། ཁོ་ཚོས་ལས་ཀ་གང་མིན་ཚད་ཡག་པོ་བྱེད་ཀྱི་ཡོད་པ་རེད་ They are working extraordinarily well. ། འདི་གང་མིན་ཚད་ཀྱི་ཁྲིམས་འགལ་རེད་ This is an extraordinary violation of the law. 2. extraordinarily (bad), sth. else ། མི་དེ་གང་མི་ཚད་རེད་ That man is something else. ། འདི་མ་བྱས་ན་གང་མིན་ཚད་བྱུང་ཡོང་ If (you) don't do this, something bad will happen. 3. va.—བྱེད་ idiomatic phrase conveying one's great appreciation for help (even though it may really have been little) — "it was wonderful" ། ང་ལ་ལག་རྟགས་ཆེན་པོ་འདི་འདྲ་གནང་བ་གང་མིན་ཚད་བྱས་སོང་ Giving me a big present like that—it was wonderful.
གང་མྱུར་ (kaŋñur) as soon/ quick as possible ། འདིའི་སྐོར་གང་མྱུར་བཀའ་ལན་གནང་རོགས་གནང་ Please send a reply concerning this matter as soon as possible.
གང་ཙམ་ (kaŋdzam) 1. how much, how many ། འདི་ནས་ལྷ་ས་བར་མི་ལི་གང་ཙམ་ཡོད་དམ་ How many miles is it from here to Lhasa? 2. (— + vb. པ་/ བ་ + དེ་ཙམ་) however much, that much ། ལས་ཀ་གང་ཙམ་བྱས་པ་དེ་ཙམ་གྱི་གླ་ཐོབ་ཀྱི་རེད་ However much you work, that much you will get in wages. 3. sm. གང་འཚམས་.
གང་ཙམ་སོང་ནས་ (kaŋdzam sõŋnε) after a period of time, after awhile ། གང་ཙམ་སོང་ནས་ཁོ་ཕྱིན་པ་རེད་ After awhile he left.
གང་བརྩམས་མཐར་སྐྱོལ་ (kaŋdzam tārgye) finishing/ completing whatever one has started; va.—བྱེད་ ། མི་དེ་ལས་ཀ་གང་བརྩམས་མཐར་སྐྱོལ་བྱེད་མཁན་ཞིག་རེད་ He is the kind of person who carries through to completion whatever work (he is doing or is given).
གང་འཚམ་ (kandzam) sm. གང་འཚམས.
གང་འཚམས་ (kandzam) 1. quite some ། ད་བར་ལས་ཀ་བྱས་ནས་ཉམས་མྱོང་གང་འཚམས་བྱུང་ཡོད་ They have gained quite some experience working. 2. sometime, a while ། དུས་ཚོད་གང་འཚམས་བལྟས་རྗེས་ After watching awhile. 3. sm. གང་ལ་གང་འཚམས་.
གང་འཚམས་ཤིག (kandzamjig) 1. awhile ། དུས་ཚོད་གང་འཚམ་ཤིག་རང་དཔེ་དེབ་པ་བཀླགས་པ་ཡིན་ I read the book for awhile.
གང་འཚམས་ཤིག་ནས་ (kandzam shignε) after awhile, after some time ། དུས་ཡུན་གང་འཚམས་ཤིག་ནས་ After sometime.
གང་འཚམས་སོང་ནས་ (kandzam sõŋnε) sm. གང་འཚམས་ཞིག་ནས་.
གང་ཞིག (kaŋshig) whatever, whichever ། རྒྱལ་ཁབ་ཁག་གང་ཞིག་ཕྱིན་ན་ཡང་ཁྲིམས་འཁུར་དགོས་ Whatever country you go to you have to abide by the law.
གང་ཞིག་གང་ཡིན་ (kaŋshig kaŋyin) sm. གང་ཞིག.
གང་ཞིག་དུ་ (kaŋshigdu) wherever.
གང་ཞིག་འདུག (kaŋshigduù) sm. གང་དྲུག.
གང་ཞིག་ཡིན་རུང་ (kaŋshig yinruŋ) whatever/ whichever; either ། སྟོད་ཐུང་དཀར་ནག་གང་རུང་ཞིག་གཉིགས་རོགས་གནང་ Please buy me either a black or white shirt (or Please buy me any color shirt).
གང་ཟག (kaŋsaà) 1. person, human being ། ཡོན་ཏན་ཅན་གྱི་གང་ཟག A learned person. 2. a pipe (for smoking); va.—འཐེན་ to smoke a pipe.
གང་ཟག་གི་གང་མགོ་ (kaŋsaàgi kaŋgo) bowl of a smoking pipe.
གང་ཟག་གི་ཡུ་བ་ (kaŋsaàgi yuwə) stem of a smoking pipe.
གང་ཟབ་ (kaŋsəb) as deep as possible.
གང་གཟབ་ (kaŋsəb) 1. as good as possible, whatever is best ། ལྷ་བསྐོར་བ་ཚོར་སྣེ་ལེན་གང་གཟབ་བྱས་སོང་ They gave the visitors as good a reception as was possible. 2. as carefully as one can ། ལྟ་ཞིབ་གང་གཟབ་བྱས་ཡོད་པ་རེད་ (They) have investigated it as carefully as they could.
གང་གཟབ་ཟབ་ (kaŋ səbsəb) sm. གང་གཟབ་.
གང་འོས་ (kaŋöö) whatever is suitable/ appropriate.
གང་ཡག་ཡག (kaŋ yayaà) sm. གང་གཟབ་, 1.
གང་ཡང་ (kaŋyaŋ) 1. anything, whatever, whichever ། ཁོང་གང་ཡང་བྱེད་ཐུབ་ཀྱི་རེད་ He can do anything. 2. (— + neg.) nothing, none at all, not at all ། འདི་ཕན་ཐོགས་གང་ཡང་བྱུང་མི་འདུག This was no benefit at all. ། དེ་སྐོར་ཁོས་གང་ཡང་ཤེས་མི་འདུག He knew nothing at all about that.
གང་ཡང་རུང་ (kaŋyaŋruŋ) sm. གང་རུང་.
གང་ཡང་རུང་བ་ (kaŋyaŋ ruŋwa) sm. གང་རུང་.
གང་ཡིན་ཅེ་ན་ (kaŋyin jēna) sm.* གང་ཡིན་ཞེ་ན་.
གང་ཡིན་འདི་ཡིན་མེད་པ་ (kaŋyin diyin meèba) 1. without any rhyme or reason ། ཁོ་དོན་དག་གང་ཡིན་འདི་ཡིན་མེད་པར་སླེབས་བྱུང་ He arrived without any reason. 2. a bit lost, not knowing what is what. 3. odd, unusual, weird ། ཁོ་གང་ཡིན་འདི་ཡིན་མེད་པའི་དྲུག་ལོག་ཅིག་གོན་བཞག He wore weird clothes.
གང་ཡིན་ན་ (kaŋyinna) why, for what reason ། ཁོ་མ་ཡོང་བ་གང་ཡིན་ན་ Why didn't he come?
གང་ཡིན་པ་བྱས་དགོ་ (kaŋyinba cεὲgo) slang. I bet sth. will occur ། ཁོ་སླེབས་མ་སོང་ན་ངས་གང་ཡིན་པ་

ཐུབ་དགོ་ I bet he will come.

གང་ཡིན་ཞི་ན་ (ka̲ŋyin she̲na) if you ask why, it is because ¶ ལུང་པ་འདི་ར་མི་མང་པོ་ཡོད་པ་འདི་གང་ཡིན་ཞི་ན་ཐོན་སྐྱེད་ཡག་པོ་ཡོད་པ་རེད་ If you ask why there are so many people in that area, it is because production is good.

གང་ཡིན་ཟེར་ན་ (ka̲ŋyin se̲na) sm. གང་ཡིན་ཞི་ན་.

གང་ཡོད་ (ka̲ŋyöö) all there is, whatever there is ¶ ནང་གི་ཅ་ལག་གང་ཡོད་བཙོང་པ་ཡིན་ I sold whatever things we had in the house.

གང་ཡོད་རུང་ (ka̲ŋ yö̲ruŋ) sm. གང་ཡོད་ཀྱང་.

གང་ཡོད་ཀྱང་ (ka̲ŋyögyaŋ) whatever there is, whatever you have.

གང་རིལ་ (ka̲ŋrii) sm. སྒང་རིལ་.

གང་རུང་ (ka̲ŋruŋ) 1. whatever, whichever, any kind ¶ ལས་ཀ་གང་རུང་ཞིག་ཐོབ་ཐབས་བྱེད་ཀྱི་ཡོད་ (I) am trying to get any (whatever) kind of job. 2. either ¶ སྟོད་ཐུང་དཀར་ནག་གང་རུང་ཞིག་གཉིས་རོགས་གནང་ Please buy me a either a black or white shirt.

གང་རུང་རུང་ (ka̲ŋruŋruŋ) sm. གང་བྱུང་བྱུང་.

གང་ལ་ (ka̲ŋla) sm. ག་པར་.

གང་ལ་གང་འཚམས་ (ka̲ŋla ka̲ndzam) 1. appropriate, proper and fitting, in accordance with (a need/ capacity/ capability/ etc.) ¶ མི་དེ་ཚོར་གང་ལ་གང་འཚམས་ཀྱི་ལས་ཀ་སྤྲད་ཡོད་པ་རེད་ Those people were given appropriate jobs. 2. quite good, not bad ¶ ད་བར་ཡར་རྒྱས་གང་ལ་གང་འཚམས་བྱུང་ཡོད་ Up to now there has been quite good progress.

གང་ལ་གང་འོས་ (ka̲ŋla ka̲ŋwöö) sm. གང་ལ་གང་འཚམས་.

གང་ལ་ཅི་འོས་ (ka̲ŋla jīwöö) sm. གང་ལ་གང་འཚམས་.

གང་ལ་ཇི་འོས་ (ka̲ŋla ji̲wöö) sm. གང་ལ་གང་འཚམས་.

གང་ལ་བརྟེན་ནས་ (ka̲ŋla dēnnɛ) because of what, why ¶ གང་ལ་བརྟེན་ནས་དཔལ་འབྱོར་ཡར་རྒྱས་གཏོང་མ་ཐུབ་པ་རེད་དམ་ Why haven't (they) been able to improve the economy?

གང་ལ་ཐུག་ཀྱང་ (ka̲ŋla tūggyaŋ) whatever happens ¶ གནས་ཚུལ་གང་ལ་ཐུག་ཀྱང་ཁ་མཆུ་འདི་མཐར་ཕྱིན་པ་ཞིག་རྒྱག་དགོས་ Whatever events happen (we will) carry the case to its conclusion.

གང་ལ་ཏེ་འཚམས་ (ka̲ŋla te̲dzam) sm. གང་ལ་གང་འཚམས་.

གང་ལ་ཏེ་འོས་ (ka̲ŋla te̲wöö) sm. གང་ལ་གང་འཚམས་.

གང་ལ་ཡང་མ་འཛེམས་པར་ (ka̲nlayaŋ ma̲ndzembar) brazenly, without fear ¶ གང་ལ་ཡང་མ་འཛེམས་པར་མང་ཚོགས་ཁྲོམ་སྐོར་བྱས་པ་རེད་ The masses demonstrated without fear (of the consequences).

གང་ལགས་ཟེར་ན་ (ka̲ŋla se̲na) sm. གང་ཡིན་ཞི་ན་.

གང་ལགས་ཤི་ན་ (ka̲ŋla shēna) sm. གང་ཡིན་ཞི་ན་.

གང་ལབ་ལབ་ (ka̲ŋ lə̲bləb) a person who believes anything, a gullible person ¶ མི་ལྐུགས་པ་འདི་ལ་གང་ལབ་ལབ་ཡོད་པ་རེད་ This stupid person believes anything you say. 2. a tolerant person ¶ ངའི་གྲོགས་པོ་འདི་ལ་གང་ལབ་ལབ་ཡོད་ My friend is tolerant (I can say anything). 3. sb. with whom one can talk freely/ candidly.

གང་ལས་ (ka̲nlɛɛ̀) from where (usu. with respect to origins) ¶ གང་ལས་ཆར་པ་བྱུང་ངམ་ Where does the rain come from?

གང་ལེགས་ (ka̲ŋleg) 1. whatever is best, as good as possible ¶ གནད་དོན་དེ་ཁྱེད་རང་གིས་ཐག་གཅོད་གང་ལེགས་ཤིག་གནང་རོགས་གནང་ Please settle this matter as best as you can. 2. very/ extremely good ¶ ཕྲུ་གུ་འདི་སློབ་སྦྱོང་ཡར་རྒྱས་གང་ལེགས་བྱུང་བཞག This child has made an extremely good improvement.

གང་ལེགས་གང་ཟབ་ (ka̲ŋleg ka̲ŋsəb) doing the best ¶ ལས་ཀ་གང་ལེགས་གང་ཟབ་བྱས་ན་འབྲས་བུ་ཕུལ་བྱུང་ཐོན་ If you do the best you can, the outcome will be good.

གང་ལེགས་ལེགས་ (ka̲ŋ legleg) sm. གང་ལེགས་.

གང་ལོ་ (ka̲nlo) empty pod.

གང་ལོན་བྱེད་ (ka̲nlön cɛ̲ɛ̀) sm. གང་ལོན་ལོན་བྱེད་.

གང་ལོན་ལོན་བྱེད་ (ka̲n lönlön cɛ̲ɛ̀) va. to get/ take/ achieve as much as possible ¶ ཡིག་ཚད་གང་ལོན་ལོན་བྱས་པ་རེད་ (He) tried to get (as high a score) as possible on his exam.

གང་ཤེས་ (ka̲ŋsheè) whatever one knows, to the best of one's knowledge/ ability; va.—བྱེད་ to do the best according to one's ability/ knowledge.

གང་ཤེས་གང་ངེས་ (ka̲ŋsheè ka̲ŋŋeè) whatever one knows one remembers.

གང་ཤེས་ཅི་ཤེས་ (ka̲ŋsheè jīsheè) sm. གང་ཤེས་.

གང་ཤེས་ཤེས་ (ka̲ŋ shēsheè) all known, everything one knows, everyone known ¶ ང་གང་ཤེས་ཤེས་ལ་སྐད་ཆ་དྲིས་ཀྱང་ཁང་པ་དེ་བརྙེད་ཚད་མ་སོང་ I asked everyone I know, but couldn't find the house.

གང་ཤོད་འདི་ཤོད་མེད་པ་ (ka̲ŋshöö di̲shöö me̲èba) sm. ག་ཤོད་འདི་ཤོད་མེད་པ་.

གང་ས་ (ka̲ŋsa) sm. གང་སར་.

གང་ས་གང་ལ་ (ka̲ŋsa ka̲ŋla) everywhere ¶ ཁོས་གང་ས་གང་ལ་ཕྱིན་པ་རེད་ He went everywhere.

གང་ས་ཅི་ཐད་ནས་ (ka̲ŋsa jīdɛnɛ) sm. གང་ཅིའི་ཐད་ནས་.

གང་ས་ནས་ (ka̲ŋsanɛ) sm. གང་ཅིའི་ཐད་ནས་.

གང་སར་ (ka̲ŋsaa) all over, everywhere, wherever ¶ རྒྱལ་སའི་ས་ཕྱོགས་གང་སར་ Everywhere in the capital. ¶ གང་སར་ཁྱབ་ (It) spread everywhere.

གང་གསུང་ཅི་སྒྲུབ་ (ka̲ŋsuŋ jīdrub) adhering to or doing what one is told to do; va.—བྱེད་ ¶ ཕྲུ་གུས་ཕ་མའི་གང་གསུང་ཅི་སྒྲུབ་བྱས་ཙང་ཕ་མ་དགའ་པོ་བྱུང་པ་རེད་ The parents were happy because the children did whatever they said.

གང་གསུང་ཏེ་སྒྲུབ་ (ka̲ŋsuŋ te̲drub) sm. གང་གསུང་ཅི་སྒྲུབ་.

གང་བསམ་ (ka̲ŋsam) whatever one is thinking; va.—བྱེད་ to do whatever one is thinking or thinks ¶ རྩོམ་པ་པོས་གང་བསམ་བཤད་ཙང་རྙོག་དྲ་མང་པོ་བྱུང་བ་རེད་ Because the writer said what was on his mind he got into trouble.

གང་བསམ་འདི་བསམ་མེད་པ་ (ka̲ŋsam di̲sam me̲èba) not having any thoughts (about sth.).

གང་བསམ་འདོད་དོན་ལྷུན་གྱིས་གྲུབ་ (ka̲ŋsam dö̲ödön lhūngi dru̲b) shung. having one's wishes fulfilled ¶ གང་བསམ་འདོད་དོན་ལྷུན་གྱིས་འགྲུབ་པའི་ཐུགས་སྨོན་སྐྱབས་འཇུག་ཡོད་པ་ཞུ་ I pray that our wishes will be fulfilled.

གང་བསམ་ལྷུག་བརྗོད་ (ka̲ŋsam lhūgjöö) saying freely what one thinks.

གང་ཧྲིལ་ (kə̲ŋhril) sleeping with one's clothes on ¶ ཕྲུ་གུ་འདི་གང་ཧྲིལ་ཉལ་བསྡད་བཞག The child slept with his clothes on.

གངས་ (ka̲ŋ) snow; vi.—འབབ་; —རྒྱག་; —འཐུལ་ to snow; vi.—ཆད་ to stop snowing ¶ ས་གནས་དེ་ཚོར་སྤྱི་ཟླ་བཅུ་པའི་ནང་གངས་རྒྱག་གི་འདུག In those regions, it snows in October.

གངས་ཀྱི་འཁྲོལ་འཛིན་ (ga̲ŋgi trȫndzin) shung. a certificate giving permission to sweep snow (during the Monlam Prayer Festival in Lhasa).

གངས་དཀར་ (ga̲ŋgar) 1. white snow. 2. a snow mountain.

གངས་དཀར་ཏི་སེ་ (ka̲ŋgar di̲si) 1. Mt. Kailash. 2. the Gangdis mountain range.

གངས་སྐྱེལ་ (ka̲ŋgyee) a custom in tt. wherein people sent a paper package of snow to close friends or relatives with the meaning that they should give a party during the snowy season.

གངས་སྐྱེས་ (ka̲ŋgyeè) sth. that grows in the snow.

གངས་སྐྱོན་ (ka̲ŋgyön) damage from snowfall, snow disaster; vi.—ཕོག་ to get/ undergo damage from snowfall.

གངས་འཁྱག (ka̲ŋkyaà) sm. གངས་འཁྱགས་.

གངས་འཁྱགས་ (ka̲ŋkyaà) snow and ice ¶ རི་ལུང་གངས་འཁྱགས་ཀྱི་ཁེབས་པ་ Hills and valleys filled with snow and ice.

གངས་གྲུ་ (ka̲ndru) snow sled, sleigh.

གངས་རྒྱན་པད་མ་ (ga̲ŋgyɛn bɛ̄ɛma) snow lotus (savssurea involucrata).

གངས་ཅན་ (ka̲njɛn) 1. Tibet. 2. snowy.

གངས་ཅན་ལྗོངས་ (ka̲njɛnjoŋ) Tibet.

གངས་ཅན་པ་ (ka̲ŋjɛnba) Tibetan.
གངས་ཆར་ (ka̲ŋcar) snow and rain mixed, slush.
གངས་ཆུ་ (ka̲ŋju) water from snow mountains/ glaciers.
གངས་ཆེན་མཛོད་ལྔ་ (ka̲ŋcen jö̲ö̲ŋa) Mount Kanchenjunga.
གངས་ལྗོངས་ (ka̲ŋjoŋ) Tibet [Lit. land of snow].
གངས་ལྗོངས་ཡུལ་ (ka̲ŋjoŋyüü) sm. གངས་ལྗོངས་.
གངས་དི་སེ་ (ka̲ŋ dīsi) Mt. Kailash.
གངས་ཐང་ (kə̲ŋdaŋ) a plain of snow.
གངས་ཐིག (kə̲ŋdig) snow line.
གངས་ཐིགས་ (kə̲ŋdig) 1. calamina. 2. dripping/ melting snow.
གངས་ཐིབས་ (ka̲ŋdib) heavy snow; vi.—རྒྱག to snow heavily.
གངས་ཐོག་སད་བརྒྱབ་ (ka̲ŋtɔɔ̀ sɛ̲ɛ̀gyəb) one misfortune piled on top of another [Lit. on top of snow, frost].
གངས་འདུལ་ (ka̲ŋdṻṻ) see གངས་.
གངས་མདོག (ka̲ŋdɔɔ̀) the color of snow.
གངས་འདབ་ (ka̲ŋdəb) 1. snow flake. 2. near/ under a snow mountain.
གངས་དིབ་ (ka̲ŋdib) an avalanche; vi.—རྒྱག to have an avalanche.
གངས་དོག (ka̲ŋdog) snow ball.
གངས་ལྡན་ (ka̲ŋdɛn) 1. snow mountain. 2. Tibet. 3. white calamus, sweet sedge. 4. snowy.
གངས་ཕྱིད་ (kə̄ŋjii) 1. snow blindness; vi.—ཐེབས་ to get snowblind. 2. frostbite; vi.—རྒྱག; —ཐེབས་ to get frostbitten.
གངས་ཕྱེ་ (kə̄ŋje) powder snow.
གངས་བྱིའུ་ (ka̲ŋciwu) snow finch.
གངས་འབབ་ (ka̲ŋ bə̲b) see གངས་.
གངས་སྦལ་ (ka̲ŋbɛɛ) snow lizard.
གངས་མ་ཆར་ (ka̲ŋmacar) rain and snow mixed.
གངས་མི་ (kə̲ŋmi) snowman.
གངས་རྩེད་ (ka̲ŋdze) games played in the snow, playing in the snow; va.—རྩེ་ to play in the snow.
གངས་ཚུབ་ (kə̲ŋdzub) sm. གངས་ལྷུང་.
གངས་མཚམས་ (kə̲ŋdzam) snow line.
གངས་མཚོ་ (ka̲ŋdzo) snow covering everywhere [Lit. a sea of snow].
གངས་འཚུབ་ (kə̲ŋdzub) snow storm; vi.—རྒྱག to have a snow storm.
གངས་འཛེགས་ (ka̲ŋ dze̲g) mountain climbing, mountaineering; va. གངས་འཛེགས་; —བྱེད་.
གངས་འཛེགས་ཚོགས་པ་ (ka̲ŋdzeg tsōgba) mountaineering club.
གངས་འཛེགས་རུ་ཁག (ka̲ŋdzeg ru̲gaà) mountaineering team.
གངས་ཞོད་ (ka̲ŋshöö̀) degree/ amount of snowfall ¶ ད་ལོ་གངས་ཞོད་ཆེན་པོ་བྱུང་སོང་ This year we had heavy snowfall.
གངས་བཞུ་རྫ་ཆག (ka̲ŋ shu̲ dza̲ cāà) finished, collapsed, ended [Lit. snow melt, pot crack].
གངས་གཟིག (kə̲ŋsiì) snow leopard.
གངས་འུར་ (ka̲ŋwur) 1. blizzard; vi.—རྒྱག to have a blizzard. 2. avalanche; vi.—རྒྱག to have an avalanche.
གངས་རི་ (kə̲ŋri) snow mountain; vi.—ཉིལ་ to avalanche.
གངས་རིའི་ར་བ་ (kə̲ŋri ra̲wa) a chain of snow mountains.
གངས་རིལ་ (ka̲ŋrii) snowball; va.—འགྲིལ་ to roll a snowball.
གངས་རུད་ (ka̲ŋrṻṻ) avalanche, snowslide; vi.—རྒྱག to have an avalanche.
གངས་ལྷུང་ (kə̲ŋluŋ) snow storm.
གངས་ལོང་ (ka̲ŋloŋ) snow blindness; vi.—ཐེབས་ to get snow-blind.
གངས་ཤུད་ (kə̲ŋshṻṻ) skiing; va.—རྒྱག་; —གཏོང་ to ski.
གངས་ཤུད་འཁོར་ལོ་ (kə̲ŋshṻṻ kɔ̄ɔ̄lo) a vehicle that goes on the snow such as a snowmobile.
གངས་ཤེལ་ (ka̲ŋshee) snow goggles.
གངས་སེང་ (ka̲ŋseŋ) snow lion.
གངས་སྲུལ་ (ka̲ŋsüü) 1. avalanche, snowslide. 2. skiing.
གངས་ཧྲག (ka̲ŋhrag) a place filled with snow.
གངས་ལྷགས་ (ka̲ŋlhaà) snow storm, wind with accompanying snow.
གད་ (kɛ̲ɛ̀) 1. sweeping; va.—རྒྱག ¶ ཞོགས་ལྟར་ཁྲོམ་ལམ་དུ་གད་རྒྱག་པ་རེད་ (They) swept the streets every morning. 2. abbr. of གད་མོ་.
གད་ཀ་ (kɛ̲ɛ̀ga) cliff, precipice.
གད་སྐྱིབས་ (kɛ̲ɛ̀gyib) cave under an overhanging cliff.
གད་ཁ་ (kɛ̲ɛ̀ga) sm. གད་ཀ་.
གད་ཁང་ (kɛ̲ɛ̀gaŋ) shung. abbr. sweepers and house caretakers.
གད་ཁུངས་ (kɛ̲ɛ̀guŋ) an area/ section where a person has the responsibility to sweep.
གད་མཁན་ (kɛ̲ɛ̀ñen) sweeper, janitor.
གད་དགོད་ (kɛ̲ɛ̀göö̀) laughing, laughter; va. གད་དགོད་; —བྱེད་.
གད་གླ་ (kɛ̲ɛ̀la) sweeper's fee/ wage.
གད་རྒྱག་མཁན་ (kɛ̲ɛ̀gyañen) sm. གད་མཁན་.
གད་རྒྱངས་ཤོར་ (kɛ̲ɛ̀gyaŋ shɔ̄ɔ̄) bursting out into loud laughter, roaring with laughter.
གད་སྒྲ་ (kɛ̲ɛ̀dra) sound of laughter; vi.—ཤོར་ to burst out into laughter.
གད་ཆུ་ (kɛ̲ɛ̀ju) water that is sprinkled on the ground before sweeping; va.—གཏོར་ to sprinkle water before sweeping.
གད་ཆུང་གོད་ (kɛ̲ɛ̀juŋ gö̲ö̀) va. to laugh slightly/ a little.
གད་སྙིགས་ (kɛ̲ɛ̀ñiì) garbage, rubbish, trash; va.—གཡུག་ to dispose of garbage.
གད་སྙིགས་འགྲོལ་འཛིན་ (kɛ̲ɛ̀ñiì trǖndzin) shung. certificate issued during Monlam giving permission to throw away garbage.
གད་སྙིགས་ཕུང་པོ་ (kɛ̲ɛ̀ñiì pūŋbo) garbage heap.
གད་སྙིགས་ལྕུག་སྣམ་ (kɛ̲ɛ̀ñiì lūgam) garbage pail, trash container.
གད་སྙིགས་དོར་འཁོར་ (kɛ̲ɛ̀ñiì wɔ̄rgɔɔ) garbage truck.
གད་སྙིགས་འཇོ་སྣོད་ (kɛ̲ɛ̀ñiì jo̲nöö̀) garbage can.
གད་བདར་ (kɛ̲ɛ̀dar) 1. cleaning up, sweeping up (physicallyt); va.—རྒྱག; —བྱེད་ to clean up, to sweep up. 2. liquidating, sweeping away (in a political sense); va.—རྒྱག; —བྱེད་.
གད་པ་ (kɛ̲ɛ̀ba) 1. sm. གད་ཀ་. 2. sweeper, janitor.
གད་ཕུག (kɛ̲ɛ̀pug) a crevice/ crack in a rock, rock cave (under a cliff).
གད་ཕྱིས་ (kɛ̲ɛ̀jiì) sm. གད་བདར་.
གད་ཕྱིས་ཆེན་པོ་ (kɛ̲ɛ̀jiì cēmbo) the big/ great cleanup (in a political sense).
གད་འཕྱིད་ (kɛ̲ŋjii) sm. གད་བདར་.
གད་མོ་ (kɛ̲ɛ̀mo) laughter, laughing; va.—དགོད་; —གོད་ to laugh; va.—སློང་ to make sb. laugh; vi.—ཤོར་ to burst out into laughter; vi.—སྣེ་ to feel like laughing.
གད་མོ་ཁྲོད་ཁོག་ན་ (kɛ̲ɛ̀mo tro̲gɔɔ̀ na̲) vi. to laugh so hard it hurts.
གད་མོ་ཁྲོ་པོ་ (kɛ̲ɛ̀mo tro̲bo) funny.
གད་མོ་ཚད་ཚད་ (kɛ̲ɛ̀mo tsɛ̄ɛ̀dzɛɛ̀) smiling, grinning; va.—བྱེད་.
གད་རེས་ (kɛ̲ɛ̀rɛɛ̀) on duty, one's turn to do sth.
གད་རོ་ (kɛ̲ɛ̀ru) garbage.
གན་ (kɛ̲n) abbr. of གན་རྒྱ་.
གན་ཀྱལ་ (kɛ̲ngyɛɛ) sm. གན་རྒྱལ་.
གན་རྒྱལ་ (kɛ̲ngyɛɛ) supine, lying on one's back; va.—སྒྱིག to lie on one's back; vi.—ལོག to be lying on one's back, to fall back onto one's back ¶ ཁོས་གན་རྒྱལ་བསྒྱིགས་ནས་ཉལ་བ་རེད་ He slept lying on his back. ¶ འབུ་འདི་གན་རྒྱལ་ལོག་བཞག The bug has fallen over onto its back.
གན་ཁྲལ་ (kɛ̲ndrɛɛ) tax on a contract/ agreement.
གན་འགལ་ (kɛ̲ngɛɛ) in violation of a contract/

agreement.

གན་རྒྱ་ (kɛngya) agreement, contract, guarantee; va.—འཇོག; —འཛུགས་; —བཟོ་ to make an agreement; va.—བསྡུ་ to annul an agreement/ contract.

གན་རྒྱ་ཐིམ་དུས་ (kɛngya timdüù) the expiration date of a contract/ agreement; vi.—གཙང་; —རྫོགས་ to be expired (a contract/ agreemen).

གན་རྒྱ་ཐེ་འཛུགས་ (kɛngya tēndzuù) shung. putting a seal on a contract/ agreement ། གན་རྒྱ་ཐེ་འཛུགས་ཀྱི་རྗེས་འབྲེལ་ In accordance with affixing the seal on the contract.

གན་རྒྱ་སེལ་འགོད་ (kɛngya sēlköö) shung. writing on a loan note that it has been repaid (or a part has been repaid).

གན་བསྒྱུར་ནང་སྦྱོར་ (kɛngyur naŋjɔɔ) shung. transferring a loan agreement to sb. else.

གན་ཇི་ར་ (kɛnjira) a type of rooftop decoration found on temples and monasteries.

གན་འཇོག (kɛnjɔɔ̀) abbr. of གན་རྒྱ་འཇོག.

གན་འཇོག་གཏན་འཁེལ་ (kɛnjɔɔ̀ dɛngee) shung. signing a pledge or contract.

གན་འཇོག་བཟོ་པ་ (kɛnjɔɔ̀ soba) contract worker.

གན་དར་ (kɛndar) a type of brocade.

གན་དུ་ (kɛndu) nearby, close to.

གན་དུ་ཕུལ་ (kɛndu pūü) shung. to sign as a contract/ agreement, to gave sth. as a contract/ agreement.

གན་དོན་ (kɛndön) the terms or content of a contract/ guarantee/ agreement ། གན་དོན་དང་འགལ་རིགས་ཕྲ་མོ་ཙམ་ཤར་ཚེ་ If there is a slightest violation of the content of the agreement.

གན་འདོམས་ (kɛndom) shung. making a vow/ agreement/ pledge in a law case; va.—བྱེད་.

གན་ད་བ་དྲ་ (kɛnda badra) affine cudweed (used in Tibetan medicine).

གན་ལྡེ་ (kɛnde) a type of bag that is put on a the backs of sheep or goats when they are used for transporting goods.

གན་པ་ (kɛmba) arc. steward.

གན་སྤོས་ (kɛmböö) shung. making a new loan agreement after adding the interest of the previous year to the principal; va.—རྒྱག.

གན་སྦུབ་ (kɛnbub) abbr. lying on one's back and lying on one's stomach.

གན་མཛོད་ (kɛndzöö) storehouse, treasury.

གན་འཛིན་ (kɛndzin) contract, agreement letter, guarantee document; va.—བཟོ་ to make a contract/ agreement/ guarantee.

གན་འཛིན་གཅིག་བསྡུས་ (kɛndzin jīgdüü) 1. a type of written contract/ agreement. 2. a receipt of a contract/ agreement.

གན་ལྡ་ (kɛnda) a rectangular carrying bag with an opening in the middle.

གན་ཡིག (kɛnyiì) an agreement/ guarantee/ contract letter.

གན་ཤོག (kɛnshɔɔ̀) sm. གན་ཡིག.

གབ་ (kəb) va. to hide/ conceal (oneself).

གབ་སྒོར་འཐབ་ར་ (kəbgɔɔ tābra) bunker, trench, foxhole.

གབ་ཁུང་ (kəbguŋ) hiding place, hideout.

གབ་རྒྱ་ (kəbgya) secret command/ teaching.

གབ་ཉུལ་ (kəbñül) going/ wandering while hiding; va.—བྱེད་ ། ཇག་པ་རྣམས་ཤིང་ནགས་ནང་གབ་ཉུལ་བྱས་འདུག The bandits were hiding and going around in the forest.

གབ་དོང་ (kəbdoŋ) tunnel, trench.

གབ་བདེ་འཕེན་བདེ་ (kəbde pēnde) easy to hide and easy to shoot.

གབ་སྡོད་ (kəbdöö) sm. གབ་ནས་སྡོད་.

གབ་ནས་ལྟ་ (kəbnɛ dā) va. to look from a hiding place.

གབ་ནས་སྡོད་ (kəbnɛ döö) va. to stay hidden, to stay in seclusion ། མི་དེ་ཚོས་ལོ་མང་ཕྱི་རྒྱལ་དུ་གབ་ནས་བསྡད་པ་རེད་ Those people stayed hidden abroad for many years.

གབ་པས་བཙན་རྫོང་མ་ཟིན་བྲོས་པས་ལམ་སྣེ་མ་ཆོད་ (kəbbɛ dzēndzoŋ masintrööbɛ lamne macöö) a hopeless situation [Lit. if one hides (unable) to hold one's fort, if one flees (unable) find the road].

གབ་ཕྱི་ཀོ་ལོག (kəbji kolɔɔ̀) sm. གབ་ཕྱི་ལོག.

གབ་ཕྱི་ལོག (kəbji lɔɔ̀) vi. to be reversed/ backwards/ opposite, to be topsy -turvy/ upside down ། མི་ཚང་མས་སྤྱི་ཚོགས་རིང་ལུགས་ཡག་པོ་འདུག་ཟེར་དུས་ཁོས་གབ་ཕྱི་བསློགས་ནས་ཡག་པོ་མ་རེད་ཟེར་སོང་ When everyone said, "socialism is good," he made things topsy-turvy by saying, "It is not good."

གབ་ཕྱི་སློག (kəbji lɔ̄ɔ̀) va. to reverse a position, to do the opposite, to act contrary, to do backward, to turn topsy-turvy. to put on (clothes) inside out ། ཁོས་རྟ་ཐོག་གབ་ཕྱི་སློག་ནས་བཞོན་པ་རེད་ He rode on the horse sitting backward. ། ངས་ཁོང་སྣ་རིལ་བཞོན་ལབ་ཀྱང་ཁོས་གབ་ཕྱི་སློགས་བྱས་རྟ་བཞོན་བཞག I told him to ride a bicycle but he did the opposite and rode a horse. ། ཁོས་ཕྱུ་པ་གབ་ཕྱི་སློག་ནས་གོན་བཞག He put on the clothes inside out.

གབ་ཕྱུང་ (kəbjuŋ) 1. va. to clear up sth. that was unclear. 2. va. to reveal sth. that was a secret.

གབ་ཅའི་དོན་ (kəbcɛ tön) answer to a riddle.

གབ་བྲོལ་ (kəbjöö) fleeing and hiding; va.—བྱེད་ ། བསྐོར་སྲུང་པ་ཡོང་སྐབས་ཁོ་ཚོས་ས་གནས་གཞན་དུ་གབ་བྲོལ་བྱེད་ཀྱི་ཡོད་པ་རེད་ When the police come they flee and hide away in other areas.

གབ་མིང་ (kəbmiŋ) an alias, a hidden/ secret name.

གབ་དམག (kəbmaà) ambush, sneak attack; va.—རྒྱག.

གབ་ཙེ་ (kəbdze) sm. གབ་རྩེ་.

གབ་རྩ་ (kəbdza) a vein that isn't pulsating obviously.

གབ་རྩེ་ (kəbdze) 1. a food container. 2. astrological chart; va.—བརྩིངས་ to make a calculation according to the astrological chart.

གབ་ཚིག (kəbdziì) riddle, phrase with hidden meaning; va.—ཤོད་ to say sth. with a hidden meaning, to say a riddle.

གབ་འཚོལ་ (kəbdzöö) 1. searching for sth. secretly; va.—བྱེད་ 2. trying to find out sth., probing, exploring; va.—བྱེད་.

གབ་འཛུལ་ (kəb dzüü) entering/ going into sth. to hide; va.—བྱེད་ ། དམག་མི་ཡོང་དུས་མི་དམངས་ཚང་མས་སྦུབ་ནང་གབ་འཛུལ་བྱས་འདུག When the soldiers came, all the people went and hid in a tunnel.

གབ་ཡིག (kəbyiì) 1. secret code. 2. secret.

གབ་ཡིབ་ (gəbyib) hiding out; va.—བྱེད་ ། ཉིན་ཤས་ངས་རི་སྟེང་དུ་གབ་ཡིབ་བྱས་པ་ཡིན་ I hid out for a few days on the top of mountain.

གབ་གཡོལ་ (kəbyöö) hiding out to avoid sth. va.—བྱེད་ ། བུ་ལོན་ལེན་མཁན་ཡོང་བར་བརྟེན་ཁོང་གིས་གནས་སྐབས་གབ་ཡོལ་བྱས་འདུག Because the loan collector came, he temporarily hid out to avoid him.

གབ་རེས་ཁུར་རེས་ (kəbreè wurreè) hide and seek (the game); va.—རྩེ་; —བྱེད་.

གབ་རེས་ཡིབ་རེས་ (kəbreè yibreè) sm. གབ་རེས་ཁུར་རེས་.

གབ་ལན་ (kəblɛn) the meaning of riddles.

གབ་ས་ (kəbsə) hiding place.

གབ་རྡུལ་ (kəbhrüü) worn out/ tattered hem.

གམ་ (kam) 1. question particle used after final ག. ། དེ་ར་དེབ་ཅིག་འདུག་གམ་ Is there a book here? 2. the "or" particle (used after final ག) ། ལག་གམ་རྐང་ Hand or foot. 3. sm. རྡུང་. 4. pea pod. 5. vi. a type of horse disease ། ངའི་རྟ་དེ་གམ་ནས་ཤི་སོང་ My horse died from གམ་ disease.

གམ་རྒྱག (kam gyaà) va. to draw blood (from the noses of mules and horses as therapy).

གམ་བཅར་ (kamjaa) shung. attendants, servants.

གམ་བཅར་མཁན་སྡེ་ཚེ་ཆུང་ (kamjaa kēnde cējuŋ) shung. the personal retinue/ attendants of the Dalai Lama.

ཀམ་དུ་ (kamtu) sm. དུང་དུ་.

ཀམ་ན་ (kamna) sm. དུང་དུ་.

ཀམ་ནས་ (kamnɛ) sm. དུང་ནས་.

ཀམ་པ་ (kamba) name of a district.

ཀམ་པ་ལ་ (kambala) the pass separating U and Tsang in central Tibet.

ཀམ་སྦྱར་པང་ལེབ་ (kamjar bāŋleb) tongue-and-groove joined board.

ཀམ་ཤབས་ (kamshəb) sm. ཀམ་པཙར་.

ཀམ་ཡོ་ (kamyo) shung. near, close, in the presence of.

ཀམ་གཡོག (kamyɔɔ̀) shung. sm. ཀམ་པཙར་.

ཀམ་རུམ་ (kamrum) sm. གུམ་ཅེ་.

ཀའ་ན་ (kana) Ghana.

ཀའི་གནང་གི་མ་རེད་ (kɛ nāŋgi maareè) standard phrase conveying, "It doesn't matter."

ཀའི་ཅིད་ཀྱི་མ་རེད་ (kɛ cigimareè) sm. ཀའི་གནང་གི་མ་རེད་.

ཀའུ་ (kəwu) 1. small box/ pendant for keeping religious objects. 2. small jewelry box worn by women as necklace.

ཀའུ་ལི་ (kəwuli) 1. a work schedule book. 2. file, catalogue.

ཀའུ་ཁ་སྦྱར་ (kəwu kājar) a type of box/ pendant with a fitted lid or cover.

ཀའུ་གསུམ་སྒྲོམ་མ་ (kəwu sūmdromma) shung. the three-jointed pendant worn by the རྒྱན་བཟང་མ་.

ཀར་ (kar) 1. dancing; va.—འཁྲབ་; —སྦྱར་ to dance. 2. sm. ཀ་ན་. 3. abbr. of ཀར་པོ་.

ཀར་སྐྱིད་པ་ཡུལ་ སུ་བྱམས་པ་མ་ (kargyii pəyüü sūjam pāma) wherever one is happy and well treated is one's homeland [Lit. wherever one is happy is one's homeland, whoever is kind is one's parents].

ཀར་ཁང་ (karkaŋ) dance hall.

ཀར་ཁྲིད་དེར་འགྲོ་ (kartrii deedro) easily led, following other's leads; va.—བྱེད་ ། མི་དེ་སྲིད་དོན་གྱི་ལྟ་བའི་སྐོར་མི་གཞན་གྱིས་ཀར་ཁྲིད་དེར་འགྲོ་བྱེད་མཁན་ཞིག་རེད་ Regarding political views, that person is sb. who is easily led by others.

ཀར་མཁན་ (kargɛn) dancer.

ཀར་མཁན་མ་ (kargɛnma) a female dancer; actress.

ཀར་གླུ་ (karlu) a song in the repertoire of the special dance troupe of the Dalai Lama.

ཀར་དགོས་ (kargöö) going wherever there is a need ། ང་ལས་ཁུངས་ཀྱི་ནང་ཀར་དགོས་ཀྱི་ལས་ཀ་བྱེད་ཀྱི་ཡོད་ In the office, my job involves going wherever there is a need.

ཀར་དགོས་པ་ (kargööba) shung. a type of taxpayer attached to the རྩམ་པཞིས་ལས་ཁུངས་ whose job involved transporting goods.

ཀར་དགོས་ཨུ་ལག་ (kargöö wulaà) shung. corvee laborers who are sent wherever there is a need.

ཀར་འགྲོས་ (kardröö) dancing steps, body movements used in dancing.

ཀར་ཆག (karjaà) shung. the tax exemption received by families for providing a dancer for the Dalai Lama's dance troupe.

ཀར་ཆང་ (karjaŋ) very strong chang.

ཀར་འཆམ་ (kanjam) a religious dance; va.—རྒྱག.

ཀར་འཆམས་ (karcam) sm. ཀར་འཆམ་.

ཀར་མཇལ་ (kar jɛɛ) wherever sb. is meeting ། འཐུས་མི་ཚོ་ཀར་མཇལ་སར་ཡི་གེ་སྐྱེལ་བར་བཏང་བ་རེད་ (We) sent letters to be delivered wherever the delegates are meeting.

ཀར་ཉམས་ (karñam) the style/ manner of dancing.

ཀར་བཏང་གོ་ཆོད་ (kardaŋ gojöö) very capable, able ། ངའི་གཡོག་པོ་ཀར་གཏོང་གོ་ཆོད་ཡིན་ My servant is very capable. [Lit. wherever sent, capable].

ཀར་སྟབས་སྦྱར་ (kardəb) sm. ཀར་སྦྱར་.

ཀར་སྟེགས་ (kardeg) stage/ platform for dancing.

ཀར་སྟེགས་སྟོག་གི་སྒྱུ་རྩལ་ (kardegtɔɔ̀gi gyudzee) stage art.

ཀར་ཐལ་ (kartɛɛ) wherever sb. goes.

ཀར་ཐིག་དབྱངས་གསུམ་ (kardig yāŋsum) shung. the three: religious dancing, making sand mandalas and chanting prayers.

ཀར་དུ་འགྲོ་ (kardu dro) sm. ར་དུ་འགྲོ་.

ཀར་དུ་སློས་ (kardu döö) va. to act in a play ། གནའ་རབས་ཀྱི་ལོ་རྒྱུས་རྣམས་ཀར་དུ་སློས་རེད་ (They) acted out ancient history as a play.

ཀར་ནག (karnaà) the ash of pig's excrement (used in Tibetan medicine).

ཀར་པ་ (karba) a dancer in the Dalai Lama's dance troupe.

ཀར་པོ་ (karbo) thick for soups/ broths/ stews ། ཐུག་པ་ཀར་པོ་ཞིག་བསྐོལ་བ་རེད་ They cooked a thick soup. 2. strong (for drinks such as wine, tea and whisky).

ཀར་དཔོན་ (karbön) head of the Dalai Lama's dance troupe.

ཀར་ཕྱིན་རང་ཡུལ་ སུ་བྱམས་པ་མ་ (karjin raŋyüü sūjam pāma) sm. ཀར་སྐྱིད་པ་ཡུལ་ སུ་བྱམས་པ་མ་.

ཀར་ཕྲུག (kərdrug) sm. ཀར་ཕྲུག་པ་.

ཀར་ཕྲུག་པ་ (kədrugbə) young male dancers in the Dalai Lama's ceremonial dance troupe.

ཀར་འཕྱུགས་ (karjaà) shung. sm. ཀར་ཆག.

ཀར་བབ་ (karbəb) stopping for the night on journeys wherever one reaches at the end of the day (rather than at a set place) ། ང་ཚོ་དོ་དགོང་སླས་གནས་ཀར་བབ་ཅིག་དུ་སྡོད་ཀྱི་ཡིན་ This evening we will stop (overnight) wherever we reach.

ཀར་བབས་གཏོལ་མེད་ (karbəb dööme è) not knowing where sth. will fall.

ཀར་བུ་ (karbu) a lump (of sth.).

ཀར་བྲོ་ (kardro) song and dance.

ཀར་བྲོའི་ཚོམས་ཆེན་ (kardrö tsōmjen) dance hall.

ཀར་བླུགས་ (karluù) casting metals.

ཀར་འབབ་ (kambəb) tax for ཀར་ཕྲུག་པ་ that is paid by villagers.

ཀར་མ་ (karma) sm. ཀར་མཁན་མ་.

ཀར་མོ་ (karmo) sm. ཀར་པོ་.

ཀར་རྩལ་ (kardzɛɛ) the art of dancing.

ཀར་རྩེད་ (kardzeè) dancing, dancing performance.

ཀར་ཚད་ (kardzɛè) sm. ཀར་ལོས་.

ཀར་ཚིག (kardzii) words used in accompaniment to dancing.

ཀར་ཚོགས་ (kardzɔɔ̀) dance group/ troupe.

ཀར་ཞ་ (karsha) Lahul.

ཀར་བཟོས་ (karsöö) condensed ། ཀར་བཟོས་འོ་མ་ Condensed milk.

ཀར་ཡང་ (karyaŋ) anywhere, any place, no matter where.

ཀར་ཡོང་ཆ་མེད་ (karyoŋ cāmeè) arriving/ appearing out of nowhere (not knowing where sb. came from) ། མདང་དགོང་དམག་མི་མང་པོ་ཞིག་ཀར་ཡོང་ཆ་མེད་ཀྱིས་སླེབས་འདུག Last night many soldiers appeared out of nowhere.

ཀར་ཡོད་ (karyöö) wherever ། དགྲ་བོ་ཀར་ཡོད་སར་ལ་དམག་རྒྱག་དགོས་ (We) must fight the enemy wherever he is.

ཀར་ཡོལ་ (karyöö) stage curtain; va.—རྒྱག to close a stage curtain, to end a performance.

ཀར་རུ་འགྲོ་ (karru dro) vi. to become stronger/ thicker.

ཀར་རུ་གཏོང་ (garru dōŋ) va. to make thicker, to make stronger.

ཀར་རུ་ཡང་ (garru yaŋ) sm. ཀར་ཡང་.

ཀར་རོལ་ (karröö) dancing and music.

ཀར་རོལ་པ་ (kar rööba) shung. dancers and musicians of the Dalai Lama.

ཀར་ལོས་ (karlöö) degree of thickness or strength (pertaining to liquids) ། ཇ་འདི་ཀར་ལོས་ག་འདྲ་བྱུང་འདུག How strong did the tea turn out?

ཀར་ལོས་སྙོམས་པོ་ (karlöö ñōmbo) the right degree of thickness/ strength.

ཀར་ཤ་ (karsha) skin between the index finger and the thumb.

ཀར་སོང་ (karsoŋ) whereabouts, where a thing/ person has gone ། ཁོ་ཀར་སོང་སུས་ཀྱང་ཤེས་ཀྱི་མི་འདུག

No one knows his whereabouts.

གར་སོང་ཆ་མེད་དུ་སོང་ (karsoŋ cāmeèdu sōŋ) vi. to disappear, to go somewhere that is not known, to be missing.

གར་སོང་ཇི་བྱུས་ (karsoŋ jicɛɛ̀) where sb. went and what has become of (them) ༑ཁོང་ཚོ་འཛིན་བཟུང་བྱས་ནས་གར་སོང་ཇི་བྱུས་ཤེས་རྟོགས་མེད་པ་རེད་ No one knows where they are and what became of them after they were arrested.

གར་སོང་རྗེས་འབྲངས་ (karsoŋ jendraŋ) pursuing/ following sb. (who is running away).

གར་སོང་རྗེས་མེད་ (karsoŋ jemeè) disappearing/ vanishing with no trace.

གར་སོང་བསྡད་མི་འདུག (karsoŋ dɛɛ̀minduù) sm. གར་སོང་ཆ་མེད་དུ་སོང་.

གར་སླ་ (karla) 1. viscosity; consistency of liquids ༑ཚོན་འདི་གར་སླ་འགྲིག་འདུག་གམ་ Is the thickness of the paint all right? 2. strength of drinks/ foods ༑ཁྱེད་རང་གསོལ་ཇ་གར་སླ་གང་འདྲ་ཡོད་ How strong is your tea? [Lit. thick and thin].

གར་སླའི་ཚད་ (karlɛ tsɛ̄ɛ̀) 1. viscosity, thickness, consistency. 2. strength.

གར་ལྷམ་ (karlham) a type of traditional boot.

གལ་ (kɛɛ) important ༑ཁོང་དམིགས་བསལ་མཇལ་འཕྲད་གནང་གལ་ཨ་ཡོད་ (I) don't think it's important to go specially to meet him.

གལ་གྱིས་ (kɛɛ̀gi) by force.

གལ་འགག (kɛngàa) sm. གལ་འགངས་.

གལ་འགངས་ (kɛngaŋ) importance, significance, essentiality ༑གནད་དོན་གལ་འགངས་ཆེན་པོ་ A matter of great importance.

གལ་ཆུང་ (kɛɛjuŋ) 1. less important, secondary, not critical, unimportant. 2. a small bag.

གལ་ཆེ་ (kɛɛje) important, essential ༑གནད་དོན་གལ་ཆེ་ An important issue.

གལ་ཆེ་དུས་གཏུགས་ (keece tüüdug) important and urgent.

གལ་ཆེ་བ་ (kɛɛcewa) very important.

གལ་ཆེ་ཡུལ་གཉན་ (kɛɛche yüüñɛn) very important and risky/ dangerous ༑ཆིངས་ཡིག་འཛུགས་རྒྱུའི་གཞུང་དོན་གལ་ཆེ་ཡུལ་ཉེན་ཡིན་པར་བརྟེན་ཁྱེད་རང་གི་གཟབ་གཟབ་བྱ་དགོས་ Because making the treaty is important and risky for the government you should be careful.

གལ་ཆེན་ (kɛɛjen) sm. གལ་ཆེ་.

གལ་ཆེན་པོ་ (kɛɛ cēmbo) sm. གལ་ཆེ་.

གལ་ཆེའི་རང་བཞིན་ (kɛɛce rəŋshin) the significance of sth., the reason why sth. is important.

གལ་ཆེར་འཛིན་ (kɛɛcer dzin) va. to consider/ hold important, to regard as essential, to attach importance to, to lay stress on ༑ཁོང་ཚོ་དང་འབྲེལ་བ་ཡག་པོ་དགོས་པ་གལ་ཆེར་འཛིན་གྱི་ཡོད་པ་རེད་ (They) consider it important to have good relations with them.

གལ་ཉེན་ (kɛɛñɛn) important and dangerous.

གལ་ད་མགོ་སྒྲིལ་ (kɛɛda godrel) sm. གན་ལྡི་.

གལ་དེ་ (kɛɛde) if, in case ༑གལ་དེ་ཁྱེད་རང་ཡུལ་དེའི་གནས་ཚུལ་ཤེས་འདོད་ཡོད་ན་ If you want to know about that country.

གལ་དུ་ (kɛɛdu) important ༑ལུང་པ་དེ་ཚོར་ཕྱིན་ན་ཡུལ་སྐད་ཤེས་དགོས་གལ་དུ་བཤད་ It is said that if one goes to those places it is important to know the language.

གལ་དུ་འཛིན་ (kɛɛdu dzin) va. to consider sth. important/ serious.

གལ་མདོ་ (kɛndo) 1. critical time or point. 2. abstract, extract, key summary.

གལ་བསྡོམས་ (kɛdom) summary of the important/ main points.

གལ་གནད་ཅན་ (kɛɛnɛɛ̀jɛn) of great importance/ significant ༑ལས་ཚན་གལ་གནད་ཅན་ A very important post.

གལ་གནད་ཆེ་བ་ (kɛɛnɛɛ̀ cēwa) sm. གལ་གནད་ཅན་.

གལ་གནད་ཆེན་པོ་ (kɛɛnɛɛ̀ cēmbo) sm. གལ་གནད་ཅན་.

གལ་པོ་ཆེ་ (kɛboce) important ༑དོན་དག་དེ་གལ་ཆེན་པོ་ཡིན་སྐབས་ཁྱེད་རང་གིས་གཟབ་གཟབ་བྱ་དགོས་ Because this matter is important, you should be careful.

གལ་པོ་ཆེ་ལ་ནན་དན་ (kɛɛbocelə nɛndɛn) taking seriously what is important ༑གལ་པོ་ཆེ་ལ་ནན་དན་གྱི་དཔེ་ལྟར་ངས་ཁྱེད་རང་ལ་ཡང་སྐྱར་ཞུས་པ་ཡིན་ Like the saying one must take seriously what is important, I will tell you again.

གལ་འཛིན་ (kɛndzin) sm. གལ་དུ་འཛིན་.

གལ་འཛིན་པ་ (kɛndzinbə) hunter, trapper.

གལ་འཛུགས་ (kɛɛdzuù) 1. va. to set a trap. 2. va. to blame. 3. hypothesis (in science) ༑སྟབས་བདེའི་གལ་འཛུགས་ A simple hypothesis.

གལ་བཟུང་ (kɛɛsiŋ) sm. གལ་འཛིན་.

གལ་རོ་ (kɛɛro) waste, dregs, sediment.

གལ་སྲིད་ (kɛɛsii) sm. གལ་དེ་.

གས་ (kɛɛ̀) a crack; vi. གས་; —སོང་ to crack/ split ༑དཀར་ཡོལ་དེ་གས་བཞག The cup has cracked.

གས་ཁ་ (kɛɛ̀ka) a crack.

གས་འགྱུར་ (kɛɛ̀gyur) fission (in chemistry).

གས་འགྱུར་འགྱུར་རིག (kɛɛ̀gyur gyurriì) fission chemistry.

གས་འགྱུར་ཆག་རོ་ (kɛɛ̀gyur cāgro) fission fragments.

གས་འགྱུར་ཐོན་འབོར་ (kɛɛ̀gyur tōmbɔr) fission yield.

གས་འགྱུར་ཐོན་རྫས་ (kɛɛ̀gyur tōndzɛɛ̀) fission products.

གས་ཆག (kɛɛ̀jaà) damage, breakage, cracks.

གས་ཆག་མེད་པ་ (kɛɛ̀jaà meèba) without damage/ breakage/ cracks.

གས་གཏོར་ (kɛɛ̀dɔr) destroying, demolishing; va. གས་གཏོར་; —བྱེད་ to demolish, to destroy.

གས་ཡུན་ (kɛɛ̀yün) the time of blooming.

གས་རིས་ (kɛɛ̀rii) sm. གས་སྲུབས་.

གས་སྲུབས་ (kɛɛ̀rub) crack, split, rift.

གི་ (ki) 1. genitive particle used after final ག་ and ང་. 2. verbal particle indicating nonpast ༑ང་ལྷ་སར་འགྲོ་གི་ཡིན་ I will go to Lhasa.

གི་ཁྲོད་ (kidröö) a class of Bon deities.

གི་གུ་ (kigu) the vowel "i" in the Tibetan alphabet.

གི་གུ་ཤ་ (kigusha) glazedware, porcelain, enamel, cloisonne.

གི་ཝང་ (kiwaŋ) bezoar.

གི་ཡིན་ (giyin) first person future tense particle ༑ང་འགྲོ་གི་ཡིན་ I will go.

གི་ཡོད་ (giyöö) first person present/ usual tense particles ༑ང་འགྲོ་གི་ཡོད་ I am going.

གི་ཡོད་པ་རེད་ (giyɔ̀ɔreè) third person present/ usual tense particles ༑ཁོ་འགྲོ་གི་ཡོད་པ་རེད་ He is going.

གི་རིན་ལ་ (kirinla) Greenland.

གི་རེད་ (gireè) third person future tense particles ༑ཁོ་འགྲོ་གི་རེད་ He will go.

གི་ལིང་ (kiliŋ) sm. གྱི་ལིང་.

གི་ཧང་ (kihaŋ) sm. གི་ཝང་.

གིང་ (giŋ) a messenger for fierce deities in ritual dances.

གིན་ (gin) 1. sm. གྱིན་ (used after final ག་ and ང་). 2. (vb. + གིན་ + vb. + གིན་) while ༑འགྲོ་གིན་འགྲོ་གིན་སྐད་ཆ་བཤད་པ་ཡིན་ (I) talked to (him) while I was going.

གིས་ (kii) sm. གྱིས་ (used after final ག་ and ང).

གིས་རལ་ཐར་ (kirɛltar) Gibraltar.

གུ་ (ku) 1. inside, within ༑གུ་དོག་པོ་ Narrow space. 2. small ༑ཁྱི་གུ་ Small dog.

གུ་གུ་ཤ་ (kuggusha) enamel, enamelware, cloisonne.

གུ་གུ་ཤའི་རྩི་ (kugu shēdzi) enamel paint.

གུ་གུ་ས་འཛིན་ (kugu sāndzin) cuscuta europaea (a plant used in Tibetan medicine).

གུ་གུལ་ (kugül) benzoin (herbal medicine).

གུ་ངུར་ (kuŋur) large rhodiola root (used in Tibetan medicine).

གུ་ཐུང་ (kuduŋ) pants, trousers; va.—རྗེ་ to roll up trousers; va.—གོན་ to put on trousers.

གུ་ཐུང་དུང་ཆེན་ཁ་ (kuduŋ duŋcenka) bell-bottom pants.

གུ་དུང་ (kuduŋ) sm. གུ་ཐུང་.

ཀུ་དུང་གཅིག་ནང་ཁང་པ་བརྒྱུས་པ་ (kudun jignan gānba gyəbbə) sm. སྐྱ་ཁང་གཅིག་ནས་དབུགས་གཏོང་བ་.

ཀུ་དུར་ (kudur) large rhodiola root (used in Tibetan medicine).

ཀུ་དོག (kudɔɔ) sm. ཀུ་དོག་པོ་.

ཀུ་དོག་པོ་ (ku togbo) narrow, closed in, cramped, crowded ¶ སེམས་པ་ཀུ་དོག་པོ་ Narrow minded. ¶ ཁང་པ་ཀུ་དོག་པོ་ Small (cramped) house.

ཀུ་དོག་མི་རིགས་རིང་ལུགས་ (kudoò mirii rinluù) narrow nationalityism (placing the interests of one's nationality above that of the nation).

ཀུ་ཙི་རི་དྲུག (kudzi riduù) ch. type of soup with small cone shaped dough balls.

ཀུ་ཡང་ (kuyan) sm. ཀུ་ཡངས་.

ཀུ་ཡངས་ (kuyan) 1. open, spacious, roomy ¶ ཁང་པ་འདི་ཀུ་ཡངས་ཤིག་འདུག This house is very spacious. 2. open-minded, at ease, easygoing, carefree, liberal, lenient, magnanimous ¶ སེམས་པ་ཀུ་ཡངས་པོ་བྱས་ན་གཟུགས་པོ་ཐང་པོ་ཡོང་གི་རེད་ If you keep your mind at ease, you will be healthy. 3. a pardon, a reduction of sentence, a forgiving; va.—གཏོང་ ¶ གཞུང་གིས་བཙོན་གྲོལ་བཏང་ནས་ཁོ་ལ་ཀུ་ཡངས་ཐོབ་པ་རེད་ The government granted amnesty to prisoners so he got pardoned.

ཀུ་ཡངས་ཀྱི་སྲིད་ཇུས་ (kuyangi siijüü) policy of leniency (i.e., the policy of reducing sentences and punishments).

ཀུ་ཡངས་པོ་ (ku yanbo) 1. open-minded, at ease, easygoing, carefree, lenient, magnanimous.

ཀུ་ཡངས་དམངས་གཙོ་ཚོགས་པ་ (kuyan māndzo tsōgba) liberal democratic party.

ཀུ་ཡངས་སྲིད་ཇུས་ (kuyan siijüü) sm. ཀུ་ཡངས་ཀྱི་སྲིད་ཇུས་.

ཀུ་ཡུ་ (kuyu) betel nut.

ཀུ་ཡུ་ཤིང་ (kuyu shin) areca tree.

ཀུ་ཡུལ་ཆེན་པོ་ (kuyü cēmbo) spacious ¶ ཁང་པ་ཀུ་ཡུལ་ཆེན་པོ་འདུག The house is spacious.

ཀུ་ཡུལ་དོག་པོ་ (kuyü togbo) not spacious, cramped.

ཀུ་ཡོག (kuyog) fire poker; va.—རྒྱག; —བྱེད་ to stir a fire with a poker.

ཀུ་རུ་ (guru) teacher, guru.

ཀུ་རུ་པད་མ་སམ་བྷ་ཝ་ (guru bɛma sāmbhowa) sm. ཀུ་རུ་རིན་པོ་ཆེ་.

ཀུ་རུ་རིན་པོ་ཆེ་ (guru rimboce) Padmasambhava.

ཀུ་ལིང་ (gulin) sm. ཀུ་ལིང་དར་.

ཀུ་ལིང་དར་ (gulindar) a type of fine brocade/ silk.

ཀུ་ཤ་ (kusha) ཀུ་ཀུ་ཤ་.

ཀུ་ཤྲི་ཧན་ (kushri hān) Gushri Khan.

ཀུ་ཤྲི་བསྟན་འཛིན་ཆོས་རྒྱལ་ (kushri dɛ̄ndzin cōōgyɛɛ) Gushri Khan (1582-1654).

ཀུ་བཤདས་ (kushan) 1. letting sb. use space to live in; va.—བྱེད་ ¶ ངའི་སར་འགྲུལ་པ་ཞིག་སླེབས་སྐབས་ངའི་གྲོགས་པོས་ཁོ་རང་གི་ཁང་པ་ཀུ་བཤདས་བྱས་སོང་ A traveler arrived at my house and my friend let me use part of his house for him (the traveler). 2. va.—བྱེད་ to compromise ¶ གྱོད་དོན་འདིའི་སྐོར་ཕྱོགས་ཕན་ཚུན་གཉིས་ཀས་ཀུ་བཤདས་བྱེད་དགོས་ Concerning this case, both parties should compromise.

ཀུག (kuù) 1. vi. to get/ be bent. 2. abbr. of ཀི་ཀུ་ and ཞབས་ཀྱུ་.

ཀུག་གྱེད་ (kuggyèe) the four vowels.

ཀུག་ཀུག (kugguù) bent, hooked, curved; va.—བཟོ་ to bend (things) ¶ ལྕགས་འདི་ཀུག་ཀུག་བཟོས་བཞག (He) has bent the iron.

ཀུག་ཆུང་ (kugcun) sm. ཀུག་རྟགས་ཆུང་བ་.

ཀུག་རྟགས་ (kugdaà) brackets ([ ] or ()).

ཀུག་རྟགས་གྲུ་བཞི་ (kugdaà drubshi) square brackets.

ཀུག་རྟགས་ཆུང་བ་ (kugdaà cūnwa) parentheses.

ཀུག་སྡེམ་ (kugdem) bending gracefully; va.—བྱེད་.

ཀུག་པོ་ (kugbo) sm. ཀུག་ཀུག.

ཀུག་ཚད་ (kugdzɛɛ̀) plasticity, degree sth. can bend.

ཀུང་ (kun) 1. kind of leopard found in Tibet. 2. middle, center ¶ ཉིན་ཀུང་ Noon. 3. ch. abbr. for ཀུང་ཁྲན་. 4. ch. a high title in tt. government.

ཀུང་བཀུར་ (kun gur) ch.tib. respect the Communist Party ¶ ཀུང་བཀུར་ཆེན་པོའི་ངང་ནས་ With great respect to the Communist Party.

ཀུང་ཁྲན་ (kundren) ch. communist ¶ ཀུང་ཁྲན་ཏང་ཀྲུང་དབྱང་ Central Committee of the Communist Party.

ཀུང་ཁྲན་འགོག་པ་ (kundren gəgba) ch.tib. anticommunist.

ཀུང་ཁྲན་རྒྱལ་སྤྱི་ (kundren gyɛɛji) ch.tib. comintern.

ཀུང་ཁྲན་ཏང་ (kundren dān) ch. the Communist Party.

ཀུང་ཁྲན་ཏང་གི་བསྒྲགས་གཏམ་ (kundrenangi drāgdam) ch.tib. the Communist Manifesto.

ཀུང་ཁྲན་ཏང་མི་ (kundren dānmi) ch.tib. sm. ཀུང་ཁྲན་ཏང་ཡོན་.

ཀུང་ཁྲན་ཏང་ཡོན་ (kundren dānyön) ch. Communist Party member.

ཀུང་ཁྲན་རིང་ལུགས་ (kundren rinluù) ch.tib. communism.

ཀུང་ཁྲན་རིང་ལུགས་ཀྱི་གོ་རྟོགས་ (kundren rinluùgi kodoò) ch.tib. communist consciousness.

ཀུང་ཁྲན་རིང་ལུགས་ཀྱི་སྤྱི་ཚོགས་ (rinluicgi jītsoò) ch. tib. communist society.

ཀུང་ཁྲན་རིང་ལུགས་ཀྱི་སྤྱོད་བཟང་ (rinluùgi jöösan) ch.tib. communist ethics/ morality.

ཀུང་ཁྲན་རིང་ལུགས་ཀྱི་མི་ཚེར་ལྟ་ཚུལ་ (rinluùgi midzer dātsül) ch.tib. communist philosophy of life.

ཀུང་ཁྲན་རིང་ལུགས་ཀྱི་ལས་འགུལ་ (rinluùgi lɛngüü) ch.tib. the movement of communism, a communist movement.

ཀུང་ཁྲན་རིང་ལུགས་ཀྱི་གཤིས་ཀ་ (rinluùgi shīigə) ch.tib. the character of communist.

ཀུང་ཁྲན་རིང་ལུགས་པ་ (kundren rinluùba) ch.tib. a communist.

ཀུང་གོལ་ (kun göö) ch.tib. anticommunist; va.—བྱེད་ to oppose communism, to be anticommunist.

ཀུང་འགྲིགས་ (kundrig) suitable, appropriate.

ཀུང་བསྒྲིགས་ (kun drig) va. to arrange in sequence/ order ¶ ཁྱེད་རང་གིས་ཡིག་ཆ་འདི་རྣམས་ཀུང་བསྒྲིག་དགོས་ You should arrange these documents in sequence.

ཀུང་ཅིང་ཐོན་ (kunjin tön) ch. Communist Youth League.

ཀུང་ཅིང་ཐོན་ཡོན་ (kunjīn tönyön) ch.tib. Communist Youth League member.

ཀུང་ཇ་ (kunja) midday tea.

ཀུང་ཇག (kunjag) ch.tib. communist bandits.

ཀུང་ཐང་ (kundan) a place in Central Tibet.

ཀུང་ཐང་མེ་ཏོག་མཆོད་པ་ (kundan medog cōōba) the "flower" rite held at ཚལ་གུང་ཐང་ on the 15th day of the 4th month (the main activity is the symbolic meeting of Panden Lhamo and her consort Trib Dzongtsen).

ཀུང་ཐུན་ (kundün) the third of four parts of the day (usu.used in monastic study and meditation).

ཀུང་མདོ་ (kundo) a measurement unit equal to the distance between the tip of the middle finger and the tip of the thumb.

ཀུང་པ་ (kunba) the middle one, the one in the center ¶ ཁོའི་བུ་ཀུང་པ་དེ་ His middle son.

ཀུང་ལྤགས་ (kunbaà) the skin of a leopard.

ཀུང་བློན་ (kunlön) 1. minister. 2. abbr. of ཀུང་ and བཀའ་བློན་ or སྲིད་བློན་.

ཀུང་མོ་ (kunmo) 1. middle finger. 2. a kind of leopard.

ཀུང་དམག (kunmaà) ch.tib. communist soldiers/ army.

ཀུང་ཚིགས་ (kundzii) lunch, midday meal.

ཀུང་མཛུབ་ (kundzub) sm. ཀུང་མོ་; 1.

ཀུང་གཞོན་ཐོན་ཡོན་ (kunnshön tōnyon) ch.tib. Communist Youth League member.

ཀུང་གཞོན་ཚོགས་པ་ (kunnshön tsōgba) ch.tib. Communist Youth League.

ཀུང་ཡོལ་ (kunyöl) afternoon.

གང་རི་གང་བཙན་ (kuŋri guŋdzɛn) name of the son of Srongtsen Gampo.

གང་རིམ་གྱི་རྒྱལ་ཁྲན་ (kuŋrimgi gyɛɛtrɛn) duchy, dukedom.

གང་ལ་ཕུག (kuŋ ləbuù) carrot.

གང་སངས་ (kuŋsaŋ) sm. གང་གསེང་.

གང་གསེང་ (kuŋseŋ) 1. vacation, holiday; va.—འགྲོ་; —གཏོང་ to take a vacation ། ཁ་སང་ངས་གང་གསེང་ལ་ཕྱིན་པ་ཡིན་ Yesterday I went on vacation. 2. va. to give sb. a vacation, to give sb. time off ། ཁྲོམ་དུས་དེའི་སྐབས་བཟོ་པ་ཚོ་གང་གསེང་བཏང་པ་རེད་ (They) gave the laborers the day off on the day of the fair.

གུད་ (küǜ) sm. གོད་.

གུད་དུ་ (küǜdu) arc. separately, aside, in private.

གུད་མུན་ (küǜmün) a dark period (of deterioration).

གུད་པོ་ (küǜbo) 1. weak, frail, poor. 2. a loss.

གུན་ (kün) a loss; vi.—ཐོག to suffer a loss ། དེ་ཁྱེད་རང་ལ་གུན་ཆེན་པོ་རེད་ That is a great loss to you. ། བཟོ་གྲྭ་གསར་པ་དེས་ཁོ་ཚོར་གུན་ཆེན་པོ་ཐོག་པ་རེད་ They suffered a great loss due to the new factory.

གུན་མཐུད་ (küntüü) compensation, making up ། ཁང་པར་མེ་སྐྱོན་ཕྱུང་ཙང་གཞུང་ནས་གུན་མཐུད་དངུལ་སྤྲད་པ་རེད་ Because the house suffered fire damage the government compensated them with money.

གུན་དུམ་ (kündum) round basket.

གུན་དོད་ (kündöö) compensation for a loss.

གུན་པོ་ (kümbo) expensive.

གུན་ཚབ་ (kündzəb) sm. གུན་མཐུད་.

གུན་སེལ་ཁེ་སྒྱུར་ (künsel kẽgyur) turning losses into profits; va.—བྱེད་.

གུན་གསབ་ (künsəb) sm. གུན་མཐུད་.

གུམ་ (kum) vi. to die, to pass away ། མི་རྒན་འཁོགས་དེ་གུམ་པ་རེད་ That old man died.

གུམ་རྒྱག (kum gyaà) va. to fly a kite in a spiral maneuver, to make one's kite fly in circles.

གུམ་གུམ་པ་ (kumkumba) shriveled up, withered, shrunk.

གུམ་ཤར་ (kumshar) sm. ཞ་རི་.

གུམ་ཤིང་ (kumshiŋ) butt of a rifle.

གུར་དིག (kurdig) wild mint.

གུའང་དོང་ (guaŋdoŋ) Guangdong (Province).

གུའང་ཤིའི་ (guaŋshi) Guangshi (Province).

གུའི་ཀྲོའུ་ (güdro) Guizhou (Province).

གུར་ (kur) tent; va.—འཕུབས་; —རྒྱག; —སྒྲོན་ to pitch a tent; va.—གཏིབ་; —བཤིག to take down a tent.

གུར་གུམ་ (kurgum) saffron.

གུར་གུམ་མེ་ཏོག (kurgum medog) sm. གུར་གུམ་.

གུར་དཀར་པོ་ཕྱི་གསལ་ནང་གསལ་ (kur gãrbo cisɛɛ naŋsɛɛ) sth. that is extremely clear [Lit. a transparent tent].

གུར་ཁང་ (kurgaŋ) a room where tents are kept/ stored.

གུར་ཁེབས་ (kurgeb) canopy/ fly that goes over a tent.

གུར་གུམ་ (kurgum) sm. གུར་ཀུམ་.

གུར་རྒྱུག (kurgyuù) tent pole.

གུར་ཐག (kurdag) tent rope, guyline.

གུར་པ་ (kurbə) person responsible for putting up tents.

གུར་ཕྱིད་ (kur bii) sm.* གུར་འཕུབས་.

གུར་ཕུབ་ (kur pūb) p. of གུར་འཕུབས་.

གུར་ཕུར་ (kurbur) tent peg/ stake.

གུར་འཕུབས་ (kur bub) see གུར་.

གུར་ཤག (kurshaà) old tent.

གུར་ཤིང་ (kurshiŋ) tent pole.

གུལ་གུལ་ (küügüü) moving, shaking, slithering; va.—བྱེད་ to move, to shake/ slither ། འབུ་འདི་གུལ་གུལ་བྱེད་ཀྱི་འདུག The bug is slithering (along).

གུས་ (küǜ) 1. I (humble term) ། གུས་འདིའི་ཕྱོགས་བཅར་རྩིས་ཡོད་ I plan to come here. 2. respect, reverence ། གུས་ཞིང་བརྩེ་བའི་ངང་ནས་ཁོང་ལ་དགའ་བསུ་ཞུས་པ་རེད་ They greeted him with respect and love.

གུས་བཀུར་ (küǜgur) respect, reverence; va.—བྱེད་; —ཞུ་ to pay one's respect, to show/ demonstrate reverence/ respect ། བླ་མ་དེ་ར་ཚང་མས་གུས་བཀུར་ཞུས་པ་རེད་ (They) all respected that lama. ། ཁོང་གིས་གུས་བཀུར་གྱི་རྣམ་པའི་ངང་ནས་གསུངས་པ་རེད་ He spoke in a respectful manner.

གུས་བཀུར་ཕྱག་འཚལ་ (küǜgur cãgdzɛɛ) being respectful and prostrating.

གུས་བཀུར་བརྩི་འཇོག (küǜgur dzĩnjoò) respecting and obeying ། དབུ་འཁྲིད་དེ་ཚོར་ཁོང་ཚོས་གུས་བཀུར་བརྩི་འཇོག་བྱེད་ཀྱི་ཡོད་པ་རེད་ They are respecting and obeying those leaders.

གུས་བཀུར་ཡི་རང་ (küǜgur yiraŋ) agreeing/ liking and respecting.

གུས་གུས་འདུད་འདུད་ (küǜgüǜ düǜdüǜ) respectful; va.—བྱེད་ to show respect.

གུས་གུས་སྦྱར་སྦྱར་ (küǜgüǜ jarjar) showing respect in a flattering way, acting sycophantically; va.—བྱེད་ ། མི་དེ་རྟག་པར་འགོ་ཁྲིད་ལ་གུས་གུས་སྦྱར་སྦྱར་བྱེད་མཁན་ཞིག་རེད་ He is sb. who always flatters the leader.

གུས་གུས་ཞུམ་ཞུམ་ (küǜgüǜ shumshum) sm. གུས་གུས་འདུད་འདུད་.

གུས་སྒུར་ (küǜgur) bowing in a respectful manner; va.—ཞུ་.

གུས་བཏུད་ (küǜdüǜ) sm. གུས་བཀུར་.

གུས་རྟག་བརྩོན་པ་ (küǜdaà dzōmba) respecting and working diligently.

གུས་སྟབས་ (küǜdəb) in a respectful manner.

གུས་སྟར་ (küǜdar) a welcoming line.

གུས་བསྟོད་ (küǜdüǜ) sm. གུས་བཀུར་.

གུས་འདུད་ (küǜdüǜ) sm. གུས་བཀུར་.

གུས་འདུད་གོང་བཀུར་ (küǜdüǜ koŋgur) looking up to (someone) with respect.

གུས་འདུད་ཕྱག་རྒྱ་ (küǜdüǜ cāggyaà) a respectful hand gesture (usu. clasping hands together in front of chest).

གུས་འདུད་ཚོགས་པ་ (küǜdüǜ tsōgba) a goodwill delegation.

གུས་འདུད་ཡིད་སྨོན་ (küǜdüǜ yiimön) respecting and admiring.

གུས་འདུད་རུ་བསྲིགས་ (küǜdüǜ rudrig) guard of honor.

གུས་འདྲིས་ (küǜdrii) respectful and close (relationship).

གུས་པ་ (küǜbə) 1. respect, reverence ། ཁོ་ཚོ་ཆོས་ལ་གུས་པ་ཆེན་པོ་ཡོད་པ་རེད་ They have great respect for religion. 2. I ། གུས་པ་གནས་སྐབས་འདིར་སྡོད་ཀྱི་ཡིན་ I am going to stay here for awhile.

གུས་པར་འོས་པ་ (küǜbar wööba) worthy of respect/ reverence ། ང་ཚོའི་གུས་པར་འོས་པའི་དབུ་ཁྲིད་ Our respected leader.

གུས་པོ་ (küǜbo) respect, reverence.

གུས་ཕྲན་ (küǜtrɛn) I, your humble servant.

གུས་འབངས་ (küǜbaŋ) shung. your humble servant (a polite way to refer to oneself in letters/ reports to superiors).

གུས་མིང་ (küǜmiŋ) term or title of respect, honorific term.

གུས་མོ་ (küǜmo) I (for females).

གུས་རྩི་ (küǜdzi) abbr. of གུ་བཀུར་བརྩི་འཇོག.

གུས་བརྩེ་ (küǜdze) respecting and loving; va.—བྱེད་; —གནང་.

གུས་ཚིག (küǜdzig) 1. saying respectful things; va.—སྨྲ. 2. sm. གུས་མིང་.

གུས་ཚུལ་ (küǜdzul) greeting respectfully; va.—བྱེད་; —སྟོན་.

གུས་ཚུལ་གུས་ལན་ (küǜdzüü küǜlɛn) greeting back and forth in a respectful manner; va.—བྱེད་; va.—ཞུ་.

གུས་ཚུལ་གྱི་ཕྱག་རྒྱ་ (küǜdzulgi cāàgya) sm. གུས་འདུད་ཕྱག་རྒྱ་.

གུས་ཞབས་ (küǜshəb) sm. གུས་བཀུར་.

གུས་ཞུ་ (küǜshu) sm. གུས་བཀུར་.

གུས་ཞུའི་གློག་འཕྲིན་ (küǜshü lɔ̄gdrin) telegram of

greeting.

གུས་ཞུའི་ཚོགས་པ་ (küüshü tsōgba) goodwill delegation.

གུས་ལ་གུས་ལན་ (küüla güülɛn) reciprocal respect.

གུས་ལན་ (küülɛn) returning a greeting, returning a show of respect; va.—སློག; —གནང་; —འཇལ་ to return a greeting or a show of respect.

གུས་ལུགས་ (küüluù) sm. གུས་སྲོལ་.

གུས་ལན་ (küülɛn) return a show of respect, return a compliment; va.—འཇལ་; —ཞུ་.

གུས་ལེན་ (küülen) accepting a greeting/ salute (usu. by waving a hand); va.—གནང་.

གུས་ཤིང་གཅེས་ (küüshiŋ jēè) respect and love.

གུས་ཤིང་བརྩེ་བ་ (küüshiŋ dsēwa) dear (term used in addressing letters).

གུས་བསུ་ (küüsu) welcoming with great respect; va.—ཞུ་ to welcome with great respect.

གུས་སེམས་ (küüsem) sm. གུས་བཀུར་.

གུས་སྲོལ་ (küüsöö) requirements of etiquette, customs involving respect.

གེ་སར་ (kesar) the epic hero Gesar.

གེ་སར་གྱི་སྒྲུང་ (kesargi drum) the epic story of Gesar.

གེགས་ (keg) hindrance, impediment, obstruction, barrier; va.—བྱེད་ to hinder/ impede/ obstruct; va.—སེལ་ to remove obstacles/ hindrance/ impediments ¶ ཡུལ་གཉིས་དབར་དམག་འཁྲུག་བྱུང་བ་དེས་དཔལ་འབྱོར་ཡར་རྒྱས་ལ་གེགས་སྐྱོན་ཆེན་པོ་བྱས་པ་རེད་ The war between the two countries has impeded economic progress.

གེགས་སྐྱོན་ (keggyön) disaster ¶ ལུང་པ་དེར་ཆུ་ལོག་གི་གེགས་སྐྱོན་ཆེན་པོ་བྱུང་འདུག That area had a great flood disaster.

གེགས་སྐྱོབ་ (keggyob) disaster relief.

གེགས་ཁུལ་ (keggüü) sm. གེགས་བར་བྱུང་ཁུལ་.

གེགས་འགོག་གེགས་སྐྱོབ་ (keŋgɔ̀ɔ keggyob) disaster prevention.

གེགས་འགོག་གེགས་སེལ་ (keŋgɔ̀ɔ gegsel) overcoming a disaster.

གེགས་སྒྲོལ་ (keŋgdröl) a rite done to overcome disasters; va.—བྱེད་.

གེགས་ཆགས་ (kegjaà) sm. གེགས་སྐྱོན་.

གེགས་བར་ (kegbar) 1. sm. གེགས་. 2. disaster, calamity; va.—ཟློག to repel/ combat/ overcome a calamity (like an epidemic) ¶ རང་བྱུང་གི་གེགས་བར་ Natural calamity.

གེགས་བར་བྱུང་ཁུལ་ (kegbar cuŋgül) disaster area.

གེགས་བྱེད་ (kegjèe) obstacle, hindrance, barrier, impediment.

གེགས་དབང་ (kegwaŋ) misfortune or serious sickness (usu. caused by deities/ demons) ¶ མི་ཚང་དེས་ལྷ་ལ་ལོག་ཐུག་བཏང་རྐྱེན་གེགས་དབང་ཆེན་པོ་བྱུང་ནས་པ་མ་གཉིས་ཀ་གྲོངས་འདུག The family offended a deity and had a major misfortune in that both the father and mother died.

གེགས་དབང་བར་ཆད་ (kegwaŋ parcɛ̀ɛ) sm. གེགས་དབང་.

གེགས་མེད་ (kegmeè) without disaster/ obstacles/ misfortune/ obstructions/ problems ¶ ལས་དོན་དེ་འཆར་གཞི་བཞིན་གེགས་མེད་བསྒྲུབས་པ་རེད་ (They) completed the project as planned without any obstruction.

གེགས་དམངས་ (kegmaŋ) people in a disaster area.

གེར་རག (kegraà) arc. unpurified brass.

གེར་ལིང་ (kerliŋ) a fine horse.

གེལ་པ་ (geewa) twig, thin branch.

གེལ་པོ་ (geebo) fat, obese, portly.

གོ་ (ko) 1. vi. to hear ¶ མེ་མདའི་སྒྲ་མི་ལེ་ཁ་ཤས་ཀྱིས་ནས་གོ་གི་འདུག (One) can hear the sound of guns from several miles away. 2. term connoting "I will," at the end of a sentence ¶ ངས་བྱས་གོ་ I will do it. 3. vi. to understand ¶ ཁོའི་དབྱིན་ཇི་འདི་ངས་གོ་གི་མི་འདུག I don't understand his English. 3. numerical particle for the nineties ¶ དགུ་བཅུ་གོ་གསུམ་ Ninety three. 4. abbr. of གོ་ཁྲབ་.

གོ་བཀྲག (kodraà) armor.

གོ་སྐད་ལ་ (ko gɛɛla) it is said ¶ གོ་སྐད་ལ་རྒྱ་ནག་ལ་ས་གཡོས་བྱུང་འདུག It is said that an earthquake occurred in China.

གོ་སྐལ་ (kogɛɛ) 1. share of stock. 2. wage, salary. 3. the share stored from one's past karma.

གོ་སྐབས་ (kugəb) opportunity, chance; vi.—རྙེད་ to find an opportunity, to get a chance; va.—འཚོལ་ to look for an opportunity; vi.—ཤོར་ to miss or lose an opportunity ¶ སློབ་སྦྱོང་བྱེད་ཡས་ཀྱི་གོ་སྐབས་ཐོབ་བྱུང་ (I) got an opportunity to study.

གོ་སློན་ (kogön) making understand, advising, persuading, convincing; va.—བྱེད་ to make understand, to advise, to persuade, to convince ¶ གང་གསེང་མང་པོ་བཏང་ན་ཡག་པོ་མེད་ལུགས་གོ་སློན་བྱས་པ་རེད་ (He) made them understand that (they) shouldn't take many vacations.

གོ་སློན་གྱི་སློབ་གསོ་ (kogöngi lōbso) education aimed at persuading sb. to change ¶ དགྲ་བོར་གོ་སློན་གྱི་སློབ་གསོ་བྱས་པ་ཡིན་ (We) educated our enemy to change.

གོ་སློན་བློ་འགུག (kogön lōnguù) persuasion; va.—བྱེད་ to persuade, to convince.

གོ་སློན་གསེད་འགྲོལ་ (kogön sēndrö) persuading by explaining sth. clearly; va.—བྱེད་.

གོ་བསློན་ (kogön) sm. གོ་སློན་.

གོ་ཁ་ (koga) 1. the hole in the stove from which the ashes are removed.

གོ་ཁང་ (gogaŋ) armory. 2. near/ beside the stove.

གོ་ཁྲབ་ (kodrəb) armor, coat of mail; va.—བགོ་ to wear/ put on armor) ¶ གོ་ཁྲབ་ལྡན་པའི་རླངས་འཁོར་ An armored car.

གོ་ཁྲབ་རྨོག་གསུམ་ (kodrəb mōgsum) the three: weapons, armor and helmet.

གོ་མཁྲེགས་པོ་ (ko trāgbo) hard, solid, firm.

གོ་གོ་གསལ་གསལ་ (kogo sɛ̄ɛsɛɛ) understanding/ comprehending clearly.

གོ་གྱོན་མཚོན་ཐོགས་ (kogön tsōndɔ̀ɔ) armed to the hilt; va.—བྱེད་ [Lit. wear armor, fasten weapons].

གོ་གྲལ་ (kodrɛɛ) lines/ groups organized by ranks.

གོ་གྲི་ (kodri) chopping knife, cleaver.

གོ་བགོ (ko go) va. to wear/ put on armor.

གོ་བགོས་ (ko göò) 1. va. to divide up/ allocate/ allot/ distribute/ assign. 2. sm. གོ་བགོ.

གོ་རྒྱ་ (kogya) 1. one who has heard a lot (through travel or communication with people). 2. sb. who is well read.

གོ་རྒྱུ་ (kugyu) implication, meaning, significance; va.—གཏོང་; —ཤོད་ to imply, to say things indirectly, to hint ¶ དམངས་ཁྲོད་གཞས་ཚིག་དེ་ཚོར་གོ་རྒྱུ་ཆེན་པོ་ཡོད་ The words of the popular songs have a lot of significance. ¶ ང་ལ་ཁོང་གིས་མ་ཡོང་མདོག་མདོག་གོ་རྒྱུ་གཏོང་གི་འདུག He is hinting indirectly that I shouldn't come to his house.

གོ་རྒྱུ་འཚོར་རྒྱུ་ (kugyu tsōrgyu) information, news ¶ དེང་སང་བོད་ཀྱི་གནས་ཚུལ་གོ་རྒྱུ་འཚོར་རྒྱུ་མི་འདུག These days there is no news on the situation in Tibet.

གོ་སྒྲིག (kudrig) 1. arranging, organizing; va.—བྱེད་, —ཞུ་ ¶ ཁོང་ཚོ་ས་གནས་ལ་ལྟ་སྐོར་བྱེད་ཆེད་རླངས་འཁོར་གཅིག་གོ་སྒྲིག་བྱེད་དགོས་ (We) have to arrange a car for their tour of the area. 2. va. to line up and cut crops in an area one is assigned to.

གོ་སྒྲིགས་ (kudrig) sm. གོ་སྒྲིག.

གོ་ངན་ཀླད་ལྡུགས་ (koŋɛn) instilling evil ideas into sb.'s head.

གོ་ངན་མ་ (ko ŋɛnma) unmarried women who live at home.

གོ་ཅ་ (koja) sm. གོ་ཁྲབ་.

གོ་ཅི་གཉིས་པ་ (koji ñiibə) ch.tib. Second Internationale (1877-1918).

གོ་ཅི་དང་པོ་ (koji taŋbo) ch.tib. First Internationale (1864-1876).

གོ་ཅི་གསུམ་པ་ (koji sūmba) ch.tib. Third Internationale (1919-1943).

གོ་གཅལ་ (kojɛɛ) wooden floor.

གོ་གཅོད་ (kojöö) 1. va. to make use of, to use ། ཁོ་ཚོས་ཚགས་པར་རྙིང་པ་དེ་ཚོས་མེ་ཤིང་གི་གོ་བཅད་པ་རེད་ They used old newspapers for firewood. 2. va. to decide, to make a decision.

གོ་ཆ་ (koja) 1. weapons. 2. armor.

གོ་ཆའི་བརྩོན་འགྲུས་ (kojɛ dzǖndrüü) extremely diligently, sb. who does not lose heart in his effort.

གོ་ཆོད་ (kojöö) 1. capable, able ། ཁོ་མི་གོ་ཆོད་ཅིག་འདུག He is a capable person. 2. effective, efficacious, useful; vi. གོ་ཆོད་ to be of use, to be effective, to suffice, to serve the function ། ཐབས་ཤེས་གོ་ཆོད་ཅིག An effective method. ། འཕྲུལ་འཁོར་འདིས་བཟོ་པ་མང་པོའི་གོ་ཆོད་ཀྱི་ཡོད་པ་རེད་ This machine serves the function of many workers. ། བོད་ཡིག་འབྲི་ལས་ལ་སྨྱུག་གུ་འདིས་གོ་ཆོད་ཀྱི་རེད་ This pen will suffice for writing Tibetan.

གོ་ཆོད་པའི་ཡུན་ཚད་ (kocöbɛ yündzɛɛ̀) period of validity, effective period ། ལག་འཁྱེར་འདིའི་གོ་ཆོད་པའི་ཡུན་ཚད་རྫོགས་འདུག The period of validity of the permit has expired.

གོ་ཆོད་པོ་ (ko cööbo) useful, helpful, handy.

གོ་འཇོ་ (konjo) a county in Chamdo.

གོ་བརྗེས་ (ko jeè) exchanging; va.—རྒྱག ། ཁོང་གཉིས་ཀྱི་ཆུ་ཚོད་གོ་བརྗེས་བརྒྱབ་པ་རེད་ The two of them exchanged watches.

གོ་བརྗེས་དངུལ་འཛིན་ (kojeè ŋǖndzin) letter of credit for transferring money.

གོ་གཉིད་ (koñii) dozing off, falling asleep; vi.—རྒྱག; —ཐོག.

གོ་སྙོད་ (koñöö) cumin (seed).

གོ་རྟོགས་ (kodɔɔ̀) consciousness, awareness; understanding, comprehension; vi.—སད་ to become conscious/ aware, to understand comprehend ། དེབ་འདི་མི་དམངས་ཀྱི་གོ་རྟོགས་གང་བདེ་ཐུབ་ཡོད་པ་རེད་ This book has been written so as to be as easy to understand as possible. ། འཛམ་གླིང་མི་དམངས་ཀྱི་གོ་རྟོགས་ཉིན་རེ་བཞིན་སད་ཀྱི་ཡོད་པ་རེད་ The consciousness of the people of the world is becoming awakened more every day.

གོ་རྟོགས་ཀྱི་ཚད་ (kodɔɔ̀gi dzɛɛ̀) level of understanding/ consciousness/ awareness.

གོ་རྟོགས་མཐོ་བ་ (kodɔɔ̀ tōwa) high consciousness.

གོ་རྟོགས་བདེ་པོ་ (kodɔɔ̀ debo) easy to understand.

གོ་སྟངས་ (kodaŋ) sm. གོ་སྣང་.

གོ་སྟབས་ (kodob) ability to understand/ grasp/ understand ། ཁོང་སློབ་སྦྱོང་གི་ཐོག་གོ་སྟབས་ཆེན་པོ་ཡོད་པ་རེད་ Regarding his studies, he understands things easily.

གོ་བསྟུན་ (kodün) 1. in accordance with, in keeping with ། ཁྲིམས་ལམ་ལ་གོ་བསྟུན་གྱིས་ཡིག་ཆ་དེ་བཟོས་པ་ཡིན་ I made the document in accordance with the regulations. 2. discussing, consulting ། ཕྱག་རོགས་ལ་གོ་བསྟུན་གྱིས་ཐག་གཅོད་བྱས་པ་ཡིན་ (I) made the decision in consultation with (my) colleague.

གོ་ཐང་ (kotaŋ) shung. healthy ། མི་གོ་ཐང་ A healthy person.

གོ་ཐལ་ (kodɛɛ) ash, cinder.

གོ་ཐལ་མདོག (kotɛɛ dɔɔ̀) ash color.

གོ་ཐོབ་ (kotob) official rank/ position; va.—གནང་.

གོ་ཐོབ་དཔུང་རྟགས་ (kotob būŋdaà) rank; va.—གནང་ to give a rank/ position [Lit. the epaulet signifying rank].

གོ་ཐོས་ (kodöö) things heard, news, information, reports ། དེང་སང་བོད་ནས་གནས་ཚུལ་གོ་ཐོས་ལྟར་ན་ According to what is heard from Tibet these days.

གོ་དྭ་ག་གསུམ་ (kodaga sūm) a Tibetan Muslim exclamation conveying a promise (e.g., I swear (to God)) ། གོ་དྭ་ག་གསུམ་ ངས་ལས་ཀ་འདི་ཡག་པོ་ཞིག་བྱེད་ཀྱི་ཡིན་ I swear to God I will do the work well.

གོ་དོང་ (kodoŋ) a pit into which ashes are poured.

གོ་དོན་ (kodön) meaning, sense; vi.—འཁྱོད་ to understand the meaning ། ཁོའི་ཡི་གེ་དེའི་གོ་དོན་འཁྱོད་མ་སོང་ I didn't understand the meaning of his letter. ། ཁོའི་ཡི་གེ་དེའི་ནང་གི་གོ་དོན་གཙོ་བོ་ནི་ The main meaning of his letter.

གོ་དོན་འཁྱོད་ཙམ་ (kodön dröödzam) just barely understanding the meaning ། ངའི་དབྱིན་སྐད་ཐབས་ཆག་འདིས་གོ་དོན་འཁྱོད་ཙམ་བྱུང་སོང་ With my poor English (I) could barely understand the meaning.

གོ་དོན་ལེགས་རྟོགས་ (kodön legdɔɔ̀) good or thorough understanding/ comprehension of the meaning.

གོ་བདེ་ (kode) sm. གོ་རྟོགས་བདེ་བ་.

གོ་བདེ་པོ་ (ko debo) sm. གོ་རྟོགས་བདེ་པོ་.

གོ་བདེ་བ་ (ko dewa) sm. གོ་རྟོགས་བདེ་པོ་.

གོ་བདེ་ཤེས་སླ་ (kode sheèlā) easy to understand.

གོ་བདེར་ཕབ་ (koder pāb) va. to make sth. more easily understandable.

གོ་འདབས་ (godəb) near/ beside the stove.

གོ་འདྲ་ (kondra) a type of medicinal herb.

གོ་འདྲིས་ (kondrii) close, intimate (relationship).

གོ་ལྡོག (kodog) opposite, contrary, upside-down, reverse, counter; vi. གོ་ལྡོག; —བྱེད་ to be opposed/ contrary to, to put upside down, to reverse; vi. གོ་ལྡོག (དུ་) འགྲོ་ to become opposite/ contrary/ reversed ། ང་ཚོའི་བསམ་བློ་དང་གོ་ལྡོག་པའི་བྱེད་སྟངས་ A way of doing things that is contrary to our ideas. ། ཁོས་བྱེད་ཡ་དེ་ཁོས་ཤོད་ཡག་དང་གོ་ལྡོག་གི་འདུག What he does is contrary to what he says. ། སྐད་ཆ་ཤོད་སྟངས་དེ་འདྲ་བཤད་ན་དམངས་གཙོའི་རིང་ལུགས་དང་གོ་ལྡོག་ཏུ་འགྲོ་གི་རེད་ If you speak in this manner, it will be contrary to democracy.

གོ་ལྡོག་པའི་བསྡུར་ཚད་ (kodogbɛ durdzɛɛ̀) inverse proportion.

གོ་ལྡོག་པའི་ནུས་པ་ (kodogbɛ nüübə) counterforce.

གོ་སྡུར་ (kodur) sm. གོ་བསྡུར་.

གོ་བརྡ་ (koda) 1. notification, communication; va.—སྤྲོད་ to notify ། ཏང་གི་འབོད་བསྐུལ་གསར་པ་འདི་མི་དམངས་ལ་གོ་བརྡ་སྤྲད་པ་རེད་ (They) notified the people of the party's new appeal. vi.—འཕྲོད་ to be able to communicate ། ཁོས་བོད་སྐད་མ་ཤེས་སྐབས་གང་བཤད་གོ་བརྡ་འཕྲོད་ཀྱི་མི་འདུག He doesn't understand Tibetan so we can't communicate with (him) whatever (we) say. 2. implying, hinting; va.—གཏོང་ to imply, to hint.

གོ་བརྡ་སྟོན་རིས་ (koda dōnrii) illustration (in a book).

གོ་བསྡུར་ (kodur) 1. conferring, discussing; va.—བྱེད་ ། ལས་དོན་དེའི་སྐོར་ཚོགས་འདུར་གོ་བསྡུར་བྱས་པ་རེད་ Concerning this work, it was discussed at the meeting. 2. contrasting/ comparing; va.—བྱེད་.

གོ་ན་སྐྱི་གཡའ་བ་ (kona gyī yāwa) sensational, shocking ། གོ་ན་སྐྱི་གཡའ་བའི་གནས་ཚུལ་ Shocking news.

གོ་ནོར་ (konɔr) misunderstanding, hearing wrong; vi.—ཐེབས་ to misunderstand, to hear wrong ། དེ་ངས་གོ་ནོར་ཐེབས་པ་རེད་ I misunderstood that.

གོ་གནས་ (konɛɛ̀) position, rank, status; va.—སྤོར་ to promote; vi.—འཕར་ to get a promotion; va.—འབེབས་ to demote; va.—འཕྲོག་ to dismiss from a position ། རིམ་བཞིའི་གོ་གནས་ The rank of Rimshi.

གོ་གནས་བསྒོ་འཕྲོག་ (konɛɛ̀ gōden) hiring and firing, promoting and demoting, appointing and dismissing; va.—འཕྲོག་.

གོ་གནས་གཅིག་ཁྱོགས་ (konɛɛ̀ jīgjɔɔ̀) a person holding two positions jointly.

གོ་གནས་སྟོང་ལུས་ (konɛɛ̀ dōŋlüü) vacant position/ rank.

གོ་གནས་མཐོ་དམན་ (konɛɛ̀ tōmɛn) level of rank/ position ། ཁོ་གཉིས་གོ་གནས་མཐོ་དམན་གཅིག་པ་རེད་ The rank of those two are at the same level.

གོ་གནས་གནས་དབྱུང་ (konɛɛ̀ nɛɛ̀yuŋ) demotion; va.—གཏོང་.

གོ་སྣང་ (konaŋ) from what I heard ། ངའི་གོ་སྣང་ལ་འགོ་ཁྲིད་ཀྱིས་ཚོགས་འདུའི་ཐོག་ཁོ་ཀ་མ་ཡིན་པའི་སྐོར་བཤད་སོང་ From what I heard, the leader spoke at the meeting about him being a thief.

གོ་ཕུད་ (ko pū̀ü) p. of གོ་འབུད་.

གོ་ཕྱོགས་ནོར་ (kocoò nɔr) sm. གོ་ནོར་ཐེབས་.

གོ་ཕྲུག (kotruù) baby eagle.

གོ་འཕང་ (gombaŋ) 1. state of enlightenment. 2. sm. གོ་གནས་.

གོ་འཕེར་ (komber) sm. གོ་ཆོད་.

གོ་བ་ (kowa) comprehension; va.—རྒྱག་; —ལེན་ to understand, to comprehend; vi.—ལོག to misunderstand/ misinterpret; vi.—ཐེབས་; —ལོན་; —རྟེད་ to understand, to comprehend ¶ གཏམ་དཔེ་དེ་ཚོར་གོ་བ་རྒྱག་ཁག་པོ་རེད་ Those proverbs are hard to understand. ¶ གཞུང་ཡིག་འདི་ཚོ་གོ་བ་བརྒྱབ་ཀྱང་ཐེབས་ཁག་པོ་འདུག As for the traditional Government terminology, even though (I) try it is very difficult to understand.

གོ་བ་བསྐྱོན་ (kowa gȫn) sm. གོ་སྐྱོན་བྱེད་.

གོ་བ་ཅན་ (kowajɛn) learned, wise.

གོ་བ་ཆེན་པོ་ (kowa cēmbo) easy to understand.

གོ་བ་ལོག་པ་བྱེད་ (kowa lɔ̄gba ceè) va. to give the opposite meaning, to misinterpret.

གོ་བབ་(ས) (kobab) entitlement, right, position, status ¶ ཁོང་གིས་ང་ལ་བཀའ་བཀོད་གཏོང་ཡས་ཀྱི་གོ་བབ་ཡོད་པ་མ་རེད་ He has no right to give me orders.

གོ་བབ་ཐོབ་ཐང་ (kobab tōbdaŋ) sm. གོ་བབ་.

གོ་བབ་འདྲ་མཉམ་ (kobəb drañam) shung. equal position/ status.

གོ་བར་བྱེད (kowar cɛ̀ɛ) sm. གོ་བ་ལེན་.

གོ་བས་ཆོད་པ་ (kowɛ cȫòba) shung. to understand ¶ ཙ་ཆིག་གི་དགོངས་དོན་ཀུན་ཤེས་གོ་བས་ཆོད་པ་ལྟར་ལགས་ We all understand the contents of the proclamation.

གོ་བོ་ཀླད་དཀར (kowo lɛ̄ɛ̀gar) type of large bird of prey.

གོ་བྱུང་ཐོས་བྱུང་ (kojuŋ tȫòjuŋ) information that is secondhand ¶ ཁོའི་སྐད་ཆ་གོ་བྱུང་ཐོས་བྱུང་ཡོད་པ་མ་རེད་ His talk is not secondhand information.

གོ་བློ་ (kolo) wisdom and intelligence.

གོ་བློས་ཆོད་མིན་ (kolö̀ö cȫòmin) shung. unable to understand.

གོ་འབུད་ (ko pǜü) va. to relieve/ discharge from office.

གོ་འབྱེད་ (kojeè) 1. the stave/ walking stick of a དགེ་སློང་. 2. va. to differentiate/ separate. 3. va. to create an opportunity.

གོ་སྦུག (kobuù) the place near the stove where dried dung is kept.

གོ་མ་ (koma) unmarried woman who lives at home.

གོ་མ་ཆོད་ (ko macö̀ö) sm. གོ་མི་ཆོད་པ་.

གོ་མག (komaà) "adoptive" bridegroom (male who goes to live with his wife's family after marriage).

གོ་མང་ཆོད་པ་ (komaŋ cȫòba) useful for many purposes, multifunctional, universal.

གོ་མང་ཆོད་པའི་བདར་བྱེད་འཁོར་ལོ་ (komaŋ cȫòbɛ dajeè kɔ̄ɔ̄lo) universal sanding/ grinding machine.

གོ་མི་ (komi) skt. a monk.

གོ་མི་ཆོད་པ་ (ko micö̀öba) useless, ineffective, incapable; va.—བྱེད་ to do sth. useless/ ineffective; va.—བཟོ་ to make useless; vi.—འགྱུར་ to become useless/ ineffective, to fail ¶ ཁོང་གིས་ལས་ཀ་གོ་མི་ཆོད་པ་ཞིག་བྱས་བཞག He did a job that was useless. ¶ ཁོས་འཕྲུལ་འཁོར་དེ་གོ་མི་ཆོད་པ་འཟོས་བཞག He made the machine useless. ¶ ཁོང་ཚོ་མ་ཡོང་ཙང་ང་ཚོས་གྲ་སྒྲིག་བྱས་པ་གོ་མི་ཆོད་པར་གྱུར་པ་རེད་ Because they didn't come, all (our) preparations became useless.

གོ་མིང་ (komiŋ) title.

གོ་མིན་ཏང་ (ko mindaŋ) ch. Kuomintang Party.

གོ་མིན་ཧྲ་ཧུད་ (komin dahǜü) Kuomintang constitutional meeting of 1945-46.

གོ་མེད (komeè) 1. meaningless, useless. 2. unarmed.

གོ་མེད་ཚོར་མེད (komèe tsɔ̄rmeè) insensitive, apathetic [Lit. not knowing and not feeling].

གོ་རྩལ་ (kodzɛɛ) martial arts; va.—རྩེ་ ¶ ལག་དུ་དབྱུག་པ་ཁྱེར་ནས་གོ་རྩལ་རྩེ་གི་ཡོད་པ་རེད་ He was performing martial arts with a stick in his hand.

གོ་རྩེད (kodzeè) 1. martial arts. 2. soldiers attired in the battle dress and weapons of the era of the Kings (this occurs during the Great Monlam Prayer Festival).

གོ་རྩེད་རྩེ་ (kodzeè dzē) va. to perform martial arts.

གོ་རྩུལ་ (kodzül) sm. གོ་སྣང་.

གོ་མཚམས་ (kodzam) the line dividing an area a person has taken to harvest from those next to him/ her.

གོ་མཚོན་ (kodzön) weapons, arms.

གོ་མཚོན་ལྡན་པ་ (kodzön dɛmba) armed ¶ གོ་མཚོན་ལྡན་པའི་ངོ་ལོག Armed rebellion.

གོ་མཚོན་དཔུང་ཁག (kodzön būŋgà) armed forces/ troops.

གོ་མཚོན་རྫས་མདེལ་ (kodzön dzɛɛ̀del) weaponry.

གོ་མཛོད་ (komdzö̀ö) ammunition dump, armory.

གོ་མཛོད་གཉེར་པ་ (komdzö̀ö ñērba) an official in charge of an armory.

གོ་འཛོལ་ (komdzöö) sm. གོ་ནོར་.

གོ་ཞིང་ཤེས་པར་བྱེད་ (koshiŋ shēèbar ceè) shung. va. to let/ make sb. understand ¶ ཙ་ཆིག་གི་དགོངས་དོན་རྣམས་ཆབ་འབངས་ཀུན་གྱིས་གོ་ཞིང་ཤེས་པར་བྱེད་ Let all the subjects fully understand the contents of the proclamation.

གོ་བཟློག (kondɔɔ̀) sm. གོ་ལྡོག.

གོ་ཡས་ལ་ (koyɛla) sm. གོ་ཐོས་ལ་.

གོ་ཡུ་ (koyu) see ཀུ་ཡུ་.

གོ་གཡོག (koyɔɔ̀) a wooden poker (for fires).

གོ་ར་ (kɔra) courtyard.

གོ་རག་འཇུར་རྡ་ (kɔra jurda) army boots.

གོ་རིག (korig) intelligence.

གོ་རིག་ཅན་ (korigjɛn) an intelligent person.

གོ་རིམ་ (kurim) order, sequence, steps, rank, class, strata; va.—སྒྲིག to put in order, to rank, to stratify, to arrange; vi.—འཁྲུག to have trouble stirred up among classes/ strata/ ranks, to have disorder occur in the sequence of work. ¶ ལས་ཀའི་གོ་རིམ་ Sequence of work. ¶ སྤྱི་ཚོགས་ཀྱི་གོ་རིམ་ Social stratification. ¶ ང་ཚོ་གོ་རིམ་བསྒྲིགས་སྟེ་ཚོགས་ཆེན་དུ་ཕྱིན་པ་རེད་ We went into the meeting hall in order of our rank.

གོ་རིམ་ལྟར་རྩེག (kurim dārdzeg) va. to pile or stack sth. up in layers.

གོ་རིམ་ལྡན་པ་ (kurim dɛmba) sm. གོ་རིམ་ཡོད་པ་.

གོ་རིམ་མི་གསལ་བ་ (kurim misɛlwa) sm. མགོ་མཇུག་མི་གསལ་བ་.

གོ་རིམ་མེད་པ་ (kurim meèba) 1. without regard to rank ¶ མི་དེས་ཚོགས་འདུའི་ཐོག་གོ་རིམ་མེད་པའི་སྒོ་ནས་འགོ་ཁྲིད་ལ་འཕྱ་ལད་བརྒྱབ་སོང་ That person, without regard to rank, made fun of the leaders at the meeting. 2. disorderly, disorganized ¶ ལས་ཁུངས་དེའི་ནང་ལ་གོ་རིམ་མེད་པའི་ལས་ཀ་བྱས་བཞག Work in that office was done in a disorderly manner.

གོ་རིམ་ཡོད་པ་ (kurim yȫba) systematic, orderly.

གོ་རེ་ (kure) 1. steamed bun/ bread; va.—འཇོག to make bread. 2. va. to play/ have fun. 3. va. to fill. 4. circular, round.

གོ་ལ་ (kola) planet.

གོ་ལ་མ་གོ་ (kola mako) 1. unable to hear clearly/ distinctly. 2. not clear/ understandable/ comprehensible ¶ ཁོང་གིས་དབྱིན་ཇིའི་སྐད་གོ་ལ་མ་གོ་ཞིག་རྒྱག་གི་འདུག He speaks English that is incomprehensible.

གོ་ལག (kolaà) arms, weapons; va.—འབེབས་ to surrender one's arms, to lay down one's arms.

གོ་ལག་ཆ (ko lagja) sm. གོ་ལག.

གོ་ལེ་ (kole) slowly, sluggishly.

གོ་ལོ་གདེང་ལྡན་ (kolo deŋdɛn) shung. reliable.

གོ་ལོ་པ་ནི་ (kolo bāni) a type of woolen material.

གོ་ལོག (kolog) 1. name of a Tibetan nomad group in Amdo. 2. vi. to have a marriage fail and the in-marrying bride/ groom return home ¶ ལོ་གཅིག་ནས་མནའ་མ་འདི་གོ་ལོག་པ་རེད་ After one year the bride returned home.

གོ་ལོག་གནས་འཁྱར་ (kolɔ̄ɔ nɛ̄ɛ̀gyar) the returning of a bride to her parent's family (i.e., a failed marriage).

གོ་ལོག་མ་ (ko logma) a woman who leaves her husband and returns home.

གོ་ལོད་ (kolöö) comprehensible, understandable ¶ ངའི་སྐད་འདི་གོད་ལོད་ག་འདྲ་འདུག How understandable is my speech?

གོ་ལོབ་ (kolob) arc. shung. fast, speedy.

གོ་ཤེས་ (koshee) ability to understand, sb. who listens and understands well; va.—བྱེད་.

གོ་བཤེར་ (kosher) inspection of weapons; va.—བྱེད་.

གོ་ས་ (kosa) title, rank, position; va.—སྤར་ to promote; vi.—འཕར་ to get promoted; va.—འབེབས་ to demote.

གོ་ས་བརྒྱུད་འཛགས་ (kosa gyünjaà) shung. a title that passes from generation to generation ¶ གཞུང་སའི་ཞབས་འདེགས་གཟེངས་ཐོན་ཞུས་ངོར་ཕ་རབས་བུ་བརྒྱུད་ནས་རིམ་པ་བཞི་པའི་གོ་ས་བརྒྱུད་འཛགས་སྩལ་བ་ Because of their sincere devotion to the goverment, they were given the title of fourth rank from generation to generation.

གོ་ས་རིམ་ཕབ་ (kosa rimbəb) shung. demoting, reducing to a lower rank ¶ ལས་ཀྱི་བྱེད་པོ་སོ་སོའི་ཉེས་འཛོལ་ལ་གཞིགས་པའི་གོ་ས་རིམ་ཕབ་བྱས་པ་ The officials were demoted from their post in accordance with the crimes they committed.

གོ་སའི་སྣེ་སྡོད་དཔོན་རིགས་ (kosɛ nēdöö bönrig) shung. people of rank/ positions/ status.

གོ་སླ་ (kolā) sm. གོ་སླ་པོ་.

གོ་སླ་དོན་གསལ་ (kolā tönsɛl) sm. གོ་སླ་.

གོ་སླ་པོ (ko lābo) easy to understand/ know/ comprehend.

གོ་སླ་བ (ko lāwa) sm. གོ་སླ་པོ་.

གོ་སླ་བར་ཤོད་ (ko lāwar shöö) va. to articulate in an easy way.

གོ་གསེད་ (kosèe) explaining clearly; va.—བྱེད་.

གོ་གསེས་ (koseè) sm. གོ་གསེད་.

གོ་ཧྲུའི་གྲོས་ཚོགས་ (kohü trötsɔɔ̀) ch.tib. assembly, congress, parliament.

གོ་ཧྲུའི་རྒྱལ་ཚོགས་ (kohü gyɛɛtsɔɔ̀) ch.tib. National Assembly.

གོ་ཧྲག (kohrag) 1. sm.གོ་མཁྲེགས་པོ་. 2. well-trained and well-equipped (military troops).

གོག (kɔɔ̀) 1. vi. to come unstuck/ unglued, to peel off, to come free ¶ སྣོད་ཆས་འདིའི་ལུང་གོག་སོང་ The handle of this pot came off. 2. va. to crawl ¶ ཕྲུ་གུ་དེ་གོག་ནས་འགྲོ་གི་འདུག That child is going along crawling.

གོག་སྐྱོན་ (kɔggyön) run-down, dilapidated.

གོག་འགྲོ་ (kɔŋdro) sm. གོག་འགྲོས་.

གོག་འགྲོས་ (koŋdröö) crawling; creeping; va.—རྒྱག.

གོག་འགྲོས་རིང་ལུགས་ (koŋdröö riŋluù) "crawling mentality" (underestimating one's own capabilities in science and technology, blindly worshipping ideas from the West and believing that Chinese science can only crawl slowly behind).

གོག་འགྲོས་སྲིན་འབུ་ (koŋdröö simbu) reptile.

གོག་གཅོང་ (kogjoŋ) weak and old.

གོག་དོ་ (kobdo) 1. a sluggish/ sloppy person. 2. rundown, dilapidated (for things).

གོག་ཐལ་ (kogdɛɛ) ashes.

གོག་འདྲུད་རྒྱག (kogdrüù gyaà) sm. གོག་བུ་གོག.

གོག་པོ་ (kogbo) 1. crawling; va.—གོག to crawl ¶ ཕྲུ་གུ་ཚོ་ཐོག་མར་གོག་པོ་གོག་པའི་སྐབས་ When children first crawl. 2. in ruin, dilapidated ¶ ཁང་པ་གོག་པོ་ A dilapidated house.

གོག་པོ་ཤིག་འགྲོས་ (kogbo shīg dröö) extremely slow [Lit. as slow as lice's crawl].

གོག་བུ་གོག (kogbu kɔɔ̀) va. to crawl.

གོག་མ་ (kogma) unhusked barley.

གོག་ཞིག (kogshig) sm. གོག་སྐྱོན་.

གོག་ཧྲུལ་ (koghrül) dilapidated, rundown, ruined.

གོང་ (koŋ) 1. above, on top ¶ གོང་དུ་བཀོད་པ་བཞིན་ As written above. 2. before, prior to ¶ ལོ་1000ལྷག་གི་གོང་ Over 1000 years before. 3. price, value ¶ འདི་ལ་གོང་ག་ཚོད་རེད་ What is the price of this? 4. breast collar worn by horses.

གོང་དཀར་གནམ་གྲུ་ཐང་ (koŋgar nəmdrudaŋ) Gonggar airport (of Lhasa).

གོང་དཀར་རྫོང་ (koŋgar dzōŋ) a district just south of Lhasa.

གོང་དྲིས་ (koŋdrii) necktie; va.—རྒྱག to tie on a necktie.

གོང་བཀུར་ (koŋgur) 1. respect, veneration, esteem; va.—བྱེད་. 2. support, backing; va.—བྱེད་ ¶ གྲོས་མཐུན་དོན་ཚན་བཅུ་བདུན་ལ་མགྲིན་དབྱངས་གཅིག་ཏུ་གོང་བཀུར་བྱས་པ་རེད་ (They) gave unanimous support to the 17 Point Agreement.

གོང་བཀོད་ལྟར་ (koŋgöödar) sm. གོང་འཁོད་ལྟར་.

གོང་ཁ་ (koŋga) collarband, neckband.

གོང་ཁེ་པོ་ (koŋ kēbo) cheap, inexpensive.

གོང་འཁོད་ (koŋköö) sm. གོང་འཁོད་.

གོང་འཁོད་ལྟར་ (koŋköödar) as written/ stated above.

གོང་འཁོད་བཞིན་ (koŋkööshin) sm. གོང་འཁོད་ལྟར་.

གོང་གོང་ (koŋgoŋ) round, arched, protruding.

གོང་གྲས་ (koŋdrɛɛ̀) sm. གོང་རིམ་.

གོང་འགྲིགས (koŋ drii) vi. to settle/ agree on a price.

གོང་རྒྱག (koŋ gyaà) va. to put a price on sth. ¶ ཅ་ལག་འདི་ལ་གོང་བརྒྱབ་མི་འདུག No price has been put on this thing.

གོང་རྒྱན་ (koŋgyɛn) band of decoration made of fur and cloth worn on the lapel of Tibetan men's dress.

གོང་སྒྲིག (koŋ drii) va. to negotiate a price, to bargain for a price ¶ ཁོ་གཉིས་གོང་སྒྲིག་ཐུབ་མ་སོང་ They were unable to negotiate a price.

གོང་སྒྲིལ་ (koŋ drii) sm. སྦྲ་འགྱུར་.

གོང་གཅོག (koŋ jɔ̄ɔ̀) va. to reduce a price, to discount.

གོང་གཅོད་ (koŋ jöö) va. to fix a price.

གོང་བཅག (koŋ jāà) p. of གོང་གཅོག.

གོང་བཅད་ (koŋ jɛ̄ɛ̀) p. of གོང་གཅོད་.

གོང་ཆག (koŋ cāà) 1. on sale, at reduced price ¶ གོང་ཆག་དངོས་ཟོག Goods on sale. 2. vi. to have the price of sth. fall ¶ དེང་སང་འབྲས་ཀྱི་གོང་ཆག་བཞག These days the price of rice has fallen.

གོང་ཆུང་ (koŋjuŋ) cheap, inexpensive.

གོང་ཆེན་པོ་ (koŋ cēmbo) expensive.

གོང་བརྗོད་ (koŋ jöö) mentioned above, as said above ¶ གོང་བརྗོད་ལྟར་ As mentioned above.

གོང་གཉའ་ (koŋña) back of the neck.

གོང་གདམ་ (koŋdam) sm. གོང་སྒྲིག.

གོང་གདུག་སྙན་ཞུ་ (koŋduù ñɛ̃nshu) an appeal to higher court; va.—འབུལ་ to lodge an appeal to a higher court.

གོང་གདུག་བྱེད་མི་ (koŋduù ceèmi) plaintiff.

གོང་གདོང་ (koŋ dōŋ) va. to give a price ¶ ཚོང་པ་དེས་གོང་འདི་ཆེ་དྲགས་འདུག་ན་ཁྱེད་རང་གི་གོང་ཞིག་གདོང་དང་ཞེས་ལབ་པ་རེད་ The trader said, "If this is too expensive then you give me a price."

གོང་རྟགས་ (koŋdaà) 1. an emblem/ insignia on a shirt collar, a collar badge. 2. price tag.

གོང་བསྟོད་འོག་གནོན་ (koŋdöö wɔ̃nön) praising superiors and bullying those below [Lit. praise above, oppress below].

གོང་ཐག (koŋdaà) 1. final price, settled price; va.—ཆོད་ to settle/ finalize on a price ¶ ཁོ་གཉིས་ཅ་ལག་འདིའི་གོང་ཐག་ཆོད་མ་སོང་ Those two were unable to settle on a price. 2. a piece of horse tack that goes under the neck on the chest (breast collar).

གོང་ཐག་གཅོད་ (koŋdaà jöö) va. to decide on a price.

གོང་ཐག་ཆོད་ (koŋdaà cöö) see གོང་ཐག.

གོང་ཐང་ (koŋdaŋ) value, price.

གོང་ཐིག (koŋdig) decorative dots painted on a wall or window trim.

གོང་མཐའ་ (koŋda) at the top, at the highest level/ position.

གོང་མཐུད་འོག་འདྲེན་ (koŋdüü wondren) connecting sth. that preceded and followed.

གོང་མཐུན་ (koŋdün) 1. to agree with sth. above or that occurred before ¶ གནད་དོན་འདིའི་ཐོག་ངའི་བསམ་འཆར་གོང་མཐུན་ཡིན་ Concerning this issue, my opinion agrees with what was said/ written above. 2. reasonable/ customary price.

གོང་མཐོར་ (koŋdɔr) going up/ increasing/ going higher; vi.—འགྲོ་; —འཕེལ་ to go higher/ increase ¶ ཞིང་ལས་ཀྱི་ཐོན་སྐྱེད་གོང་མཐོར་འགྲོ་གི་ཡོད་པ་རེད་ Agricultural production is going higher. va.—གཏོང་; —སྤེལ་ to make higher/ better, to increase, to improve, to advance ¶ ཐབས་ཤེས་སྣ་ཚོགས་ཀྱིས་ཁོང་ཚོའི་ཤེས་ཚད་གོང་མཐོར་གཏོང་གི་ཡོད་པ་རེད་ (They) are improving their level of knowledge through different methods.

གོང་འདུས་ (koŋdüü) 1. sm. གོང་མཐུན་. 2. the title of the local head of Tromo.

གོང་འདྲེན་གནས་སྤར་ (koŋden nɛ̄ɛbar) transferring/ promoting to a higher position.

གོང་དུ་ (koŋdu) 1. above, before ¶ གོང་དུ་བཀོད་པ་བཞིན་ As written above. 2. higher ¶ གོང་དུ་འགྲོ་ To go higher. 3. (neg. + vb. + —) before ¶ ང་ཁ་ལག་མ་བཟས་གོང་དུ་ Before I ate.

གོང་དུ་བཀུར་ (koŋdu gūr) sm. གོང་བཀུར་ཞུ་.

གོང་དུ་ཇི་གསལ་བཞིན་ (koŋtu jisɛlshin) as stated above/ earlier.

གོང་དུ་བརྗོད་པ་ལྟར་ (koŋdu jöõbadar) sm. གོང་དུ་ཇི་གསལ་བཞིན་.

གོང་དུ་སྤེལ་ (koŋdu bēl) sm. གོང་སྤེལ་གཏོང་.

གོང་དུ་འཕེལ་ (kuŋdu pēl) sm. གོང་འཕེལ་འགྲོ་.

གོང་དུ་འཕྱུར་ (koŋdu cūr) vi. to rise (of water/ rivers).

གོང་དོན་འགལ་མེད་ (koŋdön gɛɛmeè) shung. not violating the contents mentioned above.

གོང་མདུད་ (koŋdüü) bow tie.

གོང་འདེགས་ (koŋdeg) sm. གོང་བཀུར་.

གོང་ན་དཔོན་མེད་ (koŋna bõnmeè) shung. arrogant, thinking there is no one higher than oneself.

གོང་ན་མེད་པ་ (koŋna meèba) 1. the best, unequaled ¶ ཕ་ལམ་དེ་གོང་ན་མེད་པ་ཞིག་རེད་ That is the best diamond.

གོང་ནས་ (koŋnɛ) 1. from above, from a superior ¶ ལས་ཀ་འདིའི་སྐོར་གོང་ནས་བཀའ་ཕེབས་ཀྱི་འདུག་ Regarding this work, the order is coming from above. 2. from before.

གོང་ནས་གོང་མཐོར་ (koŋnɛ koŋdɔr) sm. གོང་ནས་གོང་དུ་.

གོང་ནས་གོང་དུ་ (koŋnɛ koŋdu) higher and higher, better and better; va.—གཏོང་; —སྤེལ་ to improve, to raise, to develop, to make better/ higher, to enhance, to progress; vi.—འཕེལ་; —འགྲོ་ to get higher progress, to get better and better ¶ མི་དམངས་ཀྱི་གོ་རྟོགས་ཀྱི་ཚད་གོང་ནས་གོང་དུ་བཏང་པ་རེད་ They raised the consciousness of the people higher and higher. ¶ ཡུལ་གྱི་དཔལ་འབྱོར་གྱི་གནས་ཚད་གོང་ནས་གོང་དུ་སྤེལ་ཐབས་སུ་ For the purpose of improving the country's economy. ¶ ཞིང་ལས་ཡར་རྒྱས་ཀྱིས་མི་དམངས་ཀྱི་འཚོ་བའི་གནས་སྟངས་གོང་ནས་གོང་དུ་འཕེལ་པ་རེད་ Because of agricultural advancement the standard of living of the people has become better and better.

གོང་ནས་གོང་འཕེལ་ (koŋnɛ koŋ pēl) vi. to improve/ progress/ develop in succession.

གོང་ནས་འོག་ཏུ་ (koŋnɛ wɔgdu) from top to bottom ¶ ཡིག་ཆ་འདི་གོང་ནས་འོག་ཏུ་མི་ཚང་མར་བགྲམས་འདུག་ The document has been distributed to all the people from top to bottom.

གོང་ནས་འོག་བར་ (koŋnɛ wɔgpar) sm. གོང་ནས་འོག་ཏུ་.

གོང་པོ་ (koŋbo) 1. sm.གོང་བུ་. 2. creatures that crawl.

གོང་དཔོན་ (koŋbön) leaders/ chiefs above oneself.

གོང་སྤར་ (koŋ bār) va. to raise/ increase the price ¶ དེ་རིང་ཚོང་ཁང་ཚང་མས་གོང་སྤར་སོང་ All stores raised the price today.

གོང་སྤར་ཕྱིར་འཚོང་ (koŋbar cirdzoŋ) selling when the price is high.

གོང་སྤེལ་ (koŋbel) sm. གོང་འཕེལ་.

གོང་ཕྱེད་ (koŋjeè) half price.

གོང་འཕར་ (koŋ pār) vi. to have prices go up ¶ དེ་རིང་གོང་ཚང་མ་འཕར་བཞག་ Today all the prices went up.

གོང་འཕེལ་ (koŋbel) improvement, development, progress, advancement; va.—གཏོང་ to develop/ advance/ progress/ improve; vi.—འགྲོ་ to develop/ increase/ make progress ¶ དེ་ཕན་ལོ་ལྔའི་ནང་གི་དཔལ་འབྱོར་གོང་འཕེལ་ལ་བལྟས་ན་ If (we) look at the economic progress of the past five years.

གོང་འཕེལ་བློན་པོ་ (koŋpel lõmbo) Development Minister.

གོང་བ་ (koŋwa) collar, lapel, neckband.

གོང་བུ་ (koŋbu) 1. lump, heap, mass, ball ¶ ལྕགས་ཀྱི་གོང་བུ་ Iron ball/ lump. 2. entity ¶ ཆབ་སྲིད་ཀྱི་གོང་བུ་ Political entity.

གོང་བུ་གཅིག་གྱུར་ (koŋbu jiggyur) sm. གོང་བུ་ཆིག་སྒྲིལ་.

གོང་བུ་ཆིག་སྒྲིལ་ (koŋbu cigdril) united, unified; unity, solidarity ¶ བཙན་འཛུལ་ལ་ངོ་རྒོལ་བྱེད་པར་མི་ཚང་མའི་བསམ་ཕྱོགས་གོང་བུ་ཆིག་སྒྲིལ་དུ་གནས་ཡོད་ All the people are united in opposing aggression.

གོང་བུར་འཁྱིངས་ (koŋbur kēŋ) vi. to become solid/ coagulated, to get congealed ¶ མར་ཁུ་གོང་བུ་འཁྱིངས་བཞག་ The liquid butter has congealed.

གོང་བུར་འགྱུར་ (koŋbur gyur) sm. གོང་བུར་འཁྱིངས་.

གོང་འབབ་ (koŋbəb) price.

གོང་མ་ (koŋma) 1. emperor ¶ རྒྱ་ནག་གོང་མ་ Emperor of China. 2. the former, the previous, formerly, previously ¶ རྒྱལ་ཁབ་ཀྱི་སྲིད་འཛིན་གོང་མ་ཚོའི་སྐབས་ During the time of the former presidents of the country. 3. higher, superior ¶ ལས་ཁུངས་གོང་མ་རྣམས་ The higher offices.

གོང་མ་རྒྱ་གཞུང་ (koŋma gyashuŋ) shung. the royal/ imperial government of China.

གོང་མ་མཆོད་ཡོན་ (koŋma cõõyön) the priest-patron relationship between the Dalai Lama and the Emperors of China.

གོང་མ་བདག་པོ་ཆེན་པོ་ (koŋma dagbo cēmbo) shung. the great Emperor (of China).

གོང་མ་ཚང་ (koŋmatsaŋ) the emperor's household.

གོང་མ་སྲུང་མཁན་ (koŋma sūŋgɛn) 1. royalist. 2. one who guards the emperor.

གོང་མ་སྲེག (koŋmaseg) partridge.

གོང་མའི་བཀའ་ (koŋmɛ gā) shung. an order of the Emperor.

གོང་མའི་རྒྱལ་ཁབ་ (koŋmɛ gyɛɛgəb) kingdom.

གོང་མའི་གདུང་སྒམ་ (koŋmɛ duŋgam) imperial coffin.

གོང་མའི་ཕོ་བྲང་ (koŋmɛ pōdraŋ) imperial palace.

གོང་མའི་དབུ་བླ་ (koŋmɛ ūla) imperial preceptor.

གོང་མའི་ཡབ་གཞིས་ (koŋmɛ yəbshii) imperial estate.

གོང་མའི་ཡུམ་ཆེ་ (koŋmɛ yumdze) dowager empress, mother of the emperor.

གོང་མའི་སྲིད་གཞུང་ (koŋmɛ siishuŋ) imperial government, dynasty, kingdom.

གོང་མེད་ (koŋmeè) valueless, worthless, useless.

གོང་མོ་ (koŋmo) a kind of grouse.

གོང་སྨོས་ (koŋmöö) the above statement, what is said above ¶ གོང་སྨོས་ལྟར་ As said above.

གོང་ཙམ་ནས་ (koŋdzamnɛ) sm. གོང་ཙམ་ལ་.

གོང་ཙམ་ལ་ (koŋdzamla) just before ¶ 1912 ལོའི་གོང་ཙམ་ལ་ Just before 1912. ¶ ཁོང་མ་ཕེབས་གོང་ཙམ་ལ་ Just before he came.

གོང་བཙག (koŋ dzāā) va. to bargain on the price ¶ མི་དེས་གོང་ཞེ་དྲག་བཙག་གི་འདུག་ That person bargains a lot.

གོང་བཙག་བཙག (koŋ dzāgdzaā) sm. གོང་བཙག.

གོང་བཙག་བཙག་མེད་པ་ (koŋ dzāgdzaā meèba) price with no discount ¶ ཁོས་ཅ་ལག་དེ་གོང་བཙག་བཙག་མེད་པ་ཉོས་སོང་ He bought the thing without any discount.

གོང་ཚད་ (koŋdzɛɛ̀) price; va.—རྒྱག; —བྱེད་; —བཟོ་ to put a price on sth. ¶ ཅ་ལག་གསར་པ་འབྱུར་པ་འདི་

ཚོར་ད་ལྟ་གོང་ཚད་བཟོས་མི་འདུག Now (they) have not fixed a price on the new things that have arrived.

གོང་ཚད་འབེབས་ (koŋdzɛɛ beb) 1. va. to appraise ¶ ཅ་ལག་རྙིང་པ་དེ་ཚོར་གོང་ཚད་འབེབས་ཁག་པོ་འདུག It is difficult to appraise the price of old things. 2. va. to reduce price ¶ དེ་རིང་ཚོང་ཁང་ནས་ཅ་ལག་མང་པོ་གོང་ཚད་ཕབ་ནས་འཚོང་གི་འདུག Today the store is reducing the price on many items and selling them.

གོང་ཆེས་ཉིན་ (koŋdzēe ñin) the above mentioned date/ day.

གོང་ཚོད་ (koŋdzöö) appraisal, estimation of value/ price/ worth; va.—བྱེད་ ¶ ཅ་ལག་རྙིང་པ་དེ་ཚོར་གོང་ཚོད་བྱེད་ཁག་པོ་འདུག Making an appraisal on those old item is difficult.

གོང་མཚུངས་ (koŋdzuŋ) same as above, as/ like before, ditto.

གོང་འཚམས་པོ་ (koŋ tsāmbo) a reasonable price.

གོང་ཞུ་ (koŋshu) appealing to a superior; va.—བྱེད་ ¶ ཁྲིམས་ཁང་འོག་མ་ནས་ཐག་མ་ཆོད་སྐབས་གོང་ཞུ་བྱས་པ་རེད་ Because the lower court didn't settle the case, it was appealed above (to a higher court).

གོང་བཞིན་ (koŋshin) as above, as before ¶ གནད་དོན་འདིའི་སྐོར་ངའི་བསམ་འཆར་གོང་བཞིན་ཡིན་ Concerning this issue, my opinion is the same as (stated/ written) above.

གོང་འོག་ (koŋwɔɔ) high and low, upper and lower, top and bottom ¶ གྲོས་ཚོགས་གོང་འོག The Upper and Lower House (of Representatives). ¶ གྲལ་རིམ་གོང་འོག་ཚང་མའི་མི་སྣ་ People from high and low classes.

གོང་འོག་གཡས་གཡོན་ (koŋwɔɔ yɛɛyön) up and down and right and left.

གོང་ཡང་དིག (koŋ yaŋdii) the real/ final price.

གོང་རིམ་ (koŋrim) 1. the superior/ upper grade/ class/ strtum/ level. 2. the higher authorities.

གོང་རིམ་གྱི་མི་སྣ་ (koŋrimgi minə) 1. people in the upper strata, the upper classes. 2. the higher authorities.

གོང་རིམ་གྲལ་རིམ་ (koŋrim trɛɛrim) upper classes/ strata.

གོང་རིམ་ནས་ (koŋrimnɛ) from/ by the higher authorities.

གོང་རིམ་དཔོན་པོ་ (koŋrim bōmbo) leaders/ chiefs above oneself, the higher authorities.

གོང་རོལ་དུ་ (koŋröldu) before, earlier, prior to ¶ དམངས་གཙོའི་བཅོས་སྒྱུར་གྱི་གོང་རོལ་དུ་ཟམ་པ་དེ་བརྒྱབས་ཟིན་པ་རེད་ That bridge was built before the democratic reforms.

གོང་ལ་ (koŋla) 1. sm. གོང་དུ་. 2. a wall on a roof.

གོང་ལ་ངོ་དགའ་འགག་ལ་ཐུབ་ཚོད་ (koŋla ŋogaa gəblə tūbdzöö) sm. གོང་བསྟོད་འོག་གནོན་.

གོང་ལ་བཙག (koŋla dzāā) sm. གོང་བཙག.

གོང་ལ་བཙག་བཙག (koŋla dzāgdzaà) sm. གོང་ལ་བཙག་བཙག.

གོང་ལ་བཙག་བཙག་མེད་པ་ (koŋla meèba) sm. གོང་བཙག་བཙག་མེད་པ་.

གོང་ལ་ཤོར་ (koŋla shɔ̄r) vi. to have someone go aheadof one, to be/ get overtaken ¶ ཁོ་ངའི་གོང་ལ་ཤོར་ཡག་གི་སེམས་ཁྲལ་འདུག I am worried that he will overtake me.

གོང་ལབ་ (koŋləb) sm. གོང་བཤད་.

གོང་ལོ་ (koŋlo) the previous year.

གོང་གཤམ་ (koŋsham) 1. sm. གོང་འོག. 2. the brocade surrounding a thanka.

གོང་གཤོ་ (koŋsho) shung. sm. གོང་ཐང་.

གོང་བཤད་ (koŋshɛɛ) stated above, stated before.

གོང་ས་ (koŋsa) 1. the upper place/ position. 2. shung. the sovereign, the ruler. 3. the Dalai Lama ¶ གོང་ས་ལྔ་པ་ The Fifth Dalai Lama. ¶ གོང་ས་སྐུ་ཕྲེང་བཅུ་གསུམ་པ་ The Thirteenth Dalai Lama.

གོང་ས་སྐྱབས་མགོན་ (koŋsa gyəmgön) shung. sm. གོང་ས་སྐྱབས་མགོན་ཆེན་པོ་.

གོང་ས་སྐྱབས་མགོན་རྒྱལ་དབང་ (koŋsa gyəmgön gyɛɛwaŋ) shung. sm. གོང་ས་སྐྱབས་མགོན་ཆེན་པོ་.

གོང་ས་སྐྱབས་མགོན་ཆེན་པོ་ (koŋsa gyəmgön cēmbo) shung. the Dalai Lama.

གོང་ས་ཆེན་པོ་ (koŋsa cēmbo) shung. sm. གོང་ས་སྐྱབས་མགོན་ཆེན་པོ་.

གོང་ས་མཆོག (koŋsa cɔ̄ɔ) sm. གོང་ས་སྐྱབས་མགོན་ཆེན་པོ་.

གོང་ས་མཆོད་ཡོན་ (koŋsa cööyön) shung. 1. the Dalai Lama and the Regent. 2. the Dalai Lama and the Panchen Lama when one is tutor to the other.

གོང་སྲིད་བཀའ་གདན་དམར་ནག (koŋsii gādɛn mārnaà) shung. a land tenure document sealed with the Dalai Lama and the Regent seals (which are red and black).

གོང་སྲུང་བ་ (koŋsuŋwə) sm. གོང་མ་སྲུང་མཁན་.

གོང་སྲུང་དམག (koŋ sūŋmaà) palace guards, emperor's bodyguards.

གོང་སླ་པོ་ (koŋ lābo) cheap, inexpensive.

གོང་གསང་འོག་བརྙས་ (koŋsaŋ wɔɔ ñɛɛ) hoodwink those above and bully those below, keep things secret from those above and abuse those below.

གོང་གསང་འོག་སླུ་ (koŋsaŋ wɔɔlū) keeping things secret from one's superior and deceiving those below.

གོང་གསལ་ (koŋsɛl) above mentioned/ cited ¶ ཚོགས་པ་གོང་གསལ་ The above mentioned group.

གོད་ (köö) misfortune, disaster, calamity ¶ ད་ལོ་མི་ཚང་དེ་ར་སེམས་ཅན་ཤི་གོད་ཆེན་པོ་བྱུང་སོང་ This year that family had a great disaster with lots of animals dying.

གོད་ཀ་ (kööga) sm. གོད་ཆགས་.

གོད་ཁ་ (kööga) sm. གོད་ཆགས་.

གོད་ཆག (kööcaà) sm. གོད་ཆགས་.

གོད་ཆགས་ (kööcaà) misfortune, calamity, loss ¶ གོད་ཆག་ཚབས་ཆེན་ A serious misfortune.

གོད་ཆུང་ (kööjuŋ) 1. sm. ཟད་ཆུ་ཆུང་. 2. lesser disaster/ calamity/ misfortune.

གོད་གནད་ (köönɛɛ) sm. གོད་ཆགས་.

གོད་མ་ (kööma) remnants, remains, scraps.

གོན་ (kön) va. to wear (clothes).

གོན་ཉན་བྱེད་ཉན་མེད་པ་ (könñɛn ceèñɛn meèba) clothes that are unfit/ unsuitable/ ugly.

གོན་པ་ནང་འཚང་ཅན་ (komba naŋdzaŋjɛn) quilted/ padded clothes.

གོན་ཟད་ (konsɛɛ) worn out; vi. གོན་ཟད་; —ཐེབས་ to be/ get worn out.

གོན་ལོ་ (könlo) 1. vi. to be appropriate to wear ¶ དུག་ལོག་འདི་ཆུང་དྲག་ནས་གོན་ལོ་གི་མི་འདུག This shirt isn't appropriate to wear because it is too small.

གོན་ཤེད་ (könsheè) durable.

གོན་ཤེད་ཆེན་པོ་ (könsheè cēmbo) very durable.

གོན་ཤེད་མེད་པ་ (könsheè meèba) not durable.

གོབ་ (kob) 1. arrogant, proud, conceited. 2. old and worn out. 3. imp. of གབ་.

གོབ་དོ་ (kobdo) old, dilapidated, worn out.

གོབ་ཚ་པོ་ (kob tsābo) very arrogant/ proud/ conceited.

གོབ་ལོབ་ (komlob) sm. སྣ་བཙོས་.

གོམ་ (kom) abbr. of གོམ་པ་.

གོམ་ཁ་ (komga) style/ manner/ way of walking.

གོམ་འཁྱོར་ (komgyɔr) vi. to be lame, to limp.

གོམ་འགྲུལ་ (kom kyöö) va. to walk/ go on foot ¶ གྲོང་ཚོ་རྗེས་མ་དེ་རིང་ཉིན་མ་གཅིག་ལ་གོམ་འགྲུལ་ཐུབ་ཙམ་ཡོད་པ་རེད་ One is just able to walk to (reach) the next village by foot in one day.

གོམ་གང་ (komgaŋ) one step ¶ གོམ་གང་ཕྱིར་འཐེན་མ་བྱས་པ་རེད་ (They) did not withdraw one step.

གོམ་གང་གང་ (kom gaŋgaŋ) step-by-step; —བྱེད་.

གོམ་གང་མདུན་དུ་སྤོ་ (komgaŋ dündu bō) va. to take a step forward, to move forward ¶ ཞིང་ལས་འཕྲུལ་ཆས་ཅན་གྱི་ཕྱོགས་སུ་སྒྱུར་ཡང་གོམ་གང་མདུན་དུ་སྤོས་པ་རེད་ (They) took one step (forward) toward mechanized agriculture.

གོམ་གང་མདུན་སྤོས་ (komgaŋ dünböö) moving forward step-by-step/ gradually, steadily improving; va.—བྱེད་ ¶ རྒྱལ་ཁབ་ཁག་གི་མི་དམངས་དབར་གྱི་མཛའ་བརྩེའི་ཞི་གོམ་གང་མདུན་སྐྱོད་ཀྱིས་ས་བརྟན་དུ་འགྲོ་གི་ཡོད་པ་རེད་ The friendship of the people of the different countries is steadily becoming stronger.

གོམ་གང་ནོར་ན་གོམ་བརྒྱ་འགལ་ (ko̲mgaŋ nɔ̲ɔ̲na ko̲mgya gɛ̲ɛ̲) if one makes one mistake everything will go wrong, [a mistake of one step leads to one hundred steps].

གོམ་བགྲོད་ (ko̲mdröö̀) walking on foot; va.—བྱེད་.

གོམ་འགྲོས་ (ko̲mdröö̀) style/ manner of walking ¶ གོམ་འགྲོས་ཡང་པོ་ A light step.

གོམ་སྒྲ་ (ko̲mdra) sound of footsteps.

གོམ་སྒྲ་སིམ་པོ་ (ko̲mdra sī̀mbu) walking slowly and silently/ quietly.

གོམ་ཆེན་མདུན་སྐྱོད་ (ko̲mcɛn dü̲ngyöö̀) striding/ marching forward, forging ahead; va.—བྱེད་.

གོམ་ཆེན་མྱུར་སྐྱོས་ (ko̲mjɛn ñu̲rböö̀) going/ advancing fast; va.—བྱེད་.

གོམ་མཆོངས་ (ko̲mcoŋ) jumping/ hopping forward ¶ ཕྲུ་གུར་རྩེད་ཆས་གསར་པ་རག་ཙང་དགའ་ཐག་ཆོད་ནས་གོམ་མཆོངས་བརྒྱབ་ནས་ཡོང་གི་འདུག Because the children got new toys they were very happy and were coming jumping and hopping.

གོམ་སྟབས་ (ko̲mdəb) a step; va.—སྤོ་ to walk ¶ མདུན་སྐྱོད་ཀྱི་གོམ་སྟབས་ཆེན་པོ་ A big step forward. ¶ གོམ་སྟབས་མགྱོགས་པོ་སྤོས་ནས་ལུས་རྩལ་བྱེད་ཀྱི་ཡོད་པ་རེད་ (They) are exercising by walking fast.

གོམ་སྟབས་འཁྲུག (ko̲mdəb trūù) vi. to not march in unison, to fall out of unison marching.

གོམ་སྟབས་འགྲན་ (ko̲mdəb trɛ̲n) va. to compete in a foot race, to race.

གོམ་སྟབས་འགྲིག་པོ་ (ko̲mdəb dri̲gbu) marching in unison.

གོམ་སྟབས་གཅིག་པ་ (ko̲mdəb jī̀gbə) keeping in step/ in unison, marching in step, being unified; va.—བྱེད་ ¶ མི་དམངས་རྣམས་གོམ་སྟབས་གཅིག་པ་བྱས་ནས་ལས་འགུལ་དེའི་ནང་ཞུགས་པ་རེད་ The people, marching in unison, are participating in the campaign.

གོམ་སྟབས་ཆེན་པོས་མདུན་བསྐྱོད་ (ko̲mdəb cēmbö dü̲ngyöö̀) taking a big step forward, making great progress/ development.

གོམ་སྟབས་གཉིས་ (ko̲mdəb ñiì) "the two steps" [socialism and modern development].

གོམ་སྟབས་མཉམ་སྒྲིག (ko̲mdəb ñāmdrig) sm. གོམ་སྟབས་གཅིག་པ་.

གོམ་སྟབས་དལ་སྤོ་ (ko̲mdəb tɛ̲ɛ̲bo) walking slow.

གོམ་སྟབས་མྱུར་སྤོ་ (ko̲mdəb ñu̲rböö̀) walking fast.

གོམ་འདྲུད་འདྲིས་མ་ (ko̲mdröö̀ dre̲èma) half walking and half being dragged.

གོམ་པ་ (ko̲mba) a step; va.—སྤོ་; —རྒྱག to take a step, to walk ¶ གོམ་པ་བཞི་ཙམ་བརྒྱབ་འཕྲལ་ As soon as (he) walked about four steps.

གོམ་པ་འཁྱོར་ (ko̲mba kyōr) vi. to sway/ stagger while walking.

གོམ་པ་གང་གང་ (ko̲mba ka̲ŋgaŋ) step by step; va.—བྱེད་.

གོམ་པ་གང་གིས་གནམ་ལ་སླེབས་ (ko̲mba ka̲ŋgi nāmla lēè) in one step reach the sky [a term used during the 1955-56 Socialist Transformation campaign to indicate that China can move to socialism in one leap unlike the USSR's slower stage by stage progress].

གོམ་པ་རྒྱག (ko̲mba gya̲à) va. to walk, to take a step, to go on foot ¶ ཁོ་ཚོ་ལྷ་སར་གོམ་པ་བརྒྱབ་ནས་ཕྱིན་པ་རེད་ They went to Lhasa on foot.

གོམ་པ་སྔོན་སྤོས་ (ko̲mba ŋȫmböö̀) advancing forward, progressing, developing; va.—བྱེད་.

གོམ་པ་སྔོན་སྤོས་ཅན་ (ko̲mba ŋȫmböö̀jɛn) progressive, advanced.

གོམ་པ་བརྟན་པོ་ (ko̲mba dēmbo) sm. གོམ་ཚུགས་བརྟན་པོ་.

གོམ་པ་མདུན་སྤོས་ (ko̲mba dü̲nböö̀) 1. sm. གོམ་གང་མདུན་སྤོས་. 2. sm.གོམ་པ་སྔོན་སྤོས་.

གོམ་པ་ཡར་འདོར་ (ko̲mba ya̲ndor) sm. གོམ་གང་མདུན་སྤོས་.

གོམ་པ་རིམ་བགྲོད་ (ko̲mba ri̲mdröö̀) step by step, gradually.

གོམ་པ་རིམ་སྤོས་ (ko̲mba ri̲mböö̀) sm. གོམ་པ་རིམ་བགྲོད་.

གོམ་སྤོས་ (ko̲mböö̀) forward march! (military command).

གོམ་འཕྲས་ (ko̲mdrɛɛ̀) holding back taking a step forward, being unwilling to go forward; va. va.—རྒྱག.

གོམ་ཚུགས་བརྟན་པོ་ (ko̲mdzug dēmbo) 1. walking firmly/ steadily, walking without stumbling. 2. doing carefully; va.—རྒྱག ¶ ལས་ཀ་འགོ་ཚུགས་རྗེས་གོམ་ཚུགས་བརྟན་པོ་རྒྱག་དགོས་ After starting a job, one must do it carefully.

གོམ་ཚུལ་ (ko̲mdzul) sm. གོམ་སྟབས་.

གོམ་ཞང་ (ko̲mshaŋ) sm. གོམ་ཞེང་.

གོམ་ཞེང་ (ko̲msheŋ) the length of a step or pace, distance of a step ¶ གོམ་ཞེང་ཆེན་པོས་མདུན་སྐྱོད་བྱེད་དགོས་ By taking a big step and move forward.

གོམ་ཞེང་ཆུང་ཆུང་ (ko̲msheŋ cūŋjuŋ) short pace/ stride/ step; va. རྒྱག.

གོམ་ཞེང་ཆེན་པོ་ (ko̲msheŋ cēmbo) great/ large step; va.—རྒྱག.

གོམ་རིམ་ (ko̲mrim) by steps/ stages ¶ སློབ་གསོའི་གོམ་རིམ་ Steps in education.

གོམ་རིམ་རྗེས་མ་ (ko̲mrim je̲èma) the next step.

གོམ་རིམ་དང་པོ་ (ko̲mrim ta̲ŋbo) the first step.

གོམ་ལྡབས་ (ko̲mləb) sm. གོམ་ཞེང་.

གོམ་ལོབ་ (ko̲m lo̲b) va. to be lazy, to loaf on a job.

གོམ་ཤིང་ (ko̲mshiŋ) stock of a rifle.

གོམ་བཤོལ་ (ko̲mshöl) 1. taking a step backward, retreating, withdrawing; va.—བྱེད་ ¶ དམག་ས་ནས་གོམ་བཤོལ་བྱས་པ་རེད་ (They) retreated from the battleground. 2. compromise ¶ གྲོས་མོལ་བྱེད་སྐབས་ཕྱོགས་གཉིས་ཀས་གོམ་བཤོལ་བྱས་ན་གྲོས་ཐག་མགྱོགས་པོ་ཆོད་ཐུབ་ When you have discussions, if both parties compromise, you can settle things quickly.

གོམས་ (ko̲m) vi. to get accustomed to, to get used to, to adapt to ¶ ང་ཨ་རི་ར་ཡུན་རིང་བསྡད་ཙང་ཁོང་ཚོའི་ལུགས་སྲོལ་གོམས་འདུག Because I lived in America for a long time I got used to their customs.

གོམས་སྟོབས་ (ko̲mdob) experience, skill through practice.

གོམས་འདྲིས་ (ko̲mdriì) familiar, accustomed, used to; vi.—ཆགས་; —སུ་འགྱུར་ to become familiar with, to become a habit, to become accustomed to; va.—བྱེད་ to make familiar, to make accustomed, to make get used to ¶ ཡུལ་འདིའི་ཤེས་རིག་ལ་གོམ་འདྲིས་མེད་ (I) am not familiar with the culture of this country.

གོམས་འདྲིས་ཀྱི་ཁྲིམས་སྲོལ་ (ko̲mdriìgi trī̀msüü) customary law.

གོམས་འདྲིས་ངན་པ་ (ko̲mdriì ŋɛ̲mba) bad habit.

གོམས་འདྲིས་ཆེན་པོ་ (ko̲mdriì cēmbo) being accustomed/ used to sth.

གོམས་འདྲིས་རྙིང་པ་ (ko̲mdriì ñī̀ŋbə) old habits.

གོམས་པ་ (ko̲mba) sm. གོམས་འདྲིས་.

གོམས་པ་གློང་འགྱུར་ (ko̲mba lōŋgyur) vi. to get accustomed/ used to.

གོམས་པའི་སྐད་ཆ་ (ko̲mbɛ gɛ̄ɛ̀ca) habitual saying.

གོམས་པའི་ངང་ཚུལ་ (ko̲mbɛ ŋə̲ŋtsul) a habit.

གོམས་བྱ་ (ko̲mja) accustomed/ used to sth.; vi.—འགྱུར་; —ཆགས་ to become accustomed/ used to ¶ བོད་ལ་ལོ་མང་པོ་སྡོད་ན་རྩམ་པ་ཟ་ཡག་གོམས་བྱར་འགྱུར་གྱི་རེད་ If one lives in Tibet for many years one will get accustomed to eating tsampa.

གོམས་བྱང་ཐོན་པ་ (ko̲mjaŋ tȫmba) sm. བྱང་གོམས་ཐོན་པ་.

གོམས་སྦྱོང་ (ko̲mjoŋ) practicing to become skillful, learning to become proficient; va.—བྱེད་.

གོམས་སྦྱོང་བདར་གསུམ་ (ko̲mjoŋ dārsum) the three: getting accustomed, studying, and practicing;

va.—བྱེད་.

གོམས་ལོབས་སུ་འགྱུར་ (ko̱mlobsu gyu̱r) vi. to become habitual/ a habit.

གོམས་ཤུགས་ (ko̱mshuù) sm. གོམས་སྟོབས་.

གོམས་གཤིས་ (ko̱mshiì) sm. གོམས་འདྲིས་.

གོམས་གཤིས་དབང་ (ko̱mshiì wāŋ) a grammatical exception.

གོམས་སུ་འཇུག (ko̱msu ju̱g) va. to make oneself get used to sth. ¶ལུང་པ་གསར་པ་ཞིག་ལ་སླེབས་སྐབས་ཡུལ་དེའི་འཚོ་བའི་གཤིས་ལུགས་གོམས་སུ་འཇུག་རྒྱུ་དེ་གལ་ཆེན་པོ་ཡིན་ When (one) arrives in a new area it is very important to make yourself get used to that area's livelihood customs.

གོམས་སྲོལ་ (ko̱msöö) habits and customs.

གོར་ (kɔ̱r) 1. abbr. of གོར་ཁ་. 2. a type of livestock illness/ disease. 3. abbr. of གོ་རེ་.

གོར་ཁ་ (kɔ̱rka) 1. Gurkha (one of the ethnic groups of Nepal). 2. Nepal.

གོར་ཁ་ཀབ་ཏན་ (kɔ̱rka gəbdɛn) shung. the Nepalese Government Representative in Lhasa.

གོར་གོར་ (kɔ̱rgɔɔ) round, circular.

གོར་ཊམ་ (kɔ̱rdram) shung. Nepalese coin (tranka).

གོར་རྡོ་ (kɔ̱rdo) a water smoothed stone/ pebble.

གོར་ནད་ (kɔ̱rnɛɛ̀) rinderperst.

གོར་པ་ (kɔ̱rba) hard, tough, solid.

གོར་དཔོན་ (kɔ̱rbön) 1. shung. the Nepalese Government Representative in Lhasa. 2. a Nepalese official.

གོར་བ་ (kɔ̱rwa) a type of bread.

གོར་བུ་ (kɔ̱rbu) 1. a kind of square cushion. 2. sly, evasive.

གོར་བོད་ (kɔ̱rböö) abbr. Tibet and Nepal.

གོར་མ་ (kɔ̱rma) pebble, round cobblestone.

གོར་མ་བཀུམ་ (kɔ̱rmagum) sm. གོར་མ་ཆག.

གོར་མ་ཆག (kɔ̱rmajaà) no doubt, of course, sure, certainly ¶ཁྱེད་རང་སླར་ཡང་མཇལ་ན་ཚང་མ་དགའ་པོ་ཡོང་རྒྱུ་ཡིན་པ་གོར་མ་ཆག Of course they will all be happy to see you again.

གོར་མོ་ (kɔ̱rmo) sm. སྒོར་མོ་.

གོར་དམག (kɔ̱rmaà) Nepalese soldiers/ troops.

གོར་ལེབ་ (kɔ̱rleb) a type of bread.

གོར་ཥ་ (kɔ̱ɔ̱sha) sm. གོར་ཁ་.

གོར་ཤུགས་ (kɔ̱rshuù) shung. compensation paid to Nepal.

གོལ་ (kö̱ö̱) vi. to err, to make a mistake ¶འགྲུལ་པ་དེ་ལམ་གོལ་བ་རེད་ The traveler went on the wrong road.

གོལ་ཕི་ (kö̱lpi) eng. golf.

གོལ་མ་ (kö̱ö̱ma) hot food.

གོལ་ལམ་ (kö̱ö̱lam) shung. wrong path.

གོལ་ས་ (kö̱ö̱sa) 1. wrong road/ path. 2. error, mistake, fallacy. 3. area with precipices.

གོས་ (kö̱ö̀) 1. clothes, garments; va.—གྱོན་ to put on clothes, to wear clothes. 2. p. of འགོ་.

གོས་ཀྱིས་མི་བཟོ་ (kö̱ö̀gi mi̱ so̱) clothes make the man, clothing changes the appearance of a person.

གོས་དཀར་ཅན་ (kö̱ö̀ gārjɛn) 1. sb. wearing white/ whitish clothing. 2. tantric practitioner.

གོས་དཀར་ལྕང་ལོ་ཅན་ (kö̱ö̀gar jāŋlojɛn) a tantric practitioner (who has a long braided hair and wears white clothing).

གོས་དཀར་འཐབ་འཛིང་པ་ (kö̱ö̀gaa tāmdziŋba) a medical worker [Lit. fighter in white clothes].

གོས་རྐྱང་ (kö̱ö̀gyaŋ) unlined garment.

གོས་རྐྱོང་ (kö̱ö̀gyoŋ) a brocade covered cushion.

གོས་སྐུ་ (kö̱ö̀gu) huge applique thankas (religious banners).

གོས་སྐུད་ (kö̱ö̀güù) silk thread.

གོས་སྐུད་བརྒྱད་མ་ (kö̱ö̀güù gyɛ̱ɛ̀ma) eight ply silk/ satin thread.

གོས་ཁ་ (kö̱ö̀ga) a square brocade mat that is placed over a mattress.

གོས་ཁ་འབུས་ (kö̱ö̀gabüù) raw silk.

གོས་འཁོར་བརྒྱད་རྒྱ་སྨུག (kö̱ö̀gɔɔ gyɛ̱ɛ̀ gyə̱muù) shung. a type of maroon silk/ satin with a design of eight wheels.

གོས་འཁྲུད་འཕྲུལ་ཆས་ (kö̱ö̀drüù trüùjɛɛ̀) washing machine.

གོས་འཁྲུད་ཤིང་ལེབ་ (kö̱ö̀drüù shīŋleb) washboard.

གོས་གུར་ (kö̱ö̀gur) a tent with applique design.

གོས་གྲུམ་ (kö̱ö̀drum) cotton padded mattress with satin/ silk covering.

གོས་གྲུའུ་ (kö̱ö̀dru) tib.ch. abbr. of brocade and silk.

གོས་གྲོ་ལོ་མ་ (kö̱ö̀dro lo̱ma) shung. a type of satin/ silk with a design of wheat shoots.

གོས་སྐྱ་ (kö̱ö̀gya) a large applique thanka.

གོས་རྒྱུ་ (kö̱ö̀gyu) clothing material.

གོས་སྒབ་ (kö̱ö̀gab) hem.

གོས་སྒམ་ (kö̱ö̀gam) clothes box.

གོས་ཆེན་ (kö̱ö̀jen) brocade.

གོས་ཆེན་རྙས་ཀྱང་རི་མོའི་གཞུང་ (kö̱ö̀jen gɛ̱ɛ̀gyaŋ re̱mö shu̱ŋ) traces of beauty remain despite old age [Lit. even though the brocade has faded the pattern is still visible].

གོས་ཆེན་འཇམ་སང་ (kö̱ö̀jen ja̱msaŋ) plain brocade without design.

གོས་ཆེན་ཐགས་གྲུབ་མ་ (kö̱ö̀jen təgdrumə) brocade with woven designs of deities.

གོས་ཆེན་ཐབ་འཕྱིད་ (kö̱ö̀jen təbjiì) doing/ using sth. inappropriately [Lit. a brocade wiping cloth].

གོས་ཆེན་དར་ཆ་ (kö̱ö̀jen ta̱rca) silk banner.

གོས་ཆེན་སྤུ་མ་ (kö̱ö̀jen būmə) a type of brocade that has a velvet quality.

གོས་ཆེན་འབྲུག་རིས་མ (kö̱ö̀jen dru̱grimə) brocade with a dragon design.

གོས་ཆེན་རྩམ་ཁུག (kö̱ö̀jen dzəmguù) sm. གོས་ཆེན་རྩམ་ཁུག་ནང་ལ་སྦང་མའི་རྩམ་པ་.

གོས་ཆེན་རྩམ་ཁུག་ནང་ལ་སྦང་མའི་རྩམ་པ་ (kö̱ö̀jen dzəmguù na̱ŋla ba̱ŋmɛ dzāmba) putting sth. bad or worthless into sth. fancy (usu. for sb. who dresses beautiful but is stupid) [Lit. the worst tsamba (made from beer dregs) in a brocade tsamba pouch].

གོས་ཆེན་ཚོན་ཁྲ་ (kö̱ö̀jen tsȫndra) colored brocade.

གོས་ཆེན་གསེར་ཊམ་ (kö̱ö̀jen sērdram) gold thread brocade with a design of medallions.

གོས་ཆེན་གསེར་མ་ (kö̱ö̀jen sērma) gold brocade.

གོས་བརྗེ་ཁང་ (kö̱ö̀ jeègaŋ) dressing room, room to change clothes.

གོས་གཉིད་ (kö̱ö̀ñiì) taking a nap with one's clothes on; va.—རྒྱག.

གོས་རྙིང་ (kö̱ö̀ñiŋ) old clothes/ garments.

གོས་ཏའི་ཧུང་གི་རྣམ་སྦྱར་ (kö̱ö̀dɛ hūŋgi nāmjar) shung. a type of satin/ silk shawl worn by monks.

གོས་སྟོད (kö̱ö̀döö̀) upper vest/ garment with brocade lining on the exterior (worn by the monk officials in tt.).

གོས་ཐང་ (kö̱ö̀daŋ) an appliqué thanka; va.—བཞེངས་ to make an applique thanka.

གོས་ཐུ་ (kö̱ö̀du) front (part) of a dress/ jacket.

གོས་ཐུང་ (kö̱ö̀duŋ) 1. pants, trousers. 2. short coat.

གོས་ཐུང་གི་རྟ་ (kö̱ö̀duŋgidā) crotch of pants/ trousers.

གོས་ཐུང་ནང་འཇམ་ (kö̱ö̀duŋ na̱ŋjam) underwear, underpants.

གོས་ཐུང་ཨམ་ཕྲག (kö̱ö̀duŋ āmdraà) pant pocket.

གོས་མཐའ་ (kö̱ö̀da) the border of a dress.

གོས་གདང་ (kö̱ö̀daŋ) a horizontal hanging pole for coat hangers.

གོས་ལྡིང་ (kö̱ö̀deŋ) enough material for dress ¶གོས་ཆེན་གོས་ལྡིང་གཅིག་ལག་རྟགས་ལ་སྤྲད་བྱུང་ I was given a gift of brocade that was enough for one dress.

གོས་ནག་མ་ (kö̱ö̀ na̱gma) black clothes, people who dress in black.

གོས་སྣ་ (kö̱ö̀na) varieties of clothes.

གོས་སྣ་འཛོམས་པོ་ (kö̱ö̀na dzo̱mbo) abundant clothes.

གོས་པང་ (kü̱ö̀baŋ) woman's brocade apron.

གོས་དཔེ་གསར་ (k̲ö̲ö bēsar) new style clothes, new fashions.

གོས་དཔུད་ལྡན་ (k̲ö̲ö jɛndɛn) shung. brocade/ silk with large lotus design.

གོས་བུ་རིས་མ་ (k̲ö̲ö būrimə) velvet.

གོས་ཕོགས་ (k̲ö̲öbɔɔ̀) clothing ration/ salary.

གོས་ཕྲ་ (k̲ö̲ödra) fine quality silk.

གོས་འཕན་ (k̲ö̲öben) brocade decorative hangings used on pillars in temples and monasteries.

གོས་བེར་ (k̲ö̲öber) monk's cloak.

གོས་བྲལ་ (k̲ö̲ödrɛɛ) 1. naked. 2. unpolluted, pure.

གོས་འབོལ་ (k̲ö̲mböö) brocade covered Tibetan cushion.

གོས་འབྲུག་རིས་ཅན་ (k̲ö̲ödrug r̲i̲ijɛn) brocade with dragon designs.

གོས་འབྲུག་རིས་མ་ (k̲ö̲ödrug r̲i̲imə) sm. གོས་འབྲུག་རིས་ཅན་.

གོས་མེད་ (k̲ö̲ömeè) without clothes, naked.

གོས་ཚགས་ (k̲ö̲ödzag) style of dressing.

གོས་འཛར་ (k̲ö̲ndzar) 1. clothes (usu. shirts) with tassels at the bottom. 2. shirts that hang out, dresses that are not tied at the waist.

གོས་གཞི་འཛམ་བུ་རིས་མ་ (k̲ö̲öshi j̲a̲mbu r̲i̲mə) shung. a type of satin/ silk with textured patterns.

གོས་གཤུག (k̲ö̲öshug) hem (of a garment), lower part of a gown.

གོས་ཟས (k̲ö̲öbsɛɛ̀) 1. clothing. 2. clothing and food.

གོས་ཟེགས་ (k̲ö̲ösɛɛ̀) 1. tattered/ worn-out clothing. 2. leftover material when making clothing.

གོས་བཟོ་ (k̲ö̲öso) 1. style or design of clothing. 2. tailoring of clothing.

གོས་བཟོ་བ་ (k̲ö̲ö s̲o̲wa) tailor, seamstress.

གོས་ཡིག་རིས་མ་ (k̲ö̲öyig r̲i̲imə) brocade with Chinese characters woven into it.

གོས་ཡུག (k̲ö̲öyug) a roll/ bolt of brocade or material.

གོས་ལ་ (k̲ö̲öla) clothes.

གོས་ལོག (k̲ö̲öloò) clothes.

གོས་ལོག་ཐང་ཡུག (k̲ö̲öloò tāŋyuù) shung. a piece of brocade/ satin/ silk large enough to make a dress.

གོས་གཤམ་ (k̲ö̲ösham) sm. གོས་ཤམ་.

གོས་ཤུལ་ (k̲ö̲öshüü) folds/ pleats in the back of a Tibetan dress.

གོས་སློག (k̲ö̲ölɔɔ̀) sm. གོས་ལོག.

གོས་གསར་མ་ (k̲ö̲ö sārma) 1. clothes that are brand new. 2. a change of clothing, spare clothes.

གོས་བསུ་ (k̲ö̲ösu) clothes sent to the in-marrying bride/ bridegroom by the family into which they are marrying.

གོས་ཧྲུལ་ (k̲ö̲öhrüü) tattered/ ragged clothes.

གོས་ཧྲུལ་སྐྲ་འཛིང་ (k̲ö̲öhrul drādziŋ) disheveled hair and tattered clothes.

གོས་ལྷམ་ (k̲ö̲ölham) 1. brocade shoes. 2. clothing and shoes.

གྭ་ (gwa̲) white forehead (for yaks and horses) ། གཡག་གྭ་ཡོད་པ་ A yak with a white forehead.

གྭ་གྭ་ (gwa̲gwa) ch. melon, vegetables with seeds like cucumbers.

གྭ་ཏེ་མ་ལ་ (gwa̲dema̲la) Guatemala.

གྭ་དོར་ (gwa̲dɔɔ) sm. ཁྲག་དུ་.

གྭ་པ་ (gwa̲ba) an animal with a white forehead.

གྭ་ཤུར་ (gwa̲shur) a broad white patch that runs from the forehead of a (horse or yak) to the end of the nose.

ཀྱ་ (kya̲) numerical particles for the eighties ། བརྒྱད་བཅུ་ཀྱ་གསུམ་ Eighty three.

ཀྱ་ཀྱུ་ (kya̲gyu) deceit, guile; va.—བྱེད་ to deceive/ tricky.

ཀྱ་ཀྱུ་ཅན་ (kya̲gyüüjɛn) deceitful, devious, trickery.

ཀྱ་ཀྱུའི་བློ་ (kya̲gyü lō) sm. ཀྱ་ཀྱུར་ཅན་.

ཀྱ་ཉེས་ (kya̲ñeè) bad strategy, unwise.

ཀྱ་ཐོ་ (kya̲do) arc. earring.

ཀྱ་དོ་ (kya̲do) sm. ཀྱ་ཐོ་.

ཀྱ་ནོམ་པ་ (kya̲ nōmba) abundant, plentiful, lots, much ། ཚང་མར་ཟས་གོས་ཀྱ་ནོམ་པ་སྤྲད་པ་རེད་ (They) gave all of them lots of food and clothing.

ཀྱ་ནོམ་པོ་ (kya̲ nōmbo) sth. that satisfies one's wants, sth. that is satisfactory ། བཟོ་པ་དེ་ར་གླ་ཆ་ཀྱ་ནོམ་པོ་སྤྲད་པ་རེད་ They paid that worker a satisfactory wage.

ཀྱ་མ་ཀྱུ་ (kya̲magyu) not too upright, not too bent.

ཀྱ་རྫོམ་པ་ (kya̲ dzōmba) sm. ཀྱ་ཚོམ་.

ཀྱ་ཚོམ་ (kya̲dzom) acting without first checking sth. out, acting blindly ། མི་དེ་ཀྱ་ཚོམ་དུ་གཞན་རྗེས་སུ་འགྲོ་མཁན་ཞིག་རེད་ That man is sb. who blindly follows others.

ཀྱ་རི་ཀྱུ་རི་ (gya̲ri gyu̲ri) 1. vacillating ། བསམ་བློ་ཀྱ་རི་ཀྱུ་རི་ Vacillating thoughts. 2. sm. ཀྱ་ཀྱུ་.

ཀྱག (kya̲g) destroying, damaging.

ཀྱག་ཀྱུག (kyaggyɔɔ̀) winding, crooked.

ཀྱང་ (kya̲ŋ) a fence-like wall; va.—རྒྱག; —རྩིག to build a wall ། ཁང་པ་དེ་ར་ཀྱང་གིས་བསྐོར་བ་རེད་ That house was surrounded by a wall. 2. sm. རྒྱང་.

ཀྱང་སྐུ་ (kya̲ŋgu) paintings of the Buddha and other deities on walls.

ཀྱང་སྐོར་ (kya̲ŋgɔɔ) 1. a wall that encloses or surrounds sth. ། ཁང་པའི་མཐའ་ལ་ཀྱང་སྐོར་ཞིག་འདུག The house's perimeter is surrounded by a wall. 2. va. to surround or enclose with a wall ། ཁང་པའི་མཐའ་ལ་ཀྱང་བསྐོར་བཞག (They) built a wall to surround the house.

ཀྱང་ཁའི་རྩྭ་ (kya̲ŋgɛ dzā) sb. with no definite view/ position, one who sways with the prevailing wind [Lit. grass at the edge of a wall].

ཀྱང་གོག (gya̲ŋgɔɔ̀) ruins of a wall/ building/ house.

ཀྱང་ཀྱེང་ (kya̲ŋgyeŋ) abbr. of ཀྱང་ངེ་ཀྱེང་ངེ་.

ཀྱང་ཀྱོང་ (kya̲ŋgyoŋ) abbr. of ཀྱང་ངེ་ཀྱོང་ངེ་.

ཀྱང་འགྱེལ་དབྱུག་པས་མི་ལྡོང་ (kya̲ŋgyee yūgbɛ m̲i̲loŋ) uncontrollable/ unmanageable situation, impossible to repair or restore [Lit. one can not hold up a falling wall with a stick].

ཀྱང་འགྲེམས་ (kyāŋ drēm) va. to put/ hang on a wall.

ཀྱང་རྒྱག (kyāŋ gya̲à) va. to a build wall. 2. sm.* རྒྱང་རྒྱག.

ཀྱང་རྒྱུག (kya̲ŋgyuù) wooden implements used for building walls.

ཀྱང་རྒྱོང་ (kya̲ŋgyoŋ) va. to stuff/ pound earthen materials when building a wall.

ཀྱང་སྒམ་ (kya̲ŋgam) a closet inset in a wall, a wall chest.

ཀྱང་སྒྲོམ (kya̲ndrom) the wooden frame into which earth is pounded when building a wall.

ཀྱང་ངེ་ཀྱེང་ངེ་ (kya̲ŋŋe kye̲ŋŋe) 1. pride. 2. sm. ཀྱང་ངེ་ཀྱོང་ངེ་.

ཀྱང་ངེ་ཀྱོང་ངེ་ (kya̲ŋŋe kyo̲ŋŋe) a hard headed/ difficult person, sb. who doesn't take orders well.

ཀྱང་ངོས་ (kya̲ŋŋöö) the surface of a wall.

ཀྱང་བཅག (kya̲njaà) sm. ཀྱང་ཀྱོང་.

ཀྱང་ལྡེབས་ (kya̲ndeb) sm. ཀྱང་ངོས་.

ཀྱང་སྡེང་གི་རྩྭ་ (kya̲ndeŋgi dzā) sm. ཀྱང་ཁའི་རྩྭ་.

ཀྱང་དུང་ (kya̲ndu̲ŋ) sm. ཀྱང་རྒྱོང་.

ཀྱང་ན་ཉིང་ལོག་ནས་ཐལ་ད་ལོ་ལངས་ (kya̲ŋ n̲a̲niŋ l̲ɔ̲ɔ̀nɛ dü̲l t̲a̲lo la̲ŋ) the results of sth. do not manifest themselves until much later [Lit. although the wall collapsed last year, the dust rose this year].

ཀྱང་ནག་ཁ་སྦྱོར་ (kya̲ŋnag kājor) causing/ instigating trouble [Lit. to stick two black walls together face-to-face].

ཀྱང་པང་ (kya̲npaŋ) wall planks.

ཀྱང་ཕག (kya̲ŋpag) bricks for making walls.

ཀྱང་ཕྲེང་ (kya̲ntreŋ) vertical section of a wall.

ཀྱང་རྩ་ (kya̲ndza) foundation of wall.

ཀྱང་རྩིག (kya̲ndzig) sm. ཀྱང་.

ཀྱང་བརྩིགས་ (kya̲ŋ dzīī) see ཀྱང་.

ཀྱང་མཚམས་ (kya̲ndzam) juncture/ line at which one section of a wall ends and a new section is built on top of it.

གྱང་བཞུ་ (kya̲ŋshu) a wall lamp.

གྱང་བཞོན་རིང་ལུགས་ (kya̲ŋshön ri̲ŋluù) straddling-the-fenceism.

གྱང་ཡིག (kya̲ŋyiì) wall newspaper/ poster.

གྱང་ར་ (kya̲ŋra) a walled/ fenced in enclosure (usu. for keeping animals).

གྱང་རིས་ (kya̲ŋriì) fresco, wall painting, mural.

གྱང་རུལ (kya̲ŋrüù) a ruined/ broken down wall.

གྱང་རོ་ (kya̲ŋro) ruins.

གྱང་རོལ་ (kya̲ŋrö) sm. གྱང་རོ་.

གྱང་ལ་རྡེབ་ (kya̲ŋla de̲b) vi. to be/ get rebuffed, to run up against a stone wall [Lit. bang against a stone wall].

གྱང་ལག (kya̲ŋlaà) a wall separating two rooms.

གྱང་ལོགས་ (kya̲ŋlɔɔ̀) sm. གྱང་ངོས་.

གྱང་ཤིང་ (kya̲ŋshiŋ) the frame in which mud is pounded to construct a wall.

གྱང་གསེབ་ (kya̲ŋseb) the space between the walls.

གྱད་ (kyɛ̲ɛ̀) 1. strength; strong. 2. a short, strong man.

གྱད་ཆེན་ (kyɛ̲ɛ̀jen) extremely strong.

གྱད་སྟོབས་ (kyɛ̲ɛ̀dob) strong.

གྱད་འཐབ་ (kyɛ̲ɛ̀dəb) tests of strength in athletic competitions; va.—འགྲན་ to compete in athletic tests of strength.

གྱད་རྡོ་ (kyɛ̲ɛ̀do) a heavy stone used in a Tibetan competition of strength.

གྱད་ནར་སོན་ (kyɛ̲ɛ̀nr sõn) va. to become fully mature with the strength of a strong man.

གྱད་མི་ (kyɛ̲ɛ̀mi) a powerful/ strong man.

གྱད་འཛིང་ (kyɛ̲ɛ̀dziŋ) sm. གྱད་འཐབ་.

གྱད་ཤུགས་ (kyɛ̲ɛ̀shig) sm. གྱད་སྟོབས་.

གྱབས་ (kyə̲b) kidding, joking.

གྱམ་ (kya̲m) a recess (in a rock), a shelter (under a rock).

གྱམ་ཁ་ (kyə̲mka) bottom land, land near a river, flood plain.

གྱམ་བུ་ (kyə̲mbu) small cave.

གྱར་ (kya̲r) vi. 1. to get/ fall into a state or situation ། གནས་སྐབས་སྐྱོ་པོ་ཞིག་ལ་གྱར་བ་རེད་ (They) fell into a sad situation. 2. vi. to go astray, to get separated (from a group/ herd/ etc.) ། གཡག་གཅིག་ཁྱུ་ནས་གྱར་འདུག One yak strayed from the herd. 3. vi. to move/ wander to another place ། རང་ཡུལ་དུ་མུ་གེ་བྱུང་སྐབས་གཞན་ཡུལ་དུ་གྱར་བ་རེད་ Because there was famine in (his) own homeland he wandered off to another place. 4. va. to spread/ distribute/ disseminate ། སྐད་ཆ་འདི་ཕྱི་ལ་གྱར་མི་ཆོག It is not permitted to spread (say) this talk outside.

གྱར་འཛུལ་ (kya̲rdzül) wandering/ moving to different region; va.—བྱེད་ ། དམག་ཕོར་ཙང་རྒྱ་གར་ནས་མི་མང་པོ་བོད་དུ་གྱར་འཛུལ་བྱས་སོང་ Because they lost the war many people from India wandered into Tibet.

གྱལ་གྱོལ་ (kyɛlgyöö) winding, twisting, torturous.

གྱི་ (kyi) genitive particle used after final ན་, མ་, ར་, ལ་.

གྱི་ན་བ་ (kyi̲nawa) 1. inferior quality. 2. low ranking.

གྱི་ལིང་ (kyi̲liŋ) a fine quality horse.

གྱིག (gyi̲g) rubber.

གྱིག་སྐུད་ (gyiggüù) plastic string/ rope.

གྱིག་ཁུག (gyi̲gguù) rubber/ plastic bag.

གྱིག་འཁོར་ (gyiggɔɔ) rubber tire.

གྱིག་ཤིང་ (gyigshiŋ) rubber plant/ tree.

གྱིག་ལྷམ་ (gyi̲glham) rubber boots, rubber shoes.

གྱིན་ (gyi̲n) sm. ཀྱིན་ (but used after final ན་, མ་, ར་ and ལ་).

གྱིན་འདའ་བ་ (gyi̲ndawa) shung. a mediocre person.

གྱིམ་པོ་ (gyi̲mbu) shung. sentry, guard.

གྱིམ་ཤིང་ཀོང་ཇོ་ (kyi̲mshiŋ gõŋjo) Tang dynasty Chinese princess who married the Tibetan King Tride Tsugden in 710 A.D.

གྱིམ་ཤུང་ (gyi̲mshuŋ) shung. good and bad.

གྱིས་ (gi) 1. sm. ཀྱིས་ (but used after final ན་, མ་, ར་ and 2. imp. of བགྱི་. 3. (vb. + —) do it! (conveys imperative).

གྱུ་བ་ (gyu̲wə) shung. respectful.

གྱུག་གྱུག (kyu̲ggyug) shining, shimmering, glimmering.

གྱུར་ (kyu̲r) p. of འགྱུར་.

གྱུར་ཅིག་གུ་ (kyu̲rjigu) may it come (usu. used at the end of a prayer) ། འཛམ་གླིང་ཞི་བདེ་ཡོང་བར་གྱུར་ཅིག་གུ་ May world peace come.

གྱུར་དུག (kyu̲rdug) edible things that become poisonous.

གྱུར་མིད་ (kyu̲rmiì) sm. ཁྱུར་མིག.

གྱེད་ (kyeè) sm. འགྱེད་.

གྱེན་ (kye̲n) uphill, upwards ། ང་ཚོ་རིའི་གྱེན་དུ་འཛེགས་སྐབས་ When we were climbing up the hill.

གྱེན་འགོག (kye̲ŋgɔɔ̀) confronting, opposing; va.—བྱེད་.

གྱེན་གོལ་ (kye̲ŋgöö) sm. གྱེན་ལོག.

གྱེན་ཆུ་གྲུ་གཏོང་ (kye̲nju tru̲doŋ) a difficult task [Lit. paddling a boat upstream].

གྱེན་ཐུར་ (kye̲ndur) slopes, inclines, uphills and downhills, up and down; va.—སློག to throw into confusion/ disorder ། གྱེན་ཐུར་གཟར་པོ་ A steep slope. ། ས་ཆ་འདི་གྱེན་ཐུར་མང་པོ་ཡོད་ས་ཞིག་རེད་ This place has a lot of slopes (uphills and downhills).

གྱེན་འཐེན་ (kye̲nden) pulling/ drawing/ hauling upwards; va.—བྱེད་ to pull (haul upwards ། གཙང་པོའི་གྱེན་དུ་གྲུ་གྱེན་འཐེན་བྱེད་བཞིན་འདུག (They) are pulling the boat upwards against the river's current.

གྱེན་འཐེན་ལྕགས་ཐག་དཀྲི་སའི་འཕྲུལ་འཁོར་ (kye̲nden jãgdaà drĩsɛ trũũgɔɔ) a hoisting machine.

གྱེན་དམ་པོ་ (kye̲n da̲mbo) sm. གྱེན་གཟར་པ་.

གྱེན་དུ་ (kye̲ndu) upward, uphill, up; va.—འདེགས་ to raise/ lift up.

གྱེན་དུ་འགྲེང་ (kye̲ndu dre̲ŋ) 1. va. to erect, to raise vertically. 2. to get an erection ། ཧྲིག་པ་གྱེན་དུ་འགྲེང་སོང་ (His) penis got erect.

གྱེན་འདེགས་ (kye̲ndeg) lifting/ hoisting/ elevating; va.—བྱེད་.

གྱེན་འདྲེན་ (kye̲ndren) sm. གྱེན་འཐེན་.

གྱེན་ལོག (kye̲ndɔg) revolting against, rebelling against, rising up against; va.—བྱེད་ ། མི་དམངས་ཀྱིས་དམག་དོན་སྲིད་དབང་ལ་གྱེན་ལོག་བྱས་པ་རེད་ The people rebelled against the military dictatorship.

གྱེན་ལོག་གི་རང་བཞིན་ (kye̲ndɔggi rə̲ŋshin) the nature of rebelliousness.

གྱེན་ལོག་པ་ (kye̲ndɔgba) a rebel.

གྱེན་ལོག་ཤོག་ཁག (kye̲ndɔg shɔ̃ɔ̀gaà) rebel group/ clique.

གྱེན་བརྡོལ་ (kye̲ndöö̀) breaking/ surging through, overflowing.

གྱེན་པ་ (kye̲mba) 1. playing hard to get; va.—ཤོད་ ། ཁོ་རང་རྩེད་མོ་རྩེ་འདོད་ཡོད་ཀྱང་གྱེན་པ་བཤད་ནས་ལམ་སང་ལན་བྱེད་ཀྱི་མི་འདུག Even though he wants to play, he plays hard to get and doesn't immediately agree. 2. not obliging others when they ask a favor, declining to do sth. when asked.

གྱེན་པ་ཚ་པོ་ (kye̲nba tsābo) sb. exhibiting the characteristics of གྱེན་པ་.

གྱེན་འཕུར་ (kye̲nbur) flying upwards; va.—བྱེད་ ། གནམ་གྲུ་གྱེན་འཕུར་བྱེད་དུས་ When the plane was flying upwards.

གྱེན་འཕུར་གནམ་གྲུ་ (kye̲nbur nə̄mdru) helicopter.

གྱེན་འཕྱུར་ཆུ་མིག (kye̲njur cūmig) geyser.

གྱེན་འཕྱུར་ཆུ་རྫིང་ (kye̲njur cūdziŋ) water fountain.

གྱེན་འཕྱུར་འཐོར་ཆུ་ (kye̲njur tɔ̄rju) sm. གྱེན་འཕྱུར་ཆུ་རྫིང་.

གྱེན་མ་གསེག (kye̲nmaseg) a gentle slope/ incline.

གྱེན་བཞར་ (kye̲nshar) shaving against the grain (of hair growth); va.—རྒྱག.

གྱེན་ཟུར་ (kye̲nsur) angle of elevation/ steepness.

གྱེན་ཀློག (kye̲ndɔɔ̀) sm. གྱེན་ལྡོག.

གྱེན་གཟར་པོ་ (kye̲n sa̲rbo) a steep slope/ incline.

གྱེན་ལངས་ (kye̲nlaŋ) sm. གྱེན་ལྡོག.

གྱེན་ལན་ཐུར་སྦྲོད་ (kye̲nlɛn tūrdröö̀) people following the example of their leader.

གྱེན་ལམ་ (kye̲nlam) uphill road.

གྱེན་ལོག (kye̲nlɔɔ̀) 1. sm. གྱེན་ལྡོག. 2. name of one of the two main Red Guard groups in Tibet. 3. name of several anticommunist rebel groups who adopted the Red Guard group name and staged uprisings in and about 1969.

གྱེན་གསེག (kye̲nseg) sm. གྱེན་མ་གསེག.

གྱེར་ (kye̲r) va. to chant, to sing.

གྱེར་དབྱངས་ (kye̲ryaŋ) tune, melody.

གྱེས་ (kye̲è) p. of འགྱེ་.

གྱེས་ཁ་ (kye̲èga) at the point of departure, just prior to departure.

གྱེས་ཁར་ (kye̲ègar) sm. གྱེས་ཁ་.

གྱེས་ཆང་ (kye̲èjaŋ) ཆང་ drunk at the time of departure/ separation.

གྱེས་མཇལ་ (kye̲èjɛɛ) meeting at or just before departing/ separating.

གྱེས་སྟོན་ (kye̲èdön) farewell party/ banquet.

གྱེས་ཐོན་འགྱུར་ལྡོག (kye̲èdön gyu̲ndoò) fission (in physics).

གྱེས་རྡུལ་ (kye̲èdüü) an ion ¶ གྱེས་རྡུལ་ཕོ་ Positive ion.

གྱེས་བྲལ་ (kye̲èdrɛɛ) separating, separation.

གྱེས་འཚམས་ཞུ་ (gye̲ndzam shu̲) va. to bid farewell.

གྱེས་འཛོམས་ (kye̲ndzom) reunion; va.—བྱེད་ to make/ hold a reunion [Lit. separating, coming together].

གྱེས་རབས་ (kye̲èrəb) the history/ record of a separation.

གྱེས་སོ་ (kye̲èso) y-shaped fork of a tree or crossroad.

གྱེས་གསོལ་སྟོན་ (kye̲èsödön) farewell dinner.

གྱོ་དུམ་ (kyo̲dum) broken brick.

གྱོ་རྡུལ་ (kyo̲düü) ion.

གྱོ་རྡུལ་འབྲེལ་མདང་ (kyo̲düü dre̲e̲daŋ) ionic bond, ionic link.

གྱོ་མོ་ (kyo̲mo) brick, tile, ceramics.

གྱོ་རྫི་ (kyo̲dzi) glaze.

གྱོ་རྫིའི་རྒྱ་ཕིབས་ (kyo̲dzii gyə̲bib) tiled roof.

གྱོ་བཟོ་བ་ (kyo̲sowa) tiler, plasterer.

གྱོག་པོ་ (kyo̲gbo) crooked, curved.

གྱོང་ (kyo̲ŋ) a loss; vi.—ཕོག་; —འཕོག་; —རགས་ to incur/ suffer a loss (usu. in business); va.—གཏོང་ to make sb. suffer a loss (by cheating/ dishonesty) ¶ ད་ལོ་ཁོ་ཚོར་གྱོང་ཆེན་པོ་ཕོག་པ་རེད་ They suffered a great loss this year. ¶ ཁོ་ཕྱུག་པོ་གཞན་ལ་གྱོང་བཏང་ནས་ཆགས་པ་རེད་ He became rich by causing others to suffer losses.

གྱོང་བསྐུར་ (kyo̲ŋgur) sm. གྱོང་གཏོང་.

གྱོང་མཁྲེགས་ (kyo̲ŋdreg) hard, tough.

གྱོང་འཁེལ་ (kyo̲ŋkee) sm. གྱོང་ཕོག.

གྱོང་འཁྱེར་ (kyo̲ŋkyer) va. to accept a loss/ defeat.

གྱོང་གན་ (kyo̲ŋgɛn) sm. གྱོང་གུན་.

གྱོང་གུན་ (kyo̲ŋgün) a loss/ deficit; va.—གཏོང་; —བྱེད་; —བཟོ་ to cause sb. to suffer a loss ¶ ཁོ་ལ་གྱོང་གུན་ཆེན་པོ་བྱུང་པ་རེད་ He suffered a great loss. ¶ ཁོས་མོར་གྱོང་གུན་ཆེན་པོ་བཏང་བ་རེད་ He made her suffer a great loss.

གྱོང་གྱོང་ (kyo̲ŋkyoŋ) sm. གྱོང་པོ་.

གྱོང་རྒུད་ (kyo̲ŋgüù) sm. གྱོང་གུན་.

གྱོང་མཉམ་ཐུག་པ་ (kyo̲ŋñam tūgba) equally stubborn /unyielding, two parties each of whom will not give in to the other.

གྱོང་མཉམ་གདོང་གདུགས་ (kyo̲ŋñam do̲ŋdug) two equally stubborn/ unyielding persons coming face to face in a dispute/ fight, etc.

གྱོང་གཏོང་ (kyo̲ŋ dōŋ) see གྱོང་.

གྱོང་སྟེར (kyo̲ŋ dēr) sm. གྱོང་གུན་གཏོང.

གྱོང་པོ་ (kyo̲ŋbo) 1. strong, tough, self-sufficient, able to take care of oneself, competent ¶ མི་འདི་གྱོང་པོ་འདུག This man is able to take care of himself. 2. rough, coarse in texture and manners.

གྱོང་ཕོག (kyo̲ŋ pɔ̄ɔ̀) see གྱོང་.

གྱོང་རྩུབ་ (kyo̲ŋdzub) harsh, rough, coarse (of materials and manners).

གྱོང་རགས་ (kyo̲ŋraà) see གྱོང.

གྱོང་རལ་ (kyo̲ŋrɛɛ) foam, froth.

གྱོང་རོ་ (kyo̲ŋro) a dried-up shriveled corpse, a mummy.

གྱོང་རོལ་ (kyo̲ŋröö) sm. གྱོང་རལ་.

གྱོང་སེལ་ཁེ་སྒྱུར་ (kyo̲ŋsee kēgyur) turning loss into profit, eliminating loss and making profit.

གྱོང་གསབ་ (kyo̲ŋsəb) sm. གུན་གསབ་.

གྱོང་ཧྲག་ཧྲག (kyo̲ŋ hrāghrag) sb. who is vocally rash/ impolite and also stubborn.

གྱོད་ (kyö̲ö̀) quarrel, dispute, law case; va.—བཟོ་ to create/ make a dispute or law case; va.—གཏུག to sue, to file a complaint, to institute a law case; vi.—ཐོབ་ to win a court case/ dispute ¶ ཁོས་ཁང་བདག་ལ་གྱོད་གཏུག་པ་རེད་ He sued his landlord.

གྱོད་ཀྱི་ (kyö̲ö̀gye) sm. གྱོད་ཚ་པོ་.

གྱོད་ཁ་ (kyö̲ö̀ga) sm. གྱོད.

གྱོད་ཁོངས་ (kyö̲ö̀goŋ) sb. involved in an argument/ dispute/ quarrel.

གྱོད་འཁྲུན་ (kyö̲ö̀drün) shung. the settlement of a dispute.

གྱོད་འཁྲུན་གཅོད་ (kyö̲ö̀drɛn jȫö̀) sm. གྱོད་ཐག་གཅོད་.

གྱོད་གླ་ལེན་ (kyö̲ö̀ lā le̲n) va. to receive a fee for helping people in a law case (sth. like a lawyer).

གྱོད་མགོ་རི་ལས་ལྗི་ གྱོད་ཇ་ཆུ་ལས་རིང་ (kyö̲ö̀ngo ri̲lɛ jī kyö̲ö̀ŋa cūlɛ ri̲ŋ) court cases are long and costly [Lit. the beginning of a court case is heavier than a mountain and the end is longer a river].

གྱོད་ཇ་མ་རིང་ན་བུ་ལ་ངན་ བ་ཇ་མ་རིང་ན་དཔྱིད་ལ་ངན་ (kyö̲ö̀ ŋāma ri̲ŋnə pə̲ulə ŋɛ̲n pa̲ ŋāma ri̲ŋnə jīìlə ŋɛ̲n) leaving a law case unsettled for a long time is not good for the future/ next generation [Lit. if the tail of a law case is long it is not good for the son, if the tail of a cow is long, it is not good in spring].

གྱོད་གཅོད་ (kyö̲ö̀ jȫö̀) sm. གྱོད་ཐག་གཅོད་.

གྱོད་ཆགས་ (kyö̲ö̀jaà) misfortune/ disaster regarding a lawsuit.

གྱོད་རྙིང་གཙང་བཤེར་ (kyö̲ö̀ñiŋ dzāŋsher) clearing the docket of old cases.

གྱོད་གཏུག (kyö̲ö̀duù) see གྱོད་.

གྱོད་ཐོག་གྱོད་བརྩེགས་ (kyö̲ö̀dɔɔ̀ gyö̲ö̀deg) repeatedly blaming/ accusing in a court.

གྱོད་ཐག་གཅོད་ (kyö̲ö̀daà jȫö̀) va. to settle a law case/ lawsuit/ dispute.

གྱོད་དོན་ (kyö̲ö̀do̲n) sm. གྱོད་གཞི་.

གྱོད་འདྲེ་ (kyö̲ndrɛɛ) a derogatory term used for people who always cause law cases.

གྱོད་རྡལ་ (kyö̲ö̀dɛɛ) sm. གྱོད་བརྡལ་.

གྱོད་བརྡལ་ (kyö̲ö̀dɛɛ) blaming, accusing; va.—བྱེད་.

གྱོད་སྡོམ་ (kyö̲ö̀dom) conclusion/ settlement of a law case.

གྱོད་བསྡོམས་ (kyö̲ö̀dom) sm. གྱོད་སྡོམ་.

གྱོད་སྣ་ (kyö̲ö̀na) law case, quarrel, dispute.

གྱོད་སྣེ་ (kyö̲ö̀ne) sm. གྱོད་སྣ་.

གྱོད་སྣེ་ནང་འདྲེན་ (kyö̲ö̀ne na̲ŋdren) arguments/ troubles/ court cases start at home.

གྱོད་པ་ (kyö̲ö̀ba) a person involved in a lawsuit/ law case.

གྱོད་རྩ་ (kyö̲ö̀dza) sm. གྱོད་གཞི་.

གྱོད་ཚ་པོ་ (kyö̲ö̀ tsābo) 1. disputatious. 2. pretending or exaggerating the negative of sth. ¶ ཕྲུ་གུ་གྱོད་ཚ་པོ་འདིས་ཞི་དྲག་མ་ན་ནའི་ན་གི་འདུག་ལབ་པ་རེད་ The child who exaggerates was telling (people) that he was ill even though he was not very ill.

གྱོད་འཚོལ་ (kyö̲ö̀ tsȫö̀) va. to look for a reason to

file a lawsuit.
ཁྲོད་འཛུགས་ (kyöö dzug) starting a dispute/court case; va.—བྱེད་.
ཁྲོད་ཞིབ་ལས་ཁུངས་ (kyööshi lɛ̱ɛ̱gyuŋ) a branch of the judicial system where civil disputes are settled.
ཁྲོད་གཞི་ (kyööshi) law case, lawsuit, dispute; va.—ཞུ་ to bring a law case; va.—བཟོ་ to make/ cause a law case.
ཁྲོད་གཞི་ཁྲ་ལོག (kyööshi trālɔɔ) reversing a verdict/ decision in a (settled) law case; va.—རྒྱག.
ཁྲོད་གཞི་ཐག་གཅོད་ (kyööshi tagjöö) settling a law case, deciding/ finalizing on a verdict; va.—བྱེད་.
ཁྲོད་གཞི་འདུམ་སྒྲིག (kyööshi dumdrig) mediating a dispute, reconciling a quarrel.
ཁྲོད་གཞི་སློང་བསླང་ (kyööshi lōŋlaŋ) causing/ instigating a dispute or law case.
ཁྲོད་བཟོ་ (kyöö so) see ཁྲོད་.
ཁྲོད་ཡ་ (kyööya) defendant in a law case, the accused ¶ ཁྲོད་ཡ་རྡོ་རྗེ་. Defendent Dorje.
ཁྲོད་ཡ་སྟག་གཟིག་ཁ་སྤྲོད་ འགྲིགས་རྒྱུ་རེ་བ་བྲེད་ཟད་ (kyööya dāgsii kābdröö driggyu rewa bɛd sɛ̱ɛ̱) there is no hope of agreement in a case when each defendant is very powerful [Lit. there is no hope of agreement when the defendants are the tiger and the leopard face-to-face].
ཁྲོད་ལོག (kyöölɔɔ) sm. ཁྲོད་གཞི་ཁྲ་ལོག.
ཁྲོད་ལོག་ཁྲ་ལོག (kyöölɔɔ trālɔɔ) sm. ཁྲོད་གཞི་ཁྲ་ལོག.
ཁྲོད་ཤོད་ (kyöö shöö) giving the impression one is sh. other than what one is ¶ ཁོ་ཕྱུག་པོ་ཡིན་ན་ཡང་སྐྱོ་པོ་ཡིན་མདོག་མདོག་གི་ཁྲོད་ཤོད་ཀྱི་འདུག Even though he is rich, he is giving the impression he is poor.
གྱོན་ (kyön) va. to wear, to put on (clothes) ¶ ཁོས་སྣམ་བུའི་ཕྱུ་པ་གཅིག་གྱོན་འདུག He was wearing a woolen dress.
གྱོན་གོས་ (kyögöö) sm. གྱོན་ཆས་.
གྱོན་ཆས་ (kyöncɛɛ) clothes.
གྱོན་ཆས་ཀུང་སི་ (kyöncɛɛ gūŋsi) clothing/ apparel store.
གྱོན་ཆས་དཔེ་གསར་ཚོང་ཁང་ (kyöncɛɛ bēsar tsōŋgaŋ) boutique, store that sells fashionable clothing.
གྱོན་ཆས་བཟོ་གྲྭ་ (kyöncɛɛ sodra) clothing factory.
གྱོན་སྡེར་ (kyön dēr) see གྱོན་.
གྱོན་ལྡང་ (kyöndaŋ) enough material to make sth. piece of clothes.
གྱོན་ལྡིང་ (kyöndeŋ) sm. གྱོན་ལྡང་.
གྱོན་པ་ (kyönba) sm. གྱོན་ཆས་.
གྱོན་ཕྱིང་ (kyönjiŋ) clothes made of felt.
གྱོན་ཚལ་ (kyöndzɛɛ) a piece of torn up clothing.
ཁྲོལ་ (kyöö) vi. to be lame/ crippled (in the leg).
ཁྲོལ་ཁྲོལ་ (kyöögyöö) sm. ཁྲོལ་པོ་.
ཁྲོལ་པོ་ (kyööbo) lame, crippled (in the leg).
ཁྲོས་སྒྱུག (kyöögyuù) father- or mother-in-law.
ཁྲོས་པོ་ (kyööbo) father-in-law.
ཁྲོས་མོ་ (kyöömo) mother-in-law.
ཁྲ་ (tra) 1. sheen of animal's fur. 2. (vb. + ཁྲ་སྒྲིག) preparing to do the verbal action ¶ འགྲོ་ཁྲ་སྒྲིགས་སོང་ He prepared to go. 3. a part. 4. name of an ancient lineage.
ཁྲ་འགྲིག (tra drig) vi. to go smoothly/ without hitches, to work out well/ successfully, to go according to plan ¶ ལས་དོན་ཚང་མ་ཁྲ་འགྲིགས་སོང་ All the work went well.
ཁྲ་འགྲིག་འགྲུབ་ཚང་ (tradrig tüüdzaŋ) things done in a proper/ complete/ successful manner ¶ ལས་ཀ་འདི་ཁྲ་འགྲིག་འགྲུབ་ཚང་བྱུང་སོང་ This task was completed successfully.
ཁྲ་འགྲིག་པོ་ (tra drigbo) sm. ཁྲ་འགྲིགས་པོ་.
ཁྲ་འགྲིགས་པོ་ (tra drigbu) done well, completed successfully; va.—བཟོ་ to complete successfully/ without hitches ¶ ཁོང་ཚོའི་ལས་ཁུང་གི་ལས་ཀ་ཚང་མ་ཁྲ་འགྲིགས་པོ་འདུག All the work done in their office is done well.
ཁྲ་རྒྱས་ (tragyɛɛ) sm. ཁྲ་རྒྱས་པོ་.
ཁྲ་རྒྱས་པོ་ (tra gyɛɛbo) elaborate and good (usu. for a ceremony) ¶ དེ་རིང་ཚང་ས་འདི་ཁྲ་རྒྱས་པོ་ཞིག་བྱུང་སོང་ The wedding today was very elaborate.
ཁྲ་རྒྱས་པ་ (tra gyɛɛba) sm. ཁྲ་རྒྱས་.
ཁྲ་རྒྱས་པོ་ (tra gyɛɛbo) sm. ཁྲ་རྒྱས་.
ཁྲ་རྒྱས་ཕུན་སུམ་ཚོགས་པ་ (tragyɛɛ pūndzo tsōgba) elaborate and good.
ཁྲ་སྒྲིག (tradrii) preparing; va.—བྱེད་ to make preparations, to prepare, to arrange ¶ ཁོ་ཚོས་ལོ་གསར་གྱི་ཁྲ་སྒྲིག་ཉི་མ་མང་པོའི་སྔོན་ནས་བྱེད་ཀྱི་ཡོད་པ་རེད་ They are making preparations for New Year's Day many days in advance.
ཁྲ་སྒྲིག་འཁྲབ་སྟོན་ (tradrii trābdön) preview (of a show).
ཁྲ་སྒྲིག་གྲོས་ཚོགས་ (tradrii trööddzɔɔ) preparatory meeting.
ཁྲ་སྒྲིག་འགྲན་བསྡུར་ (tradrii drendur) preliminary contest/ heat.
ཁྲ་སྒྲིག་འགྲེམ་སྟོན་ (tradrii dremdön) preview of an exhibition.
ཁྲ་སྒྲིག་དང་ཡོན་ (tradrii daŋyön) probationary member of a party.
ཁྲ་སྒྲིག་འདེམས་བསྐོ་ (tradrii demgo) primary election.
ཁྲ་སྒྲིག་འདེམས་སྒྲུག (tradrii demdruù) preselection.
ཁྲ་སྒྲིག་ཚན་ཁག (tradrii tsɛngaà) preparatory department.
ཁྲ་སྒྲིག་ཚོགས་པ་ (tradrii tsōgba) preparatory committee.
ཁྲ་སྒྲིག་འཛིན་གྲྭ་ (tradrii dzindra) preparatory course/ class.
ཁྲ་སྒྲིག་ཡུན་ཚད་ (tradrii yundzɛɛ) probationary period.
ཁྲ་སྒྲིག་རུ་ཁག (tradrii rugaà) reserve force.
ཁྲ་སྒྲིག་ལས་དོན་ (tradrii ledön) preparatory work.
ཁྲ་སྒྲིག་ལྷན་ཚོགས་ (tradrii lhɛntsoò) preparatory committee ¶ བོད་རང་སྐྱོང་ལྗོངས་ཁྲ་སྒྲིག་ཨུ་ཡོན་ལྷན་ཁང་ The Preparatory Committee for the Tibet Autonomous Region.
ཁྲ་སྒྲིག་ཨང་བསར་ (tradrii āŋsar) all ready/ all set.
ཁྲ་སྒྲིགས་ (tra drig) imp. of ཁྲ་སྒྲིག.
ཁྲ་བསྒྲིག (tra drig) f. of ཁྲ་སྒྲིག.
ཁྲ་བསྒྲིགས་ (tra drig) p. of ཁྲ་སྒྲིག.
ཁྲ་ཆུ་ (traju) 1. a type of woven wool that is thick and strong. 2. thick/ strong sheep wool.
ཁྲ་ཉེན་མ་འཛོལ་ (traden mandzöl) a ceremony/ ritual without mistakes; va.—བྱེད་.
ཁྲ་ཉེན་ལེགས་འགྲིགས་ (traden legdrig) successful, well ¶ མཛད་སྒོ་ཁྲ་ཉེན་ལེགས་འགྲིགས་ངང་ནས་གྲོལ་སོང་ The ceremony ended successfully.
ཁྲ་དག་མོ་ (tra tagmo) tidy, well arranged (usu. for rooms, etc.).
ཁྲ་སྡེབ་ (tradeb) smoothing fur in the direction of the grain to enhance its sheen. 2. sm. ཁྲ་སྡེབ.
ཁྲ་སྤུ་ (trabu) cilium.
ཁྲ་ཕུད་ (trabüü) sm. ཁྲ་མ་.
ཁྲ་ཕུབ་ (trapub) abbr. of ཁྲ་མ་ and ཕུབ་མ་.
ཁྲ་ཕྱི་ (trapci) sm.* ཁྲ་བཞི་.
ཁྲ་བུབ་ (trapub) a kind of cymbal.
ཁྲ་སྦུག (trapug) a kind of large cymbal.
ཁྲ་མ་ (trama) 1. dried mucus/ grit in the eye. 2. awn. 3. body hair. 4. frame, lattice.
ཁྲ་མ་འགྲིགས་ (tra madrig) difficulties, mishaps ¶ ལས་ཀ་འདི་ལ་ལྭ་ཁྲ་མ་འགྲིགས་མང་པོ་བྱུང་བཞག This work has had many mishaps.
ཁྲ་ཟུར་ (trasur) corner/ side (of a frame).
ཁྲ་རུ་ (traru) wooden frame on which wood is placed when making wooden bowls on a lathe.
ཁྲ་ལོ་རྒྱས་པོ་ (tralo gyɛɛbo) prosperous, flourishing.
ཁྲ་ལོ་ཉིལ་བ་ (tralo ñiiwə) animals having good sheen.
ཁྲ་ཤར་ (tra shār) vi. to have a sheen appear.
ཁྲ་ཤར་བའི་དུས་སྐབས་ (trasharwɛ tüügəb) the best season, the period of florescence [Lit. the time when the sheen appears].
ཁྲ་བཤུར་ (trashur) 1. burning hair/ fur; va. ཁྲ་བཤུར་; —གཏོང་. 2. singing the hair of woolen cloth after

its woven so as to burn off excess hair; va. སྤུ་བཤུར་; —གཏོང་.

གྲག (trag) vi. to sound ། འབྲུག་སྐད་ཀྱི་སྒྲ་གྲག་རྗེས་ After the thunder sounded.

གྲགས་ (trag) 1. vi. to be known as ། རི་དེ་ར་ཡུལ་ལྷ་གནས་པ་གྲགས་པ་རེད་ That mountain is known as an area where gods dwell. ། སྔོན་ན་མ་གྲགས་པ་ Not known before. 2. vi. to be widespread, to be spread widely over an area/ region.

གྲགས་སྐམ་ (traggam) an empty title, a title without commensurate power or wealth.

གྲགས་འགྱུལ་ (trangüü) sounds and movements ། འཕྲུག་ཙམ་རིང་ཁྱིམ་ཚང་ནང་གྲགས་འགྱུལ་གང་ཡང་མེད་པར་གནས་ There were no sounds and movements in the family for a moment.

གྲགས་ཅན་ (tragjɛn) sm. གྲགས་པ་ཅན་.

གྲགས་ཆེན་ (tragjen) sm. གྲགས་པ་ཆེན་པོ་.

གྲགས་སྙན་ (tragñɛn) fame, reputation.

གྲགས་འདོད་ཅན་ (tragdöjɛn) ambitious.

གྲགས་ལྡན་ (tragdɛn) sm. གྲགས་པ་ཅན་.

གྲགས་པ་ (tragba) 1. fame, reputation; vi.—འགྱུར་ to become famous/ renowned; va.—བྱེད་ to act famous/ renowned. 2. man's name.

གྲགས་པ་ངན་པ་ (tragba ŋɛmba) notorious, of ill repute.

གྲགས་པ་ཅན་ (tragbajɛn) famous, renowned, well known, celebrated ། ཁོང་ནི་བོད་ཀྱི་མཁས་པ་གྲགས་པ་ཅན་ཞིག་རེད་ He is a renowned Tibetan scholar.

གྲགས་པ་ཆེན་པོ་ (tragba cēmbo) great fame/ renown.

གྲགས་པ་དོན་མཐུན་ (tragba töndün) deserving of one's reputation.

གྲགས་པའི་རྗེས་འབྲང་ (tragbɛ jeèdraŋ) blindly following the well known/ famous.

གྲགས་པའི་བ་དན་ལྷབ་ལྷུབ་དུ་གཡོ་ (tragbɛ padɛn lǝblhubdu yō) famous [Lit. the flag of fame is fluttering].

གྲགས་པའི་མཚོ་ཆེན་བཞི་ (tragbɛ tsöjen shi) the four famous lakes of Tibet.

གྲགས་མེད་ (tragmeè) unknown.

གྲགས་མེད་དཔའ་བོ་ (tragmeè bāwo) unknown heroes.

གྲགས་ཤིང་གསལ་བ་ (transhin sɛ̄ɛwa) clear sounding.

གྲང་ (traŋ) cold ། ཡུལ་དེ་དགུན་དུས་གྲང་ཞིང་དབྱར་ཁ་ཚ་བ་ཞིག་འདུག This place is cold in winter and hot in summer. 2. vi. to get cold, to be cold ། ང་གྲང་བྱུང་ I got cold.

གྲང་ཁུལ་ (traŋgüü) sm. གྲང་བའི་ས་ཁུལ་.

གྲང་ཁུལ་བྱང་མ་ (traŋgüü caŋma) Arctic Circle.

གྲང་ཁུལ་ལྷོ་མ་ (traŋgüü lhāmo) Antarctica.

གྲང་མཁྲིས་ (trandrii) a type of jaundice that diminishes appetite.

གྲང་འཁུམས་ (traŋ kūm) vi. to contract because of cold.

གྲང་འཁུམས་ཚ་སྐྲངས་ (traŋgum tsābö̤ö̤) shrinking/ contracting because of cold and swelling from heat.

གྲང་འཁྱིང་བཟོ་ (trangeŋ so) va. to make sth. coagulate (by cooling off).

གྲང་འཁྱག (traŋkyaà) cold.

གྲང་འཁྲུ་ (trantru) a type of diarrhea.

གྲང་འགོག་ནུས་ཤུགས་ (traŋgɔɔ̀ nüüshuù) ability to resist cold.

གྲང་འགོག་རང་བཞིན་ (traŋgɔɔ̀ rəŋshin) cold enduring, cold resistant.

གྲང་རྒྱུན་ (traŋgyün) cold wave.

གྲང་ངད་ (traŋŋɛɛ̀) coldness, cold ། གནམ་གྲང་ངད་ Cold weather.

གྲང་ངད་ཀྱི་དུས་རླབས་ (traŋŋɛɛ̀gi tüülǝb) sm. གྲང་རྒྱུན་.

གྲང་ངད་ཆེ་བའི་ཁུལ་ (traŋŋɛɛ̀ cēwɛküü) frigid/ arctic area.

གྲང་ངར་ (traŋŋar) sm. གྲང་ངད་.

གྲང་ངར་ཆུང་ (traŋŋar cūŋ) slightly cold.

གྲང་ངར་ཆེ་ (traŋŋar cē) very cold.

གྲང་ངར་ཆེན་པོ་ (traŋŋar cēmbo) extremely cold.

གྲང་ངར་ཐེག་ཐུབ་པ་ (traŋŋar tēgdubbǝ) cold resistant.

གྲང་རྔུལ་ (traŋŋüü) cold sweat; vi.—ཐོན་ to break out in a cold sweat.

གྲང་ཆགས་རླངས་འཁོར་འཁྲུལ་ཆས་ (tranjaà lāŋgɔɔ trü̃üjɛɛ̀) condensing type turbine.

གྲང་ཆུ་ (tranju) 1. urine from sb. with gonorrhea. 2. a kind of illness. 3. cold water va.—རྒྱག to add cold water to boiling water.

གྲང་ཉར་ (trañar) cold storage, va.—བྱེད་.

གྲང་གཏོང་སྤུ་ལུ་ (trandoŋ sūlu) a (cold) method for making hair curly that does not require heat; va.—བཟོ་.

གྲང་ཐིང་ཐིང་ (traŋ tiŋdiŋ) cool.

གྲང་ཐུབ་ (trantub) cold resistant ། གྲང་ཐུབ་ལོ་ཏོག Cold resistant crops.

གྲང་ཐོག་ལས་སྣོན་ (trandɔɔ̀ lɛɛ̀nön) cold processing.

གྲང་ཐོར་ (trandɔɔ) goose bumps.

གྲང་འཐུང་ཐང་སྨན་ (trandun tāŋmɛn) liquid medicine taken cold.

གྲང་དྲོ་ (trandro) sm. གྲང་དྲོད་.

གྲང་དྲོད་ (trandrö̤ö̤) temperature.

གྲང་དྲོད་ཆ་སྙོམས་ལྡན་པ་ (trandrö̤ö̤ cāñam demba) having an even temperature/ climate, a temperate (climate) ། གྲང་དྲོད་ཆ་སྙོམས་ལྡན་པའི་ས་ཁུལ་ཁག་གི་ཤིང་ཏོག Temperate fruit plants.

གྲང་འདར་ (trandar) shaking from cold; vi.—རྒྱག.

གྲང་ནག (trannag) sm. གྲང་གཞི་.

གྲང་ནད་ (traŋnɛɛ̀) 1. sm. གྲང་གཞི་. 2. cold illnesses.

གྲང་ནས་འཁྱེངས་ (traŋnɛ kēŋ) vi. to coagulate (due to cooling off).

གྲང་པོ་ (traŋbo) cold.

གྲང་བ་ (traŋwa) 1. sm. གྲང་པོ་. 2. cold; colder ། མཚོ་སྣ་ནི་བོད་ལྷོ་ཕྱོགས་ཁུལ་གནམ་གཤིས་གྲང་བ་ཞིག་ཡིན་ Tsöna is an area in southern Tibet that has a colder climate.

གྲང་བ་དཀར་པོ་ (traŋwa garpo) sm. གྲང་དབང་དཀར་བ་.

གྲང་བའི་ས་ཁུལ་ (traŋwɛ sāgüü) frigid/ cold area.

གྲང་དབང་དཀར་བ་ (traŋwaŋ gārwa) gonorrhea.

གྲང་མིན་དྲོ་མིན (traŋmin tromin) lukewarm.

གྲང་མོ་ (traŋmo) cold; vi.—བྱེད་; —ཆགས་ to become cold; va.—བཟོ་ to make cold.

གྲང་དམག (traŋmaà) the cold war.

གྲང་དམྱལ་ (trañɛl) the part of hell where it is cold.

གྲང་ཚ་ (trandza) cold-welding; va.—རྒྱག.

གྲང་ཚལ་ (trandzɛɛ) 1. cold dishes (in Chinese cuisine). 2. salad.

གྲང་མཛོད་ (trandzö̤ö̤) cold storage.

གྲང་གཞི་ (traŋshi) gonorrhea; vi.—འཛགས to have vaginal or penal discharge due to gonorrhea.

གྲང་ཟུག (traŋsug) freezing/ piercing/ bitter cold; vi.—རྒྱག.

གྲང་བཟོ་ (traŋso) making sth. cold, cooling; va.—བྱེད་.

གྲང་བཟོ་མཐོ་སྡེགས་ (traŋso tōdeg) cooling tower.

གྲང་བཟོའི་འཁྲུལ་འཁོར་ (traŋsö trü̃ügɔɔ) freezer.

གྲང་འོད་ (traŋwö̤ö̤) cool light.

གྲང་གཡོལ་ (traŋyöö) moving to a warmer place when cold weather comes; va.—བྱེད་.

གྲང་རིག (traŋrii) feeling/ sense of cold.

གྲང་རེད་ (traŋrii) sm. འཁྱགས་རེངས་.

གྲང་རླབས (traŋlǝb) cold wave.

གྲང་རླུང་ (traŋluŋ) 1. air conditioning va.—གཏོང་ to air condition. 2. cold air.

གྲང་རླུང་འཁྲུལ་ཆས་ (traŋluŋ trü̃üjɛɛ̀) air conditioning equipment.

གྲང་ལོས (traŋlö̤ö̤) degree of coldness ། དེ་རིང་གནམ་གྲང་ལོས་འདུག་གམ་ How cold is it today?

གྲང་ཤས (traŋshɛɛ̀) (degree) of coldness.

གྲང་ཤུམ་ (traŋshum) cold, chilly.

གྲང་ཤུར་ (traŋshur) shivering (due to fever); vi.—རྒྱག ། ཚ་བ་རྒྱས་ནས་གྲང་ཤུར་བརྒྱབ་བྱུང་ I got a fever and shivered.

གྲང་ཤུར་ཤུར་ (traŋ shūrshur) 1. cool, chilly ། དེ་རིང་གནམ་གཤིས་གྲང་ཤུར་ཤུར་ཞིག་འདུག The weather today is chilly. 2. showing disapproval or dislike ། ངས་ཁོར་ཕན་ཐོགས་པའི་སྐད་ཆ་བཤད་པ་ཡིན་ཀྱང་ཁོས་ཉམ་འགྱུར་གྲང་ཤུར་ཤུར་བསྟན་བྱུང་ I told him sth. that would benefit him, but his expression showed dislike.

གྲང་ས་ (traŋsa) cold area/ region.

གྲང་སངས་ (traŋsaŋ) cooling off; va.—གཏོང་ to cool off.

གྲང་སིལ་སིལ་ (traŋsiisii) sm. གྲང་བསིལ་བསིལ་.

གྲང་གསུམ་དྲོ་གསུམ་ (traŋsum trosum) three parts cold and three parts warm, half cold and half warm ¶ དཔྱིད་ཀྱི་ཉིན་རིང་པོ་གྲང་གསུམ་དྲོ་གསུམ་ཡིན། མི་ཚེ་རིང་པོ་སྐྱིད་གསུམ་སྡུག་གསུམ་ཡིན། The long days of spring are half cold and half warm; one's long life is half happiness and half suffering.

གྲང་གསེར་ (traŋser) specially treated gold used for painting tankas and painting the faces of statues/ icons.

གྲང་བསང་གཏོང་ (traŋsaŋ dōŋ) va. to cool sth. off.

གྲང་བསིལ་གཏོང་ (traŋsii) sm. གྲང་གསང་གཏོང་.

གྲང་བསིལ་བསིལ་ (traŋ sīisii) sm. གྲང་སིལ་སིལ་.

གྲང་ལྷགས་ (traŋlhag) cold wind.

གྲང་ལྷགས་ཤོགས་ཤོགས་ (traŋlhag) cold/ chilly wind.

གྲང་ལྷང་ལྷང་ (traŋ lhāŋlhaŋ) sm. གྲང་སིལ་སིལ་.

གྲངས་ (traŋ) 1. number, quantity ¶ མི་གྲངས་ Number of people. 2. (number particle + —) expresses ten number units, e.g., the twenties and thirties ¶ ཁོ་ལོ་སུམ་ཅུ་སོ་གྲངས་ཤིག་རེད། He is in his thirties.

གྲངས་ཀ་ (traŋga) number; va.—རྒྱག་ to count.

གྲངས་ཀ་མ་ཐེབས་པ་ (traŋga matebba) countless, so large as to be uncountable.

གྲངས་ཀ་མིང་ཅན་ (traŋga miŋjɛn) concrete number (in math).

གྲངས་ཀ་མིང་སྦྲགས་མ་ (traŋga miŋdragba) complex number (in math).

གྲངས་ཀ་མིང་མེད་པ་ (traŋga miŋmeba) abstract number (in math).

གྲངས་ཀ་ལོངས་ (traŋga loŋ) sm. གྲངས་ཀ་ལོན་.

གྲངས་ཀ་ལོན་ (traŋga lön) vi. to reach/ meet a required/ number/ target ¶ འདི་ལོ་སློབ་གྲྭའི་མི་གྲངས་ཀ་ལོན་བཞག This year the school reached the target for students.

གྲངས་ཀའི་ཁྱད་རྟགས་ (traŋgɛɛ kyɛ̄ɛ̀daà) numerical characteristics.

གྲངས་ཀྱི་འགྱུར་ལྡོག (traŋgi gyundog) quantitative change (in math).

གྲངས་ཀྱིས་མི་ཚོད་པ་ (traŋgi mijöba) countless, innumerable.

གྲངས་སྐར་མས་མང་ཡང་ སྐག་ཟླ་བས་བསལ་ (traŋ gārmɛ maŋyaŋ māg dawɛ sɛ̄ɛ̀) it is better to have quality than quantity [Lit. even though there are many stars, at night the moon shines brighter].

གྲངས་ཁྱོན་ (traŋgyön) number, quantity, amount ¶ མི་གྲངས་ཁྱོན་ཆེན་པོ་ A large number of people.

གྲངས་འགྱུར་ (trəŋgyur) quantitative change (in math).

གྲངས་ངེས་ (traŋŋe) sm. གྲངས་བཅད་.

གྲངས་ངེས་བགོ་བཤའི་ལམ་ལུགས་ (traŋŋɛ goshɛ ləmluù) quota system.

གྲངས་ངེས་ཅན་ (traŋŋɛjɛn) sm. གྲངས་བཅད་.

གྲངས་བཅད་ (traŋjɛɛ̀) the determined/ fixed/ established amount or number or size.

གྲངས་བཅད་ཀྱི་ངེས་སྲོལ་ (traŋjɛɛ̀gi ŋesöö) the principle of fixed numbers (in math).

གྲངས་བཅད་ལག་འཁྱེར་ (traŋjɛɛ̀ laggyer) permit, license.

གྲངས་ཆ་བསྡུས་བཟོ་ (traŋja düüso) reduction of fractions (in math).

གྲངས་ཆུང་ (traŋjuŋ) decimal fraction, decimal points.

གྲངས་ཆུང་གི་ཚེག་ཐིག (traŋjuŋgi tsēgdig) sm. གྲངས་ཆུང་ཐིག་ཚེག.

གྲངས་ཆུང་ཐིག་ཚེག (traŋjuŋ tēgdzeè) decimal point.

གྲངས་ཉུང་ (trəŋñuŋ) 1. minority ¶ གྲངས་ཉུང་མི་རིགས་ཁག Minority nationalities. 2. a few, a limited number ¶ ལོག་སྤྱོད་པ་གྲངས་ཉུང་ཞིག་ནས་ By a few reactionaries.

གྲངས་རྟགས་ (traŋdaà) the sign of a number (in math).

གྲངས་སྟར་ (traŋdar) a sequence of numbers.

གྲངས་ཐོ་ (traŋto) list or record of the amount/ number of sth.; va.—རྒྱག.

གྲངས་འདྲེན་ (traŋ dren) va. to count in sequence.

གྲངས་སྡུད་པ་ (traŋdüba) a grammatical term in Tibetan for particles expressing "from."

གྲངས་བརྡ་ (traŋda) number.

གྲངས་གནས་ (traŋnɛɛ̀) position of a number/ digit (e.g., 1st decimal place, 2nd decimal place).

གྲངས་སྤུས་ (traŋbüù) quantity and quality.

གྲངས་ཕྱེད་ (traŋcɛè) half (of a number).

གྲངས་ཕྲེང་ (traŋdreŋ) sm. གྲངས་སྟར་.

གྲངས་ཕྲིན་གྲངས་རིག (traŋdrin trəŋriì) numerical mathematics.

གྲངས་ཕྲིན་ཆ་ཕྲན་ (traŋdrin cādrɛn) numerical differentiation.

གྲངས་ཕྲིན་དབྱེ་ཞིབ་ (traŋdrin yēshib) numerical analysis.

གྲངས་འབོར་ (traŋbɔr) amount, number, quantity; va.—རྩིས་ to count the amount/ quantity/ number ¶ སློབ་གྲྭ་འདིའི་སློབ་ཕྲུག་གི་གྲངས་འབོར་ The number of students in this school.

གྲངས་མང་ (traŋmaŋ) 1. majority. 2. many, a lot.

གྲངས་མང་བའི་གྲས་ (traŋmaŋwe trɛ̄ɛ̀) the majority, the majority party.

གྲངས་མང་མི་རིགས་ (traŋmaŋ mirii) majority nationality.

གྲངས་མེད་ (traŋmeè) countless, innumerable ¶ དམག་དེའི་རིང་ལ་མི་གྲངས་མེད་ཤི་ཡོད་པ་རེད་ Countless numbers of people died during that war.

གྲངས་ཚང་ (traŋdzaŋ) complete in number/ amount.

གྲངས་ཚང་གཙང་འབུལ་ (traŋdzaŋ dzāŋbüü) shung. handing sth. over completely.

གྲངས་ཚད་ (traŋdzɛɛ̀) quantity, number, rate, amount ¶ གྲངས་ཚད་མེད་ན་སྤུས་ཚད་ཀྱང་ཡོང་གི་མ་རེད་ Without quantity there will not be quality. ¶ མི་རེ་ལ་ཆ་སྙོམས་སྔོ་ཚལ་གྲངས་ཚད་ The average rate/ amount of vegetables per person.

གྲངས་ཚད་ཀྱི་འགྱུར་ལྡོག (traŋdzɛɛ̀gi gyundoò) quantitative change.

གྲངས་ཚད་ཀྱི་ཚིག (traŋdzɛɛ̀gi tsīi) numeral classifier (in linguistics).

གྲངས་ཚད་འགྱུར་ (traŋdzɛɛ̀gi) sm. གྲངས་ཚད་ཀྱི་འགྱུར་ལྡོག.

གྲངས་ཚད་ངེས་པའི་དབྱེ་ཞིབ་ (traŋdzɛɛ̀gi ŋeèbɛ yɛ̄shib) quantitative analysis.

གྲངས་ཚིག (traŋtsii) numerals.

གྲངས་གཡར་ (trāŋyar) borrowed number (in math).

གྲངས་རིག (traŋriì) sm. རྩིས་རིག.

གྲངས་རིག་འཆར་འགོད་ (trəŋriì cārgöö) mathematical programming.

གྲངས་རིག་དྲིལ་ཐབས་ (traŋriì triitəb) mathematical induction.

གྲངས་རིག་དཔེ་དབྱིབས་ (traŋriì bēyib) mathematical model.

གྲངས་རིམ་ (trəŋrim) sm. གྲངས་སྟར་.

གྲངས་ལས་འདས་པ་ (traŋlɛɛ̀ dɛɛ̀ba) innumerable, countless ¶ གློག་འདོན་ནུས་ཚོགས་གྲངས་ལས་འདས་པ་གསར་འཛུགས་བྱས་པ་རེད་ (They) constructed countless power stations.

གྲངས་ལུགས་གཏན་ཚིགས་ (trəŋlug dendziì) mathematical logic.

གྲངས་ལུགས་སྡོམ་རྩིས་ (traŋlug domdziì) mathematical statistics.

གྲངས་ལོང་ (traŋloŋ) a numerical target ¶ མ་ཎི་གྲངས་ལོང་བསགས་ཚར་སོང་ I have completed the target number of mani prayers.

གྲངས་བཤེར་ (traŋsher) va. to check the amount/ number/ calculation ¶ ལས་ཁུངས་ཀྱི་རྩིས་ཁྲ་ཚང་མ་གྲངས་བཤེར་བྱས་པ་རེད་ They checked all the office's accounts.

གྲངས་བཤེར་རྩིས་སྤྲོད་ (traŋsher dzīidröö) shung.

handing over sth. item by item.

གྲངས་གསོག (trasŋsoò) reciting-prayers (like O-mani-padme-hum); va.—བྱེད་ ¶ ཚེ་གཟུངས་འགྲོ་གང་ཆེ་གྲངས་གསོག་བྱས་པ་ They recited the mantra of longevity as much as they could.

གྲབས་ (trəbdro) 1. (vb. + —) about to do the verbal action ¶ ཁོ་འགྲོ་གྲབས་འདུག He is about to go. 2. va.—བྱེད་ to make preparations ¶ ཁོ་ཚོས་ཐུགས་སྤྲོའི་གྲབས་བྱེད་ཀྱི་འདུག They are making preparations for the party. ¶ དམག་འཐབ་བྱེད་རྒྱུའི་གྲབས་བྱས་ནས་མཚོན་ཆ་ཉོ་སྒྲུབ་བྱས་པ་རེད་ (They) bought weapons in preparation for war.

གྲབས་རྒྱགས་ (trəbgyaà) provisions for traveling.

གྲབས་སྒྲིག (trəbdrig) preparations; va.—བྱེད་.

གྲབས་དངོས་ (trəbŋöö) reserve supplies/ parts/ etc.

གྲབས་ཆས་ (trəbjɛɛ̀) sm. གྲབས་དངོས་.

གྲབས་བྱེད་ (trəbjeè) see གྲབས་, 2.

གྲབས་མོལ་ (trəbmöö) preliminary/ preparatory discussions; va.—བྱེད་.

གྲབས་དམག (trəbmaà) reserve troops/ soldiers.

གྲབས་ཟོན་ (trəbsön) preparing and being alert/ cautious; va.—བྱེད་ ¶ དགྲ་བོའི་གནོད་འཚོལ་ལ་ཡོང་རྒྱུར་གྲབས་ཟོན་བྱས་ཡོད་པ་རེད་ They were prepared and alert about the enemy's attack.

གྲབས་གཞོམ་ (trəbshom) preparing, getting ready; va.—བྱེད་.

གྲབས་གཞོམ་འབྲུ་ཁང་ (trəbshom drugaŋ) reserve granary.

གྲབས་གསོག (trəbsoò) accumulating in preparation for doing sth; va.—བྱེད་ ¶ མ་དངུལ་དེ་དག་རྗེས་མའི་འཆར་གཞིའི་ཆེད་དུ་གྲབས་གསོག་བྱས་པ་རེད་ They accumulated capital in preparation for a future plan.

གྲམ་ (tram) vi. to be or get spread/ dispersed/ scattered ¶ མི་ཚང་མ་ཁ་གྲམ་བཞག All the people got scattered.

གྲམ་ཁ་ (tramga) bank (of a river).

གྲམ་སྟོང་ (tramdoŋ) vi. གྲམ་ཐང་.

གྲམ་ཐང་ (tramtaŋ) a field with many pebbles.

གྲམ་རྡོ་ (tramdo) pebble.

གྲམ་པ་ (tramba) sm. གྲམ་རྡོ.

གྲམ་ས་ (tramsa) sm. གྲམ་ཁ་.

གྲམ་གསེག (tramseg) sm. གྲམ་ཧྲུག.

གྲམ་ཧྲུག (tramhrul) small round pebbles.

གྲམས་ (tram) sm. གྲམ་.

གྲལ་ (trɛɛ) line, row, series ¶ ཁོ་ཚོ་གྲལ་ལ་བསྡད་སོང་ They sat in a line.

གྲལ་དཀྲུག་ཕུང་སྦྱོར་ (trɛɛguù pūŋjɔɔ) stirring up and causing ruin.

གྲལ་སྐེད་ (trɛɛgeè) in the middle row.

གྲལ་སྐོར་ (trɛɛgɔɔ) making/ doing the rounds of a row of people in turn (e.g., serving drinks); va.—བྱེད་ ¶ སྐུ་མགྲོན་ཚོར་མཆོད་ཆང་གྲལ་སྐོར་བྱས་ནས་བཀུག་པ་རེད་ (They) served the guests beer in turn.

གྲལ་ཁོངས་ (trɛɛgoŋ) sm. གྲལ་.

གྲལ་མགོ་ (trɛngo) the head of a line/ row, seat of honor ¶ ཁོང་གྲལ་མགོར་བཞུགས་པ་རེད་ He sat at the head of the line/ row.

གྲལ་འགོ་ (trɛngo) sm. གྲལ་མགོ་.

གྲལ་འགྲིགས་པོ་ (trɛɛ drigbo) arranged in a row, lined up in an orderly fashion.

གྲལ་སྐོར་གྲོས་ཚོགས་ (trɛɛgɔɔ trööt̄soò) round-table conference.

གྲལ་སྒྲིག (trɛɛ drig) va. to line up, to put things in rows ¶ མི་དམངས་ཀྱིས་ལམ་གྱི་གཡས་གཡོན་ལ་གྲལ་བསྒྲིགས་འདུག The people have lined up on both sides of the road. ¶ ཤིང་རྣམས་གྲལ་བསྒྲིགས་ནས་བཙུགས་ཡོད་པ་རེད་ (They) have planted the trees in rows.

གྲལ་བསྒྲིགས་ (trɛɛ drig) p. of གྲལ་སྒྲིག.

གྲལ་མཇུག (trenjuù) the end of the row/ line.

གྲལ་མཉམ་སྒྲིག (trɛɛ ñamdrig) lining up side by side; va.—བྱེད་ ¶ དེ་རིང་ཚོགས་འདུའི་ཐོག་འགོ་ཁྲིད་དང་ང་ཚོ་གྲལ་མཉམ་སྒྲིག་བྱས་ནས་བསྡད་པ་ཡིན་ Today at the meeting we sat side by side with the leaders.

གྲལ་མཉམ་གཤིབ་ (trɛɛ ñamshib) sm. གྲལ་མཉམ་སྒྲིག.

གྲལ་སྡར་ (trɛɛdar) sm. གྲལ་བསྡར་.

གྲལ་བསྡར་ (trɛɛdar) a row or line of sth., a queue; va.—སྒྲིག to arrange in a row/ line/ queue ¶ ཚོགས་འདུར་ཞུགས་མཁན་གྲལ་བསྡར་གཉིས་ཡོད་པ་ལས་གཅིག་ཏུ་སྐྱེས་པ་རྣམས་བསྡད་ཡོད་པ་དང་ཅིག་ཤོས་དེར་བུད་མེད་རྣམས་བསྡད་འདུག Of the two rows of people attending the meeting, one was women and the other men.

གྲལ་བསྡར་འགྲིག་པོ་ (trɛɛdar drigbo) sm. གྲལ་འགྲིགས་པོ་.

གྲལ་དུ་ཚུད་ (trɛɛtu tsǖü) vi. to be included as a member of a rank/ class/ category.

གྲལ་གནས་ (trɛɛnɛɛ̀) 1. rank ¶ ཁོང་གི་གྲལ་གནས་མཐོ་པོ་རེད་ His rank is high. 2. row/ line of people on the basis of some characteristic or status ¶ མཛད་སྒོའི་ཐོག་གཞུང་ཞབས་རྣམས་གོ་ས་མཐོ་དམན་གྱི་གྲལ་གནས་སོ་སོར་སྡོད་དགོས་ཀྱི་ཡོད་པ་རེད་ At the ceremony, the officials have to sit in rows in accordance with their rank.

གྲལ་པ་ (trɛɛba) a person sitting in a row/ line.

གྲལ་འཕྲོས་ (trendröö) the spaces/ gaps between rows.

གྲལ་འཕྲོས་པ་ (tredrööba) shung. two junior monk officials who sit apart from the main body and recite auspicious verses at the New Year's ceremony in the Potala.

གྲལ་མ་ (trɛɛma) beam, rafter.

གྲལ་རྩེ་འབུལ་ (trɛɛdze büü) shung. va. to present a memorial to the Emperor ¶ བོད་སྡོད་ཨམ་བན་ནས་གྱོད་དོན་དེའི་སྐོར་གོང་མར་གྲལ་རྩེ་ཕུལ་པ་ The Amban presented a memorial to the Emperor concerning that case.

གྲལ་ཚེས་ (trɛɛdzeè) date, day.

གྲལ་མཚུངས་ (trɛɛdzuŋ) 1. equal rank/ position/ class. 2. equal line/ row.

གྲལ་མཚེས་ (trɛɛdzeè) the person sitting beside sb.

གྲལ་མཚེས་པ་ (trɛɛdzɛba) sm. གྲལ་མཚེས་.

གྲལ་འཛིན་ (trɛndzin) 1. seating assignment; va.—བྱེད to assign/ reserve seats. 2. the assigning of monk's seats on the first day of Monlam.

གྲལ་འཛིན་ལྡོག་པ་ (trɛndzin dɔgba) a seating arrangement/ assignment that is opposite that of usual.

གྲལ་ཞིག (trɛɛ shii̱) vi. to have rows/ lines get broken up or disassembled.

གྲལ་གཞུག (trɛɛshuù) the end of the row.

གྲལ་རིམ་ (trɛɛrim) 1. class (social or political) ¶ གྲལ་རིམ་གྱི་འཐབ་རྩོད་ Class struggle. 2. derogatory slang term for the bad exploiting higher classes (མངའ་བདག and མངའ་ཚབ་ classes).

གྲལ་རིམ་འཁོན་འཛིན་ (trɛɛrim kōndzin) class hatred.

གྲལ་རིམ་གྱི་བཀག་རྒྱའི་རང་བཞིན་ (trɛɛrimgi gāggyɛ rəŋshin) the limitation of one's class.

གྲལ་རིམ་གྱི་གོ་རྟོགས་ (trɛɛrimgi kodoò) class consciousness.

གྲལ་རིམ་གྱི་ངོ་བོ་ (trɛɛrimgi ŋowo) class nature.

གྲལ་རིམ་གྱི་ཆབ་སྲིད་གོ་རྟོགས་ (trɛɛrim cəpsii̱ kodoò) class political consciousness.

གྲལ་རིམ་གྱི་ལྟ་བ་ (trɛɛrimgi dāwa) sm. གྲལ་རིམ་གྱི་ལྟ་ཚུལ་.

གྲལ་རིམ་གྱི་ལྟ་ཚུལ་ (trɛɛrimgi dədzüü) class viewpoint.

གྲལ་རིམ་གྱི་འཐབ་རྩོད་ (trɛɛrimgi təbdzöö) class struggle.

གྲལ་རིམ་གྱི་འཐེན་ཁྱེར་ (trɛɛrimgi tēngyer) sm. གྲལ་རིམ་གྱི་ཕྱོགས་ཞེན་.

གྲལ་རིམ་གྱི་འདུ་ཤེས་ (trɛɛrimgi dusheè) class awareness/ consciousness.

གྲལ་རིམ་གྱི་གནས་ཚུལ་ (trɛɛrimgi nēēdzüü) class situation.

གྲལ་རིམ་གྱི་སྤྱི་ཚོགས་ (trɛɛrimgi jīdzoò) class society.

གྲལ་རིམ་གྱི་ཕྱོགས་ཞེན་ (trɛɛrimgi cōgshen) class bias.

གྲལ་རིམ་གྱི་བུ་ཕྲུག (trɛɛrimgi pudruù) child of a class

enemy (མངའ་བདག and མངའ་ཆབ་ classes).

གྲལ་རིམ་གྱི་བརྩེ་གདུང་ (treerimgi dzēduŋ) class love.

གྲལ་རིམ་གྱི་མཚན་རྟགས་ (treerimgi tsēndaà) sm. གྲལ་རིམ་གྱི་མཚན་རྟགས་.

གྲལ་རིམ་གྱི་མཛའ་མཐུན་ (treerimgi dzadün) class friendship/ amity.

གྲལ་རིམ་གྱི་མཛའ་བརྩེ་ (treerimgi dzadze) class brotherhood/ love.

གྲལ་རིམ་གྱི་མཛའ་བཤེས་ (treerimgi dzasheè) sm. གྲལ་རིམ་གྱི་མཛའ་བཤེས་.

གྲལ་རིམ་གྱི་རང་ནུས་ (treerimgi raŋnüù) class instinct.

གྲལ་རིམ་གྱི་རང་བཞིན་ (treerimgi raŋshin) class nature.

གྲལ་རིམ་གྱི་རང་གཤིས་ (treerimgi raŋsheè) class nature.

གྲལ་རིམ་གྱི་ལངས་ཕྱོགས་ (treerimgi loŋjoò) class stand/ position.

གྲལ་རིམ་གྱི་ལམ་ཕྱོགས་ (treerimgi lamjoò) class line.

གྲལ་རིམ་གྱི་བཤུ་གཞོག (treerimgi shūshoò) class exploitation.

གྲལ་རིམ་གྱི་སློབ་གསོ་ (treerimgi lōbso) class education.

གྲལ་རིམ་གྱེས་པ་ (treerimgi gyeèwa) class differentiation.

གྲལ་རིམ་འགལ་བ་ (treerim geewa) class contradiction.

གྲལ་རིམ་རྟགས་ཐམ་ (treerim dāgdam) sm. གྲལ་རིམ་རྟགས་དམ་.

གྲལ་རིམ་རྟགས་དམ་ (treerim dāgdam) brand/ imprint of a class.

གྲལ་རིམ་གྱི་ཐ་དད་ (treerimgi tādεε) separate classes.

གྲལ་རིམ་འཐབ་ཕྱོགས་ (treerim tābjoò) class battle line/ front.

གྲལ་རིམ་འཐབ་རྩོད་ (treerimgi tābdzöö) class struggle.

གྲལ་རིམ་འདུམ་འགྲིག (treerim dumdrig) class conciliation.

གྲལ་རིམ་དཔུང་ཁག (treerim būŋgaà) class camp.

གྲལ་རིམ་དཔུང་སྡེ་གཙང་བཤེར་ (treerimgi būŋde dzāŋsher) purification of class ranks.

གྲལ་རིམ་བར་གྱི་འཐབ་རྩོད་ (treerimgi wargi tābdzöö) class struggle.

གྲལ་རིམ་དབྱེ་ཞིབ་ (treerim yēshib) class analysis.

གྲལ་རིམ་འབྱུང་ཁུངས་ (treerim cuŋguŋ) class status.

གྲལ་རིམ་མེད་པ་ (treerim mēèba) classless.

གྲལ་རིམ་མེད་པའི་སྤྱི་ཚོགས་ (treerim meèbε jitsoò) classless society.

གྲལ་རིམ་ལས་འདས་ (treerimlε dεè) passing beyond class.

གྲལ་རིས་ (treerii) seating order/ arrangement.

གྲལ་རོགས་ (treeroò) the person sitting next to one in a row.

གྲལ་ལ་འཁོད་ (treela kōō) va. to take seats in accordance with rank (usu. at ceremonies or meetings) ¶ ཚོགས་མི་རྣམས་གྲལ་ལ་འཁོད་པ་དང་ཚོགས་གཙོས་གསུང་བཤད་གནང་བ་རེད་ After the members took their seats, the president spoke.

གྲལ་ཤར་ (treeshar) sm. གྲལ་བསྒར་.

གྲལ་གཤིབས་ (treeshib) tightening/ closing up the gaps between rows; va.—རྒྱག.

གྲལ་གསེང་ (treeseŋ) space between lines/ rows.

གྲས་ (treè) kind, type, sort, class ¶ ཆོས་པའི་གྲས་ནས་འཐུས་མི་འདེམས་ཀྱི་མ་རེད་ (They) won't select a delegate from the ranks of religious devotees. ¶ མི་ཁྱེད་རང་ཚོའི་གྲས་ལ་ལས་ཀ་རག་གི་མ་རེད་ Your kind of person will not get a job.

གྲས་ཀ་ (treèga) གྲས་.

གྲས་རིས་ (treèrii) strata, stratum, layer.

གྲས་སུ་ (treèsu) among, in ¶ ཁོང་དང་མཉམ་དུ་ཕེབས་མཁན་གྲས་སུ་ Among the people (who) came with him.

གྲི་ (tri) knife; va.—རྒྱག; —འཛུགས་ to knife.

གྲི་ཁ་ (trigə) sm. གྲི་དངོ་.

གྲི་ཁ་འགྲན་ (trigə tren) sm. གྲི་རྩེད་རྩེ་.

གྲི་ཁ་གཉིས་མ་ (trigə ñiimə) double-edged knife.

གྲི་ཁ་འདོན་ (trigə tön) va. to sharpen a knife.

གྲི་ཁའི་སྦྲང་རྩི་ (trigε draŋdzi) making sth. harmful superficially appear good [Lit. honey on the cutting edge of a sword].

གྲི་གར་ (trigar) a dance performed by garpa while holding a sword.

གྲི་གུ་ (trigu) small knife.

གྲི་གོག་དོ་ (trigə gobdo) blunt knife.

གྲི་མགོ་ (tringo) handle of a knife/ sword; va.—གནོན་ to grab the handle of a sword (that is in one's belt) as a threat.

གྲི་འགག་གསོར་ (tri gagsoŋ) a knife/ sword hanging from a belt.

གྲི་འགོ་ (tringo) sm. གྲི་མགོ་.

གྲི་ངར་མེད་ (tri ŋarmeè) a dull or untempered knife.

གྲི་དངོ་ (triŋo) the cutting edge of a knife/ sword; va.—འདོན་ to unsheathe a sword/ knife.

གྲི་ལྕག (trijaà) 1. flat part of knife/ sword. 2. the blunt part of a knife/ sword.

གྲི་ཆག (trijaà) a broken knife.

གྲི་ཆད་ (trijεε) a fine/ penalty imposed for stabbing sb.

གྲི་ཆས་ (tricεè) cutters, cutting instruments.

གྲི་ཆུང་ (trijuŋ) sm. གྲི་གུ་.

གྲི་ཆུང་རྩེ་རྣོ་ (trijuŋ dzēno) sth. small but effective [Lit. small knife, sharp point].

གྲི་ཆུང་རྩེ་གསེག (trijuŋ dzēseg) sm. གྲི་ཆུང་རྩེ་རྣོ་.

གྲི་ཆེན་ (trijen) big sword/ knife.

གྲི་འཇམ་པོ་ (tri jambo) sm. གྲི་ངར་མེད་.

གྲི་བདོན་ (tri dön) p. of གྲི་འདོན་.

གྲི་བདོན་གཞུ་བཀང་ (tridön shugaŋ) saber rattling [Lit. unsheathe swords, pull bows].

གྲི་ལྡག (tridag) sm. གྲི་ཡི་ལྡག་པ་.

གྲི་དར་ (tridar) sm.* གྲི་བདར་.

གྲི་དོར་ (tridor) sm. གྲི་བདར་.

གྲི་བདར་ (tridar) p. and f. of གྲི་དར་.

གྲི་བསྣུན་པའི་མ་ཚད་གྲི་འགོ་འཕྱུར་འཕྱུར་ (trinünbε madzεè tri go cārcar) committing sth. evil and showing off about it [Lit. not only stabbing sb. but waving the sword over one's head].

གྲི་པ་ (triba) a swordsman, a sword-bearing soldier.

གྲི་དཔའ་དམ་ (tri bādam) a long sword.

གྲི་བུ་ (tribu) a small knife.

གྲི་རྨོ་ཕུར་འདེབས་ (trimo purdeb) not giving up, using whatever is available [Lit. plowing with a knife and planting with a stake].

གྲི་རྩལ་ (tridzεε) the art of swordsmanship.

གྲི་རྩལ་མདུང་རྩལ་ (tridzεε duŋdzεε) martial arts.

གྲི་རྩེ་ (tridze) point of a knife.

གྲི་རྩེད་ (tridzeè) fencing, va.—རྩེ་ to fence (with sword).

གྲི་རྩེའི་འཐབ་རྩལ་ (tridzee tābdzüü) "sharp knife" tactics, hand-to-hand combat.

གྲི་མཚོན་ (tridzön)1. weapons. 2. sm. གྲི་རིང་.

གྲི་འཛིང (tridziŋ) knife/ sword fighting, bayonet fighting, hand-to-hand combat.

གྲི་གཞོག (trishog) a slice; va.—རྒྱག to cut/ slice with a knife ¶ མར་གྲི་གཞོག་གཅིག A slice of butter.

གྲི་ཡི་ལྡག་པ་ (triyi dāgba) the back/ blunt side of a knife.

གྲི་ཡུ་ (triyu) knife handle.

གྲི་གཡུག (tri yūù) sm. གྲི་གཡུགས་.

གྲི་གཡུགས་ (tri yūù) 1. va. to throw a knife. 2. to swing a sword. 3. fencing; va.—རྩེད་ to fence.

གྲི་གཡུགས་རེས་གཏོང་ (tri yūùre dōŋ) va. to hit back and forth with swords.

གྲི་རི་མེ་མཚོ་ (triri metso) a dangerous place [Lit. a mountain of swords, a sea of flames].

གྲི་རིང་ (tririŋ) sword.

གྲི་རུ་བ་ (trirubə) people with knives ganging up to attack sb.; va.—རྒྱག.

གྲི་ལ་ཁུ་ཚུར་རྡེགས་ (trilə kūdzur deg) brave but stupid [Lit. punching a sword].

གྲི་ཤན་ (trishεn) knife.

གྲི་ཤི་ (trishi) killed by knife.

གྲི་ཤུབས་ (trishub) knife sheath/ scabbard.

གྲི་སོ་ (triso) sm. གྲི་དང་.

གྲི་སོ་གཉིས་མ་ (triso ñiimə) double-edged knife.

གྲིན་པ་ (trimbə) astute, shrewd, clever.

གྲིན་པོ་ (trinmbo) sm. གྲིན་པ་.

གྲིབ་ (trib) 1. contamination, defilement, pollution (in a symbolic rather than physical sense); va.—ཕོག to be/ get polluted/ defiled ༎ནད་གྲིབ་ Pollution emanating from an illness. 2. sm. གྲིབ་མ་. 3. p. of འགྲིབ་. 4. a region near Lhasa. 5. a class of demons.

གྲིབ་བསྐམ་ (tribgam) drying sth. in the shade; va.—གཏོང་.

གྲིབ་སྐྱོན་ (tribgyön) type of epileptic fit/ stroke; vi.—ཕོག to have such a fit/ stroke.

གྲིབ་ཁུང་ (tribguŋ) rooms that do not get any sunshine.

གྲིབ་ཁྲུས་ (tribtrüü) religious rite to cleanse pollution.

གྲིབ་དགའ་རྩི་ཤིང་ (tribga dzīshiŋ) plants that grow in the shade.

གྲིབ་ངོས་ (tribŋöö) area in the shadows.

གྲིབ་ཅན་ (tribjɛn) defiled, contaminated, polluted.

གྲིབ་བརྙན་ (tribñɛn) sm. གྲིབ་ནག.

གྲིབ་བརྙན་བཟོ་བ་ (tribñɛn sowa) radiography.

གྲིབ་ལྡན་ཁེ་སྤོགས་ (tribdɛn kēbɔɔ) gross profit.

གྲིབ་ལྡན་ལྗི་ཚད་ (tribdɛn jidzɛɛ) gross weight.

གྲིབ་ནག (tribnaà) shadow.

གྲིབ་ནག་འདྲེ་མཐོང་ (tribnaà drendoŋ) having suspicions/ doubts of sth. when there is no basis ༎ཁོ་རྒྱ་མིའི་སོ་པ་རེད་བསམས་ནས་གྲིབ་ནག་འདྲེ་མཐོང་ལྟར་བསད་པ་རེད་ Like seeing ghost in the shadows, (they) thought he was a Chinese spy and killed him. [Lit. seeing a ghost in the shadows].

གྲིབ་ནག་སྦར་འཛིན་ (tribnaà bandzin) groping in the dark.

གྲིབ་ནག་ཞགས་འཕེན་ (tribnaà shagben) useless/ hopeless activity [Lit. lassoing in the dark].

གྲིབ་ནད་ (tribnɛɛ) illness caused by contamination/ pollution (both physical and symbolic).

གྲིབ་གནོན་ (tribnön) nightmare (which occurs when a person sleeps with his hand on his heart); vi.—རྒྱག.

གྲིབ་པོ་ (tribbo) sm. གྲིམས་པོ་.

གྲིབ་ཕུད་ (tribbüü) va. to exclude the weight of a container when weighing sth.

གྲིབ་ཕོག (trib pɔ̄ɔ) vi. to get contaminated/ polluted/ defiled.

གྲིབ་ཕྱོགས་ (tribjɔɔ) the shady side of hill/ mountain.

གྲིབ་མ་ (tribmə) shadow, shade.

གྲིབ་མ་སྙུམ་པོ་ (tribmə nūmbo) pleasant and shady.

གྲིབ་མའི་རྒྱལ་སྲིད་སྒྱུ་ཕྲུལ་ཁང་ (tribmɛ gyɛɛsii jīgyəbgaŋ) shadow cabinet.

གྲིབ་བཙོག (tribdzog) diseases caused by dirt/ unhygienic practices/ pollution/ contamination.

གྲིབ་ཚོད་ (tribdzöö) sm. ཉི་ཚོད་.

གྲིབ་རྫོང་བཙན་ (trib dzōŋdzɛn) guardian diety of Tsecholing monastery.

གྲིབ་གཟུགས་ (tribsug) shadow figures; vi.—ཕོག to get enveloped/ covered by shadow.

གྲིབ་གཟུགས་ལྡོས་གར་ (tribsug döögar) puppet/ shadow show.

གྲིབ་གཡོགས (tribyɔɔ) a covering/ blanket that enables one to be invisible.

གྲིབ་རི་ (tribri) the shaded side of a mountain.

གྲིབ་རླུང་ (tribluŋ) a type of རླུང་ sickness caused by pollution.

གྲིབ་ལམ་ (triblam) 1. the milky way. 2. a shady path.

གྲིབ་ལིང་ (tribliŋ) a cataract-like growth on the iris caused by uncleanliness/ pollution.

གྲིབ་ལོང་ (trib loŋ) blindness caused by pollution/ contamination.

གྲིབ་ཤོར་ (trib shɔɔ) vi. to be/ get contaminated or polluted.

གྲིབ་སིལ་ (tribsil) sm. གྲིབ་བསིལ་.

གྲིབ་སོ་ (tribso) shadow; shade; vi.—ཐེབས་ to become shady, to come into shade.

གྲིབ་བསངས་ (trib sāŋ) va. to clear or clean up contamination/ pollution.

གྲིབ་བསིལ་ (trib sil) 1. shade, shadow ༎ལྗོན་པའི་གྲིབ་བསིལ་འོག In the shade of a tree. 2. under the protection/ wing of a government or ruler ༎འབྲུག་ཡུལ་དེ་རྒྱ་གར་གྱི་གྲིབ་བསིལ་འོག་ཏུ་གནས་ཡོད་པ་ཡོད་ Bhutan is under the wing of India.

གྲིམ་ (trim) rope/ thread that is spun; va.—རྒྱག to spin (thread, rope, etc.) vi.—ཐེབས་ to get spun ༎ངས་སྐུད་པ་འདི་བགྲིམས་པ་ཡིན་ནའང་གྲིམ་མི་འདུག Even though I spun the (material into) thread, it didn't take.

གྲིམ་ཅག (trimjaà) careful, cautious; va.—བྱེད་.

གྲིམ་པོ་ (trimbo) 1. astute, clever, efficient, smart ༎ཁོ་ལས་ཀ་གྲིམ་པོ་འདུག He is astute in his work. 2. stingy, miserly ༎ཁོ་ལག་པ་གྲིམ་པོ་འདུག He is stingy. 3. well spun ༎སྐུད་པ་དེ་གྲིམ་པོ་བྱུང་མི་འདུག That thread is not well spun.

གྲིམ་རིལ་རྒྱག (trimrii gyaà) sm. འདྲེ་ལྡོག་རྒྱག.

གྲིམ་ཚད་ (trimdzɛɛ) the volume of sales.

གྲིམས་པ་ (trimba) sm. གྲིམ་པོ་.

གྲིའི་ཁ་ (trii kā) sm. གྲི་ཁ་.

གྲིའི་དང་ (trii ŋō) the cutting edge of a knife/ sword.

གྲིའི་རྣོ་ (trii nō) sharpness of a blade.

གྲིའུ་ (triu) sm. གྲི་ཆུང་.

གྲིར་ཤི་ (trishi) killed by the sword/ knife.

གྲིལ་ (tril) 1. a roll ༎ཤོག་གྲིལ་ A roll of paper. 2. p. of འགྲིལ་.

གྲིལ་ཁ་ (triiga) a roll; va.—རྒྱག to roll up.

གྲིས་རྨོ་མེས་འདེབས་ (trii mō meedeb) slash and burn cultivation.

གྲིས་གཞུས་ (trii shüü) va. to hit/ slash with a sword or knife.

གྲུ་ (tru) 1. boat; va.—གཏོང་ to sail a boat. 2. angle, corner.

གྲུ་དཀར་ (trugar) jadeite.

གྲུ་སྐས (trugɛɛ) ladder used at the corner of a house.

གྲུ་སྐྱ་ (trugya) oar.

གྲུ་སྐྱེལ་ཀུང་སི་ (trugyee gūŋsi) shipping company (via boats).

གྲུ་སྐྱེལ་ཅུའུ་ (trugyee jūwu) shipping bureau (regarding boat transport).

གྲུ་ཁ་ (truga) place where boats land/ dock, e.g. a port, harbor, landing place, wharf, quay ༎རྒྱ་མཚོའི་གྲུ་ཁ་ Seaport. ༎གྲུ་ཁའི་ཁྲལ་ Wharf tax.

གྲུ་ཁང་ (trugaŋ) stateroom (in a ship), ship's cabin.

གྲུ་ཁའི་གྲོང་ཁྱེར་ (trugɛ troŋgyer) port city.

གྲུ་ཁའི་ལས་དོན་དོ་དམ་ཅུའུ་ (trugɛ lɛɛdön todam jūwu) harbor bureau, port office.

གྲུ་ཁའི་འབབ་ཚུགས་ (trugɛ bəbdzuù) port, boat landing station.

གྲུ་ཁའི་བཟོ་པ་ (trugɛ soba) stevedore, longshoreman.

གྲུ་ཁུག (trugug) crotch of the elbow.

གྲུ་ཁེབས་ (trugeb) boat cover.

གྲུ་ཁྱིམ་ (trugyem) sm. གྲུ་སྐྱ་.

གྲུ་མཁན་ (trugɛn) sm. གྲུ་པ་.

གྲུ་ག (truga) sm. ཟུར་.

གྲུ་ག་ཅན་ (trugajɛn) pyramidal shape.

གྲུ་གུ་ (trugu) 1. ball of yarn/ thread; va.—རྒྱག; —སྒྲིལ་ to roll yarn/ thread into a ball. 2. see ཀང་ཙེད་གྲུ་གུ་.

གྲུ་གླ་ (trula) boat fare, boat fee.

གྲུ་མགོ་ (truŋgo) tip of the elbow.

གྲུ་འགག (truŋgaà) canal lock.

གྲུ་འགོ་ (truŋgo) bow of boats.

གྲུ་རྒྱུག (trugyuù) oar.

གྲུ་གཅལ་ (trujɛɛ) sm. གྲུ་པང་.

གྲུ་ཆར་ (trucar) light drizzle.

གྲུ་ཆས་ (trujɛɛ) boat equipment.

གྲུ་ཚོད་ (trujöö) squares, a design consisting of squares.

གྲུ་མཇུག (trunjuù) stern of boats.

གྲུ་འཛོག་ས་ (trunjɔ̀ɔsa) dock, shipyard.

གྲུ་དུ་རུ་མོ་ (trudu rumo) sm. གྲུ་ཁུག.

གྲུ་གདོང་ (tru dōŋ) va. to row a boat, to sail a ship.

གྲུ་གདོང་མཁན་ (tru dōŋgɛn) boatman, helmsman.

གྲུ་གདོང་ཐེངས་གྲངས་ (trudoŋ tēŋdraŋ) 1. a number indicating a ship's order of departure. 2. number of voyages taken by a ship.

གྲུ་རྟ་མགོ་མ་ (truda goma) a boat whose bow is carved as a horse's head.

གྲུ་སྟར་ (trudar) line of barges/ ships, a flotilla of ships.

གྲུ་སྡེགས་ (trudeg) berth (of a ship).

གྲུ་ཐག (trudaà) a rope used for tying boats, mooring rope, a rope for towing a boat; va.—འཐེན་ to pull a rope that is tied to a boat.

གྲུ་ཐོག་གྲིག་ཆས་ (trutaà drigjɛɛ̀) sm. གྲུ་ཆས་.

གྲུ་མཐིལ་ (trutil) ship's bottom.

གྲུ་དར་ (trudar) small flags erected at the edge of nomad tents.

གྲུ་དྲང་ (trudraŋ) right angle.

གྲུ་བདག (trudaà) ship/ boat owner.

གྲུ་འདོགས་རྡོ་ཀེར་ (trundɔ̀ɔ doger) a ship tied to a stone pillar on shore.

གྲུ་ལྡན་ཀ་བ་ (trudɛn gāwa) rectangular pillar, pillar with edges.

གྲུ་སྡེ་ (trude) boat dweller, boat people community.

གྲུ་ནར་ (trunar) rectangle, rectangular.

གྲུ་ནར་ཅན་ (trunarjɛn) rectangular.

གྲུ་པ་ (truba) sailor, boatman.

གྲུ་པང་ (trubaŋ) deck of a boat.

གྲུ་དཔུང་ (trubuŋ) the wooden frame of a coracle.

གྲུ་དཔོན་ (trubün) captain (of a ship), helmsman, skipper.

གྲུ་སྤྱོད་ལོ་གྲངས་ (trujɛɛ̀ lodraŋ) age of vessel.

གྲུ་ཕྱུར་ (trujar) mat or wooden roofing of boat. 2. sail of a boat.

གྲུ་བུ་ (trubu) sm. གྲུ་གུ་.

གྲུ་བོ་ཆེ་ (truboce) ship.

གྲུ་མ་ (truma) angle; side, edge.

གྲུ་མོ་ (trumo) elbow.

གྲུ་དམག་དཔུང་སྡེ་ (trumaà būŋde) Marine Corps (U.S.A.).

གྲུ་དམར་ (trumar) red (turquoise).

གྲུ་བཙས་ (trudzɛɛ̀) sm. གྲུ་ཏྲ་.

གྲུ་བཙས་པ་ (trudzɛba) boatman.

གྲུ་ཚིགས་ (trudzii) elbow joint.

གྲུ་ཚུགས་ (trudzuù) sm. གྲུ་ཁ་.

གྲུ་ཚོགས་ (trudzoò) fleet of ships, armada of ships.

གྲུ་འཛིན་ (trundzin) 1. boat ticket. 2. Potala Palace.

གྲུ་འཛིན་གཉིས་པ་ (trudzin ñiìbə) the Potala Palace.

གྲུ་རྫིངས་ (trudziŋ) sm.* གྲུ་གཟིངས་.

གྲུ་རྫིངས་བབ་ཚུགས་ (trudziŋ bəbtsuù) port.

གྲུ་རྫོང་ (trudzoŋ) cargo for a boat/ ship; va.—རྒྱག to load a ship with cargo.

གྲུ་ཞབས་ (trushəb) 1. ship's bottom. 2. floor of a boat.

གྲུ་གཞས་ (trushɛɛ̀) song sung by boatman.

གྲུ་གཞུག (trushuù) stern of boats.

གྲུ་གཞོགས་ (trushoò) side of boat/ ship.

གྲུ་བཞི་ (trubshi) 1. square. 2. the mineral limonite.

གྲུ་བཞི་ཀྱོག་མོ་ (trupshi gyōgmo) rhombus.

གྲུ་བཞི་ཁ་གང་ (trupshi kāgaŋ) a square piece (usu. of folded material).

གྲུ་བཞི་ནར་མོ་ (trupshi narmo) rectangular.

གྲུ་བཞི་འབུར་འདོན་ (trupshi burdön) cube shaped.

གྲུ་བཞི་རིང་པོ་ (trupshi riŋbu) rectangle, rectangular.

གྲུ་བཞི་གསེག་ནར་མ་ (trupshi sēgnarma) parallelogram.

གྲུ་བཞི་ལྷམ་པ་ (trupshi lhāmba) sm. གྲུ་བཞི་འབུར་འདོན་.

གྲུ་ཟམ་ (trusam) 1. ship's bridge. 2. gangplank.

གྲུ་ཟུར་ (trusam) right angle, edge of sth.

གྲུ་གཟིངས་ (trusiŋ) ship, vessel, boat ¶ གནམ་གྲུ་འབབ་སའི་གྲུ་གཟིངས་ Aircraft carrier.

གྲུ་གཟིངས་བཀག་ས་ (trusiŋ gāgsa) anchorage, dockyard, anchoring berth.

གྲུ་གཟིངས་ཀྱི་གདིང་རྡོ་ (trusiŋgi diŋdo) ship's anchor.

གྲུ་གཟིངས་གྲམ་ཟུག (trusiŋ tramsug) running aground.

གྲུ་གཟིངས་འཛོག་ས་ (trusiŋ jɔgsa) sm. གྲུ་གཟིངས་བཀག་ས་.

གྲུ་གཟིངས་ཐོ་འགོད་གྲུ་ཁ་ (trusiŋ tōgöö trugə) port of registry.

གྲུ་གཟིངས་བདག་ཁངས་ (trusiŋ daggoŋ) home port (for ship).

གྲུ་གཟིངས་གནས་ས་ (trusiŋ nɛ̄ɛsa) ship's position (at sea).

གྲུ་གཟིངས་འབྲུག་གཟུགས་མ་ (trusiŋ drugsugmə) dragon boat.

གྲུ་གཟིངས་བཟོ་བསྐྲུན་ཀུང་སི་ (trusiŋ sogyön gūŋsi) tib.ch. shipbuilding company.

གྲུ་གཟིངས་བཟོ་གྲྭ་ (trusiŋ sodra) shipyard, dockyard, shipbuilding factory.

གྲུ་གཟིངས་རུ་ཁག (trusiŋ rugaà) barge train, convoy of ships.

གྲུ་གཟུགས་ (trusug) hull.

གྲུ་གཟུགས་ལས་ཚན་ (trusug lɛɛ̀dzɛn) hull shop.

གྲུ་བཟོ་ (truso) shipbuilding; va.—བྱེད་.

གྲུ་བཟོ་ (tru so) vi. to not conceive (usu. livestock).

གྲུ་བཟོ་པ་ (trusowa) shipbuilder.

གྲུ་གཡོར་ (truyɔr) sail (of a boat); va.—འགེལ་ to hoist sails, to set sail.

གྲུ་གཡོར་རླུང་གིས་འདེད་པ་ལྟར་ (truyɔr lūŋgi dèèbadar) without obstacles/ hindrances, smooth sailing [Lit. like sails driven by the wind].

གྲུ་རོགས་ (trurɔɔ̀) servant on a ship, manual laborer on a ship.

གྲུ་ལམ་ (trulam) shipping route/ shipping lane.

གྲུ་ལམ་འགག་སྒོ་ (trulam gaŋgo) canal lock.

གྲུ་ལས་པ་ (trulɛba) sm. གྲུ་པ་.

གྲུ་ལོག (trulɔɔ̀) capsizing; vi.—རྒྱག; —ཐེབས་ to capsize, to tip over (boats).

གྲུ་ལོགས་ (trulɔɔ̀) corner ¶ རྩིག་པའི་གྲུ་ལོགས་སུ་ At the corner of the wall.

གྲུ་ཤན་ (trushɛn) ferry boat/ ship.

གྲུ་ཤན་ཁ་ (trushɛnga) ferry landing.

གྲུ་ཤན་ཆུ་འཛིངས་སུ་སླེབས་པས་བཏོལ་ཁུང་བཀག་ཀྱང་ཕན་པ་ཅི་ (trushɛn cūnjiŋsu lēbbɛ döökuŋ gāàgyaŋ pēmba jī) its better to plan in advance [Lit. it is useless to plug a leak when the boat is in midstream].

གྲུ་ཤན་རྟ་མགོ་ (trushɛn dāŋgo) boat/ ferry with the bow carved as a horse's head.

གྲུ་ཤན་པ་ (trushɛmba) sm. གྲུ་པ་.

གྲུ་ཤན་དཔེ་དབྱིབས་ (trushɛn bēyib) model ships.

གྲུ་ཤིང་ (trushiŋ) oar, boat pole.

གྲུ་གཤོག (trushɔɔ̀) side of a ship or boat.

གྲུ་ས་ (trusə) 1. harbor, place where boats are kept. 2. a place where boats can be sailed.

གྲུ་གསུམ་ (trusum) triangle.

གྲུ་ལྷགས་ཕྱོགས་སུ་གཏོང་བ་ལྟར་ (trulhag cōgsu dōŋbadar) sm. གྲུ་གཡོར་རླུང་གིས་འདེད་པ་ལྟར་.

གྲུག (trug) 1. vi. to be broken/ chipped དཀར་ཡོལ་གྱི་ཁ་གྲུག་བཞག The cup's lip has been broken. 2. vi. the skin becoming coarse/ chapped because of the cold.

གྲུག་དུབ་ (trugdub) bracelets/ bangles worn just below the biceps.

གྲུག་རིལ་ (trugrii) ball of thread.

གྲུང་ (truŋ) adj. of གྲུང་པོ་.

གྲུང་འཁྱུག (truŋgyuù) sm. གྲུང་པོ་.

གྲུང་ཅིང་ (truŋjiŋ) Chongqing.

གྲུང་པོ་ (truŋbu) clever, smart, intelligent ¶ ཁོ་ནི་རང་བཞིན་གྱི་གྲུང་པོ་ཞིག་འདུག He is naturally intelligent.

གྲུང་ཟོན་གཉིས་ལྡན་ (truŋsön ñiìlɛn) cautious/ vigilant and alert.

གྲུང་ཤ་ (truŋsha) alertness, keenness, awareness.

གྲུང་ཤ་དོད་པོ་ (truŋsha dööbo) appearing clever, smart, intelligent.

གྲུང་ཧྲིག་ཧྲིག (tru hrighrii) alert, lively.

གྲུངས་བྱེད (truŋjeè) water purifier/ filter.

གྲུངས་མ (truŋma) clear, pure (liquid).

གྲུབ (trub) 1. p. of འགྲུབ. 2. vi. to obtain, to achieve, to attain ¶ ང་ཚོའི་རེ་དོན་གྲུབ་པ་རེད Our hopes have been achieved. 3. vi. to form, to become, to be made/ created from ¶ སྐུ་བརྙན་དེ་རྡོ་ལས་གྲུབ་པ་ཞིག་རེད That image is one that is made from stone. 4. vi. to finish, to complete ¶ གཟིགས་བསྐོར་གྲུབ་ནས After (they) completed the tour. 5. vi. to confirm or establish (an idea or fact) ¶ མེ་ཡིན་ན་ཚ་པོ་ཡིན་པས་གྲུབ If (it) is fire, this establishes (it) being hot.

གྲུབ་ཆ (trubja) element, component.

གྲུབ་ཆེན (trubjen) Buddhist tantric siddha.

གྲུབ་མཆོག (trubjoò) sm. གྲུབ་ཆེན.

གྲུབ་རྗེས (trubjeè) achievement, accomplishment.

གྲུབ་རྟགས (trubdaà) miracle; va.—སྟོན to perform a miracle.

གྲུབ་སྟོན (trubdön) a ceremony held on completion of a project/ task, etc.

གྲུབ་ཐོབ (trubdob) sm. གྲུབ་ཆེན.

གྲུབ་ཐོབ་ཆེན་པོ (trubdob cēmbo) sm. གྲུབ་ཆེན.

གྲུབ་མཐའ (trubda) religious sect.

གྲུབ་མཐའ་གོང་མ (trubta koŋma) Mahayana School of Buddhism.

གྲུབ་མཐའ་འོག་མ (trubta wɔgmaå) Hinayana school of Buddhism.

གྲུབ་མཐའི་འཛིན་འཁྱེར (trubtɛ tēnkyer) sectarianism (religious).

གྲུབ་མཐའི་ཕྱོགས་རིས (trubdɛ cɔ̄grii) sm. མཐའི་འཛིན་འཁྱེར.

གྲུབ་དོན (trubdön) sm. གྲུབ་འབྲས.

གྲུབ་ནང་སེམས་གཅིག (trunaŋ sēmjig) all having the same thoughts/ opinions [Lit. one mind in a boat].

གྲུབ་པ་ཐོབ (tubə tōb) vi. to achieve the level of siddhi.

གྲུབ་པའི་མཐའ (trubɛ tā) sm. གྲུབ་མཐའ.

གྲུབ་པའི་རྨ (trumbɛ mā) a cut/ wound caused by an accident.

གྲུབ་འབྲས (trumdrɛɛ̀) achievement, result, success; vi.ཐོབ; —སྟོན to achieve results/ success ¶ ཁོང་གིས་ལས་ཀར་གྲུབ་འབྲས་ཆེན་པོ་ཐོབ་བཞག He achieved great success in his work.

གྲུབ་འབྲས་འོད་སྡོང་འབར་བ (trumdrɛɛ̀ ö̱ödoŋ barwa) brilliant achievement, remarkable success.

གྲུབ་རྫས (trubdzɛɛ̀) finished products/ goods.

གྲུབ་གཟུགས (trubsug) 1. combine all into one, aggregate. 2. the total, the answer of a calculation (in math).

གྲུབ་གསལ (trubsɛl) sm. གྲུབ་པས་བསྟན་པ.

གྲུམ (trum) 1. abbr. for གྲུམ་བུ. 2. sm. གྲུག. 3. vi. to have a horse walk unsteadily due to losing a horseshoe.

གྲུམ་རྒྱང (trumgyaŋ) a long Tibetan rug.

གྲུམ་འཐག (trumdaà) carpet weaving ¶ གྲུམ་ཐག་བཟོ་གྲྭ.

གྲུམ་གདན (trumdɛn) carpet, rug.

གྲུམ་ནད (trumnɛɛ̀) sm. གྲུམ་བུ.

གྲུམ་པ (trumba) 1. a badger. 2. broken pieces. 3. a tiller.

གྲུམ་པ་རྒྱས (trumbə gyɛɛ̀) vi. to put forth new shoots from the root or bottom of a stalk.

གྲུམ་པོ (trumbu) 1. sm. གྲུམ་བུ. 2. lame foot.

གྲུམ་ལྤགས (trumbaà) badger skin.

གྲུམ་བུ (trumbu) arthritis, rheumatism.

གྲུམ་བུ་རྒྱ་སེར (trumbu cūser) impetigo.

གྲུམ་རྩེ (trumdze) carpet, rug.

གྲུམ་ཟེ (trumse) sm. གྲུམ་རྩེ.

གྲུའི་ཁ་ལོ (trüü kālo) boat's rudder/ steering wheel.

གྲུའི་ཉག་ཐག (trüü ñagdaà) rope used to pull a boat.

གྲུའི་དར་ཤིང (trüü tarshiŋ) (ship) mast.

གྲུའི་བང་ཞོལ (trüü paŋshöö) ship's hold/ cabin.

གྲུའུ་རྩི (trüüdzi) ch. silk.

གྲུའུ་རྫས (trüüdzüü) ch.tib. synthetic silk.

གྲུལ་ཐུབ་པ (trüüdubbə) shung. reliable ¶ སེམས་པ་གྲུལ་ཐུབ་པའི་གྲོགས་པོ་ཞིག་འཚོལ་དགོས One should find a reliable friend.

གྲུལ་བུམ (trüübum) a class of demons.

གྲུས (trüü) 1. circles on the horns of animals that indicate their age. 2. vi. to go into heat.

གྲུས་མ (trüümə) milch animals. 2. animals in heat.

གྲུས་ལོག (trüü lɔ̀ɔ̀) not coming into heat a second time (year) and conceiving (for livestock); vi.—རྒྱག.

གྲེ་འགྱུར (tregyur) tone, note.

གྲེ་སྒོ (trego) vocal cords.

གྲེ་ཆམ (trejam) cold with a sore throat; vi.—རྒྱག; —ཕོག.

གྲེ་ཐོགས (tredog) throat cancer.

གྲེ་བ (trewa) windpipe, throat; vocal cords; vi.—འཛེར; —འགགས to become hoarse.

གྲེ་པོ་མདོག (trewo dɔ̀ɔ̀) yellowish color.

གྲེ་བའི་ཚ་ནད (trewɛ tsānɛɛ̀) pharyngitis.

གྲེ་སེར་འབྲོང (treser droŋ) wild yak.

གྲེ་གསང (tresaŋ) clearing ones throat; va.—རྒྱག.

གྲེ་བསལ (tresɛl) sm. གྲེ་གསང.

གྲེའུ (trəwu) buckwheat.

གྲེས་མ (treēma) 1. iris. 2. a type of grass (strobilathes cusia).

གྲོ (tro) 1. wheat. 2. food (in the Kham dialect) ¶ གྲོ་ཟོས་ཟིན (We) have eaten.

གྲོ་དཀར (trogar) light gray color (for horses).

གྲོ་ཁ (truga) food provisions carried for a journey or when herding.

གྲོ་ཁང (trokaŋ) 1. flour mill. 2. house where wheat is stored.

གྲོ་ག (troga) the bark of a birch tree.

གྲོ་གྲོ (trodro) mixture of black and white wool.

གྲོ་གྲོན (trodrön) expenses.

གྲོ་ང་འཕྲུལ་འཁོར (troŋā trüügɔɔ) wheat harvester.

གྲོ་ཕྱོག (trojoò) bundles of wheat piled up on the fields after harvest.

གྲོ་ཆག (trojaà) pounded (flat) wheat.

གྲོ་ཆང (trojaŋ) beer made from wheat.

གྲོ་ཆན (trojɛn) porridge made from wheat.

གྲོ་ཆས (trojɛɛ̀) sm. གྲོ་ཁ.

གྲོ་ཇུ (troju) broth made from pounded wheat.

གྲོ་རྗེན (trojen) flour.

གྲོ་ལྗང (trojaŋ) wheat seedling/ shoot.

གྲོ་སྙིགས (troñii) wheat dregs/ remnant, wheat bran.

གྲོ་སྙེ (troñe) ear of wheat.

གྲོ་སྙོད (troñöö) a plant used for in Tibetan medicine (carum carvi).

གྲོ་བདགས (trodaà) grinding wheat into flour; va.—རྒྱག.

གྲོ་རྡེན (troden) money and provisions for travel/ journey.

གྲོ་ཐལ (trodɛɛ) wheat smut.

གྲོ་ཐིག (trudii) freckles, moles.

གྲོ་ཐུག (troduù) soup/ porridge made from wheat.

གྲོ་འཐག (trodaà) flour mill.

གྲོ་འཐག་བཟོ་གྲྭ (trodag sodra) wheat grinding factory.

གྲོ་འཐག་ལས་ཁངས (trodaà lɛɛ̀guŋ) flour milling office/ work unit.

གྲོ་འདེབས (tro deb) 1. va. to plant wheat. 2. va. to stop on a trip/ journey to have a noon meal.

གྲོ་ནས་སྲན་གསུམ (tro nɛɛ̀ sēnsum) the three: wheat, barley and peas.

གྲོ་ལྤགས (trobaà) skin of wheat.

གྲོ་བྱི (troji) abbr. of གྲོ་མོ་བྱི་ཁྱུབ.

གྲོ་བྱི་ཁང (trojigaŋ) residence of the གྲོ་མོ་བྱི་ཁྱུབ.

གྲོ་ཕུག (trobuù) sm. གྲོ་ཕུབ.

གྲོ་ཕུབ (trobub) hay from wheat.

གྲོ་ཕྱེ (troje) wheat flour.

གྲོ་ཕྱེ་འཐག་ཁང (troje tāagaŋ) mill (for grinding wheat).

གྲོ་ཕྱེ་སྣུམ་བརྫོས (troje nūmŋöö) cookies fried in oil or butter.

གྲོ་ཕྱེ་བཟོ་གྲྭ་ (trobce sodra) flour mill.

གྲོ་པོ་ (trowo) grayish color.

གྲོ་འབྲུ་ (trondru) 1. wheat grain. 2. abbr. wheat and grain.

གྲོ་སྦུན་ (trobün) sm. གྲོ་ཕུབ་ས.

གྲོ་མ་ (troma) wild sweet potato, potentilla anserina.

གྲོ་མ་འབྲས་སིལ་ (troma drɛɛ̀sii) a ceremonial food made from wild sweet potato, rice, sugar and butter.

གྲོ་མ་མར་ཁུ་ (tromo mərgu) a food made from boiled wild sweet potato and melted butter.

གྲོ་མར་ (tromar) butter for travel/ journey.

གྲོ་མོ་ (tromo) Yadong (a border area and town located between Phari and Sikkim).

གྲོ་མོ་སྤྱི་ཁྱབ་ (tromo jīgyəb) shung. Governor General of Yadong area (in tt. government).

གྲོ་མོ་བ་ (tromowa) people from Yadong.

གྲོ་སྨྱུག (troñuù) sm. གྲོ་ལྦང་.

གྲོ་སྨྱུག་མངར་ཆ་ (troñug ŋārja) malt sugar, maltose.

གྲོ་དམར་ (tromar) reddish gray horse.

གྲོ་རྩམ་ (trodzam) tsampa made from wheat.

གྲོ་ཞིང་ (troshiŋ) wheat field.

གྲོ་ཞིབ་ (trushii) flour; va.—རྫི་ to knead flour into dough.

གྲོ་བཞིན་ (troshin) sm. གྲོ་ཞིན་.

གྲོ་བཞིན་ཟླ་བ་ (troshin dawa) the 7th month of the Tibetan calendar.

གྲོ་ཟན་ (trosɛn) a kind of food made from cooked wheat.

གྲོ་ཟན་གནོད་འབུ་ (trosɛn nömbu) gelechild (a type of moth).

གྲོ་ཟས་ (trusɛɛ̀) sm. གྲོ་ཟན་.

གྲོ་ཡོས་ (troyöö) popped wheat.

གྲོ་རིལ་ (trorii) wheat (unmilled).

གྲོ་ལམ་ (trolam) the distance from where one leaves in the morning on a trip to where they stop for their noon meal.

གྲོ་ཤ་ (trosha) meat for travel/ journey.

གྲོ་སོ་ཕྱེ་མར་ (troso cēmar) traditional Tibetan offering box with two sections—one section is filled with a mixture of tsampa and butter and the other with popped corn.

གྲོ་སོག (trosoò) wheat straw.

གྲོ་སྲན་ཕྱེད་འཁྱེར་ (trosɛn cēègyer) shung. half wheat and half beans ། དམག་ཕོགས་གྲོ་སྲན་ཕྱེད་འཁྱེར་གྱི་རྒྱུའི་ཁལ་༡༨ For soldier's salary, 18 ཁལ་ of grain, half wheat and half beans.

གྲོ་ཧྲལ་ (trohrɛɛ) roughly ground wheat that is used for cooking porridge or stew.

གྲོག (troò) 1. sm. གྲོག་པོ་. 2. auspicious omen. 3. good opportunity. 4. abbr. of གྲོག་མ་.

གྲོག་སྐད་ (troggɛɛ̀) the cawing noise that crows make (that is considered auspicious).

གྲོག་ཁ་ནང་སླེབས་པ་ལྕེ་ཡིས་འཕུལ་ (troò kānaŋ lēèba jēè yii pǖü) sm. གྲོག་ཁ་ལ་ཡོད་པ་ལྕེས་སྣུད་རྒྱག་རྒྱག.

གྲོག་ཁ་ལ་ཡོད་པ་ལྕེས་འབུད་ (troòkāla yööba jēè bǖü) sm. གྲོག་ཁ་ལ་ཡོད་པ་ལྕེས་འབུད་.

གྲོག་ཁ་ལ་ཡོད་པ་ལྕེས་འབུད་ (troòkāla yöba jēè bǖü) va. to blow an easy opportunity, to let a good opportunity slip by; va.—རྒྱག [Lit. on the edge of the mouth, pushed out by the tongue].

གྲོག་མཁར་ (troògar) ant hill.

གྲོག་ངོ་ (trogŋo) a sign of good fortune/ luck.

གྲོག་ཆུ་ (trogju) river in a gorge.

གྲོག་ཆེན་པོ་ (trɔɔ̀ cēmbo) lucky ། ད་རྒྱུགས་ལ་ཁོང་གི་དངུལ་བཙུགས་ནས་ཁོང་ལ་གྲོག་ཆེན་པོ་བྱུང་བཞག He bet on the horse race and got lucky and won.

གྲོག་ནག (trognaà) black ant.

གྲོག་པོ་ (trogbo) sm. གྲོག་མོ་.

གྲོག་ལྷ་ (trogja) feeling the pulse of sb. to foretell/ divine; va.—བརྟག་ to foretell/ divine by feeling the pulse.

གྲོག་སྦུར་ (trogbur) sm. འབུ་སྦིན་.

གྲོག་མ་ (trɔɔ̀ma) ant.

གྲོག་མ་དཀར་པོ་ (trɔɔ̀ma gārbo) termite, white ant.

གྲོག་མ་རྟ་ཐོག་ནས་མཐོང་ (trɔɔ̀ma dādɔɔ̀nɛ ŋön) high authorities seeing the problems of poor people [Lit. seeing ants from horseback].

གྲོག་མ་ཚང་ (trɔɔ̀madzaŋ) ant hill.

གྲོག་མའི་ཚོགས་ཀྱིས་སེང་ཕྲུག་གསོད་ (trɔɔ̀mɛ tsöggiì sēŋdruù söö) strength in numbers, a united effort can accomplish a lot [Lit. a colony of ants can kill a lion cub].

གྲོག་མས་རི་བོ་ཐའི་ཧྲན་སྒྲོ་ (trɔɔ̀mɛɛ̀ riwo tēhrɛn bō) the united efforts of the masses can accomplish mighty projects [Lit. ants can move Mount Taishan].

གྲོག་མོ་ (trogmo) narrow gorge, ravine.

གྲོག་མོ་སྒམ་པོར་ཉ་རྒྱ་བདབ་ (tromo gāmbor ñagya dəb) trying to do the impossible [Lit. casting a net to catch fish in a gorge].

གྲོག་མོའི་རོང་ (trɔgmö roŋ) sm. གྲོག་མོ་.

གྲོག་དམར་ (trɔɔ̀mar) red ant.

གྲོག་ཙེ་ (trɔgdze) table.

གྲོག་ཚང་ (trɔgdzaŋ) ant hill.

གྲོག་ཟ་སྡིག་ཆགས་ (trɔgsa sōgjaà) anteater.

གྲོག་ཟན་ (trɔgsɛn) anteater.

གྲོག་གཟར་ (trɔgsar) precipitous gorge.

གྲོག་གཡང་ (trɔgyar) sm. གྲོག་གཟར་.

གྲོག་རོང་ (trɔgroŋ) gully, ravine, narrow gorge.

གྲོག་རོང་དོག་པོ་ (trɔgroŋ togbo) narrow/ deep gorge.

གྲོག་རོང་ས་ཁུལ་ (trɔgroŋ sōgüü) gorge/ ravine area.

གྲོག་ཤིང་ (trogshiŋ) moss.

གྲོག་ཤུར་ (trogshur) sm. གྲོག་རོང་.

གྲོགས་ (trog) 1. friend. 2. assistance, help; va.—བྱེད་ to assist, to help ། ཁོས་མོ་ལ་དོ་པོ་འཁྱེར་གྲོགས་བྱེད་པ་རེད་ He helped her carry the load. 3. associate, colleague, helper ། ཁོང་ངའི་ལས་གྲོགས་རེད་ He is my associate (at work). 4. when used at the end of a clause (often with གནང་ or བྱེད་) it expresses the idea 'please, would you?' ། ཁྱེད་རང་འདི་ར་འབྱུག་ཙམ་ཕེབས་གྲོགས་གནང་ Would you please come here for a moment.

གྲོགས་སྐལ་ (troggɛɛ) fortune/ luck for getting a good spouse.

གྲོགས་མགོན་ (troggön) help and protection/ support.

གྲོགས་སྒྲིག (trogdrig) making friends; va.—བྱེད་.

གྲོགས་ངན་ (trognɛn) bad friend.

གྲོགས་ཆང་ (trogcaŋ) a chang drinking party of friends; va.—རྒྱག.

གྲོགས་མཆེད་ (trogjeè) 1. friends who are as close as a relative. 2. friends and relatives.

གྲོགས་མཆོག (trogcɔɔ̀) best friend.

གྲོགས་དང་ (trogdaŋ) a friendly party (political).

གྲོགས་དང་གྲོགས་དམག (trogdaŋ trogmaà) friendly party and friendly army/ troops.

གྲོགས་དན་ (trogdɛn) sm. རོགས་རམ་.

གྲོགས་དོན་ (trogdön) friendship.

གྲོགས་སྡེབ་ (trogdeb) going/ doing with sb. as a friend.

གྲོགས་པོ་ (trogbo) friend; va.—རྒྱག; —སྒྲིག; —བྱེད་ to be friends, to make friends.

གྲོགས་པོ་མི་གཅིག་སྙིང་གཅིག (trogbo mijig ñiŋjig) very close friend.

གྲོགས་པོ་འཚོང་ (trogbo tsöŋ) va. to betray or sell out one's friends.

གྲོགས་པོ་གཡོ་འཚོང་ (trogbo yōdzoŋ) betraying one's friends; va.—རྒྱག.

གྲོགས་པོ་སློག (trogbo lɔɔ̀) va. to cease being a friend.

གྲོགས་པོའི་མདོང་མོ་ནང་ཤུགས་གདོང་ (trogbö doŋmo nəŋshugsu dōŋ) va. to lend one's wife to a good friend (for sexual intercourse) [Lit. internally selling/ trading a friend's churn].

གྲོགས་སྤུན་ (trogbün) friends and relatives.

གྲོགས་ལྷ་ (trogja) sm.* གྲོག་ལྷ་.

གྲོགས་བྲལ་ཁེར་སྡོད་ (troŋdrɛɛ kērdöö) isolated, alone.

གྲོགས་འབྲེལ་ (trogdrel) friendship; va.—བྱེད་ to make friends.

གྲོགས་འབྲེལ་དམ་པོ་ (trogdrel dambo) close/ tight

friendship.

གྲོགས་མེད་ཁེར་རྐྱང་ (trogmeè kērgyaŋ) alone, without friends, isolated ¶ གྲོགས་མེད་ཁེར་རྐྱང་དུ་གནས་ཡོད་པ་རེད་ (They) remained isolated (without friends).

གྲོགས་མེད་ཁེར་སྲུང་ (trogmeè kērsuŋ) standing alone in defense.

གྲོགས་མེད་གཅིག་འགྱུར་ (trogmeè jīgyur) sm. གྲོགས་མེད་ཁེར་རྐྱང་.

གྲོགས་མེད་གཅིག་པུ་ (trogmeè jīgbu) sm. གྲོགས་མེད་ཁེར་རྐྱང་.

གྲོགས་མེད་ཤུགས་ཞན་ (trogmeè shūgshɛn) weak and friendless.

གྲོགས་མོ་ (trɔ̄ɔmo) 1. girl friend, sweetheart. 2. female friend.

གྲོགས་དམག (trogmaà) friendly forces/ troops/ army.

གྲོགས་ཚིག (trogtsig) auxiliary word/ particle.

གྲོགས་ཟ་འཁྱེར་སོང་ (trogsa kyērsoŋ) getting sth. through luck ¶ ལས་གནས་ཡག་པོ་དེ་ཁོ་ལ་གྲོགས་ཟ་འཁྱེར་སོང་ He got that good position through luck.

གྲོགས་ཟས་ཟ་ (trogsɛɛ̀ sa) va. to eat food with friends.

གྲོགས་བཟང་ (trogsaŋ) good/ close friend.

གྲོགས་རམ་ (trogram) help, assistance, aid; va.—བྱེད་.

གྲོགས་བཤེས་ (trogsheè) a reliable/ dependable/ trusted friend.

གྲོགས་སུ་བསྟེན་ (trogsu dēn) 1. va. to take someone as one's spouse. 2. va. to make somebody one's friend.

གྲོགས་བསོད་ཆུང་ཆུང་ (trogsöö cūŋjuŋ) not having a good spouse due karma.

གྲོགས་བསོད་ཆེན་པོ་ (trogsöö cēmbo) having good spouse due karma.

གྲོང་ (troŋ) 1. village, hamlet. 2. sm.* གྲོངས་.

གྲོང་སྐད་ (troŋgɛɛ̀) 1. local dialect. 2. colloquial speech.

གྲོང་སྐད་མིན་པ་ (troŋgɛɛ̀ mimbə) formal speech/ talk (in opp. to informal style of talk).

གྲོང་སྐོར་ (troŋgɔɔ) 1. going around a town or village. 2. parading sb. around the street as a punishment and to show others he is a criminal; va.—ཁྲིད་ to take sb. around like this.

གྲོང་ཁུལ་ (troŋgüü) 1. village area. 2. urban area.

གྲོང་ཁྱིམ་ (troŋgyim) 1. household in a city. 2. household in a village.

གྲོང་ཁྱེར་ (troŋgyer) city, town, municipality.

གྲོང་ཁྱེར་འགོ་འཛིན་ (troŋgyer gondzin) mayor of a city.

གྲོང་ཁྱེར་ཆབ་སྲིད་གྲོས་ཚོགས་ཁང་ (troŋgyer cābsiì trȫötsoògaŋ) political consultative conference of a city.

གྲོང་ཁྱེར་ཆེ་གྲས་ (troŋgyer cēdrɛɛ̀) large cities.

གྲོང་ཁྱེར་ཆེ་ཆུང་ (troŋgyer cējuŋ) cities and towns, large and small cities.

གྲོང་ཁྱེར་ཉེ་འཁོར་ (troŋgyer ñegɔɔ) sm. གྲོང་ཁྱེར་ཉེ་འདབས་.

གྲོང་ཁྱེར་ཉེ་འདབས་ (troŋgyer ñedəb) suburbs.

གྲོང་ཁྱེར་ལྟེ་བ་ (troŋgyer dēwa) main city.

གྲོང་ཁྱེར་དོ་དམ་གྱི་ལས་དོན་ (troŋgyer todamgi lɛɛ̀dön) municipal affairs.

གྲོང་ཁྱེར་བདག་གཉེར་ཨུ་ཡོན་ལྷན་ཁང་ (troŋgyer dagñer üyön lhɛnkaŋ) municipal management committee.

གྲོང་ཁྱེར་ནང་ཁོངས་ (troŋgyee naŋgoŋ) municipal government.

གྲོང་ཁྱེར་སྤྱི་སྤྱོད་སྒྲིག་ཆས་ (troŋgyee jījöö drigjɛɛ̀) municipal public facilities.

གྲོང་ཁྱེར་སྤྱི་སྤྱོད་ལས་དོན་ (troŋgyee jījöö lɛɛ̀dön) city public services/ utilities.

གྲོང་ཁྱེར་པ་ (troŋgyeewa) city folk.

གྲོང་ཁྱེར་མི་དམངས་འཐུས་མི་ཚོགས་པ་ (troŋgyee mimaŋ tǖümi tsōgba) municipal people's congress.

གྲོང་ཁྱེར་མི་དམངས་སྲིད་གཞུང་ (troŋgyee mimaŋ sīishuŋ) municipal people's government.

གྲོང་ཁྱེར་མཚོན་རྟགས་ (troŋgyee tsōndaà) emblem of a city.

གྲོང་ཁྱེར་མཚོན་བྱེད་མེ་ཏོག (troŋgyee tsōnjeè medog) city flower (flower emblematic of a city).

གྲོང་ཁྱེར་འཛུགས་སྐྲུན་ཨུ་ཡོན་ལྷན་ཁང་ (troŋgye dzugdrün üyön lhɛngaŋ) committe of urban construction.

གྲོང་ཁྱེར་འཛུགས་སྐྲུན་ལག་རྩལ་སློབ་གྲྭ (troŋgye dzugdrün lagdzɛɛ lōbdra) urban development technical school.

གྲོང་ཁྱེར་ཟློས་གར་ཚོགས་པ་ (troŋgyee döögar tsōgba) municipal dance troupe.

གྲོང་ཁྱེར་ལས་དོན་པུའུ་ (troŋgyee lɛɛ̀dön būwu) department of urban works.

གྲོང་ཁྱེར་སྲིད་འཛིན་དོ་དམ་ཐྲུའུ་ (troŋgyee sīndzin todam trūwu) municipal administration department.

གྲོང་ཁྱེར་ཨུ་ཡོན་ལྷན་ཁང་ (troŋgyee üyön lhɛ̄nkaŋ) city/ municipal party committee.

གྲོང་གླིང་ (troŋliŋ) villages.

གྲོང་འགོ་ (troŋgo) city center.

གྲོང་འགྲམ་ (troŋdram) outskirts of a city/ town/ village, suburbs.

གྲོང་གཅིག་མ་ (troŋjigmə) a village consisting of one household, one household by itself.

གྲོང་ཆོག (troŋcɔɔ̀) monks going to do prayers in a lay person's home; va.—རྒྱག་; —འགྲིམ་ to go to do prayers in a lay person's house.

གྲོང་ཆོག་པ་ (troŋcɔgba) a monks who going to do prayers in a lay person's home.

གྲོང་ཆོས་པ་ (troŋcööba) a lay person who goes to perform religious rites and read scriptures in the houses of laymen.

གྲོང་འཇུག (troŋjuù) a type of tantric practice whereby a person's spirit after he dies can come to life again.

གྲོང་བསྙེན་ (troŋñen) going into retreat in one's own home.

གྲོང་གདམ་ (troŋdam) sm. གྲོང་སྐད་.

གྲོང་དྲག་དམག་སྒར་ (troŋdraà māgar) name of a regiment in tt. that was specially recruited from better families as a corvess tax.

གྲོང་བདག (troŋdaà) head of a village.

གྲོང་མདོ་ (troŋdo) the lower part of a village.

གྲོང་འདབས་ (troŋdəb) sm. གྲོང་འགྲམ་.

གྲོང་དལ་ (troŋdɛɛ) a town.

གྲོང་སྡེ་ (troŋde) village.

གྲོང་བརྡལ་ (troŋdɛɛ) sm. གྲོང་དལ་.

གྲོང་སྣེ་ (troŋne) edge of a town/ city/ village.

གྲོང་པ་ (troŋba) 1. household. 2. neighbor.

གྲོང་པ་ཁྱིམ་མཚེས་ (troŋba gyīmdzeè) neighbors.

གྲོང་པ་ཉེ་འདོད་ན་སྒོང་ལ་ཚེར་མས་སྐོར་ (troŋba ñe döōna goŋla tsērmɛ gɔ̄ɔ) if you want to have close relations with your neighbors, keep some distance from them [Lit. If you want to be friendly with your neighbors, surround the roof with thorns].

གྲོང་པའི་ཤི་ཡང་ཉ་ངན་ཞག་གསུམ་ (troŋpɛɛ shīyaŋ ñaŋɛn shagsum) one should sympathize with one's neighbor's misfortunes [Lit. even if a neighbor's cow dies one should mourn for three days].

གྲོང་དཔོན་ (troŋbön) sm. གྲོང་བདག.

གྲོང་ཕུ་ (troŋ pū) the upper part of a village.

གྲོང་འཕོ་གྲོང་འཇུག (troŋpo troŋjuù) sm. འཕོ་བ་གྲོང་འཇུག.

གྲོང་མི་ (troŋmi) a resident of a city or village.

གྲོང་མི་ཨུ་ཡོན་ལྷན་ཁང་ (troŋmi üyön lɛ̄ngaŋ) neighborhood committee (in city).

གྲོང་ཚིག (troŋdziì) 1. colloquial language. 2. dirty talk.

གྲོང་ཚོ་ (troŋdzo) village, town.

གྲོང་གཞིས་ (troŋsheè) a village household.

གྲོང་བཟོ་ (troŋso) an association of tailors in tt.

གྲོང་རོགས་ (tro̱ŋroò) neighbor.

གྲོང་གསེབ་ (tro̱ŋseè) village, the countryside ༉ཁོང་ཚོ་གྲོང་གསེབ་ལ་སྡོད་པ་རེད་ They live in the countryside.

གྲོང་གསེབ་པ་ (tro̱ŋsebba) villager.

གྲོང་གསེབ་བྱ་བའི་ཁྲུའུ་ (tro̱ŋseb ca̱wɛ trūwu) rural work department.

གྲོང་ལྷན་ (tro̱ŋlhɛn) street party comittee.

གྲོངས་ (tro̱ŋ) p. of འགྲོངས་.

གྲོངས་མཁན་ (tro̱ŋgɛn) the late, the deceased ༉ཉི་མ་གྲོངས་མཁན་དེ་ The late Nyima.

གྲོངས་པ་ (tro̱ŋba) sm. གྲོངས་མཁན་.

གྲོད་སྐྱི་ (trö̱gyi) peritoneum.

གྲོད་ཁོག (trö̱ögɔɔ) stomach; vi.—རྒྱགས་; —འགྲངས་ to be/ get full; vi.—ལྟོགས་ to be hungry; vi.—སྦོས་ to be/ feel bloated.

གྲོད་ཁོག་འཁྲོག (trö̱ögɔɔ trɔɔ) vi. to have a rumbling stomach.

གྲོད་ཁོག་སྒྲིམ་ (trö̱ögɔɔ dri̱m) sm. གྲོད་ཁོག་བཤལ་.

གྲོད་ཁོག་ང་རྒྱས་ (trö̱ögɔɔ ŋāgye) distended stomach; vi.—ཆགས་ to have the stomach be/ get/ feel distended.

གྲོད་ཁོག་གཅུས་རིལ་རྒྱག (trö̱ögɔɔ jǖrii) vi. to have a twisting of the stomach.

གྲོད་ཁོག་ཆུང་ཆུང་ (trö̱ögɔɔ cūŋjuŋ) 1. small stomach. 2. sb. who eats little, having a small appetite. 3. an official who only takes small bribes ༉ལས་བྱེད་པ་དེ་གྲོད་ཁོག་ཆུང་ཆུང་ཡོད་པ་རེད་ The cadre has a small stomach (i.e., takes only small bribes).

གྲོད་ཁོག་ཆེན་པོ་ (trö̱ögɔɔ cēmbo) 1. person with a big stomach. 2. sb. who eats a lot, large appetite. 3. sb. who takes large bribes ༉དཔོན་པོ་དེ་གྲོད་ཁོག་ཆེན་པོ་ཡོད་པ་རེད་ That official has a big stomach (takes large bribes).

གྲོད་ཁོག་ལྟོགས་ (trö̱ögɔɔ dɔɔ) see གྲོད་ཁོག.

གྲོད་ཁོག་སྦོས་ (trö̱ögɔɔ bö̱ö) see གྲོད་ཁོག.

གྲོད་ཁོག་འཚོང་ (trö̱ögɔɔ tsōŋ) 1. va. to go uninvited to the houses of friends, relatives, etc. so as to mooch a meal (negative connotation) ༉མི་དེས་རྟག་པར་གྲོགས་པོའི་སར་གྲོད་ཁོག་འཚོང་གི་ཡོད་པ་རེད་ That person always goes to his friends place to mooch a meal. 2. va. to ask or hint for a bribe ༉ཁྲིམས་དཔོན་ངན་པ་དེས་ཁ་མཆུ་རྒྱག་མཁན་ལ་རྟག་པར་གྲོད་ཁོག་འཚོང་གི་འདུག The evil judge always hints for a bribe from the disputants in cases.

གྲོད་ཁོག་བཤལ་ (trö̱ögɔɔ shɛ̄ɛ) vi. to have/ get diarrhea.

གྲོད་ཉེར་ཅན་ (trö̱ñorjɛn) a person with a pot belly.

གྲོད་སྒྲུམ་ (trö̱dum) sth. that is sewn up/ wrapped in the stomach of a sheep.

གྲོད་ད་ (trö̱da) sm. གྲོད་པ་.

གྲོད་པ་ (trö̱ba) sm. གྲོད་ཁོག.

གྲོད་པ་ཁ་ཚ་ (trö̱ba kādza) a dish made of the stomach of an animal and turmeric.

གྲོད་པ་ཅན་ (trö̱bajɛn) person with a big appetite.

གྲོད་པ་ལྷུག་ལྷུག (trö̱ba lhūgluù) person with a pot belly.

གྲོད་རིལ་ (trö̱örii) lump of butter wrapped in the stomach of an animal.

གྲོད་ལུག (trö̱luù) sm. གྲོད་པ་ལྷུག་ལྷུག.

གྲོད་ལོང་ (trö̱loŋ) sm. གྲོད་ཁོག.

གྲོད་ཤ་ (trö̱ösha) tripe.

གྲོན་ (trö̱n) expense, expenditure ༉ངལ་གྲོན་གཉིས་ཀ་ཆུད་ཟོས་སུ་ཕྱིན་པ་རེད་ Both the troubles and the expenses went to waste.

གྲོན་དངུལ་ (trö̱nŋüü) expenditure, expenses, outlay (money) ༉གྲོན་དངུལ་གཞུང་ནས་བཏང་པ་རེད་ The government paid the expenses.

གྲོན་ཅན་ (trö̱njɛn) 1. heavy expense. 2. arc. meaningless.

གྲོན་ཆུང་ (trö̱njuŋ) economical, inexpensive, thrifty; va.—བྱེད་ to economize, to be careful in spending, to be thrifty.

གྲོན་ཆུང་ཐོན་སྤེལ་ (trö̱njuŋ tōnbel) sm. ཐོན་སྤེལ་གྲོན་ཆུང་.

གྲོན་ཆུང་དམ་ཚགས་ (trö̱njuŋ da̱mdzaà) thrifty, economical.

གྲོན་ཆུང་ནན་དན་ (trö̱njuŋ nɛ̱ndɛn) strict or rigid application of thrift/ economicalness.

གྲོན་ཆེན་ (trö̱njɛn) expensive, a large expenditure/ outlay.

གྲོན་གཏོང་ (trö̱ndoŋ) paying expenditures/ expenses; va.—བྱེད་ to meet/ pay expenditures ༉ཁོང་ཚོས་འཆར་གཞི་འདིའི་གྲོན་གཏོང་བྱེད་རྒྱུ་ཁས་བླངས་པ་རེད་ They promised to pay the expenditures for this plan.

གྲོན་པ་ (trö̱mba) consumption, consuming; expenditure ༉རླངས་འཁོར་འདི་སྣུམ་གྱི་གྲོན་པ་ཆེན་པོ་འདུག The car has a high oil consumption. ༉ལོ་འདིའི་ནང་ལས་ཁུངས་ཀྱི་དངུལ་གྲོན་པ་ཆེན་པོ་བྱུང་སོང་ This year the office had a large expenditure of money.

གྲོན་མེད་ (trö̱nmeè) free.

གྲོན་འཛད་ (tröndzɛɛ̀) sm. གྲོན་པ་.

གྲོན་ཤས་ (trö̱nshɛɛ̀) item/ part of an expenditure.

གྲོའི་གཡུང་དྲུང་ (trö̱ö yūŋdruŋ) a swastika drawn with wheat during ceremonies.

གྲོལ་ (trö̱ö) 1. vi. to be free of troubles/ difficulties/ danger, to get loose/ free/ untied ༉ཉེན་ཁ་ལས་གྲོལ་པ་རེད་ (They) got out of danger. ༉འཇུར་སྒྲོག་གྲོལ་འདུག The shoelaces got loose. 2. vi. to be over, to be dismissed/ adjourned ༉ཚོགས་འདུ་གྲོལ་ནས་ After the meeting adjourned.

གྲོལ་ཇ་ (trö̱öja) tea served in offices at the end of a work day.

གྲོལ་ཉིན་ (trö̱öñin) the day a particular project is completed.

གྲོལ་སྟོན་ (trö̱ödön) closing/ completion/ graduation celebration.

གྲོལ་བདེའི་སྒོ་མོ་ (trö̱ödee go̱mo) exit.

གྲོལ་མ་ (trö̱öma) a worm that grows in the intestines.

གྲོལ་མ་དུད་ (trö̱ö mə̱düü) a knot that is easily untied, slip knot.

གྲོལ་ཚུགས་ (trö̱ödzuù) beginning and end, start and finish ༉འཛིན་གྲྭ་གྲོལ་ཚུགས་སྐབས་ At the beginning and end of the class.

གྲོལ་མཚམས་ (trö̱ndzam) intermission, adjournment, break.

གྲོལ་ཟིན་ཡུལ་གྲུ་ (trö̱ösin yü̱ü̱dru) sm. གྲོལ་ཟིན་ས་གནས་.

གྲོལ་ཟིན་ས་གནས་ (trö̱ösin sānɛɛ̀) liberated area.

གྲོལ་བསང་ (trö̱ösaŋ) incense that is burnt to indicate the duration of a party (i.e., the party ends when the incense burns out).

གྲོས་ (trö̱ö) talk, discussion, negotiations; va.—བྱེད་; —བཟོ་ to have talks/ negotiations, to discuss.

གྲོས་ཀྱི་རྒྱུ་བྱེད་ (trö̱ögi gyu̱jeè) the main (warp) focus of a discussion.

གྲོས་ཀྱི་སྤུན་བྱེད་ (trö̱ögi bǖnjeè) the secondary (woof) focus of a discussion.

གྲོས་ཁ་གཅིག་མཐུན་ (trö̱öga ji̱gdün) unanimous agreement.

གྲོས་ཁང་ (trö̱ögaŋ) parliament, assembly, congress, soviet, council, legislature (e.g., house of representatives, chamber of deputies, etc.).

གྲོས་ཁང་གི་ཁོངས་མི་ (trö̱ögaŋgi kōŋma) member of parliament, congressman, assemblyman.

གྲོས་ཁང་གོང་མ་ (trö̱ögaŋ ko̱ŋma) House of Lords (England), Senate (U.S.), House of Councilors (Japan), Upper House (in a parliament).

གྲོས་ཁང་གཅིག་གི་ལམ་ལུགས་ (trö̱ögaŋ ji̱ggi lə̱mluù) unicameral or one chamber legislative system.

གྲོས་ཁང་གཉིས་ཡོད་པའི་ལམ་ལུགས་ (trö̱ögaŋ ñīi yö̱bɛ lə̱mluù) two-chamber legislative system.

གྲོས་ཁང་འོག་མ་ (trö̱ögaŋ wɔ̱ɔma) Lower House (in a parliament), House of Commons, House of Representatives.

གྲོས་གྲོགས་ (trö̱ödrɔɔ̀) partner/ colleague/ in discussions.

གྲོས་གྲོས་ (tro̱ödröö) discussing, taking about; va.—གཏོང་ ¶ མི་གཞན་གྱིས་ཁྱེད་རང་གི་སྐོར་གྲོས་གྲོས་གཏོང་གི་འདུག Other people are talking about you.

གྲོས་གླེང་ (tro̱öleŋ) discussing; va.—ལེན་; —བྱེད་ to discuss ¶ བཟོ་གྲྭ་གསར་པའི་སྐོར་གྲོས་གླེང་བྱས་མི་འདུག They didn't discuss the matter of the new factory.

གྲོས་འགོ་ (tro̱ngo) the opening statement/ speech read at a meeting, initial comments at a meeting that are made to initiate discussion of an issue; va.—བྱེད་; —འདོན་.

གྲོས་འགོ་དང་ལེན་ (tro̱ngo ta̱ŋlen) voluntarily accepting the opening/ initial statement at a meeting; va.—བྱེད་.

གྲོས་འགྲིག་ཚོགས་པ་ (tro̱drig tsōgba) a negotiating team.

གྲོས་ངན་ (tro̱öŋɛn) plotting, scheming; va.—གཤོམ་ to plot ¶ ཁོ་གཉིས་བྲོས་བྱོལ་འགྲོ་རྒྱུའི་གྲོས་ངན་བཤམས་འདུག They plotted to run away.

གྲོས་ཆོད་ (tro̱öjöö) resolution, decision, agreement; va.—འཇོག to pass a resolution, to come to a decision, to sign an agreement ¶ ས་མཚམས་གནད་དོན་སྐོར་གྱི་གྲོས་ཆོད་ The resolution regarding the border question.

གྲོས་ཆོད་ཀྱི་འཆར་ཟིན་ (tro̱öjöögi cə̄rsin) draft resolution.

གྲོས་ཆོད་ཀྱི་ཡི་གེ་ (tro̱öjöögi yi̱gi) a protocol, a resolution/ document ¶ ཉོ་ཚོང་གྲོས་ཆོད་ཡི་གེ་ Trade protocol.

གྲོས་འཆམ་ (tro̱njam) 1. agreement, resolution; vi.—ཡོང་ to come to an agreement, to resolve, to adopt a resolution; va.—བྱེད་ to agree on a decision/ resolution ¶ ཚོགས་འདུ་དེའི་གྲོས་འཆམ་ལ་མིང་རྟགས་བཀོད་པ་རེད་ They signed the resolution of that meeting. ¶ མི་མང་བས་གྲོས་འཆམ་བྱུང་བ་རེད་ The majority of the people agreed (to the resolution). ¶ ཚོགས་འདུར་གྲོས་ཆོད་འགའ་ཤིག་ལ་གྲོས་འཆམ་བྱེད་སྐབས་ At the time of agreeing to several resolutions.

གྲོས་འཆམས་ (tro̱njam) 1. p. of གྲོས་འཆམ་. 2. sm. གྲོས་འཆམ་.

གྲོས་འཆར་ (tro̱njar) 1. agenda of a meeting; va.—འདོན་ to put forth an agenda. 2. suggestion, recommendation, proposal; va.—འདོན་ ¶ ཚོགས་འདུའི་ཐོག་མི་དམངས་ཀྱི་འཚོ་བ་ཡར་རྒྱས་གཏོང་རྒྱུའི་གྲོས་འཆར་བཏོན་འདུག They made a suggestion at the meeting for improving the livelihood of the people.

གྲོས་གཏན་འཁེལ་ (tro̱ö dɛ̄ngɛɛ) va. to come to a decision after a discussion or negotiation.

གྲོས་སྟོན་ (tro̱ö dōn) sm. གྲོས་འདོན་.

གྲོས་སྟོན་མཁན་ (tro̱ö dōngɛn) consultant.

གྲོས་སྟོན་པ་ (tro̱ö dōmba) sm. གྲོས་སྟོན་མཁན་.

གྲོས་ཐག་གཅོད་ (tro̱ödaa jöö) va. to decide, to resolve.

གྲོས་ཐག་བཅད་ (tro̱ödaa jɛ̄ɛ) p. of གྲོས་ཐག་གཅོད་.

གྲོས་ཐག་ཆོད་ (tro̱ödaa cöö) vi. to come to an agreement or conclusion, to be resolved ¶ གྲོས་བསྡུར་མང་པོའི་རྗེས་སུ་འཆར་གཞི་གསར་པ་ལག་ལེན་བསྟར་རྒྱུར་གྲོས་ཐག་ཆོད་པ་རེད་ After many discussions (they) agreed to implement the new plan ¶ གྲོས་ཐག་ཆོད་པའི་གྲོས་གཞི་ A resolution that has been approved/ passed.

གྲོས་མཐུན་ (tro̱ödün) 1. agreement, accord, concord; va.—འཇོག to sign an agreement/ accord. 2. vi. to agree through discussion.

གྲོས་མཐུན་ཆོད་ཡིག (tro̱ödün cööyii) treaty, agreement, concord, pact; va.—འཇོག to sign a treaty/ agreement/ concord/ pact.

གྲོས་མཐུན་དོན་ཚན་བཅུ་བདུན་ (tro̱ödün töndzɛn jūbdün) 17 Point Agreement (for the Peaceful Liberation of Tibet) (signed May 23, 1951).

གྲོས་མཐུན་ཡིག་ཆ་ (tro̱ödün yi̱gjə) a document containing an agreement.

གྲོས་དན་ (tro̱ndɛn) sm. གྲོས་མཐུན་.

གྲོས་དོན་ (tro̱dön) 1. subject of debate/ discussion, a topic to be discussed. 2. the point of a གྲོས་གཞི་. 3. contents of an agreement.

གྲོས་དོན་ཆོད་ཡིག (tro̱dön cööyii) resolution, decision.

གྲོས་དོན་ཡིག་ཆ་ (tro̱dön yi̱gjə) sm. གྲོས་མཐུན་ཡིག་ཆ་.

གྲོས་འདེབས་ (tro̱ndeb) sm. གྲོས་བསྡུར་.

གྲོས་འདོན་ (tro̱ö dö̱n) va. to give/ put forth an idea, to make a suggestion ¶ གནད་དོན་འདིའི་སྐོར་ཁོང་གིས་གྲོས་བཏོན་པ་རེད་ Concerning this issue, he made a suggestion.

གྲོས་འདྲི་ (tro̱ndri) va. to ask (advice), to consult, to take an issue before a council/ assembly/ etc.

གྲོས་འདྲི་ས་ (tro̱ö tri̱sə) person to whom one asks/ consults.

གྲོས་སྡུར་ (tro̱ödur) sm. གྲོས་བསྡུར་.

གྲོས་བསྡུར་ (tro̱ödur) discussion, talk; va.—བྱེད་ to discuss, to talk over ¶ ཞི་བདེའི་གྲོས་བསྡུར་ Peace talks. ¶ གྲོས་དོན་རེ་རེ་བཞིན་ཚོགས་ཆུང་གིས་གྲོས་བསྡུར་བྱས་འདུག The small group has had discussions on each subject.

གྲོས་བསྡུར་བབ་ལྟ་ (tro̱ödur bə̱bda) a discussion in which an evaluating of sth. occurs; va.—བྱེད་.

གྲོས་བསྡུར་བྱ་གཞི་ (tro̱ödur cə̱shi) a question/ agenda for discussion.

གྲོས་བསྡུར་ཚོགས་འདུ་ (tro̱ödur tsōndu) a symposium.

གྲོས་པ་ (tro̱öba) advisor, councilor, one who gives advice.

གྲོས་བྱེད་ (tro̱ö ce̱è) to discuss, to have a talk.

གྲོས་མི་ (tro̱ömi) 1. sb. with whom one discusses sth., sb. who gives advice. 2. sm. གྲོས་ཚབ་.

གྲོས་མི་ལ་འདྲི་ གྲོས་ཐག་རང་གིས་གཅོད་ (tro̱ömilə tri̱ tro̱öraŋgi jöö) one should seek other's advice but make one's own decision.

གྲོས་མེད་བསམ་མཐུན་ (tro̱ömeè sāmdün) agreeing/ thinking alike without prior discussion.

གྲོས་མོལ་ (tro̱ömöö) sm. གྲོས་བསྡུར་.

གྲོས་མོལ་སྤྱི་བསྒྲགས་ (tro̱ömöö ji̱draà) official report/ communiqué of a discussion or meeting.

གྲོས་མོལ་ཚོགས་འདུ་ (tro̱ömöö tsōndu) symposium, consultative conference.

གྲོས་ཚབ་ (tro̱ödzəb) parliamentary representative, congressman.

གྲོས་ཚབ་ལམ་ལུགས་ (tro̱ödzəb lə̱mluù) parliamentary/ representative system.

གྲོས་ཚོགས་ (tro̱ödzoò) 1. assembly, parliament, congress (U.S.A.) ¶ གྲོས་ཚོགས་ཀྱི་ཕྱི་འབྲེལ་ཚོགས་ཆུང་ The Committee on Foreign Relations of the U.S. Congress. 2. meeting, conference.

གྲོས་ཚོགས་ཁང་ (tro̱ödzoògaŋ) conference hall, meeting room.

གྲོས་ཚོགས་ཀྱི་བཀའ་ཁྲོལ་ཞུ་སྒྲོད་ཚོགས་ཆུང་ (tro̱ödzoògi gādröö shu̱dröö tsōgjuŋ) Committee on Authorization (U.S. Congress).

གྲོས་ཚོགས་ཀྱི་རྒྱལ་སྤྱིའི་ལས་དོན་ཚོགས་ཆུང་ (tro̱ödzoògi gyɛɛjii lɛ̱ɛdön tsōgjuŋ) Committee on International Relations (U.S. Congress).

གྲོས་ཚོགས་ཀྱི་རྒྱལ་ཡོངས་དཔེ་མཛོད་ (tro̱ödzoògi gyɛ̱ɛyoŋ bēndzöö) Library of Congress (U.S.A.).

གྲོས་ཚོགས་ཀྱི་སྔོན་རྩིས་ཚོགས་ཆུང་ (tro̱ödzoògi ŋöndzii tsōgjuŋ) Committee on the Budget (U.S. Congress).

གྲོས་ཚོགས་ཀྱི་ཉམས་ཞིབ་ལས་དོན་ཁང་ (tro̱ödzoògi ñə̱mshibgaŋ) Congressional Research Service (U.S.A.).

གྲོས་ཚོགས་ཀྱི་དཔལ་འབྱོར་ལས་དོན་ཚོགས་ཆུང་ (tro̱ödzoògi bɛ̄njɔɔ lɛ̱ɛdön tsōgjuŋ) Congressional Committee on Finance (U.S.A.).

གྲོས་ཚོགས་ཀྱི་ཕྱི་འབྲེལ་ཚོགས་ཆུང་ (tro̱ödzoògi ci̱dree tsōgjuŋ) Senate Committee on Foreign Relations (U.S.A.), House Committee on International Relations.

གྲོས་ཚོགས་ཀྱི་གཞུང་སྒྲོན་ཟུར་གཅོད་ཚོགས་ཆུང་ (tro̱ödzoògi shu̱ŋdrön su̱rjöö tsōgjuŋ) Senate/

House Appropriations Committees (U.S.A.).

གྲོས་ཚོགས་ཀྱི་སོ་ནམ་ལས་དོན་ཚོགས་ཆུང་ (tröödzoògi sōnam lɛ̀ɛ̀dön tsɔ̄gjuŋ) Congressional Committee on Agriculture (U.S.A.).

གྲོས་ཚོགས་གོང་འོག་ (tröödzoò koŋwɔ̀ɔ̀) Upper and Lower Houses of Parliament.

གྲོས་ཚོགས་འོག་མ་ (tröödzoò wɔ̀ɔ̀ma) Lower House of Parliament.

གྲོས་ཚོགས་ལྷན་ཚོགས་ (tröödzoò lhɛ̄ntsoò) parliament.

གྲོས་མཚམས་གཅོད་ (trööd zam joȍ) va. to adjourn (a meeting).

གྲོས་ཞིབ་ (trööshib) thorough/ detailed discussion; va.—བྱེད་ to discuss in detail.

གྲོས་ཞིབ་ཁང་ (trööshibgaŋ) sm. གྲོས་ཁང་.

གྲོས་གཞི་ (trööshi) proposal, subject for discussion, motion, topic; va.—བྱེད་; —འདོན་ to propose sth., to put forth a motion, to raise an issue/ subject (for discussion) ༑དམག་དོན་འགྲོ་སོང་ཆུང་དུ་གཏོང་དགོས་པའི་གྲོས་གཞི་དེ་སྐར་ཡང་བཏོན་པ་རེད་ They put forth once again the motion that military expenditures be decreased.

གྲོས་གཞི་འདོན་མཁན་ (trööshi döngɛn) person who moves/ proposes a resolution or motion.

གྲོས་གཞི་འདོན་ཡིག་ (trööshi dönyig) sm. གྲོས་གཞིའི་ཡི་གེ.

གྲོས་གཞིའི་ཡི་གེ་ (trööshi yigi) motion/ proposal/ resolution document.

གྲོས་འགོ་ (troŋgo) making an initiating statement at a meeting/ discussion; va.—འདོན་.

གྲོས་ཡ་ (trööya) a person with whom one consults/ discusses.

གྲོས་ཡིག་ (trööyii) abbr. of གྲོས་དོན་ཡིག་ཆ་.

གྲོས་རིམ་ (tröörim) agenda.

གྲོས་རིམ་ཉིན་ཐོ་ (trööriｍ ñinto) daily agenda.

གྲོས་གསོམ་ (trööshom) va. to discuss, to hold talks.

གྲྭ་ (tra) 1. fence, yard. 2. angle, corner. 3. abbr. of གྲྭ་པ་. 4. school.

གྲྭ་དཀྱུས་ (trəgyüü) ordinary/ common monk.

གྲྭ་རྐང་སྤ་འཐོར་ (tragaŋ ŋādɔɔ) shung. monks who have lost their celibacy.

གྲྭ་རྐྱང་ (tragyaŋ) a simple/ ordinary monk.

གྲྭ་སྐལ་ (tragɛɛ) the share of a donation that a monk receives.

གྲྭ་སྐོར་ (tragɔɔ) 1. monks who go to different monasteries to debate. 2. monastery.

གྲྭ་ཁང་ (tragaŋ) a room/ house where monks live.

གྲྭ་ཁྲལ་ (tradrɛɛ) a tax wherein a family has to provide a son to become a monk.

གྲྭ་གོང་ (tragoŋ) sm. སྣ་གོང་.

གྲྭ་གོས་ (tragöö) monk's clothes.

གྲྭ་གྲངས་ (tradraŋ) number of monks.

གྲྭ་རྒན་ (tragɛn) an old monk.

གྲྭ་རྒྱུན་ (tragyün) a young monk who has come from far away (mostly Amdo, Kham) to spend time in one of the great monasteries in Lhasa (and central Tibet) as part of a long tradition of such visits.

གྲྭ་ཇ་ (traja) tea provided by a college in a large monastery.

གྲྭ་ཐོག་ (tradog) the date when a monk joined the monastery ༑ང་གཉིས་གྲྭ་ཐོག་གཅིག་པ་རེད་ We two are from the same period (in joining a monastery).

གྲྭ་པ་ (traba) monk; va.—བྱེད་ to become a monk; va.—སློག་ to cause a monk to lose (his) celibacy); vi.—ལོག་ to lose one's celibacy (for a monk).

གྲྭ་པ་བཀའ་ལོག་ (traba gālɔɔ) sm. གྲྭ་པ་ལོག.

གྲྭ་པ་གྲྭ་རྐྱང་ (traba tragyaŋ) a typical/ quintessential monk (in attitude and deportment).

གྲྭ་པ་དར་པོ་དོག་པོ་ (traba dabedobe) monks in their twenties and thirties who do not study and do menial tasks around the monastery.

གྲྭ་དཔོན་ (trabön) abbot.

གྲྭ་ཕྲུག་ (tradrug) child monk.

གྲྭ་འཇུགས་ (trajaà) shung. custom/ process of conscripting monks to serve as monk officials in the government.

གྲྭ་བུ་སློབ་ (tra pulob) monk disciple.

གྲྭ་མང་ (tramaŋ) sm. གྲྭ་དམངས་.

གྲྭ་དམག་ (tramaà) 1. monk soldiers. 2. monk war.

གྲྭ་དམངས་ (tramaŋ) the common monks ༑ང་གྲྭ་དམངས་ཀྱི་འཐུས་མི་ཡིན་ I am a representatives of the common monks.

གྲྭ་བཙུན་ (tradzün) monk and nun.

གྲྭ་ཚང་ (tradzaŋ) college in a monastery.

གྲྭ་ཚང་ཆོས་མཛད་ (tradzaŋ cöndzɛɛ) shung. a title purchased in monastic colleges that exempts the holder from most work obligations.

གྲྭ་ཚང་སྤྲུལ་སྐུ་ (tradzaŋ drüügu) an incarnate lama of the monastic college level rank.

གྲྭ་ཚང་ཕྱག་མཛོད་ (tradzaŋ cāndzöö) manager/ steward/ financial administrator of a monastic college.

གྲྭ་ཚང་དབུ་མཛད་ (tradzaŋ ūmdzɛɛ) prayer leader of a monastic college.

གྲྭ་ཚང་ཚོགས་འདུ་ (tradzaŋ tsōŋdu) the assembly of a college (in a monastery).

གྲྭ་ཚད་ (tradzɛɛ) shung. number of monks in a monastery as fixed by the tt. government.

གྲྭ་ཚབ་ (tradzəb) substitute monk.

གྲྭ་ཚོགས་ (tradzɔɔ) assemblage of monks.

གྲྭ་ཞིང་ (trashiŋ) shung. a field whose yield is dedicated to support a monk.

གྲྭ་ཞྭ་ (trasha) monk's hat.

གྲྭ་གཞོན་ (trashön) a young monk.

གྲྭ་བཞི་ (trəpshi) 1. locale north of Lhasa and just south of Sera monastery. 2. sm. གྲྭ་བཞི་དམག་སྒར་.

གྲྭ་བཞི་གླིང་ཀ་ (trəpshi lı̄ŋga) a grove located in གྲྭ་བཞི་.

གྲྭ་བཞི་དམག་སྒར་ (trəpshi māagar) shung. the (Trapshi) Regiment (in the tt. army) that was based in Trapshi.

གྲྭ་བཞི་རྩིས་བཤེར་ (trəpshi dzı̄isher) shung. the inspection/ review of troops in Trapchi during the Great Prayer Festival in Lhasa.

གྲྭ་བཞི་ལས་ཁུངས་ (trəpshi lɛ̀ɛ̀gun) shung. the armory and mint that was located in Trapshi (in tt.).

གྲྭ་ཟུར་ (trasur) 1. corner, edge. 2. an ex-monk.

གྲྭ་གཟན་ (trasɛn) monk's upper shawl.

གྲྭ་གཡོག་ (trayɔɔ) monk servant.

གྲྭ་རིགས་ (trərig) monks.

གྲྭ་རུ་ (traru) a herd that belongs to monastery.

གྲྭ་ལུགས་ (traluù) 1. the customs of monks. 2. male homosexuality; va.—བྱེད་; —གཏོང་ [Lit. monk's customs].

གྲྭ་ལན་ (tralen) monk's vest.

གྲྭ་ཤག་ (trashaà) monk's apartment/ room/ house.

གྲྭ་ཤར་ (trashar) young monks (roughly teenagers and young adults).

གྲྭ་ས་ (trasa) 1. monastery ༑ངའི་གྲྭ་ས་སེ་ར་ཡིན་ My monastery is Sera. 2. monastic college.

གྲྭ་ས་གྲྭ་ཚང་ (trasa tradzaŋ) monastery and its colleges.

གྲྭ་སའི་སྒྲིག་སྡུག་ (trasɛ gyiduù) the monastic organization/ community; va.—(ནས་)འབུད་ to be thrown out/ expelled from monastery; va.—འཐེན་ to withdraw from monastery.

གྲྭ་ལྷམ་ (tralham) monk's boots.

གྲྭ་གསུམ་ (trasum) triangle, triangular.

གླ་ (lā) 1. wage, salary ༑ཉིན་གླ་ Daily wage. 2. rental fee, rent ༑ཁང་གླ་ The rent for the house. 3. a fare, freight fee/ charge ༑གནམ་གྲུའི་གླ་ Plane fare. 4. abbr. of གླ་པ་ and གླ་མི་.

གླ་: p. གླས་; f. གླ་; imp. གློས་ (lā) va. to hire, to rent ༑རྩྭ་མཁན་མི་གཉིས་གླས་པ་རེད་ (They) hired two people to cut the grass.

གླ་བསྐུལ་ (lāgüü) coercive/ exploitive employment ༑ཕྲུ་གུར་གླ་བསྐུལ་བཀག་སྡོམས་ Prohibition of coercive child employment.

གླ་ཁུངས་བྱེད་ (lāguŋ ceè) va. to help sb. find people

to hire.

གླ་ཁོངས་ (lāgoŋ) hired, on the payroll; va.—བྱེད་.

གླ་ཁོངས་ནས་འབུད་ (lākoŋ) va. to dismiss from employment, to take off the payroll.

གླ་ཁོལ་ (lāgöö) abbr. hired hands and servants.

གླ་གག (lāgaà) a bird of prey similar to an eagle.

གླ་གི (lāge) sm. གླ་བ་.

གླ་རྒྱུན་ (lōgyün) rawhide made from the hide of a musk deer.

གླ་སྒང་ (lāgaŋ) 1. geranium (pylzowianum maxim). 2. cyperus rotundus (the rhizome of nutgrass flatsedge).

གླ་སྒྲིལ་ལྟོ་སྒྲིལ་ (lədrii dōdrii) work where a wage is paid and meals are also provided.

གླ་རྔན་ (lāŋɛn) wages and gifts.

གླ་ཆ་ (lāja) 1. wages, salary, remuneration; va.—སྤྲོད་ to pay wages. 2. rental fee/ charge. 3. fare, freight fee/ charge.

གླ་ཆའི་ཐང་གཞི་ (lājɛ tāŋshi) the prevailing rate of wages/ fees/ fares.

གླ་ལྟོ་ (lādo) abbr. wage and food.

གླ་ཐང་ (lādaŋ) abbr. of གླ་ཆའི་ཐང་གཞི་.

གླ་ཐོབ་ (lādob) wage, salary.

གླ་བདག (lādaà) 1. employer. 2. labor and management ། གླ་བདག་གཉིས་ཀྱི་རྩོད་པ་ A labor-management dispute.

གླ་སྡོང་ (lādoŋ) trunk/ stem of geranium.

གླ་པ་ (lāba) 1. wage laborer/ worker, hired hand; va.—གླ་ to hire a wage laborer; —བྱེད་ to work as a hired hand ། སྐབས་འཕྲལ་གླ་པ་ Temporary hired hands.

གླ་སྤུ་ (ləbu) hair of a musk deer ། གླ་སྤུའི་འབོལ་གདན་ A cushion filled with the hair of musk deer.

གླ་ཕོགས་ (lābɔɔ̀) sm. གླ་ཆ་.

གླ་ཕོར་ (lābɔɔ) wooden bowl.

གླ་ཕྲུག (lədruù) young musk deer.

གླ་བ་ (lāwa) musk deer.

གླ་བ་ཅེ་བ་ཅན་ (lāwa cēwajɛn) male musk deer.

གླ་བུ་ (ləbu) sm. གླ་པ་.

གླ་བོ་ (lābo) talk; va.—བྱེད་.

གླ་བྱེད་ (lājeè) for hire (as a taxi).

གླ་བྱེད་རླངས་འཁོར་ (lājeè lāŋgɔɔ) taxi.

གླ་འབོལ་ (lāmböö) cushion made with musk deer hair.

གླ་མི་ (lāmi) sm. གླ་པ་.

གླ་མེད་ (lāmeè) without pay.

གླ་མེད་ངལ་རྩོལ་ (lāmeè ŋɛɛdzöö) unpaid/ free labor.

གླ་མེད་ལྟོ་མེད་ (lāmeè dōmeè) work/ labor with no wages or food paid.

གླ་མོ་ (lāmo) female musk deer.

གླ་རྫི་ (lādzi) musk.

གླ་རྫི་དབྱུག་ནས་གླ་ལྤགས་ཉར་ (lədzi yūùnɛ lābaà ñaa) lack of judgment [Lit. discard the musk, retain musk deer skin].

གླ་ཟན་ (lāsɛn) sm. གླ་པ་.

གླ་ཡོན་ (lāyön) sm. གླ་ཆ་.

གླ་རིན་ (lərin) abbr. wage and cost or price (of materials).

གླ་ས་ (lāsa) place to hire workers.

གླག (lāà) eagle.

གླག་ཕྲུག (ləgdruù) baby eagle.

གླག་རོག (lāàroò) black eagle.

གླགས་ (lāà) 1. coping with, managing; vi.—རྙེད་; —ཁེལ་ to be able to cope with ། ཕྲུ་གུ་འཁྱལ་པོ་དེ་ཕ་མས་གླགས་ཁེལ་གྱི་མེད་པ་རེད་ The parents are unable to cope with the naughty boy. 2. (vb. + —) time to do the verbal action ། ལས་ཀ་བྲེལ་བ་ཚ་དྲགས་ནས་ནང་ལ་སྡོད་གླགས་མི་འདུག Because I was too busy, I had no time to stay at home.

གླགས་སྐབས་འཚོལ་ (lāà gəbtsöö) va. to look for an opportune moment to get back at sb. or take revenge. 2. va. to look for a pretext.

གླགས་ཁེལ་ (lāà kēē) vi. to be able to handle ། ཁོས་རྟ་འདི་གླགས་ཁེལ་གྱི་མ་རེད་ He will not be able to handle that horse.

གླགས་རྙེད་ (lāà ñēè) sm. གླགས་ཁེལ་.

གླགས་ལྟ་ (lāà dā) 1. va. to test. 2. va. to look for faults.

གླགས་འཚོལ་ (lāà tsöö) sm. གླགས་སྐབས་འཚོལ་.

གླགས་ཡུས་བཤད་ (lāàyüü shɛɛ) va. to behave like a spoiled child.

གླང་ (lāŋ) bull, bullock.

གླང་ཀོ་ (lāŋgo) oxhide, cowhide.

གླང་གླད་ (lāŋlɛɛ̀) soap.

གླང་སྐེར་བེལ་བདགས་ (lāŋger pee dāà) a small poor family merging with a bigger family so as to be able to fulfill tax obligations; a small business merging with a bigger one [Lit. tie a calf around an ox's neck.].

གླང་ཁྱིམ་ (ləŋgyim) 1. cowshed. 2. Taurus the Bull.

གླང་གོག (lāŋgɔò) bull, bullock, ox.

གླང་རྒན་གྱིས་འཁོར་ལོ་གོག་རུལ་འཐེན་ (lāŋgɛngi kɔɔlo gɔghrül tēn) very slow [Lit. a broken down cart pulled by an old bull].

གླང་རྒོད་ (lāŋgöö) wild elephant.

གླང་རྒྱབ་ (lāŋgyəb) 1. the back of a bull. 2. the load that a bullock carries.

གླང་རྒྱུད་ཁྱུང་དཀར་ བོང་རྒྱུད་སྨུག་ཆུང་ (lāŋgyüü kyuŋgaa poŋgyüü mugjuŋ) children superior/ stronger/ more capable than their father [Lit. dzo from ox, mules from donkeys].

གླང་སྒ་ (lāŋga) ox saddle.

གླང་སྒ་རིལ་ (lāŋgarii) bullock cart; va.—གཏོང་ to drive a bullock cart.

གླང་སྐྱུར་ (lāŋgur) a liver disease.

གླང་ཆུང་ (lāŋjuŋ) young bull.

གླང་ཆེན་ (lāŋjen) elephant.

གླང་ཆེན་མཆུ་ཏོ་ (lāŋjen cūdo) trunk (of an elephant).

གླང་ཆེན་རྐང་རྔ་ (lāŋjen gāŋŋa) a drum shaped like an elephant's leg.

གླང་ཆེན་ཁ་འབབ་ (lāŋjen kəbəb) Sutlej river.

གླང་ཆེན་འཁྱིང་རེ་ (lāŋjen gyiŋre) Mt. Emei.

གླང་ཆེན་རྒྱབ་ཁལ་བེའུ་ལ་འགེལ་ (lāŋjen gyəbkɛɛ biwulə gee) overloading sb., taking advantage of sb. [Lit. loading an elephant's load on a calf].

གླང་ཆེན་མཆེ་བ་ (lāŋjen cēwa) elephant tusk.

གླང་ཆེན་ཐལ་དཀར་ (lāŋjen tɛɛgar) whitish elephant.

གླང་ཆེན་སྨྱོན་པ་ (lāŋjen ñomba) 1. mad/ rogue elephant. 2. name of a traditional Tibetan medicine.

གླང་ཆེན་རི་ཟུར་ (lāŋjen risur) the mountain "finger" extending just to the east of Sera Monastery.

གླང་ཏིག་པ་ (lāŋdigbə) prunella vulgaris.

གླང་ཐབས་ (lāŋdəb) 1. sm. གླང་འཐབ་. 2. sm. གླང་བུར་.

གླང་ཐུག (lāŋduù) stud ox, stud bull.

གླང་འཐབ་ (lāŋdəb) an excruciating pain in the stomach.

གླང་འདྲེན་འཁོར་ལོ་ (lāŋden kɔɔlo) bullock cart.

གླང་དར་མ་ (lāŋ tarma) the Tibetan king Langdarma who was assassinated in 842 A.D.

གླང་དོར་ (lāŋdɔr) pair of bullocks.

གླང་མདུན་ (ləŋdün) name of an aristocratic family.

གླང་སྣ་ (lāŋna) trunk of an elephant.

གླང་སྣ་མེ་ཏོག (lāŋna medɔɔ̀) a type of Tibetan herbal medicine.

གླང་པོ་ (lāŋbo) sm. གླང་ཆེན་.

གླང་པོ་ཆེ་ (lāŋboce) sm. གླང་ཆེན་.

གླང་པོ་གདུམ་པོ་ (lāŋbo dūmbo) wild/ untamed elephant.

གླང་པོ་རིན་པོ་ཆེ་ (lāŋbo rimboce) one of the seven auspicious symbols.

གླང་པོའི་ཁ་ལོ་པ་ (lāŋbö kāloba) sm. གླང་རྫི་.

གླང་བྲིས་ (lāŋdreè) cattle trough.

གླང་སྦལ་ (lāŋbɛɛ) bullfrog.

གླང་མ་ (lāŋma) alpine willow tree.

གླང་མ་རི་ (lāŋmari) sm. ཇོ་མོ་གླང་མ་.

གླང་མ་ཤིང་ (lāŋmashiŋ) sm. གླང་མ་.

གླང་མོ་ (lāŋmo) female elephant.

གླང་རྩིས་ (ləŋdzii) a type of astrological calculation.

གླང་ཚེར་ (lāŋdzer) a type of tree.

གླང་རྫི་ (lāŋdzi) elephant keeper/ herder.

གླང་ཟལ་པོ་ (lāŋ zɛɛbo) an ox with variegated color.

གླང་ཟླ་ (lāŋda) the 12th month of the Tibetan calendar.

གླང་གཡོག (lāŋyɔɔ̀) elephant attendant/ feeder.

གླང་ར་ (lāŋra) 1. a stable where oxen are kept. 2. elephant pen/ enclosure.

གླང་རུ་ (lāŋru) sm. གླང་རྭ་.

གླང་རོག (lāŋroò) black bull.

གླང་རྭ་ (lāŋra) ox horn.

གླང་ལ་རྭ་ཅོ་མེད་ རྟ་ལ་རྭ་ཅོ་སྐྱེས་ (lāŋla rājomeè dāla rajo gyēè) unfounded and baseless, impossible [Lit. an ox without horns, a horse with horns].

གླང་ལོ་ (lāŋlo) year of the ox.

གླང་ལོ་པ་ (lāŋloba) a male born in the year of the ox.

གླང་ལོ་པའི་ཆག་སྒོ་ཡོས་ལོ་བར་འཁེལ་ (lāŋlobɛ cāgo yöölobar kēē) blaming unjustly, making sb. into a scapegoat [Lit. misfortune of the ox year person falling on the hare year person].

གླང་ལོ་མ་ (lāŋloma) a female born in the year of the ox.

གླང་ཤ་ (lāŋsha) beef.

གླང་ཤིང་ (lāŋshiŋ) sm. གླང་མ་ཤིང་.

གླང་ཤུ་ (lāŋshu) psoriasis.

གླང་ཧྲང་ (lāŋhraŋ) bull (uncastrated).

གླན་ (lɛ̄n) a patch; va.—གླན་; —རྒྱག to patch ¶ མོས་གོས་ལོག་གི་བུག་ག་དེ་ར་ལྷན་པ་གླན་པ་རེད་ She patched up the hole in the garment.

གླན་གླེན་ (lɛ̄nlen) completely ignorant/ stupid.

གླན་རྒྱག (lɛ̄n gyaà) 1. see གླན་. 2. va. to answer/ reply/ retort.

གླམ་གྱིས་འཁྱེར་ (lāmgyi kyēr) vi. to get mildewed.

གླལ་ (lɛ̄ɛ) 1. vi. to yawn. 2. va. to stretch (hands and/ or feet).

གླལ་རིང་རྒྱག (lɛ̄ɛriŋ gyaà) vi. to yawn for a long time.

གླས་ (lɛ̀ɛ) p. of གླ་.

གླས་གླ་ (lɛ̄ɛla) wage (for a hired hand).

གླས་པའི་ངལ་རྩོལ་ (lēbɛ ŋɛɛdzöö) labor with pay on an hourly/ daily basis (rather than regular salary).

གླས་སྤྱོད་ (lɛ̄ɛjöö) renting and using.

གླས་དམག (lɛ̄ɛmaà) mercenary troops/ army.

གླས་འཚོ་བ་ (lɛ̄ɛ tsōwa) a person who depends for his livelihood on wages.

གླིང་ (līŋ) 1. island. 2. continent. 3. a part of sth. (often a section of a monastery). 4. abbr. of གླིང་བུ་. 5. abbr. of གླིང་ཁག.

གླིང་སྐོར་ (līŋgɔɔ) an outer circumambulation path/ circuit.

གླིང་སྐྱོད་ (līŋgyöö) sm. གླིང་བསྐྱོད་.

གླིང་སྐྱོད་འཕུར་མདའ་ (līŋgyöö pūndə) sm. གླིང་བསྐྱོད་འཕུར་མདའ་.

གླིང་བསྐྱོད་ (līŋgyöö) intercontinental.

གླིང་བསྐྱོད་འཕྲིད་མདའ་ (līŋgyöö trīnda) sm. གླིང་བསྐྱོད་འཕུར་མདའ་.

གླིང་བསྐྱོད་མདའ་ལམ་མེ་ཤུགས་འཕུར་མདའ་ (līŋgyöö dalam meshug pūnda) sm. གླིང་བསྐྱོད་འཕུར་མདའ་.

གླིང་བསྐྱོད་འཕུར་མདའ་ (līŋgyöö pūnda) intercontinental (ballistic) missile.

གླིང་ཁག (līŋgaà) the four major Labrangs in Lhasa: Reting, Tengyeling, Tshomoling, Kundeling.

གླིང་ཁག་བཞི་ (līŋgaà) sm. གླིང་ཁག.

གླིང་ག (līŋgə) park; va.—གཏོང་ to have a picnic.

གླིང་ག་དབྱི་ཧོ་ཡོན་ (līŋgə yīhoyön) tib. ch. the Summer Palace (in Beijing).

གླིང་གའི་སྒྲོ་ཚོགས་ (līŋgɛ drōtsoò) garden party.

གླིང་གེ་སར་ (līŋ gesar) King Gesar (the hero of the Tibetan epic).

གླིང་འགྲོད་མེ་ཤུགས་འཕུར་མདེལ་ (līŋdröö meshug pūnda) intercontinental (ballistic) missile.

གླིང་ཆེན་ (līŋjen) continent ¶ འཛམ་གླིང་གི་གླིང་ཆེན་ཁག The continents of the world.

གླིང་ཆེན་ལྔ་ (līŋjen ŋā) the five continents.

གླིང་ཆེན་ཨ་མེ་རི་ཀའི་རྒྱལ་ཁབ་ཀྱི་མཐུན་ཚོགས་ (līŋjen āmerikɛ gyɛkəbgi tündzoò) Organization of American States (OAS).

གླིང་ཆེན་ཨ་ཧྥི་རི་ཀ་ནུབ་རྒྱུད་ (līŋjen āferigə nubgyüü) West Africa.

གླིང་ལྗོངས་བདག་གཉེར་ཁང་ (līŋjoŋ dagñerkaŋ) park service.

གླིང་གཏོང་ (līŋdoŋ) abbr. of གླིང་ག་གཏོང་.

གླིང་དང་གླིང་ (līŋdaŋ līŋ) vast land.

གླིང་མདའ་ (līŋda) the lower part of a monastery or park/ garden.

གླིང་འདེབས་ (līŋdeb) planting by གླིང་ཞིང་ rather than individually owned plots of land.

གླིང་ནགས་ (līŋnaà) forest.

གླིང་སྣེ་ (līŋne) the poles.

གླིང་སྣེ་གཉིས་ (līŋne ñīī) the two poles of the earth (i.e., north and south pole).

གླིང་སྣེ་བྱང་མ་ (līŋne cāŋma) north pole.

གླིང་སྣེ་བྱང་མའི་མུ་ཁྱུད་ (līŋne caŋmɛ mugyüü) the arctic circle.

གླིང་སྣེ་བྱང་མའི་འོད་ཟེར་ (līŋne caŋmɛ öösee) aurora borealis.

གླིང་སྣེ་ས་ཁུལ་ (līŋne səgüü) the polar reigns.

གླིང་སྣེ་ལྷོ་མ་ (līŋne lhōma) the south pole.

གླིང་སྣེ་ལྷོ་མའི་མུ་ཁྱུད་ (līŋne lhōmɛ mugyüü) antarctic circle.

གླིང་སྣེའི་མུ་ཁྱུད་ (līŋnee mugyüü) arctic and antarctic circles.

གླིང་སྣེའི་འོད་ཟེར་ (līŋnee öösee) sm. གླིང་སྣེ་བྱང་མའི་འོད་ཟེར་.

གླིང་པ་ (līŋba) islander.

གླིང་ཕྲན་ (līŋtrɛn) island.

གླིང་ཕྲན་རྐྱང་མ་ (līŋtrɛn gyāŋma) an isolated island.

གླིང་ཕྲན་རྒྱལ་ཁབ་ (līŋtrɛn gyɛ̀gəb) island nation.

གླིང་ཕྲན་བརྒྱད་ (līŋtrɛn gyɛɛ̀) the eight legendary Buddhist subcontinents.

གླིང་ཕྲན་ཧྲེང་ཧྲེང་ (līŋtrɛn hrēŋgreŋ) sm. གླིང་ཕྲན་རྐྱང་པ་.

གླིང་བུ་ (līŋbu) flute; va.—གཏོང་ to play a flute.

གླིང་བུ་ལྦུ་གཉིས་མ་ (līŋbu jēñiimə) oboe.

གླིང་བུ་བ་ (līŋbuwə) flutist.

གླིང་བུ་ས་ཁེ་ (līŋbu sāke) saxophone.

གླིང་མ་ (līŋma) small piece of land (island) on a lake or river.

གླིང་མེ་ (līŋme) lamps lit on roof tops commemorating the death of Tsongkapa.

གླིང་ཙེ་ (līŋdze) ch. collar, lapel.

གླིང་ཚོམ་ (līŋdzom) archipelago, group of island, a chain of islands.

གླིང་ཞིང་ (līŋshiŋ) an area of multiple plots of land that are plowed/ planted together (although the plots are owned individually).

གླིང་བཞི་ (līŋshi) the four continents around Mt. Meru (in Buddhist legend). 2. sm. གླིང་ཁག་བཞི་.

གླིང་ལག (līŋlaà) peninsula.

གླིང་ལོག (līŋlɔɔ̀) civil war, internal rebellion.

གླིང་སྲུང་པ་ (līŋsuŋmə) caretaker of a park/ grove.

གླིང་བསེ་ (līŋse) a type of lower geshe degree.

གླིངས་སྟན་ (līŋdɛn) felt rug.

གླིངས་པ་ (līŋbə) sm. གླིངས་སྟན་.

གླུ་ (lū) song; va.—ལེན་ to sing.

གླུ་གར་ (lūgar) song and dance.

གླུ་གར་ཚོགས་པ་ (lūgar tsōgba) song and dance ensamble/ troop.

གླུ་འགྱེད་ (lū gyeè) sm. གླུ་ཤགས་.

གླུ་སྒྲ་ (lūdra) sound of singing; va.—སྒྲོག to sing.

གླུ་ཆུང་ (lūjuŋ) singing in a low/ soft tones; va.—གཏོང་.

གླུ་སྙན་པོ་ (lū ñɛ̄mbo) sweet or melodious tune/ song.

གླུ་གདངས་ (lūdaŋ) melody, tune.

གླུ་སྣེ་འཁྲིད་ (lūne trīī) va. to lead in singing a song.

གླུ་པ་ (lūba) singer.

གླུ་བ་ (lūwa) sm. གླུ་པ་.

གླུ་དབྱངས་ (lūyaŋ) song, melody; va.—ལེན་ to sing.

གླུ་དབྱངས་མཉམ་ལས་རུ་ཁག (lūyaŋ ñāmlɛɛ̀ rugaà)

sm. གླུ་གཞས་མཉམ་གཏོང་ཚོགས་པ་.

གླུ་མ་ (lūma) female singer.

གླུ་མ་གདམ་ (lūmadam) sm. གཞས་མ་གདམ་.

གླུ་ཚིག་ (lūdzig) song words, lyrics.

གླུ་གཞས་ (lūshεὲ) song; va.—གཏོང་ to sing.

གླུ་གཞས་རྐྱང་གཏོང་ (lūshεὲ gyāŋdoŋ) solo song; va.—གཏོང་.

གླུ་གཞས་མཉམ་གཏོང་ (lūshεὲ ñāmdoŋ) choral singing.

གླུ་གཞས་མཉམ་གཏོང་ཚོགས་པ་ (lūshεὲ tsōgba) chorus, choir.

གླུ་གཞས་མཉམ་ལེན་རུ་ཁག་ (lūshεὲ ñāmlen rugaà) sm. གླུ་གཞས་མཉམ་གཏོང་ཚོགས་པ་.

གླུ་གཞས་ཟློས་གར་ (lūshεὲ döögar) opera, musical play.

གླུ་ལེན་ (lū len) see གླུ་.

གླུ་ལེན་ཁྲང་ཞི་ (lūlen trāŋshi) tib.ch. opera.

གླུ་ལེན་པ་ (lūlemba) singer.

གླུ་ལེན་བྲོ་འཁྲབ་ (lūlen trodrəb) singing and dancing; va.—བྱེད་.

གླུ་ལེན་རེས་ (lū lenreè) two persons singing back abd forth; va.—བྱེད་.

གླུ་ཤགས་ (lūshaà) competing by answering the content of one song with the words/ content of another; va.—རྒྱག.

གླུད་ (lüü) 1. ransom, redemption, pawn; va.—གཏོང་. 2. objects used in "ransom" rituals.

གླུད་འགོང་ (lüügoŋ) sm. གླུད་འགོང་རྒྱལ་པོ་.

གླུད་འགོང་རྒྱལ་པོ་ (lüügoŋ gyεεbo) shung. the name of the two "scapegoats" who are ritually expelled from Lhasa bearing ransom for the ruler and populace in a ceremony held in Lhasa on 29th of the Tibetan second month (during ཚོགས་མཆོད་).

གླུད་འགོངས་རྫོང་བ་ (lüügoŋ dzoŋwa) shung. a form of excorcism which takes place on 29th of the Tibetan second month (during ཚོགས་མཆོད་).

གླུད་ཆས་ (lüüjεὲ) shung. the gifts given to the two གླུད་འགོང་རྒྱལ་པོ་.

གླུད་གཏོར་ (lüüdɔɔ) the torma given as ransom to demons when sick.

གླུད་རྫས་ (lüüdzεὲ) the objects that are used during the གླུད་ ceremony/ rite.

གླུམ་ (lūm) sm. སྦང་གླུམ་.

གླེ་ (lē) dry ground amidst water.

གླེ་པོ་ (lēbo) large basket.

གླེགས་ (lēg) flat wood.

གླེགས་ཐག་ (lēgtaà) the band/ strap used to tie traditional Tibetan books.

གླེགས་ཤིང་ (lēgshiŋ) rectangular slabs of wood that are used as covers of traditional Tibetan books.

གླེང་ (lēŋ) 1. va. to discuss, to talk, to speak (usu. follows གདམ་) ¶ བོད་ཀྱི་རིག་གནས་སྐོར་རགས་གདམ་གླེང་བ་རེད་ (They) had a brief discussion on Tibet's cultural relics.

གླེང་བརྗོད་ (lēŋjöö) 1. editorial, commentary ¶ གསར་འགོད་གླེང་བརྗོད་ News editorial. 2. talk ¶ གོང་ས་མཆོག་ནས་མཁྱེན་ཏེ་ཅུང་ཟད་དགོངས་པར་མི་ལྷན་པ་བྱུང་ཚུལ་གླེང་བརྗོད་ཡོད་པ་རེད་ There was talk that the Dalai Lama found out and was a little displeased.

གླེང་སྟེགས་ (lēŋdeg) forum ¶ བོད་དོན་གླེང་སྟེགས་ The Tibet Forum.

གླེང་ཐོན་ (lēŋdön) shung. talk, gossip.

གླེང་ཐོས་ (lēŋdöö) hearing sb. talking about sth.

གླེང་སྣེ་ (lēŋne) starting point or topic of a conversation.

གླེང་སྒྲོགས་ (lēŋjɔɔ) 1. public opinion; va.—བཟོ་; —སྤེལ་ to mold/ make public opinion ¶ དེང་སང་མང་ཚོགས་ཀྱི་གླེང་སྒྲོགས་ག་འདྲ་འདུག These days what is public opinion among the people. 2. advancing/ spreading/ propagating one's position, publicizing ¶ ཚོགས་པ་དེས་རང་ཉིད་ཀྱི་ལྟ་བའི་གླེང་སྒྲོགས་བཟོ་གི་ཡོད་ That association is propagating its views.

གླེང་མེད་ (lēŋmeè) 1. without discussion ¶ ས་མཚམས་ཀྱི་གནད་དོན་འདི་ལོ་མང་པོ་གླེང་མེད་དུ་གནས་བཞག The border issue has remained for many years without any discussion. 2. unconditional ¶ བཙན་འཛུལ་པས་གླེང་མེད་མགོ་བཏགས་ཞུ་དགོས་བྱུང་བ་རེད་ The invaders had to surrender unconditionally.

གླེང་མོ་ (lēŋmo) talk, discussion, conversation; va.—བྱེད་ to talk, to discuss ¶ ཆོས་ཀྱི་གླེང་མོ་བྱེད་ཀྱི་འདུག They are having a religious discussion.

གླེང་མོའི་ལེའུ་འཁྲུག་ (lēŋmöö lewu trūg) people talking to each other a lot.

གླེང་མོལ་ (lēŋmöö) sm. གླེང་མོ་.

གླེང་རྩོད་ (lēŋdzöö) debate, argument ¶ དེ་སྐོར་ཕན་ཚུན་གོ་བསྡུར་གླེང་རྩོད་མང་པོ་བྱུང་སོང་ There were many discussions and arguments about that.

གླེང་གཞི་ (lēŋshi) 1. forward, preface (in books). 2. basis of a quarrel/ dispute. 3. main issue/ topic in a discussion.

གླེང་ར་ (lēŋra) a place for discussion or debate.

གླེང་རིན་མེད་པ་ (lēŋrin meèba) unmentionable, not appropriate or worthy of being said ¶ ཚོགས་འདུ་འདིའི་ཐོག་སྐད་ཆ་དེ་གླེང་རིན་མེད་པ་ཞིག་རེད་ At this meeting, that comment is not appropriate.

གླེང་སློང་ (lēŋloŋ) issue, question, motion; va.—བྱེད་ to raise an issue/ question, to bring sth. up for discussion ¶ གསར་ཤོག་ཁག་ནང་གླེང་སློང་བྱས་ཡོད་པ་རེད་ The question was raised in several newspapers.

གླེང་བསླངས་ (lēŋlaŋ) p. of གླེང་སློང་.

གླེང་ལྷག་ (lēŋlhaà) 1. unfinished discussion, sth. left to be discussed ¶ མི་མཐུན་པའི་གླེང་ལྷག་ཡོད་ན་ If there are (points) of disagreement (still) to be discussed. 2. unconfirmed talk about sth., gossip ¶ མི་མདའ་སྦས་སྐུང་བྱེད་པའི་གླེང་ལྷག་བྱུང་བ་རེད་ There is unconfirmed talk that he secretly hid a gun.

གླེངས་ (lēŋ) p. of གླེང་.

གླེན་ཀླུགས་ (lēngug) sm. གླེན་པ་.

གླེན་འཆར་ (lēnjar) a phrase used to convey humbleness (e.g., as ignorant as I am, ...).

གླེན་རྟགས་ (lēndaà) 1. stupidity, idiocy; va.—སྟོན་ to act or be stupid/ idiotic ¶ གླེན་རྟགས་མ་སྟོན་ Don't be stupid. 2. very expensive ¶ ཚོང་ཁང་འདིའི་ཅ་ལག་ལ་གོང་གླེན་རྟགས་རེད་བཞག Things sold in that shop are very expensive.

གླེན་རྟགས་ཚ་པོ་ (lēndaà tsābo) stupid (often also conveys stupid in a gutsy manner) ¶ འགོ་ཁྲིད་ལ་ཁྲུང་སྟོན་རྒྱུ་དེ་གླེན་རྟགས་ཚ་པོའི་ལས་ཀ་ཞིག་རེད་ (His) showing anger at the boss, is a stupid act.

གླེན་ནད་ (lēnnεὲ) dementia.

གླེན་པ་ (lēmba) imbecile, idiot, moron, simpleton.

གླེན་པ་གླེན་ནག་ (lēmba lēnnaà) completely ignorant/ stupid.

གླེན་པ་རང་འཁྲུག་ (lēmba rəndruù) worrying about troubles created by one's own imagination.

གླེན་པ་ཨུ་ཚུགས་ (lēmba ūdzuù) sm. ལྐུགས་པ་ཨུ་ཚུགས་.

གླེན་རྫ་རྟོད་པོ་ (lēmdza töòbo) sm. ལྐུགས་རྟགས་ཚ་པོ་.

གླེབ་ (lēb) sm. གནོན་.

གླེབས་ (lēb) p. of གླེབ་.

གླེམ་ (lēm) sm. གནོན་.

གླེའུ་ (lēwu) young musk deer.

གློ་ (lō) 1. abbr. for གློ་བ་. 2. a cough; vi.—རྒྱག to cough. 3. cinch strap. 4. side ¶ གྲི་ཆུང་ཞིག་གློ་གཡས་སུ་འདོགས་ཀྱི་ཡོད་པ་རེད་ (They) carry a small knife at the right side. 5. the Mustang area of Nepal.

གློ་དཀར་ (lōgar) sm. གློ་སྐར་.

གློ་སྐར་ (lōgar) window.

གློ་ཁུག་ (lōguù) pouch worn on side.

གློ་གྲི་ (lōtri) dagger.

གློ་མགོ་ (lōngo) a type of ornament worn by women in eastern Tibet.

གློ་འགོག་སྨན་ (lō gɔgmēn) cough medicine.

གློ་རྒྱག་ (lōgyaà) see གློ་, 2.

གློ་རྒྱལ་ལང་ (lōgyεε laŋ) vi. to get/ have a cough for

a long time.

གློ་རྒྱས་ (lōgyɛɛ̀) a type of pneumonia.

གློ་གཅོང་ (lōjoŋ) lung disease.

གློ་ཆུང་རྒྱག (lōcuŋ gya̱à) va. to cough quietly to send a signal.

གློ་འཛགས་སྨན་ (lōnjaà mɛ̄n) cough medicine.

གློ་སྙིང་ (lōñiŋ) 1. abbr. lungs and heart. 2. internal organs.

གློ་སྙིང་མཆིན་གསུམ་ཁ་ལ་ཐོན་ལྟར་ (lōñiŋ cīnsum kāla tōndar) very frightened, extremely afraid [Lit. like the lungs, hearts and liver coming out of the mouth].

གློ་སྙིང་གཏོད་ས་ (lōñiŋ dōōsa) a person who is trusted completely.

གློ་ཐག (lōtaà) cinch strap.

གློ་དེ་གློ་བུར་ (lōde lōbur) sudden ། རྐྱེན་ངན་དེ་གློ་དེ་གློ་བུར་བ་ཞིག་རེད་ That was a sudden disaster.

གློ་མདོང་ (lōdoŋ) windpipe.

གློ་འདབ་ (lodəb) lobe of the lung.

གློ་དེག (lōdeg) sm. གློ་བུར་.

གློ་ཐིག་པ་ (lōdegba) pulsating heart; throbbing heart.

གློ་ནད་ (lōnɛɛ̀) tuberculosis; vi.—ན་ to be/ get sick with tuberculosis.

གློ་ནད་ཐེངས་པོ་ (lōnɛɛ̀ tēŋbo) one of eight lung diseases according to tt. medicine.

གློ་ནད་པུང་ཚང་ (lōnɛɛ̀ pu̱ŋdzaŋ) tuberculosis.

གློ་རྣག (lōnaà) pulmonary abscess.

གློ་འཕྲ་རྒྱག (lōdra gya̱à) va. to kick the hind legs toward the side (for horses).

གློ་བ་ (lōwa) lungs.

གློ་བ་དཀར་བ་ (lōwa gāāwa) loyal and sincere ། དཔོན་པོ་ལ་གློ་བ་དཀར་བའི་བྲན་གཡོག A servant who is loyal and sincere to his master.

གློ་བ་རྒྱ་ཐབ་ (lōwa gyābəb) one of eight lung diseases according to tt. medicine.

གློ་བ་དགའ་ (lōwa ga̱) va. to be happy/ joyful/ pleased.

གློ་བ་ཆུ་ཤོར་ (lōwa cūshɔɔ) one of eight lung diseases according to Tibetan medicine (something like pleurisy).

གློ་བ་ཉེ་བ་ (lōwa ñewa) very close/ friendly ། རང་ལ་གློ་བ་ཉེ་བའི་གྲོགས་པོ་ A friend who is very close.

གློ་བ་བུ་ལྔ་ (lōwa pu̱ŋa) the five sections on the front part of the lung according to tt. medicine.

གློ་བ་བུང་ཚང་ (lōwa pu̱ŋdzaŋ) one of eight lung diseases according to Tibetan medicine.

གློ་བ་མ་ལྔ་ (lōwa ma̱ ŋā) five sections on back part of the lung according to Tibetan medicine.

གློ་བ་རིང་བ་ (lōwa ri̱ŋwə) not close to, distant ། དཔོན་པོ་གསར་པ་དེས་རང་ཉིད་དང་གློ་བ་རིང་བའི་ལས་བྱེད་རྣམས་ཕུད་འདུག The new boss fired all the officials who were not close to him.

གློ་བ་ལ་མ་ཕན་མཆིན་པའི་དུག (lōwa ma̱pɛn cīmbɛ tu̱ù) sth. that is supposed to be beneficial to sb. has a bad result and harms them, let alone not helping sb. causing harm to them [Lit. not benefiting the lung, poison for the liver].

གློ་བ་ལ་མ་ཕན་མཆིན་པའི་དུག་ལ་སོང་ (lōwala ma̱ pɛ̄n cīmbɛ tu̱gsoŋ) sm. གློ་བ་ལ་མ་ཕན་མཆིན་པའི་དུག.

གློ་བར་མ་ཕན་མཆིན་པར་གནོད་ (lōwar ma̱pɛn cīmbar nōō) let alone not helping but causing a problem instead [Lit. unable to cure the lung, harming the liver].

གློ་བའི་སྡོད་རྩ་ (lōwɛ dö̱ödza) pulmonary vein.

གློ་བའི་འཕར་རྩ་ (lo̱wɛ pārdza) pulmonary artery.

གློ་བའི་ཚ་ནད་ (lo̱wɛ tsānɛɛ̀) pneumonia.

གློ་བུ་ (lōbu) sm. གློ་བ་བུ་ལྔ་.

གློ་བུག (lōbuù) holes in the lungs (e.g., due to tuberculosis).

གློ་བུར་ (lōbur) sudden, suddenly ། གློ་བུར་འགྲོ་དགོས་བྱུང་བ་རེད་ Suddenly (they) had to go. ། གློ་བུར་གྱི་ནད་ཚ་ A sudden illness/ pain.

གློ་བུར་གྱི་སྨན་བཅོས་ (lōburgi mɛ̄njöö) emergency medical aid/ treatment.

གློ་བུར་སྟག་གིས་མི་ཚུགས་ (lōbur dāāgi mi̱dzuù) it is difficult to overcome a sudden attack [Lit. (if) suddenly (attack), (even) a tiger can't cope].

གློ་བུར་ཐོག་རྒྱག (lōbur tōggyaà) suddenly, all of a sudden, unexpectedly ། ཁོའི་བསམ་བློ་དེ་གློ་བུར་ཐོག་རྒྱག་ཏུ་འགྱུར་བ་རེད་ All of a sudden he changed his mind.

གློ་བུར་ཐོག་པ་ (lōbur tōgba) sm. གློ་དེ་གློ་བུར་.

གློ་བུར་ཐོག་བབ་ (lōbur tōgbəb) sm. གློ་བུར་ཐོག་རྒྱག.

གློ་བུར་ཐོབ་རྒྱག (lōbur tōbgyaà) sm. གློ་བུར་དུ་.

གློ་བུར་དུ་ (lōburdu) suddenly ། ཁོང་ལ་གློ་བུར་དུ་སྙུན་གཞི་ཐོག་བབས་ He suddenly got sick.

གློ་བུར་རྨ་ (lōbur mā) a sudden cut or wound from a weapon such as a knife, arrow, etc.

གློ་དབུགས་ཤོང་ཚད་ (lōwug shōŋdzɛɛ̀) lung capacity.

གློ་འབུའི་ནད (lōmbü nɛ̱ɛ̀) a lung disease of cattle/ sheep/ goats.

གློ་འབུར་ (lōbur) an extension on the main wall of a house, an outer wall that enlarges a house.

གློ་འདྲས་ (lōndrɛɛ̀) throat disease.

གློ་སྦུབས་ (lōbub) inside the lung.

གློ་མ་ (lōma) the back side of lung.

གློ་མིད་བསངས་ (lōmiì sāŋ) va. to clear one's throat by coughing, etc.

གློ་མིད་ནང་ལ་ཤོར་ (lōmiìnaŋla shōr) vi. to have food accidentally get into the windpipe and choke.

གློ་སྨན་ (lōmɛn) cough medicine.

གློ་རྩ་ (lōdza) lung's pulse.

གློ་ཚད་ (lōdzɛɛ̀) pneumonia.

གློ་ཟུང་ (lōsuŋ) ornament worn on the waist by Eastern Tibetans.

གློ་བཟོ་བྱེད་ (lōso ce̱è) va. to cough on purpose as a signal or to get sb.'s attention.

གློ་ཡུ་ (lōyu) trachea, windpipe.

གློ་ཡུའི་གཉན་ཚད་ (lōyü ñɛ̃ndzɛɛ̀) tracheitis.

གློ་ཡུའི་ནད་ (lōyü nɛ̱ɛ̀) illness of trachea.

གློ་ཡུའི་ཚ་ནད་ (lōyü tsānɛɛ̀) tracheitis.

གློ་ལངས་ (lō la̱ŋ) sm. གློ་རྒྱག.

གློ་ལེན་ (lōlen) sm. གློ་ཐག.

གློ་ལོང་ (lōlaŋ) a type of ornament worn on the side of the body.

གློ་སངས་རྒྱག་པའི་བརྡ་ (lōsaŋ gya̱bɛ da̱) coughing to convey a sign/ signal.

གློ་སུབ་ (lōsub) dry coughing; vi.—རྒྱག.

གློ་གསུད་ (lōsüü) coughing endlessly.

གློག (lɔ̄ɔ) electricity ། ཕོ་གློག་དང་མོ་གློག Positive and negative electricity. 2. lightning; vi.—འཁྱུག; —རྒྱག to have lightning burst in the sky.

གློག་གི་བརྙན་རིས་ (lɔ̄ɔgi ñɛ̃nrii) sm. གློག་བརྙན་.

གློག་ཀླད་ (lɔ̄ɔlɛɛ̀) sm. གློག་ཀླད་འཕྲུལ་འཁོར་.

གློག་ཀླད་འཕྲུལ་འཁོར་ (lɔ̄ɔlɛɛ̀ trü̃ügɔɔ) computer.

གློག་སྐད་ (lɔ̄ɔgɛɛ̀) telephone.

གློག་སྐད་གྲོས་ཚོགས་ (lɔ̄ɔgɛɛ̀ trö̱ödzɔɔ̀) telephone conference.

གློག་སྐད་ཅུའུ་ (lɔ̄ɔgɛɛ̀ jüwu) tib.ch. telephone office, telephone exchange/ station.

གློག་སྐད་དྲིལ་སྒྲ་ (lɔ̄ɔgɛɛ̀ tri̱idra) electric bell.

གློག་སྐད་ཨང་གྲངས་འདྲི་ས་ (lɔ̄ɔgɛɛ̀ āŋgraŋ dri̱sə) telephone information/ directory assistance.

གློག་སྐས་ (lɔ̄ɔgɛɛ̀) abbr. of གློག་གི་སྐས་འཛེགས་.

གློག་སྐུད་ (lɔ̄ɔgüü) electric wire, telephone wire.

གློག་སྐུད་ཀ་བ་ (lɔ̄ɔgüü gāwa) sm. གློག་སྐུད་ཀྱི་ཀ་བ་.

གློག་སྐུད་ཀྱི་ཀ་བ་ (lɔ̄ɔgüügi gāwa) telegraph/ telephone pole.

གློག་སྐུད་བཟོ་གྲྭ་ (lɔ̄ɔgüü so̱dra) wire factory.

གློག་སྐུད་ཤུན་མེད་ (lɔ̄ɔgüü shūmmeè) bare wire, wire without a sheath.

གློག་སྐྱེད་ (lɔ̄ɔgyeè) sm. གློག་སྐྱེལ་.

གློག་སྐྱེད་འཕྲུལ་འཁོར་ (lɔ̄ɔgyeè trü̃ügɔɔ) generator.

གློག་སྐྱེལ་ (lɔ̄ɔgyee) electric power transmission; va.—བྱེད་ to transmit electric power.

གློག་སྐྱེལ་སྐུད་པ་ (lɔ̄ɔgyel gü̃übə) transmission line, electric line.

གློག་སྐྱེལ་སྐུད་ལམ་ (lɔ̄ɔgyel gü̃ülam) electric transmission line.

གློག་སྐྱེལ་ཀོ་རིམ་ (lɔ̄ɔgyel ko̱rim) electroproduction.

གློག་སྐྱེལ་འཕྲུལ་འཁོར་ (lɔ̄ɔ̀gyel trṹṹgɔɔ) electric generator.

གློག་སྐྱེལ་མ་འཁོར་ (lɔ̄ɔ̀gyel magɔɔ) sm. གློག་སྐྱེལ་འཕྲུལ་འཁོར་.

གློག་སྐྱེལ་གཟུགས་བརྙན་ (lɔ̄ɔ̀gyel sugñɛn) television ¶ རླུང་འཕྲིན་དང་གློག་སྐྱེལ་གཟུགས་བརྙན་བརྒྱུད་ནས་ Via television and radio.

གློག་སྐྱེལ་གཟུགས་བརྙན་ཁང་ (lɔ̄ɔ̀gyel sugñɛn gaŋ) television station.

གློག་སྐྱེལ་གཟུགས་བརྙན་འཕྲུལ་ཆས་ (lɔ̄ɔ̀gyel sugñɛn trṹṹjɛɛ̀) television equipment.

གློག་སྐྱེལ་ས་ཚིགས་ (lɔ̄ɔ̀gyel sədzig) electric/ power station.

གློག་སྐྱོད་ (lɔ̄ɔ̄gyöö̀) sm. གློག་བསྐྱལ་.

གློག་བསྐྱེད་ (lōggyeè) sm. གློག་སྐྱེལ་.

གློག་ཁ་ལོ་སྒྱུར་ཆས་ (lɔ̄ɔ̀ kālo gyurjɛɛ̀) thyristor.

གློག་ཁང་ (lɔ̄ɔ̀gaŋ) electric/ power plant.

གློག་ཁབ་ལེན་ (lɔ̄ɔ̀ kāblen) electromagnetism.

གློག་ཁབ་ལེན་ཁྱབ་འགྲོ་ (lɔ̄ɔ̀ kāblen kyāmdro) electromagnetic radiation.

གློག་ཁབ་ལེན་གྱི་རླབས་ཕྲེང་ (lɔ̄ɔ̀ kāblengi lābdreŋ) electromagnetic wave.

གློག་ཁབ་ལེན་སྒྱུར་ལྡོག་བྱུང་རྒྱལ་ (lɔ̄ɔ̀ kāblen gyundoò cundzüü) sm. གློག་ཁབ་ལེན་བསྐོར་འབྱུང་.

གློག་ཁབ་ལེན་བསྐོར་འབྱུང་ (lɔ̄ɔ̀ kāblen dɔ̄ɔ̀juŋ) sm. གློག་སྣུད་བརྙེན་སྣང་.

གློག་ཁབ་ལེན་གཡོ་འགུལ་ (lɔ̄ɔ̀ kāblen yōngüü) sm. གློག་སྣུད་འདར་གཡོ་.

གློག་ཁབ་ལེན་ར་བ་ (lɔ̄ɔ̀ kāblen rawa) electromagnetic field.

གློག་ཁབ་ལེན་རིག་པ་ (lɔ̄ɔ̀ kāblen rigba) electromagnetics.

གློག་ཁམས་ཀྱི་ནུས་པ་ (lɔ̄ɔ̀kamgi nüüba) energy of an electric field.

གློག་ཁུངས་ (lɔ̄ɔ̀guŋ) electric power source.

གློག་ཁུར་ (lɔ̄ɔ̀gur) electric charge.

གློག་ཁེམ་ (lōggem) electric shovel.

གློག་ཁྱེམ་ (lōggyem) electric shovel.

གློག་འཁོར་ (lɔ̄ɔ̀gɔɔ) 1. electric trolley/ tram. 2. electrical machinery, electric motor, electric train.

གློག་འཁྱུག་ (lōggyuù) lightning; vi. to have lightning.

གློག་འཁྱུག་འབྲུག་གྲགས་ (lōggyuù drugdraà) thunder and lightning.

གློག་འཁྱུད་ (lɔ̄ɔ̀gyüü) vi. to get an electric shock.

གློག་འཁྲིད་ (lōgdriì) electrical conductivity, conducting electricity; va. གློག་འཁྲིད་; —བྱེད་ to bring in/ conduct electricity (e.g., to one's house) ¶ ཁང་པ་གསར་པ་དེར་གློག་འཁྲིད་རྒྱུ་རེད་ They have yet to bring electricity to the new house.

གློག་འཁྲིད་སྐུད་པ་ (lōgtriì gṹṹbə) electric wire/ cable.

གློག་འཁྲིད་དངོས་རྫས་ (lōgdriì ŋɔ̃ɔ̀dzɛɛ̀) a conductor of electricity.

གློག་འཁྲིད་ལྕགས་མདའ་ (lōgdriì jāgda) lightning rod.

གློག་གི་ཀ་བ་ (lɔ̄ɔ̀gi gāā) electrical pole.

གློག་གི་ཀློད་པ་ (lɔ̄ɔ̀gi lɛ̄ɛ̀ba) computer.

གློག་གི་སྐད་པར་ (lɔ̄ɔ̀gi gɛ̄ɛ̀bar) electric phonograph.

གློག་གི་སྐས་འཛེགས་ (lɔ̄ɔ̀gi gɛ̄ndzeè) elevator/ escalator.

གློག་གི་འཁྱགས་སྒམ་ (lɔ̄ɔ̀gi kyāàgam) refrigerator.

གློག་གི་ཆུ་ཚོད་ (lɔ̄ɔ̀gi cūdzöö̀) sm. གློག་གི་ཆུ་ཚོད་འཁོར་ལོ་.

གློག་གི་ཆུ་ཚོད་འཁོར་ལོ་ (lɔ̄ɔ̀gi cūdzöö̀ kɔ̄ɔ̄lo) electric clock/ watch.

གློག་གི་བསྐོར་འབྱུང་ (lɔ̄ɔ̀gi dɔ̄ɔ̀juŋ) electric inductance.

གློག་གི་མདངས་ (lɔ̄ɔ̀gi daŋ) glow of an electric light.

གློག་གི་ལྡེ་མིག (lɔ̄ɔ̀gi dimiì) electric switch.

གློག་གི་ཕོ་སྣེ་ (lɔ̄ɔ̀gi pōne) positive (electricity).

གློག་གི་ཕྱག་མ་ (lɔ̄ɔ̀gi cāàma) electric vacuum cleaner.

གློག་གི་འཕྲུལ་འཁོར་ (lɔ̄ɔ̀gi trṹṹgɔɔ) electric motor/ machine.

གློག་གི་དབུར་དེ་ (lɔ̄ɔ̀gi wūrde) electric iron.

གློག་གི་དྲག་སྒོ་ (lɔ̄ɔ̀gi draggo) main switch, master switch.

གློག་གི་མེ་སྟག (lɔ̄ɔ̀gi medag) electric spark.

གློག་གི་མོ་སྣེ་ (lɔ̄ɔ̀gi mone) negative (electricity).

གློག་གི་རྩོལ་ཚད་ (lɔ̄ɔ̀gi dzɔ̄ɔ̄dzɛɛ̀) electric power.

གློག་གི་ཚ་ལ་ (lɔ̄ɔ̀gi tsāla) electrowelding ¶ གློག་གི་ཚ་ལའི་ལས་ཚན་ Electrowelding workshop.

གློག་གི་བཞུ་ཐབ་ (lɔ̄ɔ̀gi shudəb) གློག་ཐབ་.

གློག་གི་བཟོ་པ་ (lɔ̄ɔ̀gi soba) electrician, electrical worker.

གློག་གི་ཡོ་ཆས་ (lɔ̄ɔ̀gi yojɛɛ̀) sm. གློག་གི་ཡོ་བྱད་.

གློག་གི་ཡོ་བྱད་ (lɔ̄ɔ̀gi yobjɛɛ̀) electrical equipment/ utensils.

གློག་གི་ཤེལ་དོག (lɔ̄ɔ̀gi shēēdɔɔ̀) electric bulb.

གློག་གི་སོག་ལེ་ (lɔ̄ɔ̀gi sōle) electric saw.

གློག་གི་བསད་སྤར་ (lɔ̄ɔ̀gi sɛ̄ɛ̀bar) light switch.

གློག་གི་བསིལ་འཁོར་ (lɔ̄ɔ̀gi sīŋgɔɔ) electric fan.

གློག་གི་ཨ་མ་ (lɔ̄ɔ̀gi āma) the main generator.

གློག་གེགས་ (lɔ̄ɔ̀geg) sm. གློག་འགོག.

གློག་གྱེས་ (lɔ̄ɔ̀gyɛɛ̀) ionization.

གློག་བགོད་འཕྲུལ་ཆས་ (lɔ̄ɔ̀göö̀ trṹṹjɛɛ̀) switchboard.

གློག་འགུལ་ (lɔ̄ɔ̀güü) electric, electrically operated/ powered.

གློག་འགུལ་འཁོར་ལོ་ (lɔ̄ɔ̀güü kɔ̄ɔ̄lo) 1. electric vehicle. 2. electric motor.

གློག་འགུལ་འཕྲུལ་འཁོར་ (lɔ̄ɔ̀güü trṹṹgɔɔ) electric motor.

གློག་འགུལ་མ་འཁོར་ (lɔ̄ɔ̀güü magɔɔ) electric motor.

གློག་འགུལ་མ་འཁོར་བཟོ་གྲྭ་ (lɔ̄ɔ̀güü magɔɔ sodra) electric motor factory.

གློག་འགུལ་མེ་འཁོར་ (lɔ̄ɔ̀güü megɔɔ) electric train.

གློག་འགུལ་འཚེམ་འཁོར་ (lɔ̄ɔ̀güü tsēmgɔɔ) electric sewing machine.

གློག་འགོ་འཛུགས་ས་ (lōŋgo dzugsa) electric socket/ outlet.

གློག་འགོག (lɔ̄ŋgɔɔ̀) electric resistance.

གློག་འགོག་དཀྲིས་སྐུད་ (lɔ̄ŋgɔɔ̀ trīgüü) electric resistance coil.

གློག་འགོག་སྒྲོམ་བུ་ (lɔ̄ŋgɔɔ̀ drombu) electric resistance box.

གློག་འགོག་དངོས་པོ་ (lɔ̄ngɔɔ̀ ŋɔ̃ɔ̀bo) things used for electric resistance.

གློག་འགོག་ཐབ་ཀ་ (lɔ̄ŋgɔɔ̀ tābgə) resistance furnace.

གློག་འགོག་བྱུང་ཚད་ (lɔ̄ŋgɔɔ̀ cundzɛɛ̀) amount/ quantity of electric resistance.

གློག་འགོག་མེད་པ་ (lɔ̄ŋgɔɔ̀ meèba) superconduction.

གློག་འགོག་མེད་པའི་འདྲེན་གཟུགས་ (lɔ̄ŋgɔɔ̀ meèbɛ trensug) superconductor.

གློག་འགོག་མེད་པའི་ལག་རྩལ་ (lɔ̄ŋgɔɔ̀ meèbɛ lagdzɛɛ) superconduction technology.

གློག་འགྱུ་ (lɔ̄ngyu) arc. electric.

གློག་འགྱུ་བ་ (lɔ̄ɔ̀ guwə) lightning (discharge).

གློག་འགྱུར་ (lɔ̄ngyur) sm. གློག་སྒྱུར་.

གློག་འགྱུར་ས་ཚིགས་ (lōggyur sədzig) sm. གློག་སྒྱུར་ས་ཚིགས་.

གློག་འགྱུར་སློབ་ཁྲིད་ཁང་ (lōggyur lōbdriìgaŋ) audiovisual education room.

གློག་རྒྱ་ཚད་ (lɔ̄ɔ̀ gyadzɛɛ̀) electric flux.

གློག་རྒྱག (lɔ̄ɔ̀ gyaà) see གློག.

གློག་རྒྱུན་ (lōggyün) electric current.

གློག་རྒྱུན་རྒྱུ་ལམ་ (lōggyün gyuləm) sm. གློག་ལམ་.

གློག་རྒྱུན་གཅོད་ཆས་ (lɔ̄ɔ̀gyün jɔ̄ɔ̀jɛɛ̀) electric insulating material.

གློག་རྒྱུན་འཇལ་ཆས་ (lɔ̄ɔ̀gyün jɛɛjɛɛ̀) amperemeter.

གློག་རྒྱུན་འཕར་ཆག (lōggyün pārjaà) pulsating electric current.

གློག་རྒྱུན་ཚ་དྲོད་ནུས་པ་ (lōggyün tsādröö̀ nüüba) heating effect of electrical current.

གློག་སྒུལ་ (lōggüü) sm. གློག་འགུལ་.

གློག་སྒུལ་དཀྲིས་འདྲེགས་འཕྲུལ་འཁོར་ (lōggüü drīndeg trṹṹgɔɔ) electric capstan machine.

གློག་སྒུལ་སྐད་པར་ (lōggüü gɛ̄ɛ̀bar) electric record player.

གློག་སྒུལ་སྟོབས་ (lōg güldob) electromotive force.

གློག་སྒུལ་ཐོ་བ་ (lōggüü tɔ̄ɔ̄) electric hammer.

གློག་སྒུལ་འཕྲུལ་འཁོར་ (lōggüü trṹṹgɔɔ) electric

motor.

གློག་སྐུལ་འཕྲུལ་ཆས་ཞིག་གསོ་ཁང་ (lōggüü trűűjɛɛ̀ shigsogaŋ) electromotor repair shop.

གློག་སྐུལ་བལ་འབྲེག་འཕྲུལ་འཁོར་ (lōggüü pɛɛdreè trűűgɔɔ) electric wool-shearing machine.

གློག་སྐུལ་མེ་འཁོར་མགོ་ (lōggüü megɔɔ go) electric locomotive.

གློག་སྐུལ་ཞིང་ཆུ་འདྲེན་གཏོང་ས་ཚིགས་ (lōggüü shiŋcu drendoŋ sətsig) electric irrigation pumping station.

གློག་སྐུལ་ཡོ་བྱད་བཟོ་གྲྭ་ (lōggüü yobjeɛ̀ sodra) electric tool factory.

གློག་སྐུལ་ལྷུང་གཡབ་ (lōggüü lūŋyəb) electric fan.

གློག་སྐུལ་འོ་བཞོ་འཕྲུལ་ཆས་ (lōggüü osho trűűcɛɛ̀) electric milking equipment.

གློག་སྐུལ་ཤུགས་རིག (lōggüü shūgrig) electrodynamics.

གློག་སྒོ་ (lōggo) 1. electric door. 2. electric switchboard/ switch.

གློག་སྒྱུར་ (lōggyur) electrical transformer.

གློག་སྒྱུར་འཕྲུལ་ཆས་ (lōggyur trűűjɛɛ̀) transformer.

གློག་སྒྱུར་ཡོ་ཆས་ (lōggyur yojɛɛ̀) sm. གློག་སྒྱུར་འཕྲུལ་ཆས.

གློག་སྒྱུར་ས་ཚིགས་ (lōggyur sədzig) (electric) transformer station.

གློག་སྒྲ་ནུས་བརྗེ་ཆས་ (lɔ̄gdra nűűjejɛɛ̀) electroacoustic transducer.

གློག་སྒྲ་རིག་པ་ (lɔ̄gdra rigbə) electroacoustics.

གློག་སྒྲོན་ (lɔ̄gdrön) sm. གློག་བཞུ་.

གློག་སྒྲོན་གྱི་གློག་སྒོ་ (lɔ̄gdröngi lɔ̄ɔ̀go) electric lamp switch.

གློག་སྒྲོན་ཤེལ་དོག (lɔ̄gdrön shēēdog) light bulb.

གློག་བརྒྱུད་ (lōg gyüü) vi. to conduct electricity.

གློག་བསྐུལ་ (lɔ̄ɔ̀güü) electrically operated/ powered, electric ¶ གློག་སྐུལ་ལྷུང་གཡབ་ Electric fan.

གློག་བསྐུལ་འཕྲུལ་འཁོར་ (lɔ̄ɔ̀güü trűűgɔɔ) electric motor.

གློག་བསྐུལ་ལྷུང་ཡབ་ (lōggüü lūŋyəb) electric fan.

གློག་གཅོད་སྐམ་པ་ (lōgjöö gāmba) pliers for use in electric work.

གློག་བཅོས་ (lōgjöö) electrotherapy.

གློག་ཆད་ (lōg cɛ̄ɛ̀) vi. to have electricity get cut (e.g., due to power failure).

གློག་ཆས་ (lōgjɛɛ̀) electrical appliances.

གློག་ཅེམ་ཅེམ་ (lɔ̄ɔ̀ cīmjim) blinking, flickering (light); va.—བྱེད་.

གློག་ཆུ་ (lōgju) battery acid.

གློག་ཆོད་ (lōgjöö) electric insulator/ insulation.

གློག་ཆོད་ལྕགས་ཤོག (lōgjöö jāgshoò) vulcanized/ insulated sheet metal.

གློག་ཆོད་སྦུ་གུ (lōgjöö bugə) insulating bushing.

གློག་ཆོད་ཤོག་བུ་ (lōgjöö shōgbu) insulating paper.

གློག་འཇོར་ (lōgjɔɔ) electric hoe.

གློག་བརྙན་ (lōgñɛn) motion picture, movie; va.—སྟོན་ to show a film ¶ གློག་བརྙན་པར་གཞི་བཟོ་གྲྭ་ Film studio.

གློག་བརྙན་སྐར་མ་ (lōgñɛn gārma) movie star.

གློག་བརྙན་ཁང་ (lōgñɛngaŋ) movie theater.

གློག་བརྙན་འཁྲབ་ (lōgñɛn trəb) va. to act in movies.

གློག་བརྙན་འཁྲབ་གཞུང་ (lōgñɛn trəbshuŋ) scenario, screen play.

གློག་བརྙན་གྱི་པར་གཞི་ (lōgñɛngi bārshi) motion pictures; va.—ལེན་; —བཟོ་ to make motion pictures.

གློག་བརྙན་གྱི་པར་ཤོག (lōgñɛngi bārshoò) 1. negative (film). 2. undeveloped film.

གློག་བརྙན་གྱི་ཕེན་ཚེ་ (lōgñɛngi pēndzi) sm. གློག་བརྙན་གྱི་པར་གཞི་.

གློག་བརྙན་འགྲེམ་གཏོང་ཀུང་སི་ (lōgñɛn dremdoŋ gūŋsi) film distribution company.

གློག་བརྙན་བསྒྱུར་སྒྲུན་ཁང་ (lōgñɛn gyurdrüngaŋ) film dubbing studio.

གློག་བརྙན་མངོན་གསོན་ (lōgñɛn ŋōnsön) realistic movie, real life drama.

གློག་བརྙན་ཆེ་གྲས་ (lōgñɛn cēdrɛɛ̀) feature film.

གློག་བརྙན་སྟོན་ཁང་ (lōgñɛn dōngaŋ) movie theater.

གློག་བརྙན་སྟོན་འཁོར་ (lōgñɛn dōngɔɔ) movie projector.

གློག་བརྙན་སྟོན་བྱེད་འཕྲུལ་འཁོར་ (lōgñɛn dōnjeè trűűgɔɔ) sm. གློག་བརྙན་སྟོན་འཁོར་.

གློག་བརྙན་སྟོན་ས་ (lōgñɛn dōnsa) motion picture theater.

གློག་བརྙན་པར་གཞི་བཟོ་གྲྭ་ (lōgñɛn bārshi sodra) movie film company/ factory ¶ པེ་ཅིང་གློག་བརྙན་པར་གཞི་བཟོ་གྲྭ་ The Beijing Film Company.

གློག་བརྙན་སྤྱིན་ཤོག (lōgñɛn bīŋshoò) movie film.

གློག་བརྙན་སྤྱིན་ཤོག་པར་འབྲུའི་བཟོ་གྲྭ་ (lōgñɛn bīŋshoò bārtrü sodra) film developing and printing factory.

གློག་བརྙན་ཕྱི་སྟོན་དོ་དམ་ས་ཚིགས་ (lōgñɛn cīdün todam sədzii) film projection management/ administration station.

གློག་བརྙན་ཕྱི་སྟོན་རུ་ཁག (lōgñɛn cīdün rugaà) film projection team/ unit.

གློག་བརྙན་འཕྲུལ་ཆས་ (lōgñɛn trűűjɛɛ̀) film equipment.

གློག་བརྙན་འཕྲུལ་ཆས་ལས་གཉེར་ཁང་ (lōgñɛn trűűjɛɛ̀ lɛɛ̀ñergaŋ) film equipment management office.

གློག་བརྙན་འཕྲུལ་ཆས་གསོ་སྒྲིག་ཁང་ (lōgñɛn trűűjɛɛ̀ sōdriggaŋ) film equipment repair and installation office/ unit.

གློག་བརྙན་བྱ་བ་ (lōgñɛn cawa) film industry.

གློག་བརྙན་དབྱིབས་ཆེ་བ་ (lōgñɛn yībcewa) feature film.

གློག་བརྙན་བཙོག་པ་ (lōgñɛn dzɔ̄gba) pornographic movie.

གློག་བརྙན་བཟོ་གྲྭ་ (lōgñɛn sodra) motion picture studio/ company.

གློག་བརྙན་རིང་བ་ (lōgñɛn riŋwə) full length feature film.

གློག་བརྙན་རུ་ཁག (lōgñɛn rugaà) film projection team.

གློག་དུའུ་ (lōgdu) tib.ch. kilowatt hour.

གློག་དོག (lɔ̄gdoò) lamp/ light bulb.

གློག་བཏོན་ (lɔ̄gdön) p. of གློག་འདོན་.

གློག་སྟེགས་ (lɔ̄gdeg) elevator.

གློག་བརྟེན་ཁབ་ལེན་ (lɔ̄gden kəblen) electromagnet.

གློག་བརྟེན་བརྟེན་སྣང་ (lɔ̄gden dēnnaŋ) electromagnetic induction.

གློག་བརྟེན་དབྱེ་འབྱེད་ (lɔ̄gden yējeè) sm. གློག་འབྱེད་.

གློག་བརྟེན་སྨན་བཅོས་ (lɔ̄gden mɛnjöö) sm. གློག་བཅོས་.

གློག་བརྟེན་ཟངས་དམར་བཟོ་གྲྭ་ (lɔ̄gden saŋgar sodra) electrolytic copper factory.

གློག་བརྟེན་གསོ་ཐབས་ (lɔ̄gden sōdəb) electrotherapy, diathermy.

གློག་ཐག (lɔ̄gdaà) electric cable.

གློག་ཐད་རྒྱུད་ (lɔ̄g tɛ̄ɛ̀gyüü) direct electric current (DC).

གློག་ཐབ་ (lɔ̄gdəb) 1. hot plate, electric stove. 2. electric furnace/ stove.

གློག་མཐུད་ཡོ་བྱད་ (lɔ̄gdüü yojɛɛ̀) electric splicing equipment.

གློག་མཐེབ་ (lɔ̄gdeb) telegraph key.

གློག་འཐག (lɔ̄gdaà) electrical weaving.

གློག་དྲིལ་ (lɔ̄gdrii) electric bell/ buzzer.

གློག་དྲོད་ (lɔ̄gdröö) electric heat.

གློག་དྲོད་བྱ་ཕྲུག་སྙོལ་ཆས་ (lɔ̄gdröö cədruù ñɔ̄ɔ̀jɛɛ̀) electric incubator.

གློག་དྲོད་མལ་གདན་ (lɔ̄gdröö mɛɛdɛn) electric (heated) mattress.

གློག་དྲོད་མལ་གཟན་ (lɔ̄gdröö mɛɛsɛn) electric blanket.

གློག་འདོན་ (lɔ̄gdön) electric power production, power generation; va.—བྱེད་ to produce electricity, to generate electric power.

གློག་འདོན་སྐྱུད་ལམ་ (lɔ̄gdön güülam) electric transmission line.

གློག་འདོན་ཁང་ (lɔ̄gdöngaŋ) electric power generating plant/ station.

གློག་འདོན་འཁོར་ལོ་ (lɔ̄gdön kɔ̄ɔlo) electric power

generator.

གློག་འདོན་སྒྲིག་ཆས་ (lɔ̄gdön drigjɛ̀ɛ̀) power generating equipment.

གློག་འདོན་ཅུའུ་ (lɔ̄gdön jū) power supply bureau.

གློག་འདོན་འཕྲུལ་འཁོར་ (lɔ̄gdön trǖügɔɔ) electric generator.

གློག་འདོན་ཚད་ (lɔ̄gdön tsɛ̀ɛ̀) electricity output, electric power generating capacity.

གློག་འདོན་ས་ཚིགས་ (lɔ̄gdön sətsig) power station/ electric power generating station.

གློག་འདད་ (lɔ̄gdrɛɛ̀) electric brush.

གློག་རྡུལ་ (lɔ̄gdül) electron; electronics.

གློག་རྡུལ་སྐྱོད་ལམ་ (lɔ̄gdül gǖülam) electron circuit.

གློག་རྡུལ་སྐོར་འཁོ་ (lɔ̄gdül gōndro) electron diffraction.

གློག་རྡུལ་ཁ་སྦྱོར་འཕྲུལ་འཁོར་ (lɔ̄gdül kājɔɔ trǖügɔɔ) electronic sealing machine.

གློག་རྡུལ་གྱི་ཆེ་ཤེལ་ (lɔ̄gdülgi cēsheè) electron microscope.

གློག་རྡུལ་སྒྲིག་ཆས་བཟོ་གྲྭ (lɔ̄gdül drigjɛ̀ɛ̀ sodra) electronics equipment factory.

གློག་རྡུལ་ཅན་རྩིས་རྒྱག་འཕྲུལ་འཁོར་ (lɔ̄gdüljɛn dzīīgyaà trǖügɔɔ) sm. གློག་རྡུལ་རྩིས་འཁོར་.

གློག་རྡུལ་ཆ་ལྡན་ (lɔ̄gdüü cāndɛn) electron pairs.

གློག་རྡུལ་ཆུ་ཚོད་ (lɔ̄gdül cūdzöö) atomic clock.

གློག་རྡུལ་རྒྱུན་པོ་ (lɔ̄gdüü cǖmbo) electron beam.

གློག་རྡུལ་བརྟག་དཔྱད་ཡོ་བྱད་ (lɔ̄gdüü dāgjɛ̀ɛ̀ yobjɛ̀ɛ̀) electric instruments, electron meter.

གློག་རྡུལ་དྲ་བའི་བརྒྱུད་ལམ་ (lɔ̄gdüü trawɛ gyǖülam) the internet.

གློག་རྡུལ་དཔྱད་ཁབ་ (lɔ̄gdüü jɛ̄kəb) electronic probe.

གློག་རྡུལ་དཔྱད་ཆས་ (lɔ̄gdüü jɛ̀ɛ̀jɛ̀ɛ̀) sm. གློག་རྡུལ་བརྟག་དཔྱད་ཡོ་བྱད་.

གློག་རྡུལ་ཕོ་ (lɔ̄gdüü pō) positive election, positron.

གློག་རྡུལ་ཕྲ་མཐོང་ཆེ་ཤེལ་ (lɔ̄gdüü tradoŋ cēshel) electron microscope.

གློག་རྡུལ་ཕྲ་མཐོང་ཆེ་ཤེལ་ (lɔ̄gdüü drāgoŋ cēshee) electron microscope.

གློག་རྡུལ་འཕྲུལ་ཆས་ཀྱི་ལྷུ་ལག (lɔ̄gdüü trǖüjɛ̀ɛ̀gi lhūlaà) electronic components.

གློག་རྡུལ་མེ་མདའ་ (lɔ̄gdüü menda) electron gun.

གློག་རྡུལ་སྦུ་གུ་ (lɔ̄gdüü bugu) electron tube.

གློག་རྡུལ་མྱུར་འཕྲིན་ (lɔ̄gdüü ñundrin) fax.

གློག་རྡུལ་སྨྲ་བ་ (lɔ̄gdüü māwa) electron theory.

གློག་རྡུལ་རྩིས་འཁོར་ (lɔ̄gdüü dzīgɔɔ) electronic computer.

གློག་རྡུལ་ཞིབ་འཇུག་ཁང་ (lɔ̄gdüü shimjuùgaŋ) institute of electronics.

གློག་རྡུལ་བཟོ་གྲྭ (lɔ̄gdüü sodra) electronics factory.

གློག་རྡུལ་བཟོ་ལས་ཅུའུ་ (lɔ̄gdüü solɛɛ̀jūwu) electronics industry bureau.

གློག་རྡུལ་འོད་རིག (lɔ̄gdüü wöörig) electron optics.

གློག་རྡུལ་རང་དབང་ཅན་ (lɔ̄gdüü raŋwaŋjɛn) free electron.

གློག་རྡུལ་རིག་པ་ (lɔ̄gdüü rigbə) electronics.

གློག་རྡུལ་རོལ་ཆ་ (lɔ̄gdüü rööja) electric musical instrument.

གློག་རྡུལ་རོལ་དབྱངས་ (lɔ̄gdüü rööyaŋ) electronic music.

གློག་རྡུལ་རོལ་རྩེད་ཁང་ (lɔ̄gdüü röödzegaŋ) video game room.

གློག་རྡུལ་ཤེལ་སྦྲུབ་ (lɔ̄gdüü shēldrub) electron tube.

གློག་རྡོ་ (lɔ̄gdo) carbide, calcium carbide.

གློག་རྡོའི་རླངས་པ་ (lɔ̄gdö lāŋba) acetylene, ethyne.

གློག་རྡོའི་རླངས་པ་ (lɔ̄gdö lāŋba) acetylene.

གློག་སྡུད་ (lɔ̄gdüù) sm. གློག་ཁབ་ལེན་.

གློག་སྡུད་འགྱིན་འཁོ་ (lɔ̄gdüù gyentro) sm. གློག་ཁབ་ལེན་ཁྱབ་འཁོ་.

གློག་སྡུད་འདར་གཡོ་ (lɔ̄gdüù daryo) sm. གློག་ལེན་གཡོ་སྒུལ་.

གློག་བདར་ (lōgda) a flare.

གློག་ནུས་ (lōgnüù) electric energy.

གློག་གནས་ཧེ་བག (lɔ̄gnɛɛ̀ hēbaà) electrical (potential difference).

གློག་གནོན་ (lɔ̄gnön) voltage.

གློག་གནོན་འཇལ་ཆས་ (lɔ̄gnön jɛɛ̀jɛ̀ɛ̀) sm. གློག་གནོན་དཔྱད་ཆས་.

གློག་གནོན་དཔྱད་ཆས་ (lɔ̄gnön jɛ̀ɛ̀jɛ̀ɛ̀) voltage meter.

གློག་གནོན་ཡོ་ཆས་ (lɔ̄gnön yojɛ̀ɛ̀) sm. གློག་གནོན་དཔྱད་ཆས་.

གློག་སྣེ་ (lɔ̄gne) 1. electrode. 2. electric poles.

གློག་སྣེ་ཕོ་མོ་གཉིས་ (lɔ̄gne pōmo ñīī) the positive and negative electric poles.

གློག་སྣོད་ (lɔ̄gnöò) electric condenser, storage battery.

གློག་སྣོད་བསྒྱུར་འཁོར་ (lɔ̄gnöò gyurgɔɔ) electric transformer.

གློག་པ་ (lɔ̄gba) a type of skin disease.

གློག་པར་ (lɔ̄gbar) x rays; va.—རྒྱག to x-ray.

གློག་པར་ཁང་ (lɔ̄gbargaŋ) x-ray room.

གློག་དཔར་ (lɔ̄gbar) sm. གློག་པར་.

གློག་སྤྱད་སློབ་ཁྲིད་ (lɔ̄gjɛ̀ɛ̀ lōbdriì) teaching with electrical-visual aides.

གློག་སྤྱོད་ (lɔ̄gjöò) electricity usage.

གློག་ཕོ་མོ་ (lɔ̄ɔ̀ pōmo) positive and negative electricity.

གློག་ཕོག (lɔ̄ɔ̀ pɔ̄ɔ̀) vi. to get an electric shock.

གློག་འཕྲིན་ (lɔ̄gdrin) telegram, cable, wire; va.—གཏོང་ to send a telegram/ cable/ wire.

གློག་འཕྲིན་ཁང་ (lɔ̄gdringaŋ) telegraph office.

གློག་འཕྲིན་ཁྱབ་གཏོང་ (lɔ̄gdrin kyəbdoŋ) telegrams sent to many areas; va.—བྱེད་.

གློག་འཕྲིན་གྱི་ཡོ་བྱད་ (lɔ̄gdrin gi yobjɛ̀ɛ̀) telegraph/ wireless equipment.

གློག་འཕྲིན་གྱི་གསར་འགྱུར་ (lɔ̄gdringi sāngyur) telegram/ wireless news.

གློག་འཕྲིན་ངོས་འཛིན་ཨང་རྟགས་ (lɔ̄gdrin ŋöndzin āŋdaà) cable address, telegraphic address.

གློག་འཕྲིན་དངུལ་གཏོང་ (lɔ̄gdrin ŋǖüdoŋ) sm. གློག་འཕྲིན་ཐོག་གི་དངུལ་འསྐུལ་.

གློག་འཕྲིན་ཅུའུ་ (lɔ̄gdrin jūwu) telecommunications bureau.

གློག་འཕྲིན་ཆས་བཟོ་གྲྭ (lɔ̄gdrinjɛ̀ɛ̀ sodra) telecommunications equipment factory.

གློག་འཕྲིན་གཏོང་ལེན་འཕྲུལ་འཁོར་ (lɔ̄gdrin dōŋlen trǖügɔɔ) telegraph receiver and transmitter.

གློག་འཕྲིན་ཐོག་གི་དངུལ་འསྐུལ་ (lɔ̄gdrin tɔ̄ɔ̀gi ŋǖüdrül) telegraphic money order, telegraphic transmission of money.

གློག་འཕྲིན་བརྡ་རྟགས་ (lɔ̄gdrin dadaà) (telegraph) code.

གློག་འཕྲིན་པ་ (lɔ̄gdrimba) telegraph/ wireless operator.

གློག་འཕྲིན་འཕྲུལ་ཆས་ (lɔ̄gdrin trǖüjɛ̀ɛ̀) telegraphic equipment.

གློག་འཕྲུལ་ (lɔ̄gdrüü) electric machine.

གློག་འཕྲུལ་བཟོ་གྲྭ (lɔ̄gtrüü sodra) electrical machinery plant.

གློག་འཕྲུལ་བཟོ་བཅོས་ཁང་ (lɔ̄gtrüü sojöögaŋ) repair shop for electrical machines.

གློག་བྱེད་དངོས་པོ་ (lɔ̄gjeè ŋööbo) electrolyte.

གློག་སླུག (lɔ̄g lüù) va. to charge a battery.

གློག་འབྱེད་ (lɔ̄gjeè) electrolysis.

གློག་འབྲེལ་གཅོད་ (lɔ̄ŋdrel jöò) va. to insulate (electricity).

གློག་འབྲེལ་གཅོད་བྱེད་དངོས་པོ་ (lɔ̄ŋdrel jööjeè ŋööbo) electric insulating materials.

གློག་འབྲེལ་གཅོད་བྱེད་ཡོ་ཆས་ (lɔ̄gdrel jööjeè yobjɛ̀ɛ̀) sm. གློག་འབྲེལ་གཅོད་བྱེད་དངོས་པོ་.

གློག་སྦྱོར་ཁང་ (lɔ̄gjɔɔgaŋ) room where electric power is distributed.

གློག་མི་ཁྲིད་པའི་དངོས་རྫས་ (lōgmi trībɛ ŋöödzɛɛ̀) nonconductors of electricity.

གློག་དམར་ (lɔ̄gmar) 1. lightening; vi.—འཁྱུག to have a flash of lightening. 2. red (traffic) light; vi.—གསལ་ to be on (for a red traffic light) ༡གློག་དམར་གསལ་དུས་འགྲོ་མི་ཆོག When the traffic light is red one is not permitted to go.

གློག་སྨན་ (lɔ̄gmɛn) flashlight battery.

གློག་སྨྱུག (lɔ̄gñuù) pencil-type gauge for measuring

electricity.

གློག་རྩི་ (lɔ̄gdzi) electroplating; va.—གཏོང་.

གློག་བཙའི་སྦྱོད་ཐབས་ (lɔ̄gdzɛ jȫödəb) acupuncture with electric stimulation.

གློག་ཚད་འཁོར་ལོ་ (lɔ̄gdzɛɛ̀ kɔ̄ɔ̄lo) sm. གློག་ཚད་ལྟ་ཆས་.

གློག་ཚད་འཇལ་ཆས་ (lɔ̄gdzɛɛ̀ jɛɛjɛɛ̀) sm. གློག་ཚད་ལྟ་ཆས་.

གློག་ཚད་ལྟ་ཆས་ (lɔ̄gdzɛɛ̀ dōjɛɛ̀) electric meter.

གློག་ཚད་ལྟ་བྱེད་ (lɔ̄gdzɛɛ̀ dājɛɛ̀) sm. གློག་ཚད་ལྟ་ཆས.

གློག་ཚད་བརྟག་ཆས་ (lɔ̄gdzɛɛ̀ dāgjɛɛ̀) electroscope.

གློག་ཚད་དཔྱད་ཆས་ (lɔ̄gdzɛɛ̀ jɛ̄ɛ̀cɛɛ̀) sm. གློག་ཚད་ལྟ་ཆས་.

གློག་ཚའི་ལྕགས་མདའ་ (lɔ̄gtsɛ jāŋda) electric welding rod.

གློག་ཚིག (lɔ̄ɔ̀ tsīì) vi. to have a light bulb burn out, to have/ get an electric short.

གློག་ཚོད་ (lɔ̄ɔ̀dzöö) electric meter.

གློག་རྫ་ (lɔ̄gdza) electro porcelain/ ceramics.

གློག་རྫས་ (lɔ̄gdzɛɛ̀) sm. གློག་སྨན་.

གློག་རྫས་སྐམ་པོ་ (lɔ̄gdzɛɛ̀ gāmba) dry cell (battery).

གློག་ཞགས་འཁྱུག་བསྒྲོད་ (lɔ̄gshaà kyūùdröö) sm. གློག་འཁྱུག.

གློག་ཞུ་ (lɔ̄gshu) sm. གློག་བཞུ་.

གློག་ཞུ་ལྗང་ཁུ་ (lɔ̄gshu jaŋgu) green light (for traffic); vi.—སྤར་ to have the green light turn on. 2. doing a special favor, giving sb. the green light to do sth.

གློག་ཞུ་དམར་པོ་ (lɔ̄gshu māābo) red light (for traffic).

གློག་ཞུན་ (lɔ̄gshün) sm. གློག་བཞུ་.

གློག་ཞུའི་ཞྭ་ཁེབས་ (lɔ̄gshü shageb) lamp shade.

གློག་ཞུའི་ཤེལ་དོག (lɔ̄gshü shēdoò) electric light bulb.

གློག་བཞུ་ (lɔ̄gshu) 1. flashlight. 2. lamp, light; va.—སྤར་ to turn on a flashlight/ lamp/ light; va.—གསོད་ to turn off a flashlight/ lamp/ light.

གློག་བཞུ་དཀར་པོ་ (lɔ̄gshu gāābo) fluorescent light.

གློག་བཞུའི་ཤེལ་དོག (lɔ̄gshü shēdoò) sm. གློག་ཞུའི་ཤེལ་དོག.

གློག་ཟུང་སྣེ་དུལ་ (lɔ̄gsuŋ nēdül) electric dipole.

གློག་ཟོན་ (lɔ̄gsön) electric calculator.

གློག་བཟོ་པ་ (lɔ̄gsoba) electrical worker, electrician.

གློག་བཟོ་ལས་ (lɔ̄ɔ̀ solɛɛ̀) electrical industry.

གློག་འོད་ (lɔ̄gwöö) electric light; vi.—རྒྱག to have light shine.

གློག་འོད་གཞུ་དབྱིབས་ཅན་ (lɔ̄göö shuyibjɛn) electric.

གློག་ཡིག་ཁང་ (lɔ̄ɔ̄yigaŋ) telegraph station.

གློག་ཡོམ་གློག་གཏོང་ (lɔ̄gyom lɔ̄gdoŋ) corona discharge.

གློག་གཡིས་ (lɔ̄gyii) tib.ch. battery, electric cell ¶ གློག་གཡིས་སློབ་གྲྭ་ Battery factory.

གློག་གཡེར་ (lɔ̄gyer) microwave.

གློག་རའི་ནུས་ཚད་ (lɔ̄grɛ nüüdzɛɛ̀) sm. གློག་ཁམས་ཀྱི་ནུས་ཚད་.

གློག་རིག (lɔ̄grig) science of electricity.

གློག་རིག་སློབ་གྲྭ་ (lɔ̄grig lōbdra) electronics school.

གློག་རིན་ (lɔ̄grin) the cost of electricity, electric bill.

གློག་རླབས་ (lɔ̄gləb) electric waves.

གློག་རླུང་གི་འཁྱགས་སྒམ་ (lɔ̄gluŋgi kyāàgam) refrigerator.

གློག་ལམ་ (lɔ̄glam) electric circuit.

གློག་ལམ་ཁ་ཟུམ་གྱི་བརྙན་འཕྲིན་ (lɔ̄glam kāsumgi ñɛ̄ndrin) closed circuit television.

གློག་ལམ་མཚོན་རིས་ (lɔ̄glam tsönrii) circuit diagram.

གློག་ལས་ (lōglɛɛ̀) electrical work, electronics.

གློག་ལས་ཅན་དུ་འགྱུར་ (lɔ̄glɛɛ̀jɛndu gyur) sm. གློག་ལས་སུ་འགྱུར་.

གློག་ལས་པ་ (lɔ̄lɛɛ̀ba) sm. གློག་ལས་བཟོ་པ་.

གློག་ལས་བཟོ་པ་ (lɔ̄glɛɛ̀ soba) electrical worker, electrician.

གློག་ལས་བཟོ་ལས་ (lōglɛɛ̀ solɛɛ̀) electrical industry.

གློག་ལས་ལག་རྩལ་སློབ་གྲྭ་ (lōglɛɛ̀ lagdzɛɛ lōbdra) school of electrical engineering/ electronics.

གློག་ལས་སུ་འགྱུར་ (lɔ̄glɛɛ̀su gyur) vi. to become electrified.

གློག་ལུགས་ (lɔ̄gluù) electrotyping; va.—རྒྱག.

གློག་ཤི་ (lɔ̄ɔ̀ shī) vi. to have a light to go out.

གློག་ཤིང་ (lɔ̄gshiŋ) electric pole, telephone pole.

གློག་ཤུགས་ (lɔ̄gshuù) electric power, electric energy.

གློག་ཤུགས་བཀོད་སྒྲིག་ཁང་ (lɔ̄gshug gȫödriggaŋ) electric power control room.

གློག་ཤུགས་ཁབ་ལེན་ (lɔ̄gshug kəblen) electromagnetism.

གློག་ཤུགས་ཅན་ (lɔ̄gshugjɛn) electrified; vi.—དུ་འགྱུར་ to become electrified.

གློག་ཤུགས་ཅུའུ་ (lɔ̄gshug jūwu) Bureau of Electric Power.

གློག་ཤུགས་ཆུ་འཐེན་ (lɔ̄gshug cūnden) sm. གློག་ཤུགས་ཆུ་འདྲེན་.

གློག་ཤུགས་ཆུ་འདྲེན་ (lɔ̄gshug cūndren) electric pumping of water ¶ གློག་ཤུགས་ཆུ་འདྲེན་ས་ཚིགས་ Water pumping station.

གློག་ཤུགས་ཆུ་ཚོད་ (lɔ̄gshug cūdzöö) electric watch.

གློག་ཤུགས་གཏོང་འཛིན་འཁོར་ལོ་ (lōgshug dōŋdzin kɔ̄ɔ̄lo) electric transformer.

གློག་ཤུགས་ལྟེ་གནས་ཚོད་ལྟ་ཁང་ (lōgshug dēnɛɛ̀ tsȫödagaŋ) center for testing electric power.

གློག་ཤུགས་དྲ་བ་ (lɔ̄gshug trawa) power network.

གློག་ཤུགས་མེ་འཁོར་ (lɔ̄gshug megɔɔ) electric train.

གློག་ཤུགས་རྩི་འབྱུག (lɔ̄gshug dzīyug) electroplating.

གློག་ཤུགས་ཚ་ལའི་འཕྲུལ་འཁོར་ (lɔ̄gshug tsālɛ trǖügɔɔ) electrowelding machine.

གློག་ཤུགས་བཟོ་ལས་ (lɔ̄gshug solɛɛ̀) electric power industry.

གློག་ཤོར་ (lɔ̄ɔ̀ shɔ̄ɔ̄) vi. to have electricity leak/ get lost.

གློག་གཤོལ་ (lɔ̄gshöö) electric plow.

གློག་གསོག་སྣོད་ཆས་ (lɔ̄gsoò nȫöjɛɛ̀) storage battery.

གློག་གསོག་འཕྲུལ་ཆས་ (lɔ̄gsoò trǖüjɛɛ̀) sm. གློག་གསོག་སྣོད་ཆས་.

གློག་གསོར་ (lɔ̄gsor) electric drill.

གློག་བསྲོས་གསོ་ཐབས་ (lɔ̄gsöö sōtəb) electric heating therapy/ treatment (for illness).

གློང་ (lōŋ) 1. va. to tease/ tantalize. 2. va. to search for sth.

གློད་ (lȫö) va. to release, to let go, to let loose, to set free, to be let loose ¶ ཁོང་ཚོས་འཛིན་བཟུང་བྱས་པའི་མི་དེ་གློད་འདུག The man they arrested has been released. ¶ ང་གློད་རོགས་གནང་ Please let me go. ¶ རྐང་སྐྲ་རིལ་གྱི་འཁོར་ལོའི་ཕུ་གློད་བཞག The air in the bicycle tire has been let out (by sb.).

གློད་ཤོར་ (lȫö shɔ̄ɔ̄) vi. to escape/ run away ¶ བཙོན་པ་དེ་གློད་ཤོར་བྱུང་འདུག The prisoner escaped.

གློད་བཀྲོལ་ (lȫödröö) releasing, letting go; va.—གཏོང་ to release, to let go; vi.—ཐོབ་ to obtain release; va.—ཞུ་ to ask to be released.

གློད་འགྲོལ་ (lȫödröö) sm. གློད་བཀྲོལ་.

གློད་གཏོང་ (lȫödoŋ) 1. releasing, letting go, freeing; va. གློད་གཏོང་; —བྱེད་ to release, to let go, to free ¶ བཙོན་ཁང་ནས་བཙོན་པ་མང་པོ་ཞིག་གློད་གཏོང་བྱས་བཞག They have released many prisoners from prison. 2. launching, sending off; va. གློད་གཏོང་; —བྱེད་ to launch, to send off ¶ མི་བཟོས་སྐྱུང་སྐར་ཞིག་གློད་གཏོང་བྱས་པ་རེད་ They launched a satellite.

གློད་ཚོད་ (lȫödzöö) letting sth. go or releasing it while still maintaining control; va.—རྒྱག ¶ ཐེར་གེའི་སྒྲི་རིག་བཀག་ནས་ཐུར་ལ་གློད་ཚོད་བརྒྱབ་པ་རེད་ (He) applied the brakes of the cart and let it go down the slope while still keeping it under control.

གློན་ (lȫn) 1. sm. གླན་. 2. va. to patch.

གློན་སྨན་ (lȫnmɛn) tape that is stuck on the temple to relieve headaches, pains, etc.

གློས་ (lȫö) imp. of གླ་.

གློས་ཕབ་ (lȫö pāb) p. of གློས་འབེབས་.

གློས་ཕབ་སྙེ་ཉལ་ (lȫöpəb dēñɛɛ) va. to lay down on one's side.

གློས་འབེབས་ (lȫn beb) va. to lay on one's side.

གྷ་ནཱ་ (ghanna) Ghana.

གྷི་ཕམ་ (ghibam) gallstone.

དགག (gaà) f. of འགེག.

དགག་འགྱངས་ (gaggyaŋ) a delay due to an obstruction ¶ དམག་འཁྲུག་རྒྱ་བསྐྱེད་དེས་དཔུང་དམག་ཕྱིར་འཐེན་ལ་དགག་འགྱངས་བྱུང་ Because the war has expanded the withdrawal of troops has been delayed. [Lit. obstruction, delay].

དགག་སྒྲ་ (gagdra) sm. དགག་ཚིག.

དགག་སྒྲུབ་ (gagdrub) sm. དགག་པ་.

དགག་ཆ་ (gagja) objection, opposition; va.—བྱེད་ ¶ ཁོང་གིས་ང་ཕྱི་རྒྱལ་འགྲོ་རྒྱུར་དགག་ཆ་གནང་གི་འདུག (He) is objecting to my going abroad.

དགག་སྙི་ (gəgñi) a snare that catches animals by the neck.

དགག་གདོང་སུན་ཕྱུང་ (gagdoŋ sũnjuŋ) refuting/ rebutting and criticizing.

དགག་བདང་སུན་ཕྱུང་ (gagdaŋ sũnjuŋ) sm. དགག་གདོང་སུན་ཕྱུང་.

དགག་དྲི་ (gəgdri) belch, belching; vi.—རྒྱག to belch.

དགག་པ་ (gagba) 1. refuting, rebutting, objecting to, combating; va.—རྒྱག to refute, to rebut ¶ ཁོའི་ལྟ་བ་ལ་དགག་པ་བརྒྱབ་ཡོད་པ་རེད་ (They) refuted his ideology. ¶ ཐ་མག་འཐེན་རྒྱུར་དགག་པ་རྒྱག་དགོས་ (We) have to combat smoking.

དགག་པས་བཏུལ་ (gagbε dũl) va. to subdue/ defeat by refuting.

དགག་བྱ་ (gagja) the point or issue that is to be refuted in a debate/ argument.

དགག་ཚིག (gəgdzii) words of rebuttal/ rebutting/ refuting.

དགག་ཡིག (gəgyig) statements people had to write "opposing" things during the Cultural Revolution.

དགག་ལན་ (gaglεn) 1. reply to a refutation/ rebuttal, answer to a charge/ criticism; va.—རྒྱག; —བྱེད་; —སློད་; —སློག ¶ ཁོང་གིས་དམངས་གཙོའི་ལྟ་བའི་སྐོར་གྱི་རྩོམ་ཡིག་དེའི་དགག་ལན་ཞིག་བརྒྱབ་པ་རེད་ He refuted the article about the democratic point of view.

དགང་ (gaŋ) f. of འགེངས་.

དགང་བླུགས་ (gaŋluù) ladles used in rituals of exorcism.

དགང་གཟར་ (gaŋsar) 1. a kind of ladle used in exorcism. 2. a pipe (for smoking).

དགད་ (gεὲ) f. of འགད་.

དགན་པ་ (gεmba cḛè) sm. གྲེན་པ་.

དགན་པ་ཚ་པོ་ (gεmba tsābo) sm. གྲེན་པ་ཚ་པོ་.

དགབ་ (gəb) f. of འགེབས་.

དགའ་ (ga) 1. vi. to be glad, to be pleased, to be happy ¶ ཁྱེད་རང་འདིར་ཕེབས་ཙང་ཁོ་ཚོ་དགའ་སོང་ They were glad because you came. ¶ ང་དགའ་མ་བྱུང་ I was not pleased. 2. vi. to like, to love, to be fond of ¶ ཁོ་བཙོང་ལ་དགའ་གི་མི་འདུག He does not like onions. ¶ ཁོ་བུ་མོ་དེ་ར་ཞེ་དྲག་དགའ་པོ་འདུག He loves that girl a lot. 3. vi. to be better, to be more advantageous ¶ འདི་བཙོངས་ན་དགའ་གི་རེད་ It is better to sell it. 4. abbr. of དགའ་པོ་.

དགའ་ཀྲོག་གེར་ (ga drɔ̄gge) sm. དགའ་ལྷང་ལྷང་.

དགའ་བཀུར་ (gagur) love and respect ¶ ཁོ་མི་དགའ་བཀུར་འོས་པ་ཞིག་འདུག He is a person worthy of love and respect.

དགའ་སྐད་ (gagεὲ) cheers, shouts of joy; va.—སྒྲོག to cheer, to shout (for joy).

དགའ་སྐྱིད་ (gagyiì) abbr. for དགའ་དགའ་སྐྱིད་སྐྱིད་.

དགའ་སྐྱིད་ལྡན་པ་ (gagyiì dεmba) happy, joyful, glad.

དགའ་སྐྱེལ་ (gagyee) seeing someone off (happily); va.—ཞུ་ to see sb. off ¶ དགའ་སྐྱེལ་གྱི་ཐུགས་སྒྲོ་ A farewell/ seeing off party.

དགའ་སྐྱེལ་ཚོགས་འདུ་ (gagyee tsōndu) party given in honor of someone's departure.

དགའ་སྐྱོ་ (gagyo) joy and sorrow, happiness and sadness ¶ ལོ་རྒྱུས་དེ་ནི་དགའ་སྐྱོ་གཉིས་ཀ་ཡོད་པ་ཞིག་འདུག Their story has both happiness and sadness.

དགའ་སྐྱོ་སྐྱེ་སླ་བ་ (gagyo gyēlawa) sb. who easily feels happy or sad.

དགའ་སྐྱོ་གཉིས་ལྡན་ (gagyo ñiìdεn) simultaneous happiness and sadness.

དགའ་སྐྱོ་གཉིས་འོས་ (gagyo ñiìöò) sm. དགའ་སྐྱོ་གཉིས་ལྡན་.

དགའ་སྐྱོ་གཉིས་ཡོད་ (gagyo ñiìyöò) sm. དགའ་སྐྱོ་གཉིས་ལྡན་.

དགའ་སྐྱོ་མཉམ་འཆར་ (gagyo ñāmjar) sm. དགའ་སྐྱོ་གཉིས་ལྡན་.

དགའ་སྐྱོ་འདྲེས་མ་ (gagyo dreèma) sm. དགའ་སྐྱོ་གཉིས་ལྡན་.

དགའ་ཁུལ་ (gəgüü) pretending to like/ love; va.—བྱེད་.

དགའ་ཁྲས་ཁྲས་ (ga treèdreè) happy appearance; va.—བྱེད་ to act happy, to have a happy appearance.

དགའ་མཁན་ (gañen) one who likes, pro sb. or sth. ¶ ཨ་རིར་དགའ་མཁན་ People who are pro-U.S.A.

དགའ་འཁྱིལ་ (gəgyil) a traditional design (a circle with two crescents).

དགའ་གུས་ (gəgüü) love and respect ¶ དགའ་གུས་འོས་ཤོས་ཀྱི་དབུ་ཁྲིད་ The most respected and loved leader. ¶ དགའ་གུས་འོས་པ་ Worthy of love and respect.

དགའ་གྲོགས་ (gadroò) close friend, girlfriend, boyfriend.

དགའ་གླུ་ (galu) love song.

དགའ་དགའ་སྐྱིད་སྐྱིད་ (gaga gyīgyiì) joy, happiness; va.—བྱེད་ to be happy/ joyful ¶ དགའ་དགའ་སྐྱིད་སྐྱིད་ངང་ནས་ཐུགས་སྒྲོ་བཏང་བ་རེད་ (They) gave a joyful party.

དགའ་དགའ་སྤྲོ་སྤྲོ་ (gaga trōdro) sm. དགའ་དགའ་སྐྱིད་སྐྱིད་.

དགའ་མགུ་ (gaŋgu) sm. དགའ་མགུ་ཡིད་རང་.

དགའ་མགུ་ཡིད་རང་ (gaŋgu yiraŋ) happy and satisfied.

དགའ་མགུར་སྤྱོད་ (gaŋgur jöö) 1. va. to enjoy happiness. 2. va. to have sexual intercourse.

དགའ་སྒོམ་ (gagom) sm. དགའ་ངོམས་ཆོག་ཤེས་.

དགའ་ངུ་ (gaŋu) crying with joy; vi.—ཤོར་ to cry with joy.

དགའ་ངོམས་ཆོག་ཤེས་ (gaŋom cōgsheè) satisfied/ content with one's lot; va.—བྱེད་ to be satisfied/ content with one's lot.

དགའ་གཅེས་ (gajeè) love, affection; va.—བྱེད་.

དགའ་ཆེས་ན་ངུ་ཤོར་ (gacēna ŋu shɔ̄ɔ̄) sm. དགའ་ངུ་.

དགའ་ཆོག་ཆོག་ཁྲུག་ཆོག་ཆོག (gacōgjoò dug cōgjoò) sb. who gets happy quickly and angry quickly, temperamental.

དགའ་མཆོང་ (gajoŋ) leaping/ jumping with joy; va.—རྒྱག.

དགའ་བརྗོད་ལས་འདས་པ་ (gajööle dεèba) extremely happy [Lit. happy beyond words].

དགའ་ཉམས་ (gañam) good feelings, high spirits; vi.—སྐྱེད་ to be in high spirits, to feel good; va.—སྟོན་ to express or show liking.

དགའ་ཉེ་ (gañe) sm. དགའ་པོ་ཉེ་པོ་.

དགའ་ཉེ་བློ་དཀར་ (gañe lōgaa) sm. དགའ་པོ་ཉེ་པོ་.

དགའ་ཉེར་བརྟེན་མཁན་ (gañe dēngεn) ones who side with ¶ བཙན་རྒྱལ་རིང་ལུགས་དགའ་ཉེར་བརྟེན་མཁན་ Those who side with the imperialists.

དགའ་ཉེར་བསྟེན་ (gañee dēn) 1. va. to make friends with ¶ ཁོང་གི་མི་ཚང་ཕྱུག་པོ་རྣམས་དགའ་ཉེར་བསྟེན་གྱི་ཡོད་པ་རེད་ He makes friends with rich families. 2. va. to ally with, to side with ¶ བཙན་རྒྱལ་རིང་ལུགས་དགའ་ཉེར་བསྟེན་མཁན་ Those who side with imperialists.

དགའ་སྟོན་ (gadön) party, banquet, celebration; va.—བྱེད་; —གསོལ་; —ཞུ་ to celebrate ¶ ལོ་འཁོར་དགའ་སྟོན་ An anniversary party. ¶ འཁྲུངས་སྐར་གྱི་དགའ་སྟོན་བྱས་པ་རེད་ (They) celebrated (his) birthday.

དགའ་སྟོན་རྟེན་འབྲེལ་ (gadön dēmdree) celebration; va.—ཞུ་ to celebrate.

དགའ་སྟོན་ཚོགས་ཆེན་ (gadön tsɔ̄gjen) ¶ celebration or congratulatory meeting/ assembly, anniversary assembly/ meeting.

དགའ་སྟོན་ཚོགས་འདུ་ (gadön tsōndu) sm. དགའ་སྟོན་ཚོགས་ཆེན་.

དགའ་ཐག་ཆོད་ (gadaà cōō) vi. to be extremely happy ། ཁོང་བོད་ལ་འགྲོ་རྒྱུ་ཆོག་མཆན་ རག་ཙང་དགའ་ཐག་ཆོད་པ་རེད་ Because he received permission to go to Tibet, he was extremely happy.

དགའ་ཐལ་ (gadɛɛ) feeling too happy, excessively happy; vi.—བྱེད་.

དགའ་མཐུན་པ་ (gadümba) friends with whom one gets along well.

དགའ་དར་ (gadar) a ceremonial white scarf offered on happy occasions.

དགའ་གདོང་ (gadoŋ) the temple near Lhasa of one of Tibet's leading oracles of the same name.

དགའ་གདོང་ཆོས་སྐྱོང་ (gadoŋ cōōgyoŋ) one of Tibet's leading oracles (Drepung monastery's Gadong).

དགའ་བདེ་ (gade) sm. དགའ་དགའ་སྐྱིད་སྐྱིད་.

དགའ་མདོག་ཤང་མདོག (gandɔɔ shāŋdɔɔ) pretending to like or be friends; va.—བྱེད་.

དགའ་འདྲིས་ (gandrii) close friend.

དགའ་ལྡན་ (gandɛn) 1. happy, joyful. 2. Ganden Monastery (founded in 1408). 3. Tushita (the heaven of joy).

དགའ་ལྡན་ཁྲི་པ་ (gandɛn trība) the chief abbot at Ganden Monastery who is considered to hold the throne of Tsongkapa (he is considered the highest religious figure in the Gelugpa sect).

དགའ་ལྡན་ཁྲི་ཟུར་ (gandɛn trīsur) title of a former/ ex-abbot of Ganden Monastery.

དགའ་ལྡན་དགོན་པ་ (gandɛn gomba) see དགའ་ལྡན་, 2.

དགའ་ལྡན་ལྔ་མཆོད་ (gandɛn ŋāmjöö) festival held on the 25th day of the 10th month to commemorate the death of Tsonkapa.

དགའ་ལྡན་དར་ཆེན་ (gandɛn tarjen) shung. the tall prayer flag at the northeast corner of the Barkor.

དགའ་ལྡན་ཕོ་བྲང་ (gandɛn pōdraŋ) shung. name of the residence of the Dalai Lamas in Drepung Monastery that was built by Gendun Gyatso in the 16th century and later became the name of the Tibetan Government after the 5th Dalai Lama assumed political power in Tibet.

དགའ་ལྡན་ཕོ་བྲང་ཕྱོགས་ལས་རྣམ་རྒྱལ་ (gandɛn pōdraŋ cɔ̄ɔlɛɛ nāmgyɛɛ) shung. the full name of the tt. government.

དགའ་སྡང་ (gadaŋ) love and hate.

དགའ་སྡུག (gɔdug) happiness and sorrow.

དགའ་སྡུག་བྱེད་མི་ཤེས་པ་ (gɔdug cɛmisheèba) sb. who is incapable of showing feelings of happiness or sorrow.

དགའ་སྣང་ (ganaŋ) joyful/ happy feeling; va.—བྱེད་ to be happy/ joyous, to show happiness.

དགའ་པོ་ (gabo) 1. glad, happy, pleased ། ལྟད་མོར་འགྲོ་རྒྱུར་ཕྲུ་གུ་ཚོ་དགའ་པོ་ཡོང་གི་རེད་ The children will be happy about going to the show. ། ཁྱེད་ཚོ་ཕེབས་ནས་དགའ་པོ་བྱུང་ I am glad you all came. 2. liking, fond of, loving; va.—བྱེད་ ། ང་ཁྱི་ལ་དགའ་པོ་ཡོད་ I like dogs. ། ཁོ་ལ་མི་ཚང་མས་དགའ་པོ་བྱས་པ་རེད་ Everybody liked him.

དགའ་པོ་སྐྱིད་པོ་ (gabo gìibu) happiness and joy; va.—གཏོང་ to be happy and joyful.

དགའ་པོ་ཉེ་པོ་ (gabo ñebo) friends and relatives.

དགའ་དཔུང་ (gabuŋ) a gathering of friends and relatives at the time of a person's death for the purpose of giving donations and consolation.

དགའ་སྤོབས་ (gabob) happiness/ joy and pride.

དགའ་སྤྱོད་ (gajöö) sm. དགའ་མགུར་སྤྱོད་པ་.

དགའ་སྤྲོ་ (gadro) happiness, joy; vi.—འཁོལ་ to be happy/ joyous, to bubble over with happiness/ joy །཈ོ་ཚོར་རྒྱལ་ཁ་ཐོབ་པར་དགའ་སྤྲོ་འཁོལ་བ་རེད་ They were happy over their victory.

དགའ་སྤྲོ་འཁོལ་ (gadro kōō) see དགའ་སྤྲོ་.

དགའ་སྤྲོ་ཆེན་པོ་ (gadro cēmbo) great joy, great happiness.

དགའ་སྤྲོ་དཔག་མེད་ (gadro bāgmeè) immeasurable/ inestimable joy or happiness.

དགའ་སྤྲོ་དཔག་ཏུ་མེད་པ་ (gadro bāgmeèba) sm. དགའ་སྤྲོ་དཔག་མེད་.

དགའ་སྤྲོ་ཚད་མེད་ (gadro tsɛ̄ɛmeè) sm. དགའ་སྤྲོ་དཔག་མེད་.

དགའ་སྤྲོས་ཁེངས་ (gadröö kēŋ) vi. to be filled with joy and happiness.

དགའ་ཕྱོགས་ (gajoò) favoritism, partiality; va.—བྱེད་ to show favoritism and partiality.

དགའ་བ་ (gawa) joy, happiness; vi.—སྐྱེད་ to be joyous, happy; va.—སྒྲོག to cheer/ acclaim/ hail; va.—སྐོང་ to fulfill sb. else's pleasure.

དགའ་བ་སྐྱེ་འོས་པ་ (gawa gyē wööba) joyous, worthy of joy.

དགའ་བ་ཕྱིན་ཅི་ལོག་པ་ (gawa cīnji lɔgba) liking sth. that is not worthy of liking.

དགའ་བ་ཚད་མེད་ (gawa tsɛ̄ɛmeè) immeasurable joy.

དགའ་བ་ལ་ (gawala) how happy, how pleased/ joyful ། དགའ་བ་ལ་ ངའི་ཕ་མ་གཉིས་ཀྱི་ཡི་གེ་འབྱོར་བྱུང་ Oh, how happy (I am). I received a letter form my parents.

དགའ་བའི་སྒྲ་དབྱངས་ (gawɛ drayaŋ) cheers, acclamation, shouts of joy; va.—སྒྲོག to cheer, to acclaim, to hail ། གྲོས་མཐུན་ལ་མིང་རྟགས་བཀོད་པར་ དགའ་བའི་སྒྲ་དབྱངས་བསྒྲགས་པ་རེད་ (They) cheered the signing of the treaty.

དགའ་བའི་འབོད་དབྱངས་ (gawɛ bööyaŋ) sm. དགའ་བའི་སྒྲ་དབྱངས་.

དགའ་བའི་ཚལ་ (gawɛ tsɛ̄ɛ) sm. གླིང་ཀ.

དགའ་བའི་བཞིན་ (gawɛshin) (expression of) joy/ happiness.

དགའ་བར་རོལ་ (gawar röl) va. to enjoy/ experience pleasure.

དགའ་བོ་ (gawo) name of one of the six disciples of the Buddha.

དགའ་དབྱེ་འཛུམ་འབྲལ་ (gaye dzumdrɛɛ) separating/ parting/ splitting up amicably or in a friendly manner (i.e., without enmity); va.—བྱེད་ ། ཁྱོ་ཤུག་མ་འགྲིགས་སྟེ་དགའ་དབྱེ་འཛུམ་འབྲལ་བྱས་སོང་ The husband and wife didn't get along and separated amicably.

དགའ་འབོད་ (gaböö) sm. དགའ་བའི་སྒྲ་དབྱངས་.

དགའ་འབོད་ཅི་དགར་སྒྲོག (gaböö jīgar drog) va. to celebrate with roars/ shouts/ cheers of happiness.

དགའ་འབོད་ཆེན་པོ་ (gaböö cēmbo) shout/ cheer of joy.

དགའ་འབྲེལ་ཚོགས་འདུ་ (gandrel tsōndu) social meeting/ gathering.

དགའ་སྦུགས་ (gabug) shung. a hat worn by monk officials in winter.

དགའ་སྦུབས་ (gabub) shung. sm. དགའ་སྦུགས་.

དགའ་མ་ (gama) 1. wife. 2. girlfriend.

དགའ་མིན་དགའ་དོགས་ (gəmin gadɔg) holding a grudge/ enmity/ hatred, being biased towards sb.; va.—བྱེད་ ། འགོ་ཁྲིད་ཀྱིས་ང་ལ་དགའ་མིན་དགའ་དོགས་བྱེད་ཀྱི་འདུག The leader holds a grudge against me.

དགའ་མིན་ཞེ་བཞག (gəmin sheshaà) keeping hatred/ antipathy in mind, holding on to a dislike of sth.

དགའ་མིན་ཞེ་ལོག (gəmin shelɔg) hatred, antipathy.

དགའ་མོ་ (gamo) 1. good, nice ། མི་འདི་དགའ་མོ་ཡོད་ The man is good. 2. quite, rather ། དེང་སང་བྲེལ་བ་དགའ་མོ་ཡོད་ I am quite busy these days.

དགའ་མོས་ (gamöö) liking ། ཁོའི་བསམ་འཆར་དེ་ལ་ཚང་མས་དགའ་མོས་བྱུང་བ་རེད་ Everyone liked his suggestions.

དགའ་སྨོན་ (gamön) congratulations; va.—བྱེད་; —ཞུ་ ། ཁྱེད་རང་ལ་ལས་ཀ་གསར་པ་རག་པར་ངས་དགའ་སྨོན་བྱེད་ཀྱི་ཡོད་ I congratulate you on getting the new job.

དགའ་རྩེ་ (gadze) liking and loving.

དགའ་ཚད་ཚད་ (ga tsɛ̄ɛdzɛɛ) extremely happy/ elated/ joyful; va.—བྱེད་ to act/ show/ be extremely happy. ། གནས་ཚུལ་གོ་མ་ཐག་ཁོང་དགའ་ཚད་ཚད་བྱས་པ་རེད་ As soon as he heard the news he was extremely happy.

དགའ་ཚལ་ (gatsεε) garden, park, grove.

དགའ་ཚོར་ (gatsor) feeling of happiness/ gladness/ joy; va.—བྱེད་; vi.—སྐྱེད་; vi.—སྐྱེས་ ¶ མི་དམངས་དང་གིས་ཐུགས་ཁུར་གཉན་བཞིས་གནང་བར་དགའ་ཚོར་ཚད་མེད་བྱུང་སོང་ The people were extremely happy at the party's taking serious concern (for them).

དགའ་ཚོར་ཡིད་སྨོན་ (gatsor yimün) sm. དགའ་སྨོན་.

དགའ་འཛུམ་ (gandzum) a happy or joyful/ smile, a grin; va.—སྟོན་ to smile or grin happily.

དགའ་འཛོམས་ (gandzom) a happy/ joyful gathering or get-together; va.—བྱེད་.

དགའ་ཞིང་གུས་པ་ (gashiŋ güübə) loving and respectful, loved and respected.

དགའ་ཞེན་ (gashen) love and loyalty; va.—བྱེད་ to love and be loyal ¶ ཁོ་ཚོས་རང་གི་ཕ་ཡུལ་དགའ་ཞེན་ཚད་མེད་བྱས་པ་རེད་ They had boundless love and loyalty for their motherland.

དགའ་ཞེན་ལྔ་ (gashen ŋā) the five loves (love of motherland, the people, labor, science and socialism).

དགའ་ཞེན་སྤྱི་འཁུར་ (gashen jīgur) loving and respecting.

དགའ་བཞི་ (gabshi) shung. name of an important aristocratic family.

དགའ་བཞི་རྡོ་རིང་ (gabshi doriŋ) sm. དགའ་བཞི་.

དགའ་བཞི་འཕྲུལ་གྱི་ལྷ་ཁང་ (gabshi trüügi lhāgaŋ) shung. name of Tsuglakhang Cathedral in Lhasa.

དགའ་བཞིན་སྤྲོ་བཞིན་ (gashin drōshin) in a state of happiness, in a happy manner.

དགའ་འུར་ (gawur) the noise/ roar made by a cheering crowd; va.—རྒྱག.

དགའ་འོས་པ་ (ga wööba) worthwhile, worthy ¶ དགའ་འོས་པའི་གྲུབ་འབྲས་ཐོབ་སོང་ They achieved a worthwhile result.

དགའ་ཡ་ལི་ (ga yale) sm. དགའ་དགའ་ལྷང་ལྷང་.

དགའ་ཡལ་ཡལ་ (ga yεεyεε) sm. དགའ་ལྷང་ལྷང་.

དགའ་རབ་ (garəb) a lot ¶ ཁོང་གི་ངོས་འཛིན་དགའ་རབ་མཐོ་རུ་ཕྱིན་འདུག His understanding has increased a lot.

དགའ་རིན་ (garin) worthy/ deserving of love; vi.—ཆོག ¶ བུ་མོ་དེ་ཁྱེད་རང་དགའ་རིན་ག་རེ་འདུག་གམ How is that girl is deserving of your love?

དགའ་རོགས་ (garɔɔ̀) lover; boyfriend, girlfriend; va.—སྒྲིག to become boyfriend or girlfriend or lovers.

དགའ་ལ་ཉེ་ཕྱོགས་ (gala ñejɔɔ̀) one's side, one's friends/ associates; va.—བྱེད་ to favor/ side with one's friends or associates.

དགའ་ས་སྐྱིད་ས་ (gasa gyiisə) a happy and joyful place.

དགའ་ས་མཐུན་སྣང་ (gasa tũngaŋ) a favorite person.

དགའ་སིལ་སིལ་ (ga sīisi) happy, glad.

དགའ་སེམས་ (gasem) joy, happiness; va.—འཁོལ་ to be happy/ joyous.

དགའ་སོབ་སོབ་ (ga sōbsob) sm. དགའ་ལྷང་ལྷང་.

དགའ་བསུ་ (gəsu) welcoming; va.—བྱེད་; —ཞུ་ to welcome, to greet, to receive (people) ¶ སྤྲོ་སེམས་འཁོལ་བའི་ངང་ནས་ཁོང་ལ་དགའ་བསུ་ཞུས་པ་རེད་ (They) welcomed him warmly.

དགའ་བསུའི་དགོང་ཚོགས་ (gəsü goŋdzɔɔ̀) a welcoming evening party.

དགའ་ལྷང་ལྷང་ (ga lhāŋlhaŋ) joyous, happy, high spirits; vi.—བྱེད་ to be in high spirits.

དགར་: p. བཀར་; f. དགར་; imp. ཁོར་ (gar) 1. va. to set aside, to separate, to isolate, to quarantine (usu. follows ལོགས་སུ་) ¶ དོགས་པ་ཆེ་བ་ཡོད་པའི་མི་དེ་ཚོ་ལོགས་སུ་བཀར་ནས་དྲི་བ་བྱས་པ་རེད་ (They) separated the people (they) suspected the most and questioned them. 2. slang. va. to squeeze sb. to get information or a confession.

དགལ་ (gεε) f. of འགེལ་.

དགས་ (gεὲ) f. of དགས་.

དགུ་ (gu) 1. nine. 2. (ཡོད་ + —) all, everything ¶ ཁོ་ལ་ནོར་ཡོད་དགུ་ཤོར་བ་རེད་ He lost all his wealth. 3. (neg. + vb. + —) to do to excess ¶ མ་བྱེད་དགུ་བྱེད་བྱས་ན་ If you do this in excess. ¶ ཁ་ལག་མི་ཟ་དགུ་ཟ་ཟས་ན་ནད་གཞི་ཡོང་གི་རེད་ If you eat all sorts of things, you will get sick.

དགུ་སྐྱེག (gugeg) an inauspicious year which comes every nine years, e.g., 9. 18, 27.

དགུ་སྐྱེད་ (gugyeè) shung. 18% interest.

དགུ་འགྲིམ་ (gudrim) the coldest period in Tibet (the three coldest periods each of nine days).

དགུ་རྒྱུད་ (gugyüü) from generation to generation.

དགུ་བཅུ་ (gubju) ninety ¶ བརྒྱ་ཆ་དགུ་བཅུ་གོ་དགུ་ Ninety nine percent.

དགུ་བཅུ་འགྲོ་ (gu jū dro) shung. eleven percent interest. [Lit. 9 becomes 10].

དགུ་གཉིས་ (guñii) 9th day of 9th lunar month.

དགུ་གཉིས་པ་ (guñiibə) the second of the three coldest nine-day periods.

དགུ་གཏོར་ (gudɔɔ) an rite expelling the year's sins through a religious (cham) dance-rite performed on the 29th day of the 12th lunar month.

དགུ་ལྡེབ་ (gudeb) sth. folded in nine folds; va.—རྒྱག.

དགུ་ཐུག (gudug) broth/ stew eaten on the 29th of the 12th lunar month.

དགུ་ཐུབ་ (gudub) a bitter medicine used to counteract poison.

དགུ་ཐོག (gudɔɔ̀) nine stories (e.g., in a building).

དགུ་མཐའ་ (guda) multiplication tables in traditional Tibetan arithmetic (up to the nine times table).

དགུ་མཐའི་རེའུ་མིག (gudε riumig) multiplication chart/ table.

དགུ་དང་པོ་ (gu taŋbo) the first of the three coldest nine-day periods.

དགུ་མདའ་ (gunda) a kind of rifle that holds nine bullets.

དགུ་འདྲེན་ (gundren) sm. དགུ་འགྲིམ་.

དགུ་ཉིང་ (gūniŋ) three years ago.

དགུ་པ་ (gubə) ninth.

དགུ་ཕུད་བཅུ་ཟུར་ (gupü jūsur) shung. 10% tax in kind.

དགུ་བོག (gubɔɔ̀) sm. དགུ་མདའ་.

དགུ་ཚིག (gudzig) a verse composed with nine words.

དགུ་ཚིགས་ཀྱི་མ་ལག (gudziigi malag) the Milky Way; the galaxy.

དགུ་ཚིགས་རྒྱ་མོ་ (gudzii gyāmo) sm. དགུ་ཚིགས་ཀྱི་མ་ལག.

དགུ་ཚིགས་ཁོངས་གདོགས་ (gudzii kōŋdɔɔ̀) sm. དགུ་ཚིགས་ཀྱི་མ་ལག.

དགུ་འཛོམས་ (gundzom) all of some characteristics/ qualities combined together ¶ མི་དེ་གདུག་རྩུབ་དགུ་འཛོམས་ཤིག་རེད་ That person is sb. who has all the cruel characteristics combined.

དགུ་རྫས་ (gudzεὲ) broth that contains nine ingredients.

དགུ་ནྡ་ (gunda) sm. དགུ་མཐའ་.

དགུ་རུལ་ (gurüü) a warm spell during the 27 coldest days of the year (this is considered bad as it harms the next year's crops).

དགུ་ཤོག་རྒྱག (gusɔɔ̀ gyaà) va. to fire a volley.

དགུ་གསུམ་པ་ (gu sūmbə) the third of the three coldest nine day periods.

དགུ་གསུམ་སློབ་ཚོགས་ (gusum lōbdzoò) the "September Third Society": one of the eight democratic parties in precommunist China.

དགུ་གསོལ་ (gusüü) custome of putting white marks on the copper cauldron after cleaning the soot (on the 29th of the 12th month of the Tibetan calendar); va.—བྱེད་.

དགུག (guù) f. of འགུགས་.

དགུག་བྱང་ (gugjaŋ) wooden instrument used in rituals to attract demons to be exorcised.

དགུང་ (guŋ) 1. sky ¶ རི་མཐོན་པོ་དགུང་ལ་རེག་པ་ལྟ་བུ་ A high mountain which seemed to touch the sky. 2. middle ¶ ཉིན་གུང་ Middle of the day. 3. abbr.

of དགུང་ལོ་.

དགུང་དཀྱིལ་ (guŋkyii) in the middle of the sky.

དགུང་སྐག (guŋgaà) sm. དགུང་སྐེག.

དགུང་སྐེག (guŋgeg) 1. an unlucky year for an individual that comes every 12 years beginning at age 12. 2. a year when astrology says there is a d likelihood of misfortune.

དགུང་གྲངས་ (guŋdraŋ) sm. དགུང་ལོ་.

དགུང་སྔོན་ (guŋŋön) sky ། དགུང་སྔོན་གཡའ་དག Clear sky.

དགུང་ཆར་ (guŋjar) rain.

དགུང་ཇ་ (guŋja) afternoon tea.

དགུང་མཉམ་ (guŋñam) of the same age (h.) ། ཁོང་གཉིས་དགུང་མཉམ་རེད་ Those two are the same age.

དགུང་སྙིང་ (guŋñiŋ) h. of ལོ་རྟགས་.

དགུང་ཐིག (guŋdig) meridian line.

དགུང་ཐུན་ (guŋtün) the middle part of the three parts of a day.

དགུང་མཐོངས་ (guŋdoŋ) sky.

དགུང་དུ་བསྒྲེང་ (guŋdu dreŋ) va. to raise high, to lift up to the sky ། ཁོང་ཁྲོའི་ཁུ་ཚུར་དགུང་དུ་བསྒྲེངས་སྒྲ་སྐད་འདོན་བྱས་པ་རེད་ (They) raised their fists to the sky in anger and shouted slogans.

དགུང་དུ་འཕྱུར་ (guŋdu cūr) vi. to be rising/ curling up, to be on the upsurge ། ཁང་པའི་ཐོག་ཁ་ནས་དུ་བ་དགུང་དུ་འཕྱུར་བཞིན་འདུག The smoke is rising up from the roof of the house.

དགུང་དོ་ནུབ་ (guŋ tonub) this evening, tonight.

དགུང་གདུགས་ (guŋdug) the hot part of the day (at midday).

དགུང་བདུན་ (guŋdün) a week.

དགུང་འདེགས་ (guŋdeg) lifting up, raising, elevating; va.—བྱེད་.

དགུང་ན་ (guŋnə) age ། དགུང་ན་མཐོ་པོ་ Old age.

དགུང་དབྱིངས་ (guŋyiŋ) in the sky.

དགུང་མོ་ (guŋmo) sm. དགོང་མོ་.

དགུང་ཚ་དིང་ (guŋ tsādiŋ) sm. ཚ་དིང་.

དགུང་ཚིགས་ (guŋdzig) sm. གུང་ཚིགས་.

དགུང་ཚིགས་ཚོས་ར་ (guŋtsig cōōra) the afternoon debating session of scholar monks (དཔེ་ཆ་བ་).

དགུང་ཞག (guŋshaà) one day and night.

དགུང་ཞག་ཞེ་དགུ (guŋshaà shegu) the 49 days of mourning.

དགུང་ཞོགས་ཉིན་མཚན་ (guŋshɔɔ ñindzɛn) morning and evening, day and night.

དགུང་ཟླ་ (guŋda) sm. དགུ་མཉམ་.

དགུང་ལ་རེག་པ་ (guŋla regba) high, lofty [Lit. touching the sky].

དགུང་ལ་གཤེགས་ (guŋla shēg) vi. to die (h.).

དགུང་ལོ་ (gonlo) year, age (h.) ། དགུང་ལོ་ཉི་ཤུ Twenty years of age.

དགུང་སེང་ (guŋseŋ) reporting to or informing superiors; va.—ཞུ་ to report to/ inform superiors.

དགུང་གསར་ (guŋsar) h. of ལོ་གསར་.

དགུང་བསངས་ (guŋsaŋ) sky.

དགུང་ཨ་སྔོན་ (guŋ āŋön) the blue sky.

དགུན་ (gün) winter.

དགུན་ཀ་ (günga) winter.

དགུན་དཀྱིལ་ (güngyi) the middle of winter.

དགུན་རྒྱལ་ (güngyɛɛ) winter swimming.

དགུན་སྐྱིད་ (güngyii) shung. winter party for རྩེ་སློབ་གྲྭ་ students who are to become monk officials.

དགུན་སྐྱོལ་དཔྱིད་འགྲོས་ (güngyel jindröö) sm. དགུན་བསྐྱལ་དཔྱིད་སྒྲོལ་.

དགུན་སྐྱོལ་ལོ་ཏོག (güngyel lodoò) crops planted in winter, winter crops.

དགུན་སྐྱེས་ (güngyeè) winter grown ། དགུན་སྐྱེས་ལོ་ཏོག Winter crops.

དགུན་བསྐྱལ་ (güngyel) the passing of winter.

དགུན་བསྐྱལ་དཔྱིད་སྒྲོལ་ (güngyel jindröö) a saying that conveys managing through winter and spring (the lean times in the annual cycle) [Lit. passing winter, finishing spring].

དགུན་ཁ་ (günga) sm. དགུན་ཀ་.

དགུན་ཁའི་གུང་གསེང་ (güngɛ kuŋseŋ) winter vacation.

དགུན་གོས་ (güngöö) sm. དགུན་ཆས་.

དགུན་གྱི་ཁུ་བྱུག (güngi kūyuù) sb. who isn't talkative [Lit. a cuckoo bird in winter].

དགུན་གྲོ་ (gündro) winter wheat.

དགུན་བཀྱལ་ (güngɛɛ) sm. དགུན་བསྐྱལ་.

དགུན་བཀྱལ་དཔྱིད་སྒྲོལ་ (güngɛɛ jiidrö) sm. དགུན་བསྐྱལ་དཔྱིད་སྒྲོལ་.

དགུན་བཀྱལ་ལོ་ཏོག (güngɛɛ lodog) sm. དགུན་བསྐྱལ་ལོ་ཏོག.

དགུན་ཆས་ (günjɛɛ) winter clothes.

དགུན་ཆུ་ (günju) winter irrigation (irrigation in late fall that freezes and then melts in spring); va.—འདྲེན་; —གཏོང་ to do a winter irrigation.

དགུན་ཆོས་ (güncöö) sm. དགུན་ཆོས་ཆེན་མོ་.

དགུན་ཆོས་ཆེན་མོ་ (günjöö cēmbo) the monastic month-long debating semester held in winter.

དགུན་མཇུག་མེ་ཏོག (günjuù medog) wintersweet flower.

དགུན་ཉར་ (günñar) sth. preserved/ set aside for winter; va.—བྱེད་.

དགུན་ཉལ་ (günñɛɛ) winter hibernation; va.—བྱེད་.

དགུན་ཉི་ལྡོག (günñidɔg) winter solstice.

དགུན་སྟོད་ (gündöö) the early part of the winter.

དགུན་སྟུབ་ལོ་ཏོག (gündub lodoò) winter crops.

དགུན་ཐོག (gündɔɔ) during winter, in the winter.

དགུན་མཐའི་སྐང་ཚད་ (gündɛ gaŋdzɛɛ) the 11th month of the Tibetan lunar calendar.

དགུན་དལ་ (gündɛɛ) the slack/ leisure period for villagers during the winter.

དགུན་དལ་སློབ་གྲྭ་ (gündɛɛ lōbdra) a school held during the winter slack season.

དགུན་དུང་ (günduŋ) an area such as a river bed that is dry during the hot season where there is little rainfall.

དགུན་དུས་ (gündüü) winter time, winter; va.—སྐྱེལ་; —བཀྱལ་ to live/ pass through the winter ། དགུན་དུས་སྐྱེལ་རྒྱུའི་ཆེད་དུ་ཚལ་ས་དོང་དུ་སྦེད་དགོས་ In order to live through the winter one should bury vegetables in a pit (underground).

དགུན་འདེབས་ (gundeb) winter sowing/ planting; va.—བྱེད་.

དགུན་འདེབས་ལོ་ཏོག (gundeb lodoò) sm. དགུན་སྐྱོལ་ལོ་ཏོག.

དགུན་ནས་ (günnɛɛ) winter barley.

དགུན་དཔྱིད་ (günjii) abbr. winter and spring.

དགུན་བྲེལ་ (gündree) busy period during the winter.

དགུན་འབྲིང་ (gündriŋ) the 11th month in the Tibetan lunar calendar.

དགུན་མོ་ (günmo) winter plowing; va.—རྒྱག.

དགུན་རྨོས་ (günmöö) sm. དགུན་མོ་.

དགུན་སྨད་ (günmɛɛ) latter part of winter.

དགུན་ཚར་ (gundzar) a winter lamb's skin/ pelt.

དགུན་ཚུགས་ (gündzuù) the beginning of winter.

དགུན་མཚེར་ (gündzer) winter campsite of nomads.

དགུན་ཞྭ་ (günsha) winter hat.

དགུན་གཞུག (günshug) the end of winter.

དགུན་གཞུང་ (günshuŋ) sm. དགུན་དཀྱིལ་.

དགུན་ཟུག (günsug) the beginning of winter (the 10th month in the Tibetan lunar calendar).

དགུན་ཟོག (günsog) goods for trading/ selling in winter.

དགུན་ཟོན་བདེ་སྲུང་ (günsön desuŋ) making preparations to protect against winter (e.g., storing up hay); va.—བྱེད་.

དགུན་ཟླ་ཐ་ཆུང་ (günda tājuŋ) the end month of winter (the 12th month of the Tibetan lunar calendar).

དགུན་ཟླ་འབྲིང་པོ་ (günda driŋbo) the middle month of winter (the 11th month of the Tibetan lunar calendar).

དགུན་ཟླ་ར་བ་ (günda rawa) the beginning month of winter, the 10th month of the Tibetan lunar calendar.

དགུན་ཟླ་གསུམ་ (günda sūm) the three winter months (the 10th, 11th, and 12th Tibetan lunar months).

དགུན་ཡམས་ (günyam) winter epidemic.

དགུན་ལམ་ (günlam) a road that can be used in the winter.

དགུན་ལས་ (günlɛɛ̀) winter work/ chores.

དགུན་ལྭ་ (günla) winter woolen cloth.

དགུན་ས་ (günsa) winter residence, winter site.

དགུན་སློབ་ (günlob) winter school.

དགུན་ལྷམ་ (günlham) winter boots/ shoes.

དགུན་ཨ་རང་སྐང་རང་ (gün āraŋ gaŋraŋ) sm. དགུན་ཨ་རང་ད་རང་.

དགུན་ཨ་རང་ད་རང་ (gün āraŋ taraŋ) coldest part of winter, the depths of winter, severest part of winter.

དགུམ་ (gum) f. of འགུམ་.

དགུར་ (gur) crooked, bent over, hook shaped ¶ ཤིང་དགུར་ Bent wood.

དགུར་པོ་ (gurbo) sm. དགུར་.

དགུས་ཉིན་ (güüñin) sm. དགུས་ཉིན་ཀ་.

དགུས་ཉིན་ཀ་ (güüñingə) four days from today.

དགུས་ནིང་ (güüniŋ) three years ago.

དགེ་ (ge) 1. abbr. of དགེ་བ་. 2. (n. + —) teacher, instructor ¶ དམག་དགེ་ Military instructor. ¶ དབྱིན་དགེ་ English teacher.

དགེ་སྐུལ་ (gegüü) shung. asking for donations.

དགེ་སྐོས་ (gegöö) head discipline officer in a monastery or monastic college.

དགེ་སྐྱོན་ (gegyön) advantages and disadvantages, benefits and harm ¶ དགེ་རྒན་གྱིས་སློབ་ཕྲུག་ཚོར་སློབ་སྦྱོང་གི་སྐོར་དགེ་སྐྱོན་གསལ་པོ་བཤད་པ་རེད་ The teacher explained the advantages and disadvantages of studying clearly to the students.

དགེ་སྐྱོན་སྦྱོང་བཤད་ (gegyön joŋshɛɛ̀) explaining the advantages and disadvantages of sth.

དགེ་སྐྱོན་ཡོ་བསྲང་ (gegyön yosaŋ) constructive suggestions about the advantages and disadvantages (benefits/ harms); va.—བྱེད་ ¶ ཕ་མས་ཕྲུ་གུར་དགེ་སྐྱོན་ཡོ་བསྲང་བྱས་པ་རེད་ The parents gave constructive suggestions to their children about the advantages and disadvantages.

དགེ་སྐྱོན་སྲོང་ (gegyön sōŋ) sm. དགེ་སྐྱོན་ཡོ་བསྲང་.

དགེ་བསྐོས་ (gegöö) sm. དགེ་སྐོས་.

དགེ་གོམས་ (gegom) good/ virtuous habits; vi. དགེ་གོམས་; —ཆགས་ to acquire good habits.

དགེ་དགེ་ (gege) showing off; va.—བྱེད་.

དགེ་དགེ་ཤར་དུར་ས་ (gegeshar tursa) Chinese Muslim cemetery in Lhasa.

དགེ་རྒན་ (gegɛn) teacher ¶ དགེ་རྒན་འོས་སྦྱོང་སློབ་གྲྭ་ Teacher's college.

དགེ་རྒན་ཆེ་མོ་བ་ (gegɛn cēmowa) full professor.

དགེ་རྒན་བསྟེན་ (gegɛn dɛ̄n) va. to ask sb. to be one's teacher.

དགེ་རྒན་ཕ་མའི་སྒྲིག་འཛུགས་ (gegɛn pāmɛ drigdzuù) parent-teacher association (PTA).

དགེ་རྒན་སྦྱོང་བདར་འཛིན་གྲྭ་ (gegɛn joŋdar dzindra) teacher's training class.

དགེ་རྒན་འོས་འཕེར་ (gegɛn wömber) qualifications for teacher.

དགེ་རྒན་འོས་སྦྱོང་སློབ་གྲྭ་ (gegɛn wööjoŋ lōbdra) teacher's training college.

དགེ་རྒན་སློབ་གྲྭ་ (gegɛn lōbdra) teacher's training college.

དགེ་རྒྱུན་ (gegyün) sm. དགེ་རྒྱུན་གྱི་ཐེབས་.

དགེ་རྒྱུན་གྱི་ཐེབས་ (gegyüngi tēb) shung. a trust fund set up for making offerings ¶ གདན་ས་སེ་འབྲས་དགའ་གསུམ་ལ་དགེ་རྒྱུན་གྱི་ཐེབས་ཙ་བཞག་པ་ (They) set up a trust fund for making offerings in the three monastic seats: Sera, Drepung and Ganden.

དགེ་སྒྲུབ་ (gedrub) 1. virtue/ good karma; va.—བྱེད་ to act with virtue, to acquire good karma. 2. collecting grain for religious offerings; va.—འདེད་.

དགེ་སྒྲུབ་སྡིག་སྤོང་ (gedrub digboŋ) acquiring virtue/ good karma and giving up sin.

དགེ་བཅུ་ (geju) 1. the ten virtues of a place/ country. 2. ten meritorious deeds.

དགེ་ཆས་ (gejɛɛ̀) utensils used when praying for the deceased.

དགེ་ཆུ་ (geju) holy water.

དགེ་ཆེ་ (geje) abbr. for དགེ་རྒན་ཆེ་མོ་བ་.

དགེ་ཆོས་ (gejöö) sm. དགེ་བའི་བྱ་བ་.

དགེ་འཇུག་ (gejuù) virtuous activities.

དགེ་བསྙེན་ (geñen) religious vows taken by laymen.

དགེ་བསྙེན་སྡོམ་བཞེས་ (geñen domsheè) va. to take the laymen's religious vows.

དགེ་བསྙེན་མ་ (geñenma) female who has taken laymen's vows.

དགེ་ལྟས་ (gedɛɛ̀) auspicious signs.

དགེ་བསྟོད་སྡིག་སྨད་ (gedöö digmɛɛ̀) praising virtue and condemning sin.

དགེ་ཐོན་སློབ་གྲྭ་ (getön lōbdra) teacher's training school/ college.

དགེ་ཐོན་སློབ་གྲྭ་ཆེན་མོ་ (gedön lōbdra cēmmo) teacher's college.

དགེ་ཐོན་སློབ་ཆེན་ (getön lōbjen) abbr. of དགེ་ཐོན་སློབ་གྲྭ་ཆེན་མོ་.

དགེ་དོན་ (gedön) virtue; va.—བྱེད་; —སྒྲུབ་ to do a virtuous act.

དགེ་འདུན་ (gendün) monk (h.).

དགེ་འདུན་ཀུན་ར་ (gendün günra) courtyard where debating takes place in a monastery.

དགེ་འདུན་རྒྱ་མཚོ་ (gendün gyatso) the name of the second Dalai Lama.

དགེ་འདུན་པ་ (gendünba) monk (h.).

དགེ་འདུན་དབུལ་ཕོངས་ (gendün wüüboŋ) poor monks.

དགེ་འདོན་སྐྱོན་སེལ་ (gendün gyönsel) sm. དགེ་འདོན་སྐྱོན་བསྲང་.

དགེ་འདོན་སྐྱོན་བསྲང་ (gendön gyönsaŋ) constructive advice/ criticism [Lit. bring out the good/ right and correct the errors].

དགེ་ལྡན་ (gedɛn) virtuous.

དགེ་སྡིག (gedig) virtue and vice, good and evil.

དགེ་སྡིག་དཀར་ནག (gedig gārnag) sm. དགེ་སྡིག.

དགེ་སྡིག་ཤན་འབྱེད་ (gedig shɛ̄njeè) differentiating virtue and sin/ good and evil.

དགེ་ནས་ (genɛɛ̀) shung. restitution paid in grain to the victim's family by the killer.

དགེ་སྤེལ་སྡིག་སྤོང་ (gebel digboŋ) increase virtue, renounce sin.

དགེ་སྤྱོད་ (gejöö) religious acts/ practices.

དགེ་ཕྱོགས་ (gejɔɔ̀) in the direction of virtue ¶ མི་ཚང་འདིས་རྒྱུ་དངོས་མང་པོ་ཞིག་དགེ་ཕྱོགས་ལ་གཏོང་གི་ཡོད་པ་རེད་ That family gives much wealth to virtuous endeavors (e.g., charity).

དགེ་ཕྲུག (gedrug) students, pupils.

དགེ་འཕེལ་དབུ་རྩེ་ (gembee ūdze) the name of the top of the mountain directly behind Drepung monastery.

དགེ་འཕེལ་རི་ (gyamberi) the mountain overlooking/ behind Drepung Monastery.

དགེ་བ་ (gewa) virtue, good deeds, merit (in a religious sense); va.—གཏོང་; —བྱེད་ to be virtuous, to do good deeds, to gain merit; va.—གསོག to accumulate good deeds/ merits.

དགེ་བ་ལྔའི་སྡོམ་པ་ (gewa ŋɛ̄ domba) the five virtuous vows (for monks).

དགེ་བ་བཅུ་ (gewa jū) the ten virtues: not killing/ stealing/ fornicating/ lying/ slandering/ using harsh words/ indulging idle gossip/ being coveting/ harming others/ holding heretical views.

དགེ་བ་བདེ་བའི་རྒྱུ་ སྡིག་པ་སྡུག་པའི་རྒྱུ་ (gewa dewɛ gyu digbə dugbɛ gyu) virtue is the foundation of happiness and sin is the foundation of suffering.

དགེ་བ་ཡོང་ (gewa yoŋ) good merit will come.

དགེ་བའི་བྱ་སྤྱོད་ (gewɛ cajöö) sm. དགེ་བའི་ལས་.

དགེ་བའི་བྱ་བ་ (gewɛ cawa) sm. དགེ་བའི་ལས་.

དགེ་བའི་མཚན་མ་ (gewɛ tsɛ̄nma) sm. དགེ་མཚན་.

དགེ་བའི་ལས་ (gewɛ lɛ̱ɛ̀) good/ virtuous/ work or deeds, charitable work.
དགེ་བའི་བཤེས་གཉེན་ (gewɛ shēñen) sm. དགེ་བཤེས་.
དགེ་ཕན་ (gebeè) good use, usefulness; va.—སྤྱོད་; —འདོན་ to make good use of, to utilize a speciality ༑ཆུ་མཛོད་དེ་ལ་བརྟེན་ནས་ས་སྟོང་དེ་ཚོར་དགེ་ཕན་སྤྱོད་ཐུབ་པ་རེད་ Because of the dam they were able to make use of the virgin land.
དགེ་འབྲས་ (gendrɛɛ̀) the result of good/ virtuous deeds.
དགེ་སྦྱིན་ (gejin) religious/ virtuous charity.
དགེ་སྦྱོང་ (gejoŋ) sm. དགེ་སློང་.
དགེ་སྦྱོར་ (gejɔr) activities that bring positive merit/ good karma.
དགེ་མ་ (gema) 1. nun. 2. an old woman. 3. the deity Tara.
དགེ་མར་ (gemar) shung. butter paid to the family of a person who was killed by the killer as an act of restitution.
དགེ་རྩ་ (gedza) sm. དགེ་ལས་.
དགེ་བརྩོན་པ་ (gedzömba) a religious person.
དགེ་ཚུལ་ (gedzüü) monks with novice vows.
དགེ་མཚན་ (gendzɛn) 1. a good/ auspicious sign or omen; vi.—འཆར་; —མངོན་ to have a good sign/ omen appear; va.—ལེན་ to take what is advantageous ༑ལོ་ལེགས་ཡོང་རྒྱུའི་དགེ་མཚན་མང་པོ་མངོན་པ་རེད་ Many signs of a coming good harvest appeared. 2. advantages, good points, benefits ༑ལས་ཀ་དེ་ལ་དགེ་མཚན་ཆེན་པོ་ཞིག་ཚང་མས་མཐོང་བ་རེད་ Everybody saw great advantages in that work. ༑དགེ་མཚན་མ་མཆིས་སྐབས་ Because there was no advantage. ༑ནུབ་ཕྱོགས་པའི་ཤེས་རིག་གི་དགེ་མཚན་རྣམས་ལེན་གྱི་ཡོད་པ་རེད་ They are taking the good points of Western Culture. 3. special knowledge/ ability, a specialty ༑མི་རེ་ལ་དགེ་མཚན་རེ་ Everyone has his own speciality.
དགེ་མཚན་འདོན་སྤེལ་ (getsɛn dö̱mbel) sm. ཁྱད་ནུས་འདོན་སྤེལ་.
དགེ་མཚན་ལྡན་པ་ (getsɛn dɛ̱mba) advantageous, beneficial, constructive, useful ༑དགེ་མཚན་ལྡན་པའི་བསམ་འཆར་ Constructive criticism.
དགེ་མཚན་བླངས་ (getsɛn lāŋ) p. of དགེ་མཚན་ལེན་.
དགེ་མཚན་ལེན་ (getsɛn le̱n) see དགེ་མཚན་.
དགེ་འོས་ (gewö̱ö̀) teacher's training.
དགེ་འོས་སློབ་གྲྭ་ཆེན་མོ་ (gewö̱ö̀ lōbdra cēmmo) teacher's training college.
དགེ་ཡོན་ (geyön) good points/ qualities of people.
དགེ་གཡོག (geyɔɔ̀) assistants of the disciplinary officer (དགེ་བསྐོས་) in monastic colleges.
དགེ་ལས་ (gelɛɛ̀) 1. charitable acts, good work and deeds, virtuous work; va.—སྒྲུབ་ to accumulate virtuous deeds.
དགེ་ལུགས་པ་ (gelugba) follower of the Gelugpa sect. 2. teachers and staff.
དགེ་ལེགས་ (geleg) 1. good, fine, auspicious. 2. person's name.
དགེ་བཤད་སྡིག་བསྒྲོལ་ (geshɛɛ̀ di̱gdröö) sm. དགེ་བཤད་སྡིག་སྒྲོལ་.
དགེ་བཤད་སྡིག་སྒྲོལ་ (geshɛɛ̀ di̱gdröö) explaining in order to persuade sb. to change their ways/ faults, showing what is right and wrong (good and bad) [Lit. explain virtue, release from sin].
དགེ་བཤེས་ (gesheè) title of a monastic degree given to monks who have finished higher monastic studies.
དགེ་བཤེས་ལགས་རྟ་ནས་དབྱུགས་ བབ་མི་དགོས་ཁེ་བཟང་ (gesheèla dɛ̄ɛ̀yug bə̱bmigɔɔ̀ kēbsaŋ) a misfortune can accidently bear good result/ benefit [Lit. The geshe was thrown from the horse so didn't have to dismount].
དགེ་བཤེས་ལགས་ལ་རྩོད་པ་མ་རྒྱག ཀ་བ་ལགས་དང་དུང་ག་མ་རྒྱག (gesheèlala dzȫöba ma̱gyaà gāwaladaŋ dü̱ŋga ma̱gyaà) don't argue with a stubborn/ difficult person [Lit. do not debate with a a geshe; do not bang against a pillar].
དགེ་བཤེས་ལྷ་རམས་པ་ (geshee̱ lhāramba) the highest type of དགེ་བཤེས་.
དགེ་སེམས་ (gesem) virtuous, pious, good-hearted, kind.
དགེ་སེམས་ཆེན་པོ་ (gesem cēmbo) very pious/ devout.
དགེ་སེམས་པ་ (gesemba) a virtuous/ pious/ kind/ good-hearted person.
དགེ་སློང་ (geloŋ) monks who have taken the highest monastic vows.
དགེ་སློང་མ་ (geloŋma) a nun who has taken the highest vows.
དགེ་སློབ་ (gelob) abbr. teacher and students, master and pupil/ apprentice.
དགེའོ་དགེའོ་ (geo geo) good, good!
དགེས་ (geè) sm. དགྱེས་.
དགོ་དགོ་ (gogo) a kind of mushroom.
དགོ་བ་ (gowa) Tibetan gazelle.
དགོ་རུ་ (goru) the horn of a gazelle.
དགོ་སློག (golog) robe/ dress made from the skin of a gazelle.
དགོག (gɔɔ̀) f. of དགོག.
དགོག་པ་རྒྱག (gɔgba gya̱à) vi. to chip off a large piece of stone by mistake and ruin the work on that stone.
དགོང་ (goŋ) abbr. of དགོང་མོ་.
དགོང་ཀ་ (goŋga) sm. དགོང་དྲོ་.
དགོང་ཁ་ (goŋga) sm. དགོང་དྲོ་.
དགོང་ཁྲོམ་ (goŋdrom) afternoon market; vi.—འཚོགས་ to convene/ start an afternoon market.
དགོང་ག (goŋga) sm. དགོང་དྲོ་.
དགོང་གས་ (goŋgɛɛ̀) sunset.
དགོང་བཅད་ (goŋjɛɛ̀) fasting after lunch; va.—བྱེད་.
དགོང་ཆ་ (goŋja) one of the twelve segments that a day is divided into (in this case, the time around sunset).
དགོང་ཇ་ (goŋja) shung. the tea served to monks at their late afternoon prayer assembly.
དགོང་འཇམ་ (goŋjam) broth/ stew/ soup eaten at night.
དགོང་ཉུག (goŋñug) arc. afternoon/ early evening hunting.
དགོང་ལྟར་ (goŋdar) 1. every night. 2. every afternoon.
དགོང་ལྟར་རེ་བཞིན་ (goŋdar re̱shin) sm. དགོང་ལྟར་.
དགོང་ལྟོ་ (goŋdo) evening meal, dinner.
དགོང་ཐུན་ (goŋdün) evening prayer time.
དགོང་དག (goŋdaà) evening, night ༑ཞོགས་པ་ལས་ཁངས་སུ་ཕྱིན་ནས་དགོང་དག་མ་གཏོགས་ཚུར་ལོག་ཐུབ་ཀྱི་མེད་ (They) go to the office in the morning and can return only in the evening.
དགོང་དྲོ་ (goŋdro) evening ༑དགོང་དྲོའི་ཚགས་པར་ Evening newspaper. ༑དགོང་དྲོའི་ཆུ་ཚོད་གསུམ་པའི་ཐོག At 3 p.m.
དགོང་དྲོའི་ཁ་ལག (goŋdrö kālaà) evening meal, dinner.
དགོང་འདེབས་ (goŋdeb) halting/ staying overnight (on a trip).
དགོང་སྦྱོད་ (goŋjö̀ö) dinner; va.—བྱེད་ to eat dinner.
དགོང་སྦྱོད་རྒྱུན་རིང་ལ་ ཁ་མཆུ་རྒྱག (goŋjö̀ö gyü̱nriŋlə kə̄mju gyaà) unless one is careful in a long relationship there is a danger of trouble breaking out [Lit. at a long dinner a dispute will occur].
དགོང་ཕྱི་ (goŋji) late at night.
དགོང་མལ་ (goŋmɛɛ) halting/ staying overnight (on a trip); va.—བྱེད་.
དགོང་མོ་ (goŋmo) evening, night.
དགོང་ཚིགས་ (goŋdzii) evening meal, supper, dinner.
དགོང་ཚོགས་ (goŋdzoò) evening party/ gathering.
དགོང་ཞག (goŋshaà) a night, overnight ༑ཁོང་ངའི་ནང་ལ་དགོང་ཞག་གཅིག་བཞུགས་སོང་ He stayed at my house for one night.
དགོང་ཤོགས་ (goŋshog) morning and night.
དགོང་ཟན་ (goŋsɛn) sm. དགོང་ཟས་.
དགོང་ཟས་ (goŋsɛɛ̀ɛ̀) evening meal, dinner, supper.

དགོང་ལས་ (goŋlɛɛ̀) 1. night work; va.—བྱེད་ ། འདི་དགོང་ལས་གཅིག་གི་ལས་ཀ་རེད་ This (job) is night work. 2. an evening's work ། འདི་དགོང་ལས་གཅིག་ལ་ཚར་གྱི་རེད་ This work will be finished in one evening.

དགོང་ལས་གཅིག (goŋlɛɛ̀ jĭg) one evening's work.

དགོངས་ (goŋ) va. to think, to consider (h.) ། ཁོང་གིས་དེ་འདྲ་དགོངས་མི་འདུག He did not think like that. ། གཞན་གྱི་སྡུག་བསྔལ་དགོངས་དགོས་ One should think of others' sorrow.

དགོངས་སྐོར་ (goŋgɔɔ) asking for opinions, consulting (h.); va.—ཞུ་ to ask for an opinion ། བཀའ་ཤག་ལ་དགོངས་སྐོར་ཙམ་མ་ཞུས་པར་རང་མཚམས་ཀྱིས་ཁྲིམས་གཅོད་བྱས་པ་རེད་ (He) punished them on his own without as much as asking the opinion of the Kashag.

དགོངས་སྐོར་ཞུ་ལན་ (goŋgɔɔ shulen) answer given to a request for one's opinion ། ངའི་སྐོར་ཁོང་ལ་དགོངས་སྐོར་ཞུས་ལན་དུ་མོས་མཐུན་ཡོད་གསུངས་པ་རེད་ In answer to a request for an opinion, (he) said that (he) agreed.

དགོངས་འཁྲུག (goŋdruù) getting angry.

དགོངས་འགྲོལ་ (goŋdröö) permission (h.); va.—ཞུ་ to ask permission ། ང་གུང་སེང་ལ་འགྲོ་རྒྱུའི་དགོངས་འགྲོལ་ཞུས་པ་ཡིན་ I asked for permission to go on vacation.

དགོངས་འགལ་ (goŋgɛɛ) taking offense, getting angry (h.); va.—བཞེས་; —གནང་ to get angry, to take offense; vi.—འགྱུར་ to become angry ། ངས་སྐད་ཆ་ཕོད་ནོར་ཤུར་སོང་ དགོངས་འགལ་མ་གནང་རོགས་གནང་ I misspoke. Please don't get angry.

དགོངས་འགལ་ཐུགས་བསུན་མེད་པ་ (goŋgɛɛ tūgsün meèba) sm. དགོངས་འགལ་མེད་པ་.

དགོངས་འགལ་མེད་པ་ (goŋgɛɛ meèba) don't be angry/ offended ། ངས་སྐད་ཆ་ཕོད་ནོར་ཤུར་སོང་དགོངས་འགལ་མེད་པ་ཅིག I misspoke. Please don't get angry.

དགོངས་འགྱངས་ (goŋgyaŋ) extension of a leave of absence (h.); va.—ཞུ་ to ask for such an extension.

དགོངས་འགྲེལ་ (goŋdrel) commentary on an article, etc. (h.).

དགོངས་ངལ་གསོ་ (goŋŋɛɛ sō) va. to retire.

དགོངས་མངགས་ (goŋŋaà) sm.* དགོངས་མངའ་ལྟར་.

དགོངས་མངའ་ལྟར་ (goŋŋa dār) as you know (h.) ། ཁྱེད་རང་གི་དགོངས་མངའ་ལྟར་ང་མགྱོགས་པོ་བོད་ལ་འགྲོ་གི་ཡིན་ As you know, I am going to Tibet soon.

དགོངས་བཅངས་ (goŋjaŋ) sm. དགོངས་འཇགས་.

དགོངས་བཅད་ (goŋjɛɛ̀) thinking and deciding; va.—གནང་ to think and decide ། དོན་གནད་འདིའི་སྐོར་ཁྱེད་རང་གིས་དགོངས་བཅད་གནང་རོགས་གནང་ Concerning this issue, please think about it and make a decision.

དགོངས་བཅུད་ (goŋjüü) the essence of sb.'s thought.

དགོངས་མཆོད་ (goŋjöö) religious service done when someone dies, funeral rite.

དགོངས་འཆར་ (goŋjar) suggestion, opinion (h.); va.—འདོན་; —གནང་; —གསུང་ to make a suggestion, to express an opinion ། དོན་གནད་དེའི་སྐོར་དགོངས་འཆར་གནང་རོགས་གནང་ Please give your opinion on that issue.

དགོངས་འཆར་སྒམ་ (goŋjar gam) suggestion box.

དགོངས་འཇགས་ (goŋjaà) keeping/ bearing in mind, remembering (h.); va.—གནང་ ། ངས་ཞུས་པ་དེ་དགོངས་འཇགས་གནང་རོགས་གནང་ Please keep in mind what I said.

དགོངས་འཇགས་མཁྱེན་ (goŋjaà kyēn) sm. དགོངས་འཇགས་.

དགོངས་སྙན་ (goŋñɛn) requesting to take a leave of absence (h.); va.—འབུལ་ to give a request asking for a leave ། ང་གཟུགས་པོ་ཐང་པོ་མེད་སྐབས་ཟླ་གསུམ་རིང་དགོངས་སྙན་ཕུལ་བ་ཡིན་ Because I am not feeling well, I submitted a request asking for three months leave of absence.

དགོངས་སྙིང་ (goŋñiŋ) shung. main content/ meaning.

དགོངས་གཏད་ (goŋdɛɛ̀) shung. establishing, founding.

དགོངས་གཏེར་ (goŋder) a type of གཏེར་མ་.

དགོངས་བསྟུན་ཞུ་ (goŋdün shu) va. to do/ act according to sb.'s wish.

དགོངས་མཐུན་ (goŋdün) agreeing in thought/ opinion (h.) ། ངའི་བསམ་འཆར་དེ་ཁོང་གི་དགོངས་མཐུན་རེད་བཞག His thinking agrees with that opinion of mine.

དགོངས་དག (goŋdaà) common term of apology: "I beg your pardon," "I'm sorry," "I apologize"; va.—ཞུ་ to apologize, to ask forgiveness/ pardon.

དགོངས་དག་ཐུགས་བདེན་ཞུ་ (goŋdaà tūùden shu) sm. དགོངས་དག.

དགོངས་དྭངས་ (goŋdaŋ) sm. དགོངས་པ་དྭངས.

དགོངས་དྭངས་ཡོང་གནས་ (goŋdaŋ yoŋnɛɛ̀) shung. clear in one's mind.

དགོངས་དོན་ (goŋdön) 1. meaning, content, sense, purpose ། རྩ་ཁྲིམས་ཀྱི་དགོངས་དོན་དང་མ་མཐུན་པའི་ལས་ཀ་ Acts not in accordance with the content of the constitution. 2. thought, thinking ། ཏཱ་ལའི་བླ་མའི་དགོངས་དོན་ The thought of the Dalai Lama.

དགོངས་བདེ་ (goŋde) shung. easy to think/ consider.

དགོངས་པ་ (goŋba)1. thought, idea (h.); vi.—འཁོར་ to get a thought/ idea ། ཁོང་གི་དགོངས་པ་གཞིར་བཟུང་ངས་ལས་ཀ་བྱས་པ་ཡིན་ I did the work based on his thoughts. 2. a leave of absence; a resignation; va.—ཞུ་ to ask for a leave of absence; to resign; va.—སྩེར་, —གནང་ to give/ grant a leave of absence ། ཉི་མ་ལྔའི་དགོངས་པ་ཞུས་པ་ཡིན་ I asked for five days leave of absence. ། ཁོང་གིས་དམག་སྤྱི་ནས་དགོངས་པ་ཞུས་པ་རེད་ He resigned from the post of commander in chief.

དགོངས་པ་དཀྲུགས་ (goŋba drūg) va. to make/ cause anger ། ཕྲུ་གུ་དེས་རྟག་པར་ཕ་མའི་དགོངས་པ་དཀྲུག་གི་ཡོད་པ་རེད་ The child always makes his parents angry. ། དེ་རིང་མ་ཇོང་རྒྱག་སྐབས་ང་ལ་མང་པོ་ཐོབ་ཙང་མ་ཇོང་རྒྱག་མཁན་གཞན་དག་དགོངས་པ་དཀྲུགས་པ་ཡིན་ Because I won a lot today when I was playing mahjong, I made the other mahjong players angry (usu. said in a joking manner).

དགོངས་པ་སྐོར་ (goŋba gɔ̄ɔ̄) va. to ask for opinions, to consult.

དགོངས་པ་འགྲོལ་ (goŋba trǒǒ) vi. to get permission/ consent/ approval to take a leave of absence or a resignation (h.).

དགོངས་པ་འགལ་ (goŋba gɛɛ) sm. དགོངས་འགལ་.

དགོངས་པ་འགྲེལ་ (goŋba drel) va. to explain/ clarify the main meaning (h.).

དགོངས་པ་ཅན་ (goŋbajɛn) thoughtful.

དགོངས་པ་ཆེན་པོ་ (goŋba cēmbo) thoughtful.

དགོངས་པ་ཆོས་དབྱིངས་སུ་ཐིམས་ (goŋba cöòyiŋsu tīm) shung. vi. to die (h.).

དགོངས་པ་གཏོང་ (goŋba dōŋ) see དགོངས་པ.

དགོངས་པ་སྟེར་ (goŋba dēr) see དགོངས་པ་.

དགོངས་པ་དྭངས་ (goŋba taŋ) vi. to have one's anger allayed/ subside ། ངས་ཕ་མའི་གཉིས་ལ་དགོངས་དག་ཞུས་སྐབས་ཕ་མ་གཉིས་དགོངས་པ་དྭངས་སོང་ Because I apologized to my parents, their anger subsided.

དགོངས་པ་གནང་ (goŋba nāŋ) sm. དགོངས་པ་གཏོང.

དགོངས་པ་མནལ་ (goŋba nēl) sm. དགོངས་པ་རྫོགས་.

དགོངས་པ་གཙང་ཞུ་ (goŋba dzāŋshu) sm. དགོངས་པ་རྩ་ཞུ་.

དགོངས་པ་རྩ་ཞུ་ (goŋba dzāshu) permanent withdrawal/ resignation (from a job/ position); va.—བྱེད་.

དགོངས་པ་རྩ་ཡང་ཞུ་ (goŋba dzāyaŋ shu) shung. va. to take leave from work for good, to retire.

དགོངས་པ་ཚོམ་ (goŋba tsōm) vi. to be angry.

དགོངས་པ་རྫོགས་ (goŋba dzɔ̄ɔ̀) 1. vi. to accomplish fully, to fulfill all one's wishes (intentions) ། ཕ་མའི་དགོངས་པ་རྫོགས་པའི་ཆེད་དུ་ངས་སློབ་སྦྱོང་ཏུར་ཐག་བྱེད་ཀྱི་ཡིན་ In order to fulfill all my parent's wishes, I am studying diligently. 2. vi. to die ¶ ཁོང་ལ་སྙུན་གཞི་ཕོག་ནས་དགོངས་པ་རྫོགས་བཞག He got sick and died.

དགོངས་པ་ཞི་བར་མཉལ་བ་ (go̲ŋba shi̲war nɛ̄ɛ̄) shung. vi. to die (h.).

དགོངས་པ་ཞི་དབྱིངས་སུ་མཉལ (go̲ŋba shi̲yiŋsu nɛ̄ɛ̄) vi. to die (h.).

དགོངས་པ་ཞུ་ (go̲ŋba shu̲) see དགོངས་པ་.

དགོངས་པ་གཞན་དོན་དུ་གཤེགས་ (go̲ŋba she̲ndöntu shēg) vi. to die (h.).

དགོངས་པ་བཞེས་ (go̲ŋba she̲è) va. to think over, to consider (h.).

དགོངས་པ་ཟབ་པོ་ (go̲ŋba sa̲bu) profound or deep meaning/ thought (h.) ¶ རྩོམ་ཡིག་འདིའི་དགོངས་པ་ཟབ་པོ་ཡིན་སྟབས་གོ་བ་ལེན་ཁག་པོ་ཡོད་ Because the article is profound, it is hard to understand.

དགོངས་པ་ཟབ་བཞེས་ (go̲ŋba sa̲bsheè) careful consideration, thorough investigation/ thinking over (h.); va.—གནང་ to consider carefully, to think over thoroughly.

དགོངས་པ་ཡངས་པོ་ (go̲ŋba ya̲nbo) open-minded, broad-minded (h.).

དགོངས་པ་རང་ཞུ་ (go̲ŋba ra̲ŋshu) va. to ask to be fired/ let go/ dismissed ¶ མི་དེས་ནོར་འཁྲུལ་མང་པོ་བྱུང་ཙང་ཁོང་རང་ལས་ཁུངས་ནས་དགོངས་པ་རང་ཞུས་པ་རེད་ Because that person made mistakes, he asked to be let go from the office.

དགོངས་པའི་ཀློང་ (go̲ŋbɛ lōŋ) 1. in thought/ mind ¶ དོན་དག་འདི་དགོངས་པའི་ཀློང་ལ་འཇགས་རོགས་ Please keep this in mind. 2. the broadness (of a person's mind).

དགོངས་པར་རྟོགས་ (go̲ŋbar dɔ̄ɔ̀) va. to know/ understand ¶ གནས་ཚུལ་དེ་ཁོང་གི་དགོངས་པར་རྟོགས་གི་ཡོད་ He understands that situation.

དགོངས་པར་མི་ལྷན་པ་ (go̲ŋbar mi̲dɛmba) displeased ¶ ངའི་སྐད་ཆ་དེ་ཁོང་གི་དགོངས་པར་མི་ལྷན་པ་བྱུང་འདུག My comments displeased him.

དགོངས་དཔྱད་ (go̲ŋjɛ̄ɛ̀) thinking and investigating (an issue); va.—བྱེད་; —གནང་ ¶ ཚོང་འདི་འགྲིག་གི་ཡོད་མེད་ཁྱེད་རང་གིས་དགོངས་དཔྱད་གནང་རོགས་གནང་ Please investigate whether this business deal is okay or not.

དགོངས་ཕུགས་ (go̲ŋbuù) final thought/ idea.

དགོངས་ཕོག (go̲mbɔ̄ɔ̀) demotion; va.—གཏོང་ ¶ ཁོང་ནོར་འཁྲུལ་ཤོར་ཙང་དགོངས་ཕོག་བཏང་བ་རེད་ Because he made a mistake, he was demoted.

དགོངས་ཕྱོགས་ (go̲njɔ̄ɔ̀) displeased, angry; va.—གཏད་ to be/ get angry.

དགོངས་འབྲེལ་ (go̲ndree) in accordance with an idea/ thought/ purpose ¶ རྩ་ཁྲིམས་ཀྱི་དགོངས་འབྲེལ་ In accordance with the constitution.

དགོངས་ཚུལ་ (go̲ndzül) opinion, thought ¶ གནས་ཚུལ་དེའི་སྐོར་ཁྱེད་རང་ལ་དགོངས་ཚུལ་ག་རེ་ཡོད་དམ་ What is your opinion on that matter?

དགོངས་ཚོམ་ (go̲ndzom) anger, angry (h.); va.—གནང་ ¶ དགོངས་ཚོམ་མ་གནང་རོགས་གནང་ Please don't be angry.

དགོངས་རྫོགས་ (go̲ŋdzɔ̄ɔ̀) dying, death va.—སྒྲུབ་ to have a funeral/ memorial service ¶ དགོངས་རྫོགས་མཆོད་འབུལ་ Religious offerings done for the dead.

དགོངས་རྫོགས་སྒྲུབ་ཐེབས་ (go̲ŋdzɔ̄ɔ̀ dru̲bteb) shung. a trust fund for an annual religious offering for a deceased person.

དགོངས་རྫོགས་རྗེས་དྲན་ (go̲ŋdzɔ̄ɔ̀ je̲ndren) death anniversary, death memorial rite/ service.

དགོངས་རྫོགས་དུས་མཆོད་ (go̲ŋdzɔ̄ɔ̀ tü̲üjöö) religious rites conducted on the death anniversary of a person.

དགོངས་ཞག (go̲ŋshaà) vacation time, vacation days; vi.—འཁོར་; —གཙང་ to have one's vacation be finished ¶ ད་ངའི་དགོངས་ཞག་ཐིམས་སོང་ Now my vacation time is finished.

དགོངས་ཞུ་ (go̲ŋshu) 1. request for a leave of absence; va.—འབུལ་ to ask for a leave of absence; va.—གནང་ to grant a leave of absence ¶ ངས་ད་རིང་ཉི་མ་གསུམ་གྱི་དགོངས་ཞུ་ཕུལ་པ་ཡིན་ Today I asked for a leave of absence of three days. 2. resignation; va.—འབུལ་; —གནང་ to resign ¶ དམག་སྤྱི་ནས་དགོངས་ཞུ་གནང་གི་ཡོད་པ་རེད་ (He) is resigning from (the post of) commander in chief.

དགོངས་གཞི་ (go̲ŋshi) intention, plan, idea, thought; va.—བསྡུར་ to examine/ consider/ discuss an issue, to inquire into a matter ¶ གནས་སྐབས་ཕྱི་རྒྱལ་ཐེབས་ཡས་ཀྱི་དགོངས་གཞི་མེད་གསུངས་འདུག (He) said that for the time being he did not have plans to go abroad.

དགོངས་བཞེད་ (go̲ŋshɛɛ̀) wish ¶ བླ་མའི་དགོངས་བཞེད་འགྲུབ་པའི་སྨོན་ལམ་རྒྱག་གི་ཡོད་ I am praying that the lama achieves his wish.

དགོངས་བཞེས་ (go̲ŋshɛɛ̀) thinking, considering (h.); va.—གནང་ to think over/ consider ¶ འཆར་གཞི་དེའི་སྐོར་ལ་དགོངས་བཞེས་གནང་ཡུས་རེད་ (They) are considering the plan.

དགོངས་བཞེས་ཚད་མེད་ (go̲ŋsheè tsɛ̄ɛ̄meè) giving great consideration/ attention/ thought.

དགོངས་ཟབ་ (go̲ŋsəb) deep/ profound thoughts or ideas.

དགོངས་ཟབ་རྒྱས་དཔྱད་ (go̲ŋsəb gyɛ̲ɛ̄jɛɛ̀) shung. deliberating through deep thoughts and detailed investigation.

དགོངས་བཟང་མཐོ་སྒྲོན་ (go̲ŋsaŋ tōdrön) shung. thinking clearly and kindly.

དགོངས་ཡངས་ (go̲ŋyaŋ) forgiving, forgiveness (h.); va.—གནང་ to forgive ¶ དགེ་ཕྲུག་གིས་ནོར་འཁྲུལ་གྱི་ལས་ཀ་བྱས་ཀྱང་བླ་མས་དགོངས་ཡངས་གནང་བཞག Even though the disciple did the work wrong, the lama forgave him.

དགོངས་སུ་གསོལ་ (go̲ŋba sȫö̀) please listen to me (e.g., when a monk is taking vows each phrase starts with དགོངས་སུ་གསོལ་).

དགོངས་སེལ་ (go̲ŋsel) apology, pardon (h.); va.—ཞུ་ to apologize, to ask for forgiveness/ pardon.

དགོངས་བསམ་ (go̲ŋsam) sm. དགོངས་, 1.

དགོད་: p. བགད་; f. བགད་; imp. དགོད་ (gö̲ö̀) 1. va. to laugh (usu. གད་མོ་ +—) ¶ ཁོ་གད་མོ་དགོད་ཀྱི་འདུག He is laughing. 2. f. of འགོད་.

དགོད་ཁར་བལྟས་ན་དགོད་བློ་ ངུ་ཁར་བལྟས་ན་ངུ་བློ་ (gö̲ö̀gar dɛ̄ɛ̄na gö̲ndro ŋu̲kar dɛ̄ɛ̄na ŋu̲dro) emulating, copying, influenced by sth. [Lit. if one sees laughter one feels like laughing, if one sees crying one feels like crying].

དགོད་ངུ་གང་མིན་ (gö̲ö̀ŋu ka̲nmin) not knowing what to do or how to react, not quite laughing, not quite crying [Lit. neither laughing nor crying].

དགོད་གཏམ་ (gö̲ö̀dam) humorous talk/ speech/ story; va.—ཤོད་.

དགོད་ཐལ་ (gö̲ö̀dɛɛ) laughing too much or too long.

དགོད་གནས་ (gö̲ö̀nɛɛ̀) butt/ brunt of a joke, laughingstock; vi.—ཆགས་ to become the butt/ brunt of a joke, to become a laughingstock.

དགོད་བག་ཅན་ (gö̲ö̀baàjɛn) a smiling countenance/ appearance.

དགོད་བྲོ་ (gö̲ö̀tro) sm. དགོད་བྲོ་བ་.

དགོད་བྲོ་པོ་ (gö̲ö̀ tro̲bo) sm. དགོད་བྲོ་བ་.

དགོད་བྲོ་བ་ (gö̲ö̀ tro̲wa) funny, humorous, laughable ¶ དགོད་བྲོ་བའི་སྒྲུང་ Humorous stories.

དགོད་བྲོའི་གཏམ་གླེང་ (gö̲ö̀drö dāmleŋ) a kind of comic performance in which two people talk humorously back and forth in an exchange.

དགོད་མ་འཚོགས་ (gö̲ö̀ ma̲dzɔ̄ɔ̀) vi. to be unable to control laughing ¶ གསོལ་དོན་སྟོག་དགོད་མ་འཚོགས་པར་གད་མོ་ཤོར་སོང་ He couldn't control himself and broke out into laughter at the party.

དགོད་མི་འཚོགས་ (gö̲ö̀ mi̲dzɔ̄ɔ̀) sm. དགོད་མ་འཚོགས་.

དགོད་མ་འཛུམ་ (gö̲ö̀ ma̲ dzu̲m) half laughing and half smiling.

དགོད་མ་ཤེས་ངུ་མ་ཤེས་ (gö̲ö̀ ma̲sheè ŋu̲ ma̲sheè) not knowing whether to cry or to laugh.

དགོད་འཚེར་འཚེར་ (g̲öö tsērdzer) laughingly ¶ དགོད་འཚེར་འཚེར་ངང་བཤད་པ་རེད་ He said it in a laughing manner.

དགོད་གཞི་ (g̲ööshi) 1. the cause/ reason for laughing. 2. sm. དགོད་གཞས་.

དགོད་བཞིན་ཤོད་ (g̲ööshin shōö) va. to laugh as one speaks, to speak laughingly.

དགོད་སློང་ (göö lōŋ) va. to make sb. laugh.

དགོད་སློང་རྫས་འགྱུར་རླངས་པ་ (g̲ööloŋ dzɛ̱ɛgyur lāŋba) laughing gas, nitrous oxide.

དགོན་ (g̲ön) abbr. of དགོན་པ་.

དགོན་ཁག་ (g̲öngaà) monasteries ¶ དགོན་ཁག་མང་པོའི་གྲྭ་པ་འཛོམས་ཡོད་པ་རེད་ Monks from many monasteries gathered.

དགོན་སྡེ་ (g̲öndrig) shung. དགོན་པའི་སྒྲིག.

དགོན་ཆག་ (g̲önjaà) a destroyed monastery, a monastery in ruins.

དགོན་གཉེར་ (g̲önñer) monastery steward/ manager.

དགོན་འདུས་ (g̲öndüü) abbr. of དགོན་པའི་འདུས་མི་.

དགོན་དུང་ (g̲önduŋ) sm. དཀུན་དུང་.

དགོན་བདག་ (g̲öndaà) patron of a monastery.

དགོན་སྡེ་ (g̲önde) monastery, monastic community.

དགོན་ནོར་ (g̲önnɔɔ) monastic wealth/ property.

དགོན་གནས་ (g̲önnɛɛ̀) sm. དགོན་སྡེ་.

དགོན་པ་ (g̲omba) 1. monastery. 2. wilderness area, a place far away from towns/ villages.

དགོན་པ་གྲྭ་ཚང་ (g̲omba tr̲adzaŋ) monastery and monastic college (within a monastery).

དགོན་པའི་ཁྱི་ལ་གཞུས་ན་ བླ་མའི་ཐུགས་ལ་ཐོག་ཡོང་ (g̲ombɛ kyīlə sh̲üünə lāmɛ tūùlə pɔ̄ɔyoŋ) hurting a superior by harming a subordinate [Lit. if you beat a dog of the monastery, it will hurt the feelings of the lama].

དགོན་པའི་སྒྲིག (g̲ömbɛ dri̲g) shung. the organization of a monastery (that which a monk belongs to).

དགོན་པའི་བཅའ་ཡིག (g̲ömbɛ jāyii) shung. the charter of a monastery.

དགོན་པའི་མཆོད་ཐེབས་ཐབ་དེན་ (g̲ömbɛ cōōdeb tə̄bden) shung. a trust fund for making offerings in a monastery.

དགོན་པའི་ཇ་མེད་ལ་ཞོལ་གྱི་ཐུག་པ་ཡང་མེད་ (g̲ombɛ c̲a me̱ɛla shöögi tūgbəyaŋ me̱ɛ) sm. ཕ་རིའི་ལྤྱི་བ་མེད་པ་ ཚུར་རིའི་སྤྱི་པོ་ཡང་མེད་.

དགོན་པའི་འདུས་མི་ (g̲ombɛ tüümi) monastic delegate/ representative.

དགོན་འབངས་ (g̲ömbaŋ) monastery and subjects.

དགོན་མ་ལག (g̲ön m̲alaà) the main monastery and its branch monasteries.

དགོན་གཞི་ (g̲önshi) 1. monastic wealth/ property. 2. wilderness area.

དགོན་གཞིས་ (g̲önshii) manorial estate of a monastery.

དགོན་ལག (g̲önlaà) a branch/ affiliate monastery.

དགོན་ཤུལ་ (g̲önshüü) ruins/ rubble/ traces of a destroyed monastery.

དགོས་ (g̲öö) 1. vi. to need, to require ¶ ང་ལ་རོགས་པ་ཞིག་དགོས་ཀྱི་འདུག I need a helper.

དགོས་མཁོ་ (g̲ööko) a need, a necessity; va.—སྐོང་ to fill a need ¶ དགོས་མཁོའི་ཅ་རག Needed/ necessary things. ¶ ང་ཚོར་མཚོན་ཆའི་དགོས་མཁོ་མེད་ We do not have a need for weapons.

དགོས་མཁོ་སྒྲུབ་སྦྱོར་ (g̲ööko dr̲ubdröö) supplying needs, procuring supplies/ provisions; va.—བྱེད་ ¶ དགོས་མཁོ་སྒྲུབ་སྦྱོར་ལས་ཁུངས་ Supply office.

དགོས་མཁོ་ལྡིང་ངེས་ (g̲ööko de̱ŋŋeè) self-sufficient ¶ ཨ་མེ་རི་ཀ་དགོས་མཁོ་ལྡིང་ངེས་ཀྱི་ལུང་པ་ཞིག་རེད་ America is a self-sufficient country.

དགོས་མཁོ་ཟད་ལེན་ (g̲ööko s̲ɛ̱ɛlen) taking/ replacing sth. as it becomes exhausted; va.—བྱེད་ ¶ སློབ་ཕྲུག་དེས་ཨ་ཁུའི་ས་ནས་དགོས་མཁོ་ཟད་ལེན་བྱེད་ཀྱི་ཡོད་པ་རེད་ The student takes whatever he needs from his uncle (as he runs out).

དགོས་གལ་ (g̲öökɛɛ) a need, a necessity ¶ ཁོ་ཚོས་སྐད་བསྒྱུར་གྱི་དགོས་གལ་མ་མཐོང་བ་རེད་ They didn't see the need for an interpreter.

དགོས་གལ་དང་པོ་ (g̲öökɛɛ t̲aŋbo) the primary/ foremost/ most essential need.

དགོས་དགོས་པ་ (g̲öögöba) must, should, ought ¶ ཁོང་ལ་སྐད་སྒྱུར་དགོས་དགོས་པ་ཡིན་པ་དེ་ཡོད་མི་དགོས་པ་རེད་ That he must have a translator is sth. that is not a question.

དགོས་རྒྱུ་ཐུགས་ལ་ཐུགས་ཁུ་དར་བ་ (g̲öögyu bāgla bəku t̲arwa) having supporting elements that are essential [Lit. the tsamba ball that one needs requires liquid whey (for mixing the tsamba into an eating ball)].

དགོས་ངེས་ (g̲ööŋeè) absolutely needed/ necessary ¶ དེ་བྱེད་དགོས་ངེས་ཤིག་རེད་ This is sth. that is absolutely necessary to do.

དགོས་ངེས་བབ་ཆགས་ (g̲ööŋeè p̲əbjaà) necessary and appropriate.

དགོས་དངུལ་ (g̲ööŋüü) money used for official purposes, money for a particular official project.

དགོས་ཆ་ (g̲ööja) sm. དགོས་ཆས་.

དགོས་ཆས་ (g̲ööjɛɛ̀) essentials, necessities, required things.

དགོས་ཆེད་ (g̲ööjeè) purpose, aim, goal.

དགོས་ཆེད་ཀྱི་སྒྲ་ (g̲ööjeègi dr̲a) the 4th of the 8 parts of speech in Tibetan grammar (conveys "purpose").

དགོས་ཉུང་ཐོན་མང་ (g̲ööñuŋ tōnmaŋ) production exceeding demand.

དགོས་གདུགས་ (g̲ööduù) urgently/ greatly needed ¶ སྨན་བཅོས་ཀྱི་དགོས་གདུགས་ཆེན་པོ་ཡོད་པ་རེད་ There is an urgent need for medical treatment.

དགོས་ཐོབ་སྦྲད་མཆན་ (g̲öödob drɛ̄ɛjɛn) shung. a notation made on a document that a supply of sth. was given.

དགོས་དོད་ (g̲öödöö) shung. money paid as a substitute for sth. ¶ སད་སྲུང་སོགས་ཀྱི་དགོས་དོད་ཁྱོན་བསྡོམས་དངུལ་སྲང་བཅུ་ The total of money paid as a subsitute (for the required food, etc.) to the person who protects the fields from hail is ten སྲང་.

དགོས་དོན་ (g̲öödön) the reason for a need, the reason sth. is needed; va.—སྟོན་ to indicate/ show a reason why sth. is needed ¶ འདིའི་སྐོར་རྩོམ་ཡིག་བྲིས་པའི་དགོས་དོན་ནི་ As for the reason why there was a need to write about this.

དགོས་དོན་མེད་པ་ (g̲öödön me̱ɛba) inessential, unnecessary, unrequired, not needed.

དགོས་འདུན་ (g̲öndün) wish, hope; —འདོན་ to make a wish, to express a hope, to request sth. ¶ ཕྱི་རྒྱལ་གྱི་རྒྱབ་སྐྱོར་ཐོབ་པའི་དགོས་འདུན་བཏོན་པ་རེད་ (They) made a request to get foreign support.

དགོས་འདོད་ (g̲öndöö) a want/ desire (to have things), things wanted/ needed; va.—བྱེད་ ¶ ཁོས་མོ་ཊ་ཞིག་དགོས་འདོད་བྱེད་ཀྱི་འདུག He wants to have a car.

དགོས་འདོད་ཀུན་འབྱུང་ (g̲öödöö g̃ünjuŋ) sth. that fulfills all want/ desires ¶ ནོར་བུ་དགོས་འདོད་ཀུན་འབྱུང་ A wish-fulfilling jewel.

དགོས་གནས་ (g̲öönɛɛ̀) need, necessity ¶ སྨྱུ་གུ་ཞིག་དགོས་གནས་འདུག I need a pen.

དགོས་པ་ (g̲ööba) 1. need, necessity, purpose ¶ ང་ལ་ཁང་པ་ཆེན་པོའི་དགོས་པ་མེད་ I don't need a big house. ¶ ལས་ཀ་དེ་ལ་དགོས་པ་ག་རེ་ཡོད་པ་རེད་དམ་ What is the purpose of this work?

དགོས་པ་དགེ་ཚན་ (g̲ööba g̲edzɛn) benefit, purpose.

དགོས་དབང་ (g̲ööwaŋ) purposely, on purpose, intentionally ¶ ནོར་འཁྲུལ་འདི་དགོས་དབང་གིས་བཟོས་པ་མ་རེད་ (He) did not make this mistake on purpose.

དགོས་དབང་སྦྲུག་འདྲེན་ (g̲ööwaŋ b̲undren) shung. keeping sth. secret purposely.

དགོས་འདྲས་ (g̲öndrɛɛ̀) shung. sth. that one should do ¶ ཕན་རྒྱུར་འགྲོ་ལམ་གང་ཆེ་ཞིག་དགོས་འདྲས་ཀྱང་ It is deemed necessary to help as much as one can, but.

དགོས་འབྲུ་ (g̲öndru) shung. grain that is needed for sth. ¶ ཨར་ལས་ཀྱི་དགོས་འབྲུ་ The grain supply for the construction work.

དགོས་མང་གྲོན་ཉུང་ (gö̱ömaŋ tõññuŋ) demand exceeding supply, much needed but few produced.

དགོས་མེད་ (gö̱ömeè) unnecessary, unneeded ॥ཁོས་དགོས་མེད་ཅ་ལག་མང་པོ་ཉོས་པ་རེད་ He bought many unnecessary things.

དགོས་མེད་ཁ་གསབ་ (gö̱ömeè kǝ̄sǝb) an unnecessary supplement/ embellishment.

དགོས་མེད་འཕྲོལ་པ་ (gö̱ömeè tȫōba) sth. extra that is unnecessary/ unneeded.

དགོས་མེད་མཛེས་ཆོས་ (gö̱ömeè dze̱èjöö) unnecessary decorations.

དགོས་མེད་འཛེམ་ཟོན་ (gö̱ömeè dze̱msön) unnecessary caution in saying or doing sth.

དགོས་མེད་རིང་ལུགས་ (gö̱ömeè ri̱ŋluù) liquidationism.

དགོས་མེད་ལྷག་འཁྱིལ་ (gö̱ömeè lhāgkyii) sm. དགོས་མེད་འཕྲོལ་པ་.

དགྱེ་ (gye̱) 1. vi. to sit/ stand upright or erect, to hold upright/ erect ॥མགོ་ཡར་དགྱེས་ Hold your head upright.

དགྱེ་གུག (gye̱guù) bending over and standing/ sitting erect; va.—བྱེད་ ॥ང་སྒལ་པ་ན་ནས་གཟུགས་པོ་དགྱེ་གུག་བྱེད་ཁག་པོ་འདུག After my back was injured, it was difficult for me to stand erect or bend over.

དགྱེ་དགུ་ (gye̱gu) sm. འགུལ་སྐྱོད་.

དགྱེ་དགྱེ་ (gye̱gye) sm. དགྱེ་.

དགྱེ་དགྱེ་གུག་གུག (gye̱gye gu̱ùguù) sm. དགྱེ་གུག.

དགྱེ་པོ་ (gye̱bo) upright, erect; va.—རང་ལངས་ to sit/ stand erect or upright.

དགྱེ་བོ་ (gye̱wo) 1. a person with a protruding (pigeon) breast. 2. sm. དགྱེ་པོ་.

དགྱེད་ (gye̱è) 1. sm. དགྱེ་. 2. f. of བགྱེད་.

དགྱེད་དགུར་ (gye̱gur) sm. དགྱེ་དགུ་.

དགྱེད་དགྱེད་ (gye̱gyeè) sm. དགྱེ་དགྱེ་.

དགྱེས་ (gye̱è) vi. to be pleased/ glad/ happy.

དགྱེས་སྐྱེམ་གསོལ་སྟོན་ (gye̱ègyem söödön) sm. ཆང་སྟོན་.

དགྱེས་དགུར་སྤྱོད་ (gye̱ègur jöö) va. to have fun, to enjoy oneself.

དགྱེས་གུར་སྤྱོད་ (gye̱ègur jöö) sm. དགྱེས་དགུར་སྤྱོད་.

དགྱེས་ཉམས་མཛད་ (gye̱èñam dzɛ̱̀ɛ̀) to show a happy appearance.

དགྱེས་མཉེས་ (gye̱ènyeè) happy, glad, joyous.

དགྱེས་སྟོན་ (gye̱èdön) 1. sm. དགའ་སྟོན་. 2. epithet for the Monlam Chemmo.

དགྱེས་སྟོན་རྟེན་འབྲེལ་ (gye̱èdön dēmdree) sm. དགའ་སྟོན་རྟེན་འབྲེལ་.

དགྱེས་པའི་མདངས་ (gye̱èbɛ da̱ŋ) happy/ joyous appearance.

དགྱེས་ཚོར་ (gye̱èdzɔɔ) sm. དགྱེས་ཉམས་མཛད་.

དགྱེས་འཛུམ་ (gye̱èdzum) smiling with happiness/ joy.

དགྱེས་འཛུམ་ལྷུག་འཕྲོལ་ (gye̱èdzum) smiling with a happy/ cheerful face.

དགྱེས་ཞལ་ (gye̱èzhɛɛ) a happy/ cheerful face.

དགྲ་ (dra̱) 1. enemy, foe; va.—བྱེད་ to become enemies; to harm ॥ས་ཆ་འདིར་རི་དྭགས་ལ་དགྲ་བྱེད་ཆོག་གི་མེད་པ་རེད་ In this area, it is not permitted to harm animals. 2. va.—རྒྱག to make war on enemies.

དགྲ་ཁ་གདོང་ (dra̱ kāb dɛ̱̀ɛ̀) the enemy, the opponents; va.—བྱེད་ to become an enemy/ opponent.

དགྲ་ཁང་ (dra̱gaŋ) 1. watchtower. 2. place where one's enemy stays.

དགྲ་གྲོགས་རང་གསུམ་ (dra̱ tro̱g ra̱ŋsum) the three: enemy, friend and self.

དགྲ་དགའ་གཉེན་སྐྱོ་ (dra̱ga ñēngyo) sm. དགྲ་དགའ་གཉེན་སྡུག.

དགྲ་དགའ་གཉེན་སྡུག (dra̱ga ñēnduù) pleasing one's enemies and enraging/ saddening/ harming one's friends.

དགྲ་བགེགས་ (dra̱geg) a harmful demon/ spirit; an enemy.

དགྲ་མགོ་ (dra̱ŋgo) head or leader of one's foes/ enemy.

དགྲ་འགོག (dra̱ŋgɔɔ̀) resisting the enemy.

དགྲ་འགོག་དམག་འཁྲུག (dra̱ŋgɔɔ̀ mǝ̄gtruù) war of resistance.

དགྲ་འགོག་ལས་འགུལ་ (dra̱ŋgɔɔ̀ lɛ̱ngüü) resistance movement.

དགྲ་འགོག་ས་འོབས་ (dra̱ŋgɔɔ̀ sāwob) moat.

དགྲ་རྒྱག (dra̱gyaà) see དགྲ་.

དགྲ་ངན་དཔུང་ཚོགས་ (dra̱ŋɛn bū̱ŋdzɔɔ̀) an army/ group of evil enemies.

དགྲ་ངོམ་ (dra̱ŋom) va. to show off to one's enemy through parades/ military exercises/ maneuvers; va.—བྱེད་.

དགྲ་སྔ་རྒྱག (dra̱ ŋā gya̱à) va. to attack an enemy first.

དགྲ་བཅོམ་པ་ (dra̱jomba) arhat.

དགྲ་ཆ་ (dra̱ja) sm. དགྲ་ཆས་.

དགྲ་ཆས་ (dra̱jɛ̱̀ɛ̀) weapons, arms, war equipment.

དགྲ་ཆས་ཅན་ (dra̱jɛ̱̀ɛ̀jɛn) armed ॥དགྲ་ཆས་ཅན་གྱི་དཔུང་དམག Armed forces.

དགྲ་ཆོས་ (dra̱jöö) defeating the enemy by casting an evil spell on them.

དགྲ་འཆི་བདག་ནམ་ཡོང་ངེས་པ་མེད་ (dra̱ cīdag na̱m yo̱ŋ ŋe̱èba me̱è) a saying that conveys the idea of uncertainty and the need to be prepared [Lit. it is uncertain when the enemy, the lord of death will come].

དགྲ་ཇག (dra̱jaà) bandit enemy.

དགྲ་འཇོམས་གནམ་གྲུ་ (dra̱jom nǝ̄mdru) fighter plane.

དགྲ་གཉེན་ (dra̱ñen) enemies and friends.

དགྲ་གཉེན་མགོན་གསུམ་ (dra̱ñen gö̱nsum) the three: foes, friends, and protective deities.

དགྲ་གཉེན་དབྱེ་འབྱེད་ (dra̱ñen yē̱jeè) differentiating between friends and enemies; va.—བྱེད་.

དགྲ་གཉེན་གསལ་འབྱེད་ (dra̱ñen sɛ̄ɛ̄jeè) sm. དགྲ་གཉེན་དབྱེ་འབྱེད་.

དགྲ་སྟ་ (dra̱da) an ax-like weapon.

དགྲ་ཐབས་ (dra̱dǝb) a strategy to subdue/ defeat (one's) enemy.

དགྲ་གདོན་ (dra̱dön) enemy and demon.

དགྲ་གདོས་ (dra̱döö) shung. being/ acting hostile; va.—བྱེད་.

དགྲ་མདའི་ལྡིའུ་ (dra̱ndɛ di̱wu) shung. sm. མེ་མདའི་ལྡིའུ་.

དགྲ་འདུལ་ (drǝ̱ndül) 1. subduing/ conquering the enemy; va.—བྱེད་. 2. a man's name.

དགྲ་འདུལ་གཉེན་སྐྱོང་ (drǝ̱ndül ñēngyoŋ) subdue/ conquer/ attack one's enemy and protect/ take care of one's friends; va.—བྱེད་.

དགྲ་འདུལ་དཔའ་རྩལ་ (drǝ̱ndül bādzɛɛ) defeating the enemy with skill and bravery; va.—བྱེད་.

དགྲ་འདུལ་དཔུང་འཛུག (drǝ̱ndül bū̱ŋjuù) deploying soldiers to defeat the enemy; va.—བྱེད་.

དགྲ་འདེད་ (drǝ̱ndeè) driving the enemy away; va.—བྱེད་.

དགྲ་སྡང་ (dra̱daŋ) sm. དགྲ་སྡང་པོ་.

དགྲ་སྡང་པོ་ (dra̱ da̱ŋbo) intense/ strong dislike or hate; va.—བྱེད་ ॥དོན་དག་ཆུང་ཆུང་ཞིག་ལ་ཡང་ཁོ་ལ་དགྲ་སྡང་པོ་བྱེད་ཀྱི་འདུག Even though it is for a minor reason, they dislike him intensely.

དགྲ་ནག (dra̱nag) an evil enemy, a bitter enemy.

དགྲ་དཔུང་ (dra̱buŋ) enemy army/ force.

དགྲ་དཔོན་ (dra̱bön) enemy leader/ chief.

དགྲ་ཕྱ་ (dra̱ja) feeling/ checking the pulse of the leader to determine the outcome of a war/ battle.

དགྲ་ཕྱི་རྒྱག (dra̱ji gya̱à) va. to attack an enemy in retaliation.

དགྲ་ཕྱོགས་ (dra̱jɔɔ̀) the enemy side.

དགྲ་ཕྱོགས་གྲལ་རིམ་ (dra̱jɔɔ̀ tre̱èrim) the enemy class, the opposition class.

དགྲ་བོ་ (dra̱wo) enemy, foe, opponent.

དགྲ་བོའི་དྲངས་མ་ (dra̱wo da̱ŋma) the main enemy/ foe.

དགྲ་བྱུང་ན་གྲི་ཀ་མཉམ་འདོན་དང་ གྲོགས་བྱུང་ན་ཕོར་པ་མཉམ་འཛུགས་ (dra cuŋna trigu ñamdöntaŋ trog cuŋna pōr ñamdzug) sharing good and bad together [Lit. if an enemy comes take out one's knife together, if a friend comes take out one's cup together].

དགྲ་བྱེད་ (drajeè) see དགྲ་.

དགྲ་མི་ཤ་བོ་ (drəmi shāwo) hated foe/ enemy.

དགྲ་མིས་བསད་པས་མགོ་ལག (drəmi sɛ̀ɛbɛ golag) taking credit for sb. else's achievement/ victory [Lit. (showing) the head and hand of an enemy killed by other people].

དགྲ་དམག (dramaà) enemy troops.

དགྲ་ཚང་ (dradzaŋ) enemy's den/ hideout.

དགྲ་ཚུལ་རྩད་གཅོད་ (dradzül dzɛ̀ɛjöö) investigating the enemy's situation; va.—བྱེད་.

དགྲ་འཛིན་ (drəndzin) holding/ considering as the enemy; va.—བྱེད་ ༎ མེས་རྒྱལ་དགྲ་འཛིན་གྱིས་གྲོས་མཐུན་ལ་ངོ་རྒོལ་བྱས་སོང་ Holding the motherland as the enemy, (they) opposed the agreement.

དགྲ་འཛིན་གྲལ་རིམ་ (drəndzin trɛɛrim) enemy class.

དགྲ་ཟུན་ (drasün) sm. དགྲ་གཉེན་.

དགྲ་ཟོན་ (drasön) vigilance or precaution (against enemies); va.—བྱེད་ to take precautions, to be vigilant/ on guard.

དགྲ་ཟླ་ (dranda) enemy, foe, opponent; va.—འཛིན་ to consider as an enemy; —ལངས་ to become an enemy/ foe.

དགྲ་ཟླར་འགྱུར་བའི་གྲལ་རིམ་ (dranda gyurwɛ treerim) the enemy class.

དགྲ་ཡ་ (draya) enemy, foe, opponent, rival, adversary, antagonist.

དགྲ་ཡ་འགག་ཐུག (draya gagduù) running into unexpected bad luck ༎ ང་ལ་དགྲ་ཡ་འགག་ཐུག་བརྒྱབ་པ་ལྟར་གྱི་རྐྱེན་ངན་འཕྲད་བྱུང་ Like running into one's enemy on a narrow precipice trail, I met unexpected disaster. [Lit. meet enemies on narrow precipice/ defile].

དགྲ་ཡའི་རྒྱབ་ཕྱོགས་ (drayɛ gyəbjɔɔ) behind enemy lines.

དགྲ་རུ་ལང་ (drəru laŋ) vi. to become an enemy.

དགྲ་ལ་དགྲ་ལན་ ཀི་ལ་ཀི་ལན་ (drala dralɛn gīla gīlɛn) taking revenge, taking an eye for an eye.

དགྲ་ལ་དགྲ་ལན་ བུན་ལ་བུན་བདག (drala dralɛn pünla pündaà) taking revenge [Lit. revenge should be taken, a debt should have a debt holder].

དགྲ་ལ་ལང་ (drəla laŋ) sm. དགྲ་རུ་ལང་.

དགྲ་ལང་ (dra laŋ) sm. དགྲ་རུ་ལང་.

དགྲ་ལན་ (dralɛn) retaliation, revenge, counterattack; va.—རྒྱག; —སློག to take revenge, to retaliate.

དགྲ་ལན་རིང་ལུགས་ (dralɛn riŋluù) revanchism.

དགྲ་ཤ་ (drasha) revenge, vengeance; va.—ལེན་; va.—སྒྲུབ་ to take revenge, to avenge.

དགྲ་ཤོར་ (dra shɔ̄ɔ) vi. to be lost, to/ be killed by the enemy ༎ རུ་དཔོན་སྐད་གྲགས་ཅན་དེ་ཡང་དགྲ་ཤོར་བྱུང་ The famous Rupon was lost to the enemy.

དགྲ་གཤེད་ (drasheè) the enemy.

དགྲ་སེམས་ (drasem) considering/ regarding as an enemy; vi.—སྐྱེད་; —འཆང་ to regard/ consider as an enemy.

དགྲ་སྲི་ལངས་ (drasi laŋ) vi. to be confronted by an enemy or to be robbed at same time of the year as before.

དགྲ་གསོག (dra sɔ̄g) va. to make/ accumulate enemies.

དགྲ་གསོད་ནུས་རྩལ་ (drasöö nüüdzɛɛ) fighting techniques, skills/ techniques for killing one's enemies.

དགྲ་ལྷ་ (dralha) warrior deity.

དགྲད་ (drɛɛ) sm. བགྲད་.

དགྲམ་ (dram) f. of འགྲེམས་.

དགྲར་ལྟ་ (draa dā) va. to regard as an enemy.

དགྲར་བཏེན་དགྲ་འདུལ་ (draadēn drandül) vanquishing an enemy by using an enemy.

དགྲར་འཛིན་ (draa dzin) sm. དགྲར་ལྟ་.

དགྲར་འཛིན་གྲལ་རིམ་ (drəndzin treerim) the hostile/ enemy class.

དགྲར་འཛིན་བྱ་སྤྱོད་ (drəndzin cajöö) hostilities, hostile acts.

དགྲར་ལང་ (draa laŋ) sm. དགྲར་ལྟ་.

དགྲས་བཟུང་ས་ཁུལ་ (drasuŋ sāgüü) enemy occupied area/ territory.

དགྲོང་: p. བགྲོངས་; f. དགྲོང་; imp. དགྲོངས་ (droŋ) va. to kill (h.) ༎ ཁོང་བགྲོངས་བར་ཕེབས་སོང་ (He) came to kill him.

དགྲོངས་ (droŋ) imp. of དགྲོང་.

དགྲོལ་ (dröl) f. of འགྲོལ་.

བགག: p. བགགས་; f. བགག; f. བགོགས་ (gag) va. to block, to obstruct, to choke ༎ དགུན་ཁ་གངས་ཀྱིས་ལ་བགག་གི་ཡོད་པ་རེད་ The mountain passes are blocked by snow in the winter.

བགགས་ (gag) p. of བགག.

བགད་ (gɛɛ) p. of དགོད་.

བགམ་: p. བགམ་; f. བགམ་; imp. བགོམ་ (gam) va. to test, to estimate (usu. follows ཚོད་) ༎ ཁོས་ལས་ཀ་དངོས་བྱེད་ནུས་མིན་ཚོད་བགམས་པ་རེད་ (They) tested him (to see) if he would really dare to do the job.

བགམས་ (gam) p. of བགམ་.

བགས་ (gɛɛ) va. to cut, to carve.

བགེགས་ (geg) 1. misfortune, disaster, mishap, calamity, obstacle, hindrance, obstruction; va.—སེལ་ to remove an obstruction/ hindrance ༎ ང་ཚོའི་ལས་འགུལ་དེར་བགེགས་ཆེན་པོ་བྱུང་བ་རེད་ We had many misfortunes in our campaign. 2. sm. བགག.

བགེགས་རྐྱེན་ (geggyen) cause of a disaster/ misfortune/ mishap.

བགེགས་སྐྱོན་ (geggyön) sm. བགེགས་.

བགེགས་བསྐྲད་ (gegdrɛɛ) exorcising/ expelling a demon or evil spirit; va.—བྱེད་.

བགེགས་གཏོར་ (gegdɔr) a གཏོར་མ་ offering to demons.

བགེགས་བར་ (gegbar) sm. བགེགས་.

བགེགས་བར་ཆད་བྱུང་ (gegbar cɛ̀ɛjuŋ) having or experiencing misfortune/ mishap.

བགེགས་དབང་བར་ཆད་ (gegwaŋ parjɛɛ) calamity, disaster, obstacle, misfortune caused by demons.

བགེགས་མང་དགེ་ཉུང་ (gegmaŋ geñuŋ) many obstacles and few benefits.

བགེགས་འཚུབ་ (gegdzub) sm. བགེགས་དབང་བར་ཆད་.

བགོ་: p. བགོས་; f. བགོ; imp. བགོས་ (go) 1. va. to divide. 2. va. to wear, to put on (clothes). 3. f. of བགོད་.

བགོ་སྐལ་ (gogɛɛ) share, quota.

བགོ་འགྲེམས་ (gondrem) 1. sm. བགོད་འགྲེམས་ 2. sm. ཐོབ་ཆ་.

བགོ་ཉེས་ (goñeè) error in dividing/ sharing; vi.—ཤོར་ to make an error in dividing/ sharing.

བགོ་རྟགས་ (godaà) division sign (in math).

བགོ་ཐབས་ (godəb) division (in math).

བགོ་བ་ (gowa) clothes.

བགོ་བྱ་ (goja) dividend (in math).

བགོ་བྱེད་ (gojeè) sm. བགོ་ཐབས་.

བགོ་བྱེད་གྲངས་ (gojeèdraŋ) divisor (in math).

བགོ་རྩིས་ (godzii) division (in math).

བགོ་ཚུལ་ (godzül) manner of dividing, schedule/ timetable (for dividing sth.).

བགོ་གཞི་ (goshi) things that are to be divided.

བགོ་རིས་སུ་གཅོད་ (go riisu jöö) va. to divide into individual portions.

བགོ་རེ་ (gore) square house.

བགོ་ལུགས་ (golug) sm. བགོ་ཚུལ་.

བགོ་བཤའ་ (gosha) apportionment, allocation, division; va.—རྒྱག; —བགོད་ to divide, to allocate, to apportion ༎ སྐལ་བ་བརྒྱད་ལ་བགོ་བཤའ་བརྒྱབ་པ་རེད་ (They) divided (it) into eight portions.

བགོ་སྲོལ་ (gosöö) distributive law (in math).

བགོད་: p. བགོས་; f. བགོ; imp. བགོས་ (göö) va. to divide, to allocate, to apportion ༎ བཟོ་པ་རྣམས་ཚོ་ཁག་གསུམ་ལ་བགོས་པ་རེད་ (They) divided the workers into three groups.

བགོད་འགྲེམས་ (göndrem) distribution, allocation; va.—རྒྱག to distribute, to allocate ། ས་ཞིང་རྣམས་མི་དམངས་ལ་ཆ་སྙོམས་བགོད་འགྲེམས་བྱས་ཡོད་པ་རེད་ They distributed the land equally among the people.

བགོད་གདུབ་ (göödub) divisor (in math).

བགོད་བྱེད་ (gööceè) division (in math).

བགོད་བྱེད་གྲངས་ (gööceèdraŋ) divisor (in math).

བགོད་རྩིས་ (göödzii) division (in math).

བགོད་ར་ (gööra) share, part, quota.

བགོད་རུང་ (gööruŋ) algebraic division.

བགོམ་ (gom) f. of འགོམ་.

བགོམས་ (gom) p. and imp. of འགོམ་.

བགོར་ (gɔr) 1. sm. འགོར་. 2. va. to keep nearby/ around. 3. va. to delay ། སོན་འདེབས་པའི་དུས་ཚོད་བགོར་མི་རུང་ It is not okay to delay the planting of seeds.

བགོས་ (göö) p. of བགོད་ and བགོ་.

བགོས་བསྐོ་ (töögo) dividing and appointing (e.g., into areas and jobs); va.—བྱེད་ ། སློབ་གྲྭ་ཐོན་པ་རྣམས་བོད་ཀྱི་ས་གནས་ཡོངས་ཀྱི་ལས་གནས་ཁག་ལ་བགོས་བསྐོས་བྱས་པ་རེད་ They divided up the graduates of school and appointed them to different positions all over Tibet.

བགོས་འགྲེམས་ (göndrem) sm. བགོད་འགྲེམས་.

བགོས་ཐོབ་ (göödob) 1. share/ portion of sth. to be divided. 2. the sum/ number that results from division (in math).

བགོས་བེད་སྤྱོད་ (gööbeè jɛ̀ɛ̀) shung. va. to divide and use.

བགོས་འབབ་ (gööbəb) sm. བགོས་ཐོབ་.

བགོས་འཚོང་ (göödzoŋ) a ration or quota in selling goods; va.—རྒྱག to sell goods by allotment/ quota/ ration.

བགོས་ཞིང་ (gööshiŋ) shung. divided field.

བགོས་ར་ (gööra) shung. dividing; va.—བྱེད་; va.—བགྱིས་.

བགྱང་: p. **བགྱངས་**; f. **བགྱང་**; imp. **བགྱོངས་** (gyaŋ) va. to postpone, to delay ། ཉིན་ཤས་ཚོགས་འདུ་བགྱངས་པ་རེད་ (They) postponed the meeting for a few days.

བགྱངས་ (gyaŋ) p. of བགྱང་.

བགྱི་ (gyi) 1. f. of བགྱིད་. 2. genitive particle (sm. གི་).

བགྱི་སྒོ་ (gyigo) sm. བྱེད་སྒོ་.

བགྱིད་: p. **བགྱིས་**; f. **བགྱི་**; imp. **གྱིས་** (gyii) va. to do ། ལས་ཀའི་ཐོག་གཟབ་ནན་གྱིས་ཤིག Be careful in doing (your) work.

བགྱིད་འདུན་ (gyindün) shung. a wish to do sth.

བགྱིད་འོས་ (gyiiwöö) shung. appropriate to do

བགྱིས་ (gyii) p. of བགྱིད་.

བགྱེས་ (gyeè) p. of འགྱེད་.

བགྲང་: p. **བགྲངས་**; f. **བགྲང་**; imp. **བགྲོངས་** (draŋ) va. 1. to count, to enumerate, to compute, to calculate ། ཚོགས་འདུར་ཞུགས་པའི་མི་གྲངས་བགྲངས་སྐབས་ When (they) counted the people who participated in the meeting. 2. va. to tell, to give an account of, to relate, to list/ enumerate ། ཁོའི་བྱས་ཉེས་རྣམས་རིམ་པ་བཞིན་དུ་བགྲངས་པ་རེད་ (They) enumerated his crimes one by one.

བགྲང་དུ་མི་བཟོད་ (draŋdu misöö) countless, innumerable, uncountable.

བགྲང་དུ་མེད་པ་ (draŋdu meèba) sm. བགྲང་དུ་མི་བཟོད་.

བགྲང་ཕྲེང་ (daŋdreŋ) sm. བགྲང་འཕྲེང་.

བགྲང་འཕྲེང་ (daŋdreŋ) rosary.

བགྲང་བྱ་ཁམས་ཀྱི་ཐོག་ཏུ་སོན་པ་ (traŋja kāmgi tɔ̄gdu sɔ̄mba) shung. having reached the age of 18.

བགྲང་ཡས་ (draŋyɛɛ̀) countless.

བགྲང་སེ་ (draŋse) eng. dance; va.—རྒྱག to dance.

བགྲངས་ (draŋ) p. of བགྲང་.

བགྲད་ (drɛɛ̀) va. to spread apart, to open wide ། རྐང་པ་བགྲད་དེ་བསྡད་ (He) sat with his legs spread apart.

བགྲད་བགྲད་ (drɛɛ̀drɛɛ̀) sm. བགྲད་.

བགྲིལ་ (drii) va. to roll down ། རི་སྟེང་ནས་རྡོ་ཐུར་དུ་བགྲིལ་བ་རེད་ (They) rolled the stone down from top of the hill.

བགྲུ་: p. **བགྲུས་**; f. **བགྲུ་**; imp. **བགྲུས་** (dru) va. to husk, to hull.

བགྲུ་འཁོར་ (drugɔɔ) husking wheel/ machine.

བགྲུ་འཁོར་ར་བ་ (drugɔɔ rawa) mill for husking grains.

བགྲུ་རྒྱག (dru gyaà) va. to husk.

བགྲུ་རྡོ་ (drudo) stone used to husk grain.

བགྲུ་གཞོང་ (drushoŋ) basin for husking grain.

བགྲུང་: p. **བགྲུངས་**; f. **བགྲུང་**; imp. **བགྲུངས་** (druŋ) vi. to filter water to make it clear, to purify liquids.

བགྲུངས་ (druŋ) p. and imp. བགྲུང་.

བགྲུད་ (drüü) sm.* བགྲུ་.

བགྲུད་འཁོར་ (drüükɔɔ) sm.* བགྲུ་འཁོར་.

བགྲུ་རྒྱག (dru gyaà) sm.* བགྲུ་རྒྱག.

བགྲུད་རྡོ་ (drüüdo) sm.* བགྲུ་རྡོ་.

བགྲུད་གཞོང་ (drüüshoŋ) sm.* བགྲུ་གཞོང་.

བགྲུས་ (drüü) 1. p. of བགྲུ་. 2. husking/ hulling grain; va.—རྒྱག.

བགྲུས་ཁང་ (drüügaŋ) husking mill.

བགྲུས་མ་ (drüüma) husked grain.

བགྲེ་ (dre) va. to roll on one's back.

བགྲེས་ (dreè) 1. vi. to age, to grow old (h.) ། ཁོང་དེང་སང་ཞེ་དྲག་བགྲེས་བཞག He has aged a lot these days. 2. vi. to lose weight/ health, to become physically weak (h.) ། ཁོང་སྙུན་པའི་རྗེས་སུ་ཞེ་དྲག་བགྲེས་བཞག After his illness he looks thin and weak.

བགྲེས་འགོགས་ (dreŋgɔɔ) old, aged.

བགྲེས་གྲས་ (dreèdɛɛ) the older/ elderly ones ། གཞུང་ཞབས་བགྲེས་གྲས་ The older government officials.

བགྲེས་པ་ (drɛɛ̀ba) older, senior (in age) (h.) ། ཁོང་གི་སྐུ་མཆེད་བགྲེས་པ His older relatives.

བགྲེས་པོ་ (dreèbo) old, aged (h.) ། ཁོང་བགྲེས་པོ་རེད་ He is old.

བགྲེས་མོ་ (dreèmo) old (for females). (h.) ། ཁོང་གི་ཡུམ་བགྲེས་མོ་དེ་ His old mother.

བགྲེས་གཞོན་ (dreèshön) older and younger, senior and junior, main and secondary ། སྐུ་མཆེད་བགྲེས་གཞོན་ Older and younger relatives ། སྲིད་འཛིན་བགྲེས་གཞོན་ The president and the vice-president.

བགྲེས་ཤོས་ (dreèshöö) oldest, the most senior (h.) ། བཀའ་བློན་བགྲེས་ཤོས་ The most senior minister.

བགྲེས་སོང་ (dreèsoŋ) old, aged, veteran ། བཟོ་པ་བགྲེས་སོང་ Veteran workers.

བགྲེས་སོན་ (dreèsön) reaching old age ། བཟོ་པ་བགྲེས་སོན་རྣམས་ནུས་གསོལ་བྱས་པ་རེད་ The workers who reached old age retired.

བགྲོ་: p. **བགྲོས་**; f. **བགྲོ་**; imp. **གྲོས་** (dro) va. to discuss, to confer ། ལན་མང་བགྲོས་ཀྱང་ཐག་གཅོད་མ་ཐུབ་པ་རེད་ (They) could not decide even though (they) discussed it many times.

བགྲོ་གླེང་ (droleŋ) conversation, debate, discussion (h.); va.—གནང་.

བགྲོ་གླེང་པ་ (droleŋba) shung. the two geshe who do debating at the New Year's celebration in the Potala Palace.

བགྲོ་འདེབས་ (dro deb) va. to discuss/ parley/ confer.

བགྲོངས་ (droŋ) see བགྲང་.

བགྲོད་ (dröö) 1. va. to cross, to pass, to get through, to go beyond/ past ། རི་མཐོ་པོ་དང་ཆུ་ཆེན་པོ་བཅས་བགྲོད་དགོས་ཡོད་ One has to cross high mountains and large rivers. ། དཀའ་ངལ་མང་པོ་ལ་བགྲོད་ནས་ཡོང་པ་རེད་ Passing through many difficulties, (they) came here. 2. va. to have sexual intercourse ། བུད་མེད་ལ་བགྲོད་པ་རེད་ (He) had intercourse with women.

བགྲོད་སྒྲ་ (dröödra) the sound of a watch ticking.

བགྲོད་མཐའ་ (drööda) the final point/ destination.

བགྲོད་མཐའི་ས་ཚིགས་ (drööte sɔ̄dzig) terminus, the last station.

བགྲོད་པ་གཅིག་པ་ (drööba jigbə) 1. the same road/ path. 2. walking/ marching in step.

བགྲོད་པའི་དུས་སྐབས་ (drööbɛ tüügəb) transition

period.

བགྲོད་ཕྱོགས་ (drööjɔɔ̀) sm. འགྲོ་ཕྱོགས་.

བགྲོད་རིམ་ (drööriṃ) steps, stages ¶ ལས་ཀ་འདི་ལ་བགྲོད་རིམ་བཞི་ཡོད་པ་རེད་ There are four stages in this work.

བགྲོད་ལམ་ (dröölam) 1. road, way, path; va.—གཅོད་ to cross a road ¶ བགྲོད་ལམ་མི་གཅིག་ཀྱང་དམིགས་ཡུལ་གཅིག་པ་ Though they went on different roads, their destination was the same. 2. vagina.

བགྲོད་ཤུལ་ (drööshöö) track/ trace of where sb. or sth. has gone (e.g., cars, troops, horses).

བགྲོས་ (dröö) p. of བགྲོ་.

བགྲོས་ངན་ (drööŋɛn) plot; va.—གཡོས་ to plot.

མགར་ (gar) 1. abbr. of མགར་བ་. 2. name of a famous minister during the ancient Tibetan kingdom.

མགར་སྐྱག (gargyaà) pieces of charcoal.

མགར་ཁང་ (gargaŋ) blacksmith's shop.

མགར་ཆས་ (garjɛɛ̀) sm. མགར་སྤྱ་.

མགར་ནག (garnag) name of a protective deity.

མགར་སྤྱ་ (garca) blacksmith tools/ equipment.

མགར་བ་ (gara) blacksmith; va.—བྱེད་ to work as blacksmith.

མགར་བ་སོལ་རྡོག (garwa söödoò) sm. མགར་སྐྱག.

མགར་བྱད་ (garcɛɛ̀) sm. མགར་སྤྱ་.

མགར་ལྡུག (garluù) blacksmith's mold/ crucible.

མགར་ར་ (garra) sm. མགར་བ་.

མགར་རུ་ (garru) vase with a long lip.

མགལ་ (gɛɛ) jaw ¶ ཡ་མགལ་ The upper jaw. ¶ མ་མགལ་ The lower jaw.

མགལ་མཆུ་ (gɛɛju) sm. མགལ་དུམ་.

མགལ་དུམ་ (gɛɛdum) charcoal.

མགལ་པ་ (gɛɛba) 1. sm. མགལ་དུམ་. 2. tree branch.

མགལ་མེ་ (gɛɛme) firebrand.

མགུ་ (gu) vi. to be glad/ pleased/ content/ satisfied ¶ ང་ཚོས་ལས་ཀ་བྱེད་སྟངས་ལ་ཡིད་མགུ་སོང་ (They) were pleased with our way of working.

མགུ་པོ་ (gubo) satisfied, pleased, content; va.—བྱེད་ ¶ ཁོའི་ལས་ཀ་འདིར་འགོ་ཁྲིད་ཀྱིས་མགུ་པོ་བྱེད་ཀྱི་འདུག The boss is pleased with his work.

མགུ་སྤྲོ་ (gudro) happy, joyful.

མགུ་བ་སྐྱེ་ (guwa gyē) va. to be happy/ glad.

མགུ་སེམས་ (gusem) pleased, glad, satisfied, content; vi.—འཆང་ to be pleased, satisfied, content.

མགུར་ (gur) classical/ religious song; va.—གསུང་; —བཞེས་; —འཐེན་ to sing མགུར་.

མགུར་གླུ་ (gurlu) sm. མགུར་.

མགུར་ཆུ་ (gurju) the flat base of a stupa.

མགུར་དུ་གསུངས་ (gurdu sūŋ) va. to say/ sing a མགུར་.

མགུར་དབྱངས་ (guryaŋ) melody.

མགུར་འབུམ་ (gurbum) the Hundred Thousand Songs of Milarepa.

མགུར་མ་ (gurma) sm. མགུར་.

མགུར་མོ་ (gurmo) eight trankas (ཏམ་ཀ་) in the tt. system of currency.

མགུར་ཞོ་ (gursho) a weight measurement used for gold, silver, etc. that is equal to about 7 སྐར་མ་ (i.e., a little less than one ཏམ་ཀ་.

མགུལ་ (gül) neck, throat (h.).

མགུལ་ཁབ་ (gülgəb) needle (h.).

མགུལ་གའུ་ (gülgəwu) Tibetan charm box worn around the neck (h.).

མགུལ་གློ་ (güülo) coughing (h.); vi.—སྐྱོན་ to cough.

མགུལ་འགགས་ (güŋgaà) 1. a hoarse/ hissing voice. 2. a throat disease.

མགུལ་རྒྱན་ (güügyɛn) necklace (h.).

མགུལ་ཆམ་ (güujam) a cold, the flu (h.); vi.—སྐྱོན་ to get a cold/ flu.

མགུལ་ཆིངས་ (güüjiŋ) scarf, tie (h.).

མགུལ་མཇིང་ (güüjiŋ) neck (h.).

མགུལ་ཐབ་ (güüdəb) button (h.); va.—སྐྱོན་ to button.

མགུལ་ཐོབ་ (güüdob) sm. མགུལ་ཐབ་.

མགུལ་དམ་ (güüdam) shung. h. of དམ་ཕྱུག.

མགུལ་དར་ (güldar) Tibetan ceremonial scarf (h.); va.—སྐྱོན་ to put on such a scarf.

མགུལ་གདུབ་ (güldub) sm. མགུལ་འཕྲེང་.

མགུལ་འཕྲེང་ (güldreŋ) necklace (h.).

མགུལ་གཟི་ (gülsi) h. of གཟི་.

མགུལ་གཡུ་ (gülyu) turquoise necklace (h.).

མགུལ་བཤལ་ (gülsam) clearing one's throat (h.); va.—གནང་.

མགོ་ (go) 1. head. 2. top, summit ¶ རིའི་མགོ་ The top of the mountain.

མགོ་བཀྱག (go gāà) va. to lift up one's head ¶ གསར་བརྗེ་བྱུང་ཙང་དབུལ་པོངས་མགོ་ཀྱག་ཐུབ་པ་རེད་ Because there was revolution the poor were able to lift their heads (high).

མགོ་བཀྱག་དུས་བྱུང་ (go gyāàtüǜ) a time/ opportunity when one is able to raise up one's head ¶ དམངས་གཙོའི་ལམ་ལུགས་ཀྱི་འོག་ཏུ་ངལ་རྩོལ་མི་དམངས་ལ་མགོ་ཀྱག་དུས་བྱུང་བ་རེད་ Under democracy, the working class got the opportunity to lift their heads (high).

མགོ་དཀར་པོ་ (go gāābo) white/ gray hair.

མགོ་དཀྱིལ་ (gogyii) center of the crown/ head, top of the head.

མགོ་དཀྲིས་ (godrii̇̀) turban, scarf wrapped around head.

མགོ་དཀྲུགས་ལུས་དཀྲུགས་ (godrug lüüdrug) shaking one's head and body (expressing dislike).

མགོ་དཀྲུགས་དཀྲུགས་ (go drūgdruù) shaking one's head (expressing dislike); va.—བྱེད་.

མགོ་དཀྲོགས་བཟོ་ (godrog so) 1. va. to cause a mishap/ calamity/ disaster ¶ ཕྲུ་གུ་འདིས་སློབ་ཁང་གི་ཤེལ་སྒོ་བཅག་ནས་མགོ་དཀྲོགས་བཟོས་བཞག The child caused a mishap by breaking the school's window.

མགོ་དཀྲོགས་སློང་ (godrog lōŋ) sm. མགོ་དཀྲོགས་བཟོ་.

མགོ་བཀྲུས་མཇིང་དག (godrüǜ jiŋdag) one must perform all of one's duties/ responsibilities completely, one must follow through to completion (can convey putting up proof for an accusation); va.—བཟོ་ [Lit. wash head, clean neck].

མགོ་བཀྲུས་གདོང་དག (godrüǜ doŋdag) sm. མགོ་བཀྲུས་མཇིང་དག.

མགོ་སྐེ་འབྲལ་མེད་ (goge trɛɛmeè) inseparable, close (i.e., friends or relatives) [Lit. head and neck inseparable].

མགོ་སྐོགས་ (gogɔɔ̀) a skeleton of a skull.

མགོ་སྐོན་ (gogön) a coppersmith's tool.

མགོ་སྐོར་ (gogɔɔ) 1. duping, tricking, fooling; va. མགོ་སྐོར་; —གཏོང་ to dupe, to fool, to trick, to deceive; vi.—ཐེབས་; —གཟིད་ to be tricked/ duped/ deceived. 2. amusing/ diverting sb.; va.—གཏོང་.

མགོ་སྐོར་བཙན་བཅོས་ (go gɔ̄ɔ ñɛɛjöö) deceiving and bullying; va.—བྱེད་.

མགོ་སྐོར་གཡོ་འཁྲུལ་ (go gɔ̄ɔ yöndrüü) tricking and deceiving, cheating, swindling; va.—བྱེད་.

མགོ་སྐྱ་ཕྱེད་སྔོ་ཕྱེད་ (go gyācēè ŋōceè) salt and pepper hair, greying hair.

མགོ་སྐྱེས་ (gogyeè) sm. སྐྲ་.

མགོ་སྐྱོང་ (gogyoŋ) sm. མགོ་འདྲེན་བྱེད་.

མགོ་སྐྱོབ་ (gogyob) helmet.

མགོ་སྐྲ་ (godra) head hair; vi.—བྱི་ to get bald, to lose (one's head) hair.

མགོ་ཁེབས་ (gokeb) sm. མགོ་རས་.

མགོ་ཁྱག་ཁྱག (go kyāggyaà) sm. མགོ་བཀྱག.

མགོ་ཁྲ་ (godra) 1. (for cattle) a head with a different color than the body. 2. for humans, different color skin on head due to disease or scars.

མགོ་ཁྲིད་ (gudrii̇̀) sm. འགོ་ཁྲིད་.

མགོ་ཁྲོག (godrog) sm. མགོ་དཀྲོགས་.

མགོ་མཁྲེགས་གྲམ་པའི་ཆུ་རྡོ་ (godreg trambɛ cūdo) stubborn, hardheaded [Lit. hard head (like) a stone on a river bank].

མགོ་མཁྲིགས་པོ་ (go tragbo) stubborn, obstinate.

མགོ་འཁོར་ (gogɔɔ) 1. vi. to be fooled, to be duped, to be deceived, to be conned. 2. vi. to be amused with/ absorbed in sth.

མགོ་འཁོར་པོ་ (go kɔ̄ɔ̄bo) interesting, amusing.

མགོ་འཁོར་ས་ (go kɔ̄ɔ̄sa) sth. to amuse/ interest.

མགོ་འཁྲིད་ (gudrii) see འགོ་ཁྲིད.

མགོ་འཁྲུད་མཇིང་དག (godrüü jiŋdaà) sm. མགོ་བཀྲུས་མཇིང་དག.

མགོ་འཁྲུད་མདོང་དག (godrüü doŋdaà) sm. མགོ་བཀྲུས་མཇིང་དག.

མགོ་འཁྲུལ་ (go trüü) vi. to be confused ¶ ཁོང་གི་སྐད་ཆ་དེས་ང་མགོ་འཁྲུལ་སོང་ I got confused by his comments.

མགོ་གུག (go guù) 1. va. to bow/ hang down one's head. 2. to surrender/ yield/ give in.

མགོ་གུག་གུག (go guguù) 1. hanging one's head down, bowing one's head; va.—བྱེད་. 2. surrendering, yielding; va.—བྱེད་.

མགོ་གྲངས་ (godraŋ) the number of individuals (in a group/ herd) ¶ ཕྱུགས་རིགས་མགོ་གྲངས་ཁྲི་ཙམ་སོན་པ་རེད་ Ten thousand head of cattle survived.

མགོ་གྲུང་པོ་ (go truŋbu) clever, bright, shrewd, smart.

མགོ་དགུ་ (gogu) sm. མགོ་གུག.

མགོ་དགུ་མཇུག་དགུ་ (gogu juggu) sm. མགོ་གུག.

མགོ་དགུར་ (gogur) sm.* མགོ་དགུ.

མགོ་དགུར་དགུར་ (go guguù) sm.* མགོ་གུག་གུག.

མགོ་རྒྱིག་རྒྱག (gogyig gyaà) va. to raise one's head while walking (for horses).

མགོ་རྒྱན་ (gogyɛn) head ornaments.

མགོ་རྒུག་གཞུ་ (goguù shu) 1. va. to hit on the head with a stick. 2. va. to hold/ keep sb. down ¶ ལས་བྱེད་པ་གཞོན་ནུ་དེ་གནས་སྤར་མ་བྱུང་བ་དེ་ནི་དཔོན་པོ་ཞིག་གིས་མགོ་རྒུག་གཞུས་པའི་རྐྱེན་གྱིས་རེད་ The young cadre's not getting promoted is because the boss was holding him down.

མགོ་རྒྱུད་ (gogyüü) sm. མགོ་བརྒྱུས་.

མགོ་རྒྱུས་ (gogyüü) va. to immerse oneself on sth., to be spend all one's time on sth. ¶ ཉིན་ལྟར་དཔེ་ཆའི་ནང་མགོ་བརྒྱུས་བྱས་ནས་མ་སྡོད་ Don't immerse yourself in religious books everyday.

མགོ་སྒུར་ (go gur) 1. va. to surrender, to submit ¶ ཤི་ཡང་མགོ་སྒུར་གྱི་མ་རེད་ (They) will not surrender even if they have to die. 2. va. to bow one's head.

མགོ་སྒུར་སྒུར་ (go gugur) va. to kowtow, to bow down before sb. ¶ མགོ་སྒུར་སྒུར་ལན་གསུམ་བྱེད་བཅུག་པ་རེད་ We were made to bow down three times.

མགོ་སྒུར་ངོས་ལེན་ (gogur ŋöölen) surrendering and acknowledging/ admitting/ confessing one's faults or crimes; va.—བྱེད་.

མགོ་སྒུར་ལྕེ་སྣར་ (gogur jēnar) showing respect [Lit. bowing one's head and sticking out one's tongue].

མགོ་སྒུར་ཕྱག་འཚལ (gogur cāàdzɛɛ) bowing one's head and prostrating.

མགོ་སྒྲིམ་པོ་ (go drimbu) sm. མགོ་གྲུང་པོ་.

མགོ་སྒྲོག (godrɔɔ̀) sm. ཡོག་སྒྲོག.

མགོ་སྒྲོམ་ (godrom) forward/ preface of a book.

མགོ་བརྒྱུས་ (gogyüü) sm. མགོ་རྒྱུས་.

མགོ་བསྒྲེ་ (godre) sm. མགོ་བསྒྲེས་.

མགོ་བསྒྲེས་ (godreè) sm. རིག་འགྲེ་.

མགོ་ང་ (goŋa) head and tail.

མགོ་ང་གཉིས་མཐུད་ (goŋa ñiidüü) adjacent, sharing a border [Lit. head and tail joined together].

མགོ་ང་མེད་པ་ (goŋa meèba) sm. མགོ་མཇུག་མེད་པ་.

མགོ་ང་ཡོད་པ་ (goŋa yööba) orderly, well-arranged; va.—བྱེད་ [Lit. having a head and a tail].

མགོ་ངོ་ཅན་ (goŋojɛn) a person affected with head mange or scalp disease.

མགོ་ཐུས་སྦྲེལ་ (goŋɛɛ̀ dree) vi. to be inseparable.

མགོ་སྔོ་ཆོབ་ཙམ་ (goŋa cōbdzam) salt-and-pepper hair.

མགོ་ཅན་ (gojɛn) the three letters that are used as suffixes: ར་, ལ་, ས་.

མགོ་ཅོག་ཅོག (go jogjoò) sm. མགོ་ལྡུག་ལྡུག.

མགོ་གཅོད་ (gojöö) sm. སྐྲ་གཅོད་.

མགོ་བཅད་མཇུག་གཏུབས་ (gojɛɛ̀ jugdub) censoring; va.—བྱེད་ ¶ ལུང་པ་དེའི་ནང་རྩོམ་ཡིག་ཚང་མ་མགོ་བཅད་མཇུག་གཏུབ་མ་བྱས་གོང་འདོན་ཆོག་གི་མེད་པ་རེད་ In this country, no article can be published before being censored. [Lit. cut head, cut tail].

མགོ་བཅོལ་ (go jöö) va. to place oneself under the protection of another, to seek asylum ¶ མོས་རྒྱ་ནག་ལ་མགོ་བཅོལ་སོང་ She sought asylum from China.

མགོ་ལྡུག་བདེ་པོ་ (gojoò debo) sm. མགོ་བདེ་པོ་.

མགོ་ལྕག་གཞུ་ (gojaà shu) 1. va. to slap on the head. 2. va. to have a better hand than one's opponent's (in a card game such as poker).

མགོ་ལྡུག (gojoò) 1. sm. མགོ་ལྡུག་ལྡུག. 2. hair worn in a bun on top of the head.

མགོ་ལྡུག་ཁས་ལེན་ (gojoò kɛ̄ɛlen) showing approval by nodding; va.—བྱེད་.

མགོ་ལྡུག་ལྡུག (gojogjoò) nodding one's head (conveying yes); va.—བྱེད་.

མགོ་ལྡུགས་ (gojoò) the head of a stalk/ flower hanging over because it is full with grain/ flower; vi.—ཕྱིམ་ to have a stalk/ flower bend or sway.

མགོ་ཆུ་ (goju) amniotic fluid; vi.—རོལ་ to break water (before birth).

མགོ་ཆེན་པོ་ (go cēmbo) big head.

མགོ་མཆན་ (gojɛn) sm. འགོ་མཆན་.

མགོ་འཆིང་ (gojiŋ) leader, director, commander.

མགོ་མཇུག (gomjuù) 1. beginning and end, start and finish. 2. order, discipline.

མགོ་མཇུག་གོ་ལྡོག (gomjuù kodoò) sm. མགོ་མཇུག་ལྡོག.

མགོ་མཇུག་ལྡོག (gomjuù dɔɔ̀) sm. མགོ་མཇུག་སློག.

མགོ་མཇུག་བར་གསུམ་ (gomjuù parsum). beginning, middle and end.

མགོ་མཇུག་མེད་པ་ (gomjuù meèbə) anarchic, disorderly, leaderless, chaotic, topsy-turvy.

མགོ་མཇུག་ལོག (gomjuù lɔɔ̀) vi. to be overthrown, to be turned upside down, to get upset.

མགོ་མཇུག་སློག (gonjuù lɔ̄ɔ̀) va. to overthrow, to upset, to bring down, to put/ turn upside down ¶ སྲིད་གཞུང་རྙིང་པ་མགོ་མཇུག་བསློགས་པ་རེད་ (They) overthrew the old government.

མགོ་འཇོག་བྱེད་ (gonjoò cee) sm. མགོ་ལྡུག་ལྡུག་བྱེད་.

མགོ་བརྗོད་ (gojöö) sm. འགོ་བརྗོད་.

མགོ་ཉུག་ཉུག (go ñugñuù) poking one's head in or out of a window/ door; va.—བྱེད་.

མགོ་ཉོག (goñog) sm. མགོ་རྙོག.

མགོ་གཉིས་མ་ (go ñimə) deceitful, two faced, double-dealing, untrustworthy.

མགོ་གཉིས་མ་ཚ་པོ་ (goñimə tsābo) unreliable, untrustworthy, undependable, two-faced.

མགོ་མཉམ་ (goñam) same rank/ level/ height.

མགོ་རྙོག (goñog) complicated, confused, muddled, messed up; va.—བཟོ་ to confuse, to muddle, to make a mess, to disorganize ¶ ལས་ཀ་འདི་མགོ་རྙོག་ཡོད་པ་རེད་ This work is complicated. ¶ ལས་བྱེད་པ་གསར་པ་དེས་ལས་ཀའི་ཐོག་མགོ་རྙོག་བཟོས་བཞག The new cadre messed up the work (could be intentional or out of ignorance).

མགོ་རྙོག་ཆེན་པོ་ (goñoò cēmbo) muddled, confused, messed up, disorganized; va.—བཟོ་ to mess sth. up, to cause to be muddled/ confused/ disorganized.

མགོ་རྙོག་པོ་ (go ñōgbo) sm. མགོ་རྙོག.

མགོ་རྙོག་ཚ་པོ་ (goñoò tsābo) sm. མགོ་རྙོག་ཆེན་པོ་.

མགོ་རྙོག་ལུང་པ་གང་ (goñoò luŋbə kaŋ) a big mess, a hopeless muddle.

མགོ་སྙོམས་ (go ñōm) va. to equalize, to even out/ balance, to make to the same height.

མགོ་བརྙན་ (goñɛn) model/ sculpture of a head; mask.

མགོ་གདད་ (godɛɛ̀) sm. མགོ་བདགས་.

མགོ་གདུག (go̲duù) 1. two actions offsetting/ balancing each other; va.—གཏོང་ ། མི་ཚང་དེ་གཉིས་ཀྱི་ཕྲུ་གུས་ཕན་ཚུན་ཉིས་རྡུང་བརྡང་བ་དེའི་སྐོར་རྩོད་པ་རྒྱག་མ་དགོས་པར་མགོ་གདུགས་བཏང་བ་རེད་ As for the two households children hitting each other (back and forth), there is no need to have a dispute as the actions offset each other. 2. va. to touch foreheads (as a gesture of greeting.

མགོ་བདགས་ (go̲daà) 1. surrendering; va.—ཞུ་ to surrender, to capitulate; va.—ལེན་ to accept/ receive surrender ། དགྲ་བོའི་དམག་མིས་ང་ཚོར་མགོ་བདགས་ཞུས་པ་རེད་ The enemy soldiers surrendered to us.

མགོ་བདགས་ཞུ་རྟེན་ (go̲daà shu̲den) shung. an offering of gifts after surrendering.

མགོ་ཏིང་སློག (gu̲diŋ lɔ̄ɔ̀) sm. མགོ་མཇུག་སློག.

མགོ་ལྟག (go̲daà) sm. ལྟག་ཁུང་.

མགོ་སྟོང་པ་ (go̲ dōŋbo) empty-headed.

མགོ་སྟོད་ཨ་གསར་ (go̲döö āsar) being excited or infatuated with sth. at the start or in the beginning.

མགོ་སྟོན་ (go̲dön) sm. མགོ་འདོན་འཚོ་སྟོན་.

མགོ་ཐག (go̲daà) 1. a collar tied on animals. 2. a leash.

མགོ་ཐག་ཕུད་ (go̲daà pǖù) p. of མགོ་ཐག་འབུད་.

མགོ་ཐག་འབུད་ (go̲daà bü̲ü̲) vi. to complete one's duty/ work in a certain time period ། ཉི་མ་རེ་རེའི་ལས་ཀ་དེ་ཉིན་དེ་རང་མགོ་ཐག་འབུད་དགོས་ Each day's work has to be completed that very day.

མགོ་ཐར་དཔུང་འཛུག (go̲dar būŋjuù) giving sb. an inch and he takes a mile [Lit. heads get in, insert the shoulder].

མགོ་ཐར་དཔུང་ཐར་ (go̲dar būŋdar) sm. མགོ་ཐར་དཔུང་འཛུག.

མགོ་ཐར་དཔུང་འཛུད་ (go̲dar būŋdzüü) sm. མགོ་ཐར་དཔུང་འཛུག.

མགོ་ཐར་དཔུང་འཛུལ་ (go̲dar būŋdzüü) sm. མགོ་ཐར་དཔུང་འཛུག.

མགོ་ཐུག (go̲ tūg) 1. vi. to tally, to agree, to come out right (in accounting) ། ཁོས་བཤད་ཡས་དང་ང་ཚོས་གོ་བ་མགོ་ཐུག་གི་མི་འདུག What he says and what we heard do not tally. 2. exchanging evenly in barter; va.—གཏོང་ to make an even exchange of goods ། ཁོང་གི་རྟ་དང་ངའི་ཐུག་ཐུག་དེ་མགོ་ཐུག་བཏང་བ་ཡིན་ I exchanged my motorcycle for his horse (in an even exchange).

མགོ་ཐུག་དཔུང་སྦྱོར་ (go̲dug būŋjɔɔ) a crowd, a mass of people together.

མགོ་ཐོ་ (go̲do) banging heads together (for sheep, etc.); va.—རྒྱག.

མགོ་ཐོག་གི་བུམ་པ་ ལྕེ་ཐོག་གི་བདུད་རྩི་ (go̲dɔ̀ɔgi pu̲mbɔ jēdɔ̀ɔgi dü̲ü̲dzi) holding sth. as very dear/ precious [Lit. vase on head, ambrosia on tongue].

མགོ་ཐོག་མགོ་བརྩེགས་ (go̲dɔ̀ɔ go̲dzeg) one on top of another.

མགོ་ཐོག་གཡམ་སེལ་ (go̲dɔ̀ɔ yāmsel) accomplishing the work one is responsible for; va.—བྱེད་.

མགོ་ཐོག་ལ་སྡོད་ (go̲dɔ̀ɔla dö̲ö̲) va. to ride roughshod over, to bully [Lit. sit on sb.'s head].

མགོ་ཐོག་ལག་བཞག (go̲dɔ̀ɔ la̲gshaà) empty-handed ། བཟའ་ཚང་དེ་གཉིས་ཁག་ཁག་བྱེད་སྐབས་ཁྱོ་ག་དེ་མགོ་ཐོག་ལག་བཞག་གིས་ཕྱིར་བཏང་བ་རེད་ When the couple divorced the man was sent out (of the household) empty-handed.

མགོ་ཐོད་ (go̲döö) forehead ། མགོ་ཐོད་རི་མོ་ Wrinkles on the forehead.

མགོ་ཐོན་ (go̲dön) vi. to be able to take care of oneself, to be able to do things independently, to be independent ། ཕྲུ་གུར་ལས་ཀ་རག་ནས་མགོ་ཐོན་སོང་ After the youth got work he was able to take care of himself.

མགོ་ཐོན་གདོང་སྟོན་ (go̲dön do̲ŋdön) appearing publicly, being in the limelight.

མགོ་ཐོན་པོ་ (go̲ tōmbo) able, capable, a person who is able to look after himself.

མགོ་མཐོ་པོ་ (go̲ tōbo) carrying one's head high.

མགོ་འཐུ་པོ་ (go̲ tūwo) witness.

མགོ་འཐོག་མཇུག་འཐོག (go̲dɔ̀ɔ ju̲ùdɔ̀ɔ) taking a little here and there (commonly used for women who get their boyfriends to buy them things); va.—རྒྱག ། ངའི་གྲོགས་མོ་འདིས་མགོ་འཐོག་མཇུག་འཐོག་བརྒྱབ་ནས་ང་ལ་དཀའ་ངལ་ཆེན་པོ་བཟོས་སོང་ My girl friend is making me buy a little here and there and this is causing me a lot of difficulties. [Lit. taking from the top, taking from the bottom].

མགོ་འཐོག་གཞུག་འཐོག (go̲dɔ̀ɔ shu̲gdɔ̀ɔ) sm. མགོ་འཐོག་མཇུག་འཐོག.

མགོ་འཐོན་ (go̲dön) sm. མགོ་ཐོན་.

མགོ་འཐོམ་ (go̲ tōm) vi. to be confused/ stunned/ puzzled/ dazed/ lost ། ཁ་ཚོས་སྐབས་རེ་ཐད་དེ་མགོ་འཐོམས་པའི་རྟགས་བསྟན་གྱི་འདུག Sometimes they show signs that they are completely confused.

མགོ་འཐོམས་ (go̲ tōm) p. of མགོ་འཐོམ་.

མགོ་འཐོམས་ཕྱོགས་འཁྱམ་ (go̲dom cɔ̄ndrüü) losing one's bearings, being utterly confused/ lost.

མགོ་འཐོམས་ཕྱོགས་འཛོལ་ (go̲dom cɔ̄ndzöö) sm. མགོ་འཐོམས་ཕྱོགས་འཁྱམ་.

མགོ་དམ་འཇུག་ལྷོད་ (go̲dam ju̲glhöö) incongruous, unmatched [Lit. tight in the beginning; loose/ lenient at the end].

མགོ་དམ་པོ་ (go̲ ta̲mbo) 1. strict, not loose, easygoing. 2. sb. who cannot be fooled easily.

མགོ་དོ་གེར་ཅན་ (go̲do ge̲rjɛn) hair tied in a bundle on top of the head.

མགོ་བདེ་ (go̲de) sm. མགོ་བདེ་པོ་.

མགོ་བདེ་སྐབས་འཚོལ་ (go̲de gābdzöö) seizing every chance to gain advantage by cunning/ craftiness, shrewdness, being opportunistic.

མགོ་བདེ་འཁྲབ་ (go̲de trɔ̄b) va. to be or act cunning/ shrewd/ crafty.

མགོ་བདེ་གླགས་ཚོང་ (go̲de lāàdzoŋ) seizing every opportunity to gain advantage in business by cunning/ craftiness/ shrewdness.

མགོ་བདེ་དྲན་འཕྲུལ་ (go̲de tre̲ndrüü) sm. མགོ་བདེ་སྐབས་འཚོལ་.

མགོ་བདེ་པོ་ (go̲ de̲bo) shrewd, sharp, clever, cunning.

མགོ་བདེ་པོས་ཞྭ་མོ་བརླགས་ (go̲ de̲bo sha̲mo lāà) too clever for one's own good [Lit. by cleverness, losing one's hat].

མགོ་བདེ་རྩེད་ (go̲de dzēè) va. to be or act cunning/ shrewd/ crafty.

མགོ་འདོགས་ (go̲ dɔ̲ɔ̀) va. to surrender, to capitulate.

མགོ་འདར་རྒྱག (go̲dar gya̲à) vi. to have one's head shake/ tremble (usu. due to old age).

མགོ་འདོགས་ཞུ་ཡིག (go̲dɔ̀ɔ shu̲yiì) letter of surrender.

མགོ་འདོགས་རིང་ལུགས་ (go̲dɔ̀ɔ ri̲ŋluù) capitulationism.

མགོ་འདོགས་ལུས་འབུལ་ (go̲dɔ̀ɔ lü̲mbüü) surrendering, capitulating; va.—བྱེད་.

མགོ་འདོན་ (go̲ndön) bringing up, caring for, raising, rearing; va. མགོ་འདོན་; —བྱེད་ ། ཕ་མའི་གནས་སྟངས་ཞན་པས་ཕྲུ་གུ་མགོ་འདོན་ཤིན་ཏུ་ཁག་པོ་རེད་ Because of the parent's poverty, it is very hard (for them) to bring up the children.

མགོ་འདོན་འཚོ་སྐྱོང་ (go̲ndön tsōgyoŋ) sm. མགོ་འདོན་.

མགོ་འདོན་འཚོ་སྟོན་ (go̲ndön tsōdön) sm. མགོ་འདོན་.

མགོ་འདོན་འཚོ་ཕན་ (go̲ndön tsōbɛn) sm. མགོ་འདོན་.

མགོ་དྲིན་ (go̲drin) shung. guidance.

མགོ་འདྲེན་ (go̲ndren) 1. protector, patron, backer, supporter; va.—བྱེད་; —གཏོང་ to act as a protector/ patron/ backer; va.—འཚོལ་ to seek a protector/ patron/ backer; va.—ཞུ་ to seek help/ support/ protection from sb. in a position of power/ influence; va.—རྒྱུད་ to go through sb.'s relationship to get a patron/ protector/ supporter/ backer ། ལུང་པ་འདིའི་ནང་མགོ་འདྲེན་མེད་ན་ལས་ཀ་བྱེད་ཁག་པོ་རེད་ In this place, if one doesn't have a supporter, it is difficult get things done. ། ལས་བྱེད་པ་དེ་མགོ་འདྲེན་བདང་ནས་གནས་སྲུར་བྱུང་བ་ཞིག་རེད་ That official is sb. who was promoted as a result of help from a patron/ backer.

མགོ་འདྲེན་མཁན་ (go trɛññɛn) sm. མགོ་འདྲེན་པ་.

མགོ་འདྲེན་པ་ (go trɛmba) 1. sb. who helps/ supports. 2. sb. who leads.

མགོ་རྡུང་ (go duŋ) va. to cheat, to beat (in business) ། ཚོང་པ་འདིས་ཅ་ལག་བརྫུས་མ་བཙོང་ནས་ངའི་མགོ་བརྡུངས་བྱུང་ The trader cheated me in business by selling me fake goods.

མགོ་རྡོག་རྡོག (go dogdoò) sm. མགོ་ཀྲག་ཀྲག.

མགོ་ལྡོག (go dɔ̀ɔ) 1. sm. མགོ་མཇུག་ལོག. 2. sm. ཕྱིན་ཅི་ལོག་པ་.

མགོ་བརྡུངས་ (go duŋ) p. of མགོ་རྡུང་.

མགོ་བསྡུར་ (go dur) va. to compare/ contrast/ correlate.

མགོ་ན་ (go na) vi. to have a headache, to have one's head hurt ། ངའི་མགོ་ན་གི་འདུག My head hurts.

མགོ་ན་པོ་ (go nabo) 1. sm. མགོ་ན་. 2. complex, complicated, perplexing, a headache; va.—བཟོ་ to make (sth.) complex/ complicated/ perplexing or to give a headache ། ལས་ཀ་འདི་མགོ་ན་པོ་ཞི་དྲག་འདུག This work is very complex. ། ལས་ཀ་འདིས་ང་མགོ་ན་པོ་བཟོས་བྱུང་ This work gave me a headache.

མགོ་ནག (gonag) humans, mankind.

མགོ་ནད་ (gonɛɛ̀) head illness, headache.

མགོ་ནས་ (go nɛɛ̀) sm. འགོ་ནས་.

མགོ་ནས་འཇུག་བར་ (gonɛɛ̀ jugbar) from beginning to end, from top to bottom.

མགོ་གནོན་ (gonön) oppression, bullying, abusing, suppressing; va.—གཏོང་; —བྱེད་.

མགོ་པ་ (goba) leader, chief.

མགོ་པང་ (gobaŋ) putting the head on sb.'s lap.

མགོ་སྐྲ་ (gobu) head hair.

མགོ་སྐྲ་ལག་འཛིངས་ (gobu lɔŋdzin) fighting by pulling each other's hair.

མགོ་སྤྲོད་ (godröö) placing/ putting face-to-face; va.—བྱེད་.

མགོ་ཕིབས་ (gobib) small tent.

མགོ་ཕོར་ (gobur) bowl of a pipe.

མགོ་ཕྱོགས་དཔུང་ཉེ་ (gojɔɔ̀ būŋñe) siding with one's boss or leader in a fight/ dispute.

མགོ་འཕང་ (gombaŋ) pride and power/ prestige.

མགོ་འཕྲུ་ (gondru) button on the top of a hat.

མགོ་བར་སྣང་ལ་ཡོད་པའི་མི་ (gowar nāŋla yööbɛ mi) people who are extremely proud [Lit. raise one's head into space].

མགོ་བོ་ (gowo) the head; va.—བཀྱགས་ to raise up one's head, to rise up; va.—སྐོར་; —འཁོར་ to be deceived, to be duped/ fooled/ conned ། དྲན་གཡོག་བསྐྱལ་བའི་ལམ་ལུགས་འོག་ནས་མགོ་བོ་བཀྱགས་ཐུབ་པ་རེད་ They were able to rise up from under the system of slavery. ། ཁོ་ཚོའི་ཁྱབ་བསྒྲགས་ལ་མགོ་བོ་འཁོར་བ་རེད་ They were duped by their publicity.

མགོ་བོ་ཡུག་ཡུག (gowo jɔ̄gjɔɔ̀) nodding one's head (conveying "yes"); va.—བྱེད་.

མགོ་བོ་སྐྲ་མེད་ལ་རལ་པའི་ཁྲལ་ (gowo būmeèla rɛɛbɛ trɛ̄ɛ̀) levying a tax on sb. who doesn't have the means to pay it [Lit. levying a tax for matted dense hair on a bald person].

མགོ་བོ་སྤྱི་ཐེར་ (gowo jīder) sm. མགོ་དམར་པོ་.

མགོ་བོ་ཅི་བོ་ (gowo ciwo) sm. མགོ་དམར་པོ་.

མགོ་བོ་རྨོངས་ (gowo mōŋ) ignorant.

མགོ་བོ་སྙུང་སྙུང་ (gowo ñūŋñuŋ) a cone shaped head, an elongated head.

མགོ་བོ་ཞོ་འདྲག (gowo shodaà) beating (head) to a pulp ། རྒྱུག་པ་གཞུས་ནས་མགོ་བོ་ཞོ་འདྲག་འདྲ་པོ་བཟོས་བཞག (He) hit him with a stick and beat his head to a pulp (made his head look like yogurt) [Lit. head like yogurt].

མགོ་བོ་ཟགས་ (gowo saà) vi. to have grain fall to the ground when harvesting due the harvest being too late.

མགོ་བོག་རྒྱག (gobog gyaà) sm. མགོ་བོ་ཟགས་.

མགོ་ཅི་བོ་ (go ciwo) sm. མགོ་དམར་པོ་.

མགོ་བྱེད་ (go cɛɛ̀) sm. འགོ་བྱེད་.

མགོ་སླང་ (go lāŋ) see མགོ་ལེན་.

མགོ་འབུར་ (gobur) 1. vi. to come out, to appear ། རྩ་མགོ་འབུལ་བ་དང་སེམས་ཅན་བཟས་སོང་ As soon as the grass came out the animals ate it. 2. vi. to have freedom to act/ decide ། འགོ་ཁྲིད་དེས་ལས་བྱེད་པ་ཚོ་མགོ་འབུལ་འཇུག་གི་མེད་པ་རེད་ The leader is not giving the officials any freedom to act.

མགོ་འབུལ་ལུས་འབུལ་ (gombüü lümbüü) surrendering, capitulating; va.—བྱེད་.

མགོ་སྦོས་ (goböö) sm. མགོ་འཐོམ་.

མགོ་སྦོས་མིག་འཁྲུལ་ (goböö miŋdrüü) sm. stunned/ dazed and hallucinating.

མགོ་སྦྱར་མིག་གི་བྱ་ར་ (gojar miìgi cara) having been given the authority, one is expected to exercise it and know what is going on ། མགོ་སྦྱར་མིག་གི་བྱ་རའི་དཔེ་ལྟར་རྫོང་འོག་གི་གནས་ཚུལ་རྣམས་རྫོང་སྡོད་ནས་རྟོགས་ཐུབ་པ་བྱ་དགོས་ Like the proverb "the eyes stuck on the head," the situation in the district is one that the district commissioner must know.

མགོ་སྦྲེད་ (godel) sm. མགོ་འཁོར་, 2.

མགོ་སྦྲེལ་ (godel) 1. tying animals side-by-side. 2. continuously, without break ། ཉིན་མཚན་མགོ་སྦྲེལ་ནས་བཟོ་གྲྭའི་ལས་ཀ་བྱེད་ཀྱི་ཡོད་པ་རེད་ They worked in the factory day and night without break.

མགོ་མ་ (goma) sm. ཐོག་མ་.

མགོ་མ་ཐོན་ (gomadön) 1. vi. to miscarry. 2. neg. of མགོ་ཐོན་.

མགོ་མ་འཚོས་གོང་ནས་ལྕེ་ལ་བརྣབ་པ་ (gomadzöögoŋnɛ jēla ñɔ̄bbɔ̀) doing sth. too early [Lit. grabbing the tongue before the head is cooked].

མགོ་མི་ (gomi) headman, leader.

མགོ་མི་ན་བ་ཐོ་གུས་བསྡམས་ (go minawa tīgüü dam) feigning, pretending [Lit. to tie one's head although one does not have a headache].

མགོ་མི་འཚོས་ (go midzöö) vi. to not understand.

མགོ་མེད་མཇུག་དུམ་ (gomɛɛ̀ jugdum) sm. མགོ་མེད་མཇུག་མེད་.

མགོ་མེད་མཇུག་མེད་ (gomɛɛ̀ jugmeè) 1. disorderly, chaotic, anarchic. leaderless, upside down, topsy-turvy. 2. disrespectful.

མགོ་མེད་ཐུག་མེད་ (gomɛɛ̀ tūùmeè) see མགོ་མེད་མཇུག་མེད་.

མགོ་མེད་དཔུང་རོང་ (gomeè būŋroŋ) anarchy, disorder, chaotic.

མགོ་མེད་གཞུག་མེད་ (gomeè shugmeè) sm. མགོ་མེད་མཇུག་མེད་.

མགོ་རྨོས་ (goñöö) sm. མགོ་འཐོམ་.

མགོ་དམར་ (go mār) 1. sm. མགོ་དམར་པོ་. 2. a type of kite with a red top.

མགོ་དམར་པོ་ (go mārbo) bald.

མགོ་དམར་སོ་བྱུད་ (gomar sōbüü) old [Lit. bald and toothless].

མགོ་རྨོངས་ (gomoŋ) sm. མགོ་བོ་རྨོངས་.

མགོ་རྨོངས་བློ་འཐོམས་ (gomoŋ lōndom) ignorant and confused/ dazed/ stunned.

མགོ་སྨད་ (go mɛ̄ɛ̀) hanging one's head down; va.—བྱེད་.

མགོ་སྨན་ (gomɛn) 1. headache medicine. 2. sm. ཡ་མ་རྐྱང་.

མགོ་ཙ་ (godza) top and bottom; va.—སྒྲིག to put things in good order (from top to bottom); vi.—འགྲིག to be arranged in good order.

མགོ་ཙ་འགྲིགས་པོ་ (godza drigbu) in good order.

མགོ་ཙ་འདྲེག (godza dreg) va. to cut the tops of plants to make them even.

མགོ་རྩིས་ (godzii) shung. a unit of taxation in tt. equal to 20 yak.

མགོ་རྩོམ་ (godzom) sm. འགོ་རྩོམ་.

མགོ་ཚང་ (godzaŋ) size (circumference) of a hat/ cap ། མགོ་ཚང་དམ་པོ་ A tight fitting hat/ cap.

མགོ་ཚོད་ (gō tsöö) vi. to know, to understand ། ངས་

འདི་ཙ་བ་ནས་མགོ་ཚོད་ཀྱི་མི་འདུག I do not understand this at all.

མགོ་ཚོད་པོ་ (go tsööbo) sb. who knows how to do things, sb. who understands things easily.

མགོ་ཚོད་ལ་མ་ཚོད་ (go tsööla madzöö) sb. who doesn't understand things clearly.

མགོ་མཚུངས་པ་ (go tsūŋba) same (race/ type/ kind).

མགོ་འཚོས་ (go tsöö) vi. to comprehend, to understand.

མགོ་འཛིན་ (go dzin) sm. འགོ་འཛིན་.

མགོ་འཛུག (go dzug) sm. འགོ་འཛུགས་.

མགོ་ཞྭ་ (gosha) hat, headgear.

མགོ་ཤགས་ཤགས་ (go shagshaà) vehemently, fiercely (usu. for arguments) ¶ དེ་རིང་ང་ཚོ་སྲིད་དོན་སྐོར་རྩོད་པ་མགོ་ཤགས་ཤགས་བརྒྱབ་པ་ཡིན་ Today we had a vehement argument on politics.

མགོ་གཞུག (gushuù) sm. མགོ་མཇུག.

མགོ་གཞུག་ལོག (gushuù lɔ̀ɔ) sm. མགོ་མཇུག་ལྡོག.

མགོ་གཞུག་སློག (gushuù lɔ̄ɔ) sm. མགོ་མཇུག་སློག.

མགོ་བཞར་ (go shar) va. to cut hair, to give a haircut.

མག་ཟླ་བ་ (go dawa) the 11th month of the Tibetan lunar calendar.

མགོ་གཟེར་ (goser) severe headache, sharp pain in the head; vi.—རྒྱག to have a severe headache.

མགོ་བཟི་འཐོམ་ལང་ (go sitom laŋ) vi. to feel dizzy/ giddy.

མགོ་འོག་མཇིང་ཚུད་ (gowɔ̀ɔ jiŋdzüü) sm. མགོ་འོག་ལུས་ཚུད་.

མགོ་འོག་ལུས་ཚུད་ (gowɔ̀ɔ lüüdzüü) getting those under one to obey or carry out orders.

མགོ་ཡང་ (goyaŋ) 1. a changeable/ unsteady person. 2. a loose woman; va.—བྱེད་.

མགོ་ཡང་འཁྱམ་མོ་ (goyaŋ kyāmbo) a loose woman.

མགོ་ཡན་ (goyɛn) a person with no respect/ regard for others.

མགོ་ཡར་བཀྱག (go yaa gyāà) va. to hold/ raise up one's head.

མགོ་ཡི་བྱ་རལ་ལ་མིག་བསྐོས་ (goyi carala miigöö) appointing a leader with vision/ ability.

མགོ་ཡུ་འཁོར་ (guyu kɔ̄ɔ) vi. to feel giddy/ dizzy ¶ ཁོ་མོ་ཊའི་ནང་མགོ་ཡུ་འཁོར་སོང་ He felt dizzy in the car.

མགོ་ཡུར་འཁོར་ (guyuu kɔ̄ɔ) sm. མགོ་ཡུ་འཁོར་.

མགོ་ཡེངས་ (go yeŋ) 1. vi. to be absorbed/ engrossed/ oblivious. 2. vi. to have one's mind wander.

མགོ་ཡོད་མཇུག་མེད་ (goyöö jugmeè) not achieving completion/ success [Lit. having a head, not having a tail].

མགོ་ཡོད་མཇུག་ཡོད་ (goyöö jugyöö) 1. achieving completion/ success. 2. orderly, top and bottom adhering to their places [Lit. having a head, having a tail].

མགོ་ཡོམ་ཡོམ་ (go yomyom) dizzy, giddy; vi.—བྱེད་.

མགོ་ཡོར་ (goyɔɔ) leaning/ moving one's head from side to side; va.—བྱེད་.

མགོ་ཡོར་ཡོར་ (go yɔɔyɔɔ) sm. མགོ་ཡོར་.

མགོ་གཡུག་གཡུག (go yūùyuù) shaking one's head (conveying "no"); va.— གཏོང་; —བྱེད་.

མགོ་གཡེང་ (go yeŋ) sm. མགོ་ཡེངས་.

མགོ་གཡོགས་ (go yɔ̀ɔ) sm. མགོ་སྐོར་.

མགོ་གཡོགས་མགོ་བསྐོར་ (goyɔ̀ɔ gogɔɔ) sm. མགོ་སྐོར་.

མགོ་རལ་ (gorɛɛ) scars on the head.

མགོ་རས་ (gorɛɛ) scarf.

མགོ་རིལ་ (gorii) 1. shaved head. 2. slang. monk.

མགོ་རུལ་རྣ་བས་མི་ཚོར་ (gorüü nawɛ midzɔɔ) unaware of what is going on around one [Lit. even though the head is rotten the ear doesn't know].

མགོ་རུས་ (gorüü) skull.

མགོ་རྡ་དམ་ (go radam) shung. a seal put on the horns of livestock so that the horn can be shown to the owner if the animal dies.

མགོ་ལ་རྣ་འབྱར་ (gola nājar) selling sth. on condition that sth. else is also bought [Lit. the ear is stuck on the head].

མགོ་ལ་སྤུ་སྐྱེས་ (gola būgyeè) human beings [Lit. hair growing on the head].

མགོ་ལ་བབ་ (gola pəb) vi. fall on one's head, to fall on oneself ¶ ལས་འགན་འདི་ངའི་མགོ་ལ་བབས་པ་ཞིག་རེད་ The responsibility for this job has fallen on me.

མགོ་ལ་མེ་ཤོར་ (gola meshɔɔ) abbr. of མགོ་ལ་མེ་ཤོར་ཡང་འཕྱུར་ལོང་མི་འདུག.

མགོ་ལ་མེ་ཤོར་ཡང་འཕྱུར་ལོང་མི་འདུག (gola meshɔɔ) very busy [Lit. even though the head catches on fire, no time to rub the head].

མགོ་ལ་གཞུས་ (gola shüü) sm. མགོ་རྔང་.

མགོ་ལ་ཤི་རྟགས་ཕོག (gola shīdaà pɔ̀ɔ) vi. to have white hair grow as a sign of impending death.

མགོ་ལག (golag) head and hands; va.—ལེན་ to cut off the heads and hands of the enemy (as proof of having killed them); va.—འཁྱེར་ to leave as bride/ groom (or to separate from one's household) with no share or property (taking only one's head and hands).

མགོ་ལས་སྐྱེས་ (golɛ gyēè) the 10th month of the Tibetan lunar calendar.

མགོ་ལས་དཔུང་པ་མཐོ་བ་ (golɛɛ būŋwa tōwa) a subordinate who tries to assume the authority of a superior; —བྱེད་ [Lit. shoulder is higher than the head].

མགོ་ལས་རྨ་ཆེ་ (golɛɛ māje) a small problem getting out of hand, a small situation becoming large and out of control [Lit. the sore/ wound is bigger than the head].

མགོ་ལུང་ (goluŋ) shung. sm. མགོ་ཁྲིད་ or འགོ་འདྲེན་.

མགོ་ལུས་མཚུངས་པོ་ (golüü tsūŋbo) a well-proportioned person.

མགོ་ལེན་ (golen) accepting submission, receiving surrender; va.—བྱེད་. 2. va. to behead.

མགོ་ལེན་བསྟེན་བསྐྱིལ་ (golen dēngyii) accepting submission/ surrender/ capitulation from sb. and then keeping and using them.

མགོ་ལེབ་ (goleb) flat head.

མགོ་ལོག (golɔg) 1. making a mess, causing trouble/ disorder; va.—བཟོ་; —རྩེ་ to make a mess of things, to cause trouble and disorder. 2. an ethnic Tibetan group living in Qinghai Province.

མགོ་ལོག་བོད་རིགས་རང་སྐྱོང་ཁུལ་ (golɔ̀ɔ pöörii raŋgyoŋgüü) Golok Tibetan Autonomous Area.

མགོ་ཤ་ (gosha) meat from head of animals.

མགོ་ཤིག (goshii) head lice.

མགོ་ཤུ་ (goshu) a sore on the head.

མགོ་ཤུབས་ (goshub) sleeveless poncho-type gown/ dress worn by the women of Kongpo.

མགོ་སུག (gosug) head and feet of animals.

མགོ་སེ་ (gose) grayish hair.

མགོ་སེར་ (goser) 1. blond hair [Lit. yellow head]. 2. derogatory term for caucasions.

མགོ་སྲ་མོ་དང་ཀོ་བ་མཐུག་པོ་ (go drāmo daŋ gōwa tūgbu) stubborn [Lit. hard head and thick skin/ leather].

མགོ་སླ་པོ་ (go lābo) a person who is easily swayed/ changeable.

མགོན་ (gön) abbr. མགོན་པོ་.

མགོན་སྐྱབས་ (göngyəb) sm. མགོན་པོ་.

མགོན་སྐྱབས་དཔུང་བྲལ་ (göngyəb būŋtrɛɛ) having no savior/ protector.

མགོན་སྐྱོབ་ (göngyob) sm. མགོན་པོ་.

མགོན་སྐྱོབ་དཔུང་གཉེན་ (göngyob būŋñen) savior, protector; va.—གནང་ to help/ protect.

མགོན་ཁང་ (göngaŋ) chapel of protective deities.

མགོན་གཉེན་ (gönñen) abbr. མགོན་སྐྱོབ་དཔུང་གཉེན་.

མགོན་པོ་ (gombo) 1. protector, defender, savior. 2. the protective deity Mahakala. 3. sm. མགོན་པོ་བ་. 4. honorific term of address for high lamas and rulers.

མགོན་པོ་གང་ (gombogaŋ) honorific term of address

for high lamas and rulers ། མགོན་པོ་གང་རིས་སྲིད་ཇུས་གསར་པ་གཏན་འཁེལ་གནང་བ་རེད་ He (the savior/ ruler) decided on a new policy.

མགོན་པོ་བ་ (gönbowa) monk who does prayers to protective deities.

མགོན་བླ་ (gönla) sm. མགོན་པོ་བ་.

མགོན་མེད་ (gönmeè) without a protector, helpless.

མགོན་མེད་སྐྱབས་མེད་ (gönmeè gyəbmeè) in a difficult situation, helpless [Lit. without a protector, without a savior].

མགྱོགས་ (gyog) abbr. of མགྱོགས་པོ་.

མགྱོགས་སྐྱོད་མེ་འཁོར་ (gyoggyöö megɔɔ) sm. express train.

མགྱོགས་སྐྱོད་རླངས་འཁོར་ (gyoggyöö lāŋgɔɔ) express bus/ car.

མགྱོགས་ཁྱད་འགྲན་ (gyoggyɛɛ̀ trɛn) va. to race competitively (usu. for horses).

མགྱོགས་འཁོར་ (gyoggɔɔ) 1. express train/ bus. 2. flywheel.

མགྱོགས་ག (gyogga) faster, quicker.

མགྱོགས་གྲུ་ (gyogdru) motorboat, speedboat.

མགྱོགས་བགྲོད་ (gyogdröö) speed.

མགྱོགས་བགྲོད་འཁོར་ལམ་ (gyogdröö kɔ̄ɔlam) express road, highway, turnpike.

མགྱོགས་བགྲོད་མེ་འཁོར་ (gyogdröö mēgɔɔ) express train.

མགྱོགས་བགྲོད་དམག་སྐྱོད་ (gyogdröö māggyöö) fast march.

མགྱོགས་བགྲོད་གཞུང་ལམ་ (gyogdröö shuŋlam) express road, highway, turnpike.

མགྱོགས་བགྲོད་རླངས་འཁོར་ (gyogdröö lāŋgɔɔ) express bus/ car.

མགྱོགས་མགྱོགས་བྱས་ན་འགོར་འགོར་ (gyogdröö cɛ̀ɛna gɔ̄ɔgɔɔ) sm. མགྱོགས་མགྱོགས་བྱས་ཙང་འགོར་འགོར་.

མགྱོགས་མགྱོགས་བྱས་ཙང་འགོར་འགོར་ (gyogdröö cɛ̀ɛdzaŋ gɔ̄ɔgɔɔ) trying to do sth. quickly causes it to take much longer, haste makes waste [Lit. because did fast, slow slow].

མགྱོགས་འགྲོ་མགྱོགས་མཇལ་ (gyogdro gyogjɛɛ) going quickly and meeting quickly.

མགྱོགས་རྒོལ་ (gyoggöö) quick attack.

མགྱོགས་བཅོས་སློད་ (gyogjöö lȫö) va. to do badly because it was done quickly/ hurriedly/ without care.

མགྱོགས་ཆང་ (gyogjaŋ) a cup of beer (chang) served as a penalty when a person finishes drinking a cup of beer before the drinking song is over.

མགྱོགས་གདམ་ (gyogdam) allegro.

མགྱོགས་གཏོར་ (gyogdɔɔ) sm. མགྱོགས་རྒོལ་.

མགྱོགས་རྟགས་ཟིན་བཀོད་ (gyogdaà siŋgöö) stenography, shorthand.

མགྱོགས་ཐོན་མྱུར་ལོག (gyogdön ñurlɔɔ) going and returning quickly.

མགྱོགས་རྡུང་བྱེད་ (gyogduŋ cèè) va. to beat a drum/ etc. quickly.

མགྱོགས་ནས་མྱུར་དུ་ (gyognɛ ñurdu) very quickly/ fast.

མགྱོགས་སྣོན་ (gyognön) acceleration.

མགྱོགས་སྣོན་ཚད་ (gyognöndzɛɛ̀) rate of acceleration.

མགྱོགས་པ་ལྕག་གིས་བསྣུན་པ་ (gyogba jāàgi nȗmba) exhorting to go/ do faster when already going fast [Lit. hitting a speeding horse with a whip].

མགྱོགས་པོ་ (gyogbo) fast, quick, rapid.

མགྱོགས་འཕྲིན་ (gyogdrin) fax; va.—གཏོང་.

མགྱོགས་ཁྲིས་ (gyogtrii) 1. sm. མགྱོགས་རྟགས་ཟིན་འགོད་. 2. sketch (drawing) ། མགྱོགས་ཁྲིས་རི་མོ་ A quick sketch.

མགྱོགས་མྱུར་ (gyoñur) quick, rapid ། ཁོ་མགྱོགས་མྱུར་ཐོན་གྱི་རེད་ He is leaving quickly.

མགྱོགས་མྱུར་དུ་ (gyoñurdu) quickly, rapidly.

མགྱོགས་ཚད་ (gyogdzɛɛ̀) 1. degree or rate of speed/ quickness/ fastness ། ལས་ཀའི་མགྱོགས་ཚད་མཐོ་རུ་བཏང་དགོས་ (You) have to increase the speed of doing the work. 2. speed limit.

མགྱོགས་ཚྭ་ (gyogdza) sm. གྲང་ཚྭ་.

མགྱོགས་ཟས་ (gyogsɛɛ̀) fast food.

མགྱོགས་ཡིག (gyogyii) cursive writing style.

མགྱོགས་རིས་ (gyogrii) sm. མགྱོགས་ཁྲིས་.

མགྱོགས་ལམ་ (gyoglam) shortcut.

མགྱོགས་ལོས་ (gyoglöö) how fast, how quick.

མགྱོགས་སུ་གཏོང་ (gyogsu dōŋ) va. to accelerate, to speed up.

མགྱོགས་སུ་གཏོང་བྱེད་འཕྲུལ་འཁོར་ (gyogsu dōŋcɛɛ̀ trȗȗgɔɔ) accelerator (machine).

མགྱོགས་སུམ་ (gyogsum) a race; va.—རྒྱུར་; —བགྲོད་ to race.

མགྲིན་ (drin) abbr. of མགྲིན་པ་.

མགྲིན་གླུ་ (drinlu) sm. མགྲིན་དབྱངས་.

མགྲིན་འགུགས་ (dringuù) sm. གདངས་འགུགས་.

མགྲིན་རྒྱན་ (dringyɛn) necklace.

མགྲིན་སྔོན་ (drinŋön) poet. power.

མགྲིན་གཅིག་གཅིག་མཐུན་ (drinjig jīgdün) sm. མགྲིན་གཅིག་ཏུ་.

མགྲིན་གཅིག་ཏུ་ (drinjigdu) as with one voice, unanimously, in unison.

མགྲིན་གཅིག་ནས་ (drinjignɛ) sm. མགྲིན་གཅིག་ཏུ་.

མགྲིན་སྙན་ (drinñɛn) a beautiful voice.

མགྲིན་སྙན་བྱ་རིགས་ (drinñɛn carig) songbird, singing bird.

མགྲིན་མདངས་ (drindaŋ) voice.

མགྲིན་ནག (drinnag) sm. མགྲིན་སྔོན་.

མགྲིན་ནད་ཚན་ཁག (drin nɛɛ̀ tsɛ̄ngaà) the ear, nose, throat, (E.N.T) department in a hospital.

མགྲིན་པ་ (drimbə) 1. neck, throat; va.—འདེགས་ to read/ sing/ talk in a loud voice.

མགྲིན་པ་འཛེར་ (drimbə dzer) sm. སྐད་འཛེར་.

མགྲིན་དབྱངས་ (drinyaŋ) voice.

མགྲིན་དབྱངས་གཅིག་གྱུར་ (drinyaŋ jīggyur) sm. མགྲིན་གཅིག་ཏུ་.

མགྲིན་མང་དབྱངས་གཅིག (drinmaŋ yāŋjii) shung. sm. མགྲིན་གཅིག་ཏུ་.

མགྲིན་ཚབ་ (drindzəb) spokesman; va.—བྱེད་ to act as spokesman, to speak on behalf of.

མགྲིན་ཚབ་པ་ (drindzəbə) spokesman.

མགྲིན་བཟང་ (drinsaŋ) a strong/ loud voice.

མགྲིན་ལམ་ཡངས་པོར་ཕྱེ་ (drinlam yaŋbor cē) va. to open the throat wide (when singing).

མགྲོན་ (drön) 1. abbr. for མགྲོན་པོ་. 2. shung. abbr. for ཤོད་མགྲོན་ or རྩེ་མགྲོན་ or མགྲོན་གཉེར་ཆེ་མོ་.

མགྲོན་སྐྱེལ་ (dröngyee) passenger transportation ། མགྲོན་སྐྱེལ་ཁང་ Passenger transportation office/ bureau.

མགྲོན་སྐྱོང་ (dröngyoŋ) taking care of/ entertaining a guest.

མགྲོན་ཁང་ (drönkaŋ) guest house, inn.

མགྲོན་གུར་ (drönkur) shung. the guest tents put up for foreign officials in Lhasa during the Opera Festival.

མགྲོན་གྱི་གཙོ་བོ་ (dröngi dzōwo) chief guest, guest of honor.

མགྲོན་བརྒྱུད་ (dröngyüü) transmitting a message via the བཀའ་མགྲོན་ or རྩེ་མགྲོན་ or ཤོད་མགྲོན་ ། ངས་བཀའ་ཤག་ལ་མགྲོན་བརྒྱུད་སྙན་ཞུ་ཕུལ་བ་ཡིན་ I sent a request to the Kashag via the Kashag's aide (བཀའ་མགྲོན་).

མགྲོན་ཆེ་ (drönce) shung. abbr. of མགྲོན་གཉེར་ཆེན་མོ་.

མགྲོན་ཇ་ (drönca) tea served to a guest; va.—གཏོང་ to serve a guest tea [Lit. guest tea].

མགྲོན་གཉེར་ (drönñer) steward of a aristocratic family or labrang.

མགྲོན་གཉེར་ཆེན་མོ་ (drönñer cēmmo) shung. Lord Chamberlain in tt.

མགྲོན་གདུག་ཁང་ (drönduùgaŋ) a room/ hall where guests are met.

མགྲོན་གཏོང་ (drön dōŋ) va. to give a party ། གཅེན་མོས་ཕྲན་ལ་མགྲོན་བཏང་སོང་ My older sister gave me a party.

མགྲོན་བསྙེན་ (drön dēn) va. to entertain a guest.

མགྲོན་ཐུག་ཁང་ (drönduùgaŋ) sm. མགྲོན་གདུག་ཁང་.

མགྲོན་དུ་འགུགས་ (dröndu guù) sm. མགྲོན་དུ་འབོད་.

མགྲོན་དུ་བོས་ (dröndu pöö) p. of མགྲོན་དུ་འབོད་.

མགྲོན་དུ་འབོད་ (dröndu böö) va. to invite.

མགྲོན་དྲུང་ཁང་ (dröndruŋgaŋ) shung. office under Kashag that consists of the བཀའ་དྲུང་ and བཀའ་མགྲོན་.

མགྲོན་བདག (dröndaà) host ¶ མགྲོན་བདག་རྒྱལ་ཁབ་ Host nation.

མགྲོན་བརྡ་ (drönda) invitation; va.— འབུལ་; —གཏོང་ to send an invitation, to invite.

མགྲོན་བརྡའི་ཤོག་ལྷེ་ (dröndee shɔ̄ɔle) sm. མགྲོན་ཤོག.

མགྲོན་གནས་ (drönnɛɛ̀) seats/ section for guests.

མགྲོན་པ་ (drömba) vocal cords.

མགྲོན་པོ་ (drömbo) 1. guest, passenger, traveler. 2. slang term for male homosexual partner.

མགྲོན་པོའི་གཙོ་བོ་ (drömbö dzōwo) guest of honor.

མགྲོན་བུ་ (drömbu) white cowry shell.

མགྲོན་པོས་ལུས་རྩལ་རུ་ཁག (drömböö lüüdzɛɛ rugaà) visiting team.

མགྲོན་བྱེད་ (drön cèè) sm. སྣེ་ལེན་བྱེད་.

མགྲོན་འབོད་ (drömböö) an invitation; va, —ཞུ་; —གནང་ to invite ¶ མགྲོན་འབོད་གནང་བ་ལྟར་བཅར་ (I) came in accordance with the invitation.

མགྲོན་ཞུགས་ (drönshuù) va. to go as a guest ¶ ཁོང་མགྲོན་ཞུགས་སུ་ཕེབས་པ་རེད་ He went as a guest.

མགྲོན་ཟས་ (drönsɛɛ̀) food for guests.

མགྲོན་ཟོག་གྲུ་གཟིངས་ (drönsɔɔ̀ trudzin) a ship that carries cargo and passengers.

མགྲོན་ཡིག (drönyii) sm. མགྲོན་ཤོག.

མགྲོན་གཡོག་ (drönyɔɔ̀) waiter, hotel servant.

མགྲོན་རོགས་ (drönroò) guest other than the guest of honor.

མགྲོན་ལས་ (drönlɛɛ̀) shung. abbr. རྩེ་མགྲོན་ and ལས་ཚན་པ་.

མགྲོན་ལོ་གཉིས་ (drönlo ñìì) abbr. རྩེ་མགྲོན་ and ལོ་ཙཱ་(བ་).

མགྲོན་ཤོག (drönsɔɔ̀) invitation card.

མགྲོན་བསུ་ཁང་ (drönsugaŋ) room or house where guests and visitors are welcomed/ met, a reception room/ house.

མགྲོན་བསུར་འགྲོ་ (drönsur dro) va. to go to receive/ welcome a guest.

འགག: p. འགགས་; f. འགག (gaà) vi. to be blocked/ stopped/ obstructed ¶ ཡུར་བུ་འགགས་བཞག The drain is blocked.

འགག་ཀྱོག (gaàgyoò) sm. ཆག་ཁྱུག, 2.

འགག་སྒོ་ (gaàgo) 1. obstacle, obstruction, barrier; va.—བརྒྱལ་ to break/ pass through a barrier or obstacle. 2. customs (the toll/ duty/ taxes) ¶ འགག་སྒོའི་ནང་གཏོང་ Custom's duty on imports.

འགག་སྒོ་བརྒྱལ་ (gaàgo gɛɛ) see འགག་སྒོ་.

འགག་སྒོ་སྤྱི་གཉེར་ལས་ཁངས་ (gaàgo jiñer lɛɛ̀guŋ) custom's head office.

འགག་སྒོ་ལས་ཁངས་ (gaàgo lɛɛ̀guŋ) custom's office.

འགག་སྒོའི་ཞིབ་བཤེར་པ་ (gaàgö shibsherba) custom's inspection officer.

འགག་སྒོའི་ནང་གཏོང་ (gaàgö nandoŋ) custom's duty on imports.

འགག་སྒོའི་ཕྱིར་གཏོང་ (gaàgö cirdoŋ) custom's duty on exports.

འགག་ཆ་ཞུ་ (gagja shu) to request to not do sth. (h.) ¶ ཁོང་བོད་ལ་ཕེབས་རྒྱུར་འགག་ཆ་ཞུས་པ་རེད་ They requested him not go to Tibet.

འགག་སྟུང་ (gagduŋ) a vest worn by monks.

འགག་དོག་པོ་ (gaà togbo) 1. narrow road on a precipice. 2. a situation of great peril. 3. sm. འགག་དྲག་པོ་. 4. critical point/ issue/ juncture.

འགག་དོན་ (gagdön) critical point, the most important issue ¶ རྩོམ་ཡིག་གི་འགག་དོན་ལ་གོ་བ་ཡག་པོ་ལེན་དགོས་ You have to be able to comprehend the most important point in the article.

འགག་དོགས་ཟས་སྤང་ (gagdog sɛɛ̀baŋ) refraining from doing sth. that is necessary due to fear, losing a good opportunity/ advantage due to a minor risk [Lit. give up eating for fear of choking].

འགག་དོགས་ཟས་སྲུང་ (gagdog sɛɛ̀suŋ) sm. འགག་དོགས་ཟས་སྤང་.

འགག་དྲི་ (gɔgdri) belch, belching; va. and vi.—རྒྱག to belch.

འགག་མདོ་ (gagdo)1. sm. འགག་རྩ་. 2. a crossroads ¶ ཤང་ཀང་དེ་ཚོང་ལས་ཀྱི་འགག་མདོ་ཞིག་ཡིན་ Hong Kong is a crossroads for business.

འགག་རྡོ་ (gagdo) obstacle, barrier, obstruction.

འགག་ནད་ (gagnɛɛ̀) a throat disease (of animals).

འགག་གནད་ (gagnɛɛ̀) sm. འགག་དོན་.

འགག་གནད་མཉམ་སྒྲོལ་ (gagnɛɛ̀ ñāmdröö) breaking a deadlock through joint effort, va.—བྱེད་.

འགག་པ་ (gagba) 1. guard. 2. shung. a guard/ aide of a high official. 3. sm. འགག.

འགག་པ་མེད་པ་ (gagba mèèba) unhindered, unobstructed.

འགག་འཕྲེང་ (gagdreŋ) gorge.

འགག་བཙིར་ (gagdzir) strangling, choking; va.—གཏོང་.

འགག་རྩ་ (gagdza) a vital/ decisive/ critical/ key point or issue; va.—ཐུག to have reached or come face-to-face with a vital/ decisive/ critical/ key issue ¶ འགག་རྩ་ཆེ་བའི་ས་གནས་ Areas that are very vital. ¶ ད་ལྟ་ལུང་པ་དེ་གཉིས་དབར་གྲོས་མོལ་བྱ་རྒྱུའི་འགག་རྩ་ཞིག་ལ་སླེབས་ཡོད་པ་རེད་ Now the discussions between the two countries had reached a critical point.

འགག་རྩའི་འགག་རྩ་ (gagdzɛ gagdza) the absolutely most vital/ decisive/ critical/ key point or issue.

འགག་ཚབ་ (gagdzəb) shung. a person acting as a substitute (འགག་པ་) guard/ aide of a high official.

འགག་རིང་ (gəgriŋ) a sleeveless robe worn by monks.

འགག་ལམ་ (gaglam) a narrow road on a precipice.

འགག་ལས་གྲོལ་ (gaglɛ dröö) sm. འགག་སྒོ་བརྒྱལ་.

འགགས་ (gaà) p. of འགག.

འགགས་དོགས་ཟས་སྤང་ (gagdɔɔ̀ sɛɛ̀baŋ) sm. འགག་དོགས་ཟས་སྤང་.

འགངས་ (gaŋ) importance, value ¶ འགངས་ཆེན་ལས་འགན་ A responsibility of great importance.

འགངས་གལ་ (gaŋgɛɛ) sm. འགངས་ཆེ་.

འགངས་ཆུང་ (gaŋjuŋ) little value/ importance.

འགངས་ཆེ་ (gaŋce) great value, important.

འགངས་ཆེན་པོ་ (gaŋ cēmbo) great value, important,valuable.

འགངས་ཆེའི་ནུས་པ་ (gancee nüüba) important result.

འགངས་གནད་ (gaŋnɛɛ̀) sm. འགངས་.

འགངས་ལ་ཐུག་ན་ཕ་སྤུན་མེད་ (gaŋla tūūnə pābün mɛɛ̀) when the matter/ issue is very important, parents and relatives should not matter.

འགད་: p. བཀད་; f. དགད་: p. ཁོད་ (gɛɛ̀) va. to crack/ split open.

འགན་ (gɛn) 1. responsibility; va.—ལེན་ to take responsibility ¶ ངས་ལས་ཀ་འདི་འགན་ལེན་ཆོག I will take responsibility for this job.

འགན་དཀྲི་ (gɛndri) 1. va. to charge/ entrust with responsibility, to hold responsible ¶ ནོར་འཁྲུལ་དེའི་འགན་ཁོ་ལ་དཀྲིས་པ་རེད་ They held him responsible for that mistake. 2. a responsibility ¶ འདི་ངའི་འགན་དཀྲི་རེད་. This is my responsibility.

འགན་དཀྲིས་ (gɛndrii) p. of འགན་དཀྲི་.

འགན་བསྐུར་ (gɛngur) sm. འགན་དཀྲི་.

འགན་ཁག (gɛn kāà) 1. responsibility, blame ¶ ཁང་པ་མེ་སྐྱོན་ཤོར་བའི་འགན་ཁག་ཁོང་ལ་བྱུང་བ་རེད་ The blame for the house catching on fire fell on him. 2. a guarantor.

འགན་ཁུར་གྱི་དགོངས་པ་ (gɛngurgi gɔŋba) sm. འགན་ཁུར་གྱི་འདུ་ཤེས་.

འགན་ཁུར་ (gɛnkur) 1. responsibility. 2. p. of འགན་འཁུར་.

འགན་ཁུར་གྱི་འདུ་ཤེས་ (gɛnkurgi tusheè) sense of responsibility.

འགན་ཁུར་གྱི་ལམ་ལུགས་ (gɛnkurgi ləmluù) system of job responsibility.

འགན་ཁུར་གྱི་བསམ་པ་ (genkurgi sāmba) sm. འགན་ཁུར་གྱི་འདུ་ཤེས་.

འགན་ཁུར་གཙོ་སྐྱོང་ (genkur dzōgyoŋ) taking the main charge/ responsibility.

འགན་ཁྱེར་ (gengyer) sm. འགན་ཁུར་.

འགན་འཁུར་ (gen kūr) 1. va. to take responsibility. 2. responsibility; va.—ལེན་; —བཞེས་ to take responsibility.

འགན་འཁུར་མཁན་ (gen kūrñen) person with responsibility, person in charge.

འགན་འཁུར་བ་ (gen kūrwa) sm. འགན་འཁུར་མཁན་.

འགན་འཁུར་བློ་མཐུན་ (genkur lōdün) comrade holding a position of responsibility.

འགན་འཁུར་མི་སྣ་ (genkur mina) people with responsibility ། འབྲེལ་ཡོད་སྡེ་ཁག་གི་འགན་འཁུར་མི་སྣ་ Officials of the related offices with responsibility.

འགན་འཁུར་ལམ་ལུགས་ (genkur ləmluù) sm. འགན་འཁུར་གྱི་ལམ་ལུགས་.

འགན་འཁུར་ལས་བྱེད་པ་ (genkur leèjeba) sm. འགན་འཁུར་མི་སྣ་.

འགན་འཁོར་རེས་ (gen kōōreè) responsibilities/ duties done in rotation or by turns; va.—བྱེད་ ། ཁང་པ་འདི་ནང་གཙང་སྦྲ་བྱ་རྒྱུ་འགན་འཁོར་རེས་བྱེད་ཀྱི་ཡོད་ In this house we do cleaning by turns.

འགན་འཁྲི་ (gentri) responsibility, duty ། ང་ལ་ཉོ་ཆ་རྒྱག་རྒྱུའི་འགན་འཁྲི་ཡོད་ I have the responsibility for doing shopping. ། འདི་ངའི་འགན་འཁྲི་རེད་ This is my responsibility.

འགན་འཁྲི་ཚད་བཀག་ཀུང་སི་ (gentri tseègaà gūŋsi) limited liability company.

འགན་འཁྲིའི་ལམ་ལུགས་ (gentrii ləmluù) "responsibility" system (implemented when communes were disbanded).

འགན་འཁྲིའི་ས་ཞིང་ (gentrii səshiŋ) a field that is part of the "responsibility" system.

འགན་བགོ་ (gen go) va. to share/ divide/ distribute responsibility.

འགན་སྒྲུབ་དམ་བཅའི་ཚོགས་ཆེན་ (gendrub tamce tsōgjen) rally at which people take an oath to fulfill their responsibilities.

འགན་ཆེ་ལམ་རིང་ (gence lamriŋ) the long road of carrying out a large responsibility.

འགན་འཇི་ (genji) hind. undershirt, T-shirt.

འགན་འཇིར་ (genjir) a brass ornament on top of temples and monasteries.

འགན་ལྗིད་ (genjii) sm. འགན་ལྗིད་པོ་.

འགན་ལྗིད་པོ་ (gen jiibu) 1. serious ། ན་ཚ་འགན་ལྗིད་པོ་ A serious illness. 2. a heavy responsibility ། ཁོ་ལ་ལས་ཀ་འགན་ལྗིད་པོ་གཅིག་སྤྲད་པ་རེད་ They gave him a job with heavy responsibility.

འགན་གཉེར་ (genñer) taking on a responsibility; va.—བྱེད་.

འགན་ནུས་ (gennüü) 1. abbr. responsibility and power ། ཁོང་གིས་རང་ཉིད་ཀྱི་འགན་ནུས་བེད་སྤྱོད་ཡག་པོ་བྱེད་ཐུབ་ཀྱི་མི་འདུག He was unable to use his responsibility and power. 2. the power or authority that adheres to a responsibility/ position; va.—བྱེད་ to exercise one's authority.

འགན་ནུས་སྡེ་ཚན་ (gennüü dedzen) an office that has power and responsibility.

འགན་བབ་ (gembəb) sm. འགན་བབས་.

འགན་བབ་བྱ་བ་ (gembəb cawa) the work for which you have responsibility.

འགན་བབས་ (gembəb) duty, responsibility.

འགན་བླངས་ (gen lāŋ) p. of འགན་ལེན་.

འགན་བློས་བཟོད་ (gen lōō söö) va. to be afraid of taking/ bearing responsibility ། ལས་ཀ་འདི་གོང་རིམ་ལ་སྙན་སེང་མ་ཞུས་པར་ངས་འགན་བློས་བཟོད་ཀྱི་མ་རེད་ Without discussing this work with the higher authorities I am afraid to take responsibility. ། ཁྱེད་རང་གིས་ལས་ཀ་འདི་འགན་བློས་བཟོད་པ་འདུག་གམ་ Can you handle the responsibility for doing this job?

འགན་དབང་ཚབ་འཛིན་ (genwaŋ tsāmdzin) acting on behalf of sb. else, holding authority in another's name ། སློབ་གྲྭའི་འགོ་ཁྲིད་བསྡད་མེད་སྐབས་སུ་རྡོ་རྗེ་ལགས་ཀྱིས་འགན་དབང་ཚབ་འཛིན་བྱས་པ་རེད་ During the time the school principal was not there, Dorje acted on his behalf.

འགན་དབང་འཛིན་ (genwaŋ dzin) va. to hold office, to hold authority ། ཁོང་གིས་སྲིད་འཛིན་འགན་དབང་ལོ་བརྒྱད་རིང་བཟུང་བ་རེད་ He held the office of president for eight years.

འགན་དབྱུག (gen yūù) va. to give up a responsibility/ responsibilities.

འགན་གཙང་ (gendzaŋ) sm. འགན་གཙང་དུད་ཚང་ལ་སྤྲད་པའི་ལམ་ལུགས་.

འགན་གཙང་དུད་ཚང་ལ་སྤྲད་པའི་ལམ་ལུགས་ (gendzaŋ tüüdzaŋla dreèbe ləmluù) system of giving families responsibility for production.

འགན་གཙང་བཞི་ (gendzaŋ shi) four types of responsibility: units take responsibility for employees; schools take responsibility for their students; parents take responsibility for their children; and neighborhoods take responsibility for society's youths [this method was proposed as a way to promote law and order in society].

འགན་གཙང་ལམ་ལུགས་ (gendzaŋ ləmluù) the system of giving families responsibility for production (implemented at the time of disbanding communes) ། འགན་གཙང་ལམ་ལུགས་མི་གྲངས་ People who hold shares of "responsibility" land.

འགན་གཙང་ལེན་གྱི་གན་རྒྱ་ (gen dzāŋlengi kengya) a contract to take full responsibility (for production).

འགན་གཙང་ལེན་གྱི་འགན་འཁྲིའི་ལམ་ལུགས་ (gen dzāŋlengi gendrii ləmluù) contract responsibility system.

འགན་འཛིན་ (gendzin) person in authority ། ཁོང་ལས་ཁུངས་འདིའི་འགན་འཛིན་རེད་ He is the person in charge of this office.

འགན་འཛིན་ (gen dzin) va. to hold authority.

འགན་འཛིན་པ་ (gendzinba) person in authority, person in charge of an office.

འགན་འཛིན་དབང་ཆ་ (gendzin wāŋja) the right to be in charge/ in authority ། ང་ལ་ལས་ཁུངས་འདིའི་འགན་འཛིན་དབང་ཆ་ཡོད་པ་མ་རེད་ I don't have authority in this office.

འགན་འཛིན་ཡུན་ཚད་ (gendzin yündzeè) term of office, period of appointment/ authority.

འགན་འཛིར་ (gendzir) sm. འགན་འཇིར་.

འགན་འཛོལ་ (gendzöö) negligent or derelict in fulfilling responsibility; vi.—ཤོར་ to be derelict in fulfilling one's responsibilities ། འགོ་ཁྲིད་ཀྱིས་འགན་འཛོལ་ཤོར་བར་བརྟེན་བཟོ་གྲྭ་འདི་ལ་མེ་སྐྱོན་བྱུང་བ་རེད་ Because the leader was negligent in carrying out his responsibility, the factory had a fire.

འགན་འཛོལ་རང་དྲི་ (gendzöö randri) holding oneself responsible for mistakes/ negligence.

འགན་བཞག་བཟོ་པ་ (genshaà soba) contract workers.

འགན་བཞེས་ (gen sheè) h. of འགན་ལེན་.

འགན་བཞེས་དབུ་ཁྲིད་ (gensheè ūtrii) person in charge (h.).

འགན་གཟན་ (gensen) sm. འགན་སྲུར་.

འགན་བཟོད་ (gensöö) sm. འགན་བློས་བཟོད་.

འགན་ལམ་ (genlam) abbr. of འགན་གཙང་ལམ་ལུགས་.

འགན་ལེན་ (genlen) 1. responsibility; va.—བྱེད་ ། ལས་ཀ་འདིའི་ཐོག་འགན་ལེན་བྱེད་མཁན་མི་འདུག Concerning this work, there is no one taking responsibility. 2. guarantee, pledge; va. འགན་ལེན་; —བྱེད་ to guarantee, to pledge ། འཕུར་སྐྱོད་བདེ་འཇགས་ཡོང་བའི་འགན་ལེན་བྱེད་ཐུབ་པ་རེད་ (They) were able to guarantee safe flights. ། ཁོ་ཚོའི་སྟེང་ལ་སྐྱོན་མི་ཡོང་བའི་འགན་བླངས་པ་རེད་ They guaranteed that no harm will come to them.

འགན་ལེན་ལྔ་ (genlen ŋā) "the five guarantee" welfare system for elderly people without children or relatives and for disabled people.

འགན་ལེན་གསུམ་ (gɛnlen sūm) the "three guarantees" for students (free food, housing and clothes).

འགན་ཤོར་ (gɛn shɔ̄ɔ) vi. to be negligent or derelict in one's duty/ responsibility ¶ འགོ་ཁྲིད་ཀྱིས་འགན་ཤོར་བར་བརྟེན་བཟོ་གྲྭ་འདི་ལ་མེ་སྐྱོན་བྱུང་བ་རེད་ Because the leader was negligent in carrying out his responsibility the factory had a fire.

འགན་ཤོར་སྐྱོན་ཆ་ (gɛnshɔɔ gyōnja) accident due to negligence.

འགན་སྲུང་ (gɛnsuŋ) sm. འགན་ལེན་, 2.

འགན་སྲུང་ལྷ་ (gɛnsuŋŋa) sm. འགན་ལེན་ལྷ་.

འགབ་ (gəb) vi. to be appropriate, to be fitting/ right/ proper ¶ གནད་དོན་ཐག་གཅོད་བྱེད་སྟངས་ཇི་འགབ་འཕྲལ་དུ་བཀའ་གསལ་ཡོད་པ་ཞུ། Please tell (me) at once what would be the proper way of settling this issue. 2. abbr. of འགབ་གཤམ་.

འགབ་ཁུང་ (gəbguŋ) back of the knee.

འགབ་ཐུང་ (gəbduŋ) a short hem (of a dress).

འགབ་མཐའ་ (gəbda) sm. འགན་གཤམ་.

འགབ་མཐུན་ (gəbdün) illicit/ secret sexual intercourse; va.—བྱེད་.

འགབ་པ་ (gəbbə) suitable, appropriate.

འགབ་པོ་ (gəbbo) appropriate, fitting ¶ བཀའ་མོལ་འགབ་པོ་གཅིག་གནང་སོང་ (He) made an appropriate speech.

འགབ་མ་ (gəbma) lower.

འགབ་མིན་ (gəbmin) inappropriate, unfitting, unsuitable.

འགབ་ལ་ (gəbla) behind, at the back, later ¶ ཁྱེད་རང་འགབ་ལ་ཕེབས་ Please come later.

འགབ་གཤམ་ (gəbsham) the hem (on clothes).

འགམ་: p. **འགམས་**; f. **འགམ་**; imp. **འགམས་** (gam) va. to eat tsamba dry without mixing in any liquid ¶ རྩམ་པ་འགམས་པ་རེད་ (He) ate dry barley tsamba flour.

འགམ་གན་ (gamgɛn) greedy, avaricious, gluttonous.

འགམ་ཕྱེ་ (gamce) tsampa (for eating dry without adding in any liquid).

འགའ་ (ga) 1. sm. འགའ་ཤིག. 2. a thick cotton material.

འགའ་ཆེན་ (gajen) quite a few, a good many, quite a lot, quite some time ¶ ང་ལྷ་སར་སླེབས་ནས་འགའ་ཆེན་ཕྱིན་སོང་ It has been some time since I came to Lhasa. ¶ ཁོས་བྱི་རིལ་འགའ་ཆེན་བཟས་སོང་ He ate quite a lot of candy. ¶ ཚོགས་འདུར་མི་འགའ་ཆེན་སླེབས་བཞག Quite a few people came to the meeting today.

འགའ་ཙམ་ (gadzam) just a few, only a little ¶ དེ་རིང་མི་འགའ་ཙམ་ལས་སླེབས་མི་འདུག Today, just a few people came.

འགའ་ཤིག (gashig) some, several, a few ¶ མི་འགའ་ཤིག་འབྱོར་འདུག A few people have arrived.

འགའ་རབ་ (garəb) sm. འགའ་ཆེན་.

འགའ་རུ་ (garu) metal pot/ jar.

འགའ་རེ་ (gare) sm. འགའ་ཤིག.

འགའ་ལོ་ (galo) a type of boot worn in Pembo.

འགའ་ཤས་ (gashɛɛ̀) sm. འགའ་ཤིག.

འགར་ (gar) some, sometimes ¶ ཁོང་སྐབས་འགར་ངའི་ནང་ལ་ཕེབས་ཀྱི་ཡོད་ Sometimes (he) comes to my house. ¶ མི་འགར་བསམ་ཚུལ་དེ་འདྲ་བྱུང་ཡོད་པ་རེད་ Some people have opinions like that.

འགལ་ (gɛɛ) vi. to be contrary, to go against, to violate, to contradict ¶ ལས་ཀ་འདི་ཁྲིམས་དང་འགལ་བ་རེད་ This action violates the law.

འགལ་རྐྱེན་ (gɛɛgyen) 1. an unfavorable condition, an obstruction/ obstacle/ hindrance/ impediment; va.—བཟོ་; —བྱེད་; —གཏོང་ to hinder, to obstruct, to harm ¶ ཁོང་ཕེབས་རྒྱུའི་འགལ་རྐྱེན་གཙོ་བོ་ནི་ As for the main obstacle to his coming. ¶ སྲིད་སྐྱོང་རིན་པོ་ཆེ་འགལ་རྐྱེན་གཏོང་རྒྱུའི་སྐོར་ Concerning doing harm to the Regent.

འགལ་སྐྱོན་ (gɛɛgyön) a violation, a breach of law, an illegal act; va.—གཏོང་ ¶ ལས་ཀ་འདི་ལས་ཁུངས་ཀྱི་སྒྲིག་ཁྲིམས་ལ་འགལ་སྐྱོན་གཏོང་བ་ཞིག་རེད་ This work is in violation of the regulations of the office.

འགལ་འཁྲུལ་ (gɛɛdrüü) violations/ contradictions and errors.

འགལ་འགོལ་ (gɛɛgöö) contrary and opposed, in disobedience of; va.—བྱེད་ to act in violation of sth., to do sth. illegal/ in disobedience of.

འགལ་ཆ་ (gɛɛja) sm. འགལ་བ་.

འགལ་ཉེས་ (gɛɛñeè) sth. illegal, a crime.

འགལ་མཐུན་ (gɛɛdön) eclectic.

འགལ་མཐུན་རིང་ལུགས་ (gɛɛdön riŋluù) eclecticism.

འགལ་འཐབ་ (gɛɛdəb) contradiction and struggle.

འགལ་འདུ་ལྷག་སྒྲོད་ (gɛndu dāgdröö) diametrically opposed/ opposite.

འགལ་འདུའི་ཕུང་པོ་ (gɛndü pūŋbo) sm. འགལ་བ་.

འགལ་སྤྱོད་ (gɛɛjöö) contrary action, disobedience.

འགལ་བ་ (gɛɛwa) a contradiction ¶ ཁོང་གིས་སྤྱི་ཚོགས་གསར་རྙིང་དབར་གྱི་འགལ་བའི་སྐོར་བཤད་སོང་ He spoke on the contradiction between the old and new societies. ¶ འགལ་བའི་གཙོ་བོ་ The principle contradiction.

འགལ་བ་གཅིག་གྱུར་ (gɛɛwa jiggyur) the identity of opposites.

འགལ་བ་གཙོ་བོ་ (gɛɛwa dzōwo) principle contradiction.

འགལ་བའི་ཆོས་ཉིད་ (gɛɛwɛ cöönii) law of contradiction.

འགལ་བའི་ལྷག་སྒྲོད་ (gɛɛwɛ dāgdröö) sm. འགལ་འདུ་ལྷག་སྒྲོད་.

འགལ་བའི་རྣམ་བཤད་ (gɛɛwɛ nāmshɛɛ̀) "On Contradiction" (an essay by Mao Zedong).

འགལ་འབྲེལ་ (gɛɛdree) a relationship of contradictions or opposites.

འགལ་མི་ (gɛɛmi) a violator.

འགལ་ཚབས་ཅན་ (gɛɛtsəbjɛn) a person guilty of violating the law, a criminal.

འགལ་འཛོལ་ (gɛɛdzöö) violation, infraction, transgression ¶ འདི་ནི་ཡུལ་ཁྲིམས་དང་འགལ་འཛོལ་ཆེན་པོ་ཞིག་རེད་ This is a great violation of local law.

འགལ་ཟླ་ (gɛnda) 1. opposite, opposition ¶ སྐྱིད་པོའི་འགལ་ཟླ་སྡུག་པོ་རེད་ The opposite of happiness is suffering. 2. contradiction ¶ འབྱོར་མེད་གྲལ་རིམ་དང་བཙུ་གཞོག་གྲལ་རིམ་གྱི་འགལ་ཟླ་ནི་ As for the contradiction between the proletarian class and the exploiting class.

འགལ་ཟླ་གཅིག་གྱུར་ (gɛnda jiggyur) unity of opposites/ contradictions ¶ འདི་ཐད་དེ་འགལ་ཟླ་གཅིག་གྱུར་རེད་ This is completely a unity of opposites. 2. opponent, rival.

འགལ་ཟླའི་ཕྱོགས་ (gɛndɛ cɔ̄ɔ) opposites, opposing sides, opponents ¶ འགལ་ཟླའི་ཕྱོགས་གཉིས་དབར་གྱི་རྩོད་གླེང་བར་འདུམ་བྱས་པ་རེད་ (They) mediated the dispute between the two opposing sides.

འགལ་ཟླའི་རང་བཞིན་ (gɛndɛ rəŋshin) opposition, antagonism.

འགལ་ཟླར་འཛིན་ (gɛndar dzin) va. to consider or hold as an opponent/ rival/ enemy ¶ མི་ཚང་དེ་གཉིས་ཕན་ཚུན་འགལ་ཟླར་འཛིན་གྱི་ཡོད་པ་རེད་ These two households consider each other as enemies.

འགལ་བཟུང་ (gɛɛsuŋ) sm. འགལ་ཟླར་འཛིན་.

འགལ་རིགས་ (gɛɛrig) things that violate/ contradict.

འགལ་གཤགས་ (gɛɛshaà) rebuttal (in a debate); va.—རྒྱག.

འགས་: p. **བཀས་**; f. **དགས་**; imp. **ཁོས་** (gɛɛ̀) va. to smash, to split, to shatter ¶ ཤེལ་དམ་དེ་དུམ་བུ་མང་པོ་བཀས་སོང་ They smashed the bottle into many pieces.

འགས་: p. **གས་**; f. **འགས་** (gɛɛ̀) vi. to get cracked/ split, to burst ¶ ཤེལ་སྒོ་དེ་གས་སོང་ The glass cracked.

འགས་མདེལ་ (gɛɛ̀dee) a bomb.

འགས་སྨན་ (gɛɛ̀mɛn) explosive powder, gunpowder ¶ འགས་སྨན་མཛོད་ཁང་ Powder magazine.

འགི་ (gi) a verb of existence in the Kham dialect.

འགི་གང་ (gigaŋ) sm. ཐེ་བན་.

འགི་ཝང་ (giwaŋ) sm. གི་ཝང་.

འགི་ཧང་ (gihaŋ) sm. འགི་ཝང་.

འགིའུ་ཝང་ (giuwaŋ) sm. འགི་ཝང་.

འགུག (guù) sm. འགུགས་.

འགུགས་: p. བཀུག; f. དགུག; imp. ཁུག (guù) 1. va. to summon, to call, to send for, to recall ¶ གྲོང་གསེབ་ཁག་ནས་ལག་རྩལ་པ་མང་པོ་བཀུག་པ་རེད་ They summoned many craftsmen from the various villages. 2. va. to interest, to attract, to turn on (usu. follows a word for "mind" such as སེམས་) ¶ མི་མང་པོའི་སེམས་འགུགས་ཐུབ་པའི་ཟློས་གར་ Plays that are able to interest many people.

འགུགས་རྒྱ་ (guggya) written summons; va.—གཏོང་ to send a written summons.

འགུགས་རྒྱག (gugyaà) 1. va. to make the color of a newly dyed woolen cloth more rich/ shinny (usu. by laying it out on grass). 2. va. to hook sth. 3. va. to stir up brewed tea with a ladel.

འགུགས་སྔགས་ (gugŋaà) a tantric practice to summon demons and evil spirits.

འགུགས་འདུལ་ (guŋdüü) conquering by persuading to surrender; va.—བྱེད་.

འགུགས་སྡུད་ (gugdüü) summoning/ assembling/ collecting/ calling people; va.—བྱེད་.

འགུགས་བརྡ་ (gugda) a message to recall/ summon; va.—གཏོང་.

འགུགས་ནུས་ (gugnüü) the power to attract/ interest/ turn on ¶ ཁོང་གི་གསུང་བཤད་དེ་ལ་མི་སེམས་འགུགས་ནུས་ཆེན་པོ་ཡོད་པ་རེད་ His speech has the power to attract many people.

འགུགས་འབོད་ (guŋböö) summoning/ calling to come; va.—བྱེད་ ¶ ཁོ་ལས་ཁུངས་སུ་འགུག་འབོད་བྱས་པ་རེད་ (They) called him to (their) office.

འགུགས་ཚྭ་ (gugtsa) a type of salt used in འགུགས་རྒྱག.

འགུགས་ལུང་ (gugluŋ) sm. གློག་ལུང་.

འགུགས་ལེན་ (guglen) summoning, recruiting; va.—བྱེད་ to summon/ recruit.

འགུགས་ཤུགས་ (gugshuù) sm. འགུགས་ནུས་.

འགུད་ (güü) sm. གུད་.

འགུམ་: p. གུམ་; f. འགུམ་ (gum) 1. vi. to die. 2. vi. to have a leg/ hand contract.

འགུམས་: p. བཀུམ་ f. དགུམ་ imp. ཁུམས་ (gum) va. to kill.

འགུར་ཞོ་ (gursho) sm. མགུར་ཞོ་.

འགུལ་ (güü) vi. to move/ shake, to quake ¶ མི་མང་པོའི་སེམས་འགུལ་བའི་བཀའ་སློབ་ཞིག་གནང་སོང་ (He) gave a talk that moved many people.

འགུལ་སྐྱོད་ (güügyöö) 1. moving, movement, shaking; va.—བྱེད; —རྒྱག ¶ རྙི་ལ་ཚུད་དེ་འགུལ་སྐྱོད་བྱེད་མ་ཐུབ་པའི་སྐབས་ When (it) was caught in a trap and could not move. ¶ བོད་ལ་དབྱིན་ཇི་ས་འགུལ་སྐྱོད་ཇི་བྱེད་བརྟག་དཔྱད་བྱེད་དགོས་ (You) must investigate what movements the British are making in Tibet. 2. the way of functioning/ operating ¶ བཙན་རྒྱལ་རིང་ལུགས་པས་འགུལ་སྐྱོད་བྱས་ལུགས་ང་ཚོས་མཐོང་མྱོང་ We have seen how the imperialists operate.

འགུལ་སྐྱོད་འཕྲུལ་འཁོར་ (güügyöö trüügɔɔ) motor, engine.

འགུལ་སྐྱོབ་ (güügyob) sm. འགེབས་སྲུང་.

འགུལ་བསྐྱོད་ (güügyöö) sm. འགུལ་སྐྱོད་.

འགུལ་ཁྱུག་ཁྱུག (güü kyüùgyuù) moving, wiggling, shaking.

འགུལ་འགུལ་གཏོང་ (güügüü dōŋ) va. sm. འགུལ་སྐྱོད་.

འགུལ་ཐྲིག (güüdeg) moving up and down, pulsating.

འགུལ་བྱེད་འཕྲུལ་འཁོར་ (güüjeè trüügɔɔ) motor, engine.

འགུལ་མེད་ (güümeè) not moving.

འགུལ་མེད་གློག (güümeè lɔ̃ɔ̀) static electricity.

འགུལ་མེད་དངོས་པོ་ (güümeè ŋö̃öbo) inanimate object.

འགུལ་མེད་རེངས་པོ་ (güümeè reŋbo) unchanging, static.

འགུལ་མེར་མེར་ (güü meemee) shaking, trembling (as in an earthquake).

འགུལ་ཙམ་ (güüdzam) moving slightly; va.—བྱེད་.

འགུལ་རྩ་ (güü dza) sm. འཕར་རྩ་.

འགུལ་ཚད་ (güüdzɛɛ̀) frequency ¶ འགུལ་ཚད་མཐོ་བ་ High frequency.

འགུལ་ཚད་མྱུར་བའི་གློག་རླབས་ (güüdzɛɛ̀ ñurwɛ lɔ̃gləb) high frequency waves.

འགུལ་འཆེར་ (güüdzee) lazy; va.—བྱེད་ to act lazy.

འགུལ་ཤུགས་ (güüshuù) power/ force of movement, energy.

འགུལ་ཤུགས་འཕྲུལ་ཆས་ (güüshuù trüüjɛɛ̀) power machinery.

འགུལ་ཤུགས་འབར་རྫས་ (güüshuù bardzɛɛ̀) fuel for motors/ engines.

འགུལ་སིག་བྱེད་ (güüsiì ceè) vi. shaking with anger.

འགུལ་སློ་ (güüle) cradle.

འགེགས་ (geg) 1. va. to choke, to strangle. 2. p. of འགོག.

འགེགས་སྒྲོམ་ (gegdrom) gallows.

འགེགས་ཐག (gegdaà) noose.

འགེགས་གསོད་ (gegsöö) killing by strangulation, va.—གཏོང་ to hang, to strangle, to garrote.

འགེགས་གསོད་ཀྱི་ཆད་པ་ (gegsöögi cɛ̃ɛba) capital punishment by hanging, sentencing to the gallows.

འགེངས་: p. བཀང་; f. དགང་; imp. ཁོང་ (geŋ) va. to fill up ¶ སྣོད་ཆས་དེ་ཆུས་བཀང་པ་རེད་ (They) filled the pot with water.

འགེངས་ཤོག (geŋshɔɔ̀) a form.

འགེབས་: p. བཀབ་; f. དགབ་; imp. ཁོབ་ (geb) 1. va. to cover, to conceal ¶ ཁོ་ཚོས་དམིགས་ཡུལ་ངན་པ་དེ་འགེབས་ཀྱི་ཡོད་པ་རེད་ (They) are concealing their evil aims. ¶ རི་རྣམས་ཁ་བས་འགེབས་འདུག The mountains are covered with snow. 2. va. to put on a roof/ covering ¶ ཁང་པ་དེ་ར་ཐོག་འགེབས་ཀྱི་འདུག They are putting a roof on the house.

འགེབས་སྐྱོབ་ (gebgyob) sm. འགེབས་སྲུང་.

འགེབས་བྱེད་ (gebjɛɛ̀) lid, cover.

འགེབས་སྦས་ (gebbɛɛ̀) covering, hiding, concealing; va.—བྱེད་ ¶ མེ་མདའ་དེ་ཚོ་འགེབས་སྦས་བྱེད་དགོས་བྱུང་པ་རེད་ (They) had to hide the guns.

འགེབས་རས་ (gebrɛɛ̀) covering cloth, tarpaulin.

འགེབས་སྲུང་ (gebsuŋ) defending, protecting, concealing, sheltering ¶ འགེབ་སྲུང་འཛིང་དོ་ Military trenches for defense. 2. (— + འོག) under the cover/ protection of, screening, covering ¶ མེ་སྒྱོགས་ཀྱི་འགེབ་སྲུང་འོག Under the cover of artillery.

འགེམ་མེ་ (gemme) protruding lips.

འགེམས་ (gem) va. to subdue/ conquer/ defeat ¶ དགྲ་བོར་ཀླད་པ་འགེམས་པའི་དུང་རྡེག་བརྡུང་པ་རེད་ (They) defeated the enemy [Lit. struck a blow to the brain that defeated the enemy].

འགེལ་: p. བཀལ་; f. དགལ་; imp. ཁོལ་ (gee) 1. va. to load on, to put on, to impose ¶ རྟ་ལ་དོ་པོ་བཀལ་པ་རེད་ (They) loaded the horse. ¶ ཉེས་ཆད་ཆེན་པོ་འགེལ་གྱི་རེད་ They will impose a big penalty on (them). 2. va. to hang (on walls, etc.) ¶ རྩིག་པའི་ལྡེབས་ལ་པར་བཀལ་སོང་ They hung pictures on the wall.

འགེལ་དགྲི་ (geedri) a responsibility; duty; va.—བྱེད་ to give sb. a responsibility ¶ ཁོང་ལ་ལས་འགན་ཆེན་པོ་ཞིག་འགེལ་དགྲི་བྱས་སོང་ (They) gave him a big responsibility.

འགེལ་དགྲིས་ (geedrii) sm. འགེལ་དགྲི་.

འགེལ་བཀོད་ (gee göö) shung. va. to impose ¶ ཁྲལ་རིགས་མི་སྐྱིར་འགེལ་འགོད་མི་ཆོག་ཅིང་ No one is allowed to impose new taxes on the commoners.

འགེལ་ཁལ་ (geekɛɛ) transport animals.

འགེལ་འགྲེམས་ (gendrem) displaying and hanging, hanging to display; va.—བྱེད་ to hang and display.

འགེལ་ཉེས་ (geeñeè) 1. a mistake in giving responsibility; vi.—ཤོར་ to have such a mistake inadvertently come about. 2. a mistake in levying a tax; vi.—ཤོར་ to have such a mistake inadvertently come about.

འགེལ་དྲེལ་ (geedree) transport mules.

འགེལ་གདངས་ (geedaŋ) 1. coat hanger, coat rack. 2. string or rope for hanging clothes to dry.

འགེལ་གདན་ (geedɛn) rugs for hanging on walls.

འགེལ་གཙེར་ (geedzer) imposing sth.; va.—བྱེད་ ། ཁོང་ལ་ཁྲལ་རིགས་གསར་པ་འགེལ་གཙེར་བྱས་སོང་ (They) imposed new taxes on him.

འགེལ་ཚད་ (geedzɛ̀ɛ) load capacity, load limit (for a carrying animal).

འགེལ་བཞོན་ (geeshön) animals for carrying/ transporting and riding.

འགེལ་གཡག (geeyaà) transport/ carrying yaks.

འགེལ་རིལ་ (geerii) a scroll or hanging picture.

འགེལ་ལུག (geelug) transport/ carrying sheep.

འགེལ་ལུང་ (geeluŋ) a hanger.

འགེལ་ལེན་ (geelen) levying and collecting; va.—བྱེད་ ། གཞུང་གིས་ཁྲལ་རིགས་གསར་པ་མང་པོ་འགེལ་ལེན་བྱས་འདུག The government levied and collected many new taxes.

འགོ་ (go) 1. start, beginning, initial stage; va.—འཛུགས་ to start/ begin/ commence ། ལས་ཀའི་འགོར་ At the start of work. ། ཁོས་ལས་ཀ་འགོ་འཛུགས་དུས་ When he started the work. 2. head, chief, leader, foreman; va.—བྱེད་ to head, to be in charge, to act as the leader foreman ། ཚོགས་པའི་འགོ་ Leader of the group.

འགོ་: p. གོས་; f. འགོ་ (go) 1. vi. to have a substance like ashes, dust, etc. involuntarily stick to sth., to inadvertently get sth. on oneself ། ལག་པར་ཚོན་གོས་འདུག Paint got on (his) hands. 2. vi. to catch an (illness), to get infected ། ང་ལ་ཁོའི་ཆམ་པ་དེ་གོས་འདུག I caught his cold.

འགོ་སྐྱལ་ (go gǖü) va. to take the lead in starting/ opening a song, prayer, etc.

འགོ་ཁྲིད་ (gudriì) 1. leader, head, boss; va.—བྱེད་ to lead/ head, to act as leader ། ཁོས་ཚོགས་པ་འདི་འགོ་ཁྲིད་བྱས་སོང་ He headed the group. 2. sm. འགོ་འཁྲིད་.

འགོ་ཁྲིད་ཀྱི་སྒྱུ་རྩལ་ (gudriìgi gyudzɛɛ) the art of leadership.

འགོ་ཁྲིད་ཀྱི་ལྡེ་བ་ (gudriìgi dēwa) the core of leadership.

འགོ་ཁྲིད་ཀྱི་ཐབས་རྩལ་ (gudriìgi tābdzɛɛ) methods of leadership.

འགོ་ཁྲིད་ཀྱི་དབང་ཆ་ (gudriìgi wāŋja) the might/ power/ authority of leadership.

འགོ་ཁྲིད་ཀྱི་ལས་གནས་ (gudriìgi lɛ The light is glittering.

འགོ་ཁྲིད་ཀྱི་སྲོག་ཤིང་ (gudriìgi sōgshiŋ) nucleus/ core of leadership.

འགོ་ཁྲིད་ཀང་འཛིན་ (gudriì gāŋdzin) the key members or backbone of the leadership.

འགོ་ཁྲིད་ཁོངས་མི་ (gudriì kōŋmi) members of the leadership.

འགོ་ཁྲིད་གྲལ་རིམ་ (gudriì trɛɛrim) ruling/ leading class.

འགོ་ཁྲིད་ཉིས་བརྩེགས་ (gudriì ñiìdzeg) dual leadership.

འགོ་ཁྲིད་པ་ (gudriìbə) leader.

འགོ་ཁྲིད་བྱེད་ཐབས་ (gudriì ceèdəb) method of leadership.

འགོ་ཁྲིད་ཚོགས་ཁག (gudriì tsōgba) leading clique.

འགོ་ཁྲིད་ལས་ཁུངས་ (gudriì lɛ̀ɛguŋ) headquarters/ offices of leader(s) ། ཏང་གི་འགོ་ཁྲིད་ལས་ཁུངས་ The party headquarters.

འགོ་ཁྲིད་ལས་བྱེད་པ་ (gudriì lɛ̀ɛceèba) the leading cadre.

འགོ་འཁྲིད་: p. འགོ་ཁྲིད་ (gu triì) va. to lead, to head ། ཁོང་གིས་ཚོགས་པའི་འགོ་ཁྲིད་པ་རེད་ He led the group.

འགོ་མཆན་ (gojɛn) shung. a note written by a superior office/ official on a report submitted by a subordinate office/ official that indicates the superior's decision or answer; va.—འགོད་; —གནང་ to write such a note; —ཞུ་ to ask to write such a note.

འགོ་མཇུག (gonjuù) beginning to the end, start to finish, top to bottom.

འགོ་མཇུག་བར་ (gonjuù par) sm. འགོ་མཇུག.

འགོ་འཛུ་ (go ju) sm. འགོ་ཚུགས་.

འགོ་བརྗོད་ (gojöö) preface, foreword, introduction; heading, title.

འགོ་བརྗོད་སྙིང་གཞི་ (gojöö gēŋshi) preface, foreword.

འགོ་གདེ་ (gode) chieftain, headman, ringleader.

འགོ་བཏོག (gobdɔɔ̀) picking/ plucking the heads of crops; va.—རྒྱག.

འགོ་སྟོད་ (godöö) in the beginning, at the start, in the initial stage ། འགོ་སྟོད་དུ་བཟོ་གྲྭ་དེར་བཟོ་པ་ཉུང་ཤས་ལས་མེད་ In the beginning the factory had only a few workers.

འགོ་སྟོན་ (godön) sm. མགོ་སྟོན་.

འགོ་ཐུག (goduù) sm. མགོ་ཐུག.

འགོ་ཐོན་ (godön) sm. མགོ་ཐོན་.

འགོ་མཐོ་ (godo) shung. powerful ། མི་རྩ་ཁག་ཅིག་སྔར་ཆོས་འགོ་མཐོ་ཁ་ཤས་ལ་མགོ་འབུལ་བྱས་པ་ Some serfs left their previous lords and decided to become the serfs of some powerful aristrocrats and monasteries.

འགོ་འདོགས་རིང་ལུགས་ (godɔɔ̀ riŋluù) sm. མགོ་འདོགས་རིང་ལུགས་.

འགོ་འདོན་ (godön) 1. the opening statement at a meeting; va.—བྱེད་ ། ཚོགས་འདུའི་སར་ཁོང་གི་འགོ་འདོན་བྱས་པ་རེད་ He made the opening statement at the meeting. 2. sm. མགོ་འདོན.

འགོ་འདོན་འཚོ་སྐྱོང་ (godön tsōgyoŋ) sm. མགོ་འདོན་.

འགོ་འདོམས་ (gondom) head, leader; va.—བྱེད་ to lead, to head ། གྲྭ་གཡབ་དམག་གི་འགོ་འདོམས་ The head of the Trayab troops.

འགོ་འདོམས་ལས་ཆེན་ (gondom lɛ̀ndzɛn) shung. sm. འགོ་འདོམས་.

འགོ་འདྲེན་ (gondren) sm. མགོ་འདྲེན་.

འགོ་ནས་མཇུག་བར་ (gonɛ jugbar) from start to finish.

འགོ་ནད་ (gonɛɛ̀) infectious disease.

འགོ་ནད་སྔོན་འགོག (gonɛè ŋöngɔɔ̀) inoculation; va.—བྱེད་.

འགོ་ནད་ཐར་མ་ (gonɛɛ̀ tārma) immunity from a disease (as a result of getting it once and not dying from it).

འགོ་ནད་སྨན་ཁང་ (gonɛɛ̀ mēngaŋ) isolation/ quarantine hospital, hospital for infectious diseases.

འགོ་ནན་ (gonɛn) shung. starting, beginning.

འགོ་ནས་ (gonɛɛ̀) from the beginning, from the start.

འགོ་ནས་མཇུག་བར་ (gonɛɛ̀ jugbar) sm. མགོ་ནས་འཇུག་བར་.

འགོ་ནོན་ (gonön) sm. འགོ་གནོན་.

འགོ་གནོན་ (gonön) suppressing, oppressing; va.—རྒྱག ། མི་སེར་ཐོག་འགོ་གནོན་གི་གནས་ཚུལ་མང་པོ་ཅིག་བྱུང་འདུག A lot of news has been received concerning (their) oppressing the people.

འགོ་སྣམ་ (gonam) a kind of woven woolen cloth.

འགོ་པ་ (goba) foreman, headman, chief, leader, officer-in-charge.

འགོ་དཔོན་ (gobön) sm. འགོ་པ་.

འགོ་སྤྱི་ (goji) shung. headman.

འགོ་བའི་རིམས་ (gowɛ rim) epidemic.

འགོ་བའི་ལྷ་ (gowɛ lhā) a protective deity.

འགོ་བྱེད་ (gojeè) sm. འགོ་པ་.

འགོ་བྱེད་མཁན་ (gojeèñɛn) one who heads/ leads.

འགོ་བྱེད་གནམ་གྲུ་ (gojeè nāmdru) leading aircraft.

འགོ་བྱེད་པོ་ (gō ceèbo) sm. འགོ་པ་.

འགོ་བྱེད་མི་སྣ་ (gojeè minə) leaders, ones who lead.

འགོ་བྱེད་སེར་སྐྱ་ (gojeè sērgya) shung. a headman of both monks and layman.

འགོ་འབྱེད་ (go ceè) va. to open, to inaugurate ། འགོ་འབྱེད་ཚོགས་འདུ་ The inaugurating session of a larger meeting.

འགོ་མ་ (goma) starting, beginning, at first ། ང་ཚོའི་ལས་ཀ་འདི་མགོ་མ་རེད་ Our work is at the starting point.

འགོ་མང་ (gomaŋ) sm. འགོ་དམངས་.

འགོ་མའི་ལེ་ཚན་ (gomɛ ledzɛn) prologue.

འགོ་མི་ (gomi) sm. མགོ་མི་.

འགོ་དམག་ (gomaà) officers and ordinary soldiers.

འགོ་དམངས་ (gomaŋ) leaders and people/ masses/ commoners.

འགོ་གཙོ་ (godzo) sm. འགོ་པ་.

འགོ་གཙོ་གཅིག་གཅོད་ཀྱི་ལམ་ལུགས་ (godzo jigjöögi ləmluù) the system of dictatorship/ autocracy.

འགོ་གཙོའི་ལྷན་འཛོམས་གྲོས་མོལ་ (godzö lhɛ̄ndzom tröömöö) summit conference.

འགོ་བཙུགས་ (go dzūù) p. of འགོ་འཛུགས་.

འགོ་ཙ་ (godza) the start, the beginning.

འགོ་རྩོམ་ (godzom) va. to begin, to start ། ལས་ཀའི་འགོ་རྩོམ་དུས་གཟབ་གཟབ་བྱེད་དགོས་ When one starts a job one must be careful.

འགོ་བརྩམས་ (go dzām) p. of འགོ་རྩོམ་.

འགོ་ཚུགས་ (go tsūù) vi. to begin, to start ། སློབ་གྲྭ་འདི་ནས་སློབ་གྲྭ་འགོ་ཚུགས་པ་རེད་ The school began from this month. ། ལས་ཀ་བྱེད་འགོ་ཚུགས་ནས་ཉི་མ་ཁ་ཤས་སོང་པ་རེད་ It has been a few days since his work started.

འགོ་ཚུགས་པའི་གླུ་དབྱངས་ (godzugbɛ lūyaŋ) prelude, overture (in music).

འགོ་ཚུགས་པའི་ལེ་ཚན་ (godzugbɛ ledzɛn) preface.

འགོ་ཚུགས་མཛད་སྒོ་ (godzuù dzɛ̄ɛgo) opening ceremony.

འགོ་ཚུགས་རོལ་མོ་ (godzuù röömo) musical overture, music played at the start of a show.

འགོ་ཚུགས་ས་ (go tsūgsə) the starting point, the departure point.

འགོ་ཚོང་ (godzoŋ) the first sale with a client, the first sale of a day; va.—རྒྱག.

འགོ་མཚལ་ (godzɛɛ) shung. red serge.

འགོ་འཚེམ་ (go dzēm) va. to stitch/ sew the upper part of sth.

འགོ་འཚོ་བྱེད་ (gotso cɛ̄ɛ) sm. འགོ་འདོན་འཚོ་སྐྱོང་བྱེད་.

འགོ་འཛིན་ (gondzin) leader, head, chief; va.—བྱེད་ to head, to preside over, to lead ། ཁོང་གིས་ཚོགས་འདུ་འདིའི་འགོ་འཛིན་གནང་བ་རེད་ He presided over the meeting.

འགོ་འཛུགས་ (go dzuù) va. to start, to begin ། གྲོས་མོལ་འགོ་མ་བཙུགས་གོང་ Before they started discussions.

འགོ་འཛུགས་མཁན་ (go dzuùñɛn) initiator, starter.

འགོ་རྫས་ (godzɛɛ) antigen.

འགོ་ཞབས་ (goshəb) sm. འགོ་ནས་མཇུག་བར་.

འགོ་ཟིན་ (go sin) 1. va. to start, begin (work) ། ལས་ཀའི་འགོ་ཟིན་བཞག The work has started.

འགོ་ཡག་པོ་ (go yagbo) a good place to start.

འགོ་ཡིག (goyii) heading, title.

འགོ་ཡོད་ (goyöö) shung. foreman, chief.

འགོ་ཡོད་མཇུག་མེད་ (goyöö jugmeè) starting sth. but failing to carry it though to the end, not getting a good result.

འགོ་རན་མ་ནས་ཉེས་ན་ གོས་ནམ་ཟད་བར་ (gorɛnmanɛ ñɛ̄ɛna kȫö nam sɛ̄ɛdar) if there is a mistake at the beginning it remains until the end [Lit. if there is an error when setting up the yarn it remains until the clothes are worn out].

འགོ་རིལ་ (gorii) 1. a type of round barley. 2. an inferior type of woolen material.

འགོ་རིམས་ (gorim) an epidemic.

འགོ་ལིང་རྒྱས་ (goliŋ gyɛ̄ɛ) vi. to sprout branches/ shoots.

འགོ་ལེན་བསྟེན་སྐྱོབ་ (golen dēngyob) shung. accepting people and giving them protection as one's subject/ serf ། སྐྱེར་པའི་མི་སེར་མང་པོ་ཞིག་བླ་བྲང་ཁག་ནས་འགོ་ལེན་བསྟེན་སྐྱོབ་བྱས་པ་ Many subjects of aristocrats were accepted by different Labrangs which henceforth gave them protection as their own serfs.

འགོ་ཤོག (goshoò) the empty space left on top of letters in tt. (as a sign of respect).

འགོ་བཤད་ཀུབ་བརླག (goshɛɛ̄ gūblaà) starting a topic in a conversation and then losing the thread of one's thought while speaking.

འགོ་སེར་ (goser) yellow serge.

འགོག: p. བཀོག; f. དགོག; imp. ཁོག (gɔɔ̀) to pluck, to dig up, to rip off ། ཁོས་ཡིག་བསྐྱར་དེ་སྒོ་ནས་བཀོག་རྗེས་བཀའ་ཤག་ལ་སྤྲད་སོང་ He ripped the protest poster from the door and gave it to the Kashag.

འགོག: p. བཀག or འགོགས་; f. དགག; imp. ཁོག (gɔɔ̀) 1. va. to ban, to block, to obstruct, to stop ། ལམ་ཁ་དེ་བཀག་འདུག They blocked the road ། གོང་མའི་བཀའ་ཡིག་དང་དུ་ལེན་རྒྱུར་ཐབས་སྣ་ཚོགས་ཀྱིས་བཀག་འདུག (He) did various things to obstruct accepting the Emperor's order. 2. va. to resist, to hold out against ། རི་འགོག་དམག་འཁྲུག War of resistance against the Japanese. 3. va. to set a time, to set an alarm ། སང་ཉིན་ཆུ་ཚོད་དྲུག་པར་ཐིར་བཀག་དགོས་ (I) have to set the alarm for 6 am tomorrow. ། ང་གཉིས་འཛོམས་དུས་ཆུ་ཚོད་གསུམ་པ་བཀག་ཡོད་ We are set to meet at three o'clock.

འགོག་རྐྱེན་ (gɔggyen) obstacle, barrier, hindrance, misfortune; va.—གཏོང་; — བཟོ་ to obstruct, to hinder, to prevent, to block ། ཆར་འབོད་ཆེན་པོ་བྱུང་བ་དེས་ཁང་པ་རྒྱག་རྒྱུར་འགོག་རྐྱེན་བཟོས་པ་རེད་ The heavy monsoon rain obstructed the building of houses.

འགོག་སྐྱོང་ (gɔggyoŋ) protecting, defending.

འགོག་སྐྱོབ་ (gɔggyob) sm. འགོག་སྐྱོང་.

འགོག་འཁྲུག (gɔgdruù) war of resistance.

འགོག་གྱང་ (gɔggyaŋ) a wall used as a barrier.

འགོག་རྒོལ་ (gɔggöö) resistance, resisting; va.—བྱེད་ to resist, to fight ། དྲག་པོའི་འགོག་རྒོལ་ Armed resistance.

འགོག་བཅོས་ (gɔgjöö) prevention and cure/ correction/ eradication; va.—གཏོང་; —བྱེད ། ལོ་ཏོག་ལ་གནོད་པའི་འབུ་རིགས་འགོག་བཅོས་བྱ་བར་བརྟག་དཔྱད་བྱས་པ་རེད་ They are doing research to prevent and eradicate the insects that harm crops.

འགོག་མཆན་ (gɔgjɛn) a rebuttal, a refutation, a note that prohibits/ bans/ stops; va.—འགོད་ to issue or write a rebuttal/ refutation/ ban/ prohibition.

འགོག་གདམ་ (gɔgdam) sm. རྒོལ་གདམ་.

འགོག་ཐབས་ (gɔgdəb) method of prevention, means of resistance.

འགོག་འདོམས་ (gɔgdom) sm. འགོག་སྡོམ་.

འགོག་སྡོམ་ (gɔgdom) 1. restriction, ban, prohibition, blockade; va.—བྱེད་. 2. monopolizing; va.—བྱེད་.

འགོག་གནོན་ (gɔgnön) suppression, putting down, subjugating; va.—བྱེད་.

འགོག་དམག་ (gɔgmaà) war of resistance.

འགོག་ཙེ་ (gɔgdze) ch. an outer garment (coat, etc.).

འགོག་རགས་ (gɔgraà) a dam.

འགོག་ལུང་གི་ལམ་ཐིག (gɔgluŋgi lamdig) defense line.

འགོག་ཤུགས་ (gɔgshuù) resisting, obstructing ། ཐན་པ་འགོག་ཤུགས་ Drought resistant.

འགོག་བཤོལ་ (gɔgshöö) resisting, obstructing; va.—བྱེད་.

འགོག་ས་ (gɔgsa) sm. འགོག་རྐྱེན་.

འགོག་སྲུང་ (gɔgsuŋ) defending, guarding against, protecting; va.—བྱེད་ to defend, to guard against, to protect ། བཀའ་འཁྲོལ་མེད་པའི་མི་སྣར་འགོག་སྲུང་ Protecting against people (coming) without permission.

འགོག་སྲུང་གི་ལས་དོན་ (gɔgsuŋgi lɛ̄ɛdön) defensive measures.

འགོག་སྲུང་སྒྲིག་ཆས་ (gɔgsuŋ drigjɛɛ̄) defense installations.

འགོག་སྲུང་འཐབ་ར་ (gɔgsuŋ tābra) defensive installation/ fortification.

འགོག་སྲུང་ནུས་ཤུགས་ (gɔgsuŋ nüüshug) defensive force/ power.

འགོག་སྲུང་དམག་འཐབ་ (gɔgsuŋ māgdəb) defensive war.

འགོག་སྲུང་འཛིང་རགས་ (gɔgsuŋ dziŋraà) defense installation/ fortification.

འགོག་སྲུང་ཤིང་ནགས་ (gɔgsuŋ shiŋnaà) protected forest.

འགོག་གསོག (gɔgsɔɔ̀) hoarding, holding back; va.—བྱེད་.

འགོང་: p. འགོངས་; f. འགོང་ (goŋ) 1. v. to be afraid. 2. va. to violate/ contradict. 3. va. to compete with. 4. vi. to exceed (a number/ unit). 5. vi. to escape (from danger, etc.).

འགོང་ (goŋ) sm. འགོང་པོ་.

འགོང་པོ་ (goŋbo) a type/ class of demons.

འགོད་: p. བཀོད་; f. དགོད་; imp. ཁོད་ (göö) 1. va. to draw up, to formulate, to plan ¶ གཞུང་ལམ་གསར་པ་བཟོ་བའི་འཆར་གཞི་འགོད་ཀྱི་ཡོད་པ་རེད་ (They) are formulating a plan for building a new highway. 2. va. to record, to write down, to sign ¶ ཡིག་ཆ་དེ་ཚོའི་ནང་ལོ་མང་པོའི་ལོ་རྒྱུས་བཀོད་ཡོད་པ་རེད་ (They) have recorded the history of many years in those documents. 3. va. to put into, to insert ¶ ཚན་རིག་གིས་མི་རྣམས་བདེ་སྐྱིད་ལ་འགོད་ཐུབ་པའི་ཡིད་ཆེས་བྱེད་ཀྱི་ཡོད་པ་རེད་ (They) believe that science is going to put men into a state of peace and happiness. ¶ ཁྱེད་རང་གི་བཀའ་སློབ་རྣམས་ངའི་སྙིང་ལ་བཀོད་ཡོད་ I have taken your advice to heart.

འགོད་ཐོ་ (göödo) a record, register; va.—འགོད་ to set a record ¶ མཆོང་རྒྱག་མཁན་དེས་འགོད་ཐོ་གསར་པ་བཀོད་པ་རེད་ That jumper set a new record.

འགོད་དེབ་ (göödeb) notebook.

འགོད་གནང་མཛད་ (göö nāŋdzɛɛ̀) h. of འགོད་.

འགོད་ཨང་ (göö āŋ) sm. ཐོ་འགོད་ཨང་གྲངས་.

འགོམ་: p. བགོམས་; f. བགོམ་; imp. བགོམས་ (gom) va. to walk/ step over, to cross/ pass over ¶ ཆུ་ཡུར་བགོམས་སོང་ (He) stepped over the ditch.

འགོམ་རྫི་ (gomdzi) trampling, stamping; va.—གཏོང་.

འགོམ་ཡུག་གཏོང་ (gomyuù dōŋ) sm. འགོམ་.

འགོམས་ (gom) shung. va. to aid.

འགོའུ་ཏ་མ་ (godama) Gautama (Buddha).

འགོར་ (gɔɔ) vi. to take (time), to elapse ¶ སྐར་མ་ལྔ་ཙམ་འགོར་གྱི་རེད་ (This) will take about five minutes.

འགོར་སྐྱོན་ (gɔɔgyön) sm. འགོར་འགྱངས་.

འགོར་གྲས་ (gɔɔdrɛɛ̀) slow, nonexpress ¶ མེ་འཁོར་འགོར་གྲས་ Nonexpress train.

འགོར་འགྱངས་ (gɔɔgyaŋ) delaying, procrastinating; va.—བྱེད་ ¶ ཡིག་ལན་དེ་འགོར་འགྱངས་ཆེན་པོ་བྱུང་སོང་ The reply was delayed for a long time.

འགོར་རྒྱུན་ (gɔɔgyün) duration/ time elapsed ¶ ཁྱེད་རང་གི་གུང་སེང་ལ་འགོར་རྒྱུན་ག་འདྲ་ཡོང་གི་རེད་དམ་ How long of a duration will your vacation be?

འགོར་ཆང་ (gɔɔjaŋ) a cup of beer (ཆང་) served as a penalty when a person has not finished drinking his cup of chang by the time a drinking song is over.

འགོར་ཐོགས་ (gɔɔdog) sm. འགོར་འགྱངས་.

འགོར་པོ་ (gɔɔbo) slow, time-consuming ¶ ཁོ་ལས་ཀ་འགོར་པོ་འདུག He is slow in his work.

འགོར་གཞི་མེད་པ་ (gɔɔshi meèba) sm. འགྱངས་མེད་.

འགོར་ཡུན་ (gɔɔyün) sm. འགོར་རྒྱུན་.

འགོར་ལམ་ (gɔɔlam) a longer route/ road, a detour.

འགོལ་ (göö) 1. vi. to be remote/ isolated/ secluded ¶ ས་ཆ་འདི་ལས་དེ་འགོལ་གྱི་རེད་ This place is more remote than that. 2. time ¶ ང་ཁྱེད་རང་གི་ཐུ་ལ་ཡོང་རྒྱུའི་འགོལ་བ་བྱུང་མ་སོང་ I didn't have time to come to see you. 3. relaxed, at ease.

འགོལ་གནས་ (göönɛɛ̀) 1. a remote/ secluded/ isolated place. 2. mistakes, faults, errors ¶ གཞན་གྱི་འགོལ་ས་གཙང་ལ་ཐབས་མཁས་དགོས་ To do away with other's faults one must be very diplomatic.

འགོལ་པོ་ (gööbo) relaxed, at ease.

འགོལ་ས་ (göösa) sm. འགོལ་གནས་.

འགོལ་ས་འཚོལ་ལས་ (göösa tsöölɛɛ̀) searching for faults/ errors/ mistakes.

འགོལ་གསེང་ (gooseŋ) sm. འགོལ་, 2.

འགོས་ (goò) 1. p. of འགོ་. 2. name of an ancient lineage in Lhoka.

འགོས་ཁུངས་ (göòguŋ) the origin or source of an epidemic.

འགོས་ནད་ (göònɛɛ̀) contagious/ infectious disease, epidemic.

འགོས་ནད་སྔོན་འགོག་དང་འགོག་ཐབས་ལས་དོན་ཁང་ (göònɛɛ̀ ŋöngɔɔ̀daŋ gɔgdəb lɛɛ̀döngaŋ) Centers for Disease Control and Prevention.

འགོས་ནད་སྨན་ཁང་ (göònɛɛ̀ mēngaŋ) hospital for contagious/ infectious diseases.

འགོས་ཚབས་ (göödzəb) a dangerous contagious disease/ infection, a dangerous epidemic.

འགྱངས་: p. འགྱངས་; f. འགྱང་ (gyaŋ) vi. to be delayed, to be postponed ¶ གནམ་གྲུ་དེ་འབྱོར་རྒྱུ་ཆུ་ཚོད་ཁ་ཤས་འགྱངས་པ་རེད་ The arrival of the plane was delayed by a few hours.

འགྱངས་སྐྱེད་ (gyaŋgyeè) shung. the interest charged for delaying either the payment of a loan or the interest payment on a loan.

འགྱངས་འཁྲི་ (gyaŋdri) shung. fine for delaying the payment of a loan or the interest on a loan.

འགྱངས་ཆ་ (gyaŋja) delaying; va.བྱེད་ to delay.

འགྱངས་ཆད་ (gyaŋjɛɛ̀) a fine/ penalty for being late with a payment; vi.—འཁྲི་ to be fined for being late in payment.

འགྱངས་ཆད་ཁྲལ་དངུལ་ (gyaŋjɛɛ̀ trɛ̄ɛ̄ŋüü) fine in money for being late with a payment.

འགྱངས་འཐེན་ (gyaŋden) postponing, delaying; va.—བྱེད་ ¶ ཁོ་ཐོན་རྒྱུ་གནས་སྐབས་འགྱངས་འཐེན་བྱས་པ་རེད་ (He) is postponing his departure for the time being.

འགྱངས་མེད་ (gyaŋmeè) without delay ¶ ཡིག་ལན་འགྱངས་མེད་གནང་རོགས་གནང་ Please reply to the letter without delay.

འགྱངས་ཞུ་ (gyaŋ shu) shung. va. to ask permission to delay sth.

འགྱངས་བཤོལ་ (gyaŋshöö) shung. delaying, postponing.

འགྱངས་བསྲིང་ (gyaŋsiŋ) sm. འགྱངས་འཐེན་.

འགྱར་འགྱུར་ (gyaŋgyur) unsteady, unstable, not firm, changeable.

འགྱར་རེ་འགྱུར་རེ་ (gyare gyurre) sm. འགྱར་འགྱུར་.

འགྱིག (gyig) 1. rubber. 2. plastic.

འགྱིག་ཀོ་ (gyiggo) sm. འགྱིག.

འགྱིག་ཁུག (gyiggug) rubber/ plastic bag.

འགྱིག་འཁོར་ (gyiggɔɔ) rubber tire.

འགྱིག་འཁོར་གྱི་ནང་པགས་ (gyiggɔɔgi naŋbaà) inner tube.

འགྱིག་འཁོར་གྱི་ནང་མའི་སྦྲུར་རས་ (gyiggɔɔgi naŋmɛ jarrɛɛ̀) cord fabric (in tires).

འགྱིག་འཁོར་བཟོ་གྲྭ་ (gyiggɔɔ sodra) tire factory.

འགྱིག་འཁོར་ཤིང་རྟ་ (gyiggɔɔ siŋda) cart with rubber wheels.

འགྱིག་གི་ལྒང་བུ (gyiggi gaŋbuù) rubber balloon.

འགྱིག་གི་སྤོ་ལོ་ (gyiggi bōlo) rubber ball.

འགྱིག་གི་སྦུ་གུ (gyiggi bugu) sm. འགྱིག་སྦུག.

འགྱིག་གི་སུབ་བྱེད་ (gyiggi sūbjeè) rubber eraser.

འགྱིག་གྲུ་ (gyigdru) rubber boat.

འགྱིག་ཆས་ (gyigjɛɛ̀) rubber goods, rubberware.

འགྱིག་འཇུར་ (gyiŋjur) sneakers, gym shoes.

འགྱིག་ཐག (gyigdaà) rubberband.

འགྱིག་ཐམ་ (gyigdam) rubber stamp.

འགྱིག་དམ་ (gyigdam) hot water bottle/ bag.

འགྱིག་དྭངས་མ་ (gyig taŋma) clear plastic.

འགྱིག་དེམ་ (gyigdem) sm. འགྱིག་དམ་.

འགྱིག་གདན་ (gyigdɛn) foam mattress/ cushion.

འགྱིག་མདའ་ (gyiŋda) rubber slingshot; va.—རྒྱག to shoot a rubber slingshot.

འགྱིག་མདོང་ (gyiŋdoŋ) rubber pipe/ hose.

འགྱིག་སྡོང་ (gyigdoŋ) rubber tree.

འགྱིག་པར་ (gyigbar) rubber stamp.

འགྱིག་ཕྱགས་ (gyigbaà) inner tube (of tire).

འགྱིག་སྦྱིན་ (gyigjin) glue for rubber (tires, etc.).

འགྱིག་ཕད་ (gyigpɛɛ̀) rubber or plastic pack/ pouch.

འགྱིག་ཕོར་ (gyigbɔɔ) plastic cup/ bowl.

འགྱིག་བྱི་རིལ་ (gyig cirii) chewing gum.

འགྱིག་ལྦུ་བ་ཅན་ (gyig buwəjɛn) foam rubber.

འགྱིག་སྦུག (gyigbuù) rubber pipe, plastic tube.

འགྱིག་ཟོན་ (gyigsön) Tibetan-style woolen boots with rubber soles.

འགྱིག་བཟོས་ལག་ཤུབས་ (gyigsöö ləgshub) rubber gloves.

འགྱིག་རས་ (gyigrɛɛ̀) rubber/ plastic cloth.

འགྱིག་རློན་ (gyiglön) rubber gum.

འགྱིག་ཤིང་ (gyigshiŋ) rubber tree.

འགྱིག་ཤོག (gyigshɔɔ̀) plastic paper, plastic cloth.

འགྱིག་སུབ་ (gyigsub) abbr. འགྱིག་གི་སུབ་བྱེད་.

འགྱིག་ལྷམ་ (gyiglham) rubber boots/ shoes/ galoshes.

འགྱིགས་ (gyig) sm. འགྱིག.

འགྱིང་: p. འགྱིངས་; f. འགྱིང་; imp. འགྱིངས (gyiŋ) va. to act haughty, to put on airs.

འགྱིང་འགྲོས་ (gyiŋdröö) a pompous/ haughty way of walking.

འགྱིང་ངེར་སྡོད་ (gyiŋŋer döö) va. to sit tall/ straight/ erect.

འགྱིང་ངེར་ལངས་ (gyiŋŋer laŋ) va. to stand tall/ straight/ erect.

འགྱིང་འཆམ་ (gyiŋcam) a slow type of འཆམ་.

འགྱིང་ཉམས་ (gyiŋñam) 1. grand, imposing, haughty, arrogant, pretentious, pompous; va.—སྟོན་.

འགྱིང་སྟབས་ (gyiŋdəb) sm. འགྱིང་ཉམས་.

འགྱིང་བག (gyiŋbaà) sm. འགྱིང་ཉམས་.

འགྱིང་ཐིག (gyiŋdig) the line outlining the posture of a body in tangka painting.

འགྱིང་བྱེད་ (gyiŋjeè) sm. འགྱིང་.

འགྱིང་ཚུགས་ཆེ་ཉམས་ (gyiŋdzuù cẽñam) sm. འགྱིང་ཉམས་.

འགྱིང་ཚུལ་ (gyiŋdzüü) sm. འགྱིང་ཉམས་.

འགྱིངས་ (gyiŋ) p. of འགྱིང་.

འགྱུ་: p. འགྱུས་; f. འགྱུ་ (gyu) sm. འཆར་.

འགྱུར་: p. གྱུར་; f. འགྱུར་ (gyur) 1. vi. to be changed, to be transformed, to become ¶ རྣམ་པ་རྩ་བ་ནས་གྱུར་པ་རེད་ The appearance changed completely. ¶ བཟོ་ལས་ཅན་གྱི་གྲོང་ཁྱེར་ཞིག་ཏུ་གྱུར་བ་རེད་ (It) has changed into an industrial city/ town. ¶ ཉེན་ཁ་ཤིན་ཏུ་ཆེ་བར་འགྱུར་བའི་སྐབས་ When it becomes extremely dangerous. 2. times ¶ འཕྲུལ་འཁོར་གསར་པ་དེས་ཐོན་སྐྱེད་བརྒྱ་འགྱུར་གྱི་མགྱོགས་པར་བྱེད་ཐུབ་ཀྱི་ཡོད་པ་རེད་ The new machine can produce things a hundred times faster.

འགྱུར་སྐད་ (gyargɛɛ̀) sm. འགྱུར་ཁུག.

འགྱུར་སྐུལ་དངོས་རྫས་ (gyurgüü ŋöödzɛɛ̀) a catalyst ¶ འགྱུར་སྐུལ་དངོས་རྫས་བཟོ་གྲྭ Catalyst factory.

འགྱུར་ཁུག (gyarguù) melody.

འགྱུར་གྲངས་ (gyurdraŋ) variable number (in math).

འགྱུར་གློག (gyurlɔɔ̀) alternating current.

འགྱུར་འགོད་ (gyurgöö) transforming, transformation ¶ སྤྱི་ཚོགས་རིང་ལུགས་ཀྱི་འགྱུར་འགོད་ Socialist transformation.

འགྱུར་འགྲོས་ (gyurdröö) changes (in a situation).

འགྱུར་བཅོས་ (gyurjöö) correcting a translation; va.—བྱེད་. 2. reform, reforming; va.—བྱེད་.

འགྱུར་བཅོས་སྒོ་ཕྱེ་སྲིད་ཇུས་ (gyurjöö goce siijüü) the policy of "reform and open door".

འགྱུར་ཅན་ (gyurjɛn) variable, changeable.

འགྱུར་ཅན་གློག་འགོག (gyurjɛn lɔ̃ŋgɔɔ̀) variable resistance.

འགྱུར་ཅན་གློག་གསོག་སྣོད་ཆས་ (gyurjɛn lɔ̃gsɔɔ̀ nööcɛɛ̀) adjustable capacitor, variable condenser.

འགྱུར་ཅན་རྒྱུན་འཁོར་མ་རྩ་ (gyurjɛn gyüngɔɔ madza) circulating capital.

འགྱུར་ཅན་མ་རྩ་ (gyurjɛn madza) variable capital.

འགྱུར་བའི་ཆོས་ (gyurwɛ cöö) impermanence, change.

འགྱུར་བརྗེ་ (gyurje) sm. བརྗེ་ལེན་.

འགྱུར་ད་རེ་ (gyurdare) idiom indicating that (it/ sth.) will certainly happen.

འགྱུར་རྟེན་ (gyurden) deposit, down payment; va.—འཇོག to leave a deposit/ down payment ¶ ཚོང་ཁང་ནས་ཅ་ལག་དེ་ཉོ་རྒྱུའི་འགྱུར་རྟེན་བཞག་སྟེ་ནང་ལ་དངུལ་ལེན་པར་ཕྱིན་པ་ཡིན་ I left a deposit at the store for buying the goods, and went home to get the (rest of the) money.

འགྱུར་རྟེན་དང་ཚོང་རྩ་བརྗེ་བསྒྱུར་གྱི་འགན་འཛིན་ཁང་ (gyurdendaŋ tsõŋ dza jegyurgi gɛndzingaŋ) Securities and Exchange Commission (SEC).

འགྱུར་རྡོ་ (gyurdo) fossil.

འགྱུར་ལྡོག (gyundɔɔ̀) 1. change, transformation ¶ འགྱུར་ལྡོག་ཏུ་ཅང་ཆེན་པོ་ཡོང་བཞིན་པའི་དུས་སྐབས་ཤིག A time of great change. 2. a chemical reaction.

འགྱུར་ལྡོག་གི་འགག་རྩ་ (gyundɔɔgi gagdza) turning point.

འགྱུར་ལྡོག་ཚ་པོ་ (gyundɔɔ tsãbo) changeable, not stable.

འགྱུར་དཔེ་ (gyurbe) translated book/ text/ scripture.

འགྱུར་ཕྱག (gyurjaà) prostrating to a deity before translating a religious scripture; va.—བྱེད་.

འགྱུར་བ་ (gyurwa) a change; va.—གཏོང་ to change; vi.—འགྲོ་ to get/ be changed ¶ དུས་ཚོད་ཐུང་ཐུང་ཞིག་གི་ནང་འགྱུར་བ་མང་པོ་ཞིག་བྱུང་བ་རེད་ There were many changes during a short time. ¶ ལས་ཀ་བྱེད་སྟངས་ལ་འགྱུར་བ་ཆེན་པོ་ཞིག་བཏང་བ་རེད་ (They) made a big change in their procedure. ¶ ཁོ་ཚོའི་བསམ་བློར་འགྱུར་བ་ཆེན་པོ་ཕྱིན་ཡོད་པ་རེད་ Their ideas changed a great deal.

འགྱུར་བ་མ་ནིང་ (gyurwa maniŋ) a Tibetan belief that hermaphrodites change sex every 15 days.

འགྱུར་བ་མེད་པ་ (gyurwa meèba) sm. འགྱུར་མེད་.

འགྱུར་བག (gyurbaà) the appearance of change.

འགྱུར་བའི་མི་རྟག་པ་ (gyurwɛ midagba) impermanence.

འགྱུར་བྱང་ (gyurjaŋ) section at the end of a book where the translator's name appears.

འགྱུར་བྱེད་ (gyurjeè) 1. senseless, silly, stupid. 2. sm. ལན་ཚྭ་.

འགྱུར་མིང་ (gyurmiŋ) a new name that is taken, a name that has been changed.

འགྱུར་མེད་ (gyurmeè) 1. unchanging, permanent ¶ འགྱུར་མེད་སྲིད་ཇུས་ Unchanging policy. 2. a person's name.

འགྱུར་མེད་དངོས་གཙོའི་རིང་ལུགས་ (gyurmeè ŋöödzö riŋluù) mechanistic materialism.

འགྱུར་མེད་བརྟན་སྲུང་ (gyurmeè dɛ̃nsuŋ) sticking to one's promise/ word; va.—བྱེད་.

འགྱུར་མེད་རྣམ་རྒྱལ་ (gyurmeè nãmgyɛɛ) shung. the son of Polha Sonam Togyal who ruled Tibet from 1747 to 1750.

འགྱུར་མེད་མ་རྩ་ (gyurmeè madza) fixed capital.

འགྱུར་མེད་འཚོ་རྟེན་ (gyurmeè tsõden) immovable or fixed assets/ property.

འགྱུར་མེད་ཡུལ་གནས་ (gyurmeè yüünɛɛ̀) unchanging, stable.

འགྱུར་མེད་རབ་བརྟན་ (gyurmeè rəbdɛn) constant, steady, unchangeable.

འགྱུར་མེད་རིན་གོང་ (gyurmeè ringoŋ) constant/ stable price, fixed price.

འགྱུར་ཚིག (gyurdzii) translated words.

འགྱུར་ཚུལ་ (gyurdzüü) manner of change.

འགྱུར་མཚམས་ཀྱི་ཁུག་ཆ་ (gyundzamgi kũgja) critical angle (in math).

འགྱུར་མཚམས་ཀྱི་དྲོད་ཚད་ (gyundzamgi trööddzɛɛ̀) critical temperature.

འགྱུར་མཚམས་ཀྱི་གནད་ (gyundzamgi nɛɛ̀) critical point, turning point.

འགྱུར་རྫས་བཟོ་ལས་ (gyurdzɛɛ̀ solɛɛ̀) chemical industry.

འགྱུར་ཞུས་པ་ (gyursüüba) proofreader for a translation.

འགྱུར་སྲིད་པའི་རང་བཞིན་ (gyursiibɛ rəŋshin) alterability, changeability.

འགྱུས་ (gyüü) p. of འགྱུ་.

འགྱེངས་ངེར་ལངས་ (gyeŋŋer laŋ) sm. འགྱིང་.

འགྱེད་ (gyeè) 1. alms (given to monks); va.—གཏོང་;

—རྒྱག to give alms ། གྲྭ་པ་ཚོར་འགྱེད་བཏང་སོང་ He gave alms to the monks.

འགྱེད་: p. བཀྱེས་; f. བཀྱེ་; imp. ཁྱེས་ (gyḛè) 1. va. to send ། ངས་བང་ཆེན་བཀྱེས་པ་ཡིན་ I sent a messenger. 2. va. to fight/ contest/ debate ། རྩོད་པ་འགྱེད་ To debate ། འཐབ་མོ་འགྱེད་ To fight. 3. vi. to shine ། འོད་ཟེར་བཀྱེས་དུས་ When the light shone. 4. va. to give.

འགྱེད་དངུལ་ (gyḛèŋüü) money given as alms.

འགྱེད་ཉུང་བན་མང་ (gyḛèñuŋ pḛnmaŋ) not enough to go around [Lit. few alms, many monks].

འགྱེད་ཕོགས་ (gyḛèpɔ̀ɔ) alms and salary.

འགྱེད་ཡོན་ (gyḛèyön) alms.

འགྱེར་ (gyḛr) arc. to renounce/ give up.

འགྱེལ་ (gyḛe) vi. to fall, to collapse ། སྡོང་བུ་ར་དུ་ཤིང་དེ་འགྱེལ་སོང་ The tree fell down suddenly.

འགྱེལ་ཐོག་རྡོག་བརྫིས་ (gyḛetɔ̀ɔ dḛgdzii) hitting sb. when he is down, taking advantage of someone's precarious situation [Lit. stomp on sb. who has fallen].

འགྱེལ་རྡབ་རྨས་སྐྱོན་ (gyḛedəb mɛ̀ɛgyön) an injury from a fall.

འགྱེལ་བའི་སྒང་ལ་རྡོག་བརྫིས་ (gyḛlwɛ gḛŋla dḛgdzi) sm. འགྱེལ་ཐོག་རྡོག་བརྫིས་.

འགྱེལ་བའི་ཐོག་ལ་རྡོག་བརྫིས་ (gyḛlwɛ tɔ̄ɔla dḛgdzi) sm. འགྱེལ་ཐོག་རྡོག་བརྫིས་.

འགྱེལ་ལོག (gyḛelɔ̀ɔ) rolling over; va.—རྒྱག.

འགྱེས་: p. གྱེས་; f. འགྱེས་ (gyḛè) vi. to be separated, to part, to get split up, to break up ། ཁོང་ཚོ་ཚོགས་ཁག་མང་པོ་གྱེས་པ་རེད་ They split up into many groups. ། གྲོགས་པོ་འགྱེས་ལ་ཉེ་བའི་སྐབས་ When the friends were about to part.

འགྱོགས་: p. བཀྱགས་; f. བཀྱག (gyɔ̀ɔ) 1. va. to lift up ། རྡོ་ཡར་བཀྱག་དགོས་ (We) have to lift the stone. 2. va. to serve a drink ། གཞོན་ནུ་མ་དེས་མཆོད་ཆང་བཀྱགས་སོང་ The young woman served beer. 3. vi. to float ། པོ་ལོ་ཆུ་ཁར་བཀྱག་བསྡད་འདུག The ball is floating on the water. 4. va.—རྒྱག to put sth. under something else (e.g., the leg of a table) to make it higher or to level it.

འགྱོགས་སྣས་ (gyɔ̀ɔŋɛ̀ɛ) a wood or stone support used as leverage to jack up a pillar so that it can be changed.

འགྱོགས་ཐག (gyɔgdaà) a rope used when jacking up a pillar.

འགྱོགས་གདུང་ (gyɔgduŋ) a pole/ lever used for raising a pillar.

འགྱོགས་མདའ་ (gyɔŋda) sm. འགྱོགས་གདུང་.

འགྱོགས་གནོན་ (gyɔgnön) a heavy object used to add weight to a pole (lever) that is being used to jack sth. up (usu. a pillar).

འགྱོགས་དཔྱང་ (gyɔgjaŋ) sm. འགྱོགས་འཕྱང་.

འགྱོགས་འཕྱང་ (gyɔgjaŋ) palanquin, stretcher, litter; va.—འཁྱེར་ to carry a palanquin/ stretcher/ litter.

འགྱོགས་བྱམས་ (gyɔgjam) sm. འགྱོགས་འཕྱང་.

འགྱོགས་བྱམས་པ་ (gyɔgjamba) palanquin bearer.

འགྱོགས་རྩུགས་ (gyɔgdzuù) a temporary support used when replacing an old pillar with a new one.

འགྱོགས་ཤིང་ (gyɔgshiŋ) a pillar/ brace/ piece of timber used to prop sth. up.

འགྱོད་ (gyö̱ö) sm. འགྱོད་པ་སྐྱེ་.

འགྱོད་བཅོས་ (gyö̱öjöö) regretting and then correcting/ reforming; va.—བྱེད་ ། སྔོན་ཆད་ཀྱི་ནོར་འཁྲུལ་ལ་འགྱོད་བཅོས་བྱ་དགོས་ As for past mistakes, one should regret and then correct them.

འགྱོད་རྟོགས་ (gyö̱ödɔɔ) regreting; vi.—བྱེད་ to regret.

འགྱོད་གདུང་ (gyö̱öduŋ) suffering from regret; vi.—བྱེད་ to suffer from regret.

འགྱོད་པ་ (gyö̱öba) regret, remorse; va.—བྱེད་ to repent, to regret; vi.—སྐྱེ་ to feel regret/ remorse ། ཁོང་ཚོས་ནོར་འཁྲུལ་དེ་ཚོར་འགྱོད་པ་བྱེད་ཀྱི་ཡོད་པ་རེད་ They are regretting those mistakes. ། སྔོན་ཆད་ཀྱི་ནོར་འཁྲུལ་ལ་འགྱོད་པ་སྐྱེ་གི་འདུག I feel regret for past mistakes.

འགྱོད་པས་གནོང་ (gyö̱öbɛ nōŋ) vi. to feel remorse/ regret.

འགྱོད་པས་མནར་ (gyö̱öbɛ nār) vi. to be tormented by regret, to be burdened/ suffer from regret.

འགྱོད་ཚངས་ (gyö̱ödzaŋ) regretting, being remorseful.

འགྱོད་བཤགས་ (gyö̱öshaà) repenting; va.—བྱེད་ to repent.

འགྱོད་སེམས་ (gyö̱ösem) sm. འགྱོད་པ་.

འགྲང་: p. འགྲངས་; f. འགྲང་ (dra̱ŋ) vi. to be full (regarding eating), to be satisfied/ satiated.

འགྲང་སྣོན་ (dra̱ŋnön) supplementary hay/ fodder given to animals after returning from a day of grazing.

འགྲངས་ (dra̱ŋ) p. of འགྲང་.

འགྲངས་ལྟོགས་ (dra̱ŋdɔɔ) hungry and full, hungry and satiated.

འགྲངས་ཕྱེད་ལྟོགས་ཕྱེད་ (dra̱ŋjeè dōgjeè) underfed, half full and half hungry.

འགྲན་ (drḛn) va. to compete, to contest, to vie with, to contend ། ལུས་རྩལ་མང་པོ་འགྲན་ཡོད་པ་རེད་ (They) have competed in many sporting events.

འགྲན་གྱི་ཏོ་མེད་ (drḛngi tomɛɛ) sm. འགྲན་ཡ་མེད་པ་.

འགྲན་གྱི་དོ་ཟླ་ (drḛngi tonda) sm. འགྲན་ཡ་མེད་པ་.

འགྲན་གྱི་ཟླ་མེད་ (drḛngi da̱meè) sm. འགྲན་ཟླ་མེད་པ་.

འགྲན་གླིང་ (drḛnleŋ) competing, contesting, contending ། མཁས་བརྒྱ་འགྲན་གླིང་ Let 100 (schools) of thought contend.

འགྲན་གྲོལ་ (drḛngöö) antagonism, confrontation, opposition; va.—བྱེད་ to antagonize, to confront, to oppose ། གྲལ་རིམ་གྱི་འགྲན་གྲོལ་ Class antagonism.

འགྲན་གྲོལ་གྱི་འགལ་བ་མ་ཡིན་པ་ (drḛngöögi gḛḛwa ma̱ yi̱mbə) nonantagonistic contradiction.

འགྲན་གྲོལ་གྱི་རང་བཞིན་ (drḛngöögi ra̱ŋshin) antagonism, antagonistic nature.

འགྲན་གྲོལ་ཅན་གྱི་འགལ་བ་ (drḛngööjɛngi gḛḛwa) antagonistic contradiction.

འགྲན་ང་ཕྲག་དོག (trḛnŋa trāàdɔɔ) shung. rivalry and jealousy.

འགྲན་ཐང་ (drḛndaŋ) an area or field for holding competitions.

འགྲན་དོ་ (drḛndo) sm. འགྲན་ཟླ་.

འགྲན་བདར་ (drḛnda) a challenge to compete; va.—གཏོང་.

འགྲན་བསྡུར་ (drḛndur) competing, contesting; competition, match, contest; va.—བྱེད་ to compete, to contest; va.—སློང་ to bring about/ provoke a contest ། ཐོན་སྐྱེད་སྤུས་ཚད་ཀྱི་འགྲན་བསྡུར་ Competition in the quality of production.

འགྲན་བསྡུར་ཁས་ལེན་གྱི་ཡི་གེ་ (drḛndur kɛ̀ɛlengi yi̱gi) a letter accepting a challenge to a contest.

འགྲན་བསྡུར་ཆུ་ཚོད་ (drḛndur cūdzöö) a stopwatch.

འགྲན་བསྡུར་སློང་ཡིག (drḛndur lōŋyii) letter of challenge for a (contest).

འགྲན་དཔང་ (drḛnbaŋ) judge in a competition or performance; va.—བྱེད་.

འགྲན་སྤྲལ་ (drḛndrɛɛ) sm. འགྲན་ཟླ་མེད་པ་.

འགྲན་མེད་ (drḛnmeè) abbr. of འགྲན་ཟླ་མེད་པ་.

འགྲན་རྩོད་ (drḛndzöö) contending, competing; va.—བྱེད་.

འགྲན་རྩོད་བྱེད་ས་ (drḛndzöö cḛ̀ɛsa) a bone/ object of contention.

འགྲན་ཟླ་ (drḛnda) rival, competitor, match ། ཁོ་གཉིས་འགྲན་ཟླ་རེད་ Those two are rivals. 2. competing, contesting, vying; va.—བྱེད་ to compete, to contest, to vie ། ས་གནས་ཀྱི་སྤོ་ལོའི་རུ་ཁག་གིས་རྒྱལ་སའི་སྤོ་ལོའི་རུ་ཁག་གི་འགྲན་ཟླ་བྱེད་ཐུབ་ཀྱི་མ་རེད་ The local ball team cannot compete with the capital's ball team. ། དབང་ཤུགས་འགྲན་རྩོད་བྱེད་རྒྱུ་ Competing for power.

འགྲན་ཟླ་ཆོག (drḛnda cɔ̄ɔ) 1. vi. to be capable of competing with ། ས་གནས་ཀྱི་སྤོ་ལོའི་རུ་ཁག་གིས་རྒྱལ་སའི་སྤོ་ལོའི་རུ་ཁག་གི་འགྲན་ཟླ་ཆོག་གི་མ་རེད་ The local ball team cannot compete with the capital's ball team.

འགྲན་ཟླ་བྲལ་བ་ (drenda treewa) sm. འགྲན་ཟླ་མེད་པ་.

འགྲན་ཟླ་མེད་པ་ (drenda meèba) unrivaled, matchless, unequaled, unsurpassed, incomparable.

འགྲན་ཡ་ (drenya) sm. འགྲན་ཟླ་.

འགྲན་ཡ་མེད་པ་ (drenya meèba) sm. འགྲན་ཟླ་མེད་པ་.

འགྲན་ར་ (drenra) place where competition/ games take place.

འགྲན་ལེན་ (drenlen) accepting a challenge; va.—བྱེད་ to accept a challenge.

འགྲན་ལེན་འཇལ་ཡིག (drenlen jeeyiì) letter accepting a challenge/ match.

འགྲན་སེམས་ (drensem) competitiveness, having the thought of competing; vi.—སྐྱེད་ to have a competitive feeling arise; va.—འཆང་ to hold competitive thoughts.

འགྲན་སློང་ (drenloŋ) abbr. of འགྲན་བསྡུར་སློང་ཡིག.

འགྲམ་ (dram) 1. near, by the side of ༑ ཁོ་ཚོའི་ཁང་པའི་འགྲམ་ལ་ Near their house. 2. bank, shore ༑ གཙང་པོའི་ལྷོ་འགྲམ་ The southern bank of the river. 3. abbr. of འགྲམ་པ་.

འགྲམ་དཀྱུས་ (dramgyüù) the cheeks.

འགྲམ་སྐྱོར་ (dram gyōr) va. to sit with one's hands holding the side of one's face while one's elbows are placed on a table/ desk.

འགྲམ་ཁུག (dramguù) the inside of the cheeks.

འགྲམ་ངོགས་ (dramŋɔ̀ɔ) shore, bank.

འགྲམ་ལྕག (dramjaà) 1. a slap on the cheek/ face; va.—རྒྱག; —གཞུ་ to slap the cheek/ face. 2. an instrument made of leather that is used to slap the cheek (as punishment).

འགྲམ་ལྕག་བཞུས་ནས་རྒྱགས་པ་ཡིན་ཁུལ་བྱེད་པ་ (dramjaà shüünɛ gyagba yingüü ceèba) putting on a good front even though sth. bad has happened [Lit. slapping on the face, pretending to be fat].

འགྲམ་ཆང་ (drajaŋ) sm. འགྲམ་ཆུ་.

འགྲམ་ཆུ་ (dramju) saliva; spittle vi.—འཁོར་; —ལྷུང་; —ཁོལ་; —ཤོར་ to have one's mouth water (to eat), to salivate.

འགྲམ་སྟེགས་ (dramdeg) platform near sth.

འགྲམ་སྟོང་ (dramdoŋ) sunken cheek.

འགྲམ་དུ་ (dramdu) near, by the side/ bank of.

འགྲམ་ན་ (dramna) sm. འགྲམ་དུ་.

འགྲམ་པ་ (dramba) cheek ༑ བུ་འདིའི་འགྲམ་པ་བྱིལ་བྱིལ་བྱས་ (He) stroked the boy's cheeks.

འགྲམ་པ་ཉམས་པ་ (dramba ñamba) a type of Tibetan wind disease characterized by locked jaws.

འགྲམ་པ་ས་ཕབ་ (dramba sāpəb) with humility and sincerity ༑ ངང་ཉིད་ནས་འགྲམ་པ་ས་བབ་ཀྱི་རེ་འདུན་ཞུས་ཀྱང་དོན་སྨིན་མ་བྱུང་ Even though I requested (it) with humility and sincerity, they didn't agree. [Lit. putting the cheek on the ground].

འགྲམ་ཕུག (drampug) the inside of the mouth.

འགྲམ་སྦྱོར་ (dramjɔɔ) pieces of wood that enclose the plough blade. 2. sm. འགྲམ་པ་, 2.

འགྲམ་སྨིན་ཚ་ནད་ (drammen tsānɛɛ̀) parotitis.

འགྲམ་གཞི་ (dramshi) foundation, basis.

འགྲམ་རུས་ (dramrüù) jaw, cheekbone.

འགྲམ་ལ་བཅར་ (dramla jāā) va. to draw near, to come close/ near to ༑ དགྲ་བོ་འགྲམ་ལ་བཅར་སྐབས་གཞི་ནས་མེ་མདའ་བརྒྱབ་འདུག (They) fired only when the enemy came close.

འགྲམ་ལོགས་ (dramlɔ̀ɔ) near, adjacent, close to.

འགྲམ་ཤ་ (dramsha) fleshy part of the cheek; va.—འཕྱུག to rub one's cheek (when feeling embarrassed).

འགྲམ་ཤ་ཕིག་ཕིག་ཏུ་འདར་ (dramsha pigbiìdu dar) phrase connoting anger [Lit. cheek flesh shaking].

འགྲམ་གཤོག (dramshoò) side.

འགྲམ་སོ་ (dramso) molar teeth.

འགྲམ་སོ་སྦུག་མ་ (dramso bugma) wisdom tooth.

འགྲམ་སྲུང་ཤིང་ནགས་ (dramsuŋ shiŋnaà) erosion protection forest (usu. planted on river banks).

འགྲམས་ (dram) sm. གྲམ་.

འགྲས་ (drɛɛ̀) vi. to hate/ dislike.

འགྲས་འགྲུས་ (drɛɛ̀drüù) shung. a cunning/ tricky person.

འགྲིག་ཀ་ (drigə) id. "its okay." ༑ ལྷ་སར་ཕེབས་ན་འགྲིག་ཀ་ Its okay to go to Lhasa.

འགྲིག་ཁྲིམས་ (drigtrim) sm.* སྒྲིག་ཁྲིམས་.

འགྲིག: p. **འགྲིགས་**; f. **འགྲིག** (drig) 1. vi. to be all right, to be okay, to be right ༑ ཁང་མིག་མང་པོ་མེད་ན་ཡང་འགྲིག་གི་རེད་ It will be okay even if there are not many rooms. 2. vi. to fit, to suit, to match, to be suitable with, to be in conformity with ༑ པར་དེ་པར་སྒྲོམ་ནང་ལ་འགྲིག་གི་མི་འདུག The picture does not fit the frame.

འགྲིག་འགྲོ་གི་རེད་ (drig drugireè) things will sort themselves out, it will be okay ༑ གནད་དོན་འདིའི་སྐོར་སེམས་ཁྲལ་མ་བྱེད་ འགྲིག་འགྲོ་གི་རེད་ Concerning this issue, don't worry. It will be okay.

འགྲིག་ཆ་ (drigca) sm. འགྲིག་ཆགས་.

འགྲིག་ཆགས་ (drigcaà) an arrangement (to settle sth.); va.—བྱེད་ ༑ ཕྱོགས་གཉིས་བར་གྱི་རྩོད་གཞི་འགྲིག་ཆགས་ཡོང་ཐབས་གནང་བ་རེད་ (They) tried to work out an arrangement to settle the dispute between the two parties.

འགྲིག་རྟགས་ (drigdaà) the sign/ symbol indicating correct, a check mark.

འགྲིག་ཐབས་ (drigtəb) means/ methods/ strategies for reconciliation or compromise or agreement; va.—བྱེད་ to reconcile, to compromise, to bring about an agreement ༑ ཚོགས་ཁག་དེ་གཉིས་དབར་གྱི་རྩོད་རྙོག་དེ་འགྲིག་ཐབས་བྱེད་ཀྱི་ཡོད་པ་རེད་ (They) are making an effort to reconcile the dispute between the two groups.

འགྲིག་མཐུན་ (drigtün) reconciling, working out, arranging, settling; va.—བྱེད་ ༑ ཁ་མཆུ་དེ་འགྲིག་མཐུན་བྱས་པ་རེད་ (They) settled the dispute.

འགྲིག་པོ་ (drigbo) 1. friendly, on good terms, in harmony ༑ ཁོ་གཉིས་འགྲིག་པོ་འདུག They are on friendly terms. 2. fitting, suitable, a good match ༑ ན་བཟའ་དེ་དང་དབུ་ཞྭ་དེ་འགྲིག་པོ་འདུག That dress and that hat match (well).

འགྲིག་མིན་ (drigmin) whether sth. is right or not ༑ ཁྱེད་རང་བོད་ལ་ཕེབས་ན་འགྲིགས་མིན་གོང་རིམ་ལ་བཀའ་འདྲི་ཞུས་པ་ཡིན་ I asked the superior officials whether it is all right for you to go to Tibet or not. 2. it is not all right ༑ གོང་རིམ་ནས་ཁྱེད་རང་བོད་ལ་ཕེབས་ན་འགྲིགས་མིན་ཞེས་བཀའ་ཕེབས་བྱུང་ The superior officials said "It is not all right for you to go to Tibet."

འགྲིག་མེད་ (drigmeè) whether sth. is all right or not ༑ ལྷ་སར་འགྲོ་རྒྱུའི་ལག་ཁྱེར་དེ་འགྲིག་མེད་ཤེས་ཀྱི་ཡོད་པས་ Do you know whether the visa for going to Tibet is all right or not?

འགྲིག་མེད་བཟའ་ཟླ་ (drigmeè sanda) a couple that have problems.

འགྲིགས་ (drig) p. of འགྲིག.

འགྲིགས་འཇགས་ (drig jaà) sm. འགྲིག་ཆགས་.

འགྲིགས་དབང་བཀའ་མཐུན་ (driwaŋ kādün) shung. agreeing upon sth.

འགྲིགས་ཤོ་སྦག (drig shōbaà) shung. gambling paraphernalia.

འགྲིབ་ (drib) 1. vi. to decline, to go down, to decrease, to decay ༑ ཐན་པ་བསྟན་རྗེས་གཙང་པོ་གྲིབ་བཞག After the drought the water in the river went dry. 2. vi. to block, to cover/ shade ༑ སྒེའུ་ཁུང་མདུན་གྱི་ཤིང་སྡོང་དེས་ཉི་མ་འགྲིབ་ཀྱི་འདུག The tree in front of the window blocks the sun.

འགྲིབ་དུས་ (dribdüù) time/ period of decline.

འགྲིམ་: p. **འགྲིམས་**; f. **འགྲིམ་**; imp. **འགྲིམས་** (drim) 1) va. to journey, to travel ༑ ཁོས་ལུང་པ་མང་པོ་འགྲིམས་ཡོད་པ་རེད་ He has traveled through many countries. 2. va. to go, to pass through ༑ མོས་ལོ་མང་སློབ་གྲྭ་འགྲིམས་ཡོད་པ་རེད་ She went through many years of school.

འགྲིམ་སྐོར་ (dri̲bgɔɔ) sm. ལྷ་སྐོར་.

འགྲིམ་འགྲུལ་ (dri̲mdrüü) 1. communication, travel, intercourse, traffic; va.—བྱེད་ ¶ རྒྱལ་ཁབ་གཉིས་དབར་ཚོང་ཐོག་ནས་འགྲིམ་འགྲུལ་སྔར་ནས་ཡོད་པ་རེད་ There was commercial intercourse between the two countries from before. ¶ འགྲིམ་འགྲུལ་གྱི་སྐོར་སྲུང་པ་ A traffic policemen. ¶ མཐའ་འཁོབ་ས་གནས་དེ་ཚོར་འགྲིམ་འགྲུལ་བྱེད་རྒྱུ་དེང་སང་ཡང་ཁག་པོ་ཡོད་ Even these days it is difficult to travel to the remote areas.

འགྲིམ་འགྲུལ་སྐྱེལ་འདྲེན་ (dri̲mdrüü gyēndren) 1. transportation, transporting. 2. communications and transportation.

འགྲིམ་འགྲུལ་མཁོ་ཆས་ (dri̲mdrüü kōcεὲ) equipment for traveling, things needed when traveling.

འགྲིམ་འགྲུལ་གྱི་ཁྲལ་ (dri̲mdrüügi trε̄ε) traveling tax.

འགྲིམ་འགྲུལ་གྱི་ཅིང་ཁྲ་ (dri̲mdrüügi jīŋdra) tib. ch. traffic policeman.

འགྲིམ་འགྲུལ་གྱི་མཚོན་རྟགས་ (dri̲mdrüügi tsōndaà) traffic signs/ signals.

འགྲིམ་འགྲུལ་གྱི་ལས་འཛོལ་ (dri̲mdrüügi lε̲ὲdzöö) traffic accident.

འགྲིམ་འགྲུལ་ཉེན་རྟོག་ཁང་ (dri̲mdrüü ñe̲ndɔggaŋ) traffic police office.

འགྲིམ་འགྲུལ་ཉེན་རྟོག་པ་ (dri̲mdrüü ñe̲ndɔgba) traffic policeman.

འགྲིམ་འགྲུལ་ཐིང་ (dri̲mdrüü tīŋ) tib.ch. bureau of communications/ traffic.

འགྲིམ་འགྲུལ་དྲ་བ་ (dri̲mdrüü tra̲wa) communication net/ network.

འགྲིམ་འགྲུལ་བདེ་འཇགས་ (dri̲mdrüü de̲jaà) traffic safety ¶ འགྲིམ་འགྲུལ་བདེ་འཇགས་ཀྱི་སློབ་གསོ་གཏོང་དགོས་ (We) must teach about traffic safety.

འགྲིམ་འགྲུལ་བདེ་འཇགས་ཨུ་ཡོན་ལྷན་ཁང་ (dri̲mdrüü de̲jaà ūyön lhε̄ngaŋ) traffic safety committee.

འགྲིམ་འགྲུལ་པུའུ་ཁང་ (dri̲mdrü būkaŋ) tib. ch. ministry of communications, department of transportation.

འགྲིམ་འགྲུལ་དཔུང་སྡེ་ (dri̲mdrü būŋde) transportation unit (military).

འགྲིམ་འགྲུལ་ལས་ཁུངས་ (dri̲mdrü lε̲ὲguŋ) Department of Transportation.

འགྲིམ་འགྲུལ་སོ་ལྟ་ཁང་ (dri̲mdrü sōdagaŋ) traffic police stand/ booth.

འགྲིམ་སྒོ་ (dri̲mgo) exit (door).

འགྲིམ་རྟོག་གྲུ་གཟིངས་ (dri̲mdog tru̲dziŋ) patrol boat.

འགྲིམ་འབད་ (dri̲mbεὲ) shung. working tirelessly ¶ དབུས་གཙང་གི་སྐྱ་སེར་རང་རང་སོ་སོ་ནས་བདེ་སྐྱིད་དཔལ་ལ་འགོད་པའི་འགྲིམ་འབད་ཀྱིས་ You should work tirelessly so that all the monks and common people in Tibet can live in happiness.

འགྲིམས་ (dri̲m) p. of འགྲིམ་.

འགྲིལ་ (dri̲i̲) 1. vi. to be accumulated/ concentrated/ collected/ merged/ summarized (main points) ¶ ཁོང་གི་རྩོམ་ཡིག་དེའི་ནང་དོན་འགྲིལ་བ་རེད་ He summarized the main points of the article. 2. vi. to roll (by itself). 3. sm. ཁ་འགྲིལ་.

འགྲིལ་པོ་ (dri̲i̲bu) collected/ accumulated/ concentrated entirely.

འགྲུབ་: p. གྲུབ་; f. འགྲུབ་ (dru̲b) vi. to achieve, to fulfill, to complete ¶ ང་ཚོའི་དམིགས་ཡུལ་དེ་ག་དུས་འགྲུབ་ཀྱི་རེད་དམ་ When will we achieve our aims?

འགྲུབ་ཐུབ་ཚོད་ (dru̲b tūbdzöὸ) sas much as one can achieve.

འགྲུབ་སྦྱོར་ (dru̲bjɔɔ) conjunction of a star in astrology (can be a good or bad conjunction/ date).

འགྲུབ་དམིགས་ (dru̲bmiì) shung. means to accomplish sth. ¶ གཙུག་ལག་ཁང་གི་ཞིག་གསོ་སྐྱོན་ཆོས་འགྲུབ་དམིགས་མེད་པ་སེམས་གསལ་བཞིན་ We are fully aware that we don't have the means to renovate the Lhasa Cathedral.

འགྲུབ་རེ་ (dru̲bre) hope of getting/ finishing/ accomplishing.

འགྲུབ་རེའི་དམིགས་ཚད་ (dru̲bree mīgtsεὲ) production quota/ target/ goal.

འགྲུལ་ (drü̲ü̲) 1. traveling, taking a trip; va.—རྒྱག to travel, to take a trip/ journey ¶ ལྷ་ས་ནས་ཁམས་ཁུལ་འགྲུལ་ཐེངས་ཁ་ཤས་རྒྱག་སོང་ (We) have traveled several times from Lhasa to Kham. 2. abbr. of འགྲུལ་པ་.

འགྲུལ་སྐྱེལ་ (drü̲ü̲gyel) transporting travelers; va.—བྱེད་ ¶ འགྲུལ་སྐྱེལ་གནམ་གྲུ་ Passenger aircraft.

འགྲུལ་སྐྱེལ་འཁོར་ལོ་ (drü̲ü̲gyel kɔ̄ɔlo) passenger vehicle.

འགྲུལ་སྐྱེལ་གྲུ་གཟིངས་ (drü̲ü̲gyel tru̲dziŋ) passenger ship.

འགྲུལ་སྐྱེལ་སྣུམ་འཁོར་པ་སི་ (drü̲ü̲gyel nūmkɔɔ ba̲se) tib. eng. bus.

འགྲུལ་སྐྱེལ་བབས་ཚུགས་ (drü̲ü̲gyel bə̲btsuù) traveler's station.

འགྲུལ་སྐྱེལ་མེ་འཁོར་ (drü̲ü̲gyel me̲kɔɔ) passenger train.

འགྲུལ་སྐྱེལ་གླངས་འཁོར་ (drü̲ü̲gyel lāŋkɔɔ) passenger car.

འགྲུལ་སྐྱེལ་ས་ཚིགས་ (drü̲ü̲gyel sə̲tsig) traveler's station.

འགྲུལ་སྐྱོད་ (drü̲ü̲gyöὸ) traveling, touring, journeying; va.—བྱེད་.

འགྲུལ་སྐྱོད་པ་ (drü̲ü̲gyöὸba) traveler.

འགྲུལ་བསྐྱོད་ (drü̲ü̲gyöὸ) sm. འགྲུལ་སྐྱོད་.

འགྲུལ་ཁ་ (drü̲ü̲ka) an illness caused by the arrival of a visitor.

འགྲུལ་ཁང་ (drü̲ü̲gaŋ) hotel, traveler's guesthouse.

འགྲུལ་ཁུར་ (drü̲ü̲kur) a tent for traveling.

འགྲུལ་གྲོགས་ (drü̲ü̲drɔɔ̀) co-passenger, traveling companion.

འགྲུལ་འགྲིམ་པ་ (drü̲ü̲drimbə) shung. travelers.

འགྲུལ་རྒྱུན་ (drü̲ü̲gyün) flow/ turnover/ circulation of travelers.

འགྲུལ་སྒར་ (drü̲ü̲gar) a camp of travelers.

འགྲུལ་བཅོམ་ཇག་པ་ (drü̲ü̲jom ca̲gba) bandits who rob travelers.

འགྲུལ་ཆས་ (drü̲ü̲cεὲ) travel luggage.

འགྲུལ་ཆས་དབོར་བཅོལ་ (drü̲ü̲cεὲ wɔɔjöö) checking baggage.

འགྲུལ་ཐོ་ (drü̲ü̲to) a list of visitors/ travelers; va.—རྒྱག to make a list of visitors/ travelers.

འགྲུལ་སྣ་ (drü̲ü̲na) 1. tour guide. 2. sm. འགྲུལ་ཁ་.

འགྲུལ་པ་ (drü̲ü̲bə) traveler, passenger, visitor, guest.

འགྲུལ་པ་སྐྱེལ་འདྲེན་བྱེད་ཚད་ (drü̲ü̲bə gyēndren cε̲ὲtsεὲ) sm. འགྲུལ་པ་སྐྱེལ་ཚད་.

འགྲུལ་པ་སྐྱེལ་ཚད་ (drü̲ü̲bə gyēētsεὲ) the rate of passenger/ traveler traffic.

འགྲུལ་པ་ཕར་ཚུར་འགྲོ་ཚད་ (drü̲ü̲bə pāā tsūū dro̲tsεὲ) sm. འགྲུལ་པ་སྐྱེལ་ཚད་.

འགྲུལ་པ་ཡོང་ཁུངས་ (drü̲ü̲bə yo̲ŋkuŋ) source or origin of travelers.

འགྲུལ་པ་ལམ་དུ་འགྲོ་ (drü̲ü̲bə la̲mtu dro̲) va. to start a trip/ journey.

འགྲུལ་པའི་སྦྱ་སི་ (drü̲ü̲bε bāse) tib. eng. travel tickets.

འགྲུལ་བའི་མིང་ཐོ་འགོད་ས་ (drü̲ü̲wε mi̲ŋdo gö̲ὸsa) (traveler's) registration desk.

འགྲུལ་མི་ (drü̲ü̲mi) sm. འགྲུལ་པ་.

འགྲུལ་ཚ་པོ་ (drü̲ü̲ tsābo) traveling/ going fast; va.—རྒྱག.

འགྲུལ་ཚད་ (drü̲ü̲dzεὲ) the length of one day's journey.

འགྲུལ་ཞུགས་མི་གྲངས་ (drü̲ü̲shuù mi̲draŋ) floating population (a term used in China for temporary migrant workers).

འགྲུལ་བཞུད་ (drü̲ü̲shüὺ) 1. traffic ¶ གྲོང་ཁྱེར་ནང་ལ་གླངས་འཁོར་འགྲུལ་བཞུད་ཆེན་པོ་ཡོད་ In the city there is heavy car traffic. 2. journey, trip ¶ སྲིད་དོན་གྱི་འགྲུལ་བཞུད་ A political journey.

འགྲུལ་བཞུད་འཁོར་ལོ་ (drü̲ü̲shüὺ kɔ̄ɔlo) passenger car, passenger vehicle.

འགྲུལ་བཞུད་གྲུ་གཟིངས་ (drüüshüü trudziŋ) passenger ship/ steamer.

འགྲུལ་བཞུད་ཉལ་ཁྲི་ (drüüshüü ñɛɛdri) cot, camp bed [Lit. traveler's bed].

འགྲུལ་བཞུད་གནམ་གྲུ་ (drüüshüù nəmdru) commercial/ passenger plane.

འགྲུལ་བཞུད་སྤྲོ་འཆམ་ (drüüshüù drōjam) tourist.

འགྲུལ་བཞུད་འབོག་སྒྲིལ་ (drüüshüù bɔgdrii) traveler's or passenger's baggage/ luggage.

འགྲུལ་བཞུད་མེ་འཁོར་ (drüüshüù mekɔɔ) passenger train.

འགྲུལ་བཞུད་ཀླངས་འཁོར་ (drüüshüù lāŋkɔɔ) sm. འགྲུལ་བཞུད་འཁོར་ལོ་.

འགྲུལ་ཟོག (drüüsɔɔ̀) traveler's/ passenger's baggage or luggage.

འགྲུལ་ཟོག་སྐྱེལ་འདྲེན་འཁོར་ལོ་ (drüüsɔɔ̀ gyēndren kɔ̄ɔlo) truck for delivering/ transporting passenger's luggage.

འགྲུལ་ཟོག་སྐྱེལ་འདྲེན་གནམ་གྲུ་ (drüüsɔɔ̀ gyēndren nəmdru) passenger and cargo plane.

འགྲུལ་ཟོག་གྲུ་གཟིངས་ (drüüsɔɔ̀ trudziŋ) ship for passenger's luggage.

འགྲུལ་རོགས་ (drüürɔɔ̀) 1. a person one travels with, traveling companion.

འགྲུལ་ལམ་ (drüülam) 1. communication line/ link/ route/ road. 2. journey, trip; va.—དུ་ཞུགས་ to go on a journey ¶ཁོང་མོ་ཊར་ནང་ཐག་རིང་གི་འགྲུལ་ལམ་དུ་ཞུགས་པ་རེད་ He went on a long trip by car on the road.

འགྲུས་སྐྱོང་ (drüügyoŋ) sm. འགྲུས་པ་.

འགྲུས་འགོག (drüngɔɔ̀) sm. འགྲུས་པ་.

འགྲུས་ཅན་ (drüüjɛn) diligent, industrious.

འགྲུས་པ་ (drüübə) diligent, industrious.

འགྲེ་: p. འགྲེས་; f. འགྲེ (dre) vi. to reason by analogy. 2. va. to roll over (for animals).

འགྲེ་ལྡོག (drendɔɔ̀) sm. འགྲེ་སློག.

འགྲེ་ལོག (drelɔɔ̀) sm. འགྲེ་སློག.

འགྲེ་སློག (drelɔ̄ɔ̀) 1. rolling over (e.g., animals on the ground); va.—རྒྱག to roll on the ground ¶ཁོང་གིས་མལ་ཆས་ནང་འགྲེ་སློག་ཡང་ནས་ཡང་དུ་རྒྱག་གི་འདུག Rolling over in bed again and again. 2. procrastinating; va.—རྒྱག to procrastinate.

འགྲེང་: p. འགྲེངས་; f. འགྲེང་; imp. འགྲེངས་ (dreŋ) va. to hold up ¶དར་ཆ་ཡར་འགྲེངས་སོང་ (They) held up the flag.

འགྲེང་པོ་ (dreŋbo) sm. འགྲེང་བུ་.

འགྲེང་བུ་ (dreŋbu) the name of the vowel 'e'.

འགྲེང་རྩུགས་ (dreŋdzuù) sm. རང་རྩུགས་.

འགྲེང་གཟུགས་འཁོར་སྐོགས་ (dreŋsug kɔ̄ɔlo) vertical lathe.

འགྲེང་བཞེངས་ (dreŋsheŋ) shung. officials or lamas who stand at the front of the throne of the Dalai Lama and offer prayers.

འགྲེངས་ (dreŋ) p. of འགྲེང་.

འགྲེད་ (dreè) sm. འདྲེད་.

འགྲེད་བདར་ (dreèdaa) slipping; vi.—ཤོར་ to slip.

འགྲེད་བརྡབ་ (dreèdəb) slipping and falling; vi.—ཤོར་ to slip and fall.

འགྲེད་འཕྱིད་ (dreècii) sm. འགྲེད་བདར་.

འགྲེམ་ (drem) sm. འགྲེམས་.

འགྲེམ་ཁང་ (dremgaŋ) sm. འགྲེམས་ཁང་.

འགྲེམ་ཡིག (dremyii) sm. འགྲེམས་ཡིག.

འགྲེམས་:p. བཀྲམ་; f. དཀྲམ་; imp. ཁྲོམས་ (drem) 1. va. to spread out, to display, to exhibit ¶ཁོས་ཅོག་ཙེའི་ཐོག་ཏུ་ས་བཀྲ་བཀྲམ་སོང་ He spread the map on the table. ¶འགྲེམས་སྟོན་དེ་ར་དངོས་རྫས་1,500 ཙམ་བཀྲམ་ཡོད་ In that exhibition about 1,500 things were displayed. 2. va. to distribute, to hand out ¶ཁོ་ཚོའི་དྲིལ་བསྒྲགས་ཀྱི་ཡིག་ཆ་ག་ས་གར་བཀྲམ་པ་རེད་ (They) distributed their publicity leaflets all over. ¶ཡིག་ཆ་དེ་ཚོ་གནས་མང་པོར་འགྲེམས་ཀྱི་ཡོད་རེད་ (They) are distributing the documents to many areas.

འགྲེམས་ཁང་ (dremgaŋ) 1. museum. 2. post office.

འགྲེམས་བསྒྲགས་ (dremdraà) notice, bulletin; va.—བྱེད་ to announce/ publish/ proclaim a notice.

འགྲེམས་འཛོག (dremjɔɔ̀) displaying; va.—བྱེད་ ¶ཅ་ལག་མང་པོ་འགྲེམས་འཛོག་བཞག་འདུག They displayed many new things.

འགྲེམས་སྟོན་ (dremdön) exhibition, display; va.—བྱེད་ to exhibit, to display.

འགྲེམས་སྟོན་ཁང་ (dremdöngaŋ) exhibition hall/ center.

འགྲེམས་སྟོན་ཁང་ཆེན་ (drɛ̀ɛdön kāŋcen) museum hall, exhibition hall.

འགྲེམས་སྟོན་དངོས་རྫས་ (dremdön ŋȫödzɛɛ̀) articles in an exhibition/ display.

འགྲེམས་སྟོན་ལྟེ་གནས་ (dremdön dēnɛɛ̀) sm. འགྲེམས་སྟོན་ཁང་.

འགྲེམས་འདོན་ (dreèdön) distributing; va.—བྱེད་ ¶ཚགས་པར་བོད་ཡོངས་སུ་འགྲེམས་འདོན་བྱས་བཞག The newspapers were distributed all over Tibet.

འགྲེམས་སྟོན་ཚོམས་ཁང་ (dreèdön tsɔ̄ɔgaŋ) sm. འགྲེམས་སྟོན་ཁང་ཆེན་.

འགྲེམས་སྟོན་ཚོགས་འདུ་ (dremdön tsōndu) an exhibition (with meetings or seminars).

འགྲེམས་སྤེལ་ (drembel) distributing; va.—བྱེད་ to distribute, to spread, to issue ¶ཚགས་པར་དེ་རྒྱལ་ཡོངས་ལ་འགྲེམས་སྤེལ་བྱས་པ་རེད་ (They) distributed that newspaper throughout the nation.

འགྲེམས་སྤེལ་ས་ཚིགས་ (drembel sātsig) distribution station (usu. for newspapers, etc.).

འགྲེམས་སྒྲོད་ (dremdröö) sm. འགྲེམས་སྤེལ་.

འགྲེམས་འབུལ་ (drembüü) distributing and offering/ giving; va.—མཛད་ to distribute and offer/ give (h.).

འགྲེམས་ཚོང་ (dremdzoŋ) market.

འགྲེམས་འཚོང་ (dremdzoŋ) issuing/ offering sth. for sale (e.g., a stock offering); va.—བྱེད་.

འགྲེམས་ཡིག (dremyii) 1. advertisement. 2. mail.

འགྲེལ་: p. བཀྲལ་; f. དཀྲལ་; imp. ཁྲོལ་ (drel) va. to explain, to comment ¶དགེ་རྒན་གྱིས་རྩོམ་ཡིག་དེའི་ནང་དོན་བཀྲལ་བ་རེད་ The teacher explained the meaning of the text.

འགྲེལ་ཆེན་ (dreecen) detailed explanation/ commentary.

འགྲེལ་མཆན་ (dreecɛn) footnote.

འགྲེལ་བརྗོད་ (dreejöö) sm. འགྲེལ་བཤད་.

འགྲེལ་རྟགས་ (dreedaà) dash (used in punctuation).

འགྲེལ་པ་ (dreeba) sm.འགྲེལ་བཤད་.

འགྲེལ་བ་ (dreewa) sm. འགྲེལ་བཤད་.

འགྲེལ་ལོག (dreēlɔɔ gyaà) wrong explanation; va.—རྒྱག to give a wrong explanation.

འགྲེལ་བཤད་ (dreēshɛɛ̀) explanation, commentary; va.—རྒྱག; —བྱེད་ to explain, to define, to comment on, to interpret ¶ཁོང་གི་སྲིད་ཇུས་གསར་པ་འགྲེལ་བཤད་གསལ་པོ་བརྒྱབ་སོང་ He gave a clear explanation of the new government policy.

འགྲེས་ (dreè) p. of འགྲེ་.

འགྲོ་: p. ཕྱིན་ or སོང་; f. འགྲོ་; imp. རྒྱུག (dro) va. to go, to proceed ¶ཉིན་ལྟར་ལས་ཀར་འགྲོ་གི་ཡོད་ (I) go to work every day.

འགྲོ་ (dro) abbr. of འགྲོ་བ་.

འགྲོ་ཀུན་བདེ་བ་ (drogün dewa) the happiness of all sentient beings.

འགྲོ་སྐྱོད་ (drogyöö) going, traveling; va.—བྱེད་.

འགྲོ་སྐྱོད་དམག་འཐབ་ (drogyöö māgtəb) mobile warfare.

འགྲོ་ཁ་ (droka) just about to go/ leave.

འགྲོ་ཁུངས་ (drokuŋ) 1. market ¶ཅ་ལག་འདི་ཚོ་འགྲོ་ཁུངས་ཡག་པོ་འདུག There is a good market for these goods. 2. sb. in authority one can go to seek help from, a channel ¶འགྲོ་ཁུངས་ཟབ་པོ་ A good channel. ¶ཁོང་སྲིད་གཞུང་ནང་འགྲོ་ཁུངས་ཟབ་པོ་ཡོད་སྟབས་ལས་ཀ་ཡག་པོ་ཞིག་རག་འདུག Because he had a good channel in the government, he got a good job.

འགྲོ་ཁྱབ་ (drokyəb) the extent use ¶དེང་སྐབས་འཛམ་གླིང་ནང་འགྲོ་ཁྱབ་ཆེ་ཤོས་དབྱིན་ཇིའི་སྐད་རེད་ These days English is the most used language in the world.

འགྲོ་མཁས་འདུག་ཤེས་ (drokɛɛ̀ dugsheè) behaving well/ properly; va.—བྱེད་ ¶ ལུང་པ་གསར་པ་ཞིག་ལ་སླེབས་སྐབས་འགྲོ་མཁས་འདུག་ཤེས་བྱེད་དགོས་པ་རེད་ When one arrives in a new area, one has to behave properly (i.e., not make mistakes and get into trouble) [Lit. skilled at going, knowing how to stay].

འགྲོ་འཁོར་འགྲོ་ལམ་ (drokɔɔ̀ drolam) channel of circulation.

འགྲོ་གང་ཆེ་ (dro kaŋce) shung. as much/ many as one can do sth. ¶ ཚེ་གཟུངས་འགྲོ་གང་ཆེ་སྒྲངས་གསོག་བྱས་པ་ They recited the mantra of longevity as much as they could.

འགྲོ་གང་བཟང་ (dro, kaŋsuŋ) shung. (levying taxes, etc.) as much as one can ¶ ཁྲེད་པ་པོས་འགྲོ་གང་བཟང་གིས་རང་མཚམས་འགེལ་གཅེར་མི་འབྱུང་ཞིང་ One should not impose taxes as much as one can.

འགྲོ་གྲོགས་གྲིབ་མ་ཤུལ་ལུས་རྐང་རྗེས་ (drodrɔɔ̀ tribma shūùlüù gāŋjeè) alone, without friends [Lit. traveling companion is a shadow, behind one is a footprint].

འགྲོ་གྲོན་ (drodrön) expenditure, expense; va.—གཏོང་ ¶ བཟོ་གྲྭ་དེའི་འཛུགས་བསྐྲུན་གྱི་འགྲོ་གྲོན་ཆ་ཚང་གཞུང་གིས་བཏང་བ་རེད་ The government paid all the expenses for the construction of that factory.

འགྲོ་མགོན་ (drogön) name for the Buddha.

འགྲོ་མགོན་ཕྱག་ན་ (drogön cāàna) shung. the nephew of the Sakyaba tutor of the Emperor Kublai Khan.

འགྲོ་མགོན་འཕགས་པ་ (drogön pāgba) the Sakyaba tutor of the Emperor Kublai Khan.

འགྲོ་འགྲོ་བ་ (dro drowa) always going ¶ ཁོང་རྒྱ་གར་ལ་དེང་སང་འགྲོ་འགྲོ་བ་རེད་ These days he is always going to India.

འགྲོ་རྒྱ་གོད་པོ་ (drogya göòbo) a wanderer, sb. who likes to go to different places.

འགྲོ་རྒྱུག (drogyuù) 1. marketability, demand ¶ འདིའི་ཁུལ་དགུན་དུས་པགས་པ་འགྲོ་རྒྱུག་ཆེན་པོ་ཡོད་པ་རེད་ Around here there is a big demand for skins in the winter. ¶ ཚོང་ཟོག་འདི་ལུང་པ་གང་དུ་ཡང་འགྲོ་རྒྱུག་ཆེན་པོ་ཡོད་པ་རེད་ This type of merchandise is marketable in all countries. 2. circulation.

འགྲོ་རྒྱུག་ཁྱབ་ཁོངས་ (drogyuù kyābkoŋ) circulation area.

འགྲོ་རྒྱུག་གི་ཚད་ (drogyuùgi tsɛɛ̀) the rate of circulation.

འགྲོ་རྒྱུག་ངོས་པོ་ (drogyuù ŋööbo) fast selling goods.

འགྲོ་རྒྱུག་ཐབས་ལམ་ (drogyuù tāblam) channel of circulation.

འགྲོ་རྒྱུག་འཕེར་པོ་ (drogyuù pērbo) salable, marketable.

འགྲོ་རྒྱུག་བྱེད་ཚད་ (drogyuù ceètsɛɛ̀) rate of circulation.

འགྲོ་རྒྱུག་ཡོད་པ་ (drogyuù yööba) sm. འགྲོ་རྒྱུག་འཕེར་པོ་.

འགྲོ་རྒྱུན་ (drogyün) shung. a tradition of going somewhere ¶ དེ་སྔ་ལྷ་སར་ཚོང་རྒྱག་པར་འགྲོ་རྒྱུན་ཡོད་པ་ There was a tradition of going to Lhasa for trading.

འགྲོ་སྒོ་ (drogo) sm. འགྲོ་གྲོན་.

འགྲོ་སྒོར་དམ་བསྒྲགས་ (drogor tamdraà) strictly/ tightly controlled expenditures.

འགྲོ་དངུལ་ (droŋüü) money for expenses.

འགྲོ་སྔ་བ་ (droŋawa) one who goes before/ earlier.

འགྲོ་ཆ་ (droca) sm. འགྲོ་གྲོན་.

འགྲོ་ཆས་ (drocɛɛ̀) provisions/ money for traveling or for a journey; va.—སྒྲིག་ to prepare for a journey.

འགྲོ་ཆེ་བ་ (drocewa) commodities that sell/ move well.

འགྲོ་རྗེས་ (drojeè) tracks, trail; va.—འདེད་ to follow tracks.

འགྲོ་བསྙད་ (droñɛɛ̀) shung. to bully ¶ ད་ཆ་སོག་པོ་ནས་འགྲོ་བསྙད་ཀྱིས་གཞུང་ལ་བརྩི་མེད་བྱས་པ་ The Mongols bullied and disregarded the (Tibetan) government.

འགྲོ་སྟངས་ (drodaŋ) 1. the manner of going. 2. the way things go, the manner in which one goes, the system, procedures; va.—བཟོ་ to fix a person up with a means of livelihood, to help someone to stand on his own two feet; to arrange a marriage ¶ ལས་ཀའི་འགྲོ་སྟངས་ Work procedures. ¶ ང་ཚོའི་བུ་ལ་འགྲོ་སྟངས་བཟོ་དགོས་ཡོད་ We will get a bride for our son.

འགྲོ་སྟངས་འདུག་སྟངས་ (drodaŋ dugdaŋ) sm. འགྲོ་སྟངས་སྡོད་སྟངས་.

འགྲོ་སྟངས་སྡུག་སྟངས་ (drodaŋ dugdaŋ) sm. འགྲོ་སྟངས་སྡོད་སྟངས་.

འགྲོ་སྟངས་སྡོད་སྟངས་ (drodaŋ döödaŋ) 1. the manner in which one lives, the way one leads one's life, the manner in which one subsists; va.—ཤེས་ to know how to live/ subsist ¶ ངའི་བུ་འདིས་འགྲོ་སྟངས་སྡོད་སྟངས་ཤེས་བཞག My son has learned how to lead his life.

འགྲོ་སྟངས་བཟོ་པོ་ (drodaŋ sobo) doing sth. carefully/ expertly/ cleverly/ well ¶ ཞི་མིས་ཙི་ཙི་འཛིན་པ་དང་བཞིན་འགྲོ་སྟངས་བཟོ་པོ་བྱེད་དགོས་ One must go expertly and carefully like a cat catching a mouse.

འགྲོ་སྟངས་ཤོར་ (drodaŋ shɔ̄ɔ̄) va. to be unable to make a living, to lose one's way of life ¶ ཨ་མེ་རི་ཀར་སླེབས་རྗེས་ལས་ཀ་མ་རག་པའི་རྐྱེན་གྱིས་འགྲོ་སྟངས་ཤོར་སོང་ After arriving in America, because he didn't get a job, he lost the ability of subsisting/ making a living. 2. see ལུམ་ལགས་ཀྱི་འགྲོ་སྟངས་མ་ཤེས་ང་རའི་འགྲོ་སྟངས་ཤོར་.

འགྲོ་དོན་ (drodön) 1. the welfare of all sentient beings. 2. the reason for going.

འགྲོ་བདེའི་སྒོ་མོ་ (drodee gomo) emergency exit.

འགྲོ་འདུག (drdug) going and staying.

འགྲོ་འདུག་ཀུན་སྤྱོད་ (drodug gũnjöö) behavior (all the time, when going or staying).

འགྲོ་འདྲེན་ (drondren) sm. འགྲོ་མགོན་.

འགྲོ་ལྡོག་གཉིས་དཀའ་ (drodɔɔ̀ ñiiga) able neither to advance nor retreat, a dilemma, a quandary ¶ དགྲ་བོས་ཕྱོགས་བཞི་ནས་བསྐོར་རྗེས་ང་ཚོ་འགྲོ་ལྡོག་གཉིས་དཀའི་གནས་སུ་གྱུར་སོང་ After being surrounded on four sides by the enemy, we came into the state of being unable to retreat or advance.

འགྲོ་སྡོད་ (drodöö) going and staying, movement ¶ ད་ལྟ་འགྲོ་སྡོད་གཏན་གཏན་མེད་ (I) am not certain yet whether I will go or stay.

འགྲོ་སྡོད་གཉིས་དཀའ་ (drodöö ñiiga) sm. འགྲོ་ལྡོག་གཉིས་དཀའ་.

འགྲོ་སྡོད་བྱ་གསུམ་ (drodöö casum) going/ traveling, staying and doing things.

འགྲོ་སྡོད་བྱེད་གདད་ (drodöö ceèdɛɛ̀) sm. འགྲོ་ལྡོག་གཉིས་དཀའ་.

འགྲོ་སྡོད་མ་ཤེས་ (drodöö masheè) 1. sm. འགྲོ་སྡོད་གཉིས་དཀའ་. 2. sm. འགྲོ་སྟངས་ཤོར་.

འགྲོ་པོ་ (drobo) 1. sm. འགྲོ་ཆེ་བ་. 2. able to recite well/ thoroughly.

འགྲོ་སྤྱོད་བདེ་པོ་ (drojöö debo) convenient/ easy to travel or get to places.

འགྲོ་ཕན་ (dropɛn) sm. འགྲོ་དོན་.

འགྲོ་ཕྱོགས་ (drocɔɔ̀) direction one is going, the current/ trend/ tide/ tendency ¶ ཆབ་སྲིད་ཀྱི་འགྲོ་ཕྱོགས་དང་བསྟུན་ནས་ལས་ཀ་བྱ་དགོས་ One must work in accordance with the politics current.

འགྲོ་ཕྱོགས་གནད་གཙོ་བོ་ (drocɔɔ̀ nɛ̀ɛ̀ dzōwo) main trend, chief tide/ current.

འགྲོ་བ་ (drōwo) sentient being ¶ མི་ཡི་འགྲོ་བ་ Human beings.

འགྲོ་བ་ངན་པ་ (drowa ŋɛmba) the three classes of bad sentient beings: animals, hungry ghosts and beings in hells.

འགྲོ་བ་གཉིས་ (drowa ñii) the two broad classes of sentient beings: the three good rebirths and the three bad rebirths.

འགྲོ་བ་མི་ (drowami) human beings.

འགྲོ་བ་མིའི་ཐོབ་ཐང་ (drowa mii tōbdaŋ) human

rights.

འགྲོ་བ་མིའི་ཐོབ་ཐང་ལྟ་རྟོགས་ཚོགས་པ་ (drowa mii tōbdaŋ dādɔɔ tsɔ̄gba) Human Rights Watch.

འགྲོ་བ་མིའི་གཞི་རྩའི་ཐོབ་ཐང་ (drowa mii shidzɛ tōbdaŋ) fundamental human rights.

འགྲོ་བ་མིའི་རིགས་ (drowa mirig) mankind, human beings.

འགྲོ་བ་བཟང་པོ་ (drowa saŋbo) the three good classes of sentient beings: gods, semigods, humans.

འགྲོ་བ་བཟང་མོ་ (drowa saŋmo) 1. name of a Tibetan Folk Opera. 2. name of main character in fold opera of same name.

འགྲོ་བ་རིགས་དྲུག (drowa rigtruù) the six realms of sentient beings: gods, demigods, humans, animals, hungry ghosts and beings in hell.

འགྲོ་བའི་མགོན་པོ་ (drowɛ gömbo) the Buddha.

འགྲོ་བའི་དེད་དཔོན་ (drowɛ teèbön) the Buddha.

འགྲོ་བའི་འདྲེན་མཆོག (drowɛ drenjɔɔ) shung. the savior of sentient beings ¶ འགྲོ་བའི་འདྲེན་མཆོག་སྐྱབས་མགོན་ཡབ་སྲས་རྣམ་གཉིས་ The Dalai Lama and the Panchen Lama who are the two saviors of all sentient beings.

འགྲོ་བྱམས་ (drocam) sedan chair, palanquin.

འགྲོ་བའི་བླ་མ་ (drowɛ lāma) shung. Buddha.

འགྲོ་སྦྱོང་ (drojoŋ) sm. ཉིན་མོའི་སློབ་གྲྭ་.

འགྲོ་སྦྱོང་སློབ་གྲྭ་པ་ (drojoŋ lābdraà) day student.

འགྲོ་མ་གོག (drōmagɔɔ) going in a manner that is part crawling (usu. used for infants).

འགྲོ་མ་རྒྱུག (dromagyuù) walking and running at the same time (neither completely walking nor completely running).

འགྲོ་ཚད་ (drotsɛɛ̀) 1. rate/ level of sales ¶ དེང་སང་ཕྲུ་གུའི་རྩེད་ཆས་འགྲོ་ཚད་ཆེན་པོ་འདུག These days the rate of sales of toys is high. 2. rate/ degree/ level of going, rate/ degree/ level of progress ¶ ཞིང་ལས་ཡར་རྒྱས་འགྲོ་ཚད་ཆེན་པོ་འདུག The rate of improvement in agriculture is high.

འགྲོ་ཚོད་ (drodzöö) testing to see how far one can go (usu. in the context of taking advantage); va.—བལྟ་ to see/ test how far one can go ¶ མི་དེས་འགོ་ཁྲིད་ལ་འགྲོ་ཚོད་བལྟས་ནས་ལས་ཀ་བྱེད་ཀྱི་འདུག That person works in the manner of testing the leader to see how far he can go.

འགྲོ་ཚོད་བཤར་ (drodzöö shār) va. to bully, to take advantage of, to see how far one can go.

འགྲོ་མཚམས་བལྟ་ (drodzam dā) sm. འགྲོ་ཚོད་(བལྟ་).

འགྲོ་མཚམས་རྩོད་འཛུགས་ (drodzam dzōnjuù) shung. insatiable greed.

འགྲོ་མཆེར་ (dro tsēr) sm. འགྲོ་མཆེར་པོ་.

འགྲོ་མཆེར་པོ་ (dro tsērbo) reluctant/ unwilling/ uncomfortable to go.

འགྲོ་འཚེར་པོ་ (dro tsērbo) sm. འགྲོ་མཆེར་པོ་.

འགྲོ་རྫོངས་ (drodzoŋ) farewell gift; va.—རྒྱག to give a farewell gift.

འགྲོ་ཞི་མི་ལས་མཁས་པ་ སྡོད་རི་བོང་ལས་ཙོག་པ་ (dro shimilɛ kɛ̄ɛba dӧӧ regoŋlɛɛ dzōgba) sb. who can go/ do things carefully/ cleverly/ expertly [Lit. going more skillfully than a cat, sitting more crouched than a rabbit].

འགྲོ་ཞོར་ཤོད་ཞོར་ (droshɔɔ shōōshɔɔ) talking while walking.

འགྲོ་བཟོ་སྡོད་མཁས་ (droso dӧӧkɛɛ̀) sm. འགྲོ་མཁས་འདུག་ཤེས་.

འགྲོ་བཟོད་སྡོད་བཟོད་བདེ་པོ་ (drosöö dӧӧsöö debo) safety/ security in going and staying ¶ ལུང་པའི་ནང་ཇག་པ་མང་བས་མི་དམངས་རྣམས་འགྲོ་བཟོད་སྡོད་བཟོད་བདེ་པོ་མེད་པ་རེད་ Because there are many bandits in the area, there is no safety and security for people (going and staying).

འགྲོ་འོང་ (drooŋ) coming and going; va.—བྱེད་ to come and go ¶ མགྲོན་ཁང་འདིར་འགྲུལ་པ་མང་པོ་འགྲོ་འོང་བྱེད་ཀྱི་ཡོད་པ་རེད་ That hotel has many travelers coming and going.

འགྲོ་འོང་རང་མོས་ (drooŋ raŋmöö) freedom to travel/ come and go.

འགྲོ་འོང་ལག་ཁྱེར་ (drooŋ lagkyer) gate pass, permit/ pass allowing one to travel/ come and go.

འགྲོ་རེས་ (droreè) one's turn to go or do ¶ སང་ཉིན་ལས་ཀ་འགྲོ་རེས་ཁོ་རེད་ Tomorrow it is his turn to work. ¶ ང་ཚོ་མི་ཚང་གཉིས་བར་ཕན་ཚུན་འགྲོ་རེས་ཡོད་ We two families take turns visiting back and forth.

འགྲོ་རོགས་ (drorɔɔ) 1. traveling help/ assistance. 2. traveling companion.

འགྲོ་རོགས་སྡོད་རོགས་ (drorɔɔ dӧӧrɔɔ) companion, friend.

འགྲོ་ལ་མ་འགྲོའི་རྟ་པོ་ལས་གློ་ཐག་ཆོད་པའི་རྐང་ཐང་ཡག (drola mandrö dāpolɛ lōdaà cööbɛ gāntaŋ yaà) a bird in hand is worth nine in the bush [Lit. it is better to go with certainty on foot than be uncertain about whether one can go by horse].

འགྲོ་ལམ་ (drolam) 1. road, way, path; va.—སྟོན་ to show the way, to direct; va.—འབྱེད་ to create a path/ road/ way, to open up a route ¶ རླངས་འཁོར་འགྲོ་ལམ་ Motor road. 2. prospects, opportunities; va.—སྟོན་ to show opportunities; va.—འབྱེད་ to create opportunities/ prospects ¶ བོད་སྐད་སློབ་སྦྱོང་བྱས་ན་འགྲོ་ལམ་ཆེན་པོ་མི་འདུག If you study Tibetan there are no good prospects (for jobs).

འགྲོ་ལམ་ཁ་ཞལ་ (drolam kāshɛɛ) paved road.

འགྲོ་ལམ་ཆུང་གྲས་ (drolam cūŋdrɛɛ̀) alley, back street.

འགྲོ་ལམ་འབྱེད་ (drolam ceè) see འགྲོ་ལམ་.

འགྲོ་ལམ་འཚོལ་ (drolam tsöö) va. to look for way/ path / means; to search for an opportunity.

འགྲོ་ལམ་གསར་གཏོད་བྱེད་ (drolam sārdöö) sm. འགྲོ་ལམ་འབྱེད་.

འགྲོ་ལས་ཆེ་ (dro lɛɛ̀ce) འགྲོ་ཤས་ཆེ་.

འགྲོ་ལུགས་ (droluù) procedure (for doing sth.), system, custom, way of life. ¶ ལས་ཁུངས་ནང་གི་འགྲོ་ལུགས་མ་ཤེས་ན་ནོར་འཁྲུལ་ཤོར་རྒྱུའི་ཉེན་ཁ་ཡོད་ If you do not the know the procedures of the office, there is a danger that you will make a mistake.

འགྲོ་ལུགས་སྡོད་སྟངས་ (droluù dӧӧtaŋ) sm. འགྲོ་སྟངས་སྡོད་སྟངས་.

འགྲོ་ཤས་ཆེ་ (dro shɛ̄ɛce) likely or probably will go, likely to be used ¶ ཤིང་ཆ་འདི་རྣམས་འགྲོ་ཤས་ཆེ་ This timber will probably be used. ¶ ཁོ་ལྷ་སར་འགྲོ་ཤས་ཆེ་ He will probably go to Lhasa.

འགྲོ་ཤུལ་ (droshüü) 1. road, path. 2. a trace. 3. a replacement.

འགྲོ་ཤོམ་ (droshom) sm.* འགྲོ་གཤོམ་.

འགྲོ་གཤོམ་ (droshom) preparing to go; va.—བྱེད་.

འགྲོ་ས་ (drosa) 1. place to go. 2. a way/ avenue/ path to tell or ask sth. ¶ ཆོག་མཆན་ཞུ་རྒྱུའི་སྐད་ཆ་དེ་འགོ་ཁྲིད་འདིར་འགྲོ་ས་ཡོད་པ་མ་རེད་ There is no avenue to ask the boss for approval. 3. (with neg.) being incompatible, not being able to handle/ stand, being allergic to ¶ ང་ལ་ཕག་ཤ་འགྲོ་ས་མེད་ I can't stand pork.

འགྲོ་སོང་ (drosoŋ) sm. འགྲོ་གྲོན་.

འགྲོ་སོང་འཕར་གཏོང་ (drosoŋ pārdoŋ) overspending, extra spending; va.—བྱེད་ ¶ འགོ་ཁྲིད་ཀྱི་ཆོག་མཆན་མེད་པར་འགྲོ་སོང་འཕར་གཏོང་བྱས་འདུག (They) spent extra without permission from the boss.

འགྲོ་སོང་ཕྲན་ཚེགས་ (drosoŋ trɛ̄ntseg) sm. འགྲོ་སོང་ཙག་ཙིག.

འགྲོ་སོང་ཙག་ཙིག (drosoŋ dzə̄gdzog) incidental/ small expenses.

འགྲོ་སོང་རྩིས་ཞུ་ (drosoŋ dzīishu) giving an accounting (of expenditures) va.—བྱེད་; —ཞུ་.

འགྲོགས་ (drɔɔ̀) va. to associate with, to be friends with, to be in the company of, to have a close relationship with ¶ གྲོགས་པོ་ངན་པ་དང་མ་འགྲོགས་ཤིག Do not associate with bad friends.

འགྲོགས་སྐལ་ (drɔggɛl) predestined by karma to become a couple.

འགྲོགས་བདེ་གཞིབ་བདེ་ (drɔgde shīpde) easy to get along with, compatible, amicable, amiable.

འགྲོགས་འདྲིས་ (drɔŋdrii) sm. འགྲོགས་.

འགྲོགས་ཤེས་ (drɔgsheè) shung. easy to get along with.

འགྲོགས་བཤེས་ (drɔgsheè) close friends.

འགྲོགས་སེམས་ (drɔgsem) 1. friendly/ harmonious thoughts. 2. wishing/ desiring to associate with or make friends with, desiring to be in the company of.

འགྲོང་ (droŋ) sexual organs.

འགྲོངས་: p. གྲོངས་; f. འགྲོངས་ (droŋ) vi. to die, to pass away ། ཁོང་གྲོངས་ནས་ཉི་མ་གསུམ་ཕྱིན་སོང་ It is three days since he died.

འགྲོངས་ཀ་ (droŋga) at the point of death, just before dying.

འགྲོངས་ཁ་ (droŋga) sm. འགྲོངས་ཀ་.

འགྲོན་ (drön) sm. མགྲོན་.

འགྲོན་ཁང་ (dröngaŋ) sm. མགྲོན་ཁང་.

འགྲོན་ཐལ་ (dröntɛɛ) ashes of burned shell used in medicines.

འགྲོན་པོ་ (drönbo) sm. མགྲོན་པོ་.

འགྲོན་བུ་ (drönbu) 1. small white (cowry) shell. 2. see སྒྲོམ་བུ་.

འགྲོན་ལམ་ (drönlam) road, path.

འགྲོན་ལམ་པ་ (drönlamba) 1. traveler. 2. poet. trader, merchant, businessman.

འགྲོལ་: p. བཀྲོལ་; f. དགྲོལ་; imp. ཁྲོལ་ (dröö) 1. va. to untie/ undo a knot ། མདུད་པ་བཀྲོལ་པ་རེད་ (He) untied the knot. 2. va. to set free, to release, to liberate ། བྲན་གཡོག་རིང་ལུགས་ཀྱི་འཆིང་ཐག་འགྲོལ་དགོས་ཟེར་བ་རེད་ (They) say that (they) should free them from the system of slavery. 3. va. to get consent/ permission ། ནང་ལ་འགྲོ་བ་ལ་དགེ་རྒན་གྱི་བཀའ་འགྲོལ་དགོས་ One must have permission from the teacher to go home.

འགྲོལ་ཐབས་ (dröötəb) finding a way to set free/ release/ liberate; —བྱེད་.

འགྲོལ་ཤང་ (drööshaŋ) expelling, kicking out, firing; va.—གཏོང་ ། ཁོས་ལས་ཀ་ཡག་པོ་མ་བྱས་ཙང་ལས་ཁུངས་ནས་འགྲོལ་ཤང་གཏོང་པ་རེད་ Because he didn't do his work well, the office fired (him).

འགྲོས་ (dröö) trot (gait of horses).

འགྲོས་ཁོབ་ (dröökob) trotting clumsily/ badly (for horses).

འགྲོས་སྒོ་ (dröögo) shung. expenditures.

འགྲོས་རྒྱག (dröö gyaà) va. to trot.

འགྲོས་ཆེན་རྟ་པོ་ (drööcen dābo) a horse with an excellent trot.

འགྲོས་རྒྱུར་ (dröödur) horse trotting competition; va.—བྱེད་.

འགྲོས་མ་ (drööma) a horse trained to trot.

རྒ་: p. རྒས་; f. རྒ་ (ga) 1. vi. to get old, to age ། ཁོ་རྒས་ནས་དེ་ཙམ་ཕྱུགས་བསྐྱོད་བྱས་ཡོད་པ་མ་རེད་ After he got old he did not travel much. 2. vi. to become weak (physically), to loose health ། ཁོ་ན་ནས་རྒས་འདུག He became weak after he got sick. 3. vi. to set (e.g., the sun) ། ཉི་མ་རྒས་བཞག The sun has set.

རྒ་རྒས་ཕྱུགས་ཟོག (gagɛɛ cūgsoò) old domestic animals.

རྒ་བ་ (gawa) aging, getting old ། རྒ་བའི་སྡུག་བསྔལ་ The suffering of getting old.

རྒ་བུ་ (gəbu) a calf of a cross between a female yak and bull.

རྒ་བུབ་ (gəbub gur) 1. crawling; va.—སྐྱུར་ to crawl.

རྒ་ཤི་ (ga shi) old age and death.

རྒ་ཤི་ཟླ་བ་ (gashi dawa) the 11th month of the Tibetan calendar.

རྒང་ (gaŋ) hedgehog.

རྒད་ཉམས་ (gɛɛ̀ñam) sm. རྒན་ཉམས་.

རྒད་ཉམས་ཆགས་པ་ (gɛɛ̀ñam cāgba) sm. རྒན་བཟོ་དོད་པོ་.

རྒད་པོ་ (gɛɛ̀bo) old man.

རྒད་མོ་ (gɛɛ̀mo) old woman.

རྒད་མོ་ཁྱིས་དེད་པའི་གྲལ་འགོ་ (gɛɛ̀mo kyii teèbɛ trɛngo) coming into a higher position accidently [Lit. the old woman came to the higher seat because the dog chased her].

རྒད་མོ་གསེར་འཁུར་གྱི་དུས་རབས་ (gɛɛ̀mo sērkurgi tüürəb) a safe and peaceful period (without robbers and bandits) [Lit. an era when old woman carry gold].

རྒད་གཟུགས་མངོན་པ་ (gɛɛ̀suù ŋömba) the appearance of getting old.

རྒན་ (gɛn) 1. adult, mature. 2. abbr. of རྒན་འཁོགས་.

རྒན་བཀུར་ཁང་ (gɛgurgaŋ) old people's home.

རྒན་བཀུར་རྒན་སྐྱོང་ (gɛngur gɛngyoŋ) respecting and taking care of the elderly.

རྒན་བཀུར་ཆུང་གཅེས་ (gɛngur cūnjeè) respecting the elderly and cherishing the children.

རྒན་བཀུར་གཞོན་སྐྱོང་ (gɛngur shöngyoŋ) respecting the elderly and taking care of the young.

རྒན་སྐྱོང་ཁང་ (gɛngyoŋgaŋ) old people's home.

རྒན་སྐྱོང་གླིང་ (gɛngyoŋliŋ) nursing home.

རྒན་སྐྱོར་དབུལ་སྐྱོང་ (gɛngyɔr üügyoŋ) helping the elderly and supporting the poor.

རྒན་སྐྱོར་གཞོན་ཁྲིད་ (gɛngyɔr shöntrii) helping/ supporting the elderly and leading the youngsters.

རྒན་ཁ་གཞོན་ཉན་ (gɛngɔɔ̀ shönñɛn) the young should obey their elders; va.—བྱེད་.

རྒན་ཁྲལ་ (gɛndrɛɛ) shung. a tax for older monk.

རྒན་འཁོགས་ (gɛngɔɔ̀) old, aged ། རྒན་འཁོགས་གསོ་སྐྱོང་ཁང་ Old people's home.

རྒན་གོག (gɛngɔɔ̀) sm. རྒན་འཁོགས་.

རྒན་གྲས་ (gɛntrɛɛ̀) elders, seniors.

རྒན་མགོ་དཀར་ནས་གཞོན་སོ་དཀར་མན་ཆད་ (gɛngo) people of all ages [Lit. from old people with white hair to young people with white teeth].

རྒན་འགོ་ (gɛngo) 1. elders and leaders/ heads. 2. the oldest of one's children.

རྒན་རྒོན་ (gɛngön) sm. རྒན་འཁོགས་.

རྒན་རྒོན་གཉིས་ (gɛngön ñii) an elderly couple.

རྒན་ཆོས་ (gɛncöö) living a religious life after one becomes old, turning actively to religious activities and prayers when one is old; va.—བྱེད་.

རྒན་ཆོས་ལོག (gɛncöö lɔɔ̀)vi. to lose one's celibacy after committing to a religious life when old.

རྒན་འཆལ་ (gɛncɛɛ) second youth, old people behaving like youth; vi.—ལང་ to have a second youth, to act like a youth (for elders).

རྒན་ཉམས་ (gɛnñam) appearing old/ aged in appearance.

རྒན་ཉམས་དོད་པོ་ (gɛñam döòbo) a person who looks older than he or she is.

རྒན་རྟེན་ (gɛnden) sm. རྒན་པོའི་རྟེན་.

རྒན་དར་གཞོན་གསུམ་ (gɛn tar shön sūm) elderly, adults, young—the three.

རྒན་དྲུང་ (gɛndruŋ) senior clerk (in Dharamsala).

རྒན་བདག (gɛndaà) student prefect (in school).

རྒན་ཕྱིང་ (gɛndiŋ) abbr. of རྒན་པོ་ and ཕྱིང་དཔོན་.

རྒན་པ་ (gɛmba) the older/ elder; the senior ། ངའི་ཨ་ཁུ་རྒན་པ་དེ་ My older paternal uncle.

རྒན་པོ་ (gɛmbo) 1. old (age). 2. village headman.

རྒན་པོའི་རྟེན་ (gɛmbö dēn) land held as payment for serving as headman of a village.

རྒན་སྤྱི་ (gɛnji) the main person who collects taxes.

རྒན་ཕྲུགས་ (gɛntrii) adult and children.

རྒན་མིག (gɛnmii) eyes that do not see well because of old age, presbyopia ། རྒན་མིག་མིག་ཤེལ་ Glasses for presbyopia.

རྒན་མོ་ (gɛmmo) old woman.

རྒན་མོ་གསེར་འཁུར་ (gɛmmo sērkur) peaceful/ safe place, a place without thievery and robbery [Lit. old woman carrying gold].

རྒན་དམངས་ (gɛnmaŋ) abbr. headman and the people.

རྒན་ཚབ་ (gɛntsəb) one who stands in as a prefect/ headman.

རྒན་ཞན་ནད་སྐྱོན་བཞི་ (gɛnshɛn nɛɛ̀gyön shi) the four: the old, weak, sick and disabled.

རྒན་ཞུགས་ (gɛnshuù) sm. རྒན་ཆོས་.

རྒན་གཞོན་ (gɛnshön) 1. old and young ¶ རོལ་དབྱངས་དེ་ཚོར་རྒན་གཞོན་ཚང་མས་དགའ་པོ་བྱས་པ་རེད་ All the people, young and old, liked the music. 2. age ¶ ཕོ་གཉིས་རྒན་གཞོན་གཅིག་པ་རེད་ The two of them are the same age. 3. seniority ¶ རྒན་གཞོན་གཞི་བཟུང་ By seniority.

རྒན་གཞོན་གོ་རིམ་ (gɛnshön) order by seniority by generation (e.g. from the old to the young).

རྒན་གཞོན་བར་གསུམ་ (gɛnshön parsum) all ages [Lit. the three: old, young and middle].

རྒན་གཞོན་འབྲིང་གསུམ་ (gɛnshön drinsum) sm. རྒན་གཞོན་བར་གསུམ་.

རྒན་གཞོན་མ་བརྩིས་པ་ (gɛnshön madziìbə) young people not respecting the elderly [Lit. not taking into account the difference between the old and the young].

རྒན་གཞོན་གཞི་བཟུང་ (gɛnshön) by seniority.

རྒན་བཟོ་དོད་པོ་ (gɛnso tööbo) looking/ acting older than one is.

རྒན་ཡོལ་ (gɛnyöö) sm. རྒས་ཡོལ་.

རྒན་གཡོག་ (gɛnyɔɔ̀) junior/ assistant prefect.

རྒན་རབས་ (gɛnrəb) the older/ senior generation.

རྒན་རབས་པ་ (gɛnrəbbə) elders; precursors.

རྒན་རིགས་ (gɛnriì) elder.

རྒན་རིམ་ (gɛnrim) sm. རྒན་བྲས་.

རྒན་ལ་འཚར་ (gɛnlaà tsār) vi. to grow up (for children).

རྒན་ལགས་ (gɛnlaà) polite term of address for a teacher.

རྒན་ཤོས་ (gɛnshöö) eldest, oldest ¶ ངའི་གཅེན་པོ་རྒན་ཤོས་ My oldest brother.

རྒན་ལབ་གཞོན་ཉན་ (gɛnləb shönñɛn) shung. elderly should give advise and the young people should accept it.

རྒན་གསོ་ (gɛn sō) va. to look after/ take care of the elderly.

རྒན་གསོ་ཁང་ (gɛnsogaŋ) sm. རྒས་གསོ་ཁང་.

རྒན་གསོ་དངུལ་ (gɛnsoŋüü) sm. རྒན་གསོའི་འཚོ་དངུལ་.

རྒན་གསོའི་འཚོ་དངུལ་ (gɛnsö tsōŋüü) old age pension.

རྒལ་: p. བརྒལ་; f. བརྒལ་; imp. རྒོལ་ (gɛɛ) 1. va. to cross, to traverse ¶ ལྕགས་ཟམ་དེ་བརྒལ་ནས་ལྷ་སར་སླེབས་པ་རེད་ After (they) crossed the bridge (they) reached Lhasa. 2. va. to overcome, to pass ¶ དགྲ་བོའི་འགོག་ས་མང་པ་བརྒལ་བ་རེད་ (They) overcame many of the enemies' obstacles. 3. va. to extend, to surpass, to go beyond, to exceed ¶ མི་འབོར་ནི་ས་ཡ་བདུན་བརྒལ་ཡོད་པ་རེད་ As for the population, it has exceeded seven million. ¶ ལོ་ན་དྲུག་ཅུ་བརྒལ་བའི་མི་ A person over sixty years of age. ¶ འགྲོ་སོང་འཆར་གཞི་ལས་བརྒལ་སོང་ (They) exceeded their plan with respect to expenditures.

རྒལ་སྐྱོད་ (gɛɛgyöö) crossing/ traversing a territory or place.

རྒལ་གྲུ་ (gɛɛdru) boat.

རྒལ་རབས་ (gɛɛrəb) the shallow part of a river where it is best to cross.

རྒས་ (gɛɛ̀) p. of རྒ་.

རྒས་ཀ་ (gɛɛ̀ga) at the time of getting old.

རྒས་ཀ་སྲ་བ་ (gɛɛ̀ga drāwa) a person who does not look as old as his age.

རྒས་སྐྱོར་བྱིས་ཁྲིད་ (gɛɛgyɔɔ̀ ciitrii) supporting the elderly and bringing along/ leading the youngsters.

རྒས་སྐྱོར་གཞོན་ཁྲིད་ (gɛɛgyɔɔ̀ shöntrii) sm. རྒས་སྐྱོར་བྱིས་ཁྲིད་.

རྒས་འཁོགས་ (gɛngɔɔ̀) sm. རྒན་འཁོགས་.

རྒས་འཁྱོམས་ (gɛngyom) senile.

རྒས་ཁོག་ (gɛngɔɔ̀) sm. རྒན་འཁོགས་.

རྒས་ཁུད་ (gɛngɔɔ̀) sm. རྒན་འཁོགས་.

རྒས་གཅོང་ (gɛɛ̀joŋ) old and infirm/ weak/ feeble.

རྒས་འཆོལ་ (gɛɛ̀ cöö) vi. to be/ get senile (unable to function well in body, mind, speech).

རྒས་ཉམས་དོད་པ་ (gɛɛ̀ñam tööbo) old looking (for one's age).

རྒས་གཉེར་ (gɛɛ̀ñer) the wrinkles of old age.

རྒས་མདོག་ཁ་པོ་ (gɛɛ̀ndɔɔ̀ kābo) sm. རྒན་ཉམས་.

རྒས་སྡོད་ (gɛɛ̀döö) retirement, retiring; va.—བྱེད་ ¶ རྒས་སྡོད་བཟོ་པ་ Retired worker.

རྒས་པ་སྲ་བ་ (gɛɛ̀ba drāwa) sm. རྒས་ཀ་སྲ་བ་.

རྒས་པོ་ (gɛɛ̀bo) old man.

རྒས་མེད་འཆི་མེད་ (gɛɛ̀meè cīmeè) not growing old and not dying.

རྒས་མོ་ (gɛɛ̀mo) old woman.

རྒས་རྩུགས་སྟོན་ (gɛɛ̀tsuù dön) sm. རྒས་རྩུལ་སྟོན་.

རྒས་རྩུལ་སྟོན་ (gɛɛ̀tsui dön) va. to act/ talk as if you are older than you are.

རྒས་ཡོལ་ (gɛɛ̀yöö) retiring; va.—བྱེད་ ¶ རང་ལོ་དྲུག་ཅུར་སླེབས་ན་རྒས་ཡོལ་བྱེད་ཆོག་གི་རེད་ When one reaches age sixty one is permitted to retire.

རྒས་ཡོལ་གྱི་དངུལ་ (gɛɛ̀yöögi ŋüü) old age pension.

རྒས་རབ་ཅག་ཅེན་ (gɛɛ̀rəb cāgcen) a wise old man.

རྒས་ཤེས་ནས་གོ་མ་ཤེས་པ་ (gɛɛ̀sheènɛ koma sheèba) old people who do not know or realize that they are old (understand what it means to be old) ¶ མི་དེ་རྒས་ཤེས་ནས་གོ་མ་ཤེས་པར་ཤི་ཁ་ལྷ་མོར་ཁང་པ་མང་པོ་དེ་འདྲ་བརྒྱག་གི་འདུག་ That person does not realize that he is old and when he is nearing death is building many houses.

རྒས་ཤི་ (gɛɛ̀shi) dying of old age.

རྒས་ཤིང་འཁོགས་པ་ (gɛɛ̀shiŋ kɔ̄gba) old and infirm/ weak/ feeble.

རྒས་སེམས་བྱིས་པ་ (gɛɛ̀sem cibə) 1. an old person who has become childlike or acts like a child; vi.—ཆགས་. 2. a child who thinks like an older person.

རྒས་གསོ་ཁང་ (gɛɛ̀sogaŋ) home for the aged, old people's home.

རྒས་གསོ་དངུལ་འབབ་ (gɛɛ̀so ŋüübəb) sm. རྒས་ཡོལ་གྱི་དངུལ་.

རྒུ་ (gu) see ཡོད་རྒུ་.

རྒུ་དྲུས་ (gudrüü) a plant used for herbal medicines (corydalis dasyptera maxim).

རྒུད་ (güü) vi. to go down, to decay, to decline ¶ དམག་འཁྲུག་གིས་ཕོ་ཚོའི་དཔལ་འབྱོར་རྒུད་པ་རེད་ Their economy declined because of the war.

རྒུད་སྐྱོབ་ (güügyob) aid (for poor); va.—བྱེད་.

རྒུད་སྐྱོབ་དངུལ་ (güügyob ŋüü) relief money, relief fund.

རྒུད་ཆགས་ (güücaà) a calamity/ misfortune.

རྒུད་ཉམས་ (güüñam) ruin, decline, decay, deterioration; vi.—སུ་འགྲོ་ to become ruined/ deteriorated, to decline.

རྒུད་ཚོགས་ (güüdzɔɔ̀) many calamities one after another.

རྒུད་པ་ (güüba) sm. རྒུད་ཉམས་.

རྒུད་པ་རིམ་རྩེག (güübə rimdzeg) many declines coming one after another.

རྒུད་པོ་ (güübo) sm. གུད་པོ་.

རྒུད་མུན་ (güümün) sm. རྒུད་ཉམས་.

རྒུད་ཚོགས་ (güütsɔɔ̀) many declines.

རྒུད་གསབ་ལས་སྦྱོར་ (güüsəb lɛɛ̀dröö) relieving/ assisting people in disaster areas by giving them employment; va.—བྱེད་.

རྒུན་སྐྱེམས་ (güngyem) sm. རྒུན་ཆང་.

རྒུན་སྐྱེམས་རྒུན་ཆང་ (güngyem güncaŋ) sm. རྒུན་ཆང་.

རྒུན་རྒོད་ (güngöö) wild grapes.

རྒུན་སྒྲོམ་ (gündrom) grape trellis.

རྒུན་ཆང་ (güncaŋ) wine made from grapes.

རྒུན་ཆང་བཟོ་གྲྭ་ (güncaŋ sodra) winery.

རྒུན་ཆུ་ (güncu) grape juice.

རྒུན་འབྲུ་ (gündru) sm. རྒུན་འབྲུམ་.

རྒུན་འབྲུམ་དཀར་པོ་ (gündrum gārbo) yellowish grape.

རྒུན་འབྲུམ་སྐམ་པོ་ (gündrum gāmbo) dried grapes, raisin.

རྒུན་འབྲུམ་ཁུ་བ་ (gündrum kūwa) grape juice/ extract.

རྒུན་འབྲུམ་མངར་ཁུ་ (gündrum ŋārku) grape juice.

རྒུན་འབྲུམ་མངར་ཙ་ (gündrum ŋārca) grape sugar, glucose, dextrose.
རྒུན་འབྲུམ་མདོག (gündrum dɔ̀ɔ) grape color.
རྒུན་འབྲུམ་ནག་པོ་ (gündrum nagbo) black grape.
རྒུན་འབྲུམ་སྨན་ཆུ་ (gündrum mēncu) glucose.
རྒུན་འབྲུམ་ཤིང་ (gündrum shīŋ) grape vine.
རྒུན་འབྲུམ་ཨ་རག (gündrum āraà) wine (made from grapes) ¶ རྒུན་འབྲུམ་ཨ་རག་དམར་པོ་ Red wine.
རྒུམ་བུ་ (gumbu) bird feed.
རྒུམ་འབུ་ (gumbu) a type of small insect.
རྒུར་མཐིལ་ (gurtil) sm.* ཁུར་མཐིལ་.
རྒུར་རྡོ་ (gurdo) sm.* ཁུར་རྡོ་.
རྒུས་ (güü) instrumental case of རྒུ་.
རྒོ་ལྤགས་ (gobaà) Tibetan gazelle skin.
རྒོ་བ་ (gowa) Tibetan gazelle.
རྒོ་བ་ར་ཙ་ (gowa radza) a type of coarse wool (like that of gazelle) found in sheep wool.
རྒོ་སློག (go lɔ̄ɔ) a dress/ robe made from the skin of gazelles.
རྒོད་ (göö) 1. vulture. 2. wild, untamed ¶ རྟ་རྒོད་ Wild horse. 3. laughter ¶ རྒོད་མ་སློངས་ཤིག Don't arouse laughter (in others). 4. abbr. of རྒོད་པོ་. 5. va. to laugh ¶ གད་མོ་རྒོད་དུས་ When laughing. 6. vi. to be unable to concentrate when meditating. 7. military.
རྒོད་ཀྱི་སྟོང་སྡེ་ (göögo dōŋde) shung. a military unit made up of 1000 soldiers.
རྒོད་ཀྱི་ཐུལ་ཕྲན་ (göögi tǖǖdrɛn) hair growing on the top of the ears of horses.
རྒོད་ཀྱི་ལྡེམ་འཕྲུ་ (göögi demdru) the vulture's feather that is used on top of a hat (as a symbol of a rank).
རྒོད་ཀྱི་ཕོ་བ་ (göögi pōwa) stomach of vultures (used in Tibetan medicine).
རྒོད་ཀྱི་ཤ་ཤེས (göögi shāmii) keen-sighted [Lit. the vulture's ability to sense/ know that there is a carcass from a very great distance].
རྒོད་སྐམ་མ་ (göö gāmba) a mare that cannot conceive, a barren mare.
རྒོད་རྒོད་ (göögöö) working hard/ diligently; va.—བྱེད་.
རྒོད་སྒྲོ་ (göödro) vulture feather.
རྒོད་གཏམ་ (göödam) humorous/ amusing speech.
རྒོད་ཐང་སྨུག (göötaŋ mūg) brown vulture.
རྒོད་ཐལ་ (göötɛɛ) vulture's droppings.
རྒོད་མདོག (göndɔɔ) sm. རྒོད་མདོག་མདོག.
རྒོད་མདོག་མདོག (göndɔbdɔɔ) pretending to be capable ¶ ཁོ་ལ་འཛེམ་ཐང་གང་ཡང་མེད་ཀྱང་རྒོད་མདོག་མདོག་བྱེད་ཀྱི་འདུག Even though he is not at all capable, he pretends to be capable.

རྒོད་ལྡེམ་ (göödem) sm. རྒོད་ཀྱི་ལྡེམ་འཕྲུ་.
རྒོད་པ་ (gööba) a stage when the practitioner of meditation tries to meditate but the mind wanders.
རྒོད་པོ་ (gööbo) 1. capable, able, good at (connotates aggressiveness) ¶ མི་དེ་ཚོང་ལ་རྒོད་པོ་ཡོད་པ་རེད་ The man is capable at trading/ business. 2. vulture. 3. wild ¶ རྟ་རྒོད་པོ་ ¶ Wild horse. 4. all sorts of things ¶ འགྲོ་རྒྱུ་རྒོད་པོ་ A person who goes everywhere. ¶ དྲན་རྒྱུ་རྒོད་པོ་ Sb. who thinks of all sorts of things (that other's don't).
རྒོད་པོ་དཔུང་སྒྲིག (gööbo būŋdrig) warriors/ heroes marching (together) shoulder-to-shoulder.
རྒོད་པོ་ཡོད་མདོག་མདོག (gööbo yondɔndɔɔ) sm. རྒོད་མདོག་མདོག.
རྒོད་འཕྲུ་ (gööđru) abbr. རྒོད་ཀྱི་ལྡེམ་འཕྲུ་.
རྒོད་བག (gööbaà) 1. proud but ignorant. 2. agitated mind.
རྒོད་བྲུན་ (göödrum) sm. རྒོད་ཐལ.
རྒོད་བྲོ་ (göö tro) vi. to feel like laughing.
རྒོད་བྲོ་བ་ (göö trowa) laughable, funny ¶ གནས་ཚུལ་དེ་རྒོད་བྲོ་བ་ཞིག་རེད་ That was a laughable event.
རྒོད་མ་ (gööma) mare.
རྒོད་མ་ཅན་གྱི་ཟླ་བ་ (göömajɛngi dawa) the 9th month of the Tibetan calendar.
རྒོད་ཞོར་རྩེད་ཞོར་ (gööshɔɔ dzēèshɔɔ) playing and laughing simultaneously ¶ ཕྲུ་གུ་ཚོས་རྒོད་ཞོར་རྩེད་ཞོར་དུ་ནང་ལ་སླེབས་སོང་ The children came home laughing and playing.
རྒོད་གཡེར་ཆེ་བ་ (gööyer cēwa) courageous and broad-minded.
རྒོད་གཡུང་ (gööyuŋ) 1. abbr. unyielding/ hard and gentle. 2. the strength of medicine. 3. military and civil.
རྒོད་རེངས་ (gööreŋ) sm. ངན་རེངས་.
རྒོད་སེམས་ (göösem) a wandering mind.
རྒོད་སྲུན་ (göösɛn) a person who can keep a straight face even when others are laughing.
རྒོབ་སྒྲ་ (gobdra) sound of sth. boiling in a pot.
རྒོབ་ཚ་པོ་ (gob tsābo) putting on an airs, acting in a haughty manner.
རྒོབ་ཤོད་ (gob shöö) va. to put on an airs, to act in a haughty manner.
རྒོའུ་ (gowu) baby gazelle.
རྒོལ་གླེང་ (gööleŋ) sm. རྒོལ་གཏམ་.
རྒོལ་འགོག (göŋgɔɔ) protest, objection, disagreement; va.—བྱེད་.
རྒོལ་: p. བརྒལ་; f. བརྒལ་; imp. རྒོལ་ (göö) 1. va. to oppose, to stand against ¶ གསར་བརྗེའི་ལྟ་བར་རྒོལ་མཁན་ Those who oppose the revolutionary view point. 2. va. to attack, to combat, to fight ¶ རང་ཕྱོགས་ལ་ལན་བཞི་རྒོལ་འདུག (They) attacked our side four times. 3. attack, offensive, assault ¶ ཕར་རྒོལ་ Attack (on others) ཚུར་རྒོལ་ Attack (by other's on one's own side).
རྒོལ་མཆོངས་ (göōcoŋ) attacking, assaulting; va.—བྱེད་ to attack, to assault, to launch an offensive ¶ གནམ་ས་མཚོ་གསུམ་ནས་དུས་གཅིག་ཏུ་རྒོད་མཆོངས་བྱས་པ་རེད་ (They) attacked simultaneously by air, land and sea.
རྒོལ་གཏམ་ (göödam) verbally criticizing/ protesting/ condemning; va.—སློག; —གཏོང་ to criticize/ protest/ condemn ¶ དམག་པོའི་བཙན་འཛུལ་ལ་རྒོལ་གཏམ་བསྒྲགས་པ་རེད་ (They) condemned the military invasion.
རྒོལ་གཏམ་བརྗོད་ཡིག (göödam jööyii) note of protest, protest letter.
རྒོལ་རྡུང་ (gööduŋ) striking, attacking; va.—གཏོང་; —བྱེད་.
རྒོལ་བག (gööbaà) shung. aggressive, prone to get into fights.
རྒོལ་རྩོད་ (göödzöö) opposing through argument/ debate.
རྒོལ་ཚིག (göötsig) rebutting, rebuttal; va.—བྱེད་.
རྒོལ་འཛིང་ (göödziŋ) militarily assaulting/ attacking; va.—བྱེད་ ¶ མན་ཇུ་ར་རྒོལ་འཛིང་བྱས་ཀྱང་ Even though they attacked the Manchu.
རྒོལ་ལན་ (göölɛn) counterattacking, retaliating (attacking); va.—སྤྲོད་ to retaliate, to counterattack, to return fire.
རྒོལ་ལན་རྒོལ་སྤྲོད་ (göölɛn göödröö) combating attack with attack.
རྒོལ་ལན་སྤྲོད་ (göölɛn dröö) see རྒོལ་ལན་.
རྒོལ་ལན་སློག (göölɛn lɔ̄ɔ) sm. རྒོལ་ལན་སྤྲོད་.
རྒོལ་སྲུང་ (göösuŋ) offense and defense.
རྒོལ་སྲུང་གཉིས་ཐུབ་ (göösuŋ ñiitub) capable in offense/ attacking and in defense/ defending.
རྒོལ་སྲུང་མནའ་མཐུན་ (göösuŋ nātün) 1. an offensive and defensive alliance; va.—འཛོག to make such an agreement. 2. an oath/ agreement of partners in crime; va.—འཛོག to make such an agreement.
རྒོལ་སྲུང་མནའ་སྒྲིལ་ (göösuŋ nādree) sm. རྒོལ་སྲུང་མནའ་མཐུན་.
རྒྱ་ (gya) 1. abbr. for China and for India ¶ རྒྱ་བོད་ China and Tibet (or India and Tibet). 2. extent, area, width ¶ ཁོ་ལ་ས་ཞིང་རྒྱ་ཆེན་པོ་ཡོད་པ་རེད་ He has a large area of land. ¶ བསམ་བློ་རྒྱ་ཆེན་པོ་གཏོང་དགོས་ (We) should think big. 3. a trap; va.—འཛུགས་; —འགྲེམ་ to lay/ put out a trap. 4. seal,

stamp, sign, mark. 5. name of a hair style of Dobdo monks (characterized by a strip of hair extending to their cheeks like side burns. 6. envelope. 7. see རྒྱ་རྒྱག.

རྒྱ་: p. རྒྱས་; f. རྒྱ་ (gya) vi. to get large, to increase, to get developed.

རྒྱ་ཀྱུ་ (gyagyu) the hook on which a scale is fastened/ hooked/ attached.

རྒྱ་དཀར་ (gyagar) sm. རྒྱ་གར་.

རྒྱ་དཀར་ནག་གཉིས་ (gya gārnag ñīi) India and China.

རྒྱ་བཀྲས་ (gya drɛ̄ɛ̀) abbr. of China and Tashilhunpo (monastery).

རྒྱ་སྐག (gyagaà) sm. རྒྱ་སྐྱེགས་.

རྒྱ་སྐད་ (gyagɛɛ̀) Chinese language (spoken).

རྒྱ་སྐར་ (gyagar) one of the parts of the body cavity where there are no vital organs.

རྒྱ་སྐས་ (gyagɛɛ̀) ladder.

རྒྱ་སྐོགས་ (gyagɔɔ̀) envelope.

རྒྱ་སྐྱེགས་ (gyagyeg) Laccifer lacca kerr (used in Tibetan medicine).

རྒྱ་སྐྱེགས་ཚིགས་མ་ (gyagyeg tsīgmə) the wax རྒྱ་སྐྱེགས་.

རྒྱ་སྐྱེགས་ཚོས་ (gyagyeg tsȫȍ) a paint/ dye made from རྒྱ་སྐྱེགས་.

རྒྱ་སྐྱེགས་ཤིང་ (gyagyeg shīŋ) the རྒྱ་སྐྱེགས་ tree.

རྒྱ་སྐྱེད་ (gyagyeè) sm. རྒྱ་བསྐྱེད་.

རྒྱ་སྐྱེད་ནུས་ཤུགས་ (gyagyeè nüüshuù) sm. རྒྱ་བསྐྱེད་ནུས་ཤུགས་.

རྒྱ་བསྐུམ་ (gyagum) contraction (expanding and contracting).

རྒྱ་བསྐྱེད་ (gyagyeè) expansion, expanding, extending, disseminating; va.—གཏོང་; —བྱེད་ to expand/ spread/ extend; vi.—འགྲོ་ to get spread/ extended/ disseminated ༶ རྒྱ་བསྐྱེད་ཀྱི་སྲིད་ཇུས་ An expansionist policy. ༶ བཟོ་ལས་འཛུགས་བསྐྲུན་རྒྱ་བསྐྱེད་བཏང་བ་རེད་ (They) expanded the development of industry. ༶ ད་ལོ་གཞི་ཁྱོན་ཆེན་པོའི་བསད་རྒྱས་རང་བཞིན་གྱི་མཚོན་ཆ་རྒྱ་བསྐྱེད་འགྲོ་གི་ཡོད་པ་རེད་ This year weapons of mass destruction are spreading.

རྒྱ་བསྐྱེད་སྒྱུར་གྲངས་ (gyagyeè durdraŋ) coefficient of expansion.

རྒྱ་བསྐྱེད་ནུས་ཤུགས་ (gyagyeè nüüshuù) the power of expansion or spreading.

རྒྱ་བསྐྱེད་རིང་ལུགས་ (gyagyeè riŋluù) expansionism.

རྒྱ་ཁ་ཆེ་ (gya kāce) Chinese Muslims (in contrast to Kashmiri Muslims) ༶ ལྷ་ཡོད་རྒྱ་ཁ་ཆེ་ Chinese Muslims living in Lhasa.

རྒྱ་ཁག (gyakaà) monk guards.

རྒྱ་ཁབ་ (gyakəb) sewing needle.

རྒྱ་ཁམ་ (gyakam) peach (prunus persica).

རྒྱ་ཁུག (gyākuù) pouch.

རྒྱ་ཁུར་ (gyakur) sonchus brachyotus.

རྒྱ་ཁུར་དཀར་ (gya kūrgar) dandelion.

རྒྱ་ཁུར་ནག་པོ་ (gyākur nagbo) picris hieracioides.

རྒྱ་ཁོག (gyakɔɔ̀) hot pot (Mongolian barbecue pot).

རྒྱ་ཁྱབ་ (gyakyəb) broad, widespread, everywhere, all over ༶ རྒྱ་ཁྱབ་གྲོང་གསེབ་ The broad countryside ༶ རྒྱ་ཁྱབ་གསར་བརྗེའི་ལས་བྱེད་པ་ The revolutionary cadres spread all over ༶ རྒྱ་ཁྱབ་རྫོང་གཞིས་ཚང་མ་ All districts (all over) the country.

རྒྱ་ཁྱབ་མང་ཚོགས་ (gyakyəb maŋtsɔɔ̀) the broad masses.

རྒྱ་ཁྱི་ (gyəkyi) Pekinese (breed of dog).

རྒྱ་ཁྱོན་ (gyakön) area, size, scale, extent ༶ ཤིང་ནགས་རྒྱ་ཁྱོན་ཆེན་པོ་འདུག There is a large area of forest. ༶ རྒྱ་ཁྱོན་ཆེ་བའི་འཛུགས་བསྐྲུན་གྱི་འཆར་གཞི་ Large-scale development plans.

རྒྱ་ཁྱོན་ཆེ་བ་ (gyakyön cēwa) large-scale, widespread.

རྒྱ་ཁྱོན་བསྡོམས་འབོར་ (gyakyön dombɔɔ) gross area.

རྒྱ་ཁྲ་ (gyadra) railing ༶ ཆུ་རྫིང་གི་རྒྱ་ཁྲའི་འགྲམ་དུ་ལངས་ནས་ Standing beside the railing of the pond.

རྒྱ་ཁྲག (gyātraà) a type of Tibetan medicine.

རྒྱ་ཁྲམ་ (gyatram) sm.* རྒྱ་གྲམ་.

རྒྱ་གད་ (gyāgɛɛ̀) scolding, harsh words.

རྒྱ་གར་ (gyagar) India.

རྒྱ་གར་སྐད་ (gyagar gɛ̄ɛ̀) the language of India.

རྒྱ་གར་གྲོས་ཚོགས་འོག་མ་ (gyagar trȫȍdzoò wɔ̄gma) Lok Sabha (India).

རྒྱ་གར་གྱི་གསང་བའི་ལས་ཁུངས་ (gyagargi sāŋwɛ lɛ̄ɛ̀guŋ) Intelligence Bureau (India) (IB).

རྒྱ་གར་རྒྱ་མཚོ་ (gyagar gyatso) Indian Ocean.

རྒྱ་གར་ནུབ་ལི་ (gyagar nubli) icons/ statues cast in western India.

རྒྱ་གར་སྤྱི་ཡོངས་རླུང་འཕྲིན་ཁང་ (gyagar jīyoŋ lūŋdringaŋ) All India Radio.

རྒྱ་གར་དབུས་གཞུང་གི་ཞིབ་དཔྱོད་ལས་ཁང་ (gyagar üüshuŋgi shibjöö lɛ̄ɛ̀gaŋ) Central Bureau of Investigations (India).

རྒྱ་གར་རྨ་བྱའི་གཤོག་སྒྲོ་བཙལ་ནས་མ་གཏོགས་བོད་ལ་བྱ་དེའི་གཤོག་སྒྲོ་མེད་པ་རང་དུ་མ་རེད་ (gyagar mābcɛ shugu cuŋnə sāmba məndoò pȫȍla chadɛ shugu meèbaraŋda mareè) wishing for better things from outside the country although having ordinary things in one's own country/ area [Lit. wishing to get a peacock tail in India although having chicken tails in Tibet].

རྒྱ་གར་ཞྭ་མོ་ (gyagar shamo) felt hat, Western style felt hat (with brim).

རྒྱ་གར་གཞུང་ (gyagar shuŋ) the Indian government.

རྒྱ་གར་ཤར་མའི་ཀུང་སི་ (gyagar shārmɛ gūŋsi) the East India Company.

རྒྱ་གར་ཤར་ལི་ (gyagar shārli) icons statues cast in Eastern India.

རྒྱ་གུང་ (gyaguŋ) abbr. 1. Chinese communist/ communism. 2. Indian communist/ communism.

རྒྱ་གོས་འུང་མདོག་ (gyagȫȍ aŋdɔɔ̀) drab (blue) colored clothes [Lit. Chinese clothes, pigeon color].

རྒྱ་གྲགས་བོད་གྲགས་ (gyadraà pȫȍdraà) known by everyone [Lit. known to Chinese, known to Tibetans].

རྒྱ་གྲངས་ (gyadraŋ) the number of jin.

རྒྱ་གྲམ་ (gyadram) cross (+) ༶ རྒྱ་གྲམ་དམར་པོ་ The Red Cross.

རྒྱ་གྲམ་རྟགས་ཅན་དམག་དཔུང་ (gyadram dāgjɛn məgbuŋ) the Crusades.

རྒྱ་གྲམ་དམར་པོ་ (gyadram mārbo) the Red Cross.

རྒྱ་གྲམ་དམར་པོའི་ཚོགས་པ་ (gyadram mārbö tsɔ̄gba) the Red Cross Society.

རྒྱ་གྲམ་དམར་པོའི་ལྷན་ཚོགས་ (gyadram mārbö lhɛ̄ndzoò) the Red Cross Society.

རྒྱ་གྲམ་གཟུགས་ (gyadram sug) the shape of a cross.

རྒྱ་གྲི་ (gyātri) a knife and chopstick holder/ case that is tied on the belt.

རྒྱ་གྲི་པོར་ཤུབས་ (gyatri pɔ̄ɔ̄shub) sm. རྒྱ་གྲི་.

རྒྱ་གྲུ་གུ་ (gya drugu) wild garlic.

རྒྱ་གྲོ་ (gyatro) 1. Chinese flour. 2. Chinese wheat.

རྒྱ་གྲོ་མོ་ (gya tromo) potato.

རྒྱ་གྲོལ་ (gya trȫȍ) 1. vi. to bloom, to open ༶ མེ་ཏོག་འདི་ཚོ་རྒྱ་གྲོལ་བཞག The flowers bloomed. 2. vi. to come untied/ unsealed. 3. vi. to get revealed (a secret).

རྒྱ་གླང་ (gyalaŋ) Indian ox.

རྒྱ་གླིང་ (gyəliŋ) 1. clarinet type musical instrument (used chiefly by monks during religious ceremonies); va.—གཏོང་ to play this instrument. 2. slang. children crying; va.—གཏོང་.

རྒྱ་གླིང་ཁ་ (gyəliŋgə) the opening of a རྒྱ་གླིང་.

རྒྱ་གླིང་མདའ་ (gyəliŋ da) the body of a རྒྱ་གླིང་.

རྒྱ་གླིང་པ་ (gyəliŋbə) a person/ monk who plays a རྒྱ་གླིང་.

རྒྱ་མགོ་ནག (gya gonaà) China.

རྒྱ་འགྲོགས་བྱེད་ (gyāgyɔɔ̀ ceè) va. to weigh sth. on a scale.

རྒྱ་འགྲེལ (gyandree) the commentaries by Indian Pandits on the Buddha's teachings.

རྒྱ་འགྲོལ་ (gya trȫȍ) sm. རྒྱ་གྲོལ་.

རྒྱ་རྒོལ་ (gyagȫȍ) antichinese, opposing China.

རྒྱ་རྒྱག (gya gyaà) va. to seal, to stamp.

རྒྱ་རྒྱུགས་པོད་རྒྱུགས་ (gyəgyuù pȫȍgyuù) 1. can go

everywhere and it is fitting. 2. can sell everywhere (best selling).

རྒྱ་སྒ་ (gyā ga) saddle from China or India.

རྒྱ་སྒོ་ (gya go) 1. gate, the main entrance gate, the main door. 2. Chinese-style door with rounded sides.

རྒྱ་སྒོག (gyagɔɔ̀) a type of garlic (from China).

རྒྱ་བསྒྲགས་བོད་བསྒྲགས་ (gyadraà pöödraà) publicizing/ advertising everywhere va.—བྱེད་ [Lit. publicizing in China publicizing in Tibet].

རྒྱ་དངུལ་ (gya ŋüü) Chinese silver.

རྒྱ་རྔོན་ (gyaŋön) a trapper.

རྒྱ་བཅད་རྒྱག (gyajɛɛ̀ gyaà) 1. va. to paint along the edge of a figure/ drawing with another color. 2. va. to affix a seal on an envelope.

རྒྱ་ལྕགས་ (gyajaà) abbr. of རྒྱ་ནག་ལྕགས་རི་.

རྒྱ་ལྕང་ (gyajaŋ) weeping willow tree.

རྒྱ་ལྕང་སྡོང་པོ་ (gyajaŋ doŋbo) sm. རྒྱ་ལྕང་.

རྒྱ་ལྕང་ཕྱུགས་མོ་ (gyajaŋ cūgmo) sm. རྒྱ་ལྕང་.

རྒྱ་ལྕོག (gyajɔɔ̀) Tibetan style low table.

རྒྱ་ཆད་ (gyacɛɛ̀) 1. bias, prejudice. 2. uneven.

རྒྱ་ཆས་ (gyacɛɛ̀) Chinese or Indian clothes.

རྒྱ་ཆུང་ (gyacuŋ) narrow, limited, small.

རྒྱ་ཆེ་ (gyace) 1. vast, large, broad, extensive (in number or size). 2. the general (public).

རྒྱ་ཆེ་ཁ་མ་འདུས་ (gyace kūmaduoò) sm. རྒྱ་ཆེ་སྐྱེ་སྟོང་གླིང་བུའི་རྫོང་.

རྒྱ་ཆེ་སྐྱེ་སྟོང་གླིང་བུའི་རྫོང་ (gyace gyedoŋ līŋbü dzōŋ) having sth. that looks rich and great but really being broke/ bankrupt [Lit. large empty sack, (but) playing the flute].

རྒྱ་ཆེ་གཏིང་ཟབ་ (gyace dīŋsəb) far-reaching and deep/ profound.

རྒྱ་ཆེ་དཔངས་མཐོ་ (gyace bāŋto) 1. a mansion, a large house. 2. great variety and quantity/ amount.

རྒྱ་ཆེ་བ་ (gyacewa) sm. རྒྱ་ཆེ་.

རྒྱ་ཆེ་མུ་མེད་ (gyace mumeè) limitless, boundless.

རྒྱ་ཆེ་གཟབ་རྒྱས་ (gyace səbgyɛɛ̀) grand, magnificent.

རྒྱ་ཆེན་ (gyacen) sm. རྒྱ་ཆེན་པོ་.

རྒྱ་ཆེན་པོ་ (gya cēmbo) broad, wide, extensive, large-scale.

རྒྱ་ཆེའི་མི་མང་ (gyacee mimaŋ) sm. རྒྱ་ཆེའི་མི་དམངས་.

རྒྱ་ཆེའི་མི་དམངས་ (gyacee mimaŋ) the broad masses, the general public.

རྒྱ་ཆེའི་མི་དམངས་མང་ཚོགས་ (gyacee mimaŋ māŋtsɔɔ̀) sm. རྒྱ་ཆེའི་མི་དམངས་.

རྒྱ་ཆེར་ (gyacer) larger, more extensive; va.—གཏོང་; —སྤེལ་ to enlarge, to expand, to broaden, to widen ¶ སྔོ་ཚལ་འདེབས་ཡག་མུའུ་100 ཙམ་རྒྱ་ཆེར་བཏང་སོང་ (They) increased cultivation of vegetables by about 100 mu.

རྒྱ་ཆེར་འགྲེམ་ (gyacer drem) sm. རྒྱ་ཆེར་གཏོང་.

རྒྱ་ཆེར་འགྲེལ་བ་ (gyacer dreewa) detailed and comprehensive commentary.

རྒྱ་ཇ་ (gyaca) Chinese tea.

རྒྱ་རྗེ་ (gyaje) Emperor of China.

རྒྱ་ཉི་ (gyañi) trap, snare.

རྒྱ་རྙིང་ (gyañiŋ) old.

རྒྱ་ཏ་ (gyada) 1. horse from India or China. 2. a horse's whose mane and tail are cut very short.

རྒྱ་རྟགས་ (gyadaà) signing on the back of the envelope instead of using a seal.

རྒྱ་སྟག (gyadaà) tiger.

རྒྱ་སྟག་ང་རོ་ངར་ གངས་སེང་འགྱིང་འགྱིང་ (gyadaà ŋarŋar tarsem gyiŋgyiŋ) powerful and imposing [Lit. ferocious as a tiger, haughty as a snow lion].

རྒྱ་སྟག་ར་མོ་ཆེ་ (gyadaà ramoce) Ramoche temple (in the north of Lhasa).

རྒྱ་ཐགས་ (gyadaà) Chinese woven materials.

རྒྱ་ཐག (gyadaà) the cord/ rope/ string used for lifting things on a རྒྱ་མ་ scale.

རྒྱ་ཐང་ (gyadaŋ) a vast plain/ flat area.

རྒྱ་ཐིག (gyadig) a dot/ cross design used on woolen materials, woolen materials with that design.

རྒྱ་ཐུག (gyəduù) noodles (Chinese style).

རྒྱ་ཐུག་ཁུ་བ་ (gyaduù kōwa) soup/ broth for noodles.

རྒྱ་ཐུར་ (gyadur) a small scale used to weigh gold and silver; va.—བཀུག to weigh gold/ silver on such a scale.

རྒྱ་ཐུར་སྐར་ཚོམ་ (gyatur gārdzom) the constellation Libra.

རྒྱ་ཐེར་ (gyater) serge made in India.

རྒྱ་ཐེལ་ (gyatel) a Chinese seal.

རྒྱ་ཐོན་ (gyadön) produced in China ¶ རྒྱ་ཐོན་གྱི་དངོས་ཟོག Chinese made products.

རྒྱ་ཐོར་ (gyadɔɔ) sm. ཤུ་བ་.

རྒྱ་མཐོངས་ (gyadoŋ) open roof, skylight.

རྒྱ་དར་ (gyadar) Chinese silk.

རྒྱ་དོགས་པ་ བོད་རེ་བ་ (gya tɔgba pöö rewa) a saying used to convey a fundamental Cultural difference between Chinese and Tibetans: Chinese are suspicious and Tibetans are hopeful.

རྒྱ་དོན་ (gyadön) abbr. of name of Dalai Lama's older brother (Gyalo Thondrup).

རྒྱ་དོར་ (gyadɔɔ) Chinese trousers/ pants.

རྒྱ་མདའ་ (gyamda) rifle made in China.

རྒྱ་མདུད་ (gyəndüü) knotted and braided.

རྒྱ་འདེགས་ (gyandeg) weighing on a scale; va.—བྱེད་.

རྒྱ་འདོན་ (gyandön) shung. the field from which a corvee soldier was recruited by the རྒྱ་སྲུང་དམག་སྐོར་.

རྒྱ་འདྲ་ (gyandra) a kind of brocade.

རྒྱ་འདྲེ་ (gyandre) sm. རྒྱབ་འདྲེ་.

རྒྱ་རྡོ་ (gyado) the stone that is used as a weight on རྒྱ་མ་ scales.

རྒྱ་སྡེ (gyade) territory controlled by China (usu. for those parts of Kham and Amdo under China control).

རྒྱ་སྡེར་ (gyader) the plate of a རྒྱ་མ་ scale on which items to be weighed are placed.

རྒྱ་ནག (gyanaà) China.

རྒྱ་ནག་གོང་མ་ (gyanaà koŋma) Emperor of China.

རྒྱ་ནག་གླང་ཆེན་ (gyanaà lāŋcen) Mt. Emei.

རྒྱ་ནག་ལྕགས་རི་ (gyanaà jāəri) 1. the Great Wall of China. 2. a type of design used in Tibetan and Chinese rugs and furniture.

རྒྱ་ནག་ཉིན་རེའི་ཚགས་དཔར་ (gyanaà jāəri) China Daily.

རྒྱ་ནག་སྣག་ཚ་ (gyanaà nāgdza) ink from China.

རྒྱ་ནག་མི་དམངས་སྤྱི་མཐུན་རྒྱལ་ཁབ་ (gyanaà mimaŋ jīdün gyɛɛgəb) People's Republic of China.

རྒྱ་ནག་ཤེལ་སྒོ་ (gyanaà shēēgo) Chinese mirror.

རྒྱ་ནག་སེ་བའི་མེ་ཏོག (gyanaà sēwɛ metog) rose.

རྒྱ་ནད་ (gyanɛɛ̀) syphilis.

རྒྱ་སྣག (gyanag) ink from China.

རྒྱ་སྣེ་ (gyane) chenopodium album.

རྒྱ་པ་ (gyaba) 1. a trapper. 2. swindler, con man, impostor.

རྒྱ་དཔང་ (gyabaŋ) 1. mediator. 2. witness.

རྒྱ་དཔངས་ (gyabaŋ) cube.

རྒྱ་དཔངས་གྲུ་བཞི་ (gyabaŋ trubshi) cube, cubic ¶ སྨི་རྒྱ་དཔང་གྲུ་བཞི་གཅིག A cubic meter.

རྒྱ་དཔེ་ (gyabe) scriptures written in Sanskrit.

རྒྱ་དཔོན་ (gyabön) Chinese officials; Indian officials.

རྒྱ་སྤོས་ (gyaböö) 1. incense from China/ India. 2. melilotus suaveolens ledeb (a plant used in Tibetan medicine).

རྒྱ་སྤོས་སེར་པོ་ (gyaböö sērbo) a plant used for herbal medicines (melilotus suaveolens).

རྒྱ་སྤོས་དཀར་པོ་ (gyaböö gārbo) valeriana officinalis (a plant used for herbal medicines).

རྒྱ་ཕིགས་ (gyəpig) sm.* རྒྱ་ཕིབས་.

རྒྱ་ཕིབས་ (gyəbib) roof (usu. a gilded, pagoda-like roof) ¶ འཛམ་གླིང་རྒྱ་ཕིབས་ The roof of the world.

རྒྱ་ཕུབས་ (gyabub) sm. རྒྱ་ཕིབས་.

རྒྱ་ཕྱིར་ (gyajir) shung. a type of cotton cloth.

རྒྱ་ཕྱོགས་ (gyajɔɔ̀) the Chinese side/ position, the Chinese.

རྒྱ་ཕྲུག་སློབ་གྲྭ་ (gyadruù lōbdra) the Chinese language track/ class in some Tibetan elementary and secondary schools.

རྒྱ་ཕྲེང་ (gyadreŋ) shung. necklace of beads (worn by Chinese Imperial Officials).

རྒྱ་བལ་འབྲས་འབྲུག (gya pɛɛ drɛɛ̀ drug) abbr. India, Nepal, Sikkim, and Bhutan.

རྒྱ་བལ་འབྲུག (gya pɛɛ drug)) abbr. India, Nepal, and Bhutan.

རྒྱ་བོ་ (gyəwu) 1. bearded (for people) ¶ མི་རྒྱ་བོ་ A bearded man. 2. a type of coloring for dogs: a black dog with yellow spots over its eyes and a yellow mouth.

རྒྱ་བོད་ (gyapöö) China/ India and Tibet.

རྒྱ་བོད་བདེ་འཁོད་ (gyaböö degöö) shung. Chinese and the Tibetans living in peace.

རྒྱ་བོད་དཔྱད་མཚམས་ (gyaböö jɛɛ̀dzam dzɛ̀ɛrii) shung. verdicts signed by China and Tibet (Chinese and Tibetan officials).

རྒྱ་བོད་འཛུགས་སྐྲུན་ཐེབས་རྩ་ཁང་ (gyaböö dzugdrön tēbdzagaŋ) China Tibet Development Foundation.

རྒྱ་བོད་ཞི་དོན་ (gyaböö shidön) shung. peaceful matters regarding China and Tibet.

རྒྱ་བོད་ཞི་དྲག་དཔོན་འབངས་ (gyaböö shidraà bõnbaŋ) shung. Chinese and Tibetan civil and military Officials and the subjects/ commoners.

རྒྱ་བྱ་ (gyaja) phoenix.

རྒྱ་བྱེར་ (gya cer) broad, extensive, wide.

རྒྱ་བྲ་ (gyadra) buckwheat.

རྒྱ་དབྱིན་ཨ་ (gya ĩn ā) abbr. China, Britain, U.S.A.

རྒྱ་དབྱུག (gyayug) threshing stick (with a revolving striker); va.—རྒྱག to thresh with a revolving stick.

རྒྱ་འབྱམས་ (gya cam) vi. to be unable to manage a task because it's too big/ large.

རྒྱ་འབྲས་ (gyamdrɛɛ̀) Chinese or Indian rice.

རྒྱ་འབྲུ་ (gyandru) shung. grain for supplying to the Chinese.

རྒྱ་སྦུག (gyəbuù) a cymbal made in China.

རྒྱ་སྦྱོང་དམག་སྒར་ (gyajoŋ māàgar) a Tibetan regiment started in Tibet during by the Manchu Amban in 1752 (also known as the ཁ་དང་ or Trapchi regiment) [Lit. Chinese trained regiment].

རྒྱ་མ་ (gyama) ch. 1. a jin (=0.5 kilograms or 1.1023 pounds); va.—བརྒྱག་; —འདེགས་; —འགྱོགས་ to weigh sth. [Lit. measure the number of jin]. 2. a hand-held scale, a steelyard. 3. va. to test sb. to find out what the person thinks/ feels ¶ ཁོའི་གནས་ཚུལ་དེ་ཤེས་ཡོད་མེད་ངས་རྒྱ་མར་བཀུག་པ་ཡིན་ I tested to see whether he knew about the news or not. 4. an envelope.

རྒྱ་མ་དངུལ་ཆུ་ (gyama ŋũũcu) sm. རྒྱ་མོ་རྔུལ་ཆུ་.

རྒྱ་མ་བོད་ (gya ma pöö) a person of mixed Chinese and Tibetan ancestry.

རྒྱ་མའི་མདའ་ (gyamɛ da) the arm of a hand-held scale/ steelyard.

རྒྱ་མའི་འཁྲོལ་འཛིན་ (gyamɛ trõndzin) shung. a permit allowing one to use scales during the Monlam Festival.

རྒྱ་མི་ (gyəmi) a Han (ethnic) Chinese.

རྒྱ་མི་ཕྱུགས་ན་དམག བོད་པ་ཕྱུགས་ན་ཁང་ (gyəmi gyaàna māà pööba gyaàna kãŋ) a saying conveying cultural differences between Chinese and Tibetans: if Chinese get rich they go to war; if Tibetans get rich they build a house.

རྒྱ་མིག (gyamii) the marks/ measures on the arm of a hand-held scale/ steelyard.

རྒྱ་མེན་ (gyamen) a herbal medicine (papaver rhoeas).

རྒྱ་མོ་ (gyamo) 1. a Han (ethnic) Chinese woman. 2. a mule with yellow spots over its eyes.

རྒྱ་མོ་རྐང་རིལ་ (gyamo gãŋrii) Chinese women with bound feet.

རྒྱ་མོ་རྔུལ་ཆུ་ (gyamo ŋũũju) the name of the part of the Upper Yangtze River that formed the Sino-Tibetan border in Eastern Tibet in 1951.

རྒྱ་མོ་བཟའ་ (gyamo sa) sm. རྒྱ་མོ་ཨོང་ཇོ་.

རྒྱ་མོ་ཨོང་ཇོ་ (gyamo õŋjo) Chinese wives of Srongtsen Gampo and Mes Agtsom.

རྒྱ་དམག (gyamaà) Chinese soldier, Chinese army.

རྒྱ་དམར་ (gyamar) 1. Red China, Communist China. 2. purplish red.

རྒྱ་དམར་ནག (gya mārnaà) Communist and Goumingdang China/ Chinese.

རྒྱ་སྨུག (gyəmuù) purple.

རྒྱ་ཙོང་ (gyadzoŋ) onion.

རྒྱ་བཙུན་ (gyadzün) a Chinese monk.

རྒྱ་ཙ་ (gyadza) the name of a large artery in Tibetan medicine.

རྒྱ་རྩི་ (gyədzi) 1. lacquer. 2. Western style paint.

རྒྱ་རྩི་གོད་པ་ (gyədzi gööbo) a plant used in Tibetan medicine (cimicifuga foetida).

རྒྱ་རྩི་དྲུག་ལོ་ (gyədzi truglo) a plant used in Tibetan medicine.

རྒྱ་རྩི་གཡུང་བ་ (gyədzi yũŋwa) a plant used for herbal medicines (adonis coerulea maxim).

རྒྱ་རྩི་ཤིང་ (gyədzi shĩŋ) a tree from which lacquer is made.

རྒྱ་རྩིས་ (gyadzii) a kind of astrology that was introduced to Tibet from China, Chinese astrology.

རྒྱ་བརྩོན་འགྲུས་སེང་གེ་ (gya dzõndröö sẽŋge) one of the Tibetan translators who brought Atisha to Western Tibet in the 11th century.

རྒྱ་ཚ་ (gyadza) 1. a Tibetan of mixed Chinese and Tibetan ancestry. 2. name of a Dzong.

རྒྱ་ཚྭ་ (gyadza) a kind of salt (sal ammoniacum).

རྒྱ་ཚྭ་ལྕེ་འབིག (gyatsa jẽmbig) sm. རྒྱ་ཚྭ་.

རྒྱ་ཚད་ (gyadzɛɛ̀) size of an area/ expanse. 2. disease caused by heat/ hot climates.

རྒྱ་ཚིགས་ (gyədzii) metatarsal bone.

རྒྱ་ཚུགས་ (gyadzuù) a postal station (that was part of the Qing transport system in which stations were set up one day apart).

རྒྱ་ཚེམ་ (gyadzem) the Chinese way of stitching/ sewing (with the needle pointing away from the body).

རྒྱ་ཚོང་ (gyadzoŋ) 1. trade, business; va.—རྒྱག. 2. trade with China/ India; va.—རྒྱག.

རྒྱ་ཚོས་ (gyadzöö) 1. red ink, Chinese vermilion. 2. dyes from India/ China.

རྒྱ་མཚལ་ (gyadzɛɛ) sm. རྒྱ་ཚོས་.

རྒྱ་མཚལ་ལྗོག་ལ་ (gyadzɛɛ jōgla) sm. རྒྱ་མཚལ་.

རྒྱ་མཚོ་ (gyatso) 1. the ocean ¶ ཕྱི་པའི་རྒྱ་མཚོ་ The open seas.

རྒྱ་མཚོ་སྐམ་ནུས་ན་སྦལ་པ་ཤི་ནུས་ (gyatso gāmnüùnə bɛɛba shĩnüù) if the high authorities can make sacrifices so too should the lower people [Lit. if the ocean is able to dry up, the frogs are able to die].

རྒྱ་མཚོ་གན་པོ་ (gyatso gɛmbo) shung. a type of local district official who was below District Commissioner and above village headman (he was involved in tax collection).

རྒྱ་མཚོ་ཅུའུ་ (gyatso cū) tib.ch. oceanography bureau.

རྒྱ་མཚོ་ཆུ་ཐིགས་ (gyatso cūdig) a tiny amount [Lit. a drop in the ocean].

རྒྱ་མཚོ་ཆུ་ཐིགས་ཀྱི་འབྲེལ་བ་ (gyatso cūdiggi dreewa) a karmic relation/ connection [Lit. relations of drops in the ocean].

རྒྱ་མཚོ་ཆེན་པོ་ (gyatso cēmbo) the ocean.

རྒྱ་མཚོ་ཉ་ལས་ (gyatso ñalɛɛ̀) ocean/ marine fishing industry ¶ རྒྱ་མཚོ་ཉ་ལས་བཟོ་གྲྭ Ocean fishery company.

རྒྱ་མཚོ་རྡོ་དབྱུག (gyatso doyuù) difficult to find/ investigate [Lit. throwing a rock into the ocean].

རྒྱ་མཚོ་དམར་པོ་ (gyatso māābo) the Red Sea.

རྒྱ་མཚོ་གཡོ་ (gyatso yō) vi. to get an earthquake under the ocean.

རྒྱ་མཚོ་ཤར་མ་ (gyatso shārma) the East China Sea.

རྒྱ་མཚོ་ས་གཤིས་ (gyatso sɔ̄shiì) marine geology ¶ རྒྱ་མཚོ་ས་གཤིས་རྟོག་དཔྱོད་རུ་ཁག Marine geological survey team.

རྒྱ་མཚོ་སེར་པོ་ (gyatso sērbo) Yellow Sea.

རྒྱ་མཚོའི་གོས་ཅན་ (gyatsö kööjɛn) shung. earth.

རྒྱ་མཚོའི་འགྲམ་ཐིག (gyatsö dramdig) coastline.

རྒྱ་མཚོའི་རྒྱལ་པོ་ (gyatsö gyɛɛbo) ocean.

རྒྱ་མཚོའི་ངོས་ (gyatsö ŋöö) sea level.

རྒྱ་མཚོའི་ངོས་ལས་ (gyatsö ŋöölɛ) above sea level.

རྒྱ་མཚོའི་ངོས་ལས་མཐོ་ཚད་ (gyatsö ŋöölɛ tödzɛɛ̀) height above sea level.

རྒྱ་མཚོའི་མངའ་དབང་ (gyatsö ŋāwaŋ) territorial rights in the ocean.

རྒྱ་མཚོའི་ཆུ་སྐྱར་ (gyatsö cūgyar) seagull.

རྒྱ་མཚོའི་མཚིང་ (gyatsö ciŋ) in the middle of the ocean.

རྒྱ་མཚོའི་དུས་རླབས་ (gyatsö tüüləb) sea tide.

རྒྱ་མཚོའི་ནང་གི་ཐིགས་པ་ (gyatsö naŋgi tīgbə) a drop in the ocean.

རྒྱ་མཚོའི་ནང་གི་རྡོ་དབྱུག (gyatsö naŋgi doyuù) sm. རྒྱ་མཚོ་རྡོ་དབྱུག.

རྒྱ་མཚོའི་ཕ་རོལ་ (gyatsö pārol) across the ocean, overseas.

རྒྱ་མཚོའི་འཕེལ་འགྲིབ་ (gyatsö pēndrib) morning and evening tide.

རྒྱ་མཚོའི་བླ་མ་ (gyatsö lāma) the Dalai Lama.

རྒྱ་མཚོའི་ལྦུ་བ་ (gyatsö buwa) ocean froth.

རྒྱ་མཚོའི་རང་བཞིན་གྱི་གནམ་གཤིས་ (gyatsö rəŋshingi nəmshiì) marine climate.

རྒྱ་མཚོའི་རིག་པ་ (gyatsö rigbə) oceanography.

རྒྱ་མཚོའི་རླུང་འཚུབ་ (gyatsö lūŋdzub) typhoon, hurricane.

རྒྱ་མཚོར་སྐོར་གཡེང་དམག་གྲུ་ (gyatsɔɔ gɔ̄ɔyeŋ məgdru) cruiser (warship).

རྒྱ་མཚོར་འགྲོ་ (gyatsɔɔ dro) va. to go to sea.

རྒྱ་མཚོར་རྡོ་བསྐྱུར་ (gyatsɔɔ do gyūr) receiving no response /reply to an action. 2. disappearing, not knowing where sth. went [Lit. casting a stone into the ocean].

རྒྱ་མཚོར་རྡོ་དབྱུགས་ (gyatsɔɔ do yūù) sm. རྒྱ་མཚོར་རྡོ་བསྐྱུར་.

རྒྱ་མཚོར་ཞུགས་ (gyatsɔɔ shuù) (slang) intellectuals/ officials going into business [Lit. entering the ocean].

རྒྱ་ཞིབ་ (gyəshib) 1. buckwheat flour. 2. sieve; va.—རྒྱག to strain/ sieve.

རྒྱ་ཞྭ་ (gyasha) a kind of felt hat.

རྒྱ་གཞུང་ (gyashuŋ) Indian or Chinese Government.

རྒྱ་བཞར་སྤུ་གྲི་ (gyashar būdri) razor.

རྒྱ་ཟས་ (gyasɛɛ̀) Chinese food.

རྒྱ་ཟས་མ་བྱན་ (gyaseè majɛn) chef/ cook for Chinese cuisine.

རྒྱ་ཟོག (gyasɔɔ̀) Chinese or Indian goods.

རྒྱ་ཟོང་ (gyasoŋ) sm. རྒྱ་ཟོག.

རྒྱ་གཟེབ་ (gyaseb) see རྒྱལ་གཟེབ་.

རྒྱ་གཟེར་ (gyaser) nails from India.

རྒྱ་བཟའ་ (gyāsa) the Chinese wife of king Srongtsen Gampo.

རྒྱ་བཟའ་བལ་བཟའ་ (gyasa bɛɛsa) the Chinese and the Nepalese wives of king Srongtsen Gampo.

རྒྱ་བཟོ་ (gyaso) Chinese style or shape.

རྒྱ་འུབ་འདུ་ (gyawub du) sm. རྒྱ་འུབས་འདུ་.

རྒྱ་འུབས་འདུ་ (gyawub du) vi. to be able to cope with, to be able to handle/ manage, to be able to compete ¶ ཕྱི་ནང་སྐྱིན་བུན་གྱིས་རྐྱེན་པས་ཁྱིམ་ཚང་རྒྱ་འུབས་མི་འདུས་པའི་གནས་སུ་གྱུར་བ་རེད་ Because of their internal and external loans (they) were unable to manage the household well.

རྒྱ་ཡངས་པོ་ (gya yaŋbo) wide, broad.

རྒྱ་ཡན་ (gyayɛn) laissez faire, overly lenient, spoiling, letting sb. continue to do bad things, allowing sb. to get away with bad actions; va. (དུ་) —གཏོང་ ¶ ཁྲིམས་འགལ་བྱེད་མཁན་རྒྱ་ཡན་དུ་གཏོང་རྒྱུ་མེད་ One shouldn't let violators of the law get away with that.

རྒྱ་ཡན་དུ་འཇོག (gyayɛndu jɔɔ̀) shung. va. to let somebody get away with bad acts/ behavior.

རྒྱ་ཡན་ཚ་པོ་ (gyayɛn tsābo) sb. who spoils another, sb. who is overly lenient, sb. who lets others get away with things.

རྒྱ་ཡན་རིང་ལུགས་ (gyayɛn riŋluù) laissez faireism.

རྒྱ་ཡིག (gyəyiì) Chinese written language.

རྒྱ་ཡིག་སྒྲ་སྦྱོར་བྱེད་སྟངས་ (gyəyiì drajɔɔ cēdaŋ) Chinese phonetic alphabet (proposed as a substitute for characters).

རྒྱ་ཡིག་སྡེ་ཁག (gyəyiì degaà) department of Chinese language and literature.

རྒྱ་ཡུལ་ (gyəyüü) China, India.

རྒྱ་ར་ (gyara) mountain goat.

རྒྱ་རག (gyaraà) 1. alcoholic beverages from China or India. 2. brass.

རྒྱ་རིགས་ (gyərii) ethnic Chinese (Han), ethnic Indians.

རྒྱ་རིགས་ཆེན་པོའི་རིང་ལུགས་ (gyərii cēmbö riŋluù) great Han chauvinism.

རྒྱ་རུ་ (gyaru) the horns of a mountain goat.

རྒྱ་རུམ་ (gyarum) Chinese (knotted) carpet.

རྒྱ་རོ་ (gyaro) derogative term for a Chinese person [Lit. Chinese corpse].

རྒྱ་ལ་ (gyala) if ¶ རྒྱ་ལ་ཁྱེད་རང་བོད་ལ་ཕེབས་ན་ལན་ཞིག་སྐྱོམ་རོགས་གནང་ If you are going to Tibet please take a message for (me).

རྒྱ་ལ་ཕུག (gya ləbuù) radish.

རྒྱ་ལྭ་ (gyala) sm. རྒྱ་ཆས་.

རྒྱ་ལབ་ (gyaləb) abbr. of རྒྱ་ལ་ཕུག.

རྒྱ་ལམ་ (gyalam) highway, a main/ broad street ¶ རྒྱ་ལམ་ཁོད་སྙོམས་ A level highway.

རྒྱ་ལམ་སྐྱ་མོ་ (gyalam gyāmo) a dirt highway.

རྒྱ་ལམ་འགྲུལ་བས་བལྟས་ན་ཆ་ལོ་ཉི་མ་དྲོ་བ་ ཆ་ལོ་ངར་རས་བལྟས་ན་བྲག་ལ་རླུང་བུ་སྣང་བ་ (gyalam drüübɛ dɛɛ̀na cōlo ñimə trowa cōlo ŋarɛɛ̀ dɛɛ̀na tragla lūŋbu daŋwa) people always see others as better off/ happier [travelers on the road see the moss as enjoying the sunshine; the moss itself feels it is very windy on the hill].

རྒྱ་ལས་ཐར་ (gyalɛɛ̀ tār) sm. རྒྱ་ལས་ཤོར་.

རྒྱ་ལས་ཤོར་ (gyalɛɛ̀ shɔ̄ɔ) vi. to escape from a trap/ net, to escape unpunished, to slip through a net.

རྒྱ་ལུ་ (gyalu) prince.

རྒྱ་ལུ་ཆས་ (gyəlu cɛɛ̀) a traditional Tibetan dress worn by lay government officials.

རྒྱ་ལུ་བ་ (gyəluwa) a performer in the Tibetan opera.

རྒྱ་ལུགས་ (gyəluù) Chinese custom ¶ རྒྱ་ལུགས་གུས་བཏུད་ The Chinese custom of showing respect.

རྒྱ་ལུགས་སྨན་པ་ (gyəluù mēmba) a physician trained in Chinese herbal medicine.

རྒྱ་ལུའི་གྲི་ (gyəlü tri) a knife worn with the རྒྱ་ལུ་ཆས་ costume.

རྒྱ་ལུའི་སྟོད་གོས་ (gyəlü döögöö) an upper garment worn by the རྒྱ་ལུ་བ་ in the Tibetan opera.

རྒྱ་ལོ་ (gyalo) the stick/ pole that is used to churn butter tea.

རྒྱ་ལོ་བོད་ལོ་ (gyalo pöölo) 1. Chinese year and Tibetan year. 2. ordinary looking.

རྒྱ་ཤིང་ (gyashiŋ) 1. arm of a hand-held scale/ steelyard. 2. a type of tree (from which churns are made).

རྒྱ་ཤིང་བརྔོས་གསུམ་ (gya shīŋ ŋöö sūm) shung. name of a three part tax in tt. that included grain, firewood and tsamba.

རྒྱ་ཤུག (gyəshug) 1. cypress tree. 2. jujube tree.

རྒྱ་ཤུག་འབྲས་བུ་ (gyəshug drɛɛbu) 1. date. 2. the (fruit) of the cypress tree (used for medicinal purposes).

རྒྱ་ཤེལ་ (gyashel) rock candy.

རྒྱ་ཤོ་ (gyasho) rumex crispus (used in Tibetan medicine).

རྒྱ་ཤོག (gya̲shog) Chinese paper.

རྒྱ་བཤིག (gya̲shii) va. to open an envelope.

རྒྱ་སེ་ (gya̲se) 1. rose. 2. a thick brocade used in making hats.

རྒྱ་སེ་མདོག (gya̲se d̲ɔ̀ɔ) rose color.

རྒྱ་སེ་སྐྱེ་གླིང་ (gya̲se jīliŋ) Rose Garden (of the U.S. White House).

རྒྱ་སེའི་མེ་ཏོག (gya̲see me̲dog) rose.

རྒྱ་སེར་ (gya̲ser) 1. Russia. 2. a yellowish beard. 3. fissure, gap, crack.

རྒྱ་སོག (gya̲sɔ̀ɔ) abbr. of Chinese and Mongolians, China and Mongolia.

རྒྱ་སྲང་ (gya̲saŋ) 1. small hand-held scale/ balance/ steelyard. 2. street.

རྒྱ་སྲན་ (gya̲drɛn) a type of bean (vicia faba).

རྒྱ་སྲན་མ་ (gya̲ drɛ̄ma) sm. རྒྱ་སྲན་.

རྒྱ་གླེབས་བོད་དྲིན་ (gya̲leb pö̲ödrin) shung. the benefits gained by China are due to the grace of Tibet.

རྒྱ་གསར་ (gya̲sar) a dye for woolen cloth.

རྒྱ་གསེར་ (gya̲see) brocade.

རྒྱ་ལྷ་ཁང་ (gyā lhāgaŋ) a mosque of Chinese Muslims.

རྒྱ་ཨ་སོབ་ (gya̲ āsob) sm. རྒྱུའུ་.

རྒྱག་: p.བརྒྱབ་ or རྒྱབ་; f. རྒྱག; imp. རྒྱོབ་ (gya̲à) verbalizer of nominals ¶ཁང་པ་རྒྱག To build a house. ¶དམག་རྒྱག To make war. ¶སྒོ་རྒྱག To close a door.

རྒྱག་སྐོར་ (gya̲àgɔɔ) 1. repeating sth., doing again; va.—ཤོད་ to repeat sth. over and over again. 2. straining a batch of ཆང་ (beer) a second time to make the ཆང་ more potent; va.—རྒྱག. 3. a round (of playing a game such as cards).

རྒྱག་སྐྱོར་རྒྱག (gya̲àgyɔɔ gya̲à) va. to do sth. again ¶ ཐེར་རྫོང་རྒྱག་སྐྱོར་རྒྱག To load the cart again.

རྒྱག་གཅིག་མཆོངས་གཅིག (gya̲jig cōŋjig) 100% commitment, doing sth. without hesitation ¶ང་ཚོ་བཙན་འཛུལ་བ་དང་དམག་རྒྱག་ཡག་ལ་རྒྱག་གཅིག་མཆོངས་གཅིག་བྱེད་དགོས་རེད་ We have to be 100% committed to wage war against the invaders.

རྒྱག་ཇ་ (gya̲àja) tea for one's own use (rather than for sale).

རྒྱག་ཉེས་ཕོག་ཉེས་ཤོར་ (gya̲gñeè pōgñeè shɔ̄ɔ) vi. to hit sb. accidently.

རྒྱག་གདམ་ (gya̲gdam) a sarcastic/ biting remark; va.—རྒྱག་; —ཤོད་.

རྒྱག་སྡེའུ་ (gya̲àdewu) a carpenter's tool.

རྒྱག་ཐེངས་གཅིག (gya̲àdeŋjig) in one stroke, in one shot ¶དམག་རྒྱག་ཐེངས་གཅིག་ལ་རྒྱལ་ཁ་ཐོབ་པ་རེད་ In one stroke (battle) they won the war.

རྒྱག་ཐོ་ (gya̲àdo) a kind of large hammer.

རྒྱག་མདོང་ (gya̲doŋ) mortar (the weapon).

རྒྱག་འདྲེ་གོད་པོ་ (gya̲ndre gö̲öbo) belligerent, pugnacious.

རྒྱག་རྡུང་ (gya̲gduŋ) beating, hitting; va.—བྱེད་.

རྒྱག་དགུག (gya̲gyuù) see རྒྱ་དགུག.

རྒྱག་འབེན་ (gya̲ŋben) sm. རྒྱང་འབེན་.

རྒྱག་མར་ (gya̲gmar) butter for one's own use.

རྒྱག་མཛོག (gya̲ŋdzɔ̀ɔ) shung. va. to beat ¶དུད་འགྲོ་རྒྱག་མཛོག་སོགས་བྱུང་ན་ If he does things such as beating the animals.

རྒྱག་ཟིང་ (gya̲gsoŋ) sm. རྒྱགས་ཆས་.

རྒྱག་རེས་ (gya̲greè) sm. རྒྱབ་འདྲེ་.

རྒྱགས་ (gya̲à) provisions, food supplies ¶ལམ་རྒྱགས་ Food provisions for a journey ¶དམག་རྒྱགས་ Military food provisions.

རྒྱགས་: p. བརྒྱགས་; f. བརྒྱག (gya̲à) 1. vi. to be full/ satisfied ¶གྲོད་པ་མ་བརྒྱགས་བར་བཟས་པ་རེད་ They ate until they were full. 2. vi. to be proud.

རྒྱགས་སྐྱེལ་ (gya̲ggyee) delivering provisions; va.—བྱེད་.

རྒྱགས་ངན་ (gya̲àŋɛn) gifts/ presents of provisions to travelers.

རྒྱགས་བངན་ལྷ་བསངས་ (gya̲àŋɛn lhābsaŋ) shung. gift of incense offered to the deities.

རྒྱགས་ཆས་ (gya̲gjɛɛ̀) sm. རྒྱགས་.

རྒྱགས་ཆུ་ (gya̲gju) food and drink.

རྒྱགས་ཆེ་བའི་ཡོ་བྱད་ (gya̲gcewɛ yo̲jɛɛ̀) luxury goods/ items.

རྒྱགས་རྟེན་ (gya̲gden) living expenses; va.—སྤྲོད་ to give living expenses.

རྒྱགས་ལྟོགས་ (gya̲gdɔɔ̀) full or satiated and hungry.

རྒྱགས་པ་ (gya̲gba) fat ¶ཁོ་རྒྱགས་པ་ཆགས་འདུག He has become fat.

རྒྱགས་སྤྱོད་ (gya̲gjöö̀) sm. རྒྱགས་ཤ་.

རྒྱགས་ཕྱེ་ (gya̲gje) tsampa/ flour for traveling.

རྒྱགས་སྦྱངས་ (gya̲gjaŋ) va. to feed/ give food (continuously).

རྒྱགས་ཚད་ (gya̲gdzɛɛ̀) a lot, a great deal, until one is full/ stuffed, as much as one wants to satisfy one's needs/ desires ¶ལུང་པ་འདི་ར་ཤིང་ཏོག་རྒྱགས་ཚད་ཡོད་པ་རེད་ This place has a lot of fruit. ¶ཁོས་ཤ་རྒྱགས་ཚད་བཟས་སོང་ He ate meat until he was completely full.

རྒྱགས་རང་འཁུར་ (gya̲g ra̲ŋgur) taking/ bringing (supplying) one's own food; va.—བྱེད་ ¶སང་ཉིན་ཡུལ་དམག་རྒྱགས་རང་འཁུར་བྱས་ནས་ཐོན་དགོས་ Tomorrow the militia have to depart taking their own food.

རྒྱགས་རིལ་ (gyə̲grii) sm. རྒྱགས་ལེབ་.

རྒྱགས་ལེབ་ (gya̲gleb) fat and short (in stature).

རྒྱགས་ལོས་སྙོམས་པོ་ (gya̲glöö̀ ñōmbo) just the right weight, not fat-not thin.

རྒྱགས་ལོས་པ་ (gya̲glöö̀ba) a fat person.

རྒྱགས་ཤ་ (gya̲gsha) over-indulging in pleasure.

རྒྱགས་ཤེད་ཆེན་པོ་ (gya̲gshɛɛ̀ cēmbo) foods that satisfy one's hunger quickly and quench one's hunger for a long time.

རྒྱགས་ལྷུག་པ་ (gya̲à lhūgba) sm. རྒྱགས་ལྷུག་ལྷུག.

རྒྱགས་ལྷུག་ལྷུག (gya̲à lhūglhuù) fat, fatty.

རྒྱང་ (gya̲ŋ) distance, span, space, range ¶འདི་ནས་ཁོང་བཞུགས་ས་རྒྱང་རིང་པོ་མེད་ His home is not a long distance from here.

རྒྱང་ཤིང་ (gya̲ŋshiŋ) wooden cross, crucifix.

རྒྱང་བཀྲག (gya̲ŋdraà) noticeable/ striking/ attractive from a distance ¶ཚོན་གཞི་འདི་རྒྱང་བཀྲག་ཆེན་པོ་འདུག This color is very striking from a distance.

རྒྱང་བཀྲག་དོད་པོ་ (gya̲ŋdraà tö̲öbo) attractive /good-looking/ striking from a distance.

རྒྱང་སྐད་པབ་ཅོལ་ (gya̲ŋgɛɛ̀ pə̲bjöö) shung. loud noice from a distance.

རྒྱང་སྐྱོད་ (gya̲ŋgyöö̀) 1. a long distance trip/ expedition; va.—བྱེད་ to go on an expedition, to take a long journey. 2. the Long March (of the Chinese Communists in 1934-35) ¶དམར་དམག་རྒྱང་སྐྱོད་ Red Army's "Long March."

རྒྱང་སྐྱོད་དམག་སྦྱོང་ (gya̲ŋgyöö̀ māgjoŋ) long distance military drill; va.—བྱེད་.

རྒྱང་སྐྱོད་མཚོ་གྲུ་ (gya̲ŋgyöö̀ tsōdru) oceangoing ship, long distance ship.

རྒྱང་བསྒྱུར་རྩིས་མེད་ (gya̲ŋgyur dzīìmeè) irresponsible in work; va.—བྱེད་.

རྒྱང་བསྐྱོད་ (gya̲ŋgyöö̀) sm. རྒྱང་སྐྱོད་.

རྒྱང་ཁད་ (gya̲ŋgɛɛ̀) sm. རྒྱང་ཁྱད་.

རྒྱང་ཁྱད་ (gya̲ŋgyɛɛ̀) the distance between things ¶ས་ཆ་དེ་གཉིས་དབར་རྒྱང་ཁྱད་ཆེན་པོ་ཡོད་པ་རེད་ There is a great distance between those two places.

རྒྱང་ཁྲ་ (gya̲ŋdra) the ornamental lining put on the hem of fur gown's worn in Eastern Tibet.

རྒྱང་གྲགས་ (gya̲ŋdraà) sm. རྒྱང་བསྒྲགས་.

རྒྱང་གྲགས་ཅན་ (gya̲ŋdraàjɛn) well-known, famous.

རྒྱང་མགོ་ (gya̲ŋgo) shoe tree; hat block; va.—རྒྱག to put in a shoe tree/ hat block.

རྒྱང་འགྲུལ་ (gya̲ŋdrüü) long distance travel.

རྒྱང་འགྲུལ་སྣངས་འཁོར་ (gya̲ŋdrüü lāŋgɔɔ) long distance bus.

རྒྱང་རྒྱག (gya̲ŋgyaà) va. to stretch out.

རྒྱང་རྒྱུགས་ (gya̲ŋgyuù) long distance race, long distance running; va.—གཏོང་ to run a long distance race.

རྒྱང་སྒྲིབ་ (gya̱ŋdrib) nearsighted, shortsighted.

རྒྱང་སྒྲོག (gya̱ŋdrɔɔ̀) see རྒྱང་བསྒྲགས་.

རྒྱང་སྒྲོམ་ (gya̱ŋdrom) wooden frame (used to stretch cloth to paint tankas).

རྒྱང་བསྒྲགས་ (gya̱ŋdraà) 1. broadcasting; va.—བྱེད་; —ཕོད་; —གཏོང་ to broadcast ¶ གསར་འགྱུར་དེ་ལམ་སེང་རྒྱང་བསྒྲགས་བྱས་པ་རེད་ They broadcast the news at once. 2. loudspeaker, public address system; va.—བྱེད་; —གཏོང་ to say through a loud speaker. 3. an ancient distance measurement equal to 2,000 cubits.

རྒྱང་བསྒྲགས་ཁང་ (gya̱ŋdraàgaŋ) broadcast studio.

རྒྱང་བསྒྲགས་སྒྱུ་ཆས་ (gya̱ŋdraà gyu̱jɛ̀ɛ̀) broadcasting equipment.

རྒྱང་བསྒྲགས་སྒྲིག་ཆས་ (gya̱ŋdraà dri̱gjɛ̀ɛ̀) broadcasting equipment.

རྒྱང་བསྒྲགས་བརྙན་འཕྲིན་ (gya̱ŋdraà ñɛ̃ndrin) radio and television, broadcasting.

རྒྱང་བསྒྲགས་བརྙན་འཕྲིན་ལས་དོན་ཅུས་ (gya̱ŋdraà ñɛ̃ndrin lɛ̱̀ɛdönju) tib.ch. bureau of radio and television, broadcast bureau.

རྒྱང་བསྒྲགས་གཏོང་ཁང་ (gya̱ŋdraà dōŋgaŋ) broadcast station.

རྒྱང་བསྒྲགས་གཏོང་མཁན་ (gya̱ŋdraà dōŋgɛn) broadcaster.

རྒྱང་བསྒྲགས་པ་ (gya̱ŋdraàba) sm. རྒྱང་བསྒྲགས་གཏོང་མཁན་.

རྒྱང་བསྒྲགས་འཕྲུལ་ཆས་ (gya̱ŋdraà trṻṻjɛ̀ɛ̀) broadcast equipment.

རྒྱང་བསྒྲགས་རླུང་འཕྲིན་ (gya̱ŋdraà lūŋdrin) radio ¶ རྒྱང་བསྒྲགས་རླུང་འཕྲིན་ཁང་ Radio/ broadcasting station.

རྒྱང་བསྒྲགས་རླུང་འཕྲིན་རོལ་མོ་ཚོགས་པ་ (gya̱ŋdraà lūŋdrin röömo tsōgba) radio orchestra.

རྒྱང་བསྒྲགས་ལས་ཁུངས་ (gya̱ŋdraà lɛ̱̀ɛguŋ) radio broadcasting station.

རྒྱང་བསྒྲགས་ལུས་སྦྱོང་ (gya̱ŋdraà lṳ̈̀joŋ) exercising to music from the radio.

རྒྱང་བསྒྲགས་ལུས་རྩལ་ (gya̱ŋdraà lṳ̈̀dzɛɛ) sm. རྒྱང་བསྒྲགས་ལུས་སྦྱོང་.

རྒྱང་བསྒྲགས་ས་ཚིགས་ (gya̱ŋdraà sədzii) radio/ broadcast station.

རྒྱང་ངེ་ (gya̱ŋŋe) at the head of a group/ pack.

རྒྱང་ཆོད་ (gya̱ŋdzöö) vi. to be separated by a long distance (in time or space) ¶ གྲོང་སྡེ་དེ་མེ་འཁོར་འབབས་ཚུགས་ནས་མེ་ལི་ 20 ཙམ་གྱིས་རྒྱང་ཆོད་ཡོད་ The town is twenty miles away from the railway station ¶ དམག་འཁྲུག་དེ་གཉིས་དབར་མི་རབས་ཁ་ཤས་ཀྱིས་རྒྱང་ཆོད་ཡོད་པ་རེད་ The two wars were separated by a few generations.

རྒྱང་མཆོང་ (gya̱ŋjoŋ) long jump, broad jump (sports); va.—རྒྱག.

རྒྱང་མཆོངས་ (gya̱ŋjoŋ) sm. རྒྱང་མཆོང་.

རྒྱང་མཇལ་ (gya̱ŋjɛɛ) seeing/ visiting a statue or a lama or holy place from a distance ¶ ༸གོང་ས་ལྷ་མིའི་རྣམ་འདྲེན་མཆོག་ནས་གསུང་ཆོས་བཀའ་དྲིན་ཆེ་སྐབས་མང་འབངས་རྣམས་ལ་རྒྱང་མཇལ་གྱི་སྐལ་བཟང་ཐོབ་པ་ When H.H. the Dalai Lama gave teachings to the masses they got a chance to see the Dalai Lama from a distance.

རྒྱང་བསྙལ་ (gya̱ŋñɛɛ) marinated, pickled.

རྒྱང་ལྟ་ (gya̱ŋda) watching/ looking from a distance; va. རྒྱང་ལྟ་; —ལྟ་.

རྒྱང་ལྟ་སོ་པ་ (gya̱ŋda sōba) a lookout, sb. watching sth. from a distance.

རྒྱང་ལྟའི་མཐོ་སྒྲིགས་ (gya̱ŋdɛ tōdeg) observation tower.

རྒྱང་བལྟས་ (gya̱ŋdɛ̀ɛ) sm. རྒྱང་ལྟ་.

རྒྱང་ཐག (gya̱ŋtaà) distance ¶ རྒྱང་ཐག་ལི་དབར་ 200 ཡོད་པ་རེད་ There is a distance of 200 kilometers.

རྒྱང་ཐག་ཚད་ (gya̱ŋ tāàjöö) sm. རྒྱང་ཚད་.

རྒྱང་ཐག་ཚད་ལེན་འཕྲུལ་ཆས་ (gya̱ŋdaà tsēèlen trṻṻjɛ̀ɛ) an instrument for measuring distances.

རྒྱང་ཐག་རིང་བའི་ས་ཁུལ་ (gya̱ŋdaà riŋwɛ səgüü) remote border area/ region, a far away place.

རྒྱང་ཐུང་ཐུང་ (gya̱ŋ tūŋduŋ) a short distance.

རྒྱང་མཐོང་ (gya̱ŋdoŋ) skylight.

རྒྱང་དུ་འགྲོ་ (gya̱ŋtu dro̱) vi. to become more distant in relations ¶ གཅེན་གཅུང་གཉིས་ཀྱི་འབྲེལ་བ་རྒྱང་དུ་སོང་ཡོད་པ་རེད་ The relationship between the older and the younger brother became distant.

རྒྱང་དེང་ཕུགས་གསུམ་ (gya̱ŋ te̱ŋ pūg sūm) sm. འཕུལ་ཕུགས་རྒྱང་གསུམ་.

རྒྱང་མདའ་ (gya̱ŋda) long range arrow.

རྒྱང་མདོང་ (gya̱ŋdoŋ) sm. རྒྱག་མདོང་.

རྒྱང་འདུལ་ (gya̱ŋdüü) expedition, expeditionary force.

རྒྱང་འདུལ་དམག (gya̱ŋdüümaà) expeditionary army.

རྒྱང་བརྡ་ (gya̱ŋda) a signal sent from a distance; va.—གཏོང་.

རྒྱང་ཕུགས་ (gya̱ŋbuù) sm. ཕུགས་རྒྱང་.

རྒྱང་ཕུད་ (gya̱ŋbüü) expelling, banishing; va.—གཏོང་ ¶ ཁོ་ལྷ་ས་ནས་རྒྱང་ཕུད་བཏང་བཞག (They) banished him from Lhasa.

རྒྱང་འཕེན་ (gya̱ŋben) long-range ¶ རྒྱང་འཕེན་མེ་སྒྱོགས་ Long-range artillery.

རྒྱང་འཕེན་འཕུར་མདའ་ (gya̱ŋben pūnda) long-range missile.

རྒྱང་འཕེན་འཕུར་མདེལ་ (gya̱ŋben pūndel) sm. རྒྱང་འཕེན་འཕུར་མདའ་.

རྒྱང་འཕེན་མེ་སྒྱོགས་ (gya̱ŋben me̱gyɔɔ̀) long-range cannon, long-range artillery.

རྒྱང་འཕེན་མེ་ཤུགས་འཕུར་མདའ་ (gya̱ŋben me̱shuù pūnda) long-range rocket.

རྒྱང་འཕེན་མཚོན་ཆ་ (gya̱ŋben tsōnja) long-range weapon.

རྒྱང་འཕོ་བ་ (gya̱ŋ pōwa) doing འཕོ་བ་ from a distance (i.e., monks not coming in person); va.—རྒྱག.

རྒྱང་འབུད་ (gya̱ŋbüü) exiling, banishing, deporting, extraditing; va.—གཏོང་ to exile/ banish/ deport/ extradite.

རྒྱང་འབེན་ (gya̱ŋben) a target.

རྒྱང་འབོད་ (gya̱ŋböö) calling from a distance; va.—བྱེད་.

རྒྱང་འབྲོག (gya̱ŋdrog) nomads who live far away from villages/ administrative centers.

རྒྱང་མ་ (gya̱ŋma) 1. sm. རྒྱང་. 2. an arrow used for long distances.

རྒྱང་མིག (gya̱ŋmii) farsighted (with regard to vision).

རྒྱང་མིག་གསལ་པོ་ (gya̱ŋmii sɛ̄ɛbo) good eyesight.

རྒྱང་ཚད་ (gya̱ŋdzɛ̀ɛ) range, distance; va.—འཇལ་ to measure range/ distance.

རྒྱང་ཚད་ཐིག་ཤིང་ (gya̱ŋdzɛ̀ɛ tīgshiŋ) surveyor's pole.

རྒྱང་གཞས་ (gya̱ŋshɛɛ̀) a slow song (the slow portion of a Tibetan song).

རྒྱང་བཞུད་ (gya̱ŋshüü) sm. རྒྱང་སྐྱོད་.

རྒྱང་གཡེར་ཆེ་བ་ (gya̱ŋyer cēwa) sm. རྒྱང་གྲགས་ཆེ་བ་.

རྒྱང་ར་རྒྱང་སྐོར་ (gya̱ŋra gya̱ŋgɔɔ) circling around sb. or sth. at a distance; va.—བྱེད་.

རྒྱང་རིང་ (gya̱ŋriŋ) far, distant, long-range, long-term ¶ རྒྱང་རིང་གི་དམིགས་ཡུལ་ Long-term aim/ goal. ¶ རྒྱང་རིང་དམིགས་ཡུལ་གྱི་འཆར་འགོད་ Long-term plan.

རྒྱང་རིང་གློག་སྐད་ཁང་ (gya̱ŋriŋ lōggɛ̀ɛ kāwo) long distance telephone section/ office/ department.

རྒྱང་རིང་གློག་འཕྲིན་ཁང་ (gya̱ŋriŋ lōgdrin kāwo) long distance telecommunications section/ office/ department.

རྒྱང་རིང་གཏིང་ཟབ་ (gya̱ŋriŋ dīŋsəb) deep and profound.

རྒྱང་རིང་དུ་ལས་ (gya̱ŋriŋdu lɛ̱̀ɛ) sm. རྒྱང་རིང་དུ་ལུས་.

རྒྱང་རིང་དུ་ལུས་ (gya̱ŋriŋdu lṳ̈̀) vi. to be left behind.

རྒྱང་རིང་སྨྲ་བ་ (gya̱ŋriŋ māwa) the theory of remoteness.

རྒྱང་རིང་མཚོ་ལམ་ (gya̱ŋriŋ tsōlam) cross-ocean shipping route.

རྒྱང་རིང་ལུང་ཁུག (gya̱ŋriŋ lu̱ŋguù) a remote and

isolated area.

རྒྱང་ཤར་ (gya̲ŋshar) the Far East.

རྒྱང་ཤར་ས་ཁུལ་ (gya̲ŋshar sāgüü) the Far East area/ region.

རྒྱང་ཤར་ཨེ་ཤེ་ཡའི་དཔལ་འབྱོར་དཔྱད་ཞིབ་ཀྱི་གསར་དེབ་ (gya̲ŋshar ēshye bēnjɔɔ jɛ̄ɛ̄shibgi sāādeb) Far Eastern Economic Review (magazine).

རྒྱང་ཤིང་ (gya̲ŋshiŋ) sm.* རྒྱངས་ཤིང་.

རྒྱང་ཤེལ་ (gya̲ŋshee) telescope.

རྒྱང་སོ་ (gya̲ŋso) spying/ watching secretly from a distance; va.—འཛུགས་ to spy on, to watch secretly from a distance; —ལྟ་ to look far into the distance.

རྒྱང་བསངས་ (gya̲ŋsaŋ) burning incense from a distance; va.—གཏོང་.

རྒྱང་སྲིང་ (gya̲ŋsiŋ) sm. རྒྱང་བསྒྲགས་.

རྒྱང་སྲིང་མཉམ་སྦྲེལ་ (gya̲ŋsiŋ ña̲mdree) broadcast corporation/ company.

རྒྱང་བསྲིང་ (gya̲ŋsiŋ) sm. རྒྱང་བསྒྲགས་.

རྒྱང་བསྲིང་ཡིག་པར་ (gya̲ŋsiŋ yi̲gbar) fax.

རྒྱངས་མགོ་ (gya̲ŋgo) sm. རྒྱང་མགོ.

རྒྱངས་རྒྱག (gya̲ŋ gya̲à) va. to stretch/ spread out objects such as clothes when hanging them outside in the sun to dry.

རྒྱངས་ཤ་ (gya̲ŋsha) meat filling (for sausages).

རྒྱངས་ཤིང་ (gya̲ŋshiŋ) wooden cross/ crucifix used for punishment; va.—རྒྱག to put on a cross (as a punishment).

རྒྱན་ (gye̲n) 1. ornament, decoration; va.—སྤྲས་; —བྱས་ to adorn, to ornament, to decorate. 2. a bet, wager, stake; va.—འཛུགས་; —འགྱེད་; —འཕེན་ to bet; vi.—ཐོབ་ to win a bet; vi.—ཤོར་ to lose a bet. 3. a lot (in a lottery); va.—རྒྱག to draw lots.

རྒྱན་གླུབས་ (gye̲nlub) sm. རྒྱན་སྤྲས་.

རྒྱན་བཀོད་ (gye̲ngöö) ornamentation, decoration.

རྒྱན་སྐོར་ (gye̲ngɔɔ) a large decorative nail used to pin down cushions on saddles.

རྒྱན་ཁ་ (gye̲nga) a bet/ wager; va.—འཛུགས་ to gamble/ wager/ bet.

རྒྱན་མཁན་པོ་ (gye̲n kēmbo) sb. expert in poetics.

རྒྱན་འཁེལ་ (gye̲n kēē) vi. to get the winning number in a drawing of lots, etc. ¶རྒྱན་འཁེལ་ཨང་གྲངས་ The winning number in a lottery.

རྒྱན་གོས་ (gye̲ngöö) fancy clothes.

རྒྱན་གོས་དཔེ་གསར་གཞོན་ནུ་མ་ (gye̲ngöö bēsar shö̲nnuma) a fashionable young woman.

རྒྱན་གྱི་རྡོ་རྗེ་ (gye̲ngi dɔ̲ɔje) a vajara-shaped design.

རྒྱན་གྲིས་རྒྱན་ (gye̲ngi gye̲n) sm. རྒྱན་སྤྲས་.

རྒྱན་འགྱེད་ (gye̲n gye̲è) sm. རྒྱན་འཕེན་པ་.

རྒྱན་རྒྱག (gye̲n gya̲à) see རྒྱན་, 3.

རྒྱན་: p. བརྒྱན་; f. བརྒྱན་; imp. རྒྱན་ (gye̲n) va. to decorate, to adorn, to ornament.

རྒྱན་དངུལ་ (gye̲nŋüü) money wagered, money bet.

རྒྱན་ཅན་ (gye̲njɛn) decorated/ ornamented.

རྒྱན་ཆ་ (gye̲nja) ornament, jewelry; va.—འདོགས་ to wear jewelry/ ornaments.

རྒྱན་ཆས་ (gye̲njɛɛ̀) sm. རྒྱན་ཆ་.

རྒྱན་མཆོར་ (gye̲njɔɔ) ornament, decoration; va.—བརྒྱན to decorate.

རྒྱན་འཇོག (gye̲njɔɔ̀) sm. རྒྱན་.

རྒྱན་ཐོབ་ (gye̲ndob) vi. to win (a prize, bet, etc.).

རྒྱན་དུ་བྱེད་ (gye̲ndu ce̲è) va. to use sth. as an ornament.

རྒྱན་དོར་ (gye̲n tɔ̲r) 1. va. to bet, to wager. 2. va. to give up/ abstain from wearing jewelry.

རྒྱན་འདོགས་ཆ་ (gye̲n tɔ̲gja) ornaments.

རྒྱན་པོ་ (gye̲mbo) gambling; va.—འགྱེད་ to gamble.

རྒྱན་པོ་བ་ (gye̲mbowa) gambler.

རྒྱན་སྤྲས་ (gye̲ndrɛɛ̀) sm. རྒྱན་.

རྒྱན་སྤྲོས་ (gye̲ndröö) sm. རྒྱན་སྤྲས་.

རྒྱན་ཕྲེང་ (gye̲ndreŋ) sm. རྒྱན་འཕྲེང་.

རྒྱན་འཕེན་ (gye̲n pēn) va. to gamble, to bet.

རྒྱན་འཕྲེང་ (gye̲ndreŋ) 1. abbr. rosary and ornaments. 2. a necklace, a string of beaded jewelry.

རྒྱན་དབྱུག (gye̲n yūù) va. to place a bet, to wager, to gamble.

རྒྱན་བཙུགས་ (gye̲n dzūù) p. of རྒྱན་འཛུགས་.

རྒྱན་ཚིག (gye̲ndzii) adjective.

རྒྱན་འཛུགས་ (gye̲n dzu̲ù) see རྒྱན་.

རྒྱན་འཛུགས་མ་རྩ་ (gye̲ndzuù ma̲dza) capital for gambling.

རྒྱན་བཞག (gye̲n sha̲à) p. of རྒྱན་འཇོག.

རྒྱན་བཞི་ (gye̲nshi) 1. brocade material that has four auspicious symbols: water, rocks, dragons and clouds.

རྒྱན་བཟང་མ་ (gye̲n sa̲ŋma) 1. shung. the women who serve ཆང་ to the Yasor at Monlam. 2. a richly attired woman.

རྒྱན་གཡེར་ (gye̲nyer) small bell ornament.

རྒྱན་གཡོག (gye̲nyɔɔ̀) shung. assistant of the རྒྱན་བཟང་མ་ who serves ཆང་ to the Yasor at Monlam.

རྒྱན་རིས་ (gye̲nrii) design, pattern, decoration.

རྒྱན་ཤོག (gye̲nshog) lottery, lottery ticket.

རྒྱན་ཤོར་ (gye̲n shɔ̄ɔ) see རྒྱན་.

རྒྱབ་ (gyə̲b) 1. back, behind, after; va.—བྱེད་ to back, to give support ¶ལག་པའི་རྒྱབ The back of the hand. ¶ཁོའི་རྒྱབ་ལ་སྐད་ཆ་མང་པོ་ཤོད་ཀྱི་འདུག (They) talk a lot behind his back. 2. sm. བརྒྱབ་. 3. a load ¶ཕྱེ་ཞིབ་རྒྱབ་གཅིག One load of flour.

རྒྱབ་ཀྱི་ཐེག་པ་ (gyə̲bgi tēgba) a burden, a load.

རྒྱབ་དཀར་ (gyə̲bgar) buzzard.

རྒྱབ་སྐྱུར་ (gyə̲bgyur) discarding, abandoning, throwing/ casting away; va.—བྱེད་ ¶མི་དེས་ཁས་ལེན་རྒྱབ་སྐྱུར་བྱས་ནས་མགོ་སྐོར་སྐྱེར་བ་རེད་ That person tricked them and abandoned the agreement.

རྒྱབ་སྐྱོར་ (gyə̲bgyɔɔ) supporting, backing, aiding, helping; va.—བྱེད་ ¶ཁོ་ཚོའི་རང་བཙན་གྱི་འཐབ་འཛིང་ལ་རྒྱབ་སྐྱོར་གཙང་མ་བྱེད་ཀྱི་ཡོད་ (We) are supporting their struggle for independence.

རྒྱབ་སྐྲ་ (gyə̲bdra) back side of the hair.

རྒྱབ་བསྐྱུར་ (gyə̲bgyur) sm. རྒྱབ་སྐྱུར་.

རྒྱབ་ཁལ་ (gyə̲bgɛɛ) a load (that is carried by animals on their backs).

རྒྱབ་ཁུག (gyə̲bguù) bag, backpack.

རྒྱབ་ཁུར་ (gyə̲bgur) a load for carrying va.—འཁུར་ to carry a load ¶རྒྱབ་ཁུར་ལྗིད་པོ་ A heavy load.

རྒྱབ་ཁེབས་ (gyə̲bgeb) an apron worn on the back (by women in some parts of Tibet).

རྒྱབ་ཁྱེར་ (gyə̲bgyer) carrying on the back; va.—བྱེད་.

རྒྱབ་འཁུར་ (gyə̲b kūr) va. to carry on one's back.

རྒྱབ་གོན་པ་ (gyə̲bgönba) clothing.

རྒྱབ་འགལ་ (gyə̲bgɛɛ) 1. contrary, defying, opposite, contradictory, not in conformity with; va.—བྱེད་ to go against, to act contrary to, to defy ¶དེ་ནི་ལོ་རྒྱུས་ཀྱི་འཕེལ་ཕྱོགས་དང་རྒྱབ་འགལ་རེད་ That is contrary to the trend of history. 2. violating (a law, rule, etc.); va.—བྱེད་ ¶ཁྲིམས་ལ་རྒྱབ་འགལ་བྱས་ན་བཙོན་ཁང་ལ་བཏང་གི་རེད་ If you violate the law you will be sent to prison.

རྒྱབ་འགྲོས་ (gyə̲mdröö) walking backward as a sign of respect and reverence; va.—བྱེད་.

རྒྱབ་སྒུར་པོ་ (gyə̲b gu̲rbu) a hunched over back.

རྒྱབ་སྒོ་ (gyə̲bgo) back door.

རྒྱབ་སྒྱུར་ (gyə̲bgyur) about face! (a military command).

རྒྱབ་བསྒར་གློག་ཞུ་ (gyə̲bgar lɔ̄gshu) taillight.

རྒྱབ་ངོས་ (gyə̲bŋöö) back side, behind ¶རྩེ་པོ་བྲང་གི་རྒྱབ་ངོས་ The back side of the Potala.

རྒྱབ་སྔས་ (gyə̲bŋɛɛ̀) sm. རྒྱབ་སྙེས་.

རྒྱབ་གཅིག་སྒ་གཉིས་ (gyə̲bjig ga̲ñii) shung. levying double taxes on one person [Lit. putting two saddles on one back].

རྒྱབ་བཅའ་ (gyə̲bjaa) sm. རྒྱབ་རྟེན་.

རྒྱབ་ཆ་ (gyə̲bja) a load.

རྒྱབ་ཆད་ (gyə̲bjɛɛ̀) without backing/ assistance/ support ¶དམག་དཔུང་དེ་རྒྱབ་ཆད་དུ་གྱུར་ནའང་མཐར་ཐུག་རྒྱལ་ཁ་ཐོབ་པ་རེད་ Even though the soldiers came to be without any support, ultimately they were victorious.

རྒྱབ་ཆོས་ (gyə̱bjöö̀) religious services conducted after a sky burial.

རྒྱབ་ཇ་ (gyə̱bja) afternoon tea prayer session (in a monastery).

རྒྱབ་ལྗོངས་ (gyə̱bjoŋ) background scenery, backdrop (of a stage).

རྒྱབ་ཉལ་ (gyə̱bñɛɛ) lying on one's back; va.—བྱེད་.

རྒྱབ་གཉེར་ (gyə̱bñer) support, backing; va.—བྱེད་.

རྒྱབ་གཉེར་ལས་དོན་ (gyə̱bñer lɛ̱ɛ̀dön) the task or job of supporting/ backing.

རྒྱབ་སྙེ་ (gyə̱bñe) sm. རྒྱབ་སྙེས་.

རྒྱབ་སྙེས་ (gyə̱bñeè) cushion, pillow (for the back); va.—བྱེད་; —རྒྱག to lean back, to rest against ¶ ཁོས་རྩིག་པར་རྒྱབ་སྙེས་བྱས་འདུག He is leaning back against the wall.

རྒྱབ་བསྙེས་ (gyə̱bñeè) sm. རྒྱབ་སྙེས་.

རྒྱབ་བསྙེས་ཀུབ་ཀྱག (gyə̱bñeè gūbgyaà) chair.

རྒྱབ་བསྙེས་ཀུབ་སྟེགས་ (gyə̱bñeè gūbdeg) sm. རྒྱབ་སྙེས་ཀུབ་ཀྱག.

རྒྱབ་ཏུ་སྐྱུར་ (gyə̱bdu gyūr) va. to abandon, to turn one's back on, to leave behind.

རྒྱབ་ཏུ་བསྙེས་ (gyə̱bdu ñēè) sm. རྒྱབ་སྙེས་.

རྒྱབ་ཏུ་དབྱུག (gyə̱bdu yūù) sm. རྒྱབ་སྐྱུར་.

རྒྱབ་ཏུ་རི་འགུལ་བ་མ་ཤེས་ མདུན་དུ་སྤུ་འགུལ་བ་མཐོང་ (gyə̱bdu ri̱ngüüwə ma̱sheè dü̱ndu būgüüwa dōŋ) seeing things only on the surface. [Lit. oblivious of a mountain moving behind, seeing a piece of hair moving in front].

རྒྱབ་གཏད་ (gyə̱bdɛɛ̀) p. of རྒྱབ་གཏོད་.

རྒྱབ་གཏོད་ (gyə̱bdöö̀) 1. betraying, acting traitorous; va.—བྱེད་ to betray, to turn traitor ¶ གཞུང་དང་རྒྱལ་ཁབ་ལ་རྒྱབ་གཏོད་བྱས་པ་རེད་ (They) betrayed their government and country. 2. showing/ turning one's back; va.—བྱེད་.

རྒྱབ་གཏོད་པ་ (gyə̱bdöö̀ba) betrayer, traitor.

རྒྱབ་རྟེན་ (gye̱bden) support, backing; va.—བཙོལ་ to depend/ rely on a supporter or backer ¶ རྒྱལ་ཁབ་ཆུང་བས་རྒྱལ་ཁབ་ཆེ་བར་རྒྱབ་རྟེན་བཙོལ་བ་རེད་ Small countries depend on the support of big countries. ¶ ལས་ཀ་ཡག་པོ་ཞིག་རག་དགོས་ན་རྒྱབ་རྟེན་ཞིག་དགོས་པ་རེད་ If you want a good job you need a good backer.

རྒྱབ་རྟེན་ཐུབ་པ་ (gyə̱bden tūbbə) dependable, reliable, trustworthy.

རྒྱབ་ལྟོས་ (gyə̱bdöö̀) sm. རྒྱབ་གཏོད་.

རྒྱབ་སྟན་ (gyə̱bdɛn) sm. རྒྱབ་སྙེས་.

རྒྱབ་སྟར་ (gyə̱bdar) the last/ back row.

རྒྱབ་སྟོན་ (gyə̱bdön) sm. རྒྱབ་གཏོད་.

རྒྱབ་བལྟབ་ (gyə̱b dāb) va. to fold/ turn to the back, to wear a hat backwards.

རྒྱབ་དར་ (gyə̱bdar) shung. long piece of colored silk hung behind the back of Tibetan opera performers.

རྒྱབ་དོད་ (gyə̱bdöö̀) shung. a money substitute for a payment in kind.

རྒྱབ་གདན་ (gye̱bdɛn) vest-like garment that is worn when carrying loads to prevent sores on the back.

རྒྱབ་མདུན་ (gyə̱mdün) front and back, both sides; va.—སློག to reverse back and front.

རྒྱབ་འདྲེ་ (gya̱mdre) fighting, quarreling, disputing; va.—རྒྱག to fight/ quarrel/ dispute; vi.—ཤོར་ to have a dispute/ fight / quarrel break out ¶ ཁོ་གཉིས་ཀྱིས་ཉིན་ལྟར་བརྒྱབ་འདྲེ་རྒྱབ་པ་རེད་ They fought all the time.

རྒྱབ་འདྲེ་རྒོད་པོ་ (gya̱mdre gö̱ö̀bo) sb. who fights a lot, a quarrelsome person.

རྒྱབ་འདྲེ་ཚ་པོ་ (gya̱mdre tsābo) sm. རྒྱབ་འདྲེ་རྒོད་པོ་.

རྒྱབ་འདྲེ་འཚུབ་འཚུབ་ (gya̱mdre tsūbdzub) fighting/ quarreling/ disputing all the time; va.—བྱེད་.

རྒྱབ་རྡོ་དབྱུག (gyə̱bdo yūù) 1. a sport competition involving monks tossing a large stone backward to see who can throw it the furthest. 2. slang. va. to defecate.

རྒྱབ་ལྡན་ (gyə̱mdɛn) sm. རྒྱབ་ཤ་.

རྒྱབ་གནོན་ (gye̱bnön) sm. རྒྱབ་སྐྱོར་.

རྒྱབ་གནོན་ཐམ་ཀ་ (gyə̱bnön tāmga) shung. an order with a seal that indicates support/ approval.

རྒྱབ་སྣོན་ (gyə̱bnön) 1. supporting from the rear, reinforcing, resupplying; va.—གཏོང་; —བྱེད་ ¶ རྒྱབ་སྣོན་དམག་མི་ Reinforcement troops (or troops in a rear area that support the frontline troops).

རྒྱབ་དཔུང་ (gyə̱bbuŋ) sm. རྒྱབ་དམག.

རྒྱབ་སྤྱོད་ (gyə̱bjöö̀) sm. རྒྱབ་འགལ་.

རྒྱབ་སྦྱོད་ (gyə̱bjöö̀) sitting back-to-back; va.—བྱེད་.

རྒྱབ་ཕྱོགས་ (gyə̱bjɔɔ̀) rear area, back area.

རྒྱབ་ཕྱོགས་ཀྱི་སྐྱེལ་འདྲེན་ (gyə̱bjɔɔ̀gi gyēndren) supplying from the rear area; va.—བྱེད་.

རྒྱབ་ཕྱོགས་ཆེན་པོ་ (gyə̱bjɔɔ̀ cēmbo) the "great rear area" (the area of China not occupied by the Japanese during the Sino-Japanese war).

རྒྱབ་ཕྱོགས་ཞབས་འདེགས་པུའུ་ (gyə̱bcɔɔ̀ sha̱mdeg bū) tib.ch. rear service department/ bureau.

རྒྱབ་ཕྱོགས་སི་ལིང་པུའུ་ (gyə̱bcɔɔ̀ si̱liŋ bū) tib.ch. rear area military headquarters.

རྒྱབ་བོད་ (gyə̱bpöö̀) shung. "Back Tibet" (the term used by the Qing Dynasty to denote the area of the Panchen Lama in གཙང་).

རྒྱབ་བེད་ (gyə̱bbeè) shung. using animals for transportation.

རྒྱབ་འབེན་ (gyə̱bben) see རྒྱང་འབེན་.

རྒྱབ་འབུད་མདུན་འདྲུད་ (gyə̱mböö dü̱ndrüù) pushing from the back and dragging from the front (usu. used with respect to apprehending criminals); va.—བྱེད་.

རྒྱབ་འབོལ་ (gyə̱mböö) sm. རྒྱབ་སྙེ་.

རྒྱབ་བྱེད་ (gyə̱b ce̱è) va. to back, to support ¶ ཨ་མས་པ་ཕའི་རྒྱབ་བྱས་ནས་བུ་གུར་གཤེ་གཤེ་གཏོང་གི་འདུག The mother, backing the father, is scolding the child.

རྒྱབ་མ་ (gyə̱bma) 1. the back one, the one on the back side. 2. later, after.

རྒྱབ་དམག (gyə̱bmaà) troops that support the front from the rear, reinforcement troops, reserve troops.

རྒྱབ་རྨ་ (gyə̱bma) a sore/ wound on the back.

རྒྱབ་རྩ་ (gyə̱bdza) a backer, a supporter; va.—བྱེད་; —གཉེན་ to act as a supporter, to back.

རྒྱབ་ཚོམས་ (gyə̱bdzom) a hall located in the back of sth.

རྒྱབ་རྫི་ (gyə̱bdzi) the person who represents the deceased family at the sky burial to ensure the corpse is properly disposed of. 2. person in charge of accompanying prisoners. 3. foreman/ supervisor of a work unit.

རྒྱབ་བཞེངས་ (gyə̱bsheŋ) a full load for a carrying animal.

རྒྱབ་གཞུང་ (gyə̱bshuŋ) sm. རྒྱབ་རུས་.

རྒྱབ་གཞུང་ཀུབ་སྟེགས་ (gyə̱bshuŋ gūbdeg) sm. རྒྱབ་སྙེས་ཀུབ་ཀྱག.

རྒྱབ་ཡོལ་ (gyə̱byöö) 1. a curtain that separates the back of a room. 2. a curtain put up on back walls when important persons visit.

རྒྱབ་རི་ (gyə̱bri) mountain located at the back of a village or house.

རྒྱབ་རི་མདུན་ཆུ་ (gyə̱bri dü̱nju) having backing/ support from high people [Lit. behind is a hill, in front is water].

རྒྱབ་རིམ་བསྙེན་ཡོན་ (gyə̱brim ñēnyön) shung. offerings to monks who perform prayers/ rites.

རྒྱབ་རུ་ (gyə̱bru) rear area/ side soldiers.

རྒྱབ་རུས་ (gyə̱brüù) backbone, spine.

རྒྱབ་རོགས་ (gyə̱brɔɔ̀) reinforcing/ backing/ supporting from the rear; va.—བྱེད་.

རྒྱབ་རོལ་ (gyə̱bröö) sm. རྒྱབ་ཕྱོགས་.

རྒྱབ་ལ་དབྱུགས་ (gyə̱bla yūù) sm. རྒྱབ་སྐྱུར་.

རྒྱབ་ལག (gyə̱blaà) 1. backhand (in tennis or table tennis). 2. hands behind one's back; va.—བྱེད་ to put one's hands behind one's back.

རྒྱབ་ལངས་ (gyə̱blaŋ) sm. རྒྱབ་རྩ.

རྒྱབ་ལབ་ (gyə̱bləb) sm. རྒྱབ་བཤད་.

རྒྱབ་ལོག (gyəblɔɔ̀) sm. རྒྱབ་གཏོད་.

རྒྱབ་ལོགས་ (gyəblɔɔ̀) back, behind, rear ¶ ཁང་པའི་རྒྱབ་ལོགས་ལ་ལྡུམ་ར་ཆུང་ཆུང་ཞིག་འདུག There is a small garden behind the house.

རྒྱབ་ཤ་ (gyəbsha) an outer lining/ covering, va.— རྒྱག to cover sth. with an outer lining.

རྒྱབ་ཤིག (gyəbshiì) moving backward; va.—རྒྱག to move backwards ¶ ཚོགས་ཁང་གི་རྒྱབ་ལ་ས་ཆ་སྟོང་པ་འདུག་པས་ཚང་མ་རྒྱབ་ཤིག་རྒྱག་རོགས་གནང་ The back portion of the hall is empty so please all move backwards.

རྒྱབ་ཤོག (gyəbsɔɔ̀) the back cover (of a book).

རྒྱབ་ཤོག་དཀར་པོའི་དེབ་ (gyəbsɔɔ̀ gārbö teb) white paper (special report issued by a government).

རྒྱབ་ཤོག་སྔོན་པོའི་དེབ་ (gyəbsɔɔ̀ ŋōnbö teb) blue book (special issued by a government).

རྒྱབ་ཤོག་ནང་མ་ (gyəbsɔɔ̀ naŋma) inside back cover.

རྒྱབ་བཤད་ (gyəbshɛ̀ɛ) talking behind someone's back, backbiting; va.— བྱེད་; —གཏོང་; —རྒྱག.

རྒྱབ་བཤུལ་ (gyəbshüü) sm. རྒྱབ་གཞུང་.

རྒྱབ་སྲུང་ (gyəbsuŋ) 1. rear guard. 2. a defensive back (in sports like soccer).

རྒྱབ་སྲུང་བར་མ་ (gyəbsuŋ parma) center half back (in soccer).

རྒྱབ་སློག (gyəb lɔ̄ɔ̀) va. to turn one's back.

རྒྱབ་ལྷག (gyəblhaà) tailwind, rear wind.

རྒྱམ་ཚྭ་ (gyəmtsa) a type of mineral used in Tibetan medicine (sallucidum).

རྒྱའི་མི་རིགས་ (gyɛ mirii) Han (Chinese) ethnic group.

རྒྱའུ་ (gyəwu) 1. beard. 2. a person with a beard.

རྒྱའུ་ཨ་སོབ་ (gyəwu āpso) a large/ bushy beard.

རྒྱར་ཤ་ (gyarsha) shung. meat to be eaten with Tsampa.

རྒྱལ་ (gyɛɛ) 1. vi. to be victorious, to overcome, to win. 2. abbr. of རྒྱལ་ཁབ་. 3. sm. རྒྱན་.

རྒྱལ་སྐྱོང་དམངས་བདེ་ (gyɛɛgyoŋ māŋde) administer the country effectively and give the people peace and security.

རྒྱལ་སྐྱོབ་ (gyɛɛgyob) saving the nation, national salvation; va.—བྱེད་ to save the country/ nation ¶ ཁྱིམ་སྲུང་རྒྱལ་སྐྱོབ་བྱེད་ To defend the home and save the nation.

རྒྱལ་སྐྱོབ་འཐབ་ཕྱོགས་ (gyɛɛgyob tābjɔɔ̀) national salvation front.

རྒྱལ་སྐྱོར་དམངས་ཕན་ (gyɛɛgyɔr māŋpɛn) support the nation, benefit the people/ masses.

རྒྱལ་ཁ་ (gyɛɛga) victory, success, triumph; vi.—ཐོབ་ to be victorious, to win, to obtain a victory; va.—ལེན་; —ལོན་ to win, to gain victory ¶ མཐའ་མའི་རྒྱལ་ཁ་ང་ཚོར་ཐོབ་རྒྱུ་རེད་ We will have the final victory.

རྒྱལ་ཁ་མཚོན་བྱེད་ཀ་བ་ (gyɛɛga tsōnjeè gāā) a pillar erected to commemorate a victory.

རྒྱལ་ཁག (gyɛɛgaà) nations.

རྒྱལ་ཁང་ (gyɛɛgaŋ) palace, castle.

རྒྱལ་ཁབ་ (gyɛɛgəb) state, country, nation.

རྒྱལ་ཁབ་ཀྱི་དཀའ་ཉེན་ (gyɛɛgəbgi gāñen) sm. རྒྱལ་ཁབ་འཇིག་ཉེན་.

རྒྱལ་ཁབ་ཀྱི་འཁོས་བབ་ (gyɛɛgəbgi kööbəb) national financial strength.

རྒྱལ་ཁབ་ཀྱི་ངོ་བོ་ (gyɛɛgəbgi ŋowo) form/ structure of a nation.

རྒྱལ་ཁབ་ཀྱི་མངའ་ཁོངས་ (gyɛɛgəbgi ŋāgoŋ) national territory.

རྒྱལ་ཁབ་ཀྱི་ཆོས་ལུགས་ (gyɛɛgəbgi cöōluù) state religion.

རྒྱལ་ཁབ་ཀྱི་རྗེས་གཞི་ཆེན་པོ་ (gyɛɛgəbgi jüüshi cēmbo) sm. རྒྱལ་རྗེས་.

རྒྱལ་ཁབ་ཀྱི་རྟགས་མཚན་ (gyɛɛgəbgi dāgdzɛn) national emblem/ insignia.

རྒྱལ་ཁབ་ཀྱི་འདས་འཇུག་མཛད་སྒོ་ (gyɛɛgəbgi dɛnjuù dzɛ̄ègo) state funeral.

རྒྱལ་ཁབ་ཀྱི་གནས་ཚུལ་ (gyɛɛgəbgi nɛ̄ɛ̄dzüü) the condition/ state/ situation of a country.

རྒྱལ་ཁབ་ཀྱི་གནས་ཚུལ་ཞུ་ཡིག (gyɛɛgəbgi nɛ̄ɛ̄dzüü shuyiì) state of the union message (in U.S.A.).

རྒྱལ་ཁབ་ཀྱི་སྤྱི་སྐད་ (gyɛɛgəbgi jīgɛ̀ɛ) the national language, the common language used in a multilinguistic state.

རྒྱལ་ཁབ་ཀྱི་བང་མཛོད་ (gyɛɛgəbgi paŋdzöö) state/ nation's treasury or exchequer.

རྒྱལ་ཁབ་ཀྱི་བྱ་བ་ (gyɛɛgəbgi cawa) national affairs.

རྒྱལ་ཁབ་ཀྱི་དབང་འཛིན་ལས་ཁུངས་ (gyɛɛgəbgi wāŋdzin lɛ̄ɛ̀guŋ) power organs/ offices of the state.

རྒྱལ་ཁབ་ཀྱི་དབུ་བཞུགས་ (gyɛɛgəbgi wūshuù) head of state.

རྒྱལ་ཁབ་ཀྱི་མིང་ (gyɛɛgəbgi miŋ) 1. name of a country. 2. name of a reigning dynasty.

རྒྱལ་ཁབ་ཀྱི་གཙོ་བོ་ (gyɛɛgəbgi dzōwo) head of state, chief executive/ ruler of a country.

རྒྱལ་ཁབ་ཀྱི་གཙོ་འཛིན་ (gyɛɛgəbgi dzōndzin) sm. རྒྱལ་ཁབ་ཀྱི་གཙོ་བོ་.

རྒྱལ་ཁབ་ཀྱི་ཟིལ་རྔམ་ (gyɛɛgəbgi siiŋam) national prestige.

རྒྱལ་ཁབ་ཀྱི་གཟི་བཤུགས་ (gyɛɛgəbgi sishuù) sm. རྒྱལ་ཁབ་ཀྱི་ཟིལ་རྔམ་.

རྒྱལ་ཁབ་ཀྱི་ལ་རྒྱ་ (gyɛɛgəbgi lagya) national loyalty/ patriotism.

རྒྱལ་ཁབ་ཀྱི་ལམ་ལུགས་ (gyɛɛgəbgi ləmluù) state system.

རྒྱལ་ཁབ་ཀྱི་ཤན་འབྱེད་པ་ (gyɛɛgəbgi sɛnjeèba) national referee.

རྒྱལ་ཁབ་ཀྱི་ས་ཁོངས་ (gyɛɛgəbgi sāgoŋ) national territory.

རྒྱལ་ཁབ་ཀྱི་གསོལ་སྟོན་ (gyɛɛgəbgi sȫȫdön) state banquet.

རྒྱལ་ཁབ་ཁག (gyɛɛgəb kāà) countries, nations.

རྒྱལ་ཁབ་དགའ་སྟོན་ (gyɛɛgəb gadön) 1. state banquet. 2. a national celebration (e.g., Labor Day).

རྒྱལ་ཁབ་སྒེར་སྡམ་མ་རྩའི་རིང་ལུགས་ (gyɛɛgəb gerdam madzɛ riŋluù) state monopoly capitalism.

རྒྱལ་ཁབ་རྒྱ་མཚོ་ཅུའུ་ (gyɛɛgəb gyadzo jūwu) tib.ch. national bureau of oceanography.

རྒྱལ་ཁབ་བརྒྱད་ཀྱི་མཉམ་འབྲེལ་དམག (gyɛɛgəb gyɛ̀ègi ñamdre māà) allied army of the eight states (during the Boxer Rebellion).

རྒྱལ་ཁབ་ངལ་རྩོལ་སྤྱི་ཁྱབ་ཅུའུ་ (gyɛɛgəb ŋɛɛdzöö jīgyəb jūwu) tib.ch. state general labor bureau.

རྒྱལ་ཁབ་ངེས་རྩིས་ (gyɛɛgəb ŋeèdziì) national economic statistics ¶ 1996 ལོའི་རྒྱལ་ཁབ་ངེས་རྩིས་སྐོར་ About the national economic statistics for 1996.

རྒྱལ་ཁབ་ཆེན་པོའི་རིང་ལུགས་ (gyɛɛgəb cēmbö riŋluù) big nation chauvinism.

རྒྱལ་ཁབ་འཆར་འགོད་ཨུ་ཡོན་ལྷན་ཁང་ (gyɛɛgəb cārgöö ūyön lhɛ̄ngaŋ) state planning commission.

རྒྱལ་ཁབ་འཇིག་ཉེན་ (gyɛɛgəb jiŋñen) national crisis/ danger (usu. used with respect to an invasion/ aggression).

རྒྱལ་ཁབ་མཉམ་འབྲེལ་ (gyɛɛgəb ñamdree) confederation.

རྒྱལ་ཁབ་ཏུ་བསྡུ་ལེན་ (gyɛɛgəbdu dulen) nationalization, nationalizing; va.—བྱེད་ to nationalize.

རྒྱལ་ཁབ་རྟགས་མཚན་ (gyɛɛgəb dāgdzɛn) state/ national emblem or insignia.

རྒྱལ་ཁབ་སྟོངས་ (gyɛɛgəb dōŋ) vi. to become extinct (for a country) ¶ དམག་འཁྲུག་མང་པོ་བྱུང་ནས་རྒྱལ་ཁབ་སྟོངས་རྒྱུའི་ཉེན་ཁ་བྱུང་བ་རེད་ Because they experienced many wars there was a danger the country would become extinct.

རྒྱལ་ཁབ་དུས་ཆེན་ (gyɛɛgəb tüüjen) national day.

རྒྱལ་ཁབ་ཕྱིར་བཙོང་ (gyɛɛgəb ciīdzoŋ) sm. རྒྱལ་གཏོད་.

རྒྱལ་ཁབ་འཕྲུལ་འཁོར་ (gyɛɛgəb trūūgɔɔ) state apparatus/ machinery.

རྒྱལ་ཁབ་དབུ་བརྙེས་པའི་དུས་ཆེན་ (gyɛɛgəb ūñeèbɛ tüüjen) sm. རྒྱལ་ཁབ་དུས་ཆེན་.

རྒྱལ་ཁབ་འབྲེལ་ལམ་ (gyɛɛgəb dreelam) diplomatic relations.

རྒྱལ་ཁབ་མ་རྩའི་རིང་ལུགས་ (gyɛɛgəb madzɛ riŋluù) state capitalism.

རྒྱལ་ཁབ་ཚད་ལྡན་ཚད་འཇལ་ཅུའུ་ (gyɛɛgəb tsɛ̄ndɛn tɛ̄njɛɛ jūwu) tib.ch. state bureau of standards and measures.

རྒྱལ་ཁབ་ཚན་རིག་ལག་རྩལ་ཡུ་ཡོན་ལྷན་ཁང་ (gyɛɛgəb tsɛ̄nriì lagdzɛɛ ūyön lhɛ̄ngaŋ) state commission on science and technology.

རྒྱལ་ཁབ་འཚོང་ (gyɛɛgəb tsōŋ) sm. རྒྱལ་གཏོད་.

རྒྱལ་ཁབ་འཛུགས་ (gyɛɛgəb dzuù) va. to found/ establish a state.

རྒྱལ་ཁབ་འཛུགས་བསྐྲུན་ (gyɛɛgəb dzugdrön) national construction.

རྒྱལ་ཁབ་འཛུགས་ཁྲིམས་ (gyɛɛgəb dzugdrim) state/ national law, constitutional law.

རྒྱལ་ཁབ་འཛུགས་པའི་སྒྲིག་གཞི་ (gyɛɛgəb dzugbɛ drigshi) state/ national structure.

རྒྱལ་ཁབ་ཡིག་ཆ་ (gyɛɛgəb yigja) diplomatic credentials.

རྒྱལ་ཁབ་ལ་གཅེས་ (gyɛɛgəblə jēè) va. to be patriotic, to love one's country.

རྒྱལ་ཁབ་ལ་ བློ་ལོག (gyɛɛgəblə lōlɔɔ̀) va. to betray/ turn against one's country.

རྒྱལ་ཁབ་ལ་དབང་ (gyɛɛgəblə wāŋ) to be owned by the nation, state ownership; va. རྒྱལ་ཁབ་ལ་དབང་; —བྱེད་ to nationalize, to put under state ownership ། ས་ཆ་ཚང་མ་རྒྱལ་ཁབ་ལ་དབང་བ་རེད་ All the land was nationalized.

རྒྱལ་ཁབ་ལ་དབང་བའི་ཁེ་ལས་ (gyɛɛgəblə wāŋwɛ kēlɛɛ̀) state enterprise.

རྒྱལ་ཁབ་ལ་དབང་བའི་ལམ་ལུགས་ (gyɛɛgəblə wāŋwɛ ləmluù) system of state/ national ownership.

རྒྱལ་ཁབ་ལས་ཁུངས་ (gyɛɛgəblə lɛɛgun) state organs, government offices.

རྒྱལ་ཁབ་ཤོར་ (gyɛɛgəb shɔ̄ɔ) vi. to lose one's country.

རྒྱལ་ཁབ་སློབ་ཕྱུ་ (gyɛɛgəb lōbu) tib.ch. state education bureau.

རྒྱལ་ཁབ་བསམ་ (gyɛɛgəblə sām) va. to be patriotic.

རྒྱལ་ཁམས་ (gyɛɛgam) territory/ area of a nation or state; va.—སྐོར་; —རྒྱུ་ to travel/ wander around to many countries.

རྒྱལ་ཁམས་ཀྱི་ཁ་ལ་ཡེ་ཤེས་ཀྱི་སྤྱན་ཡོད་ (gyɛɛkamgi kāla yesheègi jɛ̄nyöö) sb. who has traveled the world can see true wisdom.

རྒྱལ་ཁམས་པ་ (gyɛɛgamba) sb. who goes to many countries/ places.

རྒྱལ་ཁམས་སྤྱི་སྤྱི་འདྲེས་ (gyɛɛgam jījidreè) shung. like every one in the country ། རྒྱལ་ཁམས་སྤྱི་སྤྱི་འདྲེས་ཀྱི་ཡུལ་ཁྲིམས་འཁུར་ཤེས་དགོས་རྒྱུ་ One should observe the law of the country like every one in the country.

རྒྱལ་ཁའི་གླུ་དབྱངས་ (gyɛɛgɛ lūyaŋ) song celebrating a victory or a triumph.

རྒྱལ་ཁའི་སྒོ་ (gyɛɛgɛ go) gate erected to commemorate a victory.

རྒྱལ་ཁོངས་ (gyɛɛgoŋ) belonging to or part of a nation ། ནང་སོག་ནི་ཀྲུང་གོའི་རྒྱལ་ཁོངས་རེད་ Inner Mongolia is part of China.

རྒྱལ་ཁོངས་ཀྱི་བཅའ་ཁྲིམས་ (gyɛɛgoŋgi jādrim) citizenship/ naturalization laws.

རྒྱལ་ཁོངས་རྒྱབ་སྐྱུར་ (gyɛɛgoŋ gyəbgyur) giving up one's citizenship.

རྒྱལ་ཁོངས་གཉིས་འཛིན་ (gyɛɛgoŋ ñīndzin) dual nationality/ citizenship.

རྒྱལ་ཁོངས་གཉིས་སུ་གཏོགས་པ་ (gyɛɛgoŋ ñīīsu dōgba) sm. རྒྱལ་ཁོངས་གཉིས་འཛིན་.

རྒྱལ་ཁྲི་ (gɛɛdri) throne.

རྒྱལ་ཁྲིམས་ (gyɛɛdrim) national law.

རྒྱལ་ཁྲིམས་བཅོ་ལྔ་ (gyɛɛdrim jōŋa) the fifteen national laws established by King Srongtsen Gambo.

རྒྱལ་ཁྲིམས་དང་བྱ་དགའ་སྦྱོང་བ་ (gyɛɛdrim daŋ caga gyōŋwa) shung. to demonstrate the magnanimity of my administration ། ད་ལྟ་བདག་གིས་གནམ་ས་འི་ཚུལ་དང་མཐུན་པར་རྒྱལ་ཁྲིམས་དང་བྱ་དགའ་སྦྱོང་བ་ལ་ In complying with the will of heaven and earth and to demonstrate the magnanimity of my administration.

རྒྱལ་ཁྲིམས་འདད་འདེད་ (gyɛɛdrim dɛndeè) shung. pursuing and enforcing the law ། མིག་ལྟོས་ལ་ཕན་པའི་རྒྱལ་ཁྲིམས་འདད་འདེད་ཡིན་པར་མ་སོང་བ་སྙད་ལམ་འདོམས་པ་ཡོང་བ་ In order to set up an example for the future we appeal (to the government) to pursue and enforce the law.

རྒྱལ་མཁར་བ་ (gyɛngara) an opera dance troupe that performs at Shöton.

རྒྱལ་གླུ་ (gyɛɛlu) national anthem.

རྒྱལ་མགྲོན་ (gyɛndrön) 1. state guest. 2. aide to the King of Bhutan.

རྒྱལ་མགྲོན་ཁང་ (gyɛndröngaŋ) state guest house.

རྒྱལ་འགོང་ (gyɛngoŋ) a type of demon.

རྒྱལ་འགྲན་ (gyɛndrɛn) 1. competing; va.—བྱེད་ to compete. 2. gambling, betting; va.—བྱེད་ to gamble/ place a bet.

རྒྱལ་རྒྱལ་རྒྱལ་པ་ (gyɛɛgyɛɛ gyɛɛba) victorious in one battle after another. ། དེ་ནས་ཆུ་བཞི་སྒང་དྲུག་རྒྱལ་རྒྱལ་རྒྱལ་པ་ཕྱིན་པ་རེད་ After that, Chushigandru (the Tibetan rebel group) won one battle after another.

རྒྱལ་རྒྱུད་ (gyɛɛgyüü) royal lineage ། རྒྱལ་རྒྱུད་སྲས་མོ་ Princess.

རྒྱལ་རྒྱུད་འཛིན་ (gyɛɛgyüü dzin) va. to succeed to a throne.

རྒྱལ་སྒོ་ (gyɛɛgo) main gate.

རྒྱལ་སྒོ་ཤར་སྒོ་ (gyɛɛgo shārgo) the east gate of ཞོལ་ town.

རྒྱལ་ངན་ (gyɛɛŋɛn) evil king.

རྒྱལ་ང་ (gyɛɛŋa) drum that is beat to indicate triumph/ victory.

རྒྱལ་གཅེས་ (gyɛɛjeè) patriotism ། རྒྱལ་གཅེས་ཀྱི་བསམ་པ་ Patriotic thoughts.

རྒྱལ་གཅེས་ཁྲིམས་སྲུང་ (gyɛɛjeè trīmsuŋ) being patriotic/ loving the nation and being law-abiding.

རྒྱལ་གཅེས་ཆོས་གཅེས་ (gyɛɛjeè cōōjeè) loving the nation/ being patriotic as well as loving religion.

རྒྱལ་གཅེས་ཆོས་བྱེད་ (gyɛɛjeè cōōjeè) being patriotic and practicing religion (slogan for monks).

རྒྱལ་གཅེས་འཐབ་ཕྱོགས་ (gyɛɛjeè tābjɔɔ̀) patriotic front.

རྒྱལ་གཅེས་འཐབ་རྩོད་ (gyɛɛjeè tābdzöö) patriotic struggle.

རྒྱལ་གཅེས་སྦུས་ཚོང་ (gyɛɛjeè bǖǖdzoŋ) grain sold to the government at less than the market price as a patriotic gesture (a kind of tax).

རྒྱལ་གཅེས་སྤྱི་ཆིངས་ (gyɛɛjeè jījiŋ) patriotic pact.

རྒྱལ་གཅེས་སྤྱི་འབྲུ་ (gyɛɛjeè jīndru) grain that was donated to the government as a patriotic act (a kind of tax) [Lit. patriotic common grain].

རྒྱལ་གཅེས་ཕྱིར་སྡོད་སྤུན་ཟླ་ (gyɛɛjeè cīdöö būnda) patriotic overseas brothers.

རྒྱལ་གཅེས་འཕྲོད་བསྟེན་ལས་འགུལ་ (gyɛɛjeè trööden lɛngüü) sm. རྒྱལ་གཅེས་གཙང་སྦྲའི་ལས་འགུལ་.

རྒྱལ་གཅེས་མ་དངུལ་ (gyɛɛjeè mənüü) sm. རྒྱལ་དོན་མ་དངུལ་.

རྒྱལ་གཅེས་མི་སྣ་ (gyɛɛjeè mina) patriots, patriotic elements.

རྒྱལ་གཅེས་གཙང་སྦྲའི་ལས་འགུལ་ (gyɛɛjeè dzāŋdrɛ lɛngüü) patriotic campaign for better sanitation/ hygiene.

རྒྱལ་གཅེས་རིང་ལུགས་ (gyɛɛjeè riŋluù) patriotism.

རྒྱལ་ཆས་ (gyɛɛjɛɛ̀) 1. king's robe/ dress, royal clothes. 2. robe worn by oracles.

རྒྱལ་ཆེན་ (gyɛɛjen) 1. the four great guardian deities. 2. a great king.

རྒྱལ་ཆེན་རིགས་བཞི་ (gyɛɛjen rigshi) the four great guardians deities.

རྒྱལ་མཆོག (gyεεjɔɔ̀) 1. the enlightened one, the Buddha. 2. epithet for the Dalai Lama.

རྒྱལ་མཆོག་ཡབ་སྲས་ (gyεεcɔɔ̀ yəbsεὲ) the Dalai Lama and the Panchen Lama.

རྒྱལ་ཇུས་ (gyεὲjüü) government/ national policy, affairs of state, matters of national importance.

རྒྱལ་རྗེ་ (gyεεje) sm. རྒྱལ་པོ་.

རྒྱལ་གཉེར་ (gyεεñer) state owned, state run/ managed ¶ རྒྱལ་གཉེར་སློབ་གྲྭ་ State-run schools.

རྒྱལ་གཉེར་ཁེ་ལས་ (gyεεñer kēlεὲ) state enterprise.

རྒྱལ་གཉེར་ནགས་ར་ (gyεεñer nagra) state forest.

རྒྱལ་གཉེར་དཔལ་འབྱོར་ (gyεεñer bēnjɔɔ) state-owned economy, state section of the economy.

རྒྱལ་གཉེར་ཕྱུགས་ར་ (gyεεñer cūgrə) state livestock farm.

རྒྱལ་གཉེར་ཚོང་ལས་ (gyεεñer tsōŋlεὲ) state trade/ commerce.

རྒྱལ་གཉེར་ཞིང་ར་ (gyεεñer shiŋrə) state farm.

རྒྱལ་གཉེར་བཟོ་ལས་ (gyεεñer solεὲ) state industry.

རྒྱལ་རྟགས་ (gyεεdaà) state or national emblem/ insignia.

རྒྱལ་སྟོན་ (gyεεdön) 1. national day. 2. party given to celebrate a victory.

རྒྱལ་སྟོན་དུས་ཆེན་ (gyεεdön tüücen) National Day (October 1st for the mainland and October 10th for Taiwan).

རྒྱལ་བསྟན་ (gyεεdεn) Buddhism.

རྒྱལ་བསྟན་དགུང་འདེགས་ (gyεεdεn guŋdeg) shung. elevating Buddhism.

རྒྱལ་བསྟན་དར་རྒྱས་ (gyεεdεn targyεὲ) shung. the spreading/ flourishing of Buddhism.

རྒྱལ་ཐབས་ (gyεεdəb) strategies of the state.

རྒྱལ་ཐོག (gyεεdɔɔ̀) 1. during the reign (of) a regent or king ¶ ཀུན་བདེ་གླིང་རྟ་ཚག་རྒྱལ་ཐོག་སྐབས་ At the time of the reign of the Kundeling Regent. 2. story (of a building) ¶ འཇམ་པའི་ཐུབ་ཆེན་ཞལ་ཁྲིམ་གྲང་གསེར་ལེབ་སྒྲོན་རྒྱལ་ཐོག་གཉིས་ཡོད་ A two story high clay statue of the Buddha.

རྒྱལ་དར་ (gyεεdar) national flag.

རྒྱལ་དར་ཕྱེད་འཕེབས་ (gyεεdar cēèmbeb) a flag at half mast.

རྒྱལ་དོན་ (gyεεdön) for or pertaining to the state/ nation; national ¶ རྒྱལ་དོན་སྲུང་སྐྱོབ་འགྲོ་སོང་ National defense expenditure.

རྒྱལ་དོན་ཁང་ (gyεεdöngaŋ) State Department (U.S.A.).

རྒྱལ་དོན་གྲོས་ཚོགས་ (gyεεdön tröödzoò) national assembly, parliament, congress.

རྒྱལ་དོན་བདེ་འཇགས་ལས་ཁང་ (gyεεdön denjaà lεὲgaŋ) State Security Bureau.

རྒྱལ་དོན་བསྡུ་འབབ་ (gyεεdön tüübəb) sm. རྒྱལ་དོན་མ་དངུལ་.

རྒྱལ་དོན་བློན་ཆེན་ (gyεεdön lönjen) Secretary of State (U.S.A.).

རྒྱལ་དོན་མ་དངུལ་ (gyεεdön məŋüü) national capital (financial).

རྒྱལ་དོན་མཚམས་འདྲི་ (gyεεdön tsəmdri) state visit.

རྒྱལ་དོན་ཞལ་འདེབས་ (gyεεdön shεndeb) 1. national contribution/ donation. 2. a money contribution collected by the Tibetan government in exile in India).

རྒྱལ་དོན་གཞུང་ཡིག (gyεεdön shuŋyiì) a government communiqué/ letter.

རྒྱལ་དོན་ཨུ་ཡོན་ (gyεεdön üyön) sm. རྒྱལ་སྲིད་ཨུ་ཡོན་.

རྒྱལ་ལྡན་རྒྱལ་ཁབ་ (gyεεdön gyεεgəb) kingdom.

རྒྱལ་སྡེ་ (gyεεde) citizen, subject.

རྒྱལ་སྡེ་ཁྲོམ་བསྒྲགས་ (gyεεde trōmdraà) known by all.

རྒྱལ་བྱང་ (gyεεda) a notice proclaiming victory; va.—གཏོང་ to issue a notice proclaiming victory.

རྒྱལ་ནང་ (gyεεnaŋ) inside the country/ nation, domestic, internal ¶ རྒྱལ་ནང་རྒྱལ་སྤྱི་ Domestic and foreign.

རྒྱལ་ནང་ཁྲལ་བསྡུ་ལས་ཁང་ (gyεεnaŋ trεὲdu lεὲgaŋ) Internal Revenue Service (IRS, in U.S.A.).

རྒྱལ་ནང་གི་ཁྲིམས་ (gyεεnaŋgi trim) domestic law.

རྒྱལ་ནང་གི་ཉོ་ཚོང་ (gyεεnaŋgi ñodzoŋ) domestic trade.

རྒྱལ་ནང་གི་དམག་འཁྲུག (gyεεnaŋgi məgdru) civil war.

རྒྱལ་ནང་ཚོང་ཁྲོམ་ (gyεεnaŋ tsōŋdrom) domestic market.

རྒྱལ་ནང་ས་ཞིབ་ལས་ཁུངས་ (gyεεnaŋ səshib lεὲguŋ) Department of the Interior (U.S.A.).

རྒྱལ་ནང་གསར་བརྗེའི་དམག་འཁྲུག (gyεεnaŋ sārjee məgdruù) revolutionary civil war.

རྒྱལ་གནས་ཞུ་ཡིག (gyεεnεὲ shuyiì) state of the union message (U.S.A.).

རྒྱལ་པོ་ (gyεεbo) king.

རྒྱལ་པོ་ཁྲི་ཁ་ན་ཡོད་ཀྱང་སྣུན་མིག་ཕོར་ཁ་ (gyεεbo trikana yöögyaŋ jεnmiì pōrga) a leader should be able to see the problems of his subjects [Lit. even though the king is seated on the throne he should see the amount of food in the subject's bowls].

རྒྱལ་པོ་གྲོ་ཁྲལ་ (gyεεbo trodrεε) shung. a type of wheat tax paid to the government at the time of Tibetan New Year.

རྒྱལ་པོ་འགན་སྡིག (gyεεbo gεndrig) a board game (somewhat similar to checkers or chess); va.—རྒྱག.

རྒྱལ་པོ་རྒྱན་འདེབས་ (gyεεbo gyεndeb) sm. རྒྱལ་པོ་འགན་སྡིག.

རྒྱལ་པོ་དང་ཚ་ཁྲིམས་གཉིས་ལྡན་ (gyεεbotaŋ dzədrim ñiidεn) constitutional monarchy.

རྒྱལ་པོ་དྲག་ཤུལ་ཅན་ (gyεεbo trəgshüjεn) tyrant, despot, autocrat.

རྒྱལ་པོ་ལྡེ་བརྒྱད་ (gyεεbo degyεὲ) the eight Tibetan kings whose name contains the word ལྡེ་.

རྒྱལ་པོ་དབུ་གཉིས་པ་ (gyεεbo ūñiibə) a name for Songtsen Gampo [Lit. king with two heads].

རྒྱལ་པོ་ཚང་ (gyεεbodzaŋ) imperial clan, royal family.

རྒྱལ་པོ་ཟས་གཙང་ (gyεεbo sεὲdzaŋ) name of the king who was the Gautama Buddha's father.

རྒྱལ་པོ་ཡོད་པའི་རྒྱལ་ཁབ་ (gyεεbo yööbε gyεεgəb) sm. རྒྱལ་པོའི་རྒྱལ་ཁབ་.

རྒྱལ་པོ་རོལ་སྟབས་ (gyεεbo röödab) a sitting position of deities in tankas and icons where one leg is stretched and the other brought towards the body.

རྒྱལ་པོ་ལུགས་ཀྱི་བསྟན་བཅོས་ (gyεεbo luggi dεnjöö) a legal code.

རྒྱལ་པོ་ལོ་གསར་ (gyεεbo losar) the "King's New Year," celebrated on the 1st day of the 1st Tibetan month.

རྒྱལ་པོའི་དཀོར་མཛོད་ (gyεεbö gɔndzöö) shung. royal treasury/ storehouse.

རྒྱལ་པོའི་བཀའ་ནི་རི་གཟར་གྱི་ཐབ་རྡོ་འདྲ་ (gyεεbö gāni risagi bəbdo dra) no one can go against/ block/ stop orders from above [Lit. the king's order is like a rock rolling down a mountain].

རྒྱལ་པོའི་ཁབ་ (gyεεbö kəb) 1. king's palace/ castle. 2. one of the six great cities of India.

རྒྱལ་པོའི་ཁྲི་སྟོན་ (gyεεbö tridön) coronation.

རྒྱལ་པོའི་རྒྱལ་ཁབ་ (gyεεbö gyεεgəb) monarchy, kingdom ¶ ནེ་པ་ལ་རྒྱལ་པོའི་རྒྱལ་ཁབ་ The kingdom of Nepal.

རྒྱལ་པོའི་གདུང་ (gyεεbö duŋ) lineage of kings, descendents of kings.

རྒྱལ་པོའི་དཔྱ་ (gyεεbö jā) shung. taxes collected by the king.

རྒྱལ་པོའི་ལུང་ (gyεεbö luŋ) shung. order of the king.

རྒྱལ་པོའི་སྲས་ (gyεεbö sεὲ) prince.

རྒྱལ་སྤྱི་ (gyεεji) 1. international. 2. abbr. of UN. ¶ རྒྱལ་སྤྱིའི་རོགས་རམ་ཚོགས་པ་ UN Relief Organization.

རྒྱལ་སྤྱི་གུང་ཁྲན་རིང་ལུགས་ (gyεεji kuŋdrεn riŋluù) tib.ch. the internationale ¶ རྒྱལ་སྤྱི་གུང་ཁྲན་རིང་ལུགས་གསུམ་པ་ The Third Internationale.

རྒྱལ་སྤྱི་ཅན་དུ་འགྱུར་ (gyεεjijεndu gyur) vi. to internationalize.

རྒྱལ་སྤྱི་གཉིས་པ་ (gyɛɛji ñiìbə) the Second Internationale.

རྒྱལ་སྤྱི་དང་པོ་ (gyɛɛji taŋbo) the First Internationale.

རྒྱལ་སྤྱི་རིང་ལུགས་ (gyɛɛji riŋluù) internationalism.

རྒྱལ་སྤྱི་གསུམ་པ་ (gyɛɛji sūmbə) the Third Internationale.

རྒྱལ་སྤྱིའི་ཁྱོན་ (gyɛɛjii kyȫn) international sphere, global.

རྒྱལ་སྤྱིའི་ཁྲིམས་དམག (gyɛɛjii trīmmaà) international peace keeping force.

རྒྱལ་སྤྱིའི་ཁྲིམས་ཁང་ (gyɛɛjii trīmgaŋ) International Court of Justice.

རྒྱལ་སྤྱིའི་ཁྲིམས་ར་ (gyɛɛjii trīmra) International Court of Justice.

རྒྱལ་སྤྱིའི་ཁྲིམས་ལུགས་ (gyɛɛji trīmluù) international law.

རྒྱལ་སྤྱིའི་ཁྲོམ་ར་ (gyɛɛjii trōmra) international markets.

རྒྱལ་སྤྱིའི་གོ་གནས་ (gyɛɛjii konɛɛ̀) international position/ status/ prestige.

རྒྱལ་སྤྱིའི་གོམས་སྲོལ་ (gyɛɛjii komdröö) international custom.

རྒྱལ་སྤྱིའི་གྲོས་མཐུན་ (gyɛɛjii tröödün) international agreement.

རྒྱལ་སྤྱིའི་གླུ་དབྱངས་ (gyɛɛjii lūyaŋ) "the international" (song).

རྒྱལ་སྤྱིའི་རྒྱ་གྲམ་དམར་པོའི་ཚོགས་པ་ (gyɛɛjii gyadram mārbö tsōgba) International Red Cross.

རྒྱལ་སྤྱིའི་སྒེར་ཁྲིམས་ (gyɛɛjii gerdrim) international private law.

རྒྱལ་སྤྱིའི་སྒྲ་རྟགས་ (gyɛɛjii dradaà) international phonetic symbols, international phonetic alphabet.

རྒྱལ་སྤྱིའི་ངལ་རྩོལ་དུས་ཆེན་ (gyɛɛjii ŋɛɛdzöö tüüjen) International Labor Day, May Day (May 1st).

རྒྱལ་སྤྱིའི་དངུལ་ལོར་ (gyɛɛjii ŋüülɔr) convertible foreign exchange, international currency.

རྒྱལ་སྤྱིའི་དངོས་མང་བཤམས་སྟོན་འདུ་ཚོགས་ (gyɛɛjii ŋüümaŋ shāmdön dudzoò) international fair.

རྒྱལ་སྤྱིའི་བཅའ་ཁྲིམས་ (gyɛɛjii jādrim) international law.

རྒྱལ་སྤྱིའི་ཆུ་ཚད་ (gyɛɛjii cūdzɛɛ̀) world level/ standard, international standard.

རྒྱལ་སྤྱིའི་འཇལ་ཚད་རྩིས་གཞི་ལམ་ལུགས་ (gyɛɛjii jɛɛdzɛɛ̀ dzīshi ləmluù) international system of units.

རྒྱལ་སྤྱིའི་ལྗོངས་སྐྱུ་ལས་དོན་ཁང་ (gyɛɛjii jōŋgyu lɛɛ̀döngaŋ) international travel service.

རྒྱལ་སྤྱིའི་ཉིན་ཚེས་འགྱུར་ལྡོག་ས་ཐིག (gyɛɛjii ñindzeè gyundɔɔ sādig) international date line.

རྒྱལ་སྤྱིའི་ཉེན་རྟོག་པའི་ལས་ཁང་ (gyɛɛjii ñendogbɛ lɛɛ̀gaŋ) interpol.

རྒྱལ་སྤྱིའི་ཉེས་ཡང་ཚོགས་པ་ (gyɛɛjii ñeèyaŋ tsɔ̄gba) Amnesty International.

རྒྱལ་སྤྱིའི་ཉོ་ཚོང་ (gyɛɛjii ñodzoŋ) international/ world trade.

རྒྱལ་སྤྱིའི་ཉོ་ཚོང་རྒྱས་སྤེལ་ཚོགས་པ་ (gyɛɛjii ñotsoŋ gɛ̄ɛ̄bel tsɔ̄gba) council for the promotion of international trade.

རྒྱལ་སྤྱིའི་རྡུལ་ཕྲན་ནུས་ཤུགས་ལས་དོན་ཁང་ (gyɛɛjii tüdrɛn nüüshuù lɛɛ̀dongaŋ) International Atomic Energy Agency.

རྒྱལ་སྤྱིའི་གནད་དོན་ (gyɛɛjii nɛɛ̀dön) international issues/ affairs.

རྒྱལ་སྤྱིའི་གནད་ཡོད་མི་སྣ་བརྒྱ་ལས་གྲུབ་པའི་བོད་དོན་ཚོགས་པ་ (gyɛɛjii nɛɛ̀yöö mina gyalɛ drubbɛ pöödön tsōgba) Committe of 100 for Tibet.

རྒྱལ་སྤྱིའི་གནས་ཚུལ་ (gyɛɛjii nɛɛ̄dzüü) international situation.

རྒྱལ་སྤྱིའི་མནའ་འབྲེལ་ (gyɛɛjii namdrel) League of Nations.

རྒྱལ་སྤྱིའི་དཔུང་སྒྲིལ་ (gyɛɛjii būŋdrel) international brigade (in Spanish Civil War).

རྒྱལ་སྤྱིའི་སྤྱི་ཁྲིམས་ (gyɛɛjii jīdrim) international law.

རྒྱལ་སྤྱིའི་འཕྲོད་བསྟེན་ལྷན་ཁང་ (gyɛɛjii tröödengaŋ) World Health Organization (WHO).

རྒྱལ་སྤྱིའི་བུད་མེད་དུས་ཆེན་ (gyɛɛjii püümeè tüüjen) International Women's Day (March 8th).

རྒྱལ་སྤྱིའི་བོད་དོན་ལས་འགུལ་ཚོགས་པ་ (gyɛɛjii pöödön lɛngüü tsōgba) International Campaign for Tibet (ITC).

རྒྱལ་སྤྱིའི་བོད་ཀྱི་ལོ་ (gyɛɛjii pöögi lo) International Year of Tibet.

རྒྱལ་སྤྱིའི་བྱིས་པའི་དུས་ཆེན་ (gyɛɛjii cibɛ tüücen) International Children's Day (June 1st).

རྒྱལ་སྤྱིའི་མ་དངུལ་ཐེབས་རྩ་ (gyɛɛjii məŋüü tēbdza) International Monetary Fund (IMF).

རྒྱལ་སྤྱིའི་མ་དངུལ་ཐེབས་རྩ་ (gyɛɛjii məŋüü tēbdza) International Monetary Fund (IMF).

རྒྱལ་སྤྱིའི་དམག་སྲིད་ཉེན་རྟོག་དམག (gyɛɛjii məgsiì ñendɔgmaà) international peace keeping force.

རྒྱལ་སྤྱིའི་དམངས་གཙོའི་བུད་མེད་མནའ་འབྲེལ་ཚོགས་པ་ (gyɛɛjii māŋdzö püümeè namdrel) Women's International Democratic Federation (WIDF).

རྒྱལ་སྤྱིའི་རྩིས་གཞིའི་སྤྱི་ལུགས་ (gyɛɛjii dzīishii jīluù) metric system.

རྒྱལ་སྤྱིའི་ཚོང་ར་ (gyɛɛjii tsōŋra) international market.

རྒྱལ་སྤྱིའི་ཚོང་དོན་དང་དགག་སྒོའི་དཔྱ་ཁྲལ་ཆ་སྙོམས་གྲོས་མཐུན་ (gyɛɛjii tsōŋdön daŋ gagö jādrɛɛ cāñom tröödün) GATT (General Agreement on Tariffs and Trade).

རྒྱལ་སྤྱིའི་ཚོང་ལས་ཀྱི་བཅའ་ཁྲིམས་ (gyɛɛjii tsōŋlɛɛ̀gi jədrim) international trade/ commerce law.

རྒྱལ་སྤྱིའི་ཞི་བདེ་ (gyɛɛjii shide) international peace.

རྒྱལ་སྤྱིའི་བཟོ་ལས་པའི་མཉམ་འབྲེལ་ (gyɛɛjii solɛɛ̀bɛ ñamdree) International Workers of the World (IWW).

རྒྱལ་སྤྱིའི་ཡར་རྒྱས་ལས་དོན་ཁང་ (gyɛɛjii yargyɛɛ̀ lɛɛ̀döngaŋ) Agency for International Development (AID).

རྒྱལ་སྤྱིའི་རིང་རྒྱུག་འགྲན་ཚོགས་ (gyɛɛjii riŋgyuù trɛndzoò) international marathon.

རྒྱལ་སྤྱིའི་རིང་ལུགས་ (gyɛɛjii riŋluù) internationalism.

རྒྱལ་སྤྱིའི་ལས་དོན་ཚོགས་པ་ (gyɛɛjii lɛɛ̀dön tsɔ̄gba) Committee on International Relations.

རྒྱལ་སྤྱིའི་ཤན་འབྱེད་པ་ (gyɛɛjii shɛnjeba) international referee.

རྒྱལ་སྤྱིའི་སྲིད་དོན་སློབ་སྦྱོང་ (gyɛɛjii siìdön lōbjoŋ) international studies.

རྒྱལ་སྤྱིའི་སློབ་གྲྭ་བའི་མཉམ་འབྲེལ་ཚོགས་པ་ (gyɛɛjii lōbdrɛ ñāmdree tsōgba) International Union of Students (IUS).

རྒྱལ་སྤྱིའི་སློབ་མའི་མཉམ་འབྲེལ་ལྷན་ཚོགས་ (gyɛɛjii lōbmɛ ñāmdree lhɛndzoò) sm. རྒྱལ་སྤྱིའི་སློབ་གྲྭ་བའི་མཉམ་འབྲེལ་ཚོགས་པ་.

རྒྱལ་སྤྱིའི་གསོ་རིག་ཡིག་ཆ་ (gyɛɛjii sōrig yigja) international medical records.

རྒྱལ་སྤྱིའི་ཨོ་ལིམ་པིག་རྩེད་འགྲན་འཛིན་སྐྱོང་ཁང་ (gyɛɛjii ōlembi dzēndrɛn dzingyoŋgaŋ) international olympic committee (IOA).

རྒྱལ་སྤྲུལ་ (gyɛɛdrüü) lamas whose predecessors have been regents of Tibet.

རྒྱལ་ཕམ་ (gyɛɛpam) victory or defeat, gain or loss; va.—འབྱེད་ to see who will win and lose, to decide victory and defeat ། སུ་ལ་ཡང་རྒྱལ་ཕམ་བྱུང་མེད་ No one has won or lost.

རྒྱལ་ཕམ་ཐག་གཅོད་འགྲན་སྡུར་ (gyɛɛbam tāgjöö drɛndur) finals of a sports event/ competition.

རྒྱལ་ཕམ་དབྱེ་འབྱེད་ཀྱི་འགྲན་སྡུར་ (gyɛɛbam yeceègi drɛnduu) sm. རྒྱལ་ཕམ་ཐག་གཅོད་འགྲན་སྡུར་.

རྒྱལ་ཕམ་མེད་པ་ (gyɛɛbam meèba) a draw, a tie, neither winning nor lose.

རྒྱལ་ཕམ་མེད་ཕྱིད་ (gyɛɛbam meèjeè) sm. རྒྱལ་ཕམ་མེད་པ་.

རྒྱལ་ཕྱི་ (guɛɛji) abroad, external.

རྒྱལ་ཕྲན་ (gyɛɛdrɛn) small nation/ country.

རྒྱལ་ཕྲན་མཉམ་འབྲེལ་ (gyɛɛdrɛn ñāmdree) federation, federal union, union commonwealth ། རྒྱལ་ཕྲན་མཉམ་འབྲེལ་དེ་མོ་ Federal Republic of

Germany.

རྒྱལ་ཕྲན་མཉམ་འབྲེལ་གྱི་དབྱི་ཧུའི་གྲོས་ཚོགས་ (gyɛɛtrɛn ñāmdreegi yihue trööd̄zoò) tib.ch. federal parliament.

རྒྱལ་ཕྲན་མཉམ་འབྲེལ་སྤྱི་མཐུན་རྒྱལ་ཁབ་ (gyɛɛtrɛn ñāmdree jīdün gyɛɛgəb) federal republic, federated republic.

རྒྱལ་ཕྲན་མཉམ་འབྲེལ་ལམ་ལུགས་ (gyɛɛdrɛn ñāmdree ləmluù) federal system, commonwealth system.

རྒྱལ་བ་ (gyɛɛwa) 1. the victorious, the conqueror, the Buddha ¶ རྒྱལ་བའི་བསྟན་པ་ the Buddha's teaching. 2. the Dalai Lama ¶ རྒྱལ་བ་ལྔ་པ་ the 5th Dalai Lama.

རྒྱལ་བ་སྐུ་འཕྲེང་ (gyɛɛwa gūdreŋ) the reincarnation series of the Dalai Lamas, a Dalai Lama ¶ རྒྱལ་བ་སྐུ་འཕྲེང་བཅུ་གསུམ་པ་ཐུབ་བསྟན་རྒྱ་མཚོ་ Thubtan Gyatso, the 13th Dalai Lama.

རྒྱལ་བ་དགྱེས་པའི་མཆོད་སྦྱིན་ (gyɛɛwa gyeèbɛ cöödrin) good works/ deeds done for the purpose of pleasing a superior [Lit. offerings made for pleasing a god].

རྒྱལ་བ་གཉིས་པའི་རིང་ལུགས་ (gyɛɛwa ñiìgi riŋluù) shung. sm. དགེ་ལུགས་པ་.

རྒྱལ་བ་བྱམས་པ་ (gyɛɛwa camba) the Buddha Maitreya.

རྒྱལ་བ་ཡབ་སྲས་རྣམ་གཉིས་ (gyɛɛwa yəpsɛɛ̀ nāmñiì) shung. the Dalai Lama and the Panchen Lama.

རྒྱལ་བ་རིན་པོ་ཆེ་ (gyɛɛwa rimpoce) the Dalai Lama.

རྒྱལ་བའི་བཀའ་ (gyɛɛwɛ gā) the teachings of the Buddha.

རྒྱལ་བའི་ཁྲིམས་ལུགས་ (gyɛɛwɛ trīmluù) shung. monastic rules.

རྒྱལ་བའི་བསྟན་པ་ (gyɛɛwɛ dēmba) the Buddha's teachings.

རྒྱལ་བའི་ཐུགས་སྲས་ (gyɛɛwɛ tūgsɛɛ̀) 1. disciples of the Buddha. 2. bodhisattvas.

རྒྱལ་བའི་ཡང་སྲིད་ (gyɛɛwɛ yəŋsii) incarnation of the Dalai Lama.

རྒྱལ་བའི་རིང་བསྲེལ་ (gyɛɛwɛ riŋsɛɛ̀) relics/ remains of the Buddha.

རྒྱལ་བའི་གསུང་ (gyɛɛwɛ sūŋ) the teachings of the Buddha.

རྒྱལ་བའི་གསུང་རབ་ (gyɛɛwɛ sūŋrəb) the teachings and scriptures of the Buddha.

རྒྱལ་བུ་ (gyɛɛbu) prince.

རྒྱལ་བུ་དོན་གྲུབ་ (gyɛɛbu töndrup) prince Siddhartha.

རྒྱལ་བུན་ (gyɛɛbün) national debt.

རྒྱལ་པོ་ (gyɛɛwo) sm. རྒྱལ་པོ་.

རྒྱལ་བློན་ (gyɛɛlön) 1. the king and his ministers. 2. shung. the regent and the prime minister (in tt.). 3. the ruling circle.

རྒྱལ་བློན་བཀའ་ (gyɛɛlön gā) shung. regent, the prime minister and the council ministers (བཀའ་ཤག་) (in tt.).

རྒྱལ་བློན་གྲོས་ཚོགས་ (gyɛɛlön trööd̄zoò) sm. རྒྱལ་བློན་ལྷན་ཚོགས་.

རྒྱལ་བློན་སྲིད་ཚོགས་ (gyɛɛlön siidzoò) ruling clique or circle, the ruling elite.

རྒྱལ་བློན་ལྷན་ཚོགས་ (gyɛɛlön lhēndzoò) shung. a meeting/ session of the Tibetan Council of Ministers (བཀའ་ཤག་) and the Dalai Lama.

རྒྱལ་དབང་ (gyɛɛwaŋ) title used for the highest lamas of Tibet.

རྒྱལ་དབང་ཀརྨ་པ་ (gyɛɛwaŋ gārmaba) the Karmapa Lama.

རྒྱལ་འབངས་ (gyɛmbaŋ) 1. citizen, subject. 2. people and country; national.

རྒྱལ་འབངས་དཔལ་འབྱོར་ (gyɛmbaŋ bēnjɔɔ) national economy.

རྒྱལ་འབངས་ཡོང་འབབ་ (gyɛmbaŋ yoŋbəb) national income.

རྒྱལ་འབངས་སློབ་གསོ་ (gyɛmbaŋ lōbso) national education.

རྒྱལ་འབངས་གསར་བརྗེ་ (gyɛmbaŋ sārje) national revolution.

རྒྱལ་འབྲེལ་ (gyɛndree) 1. international ¶ རྒྱལ་འབྲེལ་འཆིང་ཡིག International treaty. 2. relations with other governments, foreign relations.

རྒྱལ་འབྲེལ་རིང་ལུགས་ (gyɛndree riŋluù) internationalism.

རྒྱལ་མ་ (gyɛɛma) Tara.

རྒྱལ་མང་ཀུང་སི་ (gyɛɛmaŋ gūŋsi) multinational corporation.

རྒྱལ་མིང་ (gyɛɛmiŋ) the name of a dynasty, dynastic name.

རྒྱལ་མོ་ (gyɛɛmo) 1. queen. 2. goddess.

རྒྱལ་མོ་ཀ་གོན་ (gyɛɛmo kagön) a type of large turnip.

རྒྱལ་མོ་དངུལ་ཆུ་ (gyɛɛmo ŋüju) Upper Yangtse River in Eastern Tibet.

རྒྱལ་དམངས་ (gyɛɛmaŋ) 1. the people, the populace of a nation. 2. abbr. the state and the people.

རྒྱལ་དམངས་གྲོས་ཁང་ (gyɛɛmaŋ tröögaŋ) people's assembly hall.

རྒྱལ་དམངས་གཉིས་ཕན་ (gyɛɛmaŋ ñiìbɛn) beneficial to the state and the people.

རྒྱལ་དམངས་ཐོན་སྐྱེད་ཀྱི་རིན་ཐང་བསྡོམས་འབོར་ (gyɛɛmaŋ tōŋgyɛɛ̀gi rindaŋ dombɔɔ) gross national product.

རྒྱལ་དམངས་དཔལ་འབྱོར་ (gyɛɛmaŋ bēnjɔɔ) national economy.

རྒྱལ་དམངས་ཚོགས་པ་ (gyɛɛmaŋ tsōgba) the Koumintang Party.

རྒྱལ་དམངས་ཚོགས་ཆེན་ (gyɛɛmaŋ tsōgjɛn) national assembly (of KMT).

རྒྱལ་རྩེ་ (gyandze) Gyantse.

རྒྱལ་རྩེ་བ་ (gyandzewa) person from Gyantse.

རྒྱལ་རྩེ་དམག་སྒར་ (gyandze māàgar) shung. the Gyantse Regiment.

རྒྱལ་རྩེ་ཚོང་དོན་སྤྱི་ཁྱབ་པ་ (gyandze tsōŋdön jīgyəbbə) Gyantse Trade Agent (British).

རྒྱལ་ཚང་ (gyɛɛdzaŋ) royalty, royal family.

རྒྱལ་ཚབ་ (gyɛɛdzəb) shung. regent.

རྒྱལ་ཚོགས་ (gyɛɛdzoò) the United Nations (abbr. for འཛམ་གླིང་མཉམ་འབྲེལ་རྒྱལ་ཚོགས་).

རྒྱལ་ཚོགས་ཚོགས་ཆེན་ (gyɛɛdzoò tsōgjɛn) General Assembly of the UN.

རྒྱལ་ཚོགས་སྲུང་སྐྱོབ་ལྷན་ཚོགས་ (gyɛɛdzoò sūŋgyəb lhēndzoò) the UN Security Council.

རྒྱལ་ཚོགས་ལྷན་རྒྱས་ (gyɛɛdzoò lhēngyɛɛ̀) General Assembly of the UN.

རྒྱལ་ཚོང་ (gyɛɛdzoŋ) national traitor ¶ རྒྱལ་ཚོང་སྒེར་གཅོད་ཀྱི་སྲིད་གཞུང་ Traitorous dictatorial government.

རྒྱལ་ཚོང་ནང་རུལ་བ་ (gyɛɛdzoŋ nəŋrübə) sm. རྒྱལ་ཚོང་.

རྒྱལ་མཚན་ (gyɛndzɛn) 1. a type of roof ornament found on monasteries and temples. 2. man's name.

རྒྱལ་མཚན་མཐོན་པོ་ (gyɛndzɛn tōbo) shung. name of the labrang of the Panchen Lama.

རྒྱལ་མཚམས་ (gyɛndzam) national boundary.

རྒྱལ་མཚམས་སྒྲོལ་འཕྲུས་ལག་ཁྱེར་ (gyɛndzam trööṯüü laggyer) exit visa.

རྒྱལ་མཚམས་རིས་མེད་རིང་ལུགས་ (gyɛndzam rimeè riŋluù) internationalism.

རྒྱལ་མཚམས་ས་ཐིག (gyɛndzam sədig) the boundary line of a country.

རྒྱལ་འཚོང་ (gyɛɛdzoŋ) sm. རྒྱལ་ཚོང་.

རྒྱལ་འཚོང་ཁེ་གཉེར་ (gyɛɛdzoŋ kēñer) traitor for profit.

རྒྱལ་འཚོང་ཆོམ་རྐུན་ (gyɛɛdzoŋ cōmgün) a person who sells/ betrays his country.

རྒྱལ་མཛོད་ (gyɛndzöö) national treasury/ exchequer.

རྒྱལ་མཛོད་བུན་འཛིན་ (gyɛndzöö pündzin) treasury bill (bond).

རྒྱལ་མཛོད་ཚབ་ལོར་ (gyɛndzöö tsəblɔr) sm. རྒྱལ་མཛོད་བུན་འཛིན་.

རྒྱལ་འཛིན་ (gyɛndzin) sm. རྒྱལ་གཉེར་.

རྒྱལ་འཛུགས་ (gyɛɛdzug) state owned, state established.

རྒྱལ་རྫས་ (gyɛɛdzɛɛ̀) materials/ things gained from victory.

རྒྱལ་ཞྭ་ (gyɛɛsha) crown.

རྒྱལ་ཞེན་ (gyɛɛshen) patriotism.

རྒྱལ་གཞིས་ (gyɛɛshiì) 1. territory of the nation. 2. royal estates.

རྒྱལ་གཞིས་འཛིན་ (gyɛɛshiì dzin) va. to succeed to a throne.

རྒྱལ་ཟུར་ (gyɛɛsur) shung. exregent.

རྒྱལ་ཟླ་བའི་བརྒྱད་ཀྱི་ཐུག་པ་ (gyɛɛ dawɛ gyɛ̀ɛgi tūgbə) rice porridge made with nuts and dried fruits that is eaten on the eighth day of the twelfth lunar month (Chinese custom).

རྒྱལ་གཟིམ་ (gyɛɛsim) Private Secretary of the King of Bhutan.

རྒྱལ་གཟེབ་ (gyɛɛseb) a rake.

རྒྱལ་ཡབ་ (gyɛɛyəb) shung. title/ term of address for the Dalai Lama's father.

རྒྱལ་ཡིག (gyɛɛyiì) diplomatic credentials.

རྒྱལ་ཡུམ་ (gyɛɛyum) shung. title/ term of address for the Dalai Lama's mother.

རྒྱལ་ཡོངས་ (gyɛɛyoŋ) nationwide, pertaining to the nation as a whole, national ¶ རྒྱལ་ཡོངས་གཞོན་ནུའི་འཐུས་མི་ National youth representatives.

རྒྱལ་ཡོངས་ཀྱི་ཁྱོན་ (gyɛɛyoŋgi kyȭn) all over the nation, nationwide.

རྒྱལ་ཡོངས་མཁའ་འགྲུལ་དང་མཁའ་དབྱིང་ལས་དོན་ཁང་ (gyɛɛyoŋ kəndrüü daŋ kəyiŋ lɛ̀ɛdöngaŋ) NASA (National Aeronautics and Space Administration) (U.S.A.).

རྒྱལ་ཡོངས་གྲོས་ཚོགས་ (gyɛɛyoŋ tröödzoò) Congress (U.S.A.).

རྒྱལ་ཡོངས་གླིང་ལྗོངས་བདག་གཉེར་ཁང་ (gyɛɛyoŋ lìŋjoŋ dagñergaŋ) National Park Service.

རྒྱལ་ཡོངས་སྒྱུ་རྩལ་གོང་འཕེལ་ལས་ཁང་ (gyɛɛyoŋ gyudzɛɛ koŋpel lɛ̀ɛgaŋ) National Endowment for the Arts (U.S.A.).

རྒྱལ་ཡོངས་བཅིང་འགྲོལ་མདུན་བསྐྱོད་ཚོགས་པ་ (gyɛɛyoŋ jiŋdröö düngyöö tsōgba) National Liberation Front.

རྒྱལ་ཡོངས་མཐོ་སློབ་ཁག་གི་རྩེད་རིགས་འཛིན་སྐྱོང་གི་མཐུན་ཚོགས་ (gyɛɛyoŋ tũũmii tsōgba) National Collegiate Athletic Association (NCAA).

རྒྱལ་ཡོངས་འཐུས་མིའི་ཚོགས་ཆེན་ (gyɛɛyoŋ tũũmii tsōgba) national assembly/ congress, representatives from all over the nation.

རྒྱལ་ཡོངས་དྲུང་ཆེ་ (gyɛɛyoŋ trunje) Secretary of State (U.S.A.).

རྒྱལ་ཡོངས་ནགས་གསེབ་ལས་དོན་ཁང་ (gyɛɛyoŋ nagseb lɛ̀ɛdöngaŋ) National Forest Service.

རྒྱལ་ཡོངས་ནང་བསྟན་མཐུན་ཚོགས་ (gyɛɛyoŋ naŋdɛn tũndzɔɔ̀) Buddhist Association of China.

རྒྱལ་ཡོངས་གནམ་གཤིས་ལས་དོན་ཁང་ (gyɛɛyoŋ nāmshiì lɛ̀ɛdöngaŋ) National Weather Service.

རྒྱལ་ཡོངས་གནའ་བོའི་ཡིག་ཚགས་ཁང་ (gyɛɛyoŋ nāwö yigdzaŋgaŋ) National Archives (U.S.A.).

རྒྱལ་ཡོངས་སྤྱི་ཚོགས་རིག་གནས་གོང་འཕེལ་ལས་ཁང་ (gyɛɛyoŋ jītsoõ rignɛɛ̀ koŋpel lɛ̀ɛgaŋ) National Endowment for the Humanities (NEH).

རྒྱལ་ཡོངས་འཕྲོད་བསྟེན་ཞིབ་འཇུག་ཁང་ (gyɛɛyoŋ trȫȫdɛn shimjuùgaŋ) National Institutes of Health.

རྒྱལ་ཡོངས་བུད་མེད་ཀྱི་སྒྲིག་འཛུགས་ (gyɛɛyoŋ pũũmeègi drigdzüü) National Organization for Women (NOW).

རྒྱལ་ཡོངས་བོད་ཀྱི་དམངས་གཙོ་ཚོགས་པ་ (gyɛɛyoŋ pöögi māŋdzo tsōgba) Tibetan National Democratic Party.

རྒྱལ་ཡོངས་མི་མང་རླུང་འཕྲིན་ཁང་ (gyɛɛyoŋ mimaŋ lūŋdringaŋ) National Public Radio.

རྒྱལ་ཡོངས་མི་དམངས་འཐུས་མིའི་ཚོགས་ཆེན་ (gyɛɛyoŋ mimaŋ tũũmi tsōgba) National People's Congress (PRC).

རྒྱལ་ཡོངས་མི་རིགས་ནག་པོའི་བདེ་དོན་གོང་འཕེལ་གྱི་སྒྲིག་འཛུགས་ (gyɛɛyoŋ miriì nagbö dedön koŋbelgi drigdzuù) National Association for the Advancement of Colored People (NAACP).

རྒྱལ་ཡོངས་མེ་མདའི་མཐུན་ཚོགས་ (gyɛɛyoŋ mendɛ tũndzɔɔ̀) National Rifle Association (NRA).

རྒྱལ་ཡོངས་ཚན་རིག་སློབ་གཉེར་ཁང་ (gyɛɛyoŋ tsɛ̄nriì lōññergaŋ) National Academy of Sciences.

རྒྱལ་ཡོངས་མི་དམངས་འཐུས་མིའི་ཚོགས་ཆེན་ (gyɛɛyoŋ mimaŋ tũũmii tsōgjen) National People's Congress ¶ རྒྱལ་ཡོངས་མི་དམངས་འཐུས་མིའི་ཚོགས་ཆེན་གྱི་རྒྱུན་ཨུ་ཡོན་ལྷན་ཁང་ Standing Committee of the National People's Congress.

རྒྱལ་ཡོངས་ཚན་རིག་ལྟེ་གནས་ (gyɛɛyoŋ tsɛ̄nrig dēnɛɛ̀) National Science Foundation.

རྒྱལ་ཡོངས་ཚོགས་ཆེན་ (gyɛɛyoŋ tsōgjen) National Assembly.

རྒྱལ་ཡོངས་ཚོགས་འདུ་ (gyɛɛyoŋ tsōndu) National Assembly (of Bhutan).

རྒྱལ་ཡོངས་ཡོང་འབབ་ (gyɛɛyoŋ yoŋbəb) national income.

རྒྱལ་ཡོངས་ལས་དོན་གྲོས་ཚོགས་ (gyɛɛyoŋ lɛ̀ɛdön tröötsoò) National Working Conference.

རྒྱལ་ཡོངས་ལས་རྩོལ་ཞིབ་འཇུག་དང་འབྲེལ་བའི་ལས་ཁང་ (gyɛɛyoŋ lɛ̀ɛdzöö shimjuù daŋ dreewɛ lɛ̀ɛgaŋ) National Labor Relations Board (NLRB).

རྒྱལ་ཡོངས་ཤེས་ཡོན་སློབ་གསོའི་མཐུན་ཚོགས་ (gyɛɛyoŋ shɛ̄ɛyön lōbsö tũndzoò) National Education Association (NEA).

རྒྱལ་ཡོངས་སྲུང་སྐྱོབ་ (gyɛɛyoŋ sūŋgyob) national defense.

རྒྱལ་ཡོངས་གསང་བའི་སྲུང་སྐྱོབ་ལས་དོན་ཁང་ (gyɛɛyoŋ sāŋwɛ sūŋgyob lɛ̀ɛdöngaŋ) National Security Agency.

རྒྱལ་རབས་ (gyɛɛrəb) 1. history ¶ རྒྱ་ནག་གི་རྒྱལ་རབས་ Chinese history. 2. dynasty, royal lineage ¶ ཆིང་རྒྱལ་རབས་འགོ་ཚུགས་པ་ནས་ From the beginning of the Qing Dynasty.

རྒྱལ་རབས་གསལ་བའི་མེ་ལོང་ (gyɛɛrəb sɛ̄lwɛ meloŋ) title of a history of Tibet written by Sakya Sonam Gyaltsan.

རྒྱལ་རིགས་ (gyɛɛrig) lineage of kings.

རྒྱལ་ལོ་ (gyɛɛlo) 1. year in the Tibetan system of counting. 2. year in the reign of a dynasty.

རྒྱལ་ཤོར་བྲན་གཡོག (gyɛɛshɔɔ trɛnyɔɔ̀) conquered and enslaved people.

རྒྱལ་ས་ (gyɛɛsa) capital.

རྒྱལ་སའི་མཁར་སྒོ་ (gyɛɛsɛ kārgo) the gateway of a country.

རྒྱལ་སྲས་ (gyɛɛsɛɛ̀) 1. prince. 2. bodhisattva.

རྒྱལ་སྲས་བྷ་ཀུ་ལ་རིན་པོ་ཆེ་ (gyɛɛsɛɛ̀ bhagala rimpoce) title of a reincarnation Lama from Ladakh (Bakula Rimpoche).

རྒྱལ་སྲས་སེམས་དཔའ་ཆེན་པོ་ (gyɛɛsɛɛ̀ sēmba cēmbo) the great bodhisattvas.

རྒྱལ་སྲིད་ (gyɛɛsiì) state affairs, government, political power; va.—སྐྱོང་; —འཛིན་ to rule/ govern.

རྒྱལ་སྲིད་གྲོས་ཚོགས་ (gyɛɛsiì tröödzoò) parliament, congress.

རྒྱལ་སྲིད་ཆོས་སྲིད་ (gyɛɛsiì cȫȫsiì) shung. system of government where the political and the religious powers are merged, theocracy.

རྒྱལ་སྲིད་རྣམ་གཉིས་ (gyɛɛsiì nāmñiì) shung. the Dala Lama and the regent.

རྒྱལ་སྲིད་སྣ་བདུན་ (gyɛɛsiì nādün) seven auspicious royal symbols.

རྒྱལ་སྲིད་སྤྱི་ཁྱབ་ཁང་ (gyɛɛsiì jīgyəbgaŋ) 1. State Council (P.R.C.). 2. State Department.

རྒྱལ་སྲིད་འཛིན་སྐྱོང་ (gyɛɛsiì dziŋgyoŋ) administrating/ ruling a country; va.—མཛད་; —བྱེད་ to rule a country.

རྒྱལ་སྲིད་ཡུན་རིང་དུ་བརྟན་པ་ (gyɛɛsiì yünriŋdu dɛ̄mba) shung. long lasting government.

རྒྱལ་སྲིད་ཨུ་ཡོན་ལྷན་ཁང་ (gyɛɛsiì ūyün lhɛ̄ngaŋ) state

council.

རྒྱལ་སྲུང་ (gyɛ̲ɛ̲suŋ) national defense.

རྒྱལ་སྲུང་དམངས་སྐྱོབ་ (gyɛ̲ɛ̲suŋ māŋgyob) defend the nation, protect the people/ masses.

རྒྱལ་སྲུང་དེང་རབས་ཅན་ (gyɛ̲ɛ̲suŋ te̲ŋrəbjɛn) modernization of national defense.

རྒྱལ་སྲུང་པུའུ་ (gyɛ̲ɛ̲suŋbu) tib.ch. Defense Department (U.S.A.), Ministry of Defense.

རྒྱལ་སྲུང་འབྲེལ་གཏུག་པུའུ་ (gyɛ̲ɛ̲suŋ dre̲e̲duù būwu) tib.ch. national defense liason department.

རྒྱལ་སྲུང་དམག་འཁྲུག (gyɛ̲ɛ̲suŋ māgdruù) war of national defense.

རྒྱལ་སྲུང་དམག་དཔུང་ (gyɛ̲ɛ̲suŋ māgbuŋ) national defense army.

རྒྱལ་སྲུང་འཛུགས་སྐྲུན་ (gyɛ̲ɛ̲suŋ dzu̲gdrön) national defense construction.

རྒྱལ་སྲུང་བཟོ་ལས་ (gyɛ̲ɛ̲suŋ so̲lɛɛ̀) national defense industry.

རྒྱལ་སྲུང་གཡུལ་ས་ (gyɛ̲ɛ̲suŋ yǖǜsə) national defense line.

རྒྱལ་སྲུང་ལུས་རྩལ་ (gyɛ̲ɛ̲suŋ lü̲ǜdzɛɛ̀) national defense physical.

རྒྱལ་སྲུང་ས་མཚམས་ (gyɛ̲ɛ̲suŋ sāndzam) national defense line.

རྒྱལ་སྲུང་སློབ་གྲྭ་ཆེན་པོ་ (gyɛ̲ɛ̲suŋ lōbdra cēmbo) national defense university.

རྒྱལ་སྲུང་ཨུ་ཡོན་ལྷན་ཁང་ (gyɛ̲ɛ̲suŋ ūyön lhēngaŋ) National Defense Council/ Commission.

རྒྱལ་བསམ་ (gyɛ̲ɛ̲sam) patriotism.

རྒྱལ་བསམ་ཁྱིམ་བརྗེད་ (gyɛ̲ɛ̲sam kyīmjeè) patriotic [Lit. to think of state and forget household].

རྒྱལ་བསམ་ཅན་ (gyɛ̲ɛ̲samjɛn) patriotic person.

རྒྱལ་བསེན་ (gyɛ̲ɛ̲sen) ghost.

རྒྱལ་པོའི་ (gyɛ̲ɛ̲bö) shung. abbr. of རྒྱལ་པོའི་.

རྒྱལ་སྲིད་ (gyɛ̲ɛ̲sii̇) shung. abbr. of རྒྱལ་སྲིད་.

རྒྱས་ (gyɛ̲ɛ̀) 1. vi. to flourish, to thrive, to prosper, to bloom ¶ མེ་ཏོག་རྒྱས་པའི་སྐབས་ When the flowers are blossoming. ¶ རྒྱལ་ཁབ་ཀྱི་དཔལ་འབྱོར་རྒྱས་པ་ལ་བརྟེན་ནས་ Because of the prospering of nation's economy. ¶ སྒོ་ཕྱུགས་རྣམས་ཤ་ཤེད་རྒྱས་འདུག The livestock have thrived [Lit. become fat]. 2. vi. to swell, to rise, to overflow (as with river/ water) ¶ གཙང་པོ་རྒྱས་འདུག The river has risen. 3. abbr. of རྒྱས་པོ་.

རྒྱས་བསྐྲུན་ (gyɛ̲ɛ̀drün) 1. expansion, extension; va.—བྱེད་ to expand, to extend, to add new things to, to elaborate ¶ ལྷ་ཁང་ཁག་རྒྱས་བསྐྲུན་བྱེད་བཞིན་འདུག (They) are expanding the temples.

རྒྱས་བསྐྲུན་ཨར་ལས་ (gyɛ̲ɛ̀drün ārlɛɛ̀) expansion/ extension construction project.

རྒྱས་ཁེབས་ (gyɛ̲ɛ̀geb) shung. sm. རྒྱས་འགེབས་.

རྒྱས་གྲས་ (gyɛ̲ɛ̀drɛɛ̀) full length ¶ པ་ལེའི་ཞབས་བྲོ་རྒྱས་གྲས་ Full length ballet.

རྒྱས་འགེབས་ (gyɛ̲ɛ̀ ge̲b) 1. va. to affix a government seal. 2. va. to argue by analogy, to infer.

རྒྱས་འགྲེལ་ (gyɛ̲ndree) an elaborate or detailed explanation/ commentary.

རྒྱས་བཅད་ (gyɛ̲ɛ̀jɛɛ̀) 1. fixed, standardized (price, schedule, tax, etc.); va.—བྱེད་ to fix (prices, etc.) ¶ རྒྱས་བཅད་སྐྱེད་ཀ་ fixed interest ¶ བཟའ་ཆའི་རིན་གོང་གཞུང་ནས་རྒྱས་བཅད་བྱས་པ་རེད་ The government fixed the prices of food articles. 2. setting a time to finish work ¶ ཉིན་བདུན་ཡས་མས་ཀྱི་ལས་འགན་ཉིན་གྲངས་རྒྱས་བཅད་ཀྱི་སྤྲད་སོང་ (They) were given a work plan (to do) the job in about 7 days. 3. a eform policy on loans that reduced the burden of old debts (in the 1950's).

རྒྱས་བདབ་ (gyɛ̲ɛ̀dəb) 1. sm. རྒྱས་འགེབས་. 2. va. to join together, to seal.

རྒྱས་བདབ་ར་མོ་ཆེ་ (gyɛ̲ɛ̀dəb ra̲moce) Ramoche temple (in Lhasa).

རྒྱས་བསྡུས་ (gyɛ̲ɛ̀düǜ) elaborating and abbreviating, elaborateness ¶ མཛད་སྒོ་རྒྱས་བསྡུས་རན་པོ་ཞིག་གནང་ཡོད་པ་རེད་ (They) had a ceremony of appropriate elaborateness.

རྒྱས་པ་ (gyɛ̲ɛ̀ba) 1. more elaborate/ detailed/ extensive, more comprehensive ¶ བོད་ཀྱི་རྒྱལ་རབས་རྒྱས་པ་ཞིག་སྒྲིག་རྩོམ་བྱས་པ་རེད་ They compiled a more comprehensive book of Tibetan history. 2. general, full, elaborate (usu. of meetings) ¶ ཚོགས་འདུ་རྒྱས་པ་ A full meeting (of all the delegates).

རྒྱས་པར་བྱེད་ (gyɛ̲ɛ̀bar cɛ̲ɛ̀) va. to enlarge/ expand/ increase ¶ དེ་སྔའི་བཟོ་གྲྭ་དེ་རྒྱས་པར་བྱས་པ་རེད་ The previously built factory was expanded.

རྒྱས་པོ་ (gyɛ̲ɛ̀bo) elaborate, detailed, extensive ¶ ཚིག་རེ་རེར་འགྲེལ་བཤད་རྒྱས་པོ་སྒྲོན་གྱི་འདུག (He) gives elaborate explanations of each word. ¶ གསོལ་ཚོགས་རྒྱས་པོ་ An elaborate meal.

རྒྱས་དཔྱད་ (gyɛ̲ɛ̀jɛɛ̀) sm. རྒྱས་བཅད་.

རྒྱས་དཔྱད་རྩ་ཚིག (gyɛ̲ɛ̀jɛɛ̀ dzədzii̇) shung. proclamation.

རྒྱས་སྤྱོད་ (gyɛ̲ɛ̀jöö̀) extravagant/ elaborate life style.

རྒྱས་སྤྲོས་ (gyɛ̲ɛ̀dröö̀) elaborate, sumptuous, stylish, ostentatious; va.—བྱེད་.

རྒྱས་སྤྲོས་རྒྱས་གཤོམ་ (gyɛ̲ɛ̀dröö̀ gyɛ̲ɛ̀shom) ostentatious and extravagant/ elaborate.

རྒྱས་སྤྲོས་དངོས་རིགས་ (gyɛ̲ɛ̀dröö̀ ŋöö̀rig) luxury items/ goods/ products.

རྒྱས་སྤྲོས་ཆུད་ཟོས་ (gyɛ̲ɛ̀dröö̀ cǖǜsöö̀) extravagant and wasteful.

རྒྱས་སྤྲོས་འཕྲོ་བརླག (gyɛ̲ɛ̀dröö̀ trōlaà) sm. རྒྱས་སྤྲོས་ཆུད་ཟོས་.

རྒྱས་སྤྲོས་མེད་པ་ (gyɛ̲ɛ̀dröö̀ me̲èba) simple, not elaborate.

རྒྱས་སྤྲོས་ལོངས་སྤྱོད་ (gyɛ̲ɛ̀dröö̀ la̲ŋdröö̀) sm. རྒྱས་བཟའ་རྒྱས་འཐུང་.

རྒྱས་འབྲི་ (gyɛ̲ɛ̀dri) elaborate/ detailed writing.

རྒྱས་འབྲིང་བསྡུས་གསུམ་ (gyɛ̲ɛ̀driŋ dü̲ǜ sūm) the three: elaborate, moderate and simple.

རྒྱས་རྩོད་ (gyɛ̲ɛ̀dzöö̀) a big/ grand debate.

རྒྱས་རྩོད་རྒྱས་གླིང་ (gyɛ̲ɛ̀dzöö̀ gyɛ̲ɛ̀leŋ) sm. རྒྱས་རྩོད་.

རྒྱས་འཛོམས་ (gyɛ̲ndzom) plenary/ large session ¶ ཚོགས་འདུ་རྒྱས་འཛོམས་ Plenary session.

རྒྱས་འཛོམས་གྲོས་ཚོགས་ (gyɛ̲ndzom trö̲ö̀dzoò) plenary session, full or large session/ meeting/ conference.

རྒྱས་འཛོམས་ཚོགས་འདུ་ (gyɛ̲ndzom tsōndu) sm. རྒྱས་འཛོམས་གྲོས་ཚོགས་.

རྒྱས་ཟ་རྒྱས་སྤྲོས་ (gyɛ̲ɛ̀sa gyɛ̲ɛ̀dröö̀) doing sth. extravagantly; va.—བྱེད་.

རྒྱས་བཟའ་རྒྱས་འཐུང་ (gyɛ̲ɛ̀sa gyɛ̲ɛ̀duŋ) eating and drinking elaborately/ sumptuously/ extravagantly.

རྒྱས་གཤོམ་ (gyɛ̲ɛ̀shom) sm. རྒྱས་སྤྲོས་.

རྒྱས་བཤད་ (gyɛ̲ɛ̀shɛɛ̀) detailed/ elaborate explanation; va.—བྱེད་.

རྒྱས་བཤད་རྒྱས་གླིང་ (gyɛ̲ɛ̀shɛɛ̀ gyɛ̲ɛ̀leŋ) 1. airing one's views, expressing one's opinions, arguing or debating things out. 2. elaborate speech/ discussion, explaining in detail.

རྒྱས་བཤད་རྒྱས་གླིང་རྒྱས་རྩོད་ (gyɛ̲ɛ̀shɛɛ̀ gyɛ̲ɛ̀leŋ gyɛ̲ɛ̀dzöö̀) sm. རྒྱས་བཤད་རྒྱས་གླིང་.

རྒྱསར་ (gyɛ̲ɛ̀bar) shung. abbr. of རྒྱས་པར་.

རྒྱུ་ (gyu̲) 1. matter, substance, material ¶ རྒྱུ་ལེགས་ཉེས་ The quality of the materials/ things. 2. wealth, possessions ¶ རང་རྒྱུ་ One's own possessions. 3. cause (primary or direct) ¶ རྩྭ་ཤིང་རྣམས་སྐྱེ་བའི་རྒྱུ་ The cause of the plant's growth. 4. (vb. + — + linking verb) future action ¶ ང་ཚོ་སང་ཉིན་འགྲོ་རྒྱུ་ཡིན་ We are going tomorrow. 5. (vb. + — + linking verb) conveys the idea that the verbal action "has yet to be done" ¶ཁོ་ད་ལྟ་ཁ་ལག་བཟའ་རྒྱུ་རེད་ He has yet to eat. 6. (vb. + — + བྱུང་) there was a chance or possibility to do the verbal action ¶ ཁོ་ཁྲོམ་ལ་འགྲོ་རྒྱུ་བྱུང་སོང་ He had a chance to go to the market. 7. (vb. + — + neg. existential vb.) a. shouldn't do the verbal action ¶ ཁ་ལག་ཞེ་དྲག་ཟ་རྒྱུ་ཡོད་པ་མ་རེད་ (One) shouldn't eat a lot of food. b. conveys nonexistence ¶ འདིར་

སྤྲང་པོ་གཏན་ནས་མཐོང་རྒྱུ་མེད་ One never sees beggars here. 8. (vb.+ — + positive existential vb.) conveys existence of sth. or sb. ༈ དེང་དུས་ཁོ་ཚོར་འབྲས་བཟའ་རྒྱུ་ཡོད་པ་རེད་ These days they have rice to eat. 9. (vb. + —) future nominalizing particle ༈ ཁོས་དེབ་ཉོ་རྒྱུའི་དངུལ་བརླགས་པ་རེད་ He lost the money for buying the book. ༈ དམག་རྒྱག་རྒྱུ་དེ་ཤུགས་ཆེ་རུ་གཏོང་དགོས་ (We) must intensify the fighting of the war. ༈ ཁ་ལག་བཟོ་རྒྱུར་ཚལ་འདི་ཡག་པོ་འདུག This vegetable is good for making food. 10. wealth, riches ༈ ཨ་རི་ར་རྒྱུ་ཡོད་པའི་ཁྱིམ་ཚང་མང་པོ་ཡོད་པ་རེད་ There are many wealthy families in America. 11. warp (in weaving); va.—ཡོག to spin wool into thread.

རྒྱུ་དཀར་ (gyugar) the large intestine.

རྒྱུ་དཀྲིས་ (gyudrii) the wooden frame on which the warp is attached.

རྒྱུ་རྐྱེན་ (gyugyen) 1. cause, reason ༈ ཁོ་སེམས་སྐྱོ་བའི་རྒྱུ་རྐྱེན་ག་རེ་རེད་དམ་ What is the reason for his sadness? 2. va.—ཞུ་ to appeal/ petition to a higher official ༈ ཁ་མཆུ་འདིའི་སྐོར་ངས་རྫོང་ལ་རྒྱུ་རྐྱེན་ཞུས་པ་ཡིན་ Concerning this dispute, I made a petition to the district.

རྒྱུ་རྐྱེན་མི་རྟག་པ་ (gyugyen midagba) the impermanence of cause and effect.

རྒྱུ་རྐྱེན་མེད་ (gyugyen meè) without reason, without cause ༈ རྒྱུ་རྐྱེན་མེད་ན་མི་ཤི་གི་མ་རེད་ Without a cause, a person will not die.

རྒྱུ་རྐྱེན་གཙོ་བོ་ (gyugyen dzōwo) the main cause/ reason.

རྒྱུ་རྐྱེན་བཟང་པོ་ (gyugyen saŋbo) benevolent/ good cause.

རྒྱུ་རྐྱེན་གསལ་རྗེན་བཀོད་པ་ (gyugyen sɛ̄ɛjen gōōba) shung. the causes and reasons being clearly mentioned ༈ ད་ལམ་ཕྱོགས་གཉིས་ཀའི་རྒྱུ་རྐྱེན་གསལ་རྗེན་བཀོད་པའི་སྙན་ཞུ་འབུལ་འབྱོར་བྱུང་དོན་ Recently we received the report in which the causes and reasons were clearly mentioned.

རྒྱུ་རྐྱེན་ཨ་འཐས་ཞུ་འཛུར་ (gyugyen āndɛɛ̀ shunjɔɔ) shung. being very insistant in making a plea/ petition in which the causes and reasons for sth. are conveyed ༈ མི་སེར་ཚགས་རྟེན་བྲལ་ཚུལ་སོགས་རྒྱུ་རྐྱེན་ཨ་འཐས་ཞུ་འཛུར་ལ་ཞིབ་པར་ Investigating the insistant plea to look into the hardship of the subject's livelihood.

རྒྱུ་ཀླུགས་ (gyuguù) a disease of the intestines.

རྒྱུ་སྐར་ (gyugar) star, planet, constellation.

རྒྱུ་སྐར་འགྱུལ་སྐྱོད་ (gyugar güügyöö) planetary motion.

རྒྱུ་སྐར་དབུས་ན་ཟླ་བ་ཤར་ (gyugar üüna dawa shār) sth. outstanding, sth. that stands out [Lit. among the constellations, the moon shines].

རྒྱུ་སྐར་ལམ་ (gyugar lam) the Milky Way.

རྒྱུ་ཁུ་ (gyuku) intestinal fluid.

རྒྱུ་མཁྲིས་ (gyutrii) a type of herbal medicine.

རྒྱུ་འཁྲིལ་ (gyutrii) sm. རྒྱུ་འཁག.

རྒྱུ་གང་སོང་གི་འབྲས་བུ་ (gyukaŋ sōŋgi drɛɛ̄bu) results come according to the expenditure, the more you spend the better the result.

རྒྱུ་གྲོ་ (gyudro) shung. wheat for grinding into flour.

རྒྱུ་སྒྲོན་ (gyudrön) expenses, costs, va.—གཏོང་ ༈ རྒྱུ་སྒྲོན་ཆེན་པོ་བཏང་ནས་ཐུགས་སྐྱིད་བཏང་བ་རེད་ They paid out a lot of expenses and gave a party.

རྒྱུ་འགག (gyuŋgaà) blockage in the intestines (a type of disease).

རྒྱུ་འགྲན་ (gyundrɛn) foot race; va.—རྒྱུར་ to race (on foot).

རྒྱུ་འགྲུལ་ (gyundrüü) traveling; va.—བྱེད་ ༈ དེང་སང་ཇག་པ་མང་པོ་ཡོད་སྟབས་མཚན་མོ་རྒྱུ་འགྲུལ་བྱེད་མཁན་མེད་པ་རེད་ These days because there are many bandits no one goes traveling at night.

རྒྱུ་འགྲོ་མ་དགོས་པའི་ལྷ་དབུ་ཆེན་པོ་ (gyundro magööbɛ lhā ū cēmbo) hoping to achieve sth. big without paying the cost [Lit. hoping to build a large statue with a big head without expending the building materials].

རྒྱུ་འགྲོ་རང་གཞོམས་ (gyundro raŋshom) making sth. under an arrangement in which the craftsman is provided with all the materials; va.—བྱེད་ ༈ ངས་རྒྱུ་འགྲོ་རང་གཞོམ་བྱས་ནས་ཤིང་བཟོ་བ་ཞིག་གླས་པ་རེད་ I hired a carpenter on the arrangement that I provide all the materials (for what he will make).

རྒྱུ་འགྲོའི་བྱེ་མ་ (gyudrö cema) shifting sand.

རྒྱུ་རྒྱངས་ (gyugyaŋ) sm. རྒྱུ་མ་རྒྱངས་.

རྒྱུ་རྒྱུ་བ་ (gyu gyuwa) sm. འགྲོ་འགྲོ་བ་.

རྒྱུ་སྒྲིག་འཕྲུལ་འཁོར་ (gyudrig trüügɔɔ) warping machine.

རྒྱུ་ངན་སྤུན་རྩུབ་ (gyuŋɛn bündzub) a harsh/ rough/ crude person, people who behave badly; va.—བྱེད་.

རྒྱུ་ངོམ་ (gyuŋom) boasting/ showing off one's wealth; va.—བྱེད་.

རྒྱུ་དངུལ་ (gyuŋüü) riches, wealth.

རྒྱུ་དངོས་ (gyuŋöö) property, wealth, possessions, goods.

རྒྱུ་དངོས་རྩིས་བཤེར་ (gyuŋöö dziisher) checking the amount of goods/ property/ possessions; va.—བྱེད་.

རྒྱུ་རྔན་ (gyuŋɛn) a bribe, bribing; va.—སྤྲོད་; —སྦྱིན་ to give a bribe.

རྒྱུ་ཧམ་མི་གསོད་ (gyuŋam misöö) murdering for money/ greed.

རྒྱུ་ཅ་ལག (gyu jālaà) sm. རྒྱུ་དངོས.

རྒྱུ་ཅན་ (gyujɛn) a rich/ wealthy person.

རྒྱུ་གཅིག་སྨྲ་བ་ (gyujig māwa) monastic theory of origins, monism.

རྒྱུ་གཅོང་ (gyujoŋ) chronic disease of intestines.

རྒྱུ་ཆ་ (gyuja) materials ༈ གོས་ལོག་གི་རྒྱུ་ཆ་ Dress material.

རྒྱུ་ཆ་བཟོ་གྲྭ་ (gyuja sodra) raw material factory.

རྒྱུ་ཆད་ (gyujɛɛ̀) a fine paid in goods.

རྒྱུ་ཆས་ (gyujɛɛ̀) 1. raw material. 2. things.

རྒྱུ་ཆུ་ (gyuju) sm. རྒྱུ་ཁུ་.

རྒྱུ་ཆུང་འཁྲུག་ལང་ (gyujuŋ trōglaŋ) shung. causing trouble over a small reason.

རྒྱུ་ཆེན་པོ་ (gyu cēmbo) wealthy, rich.

རྒྱུ་གཉིས་སྨྲ་བ་ (gyuñii māwa) dualism, dualistic theory.

རྒྱུ་རྟགས་ (gyudaà) the symbol of an element.

རྒྱུ་སྟོང་ (gyudoŋ) empty intestines (intestines not filled with food).

རྒྱུ་སྟོབས་ (gyudob) rich and powerful.

རྒྱུ་དག (gyudag) 1. character ༈ མི་དེ་རྒྱུ་དག་ཡག་པོ་འདུག This man has a good character. 2. quality (of materials) ༈ རས་ཆ་འདི་རྒྱུ་དག་ཡག་པོ་འདུག This material is of good quality.

རྒྱུ་དག་མེད་(པ་) (gyudag meèba) 1. bad personality/ character. 2. an ungrateful person ༈ མི་དེ་རྒྱུ་དག་མེད་ཙང་ཕ་མར་གཡོག་པོ་ཡག་པོ་རྒྱུགས་མ་སོང་ Because that person is ungrateful he didn't help his parents well.

རྒྱུ་དུས་ (gyudüü) a seed that has been planted but not yet sprouted.

རྒྱུ་འདྲི་ (gyu drii) va. to ask the reason.

རྒྱུ་ནག (gyunag) small intestine.

རྒྱུ་ནག་སོར་བཅུ་གཉིས་མ་ (gyunag sōr jūñiimə) duodenum.

རྒྱུ་ནད་ (gyunɛɛ̀) enteritis.

རྒྱུ་ནོམ་ (gyunom) sm. རྒྱུ་ནོར་.

རྒྱུ་ནོར་ (gyunɔɔ) wealth, riches, property, valuables, possessions; va.—སྤེལ་ to increase one's wealth; vi.—འཕེལ་ to have one's wealth increase.

རྒྱུ་ནོར་ལྐོག་ཟ་ (gyunɔɔ gɔ̄gsa) embezzling, stealing, being corrupt; va.—བྱེད་.

རྒྱུ་ནོར་ལ་ཧམ་ (gyunɔɔla ŋām) vi. to strive/ seek wealth in a greedy fashion.

རྒྱུ་སྤུན་ (gyubün) warp and wool.

རྒྱུ་སྤུས་ (gyubüü) quality ༈ རྒྱུ་སྤུས་དག་པོ་ Good quality.

རྒྱུ་ཕྱོགས་ (gyucɔɔ) the direction from which the

wind is blowing.

རྒྱུ་འཕྲི་གླ་བཅོས་ (gyutri lājöö) stinting on materials and doing shoddy work.

རྒྱུ་འཕྲོག (gyundrɔɔ̀) looting, plundering, stealing; va.—བྱེད་.

རྒྱུ་བ་ (gyuwa) movement, circulation ¶ ཁྲག་གི་རྒྱུ་བ་ Blood circulation.

རྒྱུ་འབྱོར་ (gyunjɔɔ) sm. རྒྱུ་ནོར་.

རྒྱུ་དབང་གཉིས་ལྡན་ (gyuwaŋ ñiidɛn) having both wealth and power/ authority.

རྒྱུ་དབང་དཔའ་དཔུང་ཤེད་ཁྱེར་ (gyuwaŋ bābuŋ sheēgyer) shung. displaying in an arrogant manner one's power and wealth; va.—བྱེད་ ¶ ཁོ་པས་རྒྱུ་དབང་དཔའ་དཔུང་ཤེད་ཁྱེར་ཁོ་ན་བྱེད་པ་དང་མི་སེར་ལ་བདག་གསིག་གཏོང་བ་ He always arrogantly displays his power and wealth and abused the subjects.

རྒྱུ་འབྲས་ (gyumdrɛɛ̀) cause and effect (karmic); vi.—འཁོར་ to reap the result of one's past action; va.—བརྩི་ to act morally taking into account the law of karma ¶ ཕྲུ་གུ་དེས་རྒྱུ་འབྲས་བརྩིས་ནས་ཕ་མ་གཉིས་ལ་ཞབས་ཕྱི་ཡག་པོ་ཞུས་སོང་ The child acted morally and served his parents well.

རྒྱུ་འབྲས་ཀྱི་འབྲེལ་བ་ (gyumdrɛɛ̀gi dreewa) relationship between cause and effect.

རྒྱུ་འབྲས་ཁྱད་གསོད་ (gyumdɛɛ kyɛɛ̀söö) sm. རྒྱུ་འབྲས་མེད་པ་.

རྒྱུ་འབྲས་མིག་མེད་ (gyumdɛɛ̀ migmeè) sm. རྒྱུ་འབྲས་མེད་པ་.

རྒྱུ་འབྲས་མེད་པ་ (gyumdɛɛ̀ meèba) without conscience, immoral, disregarding the law of karma ¶ མི་དེས་རྒྱུ་འབྲས་མེད་པའི་ལས་ཀ་བྱས་ནས་རང་ཉིད་ཀྱི་བཟའ་ཟླ་ནད་པ་དེ་ཕུད་སོང་ That man acted immorally by kicking out his sick wife.

རྒྱུ་འབྲས་སྨྲ་བ་ (gyumdɛɛ̀ māwa) theory of cause and effect.

རྒྱུ་འབྲས་རྩི་མེད་ (gyumdɛɛ̀ dzīmeè) sm. རྒྱུ་འབྲས་མེད་པ་.

རྒྱུ་འབྲེལ་སྐྱི་མོ་ (gyumdee gyīmo) mesentery.

རྒྱུ་སྦྱོར་ (gyujɔɔ) sponsoring, acting as a patron ¶ ཁོང་གིས་རྒྱུ་སྦྱོར་བྱས་ནས་དཔེ་ཆ་འདི་དཔར་བསྐྲུན་པ་རེད་ He acted as a patron and printed the book.

རྒྱུ་སྦྱོར་བ་ (gyujɔɔwa) patron/ sponsor.

རྒྱུ་མ་ (gyuma) intestine.

རྒྱུ་མ་དཀར་ནག (gyuma gārnag) intestines.

རྒྱུ་མ་འཁུམ་ (gyuma kūm) vi. to get/ or have an intestinal spasm.

རྒྱུ་མ་ཕུ་འདེད་ (gyuma pūndeè) making a thorough or exhaustive inquiry/ investigation; va.—བྱེད་ to probe in detail [Lit. to blow in the intestine].

རྒྱུ་མ་རིང་པོ་ (gyumə riŋbu) 1. a patient person, sb. who is tolerant and does not easily lose his/ her temper. 2. sb. who is lazy, a procrastinator.

རྒྱུ་མང་འདུས་གཞི་ (gyumaŋ dǖüshi) complex root (in chemistry).

རྒྱུ་མང་ཕྱིར་ལྡོག་དཔྱད་ཞིབ་ (gyumaŋ cīdɔɔ̀ yēshib) multiple regression analysis.

རྒྱུ་མང་དཔྱད་ཞིབ་ (gyumaŋ yēshib) multivariate analysis.

རྒྱུ་མང་སྨྲ་བ་ (gyumaŋ māwa) pluralism.

རྒྱུ་མའི་གླང་འཐབ་ (gyumɛ lāŋdəb) an illness characterized by excruciating pain in the stomach.

རྒྱུ་མེད་རྐྱེན་མེད་ (gyumeè gyenmeè) without reason/ cause ¶ གནད་དོན་འདི་རྒྱུ་མེད་རྐྱེན་མེད་ལ་བརྟེན་ནས་བྱུང་མ་སོང་ This matter did not occur without cause.

རྒྱུ་སྨད་ (gyumɛɛ̀) lower part of the stomach.

རྒྱུ་གཙང་ (gyudzaŋ) sm. རྒྱུ་ལེགས་.

རྒྱུ་གཙང་སྦུས་གཙང་ (gyudzaŋ bǖüdzaŋ) high quality.

རྒྱུ་གཙོ་བོ་ (gyu dzōwo) main or essential element/ ingredient ¶ ཀམ་པ་ལི་དེའི་རྒྱུ་གཙོ་བོ་བལ་རེད་ The main ingredient in the blanket is wool.

རྒྱུ་རྩ་ (gyudza) 1. the origin, the source, the root. 2. a vein.

རྒྱུ་ཚད་ (gyudzɛɛ̀) enteritis of the intestine; typhoid fever.

རྒྱུ་ཚད་འབྲུམ་བུ་ཅན་ (gyudzɛɛ̀ drumbujɛn) typhus, typhoid fever.

རྒྱུ་ཚིལ་ (gyudzii) intestinal fat.

རྒྱུ་མཚན་ (gyumdzɛn) reason ¶ དེ་བྱེད་དགོས་པའི་རྒྱུ་མཚན་ག་རེ་རེད་ What is the reason for having to do this?

རྒྱུ་མཚན་གྱིས་སེམས་འགུགས་ (gyumdzɛngi sēmguù) convincing by reason.

རྒྱུ་མཚན་དུ་འཁྱེར་ (gyumdzɛndu kyēr) sm. རྒྱུ་མཚན་དུ་བྱེད་.

རྒྱུ་མཚན་དུ་བྱེད་ (gyumdzɛndu cee) va. to use a pretext ¶ རྒྱལ་སྲུང་ལ་རོགས་རམ་བྱེད་ཡས་རྒྱུ་མཚན་དུ་བྱས་ནས་བཙན་འཛུལ་བྱས་པ་རེད་ Using national defense as a pretext, (they) invaded (the country).

རྒྱུ་མཚན་མེད་པ་ (gyumdzɛn meèba) without reason/ cause, senseless.

རྒྱུ་མཚན་ཡང་དག (gyumdzɛn yaŋdaà) reasons that are unimpeachable/ unquestionable/ irreproachable.

རྒྱུ་རྫས་ (gyudzɛɛ̀) sm. རྒྱུ་ནོར་.

རྒྱུ་ཞགས་ (gyushaà) small intestines.

རྒྱུ་ཟ་ (gyusa) va. to take a bribe ¶ དཔོན་པོ་དེས་རྒྱུ་ཞི་དྲག་ཟ་གི་ཡོད་པ་རེད་ That boss takes a lot of bribes.

རྒྱུ་ཟས་ (gyusɛɛ̀) p. of རྒྱུ་ཟ་.

རྒྱུ་ཟས་ཕྱོགས་ལྷུང་ (gyusɛɛ̀ cɔ̄ɔ̀lhuŋ) shung. being biased as a result of taking a bribe; va.—བྱེད་ ¶ ས་གནས་སྣེ་སྒོད་ནས་རྒྱུ་ཟས་ཕྱོགས་ལྷུང་གིས་གྱོད་དོན་ཐག་གཅོད་དྲང་མིན་གྱིས་རྐྱེན་པས་བསྐྱོས་ཡ་རྒྱལ་ཁབ་ཏུ་མི་བཙར་མཐུ་མེད་བྱུང་བ་ The district heads were biased regarding settling the case because they had taken a bribe so one party had to go the capital to appeal.

རྒྱུ་གཟུགས་བཞི་ (gyusug shi) the four elements: earth, water, fire and air.

རྒྱུ་གཟེར་ (gyuser) sharp pain in stomach/ intestine; vi.—རྒྱག.

རྒྱུ་བཟང་གོང་ཁེ་ (gyusaŋ koŋge) high quality with low price.

རྒྱུ་བཟས་ཕྱོགས་ལྷུང་ (gyusɛɛ̀ cɔ̄ɔ̀lhuŋ) sm. རྒྱུ་ཟས་ཕྱོགས་ལྷུང་.

རྒྱུ་བཟོའི་འཁོར་ཁང་ (gyusöö kɔ̄ɔ̀gaŋ) beam mill.

རྒྱུ་ཡོད་མཁན་ (gyu yöngɛn) a rich person.

རྒྱུ་རླུགས་ (gyuluù) hernia.

རྒྱུ་ལ་རྔམ་ (gyula ŋām) vi. to be greedy for wealth.

རྒྱུ་ལམ་ (gyulam) sm. འགྲོ་ལམ་.

རྒྱུ་ལེགས་ (gyuleg) good quality.

རྒྱུ་ཤ་ (gyusha) sm. རྒྱུ་ཞགས་.

རྒྱུ་ཤུགས་ (gyushug) financial strength.

རྒྱུ་ཤེད་ཅན་ (gyusheèjɛn) plutocrat.

རྒྱུ་ཤེད་དབང་ཤེད་ (gyusheè wāŋsheè) shung. sm. རྒྱུ་དབང་དཔའ་དཔུང་ཤེད་ཁྱེར་.

རྒྱུ་ཤེལ་ (gyushek) thin lens.

རྒྱུ་གཤིས་ (gyushiì) nature, character (usu. of things).

རྒྱུ་ས་ (gyusə) sm. རྒྱུ་ལམ་.

རྒྱུ་སྲང་ (gyusaŋ) narrow street/ lane.

རྒྱུ་སྲིན་ (gyusin) worms in the intestine.

རྒྱུ་སྲིན་ལེབ་མོ་ (gyusin lebmo) tapeworm.

རྒྱུ་གསུམ་ (gyusum) the three: innate ability, learned ability (receiving many teachings, reading many books) and diligence. 2. the three Tibetan diseases: རླུང་, མཁྲིས་, བད་ཀན་.

རྒྱུ་ལྷག (gyulhaà) appendix; vi.—ན་ to get appendicitis.

རྒྱུ་ལྷག་གི་ནད་ (gyulhaàgi nɛɛ̀) sm. རྒྱུ་ལྷག་གཉན་ཚད་.

རྒྱུ་ལྷག་གཉན་ཚད་ (gyulhaà ñēntsɛɛ̀) appendicitis.

རྒྱུ་ལྷག་ཚ་ནད་ (gyulhaà tsānɛɛ̀) sm. རྒྱུ་ལྷག་གཉན་ཚད་.

རྒྱུག་ཁུལ་ (gyuùküü) the area over which water has flowed ¶ ཆུ་ལོག་རྒྱུག་ཁུལ་ The flood area.

རྒྱུག་ཁྱི་ (gyuùgyi) stooge, running dog.

རྒྱུག་ཁྲ་ (gyugdraà) fence, banister, balustrade.

རྒྱུག་གུག (gyugguù) backpack, rucksack.

རྒྱུག་མགྱོགས་ (gyuggyoò) fast-moving, quick ༡ རྒྱུག་མགྱོགས་ཚོང་ཟོག Fast-moving (selling) merchandise.

རྒྱུག་འགྲོ་ (gyugdro) va. to run ༡ སྐད་རྒྱག་ས་དེ་ལ་རྒྱུག་ཕྱིན་སོང་ (They) ran to the place where there was shouting.

རྒྱུག་འགྲོ་བའི་བྱེ་མ་ (gyugdrö cema) sm. རྒྱུག་འགྲོའི་བྱེ་སྡོང་.

རྒྱུག་འགྲོའི་བྱེ་སྡོང་ (gyugdrö cedoŋ) shifting sand.

རྒྱུག: p. བརྒྱུགས་; f. བརྒྱུག་; imp. རྒྱུགས་ (gyuù) va. to run, to race ༡ ཞོགས་ལྟར་མི་ལི་གཉིས་ཙམ་རྒྱུག་གི་ཡོད་ས་རེད་ (They) run about two miles every morning. 2. va. to work for, to serve, to work as a servant ༡ མི་ཚང་འབྱོར་ལྡན་ཞིག་གི་གཡོག་པོ་རྒྱུགས་པ་རེད་ He served as a servant for a wealthy family. 3. vi. to sell, to move (in terms of sales) ༡ དཀར་ཡོལ་གྱི་དངོས་ཆས་དེ་ཚོ་རྒྱུག་གི་མིན་འདུག The chinaware is not selling. 4. vi. to flow, to circulate, to run (water, blood, etc.) ༡ གཙང་པོ་དེ་ལྷོ་ཕྱོགས་སུ་རྒྱུག་གི་ཡོད་པ་རེད་ The river runs south. 5. a test; va.—སྤྲོད་ to take a test; —ལེན་ to give a test.

རྒྱུག་ཁྲ་ (gyugdra) a surveyor's measuring pole.

རྒྱུག་ཆུ་ (gyugju) fast running stream.

རྒྱུག་ཅེ་བ་ (gyugjewa) fast-selling goods འདི་རྒྱུག་ཅེ་བའི་ཚོང་ཟོག་རེད་ This is a fast-selling commodity.

རྒྱུག་ཆེན་པོ་ (gyug cēmbo) sm. རྒྱུག་ཅེ་བ་.

རྒྱུག་མཆོང་ (gyugjoŋ) running and jumping; va.—བྱེད་.

རྒྱུག་རྟ་ (gyugda) race horse.

རྒྱུག་ཐང་ (gyugdaŋ) a stick with a tsamba bag that is carried by beggars.

རྒྱུག་དུམ་ (gyugdum) a short piece of wood/ stick.

རྒྱུག་དུས་ (gyugdüù) busy season ༡ དེང་སང་དགུན་ཁའི་ཚོང་ཟོག་རྒྱུག་དུས་རེད་ Nowadays is the busy season for (selling) winter goods.

རྒྱུག་ར་ (gyugdra) a fence or wall made of poles.

རྒྱུག་གདང་ (gyugdaŋ) railing (on stairs).

རྒྱུག་དུང་ (gyugduŋ) beating with a stick; vi.—ཐོབ་ to get beaten with a stgick; va.—གཏོང་ to beat with a stick.

རྒྱུག་པ་ (gyugba) cane, staff.

རྒྱུག་པ་འཁྲུག་ལངས་ (gyugbə trɔ̄glaŋ) disorder/ trouble/ problem caused by rumors.

རྒྱུག་པ་བྱི་རིལ་ (gyugbə cirii) lollipop.

རྒྱུག་པ་ལེབ་འདུར་ (gyugbə lebdur) without exceptions/ exemptions ༡ ཁྲལ་གསར་པ་འདི་གཞུང་གྲྭ་སེར་ཆོས་གསུམ་ཚང་མ་རྒྱུག་པ་ལེབ་འདུར་དུ་བསྐུལ་འདུག This new tax has been levied on all religious, government and aristocratic subjects without exceptions.

རྒྱུག་པོ་ (gyugbo) things that sell well, popular (in business), good sales ༡ ཟ་ཁང་འདི་རྒྱུག་པོ་ཡོད་པ་རེད་ This is a popular restaurant.

རྒྱུག་བྱེ་ (gyugje) shifting sand.

རྒྱུག་སྦོམ་ (gyugbom) dynamite stick.

རྒྱུག་མ་ (gyuŋma) sm. རྒྱུག་རྟ་.

རྒྱུག་མ་ཞལ་ངོ་ (gyuŋmə shɛɛŋo) shung. the person in charge of the horse race held after Monlam.

རྒྱུག་རྩལ་ (gyugdzɛɛ) 1. track event; va.—འགྲན་ to take part/ compete in track events. 2. shung. riding or running skill.

རྒྱུག་ཟམ་ (gyugsam) a plank or tree trunk used as a bridge.

རྒྱུག་གཟུགས་ཤུགས་རིག (gyugsuù shūgrii) fluid mechanics.

རྒྱུག་ཡིག (gyuùyii) cursive (writing style in Tibetan).

རྒྱུག་རིང་ (gyugriŋ) shung. the long distance race after Monlam.

རྒྱུག་རིལ་ (gyugrii) javelin; va.—དབྱུགས་ to throw the javelin.

རྒྱུག་ལམ་ (gyuglam) a track (for racing).

རྒྱུག་ཤད་ (gyugshɛɛ̀) comb; va.—རྒྱག to comb.

རྒྱུག་ཤན་པ་ (gyug shɛmba) shung. person who whips prisoners.

རྒྱུག་ཤར་ (gyugshar) running; va.—སློད་; —སློད་ to run, to race.

རྒྱུག་ཤུགས་ (gyugshuù) force of water current.

རྒྱུག་ཤུར་ (gyugshur) 1. wooden stick used in weaving. 2. the concave channel in which horses ran during the tt. ceremony when riders had to shoot at targets.

རྒྱུག་ཤེད་ (gyugsheè) running strength/ power.

རྒྱུག་སུག (gyugsuù) poking (a person or thing) with a stick; va.—གཏོང་.

རྒྱུག་ཧྲིལ་ (gyughrii) rolling pin.

རྒྱུག་ཧྲིང་ (gyughraŋ) vegetables becoming tall and hard ༡ པད་ཚལ་རྒྱུག་ཧྲིང་ཆགས་བཞག The cabbage has become tall and hard.

རྒྱུགས་ (gyuù) 1. imp. of རྒྱུག. 2. go away! 3. test, examination; va.—སྤྲོད་ to take a test/ exam; va.—ལེན་ to give a test; va.—ཐོན་ to pass a test/ exam.

རྒྱུགས་གྲངས་ (gyugdraŋ) examination marks/ grades.

རྒྱུགས་གྲལ་ (gyugdrɛɛ) a line of people attending an exam.

རྒྱུགས་འགྲོ་ (gyugdro) va. to run.

རྒྱུགས་གཅལ་ (gyugjɛɛ) shung. laying sticks to make a floor; va.—སྒྲིག.

རྒྱུགས་ཆུང་སློད་ (gyugjuŋ lȫȍ) va. to run at a slow speed.

རྒྱུགས་ཆེན་ (gyugjen) final examination; va.—ལེན་ to give a final examination; va.—སྤྲོད་ to take a final exam.

རྒྱུགས་ངོ་བཀོད་ (gyuùdo gȍȍ) va. to present oneself for an examination, to register oneself for an examination.

རྒྱུགས་འདུར་ཀོད་ (gyugdur gȍȍ) way of running fast (like a wolf).

རྒྱུགས་དཔོན་ (gyugbön) person in charge of a test, test master/ proctor.

རྒྱུགས་སྤྲོད་ (gyug drȍȍ) va. to take an examination.

རྒྱུགས་སྤྲོད་བྱེད་ (gyugdrȍȍ ceè) sm. རྒྱུགས་སྤྲོད་.

རྒྱུགས་སྤྲོད་ཡི་གེ་ (gyugdrȍȍ yigi) examination paper.

རྒྱུགས་སྤྲོད་སློབ་གྲྭ་བ་ (gyugdrȍȍ lōbdrawa) sm. རྒྱུགས་འབུལ་སློབ་མ་.

རྒྱུགས་ཕྱིན་ (gyugjin) p. of རྒྱུགས་འགྲོ་.

རྒྱུགས་འཕྲོད་ (gyug trȍȍ) vi. to pass an examination (oral or written).

རྒྱུགས་འཕྲོད་རིམ་པ་ (gyugtrȍȍ rimbə) ranking of grades on an examination.

རྒྱུགས་འབུལ་ (gyug büü) h. of རྒྱུགས་སྤྲོད་.

རྒྱུགས་འབུལ་ཡི་གེ་ (gyugbüü yigi) examination paper (h.).

རྒྱུགས་འབུལ་སློབ་མ་ (gyugbüü lōbma) candidate for an examination, examinee.

རྒྱུགས་མ་འདུར་ (gyug madur) neither galloping nor going slowly.

རྒྱུགས་མ་འཕྲོད་ (gyug madrȍȍ) vi. to fail an exam.

རྒྱུགས་ཚད་ (gyugdzɛɛ̀) sm. རྒྱུགས་, 3.

རྒྱུགས་གཞི་ (gyugshi) sm. རྒྱུགས་ཡིག.

རྒྱུགས་བཞེས་ (gyug shɛɛ̀) h. of རྒྱུགས་ལེན་.

རྒྱུགས་ཡིག (gyugyiì) examination/ test paper.

རྒྱུགས་ཡིག་དཔྱད་བསྡུར་ (gyugyiì jɛɛ̀dur) grading examination papers; va.—བྱེད་.

རྒྱུགས་ལེན་ (gyuùlen) giving an examination/ test; va. རྒྱུགས་ལེན་; —བྱེད་.

རྒྱུགས་ལེན་འཛུགས་སྐད་ (gyuùlen gugdüù) test/ exam for entrance to a school or a job; va.—བྱེད་.

རྒྱུགས་ལེན་དུས་ཚོད་ (gyuùlen tüüdzöò) exam period.

རྒྱུགས་ལེན་འདེམས་སྒྲུག (gyuùlen demdruù) testing and selection; va.—བྱེད་.

རྒྱུགས་ལེན་མིང་གདངས་ (gyuùlen miŋdaà) imperial examination in China.

རྒྱུགས་ལེན་ཡི་གེ་ (gyuùlen yīgi) test paper, examination paper.

རྒྱུགས་ལེན་ར་བ་ (gyuùlen rawa) examination room/ place.

རྒྱུགས་ལེན་ས་ (gyūù lensa) sm. རྒྱུགས་ལེན་ར་བ་.

རྒྱུགས་ཤར་ (gyuù shār) sm. རྒྱུག་ཤར་.

རྒྱུགས་ཤོག (gyuùshoò) exam paper.

རྒྱུངས་པ་ (gyuŋbə) spinal cord.

རྒྱུད་: p. **བརྒྱུས་**; f. **བརྒྱུ་**; imp. **རྒྱུས་** (gyüü) va. to string/ thread a needle ¶ཁབ་སྐུད་པ་རྒྱུད་ཀྱི་འདུག He is threading a needle.

རྒྱུད་ (gyüü) 1. character, trait, nature ¶མི་འདི་གཤིས་རྒྱུད་བཟང་པོ་འདུག That man's character is good. 2. bank, shore, coast, edge, side, range ¶རྒྱ་མཚོའི་རྒྱུད་ཀྱི་གྲོང་ཁྱེར་ Coastal cities. ¶ཆུ་བོའི་རྒྱུད་དུ་ On the banks of the river. ¶རི་རྒྱུད་ Mountain range. 3. tantra ¶མདོ་རྒྱུད་ Sutra and tantra. 4. lineage, descent line ¶ཁོང་རྒྱལ་པོའི་རྒྱུད་རེད་ He is descended from kings. 5. string (e.g., of a musical instrument).

རྒྱུད་སྐུད་ (gyüügüü) string (e.g., of a musical instrument).

རྒྱུད་སྐུལ་ (gyüügüü) entreating, appealing, inciting, encouraging; va.—བྱེད་ to entreat/ appeal/ encourage ¶རོགས་རམ་གྱི་རྒྱུད་སྐུལ་བྱས་པ་རེད་ (He) appealed for aid. ¶སྐབས་དེར་བཙན་རྒྱལ་རིང་ལུགས་པའི་རྒྱུད་སྐུལ་འོག At that time, due to the urging of the imperialists.

རྒྱུད་བསྐུལ་ (gyüügüü) sm. རྒྱུད་སྐུལ་.

རྒྱུད་ཁང་ (gyüügaŋ) a house owned by one of the two tantric colleges in Lhasa.

རྒྱུད་འཁྲིད་ (gyüü trii) vi. to inherit characteristics ¶ཕྲུ་གུ་འདི་གཟུགས་པོ་ཆེན་པོ་ཡོད་པ་དེ་པ་ཕའི་རྒྱུད་འཁྲིད་པ་རེད་ This child's tallness was inherited from his father.

རྒྱུད་གྱོང་པོ་ (gyüü gyoŋbo) rough/ brutal/ hardheaded in character or nature.

རྒྱུད་གྲྭ་ (gyüüdra) monastery/ college specializing in tantric studies, tantric college (in a monastery).

རྒྱུད་གྲྭ་སྟོད་སྨད་ (gyüüdra döömeè) the upper and lower tantric colleges in Lhasa.

རྒྱུད་རྒྱང་གཉེན་ཚན་ (gyüügyaŋ ñɛndzɛn) distant relative.

རྒྱུད་ལྔ་ (gyüüŋa) shung. the five realms of beings/ rebirths: beings in hell, animals, hungry ghosts, humans, and gods.

རྒྱུད་གཅིག་པ་ (gyüü jĩgbə) 1. (of the) same clan, lineage, ancestry. 2. same character or personality. 3. an instrument with only a single string.

རྒྱུད་ཆགས་ (gyüü cãà) vi. to conceive, to be/ get pregnant.

རྒྱུད་གཉིས་ (gyüü ñĩi) paternal and maternal lineages/ relatives.

རྒྱུད་འདྲེས་ (gyündreè) crossbreed, crossbreeding, hybridization; va.—བྱེད་ to crossbreed, to hybridize.

རྒྱུད་འདྲེས་ཆུ་འབྲས་ (gyündreè cündrɛɛ̀) hybrid wet paddy rice.

རྒྱུད་འདྲེས་སྡེབ་སྦྱོར་ (gyündreè debjɔɔ) crossbreeding, hybridization.

རྒྱུད་འདྲེས་ཕྲུ་གུ་ (gyündreè trũgu) hybrid/ or mixed race children.

རྒྱུད་འདྲེས་སྦྱོར་སྡེབ་ (gyündreè jɔɔdeb) crossbreeding, hybridization.

རྒྱུད་འདྲེས་ལུག (gyündreè luù) hybrid sheep.

རྒྱུད་འདྲེས་ལེགས་བཅོས་ (gyündreè legjöö) improving via crossbreeding/ hybridization.

རྒྱུད་འདྲེས་སོན་གསོ་ (gyündreè sõnso) method/ process of producing hybrid seeds.

རྒྱུད་ལྡན་རོལ་ཆ་ (gyündɛn rööja) stringed instruments.

རྒྱུད་ལྡན་རོལ་མོ་ (gyündɛn rööma) music by a stringed instruments.

རྒྱུད་སྡེ་ (gyüüde) 1. tantra section/ part. 2. the 18 tantras of Mahayoga.

རྒྱུད་སྡེ་གོང་མ་ (gyüüde koŋma) the yoga and annuttarayoga tantras.

རྒྱུད་སྡེ་བཞི་ (gyüüde shi) the four sections/ classes of tantra: kriya tantra, carya tantra, yoga tantra, annuttarayoga tantra.

རྒྱུད་སྡེ་འོག་མ་ (gyüüde wɔɔma) the kriya and carya tantra.

རྒྱུད་པ་ (gyüübə) lineage, race, breed, species; vi.—འཕེལ་ to multiply/ increase by breeding ¶ལུང་པ་འདིའི་ནང་ལ་རྟ་བཟང་པོའི་རྒྱུད་པ་འཕེལ་བཞག In this area the good breed of horses has multiplied.

རྒྱུད་པ་གྲྭ་ཚང་ (gyüübə tradzaŋ) sm. རྒྱུད་གྲྭ་.

རྒྱུད་སྤེལ་ (gyüübel) 1. breeding, producing offspring; va.—བྱེད་ ¶ཕག་པ་མང་པོ་རྒྱུད་སྤེལ་བྱས་སོང་ They bred many pigs.

རྒྱུད་སྤེལ་ས་ཚིགས་ (gyüübel sədzii) breeding station.

རྒྱུད་སྤེལ་ར་བ་ (gyüübel rawa) breeding ground.

རྒྱུད་འཕེལ་ (gyüüpel) sm. རྒྱུད་པ་.

རྒྱུད་འབྲེལ་སྤུན་མཆེད་ (gyündree bũnceè) collateral relatives.

རྒྱུད་མང་ (gyüümaŋ) many-stringed instruments.

རྒྱུད་མང་བཞི་སྦྲེལ་ (gyüümaŋ shidree) string quartet.

རྒྱུད་མང་རོལ་ཆ་ (gyüümaŋ rööca) sm. རྒྱུད་མང་.

རྒྱུད་མངས་ (gyüümaŋ) sm. རྒྱུད་མང་.

རྒྱུད་གཙང་ (gyüüdzaŋ) thoroughbred, pure blood.

རྒྱུད་ཙ་ (gyüüdza) offspring, descendants; vi.—ཆད་ to have a lineage die out.

རྒྱུད་ཚིག (gyüü tsĩi) vi. to be angry/ agitated.

རྒྱུད་འཛར་ (gyünjar) sm. རྒྱུད་ཙ་.

རྒྱུད་འཛིན་ (gyündzin) 1. inheriting, succeeding; va.—བྱེད་ to inherit a status/ role ¶རྒྱུད་འཛིན་དབང་ཆ་ Hereditary rule/ power. 2. successor ¶ཁོང་བླ་མ་དེའི་རྒྱུད་འཛིན་གྱི་སློབ་མ་རེད་ He is the lama's successor (disciple).

རྒྱུད་འཛིན་གྱི་རང་བཞིན་ (gyündzingi rəŋshin) heredity.

རྒྱུད་འཛིན་གྱི་རིག་པ་ (gyündzingi rigba) the study or field of hereditary/ genetics.

རྒྱུད་འཛིན་རྒྱལ་ལྡན་ལམ་ལུགས་ (gyündzin gyɛndɛn ləmluù) system of hereditary monarchy.

རྒྱུད་འཛིན་རྒྱལ་པོའི་སྲིད་གཞུང་ (gyündzin gyɛɛbö sĩishuŋ) hereditary monarchy.

རྒྱུད་འཛིན་དཔོན་གནས་ (gyündzin bõnnɛɛ̀) an inherited official position.

རྒྱུད་འཛིན་བློན་པོ་ (gyündzin lõmbo) hereditary minister.

རྒྱུད་འཛིན་དབང་ཆ་ (gyündzin wãŋja) hereditary power/ authority.

རྒྱུད་བཞི་ (gyüüshi) the name of the basic Tibetan medical text.

རྒྱུད་བཟང་ (gyüüsaŋ) good stock/ lineage, a fine or good breed.

རྒྱུད་བཟང་ཕྱུགས་གསོ་ར་བ་ (gyüüsaŋ cũgso rawa) animal breeding farm.

རྒྱུད་བཟང་གསོ་སྤེལ་ས་ཚིགས་ (gyüüsaŋ sõbel sədzii) breeding station.

རྒྱུད་རབས་ (gyüürəb) pedigree, genealogy.

རྒྱུད་རབས་དེབ་ཐེར་ (gyüürəb tebder) book of pedigrees.

རྒྱུད་རིམ་ (gyüürim) stage in a sequence/ line.

རྒྱུད་རིམ་ལྡན་པ་ (gyüürim dɛmba) systematic, methodical.

རྒྱུད་ལ་ (gyüüla) around, in the vicinity of ¶ལུང་པ་ཕ་གིའི་རྒྱུད་ལ་རི་དྭགས་མང་པོ་ཡོད་པ་རེད་ There are many animals around that place.

རྒྱུད་གསུམ་མ་ (gyüü sũmma) three-stringed (for instruments) ¶སྒྲ་སྙན་རྒྱུད་གསུམ་མ་ Three-stringed lute.

རྒྱུད་སློབ་ (gyüülob) disciple.

རྒྱུན་ (gyün) 1. continuity, continuously ¶རྒྱུད་བཟང་འཕེལ་བའི་རྒྱུན་ The continuity of increasing good stock. 2. duration, period, time ¶ཁྱེད་རང་འདིར་བཞུགས་རྒྱུན་རིང་ During the time of your stay here. ¶རྒྱུན་རིང་བསྒུགས་པ་ཡིན་ (I) waited for a long time. 3. usual, customary ¶སློབ་གྲྭ་འདིའི་ནང་བོད་ཡིག་སློབ་རྒྱུན་འདུག It is customary to teach Tibetan in this school. 4. oral ¶ཁ་རྒྱུན་ Oral tradition.

རྒྱུན་བཀག་མཆོད་མེ་ (gyüngaà cõõme) a butter lamp that burns continuously.

རྒྱུན་བཀོལ་ཞབས་འབྲིང་ (gyüngöö shəmdriŋ) servants

who serve permanently.

རྒྱུན་སྐྱོང་ (gyüngyoŋ) maintaining, perpetuating, keeping up; va. རྒྱུན་སྐྱོང་; —བྱེད་ ¶ཁོ་ཚོས་དྲང་བདེན་རྒྱུན་སྐྱོང་བྱེད་ཀྱི་ཡོད་པ་རེད་ (They) are keeping up their support for the just struggle.

རྒྱུན་ཁྲིགས་ (gyündrig) sm. རྒྱུན་ཁྲིགས་སུ་.

རྒྱུན་ཁྲིགས་སུ་ (gyün trigsu) continuously, one after another, without a break ¶ཁོང་གིས་རྒྱུན་ཁྲིགས་སུ་སློབ་སྦྱོང་བྱེད་ཀྱི་ཡོད་པ་རེད་ He studies continuously.

རྒྱུན་མཁོ་ (gyüngo) 1. daily/ everyday needs. 2. applied.

རྒྱུན་མཁོ་དངོས་རྫས་ཚོང་ཁང་ (gyüngö ŋöödzɛɛ̀ tsöŋgaŋ) store that sells daily necessities.

རྒྱུན་མཁོའི་དངོས་རྫས་ (gyüngö ŋöödzɛɛ̀) daily necessities, things used everyday.

རྒྱུན་མཁོའི་རྩིས་རིག (gyüngö dziirii) applied mathematics.

རྒྱུན་མཁོའི་རྫས་དཀར་ (gyüngö dzɛɛ̀gar) porcelain for everyday use.

རྒྱུན་མཁོའི་ཤེས་བྱ་ (gyüngö shēèja) sm. རྒྱུན་མཁོའི་རྩིས་རིག.

རྒྱུན་མཁོའི་ཤེས་རིག (gyüngö shēèrig) common/ everyday/ applied knowledge.

རྒྱུན་འཁོར་ (gyüngɔɔ) rotating, revolving, circulating.

རྒྱུན་འཁོར་མ་རྩ་ (gyüngɔɔ madza) circulation/ rotating/ revolving capital.

རྒྱུན་འཁྱོང་ (gyün kyöŋ) vi. to be able to keep up/ continue/ perpetuate/ endure; va. རྒྱུན་མ་འཁྱོང་; —བྱེད་; —གཏོང་ to continue, to perpetuate, to keep up, to endure ¶ཁོས་སློབ་སྦྱོང་རྒྱུན་མ་འཁྱོངས་པ་རེད་ He could not continue his studies. ¶བོད་ཀྱི་སྔར་ཡོད་ཆབ་སྲིད་ལམ་ལུགས་རྒྱུན་འཁྱོང་བྱེད་རྒྱུ་ Perpetuating the past political system in Tibet. ¶ཡུལ་ནང་ཞི་བདེ་རྒྱུན་འཁྱོང་བ་ཞིག་ཡོང་ཐབས་སུ་ In order to achieve an enduring peace in the country. ¶སྦྱོང་བརྡར་རྒྱུན་འཁྱོང་ Continuous training.

རྒྱུན་འཁྲིགས་སུ་ (gyün trigsu) sm. རྒྱུན་ཆད་མེད་པར་.

རྒྱུན་གོས་ (gyüngöö) everyday clothes.

རྒྱུན་གོས་གྱོན་པའི་ཉེན་རྟོག་པ་ (gyungöö kyönbɛ ñendogba) plainclothes police.

རྒྱུན་འགག (gyün gaà) vi. to be constipated.

རྒྱུན་འགྲེམས་ (gyündrem) shung. sth. that is hung/ displayed all the time.

རྒྱུན་འགྲོ་ (gyündro) daily, recurring ¶རྒྱུན་འགྲོའི་མ་དངུལ་ Daily expenses.

རྒྱུན་སྒྲོག་རྒྱག (gyündroò gyaà) va. to tie up loads with leather straps.

རྒྱུན་ངན་ (gyünŋɛn) a bad tradition.

རྒྱུན་གཅིག (gyünjig) 1. continuously ¶ལམ་ལུགས་དེ་ལོ་མང་རིང་རྒྱུན་གཅིག་ཏུ་དར་ཡོད་པ་རེད་ That system has spread continuously for many years. 2. single strand/ string.

རྒྱུན་བཅངས་ (gyünjaŋ) continuously holding on to or keeping in mind; va.—བྱེད་ ¶ཁྱེད་རང་གི་བཀྲིན་དའི་སེམས་ནང་རྒྱུན་བཅངས་བྱེད་ཀྱི་ཡོད་ I continuously keep your kindness in mind.

རྒྱུན་ལྕག (gyünjaà) leather whip.

རྒྱུན་ཆགས་ (gyün cāà) vi. to be continuous/ unbroken/ uninterrupted.

རྒྱུན་ཆང་ (gyünjaŋ) regular/ everyday beer.

རྒྱུན་ཆད་ (gyün cɛɛ̀) vi. to be interrupted/ broken off/ cut off/ not continuous ¶སློབ་ཁྲིད་ཀྱི་རྒྱུན་ཆད་ནས་ཟླ་བ་གསུམ་སོང་བ་རེད་ Three months have passed since my teaching was interrupted.

རྒྱུན་ཆས་ (gyünjɛɛ̀) regular/ everyday clothes, standard uniform.

རྒྱུན་མཆོད་ (gyünjöö) offerings that are made all the time/ daily (to gods).

རྒྱུན་ཇ་ (gyünja) regular/ everyday tea.

རྒྱུན་འཛགས་ (gyün jaà) 1. sm. རྒྱུན་གཏན་. 2. vi. to maintain/ preserve/ perpetuate a custom or tradition for a long time ¶བོད་ཀྱི་ཁྲིམས་སྲོལ་མ་ཉམས་རྒྱུན་འཛགས་ To preserve Tibet's legal tradition without decline.

རྒྱུན་ལྗང་རྩི་ཤིང་ (gyünjaŋ dzīshiŋ) evergreen plant.

རྒྱུན་ཉར་ (gyünñar) regular, standing ¶རྒྱུན་ཉར་དམག་དཔུང་ Regular standing army.

རྒྱུན་གཏན་ (gyündɛn) usual, normal, regular, at all times ¶ཁོའི་རྒྱུན་གཏན་ལས་ཀ་ His normal work ¶རྒྱུན་གཏན་ཁོ་གྲོང་ཁྱེར་ནང་ལ་སྡོད་པ་རེད་ He normally lives in the city.

རྒྱུན་གཏན་གྱི་རྣམ་པ་ (gyündɛngi nāmba) sm. རྒྱུན་ལུགས་.

རྒྱུན་གཏན་ལྟར་ (gyündɛndar) as usual, as normal ¶རྒྱུན་གཏན་ལྟར་བྱས་ན་ If (I) do as (I) normally would.

རྒྱུན་གཏན་ཚོང་འབྲེལ་ (gyündɛn tsōdree)permanent/ regular/ normal trade relations.

རྒྱུན་གཏན་བཞིན་ (gyündɛnshin) as usual, as normal.

རྒྱུན་གཏན་ལམ་ལུགས་ (gyündɛn ləmluù) usual/ normal/ everyday custom.

རྒྱུན་གཏོར་ (gyündɔr) torma that are offered all the time/ daily.

རྒྱུན་ལྟར་ (gyündar) sm. རྒྱུན་གཏན་བཞིན་.

རྒྱུན་ལྟར་མ་ཡིན་པ་ (gyündar məyimbə) not usual/ normal/ regular, abnormal.

རྒྱུན་ལྟོ་ (gyündo) 1. ordinary/ regular/ everyday food. 2. a common occurrence.

རྒྱུན་ལྟོར་འགྲོ་ (gyündɔr dro) vi. to become ordinary/ regular/ customary ¶འགོ་ཁྲིད་དེས་རྟག་པར་གཤེ་གཤེ་གཏོང་བ་དེ་རྒྱུན་ལྟོར་ཕྱིན་ནས་བརྩི་མཁན་མེད་པ་རེད་ The constant scolding of the boss has become ordinary so no one pays attention to it.

རྒྱུན་མཐུད་ (gyündüü) continuous, perpetual, persistent ¶ལོ་བརྒྱད་ཙམ་སློབ་གྲྭར་རྒྱུན་མཐུད་ཕྱིན་པ་རེད་ (He) went to school continuously for eight years.

རྒྱུན་མཐུད་ངང་ (gyündüüŋaŋ) continuously, perpetually, persistently; va.—གཏོང་.

རྒྱུན་མཐུད་རང་བཞིན་ (gyündüü rəŋshin) sm. འབྲེལ་ཆགས་རང་བཞིན་.

རྒྱུན་མཐུད་ལས་སྒྲུབ་ (gyündüü lɛɛ̀drub) assembly line type of production.

རྒྱུན་མཐུད་ལས་རིམ་ (gyündüü lɛɛ̀rim) sm. རྒྱུན་མཐུད་ལས་སྒྲུབ་.

རྒྱུན་མཐོང་ (gyündoŋ) commonly seen.

རྒྱུན་མཐོང་དངོས་པོ་ (gyündoŋ ŋööbo) (things) commonly seen.

རྒྱུན་དུ་ (gyündu) always, at all times, continuously ¶ང་རྒྱུན་དུ་ལུས་རྩལ་བྱེད་ཀྱི་ཡོད་ I always exercise.

རྒྱུན་དྲུང་ (gyündruŋ) permanent/ standing secretary.

རྒྱུན་ལྡན་ (gyündɛn) sm. རྒྱུན་གཏན་.

རྒྱུན་ལྡན་གྱི་གཞུང་དོན་ (gyündɛngi shundön) routine or daily office work.

རྒྱུན་ལྡན་ལྟར་ (gyündɛndar) sm. རྒྱུན་གཏན་བཞིན་.

རྒྱུན་ལྡན་དུ་འགྱུར་ (gyündɛndu gyur) vi. to normalize, to become normal/ customary/ usual/ habitual ¶ཁོང་གིས་ཨ་རག་འཐུང་རྒྱུ་དེ་རྒྱུན་ལྡན་དུ་གྱུར་བཞག His drinking alcohol became habitual.

རྒྱུན་སྡོད་ (gyündöö) permanent resident, permanently stationed.

རྒྱུན་སྡོད་མི་གྲངས་ (gyündöö midraŋ) permanent residents.

རྒྱུན་ནད་ (gyünnɛɛ̀) chronic disease.

རྒྱུན་ནས་ (gyünnɛɛ̀) (— + neg. vb.) emphatic negative (not at all, never) ¶འདི་ངས་རྒྱུན་ནས་མ་བྱས་ I never did this.

རྒྱུན་ནུ་ (gyünnu) sm. རྒྱུན་དུ་.

རྒྱུན་གནས་ (gyünnɛɛ̀) existing continuously/ permanently ¶རྒྱུན་གནས་དམག་དཔུང་ Permanent army.

རྒྱུན་པ་ (gyümba) 1. always, at all times ¶ཁོང་རྒྱུན་པར་ས་གནས་འདིར་བཞུགས་ཀྱི་མེད་པ་རེད་ He doesn't always stay here. 2. monks who pray while the deceased is kept in the house.

རྒྱུན་པ་འཛིན་པ་ (gyümba dzimbə) sm. རྒྱུན་འཛིན་.

རྒྱུན་སྤྱོད་ (gyünjöö) sm. རྒྱུ་མཁོ་.

རྒྱུན་སྤྱོད་སྐད་ཆ་ (gyünjöö gɛɛ̀ja) everyday language.

རྒྱུན་སྤྱོད་ཡིག་རིགས་ (gyünjöö yigrii) the normal

heading of letters and documents.

རྒྱུན་ཕྱོགས་ (gyünjɔ̀ɔ) with the current of a river.

རྒྱུན་བུ་ (gyümbu) rawhide string/ strap/ rope.

རྒྱུན་བུ་ཀོ་འདྲེག (gyünbu gōndreè) 1. rawhide string/ rope made by cutting thin strips of leather. 2. giving one's possession as an offering [Lit. cutting rawhide strips from a skin].

རྒྱུན་འབྱམས་ (gyünjam) a practice/ habit/ custom (usu. bad) spreading and becoming habitual.

རྒྱུན་འབྱམས་ཀྱི་སྐྱོན་ཆ་ (gyünjamgi gyōnja) corrupt or evil practices that have become habitual/ chronic/ usual.

རྒྱུན་མ་ཆད་པར་ (gyün macɛɛ̀bar) sm. རྒྱུན་ཆད་མེད་པར་.

རྒྱུན་མར་ (gyünmar) 1. sm. རྒྱུན་ཆད་མེད་པར་. 2. everyday butter.

རྒྱུན་མི་ཆད་པར་ (gyün micɛɛ̀bar) sm. རྒྱུན་ཆད་མེད་པར་.

རྒྱུན་བཙུགས་ (gyün dzüù) va. to set up sth. to be done regularly/ continuously/ permanently ། ཁོང་གིས་དགོན་པའི་ནང་མང་ཇ་གཏོང་རྒྱུན་བཙུགས་པ་རེད་ He set up (a fund) to have tea served at the monastery's prayer sessions regularly.

རྒྱུན་རྩ་ (gyündza) regular/ normal pulse.

རྒྱུན་ཚུགས་ (gyündzuù) sm. རྒྱུན་གནས་.

རྒྱུན་ཚུལ་ (gyündzüü) normality, normal custom/ condition.

རྒྱུན་ཚོགས་ (gyündzoò) 1. standing committee. 2. regular meeting.

རྒྱུན་འཛིན་ (gyündzin) 1. persistence, maintenance, continuity; va.—བྱེད་ to persist, to maintain, to continue ། ཧན་རྒྱལ་རབས་ཀྱི་དུས་ནས་རྒྱུན་འཛིན་བྱས་པའི་ཏའི་ཙའོ་ཆོས་ལུགས་ The Tao religion which has persisted since the Han dynasty. 2. sm. རྒྱུད་འཛིན་.

རྒྱུན་འཛིན་གྱི་རྒྱུན་གྲངས་ (gyündzingi gyēndraŋ) genetic factor.

རྒྱུན་འཛིན་པ་ (gyündzinbə) successor.

རྒྱུན་འཛིན་བཟོ་སྐྲུན་ (gyündzin sodrün) genetic engineering.

རྒྱུན་འཛིན་རིག་པ་ (gyündzin rigbə) study of genetics/ heredity.

རྒྱུན་འཛུགས (gyündzuù) sm. རྒྱུན་གནས་.

རྒྱུན་བཞུགས་ (gyünshuù) h. of རྒྱུན་སྡོད་.

རྒྱུན་བཞུགས་སྐུ་ཚབ་ (gyünshuù gūdzəb) permanent representative.

རྒྱུན་ཟས་ (gyünsɛɛ̀) regular/ usual food.

རྒྱུན་ཟིན་ (gyünsin) shung. to be consistent ། གོང་འཕེལ་ལོ་རེ་ནས་ལོ་རེ་འགྲོ་པའི་རྒྱུན་ཟིན་མཇུག་མཐོན་ཞུ་རྒྱུ་ One should consistently make progress year by year.

རྒྱུན་བཟང་ (gyünsaŋ) good tradition/ custom.

རྒྱུན་རིང་ (gyünriŋ) long time ། རྒྱུན་རིང་མཇལ་ཡོད་པ་མ་རེད་ (We) have not met for a long time.

རྒྱུན་རིང་པོ་ (gyün riŋbu) sm. རྒྱུན་རིང་.

རྒྱུན་རིམ་ (gyünrim) timetable, schedule.

རྒྱུན་ལམ་ (gyünlam) sm. རྒྱུན་སྲོལ་.

རྒྱུན་ལས་ (gyünlɛɛ̀) 1. standing committee. 2. permanent work.

རྒྱུན་ལས་སྐུ་ཚབ་ (gyünlɛɛ̀ gūdzəb) representative of a standing committee.

རྒྱུན་ལས་ལས་འཛིན་ (gyünlɛɛ̀ lɛ̱ndzin) permanent staff.

རྒྱུན་ལས་ཨུ་ཡོན་ (gyünlɛɛ̀ ūyön) member of a standing committee.

རྒྱུན་ལས་ལྷན་ཚོགས་ (gyünlɛɛ̀ lɛ̄ndzoò) standing committee.

རྒྱུན་ལས་ཨུ་ཡོན་ལྷན་ཁང་ (gyünlɛɛ̀ ūyön lhɛ̄ngaŋ) standing committee.

རྒྱུན་ལུགས་ (gyünluù) normal/ traditional way of doing sth.

རྒྱུན་ལུགས་ལྡན་པ་ (gyünluù dɛ̱mba) calm and at ease.

རྒྱུན་ལོ་ (gyünlo) non leap year.

རྒྱུན་ཤིང་ (gyünshiŋ) fuel/ wood that is used all the time, fuel for everyday use.

རྒྱུན་ཤིང་ཤིང་གཉེར་ (gyünshiŋ shīŋñer) shung. traditional Tibetan Government official in charge of firewood for everyday use.

རྒྱུན་ཤིང་ཤིང་གཉེར་ལས་ཁུངས་ (gyünshiŋ shīŋñer lɛ̱ɛ̀guŋ) shung. the office in charge of fuel for everyday use.

རྒྱུན་ཤེས་ (gyünsheè) common/ everyday/ ordinary knowledge, common sense.

རྒྱུན་གཤིས་ (gyünshiì) character, nature.

རྒྱུན་སྲིད་ (gyünsiì) sm. རྒྱུན་བསྲིང་.

རྒྱུན་སྲོལ་ (gyünsöö) tradition, convention, custom, normal procedure ། རྒྱུན་སྲོལ་རང་ལ་བརྟེན་ནས་མ་གཏོགས་འགྲོ་མི་ཤེས་མཁན་ One who cannot do things except by following what is traditional.

རྒྱུན་སྲོལ་དོར་ (gyünsöö tɔ̱ɔ) va. to break or eliminate a rule/ custom/ convention.

རྒྱུན་སྲོལ་མཚོན་ཆ་ (gyünsöö tsōnja) conventional weapon.

རྒྱུན་བསྲིང་ (gyünsiŋ) continuously ། ལས་ཀ་རྒྱུན་བསྲིང་བྱེད་དགོས་ (You) have to work continuously.

རྒྱུན་བསྲིང་དམག་འཐབ་ (gyünsiŋ māgdəb) protracted warfare.

རྒྱུན་ཨུད་ (gyünüü) sm. རྒྱུན་ལས་ཨུ་ཡོན་ལྷན་ཁང་.

རྒྱུའི་གཙོ་བོ་ (gyüü dzōwo) basic element.

རྒྱུས་ (gyüü) 1. familiarity, knowledge, being well acquainted ། གནས་དེ་ང་ལ་རྒྱུས་མེད་ I am not familiar with that area.

རྒྱུས་མངའ་ (gyüü ŋā) 1. sm. རྒྱུས་, 1. 2. imp. of རྒྱུ་. 3. རྒྱུ་ + inst.

རྒྱུས་ཅན་ (gyüüjɛn) knowledgeable, familiar.

རྒྱུས་སྟོན་ (gyüüdön) a guide, guiding; va.—བྱེད་ to guide ། ང་ལ་ལམ་ཁ་རྒྱུས་སྟོན་ཞིག་དགོས་ I need a guide for the trip.

རྒྱུས་འཕྱིངས་ (gyüüdiŋ) knowing/ understanding/ comprehending well.

རྒྱུས་གནད་ (gyüünɛɛ̀) 1. important knowledge. 2. important tendons/ muscles.

རྒྱུས་པ་ (gyüüba) muscle, sinew, tendon.

རྒྱུས་མེད་ (gyüümeè) having no knowledge/ familiarity ། དེའི་སྐོར་ང་ལ་རྒྱུས་མེད་ I have no knowledge regarding that matter.

རྒྱུས་མེད་ཅན་ (gyüümeèjɛn) not familiar, unfamiliar, not knowing.

རྒྱུས་ཤིབ་ཡོད་པ་ (gyüüshub yö̱öba) being familiar, knowing the situation.

རྒྱུས་ཡོད་ (gyüüyöö) 1. knowledge, familiarity ། ཁོ་ལ་ས་གནས་དེ་ཚོའི་ཞིང་ལས་སྐོར་རྒྱུས་ཡོད་ཆེན་པོ་ཡོད་པ་རེད་ He has a great deal of knowledge about agriculture in those areas. 2. va.—བྱེད་ to act as a guide, to show someone around ། གྲོང་འཁྱེར་ནང་ཁོས་རྒྱུས་ཡོད་བྱས་བྱུང་ He showed (me) around the city.

རྒྱུས་རུས་ (gyüürüü) muscle and bone.

རྒྱུས་ལེན་ (gyüü le̱n) 1. va. to test to see if sb. knows sth. 2. va. to get knowledge of, to get to be familiar with.

རྒྱུས་ལོན་ (gyüü lö̱n) vi. to come to have knowledge of, to be familiar with, to come to know intimately.

རྒྱོ་ (gyo̱) sexual intercourse, copulation; va.—རྒྱག.

རྒྱོ་: p. བརྒྱོས་; f. རྒྱོ་; imp. རྒྱོས་ (gyo̱) va. to have sexual intercourse, to copulate.

རྒྱོང་: p. བརྒྱངས་; f. བརྒྱང་; imp. རྒྱོངས་ (gyo̱ŋ) 1. to stretch/ extend ། ཀོ་བ་ས་སྟེང་བརྒྱངས་ནས་ཟླ་བ་གཅིག་བཞག་སོང་ They stretched the leather on the ground and left it for a month. 2. va. to fill up, to stuff ། ཐུལ་ཀྱི་ནང་ལ་སྔས་བལ་བརྒྱངས་བཞག (They) stuffed the pillow with cotton.

རྒྱོང་སྐུད་ (gyo̱ŋgüü) the strings that are used to tie (stretch) a canvas to its frame (when painting thankas).

རྒྱོང་ཁང་ (gyo̱ŋgaŋ) the wooden frame that is used for thanka painting.

རྒྱོང་འགོ་ (gyo̱ŋgo) shoe tree.

རྒྱོང་སྒྲོམ་ (gyo̱ŋdrom) sm. རྒྱོང་ཁང་.

རྒྱོང་ཤིང་ (gyo̱ŋshiŋ) sm. རྒྱོང་ཁང་.

རྒྱོང་གཤར་ (gyo̱ŋshar) basting (in sewing); va.—རྒྱག.

རྒྱོངས་ (gyo̱ŋ) imp. of རྒྱངས་.

རྒྱོབ་ (gyo̱b) sm. རྒྱོབས་.

རྒྱོབས་ (gyo̱b) imp. of རྒྱག.

རྒྱོབས་ཟེར་ན་པ་མགོ་ལ་རྒྱག སོང་ཟེར་ན་དམྱལ་བར་འགྲོ་ (gyo̱b se̱rna pāgola gyaà sõŋ se̱rna ñɛlaa dro̱) to obey someone's order absolutely [Lit. if one is ordered to hit, hit one's father's head; if one is ordered to go, go to hell].

རྒྱོས་ (gyö̱ö) imp. རྒྱོ་.

སྒ་ (ga̱) 1. sm. སྒ་. 2. ginger.

སྒ་སྐྱ་ (gagya) sm. སྒ་སྐྱ་.

སྒ་སྨུག (gəmuù) ginger.

སྒ་སེར་ (gaser) sm. སྒ་སེར་.

སྒང་རྒྱང་རུ་ཁག (gaŋgyaŋ ru̱gaà) ball team.

སྒང་པ་ (ga̱ŋba) sm. སྒང་བུ་.

སྒང་པའི་གཉན་ཚད་ (ga̱ŋbɛ ñɛ̃ndzɛɛ̀) cystitis.

སྒང་ཕུག (gəŋbuù) sm. སྒང་བུ་.

སྒང་བུ་ (gəŋbu) 1. bladder (of stomach). 2. balloon.

སྒང་སྦུག (gəŋbuù) sm. སྒང་བུ་.

སྒང་ཞུ་ (gəŋshu) lantern ། སྒང་ཞུ་དམར་པོའི་སྒྲུང་ "The Tale of the Red Lantern".

སྒང་ཞུའི་དུས་ཆེན་ (gəŋshü tüüjen) the Lantern Festival (15th of the first lunar month).

སྒང་ལི་ (gəŋli) sm. སྒང་བུ་.

སྒོ་སྒོ་ (gogo) a type of herbal medicine.

སྒ་ (ga̱) 1. saddle; va.—རྒྱག to saddle ། རྟ་སྒ་ A horse saddle. 2. a type of blanket woven from colored cotton.

སྒ་སྐྱ་ (gaya) ginger.

སྒ་ཁེབས་ (ga̱keb) saddle covering.

སྒ་ཁོག (gagɔɔ̀) the arch of a (underside) saddle.

སྒ་ཁྲལ་ (gadrɛɛ) a tax on saddled animals.

སྒ་འཁོར་བཅས་ (ga kɔ̃ɔjɛɛ̀) paraphernalia that goes with saddles.

སྒ་གློ་ (ga̱lo) girth, cinch strap.

སྒ་གློ་གསུམ་མ་ (ga̱lo sũmmə) a saddle with three cinch straps.

སྒ་གོད་ (gagöö) Chinese toon (toona sinensis).

སྒ་རྒྱག (gagyaà) 1. name for three year old horses, mules or donkeys (for horses this conveys that this is the time for first saddling). 2. see སྒ་.

སྒ་སྒྲོམ་ (ga̱drom) a frame put on a saddle to which small children are tied when they ride horseback.

སྒ་ཆས་ (ga̱jɛɛ̀) sm. སྒ་འཁོར་བཅས་.

སྒ་ཆུང་ (ga̱juŋ) an herbal medicine.

སྒ་ཉག (ga̱ñaà) the part of the saddle where the rider sits.

སྒ་ཉལ་ (ga̱ñɛɛ) lying back in the saddle; —རྒྱག.

སྒ་ཉིས་འཁེལ་ (ga̱ ñii kēl) shung. being levied double taxes [Lit. putting two saddles on sth.].

སྒ་ཏིག (ga̱dig) a plant used in Tibetan medicine (androsace maxiae).

སྒ་སྟན་ (ga̱dɛn) sm. སྒ་གདན་.

སྒ་སྟན་སྲབ་གསུམ་ (ga̱dɛn drābsum) abbr. the three: saddle, saddle rug and bit.

སྒ་སྟོང་ (ga̱doŋ) saddled horse that is riderless.

སྒ་བསྟན་ (ga̱dɛn) sm. སྒ་, 1.

སྒ་ཐག (ga̱daà) saddle rope, cinch strap.

སྒ་ཐོད་ལོ་ (ga tȭolo) a type of saddle with a rounded front and arches.

སྒ་མཐོངས་ (ga̱doŋ) the pommel and cantle of a saddle.

སྒ་གདན་ (ga̱dɛn) 1. saddle cushion. 2. abbr. saddle and saddle cushions.

སྒ་འདྲ་ (ga̱ndra) a plant used in Tibetan medicine (kaempferia galanga).

སྒ་ལྡེབས་ (ga̱ndeb) the wooden frame that holds the cantle of a saddle together.

སྒ་ཕྱར་ (ga̱jar) multicolored raw silk (commonly worn by Bhutanese).

སྒ་དབྱིབས་ (gəyib) the shape of a saddle, saddle-shaped.

སྒ་དབྲག (ga̱braà) the space between the saddle and the saddle rug (under the saddle).

སྒ་འབོར་ (ga̱mbɔɔ) decorative nail on the cushion of the saddle for attaching one's hat.

སྒ་འབོལ་ (ga̱mböö) the padding/ covering that is fastened to the top of a saddle.

སྒ་འབྱར་ (ga̱njaa) saddled animals ། དྲེལ་སྒ་འབྱར་ Saddled mules.

སྒ་སྨུག (gəbuù) shung. winter hat worn by monk officials when they accompany the Dalai Lama on horseback.

སྒ་མ་རྟ་སྒ་ (ga̱madaga) saddle on which a person can ride as well as carry baggage.

སྒ་མིག (gəmii) the space/ holes through which the front and back end of saddle are held together.

སྒ་དམར་ (ga̱mar) a type of ginger.

སྒ་སྨུག (gəmuù) ginger.

སྒ་བཙུག (ga̱dzaà) cushion placed under the saddle (usu. for carrying animals).

སྒ་ཚ་ (ga̱tsa) ranunculus japonicus thunb. (used in Tibetan medicine).

སྒ་ཚ་བཤུས་རྒྱག (ga tsəshüü gya̱à) va. to unsaddle a sweating animal (horses, mules, etc.) so that it doesn't fall ill.

སྒ་ཚང (ga̱dzaŋ) the underside of a saddle.

སྒ་ཞགས་ (ga̱shaà) sm. སྒ་ཐག.

སྒ་ཡག (ga̱yaà) the part of a saddle that sits on the back of the animal.

སྒ་རི་ (gəri) hind. vehicle, car.

སྒ་རིལ་ (gərii) sm. སྒ་རི་.

སྒ་རུ་ (ga̱ru) 1. the arches of a saddle, the front and the back end of a saddle. 2. a blacksmith's tool. 3. a type of cloud that looks like the arch of a saddle.

སྒ་རློན་ (ga̱lön) fresh ginger.

སྒ་ལ་སྤུན་དོག (ga̱la bũndɔɔ̀) wool for knitting.

སྒ་ལོག (ga̱lɔɔ̀) having the saddle slip and overturn; vi.—རྒྱག.

སྒ་སློག (ga̱lɔɔ̀) making a saddle slip and overturn; va.—རྒྱག.

སྒ་ཤ་ (ga̱sha) sm. སྒ་གཤེར་.

སྒ་ཤན་ (gāshɛn) decorations (usu. silver or bronze) on the front and back of saddle arches.

སྒ་ཤུབས་ (gəshub) shung. a scarlet red rug that goes over the saddle denoting officials of the 4th rank and above in tt.

སྒ་ཤུབས་མཚལ་ཀ་ (gəshub tsɛ̃ɛga) shung. sm. སྒ་ཤུབས་.

སྒ་ཤོ་ (ga̱sho) cremanthodium sp.(used in Tibetan medicine).

སྒ་ཤོ་རིང་བ་ (ga̱sho ri̱ŋwə) sm. སྒ་ཤོ་.

སྒ་གཤེར་ (ga̱sher) ginger.

སྒ་སེར་ (ga̱see) tumeric.

སྒག (ga̱à) va. to strangle, to choke.

སྒག་སྒྲིགས་ (gəgdreg) sm. སྒག་ཐུད་.

སྒག་ཐུད་ (gəgdüù) belching; va.—རྒྱག.

སྒང་ (ga̱ŋ) 1. a ridge. 2. on, on top of, over ། རིའི་སྒང་ལ་ On top of the hill. 3. while, in the course of, in the midst of ། ཁོ་ཚོ་ལས་ཀ་བྱེད་པའི་སྒང་རེད་ They are in the midst of their work. ། གནས་ཚུལ་དེ་ང་ཉལ་པའི་སྒང་ལ་བྱུང་བ་རེད་ It happened while I was sleeping. 4. porcupine.

སྒང་ཁ་ (ga̱ŋga) sm. ཚང་མ་.

སྒང་ཁ་ལོགས་ (ga̱ŋ kālɔɔ̀) sm. ཚང་མ་.

སྒང་རྒྱུད་ (ga̱ŋgyüù) along the ridge/ mountain top.

སྒང་ཏོག (ga̱ŋdɔɔ̀) Gangtok.

སྒང་སྟོན་ (ga̱ndön) the traditional party held in the middle of a building project.

སྒང་ཐུར་ (ga̱ŋdur) hedgehog.

སྒང་ཐོབ་ (ga̱ŋdob) shung. the whole amount.

སྒང་དྲུག (gəŋdruù) the six mountain ranges in Kham.

སྒང་མདུད་ (ga̱ndüù) a ཁ་བཏགས་ that has been blessed and knotted like a སྲུང་མདུད་.

སྒང་པ་ (ga̱ŋba) mountain men, people who live in

the mountains.

སྒང་པ་བོད་ (gaŋba pöö) Tibet, the highlands of Tibet.

སྒང་བལ་ (gaŋpɛɛ) wool from one sheep.

སྒང་བྲལ་ཟླ་ཤོལ་ (gaŋdrɛɛ dashöö) intercalary month of the lunar calendar.

སྒང་འབབ་ (gaŋbəb) sm. སྒང་ཚང་.

སྒང་འབུར་ (gaŋbur) a protruding part/ area.

སྒང་མ་ (gaŋma) older siblings ༑ཁྱེད་རང་ལ་སྤུན་མཆེད་སྒང་མ་ག་ཚོད་ཡོད་དམ་ How many older siblings do you have?

སྒང་ཚང་ (gaŋdzaŋ) 1. all, entire, complete, full. 2. sm. སྒང་རིལ་མ་, 2.

སྒང་ཚད་ (gaŋdzɛɛ̀) sm. སྒང་ཚང་.

སྒང་ཞིང་ (gaŋshiŋ) field on a ridge, field in a high area.

སྒང་གཟུགས་ (gaŋsuù) hedgehog.

སྒང་འོག་ (gaŋwɔɔ̀) above and below, upper and lower, up and down ༑ངས་ཉལ་གདན་(ཅག་དར་)སྒང་འོག་བརྗེས་པ་ཡིན་ I changed the upper and lower sheets.

སྒང་རིལ་ (gəŋrii) sm. སྒང་རིལ་མ་, 1.

སྒང་རིལ་མ་ (gəŋrimə) 1. sleeping with one's clothes on ༑ཕྲུ་གུ་དེ་དུག་ལོག་མ་ཕུད་པར་སྒང་རིལ་མར་གཉིད་ཁུག་བཞག The child fell asleep with all his clothes on. 2. sm. སྒང་ཚང་, 1. (can only be used in reference to a carcass of meat) ༑ལུག་ཤ་ཁོག་སྒང་རིལ་མ་ཞིག་ཉོས་བཞག (He) bought a complete sheep carcass.

སྒང་ལ་ (gaŋla) see སྒང་, 2.

སྒང་ལམ་ (gaŋlam) mountain path/ road, path on a ridge.

སྒང་གཤགས་ (gaŋshaà) a method of bleeding a patient as a treatment.

སྒང་གཤོང་ (gaŋshoŋ) low areas and high areas, ridges and valleys.

སྒང་གཤོང་མུ་འབྲེལ་ (gaŋshoŋ mundree) rolling hills (and valleys).

སྒང་གཤོངས་ (gaŋshoŋ) sm. སྒང་གཤོང་.

སྒང་ས་ (gaŋsa) highland area, a plateau, a ridge.

སྒང་གསུམ་ (gaŋsum) three highland areas in Kham and Amdo.

སྒབ་: p. and f. བསྒབ་; imp. སྒོབ་ (gəb) 1. va. to cover, to hide. 2. va. to support, to assist, to aid.

སྒབ་ (gəb) 1. lap/ hem of a garment ༑གོས་སྒབ་རིང་པོ་ A garment with a long hem. 2. afterwards, later, behind ༑ང་སྒབ་ལ་སླེབས་ཡོང་ I will arrive later.

སྒབ་བྱི་ (gəbgyi) lackey.

སྒབ་མོ་ (gəbmo) shung. city people.

སྒབ་མཚལ་ (gəbdzɛɛ) the red painted lower part of the inside wall (in many traditional Tibetan homes).

སྒབ་གཞུག (gabshuù) hem of garment.

སྒབ་གཞུང་ (gəbshuŋ) sm. སྒབ་གཞུག.

སྒབ་ཟོར་ (gəbsor) heaviness of the body.

སྒབ་ཟོར་ཡང་པོ་ (gəbsor yaŋbo) a person who is quick to volunteer to do things.

སྒབ་ཡོལ་གདོང་ (gəbyöö dōŋ) sm. འགོམ་.

སྒབ་གཤམ་ (gəbsham) hem or edge of a dress/ gown/ robe; va.—སུམ་ to hold the sides of one's dress when walking through a seated crowd so that the dress doesn't brush against the people seated.

སྒམ་ (gam) box, trunk; va.—རྒྱག to pack in a box.

སྒམ་ཀྱག (gamgya) a box used as a cupboard.

སྒམ་དཀྱིལ་ (gamgyee) shung. reserved/ profound and broad-minded ༑སྒམ་དཀྱིལ་ཆེན་པོས་ནི་ཆོས་སྲིད་ཟུ་ལ་ཡང་མཁས་ཤིང་གསལ་ A person who is broad-minded and reserved will be good at both at religious and political matters.

སྒམ་སྐས་ (gamgyɛɛ̀) wooden stairs that are shaped like boxes.

སྒམ་ཁྲི་ (gə̄mdri) a container (for shipping), a large box/ bale; va.—རྒྱག to pack such a box/ bale.

སྒམ་གླུ་ (gəmlu) tape recorder.

སྒམ་སྒོ་མང་ (gam gomaŋ) chest of drawers.

སྒམ་སྒྲོམ་ (gamdrom) large cupboard.

སྒམ་ཆུང་ (gəmjuŋ) small box, packet ༑མུ་སིའི་སྒམ་ཆུང་ A match box.

སྒམ་མཆོང་ (gamjoŋ) vaulting horse (in gymnastics).

སྒམ་ཇ་ (gamja) box of tea.

སྒམ་པོ་ (gambo) reserved, serious ༑མི་དེ་སྒམ་པོ་ཡིན་སྐབས་གཞིབ་བདེ་པོ་མེད་པ་རེད་ He is very reserved so it is hard to make friends with him.

སྒམ་སྦུད་ (gambüü) an elongated type of bellows in a box (used by blacksmiths).

སྒམ་གཙང་མ་ (gam dzāŋma) clean, neat ༑ཕྲུ་གུ་དེས་དུ་ལོག་སྒམ་གཙང་མ་གྱོན་བཞག The child was wearing clean clothes (was neatly dressed).

སྒམ་ཚིག (gamdzig) words said in a serious manner.

སྒམ་ཚུགས་ལྡན་པ་ (gamdzuù dɛmba) sm. སྒམ་པོ་.

སྒམ་རྫོང་རྒྱག (gamdzoŋ gyaà) va. to pack a box/ trunk.

སྒམ་ཤུ་ (gəmshu) lantern.

སྒམ་སྙིང་ (gəmliŋ) serious, deep, reserved ༑སྒམ་བརྙིང་གི་ཉམས་འགྱུར་ A serious appearance.

སྒམ་ཤག (gamshaà) a wooden crate.

སྒམ་ཤུབས་ (gəmshub) covering for a trunk/ box.

སྒམ་བཤད་ (gamshɛɛ̀) 1. phonograph. 2. radio. 3. loudspeaker.

སྒར་ (gar) camp, encampment; va.—རྒྱག; —འདེབས་; —འབབ་; —བཀོད་; —སྒྲིག; —བཅའ་ to camp, to make camp, to encamp ༑སྐྱབས་བཅོལ་བའི་སྡོད་སྒར་ Refugee camp.

སྒར་: p. and f. བསྒར་; imp. སྒོར་ (gar) 1. va. to let coagulate ༑བུ་རམ་བསྐོལ་དེ་རིལ་མོར་སྒར་དགོས་ You have to boil the brown sugar and then let it coagulate. 3. va. to insert, stick in/ on ༑སོ་ཚབ་སྒར་ To insert a false tooth.

སྒར་སྒྲིག (gar drig) sm. སྒར་བཀོད་.

སྒར་བཀོད་ (gar göö) arranging/ setting up an encampment, putting up/ making a camp; va.—བྱེད་ ༑སྒར་བཀོད་བྱེད་མཁན་སུ་རེད་ Who is the person arranging the encampment?

སྒར་སྐད་ (gargɛɛ̀) codeword, password.

སྒར་གྲྭ་ (gardra) monks sent to distant places to preach and do religious activities so that they can collect donations/ alms for their monastery.

སྒར་འགོ་ལ་ཁྲལ་ (gargo ladrɛɛ) shung. taxes collected on mountain passes.

སྒར་རྒྱག (gar gyəb) va. to set up camp.

སྒར་བཅའ་ (gar jā) sm. སྒར་རྒྱག.

སྒར་ཏོག (gardog) Gartok.

སྒར་གཏོར་མཁར་བཅོམ་ (gardɔr kārjom) causing mayhem [Lit. destroying the camp, robbing the houses].

སྒར་པ་ (garba) person in an encampment/ camp.

སྒར་དཔོན་ (garbön) 1. leader or chief of an encampment/ camp. 2. shung. Tibetan government official in charge of the མངའ་རིས་ area.

སྒར་དབྱར་ས་ (gar yārsa) shung. summer encampment/ camp/ barracks.

སྒར་མིང་ (garmiŋ) sm. སྒར་སྐད་.

སྒར་མེ་ (garme) campfire; va.—སྦར་ to light a campfire.

སྒར་ཚར་དུ་ (gardzardu) sm. སྒང་རིལ་མར་.

སྒར་ས་ (garsa) camp site, encampment; va.—འདེབས་ to set up a camp ༑ངལ་རྩོལ་གྱི་སྒར་ས་ A hard labor camp.

སྒལ་ (gɛɛ) the back (of a person or animal).

སྒལ་གླད་ (gɛɛlɛɛ̀) sm. རྒྱངས་པ་.

སྒལ་དཀྱིལ་ (gɛɛgyii) middle of the back.

སྒལ་ཁེབས་ (gɛɛgeb) 1. a covering for the back of animals. 2. sm. རྒྱབ་གདན་.

སྒལ་རྒྱུག (gɛɛgyuù) a stick used to whip people on the back.

སྒལ་བཅོས་ (gɛɛjöö) treating sores on the back of animals; va.—བྱེད་.

སྒལ་རྟ་ (gɛɛda) pack horse.

སྒལ་ནག (gɛɛnag) sm. རྒྱངས་པ་.

སྒལ་པ་ (gɛɛba) 1. the back ¶ ཁོའི་སྒལ་པ་སྐྲངས་བཞག His back was swollen. 2. sm. སྒལ་རལ་.

སྒལ་པ་ལེབ་ལེབ་ (gɛɛba lebleb) insatiable.

སྒལ་པར་འཁྱེར་ (gɛɛba kyēr) va. to carry on the back ¶ ཁོས་དོ་པོ་སྒལ་པར་ཁྱེར་བ་རེད་ He carried the load on his back.

སྒལ་པས་འདྲོངས་ཀྱང་རྩིབས་མས་འདྲོངས་ས་མ་རེད་ (gɛɛbɛ drongyaŋ dzībmɛ dronsa mareè) unbearable [Lit. even if the back can bear it, the ribs can not bear it].

སྒལ་འཕང་ (gɛɛ pāŋ) va. to throw off a load.

སྒལ་བོང་ (gɛɛbuŋ) shung. draught donkey.

སྒལ་མ་ (gɛɛma) sm. ཁལ་མ་.

སྒལ་མིག (gɛɛmii) sm. སྒལ་རྨ་.

སྒལ་རྨ་ (gɛɛ mā) sores on the back (usu. from carrying loads); vi.—ཤོར་ to get back sores (from carrying loads).

སྒལ་ཚགས་ (gɛɛdzaà) sm. སྒལ་བཙེམས་.

སྒལ་ཚིགས་ (gɛɛdzii) backbone, vertebrae.

སྒལ་ཚིགས་ཅན་གྱི་སྲོག་ཆགས་ (gɛɛdziijɛngi sōgjaà) vertebrates.

སྒལ་ཚིགས་མེད་པའི་སྲོག་ཆགས་ (gɛɛdzii meèbɛ sōgjaà) invertebrates, invertebrate animals.

སྒལ་གཞུང་ (gɛɛshuŋ) the middle section of the back (of the human body).

སྒལ་རལ་ (gɛɛrɛɛ) insubordinate, rebellious, refusing to listen to superiors; va.—འཆོང་; —བྱེད་ ¶ མི་དེ་ས་རྟག་པར་སྒལ་རལ་བཙོངས་པར་བརྟེན་ལས་ཁུངས་ནས་ཕུད་འདུག He always refused to listen to his superiors so he was fired.

སྒལ་རལ་ཉག་རྒྱང་ (gɛɛrɛɛ ñaggyaŋ) sm. སྒལ་རལ་ཚ་པོ་.

སྒལ་རལ་ཚ་པོ་ (gɛɛrɛɛ tsābo) sb. who is unwilling to listen to orders from above, sb. who is insubordinate, rebellious.

སྒལ་རིལ་ (gyɛɛrii) rolling about/ around/ over on their backs; va.—རྒྱག ¶ རྟ་དྲེལ་རྣམས་སྤང་གི་སྟེང་དུ་སྒལ་རིལ་རྒྱག་གི་འདུག The horses and the mules are rolling over on the meadow.

སྒལ་རུས་ (gyɛɛrüù) sm. སྒལ་ཚིགས་.

སྒལ་རུས་ནང་ཤ་ (gyɛɛrüù naŋsha) spinal cord.

སྒལ་ཤོར་ (gyɛɛ shɔ̄ɔ) sm. སྒལ་རྨ་ཤོར་.

སྒུ་སྟེགས་ (gudeg) 1. stool, foot rest. 2. flirtatious. 3. the milky way.

སྒུ་དོ་ (gudo) 1. slingshot; va.—རྒྱག to shoot a slingshot. 2. a water container. 3. a target.

སྒུ་རྡོ་ (gudo) sm. སྒུ་དོ་.

སྒུ་བ་ (guwa) sm. སྒུ་བོ་.

སྒུ་བོ་ (guwo) hunchback (person, man).

སྒུ་རུ་མ་ (guruma) hunchback women.

སྒུ་རུ་རུ་ (gu ruru) walking in a hunched manner ¶ རྒན་མོ་རྣམས་སྒུ་རུ་རུར་གྲོང་སྐོར་ལ་འགྲོ་གི་འདུག The old women are circumambulating the city in a hunched over manner.

སྒུག་: p. བསྒུགས་; f. བསྒུག; imp. སྒུགས་ (guù) va. to wait ¶ ཡུན་རིང་བསྒུགས་པ་ཡིན་ (We) waited a long time.

སྒུག་རྒྱག (guù gyaà) va. to lay in wait, to ambush.

སྒུག་དུས་བཟོ་ (guùdöö so) va. to make an appointment.

སྒུག་སྡོད་ (guùdöö) staying/ waiting for sb. or sth.; va.—བྱེད་.

སྒུག་སྡོད་ཁང་ (guùdöögaŋ) waiting room.

སྒུག་འབོད་ཁ་པར་ (gumböö kābar) a phone where one has to go through an operator to dial, an operator-dialed phone.

སྒུག་བཞུགས་ (guù shuù) h. of སྒུག་སྡོད་.

སྒུག་ཡུན་མ་ཐེག་པ་ (guùyün madegba) unable to wait any more.

སྒུག་ཡུན་མི་ཐུབ་ (guùyün mijog) sm. སྒུག་ཡུན་མ་ཐེག་པ་.

སྒུག་ར་ (guùra) waiting to ambush, va.—སྡོད་ to wait in ambush ¶ ཇག་པས་ལམ་ག་ལ་སྒུགས་ར་སྡོད་ནས་འཕྲོག་བཅོམ་བྱས་པ་རེད་ The bandits waited in ambush on the road and robbed them.

སྒུག་རེས་ (gurɛɛ) 1. taking turns waiting; va.—བྱེད་ ¶ ང་གཉིས་འགྲུལ་པ་སྒུག་རེས་བྱེད་དོ་ Lets us two wait for the traveler by turns. 2. va. to wait for each other ¶ ང་གཉིས་སུ་སྔོན་ལ་སླེབས་ན་ཡང་སྒུག་རེས་བྱེད་དོ་ Whoever arrives first, lets wait (for the other).

སྒུགས་ (guù) imp. of སྒུག.

སྒུད་པོ་ (güübu) father-in-law.

སྒུད་མོ་ (güümu) mother-in-law.

སྒུམ་རྒྱག (gum gyaà) vi. to turn/ spin (refers to a kite).

སྒུམ་མདའ་ (gumda) a slingshot; va.—རྒྱག to shoot a slingshot.

སྒུམ་ཙམ་ (gumdzam) ordinary, mediocre.

སྒུམ་ཤིང་ (gumshiŋ) stock of a gun, gun-butt, catapult.

སྒུར་: p. and f. བསྒུར་; imp. བསྒུར་ (guu) 1. va. to bend over/ down. 2. (with མགོ་) va. to surrender ¶ དགྲ་བོ་མགོ་སྒུར་བ་རེད་ The enemy surrendered. 3. va. to empty out a container by pouring.

སྒུར་འཁྱོག (gurgyoò) hunched over and crooked.

སྒུར་སྒུར་ (guuguu) 1. bent down, hunched over; va.—བྱེད་ to bend down ¶ ང་ཡོང་དུས་མོས་མགོ་སྒུར་སྒུར་བྱས་སོང་ When I came she bent her head down. 2. hunched back (person).

སྒུར་བཅོས་ (guujöö) a treatment for humnched back.

སྒུར་སྒུར་པོ་ (guuguubo) sm. སྒུར་པོ་.

སྒུར་དོ་ (guudo) sm. སྒུར་མདའ་.

སྒུར་ཕྱག (guujaà) bowing as a sign of respect (in contrast to full prostration).

སྒུལ་: p. and f. བསྒུལ་; imp. སྒུལ་ (güü) va. to move, to shake, to put into motion ¶ འཕྲུལ་འཁོར་དེ་ཚོ་གློག་གི་སྒུལ་གྱི་ཡོད་པ་རེད་ Those machines are moved (operated) by electricity.

སྒུལ་སྐྱོད་ (güügyüü) movement, motion; va.—རྒྱག—བྱེད་; —གཏོང་ to move ¶ སྒུལ་སྐྱོད་མ་རྒྱབ་ ཁབ་རྒྱག་གི་ཡིན་ Don't move. I am going to give you an injection. 2. va. to act on sth., to obey ¶ ང་ཚོས་བསམ་འཆར་བཏོན་ན་ཡང་ཁོ་ཚོས་སྒུལ་སྐྱོད་རྒྱག་གི་མི་འདུག Even though we made a suggestion they aren't taking action on it.

སྒུལ་བསྐྱོད་འཁོར་ལོ་ (güügyüü kɔ̄ɔlo) motor, engine.

སྒུལ་སྒུལ་གཙུས་གཙུས་ (güügyüü jüüjüü) moving around; va.—བྱེད་ ¶ བཙོན་པ་རྣམས་བཙོན་ཁང་ནང་སྒུལ་སྒུལ་གཙུས་གཙུས་བྱེད་འཇུག་གི་མེད་པ་རེད་ ¶ (They) do not let the prisoners move around in the prison.

སྒུལ་སྒྲིལ་ (güüdril) rolling sth. onto sth. else; va.—བྱེད་.

སྒུལ་ཕྱོགས་ (güüjɔɔ) trend, tendency.

སྒུལ་བྱེད་འཕྲུལ་འཁོར་ (güüjeè trüügɔɔ) motor.

སྒུལ་རྫས་ (güüdzɛɛ) movable property/ assets.

སྒུལ་ཤུགས་ (güüshuù) energy, motivating force ¶ ལས་འགུལ་འདིའི་ནང་གི་སྒུལ་ཤུགས་གཙོ་བོ་དེ་གཞོན་ནུ་ཚོགས་པ་རེད་འདུག In this campaign, the main motivating force is the Youth League.

སྒུལ་ཤུགས་འཕྲུལ་འཁོར་ (güüshuù trüügɔɔ) energy/ power producing machine.

སྒེ་ཁུང་ (giguŋ) window.

སྒེ་ཁུང་ཉིས་ཧྲལ་ (giguŋ ñiihrɛɛ) two windows (side by side).

སྒེ་སྒུ་ཅན་ (gigujɛn) not straight, bent, crooked.

སྒེ་མོ་ (gemo) sm. སྒྱེ་མོ་.

སྒེ་གཤེར་ (gesher) fresh ginger.

སྒེག (geg) vi. to be charming, to be graceful ¶ ལང་ཚོས་སྒེག་ནས་ Graceful with the beauty of youth.

སྒེག་འགྲོས་ (gendröö) graceful walking style (of women).

སྒེག་ཆོས་ (gegjöö) 1. charming and elegant countenance/ manner/ behavior/ appearance; va.—སྟོན་ to exhibit/ charm/ elegance/ grace. 2. coquettish.

སྒེག་འཆོས་ (gegjöö) sm. སྒེག་ཉམས་སྟོན་.

སྒེག་འཆོས་ཅན་ (gegjööjɛn) charming, graceful, elegant.

སྒེག་ཉམས་ (gegñam) sm. སྒེག་ཆོས་.

སྒེག་ཉམས་ལྡན་པ་ (gegñam dɛmba) sm. སྒེག་འཆོས་ཅན་.

སྒེག་ལྡན་ (gegdɛn) sm. སྒེག་ཆས་ཅན་.

སྒེག་སྤྱོད་ (gegjöö) sm. སྒེག་ཆས་.

སྒེག་མ་ (gegma) a woman having སྒེག་ཆས་.

སྒེག་མོ་ (gegmo) sm. སྒེག་མ་.

སྒེག་ཆས་ (gegdzöö) cosmetics, makeup.

སྒེག་རྫས་ (gegdzɛɛ̀) 1. cosmetics. 2. fine/ beautiful clothes.

སྒེའུ་ (geu) 1. sm. སྒེའུ་ཁུང་. 2. a small door. 3. arc. onion.

སྒེའུ་ཁུང་ (giguŋ) window.

སྒེའུ་གཤེར་ (gesher) fresh ginger.

སྒེར་ (ger) 1. private, individual personal ¶ སྤྱི་སྒེར་ Public and private. 2. (abbr. of སྒེར་པ) ¶ སྒེར་དགའ་བཞི་ The aristocratic family Gabshi.

སྒེར་སྐྱོང་ (gergyoŋ) sm. སྒེར་གཉེར་.

སྒེར་ཁག (gerkaà)1. the aristocracy, aristocratic families (in the old society). 2. private sector.

སྒེར་ཁྲིམས་ (gerdrim) private law.

སྒེར་འཁོན་ཞེ་འཛིན་ (gergön shendzin) personal grudge.

སྒེར་འཁོར་ (gerkɔr) private car/ vehicle.

སྒེར་གྱི་ཀུན་སྤྱོད་ (gergi gũnjöö) individual behavior.

སྒེར་གྱི་ཫང་དངུལ་ (gergi gāŋŋüü) private shares/ stocks.

སྒེར་གྱི་ཁེ་ཕན་ (gergi kēbɛn) personal/ private gain or benefit.

སྒེར་གྱི་ངོ་ཚབ་ (gergi ŋodzəb) personal representative.

སྒེར་གྱི་བདག་དབང་ (gergi dawaŋ) private ownership.

སྒེར་གྱི་ཕྱོགས་ (gergi cɔ̄ɔ̀) private side/ sector.

སྒེར་གྱི་འབྲེལ་བ་ (gergi dreewa) private relations.

སྒེར་གྱི་མ་ཫང་ (gergi magaŋ) private stock/ shares.

སྒེར་གྱི་མ་རྩ་ (gergi madza) private capital.

སྒེར་གྱི་མ་རྩའི་རིང་ལུགས་ (gergi madzɛ riŋluù) private capitalism.

སྒེར་གྱི་ཚོང་པ་ (gergi tsōŋba) private merchant/ trader.

སྒེར་གྱི་འཚམས་འདྲི་ (gergi tsəmdri) personal visit.

སྒེར་གྱི་འཚོ་ཐབས་ (gergi tsōdəb) private livelihood.

སྒེར་གྱི་འཚོ་བ་ (gergi tsōwa) private life.

སྒེར་གྱི་མཛའ་བརྩེ་ (gergi dzadze) personal relationship, personal consideration.

སྒེར་གྱི་བྲན་གཡོག་ (gergi dadrɛɛ̀) shung. private servants.

སྒེར་གྱི་སློབ་གྲྭ་ (gergi lōbdra) private school.

སྒེར་གྱི་གསོག་འཇོག (gergi sōnjɔɔ̀) private savings.

སྒེར་འགྲོན་ (gerdrön) personal/ private expenses.

སྒེར་དངོས་ (gēŋöö) personal belongings/ wealth.

སྒེར་གཅོད་ (gerjöö) dictatorship, dictatorial, autocratic; va.—བྱེད་ to act in a dictatorial/ autocratic manner ¶ སྒེར་གཅོད་སྲིད་གཞུང་ Dictatorial government.

སྒེར་གཅོད་ཀྱི་སྲིད་དབང་ལམ་ལུགས་ (gerjöögi sīiwaŋ ləmluù) autocratic system of government.

སྒེར་གཅོད་དབང་བསྒྱུར་ (gerjöö wəŋgyuu) dictatorship.

སྒེར་གཅོད་རིང་ལུགས་ (gerjöö riŋluù) dictatorism.

སྒེར་གཅོད་ལམ་ལུགས་ (gerjöö ləmluù) autocratic system.

སྒེར་གཅོད་སྲིད་དབང་ (gerjöö sīiwaŋ) autocratic political power.

སྒེར་ཆོས་ (ger cöö) shung. abbr. aristocratic and monastic/ religious.

སྒེར་ཆོས་རང་དཔོན་ (raŋbön) shung. the aristocrats and monasteries who are (their) own lords.

སྒེར་མཇལ་ (gerjɛɛ) private interview/ audience.

སྒེར་གཉེར་ (gerñyer) privately owned/ managed ¶ སྒེར་གཉེར་ཁེ་ལས་ Private enterprise (the opposite of རྒྱལ་གཉེར་).

སྒེར་གཉེར་ཁེ་ལས་ (gerñyer kēlɛɛ̀) privately owned enterprise, privately managed enterprise.

སྒེར་གཉེར་དཔལ་འབྱོར་ (gerñyer bɛ̄njɔɔ) private enterprise economy, private sector of the economy.

སྒེར་གཉེར་གཡོ་ཟོལ་ (gerñyer yōsöö) corrupt practices/ management.

སྒེར་གཏོར་སྤྱི་འཛུགས་ (gerdɔr jīndzuù) overcome selfishness/ individualism and foster public spirit.

སྒེར་ཐམ་ (gerdam) a private seal (in contrast to a government or official seal).

སྒེར་ཐེལ་ (gertel) sm. སྒེར་ཐམ་.

སྒེར་འཐབ་བཅོས་དགག (gertab jöögaà) sm. སྒེར་འཐབ་བཟོ་དགག.

སྒེར་འཐབ་བཟོ་དགག (gerdab sogaà) fight selfishness, repudiate revisionism.

སྒེར་དུ་ (gerdu) privately, personally ¶ ངས་ཁོང་ལ་སྒེར་དུ་བཀའ་མོལ་ཞུས་པ་ཡིན་ I spoke with him privately.

སྒེར་དོན་ (gerdön) in the interest of or pertaining to private/ personal business, private interests ¶ ཁོ་རྒྱ་གར་ལ་སྒེར་དོན་དུ་ཕྱིན་པ་རེད་ He went to India on private business.

སྒེར་དོན་གཉེར་མཁས་ (gerdön ñērgɛɛ̀) skillful in achieving one's interests/ goals/ ends.

སྒེར་དོར་གཞན་སྒྲུབ་ (gerdɔr shendrub) selflessness ¶ སྒེར་དོན་གཞན་སྒྲུབ་ཀྱི་བསམ་པ་ Selfless thoughts. [Lit. setting aside one's private interests and working for others].

སྒེར་དོར་གཞུང་སྒྲུབ་ (gerdɔr shuŋdrub) sacrificing one's interest to work for the public good or state welfare.

སྒེར་བདག (gerdaà) privately owned.

སྒེར་འདོད་ (gendöö) a selfish desire, wishing/ desiring for one's own benefit.

སྒེར་སྡེམ་ (gerdem) monopoly; va.—བྱེད་ to monopolize.

སྒེར་སྡེམ་རིན་གོང་ (gerdem riŋgoŋ) monopoly price.

སྒེར་སྡོམ་མ་རྩ་ (gerdom madza) monopoly capital.

སྒེར་སྡོམ་མ་རྩའི་རིང་ལུགས་ (gerdom madzɛ riŋluù) monopoly capitalism.

སྒེར་ནད་གཟེར་སྡུང་ (gernɛɛ̀ serduŋ) shung. holding a personal grudge.

སྒེར་ནོར་ (gernɔɔ) private wealth/ fortune.

སྒེར་པ་ (gerba) shung. nobility, aristocracy, aristocratic family ¶ ལུང་ཤར་ནི་སྒེར་པ་ཞིག་རེད་ Lungshar is one of the aristocracy.

སྒེར་པ་དྭ་རྒྱང་ (gerba dāgyaŋ) shung. the class of poorer aristocrats in tt. who held only very small estates.

སྒེར་པ་དྲུང་འཁོར་ (gērba truŋgɔɔ) shung. lay aristocratic officials.

སྒེར་པའི་མི་སེར་ (gerbɛ misee) shung. the subjects/ serfs of aristocrats.

སྒེར་དཔོན་ (gerbön) shung. the aristocratic lord of an estate (to whom peasants belonged) ¶ ངའི་སྒེར་དཔོན་གཡུ་ཐོག་རེད་ My lord is Yuthok.

སྒེར་སྤྱོད་ (gerjöö) private use; va.—བྱེད་ to use/ enjoy privately ¶ སྤྱི་ནོར་སྒེར་སྤྱོད་བྱེད་མི་ཆོག One may not make private use of public property.

སྒེར་ཕན་ (gerbɛn) private profit/ gain/ benefit.

སྒེར་ཕན་གཉེར་ (gerbɛn ñēr) va. to seek personal interest or gain.

སྒེར་ཕན་དོན་གཉེར་ (gerbɛn tönñer) sm. སྒེར་ཕན་གཉེར་.

སྒེར་དབང་ (gerwaŋ) private ownership (of property), individual rights.

སྒེར་དབང་རྒྱུ་ནོར་ (gerwaŋ gyunɔɔ) sm. སྒེར་ནོར་.

སྒེར་དབང་སྒེར་འཛིན་ (gerwaŋ gendzin) sm. སྒེར་དབང་.

སྒེར་དབང་ཆུང་བའི་ལམ་ལུགས་ (gerwaŋ cūŋwɛ ləmluù) the system of small private ownership.

སྒེར་དབང་འདུ་ཤེས་ (gerwaŋ dusheè) private ownership mentality.

སྒེར་དབང་པ་ཆུང་བ་ (gerwaŋba cūŋwa) small private owner.

སྒེར་དབང་ལམ་ལུགས་ (gerwaŋ ləmluù) sm. སྒེར་ལ་དབང་བའི་ལམ་ལུགས་.

སྒེར་མིའི་བོགས་མ་ (germii bɔɔma) private lease/ contract.

སྒེར་བཙན་ (gerdzɛn) shung. 1. the right of aristocrats and religious entities in tt. to settle criminal and civil disputes among their subjects. 2. private ownership.

སྒེར་བཙུགས་སློབ་གྲྭ་ (gerdzuù lōbdra) private school.

སྒེར་རྩེ་ (gerdze) a nomad district/ xian in northwest Tibet.

སྒེར་བརྩམས་དེབ་ཐེར་ (gerdzam tebder) unofficial history.

སྒེར་ཚོང་ (gerdzoŋ) private trade/ commerce, private business; va.—རྒྱག.

སྒེར་མཛོ་ (gerdzo) privately owned མཛོ་.

སྒེར་འཛིན་ (gendzin) held or owned privately (in contrast to being held by the government); va.—བྱེད་ ¶ ཚོང་ཁང་འདི་སྒེར་འཛིན་བྱེད་ཀྱི་ཡོད་ This store is privately owned.

སྒེར་ཞིང་ (gershiŋ) a private field/ farm.

སྒེར་གཞིས་ (gershiì) shung. aristocratic estate.

སྒེར་བཞག་ས་ཞིང་ (gershaà sāshiŋ) privately held/ owned land.

སྒེར་ཟོག (gersoò) privately owned cattle/ livestock.

སྒེར་བཟུང་ (gersuŋ) 1. privately held (in contrast to held by the government). 2. a monopoly; va.—བྱེད་ to monopolize.

སྒེར་བཟུང་མ་རྩ་ (gersuŋ madza) monopoly capital.

སྒེར་གཡོག (geryɔɔ̀) shung. servants of the nobility/ aristocracy.

སྒེར་རུ་ (ger ru) a herd belonging to an aristocrat.

སྒེར་ལ་དབང་བ་ (gerla wāŋwa) sm. སྒེར་དབང་.

སྒེར་ལ་དབང་བའི་རྒྱུ་ནོར་ (gerla wāŋwɛ gyunɔɔ) private property.

སྒེར་ལ་དབང་བའི་ལམ་ལུགས་ (gerla wāŋwɛ lɔmluù) system of private ownership (of property).

སྒེར་ལངས་ (gerlaŋ) an uprising/ revolt seeking independence from a government or country; va.—བྱེད་ ¶ རང་དབང་སྒེར་ལང་ An uprising for freedom. ¶ མི་རིགས་སྒེར་ལངས་ An uprising on behalf of one's nationality.

སྒེར་ལས་དམངས་གཅེས་ (gerlɛɛ̀ māŋjeè) holding or putting the interests of the people/ masses above that of oneself.

སྒེར་ལུགས་ (gerluù) abbr. of སྒེར་དབང་ལམ་ལུགས་.

སྒེར་ཤག (gershaà) private quarters/ residence (in contrast to office quarters).

སྒེར་སེམས་ (gersem) thinking of one's own interests; selfishness, self-interest; va.—འཆང་ to be selfish, to think of one's own interests only.

སྒེར་སེམས་ཆེན་པོ་ (gersem cēmbo) sm. སྒེར་སེམས་ཚ་པོ་.

སྒེར་སེམས་མེད་པ་ (gersem mɛɛ̀ba) without ulterior motives, altruistic, selfless.

སྒེར་སེམས་ཚ་པོ་ (gersem tsābo) selfish, thinking only of one's own interests.

སྒེར་སེམས་རིང་ལུགས་ (gersem riŋluù) egoism.

སྒེར་སློབ་ (gerlob) private school.

སྒེར་གསལ་མ་བདེ་ (gersɛɛ made) shung. feeling uneasy/ uncomfortable about making an exception ¶ ཁྲལ་རིགས་རྒྱུག་པ་ལེབ་འདུར་ཞུ་རྒྱུའི་ཁོངས་ནས་རེ་ཟུང་ལ་ཆག་ཡང་སྒེར་གསལ་མ་བདེ་བས་ (They) feel uneasy about making an exception of a few people when the taxes are supposed to be paid without any exceptions.

སྒེར་གསལ་དོན་སྨིན་མ་བདེ་ (gersɛɛ tönmin made) shung. feeling uneasy/ uncomfortable about meeting sb.'s request and making an exception ¶ མངའ་ཞབས་ཀྱི་ཡོངས་ནས་སྤྲབ་རྒྱུགས་ཞུ་སྒོའི་རིགས་ཡིན་ཕྱིན་དམིགས་བསལ་ཆག་ཡང་ཞུ་མི་རེ་ཟུང་ལ་སྒེར་གསལ་དོན་སྨིན་མ་བདེ་བས་ Since the taxes are to be paid by all subjects without exception, (they) feel uneasy about meeting their request and making an exception for a few people.

སྒེར་གསོག (gersoò) private fund.

སྒེར་ལྷ་ (gerlha) personal deity, patron deity.

སྒོ་ (go) 1. door, entrance; va.—རྒྱག to close a door; to shut/ close down ¶ ཁང་པའི་སྒོ་ Door of a house. ¶ ནམ་རྒྱུན་ཆུ་ཚོད་གཉིས་པ་ལ་དངུལ་ཁང་སྒོ་རྒྱག་གི་ཡོད་པ་རེད་ Usually the banks closes at 2 o'clock. 2. means, method, medium ¶ ཡོན་ཏན་སྦྱོང་བའི་སྒོ་ནི་བརྩོན་འགྲུས་ཡིན་ The means (door) to becoming learned is diligence. 3. room number in an address ¶ ཁང་གསུམ་སྒོ་གཉིས་ House number three, room number two. 4. a cangue; va.—གཡོག to put a cangue on a prisoner ¶ རྐུ་མ་ཡི་སྐེ་ལ་སྒོ་ཞིག་གཡོགས་བཞག (They) have put a cangue on the thief's neck.

སྒོ་ p. བསྒོས་; f. བསྒོ་; imp. སྒོས་ (go) va. to give an order or instruction ¶ ད་ལྟ་འགྲོ་དགོས་པའི་བཀའ་བསྒོས་སོང་ (He) ordered that (they) should leave now.

སྒོ་ཀུན་ (gogün) every direction, all aspects, overall ¶ སྒོ་ཀུན་ནས་འཆར་འགོད་ Overall planning.

སྒོ་ཀུན་གྱི་ཉེན་ཁ་ (gogüngi ñenga) general crisis (a danger from all directions).

སྒོ་ཀུན་ནས་ (gogünnɛ) 1. in every respect, by all means, in every way ¶ སྒོ་ཀུན་ནས་རྒྱབ་སྐྱོར་བྱེད་ཀྱི་རེད་ They say that they will give their support in every way. 2. completely, totally ¶ འཆར་གཞི་དེ་སྒོ་ཀུན་ནས་བསྒྲུབས་ཟིན་པ་རེད་ The plan has been completely accomplished.

སྒོ་ གླད་ (golɛɛ̀) door beam.

སྒོ་དཀྱིལ་མ་ (go kīimə) the middle/ center door.

སྒོ་བཀག (gogaà) the wooden inside door bolt/ lock that prevents the door from being opened.

སྒོ་བཀག་རྟ་མགོ་གཟུགས་ (gogaà dāgosug) shung. door bolt shaped like a horse's head.

སྒོ་བཀག་རང་བརྟེན་ (gogaà randen) sm. སྒོ་བཀག་རང་སྲུང་.

སྒོ་བཀག་རང་སྲུང་ (gogaà ransuŋ) isolationism, closed-doorism, closed door policy.

སྒོ་སྐྱིབས་ (gogyib) a shelter/ overhang just outside a door.

སྒོ་སྐྱེས་ (gogyeè) 1. sm. ཨ་ཕྱིང་. 2. sm. རྟ་བབ་.

སྒོ་སྐྱོང་ (gogyoŋ) sm. སྒོ་སྲུང་.

སྒོ་སྐྱོར་ (gogyɔr) a wooden screen placed behind a door.

སྒོ་ཁ་ (goga) doorway, doorstep (the areas in front of a door).

སྒོ་ཁ་སྤྲོད་ (go kābdröö) opposite doors, doors facing each other.

སྒོ་ཁང་ (gogaŋ) house situated on top of a large wall/ gate.

སྒོ་ཁང་གད་གསུམ་ (go kāŋ kɛɛ̀ sūm) abbr. the three: custodian, sweeper, gatekeeper.

སྒོ་ཁུང་ (goguŋ) door opening.

སྒོ་ཁེབས་ (gogeb) cloth hung over the opening of a door.

སྒོ་ཁྱམས་ (gogyam) porch.

སྒོ་ཁྱི་ (gogyi) watch dog, guard dog tied by the entrance door.

སྒོ་ཁྱིམ་ (gogyim) an arch with a pointed top (similar to the shape of the Taj Mahal).

སྒོ་ཁྱུད་ (gogyüù) a wall with doors that surrounds a house.

སྒོ་ཁྲ་ (godra) shung. list/ registry/ census of houses, fields and people.

སྒོ་ཁྲ་ཐེམ་གཞུང་ (godra tēmshuŋ) shung. census list ¶ མི་རྩ་ཕོ་མོ་སྒོ་ཁྲ་ཐེམ་གཞུང་རྫོང་སྲིད་ཁུངས་སུ་ཡོད་པ་ Among the documents of the district there is a census list (of male and female serfs and households).

སྒོ་ཁྲ་ཐེལ་བཤེར་ (godra tēēsher) shung. investigation/ inspection/ census of the number of households and/ or people.

སྒོ་ཁྲལ་ (godrɛɛ) custom's tariff/ duty/ tax.

སྒོ་ཁྲལ་ལས་ཁུངས་ (godrɛɛ lɛɛ̀guŋ) custom's office.

སྒོ་ཁྲི་ (godri) stretcher, litter ¶ ནད་པ་ཞིག་སྒོ་ཁྲིའི་སྟེང་དུ་འཁྱེར་སོང་ (They) carried a sick person on a stretcher.

སྒོ་ཁྲིའི་རུ་ཁག (godrii rugaà) stretcher-bearer team.

སྒོ་འཁོར་ (gogɔɔ) door hinge/ pivot.

སྒོ་འཁྲིས་ (go trii) near a door.

སྒོ་འགྲོལ་ (gondröö) shung. the customary final

whipping that is given when a prisoner's wooden cangue is taken off and the prisoner released.

སྒོ་གྲངས་ (godraŋ) number on a door.

སྒོ་གླིང་ (goliŋ) the door of a cupboard.

སྒོ་གླེགས་ (goleg) door opening; door plank, door leaf.

སྒོ་འགག (gongaà) sm. སྒོ་ཁ་.

སྒོ་འགྲམ་ (gondram) sm. སྒོ་ཁ་.

སྒོ་རྒྱ་ (gogya) shung. seal placed on a door to prevent unauthorized entrance; va.—འཐེན་; —རྒྱག to seal a door; va.—བཤིག to break a door seal.

སྒོ་རྒྱ་ཐེབ་སྟོན་ (gogya tēēnön) sm. སྒོ་རྒྱ་.

སྒོ་རྒྱག (gogyaà) 1. va. to close/ shut a door ། ཕྱི་ལོགས་ལ་འགྲོ་དུས་སྒོ་རྒྱག་དགོས་ When you go outside you must close the door. 2. va. to close (down) ། ནམ་རྒྱུན་ཆུ་ཚོད་གཉིས་པ་དངུལ་ཁང་སྒོ་རྒྱག་གི་ཡོད་པ་རེད་ Usually the banks closes at 2 o'clock.

སྒོ་རྒྱག་རིང་ལུགས་ (gogyaà riŋluù) isolationism, close-doorism.

སྒོ་རྒྱན་ (gogyɛn) decoration on doors.

སྒོ་རྒྱབ་ (gogyəb) behind a door.

སྒོ་རྒྱུག (gogyuù) a long wooden door bolt.

སྒོ་སྒྲིག (godrig) shung. va. to lay the framework for sth. ། ངེས་འཛིན་གྱི་སྒོ་སྒྲིག་པའི་སྐད་དུ་བཀའ་ཤག་གིས་ For laying the framework for finding the reincarnation, the Council of Ministers ....

སྒོ་སྒྲོམ་ (godrom) a table of merchandise for sale outside the door of a store which also sells its goods inside the shop ། སྒོ་སྒྲོམ་གཉིས་ལྡན་གྱི་ཚོང་ཁང་ A store having merchandise for sale both inside and outside.

སྒོང་ (goŋa) egg; va.—གཏོང་ to lay eggs.

སྒོང་སྙོལ་ (go ñöö) sm. སྒོང་རུམ་.

སྒོང་བསྙོལ་ (go ñöö) p. of སྒོང་སྙོལ་.

སྒོང་བསྙོལ་མ་ (go ñööma) eggs that have embryos in them.

སྒོང་གཏོང་ (goŋa dōŋ) see སྒོང་.

སྒོང་དྭངས་མའི་ཁུ་བ་ (goŋa taŋmɛ kōō) egg white.

སྒོང་བཙོས་མ་པགས་པ་བཤུས་པ་ལྟར་ (goŋa dzööma bāgba shüübadar) a pleasing looking skin [Lit. like a boiled egg whose shell has been peeled].

སྒོང་ཡི་ཙི་ (goŋa yidzi) a type of soap that is shaped like an egg.

སྒོང་རུམ་ (goŋa rum) va. to sit on eggs to hatch them, to incubate eggs.

སྒོང་ངའི་དཀར་པོ་ (goŋɛ gārbo) egg white.

སྒོང་ངའི་ནང་གི་སེར་རིལ་ (goŋɛ naŋgi sēērii) 1. the yolk of an egg. 2. the cream of the crop [Lit. the yolk of the egg].

སྒོང་ངའི་སྤྲི་དཀར་ (goŋɛ drigar) sm. སྒོང་ངའི་སྤྲི་མ་.

སྒོང་ངའི་སྤྲི་མ་ (goŋɛ drimə) egg white.

སྒོང་ངའི་བག་ལེབ་ (goŋɛ paàleè) bread/ cake made with flour mixed with eggs.

སྒོང་ངའི་སེར་རིལ་ (goŋɛ sēērii) egg yolk.

སྒོ་བཅད་རིང་ལུགས་ (gojɛɛ̀ riŋluù) sm. སྒོ་རྒྱག་རིང་ལུགས་.

སྒོ་ལྕགས་ (gojaà) door lock; va.—རྒྱག to lock a door.

སྒོ་ལྕིབས་ (gojib) the upper and lower holes into which a door fits (these function like a door hinge).

སྒོ་མཆོར་ (gojɔɔ) an area outside the main gate of a monastery/ temple that is supported by pillars.

སྒོ་ཉུལ་ (go ñüü) va. to beg door-to-door.

སྒོ་གཉའ་ (goña) the upper part of a door.

སྒོ་གཉིས་སྒྲིག (go ñiidrig) a door with double doors.

སྒོ་གཏན་ (godɛn) 1. wooden bolt on a door; va.—རྒྱག to close the bolt of a door.

སྒོ་རྟགས་ (godaà) house number, address.

སྒོ་བསྟེན་ (goden) 1. retail. 2. outpatient.

སྒོ་བསྟེན་སྨན་བཅོས་ (goden mēnjöö) outpatient service.

སྒོ་བསྟེན་སྨན་བཅོས་ཁང་ (goden mēnjöögaŋ) outpatient department/ clinic.

སྒོ་བསྟེན་ཚོང་ཁང་ (goden tsōŋgaŋ) retail sales store.

སྒོ་བསྟེན་ཚོང་ལས་ (goden tsōŋlɛɛ̀) retail sales work.

སྒོ་ཐམ་ (godam) sm. སྒོ་ཐེབ་.

སྒོ་ཐེམ་ (godem) threshold of door, doorstep.

སྒོ་ཐེབ་ (godee) sm. སྒོ་རྒྱ་.

སྒོ་ཐོད་ (godöö) door beam.

སྒོ་ཐོད་མཛེས་རྒྱན་ (godöö dzeègyɛn) decorations above a door.

སྒོ་འཐེན་ཡག (go tēnyaà) door knob, door handle.

སྒོ་དང་ཐེམ་པ་ཁ་སྤྲོད་ (godaŋ tēmba kābdröö) two houses face-to-face.

སྒོ་དམ་ (godam) hind. godown, warehouse.

སྒོ་དར་ (godar) ceremonial scarf put on a door (e.g., when a new house is built).

སྒོ་དེབ་ (godeb) sm. སྒོ་ཁྲ་.

སྒོ་དེབ་དམ་འབྱར་མ་ (godeb damjarma) shung. an official census list (with a seal affixed).

སྒོ་དེབ་ཞིབ་གཞུང་ (godeb shibshuŋ) shung. census list.

སྒོ་དོད་ (godöö) shung. to be apparent ། ཚངས་པ་དང་ཐོད་ཅན་ལ་དྲི་བ་ཞུས་པ་སོགས་ཀྱང་མཚུངས་པ་ནས་གསར་བཀོད་ཀྱི་སྒོ་དོད་པ་ After consulting the Tsangpa oracle etc., finding the new incarnation became apparent.

སྒོ་དོན་ (go tön) va. to leave (a door/ house) ། ང་སྒོ་དོན་དུས་ཁོང་ཕེབས་ཀྱི་འདུག When I left the house (door) he was coming in.

སྒོ་དྲུང་ (go truŋ) sm. སྒོ་ཁ་.

སྒོ་གདངས་ (godaŋ) va. to open a door.

སྒོ་གདོང་ (godoŋ) sm. སྒོ་ཁ་.

སྒོ་མདོ་ (godo) sm. སྒོ་འགག.

སྒོ་འདོན་བྱེད་ (godön cee) va. to take a baby outside the house for the first time since its birth.

སྒོ་རྡུང་ (go duŋ) va. to knock on a door.

སྒོ་སྡེམ་ (godem) sm. སྒོ་རྒྱག.

སྒོ་སྡོམ་ (go dəom) sm. སྒོ་རྒྱག.

སྒོ་སྡོམ་རིང་ལུགས་ (godom riŋluù) sm. སྒོ་རྒྱག་རིང་ལུགས་.

སྒོ་བསྡམས་ (godam) p. of སྒོ་སྡོམ་.

སྒོ་ན་ (gona) at the door ། སྒོ་ན་མི་ཞིག་འདུག There is a man at the door.

སྒོ་ནག (gonag) the family of a deceased person whose demise has not yet been a year.

སྒོ་ནས་ (gonɛɛ̀) 1. by means of, in the manner of ། ཁོས་ཚན་རིག་གི་སྒོ་ནས་བཤད་པ་རེད་ He discussed it scientifically. ། དགའ་སྤྲོ་གི་སྒོ་ནས་ Happily. 2. from the door.

སྒོ་ནོར་ (gonɔɔ) sm. སྒོ་ཕྱུགས་.

སྒོ་ནོར་ (go nɔɔ) vi. to enter the wrong door, to get lost finding a house.

སྒོ་ནོར་ལམ་འཁྲུལ་ (gonɔɔ lamdrüü) dishonest/ wrong behavior [Lit. entering the wrong door, taking the wrong path].

སྒོ་ནོར་ལས་ཁུངས་ (gonɔɔ lɛɛ̀guŋ) department/ office of animal husbandry.

སྒོ་པ་ (goba) sm. སྒོ་སྲུང་.

སྒོ་པང་ (gobaŋ) sm. སྒོ་གླེགས་.

སྒོ་དཔོན་ (gobön) chief of guards/ doorkeepers.

སྒོ་སྤེ་ (gobe) room built above the main door.

སྒོ་ཕིབས་ (gobib) small roof extending out from the top of the door, a roofed gateway.

སྒོ་ཕོར་ (gobɔɔ) shung. door knocker.

སྒོ་ཕྱིར་ཐོན་ (gojir tōn) va. to leave/ exit a room or house.

སྒོ་ཕྱུགས་ (gojuù) domestic livestock/ animals.

སྒོ་ཕྱུགས་ཀྱི་ར་བ་ (gojuùgi rawa) cattle corral/ enclosure.

སྒོ་ཕྱུགས་དུད་འགྲོ་ (gojuù tündrɔ) domestic animals.

སྒོ་ཕྱུགས་སྨན་བཅོས་ཁང་ (gojuù mēnjögaŋ) veterinary clinic.

སྒོ་ཕྱུགས་སྨན་པ་ (gojuù mēmba) veterinarian.

སྒོ་ཕྱུགས་གསོ་མཁན་ (gojuù sōngɛn) cattle breeder.

སྒོ་ཕྱུགས་ཨེམ་ཆི་ (gojuù ēmci) sm. སྒོ་ཕྱུགས་སྨན་པ་.

སྒོ་ཕྱེ་ (goje) p. of སྒོ་འབྱེད་.

སྒོ་ཕྱོགས་ནད་དཔྱད་ས་ཚིགས་ (gojɔɔ̀ nɛɛ̀jɛɛ̀ sədzii)

livestock quarantine station.

སྒོ་ཕྱུགས་སྤོང་ (gojɔɔ bōŋ) va. to stop visiting sb. ¶ དེང་སང་ངའི་གྲོགས་པོས་ངའི་སྒོ་ཕྱུགས་སྤངས་བཞག Nowadays my friend has stopped visiting me.

སྒོ་ཕྱུགས་གཟན་ཆས་ཁང་ (gojɔɔ sɛnjɛɛgaŋ) livestock fodder office.

སྒོ་ཕྱུགས་ལེགས་བཅོས་ས་ཚིགས་ (gojɔɔ legjöö sādzii) livestock breeding station.

སྒོ་འཕར་ (gombar) door opening.

སྒོ་འཕྱུར་ (gonjɔɔ) sm. སྒོ་མཆོར་.

སྒོ་བབས་ (gobəb) shung. corvee labor that is decreed.

སྒོ་བྱང་ (gojaŋ) 1. a narrow rectangular board hung beside a door that indicates what the house or the office is, a nameplate on a door; va.—འགེལ་; —སྦྱར་ to put up a house number. 2. sign outisde of a store.

སྒོ་དབྱེ་ (go cē) f. of སྒོ་འབྱེད་.

སྒོ་དབྱེའི་དར་ཚོན་ (gocee tardzön) ribbon at an opening/ inaugural ceremony.

སྒོ་དབྱེ་བའི་སྲིད་ཇུས་ (go cēwɛ sīijöö) open door policy.

སྒོ་འབོར་ (gombɔɔ) door knocker.

སྒོ་འབོར་ཨ་ལོང་ (gombɔɔ āloŋ) the ring of a door knocker.

སྒོ་འབྱེད་ (go ce) 1. va. to open/ unlock a door.

སྒོ་འབྱེད་ (goje) inauguration, opening ¶ སྒོ་འབྱེད་རྟེན་འབྲེལ་ Inaugural ceremony; va.—གནང་; —མཛད་ to inaugurate, to open ¶ སྲིད་བློན་མཆོག་ནས་འགྲེམས་སྟོན་དེའི་སྒོ་འབྱེད་མཛད་པ་རེད་ The Prime Minister opened the exhibition.

སྒོ་འབྱེད་མཛད་སྒོ་ (goje dzɛɛgo) inaugural ceremony.

སྒོ་མ་ (goma) 1. a type of vein. 2. a protective goddess in the Tibetan mandala.

སྒོ་མང་ (gomaŋ) abbr. of སྒོ་མང་གྲྭ་ཚང་.

སྒོ་མང་གྲྭ་ཚང་ (gomaŋ tradzaŋ) a large college in Drepung monastery.

སྒོ་མང་པོ་ (go maŋbo) 1. multipurpose. 2. many doors.

སྒོ་མིང་འབྱར་མ་ (gomiŋ jarma) doors that have name tags.

སྒོ་མོ་ (gomo) door.

སྒོ་མོ་ཆེ་ (gomoje) large gate/ door (usu. of a castle or walled city).

སྒོ་ཙ་ (godza) the area in front of a door.

སྒོ་ཙར་ (godzar) at the door ¶ ཚགས་པར་ཉིན་ལྟར་སྒོ་ཙར་སྐྱེལ་གྱི་ཡོད་པ་རེད་ They deliver the newspaper at the door every day.

སྒོ་ཚད་ (godzɛɛ) size of a door.

སྒོ་ཚད་མ་ (godzɛma) traditional Tibetan paper that is the size of a door.

སྒོ་ཚོང་ (godzoŋ) 1. retail sales; va.—རྒྱག; —བྱེད་ to sell retail. 2. door-to-door sales; va.—རྒྱག; —བྱེད་ to sell retail, to sell door-to-door.

སྒོ་མཛམས་ (gomdzam) sm. སྒོ་ཙ་.

སྒོ་འཛིན་ (gondzin) admission ticket/ pass, entrance ticket.

སྒོ་འཛུལ་ (go dzüü) va. to enter a door, to go through a door.

སྒོ་ཟམ་ (gosam) sm. སྒོ་རྒྱ་.

སྒོ་ཟམ་འབྲིང་སྒྲོག (gosam dreŋdrɔɔ) shung. leather strap used to seal sth. off ¶ བཀར་ཁང་ནང་བཙུག་ཡོག་སྒོ་ཟམ་འབྲིང་སྒྲོག་དང་འགྲིལ་ It was put into the granary and locked with a leather strap and sealed.

སྒོ་ཟོག (gosɔɔ) livestock, domestic animals.

སྒོ་ཟོག་སེམས་ཅན་ (gosɔɔ sēmjɛn) sm. སྒོ་ཟོག.

སྒོ་ཡིག (goyii) shung. edict written on paper that is stuck on a wooden board and placed in various parts of a city. 2. writing on the wooden cangue that prisoners wear indicating their crime.

སྒོ་ཡོལ་ (goyöö) curtain (over a door); door-drape; va.—རྒྱག to put down/ close the door curtain/ drape.

སྒོ་གཡོག (goyɔɔ) sm. སྒོ་, 4.

སྒོ་ར་ (gora) 1. courtyard. 2. the apartments around a courtyard.

སྒོ་ར་རྒྱབ་མ་ (gora gyəbmə) backyard.

སྒོ་ར་ཅན་ (gorajɛn) a house that has a courtyard.

སྒོ་ར་མདོ་སྦུག (gora dobuù) the front and inside door of a house compound.

སྒོ་ར་ནང་མ་ (gora naŋma) inside the yard, inside a courtyard; an inner courtyard.

སྒོ་ར་ཕྱི་མ་ (gora cīmə) the front yard; the outer courtyard.

སྒོ་ར་བ་ (gorawa) 1. gatekeeper. 2. soccer goalie.

སྒོ་ར་སྦུག་མ་ (gora bugmə) sm. སྒོ་ར་ནང་མ་.

སྒོ་རུ་ (goru) the door frame.

སྒོ་རུ་གཞི་ (goru shi) sm. སྒོ་རུ་.

སྒོ་ལུང་ (goluŋ) sm. ཀུ་ལུགས་.

སྒོ་ལེབ་ (goleb) sm. སྒོ་གླེགས་.

སྒོ་ལོགས་ (golɔɔ) the walls beside a door.

སྒོ་བཤད་ (gobshɛɛ) ceremonial words spoken as a part of a wedding ceremony before the new bride enters the house.

སྒོ་བཤན་ (goshɛn) shung. iron bands put on doors.

སྒོ་སྲུང་ (gosuŋ) doorkeeper, gatekeeper.

སྒོ་སྲུང་ཁང་ (gosuŋgaŋ) 1. a room where the doorkeeper/ gatekeeper stays. 2. two small temples on the two sides of a main temple in which guardian deities are placed.

སྒོ་སྲུང་ཉེན་རྟོག་པ་ (gosuŋ ñendogba) police guard at an entrance door.

སྒོ་སྲུང་བ་ (gosuŋwə) sm. སྒོ་སྲུང་.

སྒོ་སྲུབས་ (gosub) crack/ space in a door.

སྒོ་གསུམ་ (gosum) the three doors: the body, speech, and mind.

སྒོ་གསེང་ (goseŋ) a crack/ slit/ opening in a door.

སྒོ་གསེང་ཤོར་ (goseŋ shɔɔ) 1. vi. to have a thief slip in while the door is left open. 2. vi. to have one's wife have an affair during the absence of her husband.

སྒོ་ལྷ་ (golha) a deity residing in a door, a door-god.

སྒོ་ཨང་ (goaŋ) door number.

སྒོག: p. བསྒོགས་; f. བསྒག་; imp. སྒོགས་ (gɔɔ) va. to make sb. take an oath.

སྒོག་སྐྱ་ (gɔggya) a kind of garlic (allium sativum).

སྒོག་མཁར་བ་ (gɔɔkarwa) name of an aristocratic family.

སྒོག་སྔོན་ (gɔgŋön) sm. རི་སྒོག.

སྒོག་ཆབ་ (gɔgjəb) boiled garlic extract used as medicine.

སྒོག་ཏིང་ (gɔgdiŋ) mortar and pestle.

སྒོག་ཏིང་ལག་རྒྱག (gɔgdiŋ yɛɛgyaà) pestle.

སྒོག་གཏུན་ (gɔgdün) sm. སྒོག་ཏིང་.

སྒོག་ཐལ་ (gɔgdɛɛ) powdered garlic (used as medicine).

སྒོག་དྲི་ (gɔgdri) smell of garlic.

སྒོག་འདོན་ (gɔgdön) boiled garlic mixed with butter (used as a medicine).

སྒོག་རྡོག (gɔgdog) bulb of garlic.

སྒོག་པ་ (gɔgba) garlic; va.—སིལ་ to take apart the cloves of a garlic bulb.

སྒོག་པ་ཅིག་སྒྲིལ་ (gɔgba ciggyeè) a ball of solid garlic with no separate cloves.

སྒོག་པ་རྩ་འདོན་ (gɔgba dzādön) shung. to eradicate/ destroy completely ¶ ཁོ་པ་ཕྱིས་བཙས་སྒོག་པ་རྩ་འདོན་གནང་ཅེ་ཁོ་པའི་རྒྱུ་དངོས་མཁར་དབང་གཞུང་བཞེས་ཡོང་བ་ (We) requested the government to destroy him and confiscate his wealth and property. [Lit. to pull the garlic from the root].

སྒོག་པ་རྫོག (gɔgba dzɔɔ) 1. va. to pound garlic. 2. vi. to dance in an uncoordinated/ clumsy fashion.

སྒོག་པ་རི་སྒོག (gɔgba rigɔɔ) a kind of mountain garlic.

སྒོག་པ་སིལ་དུང་ (gɔgba sīlduŋ) sm. སྒོག་པ་སིལ་བདུངས་.

སྒོག་པ་སིལ་བདུངས་ (gɔgba sīlduŋ) splitting up the enemy and destroying them one by one; settling things one by one [Lit. taking apart the cloves of garlic and pulverizing them].

སྒོག་པོར་ (gɔgbɔr) see སྒོར་པོར་.

སྒོག་འབྲུ་ (gɔŋdru) clove of garlic.

སྒོག་བཙོང་ (gɔg dzōŋ) garlic and onions.

སྒོག་ཚི་ (gɔgdzi) extract of garlic, garlic juice.

སྒོག་ལོ་ (gɔglo) garlic shoot.

སྒོག་བསིལ་ (gɔgsil) edible tulip.

སྒོགས་ (gɔ̀ɔ̀) imp. of སྒོག.

སྒོང་: p. བསྒོངས་; f. བསྒོང་; imp. སྒོངས་ (goŋ) 1. va. to knead dough into balls. 2. va. to add fuel to a fire. 3. abbr. of སྒོ་ང་.

སྒོང་སྐོགས་ (goŋgɔ̀ɔ̀) egg shell.

སྒོང་སྐྱེས་ (goŋgyeè) oviparous, produced/ born from an egg.

སྒོང་སྐྱེས་སྲོག་ཆགས་ (goŋgyeè sɔ̄gjaà) animals that reproduce by laying eggs.

སྒོང་ཆུ་ (goŋju) the white of an egg.

སྒོང་སྙོལ་འཕྲུལ་ཆས་ (goŋñöö trüüjɛɛ̀) sm. སྒོང་རུམ་འཕྲུལ་ཆས་.

སྒོང་གཏོང་བྱ་མོ་ (goŋdoŋ camo) egg-laying hen.

སྒོང་ཐོག་པ་ (goŋtɔ̄gba) sisymbrium heteromallum (used in Tibetan medicine).

སྒོང་དུག (goŋdug) spoiled/ rotten egg; vi.—ཕོག to get sick from eating a rotten egg.

སྒོང་དྲི་ (goŋdri) egg smell; vi.—ཁ་ to smell the aroma of eggs.

སྒོང་སྒྲིལ་ (goŋ trii) va. to roll dough or other substances into the shape of a ball.

སྒོང་རྡོག (gondoò) testicles.

སྒོང་ལྤགས་ (goŋbaà) egg shell.

སྒོང་སྤྲིས་ (goŋdrii̇) egg white.

སྒོང་སྤྲིས་དཀར་པོ་ (goŋdrii̇ gāābo) sm. སྒོང་སྤྲིས་.

སྒོང་ཕྱེ་ (goŋje) powdered egg.

སྒོང་བུ་ (goŋbu) ball-shaped.

སྒོང་བྱ་ (goŋja) a hen that lays eggs.

སྒོང་དབྱིབས་ (goŋyib) eggshaped.

སྒོང་འབྲས་ (goŋdɛɛ̀) scrambled eggs; va.—རྔོ་ to fry scrambled eggs.

སྒོང་མ་སྒུར་ (goŋma gur) half bending and half crawling.

སྒོང་བཙོས་ (goŋdzöö̀) boiled eggs; va. སྒོང་བཙོས་; —རྒྱག to boil eggs.

སྒོང་གཟུགས་མ་ (goŋsugmə) egg-shaped.

སྒོང་བཟོས་ཐོན་རྫས་ (goŋsöö̀ tōndzɛɛ̀) foodstuffs made from eggs.

སྒོང་བཟོས་ཟས་རིགས་ (goŋsöö̀ sɛɛ̀rii̇) sm. སྒོང་བཟོས་ཐོན་རྫས་.

སྒོང་རིལ་ (goŋrii) sm. སྒོང་བུ་.

སྒོང་རུམ་འཕྲུལ་ཆས་ (goŋrum trüüjɛɛ̀) incubator (for eggs).

སྒོང་ཤུན་ (goŋshün) egg shell.

སྒོངས་ (goŋ) imp. of སྒོང་.

སྒོབ་ (gob) proud, haughty; va.—བྱེད་ to act haughty/ proud.

སྒོབ་རྒྱུག (gob gyaà) va. to trot in a bumpy/ bouncy manner that is considered bad.

སྒོབ་ཚ་པོ་ (gob tsābo) 1. arrogant, disdainful. 2. sb. who plays hard to get.

སྒོམ་: p. བསྒོམས་; f. བསྒོམ་; imp. སྒོམས་ (gom) va. to meditate.

སྒོམ་ (gom) meditation; va.—རྒྱག to meditate.

སྒོམ་ཁང་ (gomgaŋ) meditation room.

སྒོམ་ཁྲི་ (gomdri) a throne for doing meditation.

སྒོམ་གྲྭ་ (gomdra) meditation center, a place for meditation.

སྒོམ་ཆེན་ (gomjen) 1. yogi, ascetic, hermit. 2. marmot.

སྒོམ་ཐག (gomdaà) the rope meditators wear draped across the chest.

སྒོམ་ཐབས་ (gomdəb) ways/ methods to meditate.

སྒོམ་སྡེ་ (gomde) sm. སྒོམ་གྲྭ་.

སྒོམ་སྡོད་ (gom döö̀) va. to endure, to tolerate ¶ མི་དེ་ལ་གཞན་གྱིས་གཤེ་གཤེ་ག་ཚོད་བཏང་ནའང་སྒོམ་སྡོད་ཐུབ་མཁན་ཞིག་རེད་ However much the others scold him, he is someone who can tolerate it.

སྒོམ་གནས་ (gomnɛɛ̀) place of meditation.

སྒོམ་པའི་ལམ་ (gombɛlam) path of meditation.

སྒོམ་ཞྭ་ (gomsha) a cap worn when meditating.

སྒོམ་བཟོད་ (gomsöö̀) sm. བཟོད་སྒོམ་.

སྒོམ་བཟླས་ (gomdɛɛ̀) meditating and reciting mantras simultaneously.

སྒོམ་རིམ་ (gomrim) meditative stage.

སྒོམ་ལམ་ (gomlam) sm. སྒོམ་པའི་ལམ་.

སྒོམ་ལུང་ (gomluŋ) initiation for meditation.

སྒོམ་ཤིང་ (gomshiŋ) 1. rifle butt. 2. a stick used to support the chin when meditating.

སྒོམས་ (gom) imp. of སྒོམ་.

སྒོའི་འགྲམ་པ་ (göö dramba) the two sides of a door.

སྒོའི་རྒྱབ་རྟེན་ (göö gyəbden) wooden stick (or chair) used to brace a door to keep someone from breaking in.

སྒོའི་ལྕགས་སྒོར་ (göö jāàgɔɔ) door hasp.

སྒོའི་ཏིང་ཀ་ (göö dīŋgə) door axle.

སྒོའི་མེ་ལོང་ (göö meloŋ) sm. སྒོ་གླེགས་.

སྒོའི་མེལ་ཚེ་མཁན་ (göö meetsegɛn) sm. སྒོ་སྲུང་བ་.

སྒོའི་རུ་མེ་མཛོ་དྲི་ (göö rume dzodri) abbr. door frame, door leaf, door hasp, door latch.

སྒོའི་རུ་བཞི་ (göö rushi) door frame.

སྒོའི་ཨ་ལོང་ (göö āloŋ) a door knocker.

སྒོའི་ཨང་གྲངས་ (göö āŋdraŋ) sm. སྒོ་གྲངས་.

སྒོར་ (gɔɔ) 1. imp. of སྒར་. 2. (with ཕྱུག་འཆག) va. to thresh grains by driving animals over the stalks. 3. abbr. of སྒོར་མོ་.

སྒོར་རྐྱང་ (gɔɔgyaŋ) 1. completely round. 2. hard currency, cash.

སྒོར་འཁྱིལ་འཁྱིལ་ (gɔɔ kyīīgyii) round.

སྒོར་འཁྱིལ་ལེ་ (gɔr kyīle) curled/ coiled in a circular shape ¶ ཁྱི་དེ་སྒོ་འཁྱིལ་ལེར་ཉལ་བསྡད་འདུག That dog lay curled up in a circle.

སྒོར་སྒོར་ (gɔɔgɔɔ) round, circular; va.—ལ་གཏོང་; va.—རྒྱག to do sth. in a circular manner (e.g., by passing it around in a circle) ¶ སྣུ་མགྲོན་ཚོར་ཞལ་ཏོག་སྒོར་སྒོར་ལ་བཏང་སོང (He) passed the snacks around to the guests.

སྒོར་ཆང་རྒྱག (gɔɔjaŋ gyaà) 1. va. to drink (ཆང་) in a circle (passing it around). 2. va. to play a game involving each person putting out fingers of the right hand.

སྒོར་རྟ་གཞུ་ (gɔɔda shu) va. to pull down a kite to attack another kite below it and cut its string.

སྒོར་རྟགས་ (gɔɔdaà) parenthesis; va.—རྒྱག to put in parentheses.

སྒོར་ལྟེ་ (gɔɔde) sm. སྒོར་དབྱིབས་ཀྱི་ལྟེ་བ་.

སྒོར་ལྟེའི་ཟུར་ (gɔɔdee sur) central angle.

སྒོར་ཐིག (gɔɔdig) circumference.

སྒོར་ཐིག་རྒྱག་ཆས་ (gɔɔdig gyaàjɛɛ̀) compass.

སྒོར་མཐའ་ (gɔɔda) circumference.

སྒོར་མཐའི་གྲངས་ཚད་ (gɔɔdɛ traŋdzɛɛ̀) pi (the ratio of the circumference of a circle to its diameter).

སྒོར་མཐའི་འགུལ་སྐྱོད་ (gɔɔdɛ güügyöö̀) circular motion.

སྒོར་མཐའི་ཟུར་ (gɔɔdɛ sur) circumferential angle.

སྒོར་མཐའི་རིང་ཚད་ (gɔɔdɛ riŋdzɛɛ̀) 1. (length of) circumference. 2. sm. སྒོར་མཐའི་གྲངས་ཚད་.

སྒོར་དུང་ (gɔɔduŋ) French horn.

སྒོར་ཕོར་ (gɔɔbɔɔ) wooden eating bowl.

སྒོར་བྲོ་ (gɔɔdro) circle dance.

སྒོར་དབྱིབས་ (gɔɔyib) circular in shape, circle.

སྒོར་དབྱིབས་ཀྱི་ལྟེ་བ་ (gɔɔyibgi dēwa) center of a circle.

སྒོར་དབྱིབས་ཀྱི་སྨུ་ཁྱུད་ (gɔɔyibgi mugyüǜ) sm. སྒོར་མཐའ་.

སྒོར་དབྱིབས་ཀྱི་མཐའ་འཁོར་ (gɔɔyibgi tāgɔɔ) the circumference of a circle.

སྒོར་དབྱིབས་ཀྱི་མཐའ་འཁོར་གྱི་གྲངས་ཚད་ (gɔɔyibgi tāgɔɔgi traŋdzɛɛ̀) sm. སྒོར་མཐའི་གྲངས་ཚད་.

སྒོར་དབྱིབས་ཅན་ (gɔɔyibjɛn) circular.

སྒོར་མིག (gɔɔmii̇) shape of a round hole.

སྒོར་མོ་ (gɔɔmo) 1. basic currency unit (dollar, rupee, pound, yuan, etc.) ¶ རྒྱ་གར་སྒོར་མོ་ Indian rupee. ། ཨ་རིའི་སྒོར་མོ་ U.S. dollar. 2. round, circular ། དབྱིབས་སྒོར་མོ་ Round shape. 3. money.

སྒོར་མོའི་ཚངས་ཐིག (gɔ̱ɔmö tsāŋdig) diameter.

སྒོར་མོའི་ཚངས་ཕྱེད་ (gɔ̱ɔmö tsāŋjeè) radius.

སྒོར་ཅག (gɔ̱ɔdzaà) small/ loose change.

སྒོར་འཛིན་ (gɔ̱ndzin) 1. a check (in dollars, etc.). 2. a bond.

སྒོར་གཞས་ (gɔ̱ɔshɛɛ̀) song that accompanies a circle dance; va.—རྒྱག.

སྒོར་ཟུར་ (gɔ̱ɔsur) one tenth of a སྒོར་མོ་ (10 cents or 1 མོ་ཚེ་) ། སྒོར་མོ་དགུ་དང་སྒོར་ཟུར་བདུན་སྐར་མ་བདུན་ 9.77 dollars.

སྒོར་ཟུར་གཅིག་གཉིས་ (gɔ̱ɔsur jīgñii) loose change (money).

སྒོར་སྲོལ་ (gɔ̱ɔsöö) currency system.

སྒོས་ (gö̱ö) 1. imp. of སྒོ་. 2. private ། སྤྱི་སྒོས་ཀྱི་དགོས་པ་ General and private needs. 3. special.

སྒོས་སྐལ་ (gö̱ögɛɛ) a individual's share, a personal share.

སྒོས་དགྲ་ (gö̱ödra) a personal enemy.

སྒོས་བདག (gö̱ödaà) privately owned.

སྒོས་དཔོན་ (gö̱öbön) sm. སྒེར་དཔོན་.

སྒོས་དབང་ (gö̱öwaŋ) shung. initiation given to private families and individuals.

སྒོས་མི་ (gö̱ömi) serfs/ subjects belonging to a lord or estate.

སྒོས་ཚ་ (gö̱ödza) great great grandson.

སྒོས་གཞིས་ (gö̱öshi) one's private estate, an aristocrat's estate.

སྒོས་སུ་ (gö̱ösu) particularly, in particular, specially.

སྒྱིང་ (gyi̱ŋ) va. to stretch one's limbs.

སྒྱིད་ (gyi̱i) vi. to be active/ energetic/ diligent.

སྒྱིད་སྒྱུར་ (gyi̱igyur) abbr. of སྒྱིད་པ་སྒྱུར་.

སྒྱིད་ཁུག (gyi̱iguù) sm. སྒྱིད་ཁུང་.

སྒྱིད་ཁུང་ (gyi̱iguŋ) the crook of the knee.

སྒྱིད་ཁུང་ཆུང་བ་ (gyi̱iguŋ cūŋwə) sm. སྒྱིད་ཁུང་.

སྒྱིད་ཁུམ་པ་ (gyi̱i kūmbə) sm. སྒྱིད་ལུག.

སྒྱིད་འཁྱིལ་ (gyi̱i trī̱i) vi. to have one's clothes cling/ stick to the body.

སྒྱིད་འཁྲིས་ (gyi̱i trī̱i) va. to walk with one's knees touching one another.

སྒྱིད་སྒྱིད་ཁུག་ཁུག (gyi̱igyi̱i kūùguù) sm. སྒྱིད་ཁུག.

སྒྱིད་སྒྱུར་: p. སྒྱིད་བསྒྱུར་; f. སྒྱིད་སྒྱུར་ (gyi̱i gyu̱r) 1. vi. to have muscular pains or cramps in the legs. 2. sm. སྒྱིད་ལུག.

སྒྱིད་ངན་ (gyi̱iŋɛn) lazy, idle, apathetic.

སྒྱིད་འཇུ་ (gyinju) sm. སྒྱིད་པ་.

སྒྱིད་སྙོམས་པ་ (gyi̱i ño̱mba) sm. སྒྱིད་ལུག་ཅན་.

སྒྱིད་པ་ (gyi̱ibə) 1. muscle/ tendon running from the ankle to the thigh; vi.—སྒྱུར་ to feel tired/ worn out/ fed up (with work, etc.). 2. active, energetic, diligent.

སྒྱིད་པོ་ (gyi̱ibu) active, energetic, diligent, keen, earnest.

སྒྱིད་པོ་མེད་པ་ (gyi̱ibu me̱èba) not active/ energetic/ diligent/ earnest/ keen.

སྒྱིད་དཔྲག (gyi̱idraà) the space between the knees.

སྒྱིད་འདྲེག (gyi̱i dre̱g) a form of corporal punishment where the muscle/tendon behind the knee is severed.

སྒྱིད་ཙ་གཅོད་ (gyi̱idza jö̀ö) sm. སྒྱིད་འདྲེག.

སྒྱིད་ལ་ངན་པོ་ (gyi̱ila ŋe̱mba) sm. སྒྱིད་ལུག.

སྒྱིད་ལ་ཉེས་པོ་ (gyi̱ila ñe̱èbo) sm. སྒྱིད་ལུག.

སྒྱིད་ལུག (gyi̱iluù) lazy, idle, indolent; va.—བྱེད་.

སྒྱིད་ལུག་གི་རང་བཞིན་ (gyi̱iluùgi ra̱ŋshin) 1. inertia. 2. laziness.

སྒྱིད་ལུག་ཅན་ (gyi̱iluùjɛn) a lazy person.

སྒྱིད་ལུག་བག་གཡེང་ (gyi̱iluù pa̱gyeŋ) lazy, idle, indolent.

སྒྱུ་ (gyu̱) false, deceptive, illusory.

སྒྱུ་གར་ཚོགས་པ་ (gyu̱gar tsōgba) sm. སྒྱུ་རྩལ་ཚོགས་པ་.

སྒྱུ་ཐབས་ (gyu̱dəb) sm. བསླུ་ཐབས་.

སྒྱུ་འཕྲུལ་ (gyu̱ndrüü) sm. སྒྱུ་མ་.

སྒྱུ་འཕྲུལ་མ་ (gyu̱ trǖǖmə) the mother of Siddhartha (Buddha).

སྒྱུ་འཕྲུལ་ཚོགས་པ་ (gyu̱drüü tsōgba) circus troupe.

སྒྱུ་མ་ (gyu̱mə) illusion, fantasy, magic, conjuring.

སྒྱུ་མ་མཁན་ (gyu̱məgɛn) magician, conjurer.

སྒྱུ་མའི་ནོར་ (gyu̱mɛ nɔ̱ɔ) illusion, false perception of worldly matters.

སྒྱུ་མའི་རྫས་ (gyu̱mɛ dzɛ̱ɛ̀) 1. magician's paraphernalia. 2. illusory matter.

སྒྱུ་རྩལ་ (gyu̱dzɛɛ) 1. art ། རོལ་མོའི་སྒྱུ་རྩལ་ The art of music. 2. magic, conjuring.

སྒྱུ་རྩལ་ཁྲུའུ་ (gyu̱dzɛɛ trū) art division.

སྒྱུ་རྩལ་མཁན་ (gyu̱dzeŋgɛn) artist.

སྒྱུ་རྩལ་མཁས་པ་ (gyu̱dzɛɛ kɛ̄ɛba) artist.

སྒྱུ་རྩལ་འཁྲབ་སྟོན་ཚོགས་པ་ (gyu̱dzɛɛ trəbdön tsōgba) performing art troupe.

སྒྱུ་རྩལ་གྱི་གློག་བརྙན་ (gyu̱dzɛɛgi lɔ̄ɔñɛn) art film/ movie.

སྒྱུ་རྩལ་གྱི་ཉམས་འགྱུར་ (gyu̱dzɛɛgi ña̱mgyur) artistic style.

སྒྱུ་རྩལ་གྱི་ནུས་པ་ (gyu̱dzɛɛgi nü̱übə) artistic effect.

སྒྱུ་རྩལ་གྱི་རྣམ་པ་ (gyu̱dzɛɛgi nāmbə) artistic form.

སྒྱུ་རྩལ་གྱི་ཕན་ནུས་ (gyu̱dzɛɛgi pɛ̄nnüü) sm. སྒྱུ་རྩལ་གྱི་ནུས་པ་.

སྒྱུ་རྩལ་གྱི་ཕན་འབྲས་ (gyu̱dzɛɛgi pɛ̄ndrɛɛ̀) sm. སྒྱུ་རྩལ་གྱི་ནུས་པ་.

སྒྱུ་རྩལ་གྱི་རང་བཞིན་ (gyu̱dzɛɛgi ra̱ŋshin) artistic quality, artistry; artistic nature.

སྒྱུ་རྩལ་གྱི་ལས་རིགས་ (gyu̱dzɛɛgi lɛ̱ɛ̀rii) artistic professions.

སྒྱུ་རྩལ་གློག་བརྙན་ (gyu̱dzɛɛ lɔ̄ɔñɛn) artistic movie.

སྒྱུ་རྩལ་དངོས་རྫས་ (gyu̱dzɛɛ ŋö̱ödzɛɛ̀) sm. སྒྱུ་རྩལ་ཐོན་རྫས་.

སྒྱུ་རྩལ་སྟོན་ (gyu̱dzɛɛ dö̃n) va. to give an artistic performance.

སྒྱུ་རྩལ་ཐོན་རྫས་ (gyu̱dzɛɛ tö̃ndzɛɛ̀) artifacts.

སྒྱུ་རྩལ་སྡེ་ཁག (gyu̱dzɛɛ de̱gaà) department of art.

སྒྱུ་རྩལ་པ་ (gyu̱dzɛɛba) actor, artist, performer.

སྒྱུ་རྩལ་རྩོམ་རིག (gyu̱dzɛɛ dzōmrii) artistic works.

སྒྱུ་རྩལ་ཚན་རིག་ཁང་ (gyu̱dzɛɛ tsɛ̄nriìgaŋ) academy of fine arts.

སྒྱུ་རྩལ་ཚོགས་པ་ (gyu̱dzɛɛ tsōgba) troupe of musicians and artists.

སྒྱུ་རྩལ་འཚོང་ (gyu̱dzɛɛ tsōŋ) va. to make a living as a performer.

སྒྱུ་རྩལ་ཟློས་གར་ཁང་ (gyu̱dzɛɛ dö̱ögargaŋ) art theater.

སྒྱུ་རྩལ་ལུས་སྦྱོང་ (gyu̱dzɛɛ lü̱üjoŋ) artistic gymnastics.

སྒྱུ་རྩལ་སློབ་གྲྭ་ (gyu̱dzɛɛ lōbdra) art.

སྒྱུ་རྩལ་སློབ་གྲྭ་ཆེན་མོ་ (gyu̱dzɛɛlābdra cēmmo) university/ academy of fine arts.

སྒྱུ་རྩལ་གསར་སྒྲུན་ (gyu̱dzɛɛ sārdrön) artistic creation.

སྒྱུ་རྩལ་གསར་གཏོད་ (gyu̱dzɛɛ sārdöö) sm. སྒྱུ་རྩལ་གསར་སྒྲུན་.

སྒྱུ་ཟོག (gyu̱soò) sm. སྒྱུ་མའི་ནོར་.

སྒྱུ་ཤོམ་ (gyu̱shom) bragging/ boasting/ showing off one's knowledge; va.—བྱེད་.

སྒྱུག་པོ་ (gyu̱gbo) father-in-law.

སྒྱུག་པོ་སྒྱུག་མོ་ (gyu̱gbo gyu̱mo) father-in-law and mother-in-law.

སྒྱུག་མོ་ (gyu̱gmo) mother-in-law.

སྒྱུར་: p. and f. བསྒྱུར་; imp. སྒྱུར་ (gyu̱r) 1. va. to change, to transform, to alter ། ཁོ་ཚོའི་བསམ་བློ་སྒྱུར་ཐུབ་ཀྱི་མ་རེད་ (They) will not be able to change their mind. ། ཁོས་ཁ་ཕྱོགས་བསྒྱུར་བ་རེད་ (He) changed direction. ། ཁོས་འབྲུ་དངུལ་ལ་བསྒྱུར་བ་རེད་ He changed/ converted grain to money. 2. va. to translate, to interpret ། ཁོས་རྒྱ་སྐད་ནས་བོད་སྐད་དུ་དཔེ་དེབ་མང་པོ་བསྒྱུར་ཡོད་པ་རེད་ He has translated many books from Chinese to Tibetan. 3. va. to multiply ། བཞི་གཉིས་ཀྱིས་བསྒྱུར་བས་བརྒྱད་. Four times two equals eight. 4. times ། གྲོང་འདིར་རྒྱལ་རྩེ་ལས་བཅུ་སྒྱུར་གྱིས་མི་མང་བ་ཡོད་པ་རེད་ This town has ten times more people than Gyantse. 5. va. to bring under control, to rule ། ཕྱིའི་རྒྱལ་

ཕྱན་མང་པོ་དབང་དུ་བསྒྱུར་བ་རེད་ (They) brought many foreign kingdoms under their control.

སྒྱུར་བཀོད་ (gyurgöö) transformation, rebuilding, reconstruction, reorganization, reform; va.—བྱེད་; —གཏོང་ ༡ སྤྱི་ཚོགས་རིང་ལུགས་ཀྱི་སྒྱུར་བཀོད་ Socialist transformation.

སྒྱུར་ཁྱུ་ (gyurgyu) multiplication group, times table.

སྒྱུར་བཅོས་ (gyurjöö) reform, reforming; va.—བྱེད་; —གཏོང་ to reform ༡ སྤྱི་ཚོགས་རྙིང་པའི་ལམ་ལུགས་སྒྱུར་བཅོས་བཏང་བ་རེད་ They reformed the old society's way of life.

སྒྱུར་རྟགས་ (gyurdaà) multiplication sign.

སྒྱུར་ཐབས་ (gyurdəb) multiplying, multiplication.

སྒྱུར་མཐའ་རིའུ་མིག (gyurda rumig) multiplication table.

སྒྱུར་དེབ་ (gyurdeb) a translated book.

སྒྱུར་པ་པོ་ (gyurbəbo) translator.

སྒྱུར་ཕྱོགས་ (gyurjɔ̀ɔ̀) 1. manipulating, controlling; va.—བྱེད་ ༡ རྒྱལ་པོའི་བློན་པོས་སྒྱུར་ཕྱོགས་བྱེད་ཀྱི་ཡོད་པ་རེད་ The minister is controlling the king. 2. way/ manner of translation ༡ ཐ་སྙད་འདི་ལ་སྒྱུར་ཕྱོགས་མང་པོ་འདུག There are many different ways to translate this term.

སྒྱུར་བྱེད་གྲངས་ (gyurjeè traŋ) multiplier, multiplicator.

སྒྱུར་རྩིས་ (gyurdziì) multiplication; va.—རྒྱག to multiply.

སྒྱུར་རྩིས་ཀྱི་རྟགས་ (gyurdzigi dāà) multiplication sign.

སྒྱུར་རྩིས་དགུ་མཐའ་རིའུ་མིག (gyudziì guda rumig) nine times table.

སྒྱུར་རྩིས་སྤྱི་འགྲོས་ (gyurdziì jīndröö) multiplication formula.

སྒྱུར་རྩིས་མན་ངག (gyurdziì mɛnŋaà) oral recitation of the multiplication table.

སྒྱུར་རྩིས་རྩིས་དུལ་ (gyurdziì dzīìdüü) multiplication operation.

སྒྱུར་རྩིས་རིའུ་མིག (gyurdziì rumig) multiplication table.

སྒྱུར་རྩོམ་ (gyurdzom) 1. translations. 2. abbr. translating and writing/ composing.

སྒྱུར་ཞུས་པ་ (gyurshübə) translator and proofreader.

སྒྱུར་གཞི་ཉིས་རྩིས་ (gyurshi ñīìdziì) square root.

སྒྱུར་གཞི་གསུམ་རྩིས་ (gyurshi sūmdziì) cube root, 3rd power.

སྒྱུར་ཡིག (gyuryiì) a translation.

སྒྱུར་ཡོན་ (gyuryön) the fee/ wages for translating sth.

སྒྱེ་ (gye) sm. སྒྱེ་མོ་.

སྒྱེ་སྒྱེའུ་ (gye gyewu) big and small bag/ sack.

སྒྱེ་སྟོང་ (gyedoŋ) an empty sack/ bag.

སྒྱེ་ཐག (gyedaà) strap for bag/ sack.

སྒྱེ་སྣོད་ (gyenöö) sm. སྒྱེ་མོ་.

སྒྱེ་མོ་ (gyemo) bag, sack.

སྒྱེ་ཚད་ (gyedzɛɛ̀) shung. standard size of sack/ bag.

སྒྱེ་ཟླ་ (gyenda) long rectangular bag.

སྒྱེད་དོ་ (gyeèdo) sm. སྒྱེད་བུ་.

སྒྱེད་པུ་ (gyeèbu) sm. སྒྱེད་བུ་.

སྒྱེད་བུ་ (gyeèbu) stove made out of three stones or three pieces of iron (usu. used when traveling).

སྒྱེལ་: p. and f. བསྒྱེལ་; imp. སྒྱེལ་ (gyel) va. to cause to fall down, to pull or knock down, to bring down, to overthrow ༡ ཁོ་ཚོས་ལྕགས་རི་བསྒྱེལ་ནས་གྲོང་ཁྱེར་ནང་འཛུལ་པ་རེད་ They pulled down the wall and entered the city.

སྒྱོ་སྒྱེ་སྒྱེའུ་གསུམ་ (gyo gye gyewu sūm) large, medium and small sack/ bag.

སྒྱོ་བ་ (gyowa) a large sack/ bag.

སྒྱོགས་ (gyɔ̀ɔ̀) artillery, cannon, catapult.

སྒྱོགས་ཁྲི་ (gyɔ̀ɔ̀dri) cannon or artillery mount, platform for a cannon.

སྒྱོགས་མཁན་ (gyɔ̀ɔ̀gɛn) artillery man.

སྒྱོགས་འཁོར་ (gyɔ̀ɔ̀gɔɔ) cannon carriage.

སྒྱོགས་གྲུ་ (gyɔgdru) frigate, gunboat.

སྒྱོགས་གྲུ་ཆུང་གྲས་ (gyɔgdru cūŋdrɛɛ̀) small gunboat.

སྒྱོགས་གྲུའི་ཤུགས་ངོམ་ཕྱི་འབྲེལ་ (gyɔ̀ɔ̀drü shūgŋom cīndrɛɛ) gunboat diplomacy.

སྒྱོགས་སྒྲ་ (gyɔ̀ɔ̀dra) sound of artillery fire.

སྒྱོགས་སྒྲོམ་ (gyɔ̀ɔ̀drom) sm. སྒྱོགས་ཁྲི་.

སྒྱོགས་སྒྲ་ལྡིང་ལྡིང་ (gyɔ̀ɔ̀dra diŋdiŋ) roar of artillery fire.

སྒྱོགས་སྟེགས་ (gyɔ̀ɔ̀ded) sm. སྒྱོགས་ཁྲི་.

སྒྱོགས་ཐལ་ (gyɔ̀ɔ̀dɛɛ) cannon fodder.

སྒྱོགས་འཐབ་ (gyɔ̀ɔ̀dəb) artillery battle.

སྒྱོགས་མདའ་ (gyɔnda) sm. སྒྱོགས་མདེལ་.

སྒྱོགས་མདེལ་ (gyɔndel) cannon ball, artillery shell.

སྒྱོགས་མདོང་ (gyɔndoŋ) cannon barrel.

སྒྱོགས་རྡོ་ (gyɔ̀ɔ̀do) stone used in a sling/ catapult.

སྒྱོགས་བརྡ་ (gyɔ̀ɔ̀da) a signal given by artillery.

སྒྱོགས་ཕྲུག (gyɔgdrug) small scale artillery.

སྒྱོགས་སྦུབས་ (gyɔgbub) sm. སྒྱོགས་མདོང་.

སྒྱོགས་མེ་ (gyɔgme) artillery fire.

སྒྱོགས་དམག (gyɔgmaà) artillery force/ corps/ troops.

སྒྱོགས་རྫོང་ (gyogdzoŋ) fortress, fort, blockhouse, fortification, gun bunker.

སྒྱོང་: p. བསྒྱོངས་; f. བསྒྱོང་; imp. སྒྱོངས་ (gyoŋ) va. to hide/ cover up a crime.

སྒྲ་ (dra) 1. sound; va.—སྒྲོག to make/ produce sounds ༡ ཆུའི་སྒྲ་ The sound of water. 2. pronunciation ༡ ཚིག་གི་སྒྲ་ The pronunciation of a word.

སྒྲ་རྐྱང་ཐ་སྙད་ (dragyaŋ tãñɛɛ̀) monosyllabic word.

སྒྲ་རྐྱང་པའི་ཚིག (dragyaŋbɛ tsīg) monosyllabic word.

སྒྲ་སྐད་ (dragɛɛ̀) 1. sound ༡ དྲག་དུ་རྒྱུག་པའི་ཆུ་ཀླུང་གི་སྒྲ་སྐད་ The sound of a raging river. 2. voice ༡ ཨ་རིའི་སྒྲ་སྐད་ Voice of America.

སྒྲ་སྐད་རིག་པ་ (dragɛɛ̀ rigbə) linguistics.

སྒྲ་སྐྱུང་ (dra gyūŋ) 1. va. to lower/ reduce the sound. 2. va. to refrain from talking.

སྒྲ་སྐྱེད་གློག་དུང་ (dragyeè lɔ̄gduŋ) loudspeaker.

སྒྲ་སྐྱེད་འཕྲུལ་ཆས་ (dragyeè trũũjɛɛ̀) loudspeaker, amplifying equipment.

སྒྲ་སྐྱེལ་ (dragyee) broadcasting; va.—བྱེད་.

སྒྲ་སྐྱེལ་འཁོར་ལོ་ (dragyee kɔ̄ɔ̄lo) sm. སྒྲ་སྐྱེལ་འཕྲུལ་ཆས་.

སྒྲ་སྐྱེལ་འཕྲུལ་ཆས་ (dragyee trũũjɛɛ̀) microphone, megaphone.

སྒྲ་སྐྱོན་ (dragyön) static (in noise).

སྒྲ་བསྐྱེད་གློག་དུང་ (dragyeè lɔ̄gduŋ) sm. སྒྲ་སྐྱེད་གློག་དུང་.

སྒྲ་གོང་ (dragoŋ) deaf, deafness.

སྒྲ་མགྱོགས་ (dragyɔ̀ɔ̀) faster than sound.

སྒྲ་མགྱོགས་གནམ་གྲུ་ (dragyɔ̀ɔ̀ nɔ̄mdru) supersonic plane.

སྒྲ་འགོག་རྒྱུ་ (dra gɔ̀ɔ̀gyu) sound-proofing materials.

སྒྲ་རྒྱུ་ (drəgyu) phoneme.

སྒྲ་རྒྱུ་ཅན་གྱི་ཡི་གེ (drəgyujɛngi yigi) phonemic notation.

སྒྲ་སྒྱུར་ (drəgyur) transcription; transliteration; va.—བྱེད་; —འབྲི་ to transcribe/ transliterate.

སྒྲ་སྒྲིག (dra drig) va. to dub/ synchronize sound (for movies, etc.).

སྒྲ་ངན་ (draŋɛn) 1. an unpleasant sound. 2. bad news.

སྒྲ་ངར་ངར་པོ་ (draŋar ŋarbo) 1. sound of anger. 2. husky voice.

སྒྲ་དངོས་སྣང་ (dra ŋöönaŋ) stereophonic sound, stereo.

སྒྲ་གཅོད་ (dra jöö) dividing by syllables.

སྒྲ་གཅོད་མཚན་རྟགས་ (drajöö tsɛ̄ndaà) the syllable dividing dot "་".

སྒྲ་བཅུག (drəjuù) recorded sound (e.g., tape recorded).

སྒྲ་བཅུག་བཅར་འདྲི་ (drəjuù jəndri) recording an interview, a recorded interview.

སྒྲ་བཅུག་ཆེད་རྩོམ་ (drəjuù cēèdzom) recorded commentary/ editorial.

སྒྲ་བཅུག་གསར་འགྱུར་ (drəjuù sə̄ngyur) recorded news.

སྒྲ་ཆེན་འཁོར་ལོ་ (dracen kɔ̄ɔ̄lo) loudspeaker.

སྒྲ་ཇི་བཞིན་པ་ (dra jĩ shimbə) conveying/ translating the meaning of what was said ། དབྱིན་སྐད་དེ་སྒྲ་ཇི་བཞིན་པ་བོད་ཡིག་ནང་བྲིས་པ་རེད་ He conveyed the meaning of what was said in English into Tibetan.

སྒྲ་ཇི་བཞིན་མ་ཡིན་པ་ (dra jĩ shin məyimbə) unable to convey/ translate what was said.

སྒྲ་འཇུག (dranjuù) 1. recording on tape; va. སྒྲ་འཇུག; —བྱེད་. 2. abbr. of the name of a commentary by Sakya Pandita on Sanskrit grammar.

སྒྲ་འཇུག་འཁྲུལ་འཁོར་ (drajuù trũũgɔɔ) tape recorder.

སྒྲ་ཉམས་ (dra ñam) vi. to have a sound get lower. 2. vi. to get a change in pronunciation.

སྒྲ་སྙན་ (dramñɛn) Tibetan lute; va.—གཏོང་ to play the lute.

སྒྲ་སྙན་གྱི་སི་རྒྱུད་ (dramñɛngi sĩgyüü) silk strings (for Tibetan lute).

སྒྲ་སྙན་ཅིན་ཧུ་ (dramñɛn jĩnhu) tib. ch. string instruments.

སྒྲ་སྙན་གཅུས་བུར་ (dramñɛn jũübur) the knob that is used for tightening the strings of a lute.

སྒྲ་སྙན་གཏོང་ (dramñɛn dõŋ) see སྒྲ་སྙན་.

སྒྲ་སྙན་ཨེར་ཧུ་ (dramñɛn ērhu) tib.ch. two-stringed lute (large hocin).

སྒྲ་བརྙན་ (drañɛn) 1. echo. 2. gramophone.

སྒྲ་གཏོང་ (dra dõŋ) va. to transmit sound, to make sounds.

སྒྲ་རྟགས་ (dradaà) phonetic symbols.

སྒྲ་བརྟེན་ཚད་ལེན་འཁྲུལ་ཆས་ (draden tsɛ̃ɛlen trũũjɛɛ) sonar.

སྒྲ་མཐུན་ (dra tũn) va. to write words using colloquial pronunciations. 2. sm. སྒྲ་མཐུན་ཡི་གེ་.

སྒྲ་མཐུན་ཡི་གེ་ (dratün yigi) homonym.

སྒྲ་དག (dradag) sm. སྒྲ་དག་པོ་.

སྒྲ་དག་སྒྲོས་གཙང་ (dradag drõõdzaŋ) enunciating clearly.

སྒྲ་དག་པོ་ (dra tagbo) correct/ good pronunciation ། བོད་སྐད་སྒྲ་དག་པོ་ཞིག་རྒྱག་གི་འདུག (He) speaks Tibetan with a good pronunciation.

སྒྲ་དག་གསལ་གསུམ་ (dradaà sɛ̃ɛsum) shung. reading clearly and pronouncing well ། རྩ་ཚིག་སྒྲོག་སྒྲུངས་སྒྲ་དག་གསལ་གསུམ་དགོས་རྒྱུ་ The proclamation should be read clearly and pronounced well.

སྒྲ་དུང་ (draduŋ) megaphone, microphone.

སྒྲ་དོད་ཡི་གེ་ (dradöö yigi) phonetic alphabet.

སྒྲ་དོན་ (dradön) 1. abbr. pronunciation and meaning. 2. meaning of what is said.

སྒྲ་དྲག་པ་ (dra tragba) the Tibetan letters: ཀ་ཅ་ཏ་པ་ཙ་.

སྒྲ་གདངས་ (dradaŋ) tone, pitch, tune.

སྒྲ་གདངས་ཀྱི་མཚོན་རྟགས་ (dradaŋgi tsõndaà) phonetic signs/ symbols.

སྒྲ་གདངས་ཀྱི་གཞི་ཁྱོན་ (dradaŋgi shigyön) the range/ register of a sound or voice.

སྒྲ་གདངས་མཐོ་དམན་ (dradaŋgi tõmɛn) the volume (of sound).

སྒྲ་གདངས་དཔྱད་ཆས་ (dradaŋ jɛ̃ɛjɛɛ) sm. སྒྲ་སྤྱད་.

སྒྲ་གདངས་བཞི་ (dradaŋshi) the four tones.

སྒྲ་གདངས་རིག་པ་ (dradaŋ rigbə) phonetics.

སྒྲ་གདངས་སུ་ཕབ་ (dradaŋsu pəb) va. to transcribe sounds.

སྒྲ་གདངས་སྒྲོངས་ཤུགས་ཅན་ (dradaŋ dõŋshuùjɛn) loud and clear (speech).

སྒྲ་མདའ་ (drāda) a whistling arrow.

སྒྲ་མདོ་བཞི་ (dradoshi) four texts on Sanskrit grammar.

སྒྲ་འདས་སྐྱོན་ཞིབ་ (dradɛɛ gyõnshib) detecting flaws via ultrasound; va.—བྱེད་.

སྒྲ་འདས་བརྟག་དཔྱད་ (dradɛɛ dāgjɛɛ) examination via ultrasound; va.—བྱེད་.

སྒྲ་འདས་ནད་བརྟག (dradɛɛ nɛ̃ɛdaà) diagnosis through ultrasound; va.— བྱེད་.

སྒྲ་འདོན་ (dra dön) va. to pronounce, to make a sound.

སྒྲ་འདོན་དབང་པོ་ (dradön wāŋbo) vocal organs.

སྒྲ་འདྲ་བའི་ཚིག (dra drawɛ tsĩg) homophone, words with similar sounds.

སྒྲ་ལྡན་ (drandɛn) having sound/ talking.

སྒྲ་ལྡན་གློག་བརྙན་ (drandɛn lɔ̃ɔñɛn) talking film, sound film.

སྒྲ་ལྡན་མདའ་མོ་ (drandɛn damo) a arrow that makes a sound when it is in flight.

སྒྲ་སྡུད་ (drədüü) sound reception, acoustics.

སྒྲ་སྡུད་སྒྲ་ཕབ་གཉིས་སྦྱོར་ (drədüü drabəb ñĩijöö) combined radio and tape recorder.

སྒྲ་སྡུད་འཁྲུལ་འཁོར་ (drədüü trũũgɔɔ) radio.

སྒྲ་སྡེབ་ (dradeb) the construction of a Tibetan word from suffixes, prefixes, etc.

སྒྲ་བསྡུས་སྒྲ་བབས་ (drədüü drabəb) tape recording.

སྒྲ་ནུས་ (dranüü) sonics.

སྒྲ་ནུས་འཇལ་ཆས་ (dranüü jɛɛjɛɛ) sound measuring equipment.

སྒྲ་པར་ (drabar) sm. སྒྲ་དཔར་.

སྒྲ་དཔར་ (drabar) phonograph record, tape recording; va.—རྒྱག; —འདེབས་ to record (on record or tape).

སྒྲ་སྤྱད་ (drajɛɛ) tuning fork.

སྒྲ་ཕབ་ (dra pəb) p. of སྒྲ་འབེབས་.

སྒྲ་ཕབ་འཁོར་ལོ་ (drabəb kɔ̃ɔlo) tape recorder.

སྒྲ་བོ་ཆེ་ (draboje) loud sound/ noise.

སྒྲ་བྱེད་ (drajeè) sm. སྒྲ་སྒྲོག.

སྒྲ་བླུག་སྦྱིན་ཤོག (drəluù jĩnshoò) audio recording tape.

སྒྲ་དབྱངས་ (drayaŋ) melodious/ harmonious sound, musical sound; va.—སྒྲོག to make musical sounds.

སྒྲ་དབྱངས་ཀྱི་མྱུར་ཚད་ (drayaŋgi ñurdzɛɛ) speed of sound.

སྒྲ་དབྱངས་ཀྱི་རིག་པ་ (drayaŋgi rigbə) study of phonetics, phonology.

སྒྲ་དབྱངས་ལྷ་མོ་ (drayaŋ lhāmo) sm. ལྷ་མོ་དབྱངས་ཅན་མ་.

སྒྲ་འབེབས་ (dra beb) 1. va. to record. 2. va. to transcribe sounds.

སྒྲ་འབེབས་ཁབ་ལེན་སྦྱིན་ཤོག (drabeb kāblen jĩnshoò) magnetic recording tape.

སྒྲ་འབེབས་བརྙན་འབེབས་ (drabeb ñɛ̃nbeb) recording sound and recording film/ video.

སྒྲ་འབེབས་འཁྲུལ་འཁོར་ (drabeb trũũgɔɔ) tape recorder.

སྒྲ་འབེབས་འཁྲུལ་ཆས་ (drabeb trũũjɛɛ) sm. སྒྲ་འབེབས་འཁྲུལ་འཁོར་.

སྒྲ་འབེབས་སྦྱིན་ཤོག (drabeb jĩnshoò) audio recording tape.

སྒྲ་སྦྱོར་བམ་གཉིས་ (drajor bamñii) an 8th century work on Tibetan grammar.

སྒྲ་སྦྱོར་ (drajɔɔ) 1. phonetics, romanization. 2. rules for the spelling of the grammatical particles. 3. dubbing (a film); va.—བྱེད་.

སྒྲ་སྦྱོར་གྱི་དབྱངས་གསལ་ (drajɔɔgi yāŋsɛl) phonetics.

སྒྲ་སྦྱོར་གྱི་ཡི་གེ་ (drajɔɔgi yigi) phonetic notation/ alphabet.

སྒྲ་སྦྱོར་བྱེད་སྟངས་ (drajɔɔ ceèdaŋ) system of phonetics.

སྒྲ་མི་སྙན་ (dramiñɛn) one of the four continents surrounding Mount Meru.

སྒྲ་མེད་གློག་བརྙན་ (drameè lɔ̃gñɛn) silent film.

སྒྲ་མེད་འཇམ་ཐིང་ (drameè jamdiŋ) quiet.

སྒྲ་ཚད་དཔེ་རིས་ (dradzɛɛ bēri) sound spectrum.

སྒྲ་ཚིགས་ (drədzii) syllable.

སྒྲ་ཚིགས་རྐྱང་མ་ (drədzii gyāŋmə) monosyllable.

སྒྲ་ཆེ་ (dradze) shung. memorial to the Emperor ། བོད་བཞུགས་ཨམ་བན་ཆེན་ལ་བཀྲས་རབ་བརྒྱུད་སྙན་ཞུས་སྒྲ་ཆེ་ཕེབས་པ་ The Ambans residing in Tibet sent a memorial to the Emperor through Trɛrəb.

སྒྲ་མཚམས་འཇོག་རྟགས་ (dradzam jɔgdaà) musical rest sign.

སྒྲ་མཚུངས་ཚིག་མཛོད་ (drədzuŋ tsĩŋdzöö) homonym dictionary.

སྒྲ་མཚོན་པའི་ཚིག (dradzönbɛ tsĩi) onomatopoetic word.

སྒྲ་འཛིན་ (drəndzin) 1. poet. ears. 2. sm. སྒྲ་ཕབ་.

སྒྲ་འཛིན་འཁོར་ལོ་ (drəndzin kɔ̄olo) sm. སྒྲ་ཕབ་འཁོར་ལོ་.

སྒྲ་འཛིན་བུ་ག (drəndzin buga) poet. ear.

སྒྲ་ཞན་པ་ (drashɛmba) labial sounds.

སྒྲ་ཞི་བ་ (dra shiwə) a soft/ low tone.

སྒྲ་གཞུང་ (drashaŋ) a text on Sanskrit grammar.

སྒྲ་ཟུར་ཆགས་ (dra surcaà) language change.

སྒྲ་ཡང་བ་ (dra yaŋwa) sm. སྒྲ་ཞན་པ་.

སྒྲ་རིག་པ་ (dra rigbə) 1. linguistics. 2. Sanskrit grammar.

སྒྲ་རིག་པའི་བསྟན་བཅོས་ (dra rigbɛ dɛ̄njöö) sm. སྒྲ་གཞུང་.

སྒྲ་རིམ་ (drarim) a part (in music).

སྒྲ་རླབས་ (drələb) sound wave, acoustic wave.

སྒྲ་རླབས་ལས་བརྒལ་བ་ (drələblɛ gɛɛwa) sm. སྒྲ་ལས་མྱུར་བ་.

སྒྲ་ལན་ (dralɛn) echo; vi.—འཁོར་ to echo.

སྒྲ་ལས་མྱུར་བ་ (dralɛ ñurwə) supersonic speed, faster than sound.

སྒྲ་ལས་མྱུར་བའི་གནམ་གྲུ་ (dralɛ ñurwɛ nəmdru) supersonic plane.

སྒྲ་ལེན་འཁོར་ལོ་ (dralen kɔ̄olo) radio.

སྒྲ་ལེན་འཕྲུལ་ཆས་ (dralen trũũjɛɛ̀) radio, radio equipment.

སྒྲ་ལེན་རུས་པ་ (dralen rũũbə) ear bones.

སྒྲ་ཤེལ་ (drashee) cassette tape, video tape ¶ སྒྲ་ཤེལ་བཟོ་གྲྭ Cassette tape factory.

སྒྲ་བཤད་ (drashɛɛ̀) explaining a word; va.—རྒྱག.

སྒྲ་སིལ་སིལ་ (dra sĩĩsii) sound of bells ringing.

སྒྲ་སེང་ངེ་བ་ (dra sēŋŋewa) a ringing sound.

སྒྲ་གསང་ (drasaŋ) sound, noise.

སྒྲ་གསལ་ (drasɛl) clear sound.

སྒྲ་གསལ་ཞིང་ཚིགས་དང་ལྡན་པ་ (drasɛl shiŋ tsĩĩdaŋ dɛmba) clear and precisely enunciated.

སྒྲ་ལྷད་ (dralhɛɛ̀) noisy, staticy.

སྒྲ་ལྷོད་ (dralhöö) low and slow voice.

སྒྲབ་སྒྲོབ་ (drəbdrob) sm. སྒྲབ་བེ་སྒྲོབ་བེ་.

སྒྲབ་བེ་སྒྲོབ་བེ་ (drəbbe drobbe) 1. a pile/ heap of miscellaneous things. 2. pretending to be sth. one is not; va.—བྱེད་.

སྒྲའི་སྐྱེ་གནས་ (drɛ gyēnɛɛ̀) points of articulation (in phonetics).

སྒྲའི་མགྱོགས་ཚད་ (drɛ gyogdzɛɛ̀) the speed of sound.

སྒྲའི་འགྱུལ་ཚད་ (drɛ güüdzɛɛ̀) 1. audio frequency. 2. sm. སྒྲ་དབྱངས་ཀྱི་མྱུར་ཚད་.

སྒྲའི་རྒྱན་ (drɛ gyɛn) metaphor.

སྒྲའི་ང་རོ་ (drɛ ŋaro) sm. སྒྲ་གདངས་.

སྒྲའི་འཇུག་ཚུལ་ (drɛ jugdzüü) rules for spelling of grammatical particles after different final letters.

སྒྲའི་འདར་ཚད་ (drɛ dardzɛɛ̀) audio frequency.

སྒྲའི་སྡེབ་སྦྱོར་ (drɛ debjɔɔ) composition of compound words by putting together prefixes and suffixes, etc.

སྒྲའི་ནུས་པ་ (drɛ nũũbə) sonics.

སྒྲའི་འབྱུང་གནས་ (drɛ cuŋnɛɛ̀) vocal cords.

སྒྲའི་རིམ་པ་ (drɛ rimbə) sm. སྒྲ་རིམ་.

སྒྲིག: p. བསྒྲིགས་; f. བསྒྲིག; imp. སྒྲིགས་ (drig) 1. to arrange, to set up, to put in order ¶ མེ་ཏོག་དེ་ཚོ་ལེགས་པར་བསྒྲིགས་འདུག (They) arranged those flowers nicely. ¶ ཁོས་ཤོག་ལྷེའི་ཨང་ཀི་སྒྲིག་གི་ཡོད་པ་རེད་ He is putting the pages (of the book) in numerical order. 2. va. to form a line, to line up, to set in rows ¶ ཚང་མ་གྲལ་སྒྲིག་བཅུག་པ་རེད་ (They) made them all line up. 3. va. to put together, to assemble ¶ འཕྲུལ་འཁོར་དེ་སྒྲིག་གི་ཡོད་པ་རེད་ They are assembling the machine. 4. va. to compile, to edit, to compose ¶ ཚིག་མཛོད་འདི་1973 ལོ་བསྒྲིགས་པ་རེད་ (They) composed this dictionary in the year 1973.

སྒྲིག (drig) the official monastic community/ register ¶ ད་ལྟ་སྒྲིག་ལ་ཡོད་པའི་གྲྭ་པ་ ༡༠༠ འདུག There are 100 monks in the monastic community.

སྒྲིག་བཀོད་ (driggöö) arranging, ordering, laying out; organizing; va.—བྱེད་ ¶ དེ་ནས་དམག་སྒར་སྒྲིག་བཀོད་མཛད་པ་ནི་ As for the regiments that were organized after that. ¶ སྐུ་སྲུང་དམག་མི་ཡང་བསྐྱར་སྒྲིག་བཀོད་བྱས་སོང་ (They) organized the bodyguard regiment again.

སྒྲིག་ཁོངས་ (driggun) membership in a unit/ organization ¶ ཁོས་རྒྱལ་སྤྱིའི་སློབ་ཕྲུག་གི་ཚོགས་པའི་སྒྲིག་ཁོངས་སུ་ཞུགས་པ་རེད་ He joined the ranks of the International Students Association. ¶ དམག་མི་དེ་བོད་དམག་གི་སྒྲིག་ཁོངས་ནས་ཕུད་པ་རེད་ (They) expelled the soldier from the ranks of the Tibetan army.

སྒྲིག་ཁོངས་སུ་འཇུག (drig kūŋsu juù) va. to make sb. a member of an association or organization.

སྒྲིག་ཁོངས་སུ་གཏོང་ (drig kūŋsu dōŋ) va. to send/ despatch/ assign sb. to a unit or organization ¶ སློབ་གྲྭ་ཐོན་པ་རྣམས་ལས་ཁུངས་འདྲ་མིན་གྱི་སྒྲིག་ཁོངས་སུ་བཏང་བ་རེད་ They sent (assigned) graduates to different offices.

སྒྲིག་ཁྲིམས་ (drigdrim) discipline, disciplinary rules ¶ སྒྲིག་ཁྲིམས་དང་འགལ་ In violation of disciplinary rules.

སྒྲིག་ཁྲིམས་ཀྱི་ཉེས་ཆད་ (drigdrimgi ñɛɛ̀jɛɛ̀) disciplinary action, disciplinary measures.

སྒྲིག་ཁྲིམས་ཀྱི་རང་བཞིན་ (drigdrimgi rəŋshin) sense of discipline ¶ སྒྲིག་ཁྲིམས་ཀྱི་རང་བཞིན་མི་ལྡན་པ་ Lacking a sense of discipline.

སྒྲིག་ཁྲིམས་ཁུར་ཤེས་ (drigdrim kūrsheè) shung. observing/ abiding by rules ¶ ལས་བྱེད་ཡོངས་ནས་སྒྲིག་ཁྲིམས་ཁུར་ཤེས་བག་ཡོད་ཚུལ་དང་ལྡན་པ་དགོས་རྒྱུ་ All the officials should abide by the rules and regulations.

སྒྲིག་ཁྲིམས་དམ་སྲུང་ (drigdrim dəmsuŋ) highly disciplined.

སྒྲིག་ཁྲིམས་ལ་རྩིས་མེད་ (drigdrimla dzĩĩmeè) disregarding discipline; va.—བྱེད་.

སྒྲིག་ཁྲིམས་སྲུང་ (drigdrim sūŋ) va. to observe discipline, to respect rules and regulations.

སྒྲིག་མཁན་ (drigñɛn) editor.

སྒྲིག་མཁན་གཙོ་བོ་ (drigñɛn dzōwo) chief editor/ compiler.

སྒྲིག་གྲྭ་ (drigdra) monkastic order; va.—ཞུགས་ to be admitted into the order of monk.

སྒྲིག་རྒྱུགས་ (driggyuù) shung. entrance test.

སྒྲིག་རྒྱུན་སྔར་སྲོལ་ (driggyün nārsöö) shung. traditional rules.

སྒྲིག་སྒོ་ (driggo) regarding regulations and rules.

སྒྲིག་བཅད་ (drigjɛɛ̀) sth. that is fixed or set by authorities/ government/ etc. ¶ ཁོ་ཚོར་སྒྲིག་བཅད་ཀྱི་གླ་ཆ་མ་གཏོགས་མེད་པ་རེད་ They get only a fixed salary.

སྒྲིག་བཅོས་ (drigjöö) readjusting, repairing; va.—བྱེད་.

སྒྲིག་ཆ་ (drigja) preparations; va.—བྱེད་ to make preparation/ arrangements ¶ ཞིང་པ་ཚོས་གཞུང་གི་དཔོན་རིགས་ཚོར་སྡོད་སའི་སྒྲིག་ཆ་བྱས་པ་རེད་ The farmers made preparations for accommodating the government officials.

སྒྲིག་ཆ་བསྡུ་འདེད་ (grigja dundeè) shung. gathering/ collecting needed things ¶ ལྕགས་ཕག་ལོ་ཆོས་གྲྭའི་སྒྲིག་ཆ་བསྡུ་འདེད་ཕྱག་ལ་བྱེད་དགོས་གསུངས་བྱུང་བ་ In the year of Iron-Pig I was told to take charge of making preparations and gathering the needed things.

སྒྲིག་ཆས་ (drigjɛɛ̀) 1. equipment; va.—སྒྲིགས་ to equip, to install equipment ¶ བཟོ་གྲྭ་དེར་དེང་དུས་ཅན་གྱི་འཕྲུལ་འཁོར་གྱིས་སྒྲིག་ཆས་སྒྲིགས་པ་རེད་ (They) equipped the factory with modern machinery. 2. uniform; va.—གྱོན་; —སྒྲིགས་ to be in uniform, to wear a uniform ¶ སློབ་ཕྲུག་ཚང་མས་སྒྲིག་ཆས་སྒྲིགས་འདུག All the students were dressed in uniform.

སྒྲིག་ཆས་ཁྲུའུ་ (drigcɛɛ̀ trū) tib.ch. equipment office.

སྒྲིག་རྒྱུག (drigjug) shung. an orderly and regular manner/ way.

སྒྲིག་འཆལ་ (drigjɛɛ) losing/ breaking discipline.

སྒྲིག་འཆལ་ངན་བཞུགས་ (drigjɛɛ ŋɛnshuù) shung. being undisciplined ¶ དགེ་འདུན་འགའ་ཤས་སྒྲིག་འཆལ་ངན་བཞུགས་ཀྱིས་བྱེད་ཆང་འཐུང་དང་ Some monks have become undisciplined and are drinking beer.

སྒྲིག་གཉིས་འཛིན་ (drig ñii dzin) shung. va. to enroll in two monasteries (at the same time).

སྒྲིག་གཏོང་ (drig dōŋ) 1. shung. to organize to provide or render sth. ¶ ལས་འཛིན་འགྱུར་སྐབས་རྟ་ཁལ་སྒྲིག་གཏོང་དགོས་རྒྱུ་ When the manager changes, you must organize and provide the animal transportation corvee tax. 2. dispatching.

སྒྲིག་གཏོང་ཁང་ (drigdoŋgaŋ) dispatcher's office.

སྒྲིག་སྟངས་ (drigdaŋ) the manner/ way in which things are set or arranged, the style of composition/ compiling.

སྒྲིག་འཐེན་ (drig tēn) shung. va. to withdraw (from a monastery) ¶ བསླབ་སྐྱོན་ཡོད་རིགས་རང་གནོང་ངོས་ལེན་གྱིས་སྒྲིག་འཐེན་ཞུ་དགོས་ The monks who have lost their celibacy should confess and voluntarily withdraw from the monastery.

སྒྲིག་དོད་ (drigdöö) shung. money as a substitute for sth. in kind.

སྒྲིག་འདེབས་ (drig deb) typesetting and printing.

སྒྲིག་པ་ (drigbə) a type of manure that is formed in sheep pens.

སྒྲིག་པ་པོ་ (drigbəbo) editor, compiler.

སྒྲིག་འཕེན་སྦང་ལི་རུ་ཁག (drigbən ganli rugaà) volleyball team.

སྒྲིག་དབྱུག (drig yüù) va. to expel from the monastic community.

སྒྲིག་དབྱུང་ (drigyuŋ) sm. སྒྲིག་དབྱུག.

སྒྲིག་འབུལ་ (driŋbüü) tribute.

སྒྲིག་སྦྱང་ (drigjaŋ) arranging and practicing/ rehearsing; va.—བྱེད་ to arrange and practice/ rehearse ¶ འཁྲབ་ཚན་དེ་ཚོ་རང་རང་སོ་སོས་སྒྲིག་སྦྱོང་བྱས་པ་རེད་ (They) produced and rehearsed the performance themselves.

སྒྲིག་སྦྱོར་ (drigjɔɔ) assembling, installing, va.—བྱེད་ to assemble/ set up/ install ¶ བཟོ་གྲྭ་དེའི་ནང་འཕྲུལ་འཁོར་མང་པོ་སྒྲིག་སྦྱོར་བྱས་འདུག They have installed many machines in that factory.

སྒྲིག་སྦྱོར་བཟོ་སྐྲུན་ཀུང་སི་ (drigjɔɔ sodrün gūŋsi) assembling/ installing company.

སྒྲིག་མེད་ (drigmeè) 1. disorderly, disorganized, disarray, confused, in turmoil; va.—བྱེད་. 2. naughty ¶ ཕྲུ་གུ་སྒྲིག་མེད་འདི་ This naughty boy.

སྒྲིག་བཙུགས་ (drig dzuù) sm. སྒྲིག་འཛུགས་.

སྒྲིག་རྩོམ་ (drigdzom) editing; va.—བྱེད་.

སྒྲིག་རྩོམ་པར་སྐྲུན་ (drigdzom bārdrün) editing and publishing.

སྒྲིག་འཚེམ་ (drigdzem) binding (books/ papers).

སྒྲིག་འཚེམ་ལས་ཚན་ (drigdzem lɛɛdzɛn) binding shop.

སྒྲིག་འཛུགས་ (drigdzuù) 1. organizing, organization; va. སྒྲིག་འཛུགས་; —བྱེད་; —བཟོ་ to organize ¶ སྲིད་གཞུང་ནས་ལྟ་སྐོར་ཚོགས་པ་ཞིག་སྒྲིག་འཛུགས་བྱས་པ་རེད་ The government organized a tour delegation.

སྒྲིག་འཛུགས་འཁྱེར་ (drigdzuù kyēr) va. to abide by the rules/ regulations.

སྒྲིག་འཛུགས་ཕུའུ་ (drigdzuù bū) tib.ch. office in charge of personnel in an organization.

སྒྲིག་འཛུགས་མེད་པ་ (drigdzuù mɛɛba) disorderly, without rules/ regulations, not abiding by the rules/ regulations.

སྒྲིག་འཛུགས་བཟོ་ (drigdzuù so) see སྒྲིག་འཛུགས་.

སྒྲིག་ཞུགས་གན་གཞོན་ (drigshuù gɛnshön) seniority (in a monastic community).

སྒྲིག་ཞུགས་ (drigsuù) entering/ joining a monastery/ monastic community; va.—བྱེད་ ¶ དེའི་མཇུག་ལ་སེ་རར་སྒྲིག་ཞུགས་བྱས་པ་རེད་ After that (they) joined the Sera monastery.

སྒྲིག་གཞི་ (drigshi) 1. rules and regulations ¶ ལས་ཁང་འདིས་སྒྲིག་གཞི་ཞིག་བཟོ་དགོས་ཀྱི་འདུག The office needs to make rules and regulations. 2. structure, composition ¶ བོད་གཞུང་གི་སྒྲིག་གཞི་གང་ཡིན་ནམ་ What is the structure of the Tibetan Government? 3. project ¶ དཔལ་འབྱོར་མཉམ་འབྲེལ་སྒྲིག་གཞི་ཆུང་གྲས་གསུམ་ Three small cooperative economic projects.

སྒྲིག་གཞི་བསྒྱུར་བཅོས་ (drigshi gyurjöö) organizational/ structural reform.

སྒྲིག་གཞི་བཅོས་བསྒྱུར་སྨྲ་བ་ (drigshi jüügyur māwa) the theory of organizational/ structural reform.

སྒྲིག་ཡག་པོ་ (drig yagbo) well behaved, obedient.

སྒྲིག་ཡིག (drigyig) regulations, rules, bylaws.

སྒྲིག་ཡིག་སྟབས་བདེ་ (drigyig dābde) abridged regulations.

སྒྲིག་ལ་འཛུག་པ་པོ་ (drigla jugbabo) shung. a person enrolled in a monastery.

སྒྲིག་ལ་ཞུགས་ (drigla shuù) sm. སྒྲིག་ཞུགས་བྱེད་.

སྒྲིག་ལམ་ (driglam) discipline, order, rule; va.—སྲུང་ to maintain discipline, to obey orders/ rules ¶ སྒྲིག་ལམ་དམ་པོ་ Strict discipline.

སྒྲིག་ལམ་འཁྲུག (driglam trūù) vi. to be thrown into confusion/ disarray (regarding discipline).

སྒྲིག་ལམ་དམ་པོ་ (driglam tambo) strict rules/ regulations.

སྒྲིག་ལམ་ནན་སྲུང་ (driglam nɛnsuŋ) strict discipline.

སྒྲིག་ལམ་མེད་པ་ (driglam meèba) undisciplined, unruly.

སྒྲིག་ལུགས་ (drigluù) sm. སྒྲིག་སྲོལ་.

སྒྲིག་ཤས་ (drigsheè) shung. undisciplined.

སྒྲིག་གཤོམ་ (drigshom) a display, an exhibition; va.—བྱེད་ to display, to exhibit, to show ¶ ཚོང་ཁང་གི་སྒེའུ་ཁུང་ནང་ལ་ཅ་ལག་མང་པོ་སྒྲིག་གཤོམ་བྱས་འདུག (They) have displayed many things in the windows of their shops.

སྒྲིག་གཤོམ་སྟེགས་བུ་ (drigshom dēgbu) display stand.

སྒྲིག་སྲོལ་ (drigsöö) code, regulations, rules ¶ དཔལ་འབྱོར་སྒྲིག་སྲོལ་ Economic rules.

སྒྲིག་སྲོལ་ལམ་ལུགས་ (drigsöö lɔmluù) system of law/ rules.

སྒྲིགས་ (drig) 1. imp. of སྒྲིག. 2. sm. སྒྲིག.

སྒྲིགས་ཁྲིམས་ཆེན་པོ་གསུམ་ (drigtrim cēmbo sūm) the three main rules of discipline of the People's Liberation Army (obey orders, not take a single piece of thread or needle from the masses, turn in everything captured).

སྒྲིགས་མེད་ (drigmeè) sm. སྒྲིག་མེད་.

སྒྲིན་: p. and f. བསྒྲིན་; imp. སྒྲིན་ (drin) 1. va. to compare. 2. sm. འགྲན་.

སྒྲིན་པོ་ (drimbo) skillful, capable.

སྒྲིབ་: p. བསྒྲིབས་; f. བསྒྲིབ་; imp. སྒྲིབ་ (drib) va. to cover, to block from sight/ vision, to conceal ¶ མདུན་གྱི་ཁང་ཆེན་དེས་ཡུལ་ལྗོངས་སྒྲིབ་ཀྱི་འདུག The large house in the front is blocking the scenery (scenic view).

སྒྲིབ་ནད་ (dribnɛɛ) cerebral hemorrhage.

སྒྲིབ་མེད་མཐོང་ཤེལ་ (dribmɛɛ tõŋshel) fluoroscopy.

སྒྲིབ་ཡུན་ (dribyün) the length of eclipses.

སྒྲིབ་ཡོལ་ (dribyöö) a curtain that obstructs/ conceals/ hides/ blocks.

སྒྲིབ་གཡོགས་ (dribyɔɔ) a shade/ screen that blocks seeing.

སྒྲིབ་ཤིང་ (dribshiŋ) a magic wand that renders a person invisible (in folktales).

སྒྲིབ་ཤེལ་ (dribshel) frosted glass.

སྒྲིབས་ (drib) imp. of སྒྲིབ་.

སྒྲིམ་: p. བསྒྲིམས་; f. བསྒྲིམ་; imp. སྒྲིམ་ (drim) 1. va. to concentrate ¶ ཁོ་ཚོས་རིག་པ་བསྒྲིམས་ནས་ལས་ཀ་མཐར་འཁྱོལ་བ་བྱས་པ་རེད་ (They) concentrated all their efforts and saw their work through to the end. 2. a twist (on a thread, string, etc.) va. སྒྲིམ་; —རྒྱག to twist, to wind up; vi.—ཐེབས་ to get twisted, to get wound (up) ¶ སྐུད་པ་ཀ་ཧང་བཞི་མཉམ་དུ་བསྒྲིམས་འདུག They twisted four single strands of threads together.

སྒྲིམ་ཆ་ (drimja) sm. སྒྲིམ་པོ་.

སྒྲིམ་པོ་ (drimbo) 1. concentrated, concentrating. 2. twisted, tangled (for string, thread).

སྒྲིམ་ལྷོད་ (drimlhöö) abbr. tight and loose (usu. for thread).

སྒྲིམས་ (drim) imp. of སྒྲིམ་.

སྒྲིལ་: p. and f. བསྒྲིལ་; imp. སྒྲིལ་ (drii) 1. va. to roll, to wind (paper, cloth, scrolls, etc.), to wrap ། ཤོག་བུ་དེ་རྒྱུག་རིལ་ཞིག་ལ་བསྒྲིལ་སོང་ He rolled the paper onto a round stick. ། སྨན་དེ་ཚོ་རིལ་བུར་སྒྲིལ་གྱི་འདུག (They) rolled the medicine into pills. ། ཁོས་དེབ་དེ་ལག་རས་གཅིག་གི་ནང་བསྒྲིལ་སོང་ He wrapped the book with a handkerchief. 2. va. to combine together, to unite, to put together into one ། ང་ཚོས་ནུས་ཤུགས་ཚང་མ་གཅིག་ཏུ་བསྒྲིལ་ནས་ Uniting all our energy together. 3. see དབ་དུ་. 4. decorative cloth covering an edge/ hem of clothing. 5. va. to carry over a number (in mathematics). 6. ply ། སུམ་སྒྲིལ་ Three ply.

སྒྲིལ་ཁ་ (driigə) a roll (of paper, cloth, etc.), a wrapped bundle ། ཤོག་བུ་སྒྲིལ་ཁ་གཅིག A bundle of paper.

སྒྲིལ་ཁྲེ་ (driidre) tib.ch. a tape measure that winds up.

སྒྲིལ་སྒྲིལ་ (driidrii) sm. སྒྲིལ་ཁ་.

སྒྲིལ་ཉོ་སྒྲིལ་ཚོང་ (driiño driidzoŋ) state monopoly for purchasing and marketing; va.—བྱེད་.

སྒྲིལ་ཐ་ (driida) cigarette; va.—འཐེན་ to smoke a cigarette.

སྒྲིལ་ཐ་འཐེན་འཕྲོས་ (driida tëndröö) cigarette butt.

སྒྲིལ་འཐུམ་ (drindum) sm. སྒྲིལ་ཁ་.

སྒྲིལ་འཐེན་འཁྲུལ་འཁོར་ (drinden trüügɔɔ) hoisting machine, windlass, winch.

སྒྲིལ་བསྡུ་ (drii du) shung. va. to roll up sth. like a thanka.

སྒྲིལ་ལྡན་ (drindɛn) sm. གྲི་ག.

སྒྲིལ་གཟོང་ (driisoŋ) a smith's tool.

སྒྲིལ་རས་ (driirɛɛ̀) wrapping cloth.

སྒྲིལ་ཤིང་ (driishiŋ) 1. wooden stick sewn into the bottom of a thanka so that it can be rolled up. 2. rolling pin.

སྒྲིལ་ཤོག (driishoò) wrapping paper, wrapper ། ཏྲི་རིལ་སྒྲིལ་ཤོག Candy wrapper.

སྒྲུག་སྒྲུག་རྒྱག (drugdruù gyaà) va. to pick up the left over grain on fields (after the first picking).

སྒྲུག: p. བསྒྲུགས་; f. བསྒྲུག; imp. སྒྲུག (druù) va. to pick up, to gather, to collect ། ས་ནས་རྡོ་བསྒྲུགས་སོང་ (He) picked up stones from the ground. ། ཁོ་མེ་ཤིང་སྒྲུག་ཏུ་ཕྱིན་པ་རེད་ He went to collect firewood.

སྒྲུགས་ (drug) imp. of སྒྲུག.

སྒྲུང་ (drum) story; va.—ཤོད་ to tell a story.

སྒྲུང་: p. བསྒྲུངས་; f. བསྒྲུང་; imp. སྒྲུངས་ (druŋ) va. to soak (sth.) in a liquid and to have it dissolve.

སྒྲུང་མཁན་ (drumñɛn) storyteller.

སྒྲུང་གི་གློག་བརྙན་ (drumgi lɔ̈ɔ̈ñɛn) feature film.

སྒྲུང་གླུ་ལེན་ (drum lü len) va. to tell a story through songs and narration.

སྒྲུང་རྒྱུད་ (drumgyüü) story passed down from mouth to mouth.

སྒྲུང་གཏམ་ (drumdam) folklore, folktale, story.

སྒྲུང་ཐུང་ཐུང་ (drum tüŋduŋ) short story.

སྒྲུང་དེབ་ (drumdeb) sm. སྒྲུང་དཔེ་.

སྒྲུང་པ་ (drumbə) raconteur, storyteller.

སྒྲུང་བབ་ (drum bəb) vi. to have a person go into a trance where they see the events of Gesar then relate the story of Gesar.

སྒྲུང་ཡིག (drumyig) a book of Gesar tales.

སྒྲུང་རིང་ (drumriŋ) sm. སྒྲུང་རིང་པ་.

སྒྲུང་རིང་ཐུང་འབྲིང་པ་ (drum riŋduŋ driŋwə) novelette.

སྒྲུང་རིང་པ་ (drum riŋwə) full length novel.

སྒྲུངས་ (druŋ) imp. of སྒྲུང་.

སྒྲུན་: p. and f. བསྒྲུན་; imp. སྒྲུན་ (drün) sm. འགྲུན་.

སྒྲུན་དུ་མེད་པ་ (dründu meèba) sm. འགྲུན་དུ་མེད་པ་.

སྒྲུབ་: p. བསྒྲུབས་; f. བསྒྲུབ་; imp. སྒྲུབ་ (drub) 1. va. to acquire, to obtain, to achieve, to accomplish, to fulfill ། ཁོས་རྒྱ་གར་ནས་དངོས་ཆས་རྙིང་པ་ཁ་ཤས་བསྒྲུབས་ཡོད་པ་རེད་ He acquired some old goods from India. ། འཆར་གཞི་དེ་དུས་བཀག་གི་སྔོན་དུ་བསྒྲུབས་པ་རེད་ (They) accomplished the plan ahead of schedule. ། ང་ཚོའི་དམིགས་ཡུལ་དེ་ང་ཚོས་བསྒྲུབ་ཀྱི་རེད་ We are going to achieve our goals. 2. va. to perform one's duty/ service, to work for ། གཞུང་དང་མི་དམངས་ཀྱི་ཞབས་འདེགས་སྒྲུབ་ཀྱི་ཡོད་པ་རེད་ (They) are working for the government and the people. 3. va. to practice (sādhana), to meditate.

སྒྲུབ་ཀང་ (drubgaŋ) shung. sm. ཀང་.

སྒྲུབ་སྐྲ་ (drubdra) hair that has been let grow long when a person is in meditation.

སྒྲུབ་ཁང་ (drubgaŋ) cave or dwelling used for meditation.

སྒྲུབ་ཁུལ་ (drubgüü) pretending to perform one's duties, pretending to fulfill/ achieve sth. ། ཁོས་ལས་འགན་སྒྲུབ་ཁུལ་བྱེད་ཀྱི་འདུག He is pretending to do the job he is responsible for.

སྒྲུབ་ཁྲུན་ཚོད་ཡིག (drubdrün cöòyii) shung. an agreement signed following a verdict by the two parties in which they agree to accept/ abide by the judgement ། དོ་བདག་སོ་སོས་དངུལ་འབབ་ཕྱིར་སློག་བྱ་རྒྱུ་བཅས་སྒྲུབ་ཁྲུན་ཚོད་ཡིག་ཟླ་༩་ཚེས་༢༢་ཚུན་ཞུས་ཟིན་པ་དགོས་རྒྱུ་ The two parties must return the money, etc. and sign the agreement to abide by the judgment before the 22nd of the ninth month.

སྒྲུབ་མཁན་ (drubgɛn) 1. a practitioner of meditation/ sādhana, a religious pratictioner. 2. one who performs his duty/ task/ chore.

སྒྲུབ་འཁུར་ (drubgur) shung. to take a responsibility for doing sth.

སྒྲུབ་གྲྭ་ (drubdra) monks engaged in meditation.

སྒྲུབ་གྲོགས་ (drubdrog) meditation/ practice partner.

སྒྲུབ་རྒྱགས་ (drubgya) provisions for doing a meditation retreat.

སྒྲུབ་རྒྱུགས་ (drubgyuù) 1. sm. སྒྲུབ་. 2. va. to perform taxes ། ཞིང་པ་ཚོས་ཁྲལ་རིགས་མང་པོ་སྒྲུབ་རྒྱུགས་བྱེད་དགོས་ཀྱི་རེད་ The farmers have to perform many taxes.

སྒྲུབ་བརྒྱུད་ (drubgyüü) a lineage that teaches meditative/ practice (sādhana).

སྒྲུབ་ཆ་ (drubja) shung. paying (taxes); va.—བྱེད་.

སྒྲུབ་ཆག (drubjaà) abbr. taxes to be paid and taxes that are exempted.

སྒྲུབ་ཆག་འཇག་གསུམ་ (drubjaà jaàsum) abbr. the three: taxes to be paid, taxes to be exempted and taxes to be left as before.

སྒྲུབ་མཆོད་ (drubjöö) practice (sādhana) rituals/ offerings.

སྒྲུབ་འཇལ་ (drumjɛɛ) paying off a loan/ tax; va.—བྱེད་; —ཞུ་ ། ངས་ཁོང་གི་བུན་ལོན་སྒྲུབ་འཇལ་ཞུས་པ་ཡིན་ I paid off my loan from him.

སྒྲུབ་རྟེན་ (drubden) 1. source of income for people engaged in medidative retreats. 2. shung. fields given as the basis for paying taxes and corvee labor.

སྒྲུབ་ཐབས་ (drubdəb) 1. trying to achieve/ accomplish, the means to achieve sth.; va.—བྱེད་ ། བསམ་ཕྱོགས་སྒྲུབ་ཐབས་བྱེད་ To try to accomplish one's aim. 2. the method of visualization through meditation (sādhana).

སྒྲུབ་ཐུབ་ཚད་ (drub tūbdzɛɛ̀) as much as one is able to do/ accomplish ། ཁྱེད་རང་ལ་ལས་ཀ་རག་པའི་ཆེད་དུ་ངས་རང་ཉིད་ཀྱིས་སྒྲུབ་ཐུབ་ཚད་ཀྱི་ཐབས་ཤེས་བྱས་པ་ཡིན་ I did as much as I could to find you a job.

སྒྲུབ་ཐུབ་ཚོད་ (drub tūbdzöö) sm. སྒྲུབ་ཐུབ་ཚད་.

སྒྲུབ་ཐེབས་ (drubdeb) shung. trust set up for doing/ paying for sth.

སྒྲུབ་ཐོ་ (drubdo) shung. a list of religious rites that have been performed.

སྒྲུབ་ཐོ་འབྱོར་ལན་ (drubdo jɔɔlɛn) shung. a receipt listing religious rites that have been performed.

སྒྲུབ་འདོན་ (drubdün) 1. a འདོན་ (unit of land in tt.) from which taxes are collected. 2. supply and marketing.

སྒྲུབ་འདོན་ཁང་ (drubdöngaŋ) supply and marketing cooperative.

སྒྲུབ་གནས་ (drubnɛɛ̀) a place of meditation.

སྒྲུབ་པ་རྒྱག (drubbə gyaà) va. to do meditative retreat.

སྒྲུབ་པ་པོ་ (drubbəbo) sm. སྒྲུབ་མཁན་.

སྒྲུབ་པ་བ་ (drubbəwa) sm. སྒྲུབ་མཁན་.

སྒྲུབ་དཔོན་ (drubbön) meditation teacher/ master.

སྒྲུབ་སྤྲོད་ (drubdröö̀) shung. rendering service/ payment according to a pledge or obligation.

སྒྲུབ་སྤྲོད་ཆོད་ཡིག (drubdröö̀ cōö̀yig) shung. the document both parties sign accepting the verdict or the judgment in a suit.

སྒྲུབ་ཕུག (drubbuù) a cave for meditating.

སྒྲུབ་ཕྱོགས་ (drubjɔɔ̀) sm. སྒྲུབ་བྱེད་.

སྒྲུབ་བྱེད་ (drubjeè) 1. giving a reason or making a case/ argument for sth.; va.—འཛུགས་; —འདོན་ to set forth one's reasons/ argument ¶ འཆར་གཞི་འདི་བཟོ་དགོས་པའི་སྒྲུབ་བྱེད་གང་ཡིན་ནམ་ What is your reason for having to make this plan? ¶ ཁོ་རྐུ་མ་ཡིན་པའི་སྒྲུབ་བྱེད་འཛུགས་དགོས་ (You) have to make a case that he is a thief. 2. 4th month of the Tibetan calendar.

སྒྲུབ་བྱེད་ཕྱི་མ་ (drubjeè cīmə) minor premise (in logic).

སྒྲུབ་བླངས་ (drublaŋ) shung. rendering service or payment according to an obligation/ agreement.

སྒྲུབ་འབབ་ (drumbəb) shung. the amount of a payment.

སྒྲུབ་འབུལ་ཆོད་ཡིག (drumbüü cōöyii) shung. sm. སྒྲུབ་སྤྲོད་ཆོད་ཡིག.

སྒྲུབ་འབོར་ (drumbɔɔ) the amount to be paid.

སྒྲུབ་ཚད་ (drubdzɛɛ̀) 1. schedule/ target/ level to be achieved ¶ བཟོ་གྲྭ་འདིའི་ལས་འགན་གྱི་སྒྲུབ་ཚད་ལོན་མི་འདུག The factory did not achieve its target. 2. rate of progress/ achievement/ production ¶ བཟོ་གྲྭ་འདིའི་ཐོན་སྐྱེད་སྒྲུབ་ཚད་མཐོ་པོ་བྱུང་མི་འདུག This factory did not achieve a high rate of production.

སྒྲུབ་ཚོད་ (drubdzöö̀) sm. སྒྲུབ་ཐུབ་ཚད་.

སྒྲུབ་འཚོལ་ (drubdzöö) trying to find and acquire sth.; va.—བྱེད་.

སྒྲུབ་འཛིན་ (drumdzin) shung. a document giving authorization for collecting sth. (taxes, corvee labor etc.) ¶ ཁྲལ་དཔོན་བཀའ་དམ་དང་སྒྲུབ་འཛིན་སོགས་ལ་རྩི་མེད་ཁྲིམས་འགལ་དཔྱད་ཤིང་ Disregarding and violating the document giving authorization for collecting taxes.

སྒྲུབ་གཡོག (grubyɔɔ̀) a servant to sb. in meditation.

སྒྲུབ་ལས་ (drublɛɛ̀) homework (of students).

སྒྲུབ་ལོ་ (drublo) sm. སྒྲུབ་ཁྱལ་.

སྒྲུབ་གཤེན་ (drubsen) the Bon religion.

སྒྲུབས་ (drub) imp. of སྒྲུབ་.

སྒྲེ་: p. བསྒྲེས་; f. བསྒྲེ་; imp. སྒྲེས་ (dre) 1. va. to crossbreed, to hybridize. 2. (with རིག) va. to make an analogy.

སྒྲེ་བོ་ (drebo) bare, naked, bald.

སྒྲེ་ཅི་ (drēci) bald.

སྒྲེ་ལ་ (drela) boiled barley to which yeast is added to make beer.

སྒྲེ་ལོག (drelɔɔ̀) rolling over; va.—རྒྱག.

སྒྲེག (dreg) vi. to belch.

སྒྲེགས་ (dreg) sm. སྒྲེག.

སྒྲེགས་སྒྲ་ (dregdra) belching noise/ sound.

སྒྲེང་: p. བསྒྲེངས་; f. བསྒྲེང་; imp. སྒྲེངས་ (dreŋ) va. to erect, to hoist, to lift/ raise high ¶ རྒྱལ་དར་བསྒྲེངས་པ་དང་རྒྱལ་གླུ་བཏང་སོང་ As they hoisted the flag they sang the national anthem.

སྒྲེང་འཛུགས་ (dreŋdzuù) erecting (flags, etc.); va.—བྱེད་.

སྒྲེངས་ (dreŋ) imp. of སྒྲེང་.

སྒྲེན་པོ་ (drenbo) sm. སྒྲེན་མོ་.

སྒྲེན་མོ་ (drenmo) naked.

སྒྲེན་མོའི་རི་མོ་ (drenmö rimo) nude painting.

སྒྲེའུ་ (drewu) small leather pouch.

སྒྲེའུ་ཆུང་ (drewu cūŋ) 1. sm. སྒྲེའུ་. 2. a small pouch worn by monks over their penis to protect against wet dreams.

སྒྲེས་ (dreè) imp. of སྒྲེ་.

སྒྲོ་ (dro) 1. feathers. 2. leather bag. 3. see སྒྲོ་འདོགས་.

སྒྲོ་དཀར་ (drokar) white feather.

སྒྲོ་ཀང་ (drogaŋ) shaft of a feather.

སྒྲོ་སྐུར་ (drogur) abbr. སྒྲོ་བཏགས་.

སྒྲོ་ག (droga) sm. སྒྲོ་གུ་.

སྒྲོ་གུ་ (drogu) string/ cord/ lace for tying sth.

སྒྲོ་གུར་ (drogur) displaying/ spreading out tail feathers (e.g., a peacock); va.—ཕུབ་ to display tail feathers.

སྒྲོ་བརྗེ་ (dro je) vi. to molt feathers.

སྒྲོ་ཏོག (drodog) feather.

སྒྲོ་བཏགས་ (drodaà) exaggerating.

སྒྲོ་བཏགས་སྐུར་འདེབས་ (drodaà gūrdeb) exaggerating and defaming/ vilifying/ denigrating; va.—བྱེད་.

སྒྲོ་བཏགས་ཏེ་འབྲི་ (drodaà dēndri) va. to exaggerate in writing, to hyperbolize.

སྒྲོ་ཐིག (drodig) sm. སྒྲོ་མདོངས་.

སྒྲོ་གདོང་ (drodoŋ) sm. སྒྲོ་མདོངས་.

སྒྲོ་མདུང་ (droduŋ) spear with feathers attached to it.

སྒྲོ་མདོངས་ (drodoŋ) a feather crest on the head of a peacock.

སྒྲོ་འདོགས་ (drondɔɔ̀) 1. exaggeration; va.—བྱེད་ to exaggerate ¶ ཁོའི་བསམ་འཆར་ལ་སྒྲོ་འདོགས་སྣ་ཚོགས་བྱས་ཡོད་པ་རེད They exaggerated his suggestions in many ways. 2. doubting; vi.—ཆོད་ to have doubts clarified/ cleared up; va.—གཅོད་ to clarify/ clear up doubts ¶ གསར་འགྱུར་དེ་ངོ་མ་ཡིན་མིན་སོམ་ཉིའི་སྒྲོ་འདོགས་ཆོད་མ་སོང་ I have doubts about whether this news is true or not. ¶ མཁས་པ་ཚོས་རྩོད་པ་བརྒྱབ་ནས་ཐེ་ཚོམ་གྱི་སྒྲོ་འདོགས་བཅད་པ་རེད་ The experts debated and clarified all the doubts. 3. va. to accuse/ blame on a pretext.

སྒྲོ་པ་ (droba) quality, manner, nature.

སྒྲོ་བུ་ (drobu) feathers.

སྒྲོ་ཕོད་ (dropöö̀) 1. feathers used for decorations on hats, etc. 2. upright feather on the head of a bird.

སྒྲོ་ཕྱགས་ (drojaà) feather duster.

སྒྲོ་འཕྲུ་ (drodru) sm. སྒྲོ་ཕོད་.

སྒྲོ་བ་ (drowa) 1. leather bag/ pouch. 2. testicle.

སྒྲོ་བ་ཤིང་ (drowasiŋ) birch (tree).

སྒྲོ་དབྱིབས་ (droyib) feather shape.

སྒྲོ་མིག་གཉིས་ཅན་གྱི་གོ་གནས་ (drumiì ñiijɛngi konɛɛ̀) shung. sm. སྒྲོ་མིག་གཉིས་པའི་གོ་གནས་.

སྒྲོ་མིག་གཉིས་པའི་གོ་གནས་ (drumii ñiibɛ konɛɛ̀) shung. a feather crest on the head of a peacock with two circular designs.

སྒྲོ་སྨྱུག (droñug) quill pen.

སྒྲོ་བཙེམས་མ་ (drodzemma) type of hat worn by monks (Gelugba).

སྒྲོ་རྩེ་ (drodze) tip of a feather.

སྒྲོ་གཡབ་ (droyəb) fan made of feather.

སྒྲོ་གཤོག (droshɔɔ̀) 1. propeller/ blades in a turbine machine or water mill. 2. a paper making tool. 3. abbr. of feather and wings.

སྒྲོ་གཤོག་ལྡན་པའི་འཕྲུལ་འཁོར་ (droshɔɔ dɛmbɛ trüügɔɔ) turbine.

སྒྲོ་ལྷུག་མ་ (drolhugmə) type of hat worn by monks.

སྒྲོག: p. བསྒྲགས་; f. བསྒྲག; imp. སྒྲོགས་ (drɔɔ̀) va. to shout out, to call out, to read out loud ¶ ང་ཚོར་རང་དབང་དགོས་ཞེས་འབོད་ཚིག་སྒྲོག་གི་འདུག (They) are shouting: "We want freedom!" ¶ ཁོ་ཚོའི་གྲོས་ཆོད་དེ་ཚོགས་འདུ་དེར་བསྒྲགས་པ་རེད་ They read out their resolution at the meeting.

སྒྲོག: p. བསྒྲོགས་; f. བསྒྲོག; imp. སྒྲོགས་ (drɔɔ̀) 1. va. to sew up ¶ མོས་ཐེབ་ཙེ་སྒྲོག་གི་འདུག She is sewing buttons. 2. va. to tie/ strap up ¶ ཁོའི་རྐང་ལག་རྣམས་སྒྲོགས་པ་རེད་ (They) tied his hands and legs.

སྒྲོག (drɔɔ̀) 1. rope, strap, lace ¶ འཇུར་སྒྲོག Shoelaces. 2. a trap.

སྒྲོག་དཀར་ (drɔggar) special kind of bowl used for elaborate parties.

སྒྲོག་བཀྲོལ་ (drɔ̀ drȍȍ) p. of སྒྲོག་འགྲོལ་.

སྒྲོག་འགྲོལ་ (drɔ̀ drȍȍ) 1. va. to untie ། རྟའི་རྐང་པའི་སྒྲོག་བཀྲོལ་བ་རེད་ (They) untied the legs of the horse. 2. va. to clear one's doubt/ suspicion/ hesitation ། མཁས་པར་བཀའ་འདྲི་ཞུས་ནས་ཐེ་ཚོམ་གྱི་སྒྲོག་བཀྲོལ་བ་རེད་ After asking the expert the doubts were cleared up.

སྒྲོག་ཁ་ (drɔga) lace, band, cord, string, strap; vi.—འགྲོལ་ to come unlaced/ untied; va.—རྒྱག to lace, to tie/ bind a strap.

སྒྲོག་ཁུང་ (drɔguŋ) a hole that a strap goes through.

སྒྲོག་ཁེབས་ (drɔgeb) table cloth.

སྒྲོག་ག (drɔga) see སྒྲོག་ཁ་.

སྒྲོག་གུ་ (drɔgu) sm. སྒྲོ་གུ་.

སྒྲོག་གླེང་ (drɔ̄gleŋ) reading out and then discussing.

སྒྲོག་འགྲོས་ (drɔŋdröö) walking with shackled/ tied feet; va.—རྒྱག. 2. exchanging or sending/ doing in turn; va.—བྱེད་ ། ལས་ཁངས་ནས་ལས་བྱེད་པ་སྒྲོག་འགྲོས་བྱས་ཏེ་གུང་གསེང་དུ་གཏོང་གི་ཡོད་པ་རེད་ The office is sending officials on vacation by turns.

སྒྲོག་རྒྱག (drɔg gyaà) sm. སྒྲོག.

སྒྲོག་གདུགས་ (drɔgduù) mending, patching; va.—བྱེད་.

སྒྲོག་ཐག (drɔgtaà) string/ strap/ ribbon used to tie sth.

སྒྲོག་དུང་ (drɔgduŋ) white conch shell used as a bracelet/ bangle.

སྒྲོག་གདན་ (drɔgdɛn) the triangular patch on banners and the corner of women's aprons.

སྒྲོག་གདུབ (drɔgdub) bangles, bracelets.

སྒྲོག་སྒྲུག (drɔgduù) patching, mending; va.—རྒྱག.

སྒྲོག་སྦྱང་ (drɔgjaŋ) an announcement/ speech/ proclamation read in public; va.—བྱེད་.

སྒྲོག་སྦྱང་འགྲེལ་བཤད་ (drɔgjaŋ dreeshɛɛ̀) a proclamation and explanation.

སྒྲོག་མིག (drɔgmiì) button hole, lace hole.

སྒྲོག་ཅེ་ (drɔgdze) ch. table ། སྒྲོག་ཅེའི་སྟེང་ལ་སྒྲིག་ནས་ Having arranged (the top of) the table.

སྒྲོག་བཞུ་ (drɔgshu) table lamp.

སྒྲོག་བཞུགས་ཆུ་ཚོད་འཁོར་ལོ་ (drɔgshaà cūdzöö kɔ̄ɔlo) desk clock.

སྒྲོག་རས་ (drɔgrɛɛ̀) tablecloth.

སྒྲོག་རིལ་ (drɔgrii) a round lace.

སྒྲོག་རུས་ (drɔgrüù) clavicle.

སྒྲོག་རུས་གཤོངས་པ་ (drɔgrüù shōŋba) a small cavity where the two clavicle bones join.

སྒྲོག་ལུང་ (drɔgluŋ) sm. སྒྲོག་ཐག.

སྒྲོག་ལེབ་ (drɔgleb) flat straps/ laces.

སྒྲོག་སུམ་ལག (drɔg sūmlag) the rope used to tie a horse or mule's two front legs together with one hind leg.

སྒྲོག་སོ་ (drɔgso) zipper; va.—རྒྱག to zip.

སྒྲོགས་ (drɔ̀ɔ) imp. of སྒྲོག.

སྒྲོགས་སྦྱང་ (drɔgjaŋ) sm. སྒྲོག་སྦྱང་.

སྒྲོང་: p. བསྒྲངས་; f. བསྒྲང་; imp. p. སྒྲོངས་; (droŋ) va. to count/ enumerate/ calculate ། མོས་གནས་ཚུལ་ཆ་ཚང་བསྒྲངས་པ་རེད་ (She) enumerated all the events (that occurred).

སྒྲོངས་ (droŋ) imp. of སྒྲོང་.

སྒྲོད་: p. and f. བསྒྲོད་; imp. སྒྲོད་ (dröö) sm. བགྲོད་, 2.

སྒྲོན་: p. and f. བསྒྲོན་; imp. སྒྲོན་ (drön) va. 1. to put on/ in (h.) ། ཁོང་ལ་མཇལ་དར་ཞིག་བསྒྲོན་པ་ཡིན་ (We) put a ceremonial scarf on him. ། ཁྱེད་རང་གི་གསོལ་ཇར་བྱེ་མ་ཀ་ར་བསྒྲོན་མེད་ (I) have not put sugar in your tea. 2. va. to set out, to put/ lay out/ give (h.) ། ཁོང་ལ་ཞབས་ཀྱུ་གཅིག་བསྒྲོན་འདུག (They) set out a chair for him. 3. va. to tell/ report ། གནས་ཚུལ་དེ་ཁོང་གི་སྙན་དུ་སྒྲོན་པ་རེད་ (He) told the news to him. 4. abbr. of སྒྲོན་མ་.

སྒྲོན་བསྐལ་ (dröngɛɛ) an era in which a Buddha has come.

སྒྲོན་ཁེབས་ (dröngeb) lamp shade.

སྒྲོན་རྒྱག (dröngyaà) arranging or laying cushions and mattresses during formal functions in order of rank; va.—བྱེད་ ། ཁོང་གིས་མཛད་སྒོའི་སར་བཞུགས་གདན་སྒྲོན་རྒྱག་བྱས་པ་རེད་ He arranged the cushions (by rank) at the ceremony.

སྒྲོན་བརྙན་ (drönñɛn) slide projector; va.—སྟོན་ to show/ project slides.

སྒྲོན་སྟེགས་ (dröndeg) 1. beacon, lighthouse. 2. a stand for a lamp.

སྒྲོན་ཐལ་ (drondɛɛ) ashes from soot (for making ink).

སྒྲོན་དར་ (drondar) ceremonial scarf.

སྒྲོན་དྲེག (dröndreg) 1. sm. སྒྲོན་ཐལ་. 2. soot from the wick of a butter lamp.

སྒྲོན་བརྡ་ (drönda) torch or lantern signal; va.—གཏོང་; —རྒྱག.

སྒྲོན་སྣག (dronnaà) ink made from soot.

སྒྲོན་འབུ་ (drönbu) fire fly.

སྒྲོན་མ་ (drönma) lantern, lamp, torch.

སྒྲོན་མེ་ (dronme) lantern, lamp, torch.

སྒྲོན་མེ་ཤིང་ (dronme shiŋ) sm. སྒྲོན་ཤིང་.

སྒྲོན་མེའི་ཞྭ་ཁེབས་ (dronme shakeb) sm. སྒྲོན་ཁེབས་.

སྒྲོན་དམར་ (drönmar) red light/ lantern.

སྒྲོན་འཛུགས་ (drön dzuù) va. to erect/ put up (prayer flags).

སྒྲོན་ཞྭ་ (drönsha) lamp shade.

སྒྲོན་ཞུ་ (drönshu) va. to add a little ཆང་ to the cup of a guest to fill it after he takes a sip.

སྒྲོན་འོད་ (drönwöö) lamp/ lantern light.

སྒྲོན་ཤིང་ (drönshiŋ) species of sap containing trees such as pine or fir that can be used as a torch/ lantern.

སྒྲོབ་ (drob) arrogance, pretentiousness, pride, haughtiness, pompousness; va.—བྱེད་.

སྒྲོབ་ཉམས་ (drobñam) sm. སྒྲོབ་.

སྒྲོབ་བྱེད་ (drobjeè) sm. སྒྲོབ་.

སྒྲོབ་ཚ་པོ་ (drob tsābo) proud, haughty, pompous.

སྒྲོབ་རྫུ་པ་ (drob dzuwa) affected, pretentious.

སྒྲོམ་ (drom) 1. frame, outer structure ། ཁང་པའི་སྒྲོམ་ Frame of a house. 2. box, trunk. 3. a table on which merchandise is put for sale.

སྒྲོམ་སྐས་ (dromgɛɛ̀) stairs.

སྒྲོམ་སྐྱོར་ (dromgyɔr) railing, banisters; balustrade.

སྒྲོམ་གྲུ་བཞི་མ་ (drom drubshimə) square frame.

སྒྲོམ་ཆེན་པོ་ (drom cēmbo) 1. large frame. 2. large, grand ། མི་ཚང་དེ་སྒྲོམ་ཆེན་པོ་ཡིན་ན་ཡང་ནང་དོན་ཕྱུག་པོ་མེད་པ་རེད་ Even though that family looks grand (from the outside), internally it isn't rich.

སྒྲོམ་གཏེར་ (dromder) a kind of གཏེར་མ་.

སྒྲོམ་སྟེགས་ (dromdeg) a pylon/ brace.

སྒྲོམ་སྟོང་ (dromdoŋ) 1. empty frame. 2. a families without substance.

སྒྲོམ་བུ་ (drombu) 1. shuttle (for weaving). 2. a small box. 3. cowry shell.

སྒྲོམ་མེད་འདྲུད་འཁོར་ (drommeè drüùgɔɔ) a pulling cart with no sides.

སྒྲོམ་གཞི་ (dromshi) frame.

སྒྲོམ་གཞི་སྟོང་པ་ (dromshi dōŋba) sm. སྒྲོམ་སྟོང་.

སྒྲོམ་སློང་ (drom lōŋ) va. to set up a frame.

སྒྲོལ: p. and f. བསྒྲལ་ imp. སྒྲོལ་ (dröö) va. to liberate, to free, to save, to deliver ། བྲན་གཡོག་རིང་ལུགས་ཀྱི་གཉའ་གནོན་ལས་བསྒྲལ་པ་རེད་ (They) freed (them) from the oppression of the slave system. 2. va. to pass, to cross (a river, bridge, etc. ། རྒྱ་མཚོའི་ཕ་རོལ་དུ་སྒྲོལ་ཐུབ་པའི་གྲུ་ A boat that can cross to the other side of the ocean.

སྒྲོལ་དཀར་ (dröögar) 1. abbr. White Tara. 2. girl's name.

སྒྲོལ་ཆོག (dröjɔɔ̀) ritual done for Tara.

སྒྲོལ་ལྗང་ (drööjaŋ) the Green Tara.

སྒྲོལ་འདོན་ (droo dön) 1. va. to cross a river/ stream. 2. va. to recite prayers to Tara.

སྒྲོལ་མ་ (drööma) 1. the goddess Tara; va.—སྐྱོར་ to read/ intone the Tara prayer. 2. a girl's name.

སྒྲོལ་གསོལ་ (dröösöö) shung. religious rites.

སྒྲོས་ (dröö) 1. manner, way, custom ། སྐད་ཆ་འདི་འདྲ་བཤད་སྒྲོས་ཡོད་པ་མ་རེད་ There is no custom of saying sth. like that. 2. talk ། ཁ་ས་ཚོགས་འདུའི་ཐོག་ང་ཚོ་འགྲོ་དགོས་པའི་སྒྲོས་མེད་ There was no talk of us having to go to the meeting yesterday. 3. scar. 4. lips.

སྒྲོས་ཚོས་ (dröödzöö) lipstick.

བརྒལ་ (gɛɛ) p. and f. of རྒལ་ and རྒོལ་.

བརྒལ་བརྒྱུད་ (gɛɛdröö) crossing over; va.—བྱེད་ ། སིམ་ལ་ནས་རུ་ཐོག་བར་བརྒལ་བརྒྱུད་བྱས་པ་རེད་ (They) crossed over from Simla to Rutok.

བརྒལ་བརྡག་ (gɛɛdaà) rebuttal in debating; va.—བྱེད་.

བརྒལ་བ་ (gɛɛwa) over, beyond, surpassing, exceeding, going beyond; va.—གཏོང་ to go over/ beyond, to surpass/ to exceed ། འགྲོ་སོང་འཆར་གཞི་ལས་བརྒལ་བ་བཏང་འདུག They exceeded their plan with respect to expenditures.

བརྒལ་བའི་དུས་སྐབས་ (gɛɛwɛ tüügəb) transition period.

བརྒལ་བའི་གནས་སྐབས་ (gɛɛwɛ nɛɛgəb) sm. བརྒལ་བའི་དུས་སྐབས་.

བརྒྱ་ (gya) one hundred.

བརྒྱ་སྐོར་ (gyagɔɔ) 1. about a hundred. 2. a unit of hundred villages or households.

བརྒྱ་ཁ་གཅིག་གཅོད་ (gyaga jïgjöö) one person deciding for many, minority rule ། འཐུས་མི་མང་ཆེ་བའི་བསམ་འཆར་ལ་བསྟུན་དགོས་པ་ལས་མི་གཅིག་གིས་བརྒྱ་ཁ་གཅིག་གཅོད་བྱས་ན་མི་འགྲིགས་ (We) must go with the opinion of the majority of the delegates; it isn't okay for one to person to decide for many.

བརྒྱ་ཁ་གཅིག་ཆད་ (gyaga jïgcɛɛ) all one's work being spoiled by a single thing not done/ or done wrong.

བརྒྱ་ཁ་གཅིག་ཆོད་ (gyaka jïgjöö) sm. བརྒྱ་ཁ་གཅིག་ཆད་.

བརྒྱ་ཁ་ཡུག་ཆོད་ (gyaga yugjöö) sm. བརྒྱ་ཁ་གཅིག་གཅོད་.

བརྒྱ་ཁག་ (gyagaà) unit of a hundred ། མདོ་སྤྱི་འི་སྐུ་སྲུང་ཁ་དང་བརྒྱ་ཁག A unit of 100 of the Khadang Bodyguard of the Governor General of Kham.

བརྒྱ་གོ་གཅིག་ཆོད་ (gyago jïgjöö) sth. that can do many things, multipurpose [Lit. one hundred uses, one use].

བརྒྱ་འགྱུར་ (gyangyur) one hundred times ། མི་འབོར་བརྒྱ་འགྱུར་གྱིས་འཕར་བཞག The population has increased 100 times.

བརྒྱ་འགྲོ་སྟོང་འགྲོ་ (gyadro dõŋdro) popular, busy/ full with people [Lit. one hundred going, one thousand going].

བརྒྱ་འགྲོ་སྟོང་ཡོང་ (gyadro dõŋyoŋ) sm.བརྒྱ་འགྲོ་སྟོང་འགྲོ་.

བརྒྱ་བརྒྱ་སྟོང་སྟོང་ (gyagya dõŋdoŋ) very many [Lit. hundreds and hundreds, thousands and thousands].

བརྒྱ་འགྲོ་སྟོང་ཡོང་ (gyadro dõŋyoŋ) profitable [Lit. one hundred going, one thousand coming].

བརྒྱ་འགྲོ་སྟོང་འགྲོ་ (gyadro dõŋdro) sm. རྒྱ་རྒྱུག་བོད་རྒྱུག.

བརྒྱ་ཆ་ (gyaja) per cent, percentage ། བརྒྱ་ཆ་ 95 Ninety-five percent.

བརྒྱ་ཆ་བརྒྱ་ (gyaja gya) 1. one hundred percent. 2. one hundred percent correct/ okay ། ཁྱེད་རང་གིས་གསུངས་པ་དེ་བརྒྱ་ཆ་བརྒྱ་འགྲིགས་སོང་ What you said is one hundred percent correct.

བརྒྱ་ཆག་ (gyajaà) bundle of 100.

བརྒྱ་ཆའི་གྲངས་ཀ་ (gyajɛ traŋga) percentage.

བརྒྱ་ཆའི་རྟགས་ (gyajɛ dāà) percentage sign/ symbol (%).

བརྒྱ་ཆའི་བསྡུར་ཚད་ (gyajɛ durdzɛɛ) comparison of percent.

བརྒྱ་ཆའི་འཕར་ཚད་ཀྱི་གྲངས་ཀ་ (gyajɛ pārdzɛɛgi traŋga) an index (e.g., price index).

བརྒྱ་ཆའི་ཟིན་ཚད་ (gyajɛ sindzɛɛ) percentage rate/ level/ degree.

བརྒྱ་ཆའི་རེའུ་མིག (gyajɛ riumig) percentage table/ chart.

བརྒྱ་མཆོད་ (gyajöö) offerings of one hundred things like butter lamps, incense, flowers.

བརྒྱ་འཇལ་ (gya jɛɛ) punishment equal to 100 times the amount stolen.

བརྒྱ་བལྟས་ཀུན་གསལ་ (gyadöö gũnsɛl) practice makes perfect [Lit. look one hundred times, all is clear].

བརྒྱ་བསྟོད་སྟོང་བསྟོད་ (gyadöö dõŋdöö) profuse in praise, full of praise [Lit. praise one hundred, praise one thousand].

བརྒྱ་ཐམ་པ་ (gya tāmba) one hundred.

བརྒྱ་ཐམ་པའི་གྲལ་འགོར་མ་སླེབས་ཀྱང་ སྟོང་ཐམ་པའི་གྲལ་གཞུག་ལ་མ་ལུས་པ་ (gya tāmbɛ trɛɛgɔɔ malebgyaŋ dõŋtāmbɛ trɛɛshuùla malüübə) conveys that one is not too bad at sth. [Lit. even though I am not amongst the top hundred, I will not be amongst the bottom thousand].

བརྒྱ་འདུས་སྟོང་ཚོགས་ (gyadüü dõŋdzɔɔ) large numbers of people gathering together in one place.

བརྒྱ་འདེམས་སྟོང་སྒྲུག (gyandem dõŋdruù) choosing the best (from many) [Lit. selecting from one hundred, picking from one thousand].

བརྒྱ་ལྡིང་ (gyadiŋ) abbr. of བརྒྱ་དཔོན་ and ལྡིང་དཔོན་.

བརྒྱ་དཔོན་ (gyabön) 1. a leader of a unit of 100. 2. an NCO rank in the traditional Tibetan army (head of 100 soldiers).

བརྒྱ་ཕྱག་ (gyacaà) one hundred prostrations.

བརྒྱ་ཕྲག་ (gyadraà) 1. hundreds; many ། ངལ་བ་བརྒྱ་ཕྲག་བསྙེན་དགོས་བྱུང་ཡོད་ (They) had to undergo many hardships. 2. century ། འདས་ལོ་བརྒྱ་ཕྲག་བདུན་པ་ The 7th century A.D.

བརྒྱ་ཕྲག་ཉི་ཤུ་པ་ (gyadraà ñishubə) the twentieth century.

བརྒྱ་བམ་ (gyabam) sm. བརྒྱ་ཆག.

བརྒྱ་བྱིན་ (gyajin) the Hindu god Indra.

བརྒྱ་མེད་ (gyameè) a zero in the hundred slot ། ཆིག་སྟོང་བརྒྱ་མེད་བདུན་ཅུ་ One thousand and seventy (1070).

བརྒྱ་མོན་ (gyamön) shung. a system wherein the རྩམ་བཞེས་པ་ officials in tt. were permitted to buy 1 maund of wool from 100 sheep at a low price from the nomads of Nagchuka (from whom they were collecting taxes) as their compensation for expenses and losses they incurred during their term of office. [Lit.100 maunds].

བརྒྱ་སྨོན་ (gyamön) sm. བརྒྱ་མོན་.

བརྒྱ་རྩ་ (gyadza) sm. བརྒྱ་ཚར་.

བརྒྱ་ཚར་ (gyatsar) a hundred times.

བརྒྱ་ཚོ་ (gyatso) a unit of one hundred villages or households.

བརྒྱ་ཚོ་རྒན་པོ་ (gyatso gɛmbo) an official under the District Commission in tt. who was in charge of village headmen and tax collection.

བརྒྱ་ཟུར་ (gyasur) percent.

བརྒྱ་ལ་ (gyala) if, in case ། བརྒྱ་ལ་ཁྱེད་རང་བོད་ལ་ཕེབས་མཁན་ཡིན་ན་ If you are going to Tibet.

བརྒྱ་ལམ་ (gyalam) 1. at a time in the future. 2. sth. that occurs very rarely.

བརྒྱ་ལོར་ (gyalɔr) a one hundred (dollar, rupee, etc.) note or bill.

བརྒྱ་ཤི་སྟོང་ལངས་ (gyashi dõŋlaŋ) fighting to the finish or to the last man [Lit. 100 die, 1000 will rise].

བརྒྱ་ཤོག (gyashɔɔ) 1. group of one hundred (people, troops, etc.). 2. a company or unit of 100 in a Tibetan Regiment (see དམག་སྒར་).

བརྒྱ་ཤོད་ (gyashöö) abacus.

བརྒྱ་བཤད་སྟོང་ལ་བབ་ཀྱང་ ཡོས་ལ་བབ་རྒྱུ་རྩམ་པ་ (gyashɛɛ dõŋla bəbgyaŋ yööla bəbgyu dzāmba) sm. ཚིག་བརྒྱ་མདོ་གཅིག.

བརྒྱ་བཤད་སྟོང་བཤད་ (gyashɛɛ dõŋshɛɛ) talking a great deal, too much talking [Lit. 100 talks, 1000 talks].

བརྒྱ་བཤིག་སྟོང་འགུགས་ (gyashiì dõŋguù) expending a little for a big return [Lit. destroy 100, call forth 1000].

བརྒྱ་གསེས་ (gyaseè) sm. ཡང་གསེས་.

བརྒྱག (gyaà) f. of རྒྱག.
བརྒྱགས་ (gyaà) sm. རྒྱགས་.
བརྒྱང་ (gyaŋ) f. of རྒྱོང་.
བརྒྱང་མགོ་ (gyaŋgo) sm. རྒྱང་མགོ་.
བརྒྱང་ཤིང་ (gyaŋshiŋ) cross.
བརྒྱངས་ (gyaŋ) p. of རྒྱོང་.
བརྒྱངས་སྐམ་ (gyaŋgam) stretching out to dry; va.—བྱེད་.
བརྒྱངས་རྒྱག (gyaŋgyaà) sm. རྒྱངས་, 1.
བརྒྱངས་བཤད་ (gyaŋshɛɛ̀) sm. རྒྱང་བཤད་.
བརྒྱད་ (gyɛɛ̀) eight.
བརྒྱད་བཀག (gyɛɛ̀gaà) scolding, reproaching; va.—བྱེད་.
བརྒྱད་བཀུག (gyɛɛ̀guù) eight ply.
བརྒྱད་སྐྱེད་ (gyɛɛ̀gyeè) shung. 16% (interest).
བརྒྱད་དགུ་འགྲོ་ (gyɛɛ̀gu dro) shung. 12.5 % (interest).
བརྒྱད་འཇལ་ (gyɛɛ̀ jɛɛ) punishment equal to eight times the amount stolen.
བརྒྱད་དྲུག (gyɛɛ̀druù) shung. 33% interest.
བརྒྱད་བརྒྱ་ (gyɛɛ̀gya) eight hundred.
བརྒྱད་ཅུ་ (gyəju) eighty ¶ བརྒྱད་བཅུ་བརྒྱ་བརྒྱད་ Eighty eight.
བརྒྱད་ཅུ་གོས་དཀར་ (gyəju köögar) the white cloth worn by people when they reach the age of eighty (in some regions).
བརྒྱད་ཅུ་འཇལ་ (gyəju jɛɛ) punishment equal to eighty times the amount stolen.
བརྒྱད་གཅིག (gyɛɛ̀jig) 1st of August (Army Day in PRC).
བརྒྱད་གདོར་ (gyɛɛ̀dɔr) shung. ceremony held in the Potala on the 8th day of the 3rd month (when government officials formally change from winter to summer dress).
བརྒྱད་སྟོང་པ་ (gyɛɛ dõŋba) a teaching of the Buddha that consists of 800 phrases (each of four verses).
བརྒྱད་སྡེའི་དམག (gyɛɛ̀nee mãà) shung. the soldier recruited as tax from each eight འདོན་ of land.
བརྒྱད་པ་ (gyɛɛ̀ba) the eighth.
བརྒྱད་པ་མེ་ཏོག (gyɛɛ̀ba medog) chrysanthemum.
བརྒྱད་བཞོགས་མ་ (gyɛɛ̀shɔgma) sm. བརྒྱད་ཤོག་མ་.
བརྒྱད་ཟུར་བཀར་འཛུག (gyɛɛ̀sur gənjuù) shung. putting one eight of the grain in storage.
བརྒྱད་ཤོག་མ་ (gyɛɛ̀shɔgma) octagon.
བརྒྱད་བསླས་ (gyɛɛ̀lɛɛ̀) 8-ply rope/ string.
བརྒྱན་ (gyɛn) p. and f. of རྒྱན་.
བརྒྱབ་ (gyəb) p. of རྒྱག.
བརྒྱབ་གཙུས་ (gyəbjüù) a kind of twisted dried cheese.
བརྒྱབས་ (gyəb) p. of རྒྱག.
བརྒྱལ་ (gyɛɛ) vi. to faint, to become unconscious ¶ མོས་གནས་ཚུལ་དེ་གོ་བ་དང་བརྒྱལ་སོང་ As soon as she heard the news she fainted.
བརྒྱལ་གཟེར་ (gyɛɛser) epileptic fit/ attack; vi.—རྒྱག to have an epileptic fit.
བརྒྱལ་གཟེར་གྱི་ནད་ (gyɛɛsergi nɛɛ̀) sm. བརྒྱལ་གཟེར་.
བརྒྱལ་སངས་ (gyɛɛ sãŋ) vi. to come back to consciousness (after fainting).
བརྒྱུ་ (gyu) f. of རྒྱུ་.
བརྒྱུག (gyuù) f. of རྒྱུག.
བརྒྱུགས་ (gyuù) p. of རྒྱུག.
བརྒྱུངས་ (gyuŋ) sm. རྒྱངས་.
བརྒྱུད་ (gyüü) 1. va. to transmit, to conduct, to send/ channel through ¶ སྙན་ཞུ་དེ་ས་གནས་ལས་ཁུངས་བརྒྱུད་དགོས་ One must channel the report through the regional office. 2. via, through, by way of ¶ ཆུར་ལམ་ཡོ་རབ་བརྒྱུད་ཡོང་པ་ཡིན་ On (my way here) (I) came through Europe. ¶ཁོང་གིས་གནས་ཚུལ་དེ་ཞིབ་འཇུག་བྱས་པ་བརྒྱུད་གསལ་པོ་ཤེས་རྟོགས་བྱུང་བ་རེད་ He came to understand that issue clearly by means of doing research. 3. sm. བརྒྱུད་པ་.
བརྒྱུད་(བ)སྐུལ་ (gyüügüü) inciting sb. via another; va.—བྱེད་.
བརྒྱུད་ཁུངས་ (gyüüguŋ) sm. འབྱུང་ཁུངས་.
བརྒྱུད་ཁྲིད་ (gyüüdrii) passing down a teaching; va.—བྱེད་ ¶ མན་ངག་འདི་ཚོ་སློབ་དཔོན་གཅིག་ནས་གཅིག་བརྒྱུད་ནས་བརྒྱུད་ཁྲིད་བྱས་པ་རེད་ These secret teachings are ones that have been passed down from one master to another.
བརྒྱུད་སྐུལ་ཀོ་ཐག (gyüügüü gɔ̃daà) belt between two pulleys/ motors, etc.
བརྒྱུད་བསྒྲགས་ (gyüüdraà) passing on or conveying news/ orders/ information (usu. verbally); va.—བྱེད་ ¶ དགྲ་ཕྱོགས་ཀྱི་གནས་ཚུལ་བརྒྱུད་བསྒྲགས་བྱས་ནས་ Having passed on information about the enemy.
བརྒྱུད་བསྒྲགས་ས་ཚིགས་ (gyüüdraà sədzii) rebroadcast station, relay station.
བརྒྱུད་མངག (gyüüŋaà) asking for sth. through sb. else; va.—བྱེད་ ¶ ངས་ལས་ཀ་དེ་བརྒྱུད་མངག་བྱས་པ་ཡིན་ I asked sb. to get me the job.
བརྒྱུད་ཐོ་ (gyüüdo) the list a person keeps of all the teachings that he has received.
བརྒྱུད་དག (gyüüdaà) sm. བརྒྱུད་པ་.
བརྒྱུད་འདྲེན་ (gyündren) transshiping, forwarding; va.—བྱེད་.
བརྒྱུད་འདྲེན་ས་ཚིགས་ (gyündren sədzii) transshiping/ forwarding station.
བརྒྱུད་ནས་ (gyüünɛɛ̀) see བརྒྱུད་.
བརྒྱུད་ནས་འདེམས་ (gyüünɛ dem) va. to select indirectly or through sb.
བརྒྱུད་པའི་རྒྱུ་རྐྱེན་ (gyüübɛ gyugyen) the remote cause, an indirect cause.
བརྒྱུད་པའི་ཉམས་མྱོང་ (gyüübɛ namñoŋ) indirect experience.
བརྒྱུད་པའི་ཉེ་དུ་ (gyüübɛ ñedu) collateral relatives.
བརྒྱུད་པའི་བླ་མ་ (gyüübɛ lãma) a lama (guru) who is one of the teachers in a tradition or religious lineage.
བརྒྱུད་སྤྲོད་ (gyüüdröö) conveying, transmitting, passing on; va.—བྱེད་.
བརྒྱུད་བྱུང་ (gyüüjaŋ) sm. བརྒྱུད་ཐོ་.
བརྒྱུད་འཕོད་ཁ་པར་ (gyümböö kãbaa) long distance telephone that requires going through an operator.
བརྒྱུད་མ་ (gyüüma) continuance, series.
བརྒྱུད་འཚོང་ (gyüüdzoŋ) sales through intermediates; va.—རྒྱག.
བརྒྱུད་འཛིན་ (gyündzin) sm. རྒྱུན་འཛིན་.
བརྒྱུད་ཡིག (gyüüyig) sm. རྒྱུད་བྱུང་.
བརྒྱུད་རིམ་ (gyüürim) sm. རྒྱུད་རིམ་.
བརྒྱུད་ཤུལ་ (gyüüshüü) inheritance, legacy.
བརྒྱུད་ཤོག (gyüüshɔɔ̀) invoice, receipt.
བརྒྱུད་བཤད་ (gyüüshɛɛ̀) relaying/ transmitting through another person; va.—བྱེད་.
བརྒྱུས་ (gyüü) p. of རྒྱུད་.
བསྒག (gaà) f. of སྒོག.
བསྒགས་ (gaà) p. of སྒོག.
བསྒབས་ (gəb) p. of སྒབ་.
བསྒར་ (gar) p. and f. of སྒར་.
བསྒུག (guù) f. of སྒུགས་.
བསྒུག་ས་ (gugsa) station, stop ¶ རེ་ལི་བསྒུག་ས་ Railway station.
བསྒུགས་ (guù) p. of སྒུགས་.
བསྒུགས་ར་སྡོད་ (gugra böö) va. to wait.
བསྒུར་ (gur) p. of སྒུར་.
བསྒུལ་ (güü) p. and f. of སྒུལ་.
བསྒུལ་ཤུགས་ (güüshuù) sm. སྒུལ་ཤུགས་.
བསྒོ་ (go) f. of སྒོ་.
བསྒོ་བ་བསྒོས་ (gowa göö) 1. va. to say what has to be said. 2. va. to give advice.
བསྒོ་ཡིག (goyig) a document/ notice/ order.
བསྒོང་ (goŋ) f. of སྒོང་.
བསྒོངས་ (goŋ) p. of སྒོང་.
བསྒོམ་ (gom) f. of བསྒོམ་.
བསྒོམས་ (gom) p. of བསྒོམ་.
བསྒོམས་པ་ (gomba) meditation.
བསྒོར་འཛུག་པའི་ལས་དོན་ (gɔnjuùbɛ lɛ̀ɛdön) shung. work that one is responsible for.

བསྒོས་ (göö̀) p. of སྒོ་.

བསྒྱིང་ (gyiŋ) f. of སྒྱིང་.

བསྒྱིངས་ (gyiŋ) va. to act grandly/ imposingly.

བསྒྱུར་ (gyur) p. and f. སྒྱུར་.

བསྒྱུར་བྲིས་ (gyurdriì) written translation; va.—བྱེད་.

བསྒྱུར་བཀོད་ (gyurgöö̀) change, alteration, revision, transformation, reconstruction; va.—བྱེད་; —གཏོང་ to change, to make changes, to alter, to revise, to reconstruct, to transform ¶ སྤྱི་ཚོགས་རིང་ལུགས་ཀྱི་བསྒྱུར་བཀོད་ Socialist transformation.

བསྒྱུར་སྒྲུན་ (gyurdrün) sm. བསྒྱུར་བཀོད་.

བསྒྱུར་གྲངས་ (gyurdraŋ) product (in math).

བསྒྱུར་བཅོས་ (gyurjöö̀) reforming/ changing/ revising/ reconstructing/ transforming; va.—བྱེད་; —གཏོང་ to change/ alter/ revise/ reconstruct/ transform; vi.—འགྱོ་ to be reformed/ changed/ transformed/ revised/ reconstructed.

བསྒྱུར་བཅོས་སྒོ་དབྱེ་ (gyurjöö̀ goye) open door reform policy; va.—བྱེད་.

བསྒྱུར་བརྗེས་ (gyurjeè) changing, altering; va.—བྱེད་.

བསྒྱུར་ཐོབ་ (gyudob) sm. བསྒྱུར་གྲངས་.

བསྒྱུར་དེབ་ (gyurdeb) translated book.

བསྒྱུར་ནོར་ (gyurnɔɔ) translator mistake; vi.—ཤོར་; —འཐེབ་ to make a mistake in translation.

བསྒྱུར་བྲིས་ (gyurdiì) translation.

བསྒྱུར་དབྱེ་ (gyurye) open door reform policy; va.—བྱེད་.

བསྒྱུར་མིང་ (gyurmiŋ) 1. a new name. 2. translated name or term.

བསྒྱུར་གཞི་ (gyurshi) root, power (in math).

བསྒྱུར་གཞི་ཉིས་རྩིས་ (gyurshi ñiidziì) square root (in math).

བསྒྱུར་གཞི་སུམ་རྩིས་ (gyurshi sūmdziì) cube (in math).

བསྒྱུར་བཟོ་ (gyurso) sm. བསྒྱུར་བཀོད་.

བསྒྱུར་ཡིག (gyuryig) translation, translated text.

བསྒྱུར་ཡིག་ཕྱོགས་བསྡུས་ (gyuryig cɔ̄gdüü) translated articles compiled into book/ magazine.

བསྒྱེལ་ (gyee) p. and f. of སྒྱེལ་.

བསྒྱོངས་ (gyoŋ) p. of སྒྱོང་.

བསྒྲག (draà) f. of སྒྲོག.

བསྒྲག་ཐོ་ (dragdo) a document or letter to be publicized/ distributed.

བསྒྲག་ཡིག (drəgyig) sm. བསྒྲག་ཐོ་.

བསྒྲགས་ (draà) p. of སྒྲོག.

བསྒྲགས་གཏམ་ (dragdam) proclamation, manifesto, declaration, pronouncement.

བསྒྲགས་གཏམ་ཡིག་ཆ་ (dragdam yigja) letter of declaration, manifesto.

བསྒྲགས་ཚིག (drəgdzig) sm. བསྒྲགས་ཡིག.

བསྒྲང་ (draŋ) f. of སྒྲོང་.

བསྒྲངས་ (draŋ) p. of སྒྲོང་.

བསྒྲབས་ (drəb) p. of སྒྲུབ་.

བསྒྲལ་ (drɛɛ) p. and f. of སྒྲོལ་.

བསྒྲིག (drig) f. of སྒྲིག.

བསྒྲིགས་ (drig) p. of སྒྲིག.

བསྒྲིགས་བཙུགས་ (drigdzuù) sm. སྒྲིག་འཛུགས་.

བསྒྲིགས་ཚུལ་ (drigtsüü) see སྒྲིགས་.

བསྒྲིངས་ (driŋ) p. of སྒྲིང་.

བསྒྲིན་ (drin) p. and f. of སྒྲིན་.

བསྒྲིབ་ (drib) f. of སྒྲིབ་.

བསྒྲིབས་ (drib) p. of སྒྲིབ་.

བསྒྲིམ་ (drim) f. of སྒྲིམ་.

བསྒྲིལ་ (drii) p. and f. of སྒྲིལ་.

བསྒྲིལ་བསྒྲིལ་ (driidrii) packing into a bundle; va.—བཟོ་.

བསྒྲིལ་འཐུམ་ (drindum) bundle, package; va.—རྒྱག to wrap a package, to make a bundle/ package.

བསྒྲུག (druù) f. of སྒྲུག.

བསྒྲུགས་ (druù) p. of སྒྲུག.

བསྒྲུན་ (drün) p. and f. of སྒྲུན་.

བསྒྲུབ་ (drub) f. of སྒྲུབ་.

བསྒྲུབ་རྒྱུགས་ (drubgyuù) sm. སྒྲུབ་རྒྱུགས་.

བསྒྲུབ་གཅིག་སྒྲུབ་གཉིས་ (drubjig drubñiì) (with neg.) no way to do sth. ¶ ལས་ཀ་མང་པོ་འདི་འདྲ་བསྒྲུབ་གཅིག་སྒྲུབ་གཉིས་ཡོད་པ་མ་རེད་ There is no way that (I) can do as much work as this.

བསྒྲུབ་མཆོད་ (drubjöö̀) sm. སྒྲུབ་མཆོད་.

བསྒྲུབ་བྱ་ (drubja) 1. sth. remaining to be given/ paid/ done, a duty/ responsibility to be done ¶ ངའི་ལས་དོན་བསྒྲུབ་བྱ་ཁག་ལ་བསམ་བློ་གཏོང་གི་ཡོད་ I'm thinking about my work responsibilities (to fulfill them). 2. subject matter, theme.

བསྒྲུབ་བྱ་སྒྲུབ་བྱེད་ (drubja drubjɛè) work in process of being completed, work to be done in the future ¶ བསྒྲུབ་བྱ་སྒྲུབ་བྱེད་ཀྱི་ལས་ཀ་གང་དང་གང་ལའང་འཆར་གཞི་ཡག་པོ་འདིང་དགོས་ We have to make good plans for the work being done now and the work that will be done in the future.

བསྒྲུབས་འཇལ་ (drumjɛɛ) sm. སྒྲུབ་འཇལ་.

བསྒྲེ་ (dre) f. of སྒྲེ་.

བསྒྲེང་ (dreŋ) f. of སྒྲེང་.

བསྒྲེས་ (dreè) p. of སྒྲེ་.

བསྒྲོག (drɔɔ̀) f. of སྒྲོག.

བསྒྲོགས་ (drɔɔ̀) p. of སྒྲོག.

བསྒྲོད་ (dröö̀) p. of སྒྲོད་.

བསྒྲོན་ (drön) p. and f. of སྒྲོན་.

ང

ང་ (ŋa) 1. I ༈ང་དང་ངའི་ཁྱིམ་ཚང་ My family and I. 2. numerical particle used in the fifties ༈ལྔ་བཅུ་ང་གཅིག Fifty-one. 3. the letter 'ང' (used in alphabetical ordering).

ང་ཁོ་ན་ (ŋa kōna) only myself, I alone ༈ང་ཁོ་ན་བསམ་པའི་མི་ a person who thinks only of himself.

ང་ཁྱོད་མེད་པ་ (ŋa kyȫȫ mēēba) no difference between you and me.

ང་དགའ་ཁྱོད་སྐྱིད་ (ŋa ga kyȫȫ gyīī) both sides being satisfied/ content/ happy; va.—བྱེད་ [Lit. I happy; you glad].

ང་འགྲོ་ཁོ་འགྲོ་ (ŋadro kōdro) having a rush for sth., scrambling for sth. (can have negative or positive connotation); va.—བྱེད་ ༈ལས་གནས་གསར་པ་དེའི་གླ་ཕོགས་ཆེན་པོ་ཡོད་ཙང་མི་ཚང་མ་ང་འགྲོ་ཁོ་འགྲོ་རེད་ Because the new position had a high salary everyone was scrambling (to get it).

ང་རྒྱལ་ (ŋargyɛɛ̀) 1. arrogant, conceited, proud, haughty, self-important; vi.—སྐྱེ་; —སྐྱེད་ to be arrogant/ conceited/ proud ༈ཁོ་ལ་ཡོན་ཏན་མེད་ཀྱང་ང་རྒྱལ་བྱེད་ཀྱི་འདུག Even though he isn't learned he is proud and conceited. 2. aggressiveness, competitiveness; vi.—སྐྱེ་; —སྐྱེད་ to be aggressive/ competitive ༈ཁོས་སློབ་སྦྱོང་གི་ཐོག་ལ་ང་རྒྱལ་ཆེན་པོ་བྱེད་ཀྱི་འདུག Regarding his education he is very competitive (aggressive).

ང་རྒྱལ་ཁེངས་དྲེགས་ (ŋargyɛɛ̀ kēŋdreg) sm. ང་རྒྱལ་.

ང་རྒྱལ་ཁོ་ཕམ་ (ŋargyɛɛ̀ kōpam) sm. ང་རྒྱལ་གཞན་ཕམ་.

ང་རྒྱལ་ཅན་ (ŋargyɛjɛn) arrogant, proud, conceited.

ང་རྒྱལ་ཆེན་པོ་ (ŋargyɛɛ̀ cēmbo) 1. arrogant, conceited, proud vi.—སྐྱེ་; —སྐྱེད་ to be arrogant/ conceited/ proud; to be aggressive/ competitive ༈མི་འགའ་ཤས་གྲུབ་འབྲས་ཆུང་ཆུང་ལས་ང་རྒྱལ་ཆེན་པོ་སྐྱེ་གི་ཡོད་པ་རེད་ Some people become very conceited as a result of a small success. 2. aggressive, competitive ༈ཁོ་རྩེད་མོ་ག་རེ་རྩེད་ནའང་ང་རྒྱལ་ཆེན་པོ་འདུག Whatever game he plays he is very competitive/ aggressive.

ང་རྒྱལ་འཆབ་འཚུབ་ (ŋargyɛɛ̀ tsəbdzub) do sth. in an arrogant and rash/ hurried manner; va.—སྤོང་ to give up/ abstain from acting rash and arrogant/ conceited.

ང་རྒྱལ་ཚ་པོ་ (ŋargyɛɛ̀ tsābo) sm. ང་རྒྱལ་ཆེན་པོ་.

ང་རྒྱལ་ཞེ་སྡང་ (ŋargyɛɛ̀ shedaŋ) arrogance, hatred and anger.

ང་རྒྱལ་གཞན་ཕམ་ (ŋargyɛɛ̀ shembam) I win, you lose.

ང་སྙིར་ཅན་.(ŋargerjɛn) sm. སྙིར་སེམས་.

ང་ཅག (ŋajaà) we.

ང་ཆེ་ང་བཙན་ (ŋace ŋadzɛn) considering/ thinking oneself the best, egotistical, conceited ༈ཕན་ཚུན་ང་ཆེ་ང་བཙན་གྱིས་ཤོད་རེས་ཐུག་མཐར་གྲྭ་པས་ཁོ་བསད་སོང་ They spoke back and forth egoistically (i.e., neither would give in) and finally the monks killed him.

ང་ཉིད་ (ŋañīì) I myself.

ང་གཉིས་ (ŋañīi) we two, the two of us ༈ང་གཉིས་མཉམ་དུ་སྡོད་ཀྱི་ཡོད་ We two are staying together.

ང་དང་ (དམག་སྒར་) (ŋadaŋ) the "ང" or Gyantse Regiment in the traditional Tibetan army.

ང་བདག་རྩོད་འཛུགས་ (ŋadaà dzȫndzuù) shung. disputing over possession/ ownership.

ང་བདག་རྩོད་སློང་ (ŋadaà dzȫȫloŋ) shung. sm. ང་བདག་རྩོད་འཛུགས་.

ང་བདེན་ (ŋāden) considering oneself correct.

ང་བདེན་ང་ཡུས་ (ŋaden ŋayüü) tooting one's own horn, self aggrandizing.

ང་བདེན་ང་བཙན་ (ŋəaden ŋadzɛn) shung. insisting that justice is on one's side.

ང་བདེན་ཁོ་རྫུན་ (ŋaden kōdzün) I am right, others are wrong/ false/ untrue.

ང་སྡུག་ཁོ་སྡུག (ŋadug kōdug) refers to arguments where each side says the other is bad or wrong.

ང་ནེ་ངོ་ནེ་ (ŋane ŋone) unclear (talk).

ང་ཕོད་ (ŋabȫȫ) name of Tibetan aristocratic family.

ང་མིན་ཁོ་ཡིན་ (ŋamin kōyin) putting the blame on sb. else [Lit. it is not me, it is him].

ང་མིན་ན་སུ་ཡིན་ (ŋaminnə sūyin) conceited, arrogant, considering oneself the best [Lit. if not me, who].

ང་མིན་སུ་ཡིན་ (ŋamin sūyin) sm. ང་མིན་ན་སུ་ཡིན་.

ང་བཙན་ (ŋadzɛn) sm. ང་ཆེ་ང་བཙན་.

ང་ཚོ་ (ŋandzo) we, us ༈ཁོས་ང་ཚོ་འདིར་བཏང་བྱུང་ He sent us here.

ང་ཚོའི་ཁོ་ཚོ་ (ŋāndzo kōndzo) those from among us ༈ང་ཚོའི་ཁོ་ཚོས་མགོ་ལོག་ཞི་དྲགས་བཟོས་འདུག Our people (those from among us) have made a real mess of things.

ང་ཡི་ (ŋəyi) my, mine ༈ང་ཡི་དེབ་ My book.

ང་ར་ (ŋāra) 1. sm. ང་རང་. 2. sm. ང་རོ་. 3. cold, freezing.

ང་རང་ (ŋaraŋ) I, myself.

ང་རང་གཉིས་ (ŋaraŋñii) we two.

ང་རང་ཚོ་ (ŋaraŋdzo) we, ourselves.

ང་རོ་ (ŋaro) yell, roar, shout, cheer; va.—སྒྲོག་; —འབྱིན་ to shout/ roar/ yell/ cheer ༈དགའ་སྤྲོའི་ང་རོ་སྒྲོག་བཞིན་དགའ་བསུ་ཞུས་པ་རེད་ (They) were welcomed with shouts of happiness.

ང་ལན་ཁོ་འགྱོད་ (ŋalen kōngyöö) blaming and regretting.

ང་ལན་ཁོ་ལན་ (ŋalɛn kōlɛn) sm. ང་ལན་ཁྱོད་ལན་.

ང་ལན་ཁྱོད་ལན་ (ŋalen kyȫȫlɛn) blaming one another back and forth; va.—བྱེད་.

ང་ལུམ་བྱ་རར་གསུམ་ (ŋa lum jarsum) shung. the three Council Ministers during the era of the Seventh Dalai Lama: Ngapo, Lumpawa, and Jarawa.

ང་ཤོར་ཁྱོད་ཤོར་ (ŋalshɔɔ kyȫȫshɔɔ) competing, racing ༈ཁོང་གཉིས་ང་ཤོར་ཁྱོད་ཤོར་གྱིས་གདོང་འཕྲོག་རེས་བྱེད་ཀྱི་འདུག The two are competing trying to get in front of each other.

ང་ས་ཁོ་ས་མེད་པ་ (ŋasa kōsa mēēba) no demarcation line between land or property.

ངག (ŋaà) speech, words, talk ༈མི་ངག་འཇམ་པ་ A soft spoken person. ༈དེ་ཁོས་ངག་ཐོག་ནས་ཞུས་སོང་ He reported that orally.

ངག་ཀྱལ་ (ŋaggyɛl) meaningless/ idle talk.

ངག་བཀོད་ (ŋaggoȍ) orders, instructions (verbal); va.—གཏོང་; —བྱེད་ to give verbal orders/ instructions ༈ཁོ་ཚོས་ལས་མི་རྣམས་ལ་དེ་རིང་གི་ལས་ཀ་ངག་བཀོད་བྱས་པ་རེད་ They gave instructions to the laborers about today's work. ༈ངག་བཀོད་དང་ལེན་ Volunteering to do an order given verbally.

ངག་བཀྱལ་ (ŋaggyɛɛ) sm. ངག་ཀྱལ་.

ངག་སྐུགས་པ (ŋaà gūgbə) mute, dumb.

ངག་སྐད་ (ŋaggɛɛ̀) talk, conversation.

ངག་སྐྱོར་ (ŋaggyɔr) 1. reciting aloud, reciting/ repeating from memory; va.—བྱེད་. 2. accompanying sb. in singing; va.—བྱེད་; —གཏོང་.

ངག་ཁྲིད་ (ŋagtrīì) teaching orally, instructing orally; va.—བྱེད་.

ངག་ཁྲུན་ཆོད་ཟིན་པ་ (ŋagdrön cȫȍ simbə) shung. a case being settled verbally ༈གྱོད་དོན་འདི་སྐོར་ངག་ཁྲུན་ཆོད་ཟིན་ན་ཡང་ཡིག་ཆ་བསྟན་འཛུགས་བྱ་རྒྱུ་ཡིན་པ་ This case has been settled verbally, but it has not been put in a written agreement.

ངག་འཁྱལ་ (ŋaggyɛɛ) sm. ངག་འཆལ་.

ངག་འཁྲིལ་ལུས་ཁྱུག (ŋagdrii lüügyuù) obedient and efficient.

ངག་གི་སྒྲོན་མེ་ (ŋaàgi drönma) name of a traditional text that teaches Tibetan spelling.

ངག་གི་འདོད་འཇོ་ (ŋaàgi dönjo) extremely well-composed and beautiful, sth. that touches the heart.

ངག་གི་སྤྱོད་ཡུལ་ལས་འདས་པ་ (ŋaàgi jȫȍyüüle dεὲba) beyond words.

ངག་གི་དབང་ཕྱུག (ŋaàgi wə̄njuù) Manjushri.

ངག་གི་རྩལ་གསུམ་ (ŋaggi tsε̄ε̄sum) three positive verbal qualities: having a sound knowledge of history and able to articulate this; making people laugh; wining in debating.

ངག་གི་ལས་ (ŋaggi lεὲ) the three verbal negative qualities: lying, cheating, idle talk.

ངག་གེ་ངོག་གེ་ (ŋagge ŋogge) speaking unclearly/ inaudibly.

ངག་འགྲོ་ (ŋagdro) 1. sayings. 2. tone of talking.

ངག་རྒྱན་ (ŋaggyεn) stylistic manner of talking.

ངག་རྒྱུགས་ (ŋəggyuà) sm. ངག་ཐོག་ནས་རྒྱུགས་ལེན་.

ངག་རྒྱུན་ (ŋəggyün) traditional saying, legend, proverb, oral tradition.

ངག་རྒྱུན་རྩོམ་རིག་ (ŋəggyün dzōmriì) folktales, oral literature.

ངག་སྒོ་འབྱེད་ (ŋaà go jeè) va. to let sb. talk.

ངག་ངོག་ (ŋagŋog) abbr. of ངག་གེ་ངོག་གེ་.

ངག་ཅལ་ཅོལ་ (ŋag jεεjöö) sm. བབ་ཅོལ་.

ངག་གཅོད་ (ŋagjöö) staying silent, renouncing talking; va.—བྱེད་; —དུ་སྡོད་ to stay without speaking (usu. in meditation), to keep silent.

ངག་བཅད་ (ŋagjεὲ) p. of ངག་གཅོད་.

ངག་བཅད་པ་ (ŋagjεὲba) hermit, meditator who has given up talking.

ངག་འཆལ་ (ŋagjεε) raving, ranting, babbling; vi. ངག་འཆལ་; —བྱེད་ to rant, to babble, to rave.

ངག་འཛགས་ (ŋagjaà) sth. learned by heart ¶ཁོང་གིས་ངག་འཛགས་ཀྱི་སྙན་ངག་རྣམས་སྐྱོར་སོང་ He recited the poems he had learned by heart.

ངག་འཇམ་པོ་ (ŋaà jambo) soft spoken, verbally polite.

ངག་འཇམ་སྨྲ་མཁན་ (ŋagjam māgεn) a person with a gentle/ soft manner of speaking.

ངག་སྙན་པོ་ (ŋaà ñēmbo) sm. ངག་འཇམ་པོ་.

ངག་གདམ་ (ŋagdam) speech, verbal communication; va.—བྱེད་.

ངག་རྡ་ (ŋagda) tune/ melody (of a song).

ངག་བརྟན་པོ་ (ŋaà dε̄mbo) having a good memory.

ངག་བརྟན་བྱས་ནས་ཞུ་ (ŋagden cεὲnε shu) shung. va. to recommend sb. to a superior.

ངག་ཐོག (ŋagdɔɔ̀) orally, verbally ¶ཁོས་ངག་ཐོག་ནས་བཤད་པ་རེད་ He told it orally. ¶ངག་ཐོག་གི་རྒྱབ་སྐྱོར་ Verbal support.

ངག་ཐོག་བསྔགས་བརྗོད་ (ŋagdɔɔ̀ nāgjöö) oral/ verbal praise.

ངག་ཐོག་གཏུགས་བཤེར་ (ŋagdɔɔ̀ dūgsher) debating, cross-examining; va.—བྱེད་.

ངག་ཐོག་བརྡ་སྦྱོར་ (ŋagdɔɔ̀ dajɔɔ) notifying orally; va.—བྱེད་.

ངག་ཐོག་ནས་ (ŋagdɔɔ̀nε) orally, verbally.

ངག་ཐོག་ནས་སྐྱོར་ (ŋagdɔɔ̀nε gyɔ̄r) to recite orally/ verbally (from memory).

ངག་ཐོག་ཞུ་སྦྱོར་ (ŋagdɔɔ̀ shujɔɔ) reporting orally; va.—བྱེད་.

ངག་ཐོག་གཟེངས་བསྟོད་ (ŋagdɔɔ̀ seŋdöö) oral/ verbal praise.

ངག་གདངས་ (ŋagdaŋ) sm. ངག་རྡ་.

ངག་བདེ་པོ་ (ŋaà debo) sm. ཁ་བདེ་པོ་.

ངག་འདོན་ (ŋag dön) 1. va. to recite by heart/ memory. 2. sm. ཁ་འདོན.

ངག་རྡུགས་ (ŋag duŋ) having nothing to retort (in a debate).

ངག་ལྡན་ (ŋagdεn) eloquent, verbal.

ངག་ལྡབ་ལྡིབ་ (ŋag dəbdib) speech defect, stutter, stammer, lisp.

ངག་སྡོམ་ (ŋaà dom) va. to stay silent, to refrain from speaking ¶ངག་བསྡམས་ནས་བཞུགས་ཡོད་པ་རེད་ མི་སུ་གཅིག་ལ་སྐད་ཆ་ཤོད་མི་ཆོག (He) is staying silent (in retreat). (He) is not allowed to speak to anyone.

ངག་སྡོམ་ཚུལ་བཞུགས་ (ŋagdom) staying silent and still.

ངག་བསྡམས་ (ŋaà dam) p. of ངག་བསྡམས་.

ངག་ནས་ (ŋagnε) sm. ངག་ཐོག་ནས་.

ངག་ནས་འབྲི་ (ŋagnε tri) va. to write from memory.

ངག་སྤྱི་བརྟོལ་ (ŋagji dȫȍ) va. to speak arrogantly/ wildly.

ངག་འཕྲིན་ (ŋəgdrin) verbal or oral message/ news/ information.

ངག་བྲིས་ (ŋəgdriì) writing from memory; va.—བྱེད་.

ངག་བྲེལ་ (ŋagdrel) quick/ fast talker.

ངག་དབང་ (ŋawaŋ) 1. person's name. 2. abbr. of ངག་གི་དབང་ཕྱུག.

ངག་དབང་བློ་བཟང་རྒྱ་མཚོ་ (ŋawaŋ losaŋ gyadzo) shung. the Fifth Dalai Lama.

ངག་དབང་ལྷ་མོ་ (ŋawaŋ lhāmo) 1. a female deity. 2. female's name.

ངག་མ་ (ŋagma) sm. ངག་འཕྲིན་.

ངག་མི་གསལ་བ་ (ŋaà misεlwa) not clear in speech/ talking.

ངག་མེད་ (ŋagmeè) speechless, without speech.

ངག་ཙམ་ (ŋagdzam) in word only (i.e., not in deed).

ངག་བཙན་ (ŋagdzεn) 1. reliable works, precise speech. 2. stern words.

ངག་རྩལ་ (ŋagdzεε) eloquent, eloquence in speech.

ངག་ཚབ་ (ŋəgdzəb) 1. a letter. 2. a verbal/ oral message.

ངག་ཚིག (ŋəgdzig) sm. ངག་གདམ་.

ངག་མཚུངས་ (ŋəgdzuŋ) talking in a similar/ harmonious/ compatible manner.

ངག་འཛིན་ (ŋəŋdzin) sm. ངག་སྐྱོར་.

ངག་ཞུ་ (ŋagshu) shung. verbal report.

ངག་ཟེར་ཡི་གེར་བཀོད་པ་ (ŋagser yige gȫȍba) shung. writing down what ever was said.

ངག་བཟོ་ (ŋagso) everything that is done through the medium of speech.

ངག་ལ་ (ŋagla) in speech, orally.

ངག་ལ་སྐྱོར་ (ŋaàla gyōr) va. to recite by heart.

ངག་ལ་འབྲི་ (ŋaàla tri) va. to write from memory.

ངག་ལ་ཟིན་ (ŋaàla sin) va. to memorize.

ངག་ལ་ཟིམ་ (ŋaàla sim) va. to memorize.

ངག་ལན་ (ŋaàlεn) sm. ཁ་ལན་.

ངག་ལམ་ (ŋaglam) speech, words ¶འགྲུལ་པ་ཚོའི་ངག་ལམ་ལྟར་བྱས་ན་བོད་ནང་བསྐྱར་དུ་མི་མང་པོ་འཛིན་བཟུང་བྱས་ཡོད་འདུག According to the travelers' accounts, (they) have again arrested many people in Tibet.

ངག་ལམ་བདེ་པོ་ (ŋaglam debo) eloquent in speech.

ངག་ཤོར་ (ŋaà shɔ̄ɔ̄) vi. to have a slip of the tongue.

ངག་བཤེར་ (ŋagsher) cross-examination, interrogation va.—བྱེད་.

ངག་སློབ་ (ŋaglob) verbal teaching/ instructions; va.—བྱེད་.

ངག་སློབ་སྤྱོད་ཁྲིད་ (ŋaglob jȫȍdriì) showing/ setting an example in speech as well as action.

ངག་སློབ་ལུས་ཁྲིད་ (ŋaglob lüütriì) sm. ཁ་བཤད་དཔེ་སྟོན་.

ངག་གསལ་ (ŋagsεε) lucid/ clear speech.

ངང་ (ŋaŋ) 1. nominal adverbializer—in the manner of, in the state of (usu. gen. + —) ¶ཁོ་ཚོས་དགའ་པོའི་ངང་ནས་ཁོང་ལ་དགའ་བསུ་ཞུས་པ་རེད་ (They) welcomed (him) warmly (joyfully). 2. gradually, slowly ¶རྒྱ་བོད་མཛའ་འབྲེལ་ངང་ནས་མཐུན་འབྲེལ་བྱུང་བ་རེད་ Friendly relations between Tibet and China gradually (came to) exist. 3. abbr. of ངང་པ་.

ངང་དཀར་ (ŋaŋgar) 1. grey-white duck/ swan. 2. grey-whitish color.

ངང་དཀར་སྐར་ཚོམ་ (ŋaŋgar gārdzom) Cygnus (the swan constellation).

ངང་སྐྱ་ (ŋaŋgya) milky white in color.

ངང་ཁུལ་ (ŋəŋgüü) goose down.

ངང་ཁྱུ་ (ŋəŋgyu) flock of wild ducks/ geese/ swans.

ངང་གིས་ (ŋaŋgi) gradually, slowly ¶ངང་གིས་གོ་དོན་རྟོགས་ཀྱི་རེད་ (We) will gradually come to know the meaning.

ངང་རྒྱུ་རིང་པོ་ (ŋəŋgyu riŋgu) 1. patient, tolerant, able to endure ། ཁོ་ནི་ངང་རྒྱུ་རིང་པོ་འདུག He is a patient person. 2. sb. who is able to think deeply and plan carefully, sb. who is circumspect and farsighted.

ངང་རྒྱུད་ (ŋəŋgyüü) 1. patience, endurance ། ཁོ་ནི་ངང་རྒྱུད་ཙ་བ་ནས་མེད་པ་ཞིག་འདུག He is a person who is not at all patient. 2. temperament, character ། ངལ་རྩོལ་མི་དམངས་ཀྱི་ངང་རྒྱུད་ The temperament of the laboring people.

ངང་རྒྱུད་འཇམ་པོ་ (ŋəŋgyüü jambo) patient in character/ temperament.

ངང་རྒྱུད་ཐུང་ཐུང་ (ŋəŋgyüü tüŋduŋ) impatient, short-tempered, impulsive, irritable.

ངང་རྒྱུད་བལ་ལས་འཇམ་པ་ གཞུང་རྒྱུད་མདའ་ལས་དྲང་བ་ (ŋəŋgyüü pɛɛlɛ jam shuŋyüü dalɛ traŋwa) a patient/ good-natured character as smooth as wool and honesty as straight as an arrow.

ངང་རྒྱུད་བཟང་པོ་ (ŋəŋgyüü saŋbo) good-natured.

ངང་རྒྱུད་རིང་པོ་ (ŋəŋgyüü riŋgu) 1. patient, tolerant, able to endure. 2. sb. who is able to think deeply and plan carefully, sb. who is circumspect and farsighted.

ངང་རྒྱུན་ཐུང་ཐུང་ (ŋəŋgyün tüŋduŋ) sm.* ངང་རྒྱུད་ཐུང་ཐུང་.

ངང་རྒྱུན་རིང་པོ་ (ŋəŋgyün riŋgu) sm.* ངང་རྒྱུད་རིང་པོ་.

ངང་སྒུག་བྱེད་ (ŋəŋguù) waiting patiently; va.—བྱེད་ ། ཉིན་མང་རིང་ནང་མི་ཚོ་འཁོར་རྒྱུ་ངང་སྒུག་བྱས་པ་ཡིན་ (We) waited patiently for many days for the arrival of (our) family members.

ངང་འགྲོ་ངང་སྡོད་ (ŋandro ŋandöö) doing/ living patiently [Lit. going patiently; staying patiently].

ངང་ངང་ (ŋaŋŋaŋ) in a slow/ patient manner.

ངང་ངུར་ (ŋaŋŋur) swan and goose.

ངང་ཆུ་ (ŋəŋju) a yellow natural dye.

ངང་ཆེན་ (ŋanjen) swan.

ངང་ངན་ (ŋaŋŋɛn) evil/ bad in nature.

ངང་ཐུང་ (ŋənduŋ) sm. ངང་རྒྱུད་ཐུང་ཐུང་.

ངང་ཐུང་ཐལ་སྐྱོད་ (ŋənduŋ tɛɛgyöö) impetuosity, rashness; va.—བྱེད་ to act impetuously/ rashly.

ངང་ཐུང་འཚབ་འཚུབ་ (ŋənduŋ tsəbdzəb) impatient, overanxious, nervous.

ངང་འཐེན་ (ŋanden) temporarily delaying/ deferring/ postponing/ halting; va.—བྱེད་ to halt/ delay for a short time or temporarily ། ང་བོད་ལ་འགྲོ་རྒྱུ་ངང་འཐེན་བྱས་པ་ཡིན་ (I) delayed my going to Tibet. ། མེ་མདའ་རྒྱག་རྒྱུ་ངང་འཐེན་བྱས་པ་རེད་ (He) delayed a little before firing his gun.

ངང་ནས་ (ŋanɛ) see ངང་.

ངང་པ་ (ŋanba) wild duck, swan, goose.

ངང་པ་དཀར་པོ་ (ŋanba gārba) greyish-white wild duck/ swan/ goose.

ངང་པ་ཆུ་ལ་དགའ་བ་ལྟར་ (ŋanba cūla gaba dār) very glad/ pleased, liking a lot [Lit. like a duck likes water].

ངང་པ་པད་མཚོར་འཇུག་པ་ལྟར་ (ŋanba bɛ̄ɛdzor jugba dār) very glad/ pleased, liking a lot [Lit. like a duck entering a lotus lake].

ངང་པ་སེར་ལྡན་ (ŋanba sērdɛn) sm. ངང་པ་སེར་པོ་.

ངང་པ་སེར་པོ་ (ŋanba sērbo) yellow wild duck.

ངང་པའི་མཚོའུ་ (ŋanbɛ tsēwu) the ballet “Swan Lake”.

ངང་ཕྲུག (ŋandruù) baby swan/ goose/ duck.

ངང་མོ་ (ŋanmo) female swan/ goose/ duck.

ངང་དམར་ (ŋanmar) redish goose.

ངང་ཙམ་ནས་ (ŋandzamnɛ) after a while.

ངང་ཙམ་སོང་ནས་ (ŋandzam sōŋnɛ) 1. gradually, slowly. 2. after a while.

ངང་ཚུལ་ (ŋəndzüü) 1. atmosphere, feeling, disposition, character ། སེམས་སྐྱོ་བའི་ངང་ཚུལ་ A feeling of sadness. 2. likeness.

ངང་རིང་ (ŋəŋriŋ) sm. ངང་རྒྱུད་རིང་པོ་.

ངང་རིང་ཟོལ་མེད་ (ŋəŋriŋ söömeè) patiently and honestly.

ངང་ལག (ŋaŋlaà) banana.

ངང་སེར་ (ŋanser) sm. ངུར་པ་.

ངང་སེར་ཡོན་དབྱང་ (ŋanser yönyaŋ) tib.ch. mandarin duck.

ངང་བསྲིང་ (ŋansiŋ) sm. རྒྱུན་བསྲིང་.

ངད་ (ŋɛ̀ɛ) 1. smell, odor, fragrance. 2. effect ། སྨན་ངད་ Effect of the medicine.

ངད་ཅན་ (ŋɛ̀ɛjɛn) sm. ངད་ལྡན.

ངད་ལྡན་ (ŋɛ̀ɛdɛn) fragrant, odorous.

ངད་པ་ (ŋɛ̀ɛba) a smell/ aroma.

ངད་བཟང་ (ŋɛ̀ɛsaŋ) aromatic/ fragrant smell.

ངད་གསོད་ (ŋɛ̀ɛsöö) deodorizing; va.—བྱེད་ to deodorize, to get rid of odors/ smells.

ངན་ (ŋɛn) abbr. of ངན་པ་.

ངན་ཁང་ (ŋɛngaŋ) destitute people.

ངན་སྐུལ་ (ŋɛngüü) instigating, inciting; va.—བྱེད་ to instigate, to incite ། ལོག་སྤྱོད་པ་དེ་ཚོས་མི་དམངས་ཀྱིས་ཏང་ལ་ངོ་རྒོལ་བྱེད་དགོས་པའི་ངན་སྐུལ་བྱས་པ་རེད་ The reactionaries incited the people to oppose the party.

ངན་བསྐུལ་ (ŋɛngüü) sm. ངན་སྐུལ་.

ངན་བསྐུལ་དཀྲུག་ཤིང་ (ŋɛngüü drūgshiŋ) causing trouble by inciting and instigating; va.—རྒྱག.

ངན་སྐྱུགས་ (ŋɛngyuù) vomiting.

ངན་སྐྱོར་ (ŋɛngyɔr) helping/ assisting for evil purposes; va.—བྱེད་.

ངན་ཁག་དྲི་ (ŋənka drī) va. to blame sb.

ངན་ཁྲག (ŋɛndraà) the kind of blood according to Tibetan medicine that is considered bad (e.g., the blood associated with childbirth and menstruation and nose bleeds).

ངན་ཁྲིད་ (ŋəndrii) leading astray, taking sb. with you for some improper reason/ bad purpose; va.—བྱེད་.

ངན་ཁྲེབ་ (ŋɛndreb) 1. sb. who ignores the admonitions of people in authority, sb. who passively resists bosses; va.—བྱེད་ ། འགོ་ཁྲིད་ཀྱིས་སློབ་གསོ་ག་ཚོད་བརྒྱབ་ཀྱང་ཁོས་ངན་ཁྲེབ་བྱས་ནས་ལས་ཀར་འགྲོ་གི་མི་འདུག No matter how much the leader advises him, he ignores this and doesn’t go to work. 2. sly, cunning.

ངན་ཁྲེབ་སྐྱལ་རལ་ (ŋɛndreb gɛɛrɛɛ) sm. ངན་ཁྲེབ་.

ངན་གོམས་ (ŋɛngom) bad habit/ custom.

ངན་གྱུར་པ་ (ŋəngyurba) sm. ངན་པར་འགྱུར་བ་.

ངན་གྲ་སྔོན་བསྒྲིགས་ (ŋɛndra ŋöndrig) plotting, conniving.

ངན་གྲོགས་ (ŋəndraà) sm. ངན་རོགས་.

ངན་གྲོས་ (ŋɛndröö) 1. bad news. 2. bad reputation.

ངན་དགུ་ (ŋɛngu) all the evil/ bad things (there) are, every possible evil, extremely evil ། འཛམ་གླིང་ནང་ངན་དགའི་དཀྲུག་ཤིང་བྱེད་མཁན་ཆེས་གདུག་རྩུབ་ཅན་ཞིག་རེད་ (He) is the chief instigator of all the evil in the world.

ངན་དགུ་ཚང་བ་ (ŋɛngu tsāŋwa) thoroughly wicked, unmitigatedly evil ། བཙན་རྒྱལ་གྱི་ངན་དགུ་ཚང་བ་བྲན་གཡོག་ལམ་ལུགས་ The thoroughly evil slavery system of the imperialists.

ངན་དགུ་འཛོམས་པོ་ (ŋɛngu dzombo) sm. ངན་དགུ་ཚང་བ་.

ངན་དགུ་ལུས་ཚང་ (ŋɛngui lüüdzaŋ) sm. ངན་དགུ་ཚང་བ་.

ངན་འགྱུར་ (ŋɛngyur) sm. ངན་པར་འགྱུར་.

ངན་འགྱུར་པ་ (ŋɛngyurbə) a degenerate/ wicked/ evil person, a troublemaker.

ངན་འགྲོ་གསུམ་ (ŋɛndru sūm) the three bad rebirths (into hell or the yidag or animal realm).

ངན་རྒུ་ (ŋɛngu) sm. ངན་དགུ་.

ངན་རྒོལ་ (ŋɛngöö) opposing sb. in an evil manner; va.—བྱེད་.

ངན་རྒྱབ་ (ŋɛngyəb) supporting sth. bad/ evil, acting as an accomplice for sth. bad; va.—བྱེད་ to act as an accomplice ། ངན་རྒྱབ་བྱེད་མི་ An accomplice.

ངན་རྒྱབ་ངན་སྐྱོར་ (ŋɛngyəb ŋɛngyɔɔ) the wicked/ evil/ bad mutually backing and supporting each other; va.—བྱེད་.

ངན་རྒྱུས་ (ŋɛngyüü) giving sb. a bad idea,

introducing sb. to do sth. bad; va.—བྱེད་.

ངན་སྐུལ་ (ŋɛngɛɛ) abbr. of ངན་ཤིད་སྐུལ་རལ་.

ངན་སློག་ཕྲ་མ་ (ŋɛndrɔɔ trāma) causing trouble by talking behind people's backs.

ངན་ངོན་ (ŋənŋön) very poor, terrible, the worst conditions ། ཟས་གོས་ངན་ངོན་ལ་ཆོག་ཤེས་ཀྱིས་གནས་ཀྱི་ཡོད་པ་རེད་ (They) are content with the worst living conditions.

ངན་སྔགས་ (ŋɛnŋaà) casting an evil spell, putting a curse on sb.; va.—རྒྱག.

ངན་སྔགས་མཐུ་གཏད་ (ŋɛnŋaà tūdɛɛ) sm. ངན་སྔགས་.

ངན་འཆང་ (ŋɛnjaŋ) having evil/ wicked thoughts.

ངན་འཆར་ (ŋɛnjar) plot, scheme, conspiracy.

ངན་ཇུས་ (ŋɛnjüü) evil/ wicked conspiracy, machination, plot; va.—འདིངས་; —བྱེད་; —གཤོམ་ to conspire, to plot ། སྲིད་གཞུང་དེ་ཕྱིར་འབུད་བྱེད་རྒྱུའི་ངན་ཇུས་འདིངས་ཀྱི་ཡོད་པ་རེད་ They are plotting to overthrow the government.

ངན་ཇུས་མཉམ་འགོད་ (ŋɛnjüü ñəmgöö) jointly plotting a conspiracy; va.—བྱེད་ to plot/ engineer a conspiracy.

ངན་ཇུས་མཉམ་འགོད་བྱེད་མཁན་ (ŋɛnjüü ñamgöö cɛngɛn) conspirator, plotter.

ངན་སྙིགས་ (ŋɛnñig) dreg, sludge.

ངན་ཏགས་ (ŋɛndaà) bad omen, evil sign.

ངན་ལྟས་ (ŋɛndɛɛ) sm. ངན་ཏགས་.

ངན་གཏད་ (ŋɛndɛɛ) sm. ངན་སྔགས་མཐུ་གཏད་.

ངན་ཐབས་ (ŋɛndəb) dishonest/ wicked/ evil means or methods, deceitful or treacherous tactics ། མི་དེ་ཚོ་དགྲ་བོའི་ངན་ཐབས་ལ་མགོ་འཁོར་བ་རེད་ Those people were duped by the deceitful tactics of the enemy.

ངན་མཐའ་ (ŋɛnda) evil end.

ངན་མཐུ་ (ŋɛndu) the force/ power of evil.

ངན་མཐུན་ (ŋɛndün) evil association.

ངན་མཐུན་ལག་སྒྲིལ་ (ŋɛndün la̱ndee) collaborating to do evil; va.—བྱེད་.

ངན་མཐུན་གཡོ་འཕྲུལ་ (ŋɛndün yōndrüü) conspiring to deceive/ trick.

ངན་སྡུག (ŋənduù) 1. bad, mean. 2. sad, sorrowful.

ངན་དོག (ŋəndog) misfortune, disaster.

ངན་དོར་དགེ་སྤེལ་ (ŋɛndɔɔ ge̱bel) sm. ངན་དོར་ལེགས་སྤེལ་.

ངན་དོར་ལེགས་སྤེལ་ (ŋɛndɔɔ la̱gbel) weeding out evil/ bad/ corrupt practices and spreading good ones, forsaking evil and acting virtuously.

ངན་དྲེགས་ (ŋɛndreg) evil and proud/ conceited/ arrogant.

ངན་འདྲིས་ (ŋɛndrii) sm. ངན་གྲོགས་.

ངན་ནེ་ངོན་ནེ་ (ŋənne ŋönne) very poor, terrible (usu. for living conditions).

ངན་ནེ་བ་ (ŋənnewa) sm. ངན་ནེ་ངོན་ནེ་.

ངན་པ་ (ŋɛmba) 1. evil, bad ། ཁོ་ལ་བསམ་བློ་ངན་པ་ཞིག་འཁོར་བ་རེད་ He had an evil thought. 2. ugly, awful, terrible, bad ། བཟོ་ལྟ་ངན་པ་ An ugly shape ། དྲི་མ་ངན་པ་ An awful smell.

ངན་པ་བཀྲུས་ནས་མི་དག་པ་སོལ་བ་ལྟ་བུ་བཟོ་བ་ (ŋɛmba drüüne mi̱dagba sööwa dəbu so̱wa) spoiling sb. so badly that they can never correct their behavior [Lit. making sb. like charcoal that can never be washed clean].

ངན་པ་སྐུལ་སློང་ (ŋɛmba gūūloŋ) va. to incite, to instigate.

ངན་པ་ཁ་འགྲིལ་ (ŋɛmba kāndrii) collaborating, conspiring (to do evil); va.—བྱེད་.

ངན་པ་ཁ་སྒྲིག (ŋɛmba kādrii) sm. ངན་པ་ཁ་མཐེན.

ངན་པ་ཁ་སྒྲིལ་ (ŋɛmba kādrii) sm. collaborating, conspiring (to do evil), evil people uniting; va.—བྱེད་.

ངན་པ་ཁ་མཐུན་ (ŋɛmba kāndün) conspiring, plotting, collaborating (for evil); va.—བྱེད་ ། བཅོ་བཅོས་རིང་ལུགས་པ་དང་བཙན་རྒྱལ་རིང་ལུགས་པ་ཚོའི་ངན་པ་ཁ་མཐུན་འཛམ་གླིང་ཡོངས་ལ་ཐེར་འདོན་བྱས་པ་རེད་ The conspiracy of the revisionists and imperialists was exposed to the whole world. ། ཨ་རིས་ལི་ཁྲིན་ཧྲོན་ཕྱོགས་ཁག་དང་ངན་པ་ཁ་མཐུན་བྱས་པ་རེད་ The U.S. collaborated with the Syngman Rhee clique.

ངན་པ་ཁ་གཡོགས་ (ŋɛmba kāyɔɔ) placing the blame on others; va.—བྱེད་.

ངན་པ་ཁྱུ་སྒྲིག (ŋɛmba kyūdrig) ganging up to do evil; va.—བྱེད་.

ངན་པ་ཁྱུ་འདྲེས་ (ŋɛmba kyūndreè) sm. ངན་པ་ཁ་མཐུན་.

ངན་པ་ཁྲི་ཐོག ཁྱི་མགོ་སྡེར་ཐོག (ŋɛmba krīdɔɔ kyīngo de̱rdɔɔ) inappropriate behavior/ situation [Lit. a wicked person on the throne, the head of a dog on a plate].

ངན་པ་དགུ་འཛོམས་ (ŋɛmba gu̱dzom) the 6th and 7th days of the 11th month of the Tibetan calendar (highly inauspicious dates when bad luck abounds).

ངན་པ་རྒྱུས་ཡོད་ (ŋɛmba gyüüyöö) passing on information to a thief or evil person enabling him to commit a crime; va.—བྱེད་.

ངན་པ་ངན་ནག (ŋɛmba ŋɛnnaà) rotten to the core, totally corrupt/ bad.

ངན་པ་བརྒྱུད་བསྐུལ་ (ŋɛmba gyüügüü) sm. ངན་སྐུལ་.

ངན་པ་གཅིག་མཐུན་ (ŋɛmba jīgdün) evil accomplice, evil people collaborating, a gang of scoundrels.

ངན་པ་གཅིག་འདྲ་ (ŋɛmba jīgdra) alike/ same in evilness.

ངན་པ་ཆ་སྒྲིག (ŋɛmba cādrig) sm. ངན་པ་ཁ་མཐུན་.

ངན་པ་གཉའ་རངས་ (ŋɛmba ñāraŋ) sm. ངན་པ་གཉའ་རེངས་.

ངན་པ་གཉའ་རེངས་ (ŋɛmba ñāreŋ) extremely evil/ bad/ wicked, incorrigible, guilty of all kind of evils.

ངན་པ་མཉམ་གྲོགས་ (ŋɛmba ñəmdrog) sm. ངན་པ་གཅིག་མཐུན་.

ངན་པ་མཉམ་འདུ་ (ŋɛmba ñāmdu) sm. ཁྱི་སྤྱང་ངན་འགྲིལ་.

ངན་པ་མཉམ་རོགས་ (ŋɛmba ñəmrɔɔ) sm. ངན་པ་གཅིག་མཐུན་.

ངན་པ་བསྟོད་ན་མཉམ་ཕུང་ (ŋɛmba dööna ñāmbuŋ) praising a wicked person will bring harm to oneself.

ངན་པ་སྣ་དགུ་ (ŋɛmba nāgu) sm. ངན་པ་གཉའ་རེངས་.

ངན་པ་ཕྱོགས་སྒྲིག (ŋɛmba cɔ̄gdrii) evil/ bad people ganging up or allying with one another, bad people acting as accomplices for one another; va.—བྱེད་.

ངན་པ་ཕྱོགས་སྡེབ་ (ŋɛmba cɔ̄gdeb) sm. ངན་པ་ཕྱོགས་སྒྲིག.

ངན་པ་བྱས་རྒྱལ་ (ŋɛmba cɛ̀ɛgyɛɛ) profiting by one's evil ways.

ངན་པ་སྦུག་མཐུན་ (ŋɛmba bu̱gdün) sm. ངན་པ་ལག་འགྲིལ་.

ངན་པ་ལག་འགྲིལ་ (ŋɛmba la̱ndree) evil/ bad people ganging up or allying with one another, bad people acting as accomplices for one another; va.—གཏོང་.

ངན་པ་ལང་ཤོར་ (ŋɛmba lāŋshɔɔ) falling into evil ways or habits.

ངན་པའི་ཕྱོགས་ (ŋɛmbɛ cɔ̄ɔ) the dark/ seamy/ evil side.

ངན་པར་འགྱུར་ (ŋɛmbar gyu̱r) vi. to deteriorate, to worsen, to degenerate.

ངན་པར་ངོ་སྲུང་ (ŋɛmbar ŋosuŋ) flattering evil people; va.—བྱེད་.

ངན་པས་རང་བསྟོད་ ཁ་ཏས་སྒྲོ་བསྟོད་ (ŋɛmbɛ ra̱ndöö kādɛɛ dro̱döö) praising oneself [Lit. evil people praise themselves; crows praise their feathers].

ངན་པོ་ (ŋɛmbo) mean, evil.

ངན་སྤེལ་ (ŋɛmbel) spreading evil; va.—བྱེད་ to spread/ disseminate evil.

ངན་སྤྱོད་ (ŋɛnjöö) evil actions, malevolent/ immoral deeds; va.—བྱེད་.

ངན་སྤྱོད་ཅན་ (ŋɛnjööjɛn) wicked, evil, malevolent.
ངན་སྤྲང་ (ŋɛmdraŋ) beggar.
ངན་ཕྱིད་ (ŋɛnjiì) living in poor/ destitute conditions.
ངན་འཕྲིན་ (ŋɛndrin) a threatening message/ communication; va.—བྱེད་.
ངན་བུ་ (ŋɛmbu) I, we.
ངན་བྱས་ (ŋɛnjɛɛ̀) doing evil, bad acts/ deeds.
ངན་བྱས་ངོ་འཕྱེར་ (ŋɛnjɛɛ̀ ŋogyer) praising one's own evil deeds, doing evil deeds and boasting of it; va.—བྱེད་.
ངན་བྱས་ངོ་སོ་ (ŋɛnjɛɛ̀ ŋoso) sm. ངན་བྱས་ངོ་འཕྱེར་.
ངན་བྱས་སྣ་དགུ་ (ŋɛnjɛɛ̀ ŋəgu) a multiplicity of bad/ evil acts or misfortunes; va.—གཏོང་.
ངན་བྱུས་ (ŋɛnjüü) sm. ངན་ཇུས་.
ངན་དབང་ནང་གྲོས་ (ŋɛnwaŋ naŋdröö) evil people in power plotting/ conspiring; va.— བྱེད་.
ངན་འབྲས་ (ŋɛndrɛɛ̀) 1. bad karma, evil consequence, bad/ disasterous effect; vi.—འཁོར་ to get karmic retribution for one's misdeeds.
ངན་འབྲེལ་ (ŋɛndree) sm. ངན་པ་ཁ་མཐུན་.
ངན་སྦྲེལ་ (ŋɛndree) sm. ངན་པ་ཁ་མཐུན་.
ངན་མི་བྱེད་ (ŋɛn mijeè) v. to not harm sb.
ངན་སྨོས་ (ŋɛnmöö) bad or derogative comments.
ངན་སྨས་ (ŋɛnmɛɛ̀) 1. talking badly (of others), criticizing, reviling, defaming, slandering; va.—བྱེད་; —གཏོང་; —རྒྱག. 2. bad words/ language, cursing, swearing; va.—བྱེད་; —གཏོང་; —རྒྱག.
ངན་སྨས་ལོག་སྒྲུབ་ (ŋɛnmɛɛ̀ logdrub) shung. using bad or insulting language and doing evil or bad or harmful things.
ངན་རྫ་དོད་པོ་ (ŋɛndza töobo) sm. ངན་པོ་.
ངན་ཚོགས་ (ŋɛntsoò) a meeting for a bad/ evil purpose; va.—བྱེད་.
ངན་ཞེན་ (ŋɛnshen) desire/ liking/ motivation to do evil.
ངན་ཞོར་རྒྱུག་དུང་ (ŋɛnshɔɔ gyugduŋ) having sth. bad happen as a result of a casual association with sb. [Lit. incidentally associating with bad people, getting beaten with a stick].
ངན་གཡོ་ (ŋɛnyo) deceiving/ tricking for a bad reason; va.—བྱེད་.
ངན་གཡོ་ཅན་ (ŋɛnyojɛn) deceptive, deceitful, duplicitous, treacherous.
ངན་གཡོ་དུག་གསུམ་ (ŋɛnyo tugum) shung. the three: evil, deceitful, poisonous
ངན་གཡོ་དྲན་འཁྱུལ་ (ŋɛnyo trɛndrüü) sm. ངན་གཡོ་.
ངན་རུལ་ (ŋɛnrüü) malevolent, rotten, degenerate, decadent; vi.—ཆགས་; —དུ་འགྱུར་ to become corrupt/ decadent/ degenerate.
ངན་རེངས་ (ŋɛnreŋ) stubbornly evil/ bad, hardened (as in hardened criminal), morally corrupt, degenerate.
ངན་རེངས་འགྱུར་མེད་ (ŋɛnreŋ gyurmeè) incorrigibly bad.
ངན་རེངས་པ་ (ŋɛnreŋba) a stubborn/ diehard person.
ངན་རེངས་རྩེར་སོན་ (ŋɛnreŋ dzēr) the most evil/ wicked/ incorrigibly hardened height.
ངན་རོགས་ (ŋɛnrɔɔ̀) cohort, accomplice, puppet (in a bad activity); va.—བྱེད་ to cohort with, to be an accomplice ¶ ཨ་མེ་རི་ཀ་བཙན་རྒྱལ་རིང་ལུགས་དང་དེའི་ངན་རོགས་ཟ་ཏོའི་སྲིད་གཞུང་ The U.S. imperialists and their puppets, the Sato government. ¶ ཁོས་བུ་དེར་ངན་རོགས་བྱས་ནས་ཉིན་ལྟར་སྦག་ཁང་ལ་ཕྱིན་སོང་ He acted as an accomplice to the boy and went (with him) to the gambling house everyday.
ངན་རོགས་བསྡུ་རུབ་ (ŋɛnrɔɔ̀ durub) cohorts and accomplices gathering together; va.—བྱེད་.
ངན་ལ་སྐྱོང་པ་ (ŋɛnla kyoŋbo) shung. headstrong/ aggressive in evil activities.
ངན་ལང་ (ŋɛnlaŋ) spoiled (behaviorally), bad habits; va.—དུ་གཏོང་ to spoil, to indulge; vi.—ཤོར་ to get spoiled (behaviorally) ¶ འདི་འདྲ་བྱས་ན་ཕྲུ་རང་གི་ཕྲུ་གུ་འདི་ངན་ལང་དུ་གཏོང་གི་རེད་ If you do this you will spoil the child.
ངན་ལན་ (ŋɛnlɛn) repaying/ revenging evil deeds, making retribution; va.—བྱེད་.
ངན་ལན་ངན་ལན་ (ŋɛnlɛn ŋɛnjɛɛ) responding to sth. bad tit for tat.
ངན་ལན་བཟང་གིས་འཇལ་ (ŋɛnlɛn saŋgi jɛɛ) sm. ངན་ལན་བཟང་འཇལ་.
ངན་ལན་བཟང་འཇལ་ (ŋɛnlɛn saŋjɛɛ) repaying evil with good, returning injury/ ingratitude with kindness.
ངན་ལན་སློག (ŋɛnlɛn lɔɔ̀) va. to take revenge/ reprisals, to retaliate.
ངན་ལབ་ (ŋɛnləb) sm. ངན་བཤད་.
ངན་ལམ་ (ŋɛnlam) evil path/ way.
ངན་ལས་ (ŋɛnlɛɛ̀) hard/ dirty work.
ངན་ལོབ་ལང་ཤོར་ (ŋɛnlob laŋshɔɔ) having learned bad thing and become spoiled.
ངན་ཤགས་ (ŋɛnshaà) arguing using bad/ harsh language.
ངན་ཤི་ (ŋɛnshi) unpleasant/ painful death; vi.—ཐེབས་ to die (painfully/ unpleasantly).
ངན་ཤུགས་ (ŋɛnshuù) evil/ bad force; the strength or power of evil.
ངན་ཤུགས་ཧམ་ཁྱེར་ (ŋɛnshuù hāmkyer) sm. ངན་ཤེད་ཧམ་ཁྱེར་.
ངན་ཤུལ་ (ŋɛnshüü) remnants/ remains of sth. evil ¶ ཞྭན་གཡོག་ལམ་ལུགས་ཀྱི་ངན་ཤུལ་ད་དུང་ཡང་བསྡད་ཡོད་པ་རེད་ There are still remnants of the system of slavery.
ངན་ཤེད་ (ŋɛnsheè) mean/ evil and cruel.
ངན་ཤེད་སྐྱལ་རལ་ (ŋɛnsheè gɛɛrɛɛ) sm. ངན་ཤེད་སྐྱལ་རལ་ཚ་པོ་.
ངན་ཤེད་སྐྱལ་རལ་ཚ་པོ་ (ŋɛnsheè gɛɛrɛɛ tsābo) 1. a bad person who is insubordinate, a cruel and evil person who resists or is passively resistant to what is said from above; va.—བྱེད་.
ངན་ཤེད་ལྟག་འཁུར་ (ŋɛnsheè dāŋgur) shung. using someone else's power or authority in an arrogant manner.
ངན་ཤེད་ཆེན་པོ་ (ŋɛnsheè cēmbo) very cruel/ evil.
ངན་ཤེད་ཧམ་ཁྱེར་ (ŋɛnsheè hāmgyer) taking/ expropriating by force; va.—བྱེད་.
ངན་ཤོད་ (ŋɛnshöö) talking bad about people; va.—བྱེད་.
ངན་ཤོམ་ (ŋɛnshom) sm.* ངན་གཤོམ་.
ངན་གཤིས་གཅིག་མཐུན་ (ŋɛnshiì jīgdün) people with evil/ bad character are in agreement/ harmony.
ངན་གཤོམ་ (ŋɛnshom) preparing to do evil, bad/ evil intentions; va.—བྱེད་.
ངན་བཤད་ (ŋɛnshɛɛ̀) talking bad about people; va.—བྱེད་.
ངན་སུངས་ (ŋɛnsuŋ) spoiled, rotted, decayed.
ངན་སེམས་ (ŋɛnsem) evil thoughts, evil-mindedness, cruelty, meanness; va.—བྱེད་ to act cruel/ mean; va.—འཆང་ to bear a grudge, to hold or harbor mean/ evil thoughts or intentions.
ངན་སེམས་ཁོག་བཅངས་ (ŋɛnsem kōgjaŋ) bear or harboring evil/ bad/ cruel/ mean thoughts or intentions; va.—བྱེད་.
ངན་སེམས་མཁྲེགས་བཟུང་ (ŋɛnsem trēgsuŋ) refusing to give up evil intentions or thoughts, incorrigibly evil/ bad; va.—བྱེད་.
ངན་སེམས་འགྱུར་མེད་ (ŋɛnsem gyurmeè) sm. ངན་སེམས་མཁྲེགས་བཟུང་.
ངན་སེམས་རྒྱུན་བཅངས་ (ŋɛnsem gyünjaŋ) sm. ངན་སེམས་རྒྱུན་འཆང་.
ངན་སེམས་རྒྱུན་འཆང་ (ŋɛnsem gyünjaŋ) always having evil/ mean/ nasty thoughts; va.—བྱེད་.
ངན་སེམས་དགུ་ཚང་ (ŋɛnsem gudzaŋ) totally evil/ cruel.
ངན་སེམས་རིང་བཅངས་ (ŋɛnsem rīnjaŋ) holding bad/ evil thoughts for a long time.
ངན་སེལ་ (ŋɛnsel) 1. removing/ overcoming evil. 2. kusha grass.
ངན་སོང་ (ŋɛnsoŋ) 1. lower realms of existence; vi.—ལ་ལྷུང་ to get reborn into the lower realms of existence ¶ ཚེ་འདི་ལ་སེམས་པ་བཟང་པོ་བྱས་ན་ཚེ་ཕྱི་

མ་ངན་སོང་ལ་ལྟུང་གི་མ་རེད་ If you are kindhearted in this life, you will not get reborn into the lower realms in your next life.

ངན་སོང་ཀུན་འདྲེན་ (ŋɛnsoŋ gündren) name of a bodhisattva.

ངན་སོང་གསུམ་ (ŋɛnsoŋ sūm) creatures of the three lower realms (the realms of hell, yidag and animals).

ངན་སློང་ (ŋɛnloŋ) beggars.

ངན་སློད་ (ŋɛnlöö) 1. spoiled (behaviorally). 2. shamelss or base in character ༈ངན་སློད་མ་རབས་ཀྱི་ དྲི་མས་མ་གོས་ཤིང་ཡ་རབས་བཟང་སྤྱོད་ཀྱི་ངང་ཚུལ་ལྟར་ བཞིས་ (A person) not having the slightest hint of being base or shameless but instead being of good character.

ངན་སློབ་ (ŋɛnlob) instigating/ inciting to do evil; va.—རྒྱག.

ངན་སློབ་ཁོག་ཞུགས་ (ŋɛnlob kōgshuù) sm. ངན་སློབ་.

ངན་གསོ་ (ŋɛnso) recovering/ recuperating from sth. bad, overcoming decline/ degeneration; va.—བྱེད་.

ངན་བསླབས་ (ŋɛnlab) sm. ངན་སློབ་.

ངན་ཧྲུལ་ (ŋɛnhrüü) 1. destitute, poor ༈མི་ཚང་ངན་ ཧྲུལ་ A destitute household. 2. (with clothes) attired shabbily/ poorly. 3. sm. ངན་རེངས་.

ངན་ཧྲིང་ (ŋɛnhrüü) sm. ངན་རེངས་.

ངན་ཧྲིབ་སྐྱལ་རལ་ (ŋɛnhreb gɛɛrɛɛ) shung. sm. ངན་ ཤེད་སྐྱལ་རལ་.

ངན་ལྷུང་རུལ་འགྱུར་ (ŋɛnlhuŋ rüngyur) degenerate and corrupt.

ངམ་ (ŋam) 1. question particle for words ending in ང་ ༈ཁོས་ཡི་གེ་འདི་བཏང་ངམ་ Did he send the letter? 2. 'or' particle ༈གླང་ངམ་ལུག Oxen or sheep. 3. color. 4. ravine, canyon.

ངམ་རྒྱག (ŋam gyaà) vi. to get sick of a particular food (due to eating it all the time).

ངམ་གྲོག (ŋamdrog) ravine, canyon.

ངམ་ངམ་ཤུགས་ཤུགས་ (ŋamŋam shūgshug) understanding without being told directly, implied, insinuated ༈ཁྱེད་རང་གི་སྐད་ཆའི་ཐོག་ནས་ང་ ལ་རོགས་རམ་གནང་འདོད་མེད་པ་ངམ་ངམ་ཤུགས་ཤུགས་ ཀྱིས་ཧ་གོ་གི་འདུག I understand that you don't want to help me indirectly from what you said. 2. sm. ངམ་ཤུགས་.

ངམ་ནག (ŋamnag) angry look/ expression.

ངམ་གནག (ŋamnag) sm. ངམ་ནག.

ངམ་རིང་ (ŋəmriŋ) a district/ xian in Tsang.

ངམ་རུ་ (ŋəmru) a throat disease.

ངམ་རོང་ (ŋamroŋ) a narrow passage way, gorge.

ངམ་ལ་རྒྱག (ŋamla gyaà) sm. ངམ་རྒྱག.

ངམ་ཤུགས་(ཀྱིས་) (ŋəmshug) 1. naturally, automatically, involuntarily ༈ད་ལོ་སྟོན་ཐོག་ཡག་པོ་ བྱུང་ཙང་ངམ་ཤུགས་ཀྱིས་ཟ་ཆས་ཀྱི་རིན་ཐང་ཆག་པ་རེད་ Because there was a good crop this year, food prices have naturally gone down. 2. sm. ངམ་ངམ་ ཤུགས་ཤུགས་.

ངམ་ཤོད་ (ŋamshöö) 1. sm. སྙིང་འོག. 2. place in Lhoka, Central Tibet.

ངར་ (ŋar) 1. aggressive, volatile, vigorous (personality) ༈ཁོ་ངར་ཆེ་བའི་སྐྱོན་འདུག He has the fault of being too aggressive. 2. temper (of metals); va.—གཏོང་ to temper (metals) ༈གྲི་འདི་ལ་ ངར་མི་འདུག This knife has no temper. ༈གྲི་དང་ དེར་ངར་བཏང་བ་རེད་ (They) tempered the blade of this knife. 3. vi. to be fired up, to be excited/ stimulated ༈དམག་མོས་སླར་ཡང་རང་ཕྱོགས་ལ་རྒོལ་རྒོལ་ བྱས་པ་གོ་བས་དམག་མི་རྣམས་རབ་ཏུ་ངར་བ་རེད་ The soldiers were fired up because they heard that the enemy had attacked again. 4. intensity, strength, force ༈གྲང་ངར་དྲག་ཅང་ཆེ་བའི་ས་ཆ་ A place of very intense cold. 5. ང་ + dat.-loc. 7. front side/ part ༈ལག་ངར་ Forearm.

ངར་སྐད་ (ŋargɛɛ) a roar, an angry yell/ shout; va.—འདྲེན་; —སྒྲོག; —རྒྱག to roar/ yell/ shout angrily ༈བཙན་རྒྱལ་རིང་ལུགས་ལ་ངོ་རྒོལ་གྱི་ངར་སྐད་ འབྲུག་སྒྲ་ལྟར་བརྒྱབ་པ་རེད་ They yelled like thunder in opposition to imperialism.

ངར་སྐྱེད་ (ŋargyeè) sm. ངར་བསྐྱེད.

ངར་སྐྱོད་ (ŋārgyöö) marching/ advancing in a fired up state (usually to battle); va.—བྱེད་ to march, to advance.

ངར་བསྐྱེད་ (ŋargyeè) 1. vi. to be driven/ fired up/ stimulated/ stirred up, to exert oneself ༈སློབ་སྦྱོང་ ལ་ངར་བསྐྱེད་ནས་ཡིག་ཚད་ལོན་པ་བྱ་དགོས་ One should be driven regarding studying and try to pass the exam. 2. arrogant ༈མི་ངན་དེ་ངར་བསྐྱེད་ནས་གཞན་ལ་ གཤེ་གཤེ་གཏོང་གི་འདུག The evil person acts arrogantly scolding other people.

ངར་འགྲོས་ (ŋardröö) 1. walking fast in a fired up manner; va.—བྱེད་. 2. the gait/ walk of an angry person.

ངར་རྒྱུག (ŋargyuù) running fast in a fired up manner, running with a feeling of competitiveness; va.—བྱེད་.

ངར་སྒོང་ (ŋargoŋ) an abnormal (small) egg.

ངར་སྒྲ་ (ŋardra) sm. ངར་སྐད་.

ངར་ངར་ (ŋarŋar) sm. ངར་, 1 and 3.

ངར་ངར་འཁུན་སྒྲ་ (ŋarŋar kündra) sound of heavy breathing/ panting/ wheezing when angry.

ངར་ངར་གོད་གོད་ (ŋarŋar göögöö) sm. ངར་ངར་འཕྱེར་ འཕྱེར་.

ངར་ངར་པོ་ (ŋar ŋarbo) 1. sm. ངར་པོ་. 2. sm. ངར་ངར་ འཁུན་སྒྲ་.

ངར་ངར་ཕོད་ཕོད་ (ŋarŋar pɛ̄ɛ̀bɛɛ̀) sm. ངར་ངར་འཕྱེར་ འཕྱེར་.

ངར་ངར་འཕྱེར་འཕྱེར་ (ŋarŋar pērber) volatile, truculent, aggressive, overbearing, displaying ferocity and anger.

ངར་ངར་བད་བད་ (ŋarŋar pɛ̄ɛ̀bɛɛ̀) sm. ངར་ངར་འཕྱེར་ འཕྱེར་.

ངར་ངར་སྦད་སྦད་ (ŋarŋar bɛ̄ɛ̀bɛɛ̀) sm. ངར་ངར་འཕྱེར་ འཕྱེར་.

ངར་ངར་ཁྲིལ་ཁྲིལ་ (ŋarŋar dreedree) volatile/ trucluent/ fierce and in a rush.

ངར་ངར་ཤོར་ཤོར་ (ŋarŋar shɔ̄ɔ̄shɔɔ) sm. ངར་ངར་ འཕྱེར་འཕྱེར་.

ངར་ངར་སིག་སིག (ŋarŋar shīgsii) sm. ངར་ངར་འཕྱེར་ འཕྱེར་.

ངར་ཅན་ (ŋarjɛn) strong, powerful, vigorous.

ངར་ལྕགས་ (ŋarjaà) steel.

ངར་ལྕགས་ཀུང་སི་ (ŋarjaà gūŋsi steel company.

ངར་ལྕགས་ཀྱི་ཆུ་ (ŋarjaàgo cū) molten steel.

ངར་ལྕགས་མཁས་པ་ཅན་ (ŋarjaà kyɛ̄ɛ̀barjɛn) metallurgist.

ངར་ལྕགས་ཁྲོ་ཆ་ (ŋarjaà trōja) sm. ངར་ལྕགས་ཀྱི་ཆུ་.

ངར་ལྕགས་རྒྱུ་ཆ་ (ŋarja gyubja) raw materials for making steel.

ངར་ལྕགས་རྒྱུ་ཆས་ (ŋarjaà gyujɛɛ̀) sm. ངར་ལྕགས་རྒྱུ་ཆ་.

ངར་ལྕགས་ལྕགས་རྒྱུད་ (ŋarjaà jāàhreŋ) steel framework/ reinforcement.

ངར་ལྕགས་རྗེན་པ་ (ŋarjaà jemba) raw steel.

ངར་ལྕགས་མཉམ་འབྲེལ་ཁེ་ལས་ (ŋarjaà ñamdree kēlɛɛ̀) integrated steel plant/ works.

ངར་ལྕགས་དུམ་བུ་ (ŋarjaà dumbu) steel ingot/ bar.

ངར་ལྕགས་གནོན་བྱེད་འཕྲུལ་འཁོར་ (ŋarjaà nōnjeè trūūgɔɔ) sm. ངར་ལྕགས་བཙིར་གནོན་འཕྲུལ་འཁོར་.

ངར་ལྕགས་སྤུས་དག (ŋarjaà būūdag) high grade steel.

ངར་ལྕགས་མྱུར་དུ་འདོན་ཐབས་ (ŋarjaà ñurtu dōntəb) high-speed steel producing method.

ངར་ལྕགས་བཙིར་ཆས་ (ŋarjaà dzīrjɛɛ̀) steel roller.

ངར་ལྕགས་བཙིར་གནོན་ (ŋarjaà dzīrnön) rolling steel; va.—བྱེད་ to roll steel.

ངར་ལྕགས་བཙིར་གནོན་འཕྲུལ་འཁོར་ (ŋarjaà dzīrnön trūūgɔɔ) steel rolling machine.

ངར་ལྕགས་བཙོ་སྦྱོང་ (ŋarjaà dzōjaŋ) steel smelting.

ངར་ལྕགས་ཞུ་ཐབ་ (ŋarjaà shudəb) steel-smelting furnace.

ངར་ལྕགས་བཞུ་ཐབ་ (ŋarjaà shudəb) sm. ངར་ལྕགས་ཞུ་ ཐབ་.

ངར་ལྕགས་བཞུ་བའི་བཟོ་གྲྭ་ (ŋarjaà shuwɛ sodra) steel

factory/ plant.

ངར་ལྕགས་བཟོ་གྲྭ (ŋarjaà sodra) sm. ངར་ལྕགས་བཟོ་བའི་བཟོ་གྲྭ.

ངར་ལྕགས་བཟོ་ལས (ŋarjaà solɛɛ̀) steel worker.

ངར་ལྕགས་ལུགས་མ (ŋarjaà luŋma) cast steel.

ངར་གཅོམ (ŋar jɔ̀ɔ) 1. va. to dull/ blunt knives, swords, etc. 2. va. to pacify aggression. 3. va. to break (a person's) pride/ arrogance. 4. to anneal a metal.

ངར་ཆ (ŋarja) 1. sharpness (for knives, etc.). 2. sharpness (with regard to intellect/ mind).

ངར་ཆེ་ཆེ་ཞེ་སྡང་སྡང (ŋar cēce she daŋdaŋ) aggressively, angrily.

ངར་ཆེན་འཕེལ (ŋarjen pēl) vi. to be extremely motivated/ stimulated.

ངར་མཆོང (ŋarjoŋ) suddenly swooping down on; va.—རྒྱག.

ངར་གདོང (ŋardoŋ) see ངར.

ངར་བདགས (ŋardaà) unroasted flour.

ངར་གདོང (ŋərdoŋ) shinbone.

ངར་གདོང་ཁྲག་སྐྱེས (ŋardoŋ trāggyeè) sm. ངར་ཤུགས.

ངར་ལྡན (ŋardɛn) sm. ངར་ཅན.

ངར་ལྡུད (ŋar düü) 1. va. to temper steel. 2. va. to stimulate a person's motivation/ enthusiasm/ energy (e.g., to learn, fight).

ངར་སྣབས (ŋarnəb) nose mucus.

ངར་པ (ŋarba) sm. ངར་གདོང.

ངར་པོ (ŋarbo) 1. aggressive, vigorous, volatile ¶ ཁྱི་འདི་ངར་པོ་འདུག This dog is very aggressive. 2. fired up, stirred up. 3. well-tempered (of metals). 4. good memory (when used with སེམས).

ངར་བ (ŋarwa) strength, vigor.

ངར་སླུད (ŋarlüü) sm. ངར་གདོང.

ངར་མ (ŋarma) 1. sm. ངར་པོ. 2. unrestrainable, uncontrollable (e.g., a horse).

ངར་མེད (ŋarmeè) weak.

ངར་འཛིན (ŋandzin) holding on to the ego, ego fixation.

ངར་ཤགས (ŋashaà) roaring in anger (usu. for wild animals).

ངར་ལང (ŋalaŋ) vi. to get fired up/ stirred up/ excited.

ངར་ཤ (ŋarsha) vigor, vitality; va.—སློང to stimulate to achieve/ accomplish, to motivate, to fire or stir up; vi.—ལངས to get stimulated to achieve/ accomplish, to get motivated, to get fired or stirred up.

ངར་ཤ་ཆེན་པོ (ŋarsha cēmbo) sm. ངར་ཤ་དོད་པོ.

ངར་ཤ་དོད་པོ (ŋarsha tö̀öbo) energetic, vigorous, vital; easily fired up.

ངར་ཤག་ཤག་ཕུ་ཤོར་ཤོར (ŋər shāàshaà pū shɔ̄ɔshɔɔ) aggressively, angrily.

ངར་ཤུགས (ŋərshug) vigorous, strong, energetic, enthusiastic, zealous, motivated; vi.—སྐྱེས to get worked up/ stimulated/ excited/ inspired; vi.—ཆག to be deflated, to lose vigor/ enthusiasm/ zeal; va.—སློང to encourage, to stimulate, to fire up/ rouse, to invigorate ¶ གསར་བརྗེའི་ངར་ཤུགས་ཆེན་པོ་དང་བཅས With great revolutionary vigor.

ངར་ཤུགས་གཅིག་སྒྲིམ (ŋərshug jīgdrim) going all out, giving it one's complete effort; va.—བྱེད to go all out ¶ མི་ལི་སྟོང་ཕྲག་མང་པོའི་ས་ཆ་ཞིང་ཁ་བཟོ་བར་ངར་ཤུགས་གཅིག་སྒྲིམ་བྱས་པ་རེད They went all out to make many thousands of miles of land into agricultural fields.

ངར་སེམས (ŋarsem) sm. ངར་ཤུགས.

ངར་སློང (ŋarloŋ) encouraging, stimulating, firing up. invigorating; va.—བྱེད.

ངར་སློང་མཁན (ŋarloŋgɛn) sb. who motivates/ cheers on/ stimulates/ encourages.

ངར་སློང་རུ་ཁག (ŋarloŋ rugaà) cheering squad, rooters.

ངར་སློབ (ŋarlob) sm. ངར་སློང.

ངར་གསོད (ŋar sȫö) sm. ངར་གཅོམ.

ངལ (ŋɛɛ) 1. difficulty, hardship ¶ ངལ་གྲོན་ལ་མ་འཛེམས་པར Not shying away from hardships and expenses. 2. vi. to be tired/ exhausted ¶ ཚང་མ་ཉིན་གང་གོམ་པ་བརྒྱབ་ཙང་དཀའ་ངལ་གྱིས་ཉལ་བཞག Everyone is in bed exhausted from walking all day.

ངལ་སྐྱེན་པོ (ŋɛə gyēnbo) easy to tire.

ངལ་གྲོན (ŋɛɛdrön) hardships/ difficulties and expenses ¶ ངལ་གྲོན་ཆུང Small expenses and hardships.

ངལ་ཆད (ŋɛɛ cɛɛ̀) vi. to be tired/ weary.

ངལ་རྗེས (ŋɛɛjeè) the result of one's hard work.

ངལ་ལྟོགས (ŋɛɛdog) hardship and hunger ¶ ངལ་ལྟོགས་ཀྱིས་ཤི་གྲབས་ཡོད་པ་རེད (They) were about to die from hardship and hunger.

ངལ་སྟོང (ŋɛɛdoŋ) fruitless effort, labor in vain; vi.—དུ་འགྱུར to become a fruitless effort.

ངལ་བསྟུན་གླ་སྤྲོད (ŋɛɛdün lādröö) payment in accordance with work.

ངལ་དུ་འཇུག (ŋɛɛtu jug) va. to make tired/ weary.

ངལ་དུབ (ŋɛɛdub) fatigue, tiredness, exhaustion; va.—སེལ to overcome tiredness.

ངལ་དུབ་ཆེ (ŋɛɛdubje) fatigued, tired, weary, exhausted.

ངལ་བརྡབས (ŋɛɛdəb) causing hardship and oppression.

ངལ་ནུས (ŋɛɛnüü) abbr. of ངལ་རྩོལ་ནུས་ཤུགས.

ངལ་ནུས་འཚོང (ŋɛɛnüü tsōŋ) va. to sell one's labor, to hire out for manual labor.

ངལ་སྣང (ŋɛɛnaŋ) the appearance of being tired.

ངལ་སྤངས་བརྩོན་པ (ŋɛɛbaŋ dzōmba) diligent and industrious/ energetic/ untiring.

ངལ་བ (ŋɛɛwa) 1. hardship, difficulty ¶ ཚང་མ་ཉིན་གང་གོམ་པ་བརྒྱབ་པའི་ངལ་བས་སླེབས་པ་དང་ཉལ་སོང Because of the hardship of walking all day they went to sleep as soon as they arrived. 2. weariness, fatigue; va.—འཇུག to make tired/ weary.

ངལ་བ་ཁྱད་དུ་གསོད (ŋɛɛwa kyɛ̄ɛtu sȫö) va. to ignore hardships/ difficulties ¶ ཁོང་གིས་ངལ་བ་ཁྱད་དུ་བསད་ནས་དམག་ས་རང་ལ་ཕེབས་པ་རེད Ignoring hardships, he went to (give) medical treatment at the battlefield.

ངལ་བ་ཁྱད་བསད (ŋɛɛwa kyɛ̄ɛtu sɛɛ̀) p. of ངལ་བ་ཁྱད་དུ་གསོད.

ངལ་བ་སྟོང་ཟད (ŋɛɛwa dōŋsɛɛ̀) fruitless labor/ effort; vi.—(དུ་) འགྱུར; —འགྲོ to go down the drain, to labor/ work in vain.

ངལ་བ་སྤངས (ŋɛɛwa pāŋ) va. to renounce concern with hardships/ difficulties/ fatigue ¶ ཁོ་ཚོས་ངལ་བ་སྤངས་ནས་ཡར་རྒྱས་འགྲོ་རྒྱུའི་ས་གནས་ཚོར་ལས་ཀར་ཕྱིན་པ་རེད Renouncing concern with hardships, they went to work in the underdeveloped areas (areas to be developed).

ངལ་བ་འབྲས་མེད (ŋɛɛwa drɛɛ̀meè) working but getting no fruits/ benefits/ results/ accomplishments (from one's labor).

ངལ་བ་མེད་པ (ŋɛɛwa meèba) inexhaustible, indefatigable, untireable.

ངལ་བ་ཚད་མེད (ŋɛɛwa tsɛɛ̀meè) endless hardship/ difficulty; va.—མྱོང to undergo endless hardship or difficulty.

ངལ་བ་བཟོད (ŋɛɛwa sȫö) va. to bear/ endure difficulty or hardship.

ངལ་བས་དུབ (ŋɛɛwɛ tub) vi. to be tired, to be exhausted.

ངལ་བའི་རྒྱུ (ŋɛɛwɛgyu) only hardship/ difficulties with no gain ¶ ལས་ཀ་དེ་བྱས་ན་རང་ཉིད་ངལ་བའི་རྒྱུ་ཡིན If one does that work, then it will be only hardships without any gains.

ངལ་འབུངས (ŋɛmbuŋ) persevering, being industriousness.

ངལ་མེད (ŋɛɛmeè) abbr. of ངལ་བ་མེད་པ.

ངལ་མེད་འབྲས་ཐོབ (ŋɛɛmeè drɛɛ̀dob) vi. to reap without sowing, to benefit without hard work/ difficulties.

ངལ་མེད་འབྲས་མེད་ (ŋɛɛmeè drɛɛ̀meè) without hard work/ toiling/ difficulty there can be no accomplishment or success or profit.

ངལ་མེད་འབྲས་ལེན་ (ŋɛɛmeè drɛɛ̀len) sm. ངལ་མེད་འབྲས་ཐོབ་.

ངལ་རྩོལ་ (ŋɛɛdzöö) work, labor, toil; va.—བྱེད་ to work, to labor, to toil.

ངལ་རྩོལ་མཁས་པ་ (ŋɛɛdzöö kɛ̄ɛ̀ba) skilled laborer.

ངལ་རྩོལ་སྐོར་གྱི་བཅའ་ཁྲིམས་ (ŋɛɛdzöögɔrgi jə̄drim) labor law.

ངལ་རྩོལ་གྱི་ཁེ་དབང་ (ŋɛɛdzöögi kēwaŋ) right of work.

ངལ་རྩོལ་གྱི་འགྲན་བསྡུར་ (ŋɛɛdzöögi drɛndur) labor emulation drive.

ངལ་རྩོལ་གྱི་ཉི་མ་ (ŋɛɛdzöögi ñimə) workday, working day.

ངལ་རྩོལ་གྱི་ཉིན་གྲངས་ (ŋɛɛdzöögi ñindraŋ) sm. ངལ་རྩོལ་གྱི་ཉི་མ་.

ངལ་རྩོལ་གྱི་ཐོབ་ཆ་ (ŋɛɛdzöögi tōbja) payment/ remuneration for labor.

ངལ་རྩོལ་གྱི་མཐུན་རྐྱེན་ (ŋɛɛdzöögi tǖngyen) working conditions.

ངལ་རྩོལ་གྱི་ནུས་པ་ (ŋɛɛdzöögi nüǜba) ability/ capacity to work.

ངལ་རྩོལ་གྱི་ནུས་ཤུགས་ (ŋɛɛdzöögi nüǜshug) labor force, manpower.

ངལ་རྩོལ་གྱི་རྣམ་འགྱུར་འཛིན་སྟངས་ (ŋɛɛdzöögi nə̄mgyur dzindaŋ) labor attitude.

ངལ་རྩོལ་གྱི་ཚོང་ར་ (ŋɛɛdzöögi tsōŋra) labor market.

ངལ་རྩོལ་གྱི་འཚོ་སྲུང་ (ŋɛɛdzöögi tsōsuŋ) protection of labor.

ངལ་རྩོལ་གྱི་རིན་ཐང་ (ŋɛɛdzöögi rindaŋ) labor value.

ངལ་རྩོལ་གྱི་ལག་རྩལ་ (ŋɛɛdzöögi lagdzɛɛ) labor skills.

ངལ་རྩོལ་གྱི་ལས་བགོ་ (ŋɛɛdzöögi lɛɛ̀go) division of labor.

ངལ་རྩོལ་གྱི་གླ་པ་ (ŋɛɛdzöögi lāba) hired labor.

ངལ་རྩོལ་རྒྱལ་སྲུང་གི་ལུས་སྦྱོང་ལམ་ལུགས་ (ŋɛɛdzöö gyɛɛsuŋgi lüǜjoŋ ləmluù) labor-defense training system.

ངལ་རྩོལ་གླ་ཐོབ་ (ŋɛɛdzöö lādob) payment for work.

ངལ་རྩོལ་འགྲན་སྡུར་ (ŋɛɛdzöö drɛndur) competition at work, labor campaign.

ངལ་རྩོལ་སྒྲིག་ཁྲིམས་ (ŋɛɛdzöö drigdrim) labor discipline.

ངལ་རྩོལ་སྒྲིམ་ཚད་ (ŋɛɛdzöö drimdzɛɛ̀) intensity of labor.

ངལ་རྩོལ་བསྒྱུར་བཀོད་ (ŋɛɛdzöö gyurgöò) reform through labor (a type of incarceration in the PRC).

ངལ་རྩོལ་ངེས་ཚད་ (ŋɛɛdzöö ŋeèdzɛɛ̀) sm. ངལ་རྩོལ་བཅད་གྲངས་.

ངལ་རྩོལ་བཅད་གྲངས་ (ŋɛɛdzöö jɛ̄ɛ̄draŋ) work quota, work norm.

ངལ་རྩོལ་བཙོས་བསྒྱུར་ (ŋɛɛdzöö jöögyur) 1. reform through labor (a type of incarceration in the PRC). 2. reforming labor.

ངལ་རྩོལ་འཛོན་པོ་ (ŋɛɛdzöö jombo) sm. ངལ་རྩོལ་མཁས་པ་.

ངལ་རྩོལ་ཉིན་གྲངས་ (ŋɛɛdzöö ñindraŋ) work days, a working day.

ངལ་རྩོལ་ཉེན་སྲུང་ (ŋɛɛdzöö ñensuŋ) labor insurance.

ངལ་རྩོལ་ཉེན་འགོག (ŋɛɛdzöö ñengɔɔ̀) sm. ངལ་རྩོལ་ཉེན་སྲུང་.

ངལ་རྩོལ་ཏང་ (ŋɛɛdzöö dāŋ) Labor Party.

ངལ་རྩོལ་ལྟ་ཚུལ་ (ŋɛɛdzöö də̄dzüü) labor viewpoint.

ངལ་རྩོལ་ཐོན་སྐྱེད་ཀྱི་ནུས་ཚད་ (ŋɛɛdzöö tȫngyeègi nüǜdzɛɛ̀) sm. ངལ་རྩོལ་ཐོན་སྐྱེད་ལས་ཚད་.

ངལ་རྩོལ་ཐོན་སྐྱེད་ནུས་ཤུགས་ (ŋɛɛdzöö tȫngyeè nüǜshug) labor production capacity.

ངལ་རྩོལ་ཐོན་སྐྱེད་ལས་ཚད་ (ŋɛɛdzöö tȫngyeè lɛɛ̀cöò) productivity of labor, labor output.

ངལ་རྩོལ་ཐོན་སྐྱེད་ལས་ཕྱོད་ (ŋɛɛdzöö tȫngyeè lɛɛ̀cöò) sm. ངལ་རྩོལ་ཐོན་སྐྱེད་ལས་ཚད་.

ངལ་རྩོལ་དུས་ཆེན་ (ŋɛɛdzöö tüǜjen) sm. ངལ་རྩོལ་དུས་ཚིགས་.

ངལ་རྩོལ་དུས་ཚིགས་ (ŋɛɛdzöö tüǜdzig) labor holiday (May 1).

ངལ་རྩོལ་བདེ་སྲུང་ (ŋɛɛdzöö desuŋ) protection of labor.

ངལ་རྩོལ་ནུས་ཤུགས་ (ŋɛɛdzöö nüǜshug) 1. labor force. 2. capacity for physical labor. 3. able-bodied person/ worker.

ངལ་རྩོལ་ནུས་ཤུགས་ཕྱེད་ཙམ་ (ŋɛɛdzöö nüǜshug cēèdzam) people who can fulfill only half the quota of work.

ངལ་རྩོལ་པ་ (ŋɛɛdzööba) worker, manual laborer.

ངལ་རྩོལ་པ་དཀྱུས་མ་ (ŋɛɛdzööba gyǖǜmə) common laborer.

ངལ་རྩོལ་པ་གོ་ཐང་ (ŋɛɛdzööba kodaŋ) able-bodied laborer.

ངལ་རྩོལ་པུའུ་ (ŋɛɛdzöö bū) tib.ch. Ministry of Labor.

ངལ་རྩོལ་དཔའ་བོ་ (ŋɛɛdzöö bāwo) labor hero.

ངལ་རྩོལ་དཔེ་ལྡན་ (ŋɛɛdzöö bēdɛn) sm. ངལ་རྩོལ་དཔེ་བཟང་.

ངལ་རྩོལ་དཔེ་བཟང་ (ŋɛɛdzöö bēsaŋ) exemplary/ model worker, heroic laborer.

ངལ་རྩོལ་དཔེ་ལེགས་ (ŋɛɛdzöö bēleg) sm. ངལ་རྩོལ་དཔེ་བཟང་.

ངལ་རྩོལ་བ་ (ŋɛɛdzööwa) sm. ངལ་རྩོལ་པ་.

ངལ་རྩོལ་བྱ་ཡུལ་ (ŋɛɛdzöö cəyüü) labor target.

ངལ་རྩོལ་བྱང་ཆུབ་ (ŋɛɛdzöö caŋcub) experienced/ skilled laborer.

ངལ་རྩོལ་བྱང་མ་ (ŋɛɛdzöö caŋma) ངལ་རྩོལ་བྱང་ཆུབ་.

ངལ་རྩོལ་བྱས་པའི་འབྲས་བུ་ (ŋɛɛdzöö cɛɛ̀bɛ drɛɛ̀bu) the fruit of one's labor.

ངལ་རྩོལ་བྱེད་དབང་ (ŋɛɛdzöö ceèwaŋ) sm. ངལ་རྩོལ་གྱི་ཁེ་དབང་.

ངལ་རྩོལ་སྦྱང་སོན་ (ŋɛɛdzöö jaŋsön) sm. ངལ་རྩོལ་བྱང་ཆུབ་.

ངལ་རྩོལ་སྦྱོང་བརྡར་ (ŋɛɛdzöö joŋdar) practice through labor.

ངལ་རྩོལ་མི་དོན་ཅུའུ་ (ŋɛɛdzöö midün jū) bureau of labor and personnel.

ངལ་རྩོལ་མི་དམངས་ (ŋɛɛdzöö mimaŋ) laboring/ working masses or people.

ངལ་རྩོལ་ཚོགས་པ་ (ŋɛɛdzöö tsōgba) Labor Party (in England).

ངལ་རྩོལ་ཞབས་ཕྱི་ཀུང་ཟི་ (ŋɛɛdzöö shəbji gūŋsi) employment service company.

ངལ་རྩོལ་ཡོ་བྱད་ (ŋɛɛdzöö yobjɛɛ̀) working tools, implements needed for work.

ངལ་རྩོལ་རས་ (ŋɛɛdzöö rɛɛ̀) jean material.

ངལ་རྩོལ་རུ་ཁག (ŋɛɛdzöö rugaà) labor brigade.

ངལ་རྩོལ་ལས་གཙུན་ (ŋɛɛdzöö lɛɛ̀jün) labor discipline.

ངལ་རྩོལ་ལས་ཕྱོད་ (ŋɛɛdzöö lɛɛ̀jöò) sm. ངལ་རྩོལ་ལས་ཚད་.

ངལ་རྩོལ་ལས་ཚད་ (ŋɛɛdzöö lɛɛ̀jöò) labor efficiency/ output/ capacity.

ངལ་རྩོལ་ལས་ཞུགས་ (ŋɛɛdzöö lɛɛ̀shug) labor employment.

ངལ་རྩོལ་ཤེད་ཤུགས་ (ŋɛɛdzöö shɛ̄ɛ̀shuù) sm. ངལ་རྩོལ་ནུས་ཤུགས་.

ངལ་རྩོལ་ཤེས་ཡོན་ཅན་ (ŋɛɛdzöö shēèyönjɛn) labor intellectual.

ངལ་རྩོལ་སེམས་ཤུགས་ (ŋɛɛdzöö sēmshuù) the will/ enthusiasm/ motivation for hard work, working with enthusiasm.

ངལ་རྩོལ་སློབ་སྐྱོང་ (ŋɛɛdzöö lōbgyoŋ) sm. ངལ་རྩོལ་སློབ་གསོ་.

ངལ་རྩོལ་སློབ་གཙུན་ (ŋɛɛdzöö lōbjün) reeducation (of juvenile delinquents, etc.) through labor.

ངལ་རྩོལ་སློབ་གསོ་ (ŋɛɛdzöö lōbso) labor education.

ངལ་རྩོལ་ལྷག་མ་ (ŋɛɛdzöö lhāgba) surplus work (work producing profit for the employer), surplus labor.

ངལ་བརྩོན་ (ŋɛɛdzön) industrious, diligent (with regard to work), hardworking.

ངལ་བརྩོན་ཆེན་པོ་ (ŋɛɛdzön cēmbo) very industrious/ diligent workers.

ངལ་ཚོགས་ (ŋɛɛtsɔ̀ɔ̀) sm. ངལ་བ་.

ངལ་འཚོ་ (ŋɛntso) abbr. of ངལ་གསོ་འཚོ་གནས་.

ངལ་བཟོད་ (ŋɛɛsöö) tolerating, enduring (hardship).

ངལ་ལས་ (ŋɛɛlɛɛ̀) labor.

ངལ་ལས་ཀྱི་གླ་ཆ་ (ŋɛɛlɛɛ̀gi lāja) labor cost, labor wages.

ངལ་ལས་མཉམ་ལས་ (ŋɛɛlɛɛ̀ ñamlɛɛ̀) labor cooperation/ sharing.

ངལ་ལས་པ་ (ŋɛɛlɛɛ̀ba) laborer (usu. manual).

ངལ་ལས་ཚོང་ར་ (ŋɛɛlɛɛ̀ tsōŋra) labor market (where jobs are arranged).

ངལ་ལས་གླ་ཆ་ (ŋɛɛlɛɛ̀ lāja) wage for labor.

ངལ་ལས་ཞབས་འདེགས་ (ŋɛɛlɛɛ̀ shəmdeg) service industry. 2. service work.

ངལ་ལས་ཞབས་འདེགས་ཚོང་ར་ (ŋɛɛlɛɛ̀ shəmdeg tsōŋra) sm. ངལ་ལས་ཚོང་ར་.

ངལ་ལས་ཞབས་འདེགས་གླ་ཆ་ (ŋɛɛlɛɛ̀ shəmdeg lāja) sm. ངལ་ལས་གླ་ཆ་.

ངལ་ལས་ཞབས་ཞུའི་རང་བཞིན་ལྡན་པའི་ཐོན་ལས་ (ŋɛɛlɛɛ̀ shəbshü rəŋshin dəmbɛ tōnlɛɛ̀) service production, service work, service industry.

ངལ་གསོ་ (ŋɛɛso) rest, resting; va.—རྒྱག་; —བྱེད་ to rest; vi.—ཐེབས་ to get rested ། ཆུ་ཚོད་གཉིས་ཙམ་ངལ་གསོ་བརྒྱབ་པ་ཡིན་ (I) rested about two hours. 2. day off, work break ། དེ་རིང་ངལ་གསོ་ཡིན་པས་ Is today your day off? ། ངས་ངལ་གསོའི་བར་ལ་ཟ་འཐུང་བྱེད་པར་ཕྱིན་པ་ཡིན་ I went to eat and drink during the break.

ངལ་གསོ་སྐྱོན་ (ŋɛɛso gyön) h. of ངལ་གསོ་རྒྱག.

ངལ་གསོ་ཁང་ (ŋɛɛsogaŋ) rest home.

ངལ་གསོ་རྒྱག (ŋɛɛso gyaà) va. to rest.

ངལ་གསོ་ཐེབས་ (ŋɛɛso tēb) vi. to get rested.

ངལ་གསོ་འཚོ་གནས་ (ŋɛɛso tsōnɛɛ̀) taking it easy, taking a rest, survivig peacefully.

ངལ་གསོ་འཚོ་གནས་ཀྱི་སྲིད་ཇུས་ (ŋɛɛso tsōnɛɛ̀gi sīijüù) the policy of taking it easy that was propounded by Hu Yaobang.

ངལ་གསོ་རེས་མོས་ (ŋɛɛso remöö) resting alternately/ in turn, being off alternately/ in turn.

ངལ་གསོའི་ཁེ་དབང་ (ŋɛɛso kēwaŋ) right to have rest/ time off.

ངལ་གསོ་དགོངས་འགྲོལ་ (ŋɛɛsö goŋdröö) leave of absence, furlough.

ངལ་གསོའི་རྒྱག་ཐང་ (ŋɛɛsö gyaàdaŋ) rest site, rest area.

ངལ་གསོའི་ཉི་མ་ (ŋɛɛsöö ñimə) day off from work, e.g., Sunday in the U.S.

ངལ་གསོའི་ཉིན་མོ་ (ŋɛɛsöö ñinmə) sm. ངལ་གསོའི་ཉི་མ་.

ངལ་གསོའི་དངོས་རྫས་ (ŋɛɛsö ŋöödzɛɛ̀) comfort articles, things used for rest/ leisure.

ངལ་གསོས་ (ŋɛɛsö) 1. p. of ངལ་གསོ་. 2. in compounds, sm. ངལ་གསོ་.

ངལ་གསོར་གནས་པ་ (ŋɛɛsɔr nɛɛ̀ba) sitting cross-legged with both hands on the knees.

ངལ་བསོ་ (ŋɛɛso) 1. f. ངལ་གསོ་. 2. in compounds, sm. ངལ་གསོ་.

ངལ་བསོ་བ་ (ŋɛɛsowa) a break in a phrase or sentence (e.g., a comma).

ངས་ (ŋɛɛ̀) 1. sm. ང་ཡིས་ (ང་ + inst.) ། ངས་བཤད་པ་ཡིན་ I said it. 2. interrogative particle for verbs ending in ང ། ཁོ་འདིར་སླེབས་བྱུང་ངས་ Did he come here?

ངས་ཁྱོད་ལས་རྩམ་པ་ཟོས་པ་མང་ཞིང་ཟ་ཡུན་ཀྱང་རིང་ (ŋɛɛ̀ kyöölɛ dzāmba sööba maŋshiŋ sayüngyaŋ riŋ) I have more experience than you [Lit. I ate more tsamba than you and for a longer time].

ངས་བྱས་ན་ (ŋɛɛ̀ cɛɛ̀na) I think, in my opinion, in my viewpoint ། ངས་བྱས་ན་ཁོང་ཕེབས་འདོད་གནང་གི་རེད་ I think he would like to come.

ངས་བལྟས་ན་ (ŋɛɛ̀ dɛ̄ɛna) sm. ངས་བྱས་ན་.

ངུ་: p. ངུས་; f. ངུ་; imp. ངུས་ (ŋu) vi. to cry, to weep ། ཕྲུ་གུ་འདི་ངུ་སྐབས་ When the child is crying.

ངུ་སྐད་ (ŋugɛɛ̀) sobbing/ weeping/ lamenting while talking; va.—འདོན་; —རྒྱག་; vi.—ཤོར་; vi.—འགག to be choked with sobs.

ངུ་སྐད་ཤུབ་ཤུབ་ (ŋugɛɛ̀ shūbshub) sobbing.

ངུ་སྐྱིགས་ཤུབ་ཤུབ་ (ŋugyiì shūbshub) sm. ངུ་སྐད་ཤུབ་ཤུབ་.

ངུ་རྒྱངས་བྱེད་ (ŋugyaŋ cee) sm. ངུ་ཤར་རྒྱག.

ངུ་རྒྱུ་གོད་པོ་ (ŋugyu gööbo) a crybaby, one who is inclined to or in the habit of crying a lot ། ཕྲུ་གུ་འདི་ངུ་རྒྱུ་གོད་པོ་འདུག This child is a crybaby.

ངུ་རྒྱུར་དགའ་པོ་ (ŋugyu gabo) sm. ངུ་རྒྱུ་གོད་པོ་.

ངུ་བརྒྱལ་ (ŋu gyɛɛ) vi. to cry, to weep.

ངུ་སྒྲ་ (ŋudra) sm. ངུ་སྐད་.

ངུ་དགོད་ (ŋugöö) crying and laughing at the same time; va.—བྱེད་.

ངུ་ངག (ŋuŋaà) sm. ངུ་སྐད་.

ངུ་སྔངས་ (ŋuŋaŋ) crying/ wailing from fear or anger; va.—བྱེད་.

ངུ་དངགས་ (ŋuŋag) sm. ངུ་ངག.

ངུ་ཅོ་ (ŋujo) sm. ངུ་ཅོར་.

ངུ་ཅོ་དིག་དིག (ŋujo dēgdeg) sm. ངུ་ཅོར་.

ངུ་ཅོ་ཐིང་ཐིང་ (ŋujo tiŋdiŋ) sm. ངུ་ཅོར་.

ངུ་ཅོར་ (ŋujor) wailing, sound of crying/ weeping (implies several people crying/ weeping at once).

ངུ་ཐག་གཅོད་ (ŋu tāgjöö) va. to stop crying.

ངུ་ཐག་ཆོད་ (ŋu tāàjöö) vi. to stop crying.

ངུ་གདོང་ (ŋudoŋ) a sad face/ demeanor, a long face; va.—སྟོན་ to show/ put on a long face.

ངུ་བྱང་ལངས་པོ་ (ŋujaŋ laŋbo) sm. ངུ་རྒྱུ་གོད་པོ་.

ངུ་འདྲོ་ (ŋu dro) vi. to feel like crying ། གནས་ལུགས་སྐྱོ་པོ་དེ་མཐོང་དུས་ང་ངུ་འདྲོ་བྱུང་ When I saw that sad situation I felt like crying.

ངུ་འབོད་ (ŋumböö) crying accompanied by calling out a request; va.—བྱེད་ ། མི་སེར་ཁྲིམས་འགོ་ཁྲིད་ལ་ངུ་འབོད་བྱས་ནས་བདེ་སྡུག་ཞུས་པ་རེད་ The subjects (miser) complained to the leader of their hardship in a crying manner.

ངུ་འབོད་གནས་ (ŋumböö nɛɛ̀) shung. one of the eighteen realms of hell.

ངུ་འབོད་འོ་དོད་ (ŋumböö ödöö) crying/ wailing for help.

ངུ་མ་དགོད་ (ŋu magöö) sm. ངུ་མ་ཤེས་དགོད་མི་ཤེས་.

ངུ་མ་ངག (ŋu maŋaà) half talking and half crying, talking while crying.

ངུ་མ་ལབ (ŋu maŋaà) sm. ངུ་མ་ངག.

ངུ་མ་ཤེས་དགོད་མི་ཤེས་ (ŋu mashɛɛ̀ göö mishɛɛ̀) not knowing what to do, uncertain how to respond [Lit. not knowing whether to laugh or cry].

ངུ་མེད་བགད་མེད་ (ŋumeè gɛɛ̀meè) not knowing what to do or how to act, embarrassed [Lit. not crying and not laughing].

ངུ་ཚད་ཚད་ (ŋu tsɛɛ̀dzɛɛ̀) on the verge of tears/ weeping; va.—བྱེད་.

ངུ་མཚམས་ (ŋundzam) stopping crying; va.—འཇོག to stop crying.

ངུ་རྫུ་ (ŋudzuù) pretending to cry; va.—འདེབས་.

ངུ་ཟུག (ŋusug) the yelping/ crying of a dog.

ངུ་རུ་འཇུག (ŋuru juù) va. to make cry.

ངུ་ལབ་ (ŋuləb) sm. ངུ་སྐད་.

ངུ་སླ་པོ་ (ŋu lābo) a crybaby, sb. who cries easily.

ངུ་ཤགས་ (ŋushaà) sm. ངུ་ཤར་.

ངུ་ཤར་ (ŋushar) wailing, crying loudly; va.—རྒྱག.

ངུ་ཤི་ཁ་ལུག (ŋushi kāluù) sm. ངུ་སླ་པོ་.

ངུ་ཤུབ་ (ŋushub) weeping, sobbing, whimpering, crying with panting; va.—རྒྱག་; —བྱེད་.

ངུ་ཤུམ་ (ŋushum) weeping/ crying (conveys with tears streaming from the eyes); va.—རྒྱག.

ངུ་ཤུལ་ (ŋushüü) signs of crying, tear stains.

ངུ་ཤུལ་མིག་ཆུ་ (ŋushüü migju) sm. ངུ་ཤུལ་.

ངུ་ཤོར་ (ŋu shɔ̄ɔ) vi. to burst into tears, to cry spontaneously.

ངུ་ཤོར་པོ་ (ŋu shōrbo) bringing one to tears, easy to cry.

ངུ་བཤད་ (ŋushɛɛ̀) speaking or saying sth. while crying, va.—རྒྱག.

ངུ་བཤུམ་འཛར་འཛར་ (ŋushum dzardzar) sm. ངུ་ཤུམ་.

ངུ་ལྷུབ་ (ŋuhub) talking while crying; va.—བྱེད་.

ངུད་མོ་ (ŋüümo) sobbing, wailing, moaning.

ངུར་ (ŋur) 1. a type of duck. 2. vi. to make a grunting noise (like a pig or yak).

ངུར་སྐད་ (ŋurgɛɛ̀) 1. a grunting sound (like a pig or yak), the roaring sound of a wild animal like a tiger; va.—རྒྱག.

ངུར་ཁ་ (ŋurga) yellowish-orange color.

ངུར་ཁ་མ་ (ŋurkama) sm. ངུར་ཁ་.

ངུར་ཁམ་ (ŋurkam) sm. ངུར་ཁ་.

ངུར་སྒྲ་ (ŋurdra) sm. ངུར་སྐད་.

ངུར་དིར་ (ŋurdir) sm. ངུར་སྐད་.

ངུར་ཁྲིར་ (ŋurdir) sm. ངུར་སྐད་.

ངུར་པ་ (ŋurba) a yellow duck.

ངུར་པའི་ཤ་ (ŋurbɛsha) the meat of the yellow duck (used for medicinal purposes).

ངུར་སྨིག (ŋurmig) saffronish (color).

ངུར་སྨིག་འཛིན་པ་ (ŋumig dzimbə) monk (Buddhist).

ངུས་ (ŋüü) p. of ངུ་.

ངུས་ནས་བརྒྱལ་ (ŋüünɛ gyɛɛ) va. to throw a temper tantrum.

ངུས་ཤུལ་མིག་ཆུ་ (ŋüüshüü migju) sm. ངུ་ཤུལ་.

ངེད་ (ŋeè) sm. ང་.

ངེད་ཅ་ (ŋeèja) sm. ང་.

ངེད་ཅག (ŋeèjaà) we.

ངེད་ཉིད་ (ŋeèñii) sm. ང་ཉིད་.

ངེད་ཚོ་ (ŋeèñii) sm. ང་ཚོ་.

ངེད་རང་ (ŋeèñii) sm. ང་རང་.

ངེར་ (ŋer) vi. to growl.

ངེར་སྐད་ (ŋergɛɛ̀) growling.

ངེས་ (ŋeè) 1. vi. to be certain/ sure ¶ ང་ཚོ་ཚེས་བཅུ་ལ་འདི་ནས་ཐོན་རྒྱུར་ངེས་སོང་ It is certain that we will leave here on the 10th. ¶ འདི་འདྲ་བྱས་ན་ཁོ་ཚོ་དགའ་པོ་ཡོང་རྒྱུར་ངེས་ If we did that, they are certain to be happy. 2. (vb. + —) certainly, definitely ¶ ཁྱེད་རང་གིས་གསུངས་ན་ཁོ་ཚོས་བྱེད་ངེས་རེད་ If you tell (them), they will certainly do it. ¶ ཚུར་རྒོལ་བྱས་ན་ཕར་རྒོལ་བྱེད་ངེས་ཡིན་ If (they) attack (us) we will certainly attack (them back). 3. vi. to remember, to recollect, to recall; to keep in mind ¶ དེ་དུས་ཁོ་རྒྱ་གར་ལ་ཕྱིན་པ་ངེས་ཀྱི་མི་འདུག (I) don't recall that he went to India at that time.

ངེས་ཁུངས་ (ŋeèguŋ) shung. a reliable source ¶ གནས་ཚུལ་དེ་ངེས་ཁུངས་ཡིན་ན་ཚེ་བདེན་པར་འཛིན་ཆོག If this information is from a reliable source we can trust it.

ངེས་མཁོ་ (ŋeègo) necessary, essential, indispensable.

ངེས་ངེས་ (ŋɛèŋeè) definitely keep in mind, remember va.—བྱེད་ ¶ ཁྱེད་རང་གིས་གོང་རིམ་གྱི་བཀའ་སློབ་དེ་སེམས་ལ་ངེས་ངེས་བྱེད་དགོས་ You must keep in mind the advice of your superiors.

ངེས་ངེས་ཏིག་ཏིག (ŋɛ̀ɛ̀ŋeè dìgdig) 1. sm. ངེས་ངེས་. 2. definite, certain, sure ¶ གནས་ཚུལ་དེ་ངེས་ངེས་ཏིག་ཏིག་རེད་དམ་ Are (you) really certain about this information?

ངེས་ངེས་པོ་ (ŋɛè ŋeèbo) sm. ངེས་ངེས་.

ངེས་ཅན་ (ŋeèjɛn) certain, definite, sure ¶ གནས་ཚུལ་ངེས་ཅན་གང་ཡང་གསུངས་མ་སོང་ He didn't say anything certain.

ངེས་ཅན་ཞིག (ŋeèjɛnjig) sth. that is certain/ definite/ sure ¶ གནས་ཚུལ་ངེས་ཅན་ཞིག་གང་ཡང་གསུངས་མ་སོང་ He didn't say anything certain.

ངེས་བརྗོད་ (ŋeèjöö) defining with a metaphor.

ངེས་རྙེད་ (ŋeèñeè) vi. to definitely know ¶ ཁོས་བོད་ལ་དབང་བསྒྱུར་བྱེད་རྩིས་ཡོད་པ་ངེས་རྙེད་བྱུང་ We definitely knew that he planned to dominate/ rule Tibet.

ངེས་ཏིག (ŋeèdig) abbr. of ངེས་ངེས་ཏིག་ཏིག.

ངེས་གཏན་ (ཞིག་) (ŋeèdɛn) certainty, certainly ¶ ངེས་གཏན་མེད་པར་ཐལ་སྐྱོད་བྱེད་ཡས་འཛེམ་ཆ་བྱེད་དགོས་ (We) should avoid advancing head on unless we are certain.

ངེས་རྟོགས་ (ŋeèdɔ̀ɔ̀) knowing/ understanding for sure or definitely; va.—བྱེད་.

ངེས་བརྟན་ (ŋeèdɛn) sm. ངེས་གཏན་.

ངེས་བརྟན་དོགས་མེད་ (ŋeèdɛn tɔgmeè) no need for further confirmation.

ངེས་བརྟན་མེད་པ་ (ŋeèdɛn meèba) not definite, uncertain.

ངེས་དོན་ (ŋeèdön) absolute truth, true meaning/ significance.

ངེས་ལྡན་ (ŋeèdɛn) sm. ངེས་ཅན་.

ངེས་འདྲོངས་ (ŋendroŋ) definite, certain. 2. understood, comprehended.

ངེས་གནས་ (ŋeènɛɛ̀) existing, real, actual.

ངེས་པ་ (ŋeèba) certainty, definiteness, sureness; vi.—རྙེད་ to be certain/ definite, to know for sure ¶ ཉམས་མྱོང་ལ་བརྟེན་ནས་རྒྱལ་ཁ་ཐོབ་རྒྱུའི་ངེས་པ་གཅིག་རྙེད་པ་རེད་ Because of (their) experiences they were certain that they would be victorious.

ངེས་པ་ཅན་ (ŋeèbajɛn) certain, sure, definite, real ¶ བོད་མི་ཚོའི་གནས་སྟངས་སྐོར་ལོ་རྒྱུས་ངེས་པ་ཅན་ཁ་ཤས་ཤོད་ཡས་འདུག (They) have some definite accounts of the living conditions of the Tibetans that they can tell.

ངེས་པ་ཉིད་དུ་ (ŋeèba ñiidu) sm. ངེས་པར་དུ་.

ངེས་པ་འདྲེན་པ་ (ŋeèba trenba) having complete/ thorough understanding.

ངེས་པ་མེད་པ་ (ŋeèba meèba) uncertain, unsure, changeable ¶ ཁོ་སུ་ཡིན་ངེས་པ་མེད་པར་བརྟེན་ལམ་སེང་ཡིད་ཆེས་བྱེད་ཁག་པོ་རེད་ Because it was uncertain who he was, it was difficult to immediately trust him.

ངེས་པའི་རྒྱུ་ཡིན་ (ŋeèbɛ gyuyin) definitely (will do) ¶ ས་ཆ་དེ་མི་དམངས་ཀྱིས་སྲུང་སྐྱོབ་བྱ་རྒྱུ་ནི་ངེས་པའི་རྒྱུ་ཡིན་ It is definite that the people will protect that place.

ངེས་པའི་ཚིག (ŋeèbɛ tsïg) derived nouns (e.g., two words/ morphemes like "sky" and "boat" joined together to make another word like "airplane").

ངེས་པར་ (ŋeèbar) sm. ངེས་པར་དུ་.

ངེས་པར་དུ་ (ŋeèbartu) certainly, definitely, for sure ¶ ལས་ཀ་འདི་ཉི་མ་བདུན་གྱི་ནང་ངེས་པར་དུ་ཚར་གྱི་རེད་ This job will certainly be done in seven days. ¶ ཚོགས་འདུ་དེར་ང་ཚོ་ཚང་མ་ངེས་པར་དུ་འགྲོ་དགོས་རེད་ We all definitely have to go to that meeting. ¶ དང་མི་རྣམས་ཀྱི་ངེས་པར་དུ་ངོ་རྒོལ་བྱེད་དགོས་རེད་ Party members must oppose (it).

ངེས་པའི་མང་ཤོས་ (ŋeèbar maŋshöö) absolute majority.

ངེས་པོ་ (ŋeèbo) 1. remembering well, good memory/ recall ¶ ཁྱེད་རང་ལ་ཁོས་ག་རེ་ཞུས་མེད་ངེས་པོ་གསུང་ཡས་འདུག་གམ་ Do you remember specifically what he said to you? ¶ ཁོ་ངེས་པོ་ཞེ་དྲག་འདུག He has a good memory.

ངེས་འབྱུང་ (ŋenjuŋ) the awakening of religious seeking/ renunciation, getting the thought of seeking religious salvation; vi.— སྐྱེ་ to have the idea awaken of seeking religious salvation/ renunciation.

ངེས་འབྱུང་སྦུ་སུད་ (ŋɛnjuŋ būsüü) not real/ superficial ངེས་འབྱུང་.

ངེས་མེད་ (ŋɛèmeè) 1. sm. ངེས་པ་མེད་པ་. 2. anonymous ¶ སྦྱིན་བདག་ངེས་མེད་ཅིག་ནས་ From an anonymous donor.

ངེས་མེད་གུང་སེང་ (ŋɛèmeè guŋseŋ) casual/ nonemergency leave of absence.

ངེས་མེད་རྒོལ་རྡུང་ (ŋɛèmeè gööduŋ) guerrilla warfare.

ངེས་མེད་རྒོལ་རྡུང་ས་ཁུལ་ (ŋɛèmeè gööduŋ sәgüü) an area where guerrilla warfare exists.

ངེས་མེད་རྒོལ་རྡུང་དམག་འཐབ་ (ŋɛèmeè gööduŋ mәgtәb) guerrilla warfare.

ངེས་མེད་རྒོལ་རྡུང་རུ་ཁག (ŋɛèmeè gööduŋ rugaà) guerrilla bands/ troop.

ངེས་མེད་དགྲ་འཐབ་ (ŋɛèmeè dratәb) sm. ངེས་མེད་རྒོལ་རྡུང་.

ངེས་མེད་ཆ་བསགས་ (ŋὲ̱meè cāsaà) indefinite integral (in math).

ངེས་མེད་མཉམ་བྱ་ (ŋὲ̱meè ñamja) indeterminate equation (in math).

ངེས་མེད་དམག་འཁྲུག་ (ŋὲ̱meè māgdruù) guerrilla warfare; va.—རྒྱག.

ངེས་མེད་དམག་འཐབ་ (ŋὲ̱meè māgdəb) sm. ངེས་མེད་དམག་འཁྲུག.

ངེས་མེད་དམག་འཐབ་རུ་ཁག (ŋὲ̱meè māgdəb ru̱gaà) guerrilla band/ force.

ངེས་མེད་དམག་འཐབ་ས་ཁུལ་ (ŋὲ̱meè māgdəb sāgüü) area where there is guerrilla warfare.

ངེས་མེད་དམག་རུ་ (ŋὲ̱meè māgru) sm. ངེས་མེད་དམག་འཐབ་རུ་ཁག.

ངེས་རྩིས་ (ŋe̱èdzii) final account/ balance sheet, financial report/ accounting of revenue and expenditures.

ངེས་ཚད་ (ŋe̱èdzεὲ) norm, standard, ration.

ངེས་ཚིག (ŋe̱ètsii) abbr. of ངེས་པའི་ཚིག.

ངེས་འཛོམས་ (ŋe̱èdzom) definitely meeting/ gathering/ assembling; va.—བྱེད་.

ངེས་གཟུང་ (ŋe̱èsuŋ) 1. definite, conclusive. 2. bearing/ keeping in mind, remembering.

ངེས་བཟུང་ (ŋe̱èsuŋ) sm. ངེས་གཟུང་.

ངེས་བཟུང་སྒྲ་ (ŋe̱èsuŋ dra̱) the grammatical particle ནི་ (that points out a particular person or thing).

ངེས་བཟོ་ (ŋe̱èso) (vb. + —) certain, sure ¶ འགྲོ་སོང་རག་རྒྱུའི་ངེས་བཟོ་མི་འདུག It is not certain we will obtain the money for expenses.

ངེས་ལེགས་ (ŋe̱èleg) 1. definite or true goodness. 2. nirvana, enlightenment.

ངེས་ཤེས་ (ŋe̱èsheè) certain knowledge, confidence, conviction, assurance; vi.— སྐྱེ་; —བསྐྱེད་ to be/ get/ grow confident/ assured, to believe, to trust ¶ ཆབ་འབངས་རྣམས་ངེས་ཤེས་འདྲོངས་པའི་གནས་ལུགས་གསེད་འགྲེལ་དགོས་རྒྱུ་ One should explain the matter clearly so that the subjects can believe it.

ངེས་ཤེས་རྙེད་ (ŋe̱èsheè ñēè) vi. to get/ find certain knowledge, to get confidence/ assuredness with respect to knowledge, to believe, to trust.

ངེས་གཤིས་ (ŋe̱èshii) shung. because of being confirmed ¶ བློ་ནམ་ལ་ཛ་སག་ངེས་གཤིས་ Because Lonam was confirmed as a dzasa.

ངེས་སུ་ (ŋe̱èsu) definitely, certainly.

ངེས་སྲོལ་ (ŋe̱èsöö) law, regulation, rule.

ངེས་སྲོལ་རང་བཞིན་ (ŋe̱èsöö ra̱ŋshin) objective laws.

ངེས་གསལ་ (ŋe̱èsεl) clear, distinct ¶ ཤར་ནུབ་བར་གྱི་རིང་ཚད་ངེས་གསལ་བརྗོད་རྒྱུ་མེད་ (I) can't say clearly what the distance is between east and west.

ངེས་བསྐུར་ (ŋe̱è siŋ) va. to send definitely, to be sure to send ¶ ས་གནས་ཀྱི་ཆ་བབས་གནས་ཚུལ་འཕྲལ་འཕྲལ་ངེས་བསྐྱོངས་དགོས་རྒྱུ་ One should be sure to send the information regarding the situation right away.

ངོ་ (ŋo̱) 1. the face, the front (side) ¶ ངོ་ལ་དཀར་པོ་དམར་པོ་བྱུགས་འདུག (She) was wearing makeup on (her) face. 2. the real, the actual, the essence (often conveys the true members of a family as opposed to servants or distant relatives) ¶ ལྷ་ཀླུ་ངོ་གཡོག Lhalu family, members and servants. 3. page (in books, etc.) ¶ ངོ་བདུན་པའི་ཕྲེང་བརྒྱད་པ་ The eighth line on page seven. 4. principal (in a loan) ¶ ངོ་སྐྱེད་ Principal and interest. 5. (— + vb.) in person, face-to-face ¶ བླ་མའི་སྐུ་མདུན་ལ་ངོ་བཅར་ཞུ་དགོས་ You have to meet the lama in person.

ངོ་དཀར་ (ŋogar) 1. cheerful, happy (face/ expression); va.—སྟོན་ to show a cheerful/ happy face, to look happy/ cheerful/ pleased ¶ ཁོས་ངོ་དཀར་སྟོན་པ་མཐོང་མ་བྱུང་ (I) haven't seen him look cheerful. 2. white face.

ངོ་དཀར་བ་ (ŋo̱ gārwa) slightly better ¶ ངའི་ལྷམ་གོག་འདི་ཁྱེད་བུའི་ངོ་དཀར་བ་ཡོད་ My shoes is slightly better (than his).

ངོ་དཀར་པོ་ (ŋo̱ gārbo) sm. ངོ་དཀར་.

ངོ་ལྐོག (ŋogɔg) deceitful, two-faced, double dealing; va.—བྱེད་ to act two-faced/ deceitful, to double-deal.

ངོ་ལྐོག་གཉིས་མེད་ (ŋo̱gɔg ñiìmeè) sm. ངོ་ལྐོག་མཚུངས་པ་.

ངོ་ལྐོག་འཕེར་བ་ (ŋo̱gɔg pērwa) sm. ངོ་ལྐོག་མཚུངས་པ་.

ངོ་ལྐོག་མེད་པ་ (ŋo̱gɔg me̱èba) sm. ངོ་ལྐོག་མཚུངས་པ་.

ངོ་ལྐོག་ཚིག་མཚོན་ (ŋo̱gɔg tsīgdzön) using words to attack overtly and covertly.

ངོ་ལྐོག་མཚུངས་པ་ (ŋo̱gɔg tsūŋbə) undeceitful, straightforward, honest.

ངོ་ལྐོག་གཡོ་ལྷད་ (ŋo̱gɔg yōlhεὲ) two-faced and deceitful.

ངོ་སྐལ་ (ŋo̱gεε) share, portion.

ངོ་སྐུལ་ཞུ་ (ŋo̱güü shu̱) shung. to encourage/ insist ¶ དཔལ་འབར་བླ་མ་ནས་ངོ་བསྐུལ་ཞུས་འགྲེལ་ At the insistence of Pembar Lama.

ངོ་སྐྱེངས་ (ŋogyeŋ) 1. sm. ཁ་སྐྱེངས་ 2. disappointment, disenchantment.

ངོ་སྐྱེངས་ཟིལ་པ་ཆགས་ (ŋogyeŋ si̱lbə cāà) vi. to sweat due to embarrassment.

ངོ་སྐྱེད་ (ŋo̱gyeè) 1. principal and interest (on a loan). 2. va.—ལེན་ to start/ begin to recover from an illness.

ངོ་སྐྱེད་གྲངས་གཙང་ (ŋogyeè tra̱ndzaŋ) shung. (paying) the principle and the interest completely ¶ ངོ་སྐྱེད་གྲངས་གཙང་དུས་གཅིག་ལ་འབུལ་རྒྱུ་ (We) will pay the principle and the interest completely at once.

ངོ་སྐྱེད་རྩ་ཡང་ (ŋo̱gyeè dzāyaŋ) shung. the principal and interest both being completely written off.

ངོ་སྐྱོད་ (ŋo̱ gyöö) sm. ང་བསྐྱོད་.

ངོ་བསྐྱོད་ (ŋo̱ gyöö) going in person/ first hand; va.—བྱེད་ to go in person ¶ ཁོ་ཚོ་བསུ་བར་གནམ་ཐང་དུ་ང་རང་ངོ་བསྐྱོད་བྱས་པ་ཡིན་ I went to the airport in person to receive them.

ངོ་ཁ་སྐྱེང་ (ŋo̱ gyöö) sm. ངོ་སྐྱེངས་.

ངོ་ཁར་ (ŋo̱gar) in front of, in the presence of ¶ ཁོའི་ངོ་ཁར་དེ་ཚོ་ཤོད་ནུས་ཀྱི་མི་འདུག (They) don't dare say those things in front of him.

ངོ་ཁབས་ (ŋo̱gam) virtaligo.

ངོ་ཁེབས་ (ŋo̱geb) a veil used to cover the face (usu. by Muslim women).

ངོ་ཁེབས་གྲོ་ཐིག (ŋo̱geb dro̱dig) freckles.

ངོ་ཁྱུག་པ་ (ŋo̱kyagba) sm. ངོ་དཀར་བ་.

ངོ་ཁྲ་བྱི་ལ་ (ŋo̱tra ci̱lə) a tiger-striped cat.

ངོ་ཁྲ་ཞུམ་བུ་ (ŋo̱dra zhu̱mbu) sm. ངོ་ཁྲ་བྱི་ལ་.

ངོ་ཁྲལ་ (ŋo̱drεε) shung. tax on aristocratic families who were unable to provide a government office at a given time. 2. head tax.

ངོ་འཁོར་ (ŋo̱gɔɔ) master and servant, head and servants/ retinue.

ངོ་མཁྱེན་ (ŋo̱ kyēn) vi. to know, to recognize (h.) ¶ ང་ཐོག་མར་གཟིགས་དུས་ངོ་མཁྱེན་བྱུང་ངམ་ Did (you) recognize me when (you) first saw me?

ངོ་མཁྱེན་འདྲིས་གྲོགས་ (ŋo̱gyen tri̱idrɔɔ) h. of ངོ་ཤེས་འདྲིས་གྲོགས་.

ངོ་འཁྱེར་ (ŋo̱ kyēr) 1. va. to use one's relationship/ friendship (to get sth.) ¶ དེ་རིང་ངའི་ངོ་འཁྱེར་ནས་ཁོང་གི་ས་ནས་དངུལ་གཡར་བ་ཡིན་ Today I used my relationship with him to get a loan. ¶ ངའི་ངོ་འཁྱེར་ནས་རྡོ་རྗེ་ལགས་ཀྱིས་ཟ་ཁང་ལ་མི་ཞིག་བཙུག་པ་ཡིན་ I used my relationship with Dorjela to (get him to) put (hire) a person in his restaurant. 2. making a big deal.

ངོ་འཁྲུད་ཁང་ (ŋo̱trüügaŋ) wash room.

ངོ་གྲངས་ (ŋo̱draŋ) number, quantity ¶ རྒྱལ་ཁབ་དེས་གནམ་གྲུ་ངོ་གྲངས་ 50 སྐོར་ཉོས་པ་རེད་ That country bought about fifty planes.

ངོ་དགའ་ (ŋo̱gar) flattery, sycophancy, boot licking; va.—བྱེད་; —རྒྱག.

ངོ་དགའ་ངོ་བསྟོད་ (ŋo̱gar ŋo̱döö) sm. ངོ་དགའ་.

ངོ་དགའ་པད་ལད་ (ŋo̱gar bēèlεὲ) flattering, being sycophantic; va.—བྱེད་.

ངོ་དགའ་སྦྲིལ་ལབ་ (ŋo̱ga bēlεὲ) sm. ངོ་དགའ་པད་ལད་.

ངོ་དགའ་སྤྲིལ་ལད་ཚ་པོ་ (ŋoga bēlɛɛ tsābo) sb. who is a flatterer/ sycophant.

ངོ་དགའ་ཕྱོགས་འཛིན་ (ŋoga cɔ̄gten) shung. showing/ practicing favoritism or nepotism, acting biased or partial; va.—བྱེད་ ¶ ཞིབ་ས་ནས་ངོ་དགའ་ཕྱོགས་འཛིན་མེད་པའི་དྲང་པོའི་ཁྲིམས་སྲོལ་རྒྱུན་སྐྱོང་དགོས་རྒྱུ་ The special office for investigating the case should practice the law justly, and should not practice favoritism.

ངོ་འགྲོ་ (ŋodro) shung. to go/ attend in person ¶ ཚོགས་འདུར་ངོ་འགྲོ་མ་ཐུབ་པར་ངོ་ཚབ་བཏང་བ་ Because of being unable to attend the meeting in person, (he) sent a representative.

ངོ་རྒོལ་ (ŋogöö) opposition, opposing, protesting; va.—བྱེད་ to oppose, to protest, to stand up against ¶ གྲོས་ཆོད་དེ་ལ་འཐུས་མི་ཁ་ཤས་ནས་ངོ་རྒོལ་བྱས་ཡོད་པ་རེད་ Some representatives opposed the resolution. 2. anti-, counter- ¶ གསར་བརྗེ་ར་ངོ་རྒོལ་ Counterrevolutionary.

ངོ་རྒོལ་སྐད་འབོད་ (ŋogöö gēmböö) demonstrating in opposition to sth. (by shouting slogans, etc.); va.—བྱེད་.

ངོ་རྒོལ་སྐྱོན་བརྗོད་ (ŋogöö gyōnjöö) criticism in opposition of sth.; va.—བྱེད་.

ངོ་རྒོལ་སྒེར་ལངས་ (ŋogöö gerlaŋ) uprising, rebellion, insurrection; va.—བྱེད་.

ངོ་རྒོལ་ལྔ་ (ŋogöö ŋā) the five anti's movement (against bribery, against tax evasion, against theft of state property, against cheating on government contracts, and against stealing economic information).

ངོ་རྒོལ་ཕྱོགས་ཁག (ŋogöö cɔ̄gaà) opposition faction/ party.

ངོ་རྒོལ་གསུམ་ (ŋogöö sūm) polit. the three antis campaign of 1951-1952—the campaign against corruption, waste and bureaucracy within the party, government, army and mass organizations.

ངོ་རྒྱ་ (ŋogya) page, leaf (of a book).

ངོ་རྒྱབ་གཉིས་ (ŋogyab ñīi) front and back.

ངོ་རྒྱུག (ŋogyuù) shung. corvee labor that a person must carry out himself/ in person ¶ རྟ་ཁལ་མི་གསུམ་གྱི་ཁྲལ་རིགས་ངོ་རྒྱུག་དགོས་པ་ལས་ཚབ་སྤྲོད་དང་དངོས་སྤྲོད་སོགས་མི་ཆོག་པ་ One should provide the riding horses and accompanying person corvee tax as demanded in person, and it is not allowed to make a substitute and a money payment in place of the performing this in person.

ངོ་སྒྲུབ་ (ŋodrub) shung. to pay whatever the tax is ¶ ཐྲར་རྒྱུན་ངོ་སྒྲུབ་དགོས་ངེས་ཞིབ་དེབ་གཞིར་བཟུང་ངོ་སྒྲུབ་དགོས་རྒྱུ་ One should pay whatever the tax is in accordance with the tax investigation book.

ངོ་ཅག (ŋojag) sm. ངར་ཚོ་.

ངོ་གཅོམ་ (ŋo jɔ̄ɔ) va. to crush another's hopes/ wishes/ desires.

ངོ་བཅར་ (ŋojar) reporting in person, meeting in person (h.); va.—ཞུ་ ¶ ཁྱེད་ན་ཟུ་བཏབ་ནས་ངོ་བཅར་མ་ཞུས་ཙང་ Because you feigned illness and didn't report in person.

ངོ་ཆག (ŋojaà) shung. a reduction in taxes because a family has a member serving as a government official ¶ གཞུང་གི་ཞབས་སྒེར་འཁོད་པ་རྣམས་ལ་ངོ་ཆག་ཐོབ་ཐང་ཡོད་ Government officials have the right to get a tax deduction for going into government service.

ངོ་ཆང་ (ŋojaŋ) beer (ཆང་) served by sb. in person (rather than by a servant) (implies that the person served has to drink the beer).

ངོ་ཆེ་ངོ་ཆུང་ (ŋoje ŋojuŋ) favoritism, nepotism, showing partiality; va.—བྱེད་.

ངོ་ཆེན་ (ŋojen) sb. of influence/ power, a patron; va.—ཞུ་; —གནང་རོགས་ཞུ་ to ask a favor of sb. of influence/ power, to ask sb. in power to intercede; va.—གནང་ to grant a favor.

ངོ་ཆེན་ངོ་བརྒྱུད་ (ŋojen ŋogyüü) seeking a favor through an influential person, asking sb. who is powerful to intercede; va.—བྱེད་.

ངོ་ཆེན་ངོ་ཆུང་ (ŋojen ŋojuŋ sm. ངོ་ཆེ་ངོ་ཆུང་.

ངོ་ཆེན་ཞུ་བརྒྱུད་ (ŋojen shugyüü) sm. ངོ་ཆེན་ངོ་བརྒྱུད་.

ངོ་ཆེན་ཞུ་མི་ (ŋojen shumi) a person who intercedes with an influential person on behalf of the another; va.—གཏོང་ to send such a person.

ངོ་ཆོད་ (ŋo cöö) abbr. ངོ་ཐག་ཆོད་.

ངོ་མཆིལ་འདེབས (ŋo cii deb) va. to spit on sb.'s face.

ངོ་མཇལ་ (ŋo jɛɛ) h. of ངོ་འཕྲད་.

ངོ་ཉར་སྐྱིད་འཇལ (ŋoñar gyēnjɛɛ) sm. མ་ཉར་སྐྱིད་འཇལ་.

ངོ་གཉིས་པ་ (ŋoñiibə) a two-faced person, a double dealer.

ངོ་གཉིས་མ་ (ŋo ñiimə) 1. dual ¶ འཐབ་ཇུས་ངོ་གཉིས་མ་ A dual strategy. 2. two-faced person, double-dealer.

ངོ་གཉེར་མ་ མིག་མཆི་མ་ (ŋo ñērma mii cīmə) great sadness or suffering [Lit. wrinkled face, tearful eyes].

ངོ་གཉེར་མ་ གདོང་མཆི་མ་ (ŋo ñērma doŋ cīmə) great sadness or suffering [Lit. wrinkled face; tearful face].

ངོ་གཏད་ (ŋodɛɛ) sm. ཁ་གཏད་.

ངོ་གཏུག (ŋoduù) meeting face-to-face, meeting in person; va.—བྱེད་ ¶ ཁོས་ང་དང་ངོ་གཏུག་ཏུ་ཡོང་བ་རེད་ He came to meet me in person. ¶ ངས་ཁོང་ངོ་གཏུག་བྱས་ནས་བཤད་པ་ཡིན་ I went to tell him in person.

ངོ་གཏུག་ངོ་གདོང་ (ŋoduù ŋodoŋ) meeting face-to-face, in person.

ངོ་གདོང་བསུ་ལེན་ (ŋodoŋ sūlen) the welcoming done by the main members of a family to an in-marrying bride or groom; —བྱེད་ ¶ གཟའ་སྐར་འཕྲོད་སྦྱོར་དགེ་བའི་ཉིན་བག་མ་ངོ་གདོང་བསུ་ལེན་བྱ་རྒྱུ་ On an auspicious day, the main members of the family will welcome the bride.

ངོ་རྟགས་ (ŋodaà) identification sign/ mark; vi.—རྒྱག་; vi.—ཆོད་; vi.—ཟིན་ (ཟིམ་) to be identified/ recognized; va.—གཙོད་ to identify.

ངོ་རྟགས་རྒྱག་པོ་ (ŋodaà cūgbo) sm. ངོ་ཐག་ཆོད་པོ་.

ངོ་རྟགས་ཆོག་ཐམ་ (ŋodaà cōgdam) identity card/ certificate.

ངོ་བརྟན་པོ་ (ŋo dēmbo) sm. གདོང་བརྟན་པོ་.

ངོ་ལྡ་ (ŋoda) 1. vi. to recover/ get well/ take a turn for the better (usu. regarding an illness) ¶ ན་ཚ་དྲག་ངོ་ལྡ་གི་འདུག He is starting to recover from the illness. 2. abbr. ངོ་ལ་ལྡ. 3. mirror. 4. sm. ཕྱོགས་སུ་ལྡང་.

ངོ་ལྡོས་ (ŋodöö) shung. all members of a family (the family head and everyone else) ¶ ཁྱིམ་ཚང་ངོ་ལྡོས་དང་བཅས་པ་ཚང་མ་ཡོང་བ་རེད་ All the members of the family came.

ངོ་བལྟས་ (ŋo dɛɛ) sm. ངོ་ལ་ལྡ་.

ངོ་སྟོན་ (ŋo dōn) va. to show one's face; to appear in public.

ངོ་བསྟོད་ (ŋodöö) sm. ངོ་དགའ་.

ངོ་བསྟོད་ངོ་དགའ་ (ŋodöö ŋoga) sm. ངོ་དགའ་.

ངོ་ཐག་ཆོད་ (ŋodaà cöö) 1. vi. to know, to recognize ¶ ཁྱེད་རང་མི་འདི་ངོ་ཐག་ཆོད་སོང་ངས་ Did you know this man? ¶ མིག་ཡོད་ཀྱང་ཡག་ཉེས་ངོ་ཐག་མི་ཆོད་ Even though he has eyes, he doesn't know good from bad.

ངོ་ཐག་ཆོད་པོ་ (ŋodaà cööbo) recognizable ¶ ཡི་གེ་དེ་ངོ་ཐག་ཆོད་པོ་མི་འདུག I can't recognize the letters (e.g., they are printed unclearly).

ངོ་ཐང་ (ŋodaŋ) a person's standing with regards to respect and honor.

ངོ་ཐུག (ŋodug) meeting in person; va.—བྱེད་ ¶ ཁོ་གཉིས་ 1959 ནས་ངོ་ཐུག་བྱུང་ཡོད་པ་མ་རེད་ They have not met (each other) in person since 1959.

ངོ་ཐུག་གྲོས་ཚོགས་ (ŋodug tröödzoò) a face-to-face gathering/ meeting.

ངོ་ཐུག་ངོ་འཕྲད་ (ŋodug ŋodrɛɛ) a face-to-face gathering/ meeting.

ངོ་ཐུག་གདོང་འཕྲད་ (ŋodug doŋdröö) face-to-face, in person.

ངོ་ཐུག་དྲི་ལན་ (ŋodug trilen) interviewing, asking questions face-to-face; va.—བྱེད་.

ངོ་ཐུག་གླེང་མོལ་ (ŋodug lēŋmöö) sth. told in person, a face-to-face discussion/ conversation.

ངོ་ཐོག་ (ŋodog) 1. real, true, actual ¶འདི་ཁོའི་བསམ་བློ་ངོ་ཐོག་དེ་མ་རེད་ This is not his real idea. 2. really, truly, actually ¶ཁོ་བོད་ལ་ངོ་ཐོག་འགྲོ་གི་ཡོད་པ་རེད་ He is really going to Tibet.

ངོ་ཐོག་འབྲི་ (ŋodog dri) va. to write realistically, to record the true situation, to describe actual conditions.

ངོ་ཐོན་ (ŋo tōn) 1. abbr. ངོ་སོ་ཐོན་. 2. abbr. ངོ་མ་ཐོན.

ངོ་ཐོན་དཔང་པོ་ (ŋodön pāŋbo) a witness who comes in person (to court); va.—བྱེད་.

ངོ་མཐོ་ (ŋo tō) sm. ངོ་མཐོ་བ་.

ངོ་མཐོ་བ་ (ŋo tōwa) 1. valuable, precious ¶ཁོ་ཚོས་དངོས་ཆས་ངོ་མཐོ་བ་རེ་གཉིས་མ་གཏོགས་དེ་མིན་སྤྲེར་བ་རེད་ Except for a few valuable things they gave everything away. 2. pride in an accomplishment ¶ཕྲུ་གུའི་ལོ་འཛུག་ཡིག་ཚད་ལོན་པས་ཕ་མ་གཉིས་ངོ་མཐོ་བ་བྱུང་བ་ Because the child passed the final exam, the parents were proud in an accomplishment. 3. respected, well thought of, well considered.

ངོ་མཐོ་པོ་ (ŋo tōbo) 1. having pride in an accomplishment ¶ཕྲུ་གུའི་ལོ་འཛུག་ཡིག་ཚད་ལོན་པས་ཕ་མ་གཉིས་ངོ་མཐོ་པོ་བྱུང་བ་ Because the child passed the final exam, the parents were proud. 2. respecting, considering well.

ངོ་འཐེན་ (ŋəoden) shung. abbr. of ངོ་དགའ་ཕྱོགས་འཐེན་.

ངོ་དག་ཆོས་ (ŋodaà cöö) vi. to be identified ¶ཁྱེད་ངོ་དག་མི་ཆོས་པར་འབྲི་རྒྱུ་ཡིན་ We will not identify you in (our) writings).

ངོ་དོད (ŋodöö) shung. the payment made when a family doesn't have a worker to provide, e.g., aristocratic families when they have no male of the right age to send as a government official.

ངོ་གདོང་ (ŋodoŋ) 1. face. 2. appearance.

ངོ་གདོང་ནག་པོ་ (ŋodoŋ nagbo) 1. black face. 2. angry face.

ངོ་གདོང་ལ་འབྲོང་ལྤགས་གཡོག (ŋodoŋla droŋbaà yɔ̄ɔ) shameless [Lit. putting a wild yak hide on one's face].

ངོ་མདངས་ (ŋodaŋ) facial complexion.

ངོ་མདངས་བཀྲ་བ་ (ŋodaŋ) one's face glowing with health.

ངོ་མདོག (ŋodog) facial color/ complexion; vi.—སྐྱར་ to turn white/ pale (e.g., from illness).

ངོ་འདེགས་ཞུ་ (ŋodeg shu) shung. va. to weigh (whatever had to be paid as a tax, such as wool butter, etc.).

ངོ་འདོན་ (ŋondön) shung. the estate and its subjects ¶ངོ་འདོན་གྱི་འཛིན་དབང་བྱིངས་ཆོས་སྡེ་རང་ནས་འཛིན་སྐྱོང་གིས་ The Chode Monastery shall manage and take possession of the estate and its subjects.

ངོ་འདོན་འཛིན་བདག (ŋondön dzindaà) shung. the office/ or institution in charge of both an estate and its attached subjects ¶ངོ་འདོན་འཛིན་བདག་ལྟེ་བ་རྩེ་ཡིག་ཚང་ཡིན་ཀྱང་ཤེལ་ཆོས་སྡེ་ཁ་འཛིན་བསྐུལ་དོན་ Although the main owner of the estate and its subjects is the Yigtsang Office, that office granted possession to Chode Monastery.

ངོ་འདྲ་ (ŋondra) 1. the original and the copy. 2. sth. that looks like the original/ real thing.

ངོ་ནག (ŋonag) an angry or stern or grave expression/ countenance; va.—སྟོན་; va.—སྡུད་ to make an angry/ stern face ¶མགྲོན་པོའི་དཀྱིལ་དུ་གཤེ་གཤེ་གཏོང་མི་ཐོད་ཀྱང་ངོ་ནག་བསྟུས་སོང་ Even though (he) couldn't scold (him/her) in the midst of guests, (he) showed an angry face.

ངོ་ནག་པོ་ (ŋo nagbo) sm. ངོ་ནག.

ངོ་ནོར་ (ŋonɔɔ) error, mistake.

ངོ་ནོར་སྦས་བསྐུངས་ (ŋonɔr bɛ̄ɛ̀guŋ) shung. switching inferior quality for good quality, having a mixup occur; va.—བྱེད་ ¶ངོ་ནོར་སྦས་བསྐུངས་མེད་པར་སྤྲོད་དགོས་ (You) should give things without switching some.

ངོ་ནོར་འཁྲུམ་ལུས་མེད་པ་ (ŋonɔɔ kūmlüü meèba) shung. to not make mistakes/ errors that leave sth. out ¶ས་ཞིང་རྣམས་འདི་ལོ་འདེབས་རྗེ་ནས་ངོ་ནོར་འཁྲུམ་ལུས་མེད་པ་སྤྲོད་ལེན་དགོས་རྒྱུ་ There should be no mistakes made that leave things out when handing over the fields after planting.

ངོ་གནག་པ་ (ŋonagba) sm. ངོ་ནག.

ངོ་གནོང་ (ŋo nōŋ) vi. to feel ashamed/ unworthy/ unsuitable, to regret ¶ངོ་གནོང་དགོས་པའི་བྱ་བ་ A deed that troubles one's conscience. ¶ངོ་གནོང་མི་དགོས་པ་ There is no need to be ashamed/ embarrassed.

ངོ་གནོངས་ (ŋo nōŋ) p. of ངོ་གནོང་.

ངོ་ལྤགས་མཐུག་པོ་ (ŋobaà tūgbo) shameless, not easily embarrassed, thick-skinned.

ངོ་སྤྲགས་ (ŋobdraà) confronting face-to-face; va.—བྱེད.

ངོ་སྤྲོད་ (ŋodröö) introducing, acquainting; va.—བྱེད་; —ཞུ་ to introduce, to acquaint ¶ཚོགས་སར་ཚོགས་མི་གསར་པ་རྣམས་ངོ་སྤྲོད་བྱེད་ཀྱི་རེད་ They will introduce the new members at the meeting place. ¶བརྙན་པར་ཁང་གིས་རིང་མིན་དེའི་སྐོར་ཞིབ་རྒྱས་ངོ་སྤྲོད་ཞུ་རྒྱུ་ཡིན་ The Pictorial (magazine) office will soon acquaint you in detail about this.

ངོ་སྤྲོད་མིང་བྱང་ (ŋodröö miŋjaŋ) name card.

ངོ་སྤྲོད་ཡི་གེ་ (ŋodröö yigi) letter of introduction.

ངོ་སྤྲོད་ལག་འཁྱེར་ (ŋodröö laggyer) sm. ངོ་སྤྲོད་ཡི་གེ་.

ངོ་ཕན་ (ŋobɛn) repaying a part of the principal of a loan; va.—བྱེད་ ¶དངུལ་སྲང་ ༥༠ ངོ་ཕན་ཐོག་འབུལ་རྒྱུ་ Paying 50 sangs towards the principal of the loan.

ངོ་ཕེབས་ (ŋopeb) h. of ངོ་བསྐྱོད་.

ངོ་འཕང་མཐོ་པོ་ (ŋobaŋ tōbo) sm. ངོ་སོ་ཆེན་པོ་.

ངོ་འཕྲད་ (ŋondrɛɛ̀) meeting in person ¶ཁོ་ངོ་འཕྲད་མ་བྱུང་ I haven't met him in person.

ངོ་འཕྲད་གྲོས་བསྡུར་ (ŋondrɛɛ̀ trööddur) having a face-to-face discussion/ conversation; va.—བྱེད.

ངོ་འཕྲད་གྲོས་མོལ་ (ŋondröö trööm öö) sm. ངོ་འཕྲོད་གྲོས་བསྡུར་.

ངོ་འཕྲོད་ (ŋo dröö) vi. to have sb. be introduced. 2. sm. ངོ་ཐག་ཆོད་. 3. vi. to receive the original or main (usu. a letter or document).

ངོ་བོ་ (ŋowo) 1. nature, essence, character, attitude; vi.—འགྱུར་ to get changed, to have the nature/ essence/ character/ attitude change (with food conveys to spoil) ¶བཙན་རྒྱལ་རིང་ལུགས་ཀྱི་ལམ་ལུགས་ཀྱི་ངོ་བོ་ The nature of the system of imperialism. ¶ངོ་བོ་ཡང་ཉིན་བཞིན་ཚབས་ཆེར་འགྲོ་གི་ཡོད་པ་རེད་ (It) gets more serious in nature everyday. ¶ཧྲང་མི་འདི་ཧོབ་ཏེ་ཁ་ལ་ངོ་བོ་འགྱུར་ནས་གསར་བརྗེ་ར་ངོ་ལོག་པ་ཆགས་བཞག The character of party members has suddenly changed and become counterrevolutionary.

ངོ་བོ་འགྱུར་ནས་ངན་པ་ཆགས་ (ŋowo gyurnɛ ŋɛmba cāà) vi. to degenerate, to become bad.

ངོ་བོ་ངེས་པའི་དབྱེ་ཞིབ་ (ŋowo ŋebɛɛ yēship) qualitative analysis.

ངོ་བོ་གཅིག་པ་ (ŋowo jīgbɔ) the same or similar nature.

ངོ་བོ་གཉིས་ལྡན་ (ŋowo ñīidɛn) dual nature/ character; duality.

ངོ་བོ་གཉིས་ལྡན་གྱི་རང་བཞིན་ (ŋowo ñīidɛngi rəŋshin) the nature of duality.

ངོ་བོ་ཉིས་བརྩེགས་ (ŋowo ñīidzeg) sm. ངོ་བོ་གཉིས་ལྡན་.

ངོ་དབྱིབས་ (ŋoyib) sm. གདོང་དབྱིབས་.

ངོ་འབག (ŋobaà) mask.

ངོ་འབངས་ (ŋombaŋ) shung. the estate owner/ lord and the subjects or serfs ¶ངོ་འབངས་གྱོད་གཞི་དབྱེ་བ་མ་ཆོད་པར་གཞུང་ཞིབ་བྱེད་མུས་ཡིན་བཞིན་པར་ The case between the estate owner and the subjects has not been settled yet and they are still in the process of investigating.

ངོ་འབུད་ཀྱིས་མཐར་བསྒྲོད་ (ŋombüügi tādröö) shung. expelling the chief culprit/ offender.

ངོ་འབུལ་ (ŋombüü) giving sth. in person; va.—ཞུ་.

ངོ་འབྱོར་ (ŋonjɔr) sm. ངོ་བཅར་.

ངོ་སྦྱོར་ (ŋojɔr) recommending; va.—བྱེད་.

ངོ་འབྲུ་ (ŋondru) shung. principal in a grain loan.

ངོ་མ་ (ŋoma) 1. real, actual, true ¶ གྲོགས་པོ་ངོ་མ་ A real friend. ¶ གུང་ཁྲན་ངོ་མའི་བསམ་བློ་ Real communist ideas. 2. the master, the main family members ¶ ཟུར་ཁང་ངོ་མ་དང་གཡོག་པོ་ཚོ་ the Surkhang family members and servants. 3. in person, in the real, actually ¶ ཁྱེད་རང་ངོ་མ་ཕེབས་པས་ Did you go in person?

ངོ་མ་བརྒྱགས་ནས་གཡག་ཤོར་སྐྲག་ནས་ཚིག་ཤོར་ (ŋoma gyaànɛ yāàshɔɔ dāànɛ tsiìshɔɔ) forcing people to do sth. [Lit. when people are full they can't help but fart, when people are afraid they can't help but say sth.].

ངོ་མ་ངོ་བཤུས་ (ŋoma ŋoshüü) the original and the copy.

ངོ་མ་གཅོག (ŋoma jōg) sm. ངོ་མ་ཆོག.

ངོ་མ་ཆོག (ŋoma cōg) vi. to do sth. because it is hard to refuse sb's request; to do something so another won't lose face ¶ ངོ་མ་ཆོག་པར་ཁས་ལེན་དགོས་བྱུང་ In order for her not to lose face I had to agree.

ངོ་མ་ཆོད་ (ŋoma cöö) vi. to be unable to distinguish/ know.

ངོ་མ་ལྡོག (ŋoma dɔɔ) sm. ངོ་མ་ཆོག.

ངོ་མ་བཟློག (ŋoma dɔɔ) sm. ངོ་མ་ཆོག.

ངོ་མར་འགྱུར་ (ŋomar gyur) vi. to get changed from temporary to permanent/ full status (e.g., after a probationary period at work).

ངོ་མའི་རང་བཞིན་ (ŋomɛ raŋshin) the nature of truth/ reality.

ངོ་མི་གཅོག (ŋomijɔɔ) sm. ངོ་མ་ཆོག.

ངོ་མི་དྲག་པ་ (ŋo midagba) temperamental, highly sensitive.

ངོ་མི་ཚོར་བ་ (ŋo midzorwa) 1. vi. to not recognize. 2. vi. to be straightforward, to be uninhibited.

ངོ་མིང་ (ŋo miŋ) real name (i.e., not a nickname).

ངོ་མེད་ལྐོག་མེད་ (ŋomɛɛ gōgmeè) straightforward, honest.

ངོ་མེད་དོན་མེད་ (ŋomeè tönmeè) not achieving a good result, not getting recognition/ acclaim.

ངོ་ཚ་ (ŋo tsā) vi. to be ashamed/ embarrassed ¶ མོ་ཐུག་སྐབས་ངོ་ཚ་བྱུང་ I was embarrassed when I met her.

ངོ་ཚ་ཁ་སྐྱེངས་ (ŋotsa kāgyeŋ) 1. embarrassment; vi.—ཚག to be/ get embarrassed. 2. vi. to be ashamed and embarrassed.

ངོ་ཚ་ཁྲེལ་འདྲེས་ (ŋotsa trēndɛɛ) sm. ངོ་ཚ་ཁྲེལ་མེད་.

ངོ་ཚ་ཁྲེལ་མེད་ (ŋotsa trēēmeè) shameless, brazen, having no sense of shame/ embarrassment.

ངོ་ཚ་ཁྲེལ་གཞུང་ (ŋotsa trēēshuŋ) sm. ངོ་ཚ་ཁྲེལ་ཡོད་.

ངོ་ཚ་ཁྲེལ་ཡོད་ (ŋotsa trēēyöö) honest, moral, upright, having a conscience, having a sense of embarrassment/ shame.

ངོ་ཚ་ཁྲེལ་སེམས་ (ŋotsa trēēsem) sm. ངོ་ཚ་ཁྲེལ་ཡོད་.

ངོ་ཚ་འགེབས་རས་ (ŋotsa gebrɛɛ) loin cloth, fig leaf.

ངོ་ཚ་རྒྱབ་སྒྱུར་ (ŋotsa gyəbgyur) sm. ངོ་ཚ་ཁྲེལ་མེད་.

ངོ་ཚ་རྒྱབ་ཏུ་སྒྱུར་ (ŋotsa gyəbdu gyūr) sm. ངོ་ཚ་ཁྲེལ་མེད་.

ངོ་ཚ་རྒྱུ་མེད་ (ŋotsa gyumeè) sb. who does not feel ashamed, shameless.

ངོ་ཚ་ཅན་ (ŋotsajɛn) shy, bashful.

ངོ་ཚ་ཆེན་པོ་ (ŋotsa cēmbo) sm. ངོ་ཚ་སྨིན་པོ་.

ངོ་ཚ་ཉོ་ (ŋotsa ño) va. to disgrace/ shame oneself [Lit. to buy embarrassment].

ངོ་ཚ་གཉིས་མཉམ་ (ŋotsa ñiiñam) together in good and bad.

ངོ་ཚ་པོ་ (ŋo tsābo) ashamed, embarrassed.

ངོ་ཚ་སྤྲོད་རིན་ (ŋotsa drērin) provisions provided to a thief by his captors when he is sent home.

ངོ་ཚ་ཕབ་ (ŋotsa pāb) va. to humiliate, to make sb. feel ashamed.

ངོ་ཚ་མེད་པ་ (ŋotsa meèba) sm. ངོ་ཚ་ཁྲེལ་མེད་.

ངོ་ཚ་དམའ་འབེབས་ (ŋotsa māmbeb) embarrassing and defaming; va.—བྱེད་.

ངོ་ཚ་སྨིན་པོ་ (ŋotsa mīmbu) 1. a shy person. 2. sb. who is easily embarrassed/ ashamed, sb. who is very sensitive.

ངོ་ཚ་ཞེ་ཁྲེལ་མེད་པ་ (ŋotsa shedree meèba) sm. ངོ་ཚ་རྒྱུ་མེད་.

ངོ་ཚ་རང་ཉོ་ (ŋotsa raŋño) making a fool of oneself, bringing shame/ disgrace on oneself.

ངོ་ཚ་ལྷུང་ལངས་ (ŋotsa lūŋlaŋ) vi. to become angry from being embarrassed.

ངོ་ཚན་ (ŋotsɛn) sm. གདོང་ཚན་.

ངོ་ཚབ་ (ŋotsəb) agent, representative; va.—གཏོང་ to send as a representative/ agent; va.—བྱེད་ to act as a representative/ agent ¶ རྒྱ་གར་དུ་ཡོད་པའི་རྒྱ་དམར་གྱི་ངོ་ཚབ་ The Red Chinese representative in India.

ངོ་མཚང་འབྲུ་ (ŋotsaŋ dru) va. to expose an error/ fault.

ངོ་མཚར་ (ŋotsar) miraculous, wondrous, marvelous.

ངོ་མཚར་ཅན་ (ŋotsarjɛn) miraculous, wondrous, marvelous ¶ མི་ཡུལ་གྱི་བྱས་རྗེས་ངོ་མཚར་ཅན་ A miraculous human accomplishment.

ངོ་མཚར་ཆེན་པོ་ (ŋotsar cēmbo) wondrous, marvelous.

ངོ་མཚར་པོ་ (ŋo tsābo) handsome, good-looking, beautiful.

ངོ་མཚར་ཟླ་མེད་ (ŋotsa dameè) supreme, unequaled, unrivaled.

ངོ་འཚལ་ (ŋo tsɛɛ) sm. ངོ་ཤེས་.

ངོ་འཚོ་ (ŋo tsō) sm. ངོ་འཛིན་.

ངོ་འཛིན་ (ŋundzin) sm. ངོ་སྤྲོད་, 1.

ངོ་འཛིན་ཟོལ་འཛུགས (ŋundzin sönjoò) sm. ངོ་འཛིན་.

ངོ་འཛུམ་ (ŋo dzum) sm. ངོ་དཀར་.

ངོ་འཛུམ་དཀར་པ་ (ŋodzum gāābo) a smiling face.

ངོ་འཛུམ་དཀར་ནག (ŋo dzum gārnag) expressing happiness and sadness, expressing anger and joy.

ངོ་འཛུམ་གདོང་ནག (ŋo dzum dīŋnag) a smiling face with evil intent.

ངོ་འཛོམས་ (ŋodzom) getting together (in person), several people meeting face-to-face; va.—བྱེད་.

ངོ་རྫུན་བརྗེ་ (ŋodzün je) va. to exchange the original/ genuine/ authentic one with a false one.

ངོ་ཟིལ་ (ŋosil) healthy looking (face).

ངོ་ཟུམ་ (ŋo sum) va. to look stern, to show anger facially.

ངོ་ཟློག (ŋo dɔɔ) refusing sb.'s request; va.—བྱེད་ ¶ ཁོས་ངའི་རེ་འདུན་ལ་ངོ་ཟློག་བྱས་བྱུང་ He refused my request.

ངོ་ཡ་ (ŋoya) sm. ཁ་ཡ་.

ངོ་ཡོད་ (ŋoyöö) present, in person ¶ འཐུས་མི་ངོ་ཡོད་ཐག་གཅོད་གནང་གི་ཡོད་པ་རེད་ The representatives who are present are making the decision.

ངོ་ཡོད་ངོ་དང་ ངོ་མེད་རིན་ (ŋöyöö ŋodaŋ ŋomeè rin) shung. replacing (a lost item) or if one can not find a replacement then substitute with something else (e.g., money) ¶ དངོས་ཐོར་ཉེ་བག་མེད་པ་སྤྲོད་རྒྱུར་བསྟུད་ཕྱིན་ངོ་ཡོད་ངོ་དང་ ངོ་མེད་རིན་འབབ་བཅས་སྤྲོད་ལེན་དགོས་རྒྱུ་ In accordance with the list, one should find a replacement for the items, and if not, should find a substitute (e.g., money).

ངོ་གཡོག (ŋoyɔɔ) master and servant.

ངོ་རིས་ (ŋorii) face.

ངོ་རིས་དཔྱད་ (ŋorii jɛɛ) va. to examine the face and wrinkles to tell fortunes.

ངོ་རེ་གནོངས་ (ŋore nōŋ) sm. ངོ་གནོངས་.

ངོ་རེ་ཚ་ (ŋore tsā) vi. to be embarrassed.

ངོ་ལ་ལྟ་ (ŋola dā) 1. to take into account sb.'s feelings ¶ ཁོ་ལ་ཁྲིམས་གཅོད་བྱེད་དགོས་ཀྱང་ཁྱེད་རང་གི་ངོ་ལ་བལྟས་ནས་བྱེད་ཀྱི་མིན་ (I) should punish him, but taking you into account, I won't. 2. doing sth. because of friendship or a relationship; doing sth. to save the feelings/ face of another.

ངོ་ལག་ཁྲུས་ཆུ་ (ŋolaà trüüju) water for washing face and hands.

ངོ་ལབ་ཤག་ལབ་ (ŋoləb pāgləb) talking behind sb.'s back and talking face-to-face.

ངོ་ལམ་ངོ་རྒྱུད་ (ŋolam ŋōgyüü) doing sth. through a friend of a friend.

ངོ་ལས་ (ŋolɛɛ̀) the leader and the staff/ officials ¶ མདོ་སྤྱི་ངོ་ལས་ས་གནས་སུ་ཕེབས་འབྱོར་བྱུང་འཕྲལ་ As soon as the Governor of Kham and his staffs arrived there.

ངོ་ལས་རྗེས་འབྲངས་ (ŋolɛɛ̀ jeèdraŋ) leaders, officials/ workers and followers.

ངོ་ལེན་ (ŋolen) sm. སྣ་ལེན་.

ངོ་ལོག་ (ŋoloò) rebellion, revolt, uprising; va.—རྒྱག་; —བྱེད་ to rebel, to revolt, to rise up against ¶ སྲིད་གཞུང་ལ་ངོ་ལོག་རྒྱག་རྒྱུའི་གློག་གྲོས་བྱས་ཡོད་པ་རེད་ They plotted to rebel against the government.

ངོ་ལོག་འཁྲུག་ཟིང་ (ŋoloò trūgsiŋ) sm. ངོ་ལོག་ཟིང་འཁྲུག.

ངོ་ལོག་རྒྱབ་གཏོད་ (ŋoloò gyəbdöö) treachery, treason; va.—བྱེད་.

ངོ་ལོག་ཇག་ཀུན་ (ŋoloò jəggün) rebel bandit.

ངོ་ལོག་ཇག་པ་ (ŋoloò jagba) sm. ངོ་ལོག་ཇག་ཀུན.

ངོ་ལོག་ཇུས་འགོད་ (ŋoloò jüügüü) plotting/ planning a rebellion.

ངོ་ལོག་པ་ (ŋologba) rebel, renegade, mutineer.

ངོ་ལོག་དམག་མི་ (ŋoloò māāmi) rebellious or mutinous soldier.

ངོ་ལོག་ཟིང་འཁྲུག (ŋoloò siŋdru) revolt, rebellion, insurrection; vi.—ལངས་ to have a revolt/ rebellion/ insurrection break out. va.—རྒྱག to revolt/ rebel.

ངོ་ལོག་ཟིང་འཁྲུག་པ་ (ŋoloò siŋdrubə) rebel.

ངོ་ལོག་གསང་འཛོང་ (ŋoloò sāŋdzoŋ) betraying, selling out; va.—རྒྱག.

ངོ་ཤ་སྨིན་པོ་ (ŋosha mi̋mbo) sm. ངོ་ཚ་སྨིན་པོ་.

ངོ་ཤིག (ŋoshii) a facial disease characterized by lots of pimples.

ངོ་ཤེས་ (ŋosheè) vi. to know, to be acquainted with, to recognize; va.—གཏོང་ to make friends, to introduce (people); va.—སྤྲོག to make known to each other, to introduce to one another ¶ ཁོ་ངས་ངོ་ཤེས་ཀྱི་མེད་ I don't know him. ¶ ཁོས་ང་ཐག་རིང་པོ་ནས་ངོ་ཤེས་སོང་ He recognized me from far away. ¶ ཁོས་གྲོང་པ་མང་ཆེ་བ་ངོ་ཤེས་བཏང་བ་རེད་ He made friends with most of the neighbors.

ངོ་ཤེས་འགབ་མཐུན་ (ŋosheè gəbdün) secret sexual intercourse between acquaintances.

ངོ་ཤེས་འདྲིས་གྲོགས་ (ŋosheè triidrog) friends and acquaintances

ངོ་ཤེས་པ་ (ŋosheèba) an acquaintance.

ངོ་ཤོར་ (ŋo shɔ̄ɔ) vi. to lose face.

ངོ་བཤུས་ (ŋoshüü) copying, transcribing, duplicating; va.—བྱེད་; —རྒྱག.

ངོ་བཤུས་འཁྲུལ་མེད་ (ŋoshüü trüümeè) shung. a real/ genuine copy.

ངོ་སོ་ (ŋoso) 1. respect, appreciation, praise; va.—བསྟོད་ to praise, to express respect/ appreciation; —འཁྱེར་ to feel grateful to sb., to appreciate sb.'s kindness ¶ ཁོར་ཡག་པོ་བྱས་ཀྱང་ངོ་སོ་མི་འདུག Even though (I am) good to him (he) has no respect (appreciation) for me. 2. taking credit for sb.'s work/ idea; va.—འཁྱེར་ ¶ དེ་རིང་ལས་ཀ་འདི་ངས་བྱས་ཀྱང་ངོ་སོ་ཁོས་ཁྱེར་སོང་ Although I did the work today, he took the credit (for it). 3. reminding sb. what you did for them; making too much (a big deal) out of help/ aid/ favors; va.—གཏོང་; —ཤོད་ ¶ ཨུ་རུ་སུས་ཀྲུང་གོར་རོགས་བྱེད་དུས་ངོ་སོ་ཞེ་དྲག་བཏང་བ་རེད་ When the Russians helped China they reminded them of what they did a lot. ¶ ཁོས་རོགས་དོག་ཙམ་བྱས་ཀྱང་ངོ་སོ་ཆེན་པོ་གཏོང་གི་འདུག Even though he helps only a little, he makes a big deal out of it. 5. making use of another's name for sth. ¶ ཡིད་བཞིན་ནོར་བུའི་ངོ་སོ་འཁྱེར་ནས་ཨ་རི་སྲིད་གཞུང་ནས་དངུལ་གཡར་པ་རེད་ Making use of the Dalai Lama's name, (they) borrowed money from the American Government. 6. an achievement/ accomplishment, good work that produces a good reputation; vi.—ཐོན་ to have a good result, to be successful, to have a beneficial outcome ¶ སྤྲང་པོར་རོགས་བྱས་ན་ངོ་སོ་ཡོང་གི་རེད་ If you help the beggars you will get a good reputation. ¶ ཁོའི་ལས་ཀ་ངོ་སོ་ཐོན་པ་རེད་ His work was successful.

ངོ་སོ་ཆེན་པོ་ (ŋoso cēmbo) respected, appreciated.

ངོ་སོ་བསྟོད་ (ŋoso dȍȍ) see ངོ་སོ་.

ངོ་སོ་ཐོན་པོ་ (ŋoso tȍmbo) 1. beneficial, having a good result ¶ སྨན་དེ་ངོ་སོ་ཐོན་པོ་བྱུང་སོང་ The medicine was beneficial. 2. (with regards to gifts) just what the person wanted.

ངོ་སོ་སྣོམ་(བསྣམས་) (ŋoso nōm) va. to feel grateful to sb., to be appreciative (h.).

ངོ་སོང་འཕྲོས་ (ŋosoŋ trȍȍ) shung. a leftover of sth. spent ¶ ཟླ་ཕོགས་ཇ་འདི་ནས་ངོ་སོང་འཕྲོས་ The leftover of the monthly tea salary.

ངོ་སོར་ལྟ་ (ŋosor dā) va. to do sth. thinking you will get acclaim/ recognition ¶ རོགས་རམ་བྱེད་དུས་ངོ་སོར་ལྟ་རྒྱུ་ཡོད་པ་མ་རེད་ When helping (others) you shouldn't look for recognition.

ངོ་སྲུང་ (ŋosuŋ) 1. saving face, not embarrassing; va.—བྱེད་ ¶ ནོར་འཁྲུལ་རྣམས་གསལ་ཇེན་དུ་བཏོན་པ་ལས་ངོ་སྲུང་བྱེད་རྒྱུ་མེད་ (We) must expose (their) mistakes not save face (for them). 2. agreeing with sb. due to their superior position ¶ རང་ཉིད་ཀྱི་ལྟ་བ་མཐའ་འཁྱོངས་བྱེད་དགོས་པ་ལས་མི་གཞན་དག་གི་ངོ་སྲུང་བྱེད་རྒྱུ་མེད་ One should continue doing things according to one's own view rather than agree with another because of his superior position.

ངོ་སྲུང་ཁ་གསག (ŋosuŋ kāsaà) flattery, sycophancy.

ངོ་སྲུང་མཐུན་འཇུག (ŋosuŋ tűnjuù) sm. ངོ་སྲུང་.

ངོ་གསུམ་འཛོམས་ (ŋosum dzom) three people meeting together.

ངོག་ན་ (ŋogna) arc. sm. སོང་ན་.

ངོགས་ (ŋɔɔ̀) shore, bank.

ངོམ་: p. ངོམས་; f. ངོམ་; imp. ངོམས་ (ŋom) 1. vi. to be satisfied/ satiated/ quenched (thirst). 2. va. to show off, to act ostentatious ¶ ཁོ་རྒྱུ་ནོར་ངོམ་པར་དགའ་པོ་འདུག He likes to show off his wealth. 3. using sb.'s name for one's own gain ¶ ཏ་ལའི་བླ་མ་ངོམ་ནས་ཁྲིམས་མེད་ལུགས་མེད་བྱས་པ་རེད་ Using the name of the Dalai Lama, he acted lawlessly.

ངོམ་ཁྱེར་ (ŋom kyēr) showing off; va.—བྱེད་.

ངོམ་ངོམ་བྱེད་ (ŋomŋom chɛɛ̀) sm. ངོམ་, 2.

ངོམ་འཕྱར་ (ŋomjar) showing off, flaunting; va.—བྱེད་.

ངོམ་འཕྱར་ཁྲེལ་མེད་ (ŋomjar trēēmeè) shamelessly showing off.

ངོམ་བཟོ་ (ŋomso) showing off, flaunting, bragging; va.—རྒྱག་; —འཕྱར་; —སྐྱེལ་; —བྱེད་; —སྟོན་.

ངོམ་ཟིལ་ (ŋomsil) sm. ངོམ་བཟོ་.

ངོམ་སོ་ (ŋomso) sm. ངོམ་བཟོ་.

ངོམས་ (ŋom) 1. p. of ངོམ་. 2. vi. to be satiated/ quenched ¶ ཆུ་ངོམས་པར་བཏུང་བ་རེད་ (He) drank until satiated.

ངོམས་རྒྱུ་མེད་པ་ (ŋomgyu meèba) sm. ངོམས་མེད་.

ངོམས་པ་མེད་པ་ (ŋomba meèba) sm. ངོམས་མེད་.

ངོམས་མེད་ (ŋommeè) unquenchable, insatiable.

ངོམས་ཡག་མེད་པ་ (ŋomyaà meèba) sm. ངོམས་མེད་.

ངོམས་སེམས་ (ŋomsem) satisfaction, satiation, quenchment.

ངོའི་དབང་རྩ་ (ŋöö wāŋdza) facial nerve.

ངོའོ་ (ŋowo) sm.* ངོ་བོ་.

ངོར་ (ŋɔr) in the face (of), in person, in front of.

ངོར་ལྡང་ (ŋɔrdaŋ) va. to be proud/ arrogant.

ངོས་ (ŋöö) 1. I ¶ ངོས་འདི་ཕྱོགས་མགྱོགས་པོ་ཡོང་གི་ཡིན་ I am coming here soon. 2. side, direction ¶ ཤར་ངོས་ནས་ From the eastern side. ¶ རྒྱ་རིགས་ཀྱི་ངོས་

ནས་བཤད་ན་ If we say it from the side (point of view) of the Chinese. 3. the surface or face of sth. ༑ རྩིག་པའི་ངོས་ཀྱི་རི་མོ་དེ་ཚོ་ The paintings on the surface of the wall. ༑ རྒྱ་མཚོའི་ངོས་ལས་ From or above sea level.

ངོས་འགྲོ་རྡོག་སྐོར་ (ŋöndro dɔɔgɔɔ) shung. investigation done personally/ on the spot. ཕན་ཚུན་ས་བརྗེས་བྱས་པའི་ཁེ་གྱོང་ཡོད་མེད་ཞིབ་རྟོགས་ངོས་འགྲོ་རྡོག་སྐོར་བྱས་ In order to find out if there are any gains or losses regarding exchanging the land, the investigation was done personally on the spot.

ངོས་ཅག (ŋöjaà) we, our ༑ ངོས་ཅག་ལྷ་ས་ནས་ཡོང་དུས་ When we came from Lhasa.

ངོས་ཚོད་ (ŋocöö) sm. ངོ་ཚོད་.

ངོས་མཇལ་ (ŋönjɛɛ) meeting in person; va.—ཞུ་ to meet/ see (in person) ༑ ངོས་མཇལ་སྐབས་བཀའ་མོལ་བྱུང་དོན་བཞིན་ As per our conversation when we met in person.

ངོས་འཇམ་ (ŋönjam) sm. ངོས་འཇམ་པོ་.

ངོས་འཇམ་པོ་ (ŋöö jambo) smooth surface.

ངོས་འཇམ་པོའི་ཚད་ (ŋöö jambö tsɛ̄ɛ) the degree of smoothness.

ངོས་འཇམ་འོད་འཚེར་ (ŋönjam wöndro) smooth and shinny/ glistening/ glittering.

ངོས་མཉམ་ (ŋönñam) even or level (surface).

ངོས་མཉམ་མེ་ལོང་ (ŋönñam meloŋ) a plane mirror (in physics).

ངོས་མཉམ་དར་སྡིགས་ (ŋönñam dardeg) surface grinder, flat grinder.

ངོས་ཉེས་པོ་ (ŋöö ñeèbo) ugly.

ངོས་སྙོམས་ (ŋöö ñōm) 1. va. to make level/ even. 2. a level/even surface.

ངོས་སྙོམས་ལྷ་ཆས་ (ŋöñom dājɛɛ) a gauge to determine if sth. is level.

ངོས་སྙོམས་དབྱིབས་རྩིས་ (ŋöñom yibdzii) plane geometry (math).

ངོས་བརྟག (ŋöö dāà) va. to examine.

ངོས་ཐུག (ŋöö tūù) va. to meet in person, to meet face-to-face.

ངོས་ནས་བཤད་ན་ (ŋöönɛ shɛ̄ɛna) from (sb.'s) point of view.

ངོས་སྤྲོད་ (ŋöö dröö) va. to introduce sb. in person.

ངོས་ཕྱོགས་ (ŋöjɔɔ) edge, side, bank (of river).

ངོས་འཕྲད་ (ŋöndrɛɛ̀) meeting in person, meeting face-to-face.

ངོས་བླངས་ (ŋöö lāŋ) 1. p. of ངོས་ལེན་. 2. sm. ངོས་ལེན་.

ངོས་འབྱོར་ (ŋönjɔr) sm. ངོ་བཅར་.

ངོས་སྦྱོར་ (ŋöjɔr) recommending, introducing ༑ ངོས་སྦྱོར་གྱི་ཡི་གེ་ A letter of recommendation/ introduction.

ངོས་མ་ཕྱོག་པ་ (ŋöö majogba) sm. ངོས་མ་ཐོག་པ་.

ངོས་མང་གི་གཟུགས་ (ŋömaŋgi sūg) polyhedron.

ངོས་མི་ལེན་ (ŋöö milen) va. to deny, to not accept/ admit/ acknowledge ༑ ཁོ་ཚོ་ཇག་ལོག་རྒྱག་པ་དང་འབྲེལ་བ་ངོས་མ་བླངས་པ་རེད་ They denied having any relations with the rebel bandits.

ངོས་ཚོ་ (ŋöndzo) we.

ངོས་ཚོགས་ (ŋöndzoò) advance/ front force or unit.

ངོས་འཛིན་ (ŋündzin) 1. recognizing, regarding, accepting; va. ངོས་འཛིན་; va.—བྱེད་ to recognize, to regard, to accept, to identify ༑ ངས་ཁོ་པར་གྱི་ནང་ལ་མི་དེ་ངོས་འཛིན་ཐུབ་མ་བྱུང་ I was unable to recognize him in the photograph. ༑ བཟོ་པ་ཚོས་ཁོང་འགོ་ཁྲིད་ཡག་པོ་ཞིག་ལ་ངོས་བཟུང་བ་རེད་ The workers accepted/ regarded him as a good leader. ༑ ཁོ་སྤྲུལ་སྐུ་ཡིན་པ་མི་ཚང་མས་ངོས་འཛིན་བྱེད་ཀྱི་ཡོད་པ་རེད་ Everyone recognizes him as a incarnate lama. ༑ རྒྱ་གར་གཞུང་གིས་གཞུང་འདི་ངོས་འཛིན་བྱེད་བཟོ་མེད་པ་རེད་ It doesn't seem like the Indian government will recognize this government. 2. va. to know, to understand ༑ ཁོས་དཔྱ་ཁྲལ་སྤྲོད་སྟངས་སྐོར་ངོས་འཛིན་ཐུབ་མེད་པ་རེད་ He wasn't able to understand how to pay the taxes. ༑ ལས་འགུལ་འདིའི་ནང་ལ་ཁོར་ངོས་འཛིན་གསལ་པོ་ཡོད་པ་མ་རེད་ He doesn't understand clearly about this campaign. 3. opinion, view ༑ ངའི་ངོས་འཛིན་དེ་ག་རང་ཡིན་ My opinion is exactly that.

ངོས་འཛིན་ཁས་ལེན་ (ŋündzin kēlen) sm. ངོས་འཛིན་, 1.

ངོས་འཛིན་འཁྲུལ་ (ŋündzin trüū) 1. vi. to misunderstand. 2. vi. to err in recognizing a reincarnation.

ངོས་འཛིན་གཅིག་གྱུར་ (ŋündzin jiggyur) complete agreement with regard to a position/ view/ doctrine.

ངོས་འཛིན་རྩིས་ལེན་ (ŋündzin dzīlen) sm. ངོས་འཛིན་.

ངོས་འཛིན་ཕྱོགས་རེ་བ་ (ŋündzin cɔɔrewa) looking at/ considering only one side of sth. (a situation/ person/ question), a biased or unbalanced view of a situation, an unbalanced perspective; va.—བྱེད་ ༑ དེས་པ་ལ་ངོས་འཛིན་ཕྱོགས་རེ་བ་བྱེད་མི་རུང་ You should not have a biased view of a situation.

ངོས་འཛིན་བྱས་འཐུས་ཡོང་འགྲོ་ (ŋündzin cɛ̀ɛdüü yoŋdro) shung. can be recognized as an incarnation ༑ ཏཱ་ལའི་བླ་མ་རིན་པོ་ཆེའི་མཆོག་སྤྲུལ་དུ་ངོས་འཛིན་བྱས་འཐུས་ཡོང་འགྲོ་ཞེས་བཀའ་བཞིས་བཟང་པོ་ཐོབ་ We got the approval, saying that (he) can be recognized as the reincarnation of the Dalai Lama.

ངོས་ཞིང་ (ŋöshiŋ) a field on a slope/ hill.

ངོས་བཞེས་ (ŋöö sheè) h. of ངོས་ལེན་.

ངོས་ཟིན་ (ŋösin) 1. vi. to recognize/ identify ༑ མིང་དེ་ངོས་ཟིན་ནས་ Having recognized the name. 2. vi. to understand, to comprehend.

ངོས་གཟུང་ (ŋöö suŋ) f. of ངོས་འཛིན་.

ངོས་བཟུང་ (ŋöö suŋ) p. of ངོས་འཛིན་.

ངོས་ར་ (ŋööra) we, our ༑ ངོས་རའི་དམག་མི་ Our soldiers.

ངོས་རང་ (ŋööraŋ) 1. I myself, my. 2. our.

ངོས་རོལ་ (ŋöröö) sm. ངོས་.

ངོས་ལ་ (ŋööla) in front of, face-to-face, in person.

ངོས་ལམ་ (ŋöölam) sm. ལམ་ཡིག.

ངོས་ལེན་ (ŋöölen) confession, acknowledgment; va. ངོས་ལེན་; —བྱེད་ to confess/ admit/ accept/ acknowledge, to confess ༑ ཁོས་ཇ་ལོག་པ་དང་ལག་འབྲེལ་བྱས་པ་ངོས་ལེན་བྱས་པ་རེད་ He admitted that he collaborated with the rebels. ༑ དེ་མགོ་བཏགས་ཡིན་པའི་ངོས་ལེན་གྱི་ཡོད་པ་མ་རེད་ (They) do not accept it as surrender. 2. sm. ངོས་འཛིན་.

ངོས་ལེན་གྱི་ཞུ་ཡིག (ŋöölengi shuyig) 1. written confession/ admission. 2. written deposition (in law).

ངོས་ལེན་སྐྱོན་འཛུགས་ (ŋöölen ñōmdzuù) accusing sb. in one's own confession.

ངོས་ལེབ་དར་སྡིགས་ (ŋöleb dardeg) surface grinder, flat grinder.

ངོས་ཤེས་ (ŋööshee) sm. ངོ་ཤེས་.

ངོས་བཤེར་ (ŋöösher) confronting an opponent in a dispute face-to-face; va.—རྒྱག་; —བྱེད་; —གཏོང་.

ངོས་སུ་ (ŋöösu) in front of, openly, frankly.

དངགས་ (ŋāà) sm. ངག.

དངངས་ (ŋāŋ) vi. to gasp (from surprise/ fear/ shock) ༑ ས་གཡོས་རྒྱག་སྐབས་དངངས་བྱུང་ I gasped when the earthquake (suddenly occurred).

དངངས་སྐྲག (ŋāmdraà) terror, fear, dread, fright, panic; vi.—བྱེད་ to be afraid, to be frightened; to dread; vi.—ལང་; —སྐྱེ་ to become/ get afraid/ frightened.

དངངས་སྐྲག་ཐེ་ཚོམ་ (ŋāmdraà tēdzom) fearing and doubtful; va.—བྱེད་.

དངངས་སྐྲག་ཚབ་ཚུབ་ (ŋāmdraà tsəbdzub) being afraid and nervous.

དངངས་འདྲོག་སྐྱེ་ (ŋāmdrog) vi. sm. དངངས་སྐྲག.

དངངས་འདར་ (ŋāŋdar) shivering with fear; vi.—རྒྱག.

དངངས་འཚབ་ (ŋāŋtsəp) 1. sm. དངངས་སྐྲག. 2. anxious, worried.

དངན་འཐེན་ (ŋɛ̄nden) misappropriation, mishandling of money or things of others; va.—བྱེད་.

དངན་པ་འཐེན་ (ŋɛ̄mba tēn) va. to misappropriate/ mishandle money or things of others.

དངར་ (ŋār) va. to arrange (well/ neatly) ¶ ཚར་དུ་དངར་ To arrange nicely in a line.

དངར་ཁ་ (ŋārga) a line, a queue.

དངར་རོ་ (ŋārro) the part of the flower where bees gather honey.

དངུད་མོ་ (ŋüümo) sm. ངུད་མོ་.

དངུལ་ (ŋüü) 1. silver. ¶ དངུལ་གྱི་རྣ་རྒྱན་ A silver earring. 2. money, currency ¶ བོད་དངུལ་ Tibetan money (traditional Tibetan currency units = 10 སྐར་(མ་) = 1 ཞོ་; 10 ཞོ་ = 1 སྲང་; 50 སྲང་ = 1རྡོ་ཚད་); va.—གཏོང་ to use/ spend money ¶ དེ་དོན་དུ་གཞུང་གིས་དངུལ་འབོར་ཆེན་བཏང་སོང་ The government spent a lot of money for that purpose.

དངུལ་ཀོང་ (ŋüügoŋ) a silver "butter" lamp.

དངུལ་ཀྱག (ŋüügyaà) a silver stand (for cups).

དངུལ་དཀར་ (ŋüügaa) a silver bowl/ cup.

དངུལ་སྐར་མ་ (ŋüü gārma) the smallest denomination of Tibetan currency, see དངུལ་.

དངུལ་སྐུ་ (ŋüügu) a silver statue.

དངུལ་སྐུད་ (ŋüügüü) 1. silver thread, silver wire. 2. a kind of herbal medicine.

དངུལ་སྐུར་ (ŋüü gūr) va. to send/ remit money.

དངུལ་རྐྱང་ (ŋüügyaŋ) 1. pure silver. 2. hard cash.

དངུལ་རྐྱན་ (ŋüügyɛn) a type of large silver pot with a large mouth that is used for beer.

དངུལ་སྐྱེད་ (ŋüügyeè) interest (on loans).

དངུལ་སྐྱོགས་ (ŋüügyɔɔ̀) a silver ladle.

དངུལ་ཁ་ (ŋüüga) 1. silver mine. 2. a silver rim/ border on a wooden bowl.

དངུལ་ཁ་མ་ (ŋüü kāma) a wooden bowl with a silver rim/ border.

དངུལ་ཁང་ (ŋüügaŋ) a bank.

དངུལ་ཁུག (ŋüüguù) a money purse/ belt, a wallet.

དངུལ་ཁུག་ཐང་པོ་ (ŋüüguù tāŋbo) having a lot of money.

དངུལ་ཁོངས་ཁ་སྒྱུར་ (ŋüügoŋ kāgyur) transferring a bank account; va.—བྱེད་.

དངུལ་ཁྱད་ (ŋüügyɛɛ̀) a fraction (of a dollar, etc.).

དངུལ་འཁྲོལ་ (ŋüüdröö) leftover money, money balance, spare money ¶ རྗེས་སུ་དངུལ་འཁྲོལ་བྱུང་མཚམས་ཚབ་རྒྱུན་ངེས་འབུལ་ཞུ་འཇུས་ཆོག་པ་ཞུ་རྒྱུ་ In the future, whenever I have spare money I will pay the loan.

དངུལ་གྱི་ཁུ་བས་བྱུག་པ་ (ŋüügi kūwɛ jugbə) everywhere is covered with a layer of snow [Lit. like applying liquid silver].

དངུལ་གྱི་འཇའ་ (ŋüügi dza) the value/ rate of a currency.

དངུལ་གྱིས་ཤན་ (ŋüügi shɛ̄n) banded with silver bands (e.g., a wooden bowls).

དངུལ་གྲངས་ (ŋüüdraŋ) amount of money.

དངུལ་མགར་ (ŋüügar) silversmith.

དངུལ་མགུ་མོ་ (ŋüü gumu) shung. silver coins.

དངུལ་འགྱངས་ (ŋüügyaŋ) deferred (payment of money).

དངུལ་འགྱེད་ (ŋüügyeè) a donation in money/ cash.

དངུལ་འགྲུལ་ (ŋündrüü) a money order, money exchange/ transfer; va.—གཏོང་ to exchange currency/ money, to send a money order.

དངུལ་འགྲུལ་གཏོང་གླ་ (ŋündrüü dōŋla) the fee for sending a money order.

དངུལ་འགྲུལ་འཛིན་ཡིག (ŋündrüü dzinyig) a money order, a bank draft.

དངུལ་རྒྱན་ (ŋüügyɛn) silver ornamentation on wooden drinking bowls; va.—རྒྱག.

དངུལ་སྒམ་ (ŋüügam) a money or cash box.

དངུལ་སྒོར་ (ŋüügɔɔ) a silver dollar.

དངུལ་སྒྱུར་གཏོང་ (ŋüügyur dōŋ) va. to change/ convert sth. into money ¶ ཁོས་འབྲུ་དངུལ་སྒྱུར་བཏང་སོང་ He converted the grain into money.

དངུལ་སྒྱུར་འཛིན་ (ŋüügyur dzin) a receipt for money changed.

དངུལ་ངན་པོ་ (ŋüü ŋɛmbo) silver mixed/ alloyed with other metals.

དངུལ་དངོས་ (ŋüüŋöö) money and goods/ things.

དངུལ་བཅོལ་ (ŋüü jöö) 1. va. to deposit money, to put money in the bank. 2. a deposit (in a bank).

དངུལ་བཅོལ་ཁང་ (ŋüüjögaŋ) bank.

དངུལ་བཅོལ་བའི་འཛིན་ཡིག (ŋüüjöwɛ dzinyii) bank passbook.

དངུལ་ཆད་ (ŋüüjɛɛ̀) 1. a fine (in money); va.—འགེལ་; —གཅོད་ to fine (in money) ¶ སྤྱི་པའི་ལས་ཀར་འགྲོ་མ་ཐུབ་ན་དངུལ་ཆད་སྤྲོད་དགོས་རེད་ If (one) can't go to communal work (one) has to pay a fine in money. 2. a deficit/ shortage in a payment.

དངུལ་ཆས་ (ŋüüjɛɛ̀) silverware.

དངུལ་ཆུ་ (ŋüüju) mercury.

དངུལ་ཆུ་གྲང་འདུལ་ (ŋüüju traŋdüü) cold smelted mercury.

དངུལ་ཆུ་ཚ་འདུལ་ (ŋüüju tsəndüü) heat smelted mercury.

ངུལ་ཆུའི་རླུང་གནོན་དཔྱད་ཆས་ (ŋüüjü lüŋnün jɛ̀ɛ̀cɛɛ̀) mercury barometer.

དངུལ་ཆོས་ (ŋüüjüü) a religious scripture written in silver.

དངུལ་འཇུག (ŋüü juù) sm. དངུལ་བཅོལ་.

དངུལ་འཇོག (ŋüü jɔɔ̀) va. to deposit money.

དངུལ་འཇོག་མཁན་ (ŋüü jɔnñɛn) a depositor (of money).

དངུལ་བརྗེ་ (ŋüü je) sm. དངུལ་བརྗེས་.

དངུལ་བརྗེས་ (ŋüü jeè) changing/ exchanging money; va.—གཏོང་ to change/ exchange money.

དངུལ་བརྗེས་གཏོང་གླ་ (ŋüüjeè dōŋla) fee for changing/ exchanging money.

དངུལ་བརྗེས་འཛིན་ཡིག (ŋüüjeè dzinyii) check, money order, bank draft.

དངུལ་གཉེར་ (ŋüüñer) 1. taking care of money, bookkeeping, accounting; va.—བྱེད་. 2. an accountant, cashier, bookkeeper, teller.

དངུལ་གཉེར་པ་ (ŋüüñerba) accountant, bookkeeper, cashier, teller.

དངུལ་ཏིག (ŋüüdig) a type of herbal medicine.

དངུལ་ཏིང་ (ŋüüdiŋ) silver chalice/ cup.

དངུལ་ཏིབ་ (ŋüüdib) a silver vessel with a spout.

དངུལ་ཏིལ་ (ŋüüdee) silver brand used for moxibustion.

དངུལ་ཏམ་ (ŋüüdram) a Tibetan silver coin (tranka).

དངུལ་གཏེར་ (ŋüüder) silver mine.

དངུལ་གཏོང་ (ŋüü dōŋ) see དངུལ་.

དངུལ་གཏོང་ཁའི་ (ŋüü dōŋkāwo) loan section/ unit.

དངུལ་གཏོང་གླ་ (ŋüü dōŋla) the fee for sending money.

དངུལ་གཏོང་ས་ (ŋüü dōŋsa) the money order section of the post office.

དངུལ་གཏོར་ (ŋüü dɔ̄r) sm. དངུལ་སྟོར་.

དངུལ་གཏོར་སྐྱེལ་བྱེད་ (ŋüüdɔr gyējeè) spending money like a spend thrift.

དངུལ་རྟ་རྨིག་མ་ (ŋüüda mīgmə) a silver ingot; an ancient Chinese silver coin shaped like a horse hoof.

དངུལ་རྟེན་ (ŋüüden) a money deposit.

དངུལ་ལྟིར་ (ŋüüdir) sm. དངུལ་ཏིབ་.

དངུལ་སྟོར་ (ŋüü dɔ̄r) to spend money extravagantly, to waste/ squander money.

དངུལ་བརྟིམས་ཚག་མ་ (ŋüüdim tsāgma) silver bas-relief carving.

དངུལ་ཐག (ŋüüdaà) silver chain.

དངུལ་ཐང་ (ŋüüdaŋ) the value of money/ currency, the exchange rate of a currency ¶ དེང་སང་དངུལ་ཐང་ཆེན་པོ་ཡོད་པ་རེད་ The value of money is high these days.

དངུལ་ཐལ་ (ŋüütɛɛ) silver ash used in medicine.

དངུལ་ཐུམ་ (ŋüüdum) a gift in which the money is wrapped in a traditionally folded white cloth.

དངུལ་སྦུར་ (ŋǖǖdur) silver spoon.

དངུལ་སྒོ་ཟུར་གསལ་ (ŋǖǖto sursɛɛ) shung. as written in a list of gifts of money.

དངུལ་དམ་ (ŋǖǖdam) a seal made of silver.

དངུལ་དུང་ (ŋǖǖduŋ) a silver trumpet/ horn.

དངུལ་དུལ་མ་ (ŋǖǖ düümə) melted/ molten silver.

དངུལ་དོང་ (ŋǖǖdoŋ) shung. silver vessel.

དངུལ་གདུང་ (ŋǖǖduŋ) a silver stupa/ tomb.

དངུལ་མདོག (ŋǖǖdɔɔ̀) silver color.

དངུལ་མདོང་ (ŋǖǖdoŋ) 1. shung. a silver cylinder for keeping documents. 2. a churn with silver bands (around the wood).

དངུལ་འདེད་ (ŋǖǖ teè) shung. va. to chase after money (usu. when trying to collect an outstanding loan).

དངུལ་འདོན་ (ŋǖǖ dön) va. to spend/ use/ give money.

དངུལ་རྡོ་ (ŋǖǖdo) 1. silver nugget. 2. a type of stone used in Tibetan medicine.

དངུལ་རྡོ་ཚད་ (ŋǖǖ dodzɛɛ̀) Tibetan currency unit equal to 50 srang.

དངུལ་རྡོག (ŋǖǖ dog) a piece of silver.

དངུལ་སྡེར་ (ŋǖǖder) a plate made of silver.

དངུལ་ནོར་ (ŋǖǖnɔɔ) money.

དངུལ་པར་ (ŋǖǖbar) sm. དངུལ་དཔར་.

དངུལ་དཔར་ (ŋǖǖbār) printing/ minting money; va.—རྒྱག.

དངུལ་དཔར་ཁང་ (ŋǖǖ bārgaŋ) a mint.

དངུལ་པར་དོ་དམ་ (ŋǖǖbar todam) shung. person in charge of a mint/ treasury.

དངུལ་སྤྱད་ (ŋǖǖjɛɛ̀) silverware.

དངུལ་སྤྱོད་ (ŋǖǖjöö̀) utilization of money.

དངུལ་སྤྲོད་འཛིན་ཤོག (ŋǖǖdröö dzinshoò) a check (for money), a draft, a money order.

དངུལ་ཕག (ŋǖǖbaà) silver bullion brick.

དངུལ་ཕོགས་ (ŋǖǖpɔɔ̀) salary (in cash).

དངུལ་ཕོར་ (ŋǖǖbɔɔ) a silver bowl/ cup.

དངུལ་འཕྲི་ (ŋǖǖ drī) vi. to deduct money, to subtract money.

དངུལ་འཕྲི་འཐེན་ (ŋǖǖ drīden) va. to deduct/ subtract money.

དངུལ་བུན་ (ŋǖǖbün) a loan in money; va.—གཏོང་ to give a loan in money; va.—ལེན་ to take a loan.

དངུལ་བོགས་ (ŋǖǖbɔɔ̀) cash payment made on a lease.

དངུལ་བྲན་ (ŋǖǖdrɛn) sb. who is tight with spending money.

དངུལ་བྲིས་ (ŋǖǖdriì) sm. དངུལ་ཆོས.

དངུལ་འབབ་ (ŋǖmbəb) income, amount (in money).

དངུལ་འབུམ་ (ŋǖǖbum) 1. a silver stupa/ tomb. 2. a religious text written in silver.

དངུལ་འབོར་ (ŋǖmbɔr) amount of money ། དངུལ་ཁང་ལ་དངུལ་འབོར་ཆེན་པོ་བཞག་ཡོད་པ་རེད་ (They) have put a large amount of money in the bank.

དངུལ་སྦྱངས་མ་ (ŋǖǖ jaŋma) pure silver, one hundred percent silver.

དངུལ་སྦྲུལ་ (ŋǖǖdrüü) a kind of silver colored snake found in the Yarlung R. gorge area.

དངུལ་དམར་ (ŋǖǖmar) hard currency, cash.

དངུལ་དམར་རྐྱང་ (ŋǖǖ mārgyaŋ) hard currency, cash.

དངུལ་སྨར་རྐྱང་ (ŋǖǖ mārgyaŋ) sm. དངུལ་དམར་རྐྱང་.

དངུལ་རྩ་ (ŋǖǖdza) 1. finance, capital. 2. an endowment, a fund.

དངུལ་རྩའི་སྒེར་སྡོམ་པ་ཉུང་ཤས་ (ŋǖǖdzɛ gerdomba ñuŋshɛɛ̀) financial oligarch.

དངུལ་རྩིས་བློན་པོ་ (ŋǖǖdzi lōmbo) finance minister.

དངུལ་རྩིས་ལས་ཁུངས་ (ŋǖǖdzi lɛɛ̀guŋ) Ministry of Finance.

དངུལ་ཚག (ŋǖǖdzaà) 1. bas-relief silverwork; va.—རྒྱག. 2. engraving on silver; va.—རྒྱག.

དངུལ་ཚགས་ (ŋǖǖdzaà) sm. དངུལ་ཚག.

དངུལ་ཚད་ (ŋǖǖdzɛɛ̀) shung. a sample of coins.

དངུལ་མཛོད་ (ŋǖmdzöö̀) treasury.

དངུལ་འཛའ་ (ŋǖǖ dza) rate of exchange (of money).

དངུལ་འཛིན་ (ŋǖndzin) 1. money receipt. 2. a check, a bank draft (for money), money order; va.—གཏོང་ to issue a receipt for money, to issue a check/ draft/ money order ། ལས་བྱེད་པའི་ཕོགས་ཀྱི་དངུལ་འཛིན་ཚང་མ་འདི་ནས་གཏོང་གི་ཡོད་པ་རེད་ All the salary checks for the staff are issued from here.

དངུལ་འཛུགས་ (ŋǖǖ dzuù) va. to make a bet, to gamble.

དངུལ་ཞུན་མ་ (ŋǖǖ shumə) molten silver.

དངུལ་བཞག (ŋǖǖshaà) a deposit (in a bank).

དངུལ་ཟིལ་ (ŋǖǖsil) a type of Tibetan medicine.

དངུལ་ཟོ་ (ŋǖǖso) a silver bucket.

དངུལ་བཟོ་ (ŋǖǖsoò) a silversmith.

དངུལ་བཟོ་ (ŋǖǖ so) 1. va. to make money ། ཚོང་ལས་དེ་ནས་དངུལ་ཡག་པོ་བཟོས་ཡོད་པ་རེད་ (They) made good money from that business. 2. va. to make silver/ silverware.

དངུལ་བཟོ་བ་ (ŋǖǖsoò) sm. དངུལ་བཟོ་.

དངུལ་འོ་ཁ་མ་ (ŋǖǖ okāma) whitish silver color.

དངུལ་གཡར་ (ŋǖǖ yāā) va. to borrow money, to lend money.

དངུལ་གཡོ་ (ŋǖǖyo) financial swindle, swindling sb. out of money; va.— ལེན་.

དངུལ་ལུགས་ (ŋǖǖluù) currency system.

དངུལ་ལུགས་མ་ (ŋǖǖ lugmə) silver that has been cast/ molded, silver ingot.

དངུལ་ལེན་ (ŋǖǖ len) 1. va. to collect/ take money. 2. va. to take out/ withdraw money (from a bank account).

དངུལ་ལེབ་ (ŋǖǖleb) paper currency.

དངུལ་ལོར་ (ŋǖǖlɔɔ̀) 1. paper money, paper dollar. 2. currency.

དངུལ་ལོར་རྒྱུན་འཁོར་ (ŋǖǖlɔɔ̀ gyüngɔɔ) currency in circulation.

དངུལ་ལོར་མ་རྩ་ (ŋǖǖlɔɔ̀ madza) financial capital.

དངུལ་ལོར་ཚད་ཡོལ་ (ŋǖǖlɔɔ̀ tsɛ̄yöö) exceeding a limit/ standard in the circulation of money, inflation.

དངུལ་ལོར་ཚོད་མེད་བཀྲམ་པ་ (ŋǖǖlɔɔ̀ tsǖǖmeè drāmba) inflation.

དངུལ་ལོར་ཚོད་མེད་འདོན་པ་ (ŋǖǖlɔɔ tsōmeè tömba) sm. དངུལ་ལོར་ཚོད་མེད་བཀྲམ་པ་.

དངུལ་ལོར་ས་བོགས་ (ŋǖǖlɔɔ̀ sābɔɔ̀) renting/ leasing land for cash (rather than labor).

དངུལ་ཤན་ (ŋǖǖshɛn) silver band (put around churns and other objects to hold them together); va.—རྒྱག.

དངུལ་ཤན་ཅན་ (ŋǖǖ shɛ̄mjɛn) དངུལ་ཤན་མ་.

དངུལ་ཤན་མ་ (ŋǖǖ shɛ̄mmə) wooden bowl covered with silver in the interior as well as part of the exterior.

དངུལ་ཤོག (ŋǖǖshoò) silver foil.

དངུལ་གཤོག་མ་ (ŋǖǖ shɔ̄gma) shung. silver wing attached to a white conch shell.

དངུལ་སིལ་ (ŋǖǖsil) sm. དངུལ་སིལ་མ་.

དངུལ་སིལ་མ་ (ŋǖǖ siīmə) loose change, coins.

དངུལ་སོ་ (ŋǖǖso) silver sheath put over teeth for looks; va.—གཡོགས་ to cover a teeth with a silver sheath.

དངུལ་སྲོལ་ (ŋǖǖsüü) currency system.

དངུལ་གསོག (ŋǖǖsoò) va. to save money, to deposit money ། མོས་དངུལ་མང་པོ་བསགས་པ་རེད་ She has saved a lot of money.

དངུལ་གསོག་ཁང་ (ŋǖǖsogaŋ) bank, savings bank.

དངུལ་གསོག་ཛ་སྣོད་ (ŋǖǖso dzanöö̀) jar/ pot in which money is kept.

དངུལ་བསགས་ (ŋǖǖ sāà) p. of དངུལ་གསོག.

དངུལ་སྲང་ (ŋǖǖsaŋ) silver coin in traditional Tibetan currency.

དངུལ་ཧྲོབ་ཧྲོབ་ (ŋǖǖ hrōbhrob) small pieces of silver.

དངུལ་ལྷད་ཅན་ (ŋǖǖ lhɛ̄jɛn) silver mixed/ alloyed with other metals; silver that is not hundred percent pure.

དངོ་ (ŋō) 1. blade/ edge of knife or sword. 2. shore, bank ¶ ཆུ་དངོ་ River bank.

དངོ་མདུང་ (ŋōduŋ) a kind of spear.

དངོ་བཟོ་ (ŋōso) 1. shoemaking. 2. leatherwork.

དངོ་བཟོ་བ་ (ŋōsowa) 1. cobbler, shoemaker. 2. leather worker.

དངོམ་: p. དངོམས་ (ŋōm) va. to boast, to show off.

དངོམ་ཆེན་པོ་ (ŋōm chēmbo) precious, expensive, costly.

དངོམས་ (ŋōm) p. of དངོམ་.

དངོས་ (ŋȫȫ) real, genuine ¶ ཁོ་ཚོའི་གནས་སྟངས་དངོས་དེ་མཐོང་ཐུབ་པ་རེད་ They saw the real living conditions of those people.

དངོས་སྐྱེས་ (ŋȫȫgyeè) present, gift.

དངོས་སྐྱོང་ (ŋȫȫgyoŋ) directly under the jurisdiction of, directly controlling.

དངོས་སྐྱོང་གྲོང་ཁྱེར་ (ŋȫȫgyoŋ troŋgyer) town/ city directly under the central government.

དངོས་ཁམས་ (ŋȫȫgam) 1. physics. 2. physical.

དངོས་ཁམས་ཀྱི་འགྱུར་བ་ (ŋȫȫgamgyi gyurwə) physical changes.

དངོས་ཁམས་ཀྱི་རིག་པ་ (ŋȫȫgamgyi rigbə) physics.

དངོས་ཁམས་སྡེ་ཁག (ŋȫȫgam degaà) department of physics.

དངོས་ཁམས་ནད་གསོ་ཚན་ཁག (ŋȫȫgam nɛ̱ɛ̱so tsɛ̄ngaà) department of physical therapy.

དངོས་ཁམས་ཞིབ་འཇུག་ཁང་ (ŋȫȫgam shimjuùgaŋ) physics research institute.

དངོས་ཁམས་རིག་པ་ (ŋȫȫgam rigbə) physics.

དངོས་ཁམས་ལ་བརྟེན་པའི་གསོ་ཐབས་ (ŋȫȫkamlə dēmbɛ sōdəb) physical therapy.

དངོས་འཁོད་གློག་བརྙན་ (ŋȫȫgöö lɔ̄ɔ̄ñɛn) newsreel, documentary film.

དངོས་གྲངས་ (ŋȫȫdraŋ) 1. the actual amount or number. 2. positive number, real number (in math).

དངོས་གྲུབ་ (ŋȫȫdrub) 1. name of a person. 2. accomplishment, attainment, siddhi.

དངོས་གྲུབ་བརྒྱད་ (ŋȫȫdrub gyɛ̱ɛ̀) the eight siddhis.

དངོས་འགལ་ (ŋȫngɛɛ) contradiction, antagonism.

དངོས་རྒྱུ་ (ŋȫȫgyu) direct cause.

དངོས་རྒྱུད་ (ŋȫȫgyüü) orthodox ¶ དངོས་རྒྱུད་གྲུབ་མཐའ་ An orthodox sect.

དངོས་རྒྱུད་ཆོས་ལུགས་ (ŋȫȫgyüü cȫluù) 1. orthodox teaching/ church/ religion. 2. the Catholic Church.

དངོས་ངན་ (ŋȫȫŋɛn) bad in shape/ form/ color, ugly.

དངོས་བརྒྱུད་ (ŋȫȫgyüü) directly and indirectly.

དངོས་བསྒྲགས་ (ŋȫȫdrag) publication, proclamation, declaration; va.—བྱེད་ to publish, to proclaim, to announce.

དངོས་ངན་ (ŋȫȫŋɛn) 1. ugly, repulsive. 2. thin, skinny.

དངོས་ངན་པོ་ (ŋōm ŋɛmbo) sm. དངོས་ངན་.

དངོས་དངོས་རྗེན་རྗེན་ (ŋȫȫŋȫȫ jenjen) the whole/ naked truth, candidly, very clearly ¶ ཁོ་རའི་བསམ་ཚུལ་རྣམས་དངོས་དངོས་རྗེན་རྗེན་བཤད་པ་རེད་ He spoke his opinion candidly.

དངོས་བཅོལ་ཁང་ (ŋȫȫjöögāŋ) checkroom, left luggage room.

དངོས་ཆས་ (ŋȫȫjɛ̱ɛ̀) materials/ articles/ things for use, utensils ¶ དངུལ་གྱི་དངོས་ཆས་མང་པོ་བཟོ་གི་ཡོད་པ་རེད་ (They) make a lot of silverware.

དངོས་འཇལ་དཔྱ་ཁྲལ་ (ŋȫȫjɛɛ jādrɛɛ) direct tax.

དངོས་རྗེན་ (ŋȫȫjen) abbr. for དངོས་དངོས་རྗེན་རྗེན་.

དངོས་རྗེན་ཟོལ་མེད་ (ŋȫȫjen sö̱ö̱meè) sm. དངོས་དངོས་རྗེན་རྗེན་.

དངོས་ཉིད་ (ŋȫȫñii) actual, true, real.

དངོས་ཉེས་པོ་ (ŋȫȫ ñe̱èbo) ugly.

དངོས་བརྙན་ (ŋȫȫñɛn) real image.

དངོས་གཏན་ (ŋȫȫdɛn) shung. it is definite, definitely ¶ ངོས་ནས་ཀྱང་གཞུང་དོན་སྐྱང་ལ་ར་བསམས་ནས་དེ་རྒྱབ་གཉེར་བྱེད་དགོས་དངོས་གཏན་བཅས་ Considering it is official work, I would definitely support it.

དངོས་གཏོགས་ (ŋȫȫdɔɔ̀) sm. དངོས་སྐྱོང་.

དངོས་གཏོགས་གྲོང་ཁྱེར་ (ŋȫȫdɔɔ̀ troŋgyer) sm. དངོས་སྐྱོང་གྲོང་ཁྱེར་.

དངོས་གཏོགས་ལས་ཁུངས་ (ŋȫȫdɔɔ̀ lɛ̱ɛ̀guŋ) a department directly under the control of the central government.

དངོས་བདགས་ (ŋȫȫdag) 1. real and false. 2. abbr. of དངོས་མིང་ and བདགས་མིང་.

དངོས་རྟགས་ (ŋȫȫdaà) plus sign.

དངོས་རྟགས་སྨྲ་བའི་རིང་ལུགས་ (ŋȫȫdaà māwɛ ri̱ŋluù) positivism.

དངོས་རྟེན་ (ŋȫȫden) a gift.

དངོས་ལྟར་སྣང་ (ŋȫȫdar nāŋ) vi. to see/ feel that sth. is real when it is not.

དངོས་བསྟན་ (ŋȫȫdɛn) showing sth. really/ actually.

དངོས་ཐག (ŋȫȫdaà) actual distance.

དངོས་ཐིག (ŋȫȫdig) actual line.

དངོས་ཐོ་ (ŋȫȫdo) list of things/ articles/ items; va.—རྒྱག; —འབྲི་ to write down a list of articles/ things.

དངོས་ཐོག་ཏུ་སྦྱོང་ (ŋȫȫdogdu jōŋ) sm. དངོས་སྦྱོང་བྱེད་.

དངོས་ཐོག་བདེན་འཚོལ་ (ŋȫȫdog de̱ndzöö) finding truth through facts, seeking truth from facts.

དངོས་ཐོབ་ཉམས་མྱོང་ (ŋȫȫtob ña̱mñoŋ) firsthand experience, direct experience.

དངོས་ཐོས་བདེན་འཚོལ་ (ŋȫȫdöö de̱ndzöö) seeking truth through facts (Deng Xiaoping's statement).

དངོས་མཐོང་ (ŋȫȫdoŋ) firsthand, eyewitness ¶ དངོས་མཐོང་གནས་ཚུལ་ An eyewitness account.

དངོས་མཐོང་བདེན་རྟོགས་ (ŋȫȫdoŋ dēndɔɔ̀) knowing the truth via firsthand experience.

དངོས་མཐོང་གཟུགས་གྲུབ་ (ŋȫȫdoŋ su̱gdrub) sm. དངོས་མཐོང་.

དངོས་མཐོང་ལག་འཛིན་ (ŋȫȫdoŋ la̱ŋdzin) sm. དངོས་མཐོང་.

དངོས་མཐུན་རིང་ལུགས་ (ŋȫȫdün ri̱ŋluù) realism.

དངོས་འཐབ་ (ŋȫȫdəb) actual combat.

དངོས་འཐེན་ནུས་པ་ (ŋȫȫden nü̱übə) gravity ¶ ཟླ་བའི་དངོས་འཐེན་ནུས་པ་ The gravity of the moon.

དངོས་དུག (ŋȫȫdug) real poison.

དངོས་དོད་ (ŋȫȫdöö) 1. gifts of money given instead of items in kind. 2. sm. དངོས་དོན་.

དངོས་དོན་ (ŋȫȫdön) real, true, factual, actual, true, apparent ¶ ལོ་རྒྱུས་ཀྱི་དངོས་དོན་ Historical fact.

དངོས་དོན་ངོ་མ་ (ŋȫȫdön ŋo̱ma) fact, factually true/ real/ actual.

དངོས་དོན་གནས་སྟངས་ (ŋȫȫdön nɛ̄ɛ̀daŋ) real/ actual situation.

དངོས་དོན་ཟུང་འབྲེལ་ (ŋȫȫdön su̱ndrel) linked with reality, true, factual.

དངོས་དོན་འུད་བཤད་ (ŋȫȫdön wu̱rshɛɛ̀) exaggeration.

དངོས་དོན་ལ་ (ŋȫȫdönla) actually, really.

དངོས་བདག (ŋȫȫdaà) the owner of goods/ things.

དངོས་བདེན་ (ŋȫȫden) true, factual, real, actual ¶ གསང་བའི་ཚོགས་འདུ་དེའི་ནང་དངོས་བདེན་གྲོས་ཐག་ག་རེ་བཅད་མེད་སུས་ཀྱང་ཤེས་ཀྱི་ཡོད་པ་མ་རེད་ Nobody knows what they actually decided in the secret meeting.

དངོས་མདོག་སྟོན་ (ŋȫȫdɔɔ̀ dȫn) va. to reveal the true character/ nature.

དངོས་ལྡོག (ŋȫȫdɔɔ̀) positive and negative.

དངོས་ནས་ (ŋȫȫnɛ) actually, really, truly.

དངོས་ནོར་ (ŋȫȫnɔɔ) wealth, possessions.

དངོས་སྣ་ (ŋȫȫna) a variety of goods/ things.

དངོས་གནས་ (ŋȫȫnɛɛ̀) real, true ¶ འདི་པ་ལམ་དངོས་གནས་རེད་དམ་ Is this diamond real? ¶ ཁོས་ཟེར་བ་དེ་དངོས་གནས་རེད་ What he says is true.

དངོས་གནས་ཁུངས་དག (ŋȫȫnɛɛ̀) shung. reliable source.

དངོས་གནས་དྲང་གནས་ (ŋȫȫnɛɛ̀ tra̱ŋnɛɛ̀) really/ completely true, positively factual/ certain ¶ དེ་དངོས་གནས་དྲང་གནས་ཀྱི་བརྩེ་བ་རེད་ That is true love.

དངོས་གནས་བྱས་ན་ (ŋȫȫnɛɛ̀ cɛ̱ɛ̀na) really, truly, actually, in fact.

དངོས་གནས་སྨྲ་བ་ (ŋȫnεὲ māwa) realism.

དངོས་གནས་བཤད་ན་ (ŋȫnεε shὲὲna) actually, to tell the truth.

དངོས་པོ་ (ŋȫbo) materials, things, objects, goods.

དངོས་པོ་སྐྱེལ་འདྲེན་ (ŋȫbo gōndren) cargo, freight, transport ¶ དངོས་པོ་སྐྱེལ་འདྲེན་འཁོར་ཚད་ The amount of freight traffic.

དངོས་པོ་འཕྲོ་ལྷག་ (ŋȫbo drōlaà) waste product.

དངོས་པོ་མངོན་བརྗོད་ (ŋȫbo ŋōndɔ̄ɔ) sm. དངོས་པོ་.

དངོས་པོ་གཉིས་ (ŋȫbo ñı̄i) cause and effect, action and its consequences.

དངོས་པོ་གཏན་གནས་ཀྱི་ངེས་སྲོལ་ (ŋȫbo dε̄nnεὲgi ŋe̱èsöö) law of the conservation of matter.

དངོས་པོ་སྟོབས་ཤུགས་ (ŋȫbo dōbshug) sm. དངོས་པོའི་སྟོབས་ཤུགས་.

དངོས་པོ་བདག་ (ŋȫbo da̱à) in Tibetan grammar: the actor and the means by which the action is done.

དངོས་པོ་ཙམ་ (ŋȫbodzam) materialist ¶ དངོས་པོ་ཙམ་གྱི་རྩོད་སྒྲུབ་རིག་པ་ Materialist dialectics.

དངོས་པོ་གཞན་ (ŋȫbo she̱n) in Tibetan grammar: the object and the action done on the object.

དངོས་པོ་རང་ཉིད་ (ŋȫbo rə̱ŋñı̄i) material things/ objects.

དངོས་པོ་ལས་འདས་པ་སྨྲ་བ་ (ŋȫbolε dε̱ὲba māwa) metaphysics.

དངོས་པོ་བཤེར་ (ŋȫbo shēr) va. to check goods/ materials.

དངོས་པོ་གསོག་འཇོག་ (ŋȫbo sōgjɔ̄ɔ) storing materials/ goods; va.—བྱེད་.

དངོས་པོའི་སྐུར་མ་ (ŋȫböö gūrma) a present/ gift that is sent.

དངོས་པོའི་ཁེ་ཕན་ (ŋȫböö kēbεn) material welfare/ benefit.

དངོས་པོའི་ཆ་རྐྱེན་ (ŋȫböö cāgyen) material conditions.

དངོས་པོའི་ཆོས་ཉིད་ (ŋȫböö cǖüñı̄i) innate law of things.

དངོས་པོའི་འཇིག་རྟེན་ (ŋȫböö ji̱gden) the material world.

དངོས་པོའི་སྡེར་ཆ་ (ŋȫböö dērja) award, citation.

དངོས་པོའི་སྟོབས་ཤུགས་ (ŋȫböö dōbshug) material force.

དངོས་པོའི་མཐུན་རྐྱེན་ (ŋȫböö tǖngyen) material means and resources.

དངོས་པོའི་བདག་དབང་ (ŋȫböö da̱waŋ) right of private ownership.

དངོས་པོའི་ནུས་སྟོབས་ (ŋȫböö nü̱üdob) sm. དངོས་པོའི་སྟོབས་ཤུགས་.

དངོས་པོའི་ནུས་ཤུགས་ (ŋȫböö nü̱üshug) sm. དངོས་པོའི་སྟོབས་ཤུགས་.

དངོས་པོའི་གནས་ལུགས་ཀྱི་ཚན་རིག (ŋȫböö nε̄ὲluggi tsε̄nrii) sm. དངོས་པོའི་མཚན་ཉིད་.

དངོས་པོའི་དཔལ་ཡོན་ (ŋȫböö bε̄εyön) material culture, material civilization.

དངོས་པོའི་བྱ་དགའ་ (ŋȫböö ca̱ga) material reward/ award.

དངོས་པོའི་རྨང་གཞི་ (ŋȫböö mə̄ŋshi) material base/ foundation.

དངོས་པོའི་མཚན་ཉིད་ (ŋȫbö tsε̄nñı̄i) physics.

དངོས་པོའི་འཚོ་བ་ (ŋȫböö tsōwa) material well-being.

དངོས་པོའི་རོགས་རམ་ (ŋȫböö rɔ̱ɔ̄ram) material help/ assistance.

དངོས་པོའི་ལོངས་སྤྱོད་ (ŋȫböö lo̱ŋjöö) material enjoyment.

དངོས་པོའི་གཤིས་ལུགས་ཀྱི་རིག་པ་ (ŋȫböö shı̄iluggi ri̱gbə) sm. དངོས་པོའི་མཚན་ཉིད་.

དངོས་དཔང་ (ŋȫbaŋ) material evidence/ proof.

དངོས་དཔང་རིང་ལུགས་ (ŋȫbaŋ ri̱ŋluù) positivism.

དངོས་དཔེ་ (ŋȫbe) living example, real example.

དངོས་སྤྱད་ (ŋȫjεὲ) things (material).

དངོས་སྤྱོད་ (ŋȫjöö) putting into practice, practical/ actual application, implementation; va.—བྱེད་ to put into practice, to implement ¶ བསམ་བློ་བཟང་པོ་དེ་ཚོ་དངོས་སྤྱོད་བྱེད་མཁན་དཀོན་པོ་རེད་ People who put those noble ideas into practice are rare.

དངོས་ཕན་ (ŋȫbεn) practical use.

དངོས་ཕན་རིང་ལུགས་ (ŋȫbεn ri̱ŋluù) pragmatism.

དངོས་ཕེབས་ (ŋȫ pēè) va. to come in person (h.).

དངོས་བོང་ (ŋȫboŋ) the size of things.

དངོས་བྱུང་ (ŋȫjuŋ) 1. real, true ¶ ཡ་མཚན་དངོས་བྱུང་ Strange but true. 2. firsthand.

དངོས་བྲིས་ (ŋȫdrii) realism (in art).

དངོས་འབྲེལ་ (ŋōndree) 1. true, actual, real, genuine. 2. practical, concrete ¶ དངོས་འབྲེལ་གྱི་ཉམས་མྱོང་ Practical experience. ¶ དངོས་འབྲེལ་བཤད་ན་. If I tell you the truth. 3. in reality, in actuality, in truth ¶ དངོས་འབྲེལ་ཁོང་ཚོས་རྟག་པར་དཔོན་ལ་དངུལ་སྤྲོད་དགོས་རེད་ In truth, they always have to give money to the lord.

དངོས་འབྲེལ་དྲང་འབྲེལ་ (ŋōndree dra̱ndree) sm. དངོས་གནས་དྲང་གནས་.

དངོས་སྦྱོང་ (ŋȫjoŋ) practical studies, applied studies/ training, on the job training; va.—བྱེད་ to practice, to study first hand, to undergo practical training ¶ ཁོང་གི་དགོངས་པ་དངོས་སྦྱོང་བྱེད་ཀྱི་ཡོད་པ་རེད་ His thoughts are being studied practically (as opposed to only theoretically).

དངོས་སྦྱོང་འཁྲབ་སྟོན་ (ŋȫjoŋ trə̄bdön) formal rehearsal.

དངོས་སྦྱོང་དངོས་སྤྱོད་ (ŋȫjoŋ ŋȫjöö) practical study/ training and practical application ¶ མའོ་ཀྲུའུ་ཞིའི་གསུང་རྩོམ་དངོས་སྦྱོང་དངོས་སྤྱོད་གིས་ By studying practically and applying the works of Chairman Mao.

དངོས་སྦྱོང་བ་ (ŋȫjoŋwa) sm. དངོས་སྦྱོང་སློབ་གྲྭ་བ་.

དངོས་སྦྱོང་དམག་དཔུང་ (ŋȫjoŋ mə̄gbuŋ) formally trained soldiers (in contrast to militia).

དངོས་སྦྱོང་སློབ་གྲྭ་བ་ (ŋȫjoŋ lōbdrawa) student trainee, student undergoing practical training.

དངོས་མང་འགྲེམས་སྟོན་ཚོགས་འདུ་ (ŋȫmaŋ dre̱mdön tsōndu) fair, exhibition, expo.

དངོས་མང་རིག་པ་ (ŋȫmaŋ ri̱gba) natural history.

དངོས་མང་ཁང་ (ŋȫmaŋgaŋ) natural history museum.

དངོས་མང་བཤམས་སྟོན་ཁང་ (ŋȫmaŋ shāmdöngaŋ) sm. དངོས་མང་ཁང་.

དངོས་མིང་ (ŋȫmiŋ) 1. real name; original name. 2. name of things/ items.

དངོས་མེད་ (ŋȫmeè) abstract, not realistic.

དངོས་མེད་གྲངས་ཀ་ (ŋȫmeè tra̱ŋga) abstract number.

དངོས་མེད་རྒྱལ་ཁམས་ (ŋȫmeè gyε̱gam) abstract state.

དངོས་མེད་དུ་གཏོང་ (ŋȫmeèdu dōŋ) shung. va. to destroy/ eliminate/ spoil/ ruin ¶ ཆུ་ལོག་གིས་འདེབས་ཞིང་རྣམས་ཀྱང་དངོས་མེད་དུ་བཏང་བ་ The flood destroyed the agricultural fields.

དངོས་མྱོང་ (ŋȫñoŋ) practical/ firsthand/ personal experience.

དངོས་གཙང་ (ŋȫdzaŋ) clean and tidy, well arranged.

དངོས་གཙོ་ (ŋȫdzo) materialism, materialistic ¶ དངོས་གཙོའི་བསམ་པ་ Materialistic thinking.

དངོས་གཙོ་སྨྲ་བ་ (ŋȫdzo māwa) materialism.

དངོས་གཙོ་སྨྲ་བ་པ་ (ŋȫdzo māwaba) a materialist.

དངོས་གཙོ་སྨྲ་བ་པོ་ (ŋȫdzo māwabo) sm. དངོས་གཙོ་སྨྲ་བ་པ་.

དངོས་གཙོ་སྨྲ་བའི་ཚུར་སྣང་ (ŋȫdzö māwε tsūrnaŋ) the materialist theory of reflection.

དངོས་གཙོའི་རྩོད་སྒྲུབ་རིག་པ་ (ŋȫdzö dzȫdrub ri̱gbə) materialist dialectics.

དངོས་གཙོའི་རིང་ལུགས་ (ŋȫdzö ri̱ŋluù) sm. དངོས་གཙོ་སྨྲ་བ་.

དངོས་གཙོའི་ལོ་རྒྱུས་ལྟ་ཚུལ་ (ŋȫdzö lu̱gyüü dədzul) the viewpoint of historical materialism.

དངོས་གཙོའི་ལོ་རྒྱུས་སྨྲ་བའི་རིང་ལུགས་ (ŋȫdzö lu̱gyüü māwε ri̱ŋluù) historical materialism.

དངོས་རྩལ་ (ŋȫdzül) real facts, actual facts.

དངོས་རྩལ་གསལ་མཐོང་ (ŋȫdzül sε̄εdoŋ) the true

facts clearly seen/ revealed/ disclosed.

དངོས་མཚོན་ (ŋöö tsön) vi. to convey or express reality (realism) in an article/ story.

དངོས་མཛོད་ཁང་ (ŋöödzögaŋ) museum.

དངོས་འཛིན་ (ŋöndzin) 1. ignorance. 2. perceiving things as true reality.

དངོས་རྫས་ (ŋöödzɛɛ̀) goods, articles, materials, commodities.

དངོས་རྫས་ཀྱི་དོད་དངུལ་ (ŋöödzɛɛ̀gi dööŋüü) money used as a substitute for goods.

དངོས་རྫས་ཀྱི་རྨང་གཞི་ (ŋöödzɛɛ̀gi məŋshi) material basis/ base.

དངོས་རྫས་མཁོ་སྤྲོད་ (ŋöödzɛɛ̀ kōdröö) supplying goods; va.—བྱེད་.

དངོས་རྫས་བརྗེ་རེས་ (ŋöödzɛɛ̀ jereè) flow or interflow of goods/ materials/ commodities.

དངོས་རྫས་སྒྲགས་གཏོང་ (ŋöödzɛɛ̀ dragdoŋ) parcel post section of post office.

དངོས་རྫས་རིན་གཅོད་ཨུ་ཡོན་ལྷན་ཁང་ (ŋöödzɛɛ̀ rinjöö ūyön lhengaŋ) commodity price committee.

དངོས་རྫས་ས་བོགས་ (ŋöödzɛɛ̀ sābɔɔ̀) a type of leasing of land lease where the payment/ rent is in kind.

དངོས་ཞིབ་ (ŋööshib) on the spot or firsthand survey/ investigation.

དངོས་ཞུགས་ (ŋööshug) actual participation; va.—བྱེད་ ¶ འཛམ་གླིང་ཞི་བདེའི་ལྷན་ཚོགས་ནང་དངོས་ཞུགས་བྱས་པ་རེད་ (They) participated in the World Peace Conference.

དངོས་གཞི་ (ŋööshi) 1. main, principal ¶ ད་ལྟ་ཚོགས་འདུ་དངོས་གཞི་ཚུགས་རྒྱུ་རེད་ The main meeting is yet to begin. 2. regular, normal ¶ དངོས་གཞིའི་དམག་དཔུང་ The regular army. 3. formal, official ¶ དངོས་གཞིའི་སྒོ་འབྱེད་ The official inauguration.

དངོས་གཞིའི་གནས་སྐབས་ (ŋööshii nɛɛ̄gəb) the main period/ time.

དངོས་བཞག (āööshaà) shung. actual, real (price) ¶ ཡུལ་གྱི་ཚྭ་ཐང་དངོས་བཞག་བོད་གཏོང་ལབ་གླིང་མེད་པ་དགོས་རྒྱུ་ (You) should send the salt to Tibet without delay according to the local price.

དངོས་ཟོག (ŋöösɔɔ̀) goods, articles, commodities.

དངོས་ཟོག་སྐྱེལ་འདྲེན་ (ŋöösog gyēndrɛn) transporting freight/ goods.

དངོས་ཟོག་འགྲིམ་འགྲུལ་ (ŋöösog drimdrüü) transportation of commodities/ goods.

དངོས་ཟོག་འགེལ་ཚད་ (ŋöösog geedzɛɛ̀) cargo capacity, capacity for carrying goods.

དངོས་ཟོག་འགྲེམ་སྟོན་ཁང་ (ŋöösog dremdöngaŋ) museum.

དངོས་ཟོག་མངགས་གཏམ་ (ŋöösog ŋāàdam) ordering goods, va.—བྱེད་.

དངོས་ཟོག་སྔོན་མངག (ŋöösog ŋönŋaà) ordering/ contracting goods; va.—བྱེད་.

དངོས་ཟོག་བརྗེ་རེས་ཀྱི་འདུ་ཚོགས་ (ŋöösog jereègi dudzoò) commodities exchange fair/ show.

དངོས་ཟོག་བརྗེ་འགྲུལ་ (ŋöösog jendrül) bartering goods, va.—བྱེད་.

དངོས་ཟོག་དོམ་ལེན་ (ŋöösog domlen) credit purchasing (of goods/ commodities); va.—བྱེད་.

དངོས་ཟོག་འདྲེན་འཁོར་ (ŋöösɔɔ̀ drengɔɔ) freight train, transport truck.

དངོས་ཟོག་སྣ་འཛོམས་ཚོང་ཁང་ (ŋöösog mādzom tsōŋgaŋ) department store.

དངོས་ཟོག་དོང་འདྲེན་གྱི་གྲུ་གཟིངས་ (ŋöösog wōndrengi drusiŋ) freighter, cargo ship.

དངོས་ཟོང་ (ŋöösoŋ) sm. དངོས་ཟོག.

དངོས་གཟུགས་ (ŋöösug) body (of a thing), substance.

དངོས་ཡག་གོང་འཚམས་ (ŋööyaà koŋdzam) quality goods at a reasonable price.

དངོས་ཡིག (ŋööyiì) shung. abbr. of དངོས་པོ་ and ཡིག་ཆ་.

དངོས་ཡོད་ (ŋööyöö) real, actual, existing (as opposed to ideal) ¶ དངོས་ཡོད་དབང་ཆ་ Actual power.

དངོས་ཡོད་ཀྱི་རང་བཞིན་ (ŋööyögi rəŋshin) actuality, reality, the nature of.

དངོས་ཡོད་ཆ་རྐྱེན་ (ŋööyöö cāgyen) actual/ concrete condition.

དངོས་ཡོད་ཉམས་མྱོང་ (ŋööyöö ñamñoŋ) actual experience.

དངོས་ཡོད་གྲངས་ (ŋööyöö traŋ) 1. real number (in math). 2. the actual amount or number.

དངོས་ཡོད་དོན་སྙིང་ (ŋööyöö dönñiŋ) real meaning, real significance.

དངོས་ཡོད་གནས་ཚུལ་ (ŋööyöö nɛɛ̀dzul) actual/ real/ existing condition or situation ¶ དངོས་ཡོད་གནས་ཚུལ་དང་བསྟུན་པའི་བྱེད་ཐབས་ Methods of doing things in accordance with actual conditions.

དངོས་ཡོད་དབང་ཆ་ (ŋööyöö wāŋja) real authority.

དངོས་ཡོད་སྨྲ་བ་ (ŋööyöö māwa) realism.

དངོས་ཡོད་རིང་ལུགས་ (nööyöö riŋluù) realism.

དངོས་ར་འཕྲོད་ (ŋöö radröö) 1. vi. to be proved, to be evident ¶ ཁོ་ཚོས་དངོས་སུ་རོགས་རམ་བྱེད་འདོད་མེད་པའི་དངོས་ར་འཕྲོད་པ་རེད་ It became evident that they truly did not wish to help. ¶ ཟིང་ཆ་ལངས་ཡག་འདི་ལོ་རྒྱུས་ཐོག་ནས་དངོས་ར་འཕྲོད་ཡོད་ As for the disturbances arising, through history it [the cause] became evidence.

དངོས་ར་གསལ་འཕྲོད་ (ŋöö ra sɛɛ̄dröö) proving, demonstrating, confirming, verifying; va.—བྱེད་.

དངོས་རིག་འགྲེམས་སྟོན་ཁང་ (ŋöörii dremdöngaŋ) museum.

དངོས་རིགས་ (ŋöörii) products, articles, goods, commodities, things.

དངོས་རིགས་འཕེལ་འགྱུར་ (ŋöörii pēlgyur) evolution of a product/ commodity/ thing.

དངོས་རིན་ (ŋöörin) price (of goods).

དངོས་རིན་གནས་འཛིན་ (ŋöörin nɛ̄ndzin) invoice, bill of lading.

དངོས་ལམ་ (ŋöölam) the main road.

དངོས་ལུགས་ (ŋööluù) sm. physical.

དངོས་ལུགས་ཀྱི་འགྱུར་བ་ (ŋööluggi gyurwa) physical change.

དངོས་ལུགས་འགྱུར་ལྡོག (ŋööluù gyundoò) sm. དངོས་ལུགས་ཀྱི་འགྱུར་བ་.

དངོས་ལུགས་སྨན་བཅོས་བྱེད་ཐབས་ (ŋööluù mɛ̄njöö cedəb) sm. དངོས་ལུགས་གསོ་ཐབས་.

དངོས་ལུགས་རྫས་འགྱུར་ (ŋööluù dzɛ̄ɛ̀gyur) physical chemistry.

དངོས་ལུགས་རིག་པ་ (ŋööluù rigbə) physics.

དངོས་ལུགས་གསོ་ཐབས་ (ŋöölug sōdəb) physical therapy.

དངོས་སློབ་ (ŋöölob) disciple.

དངོས་ཤུགས་ (ŋööshuù) 1. directly and indirectly ¶ དངོས་ཤུགས་ཀྱིས་ང་ཚོའི་མཐུན་སྒྲིལ་གཏོར་བཤིག་གཏོང་ཐབས་བྱེད་ཀྱི་ཡོད་པ་རེད་ They are trying to destroy our unity directly and indirectly. 2. financial or material resources. 3. actual strength.

དངོས་ཤུགས་བརྒྱུད་གསུམ་ནས་ (ŋööshūg gyüü sūmnɛ) in all kinds of ways (directly and indirectly), by all means ¶ དངོས་ཤུགས་བརྒྱུད་གསུམ་རོགས་རམ་བྱེད་དགོས་ (We) must help in every way.

དངོས་གཤིས་རིག་པ་ (ŋööshiì rigbə) sm. དངོས་པོའི་མཚན་ཉིད་.

དངོས་གཤིས་ཚོད་ལྟ་ (ŋööshiì tsōda) experiment.

དངོས་བཤམས་ (ŋöösham) formal exhibition/ display; va.—བྱེད་.

དངོས་བཤུས་གློག་བརྙན་ (ŋööshüü lɔ̄gñɛn) documentary film.

དངོས་སུ་ (ŋöösu) 1. in reality, really, actually, real ¶ མི་སྤྱོད་ལས་འདས་པའི་སྲིད་ཇུས་ངན་པ་དེ་ལག་ལེན་དངོས་སུ་ལྟར་ཡོད་པ་རེད་ (They) actually carried out that evil, inhuman policy. 2. openly, directly ¶ ཁོས་གནས་ཚུལ་དེ་དངོས་སུ་བཤད་པ་རེད་ He openly told about that news. 3. in person, personally, firsthand ¶ ངས་འདི་དངོས་སུ་རྟོག་ཞིབ་བྱས་པ་ཡིན་ I investigated it firsthand.

དངོས་སུ་སྒྲུབ་ (ŋöösu drub) va. to realize, to materialize, to achieve.

དངོས་སུ་འདེམ་ (ŋöösu dem) va. to elect directly.

དངོས་སུ་ལག་ལེན་ (ŋöösu laglen) concrete/ actual practice.

དངོས་སོང་འགྲོ་སྒྲོན་ (ŋöösoŋ drodrön) the actual expenditure.

དངོས་གསལ་ (ŋöösεε) obvious, clear, apparent, conspicuous.

དངོས་གསལ་དོད་པོ་ (ŋöösεε tööbo) sm. དངོས་གསལ་.

དངོས་སློབ་ (ŋöölob) personal students/ disciples ༈ མི་ལ་སོགས་མར་པའི་དངོས་སློབ་རྣམས་ Marpa's personal disciples such as Mila.

མངག་: p. **མངགས་**; f. **མངག་**; imp. **མངོགས་** (ŋāà) 1. to send, to commission, to entrust ༈ བརྡ་སྤྲོད་བར་དམིགས་བསལ་བང་ཆེན་ཞིག་མངགས་སོང་ (They) sent a special messenger to deliver the notice. 2. va. to order sth. ༈ ངས་དངོ་བཟོ་བ་དེ་ལ་ལྷམ་ཆ་གཅིག་མངགས་ཡོད་ I've ordered a pair of boots from that shoemaker.

མངག་བཅོལ་ (ŋāgjöö) entrusting/ commissioning (with a task or power); va.—བྱེད་ ༈ ཚོགས་ཆུང་དེ་ར་འཕྲོད་བསྟེན་ཡར་རྒྱས་ཀྱི་འཆར་གཞི་བཟོ་རྒྱུ་མངག་བཅོལ་བྱས་པ་རེད་ (They) commissioned that committee to make a plan for the improvement of hygiene.

མངག་བཅོལ་ཁང་ (ŋāgjöögaŋ) commission shop (store where goods are left to sell on commission).

མངག་བཅོལ་ཚོང་ཁང་ (ŋāgjöö tsõŋgaŋ) sm. མངག་བཅོལ་ཁང་.

མངག་ཆ་ (ŋāgja) sm. མངགས་ཆ་.

མངག་ཉོ་ (ŋāgño) sm. མངགས་ཉོ་.

མངག་ཉོའི་གན་རྒྱ་ (ŋāgñö kεngya) a signed agreement, a contract for an order.

མངག་གཏམ་ (ŋāgdam) commissioning, entrusting; sending; va.—བྱེད་; va.—ཞུ་ to send/ commission/ entrust ༈ བརྡ་སྤྲོད་བར་དམིགས་བསལ་བང་ཆེན་ཞིག་མངགས་སོང་ (They) sent a special messenger to deliver the notice.

མངག་གཏོང་ (ŋāgdoŋ) sm. མངག་, 1.

མངག་གཏོང་ཁང་ (ŋāgdongang) police station.

མངག་གདམས་ (ŋāgdam) sm. མངགས་གདམས་.

མངག་བྱ་ (ŋāgja) sm. མངགས་ཆ་.

མངག་རྫོང་ (ŋāgdzong) sending, dispatching, transferring; va.—གཏོང་; —བྱེད་ ༈ ང་ལམ་བང་མི་མངག་རྫོང་གཏོང་ཞུ་སྐྱེའི་ཡིག་ཆ་ངེས་བསྐུར་སོང་བ་རྟེས་ལེན་གྱིས་ Take possession of the documents I send you through the messenger.

མངག་གཞུག་ (ŋāgshuù) shung. servant ༈ མངག་གཞུག་ཕོ་མོ་ Male and female servants.

མངག་གཞུག་མ་ (ŋāgshuùma) shung. female servant.

མངགས་ (ŋāà) p. of མངག་.

མངགས་ཁྱབ་ (ŋāggyəb) shung. to ask (sb.) to perform a duty/ task.

མངགས་འགན་ (ŋāggen) mission, duty, task, commission ༈ གོང་རིམ་གྱི་མངགས་འགན་དང་ལེན་ཞུ་དགོས་ One should agree to the task coming from one's superiors.

མངགས་བཅོལ་ (ŋāgjöö) sm. མངག་བཅོལ་.

མངགས་ཆ་ (ŋagja) 1. placing an order, commissioning, reserving; va.—རྒྱག་; —བྱེད་ ༈ ངས་ཁྱེད་རང་གི་གནམ་གྲུའི་པ་སི་མངགས་ཆ་བྱས་ཡོད་ I asked (him) to reserve an airline ticket for you. 2. requested, asked for ༈ རྩོམ་ཡིག་མངགས་ཆ་འདི་ The essay that was requested.

མངགས་ཉོ་ (ŋāgño) ordering, buying (in advance), subscribing; va.—བྱེད་.

མངགས་གཏམ་ (ŋāgdam) sm. མངག་གཏམ་.

མངགས་གཏོང་ (ŋāgdoŋ) sm. མངག་, 1.

མངགས་གཏོང་ཁང་ (ŋāgdoŋgang) sm. མངག་གཏོང་ཁང་.

མངགས་གདམ་ (ŋāgdam) sm. མངག་ཆ་.

མངགས་པའི་ལས་ཁུར་ (nāgbε lεεgur) shung. a task/ duty that was delegated ༈ དོན་དེ་ལ་མངགས་པའི་ལས་ཁུར་ཞུ་སྒོ་གང་ཅི་ལེ་ཕྲོག་མེད་པ་དགོས་རྒྱུ་ One should perform the tasks that were delegated.

མངགས་བྱ་ (ŋāgja) 1. request. 2. order, instructions ༈ ཁོང་གི་མངགས་བྱ་ལྟར་ According to his order/ instructions.

མངགས་འཚོང་ (ŋāgtsoŋ) asking others to sell; va.—བྱེད་.

མངགས་རེས་ (ŋāgreè) exchanging; va.—བྱེད་ ༈ ཀྲུང་སུའི་རྒྱལ་ཁབ་གཉིས་མངགས་རེས་བྱེད་པའི་རིག་གནས་སྐུ་ཚབ་ཚོགས་པ་ The cultural delegations exchanged by China and the USSR.

མངན་དཔོན་ (ŋεmbön) arc. an official in charge of a treasury/ economic affairs.

མངན་གྲངས་ (ŋεndraŋ) va. to criticize someone's errors one by one.

མངའ་ (ŋāā) 1. va. to know ༈ ཁོང་གི་ལོ་རྒྱུས་མི་མངའ་ He doesn't know history. 2. vi. to exist, to be; to have, to possess. 3. power, might, dominion.

མངའ་ཁུལ་ (ŋəgüü) sm. མངའ་ཁོངས་.

མངའ་ཁོངས་ (ŋāgoŋ) a subordinate or subject territory, a colony.

མངའ་ཁོངས་ཀྱི་བདག་དབང་ (ŋāgoŋgi dàawaŋ) sovereign right over a territory.

མངའ་ཁོངས་རྒྱ་མཚོ་ (ŋāgoŋ gyatso) territorial waters.

མངའ་ཁོངས་ཆ་ཚང་ (ŋāgoŋ cādzaŋ) territorial integrity.

མངའ་ཁོངས་ཆུ་པོ་ (ŋāgoŋ cūwo) territorial waters.

མངའ་ཁོངས་བར་སྣང་ (ŋāgong parnang) territorial air space.

མངའ་ཁོངས་ས་ཆ་ (ŋāgong sāja) sm. མངའ་ཁོངས་.

མངའ་ཁོངས་སུ་འཇུག་ (ŋāgoŋsu dzüü) va. to take over a territory, to make a territory under one's control.

མངའ་ཆོས་ (ŋājöö) shung. subjects and monastery ༈ ཤེལ་དཀར་ས་གནས་སུ་ཕེབས་ཉིན་གསོལ་དོད་མངའ་ཆོས་ཕྱེད་འགྱུར་ When he came to Shelkar, the subjects and monastery paid the substitute (money) for food fifty-fifty.

མངའ་བསྙེས་ (ŋā ñēè) va. 1. to bring under control ༈ རྒྱལ་པོ་དེས་རྒྱལ་ཁབ་མང་པོར་མངའ་བསྙེས་སོང་ That king brought many nations under his control. 2. va. to master, to become an authority ༈ ཁོང་ནི་རྒྱལ་ཁབ་མང་པོའི་སྐད་རིགས་ལ་མངའ་བསྙེས་པ་ཞིག་རེད་ He is sb. who has mastered the languages of many countries.

མངའ་ཐང་ (ŋādaŋ) 1. power, might. 2. prosperity.

མངའ་ཐང་ལོངས་སྤྱོད་ (ŋādaŋ loŋjöö) rich and powerful.

མངའ་བདག་ (ŋādaà) 1. lord, king, sovereign. 2. feudal lord, serf owner.

མངའ་བདག་ཁྲི་རལ་པ་ཅན་ (ŋādaà trī rεεbajεn) the 41st king of Tibet (Ralpachen).

མངའ་བདག་གྲལ་རིམ་ (ŋādaà trεεrim) the class of feudal lords/ serf owners.

མངའ་བདག་རྒྱལ་ཁབ་ (ŋādaà gyεεgəb) feudal countries.

མངའ་བདག་ཆེན་པོ་གསུམ་ (ŋādaà cēmbo sūm) the three great feudal lords: the Tibetan government, the aristocracy, and the monasteries.

མངའ་སྡེ་ (ŋāde) state, locality ༈ མངའ་སྡེ་གཞུང་ Local government.

མངའ་སྡེ་ནང་ཁུལ་གྱི་ཚོང་ལས་འགན་འཛིན་ལྷན་ཁང་ (ŋāde naŋgüügi tsõŋlεὲ gεndzin lhēngaŋ) Interstate Commerce Commission (ICC).

མངའ་སྡེའི་འཐུས་མི་ (ŋādee tūümi) senator (in U.S.A.), a local/ state representative.

མངའ་སྡེའི་སྲིད་སྐྱོང་ (ŋādee sīigyoŋ) governor.

མངའ་སྤྱི་ (ŋāji) shung. all the subjects.

མངའ་བ་མཁྱེན་ (ŋāwa kyēn) shung. please bear in mind ༈ དེ་དོན་དགོངས་དབྱིངས་སུ་མངའ་བ་མཁྱེན་ Please bear in mind what was mentioned above.

མངའ་བྱིངས་ (ŋājiŋ) shung. abbr. of མངའ་ཞབས་སྤྱི་བྱིངས་.

མངའ་དབང་ (ŋāwaŋ) rule, power, control; va.—སྒྱུར་ to rule, to bring under control/ power.

མངའ་འབངས་ (ŋāmbaŋ) subject, citizen.

མངའ་འབངས་ལ་བཀའ་ཁྱབ་ (nāmbaŋla gā kyəb) shung. to give orders to one's subjects.

མངའ་ཚབ་ (ŋādzəb) representatives of feudal lords (e.g., their stewards).

མངའ་ཚབ་གྲལ་རིམ་ (nādzəb trɛɛrim) the class of representatives of feudal lords.

མངའ་མཚོ་ (ŋātso) territorial waters.

མངའ་མཛད་ (ŋādzɛɛ̀) sm. མངའ་བསྐོས་.

མངའ་ཞབས་ (ŋəshəb) 1. subject of a lord/ monastery. 2. sm. མངའ་འོག.

མངའ་ཞབས་སྤྱི་ཁྱིངས་ (ŋəshəb jījiŋ) shung. sm. མངའ་ཞབས་.

མངའ་ཞབས་མི་སེར་ (ŋəshəb miser) shung. sm. མངའ་ཞབས་.

མངའ་ཞབས་ས་ཆ་ (ŋəshəb sāja) shung. territory or estate or manor (of a feudal lord).

མངའ་གཞིས་ (nəshiì) shung. an estate one owns or is under one's jurisdiction.

མངའ་འོག (ŋāwɔɔ̀) under the power of, under the lordship of, subordinate, dependent, subject. va.—གཏོགས་ to put under the power/ authority of.

མངའ་འོག་རྒྱལ་ཁབ་ (ŋāɔɔ̀ gyɛɛgəb) satellite state, dependent polity.

མངའ་རིས་ (ŋəriì) 1. the region/ province of Western Tibet. 2. sm. མངའ་ཁོངས་. 3. the people, the masses, citizens.

མངའ་རིས་སྐོར་གསུམ་ (ŋəriì gōrsum) the three regions of Western Tibet.

མངའ་རིས་ཁམ་བུ་ (ŋəriì kāmbu) peach, apricot.

མངའ་རིས་ཁུལ་ (ŋəri kǖl) sm. མངའ་རིས་, 1.

མངའ་རིས་སྤྱི་རྫོང་ (ŋəri jīdzoŋ) shung. the governor of Western Tibet in tt.

མངའ་གསོལ་ (ŋāsöö) enthronement; va. མངའ་གསོལ་; —བྱེད་ to enthrone, to install in power ¶ བློན་པོ་གསར་པ་འདི་མངའ་གསོལ་བ་རེད་ (They) installed the new minister.

མངར་ (ŋār) abbr. of མངར་མོ་.

མངར་ཁམ་ (ŋārkam) abbr. of མངའ་རིས་ཁམ་བུ་.

མངར་ཁུ་ (ŋərgu) a sugary liquid.

མངར་རྒྱུ་ (ŋərgyu) molasses.

མངར་བཅུད་ (ŋərjüü) saccharin.

མངར་ཆ་ (ŋārja) sugar, things that are sugary/ sweet.

མངར་ཆ་བསྣན་པ་ (ŋārja nēmba) adding sugar to sth.

མངར་ཆ་བཙིར་ (ŋārja dzīr) va. to extract sugar.

མངར་ཆ་བཙིར་ཁང་ (ŋārja tzirgaŋ) sugar processing plant/ factory/ refinery.

མངར་ཆ་བག་ལེབ་ (ŋārja pàaleè) sweet bread, cookies.

མངར་ཆ་བཟོ་ཁང་ (ŋārja sogaŋ) sm. མངར་ཆ་བཙིར་ཁང་.

མངར་ཆ་བཟོ་གྲྭ་ (ŋārja sōdra) sugar refinery.

མངར་ཆའི་མདེའུ་ (ŋārjɛ diwu) pleasant/ nice on the outside but deadly/ nasty/ evil on the inside [Lit. sugarcoated bullet].

མངར་ཆའི་ལས་གྲྭ་ (ŋārjɛ lɛɛ̀dra) sugar or candy factory/ plant/ workshop.

མངར་ཆའི་ལོ་ཏོག (ŋārjɛ lodoò) sugar cane.

མངར་ཆས་བཏུམས་པའི་མདེའུ་ (ŋārjɛɛ̀ dūmbɛ diwu) sm. མངར་ཆའི་མདེའུ་.

མངར་ཆས་བསྒྲུམས་པའི་མདེའུ་ (ŋārjeè dūmbe diwu) sm. མངར་ཆའི་མདེའུ་.

མངར་ཐིང་ཐིང་ (ŋār tīŋdiŋ) very sweet.

མངར་འདུས་ (ŋār düü) va. to put under one's power/ authority/ rule.

མངར་པོ་ (ŋārbo) sm. མངར་མོ་.

མངར་ཕྱུར་ (ŋārjur) a kind of Tibetan dried cheese that has sugar mixed in.

མངར་བ་ (ŋarwa) sm. མངར་མོ་.

མངར་བར་བྱེད་ (ŋārwar cɛɛ̀) va. to sweeten, to sugar.

མངར་སྦངས་ (ŋārbaŋ) candied, soaked in sugar.

མངར་མོ་ (ŋāāmo) sweet, sweetish in flavor/ taste.

མངར་ཚལ་ (ŋārdzɛɛ) sugar beet.

མངར་ཚལ་ས་ཚིགས་ (ŋārtsɛɛ sədzii) sugar beet station.

མངར་ཟས་ (ŋārsɛɛ̀) sweets, pastries.

མངར་ཟས་ཁ་ཏོག (ŋārseè kādog) sweets, sweet snacks.

མངར་རིལ་ཟ་ཁང་ (ŋārriì sagaŋ) restaurant that sells sweet dumplings.

མངར་ལོང་གོ་ལོང་ (ŋārloŋ goloŋ) sweet-like, sweetish (in flavor).

མངར་སིང་རྒྱུག (nār sīŋgyaà) vi. to be extremely sweet.

མངར་སིང་སིང་ (ŋār siŋsiŋ) sm. མངར་མོ་.

མངར་གསུམ་ (ŋārsūm) the three sweets: rock sugar, honey, molasses/ burum.

མངལ་ (ŋɛ̄ɛ) 1. uterus, womb. 2. pregnancy ¶ མངལ་ཐེངས་གཅིག་ལ་བཅུ་གཅིག་ཙམ་སྐྱེ་ཐུབ་ Some (animals) are able to bear eleven (offspring) each pregnancy.

མངལ་སྐྱེས་ (ŋɛ̄ɛgyɛ̀ɛ) viviparous birth.

མངལ་སྐྱེས་སྲོག་ཆགས་ (ŋɛ̄ɛgyeè sōgjaà) animals that are viviparous.

མངལ་སྐྱོན་ (ŋɛ̄ɛgyön) disease or infections of the uterus/ womb.

མངལ་སྐྲན་ (ŋɛ̄ɛdren) tumor in the womb, cancer of the womb.

མངལ་ཁྲག (ŋɛ̄ɛdraà) blood of/ from the womb.

མངལ་འཁོར་ (ŋɛ̄ɛ kɔ̄ɔ) vi. to conceive, to get/ become pregnant ¶ མངལ་འཁོར་ནས་ཟླ་དྲུག་ཙམ་སོང་ Six months have passed since (she) conceived.

མངལ་འཁོར་ཚད་ (ŋɛ̄ɛ kɔ̄ɔdzɛɛ̀) conception rate.

མངལ་གྲིབ་ (ŋɛ̄ɛtrip) impurity from contact with substances coming from the womb.

མངལ་གྲོལ་ (ŋɛ̄ɛ tröö) vi. to give birth.

མངལ་སྒོ་ (ŋɛ̄ɛgo) vagina.

མངལ་ཆགས་ (ŋɛ̄ɛjaà) embryo, fetus.

མངལ་ཆགས་ (ŋɛ̄ɛ caà) vi. to become pregnant, to conceive.

མངལ་ཆགས་ཕྲུ་གུ་ (ŋɛ̄ɛjaà trūgu) fetus.

མངལ་ཆགས་མ་ (ŋɛ̄ɛcama) pregnant woman.

མངལ་འཇུག (ŋɛ̄ɛ juù) consciousness (རྣམ་ཤེས་) that arises when conception takes place.

མངལ་གཏོར་ (ŋɛ̄ɛdɔɔ) aborting a fetus.

མངལ་གཏོར་ (ŋɛ̄ɛ dɔ̄ɔ) va. to abort a fetus.

མངལ་རྟགས་ (ŋɛ̄ɛdaà) birthmark.

མངལ་ཐུར་ (ŋɛ̄ɛdur) a spoon like tool used to abort/ extract a fetus.

མངལ་དུ་ཆགས་ (ŋɛ̄ɛdu caà) sm. མངལ་འཁོར་.

མངལ་དུ་འཁོར་ (ŋɛ̄ɛdu kɔ̄ɔ) sm. མངལ་འཁོར་.

མངལ་དུ་ཞུགས་ (ŋɛ̄ɛdu shuù) sm. མངལ་འཁོར་.

མངལ་དུག (ŋɛ̄ɛduù) skin rash (of infants).

མངལ་ལྡན་ (ŋɛndɛn) pregnant.

མངལ་ལྡན་མ་ (ŋɛndɛnma) sm. མངལ་ཆགས་མ་.

མངལ་འདྲད་ (ŋɛndrɛɛ̀) dilation and curettage; va.—བྱེད་.

མངལ་འདྲེན་སྐམ་པ་ (ŋɛndren gāmba) obstetrical forceps.

མངལ་འདོན་ (ŋēē dön) va. to abort (a fetus).

མངལ་ནད་ (ŋɛ̄ɛnɛɛ̀) gynecological diseases, diseases of the uterus.

མངལ་སྣོད་ (ŋɛ̄ɛnöö) womb.

མངལ་གནས་ (ŋɛ̄ɛnɛɛ̀) sm. མངལ་ཆགས་.

མངལ་གནས་ཕྲུ་གུ་ (ŋɛ̄ɛnɛɛ̀ trūgu) fetus.

མངལ་གནས་ཕྲུ་གུ་སྲོག་སྐྱོབ་སྒྲིག་འཛུགས་ (ŋɛ̄ɛnɛɛ̀ trūgü sɔ̄ɔgyob drigdzuù) Operation Rescue (U.S.A.).

མངལ་གནས་ཕྲུ་གུའི་ཤུན་པགས་ (ŋɛ̄ɛnɛɛ̀ trūgü shǖnbaà) amnion.

མངལ་འབུར་ (ŋɛmbur) the protruding stomach of a pregnant woman.

མངལ་འབྱིན་ (ŋɛ̄ɛ jin) sm. མངལ་ལྟུགས་.

མངལ་སྦུབས་ (ŋɛ̄ɛbub) the interior of the womb.

མངལ་སྦྲུམ་པར་འགྱུར་ (ŋɛ̄ɛ drumbar gyur) vi. to get pregnant.

མངལ་བཙས་ (ŋɛ̄ɛ dzɛ̄ɛ) va. to give birth.

མངལ་འཛིན་ (ŋɛ̄ɛ dzin) sm. མངལ་ཆགས་.

མངལ་གཡོལ་ (ŋɛ̄ɛ yɔ̄ɔ) va. to sterilize a woman.

མངལ་ལྟུག (ŋɛ̄ɛ lūù) 1. va. to induce an abortion. 2. an abortion.

མངལ་ལྷུགས་ (ŋɛ̃ɛ̃lug) sm. མངལ་ལྷུག

མངལ་ལ་གནས་པའི་དུས་ (ŋɛ̃ɛ̃la nɛ̃ɛ̀bɛ tü̱ü̱) the time/ duration of pregnancy.

མངལ་ལམ་ (ŋɛ̃ɛ̃lam) vagina.

མངལ་ལམ་གཉན་ཚད་ (nɛ̃ɛ̃lam ñɛ̃ndzɛɛ̀) vaginitis.

མངལ་ཤོར་ (ŋɛ̃ɛ̃ shōr) vi. to miscarry, to have a spontaneous abortion/ miscarriage.

མངལ་བཤོལ་ (ŋɛ̃ɛ̃ shȍȍ) a pregnancy longer than nine months, giving birth after the nine months period.

མངལ་སྲིན་ (ŋɛ̃ɛ̃sin) a type of disease of the womb.

མངོགས་ (ŋɔ̃ɔ̀) sm. མངག

མངོན་ (ŋȍn) vi. 1. to become visible/ evident, to appear ¶ ཡར་རྒྱས་ཀྱི་རྣམ་པ་གསར་པ་ཞིག་མངོན་པ་རེད་ A new atmosphere of development appeared. ¶ སྒེར་དོར་གཞན་ཕན་གྱི་སྙིང་སྟོབས་མངོན་ཡོད་པ་རེད་ A spirit of selflessness was visible. 2. vi. to show, to demonstrate ¶ འདི་གསལ་པོ་མངོན་གྱི་ཡོད་པ་རེད་ This shows it clearly. 3. clear, clearly.

མངོན་ལྐོག (ŋȍngɔɔ̀) 1. front and back. 2. the known and the unknown.

མངོན་ཁྱབ་ (ŋȍnkyəb) comprehensive, all-embracing.

མངོན་མཁྱེན་ (ŋȍngyen) h. of མངོན་ཤེས་.

མངོན་དགའ་ (ŋȍnga) elated, happy.

མངོན་འགྱུར་ (ŋȍngyur) 1. realization, materialization achievement; va.—བྱེད་ to make materialize, to make realize. 2. real, concrete, actual ¶ མངོན་འགྱུར་རིང་ལུགས་ Realism.

མངོན་མངོན་ལྐོག་ལྐོག (ŋȍnŋȍn gɔ̃ggɔɔ̀) not clear, not evident.

མངོན་ཆུང་ (ŋȍnjuŋ) 1. inconspicuous ¶ ཁོས་མི་དགའ་བའི་ལས་བྱེད་པ་དེ་ཚོ་མངོན་ཆུང་གནས་དབྱུང་བཏང་པ་རེད་ He inconspicuously dismissed the officials he didn't like. ¶ འདི་མངོན་ཆུང་གི་ཐོག་ནས་བྱེད་དགོས་ This should be done inconspicuously. 2. looking down on sth. or sb.

མངོན་ཆུང་དུ་ལྟ་ (ŋȍncuŋdu dā) va. to look down on sth. or sb.

མངོན་ཆེན་ (ŋȍncen) conspicuous, noticeable, evident ¶ ཏང་ནང་ཁོངས་ལ་མཐུན་སྒྲིལ་མེད་པ་མངོན་ཆེན་ཆགས་པ་རེད་ It became conspicuous that there is no unity in the party.

མངོན་བརྗོད་ (ŋȍnjöö) 1. the ancient Tibetan science that deals with words/ language. 2. flowery language/ rhetoric.

མངོན་རྟགས་ (ŋȍndaà) 1. proof, evidence. 2. a sign, mark. 3. a symptom.

མངོན་རྟོགས་ (ŋȍndɔɔ̀) sm. མངོན་ཤེས་.

མངོན་རྟོགས་རྒྱན་ (ŋȍndoggyen) abhisamaya text.

མངོན་བསྟོད་ (ŋȍndöö) praise.

མངོན་མཐོ་ (ŋȍndo) exalted, elevated, high.

མངོན་དུ་གྱུར་ (ŋȍndu gyu̱r) p. of མངོན་དུ་འགྱུར་.

མངོན་དུ་འགྱུར་ (ŋȍndu gyu̱r) vi. to realize, to materialize, to achieve, to come true ¶ ཁོང་ཚོའི་འདོད་དོན་མངོན་དུ་འགྱུར་བ་རེད་ Their wish materialized. ¶ འཛམ་གླིང་ཡོངས་ལ་ཞི་བདེ་མངོན་དུ་འགྱུར་བ་བྱེད་དགོས་ཟེར་བ་རེད་ (They) say that (we) should make peace all over the world a reality.

མངོན་དུ་འགྱུར་བ་བྱེད་ (ŋȍntu gyu̱rwə ce̱è) see མངོན་དུ་འགྱུར་.

མངོན་དུ་གྲུབ་ (ŋȍndu dru̱p) sm. མངོན་དུ་འགྱུར་.

མངོན་དུ་བྱེད་ (ŋȍndu ce̱è) sm. མངོན་དུ་འགྱུར་.

མངོན་དུ་འདུ་བར་བྱེད་ (ŋȍndu du̱war ce̱è) va. to use/ practice.

མངོན་དུ་མ་འགྱུར་བའི་སྟོབས་ཤུགས་ (ŋȍndu gyu̱rwɛ dȍbshug) reserve force, potential/ hidden strength.

མངོན་དུ་བརྩོད་ ལྐོག་ཏུ་འཐབ་ (ŋȍndu dzȍȍ gɔ̃gdu tə̄b) arguing openly and struggling against secretly.

མངོན་དོད་ (ŋȍndöö) sm. མངོན་གསལ་དོད་པོ་.

མངོན་གདམ་དུ་བུད་ (ŋȍndamdu bü̱ü̱) saying sth. openly/ undisguisedly.

མངོན་མདུང་ལྐོག་མདའ་ (ŋȍnduŋ gȍnda) attacking by overt and covert means.

མངོན་མདའ་ལྐོག་མདུང་ (ŋȍnda gȍgduŋ) sm. མངོན་མདུང་ལྐོག་མདའ་.

མངོན་མདོག (ŋȍndog) true, real, factual.

མངོན་མདོག་སྟོན་ (ŋȍndɔɔ̀ dȍn) va. to reveal the turth, to reveal one's true self.

མངོན་མདོག་རང་ (ŋȍndɔɔ̀ ra̱ŋ) truly, really.

མངོན་མདོག་ཤོད་ (ŋȍndɔɔ̀ shȍȍ) va. to tell the truth.

མངོན་འདོད་ (ŋȍndöö) wishing, desiring, wanting; va.—བྱེད་.

མངོན་པ་ (ŋȍmba) abhidharma.

མངོན་པ་མཛོད་ (ŋȍmbadzöö) abhidharmakosa.

མངོན་པར་ (ŋȍmbar) openly, overtly, manifestly.

མངོན་པར་འགྲུབ་ (ŋȍmbar dru̱b) sm. མངོན་དུ་འགྱུར་.

མངོན་པར་བསྒྲར་ (ŋȍmbar dār) va. to carry out, to realize, to achieve.

མངོན་པར་བསྟོད་ (ŋȍmbar dȍȍ) sm. མངོན་བསྟོད་.

མངོན་པར་མཐོ་བ་ (ŋȍmbar tȍwa) elevated, high, exalted ¶ མངོན་པར་མཐོ་བའི་གོ་གནས་ An exalted position.

མངོན་པར་འདུ་བྱེད་ (ŋȍmbar du̱ceè) act of doing sth.

མངོན་པར་འདུ་མ་བྱས་པ་ (ŋȍmbar tu̱maceèba) the act of not doing anything.

མངོན་པར་འདུས་བྱས་པ་ (ŋȍmbar du̱ceèba) the act of having done something.

མངོན་པར་མཚོན་ (ŋȍmbar tsȍn) sm. མངོན་དུ་འགྱུར་.

མངོན་པར་རྫོགས་ (ŋȍmbar dzɔɔ̀) vi. to have sth. be complete/ finished/ exhausted.

མངོན་སྤྱོད་ (ŋȍnjöö) a tantric practice for casting a spell on enemies or demons.

མངོན་སྤྱོད་ཀྱི་སྦྱིན་སྲེག (ŋȍnjöögi ji̱nseg) a rite of exorcism.

མངོན་ཕྱོགས་ (ŋȍnjɔɔ̀) the visible/ outward side.

མངོན་འཕར་ལྐོག་ཆག (ŋȍmbar gɔ̃gjàa) overtly increase and covertly decrease.

མངོན་བྲལ་ལྐོག་འབྲེལ་ (ŋȍndrɛɛ gɔ̃gdree) overtly severed but actually still connected, having secret contact though seemingly having cut off contact.

མངོན་བྲལ་ལྐོག་སྡུག (ŋȍndrɛɛ gɔ̃gdug) sm. མངོན་བྲལ་ལྐོག་འབྲེལ་.

མངོན་བློ་འཕྱར་ (ŋȍnlo cār) vi. to disgrace/ discredit.

མངོན་མིན་ (ŋȍnmin) hidden, not open.

མངོན་མེད་ (ŋȍnmeè) hidden, not open.

མངོན་མེད་ཕྱོགས་ལྷུང་ (ŋȍnmeè cɔ̃glhuŋ) hidden tendency, unseen bias.

མངོན་མེད་བརྡ་སྟོན་ (ŋȍnmeè da̱dȍn) sending a covert signal/ sign.

མངོན་མེད་རྨས་སྐྱོན་ (ŋȍnmeè mɛ̃ɛ̃gyön) internal injury.

མངོན་མེད་ཤུགས་འདོན་ (ŋȍnmeè shūgdün) bringing forth someone or something's potential; va.—བྱེད་.

མངོན་རྩོད་ལྐོག་འཐབ་ (ŋȍndzöö gɔ̃gdəb) striving or fighting for sth. overtly and covertly.

མངོན་བརྩི་ལྐོག་འགལ་ (ŋȍndzi gɔ̃ŋgɛɛ) pretending compliance, outwardly complying but secretly violating.

མངོན་རྩོད་ (ŋȍndzöö) open argument/ debate.

མངོན་ཚུལ་ (ŋȍndzül) rule, principle, maxim ¶ གཡོན་གྱི་མངོན་ཚུལ་བགྲངས་ To list the leftist maxims (views).

མངོན་མཚན་ (ŋȍndzɛn) openly, conspicuously, obviously, outwardly, clearly ¶ གཞུང་ལ་སྐྱོན་བརྗོད་མངོན་མཚན་ཅི་བ་བྱེད་ནུས་མཁན་མེད་ There is no one who dares to criticize the government openly.

མངོན་འཛིང་ (ŋȍndziŋ) open strife/ fight.

མངོན་འཛིང་ལྐོག་འཐབ་ (ŋȍndziŋ gɔ̃gdəb) both open strife and veiled struggle.

མངོན་ཞེན་ (ŋȍnshen) open desire.

མངོན་བཟོ་དོད་པོ་ (ŋȍndziŋ) very visible/ obvious/ conspicuous ¶ ཁོང་གི་དུག་ལོག་གྱོན་སྟངས་དེས་ཕྱི་རྒྱལ་ནས་ཡོང་བའི་མངོན་བཟོ་དོད་པོ་འདུག It is very obvious from the way he dresses that he has come from abroad.

མངོན་ལྟོམ་ (ŋŏn lōm) va. to be proud/ arrogant.

མངོན་ལྟོམ་པ་ (ŋŏn lōmba) a person who is proud/ arrogant.

མངོན་ཤེལ་ (ŋŏnshee) a screen ། ལེ་དའི་མངོན་ཤེལ་ On the radar screen.

མངོན་ཤེས་ (ŋŏnsheè) foresight, foreknowledge, prophesy; va.—ཕོད་ to prophesize, to predict the future.

མངོན་སུམ་ (ŋŏnsum) real, actual perceptible, realistic ། ཁོ་ཚོས་འཆར་གཞི་དེ་ལག་ལེན་མངོན་སུམ་དུ་བསྟར་གྱི་རེད་ They will really put the plan into practice.

མངོན་སུམ་འཁྲུལ་མེད་ (ŋŏnsum trŭmeè) the real thing.

མངོན་སུམ་གྱི་རང་བཞིན་ (ŋŏnsumgi rəŋshin) the nature of perception.

མངོན་སུམ་གྱི་ཤེས་རྟོགས་ (ŋŏnsumgi shēèdɔ̀ɔ) perceptual knowledge.

མངོན་སུམ་གྱི་ཤེས་པ་ (ŋŏnsumgi shēèba) sm. མངོན་སུམ་གྱི་ཤེས་རྟོགས་.

མངོན་སུམ་གྱི་ཤེས་ཡོན་ (ŋŏnsumgi shēèyön) sm. མངོན་སུམ་གྱི་ཤེས་རྟོགས་.

མངོན་སུམ་གྱིས་ (ŋŏnsumgii) sm. མངོན་སུམ་དུ་.

མངོན་སུམ་གསལ་རྗེན་ (ŋŏnsum sɛljen) realistic.

མངོན་སུམ་དངོས་པོ་ (ŋŏnsum ŋōbo) matter.

མངོན་སུམ་རྗེན་གཅེར་ (ŋŏnsum jenjer) sm. མངོན་སུམ་གསལ་རྗེན.

མངོན་སུམ་མཐོང་ (ŋŏnsum tōŋ) vi. to see with one's own eyes, to experience onself.

མངོན་སུམ་དུ་ (ŋŏnsumdu) really, actually ། ཁོ་ཚོས་འཆར་གཞི་དེ་ལག་ལེན་མངོན་སུམ་དུ་བསྟར་གྱི་རེད་ They will really put the plan into practice.

མངོན་སུམ་དུ་འགྱུར་ (ŋŏnsumdu gyur) vi. to become real/ actual.

མངོན་སུམ་དུ་འགྲུབ་ (ŋŏnsumdu drub) sm. མངོན་སུམ་དུ་འགྱུར་.

མངོན་སུམ་སྤྱོད་ཡུལ་ (ŋŏnsum jöòyüü) real, concrete.

མངོན་སུམ་མེད་པ་ (ŋŏnsum meèba) imperceptible, unknown.

མངོན་སུམ་འཛེམས་མེད་ (ŋŏnsum dzemmeè) in front for everyone to see, not shying away from doing sth. overtly, flagrantly, openly, without restrain/ hesitation, brazenly, audacious, impertinent ། མི་དམངས་ཀྱི་ཐོག་མངོན་སུམ་འཛེམས་མེད་ཀྱིས་མེ་མདའ་བརྒྱབ་པ་རེད་ They opened fire on the people openly and without hesitation.

མངོན་སུམ་ལག་ལེན་ (ŋŏnsum laglen) really doing, actually putting into practice.

མངོན་སུམ་གསལ་ཐོན་ (ŋŏnsum sɛ̄ɛdön) vi. to have come out absolutely clearly/ evidently, beyond a shadow of doubt.

མངོན་སུམ་གསལ་རྗེན་ (ŋŏnsum sɛ̄ɛjen) beyond a shadow of a doubt, absolutely clearly/ evidently ། ཁོ་དགྲ་བོའི་སོ་པ་ཡིན་པ་མངོན་སུམ་གསལ་རྗེན་ར་འཕྲོད་བྱུང་བ་རེད་ It was proved beyond a shadow of a doubt that he was an enemy spy.

མངོན་གསང་ (ŋŏnsaŋ) open and secret, openly and secretly.

མངོན་གསལ་ (ŋŏnsɛɛ) overt, open, public, apparent ། ཁོ་ཚོའི་དབར་མངོན་གསལ་ཞེ་འགྲས་ཡོད་པ་རེད་ There is overt hostility between them.

མངོན་གསལ་ (ŋŏnsɛl) openly, conspicuously, visibly.

མངོན་གསལ་གྱི་འབེན་ (ŋŏnsɛlgi ben) open target.

མངོན་གསལ་གྱིས་ (ŋŏnsɛɛgi) openly, overly, publicly ། ཁོ་ཚོས་མངོན་གསལ་གྱིས་གཞུང་ལ་ངོ་རྒོལ་བྱས་པ་རེད་ They openly opposed the government.

མངོན་གསལ་ཅན་ (ŋŏnsɛljɛn) openly, overtly, publicly; obvious, conspicuous.

མངོན་གསལ་ཆེ་བ་ (ŋŏnsɛl cēwa) sm. མངོན་གསལ་དོད་པོ་.

མངོན་གསལ་ཆེན་པོ་ (ŋŏnsɛl cēmbo) sm. མངོན་གསལ་དོད་པོ་.

མངོན་གསལ་དུ་ (ŋŏnsɛldu) openly, conspicuously, visibly.

མངོན་གསལ་དོད་པོ་ (ŋŏnsɛl töòbo) conspicuous, obvious, apparent ། ཡར་རྒྱས་མངོན་གསལ་དོད་པོ་ཞིག་བྱུང་ཡོད་པ་རེད་ There has been conspicuous improvement. ། ཁོས་སྐྱག་རྫུན་མངོན་གསལ་དོད་པོ་ཞིག་བཤད་སོང་ He told an obvious lie.

མངོན་གསལ་འདྲི་གཅོད་ (ŋŏnsɛl jrijöò) public trial/ investigation.

མངོན་གསལ་འཕྲིན་ཡིག (ŋŏnsɛl drĭnyig) post card.

མངོན་གསལ་འཛེམས་མེད་ (ŋŏnsɛl dzemmeè) sm. མངོན་སུམ་འཛེམས་མེད.

མངོན་གསོན་ (ŋŏnsön) real, realistic.

རྔ་ (ŋā) 1. drum. 2. abbr. of རྔ་མ་.

རྔ་: p. **བརྔས་**; f. **བརྔ་**; imp. **རྔོས་** (ŋā) va. to harvest, to cut or mow grass/ plants/ crops ། ཞིང་པ་ཚོ་བཅས་མ་རྔ་གི་འདུག The farmers are harvesting. ། ཁོས་རྩྭ་བརྔ་གི་རེད་ He will cut the grass.

རྔ་སྐོར་ (ŋāgɔɔ) dog collar.

རྔ་ཁང་ (ŋāgaŋ) a room where drums are kept.

རྔ་ཁོག (ŋāgɔɔ) name of a place in Sichuan.

རྔ་མཁན་ (ŋāgɛn) mower, harvester.

རྔ་ཁྲི་ (ŋədri) a stand where a drum is placed.

རྔ་གོར་སློང་ (ŋāgɔɔ lōŋ) va. to raise up one's tail (usu. dogs).

རྔ་རྒྱན་ (ŋāgyɛn) an ornament put on a tail (horse, yak).

རྔ་སྒྲ་ (ŋādra) sound of a drum.

རྔ་རྔོག (ŋāŋɔ̀ɔ) mane and tail (of horse/ mule/ donkey).

རྔ་ལྕག (ŋājaà) stick for striking a drum, drumstick.

རྔ་ཆིངས་ (ŋəjiŋ) drumbeat.

རྔ་ཆུང་ (ŋəjuŋ) small drum.

རྔ་ཆེན་ (ŋājen) big drum.

རྔ་ཆེན་རོལ་ཆ་ (ŋājen rööja) music accompanied by drums.

རྔ་འཆམ་ (ŋānjam) doing cham (religious dance) while playing the drum; va.—རྒྱག.

རྔ་ཐུག (ŋāduù) sm. ཐུག, 7.

རྔ་དང་འཁར་རྔ་དུང་ལུགས་ (ŋādaŋ kārŋa duŋluù) acting accordingly to situation; va.—བྱེད་ [Lit. the way to beat the gong and drum].

རྔ་དང་བསྟུན་ནས་འཁྲབ་ལུགས་ (ŋādaŋ dŭnnɛ trəbluù) acting according to the circumstance/ situation [Lit. in accordance with the drum, dance].

རྔ་དུང་ (ŋāduŋ) see རྔ་.

རྔ་དུང་དར་འཕྱར་ (ŋəduŋ tarjar) a jubilant/ elaborate celebration by a crowd or group of people; va.—བྱེད་ ། རྒྱལ་ཁབ་དབུ་བརྙེས་ཀྱི་དུས་ཆེན་ལ་རྔ་དུང་དར་འཕྱར་བྱས་པ་རེད་ (They) celebrated their "national day" with jubilation. [Lit. beat drums and wave flags].

རྔ་དུང་བྲོ་གཞས་ (ŋəduŋ troshɛɛ̀) drumming, dancing and singing.

རྔ་དུང་ལམ་བཤད་ (ŋəduŋ lamshang) clearing the road/ path by beating on the drum or gong.

རྔ་བརྡ་ (ŋāda) 1. drum signal, drum for giving signals; va.—གཏོང་ to send a drum signal. 2. drumbeat. 3. the beating of a drum or gong to open a performance.

རྔ་བདར་ (ŋādar) musk deer rubbing their tails when they are in heat.

རྔ་སྡུད་ (ŋədüù) sm. རྔ་བསྡུ་.

རྔ་བསྡུ་ (ŋədu) harvesting; va.—བྱེད་.

རྔ་བསྡུ་མཉམ་འབྲེལ་འཕྲུལ་འཁོར་ (ŋədu ñāmdree trŭ̃ŭgɔɔ) combine harvester.

རྔ་བསྡུ་འཕྲུལ་འཁོར་ (ŋədu trŭ̃ŭgɔɔ) harvester (machine).

རྔ་པ་ (ŋāba) 1. a drummer. 2. a group/ region in Sichuan province.

རྔ་པ་བོད་རིགས་རང་སྐྱོང་ཁུལ་ (ŋāba pörii rāŋgyong kŭ̃ŭ) the Ngaba Tibetan Autonomous Area (in Sichuan province).

རྔ་ལྤགས་ (ŋābaà) leather from which drums are made of.

རྔ་ཡུགས་ (ŋājaà) duster (made of animal tails), yak-tail duster; va.—རྒྱག to dust with a "tail duster."

རྔ་ཕྲུག (ŋədruù) young camel.

རྔ་འཕྲུ (ŋədruù) yak tail ornament put on helmets.

རྔ་བག (ŋābaà) the croup of a (horse, etc.).

རྔ་བོ་ཆེ (ŋāwoce) a large drum that hangs from the ceiling.

རྔ་བོང (ŋāboŋ) abbr. camel and donkey.

རྔ་བྲན (ŋādrɛn) general name for མཛོ and མཛོ་མོ.

རྔ་དབྱུག (ŋəyuù) drumstick.

རྔ་སྦུག (ŋəbuù) drums and cymbals.

རྔ་མ (ŋāma) tail (of an animal).

རྔ་མ་ཀྱག (ŋāma gyaà) 1. va. to lift the tail. 2. va. to be cocky.

རྔ་མོ (ŋāmo) 1. sm. རྔ་མོང. 2. milk.

རྔ་མོང (ŋāmoŋ) camel.

རྔ་མོང་བྱ (ŋāmoŋ cha) ostrich.

རྔ་མོང་གི་ཤ་ཚོག (ŋāmoŋgi shādzog) humps (of camel).

རྔ་དམར (ŋāmar) red colored yak tail.

རྔ་རྩིད (ŋədzii) abbr. yak tail and yak hair.

རྔ་ཚོས (ŋadzöö) camel color.

རྔ་འཛིང (ŋā dziŋ) beating drums (in Tibetan opera or in Buddhist ritual prayers).

རྔ་འཛིན (ŋāndzin) rope used for hanging a drum from the ceiling.

རྔ་གཟེངས (ŋā seŋ) va. to raise the tail (for animals).

རྔ་ཡབ (ŋəyəb) fan made from yak tails.

རྔ་ཡུ (ŋəyu) handle of yak tail duster/ fan.

རྔ་ཡོག (ŋāyɔɔ̀) drum stick.

རྔ་གཡབ (ŋāyəb) sm. རྔ་ཡབ.

རྔ་གཡེར་དྲགས་མ (ŋāyer dragma) tambourine.

རྔ་གཡོག (ŋāyɔɔ̀) drum stick.

རྔ་རུས (ŋərüü) tail bone.

རྔ་རོལ (ŋāröö) marching band.

རྔ་ལ་དཔག་པའི་འཆམ (ŋāla bāgbɛ cām) sm. རྔ་དང་བསྟུན་ནས་འཁྲབ་ལུགས་བྱེད.

རྔ་ལེབ (ŋāleb) fat-tail sheep.

རྔ་གཡབ (ŋəyəb) a yak tail used as a fan or duster.

རྔ་ཤང (ŋāshaŋ) 1. abbr. drum and flat bell. 2. tambourine.

རྔ་གཤོན (ŋāshön) folk dance in which dancers carry a drum and dance at the same time.

རྔ་གསང (ŋāsaŋ) a clear sounding drum.

རྔ་གསེབ (ŋāseb) male (breeding/ stud) camel.

རྔན (ŋɛ̄n) 1. va. to bribe. 2. criticism; va.—བགྲང to criticize by pointing out the faults/ errors one by one.

རྔན་གྱིས་ཁྲིད (ŋāmgi trii) luring with a promise of gain/ bribe/ gift.

རྔན་ཆེན (ŋɛnjen) looking down on, bullying, harassing; va.—བྱེད.

རྔན་པ (ŋɛ̄mba) 1. gift, present, tip ༑ གླ་རྔན Wages and tips. 2. bribe, gift.

རྔན་སྤྲོད་བླུ་ཁྲིད (ŋɛ̄ndröö lūdrii) giving a gift/ bride to win sb. over.

རྔན་བླུ (ŋɛ̄nlu) deceiving/ luring/ enticing/ winning over with gifts or presents or bribes.

རྔབ་རྔུབ (ŋəbŋub) 1. inhaling. 2. a swig, a gulp.

རྔབ: p. བརྔབས; f. བརྔབ (ŋəb) vi. to be hungry.

རྔབས་རྭ (ŋəbrə) medical tool made from an animal horn that is used to suck puss, etc.

རྔམ: p. བརྔམས; f. བརྔམ (ŋām) 1. vi. to desire, to want, to hunger/ thirst for ༑ ཁྲག་ལ་བརྔམས་པའི་དམག་དཔུང Blood thirsty troops. ༑ མང་རྔམ Craving for more. 2. vi. to be/ get angry.

རྔམ་སྐུལ (ŋāmgüü) forcing sb. to do sth. by scaring/ frightening them.

རྔམ་རྔམ་བརྗིད་བརྗིད (ŋāmŋam jiijii) vast and mighty/ majestic.

རྔམ་རྔམ་ཛིག་ཛིག (ŋāmŋam dzigdzig) frightening, scary; va.—སྟོན to make a frightening/ threatening demonstration or display ༑ རྔམ་རྔམ་ཛིག་ཛིག་གི་རྔམ་སྟོན A frightening demonstration.

རྔམ་ཅན (ŋāmjɛn) sm. རྔམ་བརྗིད་ཅན.

རྔམ་འཇིགས (ŋəmjig) a look of anger and ferocity.

རྔམ་བརྗིད (ŋəmjii) a threatening display (of strength); va.—སྟོན to make/ show a threatening display (of strength).

རྔམ་བརྗིད་ཅན (ŋəmjijɛn) sm. རྔམ་བརྗིད་ཆེ་བ.

རྔམ་བརྗིད་ཆེ་བ (ŋəmjii cēwa) mighty, majestic.

རྔམ་བརྗིད་སྟོན (ŋəmjii dön) see རྔམ་བརྗིད.

རྔམ་སྟབས (ŋāmdəb) a ferocious/ war-like manner.

རྔམ་སྟོན (ŋāmdön) rally, demonstration, va.—བྱེད ༑ དམག་འཁྲུག་ལ་ངོ་རྒོལ་གྱི་རྔམ་སྟོན A demonstration to protest the war.

རྔམ་སྟོན་སྐད་འབོད་ཁྲོམ་བསྐོར (ŋāmdön gɛ̄mböö trōmgɔɔ) sm. རྔམ་སྟོན་ཁྲོམ་བསྐོར.

རྔམ་སྟོན་ཁྲོམ་བསྐོར (ŋāmdön trōmgɔɔ) demonstration, march, rally; va.—བྱེད to stage a demonstration/ march/ rally.

རྔམ་སྟོན་ཚོགས་ཆེན (ŋāmdön tsōgjen) rally (political).

རྔམ་པའི་ཆ་བྱད (ŋāmbɛ cājɛɛ̀) a costume used when performing religious dances or operas or plays.

རྔམ་པོ (ŋāmbo) sm. ཛིག་རྔམ་ཆེན་པོ.

རྔམ་པོ་ཆེ (ŋāmboje) sm. རྔམ་བརྗིད.

རྔམ་མེད་སྤྱོད་གཙང (ŋāmmeè jöödzaŋ) honest and upright, upright and not corrupt.

རྔམ་གཙིགས (ŋāmdzii) threatening, baring one's fangs; va.—སྟོན to threaten by one's expression, to bare one's fangs.

རྔམ་གཙིགས་སྡོམ (ŋāmdzig dom) sm. འཆམ་གཙིགས་སྡོམ.

རྔམ་ཞིང་མི་སྡུག་པ (ŋəmshiŋ midugbə) ugly and fearsome (images in tangka painting).

རྔམ་ཟིལ (ŋəmsil) sm. རྔམ་བརྗིད.

རྔམ་གཟིར (ŋāmsir) demonstrating.

རྔམ་ཤུགས (ŋəmshuù) might, power.

རྔམ་སེམས (ŋāmsem) greed; va.—བྱེད to act greedy.

རྔམ་སེམས་ཅན (ŋāmsemjɛn) greedy.

རྔམས་བརྗིད (ŋāmjii) sm. རྔམ་བརྗིད.

རྔུ་མ (ŋūmə) gum/ crud in the eyes.

རྔུབ: p. བརྔུབས; f. བརྔུབ; imp. རྔུབས (ŋūb) va. to inhale, to breathe in ༑ ཐལ་བ་རྔུབ I inhaled dust. ༑ ངས་ཆང་ཧུབ་རྔུབ་བྱས་པ་རེད I swallowed a mouthful of beer.

རྔུབ་གཏོང (ŋūb dōŋ) breathing in and out, inhaling in and out; va.—བྱེད.

རྔུབ་གཏོང་བྱེད་ལམ (ŋūbdoŋ ceèlam) respirator.

རྔུབ་འཐུང (ŋūbduŋ) sucking sth. in.

རྔུབ་པ (ŋūbbə) snoring; va.—གཏོང to snore.

རྔུབ་རྭ (ŋūbra) sm. རྔབ་རྭ.

རྔུབས (ŋūb) imp. of རྔུབ.

རྔུར་ལྟ (ŋūr dā) va. to stare/ glare angrily.

རྔུལ (ŋǖǖ) 1. vi. to sweat, to perspire ༑ ཁོ་གཟུགས་པོ་ཞེ་དྲག་རྔུལ་གྱི་འདུག He perspires a lot. 2. sweat, perspiration.

རྔུལ་ཁྲག (ŋǖǖdraà) blood and sweat; va.—འདོན to shed sweat and blood (i.e., make sacrifices).

རྔུལ་ཁྲག་གི་ཕོགས་ཐོབ (ŋǖǖdraàgi pɔ̄ɔ̀dob) wages earned by hard work (blood and sweat).

རྔུལ་འཁྱག (ŋǖǖgyaà) feeling cold after sweating; va.—བྱེད.

རྔུལ་ཆུ (ŋǖǖju) 1. sm. རྔུལ་ནག. 2. Salween R.

རྔུལ་ཆུ་ཁྲུམ་ཁྲུམ (ŋǖǖcu trūmdrum) sm. རྔུལ་ཆུ་ཁྲོམ་ཁྲོམ.

རྔུལ་ཆུ་ཁྲོམ་ཁྲོམ (ŋǖǖcu trōmdrom) covered/ dripping with sweat.

རྔུལ་ཆུ་འབབ (ŋǖǖju bəb) vi. to sweat.

རྔུལ་ཐིག (ŋǖǖdig) a drop of sweat ༑ གདོང་ནས་རྔུལ་ཐིག་ཟགས་བཞག Drops of sweat fell from his face.

རྔུལ་དྲི (ŋǖǖdri) smell of sweat, vi.—ཁ to smell of sweat.

རྔུལ་དྲི་ཁ (ŋǖǖdri kā) vi. to smell the scent of sweat.

རྔུལ་ནག (ŋǖǖnaà) sweat, perspiration; vi.—རྒྱག; —ཤོར; —ཐོན; —འདོན; —བཞུར to sweat/ perspire.

རྔུལ་ནག་གི་ཚོས (ŋǖǖnaàgi tsöö) wet with sweat ༑ ཁོ་ཚོའི་དམག་གོས་རྔུལ་ནག་གི་ཚོས་ཡོད་པ་རེད Their uniforms were wet with sweat.

རྔུལ་ནག་འཚུབ་འཚུབ (ŋǖǖnaà tsūbdzub) sweaty, steaming with sweat (from fear or exertion).

ངུལ་ནག་འཚུབ་འཚུབ་བཟོ་ (ŋüünaà tsūbdzub so) 1. vi. to give somebody a hard time 2. to make someone sweat.

ངུལ་དབྱུང་ (ŋüü yüŋ) va. to sweat an illness out (usu. when sick with fever).

ངུལ་མ་ (ŋüümə) sm. ངུལ་ནག.

ངུལ་ཞམ་མེ་བ་ (ŋüüsham mewa) feeling sweaty.

ངུལ་ཟིལ་ (ŋüüsii) beads of sweat.

ངུལ་གཟན་གྱི་གཟན་ (ŋüüsɛngi sɛn) a type of shawl monk's wear.

ངུལ་ལེན་ (ŋüülen) undershirt, thin cotton shirt worn by monks under their robe.

ངེའུ་ (ŋēwu) sm. ང་ཕྲུག.

ངེ་ཙན་ (ŋējɛn) sm. བཀྲམ་ཆགས་.

ངོ་ (ŋō) 1. a class of skin diseases such as mange, scabies, ringworm; vi.—རྒྱག to get mange/ scabies/ ringworm. 2. sm. ངོད་.

ངོ་ངོ་སྲག་སྲག (ŋōŋo drāgdrag) deep frying in oil.

ངོ་ངོ་སྲེག་སྲེག (ŋōŋo sēgseg) sm. ངོ་ངོ་སྲག་སྲག.

ངོ་ཏོག (ŋōdɔɔ̀) sm. ངོ་ཐོགས་.

ངོ་ཐོགས་ (ŋōtɔɔ̀) 1. vi. to be able, to be capable (of). 2. useful.

ངོ་འཐག (ŋōndaà) roasting grain; va.—རྒྱག.

ངོ་འཐག་རྒྱག་མཁན་ (ŋōdaà gyagɛn) a person who roasts barley.

ངོ་ནད་ (ŋōnɛɛ̀) sm. ངོ་.

ངོ་མི་ཐོགས་ (ŋōmidɔɔ̀) 1. not useful. 2. incapable, unable.

ངོ་སྨན་ (ŋōmɛn) medicine for scabies/ sores.

ངོ་ཚང་ (ŋōdzang) place where barley is roasted.

ངོ་བཟོ་ (ŋōbso) people who work with leather, tanners.

ངོ་ལོ་ལངས་ཏེ་འཕྱུར་བ་ (ŋōlo laŋde cār) sm. ངོ་ལོ་འཕྱུར་.

ངོ་ལོ་འཕྱུར་ (ŋōlo cār) vi. to do something stupid or embarrassing, to make a fool of oneself, to bring shame on sb., to lose face.

ངོ་ཤུ་ (ŋōshu) mange.

ངོག་དཀར་ (ŋōgdɛn) horses and mules that have white manes.

ངོག་ཆུང་ (ŋōgjuŋ) sm. ཟེ་.

ངོག་སྟན་ (ŋōgdɛn) a type of rug with frilled edges.

ངོག་སྟན་གྲུམ་ཙེ་ (ŋōgma drumdze) sm. ངོག་སྟན་.

ངོག་ནག (ŋōgnaà) horses with black tails/ manes.

ངོག་མ་ (ŋōgma) mane.

ངོག་ཤད་ (ŋōgshɛɛ̀) brush or comb for manes.

ངོད་: p. བརྔོས་; f. བརྔོད་; imp. ངོས་ (ŋöö) 1. va. to fry, to roast, to parch (grains). 2. va. to seduce/ lure/ dupe.

ངོད་སྐྱོར་ (ŋōgyɔr) frying/ roasting again, va.—རྒྱག.

ངོད་སྡེགས་ (ŋöödeg) a tall stove for roasting grain.

ངོད་འཐག (ŋöödaà) abbr. roasting and grinding.

ངོད་འཐག་ཝུ་ལག (ŋöödaà wulaà) corvee labor called for roasting and grinding grains.

ངོད་འཕར་ (ŋōmbar) shung. an additional tax collected when the Dalai Lama attends the Monlam Festival.

ངོད་རྫ་ (ŋöödza) earthenware utensils for roasting grain.

ངོད་སླང་ (ŋöölaŋ) metal wok used for roasting grain.

ངོན་ (ŋōn) hunting; va.—རྒྱག to hunt ། ཁོས་རི་དྭགས་བརྔོན་སོང་ He hunted animals.

ངོན་ཁྱི་ (ŋōngyi) hunting dog.

ངོན་ཁྲ་ (ŋōndra) bird used for hunting (as in falconing).

ངོན་གྲབས་གདུང་སྒམ་ (ŋōndrəb duŋgam) doing sth. in anticipation of sth. else [Lit. a wooden box in preparation of hunting, a coffin made in advance (in preparation) of death].

ངོན་མདའ་ (ŋōnda) hunting rifle.

ངོན་པ་ (ŋōmba) hunter; va.—རྒྱག to hunt.

ངོན་པའི་བྱ་འགྲོས་ (ŋōmbɛ cadröö) a style of dance in Tibetan opera.

ངོན་པས་འདོན་རྒྱག (ŋōmbɛɛ̀ töngyaà) the opening song in the Tibetan opera.

ངོམ་ (ŋōm) see ངམས་.

ངོམ་བརྗིད་ (ŋōmjii) sm. ངམ་བརྗིད་.

ངོམ་བག (ŋōmbaà) fierce, scary looking.

ངོས་ (ŋöö) 1. imp. of ང་. 2. sometimes used for ངོད་.

ངོས་ཁྱེར་ (ŋöö kyēr) vi. to die from a skin disease (like mange, scabies).

ལྔ་ (ŋā) five ། ལྔ་བརྒྱ་ལྔ་བཅུ་ང་ལྔ་ Five hundred and fifty five.

ལྔ་སྐྱེད་ (ŋāgyeè) shung. 10% interest rate.

ལྔ་ཁང་ (ŋagaŋ) a house distributed to five people (e.g., in a refugee settlement).

ལྔ་འགར་ཐོབ་པ་ (ŋagar tōbba) five things give as relief : firewood, tsampa, clothes, tea, butter.

ལྔ་བརྒྱ་ (ŋābgya) five hundred.

ལྔ་གཅིག (ŋəjii) 1. May 1st. 2. abbr. ལྔ་གཅིག་རྒྱལ་སྤྱིའི་ངལ་རྩོལ་དུས་ཆེན་.

ལྔ་གཅིག་རྒྱལ་སྤྱིའི་ངལ་རྩོལ་དུས་ཆེན་ (ŋəjii gyɛɛjii ŋɛɛdzö tücen) May Day (May 1st)—International Labor Day.

ལྔ་གཅིག་ངལ་རྩོལ་དུས་ཆེན་ (ŋəjii ŋɛɛdzö tüüjen) sm. ལྔ་གཅིག་རྒྱལ་སྤྱིའི་ངལ་རྩོལ་དུས་ཆེན་.

ལྔ་བཅུ་ (ŋəpju) fifty.

ལྔ་ཆ་ (ŋāja) a fifth ། ལྔ་ཆ་གཉིས་ two fifths.

ལྔ་ཆ་གཅིག (ŋāja jii) one fifth.

ལྔ་མཆོད་ (ŋāmjöö) anniversary of the death of Tsongkhapa (founder of Gelug sect).

ལྔ་སྟོང་ (ŋādoŋ) five thousand.

ལྔ་དྲུག་སྐྱེད་ (ŋātrugyeè) shung. 20% interest (on loans) [Lit. pay back six ཁལ་ for each five ཁལ་ borrowed].

ལྔ་དྲུག་འགྲོ་ (ŋātruù dro) shung. 20% interest [Lit. pay back six ཁལ་ or each five ཁལ་ borrowed].

ལྔ་བདུན་ (ŋā dün) May 7th.

ལྔ་བདུན་ལས་བྱེད་སློབ་གྲྭ་ (ŋādün lɛɛ̀ceè lōbdra) May 7th cadre school (named after Mao's May 7th directive of 1966).

ལྔ་བརྒྱའི་དུས་ (ŋādö tüü) a period degeneration.

ལྔ་པ་ (ŋāba) 1. the fifth ། ཉི་མ་ལྔ་པ་ The fifth day. 2. a type of monk's attire. 3. dying, passing away.

ལྔ་པ་ཆེན་པོ་ (ŋāba cēmbo) the great fifth, i.e., the Fifth Dalai Lama.

ལྔ་པའི་ལམ་ (ŋābɛ lam) at the time of death.

ལྔ་པའི་ལམ་དུ་འགྲོ་ (ŋābɛ lamdu dro) vi. to die.

ལྔ་ཚིག་སྙན་ངག (ŋətsig ñɛ̄nŋaà) a poem with five characters/ syllables to a line.

ལྔ་བཞི་ (ŋəshi) May 4th.

ལྔ་བཞི་གཞོན་ནུའི་དུས་ཆེན་ (ŋəshi shönnü tüüjen) May 4th— Youth Day.

ལྔ་བཞིའི་ལས་འགུལ་ (ŋəshi lɛngüü) the May Fourth Movement (the demonstration in 1919 protesting the "Twenty One Demands" made by Japan).

ལྔ་རིག (ŋərig) sm. རིག་གནས་ལྔ་.

ལྔ་རིག་པ་ (ŋā rigbə) one who knows the major sciences: grammar/ Sanskrit, medicine, logic, philosophy and the arts.

ལྔ་ལམ་ (ŋālam) at the time of death.

ལྔ་ལོར་ (ŋālɔr) a kind of paper money in tt. worth five སྲང་.

སྔ་ (ŋā) abbr. of སྔ་པོ་ ། ང་སྔ་དྲགས་འདུག I was too early.

སྔ་སྐྲག་ཕྱི་སྐྲག (ŋādraà cīdraà) excessively afraid/ fearful, always afraid.

སྔ་སྐྲག་ཕྱི་འཇིགས་ (ŋādraà cījig) sm. སྔ་སྐྲག་ཕྱི་སྐྲག.

སྔ་འཁོན་ད་འཁྲུས་ (ŋāgön tandrɛɛ̀) shung. holding old and new grudges.

སྔ་འཁོན་ཞི་བཞག (ŋāgön sheshaà) nursing hatred, harboring resentment, holding an old grudge ། དཔལ་མགོད་འཁྲུན་གཙང་ཆོད་ཟིན་རྗེས་གྱོད་ཡ་གཉིས་ཀས་སྔ་འཁོན་ཞི་བཞག་གིས་འཁོན་ལན་སློག་མི་ཆོག Once the case is settled, both parties are not allowed to hold grudges and retaliate against each other.

སྔ་མགོ་ (ŋāgɔ) sm. སྔ་མ་.

སྔ་གུང་ (ŋāguŋ) morning and afternoon.

སྔ་གུང་དགོང་ (ŋāguŋ goŋ) moring, afternoon and evening.

སྔ་གོང་ (ŋāgoŋ) prior, before, beforehand.

སྔ་གོམས་སོར་གནས་ (ŋāgom sōrnɛɛ̀) old fashioned, traditional, refusing to change.

སྔ་གྲོགས་དགོང་དགྲ་ (ŋādrog goŋdra) friends in the morning and enemies by night.

སྔ་གྲོལ་ (ŋādröö) adjourning earlier than usual.

སྔ་གློ་ (ŋālo) the upper strap that goes around the legs of horses to hold the saddle.

སྔ་དགོང་ (ŋāgoŋ) morning and night/ evening.

སྔ་འགལ་ (ŋāngɛɛ) shung. (the person/ party) who violates the law first ¶ ཁྲ་དོན་རས་སུ་བོར་བའི་རིགས་གཉིས་ཐད་ནས་ཉེལ་ཤུན་ཙམ་བྱུང་སྲིད་ཚེ་སྔ་འགལ་ནས་འབབ་གསེར་སྲང་གཉིས་སྐྱབ་ཐོག If there are any violations against the verdict, the party who violates the first shall pay 2 སྲང་ of gold as a fine.

སྔ་འགྱུར་ (ŋāgyur) 1. early translations during time of the kings. 2. the Nyingma sect, the teachings of the Nyingma sect.

སྔ་འགྱེལ་རྗེས་མཐུད་ (ŋāgyee jeètüü) sending one after another, wave upon wave, to replenish those troops in the front that have been killed; va.—བྱེད་.

སྔ་འགྱོད་ངོས་ལེན་ (ŋāgyöò ŋölen) admitting/ confessing and repenting; va.—བྱེད་; — ཞུ་.

སྔ་འགྱོད་ཕྱི་འདོམས་ (ŋāgyöò cīndom) repenting/ regretting and making a fresh start, changing heart, reforming past ways; va.—བྱེད་.

སྔ་འགྱོད་ཕྱི་སྡོམ་ (ŋāgyöò cīdom) repenting/ regretting and making a fresh start, changing heart, reforming; va.—བྱེད་.

སྔ་འགྲས་ད་འཁོན་ (ŋāndrɛɛ̀ tangön) continuing to harbor enmity from the past.

སྔ་འགྲས་ཕྱི་འཁོན་ (ŋāndrɛɛ̀ cīngön) old and new enmity/ hatred, new hatred added onto old ones.

སྔ་འགྲོ་ཕྱི་ཡོང་ (ŋādro cīyoŋ) going out early and coming back late; va.—བྱེད་.

སྔ་འགྲོའི་རོལ་མོ་ (ŋādrö röömo) prelude, overture (in music).

སྔ་རྒྱག (ŋāgyaà) premature fighting/ attacking; va.—བྱེད་ to attack prematurely.

སྔ་རྒྱུན་གཞི་བཟུང་ (ŋāgyɛn shisuŋ) as before, as in the past.

སྔ་རྒྱུས་ད་རྒྱུས་ (ŋāgyüù tagyüù) chit chat, talk about this and that; va.—ཤོད་ [Lit. old events and new events].

སྔ་སྔ་ (ŋāŋa) 1. very early. 2. long long ago.

སྔ་ཆ་ (ŋāja) 1. the earlier part of the day, morning (until noon). 2. previous time period.

སྔ་ཆད་ (ŋājɛɛ̀) sm. སྔོན་ཆད་.

སྔ་ཆས་ (ŋājɛɛ̀) period costume.

སྔ་རྗེས་ (ŋājeè) 1. before and after ¶ ལས་ཀའི་སྔ་རྗེས་སུ་ Before and after work. 2. sooner or later, eventually ¶ སྔ་རྗེས་སུ་ཚང་མ་ལས་སྒོར་ཞུགས་པ་རེད་ Sooner or later they all joined to work. 3. many times, on different occasions ¶ ངས་དྲན་བསྐུལ་སྔ་རྗེས་བྱས་ཀྱང་ཁོས་བྱས་མི་འདུག Even though I reminded him many times, he didn't do it. 4. in order, one after another ¶ ཁོ་གཉིས་སྔ་རྗེས་ཀྱི་ཐེབས་པ་རེད་ They left one after the other.

སྔ་རྗེས་བར་གསུམ་ (ŋājeè parsum) at all times, throughout a process [Lit. before, in the middle, at the end].

སྔ་རྗེས་མ་གཏོགས་ (ŋājeè mandoò) sm. སྔ་རྟིང་མ་གཏོགས་.

སྔ་ཉིན་ (ŋāñin) the preceding day, the day before (some event).

སྔ་ཏོག (ŋādɔɔ̀) early crop.

སྔ་བཏབ་ (ŋədəb) early sowing.

སྔ་རྟིང་ (ŋədiŋ) 1. order, stages, steps (in doing things) ¶ ལས་ཀའི་སྔ་རྟིང་རིམ་པ་གསུམ་ཡོད་ There are three steps in doing the work. 2. in order, one after another ¶ འགྲུལ་པ་ཚོར་སྔ་རྟིང་གིས་གསོལ་ཚིགས་ཞུལ་བ་རེད་ The travelers were served one after another (in order).

སྔ་རྟིང་བརྗེ་ (ŋədiŋ je) sm. སྔ་རྟིང་ལྡོག.

སྔ་རྟིང་སྤྲོད་ (ŋədiŋ drȫò) va. to give sth. beforehand, to give in advance.

སྔ་རྟིང་མ་གཏོགས་ (ŋədiŋ məndoò) sooner or later, eventually ¶ སྔ་རྟིང་མ་གཏོགས་ང་ཚོ་ཚང་མ་འགྲོ་གི་ཡིན་ Sooner or later we are all going.

སྔ་རྟིང་འཛར་འཛར་ (ŋədiŋ dzardzar) continuously, one after another.

སྔ་རྟིང་རིམ་ (ŋədiŋ rim) sm. སྔ་སྟིང་.

སྔ་རྟིང་ལོག (ŋədiŋ lɔɔ̀) sm. སྔ་རྟིང་ཤོར་.

སྔ་རྟིང་ཤོར་ (ŋədiŋ shɔ̄ɔ̀) sm. སྔ་རྟིང་ལོག.

སྔ་རྟིང་ཤོར་ (ŋədiŋ shɔ̄ɔ̄) 1. vi. to miss (a sequence, time) to have bad timing, to fail to coincide ¶ ཁོ་གཉིས་རྒྱ་གར་ནས་ཐོན་དུས་སྔ་རྟིང་ཤོར་བཞག They weren't able to leave India at the same time. 2. vi. to get/ fall out of place or order, to be not in the right order.

སྔ་རྟིང་ལྡོག (ŋədiŋ lɔ̄ɔ̀) vi. to reverse/ invert/ change the order.

སྔ་ལྟས་ (ŋādɛɛ̀) 1. early sign, omen, portent ¶ སད་རྒྱག་པའི་སྔ་ལྟས་ An early sign of frost. 2. symptom.

སྔ་བལྟས་ཕྱི་བལྟས་ (ŋābdɛɛ̀ cīdɛɛ̀) looking to the future and the past, considering the past and future; va.—བྱེད་.

སྔ་བལྟས་ཕྱི་སྲུང་ (ŋābdɛɛ̀ cīsuŋ) looking/ considering the past to protect the future.

སྔ་བལྟས་ཕྱི་བསམ་ (ŋābdɛɛ̀ cīsam) taking into account/ looking to both the past and the future, looking to the past and thinking for the future.

སྔ་ཐག་ཕྱི་ཐག (ŋātaà cīdaà) tying (a prisoner) by a rope and having a person hold each end of the rope; va.—རྒྱག.

སྔ་ཐུན་ (ŋədün) the prayers done first thing in the morning.

སྔ་ཐོག (ŋādɔɔ̀) 1. in the morning, early, in the beginning, at the start/ early part of sth. ¶ རྩེ་ལོའི་འགྲན་བསྡུར་དེ་སྔ་ཐོག་ཁོ་ཚོར་ཐོབ་ནའང་ Even if they win the game at the start. 2. for the time being ¶ སྔ་ཐོག་འདི་གར་སྡོད་ཀྱི་ཡིན་ (We) are staying here for the time being.

སྔ་ཐོག་ནས་ (ŋādognɛ) in advance, beforehand ¶ དགོས་མཁོ་ཚང་མ་གྲ་སྒྲིག་སྔ་ཐོག་ནས་བྱས་ཟིན་པ་རེད་ They prepared all the requirements in advance.

སྔ་ཐོན་ཕྱི་ལོག (ŋādön cīlɔɔ̀) working very hard [Lit. leaving early, returning late].

སྔ་མཐུད་ཕྱི་འདྲེན་ (ŋədüù cīdren) carrying on ancestral/ ancient traditions.

སྔ་དར་ (ŋādar) the first coming of Buddhism to Tibet in the 7th century.

སྔ་དུས་ (ŋātdüù) in the old days, in former times, in the past.

སྔ་དྲན་ཕྱི་མནོ་ (ŋādrɛn cīno) remembering the past and thinking of the future.

སྔ་དྲོ་ (ŋādro) morning, a.m. ¶ སྔ་དྲོ་ཆུ་ཚོད་10 ཐོག At 10 a.m.

སྔ་དྲོ་དགོང་ལ་སྐྱེལ་ (ŋādro goŋla gyēē) from morning to evening.

སྔ་དྲོ་རྟ་ཕོ་ཆས་ཀྱིས་གསོས་ན་ ཕྱི་དྲོ་དྲིན་ལན་འཕྲ་ཡིས་འཇལ་ (ŋādro dābo cɛɛ̀gi sȫòna cīdro trinlɛn trāyi jɛɛ) if one helps evil people they will be ungrateful or harm you in return [Lit. if you feed the stallion in the morning it will kick you in the afternoon].

སྔ་དྲོ་བདེ་ལེགས་ (ŋādro deleè) a new greeting said in the morning: "good morning."

སྔ་དྲོའི་ཆར་ (ŋādrö cār) shung. in the morning.

སྔ་འདང་རྒྱག (ŋādaŋ gyaà) va. to think about the past.

སྔ་འདོན་ (ŋādön) prepayment, advance/ down payment; va.—བྱེད་; —སྤྲོད་; —གཏོང་ to advance (money), to make a down payment.

སྔ་(བ)སྣུར་ (ŋā nūr) 1. ahead/ in advance of

schedule ། ཁོ་ཚོའི་ལས་སྣལ་དུས་བཀག་གི་སྔ་བསྐུར་དུ་ཚར་པ་རེད་ They finished their share of the work ahead of schedule. 2. an advance, a short term loan; va.—བྱེད་ ། ཁོའི་གླ་ཕོགས་ཐོབ་རྒྱུར་བརྟེན་དངུལ་ཕྲན་བུ་སྔ་བསྐུར་བྱས་པ་ཡིན་ I loaned him some money because he hasn't received his salary yet.

སྔ་ན་ (ŋāna) before, in the past ། སྔ་ན་མ་གྲགས་པ་ Never known before.

སྔ་ན་མེད་པ་ (ŋāna me̱èba) unprecedented, not known or happened in the past.

སྔ་ནུབ་ (ŋə̄nub) 1. last night. 2. (on the) eve (of) ། རྒྱལ་ཡོངས་བཅིངས་འགྲོལ་གཏོང་བའི་སྔ་ནུབ་ On the eve of the liberation of the nation.

སྔ་པོ་ (ŋābo) early, in advance ། ཁོ་ཚོས་གྲ་སྒྲིག་སྔ་པོར་བྱས་པར་བརྟེན་ Because they prepared (themselves) in advance. ། ཁོ་སྔ་པོ་ལང་གི་འདུག He gets up early.

སྔ་པོ་སྔ་པོ་ (ŋābo ŋābo) very early.

སྔ་དཔེ་ (ŋābe) a precedent.

སྔ་སྤྱོད་ (ŋājöö) using sth. (usu. provisions) too early; va.— བྱེད་.

སྔ་ཕྱི་ (ŋə̄ji) before and after, early and late, past and future, previous and next, on multiple occasions ། ཚེ་སྔ་ཕྱི་ The past life and the next life. ། ད་ཚོད་སྔ་ཕྱི་གང་ལ་ཕེབས་ཀྱང་འགྲིགས་ཀྱི་རེད་ It's all right whatever time you come (earlier or later). ། བོད་ཀྱི་ནང་སྲིད་ལ་ཐེ་རྫུས་སྔ་ཕྱི་བྱས་ཡོད་པ་རེད་ They interfered in the internal affairs of Tibet time and time again (earlier and later).

སྔ་ཕྱི་ཀུན་དུ་ (ŋə̄ji gǖntu) from beginning to end, throughout, all the time ། ཁོ་ཚོ་སྔ་ཕྱི་ཀུན་དུ་གཉའ་གནོན་བྱས་ཡོད་པ་རེད་ (They) oppressed them all the time.

སྔ་ཕྱི་གོ་ལྡོག (ŋə̄ji ko̱dɔɔ̀) reversing or changing the order/ priority, reversing that which comes earlier and later.

སྔ་ཕྱི་འགལ་འཁྲུལ་ (ŋə̄ii trɛ̄ŋgɛɛ) contradiction between past and future.

སྔ་ཕྱི་བར་གསུམ་ (ŋə̄ji pa̱rsum) always, all the time.

སྔ་ཕྱི་མེད་ (ŋə̄ji me̱è) sm. སྔ་ཕྱི་ཀུན་དུ་.

སྔ་ཕྱི་འཛར་འཛར་ (ŋə̄ji dza̱rdzar) continuously, one after another.

སྔ་ཕྱི་རན་པོ་ (ŋə̄ji rɛ̱mbo) a suitable time, neither late or early.

སྔ་ཕྱི་ལ་མ་བལྟོས་པར་ (ŋə̄jilə ma̱dȫöbar) sooner or later, regardless of when ། སྔ་ཕྱི་ལ་མ་བལྟོས་པར་དེ་བྱེད་དགོས་རེད་ Sooner or later (we) will have to do it.

སྔ་ཕྱིའི་ཡོང་རྐྱེན་ (ŋə̄jii yo̱ŋgyen) shung. events that happened in the past and later on, all the things that happened ། སྔ་ཕྱིའི་ཡོང་རྐྱེན་གསལ་འཁོད་ཀྱི་སྙན་ཞུ་འབུལ་འབུལ་དགོས་རྒྱུ་ (You) must send a report in which all the events that happened are written clearly.

སྔ་ཕྱིར་ (ŋə̄jir) sm. སྔ་ཕྱི་.

སྔ་ཕྱིར་སྡེ་བརྗེ་ (ŋə̄jir de̱je) sm. སྔ་ཕྱིར་གོ་ལྡོག.

སྔ་ཕྱིར་མ་བལྟོས་པར་ (ŋə̄jir ma̱dȫöbar) sm. སྔ་ཕྱི་ལ་མ་བལྟོས་པར་.

སྔ་ཕྱེད་ (ŋə̄jeè) the period of morning until afternoon.

སྔ་འདྲོ་ (ŋāndro) leftover, remnant, remainder.

སྔ་འདྲོས་ (ŋāndröö) 1. temporarily, for the time being ། སྔ་འདྲོས་ཨ་རི་ར་སྡོད་མཁན་ཡིན་ For the time being, (I) am staying in America. 2. at first, for the time being ། ཡུལ་དམག་མ་བཏང་ན་མི་འགྲིགས་སྔ་འདྲོས་ཉི་ཤུ་སུམ་བཅུ་ཙམ་གཏོང་གི་ཡིན་ It's not okay not to send the militia (so) for the time being (we) will send about 20 to 30.

སྔ་བ་ (ŋāwa) earlier ། སང་ཉིན་སྔ་བ་ར་ལང་དགོས་ཡོད་ (I) have to get up earlier tomorrow.

སྔ་བར་ཕྱི་གསུམ་ (ŋā pa̱r cī sūm) all the time, always [Lit. earlier, middle, later].

སྔ་བས་རྟ་ཁྲིད་ན་གཞུག་མ་མཛོ་ཁྲིད་ (ŋāwɛ dā triīnə su̱ùma dzo̱ triì) if you allow sb. to do sth. then you should allow others to do that also (i.e., give all the same opportunities) [Lit. if the former brings a horse, the latter will bring a dzo].

སྔ་བྱས་རྒྱབ་སྒྱུར་ (ŋājɛɛ̀ gyə̱bgyur) repenting/ rectifying/ mending one's ways (for the better); va.—བྱེད་.

སྔ་བྱས་རྒྱབ་བསྒྱུར་ (ŋājɛɛ̀ gyə̱bgyur) sm. སྔ་བྱས་རྒྱབ་སྒྱུར་.

སྔ་འབྱོར་ཕྱི་ལོག (ŋājɔɔ cīlɔɔ̀) working very hard [Lit. arriving early and leaving late].

སྔ་འབྲས་ (ŋāndrɛɛ̀) early rice, quick ripening rice.

སྔ་མ་ (ŋāma) before, in the past, formerly ། སྔ་མ་སྲིད་གཞུང་རྙིང་པའི་སྐབས་ Formerly, during the time of the old government.

སྔ་མ་སྔ་དིང་ (ŋāma ŋədiŋ) one after another in order.

སྔ་མ་སྔ་མ་ (ŋāma ŋāma) see སྔ་མོ་སྔ་མོ་.

སྔ་མའི་རྗེས་སུ་དཔག་པ་ (ŋāmɛ je̱èsu bāgba) using an analogy from the past.

སྔ་མའི་གནའ་རབས་ (ŋāmɛ nārəb) antiquity.

སྔ་མའི་མི་ཆེད་ (ŋāmɛ mi̱dzɛɛ̀) giants (of antiquity).

སྔ་མའི་ལས་ (ŋāmɛ lɛ̱ɛ̀) karma, cause and effect, fate from previous existence.

སྔ་མིང་ (ŋəmiŋ) former name/ title.

སྔ་མིན་ཕྱི་མིན་ (ŋəmiŋ cīmin) not early and not late.

སྔ་མོ་ (ŋāmo) 1. sm. སྔ་མ་. 2. sm. སྔར་.

སྔ་མོ་སྔ་མོ་ (ŋāma ŋāmo) long long ago.

སྔ་མོ་རྗེས་ཤུལ་ (ŋāmo je̱èshüü) relics, ruins.

སྔ་མོའི་ཅ་ལག (ŋāmö ja̱laà) antiques, things from the past.

སྔ་སྣུར་ཕྱི་འགྱངས་མེད་པ་ (ŋəñur cīngyaŋ me̱èba) to neither do sth. ahead of time nor delay doing it (doing it just at the right time) ། སྐབས་འཁེལ་སོ་སོའི་ཞུ་བྲོ་སྔ་སྣུར་ཕྱི་འགྱངས་མེད་པ་དགོས་རྒྱུ་ The scheduled works should not be done ahead of time nor be delayed.

སྔ་སྨིན་ (ŋəmin) 1. vi. to ripen/ mature early. 2. early ripening/ maturing crops.

སྔ་སྨིན་གྱི་འབྲས་ (ŋəmingi drɛ̱ɛ̀) early ripening rice.

སྔ་སྨིན་འབྲས་རིགས་ (ŋəmin drɛ̱ɛ̀rig) early ripening rice strains.

སྔ་ཙམ་ (ŋādzam) early, before too late ། ང་ཚོས་སྔ་ཙམ་བཙོངས་ན་ If we sell it early.

སྔ་ཚར་ (ŋātsar) stepchild.

སྔ་ཚིག་ཕྱི་འགལ་ (ŋādzii cīngɛɛ) a contradiction in what was said previously and what was said later (or is being said now).

སྔ་རྩོལ་རང་འཇོག (ŋədzul ra̱ŋjɔɔ̀) leaving sth. as it was before.

སྔ་འཛར་ (ŋāndzar) stepchild.

སྔ་ཞོགས་ (ŋāshɔɔ̀) morning.

སྔ་གཞུག (ŋəshuù) sm. སྔ་རྗེས་.

སྔ་བཞེངས་ཕྱི་གཟིམ་ (ŋāsheŋ cīsim) h. of སྔ་ལངས་ཕྱི་ཉལ་.

སྔ་ཟས་ (ŋāsɛɛ̀) breakfast.

སྔ་ཟས་ཐེབས་ (ŋāsɛɛ̀ tēb) vi. to run out of food at the end of the year (before the next harvest).

སྔ་གཡར་ (ŋāyar) an advance, a loan; va.—སྤྲོད་ to give a loan/ advance ། གཞུང་འབྲུ་སྐྱེད་མེད་སྔ་གཡར་སྤྲད་སོང་ (They) gave a no interest loan of government grain.

སྔ་རབས་ (ŋərəb) ancient.

སྔ་རབས་ཀྱི་སྐྱེ་དངོས་མཁས་པ་ (ŋərəbgi gyēŋöö kɛ̄ɛ̀ba) paleontologist.

སྔ་རབས་ཀྱི་སྐྱེ་དངོས་རིག་པ་ (ŋərəbgi gyēŋöö ri̱gbə) paleontology.

སྔ་རབས་ཀྱི་མི་ (ŋərəbgi mi̱) forefathers.

སྔ་རབས་ད་རབས་ (ŋərəb ta̱rəb) past and present events, old and new accounts/ histories.

སྔ་རབས་ཕྱི་འབྱུང་ (ŋərəb cījuŋ) things of the past and the future; past history and the future results.

སྔ་རུ་ (ŋəru) 1. the front of a Tibetan saddle. 2. earlier.

སྔ་རོལ་ (ŋāröl) before, prior, in the past, in days gone by ། སངས་རྒྱས་མ་བྱོན་པའི་སྔ་རོལ་ Before the Buddha came.

སྔ་རོལ་དུ་ (ŋāröldu) before, prior ། སངས་རྒྱས་མ་བྱོན་

པའི་སྔ་རོལ་དུ་ Before the Buddha came.

སྔ་ལག་དར་བཀོན་ (ŋālaà targön) shung. giving a ceremonial scarf (kata) in return for a gift ¶ བག་མའི་དགའ་སྟོན་ཟབ་རྒྱས་ཐོག་སྔ་ལག་དར་བཀོན་ At the wedding party they gave many ceremonial scarfs to those who gave gifts.

སྔ་ལངས་ (ŋālaŋ) rising early; va.—རྒྱག to rise early ¶ སང་ཉིན་སྔ་ལངས་བརྒྱབ་ནས་འགྲོ་ Tomorrow morning let's get up early and go.

སྔ་ལངས་ཕྱི་ཉལ་ (ŋālaŋ cīñɛɛ) working very hard, working long hours; va.—བྱེད་ [Lit. rising early, going to sleep late].

སྔ་ལམ་ (ŋālam) ancient/ previous customs and traditions.

སྔ་ལུས་ (ŋālüü) former structure/ organization.

སྔ་ལོ་ (ŋālo) last year.

སྔ་ལོགས་ (ŋālɔɔ) sm. སྔ་རོལ་.

སྔ་ཤ་ཕྱི་ཤ་ (ŋəsha cīsha) the front and back side of a saddle.

སྔ་ཤུ་ (ŋəshu) sm. སྔ་ར.

སྔ་ཤུག (ŋəshug) lending grain and other items to people in need; va.—གཏོང་.

སྔ་ཤུལ་ (ŋəshül) historical ruin/ relic, an ancient site.

སྔ་ཤོས་ (ŋāshöö) earliest, the first.

སྔ་ས་ (ŋāsa) earlier.

སྔ་ས་སྔ་གནས་ (ŋāsa ŋānɛɛ) remaining/ existing as before ¶ བོད་སྔ་ས་སྔ་གནས་ཡོང་གི་རེད་ Tibet will be as it was before.

སྔ་ས་ད་གནས་ (ŋāsa tanɛɛ) remaining/ keeping as before, maintaining the status quo; va.—ལ་འཇོག to leave as before, to leave intact, to maintain the status quo.

སྔ་ས་ནས་ (ŋāsanɛɛ) from before, from long ago, in advance, beforehand ¶ ཁོ་ཚོ་སྡོད་སའི་གྲ་སྒྲིག་སྔ་ས་ནས་བྱས་པ་རེད་ (They) made preparations for a place to stay beforehand. ¶ མའོ་ཙེ་ཏུང་གི་དགོངས་པའི་ཤུགས་རྐྱེན་དེ་སྔ་ས་ནས་ཀྲུང་གོའི་རྒྱལ་མཚམས་ལས་བརྒལ་ཟིན་པ་རེད་ The influence of Chairman Mao's thought extended beyond China's borders from long ago.

སྔ་སང་སང་ནས་ (ŋāsaŋ sāŋnɛ) sm. སྔ་ས་ནས་.

སྔ་སར་སར་ནས་ (ŋāsar sārnɛ) sm. སྔ་ས་ནས་.

སྔ་སོ་ (ŋāso) 1. in front, ahead. 2. in the past.

སྔ་སོར་ཆུད་ (ŋāsɔr cüü) va. to restore, to rebuild ¶ ཁོ་ཚོའི་ཡུལ་གཉིས་དབར་གྱི་མཐུན་འབྲེལ་སྔ་སོར་ཆུད་ཐབས་བྱས་པ་རེད་ (They) tried to restore friendly relations between the two countries.

སྔ་གསར་གསར་ (ŋā sārsar) beforehand, in advance.

སྔ་བསམ་ཕྱི་བལྟས་ (ŋāsam cīdɛɛ) sm. སྔ་བསམ་ཕྱི་དྲན་.

སྔ་བསམ་ཕྱི་དྲན་ (ŋāsam cīdrɛn) recalling over and over again; va.—བྱེད་.

སྔ་བསམ་ཕྱི་བསམ་ (ŋāsam cīsam) thinking over again and again; va.—བྱེད་.

སྔ་སྲོལ་ (ŋāsöö) old fashioned, traditional.

སྔ་སྲོལ་རྒྱུན་འཇགས་ (ŋāsöö gyünjaa) continuing as in the past or as usual, maintaining old customs/ traditions.

སྔ་སྲོལ་ལྟར་ (ŋāsöödar) as usual.

སྔ་བསླབས་ཕྱི་འདོམས་ (ŋāləb cīndom) learning from past experience, learning from past errors to avoid future mistakes.

སྔགས་ (ŋāà) mantra, tantra.

སྔགས་ཀྱི་ཐེག་པ་ (ŋāàgi tēgba) tantrayana.

སྔགས་སྐད་ (ŋāàgɛɛ) chanting mantras, the sound of mantras being chanted.

སྔགས་གྲྭ་ (ŋāàtra) tantric college.

སྔགས་རྒྱག (ŋāà kaà) va. to effect/ cause changes through the chanting of mantras.

སྔགས་རྒྱུད་ (ŋəgyüü) 1. tantric, tantra. 2. tantric scriptures.

སྔགས་ཆས་ (ŋəgjɛɛ) the clothing/ garb worn by tantric practitioners.

སྔགས་ཆུ་ (ŋəgju) water that has been blessed through the chanting of mantras.

སྔགས་འཆང་ (ŋāgjaŋ) tantric practitioners.

སྔགས་རྙིང་མ་ (ŋāà ñīŋmə) the Ningma sect.

སྔགས་ཐབས་ (ŋāgdəb) mantric/ tantric methods.

སྔགས་ཐུ་ (ŋāgtu) putting spit on sth. while doing a mantra/ tantra for curing illnesses; va.—རྒྱག.

སྔགས་དྲུང་ (ŋāgdruŋ) shung. abbr. the two representatives sent by the 9th. Panchen Lama to Lhasa in 1933 (སྔགས་ཆེན་བདར་པ་ཧོ་ཐོག་ཐུ་ and མཁན་དྲུང་མདངས་ཆེན་པ་).

སྔགས་སྡོམ་ (ŋāgdom) mantric/ tantric vows.

སྔགས་པ་ (ŋāgba) exorcist (usu. concerned with weather control).

སྔགས་པ་གྲྭ་ཚང་ (ŋāgba tradzaŋ) a college in larger monasteries such as Drepung where mantric rituals are taught.

སྔགས་ཕུར་ (ŋāgpur) pegs placed on the edge of fields that have been blessed with mantras to protect the fields.

སྔགས་ཚིག (ŋəgdzii) sm. སྔགས་སྐད་.

སྔགས་ཟོར་ (ŋāgsor) sacrificial (triangular) tormas that are used for driving away demons and evil spirits.

སྔགས་བཟླ་ (ŋāg da) va. to recite mantras.

སྔགས་བཟླས་ (ŋāg dɛɛ) p. of སྔགས་བཟླ་.

སྔགས་ཡིག (ŋāgyii) letters or notes containing mantric/ tantric incantations; va.—བྱེད་.

སྔགས་རམས་པ་ (ŋāgramba) 1. mantric initiate. 2. a type of Geshe degree.

སྔགས་རིགས་ (ŋāgrii) sm. སྔགས་རྒྱུད་.

སྔགས་ལུགས་ (ŋāgluù) mantric/ tantric tradition.

སྔགས་ས་ (ŋāgsa) sm. ས་སྔགས་.

སྔགས་གསར་མ་ (ŋāà sārma) sm. གསང་སྔགས་གསར་མ་.

སྔངས་ (ŋāŋ) sm. དངངས་.

སྔངས་སྐྲག (ŋāgdraà) see དངངས་སྐྲག.

སྔན་ཆད་ (ŋɛ̄njɛɛ) sm. སྔོན་ཆད་.

སྔན་དང་པོ་ (ŋɛ̄n tanbo) sm.* སྔོན་དང་པོ་.

སྔན་མ་ (ŋɛ̄nma) sm.* སྔོན་མ་.

སྔན་མ་ནང་བཞིན་ (ŋɛ̄nma nəŋshin) just like before.

སྔར་ (ŋār) formerly, in the past, before.

སྔར་བཀོད་འཆར་གཞི་ (ŋārgöö cəəshi) plans laid out beforehand/ in advance.

སྔར་ཁུངས་ (ŋārguŋ) belonging to the past.

སྔར་ཁོན་གཏིང་ནན་ (ŋārgön dīŋnɛɛ) an old and deep hatred/ animosity.

སྔ་འཁོན་ད་འགྲུས་ (ŋāgön tandrɛɛ) shung. holding old and new grudges.

སྔ་འཁོན་ཞི་བཞག (ŋāgön sheshaà) nursing hatred, harboring resentment, holding an old grudge ¶ ད་ལམ་གྱོད་འཁྲུན་གཙང་ཆོད་ཟིན་རྗེས་གྱོད་ཡ་གཉིས་ཀས་སྔ་འཁོན་ཞི་བཞག་གིས་འཁོན་ལན་སློག་མི་ཆོག Once the case is settled both parties are not allowed to hold grudges and retaliate against each other.

སྔར་གྱི་རྗེས་ཤུལ་ (ŋārgi jeèshül) old historical sites/ relics.

སྔར་འགྱོད་ཕྱི་འདོམས་ (ŋārgyöö cīndom) repenting and correcting oneself.

སྔར་རྒྱས་ (ŋārgɛɛ) the early/ prior diffusion (refers to first diffusion of Buddhism to Tibet).

སྔར་རྒྱུན་ལྟར་ (ŋərgyündar) as usual in the past, like before.

སྔར་རྒྱུན་ལྟར་འགྱུར་ (ŋərgyündar gyur) vi. to be restored like it was in the past, to return to what sth. was before.

སྔར་རྒྱུན་ནང་བཞིན་ (ŋərgyün nəŋshin) just as before.

སྔར་རྒྱུན་འཛིན་ (ŋəgyün dzin) va. to follow one's customs/ traditions.

སྔར་སྔ་མོ་ (ŋār ŋāmo) a long long time ago, in antiquity.

སྔར་ཆགས་ནགས་ཚལ་ (ŋārjaà nagdzɛɛ) virgin forest.

སྔར་ཆད་ (ŋārjɛɛ) sm. སྔར་.

སྔར་རྗེས་གཅོད་ (ŋārjeè jöö) va. to investigate the past, to look into the past.

སྔར་འཇགས་ (ŋārjaà) as before; va.—འཇོག to leave as before ¶ སྔོན་ཁ་སྔར་འཇགས་འཇོག་རྒྱུ་ལས་བསམ་བློ་མེད་ (I) have no thoughts other than leaving the hospital as before.

སྔར་ཉེས་ (ŋārñeè) crimes/ misdeeds of the past.

སྔར་ལྟར་ (ŋārdar) like before, as before.

སྔར་ལྟར་འགྱུར་ (ŋārdar gyu̱r) sm. སྔར་རྒྱུན་ལྟར་འགྱུར་.

སྔར་འདས་ (ŋārdɛɛ̀) those who died before.

སྔར་དྲན་དེང་སྡུར་ (ŋārdrɛn de̱ŋdur) comparing the past with the present.

སྔར་འདྲིས་ (ŋārtriì) familiar/ known in the past, an acquaintance long ago.

སྔར་ན་མ་གྲགས་པ་ (ŋārna ma̱ tra̱gba) sm. སྔར་བྱུང་མ་མྱོང་བ་.

སྔར་ན་མེད་པ་ (ŋārna me̱èba) unprecedented, not known before.

སྔར་ནས་ (ŋārnɛɛ̀) from before, from the past/ previously.

སྔར་ནས་ད་བར་ (ŋārnɛ ta̱bar) from the past until now.

སྔར་གནས་སོར་བཞག (ŋārnɛɛ̀ sōrshaà) keeping as before, allowing to remain as it was before, maintaining tradition.

སྔར་ཕན་ (ŋārbɛn) from the past till now.

སྔར་ཕན་ཆད་ (ŋār pɛ̄njɛɛ̀) sm. སྔར་ཕན་.

སྔར་འཕྲོས་ (ŋāndröò) the earlier part/ section.

སྔར་བས་ (ŋārwɛɛ̀) more than before ¶ སྟོབས་ཤུགས་སྔར་བས་ཆེ་བ་ཡོད་པ་རེད་ (Their) power is greater than before.

སྔར་བས་ཀྱང་ (ŋārwɛgyaŋ) even more than before.

སྔར་བྱས་ (ŋārcɛɛ̀) past deeds/ actions ¶ སྔར་བྱས་ཀྱི་ལོ་རྒྱུས་ The history of (one's) past deeds.

སྔར་བྱས་ལ་རྩད་གཅོད་མི་བྱེད་ (ŋārcɛɛ̀la dzɛ̄jöò mi̱ceè) no investigation of past actions.

སྔར་བྱས་ལོ་རྒྱུས་ (ŋārcɛɛ̀ lu̱gyüù) one's past/ prior experience.

སྔར་བྱུང་ (ŋārjuŋ) occurred in the past/ previously ¶ སྔར་བྱུང་གོང་མ་རྣམས་ The emperors of the past.

སྔར་བྱུང་ད་གནས་ (ŋārjuŋ ta̱nɛɛ̀) sth. existed/ occurred in the past and still exists now.

སྔར་བྱུང་ཕྱི་ལྟ་ (ŋārjuŋ cīda) looking back at the past, viewing in retrospect, thinking about what happened in the past; va.— བྱེད་.

སྔར་བྱུང་མ་མྱོང་བ་ (ŋārjuŋ ma̱ñoŋwa) unprecedented, unheard of ¶ སྔར་བྱུང་མ་མྱོང་བའི་ལོ་ལེགས་ An unprecedented good yield. [Lit. never occurred in the past].

སྔར་བྱུང་མྱོང་མེད་ (ŋārjuŋ ñu̱ŋmeè) sm. སྔར་བྱུང་མ་མྱོང་བ་.

སྔར་མ་གྲགས་པ་ (ŋār madra̱gba) sm. སྔར་བྱུང་མ་མྱོང་བ.

སྔར་མི་གྲགས་ (ŋār mi̱drag) unknown/ not known in the past (never happened before).

སྔར་མུས་བཞིན་ (ŋārmüshin) as/ like before.

སྔར་མེད་ (ŋārmeè) sm. སྔར་བྱུང་མ་མྱོང་བ་.

སྔར་མེད་རྒྱས་སྤྲོས་ (ŋārmeè gye̱ɛ̀dröò) unprecedented lavishness.

སྔར་མེད་ལ་རྗེས་སུའང་མི་མཐོང་བ་ (ŋārmeèla je̱èsuaŋ mi̱toŋwa) existing at this moment only.

སྔར་མེད་གསར་སྤྲོས་ (ŋārmeè sārdröò) innovating, inventing.

སྔར་མེད་གསར་གཏོད་ (ŋārmeè sārdöò) innovating, inventing.

སྔར་མེད་གསར་དར་ (ŋārmèe sārdar) a new custom/ rule which is widely spread but did not exist in the past.

སྔར་མེད་གསར་སྤྲོས་ (ŋārmèe sārsöö) making sth. new (usu. a rule/ regulation) that did not exist in the past.

སྔར་མེད་གསར་སྲོལ་ (ŋārmèe sārsöö) a new custom that never existed in the past.

སྔར་དམིགས་ (ŋārmig) fixing in advance, predetermining.

སྔར་རྫོམ་ (ŋārdzom) ancient literature/ writings.

སྔར་བཞིན་ (ŋərshin) sm. སྔར་ལྟར་.

སྔར་བཞིན་རང་འཇགས་ (ŋərshin ra̱ŋjaà) just as before.

སྔར་ཡོད་ (ŋāryöö) existing in the past/ previously, formerly existed ¶ བོད་ནང་གི་མི་མང་ཚོ་སྔར་ཡོད་ས་གནས་སུ་སྡོད་ཆོག་གི་མ་རེད་ The people in Tibet are not allowed to stay in the places where they lived before. ¶ སྔར་ཡོད་དམག་སྒར་ Those regiments which existed previously.

སྔར་ལམ་ (ŋārlam) old ways, traditional customs, past customs ¶ སྔར་ལམ་ལྟར་མཛད་སྒོའི་གྲ་སྒྲིག་ཞུས་པ་རེད་ They made preparations for the ceremony according to the traditional custom. ¶ སྔར་ལམ་ལྟར་ In accordance with past customs.

སྔར་ལས་ལྷག་པ་ (ŋārlɛɛ̀ lhāgba) more than before.

སྔར་ལུགས་ (ŋərluù) old system, old customs/ traditions.

སྔར་ལུགས་སྦུག་འདྲེན་ (ŋərluù bu̱ŋdren) shung. taking or embezzling as was the custom before; va.— བྱེད་ ¶ གཞུང་རྩིས་ཞུ་སྒོ་གང་ཅི་སྔར་ལུགས་སྦུག་འདྲེན་དུ་མ་སོང་བ་དགོས་རྒྱུ་ On government accounting, there should be no embezzling as in the past.

སྔར་ཤུལ་ (ŋārshül) traces of the past, historic ruin/ site, place of historic interest.

སྔར་བཞགས་གསར་བཙོས་ (ŋārshag sārjöö) sm. སྔ་འགྱོད་ཕྱིས་འདོམས་.

སྔར་ས་ད་འཇགས་ (ŋārshag ta̱njöö) shung. to leave the land as before ¶ སྔར་ས་ད་འཇགས་ཀྱི་གཞུང་བསྐུལ་བཀའ་དཔྱད་འདྲ་གཉིས་ Two copies of the verdict was issued by the government for leaving the land as it was before

སྔར་ས་ད་གནས་ (ŋārsa ta̱nɛɛ̀) sm. སྔར་ས་ད་འཇག.

སྔར་སོང་ (ŋārsoŋ) past, elapsed ¶ སྔར་སོང་ལོ་རྒྱུས་ Past history.

སྔར་སོང་སྔ་མོ་ (ŋārsoŋ ŋāmo) sm. སྔར་.

སྔར་སོང་ཉི་མ་ (ŋārsoŋ ñi̱mə) previous day(s).

སྔར་སོང་ད་འགྲོ་ (ŋārsoŋ ta̱ndro) (a person thinking he will) get away with his (behavior) again as he has done before.

སྔར་སྲོལ་ (ŋārsöö) old custom/ convention/ tradition.

སྔར་སྲོལ་གཅེས་འཛིན་ (ŋārsöö jēèdzin) conservative, adhering to old ways and customs.

སྔར་སྲོལ་ལད་རྒྱིན་ (ŋārsöö lɛ̱ɛ̀gyen) old customs deteriorating/ declining.

སྔར་ལྷག (ŋārlhag) more than before.

སྔས་ (ŋɛ̄ɛ̀) pillow, cushion.

སྔས་ཁེབས་ (ŋɛ̄ɛ̀geb) pillow case.

སྔས་མགོ་ (ŋɛ̄ŋgo) 1. pillow. 2. head of a bed.

སྔས་མགོ་སྦྲེལ་ (ŋɛ̄ŋgo dre̱e̱) two people sleeping with pillows head to head.

སྔས་སྟན་ (ŋɛ̄ɛ̀dɛn) 1. pillow and mattress. 2. mattress.

སྔས་གདུག་དུ་ཉལ་ (ŋɛ̄ɛ̀dugtu ñɛ̱ɛ̱) va. to have two people sleep with their pillows head-to-head.

སྔས་གདན་ (ŋɛ̄ɛ̀dɛn) sm. སྔས་སྟན་.

སྔས་འབོལ་ (ŋɛ̄mböö) sm. སྔས་.

སྔས་མལ་ (ŋɛ̄ɛ̀mɛɛ) abbr. pillow and bedding.

སྔས་བརྫངས་ (ŋɛ̄ɛ̀dzaŋ) pillow.

སྔས་རིལ་ (ŋɛ̄ɛ̀rii) a pillow that has a long cylindrical shape.

སྔས་ལེབ་ (ŋɛ̄ɛ̀leb) flat pillow.

སྔས་ཤུབས་ (ŋɛ̄ɛ̀shub) pillow case.

སྔུན་ (ŋǖn) front.

སྔུན་བསུ་ (ŋǖnsu) a person who walks with incense, ceremonial scarf, etc. ahead of a high lama.

སྔུར་སྒྲ་ (ŋūrdra) sound of snoring.

སྔུར་སྔུར་པ་ (ŋūrŋurba) snoring; vi.—རྒྱག་; —གཏོང་ to snore.

སྔུར་ལྟ་ (ŋūr dā) va. to stare or glare angrily.

སྔུར་པ་ (ŋūrba) snoring; vi.—རྒྱག་; —གཏོང་ to snore.

སྔུར་ཛིག་ཛིག (ŋūr dzi̱gdzig) staring or glaring angrily.

སྔེ་ (ŋē) sm.* སྙེ་.

སྔེའུ་ (ŋēwu) a type of bean/ lentil.

སྔོ་ (ŋō) 1. vegetables, greens. 2. green, blue.

སྔོ་: p. བསྔོས་; f. བསྔོ་; imp. སྔོས་(ŋō) 1. va. to do a mental calculation. 2. va. to dedicate.

སྔོ་དཀར་ (ŋōgar) pale/ light blue.

སྔོ་སྐྱ་ (ŋōgya) light blue.

སྔོ་ཁ་ (ŋōga) sm. ཕྱུར་ཁུ་.

སྔོ་ཁྲ་ (ŋōdra) 1. cymbidium, orchid. 2. blue checkered material.

སྔོ་ཁྲིམས་ (ŋōdrim) shung. law/ regulation regarding protecting crops when they are green seedlings ¶ སྔོ་ཁྲིམས་སྐབས་རང་གཞན་སུས་ཀྱང་ཞིང་དབར་ར་ལུག་གཏོང་མི་ཆོག་པ་ No one is allowed to graze goats and sheep between the fields while the regulation regarding crops is in force.

སྔོ་ཁྲོད་ (ŋōdröö) shung. in/ among the crops (when they are green seedlings).

སྔོ་གན་ (ŋōgɛn) shung. a pledge signed concerning protecting crops when they are green seedlings.

སྔོ་གྲིག་ (ŋōdrig) shung. sm. སྔོ་གན་.

སྔོ་སྒོག་ (ŋōgɔɔ̀) garlic stems, plant greens.

སྔོ་ངད་ (ŋōŋɛɛ̀) the smell of vegetables.

སྔོ་ཅེ་རེ་ (ŋō jēre) the staring look of animals just before they die.

སྔོ་བཅད་ (ŋōjɛɛ̀) a blue outline (technique used in Tibetan painting).

སྔོ་ལྕ་བ་ (ŋō jāwa) a type of medicinal herb.

སྔོ་ལྕུག་གུ་ (ŋō jōggyu) a type of medicinal herb.

སྔོ་ལྕག་ལྕིག (ŋō jāgjig) patches of grass.

སྔོ་ཆས་ (ŋōjɛɛ̀) jewelry, ornaments.

སྔོ་ཆས་ཚོང་མཁན་ (ŋōjɛɛ̀ tsōŋgɛn) middlemen who sell jewelry and ornaments.

སྔོ་ཆུ་ (ŋōju) the first irrigation of seedlings; va.—གཏོང་.

སྔོ་ཆུ་ལོ་ (ŋō cūlo) rhubarb leaf.

སྔོ་ཆུང་ཉིབ་རལ་ (ŋōjuŋ ñībrɛɛ) a kind of edible herb.

སྔོ་ཆོས་ (ŋōjöö) religious texts written on dark blue paper with gold or silver letters.

སྔོ་ལྗང་ (ŋōjaŋ) emerald green, jade green, verdant.

སྔོ་ལྗང་ཅན་དུ་འགྱུར་ (ŋōjaŋ jɛ̄ndu gyu̱r) vi. to become green (by vegetation and trees having been planted).

སྔོ་ལྗང་ཅན་དུ་སྒྱུར་ (ŋōjaŋ jɛ̄ndu gyu̱r) va. to make green (by planting vegetation/ trees).

སྔོ་ལྗང་ཞི་བདེའི་ཁོར་ཡུག་སྲུང་སྐྱོབ་ཀྱི་ཚོགས་པ་ (ŋōjaŋ shi̱dee kōryug sūŋgyobgi tsōgba) Greenpeace.

སྔོ་དོག (ŋōdɔɔ̀) unripe fruit.

སྔོ་ཐིང་ངེར་ (ŋōtiŋ ŋer) sm. སྔོ་ཐིང་ཐིང་.

སྔོ་ཐིང་ཐིང་ (ŋō tīŋdiŋ) completely green/ blue, all green/ blue ¶ དེ་རིང་གནམ་སྔོ་ཐིང་ཐིང་འདུག The sky is completely blue today. ¶ ཤིང་ནགས་དེ་སྔོ་ཐིང་ཐིང་འདུག That forest is completely green.

སྔོ་ཐོག (ŋōdog) 1. unripe/ green (vegetables, fruits and crops). 2. the stage when crops are green seedlings.

སྔོ་ཐོག་རྩིས་ལེན་ (ŋōdog dzīilen) taking possession of a field during the time when the crop is still in the seedling stage; va.—བྱེད་.

སྔོ་འཐོག (ŋōtog) 1. weeding; va.—རྒྱག. 2. picking crops before they are fully ripe because of a shortage of grain; va.—རྒྱག.

སྔོ་དྲེག (ŋōdreg) moss, bryophyte.

སྔོ་མདངས་ (ŋōdaŋ) bluish/ greenish luster.

སྔོ་བདག (ŋōdaà) shung. the person who has the possesion when the crops are green seedlings ¶ སྔོ་བདག་སར་རྒྱུ་རྐྱེན་གང་སང་མེད་པར་སྔོ་ཁྲོད་དུ་སེམས་ཅན་འཚོས་རྐྱེན་བསྣམས་བཀྱིག་བྱས་པ་ (He) was tied up because the grazing animals went into the crops without seeking the permission of the person who has possession of the crops when they are green seedlings.

སྔོ་རྡོ་ (ŋōdo) bluish color stones.

སྔོ་རྡོག (ŋōdog) unripe fruits.

སྔོ་ལྡུམ་ (ŋōdum) the herbaceous family.

སྔོ་ནག (ŋōnaà) dark blue.

སྔོ་ནེ་ (ŋōne) bead (made of glass).

སྔོ་སྤྱི་ (ŋōji) vegetation.

སྔོ་སྤྱི་བཞུར་ (ŋōji shu̱r) an herbal medicine.

སྔོ་སྤྲིན་ (ŋōdrin) cloud with bluish luster (in Tibetan painting).

སྔོ་སྤྲིན་དམན་པ་ (ŋōdrin mɛ̄mba) an herbal medicine.

སྔོ་ཕིག་ཕིག (ŋō pīgbiì) dark in color (for example due to sunburn).

སྔོ་ཕྱུར་ (ŋōjur) a type of cheese.

སྔོ་ཕྱུར་ཕྱུར་ (ŋō cūrjur) rising smoke.

སྔོ་ཕྱུར་རེ་ (ŋō cūrre) sm. སྔོ་ཕྱུར་ཕྱུར་.

སྔོ་ཕྲིག་ཕྲིག (ŋō drīgdriì) sm. སྔོ་ཐིང་ཐིང་.

སྔོ་ཕུན་ནེ་ (ŋōbünni) sm. སྔོ་ཕྱུར་རེ་.

སྔོ་ཕྱུག་ཕྱུག (ŋō cūgjuù) 1. bluish. 2. salt and pepper for hair/ beard.

སྔོ་སྦེག་སྦེག (ŋō be̱gbeè) bluish or dark skin color.

སྔོ་སྦྱོར་ (ŋōjɔr) compounding herbal medicines.

སྔོ་སྨན་ (ŋōmɛn) herbal medicines.

སྔོ་རྩྭ་ (ŋōdza) green grass.

སྔོ་ཚལ་ (ŋōdzɛɛ) green vegetables.

སྔོ་ཚོད་ (ŋōdzöö) vegetables, fresh vegetable, wild herbs.

སྔོ་ཚོད་ཀུང་སི་ (ŋōdzöö gūŋsi) vegetable company.

སྔོ་ཚོད་ཁྲོམ་ར་ (ŋōdzöö trōmra) vegetable market.

སྔོ་ཚོད་ཞིང་ར་ (ŋōdzöö shi̱ŋrə) vegetable farm.

སྔོ་ཚོས་ (ŋōdzöö) indigo blue.

སྔོ་འཛིམ་ (ŋōdzim) wild garlic, chives.

སྔོ་གཟན་ (ŋōsɛn) green fodder.

སྔོ་གཡོ་ (ŋō yō) va. to cause a disturbance, to instigate trouble.

སྔོ་གཡོས་རྒྱག (ŋōyöö gyaà) sm. སྔོ་གཡོ་.

སྔོ་རིབ་ (ŋōrib) glaucoma.

སྔོ་རེངས་ (ŋōreŋ) twilight.

སྔོ་རོམ་རྒྱག (ŋōram gyaà) vi. to begin to rot/ turn rancid.

སྔོ་ལུད་ (ŋōlüü) green manure, plant fertilizer.

སྔོ་ལུད་སྐྱེ་དངོས་ (ŋōlüü gyēŋöö) green-manure crops.

སྔོ་ལོ་ (ŋōlo) 1. green leaves 2. disgrace, humiliation; vi.—ཕྱུར་ to disgrace/ humiliate oneself, to make a fool of oneself ¶ གསོལ་ཚིགས་ཟ་དུས་ངས་རྟག་དྲི་ཤོར་ནས་སྔོ་ལོ་ཕྱུར་སོང་ I disgraced myself by farting while eating.

སྔོ་ལོ་འཕྱུར་ (ŋōlo cār) see སྔོ་ལོ་.

སྔོ་ལོང་ངེ་ (ŋō lo̱ŋŋe) gleaming blue (usu. for water).

སྔོ་ཤུར་ཤུར་ (ŋō shūrshur) greenish, bluish.

སྔོ་ས་རྒྱ་ས་ (ŋōsa gyāsa) sm. དབྱར་ས་དགུན་ས་.

སྔོ་སང་སང་ (ŋō sāŋsaŋ) sm. སྔོ་ཐིང་ཐིང་.

སྔོ་སངས་ (ŋōsaŋ) sky blue (color).

སྔོ་སངས་མ་ (ŋōsaŋma) poet. sky.

སྔོ་སངས་སངས་ (ŋō sāŋsaŋ) sm. སྔོ་སང་སང་.

སྔོ་སི་ལི་བ་ (ŋō sīlewa) glittering/ sparkling/ gleaming blue.

སྔོ་སིང་སིང་ (ŋō sīŋsiŋ) sm. སྔོ་ཐིང་ཐིང་.

སྔོ་སེར་རེ་ (ŋō sērre) lush green (vegetation).

སྔོ་གསལ་ (ŋōsɛɛ) clear, bright.

སྔོ་བསངས་ (ŋōsaŋ) sm. སྔོ་སངས་.

སྔོ་ཧང་ཧང་ (ŋō hāŋhaŋ) bluish.

སྔོ་ཧམ་མེ་ (ŋō hāmme) looking sickly grey; turning "blue" with fright.

སྔོག : p. བསྔོགས་; f. བསྔོག ; imp. སྔོགས་ (ŋɔ̄ɔ̀) va. to dig into, to search/ rummage through ¶ ཆུ་རྒྱུད་ཀྱི་ས་ཆ་བསྔོགས་ནས་སྔར་གྱི་དངོས་རྫས་མང་པོ་རྙེད་པ་རེད་ They dug up the area along the river and found many ancient artifacts.

སྔོག་འཁྲོལ་ (ŋɔ̄ndröö) va. to rummage, to ransack.

སྔོག་ལྟ་ (ŋɔ̄gda) sm. སྔོག་བཤེར་.

སྔོག་འདོན་ (ŋɔ̄gdön) excavating, extracting, mining; va. སྔོག་འདོན་; —བྱེད་ to excavate, to extract, to mine ¶ རི་རྒྱུད་དེ་ཚོ་ནས་རྡོ་སོལ་ཁྱོན་ཆེ་སྔོག་འདོན་བྱེད་ཀྱི་ཡོད་པ་རེད་ They mine lots of coal from those mountains.

སྔོག་བྲུས་ (ŋɔ̄g dru̱ù) va. to dig.

སྔོག་ཞིབ་ (ŋɔ̄gshib) sm. སྔོག་བཤེར་.

སྔོག་བཤེར་ (ŋɔ̄gsher) searching, rummaging through sth. to search/ inspect; va.—བྱེད་.

སྔོག་བཤེར་འཛིན་བཟུང་ (ŋɔ̄sher dzi̱nsuŋ) searching and arresting; va.—བྱེད་ to search and arrest.

སྔོགས་ (ŋɔ̄ɔ̀) imp. of སྔོག.

སྔོན་ (ŋōn) 1. (— + gen.) before, prior to, formerly ¶ ལོ་བཅུའི་སྔོན་ལ་ Ten years ago. 2. ancient ¶ སྔོན་

ཀྱི་རྒྱལ་རབས་ Ancient history.

སྔོན་བཀག (ŋȫngaà) 1. arranging early/ in advance; va.—བྱེད་. 2. target, schedule, goal, predetermined time; va.—བྱེད་. 3. intercepting in advance. 4. taking preventive measures.

སྔོན་བཀོད་ (ŋȫngöò) sm. སྔོན་བཀག.

སྔོན་སྐྱེས་ཀྱི་རྣ་བ་དང་རྗེས་སྐྱེས་ཀྱི་རྭ་ཅོ་ (ŋȫngyeègi nāwa ta̱ŋ je̱ègyeègi ra̱jo) conveys seniority [Lit. first ears are grown, later horns are grown].

སྔོན་སྐྱོད་ (ŋȫngyöò) advanced, progressive, forward; va.—བྱེད་ to advance, to progress, to go forward ། སྤྱི་ཚོགས་རིང་ལུགས་ཀྱི་ཕྱོགས་ལ་མགྱོགས་ནས་མྱུར་དུ་སྔོན་སྐྱོད་བྱེད་ཀྱི་ཡོད་པ་རེད་ (They) are advancing with great speed towards socialism.

སྔོན་སྐྱོད་དུད་ (ŋȫngyö dǖǜ) tib.ch. advance soldiers/ scouts.

སྔོན་སྐྱོད་དམག་དཔུང་ (ŋȫngyö mǝgbuŋ) sm. སྔོན་མངགས་རུ་ཁག.

སྔོན་སྐྱོད་ཐོན་སྐྱེད་རུ་ཁག (ŋȫngyö tȫngye ru̱gaà) advanced/ progressive production brigade.

སྔོན་བསྐྱོད་ (ŋȫngyö) sm. སྔོན་སྐྱོད་.

སྔོན་བསྐྱོད་པ་ (ŋȫngyöòba) advanced/ progressive person.

སྔོན་གན་གསལ་བཅག (ŋȫngaà sēljaà) shung. a notation made on a promissory loan note indicating full or partial payment.

སྔོན་གྱི་མཐའ་ (ŋȫngyi tā) the dawn of history of the earth; the beginning of life.

སྔོན་གྱི་སྨོན་ལམ་ (ŋȫngi mȫnlam) prayers from a previous life.

སྔོན་གྱི་ལས་ (ŋȫngi le̱è) karma from previous life.

སྔོན་གྱི་སློབ་དཔོན་ (ŋȫngi lōpbön) past scholars/ pandits.

སྔོན་གྲབས་ (ŋȫndrab) sth. prepared in advance.

སྔོན་གྲལ་ (ŋȫndrɛɛ) front line, front row.

སྔོན་གྲུབ་ཆ་རྐྱེན་ (ŋȫndrub cāgyen) precondition, prerequisite.

སྔོན་གླེང་ (ŋȫnleŋ) sm. སྔོན་བརྗོད་.

སྔོན་བགོ་ (ŋȫngo) giving a share/ portion in advance.

སྔོན་འགལ་ (ŋȫngɛɛ) previous mistakes/ violations.

སྔོན་འགོག (ŋȫngaà) prevention, precautions, preventive measures; va.—བྱེད་ to prevent, to take precautionary steps, to take preventive measure ། ནད་རིམས་སྔོན་འགོག་སྔར་ལས་ཚགས་ཚུད་པ་བྱས་པ་རེད་ They took preventive measures against epidemics much more efficiently than before.

སྔོན་འགོག་སྨན་ཁབ་ (ŋȫngaà) inoculation, vaccination; va.—འཛུགས་; —རྒྱག to inoculate/ vaccinate ། སློབ་ཕྲུག་ཚང་མར་ལྷ་འབྲུམ་སྔོན་འགོག་སྨན་ཁབ་ (They) inoculated the school children against smallpox.

སྔོན་འགྲུལ་རྗེས་མཐུད་ (ŋȫngye je̱ètüǜ) following wave after wave, going one after another; va.—བྱེད་.

སྔོན་འགྲོ་ (ŋȫndro) introductory, primary, preliminary ། སྔོན་འགྲོའི་སློབ་ཚན་ Primary/ introductory course (or lesson).

སྔོན་འགྲོ་བ་ (ŋȫndrowa) scout, one who goes ahead of the main party to look for a place to stop or to look ahead for enemies.

སྔོན་འགྲོའི་གླུ་དབྱངས་ (ŋȫndrö lūyaŋ) prelude, overture.

སྔོན་འགྲོའི་ཆ་རྐྱེན་ (ŋȫndrö cāgyen) sm. སྔོན་གྲུབ་ཆ་རྐྱེན་.

སྔོན་འགྲོའི་དཔུང་ཚོགས་ (ŋȫndrö būŋdzɔɔ̀) sm. སྔོན་འགྲོའི་རུ་དཔུང་.

སྔོན་འགྲོའི་རུ་དཔུང་ (ŋȫndrö ru̱buŋ) vanguard, advance force.

སྔོན་འགྲོའི་གཏམ་ (ŋȫndrö dām) foreword, introduction to a book/ story.

སྔོན་བགྲོད་མི་སྣ་ (ŋȫndröò mi̱na) advance personnel, people who go in advance.

སྔོན་རྒྱུ་རྗེས་འབྲས་ (ŋȫngyu je̱ndrɛɛ̀) antecedent and consequent, cause and effect.

སྔོན་བསྒུགས་རྗེས་དེད་ (ŋȫnguù je̱èdeè) driving the enemy into troops/ soldiers waiting in ambush.

སྔོན་བསྒྲགས་ (ŋȫndraà) forecasting, predicting, projecting; va.—བྱེད་ to forecast, to predict, to project.

སྔོན་མངག (ŋȫn ŋāà) va. to order ahead of time/ in advance, to make a reservation.

སྔོན་མངགས་ (ŋȫnŋaà) ordering in advance, reserving, subscribing; va.—བྱེད་ ། དངོས་ཟོག་རྣམས་བདུན་གཅིག་གོང་སྔོན་མངགས་བྱེད་གྲུབ་པ་དགོས་ The goods should be ordered a week in advance.

སྔོན་མངགས་དངོས་ཟོག (ŋȫnŋaà ŋȫòsoò) ordered goods/ merchandise.

སྔོན་མངགས་རུ་ཁག (ŋȫnŋaà ru̱gaà) vanguard group, advance group.

སྔོན་སྔོན་ནས་ (ŋȫn ŋȫnnɛ) long long ago.

སྔོན་གཙོད་དོན་ཆན་ (ŋȫjöò tö̱ndzɛɛ̀) prerequisite, necessary/ obligatory condition.

སྔོན་ཆུ་གཏོང་ (ŋȫnju dōŋ) va. to have sexual intercourse before marriage [Lit. to irrigate early].

སྔོན་ཆད་ (ŋȫnjɛɛ̀) 1. in the past, previously, formerly ། སྔོན་ཆད་ཁོ་ཚོ་ཞིང་པ་རེད་ Formerly they were farmers. 2. in arrears ། སྔོན་ཆད་ངོ་འབྲུ་ Grain in arrears of payment.

སྔོན་འཇུག (ŋȫnjuù) prefix letters.

སྔོན་རྗེས་ (ŋȫnjeè) 1. before and after. 2. prefix and suffix.

སྔོན་རྗེས་མིང་གསུམ་ (ŋȫnjeè mi̱ŋsum) prefix, suffix and the main letter.

སྔོན་རྗེས་སུ་ (ŋȫnjeèsu) sm. སྔོན་རྗེས་.

སྔོན་བརྗོད་ (ŋȫnjöò) preface.

སྔོན་ཉིན་ (ŋȫnñin) previous day.

སྔོན་གཏོང་ (ŋȫn dōŋ) va. to pay/ send in advance.

སྔོན་རྟོགས་ (ŋȫndɔɔ̀) 1. foreknowledge, foresight. 2. forecast ། གནམ་གཤིས་ཀྱི་སྔོན་རྟོགས་ Weather forecast.

སྔོན་རྟོགས་ཀྱི་རིག་པ་ (ŋȫndɔɔ̀gi ri̱gbɔ) the art of foreknowledge, foresight, forecasting.

སྔོན་བརྟག (ŋȫndàa) sm. སྔོན་རྟོགས་.

སྔོན་ཐལ་ (ŋȫndɛɛ) doing sth. before it needs to be done (e.g., before an order is given or before the due date), going excessively ahead.

སྔོན་ཐལ་རྗེས་སྡོད་ (ŋȫndɛɛ je̱èdöò) going excessively ahead and delaying or staying behind.

སྔོན་ཐོན་ (ŋȫndön) advanced, progressive, outstanding, foremost ། སྔོན་ཐོན་བཟོ་པ་ An outstanding worker.

སྔོན་ཐོན་གྱི་བཅད་གྲངས་ (ŋȫntöngi jɛ̃ɛ̀draŋ) advanced quota or norm.

སྔོན་ཐོན་ངལ་རྩོལ་བཟོ་པའི་ཏང་ (ŋȫndön ŋɛ̱ɛdzö so̱bɛ dāŋ) Progressive Labor Party.

སྔོན་ཐོན་ཅན་ (ŋȫndönjɛn) advanced, outstanding, first class ། ཐོན་སྐྱེད་སྔོན་ཐོན་ཅན་དུ་གྱུར་པ་རེད་ (He) became an outstanding producer (worker).

སྔོན་ཐོན་ཉམས་མྱོང་ (ŋȫndön ñamŋon) advanced experience or know-how.

སྔོན་ཐོན་ཐོན་སྐྱེད་པ་ (ŋȫndön tȫngyeba) advanced producer, outstanding worker, stakhanovite.

སྔོན་ཐོན་སྡེ་ཁག (ŋȫndön de̱gaà) outstanding unit/ group.

སྔོན་ཐོན་མི་སྣ་ (ŋȫndön mi̱na) advanced/ outstanding people (personnel).

སྔོན་ཐོན་ལ་དཔེ་ལྟ་ སྔོན་ཐོན་དང་འགྲན་སྡུར་ སྔོན་ཐོན་གྱི་རྗེས་སྙེག རྗེས་ཡོང་ལ་རོགས་རམ་ (ŋȫndönla bēda ŋȫndöntaŋ tre̱ndur ŋȫngi je̱èñeg je̱èyoŋla rɔ̱gram) learn from the advanced, compete with the advanced, catch up with the advanced, and help the backward.

སྔོན་ཐོན་ལག་རྩལ་ (ŋȫndön la̱gdzɛɛ) advanced techniques.

སྔོན་ཐོབ་ (ŋȫndob) obtaining the lead/ leadership, reaching an advanced/ progressive state.

སྔོན་མཐོང་ (ŋȫndoŋ) sm. སྔོན་རྟོགས་.

སྔོན་དང་པོ་ (ŋȫn ta̱ŋbo) at first, at the beginning.

སྔོན་དུ་ (ŋõndu) before, prior to, formerly ། དེའི་སྔོན་དུ་འདི་བྱེད་དགོས་རེད་ (We) should do this prior to that.

སྔོན་དུ་འགྲོ་བ་ (ŋõndu drowa) 1. sm. སྔོན་འགྲོ་. 2. va. to go forward, to advance, to go ahead.

སྔོན་དུ་བརྗོད་པ་ (ŋõndu jööba) sm. སྔོན་བརྗོད་.

སྔོན་དུས་ (ŋõndüü) former times, formerly, in the past.

སྔོན་དོན་དྲན་ (ŋõndön trɛn) sm. སྔོན་དྲན་.

སྔོན་དྲན་ (ŋõndrɛn) va. to know what is to come or happen.

སྔོན་འདུན་ཞུ་ (ŋõndün shu) 1. va. to pray for in advance. 2. to congratulate in advance.

སྔོན་སྒྲིག (ŋõndɔɔ̀) things gotten ready beforehand; —བྱེད་.

སྔོན་བརྡ་ (ŋõnda) advance notice/ warning, forecast; va.—གཏོང་ to give advance notice/ warning, to foretell, to forecast.

སྔོན་ན་མེད་པ་ (ŋõnna meèba) sm. སྔོན་མེད་.

སྔོན་ནས་ (ŋõnnɛ) from before, from long ago ། ཁོ་ཚོ་ནི་སྔོན་ནས་ཞིང་པ་རེད་ They have been farmers since long ago.

སྔོན་ནས་ཚོད་དཔག་བྱེད་ (ŋõnnɛ tsööbaà) sm. སྔོན་དཔག.

སྔོན་ནས་ཚོར་ (ŋõnnɛ tsɔ̃r) vi. to forebode, to sense/ feel beforehand.

སྔོན་གནས་རྗེས་དྲན་གྱི་མངོན་ཤེས་ (ŋõnnɛɛ̀ jeèdrengi ŋõnshɛɛ̀) ability to remember previous existence.

སྔོན་པོ་ (ŋõmbo) 1. blue ། སྔོན་པོ་གཡུ་ Blue turquoise. 2. (with plants) green ། ཚལ་སྔོན་པོ་ Green vegetables.

སྔོན་དཔག (ŋõmbaà) estimating, forecasting, prognosticating; va.—བྱེད་ ། ཨ་རིའི་དམག་མི་ཡི་ཏ་ནམ་ནས་ཕྱིར་འཐེན་བྱས་རྗེས་ཡི་ཏ་ནམ་ནང་གནས་ཚུལ་གང་འདྲ་ཞིག་ཡོད་མེད་སྔོན་དཔག་བྱེད་ཐུབ་ཀྱི་ཡོད་པ་མ་རེད་ We can't forecast what will happen in Vietnam after the American troops withdraw.

སྔོན་དཔེ་ (ŋõmbe) previous example.

སྔོན་ཕམ་རྗེས་དཔེ་ (ŋõnbam jeèbe) learn from previous failures.

སྔོན་འཕྲོས་ (ŋõndröö) continued from before.

སྔོན་བུ་ (ŋõmbu) a type of brewed medicine.

སྔོན་བྱས་ (ŋõncɛɛ̀) 1. past actions ། སྔོན་བྱས་ལ་འདྲི་བརྩད་མེད་ (We have) no questions to ask about (one's) past actions. 2. experiences of previous lives. 3. rehearsing, practicing.

སྔོན་བྱུང་ (ŋõnjuŋ) occurred/ existed before or in the past ། སྔོན་བྱུང་འཆར་གཞི་ A plan that existed in the past.

སྔོན་བྱུས་ (ŋõnjüü) precautionary strategy/ policy; va.—བྱེད་ to take precautions ། འོས་འདེམས་སྐབས་ཞིང་འཁྲུག་ཆེན་པོ་མི་ཡོང་བའི་སྔོན་བྱུས་བྱེད་པ་རེད་ (They) took precautions to avoid disturbances at the time of the election.

སྔོན་འབྱོན་ (ŋõnjön) predecessor, forerunner, precursor, pioneer.

སྔོན་འབྱོན་ཡབ་ (ŋõnjön yəb) shung. forefathers.

སྔོན་དབང་འཕུད་རྐྱེན་ (ŋõnwaŋ drɛɛ̀gyen) shung. sth. caused by previous karma ། སྔོན་དབང་འཕུད་རྐྱེན་གྱིས་མི་འདོད་ཉེར་འཚེ་ Harm caused by previous karma.

སྔོན་འབེབས་དོན་སྙིང་ (ŋõnbeb tönñiŋ) 1. assumption, premise, supposition. 2. prerequisite, precondition.

སྔོན་སྦྱངས་ (ŋõnjaŋ) propensities from a pervious life.

སྔོན་སྦྱོང་ (ŋõnjoŋ) advance preparation/ study; rehearsing; va.—བྱེད་.

སྔོན་མ་ (ŋõnma) formerly, in the past.

སྔོན་མ་ནང་བཞིན་ (ŋõnma nəŋshin) as in the past, as before.

སྔོན་མེད་ (ŋõnmeè) not existing in the past.

སྔོན་མེད་གསར་བསྐྲུན་ (ŋõnmeè sərdrün) new creation, invention; va.—བྱེད་.

སྔོན་མེད་གསར་གཏོད་ (ŋõnmeè sərdöö) sm. སྔོན་མེད་གསར་བསྐྲུན་.

སྔོན་མོ་ (ŋõnma) 1. blue. 2. blue-grey for horses/ mules.

སྔོན་མོ་ཅབ་འདྲེན་ (ŋõnmo cəbdren) sm. སྔོ་སྐྱི་བཞུར་.

སྔོན་མོ་ལྷོག་ཟན་ (ŋõnmo lhõgsɛn) a herbal medicine.

སྔོན་སྨོན་ཞུ་ (ŋõnmön shu) sm. སྔོན་འདུན་ཞུ་.

སྔོན་ཙམ་ (ŋõndzam) a little ahead/ before.

སྔོན་ཙམ་ལ་ (ŋõndzamla) a little ahead/ before ། ངས་འདིར་སྔོན་ཙམ་ལ་བཅར་པ་ཡིན་ I came here a little ahead (of them).

སྔོན་རྩིས་ (ŋõndzii) budgeting, budget; va.—རྒྱག.

སྔོན་རྩིས་གྲོ་འཆར་ (ŋõndzii dronjar) the expenditure plan of the budget.

སྔོན་རྩིས་བདང་འཛིན་ལས་དོན་ཁང་ (ŋõndzii dəŋdzin lɛɛ̀döngaŋ) Office of Management and Budget (OMB).

སྔོན་རྩིས་ཚོགས་ཆུང་ (ŋõndzii tsɔ̃gjuŋ) Committee on the Budget.

སྔོན་རྩིས་ཡོང་འཆར་ (ŋõndzii yoŋjar) the income plan of the budget.

སྔོན་རྩིས་ཨུ་ཡོན་ལྷན་ཁང་ (ŋõndzii ũyön lhẽngaŋ) budget commission/ committee.

སྔོན་ཚིག་ཕྱིས་འགལ་ (ŋõndzii cĩŋgɛɛ) contradicting what one said earlier.

སྔོན་ཚུད་ (ŋõndzüü) beforehand, in advance ། གང་ཞིག་དགོས་ཡོད་ན་སྔོན་ཚུད་ནས་ལས་ཁུངས་ལ་སྙན་སེང་ཞུ་དགོས་ If you want a vacation, you should make a request in advance.

སྔོན་ཚུད་བརྡ་སྒྲོད་ (ŋõndzüü dadröö) announcing in advance, giving advance notice; va.—བྱེད་.

སྔོན་ཚུད་ནས་ (ŋõndzüünɛ) sm. སྔོན་ཚུད་.

སྔོན་ཚེ་ (ŋõndze) in the past, long ago.

སྔོན་ཚོད་ (ŋõndzöö) prediction, forecast, estimate; va.—བྱེད་ to predict, to forecast, to estimate.

སྔོན་འཛོམས་རྒྱུ་རྐྱེན་ (ŋõndzom gyugyen) sm. སྔོན་གཙོད་དོན་ཆེན་.

སྔོན་རྫས་ (ŋõndzɛɛ̀) antiques.

སྔོན་བཞིན་ (ŋõnshin) just as before.

སྔོན་ཟོན་ (ŋõnsön) precautions, care; va.—བྱེད་ to take precautions, to be careful.

སྔོན་ཟླ་ (ŋõnda) last month.

སྔོན་བསྒྲིགས་འདུམ་འཛིན་ (ŋõndöö dumdzin) shung. the mediating agreement/ settlement of a previous lawcase ། སྔོན་བསྒྲིགས་འདུམ་འཛིན་ཉེ་མེད་བྱས་པར་འགལ་འདེད་ཡན་སོང་མེད་པ་ Please do not let (him) evade the fine/ punishment for violating the previous lawcase agreement.

སྔོན་ཡོད་ (ŋõnyöö) existing/ present in the past.

སྔོན་རབས་ (ŋõnrəb) ancient times.

སྔོན་རབས་པ་ (ŋõnrəbbə) forerunner, precursor, ancestor, elder ། གསར་བརྗེའི་སྔོན་རབས་པ་ Revolutionary forerunners.

སྔོན་རོལ་ (ŋõnröö) sm. སྔ་རོལ་.

སྔོན་ལ་ (ŋõnla) at first.

སྔོན་ལ་གང་གཟབ་ (ŋõnla kəŋsəb) doing all one can to get ahead/ progress/ advance.

སྔོན་ལ་དྲན་ལ་བློ་དང་རྗེས་ལ་དྲན་ན་འགྱོད་པ་ (ŋõnla trɛnla lõ dəŋ jeèla trɛnna gyööba) one should plan things in advance [Lit. remebering beforehand is an idea, remembering afterwards is regret].

སྔོན་ལས་ (ŋõnlɛɛ̀) sm. སྔོ་མའི་ལས་.

སྔོན་ལོགས་ (ŋõnlɔɔ̀) sm. སྔ་རོལ་.

སྔོན་ཤེས་ (ŋõnsheè) prophetic, having the ability to forecast the future.

སྔོན་གཤེགས་ (ŋõnsheg) ancestors [Lit. those who died before].

སྔོན་གཤེགས་དཔའ་བོ་ (ŋõnsheg bãwo) martyr.

སྔོན་བསགས་ (ŋõnsaà) saved/ accumulated (from the past).

སྔོན་བསུ་ (ŋõnsu) preparing to welcoming; va.—བྱེད་.

སྔོན་བསྡུས་ (ŋõnsüü) shung. a phrase used to introduce what the writer will say below.

སྔོས་ (ŋöö) imp. of སྔོ་.

སྔོར་དོག (ŋõrdog) see སྔོ་ཐོག.

བཇ་ (ŋā) f. of ཇ་.

བཇ་སྣུད་འཕྲུལ་འཁོར་ (ŋədüü trũũgɔɔ) harvesting machine.

བཇ་བསྡུ་ (ŋədu) harvesting; va.—བྱེད་ to harvest.

བཇ་བསྡུ་མཉམ་བྱེད་འཕྲུལ་འཁོར་ (ŋədu ñ͟amjeè trũũgɔɔ) combine harvest.

བཇ་རྩ་ (ŋādza) shung. pasture set aside for cutting hay.

བཇ་གསོག (ŋāsoò) gathering, collecting (crops); va.—བྱེད་.

བཇན་ (ŋēn) p. and f. of ཇན་.

བཇབ་པ་ (ŋəb) f. of ཇབ་.

བཇབས་ (ŋəb) p. of ཇབ་.

བཇམ་ (ŋām) f. of ཇམ་.

བཇམས་ (ŋām) p. of ཇམ་.

བཇས (ŋɛ̄ɛ̀) p. of ཇ་.

བཇུབ་ (ŋūb) f. of ཇུབ་.

བཇུབས་ (ŋūb) p. of ཇུབ་.

བཇོ་ (ŋō) f. of ཇོ་.

བཇོད་ (ŋȫȍ) sm. ཇོད་.

བཇོན་ (ŋȫn) p. and f. of ཇན་.

བཇོས་ (ŋȫȍ) p. of ཇོད་.

བསྔགས་ (ŋāà) va. to praise, to hail, to eulogize, to glorify །ཁོང་གི་སྙིང་པོ་ཀུན་ལ་བརྩེ་བ་དང་བྱམས་པའི་ཐུགས་ལ་ནི་ཐམས་ཅད་ཀྱིས་བསྔགས་སོང་ His love and compassion for all the people was praised by all.

བསྔགས་སྐུལ་ (ŋāàgüü) encouraging.

བསྔགས་བརྗོད་ (ŋāgjȫȍ) praising, complimenting, exaltating; va.—བྱེད་ to praise, to compliment, to exalt ། ཕྱི་རྒྱལ་ནས་ཡོང་བའི་གྲོགས་པོ་ཚོས་རང་རྒྱལ་གྱི་ཡར་རྒྱས་ལ་བསྔགས་བརྗོད་ཆེན་པོ་བྱས་པ་རེད་ The friends from abroad praised greatly our country's progress.

བསྔགས་བརྗོད་ཡོད་ཀྱུ་འཁོར་ (ŋāgjȫȍ y͟ȫȍgu tɔ̄r) vi. to be showered with praise.

བསྔགས་གདམ་ (ŋāgdam) sm. བསྔགས་བརྗོད་.

བསྔགས་བསྟོད་ (ŋāgdȫȍ) sm. བསྔགས་བརྗོད་.

བསྔགས་འོས་ (ŋāgwȫȍ) praiseworthy.

བསྔགས་འོས་སྐྱོ་འོས་ (ŋāwgȫȍ gyōwȫȍ) worthy of praise and worthy of feeling sad/ sorry for.

བསྔལ་ (ŋɛ̄ɛ) suffering.

བསྔོ་ (ŋō) f. of སྔོ་.

བསྔོ་བགྲང་ (ŋōdraŋ) counting, checking; va.—བྱེད་.

བསྔོ་ (ŋō) dedication prayer ། འདས་བསྔོ་ A prayer dedicating merit on behalf of someone who has died.

བསྔོ་རྟེན་ (ŋōden) dedication offering given by relatives of a dead person to monasteries or lamas (usu. clothing or jewelry or money).

བསྔོ་བ་ (ŋōwa) dedication prayer; va.—བྱེད་.

བསྔོ་བ་སྨོན་ལམ་ (ŋōmön) dedication prayer, a prayer that dedicates merit.

བསྔོ་སྨོན་ (ŋōmön) abbr. of བསྔོ་བ་སྨོན་ལམ་.

བསྔོ་ཡིག (ŋōyiì) letter requesting prayers to dedicate merit to sb.

བསྔོག (ŋɔ̄ɔ̀) f. of སྔོག.

བསྔོགས་ (ŋɔ̄ɔ̀) p. of སྔོག.

བསྔོགས་ཞིབ་ (ŋɔ̄gshib) searching thoroughly; va.—བྱེད་.

བསྔོགས་བཤེར་ (ŋɔ̄gsher) sm. སྔོག་བཤེར་.

བསྔོས་ (ŋȫȍ) p. of སྔོ་.

བསྔོས་ཤ་ (ŋȫȍsha) sm. དམིགས་ཤ་.

ཅ་ (jā) the letter ca (used in alphabetical numbering).

ཅ་ཁུག (jāguù) sm. ཆག་ཁུག, 2.

ཅ་ག (jāga) sm. ཅག་ག.

ཅ་ག་བྱེད་ (jāga cɛ̀ɛ) va. to look after, to care for.

ཅ་གེ་ (jāge) sm. ཅག་གེ་.

ཅ་དགུ་ (jāgu) nine tenths.

ཅ་དངོས་ (jāŋöö) goods, things.

ཅ་ཅོ་ (jājo) 1. abbr. of ཅ་ལི་ཅོ་ལི་ 2. sound made by a crowd/ assembly of people, clamor, noise; chatter; va.—སྒྲོག ། ཅ་ཅོ་བར་མེད་དུ་སྒྲོག་པའི་ཟ་ཁང་ནང་ In the restaurant where (people) clamor continuously. 3. sound of laughter.

ཅ་ཅོ་མེད་པ་ (jājo m̱eèba) noiseless, silent.

ཅ་ཅོ་ལབ་ (jājoləb) quarreling, bickering, arguing; va.—བྱེད་.

ཅ་དར་ (jādar) hind. bed sheet.

ཅ་དང་དམག་སྒར་ /jādaŋ māgar/ the Dingri Regiment in traditional Tibetan army.

ཅ་ལྡན་ཟེ་རྩའི་སྐྱུར་ (jādɛn s̱etsa gyūr) ch.tib. potassium nitrate.

ཅ་སྡེ་ (jāde) the second group of four letters in the Tibetan alphabet that starts with ཅ་.

ཅ་ན་ (jāna) Ghana.

ཅ་ན་ད་ (jānada) Canada.

ཅ་ནེ་ (jāne) sm. ཅན་ཅེ་.

ཅ་ནོར་ (jānɔr) wealth, goods, belongings.

ཅ་པོ་ (jāwo) sm. ཅ་ནོར་.

ཅ་མ་ཟིང་ (jāmasiŋ) what a nuisance, how annoying ། ཅ་མ་ཟིང་མི་དེ་རྟག་པར་ངའི་སར་ཡོང་གི་འདུག What a nuisance. That person always stops by.

ཅ་ཟིང་པོ་ (jā s̱iŋbu) troublesome, bothersome, nuisance, annoying, irritating, agitating ། ལས་ཀ་འདི་ཅ་ཟིང་པོ་ཞིག་འདུག This work is quite troublesome; va.—བཟོ་;—བྱེད་ to bother, to give problems, to be troublesome/ bothersome ། ཅ་ཟིང་པོ་མ་བཟོ་རོགས་གནང་ Please don't be bothersome.

ཅ་རཁང་ (jārakuŋ) a concave area between the shoulder blades.

ཅ་རེ་ (jāre) always, continually.

ཅ་རེ་ཉ་རེ་ (jāre ñāre) a few.

ཅ་ལག (jālaà) things, objects, belongings ། ཁོང་ཚོའི་ནང་གི་ཅ་ལག་མང་པོ་འཚོང་གི་འདུག They are selling many of their household goods.

ཅ་ལག་ཆུང་རིགས་བཅོལ་ས་ (jālaà cūŋrig jǖǖsa) left-luggage check room.

ཅ་ལག་ཉོ་འཛིན་ (jālaà ṉondzin) purchase receipt.

ཅ་ལག་བཟོ་གྲྭ་ (jālaà s̱odra) furniture factory.

ཅ་ལིའི་པིའི་མཚོ་ (jālibitso) ch.tib. Caribbean Sea.

ཅ་ལྱུད་ (jālüü) ch.tib. potassium fertilizer, potash fertilizer.

ཅ་ལི་ཅོལ་ལི་ (jāle jööle) talk that isn't meaningful, sth. said without careful thought, idle talk; va.—ཤོད་ to speak in such a way ། ཁོའི་སྐད་ཆ་ཅ་ལི་ཅོ་ལི་རེད་ His talk was nonsensical.

ཅ་ལེ་བ་ (jālewa) sm. ཅ་ལི་ཅོ་ལི་.

ཅ་སྨུན་པོ་ (jā sūnbu) troublesome, bothersome, a nuisance; vi.—བཟོ་ to bother, to be troublesome, to be a nuisance.

ཅ་སུའུ་ཆིས་ (jā sūci) ch. accelerator, cyclotron.

ཅག (jāà) plural particle ། ཁྱེད་ཅག You (plural).

ཅག་ག (jāàga) caring for, looking after; va.—བྱེད་ ། ལྡུམ་རར་ཅག་ག་ཡག་པོ་བྱེད་ཀྱི་འདུག (He) is taking good care of the garden.

ཅག་ག་དག་པོ་ (jāàga t̲agbo) sb. who takes good care of things ། གོ་གོས་ལོག་ལ་ཅག་ག་དག་པོ་ཡོད་པ་རེད་ He takes good care of his clothes.

ཅག་ག་ཚ་པོ་ (jāàga tsābo) sm. ཅག་ག་དག་པོ་.

ཅག་གེ་ (jāàge) entire, all, full of ། ཚོང་ཁང་ནང་ཚོང་ཟོག་ཅག་གེ་ཁེང་འདུག The store was full of commodities.

ཅག་ཅག (jāgjaà) 1. sound of chewing/ eating; va.—བྱེད་ to chew. 2. taking good care of; va.—བྱེད་. 3. pressing down; va.—བྱེད་.

ཅག་ཅག་དྲུང་དྲུང་ (jāgjaà tr̲uŋdruŋ) living thriftly/ economically; va.—བྱེད་.

ཅག་ཅག་པོ་ (jāà jāgbo) reliable, dependable ། མི་དེ་རྒྱུན་གཏན་ནས་ལས་ཀ་ཅག་ཅག་པོ་བྱེད་མཁན་ཞིག་རེད་ That person is sb. who is always reliable at work.

ཅག་ཅེར་རེ་ (jāg jērre) closely pressed together, crowded.

ཅག་དར་ (jāgdar) hind. bed sheet.

ཅག་སྟོན་པོ་ (jāg tōnbo) 1. sm. ཅག་ཅག་པོ་. 2. sm. ཅག་ག་དག་པོ་.

ཅག་པོ་ (jāgbo) 1. stingy, miserly ། མི་འདི་ལག་པ་ཅག་པོ་འདུག This man is stingy. 2. efficient, doing on time. 3. quick, rapid, soon; va.—བྱེད་ to be quick, to hurry up ། ཅག་པོ་ཤོག Come quickly.

ཅག་ཙེ་ (jāgdze) wicker basket.

ཅག་ཟོན་ (jāgsön) careful, alert; va.—བྱེད་ ། ལམ་བར་ཀུན་མ་ལ་ཅག་ཟོན་གནང་དགོས་ Be careful of thieves on the road.

ཅང་ (jāŋ) 1. anything, whatever ། ཁོས་ཡུན་རིང་ཅང་མི་ཟེར་བར་བསྡད་པ་རེད་ He remained for a long time without saying anything. 2. abbr. of ཅང་ཅེ་ཧྲི་. 3. a flat bell used by the practitioners of the Bon religion. 4. undersalted (for tea) ། ཇ་ལ་ཚྭ་ཅང་བཞག There is not enough salt in the tea.

ཅང་གེ་ཤག (jāŋgeshaà) sm. ཅང་ཅེ་ཧྲི་.

ཅང་སྐྱོར་གུང་གྲོལ་ (jāŋgyɔr k̲uŋgöö) aide Chiang Kaishek, oppose the communists (political slogan).

ཅང་གྲུང་ (jāŋdruŋ) intelligence, cleverness.

ཅང་གྲུང་དོད་པོ་ (jāŋdruŋ t̲ööbo) intelligent, clever.

ཅང་ངེ་ཅོག་གེ་ (jāŋŋe jōgge) arc. at a distance.

ཅང་མངར་མོ་ (jāŋ ŋāābo) a sweet sauce made of fermented flour.

ཅང་ཅང་ (jāŋjaŋ) 1. tasteless (food). 2. lonely.

ཅང་ཅང་ཁྲུག་ཁྲུག (jāŋjaŋ trūgtruù) sm. བཅང་བཅང་ཁྲུག་ཁྲུག.

ཅང་ཅུན་ (jāŋjün) ch. general.

ཅང་ཅེ་ཧྲི་ (jāŋ jēhri) Chiang Kaishek.

ཅང་ཅའི་ཧྲི་ (jāŋjɛhri) sm. ཅང་ཅེ་ཧྲི་.

ཅང་ཅོང་ (jāŋjoŋ) abbr. flat bell and (cone shaped) bell.

ཅང་ཆིང་ (jāŋciŋ) Jiang Qing (Mao Zedong's wife).

ཅང་ཇག (jāŋjaà) ch.tib. Chiang's (Kaishek) bandits.

ཅང་ཇག་ཚོགས་ཁག (jāŋjaà tsɔ̄ɔ̄gaà) ch.tib. Chiang's bandit clique.

ཅང་དེའུ་ (jāŋdewu) a small drum used for religious purpose.

ཅང་པོ་ (jāŋbo) smart, clever, intelligent; va.—བྱེད་.

ཅང་དཔོན་ (jāŋbön) ch.tib. 1. general. 2. Chiang's officers.

ཅང་དམག (jāŋmaà) Chiang's Kaishek's army.

ཅང་ཙམ་ (jāŋdzam) not quite enough salt (in tea).

ཅང་ཚལ་ (jāŋtsɛɛ) ch. pickled vegetables.

ཅང་ཞི་ (jāŋshi) Jiangxi (Province).

ཅང་ཞི་ཞིང་ཆེན་ (jāŋshi sh̲iŋjen) sm. ཅང་ཞི་.

ཅང་ཤིས་ (jāŋshii) sm. ཅང་ཞི་.

ཅང་ཡིའུ་ (jāŋyiwu) ch. soy sauce.

ཅང་ལིང་ (jāŋliŋ) ch. general.

ཅང་ཤེས་ (jāŋsheè) 1. clever, intelligent (for horses) ། ཅང་ཤེས་རྟ་ A clever horse. 2. va. to know everything, to know all.

ཅང་སུའུ་ཞིང་ཆེན་ (jāŋsu sh̲iŋjen) Jiangsu province.

ཅང་སྲིད་ (j̲aŋsii) is it possible, is it feasible? ། ཉི་མ་ནུབ་ནས་ཤར་བ་ཅང་སྲིད་དམ་ Is it possible for the sun to rise from the west?

ཅང་ཧྲི་ (jāŋhri) ch. lecturer.

ཅང་ཧྲེ་ (jāŋhre) sm. ཅང་ཧྲི་.

ཅན་ (jɛ̄n) 1. nominal adjectivizer, having, possessing ¶ གསར་ཤོག་ཤོག་ངོས་བཅུ་གཉིས་ཅན་ཞིག A newspaper having twelve pages. ¶ ཤེས་ཡོན་ཅན་ Having knowledge (an intellectual). 2. used after titles and personal names ¶ ཚེ་རིང་ལགས་ཅན་མཁས་པ་ཁག་ཅིག་ཕེབས་འདུག A group of scholars came with Tsering. 3. near, presence ¶ ང་ཁོང་ཅན་དུ་ཕྱིན་པ་ཡིན་ I went into his presence.

ཅན་ཁ་ (jɛ̄nga) sm. ཞོར་ཁ་.

ཅན་ཅེ་ (jɛ̄nje) small bowl.

ཅན་དུ་འགྱུར་ (jɛ̄ntu gyur) (noun + —) to become —ized ¶ ཀུང་ཧྲེ་ཅན་དུ་འགྱུར་བ་རེད་ It became communized. ¶ མི་རིགས་ཅན་དུ་འགྱུར་ To be nationalized.

ཅན་ནེ་ (jɛ̄nne) sm. ཅན་ཅེ་.

ཅན་པུ་ཀྲེ་ (jɛ̄nbudre) ch. Cambodia.

ཅན་བཞི་ (jɛ̄nshi) four modernizations (modernization of agriculture, industry, defense and science/technology).

ཅན་བཞི་དུ་འགྱུར་ (jɛ̄nshitu gyur) vi. to undergo the four modernizations.

ཅབ་ཅབ་ (jəbjəb) 1. sound of eating food. 2. clapping; va.—རྒྱག to clap.

ཅབ་ཅོབ་ (jəbjob) sm. ཅབ་ཅབ་.

ཅབ་བཅུ་ཞིག (jəbjushig) about ten ¶ མི་ཅབ་བཅུ་ཞིག་སླེབས་བྱུང་ About ten people came.

ཅབ་ད་སྒྲིག (jəbda drig) va. to prepare, to get ready, to make arrangements ¶ སང་ཉིན་ངའི་གྲོགས་མོ་ཐུག་རྒྱུའི་ཅབ་ད་བསྒྲིགས་བཞག་ཡོད་ I have made arrangements to meet my girl friend tomorrow.

ཅབ་ལང་སྐྱོལ་ (jəblaŋ gũũ) va. to make all work.

ཅབས་ཐེངས་ (jəbteŋ) times ¶ ཅབས་ཐེངས་མང་པོ་ཕེབས་བྱུང་ He came many times.

ཅམ་ (jām) 1. slow. 2. completely, altogether ¶ ཁོང་ཁྲུང་ལངས་ནས་ལས་ཀ་ཅམ་སྐྱི་བཞག་ནས་ཕྱིན་སོང་ He got angry and left his work completely.

ཅམ་ཅམ་ལ་འགྲོ་ (jāmjamla dro) va. to go for a walk, to take a walk.

ཅམ་འཇོག (jāmjɔɔ̀) giving up completely, refraining from leaving; va.—བྱེད་ ¶ ཐ་མག་འཐེན་རྒྱུ་ཅམ་འཇོག་བྱས་པ་རེད་ (He) gave up smoking completely. ¶ རང་གི་ནང་མི་རྒྱུ་ནོར་ཅི་ཡོད་ཅམ་འཇོག་བྱེད་དགོས་བྱུང་ I had to completely leave all my family and wealth.

ཅམ་པོ་ (jāmbo) sm. ཅམ་.

ཅམ་མེ་བ་ (jāmmewa) sm. ཅམ་.

ཅམ་མེར་འཇོག (jāmee jɔ̀ɔ) va. to leave off/ stop/ cease doing sth. on the spot ¶ འདིར་ཡོང་རྒྱུ་དེ་ཛ་དྲག་ཆེ་བར་བརྟེན་ནང་གི་ལས་ཀ་ཅམ་མེར་འཇོག་དགོས་བྱུང་ Because (it) was so urgent to come here (I) stopped doing my housework on the spot.

ཅམ་ཚེ་ (jāmdze) sm. ཚམ་ཚེ་.

ཅམ་བཞག་བྱེད་ (jāmshaà cèè) sm. ཅམ་འཇོག་བྱེད་.

ཅའོ་ཁྲེ་ (jāwotre) ch. passenger car, sedan.

ཅའོ་དན་ས་ཚིགས་ (jāwo dɛ̄n sādzii) ch.tib. power station.

ཅའོ་དབྱི་སུའོ་ (jāwo yīsuo) ch. stock exchange.

ཅའོ་ཧྲའོ་ (jāwo hraqo) ch. professor.

ཅའོ་ཕེན་ (jāwopen) ch. film.

ཅའོ་ཧྲོའུ་ (jāwoshö) ch. professor.

ཅའོ་ཧྲོའུ་གཞོན་པ་ (jāwoshö shömba) ch.tib. associate professor.

ཅར་ (jāe) (number + —) all together ལྔ་ཅར་ ¶ All five together.

ཅར་རྒྱག་ཉར་རྒྱག (jārgyaà ñargyaà) sm. གཅིག་རྗེས་གཉིས་མཐུད་.

ཅར་མར་ (jārmar) 1. permanently, all the time, always ¶ ཁོ་འདིར་ཅར་མར་སྡོད་པ་རེད་ He lives here permanently. 2. continuously, repeatedly, one after another ¶ དམག་ཐེངས་བཅུ་སྐོར་ཅར་མར་རྒྱབ་རྗེས་ After fighting about ten battles one after another.

ཅར་རེ་ (jārre) damp, moist, soaked, wet.

ཅལ་ (jɛ̄ɛ) splashing sound.

ཅལ་སྒྲོག (jɛ̄ɛdrɔɔ̀) 1. sound of splashing; vi.—བྱེད་. 2. causing trouble/ quarrels.

ཅལ་ཅོལ་ (jɛ̄ɛjöö) abbr. of ཅ་ལི་ཅོ་ལི་.

ཅལ་གཏམ་ (jɛ̄ɛdam) nonsensical/ absurd/ senseless talk.

ཅལ་འདྲོགས་ (jɛ̄ndrɔɔ̀) splashing sound of (sth.) falling in the water that causes fright.

ཅལ་ལེ་ཅོ་ལེ་ (jɛ̄ɛle jōle) sm. ཅལ་གཏམ་.

ཅས་ཅུས་ (jɛ̀ɛjüü) crooked, not straight, bent.

ཅི་ (jī) 1. what འདི་ཅི་རེད་ ¶ What is this? 2. (—+adj.) སྐྱོན་གོད་ཅི་ཆེ་བྱུང་ We got damaged greatly. ¶ མོས་ཁོ་ལ་རོགས་པ་ཅི་ཆེ་བྱས་སོང་ She helped him as much as possible. 3. (— + vb.) whatever ¶ ངས་ཅི་བྱས་ལ་སྐྱོན་བརྗོད་མ་བྱེད་ཅིག Don't criticize whatever) I did. ¶ ང་ལ་དངུལ་ཅི་ཡོད་མོར་སྤྲད་པ་ཡིན Whatever money I had, I gave it to her. 4. Hebei.

ཅི་གོན་ཆང་ (jīgöncaŋ) sm. ཅི་ཆང་.

ཅི་ཀོང་ (jīgoŋ) ch. laser.

ཅི་ཀོང་འོད་ (jīgoŋ öö) ch.tib. laser ray.

ཅི་ཀྲང་ (jīdraŋ) ch. head pilot, captain (pilot).

ཅི་བཀོལ་ལས་ལ་འཛུག (jīgöö lɛ̀ɛla jùù) doing whatever one is ordered to do.

ཅི་ཁུག་རིན་འཇལ་ (jīkuù rinjɛɛ) paying what sth. is worth, paying whatever the price is.

ཅི་ག (jīgə) arc. sm. དེ་སྐད་.

ཅི་གར་ (jīgar) sm. གང་ལྟར་ཇི་ལྟར་.

ཅི་གོ་ (jīgo) sm. གང་འདྲ་.

ཅི་གྲོས་མིན་གྲོས་ (jindröö mindröö) sm. ཅི་གྲོས་མོལ་གྲོས་.

ཅི་གྲོས་མོལ་གྲོས་ (jīdröö möödröö) chit chat, prattle, small talk; va.—ཤོད་.

ཅི་དགའ་ (jīga) whatever (one) likes ¶ ཁོས་ཅི་དགའ་བྱས་པ་རེད་ He did whatever he liked. ¶ ཨ་མ་ཅི་དགའ་མཛོད་ Mother, do whatever you like.

ཅི་དགར་ (jīgar) sm. ཅི་དགའ་.

ཅི་དགར་ལུས་སྦྱོང་ (jīgar lüüjoŋ) free exercise (gymnastics).

ཅི་དགུ་ (jīgu) everything, whatever there is ¶ ཁོ་ཚོ་འདིར་ཡོང་ཐབས་ཅི་དགུ་བྱས་པ་ཡིན (We) did everything we could so that they could come here.

ཅི་བགྱི་བཀའ་ཉན་ (jīgyi gāñɛn) doing whatever is asked obediently.

ཅི་འགྱུར་ (jī gyur) shung. to do one's best ¶ རང་གི་ནུས་པས་ཅི་འགྱུར་ཞབས་ཕྱི་ཞུ་རྒྱུ་ I will do my best to serve you.

ཅི་ཅི་ཅིག (jījijig) 1. so and so, someone, some body ¶ མི་ཅི་ཅི་ཅིག་སླེབས་པ་རེད་ (He) told me so and so came. 2. somewhere ¶ ཁོ་ས་ཆ་ཅི་ཅི་ཅིག་ལ་བསྡད་ཡོད་པ་རེད་ཟེར་གྱི་འདུག People say he lives somewhere (but I don't know the name).

ཅི་ཅི་མ་མ་ཀོ་ཀོ་ (jīji mama gōgo) sb., sth., so and so person ¶ ཁོས་མི་ཅི་ཅི་མ་མ་ཀོ་ཀོ་ལ་སྤྲད་པ་རེད་ཟེར་གྱི་འདུག I heard he gave it to someone.

ཅི་ཅུ་གློས་གར་ཚོགས་པ་ (jīju döögar tsōgba) Hebei opera troupe.

ཅི་ཅོག (jījɔɔ̀) sm. ཅི་དགུ་.

ཅི་ཆ་མེད་པ་ (jīca meèba) uncertain, indefinite.

ཅི་ཆང་ (jīcaŋ) ch. machine gun ¶ ཅི་ཆང་ལྕི་བ་ Heavy machine gun.

ཅི་ཆེབ་ (jīcəb) shung. sm. ཅི་མ་རུང་.

ཅི་ཆེ་ (jīce) 1. as big/ much as possible ¶ གནོད་སྐྱོན་ཅི་ཆེ་གཏོང་དགོས་ (You) have to create as much harm/ damages as possible. 2. huge/ very large ¶ གནོད་སྐྱོན་ཅི་ཆེར་ཕོག་འདུག (They) suffered huge damage.

ཅི་མཆིས་ (jīcii) whatever there is ¶ གསུང་འདོས་ཅི་མཆིས་ལྷུག་པོར་གསུངས་རོགས་གནང་ Please say freely whatever there is to say.

ཅི་འཇིགས་མེད་ (jī jigmee) name of a high Tibetan official in the Panchen Lama's government.

ཅི་མཉེས་ (jīñee) whatever one likes (to do).

ཅི་སྙམ་ (jīñam) 1. whatever one thinks. 2. wondering, guessing.

ཅི་ལྟ་འདི་ལྟ་མེད་པ་ (jīda dida meèba) not be able to take it all in; too many things for the eye to take in.

ཅི་ལྟ་བ་བཞིན་ (jīdawa shin) exactly like that ། ཁོང་གིས་གསུངས་པ་ཅི་ལྟ་བ་བཞིན་ངས་ལན་བསྐྱལ་བ་ཡིན་ I gave the message exactly as he said.

ཅི་ལྟ་བུ་ (jī dəbu) sm. ཇི་ལྟ་བུ་.

ཅི་ལྟར་ (jīdar) sm. གང་འདྲ་.

ཅི་སྡེ་ (jīde) sm. ག་ལ་དེ་.

ཅི་བདབ་ཅི་ཐོབ་ (jīdəb jītob) good deeds beget good rewards.[Lit. what one says is what one reaps].

ཅི་བརྟོལ་ (jīdöö) 1. a casual/ rough guess, a conjecture ། ངས་ཅི་བརྟོལ་དུ་བཤད་པ་མ་ཡིན་པར་བརྟག་དཔྱད་བྱས་ནས་བཤད་པ་ཡིན་ I did not say this as a conjecture, I researched it. 2. sm. ཉམས་པ་ཆ་པོ་.

ཅི་ཐུབ་ཐུབ་ (jī tūbdub) sm. གང་ཐུབ་ཅི་ཐུབ་.

ཅི་ཐོད་ཐོད་ (jītöödöö) sm. གང་བྱུང་མང་བྱུང་.

ཅི་དག་ (jīdag) such as, so forth, etc. ། ཁོས་སློབ་གྲྭར་ཕྱིན་ཅི་དག་བྱས་པ་རེད་ He went to school, etc.

ཅི་དྲག་ (jītrag) whatever is best ། ཐབས་ཤེས་ཅི་དྲག་བསམ་བློ་མང་པོ་བཏང་བ་རེད་ He pondered a lot on what was the best method.

ཅི་དྲག་གང་དྲག་ (jītrag kaŋtraà) sm. ཅི་དྲག.

ཅི་དྲགས་ (jītrag) sm. ཅི་དྲག.

ཅི་དྲན་ལྷུག་གླེང་ (jītrɛn lhūnleŋ) saying whatever comes to mind, speaking without inhibitions.

ཅི་གདའ་ (jī da) what is there?

ཅི་འདོད་གང་འདོད་ (jīdöö kaŋdöö) doing whatever (one) wants, letting oneself go; va.—བྱེད་ ། སྐུ་མགྲོན་ཚང་མ་ཅི་འདོད་གང་འདོད་བྱས་ནས་བཞུགས་རོགས་གནང་ You guests, please enjoy yourselves however you wish.

ཅི་འདྲ་ (jīndra) sm. གང་འདྲ་.

ཅི་འདྲ་ཞིག་ (jīndrashig) sm. གང་འདྲ་ཞིག.

ཅི་ནན་ (jīnɛn) Jinan (capital of Shandong Province).

ཅི་ནར་ (jīnar) sm. ཅི་ཀྱང་.

ཅི་ནས་ (jīnɛɛ̀) sm. ཅི་ནས་ཀྱང་.

ཅི་ནས་ཡོད་པ་ (jīnɛ yööba) whatever (type, kind) there is.

ཅི་ནས་ཀྱང་ (jīnɛgyaŋ) must, certainly ། ཚུར་ལམ་གསུམ་པའི་ནང་དུ་ཅི་ནས་ཀྱང་ཆིབས་བསྒྱུར་གནང་རོགས་གནང་ You must (by all means) visit my house on (your) way (here).

ཅི་ནི་ (jīni) hind. sugar.

ཅི་ནིའི་ན་ཚ་ (jīnii nadza) diabetes.

ཅི་ནུས་གང་ནུས་ (jīnüü kaŋnüü) as well as one can, as good as possible ། ངས་ལས་ཀ་ཅི་ནུས་གང་ནུས་བྱེད་ཀྱི་ཡོད་ I am working as well as possible.

ཅི་ནེ་ཡ་ (jīneya) Guinea.

ཅི་ཕུའུ་ཁྲི་ (jīpudre) ch. jeep.

ཅི་ཕོད་ (jī pöö) how does one dare ། གོང་རིམ་ལ་ཁ་ལན་སློག་ཅི་ཕོད་ How does one dare to answer back to one's superiors.

ཅི་ཕྱིར་ (jī cir) why, for what reason ། ཁྱོད་ཅི་ཕྱིར་ལས་ཀར་མ་ཡོང་བ་ཡིན་ Why didn't you come to work?

ཅི་འཕྲོས་མོལ་འཕྲོས་ (jīndröö möndröö) chitchat, prattle, small talk.

ཅི་བྱ་གཏོལ་བྲལ་ (jīca döötrɛɛ) sm. ཅི་བྱ་གཏོལ་མེད་.

ཅི་བྱ་གཏོལ་མེད་ (jīca döötmɛɛ̀) 1. helpless, not knowing what to do ། དེང་རབས་ཅན་གྱི་འགྲིམ་འགྲུལ་གྱི་ཡོ་བྱད་མེད་སྟབས་དགྲ་བོ་དེ་དག་གི་མདུན་དུ་ཅི་བྱ་གཏོལ་མེད་དུ་གྱུར་པ་རེད་ Because (they) didn't have modern transportation facilities, (they) became helpless in the face of their enemies.

ཅི་བྱེད་འདི་བྱེད་མེད་ (jīceè diceè meè) not knowing what to do.

ཅི་བྱས་ལམ་ལྷོངས་ (jīceè lamlhoŋ) being lucky in whatever one does.

ཅི་མ་ཡིན་ (jī məyin) 1. རང་གར་. 2. sm. ཅི་འདོད་གང་འདོད་.

ཅི་མ་རུང་ (jī məruŋ) how good/ nice it would be, how I wish [an expression of one's deep desire] ། ངའི་ནང་མི་ཚོ་ད་ལྟ་འདིར་ཡོད་ན་ཅི་མ་རུང་ How I wish that my family was here now.

ཅི་མི་ཆོག་ (jīmicɔɔ̀) sm. ཅི་མ་རུང་

ཅི་མི་སྙམ་ (jīmiñam) not bothering/ caring about sth. ། དབུལ་པོངས་རྣམས་ཀྱི་སྡུག་བསྔལ་ཅི་མི་སྙམ་པར་འཇོག་རྒྱུ་མེད་ As for the suffering of the poor, one should not leave it without caring about it.

ཅི་མི་འདྲ་ (jī mindra) what is the difference ། ད་ལྟའི་ལམ་ལུགས་འདི་དེ་སྔའི་ལམ་ལུགས་དང་ཅི་མི་འདྲ་ What is the difference between this system and the previous one?

ཅི་མི་ལེགས་ (jī mileg) what is better ། མི་དམངས་ལ་བདེ་སྐྱིད་བྱུང་ན་ཅི་མི་ལེགས་ What is better than the happiness of the people.

ཅི་མིན་འདི་མིན་ (jīmin dimin) 1. without a clear/ explicit reason ། མི་དེ་དོན་དག་ཅི་མིན་འདི་མིན་ཞིག་ལ་ངའི་སར་སླེབས་བྱུང་ That person came to me without any explicit reason. 2. an inappropriate or incorrect time ། དེ་རིང་སྐུ་མགྲོན་ཚོ་དུས་ཚོད་ཅི་མིན་འདི་མིན་ཞིག་ལ་ཕེབས་ཙང་སྣེ་ལེན་ཞུ་དཀའ་པོ་བྱུང་ Because the guests came at the wrong time today, it was hard to entertain them.

ཅི་མེད་ཅང་མེད་ (jīmeè jāŋmeè) having nothing, having no substance.

ཅི་མྱུར་ (jīnyur) as quick as possible ། ཁྱོད་ཅི་མྱུར་ཕེབས་རོགས་ Come as quick as possible.

ཅི་ཙམ་ (jīdzam) how much, how many? ། འདི་ནས་ཁྲོམ་བར་དུ་ལམ་ཐག་ཅི་ཙམ་ཡོད་དམ་ How far is it from here to the market?

ཅི་ཙུག་ (jīdzug) sm. ཅི་ཚུག.

ཅི་ཚུག་ (jītsug) how, in what way ། ཁོ་ལ་ཅི་ཚུགས་ཟེར་དགོས་སམ་ How should (I) tell him?

ཅི་ཚེ་ (jītser) (a type of) millet.

ཅི་མཛད་ལེགས་མཐོང་ (jīdzɛɛ̀ legtoŋ) seeing/ regarding whatever sb. does as good ། རང་ཉིད་ཀྱི་རྩ་བའི་བླ་མར་ཅི་མཛད་ལེགས་མཐོང་བྱ་དགོས་ You should regard whatever your root lama does as good.

ཅི་ཞིག་ (jīshig) what.

ཅི་ཞིག་ལྟར་ (jīshigdar) sm. ཇི་ལྟར་.

ཅི་ཞིག་དྲག་ (jīshigdra) sm. གང་ཞིག་དྲག.

ཅི་འོས་ (jōwöö) sm. གང་འོས་.

ཅི་ཡང་ (jīyaŋ) anything, whatever ། ཅི་ཡང་མི་སྨྲ་བར་ Not saying anything at all.

ཅི་ཡང་མེད་པ་ (jīyaŋ meèba) sm. གང་ཡང་མེད་པ་.

ཅི་ཡིན་ (jīyin) what, why ། ཁྱེད་རང་ཡོང་དགོས་པའི་དོན་ཅི་ཡིན་ What is the reason for your coming?

ཅི་ཡིན་འདི་ཡིན་མེད་པ་ (jīyin diyin meèba) sm. ཅི་མིན་འདི་མིན་.

ཅི་ཡིས་ (jīyii) by what, for what. ། དོན་དག་ཅི་ཡིས་ལས་ཀ་ཤོར་བ་རེད་ For what reason did you lose your job?

ཅི་ཡོད་ (jīyöö) whatever there is; va.—འདོན་ to put forth whatever there is, to go all out ། ངའི་དངུལ་ཅི་ཡོད་བཏོན་ནས་རོགས་བྱས་པ་ཡིན་ I helped with whatever money I had.

ཅི་རང་དྲག་ (jīraŋdraà) what a shame, what to do ། ཕྲུ་གུ་འདི་སྣགས་འཁིལ་གྱི་མི་འདུག་ཅི་རང་དྲག This child is uncontrollable. What to do?

ཅི་རིགས་ (jīrig) all kinds/ sorts ། སྲིད་གཞུང་ལ་ངོ་ལོག་བྱེད་པའི་ཐབས་ཤེས་ཅི་རིགས་བྱས་ཡོད་པ་རེད་ (They) have tried all kinds of methods of rebelling against the government.

ཅི་ལ་ (jīlə) how could ། ལས་ཀ་སྡུག་ཅག་འདི་འདྲ་ཁོང་གིས་ཅི་ལ་བྱེད་ How could he do such a bad thing (conveys he didn't do it).

ཅི་ལ་བརྟེན་ནས་ (jīlə dɛ̄nnɛ) because of what ། དོན་ཅི་ལ་བརྟེན་ནས་ཁོས་རྐུ་མ་བརྐུས་པ་རེད་ For what reason did he steal?

ཅི་ལ་ཟེར་ན་ (jīlə serna) if you ask why ། མི་དེ་ཡག་པོ་མེད་པ་རེད་ ཅི་ལ་ཟེར་ན་ ཁོས་སྔོན་མ་རྐུ་མ་རྐུ་སྒྱོང་པ་རེད་ That person is not good. If you ask why, previously he stole.

ཅི་ལ་སྲིད་ (jīləsii) how could it happen, how could it be possible ། ཚ་བའི་ས་ཁུལ་ལ་གངས་བབ་པ་ཅི་ལ་སྲིད་ How is it possible for snow to fall in a tropical area?

ཅི་ལབ་འདི་ལབ་མེད་པ་ (jīləb diləb meèba) sm. ཅི་ཤོད་འདི་ཤོད་མེད་པ་.

ཅི་ལས་སེམས་ (jīlε sēm) shung. for what other (reason), how else.

ཅི་ལིན་ཞིང་ཆེན་ (jīlin shinjen) Jilin Province.

ཅི་ཤོད་འདི་ཤོད་མེད་པ་ (jīshöö dishöö meèba) not knowing what to say; va.—བྱེད་.

ཅི་བཤད་ཅི་བརྗོད་ (jīshεὲ jījöö) whatever one says.

ཅི་གསུང་བཀའ་སྒྲུབ་ (jīsuŋ gādrub) doing whatever is asked of, accomplishing what (one) is ordered, complying, carrying out orders.

ཅི་གསུང་ཉན་པ་ (jīsuŋ ñεmba) va. to obey or listen.

ཅི་སླད་ (jīlεὲ) why, for what?

ཅི་གསུང་དང་ལེན་ (jīsuŋ taŋlen) sm. ཅི་གསུང་བཀའ་སྒྲུབ་.

ཅི་གསུང་ཞུ་ (jīsuŋ shu) sm. ཅི་གསུང་ཉན་.

ཅི་བསམ་ལྟར་འགྲུབ་ (jīsam dārdrub) getting/ achieving what one wishes, having one's dream come true ། གསར་བརྗེའི་རྒྱལ་ཁ་དེ་ནི་ཁོ་ཚོའི་ཅི་བསམ་ལྟར་འགྲུབ་པ་ཞིག་རེད་ The victory of the revolution is a dream come true for them.

ཅི་བསམ་དེ་འགྲུབ་ (jīsam tedrub) obtaining whatever one wants, getting what one wishes to have.

ཅི་བསམ་འདི་དྲན་མེད་པ་ (jīsam didrεn meèba) sm. ཅི་བསམ་འདི་བསམ་མེད་པ་.

ཅི་བསམ་འདི་བསམ་མེད་པ་ (jīsam disam meèba) not knowing what to think.

ཅི་ཧོ་རིག་པ་ (jīho rigbə) ch.tib. geometry.

ཅི་ཧོའི་དབྱིབས་རིས་ (jīho yībrii) ch.tib. geometric lines/ figures.

ཅི་ལྷག་གང་ལྷག་ (jīlhaà kaŋlhaà) leaving as much leftover as possible; va.—བྱེད་.

ཅིག (jīg) 1. one, a (used after final g, d, b) དེབ་ཅིག ། One book. 2. imperative particle ། ཁོ་ལ་སྐད་ཆ་ཤོད་ཅིག Talk to him.

ཅིག་ཅར་ (jīgjar) at the same time, simultaneously, all at once ། མི་མང་པོ་ཁོའི་སྒོ་ཁར་ཅིག་ཅར་དུ་ཡོང་པ་རེད་ Many people come to his door at the same time.

ཅིག་ཆར་ (jīgcar) sm. ཅིག་ཅར་.

ཅིག་ཤོས་ (jīgshöö) 1. the other of a pair/ match/ couple ། གྲོགས་པོ་གཉིས་ཁྲོམ་ལ་འགྲོ་དུས་གྲོགས་པོ་རྒན་པ་དེར་ཅིག་ཤོས་དེས་སྐད་ཆ་བཤད་པ་རེད་ When the two friends went to the market, the other one said sth. to the older friend. 2. the other one ། སློབ་ཕྲུག་ཅིག་ཤོས་དེ་གང་དུ་ཡོད་དམ་ Where is the other student?

ཅིང་ (jīŋ) sm. ཞིང་.

ཅིང་ཁྲ་ (jīŋtra) ch. policeman.

ཅིང་མི་སུའུ་ (jīŋmisu) ch. penicillin.

ཅིང་ཙི་ལི་ (jīŋdzili) ch. morning glory.

ཅིང་ལི་ (jīŋli) ch. manager.

ཅིན་ (jīn) abbr. of པེ་ཅིན་.

ཅིན་ཁྲ་ཅི་གསུམ་ (jīntra jīsum) Shanxi-Chahar-Hebei.

ཅིན་ཇུ་ (jīnju) sm. ཅིན་ཇུས་.

ཅིན་ཇུས་ (jīnjüü) ch. Beijing Opera.

ཅིན་ཇུས་ཟློས་གར་ (jīnjüü döögar) sm. ཅིན་ཇུས་.

ཅིན་དུང་ས་ཁུལ་ (jīnduŋ sākü̈ü) ch.tib. the near east.

ཅིན་སྡོད་ (jīndöö) residents living in Beijing ། ཅིན་སྡོད་དོན་གཅོད་ལས་ཁངས་ Resident delegation in Beijing.

ཅིན་ཙི་ལིན་ (jīndzilin) ch. morning glory.

ཅིན་ཤི་ (jīnshi) ch. Beijing Opera.

ཅིན་ལི་ (jīnli) sm. ཅིང་ལི་.

ཅིའང་ (jīaŋ) sm. གང་ཡང་.

ཅིའང་ཤིའི་ (jīaŋshi) Jiangxi Province.

ཅིའི་ཕུ་ཀྲི་ (jīipudre) ch. Cambodia.

ཅིའི་ཁྲིའི་ (jīitre) ch. locomotive.

ཅིའི་ཆེད་ (jiī cēè) for what reason, for the purpose of what, why? ། ཅིའི་ཆེད་ཡོང་པ་རེད་ Why did you come?

ཅིའི་ཐད་ནས་ (jīitεnε) by all means, in all ways/ things ། ཁོ་ཅིའི་ཐད་ནས་མཁས་པོ་ཡོད་པ་རེད་ He is an expert in all things.

ཅིའི་དོན་ (jīitön) sm. ཅིའི་ཆེད་.

ཅིའི་ཕྱིར་ (jīicir) sm. ཅིའི་ཆེད་.

ཅིའི་ཕྱིར་ཞེ་ན་ (jīicir shena) sm. གང་ཡིན་ཟེར་ན་.

ཅིའི་སླད་ (jīilεὲ) sm. ཅིའི་ཆེད་.

ཅིའུ་ཅིན་ཧྲན་ (jīu jīndrεn) San Francisco.

ཅིར་ (jīr) to what, to which, to where?

ཅིར་འགྱུར་གཏོལ་མེད་ (jīrgyur döömeè) sm. གང་ལ་ཡང་མ་འཛེམས་པར་.

ཅིར་ཅིར་ (jīrjīr) chirping sounds of birds/ insects.

ཅིར་ཡང་ (jīryaŋ) sm. གང་ཡང་.

ཅིལ་ཅིལ་ (jīicii) abbr. of ཅིལ་ལི་ཅིལ་ལི་.

ཅིལ་ལི་ཅིལ་ལི་ (gīili cīili) sound of birds chirping.

ཅིས་ (jīi) by what, why ། སྤྱི་འབངས་མི་སེར་ལ་ཕན་པའི་ལས་ལ་ཅིས་མི་འཇུག Why not do sth. that benefits the people?

ཅིས་ཀྱང་ (jīigyaŋ) by all means ། ངས་ཞུ་འོས་ག་རེ་ཡོད་ན་ཡང་ལམ་སེང་ཕྱག་བྲིས་ཅིས་ཀྱང་གནང་རོགས་ If there is anything I can do (for you) by all means write to me at once.

ཅིས་ན་ (jīinə) if you ask why.

ཅིས་མི་འདྲ་ (jīi mindra) sm. ཅིས་མི་འདྲ་.

ཅིས་ལིན་ (jīilin) Jilin Province.

ཅིས་ཤེ་ན་ (jīi shena) if you ask why.

ཅུ་ (jū) ten ། དྲུག་ཅུ་ Sixty.

ཅུ་གང་ (jūgaŋ) gypsum, plaster.

ཅུ་གང་དུལ་མ་ (jūgaŋ tüümə) plaster of paris.

ཅུ་ལི་ (jūli) ch. plum (fruit).

ཅུ་ལི་སྔོན་པོ་ (jūli ŋömbo) ch.tib. green plum.

ཅུང་ (jūŋ) 1. a bit, some, a little, not many. 2. rather, quite ། ཅུང་ལེགས་པོ་ A little good.

ཅུང་དྲག་པ་ (jūŋ tragba) a little better.

ཅུང་པིང་ (jūŋbiŋ) sm. ཆང་བུ་.

ཅུང་པོ་ (jūŋbo) sm. གཅུང་པོ་.

ཅུང་མོ་ (jūŋmo) sm. གཅུང་མོ་.

ཅུང་ཙམ་ (jūŋdzam) sm. ཅུང་ཟད་.

ཅུང་ཞིག (jūŋshig) sm. ཅུང་ཟད་.

ཅུང་ཟད་ (jūŋsεὲ) a little, a few, slightly (in number or time) ། ང་ལས་ཅུང་ཟད་རྒན་པ་རེད་ He is a little older than I. ། དེ་ལས་ཅུང་ཟད་ཆེ་བ་ཞིག་དགོས་ (I) need one a little bigger than that.

ཅུང་ཟད་ཙམ་ (jūŋsεὲdzam) sm. ཅུང་ཟད་.

ཅུང་སེང་ (jūŋseŋ) sm. ཅུང་པིང་.

ཅུད་མིག (jüümii) ch. steamed rice mixture with eight ingredients.

ཅུན་ (jūn) ch. an army corps ། ཅུན་བཞི་པ་ The Fourth Army.

ཅུན་ཀྲང་ (jūndraŋ) ch. commander of an army corps.

ཅུན་ཇུས་ (jūnjüü) tib.ch. commando.

ཅུན་ཧྲི་ (jūnhri) ch. a sergeant.

ཅུན་ཨུ་ (jūn ū) ch. army committee.

ཅུམ་སྡེ་ཉལ་ (jūmde ñεε) va. to lay down (for horses).

ཅུའུ་ (jūwu) sm. ཅུས་.

ཅུའུ་སན་ཞུའི་ཧྲི་ (jūwu sēn shühri) ch. Nine-Three Association.

ཅུར་ནིས་ (jūrnii) ch. a type of powdered medicine.

ཅུས་ (jüü) ch. bureau, board, office.

ཅུས་ཀྲང་ (jüüdraŋ) ch. director or head of a bureau/ board/ office.

ཅུས་ཙི་ (jüüdzi) ch. cigarette holder.

ཅེ་ཁེ་སི་ལོ་ཕ་ཁེ་ (jēkese lofake) Czechoslovakia.

ཅེ་ཅང་ (jējaŋ) jackal.

ཅེ་ན་ (jēna) sm. ཟེར་ན་.

ཅེ་སྤྱང་ (jējaŋ) jackal.

ཅེ་རེ་ (jēre) wide-eyed, glaringly; va.—ལྟ་ to stare/ look glaringly.

ཅེ་རེ་ལོང་བ་ (jēre loŋwa) a blind person (whose eyes are wide open).

ཅེ་ལ་ (jēla) ch. apricot.

ཅེ་ལི་ཅོལ་ལི་ (jēle jööle) sm. ཅ་ལི་ཅོལ་ལི་.

ཅེ་ལེ་བ་ (jēlewa) scattered, dispersed, strewn about.

ཅེ་ཧེ་ནད་ (jēhe nεὲ) ch.tib. tuberculosis.

ཅེ་ཧེ་ནད་གསོ་གླིང་ (jēhe nεὲsoliŋ) ch.tib. tuberculosis sanatorium.

ཅེ་ཧེ་ནད་གསོ་སྨན་ཁང་ (jēhe nε̱ὲso mēngaŋ) ch.tib. tuberculosis hospital.

ཅེ་ཧོ་ནད་ (jēho nε̱ὲ) ch.tib. tuberculosis.

ཅེམ་ཅེ་ལྷ་མོ་ (jēmje lhāmo) butterfly.

ཅེམ་ཅེམ་ (jēmjem) thin, light.

ཅེམ་ཅེམ་མ་ (jēmjemma) sm. ཅེམ་ཅེ་ལྷ་མོ་.

ཅེམ་འདྲེན་མ་ (jēm dre̱mma) sm. ཅེམ་ཅེ་ལྷ་མོ་.

ཅེམ་པོ་ (jēmbo) sm. ཅེམ་ཅེམ་.

ཅེམ་ཙེ་ (jēmdze) scissors.

ཅེའི་འཇིགས་མེད་ (jēē jigme) a leading official of 9th and 10th Panchen Lamas.

ཅེར་ལྟ་ (jēr dā) va. to stare.

ཅེར་རེ་ (jērre) sm. ཅེ་རེ་.

ཅེས (jēè) sm. ཞེས་ (occurs after final g, d, b).

ཅེས་པ་ (jēèba) sm. ཞེས་པ་.

ཅེས་བྱ་བ་ (jēècawa) sm. ཞེས་བྱ་བ.

ཅོ་ (jō) sm. སྐྱོ་.

ཅོ་ཀ་ (jōga) skylark.

ཅོ་ཀ་གླད་སྨན་ (jōga lε̄ὲmen) a Tibetan herbal medicine.

ཅོ་ག (jōga) sm. ཅོ་ཀ་.

ཅོ་གྲུས་ (jōDrεὲ) yearling colt.

ཅོ་སྒྲིག (jōdrig) preparing to do sth.; va.—བྱེད་.

ཅོ་ཅོ་ (jōjo) older brother, older cousin.

ཅོ་ཏོ་ (jōdo) arc. hair.

ཅོ་ཐོ་ (jōdo) sm. ཅོ་ཏོ་.

ཅོ་དིར་ (jōdir) rumbling/ mumbling sound of many people.

ཅོ་འདྲི་ (jō dri̱) 1. va. to ridicule, to make fun of. 2. va. to compete. 3. va. to weigh (what sb. said or did).

ཅོ་ནེ་ (jōne) name of a place and principality in Gansu.

ཅོ་ནེ་དགོན་ཆེན་ (jōne gö̱nJen) name of a monastery in Chone.

ཅོ་གཡོལ་སྦོ་གཡོལ་ (jōyöö bo̱yöö) sm. ཡང་ངེ་ཡིང་ངེ་.

ཅོ་པ་ (jōba) a two year colt.

ཅོ་བྲེགས་ (jōdreg) a two year colt whose mane and tail have been cut off.

ཅོ་རིལ་རིལ་ (jō ri̱irii) tidy, in good order.

ཅོ་རེ་ (jōre) 1. sound made while drinking or pouring (liquids). 2. sour.

ཅོ་ལེ་བ་ (jōlewa) scant, few.

ཅོ་ལོ་ (jōlo) chattering, babbling.

ཅོག (jōg) 1. all, every ¶ བོད་རིགས་སུ་གཏོགས་སོ་ཅོག All the people belonging to the Tibetan race. ¶ སློབ་གྲྭ་བ་ཡིན་ན་ཅོག Every one who is a student. ¶ ཁོས་ལས་ཀ་བྱས་སོ་ཅོག All the things he did. 2. Mr., hey you (for males) ¶ ཅོག ཟ་ཁང་གསར་པ་དེ་ག་པར་ཡོག་རེད་ Hey, mister, where is that new restaurant?

ཅོག་ཁེབས་ (jōggeb) table cover, tablecloth.

ཅོག་གུར་ (jōggur) a small tent for one person.

ཅོག་གེ་ (jōgge) upright.

ཅོག་ཅོག་པ་ (jōgjogba) an insect that feeds on leaves.

ཅོག་པ་ (jōgba) a person who dwells in a single-person tent.

ཅོག་པུ་ (jōgbu) sm. ཅོག་གུར་.

ཅོག་པུ་བ་ (jōgbuwa) sm. ཅོག་པ་.

ཅོག་པོ་ (jōgbo) sm. ཅོག་གེ་.

ཅོག་བུ་ (jōgbu) sm. ཅོག་པུ་.

ཅོག་ཅེ་ (jōgdze) sm. ཅོག་ཙེ་.

ཅོག་ཙེ་ (jōgdze) table.

ཅོག་ཙེ་ཕྲང་བུ་བཟོ་གྲྭ (jōgdze gə̱ŋbu so̱dra) table tennis ball factory.

ཅོག་ལ་ (jōgla) a type of medicine.

ཅོག་ལ་མ་ (jōglama) sm. ཅོག་ལ་.

ཅོག་ལེ་ (jōgle) eng. chocolate.

ཅོང་ (jōŋ) 1. bell, gong; va.—དཀྲོལ་ to ring a bell. 2. sm.* གཅོང་.

ཅོང་ཁང་ (jōŋgaŋ) bell tower, belfry.

ཅོང་བརྡ་ (jōŋda) signal (with a bell or gong), death knell; va.—གཏོང་ to signal (with bell/ gong); to sound the death knell ¶ ལོག་སྤྱོད་ཕྱོགས་ཁག་མཐའ་དག་རྩ་མེད་གཏོང་རྒྱུའི་ཅོང་བརྡ་ཞིག་བཏང་བ་རེད་ (They) sounded the signal for the extermination of all the reactionaries.

ཅོང་ཞི་ (jōŋshi) a type of stone used in Tibetan medicine.

ཅོང་གཡང་ (jōŋyaŋ) precipice, cliff.

ཅོད་པན་ (jōŋbεn) tiara, crown, diadem.

ཅོད་པན་དར་དཔྱང་ (jōŋbεn ta̱rjaŋ) a long piece of brocade/ silk that hangs around the ears of a statue.

ཅོབ་བརྡོལ་ (jōbdöö) piercing a hole; va.—གཏོང་.

ཅོལ་ (jöö) containers that have a wide bottom.

ཅོལ་གྲུས་མོལ་གྲུས་ (jöödröö mö̱ödröö) sm. ཅེ་གྲུས་མོལ་གྲུས་.

ཅོལ་བགྲུས་མོལ་བགྲུས་ (jöödröö mö̱ödröö) sm. ཅེ་གྲུས་མོལ་གྲུས་.

ཅོལ་ཆུང་ (jööjuŋ) silly, foolish, stupid ¶ མི་ཆ་ཅོལ་ཆུང་ A foolish person.

ཅོལ་གཏམ་ (jöödam) silly/ foolish talk.

ཅོལ་པོ་ (jööbo) sm. ཅོལ་ཆུང་.

ཅོལ་ལེ་ (jööle) standing erect.

ཅོལ་ལོ་ (jöölo) teasing, taunting; va.— བྱེད་.

གཅག (jāà) f. of གཅོག.

གཅག་གཅོག (jāgjoò) breaking, damaging; va.—བྱེད་.

གཅགས་ (jāà) va. to remember, to keep in one's mind) ¶ ཐུགས་ཀྱི་ཀློང་དུ་གཅགས་ནས་བཀའ་གནང་ཐེབས་ཚོགས་རྒྱུ་བོའི་རྒྱུན་བཞིན་ཞུ་ Please keep this in mind and give me advise continuously.

གཅགས་པོ་ (jāgbo) sm.* ཅག་པོ་.

གཅང་ངེ་གཅོང་ངེ་ (jāŋŋe jōŋŋe) physically weak through illness.

གཅང་གཅོང་ (jāŋjoŋ) sm. གཅང་ངེ་གཅོང་ངེ་.

གཅང་པོ་ (jāŋbo) eloquent, smooth, gentle (in speech).

གཅད་ (jε̄ὲ) f. of གཅོད་.

གཅན་ (jε̄n) 1. arc. checkpost, custom post. 2. duty, tax.

གཅན་སྒོ་ (jε̄ngo) arc. sm. གཞུང་ཁང་.

གཅན་པ་ (jε̄mba) lookout person, scout.

གཅན་འཕྲང་ (jε̄ndraŋ) a precipitous mountain road.

གཅན་གཟན་ (jε̄nsεn) carnivorous animal.

གཅན་གཟན་གྱི་རང་བཞིན་ (jε̄nsεngi ra̱ŋshii) brutal/ cruel nature.

གཅབ་ (jāb) va. to clap hands or beat drums or stomp one's feet along with music.

གཅམ་བསྟོད་ (jāmdöö) flattering through praise, being sycophantic; va.—སྒྲོག.

གཅམ་ནས་འཛོག (jāmnε jɔ̱ɔ̀) va. to get things ready ¶ ང་མ་ཐོན་གོང་ཅ་ལག་ཚང་མ་གཅམ་ནས་བཞག་ཡོད་ I got all my things ready before my departure.

གཅམ་བུ་ (jāmbu) false, untrue; artificial ¶ གཅམ་བུའི་ཚིག False words.

གཅམ་བུ་ངོ་སྲུང (jāmbu ŋo̱suŋ) sm. ངོ་སྲུང་མཐུན་འཇུག.

གཅམ་བུ་བ་ (jāmbuwa) sb. who lies/ falsifies/ cheats.

གཅམ་གསག (jāmsaà) sm. གཅམ་བསྟོད་.

གཅར་ (jār) f. of གཅོར་.

གཅར་རྡུང་ (jārduŋ) sm. རྡུང་.

གཅལ་ (jε̄ε̄) abbr. of གཅལ་མ་.

གཅལ་དུ་འགྲེས་ (jε̄ε̄du dre̱è) va. to spread out, to lay out flat.

གཅལ་མ་ (jε̄ε̄ma) sth. laid down flat.

གཅི་: p. གཅིས་ (jī) va. to urinate.

གཅིག (jīg) one; a ¶ དེར་མི་གཅིག་འདུག There is a person there. ¶ མེ་མདའ་གཅིག One gun. ¶ ངས་གཅིག་ཉོས་པ་ཡིན་ I bought one.

གཅིག་ཀ་ (jīggə) single, only one.

གཅིག་རྐྱང་ (jīggyaŋ) alone, solo ¶ བུད་མེད་གཅིག་རྐྱང་ཡིན་ཡང་མཚན་མོར་ཁྲོམ་ལ་འགྲོ་ནུས་ཀྱི་ཡོད་པ་རེད་ Even a woman alone is able to go the market at night.

གཅིག་ཀྱང་མ་ལུས་པ་ (jīggyaŋ ma̱lüùbə) all, everything, without remainder.

གཅིག་རྐྱེན་གཅིག་བྱེད་ (jīggyen jīgjeè) va. to effect one another.

གཅིག་སྐྱེས་དབང་ལག (jīggyeè wāŋlaà) sm. ཅིག་སྐྱེས་

དབང་ལག.

གཅིག་ཁག་གཅིག་ཁུར་ (jīggaà jīggur) joined hand-in-hand, jointly responsible, acting as guarantor for each other ¶ ང་གཉིས་གཅིག་ཁག་གཅིག་ཁུར་བྱས་ནས་བུ་ལོན་བླངས་པ་ཡིན་ We took a loan both guaranteeing for each other.

གཅིག་ཁོ་ན་ (jīg kōna) sm. གཅིག་པུ་.

གཅིག་འཁྲབ་ (jīgdrəb) solo performance.

གཅིག་གི་མགོ་ལ་གཉིས་ བརྒྱ་ཡི་མགོ་ལ་སྟོང་ (jīggigola ñīì gya̲yi go̲la dōŋ) exaggerating too much [Lit. adding two on one, adding a thousand on a hundred].

གཅིག་གིས་གཅིག་ལ་ (jīggiì jīlə) each other, one another, by one to another ¶ ཁོ་ཚོས་གཅིག་གིས་གཅིག་ལ་རོགས་བྱས་པ་རེད་ They helped each other. ¶ གཅིག་ཁག་གཅིག་ཁུར་འགན་ལེན་གན་འཛུལ་ཞུས་པའི་འགྲུ་དོན་བརྡལ་གཤིག་བཏང་བ་ (They) violated the contents of the pledge in which both parties had agreed to be guarantor for each other.

གཅིག་གོ་བཅུ་ཆོད་ (jīggo jūjöò) one person doing the work of ten, one person being adequate for ten; multipurpose.

གཅིག་གོ་གཉིས་ཆོད་ (jīggo ñīìjöò) 1. one article that has two uses, one person doing the work of two. 2. killing two birds with one stone.

གཅིག་གོ་མང་ཆོད་ (jīggo ma̲ŋjöò) 1. one article that has many uses, one person doing the work of many, multipurpose. 2. attaining many advantages with one move.

གཅིག་གྱུར་ (jīggyur) 1. unifying, unity ¶ གཅིག་གྱུར་འཆར་འགོད་ Unified planning. ¶ རྒྱལ་ཡོངས་གཅིག་གྱུར་གྱི་ཆེད་དུ་ For the purpose of having nationwide unity. 2. same as, one with ¶ ཁོ་ཚོའི་སྲིད་བྱུས་སྐྱོང་སྟངས་དེ་ནི་ཧི་ཊི་ལར་དང་གཅིག་གྱུར་རེད་ The manner in which they rule is the same as Hitler. 3. altogether.

གཅིག་གྱུར་གྱི་བཀོད་སྒྲིག (jīggyurgi gōòdrig) unified arrangement, coordinated/ centralized action.

གཅིག་གྱུར་གྱི་འགོ་ཁྲིད་ (jīggyurgi go̲driì) overall/ unified leadership.

གཅིག་གྱུར་གྱི་ཉོ་སྒྲུབ་ (jīggyurgi ño̲drub) unified (centralized) purchasing.

གཅིག་གྱུར་འཆར་འགོད་ (jīggyurgi cārshi) overall/ unified planning.

གཅིག་གྱུར་གཉིས་སུ་མེད་པ་ (jīggyurgi ñīìsu me̲èba) sm. གཅིག་གྱུར་.

གཅིག་གྱུར་ལྟར་ (jīggyurdar) like/ as one.

གཅིག་གྱུར་དོ་དམ་ (jīggyur to̲dam) centralized/ unified control or supervision.

གཅིག་གྱུར་སྟོབས་བརྟན་ (jīggyur drādɛn) strength in unity.

གཅིག་གྲས་ (jīgdrɛɛ̀) of the same kind.

གཅིག་གྲུབ་ཀུན་གྲུབ་ (jīgdrub gūndrub) sm. གཅིག་གྲུབ་བརྒྱ་གྲུབ་.

གཅིག་གྲུབ་བརྒྱ་གྲུབ་ (jīgdrub gya̲drub) all troubles end when the main trouble ends.

གཅིག་གྲོགས་གཅིག་བྱེད་ (jīgdrɔɔ̀ jīgceè) sm. གཅིག་ཕན་གཅིག་གྲོགས་.

གཅིག་འགྱུར་ (jīggyur) sm. གཅིག་གྱུར་.

གཅིག་རྒྱབ་གཅིག་མཐུད་ (jīggyəb jīgtdüù) one after another.

གཅིག་རྒྱབ་གཅིག་འཚོ་ (jīggyəb jīgdzo) backing up/ supporting each other.

གཅིག་རྒྱབ་གཉིས་སྣོན་ (jīggyəb ñīìnön) one backing or augmenting another.

གཅིག་རྒྱུད་གཅིག་འཛིན་ (jīggyüù jīgdzin) in succession, handed down through generations.

གཅིག་སྒྲིལ་ (jīgdrii) 1. unity, solidarity ¶ ངལ་རྩོལ་མི་དམངས་ཡོངས་ཀྱི་གཅིག་སྒྲིལ་ཆེན་པོ་ The great unity of all the working people of the world. 2. united ¶ འཐབ་ཕྱོགས་གཅིག་སྒྲིལ་ United front.

གཅིག་སྒྲིལ་གྱི་འགོ་ཁྲིད་ (jīgdriigyi gu̲driì) unified leadership.

གཅིག་སྒྲིལ་གྱི་ཉོ་སྒྲུབ་ (jīgdriigi ño̲drub) unified purchasing.

གཅིག་སྒྲིལ་དོ་དམ་ (jīgdrii to̲dam) unified supervision control/ rule.

གཅིག་སྒྲིལ་ཚོགས་པ་ (jīgdrii tsɔ̄gba) name of a Tibetan Association in India.

གཅིག་བསྒྲུབས་གཉིས་ཕན་ (jīgdrub ñīìbɛn) achieving one thing that benefits two (many).

གཅིག་མགོ་གཅིག་གཡོག (jīggo jīgyɔɔ̀) deceiving/ cheating/ swindling each other.

གཅིག་ངག་གཅིག་སྐྱོར་ (jīgŋaà jīggyɔɔ) sm. གཅིག་རམ་གཅིག་འདེགས་.

གཅིག་ངན་གཅིག་བཀག (jīgŋɛn jīggyɔr) shung. being biased (supporting one and being against one) ¶ ཟ་འཐུང་ལ་ཞིམ་མང་ར་གཏོང་བ་སོགས་གཅིག་ངན་གཅིག་བཀག་བྱེད་མི་ཆོག One should not be biased in distributing foodstuffs.

གཅིག་ངན་གཅིག་སྐྱེལ་ (jīgŋɛn jīggyee) shung. harming each other back and forth.

གཅིག་ངར་གཅིག་སློང་ (jīgŋar jīgloŋ) several people inciting/ goading each other ¶ ཁོ་པ་གཉིས་གཅིག་ངར་གཅིག་སློང་གི་རྩོད་འགྲན་ནང་ཞུགས་པ་ The two of them goaded each other and finally competed.

གཅིག་ངེས་པ་ (jīgŋeèba) sm.* གཅིག་ཏུ་ངེ་པ་.

གཅིག་ངོ་གཅིག་ལ་ལྟ་ (jīgŋo jīgla dā) va. to look at each other.

གཅིག་གཅིག་གཉིས་གཉིས་ (jīgjig ñīìñii) thoroughly, precisely ¶ ཅ་ལག་ཚང་མ་གཅིག་གཅིག་གཉིས་གཉིས་ཁོང་ལ་རྩིས་སྤྲད་པ་ཡིན་ I handed over all the items one by one.

གཅིག་གཅོད་ (jīgjöò) dictatorial/ autocratic rule.

གཅིག་གཅོད་ཀུན་འདོམས་ (jīgjöò gūndom) punishing one to warn/ intimidate the rest.

གཅིག་ལྕོགས་ (jīgjɔɔ̀) combined (with regard to positions/ jobs/ functions/ uses); va.—བྱེད་ ¶ སྐད་བསྒྱུར་དང་དྲུང་ཡིག་གཅིག་ལྕོགས་ Combined interpreter and secretary ¶ ཆུ་ཚོད་དེ་རྒྱན་ཆ་དང་དུས་ཚོད་ལྟ་བྱེད་གཅིག་ལྕོགས་ཡིན་ This watch has combined functions as an ornament and for telling time.

གཅིག་ཆོག (jīgcɔɔ̀) sm. གཅིག་ལྕོགས་.

གཅིག་ཆོད་ (jīgcöò) an arbitrary/ unilateral decision or action.

གཅིག་ཆོད་གཅིག་སྒྲུབ་ (jīgcöò jīgdrub) sm. གཅིག་ཆོད་.

གཅིག་མཇུག་གཉིས་མཐུད་ (jīgjuù ñīìtüù) successively, one after another, continuous, in succession ¶ སྐྱ་མགྲོན་རྣམས་གཅིག་མཇུག་གཉིས་མཐུད་ཀྱིས་ཐེབས་པ་རེད་ The guests arrived one after another.

གཅིག་མཇུག་གཉིས་འབྲེལ་ (jīgjuù ñīìdrel) continuously, one after another without break.

གཅིག་འཛགས་གཅིག་ལངས་ (jīgjaà jīglaŋ) one rising after one goes down.

གཅིག་འཛགས་གཉིས་ལངས་ (jīgjaà ñīìlaŋ) sm. གཅིག་འཛགས་གཅིག་ལངས་.

གཅིག་རྗེས་གཉིས་མཐུད་ (jīgjeè ñīìtüù) sm. གཅིག་མཇུག་གཉིས་མཐུད་.

གཅིག་ཉིད་ (jīgñiì) sm. གཅིག་པུད་.

གཅིག་གཉིས་ (jīgñiì) one or two.

གཅིག་གཉིས་གཅིག (jīgñiì jīg) sm. གཅིག་གཉིས་.

གཅིག་རྙེད་ལྟ་ཚུལ་ (jīgñiì dədzüü) personal/ individual opinion.

གཅིག་སྙིང་གཅིག་གཏད་ (jīgñiŋ jīgdɛɛ̀) trusting/ depending on one another.

གཅིག་ཏུ་ (jīgdu) in one ¶ ཕྱོགས་གཅིག་ཏུ་ In one direction. 2. insistingly, emphatically ¶ འདི་མ་རེད་གཅིག་ཏུ་ཞུ་གི་མེད་ I am not emphatically saying, “This is not it”. 3. completely ¶ གཅིག་ཏུ་མཛེས་པོ་ Completely beautiful.

གཅིག་ཏུ་དགྱེས་ (jīgdu gye̲è) sm. གཅིག་མཐུན་.

གཅིག་ཏུ་འགྱུར་ (jīgdu gyu̲r) vi. to become one/ united ¶ དམག་འཁྲུགས་དེའི་རྗེས་ལྷོ་བྱང་ས་གནས་རྣམས་རྒྱལ་ཁབ་གཅིག་ཏུ་གྱུར་པ་རེད་ After that war the southern and northern areas became one country.

གཅིག་ཏུ་རྒྱས་ཁེབས་ (jīgdu gyɛ̲ɛ̀geb) shung. applying one example/ model for all situations; va.—བྱེད་ ¶ ལམ་ལུགས་གང་ཞིག་ཡིན་རུང་གཅིག་ཏུ་རྒྱས་ཁེབས་བྱེད་མི་རུང་ One should not apply one example/ model for all other systems.

གཅིག་ཏུ་སྒྲིམ་ (jīgdu dri̲m) va. to concentrate/ unite/ bring together into one.

གཅིག་ཏུ་བསྒྲིམས་ (jīgdu dri̲m) p. of གཅིག་ཏུ་སྒྲིམ་.

གཅིག་ཏུ་སྒྲིལ་ (jīgdu dri̲l) va. to unite ། རྒྱལ་པོ་དེས་བོད་ཡུལ་གཅིག་ཏུ་བསྒྲིལ་བ་རེད་ That king united Tibet into one country.

གཅིག་ཏུ་ངེས་པ་ (jīgtu ŋe̲èba) for certain, for sure, with certainty ། ཚིག་འདིའི་དག་ཆ་གཅིག་ཏུ་ངེས་པ་ཞུ་རྒྱུ་མེད་ I can't say for certain what the spelling of that word is.

གཅིག་ཏུ་འདུ་ (jīgtu du̲) vi. to be/ get gathered together, to be/ get concentrated ། ས་ཆ་དེ་ར་ལུང་པ་མང་པོའི་མི་གཅིག་ཏུ་འདུ་བའི་ས་ཆ་གཅིག་རེད་ That place is one where people from many areas are gathered.

གཅིག་ཏུ་འདྲེ་ (jīgdu dre̲) va. to mix together, to combine, to join together ། མི་རིགས་ཁག་གི་སློབ་ཕྲུག་མང་པོ་གཅིག་ཏུ་འདྲེས་ནས་སློབ་སྦྱོང་བྱེད་ཀྱི་ཡོད་པ་རེད་ Many students from different nationalities are studying together.

གཅིག་ཏུ་འདྲེ་ (jīgdu dre̲) p. of གཅིག་ཏུ་འདྲེ་.

གཅིག་ཏུ་བསྡུ་ (jīgdu du̲) va. to gather/ collect together, to concentrate ། ཁོང་གི་རྩོམ་ཡིག་ཚང་མ་གཅིག་ཏུ་བསྡུ་གི་ཡོད་པ་རེད་ (They) are collecting all his writings.

གཅིག་ཏུ་སྦྲེལ་ (jīgdu dre̲l) va. to unite, to join together ། ཟམ་ཆེན་གཅིག་གིས་ལྷོ་བྱང་གཅིག་ཏུ་སྦྲེལ་གྱི་ཡོད་པ་རེད་ A big bridge joins the south and north together.

གཅིག་ཏུ་སྨད་ (jīgdu mɛ̄ɛ̀) shung. outstanding, excellent.

གཅིག་གཏོང་གཉིས་མཉམ་ (jīgdoŋ ñīìñam) a policy implemented at the start of communes of moving people from one area to another to equalize the numbers in brigades and communes.

གཅིག་གཏོད་ (jīgdöö) concentrating, focusing attention.

གཅིག་རྟོགས་ཀུན་ཤེས་ (gūnsheèjīgdɔɔ̀) understanding the whole from knowing one sample.

གཅིག་བརྟེན་གཅིག་དྲན་ (jīgden jīgdrɛn) one thing sparking the memory of another.

གཅིག་ཐད་ནས་ (jīgdɛnɛ) firstly, on the one hand ། གཅིག་ཐད་ནས་ང་ཚོ་བོད་རིགས་རེད་ On the one hand we are Tibetans.

གཅིག་ཐོག་གཉིས་བརྩེགས་ (jīgtɔɔ̀ ñīìdzeg) one on top of another, piled up, having one thing occur on top of another ། ཁོ་ཚོར་དཀའ་ངལ་གཅིག་ཐོག་གཉིས་བརྩེགས་བྱུང་སོང་ (They) ran into difficulties one on top of another.

གཅིག་མཐུན་ (jīgtün) 1. in agreement, unanimous ། གཅིག་མཐུན་གྱི་བསམ་བློ་ An idea that is unanimous. 2. common ། སྐད་ཆ་གཅིག་མཐུན་ A common language.

གཅིག་མཐུན་གྱི་བྱ་སྤྱོད་ (jīgtüngi caj̲öö) unanimous action.

གཅིག་མཐུན་གྱི་རང་བཞིན་ (jīgtüngi rə̲ŋshin) unanimity.

གཅིག་མཐོང་གཅིག་དྲན་ (jīgtoŋ jīgdrɛn) sm. གཅིག་བརྟེན་གཅིག་དྲན་.

གཅིག་འཐུས་ (jīgdüü) sm. གཅིག་ལྕོག.

གཅིག་དང་གཉིས་ཀྱིས་ (jīgdaŋ ñīìgi) minute, in detail ། གཅིག་དང་གཉིས་ཀྱིས་བརྩིས་པ་རེད་ (They) made a minute accounting.

གཅིག་དུ་ (jīg tu̲) abbr. one and many.

གཅིག་དྲིལ་ (jīgdrel) a cart drawn by one horse or mule.

གཅིག་འདུ་ (jīgdu) sm. གཅིག་སྡུད་.

གཅིག་འདུའི་ཕུང་པོ་ (jīgdü pūŋbo) united body/ entity.

གཅིག་དུང་གསུམ་རྒོལ་ (jīgduŋ sūmgöö) beat one, oppose three (beat those who oppose the revolution; oppose taking advantage of the state, oppose hedonism and extravagance, oppose chicanerous selling and losing).

གཅིག་དུང་གསུམ་རྒོལ་གྱི་ལས་འགུལ་ (jīgduŋ sūmgöögi le̲ngüü) the campaign to attack one thing and oppose three things (to attack the destructive activities of contemporary counterrevolutionaries, to oppose corruption and thievery, to oppose renegadism, and to oppose extravagance and waste).

གཅིག་སྡུད་ (jīgdüü) concentrating/ assembling in one place, centralizing; va.—བྱེད་ ། མི་ཤུགས་དང་མདེལ་ཤུགས་གཅིག་སྡུད་བྱས་ནས་ Having concentrated manpower and firepower.

གཅིག་སྡུད་སྐྱེལ་འདྲེན་ (jīgdüü gyēndren) containerized transport, container shipping.

གཅིག་སྡུད་འགོ་ཁྲིད་ (jīgdüü gu̲drii) centralized leadership.

གཅིག་སྡུད་བཙོན་སྒར་ (jīgdüü dzōngar) concentration camp.

གཅིག་སྡུད་བཙོན་ར་ (jīgdüü dzōnra) sm. གཅིག་སྡུད་བཙོན་ར་.

གཅིག་སྡུད་རིང་ལུགས་ (jīgdüü ri̲ŋluù) sm. གཅིག་སྡུད་ལམ་ལུགས་.

གཅིག་སྡུད་ལམ་ལུགས་ (jīgdüü lə̲mluù) centralism ། དམངས་གཙོའི་གཅིག་སྡུད་ལམ་ལུགས་ Democratic centralism.

གཅིག་སྡོམ་ (jīgdom) sum, total ། ད་ལོའི་ཐོན་སྐྱེད་ཀྱི་གཅིག་སྡོམ་གྱི་གྲངས་འབོར་ The sum total of this year's production.

གཅིག་ནས་ (jīgnɛɛ̀) 1. on the one hand ། གཅིག་ནས་ལས་སླ་བ་ཡོང་རྒྱུ་ཡང་གཉིས་ནས་སྤུས་ཚད་སྔར་ལྟར་ཡོང་གི་མ་རེད་ On the one hand it will be easier but on the other hand the quality will not be as good as before. 2. from one, from a ། མི་གཅིག་ནས་གཉིས་བར་དུ་ From one person to two.

གཅིག་ནས་གཅིག་ཏུ་ (jīgnɛ jīgtu) from one to another, in succession.

གཅིག་ནས་གཉིས་སུ་གྱེས་ (jīgnɛ ñīìsu gye̲è) sm. ཕྱོགས་གཉིས་སྒྲ་བ་.

གཅིག་གནས་ (jīgnɛɛ̀) the first decimal place.

གཅིག་གནོད་གཅིག་སྐྱེལ་ (jīgnöö jīggyee) harming each other back and forth.

གཅིག་སྣ་གཅིག་མཐུད་ (jīgna jīgdüü) connected as chain, linked/ tied to one another ། རྔ་མོང་མང་པོ་གཅིག་སྣ་གཅིག་མཐུད་བྱས་ནས་བྱེ་ཐང་ཐོག་འགྲོ་གི་འདུག Many camels are going on the sand dunes one tied to another (in single file).

གཅིག་སྣེར་གཅིག་མཐུད་ (jīgner jīgdüü) sm. གཅིག་སྣ་གཅིག་མཐུད་.

གཅིག་པ་ (jīgbə) same ། འདི་གཉིས་གཅིག་པ་རེད་ These two are the same.

གཅིག་པ་གཅིག་རྒྱང་ (jīgbə jīggyaŋ) completely the same, identical.

གཅིག་པར་ཁྲམས་ (jīgbar kūm) shung. all are same.

གཅིག་པུ་ (jīgbu) alone ། དེང་སང་ཁོང་གཅིག་པུ་ནང་དུ་བཞུགས་བཞག These days he is alone at home.

གཅིག་པུ་མ་ (jīgbuma) sb. who is alone (for females).

གཅིག་པུའི་རང་མཐོང་ (jīgbü ra̲ndoŋ) self-pride, self-esteem.

གཅིག་པུར་ (jīgbur) alone, singly ། ཁོང་གཅིག་པུར་ཕེབས་བྱུང་ He came alone.

གཅིག་པུར་གླུ་ལེན་མཁན་ (jīgbur lūlen gɛ̲n) soloist (vocal).

གཅིག་པུར་དབང་བའི་ཁེ་དབང་ (jīgbur wāŋwɛ kēwaŋ) the right of individual ownership.

གཅིག་པུར་རང་ཞིབ་ (jīgbur rə̲ŋshib) self examination.

གཅིག་པུས་ཉམས་བཟུང་ (jīgbüü ña̲msuŋ) taking exclusive possession of sth.

གཅིག་པོ་ (jīgbo) 1. single, sole, alone ། ཁོང་ནང་ལ་གཅིག་པོ་རེད་ He is alone at home. 2. the other (person).

གཅིག་པོ་ཁོ་ན་ (jīgbo kōna) sm. གཅིག་ཁོ་ན་.

གཅིག་པོར་ (jīgbor) alone.

གཅིག་པོས་བཙན་གཅོད་ (jīgböö dzɛnjöö) ruling as a dictator; va.—བྱེད་.

གཅིག་དཔུང་གཅིག་གཞིབ་ (jīgbuŋ jīgshib) crowded,

squeezed together, shoulder-to-shoulder.

གཅིག་དཔེ་བརྒྱ་འགེབས་ (jīgbe gyageb) using one incident or example and generalizing from it, one model applied to hundreds.

གཅིག་དཔེ་གཅིག་ལ་ལེན་ (jīgbe jīglə len) va. to imitate/ follow each other.

གཅིག་སྐྱོད་ཁྲིམས་ཡིག (jīgjöö trīmyiì) laws issued independent of government, local laws/ regulations.

གཅིག་སྐྱོད་ལམ་སྲོལ་ (jīgjöö lamsöö) sm. གཅིག་སྐྱོད་ཁྲིམས་ཡིག.

གཅིག་ཕན་གཅིག་གྲོགས་ (jīgbɛn jīgdrɔɔ̀) mutual help/ cooperation.

གཅིག་ཕན་གཅིག་རོགས་ (jīgbɛn jīgrɔɔ̀) sm. གཅིག་ཕན་གཅིག་གྲོགས་.

གཅིག་འཕར་གཅིག་ཆག (jīgpar jīgjaà) some (prices) rising while others fall.

གཅིག་འགྲོར་གཅིག་མཐུད་ (jīgdrɔr jīgdüù) succeeding or continuing one after another without break, ongoing ¶ གྲོང་ཁྱེར་ནང་ཁང་པ་གསར་པ་གཅིག་འགྲོར་གཅིག་མཐུད་ཀྱིས་བརྒྱབ་པ་རེད་ In the city they built new houses one after another without stop.

གཅིག་བྱས་གཉིས་གྲུབ་ (jīgceè ñīìdrub) killing two birds with one stone.

གཅིག་བྱས་ན་ (jīgjɛna) perhaps, maybe ¶ གཅིག་བྱས་ན་ངས་ཁོང་སློབ་གྲྭར་མཇལ་གྱི་རེད་ Maybe I'll meet him in school.

གཅིག་མིག་གཅིག་ལ་ལྟ་ (jīgmiì jīglə dā) va. to look at each other.

གཅིག་མིན་གཉིས་མིན་ (jīgmin ñīìmin) often, frequently, many times ¶ ཁོ་ཚོར་སྐྱོན་བརྗོད་གཅིག་མིན་གཉིས་མིན་བྱས་ཡོད་ཀྱང་ Even though (they) criticized them many times.

གཅིག་མིན་དོ་ཡོད་ (jīgmin toyöö) not single but in pairs.

གཅིག་སྨིན་འབྲས་ (jīgmindrɛɛ̀) strains of rice that produce only one crop per year.

གཅིག་ཚབ་གཅིག་བྱེད་ (jīgdzəb jīgjeè) one substituting for another; va.—བྱེད་.

གཅིག་ཚན་ཟློས་གར་ (jīgdzɛn döögar) one act play.

གཅིག་ཚར་བརྒྱ་ཚར་ (jīgdzar gyadzar) sm. གཅིག་གྲུབ་བརྒྱ་གྲུབ་.

གཅིག་ཚིག (jīgdziì) singular (in grammar).

གཅིག་མཚང་གཅིག་འདྲུ་ (jīgdzaŋ jīŋdru) exposing one another's wrong doings/ faults.

གཅིག་མཚུངས་ (jīgdzuŋ) equal, same ¶ ཁོ་ཚོས་གཅིག་མཚུངས་ཀྱི་སྒོ་ནས་བྱས་པ་རེད་ They did it equally.

གཅིག་འཛིན་ (jīgdzin) dictatorial, absolute ¶ གཅིག་འཛིན་སྲིད་དབང་ Absolute power.

གཅིག་འཛོམས་ (jīgdzom) sm. གཅིག་སྡུད་.

གཅིག་སྡུམ་ (jīgdum) merging/ making into a single bundle.

གཅིག་བཟུང་གཉིས་ཤོར་ (jīgsuŋ ñīìshɔɔ) one step forward, two steps backward [Lit. take one and lose two].

གཅིག་གཞོན་ (jīgshön) wife or husband who is one year younger than the other.

གཅིག་ཡའི་ (jīiyɛ) (with negatives) not even one ¶ ནང་ལ་མི་གཅིག་ཡའི་མི་འདུག There is not even one person at home.

གཅིག་ཡིད་གཅིག་ཆེས་ (jīgyiì jīgjeè) mutual belief/ trust.

གཅིག་ཡིད་གཅིག་ལ་ཆེས་པ་ (jīgyiì jīgla cēèba) sm. གཅིག་ཡིད་གཅིག་ཆེས་.

གཅིག་རང་གཅིག (jīìraŋ jīì) only one, just one.

གཅིག་རམ་གཅིག་འདེགས་ (jīìram jīìdeg) mutually helping/ assisting, supporting/ helping back and forth ¶ སློབ་ཕྲུག་དེ་གཉིས་ཀྱིས་གནད་དོན་དེའི་ཐོག་གཅིག་རམ་གཅིག་འདེགས་བྱེད་ཀྱི་འདུག The two students are supporting each other on this issue.

གཅིག་རེ་གཉིས་རེ་ (jīìre ñīìre) one or two, just a few.

གཅིག་ལ་གཅིག་མཐུད་ (jīgla jīg tüù) sm. གཅིག་ལ་གཅིག་སྦྲེལ་.

གཅིག་ལ་གཅིག་དང་གཉིས་ལ་གཉིས་ (jīgla jīg daŋ ñīìlə ñīì) sm. གཅིག་ལན་གཉིས་ལན་.

གཅིག་ལ་གཅིག་འབྱར་ (jīgla jīgjaa) placing closely one next to another.

གཅིག་ལ་གཅིག་འབྲེལ་ (jīgla jīŋdree) sm. གཅིག་ལ་གཅིག་སྦྲེལ་.

གཅིག་ལ་གཅིག་སྦྲེལ་ (jīgla jīgdree) joined/ attached one to another ¶ ཁང་པ་མང་པོ་གཅིག་ལ་གཅིག་སྦྲེལ་གྱིས་བརྒྱབ་ཡོད་པ་རེད་ (They) have built many attached houses.

གཅིག་ལ་གཉིས་འགྲན་ (jīglə ñīìdrɛn) shung. wanting to follow the example of sth. ¶ ཕྱིས་སྲིད་གཞུང་ཁོངས་ནས་སྐེར་ཚོས་ཁག་ལ་ཕྱིར་ཚོད་མང་ཁར་གཅིག་ལ་གཉིས་འགྲན་བྱེད་མཁན་མང་བ་ Nowadays there are many government owned estates that were granted to aristrocrats and monasteries, so many people want to follow their example.

གཅིག་ལན་གཉིས་རྒྱག (jīglə ñīìgyaà) shung. answering back or retorting by saying more than was said originally.

གཅིག་ལབ་ (jīgləb) talking to oneself; va.—རྒྱག.

གཅིག་ལན་གཉིས་འདེབས་ (jīglɛn ñīndeb) talking/ answering back; va.—བྱེད་.

གཅིག་ལན་གཉིས་ལན་ (jīglɛn ñīìlɛn) sm. གཅིག་ལན་གཉིས་འདེབས་.

གཅིག་ལམ་ (jīglam) one-way road.

གཅིག་ལས་གཅིག་ཐོས་ (jīglɛɛ̀ jīgdöö) hearing news one from another.

གཅིག་ཤད་ (jīgshɛɛ̀) Tibetan vertical line indicating a full stop at the end of a sentence/ clause.

གཅིག་ཤུལ་གཅིག་འཛིན་ (jīgshül jīgdzin) sm. གཅིག་རྒྱུད་གཅིག་འཛིན་.

གཅིག་ཤི་གཅིག་ཞ་ (jīgshül jīgsha) one dies and another is wounded.

གཅིག་ཤི་གཅིག་སོན་ (jīgshi jīgsön) one dies and another lives.

གཅིག་ཤེས་ཀུན་གྲོལ་ (jīgsheè gündröö) drawing inference about other cases from one instance.

གཅིག་ཤེས་ཀུན་རྟོགས་ (jīgsheè gündɔɔ̀) sm. གཅིག་ཤེས་ཀུན་གྲོལ་.

གཅིག་ཤོས་ (jīgshöö) 1. the other one ¶ གཅིག་ཤོས་ཀྱིས་བཤད་པ་རེད་ The other one said it. 2. the only, the sole.

གཅིག་ཤོར་དགུ་ཐོབ་ (jīgshɔɔ gudob) a small investment yielding a great profit, expending a small resources to obtain a large gain.

གཅིག་ཤོར་གཉིས་ཤོར་ (jīgshɔɔ ñīìshɔɔ) going somewhere one after another ¶ ཕྲུ་གུ་ཚོ་གློག་བརྙན་ལྟ་བར་གཅིག་ཤོར་གཉིས་ཤོར་གྱིས་ཕྱིན་སོང་ The children went to watch one movie after another.

གཅིག་བཤད་གཅིག་འཁྲབ་ཀྱི་ལྷ་མོ་ལ (jīgshɛɛ̀ jīgdrəbgi lhāmo) a Chinese show involving one person acting in front and another speaking in back.

གཅིག་སུ་མ་ངེས་པ་ (jīgsu maŋeèba) sm. གཅིག་དུ་མ་ངེ་པ་.

གཅིག་སེམས་གཅིག་གདད་ (jīgsem jīgdɛɛ̀) depending on each other, completely trusting/ relying on one another.

གཅིག་སེམས་གཅིག་ལ་རྟེན་ (jīgsem jīgladen) sm. གཅིག་སེམས་གཅིག་གདད་.

གཅིག་སེམས་གཅིག་མཐུན་ (jīgsem jīgtün) mutually agreeing, having the same thoughts/ views/ ideas.

གཅིག་བསད་ཀུན་འདོམས་ (jīgsɛɛ̀ gündom) executing a person as a warning to all others.

གཅིག་བསད་ཀུན་འདུལ་ (jīgsɛɛ̀ gündül) executing a person as a way to control others.

གཅིན་ (jīn) abbr. གཅིན་པ་.

གཅིན་ཀྱི་ (jīngye) bed wetting child.

གཅིན་སྐྱུར་ (jīngyur) uric acid.

གཅིན་ཁ་ (jīnga) urinary tract opening.

གཅིན་འགག (jīngaà) blockage of urine, being unable to urinate.

གཅིན་འགགས་ (jīngaà) sm. གཅིན་འགག.

གཅིན་རྒྱུ་ (jīngyu) urea.

གཅིན་ཆུ་ (jīncu) urine.

གཅིན་བཅུད་ (jīnjüù) urea.

གཅིན་སྙི་ (jĩnñi) retention of urine.

གཅིན་གཏོང་བདེ་བའི་སྨན་རྫས་ (jĩndoŋ dewɛ mɛ̃ndzɛɛ̀) diuretic medicine to induce urination.

གཅིན་ནོལ་ནད་ (jĩndöönɛɛ̀) sm. གཅིན་སྙི་.

གཅིན་སྐྱག (jĩndug) urine and stool.

གཅིན་དོན་དབང་པོ་ (jĩndön wãŋbo) urinary organs.

གཅིན་དུག (jĩndug) uremia.

གཅིན་དྲི་ (jĩndri) the odor/ smell of urine; vi.—ཁ་ to smell of urine.

གཅིན་རྡེག (jĩndreg) kidney stone.

གཅིན་སྣོད་ (jĩnnöö) sm. གཅིན་བཟེད་.

གཅིན་པ་ (jĩmbə) urine; va.—གཏོང་; vi.—འབབ་ to urinate; vi.—འགག to be unable to urinate; vi.—ཤོར་ to urinate involuntarily/ accidentally.

གཅིན་པ་འགག (jĩmbə gaà) see གཅིན་པ་.

གཅིན་པ་རྒྱུག་ཙ་ (jĩmbə gyugdza) ureter.

གཅིན་པ་གྱེན་ལ་བཏང་ན་ ལག་གཡོག་ཐུར་ལ་བརྒྱབ་ཡོང་ (jĩmbə gyenla dãŋna lagyɔ̀ɔ tũrla gyəbyoŋ) if one does sth. unsuitable/ stupid it comes back to harm oneself [Lit. if one pisses uphill it will come back down onto your hand].

གཅིན་པ་མངར་འགྱུར་གྱི་ནད་ (jĩmba ŋãrgyurgi nɛɛ̀) diabetes.

གཅིན་པ་འདྲེན་སྦུབས་ (jĩmbə drenbub) ureter, urinary tract.

གཅིན་པ་དྲོ་ (jĩmbə tro) vi. to feel the need to urinate.

གཅིན་པ་དྲོ་པོ་ (jĩmbə trobo) feeling like urinating.

གཅིན་པ་དྲོ་པོ་དུས་གསང་སྤྱོད་དྲན་ (jĩmbə trobo tüüsaŋ jöödrɛn) not planning in advance [Lit. remember the toilet when one wants to urinate].

གཅིན་པ་མི་འཚོག་པའི་ནད་ (jĩmbə midzɔgbɛ nɛɛ̀) incontinence.

གཅིན་པ་ཤོར་ (jĩmbə shɔ̃ɔ) sm. གཅིན་ཤོར་.

གཅིན་ཕྱི་ས་ (jĩn cĩsə) sm. གཅིན་སྐྱག.

གཅིན་ཟགས་སྡེ་ཁོངས་ (jĩnsaà degoŋ) urinary system.

གཅིན་བཟེད་ (jĩnseè) urinal pot, bedpan for urine.

གཅིན་ལམ་ (jĩnlam) the urethra.

གཅིན་ལམ་གྱི་གཉན་ཚད་ (jĩnlamgi ñɛ̃ntsɛɛ̀) inflammation of the urine passage.

གཅིན་ལམ་རྡེའུ་སྐྲན་ (jĩnlam deudrɛn) kidney stone.

གཅིན་ལམ་རྡེའུ་འཕེལ་ (jĩnlam deubel) sm. གཅིན་ལམ་རྡེའུ་སྐྲན་.

གཅིན་ལུད་ (jĩnlüù) urea fertilizer.

གཅིན་ཤ་ (jĩnsha) a type of mushroom (that grows where people or animals urinate).

གཅིན་ཤོར་ (jĩnshɔɔ) see གཅིན་.

གཅིན་སྲི་ (jĩn sĩi) vi. to be unable to urinate.

གཅིའུ་ (jĩwu) sm. གཅེའུ་.

གཅིའུ་རྨ་བཀྲུ་ (jĩwu mãdru) a pump to wash sores in the anus, enema pump.

གཅིར་ (jĩr) va. to squeeze, to squash by squeezing.

གཅིལ་ (jĩl) va. to destroy, to spoil.

གཅིས་ (jĩi) p. of གཅི་.

གཅུ་: p. གཅུས་; f. ཆུས་; imp. (jū) 1. va. to turn/ change (direction), to steer ། མོ་ཊ་དེ་ཁ་གཡས་ལ་གཅུས་པ་དང་ As he turned the car to the right 2. va. to twist, to turn around, to screw on ། ཁོའི་ལག་པ་གཅུས་སོང་ (They) twisted his arm. 3. va. to draw water (from a canal/ river). 4. va. to pinch (with ཤ་ + — + རྒྱག).

གཅུ་འཁོར་ (jūgɔɔ) twisted.

གཅུ་གལ་ (jūgɛɛ) important.

གཅུ་འཛེར་ (jūdzer) a twisted burl of wood.

གཅུ་པོ་ (jūbo) not straight, crooked, bent.

གཅུ་ཚེམ་ (jūdzem) a way of stitching.

གཅུ་རུ་ཙ་པོ་ (jūru tsābo) hardheaded and selfish.

གཅུགས་ (jūù) sm. གཅུགས་པ་.

གཅུགས་ལྡན་ (jūgdɛn) harmony, friendly.

གཅུགས་པ་ (jūgba) beloved, dear, loved ། ཤིན་ཏུ་གཅུགས་པའི་སྙིང་སྡུག Beloved sweetheart.

གཅུགས་པ་སྨྲ་ (jūgba mā) va. to talk in peace/ harmony/ love.

གཅུགས་མེད་ (jūgmeè) enmity, hostility, hate, disagreement.

གཅུང་དགའ་བོ་ (jūŋ gawo) the younger brother of the Buddha.

གཅུང་དོན་ཡོད་དོན་གྲུབ་ (jūŋ tönyöö töndrub) name of a Tibetan opera.

གཅུང་པ་བ་ (jūŋbəwa) name of a traditional opera troupe from སྐྱིད་ in Tibet.

གཅུང་པོ་ (jūŋbo) younger male relative, younger brother.

གཅུང་མོ་ (jūŋmo) younger female relative, younger sister.

གཅུན་: p. བཅུན་; f. གཅུན་; imp. ཆུན་ (jũn) 1. va. to discipline ། མོས་ཕྲུ་གུ་འདི་གཅུན་ཐུབ་ཀྱི་མི་འདུག She is unable to discipline the child. 2. va. to tame, to break in, to train ། རྟ་རྒོད་དེ་ཚོ་གཅུན་ནས་ཚོང་གི་ཡོད་པ་རེད་ (They) tame wild horses and sell them.

གཅུན་མཁས་པོ་ (jũn kɛ̃ɛbo) a good discipliner/ trainer.

གཅུར་ p. བཅུར་; f. གཅུར་; imp. ཆུར་ (jūr) 1. vi. to be squeezed in between things. 2. f. of འཇུར་. 3. vi. to come/ get into a difficult situation or state or circumstance.

གཅུར་བཀག (jūrgaà) blocking by converging; va.—གཏོང་.

གཅུར་དུང་ (jūrduŋ) sm. བཙིར་དུང་.

གཅུས་ (jũù) p. of གཅུ་.

གཅུས་སྐོར་ (jũũgɔɔ) screwing in sth.; va.—རྒྱག ། གཅུས་གཟེར་གཅུས་སྐོར་རྒྱག་གི་འདུག (They) are screwing in the screw.

གཅུས་སྒོ་ (jũũgo) tap, regulator ། ཆུའི་གཅུས་སྒོ་ A water tap.

གཅུས་སྒྲིལ་མ་ (jũũ driimə) twisted.

གཅུས་ཉིན་ཀ་ (jũũ ñiŋga) five days from now.

གཅུས་ཐིག (jũũtig) a curved line.

གཅུས་དུང་ (jũũduŋ) a washer (for screws).

གཅུས་གདན་ (jũũdɛn) 1. nut. 2. female socket.

གཅུས་ཕུར་ (jũũbur) screw, bolt; va.—རྒྱག 1. to screw sth. in, to bolt. 2. to say negative things about sb. to his superior.

གཅུས་བུར་ (jũũbur) sm. གཅུས་ཕུར་.

གཅུས་གཟེར་ (jũũsee) screw; va.—རྒྱག; —སྐོར་; —སྒྲིམ་ to screw sth. in.

གཅུས་གཟེར་སྐོར་ཆས་ (jũũsee gɔ̃ɔcɛɛ̀) sm. གཅུས་གཟོང་.

གཅུས་གཟོང་ (jũũsoŋ) screwdriver.

གཅུས་རིལ་ (jũũrii) twisting, turning; va.—རྒྱག; —སྐོར་ to twist, to turn; vi.—ཐེབས་ to get twisted/ sprained ། ཁོས་ངའི་ལག་པ་གཅུས་རིལ་བརྒྱབ་བྱུང་ He twisted my hand. ། ཁོའི་ལག་པ་གཅུས་རིལ་ཐེབས་སོང་ He twisted his hand.

གཅུས་རིས་ (jũũrii) thread (on a screw).

གཅུས་རིས་དཀྲུག་བྱེད་ (jũũrii drūgjeè) machine that threads screws.

གཅུས་རིས་ཀྱི་བར་ཐག (jũũriigi pardaà) distance between threads (on a screw).

གཅུས་ཡོད་ཤེལ་དོག (jũũyöö shẽẽdɔɔ̀) light bulb with threads (that screws into a ssocket).

གཅུས་གསོར་ (jũũsɔɔ) drilling head/ bit.

གཅེ་ (jẽ) ancient Tibetan lineage.

གཅེན་གཅུང་ (jẽnjuŋ) older and younger siblings.

གཅེན་མཆོག (jẽnjɔɔ̀) older brother.

གཅེན་ཐོར་ (jẽndɔɔ) sore in the mouth.

གཅེན་པོ་ (jẽnbo) elder brother.

གཅེན་འབོད་གཅུང་འབོད་ (jẽnböö jũŋböö) sm. གཅེན་འཚོལ་གཅུང་འཚོལ་.

གཅེན་མོ་ (jẽnmo) older sister.

གཅེན་འཚོལ་གཅུང་འཚོལ་ (jẽnmo) relatives/ family members searching for each other (in a war/ earthquake, etc.) [Lit. search for older brother, search for younger brother].

གཅེམ་པོ་ (jẽmmo) light, thin (for clothing).

གཅེའུ་ (jẽwu) 1. a long pipe for smoking. 2. a long pipe (a medical tool) made of either brass or steel that is used to blow medication into the anus.

གཅེར་ (jẽr) 1. abbr. of གཅེར་བུ་. 2. clothing.

གཅེར་ཉལ་ (jẽrñɛɛ) lying down naked; va.—བྱེད་.

གཅེར་པར་ (jērbar) picture/ photo of a nude figure.

གཅེར་བུ་ (jērbu) 1. naked ། ཁོ་ཕྱི་རུ་གཅེར་བུར་ཡོང་སོང་ He came outside naked. 2. Jainism.

གཅེར་བུ་མ་ (jērbumə) 1. sm. གཅེར་བུ་. 2. a naked female.

གཅེར་བུའི་རི་མོ་ (jērbü rimə) a nude painting.

གཅེར་མོ་ (jērmo) sm. གཅེར་བུ་མ་.

གཅེར་འཛིན་ (jērdzin) accepting sth. as factual/ authentic/ real; va.—བྱེད་.

གཅེར་ཧྲང་ (jērhraŋ) naked.

གཅེར་ཧྲེང་དམར་ཧྲེང་ (jērhreŋ mārhreŋ) naked.

གཅེས་ (jēè) va. to love, to have affection for ། རང་གི་ཕྲུ་གུར་གཅེས་པོ་བྱེད་ཀྱི་ཡོད་རེད་ He loves his child.

གཅེས་སྐྱོང་ (jēègyoŋ) taking care of with love, looking after/ keeping with love; va.—བྱེད་ to take care, to look after ། ཕྲུ་གུ་ཚོར་རང་ཉིད་ཀྱི་ཕྲུ་གུ་ཡིན་པ་བཞིན་གཅེས་སྐྱོང་བྱེད་ཀྱི་ཡོད་རེད་ (They) are looking after the children with love as if they were their own.

གཅེས་སྐྱོང་ཐོབ་ (jēègyoŋ tōb) see གཅེས་སྐྱོང་.

གཅེས་ཀུས་སྐྱོང་ (jēègyoŋ) sm. གཅེས་སྐྱོང་.

གཅེས་བསྒྲིགས་ (jēèdrig) collection, collecting ། རྩོམ་པ་པོའི་རྩོམ་ཐུང་གཅེས་བསྒྲིགས་ A collection of the author's short essays.

གཅེས་དངོས་ (jēèŋöö) things that one loves/ cherishes/ treasures.

གཅེས་ཉར་ (jēèñar) sm. གཅེས་སྐྱོང་.

གཅེས་བདུས་ (jēèdüü) sm. གཅེས་བསྡུས་.

གཅེས་མཐོང་ (jēèdoŋ) valuing, cherishing, prizing; va.—བྱེད་.

གཅེས་ལྡན་ (jēndɛn) beloved, dear ། ངའི་གཅེས་ལྡན་ཨ་མ་ལགས་སུ་ To my dear mother (a letter heading).

གཅེས་བསྡུས་ (jēèdüü) 1. selected, condensed, chosen ། མའོ་ཙེ་ཏུང་གི་རྩོམ་ཡིག་གཅེས་བསྡུས་ The selected works of Mao Zedong.

གཅེས་ནོར་ (jēènɔɔ) 1. a treasure, a precious possession. 2. a term of endearment for one's children.

གཅེས་ནོར་ལ་ཉར་ (jēènɔɔla ñaa) va. to treasure sth.

གཅེས་པར་འཛིན་ (jēèbar dzin) sm. གཅེས་འཛིན་བྱེད་.

གཅེས་པར་འོས་པ་ (jēèbar wööba) worthy of love, beloved.

གཅེས་པོ་ (jēèbo) love, cherished; va.—བྱེད་ ། རང་གི་ཕ་མར་གཅེས་པོ་བྱེད་དགོས་ One must love one's parents.

གཅེས་སྤྲས་ (jēèdrɛɛ̀) 1. taking care of, looking after; va.—བྱེད་ ། རྒྱལ་ཁབ་ཀྱི་རྒྱུ་ནོར་ལ་གཅེས་སྤྲས་ཡག་པོ་བྱེད་དགོས་ One must take good care of state property. 2. loving, revering ། ཆོས་ལ་གཅེས་སྤྲས་བྱས་སྟབས་ Because (she) revered the dharma.

གཅེས་ཕྲུག (jēèdruù) favorite child, loved child.

གཅེས་ཕྲུག་མ་ (jēèdrugma) a favorite/ loved daughter.

གཅེས་ཕྲུག་ལང་ཤོར་ (jēèdrug laŋshɔɔ) a spoiled, favorite child.

གཅེས་བློན་ (jēèlön) favorite minister, beloved minister.

གཅེས་མིང་ (jēèmiŋ) pet/ affectionate name.

གཅེས་མེད་ (jēèmeè) careless; va.—བྱེད་ ། སྤྱི་རྫས་ལ་གཅེས་མེད་བྱེད་ཀྱི་འདུག (They) are careless about common property.

གཅེས་ཚགས་ (jēètsaà) sm. གཅེས་འཛིན་.

གཅེས་འཛིན་ (jɛ̄ɛ̀dzin) holding dear, loving, cherishing, treasuring, esteeming; va.—བྱེད་ to hold dear, to treasure, to love, to esteem ། རང་གི་རིག་གཞུང་གཅེས་འཛིན་བྱེད་ཀྱི་ཡོད་པ་རེད་ (They) cherish their own culture.

གཅེས་ཞེན་ (jēèshɛn) love and loyalty/ devotion; va.—བྱེད་ ། ཕ་མ་ལ་གཅེས་ཞེན་བྱེད་དགོས་ One should show love and devotion to one's parents.

གཅེས་ཞེན་གུས་འདུད་ (jēèshɛn küüdüü) love, loyalty, devotion and respect; va.—བྱེད་.

གཅེས་ལང་ (jēèlaŋ) spoiling (behaviorally); va.—གཏོང་ to spoil; vi.—ཤོར་ to get/ become spoiled.

གཅེས་སུ་འོས་པ་ (jēèsu wööba) beloved ། ངའི་གཅེས་སུ་འོས་པའི་ཕ་ཡུལ་ My beloved motherland.

གཅེས་སུ་རུང་བ་ (jēèsu ruŋwa) sm. གཅེས་པར་འོས་པ་.

གཅེས་སེམས་ (jēèsem) love, affection.

གཅེས་སྲུང་ (jēèsuŋ) loving and protecting/ defending; —བྱེད་ ། ཡུལ་གྱི་རང་བཙན་གཅེས་སྲུང་བྱས་པ་རེད་ (They) loved and defended the country's independence.

གཅེས་བསླད་ཤོད་ (jēèlɛɛ̀ shöö) sm. སྤུ་གཡོས་ཤོད་.

གཅོག: p. **བཅག**; f. **གཅག**; imp. **ཆོག** (jɔ̄ɔ̀) 1. va. to break ། དཀར་ཡོལ་བཅག་པ་རེད་ He broke the cup. 2. va. to violate, to disobey (orders) ། རྒྱལ་པོའི་བཀའ་བཅག་ན་ཉེས་པ་གཏོང་གི་རེད་ If one violates the king's orders you will be punished. 3. va. to lower, to reduce, to deduct ། ནང་ཆས་ཀྱི་རིན་གོང་བརྒྱ་ཆ་ ༢༠ བཅག་པ་རེད་ They reduced the price of the household goods by 20%.

གཅོག་ཆ་ (jōgca) reducing, diminishing, discounting; va.—བྱེད་ to reduce/ diminish; to discount ། སྲིད་འཛིན་གསར་པས་ཁྲལ་རིགས་གཅོག་ཆ་བྱས་པ་རེད་ The new president reduced taxes.

གཅོག་རྩིས་ (jɔ̄gdzi) 1. sm. འཕྲིན་རྩིས་. 2. depreciation account.

གཅོང་ (jōŋ) abbr. གཅོང་ནད་.

གཅོང་ཀྱེ་ (jōŋgye) frail, weak ། ཕྲུ་གུ་འདི་གཅོང་ཀྱེ་རེད་ The child is frail.

གཅོང་སྐད་ (jōŋgɛɛ̀) cry/ moan of pain; vi.—རྒྱག.

གཅོང་ཆགས་ (jōŋ cāà) vi. to become frail/ weak ། ཁོ་ན་པའི་རྗེས་སུ་གཟུགས་པོར་གཅོང་ཆགས་པ་རེད་ He became weak after his illness.

གཅོང་ཆེན་ (jōŋcen) chronic/ old illness.

གཅོང་ཆེན་པོ་ (jōŋ cēmbo) 1. sm. གཅོང་ཆེན་. 2. dilapidated, ruined, run-down (for a building).

གཅོང་ནད་ (jōŋnɛɛ̀) a chronic disease, an old illness.

གཅོང་པ་ (jōŋba) physically weak.

གཅོང་པོ་ (jōŋbo) sm. གཅོང་སྐྱེ་.

གཅོང་བྱེད་ (jōŋ ce̱è) vi. to get injured ། མོ་ཊ་བརྡབ་སྐྱོན་བྱུང་ནས་ཁོང་གི་གཟུགས་པོར་གཅོང་བྱས་བཞག There was a car accident and he got injured.

གཅོང་མེད་ (jōŋmeè) healthy, well ། གཅོང་མེད་པའི་དམག་མི་ Healthy soldiers.

གཅོང་ཟོམ་ (jōŋsom) sm. གཅོང་ཆེན་པོ་, 2.

གཅོང་གཡང་ (jōŋyaŋ) precipice, steep cliff.

གཅོང་རོ་ (jōŋro) unhealthy, ill.

གཅོང་རོང་ (jōŋroŋ) sm. གཅོང་གཡང་.

གཅོད་; p. **བཅད་**; f. **གཅད་**; imp. **ཆོད་** (jöö) 1. va. to cut, to break ། ཐག་པ་དེ་བཅད་པ་རེད་ (He) cut that rope. 2. va. to cross a river ། ཁོས་གཙང་པོ་བཅད་ནས་བྲོས་ཕྱིན་པ་རེད་ He crossed the river and fled. 3. (ཤྭ་སི་ + —) va. to buy a ticket ། མི་གཅིག་གནམ་གྲུའི་ཤྭ་སི་གཅོད་པར་བཏང་བ་རེད་ (They) sent a person to buy an airplane ticket. 4. va. to pass an exam, to graduate ། ཁོང་གིས་སློབ་གྲྭ་ཆེན་མོའི་ཤྭ་སི་བཅད་པ་རེད་ He graduated from the university.

གཅོད་གུར་ (jöögur) the tent in which a person who is doing གཅོད་ ritual lives.

གཅོད་སྒོ་ (jöögo) shung. killing animal (for meat); va.—བྱེད་ ། ལོ་གསར་སྐབས་སྔར་སྲོལ་གང་ཡོད་གཅོད་སྒོ་བྱེད་བཅུག་པ་ They let them slaughter animals during the New Year (celebration) according to tradition.

གཅོད་རྒྱ་ (jöögya) 1. verdict, judgment, sentence in a lawsuit ། གྱོད་གཞི་འདིའི་སྐོར་གཅོད་རྒྱ་གཏོང་བཞིན་པ་རེད་ (They) issued a verdict concerning this case. 2. fixing a monetary value on goods that are being given in lieu of money to pay a debt. 3. sm. བཅད་རྒྱ་.

གཅོད་གཏུབ་ (jöödub) cutting, chopping off; va.—བྱེད་ ། ཤ་གཅོད་གཏུབ་ཀྱི་འཕྲུལ་འཁོར་ Meat-cutting machine.

གཅོད་ཐབས་ (jöödəb) 1. method of cutting. 2. method of making a decision.

གཅོད་འཐོག (jöödɔɔ̀) cutting and picking up.

གཅོད་པིར་ (jööbir) a fine brush used for painting.

གཅོད་འདྲེག (jöödreg) sm. གཅོད་གཏུབ་.

གཅོད་འབྲེག་གི་ཁྲིམས་ (jöödreggi trim̄) shung. corporal punishment involving the cutting off of limbs.

གཅོད་མིག (jöömii) shung. toilet hole.

གཅོད་མཚམས་ (jöndzam) 1. the break between words ༑ ཚིག་གི་གཅོད་མཚམས་ནོར་ན་གོ་བ་ལོག་གི་རེད་ If you make mistakes breaking syllables into words, the meaning will get lost. 2. sm. བཅད་མཚམས་.

གཅོད་གཞོང་ (jöösoŋ) an iron block used for cutting.

གཅོད་ལུགས་ (jööluù) 1. methods of cutting sth. 2. way of settling/ deciding sth. (e.g., a lawsuit/ dispute).

གཅོད་ལེན་ (jöölen) cutting and taking; va.—བྱེད་.

གཅོམ: p. **བཅོམས་**; f. **བཅོམ་**; imp. **གཅོམས་** (jōm) va. to make an appointment/ agreement ༑ཁོང་གཉིས་ཚོང་རྒྱག་རྒྱུའི་ཁ་ནན་བཅམས་པ་རེད་ Those two made an agreement to do business.

གཅོམ་ (jōm) 1. pride, arrogance. 2. body strength.

གཅོམ་བསྐྱུངས་ (jōmgyuŋ) 1. remaining pride/ arrogance. 2. speaking in low tone, speaking quietly.

གཅོམ་ཆུང་ (jōmjuŋ) speaking in low tones, speaking quietly.

གཅོམ་ཟླ་ (jōmda) friends/ pals—usually refers to friends who go around together running after women.

གཅོར་; p. **བཅར་**; f. **གཅར་**; imp. **གཅོར་** (jōr) 1. va. to go to meet sb. (h.) ༑ངས་བླ་མའི་སྐུ་མདུན་ལ་བཅར་བ་ཡིན་ I went to meet the lama. 2. va. to squeeze/ squash/ smash ༑རྣག་བཅར་ནས་བཏོན་པ་རེད་ (He) squeezed the puss so it would come out.

གཅོལ་ (jöö) va. to scatter/ disperse/ spread.

བཅག (jāà) p. of གཅོག.

བཅག་སྐྱོན་ (jāggyön) damage, breakage; va.—གཏོང་.

བཅག་བཅག (jāgjaà) 1. pressing down; va.—གཏོང་ ༑ས་བཅག་བཅག་བཏང་ནས་ལམ་ཁ་བཟོས་པ་རེད་ They pressed down the earth and made a road. 2. patting; va.—གཏོང་ ༑པ་ཕས་ཕྲུ་གུའི་མགོ་ལ་བཅག་བཅག་བྱས་པ་རེད་ The father patted the child's head. 3. sm.* ཅག་ཅག.

བཅག་བཅོག (jāgjoò) breaking things; va.—བྱེད་.

བཅག་གཏོར་ (jāgdɔɔ) sm. བཅག་སྐྱོན་.

བཅག་དུང་ (jāgduŋ) breaking and smashing.

བཅག་ཕྲི་ (jāgdri) shung. reducing, lowering (taxes) ༑རྫོང་གཞིས་རྒྱ་ཁྱབ་ཏུ་ཁྲལ་རིགས་བཅག་འཕྲི་མཛད་པ་ The government made tax reductions nationwide.

བཅག་མ་ (jāgma) overstaying a day or a few days on a journey or trip, staying an extra day ༑རྒྱར་ལམ་ལྡི་ལིར་བཅག་མར་བསྡད་པ་ཡིན་ On (our) way here we stayed in Delhi an extra day.

བཅག་མལ་ (jāgmɛɛ) a place where sb. stays an extra night.

བཅག་ཞག (jāgshaà) sm. བཅག་མ་.

བཅག་བཞུགས་ (jāgshuù) sm. བཅག་མ་.

བཅག་ལྷམ་ (jāglham) boot.

བཅགས་ (jāà) p. of འཆག.

བཅགས་བཅགས་ནན་ནན་ (jāgjag nɛnnɛn) careful in doing sth., e.g., working, traveling ༑ལས་ཀ་འདི་གལ་ཆེན་པོ་ཡིན་པས་བཅགས་བཅགས་ནན་ནན་བྱེད་དགོས་ Because this work is very important you must be very careful doing it.

བཅགས་པོ་ (jāgbo) compressed, compact, packed tight; va.—བཟོ་ to compress, to compact, to pack tight.

བཅང་ (jāŋ) f. of འཆང་.

བཅང་བཅང་ཁྲུག་ཁྲུག (jāŋjaŋ trūgtruù) shaking hands; va.—བྱེད་.

བཅངས་ (jāŋ) p. of འཆང་.

བཅད་ (jɛ̄ɛ) p. of གཅོད་.

བཅད་ཁ་ (jɛ̄ɛga) the surface left after sth. is cut off.

བཅད་ཁང་ (jɛ̄ɛgaŋ) a small room.

བཅད་ཁྲ་ (jɛ̄ɛtra) written judgement/ decision/ verdict; va.—གཏོང་; —འདོན་ ༑ཁོ་ལ་ཉེས་པ་མེད་པའི་བཅད་ཁྲ་བཏང་ཡོད་པ་རེད་ (They) rendered a not guilty verdict for him.

བཅད་གོང་ (jɛ̄ɛgoŋ) fixed price, fixed rate; va.—བཟོ་ to fix/ establish a price/ rate.

བཅད་གྲངས་ (jɛ̄ɛdraŋ) fixed number/ norm/ allotment, quota, targeted amount ༑སེ་ར་དགོན་པའི་དགེ་འདུན་བཅད་གྲངས་ལྔ་སྟོང་ལྔ་བརྒྱ་རེད་ The quota of monks for Sera is 5,500 monks.

བཅད་རྒྱ་ (jɛ̄ɛgya) 1. retreat for meditation; va.—སྡོད་ to stay in retreat. 2. limit, boundary of an area; va.—བཟོ་ to establish a limit or boundary of an area.

བཅད་རྒྱག (jɛ̄ɛ gyaà) 1. va. to partition/ divide ༑ཁང་པ་ཆེན་པོ་བཅད་བརྒྱབ་ནས་ཁང་མིག་གསུམ་བཟོས་བཞག (They) divided the big room into three rooms. 2. va. to draw an outline/ contour, to make a rough sketch.

བཅད་ངོས་ (jɛ̄ɛŋöö) sm. བཅད་ཁ་.

བཅད་བཅད་ཁྲིག་ཁྲིག (jɛ̄ɛjɛ̄ɛ trīgdrig) doing one's responsibility, work, etc. in a thorough and conscientious manner; va.—བྱེད་.

བཅད་གཏམ་ (jɛ̄ɛdam) resolution, decision.

བཅད་འཐེན་ (jɛ̄ɛten) sm. བཅད་རྒྱག.

བཅད་དུམ་ (jɛ̄ɛdum) pieces of cut wood or other materials.

བཅད་དོན་ (jɛ̄ɛdön) contents of a settlement/ decision.

བཅད་གདོང་ (jɛ̄ɛdoŋ) the outer corner of a house/ wall.

བཅད་འདོམས་ (jɛ̄ndom) shung. passing sentence on a criminal ༑དམར་གསོད་ཀྱི་ཉེས་ཅན་ལ་བཅད་འདོམས་ཉེས་འགེལ་ཡོང་ངེས་ཡིན་ It is certain they will pass sentence on the murderer.

བཅད་ལྡན་ (jɛ̄ɛndɛn) a brocade with a lotus design.

བཅད་བདར་ (jɛ̄ɛdar) cutting sth. and then grinding it up; va.—བྱེད་.

བཅད་ནས་སྤྲོད་ (jɛ̄ɛnɛ drōō) va. to cede (territory) ༑ཁོ་ཚོའི་འདོད་པ་ལྟར་ཁོས་ས་ཆ་ཆེན་པོ་བཅད་ནས་སྤྲོད་དགོས་བྱུང་བ་རེད་ According to their wishes, he had to cede a great deal of land to (them).

བཅད་པིར་ (jɛ̄ɛbir) a fine-tipped paint brush.

བཅད་འཕྲོ་ (jɛ̄ndro) sm. བཅད་འཕྲོས་.

བཅད་འཕྲོད་ (jɛ̄ndröö) the remainder of sth. cut.

བཅད་འབོར་ (jɛ̄ɛbɔɔ) sm. བཅད་གྲངས་.

བཅད་མ་ (jɛ̄ɛma) sm. ཚིག་བཅད་.

བཅད་རྨ་ (jɛ̄ɛma) a cut/ wound caused by a sharp weapon like a knife.

བཅད་ཚད་ (jɛ̄ɛtsɛɛ) sm. བཅད་གྲངས་.

བཅད་མཚམས་ (jɛ̄ɛdzam) 1. sm. བཅད་ཁྲ་. 2. demarcation/ boundary line; va.—བཟོ་ to make or fix a boundary line.

བཅད་བཟུང་ (jɛ̄ɛsuŋ) annexing/ occupying a territory; va.—བྱེད་ to occupy/ annex a territory ༑ས་མཚམས་མཐའ་ཁུལ་བཅད་བཟུང་བྱས་པ་རེད་ They annexed the border territory. [Lit. cutting off and seizing].

བཅད་བཟུང་ས་ཁུལ་ (jɛ̄ɛsuŋ sāgüü) an annexed/ occupied area.

བཅད་ལེན་ (jɛ̄ɛlen) annexing, occupying; va.—བྱེད་.

བཅད་ཤུལ་ཤིང་ རྩ་ (jɛ̄ɛshüü shīŋdza) tree stump.

བཅད་ལྷག (jɛ̄ɛlhaà) left over pieces of sth. cut.

བཅད་ལྷུག (jɛ̄ɛlhug) poetry and prose.

བཅད་ལྷུག་སྤེལ་མ་ (jɛ̄ɛlhug bēēma) style of writing where prose and verse are alternated.

བཅད་ལྷུག་སྤེལ་མའི་སྙན་ཚིག (jɛ̄ɛlhug bēēmɛ ñɛ̄ntsig) sm. བཅད་ལྷུག་སྤེལ་མ་.

བཅད་ལྷུག་སྤེལ་གསུམ་ (jɛ̄ɛlhug bēēsum) abbr. prose, poetry and prose-poetry combined.

བཅབ་ (jāb) f. of འཆབ་.

བཅབས་ (jāb) 1. p. of འཆབ་. 2. secret, hidden, concealed ༑ཉེས་པ་བཅབས་ Covert/ hidden crime.

བཅམ་ (jām) f. of གཅོམ་.

བཅའ་ (jāā) 1. f. of འཆའ་ and འཆོས་. 2. abbr. of བཅའ་བ་.

བཅའ་ཀ་ (jāāga) utensils (usu. used for monk's consecration rite).

བཅའ་ཁྲིམས་ (jāətrim) charter of a monastery, disciplinary laws/ regulations of a monastery.

བཅའ་ཁྲིམས་ཀྱི་གློ་འདྲིས་ (jāədrimgi lōndrii) legal advisor, legal counsel.

བཅའ་ཁྲིམས་ཀྱི་རིག་པ་ (jāədrimgi rigbə) jurisprudence, study of the law.

བཅའ་ཁྲིམས་བློ་འདྲི་ས་ (jāətrim lōdrisə) legal counsel/ advisor's office.

བཅའ་སྒ་ (jāāga) fresh ginger.

བཅའ་སྒྲིག (jāā drig) 1.va. to make advance preparations/ arrangements ¶ སང་ཉིན་གྱི་ལས་ཀའི་བཅའ་སྒྲིག་དགོས་རེད་ (We) should make preparations for tomorrow's work. 2. rules, regulations.

བཅའ་དགུ་ (jāəgu) sm. ཅ་དགུ.

བཅའ་འགྲིགས་ (jāā drig) vi. to make/ finish preparations ¶ ལས་ཀའི་བཅའ་འགྲིགས་སོང་ The preparations for the work was finished.

བཅའ་དངོས་ (jāāŋöö) things, goods.

བཅའ་བཅུ་ (jāāju) around/ about ten ¶ མི་བཅའ་བཅུ་ About ten people.

བཅའ་ཆས་ (jāājɛɛ̀) sm. བཅའ་དངོས་.

བཅའ་ཐོབ་ (jādob) shung. one's share ¶ གུས་ལ་ཡང་དེ་གའི་བཅའ་ཐོབ་ཡོང་བ་ཞུ་ཐུད་ He was saying that he also wants his own share.

བཅའ་སྡོད་ (jāādöö) permanent residence; va.—བྱེད་ to reside/ stay permanently ¶ བོད་མི་དེ་ཚོ་ཨ་རི་ར་བཅའ་སྡོད་བྱེད་ཀྱི་ཡོད་པ་རེད་ Those Tibetans are staying permanently in America.

བཅའ་སྡོད་དམག (jāādöö māà) occupation troops/ army, permanently stationed troops.

བཅའ་གནས་ (jāānɛɛ̀) sm. བཅའ་སྡོད་.

བཅའ་འཕྲང་ (jāādraŋ) sm. འཕྲང་ལམ་.

བཅའ་ཞག (jāāshaà) an overnight stop on a trip.

བཅའ་བཞུགས་སྐུ་ཚབ་ (jāāshuù gūdzəb) permanent representative.

བཅའ་ཟམ་ (jāāsam) bridge over a gorge.

བཅའ་ཡང་ (jāāyaŋ) sm. ཚག་ཡང་.

བཅའ་ཡིག (jāəyig) shung. constitution, legal document, charter.

བཅའ་ཡོས (jāāyöö) parched/ popped/ roasted grains.

བཅའ་ལག (jāālaà) sm. ཅ་ལག.

བཅའ་སྲུང་ (jāāsuŋ) garrison, defense force; va.—བྱེད་ to garrison, to defend permanently.

བཅའ་སྲུང་དཔོན་ (jāāsuŋ bōn) leader of a garrison/ defense force.

བཅའ་གསུམ་ (jāsum) shung. one third ¶ རྒྱུ་དངོས་བཅའ་གསུམ་ One third of the property.

བཅར་ (jāā) 1. va. to call on/ meet sb. higher in status ¶ ངས་ཁོང་གི་སྐུ་མདུན་དུ་བཅར་བ་ཡིན་ I called on him. 2. close, dear (with regard to a relationship) ¶ ཤིན་དུ་བཅར་བའི་གྲོགས་པོ་ A very close friend. 3. va. to get close to, to come in close contact with ¶ དགྲ་བོའི་དམག་མིས་ང་ཚོའི་ཉེ་འགྲམ་དུ་བཅར་ནུས་ཀྱི་མ་རེད་ The enemy forces will not dare come near us.

བཅར་བཅར་པོ་ (jāā jāābo) flat.

བཅར་རྟེན་ (jāāden) gift/ present given when calling on sb.

བཅར་འདྲི་ (jāndri) an interview (sb. going to ask questions of another); va.—བྱེད་ to interview.

བཅར་བ་གནང་ (jāāwa nāŋ) h. of བཅར་.

བཅར་འབྱོར་ (jānjɔɔ) reporting to/ notifying one's office or boss when one arrives somewhere ¶ འཐུས་མི་རྣམས་འདི་གའི་ལས་ཁུངས་སུ་བཅར་འབྱོར་བྱུང་ The representatives have reported to the office here.

བཅར་མིག (jāāmii) the eye of a blind person.

བཅར་ཞུགས་ (jāāshuù) 1. going and participating; va.—བྱེད་ ¶ འཚོགས་འདུ་ལ་བཅར་ཞུགས་བྱས་སོང་ (They) went and participated in the meeting. 2. h. of བཅར་སྡོད་.

བཅར་ལེབ་ (jāāleb) sm. བཅར་བཅར་པོ་.

བཅལ་ (jɛɛ̀) p. of འཇལ་.

བཅས་ (jɛɛ̀) 1. p. of འཆའ་. 2. term used to indicate inclusion ¶ ལས་ཁུངས་ནང་དགེ་རྒན་གཅིག་དང་ དྲུང་ཡིག་གཉིས་སློབ་ཕྲུག་ཁ་ཤས་བཅས་འདུག There was a teacher, two secretaries and a few students in the office (indicates that there are no other people in the office). ¶ ཁོང་སྐུ་འཁོར་དང་བཅས་རྒྱ་གར་ལ་ཕེབས་པ་རེད་ He, together with (his) retinue, left for India. 3. with ¶ དགའ་སྤྲོ་ཚད་མེད་དང་བཅས་ཁོང་ལ་དགའ་བསུ་ཞུས་པ་རེད་ They greeted him with great joy.

བཅས་བཅོས་ (jɛɛ̀jöö) reforming, revising, correcting; va.—བྱེད་.

བཅིང་ (jiŋ) f. of འཆིང་.

བཅིངས་ (jiŋ) p. of འཆིང་.

བཅིངས་བཀྱིགས་ (jiŋgyig) tying up; va.—བྱེད་.

བཅིངས་བཀྲོལ་ (jiŋdröö) sm. བཅིངས་འགྲོལ་.

བཅིངས་བཀྲོལ་ས་ཁུལ་ (jiŋdröö səküü) sm. བཅིངས་འགྲོལ་ས་ཁུལ་.

བཅིངས་འགྲོལ་ (jiŋdröö) liberation; liberating; va.—གཏོང་ to liberate; vi.—ཐོབ་ to be liberated ¶ བཅིངས་འགྲོལ་གཏོང་བཞིན་པའི་ས་ཁུལ་ Liberated areas. ¶ བཅིངས་འགྲོལ་བཏང་རྗེས་ After liberating (them).

བཅིངས་འགྲོལ་རྟགས་ཅན་ (jiŋdröö dāgjɛn) a brand of truck used in use in Tibet.

བཅིངས་འགྲོལ་འཐབ་ཕྱོགས་ (jiŋdröö tābjɔɔ) liberation front.

བཅིངས་འགྲོལ་དམག (jiŋdröö māà) liberation army.

བཅིངས་འགྲོལ་དམག་འཁྲུག (jiŋdröö məgdruù) war of liberation.

བཅིངས་འགྲོལ་དམག་མི་ (jiŋdröö məəmi) liberation army soldier.

བཅིངས་འགྲོལ་ལས་འགུལ་ (jiŋdröö lengüü) liberation movement/ campaign.

བཅིངས་འགྲོལ་ས་ཁུལ་ (jiŋdröö səgüü) an area/ regioon that has been liberated.

བཅིངས་ཐག (jiŋdaà) binds, fetters, chains; va.—རྒྱག to bind, to fetter, to chain; vi.—འགྲོལ་ to get untied/ unshackled, to get liberated from bondage.

བཅིངས་པ་ (jiŋbə) sm. བཅིངས་ཐག.

བཅིངས་བཙིར་ (jiŋdzir) an instrument of torture (for fingers).

བཅིངས་ཞགས་ (jiŋshaà) sm. བཅིངས་ཐག.

བཅིངས་ལུམས་ (jiŋlum) a Tibetan method of medical treatment—wrapping medication in a piece of cloth and after soaking it in water, applying the cloth to the pain.

བཅིབ་ (jib) f. of འཆིབ་.

བཅིབ་རེས་ (jibreè) sm. ཆིབ་རེས་.

བཅིབས་ (jib) p. of འཆིབ་.

བཅིར་ (jir) p. and f. of འཆིར་.

བཅིལ་ (jii) p. of འཇིལ་.

བཅུ་ (jū) 1. ten. 2. f. of འཆུ་.

བཅུ་སྐོར་ (jūgɔɔ) 1. almost/ about ten ¶ མི་བཅུ་སྐོར་ཕེབས་བཞག About ten people came. 2. a yield of ten times the seeds sown.

བཅུ་སྐྱེད་ (jūgyeè) shung. 20% interest.

བཅུ་ཁ་ (jūga) at least ten, ten or above; vi.—ལོན་; —ཚང་ to have reached (the amount of) ten ¶ ང་ལ་སྒོར་བཅུ་ཁ་ལོན་ཡོད་ My money has reached at least ten dollars.

བཅུ་ཁ་བུད་ (jūka büü) an old horse (over 14 years old).

བཅུ་ཁོག (jūgɔɔ̀) sm. བཅུ་སྐོར་.

བཅུ་ཁྲལ་ (jūdrɛɛ) shung. a tax levied for every ten animals.

བཅུ་དགུ་ (jūrgu) nineteen.

བཅུ་འགྱུར་ (jū gyur) ten times, tenfold ¶ སེམས་ཅན་བཅུ་འགྱུར་གྱིས་འཕར་བཞག The animals have increased tenfold.

བཅུ་གྲངས་ (jūdraŋ) ten, a unit of ten.

བཅུ་སྒོར་ (jūgɔɔ) shung. a ten སྒོར་ coin.

བཅུ་གཅིག (jūgjii) eleven.

བཅུ་གཅིག་ཞལ་ (jūgjii shɛɛ) eleven headed ikon/ statue of Avalokitesvara.

བཅུ་ཆ་ (jūca) one tenth ། བཅུ་ཆ་གསུམ་ Three tenths.
བཅུ་གཉིས་ (jūñii) twelve.
བཅུ་གཉིས་དྲུག་སྣ་ (jūñii trugna) shung. a system of conscripting soldiers as a corvee tax (one conscript from every 12 kang of land).
བཅུ་གཉིས་དྲུག་སྣའི་དམག (jūñii trugnε māà) shung. sm. བཅུ་གཉིས་དྲུག་སྣ་.
བཅུ་གཉིས་པའི་ཚེས་དགུའི་ལས་འགུལ་ (jūñiibε tsēègü lεngüü) the December 9th Movement (a demonstration staged on December 9, 1935 by Beijing students calling for resistance to Japanese aggression).
བཅུ་ལྡིར་ (jūdir) a ten སྲང་ size pot of chang.
བཅུ་ཐམ་པ་ (jūtamba) ten.
བཅུ་དེབ་ (jūdeb) a book/ set of paper that has 10 sheets.
བཅུ་དྲུག (jūdruù) sixteen.
བཅུ་དྲུག་ཆ་ (jūdruùca) one sixteenth.
བཅུ་བདུན་ (jūbdün) seventeen.
བཅུ་ལྡབ་ (jūdəb) ten times, tenfold.
བཅུ་ཉིང་ (jūniŋ) ten years ago.
བཅུ་པ་ (jūbə) the tenth ། ཟླ་བ་བཅུ་པ་ The tenth month.
བཅུ་པའི་ཚེས་གཅིག་གི་དུས་ཆེན་ (jūbε tsēèjiigi tüüjen) October 1st holiday —Chinese National Day.
བཅུ་པའི་གསར་བརྗེ་ (jūbε sārje) the October Revolution.
བཅུ་པོ་ (jūbo) the ten together ། ང་ཚོ་མི་བཅུ་པོ་དེ་བོད་ཀྱི་འཐུས་མིར་གཏོང་རྒྱུའི་ཁས་བླངས་ It was decided that the ten of us together should be the Tibetan representatives.
བཅུ་དཔོན་ (jūbön) head of a squad/ unit of ten.
བཅུ་ཕོགས་ (jūpɔ̄ɔ̀) shung. ten days ration of grain or money.
བཅུ་ཕྲག (jūdraà) 1. tens ། མི་བཅུ་ཕྲག་ཁ་ཤས་སླེབས་བཞག Several tens of people have come (could be between 20 and 100). 2. a decade ། དུས་རབས་ཉི་ཤུ་པའི་ལོ་བཅུ་ཕྲག་ལྔ་པའི་ནང་ In the 5th decade of the 20th century.
བཅུ་འཕར་རྩིས་སྟངས་ (jūpar dzīdaŋ) decimal system.
བཅུ་བུད་ (jūbüü) sm. བཅུ་ཁ་བུད་.
བཅུ་བོགས་ (jūbɔ̄ɔ̀) a10% lease fee of grain (collected by the Agriculture Department).
བཅུ་འབོ་ (jū bo) shung. a square wooden container which hold ten བྲེ་.
བཅུ་འབོར་འབྲུ་ཟན་ (jūmbɔɔ drusεn) shung. a 10% lease fee of grain.
བཅུ་མེད་ (jūmeè) zero (in the ten decimal place) ། བརྒྱ་དང་བཅུ་མེད་ལྔ་ One hundred and five [Lit. one hundred and zero five].
བཅུ་རྫ་ (jūdza) clay pot that holds ten བྲེ་ of grain (for making chang).
བཅུ་བཞི་ (jūbshi) fourteen.
བཅུ་ཟུར་ (jūsur) sm. བཅུ་ཆ་.
བཅུ་ཟུར་དཔྱ་ཁྲལ་ (jūsur jε̄εtrεε) shung. 10% tax.
བཅུ་ཟུར་འབྲུ་འབབ་ (jūsur drumbəb) shung. sm. བཅུ་བོགས་.
བཅུ་ལོར་ (jūlɔɔ) shung. a currency note worth ten སྲང་.
བཅུ་ཤད་ (jūshεὲ) marker on a rosary placed after every ten beads.
བཅུ་ཤིང་ (jūshiŋ) shung. a piece of wood representing ten in the old Tibetan system of accounting.
བཅུ་ཤོག (jūshɔ̄ɔ̀) group of ten, squad of ten. 2. shung. the smallest unit in the traditional Tibetan army.
བཅུ་ཤོད་ (jūshöö) abacus.
བཅུ་གསུམ་ (jōgsom) thirteen.
བཅུག (jūù) p. of འཇུག.
བཅུག་ཁྲ་ (jūgdra) list of stored goods.
བཅུག་བཏོན་ (jūgdön) deposits and withdrawals (in banking/ accounting) ། བཅུག་བཏོན་དེབ་ Passbook (for a bank account).
བཅུག་བཏོན་ཁ་འཐབ་ (jūgdün kādəb) shung. balancing the putting of sth. into storage with taking it out ། བུ་དེབ་ནས་བཅུག་བཏོན་ཁ་འཐབ་བཏང་སྟེ་ (They) balanced the storing and taking out (of grain) in the copy book of the master book.
བཅུག་བདེ་པོ་ (jūg debo) easy to put in, easy to pack.
བཅུག་རེག (jūgreg) the sensation of sexual intercourse.
བཅུད་ (jüü) 1. juice, sap, extract. 2. nutrition, nutrient ། ཚལ་དེ་ཚོ་གོང་ཁེ་ལ་བཅུད་ཆེ་བ་ར་མ་ཟད་ Not only were the vegetable dishes cheap and nutritious. 3. the content (of a bottle/ cup/ bowl) ། སྣོད་བཅུད་ A vessel and its content.
བཅུད་ཀྱི་མི་ (jüügi mi) human beings.
བཅུད་ཀྱི་འཇིག་རྟེན་ (jüügi jigden) all living beings on earth.
བཅུད་འགུགས་ (jüŋguù) arc. butter lamp.
བཅུད་རྒྱལ་ (jüügyεε) mercury.
བཅུད་དངོས་ (jüüŋöö) sm. བཅུད་རྫས་.
བཅུད་ཅན་ (jüüjεn) sm. བཅུད་ལྡན་.
བཅུད་ཆ་ (jüüja) nutrition.
བཅུད་ཆེན་པོ་ (jüü cēmbo) nutritious.
བཅུད་དོར་སྙིགས་ལེན་ (jüü dɔ̄ɔ ñīglen) lack of judgment [Lit. throw out the nutrition, take the dregs].
བཅུད་ལྡན་ (jüüdεn) nutritious ། ལྟོ་ཆས་བཅུད་ལྡན་ Nutritious food.
བཅུད་ལྡན་དངོས་རིགས་ (jüüdεn ŋöörig) sm. བཅུད་རྫས་.
བཅུད་ལྡན་ཞིང་ས་ (jüüdεn shiŋsə) rich soil/ land/ field.
བཅུད་ལྡན་ཟས་རིགས་ (jüüdεn sε̄εrig) nutritious foods.
བཅུད་བྲལ་ (jüüdrεε) having no nutritional value.
བཅུད་མེད་ (jüümeè) sm. བཅུད་བྲལ་.
བཅུད་སྨན་ (jüümεn) 1. vitamin. 2. ripe.
བཅུད་རྩི་ (jüüdzi) nutrient.
བཅུད་ཚོར་ (jüüdzɔr) va. to taste.
བཅུད་རྫས་ (jüüdzεὲ) nutrient, nutritional substance.
བཅུད་ལེན་ (jüülen) 1. extracting nutrients (from foods, plants, etc.). 2. a type of tree. 3. va. to take/ keep the good ། གཞན་གྱི་ཉམས་མྱོང་ལས་བཅུད་ལེན་བྱས་དགོས་ One should take the good from other's experience.
བཅུན་ (jün) p. of འཛུན་.
བཅུན་གམ་ (jüngam) eng. chewing gum.
བཅུམ་ (jüm) p. of འཛུམ་.
བཅུམས་བཅུམས་ (jūmjum) narrower; va.—བཟོ་ to make narrower.
བཅུར་ (jür) 1. p. and f. of གཅུར་. 2. p. of འཛུར་.
བཅུས་ (jüü) 1. p. of འཆུ་. 2. arc. va. to water flowers and plants.
བཅུས་དཀྲུག (jüüdrug) lathe work ། བཅུས་དཀྲུག་བཟོ་པ་ Lathe worker.
བཅེམ་: p. **བཅེམས་**; f. **བཅེམ་**; imp. **བཅེམས་** (jēm) va. to chew.
བཅེམ་རྩེ་ (jēmdze) sm.* ཅེམ་ཅེ་.
བཅེམས་ (jēm) p. of བཅེམ་.
བཅེར་ (jēr) va. to pile up, to stack up ། འབྲུ་ཕུང་མཐོན་པོར་བཅེར་ནས་ Having piled up the grains in a big heap.
བཅེས་ (jēè) p. of འཆེ་.
བཅོ་ (jō) 1. ten ། བཅོ་ལྔ་ Fifteen. 2. a two year old horse or donkey.
བཅོ་བརྒྱད་ (jōbgyεὲ) eighteen.
བཅོ་བརྒྱད་ཐོག་མདའ་ (jōbgyεὲ tōnda) shung. an archery contest held behind the Potala Palace on the 18th day of the 1st month of the Tibetan calendar.
བཅོ་བརྒྱད་དྲུག་བཅུ་ (jōbgyεὲtrugju) shung. a system in tt. of conscripting people from age 18 to 60 in emergencies.
བཅོ་ལྔ་ (jōŋa) fifteen.
བཅོ་ལྔ་མཆོད་པ་ (jōŋa cōōba) shung. "Butter sculpture" festival on the 15th of 1st Tibetan month.
བཅོམ་ (jōm) 1. p. of འཇོམས་. 2. va. to loot, to

plunder ། གསོད་བསྲེག་བཅོམ་གསུམ་ Killing, burning, and plundering. 3. va. to defeat, to conquer.

བཅོམ་བསྐྱངས་ (jōmgyuŋ) sm. གཅོམ་བསྐྱངས་.

བཅོམ་ལྡན་འདས་ (jōmdɛn dɛ̱ɛ̀) an epithet of the Buddha.

བཅོམ་ལྡན་འདས་ཀྱི་ཉན་ཐོས་ (jōmdɛn dɛ̱ɛ̀gi ñɛntöö) the disciples of Buddha while he was alive.

བཅོམ་འཕྲོག (jōmdrɔɔ̀) robbery, looting, plundering; va.—བྱེད་ to rob/ loot/ plunder; vi.—ཕོར་ to be robbed/ plundered/ looted. ། ས་གནས་དེ་ཚོར་འགྲུལ་པ་མང་པོའི་དངུལ་དང་ཅ་ལག་བཅོམ་འཕྲོག་བྱས་འདུག In those areas many travelers were robbed of their money and possessions.

བཅོམ་བརླག (jōmlaà) robbing and destroying; va.—བྱེད་.

བཅོལ་ (jōō) p. of འཚོལ་.

བཅོལ་དངུལ་ (jōōŋüü) money left with sb. 2. bank deposit.

བཅོལ་འཇོག (jōnjɔɔ̀) entrusting/ leaving in sb.'s charge; va.—བྱེད་ ། ང་གུང་སེང་ལ་འགྲོ་ཤུལ་ངའི་ཅ་ལག་གྲོགས་པོའི་སར་བཅོལ་འཇོག་བྱས་པ་ཡིན་ When I was gone on vacation I left my things with a friend.

བཅོལ་བདམས་ (jōōdam) giving instructions/ orders about work to be done; va.—བྱེད་.

བཅོལ་གདམས་ (jōōdam) sm. བཅོལ་བདམས་.

བཅོལ་ནོར་ (jōōnɔɔ) 1. yaks that have been left with another for keeping. 2. wealth/ possessions left with another for keeping.

བཅོལ་མ་ (jōōma) things entrusted/ left with another ། རི་མོ་འདི་ངའི་མ་རེད་བཅོལ་མ་རེད་ This painting is not mine. (I'm) keeping it for someone.

བཅོལ་བཞག (jōōshaēa) sm. བཅོལ་འཇོག.

བཅོལ་ཡུལ་ (jōōyüü) place of refuge/ shelter/ protection; va.—བྱེད་ to hold/ consider as (one's) place of refuge/ shelter/ protection. ། ང་ཚོའི་རེ་བ་བཅོལ་ཡུལ་ཁྱེད་རང་རང་ཡིན་ You are the one in whom we place our hope.

བཅོལ་ལེན་ (jōōlen) entrusting and accepting; va.—བྱེད་ ། བུ་བཅོལ་ཁང་དེ་རང་ཕྲུ་གུ་ ༣༠ ལྷག་ཙམ་བཅོལ་ལེན་བྱེད་ཐུབ་ཀྱི་ཡོད་པ་རེད་ That nursery takes care of over thirty children (people bring them to keep and they accept them).

བཅོལ་ས་ (jōōsa) sm. བཅོལ་ཡུལ་.

བཅོས་ (jōō) 1. p. of འཆོས་. 2. abbr. of བཅོས་མ་.

བཅོས་ཀ་ (jōōga) sm. བཅོས་ཐབས་.

བཅོས་སྒྱོང་ (jōōgyoŋ) reforming/ correcting and practicing.

བཅོས་རྒྱག (jōō gyaà) va. to correct ། ངའི་རྩོམ་ཡིག་འདི་ལ་བཅོས་རྒྱག་རོགས་གནང་ Please correct my article (manuscript).

བཅོས་རྒྱག་ཞུས་དག (jōō gya̱à shü̱ü da̱à) correcting and proofreading; va.— གཏོང་.

བཅོས་སྒྱུར་ (jōōgyur) sm. བཅོས་བསྒྱུར་.

བཅོས་སྒྲིག (jōō dri̱g) 1. reorganizing, rearranging, reshuffling ། ཏང་ནང་གི་བཅོས་སྒྲིག Reorganizing within the party. 2. repairing and assembling (of machines); va.—བྱེད་ ། འཕྲུལ་འཁོར་བཅོས་སྒྲིག་ཁང་ Machine repair and assembly workshop.

བཅོས་བསྒྱུར་ (jōōgyur) reforms, changes; va.—གཏོང་; —བྱེད་ to reform, to change, to transform ། སྲིད་གཞུང་གསར་པས་ས་ཞིང་བཅོས་བསྒྱུར་བྱས་པ་རེད་ The new government made land reforms.

བཅོས་བསྒྲིགས་ (jōōdrig) sm. བཅོས་སྒྲིག.

བཅོས་བརྗེ་ (jōōje) sm. བཅོས་བསྒྱུར་.

བཅོས་ཐབས་ (jōōdəb) remedy, cure, help ། ནད་དེ་བཅོས་ཐབས་ཡོད་པ་མ་རེད་ There is no cure for this illness.

བཅོས་ཐབས་མེད་པ་ (jōōdəb me̱èba) incurable, incorrigible, hopeless.

བཅོས་ཐབས་མེད་པའི་ནད་ (jōōdəb me̱èbɛ nɛ̱ɛ̀) terminal illness.

བཅོས་པའི་ཆང་ (jōōbɛ cāŋ) fermented barley that has been dried and then had water added to it to make a kind of chang.

བཅོས་པའི་ཆུ་ (jōōbɛ cū) drain/ irrigation canal/ reservoir water.

བཅོས་པའི་ཆོས་ (jōōbɛ cöö) false dharma, false religion.

བཅོས་པའི་ཐབས་ཤེས་ (jōōbɛ təbsheè) method for curing/ correcting.

བཅོས་པའི་ནགས་ (jōōbɛ na̱g) man-made park/ grove.

བཅོས་པའི་མ་ནིང་ (jōōbɛ ma̱niŋ) eunuch, a castrated person.

བཅོས་བུ་ (jōōbu) unauthentic, false, artificial.

བཅོས་བྱེད་ (jōō cɛ̱ɛ̀) va. to rectify/ correct.

བཅོས་མ་ (jōōma) 1. artificial, unnatural, fake, false, hypocritical. 2. a correction.

བཅོད་མ་མིན་པ་ (jōōma mi̱mbə) natural, not artificial, genuine.

བཅོས་མིན་ (jōōmin) real, true, genuine ། ཁོ་ཚོ་བཅོས་མིན་དགའ་པོ་བྱུང་བའི་རྣམ་པ་བསྟན་པ་རེད་ They showed that (they) were truly pleased. ། བཅོས་མིན་བརྩེ་བ་ True love.

བཅོས་མིན་སྙིང་ནས་ (jōōmin ñiŋnɛ) truly, really, from the bottom of the heart, sincerely ། བཅོས་མིན་སྙིང་ནས་ཐུགས་རྗེ་ཆེ་ཞུ་གི་ཡོད་ (We) thank you from the bottom of our hearts.

བཅོས་མིན་ལྷག་བསམ་ (jōōmin lhāgsam) genuine, true, sincere.

བཅོས་འཛུགས་ (jōndzug) reconstructing, reorganizing (correcting and establishing); va.—བྱེད་.

བཅོས་འཛུམ་ (jōndzum) a false smile.

བཅོས་བཟོ་ (jōōso) repairing, altering; va.—བྱེད་ to repair, to alter ། བཟོ་པ་ཚོས་སྒྲིག་ཆས་བཅོས་བཟོ་བྱས་པ་རེད་ The workers repaired the equipment.

བཅོས་བཟང་ (jōōsaŋ) improving, revising, correcting, repairing, reforming; va.—བྱེད་.

བཅོས་ཡུན་ (jōōyün) period of correction/ repair/ revision/ treatment.

བཅོས་རབ་ (jōōrəb) a record of sth. that has been repaired/ renovated.

བཅོས་རི་ (jōōri) artificial hill, man-made mountain.

བཅོས་ལས་ (jōōlɛɛ̀) processing, treating; va.—བྱེད་ ། བཅོས་ལས་མ་བྱས་པའི་ཤིང་ཆ་ Unprocessed timber.

ལྕ་རྒོད་ (jāgöö) selinum lenifolium (used in Tibetan medicine).

ལྕ་བ་ (jāwa) angelica sinensis (used in Tibetan medicine).

ལྕ་གཡུང་ (jāyuŋ) changium smyrnioides (used in Tibetan medicine).

ལྕག (jāà) 1. whip. 2. abbr. of ལྕག་པོ་.

ལྕག་སྐྱུལ་ (jəgüü) sm. ལྕག་བསྐྱུལ་.

ལྕག་བསྐྱུལ་ (jəgüü) encouragement, urging, prompting; va.—གཏོང་ —བྱེད་ to encourage, to urge, to prompt, to press on ། ཁོ་ཚོའི་ལས་ཀར་ལྕག་བསྐུལ་གཏོང་ཟེར་མངགས་པ་ཡིན་ (I) instructed (him) to urge them on with regard to their work.

ལྕག་གི་ལྕིག་གི་ (jəgi ji̱gi) scattered (people, trees, shops, etc.).

ལྕག་འགུལ་མི་བདེ་བ་ (jəgüü mi̱dewa) having difficulty walking/ moving.

ལྕག་ལྕིག (jāgjig) 1. abbr. of ལྕག་གི་ལྕིག་གི་. 2. muddy/ murky water.

ལྕག་རྡོ་ (jāgdo) flint stone.

ལྕག་བརྡ་ (jāgda) 1. clapping hands to call servants; va.—གཏོང་. 2. sm. ལྕག་བསྐྱུལ་.

ལྕག་པོ་ (jāgbo) quick, rapid, fast.

ལྕག་འབྲིང་ (jāŋdreŋ) the leather tail of a whip.

ལྕག་ཙམ་ལྕོག་ཙམ་ (jāgdzam jōgdzam) shaking the head; va.—བྱེད་.

ལྕག་ཚན་ (jāgdzɛn) sm. ལྕག.

ལྕག་ཞུ་བ་ (jāgshuwə) sb. who whips prisoners.

ལྕག་ཡུ་ (jəgyu) whip handle.

ལྕག་ཤད་ (jāgshɛɛ̀) sm. ལྕག་ཚན་.

ལྕགས་ (jāà) 1. iron; metal. 2. handcuffs, shackles 3. one of the five astrological elements used for calculating years. 4. IUD (contraceptive device); va.—འགར་.

ལྕགས་བརྒྱག (jāàgya) barbell (for weight lifting).

ལྕགས་ཀྱི་ཁྲ་མ་ (jāàgi trāma) sm. ལྕགས་ཀྱི་སྒེའུ་ཁུང་.

ལྕགས་ཀྱི་གློ་བ་ (jāàgi lōwa) iron lung machine.

ལྕགས་ཀྱི་སྒེའུ་ཁུང་ (jāàgi giguŋ) window with iron bars.

ལྕགས་ཀྱི་ཏི་ཙ་ (jāàgi dīdza) anvil.

ལྕགས་ཀྱི་གཏེར་ཁ་ (jāàgi dērma) iron mine.

ལྕགས་ཀྱི་དོམ་དོམ་དཀྲོལ་མ་ (jāàgi domdom drōōma) shung. a tassel holder made with engraved iron.

ལྕགས་ཀྱི་འཁྲུལ་འཁོར་ (jāàgi trōōgɔɔ) locomotive.

ལྕགས་ཀྱི་མེ་མདག (jāàgi medaà) red hot iron.

ལྕགས་ཀྱི་ཟོ་ལག (jāàgi solaà) iron bucket.

ལྕགས་ཀྱི་ཡོལ་བ་ (jāàgi yööwa) "the iron curtain."

ལྕགས་ཀྱི་སྲན་མ་ (jāàgi tremma) iron pellets/ balls.

ལྕགས་ཀྱུ་ (jāgyu) 1. an iron hook; va.—འདེབས་; —རྒྱག to hook. 2. slang. using flattery, gifts, and other enticements to win someone over; va.—རྒྱག ¶ བློ་བཟང་གིས་བུ་མོ་མཛེས་མ་འདི་ལ་ལྕགས་ཀྱུ་བརྒྱབ་པ་རེད་ Lobsang won over the pretty girl.

ལྕགས་ཀྱུ་མ་ (jāgyuma) one of the four female guardians of the mandala.

ལྕགས་ཀྲིང་ (jāgdriŋ) sm. ལྕགས་ཀྲིན་.

ལྕགས་ཀྲིན་ (jāgdrin) tin can, metal can.

ལྕགས་ཀྲིན་ཟས་རིགས་བཟོ་གྲྭ (jāgdrin sɛ̀ɛrii sodra) cannery.

ལྕགས་དཀར་ (jāàgar) tin, stannum.

ལྕགས་དཀྲོལ་ (jāgdröö) engraving on iron.

ལྕགས་བཀོས་མ་ (jāàgööma) engraving on iron.

ལྕགས་སྐམ་ (jāàgam) pincers, tongs.

ལྕགས་སྐུད་ (jāāgüü) iron wire, telegraph wire.

ལྕགས་སྐུད་ཀྱི་དྲ་རྒྱ་ (jāāgüügi tragya) wire mesh.

ལྕགས་སྐུད་སྒྲིམ་ (jāāgüü drim) 1. va. to twist steel wire. 2. va. to be stingy.

ལྕགས་སྐུད་འཇུར་འཐེན་ (jāāgüü jurden) wire drawing.

ལྕགས་སྐུད་འཐེན་འཁོར་ (jāāgüü tēngɔɔ) wire-drawing machine.

ལྕགས་སྐུད་མེད་པའི་ཏར་ (jāāgüü meèbɛ dār) wireless telegram, radiogram.

ལྕགས་སྐུད་ཙི་མ་ (jāāgüü dzīmɔ) enamel covered wire, enamel insulated wire.

ལྕགས་སྐུད་ཟེ་མ་ར་མགོ་ (jāāgüü sema raŋgo) barbed wire.

ལྕགས་སྐོར་ (jāàgɔɔ) 1. hasp/ chain for door that goes on a hook; va.—རྒྱག; to fasten with a chain or hasp; va.—འབྱེད་ to open a hasp/ lock. 2. patrolling around a fence/ wall.

ལྕགས་སྐྱོག (jāāgyɔɔ̀) sm. ལྕགས་སྐྱོགས་.

ལྕགས་སྐྱོགས་ (jāāgyɔɔ̀) iron ladle.

ལྕགས་བཀོས་དཀྲོལ་མའི་ཤན་ (jāggöö drōōmɛ shɛ̄n) shung. an engraved iron band.

ལྕགས་ཁ་ (jāgga) 1. steel gray (color). 2. the point at which a piece of iron has been cut. 3. the head or end of bridge.

ལྕགས་ཁབ་ (jāəkəb) iron needle/ pin.

ལྕགས་ཁབ་ལེན་ (jāà kāblen) magnetic iron, magnet.

ལྕགས་ཁམས་ (jāàgam) the element iron.

ལྕགས་ཁུ་ (jāəgu) 1. molten iron. 2. the liquid resulting from soaking iron in the juice of the myrobalan plant (used in traditional Tibetan medicine).

ལྕགས་ཁེམ་ (jāàgem) iron shovel/ spade.

ལྕགས་ཁོག (jāàgɔɔ̀) iron pot.

ལྕགས་ཁྱི་ (jāàgyi) iron-dog (year).

ལྕགས་ཁྱེམ་ (jāàgyem) 1. spoon (iron). 2. iron shovel/ spade.

ལྕགས་ཁྲ་ (jāgdra) iron grating/ grill/ railing ¶ སྒེའུ་ཁུང་གི་ལྕགས་ཁྲ་ The iron grill on a window. 2. cage, bars (as in prison).

ལྕགས་ཁྲབ་ (jāgdrəb) iron armor, plate armor.

ལྕགས་ཁྲབ་འཁོར་ལོ་ (jāgdrəb kɔ̄ɔ̄lo) armored vehicle.

ལྕགས་ཁྲབ་རླངས་འཁོར་ (jāgdrəb lāŋkɔɔ) armored car.

ལྕགས་ཁྲབ་དམག་དཔུང་ (jāgdrəb māgbuŋ) armored force/ division.

ལྕགས་ཁྲོ་ (jāgdro) 1. iron kettle/ cauldron 2. ferroalloy.

ལྕགས་ཁྲོལ་ (jāgdröö) sm. ལྕགས་དཀྲོལ་.

ལྕགས་མཁར་ (jāggar) tin/ metal house or shacks.

ལྕགས་འཁོར་ (jāggɔɔ) 1. door latch; sprocket, cog wheel; wheel/ tire rim. 2. abbr. of ལྕགས་ཁྲབ་འཁོར་ལོ་.

ལྕགས་གོང་ (jāggoŋ) iron ball.

ལྕགས་གོས་ (jāàgöö) armor.

ལྕགས་གྲོགས་ཤིང་ (jāgdrɔɔ̀shiŋ) astrological term indicating that iron and wood go together or are compatible astrologically.

ལྕགས་དགྲ་མེ་ (jāgdra me) astrological term indicating that iron and fire do not go together astrologically.

ལྕགས་འགུ་ (jāŋgu) iron bowl/ container.

ལྕགས་གླང་ (jāglaŋ) 1. iron-ox year. 2. the large size tractor in use in Tibet.

ལྕགས་གླིང་ (jāgliŋ) iron flute.

ལྕགས་གླེགས་ (jāgleg) flat/ rolled steel.

ལྕགས་མགར་ (jāggar) blacksmith.

ལྕགས་རྒྱུག (jāggyuù) 1. an iron rod/ bar/ staff, barbell. 2. ferromagnetics.

ལྕགས་རྒྱུས་ (jāggyüü) reinforcing iron bar.

ལྕགས་སྒམ་ (jāàgam) iron or metal box/ chest.

ལྕགས་སྒམ་པར་བུ་ (jāàgam bārbu) small iron or metal box.

ལྕགས་སྒོ་ (jāàgo) iron/ steel door.

ལྕགས་སྒོར་ (jāàgɔɔ) discus (in sports); va.—འཕེན་ to throw/ fling the discus.

ལྕགས་སྒོར་དོངས་ཙེ་ (jāàgɔɔ toŋdze) a round Chinese coin with a hole in the middle.

ལྕགས་སྒྱེད་ (jāàgyeè) iron or metal tripod, three-legged stove, tripod stove.

ལྕགས་སྒྲོག (jāgdrɔɔ̀) iron chains/ shackles/ fetters; iron treads.

ལྕགས་སྒྲོག་མ་ (jāgdroma) one of the female guardian deities of the mandala.

ལྕགས་སྒྲོམ་ (jāgdrom) iron cage.

ལྕགས་བརྒྱད་ (jāà gyɛ̀ɛ) the eight types of metal: gold, silver, copper, iron, tin, brass, lead, bronze.

ལྕགས་ངར་ (jāàŋar) steel; va.—གཏོང་ to temper steel.

ལྕགས་ངར་པོ་ (jāà ŋarbo) tempered steel.

ལྕགས་གཅུས་ (jāgjüü) iron screw.

ལྕགས་བཅད་པ་ནང་བཞིན་ (jāgjɛ̀ɛba nəŋshin) resolute, decisive, determined [Lit. like cutting iron].

ལྕགས་ཆས་ (jāgjɛ̀ɛ) ironware, hardware.

ལྕགས་ཆས་ཆུང་རིགས་ (jāgcɛ̀ɛ cūŋrig) small-sized ironware/ hardware.

ལྕགས་ཆས་སྤྱོད་པའི་དུས་རབས་ (jāgcɛ̀ɛ jööbɛ tüürəb) the iron age.

ལྕགས་ཆས་བཟོ་གྲྭ (jāgcɛ̀ɛ sodra) ironware factory.

ལྕགས་ཆུ་ (jāgju) molten iron.

ལྕགས་མཆིག (jāgjig) iron grinder.

ལྕགས་མཆུ་ (jāgŋju) iron mouth of a bellows.

ལྕགས་རྗེན་ (jāgjen) pig iron.

ལྕགས་ཐིད་འདེགས་འཁྲུལ་འཁོར (jāg jīìdeg trūūgɔɔ) mobile crane.

ལྕགས་འཇོར་ (jānjɔɔ) an iron rake.

ལྕགས་སྙི་ (jāàñi) iron trap.

ལྕགས་སྙིགས་ (jāàñig) iron slag, iron trash/ waste.

ལྕགས་ཏར་ (jāgdar) cable, telegram.

ལྕགས་ཏིག (jāgdig) gentianopsis paludosa (used in Tibetan medicine).

ལྕགས་ཏིག་དཀར་པོ་ (jāgdig gāābo) white gentianopsis paludosa (used in Tibetan medicine).

ལྕགས་ཏིག་ནག་པོ་ (jāgdig māābo) black gentianopsis paludosa (used in Tibetan medicine).

ལྕགས་གཏུན་ (jāgdün) iron mortar and pestle.

ལྕགས་གཏེར་ (jāgder) 1. iron ore. 2. iron mine.

ལྕགས་གཏེར་དམར་པོ་ (jāgder māābo) hematite, red iron ore.

ལྕགས་གཏེར་སེར་ནག (jāgder sērnaà) brown

hematite.

ལྕགས་རྟ་ (jāgda) 1. iron-horse year. 2. bicycle.

ལྕགས་རྟ་ཞིག་གསོ་ཁང་ (jāgda shigsogaŋ) bicycle repair shop.

ལྕགས་རྟ་བཟོ་གྲྭ (jāgda sodra) bicycle factory.

ལྕགས་རྟ་ལོའི་དམག་འཁྲུག (jāgda lö māgdruù) war of the iron-horse year (i.e., the Sino-Japanese War of 1894).

ལྕགས་སྟག (jāgdaà) iron-tiger year.

ལྕགས་སྟག་ཞིབ་གཞུང་ (jāgdaà shibshuŋ) shung. the land ennumeration of the ལྕགས་སྟག year.

ལྕགས་སྟེགས་ (jāgdeg) metal axle.

ལྕགས་ཐག (jāgdaà) chain (iron); va.—རྒྱག to chain.

ལྕགས་ཐག་གི་འཁོར་ལོ་ (jāgdaàgi kɔ̄ɔlo) cog wheel.

ལྕགས་ཐག་མཐུད་མ་ (jāgdaà tũũmə) connected chains, chain link.

ལྕགས་ཐག་ཟམ་ (jāgdaà sam) iron/ chain link bridge.

ལྕགས་ཐག་བཟོ་གྲྭ (jāgdaà sodra) iron chain factory.

ལྕགས་ཐག་ལག་འབྲེལ་ (jəgdaà mãŋdrel) sm. ལྕགས་ཐག་ལག་སྦྲེལ་.

ལྕགས་ཐག་ལག་སྦྲེལ་ (jāgdaà lagdree) forming a united front, hand-in-hand like a chain; va.—བྱེད་; to form a united front [Lit. linked holding hands as in a chain].

ལྕགས་ཐབ་ (jāgdəb) iron stove; va.—གཏོང་ to start the fire in an iron stove.

ལྕགས་ཐམ་ (jāgdam) iron seal/ stamp.

ལྕགས་ཐལ་ (jāgtɛɛ) iron dust/ powder.

ལྕགས་ཐུར་ (jāgtur) 1. spoon (metal). 2. a long piece of iron.

ལྕགས་ཐོ་ (jāgdo) iron hammer.

ལྕགས་ཐོ་བ་ (jāgdowa) iron hammer; va.—གཞུ་ to hammer.

ལྕགས་དམ་ (jāgdam) iron/ metal can.

ལྕགས་དུམ་ (jāgdum) pieces of cut iron/ metal/ steel.

ལྕགས་དོམ་ (jāgdom) shung. red tassel holder made from iron.

ལྕགས་དོམ་དཀྲོལ་མ་གསེར་ཆགས་ཅན་ (jāgdom drōōma sērdzaàjɛn) shung. red tassel holder made from iron that has been engraved and gilded.

ལྕགས་དྲ་ (jāgdra) wire mesh, wire net, wire fencing; va.—གཏོང་ to put up wire mesh/ net/ fencing.

ལྕགས་དྲིལ་ (jāgdrii) iron bell.

ལྕགས་དྲེག (jāgdreg) 1. sm. ལྕགས་དྲ་. 2. a type of disease of the digestive system in Tibetan medicine.

ལྕགས་གདུང་ (jəgduŋ) iron/ steel beam.

ལྕགས་མདའ་ (jāŋda) 1. any iron (metal) rod, knitting needle, medical probe, iron arrow. 2. shung. a type of summer hat worn by officials of the traditional Tibetan Government of the 4th rank and above.

ལྕགས་མདས་སླ་བ་ (jāŋdɛɛ̀ lāwa) knitting, embroidery.

ལྕགས་མདོང་ (jāŋdoŋ) metal pipe/ pipeline ¶ རྡོ་སྣུམ་འདྲེན་བྱེད་ལྕགས་མདོང་ Oil pipeline.

ལྕགས་དར་མཉམ་ཟད་ (jāàdar ñamsɛɛ̀) two sides facing problems/ hard times because of one trying to help the other, being dependent on (sb.) and causing them financial problems/ hardships, two parties causing each other hardships in lawsuits, etc.). [Lit. whetstone wears out, iron wears out].

ལྕགས་རྡུང་ (jāà duŋ) va. to hammer iron into shape.

ལྕགས་རྡུལ་ (jəgdüü) subatomic particles according to Buddhist philosophy which come together to constitute elements.

ལྕགས་རྡོ་ (jāgdo) iron ore.

ལྕགས་རྡོ་དམར་པོ་ (jāgdo mārbo) hematite.

ལྕགས་རྡོ་སེར་པོ་ (jāgdo sērbo) iron pyrite, fool's gold.

ལྕགས་ལྡེལ་ (jāàdee) lock and key.

ལྕགས་ནག (jāànaà) chromite.

ལྕགས་ནན་ཐར་གསུམ་ (jāà nɛn tārsum) careful, cautious, watchful; va.—བྱེད་ to be very careful/ cautious/ watchful.

ལྕགས་པང་ (jāàbaŋ) sm. ལྕགས་སྤང་.

ལྕགས་པར་ (jāgbar) 1. type for typesetting/ printing. 2. typewriter; va.—རྒྱག to type on a typewriter.

ལྕགས་པར་འཕྲུལ་འཁོར་ (jāgbar trũũgɔɔ) 1. typewriter. 2. printing press.

ལྕགས་པོ་རི་ (jāgbori) 1. one of the four famous hills in Lhasa. 2. name of one of the two traditional Tibetan medical schools in Lhasa (that is located on the Cagpori hill).

ལྕགས་པོད་ (jāgböö) sm. ལྕགས་ཕོད་.

ལྕགས་དཔར་ (jāgbar) sm. ལྕགས་པར་.

ལྕགས་སྤང་ (jāgbaŋ) iron or steel board/ plank.

ལྕགས་སྤྲེ་ (jāgdre) iron-monkey year.

ལྕགས་ཕག (jāgpaà) iron-hog year.

ལྕགས་ཕག་ལོའི་གསར་བརྗེ་ (jāgpaà lö sārje) the Chinese revolution of 1911.

ལྕགས་ཕུར་ (jəgpur) iron spike/ stake/ peg; va.—རྒྱག to peg/ stake with an iron stake.

ལྕགས་ཕོ་ (jāgpo) the male iron (year).

ལྕགས་ཕོད་ (jāgböö) 1. belt woven from fibers. 2. belt buckle. 3. a belt with a tassle on the end.

ལྕགས་ཕོར་ (jāgbɔɔ) 1. iron bowl. 2. a permanent job from which one can not be fired [Lit. the iron bowl].

ལྕགས་ཕྱེ་ (jāgje) powdered iron, iron filings, iron dust.

ལྕགས་འཕྲིན་ (jəgdrin) telegram, wire; va.—གཏོང་ to send a telegram/ wire.

ལྕགས་བན་ (jāgbɛn) iron water bucket.

ལྕགས་བྱེ་ (jāgje) iron filings coarser than ལྕགས་ཕྱེ་.

ལྕགས་བྱི་ (jəgji) iron-mouse year.

ལྕགས་བྱ་ (jāgja) iron-bird year.

ལྕགས་འབྲུག (jəgdruù) iron-dragon year.

ལྕགས་སྦར་ (jāgbar) iron rake.

ལྕགས་སྦུག (jəgbuù) iron pipe/ tube.

ལྕགས་སྦྲུལ་ (jəgdrüü) 1. iron-snake year. 2. a type of snake used in preparing traditional eye medicines.

ལྕགས་མིག (jəgmii) iron awl.

ལྕགས་མིན་གྱི་དངོས་པོ་ (jəgmingi ŋōōbo) nonmetallic things.

ལྕགས་མོ་ (jāgmo) the female iron year.

ལྕགས་དམར་ (jāgmar) 1. copper. 2. red hot iron.

ལྕགས་དམར་སྐམ་གཙུན་ (jāgmar gāmjün) disciplining, controlling; to strike while the iron is hot [Lit. to shape iron while it is hot].

ལྕགས་དམར་སྐམ་འཚུན་ (jāgmar gāmjün) sm. ལྕགས་དམར་སྐམ་གཙུན་.

ལྕགས་དམར་གཏེར་ཁ་ (jāgmar dērga) copper mine.

ལྕགས་དམར་ཚ་ཐོག་ལ་རྡུང་བ་ (jāgmar tsādɔɔla duŋwa) sm. ལྕགས་ཚ་ཐོག་ལ་རྡུང་བ.

ལྕགས་རྨིག (jəmig) horseshoe.

ལྕགས་རྨོག (jāàmog) iron helmet.

ལྕགས་སྨྱུག (jəñuù) fountain pen.

ལྕགས་བཙའ་ (jāàdza) rust.

ལྕགས་རྩི་ (jəgdzi) enamel pain/ lacquer used on ironware.

ལྕགས་རྩི་མཚལ་ཁ་ (jəgdzi tsɛ̄ɛga) red enamel/ lacquer paint used on ironware.

ལྕགས་རྩིབས་ (jəgdzib) iron rods/ ribs (used to reinforce concrete).

ལྕགས་རྩིབས་ཅན་གྱི་ཨར་འདམ་ (jəgdzibjɛngi ārdam) reinforced concrete.

ལྕགས་བཙོ་མ་ (jāà dzōma) molten iron.

ལྕགས་ཚ་ཐོག་ལ་རྡུང་ (jāgdza tɔ̄ɔla duŋ) va. to strike while the iron is hot, to do at the appropriate time.

ལྕགས་ཚགས་ (jāgdzaà) iron sieve/ sifter/ strainer.

ལྕགས་མཛོ་ (jāgdzo) tractor (for plowing) [Lit iron dzo].

ལྕགས་ཞྭ་ (jāgsha) sm. ལྕགས་རྨོག.

ལྕགས་ཞིབ (jəgshib) 1. sm. ལྕགས་ཕྱེ་. 2. shung. abbr. of ལྕགས་སྟག་ཞིབ་གཞུང་.

ལྕགས་ཞུ་ (jāgshu) 1. iron lantern. 2. sm. ལྕགས་བཞུ་.
ལྕགས་གཞོག་འཁོར་སྡེགས་ (jāgshɔ̄ɔ kōrdeg) milling machine.
ལྕགས་གཞོག་བཟོ་པ་ (jāgshɔ̄ɔ soba) milling machine operator.
ལྕགས་གཞོང་ (jāgshoŋ) iron or metal basin/ tub.
ལྕགས་བཞུ་ (jəgshu) metallurgy, iron smelting; va.—གཏོང་ to smelt iron (metals).
ལྕགས་བཞུ་ཐབ་ (jāgshutəb) metal smelting furnace.
ལྕགས་བཞུ་ཐབ་ཀ་ (jāgshu təbga) iron-smelting furnace; blast furnace.
ལྕགས་བཞུ་མཐོ་ཐབ་ (jəgshu tōtəb) blast furnace.
ལྕགས་བཞུ་ཞིབ་འཇུག་ཁང་ (jəgshu shimjugaŋ) institute of metallurgy.
ལྕགས་བཞུ་བཟོ་གྲྭ (jəgshu sodra) blast furnace plant, metallurgical/ smelting factory.
ལྕགས་བཞུ་བཟོ་ལས་པུའུ་ (jəgshu solɛɛ̀bu) tib.ch. Ministry of Metallurgical Industry.
ལྕགས་བཞུ་རིག་པ་ (jəgshu rigbə) metallurgy.
ལྕགས་བཞུའི་སྒྲིག་ཆས་ (jəgshü drigcɛɛ̀) metallurgical/ smelting equipment.
ལྕགས་བཞུའི་ཐབ་ཀ་ (jəgshü təbga) smelting furnace.
ལྕགས་ཟངས་ (jāgsaŋ) 1. iron caldron. 2. abbr. of iron and copper.
ལྕགས་ཟད་རྡིའུ་ཟད་ (jāgsam) sm. ལྕགས་དར་མཉམ་ཟད་.
ལྕགས་ཟམ་ (jāgsam) iron bridge.
ལྕགས་ཟམ་ཁ་ (jāgsamka) 1. name of a bridge and place in Ganze. 2. by the bank of an iron bridge.
ལྕགས་ཟོག (jāgsɔɔ̀) ironware, merchandise made from iron.
ལྕགས་ཟོམ་ (jāgsom) iron cauldron.
ལྕགས་གཟར་ (jāgsar) iron ladle.
ལྕགས་གཟེར་ (jāgser) iron nail; va.—རྒྱག to nail.
ལྕགས་གཟོང་ (jāgsoŋ) iron peg/ bar (used for splitting rocks).
ལྕགས་བཟོ་ (jāgso) iron smithy; va.—བྱེད་ to do blacksmith work.
ལྕགས་བཟོ་བ་ (jāgsoò) blacksmith.
ལྕགས་ཡོས་ (jāgyöò) iron-hare year.
ལྕགས་གཡའ་ (jāgya) iron rust, iron oxide.
ལྕགས་རི་ (jəəri) wall, fence; va.—རྒྱག to build/ put up a fence or wall; va.—སྐོང་ to put up a fence/ wall around sth.
ལྕགས་རི་རིང་པོ་ (jəəri riŋbu) the Great Wall (of China).
ལྕགས་རིས་བསྐོར་ (jəərii gɔ̄ɔ) va. to surround with a fence/ wall.
ལྕགས་རིགས་ (jəərii) metals, iron items ¶ལྕགས་རིགས་རྩེད་ཆས་ Metal toys.
ལྕགས་རིགས་ཀུང་སི་ (jəərii gūŋsi) metal products/ hardware company.
ལྕགས་རིགས་ཁྱད་པར་ཅན་ (jəərii kɛ̄ɛ̀barjɛn) special metals.
ལྕགས་རིགས་གློག་རྒྱུ་ཀུང་སི་ (jəərii lɔ̄ɔ̀gyu gūŋsi) hardware and electric factory.
ལྕགས་རིགས་གློག་རྒྱུ་ཚོང་ཁང་ (jəərii lɔ̄ɔ̀gyu tsōŋgaŋ) hardware and electric/ electronic store.
ལྕགས་རིགས་གློག་རྒྱུ་རྫས་བཟོ་ཚོང་ཁང་ (jəərii lɔ̄ɔ̀gyu dzɛ̄ɛ̀so tsōŋgaŋ) hardware, electric/ electronic and chemical products store.
ལྕགས་རིགས་གཏུབ་གཞོག་འཕྲུལ་སྡེགས་ (jəərii dūbshɔ̄ɔ trũũdeg) metal cutting machine.
ལྕགས་རིགས་གཏེར་རྫས་ (jəərii dērdzɛɛ̀) metals and minerals.
ལྕགས་རིགས་ཐུག་པའི་སྒྲ་ (jəərii tūgbɛ dra) clanking/ clanging sound of iron or metals banging.
ལྕགས་རིགས་འདྲེས་མ་ (jəərii dreèma) metal alloy.
ལྕགས་རིགས་ལྔ་ (jəərii nāŋa) the five metals: gold, silver, copper, iron, and tin/ pewter.
ལྕགས་རིགས་དྲེ་བྲག་བརྒྱད་ (jəərii cedraà gyɛɛ̀) sm. ལྕགས་བརྒྱད་.
ལྕགས་རིགས་བཙོ་སྦྱང་བཟོ་གྲྭ (jəərii dzōjaŋ sodra) metal smelting factory.
ལྕགས་རིགས་བཟོ་གྲྭ (jəərii sodra) ironwork/ metal-products factory.
ལྕགས་རིགས་བཟོ་ལས་ (jəərii solɛɛ̀) metallurgical industry.
ལྕགས་རིགས་ལས་ཚན་ (jəərii lɛɛ̀dzɛn) metalsmith workshop.
ལྕགས་རིགས་བསྲེས་མ་ (jəərii drēèma) sm. ལྕགས་རིགས་འདྲེས་མ་.
ལྕགས་རིའི་ཏ་སོ་ (jəərii dāso) parapet.
ལྕགས་རིལ་ (jɛ̄ɛ̀ril) iron/ steel ball. 2. shotput ball; va.—དབྱུག to throw the shotput.
ལྕགས་རིལ་ཐག་སྦྲགས་ (jəərii tāgdraà) iron ball with an attached rope that is used as a weapon.
ལྕགས་ལམ་ (jāglam) railway, railroad; va.—སྒྲིག་; —འདིང་ to lay railroad tracks.
ལྕགས་ལམ་རྐྱང་མ་ (jāglam gyāŋma) monorail, single track railroad.
ལྕགས་ལམ་གུ་དོག་པོ་ (jāglam kudɔgbo) narrow-gauge railroad.
ལྕགས་ལམ་གྱི་གདན་ཤིང་ (jāglamgi dɛnshiŋ) railroad tie.
ལྕགས་ལམ་སྒྲིག (jāglam drig) see ལྕགས་ལམ་.
ལྕགས་ལམ་གྱི་དྲ་བ་ (jāglamgi trawa) railway network, rail network.
ལྕགས་ལམ་ཆུང་ཆུང་ (jāglam cūŋjuŋ) narrow-gauge railway.
ལྕགས་ལམ་ཉེན་རྟོག་པ་ (jāglam ñendɔgba) railway police.
ལྕགས་ལམ་གཉིས་གཤིབ་ཅན་ (jāglam ñiishibjɛn) double-track railway.
ལྕགས་ལམ་ཐུའུ་ (jāglam todam jū) tib.ch. railway management bureau.
ལྕགས་ལམ་འདིང་ (jāglam diŋ) see ལྕགས་ལམ་.
ལྕགས་ལམ་པུའུ་ (jāglambu) tib.ch. Ministry of Railways.
ལྕགས་ལམ་མ་ཤིང་ (jāglam məshiŋ) sm. ལྕགས་ལམ་ཤིང་གདན་.
ལྕགས་ལམ་དམག (jāglam māà) railway corps.
ལྕགས་ལམ་ཞིང་ཕྲ་མོ་ (jāglam sheŋ drāmo) sm. ལྕགས་ལམ་གུ་དོག་པོ་.
ལྕགས་ལམ་གཞི་རྐང་ (jāglam shigaŋ) sm. ལྕགས་ལམ་གཞུང་ཐིག.
ལྕགས་ལམ་གཞུང་ཐིག (jāglam shuŋtig) main line, trunk line.
ལྕགས་ལམ་ཟུར་ཐིག (jāglam surdig) branch rail line, arterial line.
ལྕགས་ལམ་ལས་བཟོ་སྨན་ཁང་ (jāglam lɛɛ̀so mēngaŋ) railway worker's hospital.
ལྕགས་ལམ་ཤར་བསྐྱོད་ (jāglam shārgyöò) direct rail traffic, through rail traffic.
ལྕགས་ལམ་ཤིང་གདན་ (jāglam shiŋdɛn) a rail tie.
ལྕགས་ལམ་ས་ཚིགས་ (jāglam sətsii) railway station.
ལྕགས་ལམ་སློབ་གྲྭ (jāglam lōbdra) railway school.
ལྕགས་ལས་བཟོ་གྲྭ (jāàlɛɛ̀ sodra) iron-working factory.
ལྕགས་ལུག (jəgluù) iron-sheep year.
ལྕགས་ལུག་རྒྱས་དཔྱད་ (jəgluù gyɛɛ̀jɛɛ̀) shung. a document issued in the iron sheep year concerning taxes.
ལྕགས་ལུང་ (jəgluŋ) iron handle.
ལྕགས་ལེབ་ (jāgleb) 1. iron/ steel plate, sheet iron. 2. discus; va.—དབྱུག to throw the discus.
ལྕགས་ལེབ་བཙིར་འཁོར་ (jāgleb dzīrgɔɔ) iron/ steel plate rolling machine.
ལྕགས་ལོང་ (jāgloŋ) iron rings (connected together).
ལྕགས་ལོང་སྒྲིལ་ཁྲབ་ (jāgloŋ dreedrəb) armor made of iron rings (connected together).
ལྕགས་ཤད་ (jāgshɛɛ̀) carding brush, iron brush; va.—རྒྱག to brush/ comb with such a brush.
ལྕགས་ཤན་ (jāgshɛn) metal or iron band/ hoop used to bind churns and other items; va.—རྒྱག.
ལྕགས་ཤིང་ལ་མེ་ཏོག་ཤར་ (jəgshiŋla medɔg shār) sth. seldom seen or hardly possible, sth. difficult to achieve/ accomplish [Lit. an iron tree in blossom].
ལྕགས་ཤོག (jāgshɔɔ̀) iron or metal sheet/ plate.
ལྕགས་གཤོལ་ (jaāgshöò) iron plow.

ལྕགས་སག (jāgsaà) an iron file.

ལྕགས་སང་ (jāgsaŋ) thin wire mesh/ screen/ net.

ལྕགས་སེག (jāgseg) sm. ལྕགས་སག.

ལྕགས་སོ་ (jāgso) iron rake; va.—རྒྱག to rake.

ལྕགས་སོལ་ (jāgsöö) soot accumulated on a blacksmiths oven (which traditionally was used in medicines).

ལྕགས་སླང་ (jāglaŋ) iron frying pan.

ལྕགས་གསུམ་ཐོང་གཤོལ་ (jāgsum tōŋshöö) three-pronged plow.

ལྕགས་གསོར་ (jāgsɔɔ) iron drill; va.—རྒྱག to drill with an iron drill.

ལྕགས་བསྲེས་མ་ (jāà drè̱ɛma) alloyed iron.

ལྕགས་དྲང་ (jāghraŋ) 1. iron rod/ stick/ pole (usu. used for splitting rocks etc., crowbar. 2. gun barrel.

ལྕགས་དྲུག་ཟངས་དྲུག (jəghruù sa̱ŋhruù) waste iron and copper.

ལྕགས་དྲིང་ (jāghreŋ) crowbar, iron bar.

ལྕགས་དྲིང་བདར་ནས་ཁབ་ལ་སྒྱུར་ (jāghreŋ da̱rnɛ kəbla gyu̱r) if you work hard you can achieve anything [Lit. shaving an iron bar it becomes a needle].

ལྕང་ཀང་ (jāŋgŋ) a single trunk (of a tree).

ལྕང་རྒྱ་ (jāŋgya) white poplar.

ལྕང་དཀར་ (jāŋgar) white poplar.

ལྕང་གྲི་ (jāŋdri) shung. a type of sword.

ལྕང་གླིང་ (jāŋliŋ) a park.

ལྕང་གཅོད་ (jāŋjöö) cutting down trees; va.—རྒྱག.

ལྕང་ལྕུག (jāŋjuù) sm. ལྕང་ལྕུག་མ་.

ལྕང་ལྕུག་མ་ (jāŋ jūgmə) thin branch/ stalk.

ལྕང་ལྗོང་ (jāŋjoŋ) 1. craggy, steep. 2. uneven ground, bumpy road.

ལྕང་ཆུ་ (jāŋju) irrigating trees; va.—རྒྱག.

ལྕང་སྡོང་ (jāŋdoŋ) 1. tree. 2. willow tree.

ལྕང་ནག (jāŋnaà) a type of willow tree.

ལྕང་བལ་ (jāŋpɛɛ) cotton/ catkin (of willow tree).

ལྕང་མ་ (jāŋma) 1. tree. 2. willow tree.

ལྕང་མ་མེ་ཏོག (jāŋma me̱dog) oleander.

ལྕང་མ་ལོ་གསུམ་སྐྱེས་པར་དགའ་མི་དགོས། སྦྱར་པ་ལོ་གསུམ་སྐམ་པར་སྡུག་མི་དགོས་ (jāŋma me̱dog) don't get happy because of some event too soon, and don't get sad over sth. too soon [Lit. one should not feel happy if the tree grows three years, and one should not feel sad if the poplar dries up for three years].

ལྕང་མའི་སྡོང་ཕྲུག (jāŋmɛ do̱ŋdruù) tree seedling.

ལྕང་སྙུག (jāŋñuù) 1. the thin branches/ twigs of weeping willow; thin willow branch. 2. a thin and flexible switch made from willow branches (used for cannings).

ལྕང་གཞོན་ (jāŋshön) a young tree.

ལྕང་ར་ (jāŋra) 1. an orchard. 2. a park. 3. a grove of willow trees.

ལྕང་ལོ་ (jāŋlo) 1. a leaf. 2. a braid; va.—རྒྱག to braid. 3. abbr. of ལྕང་མའི་ལོ་མ་.

ལྕང་ལོ་འཛིན་ (jāŋlo dzi̱n) va. to look for mistake/ faults (in others), to seize on shortcomings [Lit. to hold a hair braid].

ལྕང་ཤིང་ (jāŋshiŋ) sm. ལྕང་མ་.

ལྕང་ཤུན་ (jāŋshün) bark.

ལྕང་སོན་ (jāŋsön) 1. tree seed. 2. willow seed.

ལྕང་སོལ་ (jāŋsöö) charcoal from a willow tree that was used for making gun powder.

ལྕང་གསར་ (jāŋsar) tree seedlings.

ལྕང་གསེབ་ (jāŋseb) sm. ལྕང་ར་.

ལྕང་བསླས་ཆུ་ཟོམ་ (jāŋlɛɛ̀ cūsom) water bucket made from braided willow branches.

ལྕམ་ (jām) 1. wife (h.). 2. small beam/ rafter.

ལྕམ་ཁེབས་ (jāmgeb) cloth used as covering for a ceiling.

ལྕམ་སྐུ་ (jāmgu) abbr. of ལྕམ་སྐུ་ཞབས་.

ལྕམ་སྐུ་ཞབས་ (jām gūshəb) term of address for women of high position (usu. for aristocrats).

ལྕམ་བགྲེས་པ་ (jām drè̱ɛba) honorific title for a senior/ older wife (usu. for aristocrats).

ལྕམ་འགྲོས་ (jāmdröö) walking in a swaying way like aristocratic ladies; va.—རྒྱག.

ལྕམ་ཆུང་ (jāmjuŋ) honorific title for the wife of an aristocratic of lower rank; the younger wives of aristocrats.

ལྕམ་དྲལ་ (jāmdrɛɛ) rafters and the smaller wooden pieces that go across the rafters. 2. older and younger siblings.

ལྕམ་སྣེ་ (jāmne) the top/ apex of the tree.

ལྕམ་པ་ (jāmba) 1. high mallow (used in Tibetan medicine). 2. hollyhock (Althaea Rosea).

ལྕམ་པ་ཧ་ལོ་ (jāmba hālo) sm. ལྕམ་པ་.

ལྕམ་པོ་ (jāmbo) a kind of person who is not pompous or arrogant.

ལྕམ་སྤང་ (jāmbaŋ) shung. planks used on beams.

ལྕམ་མོ་ (jāmmo) wife and younger sister (h.).

ལྕམ་གཞོན་པ་ (jām shö̱mbə) the younger wife (in a polygynous marriage (usu. for aristocrats).

ལྕམ་ཤིང་ (jāmshiŋ) timber for small rafters used in making roofs/ ceilings (they are laid crossways over beams).

ལྕམ་སྲིང་ (jāmsiŋ) elder and younger sisters.

ལྕི་ (jī) sm. ལྕི་བ་.

ལྕི་ཁང་ (jīgaŋ) a place where dung is stored (for fuel).

ལྕི་འཁིང་ (jīgeŋ) frozen dung.

ལྕི་སྐམ་ (jīgam) dung patties.

ལྕི་ཆས་མཚོན་ཆ་ (jīcɛɛ̀ tsōnja) heavy (for equipment/ machinery) ། ལྕི་ཆས་མཚོན་ཆ་ Heavy weapons.

ལྕི་དངོས་འདེགས་འཁོར་ (jīŋöö de̱gkɔɔ) crane, hoist.

ལྕི་རྙང་ (jīñaŋ) undried dung, loose dung.

ལྕི་ཐང་ (jītaŋ) field where dung is dried.

ལྕི་ཐལ་ (jīdɛɛ) ash from dung.

ལྕི་ཐིབས་ཐིབས་ (jī tībdib) sm. ལྡིད་ཏིག་གི་བ་.

ལྕི་འཐིབས་ (jī tīb) vi. to be/ get lethargic or sluggish.

ལྕི་འདག (jīdag) dung made into a paste.

ལྕི་འདེགས་ (jīdeg) weight lifting; va.—བྱེད་ to lift weights.

ལྕི་པོ་ (jību) heavy.

ལྕི་ཕག (jībaà) sm. ལྕི་སྐམ་.

ལྕི་ཕད་ (jīpɛɛ̀) bag in which dung is collected/ carried.

ལྕི་ཕྱེ་ (jīce) powdered or granulated dung.

ལྕི་བ་ (jīwə) 1. dung (of bovines). 2. heavy ། བཟོ་ལས་ལྕི་བ་. Heavy industry.

ལྕི་བའི་བཟོ་ལས་དོ་དམ་ཅུས་ (jīwɛ so̱lɛɛ̀ to̱damju) tib.ch. Bureau of Heavy Industry.

ལྕི་བའི་བཟོ་ལས་པུའུ་ (jīwɛ so̱lɛɛ̀bu) tib.ch. Ministry of Heavy Industry.

ལྕི་བའི་བཟོ་ལས་ (jīwɛ so̱lɛɛ̀) heavy industry.

ལྕི་མོ་ (ji̱mu) sm. ལྡི་པོ་.

ལྕི་ཚད་ (jīdzɛɛ̀) weight; vi.—འཕར་ to increase in weight.

ལྕི་གཟན་ (jī se̱n) shung. abbr. of ལྕི་བ་ and གཟན་པ་.

ལྕི་ཡང་ (jīyaŋ) 1. abbr. heavy and light. 2. weight.

ལྕི་ཡང་དལ་བྲེལ་ (jīyaŋ te̱e̱dree) in order of importance/ urgency, with regard to or in connection with something's importance/ significance.

ལྕི་ཡང་བསྡུར་ཚད་ (jīyaŋ du̱rtsɛɛ̀) specific gravity (in physics).

ལྕི་ཡི་རི་ (jī yi̱ri) sm. ལྡིད་ཡོར་ཡོར་.

ལྕི་ར་ (jīrə) sm. ལྕི་ཐང་.

ལྕི་རིགས་ལྕི་ཚད་ (jīrii jīdzɛɛ̀) all the heavy things.

ལྕི་རློན་ (jīlön) fresh dung.

ལྕི་ལེབ་ (jīleb) flattened dung patties.

ལྕིག་ལྕིག (jīgjii) completely covered (e.g., with ants).

ལྕིགས་ (jīg) va. to comprehend, to know, to understand.

ལྕིད་ (jīi) sm. ལྡིད་.

ལྕིད་པ་ (jībə) 1. weight. 2. sm. ལྕི་མོ་.

ལྕིད་ཕབ་ (jī pāb) va. to put a burden on someone.

ལྕིབས་ (jīb) potholder ། ཚལ་སླང་ཚ་པོ་ལྕིབས་ཀྱིས་བཟུང་ནས་ Holding the hot pan with a potholder. 2. va. to protect.

ལྕིབས་ཕུར་ (jībbur) a small knob/ hinge on which the door rotates.

ལྕིབས་མོ་ (jībmu) thimble.

ལྕུ་ཕལ་ (jūbɛɛ) sm. ལྕེ་ཕལ་.

ལྕུ་ཁང་ (jūggaŋ) sm. ལྕིག་ཁང་.

ལྕུག་གུ་ (jūggu) a thin/ slender belt.

ལྕུག་ལྕུག (jūgjuù) swaying.

ལྕུག་པ་ (jūgbə) thin, slender.

ལྕུག་ཕྲན་ (jūgdrɛn) a twig, a thin branch.

ལྕུག་མ་ (jūgmə) 1. sm. ལྕུག་ཕྲན་. 2. meat cut into thin strips (usu. to be dried).

ལྕུག་མ་ལྷས་མ་ (jūgmə lhɛ̄ɛ̀ma) thin branches or twigs that have been braided.

ལྕུང་ཀ་ (jūŋgə) jackdaw.

ལྕུང་མོ་ (jūŋmu) thimble.

ལྕུམ་ (jūm) rhubarb.

ལྕུམ་སྡོང་ (jūmdoŋ) rhubarb stalk.

ལྕུམ་བུ་ (jūmbu) a type of grass.

ལྕུམ་རྩ་ (jūmdza) rhubarb root (used in Tibetan medicine).

ལྕུམ་ཤོག་ (jūmshɔɔ̀) leaf of rhubarb (mixed with tobacco when smoking a pipe).

ལྕེ་ (jē). tongue; va.—སྐྱོང་ to stick out the tongue. 2. striker of a bell. 3. a type of decorative material with a triangular shaped bottom that hangs from doorways, pillars, etc.

ལྕེ་སྐད་ (jēgɛɛ̀) lisping; va.—རྒྱག.

ལྕེ་སྐྲང་ (jēdraŋ) a disease where the tongue swells.

ལྕེ་སྐྱོང་ (jē gyōŋ) va. to stick out one's tongue to show respect.

ལྕེ་ཁམས་ (jēkam) the sense of taste (of the tongue).

ལྕེ་བརྒྱར་སྤྲུལ་ཀྱང་བརྗོད་མི་ཚར་ (jēgya trūūgyaŋ jōò mitsar) remarks/ comments that are endless [Lit. even if a hundred tongues magically come forth, the talk cannot be finished].

ལྕེ་སྒྲོག་ཐེབས་ (jēdrɔɔ̀ tēè) vi. to become unable to speak clearly after drinking alcohol.

ལྕེ་ངོས་ (jēŋöö) surface/ blade of the tongue.

ལྕེ་ཅག་བདེ་པོ་ (jējaà debo) sm. ལྕེ་བདེ་པོ་.

ལྕེ་གཅོད་ (jē jöö) shung. va. to cut out the tongue as a corporal punishment.

ལྕེ་ཆུང་ (jējuŋ) uvula.

ལྕེ་ཆུང་བབ་ (jējuŋ bəb) vi. to have the uvula swell.

ལྕེ་གཉིས་ (jēñii) two-faced, deceitful [Lit. two tongued].

ལྕེ་གཉིས་པ་ (jē ñiìbə) 1. sb. who is a liar/ deceiver. 2. a parrot. 3. a snake.

ལྕེ་ཐེལ་ (jētɛɛ) printing a letter on an infant's tongue; va.—རྒྱག.

ལྕེ་དིག (jēdig) stuttering, stammering, lisping.

ལྕེ་དིག་པ་ (jē digbə) sb. who stutters/ stammers/ lisps.

ལྕེ་དིག་དིག (jē digdig) sm. ལྕེ་དིག.

ལྕེ་དྲུབ་མཆུ་སྐམ་ (jēdub cūgar) doing too much talking [Lit. tongue is torn, lips are parched].

ལྕེ་དྲི་ (jēdri) sm. ལྕེ་དྲེག.

ལྕེ་དྲེག (jēdreg) the coating on the tongue.

ལྕེ་བདེ་སྐད་དངས་ (jēde gɛ̄ɛ̀daŋ) having clear enunciation and voice.

ལྕེ་བདེ་པོ་ (jē debo) eloquent, verbal.

ལྕེ་མདུད་ཐེབས་ (jēdüù tēb) vi. to be unable to speak (usu. due to fear).

ལྕེ་མདུན་ (jēdün) the tip/ front of the tongue.

ལྕེ་དོག་ལ་ (jēdola) name of a mountain pass in Ganze.

ལྕེ་ལྡག (jēdaà) licking; va.—རྒྱག to lick.

ལྕེ་ལྡིག (jēdig) sm. ལྕེ་དིག.

ལྕེ་ནར་ནར་པོ་ (jēnar narbo) a person who can't keep secrets, sb. who is talkative.

ལྕེ་སྣར་ (jē nār) va. to stick out one's tongue (as a sign of respect) ། ཁ་གདངས་ལྕེ་བསྣར་གྱིས་ Opening (his) mouth and sticking out his tongue.

ལྕེ་གནོན་ཤིང་ལེབ་ (jēnön shīŋleb) tongue depressor.

ལྕེ་ཕྲུག (jētruù) uvula; vi.—རྒྱས་ to get tonsillitis.

ལྕེ་སྦྱང་ (jējaŋ) sm. ཅེ་སྦྱང་.

ལྕེ་བད་ (jē bɛ̀ɛ̀) sm. ལྕེ་བྲད་.

ལྕེ་བྲད་ (jē drɛɛ̀) scraping / cleaning one's tongue.

ལྕེ་དབང་ (jēwaŋ) sm. ལྕེ་ཁམས་.

ལྕེ་འབམ་ (jēbam) a type of sore on the tongue.

ལྕེ་འབལ་ (jēbɛɛ) talking too much.

ལྕེ་སྦྱང་ (jējaŋ) phrases with similar sounds that are used to practice diction.

ལྕེ་མང་ (jēmaŋ) talkative.

ལྕེ་མྱང་ཚ་ (jē ñaŋtsa) a type of salt.

ལྕེ་རྩ་ (jēdza) root of the tongue.

ལྕེ་རྩལ་ (jēdzɛɛ) eloquent, skilled in talking, verbal.

ལྕེ་རྩའི་སྒྲ་ (jēdzɛ dra) velar sound.

ལྕེ་རྩེ་ (jēdze) tip of the tongue.

ལྕེ་རྩེག (jēdzeg) shung. a part of the silk decoration on a girder.

ལྕེ་རྩེར་འཇགས་ (jēdzer jaà) becoming very fluent in speech due to practice.

ལྕེ་ཚ་ (jētsa) buttercup (used in Tibetan medicine).

ལྕེ་ཚད་ (jēdzɛɛ̀) inflammation of the tongue.

ལྕེ་ཚྭ་ཆུ་ (jē tsɔ̄cu) salted yak's tongue.

ལྕེ་ཚོར་ (jētsɔɔ) the sense of taste.

ལྕེ་འཛར་ (jēdzar) sm. ལྕེ་, 3.

ལྕེ་གཞུང་ (jēshuŋ) middle section of the tongue.

ལྕེ་བཞར་ (jēshaa) an instrument for cleaning/ scraping the tongue.

ལྕེ་འོག་དབང་རྩ་ (jēwɔɔ̀ wāŋdza) hypoglossal nerve.

ལྕེ་རལ་མཆུ་སྐམ་ (jērɛɛ cūgam) sm. ལྕེ་དྲུབ་མཆུ་སྐམ་.

ལྕེ་ལེབ་ (jēleb) 1. tongue. 2. slang. kissing with the tongue; va.—སྦྱོར་ to give a kiss with the tongue. 3. brim (of hat) ། ཞྭ་མོའི་ལྕེ་ལེབ་ Brim of a hat.

ལྕེ་ལོ་ (jēlo) stuttering, stammering, lisping.

ལྕེ་ཤེས་ (jēsheè) sense of taste.

ལྕེབ་: p. ལྕེབས་; f. ལྕེབ་; imp. ལྕེབས་ (jēb) va. to commit suicide, to take one's life ། ཁོས་གཙང་པོར་མཆོངས་ནས་ལྕེབས་པ་རེད་ He jumped in the river and took his own life.

ལྕེབ་གྲིར་ཤི་ (jēndrii shī) vi. to die by one's own hand.

ལྕེབ་འདྲི་མ་ (jēndrema) butterfly, moth.

ལྕེབས་ (jēb) p. of ལྕེབ་.

ལྕེའི་དབང་པོ་ (jēe wāŋbo) sm. ལྕེ་ཁམས་.

ལྕེའུ་ཆུང་ (jēwu cūŋ) sm. ལྕེ་ཆུང་.

ལྕེས་ལྡག (jēèdag) sm. ལྕེ་ལྡག.

ལྕོ་ (jō) sm. ལྕེ་བ་.

ལྕོ་ཕྱེ་ (jōce) 1. sm. ཐལ་བ་དུལ་ཕྲན་. 2. pulverized dung.

ལྕོག (jōg) 1. turret of house/ castle. 2. a stalk. 3. a smaller edifice on top of larger building. 4. sm. ལྕོགས་.

ལྕོག་ཁང་ (jōggaŋ) a tower house/ turret house (usu. on a wall).

ལྕོག་ཁེབས་ (jōggeb) tablecloth.

ལྕོག་ག (jōgga) lark.

ལྕོག་གུར་ (jōggur) folding tent, traveling tent.

ལྕོག་རྒྱག (jɔ̄ɔ gyaà) va. to gather the harvest and leave it in the field in elliptically-shaped heaps with the ends of the stalks sticking out and the grain part inserted into the pile.

ལྕོག་ལྕོག (jōgjɔɔ) 1. nodding/ shaking one's head in agreement (usu. preceded by མགོ་); va.—བྱེད་ to nod in agreement. 2. an elliptically-shaped mountain or hill.

ལྕོག་ཆུང་ (jōgjuŋ) a small house/ turret/ tower on top of a larger one.

ལྕོག་ཐུར་ (jōgdur) tablespoon.

ལྕོག་བུ་ (jōgbu) sm. ལྕོག.

ལྕོག་ཙེ་ (jōgdze) table.

ལྕོག་ཙེའི་ཁེབས་ (jōgdzee kēb) tablecloth, table covering.

ལྕོག་རི་ (jōgri) sm. ལྕུགས་པོ་རི་.

ལྕོག་རིང་ (jōgriŋ) long table.

ལྕོག་རིང་སྟེགས་བུ་ (jōgriŋ dēgbu) control tower,

watch tower.

ལྕོག་ཤོག་སེར་པོ་ (jōgshɔɔ̀ sērbo) a type of flower.

ལྕོགས་ (jōg) 1. vi. to be able to cope/ handle ¶ ལས་བྱེད་ལྕོགས་མིན་སྐབས་ Because the officials couldn't handle the (work). 2. vi. to have the time to do ¶ དེ་རིང་ཁྲོམ་ལ་འགྲོ་ཡས་ལྕོགས་པ་མི་འདུག (I) don't have the time to go to the market today.

ལྕོགས་རྒྱ་རྒོད་པོ་ (jōggya gö̱ö̀bo) 1. a person who interferes with other people's affairs. 2. a person who volunteers to do things he doesn't know how to do.

ལྕོགས་རྒྱ་ཚ་པོ་ (jōggya tsābo) sm. ལྕོགས་རྒྱ་རྒོད་པོ་.

ལྕོགས་པ་ (jōgba) free time ¶ རང་སང་ཉིན་ལྕོགས་པ་ཡོད་པས་ Do you have free time tomorrow?

ལྕོགས་གཟུགས་ (jōgsug) shung. a silk decoration on a girder.

ལྕོང་མོ་ (jōŋmo) tadpole, polliwog.

ཆ་ (cā) 1. the letter ཆ་ (used in alphabetical numbering). 2. fraction, part ¶ དུམ་བུ་བཞི་ལ་བཏང་བའི་ཆ་གཅིག One part out of four. ¶ བརྒྱ་ཐམ་པའི་ཆ་ One hundredth. ¶ བཞི་ཆ་གཉིས་ Two fourths. 3. pair, match ¶ ལྷམ་ཆ་གཅིག A pair of shoes. 4. a particle used to change an adjective into its abstract noun form, e.g., དཀར་པོ་ (white) to དཀར་ཆ་ (whiteness). 5. the same ¶ འདི་གཉིས་ཆ་རེད་ These two are the same. 6. together (as a pair) ¶ ཁོ་གཉིས་ཆ་ལ་ཕྱིན་པ་རེད་ They went together. 7. message; va.—སྐུར་ to send a message. 8. loose (for clothing). 9. p. and f. of ཆས་.

ཆ་ཀ་བ་ (cāgawa) sm. ཆ་ག་པ་.

ཆ་དཀར་ (cāgar) a district in Lhoka.

ཆ་རྐྱེན་ (cāgyen) conditions, circumstances, factors, facilities; vi.—འཛོམས་; —ཚང་ to be equipped, to be complete, to have what is needed ¶ དངོས་པོའི་ཆ་རྐྱེན་ Material conditions. ¶ དམག་དོན་དང་ཆབ་སྲིད་དཔལ་འབྱོར་སོགས་ཀྱི་ཆ་རྐྱེན་ Military, political, economic, and other conditions. ¶ ཁོ་ཚོར་ཆབ་སྲིད་ཀྱི་དབང་ཆའི་ཆ་རྐྱེན་མ་འཛོམ་བར་བསྒྱུར་བཅོད་གང་ཡག་གཏོང་ཐུབ་ཀྱི་མ་རེད་ Until they have the political power that is needed they will not be able to make any changes.

ཆ་རྐྱེན་ཆ་ཚང་ (cāgyen cādzaŋ) complete/ excellent conditions ¶ རང་དབང་རང་བཙན་གྱི་ཆ་རྐྱེན་ཆ་ཚང་གྲུས་ལེགས་ཡོད་པའི་རྒྱལ་ཁབ་ A country that has complete conditions for independence. ¶ བཟོ་ལས་འཛུགས་བསྐྲུན་གྱི་ཆ་རྐྱེན་ཕུན་སུམ་ཚོགས་པ་ Excellent conditions for the development of industry.

ཆ་རྐྱེན་ཕུན་སུམ་ཚོགས་པ་ (cāgyen pū̃nsum tsōgba) sm. ཆ་རྐྱེན་ཆ་ཚང་.

ཆ་རྐྱེན་ངོ་མ་ (cāgyen ŋo̱ma) sm. ཆ་རྐྱེན་ཆ་དངོས་.

ཆ་རྐྱེན་དངོས་ (cāgyen ŋȫò) specific/ concrete conditions.

ཆ་རྐྱེན་མི་དགོས་པ་ (cāgyen mi̱göòba) unconditional ¶ ཆ་རྐྱེན་མི་དགོས་པའི་ཕྱིར་འཐེན་ Unconditional withdrawal.

ཆ་རྐྱེན་མེད་པའི་མགོ་བཏགས་ (cāgyen me̱èbɛ go̱bdaà) unconditional surrender.

ཆ་རྐྱེན་ཅམ་སྨྲ་བ་ (cāgyendzām māwa) conditional theory.

ཆ་རྐྱེན་ཚུར་སྣང་ (cāgyen tsūūnaŋ) conditional reflex.

ཆ་རྐྱེན་འཛོམས་ (cāgyen dzo̱m) see ཆ་རྐྱེན་.

ཆ་རྐྱེན་འཛོམས་པོ་ (cāgyen dzo̱mbo) good/ complete conditions, well-equipped, ¶ ལུང་པ་དེར་ཆ་རྐྱེན་འཛོམས་པོ་མི་འདུག The conditions in that place are not good.

ཆ་ཁ་ (cāga) sm. ཆོ་.

ཆ་ཁ་ཡ་སྡེབ (cāga ya̱deb) va. to piece together.

ཆ་ག (cāga) 1. a piece of material sewn as an inside hem on clothes; va.—གཏོང་ to sew such a hem. 2. the epicanthic fold.

ཆ་ག་པ་ (cāgaba) locust, grasshopper.

ཆ་ག་མ་ (cāgama) hemmed clothing.

ཆ་གྲངས་ (cādraŋ) 1. point ¶ ང་ཚོའི་རུ་ཁག་ལ་ཆ་གྲངས་བཅུ་ཡོད་ Our team has ten points. 2. fraction (in math). 3. an even number.

ཆ་གྲངས་ལྷར་སྣང་ (cādraŋ dārnaŋ) improper fraction (in math).

ཆ་གྲུ་ཆབ་སྟོད་ (cədru cābdöò) shung. a shawl/ upper vest with a brocade hem that was worn by monk officials in the Tibetan government.

ཆ་བགོས་ (cāgöò) dividing into parts/ groups/ segments; va.—གཏོང་; —བྱེད་; —རྒྱག ¶ ས་ཞིང་དང་རྒྱུ་ནོར་གང་ཡོད་ཁོ་ཚོ་ཁྱིམ་ཚང་བཞི་ལ་ཆ་བགོས་བྱས་པ་རེད་ (They) divided whatever land or property there was among the four families.

ཆ་བགོས་འཐེན་ཉར་ (cāgöò tēññar) keeping a part or percent of profit (and giving rest to the state or work unit); va.—བྱེད་.

ཆ་འགྲིག (cā dri̱g) vi. to be a pair, to match ¶ ལྷམ་གོག་འདི་གཉིས་ཆ་འགྲིག་གི་མི་འདུག These shoes are not a pair.

ཆ་འགྲིག་ཉིས་འགྲིག (cədrig ñīìdrig) in pairs.

ཆ་འགྲིག་པ་ (cā drīgbə) sm. ཆ་འགྲིག་པོ་.

ཆ་འགྲིག་པོ་ (cā dri̱gbu) well-matched, well-paired, symmetrical.

ཆ་འགྲོས་ (cāndröò) shung. the gradual manner (in which the length of the days and nights change); vi.—རྒྱག ¶ དབྱར་དགུན་ཉིན་མཚན་རིང་ཐུང་གི་ཆ་འགྲོས་ཤུགས་ཀྱིས་རྒྱག་པ་ The length of the days and nights in summer and winter changes gradually.

ཆ་རྒྱག (cāgyaà) doubles (in sports); va.—རྒྱག to play doubles.

ཆ་རྒྱུས་ (cəgyüù) knowledge, familiarity ¶ ལུང་པ་འདི་ཡི་ཆ་རྒྱུས་གང་ཡང་མེད་ (I) have no knowledge at all of this place. ¶ ཁོ་ཚོར་གཞུང་གི་ལམ་སྲོལ་ཆ་རྒྱུས་ཡག་པོ་ཡོད་པ་རེད་ (They) have good knowledge of (their) system of government.

ཆ་རྒྱུས་མེད་པ་ (cəgyüù me̱èba) not familiar with, without knowledge of, foreign to, unfamiliar ¶ བོད་མི་དམངས་ཚོར་རང་དམག་ལ་ཆ་རྒྱུས་མེད་སྐབས་ Because the Tibetan people were not familiar with our troops. ¶ ང་ཆ་རྒྱུས་མེད་པའི་ལུང་པ་ཞིག་ལ་སླེབས་བྱུང་ I have arrived in an unfamiliar place.

ཆ་སྒམ་ (cāgam) a cabinet, a cupboard.

ཆ་སྒམ་མཆོད་གཤོམ་ (cāgam cȫòshom) a cupboard with an altar on top of it.

ཆ་སྒྲིག (cā dri̱g) 1. va. to pair up, to match ¶ བུ་མོ་དེ་གཉིས་དུབ་ལོག་ཆ་བསྒྲིགས་ནས་གོན་བཞག These two girls wore matching clothes. 2. va. to conjugate.

ཆ་སྒྲིག་ཡ་སྒྲིག (cədrig yə̱drig) matching or pairing up a lot of things together.

ཆ་བསྒྲིགས་ (cā dri̱g) p. of ཆ་སྒྲིག.

ཆ་བསྒྲིག (cā dri̱g) f. of ཆ་སྒྲིག.

ཆ་ངག (cāŋaà) message; va.—སྐུར་ to send a message.

ཆ་ངེ་ཆུང་ངེ་ (cāŋe cūŋŋe) small things ¶ ངའི་ནང་ལ་ཅ་ལག་ཆ་ངེ་ཆུང་ངེ་མང་པོ་ཡོད་ I have many small things in my house.

ཆ་ཅན་ (cājɛn) 1. the base to which parts are attached. 2. denominator of a fraction.

ཆ་གཅིག (cājig) one pair.

ཆ་ཆ་ (cāja) in pairs, in two's; va.—བྱེད་ to do/ go in pairs ¶ གཞོན་ནུ་མ་དེ་ཚོ་ཆ་ཆ་བྱས་ནས་ཁྲོམས་ལ་འགྲོ་གི་འདུག Those young girls are going to the market in pairs.

ཆ་ཆ་རྐྱང་ (cā cāgyaŋ) the same, identical ¶ འདི་གཉིས་ཆ་ཆ་རྐྱང་རེད་ These two are identical.

ཆ་ཆག་ཆ་ (cā cāgja) going/ traveling together ¶ ང་ཚོ་ཆ་ཆག་ཆ་ལ་རྒྱ་གར་ནས་ཡོང་བ་ཡིན་ We came from India together.

ཆ་ཆགས་ (cā cāà) 1. vi. to become paired, to become the same ¶ ཕྲུ་གུ་འདི་གཉིས་ལོ་ལ་ཧེ་བག་ཡོད་ཀྱང་གཟུགས་པོ་ཆེ་ཆུང་ཆ་ཆགས་བཞག Even though there is a difference in the age of the two children, they have become the same in size.

ཆ་ཆོ་ (cājo) crooked, not straight, zig-zag.

ཆ་ཆོ་མེད་པ་ (cājo mɛ̱ɛ̀ba) sm. ཆོ་མེད་པ་.

ཆ་འཇོག (cānjɔɔ̀) 1. believability, trustworthiness, credibility; va.—བྱེད་ to believe, to trust ¶ ཁོས་བཤད་པར་ཚང་མས་ཆ་འཇོག་བྱེད་ཀྱི་རེད་ All the people will believe what he says. ¶ སུས་ཀྱང་ཁོ་ལ་ཆ་འཇོག་ཡོད་པ་མ་རེད་ No one trusts him. 2. abiding by, honoring, respecting; va.—བྱེད་ ¶ གཞུང་གིས་གྲོས་མཐུན་དེར་ཆ་འཇོག་མི་བྱེད་མཐུ་མེད་བྱུང་ The government had no choice but to abide by the agreement.

ཆ་འཇོག་འཕེར་བ་ (cānjɔɔ̀ pērwa) honorable,

trustworthy, dependable, respectable ། ཆ་འཇོག་འཕེར་བའི་ཆིངས་ཡིག An honorable treaty.

ཆ་འཇོག་མི་རུང་བ་ (cānjɔ̀ɔ miruŋwɔ) sm. ཆ་འཇོག་མེད་པ་.

ཆ་འཇོག་མེད་པ་ (cānjɔ̀ɔ meèba) unreliable, untrustworthy, dishonorable.

ཆ་ཉམས་ (cā ñam) vi. to decrease in size (with respect to the decrease in the moon from full moon to new moon).

ཆ་ཉིན་ (cāñin) even-numbered days (of the month).

ཆ་གཉིས་དུས་ (cāñìi tüü) a day, a 24 hour period.

ཆ་གཉིས་ལྡན་པའི་དུས་ (cāñìidɛmbɛ tüü) midnight.

ཆ་མཉམ་ (cāñam) equal in size/ height, symmetrical, proportionate ། ལྕོག་ཙེ་དེ་གཉིས་མཐོ་དམན་ཆ་མཉམ་རེད་ The two tables are of equal height.

ཆ་མཉམ་དུ་ལྟ་ (cā ñamdu dā) va. to look/ consider/ place on the same or equal footing ། འགོ་ཁྲིད་དེས་མི་སེར་དབུལ་ཕྱུག་ཚང་མ་ཆ་མཉམ་དུ་ལྟ་གི་ཡོད་པ་རེད་ That leader considers the rich and the poor on the same footing.

ཆ་མཉམ་པོ་ (cā ñambo) equal ། གཞུང་གི་སྐྱིད་གསོ་མི་དམངས་ལ་བགོ་བཤའ་ཆ་སྙོམ་པོ་བརྒྱབ་འདུག The government's welfare was divided equally among the people.

ཆ་སྙོམ་ (cā ñōm) sm. ཆ་སྙོམས་.

ཆ་སྙོམས་ (cā ñōm) equal, average; va.—བྱེད་ to equalize, to even out, to average; va.—བགོ་; —བགོད་ to divide equally ། ས་ཞིང་རྣམས་ཆ་སྙོམས་བྱས་བགོས་པ་རེད་ (They) divided the land equally. ། ཆ་སྙོམས་ཀྱི་ཡོང་འབབ་མི་རེར་སྒོར་ ༦༠ ཙམ་ཡོད་ The average income per person is about sixty rupees. ། ཆ་སྙོམས་བྱས་ན་འཛིན་གྲྭ་འདིའི་སློབ་ཕྲུག་གི་ལོ་གྲངས་ ༡༥ ཡིན་ On average, the age of the students in this class is 15. ། ཆ་སྙོམས་རིན་གོང་ Average price.

ཆ་སྙོམས་ཀྱི་གྲངས་ཀ་ (cāñomgi traŋga) average number, mean.

ཆ་སྙོམས་ཀྱི་གཙང་འཕར་ (cāñom dzāŋbar) average net increase.

ཆ་སྙོམས་ཁེ་སྤོགས་ (cāñom kēbɔɔ̀) average profit/ gain.

ཆ་སྙོམས་ཁོ་ནའི་རིང་ལུགས་ (cāñom kōnɛ riŋluù) absolute egalitarianism.

ཆ་སྙོམས་གྲངས་འབོར་ (cāñom traŋbɔr) sm. ཆ་སྙོམས་གྲངས་ཀ་.

ཆ་སྙོམས་བགོད་ (cāñom göö) va. to divide equally.

ཆ་སྙོམས་བགོད་འགྲེམས་ (cāñom göndrem) even/ equal distribution.

ཆ་སྙོམས་བགོས་ (cāñom göö) p. of ཆ་སྙོམས་བགོད་.

ཆ་སྙོམས་དྲོད་གྲང་ (cāñom troödraŋ) sm. ཆ་ཉོམས་དྲོད་ཚད་.

ཆ་ཉོམས་དྲོད་ཚད་ (cāñom troödzɛɛ̀) average temperature.

ཆ་སྙོམས་ན་ (cāñomna) if one averages, on the average ། ང་རར་ལྕགས་ཐོན་ཚད་ཆ་སྙོམས་ན་ཉིན་རེར་ཀྲིན་ ༥༢༠ རེ་ཡོད་ The production of steel is on the average 520 tons per day.

ཆ་སྙོམས་པོ་ (cā ñōmbo) even, equal, well-balanced.

ཆ་སྙོམས་བྱས་ན་ (cāñom ceèna) sm. ཆ་སྙོམས་ན་.

ཆ་སྙོམས་རིང་ལུགས་ (cāñom riŋluù) egalitarianism.

ཆ་སྙོམས་རིན་གོང་ (cāñom ringoŋ) average price.

ཆ་རྟོགས་ (cā dɔɔ̀) va. to guess, to estimate ། སང་ཉིན་ཆར་པ་གཏོང་རྒྱུ་ཡིན་མིན་ཆ་རྟོགས་ཐུབ་ཀྱི་རེད་པས་ Are you able to estimate whether it will rain tomorrow?

ཆ་སྟ་ (cāda) tweezers.

ཆ་སྡིགས་ (cādeg) sm. ཆ་སྐམ་.

ཆ་སྟོན་ (cādön) pointing out, showing; va.—བྱེད་ ། ང་ཁྲོམ་ལ་འགྲོ་དུས་ལམ་ཁ་ཆ་སྟོན་བྱེད་མཁན་ཞིག་དགོས་ཀྱི་འདུག When I go to the market I need someone to show the way.

ཆ་ཐོར་ཡ་ཐོར་ (cādɔr yadɔr) disintegrated, broken up, scattered, fragmented.

ཆ་མཐུན་ (cātün) 1. well-matched ། མི་དེས་དུག་ལོག་ཆ་མཐུན་ཞིག་ཉོས་པ་རེད་ That person bought a well-matched set of clothes. 2. semi ། སྤྱི་ཚོགས་རིང་ལུགས་ཆ་མཐུན་ Semi-socialist.

ཆ་མཐུན་པོ་ (cā tũmbu) well-suited, well-matched.

ཆ་དང་(དམག་སྒར་) (cādaŋ (määgar)) shung. the "ཆ" (artillery) regiment of the traditional Tibetan army.

ཆ་དང་ཡ་ (cā daŋ ya) even and odd [Lit. a pair and single].

ཆ་དུམ་ཡ་དུམ་དུ་འགྱུར་ (cādum yadumdu gyur) vi. to get broken into pieces.

ཆ་མདའ་ (cānda) shung. commander of the ཆ་དང་ regiment.

ཆ་འདྲ་བ་ (cā drawa) sm. ཆ་མཐུན་, 1.

ཆ་འདྲེས་ (cāndreè) mixture, alloy, compound.

ཆ་བསྡུ་ཡ་བསྡུ་ (cādu yadu) collecting things from different sources and places and putting them together to do sth., scraping together bits and pieces from many sources ། ཁོ་ཚོས་འཛིན་ཆས་ཆ་བསྡུ་ཡ་བསྡུ་བྱས་ནས་སྐྱབས་བཅོལ་བ་ཚོར་གནས་སྐབས་སྡོད་ས་བཟོས་པ་རེད་ They did whatever they could to scrape together furniture from many sources for temporary residences for the refugees; va.—བྱེད་.

ཆ་བསྡུར་ (cā dur) shung. va. to compare with others.

ཆ་ལྡན་པ་ (cādɛmba) in pairs.

ཆ་ནས་ (cānɛ) 1. from the point of view/ vantage of ། དཔལ་འབྱོར་གྱི་ཆ་ནས་བཤད་ན་ If I speak from the viewpoint of the economy. 2. regarding, concerning ། དམག་དོན་གྱི་ཆ་ནས་ཁོ་ཚོ་ཡར་རྒྱས་ཕྱིན་ཡོད་པ་རེད་ Concerning military issues, they have made progress.

ཆ་ནས་བྱས་ན་ (cānɛ cɛ̀ɛna) sm. ཆ་ནས་.

ཆ་ནས་མཚོན་ན་ (cānɛ tsööna) from the point of view/ vantage of ། ཆབ་སྲིད་ཀྱི་ཆ་ནས་མཚོན་ན་ From the point of view of politics.

ཆ་གནས་བྱེད་ (cānɛɛ̀ ceè) va. to live up to an agreement, to keep one's promise/ word.

ཆ་སྣོན་ཡ་སྣོན་ (canön yanön) collecting things from difference sources to supplement sth; va.—བྱེད་ ། སྤུན་མཆེད་ཚོས་དངུལ་ཆ་སྣོན་ཡ་སྣོན་བྱས་ནས་ཁོང་གིས་སྨན་རིན་སྤྲད་པ་རེད་ The relatives collected money and he gave it to pay the medical fees.

ཆ་པེ་ཅོ་པེ་ (cābe cōbe) 1. odds and ends, junk, bits and pieces. 2. (for people) disorderly, disorganized. 3. uncertain, unsure ། ཁོ་ཆོས་དད་ཀྱི་ཐོག་ཆ་པེ་ཅོ་པེ་ཞིག་ཡོད་པ་རེད་ Regarding religion, it is uncertain whether he believes in it or not.

ཆ་དཔང་ (cābaŋ) witness.

ཆ་དཔྱད་ (cājɛɛ̀) medical tools.

ཆ་སྤྱད་ (cājɛɛ̀) 1. utensils. 2. sm. ཆ་དཔྱད་.

ཆ་ཕྲ་བ་ (cā drāwa) small bits and pieces.

ཆ་ཕྲ་མོ་ (cā drāmo) sm. ཆ་ཕྲ་བ་.

ཆ་ཕྲན་ (cādrɛn) a fraction of sth.

ཆ་འཕྲིན་ (cāndrin) a verbal/ oral message; va.—སྐུར་ to give/ send a verbal message; va.—སྤྲོད་ to deliver a verbal message.

ཆ་བེ་ཅོ་བེ་ (cābe cōbe) sm. ཆ་པེ་ཅོ་བེ་.

ཆ་བུ་ (cəbu) earring (for animals).

ཆ་བྱད་ (cājɛɛ̀) dress, costume; va.—སྤྲས་ to dress in a costume ། གཙང་མོའི་ཆ་བྱད་ Dress of women from the Tsang region.

ཆ་བྱེད་ (cā ceè) sm. ཆ་ཆ་བྱེད་.

ཆ་འབྲེལ་ (cāndree) sm. ཟུང་འབྲེལ་.

ཆ་སྦྲེལ་ (cāndree) connecting, joining; va.—བྱེད་.

ཆ་མ་ཆོ་ལོག (cāma cōlɔɔ̀) nonsensical talk, contrary/ opposite talk.

ཆ་མ་མཆིས་ (cā ma cìi) 1. vi. to be uncertain, to be unsure, to not know ། སང་ཉིན་གང་ཡོང་ཆ་མ་མཆིས་ It is uncertain what will happen tomorrow. 2. unrivaled, unequaled, unmatched. 3. only one of a pair.

ཆ་མ་རྟོགས་ (cā madɔɔ̀) sm. ཆ་མ་མཆིས་.

ཆ་མ་ཚང་ (cā madzaŋ) incomplete, inadequate །

སྒྲིག་ཆས་ཆ་མ་ཚང་ Incomplete equipment.

ཆ་མ་བཞག (cā mashaà) p. of ཆ་མི་འཇོག.

ཆ་མི་འཇོག (cā minjɔɔ̀) sm. ཆ་འཇོག་མེད་པ་.

ཆ་མི་རྟོགས་པ་ (cā mi dɔ̄gba) sm. ངེས་པ་མེད་པ་.

ཆ་མིན་གོ་ལོག (cāmin golɔɔ̀) sm. ཆ་མ་ཆོ་ལོག.

ཆ་མིན་ཆ་ལོག (cāmin cālɔɔ̀) sm. ཆ་མ་ཆོ་ལོག.

ཆ་མི་སྙོམ་པ་ (cā miñomba) unequal, unmatched.

ཆ་མི་འཚལ་ (cā midzεε) sm. ཆ་མ་འཚེས་.

ཆ་མིན་ཡ་འཐོར་ (cāmin yadɔɔ) a pair where each of the two is different.

ཆ་མེད་ (cāmeè) 1. one of a pair, a singleton ¶ ལྷམ་གོག་ཆ་མེད་མང་པོ་ཞིག་འདུག There are many single shoes (without the other half of the pair). 2. incomparable. 3. uncertain, unsure, unfamiliar ¶ གར་སོང་ཆ་མེད་དུ་སོང་ Where (he) went is uncertain.

ཆ་མེད་རྒྱུས་མེད་ (cāmeè gyüümeè) unfamiliar, with no knowledge of sth. ¶ ང་ལུང་པ་ཆ་མེད་རྒྱུས་མེད་ཅིག་ལ་སླེབས་བྱུང་ I have arrived at a place about which I have no knowledge.

ཆ་མེད་འདྲིས་མེད་ (cāmeè driimeè) sm. ཆ་མེད་རྒྱུས་མེད་.

ཆ་མེད་ཡ་འཐོར་ (cāmeè yadɔɔ) ཆ་མིན་ཡ་འཐོར་.

ཆ་ཙམ་ (cādzam) fraction of, part of ¶ ཆ་ཙམ་མ་གཏོགས་སླད་ཚང་ཤེས་མ་བྱུང་ I only understood part of it, not the whole thing.

ཆ་ཙམ་མ་ལུས་པ་ (cādzam mәlüübә) completely, totally ¶ ཁོ་ཚོའི་ཤེས་རིག་ཆ་ཙམ་མ་ལུས་པ་རྩ་མེད་བཟོ་ཐབས་བྱས་ཡོད་ (They) tried to exterminate their culture completely.

ཆ་ཚང་ (བ་) (cādzaŋ) the whole, the complete ¶ གློག་འདོན་ས་ཚིགས་ཀྱི་སྒྲིག་ཆས་ཆ་ཚང་ཐོན་སྐྱེད་བྱེད་ཀྱི་ཡོད་པ་རེད་ They produce complete equipment for a power station. ¶ ང་ལ་མོ་ཊ་བཟོ་ལས་ཀྱི་ལག་ཆ་ཆ་ཚང་ཡོད་ I have a complete set of tools for making a car.

ཆ་ཚང་གཅིག (cādzaŋjig) the whole, complete ¶ ང་ལ་གློག་བརྙན་དེའི་སྒྲིན་ཤོག་ཆ་ཚང་གཅིག་ཡོད་ I have a complete roll of film of that movie.

ཆ་ཚང་ཡོད་པ་ (cādzaŋ yöͦöba) complete, whole.

ཆ་ཚད་ (cādzεὲ) size (usu. for clothing).

ཆ་ཚུལ་འཛིན་ (cādzüü dzin) va. to disguise.

ཆ་མཚུངས་ (cā tsūŋ) vi. to be equal or balanced with, to correspond with, to be congruent with, to agree/ tally with, to go well together ¶ ང་ཚོས་གོ་ཡག་དང་ཁོས་ཤོད་ཡག་ཆ་མཚུངས་ཀྱི་མི་འདུག What we heard and what he is saying do not correspond.

ཆ་མཚུངས་པོ་ (cā tsūŋbo) sm. ཆ་མཐུན་པོ་.

ཆ་མཚོན་ (cā tsɔ̃n) va. to take as an example, to use as a case in point ¶ གནས་ཚུལ་དེ་ར་ཆ་མཚོན་ནས་བཤད་ན་ If (we) take that situation as an example.

ཆ་མཚོན་ན་ (cā tsɔ̃nna) if one uses sth. as an example, for example, for instance ¶ ཁོ་ལ་ཆ་མཚོན་ན་བོད་ལ་ཞིང་པ་ཆུང་གྲས་གཅིག་རེད་ If we use him as an example, he would be sb. classified as a small farmer in Tibet.

ཆ་འཛད་བས་ (cādzәb) width and length (for clothing).

ཆ་འཛིན་ (cәndzin) 1. a partial eclipse. 2. reliable, trustworthy, dependable ¶ མི་དེ་ཆ་འཛིན་བྱེད་ཆོག་པ་ཞིག་རེད་ He is sb. who is trustworthy. 3. a witness.

ཆ་རྫོགས་ (cā dzɔ̄ɔ) vi. to be full/ complete ¶ ཚེས་པ་བཅོ་ལྔ་ལ་ཟླ་བ་ཆ་རྫོགས་ཀྱི་རེད་ The moon will be full on the 15th.

ཆ་ཞབས་ (cāshәb) shung. under the control/ jurisdiction ¶ བབས་འགྲིག་མེད་པར་ས་ཆ་མི་སེར་སོགས་སྤྲད་པ་ཐམས་ཅད་སླར་ས་དེ་གཞུང་གི་ཆ་ཞབས་སུ་བཙུག They took back the lands and people that were given to them inappropriately and put them under the control of the government.

ཆ་བཞག (cā shaà) 1. p. of ཆ་འཇོག. 2. if we suppose, if we say hypothetically ¶ རྒྱ་དམར་གྱིས་རྒྱ་གར་ལ་བཙན་འཛུལ་བྱས་པར་ཆ་བཞག་ན་ If we suppose that Red China invaded India.

ཆ་བཞག་ནས་ (cāshaànε) 1. sm. ཆ་འཇོག. 2. relying on, based on, trusting ¶ ཁོར་ཆ་བཞག་ནས་ཉོས་པ་ཡིན་ Relying on him, I bought it.

ཆ་ཟུང་ (cāsuŋ) a pair.

ཆ་ཡ་ (cāya) 1. a pair and one half of a pair. 2. one half of a pair.

ཆ་ཡིག (cәyig) auspicious sayings written on the side of a door (a Chinese custom).

ཆ་ཡོངས་སུ་ཚང་བ་ (cā yoŋsu tsaŋwa) complete, whole, in all facets ¶ དམངས་གཙོའི་རིང་ལུགས་ཆ་ཡོངས་སུ་ཚང་བའི་སྒོ་ནས་འཕེལ་རྒྱས་གཏོང་དགོས་ (We) should develop democracy in all facets.

ཆ་ཡོད་ (cāyöö) sm. ཆ་ཡོད་རྒྱུས་ཡོད་.

ཆ་ཡོད་རྒྱུས་ཡོད་ (cāyöö gyüüyöö) familiar, well-known.

ཆ་ར་ (cāra) Himalayan oak.

ཆ་རན་པོ་ (cā rεmbo) sm. ཆ་མཐུན་པོ་.

ཆ་རེ་ (cāre) 1. some, few. 2. a pair of sth. (e.g., shoes).

ཆ་རུ་ (cәru) peg-shaped button.

ཆ་རུ་ཆབ་སྟོད་ (cәru cәbdöö) sm. ཆ་གྲུ་ཆབ་སྟོད་.

ཆ་ལ་ (cāla) 1. together. 2. (with སྡོད་) to have sexual intercourse; to live together ¶ ཁོ་གཉིས་ཆ་ལ་སྡོད་པ་རེད་ They lived together.

ཆ་ལག (cālaà) part, portion.

ཆ་ལག་ཆ་ཚང་ (cālaà cādzaŋ) entire, complete in all parts ¶ འཕྲུལ་འཁོར་ཆ་ལག་ཆ་ཚང་རང་རྒྱལ་དུ་བཟོ་ཐུབ་ཀྱི་ཡོད་པ་རེད་ (We) are able to manufacture complete machines in our country.

ཆ་ལག་ཚང་བ་ (cālaà tsāŋwa) sm. ཆ་ལག་ཆ་ཚང་.

ཆ་ལང་ (cālaŋ) cymbal.

ཆ་ལམ་ (cālam) roughly, approximately, almost, more or less ¶ གྲ་སྒྲིག་ཆ་ལམ་ཚར་སོང་ The preparations are almost finished.

ཆ་ལུགས་ (cәluù) costume, style/ custom of dressing ¶ མི་རིགས་ཀྱི་ཆ་ལུགས་ The costumes of the nationalities.

ཆ་ལེ་ཆོ་ལེ་ (cāle cōle) sm. ཆ་པེ་ཆོ་པེ་.

ཆ་ཤས་ (cāshεὲ) 1. part, portion, section, unit ¶ ཁང་པ་དེའི་ཆ་ཤས་གཅིག་ཚིག་འདུག A part of the house has been burned. 2. fraction (in math); va.—ཉུང་ to reduce a fraction (in math).

ཆ་ཤས་ཅན་ (cāshεὲjεn) sm. ཆ་ཅན་.

ཆ་སྲོལ་ (cāsöö) tradition, custom.

ཆ་གསུམ་ (cāsum) 1. three pairs. 2. one third. 3. name of a kind of ritual offering (torma).

ཆ་གསེད་ (cāseè) sm. ཆ་གསེས་.

ཆ་གསེད་བསྡུ་ལེན་ (cāseè dulen) dividing up and then collecting; va.—བྱེད་.

ཆ་གསེས་ (cāseè) dividing up; va.—བྱེད་; —རྒྱག; —གཏོང་ to divide up ¶ ལས་ཀ་དེ་ལས་ཁུངས་ཁག་བཞི་ལ་ཆ་གསེད་བྱས་ཡོད་པ་རེད་ (They) have divided the work between the four offices.

ཆ་གསེས་བགོ་འགྲེམས་ (cāseè gondrem) sm. ཆ་གསེས་.

ཆ་ཧར་ (cāhar) name of a Mongol tribe/ banner.

ཆག (cāà) 1. fodder. 2. vi. to get broken/ damaged ¶ ཁོའི་རྐང་པ་ཆག་པ་རེད་ His leg got broken. 3. vi. to get decreased/ reduced, to go down (in price, number, etc.) ¶ ཟས་གོང་ཕྲན་བུ་ཆག་འདུག The price of food has gone down a little. 4. vi. to miss (a routine activity) ¶ ཁ་ས་འཛིན་གྲྭ་ཆག་སོང་ (I) missed class yesterday. 5. abbr. of ཆག་པ་. 6. see ཆག་རྒྱུག.

ཆག་གྲུམ་ (cәgdrum) sm. ཆག་དཀྲུམས་.

ཆག་དཀྲུམས་ (cәgdrum) broken, damaged ¶ དཀར་ཡོལ་ཆག་དཀྲུམས་ A broken cup.

ཆག་སྐྱོན་ (cāggyön) damage, breakage.

ཆག་ཁུག (cәguù) 1. sm. ཆག་ཤད་. 2. the bend of a river.

ཆག་འཁྱོག (cāngyɔɔ̀) broken, damaged [Lit. broken and crooked].

ཆག་འཁྲི་ (cāgdri) shung. the reduction (of a tax) and the payment (of a tax).

ཆག་གང་ (cāggaŋ) a measurement unit equal to the width of four fingers.

ཆག་གས་ (chāàgɛɛ̀) cracked.

ཆག་གི་ཅིག་གི་ (cəgi cīgi) 1. odds and ends, bits and pieces, good and bad things mixed together. 2. in a mess, disorderly.

ཆག་གི་ཆིག་གི་ (cəgi cīgi) sm. ཆག་གི་ཅིག་གི་.

ཆག་གྲུགས་ (cəgdruù) sm. ཆག་དུམ་.

ཆག་གྲུམ་ (cəgdrum) sm. ཆག་དཀྲུམས་.

ཆག་གྲུམ་མེད་པ་ (cəgdrum m̱eèba) complete, whole, unbroken.

ཆག་གྲུམ་གས་འཁྱོག (cəgdrum ḵɛngyɔɔ̀) broken and cracked.

ཆག་རྒྱག (cāà gy̱aà) vi. to be/ get stiff, to have aches and pains (due to work).

ཆག་རྒྱུ་མེད་པ་ (cəgyu m̱ɛɛ̀ba) 1. unbreakable. 2. (for prices) irreducible.

ཆག་སྐྱོ་ (cāàgo) 1. calamity, catastrophe, misfortune; vi.—འཕྱད་;—ཐུག; —ལངས་; —བྱུང་ to meet with calamity/ catastrophe/ misfortune; va.—སློང་ to cause misfortune/ harm. ¶ མི་ཚང་དེ་ལ་ལོ་ཉེས་ཀྱི་ཆག་སྐྱོ་བྱུང་བཞག That family experienced the calamity of a bad crop harvest. 2. sm. ཆག་སྐྱོ་མ་ཆེ་. 3. va. to fine ¶ དེང་སང་དགེ་རྒན་གྱིས་ཆག་སྐྱོ་གཏོང་ཆོག་གི་མ་རེད་ These days the teachers are not allowed to fine (the students).

ཆག་སྐྱོ་མ་ཆེ་ (cāàgo m̱ace) expression of surprise when sth. bad happens.

ཆག་ཆ་ (cāgca) shung. a reduction (usu. for taxes) ¶ གཞུང་གི་ཁྲལ་ཆག་ཆ་གཏོང་དགོས་ The government should reduce taxes.

ཆག་ཆག (cāgcaà) sprinkling water to hold down dust (usu. when sweeping); va.—འདེབས་; —བྱེད་ to sprinkle water to hold down dust.

ཆག་ཆད་ (cāgcɛɛ̀) items that are broken and items that are missing or unaccounted.

ཆག་ཅིག (cəgjig) sm. ཆག་གི་ཅིག་གི་.

ཆག་ཅིངས་ (cəgjiŋ) a cast (on a broken leg/ arm).

ཆག་ཅེན་བཞི་ (cāgjen sẖi) shung. four types of reduction of taxes: 1. བཀྲུས་ཆག 2. དམག་ཆག 3. ངོ་ཆག 4. the iron hare year reduction.

ཆག་ཆོད་ (cāg cōò) shung. getting a tax reduction/ exemption.

ཆག་མཆན་ (cāgjɛn) shung. a notation/ note that gives approval for a tax reduction/ exemption.

ཆག་གཏམ་ (cāgdam) inauspicious talk, disgraceful talk.

ཆག་ཏ་ཕོས་བཟས་ ཡ་ལ་བོང་བུར་བཀལ་ (cāà dāböò s̱ɛɛ̀ y̱ala p̱uŋgur gɛ̄ɛ) blaming/ accusing wrongly [Lit. the fodder is eaten by the horse, the blame is put on the donkey].

ཆག་སྟེར་ (cāà dēr) 1. va. to give a handicap (when playing a game of skill). 2. va. to give a concession/ reduction. 3. va. to give fodder.

ཆག་གཏོང་ (cāà dōŋ) sm. ཆག་ཡང་གཏོང་.

ཆག་ཐེའུ་ (cāg twu) shung. a seal put on a document approving a reduction of taxes.

ཆག་འདེབས་ (cāà ḏeb) sm. ཆག་ཆག་འདེབས་.

ཆག་དུམ་ (cāgdum) broken piece (of sth.) ¶ ཤེལ་སྒོ་ཆག་དུམ་ཞིག A broken piece of glass.

ཆག་དོད་ (cāgdöò) shung. a money payment for a tax reduction/ exemption.

ཆག་རྡུང་ཉག་རྡུང་ (cəgduŋ ṉ̃əgduŋ) beating badly/ severely (all over); va.—གཞུ to beat badly/ severely ¶ ཇག་པས་ཁོང་ཆག་རྡུང་ཉག་རྡུང་གཞུས་བཞག The bandits beat him badly all over.

ཆག་པ་ (cāgba) bunch, bouquet ¶ མེ་ཏོག་ཆག་པ་ A bunch of flowers.

ཆག་པོ་ (cāgbo) sm. ཆག་པ་དུམ་.

ཆག་ཕད་ (cāàbɛɛ̀) feed-bag (for horses, mules, etc.).

ཆག་ཕུར་ (cəgcur) animal feed, fodder.

ཆག་བུ་ (cəgbu) a small bunch.

ཆག་མེད་ (cāàmeè) without interruption/ break, without missing sth. ¶ ཁོང་གིས་ཞོགས་ལྷར་ལུས་རྩལ་ཆག་མེད་བྱེད་ཀྱི་ཡོད་པ་རེད་ He does exercise every morning without a miss.

ཆག་མོ་ (cāgmo) sm. ཆག་པོ་.

ཆག་བསྩལ་ (cāg dzɛ̄ɛ) shung. va. to grant a reduction of taxes.

ཆག་ཚག་ཀུ་བ་ (cāgdzaà gūwə) a kind of gourd/ calabash.

ཆག་ཚད་ (cāgdzɛɛ̀) sm. ཆག་ཚེ་.

ཆག་ཚེ་ (cāgdze) a thin/ watery broth or soup (without meat).

ཆག་འཛིང་ཉག་འཛིང་ (cəgdziŋ ṉ̃əgdziŋ) tangled or chaotic warfare/ fighting, chaotic hand-to-hand combat.

ཆག་གཞོང་ (cāgshoŋ) an animal feeding trough.

ཆག་བཞག (cāgshaà) certainly, decidedly.

ཆག་འོས་ (cāgwöò) shung. worthy of a reduction of taxes.

ཆག་ཡང་ (cāàyaŋ) concession, reduction; va.—གཏོང་; —གནང་ ¶ སྲིད་འཛིན་གསར་པས་ཁྲལ་མང་པོ་ཆག་ཡང་བཏང་བ་རེད་ The new president gave reductions on many taxes.

ཆག་ཡང་གཉིས་ (cāàyaŋ ñīì) the "two exemptions" policy of 1959 (exemptions from paying lease fees and high interest loans).

ཆག་རེས་ (cāgreè) stiffness, aches and pains (usu. from work/ exercise); vi.—རྒྱག to be/ get stiff; vi.—བསངས་ to have stiffness go away.

ཆག་རོ་ (cāgro) sm. ཆག་དུམ་.

ཆག་རོ་ལྷུ་འགྲིག (cāgro lhūndrig) putting broken pieces back together.

ཆག་ལམ་བྱུང་ (cāglamjaŋ) shung. a tax reduction that has become a custom.

ཆག་ཤིང་ (cəgshiŋ) flat pieces of wood used to set broken legs, etc., a splint.

ཆགས་ (cāà) vi. 1. to get attached to, to love, to like ¶ ཁོང་པ་ཡུལ་ལ་ཆགས་ནས་ཕྱི་རྒྱལ་སློབ་གྲྭར་འགྲོ་ཐུབ་མེད་པ་རེད་ Because he was attached to his homeland he was unable to go to school abroad. 2. vi. to become ¶ ཁོ་མི་ཡག་པོ་ཞིག་ཆགས་པའི་རེ་བ་ཡོད་ (I) have hopes he will become a good person. 3. vi. to be located, situated (in a place) ¶ གྲོང་ཁྱེར་དེ་གཙང་པོའི་བྱང་ངོས་ལ་ཆགས་ཡོད་པ་རེད་ The city is situated on the northern bank of the river ¶ འདིར་ཆགས་ཐབས་བྲལ་བ་བཟོས་པ་རེད་ It was made impossible for (him) to stay here.

ཆགས་རྐྱེན་ (cāggyen) origin, source, cause of ¶ ཁོང་གི་ནོར་འཁྲུལ་དེའི་ཆགས་རྐྱེན་གསལ་པོ་ཤེས་ཀྱི་མི་འདུག He doesn't know the cause of his mistake.

ཆགས་འཁྲི་ (cəgdri) sm. ཆག་ཞེན་.

ཆགས་གླ་ (cāgla) shung. a wage for collecting dung.

ཆགས་སྐྱོ་ (cāàgo) sm. ཆག་སྐྱོ་.

ཆགས་རྒྱག (cāà gy̱aà) 1. sm. ཆགས་འཆག. 2. va. to fold.

ཆགས་ཅན་ (cāgjɛn) lustful, sexual, licentious.

ཆགས་གཅོག (cāgjog) sm. ཆག་ས་རྒྱག, 1.

ཆགས་ཅན་མ་ (cāgjenma) a lustful, sexual woman.

ཆགས་འཆག (cāg cāà) va. to soak woolen cloth/ material in water and walk on it to soften it.

ཆགས་འཇིག (cāgjig) beginning or end, creation or destruction, existing or being destroyed; a dangerous time ¶ རང་གཞུང་ཆགས་འཇིག་གི་འགག་རྩའི་དུས་སུ་ཁོང་གིས་ཞབས་ཕྱི་ཞུས་པ་རེད་ He served the government at a critically dangerous time (regarding whether it will continue to exist or be destroyed).

ཆགས་འཇོམས་ (cāgjom) epithet of the Buddha.

ཆགས་ཉམས་ (cāgñam) 1. abbr. of. ཆགས་པའི་ཉམས་. 2. the look or mannerism indicating desiring sth.

ཆགས་སྙོལ་ (cāg ñōō) shung. va. to accumulate/ amass manure in a corral/ pen ¶ ཆགས་སྙོལ་དགོས་ཚུལ་བརྗོད་པ་ (They) said (we) must accumulate manure in the sheep pen.

ཆགས་གཏམ་ (cāgdam) ribald/ sexy talk; va.—ཤོད་ to talk ribald/ sexy.

ཆགས་རྟེན་ (cāgden) foundation/ base/ basis for living or earning a livelihood, a person in whom one places one's trust/ depends on ¶ ཨ་མེ་རི་ཀའི་ནང་སྡོད་པར་ཆགས་རྟེན་ཞིག་འཚོལ་དགོས་པ་རེད་ To live in America one has to search for a basis for making a livelihood.

ཆགས་རྟེན་བྲལ་བ་ (cāgden drɛɛwa) shung. sm. ཆགས་རྟེན་མེད་པ་.

ཆགས་རྟེན་མེད་པ་ (cāgden meèba) destitute, without a basis for making a living.

ཆགས་སྣངས་ (cāgdaŋ) 1. natural situation or characteristic of a place/ area ¶ ལུང་པ་འདིའི་ནང་ཤིང་ནགས་དང་ཆུ་སོགས་ཆགས་སྣངས་ཡག་པོ་འདུག The characteristics of that place are good with regards to forest, water, etc. 2. structure, composition ¶ ས་རྒྱུའི་ཆགས་སྣངས་ The composition of the soil.

ཆགས་ཐབས་བྲལ་བ་ (cāgdəb trɛɛwa) sm. ཆགས་ཐབས་མེད་པ་.

ཆགས་ཐབས་མེད་པ་ (cāgdəb meèba) impossible to stay/ live/ remain ¶ བུ་ལོན་ཆ་འདེད་བྱས་ཙང་ཆགས་ཐབས་མེད་པ་བཟོས་སོང་ Because (they) forcibly pursued the loan repayment, it was made impossible (for him) to remain (where he was).

ཆགས་ཐོགས་ (cāgdɔɔ̀) 1. mishaps/ accidents/ problems when traveling. 2. (with negative particles) articulate, eloquent ¶ སྐད་ཆ་ཆགས་ཐོགས་མེད་པ་ Eloquent speech. 3. (with neg. and "know") knowing clearly ¶ ཚང་མ་ཁོང་གིས་ཆགས་ཐོགས་མེད་པར་མཁྱེན་འདུག He knew the complete situation clearly.

ཆགས་ལྡན་མ་ (cāgdɛnma) sm. ཆགས་ཆེན་མ་.

ཆགས་སྡང་ (cāgdaŋ) 1. love and hatred ¶ ཁོང་ལ་ཆགས་སྡང་གི་བསམ་བློ་གསལ་པོ་ཞིག་ཡོད་པ་རེད་ He is sb. who knows who to love and who to hate. 2. jealousy; vi.—ལང་ to be/ get jealous.

ཆགས་སྡང་འཐེན་འཁྱེར་ (cāgdaŋ tēngyer) discriminating, showing bias.

ཆགས་སྡང་བྲལ་བ་ (cāgdaŋ trɛɛwa) sm. ཆགས་སྡང་མེད་པ་.

ཆགས་སྡང་མེད་པ་ (cāgdaŋ mɛɛba) sm. unbiased, without prejudice.

ཆགས་སྡང་རྨོངས་གསུམ་ (cāgdaŋ mōŋsum) abbr. love, hatred, ignorance.

ཆགས་གནས་འཇིག་སྟོངས་ (cāgnɛɛ̀ jigdoŋ) the origin, the existence, and the end of the world.

ཆགས་པ་ (cāgba) attachment, lust; vi.—ལང་ to have sexual lust; vi.—སྐྱེ་ to be attached to things; va.—སྤྱོད་ to have sexual intercourse.

ཆགས་པ་དང་བྲལ་བའི་དུས་ (cāgbadaŋ trɛ̄ɛwɛ tüü) the season when animals are not in heat.

ཆགས་པའི་བསྐལ་པ་ (cāgbɛ gālba) the eon when the world originally was formed.

ཆགས་པའི་ཉམས་ (cāgbɛ ñam) lustful look of sexual desire, sexy way of looking/ acting.

ཆགས་པའི་དུས་ (cāgbɛ tüü) the time of forming/ formation.

ཆགས་པའི་རྩ་ (cāgbɛ dzā) the beginning of life—the vein that first appears (according to Tibetan medicine).

ཆགས་སྤྱོད་ (cāgjöö) sexual intercourse, sex, love-making.

ཆགས་བབ་ (cāgbəb) physical characteristics/ conditions of a place (e.g., its weather, altitude) ¶ བོད་ཀྱི་ས་ཆའི་ཆགས་བབ་ The physical nature of Tibet's territory.

ཆགས་བྲལ་ (cāgdrɛɛ) 1. free from attachments/ lust. 2. epithet for the Buddha.

ཆགས་སྦྱོར་ (cāgjɔɔ) sm. ཆགས་སྤྱོད་.

ཆགས་དབྱིབས་ (cəgyib) sm. ཆགས་སྣངས་.

ཆགས་མེད་ (cāgmeè) sm. ཆགས་བྲལ་.

ཆགས་མེད་པ་ (cāgmeèba) sm. ཆགས་རྟེན་མེད་པ་.

ཆགས་རྩེད་ (cāgdzeè) sexual intercourse, love-making; va.—བྱེད་.

ཆགས་ཚིག (cəgdzig) lover's talk.

ཆགས་ཚུལ་ (cāgdzüü) 1. the origin or way sth. came into being ¶ གུང་ཁྲན་ཏང་གི་ཐོག་མའི་ཆགས་ཚུལ་ The origin of the communist party. 2. structure/ condition/ way/ that sth. is existing ¶ ཕྱུགས་ཁྱུའི་ཆགས་ཚུལ་ The structure of the herd of cattle.

ཆགས་འཚོ་ (cāgtso) primary means of livelihood; va.—བསམ་ to consider/ think about someone's livelihood ¶ དགོན་གནས་ཆགས་འཚོར་བསམ་རྩ་རིན་སྤྲོད་ལེན་བྱུང་རྗེས་ཁ་འཛིན་སྔར་འཇགས་བྱེད་ After considering the livelihood of the monastery, as long as they pay for grazing the animals they may keep the pastureland as before.

ཆགས་གཞི་ (cəgshi) cause of sth. ¶ དགོངས་ཚོམ་ཆགས་གཞི་ The cause of their anger.

ཆགས་ཞེན་ (cāgshen) attachment, desire ¶ རྒྱུ་ནོར་ལ་ཆགས་ཞེན་ཆེན་པོ་ Great attachment to wealth.

ཆགས་ཡུལ་ (cəgyüü) sm. ཆགས་ས་.

ཆགས་རབས་ (cəgrəb) history ¶ ཆགས་རབས་ཀྱི་གློག་བརྙན་ Historical film.

ཆགས་རིམ་ (cəgrim) structure, composition, layer ¶ སའི་ཆགས་རིམ་ The composition of the soil.

ཆགས་ལར་དགོངས་ (cāglar goŋ) shung. sm. ཆགས་འཚོར་བསམ་.

ཆགས་ལུགས་ (cəgluù) sm. ཆགས་སྣངས་.

ཆགས་ལུད་ (cāglüü) shung. manure accumulated in a sheep pen/ corral.

ཆགས་ས་ (cāgsa) 1. position, site, location ¶ ལུང་པ་འདི་ཆགས་ས་ཡག་པོ་ཞིག་ལ་ཆགས་འདུག This place is situated in a good location. 2. an object to which one is attached ¶ ངའི་ནང་གི་སེམས་ཆགས་ས་ལྡུམ་ར་དེ་ཡིན་ The garden is the place at home that I am most attached to.

ཆགས་ས་རྟེན་ས་ (cāgdensa) sm. ཆགས་རྟེན་.

ཆགས་སེམས་ (cāgsem) sm. ཆགས་ཞེན་.

ཆགས་སྲེད་ (cāgseè) lustful, licentious, sexual thoughts/ desires. 2. sm. ཆགས་ཞེན་.

ཆགས་སྲེད་ཅན་ (cāgseèjɛn) having sexual thoughts/ desires/ attachments.

ཆགས་སྲོལ་ (cāgsöö) system, structure.

ཆང་ (cāŋ) Tibetan traditional beer; va.—བཟོ་; —བཙོ་ to make beer.

ཆང་ཀྱི་ (cāŋgye) drunkard, inebriate, alcoholic.

ཆང་དཀར་ (cāŋgar) 1. porcelain cup for drinking beer/ liquor. 2. white liquor.

ཆང་རྐྱན་ (cāŋgyɛn) a kind of ཆང་ container that has a spout.

ཆང་རྐྱལ་ (cāŋgyɛɛ) sm. ཆང་ཀྱི་.

ཆང་སྐད་ (cāŋgɛɛ̀) drunk/ intoxicated talk.

ཆང་སྐལ་ (cāŋgɛɛ) one's share of chang.

ཆང་སྐོར་ (cāŋgɔɔ) a round of serving chang.

ཆང་སྐྱེམས་ (cāŋgyem) sm. ཆང་.

ཆང་སྐྱོགས་ (cāŋgyɔɔ̀) ladle for pouring ཆང་.

ཆང་བསྐོལ་ (cāŋgöö) a broth/ soup made of ཆང་ and tsampa.

ཆང་ཁ་འགོག (cāŋ kā gɔɔ̀) va. to seal a pot of fermented beer for a time in order to make it stronger.

ཆང་ཁང་ (cāŋgaŋ) bar, tavern.

ཆང་ཁང་སྦག་ཁང་ (cāŋgaŋ baàgaŋ) a bar that includes a mahjong parlor.

ཆང་ཁའི་སྦང་མ་ (cāŋgɛ baŋma) few/ small in quantity [Lit. fermented grain in the chang].

ཆང་ཁོག (cāŋgɔɔ̀) chang pot.

ཆང་ཁྲལ་ (cāŋdrɛɛ) shung. chang tax, tax charged on the sales of ཆང་.

ཆང་གར་མ་ (cāŋ karma) strong chang.

ཆང་གི་ཉིང་ཁུ་ (cāŋgi ñiŋgu) 1. the liquid from fermented beer before the water is added. 2. alcohol.

ཆང་གི་སྦང་མའི་ལུམས་ (cāŋgi baŋmɛ lum) the fermented barley grain before the water is added.

ཆང་གི་ཨོབ་རྐྱལ་ (cāŋgi ōbgyɛɛ) person who consumes a lot of beer/ alcoholic beverages.

ཆང་གིས་བཟི་ (cāŋgiì sii) vi. to be intoxicated/ drunk from beer.

ཆང་གྲོགས་ (cāŋdrɔɔ̀) drinking buddies.

ཆང་གྲོགས་པོའི་ཡིན་དུང་པོ་པ་རང་གིས་རེད་ (cāŋ

drogbö yinruŋ pōwa raŋgi reè) drinking too much is bad [Lit. although the chang is one's friend's, the stomach is one's own].

ཆང་འགག (cāŋgaà) the left-over fermented chang grain after the water has been drained.

ཆང་རྒན་ (cāŋgɛn) 1. aged chang. 2. person who likes to drink ཆང་ regularly.

ཆང་རྒོད་ (cāŋgöò) the first extraction of ཆང་ from the fermented grain.

ཆང་རྒྱུ་ (cāŋgyu) raw materials (grain) that are used to make ཆང་.

ཆང་ངི་ཅུང་ངི་ (cāŋŋi cūŋŋi) sm. ཆང་ངེ་ཅུང་ངེ་.

ཆང་ངེ་ཅུང་ངེ་ (cāŋŋe cūŋŋe) miscellaneous things, odds-and-ends.

ཆང་བཅུད་ (cāŋjüù) sm. ཆང་གི་ཉིང་ཁུ་.

ཆང་བཅུད་སྒྲོན་མེ་ (cāŋjüù drönme) alcohol lamp.

ཆང་ཅུང་ (cāŋjuŋ) abbr. for ཆང་ངེ་ཅུང་ངེ་.

ཆང་ཆེམས་ (cāŋjem) arc. bar, tavern.

ཆང་ཆེམས་ཅན་ (cāŋjemjɛn) drunk, intoxicated.

ཆང་མཆོད་ (cāŋjöò) 1. ཆང་ offering to deities. 2. va. to drink ཆང་ (h.).

ཆང་གཉིས་པ་ (cāŋ ñīìbə) the ཆང་ that results from the second addition of water to the fermented grain.

ཆང་རྙིང་ (cāŋñiŋ) old beer.

ཆང་སྙལ་ལས་ཚན་ (cāŋñɛɛ lɛ̀ɛdzɛn) chang-making workshop.

ཆང་སྙིགས་ (cāŋñig) the residue that forms at the bottom of a pot of ཆང་.

ཆང་སྙིགས་སྦང་མ་ (cāŋñig baŋma) the residue of fermented ཆང་ grain after all the liquid ཆང་ has been drained off.

ཆང་སྙོལ་ (cāŋ ñōō) va. to ferment grain (to make ཆང་).

ཆང་བསྙལ་ (cāŋ ñɛ̄ɛ) p. of ཆང་སྙོལ་.

ཆང་བསྙལ་ཁང་ (cāŋñɛɛgaŋ) room where ཆང་ is fermented.

ཆང་ལྡིར་ (cāŋdir) pot in which the grain for making ཆང་ is fermented.

ཆང་སྟོན་ (cāŋdön) cocktail party, reception at which chang/ alcohol is a main item served.

ཆང་ཐབ་ (cāŋdəb) stove for making chang.

ཆང་ཐུབ་ (cāŋdub) arc. sm. གང་ཟག.

ཆང་འཐུང་ (cāŋduŋ) 1. drinking ཆང་; va.—རྒྱག to have two or more people come together to drink ཆང་. 2. va. to drink ཆང་.

ཆང་འཐུང་གྲོགས་མཆེད་ (cāŋduŋ trɔgjeè) friends who come together to drink, drinking buddies.

ཆང་འཐུང་གཏམ་ལ་ཡིད་རྟོན་མེད་ (cāŋduŋ dāmla yiìdön meè) one can't trust the talk of drunkards.

ཆང་དད་ཅན་ (cāŋdɛɛ̀jɛn) an alcoholic, a person who likes to drink ཆང་.

ཆང་དད་ཆེ་བ་ (cāŋdɛɛ̀ cēwa) sm. ཆང་དད་ཅན་.

ཆང་དམ་ (cāŋdam) sm. ཆང་སྣོད་.

ཆང་དོ་ལོག (cāŋ tolɔɔ̀) the best ཆང་ (the ཆང་ made from taking the ཆང་ produced from the first addition of water and putting that back with the fermented grain and then re-extracting it).

ཆང་དོད་ (cāŋdöò) money given as a substitute for ཆང་ that is supposed to be given.

ཆང་དྲེགས་ (cāŋ treg) va. to be drunk/ intoxicated.

ཆང་འདན་ (cāŋdɛn) sm. ཆང་བསྙོལ་.

ཆང་ནད་ (cāŋnɛɛ̀) hangover from drinking chang.

ཆང་ནད་ཆང་སེལ་(cāŋnɛɛ̀ cāŋsel) drinking ཆང་ to cure a ཆང་ hangover.

ཆང་གནས་ (cāŋnɛɛ̀) sm. ཆང་ཁང་.

ཆང་སྣོད་ (cāŋnöò) a utensil/ vessel for keeping chang.

ཆང་པ་ (cāŋba) a habitual/ regular ཆང་. drinker.

ཆང་སྤགས་ (cāŋbaà) 1. kneaded tsamba made from adding ཆང་ to tsamba. 2. va.—ཟ་ to eat while drinking ཆང་.

ཆང་ཕབས་ (cāŋpəb) the yeast/ fermentation agent for making ཆང་.

ཆང་ཕུད་ (cāŋbüù) the first ཆང་ that is given as an offering to the gods.

ཆང་ཕོར་ (cāŋbɔɔ) a cup for drinking ཆང་.

ཆང་བུམ་ (cāŋbum) ཆང་ vessel/ bottle/ jug.

ཆང་བོགས་ (cāŋbɔɔ) shung. tax on making ཆང་ (for sale).

ཆང་འབྲས་ (cāŋdrɛɛ̀) ཆང་ made from rice, rice wine.

ཆང་འབྲུ་ (cāŋdru) barley for making ཆང་.

ཆང་མ་ (cāŋma) a woman who sells ཆང་.

ཆང་མའི་འགྲོལ་འཛིན་ (cāŋmɛ trōōndzin) shung. permission to sell ཆང་ during the Monlam Festival.

ཆང་མལ་ (cāŋmɛɛ) sm. ཆང་ཁང་.

ཆང་རྩི་ (cəŋdzi) sm. ཆང་ཕབས་.

ཆང་བཙོ་ (cāŋ dzō) va. to boil barley in preparation for making ཆང་.

ཆང་ཚགས་ (cāŋdzaà) the filter/ sifter used when pouring liquid ཆང་ from the fermentation pot.

ཆང་ཚང་ (cāŋdzaŋ) sm. ཆང་ཁང་.

ཆང་ཚོང་མ་ (cāŋdzoŋma) sm. ཆང་མ་.

ཆང་འཚག (cāŋ tsāà) va. to filter ཆང་ when the liquid is being poured from the pot holding the fermented grain.

ཆང་འཚག་བཟོ་གྲྭ (cāŋdzāà sodra) brewery, winery, distillery.

ཆང་འཚོང་ (cāŋ dzōŋ) va. to sell chang.

ཆང་ཛ་ (cāŋdza) a clay container/ pot for ཆང་.

ཆང་ཞིམ་ནར་སྨིན་པ་ (cāŋshim narjimbə) aged ཆང་ that is extremely strong.

ཆང་ཞུ་བ་ (cāŋshuwə) someone who serves beer.

ཆང་ཞུ་མ་ (cāŋshumə) sm. འཁྱུངས་ཞུ་མ་.

ཆང་གཞས་ (cāŋshɛɛ̀) songs sung when drinking ཆང་, drinking songs.

ཆང་ཟས་ (cāŋsɛɛ̀) food eaten with ཆང་.

ཆང་བཟི་ (cəŋsi) drunk, intoxicated.

ཆང་གཡོག (cəŋyɔɔ̀) a servant who works making ཆང་.

ཆང་ར་ (cāŋra) sm. ཆང་ཁང་.

ཆང་རག (cāŋraà) sm. ཆང་ཨ་རག.

ཆང་རག་ལང་ཤོར་བ་ནང་ཁུལ་སྦྱང་ཐབས་ཀྱི་རྒྱལ་སྤྱིའི་སྒྲིག་འཛུགས་ (cāŋraà laŋshɔɔwa nəŋgüü bāŋdəbgi gyɛɛji drigdzuù) sm. Alcoholics Anonymous.

ཆང་རིན་ (cəŋrin) 1. price of ཆང་. 2. tip, gratuity ¶ མི་དེས་གྲོགས་པོའི་གཡོག་པོ་ལ་ཆང་རིན་སྤྲད་པ་རེད་ That man tipped his friend's servant. 3. bribe for a lower level official or worker ¶ འགག་སྒོའི་ལས་བྱེད་པར་ཆང་རིན་སྤྲད་ནས་ཕྱིག་ཚོང་བརྒྱབ་པ་རེད་ He gave the custom officer a bribe and smuggled in the goods.

ཆང་ལངས་ (cāŋ laŋ) vi. to be/ get fermented (for the grain to which yeast has been added) ¶ ཉིན་མ་གཉིས་ནས་ཆང་ལང་གི་རེད་ After two days the grain for ཆང་ will be (correctly) fermented.

ཆང་ལན་གཅིག་མ་ (cāŋlɛn jīgmə) the first/ best ཆང་.

ཆང་ལན་ཆུས་འཇལ་ (cāŋlɛn cūnjɛɛ) a poor way of returning a favor, failing to reciprocate correctly [Lit. giving water in return for ཆང་].

ཆང་ལན་འདེགས་ (cāŋlɛn deg) va. to serve ཆང་ in return (after one is served).

ཆང་ས་ (cāŋsa) marriage, wedding; va.—རྒྱག to marry ¶ ཆང་སའི་རྟེན་འབྲེལ་ Marriage ceremony. ¶ ཁོང་གཉིས་ཆང་ས་རྒྱག་གི་རེད་ The two of them will get married.

ཆང་སའི་ལག་འཁྱེར་ (cāŋsɛ laggyee) marriage certificate.

ཆང་སིང་ (cəŋsiŋ) the third or fourth extraction of ཆང་ (that is very weak).

ཆང་སིངས་ (cəŋsiŋ) sm. ཆང་སིང་.

ཆང་སློང་ (cāŋ lōŋ) va. to unwrap the covered pot of fermenting grain in anticipation of adding water to draw off the ཆང་.

ཆང་ཨ་རག (cāŋ āraà) 1. beer and liquor. 2. alcoholic beverages.

ཆངས་པ་ (cāŋba) a kneaded ball of sth. (usu. tsampa or dough).

ཆངས་བུ་ (cāŋbu) a kneaded ball of sth. like flour/ tsamba.

ཆད་ (cɛ̀ɛ̀) 1. a shortage, deficit ། ཁང་གླའི་ཆད་ཟླ་བ་རྗེས་མར་སྤྲོད་དགོས་ The rent that is short has to be paid the next month. 2. penalty, fine ། ཕྱིས་དགས་ན་ཆད་ཡོད་པ་རེད་ If (you) are late there will be a penalty. 3. vi. to be short ། ཁོ་ལ་སྤྲོད་ཡག་པད་ཤག་ ༢༠ ཆད་སོང་ (I) was short 20 cents (when I was going to pay him). 4. vi. to be cut off, to be broken off ། ཁོ་ཚོའི་འབྲེལ་བ་ཆད་ནས་ཡུན་རིང་ཕྱིན་པ་རེད་ It has been a long time since their relations were broken off. ། ཐག་པ་ཆད་ནས་ཁོ་ཟགས་པ་རེད་ The rope broke and he fell. 5. vi. to run out of ། ཁོ་ཚོ་དམག་རྒྱུགས་ཆད་ནས་ཕྱིར་འཐེན་བྱེད་དགོས་བྱུང་བ་རེད་ Because they ran out of military supplies they had to retreat. 6. vi. to lose a tradition ། ཟློས་གར་དེའི་འཁྲིད་རྒྱུན་ཆད་ནས་ལོ་མང་པོ་ཕྱིན་པ་རེད་ It has been many years since the tradition of teaching that drama has been lost. 7. (ཁ་+ — + བཟོ་) va. to make an appointment/ rendezvous ། ང་གཉིས་སང་ཉིན་འཛོམས་རྒྱུའི་ཁ་ཆད་བཟོས་པ་ཡིན་ We made an appointment to meet tomorrow. 8. vi. to be or get tired/ exhausted ། ལས་ཀའི་ཆུ་ཚོད་མང་དགས་ན་མི་ཆད་ཀྱི་རེད་ If one works too many hours, one will get tired.

ཆད་ཀ་ (cɛ̀ɛ̀ga) sm. ཆད་.

ཆད་སྐོང་ (cɛ̀ɛ̀goŋ) sm. ཆད་གྲངས་ཁ་སྐོང་.

ཆད་སྐྱོན་ (cɛ̀ɛ̀gyön) the mistake of missing/ overlooking sth.

ཆད་ཁོངས་ (cɛ̀ɛ̀goŋ) that which has not been paid or is short/ in deficit ། ཁང་གླ་ཆད་ཁོངས་ལ་དེ་རིང་ངས་སྒོར་ལྔ་བཅུ་སྤྲད་པ་ཡིན་ I gave 50 dollars on the amount I am short on the rent.

ཆད་གྲངས་ (cɛ̀ɛ̀draŋ) 1. deficit, shortage; va.— གསབ་ to make up a deficit/ shortage ། ཁང་གླའི་ཆད་གྲངས་གསབ་དགོས་ You must make up the rent deficit/ shortage. 2. negative quantity (in math).

ཆད་གྲངས་ཁ་སྐོང་ (cɛ̀ɛ̀draŋ kāgoŋ) making up a deficit/ shortage; va.—བྱེད་.

ཆད་གྲངས་མཉམ་པའི་རིམ་གྲངས་ (cɛ̀ɛ̀draŋ ñambɛ rimdraŋ) a progression (in math).

ཆད་གྲུས་ (cɛ̀ɛ̀drɛ̀ɛ̀) shung. things in arrears.

ཆད་འགེལ་ (cɛ̀ɛ̀ gee) va. to fine, to give a penalty ། མོ་ཊ་མགྱོགས་ཚད་ལས་བརྒལ་བ་བཏང་བར་བརྟེན་ཆད་བཀལ་བ་རེད་ They (fined) him for driving over the speed limit.

ཆད་འགེལ་ཉེས་སེལ་ (cɛ̀ɛ̀gɛɛ ñèèsel) clearing up a crime/ mistake by paying a fine; va.—བྱེད་.

ཆད་འགྱངས་ལེ་འགོན་ (cɛ̀ɛ̀gyaŋ legön) having problems paying back a loan and postponing it.

ཆད་བཅད་བསླབ་འདོམས་ (cɛ̀ɛ̀jɛ̀ɛ̀ ləbdom) punishing/ fining sb. to teach him a lesson.

ཆད་གཅོད་ (cɛ̀ɛ̀jöö) punishment; va.—བྱེད་ to punish. ། ཀུ་མར་ཆད་གཅོད་བྱས་པ་རེད་ They punished the thief. 2. sm. ཆད་.

ཆད་ཆད་མཐུད་མཐུད་ (cɛ̀ɛ̀jɛ̀ɛ̀ tüüdüü) not constant, stopping and starting, not continuous; va.—བྱེད་ [Lit. cutting off and rejoining].

ཆད་ཉམས་ (cɛ̀ɛ̀ñam) 1. tired, down and dejected. 2. abbr. missing/ short and deteriorated.

ཆད་རྟགས་ (cɛ̀ɛ̀daà) 1. dash (the punctuation mark indicating sth. missing).

ཆད་ལྟ་ (cɛ̀ɛ̀da) negative attitude/ viewpoint that doesn't accept the law of karma, nihilistic view.

ཆད་སྟོང་ (cɛ̀ɛ̀doŋ) vacancy.

ཆད་ཐོ་ (cɛ̀ɛ̀do) list/ record of what is missing or short or absent.

ཆད་མཐའ་ (cɛ̀ɛ̀da) a nihilistic viewpoint.

ཆད་མཐུད་ (cɛ̀ɛ̀düü) 1. making up a shortage/ deficit; va.—བྱེད་ ། ལམ་ཀ་ཆད་མཐུད་བྱས་ཟིན་འདུག They finished rejoining the road. ། ནང་ནས་དངུལ་འབྱོར་དེ་ངའི་འགྲོ་སོང་ཆད་མཐུད་བྱེད་ཐུབ་སོང་ (I) received money from home and was able to make up a deficit in my expenses. 2. joining sth. that has been cut.

ཆད་མཐུད་ཡོ་བསྒྲངས་ (cɛ̀ɛ̀düü yosaŋ) sm. ཆད་མཐུད་.

ཆད་དུས་ (cɛ̀ɛ̀düü) prison term; va.—གཙང་ to complete one's prison term.

ཆད་དོན་ (cɛ̀ɛ̀dön) 1. promise, agreement; va.—བྱེད་. 2. an appointment.

ཆད་མདོ་ (cɛ̀ɛ̀do) sm. ཆད་དོན་.

ཆད་པ་ (cɛ̀ɛ̀ba) punishment, penalty, sentence, fine; va.—གཅོད་; —གཏོང་ to punish, to fine, to sentence ། ཁོ་ལོ་ཉི་ཤུ་བཙོན་དུ་སྡོད་དགོས་པའི་ཆད་པ་བཅད་པ་རེད་ (They) gave him a sentence of twenty years in prison.

ཆད་པ་ཆད་ལན་ (cɛ̀ɛ̀ba cɛ̀ɛ̀lɛn) paying back loans or taxes or debts that were short/ in deficit; va.— སྤྲད་; —འཇལ་ to pay back loans/ taxes/ debts that were in deficit.

ཆད་པའི་ཁྲིམས་ (cɛ̀ɛ̀bɛ trim) criminal code.

ཆད་པའི་གནས་ (cɛ̀ɛ̀bɛ nɛ̀ɛ̀) 1. court. 2. criminal, law-breaker.

ཆད་པའི་མྱང་འདས་ (cɛ̀ɛ̀bɛ ñaŋdɛ̀ɛ̀) Hinayana school of Buddhism.

ཆད་པོ་ (cɛ̀ɛ̀bo) cut, severed.

ཆད་འཕྲོ་ (cɛ̀ɛ̀ trō) balance left, amount overdue, amount left/ missing (e.g., on a loan).

ཆད་འབབས་ (cɛ̀mbəb) shung. the amount of sth. in arrears ། སྔོན་སོ་སོའི་ཆད་འབབས་རྣམས་ In the future one must pay the amount in arrears.

ཆད་འབུལ་ (cɛ̀ɛ̀mbüü) paying what is owed or short; va.—བྱེད་.

ཆད་འབོར་ (cɛ̀mbɔɔ) a missing amount, an amount that is short or in deficit.

ཆད་མེད་ (cɛ̀ɛ̀meè) without skipping some part of a sequence, without leaving anything missing or in arrears ། ཉིན་ལྟར་ཆད་མེད་ Everyday without fail.

ཆད་མེད་གཙང་སྒྲིལ་ (cɛ̀ɛ̀meè dzāŋdrii) shung. paid in full without leaving any amount in arrears.

ཆད་མོལ་ཡི་གེ་ (cɛ̀ɛ̀möö yigi) letter of agreement.

ཆད་འཛར་ (cɛ̀ɛ̀dzar) balance, left-over (usu. with regard to loans/ payments).

ཆད་འཛིན་ (cɛ̀ɛ̀dzin) an IOU.

ཆད་ཚབ་རང་སྒྲིག་ (cɛ̀ɛ̀dzəb rəndrig) making up losses/ deficits/ shortages oneself.

ཆད་ཡིག་ (cɛ̀ɛ̀yig) a written agreement/ contract.

ཆད་ལས་ (cɛ̀ɛ̀lɛɛ̀) punishment, fine; va.—འགེལ་ to impose a fine/ punishment.

ཆད་ལས་ར་བ་ (cɛ̀ɛ̀lɛɛ̀ rawa) a place where sentences/ judgements are issued, a court.

ཆད་ལུས་ (cɛ̀ɛ̀lüü) an omission; vi.—ཤོར་ to inadvertently omit/ leave out ། ང་གཉིས་པར་གྱི་རྩིས་ལ་ཆད་ལུས་མེད་ We did not have any omissions in our accounts.

ཆད་ལུས་མེད་པ་ (cɛ̀ɛ̀lüü meèba) in full, complete, without omissions.

ཆད་སོ་ (cɛ̀ɛ̀so) sm. ཆད་དོན་.

ཆད་གསབ་ (cɛ̀ɛ̀səb) making up a deficiency, supplementing to make up loss/ omission; va.— རྒྱག; —བྱེད ། ངས་ཉི་མ་གཉིས་ཀྱི་ལས་ཀ་ཆད་གསབ་བྱས་པ་ཡིན་ I made up two days work.

ཆད་གསབ་སྐྱོན་བཅོས་ (cɛ̀ɛ̀səb gyōnjöö) (in editing) adding/ supplementing where things are missing and also correcting where there are mistakes.

ཆད་གསོ་ (cɛ̀ɛ̀so) sm. ཆད་གསབ་.

ཆད་གསོར་ (cɛ̀ɛ̀sor) replacing a person or animal when it is tired; va.—བྱེད་.

ཆད་ལྷག (cɛ̀ɛ̀lhaà) shortage and surplus, deficit and surplus, extra or missing, adding or omitting; va.—འཇལ་ ། ངས་ཕུལ་བའི་དངུལ་དེ་ལ་ཆད་ལྷག་ཡོད་མེད་གཟིགས་རོགས་གནང་ Please see that if there are any shortages or extras in the money I gave you. ། ཕྲུ་གུ་འདིས་ཡི་གེ་ཆད་ལྷག་མང་པོ་གཏོང་གི་འདུག That child's writing adds and omits many words and letters. 3. sm. ཆད་འཛར་.

ཆད་ལྷག་སྙོམ་སྒྲིག (cɛ̀ɛ̀lhaà ñōmdrig) making sth. even or balancing it by adding or omitting sth.

ཆད་ལྷག་མཉམ་སྙར་ (cɛ̀ɛ̀lhaà ñāmjar) sm. ཆད་ལྷག་སྙོམ་སྒྲིག.

ཆད་ལྷག་མེད་པའི་ལོ་ (cɛ̄ɛ̀lhaà me̱èbɛ lo̱) a year with neither extra nor missing months.

ཆན་ (cɛ̄n) 1. mash, pulp ¶འབྲས་ཆན་ Rice mash. 2. ch. qian (1/10 སྲང་).

ཆན་གྲི་ (cɛ̄ndri) knife used in leather work.

ཆན་ཐང་ (cɛ̄ndaŋ) Chientang River.

ཆན་ཐུག་ (cɛ̄nduù) stew/ broth made from boiling wheat or barley or rice.

ཆན་པ་ (cɛ̄mba) 1. sm. ཆན་གྲི་. 2. a surgical knife.

ཆན་ཝ་ (cɛ̄nwa) ch. kilowatt.

ཆན་ལུང་གོང་མ་ (cɛ̄nluŋ ko̱ŋma) the Qianlong Emperor of China's Qing Dynasty.

ཆབ་ (cə̄b) 1. water (h.); va.—སྐོལ་ to boil water. 2. abbr. of ཆབ་གསང་.

ཆབ་རྒྱན་ (cə̄bgyɛn) water jug/ pitcher (h.).

ཆབ་ཁང་ (cə̄bgaŋ) 1. room/ house for bathing (h.). 2. toilet. 3. a place for boiling water (h.).

ཆབ་ཁུང་ (cə̄bguŋ) 1. sewer/ drain/ canal for water. 2. urethra.

ཆབ་ཁོལ་ (cə̄bgöö) boiled water (h.).

ཆབ་ཁྲོ་ (cə̄bdro) a cast iron pot for boiling water.

ཆབ་འཁོལ་ (cə̄bgöö) sm. ཆབ་ཁོལ་.

ཆབ་འཁོལ་མ་ (cə̄bgööma) sm. ཆབ་ཁོལ་.

ཆབ་གྲོས་ (cə̄bdröö) abbr. of ཆབ་སྲིད་གྲོས་ཚོགས་.

ཆབ་འགོ་ (cə̄bgo) belt buckle.

ཆབ་བཀྲལ་གནང་ (cə̄bgɛɛ nāŋ) va. to bathe, to take a shower (h.).

ཆབ་རྒྱུན་ (cə̄bgyün) sm. ཆུ་རྒྱུན་.

ཆབ་སྒོ་ (cə̄bgo) door (of a house).

ཆབ་སྒོ་བ་ (cə̄bgowa) sm. སྒོ་སྲུང་བ་.

ཆབ་སྒྲོག་ (cə̄bdroò) sm. ཆབ་ཙེ་.

ཆབ་སྒྲོམ་ (cə̄bdrom) a seat (frame) that goes over a bedpan.

ཆབ་ལྕེ་ (cə̄bje) sm. ཆབ་འགོ་.

ཆབ་གཅིན་མ་འཁྱིལ་ (cə̄bjin ma̱kyöö) not able to defecate or urinate on one's own.

ཆབ་བཅུ་གསུམ་ (cə̄bju sūm) sm. ཆབ་ཆབ་བཅུ་གསུམ་.

ཆབ་ཆབ་ (cə̄bjəb) mediocre, not very good.

ཆབ་ཆབ་བཅུ་གསུམ་ (cə̄bjəb cōgsum) person who knows a little about a lot but nothing well, a jack-of-all-trades and master of none.

ཆབ་ཆབ་བཅོ་བརྒྱད་ (cə̄bjen jōbgɛɛ̀) sm. ཆབ་ཆབ་བཅུ་གསུམ་.

ཆབ་ཆེན་ (cə̄bjen) excrement, stool (h.); va.—གནང་ to defecate; vi.—འགག to be constipated.

ཆབ་ཆོབ་ (cə̄bjob) sm. ཆ་པེ་ཆོ་པེ་.

ཆབ་དོག་ (cə̄bdɔɔ̀) bedpan.

ཆབ་གཏོར་ (cə̄bdɔɔ) torma offered with water.

ཆབ་གཏོར་ (cə̄b dɔ̄ɔ) va. to sprinkle blessed water (done by lamas).

ཆབ་རྟགས་ (cə̄bdaà) urine specimen.

ཆབ་སྟན་ (cə̄bdɛn) diaper.

ཆབ་སྟོད་ (cə̄bdöö) upper garment of monk officials.

ཆབ་དྲེལ་ (cə̄bdree) mules that carry water (usu. refers to those that carry water for the Dalai Lama's kitchen).

ཆབ་གདན་ (cə̄bdɛn) diaper, cloth used for babies as a diaper.

ཆབ་མདོ་ (cāmdo) Chamdo.

ཆབ་མདོ་མངའ་ཁུལ་ (cāmdo ŋəgüü) an area that is part of Chamdo.

ཆབ་མདོ་བ་ (cāmdowa) person from Chamdo.

ཆབ་འདྲེན་གཞོན་ནུ་ (cə̄mdren sho̱nnu) herbal medicine for dropsy.

ཆབ་གནང་ (cə̄b nāŋ) 1. va. to bathe, to shower (h.). 2. to drink water (h.).

ཆབ་སྣོད་ (cə̄bnöö) a water vessel (h.).

ཆབ་པེ་ཆོབ་པེ་ (cə̄be cōbe) sm. ཆབ་པེ་ཆབ་པེ་.

ཆབ་བུམ་རིལ་བ་ (cə̄bbum ri̱iwə) sm. ཆབ་བླུག.

ཆབ་འབངས་ (cə̄bbaŋ) subjects (political) ¶དབྱིན་ཇིའི་ཆབ་འབངས་ Subjects of the British.

ཆབ་བླུག་ (cə̄bluù) stylized (empty) water bottle carried by monk officials.

ཆབ་འབྱིན་སྨན་ (cə̄bjin mɛ̄n) medicine to enable one to pass urine.

ཆབ་མ་ (cə̄bma) ornamented belt/ buckle.

ཆབ་མིག་ (cə̄bmig) h. of ཆུ་མིག.

ཆབ་བཙོས་ (cə̄bjöö) h. of ཆུ་བཙོས་.

ཆབ་ཙམ་ (cə̄bdzam) a bit.

ཆབ་ཙེ་ (cə̄bdze) belt buckle; va.—རྒྱག to buckle a belt.

ཆབ་ཚོད་བཟོ་གྲྭ་ (cə̄bdzöö so̱dra) water meter factory.

ཆབ་རྫིང་ (cə̄bdziŋ) swimming pool/ pond (h.).

ཆབ་ཞབས་ (cə̄bshəb) shung. citizen.

ཆབ་ཤུགས་ (cə̄bshuù) 1. shung. week-long picnic (usu. for monks and monk officials) in summer (the 8th Tibetan month). 2. bathing.

ཆབ་ཞོ་ (cə̄bsho) milk (h.).

ཆབ་ཞོ་གནང་ (cə̄bsho nāŋ) 1. va. to drink milk. 2. va. to breastfeed (h.).

ཆབ་གཞོང་ (cə̄bshoŋ) bathtub (h.).

ཆབ་བཞེས་ (cə̄b she̱e) 1. va. to drink water (h.). 2. va. to get water (h.). 3. va. to take a bath (h.).

ཆབ་གཟན་ (cə̄bsɛn) shung. a shawl worn by the monk officials of tt. government with brocade or satin lining on the hems.

ཆབ་འོག་ (cə̄bwɔɔ̀) under the power/ domain/ sovereignty of, subject or vassal to ¶བོད་རྒྱལ་ཁབ་ཀྱི་ཆབ་འོག་ཡུལ་ཚོ་ Places under the power of the Tibetan nation.

ཆབ་འོག་འཁོར་འབངས་ (cə̄bwɔɔ̀ kɔ̄ɔbaŋ) sm. ཆབ་འབངས་.

ཆབ་འོག་ཏུ་འཇུག་ (cə̄bwɔɔ̀du ju̱ù) va. to put someone under one's power/ domain.

ཆབ་འོག་པ་ (cə̄bwɔɔ̀gba) shung. citizen.

ཆབ་ཡིག་ (cə̄byiì) shung. letters or documents issued by authorities to lower offices or departments.

ཆབ་གཡོག་ (cə̄byɔɔ̀) monks who do menial tasks in monasteries such as working in the kitchen, carrying water.

ཆབ་རིལ་ (cə̄brii) 1. water bottle (h.). 2. shung. monastic college official.

ཆབ་རོམ་ (cə̄brom) glacial ice.

ཆབ་ལ་རོལ་ (cə̄blə rö̱ö) va. to go swimming, to take a bath.

ཆབ་ལོང་ (cə̄bloŋ) belt buckle.

ཆབ་ཤུབས་ (cə̄bshuù) covering for ཆབ་བླུག.

ཆབ་ཤོག་ (cə̄bshɔɔ̀) 1. official letter, notice. 2. toilet paper (h.).

ཆབ་སྲིད་ (cə̄bsiì) politics, political, rule, governing; va.—སྐྱོང་ to rule, to govern, to administrate (countries/ governments) ¶ཆབ་སྲིད་ཀྱི་ཁེ་དབང་ Political rights. ¶ཚོགས་པ་དེས་ཆབ་སྲིད་ལོ་མང་བསྐྱངས་ཡོད་པ་རེད་ That party has ruled for many years.

ཆབ་སྲིད་ཀྱི་ཁྲིག་གཡོ་ (cə̄bsiìgi gɔ̄gyo) political conspiracy.

ཆབ་སྲིད་ཀྱི་ཁྲིག་གསོམ་ (cə̄bsiìgi gɔ̄gshom) sm. ཆབ་སྲིད་ཀྱི་ཁྲིག་གཡོ་.

ཆབ་སྲིད་ཀྱི་ཁེ་དབང་ (cə̄bsiìgi kēwaŋ) political rights.

ཆབ་སྲིད་ཀྱི་གོ་རྟོགས་ (cə̄bsiìgi ko̱dɔɔ̀) political consciousness/ awareness/ understanding.

ཆབ་སྲིད་ཀྱི་གོ་གནས་ (cə̄bsiìgi ko̱nɛɛ̀) political position.

ཆབ་སྲིད་ཀྱི་འགོ་ཁྲིད་ (cə̄bsiìgi gu̱driì) political leader.

ཆབ་སྲིད་ཀྱི་འགོ་ཁྲིད་ཉུང་ཤས་ (cə̄bsiìgi gu̱driì ñu̱ŋshɛɛ̀) oligarchy.

ཆབ་སྲིད་ཀྱི་ངོ་བོ་ (cə̄bsiìgi ŋo̱wa) political nature.

ཆབ་སྲིད་ཀྱི་ཉེན་གཡོལ་ (cə̄bsiìgi ñe̱nyöö) political asylum; va.—བྱེད་ to seek political asylum.

ཆབ་སྲིད་ཀྱི་ཉེས་ཅན་ (cə̄bsiìgi ñe̱èjɛn) sm. ཆབ་སྲིད་ཀྱི་ཉེས་མེད་ཤོག་མཁན་.

ཆབ་སྲིད་ཀྱི་ཉེས་མེད་ཤོག་མཁན་ (cə̄bsiìgi ñe̱èmiŋ pɔ̄ɔgɛn) political offender/ prisoner.

ཆབ་སྲིད་ཀྱི་གཉའ་གནོན་ (cə̄bsiìgi ña̱nön) political oppression/ suppression.

ཆབ་སྲིད་ཀྱི་རྟོགས་པ་ (cə̄bsiìgi dɔ̄gba) sm. ཆབ་སྲིད་ཀྱི་གོ་རྟོགས་.

ཆབ་སྲིད་ཀྱི་ལྟ་བ་ (cə̄bsiìgi dāwa) political view/ philosophy.

ཆབ་སྲིད་ཀྱི་ལྟ་ཚུལ་ (cəbsiìgi dədzüü) political viewpoint.

ཆབ་སྲིད་ཀྱི་སྟོབས་ཤུགས་ (cəbsiìgi dōbshuù) political power/ force.

ཆབ་སྲིད་ཀྱི་ཐོབ་ཐང་ (cəbsiìgi tōbdaŋ) political rights.

ཆབ་སྲིད་ཀྱི་འཐབ་རྩོད་ (cəbsiìgi təbdzöö) political struggle.

ཆབ་སྲིད་ཀྱི་དད་མོས་ (cəbsiìgi tɛ̱ɛ̀möö) political conviction/ belief.

ཆབ་སྲིད་ཀྱི་གདོང་རིལ་ (cəbsiìgi doŋrii) sm. ཆབ་སྲིད་ཀྱི་རྣམ་པ་.

ཆབ་སྲིད་ཀྱི་དོན་སྙིང་ (cəbsiìgi tö̱nñiŋ) political significance/ meaning.

ཆབ་སྲིད་ཀྱི་གནས་ཚུལ་ (cəbsiìgi nɛ̄ɛ̀dzüü) political situation/ condition/ scene.

ཆབ་སྲིད་ཀྱི་རྣམ་འགྱུར་ (cəbsiìgi nəmgyur) political attitude.

ཆབ་སྲིད་ཀྱི་རྣམ་པ་ (cəbsiìgi nāmba) political affiliation or background.

ཆབ་སྲིད་ཀྱི་སྤྱོད་ཚུལ་ (cəbsiìgi jö̀ödzüü) political behavior/ way of acting.

ཆབ་སྲིད་ཀྱི་བྱ་བ་ (cəbsiìgi c̱awa) political work/ activity/ affairs.

ཆབ་སྲིད་ཀྱི་དམག་འཐབ་ (cəbsiìgi məgdəb) political battle/ war.

ཆབ་སྲིད་ཀྱི་ཇ་བ་ (cəbsiìgi dzāwa) sm. ཆབ་སྲིད་ཀྱི་ཇ་འཛིན་.

ཆབ་སྲིད་ཀྱི་ཇ་འཛིན་ (cəbsiìgi dzəndzin) political platform/ program.

ཆབ་སྲིད་ཀྱི་ཚོར་སྣང་ (cəbsiìgi tsōrnaŋ) political sense (ability to perceive the political nature of things).

ཆབ་སྲིད་ཀྱི་འཚོ་བ་ (cəbsiìgi tsōwa) political life.

ཆབ་སྲིད་ཀྱི་རང་རྟགས་ (cəbsiìgi ra̱ŋdaà) political nature/ character.

ཆབ་སྲིད་ཀྱི་རང་བཞིན་ (cəbsiìgi rəŋshin) political nature/ sense.

ཆབ་སྲིད་ཀྱི་རིག་པ་ (cəbsiìgi ri̱gbə) political science, politics.

ཆབ་སྲིད་ཀྱི་རོགས་པ་ (cəbsiìgi ro̱gba) political assistant/ helper.

ཆབ་སྲིད་ཀྱི་ལམ་ཕྱོགས་ (cəbsiìgi la̱mjɔɔ̀) political line/ direction/ course.

ཆབ་སྲིད་ཀྱི་ལམ་ལུགས་ (cəbsiìgi la̱mluù) political system.

ཆབ་སྲིད་ཀྱི་ལས་འགན་ (cəbsiìgi lɛ̱ngɛn) political duty/ task/ responsibility.

ཆབ་སྲིད་ཀྱི་ལས་འགུལ་ (cəbsiìgi lɛ̱ngüü) political campaign/ movement.

ཆབ་སྲིད་ཀྱི་ལས་དོན་ (cəbsiìgi lɛ̱ɛ̀dön) sm. ཆབ་སྲིད་ཀྱི་བྱ་བ་.

ཆབ་སྲིད་ཀྱི་ལས་དོན་ཚོགས་ཆུང་ (cəbsiìgi lɛ̱ɛ̀dön tsōgjuŋ) political action committee (U.S.A.).

ཆབ་སྲིད་ཀྱི་སློབ་སྟོན་པ་ (cəbsiìgi lōbdömba) political instructor (of a Peoples Liberation Army unit).

ཆབ་སྲིད་ཀྱི་ཤུགས་རྐྱེན་ (cəbsiìgi shūggyen) political influence/ effect.

ཆབ་སྲིད་ཀྱི་བསམ་པ་ (cəbsiìgi sāmba) political thought.

ཆབ་སྲིད་ཀྱི་བསམ་བློ་ (cəbsiìgi sāmlo) political thought.

ཆབ་སྲིད་ཀྱིས་དམག་སྤྱི་ (cəbsiìgi məgji) putting politics in command, making politics the commander-in-chief; va.—བྱེད་.

ཆབ་སྲིད་སྐྱིང་ (cəbsii gyīŋ) see ཆབ་སྲིད་.

ཆབ་སྲིད་སྐྱོང་ (cəbsii gyöŋ) va. to rule, to govern.

ཆབ་སྲིད་བསྐྱངས་ (cəbsii gyāŋ) p. of ཆབ་སྲིད་སྐྱོང་.

ཆབ་སྲིད་མཁས་ཅན་ (cəbsii kɛ̄ɛ̀jɛn) sm. ཆབ་སྲིད་མཁས་པ་.

ཆབ་སྲིད་མཁས་པ་ (cəbsii kɛ̄ɛ̀ba) political expert, politician.

ཆབ་སྲིད་ཁྲིད་སྟོན་པ་ (cəbsii triìdömba) political instructor (of a People's Liberation Army unit).

ཆབ་སྲིད་གྲོས་མཐུན་ཚོགས་འདུ་ (cəbsii trö̱ödün tsōŋdu) Political Consultative Congress/ Conference.

ཆབ་སྲིད་གྲོས་མོལ་ (cəbsii trö̱ömöö) political discussion/ consultation.

ཆབ་སྲིད་གྲོས་མོལ་ཨུ་ཡོན་ལྷན་ཁང་ (cəbsii trö̱ömöö ūyün lhēngaŋ) Political Consultative Congress/ Conference.

ཆབ་སྲིད་གྲོས་མོལ་ཚོགས་འདུ་ (cəbsii trö̱ömöö tsōŋdu) Political Consultative Congress/ Conference.

ཆབ་སྲིད་གྲོས་ཚོགས་ (cəbsii trö̱ödzɔɔ̀) Political Consultative Congress/ Conference.

ཆབ་སྲིད་གྲོས་ཚོགས་ཀྱི་ལོ་རྒྱུས་ཚོགས་ཆུང་ (cəbsii trö̱ödzɔɔ̀gi lu̱gyüü tsōgjuŋ) history sub-committee of the Political Consultative Conference.

ཆོས་སྲིད་གཉིས་ལྡན་ (cəbsii ñīndɛn) (involving, including, comprising) both religion and politics.

ཆབ་སྲིད་ཅུས་ (cəbsii jüü) tib.ch. political bureau.

ཆབ་སྲིད་སྟོབས་ཤུགས་ཀྱི་ཕྱོགས་ཁག (cəbsii dōbshuùgi cɔɔ̀gaà) political forces/ cliques.

ཆབ་སྲིད་ཐང་ཀྱི་ལོ་རྒྱུས་ (cəbsii tɛ̄ɛ̀gi lu̱gyüü) political history.

ཆབ་སྲིད་འཐབ་ཕྱོགས་ (cəbsii təbjɔɔ̀) political front.

ཆབ་སྲིད་དྭངས་གཙང་ (cəbsii ta̱ŋdzaŋ) politics without corruption.

ཆབ་སྲིད་པ་ (cəbsiìbə) statesman, politician.

ཆབ་སྲིད་པུའུ་ (cəbsiìbu) tib.ch. political department.

ཆབ་སྲིད་དཔལ་འབྱོར་ (cəbsii ba̱njɔɔ) political economy.

ཆབ་སྲིད་དཔལ་འབྱོར་གྱི་རིག་པ་ (cəbsii ba̱njɔɔgi ri̱gbə) study/ field/ science of political economy.

ཆབ་སྲིད་བྱ་བ་ (cəbsii c̱awa) political activity/ work/ affairs.

ཆབ་སྲིད་སྦྱོང་བརྡར་ (cəbsii jo̱ŋdar) political training.

ཆབ་སྲིད་ཇ་འཛིན་ (cəbsii dzəndzin) political platform.

ཆབ་སྲིད་རྩོད་ཡ་ (cəbsii dzö̀öya) political rival/ opponent.

ཆམ་སྲིད་འཚོ་བ་ (cəbsii tsōwa) sm. ཆབ་སྲིད་ཀྱི་འཚོ་བ་.

ཆབ་སྲིད་རིག་པ་ (cəbsii ri̱gbə) political science.

ཆབ་སྲིད་ལས་འགུལ་ (cəbsii lɛ̱ngüü) political campaign/ movement.

ཆབ་སྲིད་ལས་འདས་པ་ (cəbsiìlɛ dɛ̱ɛ̀ba) beyond politics ॥ཆབ་སྲིད་ལས་འདས་པའི་གནད་དོན་ An issue that is beyond politics.

ཆབ་སྲིད་ལས་རོགས་པ་ (cəbsii lɛ̱ɛ̀rogba) political assistant.

ཆབ་སྲིད་སློབ་སྦྱོང་ (cəbsii lōbjoŋ) 1. political study. 2. the political study sessions held in Tibet in state offices usually one afternoon a week.

ཆབ་སྲིད་ལོ་རྒྱུས་ (cəbsii lu̱gyüü) political history, politics ॥ཆབ་སྲིད་ལོ་རྒྱུས་ཚན་པ་ Department of political history.

ཆབ་སྲིད་བསམ་བློ་ (cəbsii sāmlo) political thought.

ཆབ་སྲིད་ཨུ་ཡོན་ (cəbsii ūyöö) tib.ch. political commissar (of a People's Liberation Army unit).

ཆབ་གསང་ (cābsaŋ) urine (h.); va.—གནང་/ —བྱེད་ to urinate; va.—ཕེབས་/ —འགྲོ་ to go to the toilet, to go to urinate; vi.—སྡོ་to have an urge to urinate.

ཆབ་གསང་རྒྱུས་འདུས་ (cābsaŋ gyɛ̱ndüü) urine and stool.

ཆབ་གསང་འབབ་བདེ་ (cābsaŋ ba̱bde) diuresis.

ཆབ་གསང་འབབ་སྨན་ (cābsaŋ ba̱bmɛn) diuretic.

ཆབས་ཅིག (cəbjig) together, together with ॥ང་ཨ་མེ་རི་ཀར་ཚོང་དང་ལྟ་སྐོར་ཆབས་ཅིག་ཡོང་བ་ཡིན་ I came to America to do business together with sightseeing. ॥ཚང་མ་ཆབས་ཅིག་ཡོང་པ་རེད་ They all came together.

ཆབས་སྒྲགས་ (cābdraà) sm. ཆབས་ཅིག.

ཆམ་ (cām) sm. ཅམ་.

ཆམ་འགྲམས་ (cāmdram) a cold that worsened because of eating and drinking beer and meat.

ཆམ་གྲན་ (cāmgɛn) cold/ flu that one has had for a long time.

ཆམ་ངན་ (cāmŋɛn) severe cold.

ཆམ་ཆམ་ (cāmjam) walk, stroll; va.—འགྲོ་ to go for a walk/ stroll ¶ཁོང་ཉིན་ལྟར་ཆམ་ཆམ་ལ་འགྲོ་གི་ཡོད་པ་རེད་ He goes for a stroll everyday.

ཆམ་ནད་ (cāmnɛɛ̀) sm. ཆམ་པ་.

ཆམ་པ་ (cāmba) a cold; vi.—ཐོག; —རྒྱག to catch/ have a cold.

ཆམ་ཕབ་ (cāmbəb) sm. ཆལ་ལ་འབེབས་.

ཆམ་མེ་བ་ (cāmmewa) 1. a feeling of emptiness. 2. sm. ལྷམ་མེ་བ་.

ཆམ་ཚེ་ (cāmdze) cloak.

ཆམ་བཞག (cāmshaà) sm. ཙམ་བཞག.

ཆམ་རིམས་ (cāmrim) flu epidemic.

ཆམ་ལ་ཕབ་ (cāmla pə̄b) sm. ཆམ་ལ་འབེབས་.

ཆམ་ལ་འབེབས་ (cāmla be̲b) va. to defeat, to destroy, to beat badly.

ཆོའོ་ཁེ་ལི་ (cōkeli) eng. chocolate.

ཆར་ (cār) 1. abbr. of ཆར་པ་. 2. see ད་ལྟའི་ཆར་.

ཆར་སྐྱིབས་ (cārgyib) any shelter/ protection from rain or snow.

ཆར་སྐྱོབ་ (cārgyob) 1. umbrella. 2. roof.

ཆར་ཁེབས་ (cārgeb) sm. ཆར་གོས་.

ཆར་གོས་ (cārgöö̀) raincoat, rainwear.

ཆར་གྱི་ཟེགས་མ་ (cārgi se̲gma) drizzle; vi.—བབ་ to drizzle.

ཆར་རྒྱུན་ (cārgyün) sm. ཆར་ཞོད་.

ཆར་རྒྱུན་ཟིམ་བུ་ (cārgyün si̲mbu) continuous drizzle, vi.—བབ་ to continuously drizzle.

ཆར་ཅན་ (cārjɛn) rainy.

ཆར་ཆས་ (cārjɛɛ̀) rain gear, rainwear.

ཆར་ཆུ་ (cārju) 1. rain water. 2. rainfall, rain ¶ད་ལོ་ཆར་ཆུ་ཡག་པོ་བྱུང་སོང་ This year (we) had good rainfall.

ཆར་ཆུ་བརྟག་ཆས་ (cārju dāgjɛɛ̀) rain gauge.

ཆར་ཆེན་ (cārjen) heavy rain.

ཆར་རྗེས་ཀྱི་ནམ་མཁའ་ (cārjeègi na̲mga) sth. becoming clear after some time [Lit. sky after the rain].

ཆར་རྗེས་ཀྱི་ཤ་མོ་ (cārjeègi shāmo) sm. ཆར་རྗེས་སྨྱུག་གསར་.

ཆར་རྗེས་སྨྱུག་གསར་ (cārjeè ñu̲gsar) growing up, springing up [Lit. bamboo shoots that grow after a heavy rainfall].

ཆར་ཉིན་ (cərñin) rain day.

ཆར་གཏོགས་ (cār dɔ̄ɔ̀) vi. to belong to, to be a part of ¶ས་གནས་དེ་ཚོ་བོད་དབུས་གཙང་གི་ཆར་གཏོགས་ཀྱི་རེད་ Those regions are a part of central Tibet.

ཆར་ལྟས་ (cārdɛɛ̀) a sign of rain.

ཆར་སྟོབས་ (cārdob) degree/ strength of rainfall.

ཆར་བརྟག་ཡོ་ཆས་ (cārdag yo̲bjɛɛ̀) equipment to predict rainfall, barometer, meteorological equipment.

ཆར་བརྟག་ཡོ་བྱད་ (cārdag yo̲bjɛɛ̀) sm. ཆར་བརྟག་ཡོ་ཆས་.

ཆར་ཐིགས་ (cərdig) a rain drop; vi.—རྒྱག to drizzle.

ཆར་དུ་སྙིལ་ (cārdu ñı̄ı̄) vi. to fall/ occur like rain (i.e., in abundance).

ཆར་དུས་ (cārdüǜ) rainy season.

ཆར་དྲག (cārdrag) heavy/ pouring rain, rainstorm.

ཆར་དྲག་ལྷུང་འཚུབ་ (cārdrag lūŋdzub) rain storm.

ཆར་གདུགས་ (cārduù) umbrella; va.—ཕུབས་ to open an umbrella.

ཆར་དྲུང་ (cārduŋ) rainstorm, heavy rain, vi.—གཏོང་ to rain heavily, to storm; va. —གཟེད་ to be caught in heavy rain/ rainstorm.

ཆར་དྲུང་ལྷགས་རྒྱག (cārduŋ lhāggyaà) rain and wind storm; vi.—བྱེད་.

ཆར་དྲུལ་ (cārdüü) drizzle.

ཆར་རྡོ་ (cārdo) a stone used in Bon religion to kill an animal as part of a rain making ritual.

ཆར་ལྡན་ (cārdɛn) sm. ཆར་ཅན་.

ཆར་ལྡན་དུས་ (cārdɛndüǜ) rainy season. monsoon season.

ཆར་སྡོད་བྱིའུ་ (cārdöö̀ ci̲wu) swallow (bird).

ཆར་སྣ་ཁྲིད་ (cārna trı̄ı̀) va. to bring/ cause rain.

ཆར་སྣ་ལྷུང་འཁྲིད་ (cārna lūŋdriì) sm. ཆར་སྣེ་ལྷུང་འཁྲིད་.

ཆར་སྣེ་ལྷུང་འཁྲིད་ (cārne lūŋdriì) bringing in sth. bad [Lit. the wind brings the rain].

ཆར་པ་ (cārba) rain; vi.—འབབ་; —གཏོང་ to rain; vi.—ཆད་ to stop raining.

ཆར་པ་ཆུ་གྲོགས་ (cārba cūdrog) complementing each other, helping one's own kind [Lit. rain (is) the friend of water].

ཆར་པ་སྤབས་ (cārba bə̄b) sm. ཆར་པ་འབེབས་.

ཆར་པ་འབབ་ཚད་ (cārba bə̲bdzɛɛ̀) amount of rainfall/ precipitation.

ཆར་པ་འབེབས་ (cārba be̲b) va. to cause rain to fall (part of tantric practice).

ཆར་པ་ཟིམ་ཟིམ་ (cārba si̲msim) light/ soft rain, drizzle.

ཆར་པ་སིབ་སིབ་ (cāba sı̄bsib) sm. ཆར་པ་ཟིམ་ཟིམ་.

ཆར་པ་སིམ་སིམ་ (cāba sı̄msim) sm. ཆར་པ་ཟིམ་ཟིམ་.

ཆར་པས་སྦོང་ (cārbɛ bo̲ŋ) vi. to be wet/ drenched from rain.

ཆར་སྤྲིན་ (cərdrin) 1. rain cloud. 2. rain and clouds.

ཆར་ཕི་ (cərpi) sm. ཆར་པི་.

ཆར་ཕིབས་ (cərpib) sm. ཆར་སླེ་.

ཆར་ཕྲན་ (cārtrɛn) light rainfall, drizzle.

ཆར་བུ་ (cərbu) light rainfall, drizzle.

ཆར་འབོར་ (cāmbɔr) sm. ཆར་ཚད་.

ཆར་སྦུད་ (cārbüǜ) sm. ཆར་ལྷུང་.

ཆར་སྨུན་ (cārmün) 1. darkening of sky just before rain; vi.—འཐིབས་. 2. (for people) sullen, downcast.

ཆར་མེད་ (cārmeè) drought, rainless.

ཆར་ཚད་ (cārdzɛɛ̀) quantity/ amount of rainfall.

ཆར་ཚད་དཔྱད་ཆས་ (cārtsɛɛ̀jɛ̄ɛ̀jɛɛ̀) rain gauge, rainfall measuring instrument.

ཆར་ཞོད་ (cārshöö̀) monsoon, torrential rain ¶ཆར་ཞོད་ཆེ་བའི་སྐབས་ During the heavy monsoon period.

ཆར་ཟིམ་ (cārsim) sm. ཆར་པ་ཟིམ་ཟིམ་.

ཆར་ཟིམ་པོ་ (cār si̲mbo) sm. ཆར་ཟིམ་.

ཆར་ཟིམ་བུ་ (cār si̲mbu) sm. ཆར་ཟིམ་.

ཆར་ཟིམ་ལྷུང་འཇམ་ (cārsim lūŋjam) drizzling with a gentle wind.

ཆར་ཟིལ་ (cārsii) sm. ཆར་ཟིམ་.

ཆར་ཡིབ་ (cəryib) sm. ཆར་གཡོལ་.

ཆར་གཡོགས་ (cāryɔɔ̀) sm. ཆར་ཁེབས་.

ཆར་གཡོལ་ (cār yɔ̄ɔ̄) va. to seek shelter when it is raining.

ཆར་རས་ (cārrɛɛ̀) cloth that is waterproof.

ཆར་ལྷུང་ (cərluŋ) rainstorm, hurricane ¶ཆར་ལྷུང་དྲག་པོ་ A heavy storm. [Lit. wind, rain].

ཆར་ལྷུང་བརྟག་དཔྱད་ (cərluŋ dāgjɛɛ̀) weather investigation, meteorology.

ཆར་ཤ་ (cārsha) sm. ཆར་ཞོད་.

ཆར་ཤོག (cārshɔɔ̀) rainproof plastic.

ཆར་སིམ་ (cərsim) sm. ཆར་ཟིམ་.

ཆར་སིམ་བུ་ (cər sı̄mbu) sm.* ཆར་ཟིམ་བུ་.

ཆར་སིལ་ (cərsii) light rain, drizzle.

ཆར་སླེ་ (cārle) raincoat.

ཆར་ལྷགས་ (cārlhaà) wind and rain, rainstorm; vi.—རྒྱག.

ཆར་ལྷམ་ (cārlham) rain boots, rubber boots, galoshes.

ཆལ་ (cɛɛ) soap.

ཆལ་སྒྲ་ (cɛ̄ɛ̄dra) splashing sound.

ཆལ་ཆལ་ (cɛ̄ɛ̄jɛɛ) sm. ཆལ་སྒྲ་.

ཆལ་ཆིལ་ (cɛ̄ɛ̄jii) wavering, fluctuating, pulsating ¶ཆུ་རླབས་ཆལ་ཆིལ་གཡོ་བའི་གཙང་པོའི་ཐོག On the river with pulsating waves.

ཆལ་ཆོལ་ (cɛ̄ɛ̄jöö) meaningless, aimless, senseless (talk or behavior); va.—སྨྲ་; —ཤོད་ to talk nonsense.

ཆལ་བདབ་ (cɛ̄ɛ̄dəb) sm. ཆལ་ཆིལ་.

ཆལ་མ་ (cɛ̄ɛ̄ma) evenly.

ཆལ་མར་བཀྲམ་ (cɛ̄ɛ̄mar drām) va. to spread/ scatter

evenly ། ཞལ་བའི་སྟེང་དུ་ཚགས་ཤོག་ཆལ་མར་བཀྲམ་འདུག (They) have spread newspapers evenly all over the floor.

ཆལ་མར་བརྡལ་ (cɛ̄ɛmar dɛɛ) sm. ཆལ་མར་བཀྲམ་.

ཆལ་ལི་ཅིལ་ལི་ (cɛ̄li jīli) sm. ཆལ་ཅིལ་.

ཆལ་ལེ་ཅོལ་ལེ་ (cɛ̄le jōle) sm. ཆལ་ཅོལ་.

ཆས་ (cɛ̄ɛ̀) 1. clothes, garments; va.—སྒྲས; —གྱོན་ to wear/ put on (clothes) ། བོད་ཆས་སྒྲས་འདུག (They) have put on Tibetan clothes. 2. va. to go, to leave ། ཐག་རིང་པོར་ཆས་སོང་ (They) went to far away places. 3. va. to come/ arrive ། ཁོ་ཤར་ངོས་ནས་ཆས་ཡོང་བ་རེད་ He came from the east. 4. at the point of ། ཁོ་ཚོ་འགྲོ་བར་ཆས་པ་ན་ ། As they were at the point of leaving/ going. 5. food for animals ། ཕག་པ་ལ་ཆས་སྤྲད་པ་རེད་ (They) gave food to the pigs.

ཆས་ཀ་ (cēèga) sm. ཆས་.

ཆས་ཁ་ (cɛ̄ɛ̀ga) sm. ཆས་ཀ་.

ཆས་ཁོག (cɛ̄ɛ̀gɔɔ̀) trough.

ཆས་གུར་ (cɛ̄ɛ̀gur) a tent that Tibetan opera performers use as a dressing room.

ཆས་གོས་ (cɛ̄ɛ̀göö̀) clothes, garments, costumes.

ཆས་འགྲོ་ (cɛ̄ndro) "lets go" (Eastern Tibetan dialect).

ཆས་སྒྱུར་ (cɛ̄ɛ̀ gyur) va. to change clothes.

ཆས་དངོས་ (cɛ̄ɛ̀ŋöö̀) shung. clothes and things.

ཆས་སྒྲས་ (cɛ̄ɛ̀ drɛ̄ɛ̀) va. to wear/ to put on clothing, to dress up.

ཆས་ཕོར་ (cēèbɔɔ) wooden container used for feeding animals.

ཆས་བརྫུས་ (cɛ̄ɛ̀dzüǜ) impersonating, disguising (with respect to clothing); va.—སྒྲིག; —སྒྲས་ ། ཁོས་གྲྭ་པའི་ཆས་བརྫུས་སྒྲས་ནས་དགོན་པར་ཕྱིན་པ་རེད་ He disguised himself in a monk's clothes and went to the monastery.

ཆས་ཞུགས་ (cɛ̄ɛ̀shuù) sm. ཆས་སྒྲས་.

ཆས་གཟབ་ (cɛ̄ɛ̀səb) dressing up ། དུས་ཆེན་དེ་ར་ཚང་མས་ཆས་གཟབ་སྒྲས་ཡོད་པ་རེད་ Everyone was dressed up at the festival.

ཆས་སུ་ཞུགས་ (cɛ̄ɛ̀su shuù) sm. ཆས་སྒྲས་.

ཆི་ཀང་ (cīgaŋ) ch. cylinder.

ཆི་ག (cīga) wallet.

ཆི་གེ་ (cīge) mare's milk.

ཆི་པི་ཁ་ (cībigə) sm. ཆི་པི་ཁ་.

ཆི་པི་ཁ་ (cībigə) 1. red date. 2. a type of herbal medicine.

ཆི་མན་ (cīmin) ch. yeast; va.—སྦོལ་ to ferment (dough) with yeast ། ཆི་སྨན་སྐམ་པོ་ Dry yeast.

ཆི་མན་མོག་མོག (cīmin mɔ̄ɔ̀mɔɔ̀) ch. steamed dumpling made with yeast flour.

ཆི་མན་སྦོལ་ (cīmin ñöö̀) va. to ferment yeast.

ཆི་སྨན་སྐམ་པོ་ (cīmin gāmbo) ch.tib. dry yeast.

ཆི་ཙི་ (cīdzi) ch. flat noodles.

ཆི་ཡིའུ་ (cīyü) ch. gasoline, petrol.

ཆི་ཡིའུ་དན་ (yiyüdɛn) ch. gasoline bomb.

ཆི་ལི་ (cīli) Chile.

ཆི་ལི་ལི་ (cī lili) 1. pouring rain. 2. good smelling.

ཆི་ལེན་རི་པོ་ (cīlen riwo) Chilien Mountains.

ཆི་ལེར་ (cīler) covered with sth. such as snow or blood.

ཆིག (cīg) one ། ཅིག་འབུམ་ཅིག་ཁྲི་ཅིག་སྟོང་ 111,000.

ཆིག་རྒྱ་བ་ (cīg gyāwa) sm. ཆིག་རྐྱང་.

ཆིག་རྐྱང་ (cīggyaŋ) single, alone.

ཆིག་སྐྱ་ (cīggya) sm. ཆིག་རྐྱང་.

ཆིག་སྐྱེས་ (cīggyeè) a lone growing tree or plant.

ཆིག་སྐྱེས་དབང་ལག (cīggyeè wāŋlaà) a type of herb.

ཆིག་ཁྲི་ (cīgdri) ten thousand.

ཆིག་རྒྱུ་ཉིས་སྤུན་ (cīggyu ñiibün) a type of weaving with one warp and two wefts.

ཆིག་བརྒྱ་ (cīggya) one hundred.

ཆིག་བརྒྱུད་ (cīggyüǜ) oral teachings passed on from one person to another.

ཆིག་བརྒྱུད་འབྲེལ་བ་ (cīggyüǜ dreewa) a single contact (usu. in espionage work).

ཆིག་བརྒྱུད་མ་ (cīggyüǜmə) linear ancestor.

ཆིག་སྒྲིལ་ (cīgdrii) 1. united in one, unity, solidarity. 2. a roll of one piece of sth.

ཆིག་ཚོད་ (cīgjöö) sm. གཅིག་ཚོད་.

ཆིག་སྟོང་ (cīgdoŋ) one thousand.

ཆིག་ཐུབ་ (cīgdub) able to do (sth.) alone/ on one's own.

ཆིག་དྲིལ་ (cīdrii) rolled/ wrapped/ packed in one bundle.

ཆིག་འབུམ་ (cīgbum) one hundred thousand.

ཆིག་རྫུག (cīgdzuù) sm. རང་རྒྱ་འཁྱེར་བ་.

ཆིག་ལབ་ (cīgləb) va. to talk to oneself; vi.—རྒྱག.

ཆིག་ཤད་ (cīgshɛɛ) a single ཤད་.

ཆིང་ (cīŋ) ch. 1. a unit of area equal to 100 མུའུ་ (16.474 acres). 2. the Qing dynasty in China ། ཆིང་གོང་མ་ The Qing Emperor. 3. ch. hydrogen.

ཆིང་གྲེན་ (cīŋdren) ch. Muslim, Islam.

ཆིང་ཁྲ་ (cīŋdra) (Chinese) ch. green tea.

ཆིང་དན་ (cīŋdɛn) ch. H-bomb.

ཆིང་དན་མཚོན་ཆ་ (cīŋdɛn tsōnja) ch.tib. hydrogen/ nuclear weapon.

ཆིང་རྡུལ་འབར་མདེལ་ (cīŋdüü bardee) sm. ཆིང་དན་མཚོན་ཆ་.

ཆིང་མེ་སུའུ་ (cīŋmesu) ch. penicillin.

ཆིང་དམག (cīŋmaà) ch.tib. Qing army/ troops.

ཆིང་རླུང་ (cīŋluŋ) ch.tib. hydrogen.

ཆིང་སང་ (cīŋsaŋ) ch. prime minister.

ཆིངས་ (cīŋ) 1. intervention, arbitration, mediation, negotiation (usu. regarding a treaty); va.—རྒྱག to intervene, to mediate, to negotiate; va.—འགྲིག to agree on a treaty, to sign an agreement/ treaty ། ཤོག་ཁག་གཉིས་ཀྱི་རྩོད་རྙོག་མཐུན་འགྲིག་ཆེད་ང་ཚོས་ཆིངས་བཀྱབ་པ་ཡིན་ We negotiated to settle the dispute between the two groups. ། རྒྱལ་ཁག་གཉིས་དབར་གྲོས་མོལ་བྱས་ནས་ཆིངས་འགྲིགས་བཞག The two countries held talks and agreed on a treaty. 2. a binding, a bandage; va.—རྒྱག to bind, to bandage ། རྐང་པ་ཆག་པ་ཆིངས་བཀྱབ་པ་རེད་ (They) bound up the broken leg. 3. imp. of འཆིང་. 3. abbr. of ཆིངས་ཡིག.

ཆིངས་འགྲིགས་ (cīŋdrig) negotiating an agreement/ treaty; va.—བྱེད་.

ཆིངས་དངུལ་ (cīŋŋüü) indemnity; va.—སྤྲོད་ to pay an indemnity.

ཆིངས་དོན་ (cīŋdön) contents of a treaty/ agreement.

ཆིངས་དོན་སྐུ་ཚབ་ (cīŋdön gūdzəb) representative at treaty negotiations/ signings.

ཆིངས་དོན་ཡིག་ཁག (cīŋdön yigaà) treaties.

ཆིངས་མ་ (cīŋmə) hoop.

ཆིངས་མོལ་ (cīŋmöö) conference/ negotiations for making a treaty.

ཆིངས་ཡིག (cīŋyii) treaty; va.—འཛོག to sign a treaty ། མཛའ་མཐུན་ཆིངས་ཡིག Friendship treaty.

ཆིན་ཁྲང་ (cīndraŋ) ch. Chinese tea.

ཆིན་ཁྲལ་ (jīndrɛɛ) ch. shung. amban.

ཆིན་དན་ (cīndɛn) sm. ཆིང་དན་.

ཆིན་ཙི་ལ་ཕུག (cīndzi ləbuù) ch.tib. a small red radish.

ཆིན་ཚལ་ (cīndzɛɛ) ch. type of celery.

ཆིན་ཝང་ (cīnwaŋ) ch. prince, a Chinese title.

ཆིབ་ (cīb) sm. ཆིབས་.

ཆིབས་ (cīb) 1. imp. of འཆིབ་. 2. sm. ཆིབས་པ་. 3. abbr. of ཆིབས་རྟ་.

ཆིབས་ཀྱི་སྒྱུར་ (cībgyi gyūr) h. of རྟས་དབྱུག.

ཆིབས་བཀྱག (cībgyaà) a stone used for mounting horses.

ཆིབས་སྐྱེལ་ (cībgyee) sm. ཞབས་སྐྱེལ་.

ཆིབས་བསྐྱོད་ (cībgyöö̀) going, coming (h.); va.—གནང་; —བསྐྱངས་ to go, to come (h.) ། ཁོང་ལྷ་སར་ཆིབས་བསྐྱོད་གནང་བཞག He went to Lhasa.

ཆིབས་ཁ་ (cībga) horse's mouth (h.); va.—སྒྱུར་ to change direction (when riding a horse).

ཆིབས་ཁ་ཐུབ་པ་ (cībga tūbbə) a child old enough to ride a horse.

ཆིབས་ཁལ་ (cībgɛɛ) abbr. of ཆིབས་རྟ་ and ཁལ་མ་.

ཆིབས་ཁེབས་ (cībgeb) horse blanket (h.).

ཆིབས་གྲལ་ (cibdrεε) h. of ཏ་རགས་.

ཆིབས་གློ་ (cibIo) girth (h.).

ཆིབས་འགྲོས་ (cibdröö) trotting gait of horses (h.).

ཆིབས་སྒ་ (cibga) saddle (h.); va.—སྒྲོན་ to saddle (a horse).

ཆིབས་སྒྱུར་ (cibgyur) sm. ཆིབས་བསྒྱུར་.

ཆིབས་བསྒྱུར་ (cibgyur) 1. sm. ཆིབས་བསྐྱོད་. 2. sm. ཆིབས་བསྒྱུར་ཆེན་མོ་, 2.

ཆིབས་བསྒྱུར་གནང་གོ་ (cibgyur nāŋgɔ) good-bye (said to person leaving) (h.).

ཆིབས་བསྒྱུར་ཆེན་མོ་ (cibgyur cēmbo) shung. the two processions of the Dalai Lama: from the Potala to the Norbulingka in the 1st week of the 4th Tibetan month and from Norbulingka to the Potala in the 10th Tibetan month.

ཆིབས་བསྒྱུར་ཡར་ཕེབས་ (cibgyur yarpeè) shung. the Dalai Lama's procession returning from Norbulingka to the Potala palace in the 10th Tibetan month.

ཆིབས་བསྒྱུར་མར་ཕེབས་ (cibgyur marpeè) the Dalai Lama's procession going from the Potala Palace to Norbulingka in the 4th month.

ཆིབས་སྒྲོ་ (cibdro) saddle bag (h.).

ཆིབས་གཙོག (cibjɔ̄ɔ̀) h. of ཏ་གཙོག.

ཆིབས་བདེགས་ (cib dēg) sm. ཆིབས་ཐོག་ཐོན་.

ཆིབས་ཐོག་ཐོན་ (cibdɔɔ tōn) va. to depart on a journey (h.).

ཆིབས་ལྕག (cibjaà) horse whip (h.).

ཆིབས་ཆག (cibjaà) horse fodder (h.).

ཆིབས་ཆག་ཨུ་ལག (cibjaà wu̱ùlaà) shung. corvee labor as a stable boy.

ཆིབས་ཆས་ (cibjεὲ) horse tack.

ཆིབས་ཆེ་ (cibje) shung. abbr. of ཆིབས་དཔོན་ཆེན་མོ་.

ཆིབས་ཆེན་ (cibjen) riding horse (h.).

ཆིབས་དོག (cibdɔg) an ornament put on the head of a lama's horse.

ཆིབས་ཏ་ (cibda) horse (h.); va.—འཆིབ་ to ride, to mount (a horse).

ཆིབས་སྟེགས་ (cibdeg) sm. ཆིབས་བཀུག.

ཆིབས་ཐོན་ (cibdön) departing; va.—གནང་ ¶ཁ་སང་ལྷ་ས་ནས་ཆིབས་ཐོན་གནང་བཞག (He) departed from Lhasa yesterday.

ཆིབས་དར་བ་ (cibdarwa) 1. shung. a person carrying a banner who accompanies the retinue when the Dalai Lama is going from one palace to the other. 2. riders holding banners.

ཆིབས་དྲེལ་ (cibdree) mule (h.).

ཆིབས་གདན་ (cibdεn) rug placed under the saddle (h.).

ཆིབས་དོག་ཐོན་ (cib dogdön) vi. to leave/ depart from a place (h.).

ཆིབས་འདྲ་ (cibdra) sm. ཆིབས་གསོར་.

ཆིབས་པ་ (cibbə) sm. ཆིབས་ཏ་.

ཆིབས་པ་ལྡིང་གཤོག (cibbə lūŋshɔɔ̀) speedy, fast [Lit. a horse with wings].

ཆིབས་པའི་དོག (cibε dōg) sm. ཆིབས་དོག.

ཆིབས་དཔོན་ (cibbön) manager of a stable (h.).

ཆིབས་དཔོན་ཆེན་མོ་ (cibbön cēmmo) shung. the head of the Dalai Lama's stable.

ཆིབས་བྱམས་ (cibjam) shung. palanquin, sedan chair (h.).

ཆིབས་སྦྱངས་ (cibjaŋ) practicing riding (horses/ mules) (h.).

ཆིབས་སྦྱོང་ (cibjoŋ) shung. a rehearsal of the horse procession held prior to the day the Dalai Lama goes from one palace to the other.

ཆིབས་སྨིད་ (cibmeè) shung. h. of སྨིད་.

ཆིབས་རྩྭ་ (cibdza) fodder, hay (h.).

ཆིབས་ཞལ་བསྒྱུར་ (cibshεε gyu̱r) see ཆིབས་བསྒྱུར་གནང་.

ཆིབས་ཞབས་ (cibshəb) entourage, party, retinue, people accompanying high officials on a journey (h.) ¶སྲིད་འཛིན་གྱི་ཆིབས་ཞབས་མི་བརྒྱད་ཡོད་པ་རེད་ There are eight people accompanying the president (on his journey).

ཆིབས་ཞབས་འཁོད་ (cibshəb kōò) va. to arrive (h.) ¶ཁོང་གནམ་ཐང་དུ་ཆིབས་ཞབས་འཁོད་སྐབས་ When he arrived at the airport.

ཆིབས་ཞབས་པ་ (cibshəbbə) sm. ཆིབས་ཞབས་.

ཆིབས་གཞོལ་ (cibshöö) sm. ཆིབས་བཞོལ་.

ཆིབས་ཟམ་ (cibsam) shung. h. of ཏ་ཟམ་.

ཆིབས་ཡོབ་ (cibyob) stirrup (h.).

ཆིབས་གཡོག (cibyɔɔ̀) groom (h.).

ཆིབས་ར་ (cibrə) stable (h.).

ཆིབས་ར་མདོ་ (cibrə do̱) shung. the outer section of the Dalai Lama's stable.

ཆིབས་ར་སྦུགས་ (cibrə bu̱ù) shung. the inner section of the Dalai Lama's stable.

ཆིབས་ར་ལས་ཁུངས་ (cibrə lεὲguŋ) shung. office in charge of the Dalai Lama's stable.

ཆིབས་རགས་ (cibraà) shung. a line of people on horseback (e.g., those accompanying the Dalai Lama or Regent) (h.).

ཆིབས་རེས་ (cibreè) shung. a form of tax whereby peasants have to provide horses for government officials.

ཆིབས་ལས་ (ciblεὲ) shung. abbr. of ཆིབས་ར་ལས་ཁུངས་.

ཆིབས་ཤོག (cibshɔɔ̀) sm.

ཆིབས་བཞོལ་ (cibshöö) dismounting/ getting off a horse (h.); va.—གནང་.

ཆིབས་སྲབ་ (cibdrəb) bit and head stall of a horse/ mule bridle (h.).

ཆིབས་གསེབ་ (cibseb) stallion (non-castrated) (h.).

ཆིབས་གསོར་ (cibsɔɔ) shung. spare horses that a rider takes so that he can change when one gets tired.

ཆིབས་བསུ་ (cibsu) shung. 1. a servant bringing an (extra) riderless horse to pick up (sb.), sending a person with a horse to pick up sb.; va.—འགྲོ་ to go bringing an (extra) riderless horse to pick up (sb.), va.—གཏོང་ to send a person with an (extra) riderless horse to pick up sb. 2. going or sending sb. on horseback to welcome/ greet a visitor who is arriving; va.—འགྲོ་ to go on horseback to welcome/ greet a visitor who is arriving; va.—གཏོང་ to send sb. on horseback to welcome/ greet a visitor who is arriving.

ཆིར་ (cir) imp. of བཅིར་.

ཆིར་གྱིས་ཆིར་ (cirgu cir) va. to squash/ squeeze.

ཆིར་ཆིར་ (circir) shining, glittering, sparkling.

ཆིལ་ཆིལ་ (ciljii) bubbling, rushing, splashing, dashing (sound of water).

ཆིལ་མན་ (ciimεn) see ཆི་མན་.

ཆིལ་མན་མོག་མོག (ciimεn mo̱mo) ch. dumpling made with yeast dough.

ཆིལ་ལི་ (chiile) sm. ཆིལ་ཆིལ་.

ཆིས་ཁྲི་ (ciidre) ch. vehicle, automobile.

ཆིས་ཡིའུ་ (ciiyü) ch. gasoline, petrol.

ཆིའུ་ཅིར་ (ciujil) Churchill.

ཆིའུ་ཞེ་ (ciushe) ch. gym shoes, tennis shoes, sneakers.

ཆུ་ (cū) 1. water; va.—གཏོང་ to irrigate; va.—སྐོལ་ to boil water; va.—རྒྱག to water sth. ¶དཔྱིད་ཀ་ཞིང་ཁར་ཆུ་གཏོང་དགོས་ཀྱི་རེད་ One has to irrigate the field in the spring. ¶ཇ་བཟོ་དུས་སྔོན་ལ་ཆུ་བསྐོལ་དགོས་ When making tea, first one has to boil the water. ¶ཁོས་ཞོགས་ལྟར་མེ་ཏོག་ལ་ཆུ་རྒྱག་གི་འདུག He waters the flowers every morning. 2. river ¶དེང་སང་ཆར་པ་མང་པོ་བབས་ཙང་ཆུ་རྒྱས་བཞག Because it has rained a lot these days the river has risen. 3. urine ¶ཁོང་ལ་ན་ཚ་ཕོག་ནས་དེང་སང་ཆུ་བབ་ཀྱི་མི་འདུག He has gotten sick and cannot urinate.

ཆུ་ཀ་ལ་ (cūgala) tib.hind. water tap. 2. water pipe.

ཆུ་ཀྲམ་ (cūdram) sm. ཆུ་སྲམ་.

ཆུ་ཀླུང་ (cūluŋ) river.

ཆུ་ཀླུང་ཆེན་པོ་ (cūluŋ cēmbo) great river, great current ¶རིག་གནས་གསར་བརྗེ་ཆེན་པོའི་ཆུ་ཀླུང་ཆེན་པོའི་ནང་དུ་ In the great current of the great cultural revolution.

ཆུ་ཀླུང་རབ་མེད་ (cūluŋ rəbmeè) a large river that cannot be crossed on foot or horse.

ཆུ་ཀློང་ (cūloŋ) the middle of the river.

ཆུ་དཀྱིལ་ (cūgyii) sm. ཆུ་ཀློང་.

ཆུ་དཀྱིལ་གླིང་ལག (cūgyii lĩŋlaà) peninsula.

ཆུ་དཀྲོགས་ནས་མར་མི་ཐོན་ (cūdrɔ̀ɔnɛ mar midön) futile effort, hopeless act [Lit. churning water does not produce butter].

ཆུ་བཀག (cūgaà) damming water, blocking/ stopping water; va.—གཏོང་.

ཆུ་བཀག་གཏོང་གཅུས་ཕུར་ (cūgaà dōŋ jũũbur) faucet for turning water on and off.

ཆུ་ཀ་ (cūga) irrigation ditch/ channel; va.—འཐེན་ to draw water from an irrigation ditch/ channel, to irrigate.

ཆུ་ཀ་འགོ་ལ་ཡོད་ན་ཀ་གཞུག་ལ་ཡོད་ (cūg gāgola yȫȫna gāshuùla yȫȫ) if the top does well, the lower ones will also prosper (e.g., if a business or enterprise makes good profit then workers will profit) [Lit. if there is water at the source of the irrigational canal then there is water at the end].

ཆུ་ཀེད་ (cugyeè) the middle reaches of a river.

ཆུ་ཀྱང་ (cūgyaŋ) plain water.

ཆུ་རྐྱལ་ (cūgyɛɛ) swimming; va.—རྒྱག.

ཆུ་རྐྱལ་ཁང་ (cūgyɛɛgaŋ) sm. ཆུ་རྐྱལ་རྫིང་བུ་.

ཆུ་རྐྱལ་འགྲན་བསྡུར་ (cūgyɛɛ drendur) swim meet/ competition.

ཆུ་རྐྱལ་རྫིང་བུ་ (cūgyɛɛ dziŋbu) swimming pool.

ཆུ་སྐད་ (cūgɛɛ̀) 1. the sound of rushing water. 2. in a monastery—the call announcing that the mangja or traja prayer assembly is starting.

ཆུ་སྐམ་ (cū gām) vi. to get dry. 2. abbr. of water and land ¶ ཆུ་སྐམ་གཉིས་ཐོག Via land and water.

ཆུ་སྐམ་སྐྱེལ་འདྲེན་ (cūgam gyēndren) transportation by land and water.

ཆུ་སྐམ་གྲམ་དོན་ (cūgam dramdön) revealing everything, everything coming to light. [Lit. the river dries and the bank appears].

ཆུ་སྐམ་གྲམ་ཐོན་ (cūgam dramdön) sm. ཆུ་སྐམ་གྲམ་དོན་.

ཆུ་སྐམ་གཉིས་སྤྱོད་ (cūgam ñĩĩjüü) amphibious ¶ ཆུ་སྐམ་གཉིས་སྤྱོད་ཀྱི་ཐན་ཁི་ Amphibious tank.

ཆུ་སྐམ་གཉིས་སྤྱོད་ཀྱི་འཐབ་འཁོར་ (cūgam ñĩĩjüügi tābgɔɔ) amphibious tank/ armored car.

ཆུ་སྐར་ (cūgar) a minute.

ཆུ་སྐར་ཆེན་པོ་ (cūgar cēmbo) the planet Mercury.

ཆུ་སྐེད་ (cūgeè) sm. ཆུ་ཀེད་.

ཆུ་སྐོར་ (cūgɔɔ) water mill; va.—འཐག to mill grain in a water mill.

ཆུ་སྐོར་གཉེར་པ་ (cūgɔɔ ñērba) a person in charge of a water mill.

ཆུ་སྐོལ་ (cū gȫȫ) va. to boil water.

ཆུ་སྐོལ་ཐབ་ཆེན་ (cūgöö tābjen) large hearth for boiling water.

ཆུ་སྐྱར་ (cūgyar) a type of fish eating bird.

ཆུ་སྐྱིལ་ (cū gyīl) vi. to fill up with water.

ཆུ་སྐྱུར་ (cūgyur) 1. rhubarb. 2. water burial; va.—གཏོང་. 3. the sour liquid that is vomited up. 4. a sour drink.

ཆུ་སྐྱུར་ལངས་ (cūgyur laŋ) vi. to get heart burn/ acid reflux.

ཆུ་སྐྱེགས་ (cūgyeg) sm. ཆུ་སྐྱུར་, 3.

ཆུ་སྐྱེས་ (cūgyeè) 1. lotus. 2. things that grow in water. 3. poet. wednesday. 4. poet. friday. 4. moon.

ཆུ་སྐྱེས་ཏ་མིག (cūgyeè dāmig) root of Chinese wild ginger used for headaches and toothaches.

ཆུ་སྐྱེས་པད་མ་ (cūgyeè bɛ̃ɛ̃ma) water lily.

ཆུ་སྐྱེས་དབང་ལག (cūgyeè wāŋlaà) anise, star anise.

ཆུ་སྐྱེས་ལོ་ཏོག (cūgyeè lodoò) an aquatic/ hydrophonic crop, a crop grown in water.

ཆུ་སྐྱེས་སྲོག་ཆགས་ (cūgyeè sōgjaà) aquatic creatures/ animals.

ཆུ་སྐྱོགས་ (cūgyɔɔ̀) water ladle.

ཆུ་སྐྱོན་ (cūgyön) flood damage ¶ ཆར་འབབ་ཆེ་དུས་ཆུ་སྐྱོན་ཆེན་པོ་ཡོང་གི་ཡོད་པ་རེད་ During the heavy monsoon season (they) have flood damage.

ཆུ་སྐྱོར་ (cūgɔɔ) 1. ridge or raised embankment that holds water in or channels it. 2. the ridge/ railing on a roof that prevents sb. from falling.

ཆུ་སྐྱེས་སྔོ་རིགས་ (cūgyeè ŋōrig) algae/ plants that grow in water.

ཆུ་སྐྲན་ (cūdrɛn) a cancerous liquid in the stomach.

ཆུ་བསྐྱེད་གློག་ཁང་ (cūgyeè lɔ̄ɔgaŋ) hydro-electric plant.

ཆུ་བསྐྱེད་གློག་ཤུགས་ཁང་ (cūgyeè lɔ̄ɔshugaŋ) sm. ཆུ་བསྐྱེད་གློག་ཁང་.

ཆུ་ཁ་ (cūga) 1. bank (river). 2. vagina. 3. on the surface of the water. 4. sm. གྲུ་ཁ་.

ཆུ་ཁ་སྙི་བ་ (cūga ñĩwə) a disease where the patient has to urinate often.

ཆུ་ཁ་འཕར་ཚད་ (cūga pārdzɛɛ̀) water level.

ཆུ་ཁ་ལེབ་ (cūgaleb) deerskin cloth used to polish pots.

ཆུ་ཁག (cūgaà) river basin.

ཆུ་ཁང་ (cūgaŋ) 1. bathroom, shower-room, bath house. 2. place where people went to get boiled water.

ཆུ་ཁང་གསང་གཅོད་ (cūgaŋ sānjöö) bathroom (in the American sense of a toilet and place to wash).

ཆུ་ཁེད་ (cūgɛɛ̀) bank of river/ lake.

ཆུ་ཁམས་ (cūgam) one of the five astrological elements (water).

ཆུ་ཁའི་མཉན་པ་ ལ་ཁའི་ཇག་པ་ (cūgɛ ñɛ̃mba lagɛ cagba) having power in their own sphere of authority [Lit. boatmen around the river, bandits around the mountain pass].

ཆུ་ཁུག (cūguù) cove, bay, inlet.

ཆུ་ཁུང་ (cūguŋ) sluice, weir.

ཆུ་ཁུར་ (cūgur) clouds.

ཆུ་ཁུར་བརྩེགས་པ་ (cūgur dzēgba) clouds.

ཆུ་ཁུལ་ (cūgüü) a region with rivers and lakes.

ཆུ་ཁེབས་ (cūgeb) rain protection/ covering, raincoat.

ཆུ་ཁོག (cū kɔ̄ɔ) vi. to stop water going through sth., to resist/ repel water ¶ སྟོད་ཐུང་འདིས་ཆུ་ཁོག་གི་རེད་པས་ Is this coat water resistant?

ཆུ་ཁོངས་ (cūgoŋ) sm. ཆུ་ཁུལ་.

ཆུ་ཁོལ་ (cūgöö) water that has been boiled ¶ ཆུ་ཁོལ་ཚ་པོ་ Hot boiled water.

ཆུ་ཁོལ་གྲང་ (cūgöö traŋ) cold water that had been boiled.

ཆུ་ཁོལ་མ་ (cū kȫȫma) sm. ཆུ་ཁོལ་.

ཆུ་ཁོལ་ལེན་ས་ (cūköö lensa) room where one goes to get boiled water.

ཆུ་ཁྱི་ (cūkyi) water-dog year.

ཆུ་མཁན་ (cūgɛn) sailor, boatman.

ཆུ་མཁྲིགས་ (cūdreg) sm. སེར་བ་.

ཆུ་འཁོར་ (cūgɔɔ) 1. sm. ཆུ་སྐོར་. 2. whirlpool, eddy, vortex.

ཆུ་འཁོར་གློག་འདོན་འཕྲུལ་འཁོར་ (cūgɔɔ lɔ̄gdön trũũgɔɔ̀) hydro/ water turbine generator.

ཆུ་འཁོར་གློག་འདོན་འཕྲུལ་ཆས་ (cūgɔɔ lɔ̄gdön trũũjɛɛ̀) sm. ཆུ་འཁོར་གློག་འདོན་འཕྲུལ་འཁོར་.

ཆུ་འཁོར་གཉེར་པ་ (cūgɔɔ ñēēba) person in charge of the water mill.

ཆུ་འཁོལ་ (cūgöö) sm. ཆུ་ཁོལ་.

ཆུ་འཁྱགས་ (cūgyaà) ice.

ཆུ་འཁྱིལ་ (cū kyīl) vi. to form a puddle/ pool of water ¶ ཆར་པ་བབས་རྗེས་སྒོ་རའི་ནང་ཆུ་འཁྱིལ་བཞག After it rained water puddled in the courtyard.

ཆུ་འཁྱིལ་ལི་བ་ (cū kyīlewa) 1. puddled or standing water. 2. (with མིག་) eyes full of tears.

ཆུ་གང་ (cūgaŋ) 1. arc. spirit, courage. 2. sm. ཡེགས་པ་.

ཆུ་གོས་ (cūgöö̀) raincoat, raingear.

ཆུ་གྲང་མོ་གཞོ་ (cū traŋmo shō) va. to dampen sb.'s spirits/ enthusiasm [Lit. to pour cold water].

ཆུ་གྲམ་མཉམ་འཇགས་ (cūdram ñamjag) agreeing to settle a dispute/ quarrel by both sides compromising or giving sth. up [Lit. river and bank recede together].

ཆུ་གྲི་ (cūdri) 1. a sharp knife. 2. a small curved knife.

ཆུ་གྲུབ་བྲག་རྡོ་ (cūdrub tragdo) sedimentary rock.

ཆུ་གྲོག (cūdrog) 1. ravine. 2. arc. foam/ bubbles on water. 3. cold water. 4. tsampa mixed with cold water for medical purposes.

ཆུ་གླ་ (cūla) shung. a fee for carrying water.

ཆུ་གླག (cūlaà) a large bird that preys on fish.

ཆུ་གླང་ (cūlaŋ) water-ox year.

ཆུ་གླིང་ (cūliŋ) island.

ཆུ་གླེ་ (cūle) sm. ཆུ་གླིང་.

ཆུ་གློ་ (cūlo) an animal disease characterized by water in the lungs.

ཆུ་གློག (cūlɔ̀ɔ) hydroelectric, hydropower.

ཆུ་གློག་སྒྲིག་སྦྱོར་ཀུང་ཟི་ (cūlɔ̀ɔ drigjɔɔ gūŋsi) tib.ch. hydroelectric installation company.

ཆུ་གློག་ཅུའུ་ (cūlɔ̀ɔjū) tib.ch. hydroelectric board.

ཆུ་གློག་བབས་ཚུགས་ (cūlɔ̀ɔ bəbdzuù) hydro-electric power station.

ཆུ་གློག་བཟོ་གྲྭ (cūlɔ̀ɔ sodra) hydroelectric plant.

ཆུ་གློག་ས་ཚིགས་ (cūlɔ̀ɔ sədzii) hydroelectric power station.

ཆུ་གློད་ (cū lȫö̀) 1. va. to release/ let out water. 2. va. to let down a friend or associate ¶ ད་རེས་འགག་རྩར་ཐུག་དུས་གྲོགས་པོས་ཆུ་གློད་བྱུང་ This time, when I met with an obstacle, my friend let me down.

ཆུ་མགོ་ (cūngo) 1. source/ head water of a river. 2. up-river, up-stream.

ཆུ་མགོ་གངས་ཐུག (cūngo kaŋduù) 1. the highest authority/ source/ level (usu. conveys taking a dispute/ issue to the highest level or authority) ¶ ཁ་མཆུ་འདི་ཁྲིམས་ཁང་འོག་མས་ཐག་གཅོད་དྲང་པོ་མ་བྱས་སྐབས་ཆུ་མགོ་གངས་ཐུག་གིས་གོང་རིམ་ལ་ཞུ་རྒྱུན་ཞུས་པ་རེད་ Because this dispute was not settled honestly by the lower court, like a river touching the snow, (they) petitioned to the superior officials [Lit. the river's source is the snow mountain].

ཆུ་མགོ་གྱེན་ལ་ལོག་པ་ (cūŋgo gyenla lɔgba) 1. sth. that is impossible [Lit. the head waters of a river returning uphill]. 2. sm. ཆུ་རྒྱུ་གྱེན་ལྡོག.

ཆུ་མགོ་ནས་རྙོག་ན་དྭངས་དུས་མེད་ (cūŋgonɛ ñɔgna taŋdüü meè) if people at the top don't behave, the subordinates won't [Lit. If the source of the river is muddy there won't be time for the river to become clear].

ཆུ་འགག (cūŋgaà) 1. lock, water-gate, sluice gate. 2. vi. to be unable to urinate.

ཆུ་འགུལ་གློག་སྐྱེད་མ་འཁོར་ (cūngüü lɔ̄ɔ̀gyeè magɔɔ) hydro/ water turbine generator.

ཆུ་འགུལ་སྣོ་གཤོག (cūngüü goshɔ̀ɔ) hydro/ water turbine.

ཆུ་འགུལ་མ་འཁོར་ (cūngüü magɔɔ) sm. ཆུ་འཁོར་སྣོ་གཤོག.

ཆུ་འགོ་ (cūŋgo) sm. ཆུ་མགོ་.

ཆུ་འགོ་གངས་ཐུག (cūŋgo kaŋdug) sm. ཆུ་མགོ་གངས་ཐུག.

ཆུ་འགོག (cūŋgɔ̀ɔ) water/ flood protection; waterproof ¶ ཆུ་འགོག་ལག་འདོགས་ཆུ་ཚོད་ Waterproof wrist watch.

ཆུ་འགོག་སྣོ་གླེགས་ (cūŋgɔ̀ɔ goleg) a wooden board used to control water.

ཆུ་འགྱེད་སྣོ་བཀག (cūgyeè gogaà) sluice gate.

ཆུ་འགྲམ་ (cūndram) bank, coast, shore.

ཆུ་འགྲམ་བསིལ་ཁང་ (cūdram sīīgaŋ) waterside pavilion.

ཆུ་འགྲོ་ (cūndro) drainage system, water drain/ sewer.

ཆུ་འགྲོ་མ་ཡུར་ (cūndro mayur) main water canal.

ཆུ་འགྲོས་ལྟ་བུའི་ལས་སྒྲུབ་ (cūndröö̀ dābü leèdrub) streamlined production.

ཆུ་འགྲོས་ལྟ་བུའི་ལས་རིམ་ (cūndröö̀ dābü lɛɛ̀rim) streamlined work.

ཆུ་རྐྱལ་ (cū gɛɛ) 1. va. to cross/ ford a river. 2. va. to bathe. 3. sm.* ཆུ་རྐྱལ་.

ཆུ་རྐྱལ་ཁང་ (cūgɛɛgaŋ) bathroom.

ཆུ་རྐྱལ་ས་ (cū gɛɛsa) place/ beach for swimming or bathing or fording a river.

ཆུ་རྒུན་འབྲུམ་ (cū gündrum) grapes.

ཆུ་རྒོད་ (cūgö̀ö̀) rushing/ roaring river.

ཆུ་རྒྱན་ (cūgyɛn) lotus.

ཆུ་རྒྱབ་པ་ (cūgyəbbə) person in charge of allocating irrigation water to fields.

ཆུ་རྒྱལ་(cūgyɛɛ) sm.* ཆུ་རྐྱལ་.

ཆུ་རྒྱས་ (cū gyɛɛ̀) vi. (of water) to be in spate, to rise ¶ གཙང་པོ་དེའི་ཐོག་དབྱར་དུས་ཆུ་རྒྱས་སྐབས་ཏན་ཁྲི་ཕྲག་འཁྱིག་པའི་གྲུ་གཟིངས་གཏོང་ཐུབ་ཀྱི་ཡོད་པ་རེད་ In the summer, when the river rises, ships carrying tens of thousands of tons can sail.

ཆུ་རྒྱུག (cū gyuù) vi. to be flowing (water) ¶ ཆར་པ་མང་པོ་བབ་ནས་ལམ་ཁར་ཆུ་རྒྱུག་གི་འདུག Because it rained heavily water was flowing on the road.

ཆུ་རྒྱུག་རྒྱུག (cū gyuguù) fluent ¶ ཁོས་བོད་སྐད་ཆུ་རྒྱུག་རྒྱུག་རྒྱུག་གི་འདུག He speaks fluent Tibetan.

ཆུ་རྒྱུག་ཚད་ (cū gyuùdzɛɛ̀) rate of flow of water.

ཆུ་རྒྱུག་ཤུལ་ (cū gyuùshüü) trace of running water.

ཆུ་རྒྱུག་ས་ (cū gyuùsə) river bed.

ཆུ་རྒྱུད་ (cūgyüǜ) 1. river bank, the areas beside a river ¶ འབྲི་ཆུའི་ཆུ་རྒྱུད་ལ་གྲོང་ཚོ་མང་པོ་ཡོད་པ་རེད་ Along the banks of the Yangtse River there are many villages. 2. water system.

ཆུ་རྒྱུད་དེད་ནས་འགྲོ་ (cūgyüǜ teènɛ dro) va. to go somewhere following the course of a river (upstream or downstream depending on the context).

ཆུ་རྒྱུན་ (cūgyün) 1. river, stream. 2. the flow of rivers, current; vi.—བབ་ to flow (of rivers/ stream) ¶ སྐྱིད་ཚལ་གྱི་ནང་ཆུ་རྒྱུན་མ་ཆད་པ་ར་འབབ་ཀྱི་ཡོད་པ་རེད་ The stream flows continuously through the garden; va.—གཅོད་ to stop/ cut off the flow of a river ¶ ཆུ་ཤུགས་གློག་འདོན་ས་ཚིགས་ཀྱི་ཆུ་བཀག་གིས་དྲག་དུ་རྒྱུག་པའི་གཙང་པོའི་ཆུ་རྒྱུན་བཅད་པ་རེད་ The dam of the hydroelectric station has stopped the flow of the forceful river.

ཆུ་རྒྱུན་གྱེན་ལྡོག (cūgyün gyendɔ̀ɔ) adverse current, going against the current ¶ སྤྱི་ཚོགས་རིང་ལུགས་ལ་ངོ་རྒོལ་བྱེད་པའི་ཆུ་རྒྱུན་གྱེན་ལྡོག་བཀག་འགོག་བྱེད་དགོས་ We must block the adverse current that is opposing socialism.

ཆུ་རྒྱུན་འབབ་ཡུལ་ (cūgyün bəbyüü) river valley/ basin, the place where a river descends to.

ཆུ་རྒྱུན་བཞིན་ (cūgyünshin) uninterrupted, continual [Lit. like the flow of a river].

ཆུ་རྒྱུས་ (cūgyɛɛ̀) vein.

ཆུ་སྐང་ (cūgaŋ) boil, blister; vi.—སྐྱེ་; —དོན་ to get a boil/ blister.

ཆུ་སྒང་ (cūgaŋ) abbr. of ཆུ་བཞི་སྒང་དྲུག.

ཆུ་སྒམ་ (cūgam) water tank.

ཆུ་སྒུལ་འཕྲུལ་འཁོར་ (cūgüü trṻǜgɔɔ) sm. ཆུ་འགུལ་གློག་སྐྱེད་མ་འཁོར་.

ཆུ་སྒུལ་མ་འཁོར་ (cūgüü magɔɔ) sm. ཆུ་འགུལ་མ་འཁོར.

ཆུ་སྒོ་ (cūgo) 1. water gate; va.—འབྱེད་ to open the water gate (of a dam). 2. mouth of the urethra, the opening from which males and females urinate.

ཆུ་སྒྲ་ (cūdra) sound of a river/ water.

ཆུ་སྒྲེ་(cū dre) va. to dip sth. in water/ liquids.

ཆུ་སྒྲོལ་ཟམ་བཤིག (cūdröö samshiì) not repaying kindness, being ungrateful [Lit. after crossing the river, destroying the bridge].

ཆུ་བརྐྱལ་ (cū gɛɛ) 1. p. of ཆུ་རྐྱལ་. 2. in compounds, sm. ཆུ་རྐྱལ་.

ཆུ་བརྒྱ་ཟམ་གཅིག (cūgya samjig) sm. ཆུ་བརྒྱ་ཟམ་བསྡུས་.

ཆུ་བརྒྱ་ཟམ་བསྡུས་ (cūgya samdüǜ) 1. the main or essential idea/ concept. 2. putting/ bringing many different groups under one ¶ ཚོགས་པ་འདུ་མིན་ཁག་མང་པོ་ཡོད་པ་ཚང་མ་གཞུང་གཅིག་གི་འོག་དུ་ཆུ་

བཅུ་ཐམ་བསྡུས་ཡོང་བ་བྱ་དགོས་ We have to bring all the different groups under one government like "a hundred rivers under one bridge" [Lit. hundred rivers under a bridge].

ཆུ་ང་ (cūŋe) sm. ཆུང་ངུ་.

ཆུ་ངན་ (cūŋɛn) 1. bad/ dirty/ polluted/ contaminated water. 2. flood. 3. fluid secreted in a woman's vagina when sexually aroused.

ཆུ་ངན་ལང་ཤོར་ (cūŋɛn laŋshɔɔ) sm. ཆུ་ངན་ལམ་ཤོར་.

ཆུ་ངན་ལམ་ཞུགས་ (cūŋɛn laŋshuù) sm. ཆུ་ངན་ལམ་ཤོར་.

ཆུ་ངན་ལམ་ཤོར་ (cūŋɛn lamshɔɔ) having to do sth. bad ༑ཁྲལ་རིགས་ཆུ་ངན་ལམ་ཤོར་གྱི་འབྲི་འཁེལ་བྱུང་ (We) had to pay the taxes that were imposed. [Lit. bad water spilled on the road]. 2. becoming spoiled in the sense of continuing a bad behavior/ standard ༑ཁོང་ཆུ་ཚོད་བཅུ་པར་ཡོང་ཡག་འདི་ཆུ་ངན་ལམ་ཤོར་རེད་ He has become spoiled and comes to work (only) at 10 (a.m.).

ཆུ་ངོ་ (cūŋo) sm. ཆུ་ཁ་.

ཆུ་ངོགས་ (cūŋɔɔ̀) sm. ཆུ་གྲམ་.

ཆུ་ངོགས་གཏམ་རྒྱུད་ (cūŋɔɔ̀ dəmgyüù) name of famous Chinese novel ("Outlaws of the Marsh").

ཆུ་ངོས་ (cūŋöö̀) 1. sea level. 2. the surface of water.

ཆུ་ངོས་ཀྱི་ཐིག (cūŋöö̀gi tīg) the level of water, horizon line.

ཆུ་མངར་མོ་ (cū ŋārmo) soda, pop [Lit. sweet water].

ཆུ་ཇམས་ (cūŋam) depth of water.

ཆུ་ཇམས་པ་ (cūŋamba) poet. a wave.

ཆུ་སྔོ་ (cūŋo) 1. blue water. 2. algae.

ཆུ་སྔོ་ལི་ཙའི་ (cūŋo lidzawo) tib.ch. bladder wart.

ཆུ་ཅུ་གང་ (cū jūgaŋ) a type of medicine.

ཆུ་གཅོད་ (cū jöö̀) 1. va. to stop/ cut off the flow of water. 2. va. to stop animals from drinking water.

ཆུ་གཅོག་ཚད་ (cū jöötsɛɛ̀) ship's displacement.

ཆུ་བཅད་མཚོ་བགྲལ་ (cūjɛɛ̀ tsōgɛɛ) traveling a great distance [Lit. cross river and cross lake].

ཆུ་བཅས་བྱེད་ (cūjɛɛ̀ cee̱) va. to irrigate fields.

ཆུ་བཅུ་ (cū jū) 1. f. of ཆུ་འཆུ་ 2. va. to take water out of a container with a ladle.

ཆུ་བཅུད་ (cūjüǜ) salt.

ཆུ་བཅུས་ (cūjüǜ) p. of ཆུ་འཆུ་.

ཆུ་བཅོས་ (cū jöö̀) water improvement/ purification/ control.

ཆུ་ལྕུག (cūjaà) a type of herb.

ཆུ་ལྕི་རིགས་ (cū jīrig) heavy water.

ཆུ་ཆག (cūjaà) 1. kneading rancid pieces of butter in cold water to wash away mold that has formed on it; va.—རྒྱག; —བྱེད་. 2. fodder for livestock consisting of water mixed with ground barley and lentils. 3. vi. (of water) to get lower, to go down, to recede ༑ཆར་ཞོད་ཆད་ན་ཆུ་ཆག་གི་རེད་ The river will go down when the monsoon stops. ༑ཆུ་ཆག་པའི་དུས་ Low water season.

ཆུ་ཆད་ (cū cɛɛ̀) vi. to have water be/ get cut off.

ཆུ་ཆུ་ (cūcu) an expression of feeling cold.

ཆུ་ཆུང་ཐབས་ཐམ་པ་མཐོ་ཐབས་ (cū cūŋdəb samba tōdəb) both sides compromising to reach a settlement; va.—བྱེད་ [Lit. method for making river recede, method for making bridge higher].

ཆུ་ཆུང་བའི་དུས་ (cūcuŋwɛ tüü̱) dry season.

ཆུ་ཆུང་ཟམ་མཐོ་ (cūjuŋ samto) shung. sm. ཆུ་ཆུང་ཐབས་ཟམ་པ་མཐོ་ཐབས་.

ཆུ་ཆེན་པོ་ (cū cēmbo) 1. high tide. 2. big river.

ཆུ་ཆེན་ཡུར་མ་གཤོངས་ (cūjen yu̱r ma̱shom) shung. flood water which overflows the drain/ canal.

ཆུ་ཆུའུ་ (cū cūwu) sm. ཆོ་ལོ་.

ཆུ་ཆོད་ (cū cöö̀) 1. vi. to have the flow of water stop ༑ས་ཡོམ་གྱིས་རྐྱེན་པས་གཙང་པོའི་ཆུ་ཆོད་པ་རེད་ Because of the earthquake, the flow of the river got stopped (cut off). 2. vi. to be able to cross/ ford a river ༑ཆུ་རྒྱས་སྐབས་གཙང་པོའི་ཆུ་ཆོད་ཐུབ་ཀྱི་མེད་པ་རེད་ When the river is high one is unable to cross it.

ཆུ་འཆུ་: p. **ཆུ་བཅུས་**; f. **ཆུ་བཅུ་** (cū cū) va. to ladle out water.

ཆུ་ཇ་ (cūja) a drink made from water, butter and salt.

ཆུ་འཇགས་ (cūnjaà) sprinkling water on a floor for sweeping; va.—རྒྱག.

ཆུ་འཇགས་རྡོ་གསལ་ (cūnjaà do̱sɛɛ) hidden situation coming to light [Lit. when water subsides the rocks are visible].

ཆུ་རྗེས་ (cūjeè) water mark/ stain.

ཆུ་ཉལ་ (cūñɛɛ) poet. a well.

ཆུ་ཉིན་སྲིབ་ (cū ñi̱ndrib) the mountains on two sides of a river.

ཆུ་ཉུང་ (cūñuŋ) swallow (bird).

ཆུ་ཉོག (cūñog) muddy/ dirty water.

ཆུ་གཉེར་ (cūñer) 1. ripples on water (often used to convey ceaseless action) ༑དཀའ་ངལ་ཆུ་གཉེར་བཞིན་ཐུག་པའི་སྐབས་ When one comes across ceaseless problems. 2. sm. ཆུ་སྙེར་གཉེར་པ་.

ཆུ་གཉིས་བར་ (cū ñīibar) a place between two rivers.

ཆུ་རྙོག (cūñog) 1. sm. ཆུ་ཉོག. 2. va. to stir up trouble.

ཆུ་རྙོག་ཉ་འཛིན་ (cūñog ña̱dzin) making trouble to gain profit/ benefit; va.—བྱེད་ ༑བོད་ཀྱི་སྐུ་དྲག་གིས་ཆུ་རྙོག་ཉ་འཛིན་བྱས་ནས་མི་དམངས་ཀྱི་ཁོང་ཁྲོ་བསླངས་པ་རེད་ The Tibetan aristocrats incited the people to be angry for their own gain.

ཆུ་རྙོག་མ་ (cūñogma) muddy water.

ཆུ་སྙིགས་ (cūñig) dirty water (e.g., water that has been used to wash/ rinse sth.).

ཆུ་སྙིགས་དྭངས་བཟོའི་སྒྲིག་ཆས་ (cūñig ta̱nsöö dri̱gjə) water purifying equipment.

ཆུ་སྙིང་ (cūñiŋ) salt.

ཆུ་སྙོམས་འཇལ་ཆས་ (cūñam jɛ̱ɛjɛɛ̀) a water leveling instrument (used in irrigation).

ཆུ་སྙོམས་འཇལ་བྱེད་ཁྲི་ཙེ་ (cūñam jɛ̱ɛjeè trēdze) tib.ch. instrument/ ruler for measuring water level.

ཆུ་བསྙལ་ (cūñɛɛ) a beam-like wood structure that a water mill stands on.

ཆུ་གཏིག (cū dīg) va. to allow something to drip (e.g., to drain out water).

ཆུ་གཏིག་སྦུ་བ་ (cūdig bu̱wə) burette.

ཆུ་གཏིང་ (cūdiŋ) underwater.

ཆུ་གཏིང་འགགས་མདེལ་ (cūdiŋ gɛ̱ɛ̀dee) underwater mine/ explosive.

ཆུ་གཏིང་འབར་མདེལ་ (cūdiŋ ba̱rdee) sm. ཆུ་གཏིང་འགག་མདེལ་.

ཆུ་གཏིང་ཐུང་བ་ (cūdiŋ tūŋwə) shallow water.

ཆུ་གཏིང་ཟབ་པ་ (cūdiŋ sə̱bba) deep water.

ཆུ་གཏིང་རིང་བ་ (cūdiŋ ri̱ŋwə) sm. ཆུ་གཏིང་ཟབ་པ་.

ཆུ་གཏེར་ (cūder) 1. ocean, sea. 2 an ocean mine.

ཆུ་གཏེར་མུ་ཁྱུད་ (cūder mu̱gyüù) outer-walls (used in mandalas).

ཆུ་གཏེར་བཞི་ (cūdershi) the four seas that surround Mount Meru.

ཆུ་གཏེར་ཟུར་ (cūder su̱r) bay, gulf.

ཆུ་གཏོང་ (cū dōŋ) va. to irrigate, to water.

ཆུ་གཏོང་ས་ (cūdoŋsa) place to be watered.

ཆུ་གཏོར་ (cū dɔ̄ɔ) va. to sprinkle/ splash/ scatter water.

ཆུ་གཏོར་གད་རྒྱག (cūdɔɔ kɛ̱ɛ̀ gyaà) va. to sprinkle water on the floor and then sweep.

ཆུ་གཏོར་ཁོག་ལྡིར་ (cūdɔɔ kōgdir) watering can, sprinkling can.

ཆུ་གཏོར་དམ་བེ་ (cūdɔɔ ta̱mbe) sm. ཆུ་གཏོར་ཁོག་ལྡིར་.

ཆུ་གཏོར་འཚག་ཁུང་ (cūdɔɔ tsāggun) sprinkler head (with holes).

ཆུ་གཏོར་ཡོ་བྱད་ (cūdɔɔ yo̱cɛɛ̀) watering/ spraying utensils.

ཆུ་གཏོར་མཆུ་ཏོ་ (cūdɔɔ cūdo) spraying nozzle.

ཆུ་གཏོར་ཀླངས་འཁོར་ (cūdɔɔ lāŋgɔɔ) water sprinkling car/ truck.

ཆུ་རྟ་ (cūda) water-horse year.

ཆུ་རྟ་ཞིབ་གཞུང་ (cūda shibshuŋ) shung. a government edict about land and taxes that was issued in water-horse year.

ཆུ་རྟགས་ (cūdaà) sm. ཆབ་རྟགས་.

ཆུ་སྟག (cūdaà) water-tiger year.

ཆུ་སྟེར་ (cū dēr) va. to give water.

ཆུ་སྟོད་ (cūdöö) upstream, upper reaches of a river.

ཆུ་སྟོད་སྐྱེས་ (cū döögyeè) Tuesday.

ཆུ་སྟོད་ཟླ་བ་ (cūdöö dawa) the month that goes from the 16th day of the 5th month to 15th day of the 6th month.

ཆུ་ཐག (cūdaà) the rope that connects two horses pulling a cart. 2. the rope on a plow.

ཆུ་ཐག་གཙོད་ (cūtaà jöö) va. to rinse clothes that have been washed with water.

ཆུ་ཐིགས་ (cūdig) drop of water, dripping water; vi.—རྒྱག to drip, to leak (water).

ཆུ་ཐིགས་རྡོ་ཕུག (cūdig dobuù) small amounts of diligence/ work over a long period can have a powerful effect [Lit. drops of water can wear through rocks].

ཆུ་ཐིགས་བསགས་པའི་རྒྱ་མཚོ་ (cūdig dobuù) sm. ཆུ་ཐིགས་རྡོ་ཕུག [Lit. drops of water can accumulate to make an ocean].

ཆུ་ཐུབ་ལོ་ཏོག (cūtub lodɔɔ̀) water resistant crops.

ཆུ་ཐོག (cūtɔɔ̀) via sea/ water, on the water, concerning water.

ཆུ་ཐོག་སྐྱེལ་འདྲེན་ (cūdɔɔ̀ gyēndren) shipping/ transporting by water; va.—བྱེད་.

ཆུ་ཐོག་སྐྱེལ་འདྲེན་ཀུང་སི་ (cūdɔɔ̀ gyēndren gūŋsi) tib.ch. water transport company.

ཆུ་ཐོག་སྐྱེལ་འདྲེན་ས་ཚིགས་ (cūdɔɔ̀ gyēndren sədzii̇) water transport station.

ཆུ་ཐོག་ཉེན་འགོག (cūdɔɔ̀ ñengɔɔ̀) marine insurance.

ཆུ་ཐོག་མི་ཚང་ (cūdɔɔ̀ midzaŋ) boat dwellers/ people.

ཆུ་ཐོག་འགྲིམ་འགྲུལ་ (cūdɔɔ̀ drimdrüü) water/ sea travel.

ཆུ་ཐོག་འགྲིམ་འགྲུལ་གྱི་བྱ་བ་ (cūdɔɔ̀ drimdrüügi cawa) ocean navigation.

ཆུ་ཐོག་འགྲོ་ལམ་ (cūdɔɔ̀ drolam) waterway, sea lane.

ཆུ་ཐོག་གནམ་གྲུ་ (cūdɔɔ̀ nəmdru) seaplane.

ཆུ་ཐོག་ལ་འགྲོ་ (cūdɔɔ̀la dro) va. to go by water (river/ sea/ ocean).

ཆུ་ཐོག་ལུས་རྩལ་ (cūtɔɔ̀ lüüdzεὲ) aquatic sports.

ཆུ་ཐོན་ (cūdön) marine, aquatic.

ཆུ་ཐོན་དངོས་རྫས་ (cūdön ŋöödzεὲ) marine/ aquatic products.

ཆུ་ཐོན་དངོས་རྫས་ལས་རིགས་ (cūdön ŋöödzεὲ lεèrig) aquatic products industry.

ཆུ་ཐོན་དངོས་རིགས་ (cūdön ŋöörig) sm. ཆུ་ཐོན་དངོས་རྫས་.

ཆུ་ཐོན་དངོས་རིགས་ཀྱི་ཐོན་ཁུངས་ (cūdön ŋööriggi töndzεὲ) aquatic resources.

ཆུ་ཐོན་དངོས་རིགས་གསོ་སྐྱེལ་ (cūdön ŋöörig sōbel) aquaculture.

ཆུ་ཐོན་དངོས་རིགས་གསོ་སྐྱེལ་ར་བ་ (cūdön ŋöörig sōbel rawa) aquafarm.

ཆུ་ཐོན་བྱ་བ་ (cūdön cawa) marine work/ business.

ཆུ་ཐོན་ཟ་ཆས་ (cūdön sajeὲ) seafood.

ཆུ་ཐོན་ཟམ་བརྗེད་ (cūdön samjeè) sm. ཆུ་ཐོན་ཟམ་པ་ [Lit. the water crossed, forget the bridge].

ཆུ་ཐོན་ཟམ་པ་ (cūdön samba) ungrateful, ingratitude [Lit. (forgetting) the bridge after crossing the water].

ཆུ་ཐོན་ཟམ་པ་པོར་ (cūtön samba pɔɔ) sm. ཆུ་ཐོན་ཟམ་པ་.

ཆུ་ཐོན་ཟམ་དཔེ་ (cūtön sambe) sm. ཆུ་ཐོན་ཟམ་པ་.

ཆུ་ཐོན་ཟམ་པོར་ (cūtön sam pɔɔ) sm. ཆུ་ཐོན་ཟམ་པ་པོར་.

ཆུ་ཐོབ་ (cūdob) shung. one's share of irrigation water.

ཆུ་ཐོར་ (cūdɔɔ) chicken-pox.

ཆུ་འཐག (cūdaà) water mill.

ཆུ་འཐབ་ (cūdəb) water warfare, naval fighting/ struggle.

ཆུ་འཐུང་དུས་ཆུ་ཕུགས་དྲན་དགོས་ (cū tūndü cū pūù trεngöö) not forgetting the origin/ source [Lit. when drinking water you have to remember the source of the water].

ཆུ་འཐེན་ (cū tēn) va. to drain water, to pump water.

ཆུ་འཐེན་འཁོར་ལོ་ས་ཚིགས་ (cūden kɔ̄ɔlo sədzii̇) water pumping station.

ཆུ་འཐེན་འཁོར་ལོ་ (cūden kɔ̄ɔlo) water pump.

ཆུ་འཐེན་འཕྲུལ་འཁོར་ (cūden trüügɔɔ) sm. ཆུ་འཐེན་འཁོར་ལོ་.

ཆུ་འཐེན་ས་ཚིགས་ (cūden sədzii̇) water pumping station.

ཆུ་འཐོར་ (cū tɔ̄ɔ) vi. to get scattered/ sprinkled/ splashed (of water).

ཆུ་འཐོར་རྫིང་བུ་ (cūdɔɔ dziŋbu) fountain with shooting water.

ཆུ་དང་མེ་ཕྲད་ (cūdaŋ me trεὲ) irreconcilable, incompatible [Lit. water and fire meeting].

ཆུ་དང་འོ་མ་འདྲེས་པ་ (cūdaŋ oma dreèba) getting along extremely well, compatible [Lit. water and milk mixed together].

ཆུ་དམ་ (cūdam) hot water bottle.

ཆུ་དར་ (cūdar) prayer flags situated along a river bank.

ཆུ་དིམ་ (cūtim) going underwater, diving; va.—རྒྱག to go underwater, to dive.

ཆུ་དུགས་ (cūdug) a type of Tibetan medical treatment using water.

ཆུ་དོང་ (cūdoŋ) any hole in the ground with water inside, a well, a puddle, a ditch.

ཆུ་དྭངས་ (cūdaŋ) a magical stone that makes water clear.

ཆུ་དྭངས་གྲམ་གསལ་ (cūdaŋ dramsεε) very clear [Lit. water clear, bank clear].

ཆུ་དྭངས་ཉ་གསལ་ (cūdaŋ ñamsεε) very clear [Lit. water clear, fish clear].

ཆུ་དྭངས་ནོར་བུ་ (cūdaŋ nɔɔbu) sm. ཆུ་དྭངས་.

ཆུ་དྭངས་པོ་ (cū taŋbo) clear water.

ཆུ་དྭངས་མ་ (cū taŋma) sm. ཆུ་དྭངས་པོ་.

ཆུ་དྲག (cūdrag) sm. ཆུ་དྲེག.

ཆུ་དྲངས་ (cū traŋ) p. of ཆུ་འདྲེན་.

ཆུ་དྲི་མ་ཞིམ་པོ་ (cū trimə shimbu) perfume, scent.

ཆུ་དྲེག (cūdreg) encrustation, dregs.

ཆུ་དྲོད་འཇམ་ (cū trönjam) lukewarm water.

ཆུ་དྲོད་འཇམ་གྱིས་ཤ་མི་འཚོས་ (cū trönjamgi shā midzöö) loose discipline is not effective [Lit. can't cook meat in lukewarm water].

ཆུ་དྲོན་ (cūdrön) warm water.

ཆུ་དྲོན་སོན་སྦང་ (cūdrön sönbaŋ) soaking seeds in warm water (for fast germination).

ཆུ་གདན་ (cūdεn) diaper.

ཆུ་བདེ་ཉ་སྐྱིད་ (cūde ñagyii̇) a state of being happy and well/ comfortable [Lit. water is well, fish are happy].

ཆུ་མདའ་ (cūnda) hose, water gun.

ཆུ་མདེལ་ (cūndel) torpedo.

ཆུ་མདེལ་འཕེན་བྱེད་དམག་གྲུ་ (cūndel pēnjeè məgdru) torpedo boat.

ཆུ་མདོ་ (cūndo) place where two rivers intersect.

ཆུ་མདོང་ (cūdoŋ) 1. water pipe. 2. water jug/ bucket/ pail.

ཆུ་འདལ་ (cū dεε) 1. vi. to spread water. 2. a calm/ gentle slow running river.

ཆུ་འདུར་ (cūndur) sm. ཆུ་སྣུར་.

ཆུ་འདུས་མདོ་ (cū düü do) sm. ཆུ་མདོ་.

ཆུ་འདོན་ས་ (cū dönsa) source of water.

ཆུ་འདྲེན་ (cūndren) irrigation, watering, drawing in water; va. ཆུ་འདྲེན་; —གཏོང་ ། ཞིང་ལ་ཆུ་འགོ་ནས་ཆུ་དྲངས་ཡོད་པ་རེད་ They have irrigated the field from the headwaters of the stream.

ཆུ་འདྲེན་འཁོར་ལོ་ (cūndren kɔ̄ɔlo) water wheel (irrigation device).

ཆུ་འདྲེན་ལྕགས་མདོང་ (cūndren lāgdoŋ) iron/ metal

pipe for conveying water.

ཆུ་འདྲེན་མདོང་རིང་ (cūndren do̲ŋriŋ) water conduit/ conveying pipe.

ཆུ་འདྲེན་སྦུ་གུ་ (cūndren bu̲gu) sm. ཆུ་འདྲེན་ལྦུགས་མདོང་.

ཆུ་འདྲེན་སྦུག་རིང་ (cūndren bu̲griŋ) fire hose, hose.

ཆུ་འདྲེན་ཡུར་བུ་ (cūndren yu̲rbu) irrigation canal.

ཆུ་འདྲེན་ཡུར་བཟོ་ (cūdren yu̲rso) bringing in irrigation water from a source and building irrigation canals.

ཆུ་འདྲེན་ས་ཚིགས་ (cūdren sədzii) water/ irrigation pumping station.

ཆུ་འདྲེས་ས་ (cū dre̲esa) place where several streams of water meet/ join.

ཆུ་རྡེའུ་ (cū di̲wu) small pebbles on a water bed.

ཆུ་རྡོ་ (cūdo) pebble.

ཆུ་རྡོལ་ནད་ (cū dö̲ö̲nɛɛ̀) illness characterized by inability to control urination.

ཆུ་ལྡིང་པད་མ་ (cūdiŋ bɛ̄ɛ̀ma) lotus, water lily.

ཆུ་ལྡུམ་ཨོག་དཀར་ (cūdum ɔ̄ggar) veronica javanica blume (used in Tibetan medicine).

ཆུ་ལྡུར་ (cūdur) fodder for horse/ mules (mixture of water and unroasted grains).

ཆུ་སྡོར་ (cūdɔr) ingredients such as meat, butter, and cheese that are put in soups/ stews; va.—རྒྱག; —འདེབས་ to put such ingredients into soups/ stews.

ཆུ་ནང་ཟླ་བ་འཛུ་བ་ (cūnaŋ da̲wa ju̲wə) an impractical/ useless/ vain effort [Lit. catch the moon in the water].

ཆུ་ནད་ (cūnɛɛ̀) dropsy.

ཆུ་ནུས་ (cūnüü) water power.

ཆུ་གནས་ (cūnɛɛ̀) aquatic, living in the water.

ཆུ་གནོན་འཁོར་ལོ་ (cūnön kɔ̄ɔlo) hydraulic press.

ཆུ་རྣག (cū nāg) abbr. water/ serum and pus.

ཆུ་སྣ་གར་ཁྲིད་ (cūna ka̲r trīi) gullible, led/ influenced easily [Lit. water can be led anywhere].

ཆུ་སྣ་གྱེན་འདྲེན་ (cūna gye̲ndren) impossible to drive back/ repulse [Lit. drawing water up a slope/ hill].

ཆུ་སྣ་འཛོམ་པོ་ (cūna dzo̲mbo) abundance of water/ streams.

ཆུ་སྣེ་ (cūne) sm. ཆུ་འགོ་.

ཆུ་སྣོད་ (cūnöö) water pitcher/ jug.

ཆུ་པ་ (cūbə) a person who carries water.

ཆུ་པད་ (cūbɛɛ̀) leech.

ཆུ་དཔྱད་ (cū jɛ̀ɛ) 1. investigating/ examining urine (for illness). 2. hydrology.

ཆུ་དཔྱད་ས་ཚིགས་ (cūjɛɛ sədziii) hydrometric station, hydrographic station.

ཆུ་དཔྱད་ས་གཤིས་ (cūjɛɛ̀ səshiì) hydrogeology.

ཆུ་སྤགས་ (cūbaà) སྤགས་ made from རྩམ་པ་ mixed with water.

ཆུ་སྤེ་ (cūbe) shung. railing on a roof.

ཆུ་སྤྱོད་ཚད་དཔྱད་ཆས་ (cū jō̄ò̀dzɛɛ̀ jɛ̄ɛ̀cɛɛ̀) water (use) meter.

ཆུ་སྤྲིན་ (cūdrin) rain clouds.

ཆུ་སྤྲེ་ (cūdre) water-monkey year.

ཆུ་སྤྲེལ་ (cūdrel) sm. ཆུ་སྤྲེ་.

ཆུ་ཕ་གི་ (cū pəgi) the other side of a river.

ཆུ་ཕ་རི་ (cū pəri) sm. ཆུ་ཕ་གི་.

ཆུ་ཕག (cūpag) water-pig year.

ཆུ་ཕུགས་ (cūbuù) water spring, fountain.

ཆུ་ཕུད་ (cūbüü) water offering to the gods.

ཆུ་ཕོ་ (cūpo) the male water element (in Tibetan astrology).

ཆུ་ཕྱགས་ (cūjaà) sprinkling/ spraying water (e.g., on clothes to take out wrinkles or on the floor before sweeping); va.—རྒྱག.

ཆུ་ཕྲན་ (cūdrɛn) small river/ stream.

ཆུ་འཕྱོ་ (cū cō) vi. to flood, to overflow.

ཆུ་འཕྲུལ་རྫིང་བུ་ (cūdrüü dzi̲ŋbu) mechanized reservoir.

ཆུ་བ་ (cūwa) tendon, sinew, ligament.

ཆུ་བན་ (cūbɛn) jug/ bucket for carrying water on the back.

ཆུ་བལ་ (cūbɛɛ) mud, slime, aquatic weed that looks like wool.

ཆུ་སྦུག (cūbuù) underground water drainage canal; va.—གཙང་ to clean out an underground drainage canal.

ཆུ་བུམ་ (cūbum) vase for holding water.

ཆུ་བུར་ (cūbur) 1. water bubbles. 2. blister, boil.

ཆུ་བུར་ཅན་ (cūburjɛn) one of the eight different types of cold hell.

ཆུ་བུར་རྡོལ་ (cūbur dö̲ö̲) one of the eight different types of cold hell.

ཆུ་བེད་ (cūbeè) water works, water conservancy facilities, irrigation works.

ཆུ་བེད་ཀྱི་ལྟེ་གནས་ (cūbeègi dēnɛɛ̀) a center for water control/ conservation.

ཆུ་བེད་གློག་ཤུགས་ (cūbeè lɔ̄gshuù) hydroelectric power, water resources and electric power.

ཆུ་བེད་གློག་ཤུགས་པུའུ་ (cūbeè lɔ̄gshuùbu) tib.ch. ministry of hydroelectric power, ministry of water resources and electric power.

ཆུ་བེད་གློག་ཤུགས་བབ་ཚུགས་ (cūbeè lɔ̄gshuù bə̲bdzuù) hydroelectric power station.

ཆུ་བེད་འགག་མདོའི་ཨར་ལས་ (cūbeè gagdö ārlɛɛ̀) conservation/ irrigation project.

ཆུ་བེད་ཅུའུ་ (cūbeèju) tib.ch. bureau of water resources/ works.

ཆུ་བེད་ཆུ་འདྲེན་ (cūbeè cūndren) water conservation and irrigation.

ཆུ་བེད་པུའུ་ (cūbeèbu) tib.ch. irrigation board/ department, ministry of water resources.

ཆུ་བེད་བཟོ་སྐྲུན་ (cūbeè sōdrön) sm. ཆུ་བེད་ཨར་ལས་.

ཆུ་བེད་བཟོ་བཀོད་ (cūbeè so̲göö̀) water conservation project.

ཆུ་བེད་ཨར་ལས་ (cūbeè ārlɛɛ̀) water conservancy project, irrigation works.

ཆུ་བེན་ (cūben) sm. ཆུ་བན་.

ཆུ་བོ་ (cūwo) river.

ཆུ་བོ་གྱེན་ལོག (cūwo gye̲ndɔɔ̀) sm. ཆུ་རྒྱུན་གྱེན་ལོག.

ཆུ་བོ་གྱེན་འདེད་ (cūwo gye̲ndeè) sm. ཆུ་བོ་གྱེན་ལོག.

ཆུ་བོ་བཞི་ (cūwo shi̲) 1. the four great rivers of India. 2. the four stages of life: birth, old age, sickness, death.

ཆུ་བོ་རབ་མེད་ (cūwo rə̲bmeè) an unfordable river.

ཆུ་བོའི་ཀླུང་ (cūwo lūŋ) current of a river.

ཆུ་བོའི་རྒྱུན་བཞིན་ (cūwö gyü̲nshin) sm. ཆུ་རྒྱུན་བཞིན་.

ཆུ་བོའི་མ་ལག (cūwö ma̲laà) river system/ network.

ཆུ་བོའི་སྟོད་ཁུལ་ (cūwö dō̄ò̀güü) upper reaches of a river.

ཆུ་བོའི་སྟོད་རྒྱུད་ (cūwö dō̄ò̀gyüù) sm. ཆུ་བོའི་སྟོད་ཁུལ་.

ཆུ་བྱ་ (cūbja) 1. duck, water-fowl. 2. water-bird year.

ཆུ་བྱ་མཐིང་རིལ་ (cūbja tīŋrii) sea gull.

ཆུ་བྱི་ (cūci) water-mouse year.

ཆུ་བྱི་རྒྱ་དམག (cūci gya̲maà) Tibet-Chinese war of 1912.

ཆུ་བྱིའུ་ (cū ci̲wu) aquatic bird.

ཆུ་བྱོས་ (cū cö̲ö̀) va. to pour water.

ཆུ་འབྲུག (cūdrug) water-snake year.

ཆུ་བྲུན་ (cūdrün) urine and excrement.

ཆུ་བྲུབ་ (cūdrub) p. of ཆུ་འབྲུབ་.

ཆུ་བྲོག (cūdrog) sm. ཆུ་སྡུར་.

ཆུ་བླུད་ (cū lüù) va. to give water (to an animal).

ཆུ་དབྱང་གཉིས་ཅན་ (cū yāŋ ñīìjɛn) hydrogen peroxide solution.

ཆུ་འབི་ (cūmbi) Chubi (valley).

ཆུ་འབུད་ (cū bü̲ü̲) va. to push out/ clear out water, to displace water.

ཆུ་འབུད་གྲུ་གཟིངས་ (cūmbüù tru̲ziŋ) ship displacement.

ཆུ་འབུད་འགག་སྒོ་ (cūmbüù ga̲àgo) canal, spillway.

ཆུ་འབུད་ཆུ་ཀ་ (cūmbüù cūga) sm. ཆུ་འབུད་ཡུར་བུ་.

ཆུ་འབུད་སྦུ་གུ་ (cūmbüù bu̲gu) drainage pipeline, sewer pipe.

ཆུ་འབུར་འབུར་ (cū burbur) bubbling water.

ཆུ་འབུད་ཚད་ (cū büüdzɛɛ̀) amount of displacement of water.

ཆུ་འབུད་ཡུར་བུ་ (cūbüü yurbu) drainage canal, spillway.

ཆུ་འབུར་ (cūmbur) sm.ཆུ་བུར་.

ཆུ་འབེབས་ (cū beb) 1. va. to drain the water from patients with edema. 2. to cause a flood through magic.

ཆུ་འབོམ་ (cūmbom) tib.eng. depth charge, underwater mine.

ཆུ་འབོམ་དམག་གྲུ་ (cūmbom mōgdru) tib.eng. mine dispensing warship, antisubmarine attack ship.

ཆུ་འབྲས་ (cūndɛɛ̀) wet rice, irrigated rice.

ཆུ་འབྲས་ཕུར་འདེབས་འཕྲུལ་འཁོར་ (cūndɛɛ̀ pūndeb trüügɔɔ) rice transplanting machine.

ཆུ་འབྲུག (cūdrug) water-dragon year.

ཆུ་འབྲུབ་ (cū drub) vi. to rise (water/ river).

ཆུ་འབྲུབ་པའི་དུས་སྐབས་ (cū drubɛ tüügəb) high water season, flood season.

ཆུ་འབྲུབ་པའི་ས་ཁུལ་ (cū drubɛ sōgüü) flood area.

ཆུ་འབྲུབ་ཚུལ་ (cū drubdzüü) flood situation.

ཆུ་འབྲུམ་ (cūndrum) chicken pox.

ཆུ་སྦུབས་ (cūbub) water tubes/ pipes.

ཆུ་སྦུར་ (cūbur) water bug, water beetle.

ཆུ་སྦྱིན་ (cū jin) 1. va. to give water. 2. sm. ཆུ་གཏོར་.

ཆུ་སྦྱིན་ས་ཚིགས་ (cūjin sōdzii) water supply station.

ཆུ་སྦྲུལ་ (cūdrüü) 1. a water snake. 2. the water-snake year.

ཆུ་མ་ (cūmə) 1. areas under irrigation, irrigated fields ¶ ཆུ་བེད་ཀྱི་ལས་ཀའི་གྲུབ་འབྲས་ལ་བརྟེན་ནས་ས་ཞིང་མང་བ་ཆུ་མར་གྱུར་བ་རེད་ Because of the success of the irrigation works most of the land became irrigated fields. 2. water carrier. 3. vagina.

ཆུ་མ་བདེ་ན་ཉ་མི་བདེ་ (cūmə dena ña mide) if the leaders are not well/ good/ fine, the masses will not be happy/ well-off [Lit. if water is not good, the fish are not happy].

ཆུ་མ་ཎི་ (cū mani) talking incessantly, loquaciously.

ཆུ་མ་རྩི་ (cū madzi) polygonium sibiricum laxm (used in Tibetan medicine).

ཆུ་མང་ས་ཁུལ་ (cūmaŋ sōgüü) a region of rivers and lakes.

ཆུ་མིག (cūmii) a spring.

ཆུ་མིག་གྲང་མོ་ (cūmii traŋmo) cold spring.

ཆུ་མིག་དགུ་སྒྲིལ་ (cūmii gudrii) type of sling shot with a design that has nine "eyes".

ཆུ་མེད་ཁྲོན་པ་ (cūmeè trömba) waterless well, dried-up well.

ཆུ་མོ་ (cūmo) river.

ཆུ་མོ་ཁ་ཞེང་ཆེ་ཡང་ གྲུ་ཤན་ནུ་མགོའི་འོག་རེད་ (cūmo kāsheŋ cēyaŋ trushɛn dāngö wɔɔ̀ ree) although sb. is powerful they still have to obey their superior's orders [Lit. although the river is wide, it (flows) under a wooden boat].

ཆུ་མོ་དྲངས་བཞིན་ཉ་མོ་གསལ་དུ་འགྲོ་ (cūmo daŋshin ñamo sɛldu dro) sm. ཆུ་འཛགས་རྡོ་གསལ་.

ཆུ་དམག (cūmaà) 1. sailor (in the navy). 2. navy.

ཆུ་སྨད་ (cūmɛɛ̀) downstream, lower reaches of a river.

ཆུ་སྨན་ (cūmɛn) liquid medicines.

ཆུ་སྨོག (cū mɔɔ̀) va. to dip sth. in (water, liquids).

ཆུ་སྨྱོན་ (cūñön) flood, vi.—རྒྱག to flood.

ཆུ་སྨྱོན་འགྱེད་སྒོ་ (cūñön gyeègo) sluice gate.

ཆུ་བཙོས་ (cū dzöö) boiling/ cooking in water; va.—གཏོང་; —རྒྱག to boil/ cook in water.

ཆུ་རྫངས་ (cūdzaŋ) salamander, newt.

ཆུ་རྩམ་ (cūdzam) a better quality tsamba made from washed barley that is roasted while still wet.

ཆུ་རྩལ་ (cūdzɛɛ) 1. aquatic/ swimming sports. 2. swimming skill.

ཆུ་རྩི་དཀར་པོ་ (cūdzi gāābo) root of white bidentate achyranthes.

ཆུ་རྩི་དམར་པོ་ (cūdzi māābo) root of bidentate achyrauthes.

ཆུ་རྩེད་ (cūdzeè) playing in the water, water sports; va.—རྩེ་ to play water sports.

ཆུ་རྩྭ་ (cūdza) sea weeds, algae.

ཆུ་བཙོན་ (cūdzön) water dungeon.

ཆུ་ཚགས་ (cūdzaà) sieve, strainer, filter; va.—རྒྱག.

ཆུ་ཚད་ (cūdzɛɛ̀) 1. volume of water, level of water. 2. a standard, a level ¶ ཤེས་ཡོན་གྱི་ཆུ་ཚད་ཇེ་མཐོར་འགྲོ་གི་ཡོད་པ་རེད་ The level of knowledge is going higher and higher.

ཆུ་ཚད་འཇལ་རྟོག་ས་ཚིགས་ (cūdzɛɛ̀ jɛɛdoò sōdzii)water level survey station.

ཆུ་ཚན་ (cūdzɛn) hot spring; va.—རྒྱག to bathe in a hot spring.

ཆུ་ཚན་ཁ་ (cūdzɛnka) a place where there is a hot spring.

ཆུ་ཚན་རིང་བསིལ་ (cūdzɛn riŋsii) shining round stones/ pebbles in a hot spring.

ཆུ་ཚན་རིགས་ལྔ་ (cūdzɛn rigŋa) five types of hot springs.

ཆུ་ཚའི་འཁྱིག་རྒྱལ་ (cūdzɛ gyiggyɛɛ) hot-water bottle.

ཆུ་ཚལ་ (cūdzɛɛ) watercress.

ཆུ་ཚུར་ཁ་ (cū tsūga) this side of the river.

ཆུ་ཚུར་རི་ (cū tsūūri) sm. ཆུ་ཚུར་ཁ་.

ཆུ་ཚུལ་གཞུང་ལས་ཁང་ (cūdzüü shuŋlɛɛ̀gaŋ) water regimen office.

ཆུ་ཚེ་རིང་ (cū tsēriŋ) one of the six symbols of longevity.

ཆུ་ཚོད་ (cūdzöö) 1. hour ¶ ཆུ་ཚོད་གཅིག་རིང་ For an hour. 2. clock, watch ¶ ཁོ་ལ་ཆུ་ཚོད་གཅིག་སྤྲད་འདུག (They) gave him a watch.

ཆུ་ཚོད་ཀྱི་སྐར་མ་ (cūdzöògi gārma) a minute.

ཆུ་ཚོད་ཀྱི་སྐར་ཆ་ (cūdzöògi gārja) second.

ཆུ་ཚོད་ཀྱི་གདོང་ (cūdzöògi doŋ) the face of a watch.

ཆུ་ཚོད་ཀྱི་ཐག་པ་ (cūdzöògi tāgba) a band/ strap of a wrist watch.

ཆུ་ཚོད་ཀྱི་མདའ་ (cūdzöògi da) hands of a watch or clock.

ཆུ་ཚོད་ཀྱི་མདའ་ཁབ་ (cūdzöògi dagəb) sm. ཆུ་ཚོད་ཀྱི་མདའ་.

ཆུ་ཚོད་ཀྱི་སྐང་ (cūdzöògi sāŋ) second (in time).

ཆུ་ཚོད་འཁོར་ལོ་ (cūdzöò kɔɔ̄lo) clock, watch; va.—འདོགས་ to wear a watch.

ཆུ་ཚོད་མགྱོགས་པོ་ (cūdzöò gyogbo) 1. fast (for watch/ clock). 2. for time to pass quickly/ fast ¶ སྐྱིད་པོ་བཏང་ན་ཆུ་ཚོད་མགྱོགས་པོ་འགྲོ་གི་རེད་ If (you) are having fun, time will go by fast.

ཆུ་ཚོད་འགོག་བཀག (cūdzöò gɔggaà) setting a time for sth.

ཆུ་ཚོད་འགོར་པོ་ (cūdzöò gɔɔbo) slow (for a watch/ clock).

ཆུ་ཚོད་སྒྲིག (cūdzöò drig) 1. va. to adjust/ set the (time) on a watch. 2. va. to arrange/ set a time for sth.

ཆུ་ཚོད་ཉལ་ (cūdzöò ñɛɛ) vi. to have a watch/ clock stop.

ཆུ་ཚོད་ཐིར་སྒྲིག (cūdzöò tirdrig) va. to set a clock alarm.

ཆུ་ཚོད་དང་པོ་ (cūdzöò taŋbo) one o'clock.

ཆུ་ཚོད་དྲངས་ཤེལ་ (cūdzöò taŋshel) watch crystal.

ཆུ་ཚོད་དྲིལ་བུ་ཅན་ (cūdzöò triibujɛn) alarm clock.

ཆུ་ཚོད་བུམ་པ་ (cūdzöò pumbə) hour glass.

ཆུ་ཚོད་གཡོ་ཐོ་ (cūdzöò yōdo) pendulum (clock).

ཆུ་ཚོད་ལུང་ཐག (cūdzöò luŋdaà) wrist watch band/ strap.

ཆུ་ཚོན་ (cūdzön) watercolor (paint), latex paint ¶ ཆུ་ཚོན་རི་མོ་ Watercolor painting.

ཆུ་མཚམས་འབྱེད་རི་ (cūndzam ceèri) watershed (mountain).

ཆུ་འཚག་པའི་སྐད་ཡོད་ཀྱང་གདམ་འཚག་པའི་སྐད་མེད་ (cūtsɔgbɛ nöò yöògyaŋ dāmtsɔgbɛ nöò meè) be careful not to talk about secrets as it will spread

[Lit. although there is a container to hold water, there is no container to hold talk].

ཆུ་མཛོད་ (cūdzöö) 1. reservoir. 2. ocean.

ཆུ་མཛོད་དོ་དམ་ཁང་ (cūdzöö todamgaŋ) reservoir management office.

ཆུ་འཛག (cū dzaà) vi. to leak, to drip.

ཆུ་འཛིན་ (cūndzin) poet. 1. cloud. 2. vagina.

ཆུ་འཛུལ་ (cū dzüü) 1. va. to go into/ enter the water. 2. vi. to have water get into sth.

ཆུ་འཛུལ་དམག་གྲུ་ (cūdzüü məgdru) submarine ¶ ཉིང་རྡུལ་ནུས་སྤྱོད་ཆུ་འཛུལ་དམག་གྲུ་ Nuclear powered submarine.

ཆུ་འཛོམས་ས་ (cū dzomsa) confluence of two or more rivers.

ཆུ་ཛ་ (cūdza) earthenware water pot/ pitcher.

ཆུ་ཛར་ཛར་ (cū dzardzar) water dripping from sth.

ཆུ་རྫས་ (cūdzɛɛ̀) sm. ཆུ་ཐོན་ཟ་ཆས་.

ཆུ་རྫས་ཁའོ་ (cūdzɛɛ̀ kəwo) acquatic products office/ department.

ཆུ་རྫས་མགོ་སྤྱོད་ཀུང་སི་ (cūdzɛɛ̀ kōdröö gūŋsi) tib.ch. acquatic products company.

ཆུ་རྫས་ཚོང་ཁང་ (cūdzɛɛ̀ tsōŋgaŋ) acquatic products store.

ཆུ་རྫས་ཞིབ་འཇུག་ཁང་ (cūdzɛɛ̀ shimjuùgaŋ) acquatic products research institute.

ཆུ་རྫས་ལས་སྣོན་བཟོ་གྲྭ་ (cūdzɛɛ̀ lɛɛ̀nön sodra) acquatic products processing plant.

ཆུ་རྫས་སློབ་ཚོགས་ (cūdzɛɛ̀ lōbso) Society of Fisheries.

ཆུ་རྫིང་ (cūdziŋ) pond, reservoir.

ཆུ་ལྦ་ (cūwa) roof drain pipe.

ཆུ་ལྦུ་ (cūbu) water bubbles, foam.

ཆུ་ལྦུར་ (cūbur) sm. ཆུ་ལྦ་.

ཆུ་ཞག (cūshaà) teary-eyed; vi.—འཁོར་; འཁྱིལ་ to become teary-eyed.

ཆུ་ཞིང་ (cūshiŋ) an irrigated field.

ཆུ་ཞེང་ (cūsheŋ) 1. width of a river ¶ ཆུ་ཞེང་ཆེ་རུ་ཕྱིན་ཡོད་པ་རེད The width of the river increased. 2. width and breadth.

ཆུ་ཞེང་གབ་པ་ (cūsheŋ gəbbə) well-proportioned (person, furniture or clothes, etc.).

ཆུ་གཞུག (cūshug) lower reaches of a river.

ཆུ་གཞུང་ (cūshuŋ) the middle of a stream/ river, main current.

ཆུ་གཞོང་ (cūshoŋ) 1. water basin/ trough. 2. tub for washing/ bathing.

ཆུ་བཞི་སྒང་དྲུག (cūshi gəndruù) 1. four rivers and six ranges in eastern Tibet. 2. name of the main Tibetan resistance group in the 1950's and 60's.

ཆུ་ཟངས་ (cūsaŋ) copper cauldron.

ཆུ་ཟབ་གྲུ་ཁ་ (cūsəb druga) deep water port/ harbor.

ཆུ་ཟབ་མཚོ་ཁ་ (cūsəb tsōga) sm. ཆུ་ཟབ་གྲུ་ཁ་.

ཆུ་ཟད་ཁྲོན་པ་ (cūsɛɛ̀ trōmba) in a desperate situation, at the end of one's hope [Lit. a well that has gone dry].

ཆུ་ཟིལ་ (cūsil) droplets of water.

ཆུ་ཟུར་ (cūsur) by the edge/ bank of water.

ཆུ་ཟོ་ (cūso) sm. ཆུ་ཟོམ་.

ཆུ་ཟོམ་ (cūsom) wooden barrel for storing or carrying water.

ཆུ་ཟླ་སྙོབ་པ་ (cū da ñōbba) sm. ཆུ་ནང་ཟླ་བ་འཛུ་བ་.

ཆུ་ཟླ་སྦར་འཛིན་ (cū da bardzin) sm. ཆུ་ནང་ཟླ་བ་འཛུ་བ་.

ཆུ་གཟར་ (cūsar) water ladle.

ཆུ་བཟང་ (cūsaŋ) high grade/ high quality of water.

ཆུ་འོ་གཅིག་འདྲེས་ (cūwo jiŋdreè) complete unity and harmony, completely mixed/ integrated [Lit. mixture of milk and water].

ཆུ་འོག (cūwɔɔ̀) underwater.

ཆུ་འོག་གི་འདམ་ (cūwɔɔ̀gi dam) river mud.

ཆུ་འོག་བྲག་རྡོ་ (cūwɔɔ̀ dragdo) reef, submerged rocks.

ཆུ་འོག་རྒྱུ་གྲུ་ (cūwɔɔ̀ gyudru) sm. ཆུ་འོག་དམག་གྲུ་.

ཆུ་འོག་འབར་མདེལ་ (cūwɔɔ̀ bandee) depth charge, underwater mine.

ཆུ་འོག་དམག་གྲུ་ (cūwɔɔ̀ məgdru) submarine.

ཆུ་འོག་དམག་གྲུ་གཏོར་གྲུ་ (cūwɔɔ̀ məgdru dɔ̄rdru) submarine chaser, attack submarine.

ཆུ་འོབས་ (cūwob) 1. ditch/ pit/ depression filled with water. 2. moat.

ཆུ་ཡི་འཕྲུལ་འཁོར་ (cūyi trüügɔɔ) hydrotherapy machine.

ཆུ་ཡི་ལྦུ་བ་ (cūyi buwə) water bubbles.

ཆུ་ཡིས་ཟད་ (cūyii sɛɛ̀) vi. to be eroded by water ¶ ཆུ་ཡིས་ཟད་པའི་ལུང་པ་ A water eroded area.

ཆུ་ཡུར་ (cūyur) irrigation ditch/ canal.

ཆུ་ཡུར་མ་གཞོང་ (cūyur mashoŋ) shung. sm. ཆུ་ཆེན་ཡུར་མ་གཞོང་.

ཆུ་ཡོས་ (cūyöö) water-hare year.

ཆུ་གཡེང་རྩྭ་ (cūyeŋdza) a type of lettuce.

ཆུ་ར་མ་ (cūrəmə) 1. clay water pot. 2. sm. ཆུ་ར་.

ཆུ་ར་གསུམ་སྒྲིག (cūrə sūmdrig) shung. water tank.

ཆུ་རྭ་ (cūrə) 1. sm. ཆུ་རགས་. 2. water cauldron.

ཆུ་རགས་ (cūraà) dam, dike, embankment; va.—རྒྱག to build/ make a dam.

ཆུ་རགས་ཀྱི་དགག་སྒོ་ (cūraàgi gaàgo) sluice gate.

ཆུ་རགས་ཁ་ཤོར་ (cūraà kāshɔɔ) vi. to burst/ break (of a dam, dike).

ཆུ་རགས་ཟླ་གམ་ཅན་ (cūraà dəgamjɛn) a dam with of vaulted walls.

ཆུ་རགས་འུ་ལག (cūraà wulaà) corvee labor to build a dam.

ཆུ་རང་འཁོལ་ (cū raŋgöö) shung. sth. done voluntarily, sth. that occurs on its own [Lit. water boiling by itself].

ཆུ་རབ་ (cūrəb) shallow part of the river, part of the river where it can be easily forded; va.—རྒྱག to cross/ ford a river.

ཆུ་རལ་ཉིལ་ཉིལ་ (cūrɛɛ ñiiñii) dripping water/ liquid.

ཆུ་རལ་འཛར་འཛར་ (cūrɛɛ dzardzar) sm. ཆུ་རལ་ཉིལ་ཉིལ་.

ཆུ་རས་ (cūrɛɛ̀) cloth worn when bathing, loin cloth, bathing suit, underpants, undershorts.

ཆུ་རིགས་བདུན་ (cūrig dün) seven types of water: rain water, snow water, river water, spring water, well water, salt water, water from tree roots.

ཆུ་རིས་ (cūrii) 1. ripples in water, waves. 2. water color painting. 3. painting/ drawing of water.

ཆུ་རིས་མ་ (cū riimə) brocade/ silk with a water pattern (Chinese).

ཆུ་རིས་ཤིག་ཤིག (cūrii shīgshii) rippling water.

ཆུ་རུག་སྦལ་ལག (cūruù bɛɛlaà) water hyacinth.

ཆུ་རུད་ (cūrüü) sm. ཆུ་ལོག.

ཆུ་རུམ་མ་ (cūrumba) water container.

ཆུ་རླངས་ (cūlaŋ) steam.

ཆུ་རླངས་ཀྱི་གནོན་ཤུགས་ (cūlaŋgi nönshuù) steam power, steam pressure.

ཆུ་རླབས་ (cūləb) a wave; vi.—དབ་; —རྡེབ་ to have waves beat or pound against sth.

ཆུ་ལ་བརྒྱག (cūlə gyaà) vi. to float ¶ གྲུ་དེ་ཆུ་ལ་བརྒྱག་སོང་ The boat floated.

ཆུ་ལ་སྐྲག་པའི་ནད་ (cūlə drāgbɛ nɛɛ̀) hydrophobia.

ཆུ་ལ་བརྟེན་པའི་གསོ་ཐབས་ (cūlə dēmbɛ sōdəb) hydrotherapy.

ཆུ་ལ་གདིམ་ (cūlə dim) vi. to drown.

ཆུ་ལ་དིམ་ (cūlə dim) sm. ཆུ་ལ་གདིམ་.

ཆུ་ལ་ནུབ་ (cūlə nub) sm. ཆུ་ལ་གདིམ་.

ཆུ་ལ་སྦོང་ (cūlə boŋ) va. to soak.

ཆུ་ལ་བྱིང་ (cūlə ciŋ) vi. to sink under water.

ཆུ་ལ་ཤོར་ (cūlə shɔɔ) sm. ཆུ་ལ་གདིམ་.

ཆུ་ལ་སུབ་ (cūlə sūb) va. to drown sb. by holding their head under water.

ཆུ་ལ་ལྷུང་ (cūlə lhūŋ) sm. ཆུ་ལ་གདིམ་.

ཆུ་ལག (cūlaà) sm. ཆུ་ལྡན་.

ཆུ་ལན་ཆང་འཇལ་ (cūlen cāŋ jɛɛ) repaying bad with good, returning/ repaying generously with more than one received [Lit. repay water with beer].

ཆུ་ལམ་ (cūlam) 1. waterway/ marine/ shipping route. 2. urethra. 3. the way/ path from which water is supplied or comes.

ཆུ་ལམ་གྱི་དགས་ (cūlamgi dāà) beacon, buoy, lighthouse.

ཆུ་ལམ་གྱི་སྣ་ཁྲིད་ (cūlamgi nā triì) va. to pilot a ship.

ཆུ་ལམ་གྱི་སྣ་ཁྲིད་པ་ (cūlamgi nātriìbɘ) pilot (of a ship).

ཆུ་ལམ་སྟོན་མཁན་ (cūlam dõngɛn) sm. ཆུ་ལམ་གྱི་སྣ་ཁྲིད་པ་.

ཆུ་ལམ་སྟོན་དགས་ (cūlam dõndaà) sm. ཆུ་ལམ་གྱི་དགས་.

ཆུ་ལམ་གཙང་བཤང་ (cūlam dzāŋshaŋ) clearing/ cleaning/ dredging a waterway.

ཆུ་ལམ་གཤོང་ (cūlam shōŋ) va. to clean/ clear out/ dredge a waterway.

ཆུ་ལམ་བཤང་བཅོས་ (cūlam shāŋjöö) drainage clearing, dredging, clearing out a waterway.

ཆུ་ལས་ (cūlɛɛ̀) irrigation work.

ཆུ་ལྭ་ (cūla) raincoat, poncho.

ཆུ་ལུག (cūluù) water-sheep year.

ཆུ་ལེན་བུམ་སྟོང་ (cūlen pumdoŋ) an unsuccessful action/ attempt, a failure [Lit. go to get water, (return with) empty vessel/ flask].

ཆུ་ལེན་མ་ (cūlenma) women who carry water.

ཆུ་ལོག་འཁྱིལ་ཁུལ་ (cūlɔɔ̀ kyīìgüü) a flooded area, an area with flood waters.

ཆུ་ལུད་ (cūlüù) irrigation and fertilizing; va.—རྒྱག.

ཆུ་ལུམས་ (cūlum) 1. sm. ཆུ་ཚན་ལུམས་. 2. hydrotherapy.

ཆུ་ལེན་ (cū len) va. to draw/ take water.

ཆུ་ལེན་ས་ (cūlensa) a place to get/ draw water.

ཆུ་ལོ་ (cūlo) a traditional tobacco made from mixing rhubarb and tobacco.

ཆུ་ལོག (cūlɔɔ̀) flood; vi.—ཐོན་ to flood ། དབྱར་ཁ་ཆུ་ལོག་ཡང་ཡང་ཐོན་གྱི་ཡོད་པ་རེད་ It floods again and again in the summer.

ཆུ་ལོག་བཀག་སྐྱིལ་ (cūlɔɔ̀ gāàgyii) blocking or stopping a flood/ flooding; va.—བྱེད་.

ཆུ་ལོག་གི་རྩེ་ (cūlɔɔ̀gi dzē) flood crest/ peak.

ཆུ་ལོག་འགོག (cūlɔɔ̀ gaà) sm. ཆུ་ལོག་བཀག་སྐྱིལ་.

ཆུ་ལོག་འགོག་རགས་ (cūlɔɔ̀ gograà) a dam for stopping/ blocking floods, flood control dam.

ཆུ་ལོག་སྔོན་འགོག (cūlɔɔ̀ nõngɔɔ̀) flood control/ prevention, preventing floods in advance ། ཆུ་ལོག་སྔོན་འགོག་གཞུང་ལས་ཁང་ Flood control office.

ཆུ་ལོག་ཐན་འགོག (cūlɔɔ̀ tɛ̃ngɔɔ̀) flood and drought prevention ། ཆུ་ལོག་ཐན་འགོག་བཀོད་འདོམས་ཕུའུ་ Flood and drought prevention command post.

ཆུ་ལོག་འབབ་ལམ་ (cūlɔɔ̀ bɘblam) flood diversion channel/ spillway.

ཆུ་ལོག་འབྱིད་ (cūlɔɔ̀ ceè) va. to channel off flood waters.

ཆུ་ལོག་འབྱིད་སྒོ་ (cūlɔɔ̀ cego) water gate which channels off flood water.

ཆུ་ལོག་འདྲེན་བྱེད་འགག་སྒོ་ (cūlɔɔ̀ drenjeè gaàgo) flood inlet gate.

ཆུ་ལོག་བཤང་སྒོ་ (cūlɔɔ̀ shāŋgo) water lock.

ཆུ་ལོན་ (cūlön) sm. ཆུ་རགས་.

ཆུ་ལོའི་རིགས་ (cūlö rig) yam, sweet potato.

ཆུ་ཤ་ (cūshɘ) an edible fungus.

ཆུ་ཤད་ (cūshɛɛ̀) sneakers.

ཆུ་ཤིག (cūshig) water louse.

ཆུ་ཤིང་ (cūshiŋ) driftwood.

ཆུ་ཤིང་འོམ་བུ་ (cūshiŋ wombu) tamarisk.

ཆུ་ཤུ་ (cūshu) sm. ཆུ་སླང་.

ཆུ་ཤུགས་ (cūshuù) water power, hydraulic power/ force.

ཆུ་ཤུགས་ཀྱི་སྐྱལ་ཤུགས་འཁྱུལ་འཁོར་ (cūshuùgi güüshug trüügɔɔ) hydraulic turbine.

ཆུ་ཤུགས་འཁོར་ལོ་ (cūshuù kɔɔlo) sm. ཆུ་ཤུགས་ཀྱི་སྐྱལ་ཤུགས་འཁྱུལ་འཁོར་.

ཆུ་ཤུགས་གློག་སྐྱེད་ (cūshuù lõggyeè) sm. ཆུ་ཤུགས་གློག་འདོན་.

ཆུ་ཤུགས་གློག་སྐྱེད་ཁང་ (cūshuù lõggyeègaŋ) sm. ཆུ་ཤུགས་གློག་འདོན་ས་ཚིགས་.

ཆུ་ཤུགས་གློག་སྐྱེད་ས་ཚིགས་ (cūshuù lõggyeè sɘdzii) sm. ཆུ་ཤུགས་གློག་འདོན་ས་ཚིགས་.

ཆུ་ཤུགས་གློག་བསྐྱེད་ (cūshuù lõggyeè) sm. ཆུ་ཤུགས་གློག་འདོན་.

ཆུ་ཤུགས་གློག་འདོན་ (cūshuù lõgdün) electric power generation.

ཆུ་ཤུགས་གློག་འདོན་འཁྱུལ་འཁོར་ (cūshuù lõgdün trüügɔɔ) hydroelectric power generator.

ཆུ་ཤུགས་གློག་འདོན་བབས་ཚུགས་ (cūshuù lõgdün bɘbdzüü) sm. ཆུ་ཤུགས་གློག་འདོན་ས་ཚིགས་.

ཆུ་ཤུགས་གློག་འདོན་ས་ཚིགས་ (cūshuù lõgdün sɘdziì) hydroelectric power station.

ཆུ་ཤུགས་གཏུན་བུ་ (cūshuù dũmbu) waterpowered hammer used for husking rice.

ཆུ་ཤུགས་ཐོ་བ་ (cūshuù tōwa) water hammer.

ཆུ་ཤུགས་ཐོན་ཁུངས་ (cūshuù tõnguŋ) hydraulic resources, water power resources.

ཆུ་ཤུགས་རིག་པ་ (cūshuù rigbɘ) hydraulics.

ཆུ་ཤུར་ (cūshur) 1. ravine or channel made by running water. 2. a district in central Tibet located at the confluence of the Lhasa and Tsangpo Rivers.

ཆུ་ཤུལ་ (cūshüü) 1. water spot/ stain/ mark. 2. a small amount of water left in a pot/ pan.

ཆུ་ཤུལ་གདུལ་སྒམ་ (cūshüü düügam) a stone/ crystal sarcophagus.

ཆུ་ཤེལ་ (cūshee) crystal.

ཆུ་ཤེལ་ཕོ་བྲང་ (cūshee podraŋ) the Crystal Palace.

ཆུ་ཤེལ་གཏེར་ཁ་ (cūshee dērga) crystal mine.

ཆུ་ཤེལ་རྡོ་ (cūshee do) crystal rock.

ཆུ་ཤེལ་དབང་པོ་ (cūshee wāŋbo) poet. moon.

ཆུ་ཤོག (cūshɔɔ̀) plastic bag, plastic paper.

ཆུ་ཤོངས་ (cūshoŋ) imp. of ཆུ་གཤང་.

ཆུ་ཤྭ་ (cūsha) sm. ཆུ་ལོག.

ཆུ་གཤང་: p. ཆུ་བཤངས་; f. ཆུ་བཤང་; imp. ཆུ་ཤོངས་ (cū shāŋ) va. to empty/ drain water ། ཁྲོམ་ལམ་དུ་འཁྱིལ་བའི་ཆུ་བཤངས་པ་རེད་ They drained the water that was puddled in the streets.

ཆུ་གཤམ་ (cūsham) down river, the lower reaches of a river.

ཆུ་གཤིས་ (cūshiì) nature/ type of water, characteristics of a river, lake, etc. (e.g., depth, current), hydrology.

ཆུ་གཤིས་ཞིབ་འཇུག་ཁང་ (cūshiì shimjugaŋ) institute of hydrology.

ཆུ་གཤེག་ཚད་ (cū shēgdzɛɛ̀) sm. ཆུ་འབུད་ཚད་.

ཆུ་བཤེར་གློག་སྒྲོན་ (cūsher lõgdrön) searchlight on water.

ཆུ་གཤོ་ (cū shō) va. to throw water (e.g., on a fire).

ཆུ་གཤོའི་ཡུར་བུ་ (cūshö yurbu) drainage canal/ ditch.

ཆུ་གཤོས་ (cū shöö) p. of ཆུ་གཤོ་.

ཆུ་བཤང་ཁྲེད་རགས་ (cūshaŋ trēèraà) spillway dam, water control dam.

ཆུ་བཤང་ཚད་ (cū shāŋdzɛɛ̀) sm. ཆུ་འབུད་ཚད་.

ཆུ་བཤང་ཡུར་བུ་ (cūshaŋ yurbu) a drainage canal, a spillway.

ཆུ་བཤངས་ (cūshaŋ) p. of ཆུ་གཤང་.

ཆུ་བཤལ་ (cūshɛɛ) rinsing out; va.—གཏོང་ to rinse.

ཆུ་བཤོས་རྒྱག (cūshöö gyaà) va. to throw water in a playful manner (usu. as part of the custom of throwing water at passersby to bring rainfall).

ཆུ་ས་ (cūsa) the earth beneath bodies of water.

ཆུ་སིང་ (cūsiŋ) separating stones in grain by submerging the grain in water so that the grain rises to the top, va.—རྒྱག.

ཆུ་སིམ་ (cū sĩm) vi. seep in, to soak in (water).

ཆུ་སིམ་པོ་རྒྱག (cū sĩmbu gyaà) va. to water so that the plants get well soaked.

ཆུ་སུབ་ (cūsub) drowning sb. (by keeping their head underwater); va.—གཏོང་.

ཆུ་སུབ་དུ་ཤི་ (cūsūbdu shī) vi. to die by drowning.

ཆུ་སུབ་དུ་གསོད་ (cū sūbdu söö) sm. ཆུ་སུབ་གཏོང་.

ཆུ་སུབ་གཏོང་ (cūsub dōŋ) see ཆུ་སུབ་.

ཆུ་སུབ་ཐེབས་ (cūsub tēè) vi. to accidentally drown.

ཆུ་སེར་ (cūsee) 1. lymph. 2. serum.

ཆུ་སེར་དཀར་པོ་ (cūsee gārbo) an impetigo-like skin disease.

ཆུ་སེར་སྐྱ་ཐབ་ (cūsee gyābəb) sm. ཆུ་སེར་ན་ཚ་.

ཆུ་སེར་གདོང་རྩ་ (cūsee do̱ŋdza) a vein near the ankle from which blood is drawn to treat itching in Tibetan medicine.

ཆུ་སེར་ན་ཚ་ (cūsee na̱tsa) impetigo-like skin disease accompanied by itching and postular eruptions.

ཆུ་སེར་ནག་པོ་ (cūsee na̱gbo) a leprosy-like disease which turns the skin black and causes loss of head and facial hair.

ཆུ་སེར་གཤའ་རིང་ (cūsee shāriŋ) a vein at the back of the arm from which blood is drawn to cure itching.

ཆུ་སོ་ (cūso) 1. the tip of the urethra. 2. the area below the navel.

ཆུ་སྲང་ (cūsaŋ) a minute.

ཆུ་སྲམ་ (cūdram) otter.

ཆུ་སྲི་ (cūsi) illness characterized by having difficulty urinating.

ཆུ་སྲིན་ (cūsin) 1. crocodile, alligator. 2 whale.

ཆུ་སྲིན་སྐར་ཚོམ་ (cūsin gārdzom) capricorn.

ཆུ་སྲིན་ཁྱིམ་ཅན་ (cūsin kyi̍mjɛn) the 12th month of the Tibetan calendar.

ཆུ་སྲིན་མགོ་ (cūsin go̱) head of a mythical creature that adorns the corners of the roof of the Tsuglhakang.

ཆུ་སྲིན་རྒྱལ་མཚན་ཅན་ (cūsin gyɛ̱ɛ̱jɛn) sm. ཆུ་སྲིན་མགོ་.

ཆུ་སྲིན་ཉ་མེད་ (cūsin ña̱meè) whale.

ཆུ་སྲིན་སྔོན་པོ་ (cūsin ŋȫmbo) blue whale.

ཆུ་སྲིབ་ (cūdrib) the shady side of a mountain.

ཆུ་སྲུང་ (cūsaŋ) sm. ཆུ་འགོག.

ཆུ་སྲིལ་ (cūsel) poet. ocean.

ཆུ་སྲོལ་ (cūsöö) sm. ཆུ་སྲམ་.

ཆུ་སླང་ (cūlaŋ) water bucket, water container.

ཆུ་གླིང་ (cūle) small island.

ཆུ་གླིའུ་ (cūlewu) sm. ཚར་གླི་.

ཆུ་སློང་ཆང་ཐོབ་ (cūloŋ cāŋdob) getting more than one hoped for [Lit. beg for water, get beer].

ཆུ་གསོག་ (cūsɔɔ̀) 1. storing water; va. ཆུ་གསོག་; —གཏོང་ to store water. 2. an illness where the body retains excess water, edema.

ཆུ་གསོག་མཐོ་ཁྱོག (cūsɔɔ̀ tōjɔɔ̀) water storage tower.

ཆུ་གསོག་མཐོ་སྡེགས་ (cūsɔɔ̀ tōdeg) sm. ཆུ་གསོག་མཐོ་ཁྱོག.

ཆུ་གསོག་ཚད་ (cūsɔɔ̀dzɛ̀ɛ̀) water storage capacity.

ཆུ་གསོག་རྫིང་བུ་ (cūsɔɔ̀ dzi̱ŋbu) a small water reservoir/ pond.

ཆུ་བསགས་ (cū sāà) p. of ཆུ་གསོག.

ཆུ་བསང་ས་ (cū sāŋ) burning incense on a river bank; va.—གཏོང་.

ཆུ་བསིང་ (cūsiŋ) sm. ཆུ་སིང་.

ཆུ་བསིལ་གཏོང་ (cūsil dōŋ) va. to cool sth. by pouring cold water on it.

ཆུ་ཧུབ་གང་ (cū hūbgaŋ) a sip/ mouthful of water.

ཆུ་ལྷ་ (cūlha) name of a Buddha.

ཆུ་ལྷ་མེ་ཏོག (cūlha me̱dog) narcissus.

ཆུ་ལྷ་མོ་ (cū lhāmo) a name of a star.

ཆུ་ལྷག (cūlhaà) tributary.

ཆུ་ལྷམ་ (cūlham) rain boots, galoshes, rubber boots.

ཆུ་ལྷའི་ཕྱོགས་ (cūlhɛ cɔ̄ɔ̀) the west side/ direction.

ཆུ་ལྷུང་ཁྱི་ངན་ (cūlhuŋ kyi̍ŋɛn) a vanquished enemy [Lit. bad dog fallen in the water].

ཆུ་ལྷོག (cūlhɔɔ̀) a disease characterized by extensive blisters.

ཆུག (cūù) imp. of འཇུག.

ཆུང་ (cūŋ) abbr. of ཆུང་ཆུང་.

ཆུང་གྲས་ (cūŋdrɛɛ̀) 1. smaller class/ kind/ type ། གནམ་གྲུ་ཆུང་གྲས་ Smaller type planes. 2. lower, less (important, significant) ། ལས་བྱེད་ཆུང་གྲས་ Lower ranking officials. 3. the younger, smaller, junior ། སློབ་ཕྲུ་བ་ཆུང་གྲས་རྣམས་ལ་གུང་སང་རག The younger students got a vacation.

ཆུང་གྲོགས་ (cūŋdrɔɔ̀) childhood friend.

ཆུང་གྲོགས་མ་ (cūŋdrɔɔ̀ma) childhood girlfriend/ sweetheart.

ཆུང་བརྒྱུད་ (cūŋgyüù) shung. successors, descendants, offspring.

ཆུང་ངུ་ (cūŋŋu) sm. ཆུང་ཆུང་.

ཆུང་ངམ་ཆེ་བརླག (cūŋŋam cēlaà) sm. ཆུང་ཞེན་ཆེ་བརླག.

ཆུང་བརྔམས་ཆེ་ཤོར་ (cūŋŋam cēshɔɔ) doing sth. counter productive [Lit. scare the small and lose the large].

ཆུང་ཆུང་ (cūŋjuŋ) small, tiny, young ། ཁང་པ་ཆུང་ཆུང་ A small house. ། ཁོ་ལོ་ཆུང་ཆུང་རེད་ He is young.

ཆུང་ཆུང་བློས་ཀྱིས་མ་ཐོངས་ ཆེན་པོ་གར་སོང་མི་ཤེས་ (cūŋjuŋ lȫȫgi ma̱tōŋ cēmbo ka̱rsoŋ mi̱sheè) pennywise pound foolish [Lit. not letting go of a small amount, not knowing where the large amount went].

ཆུང་ཅེས་ (cūŋjeè) too small ། ཁང་པ་འདི་ཆུང་ཅེས་བཞག The house is too small.

ཆུང་གཉེན་སྒྲིག (cūŋ ñēndrig) childhood marriage; va.—སྒྲིག to arrange a marriage of young children.

ཆུང་བརྙས་ཆེར་སྐྲག (cūŋñɛɛ̀ cēr draà) bullying the weak but fearing the strong.

ཆུང་རྟགས་ (cūŋdaà) the "less than" sign (<).

ཆུང་ཐ་ (cūŋda) the youngest child.

ཆུང་ཐོག་ཆེ་མངོན་ (cūŋdɔɔ̀ cēŋön) small in size but big in significance.

ཆུང་མཐའ་ (cūŋta) sm. ཐ་ཆུང་.

ཆུང་མཐོང་ཆེ་ཤེས་ (cūŋdoŋ cēsheè) understanding a lot from seeing only a little.

ཆུང་དུ་འགྲོ་ (cūŋdu dro̱) vi. to become smaller, to decrease ། དེང་སང་གཙང་པོའི་ཆུ་ཆུང་དུ་ཕྱིན་བཞག These days the water in the river has decreased.

ཆུང་དུ་གཏོང་ (cūŋdu dōŋ) va. to make smaller, to decrease, to reduce, to cut down ། ཁོས་ཁང་པ་རྒྱག་ཡག་གི་འགྲོ་སོང་ཆུང་དུ་བཏང་བ་རེད་ He reduced the expenses for building the house.

ཆུང་དུས་ (cūŋdüù) a youth, young ། ང་ཆུང་དུས་སློབ་གྲྭར་འགྲོ་མྱོང་ I did not go to school when I was young.

ཆུང་དུས་ནས་ (cūŋdüünɛ) from young ། ཁོ་ཆུང་དུས་ནས་ལས་ཀ་བྱས་སོང་ He worked from when he was young.

ཆུང་དོར་ཆེ་སྲུང་ (cūŋdɔɔ cēsuŋ) discarding the small to protect the big.

ཆུང་འདྲིས་ (cūŋdrii̍) 1. a lover (from a young age). 2. spouses who were raised as children in the same household.

ཆུང་འདྲིས་བྱམས་པ་ (cūŋdrii̍ ca̱mba) friends from childhood who then become lovers.

ཆུང་འདྲིས་བཟའ་ཚང་ (cūŋdrii̍ sa̱dzaŋ) sm. ཆུང་འདྲིས་.

ཆུང་བ་ (cūŋwa) 1. small ། རྒྱལ་ཁབ་ཆུང་བ་དང་དཔལ་འབྱོར་སྐྱོ་བ་ A small country and has a poor economy. 2. smaller ། ཁོ་ཁང་པ་ཆུང་བ་ཞིག་ལ་སྤོས་པ་རེད་ He moved to a smaller house. ། གཞུང་གྲོན་ཆུང་བའི་ཆེད་དུ་ For the purpose of making government expenditures smaller. 3. junior.

ཆུང་འབྲིང་ཆེ་ (cūŋ dri̱ŋ cē) 1. small, middle/ medium and large.

ཆུང་མ་ (cūŋma) the younger wife in polygamous marriage; va.—ལེན་ to take a younger wife. 2. female head of household.

ཆུང་མིང་ (cūŋmiŋ) pet name for a child.

ཆུང་ཙག (cūŋdzaà) minute, small, small-scale, miscellaneous ། བཟོ་ལས་ཆུང་ཙག Small-scale industry.

ཆུང་ཙག་གི་རིགས་ (cūŋdzaàgi ri̱gbə) odds and ends, miscellaneous.

ཆུང་བཙོན་ཆེ་དོར་ (cūŋdzön cēdɔɔ) sm. ཆུང་ཞེན་ཆེ་བརླག.

ཆུང་ཚད་ (cūŋdzɛɛ̀) degree of smallness.

ཆུང་ཚགས་ (cūŋdzaà) sm. ཆུང་རྒྱ.

ཆུང་ཚུལ་ (cūŋdzüü) seeming/ pretending to be small or little; va.—སྟོན་ ‖ཁོང་གིས་ཡོན་དན་ཆུང་ཚུལ་སྟོན་གྱི་འདུག He is pretending he has little knowledge.

ཆུང་འཛིན་ (cūŋdzin) a small eclipse.

ཆུང་ཞེན་ཆེ་བརླག (cūŋshen cē lāà) losing a lot by trying to save a little.

ཆུང་ཞེན་ཆེ་ཤོར་ (cūŋshen cēshɔɔ) sm. ཆུང་ཞེན་ཆེ་བརླག.

ཆུང་ཞིལ་ (cūŋshee) arc. low, poor, bad.

ཆུང་བཟོད་ཆེ་གཉེར་ (cūŋsöö cēñer) tolerating sth. minor for the general good.

ཆུང་རབས་ (cūŋrəb) the younger generation.

ཆུང་རབས་གཞོན་པ་ (cūŋrəb shōmba) sm. ཆུང་རབས་.

ཆུང་རུ་ (cūŋru) sm. ཆུང་དུ་.

ཆུང་ཤ་ (cūŋsha) meat of smaller animals such as sheep/ goat as opposed to cows, yaks, etc.

ཆུང་ཤོས་ (cūŋshöö) smallest.

ཆུང་ས་བ་ (cūŋsewa) slightly small, a little small ‖ སྟོད་ཐུང་འདི་ཆུང་ས་བ་ཞིག་འདུག This shirt is a little small (for you).

ཆུང་སྲི་ (cūŋsi) an evil spirit/ ghost which causes the death of infants.

ཆུང་སྲིད་ (cūŋsiì) sm. ཆུང་སྲིད་རིན་པོ་ཆེ་.

ཆུང་སྲིད་རིན་པོ་ཆེ་ (cūŋsiì rimboce) a young incarnate lama.

ཆུང་སྲིད་རྟོག་ཞིབ་ (cūŋsiì dōgshib) shung. searching for an new incarnation of a lama.

ཆུང་གསོས་མནའ་མ་ (cūŋsöö nāma) adoptive child bride (a girl who lives with groom's family since childhood with the plan being for her to later marry the boy of the house).

ཆུད་ (cüü) 1. vi. to get into, to be included in ‖ ཚིག་གསར་པ་དེ་མིང་མཛོད་འདིའི་ནང་ཆུད་མི་འདུག The new word hasn't been included in the dictionary. 2. vi. to comprehend, to understand ‖ དོན་འདི་ཁོང་དུ་ཆུད་སོང་ (He) understood the meaning. 3. vi. to be able to fit (sth. into a box, etc.) ‖ འཕྲུལ་ཆས་ཆེན་པོ་འདི་སྒམ་འདིའི་ནང་ཆུད་ཀྱི་མི་འདུག This big machine doesn't fit into this box.

ཆུད་ཚད་ (cüüdzɛɛ̀) volume, capacity (to hold/ fit sth.).

ཆུད་འཛའ་ (cündza) sm. ཆུད་ཟོས་གཏོང་.

ཆུད་འཛའ་བའི་མཚན་མ་ (cündzawɛ tsɛ̄nma) sign of death.

ཆུད་ཟ་ (cüü sa̱) vi. to get wasted, to get spoiled, to wear out ‖ མགྱོགས་པོ་མ་བཟས་ན་ཆུད་ཟ་གི་རེད་ If you don't eat the meat quickly it will spoil (and get wasted). ‖ འཕྲུལ་འཁོར་འདི་དུས་ཚོད་རིང་པོའི་རིང་ཆུད་ཟ་གི་མ་རེད་ The machine will not wear out for a long time.

ཆུད་ཟོས་ (cüüsöö) wasting, spoiling; va.—གཏོང་ to waste, to spoil; vi.—འགྲོ་ to be or get wasted/ squandered ‖ དོན་མེད་དུས་ཚོད་ཆུད་ཟོས་བཏང་བ་རེད་ (They) wasted a lot of time for no reason. ‖ དུས་ཚོད་བཟང་པོ་དེ་ཆུད་ཟོས་སྲིན་པ་རེད་ The good opportunity was wasted.

ཆུད་ཟོས་ཕོར་བརླག (cüüsöö pɔrlaà) waste and loss.

ཆུད་ཟོས་ལ་ངོ་རྒོལ་ (cüüsöölа ŋogöö) "oppose waste" (one of the "three antis" campaign of 1951-1952).

ཆུད་ཟོས་སུ་གཏོང་ (cüüsöösu dōŋ) sm. ཆུད་ཟོས་གཏོང་.

ཆུད་གཟན་ (cüüsɛn) p. of ཆུད་གཟོན་.

ཆུད་གཟོན་ (cüü sön) sm. ཆུད་ཟོས་.

ཆུན་ (cün) 1. vi. control (iso. imposing discipline) ‖ ཁོང་མི་གཤིས་བཟང་པོ་སོང་ཙང་ཕྲུ་གུ་ཚོ་ཆུན་ཐུབ་ཀྱི་མི་འདུག Because he is good natured (he) can not control the children. 2. p. of འཆུན་. 3 imp. of འཛུན་.

ཆུན་པོ་ (cümbu) 1. bunch, bundle, bouquet ‖ མེ་ཏོག་གི་ཆུན་པོ་ A bouquet of flowers. 2. being able to control/ discipline ‖ ཁོ་སློབ་ཕྲུག་ཆུན་པོ་འདུག He is able to control the students well.

ཆུན་བུ་ (cümbu) sm. ཆུན་པོ་.

ཆུན་མ་ (cünmə) the younger wife in a polygamous marriage.

ཆུབ་ (cüb) 1. vi. to comprehend/ understand completely (usu. follows ཐུགས་སུ་).

ཆུབ་གསལ་ (cübsɛɛ) shung. as you know, as you are fully aware.

ཆུམ་ (cüm) 1. vi. to shrink/ crouch with fear. 2. imp. of འཛུམ་.

ཆུའི་འཁོར་ལོ་ (cüü kɔ̄ɔlo) water wheel.

ཆུའི་གྲམ་པ་ (cüü dra̱mba) river bed.

ཆུའི་གྱེན་ (cüü gye̱n) upstream, against the current; va.—ལ་འགྲོ་ to go against the current.

ཆུའི་རྒྱུག་ཤུགས་ (cüü gyü̱nshuù) water power, the power of flowing water.

ཆུའི་འགྱུར་ཚུལ་ (cüü gyu̱rdzüü) hydrology.

ཆུའི་ཆུའི་ (cüüjüü) term used for the excrement of infants.

ཆུའི་གཉེར་མ་ (cüü ñērmə) ripples on water.

ཆུའི་མཐོ་དམན་གྱི་ཚད་ (cüü tōmɛngi tsɛ̄ɛ̀) water level.

ཆུའི་གདན་ (cüüdɛn) diaper.

ཆུའི་དྲྭ་བ་ (cüü dra̱wa) a network of rivers.

ཆུའི་དྲོད་ཚད་ (cüü trö̱ödzɛɛ̀) water temperature.

ཆུའི་གནས་ལུགས་ (cüü nɛ̀ɛ̀luù) hydrography, hydrology.

ཆུའི་སྦྲིས་མ་ (cüü driìmə) a whitish substance that forms on the surface of urine that is tested.

ཆུའི་ཕར་ཁ་ (cüü pārga) the opposite bank.

ཆུའི་བྱུག་པ་བྱུག (cüü cu̱gbə cu̱ù) doing sth. falsely [Lit. using water to massage].

ཆུའི་འབག་བཙོག (cüü ba̱gdzɔɔ̀) water pollution.

ཆུའི་འབབ་ཤུགས་ (cüü ba̱bshuù) force of descending water in a river.

ཆུའི་སྨད་རྒྱུད་ (cüü mɛ̄ɛ̀gyüü) the lower part/ reaches of a river.

ཆུའི་གཞུང་ (cüü shu̱ŋ) in the midst/ middle of a lake or river.

ཆུའི་གཞུང་ལ་འགྲོ་ (cüü shu̱ŋla dro̱) va. to go along with the current.

ཆུའི་ཟིལ་པ་ (cüü si̱ibə) drops of water.

ཆུར་ (cür) 1. (— + dat.-loc.) into/ to/ on the water ‖ ཁོ་ཆུར་མཆོངས་པ་རེད་ He jumped into the water. 2. vi. to fit into ‖ མི་གནམ་གྲུ་དེའི་ནང་ལ་མི་བརྒྱ་ཆུར་གྱི་རེད་ A hundred people will fit into the plane. 3. imp. of གཅུར་.

ཆུར་བསྐྱུར་སྒྲོན་མེ་ (cüügur drö̱nme) small lamps placed in baskets and floated on water as a type of offering.

ཆུར་ཆུར་ (cüüjuu) rhubarb.

ཆུར་ཆུང་ཆུང་ (cüü cüŋjuŋ) small capacity ‖ སྒམ་འདི་ཆུར་ཆུང་ཆུང་རེད་ This box has a small capacity.

ཆུར་ཆེན་པོ་ (cüü cēmbo) large capacity.

ཆུར་བརྟེན་གསོ་ཐབས་ (cürden sōdəb) hydrotherapy.

ཆུར་ནུབ་ (cüü nu̱b) vi to sink underwater ‖ གནམ་གྲུ་དབྱ་སྐྱོན་གྱིས་ཆུར་ནུབ་བཞག The airplane crashed and sunk underwater.

ཆུར་ནུབ་ཚད་ (cüü nu̱bdzɛɛ̀) draft (of ships).

ཆུར་གནས་སྲོག་ཆགས་ (cürnɛɛ̀ sɔ̄gjaà) aquatic animals.

ཆུར་བྱིང་ (cürjiŋ) sm. ཆུར་ནུབ་.

ཆུར་བྱིང་ནས་ཤི་ (cürjiŋnɛ shi) vi. to die by drowning.

ཆུར་འཛུལ་ (cüü dzu̱ù) 1. va. to enter the water ‖ ཆུར་འཛུལ་མ་ཐག་ཞེ་དྲག་འཁྱགས་བྱུང་ As soon as I entered the water I got very cold. 2. going/ diving under water (under water) ‖ ཆུར་འཛུལ་ནས་ཉ་རིགས་ཀྱི་ཞིབ་འཇུག་བྱས་པ་རེད་ They went underwater and did research on fish.

ཆུར་འཛུལ་གྱོན་ཆས་ (cüüdzuu gyö̱njɛɛ̀) clothes for going underwater, wet suit, diving suit.

ཆུར་འཛུལ་པ་ (cüüdzuuba) diver, frogman.

ཆུར་འཛུལ་དམག་གྲུ་ (cüüdzuu mə̄gdru) submarine.

ཆུར་འཛུལ་ཡོ་བྱད་ (cüüdzuu yo̱bjɛɛ̀) underwater equipment, scuba diving equipment.

ཆུར་ཞུའི་ཁུ་བ་ (cūū shu̲ kūwə) water/ aqueous solution.

ཆུར་བཞུར་འཕྲེད་རགས་ (cūūshur trēèraà) sm. ཆུ་བཀགས་འཕྲེད་རགས་.

ཆུར་རིང་བ་ (cūū ri̲ŋwə) long (in length).

ཆུར་ལྷུང་ནས་ཤི་ (cūū lhūŋnɛ shī) vi. to die by drowning.

ཆུར་ལྷུངས་ཁྱི་རྒན་ (cūūlhuŋ kyīgɛn) a difficult or dangerous situation [Lit. an old dog that has fallen into the water].

ཆུས་ (cūǖ) 1. by water (— + inst.) ¶ ཁྱི་དེ་ཆུས་ཁྱེར་བ་རེད་ That dog was carried away by the water. 2. ch. an administrative unit just below a county (xian) and above a township (xiang). 3. imp of འཆུ་. 4. sm. ཧུས་.

ཆུས་ཀྲང་ (cūǖdraŋ) ch. head of a ཆུས་.

ཆུས་སྐོར་ (cūǖgɔɔ) water-powered, turned by water.

ཆུས་སྐོར་བརྡུངས་འཁོར་ (cūǖgɔɔ drü̲ǖgɔɔ) water-powered husking machine.

ཆུས་སྐོར་ཆུ་འདྲེན་འཕྲུལ་འཁོར་ (cūǖgɔɔ cūndren trūǖgɔɔ) water wheel used for irrigating fields.

ཆུས་སྐོར་འཕྲུལ་འཁོར་ (cūǖgɔɔ trūǖgɔɔ) hydraulic turbine.

ཆུས་བསྐོར་གློག་འདོན་འཕྲུལ་འཁོར་ (cūǖgɔɔ lōgdön trūǖgɔɔ) hydroturbine generator.

ཆུས་ཁྱེར་རྐྱལ་རྫེམ་ (cūgyer gyɛ̄ɛlom) giving a false impression, acting as if things are going well even though they are not [Lit. pretending (one) is swimming even though (one) is being carried down (the river)].

ཆུས་འཁྱེར་ (cūǖ kyēr) vi. to be carried/ swept away by water ¶ སྟོན་ཐོག་ཁྱོན་ཆེ་ཆུས་འཁྱེར་བ་རེད་ A considerable amount of the crop was swept away by water.

ཆུས་གྲུབ་བྲག་རྡོ་ (cūǖdrub tra̲gdo) sedimentary rock.

ཆུས་འཇིག (cūǖ jig) vi. to be destroyed water.

ཆུས་གཏོར་ཤང་འཛུགས་ (cūǖdɔɔ shāŋdzuù) sm. ཆུས་དོར་ཤང་འགྲིལ་.

ཆུས་དོར་ཤང་འགྲིལ་ (cūǖdɔɔ shāŋdrii) the movement in the late 1980's in which ཆུས་ were disbanded and existing ཤང་ were made into larger ཤང་ units.

ཆུས་དུས་བྲག་ཁུང་ (cūǖdrɛɛ dra̲gguŋ) cave formed by water erosion.

ཆུས་འདེད་ (cūǖ de̲è) 1. va. to take a pill/ medicine with water ¶ སྨན་ཆུས་འདེད་ནས་གཏོང་དགོས་ You should take the medicine with water. 2. vi. to carried away by water. ¶ ཆུས་འདེད་པའི་ས་ Earth carried away by water.

ཆུས་གནོན་ (cūǖ nōn) vi. to be flooded by water ¶ ཞིང་ཁ་ཆུས་གནོན་བཞག The field has been flooded.

ཆུས་གནོན་འཕྲུལ་འཁོར་ (cūǖnön trūǖgɔɔ) hydraulic press, waterpress.

ཆུས་མནན་ (cūǖ nɛ̄n) sm. ཆུས་གནོན་.

ཆུས་སྣུབ་ (cūǖ nūb) vi. to be flooded/ submerged/ under water.

ཆུས་སྦོང་ (cūǖ bo̲ŋ) vi. to get wet, to be/ get soaked.

ཆུས་སྲིད་གཞུང་ (cūǖ sīishuŋ) the government of a ཆུས་ administrative unit.

ཆུས་ཨུ་ (cūǖ ū) abbr. ཆུས་ཨུ་ཡོན་ལྷན་ཁང་.

ཆུས་ཨུ་ཡོན་ལྷན་ཁང་ (cūǖ ūyön lhɛ̄ngaŋ) the (party) committee of a ཆུས་ administrative unit.

ཆེ་ (cē) big, large.

ཆེ་བཀུར་ (cēgur) shung. greatly respected, great respect.

ཆེ་སྐྱེད་ (cēgyeè) sm. ཆེ་བསྐྱེད་.

ཆེ་བསྐོས་ (cēgöö) a wide gap left between engraved letters (of a manuscript plate).

ཆེ་བསྐྱེད་ (cēgyeè) 1. with great ¶ འབད་བརྩོན་ཆེ་བསྐྱེད་ཀྱིས་སློབ་སྦྱོང་བྱས་ཡོད་པ་རེད་ (They) have studied with great diligence. ¶ སེམས་ཤུགས་ཆེ་བསྐྱེད་ཀྱིས་ With great enthusiasm. 2. making bigger, enlarging; va.—བྱེད་ to enlarge, to make bigger ¶ ཁོས་ཁང་པ་ཆེ་བསྐྱེད་བྱས་པ་རེད་ He enlarged the house.

ཆེ་ཁ་ (cēga) sm. ཆེ་ཁག.

ཆེ་ཁག (cēgaà) sm. ཆེ་གྲས་.

ཆེ་ཁེ་སེ་ལ་ཝ་ཁེ་ (cēge sēlawake) Czechoslovakia.

ཆེ་ཁོ་སི་ལོ་ཝ་ཁེ་ (cēgo sīlowake) sm. ཆེ་ཁེ་སེ་ལ་ཝ་ཁེ་.

ཆེ་གེ་བ་ (cēgewa) sm. ཆེ་གེ་མོ་.

ཆེ་གེ་མོ་ (cēgemo) so and so ¶ མི་ཆེ་གེ་མོ་ཞིག་སླེབས་བཞག So and so has arrived.

ཆེ་གྲས་ (cēdrɛɛ) 1. large type/ kind/ class ¶ ཆུ་གློག་ས་ཚིགས་ཆེ་གྲས་ The large class/ type of hydroelectric power station. 2. high ¶ དཔོན་རིགས་ཆེ་གྲས་ The class of high officials.

ཆེ་གྲོགས་ཆུང་གྲོགས་ (cēdroò cūŋdroò) old and new friends, close and distant friends.

ཆེ་དགུ་ (cēgu) everything that is big/ large/ high ¶ དེ་རིང་ཚོགས་འདུར་དཔོན་རིགས་ཆེ་དགུ་སླེབས་བཞག Today all the high officials have come to the meeting.

ཆེ་བགྲེས་ (cēdreè) senior, elder.

ཆེ་མགོ་ (cēngo) eldest son or daughter.

ཆེ་འགྱིང་ (cēgyiŋ) sm. ཆེ་ཉམས་དོད་པོ་.

ཆེ་འགྲོ་ཆུང་འགྲོ་ (cēdro cūŋdro) 1. putting/ fitting in sth. as much as one can ¶ སྒམ་འདིའི་ནང་ཅ་ལག་ཆེ་འགྲོ་ཆུང་འགྲོ་བྱས་ནས་བླུགས་པ་ཡིན་ I put as many things as possible in this box. 2. bullying; va.—བྱེད་ ¶ མི་དེ་དབུལ་ཕོངས་རྣམས་ལ་ཆེ་འགྲོ་ཆུང་འགྲོ་བྱེད་མཁན་ཞིག་རེད་ He is sb. who bullies the poor.

ཆེ་གུ་ (cēgu) sm. ཆེ་དགུ་.

ཆེ་རྒྱུ་གང་ཡོད་ (cēgyu ka̲ŋyöö) very many, a lot of ¶ ཁོང་དེང་སང་སྐྱ་ངལ་ཆེ་རྒྱུ་གང་ཡོད་རེད་བཞག These days he is experiencing great difficulties.

ཆེ་རྒྱུད་ (cēgyüü) royal lineage, high lineage.

ཆེ་བརྒྱུད་ (cēgyüü) asking for favors through higher rank people.

ཆེ་ཆུང་ (cījuŋ) big and small ¶ རླངས་འཁོར་ཆེ་ཆུང་མང་པོ་འདུག There were many big and small vehicles. 2. size ¶ གྲོང་ཁྱེར་དེའི་ཆེ་ཆུང་ལྷ་ས་ཙམ་ཡོད་ The size of that city is about that of Lhasa.

ཆེ་ཆུང་འཚམས་པོ་ (cījuŋ tsāmbo) just the right size.

ཆེ་ཆུང་ཤོར་ (cējuŋ shɔ̄ɔ) vi. to be/ become unequal, to be different in size ¶ ཕྲུ་གུ་འདི་གཉིས་ལོ་ན་ཡིན་ནའང་གཟུགས་པོ་ཆེ་ཆུང་ཤོར་བཞག Even though the two children are the same age they are different in body (size).

ཆེ་ཆེ་ (cēce) sm. ཆེ་གྲས་.

ཆེ་ཆེར་ (cēcer) bigger and bigger, more and more ¶ དཔལ་འབྱོར་ཡར་རྒྱས་ཆེ་ཆེར་འགྲོ་གི་ཡོད་པ་རེད་ The economy is improving more and more.

ཆེ་ཆེས་ (cēceè) too big/ large ¶ སྟོད་ཐུང་འདི་ཆེ་ཆེས་བཞག This shirt is too big.

ཆེ་མཆོག (cēcog) the very best.

ཆེ་བརྗོད་ (cējöö) sm. ཆེ་བསྟོད་.

ཆེ་ཉམས་ (cēñam) airs, acting grand; va.—བྱེད་ to put on airs, to act grand ¶ ཁོས་ཕྱི་མིའི་སར་ཆེ་ཉམས་བྱེད་ཀྱི་འདུག He puts on airs around foreigners.

ཆེ་ཉམས་དོད་པོ་ (cēñam to̲öbo) pompous, grand.

ཆེ་གདམ་མཁས་གདམ་ (cēdam kɛ̄ɛdam) talk aimed at showing one's intelligence and superiority.

ཆེ་གཏོར་ཆེ་འཛུགས་ (cēdɔɔ cēndzuù) destroying on a large scale and establishing/ developing on a large scale, breaking and setting up in a big way (a popular slogan during the Cultural Revolution regarding breaking up old customs and thoughts and establishing new ones).

ཆེ་རྟགས་ (cēdaà) 1. an emblem/ insignia indicating status or rank. 2. the sign for "greater than" (>).

ཆེ་བསྟོད་ (cēdöö) 1. praise; va.—བྱེད་ to praise ¶ དཔའ་བོར་ཆེ་བསྟོད་ཀྱི་གླུ་དབྱངས་ Song of praise to the heroes. 2. honor ¶ སྲིད་འཛིན་མཆོག་ལ་ཆེ་བསྟོད་ཀྱི་གསོལ་སྟོན་ཞིག་ཕུལ་བ་རེད་ (They) gave a banquet in honor of the President.

ཆེ་བསྟོད་ཀྱི་དཔུང་དམག་རུ་ཁག (cēdöögi būŋmaà ru̲gaà) guard of honor.

ཆེ་བསྟོད་ཆུང་སྨད་ (cēdöö cūŋmɛɛ) praising high status and deriding low status.

ཆེ་ཐག་ཆོད་ (cēdaà cöö) 1. extremely large,

immense. 2. too big.

ཆེ་ཐང་འཛོག (cēdaŋ cɔ̱ɔ̀) va. to hold in high esteem, to value.

ཆེ་ཐབས་ (cēdəb) sm. ཆེ་ཉམས་.

ཆེ་མཐོང་འཛོག (cēdoŋ jɔ̱ɔ̀) sm. ཆེ་ཐང་འཛོག.

ཆེ་འདོད་ (cēndöö) 1. ambitious, wanting to be big/ powerful/ high in rank. 2. sm. a big ego, thinking highly of oneself.

ཆེ་འདོད་ཆུང་ཤོར་ (cēndöö cūŋshɔɔ) wanting the big and losing the small.

ཆེ་འདོད་ཚ་པོ་ (cēndöö tsābo) wanting to attain high rank/ position. 1. a big ego, sb. who thinks a lot of himself.

ཆེ་འདོན་ (cē dö̱n) 1. sm. ཆེ་བསྟོད་. 2. sm. ཁྲི་འདོན་.

ཆེ་འདྲེས་ཆུང་འདྲེས་ (cēdreè cūŋdreè) able to mix with people of higher and lower status; va.—བྱེད་.

ཆེ་ནོར་ (cēnɔɔ) shung. cattle, yaks.

ཆེ་གནོན་ (cēnön) oppression by powerful people.

ཆེ་ཕྱུགས་ (cējuù) cattle, large livestock (excluding sheep and goats).

ཆེ་ཕྲ་ (cēdra) large and small, of various sizes ། གནས་ཚུལ་ཆེ་ཕྲ་ཚང་མ་ All situations large and small.

ཆེ་ཕྲ་བར་གསུམ་ (cēdra pa̱rsum) large, small and middle.

ཆེ་བ་ (cēwa) 1. great, big, large, important ། ཁང་པ་དེ་མཛེས་ལ་ཆེ་བ་ཞིག་འདུག The house is beautiful and big. 2. very ། རྙོག་དྲ་ཆེ་བའི་ལག་རྩལ་ A very complicated technique. 3. (comparative form of ཆེན་པོ་) bigger, greater, larger ། དེ་ལས་ཆེ་བ་ཡོད་པ་མ་རེད་ There is nothing bigger than that. 4. highly; va.—བརྗོད་ to speak highly of ། མི་ཚང་མས་བླ་མ་དེའི་ཆེ་བ་བརྗོད་པ་རེད་ Everyone spoke highly of that lama.

ཆེ་བ་ཤོར་ (cēwa shɔ̄ɔ) vi. to lose face.

ཆེ་བའི་ང་རྒྱལ་ (cēwɛ ŋa̱rgyɛɛ) feeling superior to others.

ཆེ་འབུལ་ཆུང་འབུལ་ (cēmbüü cūŋbüü) it is okay to give more or less (as one wishes) ། དགོན་པ་འདི་ལ་ཞལ་འདེབས་ཆེ་འབུལ་ཆུང་འབུལ་རེད་ It is okay to donate as much or little as you like to this monastery.

ཆེ་འབྲིང་ཆུང་ (cē dri̱ŋ cūŋ) large, middle, small.

ཆེ་མ་ཆུང་ (cēma cūŋ) middle size, neither large or small.

ཆེ་མིན་ཆུང་མིན་ (cēmin cūŋmin) not too big or too small.

ཆེ་མོ་ (cēmo) senior, head ། དགེ་རྒན་ཆེ་མོ་ Headmaster (in a school).

ཆེ་མོ་བ་ལགས་ (cēmɔɔlaà) shung. master (title used for the head of masons, tailors and other traditional craft groups).

ཆེ་ཙམ་ (cēdzam) slightly bigger.

ཆེ་ཙི་ (cēdzi) ch. eggplant.

ཆེ་བཙན་ (cēdzɛn) shung. high status individuals/ institutions in the old society (e.g., monasteries, aristocratic families).

ཆེ་བཙན་ཁ་འཁུར་ (cēdzɛn kāgur) relying on sb.'s power/ authority to oppress others, using the name of sb. in power/ authority to ignore the law.

ཆེ་བཙན་ལྭག་འཁུར་ (cēdzɛn dāggur) sm. ཆེ་བཙན་ཁ་འཁུར་.

ཆེ་བཙན་བདུན་ (cēdzɛn dü̱n) shung. the seven great monasteries: Sera, Ganden, Drepung, Gyuto, Gyume, Namagye Tratsang and Neyjung.

ཆེ་བཙན་ཕྲག་འཁུར་ (cēdzɛn trāggur) sm. ཆེ་བཙན་ཁ་འཁུར་.

ཆེ་རྩུགས་ (cēdzuù) sm. ཆེ་ཉམས་.

ཆེ་འཛིན་ (cēndzin) thinking highly of oneself, holding oneself in high regard.

ཆེ་ཞི་ (cēshi) arc. wife.

ཆེ་ཞེ་ (cēshe) older sister.

ཆེ་གཞི་ (cēshi) sm. ཆེ་བཞི་.

ཆེ་བཞག་ཆུང་རྡུང་ (cēshaà cūŋduŋ) avoiding/ shunning the strong and beating/ hitting the weak.

ཆེ་བཞག་ཆུང་བཤོལ་ (cēshaà cūŋshöö) leaving everything aside ། དེ་རིང་ཚོགས་འདུ་གལ་ཆེན་པོ་ཡིན་ཙང་ང་ཆེ་བཞག་ཆུང་བཤོལ་གྱིས་བཅར་པ་ཡིན་ Because the meeting today is important, I left everything aside to attend it [Lit. leaving aside the big tasks and casting aside the minor ones].

ཆེ་བཞི་ (cēshi) witness.

ཆེ་རིགས་ (cērig) high officials/ dignitaries ། རྒྱ་གར་གྱི་དཆེ་རིགས་མཇལ་འཕྲད་གནང་བ་རེད་ (They) will meet the Indian dignitaries.

ཆེ་རིམ་ (cērim) 1. one after another starting from the oldest one. 2. the main point, the crux of a matter.

ཆེ་རུ་གང་འགྲོ་ (cēru ka̱ŋdro) getting larger/ bigger, really increasing.

ཆེ་རུ་འགྲོ་ (cēru dro̱) vi. to get larger/ bigger, to increase.

ཆེ་རུ་གཏོང་ (cēru dōŋ) vi. to enlarge, to make bigger, to increase the size/ capacity/ volume/ extent/ weight ། ཞིང་ཁ་རྒྱ་ཆེ་རུ་གཏོང་དགོས་ (We) have to increase the area of the fields. ། འཆར་གཞི་དེ་ཆེ་རུ་གཏོང་གི་རེད་ (They) will make the plan bigger.

ཆེ་རུང་ཆུང་རུང་ (cēruŋ cūŋruŋ) whether big or small ། ཆེ་རུང་ཆུང་རུང་འདི་ར་བཙན་བྱོལ་གཞུང་ཞིག་ཆགས་ཡོད་ Whether big or small, we have established a refugee government.

ཆེ་ལྷོམ་ (cēlom) great conceit.

ཆེ་ལོང་ (cēloŋ) sm. ཆེ་ལོང་ཙམ་.

ཆེ་ལོང་ཙམ་ (cēloŋdzam) briefly, roughly ། བོད་ཀྱི་སྐོར་ཆེ་ལོང་ཙམ་བཀོད་པ་ཡིན་ (I) wrote briefly about Tibet.

ཆེ་ལོས་ (cēlöö) how big? ། འདི་ཆེ་ལོས་འདུག་གམ་ How big is this?

ཆེ་ཤ་ (cēsha) meat of larger animals such as ox, yak, etc.

ཆེ་ཤུལ་ཆུང་ཕྲིད་ (cēshüü cūŋdrii) dividing things with respect to their size.

ཆེ་ཤེལ་ (cēshee) magnifying glass, microscope.

ཆེ་ཤོར་ (cēshɔɔ) abbr. of ཆེ་བ་ཤོར་.

ཆེ་ཤོས་ (cēshöö) biggest, largest, greatest.

ཆེ་ས་ (cēsa) 1. high rank/ position/ title. 2. sm. ཆེ་གྲས་.

ཆེ་སང་སང་ (cē sāŋsaŋ) sm. ཆེ་སེ་བ་.

ཆེ་སེ་བ་ (cēsewa) rather big, quite big ། ཁང་པ་འདི་ཆེ་སེ་བ་འདུག That house is rather big.

ཆེད་ (cēè) 1. (vb.+ —) for the purpose of, in order to, for ། ཚོང་རྒྱག་ཆེད་དངུལ་གཡར་པ་རེད་ (They) borrowed money in order to do trading. 2. (— + vb. + བྱེད་) specially doing sth. ། ཁོང་མཇལ་བར་ཆེད་བསྐྱོད་བྱས་པ་ཡིན་ (I) went specially to see him.

ཆེད་ཀྱི་དོན་ (cēègo tö̱n) 1. special task/ reason/ purpose. 2. the part of speech in Tibetan grammar that conveys doing sth. "for".

ཆེད་བཀར་ (cēègar) sm. དམིགས་བཀར་.

ཆེད་བཀོལ་ (cēègöö) sm. ཆེད་སྐུལ་.

ཆེད་སྐུལ་ (cēègüü) specially assigned/ ordered; va.—བྱེད་ ། ཁོང་ལྷ་སར་འགྲོ་རྒྱུ་ཆེད་སྐུལ་བྱས་པ་རེད་ (They) specially ordered him to go to Lhasa.

ཆེད་བསྐུལ་ (cēègüü) sm. ཆེད་སྐུལ་.

ཆེད་བསྐོས་ (cēègöö) special appointment, specially appointing; va.—བྱེད་ ། ད་ལམ་ཆེད་བསྐོས་སེར་སྐྱ་སྤྱིལ་པོ་ས་གནས་སུ་ཕེབས་འབྱོར་བྱུང་བསྟུན་རྒྱུ་རྐྱེན་གསལ་ཞུ་དགོས་རྒྱུ་ When the specially appointed monk and lay officials arrive there you should put forward the matter of the dispute clearly.

ཆེད་བསྐོས་བརྟག་དཔྱད་པ་ (cēègöö dāgjeèba) specially appointed researcher/ investigator.

ཆེད་བསྐོས་མི་སྣ་ (cēègöö mi̱nə) specially appointed persons/ envoys.

ཆེད་བསྐོས་ལས་འགན་ (cēègöö le̱ngɛn) special duty/ assignment.

ཆེད་བསྐོས་གསར་འགྱུར་འགོད་མཁན་ (cēègöö sāngyur

gö̲ö̲ñɛn) special reporter/ correspondent.

ཆེད་བསྒྲུན་ (cēèdrün) specially made/ published.

ཆེད་བསྒྲུན་ཚགས་པར་ (cēèdrün tsāgbar) specially published issue (of a newspaper, magazine).

ཆེད་ཁེ་ (cēège) patent.

ཆེད་ཁེའི་བཅའ་ཁྲིམས་ (cēèkɛ jādrim) patent law, copyright law.

ཆེད་ཁེའི་བདག་དབང་ (cēèkɛ da̲àwaŋ) patent, copyright.

ཆེད་མཁས་ (cēèkɛɛ̀) specialist.

ཆེད་མཁས་མི་སྣ་ (cēèkɛɛ̀ mi̲nə) experts, specialists, professionals.

ཆེད་འགན་ (cēngɛn) special responsibility; va.—ལེན་; —འཛིན་ to take a special responsibility.

ཆེད་འགག་ (cēènga) sm. རེས་འགག་.

ཆེད་སྒོ་ (cēègo) sm. ཆེད་ལས་.

ཆེད་བསྒྲགས་ (cēèdrag) special announcement/ notice/ communique.

ཆེད་བསྒྲིགས་ (cēèdrig) special edition/ publication; va.—བྱེད་ to edit/ publish specially.

ཆེད་བསྒྲིགས་དུས་དེབ་ (cēèdrig tü̲ǜdeb) special issue/ edition/ supplement.

ཆེད་བསྒྲིགས་པར་ངོས་ (cēèdrig bārŋöȍ) a special edition/ publication.

ཆེད་བསྒྲིགས་ལེ་ཚན་ (cēèdrig le̲dzɛn) special column/ section (of a newspaper).

ཆེད་དངུལ་ (cēèŋüü) special funds; va.—གཏོང་ to spend/ allocate special funds.

ཆེད་དངུལ་ཆེད་སྤྱོད་ (cēèŋüü cēèjöȍ) earmarking a fund for a special purpose.

ཆེད་མངགས་ (cēèŋaà) 1. special ¶ ཆེད་མངགས་སྐུ་ཚབ་ Special envoy/ representative. 2. specially, exclusively, just for that purpose ¶ ཁོང་རྒྱ་གར་ལ་སྤུན་མཆེད་ཐུག་པར་ཆེད་མངགས་ཕྱིན་པ་རེད་ He went to India specially to see his relatives. 3. purposely, intentionally ¶ ཁྱོད་ལ་ཐེབས་པ་རེད་མ་གཏོགས་ཆེད་མངགས་གཞུ་རྒྱུ་མ་བྱུང་ (I) hit you accidentally. I did not do it purposely.

ཆེད་མངགས་སྐུ་ཚབ་ (cēèŋaà gūdzəb) special envoy/ representative.

ཆེད་མངགས་ངོ་ཚབ་ (cēèŋaà ŋo̲dzəb) sm. ཆེད་མངགས་སྐུ་ཚབ་.

ཆེད་མངགས་ཀྱིས་ (cēèŋaàgi) sm. ཆེད་མངགས་, 2. and 3.

ཆེད་མངགས་གདན་ཞུ་ (cēèŋaà de̲nshu) special invitation.

ཆེད་མངགས་པོ་ཉ་ (cēèŋaà pōña) special messenger/ envoy.

ཆེད་མངགས་འཕྲིན་སྤེལ་ (cēèŋaà drīnbel) special news dissemination.

ཆེད་མངགས་བཟོ་ (cēèŋaà so̲) va. to make or do sth. specially.

ཆེད་བཅར་གནང་ (cējar nāŋ) va. to specially go/ visit sb.

ཆེད་བརྗོད་ (cēèjöȍ) 1. editorial, commentary ¶ པྲ་ཝ་ཏའི་ཆེད་བརྗོད་ནང་ In the Pravda editorial.

ཆེད་གཉེར་ (cēèñer) specialized, professional ¶ ཆེད་གཉེར་གྱི་གསར་རྩོམ་དང་རྩོམ་ཁྲིད་མི་སྣ་ Professional composers and directors. 2. administering/ managing specially; va.—བྱེད་ ¶ ཆུ་སྐྱོན་བྱུང་བའི་ས་གནས་ལ་མི་ཁ་ཤས་ཆེད་གཉེར་བྱས་ནས་བཏང་པ་རེད་ (They) sent people to specially administer the flooded areas.

ཆེད་གཉེར་ཁྱིམ་ཚང་ (cēèñer kyīmdzaŋ) speciality households.

ཆེད་གཉེར་མཁས་པ་ (cēèñer kɛ̄ɛ̀ba) specialist, professional expert.

ཆེད་གཉེར་རྩོམ་པ་པོ་ (cēèñer dzōmbabo) professional writer.

ཆེད་གཉེར་རུ་ཁག (cēèñer ru̲gaà) specialist unit/ group.

ཆེད་གཉེར་ལས་བགོས་ (cēèñer lɛ̲ɛ̀göȍ) division of labor into specialties.

ཆེད་གདད་ (cēèdɛɛ̀) sm. ཆེད་མངགས་.

ཆེད་གཏོང་ (cēèdoŋ) specially sent ¶ ཆེད་གཏོང་གནམ་གྲུ་ A specially sent plane.

ཆེད་གཏོང་སྐུ་ཚབ་ (cēèdoŋ gūdzəb) special envoy/ representative.

ཆེད་བཏོན་དུས་དེབ་ (cēèdön tü̲ǜdeb) special issue (of a magazine).

ཆེད་བསྡད་ (cēèdɛɛ̀) shung. deliberately, purposely ¶ རྒྱ་ནག་ཏུ་འཇའ་ས་ཆེད་བསྡད་བརྩོན་པ་ཆེན་པོས་ཞུ་བར་འགྲོ་ཞིང་ They went to China deliberately to get the title.

ཆེད་ཐོ་འགོད་ (cēèdo gö̲ȍ) va. to register specially.

ཆེད་དུ་ (cēèdu) specially ¶ ཁོ་ཆོས་ཆེད་དུ་གདན་འདྲེན་ཞུས་པ་རེད་ (They) invited him here specially. 2. for the purpose of, in order to, for ¶ བུ་ལོན་འཇལ་ཆེད་དུ་ For the purpose of paying back the debt.

ཆེད་དུ་སྐོ་ (cēèdu gō) va. to appoint purposely.

ཆེད་དུ་མཁས་པ་ (cēèdu kɛ̄ɛ̀ba) specialist.

ཆེད་དུ་བྱ་བ་ (cēèdu ca̲wa) 1. special task/ work. 2. sm. ཆེད་ཀྱི་དོན་.

ཆེད་དོན་ (cēèdön) shung. 1. term used to indicate the start of the main subject in an edict or letter ¶ རྫོང་སྡོད་སེར་སྐྱ་སྤྲེལ་པོ་ལ་ ཆེད་དོན་ To the two district heads jointly, the purpose of the letter follows. 2. special reason/ meaning, special subject, special topic.

ཆེད་དོན་སྙན་ཞུ་ (cēèdön ñɛ̄nshu) special petition/ report.

ཆེད་དོན་ཞུ་ཡིག (cēèdön shu̲yig) sm. ཆེད་དོན་སྙན་ཞུ་.

ཆེད་དོན་གཞུང་ལས་ཁང་ (cēèdön shu̲ŋlɛgaŋ) office for the examination of special cases.

ཆེད་དོན་ལམ་ལུགས་ (cēèdön la̲mluù) special system.

ཆེད་དོན་ཨུ་ཡོན་ལྷན་ཁང་ (cēèdön ūyön lhɛ̄ngaŋ) special committee.

ཆེད་དྲངས་འཐུས་མི་ (cēèdraŋ tǖǜmi) specially invited representatives.

ཆེད་འདོན་ (cēè dö̲n) shung. va. to bestow great favor ¶ བསམ་པ་རྣམ་དག་གིས་མགོ་གཏོད་བྱས་པ་རྣམས་ལ་གཟེངས་བསྟོད་དང་ཆེད་འདོན་བྱ་རྒྱུ་ I grant titles and bestow great favors on those who come over to my side.

ཆེད་སྤེལ་ (cēèbel) specially spread/ disseminate; va.—བྱེད་.

ཆེད་སྤྱོད་ (cēèjöȍ) special purpose/ use ¶ སྤྱོད་ཀྱི་འཕྲུལ་སྣེགས་ A special purpose lathe.

ཆེད་སྤྱོད་ཐེབས་རྩ་ (cēèjöȍ tēbdza) special purpose fund/ endowment.

ཆེད་སྤྱོད་ཡོན་ཏན་ཅན་ (cēèjöȍ yö̲ndɛnjɛn) specialist.

ཆེད་ཕན་ (cēèbɛn) specially beneficial/ useful.

ཆེད་བྲིས་ (cēèdrii̖) specially written.

ཆེད་འབུལ་ (cēmbüü) specially given/ sent.

ཆེད་འབོད་ཀྱིས (cēmböögi) specially summoned/ called/ invited.

ཆེད་འབོད་སྐུ་ཚབ་ (cēmböȍ gūdzəb) a specially invited or summoned ambassador/ envoy/ representative.

ཆེད་འབྲུ་ཆེ་སྤྱོད་ (cēndru cējöȍ) grain used for special purposes.

ཆེད་སྦྱོང་ (cēèjoŋ) specialized study, study in a special field; va.—བྱེད་.

ཆེད་སྦྱོང་ཚན་ཁག (cēèjoŋ tsɛ̄ngaà) specialized training department or unit, professional training department.

ཆེད་སྦྱོང་ལས་རིགས་ (cēèjoŋ lɛ̲ɛ̀rig) specialized work/ jobs/ professions.

ཆེད་སྦྱོང་སློབ་གྲྭ་ (cēèjoŋ lōbdra) professional school/ college (for law, medicine, art, etc.).

ཆེད་སྦྱོང་སློབ་ཚན་ (cēèjoŋ lōbdzɛn) specialized/ professional course.

ཆེད་མིང་མཚོན་རྟགས་ (cēèmiŋ tsȫndaà) an em-dash.

ཆེད་དམིགས་ (cēèmii̖) 1. specially set aside, specially dedicated to sth. ¶ དགེ་འདུན་པའི་འཚོ་བ་ལེགས་བཅོས་ཀྱི་ཆེད་དམིགས་ཞལ་འདེབས་ཕུལ་བ་རེད་ I gave alms specially dedicated to improving the livelihood of the monks. 2. special, specially ¶ ཆེད་དམིགས་ཀྱི་ཡོན་ཏན་ Special skill/ knowledge.

ཆེད་དམིགས་དགོས་དངུལ་ (cēèmii̖ gö̲ȍŋüü) funds set

aside for a special purpose.

ཆེད་དམིགས་གླེང་བརྗོད་ (cēèmiì lēŋjöö) monograph on a special subject.

ཆེད་དམིགས་གློག་འཕྲིན་ (cēèmiì lōgdrin) special telegram.

ཆེད་དམིགས་དོན་ཚན་ (cēèmiì töndzɛn) special items (in a treaty/ agreement).

ཆེད་དམིགས་ཐ་སྙད་ (cēèmiì tãñɛɛ̀) technical/ special terms.

ཆེད་དམིགས་མི་དམངས་ཞིབ་དཔྱོད་ཁང་ (cēèmiì mimaŋ shibjöögaŋ) special people's procuratorate.

ཆེད་དམིགས་མི་དམངས་ཁྲིམས་ཁང་ (cēèmiì mimaŋ trīmgaŋ) special people's court.

ཆེད་དམིགས་ལམ་སྲོལ་ (cēèmiì lamsöö) special system.

ཆེད་རྩོམ་ (cēèdzom) thesis, dissertation.

ཆེད་རྩོམ་རྒྱུག་རྩོད་ཨུ་ཡོན་ལྷན་ཁང་ (cēèdzom gyugdzöö üyün lhɛ̄ngaŋ) dissertation defense committee.

ཆེད་བཙུགས་ (cēèdzuù) specially created/ started ¶ བོད་ཡིག་སློབ་སྦྱོང་འཛིན་གྲྭ་ཆེད་བཙུགས་བྱས་པ་རེད་ (They) specially established a class for studying Tibetan.

ཆེད་འཚོང་ཀུང་སི་ (cēèdzoŋ gūŋsi) tib.ch. an enterprise that sells specialized items.

ཆེད་འཛུགས་ (cēndzuù) specially created/ started.

ཆེད་རྫོང་ (cēèdzoŋ) specially sent; va.—བྱེད་.

ཆེད་བཟོ་ (cēèso) specially made.

ཆེད་ཞིབ་མཐའ་གསལ་ (cēèshib tāsɛl) investigating sth. so that one will understand it thoroughly ¶ གྱོད་དོན་འདི་མཇུག་ཆེད་ཞིབ་མཐའ་གསལ་ཡོང་བ་བྱེད་དགོས་ You must specially investigate the case thoroughly so that in the end you will know clearly what happened.

ཆེད་ཞུ་ (cēèshu) telling specially.

ཆེད་ལས་ (cēèlɛɛ̀) special task/ work, professional, speciality, specialized work ¶ ཆེད་ལས་ཀྱི་འཆར་འགོད་ཁང་ Special designing unit. ¶ ཆེད་ལས་ཀྱི་ཡོན་ཏན་རེ་རེ་བསླབས་ (They) each studied a specialty.

ཆེད་ལས་ཀྱི་རོལ་མོ་བ་ (cēèlɛɛ̀gi röömowa) professional musician.

ཆེད་ལས་ཀྱི་ཤེས་ཡོན་ (cēèlɛɛ̀gi shēèyön) professional knowledge or skill.

ཆེད་ལས་སྒོ་བསྡེན་ཚོང་ཁང་ (cēèlɛɛ̀ goden tsōŋgaŋ) specialized retail store.

ཆེད་ལས་པ་ (cēèlɛɛ̀ba) specialist.

ཆེད་ལས་ཐ་སྙད་ (cēèlɛɛ̀ tãñɛɛ̀) technical terms.

ཆེད་ལས་དུད་ཚང་ (cēèlɛɛ̀ tüüdzaŋ) specialized (production) households.

ཆེད་ལས་མིང་ཚིག (cēèlɛɛ̀ miŋdzii) technical term.

ཆེད་ལས་ཡོན་ཏན་ (cēèlɛɛ̀ yöndɛn) specialized knowledge/ skill; specialized field of study.

ཆེད་ལས་རུ་ཁག (cēlɛɛ̀ rugaà) specialist production unit/ brigade.

ཆེད་ལས་སུ་འགྱུར་ (cēèlɛɛ̀su gyur) vi. to become specialized/ professionalized.

ཆེད་ལས་སུ་བསྒྱུར་ (cēèlɛɛ̀su gyur) va. to specialize/ professionalize.

ཆེད་ལས་སློབ་གྲྭ་ (cēèlɛɛ̀ lōbdra) professional school, vocational school, school in which a specialization is taught.

ཆེད་སོ་ (cēèso) sm. ཆེད་དུ་.

ཆེན་ (cēn) abbr. of ཆེན་པོ་.

ཆེན་ཆུང་ (cēnjuŋ) sm. ཆེན་ཆུན་.

ཆེན་ཆུན་ (cēnjün) senior and junior (wives).

ཆེན་པོ་ (cēmbo) great, big, large ¶ ཁང་པ་ཆེན་པོ་ A big house. ¶ གལ་ཆེན་པོ་ Of great importance.

ཆེན་པོ་ཆུང་སྤྱོད་ (cēmbo cūŋjöö) wasting sb. on a petty job, not doing justice to sb.'s talents.

ཆེན་པོ་དཔོན་རྒྱུད་ (cēmbo bōngyüü) shung. aristocratic lineages.

ཆེན་པོ་ཧོར་ (cēmbo hōr) the great Mongolia/ Mongols.

ཆེན་མ་ (cēmma) senior wife.

ཆེན་མོ་ (cēmmo) sm. ཆེན་པོ་.

ཆེན་མོ་བ་ (cēmmowa) sm. ཆེ་མོ་བ་ལགས་.

ཆེན་མོ་ལགས་ (cēmmolaà) sm. ཆེ་མོ་བ་ལགས་.

ཆེན་ལུང་གནམ་ལོ་ (cēnluŋ nāmlo) shung. a year in the reign of the Emperor Qian Lung.

ཆེམ་ཆེམ་ (cēmjem) glittering ¶ འོད་ཆེམ་ཆེམ་ Glittering light.

ཆེམ་ཆེམ་འཁྱུག་འཁྱུག (cēmjem kyūggyug) glittering and shinning/ flashing.

ཆེམ་མེ་ (cēmme) 1. sm. ཆེམ་ཆེམ་. 2. (for sounds) clamor, noisy.

ཆེམས་ (cēm) will, last testament ¶ ཁོའི་ཁ་ཆེམས་ His will.

ཆེམས་ཆེམས་ (cēmjem) sm. ཆེམ་ཆེམ་.

ཆེར་ (cēē) 1. big, great, much ¶ ཁྱད་པར་ཆེར་མི་འདུག There is not a big difference. 2. bigger, greater ¶ ཁོང་གིས་ཁང་པ་ཆེ་ཆེར་བཏང་བ་རེད་ He made the house bigger.

ཆེར་བསྐྱེད་ (cēēgyeè) big, large, great, strong ¶ ཧུར་བརྩོན་ཆེར་བསྐྱེད་ཀྱིས་སློབ་སྦྱོང་བྱེད་དགོས་ (You) have to study with great diligence.

ཆེར་སྒྲོག་གློག་ཁང་ (cēēdrɔg lɔ̄ɔ̀gaŋ) broadcasting station.

ཆེར་གཏོང་སྒྲ་འཁོར་ (cēēdoŋ dragɔɔ) loud-speaker.

ཆེར་སྤེལ་ (cēēbel) enlarging/ widening/ expanding/ spreading; va.—གཏོང་;—བྱེད་ ¶ ལས་འགུལ་དེ་ཆེར་སྤེལ་གཏོང་དགོས་ (You) have to expand that campaign.

ཆེར་རློམ་ཆུང་གནོན་ (cēēlom cūŋnön) arrogant/ conceited to those above and oppressive to those below.

ཆེས་ (cēè) (— + adj.) very, extremely ¶ ཆེས་མྱུར་ Very fast.

ཆེས་ཆེ་བའི་ཚད་ (cēè cēwɛ tsɛ̄ɛ̀) the maximum or highest (e.g., value/ limit/ degree/ size).

ཆེས་ཆེར་ (cēè cēē) very much, much bigger/ larger/ greater ¶ ཞིང་ལས་ཐོན་སྐྱེད་ཆེས་ཆེར་ཕྱིན་ཡོད་པ་རེད་ Agricultural output has become much larger.

ཆེས་མགྱོགས་མེ་འཁོར་ (cēègyɔɔ̀ megɔɔ) high speed train, bullet train, express train.

ཆེས་མཐོ་ (cēèto) 1. very high, extremely high ¶ ཆེས་མཐོའི་དཔོན་རིགས་ Very high officials. 2. supreme.

ཆེས་མཐོའི་ཁྲིམས་ཁང་ (cēètö trīmgaŋ) Supreme Court (U.S.A.).

ཆེས་མཐོའི་མི་དམངས་ཁྲིམས་ཁང་ (cēètö mimaŋ trīmgaŋ) People's Supreme Court (PRC).

ཆེས་མཐོའི་མི་དམངས་རྟོག་ཞིབ་ཁང་ (cēètö mimaŋ dōgshibgaŋ) sm. ཆེས་མཐོའི་མི་དམངས་ཞིབ་དཔྱོད་ཁང་.

ཆེས་མཐོའི་མི་དམངས་ཞིབ་དཔྱོད་ཁང་ (cēètö mimaŋ shibjöögaŋ) People's Supreme Procurator's Office (PRC).

ཆེས་མཐོའི་སུའུ་ཝེའི་ཨ་ (cēètö sūwɛ ā) tib.ch. Supreme Soviet (USSR).

ཆེས་མཐོའི་སློབ་ཡོན་ཚོགས་ཆུང་ (cēètö lōbyön tsɔ̄gjuŋ) the supreme scholarship committee of the Tibetan government in exile.

ཆེས་མཐོའི་ལྷན་ཚོགས་ (cēètö lhɛ̄ndzɔɔ̀) summit conference/ meeting.

ཆེས་མང་ཤོས་ (cēè maŋshöö) majority, mostly.

ཆེས་མྱུར་ (cēèñur) 1. very fast/ quick. 2. high-speed.

ཆེས་ལོག་སྤྱོད་ (cēè lɔgjöö) completely reactionary.

ཆེས་ལྷག་པ་ (cēè lhāgba) very much/ great ¶ ཆེས་ལྷག་པའི་ཡར་རྒྱས་བྱུང་ (They) have developed greatly.

ཚོ་ (cō) 1. sense, meaning, worth ¶ སྐད་ཆ་དེ་ལ་ཚོ་མི་འདུག That talk doesn't make sense. ¶ ཚོ་མེད་པའི་ལས་ཀ་ Useless/ meaningless work. 2. situation, circumstances; va.—ལ་ལྟ་ to look at a situation/ circumstance.

ཚོ་ག (cōga) 1. rite, ritual. 2. method or way of doing sth. ¶ སྨན་བཅོས་ཀྱི་ཚོ་ག A method of treatment.

ཚོ་ངེ་ (cōŋe) wailing, lamenting; va.—འདོན་; —འདེབས་ to wail, to weep, to lament.

ཚོ་ངེ་འོ་དོད་ (cōŋe wo̱döö) sm. ཚོ་ངེ་.

ཚོ་ཆད་ (cōjɛɛ̀) arc. unsuitable, inappropriate, unfit.

ཚོ་ལྟ་ (cō dā) va. to look at a situation ¶ དང་པོ་འཛམ་གླིང་གི་འགྱུར་ལྡོག་ལ་ཚོ་ལྟ་དགོས་ First one must look at the changes throughout the world.

ཚོ་སྤྱོད་ (cōjeè) sm. ཚོ་བབ་.

ཚོ་འཕྲུལ་ (cōndrüü) miracle, miraculously; va.—སྟོན་ to perform/ manifest a miracle ¶ བླ་མས་ཚོ་འཕྲུལ་བསྟན་ནས་གནམ་ལ་འཕུར་པ་རེད་ The lama performed a miracle and flew.

ཚོ་འཕྲུལ་གྱི་བཅོ་ལྔ་ (cōndrüügi jō̃ŋa) the 15th day of the 1st month in the Tibetan calendar.

ཚོ་འཕྲུལ་མཆོད་པ་ (cōndrüü cȫöba) Monlam— the great prayer festival.

ཚོ་འཕྲུལ་དུས་ཆེན་ (cōndrüü tü̱üjen) festival of the great miracle held on the 15th of the 1st Tibetan month to commemorate the Buddha's defeat of the heretics at Sravasti.

ཚོ་འཕྲུལ་ཟླ་བ་ (cōndrüü da̱wa) the first month of the Tibetan calendar— when the Buddha defeated the heretics.

ཚོ་བབ་ (cōbəb) situation, circumstances ¶ ལས་ཀའི་ཚོ་བབ་ལ་བལྟས་ནས་སྡོད་མ་སྡོད་ཐག་གཅོད་བྱེད་ཀྱི་ཡིན་ (I) will decide to stay or go after looking at the situation of the work.

ཚོ་འབྲང་ (cōndraŋ) sm. ཚོ་རིགས་.

ཚོ་མེད་ (cōmeè) meaningless, aimless, pointless.

ཚོ་མེད་གྲོ་མེད་ (cōmeè dro̱meè) sm. ཚོ་མེད་.

ཚོ་རིགས་ (cōrig) birth status, descent ¶ ཚོ་རིགས་དམའ་བ་ Low birth or lineage.

ཚོ་རིས་ (cōrii) the eyes of dice.

ཚོ་ལེ་བ་ (cōlewa) whitish (when referring to hair it means salt and pepper).

ཚོ་ལོ་ (cōlo) 1. game of dice; va.—རྩེ་;—འགྱེད་ to play dice. 2. ch. an official position, rank given by the Chinese Emperor. 3. moss.

ཚོ་ལོ་འཇའ་ས་ (cōlo ja̱asa) shung. an order of the Emperor granting a title.

ཚོ་ལོ་པ་ (cōlowa) dice player.

ཚོ་སྲང་ལྟ་ (cōsaŋ dā) sm. ཞྱི་གསང་བྱེད་.

ཚོག (cɔ̄ɔ) 1. vi. to be allowed, to be permitted ¶ ལག་ཁྱེར་ཡོད་ན་འགྲོ་ཚོག་གི་རེད་ If (you) have a permit you are allowed to go. 2. vi. to be fit for ¶ རས་འདིས་སྟོད་ཐུང་བཟོ་ཚོག་པ་འདུག་གས་ Is this cloth fit for making a shirt? 3. (vb.+ — ཡིན་ or རེད་) ready/ set to do ¶ ང་ཚོ་འགྲོ་ཚོག་ཡིན་ We are ready to go. ¶ ཁ་ལག་ཟས་ཚོག་རེད་ The food is ready to eat. 4. a volunteering promise to do sth. (usu. "I will...") ¶ ངས་དེ་ག་རང་ཞུས་ཚོག I will do that. ¶ མ་བརྗེད་པ་བྱས་ཚོག I will not forget it. ¶ ངས་ཁ་ལག་བཟོས་ཚོག I will make the food. 5. imp. of གཙོག. 6. sm. ཚོག་ག.

ཚོག་ག (cɔ̄ɔga) I wish, I hope ¶ ང་ལ་ལས་ཀ་ཡག་པོ་ཞིག་རག་ཚོག་ག I wish I will get a good job.

ཚོག་ཚོག (cɔ̄ɔjoò) ready, about to ¶ ཁོ་ཡོང་ཚོག་ཚོག་རེད་ He is ready to come. ¶ མི་འདི་ཤི་ཚོག་ཚོག་རེད་ This man is on the verge of death.

ཚོག་མཆན་ (cɔ̄gjɛn) approval, authorization, sanction, endorsement; va.—གནང་; —འགོད་ to give approval, to authorize, to sanction, to endorse; va.—ཞུ་ to ask for approval/ authorization; vi.—ཐོབ་; —ཐོན་ to receive approval/ permission ¶ འཆར་གཞི་དེ་རུ་ཚོགས་ཆུང་གིས་ཚོག་མཆན་བཀོད་པ་རེད་ The committee approved the plan.

ཚོག་མཆན་དཔང་ཡིག (cɔ̄gjɛn bāŋyig) permission letter, letter of approval.

ཚོགས་ཐམ་ (cɔ̄gdam) 1. sm. ཚོག་མཆན་ (but conveys a seal was used for the approval).

ཚོག་འཐུས་ (cɔ̄gdüü) shung. 1. permission, approval ¶ རྒྱ་གར་ནང་ལྟ་སྐོར་བྱས་ན་ཚོག་འཐུས་ལག་ཁྱེར་ཐོབ་པ་རེད་ (They) got a document permitting them to travel inside India. ¶ བུན་འབབ་ཆད་འཇལ་རྣམས་ཟླ་གྲངས་དུས་བཅད་ཀྱིས་རིམ་འབུལ་ཚོག་འཐུས་བཀའ་བཟང་གྱི་སྒྲིན་བྱུང་དོན་ They were given permission to pay the loan in monthly payments. 2. vi. to be okay to do sth. ¶ དེ་ལྟར་བྱེད་ཚོག་འཐུས་ It is okay to do that.

ཚོག་འཐུས་དགོངས་འཁྲོལ་ (cɔ̄gdüü go̱ŋdröö) shung. permission, approval.

ཚོག་འཐུས་ལག་ཁྱེར་ (cɔ̄gdüü la̱ggyer) permission letter/ document/ permit.

ཚོག་པ་ (cɔ̄gba) sm. ཚོག.

ཚོག་པ་ཅིག (cɔ̄gbajig) May I be permitted/ allowed (to do sth.) ¶ ང་གུང་སེང་དུ་ཕྱིན་ཚོག་པ་ཅིག May I be permitted to go on vacation.

ཚོག་པའི་ལག་འཁྱེར་ (cɔ̄gbɛ la̱ggyer) license, permit.

ཚོག་པར་བྱེད་ (cɔ̄gbaa ce̱è) va. to permit, to allow ¶ ངས་ཁོ་ལྷ་སར་ཕྱིན་ཚོག་པར་བྱས་པ་ཡིན་ I permitted him to go to Lhasa.

ཚོག་རོགས་ (cɔ̄grɔɔ̀) companion for monks when praying.

ཚོག་ཤེས་ (cɔ̄gsheè) contentment (with one's lot); va.—བྱེད་ to be content ¶ རང་ལ་གང་ཡོད་པ་དེ་ར་ཚོག་ཤེས་བྱ་དགོས་ One should be content with whatever one has.

ཚོག་ཤེས་བྲལ་བ་ (cɔ̄gsheè trɛ̱ɛwa) sm. ཚོག་ཤེས་མེད་པ་.

ཚོག་ཤེས་མེད་པ་ (cɔ̄gsheè me̱èba) a person who is not content, being discontented/ dissatisfied.

ཚོགས་ (cɔ̄ɔ) imp. of འཚོག.

ཚོངས་ (cōŋ) imp. of འཚང་.

ཚོད་ (cȫö) 1. imp. of གཅོད་. 2. vi. to be cut off, to be separated, to be parted ¶ ས་གནས་དེ་གཉིས་གཙང་པོ་ཆེན་པོས་ཚོད་ཡོད་ The two regions are separated by a big river. 3. vi. to come to reach an agreement/ settlement, to be settled/ agreed ¶ ད་དུང་གོང་ཐག་ཚོད་མ་སོང་ (They) still are not able to settle the price. 4. vi. to be able to cover distances (on journeys, etc.) ¶ རྐང་ཐང་ལ་འགྲོ་དུས་ཉིན་རེ་མི་ལི་ ༢༠ ལྷག་ས་ཚོད་ཐུབ་ཀྱི་མི་འདུག (When) (we) travel on foot (we) are not able to cover more than 20 miles per day.

ཚོད་ཁྲ་ (cȫödra) judgement/ verdict; va.—གཏོང་.

ཚོད་གན་ (cȫögɛn) written agreement/ accord/ settlement; va.—འཛུགས་ to sign an agreement, to enter into an agreement.

ཚོད་གཏམ་ (cȫödam) judgement, conclusion ¶ འཛམ་གླིང་གི་འབྱོར་མེད་པ་རྣམས་བཅིངས་འགྲོལ་གཏོང་ཐུབ་ཀྱི་རེད་ཟེར་བ་དེ་མ་ལེ་རིང་ལུགས་ཀྱི་ཚོད་གཏམ་རེད་ The statement that, "We will be able to liberate the proletariat of the world," is the judgment of Marx-Leninism.

ཚོད་དན་ (cȫödɛn) sm. ཚོད་གན་.

ཚོད་དོན་ (cȫödön) resolution, decision.

ཚོད་སྡོམ་ (cȫödom) sm. ཚོད་འདོམས་.

ཚོད་འདོམས་ (cȫndom) conclusion (e.g., in a study/ experiment/ law case).

ཚོད་མ་ (cȫöma) a field that has been divided into several parts to make it easier to water.

ཚོད་ཡིག (cȫöyii) sm. ཚོད་གན་.

ཚོད་ཡིག་འབབ་ཅན་ (cȫöyii ba̱jɛn) sm. ཚོད་གན་.

ཚོད་ཡིག་འབབ་ཅན་ (cȫöyii ba̱jɛn) shung. a ཚོད་གན་ on which seals have been affixed.

ཚོད་རིགས་ (cȫörii) shung. things that have been settled/ agreed to (usu. land).

ཚོད་སེམས་ (cȫösem) determination to do sth; va.—སྟོན་ to show/ express determination; va.—འཛུགས་ to make one's mind act in a determined fashion ¶ རྒྱབ་སྐྱོར་བྱེད་ཡག་གི་ཚོད་སེམས་བསྟན་པ་རེད་ (They) expressed (their) determination to support (them).

ཚོད་སེམས་ཀྱི་ཡི་གེ (cȫösemgi yi̱gi) sm. ཚོད་སེམས་ཡིག་ཤོག.

ཚོད་སེམས་ཡིག་ཤོག (cȫösem yigshɔɔ̀) written pledge of determination.

ཚོད་སེམས་གསལ་སྟོན་ (cȫösem sēēdön) showing/ exhibiting/ expressing determination clearly.

ཚོད་སློག (cȫölɔɔ̀) veto; va.—བྱེད་ to veto.

ཚོད་སློག་དབང་ཆ་ (cȫölɔɔ̀ wāŋja) veto power.

ཚོན་ (cȫn) 1. hem of clothing. 2. Tibetan tent.

ཆོན་ཆུང་ (cõnjuŋ) a short rope used to erect the yak hair tents of Tibetan nomads.

ཆོན་ཆེན་ (cõnjen) a long rope used to erect the yak hair tents of Tibetan nomads.

ཆོན་ཐག (cõndaà) tent rope.

ཆོན་ཕུར་ (cõnbur) tent peg.

ཆོན་འབྲིང་ (cõndriŋ) the middle size rope used to erect the yak hair tents of Tibetan nomads.

ཆོན་རྩལ་ (cõndzεε) ch.tib. boxing.

ཆོབ་ཀྱེ་ (cõbgye) 1. sb. who is wild/ undisciplined/ unconventional, sb. who does all kinds of inappropriate acts. 2. a joker, sb. who makes others laugh.

ཆོབ་སྒྲོལ་ (cõb gǖǖ) 1. va. to cause laughter. 2. va. to make trouble.

ཆོབ་ཆོབ་ (cõbjob) 1. sound of blows hitting. 2. sound made when eating/ chewing.

ཆོབ་རྫེ་ (cõbdze) sm. ཆོབ་སྒྲོལ་.

ཆོབ་ཚ་པོ་ (cõb tsãbo) sm. ཆོབ་ཀྱེ་.

ཆོམ་ (cõm) 1. imp. of འཇོམས་. 2. thundering sound. 3. vi. to get/ be defeated/ subdued/ conquered.

ཆོམ་རྐུན་ (cõmgün) robber, bandit.

ཆོམ་སྒྲ་ (cõmdra) thundering sound.

ཆོམ་པོ་ (cõmbo) sm. ཆོམ་རྐུན་.

ཆོམ་པོ་བ་ (cõmbowa) bandits.

ཆོལ་ (cõõ) imp. of འཆོལ་.

ཆོལ་ཁ་ (cõõga) province.

ཆོལ་ཁ་གསུམ་ (cõõga sũm) the three traditional provinces of Tibet (དབུས་གཙང་, མདོ་སྟོད་, མདོ་སྨད་).

ཆོལ་ཁའི་ཕྱོགས་འཛིན་ (cõõgε cõŋsdzin) being partial towards one's region/ province.

ཆོལ་འགྲིགས་ (cõõ drig) vi. to be orderly. 2. vi. to be successful.

ཆོལ་འགྲིགས་པོ་ (cõõ drigbo) 1. orderly. 2. successful.

ཆོལ་སྒྲིག (cõõ drig) va. to put things in order.

ཆོལ་འདུས་ (cõõdüü) abbr. of ཆོལ་གསུམ་སྤྱི་འདུས་.

ཆོལ་ལེ་བ་ (cõõlewa) just a few, only a little bit.

ཆོལ་ལུགས་ (cõõluù) rules/ customs of the three ཆོལ་ཁ་.

ཆོལ་གསུམ་ (cõõsum) sm. ཆོལ་ཁ་གསུམ་.

ཆོལ་གསུམ་སྤྱི་འདུས་ (cõõsumgi jĩduù) elected representatives of the three provinces of Tibet (in Dharamsala).

ཆོལ་གསུམ་མི་རིགས་ (cõõsum mirii) ethnic groups in the three traditional provinces of Tibet (དབུས་གཙང་, མདོ་སྟོད་, མདོ་སྨད་).

ཆོས་ (cõõ) 1. dharma, religion; va.— འཆད་; —གོད་; —གསུང་; —སྒྲ་ to give religious teaching; va.—ཉན་ to hear/ listen to religious teaching; va.—བྱེད་ to practice religion, to live a religious life; va.—ཞུ་ to receive religious instruction, to seek/ ask for religious teaching. 2. imp. of འཆོས་ and འཆའ་.

ཆོས་ཀྱི་འཁོར་ལོ་ (cõõgi kɔ̃ɔlo) the wheel of the dharma.

ཆོས་ཀྱི་གོང་མ་ (cõõgi koŋma) 1. dharmaraja. 2. the Pope.

ཆོས་ཀྱི་སྒྲིག་ཁྲིམས་ (cõõgi drigdrim) shung. religious rules/ regulations.

ཆོས་ཀྱི་ངོ་བོ་ (cõõgi ŋowo) the true nature of the dharma.

ཆོས་ཀྱི་མངའ་བདག (cõõgi ŋadaà) one who understands/ possesses the dharma.

ཆོས་ཀྱི་ཆོལ་ཁ་ (cõõgi cõõga) the Tibetan regions of དབུས་ and གཙང་.

ཆོས་ཀྱི་ཉི་མ་ (cõõgi ñima) the name of the 9th Panchen Lama.

ཆོས་ཀྱི་སྙིང་པོ་ (cõõgi ñiŋbu) the essence of the dharma.

ཆོས་ཀྱི་ལྟ་བ་ (cõõgi dãwa) spiritual outlook, religious things.

ཆོས་ཀྱི་སྟོབས་ (cõõgi dõb) 1. name of a Buddha. 2. the power of the dharma.

ཆོས་ཀྱི་འདུན་ས་ (cõõgi dünsa) shung. the monastery.

ཆོས་ཀྱི་སྣོད་ (cõõgi nõõ) one qualified/ worthy to receive the teachings of the dharma.

ཆོས་ཀྱི་འབེལ་གཏམ་ (cõõgi bẽẽdam) conversations regarding the dharma.

ཆོས་ཀྱི་གཞུང་ (cõõgi shuŋ) the central theme of the dharma.

ཆོས་ཀྱི་ལས་རིགས་པ་ (cõõgi lεεrigbə) religious professionals/ specialists/ workers.

ཆོས་དཀར་པོ་ (cõõ gãrbo) good/ virtuous/ meritorious deeds.

ཆོས་དཀྲོལ་ (cõõdrõõ) sm.* ཆོས་འཁྲོལ་.

ཆོས་ཀློག (cõõ lɔ̃ɔ) va. to read scriptures/ prayers.

ཆོས་ཀློང་ཆེན་པོ་ (cõõloŋ cẽmbo) shung. having great knowledge of religion/ dharma.

ཆོས་སྐད་ (cõõgεὲ) classical language, bookish language, religious language.

ཆོས་སྐལ་ཡོད་པ་ (cõõgεε yööba) having the good karmic fortune to have received dharma teaching.

ཆོས་སྐོར་ (cõõgɔɔ) 1. ritual practiced by farmers in which they carry religious texts and statues around the fields so that they will get a good harvest. 2. pilgrimage.

ཆོས་སྐོར་སྐོར་ (cõõ gɔ̃ɔgɔɔ) shung. sm. ཆོས་སྐོར་.

ཆོས་སྐོར་བ་ (cõõgɔɔwa) sb. who does ཆོས་སྐོར་.

ཆོས་སྐྱིད་ (cõõgyii) name of a person.

ཆོས་སྐྱོང་ (cõõgyoŋ) defender of the faith, protective deity.

ཆོས་སྐྱོང་སྲུང་མ་ (cõõgyoŋ sũŋmə) protective deity.

ཆོས་ཁང་ (cõõgaŋ) 1. chapel, temple. 2. church.

ཆོས་ཁྲི་ (cõõdri) throne/ platform from which religious teaching or sermons are given.

ཆོས་ཁྲིམས་ (cõõtrim) religious laws, monastic laws.

ཆོས་ཁྲིམས་ཁང་ (cõõdrimgaŋ) shung. monastic court ༄ དགེ་འདུན་ཆང་འཐུང་མི་བྱུང་ན་ཆོས་ཁྲིམས་ཁང་ནས་འགུག་ར་སྦྱད་དེ་ཆང་ཉེས་ཊམ་བཞི་རེ་ཡིན་གྱི་ If a monk drinks chang he will be summoned by the monastic court and fined 4 trankas.

ཆོས་ཁྲིམས་དར་གྱི་མདུད་པ་ (cõõdrim targi düübə) religious law is gentle but strict.

ཆོས་ཁྲིམས་པ་ (cõõdrimba) sm. དགེ་བསྐོས་.

ཆོས་ཁྲིམས་གཙང་མ་ (cõõdrim dzãŋmə) shung. pure religious law/ regulations/ rules.

ཆོས་འཁོར་ (cõõgɔɔ) 1. teaching the dharma/ religion; va.—བསྐོར་ to turn the wheel of the dharma, to teach religion. 2. a vein in the heart. 3. prayer wheels (usu. many in a line).

ཆོས་འཁོར་རྒྱལ་ (cõõgɔɔgyεὲ) shung. a famous holy lake that is consulted for signs is located.

ཆོས་འཁོར་གསུམ་ (cõõgɔɔsum) 1. name of three sacred places: ལྷ་ས་, བསམ་ཡས་, ཁྲ་འབྲུག. 2. the three stages of turning the wheel of the dharma.

ཆོས་འཁྲོལ་ (cõõdröö) permission from one's lord to leave the estate and join a monastery.

ཆོས་གོས་ (cõõgöö) robe of monks, religious dress/ clothes.

ཆོས་གྲྭ་ (cõõdra) 1. school for religious study/ debate, Nyingma school of advanced religious study/ monastery. 2. ཆོས་ར་.

ཆོས་གྲོགས་ (cõõdrɔɔ) monks/ disciples who receive religious teachings from the same lama.

ཆོས་དགེ་ (cõõge) religious teacher.

ཆོས་དགོན་ (cõõgön) monastery.

ཆོས་མགོ་ཐོན་པ་ (cõõgo tõmbo) sb. who has entered the path of religion.

ཆོས་མགོ་འཁྱོངས་དུས་བླ་མ་མ་བརྗེད་ གཉེན་མགོ་འཁྱོངས་དུས་བར་པ་མ་བརྗེད་ (cõõgo kyõŋdüü lãma majeè ñẽngo kyõŋdüü parba majeè) do not forget to show gratitude to those who have helped you [Lit. when one is successful in religion do not forget one's lama; when one is successful in marriage, do not forget the intermediary].

ཆོས་རྒྱགས་ (cööӧgyaà) provisions for people engaged in religious activities, e.g., in meditation.

ཆོས་རྒྱལ་ (cöögyɛɛ) 1. dharmaraja (title given to King's who are protectors of Buddhism). 2. title of the King (Maharaja) of Sikkim.

ཆོས་རྒྱལ་ནོར་བཟང་ (cöögyɛɛ nɔrsaŋ) name of a king in a Tibetan story.

ཆོས་རྒྱལ་འཕགས་པ་ (cöögyɛɛ pāgba) religious leader from Sakya who was Imperial Tutor to Kublai Khan during the Yuan dynasty.

ཆོས་རྒྱལ་མེས་དབོན་རྣམ་གསུམ་ (cöögyɛɛ meèbön nāmsum) the three great "Buddhist" kings of Tibet (སྲོང་བཙན་སྒམ་པོ་, ཁྲི་སྲོང་ལྡེའུ་བཙན་, ཁྲི་རལ་པ་ཅན་).

ཆོས་རྒྱུགས་ (cöögyuù) reciting scriptures by heart; va.—སྤྲོད་ to take a test involving reciting scriptures from memory; va.—ལེན་ to give a test involving reciting scriptures from memory.

ཆོས་རྒྱུད་ (cöögyüü) religious tradition.

ཆོས་རྒྱུན་བླ་རབས་ (cöögyün lārəb) lineage/ line of lamas.

ཆོས་སྒར་ (cöögar) religious center; va.—ཞུགས་ to enter a monastery or nunnery, to be initiated into religious life.

ཆོས་སྒྲ་ (cöödra) 1. sound of people praying. 2. sound of monks debating.

ཆོས་སྒྲུང་ (cöödruŋ) religious story.

ཆོས་སྒྲོག (cöödrɔɔ) reading/ reciting religious scriptures or books.

ཆོས་སྒྲོམ་ (cöödrom) altar/ cabinet on which statues, etc. are placed.

ཆོས་བརྒྱད་ (cöögyɛɛ̀) abbr. of འཇིག་རྟེན་ཆོས་བརྒྱད་.

ཆོས་བརྒྱུད་ (cöögyüü) oral teachings and initiations.

ཆོས་སྒྱུར་ (cöö gyur) 1. va. to translate a religious text. 2. va. to change (one's) religion, to convert.

ཆོས་མངའ་ (cööŋa) shung. abbr. of ཕྱིལ་དཀར་ཆོས་སྡེ་ and མངའ་ཞབས་.

ཆོས་མངོན་པ་མཛོད་ (cöö ŋömba dzöö) abhidharmakosa.

ཆོས་ཅན་ (cööjɛn) 1. religious, pious. 2. a place where Buddhism/ religion flourishes.

ཆོས་ཆས་ (cööjɛɛ̀) religious garments/ clothing.

ཆོས་འཆད་ (cööjɛɛ̀) see ཆོས་.

ཆོས་འཇུག (cönjuù) making one a monk; va.—བྱེད་ ། མི་དེ་ཆོས་འཇུག་བྱེད་རྒྱུའི་སྐོར་ Concerning making that man into a monk.

ཆོས་རྗེ་ (cööje) 1. title for high lamas. 2. title for oracles (mediums).

ཆོས་རྗེ་ཟུར་པ་ (cööje surbə) ex- or former oracle/ medium.

ཆོས་ཉན་ (cöö ñɛn) va. to listen to a religious teaching.

ཆོས་ཉིད་ (cööñii) 1. law ། ཚན་རིག་ཆོས་ཉིད་ A scientific law. 2. quality, nature, characteristic, features ། རང་བྱུང་ཆོས་ཉིད་ Characteristics of nature.

ཆོས་ཉིད་ཀྱི་རང་བཞིན་ (cööñiigi rəŋshin) characteristics of nature, the nature of things ། ཉི་མ་ཤར་ནས་བཞུས་འགྲོ་ཡག་འདི་ཆོས་ཉིད་ཀྱི་རང་བཞིན་རེད་ That the sun sets after it rises is a characteristic of nature.

ཆོས་གཏེར་ (cööder) hidden scriptures.

ཆོས་སྟེགས་ (cöödeg) a shelf/ stand for placing a religious text.

ཆོས་སྟོན་ (cöödön) 1. religious festival. 2. monks begging for alms.

ཆོས་སྟོན་པ་ (cöödömba) a person who teaches dharma.

ཆོས་ཐག (cöödaà) sm. གླེགས་ཐག.

ཆོས་ཐེབས་ (cöödeb) trust fund/ endowment for the practice of a religious ritual.

ཆོས་ཐེབས་སློང་ཡིག (cöödeb lōŋyig) a letter asking for donations for a religious ritual.

ཆོས་ཐོག (cöödɔɔ) 1. a period of studying/ debating in a monastery (like a semester), the period when the dharma grove (ཆོས་ར་) is in session. 2. a practice of some monks moving from place too place over the year to debate and study religion. 3. running away from (home, school, monastery).

ཆོས་ཐོག་རྒྱུན་པ་ (cöödɔɔ gyümbə) shung. monks who goes for ཆོས་ཐོག.

ཆོས་མཐུན་པ་ (cöödümba) 1. similar characteristics. 2. the same sect/ doctrine (religion). 3. a true practitioner of the dharma.

ཆོས་དད་ (cöödɛɛ̀) religious belief/ faith.

ཆོས་དད་པ་ (cöödɛɛ̀ba) a person who believes in religion.

ཆོས་དད་མང་ཚོགས་ (cöödɛɛ̀ maŋdzɔɔ) religious masses.

ཆོས་དད་རང་དབང་ (cöödɛɛ̀ raŋwaŋ) sm. ཆོས་དད་རང་མོས་.

ཆོས་དད་རང་མོས་ (cöödɛɛ̀ raŋmöö) freedom of worship/ religion.

ཆོས་དར་ (cöö tar) 1. vi. to have religion flourish/ spread/ expand. 2. name of a person.

ཆོས་དུང་ (cööduŋ) conch horn.

ཆོས་དོད་ (cöödöö) shung. a payment made when a family that has a tax obligation to send to a son to a monastery has no one to send ། ཁོ་པར་གྲྭ་པ་ང་འཛུགས་བྱ་རྒྱ་མེད་ཀྱིན་ཆོས་དོད་སྤྲད་འབྲས་བཏོད་པ་ They were allowed to make a payment when the family did not have a monk to provide.

ཆོས་དོན་ (cöödön) religious, religious affairs, religious matters ། ཆོས་དོན་བཀའ་བློན་ Minister of Religious Affairs (in Tibetan Government).

ཆོས་དོན་ཅུས་ (cöödön jüü) tib.ch. Religious Affairs Bureau/ Commission.

ཆོས་དོན་གཉེར་མཁན་ (cöödön ñērñɛn) sb. who pursues religion.

ཆོས་དོན་ཨུ་ཡོན་ལྷན་ཁང་ (cöödön ūyön lhɛngaŋ) tib.ch. religious affairs commision/ committee.

ཆོས་དྲིན་ (cöödrin) gratitude for receiving religious teaching.

ཆོས་དྲེད་ (cöödreè) knowing the dharma but not practicing it; vi.—ཤོར་ to fall into such a state.

ཆོས་བདག (cöödaà) 1. one who adheres to the dharma. 2. one who protects the dharma. 3. a patron of a monastery.

ཆོས་འདོན་འགྲོལ་འཛིན་ (cöndön tröndzin) shung. permission to recite scriptures.

ཆོས་ལྡན་ (cöndɛn) sm. ཆོས་ཅན་.

ཆོས་ལྡན་གྱི་ཞིང་ས་ (cöndɛngi shiŋsa) a holy/ religious place.

ཆོས་ལྡན་རྒྱ་སེ་ (cöödɛn gyase) an inferior kind of brocade.

ཆོས་སྡེ་ (cööde) monastery, religious community.

ཆོས་སྡེ་རང་བཙན་པ་ (cööde raŋdzɛnba) shung. an independent religious community (one that is not subordinate to another).

ཆོས་ནག་པོ་ (cöö nagbo) sinful/ non-virtuous deeds.

ཆོས་སྣུབ་ (cöönub) eliminating/ destroying religion; va.—བྱེད་.

ཆོས་པ་ (cööba) a person who is very religious ། ཁོང་མི་ཆོས་པ་ཞིག་རེད་ He is a very religious person.

ཆོས་དཔེ་ (cööbe) religious text/ book/ scripture.

ཆོས་དཔོན་ (cööbön) priest.

ཆོས་སྤུན་ (cööbün) brethren of the same religious order/ sect.

ཆོས་སྤེལ་ (cööbee) spreading religion; va. ཆོས་སྤེལ་; —བྱེད་.

ཆོས་སྤེལ་མཁན་ (cööbeeñɛn) missionary.

ཆོས་སྤྱོད་ (cööjöö) 1. religious rites/ services/ activities (usu. involves monks invited by layman to perform prayers, etc.). 2. the act of reading religious prayers.

ཆོས་སྤྱོད་པ་ (cööjööba) one who practices the

dharma, a religious person.

ཆོས་ཕོགས་ (cööbɔ̀ɔ̀) monk's salary.

ཆོས་ཕྱི་པ་ (cööcibə) nonBuddhists.

ཆོས་ཕྱོགས་ (cööjɔ̀ɔ̀) the religious sphere/ side/ point of view ༑ཆོས་ཕྱོགས་ཀྱི་བྱ་བ་ Religious activities. ༑ཆོས་ཕྱོགས་ནས་བཤད་ནས་ Talking from the religious point of view. ༑ཆོས་ཕྱོགས་ཀྱི་མཛད་སྒོ་ Religious ceremony.

ཆོས་འཕེལ་ (cöö pēl) vi. to have religion spread. 2. name of a person.

ཆོས་བྱེད་ (cöö ceè) va. to practice religion, to live a religious life, to join a monastery ༑ཆོས་བྱེད་པར་རི་ལ་འགྲོ་མི་དགོས་ One does not have to go to the mountains to practice religion. 2. religious ༑ཆོས་བྱེད་དགེ་འདུན་པ་ Religious monks.

ཆོས་བྱེད་བགེགས་དབང་ (cööjeè gegwaŋ) an obstacle for practising the dharma.

ཆོས་བློན་ (cöölön) 1. a minister of religion/ religious affairs. 2. ministers who are pro-Buddhist.

ཆོས་དབང་ (cööwaŋ) religious authority; va.—འཛིན་ to have/ hold religious authority.

ཆོས་དབྱངས་པ་ (cööyaŋba) monks who intone prayers during the Monlam festival.

ཆོས་དབྱིངས་ (cööyiŋ) emptiness, the void, nothingness.

ཆོས་དབྱིངས་སུ་ཐིམ་ (cööyiŋsu tīm) vi. to die (be enlightened) [a term used for the death of incarnations].

ཆོས་འབག (cööbaà) religious mask/ front, outwardly religious but inwardly not.

ཆོས་འབངས་ (cööbaŋ) 1. monastic subjects, subjects on a monasteric estate. 2. the disciples of a lama.

ཆོས་འབྱུང་ (cööjuŋ) 1. book on the history/ origin of religion. 2. triangular shape.

ཆོས་འབྱུང་པདྨ་ (cööjuŋ pēèma) 1. vagina. 2. lotus cushion set in a triangle (in iconography).

ཆོས་འབྱོར་བདེ་དགེ་ (cöö jɔɔ dege) shung. having dharma, wealth, peace and happiness ༑འགྲོ་ཀུན་ཆོས་འབྱོར་བདེ་དགེས་རྟག་ཏུ་འཚོ་བ་ May all sentient beings have peace, prosperity, happiness and dharma.

ཆོས་འབྲེལ་ (cöndree) taking teachings from sb. ༑ངས་རིན་པོ་ཆེ་དེ་ནས་ཆོས་འབྲེལ་ཞུས་པ་ཡིན་ I have taken teachings from that lama. ༑ང་བླ་མ་དེ་དང་ཆོས་འབྲེལ་ཡོད་ I have taken teachings with that lama.

ཆོས་སྦེད་ (cööbeè) concealing religious teachings (from others); va. ཆོས་སྦེད་; —བྱེད་.

ཆོས་སྦྱིན་ (cöö jīn) va. to give religious teachings.

ཆོས་སྦྱིན་ཚང་འཛོམས་ (cööjin tsāŋdzom) the meeting/ gathering of monks and patrons.

ཆོས་མ་ (cööma) 1. a very religious woman. 2. nun.

ཆོས་མིང་ (cöömiŋ) new name given to people when they become monks.

ཆོས་སྨན་ (cöömɛn) pills that have been blessed.

ཆོས་སྨོ་ (cööño) sm. ཆོས་སྨྱོན་.

ཆོས་སྨྱོན་ (cööñön) a religious person who is/ becomes insane or crazy.

ཆོས་རྩོད་ (côödzöö) debating on religious philosophy.

ཆོས་གཙིགས་ (cöödzii) arc. religious vows/ regulations.

ཆོས་གཙོ་ (cöödzo) the founder/ head of a religious sect.

ཆོས་བཙུན་ (cöödzün) nun.

ཆོས་ཚན་ (cöödzɛn) chapter (in a religious text).

ཆོས་ཚབ་ (cöödzəbs) a "bad" class designation in monasteries in 1959 [Lit. representative of the religious lords].

ཆོས་ཚིག (cöödzii) religious term.

ཆོས་ཚིགས་ (cöötsii) the main places of religion/ dharma.

ཆོས་ཚུགས་ (cöö tsüù) va. to establish or organize a religious teaching.

ཆོས་ཚུལ་ (cöödzüü) religious precepts.

ཆོས་ཚོགས་ (cöödzɔ̀ɔ̀) religious association/ society/ organization, dharma center ༑འཛམ་གླིང་ནང་པའི་ཆོས་ཚོགས་ Dharma centers throughout the world.

ཆོས་མཚམས་ (cöndzam) 1. the break between prayers at a prayer or debating session of monks. 2. the break between semesters in a monastery.

ཆོས་འཚོ་མ་ཞིན་པ་ (cöö tsō məsimbə) shung. to loose one's celibacy.

ཆོས་འཚོང་བ་ (cöö tsōŋ) va. to preach the dharma for material/ financial gains [Lit. to sell religion].

ཆོས་མཛད་ (cöndzɛɛ̀) 1. title of monks who make a special offering to the monastery and are therefore exempt from having to do the manual labor required of other monks; va.—གཏོང་ to make the special offering to become a ཆོས་མཛད་. 2. h. of ཆོས་བྱེད་.

ཆོས་རྫུ་ཅན་ (cöö dzujɛn) false religious practitioners.

ཆོས་རྫུན་ (cöödzün) false religious practitioners.

ཆོས་ཞྭ་ (cöösha) religious cap.

ཆོས་ཞིང་ (cööshiŋ) shung. estates/ fields owned by a monastery.

ཆོས་ཞུགས་ (cöö shuù) 1. sm. ཆོས་སྒོར་ཞུགས་. 2. the ceremony where monks first take initiation (རབ་བྱུང་).

ཆོས་གཞིས་ (cööshii) estate of a monastery or labrang.

ཆོས་གཞིས་མི་རྩ་ (cööshiì midza) serfs belonging to the estates of monasteries and labrangs.

ཆོས་གཞིས་མི་སེར་ (cööshiì misee) sm. ཆོས་གཞིས་མི་རྩ་.

ཆོས་བཞིན་ (cööshin) in compliance/ accordance with the dharma.

ཆོས་ཟུར་ (cöösur) abbr. of ཆོས་རྗེ་ཟུར་པ་.

ཆོས་ཟོག (cöösog) religious teachings given for financial/ material gain.

ཆོས་ཡིག (cööyiì) religious writings/ scriptures.

ཆོས་ཡོན་སྦྱིན་བདག (cööyön jīndaà) priest and patron.

ཆོས་ཡོན་ཟབ་པ་ (cööyön səbbə) shung. profound knowledge ༑ཆོས་ཡོན་ཟབ་ཅིང་ཚང་མས་གུས་འདུད་ཞུ་ཡུལ་ (A person) with profound knowledge who enjoys high prestige and commands universal respect.

ཆོས་ར་ (cööra) the (dharma) grove in monasteries where monks studying theology meet to debate.

ཆོས་ར་འགྲིམ་ (cööra drim) va. to go through the debating curriculum in a monastery.

ཆོས་རིག (cöörig) abbr. religion and culture

ཆོས་ལགས་ (cöölaà) nun.

ཆོས་ལས་ (cöölɛɛ̀) religious work/ activity.

ཆོས་ལས་བྱུང་བ་ (cöölɛɛ̀ cuŋwə) Bodhisattva.

ཆོས་ལུག (cööluù) shung. sheep owned by a monastery/ labrang.

ཆོས་ལུགས་ (cüülug) a religion, a religious system, a religious denomination/ sect ༑འཛམ་གླིང་གི་ཆོས་ལུགས་ཚང་མ་ All the religions of the world.

ཆོས་ལུགས་ཀྱི་མཚན་ཉིད་རིག་པ་ (cüüluggi tsɛnñii rigbə) the science of religious philosophy/ dialectics.

ཆོས་ལུགས་གྲུབ་མཐའ་ (cüülug drubda) religious sect.

ཆོས་ལུགས་སྒྲིག་ལམ་ (cüülug driglam) religious discipline.

ཆོས་ལུགས་བཅོས་བསྒྱུར་ (cüülug jöögyur) religious reform.

ཆོས་ལུགས་ཆེ་ཁག་བཞི་ (cüülug cēgaà shi) the four main sects in Tibet (ས་སྐྱ་; དགེ་ལུགས་; བཀའ་བརྒྱུད་; རྙིང་མ་).

ཆོས་ལུགས་དད་པའི་རང་དབང་ (cüülug tɛɛ̀bɛ raŋwaŋ) sm. ཆོས་དད་རང་དབང་.

ཆོས་ལུགས་དད་མོས་ (cũülug tɛ̱ɛ̀möö) religious belief/ faith ། ཆོས་ལུགས་དད་མོས་ཀྱི་རང་དབང་ Freedom of religion belief.

ཆོས་ལུགས་དོན་གནད་ (cũülug tö̱nnɛɛ̀) religious affairs.

ཆོས་ལུགས་པ་ (cũülugba) religious person.

ཆོས་ལུགས་བྱེད་སྒོ་ (cũülug ce̱ègo) religious rituals/ activities.

ཆོས་ལུགས་དོན་བྱེད་ཨུ་ཡོན་ལྷན་ཁང་ (cũülug tö̱nceè ūyön lhɛ̄ngaŋ) sm. ཆོས་དོན་ཨུ་ཡོན་ལྷན་ཁང་.

ཆོས་ལུགས་མོངས་དད་ (cũülug mōŋdɛɛ̀) religious superstition, blind faith in religion.

ཆོས་ལུགས་ཚོགས་པ་ (cũülug tsɔ̄gba) religious party.

ཆོས་ལུགས་སྲིད་ཇུས་ (cũülug sĩijüü) religious policy.

ཆོས་ལོག (cũülɔɔ̀) heresy; va.—བྱེད་ to commit heresy.

ཆོས་ལོག་པ་ (cũülɔgba) one who has broken away from the Buddhist faith and embraced another religion, a heretic.

ཆོས་ཤོད་ (cõò shöò) va. to preach, to give a religious sermon/ teaching.

ཆོས་གཤོམ་ (cõòshom) altar.

ཆོས་བཤད་ (cõò shɛɛ̀) p. of ཆོས་ཤོད་.

ཆོས་སེམས་ (cõòsem) piety, religiosity.

ཆོས་སེམས་ཆེན་པོ་ (cõòsem cēmbo) particularly religious, highly pious.

ཆོས་སེམས་མེད་པ་ (cõòsem me̱èba) atheistic, godless.

ཆོས་སོ་ཙོག (cõò sōjoò) all the religions.

ཆོས་སྲིད་ (cũüsiì) religious and secular ། ཆོས་སྲིད་ཀྱི་ལས་དོན་གང་ལ་ཡང་ On any kind of religious and secular matter.

ཆོས་སྲིད་ཀྱི་དབང་ལུང་སྐྱུར་ (cũüsiìgi wɔ̄ŋluŋ gyu̱r) shung. va. to exercise temporal and spiritual authority.

ཆོས་སྲིད་གཉིས་ལྡན་ (cũüsiì ñĩidɛn) sm. ཆོས་སྲིད་ཟུང་འབྲེལ་.

ཆོས་སྲིད་ཐ་དད་ (cũüsiì tādɛɛ̀) separation of church and state.

ཆོས་སྲིད་ཟུང་འབྲེལ་ (cũüsiì su̱ŋdrel) combination of the religious and the secular ། བོད་ནི་ཆོས་སྲིད་ཟུང་འབྲེལ་གྱི་རྒྱལ་ཁབ་རེད་ Tibet is a country that is ruled by a system that combines the religious and the secular.

ཆོས་སྲིད་ལུགས་གཉིས་ (cũüsiì lu̱gñii) the religious and secular systems (usu. refers to Tibetan government).

ཆོས་སྲུང་ (cõòsuŋ) guardians of the faith/ dharma/ religion.

མཆད་ཀ་ (cɛ̃ɛ̀ga) graveyard, cemetery, sky-burial site.

མཆད་སྒམ་ (cɛ̃ɛ̀gam) coffin.

མཆད་གནས་ (cɛ̃ɛ̀nɛɛ̀) sm. མཆད་ཀ་.

མཆད་པ་ (cɛ̃ɛ̀ba) sm. མཆད་ཀ་.

མཆན་ (cɛ̄n) 1. footnote, note ། རྩོམ་སྒྲིག་པའི་མཆན་ The editor's note. 2. correcting (usu. in editing or proofreading); va.—རྒྱག; —འགོད་ to make corrections, to make criticisms ། ངའི་ཟིན་བྲིས་ཐོག་ཁོང་གིས་མཆན་མང་པོ་བརྒྱབ་འདུག He made many corrections on my draft. ། ཁྱེད་རང་གི་ལས་ཀའི་ཐོག་ངས་མཆན་རྒྱག་ཡས་གང་ཡང་མེད་ Concerning your work, I have no criticisms at all.

མཆན་དཀྲུག (cɛ̄ndrug) shung. ch.tib. drawing lots ། པཎ་ཆེན་ཡང་སྲིད་འོས་སྐྱོལ་གདན་འཁེལ་འཐུས་ཀྱི་མཆན་དཀྲུག་རྒྱུའི་ཆེས་གྲངས་འཕྲལ་དུ་བྱས་ནས་ Please fix a date as soon as possible for the lot-drawing ceremony for the candidates for the incarnation of the Panchen Lama.

མཆན་ཁུང་ (cɛ̄nguŋ) armpit.

མཆན་ཁེབ་ (cɛ̄ngeb) comrade-in-arms.

མཆན་གྱི་མཆིས་བྲང་ (cɛ̄ngi cĩidraŋ) beloved wife.

མཆན་གྱི་པུ་ཕྲུག (cɛ̄ngi pu̱druù) beloved child.

མཆན་འགོད་བཀའ་ལན་ (cɛ̄ngöò gālɛn) shung. a response indicating approval/ disapproval that is written on the request one has submitted.

མཆན་འགྲེལ་ (cɛ̄ndrel) notes, footnotes, annotations; va.—རྒྱག to make footnotes, to annotate.

མཆན་རྒྱག (cɛ̄n gya̱à) see མཆན་.

མཆན་བརྗོད་ (cɛ̄njöò) criticism, corrections; va.—བྱེད་ ། གནད་དོན་དེའི་ཐད་ལ་མཆན་བརྗོད་གང་ཡང་མེད་གསུངས་འདུག (He) said that he has no criticism concerning that issue.

མཆན་ཏིག (cɛ̄ndig) sm. མཆན་འགྲེལ་.

མཆན་དམ་ (cɛ̄ndam) shung. a seal put on a note in a document.

མཆན་སྤུ་ (cɛ̄mbu) underarm hair.

མཆན་ཕུག (cɛ̄mpuù) armpit.

མཆན་བུ་ (cɛ̄mbu) 1. sm. མཆན་འགྲེལ་. 2. disciple. 3. colleague (with whom one is jointly doing a job).

མཆན་འབེབས་ (cɛ̄n be̱b) shung. to add/ put a note (on a document) ། ཡིག་ཆ་ཁག་གཉིས་མཆན་འབེབས་ཟིན་གཤིས་ Because they already put notes on two documents.

མཆན་སྦུག (cɛ̄mbug) sm. མཆན་ཁུང་.

མཆན་ཤུབས་ (cɛ̄nshub) sm. མཆན་ཁུང་.

མཆན་འོག (cɛ̄nwɔɔ̀) sm. མཆན་ཁུང་.

མཆན་ཡིག (cɛ̄nyii) sm. མཆན་འགྲེལ་.

མཆི་: p. མཆིས་; f. མཆི་ (cĩ) sm. འགྲོ་.

མཆི་ཁུག (cĩguù) lachrymal sac.

མཆི་གུ་ (cĩgu) the upper stone in a stone grinding mill.

མཆི་འབྱིན་འབར་མདེལ་ (cĩjin ba̱ndee) tear gas bomb/ shell.

མཆི་མ་ (cĩmə) tears; vi.—འདོན་; —འཁྱུག; —བསྒྲིལ་; —ཤོར་; —ལྷུང་ to shed tears.

མཆི་མ་ཀོ་རོར་འགྱུར་ (cĩmə gōror gyu̱r) sm. མཆི་མ་འཁོར་.

མཆི་མ་འཁོར་ (cĩmə kɔ̄ɔ̄) vi. to have one's eyes fill with tears.

མཆི་མ་གཏོང་ (cĩmə dōŋ) va. to cry.

མཆི་མ་རིལ་རིལ་ (cĩmə ri̱irii) teardrops.

མཆི་མ་ལྷུག་ལྷུག (cĩmə lhūgluù) (eyes) brimming/ dripping with tears.

མཆི་མའི་སྦུ་གུ་ (cĩmɛ bu̱gu) lachrymal duct.

མཆི་མའི་རྩ་སྨིན་ (cĩmɛ dzāmen) sm. lachrymal gland.

མཆི་མའི་གཤེར་སྨིན་ (cĩmɛ shērmen) lachrymal gland.

མཆི་ཤག་འཁོར་ (cĩshaà kɔ̄ɔ̄) sm. མཆི་མ་འཁོར་.

མཆིག (cĩi) 1. millstone, grinding stone. 2. soft shelled turtle.

མཆིག་གུ་ (cĩigu) sm. མཆི་གུ་.

མཆིག་དོ་ (cĩgdo) grindstone, millstone, stone mill.

མཆིག་མ་ (cĩgmə) sm. མཆིག་གུ་.

མཆིང་ (cĩŋ) middle, center ། མཚོའི་མཆིང་ The middle of the lake.

མཆིང་བུ་ (cĩŋbu) a type of precious stone.

མཆིད་ (cĩi) 1. talk, discourse; va.—འཛེ་ to talk, to have a conversation. 2. correspondence/ letter.

མཆིད་ཤགས་ (cĩishaà) arguing, disputing, debating face-to-face; va.—རྒྱག.

མཆིན་ (cĩn) abbr. of མཆིན་པ་.

མཆིན་ཀ་ (cĩnga) sm. མཆིན་ཁ་.

མཆིན་སྐྲན་ (cĩndrɛn) cancer of the liver.

མཆིན་སྐྲན་ཟུགས་ཆུ་ (cĩndrɛn su̱gju) edema caused by liver cancer.

མཆིན་ཁ་ (cĩnga) liver-colored.

མཆིན་ཆུ་ (cĩnju) gastric juice.

མཆིན་དྲི་ (cĩndri) smell of liver.

མཆིན་དྲིའི་གསང་ (cĩndrii sāŋ) area on the back where moxabustion is performed to cure liver diseases.

མཆིན་མདོག (cĩndɔɔ̀) dark purple.

མཆིན་ནད་ (cĩnnɛɛ̀) diseases of the liver.

མཆིན་པ་ (cĩmbə) the liver.

མཆིན་པ་སྐྱ་ཐབ་ (cĩmbə gyābəb) a disease that causes pain in the liver.

མཆིན་པ་ཤོ་ཤ་ (cĩmbə sho̱sha) a type of liver

medicine.

མཆིན་འབྲས་ (cīndrɛɛ̀) cancer of the liver.

མཆིན་རྩ་ (cīndza) veins in the liver.

མཆིན་ཚད་ (cīndzɛɛ̀) hepatitis.

མཆིན་རླུང་ (cīnluŋ) a type of "wind" sickness in Tibetan medicine.

མཆིན་གསང་ (cīnsaŋ) sm. མཆིན་དྲིའི་གསང་.

མཆིམས་ (cīm) a lineage in ancient Tibet.

མཆིལ་ཁྲ་ (cīīdra) sparrow hawk.

མཆིལ་པ་ (cīībə) 1. sparrow. 2. iron hook.

མཆིལ་པའི་ཤ་ (cīībɛ shā) meat of a sparrow (used in Tibetan medicine).

མཆིལ་བ་ (cīīwə) sparrow.

མཆིལ་མ་ (cīīmə) 1. spit, spittle; va.—རྒྱག; vi.—གཏོར་; vi.—འདོར་ to spit (to make sth. wet); vi.—ཐོར་; vi.—འཛར་ to drool/ dribble.

མཆིལ་མ་གནམ་འཕངས་རང་ངོ་ (cīīmə nāmbaŋ ra̱ŋŋo) bringing on one's own downfall/ misfortune [Lit. if you spit at the sky it will land on yourself].

མཆིལ་མ་དབྱུག (cīīmə yūù) va. to spit.

མཆིལ་ཞགས་འཕེན་ (cīīshaà pēn) va. to spit.

མཆིལ་ལུད་ (cīī lṳ̀ü) abbr. spit and sputum.

མཆིལ་ལྷམ་ (cīīlham) 1. boot, shoe. 2. shoes worn by monks which act as a protection against snakes.

མཆིས་ (cīī) 1. existential verb that is equivalent to ཡོད་པ་རེད་ ། ང་བདེ་བར་མཆིས་ I am well. ། མཚུངས་ཟླ་མ་མཆིས་པ་ Without equal/ rival. ། འདི་ཕྱོགས་ནས་ཞབས་འཇུར་ཞུ་འོས་མཆིས་ཚེ་ནང་མའི་བཀའ་མཆིད་ལྷུག་རྩོལ་ཡོད་པ་ Please write to me without any hesitation, if there is anything I can do for you from here. 2. p. of མཆི་.

མཆིས་བྲང་ (cīīdraŋ) 1. wife. 2. residence, home, abode.

མཆིས་བྲང་མ་ (cīīdraŋmə) the lady of the house.

མཆིས་འབྲང་ (cīndraŋ) sm. མཆིས་བྲང་.

མཆིས་མལ་ (cīīmɛɛ) sm. མཆིས་བྲང་, 2.

མཆིས་མིན་ (cīīmin) whether or not ། བསྐོ་འོས་མཆིས་མིན་ Whether or not (he) is worthy of appointing.

མཆིས་སོ་ཚོག (cīīsojoò) every, all, everything, everyone ། བོད་རིགས་མཆིས་སོ་ཚོག All Tibetans.

མཆུ་ (cū) 1. lip. 2. beak.

མཆུ་སྒྲོས་ (cūdröö) sm. མཆུ་.

མཆུ་ཅན་ (cūjɛn) 1. a utensil that has a mouth or spout. 2. beings that have pointed face or beaks.

མཆུ་སྙུང་ (cūñuŋ) a swallow.

མཆུ་གཉིས་ཟུམ་པའི་སྒྲ་ (cūñiì sa̱mbɛ dra̱) bilabial sound.

མཆུ་ཏོ་ (cūdo) beak.

མཆུ་ཏོ་པད་མ་ (cūdo bɛ̄ɛ̀ma) sm. མཆུའི་གསོང་

མཆུ་ཐོ་ (cūdo) sm. མཆུ་ཏོ་.

མཆུ་ཐོ་ཐོ་བྱེད་ (cū tōdo ce̱è) va. to show a direction or point to sth. by protruding one's lips.

མཆུ་འཐོག (cūdɔɔ̀) pecking with a beak; va.—རྒྱག.

མཆུ་འདབ་ (cūndəb) sm. མཆུ་ཏོ་.

མཆུ་བརྡ་ (cūda) a signal made with one's lips; va.—གཏོང་.

མཆུ་བདར་ (cū da̱r) 1. va. to gossip, to talk a lot. 2. va. to sharpen one's beak.

མཆུ་རྣོ་ (cūno) sm. མཆུ་རྣོན་.

མཆུ་རྣོན་ (cūnön) birds with sharp beaks.

མཆུ་འཕྱང་ (cūjaŋ) 1. spout of a utensil/ vessel that is pointed downward. 2. lower lip drooping downward. 3. poet. camel.

མཆུ་ཕྱུག (cūjuù) lipstick ། མཆུ་ཕྱུག་དམར་པོ་ Red lipstick.

མཆུ་ཕྱུག་དམར་པོ་ (cūjuù mārbo) red lipstick.

མཆུ་སྦྲང་ (cūdraŋ) flute.

མཆུ་དབྱིབས་ (cūyib) lip-rounding (linguistics).

མཆུ་མེད་ཞྭ་སྒོར་ (cūmeè sha̱gɔɔ) skull cap [Lit. hat without lips (brim)].

མཆུ་དམར་ (cūmar) 1. red beak. 2. red lips.

མཆུ་ཟུམ་པའི་དབྱངས་ (cūsumbɛ yāŋ) labialized vowel (linguistics).

མཆུ་ཟླ་ (cūnda) period from the 16th of the 12th month to the 15th of the 1st month in Tibetan calendar.

མཆུ་འོག (cūwɔɔ̀) an area on the lower lip where moxibution is applied.

མཆུ་རལ་ (cūrɛɛ) sm. མཆུ་ཤོ་.

མཆུ་ཤ་ (cūsha) sm. མཆུ་ཤོ་.

མཆུ་ཤུབས་ (cūshub) halter.

མཆུ་ཤོ་ (cūsho) hare lip.

མཆུ་གསོང་ (cūshoŋ) the grove on the middle of the upper lip (philtrum).

མཆུ་སོ་ (cū sō) abbr. lip and teeth.

མཆུ་སོ་ཅན་གྱི་སྒྲ་ (cūsojɛngi dra̱) labiodental sound (linguistics).

མཆུ་སོ་བརྟེན་རེས་ (cūso dēnreè) inseparable, attached, joined ། རྒྱ་གར་དང་བོད་གཉིས་མཆུ་སོ་བརྟེན་རེས་ཀྱི་འབྲེལ་བ་ཡོད་ Tibet and India have an inseparable relationship.

མཆུ་སོར་སྡོམ་པ་ (cūsor do̱mba) a small tool/ tweezer used in Tibetan surgery.

མཆུའི་གསོང་ (cūshoŋ) sm. མཆུ་གསོང་.

མཆེ་ (cē) abbr. of མཆེ་བ་.

མཆེ་གུག (cēguù) curved canine teeth.

མཆེ་སྡེར་ (cēder) fangs and claws.

མཆེ་གཙིགས་ (cēdziì) va. to bare one's fangs, to threaten.

མཆེ་གཙིགས་སྡེར་བགྲད་ (cēdziì de̱rdrɛɛ̀) threatening, saber rattling; va.—བྱེད་ [Lit. baring one's fangs and scratching one's claws].

མཆེ་བ་ (cēwa) 1. canine teeth, fangs, tusks; vi.—སྐྱེ་ to grow fangs/ tusks; vi. —གཙིགས་ to bare one's fangs/ teeth. 2. the first shoot of a flower/ plant; vi.—གཏོང་; —འདོན་ to have the first shoot geminate/ sprout.

མཆེད་ (cēè) 1. vi. to spread, to sweep over, to become widespread ། དེ་ནས་མེ་འགྲམ་གྱི་ཁང་པ་དེར་མི་མཆེད་སོང་ After that, the fire spread to the house near it. ། གཏམ་དེ་གྲོང་ཁྱེར་ཁྲོན་ལ་མཆེད་འདུག The word spread all over the town. 2. relatives.

མཆེད་གྲོགས་ (cēèdrog) 1. monks who have studied with the same teacher/ lama. 2. abbr. relative and friend.

མཆེད་ལྕམ་ (cēèjam) brother and sister.

མཆེད་དོན་ (cēèdön) extended meaning.

མཆེད་པོ་ (cēèbo) brother.

མཆེད་མོ་ (cēèmo) sister.

མཆེད་ཟུང་ (cēèsuŋ) shung. the two brothers.

མཆེད་ཟླ་ (cēnda) relatives.

མཆེད་ཡ་ (cēèya) sm. ཆེད་ཟླ་.

མཆེར་ (cēr) abbr. of མཆེར་པ་.

མཆེར་སྐྲན་ཟགས་རྒྱུ་ (cērdrɛn sa̱gju) cancer of the spleen.

མཆེར་ནད་ (cērnɛɛ̀) disease of the spleen.

མཆེར་པ་ (cērbə) spleen.

མཆེར་པ་སྐྱ་ཐབ་ (cērbə gyābəb) a disease of the spleen.

མཆེར་འབྲས་ (cērdrɛɛ̀) cancer of the spleen.

མཆེར་རྩ་ (cērdza) a vein connected to the spleen.

མཆེར་རྩ་ཚད་རྟགས་ (cērdza cɛ̄ɛ̀daà) a sign of death (told by taking pulse).

མཆེར་གསང་ (cērsaŋ) a spot near the spleen where acupuncture is done.

མཆོག (cɔ̄ɔ̀) 1. the best, the most excellent or outstanding ། སྐྱེས་བུ་མཆོག The best human beings. 2. honorific term (used after proper names and titles) ། སྲིད་འཛིན་མཆོག The President. ། བཀའ་བློན་རྡོ་རྗེ་མཆོག The Minister Dorje.

མཆོག་དཀར་ (cɔ̄ɔ̀gar) a bow (for shooting).

མཆོག་གི་རྒྱལ་མཚན་ (cɔ̄ɔ̀gi gye̱ndzɛn) one of the 8 auspicious signs.

མཆོག་གི་དངོས་གྲུབ་ (cɔ̄ɔ̀gi ŋö̀ödrub) the complete attainment of Buddhahood.

མཆོག་གི་མཆོག (cɔ̄ɔ̀gi cɔ̄ɔ̀) creme de la creme, the best of the best.

མཆོག་གི་མཐར་ཐུག (cɔ̄ɔgi tādur) sm. མཆོག་གི་མཆོག.

མཆོག་གི་སྤྲུལ་སྐུ་ (cɔ̄ɔgi drūūgu) sm. མཆོག་སྤྲུལ་.

མཆོག་གི་བསམ་པ་ (cɔ̄ɔgi sāmba) extremely generous.

མཆོག་དགའ་ (cɔ̄ɔga) immeasurable pleasure.

མཆོག་འགྱུར་ (cɔ̄ɔgyur) the best, outstanding ¶ཁོང་ནི་མི་དམངས་ཀྱི་དབུ་ཁྲིད་མཆོག་འགྱུར་ཞིག་རེད་ He is an outstanding people's leader. ¶མཆོག་འགྱུར་གྱི་མཛེས་སྡུག The most beautiful.

མཆོག་ཉིད་ (cɔ̄ɔñii) you (h.) ¶ངས་མཆོག་ཉིད་དང་རྒྱལ་སྲིད་སྲི་ཁྲུབ་ཁང་ལ་བཀྲ་ཤིས་བདེ་ལེགས་ཞུ་གི་ཡིན་ (I) wish you and the State Council greetings.

མཆོག་གཉིས་ (cɔ̄ɔñii) the two great Buddhist masters Nagarjuna and Asanga.

མཆོག་ཏུ་འགྱུར་ (cɔ̄gdu gyur) vi. to become/ be the best ¶ཚན་རིག་ཤེས་ཤེས་ཡོན་གྱི་མཆོག་ཏུ་འགྱུར་བ་ཞིག་རེད་ Science is the best knowledge.

མཆོག་ཏུ་གྱུར་བའི་མནའ་མཐུན་ (cɔ̄gdu gyurwɛ nāmtün) the Holy Alliance (1815-1830).

མཆོག་ཏུ་འཛིན་ (cɔ̄gdu dzin) va. to hold in esteem, to regard great/ outstanding.

མཆོག་ཐུན་དངོས་གྲུབ་ (cɔ̄gdün ŋȫȫdrub) abbr. of མཆོག་གི་དངོས་གྲུབ་ and ཐུན་མོང་གི་དངོས་གྲུབ་.

མཆོག་དམ་པ་ (cɔ̄gdamba) the best of the best.

མཆོག་ནོར་ (cɔ̄gnɔɔ) treasure, wealth.

མཆོག་གནས་ (cɔ̄gnɛɛ̀) king of the gods; Brahma.

མཆོག་པ་ (cɔ̄gba) 1. best. 2. name of a person.

མཆོག་སྤྲུལ་ (cɔ̄gdrüü) an incarnate lama, a reinacarnation.

མཆོག་སྤྲུལ་ཡང་སྲིད་ (cɔ̄gdrüü yaŋsii) sm. མཆོག་སྤྲུལ་.

མཆོག་སྦྱིན་ (cɔ̄gjin) sm. དངོས་གྲུབ་.

མཆོག་མ་ (cɔ̄gma) 1. the tip/ apex/ peak. 2. the two ends of a bow.

མཆོག་དམན་ (cɔ̄gmɛn) good and bad, superior and inferior, high and low special and ordinary ¶ཁོང་ལ་སྐྱེ་བོ་མཆོག་དམན་ཚང་མས་དགའ་པོ་བྱེད་ཀྱི་རེད་ All the people, high and low, like him a lot.

མཆོག་མཛེས་ (cɔ̄gdzeè) extremely beautiful.

མཆོག་མཛེས་མ་ (cɔ̄gdzeèma) an extremely beautiful woman.

མཆོག་འཛིན་ (cɔ̄ŋdzin) sm. མཆོག་ཏུ་འཛིན་པ་.

མཆོག་འཛིན་གྱི་འདུ་ཤེས་ (cɔ̄ŋdzingi dushеè) idea/ concept that sth. is superior or the best.

མཆོག་བཞི་ (cɔ̄gshi) the four "bests," the four supreme qualities.

མཆོག་རབ་ (cɔ̄grəb) the best, the greatest, the highest.

མཆོག་ཤེས་ (cɔ̄gsheè) wisdom, great knowledge/ understanding.

མཆོག་གསུམ་ (cɔ̄gsum) sm. དཀོན་མཆོག་གསུམ་.

མཆོག་གསུམ་དཔང་འཛིན་ (cɔ̄gsum bāŋber) vow/ promise/ oath taken in the name of the three treasures: the Buddha, doctrine and the monks.

མཆོག་གསུམ་རིན་ཆེན་རྣམ་གསུམ་ (cɔ̄gsum rincen nāmsum) sm. དཀོན་མཆོག་གསུམ་.

མཆོང་: p. **མཆོངས་**; f. **མཆོང་**; imp. **མཆོངས་** (cōŋ) 1. va. to jump ¶ཁོས་ཐོག་ཁ་ནས་མཆོངས་པ་རེད་ He jumped off the roof. 2. a type of agate.

མཆོང་སྐྱོད་ (cōŋgyöö̀) sm. མཆོང་བསྐྱོད་.

མཆོང་བསྐྱོད་ (cōŋgyöö̀) leaping/ charging forward, advancing; va.—བྱེད་ ¶ན་ནིང་གི་ཐོན་སྐྱེད་ནས་བརྒྱ་ཆ་༥༠ བར་མཆོང་བསྐྱོད་བྱས་ཡོད་པ་རེད་ (They) advanced production 50% from last year.

མཆོང་བསྐྱོད་ཆེན་པོ་ (cōŋgyöö̀ cēmbo) the great leap forward (a political campaign).

མཆོང་ག་གྱེན་ལ་རྒྱག (cōŋga gyenla gyaà) shung. va. to confront (a superior) [Lit. to jump uphill].

མཆོང་འགྲིགས་མིག་མངས་ (cōŋdrig migmaŋ) Chinese checkers (a board game).

མཆོང་འགྲོ་ (cōŋdro) va. to jump/ leap forward, to advance, to dash into ¶ཁོང་ཚོས་དགྲ་བོའི་སྐར་དཀྱིལ་ལ་མཆོང་ཕྱིན་པ་རེད་ They leapt into the enemy camp.

མཆོང་སྐལ་ (cōŋgɛɛ) sm. མཆོང་བསྐྱོད་.

མཆོང་རྒྱག (cōŋgyaà) jumping; va.—རྒྱག to jump, to contest/ compete in jumping events ¶མཆོང་རྒྱག་འགྲན་བསྡུར་ Jumping competition.

མཆོང་རྒྱུག (cōŋgyuù) 1. running and jumping (usu. refers to sports events); va.—བྱེད་. 2. the hurdles (in track sports).

མཆོང་རྒྱུག་འཕེན་གསུམ་གྱི་རྩལ་ (cōŋgyuù pēnsumgi dzɛ̄ɛ̄) track and field sports (jumping, running and throwing); va.—འགྲན་ to compete in track and field sports.

མཆོང་སྒམ་ (coŋgam) the pommel horse (in gymnastics).

མཆོང་སྒྲིག་མིག་མངས་ (cōŋdrig miŋmaŋ) sm. མཆོང་འགྲིགས་མིང་མངས་.

མཆོང་སྟེགས་ (cōŋdeg) platform for jumping, diving board, ski jump.

མཆོང་གདུགས་ (cōŋdug) parachute.

མཆོང་གདུགས་དམག (cōŋdug māà) airborne (paratrooper) troops.

མཆོང་འཕེན་གྱི་རྩལ་འགྲན་ (cōŋben drɛnduu) track and field sports.

མཆོང་ལྡིང་ (cōŋdiŋ) jumping, hopping; va.—བྱེད་.

མཆོང་འཕེན་འགྲན་བསྡུར་ (cōŋpen drɛndur) track and field events (in sports competition).

མཆོང་འབུ་ (cōŋbu) grasshoppers and other insects that jump.

མཆོང་མ་རྒྱུག (cōŋ ma gyuù) going along, hopping and skipping (usu. kids), going along neither running nor jumping (but something in between these); va.—བྱེད་.

མཆོང་མ་བགྲོད་ (cōŋmadröö̀) sm. མཆོང་མ་རྒྱུག.

མཆོང་རྩལ་ (cōŋdzɛɛ) jumping sports ¶མཆོང་རྩལ་གྱི་འགྲན་བསྡུར་ Jumping competition.

མཆོང་འཛིང་ (cōŋdziŋ) assaulting, storming; va.—བྱེད་ to assault, to storm, to rush (militarily).

མཆོང་འཛིང་ སྦག་སྦག (cōŋdziŋ bagbaà) light machine gun.

མཆོང་ཟམ་ (cōŋsam) spring board, diving board.

མཆོང་ར་ (cōŋra) field for jumping events.

མཆོངས་ (cōŋ) p. of མཆོང་.

མཆོངས་རྒྱག་རྒྱག (cōŋgyaà gyaà) sm. མཆོང་.

མཆོངས་རྒྱུག་ལུས་རྩེད་ (cōŋgyuù lüüdzeè) sm. མཆོང་རྒྱུགས་འཕེན་གསུམ་གྱི་རྩལ་.

མཆོངས་རྒྱུགས་ལུས་རྩལ་ (cōŋgyuù lüüdzɛɛ) sm. མཆོང་རྒྱུགས་འཕེན་གསུམ་གྱི་རྩལ་.

མཆོངས་གདོར་ (cōŋdɔɔ) sm. གདོང་མཆོངས་དཔུང་གདོར་.

མཆོངས་འགྲོས་ (cōŋdröö̀) sm. མཆོང་མ་རྒྱུར་.

མཆོངས་སྟེགས་ (cōŋdeg) sm. མཆོང་སྟེགས་.

མཆོངས་ལྡིང་ (cōŋdiŋ) sm. མཆོང་ལྡིང་.

མཆོངས་རྩལ་ (cōŋdzɛɛ) sm. མཆོང་རྩལ་.

མཆོད་ (cȫö̀) 1. va. to give/ make offerings ¶སྤོས་དང་མར་མེ་སོགས་ཀྱིས་ལྷ་ལ་མཆོད་པ་རེད་ (He) made an offering of such things as incense and butter lamps to the deities. ¶ལྷ་མཆོད་པའི་བྱ་བ་ Rituals of giving offerings to gods/ deities. 2. va. to eat/ drink (h.) ¶ཁོང་གིས་ཤ་མཆོད་ཀྱི་མ་རེད་ He will not eat meat.

མཆོད་ཀོང་ (cȫö̀goŋ) cup used for butter lamp offerings.

མཆོད་བསྐུལ་ (cȫö̀güü) shung. making offerings.

མཆོད་ཁང་ (cȫö̀gaŋ) temple, chapel ¶ལྷ་སའི་ནང་དུ་མཆོད་ཁང་འདྲ་མི་འདྲ་མང་པོ་འདུག There are many different temples in Lhasa.

མཆོད་ཁྲི་ (cȫö̀dri) the altar where religious offerings are put.

མཆོད་གར་ (cȫö̀gar) shung. a religious dance/ offering performed at the New Year's festival in the Potala.

མཆོད་གྲྭ་ (cȫö̀dra) shung. monks who perform pujas.

མཆོད་རྒྱུན་ (cȫö̀gyün) the continuity of giving alms/ offerings (for religion) ¶འབྲུ་རིགས་འདི་ཚོ་དགོན་པའི་མཆོད་རྒྱུན་ལ་འགྲོ་གི་ཡོད་པ་རེད་ This grain is going to facilitate the continuity of the monastery's making of offerings.

མཆོད་སྒྲོམ་ (cȫö̀drom) altar.

མཆོད་ང་ (cööŋa) drum used when doing religious rites.

མཆོད་ཅན་ (cööjɛn) offering bowl.

མཆོད་ལྕོག (cööjɔg) 1. table for performing religious rites. 2. sm. མཆོད་སྟེགས་.

མཆོད་ཆང་ (cööjaŋ) h. of ཆང་.

མཆོད་ཆས་ (cööjɛɛ̀) utensils used in religious/ rituals offerings.

མཆོད་མཇལ་ (cõnjɛɛ) religious visit to a monastery or temple; va.—ཞུ་; —ལ་འགྲོ་; —ལ་ཕེབས་ to visit a place of worship (temple, monastery, etc.).

མཆོད་མཇལ་ཚོགས་པ་ (cõnjɛɛ tsɔ̃gba) a group of pilgrims going on a religious visit.

མཆོད་བརྗོད་ (cööjöö) four line poem of religious praise that appear at the start of a religious book or teaching or commentary.

མཆོད་ཏིང་ (cöödiŋ) bowls for water offerings.

མཆོད་གཏོར་ (cöödɔɔ) torma offering.

མཆོད་སྟེགས་ (cöödeg) altar.

མཆོད་སྟོན་ (cöödön) gathering of people for a religious ceremony/ offering.

མཆོད་སྟོར་ (cödɔɔ) sm. ཕུད་གཏོར་.

མཆོད་བསྟོད་ (cõndöö) a religious offering and prayers of praise.

མཆོད་ཐིགས་ (cõndig) 1. adding extra butter to a butter lamp by drips of melted butter from one's own butter lamp (when visiting a temple or monastery where there are many butter lamps). 2. sm. དཀར་ཐིགས་.

མཆོད་ཐེབས་ (cöödeb) an endowment/ trust fund for making religious offerings.

མཆོད་ཐེབས་དམིགས་ཞིང་ (cöödeb mĩgshiŋ) shung. land given for setting up a trust fund for making religious offerings.

མཆོད་ཐོབ་ (cöödob) the materials (e.g., butter, tsamba) needed to perform a certain religious offering.

མཆོད་ཐོབ་ལག་འཛིན་ (cöödob lɔ̱ndzin) shung. certificate allowing one to collect things for making a religious offerings.

མཆོད་སྡོང་ (cõndoŋ) a stupa/ tomb that contains the mummified remains of a religious person. 2. the wick of a butter lamp.

མཆོད་ནས་ (cõnnɛɛ̀) sm. མཆོད་འབྲུ་.

མཆོད་གནས་ (cõnnɛɛ̀) 1. sm. སྦྱིན་གནས་. 2. sm. སྐྱབས་གནས. 3. a monk who recites scriptures in laymen's houses.

མཆོད་གནས་ཡོན་བདག (cõnnɛɛ̀ yöndaà) patron and priest.

མཆོད་པ་ (cööba) religious offering; va.—འབུལ་ to make a religious offering.

མཆོད་པ་ཁང་ (cööbagaŋ) room where religious offerings such as torma are made.

མཆོད་པ་བརྒྱད་ (cööba gyɛɛ̀) eight kinds of religious offerings.

མཆོད་པ་དོ་དམ་པ་ (cööba to̱damba) shung. person in charge of making torma offerings.

མཆོད་པ་པོ་ (cööbabo) sb. who gives a religious offering.

མཆོད་པའི་རྫས་ (cööbɛ dzɛɛ̀) the things/ items offered to deities in religious offerings/ rites.

མཆོད་པའི་ཡོ་བྱད་ (cööbɛ yo̱bjɛɛ̀) things that are used for making religious offering.

མཆོད་པར་བྱེད་ (cööbar ceè) va. to make an offerings ། ལྷ་རྣམས་མེ་ཏོག་གིས་མཆོད་པར་བྱས་སོང་ (He) made an offering of flowers to the gods.

མཆོད་དཔོན་ (cööbön) person (monk) responsible for religious offerings and mandalas.

མཆོད་དཔོན་མཁན་པོ་ (cööbön kẽmbo) shung. monk official in charge of the religious utensils/ offerings of the Dalai Lama.

མཆོད་ཕྱད་ (cööjɛɛ̀) bowl.

མཆོད་སྤྲིན་ (cöödrin) a metaphor conveying that an offering was as much as the clouds in the sky.

མཆོད་ཕྱིར་ཐོགས་ (cööjirtɔɔ̀) a string criss-crossing from one shoulder to the arm pit of the other shoulder (used by people who meditate).

མཆོད་བྱ་ (cööja) object of worship/ offering.

མཆོད་བྱེད་ (cööceè) sm. མཆོད་པར་བྱེད་.

མཆོད་འབར་ (cöömbar) butter lamp.

མཆོད་འབུལ་ (cõmbüü) sm. མཆོད་པ་འབུལ་.

མཆོད་འབྲུ་ (cõndru) barley tossed towards the altar or put in front of the altar in a bowl (as an offering to the gods).

མཆོད་སྦྱིན་ (cööjin) 1. offerings to deities and charity/ alms to beggars. 2. Brahman caste.

མཆོད་སྦྱིན་བརྒྱ་པ་ (cööjin gya̱ba) sm. བརྒྱ་བྱིན་.

མཆོད་སྦྱིན་གནས་ (cööjin nɛɛ̀) the place where an offering or charity was/is done.

མཆོད་མར་ (cöömaa) butter used for religious offerings.

མཆོད་མེ་ (cööme) butter lamp (for offerings).

མཆོད་རྫས་ (cöödzɛɛ̀) objects/ things used in making offerings to deities.

མཆོད་རྫས་དོ་དམ་པ་ (cöödzɛɛ̀ to̱damba) shung. person in charge of objects/ things used in offerings.

མཆོད་ཞལ་ (cööshɛɛ) wooden bowl/ cup (h.).

མཆོད་གཞིས་ (cööshii) monastic/ religious estates.

མཆོད་བཞེངས་པ་ (cööshenba) the person who makes torma.

མཆོད་གཟིགས་ (cöösii) h. of མཆོད་མཇལ་.

མཆོད་བཟོ་ (cööso) the art of making torma.

མཆོད་ཡོན་ (cööyön) patron and priest (the object worthy of being given alms, and the giver of the alms).

མཆོད་ཡོན་དམ་གཙང་ (cööyön da̱mdzaŋ) a close relationship between patron and priest.

མཆོད་གཡོག (cööyɔɔ̀) an attendant who helps in the performance of religious offerings.

མཆོད་རོ་ (cööro) the leftover materials/ foods from religious offerings.

མཆོད་ཤད་ (cöösheè) appetite.

མཆོད་ཤིང་ (cööshiŋ) memorial tablet (used in Chinese ancestral worship).

མཆོད་ཤོག (cööshɔɔ̀) a type of paper offering for burning; va.—བྲེད་ to burn paper as an offering.

མཆོད་གཤོམ་ (cööshom) altar.

མཆོད་བཤམས་ (cöösham) sm. མཆོད་གཤོམ་.

མཆོར་སྒེག (cɔ̃rgeg) beauty, charm and grace.

མཆོར་སྒེག་ཅན་ (cɔ̃rgegjɛn) beautiful, charming and graceful.

མཆོར་ཆས་ (cɔ̃rjɛɛ̀) beautiful/ fine things.

མཆོར་ཉམས་ (cɔ̃rñam) sb. who is proud of his or her looks.

མཆོར་པོ་ (cɔ̃rbo) rich, expensive, elegant (in dress and ornaments), luxurious; extravagant.

མཆོར་མོ་ (cɔ̃rmo) a richly dressed/ attired woman.

མཆོར་མཛེས་ (cɔ̃rdzeè) well dressed and beautiful, beautiful and elaborately dressed.

མཆོར་མཛེས་སྒེག་ཉམས་ (cɔ̃rdzeè ge̱gñam) well-dressed and beautiful.

མཆོར་སོ་ (cɔ̃rso) the four upper and lower front teeth.

འཆག: p. བཅགས་; f. གཅག; imp. ཆོགས་ (cãà) 1. va. to step on, to walk on, to visit (usu. follows ཞབས་) (h.) ། ས་འདིར་སངས་རྒྱས་ཀྱིས་ཞབས་ཀྱིས་བཅགས་པ་རེད་ The Buddha walked on this earth. 2. va. to walk/ exercise a (horse). 3. va. to go for a walk. 4. va. to pat (sth. gently).

འཆག་སྒོར་ (cãggɔɔ) sm. ཕྱགས་འཆག་སྒོར་.

འཆག་འགྲེང་འདུག་ཉལ་ (cãg dre̱ŋ du̱g ñɛɛ̱) abbr. going for a walk, standing erect, sitting and lying down.

འཆག་ས་ (cãgsa) path, lane, place where one goes for walk/ stroll.

འཆགས: p. བཤགས་; f. བཤག; imp. བཤོགས་ (cãà) va. to confess (sins, etc.).

འཆང་: p. བཅངས་; f. བཅང་; imp. ཆོངས་ (cãŋ) 1. va. to hold, to keep ། མཐར་ཡུལ་དེ་ཚོ་མི་སེར་གྲོལ་ཡུལ་དུ་

འགྱུར་རྒྱུའི་རེ་ངན་བཅང་ཡོད་པ་རེད་ (They) have held on to the evil hope of eventually colonizing those countries. ¶ ཁོའི་ལག་པར་མདུང་ཞིག་བཅངས་འདུག (He) is holding a spear in his hand. 2. va. to touch, to handle (usu. used after ལག་པ་) ¶ དེ་ལ་ལག་པ་མ་འཆང་ Don't touch that. 3. va. to bark ¶ དགོང་དག་ཁྱིས་འཆང་གི་ཡོད་པ་རེད་ Dogs bark at night.

འཆང་བ་ (cāŋwa) handle.

འཆང་གཟུང་ (cāŋsuŋ) sm. འཆང་བ་.

འཆང་བཟུང་ (cāŋsuŋ) sm. འཆང་བ་.

འཆང་བཟུང་ཤ་གོད་ (cāŋsuŋ shāgöö) fleshy part of the hand between the thumb and the first finger.

འཆང་ས་ (cāŋsa) evidence (sth. to take hold of) ¶ མི་གསོད་ཁྲིད་དོན་དེའི་སྐོར་ལག་པ་འཆང་ས་མེད་པ་བཟོས་བཞག Regarding the murder case they eliminated the evidence.

འཆང་ས་འཛུ་ས་ (cāŋsə ju̱sə) sm. འཆང་ས་.

འཆད་: p. **ཆད་**; f. **འཆད་** (cɛ̄ɛ̄) vi. to be cut off, to be broken off/ severed ¶ ཁོ་ཚོའི་དབར་འབྲེལ་བ་ཆད་པ་རེད་ The relationship between them has broken off. ¶ ཐག་པ་འཆད་ཀྱི་རེད་ The rope will break. 2. va. to die (usu. after སྐྲག) ¶ འཇིགས་སྐྲག་གིས་སྐྲག་ཆད་པ་རེད་ (They) died out of fright.

འཆད་: p. **བཤད་**; f. **བཤད་**; imp. **ཤོད་** (cɛ̄ɛ̄) to say/ speak/ teach ¶ བླ་མ་ཆོས་འཆད་དུ་བཅུག་པ་རེད་ (They) made the lama teach religion.

འཆད་འགྲེལ་ (cēndrel) explanation, interpretation.

འཆད་ཉན་ (cɛ̄ɛ̄ñɛn) teaching/ preaching and learning; va.—བྱེད་.

འཆད་ཉན་སྒོམ་སྒྲུབ་ (cɛ̄ɛ̄ñɛn go̱mdrub) to teach/ learn/ meditate and put into practice.

འཆད་སྟེགས་ (cɛ̄ɛ̄deg) rostrum, platform.

འཆད་རྩོད་རྩོམ་གསུམ་ (cɛ̄ɛ̄dzöö dzōmsum) the three: teaching, debating and writing.

འཆབ་: p. **བཅབས་**; f. **བཅབ་**; imp. **ཆོབས་** (cə̄b) va. to hide, to conceal, to keep secret ¶ རང་སྐྱོན་འཆབ་ནས་གཞན་སྐྱོན་སྟོན་པ་ཞིག་རེད་ He is sb. who conceals his own faults and exposes other's.

འཆབ་སེམས་ (cə̄bsem) thought of hiding/ concealing.

འཆམ་: p. **འཆམས་**; f. **འཆམ་**; imp. **འཆོམས་** (cām) 1. va. to dance ¶ ཁོ་ཚོ་བྲོ་འཆམ་གྱི་འདུག They are dancing. 2. va. to get along with, to agree with, to come to an agreement ¶ ཁོ་གཉིས་ཙ་བ་ནས་འཆམ་གྱི་མ་རེད་ The two of them will never get along. ¶ གནད་དོན་དེའི་ཐོག་ཁོ་ཚོ་གྲོས་འཆམ་པ་རེད་ They came to an agreement on that issue. 3. a religious ceremonial dance; va.—རྒྱག.

འཆམ་གོས་ (cāmgöö) costumes used in the འཆམ་ dance.

འཆམ་སྒྲ་ (cāmdra) sound of dance steps.

འཆམ་སྒྲིལ་ (cāmdrii) joining two families together; va.—བྱེད་.

འཆམ་འཆམ་ (cāmjan) a stroll, a walk, an outing; va.—བྱེད་.

འཆམ་འཆམ་ལ་འགྲོ་ (cāmjanla dro̱) va. to go for a walk/ stroll.

འཆམ་འཇོམས་དཔའ་བོ་བཅུ་བཞི་ (cāmjom bāwo jūbshi) name of a of medicine for curing colds.

འཆམ་མཐུན་ (cāmdün) friendship, friendly relationship ¶ འཆམ་མཐུན་མཉམ་གནས་ Friendly coexistence.

འཆམ་པོ་ (cāmbo) harmonious, friendly; va.—བྱེད་ to be friends, to get along ¶ ཁོ་གཉིས་འཆམ་པོ་འདུག Those two are friendly.

འཆམ་དཔོན་ (cāmbön) leader/ head in འཆམ་.

འཆམ་འབག (cāmbaà) masks used in འཆམ་.

འཆམ་མིན་ (cāmmin) unfriendly.

འཆམ་ཡིག (cāmyig) dancing manual for འཆམ་.

འཆམ་ར་ (cāmra) courtyard where the monks perform འཆམ་.

འཆམས་ (cām) p. of འཆམ་.

འཆའ་: p. **བཅས་**; f. **བཅའ་**; imp. **ཆོས་** (cā) va. 1. to create, to establish ¶ ལས་ཁུངས་ཀྱི་སྒྲིག་ལམ་འཆའ་དགོས་ We must create discipline in the office. 2. va. to make a promise/ vow. ¶ རང་ཉིད་ཀྱིས་དམ་བཅས་པའི་ལས་ཀ་དེ་ངེས་པར་བསྒྲུབ་དགོས་ One should fulfill one's vows. 3. vi. to settle down ¶ ཁོང་ཚོར་གནས་འཆའ་ས་ཡག་པོ་ཞིག་རྙེད་མི་འདུག They didn't find place to settle down.

འཆའ་: p. **ཆོས་**; f. **འཆའ་**; imp. **ཆོས་** (cā) va. to bite, to chew ¶ སོ་ཡག་པོ་མེད་སྟབས་ཤ་འཆའ་ཐུབ་ཀྱི་མི་འདུག Because (he) doesn't have good teeth he is unable to chew the meat.

འཆའ་ལྒམ་ཟ་ལྒམ་ (cālom sa̱lom) greedy, avaricious.

འཆར་ (cār) 1. vi. to rise, to emerge, to appear (in sight/ mind) ¶ ཉི་མ་འཆར་བའི་སྐབས་ When the sun is rising. ¶ ཡུལ་ལྗོངས་དེ་ཁོའི་མིག་ལམ་དུ་འཆར་བ་རེད་ The scenery appeared before his eyes. 2. (vb.+ —) used to express the idea of a plan/ intention ¶ ལག་ཤེས་བཟོ་གྲྭ་ཞིག་འཛུགས་འཆར་ཡོད་ (We) have a plan to start a handicraft workshop.

འཆར་ཀ་ (cārga) just about to happen.

འཆར་བཀོད་ (cārgöö) sm. འཆར་འགོད་.

འཆར་འགོད་ (cārgöö) plan, planning, designing, mapping out; va.—བྱེད་; —སྒྲིལ་ to plan, to design ¶ བཟོ་གྲྭ་རྒྱ་བསྐྱེད་ཀྱི་འཆར་འགོད་བྱས་པ་རེད་ They made a plan for expanding the factory.

འཆར་འགོད་ཁང་ (cārgöögaŋ) designing or planning bureau/ unit/ section/ council/ office.

འཆར་འགོད་ཁྲུའུ་ (cārgöödru) planning office.

འཆར་འགོད་བུ་སྐྱེད་ཨུ་ཡོན་ལྷན་ཁང་ (cārgöö pu̱gyeè ūyün lhēngaŋ) family planning committee.

འཆར་འགོད་ཚོགས་པ་ (cārgöö tsōgba) planning committee.

འཆར་འགོད་ལས་ཁུངས་ (cārgöö lɛ̱ɛ̄guŋ) sm. འཆར་འགོད་ཁང་.

འཆར་འགོད་ལས་བྱེད་པ་ (cārgöö lɛ̱ɛ̄jeba) a planner, an official responsible for planning.

འཆར་འགོད་ལྷན་ཁང་ (cārgöö lhēngaŋ) sm. sm. འཆར་འགོད་ཁང་.

འཆར་འགོད་ཨུ་ཡོན་ལྷན་ཁང་ (cārgöö ūyün lhēngaŋ) planning committee.

འཆར་སྒོ་ (cārgo) thought, idea, conception.

འཆར་ཅན་ (cārjɛn) usually, routinely ¶ འཆར་ཅན་ཁོ་ཚོ་སློབ་གྲྭར་ཆུ་ཚོད་བརྒྱད་པར་འགྲོ་གི་རེད་ Usually they go to school at 8 o'clock. ¶ འདི་འཆར་ཅན་རེད་ This is usual.

འཆར་ཅན་གྱི་ལས་ཀ་ (cārjɛngi lɛ̱ɛ̄ga) normal/ everyday work.

འཆར་ཅན་གྱི་གཞུང་དོན་ (cārjɛngi shu̱ndön) routine business, daily office work.

འཆར་ཅན་གུང་གསེང་ (cārjɛn ku̱nsaŋ) regular/ statutory holidays.

འཆར་ཅན་གྱོན་ཆས་ (cārjɛn kö̱ncɛɛ̄) everyday clothes.

འཆར་ཅན་གནས་ཚུལ་ (cārjɛn nɛ̄ɛ̄dzüü) everyday news/ occurrences.

འཆར་ཇུས་ (cār jü̱ü) planing and strategizing ¶ འཆར་ཇུས་གང་ཡང་མེད་པའི་ལས་ཀ་ Completely unplanned work.

འཆར་ཉེར་ (cārñer) near, close.

འཆར་སྙན་ (cārñɛn) a proposal/ plan being submitted.

འཆར་བཏོན་ (cārdön) p. of འཆར་འདོན་.

འཆར་ཐོ་ (cārdo) reading notes, notes of ideas.

འཆར་དོན་ (cārdön) contents of a plan.

འཆར་མདངས་ (cārdaŋ) impression of a situation.

འཆར་འདོན་ (cār dö̱n) va. put forth a plan.

འཆར་ལྡན་བུ་སྐྱེ་ (cāndɛn pu̱dzə) sm. འཆར་ལྡན་བུ་བཙའ་.

འཆར་ལྡན་བུ་བཙའ་ (cāndɛn pu̱dzə) family planning.

འཆར་བསྡུ་ (cārdu) shung. collecting something regularly (e.g., taxes).

འཆར་སྣང་ (cārnaŋ) image, mental vision, impression, opinion, idea ¶ དེབ་དེ་ཆ་ཚང་བཀླགས་མེད་སྟབས་ང་ལ་འཆར་སྣང་གསལ་པོ་མི་འདུག Because I haven't read the book completely I don't have a clear impression (about it).

འཆར་ཤུལ་ (cārbüü) presentation of proposal, submission of a plan (usu. for approval); va.—བྱེད་; —ཞུས་ ¶ བཀའ་ཤག་ལ་འཆར་ཤུལ་ཞུས་པ་རེད་ (They) presented the proposal to the Kashag.

འཆར་ཤུལ་ཕྱག་རྟགས་དགོངས་དོན་ (cārbüü cāgdaà gondön) shung. this is a standard phrase used to indicate that a proposal has been presented to a higher authority and approved by it ¶ སྲིད་འཛིན་མཆོག་ལ་འཆར་ཤུལ་ཕྱག་རྟགས་དགོངས་དོན་ཚོགས་འདུ་ཆེན་མོ་ཟླ་ ༣ ཚེས་ ༡༠ ཉིན་ཚོགས་རྒྱུ་ As per the proposal approved by the President, the general meeting will be held on March 10th.

འཆར་འཕར་ (cārbar) 1. regular and additional/ extra/ special ¶ འཆར་འཕར་ཚོགས་འདུ་ཁག་ལ་ At the regular and the additional meetings. 2. abbr. of འཆར་ཅན་ and འཕར་མ་.

འཆར་འཕར་ཁུར་འཁྲི་ (cārbar kūrdri) the reguar and additional taxes.

འཆར་བའི་ལོ་ཟླ་ (cārwɛ loda) the coming months and years.

འཆར་འབུལ་ (cārbüü) sm. འཆར་ཤུལ་.

འཆར་དམིགས་ (cərmiì) shung. regular and special.

འཆར་རྩུལ་ (cərdzüü) feelings, sensations, impressions.

འཆར་གཞི་ (cəəshi) plan; va.—འགོད་; —འདིངས་; —བཟོ་ to plan, to work out, to design ¶ ཟམ་པ་གསར་པ་ཞིག་རྒྱག་རྒྱུའི་འཆར་གཞི་བཀོད་པ་རེད་ (They) made a plan to build a new bridge.

འཆར་གཞི་སྔོན་བཀོད་ (cəəshi ŋöngöö) preplanned, planned in advance ¶ འཆར་གཞི་སྔོན་བཀོད་ཀྱི་དཔལ་འབྱོར་ Planned economy.

འཆར་གཞི་ཅན་ (cəəshijɛn) planned.

འཆར་གཞི་ཧྲིལ་པོ་ (cəəshi hrīibu) general plan or strategy, complete plan.

འཆར་གཞིའི་དམིགས་ཚད་ (cəəshi mīgdzɛɛ) goal of a plan.

འཆར་གཞིའི་རང་བཞིན་ (cəəshii rəŋshin) sm. འཆར་གཞི་ཅན་.

འཆར་ཟིན་ (cərsin) draft of plan; va.—འགོད་ to draft/ to draw up (a plan) ¶ བཅོས་ཟིན་པའི་འཆར་ཟིན་ A corrected draft plan.

འཆར་ཟླ་ (cārda) next month.

འཆར་ཡན་ (cāryɛn) romantic.

འཆར་ཡན་ཅན་ (cāryɛnjɛn) sm. འཆར་ཡན་.

འཆར་ཡན་རིང་ལུགས་ (cāryɛn riŋluù) romanticism.

འཆར་ཡོད་བུ་བཙའ་ (cāryöö pudza) sm. འཆར་ལྷན་བུ་བཙའ་.

འཆར་ལན་མྱུར་བ་ (cārlɛn ñurwa) quick reaction.

འཆར་ལོ་ (cārlo) next year, the coming year.

འཆར་ལྷན་ (cārlhɛn) abbr. of འཆར་འགོད་ལྷན་ཁང་.

འཆལ་ (cɛ̄ɛ) 1. vi. to be/ get degenerate, to deteriorate or break down with regard to morals/ ethics; vi.—འཆལ་ ¶ དེང་སང་དགོན་པའི་ཁྲིམས་ལམ་འཆལ་བཞག These days monastic discipline has broken down. 2. crooked.

འཆལ་གླུ་ (cɛ̄ɛlu) decadent music.

འཆལ་སྒྲུང་ (cɛ̄ɛdruŋ) pornographic/ sexual story.

འཆལ་གཏམ་ (cɛ̄ɛdam) 1. rumors, gossip; va.—ཤོད་ to spread rumors; va.—བཟོ་ to fabricate rumors. 2. sexual/ dirty talk.

འཆལ་གཏམ་སྨྱོ་བཤད་ (cɛ̄ɛdam ñoshɛɛ̀) talking crazy.

འཆལ་པོ་ (cɛ̄ɛbo) a womanizer, a playboy, a promiscuous man; va.—བྱེད་; —རྒྱུག་ to run around (after women).

འཆལ་པོ་ཀྱབ་ཀྱུག (cɛ̄ɛbo) sm. འཆལ་པོ་.

འཆལ་པོ་རྒས་པོ་ (cɛ̄ɛbo gɛɛ̀bo) a womanizer who is old, an older man who chases after women.

འཆལ་པོ་འཆལ་ནག (cɛ̄ɛbo cɛ̄ɛnag) sm. འཆལ་པོ་ཀྱབ་ཀྱུག.

འཆལ་སྤྱོད་ (cɛ̄ɛjöö) sexual behavior or acts.

འཆལ་ཕྲུག (cɛ̄ɛdruù) the offspring of a sexually inappropriate relationship, illegitimate child.

འཆལ་བའི་ཚུལ་ཁྲིམས་ (cɛ̄ɛwɛ tsüüdrim) losing the vow of celibacy.

འཆལ་མོ་ (cɛ̄ɛmo) promiscuous (for women), a loose woman; va.—རྒྱུག to behave loosely/ promiscuously.

འཆལ་རྩེད་འདུས་གནས་ (cɛ̄ɛdzeè düünɛɛ̀) a place of prostitution and gambling.

འཆལ་ཚིག (cɛ̄ɛdzig) 1. talk that is rubbish. 2. sexual/ dirty talk.

འཆལ་ལེ་འཆོལ་ལེ་ (cɛ̄ɛle cōōle) sm. ཆ་ལེ་ཆོ་ལེ་.

འཆལ་ལབ་ (cɛ̄ɛləb) 1. talking nonsense; va.—རྒྱག. 2. talking sexual/ dirty; va.—རྒྱག.

འཆི་: p. ཤི་; f. འཆི་ (cī) vi. to die ¶ ཁོ་ཤི་ནས་ལོ་མང་ཕྱིན་པ་རེད་ It has been many years since he died.

འཆི་ཀ་ (cīgə) sm. འཆི་ཁ་.

འཆི་ཀའི་སེམས་ཐ་མ་ (cīgɛ sēm tāma) the final consciousness just before a person dies.

འཆི་སྐྱོན་ (cīgyön) death ¶ ཁོང་འཆི་སྐྱོན་བྱུང་བཞག He died.

འཆི་ཁ་ (cīka) the point of death.

འཆི་ཁ་མ་ (cī kāma) sm. འཆི་ཁ་.

འཆི་ཁའི་འཕག་འཛག (cīgɛ pāgdzaà) last-ditch struggle, death-bed struggle; va.—རྒྱག.

འཆི་ཁར་ཐུག (cīkaa tūù) vi. to reach the point of death.

འཆི་མཁན་ (cīñɛn) the dead, sb. who died.

འཆི་ཀུ་ (cīgu) slingshot.

འཆི་གོད་ (cīgöö) death from a disaster/ accident/ calamity ¶ ར་ལུག་འཆི་གོད་བྱུང་སོང་ Many goats and sheep died.

འཆི་ཉེ་ (cīñe) sm. འཆི་ཁ་.

འཆི་ཉེན་ (cīñen) danger of dying ¶ ནད་རིམས་ཀྱིས་མི་མང་པོ་འཆི་ཉེན་བྱུང་བའི་སྐབས་ At the time when there was a danger of many people dying from the epidemic.

འཆི་མཉམ་གསོན་མཉམ་ (cīñam sōññam) living and dying together; va.—བྱེད་.

འཆི་རྟགས་ (cīdaà) sm. འཆི་ལྟས་.

འཆི་ལྟས་ (cīdɛɛ̀) sign of death.

འཆི་འཐབ་ (cītəb) fighting to the death; va.—བྱེད་.

འཆི་དུས་ (cīdüü) at the time of death.

འཆི་དུས་ཀྱི་འོད་གསལ་ (cīdüügi wöösɛl) the bright light a dying person sees just before he dies.

འཆི་བད་ (cīda) sm. འཆི་ལྟས་.

འཆི་བདག (cīdaà) sm. འཆི་བདག་གཤིན་རྗེ་.

འཆི་བདག་གཤིན་རྗེ་ (cīdaà shīnje) the lord of hell.

འཆི་འདས་ (cī dɛɛ̀) vi. to die.

འཆི་ནད་ (cīnɛɛ̀) fatal disease/ illness.

འཆི་འཕོ་ (cī pō) vi. to die.

འཆི་འཕོའི་སྡུག་བསྔལ་ (cībö duŋŋɛɛ) sadness/ anguish of impending death.

འཆི་འཁྲུས་ (cīndrɛɛ̀) the twitching of the body just before dying; vi.—རྒྱག.

འཆི་བ་ (cīwə) death, dying ¶ འཆི་བར་འཇིགས་ནས་ Fear of death.

འཆི་བ་མི་རྟག་པ་ (cīwə midagba) uncertainty of death.

འཆི་བླུ་ (cīlu) paying money to save the life of an animal that is scheduled to be slaughtered; va.—གཏོང་.

འཆི་བློ་བདེ་ (cīlode) feeling at ease just before death.

འཆི་དབུགས་སྲིང་ཙམ་ (cīuù sīŋdzam) delaying (a person) from dying for a brief moment; va.—བྱེད་.

འཆི་མིག་དགུ་བསྒྲིགས་ (cīmiì gudriì) the nine-eyed slingshot (a sling with nine eye-like design woven into it).

འཆི་མེད་ (cīmeè) 1. immortal, not dying. 2. person's name.

འཆི་མེད་བདུད་རྩི་རིལ་བུ་ (cīmeè düùdzi riibu) a magical pill that prevents death (in tales).

འཆི་མེད་རྩིས་འཁྲིའི་སྐུ་ཐར་ (cīmeè dzīìdrii gūdar) shung. animals whose lives have been spared and given to the nomads as a lease wherein the leasee pays a fixed amount of butter to the leaser annually whether the number of animals increases or decreases.

འཆི་མེད་རིལ་བུ་ (cīmeè ri̱ibu) sm. འཆི་མེད་བདུད་རྩི་རིལ་བུ་.

འཆི་མེད་ཤི་མར་ (cīmeè shīmaa) shung. nomad lease arrangement where the leasee pays a fixed amount of butter to the leaser annually regardless of whether the original number of animal increases or decreases.

འཆི་རྨས་ (cīmɛɛ̀) casualties, dead and wounded ¶ ཕན་ཚུན་གཉིས་ཀར་འཆི་རྨས་ཆེན་པོ་བྱུང་འདུག Both sides suffered great casualties.

འཆི་རྩ་ (cīdza) the type of pulse that signals impending death.

འཆི་ཚད་ (cīdzɛɛ̀) death rate.

འཆི་ཚད་པ་ (cīdzɛèba) sm. འཆི་ལ་ཁད་.

འཆི་ལ་ངང་པ་པད་མཚོར་འཇུག་པ་བཞིན་ (cīlə ŋa̱ŋba bɛ̀ɛdzɔr ju̱gba shi̱n) very brave, courageous [Lit. (considering) death as ducks enter a lotus pond].

འཆི་ལ་ངང་པ་པད་མཚོར་ཞུགས་པ་ (cīlə ŋa̱ŋba bɛ̀ɛdzɔr shu̱gba) sm. འཆི་ལ་ངང་པ་པད་མཚོར་འཇུག་པ་བཞིན་པ་.

འཆི་ལ་ཁད་ (cīlə kɛ̀ɛ) vi. to be on the verge of death ¶ ཕོ་ཚོས་ཆུ་བྱ་འཆི་ལ་ཁད་དེ་སྲོག་སྐྱོབ་བྱས་པ་རེད་ They saved the water bird that was on the verge of death.

འཆི་ལམ་ (cīlam) the road to death.

འཆི་སེམས་ (cīsem) the thought of death.

འཆི་གསོན་ (cīsön) life and death, living and dead.

འཆིང་: p. **བཅིངས་**; f. **བཅིང་**; imp. **ཆིངས་** (cīŋ) va. 1. to bind, to tie ¶ ཁོས་རྨ་དེ་རས་ཆས་བཅིངས་པ་རེད་ He bound the wound with a piece of cloth. ¶ ཞིང་གཡོག་ལམ་ལུགས་ཀྱི་འཆིང་ཐག་གིས་བཅིངས་པའི་མི་སེར་ Serfs bound by the fetters of serfdom. 2. va. to tie wear (sth. like a belt) ¶ ཀོ་བའི་སྐེ་རགས་འཆིང་གི་འདུག (They) wear leather belts.

འཆིང་འགྲོལ་ (cīŋdröö) liberation, liberating; va.—གཏོང་ to liberate.

འཆིང་འགྲོལ་དམག (cīŋdröö māà) liberation army.

འཆིང་འགྲོལ་དམག་མི་ (cīŋdröö māəmi) liberation army, liberation army soldier.

འཆིང་རྒྱ་ (cīŋgya) 1. net, trap; va.—སྡེམ་ to trap, to net. 2. fetters, binds; va.—གཏོང་ to break fetters/ binds.

འཆིང་རྒྱག (cīŋ gya̱à) va. to bandage, to wrap.

འཆིང་སྒྲོག (cīŋdrɔ̀ɔ) sm. འཆིང་ཐག.

འཆིང་ཐག (cīŋdaà) rope for binding or tying sth., fetters, binds, shackles ¶ བཙན་རྒྱལ་རིང་ལུགས་ཀྱི་འཆིང་ཐག་ལས་གྲོལ་སོང་ (They) were freed from the shackles of imperialism.

འཆིང་སྡོམ་འཁེལ་ (cīŋdom kēē) vi. to be bound/ restrained, to be limited/ confined ¶ མི་དམངས་ལ་སྲིད་བྱུས་ཀྱི་འཆིང་སྡོམ་འཁེལ་སྟབས་རང་དབང་གིས་སྐད་ཆ་ཤོད་ནུས་ཀྱི་མེད་ Because of the policy of confining people (they) don't dare talk freely.

འཆིང་གནས་ (cīŋnɛɛ̀) prison, jail.

འཆིང་ཞགས་ (cīŋshaà) sm. འཆིང་ཐག.

འཆིབ་: p. **བཅིབས་**; f. **བཅིབ་**; imp. **ཆིབས་** (cīb) va. to ride (h.) ¶ ཁོང་ཆིབས་པ་འཆིབ་ཀྱི་འདུག He is riding a horse. ¶ མོ་ཊ་བཅིབས་ནས་ཕེབས་པ་རེད་ They came in a car.

འཆིར་: p. and f. **བཅིར་**; imp. **ཆིར་** (cīr) va. to squeeze, to press out ¶ ཤིང་ཏོག་འཆིར་གི་འདུག (They) are squeezing (the juice out of) the fruit.

འཆུ་: p. **བཅུས་**; f. **བཅུ་**; imp. **ཆུས་** (cū) va. to take/ bring/ ladle water (from a well or stream) ¶ སྔ་དགོང་བུད་མེད་ཚོ་གཙང་པོ་ནས་ཆུ་བཅུ་བར་འགྲོ་དུས་ In the morning and evening when women go to bring water from the river.

འཆུ་ (cū) administrative district in between a xiang and xian in size.

འཆུག (cūg) vi. to err, to make a mistake ¶ ལས་ཀ་འདི་ཁོས་འཆུག་པ་རེད་ He made a mistake in this work.

འཆུག་མེད་ (cūgmeè) without error.

འཆུགས་འཚབ་ཆེ་ (cūg dzɔ̄bje) a great error/ mistake.

འཆུན་: p. **ཆུན་**; f. **འཆུན་** (cǖn) vi. to discipline, to control ¶ མི་གཤིས་བཟང་བས་ཁོ་ཚོ་འཆུན་ཐུབ་ཀྱི་མི་འདུག Because (he) is good-natured, it is not possible for them to get disciplined.

འཆུན་འདོམས་ (cǖndom) controlling, imposing discipline; va.—བྱེད་ ¶ ཆོས་སྡེ་ཁག་གི་སྒྲིག་ལམ་འཆུན་འདོམས་ནན་ཏན་དགོས་རྒྱུ་ The monasteries should be well disciplined.

འཆུན་པོ་ (cǖmbo) sb. who is strict/ imposes discipline.

འཆུམ་: p. **འཆུམས་**; f. **འཆུམ་** (cūm) 1. vi. to get/ be attached to, to love, to like. 2. sm. འཁུམས་. 3. vi. to close, to get closed ¶ ཉི་མ་ཚ་དྲག་ནས་མེ་ཏོག་གི་འདབ་མ་འཆུམས་འདུག The sun was too hot and the leaves of the flowers closed.

འཆུར་ (cūr) 1. sm. གཙུར་. 2. arc. to arrive, to come.

འཆུས་ (cǖǜ) vi. to get twisted, to get sprained ¶ ཁོའི་ལག་པ་འཆུས་འདུག His hand got sprained (twisted).

འཆུས་ཀྱོག (cǖǜgyɔ̀ɔ) crooked, zigzag.

འཆུས་པོ་ (cǖǜbo) twisted, crooked.

འཆེ་: p. **འཆེས་**; f. **འཆེ་**; imp. **འཆེས་** (cē) va. to agree, to accept.

འཆེག: p. **བཤགས་**; f. **བཤག**; (cēg) va. to split (wood, etc.).

འཆེས་ (cēè) p. and imp. of འཆེ་.

འཆོབ་ཡོད་ (cōbyöö) shung. having a tassel.

འཆོབས་ (cōm) imp. of འཆབ་.

འཆོམས་ (cōm) imp. of འཆམས་.

འཆོར་: p. **ཤོར་**; f. **འཆོར་** (cɔ̄r) sm. ཤོར་.

འཆོལ་: p. **བཅོལ་**; f. **འཆོལ་**; imp. **ཆོལ་** (cȫȫ) 1. va. to entrust with, to deposit, to leave in someone's charge ¶ སྐྱེལ་འདྲེན་གྱི་ལས་ཀ་དེ་ཁོ་ལ་བཅོལ་པ་རེད་ (They) entrusted the transportation work to him. ¶ ངའི་སྒམ་དེ་མོ་ལ་བཅོལ་ཡོད་ I have left my box in her care. 2. va. to seek shelter/ protection, to place one's hope (in sb.) ¶ སྟོབས་ཆེན་རྒྱལ་ཁབ་སུ་ལ་ཡང་སྐྱབས་བཅོལ་མི་དགོས་ (They) do not have to seek protection from any powerful nation. ¶ ཁོས་ཁྱེད་རང་ལ་རེ་བ་བཅོལ་གྱི་འདུག He places his hope in you.

འཆོལ་ (cȫȫ) 1. vi. to err, to make a mistake ¶ དེ་འཆོལ་འདུག That is a mistake. ¶ འཆོལ་མེད་ Without error. 2. vi. to have delusions.

འཆོལ་གཏམ་ (cȫȫdam) delusionary talk.

འཆོལ་མ་ (cȫȫma) 1. a mentally disturbed woman. 2. immoral woman.

འཆོས་: p. **བཅོས་**; f. **བཅོས་**; imp. **ཆོས་** (cȫȫ) 1. va. to make, create ¶ ཕོ་ཚོས་ཤོག་བུའི་སྟག་གཅིག་བཅོས་འདུག They made a paper tiger. 2. va. to correct, to renovate, to repair, to revise, to reform, to treat (illness) ¶ རི་རྗེན་ཀྱང་བཟོ་བཅོས་འགོ་བཙུགས་པ་རེད་ They have begun to renovate even the bare mountains.

འཆོས་ཐབས་ (cȫȫdəb) method of reforming/ correcting.

ཇ་ (ja) 1. the letter ཇ་ (used in alphabetical ordering). 2. tea; va.—རྒྱག to put tea leaves in water for brewing ¶ བོད་ཇ་ Tibetan tea.

ཇ་ཀོ་ (cago) sm. ཇ་ཀོག.

ཇ་ཀོག (cagɔɔ̀) a leather/ hide bag used to transport tea.

ཇ་དཀར་ (cagar) porcelain tea cup.

ཇ་དཀྲུག (cadrug) a stick used to mix/ churn Tibetan tea; va.—རྒྱག to mix/ churn tea by twirling a stick.

ཇ་དཀྲུགས་མ་ (ca drūgma) sm. ཇ་བསྲུབས་མ་.

ཇ་དཀྲོགས་མ་ (ca drōgma) sm. ཇ་བསྲུབས་མ་.

ཇ་སྐྱེམས་ (cagyem) drinking tea.

ཇ་ཁ་ (caga) the color of tea, brownish red.

ཇ་ཁ་ཡ་ (caga ya) half a load of tea (= 8 བག་ཆུང་).

ཇ་ཁང་ (cagaŋ) 1. tea house, tea stall, tea parlor. 2. place where one churns/ makes tea (usu. in monasteries).

ཇ་ཁབ་ (cāgəb) needle for stitching loads of tea.

ཇ་ཁུ་ (cəgu) tea extract (the strong liquid tea resulting from boiling tea leaves); va.—རྒྱག va. to make tea extract.

ཇ་ཁུ་དང་པོ་ (cəgu taŋbo) the tea extract resulting from the first boiling of the tea leaves.

ཇ་ཁུ་གཉིས་པ་ (cəgu ñiibə) the tea extract resulting from the second boiling of the tea leaves.

ཇ་ཁུ་མདོག (cəgu dɔɔ̀) brown, the color of tea extract.

ཇ་ཁུ་སྡིར་ (cəgu dir) va. to brew tea extract.

ཇ་ཁུ་དམར་ (cəgu mār) an inferior type of reddish tea extract.

ཇ་ཁུག (caguù) tea bag.

ཇ་ཁོ་ཁོ་ (ca kōgo) tib.eng. cocoa.

ཇ་ཁོག (cagɔɔ̀) tea pot.

ཇ་ཁྲ་ (cadra) a type of tea pot used in monasteries.

ཇ་འཁོར་དྲུག (cagɔɔ truù) a bamboo basket which contains 16 བག་ཆུང་.

ཇ་གད་ (cagɛɛ̀) breaking small pieces of tea from the slab of brick tea to boil; va.—བྱེད་.

ཇ་གར་པོ་ (ca karbo) strong tea.

ཇ་གི་ཇི་གི་ (cəgi cigi) blurry.

ཇ་གོང་ (cagoŋ) price of tea.

ཇ་གོད་ (cagöö) 1. tea brewed without baking soda. 2. plain tea (without butter).

ཇ་རྒྱ་ཇ་ (ca gyaja) tea from China.

ཇ་རྒྱག (ca gyaà) see ཇ་.

ཇ་རྒྱབ་ (cagyəb) a load of tea (two boxes, one on each side of a carrying animal).

ཇ་རྒྱབ་པ་ (ca gyəbbə) shung. person in charge of loading/ transporting tea.

ཇ་སྐུགས་ (cəgyuù) one's share/ portion of tea (e.g., that is served in monastery prayer assemblies).

ཇ་སྒམ་ (cagam) box of tea.

ཇ་ངོམས་ཟས་ཚིམས་ (caŋom sɛ̀ɛ̀dzim) eating and drinking until one is full.

ཇ་མངར་མོ་ (ca ŋāāmo) English-style tea (with milk and sugar).

ཇ་མངར་ཁང་ (caŋaagaŋ) a tea house that serves English-style sweet tea.

ཇ་བརྔོས་ (caŋöö) tea boiled till all the water is absorbed by the tea leaves and then left to dry for use when traveling.

ཇ་ཆང་སྣེ་མོ་ (cajaŋ nēmo) shung. small fee paid to the person who helps one to present one's side in a law case/ dispute.

ཇ་ཆང་མཚར་གླུ་ (cajaŋ tsārlu) songs sung when having a good time drinking ཆང་ or tea.

ཇ་ཆུ་སྦྲིག (caju drig) va. to mix boiled water and brewed tea extract so that it is ready to add butter and churn.

ཇ་མཆོད་ (cajöö) an offering of tea; va.—འབུལ་ to make a tea offering to a deity.

ཇ་ཇ་མར་སྐོལ་ (caja maagöö) a child's game in which the children play at making tea.

ཇ་ལྗང་ (cajaŋ) green tea.

ཇ་གཉེར་ (cañer) abbr. of ཇ་མ་ and གཉེར་པ་.

ཇ་སྙིགས་ (jañig) 1. leftover tea 2. sm. ཇ་རོ་.

ཇ་ལྡིར་ (cadir) teapot.

ཇ་སྟོན་ (cadön) a social gathering/ party where tea and snacks (but no liquor) is served, tea party/ reception.

ཇ་སྟོན་ཚོགས་འདུ་ (cadön tsɔ̄ŋdu) a meeting at which tea is served.

ཇ་ཐང་ (cadaŋ) black tea (i.e., tea without milk or butter).

ཇ་ཐང་པགས་ལོག (cadaŋ bāglɔɔ̀) a type of winter fur hat worn by males.

ཇ་ཐུག (cādug) abbr. tea and broth/ soup/ stew.

ཇ་ཐུད་མར་གསུམ་ (ca tũũ maa sūm) the three: tea, cheese and butter.

ཇ་ཐུན་གཅིག (ca tũnjig) sm. ཇ་ཡུན་གཅིག.

ཇ་ཐེབས་ (cateb) shung. endowment fund where the interest is used to give tea to monks.

ཇ་འཐག (cadaà) tea grinder.

ཇ་དམ་ (cadam) thermos bottle, thermos, flask.

ཇ་དང་དགེ་རྒན་ཚ་ན་དགའ་ (cadaŋ gegɛn tsāna ga) a strict teacher is good [Lit. if tea and the teacher are hot that is good].

ཇ་དྭངས་ (cadaŋ) sm. ཇ་ཐང་.

ཇ་དྭངས་མདོག (cadaŋ dɔɔ̀) dark brown, the color of tea.

ཇ་དོ་ (cado) abbr. a load of tea.

ཇ་དོས་ (cādöö) a load of tea.

ཇ་བདག (cadaà) owner of a tea garden/ tea company.

ཇ་མདོང་ (cadoŋ) tea churn.

ཇ་འདན་ (cadɛn) soup/ stew made from tsampa, butter, salt and liquid tea.

ཇ་འདྲེན་ (ca dren) va. to serve tea.

ཇ་འདྲེན་ཆང་འདྲེན་ (cadren cāŋdren) good/ warm hospitality [Lit. serving tea and serving chang].

ཇ་ལྡུར་ (cadur) food made by mixing tsamba and tea (in a mushy consistency).

ཇ་སྡོང་ (cadoŋ) sm. ཇ་ཤིང་.

ཇ་སྡོར་ (cadɔɔ) butter to be used in tea.

ཇ་ནག (canaà) sm. ཇ་ཐང་.

ཇ་ནད་ (canɛɛ̀) illness caused by drinking tea.

ཇ་གནང་ཞུ་ (canaŋ shu) shung. va. to ask permission to serve tea.

ཇ་སྣོད་ (canöö) teapot.

ཇ་པ་ཏི་ (ca bədi) tib.hind. Indian tea (loose).

ཇ་པྲ་ (cadra) a kind of teapot used in monasteries.

ཇ་དཔོན་ (cabön) monk/ person in charge of making tea.

ཇ་སྤ་ཏི་ (ca bədi) sm. ཇ་པ་ཏི་

ཇ་སྤྱན་ཤེལ་ (ca jɛ̄nshee) slightly inferior tea made from the second picking.

ཇ་ཕུད་ (ca pũũ) first offering of tea to a deity.

ཇ་ཕོགས་ (cabɔɔ̀) payment/ salary/ wage in tea.

ཇ་ཕོར་ (capɔɔ) tea cup (wooden).

ཇ་ཕྱེ་ (caje) powdered tea.

ཇ་བག (cabaà) sm. ཇ་སྦྲག.

ཇ་བག་ག་ (ca paaga) sm. ཇ་སྦྲག.

ཇ་འབིང་ (canbiŋ) a type of tea pot.

ཇ་འབྲུ་ (candru) tea tree's flower.

ཇ་འབྲུ་གཉིས་ (candru ñii) tea from the second (and subsequent) picking.

ཇ་འབྲུ་གཉིས་མ་ (candru ñiimə) sm. ཇ་འབྲུ་གཉིས་.

ཇ་འབྲུ་དང་ (candru taŋ) the best tea, tea from the first picking (considered to be the best since it includes tea tips).

ཇ་བླུག (ca lūü) va. to serve/ pour tea.
ཇ་སྦག (cabaà) brick tea; a brick of tea.
ཇ་སྦག་ཆུང་ (ca bəgjuŋ) the smaller size bricks of tea.
ཇ་སྦག་ཆེན་ (ca bagjen) the larger size bricks of tea.
ཇ་སྦང་ (ca baŋ) va. to soak tea (before brewing).
ཇ་སྦོང་ (ca boŋ) sm. ཇ་སྦང་.
ཇ་སྦྱོར་གཅིག (cajɔɔjig) the time it takes to make and drink a cup of (Tibetan) tea.
ཇ་མ་ (cama) 1. cook. 2. person who makes tea.
ཇ་མན་ (camɛn) an inferior tea from southeastern Tibet (Lhopra).
ཇ་མའོ་ཅན་ (ca māwojen) tib.ch. a high quality tea.
ཇ་མར་ (camar) 1. butter for tea. 2. tea and butter.
ཇ་མར་ཚྭ་གསུམ་ (camar tsāsum) the three: tea, butter and salt.
ཇ་རྩམ་ (cadzam) tea and tsamba.
ཇ་ཚགས་ (cadzaà) tea strainer.
ཇ་ཚགས་གྲོས་མོལ་ (cadzaà trȫömöö) tea party.
ཇ་ཚོང་ (cadzoŋ) tea trade, trading in tea.
ཇ་ཚོང་མཁན་ (cadzoŋñɛn) tea trader.
ཇ་ཚྭ་ལས་ཁུངས་ (cadza lɛ̀ɛguŋ) shung. an office in tt. in charge of the collection of taxes on tea, salt and skins.
ཇ་ཞག (cashaà) the upper layer of coagulated butter in Tibetan tea that has been left standing.
ཇ་ཞིང་ (cashiŋ) tea garden, tea plantation.
ཇ་ཞིབ་ཞིབ་ (ca shibshiì) ground tea, powdered tea.
ཇ་ཞིམ་པོ་མར་གྱི་བཀའ་དྲིན་ (ca shimbu margi gədrin) sth. that is good due to another's action/ kindness [Lit. tasty tea owes gratitude to butter].
ཇ་ཞིམ་པོ་མར་གྱི་དྲིན་ (ca shimbu margi trin) sm. ཇ་ཞིམ་པོ་མར་གྱི་བཀའ་དྲིན་.
ཇ་ཞུ་ (ca shu) va. to serve tea.
ཇ་ཞུ་བ་ (ca shuwə) tea server.
ཇ་ཞོར་ཆང་ཞོར་གྱི་གྲོས་གཏམ་ (cashɔɔ cāŋshɔɔgi trȫödam) talk/ conversation while drinking tea or chang.
ཇ་ཟོག (casɔɔ̀) shung. tea.
ཇ་བཟོ་ (ca so) va. to make tea.
ཇ་ཡུན་གཅིག (cayönjig) the time it takes to drink a cup of tea (for a cup of tea to be cool enough to drink).
ཇ་གཡོག (cayɔɔ̀) monks who serve tea in the monastery.
ཇ་རིན་ (cərin) price of tea.
ཇ་རིལ་ (cərii) 1. Tibetan brick tea that is round in shape. 2. skull.
ཇ་རོ་ (caro) used tea leaves, tea leaves that have been boiled to make tea.
ཇ་ལག་གཉིས་ (calaà ñiì) abbr. tea maker and tea server.
ཇ་ལན་གཅིན་འཇལ་ (calɛn jinjɛɛ) ungrateful, inappreciative [Lit. repay tea with urine].
ཇ་ལན་གཅིན་བླུད་ (calɛn jinjɛɛ) sm. ཇ་ལན་གཅིན་འཇལ་.
ཇ་ལན་ཆུ་འཇལ་ (calɛn cūnjɛɛ) ungrateful, inappreciative [Lit. repay tea with water].
ཇ་ལས་པ་ (calɛ̀ɛba) people who work in tea shops or tea factories.
ཇ་ལས་བཟོ་གྲྭ (calɛɛ̀ sodra) tea factory.
ཇ་ལུང་ (caluŋ) leather strap for tying boxes of tea.
ཇ་ལོ་ (calo) tea leaves; va.—འཐོག to pick tea leaves.
ཇ་ལོག (cālɔɔ̀) ball of dried tea.
ཇ་ཤིང་ (cəshiŋ) tea tree/ bush.
ཇ་ཤོ་ (casho) shung. tea tax/ duty.
ཇ་ཤོག (cashoò) the paper in which bricks of tea are wrapped.
ཇ་ཤོག་སེར་པོ་ (casho sērbo) a yellow paper in which Tibetan brick tea is wrapped.
ཇ་སིག (ca siì) a brick of tea.
ཇ་སིལ་མ་ (ca siìmə) loose tea.
ཇ་སུན་རེ་ (ca sūnre) a small amount/ cup of tea for each (person).
ཇ་སོབ་ (casob) a type of low quality tea from Tibet.
ཇ་སྲུབ་ (ca sūb) va. to churn tea, to mix tea.
ཇ་སྲུབ་འཕྲུལ་ཆས་ (casub trüüjɛɛ̀) a machine for churning butter tea.
ཇ་སྲུབ་མ་ (ca sūbmə) Tibetan-style churned butter tea.
ཇ་སྲུས་མ་ (ca sūümə) sm. ཇ་སྲུབ་མ་.
ཇ་གསུར་ (casur) burning tea leaves (usu. when someone dies).
ཇ་བསྲུབས་ (ca sūb) p. of ཇ་སྲུབ་.
ཇ་ཧོང་ (cahoŋ) orange color.
ཇ་ཧྲིལ་ (cahrii) sm. ཇ་རིལ་.
ཇ་ལྷབ་སུས་ (ca lhəbsüü) Tibetan tea that has not been brewed for a long time.
ཇག (cag) abbr. of ཇག་པ་.
ཇག་དཀྱུས་ (caàgüü) common bandits.
ཇག་རྐུན་ (caàgün) bandit, brigand.
ཇག་ཁྱུ་ (caggyu) gang of bandits.
ཇག་འཁྱམས་ (cagkyam) sm. ཇག་རྐུན་.
ཇག་འགོ་ (caŋgo) bandit leader.
ཇག་བརྒྱབ་རྒྱུ་ནོར་ (cāggyəb gyunɔɔ) stolen goods, booty.
ཇག་ངན་ (cagŋɛn) sm. ཇག་རྐུན་.
ཇག་ཉུལ་ (cəgñul) sm. ཇག་སྙུལ་.
ཇག་རྟ་ (cagda) horse belonging to bandits.
ཇག་འདུལ་ (cagdüü) defeating/ conquering bandits; va.—བྱེད་.
ཇག་ནག (cagnag) sm. ཇག་རྐུན་.
ཇག་ནོམ་ (cagnom) things obtained by banditry.
ཇག་པ་ (cagba) brigand, bandit; va.—རྒྱག to rob (as a bandit).
ཇག་པ་འཇོམས་ (cagba jom) sm. ཇག་འདུལ་.
ཇག་པ་ལང་ཤོར་ (cagba laŋshɔɔ) a bandit with a long record, a hardened bandit.
ཇག་དཔུང་ (cagbuŋ) sm. ཇག་ཚོགས་.
ཇག་དཔོན་ (cagbön) boss/ ringleader of a group of bandits.
ཇག་མ་ (caàma) shovel, spade.
ཇག་མོ་ (cagmo) female bandit.
ཇག་སྙུལ་ (cəgñul) 1. spy, special agent. 2. bandit and spy.
ཇག་དམག (cagmaà) bandit army (used by the communists to refer to the Kuomintang army).
ཇག་སྨོངས་ (cagmoŋ) a derogatory term of abuse used for bandits.
ཇག་གཙོ་ (cagdzo) sm. ཇག་འགོ་.
ཇག་ཚང་ (cagdzaŋ) bandit's den/ hideaway.
ཇག་ཚོགས་ (cagdzɔɔ̀) bandit gang.
ཇག་འཛིན་པ་ (cagdzimbə) sb. who goes to arrest bandits.
ཇག་ཟིང་ (cagsiŋ) unrest caused by bandits.
ཇག་ཤོག (cagshɔɔ̀) sm. ཇག་ཚོགས་.
ཇང་ཏ་ལིང་ཏ་ (jaŋda liŋdə) swinging.
ཇང་དཔོན་ཆུང་བ་ (caŋbön cūŋwa) ch.tib. major general.
ཇང་དཔོན་ཆེ་བ་ (caŋbön cēwa) ch.tib. colonel general.
ཇང་དཔོན་འབྲིང་བ་ (caŋbön driŋwə) ch.tib. lieutenant general.
ཇང་ཡུའུ་ (cəŋyu) ch. soy sauce.
ཇན་ཅང་ (cɛnjaŋ) ch. athletic hero (master of sports).
ཇན་པུའུ་ཀྲའི་ (cɛnbudre) ch. Cambodia.
ཇབ་ཇོབ་ (cəbjob) abbr. of ཇབ་བེ་ཇོབ་བེ་.
ཇབ་བེ་ཇོབ་བེ་ (cəbbe jobbe) all mixed together in a bad way, odds and ends.
ཇམ་མུ་ (jammu) Jammu (Kashmir).
ཇར་ཇེར་དུ་འགྱུར་ (carjerdu gyur) vi. to get smashed/ crushed.
ཇར་མན་ (carmɛn) Germany, German.
ཇའི་སང་ (cɛsaŋ) shung. treasurer.
ཇི་ (ji) 1. interrogative particle: what, which ¶ དེ་ལ་གོང་ཇི་ཡིན་ནམ་ What is the price of that? 2. whatever, whichever ¶ དཔུང་དམག་ཇི་དགོས་ Whatever troops are/ were needed. ¶ སེམས་ལ་ཇི་བབས་ཤོད་ཀྱི་འདུག (He) says whatever comes into

(his) mind ། དངུལ་ཇི་ཡོད་ཁོ་ལ་སྤྲད་པ་རེད་ Whatever money (they) had (they) gave him. 3. how much, however much/ many ། མི་རེ་རེར་ད་ལྟ་ས་ཞིང་ཇི་ཡོད་ How much land does each person have now?

ཇི་སྐད་ (jigeè) 1. what/ whatever was said or written ། ཁོས་ཇི་སྐད་ཟེར་བ་བཞིན་ According to what he says. ། ཇི་སྐད་བཤད་ཀྱང་ Whatever I told him. 2. whatever was quoted from somewhere.

ཇི་ག (jigə) 1. sm. ཇི་འདྲ་. 2. never, not under any condition ། ཇི་གར་མི་བརྗེད་པ་བྱ་རྒྱུ་ཡིན་ (I) will never forget it.

ཇི་དགར་ (jigar) sm. ཅི་དགར་.

ཇི་དགུ་ (jigu) many things, all kinds of things ། གནས་ཚུལ་ཇི་དགུ་གོ་རྒྱུ་འདུག་ཀྱང་བདེན་མིན་ངས་མི་ཤེས་ One hears all kinds of things but I don't know if they are true.

ཇི་དགེ་ (jige) sm. ཇི་འགབ་.

ཇི་འགབ་ (jigəb) what is best, what is better (to do) ། གནས་ཚུལ་འདིའི་སྐོར་ཇི་འགབ་བཀའ་སློབ་ཡོད་པ་ཞུ་ Regarding this matter, please give me your advice on whatever is better.

ཇི་ཆེད་ (jijeè) for what purpose, why.

ཇི་སྙམ་ (jiñam) whatever comes to mind, whatever one thinks.

ཇི་སྙེད་ (jiñeè) however much there is, whatever there is ། ད་ཕན་ཉམས་མྱོང་ལ་གཞིགས་པའི་ཡར་རྒྱས་ཇི་སྙེད་ཅིག་བྱུང་ཡོད་ Up to now, (We) have progressed whatever was possible given our experience.

ཇི་སྙེད་ཅིག་མཆིས་ (jiñii jigjii) shung. many ། སྐབས་ཤིག་རིང་དགོན་པའི་ནང་སྒྲིག་ལམ་འགལ་བསྣད་ཀྱི་གནས་ཚུལ་ཇི་སྙེད་ཅིག་མཆིས་པ་ For a time now there have been many incidents of undisciplined behavior in the monastery.

ཇི་སྙེད་དེ་སྙེད་ (jiñeè teñeè) whatever one has/ can, that much ..., however much there is, that much... ། རང་གིས་ཇི་སྙེད་ཤེས་པ་དེ་སྙེད་གཞན་ལ་བསླབ་དགོས་ Whatever knowledge one has, that much one should teach others.

ཇི་སྙེད་ཡོད་པ་ (jiñeè yööba) sm. ཇི་སྙེད་.

ཇི་ལྟ་ཇི་ལྟར་ (jida jidar) sm. ཇི་ལྟར་

ཇི་ལྟ་ཇི་ལྟ་བུ་ (jida jidəbu) sm. ཇི་ལྟར་

ཇི་ལྟ་བ་ (ji dāwa) 1. sm. ཇི་ལྟ་བུ་. 2. authentic.

ཇི་ལྟ་བ་བཞིན་ (ji dāwashin) 1. just as, exactly, same as ། ཁོ་ཚོས་བོད་ལ་གནས་སྐབས་ཇི་ལྟ་བ་བཞིན་བྱས་ཡོད་པ་རེད་ They did it just as when they were in Tibet. ། ཁོང་གིས་གསུངས་པ་ཇི་ལྟ་བ་བཞིན་ Just like what he said. 2. whatever ། སྲོག་ཆགས་བཞི་པོ་རང་ལ་དགོས་མཁོ་ཇི་ལྟ་བ་བཞིན་ལྗོན་ཤིང་དེས་སྦྱིན་ The tree gave whatever was needed to each of the four animals.

ཇི་ལྟ་བུ་ (ji dābu) sm. ཇི་ལྟར་, 1.

ཇི་ལྟ་ཡང་ (jidayaŋ) sm. གང་ལྟར་.

ཇི་ལྟར་ (jidar) 1. how, in what way, like what ། འདི་ཇི་ལྟར་བྱེད་དགོས་རེད་ How should (one) do this? ། ཁོས་ཇི་ལྟར་ཟེར་བ་བཞིན་བྱོས་ཤིག Do as he tells (you)! 2. however, in any case, whatever, anyway ། ཇི་ལྟར་ཡང་རྒྱལ་ཁ་ང་ཚོར་ཐོབ་ཀྱི་རེད་ Anyway, we will win a victory. ། ཇི་ལྟར་བྱས་ཀྱང་ཕན་ཐོགས་ཡོད་པ་མ་རེད་ Whatever (you) do it will not help. 3. accordingly, in that manner, similar to ། སོག་པོའི་དམག་ལུགས་དང་སྒྲིག་བཀོད་ཇི་བཞིན་བཟོས་ (They) made (it) in accordance with Mongol military customs and rules.

ཇི་ལྟར་དྲང་ (jidar traŋ) how to comprehend or interpret ། རྩོམ་ཡིག་དེའི་ཚིག་ལ་བརྟེན་ནས་དོན་ཇི་ལྟར་དྲང་ Based on the words of the article, how do we comprehend the meaning?

ཇི་ལྟར་བྱེད་རྒྱུ་ (jidar cegyu) what should be done, what should we do.

ཇི་སྟེ་ (jide) if.

ཇི་འདྲ་བ་ (ji drawə) sm. གང་འདྲ་.

ཇི་འདྲ་ཞིག (ji drashig) like what, what kind ། ཁོ་མི་ཇི་འདྲ་ཞིག་ཡོད་པ་རེད་ What is he like as a person? ། མོ་ལ་ཁང་པ་ཇི་འདྲ་ཞིག་འདུག What kind of a house does she have?

ཇི་ནུས་ (ji nüü) as much as possible, to the utmost ། ཁོང་གིས་རོགས་རམ་ཇི་ནུས་བྱས་ནས་ང་ཚོར་ཕན་ཐོགས་ཆེན་པོ་བྱུང་ We got as much benefit/ assistance as possible.

ཇི་བྱེད་ (jiceè) whatever is done ། ངས་ལས་ཀ་ཇི་བྱེད་སྐྱོན་བརྗོད་བཏང་སོང་ (They) criticized whatever work I did.

ཇི་མ་ཇི་བཞིན་ (jimə jishin) exact, exactly the same, just like ། ཕྲུ་གུ་དེ་ཕ་ཇི་མ་ཇི་བཞིན་ཞིག་འདུག The child is just like his father. 2. in (real) detail. 3. whatever is.

ཇི་ཕྱིར་ (jicir) sm. ཇི་ཆེད་.

ཇི་མི་སྙམ་པར་ (jimi ñāmbar) unconcerned, indifferent, without thought of consequences, having no cares; va.—སྡོད་; —གནས་ ། དཀའ་ངལ་གྱི་མདུན་དུ་ཁོང་ཇི་མི་སྙམ་པར་གནས་པ་རེད་ He remained unconcerned when facing difficulties.

ཇི་ཙམ་ (jidzam) how much, how many, however much/ many ། ཁོ་ལ་ས་ཞིང་ཇི་ཙམ་ཡོད་པ་རེད་ How much land does he have? ། ཁྱེད་རང་ལ་ཕྱག་དེབ་ཇི་ཙམ་ཡོད་ How many books do you have? ། ཁོ་ལ་མ་རྩ་ཇི་ཙམ་ཡོད་པ་ཤོར་པ་རེད་ He lost however much (whatever) capital he had. 2. (— + vb. + པ་/ བ་ + དེ་ཙམ་) however much ... that much ། དཔེ་ཆ་ཇི་ཙམ་ཀློག་པ་དེ་ཙམ་ཤེས་ཀྱི་རེད་ However much (you) read, that much (you) will learn.

ཇི་ཙུག (jidzug) sm. གང་འདྲ་.

ཇི་ཞིག (jishig) how is it.

ཇི་བཞིན་ (jishin) sm. ཇི་ལྟར་.

ཇི་བཞིན་དུ་ (jishindu) as it is, identical ། ཁོང་གིས་སྟག་གི་གཟུགས་བརྙན་ཇི་བཞིན་དུ་བྲིས་འདུག He drew the image of the tiger identically.

ཇི་བཞིན་མ་བྱུང་བ་ (jishin məjuŋwə) not exactly like something is/ was supposed to be.

ཇི་འོས་ (jiwöö) whatever is appropriate/ fitting, whatever is right/ best ། དེ་སྐོར་ཇི་འོས་བསམ་བློ་གཏོང་གི་ཡིན་ I shall think about whatever is appropriate for that.

ཇི་ཡང་རུང་ (jiyaŋ ruŋ) anything will be okay.

ཇི་ཡོད་ (jiyöö) all, whatever there is.

ཇི་རིགས་པ་ (jirigbə) sm. ཅི་རིགས་པ་.

ཇི་རོབ་ (jirob) arc. sm. ཇི་ཆེད་.

ཇི་ལེགས་ (jileg) as good as possible.

ཇི་སོང་གཞུང་གཏོང་ (jisoŋ shuŋdoŋ) being reimbursed by the government for what was spent.

ཇི་སོང་རྩིས་དག་ཞུ་བ་ (jisoŋ dziidag shuwə) reimbursing for what was spent.

ཇི་སྲིད་ (jisii) as long as, however long ། ཇི་སྲིད་ཁྱེད་བཞུགས་པའི་བར་ As long as you live. ། ཇི་སྲིད་ལས་ཀ་མ་ཚར་བར་དུ་དེ་སྲིད་ཡར་རྒྱས་འགྲོ་གི་མ་རེད་ So long as the work is not finished there will be no development.

ཇི་སྲིད་ཉི་ཟླའི་འགྲོད་པ་མ་ནུབ་བར་ (jisii ñində drööba manubbar) shung. forever ། ཇི་སྲིད་ཉི་ཟླའི་འགྲོད་པ་མ་ནུབ་བར་ཁྲ་དོན་འདི་རང་ལ་སོར་གནས་རྒྱུན་འཁྱོངས་དགོས་རྒྱུ་ You all must abide by this verdict forever. [Lit. until the motion of the sun and moon stops].

ཇི་སྲིད་དེ་སྲིད་ (jisii tesii) doing sth. until it is done/ finished/ completed ། ཇི་སྲིད་རྒྱལ་ཁ་མ་འཐོབ་བར་དུ་དེ་སྲིད་འཐབ་འཛིང་བྱ་རྒྱུ་ཡིན་ We will fight until we are victorious.

ཇི་སྲིད་བདེ་འཁོད་ཡོང་བ་ (jisii degöö yoŋwa) to be peaceful and calm forever.

ཇི་སྲིད་ནམ་གནས་བར་ (jisii namnεèbar) shung. forever, however long ། ཇི་སྲིད་ནམ་གནས་བར་དཔའ་བོའི་མཚན་སྙན་རྒྱུན་འཇགས་སུ་གནས་རྒྱུ་ The reputation of the hero will last forever.

ཇི་སྲིད་བར་དུ་ (jisii pardu) however long ། སྐྱོན་མེད་གྲོགས་པོ་ནི་ཇི་སྲིད་བར་དུ་རྙེད་མི་སྲིད་ It is not possible to find a friend who has no faults however long (you look).

ཇི་སྲིད་འཚོ་བའི་བར་ (jisii tsōwɛ par) from birth to death.

ཇིང་གེར་ཀན་ (jiŋgee kan) Genghis Khan.

ཇིང་གེར་རྒྱལ་པོ་ (jiŋgee gyɛɛbo) Genghis Khan.

ཇིན་ཚལ་ (jindzɛɛ) ch. celery.

ཇའི་ལུད་ (jɛlüü) potash fertilizer.

ཇུ་དིག (judig) a type of divination done by Bon practitioners.

ཇུ་ཐིག (judig) sm. ཇུ་དིག.

ཇུ་པོ་ (juwo) 1. a mortar made from stone. 2. a stone, rock.

ཇུན་གར་ (juŋgar) Dzungar Mongols.

ཇུན་གར་དུས་ཟིང་ (juŋgar tüüsiŋ) shung. the Dzungar Disturbance (of 1717-18).

ཇུན་ཝང་ (junwaŋ) ch. head of a district/ area, king.

ཇུས་ (jüǜ) 1. strategy, policy, scheme, va.—གཏོང་; —འདིང་; —འདོན་ to plan, to lay out or come up with a strategy/ plan. 2. (vb.+ — + བྱེད་) to plan/ intend to do the verbal action ¶ སྡུག་བསྔལ་འབའ་ཞིག་ལ་གཏོང་ཇུས་བྱེད་ཀྱི་ཡོད་པ་རེད་ (They) plan to make only misery. 3. a type of brocade made with gold thread.

ཇུས་འཁྲི་ (jüǜdri) poking one's nose into other people's affairs, meddling in other's business, not minding one's own business; va.—བྱེད་.

ཇུས་བཀོད་ (jüǜgöö) p. of ཇུས་འགོད་.

ཇུས་བཀོད་པ་ (jüǜgööba) sm. ཇུས་འགོད་པ་.

ཇུས་སྐུལ་ (jüǜgüü) sm. ཇུས་གཏོང་.

ཇུས་མཁས་པོ་ (jüǜ kɛɛbo) crafty, ingenious, clever (with regard to planning/ strategizing).

ཇུས་མཁས་སྤྱོད་གཙང་ (jüǜkɛɛ jöödzaŋ) good at strategy and honest/upright in behavior.

ཇུས་རྒོལ་ (jüǜgöö) strategic attack; va.—བྱེད་.

ཇུས་འགོད་ (jüǜgöö) planning, making/ designing/ laying out strategies; va.—བྱེད་ to plan, to design/ laying out strategies/ policies ¶ དམག་འཁྲུག་རྒྱ་ཆེ་རུ་གཏོང་རྒྱུའི་ཇུས་འགོད་ Planning for expanding the war. ¶ མི་མང་གི་བསམ་འཆར་ལྟར་ཇུས་འགོད་བྱས་པ་རེད་ (They) designed it according to the people's suggestions.

ཇུས་འགོད་ཀྱི་དཔེ་རིས་ (jüǜgöögi bērii) model design/ drawing.

ཇུས་འགོད་ཁང་ (jüǜgöögi) a planning/ designing office.

ཇུས་འགོད་སྡེ་ཁག (jüǜgöö degaà) planning/ designing unit.

ཇུས་འགོད་པ་ (jüǜgööba) strategist, idea man, planner.

ཇུས་འགོད་བྱེད་སྟངས་ (jüǜgöö cedaŋ) designing stages, planning process.

ཇུས་འགོད་བློ་འདོན་ (jüǜgöö löndön) making strategy/ plans and giving expert advice.

ཇུས་འགོད་ཡོའན་ (jüǜgöö yoan) tib.ch. 1. planning bureau/ ministry. 2. sm. ཇུས་འགོད་ཁང་.

ཇུས་འགོད་ཞིབ་འཇུག་ཁང་ (jüǜgöö shimjuùgaŋ) institute of design.

ཇུས་འགོད་རིག་པ་ (jüǜgöö rigbə) operational studies/ science, planning studies/ research.

ཇུས་འགྲོ་ (jündro) successful (for strategies, plans, etc.).

ཇུས་ངན་ (jüǜŋɛn) bad or evil plan/ scheme/ plot; va.—བྱེད་.

ཇུས་ངན་ལམ་ལྷོངས་ (jüǜŋɛn lāmlhoŋ) successful in carrying out an evil plan/ plot.

ཇུས་ཆ་ (jüǜja) sm. ཇུས་.

ཇུས་ཆེན་ (jüǜjen) great scheme, big strategy, important plan.

ཇུས་ཉེས་ (jüǜñeè) 1. an unfortunate/ unlucky event, a tragedy, a mishap; vi.—ཕོག་ས་ ¶ སྐབས་དེར་སྐུ་བཙར་ཐུབ་བསྟན་ཀུན་འཕེལ་ཕྱོགས་གཏོགས་དང་བཅས་པར་ལམ་སེང་ཇུས་ཉེས་ཕོག་པ་རེད་ At that time the followers of Kunpela immediately came to misfortune. 2. a mistaken/ wrong/ bad strategy.

ཇུས་གདོགས་ (jüǜdɔɔ) intervention, meddling; interference; va.—བྱེད་.

ཇུས་གཏོང་ (jüǜ dōŋ) see ཇུས་.

ཇུས་ཐ་ (jüǜda) final plan.

ཇུས་ཐ་མ་ (jüǜ tāma) sm. ཇུས་ཐ་.

ཇུས་བདེ་ (jüǜde) simple method/ plan/ scheme.

ཇུས་འདིང་ (jüǜ diŋ) va. to make plans.

ཇུས་འདིང་གླིང་གི་ཐོག་ཁར་སླེབས་ (jüǜdiŋliŋgi tɔɔgaa lēè) vi. to come to a crisis/ dilemma and not know what to do [Lit. to arrive on the roof of the building called Chudingling].

ཇུས་འདོན་མཁན་ (jüǜ döŋgɛn) person who does planning.

ཇུས་འདོན་པ་ (jüǜ dömba) sm. ཇུས་འདོན་མཁན་.

ཇུས་འདྲི་ (jüǜndri) consulting; va.—བྱེད་ ¶ ཇུས་འདྲི་ཀུང་སི་ A consulting firm.

ཇུས་ནོར་ (jüǜnɔɔ) a mistaken or wrong strategy.

ཇུས་པ་ (jüǜbə) sm. ཇུས་འདོན་པ་

ཇུས་དཔོན་ (jüǜbön) the main planner, the head strategist.

ཇུས་མང་བཀོད་ཟབ་ (jüǜmaŋ göösəb) a careful plan with many strategies.

ཇུས་མེད་ཇུས་འཁྲི་ (jüǜmeè jüǜdri) uncalled for interference/ intervention, not minding one's own business, meddling into other's affairs; va.—བྱེད་ ¶ རྒྱ་དམར་གྱིས་ང་ཚོའི་ནང་སྲིད་ལ་ཇུས་མེད་ཇུས་འཁྲི་བྱེད་ཀྱི་འདུག (The) Chinese communists are meddling in our internal affairs.

ཇུས་མེད་ཇུས་གདོགས་ (jüǜmeè jüǜdɔɔ) sm. ཇུས་མེད་ཇུས་འཁྲི་.

ཇུས་རྩ་ (jüǜdza) shung. main root ¶ གཞུང་དགའ་ལྡན་ཕོ་བྲང་པའི་ཇུས་རྩ་བསིལ་ལྡན་གླིང་དགུའི་ཡ་གྱལ་གྱི་ཁམས་འདིར་ཚུགས་པ་ནས་བཟུང་ Since the main root of Ganden Photrang (the Tibetan government) was established in Tibet.

ཇུས་ཚོད་ (jüǜdzöö) controlling a plan/ scheme/ strategy.

ཇུས་འཚོལ་ (jüǜ tsöö) va. to look or search for a plan/ strategy.

ཇུས་གཞི་ (jüǜshi) plan, device, method; va.—འདོན་; —འདིང་; —སྒྲོར་ to plan, to make a plan/ strategy.

ཇུས་གཞི་མཉམ་འགོད་ (jüǜshi ñamgöö) joint planning/ strategizing.

ཇུས་གཞི་ཧྲིལ་པོ་ (jüǜshi hriìbu) complete plan or strategy.

ཇུས་ཟད་ཤུགས་རྫོགས་ (jüǜsɛè shūgdzɔɔ) at the end of one's wits/ resources [Lit. strategies worn out, strength exhausted].

ཇུས་བཟང་ (jüǜsaŋ) well planned, a good plan/ strategy.

ཇུས་བཟང་གཡུལ་རྒྱལ་ (jüǜsaŋ yüügyɛɛ) defeating one's opponent by a good strategy.

ཇུས་རབ་ (jüǜrəb) the best plan/ strategy.

ཇུས་ལ་ཇུས་ལན་ (jüǜla jüǜlɛn) a counter attack or counter response to sb.'s plot.

ཇུས་ལན་ཇུས་ཀྱིས་སློག (jüǜlen jüǜgi lɔɔ) va. to counter an opponent's strategy with one's own strategy.

ཇུས་ལེགས་ (jüǜleg) a good strategy/ plan.

ཇུས་སློབ་ (jüǜ lōb) va. to teach to plan/ strategize.

ཇེ་ (je) 1. more: augmentive particle used in comparative constructions (usu. — + adj.) ¶ ཐོན་ཚད་ཇེ་མཐོར་འགྲོ་གི་ཡོད་པ་རེད་ The level of production is going higher (increasing). ¶ ཉིན་རེ་བཞིན་གནད་དོན་དེ་ཇེ་གསལ་དུ་ཕྱིན་པ་རེད་ Each day the matter became clearer. ¶ ཁོ་ཚོས་ཐོན་ཚད་སྔར་ལས་ཇེ་མཐོར་བཏང་བ་རེད་ They increased the production level so that it was higher than before. 2. (— + adj. + — + adj.) a. with འགྲོ་ and verbs of motion: expresses the idea of becoming more and more ¶ གནམ་གྲུ་དེ་ཇེ་མཐོ་ཇེ་མཐོར་ཕྱིན་པ་རེད་ The plane went higher and higher. b. with གཏོང་: to make more and more ¶ ཁོ་ཚོས་ཐོན་སྐྱེད་ཀྱི་སྤུས་ཚད་ཇེ་ཞན་ཇེ་སྡུག་ཏུ་བཏང་བ་རེད་ They worsened the quality of the product more and more. 3. (— + vb. + — + adj.) the more the verbal action was done, the more ... it became ཁོ་ཚོའི་ངན་རྫས་དེ་ཇེ་བཀབ་ཇེ་གསལ་དུ་འགྲོ་གི་ཡོད་པ་རེད་ Their evil intention is becoming more evident the more they conceal it.

ཇེ་བཀབ་ཇེ་གསལ་ (jegəb jesɛl) making more conspicuous/ apparent by trying to hiding or conceal.

ཇེ་ངན་ཇེ་སྡུག (jeŋɛn jeduù) becoming worse and worse.

ཇེ་ཉེ་ (jeñe) closer and closer ། རྒྱལ་ཁབ་གཉིས་ཀྱི་འབྲེལ་བ་ཇེ་ཉེར་ཕྱིན་པ་རེད་ The relations between the two countries became closer and closer.

ཇེ་ཆེར་ (jecer) bigger, greater; va.—གཏོང་ to make bigger/ greater; vi.—འགྲོ་ to get or become bigger/ greater ། སྟོབས་ཤུགས་ཇེ་ཆེར་འགྲོ་གི་ཡོད་པ་རེད་ (They) are becoming more powerful.

ཇེ་ཉམས་ (jeñam) shung. declining gradually ། དགེ་འདུན་བསྙེན་བཀུར་མཆོད་རྒྱུན་ཇེ་ཉམས་བྱུང་བ་ The continuation of offerings for the monks declined gradually (more and more).

ཇེ་མཐུ་ཇེ་མང་དུ་འགྲོ་ (jedu jemaŋdu dro) vi. to become more and more serious and widespread (e.g., a rumor).

ཇེ་མཐོར་ (jedɔr) higher, greater, more ། འགྲོ་སོང་ཇེ་མཐོར་ཕྱིན་སོང་ Expenses went higher.

ཇེ་སྡུག་ཇེ་ཞན་ (jedug jeshɛn) worse and worse; vi.—འགྱུར་ to become worse and worse.

ཇེ་ནི་རལ་ (jenirel) eng. military general.

ཇེ་ཞན་ཇེ་སྡུག (jeshɛn jedug) getting worse and worse.

ཇེ་ཤིག (jeshig) sm. རེ་ཤིག.

ཇེ་བཟང་ཇེ་ལེགས་ (jeleg) better and better.

ཇེ་རིང་ཇེ་རིང་ (jeriŋ jeriŋ) longer and longer, farther and farther.

ཇེ་ལེགས་ (jeleg) getting better.

ཇེ་ལོད་དུ་འགྲོ་ (jelöödu dro) getting worse and worse ། བར་ལམ་གསུས་པའི་ནད་གཞི་ཇེ་ལོད་དུ་སོང་བས་ལས་བཅར་ཞུ་མ་ཐུབ་པ་ Recently, because my sickness got worse, I could not go to work.

ཇེམ་ཙེ་ (jemdze) scissors; va.—གཅུག to cut with scissors.

ཇོ་ཇོ་ (cojo) 1. elder brother. 2. a term used to address a man slightly older than oneself.

ཇོ་ཁང་ (cogaŋ) 1. the Tsuglagang temple in Lhasa. 2. the chapel of the Jo statue in the Tsuglagang temple in Lhasa.

ཇོ་བོ་ (cowo) 1. nobleman, man of high rank 2. elder brother, elder male relative of the same generation. 3. the Buddha.

ཇོ་བོ་མཆེད་གཉིས་ (cowo cëëñii) the two famous statues of the Buddha —ཇོ་བོ་ཤཱཀྱ་མུ་ནེ་ in the Tsulhakang and ཇོ་བོ་མི་བསྐྱོད་རྡོ་རྗེ་ in the Ramoche.

ཇོ་བོ་རྗེ་ (cowo je) Atisha.

ཇོ་བོ་དབུ་སྐྲ་ (cowo ūdra) the willow tree just outside the Tsuglagang (that is said to have been planted by Queen Wenchen).

ཇོ་བོ་མི་བསྐྱོད་རྡོ་རྗེ་ (cowo migyöö dorje) the statue in the Ramoche temple of the Buddha brought to Tibet by Songtsen Gampo's Nepalese wife.

ཇོ་བོ་རིན་པོ་ཆེ་ (cowo rimboce) the ཤཱཀྱ་མུ་ནེ་ Buddha in the Jokang.

ཇོ་བོ་ཤཱཀྱ་མུ་ནེ་ (cowo shāgya muni) the Shakyamuni Buddha.

ཇོ་བོའི་དབུ་སྐྲ་ (cowö ūdra) sm. ཇོ་བོ་དབུ་སྐྲ་.

ཇོ་དྲེགས་ (codreg) two year old mule.

ཇོ་མོ་ (como) 1. noblewoman, woman of high rank. 2. goddess. 3. nun. 4. queen. 5. the consort of a lama.

ཇོ་མོ་མཁན་པོ་ (como kɛ̄mbo) abbess.

ཇོ་མོ་གངས་དཀར་རི་ (como kāŋgarri) Mt. Everest.

ཇོ་མོ་གངས་ཅན་རི་ (como gaŋjɛnri) sm. ཇོ་མོ་གངས་དཀར་རི་.

ཇོ་མོ་གླང་མ་ (como lāŋma) Mt. Everest.

ཇོ་མོ་ལྷ་རི་ (como lhāri) Mt. Chomolhari (near Phari).

ཇོ་རྩི་ (codzi) varnish, lacquer.

ཇོ་རྩི་གསེར་ཤོག (codzi sērshɔɔ̀) varnish and golden foil.

ཇོ་ཞྭ་ (cosha) hat worn by nuns.

ཇོ་བཟང་ (josaŋ) kind, considerate (with a slightly negative connotation of being naive/ simple and unable to distinguish what is good and what is bad).

ཇོ་ལགས་ (colaà) 1. elder brother, elder male relative of the same generation. 2. shung. a term used for lower ranking clerks in the traditional Tibetan Government (a category lower than full lay government officials).

ཇོ་ལོས་པོ་ (co löökbo) sm. ཇོ་བཟང་.

ཇོ་ཤཱཀྱ་རྣམ་གཉིས་ (cosha nāmñii) sm. ཇོ་བོ་མཆེད་གཉིས་.

ཇོ་ཤཱཀྱ་རྣམ་གསུམ་ (cosha nāmsum) 1. the two main statues of the Buddha in the Ramoche and Tsuklhakhang temples (ཇོ་བོ་ཤཱཀྱ་མུ་ནེ་ and ཇོ་བོ་མི་བསྐྱོད་རྡོ་རྗེ་) and the statue of Avaloketisvara in the Potala. 2. the three statues of the Buddha in the Ramoche and Tsuklhakhang temples (ཇོ་བོ་ཤཱཀྱ་མུ་ནེ་, ཇོ་བོ་མི་བསྐྱོད་རྡོ་རྗེ་ and འཕགས་པ་ཐུགས་རྗེ་ཆེན་པོ་).

ཇོ་ཤག (coshaà) abbr. of ཇོ་བོ་ཤཱཀྱ་མུ་ནེ་.

ཇོར་དཱན་ (jɔrdɛn) Jordan.

མཇལ་; p. **མཇལ་**; f. **མཇལ་**; imp. **མཇོལ་** (jɛɛ) va. to meet, to see, to call on (h.) ། སང་ཉིན་མཇལ་གྱི་ཡིན་ (I) will meet (you) tomorrow. ། ཁོ་གཉིས་སྔོན་དུ་མཇལ་ཡོད་མ་རེད་ Those (two) haven't met before.

མཇལ་སྐལ་ (jɛɛgɛɛ) the karma to meet sb.

མཇལ་སྐོར་ (jɛɛgɔɔ) going around to visit monasteries/ temples, going to visit religious sites and do circumambulation.

མཇལ་ཁ་ (jɛɛga) an audience (h.); va.—གཏོང་; —གནང་ to grant an audience, to give an audience; va.—ཞུ་ to seek/ have an audience; va.—བཅར་ to go to have an audience ། ཕྱི་རྒྱལ་ནས་ཡོང་བའི་མི་ཚོགས་ཤིག་ལ་མཇལ་ཁ་གནང་པ་རེད་ (He) gave an audience to a group of people from abroad. ། བླ་མའི་མཇལ་ཁ་ཞུས་པ་ཡིན་ (We) had an audience with the lama.

མཇལ་ཁ་ཞུས་པ་གནང་ (jɛɛga süübə nāŋ) va. to seek an audience (h.).

མཇལ་ཁར་འབོད་ (jɛɛgar böö) va. to summon for an audience.

མཇལ་ཁྲིག (jɛɛdrig) arranging a line of audience seekers filing by a lama; va.—བྱེད་.

མཇལ་བཅར་ (jɛɛjaa) audience, visit to a superior (h.); va.—གནང་; —ཞུ་ to go for an audience, to pay a visit to a superior.

མཇལ་རྟེན་ (jɛɛden) present or gift presented when seeing/ meeting/ visiting a person (h.); va.—འབུལ་ to present or give a gift on seeing/ meeting/ visiting a person.

མཇལ་དར་ (jɛɛdar) Tibetan ceremonial scarf (h.); va.—སྔོན་; —འབུལ་ to present/ give a ceremonial scarf.

མཇལ་དར་སྣེ་སྤྲོད་ (jɛɛdar nēdröö) offering ceremonial scarves when people first meet one another.

མཇལ་དར་ལ་གཏོར་ (jɛɛdarla jɔɔ) sm. མཇལ་དར་ལ་བཅར་.

མཇལ་དར་ལ་བཅར་ (jɛɛdarla jāā) va. to go to give a ceremonial scarf.

མཇལ་དུམ་ (jɛɛdum) sm. མཇལ་འདུམ་.

མཇལ་གདན་ (jɛɛdɛn) cushion put down for people seeking audiences.

མཇལ་གནང་ (jɛɛnaŋ) va. to meet (h.).

མཇལ་འདུམ་ (jɛndum) face-to-face negotiating/ mediating; va.—བྱེད.

མཇལ་སྣ་ (jɛɛna) a go-between.

མཇལ་སྤྲོ་པོ་ (jɛɛ drōbo) pleasant to the eyes.

མཇལ་ཕྱག (jɛɛjaà) prostrating when getting an audience with a lama or ruler; va.—འབུལ་.

མཇལ་འཕྲད་ (jɛɛdrɛɛ̀) meeting (h.); va.— གནང་; —ཞུ་ to meet, to visit ¶ སྲིད་འཛིན་མཆོག་དང་མཇལ་འཕྲད་གནང་བ་རེད་ (They) met the president.

མཇལ་འཕྲད་ཁང་ (jɛɛdrɛɛ̀gaŋ) meeting room, reception room.

མཇལ་བག་སྒྲོ་པོ་ (jɛɛbaà drōbo) 1. sm. མཇལ་སྒྲོ་པོ་. 2. term used with reference to females who are plump and personable—has the slightly negative connotation of being not very pretty.

མཇལ་བར་ཞུ་ (jɛɛwar shu) va. to request an audience (h.).

མཇལ་མང་ (jɛɛmaŋ) an audience for a large group/ crowd, public audience.

མཇལ་མོལ་ (jɛɛmöö) meeting and discussing.

མཇལ་དམངས་ (jɛɛmaŋ) sm. མཇལ་མང་.

མཇལ་ཞུ་ (jɛɛshu) 1. calling on sb. of higher status to pay respects (h.); va.—ཞུ་ to call on to pay respects. 2. sm. མཇལ་རྟེན་.

མཇལ་ཡིག་མཛོད་གསུམ་ (jɛɛyii dzöösum) shung. abbr. the three: steward (མགྲོན་གཉེར་), secretary (དྲུང་ཡིག་), manager (ཕྱག་མཛོད་) of labrang and aristocratic families.

མཇལ་ལན་ (jɛɛlɛn) return visit or call; va.—བྱེད་; —གནང་; —ཞུ་.

མཇལ་སློག (jɛɛlɔɔ̀) a superior returning a gift brought by someone who has come for an audience; va.—བྱེད་; —གནང་; —ཞུ་.

མཇིང་ (jiŋ) sm. འཇིངས་.

མཇིང་ཀོང་ (jiŋgoŋ) a small indentation at the back of the neck.

མཇིང་བསྐོར་གདོང་ (jiŋgɔɔ dōŋ) va. to go with one's arm around the shoulder of another.

མཇིང་ཉག (jiŋñag) back of the neck.

མཇིང་པ་ (jiŋbə) neck; vi.—མཁྲང་ to be spoiled/ willful/ obstinate/ defiant.

མཇིང་པ་མཁྲང་པོ་ (jiŋbə trāŋbo) sm. མཇིང་པ་སྦོམ་པོ་.

མཇིང་པ་མཁྲེགས་པོ་ (jiŋbə trāgbo) sm. མཇིང་པ་སྦོམ་པོ་.

མཇིང་པ་སློད་ (jiŋbə lǒö) vi. to hang one's head down.

མཇིང་པ་སྲིང་ (jiŋbə dreŋ) va. to straighten one's neck.

མཇིང་པ་འཆུ་ (jiŋbə cū) vi. to sprain the neck.

མཇིང་པ་བརྟན་ (jiŋbə dɛn) va. to be hardheaded/ stubborn ¶ ཁྲལ་བསྡུ་དུས་མཇིང་པ་བརྟན་ཙང་གང་ཡང་སྤྲོད་དགོས་བྱུང་མ་སོང་ When taxes were being collected, because he was hardheaded he did not have to pay anything.

མཇིང་པ་བསྣར་ (jiŋbə nār) va. to work hard [Lit. to stretch one's neck].

མཇིང་པ་སྦོམ་པོ་ (jiŋbə bombo) rude, impolite, defiant, insolent, willful, obstinate.

མཇིང་པའི་རྩ་ལེབ་ (jiŋbɛ cūleb) muscle at the back of the neck.

མཇིང་པར་བཞོན་ (jiŋbar shön) va. to boss, to take advantage of (someone's inability/ weakness), to ride roughshod over [Lit. to ride on someone's neck].

མཇིང་སྦྲེལ་ (jiŋdree) putting/ fixing two (animals) together for plowing; va.—བྱེད་; —གཏོང་

མཇིང་ཚིགས་ (jiŋdzig) cervical vertebra; vi.—འཆུས་ to get a stiff neck, to twist one's neck.

མཇིང་ཡོན་ (jiŋyön) crooked/ bent neck.

མཇུག (juù) the end, the last ¶ ཟླ་བ་འདིའི་མཇུག་ལ་ At the end of this month. ¶ ལོ་མཇུག The end of the year.

མཇུག་སྐྱེལ་ (jug gyēē) va. to complete/ finish.

མཇུག་སྐྱོང་ (juggyoŋ) 1. looking after a person (until death), seeing a responsibility/ job through until it is finished, completing a task/ job; va.—བྱེད་ ¶ ཁོས་ཨ་མར་མཇུག་སྐྱོང་ཡག་པོ་བྱས་སོང་ He looked after his mother well (until her death). ¶ ལས་ཀ་འདིའི་སྐོར་མཇུག་སྐྱོང་གྲོས་མོལ་བྱེད་རྒྱུ་ལྷ་སར་རང་ལ་བྱེད་དགོས Concerning this job, we have to bring it to completion by having continuing talks in Lhasa itself. 2. sm. མཇུག་འགྲིལ་.

མཇུག་བསྐྱངས་ (jug gyāŋ) p. of མཇུག་སྐྱོང་.

མཇུག་ཁྲུན་ཆོད་ (jugdrün cöö) vi. to get wrapped up/ completed.

མཇུག་འཁྱོངས་ (juggyoŋ) completing, finishing; va.—བྱེད་.

མཇུག་གུ་ (juggu) end, last, final; va.—སྐྱེལ་ to finish, to see to the end/ completion.

མཇུག་གྲངས་ (judraŋ) the last number.

མཇུག་འགྲིལ་ (jug drii) vi. to be able to wind up/ end/ conclude/ complete (work, meetings, etc.) ¶ ཚོགས་འདུ་འདི་རྒྱལ་ཁའི་ངང་ནས་མཇུག་འགྲིལ་བ་རེད་ The meeting ended victoriously. ¶ ཛ་དྲག་གི་རོགས་རམ་མཇུག་འགྲིལ་གྱི་ཡོད་པ་རེད་ (They) are winding up the emergency aid program. ¶ ངས་ཉམས་ཞིབ་ཀྱི་ལས་ཀ་དེ་ད་དུང་མཇུག་འགྲིལ་མ་སོང་ I am not able to conclude my research even now. 2. the end.

མཇུག་འགྲིལ་མེད་པ་ (jugdrii meèba) unfinished, incomplete.

མཇུག་སྒྲིག (jugdrig) concluding compiling sth; va.—བྱེད་ ¶ ཁོང་གིས་རྒྱལ་རབས་ཀྱི་མཇུག་སྒྲིག་གནང་བ་རེད་ ¶ He finished compiling the history.

མཇུག་སྒྲིལ་ (jug drii) va. to conclude, to complete.

མཇུག་སྒྲོ་ (jugdro) tail feathers.

མཇུག་སྒྲིལ་ (jugdröö) completion, graduation, termination.

མཇུག་གཅོད་ (jug jöö) va. to discontinue/ stop, to adjourn.

མཇུག་ཆ་ (jugja) sm. མཇུག་བརྗོད་.

མཇུག་བརྗོད་ (jugjöö) epilogue.

མཇུག་མཇུག (jugjuù) the last, the final one.

མཇུག་བསྙེགས་ (jug ñēg) va. to go after, to chase.

མཇུག་ཏུ་ (jugdu) at the end, behind, after.

མཇུག་རྟོ་ (jugdo) tail.

མཇུག་གཏོང་ལྷངས་འཁོར་ (jugdoŋ lāŋgɔɔ) last bus (of the day).

མཇུག་བརྡུལ་ (jug dǖǖ) sm. མཇུག་སྒྲིལ་.

མཇུག་ཐོགས་ (jugdɔɔ̀) as soon as, immediately.

མཇུག་ཐོན་ (jug tõn) vi. to have/ be completed/ finished.

མཇུག་མཐུད་ (jug tũũ) va. to join the ends of two things.

མཇུག་དུམ་ (jugdum) 1. short tail. 2. a short period.

མཇུག་དེད་ (jugdeè) pursuing, following; va.—བྱེད་.

མཇུག་གདངས་ (jugdaŋ) (in music) conclusion, end, finale.

མཇུག་གདན་ (jugdɛn) cushion.

མཇུག་རྡུམ་ (jugdum) changeable, fickle [Lit. short tail].

མཇུག་སྡུད་ (jūgdüü) finishing, concluding; va.—བྱེད་.

མཇུག་སྡོམ་ (jugdom) concluding, conclusion, closing (usu. of a speech or meeting); va.—རྒྱག; —བྱེད་ to conclude, to close ¶ ཚོགས་མི་ཚོར་ཐུགས་རྗེ་ཆེ་ཞུའི་གསུང་བཤད་དང་བཅས་ཚོགས་འདུ་འདི་མཇུག་སྡོམ་བྱས་པ་རེད་ They concluded the meeting with a note of thanks to the delegates.

མཇུག་སྡོམ་སྙན་ཞུ་ (jugdom ñɛ̄nshu) final report, year-end report.

མཇུག་བསྡུ་ (jugdu) concluding, completing, finishing, closing; va.—རྒྱག; —བྱེད་ to conclude, to close ¶ མཇུག་བསྡུའི་གཏམ་ Closing speech. ¶ མཇུག་བསྡུའི་མཛད་སྒོ་ Closing ceremony. ¶ ངས་ལས་ཀའི་མཇུག་བསྡུས་པ་ཡིན་ I concluded my work.

མཇུག་བསྡུས་ (jugdüü) p. of མཇུག་བསྡུ་.

མཇུག་བསྡོགས་ (jugdoò) sm. མཇུག་སྒྲིལ་

མཇུག་བསྡོམས་ (jugdom) p. of མཇུག་སྡོམ་.

མཇུག་ནག (jugnag) black tail.

མཇུག་གནས་ (jugnɛɛ̀) terminal point/ destination, the last ¶ མཇུག་གནས་གྲངས་ཀ་ The last of a series of numbers.

མཇུག་གནོན་ (jugnön) keeping going, continuing; va.—བྱེད་ to continue, to keep going.

མཇུག་གནོན་རྒྱབ་གཉེར་ (jugnön gyəbñer) helping/ supporting/ assisting to continue (to function/

operate).

མཇུག་གཉོན་དོ་དམ་ (jugnön todam) shung. continuing to take care of/ look after sth. ༈ སྔོན་གཏན་འཁེལ་བའི་ལས་གཞིའི་མཇུག་གཉོན་དོ་དམ་སྐྱོང་མེད་དགོས་རྒྱུ་ One should continue to take care of the project that has been decided on earlier.

མཇུག་སྣེ་ (jugne) the tail end, the end of sth. or someplace ༈ སྐུད་པའི་མཇུག་སྣེ་ The end of the thread. ༈ མཇུག་སྣེའི་དབང་རྩ་ Nerve ending.

མཇུག་སྙོན་ (jugnön) sm. མཇུག་གཉོན་.

མཇུག་སྤོང་ཅན་ (jug pōŋjɛn) comet.

མཇུག་སྤོད་ (jugböö) the tail hair of livestock.

མཇུག་འཕྲོ་ (juŋdro) sth. unfinished, leftover; va.—སྒྲིལ་ to finish or conclude sth. that is unfinished/ leftover/ remaining ༈ ལས་ཀའི་མཇུག་འཕྲོ་ Unfinished work.

མཇུག་བྱང་ (jugjaŋ) final/ concluding section of a book, postscript.

མཇུག་དབྱངས་ (jugyaŋ) sm. མཇུག་གདངས་.

མཇུག་འབྲས་ (juŋdrɛɛ̀) final result, final outcome ༈ མཇུག་འབྲས་མི་བཟང་ A bad final result.

མཇུག་མ་ (jugmə) 1. a tail. 2. the last part of sth., the final/ end part ༈ གློག་བརྙན་དེའི་མཇུག་མ་མཐོང་མ་བྱུང་ (We) did not see the last part of the movie. 3. the one at the end, the last one ༈ ཁོ་གྲལ་གྱི་མཇུག་མ་དེ་རེད་ He is the one at the end of the row.

མཇུག་མ་བཀྱག (jugmə gyāà) va. to lift one's tail.

མཇུག་མ་སྒྲིལ་ (jug ma drii) va. to not finish.

མཇུག་མ་གཅོད་ (jugmə jöö) 1. va. to cut off a tail. 2. va. to decide sth. without looking carefully at the real situation.

མཇུག་མ་ནར་ (jugmə nar) vi. to be delayed.

མཇུག་མ་སྣར་ (jugmə nār) va. to delay.

མཇུག་མའི་རིང་ལུགས་ (jugmɛ riŋluù) backwardism; having no desire to advance, wanting to remain backward.

མཇུག་རྩིས་ (jugdzii) final accounting, final balance sheet; va.—རྒྱག.

མཇུག་རྩེ་ (jugdze) the end of a tail (of an animal).

མཇུག་ཚགས་ (jugdzaà) shung. concluding; va.—བྱེད་.

མཇུག་ཚན་ (jugdzɛn) final stage, end, last item.

མཇུག་མཚམས་ (juŋdzam) the end of ༈ ཟླ་ ༣ མཇུག་མཚམས་སུ་ At the end of the third month.

མཇུག་རྫོགས་ (jug dzɔɔ̀) vi. to end, to finish, to be over ༈ གློག་བརྙན་མཇུག་རྫོགས་སྐབས་ When the movie was over.

མཇུག་རྫོགས་ས་ (jug dzɔɔ̀sa) sm. མཇུག་གནས་.

མཇུག་འཛིན་ (juŋdzin) eclipse of the moon.

མཇུག་གཞུང་ (jugshuŋ) postscript.

མཇུག་ཟིན་ (jug sin) va. to catch up to.

མཇུག་ཟིམ་ (jug sim) sm. མཇུག་ཟིན་.

མཇུག་གཟེང་ (jugseŋ) the tail of an animal in an upright position and shaking.

མཇུག་རིང་ (jugriŋ) 1. comet. 2. long tail.

མཇུག་རུས་ (jugrüù) tail bone.

མཇུག་ཤོས་ (jugshöö) the very last/ end, the last of all.

མཇུག་སུག (jugsug) 1. hem (of a dress). 2. way/ style of dressing.

མཇུག་སྲིན་ (jugsin) hemorrhoids.

མཇེ་ (je) penis (h.); vi.—ལང་ to have an erection.

མཇེ་སྔེག (jelig) penis and scrotum.

མཇེ་ཤུབས་ (jeshub) prophylactic, contraceptive, rubber.

མཇེད་ (jeè) bothering, annoying.

མཇོར་ (jɔr) sm. འཇོར་.

མཇོར་བུ་ (jɔrbu) sm. འཇོར་བུ་.

མཇོལ་ (jöö) imp. of མཇལ་.

འཇག (jag) abbr. of འཇག་མ་.

འཇག་སྐྱ་ (jaggya) sm. འཇག་མ་.

འཇག་སྐྱ་འཕྱུར་བ་བཞིན་ (jaggya) completely destroyed [Lit. like cogon grass floating up (after being trampled)].

འཇག་ཁང་ (jaggaŋ) thatch hut.

འཇག་གི་འཇིག་གི་ (jəgi jigi) unclear/ muddy (usu. for liquids).

འཇག་གོད་ (jaggöö) hard/ stiff cogon grass.

འཇག་འཇིག (jəgjig) abbr. of འཇག་གི་འཇིག་གི.

འཇག་གདན་ (jagdɛn) cogon grass cushion/ mat.

འཇག་སྤྱིལ་ (jagjil) thatch hut.

འཇག་ཕོན་ (jagbön) pile of cogon grass.

འཇག་ཕྱགས་ (jagjaà) broom made of cogon grass.

འཇག་མ་ (jaàma) 1. a thin grass (cogon— (imperata cylindrica) used to make brooms and thatching. 2. shovel, spade; va.—རྒྱག to shovel.

འཇག་ཞྭ་ཉི་ཁེབས་ (jagsha ñigeb) a large straw hat (made from cogon grass) used for protection against the sun.

འཇགས་ (jaà) 1. vi. to be/ get calmed down, to be quelled, to settle down, to become quite/ peaceful/ tranquil ༈ ཟིང་འཁྲུག་རིམ་པས་འཇགས་རེ་ཡོད་ (We) hope the unrest will gradually settle down. 2. vi. to remain (in the mind), to remember, to stay with ༈ ཁྱེད་རང་གིས་གསུངས་པ་ངའི་སེམས་ལ་འཇགས་མ་སོང་ I don't remember what you said. ༈ སོ་སོས་སློབ་སྦྱོང་བྱས་ན་ཡོན་ཏན་སོ་སོར་འཇགས་ཀྱི་རེད་ If you study knowledge will remain with you. 3. honorific particle ༈ བཞུགས་གདན་འཇགས་ Please sit down (h.). 4. vi. to remain unchanged.

འཇགས་ཁ་ལེན་པོ་ (jagga lembo) doing sth. in a calm and orderly way.

འཇགས་ཆེ་ (jagje) shung. calm, calming down ༈ ད་ལྟ་འཐབ་གཉིས་ཀར་འཇགས་ཆེ་བྱེད་དགོས་ At present, both sides should calm down.

འཇགས་ཉལ་ (jagñɛɛ) peaceful, calm, tranquil.

འཇགས་འཇགས་ (jagjaà) 1. patting on the shoulder to convey being friendly; va.—གཏོང་ ༈ ཁོང་གིས་ངའི་དཔུང་པར་འཇགས་འཇགས་བཏང་ནས་སློབ་གསོ་བཏང་བྱུང་ He patted me on my shoulder when he gave me advice (conveys advice from high to low, old to young). 2. straightening hair that has become disheveled; va.—གཏོང་ ༈ རང་སྐྲ་ཟིངས་འདུག་པས་མགོ་འཇགས་འཇགས་གཏོང་དགོས་ Because your hair is disheveled you should straighten it out. 3. scolding/ yelling at one's employees, kids, etc.; va.—གཏོང་ ༈ དེ་ཙམ་འཇགས་འཇགས་མ་བཏང་ན་ནང་ཉམས་བྱེད་ཀྱི་རེད་ If (I) don't scold a little there will be disorder internally.

འཇགས་པོ་ (jagbo) pressed/ smoothed down.

འཇང་ (jaŋ) area in eastern Tibet (in Yunnan Province).

འཇང་ (jaŋ) 1. vi. to have diarrhea. 2. f. of འཇོང་. 3. va. to eat, to drink.

འཇང་དགུན་ཆོས་ (jaŋ günjöö) a place southwest of Lhasa where monks gather to debate on religious philosophy during the winter.

འཇང་ངེ་འཇོང་ངེ་ (jaŋŋe joŋŋe) oblong.

འཇང་འཇོང་ (jaŋjoŋ) abbr. of འཇང་ངེ་འཇོང་ངེ་.

འཇང་པ་ (jaŋba) a person from འཇང་.

འཇང་ཡུལ་ (jaŋyüü) the region of འཇང་.

འཇངས་ (jaŋ) p. of འཇོང་.

འཇད་པ་སྡེ་པ་ (jɛɛ̀ba deba) shung. title of the head of the Thongmonling estate of the Panchen Lama in tt.

འཇབ་: p. **འཇབས་**; f. **འཇབ་**; imp. **འཇོབས་** (jəb) va. to hide, to lie in wait/ ambush, to go to do sth. stealthily ༈ ཁོ་ཚོས་ས་འོག་ཏུ་འཇབས་པ་རེད་ They hid underground.

འཇབ་དཀྲུགས་ (jəbdruù) infiltrating and causing trouble/ disturbances.

འཇབ་རྐུན་ (jəbgün) thief.

འཇབ་ཁུང་ (jəbguŋ) trench, tunnel, hideout (in warfare or crime).

འཇབ་ཁྱི་ (jəbgyi) a dog that bites from behind; va.—རྒྱག to bite from behind (for dogs).

འཇབ་རྒོལ་ (jəbgöö) ambush, surprise attack, guerrilla attack; va.—བྱེད་.

འཇབ་སྒུག (jəbguù) waiting/ hiding in ambush; va.—བྱེད་.

འཇབ་སྒུག་དམག (jəbguù māg) guerrilla soldiers, guerrilla army.

འཇབ་སྒུག་དམག་འཐབ་ (jəbguù māgdəb) guerrilla warfare.

འཇབ་ལྗི་ (jəbje) sm. འཇབ་རྩེ་.

འཇབ་ཉན་ (jəbñɛn) listening surreptitiously/ secretly, bugging; va.—བྱེད་.

འཇབ་ལྟ་ (jəbda) peeping, spying; secretly looking at/ observing; va.—བྱེད་.

འཇབ་མདའ་ (jəmda) sniper-fire; va.—རྒྱག་; —འཕང་ to snipe at (with a gun).

འཇབ་དུང་ (jəbduŋ) sm. འཇབ་གྲོལ་.

འཇབ་བུ་ (jəbbu) sm. ཀུན་མ་.

འཇབ་བུ་བ་ (jəbbuwa) sm. ཀུན་མ་.

འཇབ་སྙུལ་ (jəbñul) spying, intelligence gathering; va.—བྱེད་.

འཇབ་སྙུལ་བ་ (jəbñulwa) spy, intelligence agent.

འཇབ་དམག (jəbmaà) 1. guerrilla warfare; va.—རྒྱག to engage in guerrilla warfare. 2. a guerrilla.

འཇབ་དམག་གི་འཐབ་འཁྲུག (jəbmaàgi təbdruù) guerrilla war, guerrilla warfare.

འཇབ་རྩེ་ (jəbdzi) tweezers.

འཇབ་རྩེ་ཁ་ (jəbdzeka) thin-lipped person.

འཇབ་ཚེ་ (jəbdzi) sm. འཇབ་རྩེ་.

འཇབ་འཛུལ་ (jəbdzüü) secret/ surreptitious infiltration; va.—བྱེད་.

འཇབ་གཡོལ་ (jəbyüü) hiding to avoid sth. or sb.

འཇབ་ལེན་ (jəblen) sm. འཇབ་ཀུན་.

འཇབས་ (jəb) p. of འཇབ་.

འཇམ་ (jam) 1. abbr. of འཇམ་པོ་. 2. soup, stew.

འཇམ་བཀག (jamgaà) house arrest, house detention.

འཇམ་བརྐོས་ (jamgöö) engraving, sculpturing.

འཇམ་སྐྱུགས་ (jəmgyuù) a liquid Tibetan medicine that induces vomiting.

འཇམ་ཁྲིག་གེ་ (jam triige) staying silently/ quietly/ calmly.

འཇམ་ཁྲིད་ (jam trii) taking or leading or bringing by gentle means such as coaxing/ cajoling/ persuading; va.—བྱེད་ to take/ bring sb. by noncoercive means such as coaxing/ cajoling/ persuading.

འཇམ་མཁས་ (jamgɛɛ̀) gentle/ mild and tactful.

འཇམ་མཁས་བསླུ་འདྲིད་ (jamgɛɛ̀ lūdrii) tricking by cajoling and flattery.

འཇམ་གོས་ (jamgöö) 1. silk and other soft materials/ clothing. 2. plain, designless cloth/ clothing.

འཇམ་གྲི་ (jəmdri) sm. གྲི་འཇམ་པོ་.

འཇམ་སྒྱུར་ (jəmgyur) changing/ reforming by gentle methods.

འཇམ་ཅག་གེ་བ་ (jam jāggewa) sm. འཇམ་ཆག་གེ་བ་.

འཇམ་ཆག་གེ་བ་ (jam cāgewa) sm. འཇམ་ཐིང་ཐིང་.

འཇམ་ཆར་ (jamjar) drizzle, light rain.

འཇམ་འཆགས་ (jamjaà) peaceful, calm, stable.

འཇམ་ཇུས་ (jamjüü) gentle/ peaceful/ mild tactics or plans or strategies.

འཇམ་འཇམ་ (jamjam) sm. འཇམ་པོ་.

འཇམ་ཉམས་ (jamñam) 1. a peaceful look/ countenance. 2. pretending to be generous/ good/ kind.

འཇམ་མཉེན་ (jamñen) smooth and flexible, soft and smooth.

འཇམ་མཉེན་འོད་ལྡན་ (jamñen wöndɛn) smooth and shiny.

འཇམ་བདགས་ (jamdaà) sm. འཇམ་དར་.

འཇམ་ཐབས་ (jamtəb) peaceful/ gentle/ noncoercive means; va.—བྱེད་.

འཇམ་ཐིང་ (jamdiŋ) sm. འཇམ་ཐིང་ཐིང་.

འཇམ་ཐིང་ངེ་བ་ (jam tiŋŋewa) sm. འཇམ་ཐིང་ཐིང་.

འཇམ་ཐིང་ངེར་ (jam tiŋŋe) sm. འཇམ་ཐིང་ཐིང་.

འཇམ་ཐིང་ཐིང་ (jam tiŋdiŋ) 1. extremely silent or quiet. 2. highly calm/ peaceful/ tranquil.

འཇམ་ཐུག (jəmduù) soup made from tsampa.

འཇམ་འཐབ་ (jamdəb) 1. peaceful struggle. 2. the Cold War.

འཇམ་དར་ (jamdar) 1. soft silk. 2. a type of white ceremonial scarf.

འཇམ་དལ་ (jamdɛɛ) calm and slow.

འཇམ་དུ་འགྲོ་ (jamdu dro) vi. to subside, to become more gentle in nature, to become soft (in texture) ¶ ཨ་མི་རྒོལ་འཐབ་རྩོད་དེ་བར་སྐབས་ཤིག་ལ་ཡང་བསྐྱར་འཇམ་དུ་ཕྱིན་པ་རེད་ For the time being, the anti-U.S. struggle has again subsided.

འཇམ་དོད་ (jamdöö) shung. land given for setting up a trust to serve stew in the monastery ¶ སོན་ཁལ་ ༢༠ འགྲོ་བའི་ས་འཇམ་དོད་དུ་ཕུལ་ཚུལ་ It was said land that takes 20 ke of seed was offered for serving stew (to the monks).

འཇམ་གདན་ (jamdɛn) soft mattress.

འཇམ་འདུལ་ (jamdüü) overpowering/ vanquishing by gentle means; va.—བྱེད་.

འཇམ་དྲི་ (jamdri) questioning/ interrogating in a gentle manner; va.—བྱེད་.

འཇམ་འདྲེད་ (jamdreè) 1. smooth and slippery. 2. lubricated.

འཇམ་འདྲེད་སྣུམ་རྩི་ (jamdreè nūmdzi) skin lotion ¶ གདོང་ལ་བྱུག་བྱེད་འཇམ་འདྲེད་སྣུམ་རྩི་ Skin lotion to put on the face.

འཇམ་འདྲེད་བྱེད་རྫས་ (jamdreè cèèdzɛɛ̀) lubricating materials.

འཇམ་འདྲེད་བཟོ་བྱེད་སྣུམ་ (jamdreè sojeè nūm) lubricating oil.

འཇམ་འདྲེད་ཤ་སྒྲིམ་ (jamdreè shādrim) smooth muscle.

འཇམ་འདྲོང་བབ་གསེད་ (jamdroŋ bəbseè) clarifying/ clearing up sth. in a gentle or peaceful manner.

འཇམ་སྡོད་ (jamdöö) sitting quietly; va.—བྱེད་.

འཇམ་སྡོད་ངོམ་སྟོན་ (jamdöö ŋāmdön) a "sit-down" or "sit-in" demonstration.

འཇམ་རྡར་ (jamdar) smooth whetstone; va.—རྒྱག to sharpen a knife on a whetstone.

འཇམ་ནད་ (jamnɛɛ̀) hoof and mouth disease.

འཇམ་སྣུམ་ (jamnum) lubricating oil.

འཇམ་པོ་ (jambo) 1. soft, smooth. 2. gentle, mild.

འཇམ་པོ་བྱེད་ (jambo cee) va. to do or treat smoothly/ gently/ mildly.

འཇམ་པོས་མགོ་སྐོར་ (jamböö gogɔɔ) duping/ tricking/ deceiving/ conning by gentle or mild or smooth means.

འཇམ་པོས་རྩུབ་པོ་ཐུབ་ (jamböö dzūbu tūb) gentleness overcomes aggression.

འཇམ་དཔལ་ (jambɛɛ) 1. name of a person. 2. Manjushri.

འཇམ་དཔལ་རྒྱ་མཚོ་ (jambɛɛ gyadzo) the name of the 8th Dalai Lama (1758—1804).

འཇམ་དཔལ་དབྱངས་ (jambɛɛyaŋ) Manjushri.

འཇམ་དཔྱད་ (jamjɛɛ̀) gentle methods of Tibetan medical treatment, e.g., rubbing medicines on the body.

འཇམ་དཔྱད་རྩུབ་དཔྱད་ (jamjɛɛ̀ dzūbjɛɛ̀) gentle and harsh methods of Tibetan medical treatment.

འཇམ་ཕྲུག (jamdruù) a type of good quality Tibetan wool serge.

འཇམ་ཕྲུག་ཁྲེས་ (jamdruù trēè) shung. a load of Tibetan wooden serge.

འཇམ་བྱེད་ (jam jeè) sm. འཇམ་པོ་བྱེད་.

འཇམ་དབྱངས་ (jamyaŋ) abbr. of འཇམ་དཔལ་དབྱངས་.

འཇམ་དབུར་མདངས་འདོན་འཕྲུལ་འཁོར་ (jambur daŋdön trüügɔɔ) polishing machine.

འཇམ་འབྲས་ (jamdrɛɛ̀) gorgon fruit.

འཇམ་མོ་ (jammo) sm. འཇམ་པོ་.

འཇམ་རྩུབ་ (jamdzub) 1. soft/ smooth and coarse/ rough. 2. texture. 3. gentle and harsh.

འཇམ་རྩུབ་མགོ་སྒྲིལ་ (jamdzub gondree) sm. འཇམ་རྩུབ་སྦྲེལ་སྦྱོར་.

འཇམ་རྩུབ་མཉམ་སྦྱོར་ (jamdzub ñāmjöö) sm. འཇམ་རྩུབ་སྦྲེལ་སྦྱོར་.

འཇམ་རྩུབ་སྦྲེལ་སྦྱོར་ (jamdzub bēljöö) using both harsh and gentle methods.

འཇམ་རྩུབ་ཟུང་འདྲེག (jamdzub sunjuù) sm. འཇམ་རྩུབ་

སྤེལ་སྤྱོད་.

འཇམ་ཚག (jamdzaà) engraving; va.—རྒྱག.

འཇམ་མཛེས་ (jamdzeè) soft and beautiful.

འཇམ་ཞལ་ (jamshεε) shining/ polishing/ smoothing plaster; va.—རྒྱག་; —གཏོང་.

འཇམ་ཞུམ་མེ་ (jamzhume) sm. འཇམ་ཐིང་ངེ་.

འཇམ་འོད་ (jamwöö) 1. soft/ subdued light. 2. shine; va.—འདོན་ to polish/ shine.

འཇམ་འོད་འདོན་འཁོར་ (jamwöö döngɔɔ) a machine that polishes/ shines.

འཇམ་ཡུག (jamyug) abbr. of འཇམ་དར་ཡུག་ཅིག.

འཇམ་རོལ་ (jamröö) slow tempo tunes/ music.

འཇམ་རླུང་ (jamluŋ) soft/ gentle wind.

འཇམ་ལ་འདོམས་ (jamla dom) shung. gentle but strict, soft but tight ¶ ངན་པ་རྒྱ་ཡན་དུ་མ་ལུས་པར་ཆོས་ཁྲིམས་དར་གྱི་མདུད་པ་འཇམ་ལ་འདོམས་པའི་དཔེ་ལྟར་བཀོད་འདོམས་མཐར་ཕྱིན་དགོས་རྒྱུ་ One should not let evil people evade punishment. They should be controlled under the religious law which, like the saying, is like a silk knot, gentle but strict.

འཇམ་ཤ་དོད་པོ་ (jamsha tööbo) soft, smooth.

འཇམ་ཤིག་ཤིག (jam shīgshiì) soft, smooth.

འཇམ་ཤུགས་ཤུགས་ (jam shūgshuù) quietly.

འཇམ་ཤུར་སློད་ (jam shur lȫö) vi. to slip on a smooth surface.

འཇམ་ཤོག (jamshoò) tissue paper.

འཇམ་གཤེར་འདྲེད་རྫས་ (jamsher dreèdzεὲ) lubricating materials, lubricants.

འཇམ་བཤད་ (jamshεὲ) talking gently/ smoothly/ softly; va.—བྱེད་.

འཇམ་བཤད་བློ་འགུགས་ (jamshεὲ lōŋguù) inducement, persuasion; va.—བྱེད་ to induce/ persuade.

འཇམ་བཤལ་ (jam shε̄ε) a gentle enema.

འཇམ་སེ་བ་ (jamsewa) in a gentle tone of voice.

འཇམ་གསང་ (jamsaŋ) plain, bland, without designs ¶ ཆ་སྣམ་སྒོ་སྒྲིང་གཉིས་ཚོན་མདངས་རྒྱ་སྨུག་འཇམ་གསང་རྩི་ལྡན་ A cupboard painted plain brown and varnished.

འཇམ་བསང་ས་ (jamsaŋ) sm. འཇམ་གསང་.

འཇམ་བསླུས་ (jamjüü) gentle deceiving or tricking, duping without using rough or harsh methods.

འཇའ་: p. འཇས་; f. འཇའ་ (ja) vi. to be lame.

འཇའ་ (ja) rainbow.

འཇའ་སྐེད་ (jageè) a rainbow colored belt that is worn with the རྒྱ་ལུ་ཆེ་ costume.

འཇའ་ཁ་དོག་མཚར་ཀྱང་སྙིང་པོ་མེད་ (ja kādɔgtsargyaŋ ñīŋbu meè) sth. looks good from the outside but has no substance [Lit. although the rainbow with its multicolor is beautiful, it has no core].

འཇའ་གློག (jalɔɔ̀) neon lights.

འཇའ་སྒྲིག (jadrig) matching colors; va.—གཏོང་.

འཇའ་ཆུང་ (jajuŋ) a small འཇའ་མོ་.

འཇའ་ཆེན་ (jajen) 1. shung. a type of boot with a rainbow design that is worn by officials of the traditional Tibetan government. 2. a large འཇའ་མོ་.

འཇའ་ཆེན་རྒྱ་སྨུག (jajen gyəmuù) shung. a maroon-colored boot worn by lay officials below the 5th rank in the traditional Tibetan Government.

འཇའ་ཆེན་སྔོན་པོ་ (jacen ŋömbo) shung. a blue boot with rainbow designs that was worn by government officials of the traditional Tibetan government.

འཇའ་ཆེན་སྣ་ཀེར་ (jacen nāger) shung. a boot with rainbow design and curled up toes that was worn by high ranking monk officials of the traditional Tibetan Government.

འཇའ་འདེགས་ (ja deg) jacking up the roof of houses when rebuilding the walls.

འཇའ་དེག (ja deg) sm. འཇའ་འདེགས་.

འཇའ་པན་ (jabɛn) Japan.

འཇའ་སྤྲིན་ (jadrin) rainbow and clouds.

འཇའ་པོ་ (jawo) lame.

འཇའ་དབྱིབས་ (jəyib) an arched (rainbow-like) structure/ shape.

འཇའ་དབྱིབས་ཀྱི་ཐིག (jəyibgi tīg) parabola.

འཇའ་མ་ (jama) apparel that has rainbow-like color patterns.

འཇའ་མོ་ (jamo) 1. shung. corvee labor tax that involved delivering letters and messages. 2. station (in th tt. transportation system).

འཇའ་མོ་ཏ་རྒྱུག (jamo dāgyuù) shung. delivering messages as a corvee tax with special haste.

འཇའ་ཚོན་ (jadzön) rainbow.

འཇའ་ཚོན་གློག་སྒྲོན་ (jadzön lɔ̄gdrön) neon lights.

འཇའ་ཟུག (ja suù) vi. to have a rainbow appear.

འཇའ་གཟུགས་ (jasug) sm. འཇའ་དབྱིབས་.

འཇའ་འོད་ (jawöö) the rays of a rainbow.

འཇའ་ཡལ་ (ja yεε) 1. vi. to have a rainbow disappear/ fade away. 2. vi. to lose an opportunity.

འཇའ་ཡིག (jəyig) sm. འཇའ་ས་.

འཇའ་རིས་ (jərii) rainbow design.

འཇའ་ལུས་ (jəlüü) the disappearance of the earthly body (usu. happens to very holy people according to Tibetan Buddhism).

འཇའ་ཤར་ (ja shāā) vi. to have a rainbow appear.

འཇའ་ཤོག (jashoò) sm. འཇའ་ས་.

འཇའ་ས་ (jaasa) shung. royal proclamation, imperial edict.

འཇའ་ས་མུ་ཏིག་མ་ (jaasa mudigmə) shung. a title given to Phagpa by the Yuan Dynasty.

འཇར་ (jar) 1. va. to hide ¶ གཟུགས་པོ་སར་འཇར་ནས་བསྡད་པ་རེད་ (They) stayed with (their) bodies hidden on the ground. 2. va. to go near to. 3. sm. འབྱར་.

འཇར་ཀི་ཊྲི་ (jargidri) eng. jacket.

འཇར་འཇར་ (jarjar) friendly, close; va.—བྱེད་.

འཇར་མ་ (jaama) sm.* སྦྲག་མ་.

འཇར་མན་ (jaamεn) Germany; German ¶ འཇར་མན་རྒྱལ་ཕྲན་མཉམ་འབྲེལ་རྒྱལ་ཁབ་ German Federal Republic. ¶ འཇར་མན་དམངས་གཙོ་སྤྱི་མཐུན་རྒྱལ་ཁབ་ German Democratic Republic.

འཇལ་: p. བཅལ་; f. གཞལ་; imp. འཇོལ་ (jεε) 1. va. to measure, to weigh ¶ ས་ཆའི་རྒྱ་ཁྱོན་འཇལ་གྱི་འདུག They are measuring the area of the land. 2. va. to repay, to pay back/ return ¶ ཁྱེད་རང་གི་བཀའ་དྲིན་འཇལ་གྱི་ཡིན་ (I) will repay your kindness. ¶ བུ་ལོན་འཇལ་མ་ཐུབ་པས་ Because (they) could not pay back the loan. 3. va. to pay (taxes, leases, etc.) ¶ ཁྲལ་ལྗིད་པོ་འཇལ་དགོས་རེད་ (They) have to pay heavy taxes. 4. va. to appraise, to assess, to evaluate. 5. va. to respond/ reciprocate.

འཇལ་ཁ་ (jεεga) measuring, weighing; va.—བྱེད་; —རྒྱག to measure/ weigh.

འཇལ་བགྲང་ (jεεdraŋ) counting and measuring.

འཇལ་འགྱངས་ (jεεgyaŋ) delaying paying/ repaying.

འཇལ་ཆས་ (jεεjεὲ) measuring tool/ instrument/ equipment, a gauge for measuring ¶ དྲོད་ཚད་འཇལ་ཆས་ An instrument for measuring heat. ¶ སྲབ་མཐུག་འཇལ་ཆས་ A gauge for measuring thickness.

འཇལ་འཇོལ་ (jεεjöö) abbr. of འཇལ་ལེ་འཇོལ་ལེ་.

འཇལ་ཐོབ་ (jεεdob) the amount to be paid/ repaid.

འཇལ་མདོང་ (jεεdoŋ) graduated measuring cylinder/ flask/ tube.

འཇལ་ནུས་འགན་ལེན་ (jεεnüü gεnlen) guaranteeing (payment/ repayment).

འཇལ་སྤྱད་ (jεεjεὲ) 1. weight, capacity. 2. sm. འཇལ་ཆས་.

འཇལ་སྤྲོད་ (jεεdröö) repayment, repaying; va.—བྱེད་.

འཇལ་ཕོར་ (jεεbɔɔ) measuring cup/ glass/ beaker.

འཇལ་འཕྲོ་ (jεndro) amount left to be paid, balance owed, balance due.

འཇལ་བྱེད་ (jεεjeè) 1. a month. 2. measuring, weighing.

འཇལ་བྱེད་པི་ཙི་ (jεεceè bīdzi) sm. འཇལ་མདོང་.

འཇལ་བྱེད་སྦུ་གུ་ (jεεceè bugu) sm. འཇལ་མདོང་.

འཇལ་བྱེད་ཡོ་ཆས་ (jεεceè yobjεὲ) sm. འཇལ་ཆས་.
འཇལ་བྱེད་སྲང་ (jεεceè sāŋ) scales.
འཇལ་བྱེད་སྲོལ་ལུགས་ (jεεceè sōōluù) system of weights and measures.
འཇལ་སྦུག (jεεbuù) sm. འཇལ་མདོང་.
འཇལ་ཚད་ (jεεdzεὲ) units of measurement.
འཇལ་ལི་འཇོལ་ལི་ (jεεle jööle) a Tibetan dress that's a bit long.
འཇལ་གཤོར་འདེགས་གསུམ་གྱི་ཚད་ (jεε shɔ̄ɔ degsumgi tsεὲ) weighing and measuring.
འཇས་ (jεὲ) p. of འཇལ་.
འཇི་ (ji) 1. flea. 2. sm. འཇིམ་.
འཇི་ནི་བ་ (jiniwa) Geneva.
འཇི་བ་ (jiwə) flea.
འཇི་ཨེམ་མོ་ཊ་བཟོ་ལས་ཁང་ (jiem modra solεὲgaŋ) General Motors (GM).
འཇིག: p. བཤིག་; f. བཤིག་; imp. ཤིག (jig) 1. va. to destroy, to exterminate, to extinguish, to demolish ། ཁང་ཁྱིམ་རྣམས་མེས་འཇིག་པ་མཐོང་བྱུང་ (We) saw the houses destroyed by the fire. ། ཞིང་རྣམས་ཆུས་འཇིག་པ་རེད་ Water demolished the fields.
འཇིག: p. ཞིག་; f. འཇིག (jig) vi. to come to ruin, to fall to pieces, to decay, to perish ། ཀ་བ་ཞིག་ནས་ཐོག་ཁ་རྡིབ་པ་རེད་ After the pillars fell to pieces, the roof collapsed.
འཇིག་སྐྱོབ་ (jiggyob) saving/ protecting from disaster/ ruin/ destruction.
འཇིག་སྒྲག (jigdraà) sm.* འཇིགས་སྐྲག.
འཇིག་ཁ་ (jiggə) at the verge/ point of destruction.
འཇིག་ཉེན་ (jigñεn) danger of destruction/ ruin.
འཇིག་ཉེན་ལས་སྐྱོབ་ (jigñεnlε gyōb) va. to come to the rescue, to save from destruction.
འཇིག་རྟེན་ (jigden) the external/ physical world, samsara.
འཇིག་རྟེན་ཁམས་ (jigden kām) sm. འཇིག་རྟེན་.
འཇིག་རྟེན་མཁན་པོ་ (jigden kēmbo) a monk or lama who is heavily involved in politics and secular life.
འཇིག་རྟེན་མཁའ་བགྲོད་པ་ (jigden kāgyööba) cosmonaut, astronaut.
འཇིག་རྟེན་མཁྱེན་པ་ (jigden kyēmba) epithet of the Buddha.
འཇིག་རྟེན་འཁོར་བ་ (jigden kɔ̄ɔwa) samsara.
འཇིག་རྟེན་འཁྲུགས་ཆེན་ (jigden trūgjen) world war.
འཇིག་རྟེན་གྱི་ཁྱད་ཆོས་ (jigdengi kεὲjöö) the character/ nature of the world (in contrast to higher states that transcend this world).
འཇིག་རྟེན་གྱི་ཁྲིམས་ (jigdengi trīm) law of the land.
འཇིག་རྟེན་གྱི་ཆོས་ (jigdengi cöö) 1. the behavior of secular persons. 2. sexual intercourse.
འཇིག་རྟེན་གྱི་ལྟ་སྣང་ (jigdengi dānaŋ) sm. འཇིག་རྟེན་ལྟ་ཚུལ་.
འཇིག་རྟེན་གྱི་གཏམ་ (jigdengi dām) proverbs.
འཇིག་རྟེན་གྱི་གཏམ་རྒྱུད་ (jigdengi dāmgyüü) legends, stories of the past, folklore.
འཇིག་རྟེན་གྱི་ཐ་སྙད་ (jigdengi tāñεὲ) proverbs and sayings.
འཇིག་རྟེན་གྱི་སྤྱོད་པ་ (jigdengi jööba) behavior/ nature/ character of the secular world.
འཇིག་རྟེན་གྱི་ཚུལ་ལུགས་ (jigdengi tsūūluù) the nature/ character the secular world.
འཇིག་རྟེན་གྱི་ལྷ་ (jīgdengi lhā) the gods/ spirits of this world.
འཇིག་རྟེན་གྲགས་པ་ (jigden tragba) well known/ famous throughout the world.
འཇིག་རྟེན་འགྲོ་ལུགས་ (jigden droluù) 1. the way of sentient beings; conventional ways of the world. 2. secular customs.
འཇིག་རྟེན་སྔ་མ་ (jigden ŋāma) previous existence/ life.
འཇིག་རྟེན་བཅོས་ (jigden jöö) va. to rebuild/ redo/ remake the world.
འཇིག་རྟེན་ཆགས་ཚུལ་ (jigden cəgdzüü) the manner the world came into being.
འཇིག་རྟེན་ཆོས་བརྒྱད་ (jigden cöögyεὲ) the eight worldly concerns: to profit and to lose, to hear pleasant and unpleasant things, to be flattered and be ridiculed, to be happy and unhappy.
འཇིག་རྟེན་རྙིང་པ་ (jigden ñīŋbə) the old world.
འཇིག་རྟེན་ལྟ་བ་ (jigden dāwa) sm. འཇིག་རྟེན་ལྟ་ཚུལ་.
འཇིག་རྟེན་ལྟ་ཚུལ་ (jigden dədzüü) world outlook, world ideology ། འབྱོར་ལྡན་གྲལ་རིམ་གྱི་འཇིག་རྟེན་ལྟ་ཚུལ་ The bourgeoise world outlook.
འཇིག་རྟེན་མཐུན་འཇུག (jigden tūnjuù) sm. འཇིག་རྟེན་མཐུན་སྦྱོར་.
འཇིག་རྟེན་མཐུན་སྦྱོར་ (jigden tūnjɔɔ) marriage.
འཇིག་རྟེན་མཐོང་ཚུལ་ (jigden tōŋdzüü) sm. འཇིག་རྟེན་ལྟ་ཚུལ་.
འཇིག་རྟེན་འདོད་མ་ (jigden dööma) a beautiful female.
འཇིག་རྟེན་རྣམ་གཉིས་ (jigden nāmñii) 1. the present and the next life. 2. the world and the sentient beings in it.
འཇིག་རྟེན་པ་ (jigdemba) worldly person, layman.
འཇིག་རྟེན་པའི་མི་དགེ་བ་ (jigdenbε mi gewa) the ten nonvirtuous deeds.
འཇིག་རྟེན་པའི་ཡང་དག་པའི་ལྟ་བ་ (jigdenbε yaŋdagbε dāwa) a belief in the law of cause and effect, a belief in karma.
འཇིག་རྟེན་པའི་རིག་གནས་ (jigdenbε rignεὲ) secular culture.
འཇིག་རྟེན་པའི་ལྷ་ (jigdenbε lhā) sm. འཇིག་རྟེན་གྱི་ལྷ་.
འཇིག་རྟེན་ཕ་རོལ་ (jigden pārol) future existence/ life.
འཇིག་རྟེན་ཕྱི་མའི་གཟིགས་མོར་ཕེབས་ (jigden cīmε siìmɔɔ pēè) vi. to die.
འཇིག་རྟེན་ཕྱི་མ་ (jigden cīmə) sm. འཇིག་རྟེན་ཕ་རོལ་.
འཇིག་རྟེན་འཕུར་སྐྱོད་ (jigden pūrgyöö) space travel.
འཇིག་རྟེན་འཕུར་སྐྱོད་པ་ (jigden pūrgyööba) astronaut.
འཇིག་རྟེན་འཕུར་སྐྱོད་ཀྱི་གྱོན་ཆས་ (jigden pūrgyöögi kyönjεὲ) spacesuit.
འཇིག་རྟེན་འཕུར་གྲུ་ (jigden pūrdru) space ship.
འཇིག་རྟེན་འཕྲོ་འོད་ (jigden trōwöö) cosmic rays.
འཇིག་རྟེན་འཕྲོ་ཐིག (jigden trōdig) sm. འཇིག་རྟེན་འཕྲོ་འོད་.
འཇིག་རྟེན་བར་སྟོང་ (jigden bārdoŋ) sm. འཇིག་རྟེན་བར་སྣང་.
འཇིག་རྟེན་བར་སྣང་ (jigden parnaŋ) space, universe, cosmos.
འཇིག་རྟེན་བྱེད་པོ་ (jigden ceèbo) the Creator, Brahma.
འཇིག་རྟེན་དབང་ཕྱུག (jigden wāŋjug) 1. Avalokitesvara. 2. epithet for the Dalai Lama.
འཇིག་རྟེན་མི་ཡུལ་ (jigden miyüü) the world of humans.
འཇིག་རྟེན་མི་ཇུས་ (jigden mijüü) marriage affairs.
འཇིག་རྟེན་མིག (jigden mii) great translators (of Buddhist texts).
འཇིག་རྟེན་མི་ཤུགས་འཕུར་མདའ་ (jigden meshuù pūnda) space ship/ rocket.
འཇིག་རྟེན་མེས་པོ་ (jigden meèbo) sm. འཇིག་རྟེན་བྱེད་པོ་.
འཇིག་རྟེན་གཞན་ (jigden shen) sm. འཇིག་རྟེན་ཕ་རོལ་.
འཇིག་རྟེན་ལ་ལྟ་ཚུལ་ (jigdenla dədzüü) sm. འཇིག་རྟེན་ལྟ་ཚུལ་.
འཇིག་རྟེན་ལ་སུན་སྣང་ (jigdenla sūnnaŋ) fed up with the world, pessimistic, cynical.
འཇིག་རྟེན་ལས་འདའ་ (jigdenlε da) sm. འཇིག་རྟེན་ལས་འདས་.
འཇིག་རྟེན་ལས་འདས་ (jigdenlε dεὲ) passing from or beyond the world, transcendental, supra mundane.
འཇིག་རྟེན་ས་གཞི་ (jigden sāshi) the earth.
འཇིག་རྟེན་སུན་སྣང་རིང་ལུགས་ (jigden sūnnaŋ riŋluù) pessimism, cynicism.
འཇིག་རྟེན་གསར་པ་ (jigden sāāba) the new world.
འཇིག་རྟེན་གསུམ་ (jigden sūm) the three worlds of the gods, humans and the underworld of nagas.
འཇིག་སྣུབ་ (jignub) getting destroyed/ demolished.

འཇིག་པ་རྣམ་གསུམ་ (jigba nāmsum) the three kinds of disasters: through weapon and war, through disease and epidemics and through famine and natural calamities.

འཇིག་པའི་བསྐལ་པ་ (jigbɛ gɛ̄ɛwa) eons during which destruction occurs.

འཇིག་པའི་ཆོས་ (jigbɛ cöö) impermanence, perpetual change.

འཇིག་བྱེད་རྐྱེན་གསུམ་ (jigceè gyēnsum) the three causes of the dissolution of the universe: fire, water and wind.

འཇིག་བྲལ་ (jigdrɛɛ) indestructible.

འཇིག་མེད་ (jigmeè) 1. sm. འཇིག་བྲལ་. 2. a male's name.

འཇིག་མེད་བརྟན་པོ་ (jigmeè dēmbo) indestructible and unchanging/ constant.

འཇིགས་ (jig) vi. to be afraid, to fear, to be terrorized, to be scared ¶ ཚང་མ་འཇིགས་ནས་བྲོས་སོང་ Everybody got scared and ran away.

འཇིགས་སྐུལ་ (jiggüü) intimidating, threatening, frightening; va.—བྱེད་.

འཇིགས་སྐུལ་འཕྲིན་ཡིག (jiggüü trinyii) threatening letter.

འཇིགས་སྐུལ་སྡིགས་མོ་ (jiggüü digmo) threatening, intimidating.

འཇིགས་སྐྱོབ་ (jiggyob) saving/ protecting from fear.

འཇིགས་སྐྲག (jigdraà) terror, dread, fear; va.—སྐུལ་; —སློང་ to terrorize, to frighten/ scare; vi.—སྐྱེད་; —ལང་ to be or get terrorized/ scared/ frightened.

འཇིགས་སྐྲག་གི་བསམ་རྩུལ་ (jigdraàgi sɔ̄mdzüü) atmosphere of fear/ terror.

འཇིགས་སྒྲོལ་ (jigdröö) sm. འཇིགས་སྐྱོབ་.

འཇིགས་ངོམ་བྱེད་ (jigŋom cɛè) va. to demonstrate (against sth.).

འཇིགས་དངངས་ (jigŋaŋ) sm. འཇིགས་སྐྲག.

འཇིགས་རྔམ་ཚ་པོ་ (jigŋam tsābo) very frightening/ scary/ fierce-looking.

འཇིགས་སྔངས་ (jigŋaŋ) sm. འཇིགས་སྐྲག.

འཇིགས་རྒྱུམ་ (jigjum) being scared out of one's wits.

འཇིགས་འཇིགས་ (jigjig) frightened, scared; va.—སྐུལ་; —གཏོང་ to frighten/ scare/ intimidate.

འཇིགས་བསྙེངས་ (jigñeŋ) sm. འཇིགས་སྐྲག.

འཇིགས་སྟངས་ (jigdaŋ) 1. manner of scaring/ frightening/ intimidating. 2. a look/ expression/ appearance of fright.

འཇིགས་སྟེར་ (jigder) making sb. frightened/ scared; va.—བྱེད་.

འཇིགས་འཐོམ་ (jigdom) scared out of one's wits, frightened and stunned/ shocked; va.—སྐྱེ་ to be or get scared and stunned.

འཇིགས་འཐོམས་ (jigdom) sm. འཇིགས་འཐོམ་.

འཇིགས་དོགས་ (jigdɔɔ̀) fear and suspicion/ doubt.

འཇིགས་སྣང་ (jignaŋ) fear, fright; vi.—སྐྱེད་ to fear, to be or get afraid/ scared; va.—སྐུལ་; —སློང་ to frighten, to intimidate/ threaten, to scare ¶ ང་འཇིགས་སྣང་སྐྱེད་བྱུང་ I got scared. ¶ མོས་མཐུན་མ་གནང་ཚེ་དཔུང་དམག་བོད་ལ་གཏོང་རྒྱུའི་འཇིགས་སྣང་བསྐུལ་ If (you/ they) don't agree, (they) threatened to send troops into Tibet.

འཇིགས་སྣང་ཆེན་པོ་ (jignaŋ cēmbo) sm. འཇིགས་སྣང་ཚ་པོ་.

འཇིགས་སྣང་ཚ་པོ་ (jignaŋ tsābo) frightening, terrifying, scary.

འཇིགས་གནས་ (jignɛɛ̀) a frightening place or object.

འཇིགས་པ་བྱེད་ (jigbə ceè) va. to make/ instill/ create fear, to frighten.

འཇིགས་པ་མེད་པ་ (jigbə meèba) fearless, unafraid.

འཇིགས་པ་བཞི་ (jigbə shi) the four fears: fear of sickness, old age, death, and deterioration.

འཇིགས་བྱེད་ (jigjeè) 1. the protective deity Yamantaka. 2. frightening, terrifying. 3. Vajra Yogini.

འཇིགས་བྲལ་ (jigtdrɛɛ) sm. འཇིགས་མེད་.

འཇིགས་མེད་ (jigmeè) 1. fearless, unafraid, brave. 2. person's name.

འཇིགས་འཛེར་ (jigdzer) 1. sm. འཛེར་. 2. afraid and shy.

འཇིགས་ཞུམ་ (jigshum) fright, fear; vi.—བྱེད་ to be afraid, to fear.

འཇིགས་ཞུམ་མེད་པ་ (jigshum meèba) sm. འཇིགས་མེད་.

འཇིགས་ཟིལ་ (jigsilə) frightening in a majestic sense.

འཇིགས་ཡེ་རེ་ (jigyere) in a state of fright/ fear.

འཇིགས་ཡོ་རེ་ (jigyore) sm. འཇིགས་ཡེ་རེ་.

འཇིགས་རུང་ (jigruŋ) abbr. འཇིགས་སུ་རུང་བ་.

འཇིགས་རེད་རྨ་ (jigreè mā) a sore that is said to be caused by fright.

འཇིགས་ཤུམ་ཤུམ་ (jig shūmshum) sm. འཇིགས་ཞུམ་.

འཇིགས་ས་ (jigsa) a terrifying/ frightful place.

འཇིགས་སུ་རུང་བ་ (jigsu ruŋbə) scary, frightening, terrifying, petrifying.

འཇིགས་སེལ་ཟླ་བོ་ (jigsel dawo) a companion/ friend to help one not get scared.

འཇིང་ (jiŋ) 1. abbr. of འཇིང་པ་. 2. sm. དཔྱུས་.

འཇིང་པ་ (jiŋbə) sm. མཇིང་པ་.

འཇིང་པ་སྦོམ་པོ་ (jiŋbə bombo) sm. མཇིང་པ་སྦོམ་པོ་.

འཇིང་ཟབ་ (jiŋsəb) deep.

འཇིངས་ (jiŋ) sm. འཇིང་.

འཇིན་ (jin) va. to be caught up in, to be enmeshed in.

འཇིབ་: p. འཇིབས་ or གཞིབས་; f. གཞིབ་; imp. འཇིབས་ (jib) va. to suck (sth. out of sth. else), to suckle ¶ ཨ་མའི་ནུ་མ་འཇིབས་ནས་ Having sucked (his) mother's breast.

འཇིབ་འཁོར་ (jibgɔɔ) eng.tib. automobile.

འཇིབ་གོང་ (jibgoŋ) mud ball.

འཇིབ་རྒྱག (jib gyaà) va. to treat by sucking the disease out of a patient's body.

འཇིབ་ཆས་ (jibjɛɛ̀) things used for sucking rites.

འཇིབ་འཐེན་ (jibtden) sucking out, suction.

འཇིབ་འཐུང་ (jibduŋ) sucking to drink (as with a straw).

འཇིབ་པི་ (jibi) willow flower.

འཇིབ་བུ་ (jibbu) a shoot that people suck on it because of its sweetness.

འཇིབ་རྫི་ (jibdzi) saivia prattili Hemsl (used in Tibetan medicine).

འཇིབ་ར་ (jibrə) pacifier (for babies).

འཇིབ་རུ་ (jibru) baby feeder (traditionally a horn from which milk can be sucked), baby bottle.

འཇིབ་ཤིང་ (jibshiŋ) the wooden straw used to drink millet beer.

འཇིབ་ཤུགས་ (jibshug) sucking.

འཇིབས་ (jib) imp. of འཇིབ་.

འཇིམ་ (jim) clay, mud.

འཇིམ་གོང་ (jīmgoŋ) clay butter lamp offering bowl with a long stand.

འཇིམ་སྐུ་ (jimgu) sm. འཇིམ་བརྙན་.

འཇིམ་གོང་ (jimgoŋ) sm. འཇིབ་གོང་.

འཇིམ་གླང་རྒྱ་མཚོར་འཛུལ་བ་ (jimlaŋ gyadzɔr dzüüwə) 1. not hearing from, not finding. 2. wasted effort, throwing away with no hope of return [Lit. a mud oxen entering the ocean].

འཇིམ་བརྙན་ (jimñɛn) clay/ mud image or statue.

འཇིམ་བརྙན་སྒྱུ་རྩལ་ (jimñɛn gyudzɛɛ) art of pottery, art of making clay images.

འཇིམ་རྡོག (jimdog) a lump of clay.

འཇིམ་པ་ (jimbə) clay, mud.

འཇིམ་མི་ (jimmi) clay statue of a person.

འཇིམ་རྫབ་ (jimdzəb) sm. འཇིམ་པ་.

འཇིམ་ཞལ་ (jimshɛɛ) mud plaster (for walls and floor).

འཇིམ་གཟུགས་ (jimsug) sm. འཇིམ་བརྙན་.

འཇིམ་བཟོ་ (jimso) sculpture (clay), the work of making statues from clay; va.—བྱེད་ to sculpt with clay.

འཇིམ་བཟོ་བ་ (jimsowa) sculptor who makes clay statues.

འཇིམ་ལས་པ་ (jimlɛ̀ɛbə) sm. འཇིམ་བཟོ་བ་.

འཇིལ་: p. **བཅིལ་**; f. **གཞིལ་**; imp. **ཅིལ་** (jii) 1. va. to expel/ remove/ banish. 2. va. to deteriorate/ decline/ break.

འཇུ་: p. **འཇུས་**; f. **འཇུ་**; imp. **འཇུས་** (ju) 1. va. to hold onto, to catch ། ཁོའི་ལག་པ་ནས་འཇུས་སོང་ (They) held him by the hand.

འཇུ་: p. **ཞུ་**; f. **འཇུ་** (ju) vi. to digest (food) ། ཟས་ཆས་འཇུ་མི་ཐུབ་པའི་དཀའ་ལས་ Difficulty in digesting food.

འཇུ་སྐམ་ (jugam) pliers.

འཇུ་སྐེམ་ (jugem) a type of disease in Tibetan medicine characterized by a loss of weight with a distended stomach and an insatiable appetite.

འཇུ་ཁག་པོ་ (ju kāgbo) hard to digest.

འཇུ་ཊ་ (jurda) hind. shoes.

འཇུ་སྟོབས་ (judob) digestive power/ strength ། འཇུ་སྟོབས་ཆུང་ཆུང་ Weak digestive power.

འཇུ་ཐག (judaà) a string/ strap handle.

འཇུ་བདེ་པོ་ (ju debo) easy to digest; easy to hold onto.

འཇུ་ནུས་ (junüü) capacity to digest.

འཇུ་བ་ (juwə) flea.

འཇུ་བྱེད་མཁྲིས་པ་ (jujeè trĭibə) gallbladder.

འཇུ་བྱེད་རྒྱུད་རིམ་ (jujeè gyüürim) digestion system/ process.

འཇུ་བྱེད་ནད་ (jujeè nɛ̀ɛ) digestive illnesses.

འཇུ་བྱེད་དབང་པོ་ (jujeè wāŋbo) digestive organs.

འཇུ་སྨན་ (jumɛn) medicine for digestion.

འཇུ་ཚོད་ཀྱི་ཟས། ཐེག་ཚོད་ཀྱི་ལས་ (judzöögi sɛ̀ɛ tēgdzöögi lɛ̀ɛ) one should not overdo things [Lit. food according to digestion, work according weight].

འཇུ་གཟུང་ (jusuŋ) sm. འཇུ་བཟུང་.

འཇུ་བཟུང་ (jusuŋ) arresting, capturing, seizing; va.—བྱེད་.

འཇུ་བཟུང་བཀའ་རྒྱ་ (jusuŋ kgāgya) arrest order, wanted circular/ poster.

འཇུ་རེས་ (jureè) wrestling.

འཇུ་ལུང་ (juluŋ) a handle.

འཇུ་ལུང་འཆང་བཟུང་ (juluŋ cāŋsuŋ) reliable (person, information) [Lit. sth. that has a handle and one can get a hold of it].

འཇུ་སླའི་དངོས་པོ་ (julɛ ŋöòbo) foodstuffs that are easy to digest.

འཇུ་ས་ (jusə) 1. sth. to take hold of, anything to hold on to, a handle. 2. proof, evidence.

འཇུ་སའི་ལུང་དང་འཆང་པའི་ཡུ་བ་ (jusɛluŋ daŋ cāŋbɛ yöö) sm. འཇུ་ལུང་འཆང་བཟུང་.

འཇུག: p. **ཞུགས་**; f. **འཇུག**; imp. **ཞུགས་** (jùù) 1. va. to go into, to enter, to participate ། ཁོ་ཚོས་དེ་ལོ་མཐོ་རིམ་སློབ་གྲྭར་ཞུགས་པ་རེད་ They entered college that year. ། འཛམ་གླིང་རྩེད་མོའི་འགྲན་བསྡུར་ལ་འཇུག་རྒྱུར་གྲབས་གཤོམ་བྱས་པ་རེད་ They prepared (themselves) to participate in the world sports contest. 2. va. to follow (a path, doctirne) ། ནང་པའི་བསྟན་པ་ལ་འཇུག་པའི་སྐྱེ་བོ་ A person who follows Buddhism.

འཇུག: p. **བཅུག**; f. **གཞུག**; imp. **ཅུག** (juù) 1. va. to put into, to insert, to enroll in ། ཁོས་སྡོད་དེ་ནང་ལག་པ་བཅུག་པ་རེད་ He put (his) hand into the pot. ། ཕྲུག་གུ་དེ་སློབ་གྲྭར་འཇུག་གི་རེད་ (They) are going to put the child into school. 2. va. to let, to allow, to permit ། ལག་ཁྱེར་མེད་ན་ཡང་ཁོ་ཚོ་བོད་ལ་འགྲོ་བཅུག་པ་རེད་ Even though (they) didn't have a passport (he) let them go to Tibet. ། འདི་ལྟ་རུ་མ་བཅུག་ན་ངས་རྙོག་དྲ་བཟོ་ཡོང་ If you don't allow me to look at this I will cause trouble. 3. va. to make/ force sb. to do sth. ། ཁོ་ཚོའི་བློ་འདོད་ལ་མེད་པར་འགྲོ་བཅུག་པ་རེད་ They made them go against their will. 4. va. to put under/ bring under (power, control) ། རྒྱལ་ཁབ་མང་པོ་ཁོ་ཚོའི་མངའ་འོག་ལ་བཅུག་པ་རེད་ (They) brought many nations under their control.

འཇུག་ཁྲ་ (jugdra) a list of things stored in a box or room.

འཇུག་སྒོ་ (juggo) 1. entrance, way to enter. 2. method, system, way. 3. beginning, initial stage ། ཐོག་མ་ནས་ལས་དོན་གྱི་འཇུག་སྒོ་མ་འཆོལ་བ་ཞིག་བྱ་རྒྱུ་གལ་འགངས་ཤིན་དུ་ཆེ་བས་ It is important that there should be no mistakes made at the initial stage of the work.

འཇུག་སྒོའི་སློབ་ཚན་ (juggö lōbdzɛn) beginning or introductory lesson.

འཇུག་ངོགས་ (jugŋɔ̀ɔ) sm. འཇུག་སྒོ་.

འཇུག་ལྡོག (juŋdɔ̀ɔ) 1. going away and returning, going and coming. 2. the appropriate and inappropriate, what ought to be done and what ought not to be done ། ཆོས་སྲིད་གཉིས་ཀྱི་བྱ་བའི་འཇུག་ལྡོག་མ་འཆོལ་བ་དགོས་རྒྱུ་ Regarding temporal and political matters, one should not make errors on choosing what one ought to do and what ought not to do.

འཇུག་བདེ་པོ་ (jug debo) sm. བཅུག་བདེ་པོ་.

འཇུག་སྣོད་ (jugnöö) container.

འཇུག་པ་གཅིག་པ་ (jugbə jĭgbə) in unison, in harmony/ agreement.

འཇུག་པོ་ (jugbo) efficient, fitting.

འཇུག་ཡུལ་ (jugyüü) 1. place where sth. is put/ left, place where one enters/ participates. 2. the object of sth. (nose to smell, tongue to taste, etc.) 3. prefixes and suffixes in Tibetan grammar.

འཇུང་པ་ (juŋba) sm. འཇུང་སེམས་.

འཇུང་སེམས་ (juŋsem) avarice, stinginess.

འཇུངས་པ་ (juŋba) sm. འཇུང་པ་.

འཇུངས་པ་ཅན་ (juŋbajɛn) avaricious.

འཇུད་ (jüü) va. to put inside.

འཇུད་མཐུན་མ་ (jüüdümbə) prostitute.

འཇུན་: p. **བཅུན་**; f. **གཅུན་**; imp. **ཅུན་** (jün) va. to subdue, to tame, to train/ discipline.

འཇུམ་: p. **བཅུམ་**; f. **གཞུམ་** (jüm) 1. vi. to contract/ shrink/ diminish ། ཀོ་རློན་སྐམ་ནས་མཐའ་ནས་ཆུར་བཅུམ་ When the wet leather dried it contracted from the ends. 2. vi. to shudder, to tremble.

འཇུམ་རྒྱག (jum gyaà) va. to tie horses or mules in the middle of four poles (to immobilize them for shoeing or medical treatment).

འཇུར་: p. **བཅུར་**; f. **གཅུར་**; imp. **ཅུར་** (jur) 1. va. to interrogate. 2. va. to vanquish/ overcome/ subdue/ tame. 3. va. to corral animals separately.

འཇུར་: p. **བཅུར་**; f. **གཅུར་** (jur) vi. to be/ get tangled into a knot because of too much twisting/ spinning ། སྐུད་པ་འདི་འཇུར་འདུག This thread is knotted up.

འཇུར་གེགས་ (jurgeg) impeding/ hindering sb.'s charitable act.

འཇུར་གྱིས་ (jurgi) sm. འཇུར་དེ་.

འཇུར་སྒྲོག (jurdrɔ̀ɔ) shoelace, va.—རྒྱག to tie shoelaces.

འཇུར་ཏ་ (jurdə) hind. shoe; va.—ཕྱུག to shine shoes.

འཇུར་ཏ་ཆུང་ཆུང་ (jurda cūŋjuŋ) keeping tight control on sb. subtly/ indirectly (by indirectly warning them); va.—གཡོག [Lit. (putting on) small shoes].

འཇུར་ཏ་རྟིང་ཀ་ཙོག་ཙོག (jurda dĭŋgə dzōgdzog) high-heel shoes.

འཇུར་ཏ་རྟིང་ཀ་རིང་པོ་ (jurda riŋgu) sm. འཇུར་ཏ་རྟིང་ཀ་ཙོག་ཙོག.

འཇུར་ཏ་ཡུ་རིང་ (jurda yuriŋ) Western-style riding long boots.

འཇུར་དེ་ (jurde) suddenly, all at once.

འཇུར་ཊ་ (jurda) sm. འཇུར་ཏ་.

འཇུར་ཊ་རྟིང་ཙོག (jurda dĭŋdzog) high-heel shoes.

འཇུར་ཊ་ཡུ་རིང་ (jurda yuriŋ) sm. འཇུར་ཏ་ཡུ་རིང་.

འཇུར་འདྲུག (jurduù) wrinkled.

འཇུར་མདུད་ (jurdüü) knotted up because of too much spinning/ twisting.

འཇུར་བུ་ (jurbu) sm. མཇུར་མདུད་.

འཇུར་མ་ (jurma) sm. མཇུར་མདུད་.

འཇུར་མིག (jurmii) a piece of iron with a hole that is used by blacksmiths to draw red hot iron through it to make wire. 2. harsh punishments meted out to criminals.

འཇུར་མེད་ (jurmeè) not knotted, untangled, simple, easy.

འཇུར་རྩི་ (jurdzi) shoe polish.

འཇུས་ (jüü) of འཇུ་.

འཇུས་འགོར་ (jüügɔɔ) shung. captive ། འདི་གའི་སྐྱབས་བྲན་དང་འཇུས་འགོར་དུ་མ་ཁྱེར་ These (people) are not to be owned as slaves and captives.

འཇེན་པ་ (jemba) things that one likes.

འཇེབས་ (jeb) vi. to like, to find attractive/ pleasing.

འཇེབས་པོ་ (jebbo) pleasant, attractive.

འཇེམ་ཐང་ (jemdaŋ) sm. འཇོན་ཐང་.

འཇེམ་པ་ (jemba) sm. འཇེམ་པོ་.

འཇེམ་པོ་ (jembo) able, skilled, capable.

འཇེམས་པོ་ (jembo) sm. འཇེམ་པོ་.

འཇོ་: p. བཞོས་; f. བཞོ་; imp. འཇོས་ (jo) 1. va. to milk ། མོ་བ་འཇོ་གི་འདུག She is milking a cow. 2. va. to satisfy (sb.'s needs), to yield (to sb.'s desire). 3. vi. to be infatuated.

འཇོ་གྲུབ་ (jodrub) a milking unit in a commune.

འཇོ་སྒེག (jogeg) beauty, charm.

འཇོ་སྒེག་མཛེས་ཉམས་ལྡན་པ་ (jogeg dzeèñam dɛmba) elegant, beautiful, graceful (for women).

འཇོ་སྒེག་གཡེར་བག་ཅན་ (jogeg yerbagjɛn) beautiful, elegant, charming.

འཇོ་སྟེགས་ (jodeg) a small stool used when milking.

འཇོ་བ་མོ་ (joomo) milkmaid.

འཇོ་བག་ཅན་ (jobagjɛn) beautiful, elegant, charming.

འཇོ་བག་འཆོས་ (jobagjöö) sm. སྒེག་ཉམས་སྟོན་.

འཇོ་མ་ (joma) 1. milch cow. 2. sm. འཇོ་བ་མོ་.

འཇོ་ཧལ་ལ་ནེ་རུ་ (johalla neru) Jawaharlal Nehru.

འཇོག་: p. བཞག་; f. གཞག་; imp. ཞོག (jɔɔ) 1. va. to leave, to put, to place, to put down ། ཁོས་དེབ་དེ་ལྕོག་ཙེའི་སྟེང་དུ་བཞག་འདུག He has left the book on the table. ། དེ་སྐུར་འཇོག་གི་མ་རེད་ (We) are not going to leave it like that. 2. va. to keep (in mind) ། ངས་གང་བཤད་སེམས་ལ་བཞག་མི་འདུག (You) haven't kept in mind what I said. 3. va. to sign (an agreement/ treaty) ། མི་འཁེན་མཚམས་འཇོག་གི་ཆིངས་ཡིག་ཞིག་འཇོག་གི་རེད་ (They) will sign a ceasefire agreement. 4. va. to put an end to, to cease, to stop, to halt ། ལས་ཀ་བྱེད་མཚམས་བཞག་པ་རེད་ (They) stopped working. 5. va. to lick ། ཕོར་པ་འཇོག Lick the bowl.

འཇོག་: p. བཞོགས་; f. གཞོག་; imp. ཞོགས་ (jɔɔ) va. to carve, to plane.

འཇོག་སྒྲིག (jɔgdrig) assembling, installing; va.—བྱེད་.

འཇོག་དངུལ་ (jɔgŋüü) deposited money (in a bank).

འཇོག་རྟགས་ (jɔgdaà) a punctuation mark separating syllables/ clauses/ sentences.

འཇོག་གནས་བརྗེད་ (jɔgnɛɛ jeè) vi. to forget where sth. was put/ left.

འཇོག་ཚད་ (jɔgdzɛɛ) investment, deposit.

འཇོག་ཚད་མ་དངུལ་ (jɔgdzɛɛ maŋüü) capital investment.

འཇོག་མཚམས་ (jɔgdzam) ceasing, stopping, discontinuing, suspending; va.—བྱེད་.

འཇོག་ཞབས་འཆང་ལུང་ (jɔgshab cāŋluŋ) sm. འཇུ་ལུང་འཆང་བཟུང་.

འཇོག་བཟོ་སྟོན་ (jɔgso tön) vi. to reach a result/ decision/ conclusion.

འཇོག་ས་ (jɔgsa) a place for leaving/ storing.

འཇོང་ (jɔŋ) 1. hoe, pickax. 2. sm. འཇོང་པོ་.

འཇོང་: p. འཇངས་; f. འཇང་; imp. འཇོངས་ (jɔŋ) va. to drink, to swallow.

འཇོང་འཇོང་ (jɔŋjɔŋ) sm. འཇོང་པོ་.

འཇོང་ཉམས་ཅན་ (jɔŋñamjɛn) sm. འཇོང་འཇོང་.

འཇོང་པོ་ (jɔŋbo) oblong, oval, elliptical.

འཇོང་དབྱིབས་ (jɔŋyib) sm. འཇོང་འཇོང་.

འཇོང་མོ་ (jɔŋmo) sm. འཇོང་པོ་.

འཇོང་གཟུགས་ (jɔŋsug) sm. འཇོང་པོ་.

འཇོང་རོ་ (jɔŋro) a tall idiot.

འཇོངས་ (jɔŋ) imp. of འཇོང་.

འཇོད་ཙེ་ (jöödze) ch. table.

འཇོན་ (jön) copper.

འཇོན་ཀྲང་ (jöndraŋ) a water container with a long lip.

འཇོན་ཅེ་སྤྱོད་ཆུང་ (jönce jööjuŋ) talented person made to do menial work.

འཇོན་ཐང་ (jöndaŋ) capability, ability.

འཇོན་ཐང་ཅན་ (jöndaŋjɛn) capable, able.

འཇོན་ཐང་ཆེན་པོ་ (jöndaŋ cēmbo) highly capable/ able.

འཇོན་ཐང་ལྡན་པ་ (jöndaŋ dɛmba) capable, able.

འཇོན་ཐང་ཡོད་པ་ (jöntaŋ yööba) capable, able.

འཇོན་པོ་ (jömbo) sm. འཇོན་ཐང་.

འཇོན་དམར་ (jömmar) copper.

འཇོན་ཚོད་དཔག་ཚོད་ (jöndzöö bāgdzöö) doing according to one's ability.

འཇོན་བཟོ་ཆེན་པོ་ (jönso cēmbo) appearing able/ capable.

འཇོབ་རྫ་ (jobdza) a kind of fodder.

འཇོབས་ (job) imp. of འཇབ་.

འཇོམས་: p. བཅོམ་; f. གཞོམ་; imp. ཆོམ་ (jom) 1. va. to subdue, to quell, to conquer, to defeat ། དམག་པོའི་སྟོབས་ཤུགས་ཀྱིས་ཟིང་འཁྲུག་འཇོམས་ཐབས་བྱས་པ་རེད་ They tried to quell the agitation by military force. 2. vi. to go down, to quiet down ། ན་ཚ་དེ་ཕྲན་བུ་བཅོམ་འདུག The pain has gone down a little.

འཇོར་ (jɔɔ) hoe, pickax.

འཇོར་བུ་ (jɔɔbu) sm. འཇོར་.

འཇོར་རྩེ་གསུམ་ཅན་ (jɔɔdze sūmjɛn) three-pronged hoe.

འཇོལ་ (jöö) 1. imp. of འཇལ་. 2. vi. (for dresses/ clothing) to drag on the floor, to hang down too long.

འཇོལ་འཇོལ་ (jööjöö) low/ dragging (in length of dress, etc.), hanging too long.

འཇོལ་ཉོག (jööñog) 1. unquenchable, insatiable. 2. without hesitation/ doubt. 3. troublesome, rowdy.

འཇོལ་ཐབས་ (jöödəb) sm. འཇོལ་འཇོལ་.

འཇོལ་དུ་ཀླུབ་ (jöödu lūb) va. to wear one's dress low/ dragging.

འཇོལ་པོ་ (jööbo) sm. འཇོལ་འཇོལ་.

འཇོལ་བེར་ (jööber) 1. a long gown/ cloak. 2. a sleeveless dress.

འཇོལ་མོ་ (jöömo) nightingale.

འཇོལ་ལེ་བ་ (jöölewa) hanging down.

འཇོས་ (jöö) imp. of འཇོ་.

རྗང་ (jaŋ) sm. རྗང་མ་.

རྗང་བུ་ (jaŋbu) partition in a grain storage room.

རྗང་མ་ (jaŋma) grain storeroom, grain bin.

རྗང་ཡིའུ་ (jaŋyü) ch. soy sauce.

རྗིད་པ་ (jiibə) thin, lean.

རྗིབ་ལས་ (jiblɛɛ) corvee labor.

རྗུད་ (jüü) vi. to be/ get skinny/ thin.

རྗུད་དོ་ (jüüdo) frail, skinny, bony.

རྗེ་ (je) master, lord, king, chief.

རྗེ་: p. བརྗེས་; f. བརྗེ་; imp. རྗེས་ (je) va. to change, to exchange ། ཁོས་གོས་ལོག་བརྗེས་འདུག He has changed his clothes. ། བཟོ་གྲྭ་དེ་སྒྲིག་ཆས་གསར་དུ་བརྗེ་གི་རེད་ The equipment of the factory will be changed.

རྗེ་ཁང་ལོག (jegaŋ lɔɔ) sm. འབངས་གྱེན་ལོག.

རྗེ་ཁོལ་ (jegöö) lord/ king and his subjects.

རྗེ་གོང་མ་ (je kɔŋma) deceased lord or lama.

རྗེ་ངན་ (jeŋɛn) autocratic chief/ lord/ ruler.

རྗེ་དྲུང་ (jedruŋ) 1. shung. title of monk officials from aristocratic families ། ཞོལ་ཁང་རྗེ་དྲུང་ལགས་ Sholkhang Jedrung. 2. attendant of a lama.

རྗེ་དཔོན་ (jebön) lord, chief, master, ruler, king.

རྗེ་ཕྲན་ (jedrɛn) lower ranking lords/ chiefs.

རྗེ་བོ་ (jewo) sm. རྗེ་དཔོན་.

རྗེ་བྲན་ (jedrɛn) sm. རྗེ་འབངས་.

རྗེ་བླ་མ་ (je lāma) root guru, great lama.

རྗེ་བློན་ (jelön) lord/ chief/ king and his ministers.

རྗེ་བློན་འབངས་བཅས་ (jelön baŋjɛɛ̀) abbr. king, ministers and subjects.

རྗེ་འབངས་ (jebaŋ) lord/ king and his subjects.

རྗེ་འབངས་གཉིས་ལོ་ (jebaŋ ñiilo) shung. the master and subjects both being satisfied.

རྗེ་འབུམ་ཁང་ (jebumgaŋ) a temple in Lhasa where one hundred thousand clay images of Tsongkaba are housed.

རྗེ་མོ་ (jemo) 1. female chief/ lord/ ruler. 2. wife of a lord/ chief/ king; female from the noble/ aristocratic class.

རྗེ་ཙོང་ཁ་པ་ (je dzōŋgaba) see རྗེ་རིན་པོ་ཆེ་.

རྗེ་བཙན་ (jedzɛn) king, ruler.

རྗེ་བཙུན་ (jedzün) 1. honorific title for great religious teachers (sth. like "The venerable"). 2. honorific terms for nuns of high birth).

རྗེ་བཙུན་སྐུ་ཞབས་ (jedzün gūshəb) title for a nun (usu. used for nuns of high birth).

རྗེ་བཙུན་སྒྲོལ་མ་ (jedzün drōma) Tara.

རྗེ་བཙུན་དམ་པ་ (jedzün tamba) 1. the name of the head incarnation in Mongolia. 2. a honorific title for great religious teachers (sth. like "The venerable").

རྗེ་བཙུན་བླ་མ་ (jedzün lāma) sm. རྗེ་བཙུན་དམ་པ་.

རྗེ་བཙུན་མ་ (jedzünma) 1. nun (h.). 2. a term used for women of high ranking/ aristocratic families.

རྗེ་ཞབས་ (jeshəb) master and his servants.

རྗེ་ཡབ་སྲས་གསུམ་ (je yəbsɛɛ̀ sūm) the three—the founder of the yellow hat sect and his two disciples: ཙོང་ཁ་པ་, མཁས་གྲུབ་རྗེ་ and རྒྱལ་ཚབ་རྗེ་.

རྗེ་རིགས་ (jerig) nobility, aristocracy.

རྗེ་རིགས་མ་ (jerigma) sm. རྗེ་མོ་.

རྗེ་རིན་པོ་ཆེ་ (je rimboce) 1. title for ཙོང་ཁ་པ་, the founder of the Gelugpa sect. 2. title used for high lamas.

རྗེ་ས་ (jesa) sm. ཞེ་ས་.

རྗེད་ (jeè) 1. va. to respect, to honor, to revere. 2. sm.* བརྗེད་.

རྗེད་པའི་འོས་ (jeèbɛ wö̤ö̀) worthy of respect, revered.

རྗེད་པོ་ (jeèdo) sm.* བརྗེད་པོ་.

རྗེན་ (jen) 1. abbr. of རྗེན་པ་. 2. ground unroasted barley.

རྗེན་གཅེར་ (jenjer) sm. རྗེན་ཅེར་.

རྗེན་ཆེ་ (jenje) sm. རྗེན་བདགས་.

རྗེན་ཅེར་ (jencer) 1. really, actually (usu. for visual things) ། དེ་རྗེ་ཅེར་མཐོང་བྱུང་ I actually saw it. 2. naked, bare.

རྗེན་བདགས་ (jendaà) unroasted grain that has been ground (usu. used as animal fodder).

རྗེན་ཐལ་ (jendɛɛ) sm. རྗེན་བདགས་.

རྗེན་དྲི་ (jendri) stale smell; vi.—ཁ་ to smell stale.

རྗེན་ནེ་བ་ (jennewa) 1. completely naked. 2. clear.

རྗེན་པ་ (jemba) 1. raw, unprocessed, crude ། ཤ་རྗེན་པ་ Raw meat. ། རྡོ་སྣུམ་རྗེན་པ་ Crude oil. 2. naked, anything in its real/ original form ། གནད་དོན་རྗེན་པ་མཐོང་བ་རེད་ (They) saw the naked truth (of the matter).

རྗེན་པར་འདོན་ (jembar tö̱n) va. to expose the (naked) truth.

རྗེན་བཙོས་ (jendzöö̀) abbr. raw and cooked.

རྗེན་ཚལ་ (jendzɛɛ) raw vegetables.

རྗེན་བཞོན་ (jenshön) riding an animal bareback; va.—རྒྱག.

རྗེན་ཟས་ (jensɛɛ̀) uncooked/ raw food; va.—རྒྱག to eat raw foods.

རྗེན་རིགས་ (jenrig) sm. རྗེན་ཟས་.

རྗེན་ལ་འབུད་ (jenla bṳ̈ṳ̀) va. to strip (naked).

རྗེན་ལོག (jenlɔɔ̀) semicooked, half cooked.

རྗེན་ཤ་བཙོས་ལོག (jensha dzöö̀lɔɔ̀) shung. not abiding by the verdict [Lit. cooked meat becoming raw again].

རྗེའུ་ (jewu) petty official, leader of a small principality or tribe.

རྗེའུ་རིགས་ (jewurig) one of the four races in ancient India.

རྗེས་ (jeè) 1. (vb. + —) after, later ། ང་ཚོ་ཕྱིན་རྗེས་ཁོ་ཚོ་སླེབས་པ་རེད་ They came after we left. 2. imprint, mark, track, race ། ལག་རྗེས་ Handprint. ། རྐང་རྗེས་ Footprint.

རྗེས་སྐྱེས་ (jeègyeè) youth.

རྗེས་སྐྱེས་ཕུལ་བྱུང་ (jeègyeè pṻüjuŋ) an outstanding young person.

རྗེས་ཁྲལ་ (jeèdrɛɛ) shung. taxes that are attached/ associated with sth. ། ས་ཁང་རྗེས་ཁྲལ་ The taxes attached to the house and land.

རྗེས་མཁོ་ (jeèko) necessary in the future.

རྗེས་འཁྲི་ (jeèdri) shung. (taxes and rent) that are attached/ associated with sth. ། ས་ཁང་རྗེས་འཁྲིའི་ཁྲལ་སྤྲུབ་འཇལ་བྱེད་དགོས་ One must pay the taxes attached to the land and the house.

རྗེས་འཁྲིལ་ (jeèdrii) hanging on/ clinging to sb.; va.—རྒྱག ། ཕྲུ་གུས་ཨ་མའི་རྗེས་འཁྲིལ་རྒྱག་གི་ཡོད་པ་རེད་ The child is clinging to its mother.

རྗེས་གྲབས་ (jeèdrəb) reserve/ future preparations.

རྗེས་གྲབས་དཔུང་སྡེ་ (jeèdrəb būŋde) reserve unit/ force.

རྗེས་གྲབས་མ་དངུལ་ (jeèdrəb mə ŋṻü) reserve fund/ capital.

རྗེས་གྲབས་དམག་དཔུང་ (jeèdrəb māgbuŋ) reserve force/ troops/ army.

རྗེས་གྲབས་དམག་མི་ (jeèdrəb mā̄mi) reserve soldier.

རྗེས་གྲུབ་ (jeèdrub) word derivation (the process of forming new words or phrases by combining existing words/ syllables).

རྗེས་གྲུབ་ཀྱི་མིང་ (jeèdrubgi miŋ) sm. ངེས་པའི་ཚིག.

རྗེས་འགོད་ (jengöö̀) recording/ writing afterwards; va.—བྱེད་.

རྗེས་འགྲོ་ (jendro) 1. followers. 2. similar, alike.

རྗེས་རྒལ་གཞན་འདུལ་ (jeègɛɛ shendüü) defeating/ vanquishing/ overcoming others but not striking the first blow.

རྗེས་རྒྱུགས་ (jeègyuù) sm. རྗེས་འབྲངས་.

རྗེས་སྔོ་ (jeèŋo) sm. མཇུག་བསྔོ་.

རྗེས་གཅོད་ (jeèjöö̀) 1. tracing, tracking, searching; va.—བྱེད་ ། ཀུན་མ་བྲོས་ན་ཡང་རྗེས་གཅོད་བྱས་ནས་འཛིན་བཟུང་བྱས་པ་རེད་ Even though the thief ran away (we) tracked him down and arrested him. 2. va. to eradicate/ annihilate.

རྗེས་བཅོས་ (jeèjöö̀) correcting, editing, proofing; va.—བྱེད་.

རྗེས་ཆགས་ (jeèjaà) 1. love and compassion. 2. desire, attachment.

རྗེས་ཆོད་ (jeè cöö̀) 1. vi. to be located/ found. 2. sm. རྗེས་ཟིན་.

རྗེས་འཇུག (jinjuù) 1. followers, adherents, disciples, devotees. 2. name for the ten consonants that can occur in the final (suffix) slot of a syllable.

རྗེས་འཇུག་ཕོ་ཡིག (jinjuù pōyii) the four masculine suffixed consonants (ག, ད, བ, ས).

རྗེས་འཇུག་བུ་སློབ་ (jinjuù pulob) disciples, followers, adherents.

རྗེས་འཇུག་མ་ནིང་ (jinjuù məniŋ) the three hermaphrodite suffixed consonants (ན, ར, ལ).

རྗེས་འཇུག་མོ་ཡིག (jinjuù moyig) the three feminine suffixed consonants (ང, མ, འ).

རྗེས་རྗེས་ང་ང་ (jeèjeè ŋāŋa) chasing/ following sb. continuously; va.—བྱེད་.

རྗེས་བརྗོད་ (jeèjöö̀) postscript, sth. written/ spoken after the main item.

རྗེས་ཉུལ་ (jeè ñul) va. to follow/ chase, to pursue through investigation.

རྗེས་སྙེག (jeèñeg) chasing, pursuing, following; va.—བྱེད་; —གཏོང་ chase, to pursue, to follow, to chase after.

རྗེས་སྙེགས་དུང་རྡེག (jeèñeg duŋdeg) pursuing and destroying; va.—གཏོང་.

རྗེས་བསྙེགས་ (jeèñeg) sm. རྗེས་སྙེག.

རྗེས་གདུགས་ (jeèdug) sm. རྗེས་སྙེག.

རྗེས་སྟོན་ཡོན་རྫི་ (jeèdön yondzi) tib.ch. tracer atom.

རྗེས་ཐོགས་ (jeèdɔɔ̀) as soon as.

རྗེས་ཐོན་ (jeèdön) 1. newly/ lately developed; va.—ཡོང་ to get developed, to move forward, to advance. 2. departing late.

རྗེས་མཐུན་ (jeèdün) same, identical.

རྗེས་དྲན་ (jeèdrɛn) commemoration, remembrance, anniversary; va.—བྱེད་;—ཞུ་ to commemorate, to have a remembrance ceremony ¶ རང་དབང་སྒེར་ལང་ཐེངས་བཅུ་གཅིག་པའི་རྗེས་དྲན་ The 11th commemoration of the uprising for freedom.

རྗེས་དྲན་ཁང་ (jeèdrɛngaŋ) monument, memorial hall, memorial place.

རྗེས་དྲན་གྱི་རྟགས་མ་ (jeèdrɛngi dāŋma) memorial medal.

རྗེས་དྲན་དྲུག (jedrɛn trüù) the six things to remember: one's guru (lama), the Buddha, the dharma, others, vows and charity.

རྗེས་དྲན་རྡོ་རིང་ (jeèdrɛn doriŋ) commemorative pillar.

རྗེས་དྲན་ཚོགས་འདུ་ (jeèdrɛn tsōndu) commemoration meeting/ ceremony/ celebration.

རྗེས་འདེད་ (jendeè) sm. རྗེས་སྙེག.

རྗེས་འདེད་མཁན་ (jendeèñɛn) sm. རྗེས་འབྲང་བ་.

རྗེས་འདེད་དམག་གྲུ་ (jendeè mɔgdruù) jendeè mɔgdru) destroyer (ship), pursuit frigate.

རྗེས་འདེད་ལ་འགྲོ་ (jendeèla dro) va. to follow, to pursue.

རྗེས་སྡོད་ (jeèdöö) leaving behind; va.—བྱེད་ to leave behind (a person).

རྗེས་གནང་ (jeènaŋ) permission, consent; empowerment.

རྗེས་གནོད་ (jeènöö) future problems, future harm/ damage.

རྗེས་གནོན་གཏོང་ (jeènön dōŋ) shung. va. to conduct a severe investigation and punishment ¶ ཡུལ་ཁྲིམས་རྡོག་རོལ་དུ་གཏོང་བའི་བྱ་ངན་འདི་རིགས་རྒྱ་ཡན་དུ་མ་སོང་བའི་རྗེས་གནོན་གཏོང་ངེས་ (We) will not let persons who violate the law evade punishment but will definitely conduct a severe investigation on them and put them under law.

རྗེས་གནོན་རྒྱབ་རོགས་ (jeènön gyɔbrɔɔ̀) supporting/ aiding in order to complete or finish sth. that has been started.

རྗེས་གནོན་མཐར་སྐྱེལ་ (jeènön tārgyee) completing/ finishing (sth.) that has already been started; va.—བྱེད་.

རྗེས་གནོན་བདད་འདེད་ (jeènön dandeè) shung. to investigate and impose severe punishment.

རྗེས་གནོན་ཚ་ནན་ (jeènön tsānɛn) imposing a severe punishment; va.—བྱེད་.

རྗེས་སྔོན་ (jeènön) alternate, reserve.

རྗེས་སྔོན་ཁོངས་མི་ (jeènön kōŋmi) sm. རྗེས་སྔོན་ཨུ་ཡོན་.

རྗེས་སྔོན་ཨུ་ཡོན་ (jeènön ūyün) tib.ch. alternate member of a committee.

རྗེས་དཔག (jeèbaà) reasoning, inference, rationality.

རྗེས་དཔག་གི་ཤེས་རྟོགས་ (jeèbaàgi shēèdɔɔ̀) sm. རྗེས་དཔག་གི་ཤེས་ཡོན་.

རྗེས་དཔག་གི་ཤེས་ཡོན་ (jeèbaàgi shēèyön) rational knowledge/ understanding.

རྗེས་དཔག་གི་ཤེས་པ་ (jeèbaàgi shēèba) sm. རྗེས་དཔག་གི་ཤེས་ཡོན་.

རྗེས་དཔག་ཙམ་སྨྲ་བ་ (jeèbaàdzam māwa) rationalism.

རྗེས་དཔག་ཚད་མ་ (jeèbaà tsɛɛ̀ma) inferential understanding, rational/ logical comprehension.

རྗེས་སྤྲོད་ (jeèdröö) giving/ paying later; va.—བྱེད་.

རྗེས་འབབ་སྔོན་སྔོན་ (jeèbɔb ŋōndön) spending one's income in advance of receiving it.

རྗེས་འབྱོར་ (jenjɔɔ) ones who arrived later, newly arrived ¶ རྒྱ་ནག་ནས་རྗེས་འབྱོར་བོད་རིགས་སློབ་ཕྲུག Tibetan students who arrived later from China (i.e., went into exile in India after liberalization in China in the 1980s and 1990s).

རྗེས་འབྲང་ (jeèdraŋ) sm. རྗེས་འབྲང་ས་.

རྗེས་འབྲང་ས་ (jeèdraŋ) following after, adhering to; va.—བྱེད་ to follow after, to adhere to ¶ མའོའི་རྗེས་འབྲངས་ Follower's of Mao.

རྗེས་འབྲངས་རྒྱལ་ཁབ་ (jeèdraŋ gyɛɛ̀gɔb) satellite country.

རྗེས་འབྲངས་ངན་རེངས་པ་ (jeèdraŋ ŋɛnreŋba) diehard follower.

རྗེས་འབྲངས་ཉེས་ཅན་ (jeèdraŋ ñeèjɛn) accessory (to a criminal act).

རྗེས་འབྲངས་པ་ (jeèdraŋba) follower, adherent.

རྗེས་འབྲས་ (jendɛɛ̀) result, accomplishment, achievement.

རྗེས་འབྲེལ་ (jendrel) having to do with the past, related to the past.

རྗེས་མ་ (jeèma) 1. last, final. 2. later, afterwards.

རྗེས་མ་ཟིན་ (jeè ma sin) vi. to be too late, to miss (in a time sense), to be unable to catch up ¶ འཛིན་གྲྭ་རྗེས་མ་ཟིན་པ་རེད་ They missed the class. ¶ སློབ་ཕྲུག་གཞན་དག་གི་རྗེས་མ་ཟིན་པ་རེད་ (He) could not catch up with the other students.

རྗེས་མའི་རྗེས་མ་ (jeèmɛ jeèma) the very last, in the very end.

རྗེས་མར་ (jeèmaa) afterwards, later ¶ རྗེས་མ་ང་ཚོ་ལྷ་སར་འབྱོར་སྐབས་ Later when we arrived in Lhasa. ¶ རྗེས་མར་མཇལ་ཡོང་ I'll meet you later.

རྗེས་མར་མཇལ་ཡོང་ (jeèma jɛɛyoŋ) common phrase said when departing: "meet you again".

རྗེས་མར་ལུས་ (jeèma lüü) vi. to be left behind, to fall behind.

རྗེས་མེད་ (jeèmeè) without a track/ trace/ imprint; va.—འཇིག to annihilate, to destroy completely.

རྗེས་མེད་ཤུལ་མེད་ (jeèmeè shüümeè) completely gone without a trace.

རྗེས་མྱོང་ (jeèñoŋ) firsthand experience.

རྗེས་བཙད་ (jeèdzɛɛ̀) va. to search for sb. through their tracks.

རྗེས་ཚབ་ (jeèdzɔb) relief (usu. for troops).

རྗེས་འཚོལ་ (jeèdzöö) va. to follow a trail/ track in search of sth. or sb., to trace/ look/ search for.

རྗེས་འཛིན་ (jeèdzin) 1. followers, adherents, believers; va.—བྱེད་ to follow, to adhere, to believe in ¶ ཁོ་ལ་རྗེས་འཛིན་བྱུང་ཡོད་པ་མ་རེད་ He didn't get any disciples. 2. following in sb.'s footsteps.

རྗེས་ཞིབ་ (jeèshib) retaining/ filing for later reference or examination, keeping as evidence; va.—བྱེད་.

རྗེས་ཞུ་ (jeèshu) a follow-up report.

རྗེས་བཞིན་ (jeèshin) following after; va.—འབྲང་; —འགྲོ་ to follow after.

རྗེས་ཟིན་ (jeè sim) 1. vi. to catch up with ¶ རུས་སྦལ་གཅིག་གིས་ངའི་རྗེས་ཟིན་གྱི་མ་རེད་བསམས་པ་རེད་ (He) thought that a turtle will not catch up with me. 2. vi. to do sth. in time.(usu. དུས་ཚོད་ + —).

རྗེས་ཟློས་ (jendöö) imitating, repeating after sb.; va.—བྱེད་ to imitate, to repeat ¶ རོལ་དབྱངས་དགེ་རྒན་གྱི་རྗེས་ཟློས་བྱས་པ་རེད་ (They) repeated after the music teacher.

རྗེས་ཟློས་དང་ལེན་ (jendöö tanlen) voluntarily imitating.

རྗེས་བཟུང་ (jeèsuŋ) sm. རྗེས་འཛིན་.

རྗེས་ཡི་རང་ (jeèyiraŋ) abbr. of རྗེས་སུ་ཡི་རང་.

རྗེས་ཡོང་སྔོན་དྲན་ (jeèyoŋ ŋōndrɛn) foreseeing, predicting, forecasting; va.—བྱེད་.

རྗེས་ཡོང་སྔོན་ཤེས་ (jeèyoŋ ŋōnsheè) sm. རྗེས་ཡོང་སྔོན་དྲན་.

རྗེས་ཡོང་སྔོན་སླེབས་ (jeèyoŋ ŋōnleb) come late but arrive first (conveys that although China was late in developing, it will become the best).

རྗེས་རབས་ (jeèrɔb) the younger generation.

རྗེས་ལ་ (jeèla) sm. རྗེས་སུ་.

རྗེས་ལམ་ (jeèlam) the future, the future path.

རྗེས་ལུགས་ (jeèluù) old style.

རྗེས་ལུས་ (jeèlüü) backward, underdeveloped; vi.—ཐེབས་ to fall/ lag behind, to be left behind; to be late ¶ རྗེས་ལུས་ལུང་པ་ An underdeveloped country.

རྗེས་ལུས་ཅན་ (jeèlüüjɛn) backward, underdeveloped, laggard.

རྗེས་ལོ་ (jeèlo) next year.

རྗེས་ཤུལ་ (jeèshüü) (ancient) traces, remains, ruins; va.—སྙེག་; —འདེད་ to follow a trail/ track, to trace, to track down; va.—འཛིན་ to succeed, to inherit ¶ སྔར་གྱི་མཁར་རྫོང་གི་རྗེས་ཤུལ་ Ruins of an ancient fortress.

རྗེས་ཤུལ་འཛིན་མཁན་ (jeèshüü dzingɛn) successor, inheritor.

རྗེས་སུ་ (jeèsu) later, after, afterward ¶ རྗེས་སུ་ཇི་ཡོང་ཤེས་དཀའ་ཡང་ Even though it is hard to know what will happen later. ¶ རྗེས་སུ་ཁོས་ང་ལ་ཟེར་གྱི་འདུག He told me (that) afterwards.

རྗེས་སུ་འགྱོད་ (jeèsu gyöö) va. to regret/ lament/ bemoan.

རྗེས་སུ་འགྲོ་ (jeèsu dro) 1. va. to go after, to follow, to imitate. 2. sm. རྗེས་འགྲོ་.

རྗེས་སུ་རྒྱུག (jeèsu gyuù) sm. རྗེས་སུ་སྙེག.

རྗེས་སུ་གཅགས་ (jeèsu jāà) va. to regret, lament, bemoan.

རྗེས་སུ་ཆགས་ (jeèsu cāà) vi. to get attached to.

རྗེས་སུ་སྙེག (jeèsu ñēg) 1. va. to follow sb. or sth. ¶ མོའི་སེམས་ལ་ང་ནང་ལ་ལོག་ན་ཁོ་རྗེས་སུ་བསྙེགས་ནས་ནང་དུ་ཡོང་གི་རེད་སྙམ་ She thought, if I go inside he will follow me inside. ¶ དབྱིན་ཇིའི་བརྗོད་རྗེས་སུ་བསྙེགས་ (They) were following what the British said. 2. va. to pursue, to chase.

རྗེས་སུ་སྟོན་ (jeèsu dõn) va. to open a person's eyes to sth.

རྗེས་སུ་མཐུན་ (jeèsu tũn) sm. རྗེས་མཐུན་.

རྗེས་སུ་དྲན་ (jeèsu trɛn) vi. to remember, to commemorate.

རྗེས་སུ་འདེད་ (jeèsu teè) va. to chase/ pursue, to go after.

རྗེས་སུ་གནང་བ་ (jeèsu nāŋwa) sm. རྗེས་གནང་.

རྗེས་སུ་དཔག་པ་ (jeèsu bāgba) sm. རྗེས་དཔག.

རྗེས་སུ་བྱེད་ (jeèsu ceè) 1. va. to do later/ afterwards. 2. va. to follow/ imitate.

རྗེས་སུ་བྱེད་པའི་སྒྲ་ (jeèsu ceèbɛ dra) a word or phrase used twice to make a certain point or to emphasize sth. (e.g., མ་རེད་མ་རེད་).

རྗེས་སུ་འབྲང་ (jeèsu draŋ) sm. རྗེས་སུ་སྙེག.

རྗེས་སུ་འབྲངས་ (jeèsu draŋ) p. of རྗེས་སུ་འབྲང་.

རྗེས་སུ་འབྲེལ་བ་ (jeèsu drel) sm. རྗེས་འབྲེལ་.

རྗེས་སུ་མྱོང་བ་ (jeèsu ñoŋ) vi. to experience firsthand.

རྗེས་སུ་བརྩེ་ (jeèsu dzē) va. to feel sorry, to have sympathy for.

རྗེས་སུ་འཚོལ་ (jeèsu tsöö) sm. རྗེས་འཚོལ་.

རྗེས་སུ་འཛིན་ (jeèsu dzin) va. to follow, to adhere to, to believe in.

རྗེས་སུ་བཟུང་ (jeèsu suŋ) p. of རྗེས་སུ་འཛིན་.

རྗེས་སུ་ཡི་རང་ (jeèsu yiraŋ) vi. to feel glad/ happy, to rejoice.

རྗེས་སུ་ཤེས་ (jeèsu shēè) to know/ understand/ comprehend.

རྗེས་སུ་ཤོད་ (jeèsu shöö) va. to tell/ say later.

རྗེས་སུ་ལུས་ (jeèsu lüü) vi. to lag behind, to be late (schedule), to fall behind, to be backward/ underdeveloped.

རྗེས་སུ་སློབ་ (jeèsu lōb) sm. རྗེས་སུ་སྙེག.

རྗེས་སོར་ (jeèsɔr) later, in the future, afterwards.

རྗེས་སློབ་ (jeèlob) disciple, adherent, follower.

རྗུད་དོ་ (jüüdo) dried and withered.

རྗོད་: p. བརྗོད་; f. བརྗོད་; imp. རྗོད་ (jöö) va. to say, to express ¶ ཁོ་ཚོ་འགྲོ་གི་མིན་ཞེས་རྗོད་ཀྱི་འདུག (They) say we are not going. ¶ གོང་དུ་བརྗོད་པ་ལྟར་ According to what was said earlier.

རྗོད་བཀོད་བྱེད་ (jöögöö ceè) va. to give verbal orders to subordinates.

རྗོད་དོན་ (jöödön) content/ meaning (of what was said).

རྗོད་བྱེད་ (jööceè) sm. རྗོད་དོན་.

རྗོད་ཚིག (jöödzii) 1. talk ¶ རྗོད་ཚིག་སྐམ་པོ་བྲོ་མེད་ talk that is meaningless [Lit. talk that is dry and tasteless]. 2. the predicate (in grammar).

རྗོད་རྩལ་ (jöödzüü) sm. རྗོད་དོན་.

རྗོད་གཞི་ (jööshi) topic of talk.

རྗོད་ལུགས་ (jööluù) the manner of saying.

ལྗགས་ (jaà) 1. tongue (h.). 2. term used to make nonhonorific words honorific.

ལྗགས་གློག (jaàlɔɔ) h. of གློག.

ལྗགས་གློག་གནང་ (jaàlɔɔnaŋ) h. of གློག.

ལྗགས་བཀོད་ (jaàgöö) instructions, directions (h.); va.—གནང་ to give directions, to instruct.

ལྗགས་སྐྱེད་ (jaàgyeè) interest (on a loan).

ལྗགས་སྐྱེམས་ (jaàgyem) sm. གསེར་སྐྱེམས་.

ལྗགས་ཁྲིད་ (jədrii) teaching (h.); va.—གནང་ to teach; va.—ཞུ་ to request teaching.

ལྗགས་གོང་ (jaàgoŋ) price (h.).

ལྗགས་གྲངས་ (jaàdraŋ) h. of གྲངས་ཀ་.

ལྗགས་གླིང་ (jəliŋ) a type of flute with seven fingerholes.

ལྗགས་བསྔོ་ (jaàŋo) h. of བསྔོ་བ་.

ལྗགས་ཆབ་ (jaàjəb) h. of མཆིལ་མ་.

ལྗགས་མདུད་ (jandüü) a thin scarf that lamas or oracles give to people for protection from evil spirits.

ལྗགས་འདྲིལ་ (jaà dril) va. to coil the tongue (usu. as depicted in images of Buddhist deities).

ལྗགས་ནར་ (jaànar) sticking out (one's) tongue (h.); va.—གནང་; —མཛད་.

ལྗགས་པན་ (jaàbɛn) h. of སི་པན་.

ལྗགས་ཕུ་ (jəbu) h. of ཕུ་.

ལྗགས་བྲོ་ (jaàdro) taste, tasting (h.); va.—གཟིགས་ to taste.

ལྗགས་དབུགས་ (jaàwuù) breathing, breath (h.); va.—བཏང་གནང་; to breathe; va.—འཐེན་གནང་ to inhale.

ལྗགས་མར་ (jaàmar) butter that has been blessed/ sanctified by a mantra.

ལྗགས་སྨིན་ (jaàmin) h. of ལྟོ་ཆས་.

ལྗགས་རྩིས་ (jədzii) h. of རྩིས་.

ལྗགས་རྫོམ་ (jaàdzom) h. of རྫོམ་.

ལྗགས་ཚྭ་ (jaàdza) h. of ཚྭ་.

ལྗགས་ཞིབ་ (jaàshib) h. of ཐྲུགས་.

ལྗགས་ལན་ (jaàlɛn) h. of ལན་.

ལྗགས་ལུང་ (jəluŋ) h. of ལུང་.

ལྗགས་བཤད་ (jaàshɛɛ̀) commentary/ explanation on a text (h.); va.—གནང་; —མཛད་.

ལྗགས་ཞེར་ (jaàshee) h. of ཅི་ཉི་.

ལྗགས་སི་ (jaàsi) h. of སི་པན་.

ལྗགས་སི་དམར་འདུར་ (jaàsi mərduu) paste made from ground hot pepper (h.).

ལྗགས་སིལ་ (jaàsii) sm. ལྗགས་སི་.

ལྗང་ (jaŋ) 1. abbr. of ལྗང་ཁུ་. 2. abbr. of ལྗང་བུ་.

ལྗང་ཀང་ (jaŋgaŋ) seedlings.

ལྗང་དཀར་ (jaŋgaa) light green color.

ལྗང་སྐྱ་ (jaŋgya) sm. ལྗང་དཀར་.

ལྗང་ཁུ་ (jəŋgu) green.

ལྗང་ཁུ་ཚོགས་པ་ (jəŋgu tsōgba) Green Party.

ལྗང་ཁྲ་ (jaŋdra) green pot.

ལྗང་གུ་ (jəŋgu) sm. ལྗང་ཁུ་.

ལྗང་དགུན་ཆོས་ (jaŋ günjöö) sm. འཆང་དགུན་ཆོས་.

ལྗང་འགྱུར་ (jaŋ gyur) vi. to become green by planting trees, flowers, etc.

ལྗང་སྔོན་ (jaŋŋön) bluish green.

ལྗང་ཇ་ (jaŋca) 1. green tea. 2. tea from ལྗང་.

ལྗང་ཐིག (jəŋdig) a type of material with a green base color and pluses (+) of different colors.

ལྗང་ཐིང་ (jaŋdiŋ) completely green.

ལྗང་ཐིང་ངེ་ (jaŋ tĩŋŋe) sm. ལྗང་ཐིང་.

ལྗང་ཐིང་ཐིང་ (jaŋ tĩŋdiŋ) sm. ལྗང་ཐིང་.

ལྗང་འདེམས་ (jaŋdem) selecting seedlings (for

transplanting); va.—བྱེད་.

ལྗང་དྲ་ལིང་དྲ་ (jaŋda liŋda) 1. a swing. 2. dangling, swinging back and forth.

ལྗང་དྭང་ (jaŋduŋ) pure, unadulterated.

ལྗང་དྭང་མ་ (jaŋ duŋmə) pure, unadulterated ¶ སྐུ་བརྙན་འདི་གསེར་ལྗང་དྭང་མ་རེད་ This statue is pure gold.

ལྗང་སྡོང་ (jaŋdoŋ) stalk, stem.

ལྗང་ནག (jaŋnaà) dark green.

ལྗང་པ་ (jaŋba) sm. ལྗང་བུ་.

ལྗང་སྤྲིན་ (jaŋdrin) greenish colored clouds (in Tibetan painting).

ལྗང་ཕུད་ (jaŋbüü) (villagers) giving newly cut grass to travelers for their horses (and begging for money).

ལྗང་ཕོན་ (jaŋbön) a bunch/ stack of stalks or stems.

ལྗང་བུ་ (jəŋbu) a seedling, shoot, sprout; va.—འཛུགས་ to plant/ transplant seedlings.

ལྗང་བུ་སྐམ་ནད་ (jəŋbu gāmnɛɛ̀) a plant disease that causes shriveling/ withering of new shoots and seedlings.

ལྗང་བུ་སྐྱེས་བཟང་པོ་ (jəŋbu gyēè saŋbo) flourishing young seedlings/ plants.

ལྗང་བུ་རྙིད་ནད་ (jəŋbu ñı̃ìnɛɛ̀) sm. ལྗང་བུ་སྐམ་ནད་.

ལྗང་བུ་འཐུག་སེལ་ (jəŋbu tūgsel) thinning of sprouts/ seedlings.

ལྗང་བུ་ལག་འཐེན་གྱི་སྐྱེས་རོགས་ (jəŋbu lagdengi gyēèroò) wrong kind of help, a stupid way to help [Lit. helping seedlings grow by pulling them with the hand].

ལྗང་བུ་གསོ་ (jəŋbu sō) va. to raise/ grow seedlings.

ལྗང་བུ་གསོ་ས་ (jəŋbu sōsa) a place where seedlings are raised, seedling farm.

ལྗང་མ་ (jaŋma) sm. ལྗང་བུ་.

ལྗང་སྙུག (jəŋñuù) sm. ལྗང་བུ་.

ལྗང་དམར་ (jaŋmar) dark green with a reddish hue.

ལྗང་སྨུག (jəŋmuù) sm. ལྗང་ནག.

ལྗང་འཛུགས་ (jəŋdzuù) transplanting seedlings; va.—རྒྱག.

ལྗང་འཛུགས་འཕྲུལ་ཆས་ (jəŋdzuù trũũjɛɛ̀) seedling transplanting machine.

ལྗང་གཞས་ (jaŋshɛɛ̀) work song sung when transplanting rice seedlings.

ལྗང་ལོ་ (jaŋlo) green leaves.

ལྗང་གཤར་ (jaŋshaa) greenish trimming on boots leggings.

ལྗང་སེར་ (jaŋser) yellowish green, apple green.

ལྗན་ལྗིན་ (jɛnjin) dirty, filthy.

ལྗབ་ལྗབ་ (jəbjəb) sm. ལྗབ་ལྗབ་པོ་.

ལྗབ་ལྗབ་པོ་ (jəb jəbbo) clasping one's two hands together in a hollowish shape.

ལྗར་གྱིས་ (jargi) (pressing) forcefully/ with force ¶ ལྗར་གྱིས་གནན་པ་རེད་ (They) pressed down forcefully.

ལྗར་གྱིས་གསོད་ (jargi sȍȍ) va. to kill by pressing down/ squeezing.

ལྗར་མནན་ (jarnɛn) pressing down/ squeezing forcefully.

ལྗི་པ་ (jibə) 1. flea. 2. heavy.

ལྗི་བ་ (jiwə) flea.

ལྗི་མོ་ (jimu) heavy.

ལྗིད་ (jiì) 1. heavy, heaviness ¶ དེ་ལྗིད་ག་ཚོད་འདུག How heavy is it? 2. abbr. of ལྗིད་པོ་.

ལྗིད་སྐུལ་ (jiìgüü) forcing sb. to do heavy labor.

ལྗིད་ཁུར་ (jiìgur) heavy load, heavy burden.

ལྗིད་གོག (jiìgɔɔ̀) heavy.

ལྗིད་གོག་ཚ་པོ་ (jiìgɔɔ̀ tsābo) very heavy.

ལྗིད་གྲས་ (jiìdrɛɛ̀) heavy class/ type ¶ དམག་གྲུ་ལྗིད་གྲས་ Heavy cruiser (warship).

ལྗིད་བསྐལ་ཆིང་རླུང་ (jiìgɛɛ ciŋluŋ) tritium.

ལྗིད་བསྐལ་མ་རྒྱུ་ (jiìgɛɛ məgyu) heavy elements (in physics).

ལྗིད་འགན་ (jingɛn) heavy responsibility.

ལྗིད་ཅན་ (jiìjɛn) sm. ལྗིད་ལྡན་.

ལྗིད་ཆས་ (jiìjɛɛ̀) heavy implements/ articles/ goods/ things ¶ ལྗིད་ཆས་བཟོ་ལས་ Heavy industry.

ལྗིད་ཆེ་བ་ (jiìcewa) very heavy.

ལྗིད་མཉམ་པ་ (jiì ñamba) equal weight/ heaviness.

ལྗིད་དིག་གེ་བ་ (ji dı̃ggewa) sm. ལྗིད་དིག་དིག.

ལྗིད་དིག་དིག (ji dı̃gdig) heavy (usu. for feelings).

ལྗིད་ཐིབས་ཐིབས་ (jiì tı̃bdib) dizzy.

ལྗིད་ཐེག (jiìdeg) capable of carrying a heavy weight/ load.

ལྗིད་ཐེག་གྲངས་ཚད་ (jiìdeg traŋdzɛɛ̀) loading capacity, amount of weight that can be carried, tonnage (for ships).

ལྗིད་ཐེག་སླང་འཁོར་ (jiìdeg lāŋgɔɔ) heavy capacity truck/ vehicle.

ལྗིད་ཐེག་ཆེའི་ཁྲི་ (jiìdeg cı̃dre) tib.ch. sm. ལྗིད་ཐེག་སླངས་འཁོར་.

ལྗིད་དུ་གཏོང་ (jiìdu dɔ̃ŋ) va. to add weight, to make heavier ¶ ཁོའི་ལས་འགན་ལྗིད་དུ་བཏང་བ་རེད་ (They) made his responsibility heavier.

ལྗིད་འདེགས་ (jiìdeg) lifting heavy objects, weight lifting (the sport).

ལྗིད་འདེགས་ཀྱི་ཤུགས་ (jiìdeggi shūg) lifting capacity.

ལྗིད་འདེགས་གྲུ་གཟིངས་ (jiìdeg truziŋ) crane ship.

ལྗིད་འདེགས་དབྱང་འཁོར་ (jiìdeg jāŋgɔɔ) crane, hoist, forklift.

ལྗིད་འདེགས་སྦྱོང་ཆས་ (jiìdeg jȍȍjɛɛ̀) barbell, weight-lifting equipment.

ལྗིད་འདེགས་འཕྲུལ་འཁོར་ (jiìdeg trũũgɔɔ) crane, hoist, forklift.

ལྗིད་ལྡན་ (jindɛn) heavy.

ལྗིད་ལྡན་དབྱུག་པ་ (jiìdɛn yūgbə) 1. heavy stick. 2. effectiveness.

ལྗིད་ནོད་ཚད་ (jiì nȍȍdzɛɛ̀) load-bearing capacity.

ལྗིད་གནོན་ (jiìnön) 1. oppressive. 2. heavy pressure ¶ ཆབ་སྲིད་ཀྱི་ལྗིད་གནོན་ཆེ་བས་སྐྱག་རྫུན་མ་ཤོད་ཀ་མེད་བྱུང་ (He) had no choice but to tell a lie due to the heavy political pressure.

ལྗིད་པ་ (jiìbə) weight, heaviness ¶ ལྗིད་པ་དེ་ཙམ་འདེགས་ཐུབ་ཀྱི་མ་རེད་ (One) cannot lift so much weight.

ལྗིད་པོ་ (jiìbu) heavy ¶ དེབ་འདི་ལྗིད་པོ་ཞེ་དྲགས་འདུག This book is very heavy.

ལྗིད་བ་ (jiìwə) sm. ལྗིད་པ་.

ལྗིད་བའི་བཟོ་ལས་ (jiìwɛ solɛɛ̀) heavy industry.

ལྗིད་དབྱུང་ (jiìyaŋ) heavy oxygen.

ལྗིད་མེད་ (jiìmeè) light.

ལྗིད་ཚད་ (jiìdzɛɛ̀) weight; va.—འདེགས་ to lift something heavy.

ལྗིད་ཚད་བསྐལ་བའི་མ་རྒྱུ་ (jiìdzɛɛ̀ gɛɛwɛ məgyu) sm. ལྗིད་བསྐལ་མ་རྒྱུ་.

ལྗིད་ཚད་རྩིས་གཞི་ (jiìdzɛɛ̀ dzı̃ìshi) weight unit.

ལྗིད་ཚད་ཤོར་ (jidzɛɛ̀ shɔɔ̃) vi. to be of unequal weight.

ལྗིད་རྫོབ་ཆེ་བ་ (jiìdzob cēwa) 1. heavy and big, ponderous. 2. awkward, slow.

ལྗིད་ཡང་ (jiìyaŋ) heavy and light, weight.

ལྗིད་ཡང་གོ་ལྡོག (jiìyaŋ kodɔɔ̀) putting the trivial above the important [Lit. inverting heavy and light].

ལྗིད་ཡོར་ཡོར་ (jiì yəryər) heavy.

ལྗིད་གཡོལ་ཡང་ལེན་ (jiìyöö yaŋlen) taking the easy way, choosing a light task.

ལྗིད་རིགས་ (jiìrig) heavy class/ type ¶ བཟོ་ལས་ལྗིད་རིགས་ Heavy industry.

ལྗིད་ལོས་ (jiìlöö) how heavy?

ལྗིད་ལོས་སྙོམས་པོ་ (jiìlöö ñõmbo) even/ balanced in weight.

ལྗིད་ཤོར་ (jiìshɔɔ) 1. weightlessness. 2. zero gravity.

ལྗིད་སོན་ (jiìsön) seeds that take a long time to sprout.

ལྗིན་ (jen) va. to penetrate, to enter.

ལྗོངས་ (joŋ) 1. country, province, region, area ¶ ཁ་བ་ཅན་གྱི་ལྗོངས་ A snowy country. 2. scenery. 3. abbr. རང་སྐྱོང་ལྗོངས་ (autonomous region) ¶ ལྗོངས་དང་ The communist party of the autonomous region.

ལྗོངས་བཀོད་ (joŋgöö) scenery, landscape.

ལྗོངས་རྒྱུ་ (joŋgyu) going to a far away place, traveling; va.—བྱེད་.

ལྗོངས་རྒྱུ་མཁན་ (joŋ gyuñɛn) traveler, tourist.

ལྗོངས་མཐོ་ (joŋto) highland area, high altitude place.

ལྗོངས་མི་ (joŋmi) indigenous/ local people.

ལྗོན་ (jön) abbr. of ལྗོན་པ་.

ལྗོན་ཀྲོང་ (jöndraŋ) shung. sm. འཇོན་ཀྲོང་.

ལྗོན་གྲིབ་ (jöndrib) the shade of a tree.

ལྗོན་གྲིབ་འགྲོ་ལམ་ (jöndrib drolam) tree-lined avenue/ boulevard.

ལྗོན་འདབ་ (jöndəb) leaf of tree.

ལྗོན་པ་ (jömba) woods, forest, trees ¶ ལྗོན་པའི་གྲིབ་བསིལ་ལྡན་པའི་རྒྱ་ལམ་ An avenue shaded with trees.

ལྗོན་པའི་དབང་པོ་ (jömbɛ wāŋbo) a famous book on Tibetan grammar.

ལྗོན་རྩ་ (jömdza) tree roots.

ལྗོན་ཤིང་ (jönshiŋ) sm. ལྗོན་པ་.

ལྗོན་ཤིང་སྐམ་པོར་འབྲས་བུའི་རེ་བ་མེད་པ་ (jönshiŋ gāmbɔɔ drɛɛ̀bü rewa meèba) sth. that is absolutely hopeless [Lit. hoping for fruit from a dry (dead) tree].

ལྗོན་ཤིང་གོག་པོ་ (jönshiŋ gɔgbo) a tree with its inside rotten.

ལྗོན་ཤིང་ལྡུམ་ར་ (jönshiŋ dumra) park, garden, grove.

ལྗོབ་པོ་ (jɔbbo) a faded/ muddled color.

བརྗིད་ (jii) brightness, luster, splendor.

བརྗིད་རྔམས་ (jiŋam) majestic/ grand/ glorious and awesome.

བརྗིད་རྔམས་ལྡན་པ་ (jiìŋam dɛmba) sm. བརྗིད་རྔམས་.

བརྗིད་ཆགས་ (པ་) (jiìjaà) grand, magnificent, glorious, splendid, majestic, imposing.

བརྗིད་ཆགས་ཅན་གྱི་ཚོགས་པ་རྙིང་པ་ (jiìcaàjɛngi tsōgba ñīŋbə) GOP (Republican Party, in U.S.A.) [Lit. Grand Old Party].

བརྗིད་ཆགས་ཡིད་འོང་ (jiìjaà yiìoŋ) majestic, magnificent, grand, glorious.

བརྗིད་ཆེ་ (jiìje) grand, huge, majestic.

བརྗིད་ཉམས་ (jiìñam) sm. བརྗིད་ཆགས་.

བརྗིད་ཉམས་དོད་པོ་ (jiìñam töòbo) sm. བརྗིད་ཆགས་.

བརྗིད་ཉམས་ལྡན་པ་ (jiìñam dɛmba) sm. བརྗིད་ཆགས་.

བརྗིད་པ་ (jiìbə) sm. བརྗིད་ཆགས་.

བརྗིད་པོ་ (jiìbo) sm. བརྗིད་ཆགས་.

བརྗིད་བག (jiìbaà) an attractive/ pleasing looking person.

བརྗེ་ (je) f. of རྗེ་.

བརྗེ་གྱོན་ (jegyön) changing clothing.

བརྗེ་འགྱུར་ (jegyur) sm. བརྗེ་ལེན་.

བརྗེ་འགྲུལ་ (jedrüü) changing, substituting, replacing; va.—རྒྱག་; —བྱེད་ ¶ ལས་བྱེད་མང་པོ་བརྗེ་འགྲུལ་བྱས་པ་རེད་ They replaced many officials.

བརྗེ་སྒྲིག (jedriì) transhipping, transshipment.

བརྗེ་འཐེན་ (jeden) removing/ dismissing and replacing or transferring; va.—བྱེད་.

བརྗེ་འདྲེན་ (jendren) exchange, exchanging; va.—བྱེད་ ¶ རིག་གནས་སྟེང་གི་བརྗེ་འདྲེན་ Cultural exchange.

བརྗེ་གནས་ (jenɛɛ̀) shop, store.

བརྗེ་པོ་ (jebo) changing, exchanging; va.—རྒྱག to change/ exchange; —ལྡོག to return, to exchange, to change.

བརྗེ་པོ་ལག་སྤྲོད་ (jebo lagdröö) exchanging goods right away (in contrast to giving an exchange at a later time).

བརྗེ་སྤོ་ (jeèbo) changing sth. alternatively.

བརྗེ་སྤྲོད་ (jedröö) sm. བརྗེ་འདྲེན་.

བརྗེ་འཁྲུལ་ (jedrüü) mistakenly exchange; vi.—ཐེབས་; —ཤོར་ to mistakenly exchange.

བརྗེ་བོ་ (jebo) sm. བརྗེ་པོ་.

བརྗེ་ཚོང་ (jedzoŋ) exchanging in kind, bartering; va.—རྒྱག.

བརྗེ་ཚོང་ཁང་ (jedzoŋgaŋ) a store where items are bartered/ exchanged.

བརྗེ་རེས་ (jereè) rotating, taking turns; va.—བྱེད་; —གཏོང་ ¶ དགོང་མོའི་སྲུང་ཆ་ཆུ་ཚོད་གཉིས་གཉིས་ནས་བརྗེ་རེས་བྱས་པ་རེད་ They took turns of two hours each on the night watch.

བརྗེ་རེས་བྱེད་ས་ (jereè ceèsa) exchange place/ area.

བརྗེ་ལེན་ (jelen) exchanging, substituting, replacing, interchanging; va.—བྱེད་ ¶ ཆུ་ཚོད་ ༢༤ ནང་འཁྲུལ་འཁོར་གཏོང་མཁན་ཐེངས་གསུམ་བརྗེ་ལེན་བྱས་པ་རེད་ Each 24 hours they changed the machine operator three times. ¶ ལས་བྱེད་རྙིང་པ་མང་ཆེ་བ་བརྗེ་ལེན་བྱས་པ་རེད་ Most of the old staff members were replaced.

བརྗེ་ལེན་རིན་ཐང་ (jelen rindaŋ) exchange rate/ value.

བརྗེ་སོར་ (jesɔɔ) sm. བརྗེ་ལེན་.

བརྗེད་ (jeè) va. to forget ¶ ལན་བཞག་རྒྱུ་བརྗེད་འདུག (I) forgot to leave a message.

བརྗེད་སྒུག (jeèguù) not returning things that had been borrowed, delaying returning things; va.—རྒྱག.

བརྗེད་ངད་ (jeèŋɛɛ̀) sm. བརྗེད་ངས་.

བརྗེད་ངས་ (jeèŋɛɛ̀) forgetfulness, absentmindedness.

བརྗེད་ངས་ཅན་ (jeèŋɛɛ̀jɛn) forgetful, absentminded.

བརྗེད་ངས་བརྗེད་ཆུ་ (jeèŋɛɛ̀ jeècu) a magic water that causes people to forget everything.

བརྗེད་ཆུ་ (jeècu) a magic water that causes people to forget everything.

བརྗེད་ངས་ཆེ་བ་ (jeèŋɛɛ̀ cēwa) forgetful, absentminded.

བརྗེད་ངས་ཆེན་པོ་ (jeèŋɛɛ̀ cēmbo) sm. བརྗེད་ངས་ཅན་.

བརྗེད་ངས་ཚ་པོ་ (jeèŋɛɛ̀ tsābo) sm. བརྗེད་ངས་ཅན་.

བརྗེད་སྟོར་ (jeèdɔɔ) losing/ destroying sth. because of forgetfulness.

བརྗེད་ཐོ་ (jeèto) notes (so one won't forget); va.—རྒྱག་; —བཀོད་; —འབྲི་ to keep notes/ minutes, to write down notes ¶ ང་བྱང་ལ་སྡོད་དུས་གནས་ཚུལ་ཆེ་ཆུང་མ་བརྗེད་ཐོ་བྲིས་ཡོད་ When I stayed in Northern Tibet I took notes on all the important events. ¶ ཁོས་གཏམ་བཤད་བྱེད་དུས་བརྗེད་ཐོའི་ནང་ལ་ལྟ་གི་ལྟ་གི་བཤད་པ་རེད་ When he gave his lecture, he gave it repeatedly looking at his notes.

བརྗེད་དེབ་ (jeèdeb) book for writing memo, notebook.

བརྗེད་བྱང་ (jeèjaŋ) message/ note board.

བརྗེད་བྱང་ཚིག་གཞི་ (jeèjaŋ tsīgshi) shung. memorandum, aide-mémoire.

བརྗེད་བྱེད་ (jeèjeè) alzheimer's disease.

བརྗེད་ཟན་ (jeèsɛn) magic food that causes forgetfulness.

བརྗེད་གསོ་ (jeèso) reminding; va.—གཏོང་; va.—བྱེད་.

བརྗེས་ (jeè) p. of རྗེ་.

བརྗེས་ཚབ་ (jeèdzəb) a replacement.

བརྗོད་ (jöò) p. of རྗོད་.

བརྗོད་ཀྱི་མི་ལང་བ་ (jöò milaŋwa) having nothing to say.

བརྗོད་བཀོད་ (jöò gōò) shung. to write down what is said, to record/ write the wording.

བརྗོད་གླེང་ (jöòleŋ) writings, that which was written/ said ¶ བརྗོད་གླེང་ནང་ལ་ In the writings.

བརྗོད་སྙིང་ (jöòñiŋ) the essence or main point of a conversation or speech.

བརྗོད་གཏམ་ (jöòdam) speech, talk.

བརྗོད་དུ་མེད་པ་ (jöòdu meèba) sm. བརྗོད་ཀྱི་མི་ལང་བ་.

བརྗོད་དོན་ (jöòdön) 1. used to introduce a quotation/ statement: "as was said" ¶ གསར་འགོད་པས་བརྗོད་དོན་ What the newspaper reporter said (follows immediately). 2. meaning (of what was written/ said) ¶ གྲྭ་ཚང་གི་ཡིག་ཆའི་བརྗོད་དོན་འགའ་ཤས་ Several of the meanings of the Monastic College's documents.

བརྗོད་དོན་གོང་ལྟར་ཞུ་ཞུས་ (jöòdön koŋgdar shushüù) shung. sm. འབའ་བརྗོད་གོང་ཞུར་.

བརྗོད་དོན་རྒྱང་དུ་འདོར་ (jöödön gyandu dɔɔ) vi. to digress/ deviate from the subject.

བརྗོད་དོན་རྒྱབ་སྒྱུར་ (jöödön gyəbgyur) sm. བརྗོད་དོན་རྒྱང་དུ་འདོར་.

བརྗོད་བདེ་གོ་སླ་ (jööde kola) easy to say/ pronounce/ articulate and easy to understand.

བརྗོད་བདེ་སྙན་འཇེབས་ (jööde ñɛ̃njeb) fluent.

བརྗོད་བདེ་པོ་ (jöö debo) easy to say/ articulate/ pronounce.

བརྗོད་ནན་ཆེ་བ་ (jöönɛn cēwa) insisting strongly in speech.

བརྗོད་པ་མེད་པ་ (jööba meèba) having nothing to say.

བརྗོད་པ་ཡོད་པ་ (jööba yööba) having something to say.

བརྗོད་པའི་ཉེས་པ་ (jööbɛ ñeèba) saying wrongful/ harmful things.

བརྗོད་པར་བྱེད་ (jööbar ceè) va. to comment on, to say sth.

བརྗོད་ཕྱོགས་སྒྱུར་ (jööcɔɔ̀ gyur) va. to change the topic/ subject.

བརྗོད་བབ་ (jööbəb) shung. manner of talking ¶ སྔ་ཕྱི་མི་མཐུན་པའི་བརྗོད་བབ་ལ་བརྟེན་ Because of the contradictory manner of what was said earlier and later.

བརྗོད་བྱ་ (jööja) writing style/ form.

བརྗོད་བྱ་གཙོ་བོ་ (jööja dzōwo) theme, thesis, chief subject.

བརྗོད་བྱེད་ (jööjeè) sm. རྗོད་བྱེད་.

བརྗོད་མི་ལང་བ་ (jöö milanwa) sm. བརྗོད་ཀྱི་མི་ལང་བ་.

བརྗོད་མེད་ (jöömeè) sm. བརྗོད་དུ་མེད་པ་.

བརྗོད་གཙང་ (jöödzan) shung. clearly mentioned ¶ དགོན་ལག་འཛིན་དབང་བཅས་ཇེ་སྲིད་བར་འཇགས་གནས་གསོལ་རས་གཙང་མར་གནང་ཞེས་བརྗོད་གཙང་མ་ཟད་ Not only was it clearly mentioned that the possessions of the monastery were granted forever.

བརྗོད་ཚིག (jöödzii) slogan, message ¶ འབྱར་ཡིག་ཚོའི་བརྗོད་ཚིག་ཏུ་དམག་མི་ད་ལྟ་ཕྱིར་འཐེན་བྱེད་དགོས་སོགས་འཁོད་འདུག The message written on the wall poster is that (they) should withdraw the troops now.

བརྗོད་ཚིག་འཕེལ་པོ་ (jöödzig beebo) wordy.

བརྗོད་རྩལ་ (jöödzüü) manner of speaking/ talking.

བརྗོད་གཞི་ (jööshi) 1. proposition (in logic), subject/ topic (one is writing about).

བརྗོད་གཞིའི་ནང་དོན་ (jööshi nandön) meaning of the subject/ topic.

བརྗོད་གཞིའི་གཙོ་དོན་ (jööshi dzōdön) the main subject.

བརྗོད་ལས་འདས་པ་ (jöölɛ dɛɛ̀ba) beyond words/ speech, exceptional.

བརྗོད་སྲོལ་ (jöösöö) line of argument/ reasoning.

བརྗོད་གསལ་ (jöösɛɛ) sm. བརྗོད་དོན་.

བརྗོད་གསལ་ལྷར་ན་ (jöösɛɛ dārna) sm. བརྗོད་དོན་.

ཉ

ཉ་ (ña) 1. the letter ཉ་ (used in alphabetical numbering). 2. fish; va.—འཛིན་; —ཟིན་ to fish. 3. abbr. of ཉ་གང་. 4. vi. to be full moon ¶ཟླ་བ་ཉ་བའི་སྐབས་ At the time of the full moon. 5. slang. broke ¶ང་ཉ་ཡིན་ I am broke.

ཉ་ཀྱུ་ (ñəgyu) fish hook.

ཉ་ཀང་བརྒྱད་ཅན་ (ñagaŋ gyɛ̀ɛ̀jɛn) octopus.

ཉ་རྒྱལ་ (ñagyɛɛ) fish bladder.

ཉ་ཀྲིན་ (ñadrin) canned fish.

ཉ་སྐམ་པོ་ (ña gāmbo) dried fish.

ཉ་སྐྱིབས་ (ñagyib) sm. ཉ་རྒྱབ་.

ཉ་སྐྱོགས་ (ñagyɔ̀ɔ̀) 1. gills. 2. sm. ཉ་སྐྱོབ་.

ཉ་སྐྱོབ་ (ñagyob) oyster.

ཉ་ཁ་ལེབ་ (ña kāleb) flatfish.

ཉ་ཁབ་ (ñagəb) fish hook.

ཉ་ཁྱུ་ (ñəgyu) school of fish.

ཉ་ཁྱུ་ཤར་དུས་ (ñəgyu shārdüü) the time when fish are schooling (i.e., the fishing season).

ཉ་ཁྱིའུ་ (ña kyi̊u) salamander.

ཉ་ཁྲ་ (ñadra) a type of fish-eating hawk/ falcon.

ཉ་ཁྲབ་ (ñyadrəb) fish scales.

ཉ་ཁྲབ་ཅན་ (ñyatdrəbjɛn) carp [Lit. having scales].

ཉ་ཁྲལ་ (ñadrɛɛ) fishing tax.

ཉ་ཁྲིག་ཤིང་ (ñadrigshiŋ) cherry tree.

ཉ་ཁྲོམ་ (ñadrom) fish market.

ཉ་མཁྲིས་ (ñadri̊i) fish bile gland.

ཉ་འཁྱུག (ñagyug) darting/ dashing fish.

ཉ་ག (ñaga) a hand-held weighing scale, a steelyard; va.—བཀུག to weigh on a steelyard.

ཉ་ག་གང་ (ñaga kaŋ) a unit of measurement (weight) on a ཉ་ག.

ཉ་གང་ (ñagaŋ) the 15th of a lunar month, the full moon.

ཉ་གང་བ་ (ñagaŋwa) sm. ཉ་གང་.

ཉ་གང་ཟླ་བ་ (ñagaŋ dawa) sm. ཉ་གང་.

ཉ་གེ་ཉོ་གེ (ñage ñoge) sm. ཉག་ཉོག.

ཉ་མགོ (ñaŋgo) 1. head of a fish. 2. wooden carved fish-head design.

ཉ་མགོ་གྲུ་ཁ་ (ñaŋgo trugə) name of a ferry/ boat crossing in སྐྱེ་གདོང་.

ཉ་གྲུ་ (ñadru) fishing boat.

ཉ་རྒྱ་ (ñagya) fishing net.

ཉ་རྒྱབ་ (ñagyəb) the low wall along the edge of a roof.

ཉ་རྒྱས་ (ñagyɛ̀ɛ̀) sm. ཉ་གང་.

ཉ་སྒོང་ (ñagoŋ) spawn, fish egg; va.—གཏོང་ to spawn.

ཉ་ང་ (ñaŋa) 1. fishtail. 2. rifle butt.

ཉ་ལྕིབས་ (ñajib) 1. gills. 2. oyster. 3. sm. ཉ་ཕྱིས་.

ཉ་ཆུང་ (ñajuŋ) term for fish in Tibetan songs [Lit. small fish].

ཉ་ཆེན་ཧྲ་ཡུས་ (ñacen hrəyüü) tib.ch. shark.

ཉ་མཆིན་གྱི་སྣུམ་ (ñacingi nūm) cod-liver oil.

ཉ་མཆིན་སྣུམ་སྨན་ (ñacingi nūmmɛn) cod-liver oil.

ཉ་མཆིལ་ (ñajii) sm. ཉ་ཁབ་.

ཉ་མཆོངས་ (ñajoŋ) fish jumping; va.—རྒྱག to jump out of the water (for fish).

ཉ་རྗེན་ (ñajen) 1. raw fish. 2. a kind of dish consisting of pounded raw fish mixed with hot pepper.

ཉ་ཉུང་མཉམ་བསྲེ་ (ñañuŋ ñamdre) 1. incompatible things mixed together. 2. embezzlement, mixing the funds of one's employer with one's own [Lit. fish and turnips mixed together].

ཉ་ཉོག (ñañog) children.

ཉ་ཉ་རྒྱང་ (ña ñagyaŋ) slang. completely poor/ penniless ¶ང་ཉ་ཉ་རྒྱང་ཡིན་ I am completely penniless.

ཉ་ཉུང་མཉམ་བསྲེས་ (ñañuŋ ñamseè) 1. mixing incongruous/ inappropriate things [Lit. mixing fish and turnips together]. 2. embezzlement in the sense of mixing one's money and the person you're working for.

ཉ་ཉོར་ (ñañor) abbr. of ཉ་རེ་ཉོ་རེ་.

ཉ་གཉིས་ (ñañii) on the other hand; secondly ¶ཁོས་ཕྱོགས་གཅིག་ནས་ཚོང་རྒྱག་གི་ཡོད་པ་དང་ ཉ་གཉིས་ནས་དངུལ་བུན་ལོན་གཏོང་གི་ཡོད་པ་རེད་ On the one hand he does trading, and on the other hand, he lends money.

ཉ་ལྟོ་པ་ (ñadoba) fisherman.

ཉ་སྟོང་ (ñadoŋ) the 15th and 30th of the month (auspicious days in the Tibetan calendar).

ཉ་སྟོང་བརྒྱད་གསུམ་ (ñadoŋ gyɛ̀ɛ̀sum) the 15th, 30th, and 8th of the month (three auspicious days in the Tibetan calendar).

ཉ་སྟོན་ (ñadön) party given on the 15th of the month.

ཉ་ཐང་ (ñadaŋ) fish soup.

ཉ་དང་ (ñadaŋ) shung. the ཉ་དང་ regiment in the tt. army.

ཉ་དུག་པ་ (ñādugba) vetch.

ཉ་དུང་ (ñaduŋ) conch.

ཉ་དོལ་ (ñadöö) sm. ཉ་རྒྱ་.

ཉ་དོལ་པ་ (ñadööba) sm. ཉ་པ་.

ཉ་དྲ་ (ñadra) fish net.

ཉ་དྲི་ (ñədri) smell of fish.

ཉ་དྲི་གྲོ་བའི་སྔོ་ (ñadri trowɛ ŋō) a Tibetan medicine.

ཉ་མདའ་ (ñanda) shung. general/ commander of the ཉ་དང་ regiment in the tt. army.

ཉ་འདྲིད་ཁ་ཟས་ (ñadrii kāsɛ̀ɛ̀) fish bait.

ཉ་རྡོ་ཟན་ (ña dosɛn) shark.

ཉ་ལྡིང་ (ñadiŋ) sm. ཉ་མཆོངས་.

ཉ་སྡིག་སྲིན་ (ña digsin) crab, lobster.

ཉ་ནག (ñanag) octopus, squid; black carp.

ཉ་ནད་ (ñanɛɛ̀) a disease that affects large livestock.

ཉ་སྣབས་ (ñanəb) weeds in water.

ཉ་སྣུམ་ (ñanum) fish oil.

ཉ་པ་ (ñaba) fisherman.

ཉ་པ་ཁ་ལེབ་ (ñaba kāleb) catfish.

ཉ་པེ་ཉོ་པེ་ (ñabe ñobe) lazy, inactive, lethargic.

ཉ་དཔོན་ (ñabön) head/ chief of fishermen.

ཉ་ལྤགས་ (ñabaà) fish skin.

ཉ་སྤུ་ཅན་ (ñabujɛn) a type of otter.

ཉ་སྤུ་མེད་ལ་རལ་པའི་ཁྲལ་ (ña būmeèla rɛɛbɛ trɛ̄ɛ) demanding things unjustly unfairly, inappropriate expectations [Lit. to a hairless fish, a tax on hair].

ཉ་སྤྱིན་ (ñajin) glue made from fish.

ཉ་ཕག་སྒོང་གསུམ་ (ña pāà goŋ sūm) abbr. the three: fish, pork and eggs.

ཉ་ཕྱིས་ (ñəjii) pearl.

ཉ་ཕྱིས་དུང་ (ñəcii duŋ) a pearl shaped like a conch shell or horn.

ཉ་ཕྱིས་སྣོད་ཁེབས་ (ñəcii nöökeb) lids that are made from pearl.

ཉ་ཕྱིས་སིལ་མ་ (ñəcii si̊imə) small pieces of pearl.

ཉ་ཕྱེ་ (ñəce) powdered fish.

ཉ་ཕྲུག (ñədruù) sm. ཉ་སོན་.

ཉ་འཕྱོ་ (ñaco) sm. ཉ་མཆོངས་.

ཉ་བའི་ཡར་ཚེས་ (ñawɛ yardze) shung. first part of the month.

ཉ་བྱབ་སྙུག་དྲ་ (ñajəb ñūgdra) a type of bamboo net for holding fish.

ཉ་བྱེ་རིལ་ (ña cirii) a fish-shaped sweet/ candy.

ཉ་འདྲིད་ལྕགས་ཀྱུའི་ཟས་ (ñadrii jəggyü sɛ̀ɛ̀) tricking, deceiving, duping [Lit. inducing the fish to take the bait on the hook].

ཉ་འབྲུ་ (ñadru) shung. grain given by the tt. government to fishermen as compensation for their stopping fishing.

ཉ་འབྲུག་མཉམ་འདྲིས་ (ña drug ñamdreè) good and

bad mixed together, incompatible things mixed together [Lit. fish and dragon mixed together].
ཉ་མ་ (ñama) female disciple/ adherent.
ཉ་མན་ལི་ (ña mɛnli) eel.
ཉ་མིག (ñamii) a type of chisel.
ཉ་མིག་མ་ (ña migmə) a type of brocade.
ཉ་མིད་ (ñamii) whale.
ཉ་མོ་ (ñamo) fish.
ཉ་མོ་ཁྲོ་ནང་རྒྱུ་བ་ལྟར་ (ñamo trōnaŋ gyuwa dār) in imminent danger/ peril, no way to escape [Lit. like fish swimming in a cauldron].
ཉ་མོ་ཉིན་གསུམ་འཛིན་ དྲ་བ་ཉིན་གཉིས་སྐམ་ (ñamo ñinsum dzin trawa ñinsum gām) working by fits and starts, lacking perseverance/ diligence, doing lazily [Lit. three days catching fish and two days drying the net].
ཉ་མོ་ཉུང་མས་མི་ཚོད་ (ñamo ñuŋmɛ mijöö) sth. cannot be substituted for another [Lit. a turnip can't substitute for a fish].
ཉ་མོ་མ་ཟིན་པ་མ་གཏོགས་ མཚོ་མཐའ་མ་སྐོར་བ་མེད་ (ñamo simbə mandoò tsōtaa magɔɔwa mee) trying one's best but not achieving success [Lit. going all around the ocean but not catching fish].
ཉ་མོ་རུས་མཉེན་ (ñamo rüüñen) cartilaginous fish.
ཉ་མོའི་རྣ་གཤོག (ñamö nāshog) gills.
ཉ་མོའི་དབུགས་ལམ་རྣ་གཤོག (ñamö ūglam nāshog) gill pouch.
ཉ་དམའ་པོ་ (ña mābo) embarrassed, humiliated, feeling small, feeling inferior ¶ བུ་ལོན་སྤྲོད་ཡ་མེད་ཙང་ཉ་དམའ་པོ་བྱུང་བ་རེད་ (He) felt small because he was unable to pay the loan.
ཉ་དམའ་བ་ (ña māwa) catfish.
ཉ་ཚང་ (ñadzaŋ) 1. fish nest. 2. a type of seaweed.
ཉ་ཚིལ་ (nadzii) fish fat.
ཉ་ཚེར་ (ñatser) small fish bones.
ཉ་ཚེས་ (ñadzeè) 15th day of the month in the Tibetan calendar.
ཉ་ཚོགས་ (ñadzɔɔ̀) sm. ཉ་ཁྲུ་.
ཉ་ཚོང་ (ñadzoŋ) fish selling/ trading; va.—རྒྱག.
ཉ་ཚོང་པ་ (ñadzoŋba) fishmonger, fish seller.
ཉ་འཛིན་ (ñandzin) 1. see ཉ་. 2. fisherman. 3. fishnet.
ཉ་འཛིན་གྲུ་གཟིངས་ (ñandzin trusiŋ) fishing boat/ trawler.
ཉ་འཛིན་ལྕགས་ཀྱུ་ (ñandzin jəggyu) fishing hook.
ཉ་འཛིན་འཁྲུལ་གྲུ་ (ñandzin trüüdru) fishing boat (engine driven).
ཉ་འཛིན་དབྱུག་པ་ (ñadzin yūgbə) fishing pole/ rod.
ཉ་འཛིན་དབྱུག་གུ་ (ñandzin yūggu) sm. ཉ་འཛིན་དབྱུག་པ་
ཉ་འཛིན་ཡོ་བྱད་ (ñandzin yobcɛɛ̀) fishing equipment/ tackle.
ཉ་འཛིན་རུ་ཁག (ñandzin rugaà) fishing brigade/ team.
ཉ་འཛིན་སའི་མཚོ་ཁུག (ña dzinsɛ tsōguù) fishing port.
ཉ་རྫིང་ (ñadziŋ) fish pond.
ཉ་གཞིབ་གཞིབ་ (ña shibshib) one beside the other [Lit fish side by side].
ཉ་གཞུག (ñashuù) fish tail.
ཉ་ཟན་ (ñasɛn) 1. fisherman. 2. a type of bird that eats fish.
ཉ་ཟིན་ (ña sin) see ཉ་.
ཉ་ཟིན་ས་ (ña sinsə) fishing grounds.
ཉ་ཟུང་སྐར་ཚོམ་ (ñasuŋ gɔ̄ɔ̄jom) the constellation Pisces.
ཉ་ཟླ་ (ñanda) sm. ཉ་གང་.
ཉ་གཟེབ (ñaseb) bamboo basket for fish.
ཉ་ར་ (ñara) 1. fishing grounds. 2. fishery. 3. keeping sth. for sb., looking after/ taking care of sth.; va.—བྱེད་.
ཉ་རས་ (ñarɛɛ̀) fish net.
ཉ་རི་ཉི་རིས་ (ñare ñirii) dilly dallying; va.—བྱེད་.
ཉ་རིགས་ (ñarig) types/ kinds of fish.
ཉ་རིགས་གསོ་སྐྱེལ་ (ñarig sōbel) fishery.
ཉ་རིད་ (ñarii) a type of tree.
ཉ་རིས་ (ñarii) fish scales.
ཉ་རུས་ (ñarüü) 1. fish bone. 2. sm. ཧ་རྡོ་ཙམ་.
ཉ་རེ་ཉོ་རེ་ (ñare ñore) 1. lazy, sluggish, lethargic. 2. rubbery, spongy, formless.
ཉ་ལས་ (ñalɛɛ̀) fishing industry, fishing as an occupation.
ཉ་ལས་ཀུང་སི་ (ñalɛɛ̀ gūŋsi) fishery company.
ཉ་ལས་གྲུ་ཁ་ (ñalɛɛ̀ druga) fishing port.
ཉ་ལས་མཉམ་འབྲེལ་བཟོ་གྲྭ་ (ñalɛɛ̀ ñamdree sodra) fishing cooperative factory.
ཉ་ལས་ཐོན་སྐྱེད་མཉམ་ལས་ཁང་ (ñalɛɛ̀ tōngyeè ñamlɛɛ̀gaŋ) fishing production cooperative.
ཉ་ལས་ཐོན་རྫས་ (ñalɛɛ̀ tōndzɛɛ̀) fishing products.
ཉ་ལས་དཔྱ་ཁྲལ་ (ñalɛɛ̀ jādrɛɛ) fishing tax.
ཉ་ལས་ས་ཁུལ་ (ñalɛɛ̀ səgüü) fishing area/ zone.
ཉ་ལི་ཡུས་ (ña liyü) tib.ch. carp.
ཉ་ལུ་ (ñəlu) illegitimate child.
ཉ་ལི་ཉི་ལི་ (ñale ñile) sm. ཉ་རེ་ཉོ་རེ་.
ཉ་ཤ་ (ñasha) fish flesh/ meat.
ཉ་ཤ་སྐམ་པོ་ (ñasha gāmbo) dried fish meat.
ཉ་ཤ་འཁྱགས་བག (ñasha kyāgbaà) frozen fish.
ཉ་ཤ་ཚ་ཁུ་ (ñasha tsōgu) salted fish.
ཉ་ཤི་ (ñashi) 15th and 30th of the Tibetan month.
ཉ་གཤོག (ñashog) 1. fish fin. 2. shark's fin.
ཉ་བཤོར་ (ña shɔ̄ɔ̄) va. to catch fish.
ཉ་སོག (ñasɔɔ̀) 1. dorsal fin. 2. a round ornament made from pearl.
ཉ་སོན་ (ñasön) baby fish, fry.
ཉ་སྲམ་ (ñadram) abbr. fish and otter.
ཉ་གསེར་ཉ་ (ña sērña) goldfish coy.
ཉ་གསེར་མིག (ña sērmig) a species of goldfish with prominent eyes and a large tail.
ཉ་གསོ་ (ñaso) fish raising/ rearing.
ཉ་གསོ་ཁང་ (ñasogaŋ) fish nursery, fishery.
ཉ་གསོ་ར་བ་ (ñaso rawa) sm. ཉ་གསོ་ཁང་.
ཉ་བསད་ཁྱི་སྦྱིར་ (ñasɛɛ̀ kyider) helping one person by harming another [Lit. to kill a fish and give it to the dogs].
ཉ་བསད་ནས་ཁྱི་ལ་སྦྱིར་ (ñasɛɛ̀ kyider) sm. ཉ་བསད་ཁྱི་སྦྱིར་.
ཉ་ཧྲ་དིང་ (ña hrādiŋ) sardine.
ཉ་ལྷག (ñalhaà) month with a an extra 15th day.
ཉག (ñag) 1. abbr. of ཉ་ག. 2. concave, indented.
ཉག་རྒྱང་ (ñaggyaŋ) sm. ཉག་ཅིག.
ཉག་འཁེལ་ (ñag kēl) vi. to do sth. exactly on time ¶ ངའི་ལས་ཀ་དེ་བྱེད་ཉག་འཁེལ་སོང་ (I) did my work exactly on time.
ཉག་ཁྱད་ (ñaggyɛɛ̀) differences in the weights of different (ཉ་ག) scales.
ཉག་ཁྲམ་ (ñagdram) the series of notches (measurements) on a steelyard (ཉ་ག) scale.
ཉག་ག (ñagga) 1. indentations cut into wood (e.g., on a pole so that people can climb); va.—གཏོད་. 2. the saddle-shaped indentations/ dips/ depressions along the top of mountain ranges.
ཉག་གེ་ཉོག་གེ་ (ñagge ñogge) 1. complaining, fussing about. 2. muddy, unclear ¶ ཆུ་ཉག་གེ་ཉོག་གེ་དེ་མ་འཐུངས་ Don't drink that muddy water.
ཉག་གྲངས་ (ñagdraŋ) measuring units on a steelyard (ཉ་ག་) scale.
ཉག་ཅིག (ñagjig) sm. ཉག་གཅིག.
ཉག་གཅིག (ñagjig) 1. certainly, surely, without question, inevitably ¶ དེ་ནི་དམག་དཔུང་དེའི་དམིགས་ཡུལ་ཉག་གཅིག་དེ་རེད་ That is certainly the objective of the troops. ¶ མི་ཚེའི་མཐའ་མར་ཤི་རྒྱུ་ཉག་གཅིག་རེད་ At the end of life (one) must inevitably die. 2. insistently and repeatedly ¶ གཏན་འཁེལ་དགོས་ཉག་གཅིག་བརྗོད་ (They) said insistently that (we) had to finalize (that). 3. one piece/ unit.
ཉག་ཆུ་ (ñagcu) the Nyagchu River (in western Sichuan).
ཉག་ཆུ་ཁ་ (ñagcuga) a district/ xian in Ganze Prefecture.

ཉག་ཉག (ñagñaà) bent, indented, depressed; va.—བཟོ་ i. to make an indentation/ depression. ii. to cause sb. to spend a lot of money. iii. to cause a large loss.

ཉག་ཉིག (ñagñii) dirty, filthy.

ཉག་ཉུག (ñagñuù) all sorts/ kinds, various types.

ཉག་ཉོག (ñagñog) abbr. of ཉ་གི་ཉོག་གི་.

ཉག་ཉོག་གི་མཚན་ཉིད་རིག་པ་ (ñagñoggi tsɛ̄nñii rigbə) scholasticism.

ཉག་ཐག (ñagdaà) the rope (handle) of a steelyard (ཉ་ག) scale.

ཉག་མཐིལ་ (ñagdii) the plate/ pan on which things are put on a steelyard (ཉ་ག) scale.

ཉག་མདའ་ (ñanda) the arm or wooden rod of a steelyard (ཉ་ག) scale.

ཉག་རྡོ་ (ñagdo) the sliding weight of a steelyard (ཉ་ག) scale.

ཉག་པ་ (ñagba) sm. ཉག་པོ་.

ཉག་པོ་ (ñagbo) indentation, concave shape.

ཉག་ཕྲ་ (ñagdra) 1. difficult/ bad times ། བསྟན་སྲིད་ཉག་ཕྲའི་དུས་སྐབས་ལ་ At the time of bad times for the system of joint religious and secular rule. 2. sm. ཉག་ཕྲ་བ་. 3. thin.

ཉག་ཕྲ་ཐ་ཤན་ (ñagdra tāshɛn) shung. extremely poor, penniless, destitute ། མི་སེར་ཉག་ཕྲ་ཐ་ཤན་ཞི་ཅིག་ལ་བརྟེན་བུན་རྙིང་སྤྲོད་འཇལ་ཐུབ་རེ་བྲལ་བས་ Because the subjects are extremely poor they have no means to pay the old debts.

ཉག་ཕྲ་བ་ (ñagdrawa) 1. very thin. 2. poor, destitute.

ཉག་ཕྲ་ཡང་དུང་སྐུད་གསུམ་སྒྲིལ་ཡིན་ (ñagdrayaŋ dūŋgüü sūmdree yin) even though sth. is poor/ weak it is unified [Lit. even though thin, it has three strands/ ply of silk thread].

ཉག་ཕྲན་ (ñagdrɛn) arrow.

ཉག་མ་ (ñagma) sm. ཉག་རེ་.

ཉག་ཙམ་ (ñagdzam) sm. ཉག་རེ་.

ཉག་ཚགས་ཁང་ (ñagdzaàgaŋ) storeroom.

ཉག་ཚད་ཀྱི་ཁལ་ (ñagdzɛɛ̀gi kɛ̄ɛ) shung. the weight of one ཁལ་.

ཉག་རེ་ (ñagre) a piece, a drop, a small amount, a single (strand/ blade) ། གད་སྙིགས་ཉག་རེ་ཙམ་ཡང་མཐོང་རྒྱུ་མེད་པ་རེད་ (One) couldn't see even a single piece of garbage.

ཉག་རོང་ (ñaàroŋ) Nyaong, a district/ xian in Ganze prefecture.

ཉག་ལ་བཀག་པ་ (ñagla gāgba) pressing hard on a key point (usu. in an interrogation) ། ཁྲིམས་དཔོན་གྱིས་ཁོ་ར་ཉག་ལ་བཀག་ཀྱང་ངོས་ལེན་མ་བྱས་པ་རེད་ Even though the judge pressed him, he didn't confess.

ཉག་ལུང་ (ñagluŋ) sm. ཉག་ཐག.

ཉག་ཤིང་ (ñagshiŋ) beam of a ཉག.

ཉག་ཤུར་ (ñagshur) a concave indentation in a piece of wood; va.—འདོན་ to gouge/ carve/ dig out such an indentation.

ཉག་སྲང་ (ñagsaŋ) hand-held steelyard (ཉ་ག) scale.

ཉང་ (ñaŋ) an area in Tsang.

ཉང་ཁྲི་ (ñaŋ) sm. ཉིང་ཁྲི་.

ཉང་ངེ་ཉུང་ངེ་ (ñaŋŋe ñuŋŋe) odds and ends, small items.

ཉང་ཉུང་ (ñaŋñuŋ) abbr. of ཉང་ངེ་ཉུང་ངེ་.

ཉང་ཆུ་ (ñaŋcu) a river that runs through Shigatse.

ཉང་ནོན་ (ñaŋnön) sm. ཉང་གནོན་.

ཉང་ནོན་རྟོག་ཞིབ་ (ñaŋnön dōgshib) sm. ཉང་གནོན་རྟོག་ཞིབ་.

ཉང་ནོན་པ་ (ñaŋnönba) a spy.

ཉང་གནོན་ (ñaŋnön) shung. monitoring, reconnoitering, observing clandestinely; va.—གཏོང་ ། གྲྭ་གཟུགས་མི་བདུན་རི་ལ་འཛེགས་སུ་འགྲོ་ར་མཐོང་ལ་ཉང་གནོན་བཏང་བར་ They sent someone to reconnoiter after they saw seven people climbing the mountain who looked like monks. ཉང་གནོན་རྟོག་ཞིབ་ (ñaŋnön dōgshib) investigating thoroughly; va.—བྱེད་ ། གྱོད་དོན་དེ་སྐོར་ས་གནས་སུ་ཉང་གནོན་རྟོག་ཞིབ་དང་འབྲེལ་བའི་རྒྱལ་ཁབ་ཏུ་སྙན་ཞུ་འཕྲུལ་འབུལ་དགོས་རྒྱུ་ (You) must investigate this law case thoroughly and report to the government.

ཉང་ཞིབ་ (ñaŋshib) abbr. of ཉང་ནོན་རྟོག་ཞིབ་.

ཉང་ཞིབ་ན་མར་ (ñaŋshib namar) shung. keeping up with, monitoring ། དགྲ་ཕྱོགས་ཀྱི་གནས་ཚུལ་ལ་ཉང་ཞིབ་ན་མར་བགྱིས་དགོས་ We must keep up with the enemy's situation.

ཉད་ཉོད་ (ñɛɛ̀ñöö) 1. the stretching that accompanies yawning; va.—བྱེད་. 2. secretly looking/ peeping; va.—བྱེད་.

ཉན་ (ñɛn) 1. va. to listen to ། ངས་ཁོའི་གཏམ་བཤད་ཉན་པ་ཡིན་ I listened to his speech. 2. vi. (vb. + —) to be fit for ། འདི་ཟ་ཉན་གྱི་རེད་པས་ Is this fit to eat?

ཉན་ཁ་ཡང་བ་ (ñɛnga yaŋwa) gullible.

ཉན་མཁན་ (ñɛnñɛn) audience, listener.

ཉན་ཆས་ (ñɛnjɛɛ̀) (telephone) receiver.

ཉན་འཇོག (ñenjoò) 1. obeying, heeding; va.—བྱེད་ ། ཁོང་གི་བཀའ་ལ་ཉན་འཇོག་བྱས་པ་རེད་ (They) obeyed his orders. 2. listening to; va.—བྱེད་ ། སྐབས་དེར་ངས་མའོ་ཀྲུའུ་ཞིའི་བཀའ་སློབ་ཉན་འཇོག་བྱས་པ་ཡིན་ That time I listened to Chairman Mao speak.

ཉན་སྙིང་འདོད་པོ་ (ñenñiŋ tööbo) 1. good to listen to. 2. desiring/ wishing to listen to sth.

ཉན་སྙིང་སྤྲོད་པོ་ (ñenñiŋ tröobo) sm. ཉན་སྙིང་འདོད་པོ་.

ཉན་བརྡག (ñɛndaà) sm. ཉན་བརྡག་ཡོ་བྱད་.

ཉན་བརྡག་ཡོ་བྱད་ (ñɛndaà yobjɛɛ̀) stethoscope.

ཉན་ཐོས་ (ñɛndöö) 1. listening, hearing. 2. a disciple (originally used for those disciples of the Buddha who actually listened to his teachings).

ཉན་ཐོས་མཆོག་ཟུང་ (ñɛndöö cōgsuŋ) two disciples of the Buddha.

ཉན་དུང་ (ñɛnduŋ) instrument to listen with, receiver (telephone), earphone.

ཉན་ན་ (ñɛnna) listening in secretly, eavesdropping; va.—བྱེད་.

ཉན་ན་བ་ (ñɛnnawa) eavesdropper.

ཉན་ན་སྦྲི་གསང་ (ñɛnna bisaŋ) in an alert fashion; va.—བྱེད་.

ཉན་པ་རྒྱག (ñɛmba gyaà) va. to spy, to eavesdrop, to listen secretly.

ཉན་པར་སྙོ་ (ñɛmbar drō) pleasant to listen to.

ཉན་པོ་ (ñɛmbo) obedient.

ཉན་ཕན་ཡོ་བྱད་ (ñɛnbɛn yobjɛɛ̀) hearing aid.

ཉན་བྱེད་འཕྲུལ་ཆས་ (ñɛnjeè trüüjɛɛ̀) earphone, hearing/ listening apparatus.

ཉན་བྱེད་དབང་པོ་ (ñɛnjeè wāŋbo) sense of hearing.

ཉན་ཡིག (ñɛnyii) shung. a letter given to the potential mediator of a dispute by both parties assuring that they will follow his advice if he does the mediation.

ཉན་ལེན་ (ñɛnlen) listening, accepting; va.—བྱེད་ ། བསམ་འཆར་ཉན་ལེན་བྱས་གང་ཐུབ་བྱེད་སོང་ (He) did everything possible to listen and accept the suggestions.

ཉན་ཤེས་ (ñɛnsheè) listening and understanding; va.—བྱེད་ ། ང་ཚོས་ག་རེ་ལབ་ཀྱང་ཁོས་ཉན་ཤེས་རྩ་བ་ནས་བྱས་མ་སོང་ He didn't listen to anything we said.

ཉན་ཤེས་གོ་ཤེས་ (ñɛnsheè kosheè) listening and understanding well.

ཉན་བཤད་ (ñɛnshɛɛ̀) listening and talking; va.—བྱེད་.

ཉབ་ (ñəb) 1. vi. to reach (to) ། ངའི་ལག་པས་ཉབ་ཀྱི་མི་འདུག My hand doesn't reach (it). 2. va. to collect things together.

ཉབ་ཉོབ་ (ñabñob) abbr. ཉབ་པ་ཉོབ་པེ་.

ཉབ་པ་ཉོབ་པེ་ (ñaba ñobe) sm. ཉ་པེ་ཉོ་པེ་.

ཉབ་བེ་ཉོབ་བེ་ (ñabe ñobe) 1. lazy, listless. 2. at ease, loose, relaxed.

ཉབ་ཤག (ñəbshaà) a type of cookie.

ཉབས་ (ñəb) sm. ཉབ་.

ཉམ་ (ñam) strength, power, energy.

ཉམ་ང་ (ñamŋa) 1. sm. ཉམ་ཐག. 2. fear ། དཀའ་ཚེགས་གང་འདྲ་ཞིག་ཐུག་ཀྱང་ཉམ་ང་སྣ་ཙམ་མེད་ No matter how much hardship (I) face (I) have no fear.

ཉམ་ང་བ་ (ñamŋawa) sm. ཉམ་ང་.

ཉམ་ང་བ་ཉུང་བ་ (ñamŋawa ñuŋwa) sm. ཉམ་ང་བ་ཆུང་བ་.

ཉམ་ང་བ་ཆུང་བ་ (ñamŋa cūŋwa) physical well-being, good health.

ཉམ་ང་བག་ཚ་མེད་པ་ (ñamŋa pagdza meèba) brave, courageous, fearless.

ཉམ་ཆག (ñamjaà) injury, harm; vi.—སོང་ to be/ get injured/ harmed/ damaged.

ཉམ་ཆུང་ (ñəmjuŋ) humble, weak, poor, lowly.

ཉམ་ཆུང་སྡོད་མཁས་ (ñəmjuŋ döökɛɛ̀) shung. to be modest and careful ། རྒྱལ་མཐུན་ཉམས་ཆུང་སྡོད་མཁས་དགོས་ཀྱི་ One should be modest and careful.

ཉམ་ཆུང་ཚུལ་ལྡན་ (ñəmjuŋ tsündɛn) simple and upright/ honest/ moral.

ཉམ་ཉེས་ (ñamñeè) 1. suffering, damage, loss; va.—གཏོང་ to inflict damage/ suffering ། ཁོ་ཚོས་དམག་མིར་ཉམ་ཉེས་ཆེན་པོ་བཏང་བ་རེད་ They inflicted great damage on the soldiers. 2. vi. to lessen/ diminish,/ deteriorate/ degenerate.

ཉམ་ཐག (ñamdaà) falling on bad times, leading a life of poverty/ misery.

ཉམ་ཐག་མཐར་ལྷུང་ (ñamdaà tārlhuŋ) shung. poverty stricken, poor and desperate ། ཞི་དྲག་ཁྲལ་རིགས་སྣ་མང་བཏུད་མནར་ཆེ་བས་ཆབ་འབངས་ཉམ་ཐག་མཐའ་ལྷུངས་སུ་གྱུར་པ་ Because of the oppression of many taxes the people were reduced to poverty.

ཉམ་ཐག་པ་ (ñamdagba) misery, misfortune, poverty, suffering ། དབུལ་ཞིང་ཉམ་ཐག་པའི་འཚོ་བ་སྐྱེལ་དགོས་བྱུང་བ་རེད་ (They) had to live a life of misery and poverty.

ཉམ་ཐག་མི་འཁྱར་ (ñamtaà migyar) homeless and poor.

ཉམ་ཐག་འུ་ཐུག (ñamdaà wuduù) poor and desperate, desperately poor.

ཉམ་དམན་པ་ (ñam mēmba) sm. ཉམ་ཆུང་.

ཉམ་དམའ་པོ་ (ñam māābo) feeling small, feeling inferior ། ངས་དབྱིན་ཇིའི་སྐད་མི་ཤེས་པ་དེས་ཕྱི་རྒྱལ་བ་མང་པོ་ཚོགས་སར་ཉམ་དམའ་པོ་བྱུང་ I felt small at the gathering of many foreigners because I did not speak English.

ཉམ་དམས་ (ñammɛɛ̀) 1. week, feeble; va.—གཏོང་ to make weak/ feeble ། འཇབ་དམག་མང་པོ་བརྒྱབ་ནས་དགྲ་བོའི་སྟོབས་ཤུགས་ཉམས་དམས་སུ་བཏང་བ་རེད་ They conducted much guerrilla warfare and weakened the strength of the enemy. 2. vi. to become dilapidated/ deteriorated ། ཁང་པ་འདི་ཉམ་དམས་བཞག The house became dilapidated.

ཉམ་ཞེན་ (ñamshɛn) sm. ཉམ་ཆུང་.

ཉམས་ (ñam) 1. vi. to deteriorate/ decline/ degenerate ། ལོ་ཤས་རིང་དཔལ་འབྱོར་ཉམས་བཞག The economy has declined over the past few years. 2. grandness, elegance, charm, dignity; va.—བྱེད་ (can have a negative or positive connotation depending on context); va.—གཏོང་ to make a name for oneself, to distinguish oneself ། དཔོན་པོ་དེ་ཉམས་བྱེད་ཀྱི་འདུག The official is acting very grand. ། ཁོང་གིས་ཚོགས་འདུའི་ཐོག་གཏམ་བཤད་ཏ་ཅང་ཡག་པོ་བྱས་ནས་ཉམས་བཏང་སོང་ He gave an excellent speech at the meeting and made a name for himself. 3. (adj. or vb. + — + བྱེད་) va. to show/ manifest/ exhibit a sensation or feeling ། ཁོང་གིས་དབྱལ་ལོག་མཐུག་པོ་གོན་ན་ཡང་འཁྱགས་ཉམས་བྱེད་ཀྱི་འདུག Even though he is wearing thick clothes, he gives the appearance that he is cold. ། གྲང་གློག་བཏང་ནའང་ཁོང་གིས་ཚ་དྲབ་འཚིག་ཉམས་བྱེད་ཀྱི་འདུག Even though the air condition is on, he is showing he is hot (behaving in a way that shows he is hot). 4. va. to pretend sth, to act as if ། ཡོན་ཏན་མེད་ཀྱང་ཡོད་ཉམས་བྱེད་ཀྱི་འདུག Even though he is not knowledgeable, he acts as if he is. 5. sm. ཉམས་ལོན་. 6. mind ། ལུང་པ་འདི་ཉམས་དགའ་བ་ཞིག་འདུག This place is one that is pleasing to the mind.

ཉམས་ཀྱི་ (ñamgye) grand, magnificent.

ཉམས་ཁྲིད་ (ñamdrii) teaching others through one's experience; va.—བྱེད་.

ཉམས་གུད་ (ñamgüü) sm. ཉམས་རྒུད་.

ཉམས་གོག (ñamgɔg) dilapidated ། ལྷ་ཁང་དེ་ཚོ་ཉམས་ཆེན་པོ་བྱུང་བཞག Those temples became dilapidated.

ཉམས་གླུ་ (ñamlu) sm. མགུར་གླུ་.

ཉམས་དགའ་བ་ (ñam gawa) happy, joyous.

ཉམས་དགའ་བག་དྲོ་ (ñamga pagdro) sm. ཉམས་དགའ་བ་.

ཉམས་དགའ་བློ་བདེ་ (ñam lōde) being in a happy mood and having no worries.

ཉམས་དགའ་རིང་ལུགས་ (ñamga riŋluù) optimism.

ཉམས་འགྱིང་ (ñamgyiŋ) elegant, grand, imposing, dignified; va.—བྱེད་.

ཉམས་འགྱུར་ (ñəmgyur) 1. expression, appearance, posture, acting, style (in arts) ། འཁྲབ་སྟོན་གྱི་ཉམས་འགྱུར་ Style in acting. 2. deterioration, disintegration, disintegration ། ལུང་པ་དེར་རིག་གཞུང་ཉམས་འགྱུར་གྱི་གནས་ཚུལ་མང་པོ་ཡོད་པ་རེད་ There is much news regarding cultural deterioration in that place.

ཉམས་རྒུད་ (ñəmgüü) deterioration, decline, decay; recession, depression, slump (in business); vi.—དུ་འགྲོ་; —འགྱུར་ to decline/ decay/ deteriorate; to have a recession/ depression/ slump; va.—དུ་གཏོང་ to deteriorate, to undermine, to destroy ། ལུང་པ་དེའི་ནང་དཔལ་འབྱོར་ཉམས་རྒུད་དུ་འགྱུར་བ་རེད་ In that place the economy has declined a great deal.

ཉམས་རྒུད་ཁ་ཐོར་ (ñəmgüü kādɔr) scattering and declining/ decaying/ deteriorating.

ཉམས་རྒྱུས་ (ñəmgyüü) personal experience/ familiarity/ knowledge ། བོད་སྐོར་ཉམས་རྒྱུས་ཡོད་པའི་མི་ A person with experience about Tibet.

ཉམས་རྒྱུད་ (ñəmgyüü) deteriorating, declining/ decaying/ degenerating/ worsening.

ཉམས་སྒྲོབ་ (ñamdrob) arrogant, grandiose (in a negative sense); va.—བྱེད་.

ཉམས་ང་བ་ (ñamŋawa) sm. ཉམ་ང་བ་.

ཉམས་དུས་ (ñamdüü) a period/ era of decline or deterioration.

ཉམས་དངོས་མཚོན་པ་ (ñamŋöö tsōmba) realistic, life-like ། ཁོང་གི་དེབ་འདི་ཉམས་དངོས་མཚོན་པོ་ཞིག་བྲིས་འདུག He wrote a realistic book.

ཉམས་བཙོས་ (ñamjöö) sm. ཉམས་སྒྲོབ་.

ཉམས་ཆག (ñamjaà) sm. ཉམས་རྒུད་.

ཉམས་ཆུང་ (ñəmjuŋ) sm. ཉམ་ཆུང་.

ཉམས་ཆུང་ཆུང་ (ñam cūŋjuŋ) sm. ཉམ་ཆུང་ཆུང་.

ཉམས་ཆུང་བྱེད་ (ñəmjuŋ ceè) va. to act modest/ not pompous/ humble.

ཉམས་ཆེན་པོ་ (ñam cēmbo) dignified, elegant, grand (can convey either a positive or negative connotation).

ཉམས་ཚོད་ (ñam cöö) vi. to be able to differentiate/ distinguish/ recognize what is good and bad ། ཅ་ལག་རྙིང་མའི་རིགས་ཉམས་ཚོད་ཁག་པོ་ཡོད་པ་རེད་ It is difficult to differentiate antiques.

ཉམས་ཚོད་པོ་ (ñam cööbo) a person who can differentiate/ distinguish/ recognize good from bad.

ཉམས་འཆལ་ངན་སྤྱོད་ (ñam jɛɛ ŋɛnjöö) shung. undisciplined/ unruly and bad behavior (breakdown of discipline/ law and order) ། འགོ་ཁྲིད་དོ་ནན་ཞིག་མེད་སྐབས་གཞམ་རིམ་གྱི་ནང་ནས་ཉམས་འཆལ་ངན་སྤྱོད་ཀྱི་གནས་ཚུལ་མང་པོ་ཐོན་འདུག Lacking a conscientious leader, there have been many instances of unruly and bad action by the subordinates.

ཉམས་བརྗིད་ (ñamjii) sm. ཉམས་ཆེན་པོ་.

ཉམས་ཉེན་ (ñamñen) crisis ། དཔལ་འབྱོར་ཉམས་ཉེན་

Economic crisis.
ཉམས་ཉེས་ (ñamñeè) sm. ཉམ་ཉེས་.
ཉམས་གདོང་ (ñamdoŋ) see ཉམས་, 2.
ཉམས་རྟོགས་ (ñamdog) understanding or knowledge gained through investigation/ experience.
ཉམས་སྟབས་ (ñamdəb) sm. ཉམས་འགྱུར་.
ཉམས་སྟོན་ (ñamdön) sm. རྣམ་འགྱུར་སྟོན་.
ཉམས་སྟོབས་ (ñamdob) strength, power.
ཉམས་བརྟས་ (ñamdɛɛ̀) 1. strength, power. 2. health.
ཉམས་ཐག (ñamdag) sm.* ཉམ་ཐག.
ཉམས་འཐོར་ (ñamdɔɔ) shung. a breakdown/ decline ¶ མཆོད་རྒྱུན་ཕྱི་གྲུབ་ཉམས་འཐོར་འགྲོ་རིགས་བགྱིས་ན་མི་འཐུས་ One must not do anything that causes the breakdown of supplies for religious offerings.
ཉམས་དང་པ་ (ñam taŋba) a clear mind.
ཉམས་དོད་པོ་ (ñam tööbo) elegant, dignified, stylish.
ཉམས་དྲོད་ (ñamdröö) sm. ཉམས་རྒྱས་.
ཉམས་ལྡན་ (ñamdɛn) sm. ཉམས་དོད་པོ་.
ཉམས་བདེ་པོ་ (ñam debo) at peace, happy, calm.
ཉམས་སྣང་ (ñamnaŋ) sm. ཉམས་རྟོགས་.
ཉམས་སྣང་བན་བུན་ (ñamnaŋ bɛnbün) sth. unclear that is seen (as in a vision/ dream).
ཉམས་པ་ཀུན་གསོ་ (ñamba gũnso) rebuilding/ restoring at once or all together.
ཉམས་པ་མེད་པ་ (ñamba meèba) sm. ཉམས་མེད་.
ཉམས་པ་སོར་ཆུད་ (ñamba sɔ̄rjüü) rebuilding, restoring, reinstituting.
ཉམས་པའི་རྒྱུ་ཆ་ (ñambaɛ gyubja) waste/ scrap materials.
ཉམས་པའི་མ་ནིང་ (ñambɛ məniŋ) castrated person.
ཉམས་དཔྱད་ (ñamjɛɛ̀) sm. ཉམས་ཞིབ་.
ཉམས་དཔྱོད་ (ñamjöö) sm. ཉམས་ཞིབ་.
ཉམས་བྱེད་ (ñamjeè) sm. ཉམས་བྱེད་, 2.
ཉམས་འབྲུ་ (ñamdru) sm. ཉམས་དྲོད་.
ཉམས་མེད་ (ñammeè) 1. undeteriorated, without decline/ degeneration/ damage. 2. sm. ཉམས་ཆུང་.
ཉམས་མྱོང་ (ñamñoŋ) experience ¶ ཁང་པ་རྒྱག་ལག་གི་ཉམས་མྱོང་ཞི་དྲག་ཡོད་ (I) have a lot of experience building houses.
ཉམས་མྱོང་དངོས་ (ñamñoŋ ŋöö) personal/ actual experience, practical experience/ real experience.
ཉམས་མྱོང་བརྗེ་རེས་ (ñamñoŋ jereè) exchanging experiences; va.—བྱེད་.
ཉམས་མྱོང་དང་བསླབ་བྱ་ (ñamñoŋ daŋ lābja) experience and teaching.
ཉམས་མྱོང་སྤེལ་རེས་ (ñamñoŋ bēēreè) sm. ད་ཉམས་མྱོང་རྗེས་རེས་.
ཉམས་མྱོང་ཙམ་འཛིན་པའི་རིང་ལུགས་ (ñamñoŋdzam dzimbɛ riŋluù) sm. ཉམས་མྱོང་རིང་ལུགས་.
ཉམས་མྱོང་རིང་ལུགས་ (ñamñoŋ riŋluù) empiricism.
ཉམས་མྱོང་ལེན་ (ñamñoŋ len) va. to learn/ draw from experience.
ཉམས་མྱོང་ཤོད་ (ñamñoŋ shöö) va. to talk from experience.
ཉམས་མྱོང་གསོག (ñamñoŋ sɔ̄g) va. to collect/ accumulate experiences.
ཉམས་དམན་ (ñammɛn) weak, feeble; va.—དུ་གཏོང་ to weaken, to make feeble.
ཉམས་དམའ་པོ་ (ñam māābo) sm. ཉམ་དམའ་པོ་.
ཉམས་དམས་ (ñammɛɛ̀) weak, feeble; va.—སུ་གཏོང་ to make weak/ feeble.
ཉམས་དམས་ཐོར་ཞིག (ñammɛɛ̀ tɔ̄rshiì) declining and falling apart.
ཉམས་སྨད་ (ñammɛɛ̀) sm. ཉམ་དམས་.
ཉམས་སྨོད་ (ñammöö) sm. ཉམ་དམས་.
ཉམས་རྩལ་ (ñamdzɛɛ) skill learned from practice/ practical experience.
ཉམས་ཚོད་ (ñamdzöö) experimenting, testing, trying/ feeling out; va.—ལེན་; —ལྟ་; —བྱེད་; vi.—ལོན་ ¶ གནས་ཚུལ་དེ་ཁོང་གིས་ཤེས་ཡོད་མེད་ཉམས་ཚོད་བླངས་པ་ཡིན་ I tested to see whether he knew the news or not.
ཉམས་མཚར་བ་ (ñam tsārwa) extraordinary, amazing.
ཉམས་ཞན་ (ñamshɛn) sm. ཉམས་དམན་.
ཉམས་ཞིབ་ (ñəmshib) investigating, examining, testing; va.—བྱེད་; —དཔྱོད་ to investigate, to examine, to research ¶ གྲོང་གསེབ་ཀྱི་དཔལ་འབྱོར་མི་གཅིག་ཉམས་ཞིབ་བྱེད་པར་བཏང་བ་རེད་ (They) sent one person to investigate the village economy.
ཉམས་ཞིབ་ཁང་ (ñəmshibgaŋ) research center/ institute.
ཉམས་ཞིབ་ཆུག་པོ་ (ñəmshib cūgbo) sm. ཉམས་ཚོད་པོ་.
ཉམས་ཞིབ་བརྟག་དཔྱད་རུ་ཁག (ñəmshib dāgjɛɛ̀ rugaà) research investigation team, prospecting team.
ཉམས་ཞིབ་པ་ (ñəmshibbə) researcher.
ཉམས་གཞིགས་ (ñəmshig) sm. ཉམས་ཞིབ་.
ཉམས་ཟུར་ (ñamwur) vi. to laugh or cry as a result of seeing another laugh.
ཉམས་འོག་ཚུད་ (ñamwɔɔ̀ tsüù) vi. to understand/ comprehend/ know.
ཉམས་རུལ་ (ñamrüü) corrupt, rotten, degenerate.
ཉམས་ལེན་ (ñāmlen) 1. practice (as opposed to theory), application; va.—བྱེད་ to practice, to apply ¶ ཁོང་གི་བསླབ་བྱ་ང་ཚོས་ཉམས་ལེན་བྱེད་ཀྱི་རེད་ We will put his advice into practice. 2. experience; va.—བྱེད་ to experience ¶ འཚོ་བ་ཉམས་ལེན་བྱས་ནས་ Having experienced life.
ཉམས་ལེན་པ་ (ñamlemba) one who practices/ applies sth. ¶ ཁོང་ནི་ཆོས་ཀྱི་ཉམས་ལེན་པ་ཞིག་རེད་ He is sb. who practices religion.
ཉམས་ལེན་བྱེད་སྒོ་ (ñamlen ceègo) sm. ཉམས་ལེན་ཞུ་སྒོ་.
ཉམས་ལེན་ཞུ་སྒོ་ (ñamlem shugo) shung. things to be put into practice/ applied/ implemented ¶ ཞིབ་ཕྲའི་ཉམས་ལེན་ཞུ་སྒོའི་བཀའ་རྒྱ་ཟུར་བསྐྲིངས་ལྟར་ In accordance with the detailed specifications about the implementation of the edict that has been sent separately.
ཉམས་ལོང་ཁོག་བཙུག (ñamloŋ kɔ̄gjuù) shung. sizing up/ weighing sb.'s character or ability ¶ རང་དཔོན་རྒྱལ་མཚན་མཐོན་པོར་ཉམས་ལོང་ཁོག་བཙུག་གིས་ངོ་ལོག་བརྒྱབ་གཏོད་བྱས་པ་ Having sized up our lord the Panchen's Lama, the people rebelled against him.
ཉམས་ལོན་ (ñam lön) va. to size up/ measure a situation (then act in accordance with that) ¶ ལས་བྱེད་པ་དེ་ཚོས་འགོ་ཁྲིད་ཀྱི་ཉམས་ལོན་ནས་ལས་ཀར་དུས་ཐོག་ཡོང་གི་མེད་པ་རེད་ The cadres sized up the boss (that he won't criticize/ punish them) and do not come to work on time.
ཉམས་ཤར་ (ñam shār) vi. to have the visualization of sth. appear.
ཉམས་ཤོར་ (ñam shɔ̄ɔ) 1. vi. to have one's face get thin and drawn out due to sickness or worry. 2. vi. to lose one's grandure/ grandness.
ཉམས་སད་ (ñamsɛɛ̀) sm. ཉམས་ཚོད་.
ཉམས་སུ་འགྱུར་ (ñamsu gyur) vi. to deteriorate/ decline.
ཉམས་སུ་སྒྱུར་ (ñamsu gyur) sm. ཉམས་སུ་འཇུག.
ཉམས་སུ་འཇུག (ñamsu juù) va. to harm, to cause to deteriorate/ decline, to undermine, to enfeeble ¶ སྲིད་ཇུས་གསར་པ་དེས་ཆོས་ལུགས་ཉམས་སུ་འཇུག་སྐབས་ At the time the new policy caused religion to deteriorate.
ཉམས་སུ་མྱོང་ (ñamsu ñoŋ) vi. to experience.
ཉམས་སུ་ལེན་ (ñamsu len) sm. ཉམས་ལེན་.
ཉམས་གསོ་ (ñamso) restorating, repairing, renovating; va.—བྱེད་ ¶ ཁོ་ཚོས་མགྱོགས་མྱུར་དུ་ཐོན་སྐྱེད་ཉམས་གསོ་བྱས་པ་རེད་ They quickly restored production.
ཉམས་གསོ་སྐྱོན་བསངས་ (ñamso gyõnsaŋ) sm. ཉམས་གསོ་.
ཉམས་གསོ་ལྷུ་སྒྲིག (ñamso lhūdrig) repairing and assembling, putting the parts of sth. together; va.—བྱེད་.
ཉམས་གསོག (ñamsoò) gaining/ acquiring/ accumulating experience; va.—བྱེད་.

ཉམས་གསོའི་ལག་རྩལ་ (ñamsö lagdzεε) restoring/ repairing/ renovating skill.

ཉའི་སྒོང་ (ñε goŋa) fish eggs.

ཉའི་བྲང་གཤོག (ñε draŋshog) pectoral fin.

ཉའི་ཟེ་བ་ (ñε sewa) dorsal fin.

ཉའི་གཤོག་པ་ (ñε shōgba) 1. fish fin. 2. shark's fin.

ཉར་: p. ཉར་; f. ཉར་; imp. ཉོར་ (ñaa) va. to keep ¶ ཁོས་ཁྱི་གཅིག་ཉར་བཞག He keeps a dog ¶ ངའི་ཁྱི་ཉར་རོགས་གནང་ Please keep my dog for me.

ཉར་ཁང་ (ñaagaŋ) storeroom.

ཉར་ཉོར་ (ñaañɔr) see ཉ་རེ་ཉོ་རེ་.

ཉར་བསྐྱེན་ (ñaa dēn) shung. va. to keep ¶ དགོན་ནང་དུ་རྟ་བོང་ཁྱོན་ཆེ་ཉར་བསྐྱེན་དང་ (They) kept many donkeys and horses in the monastery.

ཉར་སྤྱོད་ (ñaajöö) keeping and using; va.—བྱེད་.

ཉར་ཚགས་ (ñaadzaà) 1. keeping, taking care of; va.—བྱེད་ ¶ ལུག་དང་ཞོ་མ་བཅས་ཉར་ཚགས་བྱེད་ཀྱི་ཡོད་པ་རེད་ He keeps (takes care of) goats, sheep, and cows. ¶ ཡིག་ཆ་འདི་ཁྱིམ་ནང་ལ་ཉར་ཚགས་བྱེད་མུས་རེད་ (He) is keeping the document in (his) house. 2. conservation, preservation; va.—བྱེད་ to conserve, to preserve ¶ དམག་རྒྱག་དུས་སྟོབས་ཤུགས་ཉར་ཚགས་བྱེད་དགོས་ (One) must conserve (one's) strength in war. 3. storing up, hoarding; va.—བྱེད་ ¶ དགུན་ཟས་ཉར་ཚགས་བྱེད་ཀྱི་རེད་ (He) will store up winter food.

ཉར་འཛིན་ (ñandzin) receipt, carbon copy.

ཉར་ཡིག (ñəryig) a copy for the file, the copy one keeps; va.—སྒྲིག to file a copy.

ཉར་ཉྭོས་བཟོད་ (ñarlöö söö) va. to take a risk/ responsibility by keeping sth. ¶ ཡིག་ཆ་འདི་ང་ཉར་ཉྭོས་བཟོད་པ་མི་འདུག I am unable to take the risk of keeping this document.

ཉར་གསོ་ (ñarso) adopting (child); va.—བྱེད་ ¶ ཁོས་ཕྲུ་གུ་ཞིག་ཉར་གསོ་བྱས་པ་རེད་ He adopted a child.

ཉལ་ (ñεε) va. to lie down, to go to sleep ¶ ཁོས་ཉལ་ཁྲིའི་སྟེང་ལ་ཉལ་བ་རེད་ He laid down on the bed.

ཉལ་ཁང་ (ñεεgaŋ) 1. bedroom. 2. dormitory room (as in a school or a hostel).

ཉལ་ཁེབས་ (ñεεgeb) blanket.

ཉལ་ཁྲི་ (ñεεdri) bed.

ཉལ་འཁོར་ (ñεngɔɔ) sleeping compartment on a train.

ཉལ་གུར་ (ñεεgur) mosquito net (for a bed).

ཉལ་གོས་ (ñεεgöö) 1. bed clothes. 2. bedding.

ཉལ་སྒྲོམ་ (ñεεdrom) wooden frame for a bed.

ཉལ་གཅིན་ (ñεεjin) bed wetting; vi.—གཏོང་; —ཤོར་ to wet one's bed.

ཉལ་ཆང་ (ñεεjaŋ) ཆང་ drunk at bedtime, a nightcap.

ཉལ་ཆས་ (ñεεjεὲ) bedding.

ཉལ་ཆས་ཁེབས་ (ñεεjεὲ kēb) bed cover.

ཉལ་ཆས་སྒྲིལ་ (ñεεjεὲ drii) va. to roll up one's bedding/ bedroll.

ཉལ་ཆས་སྒྲིལ་མ་ (ñεεjεὲ driimə) bedroll, bedding.

ཉལ་འཇོ་ (ñεnjo) a case/ sheath in which to carry bedding, a bed roll case filled with bedding.

ཉལ་འཇོག (ñεnjɔɔ̀) sm. ཉལ་འཇོ་.

ཉལ་ཉལ་ཤིག་ཤིག (ñεεñεε shīshig) crumbling down (like a sand pile).

ཉལ་ཉིལ་ (ñεεñii) litter, debris, waste, rubbish, garbage.

ཉལ་ཉོལ་ (ñεεñöö) abbr. of ཉལ་ལི་ཉོལ་ལི་.

ཉལ་སྟན་ (ñεεdεn) sleeping mattress/ bed.

ཉལ་ཐ་ (ñεεda) opium; va.—འཐེན་ to smoke opium.

ཉལ་ཐག (ñεεdaà) sm. ཉལ་ཐ་.

ཉལ་ཐའི་དམག་འཁྲུག (ñεεdε mōgdruù) sm. ཉལ་ཐའི་འཐབ་འཁྲུག.

ཉལ་ཐའི་འཐབ་འཁྲུག (ñεεdε tōbdruù) the Opium War of 1840-1842.

ཉལ་ཐའི་ཡོ་བྱད་ (ñεεdε yobjεὲ) opium smoking paraphernalia/ equipment.

ཉལ་ཐུལ་ (ñεεdüü) sm. ཉལ་ཆས་.

ཉལ་དུང་ (ñεεduŋ) a bugle call signaling the time for bed; va.—གཏོང་.

ཉལ་དུད་ (ñεεdüü) sm. ཉལ་ཐ་.

ཉལ་དུད་ཀྱི་གཡུལ་འགྱེད་ (ñεεdüügi yṻügyeè) sm. ཉལ་ཐའི་འཐབ་འཁྲུག.

ཉལ་དོར་ (ñεεdɔɔ) pajamas.

ཉལ་དྲི་ (ñεεdri) the odor of a bed; vi.—ཁ་.

ཉལ་གདན་ (ñεεdεn) sleeping mattress; va.—འདིང་ to put/ lay down a sleeping mattress.

ཉལ་འདོན་ (ñεndön) reciting prayers while lying down.

ཉལ་བརྡ་ (ñεεda) a signal/ sound indicating it is time for bed; va.—གཏོང་.

ཉལ་སྡོད་ས་ (ñεεdöösa) sm. ཉལ་ཁང་.

ཉལ་པང་ (ñεεbaŋ) the planks/ boards of a bed.

ཉལ་པོ་ (ñεεbo) copulation, intercourse; va.—བྱེད་.

ཉལ་ཕུབ་ལུས་ (ñεεbub lüü) sm. ཉལ་སར་ལུས་.

ཉལ་བྱ་ (ñεεja) people on duty who sleep in their office/ post.

ཉལ་མལ་ (ñεεmεε) sm. ཉལ་ཆས་.

ཉལ་ཚལ་ (ñεεdzεε) worn out quilt/ bedding.

ཉལ་གཞུག (ñεεshug) the end of the bed.

ཉལ་གཟན་ (ñεεsεn) blanket.

ཉལ་རོགས་ (ñεεrɔɔ̀) 1. sleeping companion. 2. spouse.

ཉལ་ལངས་ (ñεεlaŋ) sleeping and getting up; va.—བྱེད་ ¶ ང་དགོང་ཉལ་ལངས་དུས་ཐོག་ལ་བྱེད་ཀྱི་ཡོད་ I go to sleep and get up in the morning on time.

ཉལ་ལི་ཉི་ལི་ (ñεεli ñili) slumped over, collapsed (usu. pertains to crops as a result of hail and rain).

ཉལ་གཤོམ་ (ñεε shōm) va. to have sexual intercourse.

ཉལ་ས་ (ñεεsa) bedroom, place to sleep; va.—བཟོ་ to make one's bed/ sleeping place.

ཉལ་ས་གཅིག་ལ་རྨི་ལམ་སོ་སོ་ (ñεεsa jīglə ñīlam sōso) being together in some unit or group but having different views/ opinions [Lit. sleeping in one bedroom, each having different dreams].

ཉལ་ས་བྱུང་ན་རྐྱོང་ས་དྲན་ (ñεεsa cuŋnə gōŋsa trεn) not satisfied/ content, greedy [Lit. after one has a place to sleep, one thinks of stretching one's legs].

ཉལ་སར་ལུས་ (ñεεsar lüü) bedridden.

ཉི་ (ñi) 1. two ¶ ཉི་བརྒྱ་ Two hundred.

ཉི་དཀྱིལ་ (ñigyii) midday, noon.

ཉི་སྐམ་ (ñigam) drying in the sun; va.—གཏོང་.

ཉི་སྐམ་ཆར་སྦང་ (ñigam cārbaŋ) things going to waste, getting ruined [Lit. dry in sun, soak in rain].

ཉི་སྐར་ (ñigar) 1. comet. 2. abbr. sun and stars.

ཉི་སྐེམ་ (ñigem) sm. ཉི་སྐམ་.

ཉི་བསྐམས་མཛོད་འཇུག (ñigam dzöòjug) drying and storing away.

ཉི་ཁ་ར་ཀ་ (ñigaraga) Nicaragua.

ཉི་ཁྱིམ་ (ñigyim) solar corona, solar halo, aureole; vi.—ཐེབས་.

ཉི་ཁྲི་ (ñitri) twenty thousand.

ཉི་འཁོར་ (ñigɔɔ) going somewhere and returning in one day; va.—གཏོང་.

ཉི་འཁོར་མེ་ཏོག (ñigɔɔ medɔg) sm. ཉི་མ་མེ་ཏོག.

ཉི་འཁྱིམས་ (ñigyim) sm. ཉི་ཁྱིམ་.

ཉི་གུང་ (ñiguŋ) sm. ཉིན་གུང་.

ཉི་གུར་ (ñigur) sm. ཉི་ཁྱིམ་.

ཉི་གྲིབ་ (ñidrib) shade ¶ ཉི་གྲིབ་ལ་བསྡད་ན་ཡག་གི་རེད་ It's better if (you) sit in the shade.

ཉི་གྲིབ་མཚམས་ཀྱི་མི་ (ñidrib tsāmgi mi) fence-sitter (in the political sense).

ཉི་དགའ་ (ñiga) 1. sm. ཉི་དགའ་མེ་ཏོག. 2. a sun lover.

ཉི་དགའ་མེ་ཏོག (ñiga medɔg) sunflower.

ཉི་དགའི་འབྲས་བུ་ (ñigε drεὲbu) sunflower seeds.

ཉི་ནུབ་ (ñigεὲ) sunset.

ཉི་ནུབ་ཐུན་མཚམས་ (ñigεὲ tṻndzam) at the point that the sun sets.

ཉི་ནུབ་མཚམས་ (ñigεὲdzam) sm. ཉི་ནུབ་ཐུན་མཚམས་.

ཉི་སྒྲིབ་ (ñidrib) shade.

ཉི་ངོས་འབར་ཐིག (ñi̱ŋöö ba̱rdig) solar flare.

ཉི་ཆ་ (ñi̱ja) 1. the sunny side. 2. day time, during the day.

ཉི་ཆད་ (ñi̱jɛɛ̀) an agreement made to work a certain number of days; va.—བཅོ་.

ཉི་འཆར་ (ñi̱ cār) at the point of first sunrise.

ཉི་བརྙན་ (ñi̱ñɛn) the reflection of the sun in the water; vi.—འཆར་.

ཉི་གདོང་ (ñi̱dɛɛ̀) facing the sun.

ཉི་ལྟེ་སྨྲ་བ་ (ñi̱de māwa) heliocentric theory.

ཉི་ཐིག (ñi̱dig) sm. ཉི་མའི་ནག་ཐིག.

ཉི་དྲོད་ (ñi̱dröö) 1. the warmth of the sun. 2. a traditional time category (about 10 a.m. in the morning when the sun begins to emit heat).

ཉི་དྲོད་སྦྱང་བུ་གསོས་ས་ (ñi̱dröö jāŋbu sōsa) greenhouse.

ཉི་དྲོད་ཐབ་ཀ་ (ñi̱dröö tābga) sm. ཉི་འོད་ཐབ་ཀ་.

ཉི་དྲོས་ (ñi̱dröö) sm. ཉི་དྲོད་.

ཉི་གདན་ (ñi̱dɛn) sun-cushion/ mattress (in. a Buddhist iconography).

ཉི་གདུགས་ (ñi̱duù) umbrella, parasol.

ཉི་གདུགས་ཀྱི་རྩིབས་མ་ (ñi̱duùgi dzībmə) the ribs of an umbrella.

ཉི་མདངས་ (ñi̱daŋ) sunlight.

ཉི་དུལ་ (ñi̱düü) abbr. of ཉི་ཟེར་གྱི་དུལ་.

ཉི་ལྡོག (ñi̱ndɔɔ̀) solstice ¶ དགུན་ཉི་ལྡོག Winter solstice.

ཉི་ནུབ་ (ñi̱nub) sunset.

ཉི་ནུབ་ལམ་ཟད་ (ñi̱nub la̱msɛɛ̀) difficult or hopeless situation [Lit. sun set, road wiped out].

ཉི་ནུས་ (ñi̱nüü) abbr. of ཉི་མའི་ནུས་པ་.

ཉི་ནུས་གློག་འདོན་ས་ཚིགས (ñi̱nüü lɔ̄gdön sādzii) solar energy electric generating power station.

ཉི་ཕྱུག་ལྡན་པ་ (ñi̱jug dɛ̱mba) a room or place that is sunny.

ཉི་ཕྱེད་ (ñi̱ceè) 1. half a day. 2. midday, noon.

ཉི་འཕྱར་ལྷག་འཕྱར་ (ñi̱jar lhāgjar) sth. that is spoiled by sunshine and wind.

ཉི་འབུད་ (ñi̱mbüü) sm. ཉི་མ་གང་འགྱོལ་.

ཉི་མ་ (ñi̱mə) 1. sun; vi.—ཤར་ to rise (sun); vi.—འགྲིབ་ to be overcast, cloudy; vi.—ནུབ་, —བཞུད་ to set (sun); va.—སྐྱེལ་ to kill time, to while away time. 2. a day ¶ ཉི་མ་ཁ་ཤས་ A few days. 3. Sunday.

ཉི་མ་ཀློ་ (ñi̱mə drō) va. to sunbathe, to bask in the sun.

ཉི་མ་སྐྱེལ་ (ñi̱mə gyēē) see ཉི་མ་, 1.

ཉི་མ་ཁ་དཀར་ངོ་དཀར་ (ñi̱mə kāgar ŋogar) broad daylight.

ཉི་མ་ཁ་རྒྱུ་ (ñi̱mə kāju) mica.

ཉི་མ་འགྱོལ་ (ñi̱mə kyöö) 1. vi. to pass/ while away time ¶ ལས་ཀ་མེད་པར་ཉིན་སྔར་ང་ཉི་མ་འགྱོལ་ཁག་པོ་འདུག It is difficult to pass away the time everyday when I am without work. ¶ སློབ་སྦྱོང་ཁོ་ནའི་ངང་ཉི་མ་འགྱོལ་གྱི་འདུག (I) passed the time studying. 2. vi. to see things to completion, to continue ¶ གོ་མིན་དང་སྲིད་དབང་ཉི་མ་འགྱོལ་དཀའ་བའི་སྐབས་ At the time when it was difficult for the Kuomintang Party to continue.

ཉི་མ་འགྱོལ་པོ་ (ñi̱mə kyööbo) easy to pass the time ¶ སློབ་སྦྱོང་བྱ་རྒྱུ་མང་པོ་ཡོད་ཙང་ཉི་མ་འགྱོལ་པོ་འདུག Because I have many things to study time passes easily.

ཉི་མ་གང་ (ñi̱mə ga̱ŋ) the whole day.

ཉི་མ་གང་འགྱོལ་ (ñi̱mə ga̱ŋgyöö) 1. passing the time of day, whiling away time. 2. working perfunctorily, killing time at work rather than working diligently.

ཉི་མ་གང་ཤར་ (ñi̱mə ga̱ŋshar) sm. ཉི་མ་ནམ་ཤར་.

ཉི་མ་དགེ་བ་ (ñi̱mə ge̱wa) an auspicious day.

ཉི་མ་དགོང་ཕྱོགས་ (ñi̱mə go̱njɔɔ̀) late afternoon.

ཉི་མ་འཁྲིབ་ (ñi̱mə tri̱b) see ཉི་མ་ 1.

ཉི་མ་གས་ (ñi̱mə gɛ̱ɛ̀) vi. to set (the sun). to be sunset.

ཉི་མ་རྒྱག (ñi̱mə gyaà) vi. to shine (sun), to have sunshine (in a location) ¶ ཁང་པ་དེ་ལ་ཉི་མ་རྒྱག་གི་མི་འདུག The sun doesn't shine on that house.

ཉི་མ་སྒྲིབ་ (ñi̱mə dri̱b) va. to block the sun (creating a shadow on sb. or sth.).

ཉི་མ་ངན་པ་ (ñi̱mə ŋɛ̱mba) an inauspicious day.

ཉི་མ་སྔ་དྲོ་ (ñi̱mə ŋādro) early morning.

ཉི་མ་གཅིག་གཉིས་ཤིག་ནས་ (ñi̱mə jīgñii shīgnɛ) after one or two days.

ཉི་མ་ཆ་འཛིན་ (ñi̱mə cāndzin) partial eclipse of the sun.

ཉི་མ་རྗེས་མ་ (ñi̱mə je̱ema) the following day, the next day.

ཉི་མ་ཉིན་གང་ (ñi̱mə ñi̱ngaŋ) all day.

ཉི་མ་ཉིན་མཚན་ (ñi̱mə ñi̱ndzɛn) sm. ཉི་མ་ཉིན་གང་.

ཉི་མ་རྟག་པར་རེ་བཞིན་ (ñi̱mə dāgbar re̱shin) all the time, every day.

ཉི་མ་རྟིང་མ་ (ñi̱mə dīŋmə) sm. ཉི་མ་རྗེས་མ་.

ཉི་མ་སྟོན་ (ñi̱mə dön) sm. ཉི་མ་རྒྱག.

ཉི་མ་དྭངས་པོ་ (ñi̱mə ta̱ŋbo) sunny day.

ཉི་མ་གདུབ་འཛིན་ (ñi̱mə du̱ndzin) solar eclipse.

ཉི་མ་ལྡེ་ (ñi̱mə de̱) va. to warm oneself in the sun, to sunbathe.

ཉི་མ་ལྡོག (ñi̱mə dɔ̱ɔ̀) vi. to have/ be a solstice.

ཉི་མ་ལྡོག་ཐིག་བྱང་མ་ (ñi̱mə dɔ̱gdig ca̱ŋmə) Tropic of Cancer.

ཉི་མ་ལྡོག་ཐིག་ལྷོ་མ་ (ñi̱mə dɔ̱gdig lhōma) Tropic of Capricorn.

ཉི་མ་ནམ་ཤར་ (ñi̱mə na̱mshar) everyday ¶ ང་སློབ་གྲྭར་ཉི་མ་ནམ་ཤར་འགྲོ་གི་ཡོད་ I go to school everyday.

ཉི་མ་ནུབ་ (ñi̱mə nu̱b) vi. to set (sun).

ཉི་མ་ནུབ་ཁ་ (ñi̱mə nu̱bga) dusk.

ཉི་མ་ནུབ་ནས་ཤར་ (ñi̱mə nu̱bnɛ shār) sth. that is impossible [Lit. the sun rises from the west].

ཉི་མ་ནུབ་ཕྱོགས་ (ñi̱mə nu̱bjɔɔ̀) shung. the west [Lit. the direction where the sun sets].

ཉི་མ་སྤྲིན་བྲལ་ (ñi̱mə drīndrɛɛ) losing one's anger ¶ ཁྲིད་ཁྲིམས་གཙང་ཆོད་ཞིན་རྗེས་ཕྱིན་ཆད་བཀོས་ཡ་གཉིས་པོ་འཁོན་མེད་ཉི་མ་སྤྲིན་བྲལ་ལྟ་བུ་དགོས་རྒྱུ་ Once the case is over both the plaintiff and the defendant should hold no grudges and should not be angry (their mind should be just as clear as the sun after the clouds pass). [Lit. the sun (shines) as the clouds part].

ཉི་མ་ཕྱི་ (ñi̱mə cē) midday, noon.

ཉི་མ་ཕྱི་དྲོ་ (ñi̱mə cīdro) afternoon.

ཉི་མ་ཕྱེད་ (ñi̱mə cēè) sm. ཉི་ཕྱེད་.

ཉི་མ་ཕྱེད་གཉིས་ (ñi̱mə cēèñii) a day and a half.

ཉི་མ་ཕྱེད་ཡོལ་ (ñi̱mə cēèyöö) afternoon.

ཉི་མ་འཕུལ་ (ñi̱mə pǖü) sm. ཉི་མ་གང་འགྱོལ་.

ཉི་མ་བྱང་བགྲོད་ (ñi̱mə ca̱ndröö) summer solstice.

ཉི་མ་བྱོན་ (ñi̱mə cɔ̱n) vi. to set (the sun), to be sunset.

ཉི་མ་མེ་གྲོགས་ ཆར་པ་ཆུ་གྲོགས་ (ñi̱mə me̱droò cārba cūdroò) helping, aiding [Lit. sun friend of fire, rain friend of water].

ཉི་མ་མེ་ཏོག (ñi̱mə me̱dog) sunflower.

ཉི་མ་དམར་ཐག་ཆོད་ (ñi̱mə mārdag cǒö) vi. the red glow in the sky after the sun sets.

ཉི་མ་འཛུམ་ཞལ་ངོམས་ (ñi̱mə dzumshɛɛ ŋo̱m) vi. to rise (sun) [Lit. the sun shines brightly (in the sky)].

ཉི་མ་བཞུད་ (ñi̱mə shü̱ü) vi. to set (sun).

ཉི་མ་བཞུད་ལ་ཁ་ (ñi̱mə shü̱üla kā) just before sunset, at the point of sunset.

ཉི་མ་བཞུད་ལ་ཁད་ (ñi̱mə shü̱ü la̱kɛɛ̀) sm. ཉི་མ་ལ་ཁར་ཐིབས་པ་.

ཉི་མ་ཟླ་བ་ཡང་དག་འགྲོགས་ (ñi̱mə da̱wa ya̱ŋdaà drɔɔ̀) the 30th day of the month in the Tibetan calendar.

ཉི་མ་གཟའ་འཛིན་ (ñi̱mə sa̱ndzin) solar eclipse.

ཉི་མ་བཟང་པོ་ (ñi̱mə sa̱ŋbo) an auspicious day.

ཉི་མ་རིང་པོ་ (ñi̱mə ri̱ŋbu) 1. a long day (iso. having nothing to do to pass the time). 2. tolerant person.

ཉི་མ་རིལ་འཛིན་ (ñimə rindzin) full solar eclipse.
ཉི་མ་རེ་གཉིས་ (ñimə renii) one or two days.
ཉི་མ་རེ་རེ་ (ñimə rere) each day, every day.
ཉི་མ་ལ་ (ñimə la) vi. to set (the sun), to be sunset.
ཉི་མ་ལ་ཁར་ཕྲིན་ (ñimə lakar lēēba) on the decline, at the end of one's rope, on the brink of death/ extinction [Lit. the sun reaching the mountain pass] ¶ བཙན་རྒྱལ་རིང་ལུགས་པའི་སྟོབས་ཤུགས་ནི་ཉི་མ་ལ་ཁར་སླེབས་པ་དང་འདྲ་བ་ཡིན་ The power of the imperialists is on the brink of extinction (it's like the sun reaching the mountain pass—i.e., about to vanish).
ཉི་མ་ལར་བཞུད་ཉེ་ (ñimə lar shüüñe) sm. ཉི་མ་ལ་ཁར་སླེབས་པ་.
ཉི་མ་ལ་སྒྲོན་མེ་ (ñimәla drönme) 1. showing off in the presence of an expert, giving advice to an expert [Lit. a lamp in the sun]. 2. a phrase used to precede a comment to show one's humility by saying my comment is like a lamp to the sun].
ཉི་མ་ལ་ལ་ཐད་ (ñimə lala tɛ̄ɛ̀) sm. ཉི་མ་ལ་ཁར་སླེབས་པ་.
ཉི་མ་ལོག (ñimə lɔ̄ɔ̀) sm. ཉི་མ་ལྷག.
ཉི་མ་ཤར་ (ñimə shār) see ཉི་མ་, 1.
ཉི་མ་ཤར་བ་སྦར་རས་མི་ཁེབས་ (ñimə shārwa barɛ migeb) an irresistible force/ power [the hand cannot cover the rising sun].
ཉི་མ་སྲོ་ (ñimə drō) sm. ཉི་མ་གྲོ་.
ཉི་མ་ཧྲིལ་འཛིན་ (ñimə hrīndzin) full solar eclipse.
ཉི་མ་ལྷོ་བགྲོད་ (ñimə lhōdröö) winter solstice.
ཉི་མའི་དཀྱིལ་ (ñimɛgyīī) during the day.
ཉི་མའི་དཀྱིལ་འཁོར་ (ñimɛ gyīngɔɔ) the sun.
ཉི་མའི་སྐར་མ་ (ñimɛ gārma) sth. that is impossible to see [Lit. stars during the day].
ཉི་མའི་ཁྱབ་འགྱེད་ནུས་པ་ (ñimɛ kyābgyeè nüübə) solar radiation energy.
ཉི་མའི་ཁྱིམ་རྒྱུད་ (ñimɛ kyīmgyüü) the solar system.
ཉི་མའི་འཁོར་ལམ་ (ñimɛ kɔ̄ɔlam) sun's orbit.
ཉི་མའི་གུང་ (ñimɛgun) noon.
ཉི་མའི་གུར་ཁང་ (ñimɛ kurgaŋ) sm. ཉི་ཁྱིམ་.
ཉི་མའི་དགུང་ལ་ (ñimɛ konla) during the day.
ཉི་མའི་རྒྱུད་རིམ་ (ñimɛ gyüürim) sm. ཉི་མའི་ཁྱིམ་རྒྱུད་.
ཉི་མའི་དུས་ཚོད་ (ñimɛ tüüdzöö) daytime.
ཉི་མའི་ནག་ཐིག (ñimɛ nəgdig) sun spot.
ཉི་མའི་ནུས་པ་ (ñimɛ nüübə) solar energy/ power.
ཉི་མའི་ཟེར་ (ñimɛ see) sm. ཉི་ཟེར་.
ཉི་མའི་འོད་ཀོར་ (ñimɛ wöögar) sm. ཉི་མའི་གུར་ཁང་.
ཉི་མའི་འོད་ཟེར་ (ñimɛ wöösee) the sun's rays.
ཉི་མའི་འོད་རིམ་ (ñimɛ wöörim) solar spectrum.
ཉི་མའི་རིགས་ (ñimɛ rig) sm. ཉི་མའི་གཉེན་.
ཉི་མར་སྟོན་ (ñimar dön) sm. ཉི་མ་སྲོ་.
ཉི་མས་སྐེམ་ (ñimɛ gēm) vi. to dry in the sun.
ཉི་སྨུར་ (ñiñur) just before sunset.
ཉི་རྩེ་ཤར་ (ñidze shār) vi. to be sunrise.
ཉི་ཚེ་བ་ (ñitsawa) 1. insects that have a life span of one day. 2. the poorest category of traders. 3. odd, fragmentary, miscellaneous.
ཉི་ཚེ་བའི་ཐེག་པ་ (ñitsewɛ tēgba) Hinayana (Buddhism).
ཉི་ཚོད་ (ñidzöö) sun dial.
ཉི་ཚོད་འཁོར་ལོ་ (ñidzöö kɔ̄ɔlo) sun dial.
ཉི་འཛིན་ (ñindzin) solar eclipse.
ཉི་འཛིན་འོད་ཀོར་ (ñindzin wöögɔɔ) solar corona during an eclipse.
ཉི་གཞོན་ (ñishön) morning sun, sunrise.
ཉི་གཞོན་མཚམས་སྤྲིན་ (ñishön tsə̄mdrin) the red clouds of sunrise.
ཉི་བཞུད་ལམ་ཟད་ (ñishüü lamsɛɛ̀) sm. ཉི་ནུབ་ལམ་ཟད་.
ཉི་ཟེར་ (ñiser) sun's rays; vi.—ཕོག to have the sun shine on sth. or sb.
ཉི་ཟེར་གྱི་དུག (ñisergi tuù) ultraviolet radiation.
ཉི་ཟླ་ (ñinda) sun and moon.
ཉི་ཟླ་སྐར་གསུམ་ (ñinda gārsum) the three: the sun, moon and the stars.
ཉི་ཟླ་འཁོར་སྐྱོད་ (ñinda kɔ̄ɔgyöö) movement of the sun and moon.
ཉི་ཟླ་འཁྱིམས་ (ñinda kyīm) vi. to have a solar corona.
ཉི་ཟླ་ནར་བསྒྱངས་ (ñinda nargyaŋ) delaying; va.—བྱེད་; —གཏོང་ to delay.
ཉི་ཟླ་ཟུང་འབྲེལ་ (ñinda suŋdree) relationship/ friendship formed between two powerful entities (countries, people, etc.) [Lit. relationship between sun and moon].
ཉི་ཟླ་གཟའ་འཛིན་ (ñinda səndzin) solar and lunar eclipses.
ཉི་ཟླ་ལ་སྒྲོན་མེའི་གསལ་སྐྱོར་ (ñindala drönmee sɛ̄ɛ gyɔ̄r) unnecessary explanation/ clarification [Lit. making the sun and moon brighter with a lamp].
ཉི་ཟླ་སྲིན་འབུའི་འོད་ཀྱིས་འགྲན་པ་འདྲ་ (ñinda sīmbü wöögi drɛmbadra) shung. trying to do the impossible, a hopeless endeavor [Lit. the fire fly trying to compete with sun and moon].
ཉི་ཟླའི་འགྲོས་ (ñīndɛ dröö) shung. the rotation of the sun and moon.
ཉི་གཟེར་ (ñiser) sm. ཉི་ཟེར་.
ཉི་བཟློག་ཞབས་སྒྲུབ་ (ñidɔɔ shəbdrub) shung. the religious rite performed during the solstices.
ཉི་འོག (ñiwɔɔ̀) under the sun.
ཉི་འོག་གི་བསྟན་སྲིད་སྤྱིའི་བདག་པོ་ (ñiwɔɔ̀gi dēnsiì jīī dagbo) shung. the Dalai Lama [Lit. the spiritual and temporal leader of all those that are under the sun and the moon].
ཉི་འོག་ཏུ་འཁོད་པའི་སྐྱེ་རྒུ་ (ñiwɔgdu kōōwɛ gyēgu) shung. phrase used at the start of orders/ edicts from the traditional government [Lit. all people existing under the sun].
ཉི་འོད་ (ñiwöö) sunshine, sunlight; vi.—འཆར་ to shine (sun), to be sunshine.
ཉི་འོད་ཀྱི་གློག་བཞུ་ (ñiwöögi lɔ̄gshu) solar lamp.
ཉི་འོད་ཀྱི་ཐབ་ (ñiwöögi tə̄b) solar furnace.
ཉི་འོད་ཀྱི་དྲུང་དུ་སྒྲོན་མེ་བཏེགས་ (ñiwöögi truŋdu drönme dēg) shung. pointless activity ¶ ཉི་འོད་ཀྱི་དྲུང་དུ་སྒྲོན་མེ་བཏེགས་པ་ལྟར་སྐྱར་ཡང་བརྟར་ཞིབ་གཅོད་དགོས་པའི་གནས་གང་ཡང་མ་མཆིས་པ་ Like raising a lantern under the sunshine, there is no need to investigate again [Lit. raising a lantern in sunlight].
ཉི་འོད་ཀྱིས་གསོ་ (ñiwöögi sō) va. to sunbathe.
ཉི་འོད་བཀྲ་བ་ (ñiwöö drāwa) the glare of the sun.
ཉི་འོད་གྲོང་ཁྱེར་ (ñiwöö troŋgyer) Lhasa.
ཉི་འོད་གློག་སྒྲོན་ (ñiwöö lɔ̄gdrön) 1. solar lamp. 2. fluorescent lamp/ light.
ཉི་འོད་གློག་སྨན་ (ñiwöö lɔ̄gmɛn) solar battery.
ཉི་འོད་གློག་ཞུ་ (ñiwöö lɔ̄gshu) sm. ཉི་འོད་གློག་སྒྲོན་.
ཉི་འོད་གློག་ཞུའི་སྦུ་གུ་ (ñiwöö lɔ̄gshü bugu) fluorescent light tube.
ཉི་འོད་གློག་ཤེལ་ (ñiwöö lɔ̄gshee) sm. ཉི་འོད་གློག་ཞུའི་སྦུ་གུ.
ཉི་འོད་ཐབ་ཀ་ (ñiwöö tə̄bga) solar stove.
ཉི་འོད་དྲོད་ཁང་ (ñiwöö drööɡaŋ) solar greenhouse.
ཉི་འོད་ནུས་པ་ (ñiwöö nüübə) solar energy/ power ¶ ཉི་འོད་ནུས་པའི་དྲོད་ཁང་ Solar heated greenhouse.
ཉི་འོད་ནུས་ཤུགས་ (ñiwöö nüüshuù) sm. ཉི་འོད་ནུས་པ་.
ཉི་འོད་ནུས་ཤུགས་ཞིབ་འཇུག་ཁང་ (ñiwöö nüüshuù shimjuùgaŋ) institute for solar energy.
ཉི་འོད་ཕོག་ཚད་ (ñiwöö pɔ̄ɔdzɛɛ̀) amount/ rate of sunshine.
ཉི་ཡོལ་ (ñiyöö) 1. screen, awning, curtain (to keep the sun off sth.). 2. umbrella.
ཉི་གཡབ་ (ñiyəb) overhanging roof, awning.
ཉི་གཡོད་ (ñiyöö) New York.
ཉི་ར་ (ñirə) veranda.
ཉི་རི་ལི་ཡ་ (ñiriliya) Nigeria.
ཉི་ལུང་ (ñiluŋ) eng. nylon.
ཉི་ཤར་ (ñishar) sunrise.
ཉི་ཤར་ནེའུ་དྲོད་ (ñishar newudröö) a little after sunrise.
ཉི་ཤུ་ (ñishu) twenty ¶ ཉི་ཤུ་རྩ་གཅིག Twenty one.
ཉི་ཤུ་རྩ་གཅིག (ñīshu dzəjii) twenty one.
ཉི་ཤུ་རྩ་གཉིས་ (ñīshu dzāñii) twenty two.

ཉི་ཤུའི་ཟུར་ (ñishü ser) one twentieth.

ཉི་གསར་ (ñisar) new sun, rising sun.

ཉི་སྲེག (ñiseg) sm. ཉི་བསྲེགས་.

ཉི་སྲེག་ཆར་རྡུང་ (ñiseg cārduŋ) suffering, hardship [Lit. sun burn, rain beat].

ཉི་སྲེག་ཆར་སྦང་ (ñiseg cārbaŋ) sm. ཉི་སྲེག་ཆར་རྡུང་ [Lit. sun burn, rain soak].

ཉི་གསར་ཐུན་མཚམས་ (ñisar tǖndzam) sunrise.

ཉི་སྲོ་ (ñi sō) sm. ཉི་བསྲེགས་.

ཉི་བསྲེགས་ (ñiseg) 1. sunbathing; va.—གཏོང་ to sun bathe; vi.—ཐེབས་ to get sun burned. 2. drying in sun.

ཉི་བསྲོས་ (ñi sȫȫ) p. of ཉི་སྲོ་.

ཉི་ཧུང་ཏིང་ (ñihuŋdiŋ) ch. neon sign.

ཉི་ཧོང་ (ñihoŋ) Japan.

ཉིག་ཉིག (ñigñīg) sm. ཉིགས་.

ཉིགས་ (ñig) dregs, slags, residue.

ཉིང་ (ñiŋ) 1. onself. 2. on top of that, moreover, furthermore.

ཉིང་སྒྱུར་སྤྲི་དཀར་འདྲེས་མ་ (ñiŋgyur drīgar dreèma) nucleoprotein.

ཉིང་ཁུ་ (ñiŋgu) essence, extract, juice.

ཉིང་འཁྲུལ་ (ñiŋ trǖǖ) vi. to be confused.

ཉིང་ཁྲི་ (ñiŋdri) a xian/ district in S.E. Tibet (in Kongpo).

ཉིང་དགོས་ (ñiŋgöö) vital, essential; essential needs and wants.

ཉིང་མངར་ (ñiŋŋar) ribose.

ཉིང་མངར་ཉིང་སྒྱུར་ (ñiŋŋar ñiŋgyur) ribonucleic acid.

ཉིང་ཏོར་ (ñiŋdɔɔ) sm. ངེས་པར་.

ཉིང་རྡུལ་ (ñiŋdüü) nucleous (of an atom), nuclear ¶ ཉིང་རྡུལ་མཚོན་ཆ་ Nuclear weapon.

ཉིང་རྡུལ་གས་འགྱུར་ (ñiŋdüü kɛ̄ègyur) nuclear reaction.

ཉིང་རྡུལ་གས་འགྱུར་སྤྲིག་ཆས་ (ñiŋdüü kɛ̄ɛ̀gyur drigjɛɛ̀) nuclear reactor.

ཉིང་རྡུལ་གློག་ཁང་ (ñiŋdüü lɔ̄ɔ̀gaŋ) nuclear power station.

ཉིང་རྡུལ་སྐྱུལ་ཤུགས་ (ñiŋdüü güüshug) nuclear power.

ཉིང་རྡུལ་དངོས་ལུགས་ཚོད་ལྟ་ (ñiŋdüü ŋȫȫlug tsȫȫda) nuclear test.

ཉིང་རྡུལ་འདུས་འགྱུར་ (ñiŋdüü düügyur) nuclear fission.

ཉིང་རྡུལ་འདུས་འགྱུར་གྱི་ནུས་པ་ (ñiŋdüü düügyurgi nüübə) nuclear energy.

ཉིང་རྡུལ་ནུས་སྤྱོད་ (ñiŋdüü nüüjöö) nuclear powered ¶ ཉིང་རྡུལ་ནུས་སྤྱོད་ཆུ་འཛུལ་དམག་གྲུ་ Nuclear powered submarine.

ཉིང་རྡུལ་ཕུ་རབ་ (ñiŋdüü trɔ̄rəb) nuclear fallout.

ཉིང་རྡུལ་འཕུར་མདེལ་ (ñiŋdüü pūndel) nuclear missile.

ཉིང་རྡུལ་འཕྲོ་ཐིག་ཁྱབ་འགྱེད་ (ñiŋdüü trōdig kyəbgyeè) nuclear radiation.

ཉིང་རྡུལ་འཕྲོ་ཐིག་ཁྱབ་མཆེད་ (ñiŋdüü trōdig kyəbjeè) sm. ཉིང་རྡུལ་འཕྲོ་ཐིག་ཁྱབ་འགྱེད་.

ཉིང་རྡུལ་འབར་མདེལ་ (ñiŋdüü bardee) nuclear warhead/ bomb/ shell.

ཉིང་རྡུལ་འབར་རྫས་ (ñiŋdüü bardɛɛ̀) nuclear fuel.

ཉིང་རྡུལ་དམག་ཆེན་ (ñiŋdüü māgjen) sm. ཉིང་རྡུལ་མཚོན་ཆའི་དམག་ཆེན་.

ཉིང་རྡུལ་དམག་གྲབས་ (ñiŋdüü məgdrəb) preparation for nuclear war; va.—བྱེད་.

ཉིང་རྡུལ་ཚ་བ་ (ñiŋdüü tsāwa) thermonuclear ¶ ཉིང་རྡུལ་ཚ་བའི་མཚོན་ཆ་ Thermonuclear weapon.

ཉིང་རྡུལ་ཚ་བའི་ཚོད་ལྟ་ (ñiŋdüü tsāwɛ tsȫȫda) thermonuclear experiment.

ཉིང་རྡུལ་མཚོན་ཆ་ (ñiŋdüü tsȫnja) nuclear weapon.

ཉིང་རྡུལ་མཚོན་ཆ་འགོག་སྲུང་ (ñiŋdüü tsȫnja gɔgsuŋ) nuclear bomb shelter.

ཉིང་རྡུལ་མཚོན་ཆ་རྒྱ་ཆེར་འགྲེམས་ (ñiŋdüü tsȫnja gyacer drem) vi. to have/ get nuclear arms proliferation.

ཉིང་རྡུལ་མཚོན་ཆ་ཉུང་འཕྲི་ (ñiŋdüü tsȫnja ñuŋdri) nuclear arms reduction; va.—བྱེད་.

ཉིང་རྡུལ་མཚོན་ཆ་ཚོད་ལྟ་ (ñiŋdüü tsȫnja tsȫȫda) nuclear arms test; va.—བྱེད་.

ཉིང་རྡུལ་མཚོན་ཆ་ཤུགས་ཆུང་དུ་གཏོང་ (ñiŋdüü tsȫnja shūgjuŋdu dōŋ) va. to reduce nuclear arms.

ཉིང་རྡུལ་མཚོན་ཆའི་རྟེན་གཞི་ (ñiŋdüü tsȫnjɛ dēnshi) nuclear arms base.

ཉིང་རྡུལ་མཚོན་ཆའི་དམག་འཁྲུག (ñiŋdüü tsȫnjɛ məgdruù) nuclear war.

ཉིང་རྡུལ་མཚོན་ཆའི་སྲུང་གདུག (ñiŋdüü tsȫnjɛ sūŋdug) nuclear (defence) umbrella.

ཉིང་རྡུལ་མཚོན་ཆས་སྡིགས་མོ་ (ñiŋdüü tsȫnjɛɛ̀ digmu) nuclear blackmail, nuclear threatening/ intimidation; va.—བྱེད་.

ཉིང་རྡུལ་མཚོན་ཤུགས་ཅེ་བའི་རྒྱལ་ཁབ་ (ñiŋdüü tsȫnshug cēwɛ gyɛɛgəb) countries with nuclear weapons.

ཉིང་སྤྲུལ་ (ñiŋdrüü) incarnation of an incarnate lama.

ཉིང་བྲན་ (ñiŋdrɛn) a servant/ serf of a servant/ serf.

ཉིང་འབངས་ (ñiŋbaŋ) subjects of subjects, serfs of serfs.

ཉིང་མེང་ (ñiŋmeŋ) sm. ཉིང་མོང་.

ཉིང་མོང་ (ñiŋmoŋ) ch. lemon.

ཉིང་ཚ་ (ñiŋdza) great grandson.

ཉིང་མཚམས་ (ñiŋdzam) the joint/ point/ connection between (two things).

ཉིང་མཚམས་སྦྱོར་ (ñiŋdzam jɔɔ) vi. to have consciousness (or the life force) attach itself to a womb.

ཉིང་ཞ་ (ñiŋshə) Ningxia (Hui Autonomous Region).

ཉིང་ཞ་ཧུའི་རིགས་རང་སྐྱོང་ལྗོངས་ (ñiŋshə hwērig raŋgyoŋjoŋ) Ningxia Hui Autonomous Region.

ཉིང་གཡོག (ñiŋyɔɔ) sm. ཉིང་བྲན་.

ཉིང་ལག (ñiŋlaà) 1. subbranch, subdivision ¶ སྔོན་འགྲོའི་ཉིང་ལག་དམག་དཔུང་ The advance subbranch military force (of the large army that went to Lhasa in 1951). ¶ ཉིང་ལག་ཚོང་ཁང་ Subbranch store. 2. parts of the body (such as finger, nose).

ཉིང་ལག་རུ་ཁག (ñiŋlaà rugaà) a group or unit that is a subdivision/ branch of a larger group.

ཉིང་ལག་ཅུས་ (ñiŋlaà jüü) tib.ch. subdivision of a branch of a main office.

ཉིང་ལག་སོར་མོ་ལྔ་ (ñiŋlaà sōrmo ŋā) the five fingers.

ཉིང་ཤ་ (ñiŋsha) 1. one's own flesh. 2. meat of an animal killed that day.

ཉིང་ཤའ་ (ñiŋsha) sm. ཉིང་ཞ་.

ཉིང་སློབ་ (ñiŋlob) a disciple of a disciple.

ཉིད་ (ñii) 1. self, oneself, itself ¶ གཅེན་པོ་ཉིད་འདིར་ཐེབས་སྐབས་ When (my) brother himself came here. ¶ ལས་ཀ་དེ་ཉིད་བྱེད་དགོས་རེད་ (We) have to do that work itself. ¶ ཁྱེད་ཉིད་ You (yourself). 2. as soon as (vb.+ —) ¶ འཐུས་མི་འབྱོར་ཉིད་ As soon as the representative arrives.

ཉིད་ཅག (ñiijaà) you (plural).

ཉིད་རང་ (ñiiraŋ) you.

ཉིན་ (ñin) 1. day ¶ ཉི་མ་གསུམ་ནས་ཡོང་གི་ཡིན་ (I'll) come after three days. 2. (vb.+ —) day of the verbal action ¶ ཚོགས་འདུ་དང་པོ་ཚོགས་ཉིན་ནས་ From the day the first meeting was held.

ཉིན་ཀ་ (ñinga) that day, the day ¶ ཁ་ཉིན་ཀ་ The day before yesterday. ¶ གནང་ཉིན་ཀ་ The day after tomorrow.

ཉིན་དཀར་ (ñingar) daytime.

ཉིན་དཀར་ལྷ་མོར་ལྷ་ལས་རོགས་ མཚན་མོ་འདྲེ་མོར་ཐགས་འཐག་རོགས་ (ñingar lhāmor lhālɛɛ̀ rɔɔ̀ tsɛ̄nmo dremor tāg tāà rɔɔ̀) openly helping good people but secretly helping evil people [Lit. in the daytime helping gods build statues, in the nighttime helping witches weave].

ཉིན་རྐུན་ (ñingün) thief who robs during the day; va.—བྱེད་.

ཉིན་སྐར་ (ñingar) 1. stars that are visible during

daytime. 2. not plentiful, rare [Lit. stars during the day].

ཉིན་སྐུང་མཚན་སྐྱོད་ (ñinguŋ tsɛ̄ngyöö) hiding during the day and traveling at night (method of fleeing).

ཉིན་སྐོར་ (ñingɔɔ) sm. ཉིན་བསྐོར་.

ཉིན་བསྐོར་ (ñingɔɔ) the roundtrip distance that can be completed in one day.

ཉིན་ཁ་དཀར་ངོ་དཀར་ (ñin kāgar ŋogar) in broad daylight ¶ཁོས་ཉིན་ཁ་དཀར་ངོ་དཀར་ལ་ཀུན་མ་བརྐུས་པ་རེད་ He stole in broad daylight.

ཉིན་ཁུག་གཏོང་ (ñinguù dōŋ) va. to start a journey in the morning and return that same evening.

ཉིན་མགོ་ (ñingo) daily/ everyday needs or necessities.

ཉིན་མགོའི་དངོས་རྫས་ (ñingö ŋöödzɛɛ̀) things needed daily, articles/ items of daily use.

ཉིན་མགོའི་ཡོ་བྱད་ (ñingö yobjɛɛ̀) articles/ items of daily use.

ཉིན་འཁལ་ཉིན་འཐག (ñingɛɛ ñindaà) starting and finishing on the same day, doing promptly [Lit. the day you spin the yarn, weave it].

ཉིན་འཁོར་ (ñingɔɔ) sm. ཉིན་བསྐོར་.

ཉིན་འགྱངས་ (ñingyoŋ) all day, the whole day ¶ཁོང་གིས་ཁ་ལག་ཉིན་འགྱངས་བཏང་བ་རེད་ He gave an all day party.

ཉིན་གང་ (ñingaŋ) the whole day, all day long ¶ཉིན་གང་ནང་ལ་བསྡད་བསྡད་པ་ཡིན་ (I) stayed home all day.

ཉིན་གང་པོ་ (ñin gaŋbo) sm. ཉིན་གང་.

ཉིན་གབ་ (ñingəb) hiding during the day.

ཉིན་གབ་མཚན་ཐོན་ (ñingəb tsɛ̄ndön) hiding during the day and coming out at night.

ཉིན་གུང་ (ñinguŋ) noon, midday ¶ཉིན་གུང་ཁ་ལག་ཟ་སྐབས་ When eating lunch.

ཉིན་གུང་ཁ་ལག (ñinguŋ kālaà) lunch.

ཉིན་གུང་གི་གཉིད་ (ñinguŋgi ñīī) siesta, midday nap, afternoon nap.

ཉིན་གུང་བདེ་ལེགས་ (ñinguŋ deleè) good afternoon (a recent term of greeting).

ཉིན་གུང་ཕྱེད་ཡོལ་ (ñinguŋ cēèyöö) past midday, afternoon.

ཉིན་གྲངས་ (ñindraŋ) number of days ¶ཉིན་གྲངས་གསུམ་ Three days.

ཉིན་བགྲོད་མཚན་སྡོད་ (ñindröö tsɛ̄ndöö) traveling during the day and stopping at night.

ཉིན་གླ་ (ñinla) daily wage, day's wages; va.—རྒྱུགས་ to work for daily wages; —རྒྱག to pay for work on a daily wage basis.

ཉིན་གླ་པ་ (ñinlabə) daily wage laborer, person hired on day-to-day basis.

ཉིན་དགུང་ཡོལ་ (ñinguŋ yöö) sm. ཉིན་དགུང་ཕྱེད་ཡོལ་.

ཉིན་འགྱངས་ཞག་ཤུད་ (ñingyaŋ shaàbüü) sm. ཉིན་འགྱངས་ཞག་འབུད་.

ཉིན་འགྱངས་ཞག་འབུད་ (ñingyaŋ shaàbüü) delaying, procrastinating ¶ཉིན་འགྱངས་ཞག་འབུད་སོང་ན་མི་ལེགས་ If you delay it is not all right.

ཉིན་སྔང་ (ñingaŋ) sm. ཉིན་གང་.

ཉིན་བརྒྱ་དུས་གཅིག་ལ་ (ñingya tüüjiglə) shung. all at once, right away ¶མི་དམངས་རྣམས་ཉིན་བརྒྱ་དུས་གཅིག་ལ་དམར་གསོད་བཏང་སོང་ They killed the people all at once. [Lit. one hundred days in one day].

ཉིན་བརྒྱའི་གློ་ནད་ (ñingyɛ lōnɛɛ̀) whooping cough.

ཉིན་གཅིག (ñinjig) one day, once.

ཉིན་གཅིག་གི་སྡོམ་པ་ (ñinjiggi domba) a vow taken for one day only.

ཉིན་གཅིག་གི་མི་ལྟར་ (ñinjiggi midar) sm. ཉིན་གཅིག་ནང་བཞིན་.

ཉིན་གཅིག་ཐོག་ཐག (ñinjig tɔ̄gdaà) from dawn to dusk.

ཉིན་གཅིག་ནང་བཞིན་ (ñinjig nəŋshin) constant, unchanging, (for people) steady, stable, reliable [Lit. doing sth. in the same manner every day].

ཉིན་གཅིག་ཟས་གཅིག (ñinjig sɛɛ̀jig) one meal per day.

ཉིན་གཅིག་ལོ་སྐྱེལ་གྱི་སྣང་བ་ (ñinjig logyeegi nāŋwa) an expression conveying boredom [Lit. a feeling where a day seems longer than a year].

ཉིན་བཅོལ་ (ñinjöö) leaving sb. or sth. on a daily basis; va.—བྱེད་.

ཉིན་ཆས་ (ñinjɛɛ̀) sm. ཉིན་མགོ་.

ཉིན་ཆད་ (ñinjɛɛ̀) sm. ཉི་ཆད་.

ཉིན་རྗེས་མ་ (ñin jeema) the next day.

ཉིན་གཉིས་པ་ (ñin ñiibə) the second day ¶ཚོགས་འདུ་ཉིན་གཉིས་པ་ The second day of the meeting.

ཉིན་ལྟར་ (ñindar) every day, daily.

ཉིན་ལྟར་རེ་བཞིན་ (ñindar reshin) sm. ཉིན་ལྟར་.

ཉིན་བསྟུད་ (ñindüü) (on) successive days, day after day, continuously ¶ང་ཚོ་ཉིན་བསྟུད་ནས་ལས་ཀ་བྱས་པ་ཡིན་ We worked continuously (day after day).

ཉིན་ཐུང་སྐབས་ (ñintuŋgəb) period of the year when the days are short (i.e., winter).

ཉིན་ཐོ་ (ñindo) diary, daily account/ record; va.—རྒྱག to keep a diary, to keep daily accounts/ records.

ཉིན་ཐོ་འགོད་དེབ་ (ñindo göödeb) diary (book).

ཉིན་ཐོག་ཏུ་སླེབས་ (ñindɔgdu lēb) vi. to arrive at the day to do sth. ¶དགོན་པ་བཞེངས་པའི་ཉིན་ཐོག་ཏུ་སླེབས་པ་རེད་ The day for building the monastery has arrived.

ཉིན་དེ་ཉིད་ (ñin teñii) that very day, the same day ¶ང་ཡོང་བའི་ཉིན་དེ་ཉིད་ལ་ཆང་ས་བརྒྱབ་པ་ཡིན་ On the very day I arrived I got married.

ཉིན་དེབ་ (ñindeb) diary, daily log book.

ཉིན་བདེ་མ་ (ñin dema) shung. a type of ceremonial scarf of the best quality.

ཉིན་ནས་ཉིན་བསྟུད་ (ñinnɛ ñindüü) day after day continuously.

ཉིན་པར་ (ñinbar) 1. everyday, daily ¶ཁོ་ཉིན་པར་ཆང་ཁང་ལ་འགྲོ་བ་རེད་ He goes to the bar everyday. 2. that day ¶དེའི་ཉིན་པར་ On that day.

ཉིན་པོའ་ (ñinbo) Ningpo.

ཉིན་ཕུད་ (ñinbüü) abbr. of ཉི་མ་འཕུལ་.

ཉིན་ཕྱེ་མཚན་ཟུམ་ (ñinje tsɛ̄nsum) a flower that opens its petals during the day and closes them at night.

ཉིན་ཕྱེད་ (ñinjeè) 1. half a day. 2. noon.

ཉིན་ཕྱེད་ཡོལ་ (ñinceè yöö) afternoon.

ཉིན་ཕྱོགས་ (ñinjɔɔ̀) the sunny part of a place/ area/ location.

ཉིན་འཕུལ་ (ñinbüü) abbr. of ཉི་མ་འཕུལ་.

ཉིན་འབྲེལ་ (ñindrel) for days on end, day after day.

ཉིན་མ་ (ñinmə) 1. a day. 2. daytime.

ཉིན་མ་གང་འཁྱོལ་ (ñinmə kaŋgyöö) sm. ཉི་མ་གང་འཁྱོལ་.

ཉིན་མེད་མཚན་མེད་ (ñinmeè tsɛ̄nmeè) sm. ཉི་མཚན་མེད་པ་.

ཉིན་མོ་ (ñinmo) 1. a day. 2. daytime.

ཉིན་མོ་ཀུ་མ་མ་རྐུ་ རི་མགོ་ཐམས་ཅད་མིག་ཡིན་ མཚན་མོ་གསང་གཏམ་མ་བཤད་ རྫིག་ཟུར་ཐམས་ཅད་རྣ་ཡིན་ (ñinmo gūmə magu ringo tāmjɛɛ̀ mig yin tsɛ̄nmo sāŋdam mashöö dzīgsur tamjɛɛ̀ nā yin) one can't keep things secret from others [Lit. Don't steal during the day as all the mountain tops are eyes; don't tell secrets at night as all the edges of walls are ears].

ཉིན་མོ་ཁ་དཀར་ངོ་དཀར་ (ñinmo kāgar ŋogar) sm. ཉི་མ་ཁ་དཀར་ངོ་དཀར་.

ཉིན་མོ་བདེ་ལེགས་ (ñinmo deleè) a type of high quality ceremonial scarf.

ཉིན་མོ་ཕར་བསྐྱལ་མཚན་མོ་ཚུར་བསུས་ (ñinmo pāāgyɛɛ tsɛ̄nmo tsūū sūū) (working/ doing sth.) day and night continuously.

ཉིན་མོའི་སྐར་མ་ (ñinmö gārma) sm. ཉིན་སྐར་.

ཉིན་མོའི་གཉིད་ལམ་ (ñinmö ñīīləm) inconceivable, impossible.

ཉིན་མོའི་མི་དང་ མཚན་མོའི་ཁྱི་ (ñinmö midaŋ tsɛ̄nmö kyī) a lot of work/ hardships [Lit. a person in the daytime, dog at night].

ཉིན་མོའི་ཟས་བཅག་ མཚན་མོའི་གཉིད་བཅག (ñi̱nmö sɛ̱ɛ̀jaà tsɛ̄nmö ñiìjaà) sorrow, sadness [Lit. unable to eat during the day and sleep at night].

ཉིན་མོའི་སློབ་གྲྭ (ñi̱nmö lōbdra) day school.

ཉིན་མོར་ (ñi̱nmɔɔ) in the daytime.

ཉིན་ཚད་ (ñi̱ndzɛɛ̀) the length of day.

ཉིན་ཚུགས་ (ñi̱ndzug) the distance one can go and return on the same day.

ཉིན་ཚེ་ཉིན་འཁོར་ (ñi̱ntse ñingɔɔ) shung. living from hand-to-mouth.

ཉིན་མཚན་ (ñi̱ndzɛn) day and night.

ཉིན་མཚན་ཀུན་ཏུ་ (ñi̱ndzɛn gũndu) sm. ཉིན་མཚན་མེད་པ་.

ཉིན་མཚན་ཁོར་ཡུག (ñi̱ndzɛn kɔ̄ryug) sm. ཉིན་མཚན་མེད་པ་.

ཉིན་མཚན་གོ་ལྡོག (ñi̱ndzɛn ko̱dɔɔ̀) doing things upside down, doing things backwards [Lit. regarding day as night].

ཉིན་མཚན་མགོ་སྦྲེལ་ (ñi̱ndzɛn go̱drel) sm. ཉིན་མཚན་མེད་པ་.

ཉིན་མཚན་གཅིག (ñi̱ndzɛn jīg) one day and one night.

ཉིན་མཚན་མཉམ་པ་ (ñi̱ndzɛn ña̱mba) equinox.

ཉིན་མཚན་ཐུན་དྲུག (ñi̱ndzɛn tü̱ndruù) sm. ཉིན་མཚན་དུས་དྲུག.

ཉིན་མཚན་བསྡུད་མ་ (ñi̱ndzɛn dü̃ümə) sm. ཉིན་མཚན་མེད་པ་.

ཉིན་མཚན་ལྡོས་མེད་ (ñi̱ndzɛn dõ̃omeè) sm. ཉིན་མཚན་མེད་པ་.

ཉིན་མཚན་བལྟོས་མེད་ (ñi̱ndzɛn dõ̃omeè) sm. ཉིན་མཚན་མེད་པ་.

ཉིན་མཚན་དུས་དྲུག (ñi̱ndzɛn dü̱ü tṟug) 1. the six parts of a 24 hour day. 2. always, all the time.

ཉིན་མཚན་ཕྱུད་པ་ (ñi̱ndzɛn cɛ̀ɛma) sm. ཉིན་མཚན་མེད་པ་.

ཉིན་མཚན་སྦྲེལ་མཐུད་ (ñi̱ndzɛn dre̱düü) sm. ཉིན་མཚན་མེད་པ་.

ཉིན་མཚན་སྦྲེལ་བ་ (ñi̱ndzɛn de̱lwa) sm. ཉིན་མཚན་མེད་པ་.

ཉིན་མཚན་མེད་པ་ (ñi̱ndzɛn me̱èba) (without distinguishing) day and night, continuously, all the time ༑ ཁོ་ཚོ་ཉིན་མཚན་མེད་པར་ལས་ཀ་བྱེད་དགོས་བྱུང་འདུག They had to work day and night.

ཉིན་མཚན་ལན་དྲུག (ñi̱ndzɛn lɛ̱ndruù) sm. ཉིན་མཚན་དུས་དྲུག.

ཉིན་ཞག (ñi̱nshaà) one 24 hour day (i.e., day with night included). 2. day and night.

ཉིན་ཞག་དག་ལོངས་ (ñi̱nshaà dāgloŋ) sm. ཉིན་ཞག.

ཉིན་ཞག་དུས་གཉིས་ (ñi̱nshaà tü̱üñiì) the two: daytime and nighttime.

ཉིན་ཞག་དུས་གསུམ་ (ñi̱nshaà tü̱üsum) 1. the six parts of a 24 hour day (3 during the day and 3 at night). 2. sm. ཉིན་མཚན་མེད་པ་.

ཉིན་ཞག་ཕྲུགས་གཅིག (ñi̱nshaà trūgjig) one day and one night, one 24 hour day, one whole day.

ཉིན་ཞག་ཚོགས་པ་ (ñi̱nshaà tsɔ̄gba) a month.

ཉིན་བཞིན་ (ñi̱nshin) every day, daily ༑ ཉིན་བཞིན་རྒྱ་ཆེར་འགྲོ་གི་ཡོད་པ་རེད་ (It) is increasing in size daily.

ཉིན་བཞིན་གོང་འཕེལ་ (ñi̱nshin ko̱ŋbel) increasing/ advancing day by day.

ཉིན་ཟླ་ (ñi̱nda) day and month.

ཉིན་ཡོལ་ (ñi̱nyöö) end of the day, evening.

ཉིན་རང་པོ་ (ñi̱n ra̱ŋbo) sm. ཉིན་རངས་པ་.

ཉིན་རངས་པ་ (ñi̱nraŋba) all day.

ཉིན་རི་ (ñi̱nri) hills or mountain where the sun hits.

ཉིན་རིང་སྐབས་ (ñi̱nriŋ gāb) time when the days are long (i.e., summertime).

ཉིན་རིམ་ (ñi̱nrim) daily agenda/ schedule.

ཉིན་རེ་ (ñi̱mre) each day, every day, daily, day by day.

ཉིན་རེ་ཉིན་འཚོལ་ (ñi̱nre ñindzöö) not having permanent job, living/ working from day to day [Lit. searching daily].

ཉིན་རེ་ཞག་རེ་ཙམ་ (ñi̱nre sha̱àredzam) for few days.

ཉིན་རེ་བཞིན་ (ñi̱nreshin) sm. ཉིན་རེ་.

ཉིན་རེ་བཞིན་གོང་འཕེལ་ (ñi̱nreshin ko̱ŋbel) sm. ཉིན་བཞིན་གོང་འཕེལ་.

ཉིན་རེ་ལས་ཉིན་རེ་ (ñi̱nrelɛ ñi̱nre) day by day, from day to day ༑ སྟོབས་ཤུགས་ཉིན་རེ་ལས་ཉིན་རེ་ཆེར་དུ་འགྲོ་གི་ཡོད་པ་རེད་ (Their) strength was increasing day by day.

ཉིན་རེའི་གྲོས་རིམ་ (ñi̱nree trö̱ö̃rim) sm. ཉིན་རིམ་.

ཉིན་རེའི་ཐོན་ཚད་ (ñi̱nree tõ̃ndzeɛ̀) a day's production.

ཉིན་རེའི་གནས་ལ་མ་བསྡད་པ་ (ñi̱nree nɛ̀ɛ̀la ma̱dɛɛ̀ba) daily flux or change ༑ ཉིན་རེའི་གནས་ལ་མ་བསྡད་པའི་གནས་ཚུལ་ཇེ་སྡུག་ཏུ་འགྲོ་གི་ཡོད་པ་རེད་ A situation that is worsening every day.

ཉིན་རེའི་ཚགས་པར་ (ñi̱nree tsāgbar) daily newspaper.

ཉིན་རེའི་ལས་ཡུན་ (ñi̱nree lɛ̱ɛ̀yün) workday, the amount of hours in a working day.

ཉིན་རེའི་ལས་རེས་ (ñi̱nree lɛ̱ɛ̀reè) duty/ assignment for a day.

ཉིན་རེའི་གསར་འགྱུར་ (ñi̱nree sɔ̄ngyur) sm. ཉིན་རེའི་ཚགས་པར་.

ཉིན་རེར་ལི་དབར་སྟོང་ཕྲག (ñi̱nree le̱war dōŋdraà) a tremendous pace [Lit. a thousand li a day].

ཉིན་ལམ་ (ñi̱nlam) a day's journey/ march.

ཉིན་ལས་ (ñi̱nlɛɛ̀) day shift, day work.

ཉིན་ལུང་ (ñi̱nluŋ) a place where there is plenty of sunshine.

ཉིན་ལོ་ (ñi̱nlo) year.

ཉིན་ལོང་གཙང་པོ་ (ñi̱nloŋ dzāŋbo) Nile River.

ཉིན་ཤ་ (ñi̱nsha) meat of an animal killed that very day.

ཉིན་ཤས་ (ñi̱nshɛɛ̀) a few days.

ཉིན་ཤད་མཚན་ཤད་ (ñi̱nshɛɛ̀ tsɛ̃ɛ̃nshɛɛ̀) traveling day and night.

ཉིན་སོ་བ་ (ñi̱nsowa) daytime sentry/ guard.

ཉིན་སྲིབ་ (ñi̱nsib) shady side of hills or mountains.

ཉིན་སྲིབས་ (ñi̱nsib) sm. ཉིན་སྲིབ་.

ཉིན་སློབ་ (ñi̱nlob) day school.

ཉིན་གསར་ཟླ་འགྱུར་ (ñi̱nsar da̱ngyur) changing with each passing day and month ༑ ཉིན་གསར་ཟླ་འགྱུར་གྱིས་ལུང་པ་འདི་ཡར་རྒྱས་འགྲོ་གི་འདུག This place is improving with each passing day and month.

ཉིན་གསོག་ཟླ་འཇོག (ñi̱nsɔɔ̀ da̱njɔɔ̀) accumulating/ storing up gradually (by days and months).

ཉིའུ་ཡུའི་ (ñi̱uyu) New York.

ཉིའུ་གཡོད་ (ñi̱uyöö) sm. ཉིའུ་ཡུའི་.

ཉིལ་ (ñi̱i) vi. to erode, to landslide ༑ རི་ཉིལ་ནས་ལམ་ཁ་འགག་བཞག The mountain had a landslide and the road has been blocked.

ཉིལ་ཉིལ་ (ñi̱iñi̱i) sm. ཉིལ་.

ཉིས་ (ñiì) two ༑ ཉིས་སྟོང་ Two thousand.

ཉིས་སྐས་ (ñiìgɛɛ̀) steps/ staircases with two sections or sides.

ཉིས་སྐལ་ (ñiìgɛɛ) 1. two shares/ portions. 2. the double share of salary and alms received by higher ranking monks in monasteries.

ཉིས་སྐྱལ་རྒྱག (ñiìgüü gya̱à) va. to levy corvee taxes twice.

ཉིས་སྐྲ་ (ñiìdra) two braids.

ཉིས་ཁྲི་ (ñiìdri) twenty thousand.

ཉིས་འཁོར་ (ñiìgɔɔ) shung. repeating, duplicating ༑ བོར་བརླག་སོང་ལུགས་ཞུ་བཞིན་ཉིས་འཁོར་མེད་པ་དགོས་རྒྱུ As it was reported that the (object) was lost, it should not be repeated (the losing).

ཉིས་འགྱུར་ (ñiìgyur) double, twice as much ༑ ཐོན་སྐྱེད་ཉིས་འགྱུར་འཕར་བཞག Production has doubled.

ཉིས་རྒྱུ་ཅིག་སྤུན་ (ñiìgyu cīgbün) type of weaving where the string is doubled on the warp and single on the weft.

ཉིས་བརྒྱ་ (ñiìgya) two hundred.

ཉིས་སྲིམ་ (ñiìdrim) double thread, two-ply.

ཉིས་ཅ་ལ་ག (ñi̱ijalaga) Nicaragua.

ཉིས་སྟོང་ (ñi̱idoŋ) two thousand.

ཉིས་ཐོག (ñiìdɔɔ̀) 1. two story. 2. second floor.

ཉིས་ལྡབ་ (ñiidəb) double, two times; va.—རྒྱག to fold into two layers.

ཉིས་སྣའི་འདོན་ (ñiinɛ dön) shung. a tax unit of land equal to two རྐང་.

ཉིས་འབུམ་ (ñiibum) two hundred thousand.

ཉིས་འབྲིལ་ཤོག་ལྷེ་ (ñiidree shɔ̃ɔle) two pieces of paper with carbon paper in the middle.

ཉིས་སྦྱོར་ (ñiijɔɔ) in pairs.

ཉིས་སྒྲགས་ (ñiidraà) two things put/ joined together.

ཉིས་སྒྲིལ་ (ñiidrel) sm. ཉིས་སྒྲགས་.

ཉིས་རྨོས་ (ñiimöö) tandem plowing; va.—རྒྱག.

ཉིས་བརྩེགས་ (ñiidzeg) one piled on top of another ། ཁང་པ་ཐོག་ས་ཉིས་བརྩེགས་ A two story house.

ཉིས་བཞོན་ (ñiishön) riding double; va.—རྒྱག.

ཉིས་ཟློས་ (ñindöö) repeating, duplicating; va.—རྒྱག to duplicate; vi.—ཐེབས་ to get duplicated ། འདི་ཉིས་ཟློས་རེད་ This is a duplicate.

ཉིས་བཟོ་ (ñiiso) sm. ཉི་བཟོ་ཁ་.

ཉིས་བཟོ་ཁ་ (ñiisoga) not certain, unsure, doubtful ། ཁོང་ཡོང་དང་མ་ཡོང་ཉིས་བཟོ་ཁ་རེད་ It is not certain whether he is coming or not.

ཉིས་བཟོ་ཁ་སྐྱོག (ñiiso kāgyɔɔ̀) sm. ཉིས་བཟོ་ཁ་.

ཉིས་བཟོ་ཤོད་ (ñiiso shö̃ö) va. to say hesitatingly/ doubtfully.

ཉིས་ཡུར་ (ñiiyur) the second weeding.

ཉིས་རིམ་ (ñiirim) 1. two story (house). 2. having two stages (in a play, plan, etc.).

ཉིས་ལས་ (ñiilɛɛ̀) having to do work twice/ a second time (i.e., not doing sth. correct the first time and so having to do it again).

ཉིས་ལུང་ (ñiiluŋ) eng. nylon.

ཉིས་ལེན་ (ñiilen) 1. taking sth. twice, taking sth. a second time (e.g., a donation, etc.); va.—རྒྱག. 2. a traditional treatment involving the draining of blood.

ཉིས་ལོག (ñiilɔɔ̀) double.

ཉིས་ཤད་ (ñiishɛɛ̀) punctuation consisting of two lines that indicates the end of a paragraph or a line of verse.

ཉིས་གཤིབ་ (ñiishib) dual, double (one beside the other) ། ལྕགས་ལམ་ཉིས་གཤིབ་ Double track.

ཉིས་གཤིབ་ལམ་ལུགས་ (ñiishib ləmluù) the system of double track (rail).

ཉུག: p. ཉུགས་; f. ཉུག; imp. ཉུགས་ (ñuù) 1. sm. སྙུག. 2. va. to grope around ། གློག་ཤི་ཙང་དངོས་པོར་ལག་པས་མ་ཉུགས་ཀ་མེད་བྱུང་བ་རེད་ Because the electricity went out, (we) had to grope around (in the dark) for the things.

ཉུག་ཉུག (ñugñuù) sm. སྨུག་སྨུག.

ཉུག་རུམ་ (ñugrum) castration; va.—བཟོ་ to castrate.

ཉུག་རུམ་པ་ (ñugrumbə) sb. who is castratesm, a eunuch.

ཉུགས་ (ñug) p. and imp. of ཉུག.

ཉུང་ (ñuŋ) abbr. of ཉུང་ཉུང་.

ཉུང་དཀར་ (ñuŋgar) sm. ཡུངས་དཀར་.

ཉུང་སྐྱེ་ལེགས་བཙའ་ (ñuŋgye legdza) lower population growth and give birth to healthy children (political slogan).

ཉུང་སྐྱོན་ (ñuŋgyön) shortage, deficit.

ཉུང་ངུ་ (ñuŋŋu) sm. ཉུང་ཉུང་.

ཉུང་ཉུང་ (ñuŋñuŋ) small amount, few; va.—གཏོང་ to diminish, to make smaller ། ཐོན་ཚད་ཉུང་ཉུང་རེད་ Production was small ། ང་ཚོ་འགྲོ་སོང་ཉུང་ཉུང་གཏོང་དགོས་ We have to expend a little in expenses.

ཉུང་ཐར་ (ñuŋdar) sm. ཉུང་མཐར་.

ཉུང་མཐའ་ (ñuŋdaa) the minimum, least (qualification, price, number, etc.) ། ལས་ཁུངས་ནང་ལས་བྱེད་པ་ལྔ་དགོས་པ་དེ་གྲངས་ཀ་ཉུང་མཐའ་ཞིག་རེད་ The need for five officials in this office is the least number.

ཉུང་མཐའ་ལ་ (ñuŋdaala) sm. ཉུང་མཐར་.

ཉུང་མཐར་ (ñuŋdaa) minimum, least (qualification, price, number, etc.) ། གྲོང་ཁྱེར་འདིར་ཉུང་མཐར་མི་འབོར་ཁྲི་བཞི་ཙམ་ཡོད་ This city has at least a population of forty thousand.

ཉུང་དུ་འགྲོ་ (ñuŋdu dro) vi. to become smaller, to get reduced/ to get small/ lesser.

ཉུང་དུ་གཏོང་ (ñuŋdu dōŋ) va. to make smaller, to reduce, to lessen, to decrease.

ཉུང་འདུ་ (ñuŋdu) a small gathering of people.

ཉུང་བསྡུས་ (ñuŋdüü) an abbreviated number, a few ། དེ་རིང་སྐུ་མགྲོན་ཉུང་བསྡུས་ཤིག་ལས་གདན་འདྲེན་ཞུས་མེད་ Today I have invited only just a few guests.

ཉུང་ཕྱོགས་ (ñuŋjɔɔ) the minority.

ཉུང་འཕྲི་ (ñuŋ) reducing, diminishing; va.—བྱེད་ to reduce, to cut down, to diminish, to lessen.

ཉུང་བ་ (ñuŋwə) smaller, fewer, less ། ང་ཚོ་ཁ་ལག་ཉུང་བ་ཟ་དགོས་ We have to eat less food.

ཉུང་མ་ (ñuŋmə) turnip.

ཉུང་མིན་ (ñuŋmin) many, not few.

ཉུང་ཙམ་ (ñuŋdzam) a little less, a little ། ཁང་གླ་ཉུང་ཙམ་ལས་མི་ལེན་པ་རེད་ (He) took only a little rent. ། དུས་ཚོད་དེ་ལས་ཉུང་ཙམ་ནང་ཚར་བ་རེད་ (They) finished in a little less time than that.

ཉུང་ཚོགས་ཅན་དུ་འགྱུར་ (ñuŋdzɔɔ̀jɛndu gyur) vi. to become smaller, to get decreased.

ཉུང་ཟད་ (ñuŋsɛɛ̀) sm. ཉུང་ཙམ་.

ཉུང་རུ་ (ñuŋru) sm. ཉུང་དུ་.

ཉུང་ལས་མང་ཐོབ་ (ñuŋlɛɛ̀ maŋdob) working less and earning more.

ཉུང་ཤས་ (ñuŋshɛɛ̀) just a few, only a little bit ། མི་ཉུང་ཤས་ཙམ་གྱིས་ By just a few people.

ཉུང་ཤོས་ (ñuŋshöö) the least, the fewest.

ཉུང་སྲེག (ñuŋseg) roasted turnips.

ཉུངས་དཀར་ (ñuŋgar) white mustard (seed).

ཉུངས་ (ñuŋ) vi. to be insufficient, to be not enough ། ཇ་འདིར་བྱེ་མ་ཀ་ར་ཉུངས་བཞག There is not enough sugar in the tea.

ཉུངས་མ་ (ñuŋmə) sm. ཉུང་མ་.

ཉུངས་མ་པོ་ཤ་ (ñuŋmə pōsha) boiled turnip stew.

ཉུངས་མར་ (ñuŋmar) mustard seed oil.

ཉུངས་གཤེར་ (ñuŋsher) fresh turnip.

ཉུལ་ (ñüü) 1. va. to wander around without a fixed residence ། མི་སེར་སྐྱོ་པོ་དེ་ཚོ་ས་ཆ་གང་སར་ཉུལ་གྱི་ཡོད་པ་རེད་ The poor subjects are wandering around all over the place. 2. va. to grope. 3. sm. གཉུལ་.

ཉུལ་ཉུལ་ (ñüüñüü) sm. ཉུལ་.

ཉུལ་པོ་ (ñüübo) wanderer, vagabond.

ཉུལ་མ་ (ñüümə) spy.

ཉུལ་མི་ (ñüümi) sm. ཉུལ་མ་.

ཉུལ་ཞིབ་ (ñüüshib) reconnaissance, espionage, spying; va.—བྱེད་ ། དམག་མི་གར་ཡོད་ཉུལ་ཞིབ་བྱས་པ་རེད་ (They) reconnoitered (to determine) where the soldiers were.

ཉེ་ (ñe) 1. abbr. of ཉེ་པོ་. 2. (vb.+ — + dat.-loc.) about to/ near to ། ང་རྒྱ་གར་ནས་ཐོན་ཉེ་ལ་གསར་འགྱུར་དེ་གོ་བྱུང་ When I was about to leave India I heard the news.

ཉེ་སྐྱལ་རིང་བརྒྱུད་ (ñegüü ringyüü) asking for sb.'s help/ favor through their close friends.

ཉེ་སྐོར་ (ñegɔɔ) 1. close by, near. 2. neighborhood, vicinity.

ཉེ་སྐྱོང་ཕྱོགས་ལྷུང་ (ñegyoŋ cɔ̃ɔlhuŋ) shung. prejudicial, biased, discriminating against ། གོང་ཐེབས་བཞིན་ཉེ་སྐྱོང་ཕྱོགས་ལྷུང་མེད་པ་དགོས་རྒྱུ་ As it was ordered by the superiors, you must not be biased and discriminate.

ཉེ་སྐྱོར་ (ñegyɔr) supporting/ backing those who are close.

ཉེ་སྐྱོར་ཕྱོགས་ལྷུང་ (ñegyɔr cɔ̃ɔlhuŋ) prejudicial, biased, discriminating, partial.

ཉེ་ཁུལ་ (ñegüü) a nearby/ neighboring area.

ཉེ་ཁུལ་བྱེད་ (ñegüü cee) va. to pretend/ act close to sb. ། ཁོས་སྤུན་མཆེད་ཕྱུག་པོ་དེ་རར་ཉེ་ཁུལ་བྱེད་ཀྱི་ཡོད་པ་རེད་ He is acting close with his rich relatives.

ཉེ་མཁོ་ (ñeko) immediate needs.

ཉེ་མཁོའི་དངོས་རིགས་ (ñekö ŋöörii) immediately necessary things, necessities.

ཉེ་འགོན་ (ñegön) sm. ཉེ་རིང་.

ཉེ་འཁོར་ (ñegɔɔ) 1. sm. ཉེ་སྐོར་. 2. retinue, attendants.

ཉེ་འཁྲིས་ (ñedrii) near ། ཁོང་ང་ཡི་ཉེ་འཁྲིས་སུ་བཞུགས་ཀྱི་ཡོད་པ་རེད་ He lives near me.

ཉེ་སྒྲིབ་མིག (ñe dribmii) sm. ཉེ་སྒྲིབ་.

ཉེ་གྲོགས་ (ñedrɔɔ̀) a close friend.

ཉེ་ཀློ་ (ñelo) beside, near to.

ཉེ་དགའ་ (ñega) close friends and relatives.

ཉེ་དགའ་ཕྱོགས་ལྷུང་ (ñega cɔ̄glhuŋ) sm. ཉེ་སྐོར་ཕྱོགས་ལྷུང་.

ཉེ་དགའ་ཕྱོགས་ཞེན་ (ñega cɔ̄gshen) sm. ཉེ་དགའ་ཕྱོགས་ལྷུང་.

ཉེ་མགོན་ (ñegön) helping/ assisting/ supporting with love; va.—བྱེད་.

ཉེ་འགྱངས་ (ñegyaŋ) distance ། ས་འདི་ནས་འདི་བར་གྱི་ཉེ་འགྱངས་ (The) distance from this place to that.

ཉེ་འགྲམ་ (ñendram) sm. ཉེ་སྐོར་.

ཉེ་རྒྱུད་ (ñegyüü) sm. ཉེ་སྐོར་.

ཉེ་སྒྲིག (ñedrig) marrying; va.—བྱེད་ to get married.

ཉེ་སྒྲིབ་ (ñedrib) farsighted (eyes).

ཉེ་རྒྱང་ (ñegyaŋ) sm. ཉེ་འགྱངས་.

ཉེ་བརྒྱུད་ (ñegyüü) sm. ཉེ་རྒྱུད་.

ཉེ་བརྒྱུད་རིང་བརྒྱུད་ (ñegyüü riŋgyüü) 1. seeking assistance from close friends and relatives as well as people not well known to you. 2. close and distant relatives.

ཉེ་སྔོན་ (ñeŋön) a short time ago (less than a month), in the recent past, lately.

ཉེ་བཅར་ (ñejar) sm. ཉེ་སྐོར་.

ཉེ་ཆར་ (ñecar) recently, lately.

ཉེ་གཉེན་ (ñeñen) relatives.

ཉེ་སྙོམ་ཚུལ་མཐུན་ (ñeñom tsüüdün) shung. unbiased and ethical/ moral ། ཕོ་མོ་རྒན་གཞོན་ཚང་མར་བྱམས་སྣང་ཕྱོགས་རིས་མེད་པ་ཉེ་སྙོམ་ཚུལ་མཐུན་ཞུ་རྒྱུ་ We will be unbiased and ethical to all people regardless of sex and age.

ཉེ་ལྡོས་ (ñedöö) relatives and friends.

ཉེ་སྙོམས་ (ñeñom) equally, unbiasedly, fairly.

ཉེ་ཐག (ñedaà) sm. ཉེ་གཉེན་.

ཉེ་མཐའ་ (ñeda) vicinity, nearby.

ཉེ་མཐོང་ (ñedoŋ) 1. nearsighted (vision). 2. respect for one's relatives.

ཉེ་དག (ñedaà) sm. ཉེ་དུ་.

ཉེ་དུ་ (ñedu) relatives, kinsmen; close associates.

ཉེ་དུ་ཛ་ལག (ñedu dzālaà) the whole expanse of one's relatives.

ཉེ་དུ་མཛའ་གྲོགས་ (ñedu dzadroò) sm. ཉེ་དུ་མཛའ་བཤེས་.

ཉེ་དུ་མཛའ་བཤེས་ (ñedu dzasheè) relatives and friends.

ཉེ་དུས་ (ñedüü) sm. ཉེ་ཆར་.

ཉེ་དོར་རིང་འཚོལ་ (ñedɔɔ riŋdzöö) sm. ཉེ་དོར་རིང་ལེན་.

ཉེ་དོར་རིང་ལེན་ (ñedɔɔ riŋlen) trying to do the impossible rather than what can be done [Lit. cast out the near, take the far].

ཉེ་དྲུང་ (ñedruŋ) sm. ཉེ་སྐོར་.

ཉེ་འདབས་ (ñedəb) sm. ཉེ་སྐོར་.

ཉེ་འདྲིས་ (ñendrii) close and friendly, close friends.

ཉེ་སྡེབ་ (ñedeb) a gathering of close friends and relatives.

ཉེ་གནས་ (ñenɛɛ̀) 1. a disciple, follower. 2. a personal attendant/ servant. 3. residing near by, local ། ཉེ་གནས་སྨན་པ་ A local doctor.

ཉེ་པོ་ (ñebo) close, near; va.—བྱེད་ to have a close (relationship) ། ཁོ་གཉིས་ཉེ་པོ་ཞེ་དྲགས་འདུག Those two are very close (relationshipwise). ། གྲོང་གསེབ་འདི་གཉིས་ཉེ་པོ་རེད་ These two villages are close (in proximity to each other).

ཉེ་པོ་དགའ་པོ་ (ñebo gabo) relatives and friends.

ཉེ་པོ་ཡིན་པ་མིན་པ་ (ñebo yimbə mimbə) not too close, not too distant.

ཉེ་སྤུན་ (ñebün) close relatives.

ཉེ་ཕྱོགས་ (ñejɔɔ̀) one's side, one's close associates/ friends; va.—བྱེད་ to side with one's friends/ associates.

ཉེ་ཕྱོགས་ཛ་ཕྱོགས་ (ñecɔɔ̀ dzājɔɔ̀) sm. ཉེ་ཕྱོགས་.

ཉེ་བ་ (ñewa) nearly, close, nearer ། ཁྲི་ཕྲག་ཉི་ཤུ་ཉེ་བ་ཞིག་གི་བར་འཕར་སྐྱོན་བྱུང་པ་རེད་ (They) increased up to nearly two hundred thousand. ། དེ་ལས་འདི་ཉེ་བ་ཡོད་པ་རེད་ This is nearer than that.

ཉེ་བ་ཉེ་རིགས་ (ñewa ñerii) relatives.

ཉེ་བ་གཉེན་འབྲེལ་ (ñewa ñēndrel) shung. relative, kinsman ། ཕ་སྤུན་རྒྱུད་ཁྲུངས་གཅིག་གྲུར་གྱི་ཉེ་བ་གཉེན་འབྲེལ་གཅིག་ཕན་གཅིག་གྲོགས་དགོས་པ་ Because of being paternal relatives, you should help each other.

ཉེ་བ་གཉེན་ཚན་ (ñewa ñendzɛn) sm. ཉེ་བ་ཉེ་རིགས་.

ཉེ་བའི་སྐབས་ (ñewɛ gɔ̄b) near/ just before ། བཅིངས་འགྲོལ་གཏོང་ཉེ་བའི་སྐབས་སུ་ Just before liberation.

ཉེ་བའི་རྐྱེན་ (ñewɛ gyēn) proximate cause.

ཉེ་བའི་རྒྱུ་ (ñewɛ gyu) basic/ fundamental cause.

ཉེ་བའི་རྒྱུ་རྐྱེན་ (ñewɛ gyugyen) proximate and basic cause.

ཉེ་བའི་ཆར་ (ñewɛ cār) sm. ཉེ་ཆར་.

ཉེ་བའི་འཆི་ལྟས་ (ñewɛ cīdɛɛ̀) a sign of dying soon.

ཉེ་བའི་འཇིག་ལྟས་ (ñewɛ jigdɛɛ̀) physical signs of imminent death.

ཉེ་བའི་དུས་རབས་ (ñewɛ düürəb) modern times, modern era.

ཉེ་བའི་ལོ་ཤས་ (ñewɛ loshɛɛ̀) the past few years.

ཉེ་བའི་སྲས་ཆེན་བརྒྱད་ (ñewɛ sɛɛ̀cen gyɛɛ̀) the eight close disciples of the Buddha.

ཉེ་བར་ (ñewar) 1. close to, near by. 2. very, extremely.

ཉེ་བར་མཁོ་བ་ (ñewar kōwa) things that are used everyday, necessities.

ཉེ་བར་སྒྲུབ་ (ñewar drub) va. to carry out, to put into practice promptly.

ཉེ་བར་འཇོག (ñewar jɔɔ̀) 1. va. to show one's respect by bowing, saluting, etc. 2. va. to place (sth.) nearby.

ཉེ་བར་དྲངས་ (ñewar traŋ) shung. to quote/ cite from sth. or someone.

ཉེ་བར་གནས་ (ñewar nɛɛ̀) va. to live/ exist close to or near.

ཉེ་བར་སྤྱོད་ (ñewar jöö) va. to make use of, to utilize.

ཉེ་བར་བྱེད་ (ñewar cee) va. to be close to/ friendly with sb.

ཉེ་བར་མྱུར་བ་ (ñewar ñurwa) extremely fast.

ཉེ་བར་མཚན་པ་ (ñewar tsɛ̄mba) well-dressed.

ཉེ་བར་མཚོན་ (ñewar tsön) va. to use as an example.

ཉེ་བར་ཞི་བ་ (ñewar shiwa) calm, peaceful, tranquil.

ཉེ་བར་ལེན་པ་ (ñewar lemba) sm. ཉེར་ལེན་.

ཉེ་དབང་ (ñewaŋ) shung. Vishnu.

ཉེ་འབྱེད་ (ñenjee) causing or instigating a quarrel; va.—བྱེད་.

ཉེ་འབྲེལ་ (ñendree) 1. close relatives, one's close associates/ friends; va.—བྱེད་ to be/ make close relations/ relationships. 2. neighboring ། ཉེ་འབྲེལ་རྒྱལ་ཁབ་ A neighboring country.

ཉེ་འབྲེལ་བརྒྱུད་ (ñedree gyüü) va. to go through one's close relationship with sb. to get sth.

ཉེ་འབྲེལ་འཛུགས་ (ñedree dzuù) va. to establish a close relationship with sb.

ཉེ་མིན་ (ñemin) not close.

ཉེ་མིན་རྒྱང་མིན་ (ñemin gyaŋmin) middle course (neither close nor distant); neither friendly nor enemies, a lukewarm relationship.

ཉེ་མིན་རིང་མིན་ (ñemin riŋmin) sm. ཉེ་མིན་རྒྱང་མིན་.

ཉེ་ཛ་ལག (ñe dzālaà) sm. ཉེ་ཚན་.

ཉེ་ཚད་ (ñedzɛɛ̀) nearness, distance.

ཉེ་ཚན་ (ñedzɛn) relatives.

ཉེ་ཚིག (ñedzig) pronoun; adjective.

ཉེ་མཚམས་ (ñedzam) near, nearby.

ཉེ་ཞོ་ (ñesho) 1. accident, mishap, disaster. 2. lack, shortage.

ཉེ་ཞོ་མེད་པ་ (ñesho meeba) 1. fine, in good shape, safe, without encountering an accident/ mishap །

ལམ་བར་ཉེ་ཞོ་མེད་པར་ནང་དུ་འབྱོར་སོང་ I arrived from the trip without encountering any mishap. 2. without shortage/ lack.

ཉེ་ཞོར་དབེན་ (ñeshöòwen) sm. ཉེ་ཞོ་མེད་པ་.

ཉེ་གཞི་ཛ་རག (ñeshi dzālaà) sm. སྣུན་གཉེན་.

ཉེ་ཟུངས་ (ñesuŋ) sm. འཁྲིགས་.

ཉེ་ཟུར་ (ñesur) adjacent angles.

ཉེ་བཟུང་མ་ (ñesuŋma) wife, female household head.

ཉེ་གཡོག (ñeyɔɔ̀) close personal servant, house-servant.

ཉེ་རབས་ (ñerəb) modern times/ era, contemporary period.

ཉེ་རབས་ཅན་ (ñerəbjɛn) modern, contemporary ༈ ཉེ་རབས་ཅན་གྱི་གོ་མཚོན་ Modern weapons.

ཉེ་རིགས་ (ñerig) friends and relatives.

ཉེ་རིང་ (ñeriŋ) 1. distance [Lit. near and far]. 2. bias, partiality, discriminating in favor of friends and relative and against enemies; va.—བྱེད་; —འཛིན་ to act biased/ partial/ discriminatory.

ཉེ་རིང་མཚོག་དམན་ (ñeriŋ cɔ̄ɔ̀mɛn) treating people according to their status/ rank and their closeness to oneself (nepotism) ༈ འགོ་ཁྲིད་ཀྱིས་ཉེ་རིང་ཕྱོགས་དམན་གྱི་དབྱེ་བ་བྱེད་རྒྱུ་ཡོད་པ་མ་རེད་ Leaders shouldn't differentiate people according to their status and nepotism.

ཉེ་རིང་དྲག་ཞན་ (ñeriŋ tragshɛn) sm. ཉེ་རིང་མཚོག་དམན་.

ཉེ་རིང་ཕྱོགས་ལྷུང་མེད་པ་ (ñeriŋ lhūŋmeèba) sm. ཉེ་རིང་མེད་པ་.

ཉེ་རིང་མི་འཛིན་ (ñeriŋ midzin) va. to be unbiased/ unprejudiced.

ཉེ་རིང་མེད་པ་ (ñeriŋ meèba) impartial, unbiased, nondiscriminatory, just, equal, fair; va.—བྱེད་ ༈ བླ་མ་དེས་སེམས་ཅན་ལ་སྙིང་རྗེ་ཉེ་རིང་མེད་པ་གནང་གི་ཡོད་པ་རེད་ The lama treats all sentient beings impartially with kindness.

ཉེ་རིང་ཙ་གསུམ་ (ñeriŋ dzāsum) relatives, close friends and ordinary friends.

ཉེ་རུ་གང་འགྲོ་ (ñeru kaŋdro) getting as close as possible to sb.; va.—བྱེད་.

ཉེ་རུ་ཉེ་རུ་ (ñeru ñeru) closer and closer.

ཉེ་རེ་ཁ་ལ་ (ñere kāla) sm. ཉེ་རེ་རེ་.

ཉེ་རེ་རེད་ (ñerereè) hanging, bulging out ༈ མི་རྒྱགས་པ་དེའི་གྲོད་ཁོག་ཉེ་རེ་རེད་བསྡད་འདུག The stomach of that fat person is bulging out.

ཉེ་ལམ་ (ñelam) sm. ཉེ་ཆར་. 2. a short cut.

ཉེ་ལོགས་ (ñelɔɔ̀) sm. ཉེ་སྐོར་.

ཉེ་ལོགས་གྲོང་ཁྱེར་ (ñelɔɔ̀ troŋgyer) sister city.

ཉེ་ཤར་ (ñeshar) the Near East.

ཉེ་ཤིང་ (ñeshiŋ) asparagus (filicinus).

ཉེ་ས་ (ñesa) a place that is near.

ཉེ་སུས་བརྒྱུད་ (ñesɛɛ̀ gyɛɛ̀) sm. ཉེ་བའི་སུས་ཆེན་བརྒྱད་.

ཉེག (ñeg) sm. ཉ་ག.

ཉེད་ (ñeè) va. to rub, to massage.

ཉེད་ཉེད་ (ñeèñeè) sm. ཉེད་.

ཉེན་ (ñen) 1. danger, risk. 2. (vb.+ —) danger/ risk of the verbal action ༈ ས་མཚམས་སུ་དམག་འཁྲུག་ལང་ཉེན་བྱུང་བ་རེད་ There was a danger of war breaking out on the border. ༈ ཁང་པ་འདི་ལོག་ཉེན་མི་འདུག There is no danger that this house will collapse. 3. vi. to suffer from (cold, hunger, etc.). ༈ མི་དམངས་བཀྲེས་ལྟོགས་ཀྱིས་ཉེན་ནས་ཡུལ་གྱུར་དགོས་བྱུང་འདུག The people suffered from hunger and had to wander off to other places.

ཉེན་ཀ་ (ñenga) 1. extra pillar (to support a beam that is unsteady). 2. sm. ཉེན་ཁ་.

ཉེན་ཀོར་ (ñengɔɔ) nearby, close to.

ཉེན་སྐྱོབ་བགེགས་གྲོལ་ (ñengyob gegdröö) saving from danger and overcoming disasters.

ཉེན་སྐྱོབ་གནས་ཐབས་ (ñengyob nɛɛ̀dəb) save from danger and ensure (its) survival.

ཉེན་སྐྱོབ་དབུལ་སྐྱོང་ (ñengyob ǖügyoŋ) saving from danger and helping the poor.

ཉེན་སྐྱོབ་སྣང་ས་འཁོར་ (ñengyob lāŋgɔɔ) ambulance.

ཉེན་ཁ་ (ñenga) danger, risk; vi.—ལས་འགྲོལ་ to be out of danger ༈ འདིར་དམག་རྒྱབ་ཡག་གི་ཉེན་ཁ་ཡོད་པ་རེད་ There is a danger of there being war here.

ཉེན་ཁ་ཅན་ (ñengajɛn) dangerous, hazardous, risky.

ཉེན་ཁ་ཆེན་པོ་ (ñenga cēmbo) very dangerous/ hazardous, a great danger/ risk.

ཉེན་ཁ་མི་མཐོང་བའི་རིང་ལུགས་ (ñenga mitoŋwɛ riŋluù) sm. ཉེན་ཁར་མི་འཛེམ་པའི་རིང་ལུགས་.

ཉེན་ཁ་མེད་པ་ (ñenga meèba) safe, secure, without danger.

ཉེན་ཁ་ཚབས་ཆེན་ (ñenga tsəbjɛn) severe/ serious danger, emergency.

ཉེན་ཁ་འཛེམས་མེད་ (ñenga dzemmeè) adventurous, fearless, not shying away from danger.

ཉེན་ཁ་འཛེམས་མེད་རིང་ལུགས་ (ñenga dzemmeè riŋluù) sm. ཉེན་ཁར་མི་འཛེམ་པའི་རིང་ལུགས་.

ཉེན་ཁ་ལ་ཁྱད་གསོད་ (ñengala kyɛɛ̀söö) sm. ཉེན་ཁར་མི་འཛེམས་པ་.

ཉེན་ཁར་མི་འཛེམ་མཁན་ (ñengar midzemñɛn) adventurist.

ཉེན་ཁར་མི་འཛེམས་པ་ (ñengar midzemba) adventurous, fearless, not shying away from danger.

ཉེན་ཁར་མི་འཛེམ་པའི་རིང་ལུགས་ (ñengar midzembɛ riŋluù) adventurism.

ཉེན་ཁར་གཡོལ་ (ñenga yöö) va. to avoid danger.

ཉེན་འགག (ñengaà) extremely dangerous juncture/ place ༈ ས་ཆ་ཉེན་འགག་ཆེ་བ་ An extremely dangerous place.

ཉེན་འགན་ (ñengɛn) danger; va.—འཁུར་ to take a risk.

ཉེན་འགན་ཅན་ (ñengɛnjɛn) dangerous ༈ གནས་སྟངས་ཉེན་འགན་ཅན་ A dangerous situation.

ཉེན་འགོག (ñengɔɔ̀) 1. stopping/ preventing danger; va.—བྱེད་ ༈ ཟིང་ཆ་མི་ཡོང་བའི་ཉེན་འགོག་བྱེད་ཀྱི་ཡོད་པ་རེད་ (They) are preventing the danger of disturbances occurring. 2. security.

ཉེན་འགོག་འགན་ལེན་ (ñengɔɔ̀ kɛnlen) insurance.

ཉེན་འགོག་འགེབ་ཆས་ (ñengɔɔ̀ gebjɛɛ̀) safety covers.

ཉེན་འགོག་སྒྲིག་ཆས་ (ñengɔɔ̀ drigjɛɛ̀) safety devices.

ཉེན་འགོག་སྒྲོན་མེ་ (ñengɔɔ̀ drönme) safety light/ lamp.

ཉེན་འགོག་དྲ་བ་ (ñengɔɔ̀ trawa) safety net.

ཉེན་འགོག་གཅུས་ཕུར་ (ñengɔɔ̀ jǖübur) safety valve bolt.

ཉེན་འགོག་ལྕགས་སྒམ་ (ñengɔɔ̀ jāàgam) a safe.

ཉེན་འགོག་ཞིབ་བཤེར་བྱེད་ས་ (ñengɔɔ̀ shibsher ceèsa) security check post.

ཉེན་འགོག་ཞྭ་མོ་ (ñengɔɔ̀ shamo) safety helmet.

ཉེན་འགོག་ཡོ་བྱད་ (ñengɔɔ̀ yobjɛɛ̀) safety equipment/ utensils.

ཉེན་ཅན་ (ñenjɛn) sm. ཉེན་ཁ་ཅན་.

ཉེན་ཆེ་ (ñence) dangerous ༈ ཉེན་ཆེའི་ཨར་ལས་ Dangerous construction work.

ཉེན་ཆེན་པོ་ (ñen cēmbo) (vb. + —) a great danger that the preceeding verbal action will occur ༈ ཁང་པ་རྙིང་པ་དེ་ལོག་ཉེན་ཆེན་པོ་འདུག There is a great danger that old house will collapse.

ཉེན་མཚོང་ (ñenjoŋ) not fearing danger or taking risks; va.—བྱེད་.

ཉེན་མཚོང་རིང་ལུགས་ (ñenjoŋ riŋluù) adventurism.

ཉེན་རྟོག (ñendog) spying/ checking/ conducting surveillance for danger; va.—བྱེད་.

ཉེན་རྟོག་ཁང་ (ñendɔggaŋ) police station.

ཉེན་རྟོག་བདེ་སྲུང་ (ñendɔg desuŋ) policing, doing security, guarding; va.—བྱེད་ to police, to patrol, to guard, to stand watch.

ཉེན་རྟོག་བདེ་སྲུང་གྲུ་གཟིངས་ (ñendɔg desuŋ trusiŋ) police boat.

ཉེན་རྟོག་པ་ (ñendɔgba) policeman.

ཉེན་རྟོག་དྲག་དཔུང་ (ñendɔg dragbuŋ) armed police.

ཉེན་རྟོག་དམག་མི་ (ñendɔg māɔ̀mi) sm. ཉེན་རྟོག་པ་.

ཉེན་རྟོག་སྲུང་སྐྱོབ་ (ñendɔg sūŋgyob) sm. ཉེན་རྟོག་བདེ་སྲུང་.

ཉེན་རྟོག་སྲུང་དམག (ñendɔg sūŋmaà) sm. ཉེན་རྟོག་པ་.

ཉེན་བརྟག་པ་ (ñendagba) adventurer, explorer.

ཉེན་དོགས་ (ñendɔɔ̀) suspecting/ fearing there is danger.

ཉེན་དོགས་དམ་བསྒྲགས་ (ñendɔɔ̀ tamdraà) being strict because one suspects impending danger (e.g., by imposing a curfew or martial law).

ཉེན་བརྡ་ (ñenda) danger alarm, warning signal; va.—རྒྱག; —སྤྲོད་; —གཏོང་ to give an alarm/ warning signal.

ཉེན་བརྡ་གཏོང་བྱེད་ས་ཚིགས་ (ñenda dōŋjeè sədzig) alarm/ warning station.

ཉེན་སྣར་སྐྱོད་ (ñennar gyȫȍ) va. to go where the danger is, to go to face danger.

ཉེན་འཕྲང་ (ñendraŋ) danger, dangerous ¶ དུ་ཚོད་ཉེན་འཕྲང་ཅན་ A dangerous time.

ཉེན་འཕྲད་རྒྱུ་འཕྲོག (ñendrɛɛ̀ gyudrɔɔ̀) stirring up trouble for one's own advantage.

ཉེན་མང་བདེ་ཉུང་ (ñenmaŋ deñuŋ) many dangers, few good things.

ཉེན་མེད་ (ñenmeè) no danger.

ཉེན་མེད་འགྲིམ་སྒོ་ (ñenmeè drimgo) escape door, emergency exit.

ཉེན་མེད་བཀོལ་སྤྱོད་ (ñenmeè gȫȫjöȍ) utilizing things safely.

ཉེན་མེད་ཁ་སྤུ་བཞར་གྲི་ (ñenmeè kəbu shaadri) safety razor.

ཉེན་ཚབས་ (ñendzəb) sm. ཉེན་ཁ་.

ཉེན་ཚོར་ས་ཚིགས་ (ñendzɔɔ sədzii̇) radar station.

ཉེན་འཚེ་ (ñendzə) danger and harm.

ཉེན་སྲུང་ (ñensön) 1. precautionary measures, va.—བྱེད་ to take precautions. 2. martial law.

ཉེན་སྲུང་སྐོར་གཡེང་ (ñensön gɔ̄ryeŋ) guard/ sentry patrolling.

ཉེན་སྲུང་གི་བཀའ་ (ñensöngi gā) martial law.

ཉེན་སྲུང་ལྕགས་ཐག (ñensön jāgdaà) safety chain.

ཉེན་སྲུང་དོ་དམ་ (ñensön todam) sm. ཉེན་སྲུང་གི་བཀའ་.

ཉེན་སྲུང་དྲིལ་བརྡ་ (ñensön treeda) alarm bell.

ཉེན་གཡོལ་ (ñenyöö) refuge, shelter, sanctuary; va.—བྱེད་ top seek refuge/ shelter/ sanctuary (to avoid danger) ¶ཁོང་ཉེན་གཡོལ་དུ་ཕེབས་པ་རེད་ (He) went to seek refuge.

ཉེན་གཡོལ་དབང་ཆ་ (ñenyöö wāŋja) right of asylum/ sanctuary.

ཉེན་གཡོལ་གནས་སྤོ་ (ñenyöö nɛ̄ɛ̀bo) moving one's residence to avoid danger and gain sanctuary; va.—བྱེད་.

ཉེན་སྲུང་ (ñensuŋ) 1. insurance. 2. security.

ཉེན་སྲུང་སྒྲི་རགས་ (ñensuŋ gēraà) seat belt; va.—སྡེམ་ to fasten the seat belt.

ཉེན་སྲུང་སྒྲོག་ཐག (ñensuŋ drɔgdaà) sm. ཉེན་སྲུང་སྒྲི་རགས་.

ཉེན་སྲུང་འགྲོ་གྲོན་ (ñensuŋ drodrön) insurance premium.

ཉེན་སྲུང་སྒྲིག་ཆས་ (ñensuŋ drigjɛɛ̀) safety/ security equipment or devices.

ཉེན་སྲུང་སྒྲོན་མེ་ (ñensuŋ drönme) safety lamp.

ཉེན་སྲུང་ལྕགས་སྐུད་ (ñensuŋ jəggüù) a fuse (for electrical circuits).

ཉེན་སྲུང་ལྕགས་སྒམ་ (ñensuŋ jāàgam) a safe.

ཉེན་སྲུང་ཡན་ལག་རུ་ཁག (ñensuŋ yɛnlaà rugaà) branch security unit.

ཉེའི་སྐབས་ (ñeegəb) sm. ཉེ་, 2.

ཉེའི་མཚམས་ (ñendzam) sm. ཉེ་, 2.

ཉེའུ་ (ñewu) 1. small fish. 2. criminal.

ཉེའུ་ཆུང་ (ñewujūŋ) sm. ཉེའུ་.

ཉེའུ་འདོན་ (ñewu dön) 1. va. to release convicts. 2. va. to release fish and animals about to be slaughtered as an act of benevolence.

ཉེར་ (ñer) 1. near, close to. 2. twenty ¶ཉེར་གཅིག Twenty one. 3. (vb.+ —) about/ near to a verbal action ¶ཁོ་འགྲོ་ཉེར་སླེབས་སྐབས་ When he was about to go. 4. va. to tan (leather).

ཉེར་མཁོ་ (ñergo) daily needs/ supplies/ necessities.

ཉེར་མཁོ་དང་གཏོང་སྒོ་ (ñergodaŋ dōŋgo) supply and demand.

ཉེར་བརྒྱད་ (ñergyɛɛ̀) twenty eight.

ཉེར་དགུ་ (ñergu) twenty nine.

ཉེར་ངན་ (ñerŋɛn) shung. making offerings, offering sacrifices.

ཉེར་ལྔ་ (ñerŋa) twenty five.

ཉེར་ལྔ་ཚེས་བཅུ་ (ñerŋa tsēèju) the 10th and 25th of the month (these are two auspicious days for religious activities).

ཉེར་བསྔོགས་ (ñerŋɔɔ̀) preparing, getting ready; va.—བྱེད་.

ཉེར་ཉེར་ (ñerñer) 1. snarling; va.—བྱེད་. 2. sm. ཉེ་རེ་རེ་.

ཉེར་ཐོབ་ (ñerdob) the darkness that occurs just before death in Tibetan beliefs.

ཉེར་དྲུག (ñerdruù) twenty six.

ཉེར་བདུན་ (ñerdün) twenty seven.

ཉེར་སྤྱད་ (ñerjɛɛ̀) daily/ necessary things.

ཉེར་སྤྱོད་ (ñerjöȍ) 1. shung. daily necessary things. 2. practical, applied.

ཉེར་སྤྱོད་ལྔ་ (ñerjöȍ ŋā) the five daily offerings: flower, incense, butter lamp, water and torma.

ཉེར་སྤྱོད་སྒྲ་རིག་པ་ (ñerjöȍ drarigbə) applied linguistics.

ཉེར་སྤྱོད་ཚན་རིག (ñerjöȍ tsɛ̄nrii̇) applied science.

ཉེར་སྤྱོད་གཏན་ཚིགས་རིག་པ་ (ñerjöȍ dɛ̄ndzig rigbə) practical logic.

ཉེར་ཕྱོགས་གཡོ་ཟོལ་ (ñerjöȍ yōsöö) favoritism.

ཉེར་འབྲས་ (ñendrɛɛ̀) result.

ཉེར་བརྩེ་ (ñerdze) shung. extremely compassionate ¶ཤེས་བྱ་མ་ལུས་ཀུན་ནས་གཟིགས་ཤིང་ཉེར་བརྩེའི་སྙིང་སྟོབས་དཔག་དཀའི་ཐུགས་ An all knowing, extremely compassionate mind and immeasurable spirit.

ཉེར་འཚེ་ (ñentse) harm, disaster ¶ཆུའི་ཉེར་འཚེ་ ¶A water disaster (e.g., a flood).

ཉེར་ལེན་ (ñerlen) the original cause of sth.

ཉེར་ལེན་གྱི་རྒྱུ་ (ñerlengi gyu) the substance that is the basic/ foundational cause.

ཉེར་ལེན་གྱི་ཕུང་པོ་ (ñerlengi pūŋbə) shung. form/ body acquired due to the karma of one's previous life.

ཉེར་ལེན་གྱིས་ (ñerlengi) because of, as a result of ¶གསུང་གླེང་བྱུང་འདུག་པའི་ཉེར་ལེན་གྱིས་ Because of the speech.

ཉེར་ལེན་ལ་བརྟེན་ (ñerlenla dēn) sm. ཉེར་ལེན་གྱིས་.

ཉེས་ (ñeè) 1. va. to beat ¶ཁོས་ཁྱི་ཉེས་པ་རེད་ He beat the dog. 2. abbr. of ཉེས་པ་. 3. (vb. + —) to be mistaken/ in error ¶ངས་སྐད་ཆ་ཤོད་ཉེས་ཤོར་སོང་ I spoke in error (misspoke).

ཉེས་བཀོད་ (ñeègöȍ) punishment, sentence; va.—གཏོང་ to punish, to sentence.

ཉེས་རྐྱེན་རང་སློང་ (ñegyen raŋloŋ) creating one's own problems; va.—བྱེད་.

ཉེས་སྐྱོན་ (ñegyön) 1. fault, crime, offense; va.—འདོན་ to accuse, to charge ¶ལས་ཁུངས་ལ་མེ་ཤོར་བ་དེ་ཁོང་གི་ཉེས་སྐྱོན་རེད་མི་འདུག The fire in the office was not his fault. 2. disaster, catastrophe, calamity ¶ཁོ་ལ་ལམ་ཁར་ཉེས་སྐྱོན་ཆེན་པོ་བྱུང་འདུག He had a disaster on the road.

ཉེས་སྐྱོན་སྒྲིག་འགེབ་ (ñegyön gɔ̄ŋgeb) hushing up, covering up (faults, crimes, etc.); va.—བྱེད་.

ཉེས་སྐྱོན་བྱུང་རྐྱལ་ (ñegyön cuŋdzüü) a disastrous/ wretched situation or condition.

ཉེས་སྐྱོན་འདོན་ (ñegyön dön) see ཉེས་སྐྱོན་, 1.

ཉེས་ཁག (ñegaà) blaming, accusing; va.—འགེལ་ to blame/ accuse.

ཉེས་ཁྲིམས་ (ñeèdrim) criminal code or law; va.—གཏོང་ to punish (by the law); vi.—ཕོག to be punished by the law ¶ཀུན་མ་དེར་ཁྲིམས་ཁང་ནས་ཉེས་ཁྲིམས་བཏང་བ་རེད་ The court punished that thief.

ཉེས་འབྲིའི་ཚིག་ལོ་ (ñendrii tsīi̇lo) shung. unnecessary wording that may cause trouble ¶ཉེ་འབྲིའི་ཚིག་ལོ་རྣམས་དོར་ནས་དོན་སྙིང་པོ་ཧྲིག་དུ་སྒྲིལ་དགོས་ One should erase those unnecessary wordings that may cause trouble and come to the point.

ཉེས་སྐྱོད་ (ñe̲ègyöö) a criminal case.

ཉེས་སྒྲོལ་ (ñe̲èdröö) sm. བཙོན་སྒྲོལ་.

ཉེས་འགན་ (ñe̲ègɛn) responsibility for misdeeds, mistakes, crimes; va.—གཡོལ་ to avoid or shirk responsibility for a crime; va.—འཁུར་ to take responsibility for one's mistakes/ crimes ༈ རང་ཉིད་ཀྱི་མ་བསམ་པའི་ཉེས་འགན་འཁུར་ཐུབ་ཀྱི་མ་རེད་ I can't take responsibility for sth. I did not do.

ཉེས་འགལ་ (ñe̲ègɛɛ) violation, crime.

ཉེས་འགལ་བ (ñe̲è ge̲ɛwa) violator, criminal.

ཉེས་འགེབས་མཛེས་བཅོས (ñe̲ègeb dze̲èjöö) disguising criminal acts with a beautiful facade.

ཉེས་འགེལ་ (ñe̲ègee) 1. blaming/ accusing of crimes of misdeeds; va.—བྱེད་. 2. imposing/ executing/ carrying out a sentence or punishment; va.—བྱེད་.

ཉེས་འགོག (ñe̲ngɔɔ) blocking/ preventing/ stopping crimes or violations; va.—བྱེད་ ༈ ལེགས་སྤེལ་ཉེས་འགོག་བྱེད་དགོས་རེད་ (We) must increase doing good deeds and stop doing bad deeds.

ཉེས་འགོག་ལེགས་སྤེལ་ (ñe̲ngɔɔ le̲gbel) stopping bad deeds/ violations/ crimes and promoting good deeds.

ཉེས་བརྒྱའི་རྒྱ་འཛིན་ (ñe̲ègyɛ cūndzin) shung. calamity, disaster.

ཉེས་བརྒྱུས་གཙེས་པ་ (ñe̲ègyɛɛ dzēèba) having had many sicknesses ༈ ཉེས་བརྒྱུས་གཙེས་པའི་གཟུགས་ཕུང་ཁ་ཁྲེར་གྱི་ངང་དུ་གནས་ལུགས་ My body, which has undergone many sicknesses, is a wreck.

ཉེས་དངུལ་ (ñe̲èŋüü) fine (in money).

ཉེས་ཅན་ (ñe̲èjɛn) criminal.

ཉེས་ཅན་གདེ་པོ་ (ñe̲èjɛn dēbo) ringleader, criminal boss.

ཉེས་ཅན་ལྟ་སྲུང་ཁང་ (ñe̲èjɛn dəsuŋgaŋ) jail, detention center (for criminals who have not yet been sentenced).

ཉེས་ཅན་དོ་དམ་ཁང་ (ñe̲èjɛn to̲damgaŋ) sm. ཉེས་ཅན་ལྟ་སྲུང་ཁང་.

ཉེས་ཅན་ཟིམ་ (ñe̲èjɛn si̲m) sm.* ཉེས་ཅན་ཟིན་.

ཉེས་ཅན་ཟིན་ (ñe̲èjɛn si̲n) va. to arrest a criminal.

ཉེས་ཅན་ལག་ཟིན་ (ñe̲èjɛn la̲gsin) sm. ཉེས་ཅན་ཟིན་.

ཉེས་ཅན་ལང་ས་ཤོར་ (ñe̲èjɛn la̲ŋshɔɔ) incorrigible criminal.

ཉེས་ཅན་ལོ་ཆུང་ (ñe̲èjɛn lo̲juŋ) juvenile delinquent.

ཉེས་གཅོད་ (ñe̲èjöö) punishment for a crime; va.—བྱེད་.

ཉེས་ཆ་ (ñe̲èja) negative trait, shortcoming.

ཉེས་ཆད་ (ñe̲èjɛɛ̀) punishment, sentence, penalty; va.—གཏོང་; —གཅོད་; —འགེལ་ to punish; va.—སྒྲོག to read out a sentence/ decision/ judgement; vi.—སྒྲུབ་ to serve a punishment; va.—ཞུ་ to confess addition to a crime; vi.—ཕོག; —རག to receive a punishment/ sentence ༈ གོ་མིན་དང་གི་དམག་འཁྲུག་ཉེས་ཅན་རྣམས་ལ་ཉེས་ཆད་བཅད་པ་རེད་ (They) punished the Komingtang war criminals.

ཉེས་ཆད་ཀྱི་ཡུན་ཚད་ (ñe̲èjɛɛ̀gi yü̲ndzɛɛ̀) term of punishment/ sentence.

ཉེས་ཆད་ཇེ་ཡང་དུ་གཏོང་ (ñe̲èjɛɛ̀ je̲yaŋdu dōŋ) va. to reduce/ commute a sentence.

ཉེས་ཆད་མཉམ་འགེལ་ (ñe̲èjɛɛ̀ ña̲mgee) punishing/ sentencing sb. along with another.

ཉེས་ཆད་གཏོང་ (ñe̲èjɛɛ̀ dōŋ) see ཉེས་ཆད་.

ཉེས་ཆད་དུས་ཐིམ་ (ñe̲èjɛɛ̀ tü̲ütim) 1. vi. to finish serving a sentence. 2. finishing/ completing a sentence; va.— བྱེད་.

ཉེས་ཆད་དུས་བསྒྱིང་ (ñe̲èjɛɛ̀ tü̲üsiŋ) postponing a sentence/ punishment; va.—བྱེད་.

ཉེས་ཆད་ནར་འཐེན་ (ñe̲èjɛɛ̀ na̲rten) sm. ཉེས་ཆད་དུས་བསྒྱིང་.

ཉེས་ཆད་ཡང་ (ñe̲èjɛɛ̀ ya̲ŋ) a light sentence/ penalty; va.—གཏོང་.

ཉེས་འཆར་ (ñe̲èjar) shung. proposal/ plan for a punishment ༈ ཁྲ་པར་ཉེས་འཆར་གསེར་སྲང་དོ་བཀོད་པ་ A fine of two སྲང་ of gold is proposed for the punishment ༈ ད་ལམ་གྱོད་དོན་དེ་སྐོར་དཔང་རྟགས་ཁུངས་བཙན་བྱུང་ཟིན་པར་བརྟེན་ཉེས་འཆར་འགོད་གནང་ཡོད་པ་ Since there is sufficient and reliable proof concerning this law case, you can make a plan for punishment.

ཉེས་གཏོང་ཕྱི་འགྱངས་ (ñe̲èdoŋ cīgyaŋ) delaying sentencing; va.—བྱེད་.

ཉེས་རྟགས་ (ñe̲èdaà) evidence (usu. in a crime).

ཉེས་རྟགས་ཁུངས་བཙན་ (ñe̲èdaà kūŋdzɛn) proof of guilt.

ཉེས་ལྷུང་ (ñe̲èlhuŋ) 1. committing a violation/ crime, sinning. 2. breaking one's monastic vows.

ཉེས་ལྷུང་བཤགས་སྡོམ་ (ñe̲rlhuŋ shāgdom) repenting for breaking one's vows and promising to abide by one's vows in the future.

ཉེས་སྟོན་ (ñe̲èdön) stating/ listing one's crimes; va.—བྱེད་.

ཉེས་འཐག (ñe̲èdaà) sm. ཉེས་དག.

ཉེས་དག (ñe̲èdaà) beating, thrashing; va.—གཏོང་ to beat/ thrash; vi.—གཟེད་ to get beaten/ thrashed.

ཉེས་དུས (ñe̲èdüü) term of sentence; vi.—ཐིམ་; —གཙང་ to have a sentence/ term be finished or expire.

ཉེས་དོན་ (ñe̲èdön) nonpolitical criminal affairs (contrasts with political crimes but includes what in the U.S. we call civil and criminal cases).

ཉེས་དོན་སྐོར་གྱི་ཁྲིམས་ལུགས་ (ñe̲èdön gɔ̄ɔ̄gi trīmluù) criminal code/ law.

ཉེས་དོན་ཁྲིམས་གཞུང་ (ñe̲èdön trīmshuŋ) sm. ཉེས་དོན་སྐོར་གྱི་ཁྲིམས་ལུགས་.

ཉེས་དོན་གྱི་གྱོད་གཞི་ (ñe̲èdöngi gyö̲öshib) criminal case.

ཉེས་དོན་གྱི་འགན་འཁྲི་ (ñe̲èdöngi ge̲ndri) criminal responsibility.

ཉེས་དོན་གྱི་ཆད་གཅོད་ (ñe̲èdöngi cɛɛ̀jöö) criminal punishment.

ཉེས་དོན་འགོད་བྱང་ (ñe̲èdön gö̲öjaŋ) a board on which a person's crimes were written and hung on the prisoner's neck before execution.

ཉེས་དོན་ཅན་ (ñe̲èdönjɛn) criminal (in nonpolitical sense).

ཉེས་དོན་ཉེས་ཅན་ (ñe̲èdön ñe̲èjɛn) sm. ཉེས་དོན་ཅན་.

ཉེས་དོན་གདུག་བཤེར་ (ñe̲èdön dūgsher) hearing/ trying a criminal action or case.

ཉེས་དོན་འདྲི་གཅོད་ཐིང་ (ñe̲èdön drijöö tīŋ) criminal judicial department.

ཉེས་དོན་བྱང་བུ་ (ñe̲èdön ca̲ŋbu) a board on which the crimes of prisoners are written.

ཉེས་འདོགས་ (ñe̲è dɔɔ̀) va. to accuse sb. of a crime/ wrongdoing.

ཉེས་འདོན་ (ñe̲èdön) exposing crimes; va.—བྱེད་.

ཉེས་འདོན་ཡི་གེ་ (ñe̲èdön yi̲ge) a letter exposing or accusing sb. of a crime/ wrongdoing.

ཉེས་འདོན་ལས་འགུལ་ (ñe̲èdön le̲ngüü) a campaign to expose crimes/ wrongdoings.

ཉེས་འདོམས (ñe̲ndom) abbr. of ཉེས་པ་སྨྲད་འདོམས་.

ཉེས་འདྲི་ཚོགས་ཆེན་ (ñe̲ndri tsɔ̄gjen) public/show trial.

ཉེས་རྡུང་ (ñe̲èduŋ) physical beating; va.—གཏོང་ to beat (physically); vi.—གཟེད་ to get a beating.

ཉེས་བརྡུང་ (ñe̲èduŋ) sm. ཉེས་རྡུང་.

ཉེས་སྣོན་ (ñe̲ènön) additional punishment/ fine.

ཉེས་པ་ (ñe̲èba) 1. punishment; va.—གཏོང་ to punish; vi.—གཟེར་; —ཕོག་; —རག to receive a punishment/ sentence ༈ ཁྲིམས་ཁང་གིས་སོ་པ་དེར་ཉེས་པ་དྲག་པོ་བཏང་སོང་ The court punished the spy severely. 2. a mistake; a crime; va.—བྱེད་; —གསོག to commit a mistake; to commit a crime.

ཉེས་པ་ཁས་ལེན་ (ñe̲èba kɛ̄ɛ̀len) confessing a crime, acknowledging guilt; va.— བྱེད་.

ཉེས་པ་སྒྲུབ་ (ñe̲èba dru̲b) 1. va. to pay a fine. 2. va. to serve one's sentence.

ཉེས་པ་ངོས་ལེན་ (ñe̲èba ŋö̲ölen) sm. ཉེས་པ་ཁས་ལེན་.

ཉེས་པ་ཧམས་པོ་ཆེ་ (ñe̲èba ŋāmboce) 1. heinous/

bold/ audacious crimes. 2. a severe punishment.

ཉེས་པ་ཅན་ (ñe̱èbajɛn) a criminal, an offender.

ཉེས་པ་ཆག་ཡང་ (ñe̱èba cāàyaŋ) lightening/ reducing the punishment, penalty or sentence; va.—གཏོང་.

ཉེས་པ་སྙོམས་པ་ (ñe̱èba ñōmba) well-being, good health.

ཉེས་པ་དག (ñe̱èba ta̱g) vi. to have paid for one's crime (e.g., served one's sentence in prison).

ཉེས་པ་དག་འབུད་ (ñe̱èba ta̱gbüü) clearing up/ vindicating an unjust accusation; va.—བྱེད་.

ཉེས་པ་འདྲི་གཅོད་ (ñe̱èba dri̱jöö) criminal hearing.

ཉེས་པ་བླུ་ (ñe̱èba lū) va. to atone for a crime.

ཉེས་པ་བབས་ཕྱི་ (ñe̱èba ba̱bji) shung. a heavy punishment/ sentence ༎ བྱེད་འཇོལ་ལ་གཞིགས་ན་ཉེས་པ་བབས་ཕྱི་ཐོབ་རུང་ཡང་བཟོད་སོང་བ་ Even though the (defendent) deserves severe punishment in accordane with the crime, (he) shall be absolved (from punishment).

ཉེས་པ་སྦོམ་པོ་ (ñe̱èba bo̱mbo) sm. ཉེས་པ་བབས་ཕྱི་.

ཉེས་པ་མེད་པ་ (ñe̱èba me̱èba) sm. ཉེས་མེད་.

ཉེས་པ་ཤེས་ (ñe̱èba shēē) va. to recognize/ know one's misdoings/ crimes.

ཉེས་པ་བཤགས་ (ñe̱èba shāà) va. to repent one's crimes.

ཉེས་པ་སླད་འདོམས་ (ñe̱èba lɛ̄ndom) shung. imposing a severe sentence as a deterrent to prevent future crimes; va.—གཅོད་ to impose a severe sentence as a deterrent to prevent future crimes ༎ སླར་ཡང་ཉེས་པ་བསགས་ན་ཉེས་པ་སླད་འདོམས་གཅོད་ངེས་ If you commit a crime again you will definitely be severely punished which will set an example for the future.

ཉེས་པ་ལེན་ (ñe̱èba le̱n) shung. va. to accuse sb. of a crime ༎ ཉེས་པ་མེད་པའི་མི་ལ་ཉེས་པ་ལེན་པ་ To accuse an innocent person of being guilty of a crime.

ཉེས་པ་གསོག (ñe̱èba sɔ̄ɔ̀) va. to commit a crime.

ཉེས་པས་ནོངས་ (ñe̱èbɛ no̱ŋ) va. to be guilty of a crime.

ཉེས་པོ་ (ñe̱èbo) ugly.

ཉེས་དཔང་ (ñe̱èbaŋ) evidence, proof (with regard to guilt/ crimes).

ཉེས་དཔང་ཁུངས་འཕེར་ (ñe̱èbaŋ kūŋber) sm. ཉེས་རྟགས་ཁུངས་བཙན་.

ཉེས་དཔང་ཁུངས་བཙན་ (ñe̱èbaŋ kūŋdzɛn) sm. ཉེས་རྟགས་ཁུངས་བཙན་.

ཉེས་སྤངས་དགེ་སྒྲུབ་ (ñe̱èbaŋ ge̱drub) renouncing crime, performing virtue/ good deeds.

ཉེས་སྤྱོད་ (ñe̱èjöö) sinful/ bad behavior, crimes; va.—བྱེད་.

ཉེས་སྦྲོད་ར་སྦྲོད་ (ñe̱èjöö ra̱dröö) 1. accusing sb. of a crime/ misdeed in face-to-face confrontation; va.—གཏོང་; —བྱེད་. 2. evidence/ proof of a crime.

ཉེས་བྱེད་ (ñe̱èjeè) sm. ཉེས་བྱས་.

ཉེས་བྱས་ (ñe̱èjɛɛ̀) a crime/ violation.

ཉེས་བབས་ཕྱི་བ་ (ñe̱èbəb jīwə) a serious crime.

ཉེས་འབྱིན་ (ñe̱èjin) sm. ཉེས་འདོན་.

ཉེས་མིང་ (ñe̱èmiŋ) name of a crime/ charge; va.—འདོགས་ to falsely accuse of a crime.

ཉེས་མེད་ (ñe̱èmeè) innocent, guiltless ༎ ཉེས་མེད་བོད་མི་ Innocent Tibetans.

ཉེས་མེད་ཁ་གཡོག (ñe̱èmeè kāyɔɔ̀) blaming the innocent; va.—བྱེད་.

ཉེས་མེད་ཁག་འགེལ་ (ñe̱èmeè kāàgee) blaming the innocent; va.—བྱེད་.

ཉེས་མེད་ཉེས་འགེལ་ (ñe̱èmeè ñe̱ègee) sm. ཉེས་མེད་ཁག་འགེལ་.

ཉེས་མེད་ཉེས་འདོགས་ (ñe̱èmeè ñe̱ndɔɔ̀) sm. ཉེས་མེད་ཁག་འགེལ་.

ཉེས་མེད་ཉེས་བཟོ་ (ñe̱èmeè ñe̱èso) sm. ཉེས་མེད་ཁག་འགེལ་.

ཉེས་མེད་དུ་གཏོང་ (ñe̱èmeèdu dōŋ) va. to pardon a crime, to absolve of a crime.

ཉེས་མེད་ནག་གཡོགས་ (ñe̱èmeè na̱gyɔɔ̀) sm. ཉེས་མེད་ཁག་འགེལ་.

ཉེས་མེད་ཞོར་འདྲུད་ (ñe̱èmeè sho̱ndrüü) innocent people being implicated/ involved/ dragged into a crime; vi.—ཐེབས་ ༎ ཁང་པ་དེའི་ནང་ལྐོག་འཚོང་རྒྱག་མཁན་ཞིག་ཡོད་ཙང་ཁྱིམ་མཚེས་ཚོ་ཡང་ཉེས་མེད་ཞོར་འདྲུད་བྱུང་ཡོད་པ་རེད་ Because there was a smuggler in the house, his innocent neighbors were implicated in the crime.

ཉེས་དམིགས་ (ñe̱èmig) wrongs, misdeeds, violations, crimes; va.—གསོག to commit a wrong/ misdeed/ crime, to sin.

ཉེས་སྨྲས་བྱེད་ (ñe̱èmɛɛ̀ ce̱è) va. to accuse, to condemn.

ཉེས་རྩད་ (ñe̱èdzɛɛ̀) criminal investigation; va.—གཅོད་ to investigate a crime.

ཉེས་ཚབས་ཆེ་ཆུང་ (ñe̱ètsəb cījuŋ) the degree of seriousness of a crime.

ཉེས་མཚང་འབྱིན་ (ñe̱èdzaŋ jin) va. to expose/ reveal/ disclose a crime.

ཉེས་འཛུགས་ (ñe̱è dzu̱ù) accusing; va.—བྱེད་.

ཉེས་འཇོལ་ (ñe̱èjöö) mistakes, wrong doing, crimes ༎ དམག་ཐོག་ཉེས་འཇོལ་རིགས་ལ་ཁྲིམས་གཅོད་བྱས་པ་རེད་ The crimes committed in the war were punished.

ཉེས་ཞུ་ (ñe̱èshu) 1. accusing, charging; va.—བྱེད་ ༎ ཁོང་གི་ལས་ཀའི་སྐོར་མི་གཞན་གྱིས་ཉེས་ཞུ་བྱས་ཡོད་པ་རེད་ Other people have accused him of crimes involving his work. 2. confessing one's crime; va.—བྱེད་ ༎ ཉེས་ཅན་དེས་རང་འགུལ་གྱིས་ཉེས་ཞུ་བྱས་པ་རེད་ That criminal voluntarily confessed.

ཉེས་ཡིག (ñe̱èyiì) a letter exposing or accusing sb. of a crime/ wrongdoing.

ཉེས་གཡོལ་ (ñe̱è yȫȫ) va. to avoid punishment for a crime.

ཉེས་ར་ངོས་འཁྲོད་ (ñe̱èra ŋȫȫdröö) solving/ proving/ clearing a criminal case.

ཉེས་ར་འཁྲོད་ངོས་ (ñe̱èra drȫȫŋöö) evidence/ proof used to solve a crime.

ཉེས་ལན་ (ñe̱èlɛn) paying back a harm, revenging, avenging; va.—སློད་ to revenge/ avenge/ pay back (a harm).

ཉེས་ལན་ཉེས་གཅོད་ (ñe̱èlɛn ñe̱èjöö) sm. ཉེས་ལན་.

ཉེས་ལས་ (ñe̱èlɛɛ̀) crimes, violations, bad deeds.

ཉེས་ཤོར་ (ñe̱è shɔ̄ɔ̀) (vb. + —) vi. to do the verbal action by mistake ༎ ཁ་ལག་བཟའ་ཉེས་ཤོར་ཙང་ན་པ་རེད་ He ate the food by mistake and got sick.

ཉེས་བཤད་ (ñe̱èshɛɛ̀) mistaken/ erroneous talk.

ཉེས་ལྷུང་ (ñe̱èlhuŋ) wrongly coming into one's hands/ possession ༎ གསང་བའི་ཡི་གེ་དེ་ཁོ་པའི་ལག་དུ་ཉེས་ལྷུང་བྱུང་བ་རེད་ The secret letter wrongly came into his hands (was delivered to him).

ཉོ་: p. ཉོས་; p. ཉོ་; imp. ཉོས་ (ño̱) va. to buy ༎ ཁོས་ཤ་ཉོས་པ་རེད་ He bought meat.

ཉོ་མཁན་ (ño̱ñɛn) customer, shopper.

ཉོ་རྒྱུ་མངག (ñu̱gyu ŋāà) va. to ask sb. to buy sth. ༎ ཁོང་ལ་ངས་དེབ་ཅིག་ཉོ་རྒྱུ་མངགས་པ་ཡིན་ I asked him to buy a book for me.

ཉོ་སྒྲུབ་ (ño̱drub) buying, purchasing; va.—བྱེད་.

ཉོ་སྒྲུབ་ཁའོ་ (ño̱drub kāwo) tib.ch. purchasing department/ section.

ཉོ་སྒྲུབ་གཅིག་བསྡུས་ (ño̱drub jīgdüü) buying/ purchasing in bulk.

ཉོ་སྒྲུབ་སྟོབས་ཤུགས་ (ño̱drub dōbshuù) sm. ཉོ་སྒྲུབ་ནུས་ཤུགས་.

ཉོ་སྒྲུབ་ནུས་ཤུགས་ (ño̱drub nü̱üshug) purchasing power.

ཉོ་སྒྲུབ་ཚན་སྒོར་ (ño̱drub tsɛ̄ngɔɔ) purchasing group.

ཉོ་སྒྲུབ་ལས་ཁུངས་ (ño̱drub lɛ̱ɛ̀guŋ) purchasing office.

ཉོ་སྒྲུབ་ས་ཚིགས་ (ño̱drub sədzii) purchasing station ༎ ཞིང་ལས་ཐོན་རྫས་ཉོ་སྒྲུབ་ས་ཚིགས་ Agricultural products purchasing station.

ཉོ་འགོད་ (ño̱göö) subscribing (e.g., for a newspaper); va.—བྱེད་ to subscribe.

ཉོ་བསྒྲུབ་ (ño̱drub) sm. ཉོ་སྒྲུབ་.

ཉོ་ཆ་ (ño̱bja) shopping; va.—རྒྱག.

ཉོ་ཆ་དཀོན་པོ་ (ño̱bja gõmbo) a shortage of goods to buy.

ཉོ་ཆ་རྒྱག་མཁན་ (ño̱bja gya̱àñɛn) buyers, shoppers.

ཉོ་ཆ་འབབ་པོ་ (ño̱bja bɛ̱ɛbo) lots of goods available for purchase.

ཉོ་ཆ་གཟེད་ (ño̱bja se̱è) slang. to get a beating ། ཁྱོད་ཉོ་ཆ་གཟེད་སྙིང་འདོད་ཀྱི་འདུག་གས་ Are you looking for beating?

ཉོ་ཆ་གཟེད་མཁན་ (ño̱bja se̱èñɛn) 1. sb. asking for a beating or trouble. 2. sb. who has been beaten.

ཉོ་ཆས་ (ño̱jɛɛ̀) goods, merchandise.

ཉོ་སྟོབས་ (ño̱dob) purchasing power.

ཉོ་ཐང་ (ño̱daŋ) market price/ rate.

ཉོ་ཐང་ཀུན་གསལ་ (ño̱daŋ günsəb) sm. ཟུར་ཐོགས་, 2.

ཉོ་ཐོ་ (ño̱do) shopping list.

ཉོ་ཐོ་འགོད་ས་ (ño̱do gö̱ösa) place where orders for purchasing are placed.

ཉོ་སྡུད་ (ño̱düü) buying, purchasing; va.—བྱེད་.

ཉོ་སྡུད་ས་ཚིགས་ (ño̱düü sədzii) purchasing station.

ཉོ་པ་ (ño̱ba) sm. ཉོ་མཁན་.

ཉོ་ཕྱོགས་ཀྱི་ཚོང་ར་ (ño̱jɔɔ̀gi tsõŋra) market for buyers.

ཉོ་ཚད་ (ño̱dzɛɛ̀) a budget/ allocation/ limit for buying; vi.—བརྒལ་ to exceed a budget/ allocation/ limit for buying.

ཉོ་ཚོང་ (ño̱dzoŋ) business, trade, commerce; va.—བྱེད་ to do business, to do trading/ commerce; to buy and sell ། དཔལ་འབྱོར་དང་ཉོ་ཚོང་འགྲེམས་སྟོན་འདུ་ཚོགས་ An economic and trade/ commerce exhibition.

ཉོ་ཚོང་ཁང་ (ño̱dzoŋgaŋ) 1. sm. ཉོ་ཚོང་མཉམ་ལས་ཁང་. 2. commerce/ trade bureau.

ཉོ་ཚོང་ཁྲོམ་ར་ (ño̱dzoŋ trõmra) 1. market, place where things are bought and sold. 2. trading pit (as in a stock exchanges).

ཉོ་ཚོང་གྲུ་ཁ་ (ño̱dzoŋ tru̱gə) trade/ commerce port.

ཉོ་ཚོང་མགོ་སྙོམས་ (ño̱dzoŋ go̱ñom) trade balance.

ཉོ་ཚོང་འགུག་ཐབས་ (ño̱dzoŋ gu̱gdəb) methods of securing orders/ business/ customers.

ཉོ་ཚོང་འགོ་སྙོམས་ (ño̱dzoŋ go̱ñom) sm. ཉོ་ཚོང་མགོ་སྙོམས་.

ཉོ་ཚོང་གཉེན་སྒྲིག (ño̱dzoŋ ñẽndrig) marriage of convenience, marriage based on money.

ཉོ་ཚོང་མཉམ་ལས་ཁང་ (ño̱dzoŋ ña̱mlɛgaŋ) commercial/ trading cooperative.

ཉོ་ཚོང་དོས་ཁང་ (ño̱dzoŋ tö̱ögaŋ) trading warehouse.

ཉོ་ཚོང་དོས་ར་ (ño̱dzoŋ tö̱öra) sm. ཉོ་ཚོང་དོས་ཁང་.

ཉོ་ཚོང་དྲང་སྙོམས་ (ño̱dzoŋ tra̱ñom) fair trade.

ཉོ་ཚོང་དྲང་བཞག (ño̱dzoŋ tra̱nshaà) sm. ཉོ་ཚོང་དྲང་སྙོམས་.

ཉོ་ཚོང་ཕུའུ་ (ño̱dzoŋ bū) tib.ch. Ministry of Commerce/ Trade.

ཉོ་ཚོང་སྤྱི་གཉེར་ཁང་ (ño̱dzoŋ jĩñergaŋ) department store.

ཉོ་ཚོང་བར་སྒྲིག (ño̱dzoŋ pa̱rdrig) arranging selling and buying.

ཉོ་ཚོང་བར་མི་ (ño̱dzoŋ pə̱rmi) middleman (in trade/ business).

ཉོ་ཚོང་ས་ཚིགས་ (ño̱dzoŋ sədzig) marketing/ trading station.

ཉོ་རོགས་ (ño̱roò) buying for sb. else, helping sb. buy sth.; va.—བྱེད་.

ཉོ་ཤུགས་ (ño̱shug) sm. ཉོ་སྟོབས་.

ཉོ་ས་ (ño̱sa) place to buy.

ཉོག (ño̱g) 1. a kind of stew/ soup. 2. abbr. of ཉོག་པ་.

ཉོག་ཅན་ (ño̱gjɛn) muddy, unclear, unclean.

ཉོག་ཆུ་ (ño̱gju) muddy water.

ཉོག་དོ་ (ño̱gdo) muddy (applies mainly to water).

ཉོག་པ་ (ño̱gba) muddy, dirty, unclean.

ཉོག་པོ་ (ño̱gbo) sm. ཉོག་དོ་.

ཉོག་བྱིང་ (ño̱gjiŋ) unclear/ muddled thinking.

ཉོག་མ་ (ño̱gma) sm. ཉོག་པ་.

ཉོག་རྫོབ་ཆེ་བ་ (ño̱gdzob cēwa) complicated, muddled (usu. regarding work).

ཉོག་སེ་བ་ (ño̱gsewa) 1. not sharp or alert (mentally) ། མདང་དགོང་གཉིད་ཡག་པོ་ཁུག་མ་བྱུང་བས་དེ་རིང་ཁམས་ཉོག་སེ་བ་ཞིག་འདུག Because I didn't sleep last night, today I am not alert. 2. slightly muddled. 3. sm. ཉོབ་པོ་.

ཉོད་པ་ (ñö̱öba) arc. food.

ཉོན་ (ñö̱n) imp. of ཉན་.

ཉོན་མོངས་ (ñö̱n mo̱ŋ) ignorance, mental defect, delusional.

ཉོབ་ (ño̱b) vi. to feel lazy/ lethargic, to be bored.

ཉོབ་ཀྱི་ (ño̱bgye) lazy, slow moving, lethargic.

ཉོབ་ཉོབ་ (ño̱bño̱b) sm. ཉོབ་ཐིང་ཐིང་.

ཉོབ་དོ་ (ño̱bdo) sm. ཉོབ་ཀྱི་.

ཉོབ་ཐིང་ཐིང་ (ño̱b tĩndiŋ) 1. lazy, slow moving, lethargic. 2. dull, languid, not alert.

ཉོབ་ཐིབས་སེ་བ་ (ño̱b tĩbsewa) sm. ཉོབ་ཐིང་ཐིང་.

ཉོབ་འཐིབ་ (ño̱btib) sm. ཉོབ་ཐིང་ཐིང་.

ཉོབ་དེ་ (ño̱bdo) sm. ཉོབ་ཀྱི་.

ཉོབ་མདངས་ (ño̱bdaŋ) 1. discouraged, sad, disheartened, low in spirits; vi.—ཐོན་; —སྟོན་ to show signs of being discouraged/ sad/ disheartened/ low in spirits. 2. sm. ཉོབ་ཀྱི་.

ཉོབ་སྤྱོད་ (ño̱bjöö) lethargic, lazy, dull/ languid behavior.

ཉོབ་སངས་ (ño̱bsaŋ) vi. to get over the feeling of laziness/ lethargy.

ཉོབས་ (ño̱b) imp. of ཉབ་.

ཉོར་ (ñɔ̱r) 1. vi. to collapse ། ལྕགས་རི་ཉར་བཞག The wall collapsed. 2. imp. of ཉར་.

ཉོར་འགྲོས་ (ñɔ̱rdröö) staggering (when walking).

ཉོལ་ (ñö̱ö) imp. of ཉལ་.

ཉོས་ (ñö̱ö) p. and imp. of ཉོ་.

ཉོས་མི་ (ñö̱ömi) a slave, a person who has been bought.

ཉྭ་ (ña̱) calf (of foot).

ཉྭ་དཀྲིས་ (ña̱drii) leggings/ wrapping worn by Chinese soldiers on their calf.

ཉྭ་ཁུག (ñə̱guù) shung. the back of the knee, the hollow of the knee; va.—འབྲེས་ to cut the tendons behind the knee (as punishment).

ཉྭ་གྲི་ (ña̱dri) knife tied/ fastened on the calf.

ཉྭ་འགྱུར་ (ña̱ gyu̱r) vi. to have/ get a cramp in the calf.

ཉྭ་རྒྱབ་ (ña̱gyəb) sm. ཉྭ་.

ཉྭ་རྒྱུས་ (ñə̱gyüü) shung. tendons of the calf; va.—གཅོད་ to cut the Achilles tendon (as punishment).

ཉྭ་སྒོར་ (ña̱gɔɔ) bowlegged.

ཉྭ་འཆུས་ (ña̱ cõö) sm. ཉྭ་འགྱུར་.

ཉྭ་སྡི་ (ña̱di) ankle bone.

ཉྭ་གདོང་ (ña̱doŋ) shin bone.

ཉྭ་མདུན་ (ña̱dün) front part of the shin.

ཉྭ་འདོན་ (ña̱ dö̱n) sm. ཉྭ་རྒྱུས་གཅོད་.

ཉྭ་འདྲིལ་གདོང་ (ña̱drii dõŋ) shung. a form of corporal punishment involving rolling a piece of wood behind the knee to destroy the use of the leg.

ཉྭ་སྦྲིད་ (ña̱ dri̱i) vi. to have one's calf become numb.

ཉྭ་རིལ་ (ñə̱rii) 1. forearm. 2. calf.

ཉྭ་ལུག (ña̱ lu̱ù) sm. ཉྭ་འགྱུར་.

ཉྭ་ལོག (ña̱ lɔ̱ɔ̀) sm. ཉྭ་འཆུས་.

ཉྭ་ཤ་ (ña̱sha) flesh on calf/ forearm.

ཉྭ་སྲུས་ (ña̱süü) flesh on the calf.

ཉྭ་ཧྲིལ་ (ñə̱hrii) sm. ཉྭ་རིལ་.

གཉག (ñāà) f. of གཉོག.

གཉགས་ (ñāà) p. of གཉོག.

གཉང་མ་ (ñāŋma) sm. རྣང་མ་.

གཉན་ (ñɛ̄n) 1. argali (a type of wild sheep). 2. an ancient lineage. 3. a kind of supernatural spirit/ demon.

གཉན་ཁ་ (ñɛ̄nga) inflammation; va.—གཅོག to decrease an inflammation; vi.—འཇོམས་ to have an inflammation decrease; vi.—བྱེད་; —རྒྱས་ to get an inflammation.

གཉན་ཆེན་ཐང་ལྷ་ (ñɛ̄njen tāŋla) a mountain. range in south Tibet.

གཉན་སྦུབ་པ་ (ñɛ̄ntubbə) sedum bulbiferum Makino (used in Tibetan medicine).

གཉན་དུག (ñɛ̄ndug) 1. a type of disease. 2. a type of poisonous plant.

གཉན་འདུལ་བ་ (ñɛ̄ndüwə) phyllophyton complanatuma (used in Tibetan medicine).

གཉན་ནད་ (ñɛ̄nnɛɛ̀) a type of illness caused by གཉན་ (demons/ spirits).

གཉན་ནད་འཁྱམ་པོ་ (ñɛ̄nnɛɛ̀ kyāmbo) a type of disease which causes the neck and chin to swell.

གཉན་པ་ (ñɛ̄mba) sm. གཉན་པོ་.

གཉན་པའི་གནད་ (ñɛ̄mbɛ nɛɛ̀) sm. གཉན་འཕྲང་.

གཉན་པོ་ (ñɛ̄mbo) stern, severe, fierce, strict, cruel.

གཉན་ཕོ་ (ñɛ̄n pō) male argali.

གཉན་ཕྲན་ (ñɛ̄ndrɛn) a small demon/ spirit.

གཉན་འཕྲང་ (ñɛ̄ndraŋ) critical, dangerous ། གཉན་འཕྲང་དུས་སྐབས་ A critical period. ། གཞུང་གི་ཆབ་སྲིད་གཉན་འཕྲང་ལ་ཐུག་པའི་སྐབས་སུ་ཕྱི་རྒྱལ་གྱི་རོགས་རམ་ཐོབ་པ་རེད་ During the critical period in the government's political life they received foreign assistance.

གཉན་བུ་ (ñɛ̄mbu) sm. གཉན་འབུར་.

གཉན་འབུར་ (ñɛ̄mbuu) boil, abscess; vi.—སྐྱེས་ to get a boil/ abscess.

གཉན་འབྲས་ (ñɛ̄ndrɛɛ̀) cancerous lymph node/ tumor/ abscess.

གཉན་ཚད་ (ñɛ̄ndzɛɛ̀) sm. གཉན་ཁ་.

གཉན་ཞན་ (ñɛ̄nshɛn) sm. དུག་ཞན་.

གཉན་རིམས་ (ñɛ̄nrim) a type of epidemic characterized by boils and abscesses.

གཉན་རྭ་ (ñɛ̄nra) horns of an argali sheep.

གཉན་ས་ (ñɛ̄nsa) 1. rugged/ rough terrain. 2. a barren, empty place.

གཉན་གསོད་ (ñɛ̄nsöö) a medicine for boils and abscesses.

གཉའ་ (ñā) back of the neck.

གཉའ་ཁྲི་བཙན་པོ་ (ñātri dzɛ̄mbo) the first King of Tibet.

གཉའ་གོང་ (ña̲goŋ) back of the neck, behind the neck.

གཉའ་རྒན་ (ña̲gɛn) rich; vi.—ཆགས་ to get rich/ wealthy.

གཉའ་སྒ་ (ñāga) yoke.

གཉའ་སྒུར་ (ñā gu̲r) va. to bow one's head down, to surrender.

གཉའ་གཅོག (ñā jɔ̄ɔ̀) va. to subdue, to put under control, to break a person (into submission).

གཉའ་ཕྱིབས་ (ñājib) the cloth wrapped around the yoke to keep the wood from rubbing against the animal's neck.

གཉའ་ཆག (ñā cāà) vi. to be down (in spirits), to be crestfallen, to feel dejected, to lose one's composure.

གཉའ་ཆག་སྐྱིད་བཀུག (ñājaà gyi̲i̲guù) sm. གཉའ་ཆག.

གཉའ་ཆག་ཉམས་ཤོར་ (ñājaà ña̲mshɔɔ) sm. གཉའ་ཆག.

གཉའ་ཆག་པོ་ (ñā cāgbo) dejected, down in spirits, crestfallen.

གཉའ་ལྟག (ñādaà) sm. གཉའ་གོང་.

གཉའ་ལྟག་གཅོག (ñā dāgjɔɔ̀) sm. གཉའ་གཅོག.

གཉའ་གདན་ (ñādɛn) sm. གཉའ་ཕྱིབས་.

གཉའ་ནང་ཤོ་པ་ (ñānaŋ shōba) shung. the official in charge of tax collection in Nyalam in tt.

གཉའ་ནང་ཤོག་བུ་ (ñānaŋ shɔ̄gbu) paper from Nyalam.

གཉའ་ནས་གནོན་ (ñānɛ nōn) va. to ride roughshod over, to suppress/ oppress.

གཉའ་གནན་སྨ་འཕེབས་ (ñānɛn māmbeb) oppressing/ suppressing and humiliating.

གཉའ་གནོན་ (ñānön) oppression, coercion, suppression; va.—བྱེད་; —གཏོང་; —མནར་ to oppress, to suppress; vi.—མྱོང་ to experience oppression/ suppression.

གཉའ་གནོན་མྱོང་མཁན་མི་དམངས་ (ñānön ño̲ŋgɛn mi̲maŋ) the oppressed people.

གཉའ་གནོན་བཤུ་གཞོག (ñānön shōshoò) oppression and exploitation.

གཉའ་ཕབ་ (ñābəb) sm. གཉའ་ཆག.

གཉའ་ཕབ་སྐྱིད་བཀུག (ñābəb gyi̲i̲guù) 1. sm. གཉའ་ཆག་སྐྱིད་བཀུག. 2. cringing, servile.

གཉའ་བ་ (ñāwa) sm. གཉའ་.

གཉའ་བ་ཧྲངས་ (ñāwa hrāŋ) vi. to be undisciplined/ incorrigible/ uncontrollable/ wild (in behavior).

གཉའ་བོ་ (ñāwo) 1. witness, guarantor; va.—བྱེད་ to act as a witness/ guarantor. 2. the person who welcomes/ receives the bride and groom at the time of marriage.

གཉའ་བྱེད་པོ་ (ñāceèbo) supporter, helper.

གཉའ་འབྲས་ (ñādrɛɛ̀) rice from Nyalam.

གཉའ་མ་ (ñāma) vagina.

གཉའ་དམའ་པོ་ (ñā māābo) sm. ཉ་དམའ་པོ་.

གཉའ་དམས་ (ñā mɛɛ̀) sm. གཉའ་ཆག.

གཉའ་ཚོག (ñādzog) red decorations decorating the neck of plowing yak/ oxen.

གཉའ་ཚིགས་ (ñādzii̲) neck joint.

གཉའ་ཞ་ཞ་ སྐྱིད་ལྷེམ་ལྷེམ་ (ñā sha̲sha gyi̲i̲ lhēmlhem) cringing with head bent and shaking (with fear).

གཉའ་ཞུམ་ (ñāshum) sm. གཉའ་ཆག.

གཉའ་རུས་ (ñārüü) neck bone.

གཉའ་རུས་ཞུམ་ (ñārüü shu̲m) sm. གཉའ་ཆག.

གཉའ་རེངས་ (ñāreŋ) sm. གཉའ་བ་ཧྲངས་.

གཉའ་རེངས་པ་ (ñā re̲ŋba) sb. who is stubborn/ obstinate/ wild/ uncontrollable.

གཉའ་ལག་བཀུག (ñālag gūù) va. to tie an animal from its neck to its legs to keep it still while working on it (e.g., cutting its hair).

གཉའ་ལམ་ (ñālam) district/ xian near the Nepalese border.

གཉའ་ཤ་ (ñāsha) the flesh around the neck.

གཉའ་ཤིང་ (ñāshiŋ) wooden yoke.

གཉའ་གཤོལ་ (ñāshöö) sm. གཉའ་ཤིང་.

གཉལ་ (ñɛ̄ɛ̄) name of a place in Southern Tibet (in Lhoga).

གཉི་ག (ñīgə) arc. sm. གཉིས་ཀ་.

གཉི་མ་ (ñīmə) arc. sm. ཉི་མ་.

གཉི་གཟེར་ (ñīser) arc. sm. ཉི་ཟེར་.

གཉིག (ñīg) arc. sm. གཅིག.

གཉིད་ (ñīì) sleep, sleeping ། གཉིད་ལས་སད་ནས་ Having awakened from sleep.

གཉིད་ཀྱི་སྙོམ་པ་ (ñīigi ñōmba) arc. sb. who likes to sleep, sb. who is lazy.

གཉིད་ཀྱིས་ཐེབ་ (ñīigi tīb) vi. to be overcome with sleepiness.

གཉིད་ཀྱིས་འཚེས་ (ñīigi tsöö) sm. གཉིད་ཀྱིས་ཐེབ་.

གཉིད་དཀྲོག (ñīi drɔ̄ɔ̀) sm. གཉིད་འདྲོག.

གཉིད་སྐོར་ (ñīigɔɔ) sm. གཉིད་.

གཉིད་སྐྱིད་པོ་ (ñīi gyi̲bu) a good sleep; vi.—ཁུག to get a good sleep.

གཉིད་སྐྱིད་ལོས་ (ñīigyilüü) good morning (a common greeting among nomads) [Lit. how was your sleep].

གཉིད་ཁུག (ñīi kūù) vi. to fall asleep.

གཉིད་སྣ་ (ñīidra) snoring; vi.—རྒྱག.

གཉིད་སྔུར་ (ñīiŋur) sm. གཉིད་སྣ་.

གཉིད་ཅན་ (ñīijɛn) sleepy.

གཉིད་ཅོག (ñīijɔɔ̀) dozing; va.—རྒྱག to doze, to fall asleep.

གཉིད་གཅོག (ñīi jɔ̄ɔ̀) va. to reduce the amount one sleeps.

གཉིད་བཅག (ñīijaà) p. of གཉིད་གཅོག.

གཉིད་བཅག་ཟས་བརྗེད་ (ñīijaà sɛ̲ɛ̀jeè) lost in one's work/ thoughts/ etc. [Lit. reduce sleep, forget food].

གཉིད་ལྕི་པོ་ (ñīi ji̲bu) deep/ heavy sleep; vi.—ཁུག to sleep deeply.

གཉིད་ཆག (ñīi cāà) vi. to be unable to sleep.

གཉིད་ཆེ་བ་ (ñīijewa) sm. གཉིད་ལྕི་པོ་.

གཉིད་འཚོལ་ (ñīijöö) sm. གཉིད་གཏམ་.

གཉིད་འཚོལ་འཁྱམས་སྨྱུལ་ (ñīijöö kyāmñul) sleepwalking and talking in one's sleep.

གཉིད་ལྗི་པོ་ (ñīì ji̱bu) sm. གཉིད་ལྕི་པོ་.

གཉིད་ལྗིད་པོ་ (ñīì ji̱bu) sm. གཉིད་ལྗི་པོ་.

གཉིད་ཉལ་ (ñīì ñɛ̱ɛ̱) va. to go to sleep ༑ཁོ་དཀའ་ལས་ཁག་ནས་གཉིད་ཉལ་སོང་ He got tired and went to sleep.

གཉིད་གཏམ་ (ñīìdam) talking in one's sleep; va.—ཤོར་ to sleep talk.

གཉིད་སྡུག་པོ་ (ñīì dūgbu) sm. གཉིད་ལྗིད་པོ་.

གཉིད་ཐལ་ཤོར་ (ñīìtəə shɔ̄ɔ̄) vi. to oversleep.

གཉིད་ཐིབ་ (ñīì tīb) vi. to be sleepy, to be overcome with sleepiness.

གཉིད་ཐིབས་ཐིབས་ (ñīì tībdib) very sleepy; vi.—བྱེད་.

གཉིད་ཐེབས་གཙོག (ñīì tēbjɔ̄ɔ̀) va. to wake up ༑ངའི་ཁྱིམ་མཚེས་ཀྱིས་སྒྲ་སྒྲུད་འཁོར་ལོ་བཏང་ཙང་ང་གཉིད་ཐེབས་བཙག་བྱུང་ Because my neighbor played his radio last night I was woken from sleep.

གཉིད་འཐིབས་ (ñīì tīb) sm. གཉིད་ཐིབ་.

གཉིད་འཐུག་པོ་ (ñīì tūgbu) sm. གཉིད་ལྷི་པོ་.

གཉིད་དུ་འགྲོ་ (ñīìdu dro̱) sm. གཉིད་ཁུག.

གཉིད་དུས་ (ñīìdüù) 1. night time. 2. while asleep.

གཉིད་དྭངས་ (ñīì ta̱ŋ) vi. to wake up.

གཉིད་འདོར་ཟས་བརྗེད་ (ñīìdɔɔ sɛ̱ɛ̀jeè) lost in one's thought/ work/ etc. [Lit. give up sleep, forget to eat].

གཉིད་འདྲོག (ñīì drɔ̱ɔ̀) vi. to be startled out of sleep, to be suddenly woken by a disturbance.

གཉིད་སྡིངས་མ་ཁུག (ñīì di̱ŋma kūù) vi. to fall deeply asleep.

གཉིད་ཕབ་ (ñīì pəb) va. to put sb. to sleep.

གཉིད་བྲོ་ (ñīì tro̱) vi. to feel sleepy.

གཉིད་མ་ཉལ་ (ñīì ma̱ñɛɛ) half asleep.

གཉིད་རྨུགས་ (ñīìmug) unclear, dazed.

གཉིད་སྨན་ (ñīìmɛn) sleeping pills, sleeping medicine.

གཉིད་རྫུ་འདེབས་ (ñīìdzü de̱b) va. to pretend to fall asleep.

གཉིད་བཟི་ལངས་བརྒྱབ་ནད་ (ñīì si̱laŋ gyə̄bnɛɛ̀) sm. གཉིད་བཟིའི་འཁྱམས་རྒྱུག.

གཉིད་བཟིའི་འཁྱམས་རྒྱུག (ñīì sii̱ kyāmgyuù) sleepwalking; vi.—བྱེད་.

གཉིད་བཟོད་བདེ་པོ་ (ñīìsöò de̱bo) sleeping soundly.

གཉིད་ཡར་ (ñīì ya̱r) sm. གཉིད་ཡེར་.

གཉིད་ཡལ་ (ñīì yɛ̱ɛ̱) sm. གཉིད་ཡེར་.

གཉིད་ཡུར་ (ñīì yu̱r) vi. to fall asleep.

གཉིད་ཡེར་ (ñīì ye̱r) vi. to lose one's sleepiness (to no longer be sleepy after first being sleepy).

གཉིད་ར་དྭངས་ (ñīìrə ta̱ŋ) vi. to be wide awake/ refreshed (after having a good sleep).

གཉིད་ར་སངས་ (ñīìrə sāŋ) sm. གཉིད་ར་དྭངས་.

གཉིད་ལ་ཤོར་ (ñīìla shɔ̄ɔ̄) vi. to fall asleep.

གཉིད་ལབ་ (ñīìləb) talking in one's sleep; vi.—རྒྱག to talk in one's sleep.

གཉིད་ལམ་ (ñīìləm) dream; vi.—གཏོང་ to dream.

གཉིད་ལམ་འཇམ་པོ་ (ñīìləm ja̱mbo) pleasant dream.

གཉིད་ལམ་སྡུག་ཅག (ñīìləm du̱gja) bad dream.

གཉིད་ལམ་རྩུབ་པོ་ (ñīìləm dzūbu) sm. གཉིད་ལམ་སྡུག་ཅག.

གཉིད་ལམ་འཚུབ་པོ་ (ñīìləm tsūbu) sm. གཉིད་ལམ་སྡུག་ཅག.

གཉིད་ལམ་ཡག་པོ་ (ñīìləm ya̱gbo) good dream.

གཉིད་ལམ་སད་ (ñīìləm sɛ̄ɛ̀) sm. གཉིད་སད་.

གཉིད་ལས་འཕགས་སྡེ་ལང་ (ñīìlɛɛ̀ pāgde la̱ŋ) vi. to wake up suddenly.

གཉིད་ལས་སློང་ (ñīìlɛɛ̀ lōŋ) va. to wake sb. up.

གཉིད་ལོག (ñīì lɔ̱ɔ̀) sm. གཉིད་ཁུག.

གཉིད་ཤོར་ (ñīì shɔ̄ɔ̄) sm. གཉིད་ལ་ཤོར་.

གཉིད་ས་ (ñīìsə) bed.

གཉིད་སངས་ (ñīìsaŋ) sm. གཉིད་ར་སངས་.

གཉིད་སད་ (ñīì sɛ̄ɛ̀) vi. to wake up ༑ང་གཉིད་སྔ་པོ་སད་བྱུང་ I woke up early.

གཉིད་སྲབ་པོ་ (ñīì drə̱bu) light sleeper, light sleep.

གཉིད་སྲུང་ (ñīì sūŋ) guarding against a sick person falling asleep (a traditional Tibetan medical practice).

གཉིད་སྲིད་ (ñīìseè) sb. who likes to sleep a lot.

གཉིད་སླེབས་ (ñīì lēè) vi. to feel sleepy [Lit. sleep arrived].

གཉིད་གསོད་ (ñīì söò) va. to wake sb. up ༑ཁོས་ང་གཉིད་བསད་བྱུང་ He woke me up.

གཉིད་ཧབ་སད་རྒྱག (ñīì həbsɛɛ̀ gya̱à) vi. to wake up suddenly (due to a noise, etc.).

གཉིད་ཧོབ་ལངས་རྒྱག (ñīì həblaŋ gya̱à) sm. གཉིད་ཧབ་སད་རྒྱག.

གཉིས་ (ñīì) two.

གཉིས་ཀ་ (ñīìgə) both, the two together ༑ཁོ་གཉིས་གཉིས་ཀར་ལས་ཀ་རག་པ་རེད་ They both got work.

གཉིས་ཀ་ར་ལོགས་ (ñīìgalɔɔ̀) both, the two of them.

གཉིས་ཀློལ་ལས་འགུལ་ (ñīì göö̱ lɛ̱ngüü) the two-antis movement: the campaign to oppose waste and conservatism (launched in the latter part of 1958 as part of the national rectification movement).

གཉིས་ཀྱི་གཉིས་སྦྲད་ (ñīìgi ñīìdrɛɛ̀) sexual intercourse.

གཉིས་གུན་མེད་པ་ (ñīìgün me̱èba) shung. incurring no loss for both sides ༑ཡུལ་སྲོལ་ཏ་གླ་གཉིས་གུན་མེད་པ་སྤྲོད་དགོས་ Cost for renting horses should be paid according to the custom of the area so that neither side losses anything.

གཉིས་སྒྲིག་བྱེད་ (ñīìdrig ce̱è) sm. ཉིས་གཤིབ་.

གཉིས་ཅ་ (ñīìja) sm. གཉིས་ཀ་.

གཉིས་ཅལ་ (ñīìjɛɛ) shung. sm. གཉིས་ཀ་.

གཉིས་ཅར་ (ñīìjaa) sm. གཉིས་ཀ་.

གཉིས་ཅར་ལོགས་ (ñīìjalɔɔ̀) sm. གཉིས་ཀ་ར་ལོགས་.

གཉིས་ཆ་ (ñīìja) sm. གཉིས་ཀ་.

གཉིས་མཇུག་གསུམ་མཐུད་ (ñīìjug sūmdüù) continuously, one after another.

གཉིས་འཇགས་བསམས་ཆེ་ (ñīìjaà sāmje) shung. considering the harmony of both sides ༑གཉིས་འཇགས་བསམས་ཆེའི་སོན་འབྲུ་གསུམ་སྐོར་བརྩིས་པའི་འབྲུ་འབབ་ཕྱིར་སྤྲོད་དུ་རྒྱུ་ Considering the harmony of both sides, (you) should return an amount of grain that is three times that used as seed.

གཉིས་ཉལ་མལ་ཁྲི་ (ñīìñɛɛ me̱ɛ̱dri) double bed (bed for two persons).

གཉིས་གཉིས་ (ñīìñīì) in pairs, by two's ༑ཁོ་ཚོས་དེབ་གཉིས་གཉིས་སྤྲད་པ་རེད་ They gave two books (each).

གཉིས་གཉིས་འཁྱུད་ (ñīìñīì kyüù) va. to embrace/ hug.

གཉིས་ཐད་ནས་ (ñīìtɛɛ̀nɛ) secondly.

གཉིས་མཐུན་རྩ་དགའ་ (ñīìdün dzāga) sexual intercourse.

གཉིས་འདོམས་ (ñīndom) the two together, both ༑ཁོང་ཁྲོ་དང་བློ་ཕམ་གཉིས་འདོམས་དང་སྐད་པས་པར་ Saying it with both anger and sadness.

གཉིས་ལྡན་ (ñīìdɛn) having two things together ༑ཆོས་སྲིད་གཉིས་ལྡན་ Both political and religious.

གཉིས་ལྡབ་ (ñīìdəb) double, two times ༑ཁོ་ཚོར་ཁེ་བཟང་གཉིས་ལྡབ་བྱུང་བ་རེད་ They got double the profit (profit two times the capital).

གཉིས་བསྡོམས་ (ñīìdom) two together.

གཉིས་ནས་ (ñīìnɛ) 1. from/ by two. 2. secondly.

གཉིས་པ་ (ñīìbə) 1. the second ༑དེབ་གཉིས་པ་ The second book. 2. (with མགོ་) deceitful, two-faced.

གཉིས་པོ་ (ñīìbo) the two (together), both ༑བློན་པོ་གཉིས་པོ་རྒྱ་གར་ལ་ཐེབས་པ་རེད་ Both ministers went to India. ༑ཀྲུང་སུའུ་རྒྱལ་ཁབ་གཉིས་པོའི་ཤུགས་པོ་ཆེའི་མནའ་འབྲེལ་ནི་ As for the great alliance of the two countries Russia and China.

གཉིས་ཕན་ (ñīìbɛn) mutually beneficial/ advantageous.

གཉིས་ཕྱོགས་ (ñīìjɔɔ̀) both sides, two sides.

གཉིས་འཕུང་ (ñīìbuŋ) sm. རང་གཞན་གཉིས་འཕུང་.

གཉིས་དབར་ (ñīìwar) between the two.

གཉིས་མ་བྱེད་པའི་སྲིད་ཇུས་ (ñīì ma̱jeèbɛ sīìjüù) the 1959-60 policy in nomad areas of not doing the "two", i.e. not separating the population into classes and not confiscating households' animals/ possessions.

གཉིས་མེད་ (ñīìmeè) nondualistic, without duality; va.—སྒྲུབ་ to achieve nonduality.

གཉིས་མེད་མཉམ་ཕུང་ (ñīìmeè ñambuŋ) both sides suffering/ losing; vi.—བྱེད་.

གཉིས་སྨིན་འབྲས་ (ñīìmin drɛɛ̀) rice which can be planted twice in a year.

གཉིས་མོས་འདོད་རྫོགས་ (ñīìmöö döödzɔɔ̀) shung. both sides being satisfied ¶ བཀའ་ཁྲིའི་དགོངས་དོན་ལ་ཕྲན་དོ་བདག་པན་ཚུན་གཉིས་མོས་འདོད་རྫོགས་བྱུང་སོང་ Both sides were satisfied with the verdict.

གཉིས་འཛིན་ (ñīndzin) holding more than one position/ view, dualistic perception.

གཉིས་འཛོམས་ (ñīndzom) in both ways, having two/ both things together ¶ བུ་མོ་འདི་གཤིས་སྤྱོད་གཉིས་འཛོམས་འདུག This girl has both (good) character and behavior.

གཉིས་ཞུགས་ གཅིག་བཅོས་ གསུམ་སྦྲེལ་འབྲེལ་ (ñīìshuù jīgjöö sūm suŋdree) two participations, one reform, three unities (this political slogan conveys: the two participants are workers participating in planning and management and cadres participating in labor; the one reform is reforming unreasonable rules and regulations; the three unities are the unity of the cadre leaders, the masses of workers and the technicians).

གཉིས་ལོ་དྲང་བཞག (ñīìlo traŋshaà) shung. an impartial decision that is acceptable to both parties/ sides; va.—བྱེད་; —དཔྱོད་ ¶ གཉིས་ལོ་དྲང་བཞག་གི་དཔྱད་མཚམས་འདིས་དཔྱད་རྗེས་ After issuing this verdict which is an impartial decision that is acceptable to both parties.

གཉིས་སུ་ (ñīìsu) in/ into two; va.—དབྱེ་ to divide/ differentiate into two.

གཉིས་སུ་བྱར་མེད་ (ñīìsu jarmeè) inseparable, indivisible.

གཉིས་སུ་མ་མཆིས་ (ñīìsu macii) sm. གཉིས་སུ་མེད་པ་.

གཉིས་སུ་མེད་པ་ (ñīìsu meèba) 1. the same, just like ¶ ཁྱེད་ཀྱིས་ཕྱག་བྲིས་འབྱོར་བས་དངོས་མཇལ་དང་གཉིས་སུ་མེད་པ་དགའ་ཚོར་ཆེན་པོ་བྱུང་ Receiving your letter made me just as happy as seeing you in person. 2. without duality.

གཉིས་སུ་སྨྲ་བ་ (ñīìsu māwa) dualism.

གཉུག་མ་ (ñūgma) 1. real, natural, innate. 2. primitive, primeval, primordial, originating in a place. 3. permanent, nontemporary.

གཉུག་མའི་གཤིས་ (ñūgmɛ shīì) innate character.

གཉུག་མར་གནས་ (ñūgmar nɛ̄ɛ̀) vi. to live permanently, to be a permanent residence.

གཉུག་དམག (ñūgmaà) a soldier posted someplace permanently.

གཉུལ་ (ñūū̀) va. to reconnoiter, to spy.

གཉེ་བོ་ (ñēbo) arc. messenger.

གཉེ་མ་ (ñēma) pancreas.

གཉེན་ (ñēn) 1. relative, kinsmen. ¶ ཕ་གཉེན་ Paternal relatives. 2. marriage.

གཉེན་ཀ་ (ñēnga) sm. གཉེན་ཁ་.

གཉེན་དཀར་ (ñēngɔr) shung. relative, kinsman.

གཉེན་སྐོར་ (ñēngɔr) relative, kinsman.

གཉེན་སྐྱར་སྒྲིག (ñēn gyārdrig) remarrying; va.—བྱེད་.

གཉེན་རྐྱེན་ (ñēngyen) fated to be married.

གཉེན་ཁ་ (ñēnga) husband and wife, couple.

གཉེན་ཁ་བྲལ་ (ñēnga trɛɛ) 1. vi. to get divorced. 2. vi. to have friendship/ harmony get destroyed.

གཉེན་ཁར་སླེབས་ (ñēnga lēb) va. to arrive/ come as a bride or a groom.

གཉེན་ཁྲིམས་ (ñēndrim) marriage law.

གཉེན་འཁོར་ (ñēngɔɔ) sm. གཉེན་སྐོར་.

གཉེན་འཁོར་ལྷོས་བཅས་ (ñēn gɔ̄ɔ̄ dṑò jɛ̀ɛ̀) relatives, associates and friends.

གཉེན་གན་ (ñēngɛn) nuptial letter signed by both families at the engagement ceremony, marriage contract/ agreement.

གཉེན་གྲོགས་ (ñēndrɔɔ̀) friend; va.—བཟོ་ to make friends.

གཉེན་འགྲིག (ñēn drig) 1. vi. to have friendly relationship, to become friends. 2. vi. to be/ get married.

གཉེན་རྒྱུད་ (ñēngyüü) lineage, clan, descent line of kinsman.

གཉེན་སྒྲིག (ñēndrig) marriage; va.—བྱེད་.

གཉེན་སྒྲིག་ཉེ་ཚན་ (ñēndrig ñedzɛn) in-laws, relatives through marriage.

གཉེན་སྒྲིག་དེབ་འབྲེལ་ (ñēndrig dēmdree) wedding/ marriage ceremony.

གཉེན་སྒྲིག་མཐུན་སྦྱོར་ (ñēndrig tū̃njɔɔ) marriage; va.—བྱེད་.

གཉེན་སྒྲིག་བཅའ་ཁྲིམས་ (ñēndrig jātrim) marriage law.

གཉེན་སྒྲིག་བར་མ་ (ñēndrig parma) matchmaker (for marriage).

གཉེན་སྒྲིག་སྤྱོན་བདེ་ (ñēndrig drönda) wedding invitation.

གཉེན་སྒྲིག་མཚམས་སྦྱོར་ལས་ཁུངས་ (ñēndrig tsāmjɔɔ lɛɛ̀guŋ) marriage bureau.

གཉེན་སྒྲིག་མཛད་སྒོ་ (ñēndrig dzɛɛ̀go) wedding/ marriage ceremony.

གཉེན་སྒྲིག་རང་མོས་ (ñēndrig raŋmöö) freedom to marry whomever one wants (as opposed to arranged marriage).

གཉེན་སྒྲིག་ལག་འཁྱེར་ (ñēndrig laggyer) marriage certificate.

གཉེན་སྒྲིག་ལམ་ལུགས་ (ñēndrig ləmluù) marriage system.

གཉེན་ཆང་ (ñēnjaŋ) wedding beer.

གཉེན་ཇ་ (ñēnja) wedding tea.

གཉེན་ཉེ་ (ñēnñe) 1. kinsmen. 2. sm. གཉེན་ཉེ་དུ་.

གཉེན་ཉེ་འཁོར་ གྲོགས་དགའ་བཤེས་ (ñēn ñegɔɔ trog gasheè) relatives and friends.

གཉེན་ཉེ་དུ་ (ñēn ñedu) friends and relatives.

གཉེན་ཉེ་བ་ (ñēn ñewa) sm. གཉེན་ཉེ་དུ་.

གཉེན་ཉེ་འབྲེལ་ (ñēn ñendree) sm. གཉེན་ཉེ་.

གཉེན་ཉེ་མཛའ་གྲོགས་ (ñēnñe dzadrɔɔ̀) relatives and friends.

གཉེན་ཉེ་རིགས་ (ñēn ñerig) sm. གཉེན་ཉེ་.

གཉེན་གདམ་ (ñēndam) wedding talks/ discussions.

གཉེན་རྫེན་ (ñēnden) wedding dowry, money or gifts given to parents of incoming bride or bridegroom; va.—འབུལ་.

གཉེན་སྟོན་ (ñēndön) wedding party.

གཉེན་ཐོ་ (ñēndo) sm. གཉེན་གན་.

གཉེན་ཐོག་གཉེན་བརྩེགས་ (ñēndog ñēndzeg) two families having marriages one after another.

གཉེན་དུ་མཐུན་སྡེབས་ (ñēndu tū̃ndeb) shung. va. to get married.

གཉེན་དོན་ (ñēndön) marriage/ marital affairs; va.—སྒྲུབ་ to make a marriage arrangement.

གཉེན་དོན་བཙན་སྒྲིག (ñēndön dzɛ̄ndrig) forced marriage.

གཉེན་འདབ་ (ñēndəb) friends and relatives.

གཉེན་འདུན་ (ñēndün) sm. གཉེན་དུ་.

གཉེན་སྡེ་ (ñēnde) sm. གཉེན་ཕྱོགས་.

གཉེན་སྡེབ་ (ñēn deb) va. to marry.

གཉེན་པོ་ (ñēmbo) remedy, antidote, cure ¶ གནོད་འབུ་སོ་སོའི་གཉེན་པོ་སྐོར་ལ་འང་བརྟག་དཔྱད་བྱས་པ་རེད་ They did research on the remedies for various harmful bugs.

གཉེན་དཔང་ (ñēnbaŋ) shung. witness at a marriage contract, a guarantor for a matrimonial contract; va.—བྱེད་.

གཉེན་དཔོན་ (ñēnbön) person who leads/ heads the marriage ceremony.

གཉེན་ཕྱོགས་ (ñēnjɔɔ̀) relatives, kinsmen.

གཉེན་འཕྱོད་ (ñēndrɛɛ̀) visiting relatives; va.—ལ་འགྲོ་ to go to visit relatives.

གཉེན་བྱེད་ (ñēn ceè) va. to marry, to wed.

གཉེན་འབྲེལ་ (ñēndree) 1. relatives, kinsmen. 2. married couple. 3. marriage arrangement; va.—གཏོང་ to match make (a marriage).

གཉེན་འབྲེལ་གདོང་མཁན་ (ñēndree dōŋgɛn) matchmaker (for marriages).

གཉེན་སྦྲོར་བྱེད་མཁན་ (ñēndree ce̱èñɛn) sm. གཉེན་འབྲེལ་གཏོང་མཁན་.

གཉེན་མི་ (ñēndzɛn) sm. གཉེན་ཉེ་.

གཉེན་ཚན་ (ñēndzɛn) relatives, kinsmen.

གཉེན་མཚམས་གཅོད་ (ñēndzam jöö) va. to divorce.

གཉེན་འཚོལ་གྲོགས་རྟེན་ (ñēndzöö tro̱gden) seeking a friend to help/ sponsor/ advocate.

གཉེན་འཛིན་པའི་བར་བ་ (ñēndzimbɛ ba̱rwa) sm. གཉེན་དཔང་.

གཉེན་ཟླ་ (ñēnda) relatives, kinsmen.

གཉེན་ཡ་ (ñēnya) one's counterpart in a marriage.

གཉེན་ཡིག (ñēnyig) sm. གཉེན་གན་.

གཉེན་རིང་ (ñēnriŋ) a distant relative/ kinsman.

གཉེན་ལམ་འཛུགས་ (ñēnlam dzu̱ù) va. to establish marriage relations.

གཉེན་ལས་གཉེན་འཁོར་ (ñēnlɛ ñēngɔɔ) several families that are connected as kinsmen.

གཉེན་ལོག (ñēnlɔɔ) the marrying-in bride or groom visiting their natal family for the first time after getting married; va.—གཏོང་; —འགྲོ་.

གཉེན་ཤ་ (ñēnsha) marriage meat.

གཉེན་གཤིན་ (ñēnshin) sm. གཉེན་བཤེས་.

གཉེན་བཤེས་ (ñēnsheè) relatives, kinsmen.

གཉེན་སྲིད་ (ñēnseè) loyalty to one's kinsmen/ relatives; va.—བྱེད་.

གཉེན་སློག (ñēnlɔɔ) divorcing.

གཉེན་སློང་ (ñēnlɔŋ) asking for the hand in marriage of a bride (or groom).

གཉེན་བསྲིས་ (ñēnseè) sm. གཉེན་འབྲེལ་.

གཉེར་ (ñēr) 1. va. to manage, to operate/ run ༎ཁོས་ཟ་ཁང་འདི་གཉེར་གྱི་ཡོད་པ་རེད་ He manages the restaurant. 2. va. to work/ strive for, to pursue an aim ༎སྙན་གྲགས་མི་གཉེར་པ་ Not working for fame. 3. scowling (facially).

གཉེར་ཀ་ (ñērga) managing, supervising, running (a business); va.—གཏོད་ to commit sth. to sb.'s management, to entrust; va.—བྱེད་ to take care of, to manage.

གཉེར་སྐྱོང་ (ñērgyoŋ) sm. གཉེར་ཀ་.

གཉེར་ཁ་ (ñērga) sm. གཉེར་ཀ་.

གཉེར་ཆུང་ (ñērjuŋ) shung. a lesser official in the ཞོལ་པ་ལས་ཁུངས་.

གཉེར་གཉེར་ (ñērñēr) scowling, a threatening facial demeanor.

གཉེར་དུ་གཏད་ (ñērdu dɛ̄ɛ) va. to entrust to take care of/ look after/ protect/ guard ༎མི་དེ་ལ་མཛོད་ཁང་གཉེར་དུ་གཏད་པ་རེད་ That man was entrusted to take care of the storage house.

གཉེར་གདམས་ (ñērdam) instructing sb. to do or look after sth.; va.—བྱེད་ ༎འགོ་ཁྲིད་གུང་སེང་དུ་འགྲོ་སྐབས་ལས་རོགས་ལ་ལས་ཁུངས་ཀྱི་ལས་ཀ་གཉེར་གདམས་བྱས་པ་རེད་ When the boss went on vacation he instructed his assistant to look after the work in the office.

གཉེར་སྡོད་ (ñērdöö) shung. sm. གཞིས་སྡོད་.

གཉེར་པ་ (ñērba) steward, manager.

གཉེར་ཕྱག (ñēr caà) abbr. of གཉེར་པ་ and ཕྱག་མཛོད་.

གཉེར་ཕྱག་མཛོད་ (ñēr cāndzöö) abbr. of གཉེར་པ་ and ཕྱག་མཛོད་.

གཉེར་བྱང་གཏད་ (ñērjaŋ dɛ̄ɛ) va. to entrust to look after/ take care of/ protect/ guard.

གཉེར་བྱང་འཛིན་ (ñērjaŋ dzi̱n) va. to take responsibility for taking care/ looking after sth.

གཉེར་མ་ (ñērma) 1. wrinkles; vi.—འཁོར་ to get wrinkles; vi.—འཁུམ་ to get wrinkled (for clothes/ cloth). 2. ripples on water.

གཉེར་མ་ཅན་ (ñērmajɛn) wrinkled.

གཉེར་མེད་ (ñērmeè) not looked after/ cared for/ managed.

གཉེར་ཚང་ (ñērdzaŋ) storehouse.

གཉེར་ཚང་པ་ (ñērdzaŋba) storehouse-keeper.

གཉེར་ཚང་ལས་ཁུངས་ (ñērdzaŋ le̱ègu̱ŋ) a treasury/ office in the tt. government.

གཉེར་འཛིན་ (ñēndzin) shung. sm. གཉེར་པ་.

གཉེར་ཤིབ་ (ñērshib) small wrinkles.

གཉེར་གཟུགས་བྲག་རྡོ་ (ñērsug tra̱gdo) rhyolite.

གཉོག: p. **གཉགས་**; f. **གཉག**; imp. **གཉོགས་** (ñōg) 1. va. to chew. 2. va. to beat up/ thrash.

གཉོད་ (ñöö) arc. value, worth.

གཉོད་ཀ་ (ñööga) 1. strong. 2. sm. འཁོས་ཀ་.

གཉོད་ཀ་ཆུང་བ་ (ñööga cūŋwa) weak, feeble.

གཉོད་ཆུང་ (ñööjuŋ) sm. གཉོད་ཀ་ཆུང་བ་.

གཉོད་ཆུང་བ་ (ñööjuŋwa) sm. གཉོད་ཀ་ཆུང་བ་.

གཉོད་ཆུང་སྟོབས་ཞན་ (ñööjuŋ dōbshɛn) sm. གཉོད་ཆུང་.

གཉོད་ཆུང་ནུས་མེད་ (ñööjuŋ nü̱ümeè) sm. གཉོད་ཆུང་.

གཉོད་མེད་ (ñöömeè) sm. གཉོད་ཆུང་.

གཉོམ་ཆུང་ (ñōmjuŋ) 1. humble, modest ༎གོང་གསལ་གནས་ཚུལ་གཉོམ་ཆུང་གི་ཐོག་ནས་ཞུས་ (He) told the above story in a humble manner. 2. weak, not strong, not powerful.

མཉན་ཉེས་ (ñɛ̄ññeè) mishearing; vi.—ཤོར་ to mishear.

མཉན་པ་ (ñɛ̄mba) 1. boatman, ferryman 2. sometimes used as p. and f. ཉན་.

མཉན་དཔོན་ (ñɛ̄mbön) sm. མཉན་པ་.

མཉན་ཡོད་ (ñɛ̄nyöö) shung. Sravasti (a holy place in India).

མཉམ་ (ñām) 1. together (with), jointly ༎ལྷ་ས་བར་ཁོ་དང་མཉམ་དུ་ཕྱིན་པ་ཡིན་ I went together with him to Lhasa. 2. like, similar, same ༎ཁོ་དུས་མཉམ་དུ་སློབ་གྲྭར་ཡོང་པ་རེད་ He came to school at the same time. 3. (vb.1. + — + vb.2. + —) doing two verbal acts together ༎ཁོ་གཉིས་ཀྱིས་ལས་ཀ་ཚུགས་མཉམ་ཚར་མཉམ་བྱས་པ་རེད་ Those two started and finished the work together. 3. (— + vb.) a verbal act occurring together ༎ལྷ་ས་ནས་མཉམ་ཐོན་བྱས་པ་ཡིན་ (We) departed together from Lhasa.

མཉམ་སྐྱིད་མཉམ་སྡུག (ñāmgyiì ñāmduù) sharing good and bad times.

མཉམ་སྐྱིད་མཉམ་སྡོད་ (ñāmgyiì ñāmdöö) sm. མཉམ་སྐྱིད་མཉམ་སྡུག.

མཉམ་སྐྱེས་མཚེ་མ་ (ñāmgyeè tsēma) twins.

མཉམ་དཀྲོལ་ (ñāmdröö) musical instruments played in unison; symphony orchestra.

མཉམ་འཁུར་ (ñāmgur) bearing together, carrying together/ jointly; va.—བྱེད་ ༎ང་གཉིས་དཀའ་ངལ་མཉམ་འཁུར་བྱེད་ཀྱི་ཡོད་ We two are bearing hardship together. ༎ང་གཉིས་ལས་འགན་མཉམ་འཁུར་བྱེད་ཀྱི་ཡོད་ We are taking responsibility (for the work) jointly.

མཉམ་འཁེལ་ (ñāmgee) coincidentally occurring at the same time.

མཉམ་འཁྱིལ་ (ñə̄mgyii) vi. to get brought/ collected/ accumulated together.

མཉམ་འཁྱེར་ (ñāmgyer) taking/ carrying together (with oneself) ༎སྲིད་དམ་ཙ་ཆེག་མཉམ་འཁྱེར་གྱིས་ Taking the order with the regents seal. ༎ཁོང་བོད་དུ་ཡོང་སྐབས་སྐད་མེད་གློག་འཕྲིན་བརྒྱ་མཉམ་འཁྱེར་པ་རེད་ When he came to Tibet he took 100 watt wireless transmitters with him.

མཉམ་གྲགས་ (ñāmdrag) 1. with one voice/ opinion, being of the same viewpoint ༎གནད་དོན་དེའི་ཐོག་ཁོ་ཚོ་ཁ་མཉམ་གྲགས་རེད་བཞག They have the same viewpoint on that issue. 2. a resonator.

མཉམ་གྲོས་ (ñāmdröö) joint discussion; va.—བྱེད་ to talk/ discuss together.

མཉམ་དགའ་མཉམ་སྡུག (ñāmga ñāmduù) sm. མཉམ་སྐྱིད་མཉམ་སྡུག.

མཉམ་བགོ་ (ña̱mgo) dividing/ distributing equally; va.—བྱེད་.

མཉམ་བགོས་ (ñāmgöö) sm. མཉམ་བགོ་.

མཉམ་འགུལ་ (ñāmgüü) moving together; va.—བྱེད་ to move together.

མཉམ་འགྲན་ (ñāmdrɛn) competing together; va.—བྱེད་.

མཉམ་འགྲོ་ (ñāmdro) going together; va.—བྱེད་.

མཉམ་འགྲོགས་ (ñāmdrɔɔ) associating together; va.—བྱེད་.

མཉམ་རྒྱག (ñāmgyaà) playing doubles/ in pairs (e.g., tennis); va.—བྱེད་.

མཉམ་སྒྲིག (ñāmdrig) arranged/ prepared together or jointly; va.—བྱེད་ ༎མཉམ་སྒྲིག་གིས་འཕུར་སྐྱོད་ Flying in formation.

མཉམ་སྒྲིལ་ (ñəmdrii) sm. མཉམ་བསྒྲིལ་.

མཉམ་སྒྲུབ་ (ñəmdrub) cooperating to achieve sth; va.—བྱེད་.

མཉམ་སྒྲུབ་ཁང་ (ñəmdrubgaŋ) co-op, cooperative store or business.

མཉམ་སྒྲུབ་ཅན་ (ñəmdrubjɛn) cooperative.

མཉམ་སྒྲུབ་ཅན་དུ་འགྱུར་ (ñəmdrubjɛndu gyur) va. to cooperativize.

མཉམ་སྒྲོག (ñām drɔ̀ɔ) 1. many sounds together; va.—བྱེད་.

མཉམ་སྒྲོག་རོལ་ཆ་ (ñām drɔ̀ɔ rööja) sm. མཉམ་སྒྲོག་རོལ་དབྱངས་.

མཉམ་སྒྲོག་རོལ་དབྱངས་ (ñām drɔ̀ɔ rööyaŋ) orchestra.

མཉམ་སྒྲོག་རོལ་མོ་ (ñām drɔ̀ɔ röömo) sm. མཉམ་སྒྲོག་རོལ་དབྱངས་.

མཉམ་སྒྲོག་རོལ་མོ་ཚོགས་པ་ (ñām drɔ̀ɔ röömo tsōgba) orchestra.

མཉམ་སྒྲོས་ (ñāmdröö) sm. མཉམ་གྲོས་.

མཉམ་བསྒྲགས་ (ñāmdraà) sm. མཉམ་གཏོང་.

མཉམ་བསྒྲགས་ལེ་ཚན་ (ñāmdraà ledzɛn) མཉམ་གཏོང་ལེ་ཚན་.

མཉམ་བསྒྲིལ་ (ñāmdrii) intertwined, combined, joined, merged; va.—བྱེད་; —གཏོང་.

མཉམ་གཅིག་འགྲོ་སྡོད་ (ñāmjig drodöö) shung. staying and going together, living together ༎དོགས་ཅན་བུད་མེད་དང་མཉམ་གཅིག་འགྲོ་སྡོད་སོགས་ He was staying and going together with a suspicious woman.

མཉམ་ལྗོགས་ (ñāmjɔ̀ɔ) doing two things at the same time/ simultaneously/ together ༎ཁོང་གིས་ཞིབ་འཇུག་དང་སློབ་ཁྲིད་མཉམ་ལྗོགས་བྱེད་ཀྱི་ཡོད་པ་རེད་ He does research and teaching at the same time.

མཉམ་འཇོག (ñāmjɔ̀ɔ) 1. leaving sth. together ༎བཀྲིས་དང་ཉི་མ་གཉིས་ལས་ཀ་མཉམ་འཇོག་བྱས་བཞག Tashi and Nyima left their work together. ༎སློབ་གྲྭ་བ་དེ་གཉིས་ཀྱི་ཅ་ལག་སྒམ་གཅིག་ནང་མཉམ་འཇོག་བྱས་པ་རེད་ The two students left their things together in one box. 2. signing jointly ༎ཆིངས་ཡིག་མཉམ་འཇོག་བྱེད་མཁན་ The one who jointly signed the treaty (with us).

མཉམ་གཉེར་ (ñāmñer) joint stock, cooperatively/ collectively/ jointly managing; va.—བྱེད་ ༎མི་ཚང་དེ་གཉིས་ཀྱིས་བཟོ་གྲྭ་མཉམ་གཉེར་བྱས་པ་རེད་ The two families jointly managed the factory.

མཉམ་གཏོང་ (ñāmdoŋ) sth. sent or done together/ jointly.

མཉམ་གཏོང་སྤྲོ་སྐྱིད་ (ñāmdoŋ drōgyii) picnicking/ partying/ having fun together; va.—གཏོང་.

མཉམ་གཏོང་རོལ་དབྱངས་ (ñāmdoŋ rööyaŋ) sm. མཉམ་གཏོང་རོལ་མོ་.

མཉམ་གཏོང་རོལ་མོ་ (ñāmdoŋ röömo) symphony ༎མཉམ་གཏོང་རོལ་མོ་དགུ་པ་ The 9th symphony.

མཉམ་གཏོང་ལེ་ཚན་ (ñāmdoŋ ledzɛn) an (symphony) orchestra.

མཉམ་མཐུན་ (ñāmdün) mutual agreement, unanimity.

མཉམ་འཐབ་ (ñāmdəb) joint struggle, joint fight; va.—བྱེད་.

མཉམ་དུ་ (ñəmdu) together ༎ཁོ་གཉིས་མཉམ་དུ་ཕྱིན་པ་རེད་ Those two went together.

མཉམ་དུ་སྒྲིག (ñəmdu drig) va. to arrange/ list/ place side by side (together).

མཉམ་དུ་སྒྲིལ་ (ñəmdu drii) va. to combine/ connect/ join/ unite together.

མཉམ་དུ་སྡོད་ (ñəmdu döö) 1. va. to live/ stay together. 2. va. to have intercourse.

མཉམ་དུ་སྤེལ་ (ñəmdu bēl) va. to promote/ develop/ spread together.

མཉམ་དུ་ཡར་འགྲོ་དང་མཉམ་དུ་ཕྱིར་བཤོལ་ (ñəmdu yardro daŋ ñāmdu cīīshöö) having the same viewpoint/ attitude/ position [Lit. going forward together, withdrawing together].

མཉམ་དུ་གཞིབ་ (ñəmdu shīb) sm. མཉམ་འགྲོགས་.

མཉམ་བདག (ñāmdaà) shung. 1. jointly owning/ possessing ༎ས་ཁང་མཉམ་བདག་བྱ་རྒྱུའི་སྐོར་གན་རྒྱར་ཞལ་གསལ་འཁོད་པ་ Regarding the joint possession of land and house, it was clearly mentioned in the contract. 2. public/ collective ownership.

མཉམ་འདུར་ (ñamdur) shung. without exemption ༎ལམ་ཐོག་ས་ཚིགས་ལ་གཞུང་སྐྱེར་ཆོས་གསུམ་ཀར་ཀྱང་མཉམ་འདུར་དང་ Corvee transportation at station posts must be performed without exemption by taxpayers, aristocrats, and monasteries.

མཉམ་འདུས་ (ñāmdüü) compound, composite, complex ༎མཉམ་འདུས་དབྱངས་ཡིག Compound vowel ༎མཉམ་འདུས་རྒྱུ་ཆས་ Composite material.

མཉམ་དོར་ (ñamdɔɔ) va. to abandon together.

མཉམ་འདྲེས་ (ñāmdreè) mixing together, incorporating, merging; va.—བྱེད་ ༎རྩམ་པ་འདི་སྲན་མ་དང་འབྲུ་མཉམ་འདྲེས་རེད་ This རྩམ་པ་ is a mixture of barley and lentil.

མཉམ་སྡེབ་ (ñāmdeb) 1. collectivization, cooperation. ༎མཉམ་སྡེབ་གཞིས་ཀ Collective farm. 2. merger.

མཉམ་སྡེབ་ཀྱིས་ (ñāmdebgi) collectively, jointly.

མཉམ་སྡེབ་ཁེ་ལས་ (ñāmdeb kēlɛɛ̀) cooperative enterprise.

མཉམ་སྡེབ་རིང་ལུགས་ (ñāmdeb riŋluù) collectivism.

མཉམ་སྡེབ་ལ་དབང་བ་ (ñāmdebla wāŋwa) collectively owned/ possessed.

མཉམ་བསྡུར་ (ñāmdur) comparing side by side; va.—བྱེད་.

མཉམ་བསྡུར་མདངས་ཉམས་ (ñəmdur daŋñam) sm. མཉམ་བསྡུར་ཞན་མཚོན་.

མཉམ་བསྡུར་ཞན་མཚོན་ (ñəmdur sheŋŋön) showing/ finding which one of sth. is bad by comparing (two or more things) together.

མཉམ་བསྡུས་སྦྱོང་བརྡར་ (ñāmdüü joŋdar) collective training.

མཉམ་བསྡོམས་ (ñāmdom) combined, composite.

མཉམ་གནས་ (ñāmnɛɛ̀) coexistence; va.—བྱེད་ ༎ཞི་བདེ་མཉམ་གནས་ Peaceful coexistence.

མཉམ་གནས་མཉམ་འཇིག (ñāmnɛɛ̀ ñāmjig) living and dying together.

མཉམ་པ་ (ñāmba) 1. equal, equivalent, same ༎ཁོང་ལ་གཟུགས་པོ་ཆེ་ཆུང་མཉམ་པའི་ཕྲུ་གུ་གཉིས་འདུག He has two children of the same height. 2. sm. སྙོམ་པ་. 3. appropriate, fitting.

མཉམ་པ་ཆ་སྒྲིག (ñāmba cādrig) well-matched.

མཉམ་པ་ཉིད་ (ñāmbañii) sm. མཉམ་ཉིད་.

མཉམ་པོར་ (ñāmbor) together ༎ང་གཉིས་མཉམ་པོར་ཕྱིན་པ་ཡིན་ We went together.

མཉམ་སྤྲོ་ (ñāmdro) enjoying or having fun together; va.—བྱེད་; —གཏོང་ to get together (for enjoyment/ fun), to gather for amusement.

མཉམ་སྤྲོ་ཁང་ (ñāmdrogaŋ) club for parties, etc.

མཉམ་སྤྲོ་དགོང་ཚོགས་ (ñāmdro goŋdzɔɔ̀) evening party.

མཉམ་སྤྲོ་ཚོགས་འདུ་ (ñāmdro tsōndu) sm. མཉམ་གཏོང་སྤྲོ་སྐྱིད་.

མཉམ་སྤྲོའི་བྱེད་སྒོ་ (ñāmdrö cēgo) festive activities, activities involved with getting together for enjoyment.

མཉམ་སྤྲོའི་ཚོགས་འཛོམས་ (ñāmdrö tsōŋdzom) sm. མཉམ་གཏོང་སྤྲོ་སྐྱིད་.

མཉམ་བྱེད་ (ñām cēe) doing sth. at the same time, using/ doing together ༎ང་གཉིས་རྒྱ་གར་ལ་མཉམ་འགྲོ་བྱས་པ་ཡིན་ We went at the same time.

མཉམ་བྱུང་ནད་རིགས་ (ñāmjuŋ neèrig) a minor sickness that follows a major illness.

མཉམ་བྲལ་ (ñāmdrɛɛ) sm. མཉམ་མེད་.

མཉམ་འབྲེལ་ (ñāmdree) 1. united, joint, combined, allied; va.—བྱེད་ to do jointly/ allied/ combined ༎དབྱིན་ཇི་རི་པིན་ཕ་རན་སི་སོགས་བཙན་རྒྱལ་རིང་ལུགས་རྣམས་མཉམ་འབྲེལ་བྱས་པ་རེད་ Imperialists such as England, Japan and France acted jointly. 2. abbr. of མཉམ་འབྲེལ་ཤོག་ཁ་.

མཉམ་འབྲེལ་ཁེ་ལས་ (ñāmdree kēlεὲ) joint enterprise.

མཉམ་འབྲེལ་གྱིས་ (ñāmdreegi) jointly ¶ མཉམ་འབྲེལ་གྱིས་མིང་ཐོ་བཏོན་པ་རེད་ (They) made nominations jointly.

མཉམ་འབྲེལ་གྱེན་ལོག (ñāmdree gyēnlɔ̀ɔ) the name of the two Red Guard groups in Tibet during the Cultural Revolution (the Grand Alliance and the Rebels).

མཉམ་འབྲེལ་གྲོགས་རམ་ (ñāmdree drɔgram) cooperative assistance/ help, joint help; va.—བྱེད་.

མཉམ་འབྲེལ་གྲོས་ཚོགས་ (ñāmdree trö̀ödzoò) joint conference/ meeting; va.—བྱེད་.

མཉམ་འབྲེལ་དགའ་སྟོན་ (ñāmdree gadön) joint celebration/ banquet; va.—བྱེད་.

མཉམ་འབྲེལ་འགོག་སྲུང་ (ñāmdree gɔgsuŋ) joint defense; va.—བྱེད་.

མཉམ་འབྲེལ་རྒྱང་བསྒྲགས་ (ñāmdree gyaŋsuŋ) broadcasting (over a radio/ T.V.) network.

མཉམ་འབྲེལ་རྒྱལ་ཚོགས་ (ñāmdree gyεεtsoò) the United Nations.

མཉམ་འབྲེལ་རྒྱལ་ཚོགས་ཀྱི་སྐྱབས་བཅོལ་བའི་ལས་དོན་ཁང་ (ñāmdree gyεεtsoògi gyə̄bjüüwε lεὲdöngaŋ) United Nations High Commissioner for Refugees (UNHCR).

མཉམ་འབྲེལ་རྒྱལ་ཚོགས་ཀྱི་འགྲོ་བ་མིའི་ཐོབ་ཐང་གི་ཚོགས་ཆུང་ (ñāmdree gyεεtsoògi drowε mii tōbdaŋ tsōgjuŋ) United Nations Subcommittee on Human Rights.

མཉམ་འབྲེལ་རྒྱལ་ཚོགས་ཀྱི་བདེ་འཇགས་ལས་འཛིན་ལྷན་ཚོགས་ (ñāmdree gyεεtsoògi denjaà lεndzin lhēndzoò) Security Council of the United Nations.

མཉམ་འབྲེལ་རྒྱལ་ཚོགས་ཀྱི་བྱིས་པའི་ཐེབས་རྩ་ (ñāmdree gyεεtsoògi cibε tēbdza) United Nations Children's Fund (UNICEF).

མཉམ་འབྲེལ་རྒྱལ་ཚོགས་ཀྱི་རྩ་ཁྲིམས་ (ñāmdree gyεεtsoògi dzə̄drim) the Charter of the United Nations.

མཉམ་འབྲེལ་རྒྱལ་ཚོགས་ཀྱི་ཤེས་རིག་དང་རིག་གཞུང་ཚན་རིག་སྡེ་ཚན་ (ñāmdree gyεεtsoògi shēèriidaŋ rigshuŋ tsēnrii dedzεn) sm. མཉམ་འབྲེལ་རྒྱལ་ཚོགས་ཀྱི་སློབ་གསོ་ཚན་རིག་རིག་གནས་ཀྱི་རྩ་འཛུགས་.

མཉམ་འབྲེལ་རྒྱལ་ཚོགས་ཀྱི་སློབ་གསོ་ཚན་རིག་རིག་གནས་ཀྱི་རྩ་འཛུགས་ (ñāmdree gyεεtsoògi lōbso cēnrig rīignεὲgi dzə̄ndzuù) United Nations Educational, Scientific and Cultural Organization (UNESCO).

མཉམ་འབྲེལ་བསྒྲགས་གཏམ་ (ñāmdree dragdam) joint declaration.

མཉམ་འབྲེལ་རྔ་བསྡུ་འཁོར་ལོ་ (ñāmdree ŋādu kɔ̄ɔlo) combine harvesting machine.

མཉམ་འབྲེལ་དཔལ་འབྱོར་ (ñāmdree bε̄njɔɔ) cooperative economy.

མཉམ་འབྲེལ་སྤྱི་བསྒྲགས་ (ñāmdree jīdraà) joint communique.

མཉམ་འབྲེལ་ཕུང་པོ་ (ñāmdree pūŋbo) a united whole/ mass/ association.

མཉམ་འབྲེལ་དམག་དཔུང་ (ñāmdree mə̄gbuŋ) allied or combined forces/ troops; united/ allied army.

མཉམ་འབྲེལ་སྨན་བཅོས་ཁང་ (ñāmdree mε̄njöögaŋ) joint clinic.

མཉམ་འབྲེལ་ཚོགས་པ་ (ñāmdree tsōgba) 1. federation, congress ¶ རྒྱལ་ཡོངས་དམངས་གཙོའི་བུད་མེད་མཉམ་འབྲེལ་ All-China Federation of Democratic Women. 2. a collective/ cooperative organization.

མཉམ་འབྲེལ་ཚོང་ཁང་ (ñāmdree tsōŋgaŋ) a cooperative store.

མཉམ་འབྲེལ་གཞུང་ (ñāmdree shuŋ) sm. མཉམ་འབྲེལ་སྲིད་གཞུང་.

མཉམ་འབྲེལ་རུ་ཁག (ñāmdree rugaà) combined team/ unit/ brigade; wing (of an air force).

མཉམ་འབྲེལ་རོགས་རམ་ (ñāmdree rɔ̀ɔram) sm. མཉམ་འབྲེལ་གྲོགས་རམ་.

མཉམ་འབྲེལ་ལས་སྣོན་བཟོ་གྲྭ (ñāmdree lεὲnön sodra) combined processing factory.

མཉམ་འབྲེལ་ཤོག་ཁ (ñāmdree shɔ̄ɔga) The Alliance (the name of one of the Red Guard Groups in Tibet during the Cultural Revolution).

མཉམ་འབྲེལ་གསལ་བསྒྲགས་ (ñāmdree sεε̄draà) joint statement/ communique.

མཉམ་འབྲེལ་སྲིད་གཞུང་ (ñāmdree sīishuŋ) coalition government.

མཉམ་འབྲེལ་ལྷན་ཚོགས་ (ñāmdree lhēndzoò) sm. མཉམ་འབྲེལ་ཚོགས་པ་.

མཉམ་སྦྲེལ་ (ñāmdree) sm. མཉམ་འབྲེལ་.

མཉམ་སྦྲེལ་གྲོས་ཚོགས་ (ñāmdree trö̀ödzoò) joint meeting.

མཉམ་སྦྲེལ་རྒྱལ་ཚོགས་ (ñāmdree gyεὲdzoò) sm. མཉམ་འབྲེལ་རྒྱལ་ཚོགས་.

མཉམ་མེད་ (ñāmmeè) unequaled, exceptional, matchless, incomparable.

མཉམ་མེད་ཟས་གཙང་གི་སྲས་པོ་ (ñāmmeè sεὲdzaŋgi sεὲbo) the Buddha.

མཉམ་མོལ་ (ñāmmöö) shung. va. to discuss together ¶ ད་ཆ་འབྱུང་རྐྱེན་ཇི་བྱུང་མཉམ་མོལ་གྱི་རྩད་གཅོད་བྱ་རྒྱུ་ Now we should discuss this together and try to find out what was the cause (of that event).

མཉམ་ཚོགས་ (ñāmdzoò) sm. མཉམ་འབྲེལ་ཚོགས་པ་.

མཉམ་ཚོགས་ཀྱི་སྤྱི་ཁང་ (ñāmdzoògi jīgaŋ) shung. public place for gathering.

མཉམ་ཚོང་ (ñāmdzoŋ) 1. cooperative commerce. 2. cooperative store.

མཉམ་ཚོང་ཁང་ (ñāmdzoŋgaŋ) sm. མཉམ་ཚོང་, 2.

མཉམ་འཚོ་བྱེད་ (ñāmdzo cee) va. to live together as a couple.

མཉམ་འཛོམས་ (ñāmdzom) congregating, gathering, meeting together; va.—བྱེད་ ¶ གདན་ས་གསུམ་གྱི་མཁན་འཐུས་མཉམ་འཛོམས་བྱས་འདུག The abbots and representatives of the three Monastic Seats have met together.

མཉམ་འཛོམས་ཚོགས་འདུ་ (ñāmdzom tsōndu) conference, general meeting, congress.

མཉམ་ཞུགས་ (ñāmshuù) joint participation; va.—བྱེད་.

མཉམ་གཞས་ (ñāmshεὲ) chorus, many people singing together; va.—གཏོང་.

མཉམ་བཞད་ཆེན་པོ་ (ñāmshεὲ cēmbo) many (flowers) blooming together (conveys many views being expressed).

མཉམ་བཞེས་ (ñāmshεὲ) sm. མཉམ་ལེན་.

མཉམ་ཟ་ (ñāmsa) eating together; va.—བྱེད་.

མཉམ་ཟ་མཉམ་འཐུང་ (ñāmsa) sm. མཉམ་ཟ་ [Lit. eating together and drinking together].

མཉམ་རུབ་ (ñəmrub) 1. working together, united effort, cooperating together; va.—བྱེད་ ¶ མཉམ་རུབ་མེད་ཙང་ Because there was no unity. 2. ganging up on sb; va.—རྒྱག.

མཉམ་རོགས་ (ñāmrɔ̀ɔ) sm. མཉམ་འབྲེལ་རོགས་རམ་.

མཉམ་ལས་ (ñāmlεὲ) cooperation (in work); va.—བྱེད་ to cooperate ¶ རྒྱལ་ཁབ་གཉིས་པོས་མཉམ་ལས་དམ་ཟབ་བྱས་པ་རེད་ The two countries cooperated closely.

མཉམ་ལས་ཁང་ (ñāmlεὲgaŋ) a co-op, cooperative ¶ ཞིང་ལས་ཐོན་སྐྱེད་མཉམ་ལས་ཁང་ Agricultural producer's co-op.

མཉམ་ལས་ཅན་ (ñāmlεὲjεn) cooperative; vi.—དུ་འགྱུར་ to become cooperativized, to become a co-op; va.—དུ་སྒྱུར་ to cooperativize.

མཉམ་ལས་བདག་གཉེར་ (ñāmlεὲ daŋñer) jointly operated, cooperative management.

མཉམ་ལས་དཔལ་འབྱོར་ (ñāmlεὲ bε̄njɔɔ) collective economy.

མཉམ་ལས་སྨན་བཅོས་ (ñāmlεὲ mε̄njöö) cooperative medical services.

མཉམ་ལས་ཚོགས་པ་ (ñāmlεὲ tsōgba) cooperative group/ society.

མཉམ་ལས་ཚོང་ཁང་ (ñāmlεὲ tsōŋgaŋ) cooperative

store, co-op store.

མཉམ་ཤི་མཉམ་གསོན་ (ñāmshi ñāmsön) shaaring good and bad together until one dies [Lit. die together, live together].

མཉམ་གཤིབ་ (ñə̄mshib) 1. side by side ། དེ་གཉིས་མཉམ་གཤིབ་ཏུ་བཞག་པ་རེད་ (They) put the two side by side. 2. living together, being closely associated with sb.; va.—བྱེད་ to live together, to closely associate with ། ཁོ་དང་མཉམ་གཤིབ་བྱེད་མ་མྱོང་ (I) have never associated with him closely.

མཉམ་གཤིབ་ཀྱིས་ (ñə̄mshibgi) sm. དཔུང་པ་མཉམ་གཤིབ་.

མཉམ་གཤིབ་མཉམ་རྒྱུད་ (ñə̄mshib ñāmgyöö) running neck and neck, equally matched.

མཉམ་གཤིབ་ཐིག་ (ñə̄mshib tīg) parallel lines.

མཉམ་གཤིབ་མཐའ་བཞི་མ་ (ñə̄mshib tāshimə) parallelogram.

མཉམ་གཤིབ་ལས་སྒྲུབ་ (ñə̄mshib lɛ̱ɛ̀drub) parallel operation.

མཉམ་གཤིབས་ (ñə̄mshib) sm. མཉམ་གཤིབ་.

མཉམ་གསུམ་ (ñāmsum) "the three togethers" (this political slogan conveys that cadres who go to the villages must do three things together with the peasants: live together, eat together, work together).

མཉམ་གསོན་མཉམ་ཤི་ (ñāmsön ñāmshi) sm. མཉམ་ཤི་མཉམ་གསོན་.

མཉམ་སྲུང་ (ñə̄msuŋ) joint defense.

མཉམ་བསྲེ་ (ñāmse) sm. མཉམ་བསྲེས་.

མཉམ་བསྲེས་ (ñāmseè) mixing, compounding, alloying; va.—བྱེད་.

མཉམ་བསྲེས་ངར་ལྕགས་ (ñāmseè ŋarjaà) alloyed steel.

མཉམ་བསྲེས་ལྕགས་རིགས་ (ñāmseè jāgrig) metal alloys, alloyed metals.

མཉམ་བསྲེས་གཟན་ཆས་ (ñāmseè sɛnjɛɛ̀) mixed feed/ fodder.

མཉམ་བསྲེས་ལུད་རྫས་ (ñāmsɛɛ̀ lüüdzɛɛ̀) mixed fertilizers.

མཉམ་ཚོང་ (ñāmdzoŋ) co-operative store.

མཉམ་འཛོམས་ (ñāmdzom) joint, jointly ། མཉམ་འཛོམས་འདྲི་གཅོད་ Joint investigation.

མཉམ་འཛོམས་འཕྲབ་སྟོན་ (ñāmdzom trə̄bdön) joint festival/ celebration.

མཉམ་འཛོམས་གྲོས་མོལ་ (ñāmdzom tröömöö) joint conversation.

མཉམ་འཛོམས་འདྲི་གཅོད་ (ñāmdzom drijöö) joint investigation.

མཉའ་སེ་ཀོ་སེ་ (ñāse gōse) 1. being a nuisance, being bothersome; va.—བྱེད་. 2. fussy.

མཉལ་ (ñɛ̄ɛ) sm.* མནལ་.

མཉེ་ (ñē) f. of མཉེད་.

མཉེད་: p. མཉེས་; f. མཉེ་; imp. མཉེས་ (ñēè) va. to tan, to soften by rubbing, to knead.

མཉེད་གྲི་ (ñēèdri) tanning knife; knife used in tanning skins.

མཉེད་འཕུར་ (ñēèbur) 1. massaging; va.—བྱེད་; —གཏོང་ to massage. 2. bothering one's parents (usu. refers to kids).

མཉེན་ལྗུག་ (ñēnjuù) sm. མཉེན་པ་.

མཉེན་ཆ་དོད་པོ་ (ñēnja töobo) flexible.

མཉེན་ལྡེམ་ (ñēndem) flexible/ pliable and swaying.

མཉེན་པ་ (ñēmba) pliable, flexible, supple, soft.

མཉེན་པའི་ཆུ་ (ñēmbɛ cū) soft water.

མཉེན་པོ་ (ñēmbo) 1. pliable, flexible, supple, soft. (for skins, leather). 2. tender (for meat).

མཉེན་འབོལ་ (ñēmböö) a cushion.

མཉེན་རྩལ་ལུས་སྦྱོང་ (ñēndzɛɛ lüüjoŋ) calisthenics, gymnastic exercises.

མཉེན་ལུས་སྲོག་ཆགས་ (ñēnlüü sōgjaà) mollusks.

མཉེན་ཤིང་ (ñēnshiŋ) 1. soft wood. 2. cork.

མཉེལ་ (ñēē) vi. to be or get tired/ fatigued (h.) ། ཁོང་སྐུ་མཉེལ་བཞག He got tired.

མཉེས་ (ñēè) 1. p. of མཉེད་ 2. vi. to be pleased, happy, glad; to like ། ཁོང་ཐུགས་རབ་ཏུ་གཉེས་ཏེ་གསུང་གཞས་གནང་གི་འདུག He is extremely happy and is singing a song. ། ཁོང་བཞེས་རག་ལ་མཉེས་ཀྱི་མ་རེད་ He doesn't like liquor.

མཉེས་དག (ñēèdaà) "bottoms up" (used as a toast) (h.); va.—གནང་; va.—ཞུ་.

མཉེས་སྣང་ (ñēènaŋ) an expression/ appearance of being pleased or glad or liking.

མཉེས་པོ་ (ñēèbo) 1. liking, being fond of (h.) ། བླ་མ་བ་འདི་སྤྱན་གཟིགས་ལ་མཉེས་པོ་ཡོད་པ་རེད་ The lama is fond of pets. 2. glad, joyful, happy, merry ། ལས་འགན་ལེགས་གྲུབ་བྱུང་ཙང་གོང་རིམ་ཚང་མ་མཉེས་པོ་བྱུང་སོང་ Because of the good work that was accomplished, all the people in authority were happy.

མཉེས་པོ་གནང་ (ñēèbo nāŋ) 1. vi. to be pleased, to like (h.). ། ཁོང་སྐུ་རྩེད་ལ་མཉེས་པོ་གནང་གི་འདུག He likes games. 2. idiom. to enjoy ། ཞལ་ལག་གཉེས་པོ་གནང་རོགས་གནང་ Enjoy the food (this phrase is said by the host to the guest).

མཉེས་ཚོར་ (ñēèdzɔr) joy, pleasure ། མཉེས་ཚོར་ཆེན་པོས་དགའ་བསུ་ཞུས་གནང་བ་རེད་ (They) welcomed (them) with great happiness.

མཉེས་ལོག (ñēè lɔ̱ɔ̀) vi. to be tired of sth., to be bored.

མཉེས་གཤིན་ (ñēèshin) a calm/ peaceful/ kind person.

རྙ་: p. བརྙས་; f. བརྙ་; imp. རྙོས་ (ñā) 1. to bully. 2. va. to lend, to borrow.

རྙ་ལོ་ (ñālo) sm. སྙ་ལོ་.

རྙང་ (ñāŋ) vi. to have diarrhea.

རྙང་རྙང་ (ñāŋ ñāŋ) vi. to have diarrhea.

རྙང་རྙིང་ (ñāŋñīŋ) old, tattered, decrepit things (clothes, etc.).

རྙང་ནད་ (ñāŋnɛɛ̀) a disease characterized by diarrhea.

རྙང་མ་ (ñāŋma) very loose diarrhea-like excrement; vi.—གཏོང་ to pass very loose stool; vi.—ཤོར་ to involuntarily pass very loose stool.

རྙད་ (ñɛ̄ɛ) va. use as pretext/ excuse for.

རྙན་ (ñɛ̄n) va. to lend.

རྙབ་ (ñə̄b) vi. to reach (e.g., with an extended hand).

རྙབ་རྙབ་ (ñə̄nñə̄b) sm. རྙབ་.

རྙབ་རྙིབ་ (ñə̄bñib) abbr. of རྙབ་བེ་རྙིབ་བེ་.

རྙབ་བེ་རྙིབ་བེ་ (ñə̄bi ñībi) 1. withered, decayed (flowers and fruits). 2. weak and feeble (for people).

རྙི་ (ñī) a trap/ snare; va.—འཛུགས་ to set a trap/ snare; va.—རྒྱག to trap, to snare; va.—འགྲིམ་; —རྙོང་ to set out a series of traps; vi.—ཐེབས་ to fall/ get caught in a trap.

རྙི་རྒྱ་ (ñīgya) sm. རྙི་རྭ་.

རྙི་ཐག (ñīdaà) string or rope used in a trap/ snare.

རྙི་ཐིག (ñīdig) sm. རྙི་ཐག.

རྙི་དོང་ (ñīdoŋ) a trap, snare (dug into the ground).

རྙི་མདེལ་ (ñīndee) the part of a trap/ snare that is a stick.

རྙི་ཞགས་ (ñīshaà) a snare/ trap made of rope.

རྙི་རྭ་ (ñīrə) trap made from the horns of animals.

རྙི་ཤིང་ (ñīshiŋ) sm. རྙི་མདེལ་.

རྙིང་ (ñīŋ) abbr. of རྙིང་པ་ ། ལུགས་སྲོལ་གསར་རྙིང་ Old and new customs.

རྙིང་ཁུངས་ (ñīŋguŋ) those whose origin is old, the older ones ། དམག་སྒར་རྙིང་ཁུངས་ཁག The older regiments.

རྙིང་གྲས་ (ñīŋdrɛɛ̀) older ones, old types.

རྙིང་དགོན་སྐྱ་འགྱུར་ (ñīŋgön gyāgyur) shung. Nyingma monasteries that had been converted into Sakya monasteries ། གདན་ཚིགས་སུ་ཕུ་དཀར་དགོན་ཟེར་བ་རྙིང་དགོན་སྐྱ་འགྱུར་གྲས་ཀྱི་དགོན་རོ་ས་ཡུལ་ཆོས་སྡེར་གནང་བ་ In the land tenure document the Nyingma Pukar Monastery was converted to a Sakya Monastery and possession of it was granted to Chode Monastery.

རྙིང་འགྱུར་ཚབ་དངུལ་ (ñīŋgyur tsə̄bŋüü) depreciation

funds.

ཉིང་ཅིང་རུལ་བ་ (ñīŋjiŋ rü̱üwa) old and rotten.

ཉིང་ཆེ་དཀའ་གསུམ་ (ñīŋ cē gā sūm) old, big and difficult (problems that have existed for a long time, that have a major impact and that cannot be solved easily).

ཉིང་རྗེ་ (ñīŋje) compassion ¶ ཉིང་རྗེ་ཚད་མེད་ Boundless/ immeasurable compassion.

ཉིང་རྗེ་ཚད་མེད་ (ñīŋje tsɛ̀ɛ̀meè) immeasurable/ boundless compassion.

ཉིང་ཆོས་ (ñīŋjöö) the Nyingma sect of Tibetan Buddhism.

ཉིང་གཏོར་གསར་འཛུགས་ (ñīŋdɔɔ sār dzṵù) destroy the old and establish the new (a political slogan during the Cultural Revolution).

ཉིང་དོར་གསར་འཛུགས་ (ñīŋdɔɔ sār dzṵù) sm. ཉིང་གཏོར་གསར་འཛུགས་.

ཉིང་དོར་གསར་ལེན་ (ñīŋdɔɔ sār le̱n) throw out the old and accept the new (a political slogan during the Cultural Revolution).

ཉིང་དྲན་ (ñiŋdrɛn) vi. to recall/ recollect/ remember past times or old acquaintances.

ཉིང་དྲི་ (ñīŋdri) smell of sth. old/ rotten/ putrid; vi.—ཁ་ to smell the smell of sth. old/ rotten/ putrid.

ཉིང་བསྟུན་བེད་སྤྱོད་ (ñīŋdün pe̱èjöö) doing things the old way.

ཉིང་པ་ (ñīŋbə) old ¶ ཁང་པ་ཉིང་པ་ An old house.

ཉིང་པ་ཉིང་རྒྱང་ (ñīŋbə ñīŋgyaŋ) very old.

ཉིང་པ་ཉིང་ནག (ñīŋbə ñīŋnaà) very old.

ཉིང་པ་བཞི་ (ñīŋbə shi̱) the four "olds": old thoughts, old customs, old culture, old habits (a slogan during the Cultural Revolution).

ཉིང་ཕུད་གསར་སྐྲུན་ (ñīŋbüü sārdrün) weed through the old and bring forth the new (a political slogan).

ཉིང་ཕུད་གསར་འདོན་ (ñīŋbüü sārdön) throw out old and bring forth the new (a political slogan).

ཉིང་ཕུད་གསར་འབྱུང་ (ñīŋbüü sārjuŋ) sm. ཉིང་ཕུད་གསར་འདོན་.

ཉིང་འབུད་གསར་སྡུད་ (ñīŋbüü sārdüù) throw out the old and collect the new (a political slogan that in Chinese originally said: exhale the old and inhale the new).

ཉིང་དབྱུག་གསར་ལེན་ (ñīŋyuù sārlen) sm. ཉིང་གཏོར་གསར་འཛུགས་.

ཉིང་མ་ (ñīŋmə) 1. ancient, old. 2. name of the "old" sect in Tibetan Buddhism. 3. antique.

ཉིང་མ་པ་ (ñīŋməbə) a follower of the ཉིང་མ་ sect.

ཉིང་ཚབ་གསར་མཐུད་ (ñīŋdzəb sērdüù) the new replacing the old.

ཉིང་ཚད་ (ñīŋdzɛɛ̀) an old infection/ disease.

ཉིང་ཞེན་ (ñīŋshɛn) conservatism; va.—བྱེད་ to be conservative, to like the old ways. ¶ ཉིང་ཞེན་བསམ་པ་ Conservative views.

ཉིང་ཞེན་ཆེན་པོ་ (ñīŋshɛn cēmbo) very conservative, liking the old ways deeply.

ཉིང་ཞེན་པ་ (ñīŋshɛnbə) a conservative person, a person who likes the old ways.

ཉིང་ཞེན་བག་ཁུམ་ (ñīŋshɛn pa̱ggum) sm. ཉིང་ཞེན་.

ཉིང་ཞེན་ཚ་པོ་ (ñīŋshɛn tsābo) sm. ཉིང་ཞེན་ཆེན་པོ་.

ཉིང་ཞེན་རིང་ལུགས་ (ñīŋshɛn ri̱ŋluù) conservatism.

ཉིང་རིགས་ (ñīŋrii) antiques, old things.

ཉིང་རིགས་བདག་གཉེར་ཁང་ (ñīŋrii da̱gñɛrgaŋ) museum.

ཉིང་རུལ་ (ñīŋrüü) old and rotten/ decayed.

ཉིང་ལ་གོག་པ་ (ñīŋlə go̱gba) old and decrepit/ shabby.

ཉིང་ལུགས་ (ñīŋluù) 1. old-fashioned, old style, obsolete. 2. the Nyingma tradition.

ཉིང་ཤུལ་ (ñīŋshüü) relics.

ཉིང་སྲུང་ (ñīŋsuŋ) defending the old, conservative; va.—བྱེད་.

ཉིང་སྲུང་རིང་ལུགས་ (ñīŋsuŋ ri̱ŋluù) sm. ཉིང་ཞེན་རིང་ལུགས་.

ཉིང་སྲོལ་ (ñīŋsöö) old ways/ customs, conservative.

ཉིང་སྲོལ་དགའ་ཞེན་ (ñīŋsöö ga̱shɛn) being partial to old ways/ customs, being conservative.

ཉིང་གསོའི་རིང་ལུགས་ (ñīŋsö ri̱ŋluù) the doctrine or principle of reintroducing/ restoring old customs and habits.

ཉིང་ཧྲུལ་ (ñīŋhrüü) old and tattered/ broken/ dilapidated, old and shabby.

ཉིངས་པ་ (ñīŋbə) old, worn out.

ཉིངས་ཚད་ (ñīŋdzɛɛ̀) sm. ཉིང་ཚད་.

ཉིད་ (ñīī) vi. to wither, to shrivel ¶ མེ་ཏོག་འདི་བཉིད་འདུག The flower has withered.

ཉིད་སྐམ་ (ñīīgam) withering, shriveling; vi.—འགྲོ་ to wither, to shrivel.

ཉིད་དོ་ (ñīīdo) withered, crumbled, worn out; vi.—ཆགས་ to become withered/ crumbled/ worn out; va.—བཟོ་ to make withered/ crumbled/ worn out.

ཉིད་ནད་ (ñīīnɛɛ̀) a disease that causes shriveling/ withering (in plants).

ཉིལ་ (ñīī) gums ¶ ཉིལ་ནད་ Diseases of the gums.

ཉིལ་སྐྲན་ (ñīīdrɛn) cancer/ tumor of the gums.

ཉེད་ (ñeè) 1. vi. to find, to discover, to get ¶ ཁོ་ལ་དངུལ་ཉེད་པ་རེད་ He found (some) money.

ཉེད་བསྐུར་ (ñēègur) bestowing gifts to show one's respect; va.—ཞུ་.

ཉེད་དཀའ་ (ñēèga) hard to come by, difficult to find.

ཉེད་རྟོགས་ (ñēèdɔg) finding out and knowing; va.—བྱེད་ ¶ ཁོང་ཚོས་ཤེས་དགོས་པ་རྣམས་ཉེད་རྟོགས་བྱ་རྒྱུར་དཀའ་ངལ་བྱུང་ཡོད་ཀྱི་མ་རེད་ It was not difficult for them to find out what they needed to know.

ཉེད་དངོས་ (ñēèŋöö) goods/ things that have been found.

ཉེད་བརྡ་ (ñēèda) advertisement for things found (lost and found); va.—གཏོང་.

ཉེད་རློམ་ (ñēèlom) ostentatious, conceited (because of one's wealth).

ཉེད་སོན་ (ñēèsön) sm. ཉེད་.

ཉོག: p. བཉོགས་; f. བཉོག; imp. ཉོགས་ (ñōg) va. to stir up, to agitate, to cause trouble ¶ ཁོས་ཆུ་བཉོགས་པ་རེད་ He stirred up the water. ¶ ཁོས་ལས་ཀའི་གོ་རིམ་ཚང་མ་བཉོགས་བཞག He has caused trouble in doing the work.

ཉོག་ཁྲ་ལུང་པ་གང་ (ñōgdra lu̱ŋbagaŋ) many disputes, full of disputes.

ཉོག་འཁྲུག (ñōgdrug) confusion, trouble, disturbances.

ཉོག་ཁྲ་ (ñōgdra) sm. ཉོག་དྲ་.

ཉོག་གླེང་ (ñōgleŋ) argument, dispute.

ཉོག་འགལ་ (ñōŋgɛɛ) angry, agitated.

ཉོག་འགལ་འཚོམས་འཁྲུགས་ (ñōŋgɛɛ tsōmdruù) shung. agitated, angry ¶ རྣམ་མཁྱེན་ཉོག་འགལ་འཚོམས་འཁྲུག་སྐད་ཅིག་ཀྱང་མི་བཞེས་པ་ Please do not hold the slightest anger even for an instant.

ཉོག་ཆེ་བ་ (ñōgcewa) sm. ཉོག་དྲ་ཚ་པོ་.

ཉོག་དྲ་ (ñōgdra) complication, trouble, problem, confusion, entanglement; va.—སློང་; —བཟོ་ to make trouble/ complications; va.—སེལ་; —སྒྲོང་ to clarify/ straighten out complications or troubles ¶ གནས་ཚུལ་འདིས་ཉོག་དྲ་ཆེན་པོ་བཟོས་པ་རེད་ The news caused a lot of trouble (confusion).

ཉོག་དྲ་ཅན་ (ñōgdrajɛn) sm. ཉོག་དྲ་.

ཉོག་དྲ་ཆེ་བ་ (ñōgdra cēwa) sm. ཉོག་དྲ་ཚ་པོ་.

ཉོག་དྲ་མེད་པ་ (ñōgdra meèba) simple, uncomplicated, without troubles/ problems.

ཉོག་དྲ་ཚ་པོ་ (ñōgdra tsābo) complicated, complex, troublesome, entangled, confused ¶ ལས་ཀ་འདི་ཉོག་དྲ་ཚ་པོ་ཞི་དྲགས་འདུག This work is very complicated.

ཉོག་དྲ་འཚང་ (ñōgdra tsōŋ) sm. ཉོག་དྲ་ཤོད་.

ཉོག་དྲ་ལང་ (ñōgdra la̱ŋ) vi. to have trouble/ problems/ confusion arise.

ཉོག་དྲ་ཤོད་ (ñōgdra shöö) va. to cause trouble verbally ¶ ཁོས་ལས་ཁུངས་ལ་གྲ་ཡོགས་སྐོར་ཉོག་དྲ་ཤོད་ཀྱི

འདུག He is causing trouble in the office (verbally) about his salary (conveys he is complaining, etc.).

ཉོག་དྲ་སེལ་ (ñōgdra sēl) see ཉོག་དྲ་.

ཉོག་དྲ་སྲོང་ (ñōgdra sōŋ) see ཉོག་དྲ་.

ཉོག་དྲ་སློང་ (ñōgdra lōŋ) see ཉོག་དྲ་.

ཉོག་དྲུལ་ (ñōgdüü) rubbish, garbage; sludge.

ཉོག་པ་ (ñōgba) 1. a dispute, quarrel. 2. anger. 2. sm. ཉོག་པོ་.

ཉོག་པའི་སེམས་ (ñōgbɛ sēm) disturbed/ agitated/ angry mind, a mind that isn't calm.

ཉོག་པོ་ (ñōgbo) 1. muddy; va.—བཟོ་ to make muddy. 2. for beer: cloudy.

ཉོག་མ་ (ñōgma) 1. unclear, dirty, muddy ༑ཆུ་ཉོག་མ་ Dirty water. 2. sludge.

ཉོག་མ་གཏིང་སློང་ (ñōgma dīŋloŋ) shung. digging up an old issue/ case again; va.—བྱེད་ ༑ཐུར་ནས་ཁྲིན་ཆོད་གཙང་མ་ཟིན་པའི་གྱོད་གཞི་ཉོག་མ་རྟིང་སློང་བྱེད་མི་ཆོག Once the law case is completely settled you are not allow to dig it up again.

ཉོག་མེད་ཉོག་བཟོ་ (ñōgmeè ñōgso) making unneccessary trouble/ problems, making trouble where there is no trouble; va.—བྱེད་.

ཉོག་ཚེགས་ (ñōgdzeg) sm. ཉོག་འཛིང་.

ཉོག་འཛིང་ (ñōgdziŋ) 1. trouble, turmoil, disturbance; va.—བཟོ་. to cause or make trouble/ turmoil/ disturbances; va.—སེལ་ to clear up trouble/ disturbance/ turmoil; vi.—ལང་ས་ to have trouble/ turmoil/ disturbances arise; va.—འཕྲད་; —ཐུག to meet with trouble. 2. intricate, complicated.

ཉོག་འཛིངས་ (ñōgdziŋ) sm. ཉོག་འཛིང་.

ཉོག་ཛོབ་ (ñōgdzob) sm. ཉོག་འཛིང་.

ཉོག་གཞི་ (ñōgshi) cause of trouble/ disturbances.

ཉོག་ཟིང་ (ñōgsiŋ) sm. ཉོག་འཛིང་.

ཉོག་བཟོ་ལབ་གཞི་ (ñōgso lə̱bshi) sm. ཉོག་གཞི་.

ཉོག་ཤེལ་ (ñōgshel) frosted glass.

ཉོག་སེ་བ་ (ñōgsewa) 1. slightly complicated. 2. slightly muddy, clouded.

ཉོགས་ (ñōg) 1. imp. of ཉོག. 2. sm. ཉོག.

ཉོགས་ཛོབ་ (ñōgdzob) sm. ཉོག་ཛོབ་.

ཉོང་: p. བརྙངས་; f. བརྙང་; imp. ཉོངས་ 1. va. to stretch out hands/ legs. 2. va. to set out traps. 3. va. to polish walls and floors.

ཉོངས་ (ñōŋ) imp. of ཉོང་.

ཉོངས་པ་ (ñōŋba) sm. ཀོང་ཀོང་.

ཉོན་ (ñōn) imp. of ཉན་.

ཉོབ་ (ñōb) vi. to be able to reach ༑ཡལ་ག་འདི་ངས་ཉོབ་ཀྱི་མི་འདུག I can't reach that branch.

ཉོས་ (ñȫȍ) imp. of ཉོ་.

སྣ་ལོ་ (ñālo) a herbal medicine.

སྣ་གི་སྣོག་གི་ (ñāge ñōgge) 1. ཉོག་དྲ་. 2. unclear speech.

སྣ་གི་སྙིགས་གི་ (ñāge ñīgge) sm. སྙིགས་མ་.

སྙག་སེ་གོ་སེ་ (ñāse g̱ose) complaining, saying things in a fussy or difficult manner, raising a lot of objections to sth., making lots of excuses; va.—གཏོང་.

སྙག་སེ་གོ་སེ་ཚ་པོ་ (ñāse g̱ose tsābo) a person who engages in a lot of སྙག་སེ་གོ་སེ་.

སྙག་ས་སྙིགས་ (ñāgsa ñīg) sm. སྙིགས་མ་.

སྙད་ (ñɛ̄ɛ̀) 1. a pretext/ excuse ༑ཁོས་ན་ཚ་ཡོད་པར་སྙད་ནས་ལས་ཁུངས་ལ་མ་ཡོང་བ་རེད་ He used being sick as a pretext and didn't come to the office (to work). 2. blaming/ accusing; va.—འཛུགས་; —འདོགས་ to blame, to accuse (falsely); to use (sth.) as a pretext/ excuse. ༑ཀུན་མ་བརྐུས་པར་སྙད་བཏགས་པ་རེད་ (They) falsely accused him of stealing.

སྙད་ཀ་ (ñɛ̄ɛ̀ga) sm. སྙད་.

སྙད་བཀོ་ (ñɛ̄ɛ̀ gō) 1. va. to tease. 2. va. to instigate/ cause/ provoke a dispute or fight.

སྙད་བརྗོད་ (ñɛ̄ɛ̀jȫȍ) sm. སྙད་གཏམ་.

སྙད་སྙོད་ (ñɛ̄ɛ̀ñȫȍ) sm. སྙད་སེ་སྙོད་སེ་.

སྙད་གཏམ་ (ñɛ̄ɛ̀dam) 1. teasing; va.—གཏོང་. 2. talk that causes quarrels; va.—གཏོང་. 3. talk that blames/ accuses; va.—གཏོང་.

སྙད་བཏགས་རྒྱུ་འཕྲོག (ñɛ̄ɛ̀dag gyu̱ndrɔɔ̀) extorting under false pretext, blackmailing; va.—བྱེད་ [Lit. accusing falsely to steal wealth/ money].

སྙད་འདོགས་ (ñɛ̄ɛ̀ dɔ̱g) va. to blame/ accuse falsely.

སྙད་མེད་སྙད་དྲི་ (ñɛ̄ɛ̀meè ñɛ̄ɛ̀dri) blaming/ accusing falsely; va.—བྱེད་; va.—གཏོང་.

སྙད་མེད་སྙད་འདོགས་ (ñɛ̄ɛ̀meè ñɛ̄ndɔɔ̀) sm. སྙད་མེད་སྙད་དྲི་.

སྙད་གཙེས་ (ñɛ̄ɛ̀dzeè) sm. སྙད་མེད་སྙད་དྲི་.

སྙད་འཚོལ་ (ñɛ̄ɛ̀ tsȫȍ) va. to try to find faults (to accuse/ blame).

སྙད་སེ་སྙོད་སེ་ (ñɛ̄ɛ̀se ñȫȍse) sm. སྙད་སེ་གོ་སེ་.

སྙན་ (ñɛ̄n) 1. ear (h.). 2. abbr. of སྙན་ཅན, སྙན་པོ་ and སྙན་ཞུ་.

སྙན་སྐད་ (ñɛ̄ngeɛ̀) pleasant/ interesting talk.

སྙན་སྐོར་ (ñɛ̄ngɔɔ) a type of large gold earring with turquoise inlay.

སྙན་བསྐུལ་ (ñɛ̄ngüü) reminding (h.); va.—ཞུ་ to remind ༑ད་བར་བླ་དཔོན་གོང་མར་སྙན་བསྐུལ་རིམ་པ་ཞུས་ཀྱང་བཀའ་གསལ་ཕེབས་རིགས་མ་བྱུང་བ་ We have been reminding our superior many times but until now we did not get any answer.

སྙན་བསྐུལ་གསོལ་འདེབས་ (ñɛ̄ngüü sȫndeb) reminding a lama about sth. one has asked or requested (h.).

སྙན་ཁུང་སླབ་པ་ (ñɛ̄nguŋ drə̄bbə) sb. who believes what anyone says, a gullible/ impressionable person.

སྙན་ཁུང་དུ་བརྒྱུད་ (ñɛ̄nguŋdu gyṳ̈ṳ̀) vi. to pass on/ transmit teachings.

སྙན་ཁོངས་ (ñɛ̄ngoŋ) included in a report ༑བཏོན་ཁྲ་བུ་དེབ་སྙན་ཁོངས་ཟུར་ཞུལ་ཞུས་པ་ A list of items taken out (from storage) was included in the report.

སྙན་ཁྲ་ (ñɛ̄ndra) sm. སྙན་སེང་.

སྙན་གྱུར་ (ñɛ̄ngyar) shung. abbr. of སྙན་ཞུ་ར་གྱུར་བ་.

སྙན་གྱི་གོང་རྒྱན་ (ñɛ̄ngi ko̱ngyɛn) earring, ear-ornament.

སྙན་གྱི་དབང་པོ་ (ñɛ̄ngi wāŋbo) ear.

སྙན་གྲགས་ (ñɛ̄ndraà) reputation, prestige, fame (h.) ༑ཁོང་ལ་སྙན་གྲགས་བྱུང་བ་རེད་ He became famous.

སྙན་གྲགས་བསྐལ་བརྒྱར་གནས་པ་ (ñɛ̄ndraà gɛ̄ɛ̄ gya̱ nɛ̄ɛ̀ba) extremely famous [Lit. fame that will live for 100 eons].

སྙན་གྲགས་ཅན་ (ñɛ̄ndraàjɛn) famous, renowned (h.).

སྙན་གྲགས་ཆེན་པོ་ (ñɛ̄ndraà cēmbo) very famous/ renowned (h.).

སྙན་གྲགས་བརྩོན་རྐྱང་ (ñɛ̄ndraà dzȫngyaŋ) striving only for fame.

སྙན་གྲགས་དམ་ལེན་ (ñɛ̄ndraà hāmlen) claiming credit/ fame that is due to another; va.—བྱེད་.

སྙན་རྒྱབ་བསེར་བུ་ (ñɛ̄ngyəb sērbu) going in one ear and out of the other, not paying attention; va.—གཏོང་.

སྙན་སྒྱོང་ (ñɛ̄n gyo̱ŋ) va. to make a report that instigates trouble for sb.

སྙན་སྒོར་ (ñɛ̄ngɔr) h. of ས་ཀོར་.

སྙན་སྒྲ་སྒྲོག (ñɛ̄ndra drɔ̱ɔ̀) va. to shout out sth. good.

སྙན་སྒྲོན་ (ñɛ̄ndrön) 1. report, message, notice (h.); va.—ཞུ་; to report, to apprise, to inform. 2. lecture, speech; va.—གནང་ to give a lecture/ speech.

སྙན་སྒྲོན་པ་ (ñɛ̄ndrönba) shung. a person who is responsible for making reports or keeping senior officials informed.

སྙན་སྒྲོན་ཡིག་ཆ་ (ñɛ̄ndrön yigjə) written report.

སྙན་བརྒྱུད་ (ñɛ̄ngyṳ̈ṳ̀) transmitting/ passing on orally.

སྙན་ངག (ñɛ̄nŋaà) poetry, verse.

སྙན་ངག་མཁན་ (ñɛ̄nŋaàgɛn) sm. སྙན་ངག་པ་.

སྙན་ངག་མཁན་པོ་ (ñɛ̄nŋaà kēmbo) sm. སྙན་ངག་པ་.

སྙན་ངག་མཁས་དབང་ (ñɛ̄nŋaà kɛ̄ɛ̄waŋ) sm. སྙན་ངག་པ་.

སྙན་ངག་གི་སྒྲ་རྒྱན་ (ñɛ̄nŋaàgi dra̱gyɛn) rhyme in

poetry.

སྙན་ངག་གི་གཞུང་ (ñɛ̃nŋaàgi shu̱ŋ) book of poems.

སྙན་ངག་སྒྲོག་སྦྱང་ (ñɛ̃nŋaà dro̱gjaŋ) poetry recitation.

སྙན་ངག་བདུན་ཚིག་རྐང་བརྒྱད་མ་ (ñɛ̃nŋaà dü̱ndzig gāŋ gyɛ̱ɛ̀ba) an eight-line poem with seven characters/ syllables per line.

སྙན་ངག་པ་ (ñɛ̃nŋagba) a poet.

སྙན་ངག་ཕྱོགས་བསྒྲིགས་ (ñɛ̃nŋaà cɔ̄ɔ̀drig) collection/ anthology of poems.

སྙན་ངག་མེ་ལོང་ (ñɛ̃nŋaà me̱loŋ) title of a book on poetics (translated from Sanskrit).

སྙན་ངག་རིག་པ་ (ñɛ̃nŋaà ri̱gbə) poetry, poetics.

སྙན་ཅོག (ñɛ̃njɔ̀ɔ̀) 1. ear (h.). 2. hearing (h.); vi.—གསན་ to hear; va.—གསན་ to listen ¶ཁ་སང་གི་གསར་འགྱུར་དེ་སྙན་ཅོག་གསན་བྱུང་ངམ་ Did you hear that news yesterday? ¶ཁོང་གི་གཏམ་བཤད་དེ་སྙན་ཅོག་གསན་རོགས་གནང་ Please listen to his speech.

སྙན་ཅོག་སྟབ་པོ་ (ñɛ̃njɔ̀ɔ̀ drə̄bu) sm. སྙན་ཁུང་སྟབ་པ་.

སྙན་ལྕག (ñe̱njaà) reminding (h.).

སྙན་ཆ་དོད་པོ་ (ñe̱nja tö̱öbo) pleasing to the ear.

སྙན་འཇམ་རོལ་མོ་ (ñe̱njam rö̱ömo) light/ soft music (h.).

སྙན་འཇེབས་ (ñɛ̃njeb) sm. སྙན་པོ་.

སྙན་འཇེབས་སྒྲ་གདངས་ (ñɛ̃njeb dra̱daŋ) pleasant tune/ melody.

སྙན་འཇེབས་ངག (ñɛ̃njeb ŋaà) pleasant talk.

སྙན་འཇེབས་ཡིད་དབང་འཕྲོག (ñɛ̃njeb yi̱iwaŋ trɔ̄ɔ̀) melodious, attractive sounding.

སྙན་བརྗོད་ (ñɛ̃njöö) sm. སྙན་གཏམ་.

སྙན་སྙན་ལེགས་ལེགས་ (ñɛ̃nñɛn le̱gleg) pleasant to the eyes and ears.

སྙན་སྣུང་ (ñɛ̃nñuŋ) shung. to interrupt/ bother.

སྙན་དཔར་ (ñɛ̃ndar) telegram that makes a report; va.—འབུལ་.

སྙན་གཏམ་ (ñɛ̃ndam) 1. pleasing/ pleasant talk. 2. talk that is interesting.

སྙན་གཏོད་ (ñɛ̃ndöö) listening to sth.

སྙན་ཐོ་ (ñɛ̃ndo) file, document, record; va.—འགོད་ to record, to note in a file/ document.

སྙན་ཐོའི་རེའུ་མིག (ñɛ̃ndö ri̱umig) table, schedule for making notes.

སྙན་དར་ (ñɛ̃ndar) shung. ceremonial scarf accompanying a petition, ceremonial scarf put on statues (h.); va.—སྐྱོན་ to give or put on such a ceremonial scarf.

སྙན་དུ་སྒྲོན་ (ñɛ̃ndu drö̱n) sm. སྙན་དུ་གསོལ་.

སྙན་དུ་གསོལ་ (ñɛ̃ndu sȫö) va. to tell/ report/ inform ¶དམག་འཁྲུགས་སྐོར་དམག་སྤྱི་ཆེ་མོའི་སྙན་དུ་གསོལ་རྒྱུ་ཡིན་ I will inform the commander in chief of the battle.

སྙན་དུ་ལྷོང་ (ñɛ̃ndu lhōŋ) vi. to get a full account/ report ¶ངའི་ཁ་མཆུ་དེའི་སྐོར་གོང་རིམ་གྱི་སྙན་དུ་ལྷོངས་བཞག Concerning my dispute, it has been fully reported to the higher authorities.

སྙན་དུ་ལྷོང་པོ་ (ñɛ̃ndu lhōŋbo) fully reported/ accounted for.

སྙན་བདར་ (ñɛ̃nda) a message/ report to a superior.

སྙན་མཉན་ (ñɛ̃n ñɛ̃n) sm. སྙན་དུ་གསོལ་.

སྙན་པ་ (ñɛ̃mba) 1. sm. སྙན་གྲགས་. 2. pleasant, interesting (to hear) ¶སྙན་པའི་སྒྲ་ Sounds that are pleasing to hear.

སྙན་པད་ (ñɛ̃nbɛɛ̀) shung. ear ornament worn by officials in tt. (with རྒྱ་ལུ་ཆས་ costumes).

སྙན་པའི་པ་དན་ (ñɛ̃nbɛɛ̀ pa̱dɛn) simile, metaphor.

སྙན་པའི་བསེར་བུ་ (ñɛ̃nbɛɛ̀ sērbu) fame spreading like wild fire.

སྙན་པར་སྨྲ་ (ñɛ̃nbɛ mā) va. to talk in soft/ gentle/ pleasant manner.

སྙན་པོ་ (ñe̱mbo) pleasant, interesting ¶ཁོའི་སྐད་ཆ་སྙན་པོ་ཞེ་དྲག་འདུག His talk is very interesting.

སྙན་ཕྲ་ (ñɛ̃ndra) shung. a report to authorities saying sth. bad about another, va.—ཞུ་; —ཕུལ་.

སྙན་ཕྲ་ཞུ་ལོག (ñɛ̃ndra shu̱lɔɔ̀) shung. a report to authorities saying sth. bad things about another ¶ཁོ་པས་བླ་དཔོན་ཆེན་པོར་སྙན་ཕྲ་ཞུ་ལོག་ཕུལ་བ་རེད་ He made a report to the superiors of bad things regarding another person.

སྙན་ཕྲིན་ (ñɛ̃ndrin) 1. a letter written in verse. 2. pleasant/ interesting talk.

སྙན་བྱིལ་ (ñe̱njil) shung. the long earring worn by tt. government officials.

སྙན་དབང་ (ñɛ̃nwaŋ) abbr. སྙན་གྱི་དབང་པོ་.

སྙན་དབང་འཕྲོག (ñɛ̃nwaŋ trɔ̄ɔ̀) vi. to be attracted by pleasant songs/ talk/ etc.

སྙན་འབུལ་ (ñɛ̃mbüü) request, petition, report, appeal (h.); va.—ཞུ་; —གནང་ ¶བོད་གཞུང་གིས་མཉམ་སྦྲེལ་རྒྱལ་ཚོགས་སུ་སྙན་འབུལ་ཞུས་པ་རེད་ The Tibetan government appealed to the UN.

སྙན་འབུལ་བཙེ་གཟིགས་ (ñɛ̃mbüü dzēsii) shung. standard phrase used on petitions requesting that it be brought before a superior to read ¶ངའི་གནད་དོན་འདིའི་སྐོར་གོང་རིམ་ནས་སྙན་འབུལ་བཙེ་གཟིགས་ཡོད་པ་ཞུ་ Concerning my situation, please look at my petition kindly.

སྙན་འབུལ་ཞུ་ཡིག (ñɛ̃mbüü shu̱yig) a written request/ appeal/ petition/ report.

སྙན་མོ་ (ñɛ̃nmo) sm. སྙན་པོ་.

སྙན་རྩོམ་ (ñɛ̃ndzom) poetry, poem.

སྙན་གཙེར་ (ñɛ̃ndzer) troublesome, annoying, bothersome (to the ear) ¶ད་རེས་ངས་ཁྱེད་ལ་སྙན་གཙེར་མི་ཞུ་མཐུ་མེད་བྱུང་སོང་ This time I have no choice but to bother you.

སྙན་ཚིག (ñɛ̃ndzig) 1. pleasant sounding words ¶གཡོ་སྒྱུའི་སྙན་ཚིག Pleasant words that are deceitful. 2. poetic language, poems.

སྙན་ཚིག་གླུ་གཞས་ (ñɛ̃ndzig lūshɛɛ̀) poems and songs.

སྙན་ཚིག་སྦྲིང་ཡིག (ñɛ̃ndzig dri̱ŋyig) sm. སྙན་འཕྲིན་.

སྙན་ཚིག་དབྱངས་རྟ་ (ñɛ̃ndzig yāŋda) reading a verse/ poem in the form of a song.

སྙན་ཚིག་ཟློས་གར་ (ñɛ̃ndzig dö̱ögar) a drama in verse.

སྙན་ཚིག་ལོ་རྒྱུས་ (ñɛ̃ndzig lu̱gyüü) 1. history of verse/ poems. 2. history written in verse.

སྙན་ཞུ་ (ñɛ̃nshu) report, account; petition, appeal, request (h.); va.—ཞུ་; —གཏོང་; —འབུལ་ to report, to give an account, to petition, to appeal, to request ¶ཁྱེད་རང་གི་གྱོད་གཞི་འདིའི་སྐོར་ལྷ་སར་སྙན་ཞུ་བཀའ་སློར་མ་ཞུས་པར་ངས་ཐག་ཆོད་ཀྱི་མ་རེད་ Concerning your case, I cannot decide without reporting to Lhasa for further instructions.

སྙན་ཞུ་བཀའ་སློར་ (ñɛ̃nshu gāgɔɔ̀) reporting and asking for further instructions.

སྙན་ཞུ་གསལ་རྗེན་ (ñɛ̃nshu sɛ̄ɛ̀jen) shung. reporting clearly to one's superior.

སྙན་ཞུ་སྐྱར་ (ñɛ̃nshu gya̱r) shung. to file a lawsuit ¶སྙན་ཞུ་སྐྱར་བ་བཀའ་ཁྲིམས་ཚོད་ལོང་ཡིན་པ་ (His) filing a lawsuit is because of his taking the measure of the court (and thinking he can win).

སྙན་ཞུས་ཀྱིས་ཞིབ་པར་ (ñɛ̃nshügi shi̱bbar) shung. investigating after reporting the matter ¶གོང་རིམ་ལ་སྙན་ཞུས་ཀྱིས་ཞིབ་པར་བྱུང་དོན་འདི་སྐོར་ཉེ་སྐོར་ཕྱོགས་ལྷུང་གི་ཐག་གཅོད་བྱུང་འདུག་དོན་ After bringing the matter before the superiors and investigating, we came to the conclusion that this matter was settled in a biased manner.

སྙན་ཟིན་ (ñɛ̃nsin) draft petition.

སྙན་གཡུ་ (ñɛ̃nyu) turquoise earring.

སྙན་ལ་འཁྱོལ་ (ñɛ̃nla kyȫö) vi. to reach sb.'s ears ¶གནས་ཚུལ་དེ་གོང་རིམ་གྱི་སྙན་ལ་འཁྱོལ་བཞག This news reached the ears of the higher authorities.

སྙན་ཤལ་ (ñɛ̃nshɛɛ) 1. white ceremonial scarf. 2. earlobe. 3. earring, ear-ornament.

སྙན་ཤས་ (ñɛ̃nshɛɛ̀) sm. སྙན་གཙེར་.

སྙན་ཤོག (ñɛ̃nshɔɔ̀) sm. སྙན་ཞུ་.

སྙན་གཤོག (ñɛ̃nshɔɔ̀) auricle (of ear).

སྙན་སུམ་ (ñɛ̃nsum) abbr. of Tibetan poetics and grammar.

སྙན་སེང་ (ñɛ̃nseŋ) a report, account; va.—ཞུ་; —བྱེད་ to report, to make an account.

སྙན་གསང་ (ñɛ̃nsaŋ) sm. སྙན་སེང་.

སྙན་གསང་པོ་ (ñɛ̃n sāŋbo) 1. a keen sense of hearing. 2. sb. who has many channels for hearing things. 3. reporting clearly/ succinctly to a superior.

སྙན་གསན་ (ñɛ̃nsɛn) sm. སྙན་ཞུ་.

སྙན་གསན་གཏོང་ (ñɛ̃nsɛn dōŋ) shung. va. to announce the coming of the Dalai Lama's procession on the road by playing the Tibetan clarinet.

སྙན་གསན་འབེབས་ (ñɛ̃nsɛn beb) va. to send a message/ report/ appeal/ petition to superior ¶ སང་ཉིན་ཚོགས་འདུར་ཕེབས་དགོས་པའི་སྙན་གསན་འབེབས་དགོས་ You should send a message to come to the meeting tomorrow.

སྙན་གསལ་ (ñɛ̃nsɛɛ) shung. as was written in the report/ petition ¶ཁང་རྙིང་རྩ་བཤིག་གིས་གསར་རྒྱག་ཞུས་དེ་སྙན་གསལ་ཁང་དེབ་གསར་བཀོད་ཞུས་པ་ We demolished the old house and built a new one as was written in the report.

སྙན་གསེང་ (ñɛ̃nsɛŋ) sm. སྙན་སེང་.

སྙན་གསོལ་ (ñɛ̃nsöö) sm. སྙན་དུ་གསོལ་.

སྙན་བསུན་ (ñɛ̃nsün) sm. སྙན་གཙེར་.

སྙན་སྲབ་ (ñɛ̃ndrəb) abbr. of སྙན་ཅོག་སྲབ་པོ་.

སྙན་ལྷན་ནེར་གསན་ (ñɛ̃nlhɛn nersɛn) listening very carefully, paying careful attention ¶ངས་ཞུས་པ་དེ་རྒན་ལགས་ཀྱི་སྙན་ལྷན་ནེར་གསན་སོང་ What I said was listened to carefully by my teacher.

སྙན་ལྷོངས་ཞུ་ (ñɛ̃nlhoŋ shu) va. to report sth. in detail.

སྙབ་སྙབ་ (ñãbñəb) sm. རྙབ་རྙབ་.

སྙམ་ (ñām) 1. vi. to think, to wonder, to imagine (h.) ¶ཚལ་ཞིང་ནང་དུ་ནས་ཏོག་ཙམ་བཏབ་པའི་རྒྱུ་མཚན་ཅི་ཡིན་ནམ་སྙམ་བྱུང་ I thought why did (they) plant a little barley in a vegetable garden. 2. (vb. "to be" + — པའི་) as if ¶ཕྱི་རྒྱལ་བ་དེ་བོད་པ་རེད་སྙམ་པའི་བོད་སྐད་ཡག་པོ་རྒྱག་གི་འདུག That Westerner speaks good Tibetan as if he were a Tibetan. ¶ངཚོར་རོགས་རམ་བྱེད་ཀྱི་རེད་སྙམ་པའི་ཡིད་ཆེས་ཡོད་པ་རེད་ We believed he would help us.

སྙམ་དུ་འཛིན་ (ñāmdu dzin) sm. སྙམ་.

སྙམ་དུ་བསམ་ (ñāmdu sām) sm. སྙམ་.

སྙམ་དུ་སེམས་ (ñāmdu sēm) sm. སྙམ་.

སྙམ་མེ་སྙོམ་མེ་ (ñāmme ñōme) empty/ idle talk.

སྙལ་ཚོད་ (ñɛɛ̄dzöö) sm. བསྙལ་ཚལ་.

སྙལ་བཟོ་ལས་ཅན་ (ñɛɛ̄so lɛɛ̀dzɛn) sm. བསྙལ་བཟོ་ལས་ཅན་.

སྙི་ (ñī) 1. name of a lineage in Dakpo. 2. sm. སྙི་. 3. abbr. of སྙི་པོ་.

སྙི་མཁྲེགས་ (ñīdreg) abbr. tender and hard.

སྙི་ནད་ (ñīnɛɛ̀) osteomalacia.

སྙི་པོ་ (ñību) soft, flexible, pliable.

སྙི་བ་ (ñīwə) 1. fresh wet dung. 2. the bulb of fritillary. 3. soft, pliable, flexible.

སྙི་བོ་ (ñību) sm. སྙི་པོ་.

སྙི་མ་ (ñīmə) sm. སྙི་མ་.

སྙི་མོ་ (ñīmu) sm. སྙི་བ་.

སྙི་ཤིང་ (ñīshiŋ) sm. མཉེན་ཤིང་.

སྙི་ཤུན་ (ñīshün) thin/ flexible/ pliant skin.

སྙི་སའི་གྲོ་མ་ (ñīsɛ troma) a bully [Lit. sweet potatoes from soft earth].

སྙི་སྲ་ (ñīdrəb) soft and hard.

སྙིག: p. **བསྙིགས་**; f. **བསྙིག**; imp. **སྙིགས་** (ñīì) va. to throw away the useless parts ¶འབྲུའི་ནང་གི་ས་རྡོ་བསྙིགས་པ་རེད་ (They) threw away (picked out or sifted) the earth and stones in the grain.

སྙིག་དྲུལ་ (ñīgdüü) garbage, refuse.

སྙིགས་ (ñīg) 1. vi. to fall/ sink to the bottom. 2. imp. of སྙིག. 3. va. to be left behind ¶ཕྲུ་གུ་དེ་ན་ཙང་སློབ་སྦྱོང་ཐོག་རྗེས་སུ་སྙིགས་སོང་ Because the child got ill he got left behind in his studies. 4. abbr. of སྙིགས་མ་.

སྙིགས་སྒམ་ (ñīggam) garbage can.

སྙིགས་སྒྲོམ་ (ñīgdrom) garbage can/ basket.

སྙིགས་གཏོར་བཅུད་ལེན་ (ñīgdɔɔ jüülen) sm. སྙིགས་འདོར་བཅུད་ལེན་.

སྙིགས་དུས་ (ñīgdüü) era/ time/ period of degeneration.

སྙིགས་འདོར་བཅུད་ལེན་ (ñīŋdɔɔ jüülen) keep the good and discard the bad ¶ཕྱི་རྒྱལ་ལ་སློབ་སྦྱོང་བྱེད་དུས་སྙིགས་དོར་བཅུད་ལེན་བྱེད་དགོས་ When you study abroad you should discard what is bad and keep what is good [Lit. discard the dregs and take in that which is nutritious].

སྙིགས་མ་ (ñīgmə) 1. sediment, refuse, siftings, dregs, scum. 2. degenerate ¶སྙིགས་མའི་དུས་ A degenerate era. 3. leftover (in negative sense) ¶ཚོང་ཟོག་སྙིགས་མ་ Leftover merchandise (goods not sold).

སྙིགས་མ་འདུལ་འཛིན་ (ñīgmə dündzin) archaeology.

སྙིགས་མ་འདུལ་འཛིན་གྱི་རྔོག་འཚོལ་ (ñīgmə dündzingi ŋɔ̄gdzöö) archaeological excavation.

སྙིགས་མའི་རྒྱུད་མདངས་ (ñīgmɛ güüdaŋ) shung. the manner of degeneration.

སྙིགས་མའི་དུས་ (ñīgmɛ tüü) sm. སྙིགས་དུས་.

སྙིགས་རོ་ (ñīgro) sm. སྙིགས་མ་.

སྙིགས་རོ་གཙང་འབུད་ (ñīgro dzāŋbüü) discarding or throwing away the dregs/ garbage.

སྙིགས་རོ་གསུམ་གྱི་འབག་བཙོག (ñīgro sūmgi bagdzön) pollution from the three industrial wastes (gas, liquids, residues).

སྙིགས་སེལ་བཟོ་ཁང་ (ñīgsel sogaŋ) refinery.

སྙིགས་བསགས་ (ñīg sāà) va. to precipitate sth. out.

སྙིང་ (ñīŋ) 1. heart. 2. mind, consciousness.

སྙིང་དཀར་ (ñīŋgar) 1. kind/ good/ generous heart. 2. white chest (usu. dogs and bears) [Lit. white heart].

སྙིང་ཀུ་མཁན་ (ñīŋ gūñɛn) sb. who has illicit sexual relations with a married man or woman.

སྙིང་སྐྱ་དབབ་ (ñīŋ gyābəb) a type of heart disease.

སྙིང་ཁ་ (ñīŋgə) heart ¶སྙིང་ཁ་འཕར་ཤུགས་ Heartbeat.

སྙིང་ཁ་ནས་དོན་གྲབས་ (ñīŋ kānɛ töndrəb) being extremely frightened [Lit. one's heart about to come out of the mouth].

སྙིང་ཁ་འཕར་གྲངས་ (ñīŋgə pārdraŋ) heart rate.

སྙིང་ཁ་འབྱེད་པའི་ཁྲག་ཤེད་ (ñīŋgə cɛ̄ɛbɛ trāgsheè) diastolic blood pressure.

སྙིང་ཁང་ (ñīŋgaŋ) atrium (of heart), ventricle.

སྙིང་ཁམས་ (ñīŋgam) 1. the heart. 2. state of mind. 3. courage, bravery.

སྙིང་ཁམས་ཀྱི་ནད་ (ñīŋgamgi nɛɛ̀) heart disease; vi.—ཡངས་ to have a heart attack, to get heart disease.

སྙིང་ཁམས་ཁྲག་རྩའི་མ་ལག (ñīŋgam trāgdzɛ malaà) cardiovascular system.

སྙིང་ཁོག (ñīŋgɔɔ̀) sm. སྙིང་ཁང་.

སྙིང་ཁོང་རུས་པའི་གཏིང་ (ñīŋgoŋ rüübɛ diŋ) from the bottom/ depth of (my) heart.

སྙིང་ཁྲག (ñīŋdraà) the blood in the heart; vi.—རྒྱས་ to suddenly get angry.

སྙིང་ག (ñīŋgə) sm. སྙིང་ཁ་.

སྙིང་གར་ཚེར་མདའ་ཕོག (ñīŋgar tsēnda pɔ̄ɔ̀) vi. to get hurt deeply (emotionally) [Lit. a thorn arrow hits the heart].

སྙིང་གས་མཁྲིས་ཐོར་ (ñīŋgɛ trīidɔɔ) sm. སྙིང་མགོ་གཞུག་ལོག.

སྙིང་གས་བླ་ཐོར་ (ñīŋgɛ lādɔɔ) sm. སྙིང་གས་བླ་འདར་.

སྙིང་གས་བླ་འདར་ (ñīŋgɛ lādar) being frightened out of one's wits, terror-stricken.

སྙིང་གི་ཆུང་ལོ་ (ñīŋgi cūŋlo) sweetheart.

སྙིང་གི་ན་ཚ་ (ñīŋgi nadza) 1. heart illness. 2. deep-seated hatred/ grudge.

སྙིང་གི་ནོར་བུ་ (ñīŋgi norbu) beloved, sweetheart.

སྙིང་གི་སྙུན་མནར་ (ñīŋgi ñünnar) heart attack, heart disease/ illness.

སྙིང་གི་འཕར་སྐྲངས་ (ñīŋgi pārdaŋ) rhythm of the heartbeat.

སྙིང་གི་འཕར་སྐྲངས་མ་སྙོམས་པ་ (ñīŋgi pārdaŋ mañomba) arrhythmia.

སྙིང་གི་འཕར་ཚད་ (ñīŋgi pārdzɛɛ̀) heart rate.

སྙིང་གི་རྩ་ (ñīŋgi dzā) valves of the heart.

སྙིང་གི་གཟུངས་སུ་བཀོད་ (ñīŋgi suŋsu göö) va. to take to heart.

སྙིང་གི་ཤ་གནད་ (ñīŋgi shānεε) sm. སྙིང་ཤ་.

སྙིང་གྲང་སྡོང་སྡེ་ (ñīŋdraŋ dōŋde) feeling of sadness.

སྙིང་གྲོགས་ (ñīŋdrɔɔ) sweetheart, boyfriend, girlfriend.

སྙིང་གློ་གྲེ་གསུམ་ (ñīŋlo dresum) the three: heart, lungs and throat.

སྙིང་མགོ་རྡིང་ལོག (ñīŋgo dīŋlɔɔ) sm. སྙིང་མགོ་གཞུག་ལོག.

སྙིང་མགོ་གཞུག་ལོག (ñīŋgo shuglɔɔ) vi. to be frightened out of one's wits.

སྙིང་འགྱུལ་ (ñīŋgüü) sm. སྙིང་འཕར་.

སྙིང་འགྱུལ་ལྷ་འདར་ (ñīŋgüü lādar) sm. སྙིང་མགོ་གཞུག་ལོག.

སྙིང་སྒྲ་ (ñīŋdra) sound of the heart beating.

སྙིང་ཅན་ (ñīŋjεn) courage, bravery ༡ མི་སྙིང་ཅན་ A brave person.

སྙིང་གཅེས་གཅེས་ (ñīŋ jēējeè) lovingly; va.—བྱེད་ to love, to cherish.

སྙིང་གཅུས་ (ñīŋjüü) untruthful, dishonest.

སྙིང་བཅང་ (ñīŋjaŋ) holding in one's heart (remembering); va.—བྱེད་ ༡ ཞེ་ཁོན་སྙིང་བཅང་བྱས་ནས་ང་ལ་ཁོན་ལན་སློག་རྩིས་བྱེད་ཀྱི་འདུག (He) holds hatred in his heart so he is planning revenge against me.

སྙིང་བཅངས་ (ñīŋjaŋ) sm. སྙིང་བཅང་.

སྙིང་བཅུད་ (ñīŋjüü) 1. crystallization. 2. the essence.

སྙིང་ཆུ་ (ñīŋju) dropsy of the heart.

སྙིང་ཆུང་ (ñīŋjuŋ) sm. སྙིང་ཆུང་ཆུང་.

སྙིང་ཆུང་ཆུང་ (ñīŋ cūŋjuŋ) timid, meek, cowardly.

སྙིང་ཆེན་ (ñīŋjen) sm. སྙིང་ཆེན་པོ་.

སྙིང་ཆེན་པོ་ (ñīŋ cēmbo) brave, courageous.

སྙིང་འཆུ་ (ñīŋ cū) sm. ཡིད་འཁྲུག.

སྙིང་རྗེ་ (ñīŋje) 1. compassion, mercy, kindness; va.—བྱེད་; —ལྟ་ to act/ treat with compassion; vi.—སྐྱེ་ to get the feeling of compassion. 2. an expression of sympathy (sth. like "poor thing" or "what a pity").

སྙིང་རྗེ་ཆེན་པོ་ (ñīŋje cēmbo) compassionate, merciful, kind.

སྙིང་རྗེ་སྙོམས་པ་ (ñīŋje ñōmba) to be compassionate equally to all.

སྙིང་རྗེ་པོ་ (ñīŋ jebo) beautiful, pretty; va.—བཟོ་ to make pretty, to dress up.

སྙིང་རྗེ་སྦྱར་ཚོད་བསྒྲིགས་པ་ (ñīŋje bardzöö giibɔ) shung. pretending to be generous but actually short changing the people by giving them less than what they are entitled.

སྙིང་རྗེ་བྲལ་བ་ (ñīŋje treewa) sm. སྙིང་རྗེ་མེད་པ་.

སྙིང་རྗེ་མི་འདོར་པ་ (ñīŋje midɔɔba) sm. སྙིང་རྗེ་མི་ལྷོད་པ་.

སྙིང་རྗེ་མི་ལྷོད་པ་ (ñīŋje milhööba) continuously acting with compassion.

སྙིང་རྗེ་མེད་པ་ (ñīŋje meèba) without compassion, inhuman, barbarous, heartless.

སྙིང་རྗེ་མོ་ (ñīŋjemo) sm. སྙིང་རྗེ་པོ་.

སྙིང་རྗེའི་དམིགས་པ་ (ñīŋjee migbɔ) the object of one's compassion.

སྙིང་རྗེའི་ཀློང་དུ་ཚུད་ (ñīŋje lōŋdu tsüü) va. to have great compassion.

སྙིང་རྗེའི་ལྷ་ (ñīŋjee lhā) the compassionate Buddha (Avaloketishvara).

སྙིང་རྗེས་མི་བཟློག་པ་ (ñīŋjeè mishööwa) va. to not abandon being compassionate.

སྙིང་ཉེ་ (ñīŋñe) close, dear, loved ༡ ང་སྙིང་ཉེ་གྲོགས་པོ་ཞིག་ཡོད་ I have a close friend.

སྙིང་ཉེ་བ་ (ñīŋñewa) sm. སྙིང་ཉེ་.

སྙིང་ཉེ་བའི་སྐད་ཆ་ (ñīŋñewε gεεja) expressing one's innermost feelings/ thoughts in speech.

སྙིང་ཉེ་བའི་ཁྲག་རྩ་མཉམ་འཁོར་ (ñīŋñewε trāgdza ñamgɔɔ) very close friends [Lit. close friends whose blood circulates together].

སྙིང་ཉེ་ལགས་ (ñīŋñelaà) term of address for the wives of middle class people such as merchants.

སྙིང་ཉེའི་གྲོགས་པོ་ (ñīŋjee trogbo) bosom friend.

སྙིང་སྙིང་ (ñīŋñiŋ) term of address for girls of middle strata.

སྙིང་ཏིག (ñīŋdig) sm. སྙིང་ཐིག.

སྙིང་གཏད་ (ñīŋ dεε) va. to trust, to reveal one's innermost thoughts and feelings to sb. ༡ ངས་ཁོ་ལ་སྙིང་གཏད་ནའང་ཁོས་ང་ལ་ཡག་པོ་བྱས་མ་བྱུང་ Even though I trusted him he didn't do well by me.

སྙིང་གཏམ་ (ñīŋdam) one's innermost feelings or thoughts; va.—ཤོད་ to tell a secret, to express/ reveal one's innermost feeling/ thoughts.

སྙིང་རྟོགས་ཐིག་རིས་ཁང་ (ñīŋdog tigriigaŋ) electrocardiograph room.

སྙིང་སྟོན་ (ñīŋdön) sm. སྙིང་གཏད་.

སྙིང་སྟོན་པའི་སྐད་ཆ་ (ñīŋdönbε gεεja) sm. སྙིང་གཏམ་.

སྙིང་སྟོབས་ (ñīŋdob) enthusiasm; spirit; va.—སྤེལ་ to do things to encourage/ increase/ spread/ instill enthusiasm; vi.—སྐྱེ་ to have enthusiasm/ spirit grow/ arise ༡ གྲྭ་པ་ཚོར་གསར་བརྗེའི་སྙིང་སྟོབས་སྤེལ་ནའང་ཁོང་ཚོས་ལག་ལེན་བསྟར་མེད་པ་རེད་ Even though they did things to increase the monk's revolutionary spirit, they (the monks) did not put it to practice.

སྙིང་སྟོབས་ཀྱིན་འཕུར་ (ñīŋdob gyenjur) full of enthusiasm.

སྙིང་སྟོབས་ཅན་ (ñīŋdobjεn) enthusiastic, spirited.

སྙིང་སྟོབས་ཆུང་ཆུང་ (ñīŋdob cūŋjuŋ) 1. not enthusiastic. 2. not brave.

སྙིང་སྟོབས་ཆེན་པོ་ (ñīŋdob cēmbo) 1. enthusiastic. 2. brave, courageous, spirited.

སྙིང་སྟོབས་དྲག་པོ་ (ñīŋdob tragbo) courageous and powerful.

སྙིང་སྟོབས་ཞན་པ་ (ñīŋdob shemba) sm. སྙིང་སྟོབས་ཆུང་ཆུང་.

སྙིང་བསྟན་ (ñīŋ dεn) p. of སྙིང་སྟོན་.

སྙིང་ཐག་པ་ (ñīŋ tāgba) sincere, genuine, earnest.

སྙིང་ཐག་པ་ནས་ (ñīŋ tāgbanε) from the bottom of the heart, sincerely, genuinely, earnestly ༡ ཁོས་མི་དམངས་ལ་སྙིང་ཐག་པ་ནས་སྐད་ཆ་བཤད་པ་རེད་ He spoke sincerely to the people.

སྙིང་ཐག་རིང་བ་ (ñīŋtaà riŋwa) not close (in relationships).

སྙིང་ཐིག (ñīŋtig) sm. སྙིང་བཅུད་.

སྙིང་ཐུམ་ (ñīŋdum) pericardium.

སྙིང་འཐིབས་ (ñīŋ tib) vi. to be or feel lethargic/ tired/ dull.

སྙིང་དུ་སྡུག་པ་ (ñīŋdu dugba) attractive, captivating, pretty, beautiful.

སྙིང་དུ་འབབ་པ་ (ñīŋdu babba) sm. སྙིང་དུ་སྡུག་པ་.

སྙིང་དོན་ (ñīŋdön) essential or main meaning/ significance, heart/ crux of the matter ༡ རྩོམ་ཡིག་འདིའི་སྙིང་དོན་ག་རེ་རེད་ What is the main meaning of this article.

སྙིང་དོན་ལྡེ་བ་ (ñīŋdön dēwa) sm. སྙིང་དོན་.

སྙིང་དོམ་ (ñīŋdom) a red tassle that hangs around a horse's chest.

སྙིང་གདོས་ (ñīŋdöö) courage, bravery.

སྙིང་འདར་ (ñīŋ dar) vi. to tremble with fear.

སྙིང་འདོད་ (ñīŋdöö) 1. desire, wish, craving. 2. (vb + —) to want to do the verbal action. ༡ ང་ཁ་ལག་ཟ་སྙིང་འདོད་གིས་ I want to eat food.

སྙིང་འདོད་པོ་ (ñīŋ dööbo) sm. སྙིང་འདོད་.

སྙིང་ལྡིང་ (ñīŋdiŋ) sm. སྙིང་འཕྱོ་.

སྙིང་སྡུག (ñīŋduù) sweetheart, girlfriend, lover.

སྙིང་བདར་བའི་སྒྲ་ (ñīŋdarwε dra) heart murmur.

སྙིང་བསྡུས་ (ñīŋdüü) summary, outline.

སྙིང་ན་ (ñīŋ na) 1. vi. to be very painful/ hurtful ༡ ཁོས་ང་ལ་སྙིང་ན་དགོས་པའི་སྐད་ཆ་བཤད་བྱུང་ He said sth. that was very painful to me (said sth. that made my heart hurt). 2. abbr. of སྙིང་གི་ན་ཚ་.

སྙིང་ནད་ (ñīŋnεε) 1. hatred, enmity, grudge; va.—བསང་ས་ to eliminate/ overcome hatred; va.—རྩོད་ to express one's hatred. 2. heart/ coronary disease ༑ སྙིང་ནད་སྨི་ཚན་ Coronary disease department.

སྙིང་ནད་ཁ་ལེ་ནག་པོ་ (ñīŋnɛɛ̀ kāle nagbo) one of seven types of heart disease in tt. medicine.

སྙིང་ནས་ (ñīŋnɛɛ̀) from the heart, really, truly ༑ སྙིང་ནས་དགའ་པོ་བྱུང་ I really liked it.

སྙིང་ནུས་ (ñīŋnüü) strength of the heart.

སྙིང་ནོར་ (ñīŋnɔɔ) the most precious ༑ ཅ་ལག་དེ་ངའི་སྙིང་ནོར་རེད་ That thing is my most precious (possession).

སྙིང་གནོན་ (ñīŋ nön) 1. va. to suppress anger. 2. a fine, punishment.

སྙིང་ན་ (ñīŋna) auricle.

སྙིང་པར་ (ñīŋbar) electrocardiogram, electrocardiograph.

སྙིང་པོ་ (ñīŋbu) sm. སྙིང་དོན་.

སྙིང་པོ་ལྔ་ (ñīŋbu ŋā) the five essentials: brown sugar, melted butter, honey, seasame oil and salt.

སྙིང་པོ་ཅེ་ (ñīŋbuje) brave, courageous.

སྙིང་པོ་ཐོ་འགོད་ (ñīŋbu tō göö) va. to take notes of the main points.

སྙིང་པོ་སྡུས་ (ñīŋbu düü) va. to collect/ condense/ the main points (of sth).

སྙིང་པོ་མེད་པ་ (ñīŋbu meèba) meaningless, pointless, nonsensical.

སྙིང་པོར་འཛིན་ (ñīŋbor dzin) to consider sth. as the essence/ central point/ main significance or task ༑ དེང་སང་འཛུགས་སྐྲུན་བྱ་རྒྱུ་ལས་དོན་གྱི་སྙིང་པོར་འཛིན་གྱི་ཡོད་པ་རེད་ These days (they) consider development as the main task.

སྙིང་པོར་དབེན་པ་ (ñīŋbor wēnba) sm. སྙིང་པོ་མེད་པ་.

སྙིང་པོས་དབེན་པ་ (ñīŋböö wēnba) sm. ནང་དོན་མེད་པ་.

སྙིང་སྤོ་ (ñīŋ bō) va. to transplant a heart.

སྙིང་ཕུར་ཐེབས་ (ñīŋbur tēb) vi. to leave an indelible mark, to be unforgettable.

སྙིང་ཕུར་འདེབས་ (ñīŋbur deb) va. to encourage sb. by giving them advice.

སྙིང་འཕག (ñīŋ pāà) 1. vi. to have one's heart beat. 2. sm. ཧྲིང་གཡུག.

སྙིང་འཕག་མཚམས་ཆད་ (ñīŋ pāà tsāmjɛɛ̀) vi. to die [Lit. to have one's heart stop beating].

སྙིང་འཕར་ (ñīŋbar) sm. ཧྲིང་འཕག.

སྙིང་འཕར་ཐླབས་རིས་ (ñīŋbar lābrii) sm. ཧྲིང་པར་.

སྙིང་འཕྱོ་ (ñīŋjo) vi. to have one's heart pound with happiness/ excitement.

སྙིང་འཕྱོ་ལྡིང་བྱེད་ (ñīŋjo diŋjeè) sm. སྙིང་འཕྱོ་.

སྙིང་འཕྱོས་ (ñīŋjöö) one of the seven heart diseases in Tibetan medicine.

སྙིང་དབང་ (ñīŋwaŋ) the heart.

སྙིང་འདྲོ་བ་ (ñīŋdrowa) (vb.+ —) to want to do the verbal action ༑ ལས་མེད་ཁྱིམ་དུ་སྡོད་སྙིང་འདྲོ་བས་ Because he wanted to stay at home without working.

སྙིང་དབུས་ (ñīŋwüü) center/ middle of the heart; va.—སུ་བཅང་ to keep in mind/ heart ༑ བླ་མའི་བཀའ་སློབ་སྙིང་དབུས་སུ་བཅངས་པ་རེད་ We kept the lama's advice in our heart/ mind.

སྙིང་དབུས་སུ་བཅང་ (ñīŋwüüsu jāŋ) va. to keep in mind/ heart ༑ བླ་མའི་བཀའ་སློབ་སྙིང་དབུས་སུ་བཅངས་པ་རེད་ We kept the lama's advice in our heart/ mind.

སྙིང་འབྲས་ (ñīŋdɛɛ̀) cancer of the heart.

སྙིང་མ་རྗེ་ (ñīŋməje) an exclamation of compassion: "what a pity/ shame."

སྙིང་མེ་ (ñīŋme) a traditional Tibetan illness characterized by symptoms such as anger/ uneasiness, rapid heart beat.

སྙིང་མེད་ (ñīŋmeè) gutless, cowardly, not brave.

སྙིང་མེད་ཁོག་སྟོང་ (ñīŋmeè kōgdoŋ) having no substance; shallow.

སྙིང་རྩ་ (ñīŋdza) a pulse used to check the heart in Tibetan medicine.

སྙིང་རྩ་འཁྲུགས་ (ñīŋdza trūù) vi. to be extremely angry.

སྙིང་རྩ་འགགས་ (ñīŋdz gaà) vi. to have a myocardial infarction.

སྙིང་རྩ་ནས་ (ñīŋdzanɛ) sm. སྙིང་ཐག་པ་ནས་.

སྙིང་རྩ་འཕག་གྲངས་འཕྲུལ་འཁོར་ (ñīŋdza pāgdraŋ trūūgɔɔ) electrocardiograph machine.

སྙིང་རྩ་འཕག་གྲངས་འབྲི་ཤོག (ñīŋdza pāgdraŋ trishoò) electrocardiograph machine paper.

སྙིང་རྩ་འཕར་ (ñīŋdza pār) vi. to be beating/ pulsating (heart).

སྙིང་རྩའི་ནད་རིགས་ (ñīŋdzɛ nɛɛ̀rig) cardiovascular diseases.

སྙིང་རྩེ་ (ñīŋdze) the apex of the heart, apex cordis.

སྙིང་བརྩེ་བ་ (ñīŋ dzēwa) beloved.

སྙིང་བརྩེ་བའི་ཞིང་ (ñīŋ dzēwɛ shiŋ) the object of one's love.

སྙིང་ཚ་སྐྱུ་རུ་རུ་ (ñīŋdza gyūruru) sm. སྙིང་ཚ་ལོང་ལོང་.

སྙིང་ཚ་བ་ (ñīŋ tsāwa) feeling disappointed/ dismayed/ troubled.

སྙིང་ཚ་ལོང་ལོང་ (ñīŋtsa loŋloŋ) extremely frightened/ scared/ afraid; vi.—བྱེད་.

སྙིང་ཚད་ (ñīŋdzɛɛ̀) one of the seven heart diseases in tt. medicine.

སྙིང་ཚིམ་ (ñīŋ tsīm) 1. vi. to have one's wishes satisfied/ fulfilled. 2. vi. to be happy at the misfortune of one's enemy.

སྙིང་ཚིམ་དཀྲུགས་ (ñīŋdzim drūù) sm. སྙིང་ཚིམ་བགྲང་.

སྙིང་ཚིམ་བགྲང་ (ñīŋdzim draŋ) va. to say sth. to sb. one dislikes like "serves you right" when sth. bad happens to them ༑ ང་ཡིག་ཚད་མ་ཐོན་ཙང་ཁོས་ང་ལ་ཕན་པོ་བྱུང་ཟེར་ནས་སྙིང་ཚིམ་བགྲང་བྱུང་ Because I did not pass the exam, he was happy at my misfortune and said "serves you right".

སྙིང་ཚིམ་བདར་ (ñīŋdzim dar) sm. སྙིང་ཚིམ་བགྲང་.

སྙིང་ཚིམ་འདེབས་ (ñīŋdzim deb) sm. སྙིང་ཚིམ་བགྲང་.

སྙིང་ཚིམ་པོ་ (ñīŋ dzīmbu) 1. satisfied, content. 2. happy at an enemy's misfortune.

སྙིང་ཚིལ་ (ñīŋdzil) fat around the heart; va.—དཀྲུག to make sb. very angry (on purpose).

སྙིང་འཚུབ་ (ñīŋdzub) nervous; excitable, apprehensive; vi.—ལང་ to get nervous/ excited/ apprehensive.

སྙིང་ཞི་ (ñīŋshi) vi. to have one's mind calm down/ cool down/ subdue.

སྙིང་ཞོ་ཤ་ (ñīŋshosha) the kernel of wild jujube.

སྙིང་བཞོས་ (ñīŋ shöö) 1. sm. སེམས་གསོ་གཏོང་. 2. va. to tell/ reveal a secret.

སྙིང་གཟེར་ (ñīŋser) pain in the heart, angina pectoris; vi.—རྒྱག; —ལང་ to have pain in the heart.

སྙིང་གཡས་ཁོག་ཆུང་ (ñīŋyɛɛ̀ kōgjuŋ) right ventricle.

སྙིང་གཡུག (ñīŋ yüù) 1. vi. to have one's heart pound (as an illness), to have the heart palpitate ༑ ཁོང་སྙིང་ཞི་དྲག་གཡུགས་ཙང་སྨན་ཁང་ལ་ཕྱིན་པ་རེད་ He went to the hospital when his heart started palpitating quickly.

སྙིང་གཡོན་ཁོག་ཆུང་ (ñīŋyön kōgjuŋ) left ventricle.

སྙིང་རིང་བ་ (ñīŋ riŋwə) no love/ affection.

སྙིང་རེ་རྗེ་ (ñīŋreje) sm. སྙིང་རྗེ་.

སྙིང་རེ་ཚིམ་ (ñīŋredzim) sm. སྙིང་ཚིམ་.

སྙིང་རུས་ (ñīŋrüü) diligence, fortitude, persistence, will power; va.—བྱེད་.

སྙིང་རུས་ཆེན་པོ་ (ñīŋrüü cēmbo) diligent, hard working, persevering, persistence, strong willed ༑ ཁོང་སྙིང་རུས་ཆེན་པོ་ཡིན་ཙང་སློབ་སྦྱོང་ཡར་རྒྱས་མགྱོགས་པོ་བྱུང་སོང་ Because he is very diligent he improved quickly in his studies.

སྙིང་ལྷུང་ (ñīŋluŋ) 1. a kind of illness characterized by being sad/ depressed; vi.—ཞུགས་; —ལང་; —སྐྱང་ to be sad/ depressed; va.—སངས་ to get over depression/ sadness ༑ མོ་སྙིང་ལྷུང་ཞུགས་ནས་ཚེ་ལས་འདས་པ་རེད་ She became depressed and died. 2. anger, angry; vi.—ལང་ to get angry; va.—དཀྲུགས་ to make sb. angry ༑ ལས་བྱེད་པ་ཚོས་ལས་ཀ་ཡག་པོ་མ་བྱས་ཙང་འགོ་ཁྲིད་སྙིང་ལྷུང་ལངས་བཞག Because the cadre didn't work well the boss got angry. 3. jealous; vi.—ལང་ to get jealous; vi.—

སྡོད་ to make sb. jealous ༎ཕོ་བརྒྱ་སེམས་ཤོར་དགོས་པ་དང་མོ་བརྒྱ་སྙིང་ཀླུང་འཚངས་དགོས་པ་ Making 100 males fall in love and 100 women jealous.

སྙིང་ཀླུང་སྡོད་འཚངས་ (ñĩŋluŋ dõõdzaŋ) a serious case of སྙིང་ལུང་.

སྙིང་བརླགས་ (ñĩŋ lāà) va. to make (sb.) unconscious.

སྙིང་ལ་བགོད་ (ñĩŋlə gõõ) sm. སྙིང་དབུས་སུ་བཅང་.

སྙིང་ལ་བཅངས་ (ñĩŋlə jāŋ) p. of སྙིང་ལ་འཆང.

སྙིང་ལ་བཅང་ (ñĩŋlə cāŋ) va. to keep in mind, to hold in your heart ༎ཁོང་གི་བཀའ་སློབ་སྙིང་ལ་འཆང་རོགས་ Keep his advice in mind.

སྙིང་ལ་བནག (ñĩŋla nāà) sm. སྙིང་ལ་འཆང་.

སྙིང་ལ་འབབ་ (ñĩŋlə bə̲b) sm. སྙིང་དུ་འབབ་.

སྙིང་ལ་ཚེར་མ་འཛུགས་ (ñĩŋlə tsēēma dzu̲ù) va. to do sth. very hurtful ༎ངའི་སྐད་ཆ་དེས་ཁོང་གི་སྙིང་ལ་ཚེར་མ་བཙུགས་པ་ལྟར་ཕོག་ཐུག་བྱུང་སོང་ What I said to him hurt him just like a thorn stuck in his heart. [Lit. stick a thorn in the heart].

སྙིང་ལ་གཟེར་རྒྱག (ñĩŋlə se̲rgyaà) sm. སེམས་ལ་རྒྱག.

སྙིང་ལགས་ (ñĩŋlaà) abbr. of སྙིང་རྗེ་ལགས་.

སྙིང་ལས་ (ñĩŋlɛɛ̀) sm. སེམས་ཁྲལ་.

སྙིང་ཤ་ (ñĩŋsha) cardiac muscle; myocardium.

སྙིང་ཤག (ñĩŋshaà) ventricle.

སྙིང་ཤུན་ (ñĩŋshün) sm. སྙིང་ཤུན་.

སྙིང་ཤུན་གཉན་ཚད་ (ñĩŋshün ñɛ̃ndzɛɛ̀) pericarditis.

སྙིང་ཤུབས་ (ñĩŋshub) pericardium.

སྙིང་སོ་ལྷར་བརྩེ་བ་ (ñĩŋsodar dzēwa) extremely loving/ endearing.

སྙིང་སྲིན་ (ñĩŋsin) one of the seven heart diseases in tt. Tibetan medicine.

སྙིང་སློག (ñĩŋsɔɔ̀) abbr. སྙིང་དང་སློག་རྩ་.

སྙིང་གསང་ (ñĩŋsaŋ) sm. སྙིང་ཁང་.

སྙིང་ཧད་ (ñĩŋ hɛ̃ɛ̀) vi. to become unconscious, to lose consciousness.

སྙིད་པོ་ (ñĩibu) 1. younger brother of one's father. 2. brother-in-law.

སྙིད་མོ་ (ñĩimu) 1. father's sister. 2. sister-in-law.

སྙིམ་གང་ (ñĩmgaŋ) sm. སྙིམ་པ་གང་.

སྙིམ་པ་ (ñĩmbə) cupped hands (two hands), handful (two hands).

སྙིམ་པ་གང་ (ñĩmbəgaŋ) one handful (made by two hands held together).

སྙིམ་པ་འདེགས་ (ñi̲mbə de̲g) va. to cup one's hands (to receive food, water or money).

སྙིམ་བུ་ (ñi̲mbu) the small cupped hands of a child.

སྙིམ་བུ་གང་ (ñĩmbugaŋ) a small handful.

སྙིལ་: p. and f. **བསྙིལ་**; imp. **སྙིལ་** (ñĩi) 1. va. to pull/ break down (e.g., a wall). 2. va. to expel, to throw out ༎དགྲ་བོ་རང་ཡུལ་ནས་བསྙིལ་བ་རེད་ (They) expelled the enemies out of our land.

སྨྱུ་ཁ་ (ñũga) point of a pen, nib.

སྨྱུ་གུ (ñũgu) sm. སྨྱུག་གུ་.

སྨྱུག: p. **བསྨྱུགས་**; f. **བསྨྱུག**; imp. **སྨྱུགས་** (ñũù) 1. va. to put on makeup. 2. vi. to throw up/ to vomit. 3. va. to throw (sth.) in the water. 4. sm. སྨྱུ་གུ་.

སྨྱུག་གྲོག (ñũgdrɔɔ̀) pen holder worn by officials of the tt. government.

སྨྱུག་གུ (ñũgu) bamboo/ reed pen.

སྨྱུག་ཅུ་གང་ (ñũgjugaŋ) sm. སྨྱུག་ཅུ་གང་.

སྨྱུག་ལྕག (ñũjaà) flat bamboo cane used to hit the cheeks of boys and the hands of girls in tt. schools.

སྨྱུག་ལྗང་ (ñũgjaŋ) bamboo green (color).

སྨྱུག་སྡོང་ (ñũgdoŋ) bamboo tree.

སྨྱུག་བྱ་ (ñũgja) sm. སྨྱུག་བྱ་.

སྨྱུག་སྦུབས་ (ñũgbub) the hollow part of a piece of bamboo.

སྨྱུག་མ་ (ñũŋmə) bamboo.

སྨྱུག་མ་མཁན་ (ñũŋməgɛn) 1. people who work with bamboo. 2. people who make bows and arrows.

སྨྱུག་མ་གཞོན་ནུ་ (ñũŋmə sho̲nnu) new bamboo shoots/ stalk.

སྨྱུག་མའི་ཝ་ཤུ་ (ñũgmɛ wə̲shu) bamboo drains on roofs.

སྨྱུག་རྩ་ (ñũgdza) bamboo shoot.

སྨྱུག་འཛིན་དབང་པོ་ (ñũŋdzin wãŋbo) calligrapher.

སྨྱུག་གཞོན་ (ñũgshön) sm. སྨྱུག་མ་གཞོན་ནུ་.

སྨྱུག་ཡོལ་ (ñũyüü) bamboo curtain.

སྨྱུག་ཤིང་ (ñũgshiŋ) sm. སྨྱུག་སྡོང་.

སྨྱུག་ཤུན་ (ñũshün) bamboo bark.

སྨྱུག་སོ་ (ñũso) sm. སྨྱུག་སེར་.

སྨྱུག་སེར་ (ñũgser) color of bamboo, darkish yellow.

སྨྱུགས་ (ñũù) 1. imp. of སྨྱུག. 2. duration, time ༎དུས་ཚོད་སྨྱུགས་རིང་དུ་ For a long time.

སྨྱུགས་ཐག་རིང་པོ་ (ñũgdaà ri̲ŋbu) 1. far, distant. 2. sb. who can endure/ tolerate a lot.

སྨྱུགས་པིད་ (ñũgbii) va. to endure/ tolerate a lot or for a long time.

སྨྱུགས་འབུད་ (ñũgbüü) sm. སྨྱུགས་པིད་.

སྨྱུགས་རིང་པོ་ (ñũg ri̲ŋbu) sm. སྨྱུགས་ཐག་རིང་པོ་.

སྨྱུགས་རུས་ཆེན་པོ་ (ñũrüù cēmbo) sm. སྨྱུགས་རུས་ཆེན་པོ་.

སྨྱུགས་རུས་ཚ་པོ་ (ñũrüù tsābo) diligent, energetic in work.

སྨྱུགས་སྲིང་ (ñũg si̲ŋ) sm. སྨྱུགས་བསྲིངས་.

སྨྱུགས་བསྲིངས་ (ñũg si̲ŋ) va. to make longer (in time), to prolong.

སྙུང་: p. **བསྙུངས་**; f. **བསྙུང་**; imp. **སྙུངས་** (ñũŋ) 1. vi. to be sick/ ill (h.) ༎ཁོང་ཤ་འདི་མཆོད་ནས་བསྙུངས་སོང་ He got sick after eating this meat. 2. va. to reduce/ diminish. ༎མི་འབོར་མང་དྲགས་པས་བསྙུང་དགོས་པ་འདུག The population is too much so we must reduce it.

སྙུང་མཁན་ (ñũŋgɛn) a patient.

སྙུང་སྙུང་ཚ་ཚ་ (ñũŋñuŋ tsādza) sb. who is frequently ill/ often sick.

སྙུང་འདས་ (ñũŋdɛɛ̀) getting sick and dying; vi.—འགྱུར་ ༎ཁོང་དུས་ཐུང་ངང་པེ་ཅིང་ལ་སྙུང་འདས་གྱུར་པ་རེད་ After being in Beijing for a short time he got sick and died.

སྙུང་གནས་ (ñũŋnɛɛ̀) fasting; va.—སྲུང་; —སྨྱུང་ to fast.

སྙུང་བུ་ (ñũŋbu) awl; va.—འཛུགས་ to make a hole with an awl.

སྙུང་བུ་ཟུར་གསུམ་མ་ (ñũŋbu su̲rsummə) triangular edged awl.

སྙུང་བྲལ་ (ñũŋdrɛɛ) well, healthy.

སྙུང་དབྱིབས་ (ñũŋyib) cone, conical shape.

སྙུང་མེད་ (ñũŋmeè) sm. སྙུང་བྲལ་.

སྙུང་གཞི་ (ñũŋshi) sickness, illness, pain (h.); vi.—གནོད་ to be ill/ in pain; vi.—དྭངས་ to be cured/ recovered.

སྙུང་ཟུག (ñũŋsug) pain, ache (h.); vi.—སྐྱོན་ to pain/ hurt.

སྙུང་རིལ་ (ñũŋrii) a round awl.

སྙུང་ལོག་སྐྱོན་ (ñũŋlɔɔ̀ gyõn) vi. to have a relapse of an illness.

སྙུངས་ (ñũŋ) imp. of སྙུང་.

སྙུན་: p. **བསྙུན་**; f. **བསྙུན་** (ñũn) sm. སྙུང་.

སྙུན་གྱི་ཟིན་ (ñũngi si̲n) sm. སྙུན་མནར་.

སྙུན་བཅོས་ (ñũnjöö) medical treatment; va.—བྱེད་.

སྙུན་སྙུན་ཚ་ཚ་ (ñũnñun tsādza) h. of ན་ན་ཚ་ཚ་.

སྙུན་དྭངས་ (ñũn ta̲ŋ) vi. to be cured, to recover from an illness.

སྙུན་གདངས་ (ñũn da̲ŋ) vi. to be cured.

སྙུན་འདས་ (ñũndɛɛ̀) sm. སྙུང་འདས་.

སྙུན་དྲག་པོ་ (ñũn tra̲gbo) severe illness.

སྙུན་འདྲི་ (ñũndri) inquiring about an illness.

སྙུན་མནར་ (ñũnnar) vi. to be sick (h.).

སྙུན་བྲལ་ (ñũndrɛɛ) sm. སྙུང་བྲལ་.

སྙུན་མེད་ (ñũnmeè) sm. སྙུང་བྲལ་.

སྙུན་མཛེ་ (ñũndze) leprosy (h.).

སྙུན་གཞི་ (ñũnshi) sm. སྙུང་གཞི་.

སྙུན་གསོལ་ (ñũnsöö) sm. སྙུན་འདྲི་.

སྙེ་ (ñē) abbr. of སྙེ་མ་.

སྙེ་: p. **བསྙེས་**; f. **བསྙེ་**; imp. **སྙེས་** (ñē) 1. va. to lean against, to rest against ༎ངས་སྒལ་པ་རྩིག་པར་བསྙེས་པ་ཡིན་ I leaned my back against the wall. 2. va.

to depend on ། ཕྲུ་གུས་ཕ་མར་བསྙེས་ནས་མ་བསྡད་པར་ལས་ཀ་འཚོལ་དགོས་ The child should go to find a job rather than stay depending on his parents.

སྙེ་དཀར་ (ñēgar) an ear of grain without any grain kernels on it.

སྙེ་ཁ་འཁྲིག (ñēga drig) vi. to have the ears of grain bloom.

སྙེ་མགོ་ (ñēngo) the head of an ear (of grain).

སྙེ་ཐོ་ (ñēdo) scarecrow.

སྙེ་ནག (ñēnaà) smut, blight (for crops).

སྙེ་ཕུང་ (ñēbuŋ) a pile of cut grain.

སྙེ་ཕྲུག (ñēdruù) shung. boys from སྙེ་མོ་ who come to Lhasa as a corvee tax to learn copying for the government.

སྙེ་བོ་ (ñewo) marriage guarantor/ witness.

སྙེ་འབོལ་ (ñēmböö) pillow.

སྙེ་འབྲུ་ (ñēndru) ear of barley.

སྙེ་མ་ (ñēma) ear of a stalk of grain; va.—རྡུང་ to thresh grain; vi.—གཏོང་; —ཐོན་; —འདོགས་; —ཤར་ to have the ears of grain appear (on a crop).

སྙེ་མ་ཕོན་གཅིག (ñēma pȭnjig) sharing the good and the hard times together [Lit. a bunch of ears (of grain)].

སྙེ་མ་མིག་བླུགས་ (ñēmə mi̱gluù) a full grown spike of grain.

སྙེ་མ་ལོང་བ་ (ñēma lo̱ŋwa) an empty ear of grain.

སྙེ་མ་ཅན་གྱི་ལོ་ཏོག (ñēmajɛngi lo̱doò) crops with ears of grain.

སྙེ་མ་སྟོང་པ་ (ñēma dōŋba) sm. སྙེ་མ་ལོང་བ་.

སྙེ་མའི་གྲ་ (ñēmɛ dra̱) tassel on an ear of grain.

སྙེ་མོ་ (ñēmo) a district in Central Tibet.

སྙེ་ཤད་ (ñēshɛɛ̀) sm. སྙེ་མ་.

སྙེ་ཤོག (ñēshoò) paper made in སྙེ་མོ་.

སྙེག: p. **བསྙེགས་**; f. **བསྙེགས་**; imp. **བསྙེགས་** (ñēg) 1. va. catch up with ། མ་རྩ་རིང་ལུགས་ཀྱི་རྗེས་སུ་སྙེག་དགོས་ (We) have to catch up with capitalism. ། ཁ་སང་ཐོན་པའི་དམག་མིའི་རྗེས་སུ་སྙེགས་དགོས་ (We) have to catch up with the soldiers who left yesterday. 2. sm. རྗེས་སྙེག. 3. pursuing/ chasing/ seeking a higher position/ status ། ཁོས་གོ་གནས་མཐོན་པོར་སྙེག་གི་ཡོད་པ་རེད་ ། He is pursuing a higher position.

སྙེག་གཏོར་ (ñēgdɔɔ) pursuing and destroying, chasing and annihilating; va.—གཏོང་.

སྙེག་དུང་ (ñēgduŋ) pursuing and destroying; va.—གཏོང་, —བྱེད་.

སྙེག་དེག (ñēgdeg) sm. སྙེག་དུང་.

སྙེང་: p. **བསྙེངས་**; f. **བསྙེང་**; imp. **སྙེངས་** (ñēŋ) 1. va. to stretch, to lean ། སྒེའུ་ཁུང་ནང་ནས་ཁོས་མགོ་བསྙེངས་སོང་ He stretched his head out of the window. 2. vi. to be afraid, to fear ། དཀའ་ངལ་ལ་བསྙེངས་ཙང་དམག་མིར་ཞུགས་པ་རེད་ Because he feared hardship, he didn't join the army.

སྙེད་ (ñēè) see ཇི་སྙེད་.

སྙེན་: p.**བསྙེན་**; f. **བསྙེན་**; imp. **བསྙེན་** (ñēn) 1. sm. སྙེན་. 2. va. to recite prayers.

སྙེན་སྙིང་ (ñēnsiŋ) sm. ཉེ་རིང་, 2.

སྙེམས་ (ñēm) vi. to be proud/ arrogant.

སྙེམས་ཆུང་ (ñēmjuŋ) humble, meek.

སྙེམས་པ་ (ñēmba) pride, arrogance.

སྙེམས་བྲལ་ (ñēmdrɛɛ) unpretentious, unassuming.

སྙེའུ་སྒོའུ་ (ñēugau) a type of garlic.

སྙེར་སྙེར་པོ་ (ñēr nērbu) appearance of an animal when it is growling/ snarling.

སྙེས་ (ñēè) p. of སྙེ་.

སྙེས་འབོལ་ (ñēmböö) sm. སྙེ་འབོལ་.

སྙེས་མ་ཚོམ (ñēma dzōg) partially leaning against sth.

སྙོག: p. **བསྙོགས་**; f. **བསྙོག**; imp. **སྙོགས་** (ñōò) 1. va. to agitate/ stir up (e.g., water) ། ཁོས་ཁྲོན་པའི་ཆུ་བསྙོགས་བཞག He has stirred up the water in the well. ། ཁོས་མི་དམངས་ཀྱི་སེམས་བསྙོགས་པ་རེད་ He stirred up anger among the people. 2. va. to pursue collecting a loan.

སྙོག་མ་ (ñōgma) slime and sludge in murky water.

སྙོགས་ (ñōg) imp. of སྙོག.

སྙོད་: p. **བསྙོད་**; f. **བསྙོད་**; imp. **སྙོད་** (ñȍȍ) 1. va. to prechew food in order to give to an infant and then give it directly from one's mouth to the infant ། ཨ་མས་ཕྲུ་གུར་ལྟོ་ཆས་སྙོད་ནས་སྤྲེར་གྱི་འདུག The mother prechewed the food and gave it [directly from her mouth] to the child. 2. va. to even the thickness of a piece of yarn.

སྙོད་: p. **བསྙོད་**; f. **བསྙོད་**; imp. **སྙོད་** (ñȍȍ) va. to say/ tell.

སྙོན་དོར་ (ñōn dɔɔ) sm. སྙོན་འཛུགས་.

སྙོན་འཛུགས་ (ñōn dzu̱ù) va. to implicate/ blame falsely, to make a false accusation; va.—བྱེད་.

སྙོན་མེད་ (ñōnmeè) sm. བསྙོན་མེད་.

སྙོབ་: p. **བསྙོབས་**; f. **བསྙོབས་**; imp. **བསྙོབས་** (ñōb) va. to reach for, to stretch out ། ཁམ་སྡོང་མཐོ་རང་དྲགས་ནས་འབྲས་བུ་སྙོབ་ཀྱི་མེད་ Because the peach tree is so tall, one can't reach the fruit.

སྙོབས་ (ñōb) imp. of སྙོབ་.

སྙོམ་: p. **བསྙམས་**; f. **བསྙམ་**; imp. **སྙོམས་** (ñōm) va. to make even, to level, to divide evenly.

སྙོམ་ (ñōm) abbr. of སྙམས་པོ་.

སྙོམ་བགོ་ (ñōmgo) dividing equally; va.—བྱེད་.

སྙོམ་སྒྲིག (ñōmdrig) adjusting to make even, evening up; va.—བྱེད་ ། རྫོང་ཚང་མར་འབྲུ་རིགས་འཕེལ་འགྲིབ་ཀུན་སྙོམ་སྒྲིག་བྱས་པ་རེད་ They adjusted the amount of grain (the abundance and scarcity) in each district to make it even.

སྙོམ་སྒྲིག་ཁ་གསབ་ (ñōmdrig kəsəb) sm. སྙོམ་སྒྲིག.

སྙོམ་སྒྲིག་དཔྱ་ཁྲལ་ (ñōmdrig jādrɛɛ) balanced/ even taxes.

སྙོམ་ཆུང་ (ñōmjuŋ) meek, humble.

སྙོམ་ཆུང་ཆུང་ (ñōm cūŋjuŋ) sm. སྙོམ་ཆུང་ཆུང་.

སྙོམ་ཆུང་བ་ (ñōmjuŋə) 1. a person who is meek. 2. a person/ household who is economically modest.

སྙོམ་ཆུང་སེམས་ཆུང་ (ñōmjuŋ sēmjuŋ) sm. སྙེམས་ཆུང་.

སྙོམ་པོ་ (ñōmbo) sm. སྙོམས་པོ་.

སྙོམ་མེད་ (ñōmmeè) diligent.

སྙོམ་ལས་ (ñōmlɛɛ̀) lazy, indifferent, indolent, careless; va.—བྱེད་ to be lazy/ indifferent/ indolent/ careless.

སྙོམས་ (ñōm) abbr. of. of སྙོམས་པོ་.

སྙོམས་སྒྲིག (ñōmdrig) sm. སྙོམ་སྒྲིག.

སྙོམས་ཆུང་ཚུལ་ལྡན་ (ñōmjuŋ tsũndɛn) humble and decent/ law abiding.

སྙོམས་འཐེན་ (ñōmden) drawing/ pulling/ withdrawing to make even; va.—བྱེད་.

སྙོམས་པར་འཇུག (ñōmbar ju̱ù) va. to mediate. 2. va. to fornicate.

སྙོམས་པར་ཞུགས་ (ñōmbar shu̱ù) sm. སྙོམས་པར་འཇུག.

སྙོམས་པོ་ (ñōmbo) equal, even; va.—བཟོ་ to make even, to equalize; va.—བྱེད་ to do sth. evenly/ equally ། ལས་ཁུངས་ནང་གི་ལས་བྱེད་པའི་གླ་ཕོགས་སྙོམས་པོ་བཟོས་བཞག (They) made the salary of the office workers even.

སྙོམས་པོར་རྫི་ (ñōmbor dzi̱) va. to knead evenly.

སྙོམས་མེད་ (ñōmmeè) unequal, uneven.

སྙོམས་ཟུར་ (ñōmsur) straight angle.

སྙོམས་ལས་ (ñōmlɛɛ̀) sm. སྙོམ་ལས་.

སྙོམས་སེམས་ (ñōmsem) equanimity.

སྙོམས་བསྒྲིད་བདེ་མིན་ (ñōmsee de̱min) shung. difficult to equalize ། ས་ཞིང་སོས་སྙོམས་ཀྱི་ལྷག་བུའི་ཆད་ལྷག་སྙོམས་བསྒྲིད་བདེ་མིན་རེགས་ When we equalized the land, it was difficult to equalize small leftover pieces of land.

སྙོར་: p. and f. **བསྙོར་**; imp. **སྙོར་** (ñɔ̄r) 1. va. to hit, to beat. 2. va. to stamp on, to squash. 3. sm. སྙོར་སྐྱོང་.

སྙོར་སྐྱོང་ (ñɔ̄rgyoŋ) looking after, taking care of (patients, etc.); va.—བྱེད་.

སྙོར་གསོ་ཁང་ (ñɔ̄rsogaŋ) nursery (for children).

སྙོལ་དང་ (ñȍȍdaŋ) sm. སྙོ་རྗེ་.

སྙོལ་: p. and f. **བསྙལ་**; imp. **སྙོལ་** (ñȍȍ) 1. va. to put to sleep, to lay down ། མོས་ཕྲུ་གུ་འདི་བསྙལ་སོང་ She put the child to sleep. 2. va. to ferment །

ཆང་བསྙལ་བ་རེད་ (They) fermented the beer. 3. va. to hatch (eggs) ¶ བྱ་དེས་སྒོང་ང་བསྙལ་བ་རེད་ The hen hatched the egg. 4. sm. དཔྱལ་.

སྙོལ་དོང་ (ñõõdoŋ) silo.

སྙོལ་ཛ་ (ñõõdza) pot for fermenting ཆང་.

སྙོལ་བཟོ་ (ñõõso) fermenting.

བརྙ་: p. **བརྙས་**; f. **བརྙ་** (ñā) to borrow.

བརྙ་སྐྱི་ (ñāgyi) lending and borrowing; va.—བྱེད་.

བརྙ་བསྐྱི་ (ñāgyi) sm. བརྙ་སྐྱི་.

བརྙང་ (ñāŋ) f. of རྙོང་.

བརྙངས་ (ñāŋ) p. of རྙོང་.

བརྙན་ (ñɛn) 1. p. and f. of ཉན་. 2. image, replica.

བརྙན་སྐྱེལ་ (ñɛngyee) 1. television broadcasting; va.—བྱེད་. 2. faxing; va.—བྱེད་.

བརྙན་སྐྱེལ་ཁང་ (ñɛngyeegaŋ) fax room.

བརྙན་སྐྱེལ་གློག་འཕྲིན་ (ñɛngyee lɔ̃gdrin) fax.

བརྙན་སྐྱེལ་འདྲ་པར་ (ñɛngyee drabar) a fax.

བརྙན་སྐྱེལ་བྱེད་ (ñɛngyee ceè) va. to send a fax, to broadcast television.

བརྙན་སྣུན་ཁང་ (ñɛndrüngaŋ) radiography room.

བརྙན་ངོས་ (ñɛnŋöö) 1. the general appearance of a picture. 2. a frame.

བརྙན་མངོན་འཁྲུལ་ཆས་ (ñɛnŋön trũũjɛɛ̀) film developing machine.

བརྙན་མངོན་སྨན་རྫ་ (ñɛnŋön mɛnju) chemicals used for developing photographic film.

བརྙན་མངོན་སྨན་ཕྱེ་ (ñɛnŋön mɛnje) sm. བརྙན་མངོན་སྨན་རྫ་.

བརྙན་དེབ་ (ñɛndeb) magazine (with photos).

བརྙན་བརྡའི་འཁྱལ་ཚད་ (ñɛndɛ güüdzɛɛ̀) television frequency.

བརྙན་པར་ (ñɛmbar) pictorial/ illustrated magazine ¶ བརྙན་པར་ལྟ་ Look at the magazine.

བརྙན་པར་སྒྲིན་ཤོག (ñɛmbar jĩnshoò) sm. གློག་བརྙན་གྱི་པར་ཤོག.

བརྙན་པོ་ (ñɛmbo) 1. substitute, replacement. 2. image. 3. a borrowed item.

བརྙན་དཔར་ (ñɛmbar) sm. བརྙན་པར་.

བརྙན་ཕབ་ (ñɛmbəb) video; va.—ལྟ་ to watch video; va.—བསྟན་ to show a video.

བརྙན་ཕབ་ཁང་ (ñɛmbəbgaŋ) video theater.

བརྙན་ཕབ་ལྟ་བསྡད་ (ñɛmbəb dādɛn) va. to watch a video show with friends.

བརྙན་ཕབ་སྟོན་ཁང་ (ñɛmbəb dõŋgaŋ) sm. བརྙན་ཕབ་ཁང་.

བརྙན་ཕབ་སྒྲིན་ཤོག (ñɛmbəb jĩnshoò) video recording tape.

བརྙན་ཕབ་འཁྲུལ་འཁོར་ (ñɛmbəb trũũgɔɔ) video playing machine.

བརྙན་འཕྲིན་ (ñɛndrin) television ¶ བརྙན་འཕྲིན་ལས་ཁངས་ Television station.

བརྙན་འཕྲིན་ཁ་པར་ (ñɛndrin kābaa) phone with picture.

བརྙན་འཕྲིན་འཁོར་ལོ་ (ñɛndrin kɔ̃ɔlo) television mobile van.

བརྙན་འཕྲིན་རྒྱང་གྲགས་ (ñɛndrin gyaŋdraà) television set.

བརྙན་འཕྲིན་སྒྲིག་ཆས་ (ñɛndrin drigjɛɛ̀) television equipment.

བརྙན་འཕྲིན་བརྒྱུད་གཏོང་ཁང་ (ñɛndrin gyüüdoŋgaŋ) television relay station/ center.

བརྙན་འཕྲིན་བརྒྱུད་གཏོང་ལྡངས་འཁོར་ (ñɛndrin gyüüdoŋ lāŋgɔɔ) mobile television broadcast van.

བརྙན་འཕྲིན་སྟོན་ཤེལ་ (ñɛndrin dõnshee) sm. བརྙན་ཤེལ་.

བརྙན་འཕྲིན་ཕབ་བཅུག (ñɛndrin pəbjuù) recording from television to video.

བརྙན་འཕྲིན་འཁྲུལ་ཆས་ (ñɛndrin trũũjɛɛ̀) television equipment.

བརྙན་འཕྲིན་ལས་ཁང་ (ñɛndrin lɛ̀ɛgaŋ) television broadcasting station.

བརྙན་འཕྲིན་ལས་ཁངས་ (ñɛndrin lɛ̀ɛguŋ) television station.

བརྙན་འཕྲིན་ལས་ཁངས་ཀྱི་ཚན་ཚན་སྒྲིར་ (ñɛndrin lɛ̀ɛguŋ ledzɛn tsɛ̃ngɔɔ) television production team/ unit.

བརྙན་འཕྲིན་སློབ་གྲྭ་ཆེན་མོ་ (ñɛndrin lõbdra cẽmmo) television university (courses aired on television).

བརྙན་འབེབས་ (ñɛ̃n beb) va. to record (on video tape).

བརྙན་འབེབས་སྒྲིན་ཐག (ñɛ̃nbeb jĩndaà) video recording tape.

བརྙན་འབེབས་འཁྲུལ་འཁོར་ (ñɛ̃nbeb trũũgɔɔ) video tape recorder.

བརྙན་རིས་ (ñɛ̃nrii) images.

བརྙན་ལེན་འཁྲུལ་ཆས་ (ñɛ̃nlen trũũjɛɛ̀ video camera.

བརྙན་ཤེལ་ (ñɛ̃nshel) television screen.

བརྙབ་ (ñə̃b) f. of རྙོབ་.

བརྙབས་ (ñə̃b) p. of རྙོབ་.

བརྙས་ (ñɛ̃ɛ̀) p. of བརྙ་.

བརྙས་དཀྲི་ (ñɛ̃ɛ̀dri) shung. va. to blame.

བརྙས་ཀོ་ (ñɛ̃ɛ̀go) 1. teasing; va. བརྙས་ཀོ་; —བྱེད་ ¶ ཁོས་བུ་མོ་ལ་བརྙས་བཀོས་བཞག He teased the girls. 2. va. to do sth. to start a fight or make sb. angry ¶ ངས་རྫུན་བཤད་པ་རེད་ཟེར་ཁོས་ང་ལ་བརྙས་བཀོས་བྱུང་ He said, "I lied" to start a fight. 3. va. to bother/ annoy ¶ ཕྲུ་གུས་ཕ་མར་དངུལ་དགོས་ཡོད་ཟེར་རྟག་པར་བརྙས་ཀོ་གི་ཡོད་པ་རེད་ The child bothered his parents all the time saying he needs money.

བརྙས་ཀོ་འཁྲུག་སློང་ (ñɛ̃ɛ̀go trũgloŋ) instigating/ starting a fight.

བརྙས་འཁུར་ (ñɛ̃ɛ̀gur) sm. བརྙས་བཙོས་འཁུར་.

བརྙས་འཁུར་འགན་སྒྲུབ་ (ñɛ̃ɛ̀gur gɛndrub) putting up with abuse to fulfill an obligation/ duty/ responsibility.

བརྙས་འཁྲུག་སློང་ (ñɛ̃ɛ̀trũg lõŋ) sm. བརྙས་ཀོ་འཁྲུག་སློང་.

བརྙས་བཙོས་ (ñɛ̃ɛ̀jöö) abusing, bullying, mistreating; va.—བཤད་; —གཏོང་; —བྱེད་ to abuse, to mistreat, to bully; va.—འཁུར་ to bear abuse/ mistreatment, bullying.

བརྙས་གདམ་ (ñɛ̃ɛ̀dam) bullying/ abusing words; va.—ཤོད་.

བརྙས་བདགས་ (ñɛ̃ɛ̀daà) p. of བརྙས་འདོགས་.

བརྙས་སྤབས་ (ñɛ̃ɛ̀dəb) sm. བརྙས་བཙོས་.

བརྙས་ཐབས་ (ñɛ̃ɛ̀dəb) sm. བརྙས་བཙོས་.

བརྙས་འདོགས་ (ñɛ̃ɛ̀ dɔ̃ɔ̀) sm.* སྨད་འདོགས་.

བརྙས་འཕྲོག (ñɛ̃ndrɔɔ̀) stealing by bullying/ abusing; va.—བྱེད་.

བརྙས་འཕྲོག་བྱེད་མཁན་ (ñɛ̃ndrɔɔ̀ ceèñɛn) bully, aggressor.

བརྙས་སྨོད་ (ñɛ̃ɛ̀möö) humiliating, disgracing, abusing verbally, shaming; va.—བྱེད་ to humiliate, to disgrace, to abuse, to shame.

བརྙས་གཙེར་ (ñɛ̃ɛ̀dzer) shung. insulting, oppressing ¶ ཆབ་འབངས་མི་སེར་ཐོག་བརྙས་གཙེར་ཇི་སྙེད་ཅིག་བྱུང་འདུག There were many events of insulting and oppressing the subjects.

བརྙས་རྩེད་རྩེ་ (ñɛ̃ɛ̀dzeè dzẽ) va. to tease, to make fun of.

བརྙས་ཚིག (ñɛ̃ɛ̀dzii) sm. བརྙས་གདམ་.

བརྙས་འཚོལ་ (ñɛ̃ɛ̀dzöö) looking for an opportunity to abuse/ bully.

བརྙས་བཞག (ñɛ̃ɛ̀ shaà) va. to insult ¶ ཁོ་པས་ཏཱ་ལའི་བླ་མ་རིན་པོ་ཆེར་བརྙས་བཞག བོད་མི་དམངས་རྣམས་ལ་བདབ་གསིག་མནར་གཅོད་ He insulted the Dalai Lama and oppressed the people.

བརྙས་སེ་གོ་སེ་ (ñɛ̃ɛ̀se kose) sm. སྣ་སེ་གོ་སེ་.

བརྙས་སེམས་ (ñɛ̃ɛ̀sem) thoughts of bullying/ abusing humiliating; va.—འཆང་.

བརྙིངས་ (ñĩŋ) sm. རྙིང་.

བརྙིས་ (ñĩi) p. of རྙེད་.

བརྙེད་ (ñẽè) p. of རྙེད་.

བརྙེས་ (ñẽè) 1. vi. to obtain/ acquire/ get. 2. vi. to begin, to start.

བརྙོག: p. **བརྙོགས་**; f. **བརྙོག** (ñõg) vi. (with ཁ་) to like the experience of sth. and want to do it again, to get hooked on sth. ¶ ཁོང་ཟ་ཁང་འདིའི་ཁ་ལག་ལ་ཁ་བརྙོག་ནས་ཡང་སྐྱར་ཟ་ཁང་དེ་ཕྱིན་སོང་ He liked the food of that restaurant and went to it again.

བརྙོགས་ (ñɔ̃ɔ̀) p. of རྙོག.

བརྙོངས་ (ñõŋ) p. of རྙོང་.

བསྙད་ (ñɛ̃ɛ̀) 1. p. of སྙོད་. 2. va. to blame, to accuse, to use as a reason for doing sth. ¶ གོམས་སྲོལ་ལོ་རྒྱུས་ཡོངས་རྫོགས་རྙིང་ལུགས་ལ་བསྙད་དེ་གཏོར་བ་རེད་ (They) destroyed all their traditions and customs accusing them of being old-fashioned. 3. va. to use as pretext, to pretend ¶ ཁོས་ན་ཚ་ཡོད་པར་བསྙད་ནས་ལས་ཀར་མ་ཡོང་བ་རེད་ He pretended to be sick and didn't go to work.

བསྙད་བཀོ་ (ñɛ̃ɛ̀go) sm. བརྙས་ཀོ་.

བསྙད་བདགས་ (ñɛ̃ɛ̀daà) p. སྙད་འདོགས་.

བསྙད་བདགས་དགོངས་ཞུ་ (ñɛ̃ɛ̀daà go̲ŋshu) va. to make excuses for doing sth., to shirk (work).

བསྙད་འདོགས་ (ñɛ̃ɛ̀ dɔ̃ɔ̀) 1. va. to blame/ accuse. 2. va. to use as a pretext/ excuse.

བསྙད་འདོགས་རྒྱུ་ཟ་ (ñɛ̃ɛ̀dɔ̃ɔ̀ gyu̲sa) va. to blackmail.

བསྙད་འདོགས་བཙན་འཁྲོག (ñɛ̃ɛ̀dɔ̃ɔ̀ dzɛ̃ndrɔ̃ɔ̀) extorting; va.—བྱེད་ to extort.

བསྙད་མེད་བསྙད་འདོགས་ (ñɛ̃ɛ̀meè ñɛ̃ɛ̀dɔ̃ɔ̀) unjustly or falsely accusing, framing.

བསྙད་འཚོལ་ (ñɛ̃ɛ̀ tsö̃ö̀) sm. སྙད་འཚོལ་.

བསྙད་གཞི་ (ñɛ̃ɛ̀shi) 1. preface (of book). 2. a basis or reason for using as an excuse/ pretext.

བསྙད་བསྲུན་བཟོད་མ་བདེ་ (ñɛ̃ɛ̀sün sö̲ö̀made) shung. to trouble, to be troublesome.

བསྙབ་ (ñɔ̃b) f. of སྙོབ་.

བསྙབ་པ་ལག་པ་སུ་རིང་ (ñɔ̃bba la̲gba sū ri̲ŋ) taking whatever one can get one's hands on [Lit. whoever's hand is longer reaches].

བསྙབས་ (ñɛ̃b) p. of སྙོབ་.

བསྙམ་ (ñam) 1. f. of སྙོམ་. 2. p. of སྙོམས་.

བསྙམས་ (ñām) f. of སྙོམ་.

བསྙལ་ (ñɛ̃ɛ̀) p. and f. of སྙོལ་.

བསྙལ་ཁང་ (ñɛ̃ɛ̀gaŋ) fermenting/ distilling workshop/ room.

བསྙལ་ཁུ་ (ñɛ̃ɛ̀gu) liquid from marinated/ pickled vegetables, the liquid from sth. that has been fermented.

བསྙལ་སྒོང་ (ñɛ̃ɛ̀goŋ) pickled egg.

བསྙལ་ཐབས་ (ñɛ̃ɛ̀dəb) a piece of string used to tie the arm (to find the vein) when drawing blood.

བསྙལ་མ་ (ñɛ̃ɛ̀ma) marinated or pickled food ¶ ཚལ་བསྙལ་མ་ Pickled vegetables.

བསྙལ་ཚལ་ (ñɛ̃ɛ̀dzɛɛ) pickled vegetables.

བསྙལ་ཚོད་ (ñɛ̃ɛ̀dzö̀ö̀) sm. བསྙལ་ཚལ་.

བསྙལ་ཟུར་ (ñɛ̃ɛ̀sur) obtuse angle.

བསྙལ་བཟོས་ཟས་རིགས་ (ñɛ̃ɛ̀sö̀ö̀ sɛ̲ɛ̀rig) marinated/ pickled foods.

བསྙལ་བཟོ་ལས་ཚན་ (ñɛ̃ɛ̀so lɛ̲ɛ̀dzɛn) a workshop where marinating or fermenting takes place.

བསྙིག (ñĩg) f. of སྙིག.

བསྙིགས་ (ñĩg) p. of སྙིག.

བསྙིལ་ (ñĩĩ) f. of སྙིལ་.

བསྙུགས་ (ñũg) p. of སྙུག.

བསྙུང་ (ñũŋ) see སྙུང་.

བསྙུང་གནས་ (ñũŋnɛɛ̀) a religious fast/ retreat.

བསྙུང་གཞི་ (ñũŋshi) sm. སྙུང་གཞི་.

བསྙུངས་ (ñũŋ) see སྙུང་.

བསྙུན་ (ñũn) p. and f. of སྙུན་.

བསྙུན་འདས་ (ñũndɛɛ̀) sm. སྙུང་འདས་.

བསྙུན་གཞི་ (ñũnshi) sm. སྙུང་གཞི་.

བསྙུན་གཤེགས་ (ñũnsheg) sm. སྙུང་འདས་.

བསྙེ་ (ñē) f. of སྙེ་.

བསྙེག (ñēg) p. and f. of སྙེག.

བསྙེགས་ (ñēg) p. of སྙེག.

བསྙེང་ (ñēŋ) f. of སྙེང་.

བསྙེངས་ (ñēŋ) p. of སྙེང་.

བསྙེངས་བྲལ་ (ñēŋdrɛɛ) 1. fearless, brave, courageous. 2. poet. hero.

བསྙེན་ (ñēn) p. and f. of སྙེན་.

བསྙེན་བཀུར་ (ñēngur) a present/ offering (such as food) given out of respect or reverence, serving sb. out of respect; va.—བྱེད་; —ཞུ་ to give presents/ offerings out of respect or reverence, to support ¶ དགེ་འདུན་པར་བསྙེན་བཀུར་དེ་ Giving presents/ offerings to the monks.

བསྙེན་བཀུར་མཇལ་ཕྱག (ñēngur jɛ̲ɛjaà) shung. making offerings/ prostrating while having an audience.

བསྙེན་བཀུར་ཞིང་མཆོག (ñēngur shi̲ŋjɔ̃ɔ̀) the object of one's respect and reverence (e.g., monks, elders).

བསྙེན་སྒྲུབ་ (ñēndrub) sm. བསྙེན་པ་.

བསྙེན་ཆེན་ (ñēnjen) 1. great respect/ reverence/ esteem. 2. a large བསྙེན་པ་.

བསྙེན་གནས་ (ñēnnɛɛ̀) a one day སྙུང་གནས་.

བསྙེན་གནས་ཚུལ་ཁྲིམས་ (ñēnnɛɛ̀ tsũũdrim) the one day vow of སྙུང་གནས་.

བསྙེན་གནས་ལ་གནས་ (ñēnnɛɛ̀la nɛ̃ɛ̀) va. to be in the state of fasting.

བསྙེན་པ་ (ñēmba) the performance of a large number of mantra prayers; va.—སྐྱེལ་; —གཏོང་.

བསྙེན་པར་རྫོགས་ (ñēmbar dzɔ̃ɔ̀) va. to take the vow of a gelong.

བསྙེན་མཚམས་ (ñēndzam) staying in retreat reciting the mantra of one's personal deity; va.—བྱེད་.

བསྙེན་རྫོགས་སྡོམ་པ་ (ñēndzɔ̃ɔ̀ do̲mba) vow of a gelong.

བསྙེན་བསྲིང་ (ñēnsiŋ) sm. ཉེ་རིང་.

བསྙེམ་ (ñēm) f. of སྙེམ་.

བསྙེམས་ (ñēm) p. of སྙེམ་.

བསྙེར་ (ñēr) p. and f. of སྙེར་.

བསྙེལ་ (ñēē) h. of བརྗེད་.

བསྙེལ་ངས་ (ñēēŋɛɛ̀) sm. བརྗེད་ངས་.

བསྙེལ་ཐོ་ (ñēēdo) a note; va.—སྒྲོན་ to make a note, to take notes.

བསྙེལ་བྱང་ (ñēējaŋ) notebook.

བསྙེལ་གསོ་ (ñēēso) h. of དྲན་གསོ་.

བསྙེས་ (ñēè) p. of སྙེ་.

བསྙེས་བཅས་ (ñēèjɛɛ̀) va. to lean against sth.

བསྙོག (ñõò) f. of སྙོག.

བསྙོགས་ (ñõò) p. of སྙོག.

བསྙོད་ (ñö̃ö̀) p. and f. of སྙོད་.

བསྙོན་ (ñõn) p. and f. of སྙོན་.

བསྙོན་དྲི་ (ñõndri) using sth. as an excuse/ pretext; va.—བྱེད་ ¶ དགོན་པ་ཉམས་གསོ་བྱ་རྒྱུ་ཡིན་ལུགས་ཀྱི་བསྙོན་དྲི་བྱས་ཏེ་དགོན་པ་ནས་འབྲུ་རིགས་མང་པོ་བླངས་འདུག Using the repair of the monastery as a pretext, (he) took much grain from the monastery.

བསྙོན་དྲི་བཙན་ལེན་ (ñõndri dzɛ̃nlen) taking sth. by force through use of a pretext.

བསྙོན་དྲི་ཚ་པོ་ (ñõndri tsābo) sb. who uses excuses/ pretexts to get things from people.

བསྙོན་དོལ་ (ñõndöö) sm. བསྙོན་དྲི་.

བསྙོན་འདིང་ (ñõndiŋ) sm. བསྙོན་དོལ་.

བསྙོན་པས་ཐོབ་ (ñõmbɛ tōb) vi. to obtain things by using a pretext.

བསྙོན་མེད་ (ñõnmeè) without a doubt, true, not false, really, truly, unquestionably ¶ རྒྱལ་ཁབ་རང་བཙན་བསྙོན་མེད་མང་པོ་བཟུང་བ་རེད་ (They) seized many unquestionably independent countries.

བསྙོན་འཛུགས་ (ñõndzuù) falsely accusing/ blaming; va.—བྱེད་.

བསྙོན་འཛུགས་ཉེས་འགེལ་ (ñõndzuù ñ̲engee) sm. བསྙོན་འཛུགས་.

བསྙོན་ཧམ་ (ñõnham) sm. བསྙོན་དྲི་.

བསྙོན་ཧམ་མནའ་དག་གི་ཞལ་ལྕེ་ (ñõnham nādaggi sh̲ɛɛje) one of sixteen ways of executing the law in the tt. judicial system whereby the accused is made to swear innocence in front of guardian deities.

བསྙོབས་ (ñōb) p. of སྙོབ་.

བསྙོར་ (ñɔ̄ɔ̄) p. and f. of སྙོར་.

བསྙོལ་ (ñȫȫ) sm. འཇེགས་.

ད

ད་ (dā) the letter ta (used in alphabetical numbering).

ད་ཀྲའི་ (dādrɛ) ch. Dazhai (name of a Chinese village that was used as a model village in state propaganda).

ད་ཁར་ཏ་ (dākarda) Jakarta.

ད་གེ་དོག་གེ (dāge dōgge) small (usu. for houses).

ད་སྒུར་ (dāgur) name for the letter ད་ (in some areas of Kham).

ད་སྒོར་ (dəgor) sm. དཱ་སྒོར་.

ད་ཅང་ (dājaŋ) ch. colonel general.

ད་ཆིང་ (dājiŋ) Daqing.

ད་ཆིང་སྣུམ་གཏེར་ (dājiŋ nūmder) ch.tib. Daqing Oilfield.

ད་ད་ག་ད་འཛིང་ (dāda gāda dziŋ) va. to argue/ dispute loudly (usu. a subordinate arguing with his superior officer).

ད་ཐ་ག་ཐ་ (dāda gada) immediately ༑གོང་རིམ་ནས་སྐྱོན་བརྗོད་བྱས་པར་ཁོས་ལན་ད་ཐ་ག་ཐ་བསྒྲིགས་སོང་ He immediately responded to the criticism of the authorities.

ད་དང་དམག་སྒར་ (dādaŋ māägar) shung. the Tadang Regiment (in the tt. army).

ད་སྡེ་ (dāde) the third category of four letters in the Tibetan alphabet (i.e., ད་ཐ་ད་ན་).

ད་པ་ན་ (dābana) Osaka.

ད་པག (dābaà) plate.

ད་དབེན་ (dāwen) sm. དཱ་དབེན་.

ད་དབྱི་ (dəji) ch. overcoat.

ད་མ་སི་ཀི་ (dāmasiki) Damascus.

ད་མིང་ (dāmiŋ) ch. the Ming Dynasty.

ད་ཙི་ཅིས་ (dādzi jii) ch. typewriter.

ད་ཛ་ (dādza) 1. coriander. 2. gold nuggets.

ད་ཤའོ་ (dāshao) ch. senior colonel.

ད་ཞི་དབྱང་རྒྱ་མཚོ་ཆེན་པོ་ (dā shiyan gyatso cēmbo) ch.tib. Atlantic Ocean.

ད་ཞིས་དབྱང་ (tā shiyaŋ) sm. ད་ཞི་དབྱང་རྒྱ་མཚོ་ཆེན་པོ་.

ད་ཟིག (dəsii) Persia.

ད་ཝེ་ (dāwe) ch. senior captain.

ད་ར་ (dāra) Tara (the female goddess).

ད་ར་ཙེ་ (dāradze) ch. a small (weighing) scale, a small steelyard.

ད་རེ་དོ་རེ་ (dāre dōre) sm. དོ་རོ་མོ་རོ་.

ད་རིག (dərig) hind. date.

ད་ལ་ (dāla) palmyra (tree).

ད་ལ་ལ་ (dālala) arc. sm. མར་མེ་.

ད་ལའི་རྒྱལ་པོ་ (dālɛ gyɛɛbo) coconut tree.

ད་ལའི་བླ་མ་ (dālɛ lāma) Dalai Lama.

ད་ལའི་ལོ་མའི་ཡི་གེ་ (dālɛ lomɛ yigi) history/ scripture recorded on palm leaves.

ད་ལའི་ཤིང་ (dālɛ siŋ) palmyra tree.

ད་ལི་ (dāli) profit.

ད་ལེ་ (dāle) 1. beauty. 2. clearly ༑སྔོན་མའི་གནས་ཚུལ་ཡིད་ལ་ད་ལེར་ཤར་བྱུང་ The past events appeared clearly in my mind.

ད་ལེ་སི་ (dālesi) Dallas.

ད་ཧུང་ (dāhuŋ) ch. red brocade.

ད་ཧུའོ་ཙི་ (dā hūwoji) ch. lighter.

ད་ཧྲི་ (dāhri) ch. consul general.

ད་ཧྲི་ལས་ཁང་ (dāhri) ch.tib. consulate.

དཱ་ (dā) ch. big, great.

དཱ་ཀོའུ་ཙི་ (dākodzi) ch. shung. long unlined Chinese gown worn in Tibet by officials of the དཱ་བླ་མ་ rank.

དཱ་སྒོར་ (dāgɔɔ) ch.tib. silver yuan (dayan).

དཱ་ཅང་ (dājaŋ) sm. ད་ཅང་.

དཱ་བླ་མ་ (dā lāma) ch.tib. shung. a monk official's rank in the traditional Tibetan government.

དཱ་དབེན་ (dāben) 1. ch. red silk 2. the Yuan Dynasty.

དཱ་དབེན་ཏི་ཧྲི་ (dāben dihri) ch. the head priest/ lama of the Yuan Dynasty.

དཱ་མིང་ (dāmiŋ) ch. sm. ད་མིང་.

དཱ་ཡང་ (dāyaŋ) ch. sm. དཱ་སྒོར་.

དཱ་ལ་ (dāla) sm. ད་ལ་.

དཱ་ལའི་ (dālɛ) 1. mong. ocean. 2. abbr. of དཱ་ལའི་བླ་མ་.

དཱ་ལའི་བླ་མ་ (dālɛ lāma) sm. ད་ལའི་བླ་མ་.

དཱ་ལའི་བླ་མར་འབོད་པའི་གདམ་ (dālɛ lāmaa bööbɛ dām) shung. an order given by (the one who is called the) Dalai Lama.

དཱ་སེ་ (dāse) playing cards; va.—རྒྱག to play cards.

དག (dāà) a weaving tool used on a loom.

དག་གི་དིག་གི་ (dāàgi diigi) small load/ package.

དག་གེ་དིག་གི་ (dāàge diige) sm. དག་གི་དིག་གི་.

དག་སྒྲ་ (dāgdra) the sound of knocking.

དག་དག (dāgdaà) 1. exactly, definitely ༑འདི་མང་ཉུང་དག་དག་རེད་ This is exactly the right amount. 2. the sound of knocking; va.—གཏོང་ to knock (e.g., on a door). 3. va. to do in, to kill; va.—བཟོ ༑ཇག་པ་དེ་དག་དག་མ་བཟོས་ན་མི་དམངས་ལ་གནོད་པ་ཆེན་པོ་སྐྱེལ་གྱི་རེད་ If we don't kill the bandits it will cause great harm to the people.

དག་དག་འཁེལ་ (dāgdaà kēē) sm. དག་དག་འགྲིག.

དག་དག་འགྲིག (dāgdaà drig) vi. to happen/ occur coincidentally or at the same time ༑ང་བོད་ལ་ཕྱིན་པ་དང་རྡོ་རྗེ་སླེབས་པ་དུས་ཚོད་དག་དག་འགྲིག་སོང་ When I went to Tibet Dorje arrived (coincidentally) at the same time.

དག་དག་དིག་དིག (dāgdaà digdii) exactly, definitely ༑འདི་མང་ཉུང་དག་དག་དིག་དིག་རེད་ This is exactly the right amount.

དག་དིག (dəddig) abbr. of དག་གི་དིག་གི་.

དག་སེ་ (dāgse) playing cards; va.—རྒྱག to play cards.

དང་ (dāŋ) ch. party (political).

དང་ཀུ (dāŋgün) ch. sm. དང་ཀུན་.

དང་ཀུན་ (dāŋgün) ch. Chinese Angelica.

དང་གྲི་པུའུ་ (dāŋ dribu) ch. party branch.

དང་གྲི་པུའུ་ཨུ་ཡོན་ལྷན་ཁང་ (dāŋ dribu ūyön lhɛngaŋ) ch. party branch committee.

དང་གྲི་ཧྲུའུ་ (dāŋ drihru) ch. secretary of a party branch.

དང་ཀྲུང་དབྱང་ (dāŋ drūŋyaŋ) ch. central committee of the party.

དང་ཀྲུང་དབྱང་ཆབ་སྲིད་ཅུས་ (dāŋ drūŋyaŋ cəbsii jüü) ch. political bureau of the central committee of the party.

དང་གི་སྐུ་ཚབ་ (dāŋgi gūdzəb) ch.tib. representative/ delegate of the party.

དང་གི་སྐྱིད་སྡུག (dāŋgi giiduù) ch.tib. party register, party membership roll.

དང་གི་སྒྲིག་ཁྲིམས་ (dāŋgi drigdrim) ch.tib. party regulations.

དང་གི་སྒྲིག་འཛུགས་ (dāŋgi drigdzuù) ch.tib. party organization.

དང་གི་སྒྲིག་ཡིག (dāŋgi drigyii) ch.tib. party constitution/ regulations.

དང་གི་གྲལ་རིམ་གྱི་ལམ་ཕྱོགས་ (dāŋgi treerimgi lamjɔɔ) ch.tib. class line of the party.

དང་གི་གྲོན་དངུལ་ (dāŋgi drönŋüü) party expenses.

དང་གི་བཅའ་ཁྲིམས་ (dāŋgi jādrim) ch.tib. sm. དང་གི་སྒྲིག་ཡིག.

དང་གི་དར་ཆ་ (dāŋgi tarja) ch.tib. party flag.

དང་གི་དམིགས་ཡུལ་ (dāŋgi migyüü) ch.tib. party program.

དང་གི་འཐུས་མི་ (dāŋgi tüümi) ch.tib. sm. དང་གི་སྐུ་ཚབ་.

དང་གི་སྤྱི་ཁྱབ་ཀྱི་པུའུ་ (dāŋgi jigyəb dribu) ch.tib. general party branch.

དང་གི་བྱེད་སྒོའི་ཉི་མ་ (dāŋgi ceègö ñimə) ch.tib. party

day.

དང་གི་རྩ་འཛིན་ (dāŋgi dzǝndzin) ch.tib. party platform/ principle/ program.

དང་གི་རྫོམ་སྣང་སྐམ་པོ་ (dāŋgi dzōmdaŋ gambo) ch.tib. party jargon, stereotyped political terminology/ writing.

དང་གི་ཚན་སྒོར་ (dāŋgi tsɛ̄ngɔɔ) leading party group (in a state organ or people's organization).

དང་གི་ཚགས་པར་ (dāŋgi tsāgbar) ch.tib. party newspaper.

དང་གི་མཚན་ཉིད་ (dāŋgi tsɛ̄nñii) ch.tib. party nature/ character.

དང་གི་ཡན་ལག་ཕུའུ་ (dāŋgi yɛnlaà bū) ch.tib.ch. sm. དང་གི་ཕུའུ་.

དང་གི་ལས་དོན་ (dāŋgi lɛ̄ɛ̀dön) ch.tib. sm. དང་དོན་.

དང་གི་ལོ་རྒྱུས་ (dāŋgi lugyur) ch.tib. party history.

དང་གི་ཤེས་བྱ་སློབ་ཁྲིད་ (dāŋgi shēèja lōndrii) ch.tib. party lecture, party class/ school.

དང་གི་སློབ་གྲྭ་ (dāŋgi lōbdra) ch.tib. party school.

དང་གི་ཨུ་ཡོན་ལྷན་ཁང་ (dāŋgi ūyön lhɛ̄ngaŋ) ch.tib. party committee.

དང་ཀློལ་ (dāŋgöö) ch.tib. antiparty ¶ དང་ཀློལ་མཐའ་འབྲེལ་ Antiparty alliance.

དང་ཀློལ་ཚོགས་ཁག་ (dāŋgöö tsɔ̄ɔ̀gaà) ch.tib. antiparty group/ faction.

དང་སྒྲིག་ (dāŋdrig) abbr. of དང་གི་སྒྲིག་ཁྲིམས་.

དང་དངུལ་ (dāŋŋüü) ch.tib. party membership fee.

དང་གཉིས་ལམ་ལུགས་ (dāŋñii lǝmluù) ch.tib. two-party system.

དང་དོང་ (dāŋdoŋ) sound of large bells clanging (usu. on yaks, donkeys, etc.).

དང་དག་ཐེར་ (dāŋ tagder) ch.tib. abbr. of དང་ནང་དག་ཐེར་.

དང་དོན་ (dāŋdön) ch.tib. party works, party affairs.

དང་ནང་གི་ཡན་ལག་བརྒྱད་པའི་རྫོམ་རྒྱལ་ (dāŋdöngi yɛnlaà gyɛ̄ɛ̀bɛ dzōmdzüü) ch.tib. sm. དང་གི་རྫོམ་སྣང་སྐམ་པོ་.

དང་ནང་གི་མར་འགྲོ་བ་ (dāŋnaŋgi mardrowa) a party official who is taking the capitalist road.

དང་ནང་དག་ཐེར་ (dāŋnaŋ tagder) ch.tib. party rectification.

དང་ནང་ཞུགས་ (dāŋnaŋ shuù) ch.tib. va. to join the party.

དང་ནང་ཞུགས་རྒྱུའི་རེ་འདུན་ཞུ་ཡིག (dāŋnaŋ shuùgyü redün shuyig) ch.tib. application for party membership.

དང་ནང་གཙང་བཤེར་ (dāŋnaŋ dzāŋsher) ch.tib. purifying the party, rectification of the party.

དང་ཕའི་ (dāŋbɛ) ch. party, clique, faction ¶ དམངས་གཙོའི་དང་ཕའི་ Democratic party.

དང་ཕྱིའི་ (dāŋcii) outside of the party ¶ དང་ཕྱིའི་མི་སྣ་ Non party members.

དང་མི་ (dāŋmi) ch.tib. party member.

དང་མི་ངོ་མ་ (dāŋmi ŋomǝ) ch.tib. full party member.

དང་ཙུང་ཀྲི་ (dāŋ dzūŋdri) ch. general party branch.

དང་ཙུང་ཀྲི་ཨུ་ཡོན་ལྷན་ཁང་ (dāŋ dzūŋdri ūyön lhɛ̄ngaŋ) ch.tib. general party branch committee.

དང་ཙུའུ་ (dāŋdzuu) ch. the leading party members, the leading group in a state organ.

དང་འཛུགས་ (dāŋ dzuù) ch.tib. va. to set up/ to establish a party.

དང་ཡོངས་ (dāŋyoŋ) ch.tib. the whole party, partywide.

དང་ཡོན་ (dāŋyön) ch.tib. sm. དང་མི་.

དང་ཡོན་གྱི་ལག་འཁྱེར་ (dāŋyöngo laggyer) ch.tib. party membership certificate.

དང་ཡོན་བགྲེས་སོང་ (dāŋyön dreèsoŋ) ch.tib. veteran/ older party members.

དང་ཡོན་སྦྱོང་བདར་འཛིན་གྲྭ་ (dāŋyön jondar dzindra) ch.tib. party members. training class/ course.

དང་ལ་ངོ་ཀློལ་ (dāŋla ŋogöö) ch.tib. sm. དང་ཀློལ་.

དང་ལུགས་རྒྱལ་ཁྲིམས་ (dāŋluù gyɛɛdrim) ch.tib. party discipline/ system and law of the land.

དང་ལོ་ (dāŋlo) ch.tib. party membership age.

དང་ཤེད་ (dāŋsheè) ch.tib. a despotic political party leader, party tyrant.

དང་ཤེད་ཅན་ (dāŋsheèjɛn) ch.tib. a despotic party boss, party tyrant.

དང་ཤོག (dāŋshoò) ch.tib. a faction in the party.

དང་གཤིས་ (dāŋshii) ch.tib. party spirit/ character.

དང་སྲིད་ (dāŋ sii) ch.tib. party and government.

དང་སྲིད་དམག (daŋ sii māà) ch.tib. party, government, army ¶ དང་སྲིད་དམག་གི་འགོ་ཁྲིད་ The leaders of the party, the government and the army.

དང་སྲིད་ལས་ཁངས་ (dāŋsii lɛ̄ɛ̀luù) ch.tib. party and government offices.

དང་སྲོལ་ (dāŋsöö) ch.tib. party's work style, party members' conduct.

དང་ཨུ་ (dāŋ ū) ch.tib. party committee.

དང་ཨུད་ (dāŋ üü) ch.tib. sm. དང་ཨུ་.

དང་ཨུའི་ལམ་ལུགས་ (dāŋüü lǝmluù) ch.tib. party committee system.

དྒང་ཀུས་ (dāŋgüü) shung. king of China.

དན་ (dēn) ch. 1. a picul (133.33 pounds). 2. nitrogen. 3. 100 liters.

དན་ཁ་ (dēnga) eng. tank.

དན་ཁེ་ (dēnge) sm. དན་ཁ་.

དན་ཉིང་སྒྱུར་ (dēn ñiŋgyur) ch.tib. tannic acid.

དན་དན་ (dēndɛn) definite, certain ¶ འདི་དན་དན་རེད་ This is certain. ¶ འདི་སྡུག་དུ་དན་དན་འགྲོ་གི་རེད་ This will definitely get worse.

དན་དན་ཨེས་ (dēndɛn ɛ̄ɛ̀) are you sure?

དན་དན་དིག་དིག (dēndɛn dīgdii) definite, certain, positive, indisputable.

དན་དིག (dēndig) sm. དན་དན་དིག་དིག.

དན་མེ་ (dēnme) Denmark.

དན་ཙེ་ (dēndze) ch. electron.

དན་ཙེ་རོལ་རྩེད་ (dēndze rööödzeè) computer/ video game.

དན་ཞིམ་ (dēnshim) ch.tib. biscuit, cake.

དན་ཞིམ་བག་ཐུག (dēnshim bǝgduù) ch.tib. a type of small biscuit that looks like བག་ཐུག.

དན་ལུད་ (dēnlüü) ch. nitrogenous manure, nitrate fertilizer.

དན་ཤིན་ (dēnshin) ch. sm. དན་ཞིམ་.

དམ་ (dām) the interrogative and "or" marker for words ending in final ན་ར་ལ་ and post final ད་.

དམ་བུ་ལ་ (dāmbula) a type of torma offered to the fire god.

དའན་ (dēn) sm. དན་.

དའི་ (dɛ) sm. ཀྲང་.

དའི་ཅི་པུར་ (dējibur) Tezpur.

དའི་ཡུས་ (dēyüü) ch. ribbon fish.

དའི་སི་དུ་ (dɛ sīdu) shung. a title given to high ranking Lamas.

དའི་པེའོ་ (dēbeo) ch. representative ¶ ཀྲང་དའི་པེའོ་ Representative Zhang.

དའོ་ཅའོ་ཆོས་ལུགས་ (dāwo jō cōōluù) ch.tib. Taoist religion.

དའོ་ཅའོ་ཆོས་པ་ (dāwo jō cōōba) ch.tib. a believer in Taoism.

དའོ་དན་ (dāwodɛn) ch. guided missile ¶ དའོ་དན་རྟེན་གཞི་ Missile base/ site.

དར་ (dār) hind. cable, telegram; va.—གཏོང་ to send a cable/ telegram.

དར་ཁང་ (dārkaŋ) hind.tib. telegraph office.

དར་གླ་ (dārla) hind.tib. telegram fee.

དར་གཏོང་འཕྲུལ་འཁོར་ (dārdoŋ trǖǖgɔɔ) hind.tib. machine/ equipment for sending telegrams.

དར་ཏོག (dārdog) hind.tib. radio tube.

དར་འཕྲིན་ (dǝrdrin) hind.tib. telegram, cable; va.—གཏོང་.

དར་འབུལ་ཞིན་ (dār bǖǖsin) shung. copy of a telegram.

དར་ཡིག (dǝryii) hind.tib. sm. དར་.

དར་ཡིག་ཁའོ་ (dǝryii kāwo) hind.tib.ch. telegraph section.

དར་ལན་ (dārlɛn) hind.tib. reply to a telegram, a

reply telegram; va.—རྒྱག; —སློག;—སྤྲོད་.

དལ་རྒྱུགས་ (dɛ̄ɛ̄gyuù) directly, straight ། ཕྲུ་གུ་དེ་ཟམ་པ་ཕྲ་པོ་དེའི་སྟེང་དུ་དལ་རྒྱུགས་ཕྱིན་པ་རེད་ The child walked straight on the narrow bridge.

དལ་གདུང་ (dɛ̄ɛ̄duŋ) a long beam used in houses that do not have pillars.

དལ་པར་ (dɛ̄ɛ̄bar) sm. དལ་རྒྱུགས་.

དལ་པོ་ (dɛ̄ɛ̄bo) a patty of fresh dung that has been stuck on a wall to dry; va.—རྒྱག.

དལ་འཕིག་ཏུ་གཏོང་ (dɛ̄ɛ̄ pi̱gdu dōŋ) va. to poke through sth. ། མདའ་དེ་གཟུགས་པོ་དལ་འཕིག་ཏུ་བཏང་འདུག The arrow poked through the body.

དལ་མར་ (dɛ̄ɛ̄mar) sm. དལ་རྒྱུགས་.

དལ་ཙམ་ (dɛ̄ɛ̄dzam) a little ། དངུལ་དལ་ཙམ་གཡར་རོགས་གནང་ Please lend me a little money.

དས་ཙམ་ (dɛ̄ɛ̀dzam) sm. དལ་ཙམ་.

དི་ཀ་ (dīgə) sm. སྡིག.

དི་ཀྲུང་དཔའི་རྒྱ་མཚོ་ (dīdruŋhe gyatso) ch.tib. Mediterranean Sea.

དི་སྐྱ་ (dīgya) silver pheasant.

དི་དི་ཐི་ (dīdi tī) eng. DDT (the insecticide).

དི་དི་རེ་ (dīdire) hind. partridge.

དི་དོ་ (dīdo) sm. དི་ལོ་.

དི་ནག (dēnag) heathcock.

དི་པི་ཅག (dībijaà) sm. དིམ་པི་ཙ་.

དི་མི་སུའུ་ (dīmisu) ch. geomycin.

དི་མུ་ས་ (dīmusa) a herbal medicine.

དི་ཙ་ (dīdza) anvil.

དི་ཚ་ (dīdza) 1. tin, stannum. 2. a type of medicine made with minerals.

དི་ཚའི་གཏེར་ཁ་ (dīdzɛ dērga) tin mine.

དི་ལ་ (dīlə) hind. sesame.

དི་ལ་ན་ (dīlɛnna) Tehran.

དི་ལོ་ (dīlo) a type of sesame.

དི་ཤྲི་ (dīshri) shung. imperial tutor ། ཀུན་དགའ་རྒྱལ་མཚན་དཔལ་བཟང་པོ་དི་ཤྲི་ནས་ཡེ་ཤེས་ཀུན་དགའ་ལ་བསྩལ་བའི་བཀའ་ཡིག The decree of the Imperial Tutor Kunga Gyaltsen Palzangpo given for the illumination and welfare of all.

དི་ས་ (dīsə) sm. དི་སེ་.

དི་སེ་ (dīse) 1. skt. snow mountain. 2. Mt. Kailash.

དིག (dīg) the essence.

དིག་གུ་ (dīggu) wine container.

དིག་ད་ (dīgdə) a type of Tibetan medicine.

དིག་དིག (dīgdig) 1. sound of dripping. 2. certain, definite.

དིག་པོ་ (dīgbu) 1. sm. དིག་དིག. 2. precise, to the point, appropriate.

དིག་མེད་ (dīgmeè) 1. uncertain, unsure. 2. not to the point, imprecise.

དིག་ཙམ་ (dīgdzam) sm. ཏོག་ཙམ་.

དིག་ཙྭ་ (dīgdzə) borax, sodium borate.

དིག་ཧྲུག (dīghruù) a minced meat broth.

དིང་ (dīŋ) 1. small water bowl used for offerings. 2. the sound of metal.

དིང་གོར་མ་ (dīŋ gōrma) sm. དིང་པར་མ་.

དིང་ཁྲི་ (dīŋdri) altar.

དིང་ཁྲོལ་ (dīŋdröö) sound made when metal is hit.

དིང་ངེ་འཛིན་ (dīŋ ŋe̱dzin) meditative concentration, meditative trance; va.—ལ་བཞུགས་ to meditate.

དིང་དིང་ (dīŋdiŋ) 1. a particle that intensifies adjectives ། སྔོ་དིང་དིང་ Completely blue. 2. a bell; va.—དུང་ to ring a bell ། རྟའི་དིང་དིང་གི་སྐད་སྒྲ The sound of a horse bell tingling.

དིང་དིང་ཅག (dīŋdiŋjaà) sm. དིང་ཤགས་, 1.

དིང་དིང་མ་ (dīŋdiŋmə) a small water bird.

དིང་དིང་ཤགས་ (dīŋdiŋshaà) 1. sm. དིང་ཤགས་. 2. wind bell.

དིང་པར་ (dīŋbar) sm. དིང་པར་མ་.

དིང་པར་མ་ (dīŋ bārma) brown sugar made in the shape of a water offering bowl.

དིང་ཕོར་ (dīŋbɔr) a bowl used for making water offerings.

དིང་བཟོ་མགོ་སྒོན་ (dīŋso go̱gön) a tool used by smiths (that is shaped sth. like a water bowl).

དིང་ལོ་ (dīŋlo) bowl made from tsampa dough to burn butter.

དིང་ཤགས་ (dīŋshaà) 1. a hand cymbal that comes in pairs, one for each hand (used by monks); va.—དུང་ to beat/ strike such cymbals. 2. idiom. va. དིང་ཤགས་དུང་ homosexual act wherein each partner take turns in being the passive and the active (male and the female roles).

དིན་དུ་ཀ་ (dīndugə) black walnut found in India.

དིབ་རིལ་ (dībrii) teapot.

དིམ་པི་ (dīmbi) thin leather hide (used as strings for string instrument as well as to decorate boots).

དིམ་པི་ཙ་ (dīmbijə) Western (nonTibetan) horses.

དིའུ་ (dīwu) lover, sweetheart; va.—གཏོང་ to be sweethearts/ in love ། ཁོ་གཉིས་དིའུ་གཏོང་གི་འདུག Those two are in love.

དིའི་ཅི་ (dīīdzi) ch. basis, foundation.

དིར་ (dīr) the sound of an alarm/ buzzer.

དིར་སྒྲ་ (dīrdra) the sound of an alarm clock.

དིར་པཱུ་ (dīrbaa) canvas.

དིར་རི་ལྦོབ་ཆས་ (dīiri dōbjɛɛ̀) a type of edible water plant.

དིལ་ (dīl) sesame; va.—འཚིར་ to extract sesame oil from sesame seeds.

དིལ་དཀར་ (dīlgar) white sesame.

དིལ་སྐྱོ་ (dīlgyo) sesame paste.

དིལ་གྱི་སྐྱོ་མ་ (dīlgi gyōma) sm. དིལ་སྐྱོ་.

དིལ་ཛང་ (dīljaŋ) compartment in a room for storing sesame seeds.

དིལ་དུང་ (dīl du̱ŋ) 1. va. to pound sesame seeds to extract oil. 2. person who extracts oil from sesame seed.

དིལ་ནག (dīlnaà) black sesame.

དིལ་སྣུམ་ (dīlnum) sesame oil.

དིལ་བག་ལེབ་ (dīl pa̱àleb) sesame cake.

དིལ་འབྲུ་ (dīndru) 1. a grain of sesame. 2. an extemely tiny amount ། ཁྱེད་རང་གི་བཀའ་མོལ་ལ་ནོར་འཁྲུལ་དིལ་འབྲུ་ཙམ་མི་འདུག Your conversation has no mistakes. [no mistakes the size of even a grain of sesame].

དིལ་འབྲུ་ཙམ་ (dīmdrudzam) even a tiny amount, not at all (+ neg.) ། དེ་ལ་ཤ་དིལ་འབྲུ་ཙམ་མ་འདྲེས་པ་བྱེད་དགོས་ (You) must not mix any meat at all in that. [Lit. as much as a grain of sesame seed].

དིལ་སྦྱང་ (dīljaŋ) sm. དིལ་ཛང་.

དིལ་མར་ (dīlmar) sesame oil.

དིལ་འཚིར་ (dīl tsīr) va. to press/ extract oil from sesame seeds.

དིལ་ཞོ་ (dīlsho) sesame paste.

དིལ་གཡིའུ་ (dīlyiwu) tib.ch. sm. དིལ་མར་.

དིལ་ཤུན་ཙམ་ (dīl shūndzam) shung. even a little, the slightest ། ཁྲ་དོན་རས་སུ་བོར་བའི་རིགས་གཉིས་ཐད་ནས་དིལ་ཤུན་ཙམ་འབྱུང་སྲིད་ན་ If there is the slightest violation against the verdict by either of the two parties... [Lit. as much as the skin of a mustard seed].

དིལ་ཤུན་ཙམ་མེད་པ་ (dīl sūndzam me̱èba) a very tiny/ small amount ། ཁོང་གི་རྩོམ་ཡིག་དེར་སྐྱོན་ཆ་དིལ་འབྲུ་ཙམ་མི་འདུག His article has no mistakes at all [Lit. not a mistake that is even the size of the husk of a sesame seed].

དིས་ལུན་ (dīīlün) ch. polyester, dacron.

དུ་ (dū) dative-locative particle used after final ག་, ད་, and བ་.

དུ་ནི་ཤི་ཡ་ (dūnishiyə) Tunisia.

དུ་ཙ་ (dūdza) sm. དི་ཙ་.

དུ་རུ་ཀ་ (dūruga) a type of incense.

དུ་རུ་གུ་ (dūrugu) Turks.

དུག་རྒྱུམ་ (dūgjum) sound of sth. heavy hitting the ground.

དུག་དུག (dūddug) a kind of low and indistinct sound.

དུག་རིང་ (dūgriŋ) a indistinct sound that lasts for a while.

དུག་རིད་ (dūgrii) 1. sm. དུག་དུག. 2. sound of hoof

beats.

ཏུང་ (dūŋ) ch. 1. east. 2. a metal composed of copper and nickel.

ཏུང་ཀ་ (dūŋgə) ch. squash.

ཏུང་ཅིན་ (dūŋjin) Tokyo.

ཏུང་ནན་ཡ་ (dūŋ nenya) ch. Southeast Asia.

ཏུང་པའི་ཁུལ་ (dūŋbɛ kǖǖ) ch.tib. the northeast area.

ཏུང་པེ་ (dūŋbe) ch. sm. ཏུང་པའི་ཁུལ.

ཏུང་ཅིང་དབན་མཚོ་ཁུག (dūŋ dzĩŋwɛn tsōgaà) ch.tib. Gulf of Tonkin.

ཏུང་ཚག (dūŋdzaà) ch.tib. ཏུང་ metal that has been carved/ engraved.

ཏུང་ཧའི་རྒྱ་མཚོ་ (dūŋhe gyatso) ch.tib. the East China Sea.

ཏུང་ཧྲེ་ (dūŋhre) ch. manager, director, trustee.

ཏུང་ཧྥི་ (dūŋfe) ch. East Africa.

ཏུན་ (dǖn) eng. ton.

ཏུན་སྤྱི་ལི་ (dǖn jile) eng.ch. ton and kilometer.

ཏུན་ཚད་ (dǖndzɛɛ̀) tonnage, limit/ standard of tons.

ཏུན་ཧྭང་ (dǖnhuaŋ) sm. ཏུན་ཧོང་.

ཏུན་ཧོང་ (dǖnhoŋ) Tunhuang.

ཏུན་ཧོང་ཡིག་རིགས་ (dǖnhoŋ) Tunhuang documents.

ཏུམ་ཏུམ་ (dǖndum) a kind of small drum.

ཏུའུ་ (dū) ch. a degree ། གྲང་ཀོར་འོག་གི་ཏུའུ་བཞི་བཅུ 40 degrees below zero (centigrade).

ཏུའུ་གྲངས་ (dūdraŋ) the number of degrees (centigrade).

ཏུའུ་ཆི་ཏན་ (dū cīdɛn) ch. tear gas bomb.

ཏུའི་ (dūwe) ch. group, team, brigade.

ཏུའི་ཀྲང་ (dūwedraŋ) ch. leader/ head of a ཏུའི་.

ཏུའི་མི་ཉ་ཅ་ (dūwe mĩ ña jā) Dominican Republic.

ཏུར་ཀི་ (dūrgi) Turkey.

ཏུར་ཏུར་ (dūrdur) 1. clear, sharp, brilliant. 2. almost finishing (doing sth.).

ཏུར་ཏུར་པོ་ (dūr dūrbo) sm. ཏུར་ཏུར་.

ཏུར་རེ་ (dūrre) sm. ཏུར་ཏུར་.

ཏེ་ (dē) sm. སྟེ་ (this particle is used after final ན་, ར་, ལ་, ས་).

ཏེ་གོ་ (dēgo) ch. Germany.

ཏེ་ཏེ་ (dēde) a small drum.

ཏེ་ཏེ་ལན་ (dēdelɛn) Teheran.

ཏེ་པ་ (dēba) a wire making tool.

ཏེ་པོར་ (dēbor) 1. arc. very, extremely. 2. good. 3. hard.

ཏེ་ཡི་ཀྲི་ (dēyidre) Germany ། ཏེ་ཡི་ཀྲི་དམངས་གཙོ་སྤྱི་མཐུན་རྒྱལ་ཁབ་ German Democratic Republic.

ཏེ་ལོ་ (dēlo) ch. skunk.

ཏེ་ལོ་པ་ (dēlopa) Tilopa: 10th century Indian tantric teacher of Naropa.

ཏེ་སེ་ (dēse) sm. ཏེ་སི་.

ཏེང་ཞའོ་ཕིང་ (dēŋ shaobiŋ) Deng Xiaoping.

ཏེན་ (dēn) sm. ཏེན་དོ་.

ཏེན་དོ་ (dēndo) ch.tib. iodine.

ཏེན་མི་འདང་བའི་གནོད་འཚེ་ (dēn midaŋwɛ nöödze) iodine deficiency sickness.

ཏེན་མེ་ (dēnme) Denmark.

ཏེན་ཙི་ (dēndzi) ch. electron. ། མོ་གློག་ཅན་གྱི་ཏེན་ཙི་ Negative electron.

ཏེན་ཙི་ཕོ་ (dēndzi pō) ch.tib. positive electron.

ཏེན་ཙི་མོ་ (dēndzi mo) ch.tib. negative electron.

ཏེན་ཙིའི་སྦུ་གུ་ (dēndzii bugu) ch.tib. electron tube.

ཏེན་ཙིའི་རྩིས་འཁོར་ (dēndzii tsĩĩgɔɔ) ch.tib. electronic computing/ calculating machine.

ཏེན་ཙིའི་ཕྲ་མཐོང་ཆེ་ཤེལ་ (dēndzii trātoŋ cēshee) ch.tib. electron microscope.

ཏེན་ཙིའུ་ (dēndziwu) ch. tincture of iodine.

ཏེན་ཚྭ་ (dēndza) ch.tib. iodized salt.

ཏེད་ཧྥང་ (dēèfaŋ) ch. iodoform.

ཏེད་ཧྥུན་ (dēèfün) ch. starch.

ཏེབ་ཙག (dēbdzaà) adze (a carpenter's tool).

ཏེབ་ཙེ་ (dēbdze) ch. plate.

ཏེའུ་ཤིང་ (dēwushiŋ) ch. a small throne/ chair.

ཏེའུ་ཤིང་ཁྲི་ (dēwu shĩŋdri) sm. ཏེའུ་ཤིང་.

ཏེབ་ལན་སློག (dēblɛn lɔ̃ɔ̃) va. to take revenge.

ཏེལ་པ་ (dēlba) branding iron.

ཏོ་ (dō) sentence final.

ཏོ་ཀེའོ་ (dōkewo) Tokyo.

ཏོ་རོ་མོ་རོ་ (dōro moro) sb. whose behavior is rash and thoughtless, disorderly, chaotic.

ཏོ་ལ་ (dōla) hind. a unit of weight (tola).

ཏོག (dōg) 1. the top/ tip of sth., the button on top of hats ། ཞྭ་མོའི་ཏོག The button (top) of a hat. 2. see ཏོག་ཙམ་. 3. sm. སྟེང་པོ་.

ཏོག་གེ་ (dōgge) a traditional measuring unit.

ཏོག་སྒྲ་ (dōgdra) cracking/ snapping sound.

ཏོག་སྡེ་ (dōgde) suddenly ། ཁོ་ཏོག་སྡེ་ལངས་ནས་ཕྱིན་པ་རེད་ He got up suddenly and went.

ཏོག་གནས་ (dōgnɛɛ̀) shung. a title/ position in the tt. government.

ཏོག་ཕུད་ (dōgpüü) the best ། ཁོ་ནི་སློབ་ཕྲུག་ནང་གི་ཏོག་ཕུད་རེད་ He is the best of the students.

ཏོག་མ་ (dōgma) a type of stick used for hitting.

ཏོག་ཙ་ (dōgdza) sm. ཏོག་ཙམ་.

ཏོག་ཙམ་ (dōgdzam) a little, some ། ཁོ་ཚོས་ཏོག་ཙམ་ཟས་པ་རེད་ They ate a little.

ཏོག་ཙམ་མ་གཏོགས་ (dōgdzam məndoò) nearly, just, almost ། ད་རེས་ནད་ཚ་འདིས་ང་ཏོག་ཙམ་མ་གཏོགས་ཤི་གྲབས་བྱས་བྱུང་ This time I nearly died from this illness. [Lit. except for a little].

ཏོག་ཙམ་མ་གཞི་ (dōgdzam məshi) sm. ཏོག་ཙམ་མ་གཏོགས་.

ཏོག་ཙམ་རིང་ (dōgdzam riŋ) for a while, for a little while ། ཏོག་ཙམ་སྒུག་རོགས་གནང་ Please wait for awhile.

ཏོག་རྩི་ (dōgdzi) needle for drawing blood.

ཏོག་རྩེ་ (dōgdze) sm. ས་འཛེར་.

ཏོག་བཙུགས་ཁྱེམ་བཙུགས་ (dōgdzug kyēmdzug) doing things haphazardly/ disorderly/ in the wrong sequence [Lit. use the shovel, use the hoe].

ཏོག་འཛར་ (dōgdzar) the tassle on the button of a hat.

ཏོག་ཞྭ་ (dōgsha) 1. a hat/ cap with a small button in the middle of the top. 2. shung. hats worn by officials of different ranks.

ཏོག་ཡུ་ (dōgyu) pick/ hoe handle.

ཏོག་རིལ་ (dōgrii) sm. མགོ་རིལ་.

ཏོང་ཏོང་ (dōŋdoŋ) large bell tied around the neck of mules and donkeys.

ཏོབ་ཀྱོག་སློག (dōbgyɔɔ̀ lɔ̃ɔ̀) va. to knock over things.

ཏོབ་ཅོག་སློག (dōbjɔɔ̀ lɔ̃ɔ̀) sm. ཏོབ་ཀྱོག་སློག.

ཏོབ་ཏོབ་ (dōbdob) sm. ཏབ་ཏོབ་.

ཏོབ་ཏོབ་སྨྲ་ (dōbdob mā) va. to talk without thinking, to talk rubbish.

ཏོམ་ (dōm) deep, depth ། ཆུ་ཏོམ་རིང་པོ་འདུག The water is deep.

ཏོམ་ཏོམ་ (dōmdom) sm. ཏོང་ཏོང་.

ཏོམ་ནག (dōmnaà) a lot, a great many, so much/ many ། ཚོགས་འདུར་མི་ཏོག་ནག་འདི་འདྲ་སླེབས་བཞག A great many people came to the meeting.

ཏོམ་ནག་འདི་གྱུད་ (dōmnaà digyɛɛ̀) a lot, a great many, much ། བུ་ལོན་ཏོམ་ནག་འདི་གྱུད་སྤྲོད་དགོས་ཙང་ཁོང་ལ་དཀའ་ངལ་ཆེན་པོ་འདུག Because (he) has to repay a great many loans, (he) is having a hard time.

ཏོའུ་ (dōwu) ch. ten liters.

ཏོའུ་ལོ་ (dōwulo) ch. polecat.

ཏོའུ་ཧྥུ་ (dōwu fū) ch. beancurd, tofu.

ཏོའུ་ཧྥུ་ལྷ་པོ་ (dōwu fū lābo) ch.tib. soft beancurd.

ཏོར་པང་ (dōrbaŋ) tool used to enlarge a hole.

ཏོལ་ (dȫȫ) suddenly ། ཁོ་ཏོལ་གྱིས་ཕྱིན་སོང་ He went suddenly.

ཏོལ་ཤེས་ (dȫȫsheè) va. to know/ comprehend/ understand with ease.

ཏམ་ཀ་ (drāŋga) a unit in Tibetan currency, see དངུལ་.

ཏམ་ཀ་དཀར་པོ་ (drāŋga gārbo) a silver ཏམ་ཀ་.

ཏམ་དཀར་ (dāŋgar) shung. abbr. of ཏམ་ཁ་དཀར་པོ་.

ཏམ་ཁབ་ (drāāgəb) a sewing needle worth one ཏམ་ཁ་ in traditional Tibetan society.

ཏམ་འཁོར་ (drāŋgɔɔ) shung. སྲིད་རབ་ཏམ་འཁོར་.

ཏམ་རྒྱན་ (drāmgyɛn) the coin design found on brocades/ silks.

ཏམ་རྒྱན་མ་ (drāmgyɛnma) sm. ཏམ་རྒྱན་.

ཏམ་ལྡིར་ (drāŋdir) a pot of ཆང་ that costs one ཏམ་ཀ་.

ཏམ་དོ་ (drāŋdo) sm. དོ་ཚད་, see དངུལ་.

ཏམ་བན་ (drāŋbɛn) a kind of ཆང་ vessel that is used on ceremonial occasions such as weddings.

ཏེའུ་གུང་གི་རྩིས་ (dīwu guŋgi dzīi) a system of astrological calculation that is used to determine whether certain days are auspicious or not for important events such as the burial of the dead, etc.

ཏྲི་ཤུལ་ (drīshüü) a trident.

ཏྲེ་བོ་ (drēwo) county/ xian in Ganze Prefecture in Sihuan.

ཏྲེ་མ་ (drēma) weasel.

ཏྲེ་ཧོར་ (drēhor) sm. ཏྲེ་བོ་.

ཏྲེ་ལྷམ་ (drēlham) a boot with a pointed toe (worn by Tibetans from Kham).

ཏྲེམ་ (drēm) a type of arthritis in Tibetan medicine.

ཏྲེམ་དཀར་ (drēmgar) a type of arthritis in Tibetan medicine.

ཏྲེམ་ནག (drēmnaà) a type of arthritis in Tibetan medicine.

ཏྲེས་སམ་ (drēèsam) an herbal medicine.

གདང་ (dāŋ) f. of གདོང་.

གདང་ཡིག (dāŋyii) letter, correspondence; va.—གཏོང་ to send correspondence.

གདང་རག (dāŋraà) a religious practice that involves giving thanks to lamas/ deities.

གདད་ (dɛ̄ɛ̀) 1. p. and f. of གདོད་. 2. va. to point ¶ མེ་མདའི་ཁ་ཁོང་ལ་གདད་དུས་ When he pointed the gun at him. 3. (with དུ་དཀའ་བྱེད་ —) difficult to do ¶ དེ་རིང་ངས་གནད་དོན་འདི་ཐག་གཅོད་དུ་རྒྱུར་དུ་དཀའ་བྱེད་གདད་ཆེན་པོ་བྱུང་ Today I had a difficult time deciding about the issue. 4. a sorcery curse (usu. hiding sth. to magically harm sb.); va.—རྒྱག; —འདུག to curse sb. ¶ ༧རྒྱལ་བ་སྐུ་ཕྲེང་བཅུ་གསུམ་པའི་ཞབས་ལྷམ་ནང་གདད་བཙུག་པ་རེད་ (He) put a sorcery curse in the 13th Dalai Lama's shoe.

གདད་ཇུས་གཞུང་ལུགས་ (dɛ̄ɛ̀jüü shuŋluù) game theory.

གདད་གཉེར་ (dɛ̄ɛ̀ñer) giving responsibility, entrusting sb.; va.—བྱེད་.

གདད་ཕྱོགས་ (dɛ̄ɛ̀jɔ̀ɔ) inclination ¶ མི་སེར་མང་ཆེ་བའི་བློ་ཁ་གདད་ཕྱོགས་གསར་བརྗེ་རེད་ The inclination of most people's minds is revolution.

གདད་ཕྲུག (dɛ̄ɛ̀druù) 1. wild, undisciplined (usu. for youths and children). 2. slang term said when angry that is something like "You bastard."

གདད་མེད་ (dɛ̄ɛ̀meè) 1. unreliable, undependable. 2. unsteady, unfirm.

གདད་རབས་ (dɛ̄ɛ̀rəb) things that have been handed down.

གདད་རུལ་ (dɛ̄ɛ̀rüü) the point when the black magic of a sorcery item that has been hidden begins to work.

གདད་ལེན་ (dɛ̄ɛ̀len) sm. སྤྲོད་ལེན་.

གདད་ས་ (dɛ̄ɛ̀sa) 1. a person in whom one trusts/ believes completely ¶ ངའི་གདད་ས་ཉི་མ་ལགས་རེད་ Nyimala is the person I trust. 2. target ¶ སྤྱི་ཚོགས་རིང་ལུགས་ཀྱི་མདུང་རྩེ་གདད་ས་དེ་མ་རྩ་རིང་ལུགས་རེད་ Socialism's target of attack is capitalism. 3. the person to whom sth. is given.

གདད་སོ་ (dɛ̄ɛ̀so) sm. གདད་ས་, 1.

གདན་ (dɛ̄n) 1. permanent. 2. (— + neg.) not at all, never ¶ ཁྱེད་འདི་འདྲ་གདན་ནས་གནང་རྒྱུ་ཡོད་པ་མ་རེད་ You should never do that.

གདན་ཁེལ་ (dɛ̄ngee) sm. གདན་འཁེལ་.

གདན་ཁྲ་ (dɛ̄ndra) shung. abbr. of གདན་ཚིགས་ཁྲ་མ་.

གདན་ཁྲ་དོག་བརྗེས་ (dɛ̄ndra dɔgdzīi) shung. to violate a verdict in an agreement document ¶ ད་ལམ་རང་མཚམས་གདན་ཁྲ་དོག་བརྗེས་ཀྱིས་ཚོང་པ་འཕར་འཛུགས་བགྱིས་སོང་བ་དང་ This time (they) violated the verdict included in the document and established additional traders.

གདན་ཁྲ་ཡིག་རིགས་ (dɛ̄ndra yigrii) shung. sm. གདན་ཚིགས་ཁྲ་མ་.

གདན་ཁྲིམས་ (dɛ̄ndrim) 1. a lifelong vow. 2. a law that has been firmly/ permanently established.

གདན་ཁེལ་གླེང་མེད་ (dɛ̄ngee lēŋmeè) definite, certain (no need for further confirmation/ discussion).

གདན་འཁེལ་ (dɛ̄ngee) settling, determining, deciding, fixing; va.—བྱེད་.

གདན་འཁེལ་ (dɛ̄n kēē) va. to settle, to determine, to decide, to fix (a rate, level) ¶ ཁོ་ཚོ་འགྲོ་ཡག་གདན་འཁེལ་བ་རེད་ It was settled that they will go. ¶ ཐོན་ཚད་གདན་འཁེལ་ནས་ After fixing the production quota.

གདན་འཁེལ་བའི་ཚད་ (dɛ̄ngeewɛ tsɛ̄ɛ̀) a fixed norm/ quota.

གདན་འཁྱོལ་ (dɛ̄n kyöö) va. to see through to the end, to complete/ finish ¶ ཁོང་གི་ལས་གཞི་དེ་གདན་འཁྱོལ་ཁག་པོ་རེད His project is difficult to finish.

གདན་ཁྱོ་ (dɛ̄nkyo) husband.

གདན་གྱི་དོན་ (dɛ̄ngi tön) future meaning/ impact ¶ རོགས་རམ་གྱི་འཆར་གཞི་དེ་གདན་གྱི་དོན་ག་རེ་ཡིན་མིན་བསམ་བློ་གཏོང་དགོས་ (One) must think about what the future impact is of that aid plan.

གདན་གྱི་འདུན་མ་ (dɛ̄ngi dünmə) the final/ ultimate goal ¶ ཁོང་ཚོའི་གདན་གྱི་འདུན་མ་དེ་རང་བཙན་རེད་ Their ultimate goal is independence.

གདན་གྲོགས་ (dɛ̄ndrɔ̀ɔ) spouse; va.—བྱེད་ ¶ ཚེ་གང་གདན་གྲོགས་ Lifelong spouse.

གདན་བགོ་ (dɛ̄ngo) permanent/ distribution; va.—རྒྱག.

གདན་འགག (dɛ̄ngaà) sm. གདན་འགོག.

གདན་འགོག (dɛ̄ngɔ̀ɔ) permanent ban or prohibition; va.—བྱེད་ to ban/ prohibit permanently.

གདན་རྒྱུག་འུ་ལག (dɛ̄ngyuù wulaà) shung. a corvee laborer who has to come to work daily (regularly).

གདན་བཅར་ (dɛ̄njaa) shung. sb. always in the presence of high personage, e.g., a favorite or a bodyguard or advisor.

གདན་ཆགས་ (dɛ̄njaà) sm. གདན་འཇགས་.

གདན་འཇགས་ (dɛ̄njaà) permanent, fixed, established, stable; va.—བྱེད་ ¶ ཁྱེད་རང་ལ་ལས་ཀ་གདན་འཇགས་ཡོད་པས་ Do you have a permanent job?

གདན་འཇགས་གླ་པ་ (dɛ̄njaà lāba) permanent employee/ worker.

གདན་འཇགས་རྒྱུ་ནོར་ (dɛ̄njaà gyunɔɔ) fixed assets.

གདན་འཇགས་སྡོད་མཁན་ (dɛ̄njaà dööñɛn) permanent resident.

གདན་འཇགས་མ་རྩ་ (dɛ̄njaà madza) fixed capital.

གདན་འཇགས་མི་གླ་ (dɛ̄njaà mila) sb. hired permanently.

གདན་འཇགས་ལམ་ཡིག (dɛ̄njaà ləmyii) shung. a permanent permit issued by the Kashag allowing sb. to requisition corvee carrying animals.

གདན་འཇགས་སློབ་གྲྭ་ (dɛ̄njaà lōbdra) boarding school.

གདན་འཇགས་ཨར་པོའི་ལས་ཁུངས་ (dɛ̄njaà ārbö lɛ̀ɛguŋ) shung. (permanent) office of building and construction (in tt. government).

གདན་ཉར་ (dɛ̄nñar) keeping/ maintaining permanently ¶ དམག་གྲངས་ ༡༠༠༠ བཙོས་དེ་གདན་ཉར་བྱས་པ་རེད་ They created 1,000 soldiers and kept them permanently.

གདན་ཉིན་སློབ་གྲྭ་ (dɛ̄nñim lōbdra) abbr. boarding school and day school.

གདན་གདན་ (dɛ̄ndɛn) certain, sure; va.—བྱེད་ to be certain/ sure of what you do, to be careful/ cautious in doing sth. ¶ འདི་གདན་གདན་རེད་ This is certain (true). ¶ གདན་གདན་མ་བྱས་ན་བཙོན་ཁང་ལ་སླེབས་ཡོང་ If (you) are not careful (you) will end up in prison.

གདན་གདན་ཏིག་ཏིག (dɛ̄ndɛn dīgdii) sm. གདན་གདན་.

གདན་གདན་མེད་པ་ (dɛ̄ndɛn meèba) unsure,

uncertain.

གཏན་གཏན་ཡོད་པ་ (dēndɛn yööba) certain, sure, definite ¶ ཅ་ལག་ཚང་མ་འཇོག་ས་གཏན་གཏན་ཡོད་པ་བྱ་དགོས་ You need to have a definite place to keep all your things.

གཏན་དུ་ (dēndu) permanently, always ¶ ཁོ་གཏན་དུ་ལྷ་སར་སྡོད་ཀྱི་ཡོད་པ་རེད་ He always stays in Lhasa.

གཏན་དུ་གནས་ (dēndu nɛ̄ɛ̀) va. to exist constantly/ everlastingly/ permanently, enduringly ¶ གཏན་དུ་གནས་པའི་མཛའ་མཐུན་ Everlasting friendship.

གཏན་དུ་བ་ (dēnduwa) permanent, everlasting.

གཏན་སྡོད་ (dēndöö) residing/ living permanently; va.—བྱེད་ ¶ ད་ས་བཞུགས་སྒར་དུ་གཏན་སྡོད་འདི་གཞི་གསར་འགྱུར་འགོད་མཁན་གྱིས་ By this reporter who resides permanently in Dharamsala. ¶ ལོ་ཆིག་སྟོང་གི་སྔོན་ནས་ཁོ་ཚོ་འདིར་གཏན་སྡོད་བྱས་ཡོད་རེད་ They have lived here from one thousand years ago.

གཏན་སྡོད་སྤོ་འཚོ་ (dēndöö bōdzo) (nomads) with permanent living quarters and (nomads) who move.

གཏན་སྡོད་ཕྱི་མི་ (dēndöö cīmi) permanent alien residents, a national of a particular country residing in another country.

གཏན་སྡོད་དམག་ (dēndöö mää) permanently billeted troops/ garrison.

གཏན་སྡོད་ཟློས་གར་ (dēndöö döögar) permanent theater, repertory theater.

གཏན་ནས་ (dēnnɛɛ̀) (— + neg.) never, not at all ¶ སྔོན་མ་ཉ་གཏན་ནས་གསོ་མ་སྐྱོང་བ་རེད་ Previously, fish were never raised (domestically).

གཏན་གནས་ (dēnnɛɛ̀) 1. permanent, eternal. 2. fixed point ¶ གཏན་གནས་རྩིས་འཁོར་ Fixed point computer (in contrast to a floating point computer).

གཏན་གནས་ངེས་སྲོལ་ (dēnnɛɛ̀ ŋɛ̀ɛsöö) law of conservation (in physics).

གཏན་གནས་མ་རྩ་ (dēnnɛɛ̀ madza) fixed assets.

གཏན་གནས་མི་ནུབ་ (dēnnɛɛ̀ minub) immortal, everlasting.

གཏན་པ་ (dēmba) lock, bolt (for a door, window).

གཏན་པ་མེད་པའི་མཆོད་སྦྱིན་ (dēmba meèbɛ cōōjin) offerings and donations not given all the time.

གཏན་པ་སྲི་བ་མེད་པའི་མཆོད་སྦྱིན་ (dēmba sēwa meèbɛ cōōjin) making offerings and donations without expecting anything in return.

གཏན་དཔྱལ་ (dēnjɛɛ) husband and wife, couple.

གཏན་ཕེབས་ (dēn pēè) sm. གཏན་ལ་ཕེབས་.

གཏན་བུ་ (dēmbu) sm. གཏན་ཤིང་.

གཏན་བོགས་ (dēmbɔɔ̀) permanent lease.

གཏན་བྲལ་ (dēndrɛɛ) 1. completely/ permanently severed or cut off, completely without; va.—བྱེད་; to separate/ part for good ¶ ང་གཉིས་བཟའ་ཚང་གཏན་བྲལ་བྱེད་དགོས་བྱུང་སོང་ The two of us had to separate (as a couple) for good. 2. (vb. + ཐབས་ + —) no way to do the verbal action ¶ འདི་འཐུང་ཐབས་གཏན་བྲལ་རེད་ There is no way one can drink (it). 3. impermanent, transitory.

གཏན་འབེབས་ (dēn beb) settled, decided, fixed; va. གཏན་འབེབས་; va.—བྱེད་ to settle, to decide, to come to a decision ¶ གཏན་འབེབས་རིན་ཐང་ Fixed value. ¶ གཏན་འབེབས་གྲངས་ཚད་ Fixed amount. ¶ ཁྲིམས་ཡིག་གཏན་འབེབས་བྱས་པ་རེད་ The law was decided.

གཏན་འབེབས་འགྱུར་མེད་ (dēmbeb gyurmeè) decided on and unchangeable, fixed/ settled and unalterable.

གཏན་འབེབས་དངུལ་བཅོལ་ (dēnbeb ŋǖüjöö) fixed/ term savings.

གཏན་མ་ (dēnma) long run, long term, future ¶ གཏན་མའི་འཚོ་ཐབས་ A livelihood strategy for the long run.

གཏན་མི་ཆགས་པ་ (dēn mi cāgba) shung. uncertain ¶ མི་རྣམས་ཀྱི་བསམ་པའི་འགྱུར་ཁུངས་གཏན་མི་ཆགས་པ་ཞིག་ཡོང་གཤིས་ Because it is uncertain whether people will change their minds.

གཏན་མེད་ (dēnmeè) sm. གཏན་བྲལ་.

གཏན་ཚིགས་ (dēndzii) 1. proof, conclusion, deduction. 2. shung. land tenure document.

གཏན་ཚིགས་ཁྲ་མ་ (dēndzii trāma) shung. a verdict included in a land tenure document.

གཏན་ཚིགས་མཁར་རུ་ (dēndzii kāru) shung. a standard volume measure equal to one ཁལ་.

གཏན་ཚིགས་མེད་པ་ (dēndzii meèba) illogical, irrational.

གཏན་ཚིགས་ཡིག་རིགས་ (dēndzii yigrii) shung. land tenure document.

གཏན་ཚིགས་རིག་པ་ (dēndzii rigbə) the science of logic.

གཏན་ཚིགས་རིག་པའི་རང་བཞིན་ (dēndzii rigbɛ rəŋshin) the nature of logic.

གཏན་ཚིགས་ས་བོན་ (dēndzii sābön) shung. draft of a land tenure document.

གཏན་རྫས་ (dēndzɛɛ̀) immovable/ fixed assets.

གཏན་ཞལ་ (dēnshɛɛ) husband and wife, couple ¶ རྡོ་རྗེ་གཏན་ཞལ་རྣམ་གཉིས་ Mr. and Mrs. Dorje.

གཏན་ཞལ་ལྷན་གཉིས་ (dēnshɛɛ dɛnñīi) husband and wife, couple.

གཏན་བཞུགས་ (dēnshuù) h. of གཏན་སྡོད་.

གཏན་ཡོད་ (dēnyöö) abbr. of གཏན་གཏན་ཡོད་པ་.

གཏན་གཡོག་ (dēnyɔɔ̀) permanent servant.

གཏན་བསླག་ (dēnlaà) overthrowing/ deposing permanently; va.—བྱེད་.

གཏན་ལ་ཕབ་ (dēnla pāb) p. of གཏན་ལ་འབེབས་.

གཏན་ལ་ཕེབས་ (dēnla pēb) va. to get decided/ settled.

གཏན་ལ་འབེབས་ (dēnla beb) sm. གཏན་འབེབས་.

གཏན་ལེགས་ (dēnleg) always good, always benevolent.

གཏན་ཤིང་ (dēnshiŋ) door bar/ bolt.

གཏན་སོ་ (dēnso) permanent tooth.

གཏན་སྲོལ་ (dēnsöö) theorem.

གཏམ་ (dām) 1. speech, talk; va.—བཤད་; —གཏོང་; —སྨྲ་ to talk. 2. news ¶ གཏམ་བཟང་ Good news.

གཏམ་སྐྱེལ་ (dām gyēē) 1. va. to deliver a message. 2. va. to tell internal matters to those on the outside ¶ ཁོས་ང་ཚོའི་ནང་དོན་གྱི་གཏམ་བསྐྱལ་བཞག He revealed our internal discussions (to others).

གཏམ་: p. **བཏམས་**; f. **བཏམ་**; imp. **གཏོམས་** (dām) va. to say, to speak.

གཏམ་སྐྱེལ་བ་ (dāmgyeewa) messenger.

གཏམ་སྐྱེལ་པོ་ (dām gyēēbo) messenger.

གཏམ་ཁ་ཁུག (dām kā kūg) va. to get sb. to talk/ speak.

གཏམ་ཁ་ལེན་ (dām kā len) va. to give an answer to sb.

གཏམ་ཁུངས་མ་ (dāmguŋ) reliable/ dependable talk.

གཏམ་ཁུངས་མེད་པ་ (dāmguŋ meèba) unreliable/ undependable/ untrustworthy talk.

གཏམ་འཁྱར་ (dāmgyar) unfounded story, rumor, gossip; vi. གཏམ་འཁྱར་ to have a rumor/ story going around; va.—བཤད་ to tell rumors/ stories.

གཏམ་གྱི་གླེང་གཞི་ (dāmgi lēŋshi) topic of a conversation/ speech.

གཏམ་གྱི་དངོས་པོ་ (dāmgi ŋööbo) sm. གཏམ་གྱི་དོན་, 1.

གཏམ་གྱི་ཉེས་པ་ (dāmgi ñēēba) the errors contained in a speech/ talk.

གཏམ་གྱི་དོན་ (dāmgi tön) the main meaning of a speech/ talk.

གཏམ་གྱི་བདུད་རྩི་ (dāmgi düüdzi) shung. interesting/ entrancing/ fascinating/ engaging speech or conversation [Lit. talk that is like ambrosia].

གཏམ་གྱི་ཟློས་གར་ (dāmgi döögar) theatrical play, drama.

གཏམ་གྱི་ཟློས་གར་ཚོགས་པ་ (dāmgi döögar tsōgba) drama troupe, theater organization.

གཏམ་གྱོང་པོ་ (dām gyoŋbo) strong/ aggressive/ tough/ belligerent in speech; va.—བཤད་.

གཏམ་གླུ་སྤེལ་མ་ (dāmlu bēlma) storytelling that includes the singing of songs as a part of the story.

གཏམ་གླེང་ (dāmleŋ) discussion, conversation; va.—བྱེད་.

གཏམ་གླེང་ཚོགས་འདུ་ (dāmleŋ tsōndu) conference, congress.

གཏམ་མགྱོགས་པོ་ (dām gyogbo) a person who talks fast.

གཏམ་འགལ་ (dāmgɛɛ) a contradiction in speech, a contradictory statement.

གཏམ་འགོ་ལས་མཇུག (dāmgo lɛnjug) (one) should complete what (one) says one will do [Lit. starting talk, finishing work].

གཏམ་འགྲིག (dām drig) vi. to come to an agreeable decision after discussion/ mediation.

གཏམ་རྒྱག (dām gyaà) sm. རྒྱག་གཏམ་.

གཏམ་རྒྱལ་ (dām gyɛɛ) vi. to win an argument/ debate.

གཏམ་རྒྱུད་ (dəmgyüü) legend, fable, tale.

གཏམ་རྒྱུན་ (dəmgyün) saying, maxim, proverb, adage.

གཏམ་སྒོ་ (dāmgo) topic of talk/ conversation.

གཏམ་སྒྲོག (dām drɔ̀ɔ) 1. va. to speak. 2. va. to read aloud to others. 3. to make known or publicize verbally.

གཏམ་བརྒྱ་བཤད་ཀྱི་སྙིང་པོ་དོན་ (dām gya shɛ̀ɛgi ñĩŋbu tön) the main point/ meaning [Lit. the main essence of one hundred talks].

གཏམ་བསྒྲགས་ (dām draà) p.of གཏམ་སྒྲོག.

གཏམ་ངན་ (dāmŋɛn) 1. bad tidings/ news/ talk. 2. unlucky talk. 3. bad reputation.

གཏམ་ངན་བསྐལ་བརྒྱར་ལུས་ (dāmŋɛn gɛ̄ɛ gyar lüü) a bad reputation will live on for a very long time [Lit. bad reputation will live for 100 eons].

གཏམ་ངན་ཕྱི་བཞག (dāmŋɛn cĩshaà) sm. གཏམ་ངན་བསྐལ་བརྒྱར་ལུས་.

གཏམ་ངན་མི་ཁ་ (dāmŋɛn miga) bad reputation; vi.—ཐོབ་ to get a bad reputation.

གཏམ་ངོ་ལྐོག་ཅན་ (dāmŋo gōgjɛn) saying nice things to sb.'s face and the opposite behind his back; va.—ཤོད་.

གཏམ་ངོས་ལ་ཤོད་སྒྲ་ལོ་རྒྱབ་ཏུ་དབྱུག (dāmŋööla shöö drālo gyəbla yüü) one should not talk behind people's back [Lit. one should talk in front of people and throw one's braid behind one's back].

གཏམ་ཇ་ (dāmŋa) sm. གཏམ་མཇུག.

གཏམ་སྔ་ཚིག་གིས་ཕྱི་ཚིག་མི་ནོན་ (dām ŋədziggi cĩdzig minön) things said that contradict things previously said.

གཏམ་ཅི་གྲག (dām jĩdraà) all/ everything that one has heard, whatever one has heard.

གཏམ་ཅོལ་ (dāmjöö) nonsensical/ meaningless talk.

གཏམ་ལྕེབས་ (dāmjeb) interrupting/ interfering with a conversation; va.—བྱེད་.

གཏམ་ཆ་པེ་ཆོ་པེ་ (dām cābe cōbe) nonsensical talk, senseless chatter.

གཏམ་ཆད་ (dām cɛ̀ɛ) 1. vi. to not get finished or concluded (a talk/ speech). 2. sm. ཁ་དན་.

གཏམ་ཆེན་ (dāmjen) talking in belligerent manner; va.—གཏོང་ ¶ཁོས་པ་རོལ་ཟིལ་གྱིས་གནོན་དགོས་བསམས་ཏེ་གཏམ་ཆེན་བཏང་བ་རེད་ He talked in a belligerent manner thinking that it would subdue his opponent.

གཏམ་འཆལ་ (dāmjɛɛ) 1. rumor ¶ཟླ་ ༡༠ ནས་རྒྱལ་ཚབ་རྭ་སྒྲེང་ཆབ་སྲིད་ཀྱི་ཐུགས་འགན་དགོངས་ཞུ་གནང་གི་ཡོད་ཚུལ་གཏམ་འཆལ་ཞིག་ལྷང་ལྷང་ཐོན་ After the 10th month a rumor clearly surfaced that Reting Regent was going to resign the Regency. 2. fabricated/ nonsensical talk; va.—ཤོད་; —བཟོ་ to spread rumors/ lies; to talk nonsensically.

གཏམ་མཇུག་སྒྲིལ་ (dāmjug dril) sm. གཏམ་མཇུག་གཅོད་.

གཏམ་མཇུག་གཅོད་ (dāmjug jöö) 1. va. to end a conversation/ talk abruptly. 2. sm. གཏམ་ལྕེབས་.

གཏམ་བརྗོད་ (dāmjöö) speech, talk; va.—འཁྲབ་ to put on a play.

གཏམ་བརྗོད་ཟློས་གར་ (dāmjöö döögar) sm. གཏམ་གྱི་ཟློས་གར་.

གཏམ་བརྗོད་ཟློས་གར་ཚོགས་པ་ (dāmjöö döögar tsōgba) modern drama theater group/ troup/ ensemble.

གཏམ་བརྗོད་རང་དབང་ (dāmjöö raŋwaŋ) freedom of speech.

གཏམ་ཉོག (dāmñog) sm. གཏམ་རྙོག.

གཏམ་རྙིང་ (dāmñiŋ) 1. old talk/ conversation. 2. old sayings.

གཏམ་རྙིང་སྐྱར་གླེང་ (dāmñiŋ gyārleŋ) sm. གཏམ་རྙིང་སྐྱར་བཤད་བྱེད་.

གཏམ་རྙིང་སྐྱར་བཤད་ (dāmñiŋ gyārshɛɛ) saying the same thing over and over again; va.—བྱེད་ [Lit. telling the old story again].

གཏམ་རྙོག (dāmñog) 1. meaningless talk ¶གཏམ་རྙོག་བསྐྱུར་ནས་དོག་དོག་བཤད་སོང་ (He) didn't talk nonsense, he said the essential things. 2. talk that causes trouble/ dissension.

གཏམ་སྙན་ (dāmñɛn) 1. pleasant talk/ conversation. 2. good news/ tidings; va.—སྐྱེལ་ to deliver good news.

གཏམ་སྙན་པོ་ (dām ñɛ̃mbo) interesting/ pleasant talk. 2. good news.

གཏམ་སྟོང་ (dāmdoŋ) empty words, meaningless talk/ conversation.

གཏམ་གཏོང་ (dām dōŋ) va. to speak/ talk. 2. va. to talk in an exaggerated and boastful manner.

གཏམ་ཐོན་ (dām tön) vi. to have a slip of the tongue, to let sth. slip out in one's speech.

གཏམ་ཐོས་ (dām töö) vi. to hear some talk/ news.

གཏམ་དང་རལ་གྲི་ཡུ་ནས་འཆང་ (dāmdaŋ rɛɛdri yunɛ cāŋ) there must be a point or reason for what one says [Lit. speech and sword should be held by the handle].

གཏམ་དང་བྱ་སྤྱོད་ (dāmdaŋ cajöö) words and deeds.

གཏམ་དང་མཆིལ་མ་གཉིས་ལ་ལེན་རྒྱུ་མེད་ (dāmdaŋ cĩĩmə ñĩĩlə lɛngyu meè) one should be careful about what one says since one can't take back one's words [Lit. speech and spit can't be taken back].

གཏམ་དོན་ (dāmdön) 1. prestige/ reputation and benefit or wealth ¶ཁོང་ལ་གཏམ་དོན་གཉིས་ཡོད་ཀྱི་ལས་ཀ་ཞིག་རག་བཞག He obtained a job that combined both prestige and wealth. 2. subject of conversation/ speech/ discussion.

གཏམ་དོན་གཉིས་མེད་ (dāmdön ñĩĩmeè) without prestige or wealth.

གཏམ་དོན་འདྲིལ་ (dāmdön drii) vi. to have a discussion come to a conclusion.

གཏམ་དོན་ཧམ་གཉེར་ (dāmdön hāmñer) seeking fame and fortune in a greedy/ unprincipled manner; va.—བྱེད་.

གཏམ་དྲངས་ (dām draŋ) p. of གཏམ་འདྲེན་.

གཏམ་དྲི་ (dām tri) sm. གཏམ་འདྲི་.

གཏམ་འདོད་ (dāmdöö) vanity, ostentation; va.—བྱེད་ to act vainly ¶ཁྱེད་རང་གཏམ་འདོད་མ་བྱས་པར་སྐྱིད་གསོ་བླངས་ན་ཡག་པོ་ཡོད་པ་རེད་ Don't be vain. It will be good if you take the welfare.

གཏམ་འདོད་ཚ་པོ་ (dāmdöö tsābo) vain, ostentatious; va.—བྱེད་ to act in an vain/ ostentatious way.

གཏམ་འདོད་ཅན་ (dāmdööjɛn) sm. གཏམ་འདོད་ཚ་པོ་.

གཏམ་འདོད་བོང་བུར་ཞོན་ནས་ རྐང་ཆུང་ས་ལ་རེག་སོང་ (dāmdöö boŋbur shönnɛ gāŋjuŋ sāla regsoŋ) trying to show off or act as if you are sb. and making a fool of yourself in the process [Lit. vanity caused (him) to ride a donkey and his feet were touching the ground].

གཏམ་འདྲི་ (dām dri) va. to question, to ask.

གཏམ་འདྲེན་ (dām dren) va. to tell a proverb or story to illustrate a point.

གཏམ་འདྲེས་ (dām dreè) talk with different topics mixed together.

གཏམ་དུགས་ (dām duù) vi. to run out of what to say, to have nothing to say.

གཏམ་ལྡིབ་ (dāmdib) stuttering talk.

གདམ་ནག (dāmnag) malicious/ vicious talk.
གདམ་རྣ་ལམ་མི་འགྲོ་ (dām nālam mindro) sm. རྣ་བར་མི་འགྲོ་, 2.
གདམ་དཔེ་ (dāmbe) proverb, saying, maxim.
གདམ་སྤྱོད་ (dāmjöö) 1. speech (all verbal activities) ¶ གདམ་སྤྱོད་རང་དབང་ Freedom of speech. 2. speech and action/ behavior.
གདམ་འཕྱུར་རྒྱག་གདེང་གསུམ་ (dāmjar gyagdeŋ sūm) talk in accordance with the situation (i.e., gentle when needed, harsh if necessary).
གདམ་བུད་ (dāmbüü) sm. གདམ་བཤད་བྱེད་.
གདམ་འབྲེལ་ཆགས་པ་ (dāmdree cāgba) speech that doesn't contradict sth. previously said.
གདམ་མི་ཁ་བརྒྱུད་ན་ཇེ་མང་ ཟས་མི་ལག་བརྒྱུད་ན་ཇེ་ཉུང་ (dāmmi kəgyüüna jemaŋ sɛ̄ɛ̀mi kāgyüüna jeñuŋ) rumors have a tendency to become elaborated/ exaggerated as they are spread [Lit. talk/ rumors become more after going through people, food becomes less after going through people].
གདམ་མེད་ཁས་ལེན་ (dāmmeè kɛ̄ɛ̀len) tacit consent/ acceptance; va.—བྱེད་.
གདམ་མེད་ཟློས་གར་ (dāmmeè döögar) pantomime.
གདམ་སྨུར་བ་ (dāmñurwa) speaking fluently, speaking quickly.
གདམ་སྨ་ (dāmma) sm. གདམ་.
གདམ་འཕྲོས་ (dāmdröö) the remaining part of a speech/ talk.
གདམ་བཙོག (dāmdzɔg) dirty talk.
གདམ་རྩུབ་ (dāmdzub) rough/ crude language.
གདམ་ཚིག (dəmdzig) words, expressions, remarks, comments.
གདམ་ཚིག་གསར་སྐྱེས་ (dəmdzig sārgyeè) shung. new remarks/ comments/ assertions ¶ ཁྲ་མ་འདེས་དཔྱད་རྗེས་གདམ་ཚིག་གསར་སྐྱེས་མི་ཆོག After the verdict has been decided no new remarks are permitted.
གདམ་ཚོགས་ (dāmdzɔɔ̀) a collection of articles/ writings/ tales. 2. name of a magazine published in India.
གདམ་གཞི་ (dāmshi) topic of a talk/ conversation.
གདམ་གཞན་འཕྲོས་ (dām shen trō) vi. to have the topic of a conversation shift/ change while talking.
གདམ་ཟད་ (dām sɛɛ̀) vi. to run out of reasons/ arguments/ points.
གདམ་བཟང་ (dāmsaŋ) good news/ tidings.
གདམ་ཡིག་རྩིས་ (dām yig dzii) the three skills: speech, writing and calculation.
གདམ་རིང་ (dāmriŋ) full-length (novel, article, etc.).
གདམ་ལ་མཚོན་ཆ་མེད་ཀྱང་ མི་སྙིང་དུམ་བུར་གཅོད་ (dāmla tsōnja meègyaŋ miñiŋ dumbur jöö) the power of speech is great [Lit. although words do not contain weapons, they nevertheless can cut the heart of a person into pieces].
གདམ་ལན་ (dāmlɛn) reply, answer; va.—སློག to answer/ reply.
གདམ་ལན་པོ་མེད་ན་ལྐུགས་པ་རེད་ དགྲ་ལན་པོ་མེད་ན་སྡར་མ་རེད་ (dāmlɛmbo meèna gūgbə reè dralɛnbo meèna tarma reè) if one doesn't respond to a comment/ question one is stupid, if one doesn't take revenge one is a coward.
གདམ་རླུང་ལ་སྐུར་ (dāmluŋla gūr) va. to spread the word about sth. with the intention that it will eventually get to the intended person [Lit. to send talk on the wind].
གདམ་བཤད་ (dāmshɛɛ̀) speech, lecture; va.—བྱེད་.
གདམ་བཤད་ཀྱི་དབང་ཆ་ (dāmshɛɛ̀gi wāŋja) sm. གདམ་བཤད་དབང་ཆ་.
གདམ་བཤད་སྟེགས་བུ་ (dāmshɛɛ̀ dēgbu) platform, dais, rostrum.
གདམ་བཤད་པ་ (dāmshɛɛ̀ba) spokesman, lecturer.
གདམ་བཤད་དབང་ཆ་ (dāmshɛɛ̀ wāŋja) freedom of speech.
གདམ་བཤེར་ (dāmsher) analyzing speech; va.—བྱེད་.
གདམ་གསུམ་སྐད་ཀྱིས་ཆོད་ (dāmsum gɛ̄ɛ̀gi cöö) vi. to become extremely famous.
གདམ་ལྷུ་འགྲིག་པོ་ (dāmlhu drigbu) sm. གདམ་འབྲེལ་ཆགས་པ་.
གདམ་ཨ་ཕས་ཤོད་རྒྱུ་ཨ་མས་ ཁྱི་བདག་པོས་བཀག་རྒྱུ་མགྲོན་པོས་ (dām ābɛɛ̀ shöögyu āmɛɛ̀ kyī dagböö gāàgyu drönböö) doing sth. inappropriately [Lit. the wife talks instead of the husband, dogs are stopped/ controlled by the guests instead of the owner].
གདམས་: p. གདམས་; f. གདམས་; imp. གདོམས་ (dām) 1.va. to fill up. 2. va. to entrust (with work/ responsibility). 3. p. of གདམ་.
གདའ་ (dā) 1. abbr. of གདའ་མ་. 2. arc. va. to beat.
གདའ་དངུལ་ (dɛ̄ŋüü) deposit, pledge, pawn, bail.
གདའ་འཇོག (dā jɔɔ̀) va. to leave as pawn/ pledge.
གདའ་འཇོག་འཛིན་ཡིག (dɛ̄njɔɔ̀ dzinyig) receipt for sth. pawned.
གདའ་ཉིས་རི་བ་ (dɛ̄ñiì riwə) to leave twice the amount of a loan as a surety/ bail.
གདའ་གཏོར་ (dādɔɔ) a type of torma.
གདའ་མ་ (dɛ̄ma) pawn, pledge, security; va.—འཇོག to leave as pawn/ pledge; va.—བླུ་ to redeem a pawn; va.—ཕྱིར་སྤྲོད་ to return or give back sb.'s pawn/ pledge/ security.
གདའ་མ་དངུལ་སྒྱུར་ (dɛ̄ma ŋüügyur) taking over an item left on pawn when repayment isn't made; va.—བྱེད་.
གདའ་མ་འཇོག་ལེན་ (dɛ̄ma joglen) taking and keeping pawn/ security/ pledges for sth.
གདའ་མ་ལྡབ་ལོག (dɛ̄ma dəblɔɔ̀) sm. གདའ་མ་ཉིས་རི་བ་.
གདའ་མ་འདས་ (dɛ̄ma dɛɛ̀) vi. to be unable to redeem one's pawn/ security/ pledge, to have one's pawn become the property of the lender.
གདའ་མ་ཕྱིར་སྤྲོད་ (dɛ̄ma cidröö) to return or give back sb.'s pawn/ pledge/ security.
གདའ་མ་བཞག (dɛ̄ma shaà) p. of གདའ་མ་འཇོག.
གདའ་མ་བཞག་ས་ (dɛ̄ma shaàsa) pawn shop.
གདའ་མར་བཞག (dɛ̄maa shaà) sm. གདའ་མ་འཇོག.
གདའ་འཛིན་ (dɛ̄ndzin) a receipt/ agreement paper for sth. that had been pawned.
གདར་: p. གདར་; f. གདར་; imp. གདོར་ (dār) va. to bleed, to draw blood (as a medical treatment).
གདར་ཁ་ (dārga) drawing blood; va.—རྒྱག.
གདར་ཁྲག (dārdraà) blood that has been drawn.
གདར་ག (dārga) sm. གདར་ཁ་.
གདར་བཅོས་ (dārjöö) blood letting as a medical treatment.
གདར་དམིགས་ (dərmiì) points from which blood is drawn.
གདར་རྩ་ (dārdza) sm. གདར་དམིགས་.
གདར་བསྲེག (dār sēg) drawing blood and doing moxibustion.
གདལ་པོ་ (dɛ̄ɛ̄bu) flat dung patties; va.—རྒྱག to make flat dung patties to set them out to dry.
གདི་ཐུག (dīduù) 1. narrow minded, shortsighted ¶ བློ་ཆུང་གདི་ཐུག་གིས་ལས་ཀ་གང་ཡང་བྱེད་ཐུབ་ཀྱི་མ་རེད་ Sb. who is narrow minded can't do any kind of work. 2. stubborn, insistent. 3. stingy.
གདི་ཐུག་ཚ་པོ་ (dīduù tsābo) sm. གདི་ཐུག.
གདི་མུག (dīmuù) ignorance, stupidity.
གདི་མུག་ཅན་ (dīmujɛn) ignorant, stupid.
གདི་མུག་རོ་ཉལ་ (dīmuù roñɛɛ) stupid, idiotic, brainless.
གདི་མུག་ཟླ་བ་ (dīmuù dawa) the 1st. month in the Tibetan calendar.
གདི་ལུམ་པ་ (dīlumbə) great/ powerful desires.
གདིག: p. བདིགས་; f. བདིག; imp. གདིགས་ (dii) va. to make sth. drip.
གདིག་འཁྱིལ་ (dīggee) titration (in chemistry).
གདིག་འཁྱིལ་བྱེད་རྫས་ (dīggee ceèdzɛɛ̀) titrant (in chemistry).
གདིག་སྦུག (dīgbug) burette (in chemistry).
གདིགས་ (dīg) imp. of གདིག.
གདིགས་པ་ (dīgbə) a drop; vi.—རྒྱག to drip, to trickle.

གཏིང་ (dīŋ) 1. bottom, depths ། རྒྱ་མཚོའི་གཏིང་ The bottom/ depths of the ocean. 2. deep down ། ཁོང་སེམས་གཏིང་ནས་རྙིང་མ་ལ་དགའ་བས་ན་ Because deep down he liked the Nyingma sect.

གཏིང་གློ་ (dīŋlo) a primitive tribe in S.E. Tibet.

གཏིང་སྐུལ་ (dīŋgüü) reminding; va.—གཏོང་.

གཏིང་སྐྱེས་རྫོང་ (dīŋgyeè dzoŋ) a district in W. Tibet.

གཏིང་སྒྱོང་ཁ་འཇམ་ (dīŋgyoŋ kānjam) soft spoken but tough on the inside.

གཏིང་ཅན་ (dīŋjɛn) 1. deep. 2. sb. who keeps things inside and doesn't speak frivolously or casually.

གཏིང་ཚོད་ (dīŋ cöö) vi. to be able to estimate the essence of sth., to get to the bottom of sth. ། གནད་དོན་དེའི་སྐོར་ཚོད་དཔག་བྱས་ཀྱང་གཏིང་ཚོད་མ་སོང་ Concerning this issue, even though we tried to estimate, we were not able to do so.

གཏིང་ཕྱིད་པོ་ (dīŋ jiibu) sm. གཏིང་ཆེན་པོ་.

གཏིང་བརྗེད་འགྲོ་ (dīŋjeè dro) vi. to forget completely.

གཏིང་ཉེ་ (dīŋñe) sm. གཏིང་ཐུང་.

གཏིང་ཉེ་བ་ (dīŋ ñewa) 1. shallow, not deep. 2. a person with whom one gets along, sb. with the same views.

གཏིང་རྟོགས་ (dīŋ dɔ̄ɔ) va. to understand sth. deeply/ thoroughly, to get to the bottom of a matter.

གཏིང་ཐག་ (dīŋdaà) anchor line; va.—སློག་ to weigh anchor.

གཏིང་ཐུང་ (dīŋduŋ) shallow, superficial.

གཏིང་ཐུང་ཐུང་ (dīŋ tūŋduŋ) sm. གཏིང་ཐུང་.

གཏིང་ཐུང་ས་ཡོམ་ (dīŋtuŋ sāyom) surface earthquake.

གཏིང་མཐའ་ (dīŋta) depth and expanse/ distance.

གཏིང་མཐའ་བྲལ་བ་ (dīŋta trɛɛwa) sm. གཏིང་མཐའ་མེད་པ་.

གཏིང་མཐའ་མེད་པ་ (dīŋta meèba) infinite, endless, deep, having no bottom/ edge.

གཏིང་དུག་ཁ་འཛེར་ (dīŋduù kādzer) having evil intentions behind a smiling face.

གཏིང་དུ་ (dīŋdu) deep, deeply; vi.—ཟུག་ to penetrate deeply; va.—ནུབ་; —སིམ་; —བྱིང་; —ནིམ་ to sink to the bottom, to permeate deeply ། ཁོང་གི་བཀའ་སློབ་འདི་ངའི་སེམས་ཀྱི་གཏིང་དུ་ཟུག་སོང་ His advise has affected me deeply. ། ཁ་སང་གི་ཆུ་དེ་ཞིང་ཁའི་གཏིང་དུ་སིམ་བཞག Yesterday's water has soaked into the field. ། རྡོ་ཆུའི་གཏིང་དུ་ནུབ་བཞག The rock has sunk to the bottom of the water.

གཏིང་དོན་ (dīŋdön) inner meaning.

གཏིང་དོན་ལེན་ (dīŋdön len) sm. གཏིང་རྟོགས་.

གཏིང་འདོན་ (dīŋdön) eliminating, cleaning up, mopping up; va.—བྱེད་.

གཏིང་འདྲི་ (dīŋ dri) va. to interrogate in detail/ thoroughly.

གཏིང་དིབ་ (dīŋdib) a hollow, a depression.

གཏིང་རྡོ་ (dīŋdo) anchor; va.—འཐེན་; —སློག་ to weigh anchor; va.—དབྱུག་ to drop/ cast anchor; va.—སྦྲགས་ to tie a stone to the body of a person who is going to be thrown into the river.

གཏིང་གནག་ཁ་ཚ་ (dīŋnaà kādza) one who speaks harshly and is also mean/ malicious/ cruel.

གཏིང་གནག་པོ་ (dīŋ nāgbo) malicious, hateful, mean, cruel, vindictive.

གཏིང་ནད་ (dīŋnɛɛ̀) deep grudge/ enmity/ hatred; va.—བྱེད་; —ཟིན་ to hold a grudge.

གཏིང་ནས་ (dīŋnɛɛ̀) from deep, deeply ། གཏིང་ནས་ཡིད་ཆེས་པ་ To believe deeply.

གཏིང་སྣ་གསུམ་ (dīŋnasum) three dimensions ། གཏིང་སྣ་གསུམ་མཐོང་བའི་རི་མོ་ A three-dimensional painting.

གཏིང་དཔག་ (dīŋbaà) p. of གཏིང་དཔོག.

གཏིང་དཔག་དཀའ་བ་ (dīŋbaà gāwa) unfathomable, difficult to get to the bottom of.

གཏིང་དཔོག་ (dīŋböö) va. to estimate the depth of sth.

གཏིང་ཕིགས་ (dīŋ pii) sm. གཏིང་རྟོགས་.

གཏིང་ཕུག་རིང་པོ་ (dīŋpuù riŋbu) 1. deep tunnel. 2. meaning that is difficult to understand.

གཏིང་ཕྱིན་པ་ (dīŋ cīmbə) sm. ཐར་ཕྱིན་.

གཏིང་བྱིང་ (dīŋjiŋ) sinking.

གཏིང་མི་དཔོགས་པ་ (dīŋ mibɔɔba) sm. གཏིང་ཚད་དཔག་མེད་.

གཏིང་མི་ཟབ་པ་ (dīŋ misəbbə) sm. གཏིང་ཐུང་.

གཏིང་མེད་ (dīŋmeè) sm. གཏིང་ཐུང་.

གཏིང་རྨོ་ (dīŋmo) deep plowing; va.—རྒྱག.

གཏིང་རྨོ་ཞིབ་ལས་ (dīŋmo shiblɛɛ̀) deep plowing and intensive cultivation.

གཏིང་རྨོད་ (dīŋmöö) sm. གཏིང་རྨོ་.

གཏིང་རྩ་ (dīŋdza) base, foundation.

གཏིང་ཚད་ (dīŋdzɛɛ̀) depth ། གཏིང་ཚད་མིས་ ༦༠༠ A depth of six hundred meters.

གཏིང་ཚད་དཔག་མེད་ (dīŋdzɛɛ̀ bāgmeè) inestimable depth, bottomless, unfathomable.

གཏིང་ཚུགས་ (dīŋ tsūù) vi. to have the foundation for sth. get laid ། དམག་འཁྲུག་རྒྱག་རྒྱུའི་རྨང་གཞི་གཏིང་ཚུགས་བཞག The foundation for a war has been laid.

གཏིང་ཚུགས་བརྟག་དཔྱད་ (dīŋdzuù dāgjɛɛ̀) comprehensive/ deep/ exhaustive research or study.

གཏིང་ཚོད་ (dīŋdzöö) guessing, estimating; va.—ལེན་ to guess, to estimate ། འདི་ལོ་ཡོང་འབབ་ག་འདྲ་ཡོང་རྒྱུ་ཡིན་མིན་ང་ཚོས་སྔོན་ནས་གཏིང་ཚོད་ལེན་དགོས་ (We) must estimate first how much yield will be gotten this year.

གཏིང་འཚོལ་ (dīŋ tsöö) sm. གཏིང་ཚོད་.

གཏིང་གཞལ་ (dīŋshɛɛ) sm. གཏིང་དཔོག.

གཏིང་ཟབ་ (dīŋsəb) deep, profound, intense; vi.—དུ་འགྲོ་ to become deeper, to become more profound; va.—བྱེད་ to deepen, to make deeper.

གཏིང་ཟབ་པོ་ (dīŋ səbbu) sm. གཏིང་ཟབ་.

གཏིང་ཟབ་མོ་ (dīŋ səbmu) sm. གཏིང་ཟབ་.

གཏིང་ཟབ་མོ་བ་ (dīŋ səbmuwa) sb. who is deep and profound.

གཏིང་རིང་ (dīŋriŋ) sm. གཏིང་རིང་པོ་.

གཏིང་རིང་ཐུང་ (dīŋ riŋduŋ) sm. གཏིང་ཚད་.

གཏིང་རིང་པོ་ (dīŋ riŋbu) deep ། མཚོ་འདི་གཏིང་རིང་པོ་འདུག This lake is deep.

གཏིང་རིང་ལོས་ (dīŋ riŋlöö) sm. གཏིང་ཚད་.

གཏིང་ལ་དིམ་ (dīŋlə dim) vi. to sink to the bottom ། རྡོ་ཆུའི་གཏིང་དུ་དིམ་བཞག The rock has sunk to the bottom of the water.

གཏིང་ལུད་ (dīŋlüü) deep fertilizer (as opposed to surface fertilizer); va.—རྒྱག་ to spread/ apply deep fertilizer.

གཏིང་ལོན་ (dīŋlön) sm. གཏིང་ཚོད་ལོན་.

གཏིང་སློག་ (dīŋlɔɔ) deep plowing; va.—རྒྱག.

གཏིབ་: p. གཏིབས་; f. གཏིབ་; imp. གཏིབས་ (dīb) vi. to make overcast with clouds/ fog.

གཏིར་མིག་ (dīrmii) a flat tool with different size holes that was used for making nails.

གཏུ་ལུམ་ (dūlum) intoxication; vi.—ཆགས་ to become intoxicated/ drunk ། གཏུ་ལུམ་པ་ A drunk.

གཏུག: p. གཏུགས་; f. གཏུག; imp. གཏུགས་ (dūg) 1. va. to reach, to touch, to come into contact with ། མཆུ་དོར་ཁ་གཏུགས་ནས་དབུགས་འབྱིན་དུ་བྱས་པ་རེད་ (He) performed mouth-to-mouth resuscitation. 2. va. to compete with, to vie ། ཕོ་གསར་དེ་གཉིས་ཨབ་དང་གཏུག་གི་འདུག The two youths are competing in wrestling. 3. va. to bring before the (law) ། གྱོད་གཞི་དེའི་སྐོར་ཁྲིམས་ཁང་ལ་བཏུགས་བཞག ། This case has been brought to court. 4. va. to see a doctor/ teacher ། ང་ཁ་ས་སྨན་ཁང་ལ་ཨེམ་ཆི་བཏུག་པར་ཕྱིན་པ་ཡིན་ I went to see a doctor at the hospital yesterday.

གཏུག་འབྲེལ་ (dūndrel) contact, relations; va.—བྱེད་ to have contact/ relations ། རྒྱལ་ཁབ་འདི་གཉིས་གཏུག་འབྲེལ་ཡག་པོ་བྱེད་ཀྱི་ཡོད་པ་རེད་ The two countries have good relations.

གཏུག་སྦྱངས་ (dūg jaŋ) va. to be tried before the law.

གཏུག་མི་ (dūgmi) a person who files a lawsuit.

གཏུག་རྩོད་ (dūgdzöö) prosecuting and arguing.

གདུག་བཤེར་ (dūgsher) lawsuit, litigation, law case; va.— གཏོང་; —རྒྱག to sue, to prosecute, to bring a law case.

གདུགས་ (dūg) p. and imp. of གདུག.

གདུན་ (dǖn) pestle and mortar; va.—བྲིས་རྡུང་ to grind/ pulverize with a mortar and pestle.

གདུན་ཁ་ (dǖnga) the mouth/ opening of a grinding stone through which the grain is poured for grinding.

གདུན་ཁུང་ (dǖnguŋ) a mortar (for grinding).

གདུན་བུ་ (dǖnbu) sm. གདུན་ཁུང་.

གདུན་རྡོ་ (dǖndo) pestle.

གདུན་ཤིང་ (dǖnshiŋ) wooden pestle.

གདུབ་ p. གདུབས་; f. གདུབ་; imp. གདུབས་ (dūb) 1. va. to cut into small pieces/ bits, to chop up, to dice ¶ ཤ་གདུབས་པ་རེད་ (He) cut up the meat into small pieces. 2. vi. to be able ¶ འགྲོ་མི་གདུབ་པའི་རྒྱུ་མཚན་ག་རེ་རེད་ What is the reason for not being able to go?

གདུབ་གྲི་ (dūbdri) knife for chopping.

གདུབ་སྟེགས་ (dūbdeg) cutting machine.

གདུབ་སྦྱེད་ (dūmjɛɛ̀) meat cutter.

གདུབ་མིན་ (dūbmin) shung. to be against sth. ¶ རང་སྐང་གང་དྲན་གྱིས་འབོ་ཉག་ཆེ་ཆུང་ངེས་མེད་འདི་ཆར་དམིགས་རྩ་ཚིག་རིན་པོ་ཆེ་དང་ཁྲིམས་འགྲུས་ལ་གདུབ་མིན་མཁྱེན་ཚོད་ལགས་ན་ As you are fully aware, making measures and scales according to one's own wish (size) is against the law.

གདུབ་གཞོག (dūbshɔɔ̀) cutting; va.—བྱེད་ to cut.

གདུབ་གཞོག་འཁོར་སྟེགས་ (dūbshɔɔ̀ kɔ̄ɔ̄deg) cutting machine/ tool ¶ ལྕགས་རིགས་གདུབ་གཞོག་འཁོར་སྟེགས་ Metal cutting machine tool.

གདུབ་གཞོག་འཕྲུལ་འཁོར་ (dūbshɔɔ̀ trǖǖgɔɔ) cutting machine.

གདུབ་ལེབ་ (dūbleb) slice.

གདུབ་ལྷེབ་ (dūblheb) sm. གདུབ་ལེབ་.

གདུབས་ (dūb) imp. and p. of གདུབ་.

གདུབས་ཚལ་ (dūbtsɛɛ) rags, tattered clothes.

གདུབས་ཤ་ (dūbsha) meat that has been cut into small pieces/ diced.

གདུམ་: p. གདུམས་; f. གདུམ་; imp. ཐུམས་ (dūm) va. to wrap. 2. va. to be fierce, harsh, stern.

གདུམ་ (dūm) abbr. of གདུམ་པོ་.

གདུམ་གད་ (dūmgɛɛ̀) laughing in an angry/ sarcastic manner; va.—བགད་.

གདུམ་རྒྱག (dūm gya̱à) sm. གདུམ་.

གདུམ་ཛམ་ (dūmŋam) stern/ intimidating looking, scary looking.

གདུམ་ཉམས་ཆེ་བ་ (dūmñam cēwa) intimidating looking, stern/ harsh looking.

གདུམ་དྲག (dūmdraà) stern, fierce.

གདུམ་པོ་ (dūmbo) intimidating, fierce, stern, harsh ¶ དགེ་རྒན་དེ་གདུམ་པོ་ཡིན་ཙང་སློབ་ཕྲུག་ཚོས་ཞེད་སྣང་བྱེད་ཀྱི་ཡོད་པ་རེད་ Because the teacher is stern the students are afraid of him.

གདུམ་པོ་གདུམ་ནག (dūmbo dūmnaà) extremely གདུམ་པོ་.

གདུམ་སྤྱོད་ (dūmjöö̀) stern/ harsh/ fierce/ intimidating in behavior or action.

གདུམ་བྱ་ (dūmja) bird of prey.

གདུམ་བྱེད་སྣོད་ཆས་ (dūmjeè nö̱ö̀cɛɛ̀) a machine that binds bales and packages with metal strips/ bands.

གདུམ་མོ་ (dūmmo) 1. a type of tantric practice (of inner heat). 2. a fierce woman.

གདུམ་བཙན་ (dūmdzɛn) sm. གདུམ་ཛམ་.

གདུམ་ཤོག (dūmshoò) wrapping paper.

གདུམས་ (dūm) p. of གདུམ་.

གདུར་བུ་ (dūrbu) a net bag.

གདུལ་ (dǖǖ) va. to make smoke (usu. by burning incense).

གདེ་ (dē) 1. (vb. + —) ringleader ¶ ངོ་ལོག་ཇག་པའི་བྱེད་གདེ་རྡོ་རྗེ་ Dorje, the ringleader of the bandits. 2. short (in height).

གདེང་པ་ (dēba) sm. གདེ་མ་.

གདེ་པོ་ (dēbo) 1. ringleader, principal criminal, chief conspirator/ schemer. 2. a short person, a shrimp.

གདེ་པོའི་དཀྱིལ་གྱི་གཟུགས་བཟང་ (dēbö gyīīgi sṳgsaŋ) good but only among the not so good [Lit. a good body among short people].

གདེ་དཔོན་ (dēbön) sm. གདེ་པོ་.

གདེ་བོ་ (dēbo) sm. གདེ་པོ་.

གདེ་འབབ་ (dēbəb) sm. གདེ་མ་.

གདེ་མ་ (dēma) sm. གདའ་མ་.

གདེ་མའི་མཛོད་ (dēmɛ dzö̱ö̀) shung. pawnshop.

གདེ་མོ་ (dēmo) a short female.

གདེ་ལེབ་པ་ (dēlebba) short person.

གཏེར་ (dēr) 1. treasure. 2. a mine.

གཏེར་ཀ་ (dērka) a support pillar in a mine.

གཏེར་ཁ་ (dērga) a mine; va.—འདོན་ to mine minerals; va.—འཚོལ་ to search for mineral deposits/ mines ¶ རྡོ་སོལ་གྱི་གཏེར་ཁ་ A coal mine.

གཏེར་ཁ་སྔོགས་འདོན་པའི་མཉམ་འབྲེལ་ (dērga ŋɔ̄gdönbɛ ña̱mdree) sm. གཏེར་ཁ་སྔོགས་འདོན་པའི་མཉམ་སྦྲེལ་.

གཏེར་ཁ་སྔོགས་འདོན་པའི་མཉམ་སྦྲེལ་ (dērga ŋɔ̄gdönbɛ ña̱mdree) United Mine Workers (in the U.S.A.).

གཏེར་ཁ་འཚོལ་ཞིབ་ (dērga tsȫȫshib) prospecting/ surveying for minerals.

གཏེར་ཁའི་ཁྱབ་རྒྱུད་ (dērgɛ kyābgyüù) mineral vein/ lode.

གཏེར་ཁའི་སྒྲིག་ཆས་ (dērgɛ dri̱gjɛɛ̀) mine facilities/ equipment.

གཏེར་ཁའི་ཆགས་རིམ་ (dērgɛ cāgrim) mineral layers, layers of a mine, ore seam.

གཏེར་ཁའི་ཐོན་ཁུངས་ (dērgɛ tö̃nguŋ) mineral resources.

གཏེར་ཁའི་ཐོན་རྫས་ (dērgɛ tö̃ndzɛɛ̀) mineral products.

གཏེར་ཁའི་སྣེ་ (dērgɛ nē) sm. གཏེར་ལྕུག.

གཏེར་ཁའི་འཕྲུལ་ཆས་ (dērgɛ trǖǖjɛɛ̀) mining equipment/ machinery.

གཏེར་ཁའི་བཟོ་པ་ (dērgɛ so̱ba) miner, mine worker.

གཏེར་ཁུང་ (dērguŋ) mineral/ ore deposit.

གཏེར་ཁུངས་ (dērguŋ) sm. གཏེར་ཁུང་.

གཏེར་ཁུལ་ (dērgüü) mine/ mining district.

གཏེར་ཁུལ་འགོ་པ་ (dērgüü go̱ba) mine foreman/ chief/ head.

གཏེར་ཁྲོན་ (dērdrün) mine shaft, mine, mine pit.

གཏེར་ཁྲོན་ཀ་བ་ (dērdrün gāā) sm. གཏེར་ཀ་.

གཏེར་ཁྲོན་གློག་ཤུ་ (dērdrün lɔ̄gshu) miner's lamp, lantern for use in mines.

གཏེར་གྱི་ཐོན་རྫས་ (dērgi tö̃ndzɛɛ̀) mineral products, minerals.

གཏེར་རྒྱུ་ (dērgyu) minerals.

གཏེར་རྒྱུ་ལྡན་པའི་ཆུ་མིག (dērgyü dɛ̱mbɛ cūmig) sm. གཏེར་རྒྱུ་ཆུ་མིག.

གཏེར་རྒྱུའི་ཆུ་མིག (dērgyü cūmig) mineral spring.

གཏེར་རྒྱུའི་ལུད་རྫས་ (dērgyü lṳ̈ṳ̀dzɛɛ̀) mineral fertilizer.

གཏེར་སྒྲོན་ (dērdrön) sm. གཏེར་ཁྲོན་གློག་ཤུ་.

གཏེར་དངོས་ (dērŋöö̀) minerals.

གཏེར་དངོས་ཀྱི་སྣུམ་ (dērŋöö̀gi nūm) mineral oil.

གཏེར་དངོས་གྲུབ་ཆ་ (dērŋöö̀ dru̱bja) mineral composition.

གཏེར་དངོས་རྡོག་པོ་ (dērŋöö̀ do̱gbo) lumps of minerals.

གཏེར་དངོས་ཚི་སྣ་ (dērŋöö̀ tsīnə) mineral fiber.

གཏེར་ཆེན་ (dērcen) great lamas who are able to find religious treasures that have been hidden in the past through their magical powers. 2. a large mine.

གཏེར་ཆུ་ (dērcu) mineral water.

གཏེར་ཆོས་ (dērjöö̀) hidden scriptures found by the magical power of a lama.

གཏེར་འཚོལ་ (dērjöö) hiding religious objects as "treasure" ¶ ས་ཞིང་འདུ་ཆེ་འོས་འགའ་དུ་སྦ་འཛུག་ཐོག་གཏེར་འཚོལ་བྱ་རྒྱུ་ (The religious objects) must be hidden as a treasure (for subsequent generations) in an appropriate place where many fields join together.

གཏེར་སྙིགས་ (dērñig) slag, the waste product of mines.

གཏེར་སྙིགས་སོ་ཕག (dērñig sōbaà) slag brick.

གཏེར་སྟོན་ (dērdön) lama who locates religious treasures hidden in the past through magical powers.

གཏེར་དོང་ (dērdoŋ) 1. mine pit. 2. mineral cave.

གཏེར་བདག (dērdaà) 1. protective/ guardian deity of a hidden religious treasure. 2. mine owner.

གཏེར་འདོན་ (dērdön) mining; va.—བྱེད་ to mine.

གཏེར་འདོན་སྒྲིག་ཆས་ (dērdön drigjɛɛ̀) mining equipment.

གཏེར་འདོན་འཕྲུལ་ཆས་ (dērdön trǖǖjɛɛ̀) mining machinery.

གཏེར་འདོན་བཙོ་སྦྱང་ (dērdön dzōjaŋ) excavating and smelting (ore).

གཏེར་འདོན་བཟོ་པ་ (dērdön soba) miner.

གཏེར་འདྲེན་འཁོར་ལོ་ (dērdren kɔ̄ɔlo) mine car/ tram (for conveying ore).

གཏེར་རྡུལ་ (dērdüü) mine dust.

གཏེར་རྡོ་ (dērdo) ore.

གཏེར་རྡོ་ཁ་གཞོག (dērdo kāshɔɔ̀) strip mining.

གཏེར་རྡོ་སྙིགས་མ་ (dērdo ñīmə) slag ore.

གཏེར་རྡོ་འདོན་བྱེད་སྒྲིག་ཆས་ (dērdo dönjeè drigjɛɛ̀) sm. གཏེར་འདོན་སྒྲིག་ཆས་.

གཏེར་རྡོ་ཞུ་ཐབ་ (dērdo shudəb) ore smelting furnace.

གཏེར་རྡོའི་སྒྲ་སྡུད་འཕྲུལ་འཁོར་ (dērdö drədüù trǖǖgɔɔ) crystal receiver/ set.

གཏེར་ལྡན་ཆུ་མིག (dērdɛn cūmig) mineral spring.

གཏེར་ལྡན་ཆུ་མིག་གི་ཆུ་ (dērdɛn cūmiggi cū) sm. གཏེར་ཆུ་.

གཏེར་སྣེ་ (dērne) outcropping, outcrop (of ore).

གཏེར་གནས་ (dērnɛɛ̀) 1. place where there are minerals. 2. storage room, warehouse treasure room.

གཏེར་དཔེ་ (dērbe) scriptures magically hidden by lamas.

གཏེར་དཔྱད་ (dērjɛɛ̀) sm. གཏེར་འཚོལ་.

གཏེར་བལ་ (dērbɛɛ) mineral wool.

གཏེར་དབོན་ (dērwön) shung. a གཏེར་སྟོན་ lama and his nephews and descendants ། གཏེར་དབོན་བརྒྱུད་བཅས་ལ་གཙུག་ལག་ཁང་གི་གནས་འཛིན་འཇགས་གནས་སུ་བསྐྱལ་བ་ The responsibility of taking care of the cathedral was permanently granted to the གཏེར་སྟོན་ lama and his nephews and descendants.

གཏེར་བྱེ་ (dērjeè) sm. གཏེར་རྡོ་.

གཏེར་འབབ་ (dērbəb) income from loan interest.

གཏེར་མ་ (dērma) hidden scriptures or relics (found by lamas through magical power).

གཏེར་སྨུག (dērñug) outcrop of mineral ore.

གཏེར་འཚོལ་ (dērdzöö) prospecting/ searching for minerals or potential mines; va.—བྱེད་.

གཏེར་འཚོལ་སྒྲིག་ཆས་ (dērdzöö drigjɛɛ̀) prospecting equipment.

གཏེར་འཚོལ་ཉེར་སྤྱད་ (dērdzöö ñerjɛɛ̀) sm. གཏེར་འཚོལ་སྒྲིག་ཆས་.

གཏེར་འཚོལ་འཕྲུལ་ཆས་ (dērdzöö trǖǖjɛɛ̀) prospecting instruments/ machines.

གཏེར་འཚོལ་རུ་ཁག (dērdzöö rugaà) prospecting team/ unit.

གཏེར་མཛོད་ (dērdzöö) treasury.

གཏེར་རྫས་ (dērdzɛɛ̀) 1. minerals, mineral products, mineral wealth. 2. things that are dear to sb.

གཏེར་རྫས་ཆགས་གཞི་ (dērdzɛɛ̀ cāgshi) mineral deposit.

གཏེར་རྫས་ཐོན་ཁུངས་ (dērdzɛɛ̀ tōnguŋ) mineral resources.

གཏེར་རྫས་ཐོན་ཡུལ་ (dērdzɛɛ̀ tōnyüü) a place where minerals are found.

གཏེར་བཟོ་ (dērso) 1. mining. 2. mine worker.

གཏེར་རི་ (dērri) a mountain containing minerals.

གཏེར་རི་སྔོག་འདོན་ (dērri ŋɔ̄gdön) excavating, mining; va.—བྱེད་.

གཏེར་རི་འཕྲུལ་འཁོར་ (dērri trǖǖgɔɔ) mining machinery.

གཏེར་རིགས་ (dērrig) all kinds of minerals.

གཏེར་རིགས་ལུད་རྫས་ (dērrig lüüdzɛɛ̀) mineral fertilizer.

གཏེར་རིའི་ས་ཤུན་བཤུ་ (dērrii sāshün shū) va. to surface/ strip mine.

གཏེར་ལས་ (dērlɛɛ̀) mining industry ། རྡོ་སོལ་གཏེར་ལས་ Coal mining industry.

གཏེར་ལས་བཟོ་པ་ (dērlɛɛ̀ soba) miner, mine worker.

གཏེར་སའི་དོང་ལམ་ (dērsɛ toŋlam) mine shaft, mine tunnel.

གཏེར་སྲུང་ (dērsuŋ) sm. གཏེར་བདག.

གཏོ་བཅོས་ (dōjöö) rituals to bring good luck or to avert misfortune/ disaster; va.—བྱེད་ ། གཏོ་བཅོས་བྱས་ཙང་ནད་གཞི་ལས་ཐར་ The sickness was cured by doing a གཏོ་བཅོས་.

གཏོ་བཅོས་ཚ་པོ་ (dōjöö tsābo) clever, inventive, ingenious.

གཏོག: p. གཏོགས་; f. གཏོག; imp. གཏོགས་ (dōg) va. to pick, to pluck ། ཁོས་མེ་ཏོག་མང་པོ་བཏོགས་པ་རེད་ He plucked many flowers.

གཏོགས་ (dɔ̄ɔ) p. of གཏོག.

གཏོགས་པ་ (dōgba) belonging to, part of ། མི་རིགས་ ༢༥ ལ་གཏོགས་པའི་གྲངས་ཉུང་མི་རིགས་ཀྱི་དགེ་རྒན་ཡོད་པ་རེད་ There are minority teachers belonging to twenty five nationalities. ། བོད་རིགས་སུ་གཏོགས་པའི་མི་མང་ People belonging to the Tibetan nationality. ། དབྱིན་གཏོགས་ Belonging to England.

གཏོང: p. བཏང་; f. གཏང་; imp. ཐོང་ (dōŋ) 1. va. to send, to give, to dispatch ། ང་ཚོས་ཁོ་ཚོར་དངུལ་གཏོང་དགོས་ We must send them money. 2. va. to let go, to dismiss ། དེ་རིང་ང་ནང་ལ་བཏང་རོགས་གནང་ (Please) let me go home today. 3. verbalizing verb ། ཁ་པར་གཏོང་ To phone. [Lit. to send a phone] ། གླུ་གཏོང་ To sing a song. [Lit. to send a song]. 4. intensifier of adjectives ། ཉུང་དུ་གཏོང་ To make fewer. ། མགྱོགས་སུ་གཏོང་ To speed up (make quicker). 5. (with རྟ་) va. to gallop. 6. va. to fly/ drive ། གནམ་གྲུ་གཏོང་ To fly a plane.

གཏོང་འགུག (dōŋguù) sending out and calling in/ summoning; va.—བྱེད་.

གཏོང་འགྲོ་བཞག་སྡོད་ (dōŋdro shagdöö) shung. sm. བཏང་འགྲོ་བཞག་སྡོད་.

གཏོང་སྒོ་ (dōŋgo) the expenses/ expenditures for a monastic rite or ritual; va.—གཏོང་.

གཏོང་སྒོའི་ལས་ཁུངས་ (dōŋgö lɛɛ̀guŋ) shung. office in tt. government that was in charge of expenses and providing supplies for religious rites.

གཏོང་ཆོད་ (dōŋjöö) shung. approval.

གཏོང་ཉར་ (dōŋñar) sending and keeping.

གཏོང་ཉུང་ཡོང་མང་ (dōŋñuŋ yoŋmaŋ) adverse trade balance, trade deficit, unfavorable balance of trade, import surplus [Lit. send out few, come in many].

གཏོང་ཐེབས་ (dōŋteb) a fund of money or things that has been set aside to be used for specific expenditures.

གཏོང་ཐེབས་ཤས་ཞིང་ (dōŋteb shɛ̄ɛ̀shiŋ) shung. land set up as a trust by leasing the land out with half the income stipulated to be used for a monastery ། སྐེར་པ་ཁག་ནས་ཕུལ་བའི་གཏོང་ཐེབས་ཤས་ཞིང་ཁག་འདེབས་སྐྱོང་ལྷོད་མེད་དགོས་རྒྱུ་ (You) must plant and take good care of the land offered for lease by the aristocrats since this is a trust wherein half of the income will go to a monastery.

གཏོང་འཛིན་ (dōŋden) controlling, manipulating; va.—བྱེད་.

གཏོང་དེབ་ (dōŋdeb) expense account/ ledger book in which items expended are listed.

གཏོང་མདོ་ཤོར་མདོ་འཕེར་བ་ (dōŋdo shōrdo pērwa) able to do all kinds of work ། ཁོང་གཏོང་མདོ་ཤོར་མདོ་འཕེར་བ་གཅིག་ཡོད་པ་རེད་ He is someone who can do all sorts of work.

གཏོང་གནང་ (dōŋnaŋ) h. of གཏོང་.

གཏོང་བསྔོན་ (dōŋnön) shung. extra provisions ། ཚེ་གླིང་དོ་དམ་ཁང་གི་གཏོང་བསྔོན་དུ་སྣ་རྩེ་ཁྲལ་བཅུ་བརྒྱད་བཀར་སྙིང་ནས་འབྲུ་ཁལ་ ༡༠༠ འདོན་རྒྱུ་ (You) should take out 100 ཁལ་ of grain from the eighteen Nangkartse grain storehouses for extra provisions for Tsechokling Monastery.

གཏོང་སྤྱིལ་ (dōŋbel) shung. sending and distributing ། ལས་འཛིན་ནས་རྩིས་ལེན་གཏོང་སྤྱིལ་གླེང་མེད་དགོས་རྒྱུ་ The manager should take possession (of it) and distribute (it) without discussion/ error.

གཏོང་ཕོད་ (dōŋbȍȍ) generosity.

གཏོང་ཕོད་ཅན་ (dōŋbȍȍjɛn) generous, philanthropic ། ཁོང་གཏོང་ཕོད་ཅན་ཡིན་ཙང་རྟག་པར་སྤྲང་པོར་དངུལ་སྟེར་གྱི་ཡོད་པ་རེད་ Because he is generous he always gives to the beggers.

གཏོང་ཕོད་ཆུང་ (dōŋ pȍȍjuŋ) stingy, miserly, tightfisted.

གཏོང་ཕོད་ཆེན་པོ་ (dōŋbȍȍ cēmbo) generous.

གཏོང་ཕྱུགས་ (dōŋcuù) livestock sent to pasture.

གཏོང་བ་གནང་ (dōŋwa nāŋ) sm. གཏོང་གནང་.

གཏོང་བློས་མ་འཁྱུད་ (dōŋlȍȍ magyȍȍ) shung. sm. གཏོང་བློས་མ་བཟོད་.

གཏོང་བློས་བཟོད་ (dōŋ lȍȍ sȍȍ) va. to dare to send a person or thing (used with negatives) ། ཕྲུ་གུ་འདི་ལོ་ཆུང་དྲགས་ནས་རྒྱ་གར་ལ་གཏོང་བློས་བཟོད་མ་བྱུང་ Because the child is too young, I didn't dare to send him to India.

གཏོང་དབྱངས་རིང་བ་ (dōŋyaŋ riŋwə) long tone (in a song/ aria).

གཏོང་འབྱོར་ (dōŋjɔɔ) sending and receiving/ arriving ། ལྷ་ས་ནས་བཏང་བའི་བང་ཆེན་འབྱོར་བྱུང་ The messenger sent from Lhasa has arrived.

གཏོང་མང་ཡོང་ཉུང་ (dōŋmaŋ yoŋñuŋ) 1. export surplus, favorable trade balance. 2. expenses exceeding income.

གཏོང་མི་ (dōŋmi) person who sent sth. ། དེབ་འདི་གཏོང་མི་སུ་རེད་ Who is the person who sent the book?

གཏོང་རྩ་ (dōŋdza) shung. a trust/ endowment set up in order to provide supplies for a monastery or a ritual ། སྔོན་དུ་འབྱོར་འབུལ་ཞུས་པའི་མཆོད་རྒྱུན་གཏོང་རྩ་རྣམས་མི་ཉམས་གོང་འཕེལ་ཡོང་བ་བྱ་དགོས་ (You) should keep up (not let decline) and increase the religious trusts that were set up earlier for ritual offerings.

གཏོང་ཡིག (dōŋyiì) a correspondence, letter.

གཏོང་ཡུལ་ (dōŋyüü) the place where (a thing) is sent.

གཏོང་ཡོང་ (dōŋyoŋ) income and expenses, revenue and expenditures.

གཏོང་ཡོང་ཁ་འཐབ་ (dōŋyoŋ kādəb) income and expenditure balancing out ། ལོ་འདིའི་ནང་ང་ཚོའི་གཏོང་ཡོང་ཁ་འཐབ་བྱུང་སོང་ This year our income and expenditure balanced.

གཏོང་ཡོང་འཁྲོལ་འཁྱིལ་ (dōŋyoŋ trȭŋgyil) an excess in income over expenditures (taking in more than expending).

གཏོང་ཡོང་ཀ་མི་འདུམ་ (dōŋyoŋ ka mindum) sm. གཏོང་མང་ཡོང་ཉུང་.

གཏོང་ཡོང་ཀ་མི་མཚུངས་ (dōŋyoŋ ka midzuŋ) sm. གཏོང་མང་ཡོང་ཉུང་.

གཏོང་ཡོང་ཀ་འཛོལ་ (dōŋyoŋ kadzöö) sm. གཏོང་མང་ཡོང་ཉུང་.

གཏོང་ཡོང་མགོ་སྙོམས་ (dōŋyoŋ goñom) sm. གཏོང་ཡོང་ཁ་འཐབ་.

གཏོང་ཡོང་མགོ་ཐུག (dōŋyoŋ godug) sm. གཏོང་ཡོང་མགོ་སྙོམས་.

གཏོང་ཡོང་མགོ་མཚུངས་ (dōŋyoŋ godzuŋ) sm. གཏོང་ཡོང་མགོ་སྙོམས་.

གཏོང་ཡོང་འགལ་འཛོལ་ (dōŋyoŋ gɛndzöö) sm. གཏོང་མང་ཡོང་ཉུང་.

གཏོང་ཡོང་རྩིས་ཐོ་ (dōŋyoŋ dzīìdo) account book/ ledger, income and expenditure book.

གཏོང་ཡོང་ཞིབ་རྩིས་ (dōŋyoŋ shibdziì) auditing/ accounting of income and expenditures; va.—བྱེད་.

གཏོང་རེས་ (dōŋreè) 1. exchanging, sending back and forth; va.—བྱེད་ ། ཁོ་གཉིས་ཡི་གེ་གཏོང་རེས་བྱས་པ་རེད་ Those two exchanged letters. 2. slang. to fight (back and forth).

གཏོང་རེས་གཏོང་ (dōŋreè dōŋ) sm. གཏོང་རེས་, 2.

གཏོང་རེས་བྱེད་ (dōŋreè ceè) see གཏོང་རེས་.

གཏོང་ལེན་ (dōŋlen) 1. receiving and sending/ transmitting. 2. in religion or meditation: to give happiness to others and to receive suffering.

གཏོང་ལེན་གློག (dōŋlen lɔ̄ɔ̀) alternating current.

གཏོང་ལེན་གློག་སྐྱེད་འཕྲུལ་འཁོར་ (dōŋlen lɔ̄ɔ̀gyeè trṻṻgɔɔ) alternating current generator.

གཏོང་ལེན་སྡེ་ཚན་ (dōŋlen dedzɛn) transport service.

གཏོང་སེམས་ (dōŋsem) having charitable thoughts.

གཏོད་: p. and f. གཏད་; imp. གཏོད་ (dȍȍ) va. 1. to hand over, to give ། ཁོས་ང་ལ་དངུལ་གཏད་བྱུང་ He gave me money. 2. va. to aim at, to direct towards, to face towards ། ཁ་ལྷོ་ལ་གཏད་ Face towards the south. 3. sm. བཙུགས་.

གཏོད་: p. བཏོད་; f. གཏོད་; imp. གཏོད་ (dȍȍ) va. to start, to begin ། ཁོ་ཚོས་ལུགས་སྲོལ་གསར་པ་ཞིག་བཏོད་པ་རེད་ They began a new system.

གཏོར་ (dɔ̄ɔ) 1. va. to destroy, to demolish, to crush, to annihilate ། ང་ཚོའི་དམག་མིས་དགྲ་བོའི་དམག་སྒར་གཏོར་བཞག Our soldiers have destroyed the enemy's regiment. 2. va. to scatter, to disperse ། ལྷག་པ་ཆེན་པོ་དེས་ར་ལུག་ཚང་མ་ཁ་གཏོར་བཞག The powerful wind scattered all the goats and sheep. 3. va. to scatter/ sprinkle ། མེ་ཏོག་ལ་ཆུ་གཏོར་གྱི་འདུག (He) is sprinkling water on the flowers. 4. abbr. of གཏོར་མ་.

གཏོར་རྐྱེན་གཏོང་ (dɔ̄ɔgyen dōŋ) va. to squander/ waste money, to be extravagant in spending money ། ཁོས་མ་ཇོང་བརྒྱབ་སྟེ་དངུལ་མང་པོ་གཏོར་རྐྱེན་བཏང་བཞག He squandered a lot of money playing mahjong.

གཏོར་སྐྱོན་ (dɔ̄ɔgyön) damage, destruction; va.—གཏོང་; —བྱེད་ to damage, to ruin, to destroy ། དགྲ་བོས་ཉ་གྲུ་གསུམ་གཏོར་སྐྱོན་བཏང་བ་རེད་ The enemy damaged three fishing boats.

གཏོར་ཁུང་ (dɔ̄ɔguŋ) sewage drain.

གཏོར་འགོག (dɔ̄ɔgɔɔ̀) destroying and obstructing/ blocking.

གཏོར་མགྲོན་ (dɔ̄rdrön) the object to which torma is offered.

གཏོར་འགྲེམས་ (dɔ̄rdrem) spraying, sprinkling.(water); va.—བྱེད་.

གཏོར་གཞོལ་ (dɔ̄ɔgöö) attacking and destroying (in war); annihilating; va.—གཏོང་ ། ང་ཚོའི་དམག་མིས་དགྲ་བོར་གཏོར་གཞོལ་བྱས་སོང་ Our soldiers annihilated the enemy.

གཏོར་གཞོལ་དམག་འཐབ་ (dɔ̄ɔgöö məgdəb) war of annihilation.

གཏོར་རྒྱག (dɔ̄ɔ gyaà) ritual where offerings are burnt to ward/ drive away evil spirits; va.—རྒྱག.

གཏོར་རྒྱན་ (dɔ̄rgyɛn) sm. དཀར་རྒྱན.

གཏོར་སྒམ་ (dɔ̄ɔgam) a box for putting torma.

གཏོར་བསྒྱིལ་ (dɔ̄ɔgyee) overthrowing; va.—གཏོང་ ། མི་དམངས་ཀྱིས་སྲིད་གཞུང་རྙིང་པ་གཏོར་བསྒྱིལ་བཏང་བ་རེད་ The people overthrew the old government.

གཏོར་བཅོམ་ (dɔ̄ɔjom) destroying and looting/ vandalizing; va.—བྱེད་.

གཏོར་ཆས་ (dɔ̄ɔjɛɛ̀) things/ equipment for making torma.

གཏོར་སྟེགས་ (dɔ̄ɔdeg) the altar on which torma is placed.

གཏོར་དར་ (dɔ̄ɔdar) banner/ flag placed on a torma.

གཏོར་གདན་ (dɔ̄ɔdɛn) a mat on which torma is placed.

གཏོར་གདུགས་ (dɔ̄ɔdug) small umbrella placed over torma.

གཏོར་འདེབས་ (dɔ̄ndeb) the broadcast method of

sowing seed; va.—བྱེད་.

གཏོར་སྐྲུགས་ (dɔ̄ɔ̄juù) destroying and expelling.

གཏོར་ཕམ་ (dɔ̄ɔ̄pam) destroying and defeating; va.—གཏོང་.

གཏོར་ཕུད་ (dɔ̄ɔ̄büü) the initial ritual offering of torma.

གཏོར་འབེན་ (dɔ̄ɔ̄ben) abbr. of གཏོར་མ་འབེན་.

གཏོར་སྦུ་ (dɔ̄ɔ̄bu) the container in which torma-offering utensils are kept.

གཏོར་བྱེད་མཆུ་ཏོ་ (dɔ̄ɔ̄jeè cūdo) nozzle of a hose/ faucet/ sprayer.

གཏོར་མ་ (dɔ̄ɔ̄ma) a cone shaped ritual offering made from tsamba; va.—འབུལ་ to make a torma offering.

གཏོར་མ་ཆུ་ལ་དབྱུག་ན་བྱ་ཁྱི་ཁོ་ཐག་ཆོད་ (dɔ̄ɔ̄ma cūlə yūùnə cə̱kyi kōdaà cȫö̀) if sth. is destroyed or given to a third party, others who seek it will have no hope of getting it [Lit. if the torma is thrown into the river, the bird and dog will lose all hope].

གཏོར་མ་གཏོང་ (dɔ̄ɔ̄ma dōŋ) to offer a type of torma.

གཏོར་མ་བཞེངས་ (dɔ̄ɔ̄ma she̱ŋ) va. to make torma.

གཏོར་རྨས་ (dɔ̄ɔ̄mɛɛ̀) damaging and injuring.

གཏོར་རྩམ་ (dɔ̄ɔ̄dzam) tsamba used for making torma.

གཏོར་རྩམ་རྗེན་ཐག (dɔ̄ɔ̄dzam je̱ndaà) shung. tsamba ground from unroasted barley that is used for making torma.

གཏོར་རྫས་ (dɔ̄ɔ̄dzɛɛ̀) dynamite, explosives.

གཏོར་གཞོང་ (dɔ̄ɔ̄shoŋ) basin in which torma offerings are placed.

གཏོར་ཟན་ (dɔ̄ɔ̄sɛn) the dough that a torma is made of.

གཏོར་ཟོར་ (dɔ̄ɔ̄sor) sm. གཏོར་རྒྱག.

གཏོར་གཟུགས་ (dɔ̄ɔ̄sug) having the triangular shape of a གཏོར་མ་.

གཏོར་གཡོག (dɔ̄ɔ̄yog) person who serves/ assists a lama or monk when offering torma.

གཏོར་ར་ (dɔ̄ɔ̄ra) place where a གཏོར་རྒྱག ritual takes place.

གཏོར་རིལ་ (dɔ̄ɔ̄ri) torma offered to ཡི་དྭགས་.

གཏོར་བརླག (dɔ̄rlaà) destroying, ruining, annihilating; va.—གཏོང་ to destroy, to ruin, to annihilate ¶ དམག་མིས་ཁང་པ་མང་པོ་གཏོར་བརླག་བཏང་སོང་ The soldiers destroyed many houses.

གཏོར་ལས་པ་ (dɔ̄ɔ̄lɛɛ̀ba) shung. person who makes torma.

གཏོར་ཤུལ་ (dɔ̄ɔ̄shüü) the aftermath/ trace/ remains of sth. destroyed.

གཏོར་བཤིག (dɔ̄ɔ̄shiì) sm. གཏོར་བརླག.

གཏོར་བཤིག་པ་ (dɔ̄ɔ̄shigba) saboteur.

གཏོར་བཤིགས་ (dɔ̄ɔ̄shiì) sm.* གཏོར་བཤིག.

གཏོར་བཤོས་ (dɔ̄ɔ̄shöö) 1. spraying or throwing (liquids), watering; va.—བྱེད་. 2. sm. གཏོར་མ་.

གཏོར་གསུམ་ (dɔ̄ɔ̄sum) the red triangular patch on the heel of Tibetan boots.

གཏོར་གསོས་ (dɔ̄ɔ̄söö) an additonal གཏོར་མ་ offering.

གཏོར་ལྷུང་ (dɔ̄ɔ̄lhuŋ) shooting down (an airplane); va.—གཏོང་ ¶ མེ་སྒྲོགས་བརྒྱབ་ནས་གནམ་གྲུ་མང་པོ་གཏོར་ལྷུང་བཏང་པ་རེད་ (They) shot down many airplanes by firing artillery.

གཏོལ་ (dȫȫ) 1. familiarity. 2. certainty, definiteness. 3. va. to expose mistakes/ errors. 4. va. to make holes.

གཏོལ་བྲལ་ (dȫȫdrɛɛ) sm. གཏོལ་མེད་.

གཏོལ་མེད་ (dȫȫmeè) 1. not knowing ¶ གྲོང་ཁྱེར་ཆེན་པོའི་ནང་གར་འགྲོ་མགོ་འཐོམས་ནས་གཏོལ་མེད་གྱུར་སོང་ He got dazed in the big city and did not know where he was going.

གཏོས་ (dȫö̀) size ¶ གཏོས་ཆེ་ལྗིད་ཆུང་ Large in size but light in weight.

གཏོས་ཆུང་ (dȫöjuŋ) small size, miniature, compact in size.

གཏོས་ཚད་ (dȫödzeɛ̀) size.

བཏག (dāà) 1. f. of འཐག. 2. tool used to tighten weaving.

བཏག་གི་སོ་ (dāàgi sō) the teeth on a བཏག.

བཏགས་ (dāā) 1. p. of འཐག. 2. p. of འདོགས་.

བཏགས་མ་ (dāgma) 1. a tool used to tighten weaving. 2. woven materials.

བཏགས་མིང་ (dāàmiŋ) a name constructed by combining two words to form a new word (e.g., "sky + boat"= airplane).

བཏགས་རྫས་ (dāgdzɛɛ̀) woven materials, textiles.

བཏང་ (dāŋ) p. of གཏོང་.

བཏང་སྐྱིལ་ (dāŋgyii) sm. བཏང་འཛིན་.

བཏང་འགྲོ་བཞག་སྡོད་ (dāŋdro sha̱gdöö) shung. able/ capable/ efficient in work, able to do whatever is asked; vi.—འཕེར་ to be efficient/ capable, to be able to do whatever is asked [Lit. (if) sent goes, if left stays].

བཏང་སྙོམས་ (dāŋñom) 1. without extremes/ excess, in moderation/ balance, equally, impartially, evenhandedly; va.—འཇོག to leave sth. alone, to take a neutral/ balanced/ evenhanded stance ¶ རང་ཉིད་ལ་ཆོས་དད་མེད་ནའང་ཆོས་ལ་དམའ་འབེབས་མ་བྱས་པར་བཏང་སྙོམ་བཞག་ན་ཡག་པོ་ཡོད་པ་རེད་ Even though one is irreligious it is good if you don't disparage religion and treat it in a balanced fashion. 2. va. to leave a game a tie.

བཏང་སྙོམས་རིང་ལུགས་ (dāŋñom ri̱ŋluù) neutralism.

བཏང་སྙོམས་པ་ (dāŋñomba) mediator.

བཏང་སྙོམས་ལ་འཇོག (dāŋñomla jɔ̱ɔ̀) va. to leave sth. alone, to take a neutral stance.

བཏང་བཏང་བྱུག་བྱུག (dāŋdaŋ cu̱gjug) sm. བཏང་བཏང་བྱུང་བྱུང་.

བཏང་བཏང་བྱུང་བྱུང་ (dāŋdaŋ cu̱ŋjuŋ) boasting.

བཏང་ཐུང་ (dāŋduŋ) sb. who does miscellaneous work, sb. sent here and there to do odd jobs; va.—རྒྱུགས་.

བཏང་ཐོ་ (dāŋdo) list of things sent.

བཏང་ན་མདའ་བཀུག་ན་གཞུ་ (dāŋna da̱guùna shu̱) sb. who is versatile/ multipurpose/ flexible.

བཏང་བྱུང་ཚ་པོ་ (dāŋjuŋ tsābo) person who shows off/ brags a lot.

བཏང་འབྱོར་ (dāŋjɔɔ) sent and received, dispatched and arrived ¶ ལྷ་ས་ནས་བལ་ཡུལ་ལ་བང་ཆེན་བཏང་འབྱོར་བྱུང་ཡོད་དམ་ Has the messenger who was sent from Lhasa to Nepal arrived?

བཏང་འཛིན་ (dəŋdzin) sm. སྣངས་འཛིན་.

བཏང་བཟུང་ (dāŋsuŋ) sm. གླང་དོར་.

བཏང་ཡིག (dəŋyig) correspondence, letter; va.—གཏོང་ to send correspondence, to communicate by letter.

བཏང་ཤོར་ (dāŋshɔɔ) shung. 1. vi. to let escape ¶ ཀུན་མ་དེ་ས་གནས་རྫོང་ལ་བཙན་འཛུག་གིས་བཏང་ཤོར་མེད་པ་བྱེད་དགོས་ That thief should be imprisoned in the district in a way so that he does not escape. 2. letting sb. intentionally go, letting escape.

བཏང་ཤོར་བཟུང་ཤོར་ (dāŋshɔɔ su̱ŋshɔɔ) intentionally and unintentionally farting.

བཏང་ཤོར་མེད་པ་ (dāŋshɔɔ me̱èba) not escaping; not letting escape.

བཏད་ (dɛɛ̀) p. of གཏོད་.

བཏབ་ (dəb) p. of འདེབས་.

བཏབ་སར་སྨིན་ (dəbsaa mi̱n) va. to do well wherever sb. is sent [Lit. to ripen wherever planted].

བཏམ་ (dām) f. of གཏམ་.

བཏམས་ (dām) p. of གཏམ་.

བཏིག (dīg) f. of གཏིག.

བཏིགས་ (dīg) p. of གཏིག.

བཏིང་ (dīŋ) p. of འདིང་.

བཏིངས་ (dīŋ) sm. བཏིང་.

བཏུ་ (dū) f. of འཐུ་.

བཏུང་ (dūŋ) f. of འཐུང་.

བཏུང་ཆུ་ (dūŋju) drinking water.

བཏུང་སྣོད་ (dūŋnoò) drinking cup/ bowl.

བཏུང་བ་ (dūŋwə) beverages; va.—བྱེད་ to use as a

beverage.

བཏུང་བ་འཇམ་པོ་ (dūŋwə jambo) soft drinks.

བཏུང་བྱ་ (dūŋja) poet. water.

བཏུངས་ (dūŋ) p. of འཐུང་.

བཏུངས་ལྷག (dūŋlhaà) leftover drinks.

བཏུད་ (dǖü) p. of འདུད་.

བཏུམས་ (dūm) p. of གཏུམ་.

བཏུམས་རྒྱ་ (dūmgya) wrapped, covered.

བཏུལ་ (dǖü) p. of འདུལ་.

བཏུལ་བཅིལ་ (dǖüjii) smelting metals; va.—བྱེད་.

བཏུལ་མ་ (dǖümə) metals that have been smelted.

བཏུས་ (dǖü) p. of འཐུ་.

བཏེག (dēg) p. of འདེགས་.

བཏེགས་ (dēg) sm. བཏེག.

བཏེགས་ཟུར་ (dēgsur) angle of elevation.

བཏོག (dōg) f. of འཐོག.

བཏོག་དེབ་ (dōgdeb) receipt book.

བཏོགས་ (dɔ̄ɔ̀) p. of འཐོག.

བཏོད་ (dȫö) p. of གཏོད་.

བཏོན་ (dōn) p. of འདོན་.

བཏོན་ཁྲ་ (dōndra) shung. list of items that were taken out of storage.

བཏོན་ཁྲ་བུ་དེབ་ (dōndeb pudeb) shung. copy book of the list of items that is taken out from storage ¶ བཏོན་ཁྲ་བུ་དེབ་སྙན་ཁོངས་ཟུར་ཕུལ་ཞུས་པ་ We attached a copy of the list of items that were taken out of storage with the petition.

བཏོན་རྒྱ་ (dōngya) an order for taking grain out of a government storehouse ¶ བཏོན་རྒྱ་གཞིར་བཟུང་བཀར་ཁང་ཁག་ནས་འདོན་རྒྱུ་ (You) shall take out grain from the storage room in accordance with the order for taking out grain.

བཏོན་ཆོག་བཀའ་རྒྱ་ (dōnjɔ̀ gāgya) shung. sm. བཏོན་རྒྱ་.

བཏོན་ཆོག་བཀའ་རྒྱ་རིན་པོ་ཆེའི་དགོངས་ (dōncɔ̀ gāgya rimpochee goŋ) shung. sm. བཏོན་རྒྱ་.

བཏོན་ཆོག་བཀའ་འཛིན་ (dōnjɔ̀ gāndzin) shung. sm. བཏོན་རྒྱ་.

བཏོན་གཏོང་ (dōndoŋ) deporting, expelling; va.—བྱེད་.

རྟ་ (dā) horse.

རྟ་ཀོས་ཕུང་བཏུམས་ (dāgöö̀ pūŋdum) dying on the battlefield [Lit. corpse wrapped in a horse's hide].

རྟ་ཀྲབ་ (dādrəb) sm.* རྟ་སྲབ.

རྟ་ཀླད་ (dālɛɛ̀) agate.

རྟ་དཀར་མི་དཀར་ (dāgar migar) rider in white on a white horse (usu. refers to the persons sent to await the bride as a sign of good fortune).

རྟ་དཀར་ལ་གདོང་ནག་དང་མི་དཀར་ལ་ཞྭ་ནག (dāgar migar) sm. མི་དཀར་ཞྭ་ནག.

རྟ་དཀྲོགས་ (dā drɔ̄ɔ̀) va. to frighten / spook horses.

རྟ་རྐང་ (dāgaŋ) 1. horse hoof. 2. a trumpet made from a horse femur bone.

རྟ་རྐྱང་ (dāgyaŋ) a lone rider on a horse ¶ ང་རྟ་རྐྱང་བྱས་ཡོང་པ་ཡིན་ I came riding alone.

རྟ་རྐྱང་མདུང་རྐྱང་ (dāgyaŋ duŋgyaŋ) a weak force [Lit. a lone rider with only a spear].

རྟ་རྐྱང་མི་རྐྱང་ (dāgyaŋ migyaŋ) without any help [Lit. a lone horse, a lone person].

རྟ་རྐྱང་ནག (dā gyaŋnaà) chestnut colored horse.

རྟ་སྐྱ་ (dā gyā) 1. va. to mount (a horse). 2. va. to ride on a horse.

རྟ་རྐྱང་པོ་ (dā gyāŋbo) purplish-red colored horse.

རྟ་རྐྱང་དམར་ (dā gyāŋmar) sm. རྟ་རྐྱང་པོ་.

རྟ་སྐད་ (dāgɛɛ̀) 1. neighing; va.—རྒྱག; —འཚེར་ to neigh. 2. shung. the report yelled by the four རྟེས་ཕྲུག་པ་ saying that the Monlam procession of riders armed with ancient weapons is complete and correct; va.—རྒྱག.

རྟ་བཀྱག (dāgyaà) a stone used for mounting a horse.

རྟ་ཁ་རྒོད་པོ་ (dā kā göö̀bo) a headstrong horse.

རྟ་ཁ་བསྒྱུར་ (dā kā gyur) va. to turn a horse (while riding); to control a horse while riding.

རྟ་ཁ་གནོན་ (dā kā nȫn) va. to hold the bit/ bridle of a horse while sb. mounts the horse.

རྟ་ཁ་གཡང་འཐེན་ (dā kā yāŋden) avoiding disaster in the nick of time [Lit. pull the horse from the abyss/ precipice].

རྟ་ཁ་ལམ་པ་བྱེད་ (dā kā lamba ceè) va. to take hold of the halter/ reins of a horse when receiving a visitor coming on horseback and lead them to the dwelling.

རྟ་ཁ་ལེན་ (dā kā len) va. to receive sb. by holding their horse halter/ reins as you walk them to the dwelling.

རྟ་ཁ་ལོ་བདེ་པོ་ (dā kālo debo) a gentle/ easy to control horse.

རྟ་ཁ་ཤོར་ (dā kā shɔ̄ɔ) vi. to have a horse get out of control while riding.

རྟ་ཁ་སྲབ་ལེན་བྱེད་ (dā kā trəblen ceè) va. to take hold of the halter/ reins of a horse when receiving a visitor coming on horseback.

རྟ་ཁང་ (dāgaŋ) stable.

རྟ་ཁམ་པ་ (dā kāmba) a tan (colored) horse, a yellowish brown horse.

རྟ་ཁལ་ (dā kɛ̄ɛ) shung. riding horses and transport/ carrying animals.

རྟ་ཁལ་ཁྲལ་འུལ་ (dāgɛɛ trɛ̄ɛwuu) shung. corvee tax consisting of providing riding horses and carrying animals.

རྟ་ཁལ་འགོ་པ་ (dāgɛɛ goba) shung. the person in charge of the system corvee taxes in riding and transport animals in an area (the person in charge of giving notice of the need for animals and people).

རྟ་ཁལ་སྤྱི་ཁྱབ་ (dāgɛɛ jīgyəb) shung. chief official in charge of the corvee riding and transport animals.

རྟ་ཁལ་མི་གསུམ་གྱི་ཁྲལ་ (dāgɛɛ misumgo trɛ̄ɛ) shung. the three human corvee labor tasks involved with fulfilling the corvee animal tax—people for riding, loading, and portering.

རྟ་ཁལ་མི་རྫིང་ (dāgɛɛ mihreŋ) shung. the people who have to assist the provision of corvee animal taxes, e.g., for loading and accompanying the animals.

རྟ་ཁལ་ལུག་དཀྲི་ (dākɛɛ lugdri) giving people work beyond their capability or capacity [Lit. making a sheep responsible for a horse's load].

རྟ་ཁེབས་ (dākeb) horse blanket; va.—གཡོགས་ to put blanket on a horse.

རྟ་ཁྱུ་ (dā kyū) a herd of horses.

རྟ་ཁྱེར་ (dā kyēr) sm. རྟ་བཞོན་.

རྟ་ཁྲ་ (dādra) 1. piebald horse. 2. zebra.

རྟ་ཁྲ་ཐིག (dā drādig) pinto colored horse.

རྟ་ཁྲབ་ (dādrəb) shung. horse armor.

རྟ་ཁྲལ་ (dādrɛɛ) sm. རྟ་འུལ་.

རྟ་ཁྲོམ་ (dādrom) horse market.

རྟ་འཁོར་ (dāgɔɔ) horse drawn cart.

རྟ་གད་ (dāgɛɛ̀) a kind of horse neigh that sounds like a laugh.

རྟ་གྭ་པ་ (dā gaba) a horse with a white face.

རྟ་གར་ཚོགས་པ་ (dāgar tsōgba) circus troupe.

རྟ་གལ་ (dāgɛɛ) saddlebag.

རྟ་གོ་ (dāgo) horse armor.

རྟ་གྲོ་དཀར་ (dā drogar) pinto colored horse.

རྟ་གྱོང་པོ་ (dā gyoŋbo) a headstrong horse.

རྟ་གྲལ་ (dā trɛɛ) a line of horsemen/ riders.

རྟ་གྲོ་དམར་ (dā tromar) red spotted horse.

རྟ་གླ་ (dāla) price to rent a horse; va.—གཏོང་; —གློ་ to rent out horses.

རྟ་གློ་ (dālo) horse cinch.

རྟ་གློད་ (dā lȫö̀) sm. རྟ་རྒྱུག་གློད་.

རྟ་མགོ་ (dāŋgo) 1. horse head. 2. a horse head shaped nail.

རྟ་མགོ་ལུག་གཞུག (dāgo lugshuù) incongruous, unmatched (usu. clothes) [Lit. horse head, sheep tail].

རྟ་མགོ་གཟུགས་ (dāgosug) Tibetan style of placing mattresses in a room in an L shape.

རྟ་མགྱོགས་པོའི་ཐོག་ལ་ལྕག (dā gyogbö tōla jāà) top/ high speed, with the greatest urgency [Lit. while the horse is going fast, whipping it].

རྟ་མགྲིན་ (dəmdrin) 1. name of a diety (that has a horse's head). 2. person's name.

རྟ་འགྱེལ་མི་འགྱེལ་ (dāgyee migyee) having all kinds of problems and setbacks [Lit. horse fall, person fall].

རྟ་འགྲོས་མ་ (dā dröòma) type of horse that trots well, a trotter.

རྟ་རྒན་ (dāgɛn) old horse.

རྟ་རྒན་གྱིས་ལམ་ཤེས་ (dāgɛngi lamsheè) experience is very important, old people are useful because of their great experience [Lit. the old horse knows the road].

རྟ་རྒན་རྨལ་བཅོས་བྱས་ན་སྡུག་ལ་མངོན་ (dāgɛn gɛɛjöö cɛɛna dugla ŋön) even though one tries to help sb. they see it as trying to harm them [Lit. treating the sores on an old horse makes the horse think people are torturing it].

རྟ་རྒན་ལམ་རྒྱུས་ (dāgɛn ləmgyüü) a person with good experience [Lit. an old horse knows the way].

རྟ་རྒན་ལམ་མངའ་ (dāgɛn lamŋa) sm. རྟ་རྒན་ལམ་རྒྱུས་.

རྟ་རྒོད་ (dā göö) sm. རྟ་རྒོད་པོ་.

རྟ་རྒོད་པོ་ (dā gööbo) a wild or untrained horse.

རྟ་རྒོད་མ་ (dā gööma) mare.

རྟ་རྒོད་རི་ཤོར་ (dāgöö rishɔɔ) an undisciplined/ wild person [Lit. an untamed/ undisciplined horse that ran away to the mountains].

རྟ་རྒྱབ་ (dāgyəb) 1. the back of a horse. 2. a load that a horse carries. 3. two riders on a horse; va.—བཞོན་; —རྒྱག to ride on the back of a horse behind the main rider, to put (a child) on the back of the horse (behind the main rider).

རྟ་རྒྱུག (dəgyuù) horse racing; va.—གཏོང་; —སློད་ to race horses.

རྟ་རྒྱུག་མཁན་ (dəgyuùñɛn) jockey.

རྟ་རྒྱུག་འགྲན་བསྡུར་ (dəgyu trɛnduu) horse race; va.—བྱེད་; —གཏོང་.

རྟ་རྒྱུག་རྒྱུག་ས་ (dəguù gyuùsə) sm. རྟ་རྒྱུག་ཐང་.

རྟ་རྒྱུག་སློད་ (dəguù lõõ) va. to have a horse race, to race horses.

རྟ་རྒྱུག་ཐང་ (dəgyuùdaŋ) race track/ course (for horses).

རྟ་རྒྱུག་མདའ་འཕེན་ (dəgyuù damben) shung. horse race that involves riders shooting arrows from the saddle.

རྟ་རྒྱུག་ན་རྒྱུག་མཉམ་དང་གུར་བརྒྱབ་ན་ཁ་སྤྲོད་ཡིན་ (dəgyuùna gyuùñamdaŋ kur gyəbna kābdröö yin) people competing head-to-head [Lit. horses in the same race, tents face-to-face].

རྟ་རྒྱུག་མི་རྒྱུག (dəgyuù migyuù) shung. a series of races that takes place after the Monlam festival (on the 25th of the 1st Tibetan month) where people and horses race.

རྟ་རྒྱུག་ཚོགས་འདུ་ (dəgyuù tsõndu) meeting pertaining to horse racing.

རྟ་རྒྱུག་ཞར་འཕེན་ (dəgyuù shamben) shung. a sport involving riding a horse at full gallop and then firing a rifle at a target and then an arrow at the next target and then a gesture of spearing at a third target.

རྟ་རྒྱུག་ར་བ་ (dəgyuù rawa) sm. རྟ་རྒྱུག་ཐང་.

རྟ་རྒྱུག་ས་ (dā gyuùsə) sm. རྟ་རྒྱུག་ཐང་.

རྟ་རྒྱུད་ (dāgyüü) 1. the character of a horse. 2. the breed of a horse.

རྟ་སྒ་ (dāga) horse saddle; va.—རྒྱག to saddle a horse; va.—ཕྲུ་ to unsaddle a horse.

རྟ་སྒ་སྒ་འཁོར་ (dāga gagɔɔ) sm. རྟ་ཆས་.

རྟ་སྒ་འབྱར་ (dā gajar) a saddled horse.

རྟ་སྒ་རིལ་ (dā gərii) horse cart/ carriage, stagecoach.

རྟ་སྒྲོ་ (dādro) saddle bag; va.—རྒྱག to put a saddle bag on a horse.

རྟ་སྒྲོག (dādrɔɔ) rope or leather strap used to tie horses feet together so that they can't go far when left out to graze.

རྟ་ངང་པ་ (dā ŋaŋba) a yellowish horse.

རྟ་ངར་པོ་ (dā ŋarbo) a horse that is difficult to control, a headstrong horse.

རྟ་རྔ་ (dāŋa) horse tail.

རྟ་རྔ་ཙམ་ (dā ŋādam) a little bit, a tiny amount ¶ཁོང་གི་བཀའ་མོལ་དེ་ར་སྐྱོན་རྟ་རྔ་ཙམ་ཡང་མི་འདུག His comments do not contain even a tiny mistake.

རྟ་རྔ་བརྒྱ་གཤག (dāŋa gyashaà) overly cautious, extremely fastidious/ careful [Lit. splitting a horses tail into one hundred strands].

རྟ་རྔོག (dāŋɔɔ) sm. རྟའི་ཤེ་.

རྟ་ཅང་ (dājaŋ) a fine horse.

རྟ་ཅང་ཤེས་ (dā jāŋsheè) a clever horse.

རྟ་གཅིག་སྒ་གཉིས་ (dājig gañii) having multiple responsibilities/ jobs (usu. conveys too many responsibilities or obligations) [Lit. one horse, two saddles].

རྟ་གཅོག (dā jōg) 1. va. to break in a horse. 2. va. to warm up a horse.

རྟ་བཅག (dā jāà) p. of རྟ་གཅོག.

རྟ་བཅོས་ (dājöö) treating horse illnesses; va.—བྱེད་.

རྟ་བཅོས་པ་ (dā jööba) veterinary doctor.

རྟ་ལྕག (dɛ̄jaà) horse whip; va.—གཞུ་; —གཏོང་ to whip.

རྟ་ལྕགས་ (dājaà) horse shoe.

རྟ་ཆག (dācaà) horse fodder.

རྟ་ཆད་ (dā cɛɛ̀) vi. to be or get exhausted/ tired/ worn out (for horses) ¶ལམ་བར་དུ་རྟ་ཆད་ནས་ང་ཚོ་གོམ་པ་རྒྱག་དགོས་བྱུང་ The horse got exhausted on the trail and we had to walk.

རྟ་ཆད་རྨལ་རལ་ (dācɛɛ̀ gɛɛrɛɛ) conveys working too hard, working like horses ¶ཁྲལ་པ་རྣམས་ཁྲལ་རིགས་བདག་གཞིག་ཆེ་བས་རྟ་ཆད་རྨལ་རལ་ལྟ་བུར་གྱུར་ཡོད་པ་རེད་ Because of heavy oppressive taxes, the taxpayer peasants were worked to exhaustion like horses (became like exhausted horses with sores on their backs). [Lit. exhausted horse with sores on its back].

རྟ་ཆས་ (dācɛɛ̀) riding equipment, saddlery, tack.

རྟ་ཆུ་སྦྱོར་ (dā cū dēr) va. to give water to a horse.

རྟ་ཆུང་ལ་བཞོན་བདེ་དང་ མི་ཆུང་ལ་བསྐུལ་བདེ་ (dā cūŋlə shönde daŋ mi cūŋlə gũũde) conveys a bad leader/ chief/ lord who takes advantage of people who are easy to boss around rather than be fair [Lit. easy to ride a small horse and easy to order a humble, ordinary person].

རྟ་མཆོག (dājɔɔ) a good horse.

རྟ་མཆོག་ཁ་འབབ་ (dājɔɔ kāmbəb) one of the four rivers that flows from Mount Kailash (it becomes the Karnali River in Nepal).

རྟ་མཆོག་ཅང་ཤེས་ (dājɔɔ jāŋsheè) a good/ fine horse.

རྟ་མཆོག་ལྕག་གིས་བསྐུལ་བ་ (dājɔɔ jāàgi gũũwa) sm. རྟ་མགྱོགས་པའི་ཐོག་ལ་ལྕག.

རྟ་མཆོག་གཙང་པོ་ (dājɔɔ dzāŋbo) sm. རྟ་མཆོག་ཁ་འབབ་.

རྟ་མཆོག་རིན་པོ་ཆེ་ (dājɔɔ rimboce) one of the seven royal Tibetan symbols.

རྟ་འཆག (dā cāà) sm. རྟ་གཅོག.

རྟ་འཇམ་སྒ་བཟོ་ (dājam gaso) sm. རྟ་བཟོ་སྒ་འཇམ་.

རྟ་ཉམས་ཚོད་པོ་ (dāñam cõõbo) a person who is expert in assessing the quality of horses.

རྟ་མཉམ་རྒྱུག (dāñam gyuù) va. to run neck and neck (horses).

རྟ་དུར་ (dādur) money collected after every round of mahjong that is used to pay for the food and drink served; va.—གསོག.

རྟ་དོག (dādɔɔ) a gilded ornament worn on top of the head of high lama's horses.

རྟ་གདུམ་པོ་ (dā dūmmo) sm. རྟ་རྒོད་པོ་.

རྟ་གདོང་ (dā dōŋ) va. to ride a horse fast, to gallop.

རྟ་གདོང་བ་ (dā dōŋwa) sm. རྟ་ཁལ་འགོ་པ་.

རྟ་སྟན་ (dādɛn) rug used under a saddle.

རྟ་ཐབ་ (dādəb) shung. abbr. of རྟ་ཐབ་གཡོག.

རྟ་ཐབ་གཡོག (dā təbyɔ̄ɔ̀) shung. peasants who as a corvee tax have to care for individuals traveling with a government travel permit when they stay overnight (this involves looking after the traveler's animals, cooking, etc.).

རྟ་ཐུག (dāduù) sm. རྟ་གསེབ་.

རྟ་ཐོ་ (dādo) shung. sm. རྟ་གཞུང་.

རྟ་ཐོ་ལོག (dā tōlɔɔ̀) a small horse, a pony.

རྟ་ཐོག་གྲུ་གུ་ (dātɔɔ̀ drugu) sm. རྟ་ཐོག་སྦོ་ལོ་.

རྟ་ཐོག་གྲོག་གཟིགས་ (dātɔɔ̀ drogsii) shung. people in high position taking an interest in the common people [Lit. to see ants while on horseback].

རྟ་ཐོག་སྦོ་ལོ་ (dādɔɔ̀ bōlo) polo; va.—རྒྱག to play polo.

རྟ་ཐོག་པོ་ལོང་ (dādɔɔ̀ pōloŋ) sm. རྟ་ཐོག་སྦོ་ལོ་.

རྟ་ཐོག་ལུས་རྩལ་ (dādɔɔ̀ lüùdzɛɛ) equestrian sports.

རྟ་མཐུར་ (dādur) a halter (for a horse's head).

རྟ་འཐེང་ (dādeŋ) a horse with a crippled leg.

རྟ་འཐེན་ (dāden) horse drawn ¶ རྟ་འཐེན་ང་བསྔུ་འཕྲུལ་འཁོར་ A horse drawn harvester.

རྟ་དར་ (dātar) shung. a horseman carrying a banner who rides before a king or high lama.

རྟ་དྲེལ་ (dādree) 1. horse and mule. 2. transport animals.

རྟ་དྲེལ་འགྲོལ་འཛིན་ (dādree trōndzin) shung. a permit allowing individual households to keep horses and mules in Lhasa during Monlam.

རྟ་དྲེལ་སྒ་འབྱར་ (dādree ganjar) horses and mules that are saddled (so are ready to go).

རྟ་དྲེལ་གྱི་གཟན་ཆག (dādreegi sɛnjaà) fodder for horses and mules.

རྟ་གདན་ (dādɛn) rug used under a saddle; va.—རྒྱག.

རྟ་བདུན་པ་ (dā dümbə) poet. sun.

རྟ་བདུན་དབང་པོ་ (dādün wāŋbo) sm. རྟ་བདུན་པ་.

རྟ་མདའ་འཕེན་ (dā da pēn) va. to shoot an arrow while galloping (on a horse).

རྟ་མདུང་ (dāduŋ) a type of short spear used on horseback.

རྟ་མདོངས་ཅན་ (dā doŋjɛn) horse with a white spot on its forehead.

རྟ་མདོངས་པ་ (dā doŋba) sm. རྟ་མདོངས་ཅན་.

རྟ་འདུར་ (dādur) slow gait (of a horse).

རྟ་འདོགས་ས་ (dā dɔgsa) a place where horses are tied.

རྟ་འདྲ་པོ་ (dā drabo) 1. like a horse. 2. slang. handsome ¶ མི་དེ་རྟ་འདྲ་པོ་ཅིག་འདུག That man is handsome.

རྟ་འདྲོགས་ (dā drɔɔ̀) vi. to get startled/ spooked (for horses).

རྟ་རྒྱུར་ (dādur) horse racing; va.—རྒྱག.

རྟ་རྟང་ (dādaŋ) a strung out or pegged out rope that is used for tying horses.

རྟ་བརྒྱུར་ (dādur) sm. རྟ་རྒྱུར་.

རྟ་ནོར་ (dānɔɔ) abbr. horse and yak.

རྟ་ནོར་ལུག་གསུམ་ (dā nɔɔ lug sūm) the three: horse, yak and sheep.

རྟ་གནས་ (dā nɛɛ̀) sm. རྟ་ཁང་.

རྟ་རྣ་ (dāna) shung. a mounted competition with bow, spear and gun that is held in front of government officials of the 4th rank and above during the དྲུང་འཁོར་རྩལ་རྒྱུགས་ ceremony.

རྟ་པ་ (dāba) a rider, a horseman.

རྟ་པང་ (dābaŋ) holding sb. (usu. an infant) on one's lap when riding; va.—ལ་རྒྱག.

རྟ་པའི་གོས་ཐུང་ (dābɛ göödùŋ) special pants worn by a jockey.

རྟ་པའི་ཉིན་ལམ་ (dābɛ ñinlam) the number of days spent traveling on horseback ¶ རྟ་པའི་ཉིན་ལམ་གཉིས་གསུམ་ A trip that takes two or three days by horse.

རྟ་པའི་དོར་མ་ (dābɛ dorma) sm. རྟ་པའི་གོས་ཐུང་.

རྟ་དཔྱ་ (dāja) shung. a government horse tax.

རྟ་དཔྱད་ (dā jɛ̄ɛ̀) checking a horse for its physical attributes; va.—བྱེད་.

རྟ་ལྤགས་ (dābaà) horse skin.

རྟ་ལྤགས་པ་ (dā bāgba) a type of Tibetan medicine.

རྟ་སྤྱི་ (dəji) shung. an official in charge of animal corvee transportation taxes.

རྟ་ཕུར་ (dābur) a stake/ peg for tying up horses; va.—རྒྱག to tie a horse to a stake/ peg.

རྟ་ཕོ་ (dābo) male horse.

རྟ་ཕོ་ལ་རྒྱུགས་ཤེད་ཡོད་ན་བྱང་ཐང་སྟོང་པ་རེད་ (dābola gyugsheè yöö̀na caŋdaŋ dōŋba reè) if one has the ability, the opportunity is there [Lit. if the horse has the strength to run, the northern plain is empty].

རྟ་ཕོ་ཆེན་ (dā pōcen) 1. a strong male horse. 2. a castrated male horse.

རྟ་ཕོ་དྲུག་ཁྲོམ་ (dāpo drugdrom) a spotted dark gray horse.

རྟ་ཕྱིང་ (dāciŋ) a high quality robe worn by lamas on special occasions.

རྟ་ཕྱུགས་ (dā cūù) horse and cattle/ livestock.

རྟ་འཕྱུགས་ (dā cāà) shung. a summoning (as a tax) by the government of horses for a special occasion; va.—རྒྱག. ¶ དམག་འཁྲུག་སྐབས་གཞུང་གིས་མི་ཚང་ཀུན་ལ་རྟ་འཕྱུགས་བརྒྱབ་པ་རེད་ At the time of war, the government issued an order to all households summoning horses from them (as a tax).

རྟ་ཕྲུག (dədrug) colt, foal.

རྟ་བབས་ (dā pəb) va. to dismount (from a horse).

རྟ་བབས་ཀྱི་སྣམ་བུ་ (dābəbgi nəmbu) a woollen material used to decorate the doors of Tibetan homes.

རྟ་བབས་བུང་གཞོན་ (dābəb puŋshön) giving up a higher position/ status for a lower one [dismouting a horse and riding a donkey].

རྟ་བོ་ཆེ་ (dāwoje) a big horse.

རྟ་བོང་རིས་མེད་ (dā boŋ riìmeè) very old [Lit. horse and donkey with no lines on their teeth].

རྟ་བོན་ (dābön) the hard part of a horse's hoof (fetock).

རྟ་བྱ་ (dāja) gold ore.

རྟ་བྱང་མ་ (dā caŋma) a horse that has not been fed before racing to enhance its performance.

རྟ་བྲ་བོ་ (dā drowa) a black horse with a white mouth and white tip of its nostrils.

རྟ་བྲན་ (dādren) riding horses.

རྟ་བྲེས་ (dādreè) trough (for horses).

རྟ་བླ་ (dāla) centipede.

རྟ་དབང་ (dāwaŋ) Tawang: town and monastery in what had been southeast Tibet but is now a part of India's Arunachal Pradesh.

རྟ་དབུགས་འཆག་བྱེད་ (dā wūgjaà ceè) va. to walk a horse (to cool it down or to rest it).

རྟ་དབྱངས་ (dāyaŋ) a kind of prayer chanting with long tones.

རྟ་འབབས་འཛེག (dā bəbdziì) mounting and dismounting a horse.

རྟ་འབོག (dāmbog) 1. large saddlebag. 2. a rug that covers large saddlebags/ bedrolls.

རྟ་སྦངས་ (dɛbaŋ) dung (of horses).

རྟ་མ་ཆད་གོང་ལ་ཁྲིད་ན་བཟང་ (dā macɛɛ̀goŋla trīìnə saŋ) prevention is better than cure [Lit. before the horse gets exhausted it is better to lead it (on foot)].

རྟ་མ་ཆད་ཙམ་ (dā macɛɛ̀dzam) just barely enough ¶ ང་ཚོའི་འཚོ་བ་རྟ་མ་ཆད་ཙམ་ཞིག་རེད་ Our livelihood is just barely enough. [Lit. just enough so a horse doesn't get exhausted].

རྟ་མེད་གོས་ཐུང་ (dāmeè köödùŋ) pants that have do not have a split in the crotch to facilitate urination and defecation.

རྟ་མེད་དོར་མ་ (dāmeè torma) sm. རྟ་མེད་གོས་ཐུང་.

རྟ་དམག (dāmaà) mounted troops, cavalry.

རྟ་དམག་དཔུང་ཁག (dāmaà būŋgaà) cavalry unit/ force.

རྟ་དམག་ཧྲག་པོ་ (dāmaà hrāgbo) strong/ powerful

cavalry.

རྟ་དམུ་རྒོད་ (dā mūgöö) sm. རྟ་སྒྱུང་པོ་.

རྟ་རྨིག་མ་ (dā mīgmə) hoof shaped silver or gold ingot.

རྟ་རྩལ་ (dādzεε) horsemanship, equestrian sports.

རྟ་རྩལ་གྱི་འགོག་རྐལ་ (dādzεεgi g̲ɔggεε) equestrian obstacle/ jumping event.

རྟ་རྩལ་ཚོགས་པ་ (dādzεε tsɔ̄gba) sm. རྟ་རྩལ་རུ་ཁག.

རྟ་རྩལ་པ་ (dādzεεba) an equestrian (sportsman).

རྟ་རྩལ་རུ་ཁག (dādzεε r̲ugaà) equestrian sports unit.

རྟ་རྩེད་ (dādzeè) 1. equestrian sports; va.—རྩེ་. 2. circus show with horses.

རྟ་ཚག (dādzaà) Kundeling Rinpoche.

རྟ་ཚག་མངགས་བཏགས་ (dādzaà ŋāàdaà) a famous type of brocade first ordered in the 18th century by the then regent, Kundeling.

རྟ་མཚལ་ལུ་ (dā tsɔ̄lu) a purplish-red horse with white heels.

རྟ་ཚུགས་ (dɔ̄dzug) shung. 1. postal station. 2. a measure of distance equal to the distance between two postal stations ། དེ་ནས་འདི་བར་རྟ་ཚུགས་གཉིས་འདུག The distance between there and here is two postal stations (roughly two days on horse).

རྟ་ཚུགས་པོ་ (dā tsūgbu) a horse that trots at a steady pace.

རྟ་འཚེར་ (dā tsēr) va. to neigh (horses).

རྟ་འཚུབ་པོ་ (dā tsūbu) mischievous/ unruly horse.

རྟ་རྫི་ (dɔ̄dzi) herder of horses, person who looks after horses.

རྟ་ཞྭ་ (dāsha) shung. a type of winter hat worn by monk officials and lamas when riding.

རྟ་ཞགས་ (dāshaà) a lasso, lassoing a horse; va.—རྒྱག to lasso a horse.

རྟ་གཞུང་ (dāshuŋ) the list of ancient cavalry displayed after their procession in the Monlam Festival.

རྟ་གཞོང་ (dāshoŋ) a water trough for horses.

རྟ་བཞོན་ (dā shö̲n) va. to mount a horse. 2. va. to ride on a horse.

རྟ་ཟམ་ (dāsam) 1. sm. རྟ་ཚུགས་. 2. postal station/ pony express system. ། ངས་སྙན་ཞུ་རྟ་ཟམ་བརྒྱུད་ནས་བཏང་བ་རེད་ I sent the petition through the postal station (system).

རྟ་ཟམ་པ་ (dāsamba) shung. a pony express messenger who takes government documents or communications.

རྟ་ཟིན་སྒ་ཟིན་ (dāsin g̲asin) touching/ holding the horse and saddle when receiving or welcoming a rider.

རྟ་ཟེག་པ་ (dā se̲gba) reddish horse.

རྟ་ཟོག (dāsog) sm. རྟ་ཟོག་སེམས་ཅན་.

རྟ་ཟོག་སེམས་ཅན་ (dāsog sēmjen) livestock.

རྟ་གཟུགས་འཁོར་སྔགས་ (dāsug kɔ̄ɔ̄ŋaà) a mantra that when put on the foot makes one go very fast.

རྟ་བཟོ་སྒ་འཇམ་ (dāso g̲ajam) satisfying both sides, satisfying rival claims, making both sides happy [Lit. careful with horse, saddle soft].

རྟ་ཟླ་ (dānda) the first month of the Tibetan calendar.

རྟ་འུལ་ (dɔ̄wuu) shung. horse corvee tax; va.—གཏོང་; —རྒྱུགས་ to pay/ perform the horse corvee tax.

རྟ་འོ་ལ་ (dā w̲ola) a black horse.

རྟ་འོལ་བ་ (dā w̲ö̲öwa) sm. རྟ་འོ་ལ་.

རྟ་ཡན་སྲབ་མེད་ (dāyön drɔ̄bmeè) a horse without reins running where it wants; va.—གཏོང་.

རྟ་ཡོད་དོར་མ་ (dāyöö t̲orma) pants that have a split in the crotch to facilitate urination and defecation.

རྟ་གཡག་མགོ་སྤྲེལ་ (dā yāà g̲odrel) conveys incompatibility (since yak will fight with horse), putting two irreconcilable persons together [Lit. putting horse and yak head to head].

རྟ་གཡུང་མོ་ (dā yūŋmu) a gentle horse.

རྟ་གཡོག (dāyɔɔ̀) stable boy, groom; va.—རྒྱག to serve as a stable boy/ groom.

རྟ་གཡོག་ཐབ་གཡོག (dāyɔɔ̀ tɔ̄byɔɔ̀) shung. sm. རྟ་ཐབ་གཡོག.

རྟ་ར་གྲུ་བཞི་ (dāra dr̲ubshi) stable.

རྟ་རག་པ་ (dā r̲agba) a pale yellowish horse.

རྟ་རགས་ (dāraà) a band of horsemen, a line of horses with riders.

རྟ་རིང་ (dāriŋ) a long opera aria in the traditional Tibetan opera.

རྟ་ལ་སྒྱོན་ (dāla gyȫn) va. to put sb. on a horse.

རྟ་ལ་འགྲོས་དང་ སྤྲེའུར་རྩལ་ (dāla drö̲ò d̲aŋ drēwu dzε̄ε̄) everyone has his own specialty [Lit. horse has gait and monkey has acrobatic skills].

རྟ་ལ་རྐལ་རྨ་མི་བཟོ་ན་སྒ་ལ་སྐལ་རྨ་ (dāla g̲εεma m̲isöna g̲ala g̲εε mā) shung. its no skin off my back ། གལ་ཏེ་ཁྲ་མ་འདིར་དན་ཞི་མེད་ཚེ་རྟ་ལ་རྐལ་རྨ་མི་བཟོ་ན་ སྒ་ལ་སྐལ་རྨའི་དཔེ་ལྟར་ཁྲ་ཐུང་ཕྱིར་ལེན་ཐོག་ནས་བླ་དཔོན་གོང་མར་སྙན་འབུལ་ཞུ་རྒྱུ་ལས་འོས་མེད་ If you do not agree with the verdict, its like the saying it makes no difference to the horse if the saddle gets a sore on its back, and we have no choice but to take back the verdict and send you to the highest authority. [Lit. if the horse does not get a sore on its back, (it makes no difference to the horse) if the saddle gets a sore on its back].

རྟ་ལ་རྒྱུག་ཤེད་ཡོད་ན་བྱང་ཐང་སྟོང་བ་རེད་ (dāla gy̲ugsheè y̲ö̀öna c̲aŋdaŋla dōŋba r̲eè) sm. རྟ་པོ་ལ་རྒྱུགས་ཤེད་ཡོད་ན་བྱང་ཐང་སྟོང་པ་རེད་.

རྟ་ལ་གཡག་འཛེམ་ (dāla yāà dz̲em) cautious, hesitating [Lit. the yak is shy with regards to the horse].

རྟ་ལམ་ (dālam) the path that is used by a rider/ horse, a horse trail/ path.

རྟ་ལམ་གྲོག་མས་བཀག (dālam tr̲ogmεὲ gāà) sm. རྟ་ལམ་གྲོག་མས་འགོག.

རྟ་ལམ་གྲོག་མས་འགོག (dālam tr̲ogmεὲ g̲ɔɔ̀) overly optimistic, not able to realistically assess one's own strength [Lit. an ant blocking the path of a horse].

རྟ་ལམ་སྒོར་མོ་ (dālam g̲ormo) shung. the horse path behind the Potala Palace.

རྟ་ལམ་བོང་བུས་འགོག (dālam b̲uŋbüü g̲ɔɔ̀) an incapable person blocking/ impeding a capable one [Lit. a donkey blocking the path of a horse].

རྟ་ལམ་བོང་བུས་བྱེད་ (dālam b̲uŋbüü c̲eè) sm. རྟ་ལམ་བོང་བུས་འགོག.

རྟ་ལས་བཞོལ་ (dālε söö) sm. རྟ་བབ་.

རྟ་ལུད་ (dālüü) horse dung.

རྟ་ལོ་པ་ (dāloba) a person born in the year of the horse.

རྟ་ཤ་ (dāsha) 1. horse meat, horse flesh. 2. buttocks.

རྟ་ཤ་ལ་སྒྲོག (dāshala dr̲ɔɔ̀) va. to tie sth. on the side of the saddle, to affix saddlebags.

རྟ་ཤད་ (dāsheè) 1. curry comb. 2. messenger, pony express; va.—གཏོང་.

རྟ་ཤར་ (dāshaa) a lone rider.

རྟ་ཤས་ (dāshεὲ) a horse shared/ owned by two (or more) owners.

རྟ་ཤུ་ (dɔ̄shu) saddle sore; vi.—སྐྱེ་ to get a saddle sore.

རྟ་ཤུགས་ (dāshuù) horsepower.

རྟ་ཤེད་ (dāsheè) sm. རྟ་ཤུགས་.

རྟ་ཤོར་ན་ཟིན་ལ་ ཚིག་ཤོར་ན་མ་ཟིན་ (dā shɔ̄ɔ̄na s̲imba tsīì shɔ̄ɔ̄na m̲asin) be careful when you speak [Lit. you can catch a horse if it gets loose, you can't catch a spoken word once it is said].

རྟ་ཤོར་ལུག་ཐོབ་ (dāshɔɔ l̲ugtob) a bad deal [Lit. lose a horse and get a sheep].

རྟ་གཤན་ (dā shε̄n) va. to let a horse cross a river.

རྟ་བཤར་ (dā shār) va. to ride horses quickly.

རྟ་སུ་བསྒྱུགས་དང་ནམ་སུ་རིང་བལྟ་ཆོག (dā sū gy̲ɔɔ̀ d̲aŋ nām sū r̲iŋ dā cɔ̄ɔ̀) we can compete/ contest/ vie/ challenge [Lit. whose horse is faster and whose night is longer we can examine].

རྟ་སོ་ (dāso) 1. horse tooth. 2. a wall built in a zigzag shape on a hill (e.g., the wall on the Potala hill).

རྟ་སོ་མ་ (dāsoma) rock candy.

རྟ་སྲབ་ (dādrəb) bit (for horse's mouth); va.—གཡོག to put the bit in a horse's mouth.

རྟ་སློག (dālɔɔ̀) shung. the person who goes with a transport corvee horse from one station to the next and then brings it back to the originating corvee station.

རྟ་གསར་ (dāsar) a colt/ young horse that has not been broken in for riding or carrying.

རྟ་གསིར་པོ་ (dā sīrbu) sm. རྟ་གསོར་པོ་.

རྟ་གསེབ་ (dāseb) a stallion; va.—གཏོང་ to breed a stallion with mares.

རྟ་གསོར་པོ་ (dā sōrbo) a horse that runs fast without prodding.

རྟ་གསོ་ (dā sō) va. to look after/ care for horses.

རྟ་གསོ་གླིང་ཕྲན་ (dāso līŋdrɛn) a riding ring for equestrian events.

རྟ་གསོ་མཚོན་བརྡར་ (dāso tsōndar) making active preparations for war [Lit. feed the horses and sharpen the weapons].

རྟ་བསུ་སྐྱེལ་མི་ (dā sūgyēē mi̱) receiving and seeing off.

རྟ་བསུ་མཛུབ་སྐྱེལ་ (dāsu dzu̱bgyee) acting nice to sb. when you need sth. but dropping them when you are finished [Lit. to send a horse to call sb. and send the person back by pointing with one's finger where to go].

རྟ་ཧྲག (dāhrag) a good horse.

རྟ་ཧྲག་དམག་ཧྲག (dāhrag māàhrag) good quality horses and soldiers.

རྟ་ཧྲག་མི་ཧྲག (dāhrag mi̱hrag) good quality horses and men.

རྟ་ཧྲེང་མི་ཧྲེང་ (dāhreŋ mi̱hreŋ) a single rider.

རྟ་ཧྲེངས་ (dāhreŋ) an untamed/ wild horse.

རྟ་ལྷིང་པོ་ (dā lhīŋbu) a gentle horse.

རྟག (dāà) 1. abbr. རྟག་པར་. 2. (— + vb. + བྱེད་) to always do sth. ། ཁོང་ལས་ཀར་རྟག་འགྲོ་བྱེད་ཀྱི་འདུག He always comes to work.

རྟག་འཁྱོངས་ (dāggyoŋ) shung. always, constantly, consistently ། སློབ་ཕྲུག་དེ་སློབ་སྦྱོང་རྟག་འཁྱོངས་བྱེད་ཀྱི་འདུག The student studies consistently (without break).

རྟག་འགྲུས་ (dəgdrüù) shung. being consistently diligent ། ཐོས་བསམ་ལ་རྟག་འགྲུས་ཀྱི་སྒྲིམ་རྒྱུན་ཐུར་སྐྱོལ་མཐའ་དག་ལས་མི་འགལ་བ་དགོས་རྒྱུ One must be consistently diligent in listening (studying) and thinking, and must not go against the regulations.

རྟག་ཆད་ (dāgjɛɛ̀) the points of view of eternalism and nihilism (the religious viewpoints that respectively assert the true existence and total nonexistence of phenomenon).

རྟག་སྙོམས་ (dāgñom) homogeneous, uniform, equal.

རྟག་ཏུ་ (dāgdu) sm. རྟག་པར་.

རྟག་ཏུ་རྒྱུན་མི་ཆད་པ་ (dāgdu gyü̱n mi̱jɛɛ̀ba) continuously, constantly, without break.

རྟག་གཏུག་བྱེད་ (dəgduù ce̱è) va. to be in touch/ contact/ communication a lot ། ཁྱེད་རང་ཚོ་སྤུན་མཆེད་དབར་རྟག་གཏུག་བྱེད་གི་ཡོད་པས Are you keeping in touch with your relatives a lot?

རྟག་གཏོར་ (dāgdɔɔ) a torma that is offered every day.

རྟག་བརྟན་མི་འགྱུར་ཕོ་བྲང་ (dāgdɛn mi̱ngyur pōdraŋ) the new palace of the 14th Dalai Lama in Norbulinga.

རྟག་བརྟན་གཡུང་དྲུང་ (dāgdɛn yūndruŋ) a swastika symbol conveying steadfastness/ unchangeablity/ permanence.

རྟག་ལྟ་ (dāgda) philosophical view of eternalism.

རྟག་ཐུབ་པ་ (dāgdubbə) unchanging, constant.

རྟག་མཐོང་མི་མཚར་ (dāgdoŋ mi̱dzar) a common sight, sth. seen everyday.

རྟག་སྡོད་ (dāgdöö) sm. གཏན་སྡོད་.

རྟག་པ་ (dāgba) permanent, unchanging.

རྟག་པར་ (dāgbar) always, all the time ། ཁོ་ཚོས་རྟག་པར་རོགས་རམ་བྱེད་པར་ཡོང་གི་ཡོད་པ་རེད་ (They) always come to help.

རྟག་པར་རེ་བཞིན་ (dāgbar re̱shin) sm. རྟག་པར་.

རྟག་པོ་ (dāgbo) always, all the time ། ཁོང་ལས་ཀར་རྟག་པོར་ཡོང་གི་འདུག He always comes to work.

རྟག་མྱོས་ (dāgñöö) one of four guardian kings.

རྟག་ཚུགས་ (dəgdzug) 1. permanently established, permanently convening/. meeting; va.—བྱེད་. 2. sm. རྟག་པར་.

རྟགས་ (dāà) 1. mark, sign, symbol, signal; va.—རྒྱག་; —འཛུགས་ to make a mark/ sign, to signal ། དད་པའི་རྟགས་ A symbol of faith. ། དོ་པོ་འདི་ཚོའི་ཐོག་རྟགས་གང་ཡང་བརྒྱབ་མི་འདུག There are no marks (signs) on these loads. 2. proof, evidence (in logic). 3. seal. 4. genitals ། ཕོ་རྟགས་ Male genitals.

རྟགས་ཀྱི་འཇུག་པ་ (dāàgi ju̱gbə) gender in grammar.

རྟགས་ཁྲངས་ (dāgguŋ) shung. putting/ affixing a seal on a (pledge) ། མི་ཆེ་རྒན་གཞོན་ཚང་མའི་རྟགས་ཁྲངས་གནང་འབུལ་ཞུས་པར་ All the elderly and younger members (of the family) put their seals on the pledge.

རྟགས་གྲགས་ཅན་ (dāàdraàjɛn) well known brands.

རྟགས་བརྒྱད་ (dāàgyɛɛ̀) the eight auspicious symbols.

རྟགས་བརྒྱད་སྤྲིན་རིས་ (dāàgyɛɛ̀ drīnrii̇) designs with eight auspicious signs and clouds.

རྟགས་བརྒྱད་བུམ་གཟུགས་ (dāàgyɛɛ̀ pu̱msuù) designs with eight auspicious signs in the shape of a vase.

རྟགས་བརྒྱད་མ་ (dāàgyɛɛ̀ma) shung. abbr. of རྟགས་བརྒྱད་རི་མོའི་ཁ་བཏགས་.

རྟགས་བརྒྱད་རི་མོའི་ཁ་བཏགས་ (dāàgyɛɛ̀ ri̱mü kādaà) a ceremonial scarf that has the eight auspicious signs.

རྟགས་ཅན་ (dāgjɛn) named, called ། གནམ་གྲུ་ B ༥༢ རྟགས་ཅན་ The plane called B-52.

རྟགས་ཅན་གྱི་གན་རྒྱ་ (dāgjɛngi kɛ̱ngya) shung. a pledge/ contract/ agreement onto which seals have been affixed.

རྟགས་ཅན་མ་ (dāgjɛnma) prostitute.

རྟགས་འཇུག (dāŋjug) an affix (in linguistics).

རྟགས་ལྟས་མཚན་བཟང་ཅན་གྱི་ཁྱིའུ་ (dāgdɛɛ̀ tsɛ̄nsaŋjɛngi kyīwu) shung. a child who has auspicious signs and omens.

རྟགས་ཐམ་ (dāgdam) imprint, brand; va.—རྒྱག to brand, to make an imprint; vi.—ཐེབས་; —ཐོག to leave a brand/ imprint ། ཁོང་གི་བསམ་བློར་འབྱོར་ལྡན་གྲལ་རིམ་གྱི་རྟགས་ཐམ་ཐོག་ཡོད་པ་རེད་ His thinking bears the brand of the bourgeois class.

རྟགས་ཐེལ་ (dāgdel) a seal/ stamp.

རྟགས་ཐོན་པ་ (dāg tōmba) the result/ sign from a ritual.

རྟགས་དམ་ (dāgdam) sm. རྟགས་ཐེལ་.

རྟགས་དར་ (dāgdar) a flag for sending signals.

རྟགས་འབྱར་ (dāŋjar) sealed with a seal ། ཡི་གེ་རྟགས་འབྱར་གཅིག་འབྱོར་བྱུང་ I received a letter sealed with a seal.

རྟགས་མ་ (dāŋma) medal, badge, insignia, emblem; va.—འདོགས་ to wear the medal/ badge/ insignia/ emblem.

རྟགས་མེད་ (dāgmeè) sexless, neuter.

རྟགས་མཚན་ (dāgdzɛn) sign; vi.—ཐོན་ to have a sign be manifested/ displayed/ appear; va.—སྟོན་ to manifest/ send/ show/ display a sign ། སྲིད་གཞུང་གཉིས་དབར་མཐུན་ལམ་ཡོང་རྒྱུའི་རྟགས་མཚན་བསྟན་པ་རེད་ The two governments sent signs of (future) friendly relations coming about.

རྟགས་རྫུས་བརྒྱབ་པའི་ཚོང་ཟོག (dāgdzüù gyə̱bbɛ tsōŋsoò) a fake/ counterfeit/ imitation of a brand name product.

རྟགས་རྫུས་མ་ (dāgdzüümə) a counterfeit/ fake brand.

རྟགས་ཡིག (dāgyig) label, logo.

རྟགས་རིམ་འབུལ་ཞུས་པ་ (dāgrim b̲ü̲ü̲ shü̲ü̲bə) shung. putting seals in sequence or in order on a pledge/ contract/ agreement.

རྟགས་གསལ་ (dāgsɛl) debating (in traditional monks' style); va.—གཏོང་.

རྟབ་: p. བརྟབས་; f. བརྟབ་ (dāb) vi. to be frightened/ scared. 2. sm. རྟབ་རྟོབ་པོ་.

རྟབ་རྟོབ་དུ་ (dāb dābdu) 1. hurriedly, quickly ¶ངས་རྟབ་རྟོབ་དུ་ཡོང་པ་ཡིན་ I came hurriedly.

རྟབ་རྟོབ་པོ་ (dāb dābbo) 1. hurriedly, quickly ¶ངས་རྟབ་རྟོབ་པོ་ཡོང་པ་ཡིན་ I came hurriedly. 2. frightened, scared.

རྟབ་བེ་རྟོབ་པོ་ (dābbe dōbe) sm. རྟབ་རྟོབ་པོ་.

རྟབ་ལ་རྒྱག (dābla gy̲a̲à) va. to carry heavy things on several people's shoulders.

རྟའི་ཀོ་བ་ (dɛ̄gɔɔ) horse hide, skin of a horse.

རྟའི་གི་ཝང་ (dɛ g̲iwaŋ) bezoar of a horse.

རྟའི་སྒ་ (dɛ̄ga) see རྟ་སྒ་.

རྟའི་ཁ་ར་ (dɛ kāra) horse stable.

རྟའི་རྔོག་མ་ (dɛ ŋɔ̄gma) sm. རྟའི་ཟེ་.

རྟའི་ཚོལ་ཁ་ (dɛ cōōga) shung. the ཚོལ་ཁ་ of the horse, i.e., མདོ་སྣོད་.

རྟའི་ཉིན་ལམ་ (d̲ɛ ñ̄inlam) sm. རྟ་པའི་ཉིན་ལམ་.

རྟའི་མཐུར་ (dɛ̄dur) horse halter.

རྟའི་ཟེ་ (dɛ̄se) horse's mane.

རྟའི་ཟེ་རྔོག (dɛ s̲e̲ŋɔɔ̀) sm. རྟའི་ཟེ་.

རྟའི་འོག་ཤ་ (dɛ w̲ɔ̲gsha) horse's tendon.

རྟའི་ཤིང་རྟ་ (dɛ shīŋda) horse drawn cart/ chariot.

རྟའི་ཨོལ་ཆམ་ (dɛ ōōjam) glanders.

རྟའུ་ (dəwu) 1. colt. 2. shung. a horse corvee tax (involving providing riding horses for travelers with permits); va.—རྒྱུགས་; —གཏོང་ to do/ perform the horse corvee tax.

རྟའུ་སྐྱུལ་ (dəwu gǖǖ) va. to levy/ impose a corvee horse tax.

རྟའུ་ཁལ་མ་ (dəwu kɛ̄ɛ̄ma) shung. the corvee animal transport tax (involving provision of riding horses and transport/ carrying animals).

རྟའུ་ལ་ (dəwula) sm. རྟའུ་.

རྟས་ (dɛ̄ɛ̀) sm. བརྟས་.

རྟས་འཐེན་ཞིང་ཆས་ (dɛ̄ɛ̀den shi̲ŋjɛɛ̀) horse drawn farm implements.

རྟས་དབྱུགས་ (dɛ̄ɛ̀yuù) va. to be thrown from a horse.

རྟས་བསུ་མཇུབ་སྐྱེལ་ (dɛ̄ɛ̀su dzu̲bgyee) sm. རྟ་བསུ་མཇུབ་སྐྱེལ་.

རྟས་འཕྲ་ (dɛ̄ɛ̀dra) being kicked by a horse; vi.—རྒྱག.

རྟི་གི་ (dīgi) colt.

རྟི་གི་ཅན་ (dīgijaà) a breed of horse in Tibet that is bigger than the average horse.

རྟིང་ (dīŋ) abbr. of རྟིང་མ་.

རྟིང་ཀ་ (dīŋgə) heel; va.—དྲང་ to say bad things about sb. behind his/ her back or about sb. who is dead ¶བསམ་འཆར་ཡོད་ན་མདུན་ལ་ཤོད་དགོས་པ་ལས་མི་གཞན་གྱི་རྟིང་ཀ་དྲང་རྒྱུ་མེད་ If you have criticisms, you should say them in front of a person not behind his back.

རྟིང་དཀར་ (dīŋgar) animal that has white hair on the fetlock.

རྟིང་སྐྱུལ་ (dīŋgüü) checking up on work to ensure it is done correctly and on time; va.—གཏོང་.

རྟིང་ཁ་རྒྱག (dīŋgə gy̲a̲à) va. to tiptoe, to stand on one's toes.

རྟིང་པ་ (dīŋbə) sm. རྟིང་ཀ་.

རྟིང་ལྕགས་ (dīŋjaà) 1. horse shoe; va.—རྒྱག to shoe a horse. 2. cleats (on the heel of a boot /shoe); va.—རྒྱག.

རྟིང་རྒྱུ་ (dīŋju) a tendon on the heel.

རྟིང་ཐག་གཅོད་ (dīŋdaà jȫȫ) va. to make a final decision.

རྟིང་དོག (dīŋdɔɔ̀) an inferior type of wool.

རྟིང་དོག (dīŋdɔɔ̀) heel of a shoe; va.—རྒྱག.

རྟིང་དུ་ (dīŋdu) afterwards, later, in the future ¶ཁོ་རྟིང་དུ་སླེབས་སོང་ He arrived later.

རྟིང་གནོན་ (dīŋnön) a support for the heel of a shoe; vi.—གཏོང་ to have a heel wear unevenly.

རྟིང་པ་ (dīŋbə) heel (of the foot); va.—ཚུགས་ to stand firmly.

རྟིང་པ་རྩད་ (dīŋbə dzɛ̄ɛ̀) va. to search/ investigate thoroughly.

རྟིང་པོ་ (dīŋbu) afterwards, later, future ¶ང་རྟིང་པོ་སླེབས་ཡོང་ I will come later.

རྟིང་མ་ (dīŋmə) 1. afterwards, later, in the future ¶ཟླ་བ་རྟིང་མ་ Next month. ¶འདི་འདྲ་བྱས་ན་རྟིང་མ་ཡག་པོ་ཡོང་གི་མ་རེད་ If you do that it will not be good in the future. 2. final, last ¶རྟིང་མའི་རྒྱལ་ཁ་ The final victory. 3. va.—ལེན་ to obtain victory in a war.

རྟིང་རྩ་ (dīŋdzə) achilles tendon; va.—གཅོད་ to cut the achilles tendon (a punishment in tt.).

རྟིང་འཚག་རྒྱག (dīŋdzaà gy̲a̲à) va. to kick with the hind legs.

རྟིང་རིལ་ (dīŋrii) sm. རྟིང་མོང་.

རྟིང་བརླག་པར་བྱེད་ (dīŋ lāàbar c̲e̲è) shung. causing destruction/ harm in the future ¶མི་ངན་འདི་ཚོས་ངོ་བསྐུས་པ་ཡིན་ཟེར་བའི་མིང་ཙམ་ལས་རྟིང་བརླག་པར་བྱེད་པ་ཞིག་འདུག These evil persons said that they had surrendered but that was just in name and in the future they will cause destruction/ harm.

རྟིང་ལ་ (dīŋlə) sm. རྟིང་དུ་.

རྟིང་ལོ་ (dīŋlo) next year.

རྟིང་ཤིང་ (dīŋsiŋ) 1. a wooden foot pedal on a lathe. 2. a shoe tree.

རྟིང་སོ་ (dīŋso) sm. རྟིང་མ་.

རྟིང་ལྷམ་ (dīŋlham) slipper.

རྟིང་ལྷན་ (dīŋlɛn) a patch behind the heel of shoe/ boot; va.—རྒྱག.

རྟིབ་གཟོང་གསེག་ཁ་ (dīŋsoŋ sēgga) a type of chisel.

རྟུག (dūg) abbr. of རྟུག་པ་.

རྟུག་སྐམ་ (dūggam) dried excrement.

རྟུག་གཅིན་ (dūgjin) excrement and urine.

རྟུག་འགགས་ (dūg g̲a̲à) vi. to be constipated.

རྟུག་པ་ (dūgbə) excrement.

རྟུག་པོ་ (dūgbo) sm. རྟུག་པ་.

རྟུག་དྲི་ (dūgdri) flatus, fart; va.—གཏོང་; vi.—ཤོར་.

རྟུན་ཅན་ (dūnjɛn) diligent.

རྟུན་པ་ (dūmbə) sm. རྟུན་ཅན་.

རྟུན་བུ་ (dūmbu) arc. stone.

རྟུལ་: p. and f. བརྟུལ་; imp. རྟུལ་ (dǖǖ) 1.va. to put together/ assemble. 2. va. to break/ tame a horse or other animal. 3. arc. diligent. 4. not smart. 5. blunt, dull.

རྟུལ་པོ་ (dǖǖbu) dull, blunt ¶གྲི་རྟུལ་པོ་ A dull/ blunt knife.

རྟུལ་ཕོད་ (dǖǖbüü) courage, bravery, heroism.

རྟུལ་ཕོད་ཆེ་བ་ (dǖǖbüü cēwa) very courageous, brave, heroic.

རྟུལ་ཕོད་ཅན་ (dǖǖbüüjɛn) brave, courageous, heroic person ¶ཁོང་མི་རྟུལ་ཕོད་ཅན་ཞིག་རེད་ He is a brave man.

རྟུལ་ཟུར་ (dǖǖsur) obtuse angle.

རྟེན་: p.and f. བརྟེན་; imp. རྟེན་ (dēn) 1. va. to depend/ rely on ¶ཁོ་ཚོའི་རོགས་དངུལ་ལ་བརྟེན་ནས་ Relying on their relief aid. 2. vi. to support/ prop up ¶མདུང་མ་ཀ་བར་རྟེན་གྱི་ཡོད་པ་རེད་ The pillar is supporting the beam. 3. shung. basis for an obligation ¶ཁྲལ་རྟེན་ The basis for paying taxes. 4. a gift/ present when going to meet sb. 5. religious object.

རྟེན་སྐལ་ (dēngɛɛ) religious objects such as statues brought along by the bride as a part of her dowry.

རྟེན་ཁེབས་ (dēngeb) a cover for religious artifacts/ items.

རྟེན་ཁྲི་ (dēndri) altar.

རྟེན་ཁང་ (dēngar) 1. chapel in a house. 2. a small

house for a protective deity (usu. on a roof top or hill).

རྟེན་འཁོར་བྱེད་ (dēngɔɔ cee̖) va. to harbor/ keep a bad person in one's house (conveys one is working in cahoots with them).

རྟེན་གྱི་གང་ཟག (dēngi gaŋsaà) shung. human form.

རྟེན་གྱི་དངོས་པོ་ (dēngi ŋōōbo) sm. རྟེན་དངོས་.

རྟེན་གྱི་གཙོ་བོ་ (dēngi dzōwo) the main/ central/ most prominent figure in a thanka or among a series of statues.

རྟེན་འགངས་ཅན་ (dēn gaŋjɛn) extremely holy/ sacred.

རྟེན་འགངས་ཅན་ (dēn gu̱ù lōŋ) a derogatory comment on poor people in the late 1990's [Lit. (they) depend, wait, beg].

རྟེན་རྒྱ་ (dēngya) a letter with a gift enclosed.

རྟེན་དངོས་ (dēnŋöö) religious objects/ things.

རྟེན་ཅིང་འབྲེལ་བ་འབྱུང་ (dēnjiŋ dre̱wa cu̱ŋ) vi. to be the result of cause and effect ༑ས་བོན་ལས་མྱུ་གུ་འབྱུང་བ་ནི་རྟེན་ཅིང་འབྲེལ་བར་འབྱུང་བ་ཞིག་ཡིན་ As for seedlings coming out of seeds, that is the result of cause and effect.

རྟེན་བཅས་ (dēnjɛɛ̀) gift, present ༑ཡི་གེ་རྟེན་བཅས་ Letter and gift.

རྟེན་ཆས་ (dēnjɛɛ̀) 1. gift, present. 2. things, belongings ༑བོད་གཞུང་རྟེན་ཆས་གོས་ཆེན་ཐང་ཀ་ An applique thanka that was a gift of the Tibetan government. 3. religious figures statues/ items/ paraphernalia for making offerings.

རྟེན་མཆོད་ (dēn cōō) sm. རྟེན་ཆས་, 3.

རྟེན་མཆོད་ཆས་ (dēn cōōjɛɛ̀) sm. རྟེན་ཆས་, 3.

རྟེན་མཇལ་ (dēn je̱e̱) going on a pilgrimage, visiting holy places; va.—ལ་འགྲོ་; —ལ་ཕེབས་ to go on pilgrimage to a holy place.

རྟེན་མཇལ་ཕྱག་མཆོད་ (dēnjɛɛ cāàjöö) abbr. visiting holy places and doing prostrations and offerings once there.

རྟེན་བརྗེས་ (dēn je̱è) 1. vi. to give up one's physical body after one dies ༑མིའི་ལུས་རྟེན་བརྗེས་ནས་ཁྱིའི་ལུས་རྟེན་བླངས་པ་རེད་ Giving up one's human body (after dying) he took the body of a dog. 2. wearing different costumes.

རྟེན་གཉིས་ (dēnñii) the two statues of the Buddha brought by the Nepalese and Chinese wives of King Srongtsen Gambo.

རྟེན་རྙིང་པ་ལ་རྟེན་བཤད་གསར་པ་ (dēnñiŋbala dēnshɛɛ̀ sārba) giving a new definition to sth. old [Lit. giving a new definition to an old statue].

རྟེན་གདན་ (dēndɛn) a gift given to an icon maker before he begins his work.

རྟེན་དང་བརྟེན་པ་ (dēndaŋ dēmba) the chapel/ temple and the religious statues/ artifacts within it.

རྟེན་དང་བརྟེན་པའི་འབྲེལ་སྒྲ་ (dēndaŋ dēmbɛ dre̱e̱dra) the function of the genitive particle that conveys sth. existing as part of sth. else.

རྟེན་མདུང་ (dēnduŋ) the spear that protective deities carry.

རྟེན་འབྲེལ་ (dēndree) shung. abbr. of རྟེན་འབྲེལ་.

རྟེན་གནས་ (dēnnɛɛ̀) one of the eight parts of speech in Tibetan grammar — conveys the place where sth. exists (in/ at).

རྟེན་འབུལ་ (dēmbüü) 1. a formal presentation/ offering/ gift; va.—ཞུ་ to make a presentation, to offer/ give a gift ༑རྟེན་འབུལ་ཚོགས་པ་ A presentation group (a delegation going to make a presentation/ offering/ gift). 2. tribute (given to the Emperor).

རྟེན་འབྱུང་ (dēnjuŋ) abbr. of རྟེན་ཅིང་འབྲེལ་བར་འབྱུང་བ་.

རྟེན་འབྱུང་བསྟར་ (dēnjuŋ dār) shung. va. to celebrate/ honor ༑ཕྱག་མཛོད་ལའང་གདན་འཕར་དང་འབྲེལ་བའི་རྟེན་འབྱུང་བསྟར་བ་ (They) honored the steward by putting out an additional cushion for him.

རྟེན་འབྲེལ་ (dēmdree) 1. ceremony, celebration, occasion ༑འཁྲུངས་སྐར་རྟེན་འབྲེལ་ Birthday celebration. 2. omen, portent ༑རྟེན་འབྲེལ་བཟང་པོ་ A good omen. 3. congratulations, congratulatory ༑རྟེན་འབྲེལ་གློག་འཕྲིན་ A congratulatory telegraph. 4. auspicious, good.

རྟེན་འབྲེལ་བྲིག (dēmdree drig) va. to make/ draw auspicious symbols.

རྟེན་འབྲེལ་གྱི་སྨོན་འདུན་ཞུ་ (dēmdreegi mōndün shu̱) a prayer said at ceremonies conveying "may good things occur."

རྟེན་འབྲེལ་འཕྲིན་ཡིག (dēmdree drīnyig) congratulatory letter.

རྟེན་འབྲེལ་འཕྱུགས་ (dēmdree cūù) shung. to be an inauspicious sign ༑དགོན་སྡེས་ལོ་འབུལ་མ་ཕུལ་བ་རྟེན་འབྲེལ་འཕྱུགས་ལུགས་དང་ It was an inauspicious sign that the monastery did not make the yearly tribute.

རྟེན་འབྲེལ་མ་འཛོམས་ (dēndree ma̱ndzom) cause and condition not being appropriate ༑རྟེན་འབྲེལ་མ་འཛོམས་པའི་རྐྱེན་གྱིས་ལས་ཀ་དེ་ཡག་པོ་མ་བྱུང་བ་རེད་ Because the conditions weren't appropriate, the work didn't go well.

རྟེན་འབྲེལ་མེ་སྒྲོགས་ (dēmdree me̱rgyoò) a salute or greeting made by firing a salvo from a cannon or rifles.

རྟེན་འབྲེལ་ཚོགས་ཆེན་ (dēmdree tsōgjen) celebration rally/ meeting.

རྟེན་འབྲེལ་མཛད་སྒོ་ (dēmdree dzɛɛ̀go) ceremony of celebration.

རྟེན་འབྲེལ་ཞུ་ (dēmdree shu̱) va. to convey/ give congratulations ༑ཕྱི་རྒྱལ་སྐུ་ཚབ་ཚོས་སྲིད་འཛིན་གསར་པར་རྟེན་འབྲེལ་ཞུས་པ་རེད་ The foreign representatives gave their congratulations to the president.

རྟེན་འབྲེལ་ཞུ་ཚིག (dēmdree shu̱dzii) congratulatory message/ speech.

རྟེན་འབྲེལ་ལ་མི་གདུབ་ (dēmdreela mi̱dub) shung. sm. རྟེན་འབྲེལ་འཕྱུགས་.

རྟེན་འབྲེལ་ལོག (dēmdree lɔ̱ɔ̀) vi. to have a bad sign/ omen occur on an auspicious day or celebration.

རྟེན་འབྲེལ་གསུང་བཤད་ (dēmdree sūŋshɛɛ̀) congratulatory speech.

རྟེན་ཕྲུགས་ (dēndraà) a letter with a gift enclosed.

རྟེན་མ་ (dēnma) prop, support.

རྟེན་དམན་པ་ (dēn mēmba) the lower rebirths.

རྟེན་མེད་ (dēnmeè) homeless.

རྟེན་མེད་ཡུལ་ཉུལ་ (dēnmeè yü̱üñüü) wandering around in a state of homelessness.

རྟེན་གཙོ་ (dēndzo) shung. main statue in a temple/ shrine.

རྟེན་རྫ་ (dēndza) sm. ཐབས་རྫ་.

རྟེན་གཞི་ (dēnshi) 1. basis, foundation ༑ང་ཚོའི་འཚོ་བའི་རྟེན་གཞི་ངོ་མ་ཞིང་ལས་ཡིན་ The main basis of our livelihood is farming. ༑གནམ་གྲུ་རྟེན་གཞི་ Air base/ installation.

རྟེན་བཟང་ (dēnsaŋ) shung. the higher/ more fortunate rebirths.

རྟེན་ཡོད་ (dēnyoò) shung. having a basis (in land) from which one pays taxes.

རྟེན་ཡོད་དམག་མི་ (dēnyöö māāmi) shung. people who serve as soldiers because they hold land as a basis for the corvee tax obligation.

རྟེན་ལན་ (dēnlɛn) return gift ༑ངའི་གྲོགས་པོར་རྟེན་ལན་ཞིག་སྤྲོད་དགོས་ཡོད་ I have to give a return gift to my friend.

རྟེན་ལེན་ (dēn le̱n) vi. to take a new physical form/ body after one dies.

རྟེན་ས་ (dēnsa) shelter, refuge, place or person in whom one depends ༑ཕྲུ་གུའི་རྟེན་ས་ཕ་མ་རེད་ The persons on whom children depend are their parents.

རྟེན་གསུམ་ (dēnsum) the three things that symbolize the Buddha's body, speech and mind: i.e., a statue, scriptures and a stupa.

རྟེན་གསུམ་མཆོད་ཆས་ (dēnsum cōōjɛɛ̀) shung. sm. རྟེན་ཆས་.

རྟེམ་ཤུར་ (dēmshur) a type of carpenter's plane.
རྟེའུ་ (dēwu) colt, foal.
རྟེའུ་ལོ་ (dēwulo) sm. རྟེ་ལོ་.
རྟོག: p. **བརྟགས་**; f. **བརྟག**; imp. **རྟོགས་** (dɔ̄ɔ̀) 1. va. to reflect on, to think over, to consider/ weigh/ deliberate. 2. va. to understand/ comprehend/ perceive/ know ¶ གསལ་པོར་རྟོགས་ཐུབ་ཀྱི་རེད་ (They) will be able to understand clearly. ¶ ཚོགས་འདུས་ནས་རྟོགས་དེ་ The assembly delegates came to know (that sth. happened).
རྟོག་གེ་ (dɔ̄gge) sophistry.
རྟོག་གེ་སྨྲ་བ་ (dɔ̄gge māwa) theory of sophistry.
རྟོག་ཅེན་པ་ (dɔ̄gjēmba) watchman, lookout, sentry.
རྟོག་འཇུག (dɔ̄ŋjuù) sm. རྟོགས་ཞིབ་.
རྟོག་པ་ (dɔ̄gba) awareness coming from meditation.
རྟོག་པ་མཐོ་པོ་ (dɔ̄gba tōbo) person who has reached a high state of religious realization (of the truth).
རྟོག་པ་འོག་འགྱུ་ (dɔ̄gba wɔggyu) distracting thoughts in meditation, impure thoughts.
རྟོག་པ་ལོག་ཤེས་ (dɔ̄gwa lɔgsheè) wrong conceptual awareness.
རྟོག་པ་ལྷ་དང་མཉམ་ཡང་སྤྱོད་པ་མི་དང་མཐུན་དགོས་ (dɔ̄gba lhādaŋ ñāmyaŋ jȫȫba mi̱daŋ tũŋgɔɔ̀) sm. རྟོག་པ་ལྷ་ལས་མཐོ་ཡང་སྤྱོད་པ་མི་དང་བསྟུན་དགོས་.
རྟོག་པ་ལྷ་ལས་མཐོ་ཡང་སྤྱོད་པ་མི་དང་བསྟུན་དགོས་ (dɔ̄gba lhālɛɛ̀ tōyaŋ jȫȫba mi̱daŋ dũŋgöö) even though one is very knowledgeable, one's behavior should be appropriate for ordinary people (should act in accordance with the norms for ordinary people).
རྟོག་པས་བཟོས་པ་ (dɔ̄gbɛ so̱öba) sm. རྟོག་བཟོ་.
རྟོག་དཔྱོད་ (dɔ̄gjȫȫ) sm. རྟོག་ཞིབ་.
རྟོག་བྲལ་ (dɔ̄gdrɛɛ) 1. without thinking/ cognition, free from thought. 2. having insight on the true nature of reality through meditation.
རྟོག་བློ་ (dɔ̄glo) sm. རྣམ་རྟོག.
རྟོག་མེད་ (dɔ̄gmɛè) sm. རྟོག་བྲལ་.
རྟོག་ཞིབ་ (dɔ̄gshib) investigation, examination, survey, inspection; va.—བྱེད་ ¶ ཞིང་པའི་ལས་འགུལ་ལ་རྟོག་ཞིབ་བྱས་པ་རེད་ (They) investigated the peasant movement.
རྟོག་ཞིབ་སྐོར་གཡེང་ (dɔ̄gshib gɔ̄ɔyeŋ) investigating by making rounds or going from place to place ¶ ཟིང་ཆ་ལངས་ཙང་ཉེན་རྟོག་པས་གྲོང་ཁྱེར་ནང་རྟོག་ཞིབ་སྐོར་གཡེང་བྱེད་ཀྱི་ཡོད་པ་རེད་ Because there was a disturbance, the police are traveling around the city investigating it.
རྟོག་ཞིབ་འཆུག་མེད་ (dɔ̄gshib cūgmeè) shung. investigating thoroughly ¶ ས་གནས་སུ་དངོས་ཡོད་གནས་ཚུལ་ཇི་བྱུང་རྟོག་ཞིབ་འཆུག་མེད་དགོས་རྒྱུ་ You must investigate thoroughly what actually happened at the actual spot.
རྟོག་ཞིབ་ལྟ་སྐོར་ (dɔ̄gshib dāgɔɔ) inspection tour; va.—བྱེད་.
རྟོག་ཞིབ་ཐིག་ལེན་རུ་ཁག (dɔ̄gshib ti̱glen ru̱gaà) surveying/ prospecting team.
རྟོག་ཞིབ་གནམ་གྲུ་ (dɔ̄gshib nāmdru) reconnaissance/ spy plane.
རྟོག་ཞིབ་སློབ་ཚོགས་ (dɔ̄gshib lōbdzɔɔ̀) research society/ association.
རྟོག་བཟོ་ (dɔ̄gso) created by imagination/ superstition ¶ མི་ཤི་གྲོང་བའི་ཁང་པའི་ནང་སྡོད་མི་རུང་ཞེར་བ་དེ་རྟོག་བཟོ་བྱས་པ་རང་རེད་ The belief that one should not live in a house in which a person has died is superstition.
རྟོགས་ (dɔ̄ɔ̀) 1. vi. to understand, to comprehend. 2. imp. of རྟོག.
རྟོགས་བརྗོད་ (dɔ̄gjȫȫ) biography.
རྟོགས་ལྡན་ (dɔ̄ŋdɛn) 1. one who has obtained realization (of the truth). 2. epithet for the Buddha.
རྟོགས་པ་ (dɔ̄gba) understanding, comprehension; va.—བྱེད་ to understand, to comprehend ¶ ཐག་མ་བཅད་གོང་གནས་ཚུལ་གསལ་པོ་རྟོགས་པ་བྱེད་དགོས་ Before making a decision, a person should understand the situation clearly.
རྟོགས་པ་བརྗོད་པ་ (dɔ̄gba jȫ̱ȫba) sm. རྟོགས་བརྗོད་.
རྟོགས་པ་མཐོ་པོ་ (dɔ̄gba tōbo) sb. with good understanding/ comprehension.
རྟོགས་པའི་སྟོབས་ (dɔ̄gbɛ dōb) the power of understanding.
རྟོགས་མ་ཐུབ་པ་སྨྲ་བ་ (dɔ̄g ma̱tubba māwa) agnosticism.
རྟོགས་དམན་ (dɔ̄gmɛn) poor understanding/ comprehension.
རྟོགས་སླ་པོ་ (dɔ̄g lābo) easy to comprehend/ know/ understand.
རྟོགས་ཞིབ་ (dɔ̄gshib) sm. རྟོག་ཞིབ་.
རྟོད་: p. and f. བརྟོད་; imp. རྟོད་ (dȫȫ) va. to tie/ stake/ fasten/ tether.
རྟོད་ཁ་ (dȫȫga) an area in which an animal tied on a stake with a leg tether can graze; va.—སྤོ་ to move the area where a horse is tethered to graze.
རྟོད་ཐག (dȫȫdaà) the rope/ tether tied to a stake to limit an animal's range of grazing.
རྟོད་པ་ (dȫȫba) sm. རྟོད་ཕུར་.
རྟོད་ཕུར་ (dȫȫbur) a stake (for tying), a peg; va.—རྒྱག to tie an animal to a stake with a long tether to allow it to graze but not move beyond the length of the rope.
རྟོན་: p. and f. **བརྟེན་**; imp. **རྟོན་** (dȭn) vi. to rely on, to depend on, to trust.
རྟོལ་: p. and f. **བརྟོལ་**; imp. **རྟོལ་** (dȫȫ) 1. va. to bore holes, to pierce, to puncture ¶ ཨི་ཁུང་བརྟོལ་ནས་ Having made a hole. 2. hybrid offspring of dzomo and yak or dzomo and bull.
རྟོལ་གོག (dȫȫgɔɔ̀) sm. རྟོལ་, 2.
རྟོལ་དྲ་ (dȫȫda) the orphan calf of a རྟོལ་མོ་.
རྟོལ་ཕོ་ (dȫȫpo) male hybrid offspring of dzomo and yak or dzomo and bull.
རྟོལ་མེད་ (dȫȫmeè) 1. sm. སྣང་མེད་. 2. uncertain, unsure. 3. having no solution, having no way out.
རྟོལ་མོ་ (dȫȫmo) female hybrid offspring of dzomo and yak or dzomo and bull.
རྟོལ་མཛོ་ (dȫȫdzo) sm. རྟོལ་ཕོ་.
རྟོལ་མཛོ་མ་ (dȫȫ dzo̱ma) sm. རྟོལ་མོ་.
རྟོལ་ཟིང་ (dȫȫsoŋ) sm.* རྟོལ་གཟིང་.
རྟོལ་གཡག (dȫȫyaà) hybrid offspring of dzomo and yak.
རྟོལ་ལེ་ (dȫȫle) sm. རྟོལ་, 2.
རྟོལ་ཤ་ (dȫȫsha) meat of hybrid offspring of dzomo and yak or dzomo and bull.
ལྟ་: p. **བལྟས་**; f. **བལྟ་**; imp. **ལྟོས་** (dā) 1. to look at/ watch ¶ ཁོ་ཚོས་པར་ལ་ལྟ་གི་ཡོད་པ་རེད་ They are looking at photos. ¶ ཁོ་དེ་རང་འདུག་མི་འདུག་ལྟོས་ཤོག Look and see whether he is there (home) or not. 2. abbr. of ལྟ་བ་.
ལྟ་ཀློག (dālɔɔ̀) reading; va.—བྱེད་ to read.
ལྟ་སྐུལ་ (dəgüü) keeping watch on, making surveillance, reconnoitering; va.—འཁུར་ to take responsibility for keeping watch on sth. or sb.; va.—བྱེད་ to keep watch on, to make surveillance on ¶ ལས་འགན་ཁག་དོན་འཁྱོལ་ཐག་གཅོད་བྱ་རྒྱུར་ལྟ་སྐུལ་བྱེད་དགོས་ They have to keep watch over the decision to implement the work.
ལྟ་སྐུལ་པ་ (dəgüübə) 1. sb. who keeps watch on sb. or sth., surveillance officer/ worker. 2. people who look after and encourage others in work (e.g., those chosen by government to wear red arm bands).
ལྟ་སྐུལ་མི་སྣ་ (dəgüü mi̱na) sm. ལྟ་སྐུལ་པ་.
ལྟ་སྐུལ་ཞིབ་བཤེར་ (dəgüü shi̱bsher) investigating, examining, surveying; va.—བྱེད་.
ལྟ་སྐོར་ (dāgɔɔ) tour, inspection, sightseeing visit ¶ ཁོ་ཚོ་ལྷ་སར་ལྟ་སྐོར་ལ་ཕྱིན་པ་རེད་ They went on a tour to Lhasa.
ལྟ་སྐོར་གྲོས་ཚོགས་ (dāgɔɔ trö̱ötsɔɔ̀) sm. ལྟ་སྐོར་ཚོགས་པ་.
ལྟ་སྐོར་སྣེ་ཤན་ (dāgɔɔ nēshɛn) tourist guide.

ལྟ་སྐོར་ཚོགས་པ་ (dāgɔɔ tsōgba) visiting/ touring group or delegation.

ལྟ་སྐོར་འཚམས་འདྲི་ (dāgɔɔ tsə̄mdri) sm. ལྟ་སྐོར་ཚོགས་པ་.

ལྟ་སྐོར་ལ་འགྲོ་ (dāgɔɔla dro) va. to go on an excursion/ tour/ trip/ visit ། སློབ་ཕྲུག་ཚོ་བཟོ་གྲྭ་ཞིག་ལ་ལྟ་སྐོར་འགྲོ་གི་རེད་ The students will go on a tour to a factory.

ལྟ་བསྐོར་ (dāgɔɔ) sm. ལྟ་སྐོར་.

ལྟ་སྐྱོང་ (dāgyoŋ) taking care of, looking after; va.—བྱེད་ to take care of, to look after, to act as guardian ། ཁོང་གིས་དྭ་ཕྲུག་ལ་ལྟ་སྐྱོང་བྱེད་ཀྱི་ཡོད་པ་རེད་ He is taking care of the orphans.

ལྟ་སྐྱོང་ཆེན་པོ་ (dāgyoŋ cēmbo) sb. who looks after/ takes care of people well.

ལྟ་སྐྱོང་པ་ (dāgyoŋba) guardian, trustee.

ལྟ་བསྐྱོད་ (dāgyöö) going to see/ watch/ look at sth.; va.—བྱེད་.

ལྟ་མཁན་ (dāñen) sb. who watches or looks, a supervisor, an overseer.

ལྟ་གར་ལ་འགྱུར་ (dāgarla gyur) how can sth. occur (its impossible) ། ལས་ཀ་མ་བྱས་པར་གླ་ཆ་ཐོབ་པ་ལྟ་ག་ལ་འགྱུར་ How can one get a high salary without working?

ལྟ་གིན་ལྟ་གིན་ (dəgin dəgin) looking/ observing all around ། ཁོ་ཚོ་ཁྲོམ་ལ་ལྟ་གིན་ལྟ་གིན་ཕྱིན་པ་རེད་ (They) went around the market looking here and there.

ལྟ་གིའི་ལྟ་གིའི་ (dəgii dəgii) sm. ལྟ་གིན་ལྟ་གིན་.

ལྟ་མགུར་ (dāgur) psalms, religious songs.

ལྟ་གྲུབ་ (dādrub) abbr. ལྟ་བ་དང་གྲུབ་མཐའ་.

ལྟ་རྒྱ་མཐོང་རྒྱ་ (dāgya tōŋgya) sm. མཐོང་རྒྱ་.

ལྟ་ངན་ (dāŋɛn) wrong view.

ལྟ་ངོ་ (dāŋo) sm. མིག་སྣང་.

ལྟ་ཅི་ (dəji) let alone, leave alone ། ཡར་རྒྱས་འགྲོ་རྒྱུ་ལྟ་ཅི་འཚོ་བ་སྡུག་ཏུ་ཕྱིན་ཡོད་པ་རེད་ Let alone getting improved, (our) livelihood has worsened.

ལྟ་ཅི་སྨོས་ (dəjimöö) no doubt, without a question ། ཐག་ཐག་བཞོན་ཤེས་ཀྱི་ཡོད་ན་རྐང་སྐྲ་རེལ་བཞོན་ཤེས་པ་ལྟ་ཅི་སྨོས་ If one can ride a motorcycle, there is no question that one can ride a bicycle.

ལྟ་ཉན་འདྲི་བརྟག་བཞི་ (dāñɛn dridaà shi) the four aspects of Tibetan medical examinations: sight, hearing, questioning, examining.

ལྟ་ཉན་ (dāñɛn) (— + neg.) very/ extremely (amazing, terrific, extraordinary; terrible, awful) ། ཕྲུ་གུ་དེ་སློབ་སྦྱོང་ཡག་པ་ལ་ལྟ་ཉན་མི་འདུག This student is amazingly good in his studies. ། ནད་པ་དེ་ན་ཚ་སྡུག་པ་ལ་ལྟ་ཉན་མི་འདུག The patient is terribly ill. ། ངོ་གདོང་མེས་འཚིགས་ནས་ལྟ་ཉན་མེད་པ་ཆགས་པ་རེད་ He looks horrible after his face was burned.

ལྟ་ཉུལ་ (dāñüü) spying, scouting, reconnoitering; va.—བྱེད་ to spy, to reconnoiter, to scout.

ལྟ་ཉུལ་པ་ (dāñüübə) spy, scout.

ལྟ་མཉམ་ (dāñam) 1. looking together. 2. looking at (sth.) simultaneously.

ལྟ་རྟོག་ (dādɔɔ) 1. inspecting, investigating, overseeing; va.—བྱེད་ to inspect, to oversee ། ང་ཚོས་ཞིང་ལས་ལ་ལྟ་རྟོག་བྱེད་དགོས་ We have to supervise agriculture. 2. supervising, looking after; va.—བྱེད་. 3. dealing with, treating; va.—བྱེད་ to treat, to deal with ། ལོག་སྤྱོད་པར་ཀ་ཡངས་ཀྱི་ལྟ་རྟོག་བྱས་པ་རེད་ (They) treated the reactionaries with leniency.

ལྟ་རྟོག་ཉན་ནན་ (dādɔɔ ñɛnna cèè) shung. investigating, doing surveillance; va.—བྱེད་ ། ས་གནས་སུ་ལྟ་རྟོག་ཉན་ནན་བྱས་པའི་འབྲས་བུར་དགྲ་བོའི་གཡོ་བྱུས་ཁག་ཅིག་ཤེས་རྟོགས་བྱུང་བ་ After investigating, we came to know some of the plots of the enemy.

ལྟ་རྟོགས་ (dādɔɔ) sm. ལྟ་རྟོག.

ལྟ་སྣངས་ (dādaŋ) opinion, view, way of looking ། ཞིང་པའི་ལྟ་སྣངས་ཀྱི་ཐོག་ནས་ཁྲིམས་ལུགས་གསར་པ་དེ་ཡག་པོ་མི་འདུག From the farmers viewpoint, the new law isn't good.

ལྟ་སྣངས་རྙིང་པ་ (dādaŋ ñiŋbə) conservative view/ idea; va.—འཛིན་ to hold conservative views/ ideas.

ལྟ་ཐུག་ (dāduù) relations; va.—བྱེད་ to have relations with, to be in touch with ། ང་ཉེ་ཉེན་དང་ལྟ་ཐུག་མེད་ I have no relations with (my) relatives.

ལྟ་དེབ་ (dādeb) magazine (with pictures), pictorial book/ magazine.

ལྟ་སྡུར་ (dādur) watching and comparing; va.—བྱེད་.

ལྟ་ན་འདོད་པ་ (dāna dööba) sm. ལྟ་ན་སྡུག་པ་.

ལྟ་ན་སྡུག་པ་ (dāna dugbə) beautiful, lovely.

ལྟ་སྣང་ (dānaŋ) impression, opinion ། ངའི་ལྟ་སྣང་ལ་མི་འདི་ཡག་པོ་ཞིག་འདུག In my opinion he is a good person.

ལྟ་སྣང་མཐོང་ཕྱོགས་ (dānaŋ tōŋjɔɔ) from one's perspective, according to one's taste ། བུ་མོའི་རྣམ་པ་ཡག་ཉེས་མི་སོ་སོའི་ལྟ་སྣང་མཐོང་ཕྱོགས་རེད་ Beauty in women (varies) according to each person's taste.

ལྟ་སྣང་མཛེས་པོ་ (dānaŋ dzeèbo) attractive, pretty.

ལྟ་དཔྱོད་ (dājöö) sm. རྟོག་ཞིབ་.

ལྟ་སྤྱོད་ (dājöö) ideology, viewpoint, attitude, position ། རྒྱ་ནག་གི་ལྟ་སྤྱོད་འགྱུར་བ་ཆེན་པོ་བྱུང་སོང་ The attitude of China changed greatly.

ལྟ་ཕྱོགས་ (dājɔɔ) sm. ལྟ་རྒྱུལ་.

ལྟ་བ་ (dāwa) 1. philosophy, doctrine, ideology ། ནང་པའི་ལྟ་བ་ Buddhist ideology. ། གུང་བྲན་གྱི་ལྟ་བ་ Communist ideology. 2. pride, proud ། ལྟ་བ་མཐོ་པོ་བྱས་ན་མི་དམངས་ཀྱི་དགའ་གི་མ་རེད་ If one acts proud the masses will not like it.

ལྟ་བ་སྒུར་ (dāwa gūr) va. to surrender/ give up, to give in to others ། ཕྲུ་གུ་འདི་ཆུང་ཆུང་ཡིན་ནའང་རྒྱུག་རེས་རྒྱག་དུས་མི་གཞན་ལ་ལྟ་བ་སྒུར་གྱི་མེད་པ་རེད་ Even though the child is small, when he fights he never gives in to others.

ལྟ་བ་གཅོག་ (dāwa jōg) va. to break down the pride/ arrogance of sb., to put down sb. ། མི་ལྟ་བ་མཐོ་པོ་དེ་ར་ཚོགས་འདུའི་ཐོག་སྐྱོན་བརྗོད་བྱས་ནས་ལྟ་བ་བཅག་པ་རེད་ At the meeting, the pompous person was put down through criticism.

ལྟ་བ་ཆག་ (dāwa caà) vi. to have pride/ arrogance be or get broken down.

ལྟ་བ་མཐོ་པོ་ (dāwa tōbo) pompous, arrogant ། ཁོ་སློབ་སྦྱོང་ཡག་པོ་ཡོད་ན་ཡང་ལྟ་བ་མཐོ་པོ་འདུག Although he is a good student he is pompous.

ལྟ་བ་གནད་ཁེལ་ (dāwa nɛ̄ɛgel) an accurate/ correct viewpoint or position.

ལྟ་བ་རྣོ་པོ་བཟོ་ (dāwa nōbo söö) va. to make sharp criticism regarding a point of view/ ideology.

ལྟ་བ་མིག་གིས་མི་ཁོམ་པ་ (dāwa miggi kōmba) very interesting visually [Lit. the eyes cannot take it all in].

ལྟ་བ་དམན་པ་ (dāwa mēmba) bad view/ idea/ ideology.

ལྟ་བ་རང་གྱེར་ (dāwa raŋgyer) sm. རང་ཤེད་ཆེ་པོ་.

ལྟ་བ་ལོག (dāwa lɔɔ) a turncoat/ renegade/ heretic.

ལྟ་བ་གསལ་སྟོན་ (dāwa sɛ̄ɛdön) expressing one's view clearly, making a clear-cut stand; va.—བྱེད་ ། ཁོང་གིས་ཚོགས་འདུའི་ཐོག་རང་ཉིད་ཀྱི་ལྟ་བ་གསལ་སྟོན་བྱས་སོང་ At the meeting, he expressed his views clearly.

ལྟ་བས་ངོམས་པ་མེད་པ་ (dāwɛɛ ŋomba meeba) sm. ལྟ་བས་མི་ངོམས་པ་.

ལྟ་བས་ཚོག་མི་ཤེས་ (dāwɛɛ cōg mishee) extremely beautiful [Lit. looking, one is not content].

ལྟ་བས་མི་ངོམས་པ་ (dāwɛɛ miŋomba) sm. ལྟ་བས་ཚོག་མི་ཤེས་.

ལྟ་བས་མི་བཟོད་ (dāwɛɛ misöö) a dreadful/ frightening sight (sth. that is unbearable to look at).

ལྟ་བུ་ (dəbu) similar, like ། ཡར་རྒྱས་འདི་ལྟ་བུ་སྔོན་མ་བྱུང་ཡོད་པ་མ་རེད་ There hasn't been progress like this before. 2. like, such as ། དབང་ཤུགས་འགྲན་རྩོད་ལྟ་བུས་ By ones as like those competing for power.

ལྟ་བྱེད་དབང་རྩ་ (dājeè wāŋdza) optic nerve.

ལྟ་སྦྱོང་ (dājoŋ) viewing and emulating/ learning; va.—བྱེད་ [Lit. look and study].

ལྟ་སྦྱོང་འཁྲབ་སྟོན་ (dājoŋ trəbdön) performance (in art) for the purpose of viewing and learning.

ལྟ་སྙུལ་ (dāñul) sm. ལྟ་ཉུལ་.

ལྟ་སྨོས་ཀྱང་ཅི་དགོས་ (dāmöögyaŋ jīgöö) sm. ལྟ་ཅི་སྨོས་.

ལྟ་སྨོས་ཅི་འཚལ་ (dāmöö jīdzεε) sm. ལྟ་ཅི་སྨོས་.

ལྟ་ཙམ་ལྟ་ཙམ་ (dādzam dādzam) looking/ glancing at quickly or discretely; va.—བྱེད་ ། མོའི་གདོང་ལ་ལྟ་ཙམ་ལྟ་ཙམ་བྱས་པ་རེད་ (He) glanced at her face repeatedly.

ལྟ་ཚུལ་ (dədzüü) viewpoint, standpoint ། དམག་དོན་ཁོ་ནའི་ལྟ་ཚུལ་ Purely military viewpoint.

ལྟ་ཚོད་ (dādzöö) experimenting, testing, surveying; va.—བྱེད་; —ལྟ་ to experiment/ test/ survey ། ལུང་པ་འདི་སྐྱིད་པོ་ཡོད་མེད་ལྟ་ཚོད་བལྟས་པ་རེད་ (They) did a trial/ test to see if the place is pleasant. ། ང་ཚོས་ཟ་ཁང་འདི་ལྟ་ཚོད་ལྟ་གི་ཡིན་ We are going to test this restaurant.

ལྟ་ཚོད་འདི་ཚོད་མེད་པ་ (dādzöö didzöö meèba) sm. ལྟ་བ་མིག་གིས་མི་ཁེམ་.

ལྟ་ཞིབ་ (dəshib) sm. རྟོག་ཞིབ་.

ལྟ་ཞིབ་ཁང་ (dəshibgaŋ) observation ward.

ལྟ་ཞོག་ (dāshog) sm. ལྟ་ཅི་.

ལྟ་བཞག་ (dā shaà) (vb. + —) leave alone, let alone ། ཞིང་ཆོས་ཞིང་བྲན་ལམ་ལུགས་ལ་གཏོར་བཤིག་གཏོང་རྒྱུ་ལྟ་བཞག་ལམ་ལུགས་དེ་སྲུང་སྐྱོང་བྱས་སོང་ Let alone destroying serfdom, they defended it.

ལྟ་བཟོ་ (dāso) 1. good looking, handsome, beautiful, attractive. 2. (with negatives) in very bad condition ། བཟོ་གྲྭ་དེ་ལ་ལྟ་བཟོ་མི་འདུག That factory is in very bad condition.

ལྟ་བཟོ་དོད་པོ་ (dāso töòbo) sm. ལྟ་བཟོ་.

ལྟ་ཡག་ཅིག་བྱེད་ (dāyajig ceè) va. to look at sb. or sth. very carefully.

ལྟ་ཡུལ་ (dəyüü) object of one's sight.

ལྟ་རུག (dəruù) sm. ལྟ་རུབ་.

ལྟ་རུབ་ (dərub) crowding around and looking; va.—རྒྱག.

ལྟ་རེག (dəreg) looking and touching ། ཕུང་པོར་ལྟ་རེག་མི་ཆོག One is not allowed to look at and touch the corpse.

ལྟ་རོགས་ (dārɔɔ̀) an onlooker, a spectator.

ལྟ་ལུགས་ (dəluù) manner/ way of looking.

ལྟ་ལོག (dālɔɔ̀) abbr. of ལྟ་བ་ལོག་པ་.

ལྟ་ཤུགས་ (dəshug) power of one's vision.

ལྟ་ཤེད་ཆེན་པོ་ (dāsheè cēmbo) person whose looks improves with time.

ལྟ་ཤེད་མེད་པ་ (dāsheè meèba) person whose looks get worse with time.

ལྟ་བཤེར་ (dāsher) searching for sth. illegal.

ལྟ་སྲུང་ (dəsuŋ) 1. surveillance, supervising, overseeing, guarding against ། ཤིང་ནགས་ལྟ་སྲུང་པ་ One who guards the forests. 2. taking into custody, detaining, placing under house arrest; va.—བྱེད་.

ལྟག (dāg) 1. behind, in back. 2. sm. ལྟག་ཁུང་.

ལྟག་ཀ་ (dāgdra) sm. ལྟག.

ལྟག་སྐྲ་ (dāgdra) hair behind the back of the neck.

ལྟག་སྐོར་ (dāggɔɔ) an attack coming from the back/ rear side; va.—རྒྱག. 2. getting sb. to do sth. by going above him to his supervisor. 3. a type of stitching.

ལྟག་ཁུང་ (dəgguŋ) back of the head/ neck.

ལྟག་ཁུར་ (dəggur) making known that one has support/ backing.

ལྟག་འཁུར་ (dāggur) sm. ལྟག་རྩ་ངོམ་.

ལྟག་འཁོར་དམག་འཐབ་ (dāggɔɔ məgdəb) roundabout warfare, attacking from the back.

ལྟག་དགྱེ་ལོག (dāg gyee lɔɔ̀) vi. to fall backwards.

ལྟག་རྒྱབ་ (dəggyəb) 1. the back of the head/ neck. 2. the back/ behind of anything.

ལྟག་རྒྱབ་ལ་དབྱུག (dāggyəbla yūù) va. to put aside, to forget/ discard ། འབྱོར་མེད་གྲལ་རིམ་གྱི་འཛམ་གླིང་ལྟ་ཚུལ་ལྟག་རྒྱབ་ལ་དབྱུག་གི་ཡོད་པ་རེད་ They are forgetting the proletarian world view.

ལྟག་སྒྲེ་ (dəgdre) baldness on top of the head.

ལྟག་སྒོ་ (dāàgo) back door, side door 2. slang. back door (to get sth. done); va.—རྒྱུད་ to go through the back door to do or get sth. ། ཁོས་འགོ་ཁྲིད་ཀྱི་ཉེ་མཚེད་ལ་ལྟག་སྒོ་བརྒྱུད་ནས་ལས་ཀ་རག་ཐབས་བྱས་པ་རེད་ He used the back door to get the job via a relative of the official.

ལྟག་སྒྲོག་མ་ (dāgdrɔɔ̀ma) a yellow hat worn by monks.

ལྟག་སྒྱེ་ (dāggye) sm. ལྟག་དགྱེ་.

ལྟག་ངོམ་ (dāgŋom) sm. ལྟག་རྩ་ངོམ་.

ལྟག་ངོམས་ (dāgŋom) sm. ལྟག་རྩ་ངོམ་.

ལྟག་ཆུ་ (dəgju) water flowing from a reservoir.

ལྟག་ཆུ་ཆད་པའི་རྫིང་བུ་ (dəgcu cεὲbε dziŋbu) cutting sth. off [Lit. a reservoir in which the flow of the water has been cut off].

ལྟག་ཆོད་ (dāgjöö) a contradictory/ opposite reply or answer.

ལྟག་ཉལ་ (dāgñεε) 1. va. to lie on one's back. 2. a small knife for drawing blood.

ལྟག་ཐེར་ (dāgder) sm. ལྟག་སྒྲེ་.

ལྟག་འཐེན་ (dāgden) cocking the hammer on a gun; va.—རྒྱག.

ལྟག་མདུད་ (dəgdüù) abbr. ལྟག་པའི་མདུད་སྒོ.

ལྟག་སྣུར་གཏོང་ (dāgnur dōŋ) va. to press down with the back of a ladle when cooking rice.

ལྟག་པ་ (dāgba) 1. back of the head/ neck. 2. behind. 3. protector, patron, backer, supporter.

ལྟག་པ་གེར་གེར་ (dāgba gērger) not hunched over, shoulders thrown back.

ལྟག་པ་ཆག (dāgba cāà) vi. to lose one's backer/ supporter.

ལྟག་པ་མཐོ་པོ་ (dāgba tōbo) person who has a strong backer/ supporter.

ལྟག་པའི་མདུད་སྒོ་ (dāgbε düùgo) the midpoint of the back of the head when a line is drawn from the tip of one ear to the other ear (a moxibustion point).

ལྟག་སྤྲོད་ (dāgdröö) back to back ། ཁོ་གཉིས་ལྟག་སྤྲོད་བྱས་བསྡད་པ་རེད་ Those two sat back to back.

ལྟག་འབིགས་ (dəgbig) chisel; va.—གཏོང་ to chisel.

ལྟག་མ་ (dāgma) upper part, above.

ལྟག་རྩ་ (dāgdza) 1. vein on the back of the head. 2. a backer or supporter in a position of power.

ལྟག་རྩ་ངོམ་ (dāgdza ŋom) va. to use the power and position and influence of sb. to get sth.

ལྟག་རྩ་བཟང་པོ་ (dāgdza saŋbo) having a strong backer in a position of authority.

ལྟག་ཚུགས་ (dāgdzuù) a way of stitching.

ལྟག་མཚར་ (dāgdzar) an ornament hung behind the head of nomad women.

ལྟག་འཛར་ (dāgdzar) sm. ལྟག་མཚར་.

ལྟག་འོག (dāg wɔɔ̀) up and down, upper and lower; va.—དང་བསྟུན་ to take into account the context (e.g., when translating) ། ང་གྲོང་ཁྱེར་ལྟག་འོག་གཉིས་ཀར་འགྲོ་སོང་ I have gone to both the upper and lower part of town.

ལྟག་ཡན་ (dāgyεn) stitching on the hem of clothes; va.—རྒྱག.

ལྟག་རལ་ (dāgrεε) a vein on the back of the head from which blood is drawn to cure headaches, earaches, etc.

ལྟག་རུས་ (dəgrüù) occipital bone.

ལྟག་ལམ་ (dāglam) a way/ road for retreat; a way out; va.—འཇོག to leave a way open for retreat.

ལྟག་ལོག (dāglɔɔ̀) 1. retreating, going/ turning back (to where one came); va.—རྒྱག ། ཁོ་ཚོ་ལྟག་ལོག་བརྒྱབ་ནས་ལྷ་སར་ཕྱིན་པ་རེད་ They turned back and went to Lhasa. 2. a kind of double stitching wherein each stitch has a second stitch sewn behind it; va.—རྒྱག.

ལྟག་ཤ་ (dāgsha) occipital muscle.

ལྟག་ཤེད་ (dāgsheè) sm. ལྟག་ཁར་.

ལྟང་ (dāŋ) a leather container used for loads on transport animals (traditionally for butter and rice) ། མར་ལྟང་གཅིག One load (leather container) of butter.

ལྟང་རྩེ་ (dāŋdze) a leather pouch.

ལྟང་ཅེའི་དེབ་ (dāŋdzee te̱b) shung. chi.tib. a record book ། འཕར་མ་འཛོག་རྒྱུའི་བཀའ་བློན་མདའ་དཔོན་རྣམས་ཀྱི་མིང་ཐོ་ལྟང་ཅེའི་དེབ་ལ་བཀོད་པ The names of the additional Kalons and Depons were written in the record book.

ལྟད་མོ་ (dɛ̀ɛmo) 1. show, performance, spectacle; va.—ལྟ་ to watch a show/ performance; va.—སྟོན་ to perform, to put on a show. 2. interesting (for shows/ movies/ etc.) ། གློག་བརྙན་འདི་ལྟད་མོ་མི་འདུག This movie is not interesting.

ལྟད་མོ་ཁང་ (dɛ̀ɛmogaŋ) theater.

ལྟད་མོ་སྟོན་མཁན་ (dɛ̀ɛmo dȍññɛn) performer, actor.

ལྟད་མོ་ལྟ་མཁན་ (dɛ̀ɛmo dāññɛn) spectators, audience.

ལྟད་མོ་ལྟོས་ (dɛ̀ɛmo dȍȍ) slang. a direct verbal threat or warning to sb. conveying that if he isn't careful "he will get it."

ལྟད་མོ་བ་ (dɛ̀ɛmowa) sm. ལྟད་མོ་ལྟ་མཁན་.

ལྟད་མོའི་རྣམ་གྲངས་ (dɛ̀ɛmö nāmdraŋ) program (of a show).

ལྟབ་ (dɔ̄b) sm. ལྟེབ་.

ལྟབ་གུག་ (dɔ̄bguù) sm. ལྟབ་མ་.

ལྟབ་གྲི་ (dɔ̄bdri) penknife.

ལྟབ་སྒྲིལ་ (dɔ̄bdrii) sm. ལྟབ་རིལ་.

ལྟབ་ཉེས་ (dɔ̄bñeè) creases caused by folding; vi.—ཐེབས་; —ཤོར་ to get creased; va.—རྒྱག to make a crease.

ལྟབ་གཉེར་ (dɔ̄bñer) sm. ལྟབ་ཉེས་.

ལྟབ་དྲིལ་ (dɔ̄bdrii) sm. ལྟབ་རིལ་.

ལྟབ་མ་ (dɔ̄bma) a fold, plait.

ལྟབ་རྩིག་ (dɔ̄bdzii) folding; va.—རྒྱག to fold ། ཉལ་ཁྲི་ལྟབ་རྩིག་རྒྱག་རྒྱུ་ཡོད་པ་ Having a folding bed.

ལྟབ་རིལ་ (dɔ̄brii) a roll of cloth/ fabric.

ལྟབ་ལག (dɔ̄blaà) centipede.

ལྟམ་ (dām) sm. བལྟམས་.

ལྟམ་མེ་ལྟེམ་མེ་ (dāme dēmme) 1. filled to the top, completely full (for liquids). 2. frail, fragile, weak and sick looking.

ལྟམ་ལྟེམ་ (dāmdem) abbr. of ལྟམ་མེ་ལྟེམ་མེ་.

ལྟར་ (dār) 1. like ། དེ་ལྟར་ Like that. ། འཕུར་བ་ལྟར་ Like flying. 2. every ། ལོ་ལྟར་ Every year. 3. according to, as, in accordance with ། གསར་ཤོག་ནང་ལ་བཀོད་པ་ལྟར་ According to what was written in the newspaper.

ལྟར་ལྟར་པོ་ (dār dārbo) 1. elongated shape. 2. a fetal stage three weeks after conception.

ལྟར་ན་ (dārna) according to, in accordance with, as ། གསར་ཤོག་ནང་བཀོད་གསལ་ལྟར་ན་ According to what was written in the newspaper.

ལྟར་སྣང་ (dārnaŋ) 1. appearance, surface looks ། བུ་མོ་དེ་ལྟ་སྣང་ལ་མཛེས་པོ་ཡོད་ཀྱང་གཤིས་ཀ་ཡག་པོ་མེད་པ་རེད་ Even though that woman is beautiful in appearance, her character is not good. 2. supposition. 3. false.

ལྟར་བྱས་ན་ (dār ce̱èna) sm. ལྟར་ན་.

ལྟར་བཞག (dārshaà) (vb. + —) leave alone, let alone ། ཁང་པ་ཉོ་རྒྱུ་ལྟར་བཞག་ད་ལྟ་ཁང་གླ་སྤྲོད་ཐུབ་ཀྱི་མི་འདུག Leave alone buying a house, (he) cannot pay (his) rent now.

ལྟས་ (dɛ̀ɛ) omen, sign.

ལྟས་སྐྱེས་ (dɛ̀ɛgyeè) slang. a derogatory term usu. used for children conveying, "rascal."

ལྟས་མཁན་ (dɛ̀ɛñɛn) person who interprets omens and signs (by divination and astrology).

ལྟས་ངན་ (dɛ̀ɛŋɛn) 1. bad omen, sign; vi.—ཤར་; —བྱུང་ to have a bad omen/ sign occur; vi.—མཐོང་ to see a bad omen/ sign. 2. sm. ལྟས་ངན་ལ་.

ལྟས་ངན་ཉེར་གཅིག་མཐོང་བ་ (dɛ̀ɛŋɛn ñe̱rjig tōŋwa) sm. མི་མཐོང་ན་མཐོང་.

ལྟས་ངན་དགྲ་ལ་འགྱུར་ (dɛ̀ɛŋɛn dra̱la gyu̱r) sm. ལྟས་ངན་ལ་.

ལྟས་ངན་ལ་ (dɛ̀ɛŋɛnla) slang. term expressing negative surprise at sth. out of the realm of expected/ appropriate behavior ། ལྟས་ངན་ལ་ བུ་མོ་དེ་ཁྲོམ་གྱི་དཀྱིལ་ལ་དམར་རྗེན་ལ་འགྲོ་གི་འདུག What the hell! The girl is going around naked in the market.

ལྟས་གནམ་ (dɛ̀ɛnam) a derogatory term for bad weather.

ལྟས་པ་ (dɛ̀ɛba) sm. ལྟས་མཁན་.

ལྟས་ཕྲུག (dɛ̀ɛdruù) a derogatory term used to scold children.

ལྟས་བཟང་ (dɛ̀ɛsaŋ) good omen/ sign.

ལྟས་རིག་པ་ (dɛ̀ɛ ri̱gbə) the art of interpreting omens and signs.

ལྟས་སུ་བལྟ་བའི་བཟོ་ (dɛ̀ɛsu dāwɛ so̱) sm. ལྟས་རིག་པ་.

ལྟི་རི་ (dĩri) a small earthenware pot (usually for tea).

ལྟིར་ (dĩr) pot for tea or beer.

ལྟིར་རིལ་དགུ་རིལ་ (dĩirii gu̱rii) stuffed, bloated ། ཁ་ལག་བཟས་ནས་གྲོད་ཁོག་ལྟིར་རིལ་དགུ་རིལ་ཆགས་པ་རེད་ (His) stomach was stuffed after eating the meal.

ལྟུང་: p. ལྟུངས་; f. ལྟུང་; imp. ལྟུང་ (dūŋ) 1. vi. to fall. 2. vi. to violate or break vows/ laws/ rules.

ལྟུང་བ་བཤགས་ (dūŋwə shāà) va. to confess/ repent one's crime, to be penitent.

ལྟུང་བཤགས་ (dūŋshaà) va. to confess/ repent one's crime; to be penitent.

ལྟབུའི་ (dəbü) shung. abbr. of ལྟ་བུའི་.

ལྟེ་ཀ་ (dēga) sm. ལྟེ་ག.

ལྟེ་ཁུང་ (dēguŋ) navel.

ལྟེ་མཁྲང་ (dēdraŋ) an illness characterized by a swelling of the navel.

ལྟེ་མཁྲེགས་ (dēdreg) an illness characterized by a hardening of the navel.

ལྟེ་འཁོར་ (dēgɔɔ) a disease of the navel usu. occurring in childhood.

སྟེ་ག (dēga) axle center, axis.

ལྟེ་གཅོད་ (dējȍȍ) cutting the umbilical cord; va.—བྱེད་.

ལྟེ་འཆལ་དབེ་འཆལ་ (dējɛɛ bējɛɛ) careless, casual, jumping from one thing to another without finishing any; va.—བྱེད་ ། མི་དེས་ལྟེ་འཆལ་དབེ་འཆལ་ཁོ་ན་བྱས་ནས་ལས་ཀ་ནན་ཏན་བྱེད་ཀྱི་མི་འདུག That person is careless and doesn't work carefully.

ལྟེ་ཐག (dēdaà) umbilical cord; va.—གཅོད་ to cut the umbilical cord.

ལྟེ་གནད་ (dēnɛɛ̀) the main/ key/ essential/ central point or issue ། ལྟེ་གནད་ནི་སྲིད་དབང་རེད་ The central issue is political power.

ལྟེ་གནས་ (dēnɛɛ̀) 1. the main city/ place/ location. 2. a center (for learning/ study/ research) ། ཞིབ་འཇུག་གི་ལྟེ་གནས་ Research center.

ལྟེ་གནས་ཚོད་ལྟ་ཁང་ (dēnɛɛ̀ tsȍȍdagaŋ) central laboratory.

ལྟེ་རྣག (dēnag) an infection on the navel (usu. infants).

ལྟེ་བ་ (dēwa) 1. middle, center, core, main, central, chief, hub; va.—བྱེད་ to act as the center/ core/ hub ། འཆར་གཞི་ལྟེ་བ་ The main plan. ། ཀྲུང་གོ་ལྟེ་བ་བྱས་པའི་སྤྱི་ཚོགས་རིང་ལུགས་ཀྱི་རྒྱལ་ཁབ་ལ་ To the socialist countries, of which China is the main one. 2. sm. ལྟེ་ཁུང་.

ལྟེ་བ་ལྟེ་བ་ (dēwa dēwa) sm. ལྟེ་གནད་.

ལྟེ་བ་བརླག (dēwa lāà) vi. to lose sight of the main issue.

ལྟེ་བ་ལས་བྲལ་བའི་ཤུགས་ (dēwalɛ trɛɛwɛ shūg) centrifugal force.

ལྟེ་བའི་མཁོ་སྤྲོད་ས་ཚིགས་ (dēwɛ kōdrȍȍ sədzii) central supply station..

ལྟེ་བའི་གྲོང་ཁྱེར་ (dēwɛ tro̱ŋgyee) main city (provincial capital).

ལྟེ་བའི་སྨན་ཁང་ (dēwɛ mēngaŋ) central hospital.

ལྟེ་བར་ཕྱོགས་པའི་ཤུགས་ (dēwar cɔ̄gbɛ shūg)

centripetal force.

ལྟེ་བྲལ་ (dēdrεε) centrifugalness.

ལྟེ་བྲལ་སྐམ་བྱེད་འཕྲུལ་ཆས་ (dēdrεε gāmjeè trű̄űjεὲ) centrifugal dessicator.

ལྟེ་བྲལ་ཆུ་འཐེན་འཕྲུལ་འཁོར་ (dēdrεε cūden trű̄űgɔɔ) centrifugal pump.

ལྟེ་བྲལ་ནུས་ཤུགས་ (dēdrεε nṳ̈ṳ̀shug) centrifugal force.

ལྟེ་འབུར་ (dēmbur) a swelling of the navel.

ལྟེ་འོག (dēwɔɔ̀) 1. anus. 2. bladder.

ལྟེང་ཀ་ (dēŋga) 1. a pool of rain water. 2. spring.

ལྟེང་ཁ་ (dēŋga) sm. ལྟེང་ཀ་.

ལྟེངས་ཀ་ (dēŋga) sm. ལྟེང་ཀ་.

ལྟེབ་: p. བལྟབས་; f. བལྟབ་; imp. ལྟོབས་ (dēb) va. to fold ། རས་འདི་བལྟབས་ནས་སྒམ་ནང་ལ་བཅུག་པ་རེད་ (He) folded the cloth and put it in a box.

ལྟེབ་འགོ་ (dēbgo) shung. a bunch of papers bound together ། ལྟེབ་འགོ་ལྔ་ཡོད་པའི་དེབ་ A bound book with five folded pages.

ལྟེབ་གྲི་ (dēbdri) sm. ལྟབ་གྲི་.

ལྟེབ་སྒྲིལ་ (dēbdrii) sm. ལྟབ་རིལ་.

ལྟེབ་སྒྲིན་ (dēbdrin) va. to fold (h.).

ལྟེབ་ཆགས་ (dēbjaà) sm. ལྟེབ་རྩེག.

ལྟེབ་པའི་ཁྲི་རྩེ་ (dēbbε trīdzi) folding ruler.

ལྟེབ་མ་ (dēbma) folded.

ལྟེབ་བརྩེག (dēbdzeè) folding; va.—རྒྱག ། ཚོང་ཁང་འདིར་ཉལ་ཁྲི་ལྟེབ་བརྩེག་རྒྱག་རྒྱུ་འདུག་གས་ Does this store have folding beds?

ལྟེབ་ཚིགས་ (dēbdziì) sm. ལྟབ་རྩིག.

ལྟེབ་རིས་ (dēbriì) a pleat, a crease.

ལྟེབ་བཤིག (dēb shīì) va. to unfold sth.

ལྟེབས་ (dēb) imp. of ལྟེབ་.

ལྟེམ་ (dēm) vi. to be sick/ ill (h.) ། ཁོང་དེང་སང་སྐུ་ལྟེམ་བཞག These days he is sick.

ལྟེམ་རྒྱང་མེད་པ་ (dēmgyaŋ m̲eèba) not in extremes, in moderation (not too much or too little).

ལྟེམ་གྱིས་གང་བ་ (dēmgi ka̲ŋwa) full with ། ཆུ་རྫིང་གི་ནང་དུ་ཆུ་ལྟེམ་གྱིས་གང་འདུག The reservoir is full with water.

ལྟེམ་ལྟེམ་ (dēmdem) sm. ལྟེམ་ཀྱིས་གང་བ་.

ལྟེམ་མེར་ (dērmer) sm. ལྟེམ་ལྟེམ་.

ལྟོ་ (dō) 1. food ། མོ་ལྟོ་སློང་བར་ཕྱིན་པ་རེད་ She went begging for food. ། ཁྱི་ལྟོ་ Dog food. 2. abbr. of ལྟོ་བ་.

ལྟོ་ཀྱོག་སློག (dōgyɔɔ̀ lɔ̄ɔ̀) va. to cause to turn upside down.

ལྟོ་དཀྲིས་ (dōdriì) woolen or cotton cloth wrapped around the waist (to keep the waist warm).

ལྟོ་བཀག (dōgaà) sm. ལྟོགས་བཀག.

ལྟོ་སྐལ་ (dōgεε) shung. an inheritance share, a share (from which one subsists) ། ཞིང་ཡོད་ལག་འདེབས་གང་ཡོད་ལྟོ་སྐལ་དུ་དག་འཐུས་ All those fields that you are working on shall henceforth be your share for subsisting.

ལྟོ་སྐོལ་ (dō gȫȫ) va. to cook ། ང་ལ་ལྟོ་སྐོལ་ཡས་ཀྱི་ཡོ་བྱད་མེད་ I have no utensils for cooking.

ལྟོ་བསྐྱུད་ (dō gyǖǜ) vi. to forget about eating (due to working or studying hard).

ལྟོ་ཁ་གཅོག (dōga jōò) va. to reduce the amount of food eaten.

ལྟོ་ཁ་སྤོར་ (dōga pɔ̄r) va. to increase the amount of food eaten.

ལྟོ་མཁན་ (dōñεn) cook.

ལྟོ་ཁྱིའི་ལྟོ་ལས་བོང་བུའི་ལས་ (dō kyīdo l̲εὲ bo̲ŋbü l̲εὲ) being fed like a dog and made to work like a donkey).

ལྟོ་གོས་ (dōgöö̀) 1. food and clothes. 2. livelihood; va.—འཚོལ་ to look for work/ livelihood, to find ways to make a livelihood ། གསར་འགྱུར་པ་རྣམས་སླེབས་མ་ཐག་ཏུ་ལྟོ་གོས་འཚོལ་དགོས་ཀྱི་ཡོད་པ་རེད་ As soon as the newcomers arrive they have to look for work. ། ལུང་པ་འདིར་ལྟོ་གོས་འཚོལ་བདེ་པོ་ཡོད་པ་རེད་ Its easy to find ways to subsist (to make one's livelihood) in this place.

ལྟོ་གོས་འགྲོ་སོང་ (dōgöö̀ dro̲soŋ) living expenses, cost of living.

ལྟོ་གོས་ངན་ངོན་ (dōgöö̀ ŋε̲nŋön) poor food and clothing, poor living conditions.

ལྟོ་གོས་གཏམ་གསུམ་ (dōgöö̀ dāmsum) food, clothing and reputation.

ལྟོ་གོས་མཉམ་དུ་ (dōgöö̀ ñə̲mdu) eating from the same hearth, sharing a livelihood/ household.

ལྟོ་གོས་ཕྱིད་ (dōgöö̀ cīì) vi. to be able to support oneself ། གླ་ཆ་ཉུང་ཉུང་ཡིན་ཙང་ལྟོ་གོས་ཕྱིད་ཀྱི་མེད་པ་རེད་ Because his wage is low, he is unable to support himself.

ལྟོ་གོས་འཛོམས་པོ་ (dōgöö̀ dzo̲mbo) well-off economically, abundant in livelihood.

ལྟོ་གོས་ལོག་བགར་ dōgöö̀ lɔ̲ggar) separate livelihood/ household.

ལྟོ་གླ་ (dōla) fee for a meal/ food.

ལྟོ་བགྲོད་སྲོག་ཆགས་ (dōdröö̀ sɔ̄gjaà) sm. ལྟོ་འགྲོའི་སྲོག་ཆགས་.

ལྟོ་འགེངས་ (dō ge̲ŋ) vi. to be full, to have one's hunger satisfied.

ལྟོ་འགྲངས་ (dō dra̲ŋ) sm. ལྟོ་འགེངས་.

ལྟོ་འགྲངས་གོས་དྲོས་ (dōdraŋ kö̲ö̀dröö̀) vi. to be satisfied/ content [Lit. full with food, warm with clothing].

ལྟོ་འགྲོ་ (dōndro) reptile, snake, crawling animals.

ལྟོ་འགྲོའི་སྲོག་ཆགས་ (dōdrö sɔ̄gjaà) species that crawl.

ལྟོ་རྒྱགས་ (dōgyaà) shung. food provisions (for a journey/ work site).

ལྟོ་རྒྱགས་རང་ཁུར་ (dōgyaà ra̲ŋgur) shung. to bring one's own food ། ཉམས་གསོ་ཆེ་ཕྲ་མི་སེར་ནས་ལྟོ་རྒྱགས་རང་ཁུར་གྱིས་ཞུ་དགོས་བྱུང་བ་ The main renovations were done by subjects who brought their own food (to the workplace).

ལྟོ་རྒྱབ་ (dōgyəb) food and clothes.

ལྟོ་རྒྱུས་ཡོད་ལས་རྒྱུས་ཡོད་ (dō gyṳ̈ṳ̀ yo̲ö̀ lε̲ὲ gyṳ̈ṳ̀ yo̲ö̀) familiar with a situation or place [Lit. familiar with the food and work].

ལྟོ་སྒོར་རྒྱག (dōgɔɔ gya̲à) va. to be seated in a circle when eating.

ལྟོ་སྒྲེ་ (dōgye) sm. ལྟོ་ཕད་.

ལྟོ་ཆག་ཤོར་ (dōjaà shɔ̄ɔ̄) vi. to get undernourished, to not get enough food ། ཕ་མ་མ་བསྡད་པའི་ཤུལ་ལ་ཕྲུ་གུ་དེ་ལྟོ་ཆག་ཤོར་ནས་ཤ་བསྐམས་འདུག While the parents were absent the child didn't get enough to eat and lost weight.

ལྟོ་ཆས་ (dōbjεὲ) 1. food, provisions; va.—བཟོ་ to prepare/ cook food; va.—སློང་ to beg for food.

ལྟོ་ཆས་འཇུ་བདེ་པོ་ (dōbjεὲ ju̲ de̲bo) food that is easy to digest.

ལྟོ་ཆས་ལས་སྣོན་བཟོ་གྲྭ་ (dōbjεὲ lε̲ὲnön so̲dra) food processing plant.

ལྟོ་ཆས་སླ་པོ་ (dōbjεὲ lābo) food that is not solid (e.g., porridge-type consistency).

ལྟོ་འཇུ་ (dō ju̲) vi. to digest food ། ཕོ་བ་ནད་པ་ཡིན་ཙང་ལྟོ་ཡག་པོ་འཇུ་ཐུབ་ཀྱི་མི་འདུག Because I have a stomach illness, I can't digest food well.

ལྟོ་ཉལ་ (dōñεε) sleeping/ napping after a meal; va.—བྱེད་.

ལྟོ་དོད་ (dōdöö̀) money given in lieu of food (usu. to workers).

ལྟོ་དུས་ (dōdüǜ) mealtime, the normal time to eat a meal ། ཁ་ལག་ལྟོ་དུས་ལ་བཟས་ན་ཡག་པོ་ཡོ་རེད It is good to eat at mealtime.

ལྟོ་དུས་གསུམ་ (dōdüǜ sūm) the three mealtimes a day (breakfast, lunch, dinner).

ལྟོ་ལྡིར་ (dōdir) protruding/ bulging stomach, potbelly ། བུད་མེད་སྦྲུམ་མ་དེ་ལྟོ་ལྡིར་ནས་སྨན་ཁང་དུ་ཕྱིན་སོང་ When the pregnant woman's stomach became protruding, she went to the hospital.

ལྟོ་སྣོད་ (dōnöö̀) a food container/ vessel.

ལྟོ་སྣུམ་པ་ (dō nūmba) nourishing/ nutritious foods (traditionally in Tibet this referred to meat and oily foods).

ལྟོ་སྣུམ་པོ་ (dō nūmbo) sm. ལྟོ་སྣུམ་པ་.

ལྟོ་སྐྱིད་ (dōjɛɛ̀) food and other necessities.

ལྟོ་ཕད་ (dōpɛɛ̀) knapsack, pack.

ལྟོ་ཕོགས་ (dōpɔ̀ɔ̀) salary, wage.

ལྟོ་ཕོར་ (dōbɔɔ) 1. a bowl for eating. 2. slang. a job; vi.—ཤོར་ to lose one's job.

ལྟོ་ཕྱིད་ (dōcii) vi. to have enough food to eat.

ལྟོ་འཕྱེ་ (dōceè) 1. earth spirits, nāga. 2. sm. ལྟོ་འཕྱེ་སྲོག་ཆགས་.

ལྟོ་འཕྱེ་ཆེན་པོ་ (dōceè cēmbo) a kind of earth spirit.

ལྟོ་འཕྱེ་སྲོག་ཆགས་ (dōceè sōgjaà) animals that crawl on their stomachs, reptiles.

ལྟོ་བ་ (dōwa) 1. stomach; vi.—ཁེངས་ to be full. 2. food.

ལྟོ་བས་འགྲོ་ (dōwɛ dro) va. to crawl (on one's stomach).

ལྟོ་བུན་ (dōbün) shung. abbr. food/ livelihood and loans.

ལྟོ་བོར་བ་ (dōbɔrwa) arc. a son born in the year his father died.

ལྟོ་སྦོས་ (dō böö) vi. to have/ get a bloated stomach.

ལྟོ་མ་འཇུ་ (dō maju) sm. ལྟོ་མི་ཞུ་.

ལྟོ་མ་འཇུ་བའི་ནད་ (dō majubɛ nɛɛ̀) dyspepsia.

ལྟོ་མི་འཇུ་ (dō miju) sm. ལྟོ་མི་ཞུ་.

ལྟོ་མི་ཞུ་ (dō mishu) vi. to have indigestion, to not digest food.

ལྟོ་ཙ་ཕྱིད་ (dōdza cii) sm. ལྟོ་གོས་ཕྱིད་.

ལྟོ་ཚང་ (dōbdzaŋ) 1. communal eating, eating and sharing costs together; va.—བྱེད་ to engage in communal eating (cooking) ། ལས་མི་རྣམས་ལྟོ་ཚང་བྱས་ནས་ཁ་ལག་ཟ་གི་ཡོད་པ་རེད་ The workers were sharing costs and eating together.

ལྟོ་ཚད་ (dōdzɛɛ̀) 1. appetite (amount of food eaten). 2. a fixed amount of food.

ལྟོ་ཚབ་ཕྱེ་མ་ (dōdzəb cēma) a flour-like food substitute.

ལྟོ་ཚེ་ཕྱིད་ (dōdze cii) sm. ལྟོ་གོས་ཕྱིད་.

ལྟོ་ཚོད་ (dōdzöö) controlling how much food is eaten; va.—བྱེད་ ། ཕྲུ་གུའི་ལྟོ་ཚད་རྒན་པས་མ་བྱས་ན་ལྟོ་ལོག་ཐེབས་ཀྱི་རེད་ If adults don't control the amount of food children (eat), they will die of overeating.

ལྟོ་ཞུ་ (dō shu) vi. to digest food.

ལྟོ་ཟ་ (dō sa) va. to eat food.

ལྟོ་ཟས་ (dōsɛɛ̀) food; va.—བཟོ་ to make food.

ལྟོ་གཡོག་ (dōyɔɔ̀) sb. who helps in cooking; va.—བྱེད་.

ལྟོ་རན་ (dōren) 1. eating moderately. 2. vi. to be the time to eat.

ལྟོ་རས་ (dārɛɛ̀) napkin.

ལྟོ་ལ་བྱེད་ (dōla ceè) va. to give a sign one wants to eat (derogatory connotation) ། ཁྱི་དེ་ཁ་ལག་མ་བྱུང་ཙང་ལྟོ་ལ་བྱེད་ཀྱི་འདུག Because the dog didn't get food it is giving signs it wants to eat.

ལྟོ་ལད་ (dō lɛɛ̀) 1. va. to eat food that has turned bad. 2. vi. to get into a bad food habit.

ལྟོ་ལོག་ཐེབས་ (dōlɔɔ̀ tēè) vi. to die of overeating.

ལྟོ་ལོང་ (dōlɔŋ) sm. ལོང་, 2.

ལྟོ་སྲིན་ (dōsin) stomach parasite/ worm.

ལྟོ་སློང་ (dō lōŋ) va. to beg for food ། ཁོའི་ནང་ལ་སྤྲང་པོ་ལྟོ་སློང་མཁན་ཞིག་ཡོང་བ་རེད་ A beggar came to his house begging for food.

ལྟོ་སུད་ (dōsüü) a snack.

ལྟོ་སོན་ (dōsün) provisions or food and seed.

ལྟོ་ལྷག (dōlhaà) leftover food.

ལྟོགས་ (dɔ̀ɔ̀) vi. to be hungry ། ཁྲོད་ཁོག་ལྟོགས་ཀྱི་འདུག (I'm) hungry.

ལྟོགས་ཀྱི་ (dɔ̀ɔ̀gye) sm. ལྟོགས་རྔམ་ཚ་པོ་.

ལྟོགས་བཀག (dɔ̀ɔ̀gaà) starvation, starving; va.—གཏོང་ to starve sb.; vi.—ཐེབས་ to get starved ། ཁོ་ཚོས་ལྟོགས་བཀག་བཏང་ནས་བཙོན་པ་མང་པོ་ཤི་བ་རེད་ They starved (them) so many prisoners died.

ལྟོགས་བཀྲེས་ (dɔ̄gdreè) hunger.

ལྟོགས་སྐད་ (dɔ̀ɔ̀gɛɛ̀) sound of stomach growling from hunger; vi.—འབྱིན་.

ལྟོགས་སྐོམ་ (dɔ̀ɔ̀gom) hunger and thirst; va.—སེལ་ to satisfy one's hunger and thirst.

ལྟོགས་ཀྱིས་མནར་ (dɔ̀ɔ̀gi nār) vi. to suffer from hunger.

ལྟོགས་ཁ་ (dɔ̀ɔ̀ga) appetite; vi.—འབྱེད་ to have one's appetite increase; vi.—འགོར་ to have one's appetite decrease/ decline ། ནད་པ་དེ་སྨན་བཅོས་བྱས་རྗེས་ལྟོགས་ཁ་ཕྱེ་བཞག After the patient got treated (his) appetite increased.

ལྟོགས་འཁྱོམས་ (dɔ̀ɔ̀ kyōm) vi. to stagger from hunger.

ལྟོགས་གྲི (dɔ̀ɔ̀dri) starvation, starving; vi.—ར་ཤི་ to die from starvation, to starve to death.

ལྟོགས་འགག (dɔ̀ɔ̀gaà) sm. ལྟོ་བཀག.

ལྟོགས་འགོག (dɔ̀ɔ̀gɔɔ̀) sm. ལྟོ་བཀག.

ལྟོགས་འགོང་ (dɔ̀ɔ̀goŋ) hungry ghost/ spirit (the term is used as a kind of metaphorical criticism for people who eat too much) ། ཨ་མས་ཕྲུ་གུར་ལྟོགས་འགོང་ཞུགས་པ་ནང་བཞིན་མ་བྱེད་ ཁ་ལག་ཚར་གྲབས་ཡོད་ཟེར་ལབ་པ་རེད་ The mother said to the child, "Don't act like you have been possessed by a hungry ghost. The food is almost ready."

ལྟོགས་རྒྱལ་ (dɔ̀ɔ̀gyɛɛ) sm. ལྟོགས་རྔམ་ཚ་པོ་.

ལྟོགས་སྒོམ་ (dɔ̀ɔ̀gom) enduring/ tolerating/ putting up with hunger; vi.—རྒྱག to endure hunger ། དམག་མི་ཚོར་ལྟོ་རྒྱགས་མ་འབྱོར་ཙང་ཉིན་གསུམ་རིང་ལྟོགས་སྒོམ་རྒྱག་དགོས་བྱུང་བ་རེད་ Because the soldiers didn't receive provisions, they had to tolerate hunger for three days.

ལྟོགས་ངལ་ (dɔ̀ɔ̀ŋɛɛ) hungry and tired.

ལྟོགས་རྔམ་ཚ་པོ་ (dɔ̀ɔ̀ŋam tsābo) 1. a derogatory term for sb. who is ravenous/ gluttonous/ extremely desirous of food ། ཕྲུ་གུ་འདི་ལྟོགས་ཀྱི་ཞི་པོ་ཅིག་འདུག This child is someone who always wants food. 2. greedy, avaricious ། རྒྱུ་ཆེན་པོ་ཞི་དག་ཡིན་ན་ཡང་ལྟོགས་རྔམ་ཚ་པོ་འདུག Even though (he) is rich, (he) is greedy.

ལྟོགས་ཅོར་ (dɔ̀ɔ̀jɔr) crying out from hunger, the cries of sb. who is hungry.

ལྟོགས་ཆད་ (dɔ̄gjɛɛ̀) tired due to lack of food; vi.—ཐེབས་ to get tired from hunger.

ལྟོགས་ཉལ་ (dɔ̀ɔ̀ñɛɛ) lying down because of hunger; va.—རྒྱག.

ལྟོགས་གཉིད་ཁུག (dɔ̀ɔ̀ ñii kūù) vi. to sleep because of hunger.

ལྟོགས་ཐག་ཆོད་ (dɔ̀ɔ̀daà cöö) vi. to be very hungry/ starving.

ལྟོགས་འདྲེ་ (dɔ̄ŋdre) sm. ལྟོགས་འགོང་.

ལྟོགས་ནད་ (dɔ̄gnɛɛ̀) illness due to hunger.

ལྟོགས་པ་ (dɔ̄gba) hunger; va.—སེལ་ to relieve one's hunger.

ལྟོགས་པར་སྡོད་ (dɔ̄gbar döö) 1. va. to fast. 2. va. to be on a hunger strike.

ལྟོགས་པར་ལུས་ (dɔ̄gbar lèè) vi. to be left or remain hungry.

ལྟོགས་སྤྲང་ (dɔ̀ɔ̀baŋ) a begger who is never satisfied.

ལྟོགས་ཕྱུག (dɔ̀ɔ̀juù) hungry and rich, poverty and wealth, poor and rich.

ལྟོགས་འབྱོར་པ་ (dɔ̄gjɔɔba) a derogatory term for a yoga practioner.

ལྟོགས་སྦྲེབས་ (dɔ̄gdreb) sm. ལྟོགས་བཀྲེས་.

ལྟོགས་མུག (dɔ̀ɔ̀mug) hunger, famine.

ལྟོགས་ཚིག (dɔ̄gdzii) anger caused by hunger; va.—ཟ་ to get angry at sth. because one is hungry.

ལྟོགས་རྩུབ་ (dɔ̄gdzub) sm. ལྟོགས་རྔམ་.

ལྟོགས་ཚོད་ (dɔ̄gdzöö) sm. ལྟོགས་.

ལྟོགས་གཟན་ (dɔ̄gsɛn) food/ provisions taken to the workplace.

ལྟོགས་གཟའ་ (dɔ̄gsa) a disease characterized by an insatiable appetite for food. 2. a derogatory term for sb. who is gluttonous.

ལྟོགས་གཟེར་ (dɔ̄gser) pain caused by hunger.

ལྟོགས་རིད་ (dɔ̄grii) sm. ལྟོགས་གྲི་.

ལྟོགས་ལ་ (dɔ̀ɔ̀la) sm.* ལྟོགས་སྣ་.

ལྟོགས་ཤི་ (dɔ̄gshi) dying by starvation; va.—གཏོང་ to starve (sb.) to death; vi.—ཐེབས་ to die of starvation.

ལྟོགས་ཤེད་ (dɔ̄gsheè) 1. sm. ལྟོགས་ཛམ་. 2. physically weak from hungry.

ལྟོགས་ཤེད་ཤོར་ (dɔ̄gsheè shɔ̄ɔ) vi. to become weak because of hunger.

ལྟོགས་ཤེས་པ་ (dɔ̄gsheèba) an newborn infant who is able to show that it's hungry.

ལྟོགས་སླ་ (dɔ̄gla) 1. a hungry person desiring/ wishing food; va.—བྱེད་. 2. very greedy, very desirous. 3. vi.—ཁ་ to feel hungry (to want to eat) when sb. else is eating, to have one's mouth water when sb. else is eating.

ལྟོགས་སླ་ཚ་པོ་ (dɔ̄gla tsābo) one who is very greedy, sb. who expects/ hopes to get things from others; va.—བྱེད་ ། མི་འདི་ལྟོགས་སླ་ཚ་པོ་ཞིག་དུག་ཡོད་ཙང་འདོད་པ་ནམ་ཡང་ཁེང་ལ་ཡོད་པ་མ་རེད་ Because the man is very greedy he will never be satisfied.

ལྟོགས་སླའི་ལོ་གསར་ (dɔ̄ɔlɛ lo̱sar) sm. སོ་ནམ་ལོ་གསར་.

ལྟོགས་གསོས་ (dɔ̄ɔsöö) a snack before a meal (to ease hunger).

ལྟོགས་བསྲན་ཆེན་པོ་ (dɔ̄gsɛn cēmbo) a person who can bear hunger for a long period of time.

ལྟོགས་རྐལ་ཀུན་བྱེད་ (dɔ̄ghrɛɛ gṹnjeè) stealing because of hunger; va.— བྱེད་.

ལྟོགས་ལྷང་ལྷང་ (dɔ̄ɔ lhāŋlaŋ) the feeling of hunger.

ལྟོང་ཀ་ (dōŋga) the notch on the arrow where the string of the bow is placed.

ལྟོང་ག (dōŋga) sm. ལྟོང་ཀ་.

ལྟོང་གཉིས་མ་ (dōŋ ñīimə) a double notched arrow.

ལྟོང་སྦྱར་ (dōŋjar) va. to place the notch of an arrow on the bow string (to be ready to shoot).

ལྟོངས་ (dōŋ) on the surface of sth. like a wall, etc.

ལྟོར་བྱུང་ (dōr ju̱ŋ) vi. to get/ be pregnant.

ལྟོབས་ (dōb) imp. ལྟེབ་.

ལྟོས་ (dōò) sm. བལྟོས་.

ལྟོས་བཅས་ (dōòjɛɛ̀) sm. བལྟོས་བཅས་.

ལྟོས་བཅས་མཐོང་སྲིད་ (dōòjɛɛ̀ jiŋdril) shung. oligarchic rule (rule through a small group of followers).

ལྟོས་ཆོས་ (dōòjöö) sm. བལྟོས་ཆོས་.

ལྟོས་གནས་ (dōònɛɛ̀) sm. བལྟོས་ས་.

ལྟོས་པའི་རྒྱུ་ (dōòbɛ gyu̱) the basis/ cause of a result.

ལྟོས་ཕྱོགས་ (dōòjɔɔ̀) sm. བལྟོས་ཕྱོགས་.

ལྟོས་མེད་ (dōòmeè) sm. བལྟོས་མེད་.

ལྟོས་མེད་རྒྱབ་བསྐྱུར་ (dōòmeè gyə̱bgyur) sm. བལྟོས་མེད་རྒྱབ་བསྐྱུར་.

ལྟོས་མེད་དོག་རོལ་ (dōòmeè do̱gröö) sm. ལྟོས་མེད་རྒྱབ་བསྐྱུར་.

ལྟོས་ས་ (dōòsa) sm. བལྟོས་ས་.

ལྟོས་ས་ལྟོས་ཆོས་ (dōòsa dōòjɔɔ̀) sm. བལྟོས་ས་བལྟོས་ཆོས་.

ལྟོས་ས་ལྟོས་འཛོག (dōòsa dōòjɔɔ̀) sm. བལྟོས་ས་བལྟོས་ཆོས་.

སྟ་གོན་ (dāgön) preparations, arrangements; va.—བྱེད་.

སྟ་གོན་འཁྲབ་སྟོན་ (dāgön trə̄bdön) preview of a show/ performance; va.—བྱེད་.

ལྟ་གོན་འགྲན་བསྡུར་ (dāgön dre̱ndur) preliminary contest/ heat.

སྟ་གོན་འགྲེམས་སྟོན་ (dāgön dre̱mdön) preliminary exhibition, preview.

སྟ་གོན་ཚོགས (dāgön cōga) shung. preparations, preparing.

སྟ་གོན་དང་མི་ (dāgön dəŋmi) candidate for membership in the communist party.

སྟ་གོན་འདྲི་གཅོད་ (dāgön dri̱jöö) preliminary investigation/ hearing.

སྟ་གོན་འཛིན་གྲྭ་ (dāgön dzi̱ndra) introductory class.

སྟ་གྲི་ (dədri) axe, hatchet; va.—གཞུ་ to hit with an axe.

སྟ་དང་ (dāŋo) the blade of an axe.

སྟ་མ་སྡིའུ་ (dāma dı̄u) pick axe; va.—རྒྱག.

སྟ་ཟུར་ (dāsur) hip.

སྟ་རེ་ (dāre) sm. སྟ་གྲི་.

སྟ་རེ་ཁ་ (dārega) a small, sharp blade used for draining blood.

སྟ་རེ་རྡོ་ལ་གཞུས་ཀྱང་སྐྱོང་ལྕགས་ལ་ཕོག་ཡོང་ (dāre do̱la shüügyaŋ gūgyoŋ jāàla pɔ̄ɔyoŋ) if one takes on too tough an opponent one will lose [Lit. hitting an axe on a stone the iron (axe head) will lose].

སྟ་རེ་ལེབ་ཆེན་ (dāre lēbjen) a large axe.

སྟ་རེ་སོ་གཉིས་མ་ (dāre sōñiìmə) double-edged axe.

སྟ་སོ་ (dāso) edge of an axe blade.

སྟག (dāà) tiger.

སྟག་ཁྱི་ (dāàgyi) fierce dog.

སྟག་གི་ཀུབ་ལ་ཐུག་པ་ (dāàgi gūblə tūgbə) daring to offend a powerful person, doing sth. dangerous/ risky [Lit. touch the tiger's ass].

སྟག་གི་ཀུབ་ལ་རེག་མི་ཉན་ (dāàgi gūblə re̱g mi̱ñɛn) not doing sth. for fear of revenge/ retribution [Lit. not daring to touch a tiger's ass].

སྟག་གི་རི་མོ་ཕྱི་དང་མིའི་རི་མོ་ནང་ (dāàgi re̱mo cı̄dan mi̱i re̱mo na̱ŋ) unable to tell what a person is like from external appearance [Lit. tiger's stripes are on the outside, human's stripes are on the inside].

སྟག་གྲུ་ཁ་ (dəgdruka) a major ferry site between Lhasa and Shigatse.

སྟག་མགོ་སྦྲུལ་མཇུག (dāàgo drũnjuù) a strong start but weak finish [Lit. head of a tiger and tail of a snake].

སྟག་མགོ་མེ་འབར་ (dāàgo me̱mbar) the southern star.

སྟག་མགོ་ར་གཞུག (dāàgo ra̱shuù) sm. སྟག་མགོ་སྦྲུལ་མཇུག [Lit. head of a tiger and tail of a goat].

སྟག་ལྕུག་དང་འགྲོལ་ (dāgjɔɔ̀ hāŋdröö) shung. carved table made from birch wood.

སྟག་རྒྱང་ (dɔ̄gjuŋ) a traditional Tibetan medicine.

སྟག་ཐོག་ནས་འབབ་དཀའ་ (dāàtɔɔ̀nɛ bə̱bgaa) a position from which it is difficult to get out of [Lit. it's difficult to dismount from a tiger's back].

སྟག་སྟོད་ (dāgdöò) upper garment made from tiger skin.

སྟག་གདན་ (dāgdɛn) tiger skin mat/ rug.

སྟག་སྟན་ (dāgdɛn) sm. སྟག་གདན་.

སྟག་སྡུལ་ (dāgdüü) a cloak made from a tiger skin.

སྟག་དང་འགྲོགས་ན་དམར་མི་ཆོད་ ཁྱི་རྗེས་ལ་འབྲངས་ན་རྡོ་ལོག་ཕོག (dāgdaŋ dro̱ɔna mār mi̱cöö kyı̄jeèla dra̱ŋna do̱lo pɔ̄ɔ) hanging around with good people will lead to profitable things, following evil people will lead to misfortune [Lit. being friends with a tiger you will get a lot of meat to eat, following dogs you will get hit by a lot of stones].

སྟག་དོང་ (dāgdoŋ) arrow quiver made from a tiger skin.

སྟག་འདྲ་གཟིག་འདྲ་ (dāgdra si̱gdra) brave, courageous [Lit. like a tiger, like a leopard].

སྟག་སྙིད་ (dāgneè) a hunched back.

སྟག་པ་ (dāgba) birch tree.

སྟག་པ་ཤིང་ (dāgba) birch tree.

སྟག་པའི་ཐོང་གཤོལ (dāgbɛ tōŋguù) shung. plow made from birch wood.

སྟག་ལྤགས་ (dāgbaà) 1. tiger skin. 2. birch bark.

སྟག་སྤྱང་གི་ཧམ་ཟ་ (dāgjaŋgi hāmsa) va. to wolf down food, to gobble/ devour food ravenously.

སྟག་ཕྲུག (dəgdruù) tiger cub.

སྟག་བྲག (dāgdraà) Taktra: name of the incarnate lama and Regent of Tibet from 1941—50.

སྟག་འབྲུག་དམར་འཛིང་ (dəgdruù māndziŋ) struggle between two evenly matched opponents; va.—བྱེད་ [Lit. bloody fight between tiger and dragon].

སྟག་མ་ (dāgma) azalea plant.

སྟག་མ་མེ་ཏོག (dāgma me̱dog) azalea flower.

སྟག་མ་ཤིང་ (dāgma shı̄ŋ) azalea tree.

སྟག་མའི་མེ་ཏོག་རྒྱང་གྲགས་ཆེ་ འཁྲིས་ལ་བཅར་ན་དུག་ལོ་རེད་ (dāgmɛ me̱dog gya̱ŋdraà cē trı̄ilə jāàna tu̱glo re̱è) some people look very good from a distance but are bad when you know them well [Lit. the azalea flower looks good from a distance but is poisonous when you get close to it].

སྟག་མོ་ (dāàmo) tigress.

སྟག་སྨད་ (dāgmɛ̀ɛ) a lower garment made of tiger skin.

སྟག་རྩེ་རྫོང་ (dāgdze dzoŋ) a county/ xian just north Lhasa.

སྟག་ཚང་ (dāgdzaŋ) tiger's den.

སྟག་ཚང་འབྲུག་མལ་ (dāgdzaŋ drugmɛɛ) an extremely dangerous place [Lit. tiger's den, dragon's sleeping place].

སྟག་ཚེར་ (dāgdzer) type of traditional medicine.

སྟག་འཚེར་ (dāgdzee) name of the place in Amdo where the 14th Dalai Lama was born.

སྟག་རྫབ་ (dāgdzəb) burl on a birch tree.

སྟག་ཞུམ་ (dəgshum) a person who is aggressive and arrogant at home but meek outside.

སྟག་གཟིག (dəgsiì) 1. Iran (Persia). 2. abbr. of tiger and leopard.

སྟག་གཟིག་ཁ་སྤྲོད་ (dəgsiì kābdröö) two powerful forces (entities) meeting face-to-face or matched in some contest [Lit. tiger and leopard face-to-face].

སྟག་གཟིག་ག་བུར་ (dəgsiì kəbuu) a type of mothball.

སྟག་གཟིག་མེ་ཏོག (dəgsiì medog) lily.

སྟག་ཟླ་ (dāŋda) the 1st Tibetan month.

སྟག་རལ་ (dāgrɛɛ) sm. སྟག་དོང་.

སྟག་རི་གཉན་གཟིགས་ (dəgri ñɛ̄nsiì) the 31st king of Tibet.

སྟག་རིས་ (dəgriì) tiger stripes.

སྟག་རུའི་ཁལ་ (dəgrü kɛ̄ɛ) shung. a type of volume measure in tt.

སྟག་རུས་ (dəgrüù) tiger's bone.

སྟག་རོ་ (dāgro) carcass of a dead tiger.

སྟག་ལོ་ (dāglo) 1. year of the tiger. 2. abbr. of the famous translator སྟག་ཚང་ལོ་ཙ་བ་.

སྟག་ལུང་ (dəgluŋ) district/ xian in Tibet.

སྟག་ལུང་བཀའ་བརྒྱུད་ (dəluŋ gəgyüù) a branch of the བཀའ་བརྒྱུད་ sect.

སྟག་ལོ་པ་ (dāgloba) sb. born in the year of the tiger (for males).

སྟག་ལོ་མ་ (dāgloma) sb. born in the year of the tiger (for females).

སྟག་ཤར་ (dāgshar) sm. སྟག་ཤར་གཞོན་པ་.

སྟག་ཤར་གཞོན་པ་ (dāgshar shönba) a young man (full of energy and vigor).

སྟག་ཤམ་ (dāgsham) a lower garment made of tiger skin.

སྟག་ཤུན་ (dāgsün) a brocade having dragon and cloud designs.

སྟག་སེང་ཁ་སྤྲོད་ (dāgseŋ kābdröö) sm. སྟག་གཟིག་ཁ་སྤྲོད་ [lit. tiger and snow lion face-to-face].

སྟག་སེང་ཁྱུང་འབྲུག (dāg sēŋ kyūŋ drug) tiger, lion, garuda and dragon.

སྟག་སེང་ང་རར་འཐབ་ (dāgseŋ ŋardəb) sm. སྟག་འབྲུག་དམར་འཛིང་.

སྟག་སེང་ང་རར་འཛིང་ (dāgseŋ ŋardziŋ) sm. སྟག་འབྲུག་དམར་འཛིང་.

སྟག་སོམ་ཕྱེད་ཁྱེར་ (dāgsom cēègyer) shung. a unit equal to half of a སྟག་རུའི་ཁལ་ and half of a སོམ་རུའི་ཁལ་.

སྟག་སློག (dāglɔ̀ɔ) a dress made of tiger skin (awarded for bravery in ancient Tibet). 2. a type of གཟི་ bead.

སྟག་གསོད་ས་མདའ་ (dāgsöö sānda) a booby trap made from a bow and arrow that is used to kill tigers.

སྟང་: p. བསྟངས་; f. བསྟང་; imp. སྟོང་ (dāŋ) va. to benefit/ help.

སྟང་རྩ་ (dāŋdza) sm. སྙིང་རྗེ་རྒྱག.

སྟང་ཚག (dāŋdzaà) sleeveless dress worn on top of the main dress by Tibetan women.

སྟང་ཟིལ་ (dāŋsil) silver ore.

སྟངས་ (dāŋ) 1.(vb.+ —) manner/ way of doing a verbal action ¶ གྲུ་གཏོང་སྟངས་ The way to sail a boat ¶ བྱེད་སྟངས་འདི་ཡག་པོ་མི་འདུག This way of doing things is not good. 2. (vb. (pres.) — + — vb. (pres.) + ལུགས་) the manner of ¶ མེ་མདའ་རྒྱག་སྟངས་རྒྱག་ལུགས་ The manner of firing a gun.

སྟངས་ཀ་ (dāŋga) sm. སྟངས་.

སྟངས་སྟབས་ (dāŋdəb) physical appearance.

སྟངས་དཔྱལ་ (dāŋjɛɛ) a married couple.

སྟངས་འཛིན་ (dəŋdzin) controlling/ managing/ administering sth.; va.—བྱེད་ ¶ མི་ཚང་གི་འགྲོ་སོང་གཏོང་ཡས་ཕ་མས་སྟངས་འཛིན་བྱེད་ཀྱི་ཡོད་པ་རེད་ The parents control the livelihood of the household.

སྟངས་འཛིན་རན་པ་ (dəŋdzin rɛmba) skillful in managing/ controlling/ administering.

སྟན་ (dɛ̄n) sm. གདན་.

སྟན་གཅིག (dɛ̄njig) a system where monks have only one meal a day.

སྟན་གཅིག་མ་ (dɛ̄njigmə) sm. སྟན་ཅིག.

སྟན་ནང་ཚངས་ཅན་ (dɛ̄nnaŋ tsāŋjɛn) stuffed or filled cushion/ matress.

སྟན་འབོལ་ (dɛ̄mböö) sm. འབོལ་གདན་.

སྟན་ཀླུམ་ (dɛ̄ndum) a small round cushion/ mat.

སྟབ་སེང་ (dəbseŋ) a herbal medicine (the bark of eucommia).

སྟབས་ (dəb) 1. because, since ¶ འདི་ར་དགུན་ཁ་ཤིན་ཏུ་གྲང་སྟབས་ལྷོ་ཕྱོགས་སུ་འགྲོ་གི་ཡོད་པ་རེད་ Because it is very cold here in the winter, (they) go south. ¶ འགྲོ་སྒྲོན་ཆེན་པོ་དེ་འདྲ་གཏོང་མི་ཐུབ་སྟབས་ Because (they) will not be able to pay such large expenses. 2. coincidence, circumstance (used only in compounds) ¶ སྟབས་ལེགས་ A good/ fortunate/ lucky coincidence or circumstance. 3. (vb. + —) manner ¶ དམག་མི་རྣམས་ཀྱི་གོམ་སྟབས་འགྲིགས་པོ་མི་འདུག The soldierùs manner of (marching) was not good (orderly).

སྟབས་ཀ་ (dəbga) 1. sm. སྟབས་, 3. 2. opportunity, chance ¶ ཚོགས་འདུའི་ཐོག་སྐད་ཆ་ཤོད་པའི་སྟབས་ཀ་ཐོབ་མ་བྱུང་ At the meeting I didn't get an opportunity to speak.

སྟབས་འཁེལ་ (dəb kēe) vi. to coincide (with) ¶ ང་འབྲས་ལྗོངས་ལ་འགྲོ་དུས་པད་མ་ལགས་ཕེབས་པ་དང་སྟབས་འཁེལ་འདུག When I went to Sikkim it coincided with Pemala's coming.

སྟབས་འགྲིག(ས་) (dəbdrig) 1. coincidence ¶ ལྷ་སར་ཡོད་སྐབས་ལ་ཚོགས་འདུ་འཚོགས་པ་དང་སྟབས་འགྲིག་ཏེ་ཚོགས་འདུར་ཞུགས་པ་ཡིན་ The meeting coincided with my being in Lhasa and I attended it. 2. slang. if it is okay/ convenient ¶ སང་ཉིན་ཁྱེད་རང་ལ་སྟབས་འགྲིགས་ན་ངའི་སར་ཕེབས་རོགས་གནང་ If it is convenient come visit me tomorrow.

སྟབས་ངན་(པ་) (dəb ŋəmba) unfortunate, unlucky ¶ སྟབས་ངན་ཞིག་ལ་ཁོའི་རྐང་པར་རྨས་སྐྱོན་བྱུང་བ་རེད་ Unfortunately, his foot got injured.

སྟབས་ཅིག (dəbjig) sm. ཆབས་ཅིག.

སྟབས་གཅིག་དོན་གཉིས་ (dəbjig tönñii) doing two things at one time, accomplishing two things at one time.

སྟབས་ཇ་ (dəbja) simple/ fast Tibetan butter tea (tea that is made of tea leaves that are only boiled for a few minutes, i.e., not brewed).

སྟབས་བསྟུན་ (dədün) 1. in accordance with ¶ འཆར་གཞི་དང་སྟབས་བསྟུན་ལས་ཀ་འགོ་འཛུགས་རྒྱུ་ཡིན་ (We) will start the work in accordance with the plan. 2. flexible, suited to particular circumstances ¶ སྟབས་བསྟུན་གྱི་སྲིད་ཇུས་ A flexible policy.

སྟབས་བསྟུན་གྱི་རང་བཞིན་ (dədüngi rəŋshin) flexibility.

སྟབས་དང་བསྟུན་ (dəbdaŋ dǖn) sm. སྟབས་བསྟུན་.

སྟབས་དོན་ (dəbdön) in brief.

སྟབས་བདེ་ (dəbde) 1. simple, convenient, easy, in brief; va.—བྱེད་ to do simply/ without elaboration; va.—བཟོ་; —གཏོང་ to simplify, to make simple ¶ སྟབས་བདེ་ས་ཁང་ Simple mud houses. ¶ ལྷ་སའི་འཁྱིམ་འགྱུལ་སྤྱར་ལས་སྟབས་བདེ་བྱུང་

Communications in Lhasa have become more convenient than before. ༡ བཟོ་པ་རྣམས་ཀྱིས་དེབ་གཡར་བར་སྟབས་བདེ་ཡོང་ཆེད་ For the purpose of making it easy for workers to borrow books. 2. (with negatives) feeling uneasy / uncomfortable ༡ མི་མང་པོ་ཡོད་སར་ལྟོ་ཆས་ཟ་རྒྱུ་སྟབས་བདེ་མ་བྱུང་བ་རེད་ He felt uneasy eating in front of all those people.

སྟབས་བདེ་ཐབས་ཆག་ (dābde tābjaà) (for goods) inferior, mediocre.

སྟབས་བདེ་པོ་ (dāb debo) easy, simple, convenient ༡ ཚོགས་འདུའི་ཐོག་རྒྱ་མི་འགའ་ཤས་སླེབས་ཡོད་ཙང་བོད་དོན་སྐོར་ཤོད་རྒྱུ་སྟབས་བདེ་པོ་མ་བྱུང་བ་རེད་ Because several Chinese came to the meeting it was not convenient to talk about the Tibetan question.

སྟབས་བདེ་ལྷ་བཅོས་ (dābde lājöö) doing sth. in a careless manner.

སྟབས་བདེའི་ཀལ་འཛུགས་ (dābdee kendzuù) simple hypothesis.

སྟབས་བདེའི་རྒྱ་ཐུག (dābdee gyəduù) instant noodles.

སྟབས་བདེའི་ངོས་མང་གཟུགས་ (dābdee ŋöömaŋ sug) simple polyhedron.

སྟབས་བདེའི་ཆ་གྲངས་ (dābdee cādraŋ) simple fraction (in math).

སྟབས་བདེའི་མཐའ་མང་དབྱིབས་ (dābdee tāmaŋ yīb) simple polygon.

སྟབས་བདེའི་བཟའ་བཅའ་ (dābde sabja) a snack, fast food.

སྟབས་བདེའི་ཡིག་གཟུགས་ (dābdee yigsuù) simplified characters (used in the PRC).

སྟབས་བདེའི་རི་མོ་ (dābdee cādraŋ) simple graph.

སྟབས་བདེའི་ལམ་ (dābdee lam) a shortcut (road).

སྟབས་བདེར་གཏོང་ (dābdee dōŋ) see སྟབས་བདེ་.

སྟབས་བདེར་བཟོ་ (dābdee so) see སྟབས་བདེ་.

སྟབས་སྦྱིལ་ (dābbel) sm. སྟབས་འབྱུལ་.

སྟབས་འབྱུལ་ (dābbüü) saying/ writing in brief (this is a phrase often used in letter headings).

སྟབས་མ་འགྲིག (dāb madrig) inconvenient, not okay.

སྟབས་མ་ལྡན་ (dāb mandɛn) sm. སྟབས་མ་འགྲིག.

སྟབས་མ་ལེགས་པ་ (dāb malegba) sm. སྟབས་མ་ལེགས་པར་.

སྟབས་མ་ལེགས་པར་ (dāb malegbar) unfortunately ༡ སྟབས་མ་ལེགས་པར་ཁོང་ལྷ་སར་སྐུ་གཤེགས་འདུག Unfortunately, (he) died in Lhasa.

སྟབས་མི་བདེ་བ་ (dāb midewə) inconvenient, difficult.

སྟབས་མི་ལེགས་པ་ (dāb milegba) sm. སྟབས་མ་ལེགས་པར་.

སྟབས་མཚུངས་སུ་ (dāb tsūŋsu) at the same time, simultaneously ༡ དེ་དང་སྟབས་མཚུངས་སུ་ At the same time as that.

སྟབས་ཞུ་ (dābshu) sm. སྟབས་འབྱུལ་.

སྟབས་ཡག (dābyaà) thank goodness, fortunately, luckily.

སྟབས་ཡག་ནས་ (dābyaànɛ) sm. སྟབས་ཡག.

སྟབས་ཡག་པོ་ (dāb yagbo) sm. སྟབས་ལེགས་.

སྟབས་རེ་ཤུ་རེ་ (dābre shūre) suddenly, unexpectedly.

སྟབས་ལ་རྒྱག (dābla gyaà) va. to carry sth. suspended on a pole over two shoulders ༡ འཕྲུལ་འཁོར་དེ་མི་བཞིས་སྟབས་ལ་བརྒྱབ་ནས་དཔོར་འདུག Four people carried the machine on (two) poles over their shoulders and moved it.

སྟབས་ལེགས་ (dābleg) fortunately, luckily; vi.—འཁེལ་ to get good fortune/ luck ༡ སྟབས་ལེགས་ཤིག་ལ་འགྲམ་ལ་ཨེམ་ཆི་ཞིག་ཡོད་པ་རེད་ Fortunately, there was a doctor nearby.

སྟབས་ལེགས་སྐབས་འཁེལ་ (dābleg gābgee) a fortunate/ lucky coincidence.

སྟབས་ལེགས་འཁེལ་ (dābleg kēē) see སྟབས་ལེགས་.

སྟབས་ལེགས་བྱུང་བ་ (dābleg cuŋwa) sm. སྟབས་ལེགས་.

སྟབས་ལེགས་རིང་ལུགས་ (dābleg riŋluù) opportunism.

སྟབས་ཤུར་ (dābshur) abbr. of སྟབས་རེ་ཤུ་རེ་.

སྟབས་གསོལ་ (dābsöö) sm. སྟབས་འབྱུལ་.

སྟར་: p. and f. **བསྟར་**; imp. **སྟོར་** (dār) 1. va. to arrange in a series or line. 2. va. (ལག་ལེན་ + —) to put into practice, to apply ༡ ཕྱི་ཚོས་སྤྱི་ཚོགས་རིང་ལུགས་ཀྱི་ལྟ་བ་དེང་སང་ལག་ལེན་བསྟར་གྱི་ཡོད་པ་རེད་ They are putting socialist ideology into practice these days.

སྟར་ཀ་ (dārga) sm. སྟར་ཁ་.

སྟར་ཀ་ཤིང་ (dārga shīŋ) walnut tree.

སྟར་ཀའི་སྡོང་པོ་ (dārgɛ doŋbo) sm. སྟར་ཀ་ཤིང་.

སྟར་ཀའི་ནང་ཚིག (dārgɛ naŋdzii) meat of a walnut.

སྟར་སྐོགས་ (dārgɔɔ) walnut shell.

སྟར་ཁ་ (dārga) walnut.

སྟར་ཁ་ཁ་བཤག (dārga kāshaà) breaking a walnut; va.—གཏོང་. 2. dividing in half/ equally; va.—གཏོང་ ༡ ཟ་ཚང་དེ་ཁག་ཁག་བྱས་ནས་རྒྱ་ནོར་རྣམས་སྟར་ཁ་ཁ་ཤག་བཏང་འདུག When that couple divorced, they divided all their wealth in half.

སྟར་ཁ་སྦག་བཤག (dārga bagshaà) sm. སྟར་ཁ་ཁ་བཤག.

སྟར་ཁའི་ཟ་ (dārgɛ sa) sm. སྟར་ཀའི་ནང་ཚིག.

སྟར་ག (dārga) sm. སྟར་ཁ་.

སྟར་འགྲིག་པོ་ (dār drigbi) 1. in a line, lined up. 2. orderly, neat, tidy.

སྟར་རྒྱུད་ (dārgyüü) sm. སྟར་ལ་རྒྱུད་.

སྟར་སྒྲིག (dār drii) va. to arrange in a line/ formation.

སྟར་གཅིག (dārjig) a string (of beads), a single line.

སྟར་གཅིག་ལ་རྒྱུད་ (dārjiglə gyüü) va. to string sth. in a single strand.

སྟར་ཆགས་ (dārjaà) one after another, continuously ༡ ལས་ཀའི་གོ་རིམ་སྟར་ཆགས་སུ་བསྒྲིགས་འདུག They arranged the work by stages one after another.

སྟར་ལྟག (dārdaà) the blunt side of an axe.

སྟར་སྡོང་ (dārdoŋ) walnut tree.

སྟར་ལྡོང་ (dārdoŋ) sm.* སྟར་སྡོང་.

སྟར་པ་ (dārba) a row/ line ༡ ནགས་ཚལ་སྟར་པ་བཙུགས་པ་རེད་ (They) planted the forest in rows.

སྟར་པ་གཅིག (dārba jīg) one line, one row, a queue.

སྟར་པ་གཅིག་ལ་རྒྱུད་ (dārba jīglə gyüü) sm. སྟར་གཅིག་ལ་རྒྱུད་.

སྟར་པང་ (dārbaŋ) walnut wood planks.

སྟར་ཕྲུགས་ (dārbaà) walnut shell.

སྟར་བ་ (dārwa) sm. སྟར་.

སྟར་བུ་ (dārbu) a fruit of a tree used in Tibetan medicine.

སྟར་མོ་ (dārmo) a large axe.

སྟར་ཞུན་ (dārshün) tree sap applied on the face for medicinal purposes.

སྟར་ཡུ་ (dāryu) axe handle.

སྟར་ལ་རྒྱུད་ (dārla gyüü) va. to string.

སྟར་ལ་བརྒྱུས་ (dārla gyüü) va. to string ༡ མུ་ཏིག་སྟར་ལ་བརྒྱུས་ནས་རྒྱན་ཆ་བཟོས་པ་བཞག (They) strung the pearls to make a piece of jewelry.

སྟར་ཤིང་ (dārshiŋ) walnut tree.

སྟར་སྦུབ་ (dārsub) the space in between lines or rows.

སྟར་སོ་ (dārso) axe edge.

སྟར་སོན་ (dārsön) walnut seed.

སྟི་: p. **བསྟིས་**; f. **བསྟི་**; imp. **སྟིས་** (dī) va. to stay somewhere in order to rest/ relax ༡ ལས་ཀ་ཉིན་ཤས་བྱས་རྗེས་སྐབས་ཤིག་རིང་ཙམ་ངལ་བསྟིས་པ་རེད་ After doing working for a few days, (he) stayed resting for awhile.

སྟི་ཀ་ (dīgə) sm. སྟི་ག.

སྟི་ག (dīgə) meat cut into small pieces, diced meat.

སྟི་སྟང་ (dīdaŋ) respect, reverence, honor; va.—བྱེད་ to respect, to show reverence, to honor.

སྟི་སྟང་ཅན་ (dīdaŋjɛn) respected, revered, honored.

སྟི་གནས་ (dīnɛɛ̀) 1. a place to stay, a home/ dwelling. 2. a central place, hub, base.

སྟིང་: p. **བསྟིངས་**; f. **བསྟིང་**; imp. **སྟིངས་** (dīŋ) 1. va. to scold, to rebuke. 2. va. to be satirical/ sarcastic.

སྟིངས་ (dīŋ) imp. of བསྟིང་.

སྟིམ་: p. **བསྟིམས་**; f. **བསྟིམ་**; imp. **སྟིམས་** (dīm) 1. va. to make (mix) two substances into one ༡ འོ་མ་ཆུ་ནང་ལ་བསྟིམས་ནས་ (He) mixed the milk into water. 2. vi. to be absorbed into sth. ༡ ཤ་ཁུ་ཤ་ལ་བསྟིམས་པ་རེད་ The meat gravy was absorbed into the meat. 3. bas-relief carving ། དངུལ་བསྟིམས་ཚག་མའི་བུམ་པ་ A vase with silver bas-relief carving. 4. va. to symbolically enter into a protective diety during meditation.

སྟིམས་ (dĩm) p.of སྟིམ་.

སྟིས་ (dĩi) imp. of སྟི་.

སྟུ་ (dū) vagina.

སྟུ་གསར་ (dūsar) sm. སོ་གསར་.

སྟུག་གེ་བ་ (dūggewa) thick, dense.

སྟུག་པོ་ (dūgbu) thick, close, dense ། ཤིང་ནགས་སྟུག་པོའི་ནང་ལ་ In a dense forest.

སྟུག་ཚད་ (dūgdzɛɛ̀) density.

སྟུག་ཚོད་ (dūgdzöö̀) density.

སྟུང་: p. བསྟུངས་; f. བསྟུང་; imp. སྟུངས་ (dūŋ) va. to make shorter.

སྟུངས་ (dūŋ) p. of སྟུང་.

སྟུད་: p. and f. བསྟུད་; imp. སྟུད་ (dũũ) va. to do continously, to do in succession ། ལོ་སྔོན་མའི་ལས་ཀའི་འཕྲོ་སྟུད་ཐུབ་པ་བྱ་དགོས་ We have to act so as to be able to continue last year's work.

སྟུད་མར་ (dũũmar) successively, in succession, one after another ། ན་ནིང་སྟུད་མར་དུས་ཚིགས་གསུམ་ལ་ཐོན་སྐྱེད་ཐོན་སྐྱོང་པར་བདམས་པ་རེད་ (He) was elected an outstanding worker last year for the third successive season. ། ཁ་ཚིག་སྟུད་མར་བསླབས་ཀྱང་ Even though they warned (them) successively.

སྟུད་མར་འགོད་ (dũũmar gö̀ö̀) va. to serialize (a story).

སྟུན་ (dũn) sm. བསྟུན་.

སྟུན་མཁས་ (dũnkɛɛ) accomodating oneself to the needs of sb.; va.—བྱེད་.

སྟུན་ཐབས་ (dũndəb) sm. སྟུན་མཁས་.

སྟུབས་ (dūb) sm. གདུབ་.

སྟེ་ (dē) a. the gerundive connective particle that is used after words ending in ག, ང, བ, མ and vowels and which generally forms relationships of the type usually glossed in English as "having" done one action another is done ། ཁོས་ཡི་གེ་འདི་ཚོ་བཏང་སྟེ་ནང་ལ་ཕྱིན་པ་རེད་ After he mailed the letters he went home. (Having mailed the letters, he went home.) ། ཁོ་ཚོས་སོན་ཚང་མ་བཏབ་སྟེ་ཁང་པ་བཟོ་བཅོས་རྒྱག་གི་ཡོད་པ་རེད་ Having planted all the crops (seeds) they are (now) fixing the house. b. linking two clauses so that the former explains the manner in which (or how) the latter occurs (the action of the two clauses is simultaneous) ། འཐུས་མི་ཚོ་ཚོགས་འདུ་ནས་གཞས་བཏང་སྟེ་ལོག་ཡོང་བ་རེད་ The delegates came back from the meeting singing. (How did they come back from the meeting? Singing they came back). ། ཁོས་སྐད་བརྒྱབ་སྟེ་ལན་བསྐྱལ་བ་རེད་ He delivered the message (by) shouting. (How did he deliver the message? In the manner of shouting he delivered the message). c. linking two clauses so that the latter defines, elaborates or tells sth. about the former; it is used both with linking and existential verbs and in place of them, and is sometimes also used with nominalized verb stems) ། སྟག་འཚེར་ནི་སོ་ནམ་པའི་ས་ཁུལ་ཞིག་སྟེ་ཟ་ཆས་གཙོ་བོ་གྲོ་དང་ཤ་རེད་ Taktser is an agricultural area. Wheat and meat are its main foodstuffs.

སྟེ་ཁ་ (dēga) 1. sharp end of an adze. 2. a Tibetan medieval tool for surgery on the head.

སྟེ་ཁ་སོ་གཉིས་ (dēga sõñĩi) double-edged medical tool for operating on the head (in Tibetan medicine).

སྟེ་པོ་ (dēbo) sm.* སྟེའུ་.

སྟེ་ལྟག་ (dēdaà) the blunt side of an axe.

སྟེ་གཙག་ (dēdzaà) a small adze.

སྟེ་གཤོག་རྒྱག་ (dēshoò gyaà) va. to pare down the side of a piece of wood with an adze.

སྟེ་ཡུ་ (dēyu) axe handle.

སྟེགས་ (dēg) sm. སྟེགས་བུ་.

སྟེགས་ཀ་ (dēgga) a device that allows the millstone in a grinding mill to raise or lower depending on how fine the grain should be ground.

སྟེགས་ཁེབས་ (dēggeb) the stand and cover (set) for a drinking cup.

སྟེགས་ཁྲི་ (dēgdri) scaffolding.

སྟེགས་རྒྱ་ (dēggya) a kind of scale.

སྟེགས་རྒྱུག་ (dēggyuù) a part of a water mill.

སྟེགས་ཅན་འཁྲུལ་འཁོར་ (dēgjɛn trũũgɔɔ) machine tools, machines for lathing [Lit. machines on platform bases].

སྟེགས་བུ་ (dēgbu) support, stand, rest, shelf, platform; va.—བརྡིག་ to undercut sb. ། ཁོས་སྟེགས་བུའི་སྟེང་དུ་འཛེགས་ནས་ཁང་པར་ཚོན་གཏོང་གི་འདུག He climbed up on a stand and painted the house.

སྟེགས་ཟམ་ (dēgsam) horizontal planks on scaffolding.

སྟེང་ (dēŋ) 1. on, on top of ། དེབ་ཀྱི་སྟེང་དུ་མེ་མདའ་གཅིག་འདུག There is a gun on top of the book. 2. upper part ། ས་ཆ་སྟེང་འོག The upper and lower part of the land. 3. on (a day/ date/ time) ། ཁོ་དུས་ཚོད་དག་དག་གི་སྟེང་དུ་སླེབས་བྱུང་ He came exactly on time.

སྟེང་ཀ་ (dēŋga) sm. ཁྲིན་པ་.

སྟེང་སྐས་ (dēŋgɛɛ̀) stairs on upper floors, the upper section of stairs/ ladder.

སྟེང་ཁང་ (dēŋgaŋ) the upper story.

སྟེང་གི་བཀོད་པ་ (dēŋgi göö̀ba) superstructure.

སྟེང་གི་བར་སྣང་ (dēŋgi parnaŋ) the sky.

སྟེང་གོས་ (dēŋgöö̀) outer layer clothing.

སྟེང་གྲིབ་ (dēŋdrib) a stroke; vi.—ཕོག to get a stroke.

སྟེང་ངོས་ (dēŋŋöö̀) on top of.

སྟེང་གཅལ་ (dēŋjɛɛ) sm. སྟེང་ཞལ་.

སྟེང་ཆས་ (dēŋjɛɛ̀) the upper part of a Tibetan woolen boot.

སྟེང་ཆས་ཀྱི་མེ་ཏོག (dēŋjɛɛ̀gi medog) the flower design on a Tibetan woolen boot.

སྟེང་ཐོག (dēŋdɔɔ̀) the upper floor/ level, upstairs.

སྟེང་དུ་ (dēŋdu) 1. on, on top of ། ཁང་པའི་སྟེང་དུ་ On top of the house. 2. to, with ། སྲིད་ཚབ་ལྷན་རྒྱས་སྟེང་དུ་དགོངས་སྐོར་ཞུས་སོང་ They consulted with the Acting Prime Minister. 3. while doing the verbal action ། སྡོད་པའི་སྟེང་དུ་ While staying there.

སྟེང་དིབ་འོག་དིབ་ (dēŋdib wɔ̀ɔ̀dib) collapsing from top to bottom.

སྟེང་རྡོ་ཡང་ན་འོག་རྡོ་འཕར་ (dēŋ doyaŋna wɔ̀ɔ̀ do pār) if the people at the top are not strict then the people below them will be undisciplined [Lit. if the stones on top are not heavy then the bottom stones will rise].

སྟེང་རྡོས་མ་ནོན་ན་འོག་རྡོ་འཕར་ (dēŋ döö̀ manönna wɔ̀ɔ̀ do pār) sm. སྟེང་རྡོ་ཡང་ན་འོག་རྡོ་འཕར་.

སྟེང་ན་ (dēŋna) sm. སྟེང་དུ་, 1.

སྟེང་ནས་ (dēŋnɛɛ̀) 1. from, from on top of. 2. by (indicates the actor in transitive constructions) ། སྲིད་ཚབ་ལྷན་སྟེང་ནས་བཀའ་གནང་བ་རེད་ The Acting Prime Minister gave an order.

སྟེང་ཕྱོགས་ (dēŋjɔɔ̀) sm. སྟེང་ངོས་.

སྟེང་མ་ (dēŋma) the above one, the one on top.

སྟེང་ཕྱོགས་ལྷ་ (dēŋjɔɔ̀ lhā) a kind of lesser diety that dwells in this world.

སྟེང་རྩ་ (dēŋdza) sm. སྟང་རྩ་.

སྟེང་རྩིག (dēŋdzeè) putting extra small bags/ cases on an animal load; va.—རྒྱག.

སྟེང་བརྩེགས་ (dēŋdzeg) sleeveless woman's dress worn over the basic dress.

སྟེང་འཛུགས་འོག་གཞུ་ (dēŋdzuù wɔ̀ɔ̀shu) stabbing from the top, hitting from the bottom (a martial arts spear maneuver).

སྟེང་ཞལ་ (dēŋshɛɛ) husband and wife, couple.

སྟེང་གཟའ་ (dēŋsa) sm. སྟེང་གྲིབ་.

སྟེང་འོག (dēŋwɔ̀ɔ̀) above and below, upstairs and downstairs, upper and lower, everywhere, all over ། ཁང་པའི་སྟེང་འོག་གང་སར་བལྟས་པ་ཡིན་ I looked all over the house. ། སྟེང་འོག་མེད་པར་

Everywhere.

སྟེང་འོག་འགྱུར་ (dēŋwɔ̀ɔ gyur) vi. to be/ get turned topsy turvy, to be overthrown.

སྟེང་འོག་སྒྱུར་ (dēŋwɔ̀ɔ gyur) va. to turn topsy turvy, to turn upside down, to overthrow.

སྟེང་འོག་བར་གསུམ་ (dēŋwɔ̀ɔ pərsum) the three: upper, bottom, and middle (usually conveys everywhere).

སྟེང་གཡོགས་ (dēŋyɔ̀ɔ) cover for putting on top of sth.

སྟེང་ལུད་ (dēŋlüü) top dressing (fertilizer); va.—རྒྱག to fertilized with top dressing fertilizer.

སྟེང་ཤོད་ (dēŋshöö) sm. སྟེང་འོག.

སྟེང་ཤོད་བར་གསུམ་ (dēŋshöö pərsum) the three: top, middle and bottom (usually conveys everywhere).

སྟེང་སོ་ (dēŋso) the upper teeth.

སྟེན་: p. and f. **བསྟེན་**; imp. **སྟེན་** (dēn) 1. va. to study with a teacher ༡ དགེ་རྒན་མང་པོ་བསྟེན་སྐབས་སྒྲུང་འབྲས་ང་ཚང་ཡག་པོ་བྱུང་ Because I studied with many teachers I got an excellent result. 2. va. to consult, to seek help/ advice ༡ ངས་ཁ་ས་ཨེམ་ཆི་བསྟེན་ཙང་ན་ཆ་དྲག་ཙམ་དྲག་བཞག Because I went to see a doctor yesterday, I have gotten a little better. ༡ ངས་ཚོང་རྒྱག་རྒྱུར་རོགས་པ་མི་གཅིག་བསྟེན་པ་ཡིན་ I sought help from a friend about doing business. ༡ བླ་མ་ལ་སྐྱབས་སུ་བསྟེན་དགོས་རེད་ You should seek refuge in a lama. 3. va. to keep/ raise/ rear ༡ ང་ཚོས་ད་ལོ་ནས་བཟུང་ར་ལུག་བསྟེན་པ་ཡིན་ We kept/ raise sheep and goats since this year.

སྟེམ་ (dēm) arc. va. to squeeze, pinch.

སྟེམས་ (dēm) va. to harm by a curse.

སྟེའུ་ (dīwu) 1. a small axe. 2. adze.

སྟེའུ་ཙག (dīwudzag) sm. སྟེ་གཙག.

སྟེར་ (dēr) va. to give ༡ ཁོ་ཚོར་དངུལ་སྟེར་བ་རེད་ (They) gave them money.

སྟེར་སྒོ་ (dērgo) dowry ༡ བུ་མོ་གཉའ་མར་གཏོང་རྒྱུའི་སྟེར་སྒོ་ཚང་མ་གྲ་སྒྲིག་བྱས་ཚར་ All the preparations have been made for the dowry when the daughter will be sent as a bride.

སྟེར་ཆ་ (dērja) things to be given (usu. as a gift/ donation).

སྟེར་ཆད་ (dērjɛɛ̀) a verbal agreement to give sth.

སྟེར་སྟེར་འཕྲོག་འཕྲོག (dērder trɔ̀ɔdrɔ̀ɔ) giving and then taking back, va.—བྱེད་ [Lit. giving giving, stealing stealing].

སྟེར་གནང་ (dērnaŋ) h. of སྟེར་.

སྟེར་སྦྱིན་རྗེས་འབྲང་ (dērjin jeèdraŋ) doing sth. as a result of being bribed or having received a gift; va.—བྱེད་.

སྟེར་ཚོང་ (dērdzoŋ) getting rid of, disposing of; va.—རྒྱག [Lit. to give and sell].

སྟེར་རེས་ (dērreè) taking turns giving ༡ སྤྲང་པོར་དངུལ་སྟེར་རེས་བྱས་པ་རེད་ (They) took turns giving money to the beggers.

སྟེར་ལན་ལྡོག (dērlɛn lɔ̀ɔ) 1. va. to reciprocate (sth. that was given to one). 2. va. to take revenge.

སྟེར་སློང་ (dērloŋ) giving and asking/ requesting; va.—བྱེད་ ༡ བོད་ཀྱི་བག་མ་སྟེར་སློང་གི་ལུགས་སྲོལ་ག་འདྲ་ཡིན་ནམ་ What is the Tibetan custom for giving and requesting brides?

སྟེས་ (dēè) sm. སྐབས་.

སྟེས་དབང་ (dēèwaŋ) spontaneous, natural, accidental ༡ ད་ལམ་གྱི་ཟིང་ཆ་དེ་སྟེས་དབང་དུ་བྱུང་བ་ཞིག་མ་རེད་ This current disturbance was not spontaneous (i.e., it was organized).

སྟེས་དབང་སྐབས་ལེགས་ (dēèwaŋ dəbleg) spontaneous, natural or accidental good luck ༡ ད་རེས་ང་ལ་ཚོང་ཡག་པོ་བྱུང་བ་དེ་སྟེས་དབང་སྐབས་ལེགས་སུ་བྱུང་བ་ཞིག་མ་རེད་ ངས་དཀའ་ལས་བརྒྱབ་ནས་བྱུང་བ་རེད་ My good fortune in business this time was not an accident. I worked hard for it.

སྟེས་དབང་ལམ་ལྷོང་ (dēèwaŋ lamlhoŋ) sm. སྟེས་དབང་སྐབས་ལེགས་.

སྟོ་ (dō) (with neg.) vi. to not matter ༡ ཆེད་མངགས་བྱས་པ་མིན་ན་ནོར་འཁྲུལ་དག་ཙམ་བྱུང་ཡང་སྟོ་མི་ཡོང་ Even if there are a few errors it does not matter so long as you didn't make them purposely.

སྟོ་ག་ (dōga) arc. a little.

སྟོང་ (dōŋ) 1. a thousand ༡ ཉིས་སྟོང་ Two thousand. 2. empty ༡ ཁང་སྟོང་ An empty house. 3. vi. to be or become empty/ finished/ exhausted ༡ མ་རྩ་སྟོང་ཞིན་ནས་ After (his) capital was finished. 4. sm. གཞིན་སྟོང་. 5. indemnity payment for murder of injury.

སྟོང་རྐང་ (dōŋgyaŋ) sm. སྟོང་སང་ས་.

སྟོང་རྐྱལ་ (dōŋgyɛɛ) swimming without a float or aid; va.—རྒྱག.

སྟོང་སྐུད་ (dōŋgüü) silk thread.

སྟོང་སྐུད་ཅབ་ཅབ་ (dōŋgüü cəbjəb) silk tassel.

སྟོང་སྐོར་ (dōŋgɔɔ) 1. shung. a chiliarchy. 2. turning around/ spinning without moving; vi.—རྒྱག.

སྟོང་སྐྱུག (dōŋgyuù) vomiting without throwing up anything; vi.—བྱེད་.

སྟོང་བསྐལ་ (dōŋgɛl) the end of the world/ eon.

སྟོང་ཁ་ (dōŋda) kilocalorie (kcal.).

སྟོང་ཁེ་ (dōŋge) kilogram (kg.).

སྟོང་ཁྲན་རྒྱལ་པོ་ (dōŋgün gyɛɛbo) ch.tib. the emperor of China.

སྟོང་ཁོག (dōŋgɔɔ) a remote/ empty place.

སྟོང་འཁོར་ (dōŋgɔɔ) sm. སྟོང་སྐོར་, 2.

སྟོང་འཁོར་ལོས་སྒྱུར་བའི་རྒྱལ་པོ་ (dōŋ kɔ̄ɔlö gyurwɛ gyɛɛbo) a universal monarch [Lit. a king who rules a thousand (realms)].

སྟོང་འཁྲུགས་ (dōŋdruù) a type of རླུང་ disease.

སྟོང་གྱོང་ (dōŋgyoŋ) a loss; vi.—ཕོག; —རག to get/ experience/ take a loss ༡ ལས་ཀ་གསར་པ་ཞིག་ཡོད་ལུགས་བཤད་ཙང་ངས་དེར་ཕྱིན་ཀྱང་ལས་ཀ་དེ་མི་འདུག་པས་ལམ་གྲོན་སྟོང་གྱོང་རག་བྱུང་ Because it was said there was a new job, I went there but there was no work so I took a loss for the travel expenses.

སྟོང་གྲངས་ (dōŋdraŋ) imaginary number (in math).

སྟོང་གླ་ (dōŋla) fare paid for an unloaded cart or sth. empty (e.g., the return trip of a taxi).

སྟོང་རྒྱུག (dōŋgyuù) doing sth. without getting any results, a fruitless act, a waste of time/ effort; vi.—བྱེད་ ༡ དེ་རིང་ཚོང་ཁང་ལ་ཕྱིན་ཀྱང་སྒོ་བརྒྱབ་པ་དང་སྐབས་འཕིལ་བས་སྟོང་རྒྱུག་བྱས་སོང་ Today I went to the store but it was closed so my going there was a waste of time. 2. running riderless (for horses/ riding mules); vi.—གློད་ ༡ རྟ་ཐང་སྟེང་དུ་དུས་སྟོང་རྒྱུག་གློད་ཀྱི་འདུག The horses are running riderless on the plain.

སྟོང་སྒྲུབ་ (dōŋ drub) 1. va. to pay an indemnity (for murder). 2. va. to pay a tax without having any tax base.

སྟོང་ཆ་ (dōŋja) 1. one thousandth. 2. blank/ empty space between sth. (e.g., words, lines).

སྟོང་ཆ་འབྲི་སྐོང་ (dōŋja trigoŋ) filling in the blank spaces (e.g., on an exam paper); va.—བྱེད་.

སྟོང་ཆམ་མེ་ (dōŋ cāmme) sm. སྟོང་སང་ངེ་.

སྟོང་མཆོད་ (dōŋjöö) a kind of offering that consists of a thousand of each of five items: flowers, incense, butter lamps, water offerings and torma.

སྟོང་མཆོད་དོ་དམ་པ་ (dōŋjöö todamba) shung. person in charge of the སྟོང་མཆོད་ offering.

སྟོང་མཇུག་མེད་པ་ (dōŋjuù meèba) sm. འགོ་མཇུག་མེད་པ་.

སྟོང་འཇལ་ (dōŋjɛɛ) shung. compensating sb. for murder; va. སྟོང་འཇལ་; —བྱེད་.

སྟོང་ཉིད་ (dōŋñii) abbr. of སྟོང་པ་ཉིད་.

སྟོང་ཉིད་རྟོགས་པའི་ཤེས་རབ་ (dōŋñii dōgbɛ shēèrəb) the knowledge /wisdom of understanding emptiness or the void.

སྟོང་ཉོ་སྟོང་འཚོང་ (dōŋño dōŋdzoŋ) speculating (in business); va.—རྒྱག.

སྟོང་སྙེག (dōŋñeg) 1. va. to chase sb. in vain. 2. shung. va. to go after sb. to obtain compensation for a killing.

སྟོང་གདམ་ (dōŋdam) empty/ meaningless talk.

སྟོང་སྟོང་ (dōŋdoŋ) a bell hung around the neck of a donkey.

སྟོང་ཐང་ (dōŋtaŋ) shung. the amount/ rate of the compensation for killing a person.

སྟོང་ཐུན་ (dōŋdün) the main points.

སྟོང་ཐོབ་ (dōŋdob) sm. སྟོང་ཐང་.

སྟོང་མཐའ་ (dōŋda) the 30th day of the Tibetan month.

སྟོང་དོན་ (dōŋdön) an ideological or abstract issue/ dimension (in opposition to a practical/ concrete/ real one).

སྟོང་སྡེ་ (dōŋde) shung. a village or a unit with a thousand households.

སྟོང་མདའ་ (dōŋda) shooting to scare off an enemy (firing at them but above their heads or into the air; va.—རྒྱག.

སྟོང་པ་ (dōŋba) empty, blank, vacant; va.—བཟོ་ to make empty/ vacant ¶ ཁང་པ་སྟོང་པའི་ནང་ལ་ In an empty house.

སྟོང་པ་ཉིད་ (dōŋbəñii) the void.

སྟོང་པ་མིན་ཙམ་ཞིག (dōŋba mi̱ndzamshig) sm. སྟོང་མིན་མཚོན་བྱེད་.

སྟོང་དཔོན་ (dōŋbön) shung. commander of a thousand (soldiers, households, etc.).

སྟོང་ཕྲག (dōŋdraà) a thousand ¶ སྟོང་ཕྲག་གཉིས་ Two thousand.

སྟོང་ཕྲག་ཁྲི་ཕྲག (dōŋdraà tri̱draà) sm. སྟོང་ཚོ་ཁྲི་ཚོ་.

སྟོང་འཕེན་ (dōŋben) a spear/ arrow that did not hit the target (or person).

སྟོང་བུ་ཆུང་ (dōŋbujuŋ) arc. a commander of less than one thousand troops/ households.

སྟོང་འབྲེལ་ (dōŋdree) empty/ meaningless relations or connections.

སྟོང་འབབ་ (dōŋbəb) the amount of money or goods paid in compensation.

སྟོང་མིན་མཚོན་བྱེད་ (dōŋmin tsōnjeè) a phrase conveying: so as not have come empty handed (I'm giving a small gift) ¶ དེ་ལམ་སྟོང་མིན་མཚོན་བྱེད་ངས་ཁྱེད་ལ་མེ་ཏོག་སོས་པ་ཞིག་འབུལ་རྒྱུ་ཡིན་ Today, so as not to be empty handed, I'm giving you a bunch of fresh flowers.

སྟོང་སྨི་ (dōŋmi) tib.ch. kilometer.

སྟོང་ཚོ་ (dōŋtso) a thousand of sth. (e.g., households, villages).

སྟོང་ཚོ་ཁྲི་ཚོ་ (dōŋtso tri̱tso) thousands and thousands, innumerable.

སྟོང་ཚོགས་ (dōŋtsɔɔ̀) a thousand religious offerings offered at one time.

སྟོང་ཚེ་རོག་པོ་ (dōŋdze rɔ̱gbo) sm. སྟོང་ཟེལ་.

སྟོང་འཚོལ་ (dōŋtsöö) fruitless search; va.—བྱེད་.

སྟོང་ཝ་ (dōŋwa) kilowatt.

སྟོང་ཟད་ (dōŋsɛɛ̀) depletion, waste, squandering; va.—གཏོང་ to deplete/ waste/ squander; vi.—འགྲོ་; —འགྱུར་ to be depleted/ wasted/ finished/ exhausted ¶ མཐར་རང་བཙན་གྱི་རེ་བ་སྟོང་ཟད་དུ་གྱུར་པ་རེད་ In the end, the hope of independence were finished. ¶ དེ་རིང་ཉིན་གང་གྲོགས་པོ་དང་སྐད་ཆ་བཤད་ནས་སྟོང་ཟད་བྱས་སོང་ Today I wasted the entire day talking to my friend. ¶ དགེ་རྒན་གསར་པ་དེས་རང་ཉིད་ཀྱི་དོན་དུ་དངུལ་ལ་སྤྱི་དངུལ་འབོར་ཆེན་སྟོང་ཟད་དུ་བཏང་བ་རེད་ The new teacher squandered a large amount of communal money on himself.

སྟོང་ཟུར་ (dōŋsur) one-thousandth.

སྟོང་འུད་ (dōŋwüü) boasting or showing off but not having any substance for doing so; va.—བྱེད་.

སྟོང་འུར་ (dōŋwur) sm. སྟོང་འུད་.

སྟོང་ར་ཅན་ (dōŋrajɛn) sm. སྟོང་ཚོ་.

སྟོང་རི་ཟིལ་པ་ (dōŋri si̱ibə) corydalis.

སྟོང་ལས་ (dōŋlɛɛ̀) work that has no result; va.—བྱེད་.

སྟོང་ལུས་ས་ཆ་ (dōŋlüù sāja) open/ unused/ empty ground.

སྟོང་ལོག (dōŋlɔɔ̀) returning empty-handed after not having accomplished (anything); va. སྟོང་ལོག; —བྱེད་.

སྟོང་བཤད་ (dōŋshɛɛ̀) sm. སྟོང་གདམ་.

སྟོང་ཤོབ་ (dōŋshob) sm. སྟོང་འུད་.

སྟོང་སང་ (dōŋsaŋ) completely empty.

སྟོང་སང་ངེ་ (dōŋsaŋŋe) sm. སྟོང་སང་.

སྟོང་སང་སང་ (dōŋ sāŋsaŋ) sm. སྟོང་སང་.

སྟོང་སངས་ (dōŋsaŋ) sm. སྟོང་སང་.

སྟོང་སེང་སེང་ (dōŋseŋseŋ) sm. སྟོང་སང་.

སྟོང་སོབ་ (dōŋsob) porous things that have no substance (like foam).

སྟོང་གསལ་ (dōŋsɛɛ) transparent.

སྟོང་བསམ་ (dōŋsam) 1. empty thought, pipe dream, wishful thinking; va.—འཆང་ to hold empty thoughts/ pipe dreams ¶ ངོ་ལོག་པས་གཞུང་མགོ་རྡིང་སློག་རྒྱུའི་སྟོང་བསམ་འཆང་གི་ཡོད་པ་རེད་ The rebels held the empty thought of (being able to) overthrow the government. 2. utopian thought.

སྟོང་བསམ་གྱི་གུང་ཁྲན་རིང་ལུགས་ (dōŋsamgi ku̱ŋdrɛn ri̱ŋluù) utopian communism.

སྟོང་བསམ་གྱི་སྤྱི་ཚོགས་རིང་ལུགས་ (dōŋsamgi ji̱dzoò ri̱ŋluù) utopian socialism.

སྟོང་བསམ་རིང་ལུགས་ (dōŋsam ri̱ŋluù) utopianism.

སྟོང་ལྷང་ལྷང་ (dōŋ lhālhaŋ) sm. སྟོང་སང་ངེ་.

སྟོངས་ (dōŋ) p. of སྟོང་.

སྟོངས་བསྐལ་ (dōŋgɛɛ) a period/ eon in which there is no Buddha.

སྟོངས་གྲོགས་ (dōŋdrɔɔ̀) sm. རོགས་པ་.

སྟོངས་གཙོད་ (dōŋjöò) sm. སྟོང་གཙོད་.

སྟོངས་གདབ་ (dōŋdəb) sm. རོགས་པ་.

སྟོངས་འདོགས་པ་ (dōŋdɔgba) sm. རོགས་པ་.

སྟོངས་པོ་ (dōŋbo) sm. བུད་སྟོངས་.

སྟོངས་མོ་ (dōŋmo) sm. རོགས་པ་.

སྟོད་ (dȍȍ) 1. the upper/ higher part ¶ གཟུགས་པོའི་སྟོད་ The upper part of the body. 2. Western Tibet.

སྟོད་: p. and f. བསྟད་; imp. སྟོད་ (dȍȍ) 1. va. to put on, to lay on ¶ རྟ་ལ་སྒ་བསྟད་ནས་ Having put a saddle on the horse. 2. sm. གདད་.

སྟོད་གོར་ (dȍȍgɔɔ) jacket.

སྟོད་ཀྱི་སྡིང་གཉིས་ (dȍȍgi dēŋñii) the two ancient kings of Tibet: ཁྲི་གུམ་བཙན་པོ་ and པུ་དེ་གུང་རྒྱལ་.

སྟོད་སྐོར་ (dȍȍgɔɔ) 1. upper part of a (valley). 2. the first part of a book, the first volume of a book.

སྟོད་སྐྱབ་ (dȍȍgyob) shirt.

སྟོད་ཁུལ་ (dȍȍgüü) upper/ higher area or region ¶ ཞིང་ཆེན་ཨ་སམ་གྱི་སྟོད་ཁུལ་ The upper part of Assam province.

སྟོད་ཁེབས་ (dȍȍgeb) a short jacket.

སྟོད་ཁོག (dȍȍgɔɔ̀) upper half of a carcass, upper part of the body.

སྟོད་ཁོག་མ་ལོང་གོང་ནས་སྨད་ཁོག་ལོང་ (dȍȍgɔɔ̀ ma̱loŋgoŋnɛ mɛɛ̀gɔɔ̀ lo̱ŋ) children having sexual desires too early [Lit. before the upper body is grown up, the lower body has grown].

སྟོད་གངས་རིན་པོ་ཆེ་ (dȍȍ ga̱n ri̱mboce) Mount Kailash.

སྟོད་གུག་གུག (dȍȍ gu̱ùguù) being hunchbacked, being hunched over.

སྟོད་གུག་ར་ (dȍȍguùrə) hunchbacked person, a person who is hunched over.

སྟོད་གོས་ (dȍȍgöö) 1. any top/ upper garment such as a shirt, vest or jacket. 2. sm. སྟོད་འགག.

སྟོད་གོས་ཕུ་མེད་ (dȍȍgöö pūmeè) any sleeveless upper garment such as a shirt/ blouse/ vest.

སྟོད་རྒྱུད་ (dȍȍgyüü) 1. upper reaches (of river). 2. sm. རྒྱུད་སྟོད་.

སྟོད་སྒག (dȍȍgaà) sm. སྟོད་འགག.

སྟོད་འགག (dȍngaà) monk's upper vest.

སྟོད་དགུར་ (dȍȍgur) sm.* སྟོད་གུག, 2.

སྟོད་སྒལ་ (dȍȍgɛɛ) the back (of humans and animals) ¶ དེ་རིང་ངའི་སྟོད་སྒལ་ན་གི་འདུག Today, my back hurts.

སྟོད་སྒུར་ (dȍȍgur) sm. སྟོད་གུག, 2.

སྟོད་སྒུར་པོ་ (dȍȍ gu̱rbu) hunchbacked, hunched over.

སྟོད་མངའ་རིས་ (dȍȍ ŋə̱rii) Western Tibet.

སྟོད་ཆ་ (dȍȍja) 1. introductory material/ forward (in a book, movie) 2. the upper part of sth. 3. the early part of a life ༑ ངའི་མི་ཚེའི་སྟོད་ཆར་སློབ་གྲྭར་འགྲོ་ལོང་མ་བྱུང་ In the early part of my life I didn't have time to go to school.

སྟོད་ཆར་ (dȍȍja) sm. སྟོད་ཆ་.

སྟོད་ཇ་ (dȍȍja) a brownish facial cosmetic made from whey that is used by women as a facial decoration/ skin protection; va.—འབྱུག to put on སྟོད་ཇ་.

སྟོད་ཇ་དཀར་པོ་ (dȍȍja kārbo) a white facial makeup worn by Tibetan women.

སྟོད་ཇ་དམར་པོ་ (dȍȍja mārbo) a red facial makeup worn by Tibetan women.

སྟོད་ཐུང་ (dȍȍduŋ) blouse, shirt.

སྟོད་ཐུང་ཧབ་ (dȍȍduŋ hāb) tib.eng. short-sleeved shirt/ blouse.

སྟོད་ད་ (dȍȍda) sm. སྟོད་ཐལ་.

སྟོད་ནད་ (dȍȍnɛѐ) diseases of the upper part of the body.

སྟོད་པ་ (dȍȍba) a person from Western Tibet.

སྟོད་པ་བ་ (dȍȍbawa) a person from Western Tibet.

སྟོད་ཕོར་ (dȍȍbɔɔ) a wooden bowl made in Western Tibet.

སྟོད་ཕྱོགས་ (dȍȍjɔɔ̀) 1. the upper part of a (valley). 2. the direction of Western Tibet.

སྟོད་འབྲས་ (dȍndrɛɛ̀) rice that comes from Western Tibet.

སྟོད་སྨད་ (dȍȍmɛɛ̀) upper and lower ༑ ཀུན་མ་ལུང་པའི་སྟོད་སྨད་གཉིས་ཀར་སླེབས་པ་རེད་ The thieves arrived in both the upper and lower part of the valley.

སྟོད་སྨད་བར་གསུམ་ (dȍȍ mɛɛ̀ parsum) the three: upper, lower and middle (usually conveys all, everything).

སྟོད་ཚ་འཚངས་པ་ (dȍȍtsa tsāŋwa) an illness characterized by fever in the upper part of the body.

སྟོད་ཚག (dȍȍdzaà) sm. སྟོད་སློག.

སྟོད་གཞས་ (dȍȍshɛɛ̀) songs from the སྟོད་ region.

སྟོད་ཟངས་ (dȍȍsaŋ) a type of copper pot made in སྟོད་.

སྟོད་ཟོག (dȍȍsoò) goods produced in Western Tibet.

སྟོད་གཟུགས་ (dȍȍsug) the upper half of a carcass.

སྟོད་གཟེར་ (dȍȍser) pain in the back.

སྟོད་གཡོག (dȍȍyɔɔ̀) a garment put on the upper body of a statue.

སྟོད་ལང་ (dȍȍlaŋ) sitting up (in bed) so that the upper half is sitting and the lower half (from waist down) is prone/ horizontal; va.—རྒྱག.

སྟོད་ལུང་ (dȍȍluŋ) district near Lhasa.

སྟོད་ལེ་ (dȍȍle) blouse, shirt.

སྟོད་སློག (dȍȍlɔɔ̀) a upper garment made of sheep/ goat skin worn with the fleece on the inside.

སྟོད་གསང་ (dȍȍsaŋ) Tibetan medical term for spaces inside the upper body where there are no vital organs.

སྟོད་གསང་ཤུལ་མོ་ (dȍȍsaŋ cɛɛ̄mo) sm. སྟོད་གསང་.

སྟོད་གསེར་ (dȍȍser) gold from the region of སྟོད་.

སྟོད་ཧོར་ (dȍȍhɔɔ) Mongolians from the region of སྟོད་.

སྟོད་ཧྲང་ (dȍȍhraŋ) the upper part of the body naked; va.—ཕུད to take off one's upper garments (so that the upper part of the body is naked).

སྟོད་ཧྲང་བ་ (dȍȍhraŋwa) person with no clothes on the upper part of the body.

སྟོད་ཧྲེང་ (dȍȍhreŋ) sm. སྟོད་ཧྲང་.

སྟོད་ཧྲེང་མ་ (dȍȍhreŋma) sm. སྟོད་ཧྲང་བ་.

སྟོད་ལྷེ་ (dȍȍlhe) sm. སྟོད་གཡོག.

སྟོད་ལྷོད་ཤིག་ཤིག (dȍȍlhoȍ shīgshiì) peaceful, relaxed.

སྟོན་: p. and f. བསྟན་; imp. སྟོན་ (dȍn) va. to show/ point out; to teach ༑ དེབ་འདིས་གསར་བརྗེའི་ཁ་ཕྱོགས་ཡང་དག་པ་སྟོན་གྱི་ཡོད་པ་རེད་ This book points out the correct revolutionary direction. ༑ འགྲོ་ལམ་བསྟན་པའི་དཔོན་པོ་འདི་ The leader who showed the way.

སྟོན་ (dȍn) 1. autumn ༑ སྟོན་དཔྱིད་ Autumn and spring. 2. banquet, feast, party ༑ བག་སྟོན་ Wedding banquet.

སྟོན་ཀ་ (dȍnga) autumn, fall ༑ སྟོན་ཀའི་བང་བསྡུ་ Autumn harvest.

སྟོན་ཀའི་མེ་ཏོག (dȍngɛ me̲dog) 1. lily. 2. things that don't last long [Lit. fall flower].

སྟོན་ཀའི་ཚ་གདུག (dȍngɛ tsəduù) sm. སྟོན་ཚད་.

སྟོན་ཀའི་མཚེར་ས་ (dȍngɛ tsērsa) sm. སྟོན་མཚེར་.

སྟོན་ཁ་ (dȍnga) sm. སྟོན་ཀ་.

སྟོན་ཁ་འབྲས་བུའི་མེ་ཏོག (dȍnga drɛ̲ɛbü me̲dog) a kind of floral design on brocade.

སྟོན་ཁའི་འབྲུབ་ཆུ་ (dȍngɛ dru̲bju) autumn floods.

སྟོན་འཁོར་ (dȍngɔɔ) shung. 1. the teacher/ lama and his retinue or servant. 2. the main person and his retinue/ servant.

སྟོན་གླུ་ (dȍnlu) songs sung during parties.

སྟོན་དགུན་མཚམས་ (dȍngün tsām) the transition period between fall and winter.

སྟོན་རྒྱབ་ (dȍngyəb) the end/ latter part of autumn.

སྟོན་རྒྱབ་པ་ (dȍngyəbba) shung. person who oversees autumn harvest work.

སྟོན་ཆེན་ (dȍnjen) shung. a heaped pile of meat and cookies set out by the tt. government at special ceremonies at which the people are allowed to rush and grab as much as they can; va.—གཤོམ་ to lay out the display of meats and cookies.

སྟོན་མཆོད་ (dȍnjöȍ) autumn religious festival where offerings are made to dieties.

སྟོན་མཇུག (dȍnjuù) the latter part of autumn.

སྟོན་མཇུག་ལོ་ཏོག (dȍnjuù l̲odoò) late autumn harvest/ crops (a crop that is harvested in late autumn).

སྟོན་ཉིན་མཚན་མཉམ་ (dȍnñin tsɛ̄nñam) sm. སྟོན་མཉམ་.

སྟོན་མཉམ་ (dȍnñam) autumn equinox (occurring during 8th month of the Tibetan calendar).

སྟོན་ཏོག (dȍndoò) sm. སྟོན་ཐོག.

སྟོན་ཐ་མ་ (dȍn tāma) the 9th month of the Tibetan calendar, the third month of autumn.

སྟོན་ཐེང་ནས་ (dȍndeŋnɛ) shung. from the harvest ༑ ཕྱི་ལོ་སྟོན་ཐེང་ནས་ངོ་སྐྱེད་བུངས་ཚང་འབུལ་ཆོག We will pay the principal and the interest of the loan from next year's harvest.

སྟོན་ཐོག (dȍndɔɔ̀) crops, harvest; va.—སྡུད་ to harvest ༑ སྟོན་ཐོག་ཡག་པོ་བྱུང་སོང་ (They) had a good crop.

སྟོན་ཐོག་བང་བསྡུ་མཉམ་འབྲེལ་འཕྲུལ་འཁོར་ (dȍndɔɔ̀ ŋədu ñāmdree trűügɔɔ) combine harvester.

སྟོན་ཐོག་སྔ་མ་ (dȍndɔɔ̀ ŋāma) the first harvest (if there are two in a year).

སྟོན་ཐོག་ཕྱི་མ་ (dȍndɔɔ̀ cīmə) the second harvest (if there are two in a year).

སྟོན་ཐའི་སྐར་ཚད་ (dȍndɛ ga̲ŋdzɛɛ̀) middle of the 9th Tibetan month.

སྟོན་ཐའི་དབུགས་ཐོབ་ (dȍtɛ ūgdob) the beginning of the 9th Tibetan month.

སྟོན་དུས་ (dȍndüȕ) autumn, fall.

སྟོན་འདེབས་ (dȍndeb) autumn planting; va.—བྱེད་.

སྟོན་དོད་ (dȍndöȍ) money given in lieu of the actual provisions for a party/ feast/ banquet.

སྟོན་སྡུད་ (dȍndüȕ) autumn harvesting; va.—བྱེད་.

སྟོན་སྡུད་འོས་ལངས་ (dȍndüȕ ö̲ölaŋ) sm. སྟོན་བསྡུའི་འོས་ལངས་.

སྟོན་བསྡུ་ (dȍndu) va. to harvest.

སྟོན་བསྡུའི་འོས་ལངས་ (dȍndü ö̲ölaŋ) the Autumn Harvest Uprising (an armed uprising led by Mao Zedong in 1927 in Hunan-Jiangxi Provinces).

སྟོན་བསྡུས་ (dȍndüȕ) p. of སྟོན་བསྡུ་.

སྟོན་ནམ་ (dȍnnam) 1. autumn night. 2. sm. སྟོན་གནམ་.

སྟོན་ནས་ (dȍnnɛ) autumn barley.

སྟོན་གནམ་ (dȍnnam) 1. the autumn sky. 2. the

autumn climate/ weather.

སྟོན་པ་ (dõmba) 1. the Buddha. 2. a religious teacher/ prophet.

སྟོན་པ་པོ་ (dõmbabo) 1. teacher of religion. 2. guide, scout.

སྟོན་པ་གཤེན་རབས་ (dõmba shēnrəb) the name of the founder of the Bon religion.

སྟོན་པ་ཤཱཀྱ་ཐུབ་པ་ (dõmba shāggya tūbbə) Shakyamuni Buddha.

སྟོན་པ་ཡེ་ཤུ་ (dõmba ye̱shu) Jesus.

སྟོན་པ་ཡེ་ཤུའི་འཁྲུངས་སྐར་ (dõmba ye̱shü trūŋgar) Christmas [Lit. the birthday of Jesus].

སྟོན་པའི་ཆོས་ལུགས་ (dõmbɛ cȭõluù) Buddhism, the Buddhist religion.

སྟོན་པའི་བསྟན་པ་ (dõmbɛ dēmba) the doctrine of the Buddha, Buddhism.

སྟོན་པའི་དབུ་ལ་བྱིས་པའི་ལག་རྩེད་ (dõmbɛ ūla ciìbɛ la̱gdzeè) ordinary people insulting/ demeaning high ranking people [Lit. children playing with the Buddha's head].

སྟོན་པའི་མཛད་པ་དུས་ཆེན་བཞི་ (dõmbɛ dzɛ̱ɛ̀ba tü̱ü̱jēnshi) four main religious festivals commemorating: the Buddha's coming down from realms of gods, his first teaching of the doctrine, his performing of miracles, and his obtaining enlightenment.

སྟོན་དཔྱིད་ (dõnjiì) autumn and spring.

སྟོན་དཔྱིད་ནི་བསྐྱལ་ (dõnjiì ni̱ gyɛ̄ɛ) having enough food to last from autumn through spring.

སྟོན་སྤྲིན་ (dõndrin) autumn clouds.

སྟོན་བལ་ (dõmpɛɛ) wool that is sheared during autumn.

སྟོན་བྱུང་ (dõnjuŋ) shung. the yield from the harvest ¶ ཆུ་སྤྲེ་ལོའི་སྟོན་བྱུང་རྩྭ་འབྲུ་རྣམས་བསྡུ་འཇུག་བྱ་རྒྱུ་ The yield in grain and hay of the Water Monkey Year shall be stored.

སྟོན་འབབ་ (dõmbəb) the yield from the harvest ¶ ད་ལོ་སྟོན་འབབ་ཡག་པོ་བྱུང་སོང་ This year we had a great harvest yield.

སྟོན་འབྲས་ (dõndrɛɛ̀) sm. སྟོན་ཐོག.

སྟོན་འབྲས་གཏའ་འཇོག (dõndrɛɛ̀ dā jɔ̱ɔ̀) shung. an autumn harvest that has been pledged as security/ pawn for repayment of a loan that was received.

སྟོན་འབྲས་བསྡུས་མཚམས་ (dõndrɛɛ̀ dü̱ndzam) shung. sm. སྟོན་སྨིང་ནས་.

སྟོན་འབྲས་ཚར་མ་ (dõndrɛɛ̀ tsārma) harvested grain with the grain still attached to the stalks.

སྟོན་འབྲིང་ (dõndriŋ) the 8th Tibetan month, the middle month of Autumn.

སྟོན་འབྲིང་དབུགས་ཐོབ་ (dõndriŋ ūùdob) beginning of the 8th (the middle) month of the Tibetan calendar.

སྟོན་མ་དབྱར་ (dõnmayar) the transition period between summer and fall.

སྟོན་མིན་ (dõnmin) the Chinese monk Mahayana who taught Buddhism in Tibet during the reign of Trisong Detsen.

སྟོན་མོ་ (dõnmo) 1. banquet, feast; va.—འདྲེན་; —གསོལ་; —འགྱེད་; —གཏོང་ to give a banquet. 2. a show, a performance (usu. with food); va.—འགྱེད་; —གཏོང་ to give a show/ performance (usu. with food).

སྟོན་རྨོ་ (dõnmo) sm. སྟོན་རྨོས་.

སྟོན་རྨོད་ (dõnmöö) sm. སྟོན་རྨོས་.

སྟོན་རྨོས་ (dõnmöö) autumn plowing; va.—རྒྱག.

སྟོན་སྨད་ (dõnmɛɛ̀) sm. སྟོན་མཇུག.

སྟོན་སྨིན་ལོ་ཏོག (dõnmin lo̱doò) crops that ripen in autumn.

སྟོན་ཙེན་རྩོད་པ་ (dõndzen dzȭõba) the great religious debate that took place during the time of Trisong Detsen between the Chinese and Indian forms of Buddhism.

སྟོན་ཚད་ (dõndzɛɛ̀) autumn heat, the heat characteristics of autumn.

སྟོན་ཚིག (dõndziì) predicate.

སྟོན་ཚུགས་ (dõndzuù) the beginning of autumn.

སྟོན་མཚམས་ (dõndzam) shung. sm. སྟོན་སྨིང་ནས་.

སྟོན་མཚེར་ (dõndzer) autumn camp/ dwelling.

སྟོན་ཞོད་ (dõnshöö) autumn rainfall.

སྟོན་གཞུག (dõnshuù) sm. སྟོན་མཇུག.

སྟོན་ཟས་ཁ་ཕྱི་དུས་སྦལ་ཁ་འཁྱིག (dõnsɛɛ̀ kācedüü bɛ̱ɛ̱ kādrig) to be not ready to make use of an opportunity [Lit. when there is lots of autumn food, the frog's mouth is stuck closed].

སྟོན་ཟུག (dõnsug) the beginning of autumn.

སྟོན་ཟླ་ (dõnda) an autumn month (the Tibetan 7th, 8th and 9th months).

སྟོན་ཟླ་ཐ་ཆུང་ (dõnda tājuŋ) the last month of autumn, the 9th Tibetan month.

སྟོན་ཟླ་འབྲིང་བ་ (dõnda driŋjuŋ) the middle month of autumn, the 8th Tibetan month.

སྟོན་ཟླ་ར་བ་ (dõnda ra̱wa) the first month of autumn, the 7th Tibetan month.

སྟོན་ཡུར་ (dõnyur) irrigation done in autumn.

སྟོན་གཡོག (dõnyɔɔ̀) workers hired for the period of fall harvest.

སྟོན་ར་བ་ (dõn ra̱wa) sm. སྟོན་ཟླ་ར་བ་.

སྟོན་རའི་སྐང་ཚད་ (dõnrɛ ga̱ndzɛɛ̀) the middle of the 7th Tibetan month.

སྟོན་རའི་དབུགས་ཐོབ་ (dõnrɛ ūùdob) the beginning of the 7th month of the Tibetan calendar.

སྟོན་ལས་ (dõnlɛɛ̀) work done during autumn.

སྟོན་ལྷུང་ (dõnluŋ) sm. སྟོན་ལྷགས་.

སྟོན་ལོག (dõnlɔɔ̀) turning over the soil in autumn; va.—རྒྱག.

སྟོན་ཤེད་ (dõnsheè) the sheen of livestock in autumn, the fatty state of animals in autumn.

སྟོན་གཤོལ་ (dõnshöö) plow used in autumn.

སྟོན་བསིལ་ (dõnsii) a cool autumn day.

སྟོན་ལྷགས་ (dõnlhaà) autumn winds.

སྟོབ་ p. བསྟབས་; f. བསྟབ་; imp. སྟོབས་ (dōb) va. to give/ offer sth. ¶ སྐུ་མགྲོན་ཚོར་གསོལ་ཚིགས་བསྟབས་པ་རེད་ (They) gave food to the guests.

སྟོབས་ (dōb) strength, force, power ¶ སྟོབས་ཆེ་ Great strength. 2. imp. of སྟོབ་.

སྟོབས་ཀྱིས་ (dōbgi) with or by strength/ force/ power, because ¶ སྟོབས་ཀྱིས་དགྲ་བོ་རྣམས་མནན་པ་རེད་ By force (they) subdued the enemy. ¶ རིག་པ་རྣོ་བའི་སྟོབས་ཀྱིས་ཡོན་ཏན་གང་ཡང་ཁོང་དུ་འཆུད་བདེ་བ་ Because (by the power) of being intelligent it is easy for (him) to study.

སྟོབས་སྐྱེད་ (dōb gyēè) vi. to increase physical strength or weight or power.

སྟོབས་བསྐྱེད་སྨན་ (dōbgyeèmɛn) vitamin.

སྟོབས་རྒྱས་ (dōbgyɛɛ̀) 1. sm. སྟོབས་སྐྱེད་. 2. man's name.

སྟོབས་རྒྱུ་ (dōbgyu) a type of nāga.

སྟོབས་འགྱེད་ (dōŋgyeè) test/ contest of strength.

སྟོབས་ངན་ (dōŋɛn) weak, frail.

སྟོབས་ཅན་ (dōnjɛn) sm. སྟོབས་ལྡན་.

སྟོབས་ཆུང་ (dōbjuŋ) weak, powerless.

སྟོབས་ཆེ་ (dōbce) great strength/ power/ might ¶ སྟོབས་ཆེ་བའི་རྒྱལ་ཁབ་ A powerful country.

སྟོབས་ཆེ་ཆུང་ (dōn ciìjuŋ) 1. degree or level or amount of strength/ power ¶ དམག་ཐོག་ལ་རྒྱ་གར་སྟོབས་ཆེ་ཆུང་ག་འདྲ་ཡོད་དམ་ Militarily, how powerful is India? 2. size of a person ¶ བུ་སྤུན་དེ་གཉིས་སྟོབས་ཆེ་ཆུང་མི་འདྲ་བ་ཡོད་ཙང་ཕྱུ་པ་ཆེ་ཆུང་མི་འདྲ་བ་བཟོ་དགོས་ཀྱི་འདུག Because the two brothers are different in size, different size clothing needs to be made. 3. wealth ¶ མི་ཚང་དེ་གཉིས་དབར་སྟོབས་ཆེ་ཆུང་ཞེ་དྲག་ཤོར་བབ There is a big difference in the size (wealth) of these two families.

སྟོབས་ཆེན་ (dōbjen) sm. སྟོབས་ཆེ་.

སྟོབས་ཆེན་ཁྱུང་དཀར་ (dōbcen kyūŋgar) unrivaled power/ strength.

སྟོབས་ཆེན་པོ་ (dōb cēmbo) 1. sm. སྟོབས་ཆེ་. 2. stout, well built.

སྟོབས་ཆེར་གཏོང་ (dōbcer dōŋ) va. to strengthen, to

increase power/ strength/ force.

སྟོབས་ཉམས་ (dōb ñam) vi. to get dissipated in strength.

སྟོབས་མཉམ་ (dōbñam) equal in strength.

སྟོབས་ལྡན་ (dōbdɛn) powerful, strong ¶ སྟོབས་ལྡན་སྤྱི་ཚོགས་རིང་ལུགས་ཀྱི་རྒྱལ་ཁབ་ Powerful socialist states.

སྟོབས་ལྡན་བོངས་ཆུང་ (dōbdɛn poŋjuŋ) short but strong/ powerful.

སྟོབས་ལྡན་ཟིལ་ཤུགས་ (dōbdɛn siishuù) powerful and fierce.

སྟོབས་ནག (dōbnaà) sm. ལས་ནག.

སྟོབས་ནུས་ (dōbnüü) strength, power, energy.

སྟོབས་སྣོན་དཔུང་གསར་ (dōbnön būŋsar) fresh troops, reinforcements.

སྟོབས་པོ་ཆེ་ (dōbboce) 1. sm. སྟོབས་ཤུགས་ཆེ་. 2. a wrathful deity. 3. name of a sutra.

སྟོབས་བྲི་ (dōbdri) sm. སྟོབས་ཉམས་.

སྟོབས་འབྱོར་ (dōmjɔɔ) 1. power and wealth/ prosperity. 2. a man's name.

སྟོབས་འབྱོར་དར་རྒྱས་ (dōmjɔɔ targyɛɛ) strong/ powerful and developed.

སྟོབས་འབྱོར་ལྡན་པ་ (dōmjɔɔ dɛmba) sm. སྟོབས་འབྱོར་ཆེ་བ་.

སྟོབས་མེད་ (dōbmeè) sm. སྟོབས་ཆུང་.

སྟོབས་མེད་འབྱོར་སྤྲལ་ (dōbmeè jɔɔdrɛɛ) physically and materially weak/ poor.

སྟོབས་རྩལ་ (dōbdzɛɛ) sports that test power and strength; va.—འགྲན་ to compete in power and strength.

སྟོབས་རྩལ་ཆེན་པོ་ (dōbdzeɛ cēmbo) one who is skilled in sports/ martial arts/ riding/ etc.

སྟོབས་རྩལ་བ་ (dōbdzɛɛwa) sm. སྟོབས་རྩལ་ཆེན་པོ་.

སྟོབས་ཚད་ (dōbdzɛè) the degree/ amount of strength.

སྟོབས་མཚུངས་པ་ (dōb tsūŋbə) a balance of power/ strength.

སྟོབས་ཞན་ (dōbshɛn) sm. སྟོབས་ཆུང་.

སྟོབས་ཞན་ཤུགས་མེད་ (dōbshɛn shūgmeè) weak, feeble.

སྟོབས་ཟད་ (dōbsɛè) sm. སྟོབས་ཉམས་.

སྟོབས་བཟང་ (dōbsaŋ) sm. སྟོབས་ཆེན་.

སྟོབས་རལ་ཆེན་པོ་ (dōbrɛɛ cēmbo) sm. སྟོབས་རྩལ་ཆེན་པོ་.

སྟོབས་ཤུགས་ (dōbshuù) strength, force, power; va.—སྤེལ་ to develop/ increase strength or power; vi.—འཕེལ་ to have strength/ power get developed; vi.—གུད་; —ཉམས་; —ཆག to have power/ strength decline; vi.—ཟད་ to have one's strength/ power fade/ wear out; vi.—རྫོགས་ to have one's power/ strength be used up/ exhausted ¶ འཐབ་འཛིང་གི་སྟོབས་ཤུགས་ Fighting strength. ¶ དམག་པོའི་སྟོབས་ཤུགས་ཆེན་པོ་ཞིག་ཏུ་འཕེལ་བ་རེད་ (They) developed into a powerful military force.

སྟོབས་ཤུགས་ཀྱི་ཁྱབ་ཡུལ་ (dōbshuùgi bēlyüü) sm. སྟོབས་ཤུགས་ཁྱབ་ཁོངས་.

སྟོབས་ཤུགས་ཁྱབ་ཁོངས་ (dōbshuù kyəbgoŋ) sphere of influence.

སྟོབས་ཤུགས་གུད་ (dōbshuù güü) vi. to decline in strength/ force/ power.

སྟོབས་ཤུགས་གསོ་སྐྱོང་ (dōbshuù sōgyoŋ) nurturing or conserving strength/ power; va.—བྱེད་.

སྟོབས་ཤེད་ (dōbsheè) sm. སྟོབས་ཤུགས་.

སྟོབས་གསར་དཔུང་སྡེ་ (dōbsar būŋde) sm. སྟོབས་གསར་དམག་དཔུང་.

སྟོབས་གསར་དམག་དཔུང་ (dōbsar məgbuŋ) reinforcements, fresh troops.

སྟོར་ (dɔ̄ɔ) sm. གཏོར་.

སྟོར་རྒྱན་ (dɔ̄ɔgyen) sm. གཏོར་རྒྱན་.

སྟོར་ཁང་ (dɔ̄ɔguŋ) sm. གཏོར་ཁང་.

སྟོར་བརླག (dɔ̄ɔlaà) sm. གཏོར་བརླག.

བརྟ་: p. བརྟས་ or རྟས་; f. བརྟ་ (dā) 1. vi. to grow (in strength/ power/ size) ¶ ཁོའི་ལུས་སྟོབས་བརྟས་བཞག His physical strength/ stature has grown. 2. vi. to be/ get happy ¶ ཁྱེད་ཀྱི་ཕྱག་བྲིས་འབྱོར་བ་ཡོད་སྤྲོ་བརྟས་ I am happy tthat your letter arrived.

བརྟག (dāà) 1. f. of རྟོག. 2. va. to examine, to study, to research ¶ གནད་དོན་ཐག་མ་བཅད་གོང་ལེགས་པར་བརྟག་དགོས་པ་རེད་ (One) must investigate the matter well before deciding.

བརྟག་ཐབས་ཀྱི་རྣམ་བཤད་ (dāgdəbgi nāmshɛè) sm. བརྟག་ཐབས་སྨྲ་བ་.

བརྟག་ཐབས་སྨྲ་བ་ (dāgdəb māwa) 1. way of examining/ studying. 2. methodology ¶ འབྱོར་ལྡན་གྲལ་རིམ་གྱི་བརྟག་ཐབས་སྨྲ་བ་ A bourgeoise methodology.

བརྟག་ཐབས་རིག་པ་ (dāgdəb rigbə) 1. the science of diagnosing. 2. the science of methodology.

བརྟག་པ་ (dāgba) divination; va.—གནང་; —ཞུ་ to ask for divination (usu. from a lama).

བརྟག་པ་མཐར་བཟུང་ (dāgba tārsuŋ) suppositional/ conjectural clause.

བརྟག་དཔྱད་ (dāgjɛè) study, research, examination; va.—བྱེད་ ¶ མའོ་ཙེ་ཏུང་གི་གཞུང་ལུགས་ལ་བརྟག་དཔྱད་བྱེད་དགོས་ One should study the theories of Mao Zedong.

བརྟག་དཔྱད་ཐིག་ལེན་ (dāgjɛè tiglen) surveying; va.—བྱེད་.

བརྟག་དཔྱད་ཐིག་ལེན་པ་ (dāgjɛè tiglenba) surveyor.

བརྟག་དཔྱད་སྡེ་ཚན་ (dāgjɛè dedzɛn) research unit/ department.

བརྟག་དཔྱད་པ་ (dāgjɛɛ̀ba) analyst, researcher ¶ རྫས་འགྱུར་བརྟག་དཔྱད་པ་ Chemical analyst.

བརྟག་དཔྱད་ཚད་ལེན་ (dāgjɛè tsɛ̄èlen) sm. བརྟག་དཔྱད་ཐིག་ལེན་.

བརྟག་དཔྱད་ཞིབ་འཇུག (dāgjɛè shimjuù) sm. བརྟག་དཔྱད་.

བརྟག་དཔྱད་ལས་ཁངས་ (dāgjɛè lɛ̄èguŋ) research institute/ office.

བརྟག་དཔྱད་ལས་རོགས་པ་ (dāgjɛè lɛ̄èrɔgba) research assistant.

བརྟག་དཔྱད་སློབ་གྲྭ་ (dāgjɛè lōbdra) research institute/ school.

བརྟག་དཔྱད་ལྷན་ཚོགས་ (dāgjɛè lhɛ̄ndzoò) research seminar/ meeting.

བརྟག་དཔྱོད་ (dāgjöö) sm. བརྟག་དཔྱད་.

བརྟག་བྱེད་ཡོ་བྱད་ (dāgjeè yobjɛè) research instrument/ apparatus.

བརྟག་གཞི་ (dəgshi) the study of research.

བརྟག་གཞིག (dəgshiì) sm. བརྟག་དཔྱད་.

བརྟག་ཞིབ་ (dəgshib) sm. བརྟག་དཔྱད་.

བརྟག་ཞིབ་མཁས་པ་ (dəgshib kɛ̄èba) expert (in research/ investigation) ¶ དམག་པོའི་བརྟག་ཞིབ་མཁས་པ་ Military intelligence expert.

བརྟག་ཞིབ་ཐིག་ལེན་ (dəgshib tiglen) sm. བརྟག་དཔྱད་ཐིག་ལེན་.

བརྟག་ཤོ་ (dāgsho) dice used for divining; va.—རྒྱག.

བརྟགས་ (dāà) p. of རྟོག.

བརྟགས་ཤིང་རྟགས་པ་ (dāgshiŋ dāgba) looking into or investigating thoroughly.

བརྟད་ (dɛ̄è) arc. suddenly.

བརྟད་མྱྱེན་ (dɛ̄ègyen) arc. fast, quick.

བརྟན་ (dɛ̄n) 1. abbr. of བརྟན་པོ་. 2. p. of རྟོན་.

བརྟནར་ (dɛ̄nbar) shung. abbr. of བརྟན་པར་.

བརྟན་སྐར་ (dɛ̄ngar) fixed stars (in Tibetan astrology).

བརྟན་སྐྱོད་ (dɛ̄ngyöö) sm. བརྟན་འགྲོ་.

བརྟན་གྲངས་ (dɛ̄ndraŋ) a constant (in math).

བརྟན་འགྲོ་ (dɛ̄ndro) proceeding step-by-step, going or advancing steadily/ stably; va.—བྱེད་ ¶ ལས་དོན་མཐའ་དག་རིམ་པར་དུ་བརྟན་འགྲོ་བྱེད་དགོས་ (You) must do all the work step-by-step.

བརྟན་ཅིང་འགྱུར་བ་མེད་པ་ (dɛ̄njiŋ gyurwə mеèba) firm and unchanging, steadfast and invariable/ unswerving.

བརྟན་འཇགས་ (dɛ̄njaà) sm. གཏན་འཇགས་.

བརྟན་བརྟན་ (dɛ̄ndɛn) sm. བརྟན་པོ་.

བརྟན་བརྟན་ཏིག་ཏིག (dɛ̄ndɛn digdiì) sm. ཏན་ཏན་ཏིག་ཏིག.

བརྟན་ལྡན་ (dɛ̄ndɛn) sm. བརྟན་པོ་.

བརྟན་གནས་ (dɛ̄nnɛ̀ɛ̀) sm. བརྟན་ཅིང་འགྱུར་བ་མེད་པ་.

བརྟན་གནས་ཡར་རྒྱས་ (dɛ̄nnɛ̀ɛ̀ yargyɛ̀ɛ̀) stable development.

བརྟན་པ་སྣོད་ཀྱི་འཇིག་རྟེན་ (dɛ̄nba nȫögi jigden) the physical world.

བརྟན་པོ་ (dɛ̄mbo) firm, steady, stable; va.—བཟོ་ to make sth. steady/ firm ¶ ཀུབ་སྒྱེགས་འདི་བརྟན་པོ་མི་འདུག This chair isn't steady.

བརྟན་པོ་མེད་པ་ (dɛ̄mbo meèba) unstable.

བརྟན་པོར་གནས་ (dɛ̄mbor nɛ̄ɛ̀) vi. to be firm/ steady/ stable, to exist stably/ firmly ¶ བརྟན་པོར་གནས་པའི་གཞུང་ A stable government.

བརྟན་པོར་ལངས་ (dɛ̄mbor laŋ) vi. to maintain a firm stand, to stand firmly ¶ ཁོང་གིས་རང་ཉིད་ཀྱི་ཚོགས་པའི་ལངས་ཕྱོགས་ལ་བརྟན་པོར་ལངས་ཡོད་པ་རེད་ He stands firmly regarding the position of his party.

བརྟན་མ་ (dɛ̄nma) 1. female protector deity ¶ བརྟན་མ་བཅུ་གཉིས་ The twelve female protector deities. 2. sm. ཀ་གདན་.

བརྟན་འཛིན་ (dɛ̄ndzin) sm. བརྟན་བཟུང་.

བརྟན་ཞིང་བརླིང་བ་ (dɛ̄nshiŋ lïŋwə) sm. བརྟན་བརླིང་.

བརྟན་བཞུགས་ (dɛ̄nshuù) long life; va.—བཀུག; —འབུལ་ to do a ritual for sb's long life ¶ མི་དམངས་ཚོས་ལ་གོང་ས་མཆོག་ལ་བརྟན་བཞུགས་ཕུལ་བ་རེད་ The people did a ritual for the long life of the Dalai Lama.

བརྟན་བཟུང་ (dɛ̄nsuŋ) holding firmly, adhering to; va.—བྱེད་ to hold firmly, to adhere to ¶ ས་ཆ་དེ་དགྲ་བོས་བརྟན་བཟུང་བྱས་འདུག That place is being held firmly by the enemy.

བརྟན་གཡོ་ (dɛ̄nyo) the physical world and the sentient beings in it.

བརྟན་བརླིང་ (dɛ̄nliŋ) stable, secure, calm, peaceful (for places); reliable, steady/ steadfast (for people) ¶ དེང་སང་ཡུལ་དེའི་ནང་བརྟན་བརླིང་གི་རྣམས་པ་ཐོན་འདུག These days there is an appearance of peacefulness in that area.

བརྟན་བརླིང་དཔའ་མཛངས་ (dɛ̄nliŋ bādzaŋ) steadfast and brave.

བརྟན་བཤིག (dɛ̄nshiì) sm. བསྟན་བཤིག.

བརྟན་སྲུང་ (dɛ̄nsuŋ) security, defence, guarding ¶ རྒྱལ་ཁབ་བརྟན་སྲུང་ National security.

བརྟན་ལྷིང་ (dɛ̄nlhiŋ) calm, peaceful.

བརྟན་ལྷིང་མཐུན་སྒྲིལ་ (dɛ̄nlhiŋ tǖndrii) peace and harmony.

བརྡབ་ (dəb) f. of རྡབ་.

བརྡབས་ (dəb) p. of རྡབ་.

བརྡས་ (dɛ̀ɛ̀) p. of བརྡ་.

བརྡབས་བརྡབས་བུ་ (dəbdəbsu) sm. རྡབ་རྡོབ་པོ་.

བརྟུན་པ་ (dǖmbə) diligent, industrious, hardworking; va.—བྱེད་ to be diligent/ industrious/ hardworking.

བརྟུལ་ཡོད་ (dǖǖbö̀ö̀) sm. རྟུལ་ཡོད་.

བརྟུལ་ཡོད་ཅན་ (dǖǖbö̀ö̀jɛn) sm. རྟུལ་ཡོད་ཅན་.

བརྟུལ་ (dǖǖ) 1. p. and f. of རྟུལ་. 2. smooth, soft. 3. shung. a traditional volume measure that is less than a དན་.

བརྟུལ་བ་བརྟན་པ་ (dǖǖwə dɛ̄mba) unchangeable zeal.

བརྟུལ་བའི་ངང་ཚུལ་ཅན་ (dǖǖwɛ ŋandzüüjɛn) gentle, humble.

བརྟུལ་ཞུགས་ (dǖǖshuù) 1. ascetic practices. 2. pretending to be sth. ¶ ཁོང་མཁས་པ་ཡིན་ཀྱང་གླེན་པོའི་བརྟུལ་ཞུགས་བཟུང་མཁན་ཞིག་ཡིན་ Even though he is an expert, he is sb. who pretends that he is a fool.

བརྟུལ་ཞུགས་མ་ (dǖǖshugmə) woman/ lady of the house.

བརྟུལ་ཟུར་ (dǖǖsur) obtuse angle (in math).

བརྟེན་ (tēn) 1. p. of རྟེན་. 2. (dat.-loc. + —) due to, because of, on account of ¶ ཁོ་ལྷ་སར་ཕྱིན་པར་བརྟེན་ Because he went to Lhasa ¶ བདུན་རེའི་གསར་ཤོག་ལ་བརྟེན་ནས་མི་དམངས་ཀྱི་ཤེས་ཡོན་ཡར་རྒྱས་ཕྱིན་པ་རེད་ The people's knowledge has improved because of the weekly newspaper. 3. (dat.-loc. + —) depending on, based on ¶ ཐོག་མར་ཚང་མས་འཕྲུལ་ཆས་ཀྱི་ནུས་ཤུགས་ལ་བརྟེན་ནས་རྗེས་ཟིན་ཐུབ་ཀྱི་རེད་སྙམ་པ་རེད་ At first everyone thought that if (they) depend on machines (they) will be able to catch up (in development).

བརྟེན་བསྐོར་ (dēngɔɔ) sm. རྟེན་འཁོར་.

བརྟེན་གནས་ (dēnnɛ̀ɛ̀) basis, foundation.

བརྟེན་པས་ (dēmbɛ̀ɛ̀) 1. sm. བརྟེན་. 2. as per, as for (used with lists) ¶ སློབ་སྤྱིར་བརྟེན་པས་ཁང་པའི་ཐོག་ཟླ་རེར་ཨོར་སྒོར་ ༥༠༠ སྤྲོད་ཀྱི་ཡོད་པ་རེད་ On top of providing the school principal a house, (they) give him 500 dollars a month.

བརྟེན་ཡུལ་ (dēnyüü) 1. sm. བརྟེན་གནས་. 2. permanent home ¶ བརྟེན་ཡུལ་མེད་པ་ Homeless.

བརྟེན་ས་ (dēnsa) sm. བརྟེན་ཡུལ་.

བརྟོད་ (dö̀ö̀) p. and f. of རྟོད་.

བརྟོལ་ (dö̀ö̀) p. and of རྟོལ་.

བལྟ་ (dā) f. of ལྟ་.

བལྟ་བསྐོར་ (dāgɔɔ) sm. ལྟ་སྐོར་.

བལྟ་སྐྱོང་ (dāgyoŋ) sm. ལྟ་སྐྱོང་.

བལྟ་བསྐྱོད་ (dāgyöö) sm. ལྟ་བསྐྱོད་.

བལྟ་མཉམ་ (dāñam) sm. ལྟ་མཉམ་.

བལྟ་རྟོགས་ (dādɔɔ) sm. ལྟ་རྟོགས་.

བལྟ་བསྡུར་ (dādur) looking and comparing; va.—བྱེད་.

བལྟ་དཔེ་ (dābe) book sample.

བལྟ་ཕྱོགས་ (dājɔɔ) sm. ལྟ་ཚུལ་.

བལྟ་བས་ཁོང་ཁྲོ་བ་ (dāwɛ kōŋdrowa) vi. to become angry the moment (one) lays eyes on sth.

བལྟ་བས་ཚོག་མི་ཤེས་ (dāwɛ cōg mi shēè) even though one looks at sth., one is not content/ satisfied ¶ བུད་མེད་དེ་བལྟ་བས་ཚོག་མི་ཤེས་པ་ཞིག་འདུག No matter (how much) one looks at that woman, one is never tired of looking (i.e., she is very beautiful).

བལྟ་བྱ་ (dāja) sth. to be looked at ¶ ཕྲུ་གུ་ཚོར་གློག་བརྙན་བལྟ་བྱ་ཡག་པོ་ཞིག་དགོས་ཀྱི་རེད་ The children need a good movie to see.

བལྟ་རྩ་ (dādza) a vein on the wrist (where Tibetan doctors feel the pulse).

བལྟ་ཚོད་ (dādzoò) sm. ལྟ་ཚོད་.

བལྟ་ཞིབ་ (dāshib) sm. ལྟ་ཞིབ་.

བལྟ་ཤེད་ (dāsheè) sm. ལྟ་ཤེད་.

བལྟ་བཤེར་ (dāsher) sm. ལྟ་བཤེར་.

བལྟབ་ (dəb) f. of ལྟབ་.

བལྟབས་ (dəb) p. of ལྟབ་.

བལྟབས་གཉེར་ (dəbñer) sm. ལྟབ་གཉེར་.

བལྟབས་དྲིལ་ (dəbdrii) a bundle/ roll (of sth.).

བལྟབས་མཛེར་ (dəbdzeè) creases (made on garments).

བལྟབས་རིལ་ (dəbrii) 1. a roller used in making woodblock prints (of Tibetan manuscripts). 2. sm. བལྟབས་དྲིལ་.

བལྟམས་ (dām) vi. to be born (h.).

བལྟས་ (dɛ̀ɛ̀) 1. p. of བལྟ་. 2. imp. of ལྟ་. 3. (མ་ + — + པར་) disregarding, regardless of, irrespective ¶ ཨུ་རུ་སུའི་བསམ་ཚུལ་ལེགས་ཉེས་ལ་མ་བལྟོས་པར་ Disregarding the opinion of Russia. ¶ དཀའ་ངལ་ཆེན་པོར་མ་བལྟོས་པར་ཁོང་གིས་ལས་ཀ་བྱེད་ཀྱི་ཡོད་པ་རེད་ Regardless of the difficulties, he is working. 4. depending/ basing on sth. ¶ བཟོ་གྲྭ་རྙིང་པ་དེ་ལ་བལྟོས་ནས་བཟོ་གྲྭ་གསར་པ་དེ་ཡར་རྒྱས་བྱུང་བ་རེད་ By basing things on the old factory, the new factory improved.

བལྟས་བལྟས་རིག་རིག (dɛ̀ɛ̀dɛ̀ɛ̀ rigrig) looking all around.

བལྟས་སྡོད་ (dɛ̀ɛ̀dö̀ö̀) va. to sit/ stay watching or looking at sth.

བལྟས་ན་ (dɛ̀ɛ̀na) sm. ངས་བལྟས་ན་.

བལྟེབས་ (dēb) p. of ལྟེབ་.

བལྟོས་ (dö̀ö̀) sm. ལྟོས་.

བལྟོས་གྲུབ་ (dö̀ö̀drub) relativity.

བལྟོས་བཅས་ (dö̀ö̀jɛ̀ɛ̀) 1. sm. བལྟོས་གྲུབ་. 2. supporters, followers. 3. sb. or sth. upon which one depends.

བལྟོས་བཅས་ཀྱི་བདེན་དོན་ (dȫȫjɛ̀ɛ̀gi dendön) relative truth.

བལྟོས་བཅས་ཀྱི་རང་བཞིན་ (dȫȫjɛɛ̀gi rəŋshin) relativity, relativism.

བལྟོས་བཅས་ཀྱི་དབུལ་པོ་ (dȫȫjɛɛ̀gi ǖūbu) relative poverty.

བལྟོས་བཅས་སྨྲ་བ་ (dȫȫjɛ̀ɛ̀ māwa) theory of relativity.

བལྟོས་ཆོས་ (dȫȫcöö) a dependent, a person who depends on sb.

བལྟོས་འཇོག (dɛ̄ɛ̀jɔɔ̀) sm. བལྟས་གྲུབ་.

བལྟོས་ཕྱོགས་ (dȫȫjɔɔ̀) a group that is partial, supporters ¶ ར་སྒྲེང་གི་ལྟོས་ཕྱོགས་ Reting's supporters (the group that was partial to Reting).

བལྟོས་མེད་ (dȫȫmeè) 1. disregarding, irrespective, regardless ¶ ཡག་ཉེས་ལྟོས་མེད་ Regardless of whether its good or bad. 2. absolute ¶ བལྟོས་མེད་བདེན་དོན་ Absolute truth. 3. sm. བལྟོས་མེད་རྒྱབ་བསྐྱུར་.

བལྟོས་མེད་རྒྱབ་བསྐྱུར་ (dȫȫmeè gyəbgyur) shung. having no regard/ respect for sth.; va.—བྱེད་ ¶ གཞིས་གཞུང་ལ་བལྟོས་མེད་བྱས་ནས་ཕྱི་རྒྱལ་ལ་བྲོས་པ་རེད་ Showing no respect for the government, he fled abroad.

བལྟོས་མེད་རང་བཞིན་ (dȫȫmeè rəŋshin) absoluteness.

བལྟོས་ས་ (dȫȫsa) person on whom sb. depends.

བལྟོས་ས་བལྟོས་ཆོས་ (dȫȫsa dȫȫjöö) depending on and being depended on ¶ ཕ་དང་བུའི་འབྲེལ་བ་ནི་བལྟོས་ས་བལྟོས་ཆོས་ཀྱི་འབྲེལ་བ་ཡིན་ As for the relationship between the father and the son, it is one of dependence and being depended upon.

བསྟང་ (dāŋ) 1. f. of སྟང་. 2. friends, supporters. 3. the essence of sth.

བསྟངས་ (dāŋ) p. of སྟང་.

བསྟད་ (dɛ̄ɛ̀) p. and f. of སྟོད་. 2. abbr. of བསྟན་པ་.

བསྟན་ (dɛ̄n) 1. p. of སྟོན་.

བསྟན་སྐྱོང་ (dɛ̄ngyoŋ) defending the faith/ religion.

བསྟན་དགྲ་ (dɛ̄ndra) one who opposes the dharma, an enemy of the Buddha's teaching.

བསྟན་འགྱུར་ (dɛ̄ngyur) the Tanjur (the collection of 225 volumes of commentary on the Buddha's teachings).

བསྟན་འགྲོ་ (dɛ̄ndro) abbr. Buddhism/ religion/ dharma and sentient beings ¶ བོད་ཁམས་བསྟན་འགྲོ་ཡོངས་ལ་ To all the sentient beings and the Buddhist religion of Tibet.

བསྟན་འགྲོར་སྨན་པའི་མཛད་པ་ (dɛ̄ndro mɛ̄mbɛ dzɛ̱ɛ̀la) shung. deeds that benefit the dharma and sentient beings ¶ སྔ་ཕྱིར་གོང་རིམ་ནས་བསྟན་འགྲོར་སྨན་པའི་མཛད་པར་ཧོ་ཐོག་ཐུའི་མཚན་བཟོས་དང་ For the deeds of the previous Lamas that had been beneficial for the dharma and sentient beings, a title of Hotoktu was given as an award.

བསྟན་འགྲོའི་གསོས་སྨན་ (dɛ̄ndrö sȫȫmɛn) shung. promotion of Buddhism and the benefit of all living beings ¶ བསྟན་འགྲོའི་གསོས་སྨན་དུ་འགྱུར་བའི་བཀའ་ལུང་བཟང་པོ་བསྩལ་བ་སྙི་བོར་ཞིབས་པས་ I learned that (Your Majesty) has issued an order for the promotion of Buddhism and benefit of all living beings.

བསྟན་རྒྱས་གླིང་ (dɛ̄ngyɛ̀ɛliŋ) name of an incarnate lama and monastery.

བསྟན་རྒྱུན་ (dɛ̄ngyün) shung. the tradition of teaching the dharma ¶ རང་ལུགས་བསྟན་རྒྱུན་གཙང་མའི་ཆོ་ག་ཕྱག་ལེན་སོགས་ཆོས་སྤྱོད་ཀྱི་བྱ་བ་གང་ཅི་ཉམས་པ་མེད་པ་དགོས་རྒྱུ་ One must keep up with the traditions of performing rituals according to the teaching of the dharma.

བསྟན་འགྲོའི་ (dɛ̄ndro) shung. abbr. of བསྟན་འགྲོའི་.

བསྟན་བཅོས་ (dɛ̄njöö) religious commentary.

བསྟན་བཅོས་ཀྱི་ཆོས་བཞི་ (dɛ̄njöögi cȫȫshi) the four types of religious commentary.

བསྟན་བཅོས་འགོ་རྩོམ་ (dɛ̄njöö godzom) the preface of a religious commentary.

བསྟན་བཅོས་ཉེ་སྦྱོར་ (dɛ̄njöö ñejɔɔ) new religious commentary.

བསྟན་ཆོས་ (dɛ̄njöö) sm. བསྟན་བཅོས་.

བསྟན་དོན་མཛད་སྒོ་ (dɛ̄ndön dzɛ̱ɛ̀go) activitie on behalf of religion.

བསྟན་པ་ (dɛ̄mba) religious teachings, the Buddhist dharma; vi.—འཇིག to have religious teachings destroyed; va.—བཤིག to destroy religion/ Buddhism. ¶ སངས་རྒྱས་ཀྱི་བསྟན་པ་ The teachings of the Buddha.

བསྟན་པ་སྔ་དར་ (dɛ̄mba ŋādar) the first spreading of Buddhism in Tibet (during the time of early kings).

བསྟན་པ་དར་རྒྱས་ (dɛ̄mba dargyɛ̀ɛ) the spread of Buddhism.

བསྟན་པ་གནས་པའི་ཞིང་མཆོག་ཁྱད་པར་ཅན་ (dɛ̄mba nɛ̄ɛ̀bɛ shiŋjɔɔ̀ kyɛ̄ɛ̀barjɛn) shung. a sacred sanctuary where the dharma flourishes.

བསྟན་པ་ཕྱི་དར་ (dɛ̄mba cīdar) the latter spread of Buddhism in Tibet.

བསྟན་པ་འཛིན་བྱེད་ (dɛ̄mba dzinjeè) shung. holding on to/ adhering to Buddhism.

བསྟན་པའི་སྒྲོན་མེ་ (dɛ̄mbɛ drönme) great lamas [Lit. the light of Buddhism].

བསྟན་པའི་མངའ་བདག (dɛ̄mbɛ ŋadaà) 1. the Buddha. 2. high lamas.

བསྟན་པའི་སྤྱི་རིམ་ (dɛ̄nbɛ jirim) shung. a religious ritual performed for the benefit of Buddhism in general.

བསྟན་པའི་གནས་ཚད་ (dɛ̄mbɛ nɛ̄ɛ̀dzɛɛ̀) a calculation which gives Buddhism 5104 years to exist before it dies out.

བསྟན་པའི་རབས་ (dɛ̄mbɛ rəb) the history of Buddhism.

བསྟན་པའི་གཞི་ (dɛ̄mbɛshi) 1. the content of sth. written ¶ རྩོམ་ཡིག་འདིའི་བསྟན་བྱའི་གཙོ་བོ་ཚན་རིག་རེད་ The main content of the article is science research. 2. the foundation/ root of the dharma.

བསྟན་པར་དམའ་འབེན་ (dɛ̄nbar mānjin) shung. insulting the dharma ¶ དགོན་ནང་ཆང་ལས་བྱེད་པ་སོགས་བསྟན་པར་དམའ་འབེན་གྱི་བྱ་ངན་ཡིན་པ་ Making ཆང་ in the monastery is a evil deed that insults the dharma.

བསྟན་སྤྱི་ (dɛ̄nji) shung. abbr. of བསྟན་པའི་སྤྱི་རིམ་.

བསྟན་བྱའི་མི་གཙོ་བོ་ (dɛ̄njɛ midzowa) main character, leading character, title role.

བསྟན་མ་ (dɛ̄nma) sm. བརྟན་མ་.

བསྟན་མེད་ (dɛ̄nmeè) nothing to show; vi.—དུ་འགྱུར་ to end up having nothing to show for sth.

བསྟན་རྩིས་ (dɛ̄ndzii) astrological calculation for when a high lama or learned scholar will be born.

བསྟན་འཛིན་ (dɛ̄ndzin) holder of the faith/ dharma.

བསྟན་འཛིན་མཁར་རུ་ (dɛ̄ndzin kāru) a standard government volume measure for grains (in ཁལ་) that equaled about 27-33 lbs. for barley.

བསྟན་འཛིན་ཆོས་ཀྱི་རྒྱལ་པོ་ (dɛ̄ndzin cȫȫgi gyɛ̱ɛbo) shung. sm. གུ་ཤྲི་བསྟན་འཛིན་ཆོས་རྒྱལ་.

བསྟན་འཛིན་སྐྱེས་བུ་ (dɛ̄ndzin gyēèbu) sm. བསྟན་འཛིན་.

བསྟན་ཡོད་ (dɛ̄nyöö) having sth. to show.

བསྟན་རབས་ (dɛ̄nrəb) sm. བསྟན་པའི་རབས་.

བསྟན་ལ་ (dɛ̄nla) shung. abbr. of བསྟན་སྲིད་ལ་རྒྱ་.

བསྟན་ཤིན་ (dɛ̄nshin) ch. cake, cookie.

བསྟན་བཤིག (dɛ̄nshiì) 1. destroyer of the faith/ dharma. 2. a joke, sth. funny; va.—སློང་ to make a joke, to make people laugh.

བསྟན་བཤིག་འཁྲབ་མཁན་ (dɛ̄nshiì trəbñɛn) clown, comedian.

བསྟན་བཤིག་ལམ་ངན་བྱེད་པོ་ (dɛ̄nshiì lamŋɛn cɛ̄ɛ̀bo) shung. person who breaks the rules and sets bad examples ¶ དགེ་བསྐོས་བསྟན་བཤིག་ལམ་ངན་བྱེད་པོ་ཞིར་འདོན་ཁྲིམས་ཉེས་པ་དགོས་གནས་ It seems appropriate that the disciplinary official who himself broke the rules and set a bad example should be exposed and punished.

བསྟན་བཞིག་སློང་མཁན་ (dɛ̄nshiì lōŋñɛn) sm. བསྟན་བཞིག་འཁྲབ་མཁན་.

བསྟན་བཞིག་ཚ་པོ་ (dɛ̄nshiì tsābo) funny, humorous.

བསྟན་བཞིག་ཟློས་གར་ (dɛ̄nshiì dö̱ögar) comedy play/ show.

བསྟན་གཤེད་ (dɛ̄nsheè) butcher of religion.

བསྟན་སྲིད་ (dɛ̄nsiì) religion and politics (used to express the Tibetan government as a combination of the religious and secular).

བསྟན་སྲིད་བདེ་རིམ་ (dɛ̄nsiì de̱rim) shung. religious rituals performed for the benefit of dharma and politics (the government) ¶ བསྟན་སྲིད་བདེ་རིམ་འཕར་མ་རྒྱུན་སྒྲུབ་དགོས་རྒྱུ་ (You) must perform additional religious rituals for the dharma and government.

བསྟན་སྲིད་སྤྱི་དོན་ (dɛ̄nsiì jīdön) religious and secular affairs.

བསྟན་སྲིད་ལ་རྒྱ་ (dɛ̄nsiì la̱gya) shung. loyalty to government and religion, loyalty to the Tibetan system of government ¶ ཨམ་བན་གྱིས་གཞུང་དཔོན་འབངས་ཚང་མའི་བསྟན་སྲིད་ལ་རྒྱར་དགོངས་ནས་གོང་མ་ཆེན་པོའི་བཀའ་འབྲེལ་ལྟར་བུ་གནང་བ་ In consideration with the government leaders and the people's loyalty towards Buddhism and government, the Amban issued the edict in accordance with the Emperor's order.

བསྟན་སྲུང་ (dɛ̄nsuŋ) guardian of doctrine/ faith/ religion.

བསྟན་སྲུང་དམག་སྒར་ (dɛ̄nsuŋ māàgar) name of the antiChinese-Tibetan rebel organization that began in 1957-58.

བསྟབ་ (dɔ̄b) f. of སྟོབ་.

བསྟབ་བསྟབས་ (dɔ̄b dɔ̄b) va. to give charity.

བསྟབས་ (dɔ̄b) p. of སྟོབ་.

བསྟར་ (dār) p. of སྟར་.

བསྟར་སྒྲིག (dārdrig) va. to line up, to place in order, to rank, to arrange in series/ line ¶ སློབ་གྲྭ་བ་རྣམས་གཟུགས་པོ་ཆེ་ཆུང་ལྟར་བསྒྲིགས་ནས་ལངས་བཞུད་འདུག The students have been lined up in accordance with their height.

བསྟར་བསྒྲིགས་ (dār dri̱g) p. of བསྟར་སྒྲིག.

བསྟར་ཆགས་སུ་ (dārjagsu) one after another, continously ¶ ལས་ཀ་འདི་བསྟར་ཆགས་སུ་བྱེད་དགོས་རེད་ (We) have to do this work continously.

བསྟར་པ་ (dārba) row, line (e.g., of houses); va.—སྒྲིག to line up/ order/ arrange in a line/ series ¶ ཁང་པ་བསྟར་པ་དང་པོ་ The first row of houses.

བསྟར་པ་སྒྲིག (dārdrig) sm. བསྟར་སྒྲིག.

བསྟར་པ་ཤིག་ཤིག (dārba shīshiì) lined up in a row/ queue/ line; va.—བྱེད་.

བསྟར་ཕྲེང་ (dārdreŋ) line, series, row ¶ ཐང་ཆེན་དུ་སློབ་གྲྭ་བའི་ཏུ་སྒྲིག་གི་བསྟར་ཕྲེང་མང་པོ་འདུག On a large field there were many rows of students lined up.

བསྟར་འབུལ་ (dār bü̱ü) sm. གཟིགས་འབུལ་བསྟར་.

བསྟར་ལ་བརྒྱུད་ (dārla gyü̱ü) va. to string out in a line/ row, to lay out one after another ¶ མུ་ཏིག་བསྟར་ལ་བརྒྱུད་ནས་རྒྱན་ཆ་བཟོས་པ་རེད་ (They) strung the pearls and made a necklace.

བསྟར་ཤོག་སྒྲིག (dārshoò dri̱g) sm. བསྟར་སྒྲིག.

བསྟི་ (dī) f. of སྟི་.

བསྟི་ཁང་ (dīgaŋ) home, residence.

བསྟི་ག (dīga) sm. སྟི་ག.

བསྟི་སྟང་ (dīdaŋ) sm. སྟི་སྟང་.

བསྟི་སྡུག་ཚ་པོ་ (dīduù tsābo) fastidious, fussy, stuffy.

བསྟི་གནས་ (dīnɛɛ̀) sm. སྟི་གནས་.

བསྟིང་ (dīŋ) 1. f. of སྟིང་. 2. va. to satirize, to make fun of.

བསྟིང་ཚིག (dīŋtsig) satirical/ sarcastic talk or speech.

བསྟིང་སླད་ (dīŋlɛɛ̀) sm. བསྟིང་ཚིག.

བསྟིངས་ (dīŋ) p. of སྟིང་.

བསྟིམ་ (dīm) f. of སྟིམ་.

བསྟིམས་ (dīm) p. of སྟིམ་.

བསྟིར་ (dīr) 1. to suffer. 2. sm. བར་མཚམས་.

བསྟིར་མེད་ (dīrmeè) arc. without rest, ceaseless.

བསྟིས་ (dīì) p. of སྟི་.

བསྟུང་ (dūŋ) f. of སྟུང་.

བསྟུངས་ (dūŋ) p. of སྟུང་.

བསྟུད་ (dūù) p. of སྟུད་.

བསྟུད་འཐབ་བསྟུད་རྒྱལ་ (dūùtəb dūùgyɛɛ) successively/ continuously victorious in battle.

བསྟུད་འདེབས་ (dūùdeb) successive sowing/ planting.

བསྟུད་བསྟུད་པར་ (dūù dūùbar) continuously, one after another ¶ ཁོང་ངའི་ནང་དུ་བསྟུད་བསྟུད་པར་སླེབས་བྱུང་ He came to my house continuously.

བསྟུད་བསྟུད་བསྟུད་པར་ (dūù dūù dūùbar) sm. བསྟུད་བསྟུད་པར་.

བསྟུད་པར་ (dūùbar) sm. སྟུད་མར་.

བསྟུད་འཕེན་ (dūù pēn) shooting/ firing continuously.

བསྟུད་མར་ (dūùmar) sm. སྟུད་མར་.

བསྟུད་ལུགས་འཕྲུལ་འཁོར་ (dūùluù trüūgɔɔ) a continuous molding machine.

བསྟུན་ (dūn) 1. va. to be or act in accordance with ¶ ཨ་མི་རི་ཀའི་བཙན་རྒྱལ་རིང་ལུགས་ཀྱི་དགོས་མཁོར་བསྟུན་ཏེ་ Acting in accordance with the needs of American imperialism. ¶ འགོ་ཁྲིད་དང་བསྟུན་ནས་ལས་ཀ་བྱེད་དགོས་རེད་ (You) have to work in accordance with the leaders (views/ orders).

བསྟུན་མཁས་པོ་ (dūn kɛ̄ɛ̀bo) ability to deal and get along with people.

བསྟུན་མཁས་བྱེད་ (dūnkeè ce̱è) va. to deal with people in a cordial and amiable manner.

བསྟུན་དྲི་ (dūn tri̱) va. to ask someone in a friendly/ cordial manner.

བསྟུན་བསྟུན་བྱེད་ (dūndün ce̱è) sm. བསྟུན་མཁས་བྱེད་.

བསྟེན་ (dēn) 1. va. to study with a teacher ¶ དགེ་རྒན་མང་པོ་བསྟེན་སྐབས་སྦྱང་འབྲས་ད་ཅང་ཡག་པོ་བྱུང་ Because I studied with many teachers I got an excellent result. 2. va. to see a doctor for medical help ¶ ངས་ཁ་ས་ཨེམ་ཆི་བསྟེན་ཅང་ན་ཚ་དྲག་ཙམ་དྲག་བཞག Because I went to see a doctor yesterday I have gotten a little better. 3. va. to consult, to seek help ¶ ངས་ཚོང་རྒྱག་རྒྱུར་རོགས་པ་མི་གཅིག་བསྟེན་པ་ཡིན་ I sought help from a friend about doing business. 4. va. to seek ¶ བླ་མ་ལ་སྐྱབས་སུ་བསྟེན་དགོས་རེད་ You should seek refuge in a lama. 5. va. to keep/ raise/ rear ¶ ངཚོས་ད་ལོ་ནས་བཟུང་ར་ལུག་བསྟེན་པ་ཡིན་ We raised sheep and goats since this year.

བསྟེན་བཀུར་ (dēngur) va. to consult and respect.

བསྟེན་སྐྱིལ་ (dēngyii) sm. བསྟེན་ཉར་.

བསྟེན་བསྐྱིལ་ (dēngyii) sm. བསྟེན་ཉར་.

བསྟེན་འགོར་ (dēngɔɔ) shung. sm. བསྟེན་ཉར་.

བསྟེན་རྒྱུན་ (dēngyün) shung. tradition of consulting/ worshipping ¶ དེ་སྔ་གཞུང་ཕྱོགས་ནས་སྲུང་མ་དེ་བསྟེན་རྒྱུན་མེད་པ་ Traditionally the government did not consult that protective deity.

བསྟེན་ཉར་ (dēnñar) keeping, raising; va. བསྟེན་ཉར་; —བྱེད་ ¶ མཆོད་ཁང་སོགས་ལ་གཡོག་མོ་བསྟེན་ཉར་མི་ཆོག་པ་ They are not allowed to keep maid servants in places such as in religious temples.

བསྟེར་ (dēr) p. of སྟེར་.

བསྟོངས་ (dōŋ) arc. 1. va. to help. 2. va. to go/ do together.

བསྟོད་ (dōò) va. to praise, to compliment.

བསྟོད་བཀུར་ (dōògur) va. to respect and praise.

བསྟོད་གླུ་ (dōòlu) praise/ compliments/ glorification in song, singing the praises of, celebrating in song; va.—གཏོང་; —ལེན་.

བསྟོད་བསྔགས་ (dōòŋaà) praising, complimenting; va.—བྱེད་; —ཞུ་.

བསྟོད་གཏམ་ (dōòdam) words of praise.

བསྟོད་པ་ (dōòba) sm. བསྟོད་བསྔགས་.

བསྟོད་པའི་ཆ་ལས་སྨད་པ་ (dōòbɛ cālɛɛ̀ mɛ̄ɛ̀ba) style of poem in which there is praise on the surface but which contains hidden meaning that is derogatory.

བསྟོད་ཕྱག (dōò cāà) praising and prostrating; va.—

འབུལ་.

བསྟོད་དབྱངས་ (dȍȍyaŋ) sm. བསྟོད་གླུ་.

བསྟོད་འབུལ་ (dȍmbüü) praising.

བསྟོད་སྨད་ (dȍȍ mɛ̀ɛ̀) praise and denunciation; va.—བྱེད་.

བསྟོད་ཚིག (dȍȍdziì) words of praise.

བསྟོད་ཚོགས་ (dȍȍdzɔɔ̀) a book that contains praise to the Buddha or Boddhisatvas.

བསྟོད་འོས་ (dȍȍwöȍ) laudable, commendable, praiseworthy.

བསྟོད་ཡིག (dȍȍyig) testimonial letter, certification of merit.

བསྟོད་བཤད་སྨད་བཤད་ (dȍȍshɛɛ̀ mɛ̀ɛ̀shɛɛ̀) praising people and saying derogatory things about people.

བསྟོད་ར་ (dȍȍra) sm. བསྟོད་བསྔགས་.

བསྟོད་རེས་ (dȍȍreè) praising one another; va.—བྱེད་.

བསྟོར་འཛིག (dɔ̃njiì) sm. གཏོར་བཤིག.

ཐ་ (tā) 1. the letter ཐ་ (used in alphabetical ordering). 2. abbr. of ཐ་མ་.

ཐ་སྐར་ཟླ་བ་ (tāgar dawa) the 9th month of the Tibetan calendar.

ཐ་སྐྱོ་ (tāgyo) poor.

ཐ་སྐྱོ་པོ་ (tā gyōbo) sm. ཐ་སྐྱོ་.

ཐ་ཁུག (tāguù) tobacco pouch/ bag.

ཐ་ཁེབས་ (tāgeb) tea cozy.

ཐ་ཁེལ་མ་ཀན་ (tā kē ma gēn) Taklamakan Desert.

ཐ་ག་པ་ (tāgaba) weaver.

ཐ་གི་ (tōgi) 1. arc. peace. 2. arc. a little. 3. arc. essence. 4. arc. distant.

ཐ་གུ་ (tōgu) small/ thin rope or string.

ཐ་གེ་ (tāge) a little bit, a small amount.

ཐ་གོག (tāgɔɔ̀) barren; va.—འཇོག to leave barren/ uncultivated ། ས་ཆ་ཐ་གོག Barren land.

ཐ་གོད་ (tāgöö) 1. sm. ཐ་གོག. 2. an unprincipled/ unethical person.

ཐ་གྲས་ (tādrɛɛ̀) 1. the lowest class/ level/ grade ། ཞིང་ཁ་ཐ་གྲས་ The lowest (poorest) grade of field. 2. a bad and dishonest/ unreliable person.

ཐ་གྲུ་ (tōdru) 1. area, place, country. 2. breadth, width, extension, size ། རྒྱ་གར་གྱི་ཐ་གྲུ་ཀུན་ལ་ All over the breadth of India.

ཐ་གཅུང་ (tājuŋ) sm. ཐ་ཆུང་.

ཐ་ཆ་ (tāja) sm. ཐ་ཆད་.

ཐ་ཆད་ (tājɛɛ̀) worst, lowest ། རིགས་ངན་ཐ་ཆད་ The lowest of the unclean castes (i.e., harijans). 2. an unprincipled/ unethical person.

ཐ་ཆུང་ (tājuŋ) 1. the youngest sibling. 2. the last ། སྟོན་ཟླ་ཐ་ཆུང་ The last month of fall. 3. pinkie (finger).

ཐ་ཇི་ཁེ་སི་དན་ (tā ji kē sī dɛ̄n) Tadjikstan.

ཐ་སྙད་ (tãñɛɛ̀) 1. name ། ཉི་མ་ལ་ཐ་སྙད་མང་པོ་ཡོད་པ་རེད་ There are many names for the sun. 2. term, jargon, terminology, concept ། ཆབ་སྲིད་ཀྱི་ཐ་སྙད་ Political terms.

ཐ་སྙད་ཀྱི་གཙུག་ལག (tãñɛɛ̀gi dzūglaà) the five sciences in tradition Tibet.

ཐ་སྙད་ཀྱི་གཞི་ (tãñɛɛ̀gi shi) the referent meaning of a name/ word.

ཐ་སྙད་མཁན་པོ་ (tãñɛɛ̀ kɛ̄ɛ̀bo) 1. one who indulges in idle/ meaningless talk. 2. a person who first named sth.

ཐ་སྙད་སྟོན་བྱེད་ (tãñɛɛ̀ dõnjeè) 1. a letter. 2. word.

ཐ་སྙད་པ་ (tãñɛɛ̀ba) 1. an ordinary layman (as opposed to a lama, monk). 2. name.

ཐ་སྙད་སྤྱོད་ཡུལ་ (tãñɛɛ̀ jöòyüü) people or things that are named.

ཐ་སྙད་ཙམ་ (tãñɛɛ̀dzam) sm. མིང་ཙམ་.

ཐ་སྙད་གསར་པ་ (tãñɛɛ̀ sārba) new term.

ཐ་སྙད་གསར་བཟོ་ (tãñɛɛ̀ sārsöö) coining new terms; va.—བྱེད་.

ཐ་བརྙས་ (tãñɛɛ̀) sm. བརྙས་བཅོས་.

ཐ་ཐ་ཤི་ (tā tāshi) a kind of rice broth with meat.

ཐ་ཐར་ (tādar) Tatar.

ཐ་ཐལ་ (tātɛɛ) sm. ཐ་མལ་བ་.

ཐ་ཐོར་ (tādɔɔ) 1. a few of sth. scattered around ། ལུང་པ་འདིའི་ནང་བོད་མི་ཐ་ཐོར་འདུག There are a few scattered Tibetans in this country. 2. a little bit, not much ། ཁོས་དབྱིན་སྐད་ཐ་ཐོར་ཞིག་རྒྱག་གི་འདུག He speaks a little bit of English. 3. shung. a type of food container.

ཐ་དང་ (tādaŋ) the Tha regiment in the traditional Tibetan army.

ཐ་དད་ (tādɛɛ̀) separate, different; vi.—དུ་འགྱུར་ to become separate/ different; va.—བྱེད་ to separate, to divorce; —དུ་གཏོང་ to make sth. separate ། མི་མང་དང་ཐ་དད་དུ་གྱུར་བ་རེད་ (He) became separated (in his views) from the people. ། ཁོ་གཉིས་ཟ་ཚང་ཐ་དད་བྱས་བཞག The couple got divorced. ། ཕ་མ་གཉིས་མནའ་མར་དགའ་པོ་མེད་ཙང་བུ་དང་མནའ་མ་ཐ་དད་དུ་བཏང་བཞག Because the parents didn't like the bride (of their son) they have made it so that the son and the bride separated (divorced).

ཐ་དད་པ་ (tādɛɛ̀ba) an active/ transitive verb.

ཐ་དམ་ཚིག (tā tamdzig) oath, pledge, promise.

ཐ་མདའ་ (tānda) the commander/ general of the ཐ་དང་ regiment.

ཐ་ན་ (tāna) 1. even, even so far as, as far as ། མི་རིགས་གཉིས་ཀྱི་དབར་ཐ་ན་ཟ་གོས་ལ་ཡང་ཡག་ཉེས་ཆེན་པོ་འདུག Even so as far as food and clothes are concerned, there was a big difference between the two races. ། སྨན་ཁང་ནང་ལ་ཐ་ན་སྨན་དཀྱུས་མ་ཞིག་ཀྱང་ད་ཅང་དཀོན་པོ་ཡོད་ In the hospital, even common medicines are very scarce. 2. roll of cotton cloth. 3. even in the least, in the minimum, in the worst.

ཐ་སྤྲག (tābaà) plate, dish.

ཐ་སྤྲིན་ (tədrin) a type of herb.

ཐ་བ་ (tāwa) 1. land (kept) out of cultivation ། ས་ཞིང་རྣམས་ལོ་མང་ཐ་བར་ལུས་པ་རེད་ The fields were kept out of cultivation for many years. 2. jealousy, anger.

ཐ་བ་སྐྱ་ཆགས་ (tāwa gyājaà) sm. ཐ་བ་, 1.

ཐ་བ་སྤངས་ (tāwa bāŋ) 1. va. to rid (oneself) of anger. 2. name of a Buddha.

ཐ་པི་འཐིབ་པི་ (tōbi tībbi) gloomy, overcast (weather).

ཐ་པི་འཐིབ་པི་ (tōbi tībbi) sm. ཐ་པི་འཐིབ་པི་.

ཐ་མ་ (tāma) 1. last, final, end ། དེ་རིང་ཚོགས་འདུའི་ཉི་མ་ཐ་མ་རེད་ Today is the final day of the meeting. 2. the worst ། སློབ་ཕྲུག་དེ་འཛིན་གྲྭའི་ནང་གི་ཐ་མ་རེད་ The student is the worst in the class.

ཐ་མ་ཁ་ (tāmaka) sm. ཐ་མག.

ཐ་མག (tāmaà) cigarettes, tobacco; va.—འཐེན་ to smoke cigarettes; va.—གཅོད་ to quit smoking.

ཐ་མག་སྒམ་ཆུང་ (tāmaà gəmjuŋ) a pack of cigarettes.

ཐ་མག་དང་ཆང་རག་མེ་མདའ་བཅས་ཉོ་བེད་བཀག་སྡོམ་ལས་ཁུངས་ (tāmaà daŋ cãŋraà menda jɛ̄ɛ̀ ñobeè gāgdom lɛɛ̀guŋ) Bureau of Alcohol, Tobacco and Firearms (U.S.A.).

ཐ་མག་ཕྲུག་ལྷག (tāmaà drūglhaà) cigarette butt.

ཐ་མག་རྡབ་ས་ (tāmaà dəbsa) ashtray.

ཐ་མག་ནག་པོ་ (tāmaà nagbo) opium.

ཐ་མག་ཞུའི་ཙ་ (tāmaà shueja) tib.ch. cigar.

ཐ་མག་རོ་དོ་ (tāmaà rodo) sm. ཐ་མག་ཕྲུག་ལྷག.

ཐ་མག་རོ་དོ་ལྷུག་ས་ (tāmaà rodo lūùsə) sm. ཐ་མག་རྡབ་ས་.

ཐ་མག་ཧྲུའི་ཡོན་ (tāmaà hrūeyön) tib.ch. water pipe (for smoking).

ཐ་མལ་གྱི་ཞེན་པ་ (tāmɛɛgi shemba) attached to worldly things.

ཐ་མལ་སྣང་བ་ (tāmɛɛ nāŋwa) worldly sensations/ feelings.

ཐ་མལ་པ་ (tāmɛɛwa) ordinary, common ། ང་མི་ཐ་མལ་པ་ཞིག་ཡིན་ I am an ordinary person (I have no degrees, titles, etc.). ། ཚོང་ཁང་འདིའི་ནང་ཅ་ལག་ཚང་མ་སྤུས་ཀ་ཐ་མལ་པ་རེད་འདུག All of the things in this store are ordinary quality.

ཐ་མལ་པའི་དངོས་གཙོའི་རིང་ལུགས་ (tāmɛɛwɛ ŋöödzö riŋluù) vulgar materialism.

ཐ་མལ་པའི་ཆབ་སྲིད་དཔལ་འབྱོར་རིག་པ་ (tāmɛɛwɛ cəbsii bɛ̄njɔɔ rigbə) vulgar political economy.

ཐ་མལ་པའི་ཕྱོགས་ (tāmɛɛwɛ cɔ̄ɔ̀) vulgar, mediocre, ordinary, common.

ཐ་མལ་པའི་འཕེལ་འགྱུར་སྨྲ་བ་ (tāmɛɛwɛ pērgyur māwa) vulgar evolutionism.

ཐ་མི་ཁ་ (tāmigə) cigarette; va.—འཐེན་ to smoke.

ཐ་མི་དད་པ་ (tā midɛɛ̀ba) involuntary/ intransitive

verb.

ཐ་དམན་ (tāmɛn) base in quality, lowest quality.

ཐ་རྫི་ (tādzi) shung. inferior land ༈ཆུ་འགྲོ་ཡུལ་མེད་པ་ཐ་རྫི་ནམས་ལ་སོན་ཁལ་ ༥ The inferior fields which can not be watered take 5 khal of seed.

ཐ་ཚིག (tādzii) 1. warning; va.—སྒྲོག; —བྱེད་ to give/ issue/ say/ shout a warning ༈ཁོ་ཚོར་ཐ་ཚིག་ནན་པོ་བསྒྲགས་པ་ཡིན་ (We) issued a firm warning to them. 2. the conclusion/ decision/ agreement of a discussion ༈ཁོ་ཚོས་གྲོས་མོལ་བྱས་པའི་ཐ་ཚིག The conclusion of their discussion.

ཐ་ཚིག་རྫིང་མ་ (tādzig dĩŋmə) ultimatum.

ཐ་ཚིག་ཡི་གེ་ (tādzig yigi) a written warning.

ཐ་ཞིང་ (tāshiŋ) 1. field where the yield is poor. 2. field that can be used only in alternate years.

ཐ་ཞན་པོ་ (tā shembo) poor, inferior ༈ཁོ་ཚོའི་ཚོ་བ་ཐ་ཞན་པོ་ཡོད་པ་རེད་ Their livelihood is poor.

ཐ་ར་ར་ (tā rara) 1. sound made by many pebbles/ marbles falling on hard surface. 2. sound of footsteps.

ཐ་ར་ཐོ་རེ་ (tāra tōre) sm. ཐ་རེ་ཐོ་རེ་.

ཐ་རམ་ (tāram) 1. cocongrass. 2. undisciplined/ bad behavior.

ཐ་རིམ་ (tārim) Tarim (Basin).

ཐ་རེ་ཐོ་རེ་ (tāre tōre) scattered, dispersed ༈ཁང་པ་ཐ་རེ་ཐོ་རེ་བྱས་ནས་བརྒྱབ་འདུག (They) have built the houses scattered about (not close together).

ཐ་རེ་ཐོར་རེ་ (tāre tōre) sm. ཐ་རེ་ཐོ་རེ་.

ཐ་ལ་ (tāla) sm. ཐལ་བ་.

ཐ་ལི་མཐའ་བཞི་ (tāli tāshi) ash-colored horses/ mules that are four years old.

ཐ་ལི་ཟུག (tālesug) shung. an outer garment worn by Tibetan government officials during special occasions (over a Mongolian dress).

ཐ་ཤལ་ (tāshɛɛ) 1. bad, inferior, base, low in quality, poor. 2. evil.

ཐ་ཤལ་ཉམ་ཐག (tāshɛɛ ñamdaà) poor ༈དཔོན་འདིའི་འོག་མི་སེར་ཐ་ཤལ་ཉམ་ཐག་མང་པོ་ཡོད་པ་རེད་ There are many poor peasants under this lord.

ཐ་ཤལ་བ་ (tā shɛ̄ɛwa) an inferior (person) ༈ལོག་སྤྱོད་དབང་སྒྱུར་གྲལ་རིམ་གྱིས་ཁོ་ཚོ་ཐ་ཤལ་བར་བརྩིས་པ་རེད་ The reactionary ruling class considered them as inferior people.

ཐ་སོན་ (tāsön) shung. lower quality seed used on inferior fields ༈ཆུ་འགྲོ་ཡུལ་མེད་པ་ཐ་རྫི་ནམས་ལ་ཐ་སོན་ཁལ་ ༥ ༈The inferior fields that can not be watered take 5 ཁལ་ of seed.

ཐ་སི་གསར་འགྱུར་ཁང་ (tāsi sāngyugaŋ) TASS news agency.

ཐ་ཧི་ཀེན་ (tāhigen) Tashkent.

ཐག (tāà) 1. distance ༈ཐག་རིང་པོ་ Far. 2. (vb.+ ma. + —) as soon as ༈ནང་ལ་སླེབས་མ་ཐག As soon as (he) arrived at home. 3. abbr. of ཐག་པ་.

ཐག་དཀར་ (tāggar) shung. rope made from grass/ reed/ hemp.

ཐག་སྐས་ (tāggɛɛ̀) a rope ladder.

ཐག་སྒྱུལ་འདྲ་གཟུགས་ (tōgüü drəsug) sm.* ཐག་སྒྱུལ་འདྲ་གཟུགས་.

ཐག་ཁྱིལ་ལེར་ (tāggyiler) the sound of shooting a slingshot.

ཐག་འཁྱུད་སྔོན་པོ་ (tōgyüü ŋōmbo) blue morning glory.

ཐག་འཁྱུད་མེ་ཏོག (tōgyüü medoò) morning glory plant, morning glory flower.

ཐག་ཁྲ་ (tāàdra) colored rope, rope woven to have stripes.

ཐག་ཁྲ་སྦྲུལ་མཐོང་ (tāàdra drüüdoŋ) 1. mistaking sth. one sees. 2. beset with imaginary fears [Lit. mistaking a colored/ striped rope for a snake].

ཐག་ཁྲི་ (tāàdri) loom for weaving.

ཐག་གི་ཐུག་གི་ (tōgi tūgi) being a nuisance by touching things (this term is especially used for children); va.—བྱེད་.

ཐག་གིས་ཆོད་ (tāàgi cȍȍ) vi. to be certain/ sure ༈ཁོ་ཚོ་ལྷ་སར་ཕྱིན་པ་ཐག་གིས་ཆོད་ (I'm) sure they went to Lhasa.

ཐག་གུ་ (tōgu) a short rope. a thin rope; va.—མཆོང་ to skip/jump rope.

ཐག་གྲུ་ (tōgdru) sm. ཐ་གྲུ་.

ཐག་འགྱངས་ (tāàgyaŋ) far, distant.

ཐག་འགྱངས་པོ་ (tāà gyaŋbo) sm. ཐག་འགྱངས་.

ཐག་རྒྱ་ (tāàgya) a rope barricade; va.—འགྲེམ་; —གཏོང་ to set up a rope barrier, to cordon off an area with rope; va.—སློད་ to take away a rope barrier/ cordon.

ཐག་རྒྱང་ (tāàgyaŋ) a measurement roughly equal to 4 arm lengths.

ཐག་སྒྱུལ་འདྲ་གཟུགས་ (tōgüü drasug) puppet ༈ཐག་སྒྱུལ་འདྲ་གཟུགས་ཀྱི་སྲིད་གཞུང་ A puppet government.

ཐག་སྒྲ་ (tāgdra) the sound of sth. banging ("tak").

ཐག་གཅོད་ (tāàjȍȍ) a decision; va. ཐག་གཅོད་; —བྱེད་ to decide, to settle ༈ཁོ་ཚོ་ག་པར་འགྲོ་མིན་ཐག་བཅད་སོང་ They decided where they would go.

ཐག་གཅོད་ཐུབ་པའི་རང་བཞིན་ (tāàjȍȍ tūbɛ rəŋshin) decisiveness.

ཐག་གཅོད་དམག་འཐབ་ (tāàjȍȍ məgdəb) decisive battle.

ཐག་བཅད་ (tāà jɛ̄ɛ̀) p. of ཐག་གཅོད་.

ཐག་ཁྱེབས་ (tāàjib) a thimble used for sewing ropes.

ཐག་ཆོད་ (tāà cȍȍ) 1. vi. to be decided/ settled/ resolved ༈སང་ཉིན་ང་ཚོ་འགྲོ་རྒྱུ་ཐག་ཆོད་པ་རེད་ It's been decided we should go tomorrow. 2. (adj. + —) intensifies adjectival meaning: extremely/ a lot/ the best of the adjective (can also convey "too" ༈མང་ཐག་ཆོད་ Very many. ༈ཡག་ཐག་ཆོད་ Extremely good. ༈གསལ་ཐག་ཆོད་ Extremely clear. ༈གྲུ་ཉུང་ཐག་ཆོད་སྐབས་ Because there were extremely few boats. ༈ཕར་རྒོལ་བྱེད་རྒྱུར་དམག་མི་ཉུང་ཐག་ཆོད་བཞག There were too few soldiers to go on the offense. 3. certainly/ definitely ༈ཁོའི་ནང་ལ་མེ་མདའ་ཡོད་ཐག་ཆོད་རེད་ He definitely has a gun at home. ༈ཁོ་སོ་པ་ཡིན་ཐག་ཆོད་རེད་ He is definitely a spy. ༈ཁོ་ཚོ་ལྷ་སར་ཕྱིན་ཐག་ཆོད་རེད་ They definitely went to Lhasa.

ཐག་ཆོད་པོ་ (tāà cȍȍbo) sb. who makes decisions quickly/ decisively.

ཐག་ཆོད་ལྷིང་པོ་ (tāàjȍȍ lhĩŋbu) a stable/ secure/ firm decision.

ཐག་མཆོང་ (tāgjoŋ) rope skipping / jumping; va.—རྒྱག to skip/ jump rope.

ཐག་ཉེ་ (tāàñe) near.

ཐག་ཉེ་གོམ་གསུམ་ (tāàñe komsum) extremely close [Lit. near (by) three steps].

ཐག་ཉེ་པོ་ (tāà ñebo) near, close by ༈ལྷ་ས་འདི་ནས་ཐག་ཉེ་པོ་འདུག Lhasa is close to here.

ཐག་ཉེ་འབྲེལ་མཚུངས་ (tāàñe dreedzuŋ) near, close, convenient ༈ངའི་སྡོད་ས་དེ་ལས་ཁུངས་དང་ཐག་ཉེ་འབྲེལ་མཚུངས་རེད་ My residence is conveniently near my office.

ཐག་ཉེ་རིང་ཀུན་ཏུ་ (tāàñeriŋ gũndu) everywhere [Lit. all over near and far].

ཐག་ཉེ་རུ་ (tāà ñeru) closer, nearer; vi.—འགྲོ་ to go or come closer/ nearer ༈དམག་འཐབ་ཀྱི་ཉེན་ཁ་ཐག་ཉེ་རུ་འགྲོ་གི་ཡོད་པ་རེད་ The threat of war is coming closer.

ཐག་ཉེ་ས་ (tāà ñesa) a place near by.

ཐག་བསྡུང་ (tāà dūŋ) va. to shorten (e.g., rope, time, travel) ༈འགྲུལ་བཞུད་བྱེད་པའི་དུས་ཚོད་བསྡུང་པ་རེད་ (They) shortened the time of travel.

ཐག་ཐག (tāgdaà) 1. knocking/ tapping on a door, etc.; va.—གཏོང་. 2. a piece of wooden rod used on a grinding stone that controls the flow of grain. 3. sm. ཐག་ཐག་ཐིག་ཐིག.

ཐག་ཐག་ཐིག་ཐིག (tāgdaà dĩgdii) exactly right, quickly and on time/ efficiently ༈མི་འདི་ལས་ཀ་གང་ཡིན་ནའང་ཐག་ཐག་ཐིག་ཐིག་བྱེད་མཁན་ཞིག་རེད་ Whatever the work, that person is sb. who does things exactly right.

ཐག་ཐིག་འཐེན་ (tōgdig tēn) va. to pull or snap a taut rope/ string (e.g., to make a guideline on the ground when building a wall).

ཐག་ཐུག (tāgduù) abbr. of ཐག་གི་ཐུག་གི.

ཐག་ཐུང་ཐུང་ (tāà tūŋduŋ) close, near.

ཐག་མཐུད་ (tāgdüü) joining two pieces of rope together; va.—རྒྱག.

ཐག་འཐེན་ལུས་རྩལ་ (tāgden lṳ̈üdzee) tug of war; va.—འགྲན་ to compete in a tug of war.

ཐག་གདང་ (tāgdaŋ) 1. long rope tied from one peg to another that is used to tie up animals. 2. clothes line (made of rope).

ཐག་མདུང་ (tāgduŋ) a rope that is attached to a short spear.

ཐག་སྡོག་རྒྱག (tāgdɔɔ̀ gyaà) sm. ཐག་བསྡོགས་རྒྱག.

ཐག་བསྡོགས་ (tāgdɔɔ̀) coiling a rope into a bundle or ball; va.—རྒྱག.

ཐག་སྣེ་ (tāgne) the end of a rope.

ཐག་པ་ (tāgba) rope, string; va.—རྒྱག; —འཆིང་; —འདོགས་ to tie, to bind (with a rope); va.—གཏོང་ to set up a rope barrier/ cordon; to throw a rope to sb. ། རྐུན་མ་དེ་ཐག་པ་བརྒྱབ་ནས་ཁྲིད་ཡོང་གི་འདུག (They) tied up the thief and are bringing him here. ། ལས་ཀ་རྒྱག་པའི་མཐའ་སྐོར་དུ་ཐག་པ་བཏང་བཞག (They) have set up a rope barrier all along the construction site.

ཐག་པ་ཆད་ (tāgba cɛ̄ɛ̀) 1. vi. to have a rope snap/ break. 2. vi. to run out of sth. (money, food, etc.) ། དེང་སང་སྐུ་མགྲོན་མང་པོ་ཕེབས་ཙང་ཁ་ལག་ཐག་པ་ཆད་སོང་ These days because many guests have come I have run out of food. 3. vi. to be out of touch.

ཐག་པ་འཐེན་ (tāgba tēn) va. to pull a rope.

ཐག་པ་འཐེན་མཁན་ (tāgba tēnñɛn) 1. a pimp. 2. sb. who acts as a go-between in an illicit affair. 3. sb. who is competing in a tug-of-war.

ཐག་པ་འཐེན་པ་ (tāgba tēmba) sm. ཐག་པ་འཐེན་མཁན་.

ཐག་པ་འཐེན་ཤར་རྒྱག (tāgba tēnshar gyaà) va. to engage in a tug-of-war.

ཐག་པ་སྡོམ (tāgba dɔ̄ɔ̀) va. to pull in/ roll up a rope.

ཐག་པ་བཞི་བསླས་ (tāgba shilɛɛ̀) a rope made of four strands, a 4-ply rope.

ཐག་པས་འདོགས་ (tāgbɛɛ̀ dɔɔ̀) va. to tie with a rope.

ཐག་དཔྱང་ (tāgjoŋ) a rappelling rope; va.— གཏོང་ to let sb. down on a rappelling rope.

ཐག་སྦྲན་ (tāgbɛn) sm. ཐག་སྤྲན་.

ཐག་སྒྲིལ་གཏོང་ (tāgdree dōŋ) va. to tie several people together with one rope.

ཐག་ཚད་ (tāgdzɛɛ̀) 1. measuring tape/ ruler. 2. length or distance of a rope. 3. sm. ཐག་རྒྱང་.

ཐག་ཞོར་ (tāgshɔɔ) sth. incidental to a main act.

ཐག་ཞོར་རྒྱུན་འདྲུད་ (tāgshɔɔ gyṳ̈ndrüü) sm. ཐག་ཞོར་འབྲེང་འདྲུད་.

ཐག་ཞོར་འབྲེང་འདྲུད་ (tāgshɔɔ dreŋdrüü) associates/ friends/ relatives of sb. getting harmed because of that person; vi.—ཐེབས་; —བྱེད་ to get punished because of one's relations with another ། ཁོ་སོ་པ་ཡིན་ཙང་བཙོན་ཁང་ལ་ཚུད་པ་མ་ཟད་ ཐག་ཞོར་འབྲེང་འདྲུད་བྱས་ནས་ཉུན་མཆེད་ཡང་བཙོན་ཁང་ལ་ཚུད་པ་རེད་ Because he was a spy not only was he put in prison, but his relatives, because of their relationship with him, were put into prison.

ཐག་ཟམ་ (tāgsam) rope bridge.

ཐག་རིང་ (tāàriŋ) distant, far.

ཐག་རིང་ཁ་པར་ (tāàriŋ kābar) long distance telephone.

ཐག་རིང་གི་འཆར་གཞི་ (tāàriŋgi cāāshi) long term plan.

ཐག་རིང་འགྲོན་པོ་ (tāàriŋ drōmbo) a guest/ visitor from a distant place.

ཐག་རིང་ཐུང་ (tāà riŋduŋ) distance ། ལྷ་ས་བར་དུ་ཐག་རིང་ཐུང་ག་ཚོད་དམ་ How far is it to Lhasa?

ཐག་རིང་ནས་ཁ་ལོ་བསྒྱུར་ (tāàriŋnɛ kālo gyur) va. to control remotely or from a distance.

ཐག་རིང་དཔུང་འཇུག (tāàriŋ būŋjuù) expedition (army).

ཐག་རིང་པོ་ (tāà riŋbu) far away, distant ། ཟ་ཁང་དེ་ཐག་རིང་པོ་འདུག That restaurant is far away.

ཐག་རིང་མོ་ (tāà riŋmu) sm. ཐག་རིང་པོ་.

ཐག་རིང་ཚོད་འཛིན་ (tāàriŋ tsōndzin) sm. ཐག་རིང་ནས་ཁ་ལོ་སྒྱུར་.

ཐག་རིང་ས་ (tāà riŋsə) a place that is far away.

ཐག་ལུང་ (tōgluŋ) a round wooden buckle/ ring at the end of a rope that is used to tighten the rope.

ཐག་ཤུར་གློད་ (tāgshur lȫö) va. to slide down a rope.

ཐགས་ (tāà) 1. weaving; va.—འཐག to weave.

ཐགས་ཀྱི་རྒྱུ་ (tāàgi gyu) warp.

ཐགས་ཀྱི་སྤུན་ (tāàgi bün) woof.

ཐགས་ཀང་ (tāàgaŋ) weaving that is tight.

ཐགས་ཁྲི་ (tōgdri) loom (for weaving).

ཐགས་མཁན་ (tāàñɛn) weaver.

ཐགས་མཁན་འབུ་ (tāàñɛnbu) spider.

ཐགས་འཁྲུགས་ (tāà drüü) vi. to get tangled up in sth.

ཐགས་གྲུ་བུ་ (tāà drubu) a ball of yarn.

ཐགས་རྒྱུད་ (tōgyüü) warp.

ཐགས་ཆས་ (tāgjɛɛ̀) weaving implements.

ཐགས་བཏགས་ (tāg dāà) p. of ཐགས་འཐག.

ཐགས་སྟེགས་ (tāgdeg) sm. ཐགས་ཁྲི་.

ཐགས་ཐོགས་ (tāgdɔɔ̀) obstacle, hindrance, impediment, obstruction ། ལམ་ཁག་ལ་ཐགས་ཐོགས་མང་པོ་བྱུང་ (We) encountered many obstacles on the trip (road). ། ཁོས་ལན་ཐགས་ཐོགས་མེད་པར་བརྒྱབ་པ་རེད་ (He) answered without any hindrances (fluently).

ཐགས་འཐག (tāà tāà) see ཐགས་.

ཐགས་འཐག་མཁན་ (tāà tāàñɛn) sm. ཐགས་མཁན་.

ཐགས་དམ་ལ་ཞིབ་ཚགས་པ་ (tāgdamla shibdzagba) tightly woven.

ཐགས་དྲུབས་མ་ (tāg drubmə) a woven thanka.

ཐགས་གནས་ (tāgnɛɛ̀) sm. ཐགས་ར་.

ཐགས་སྣལ་མ་ (tāg nɛ̄ɛma) thread, yarn.

ཐགས་བབ་ (tāgbəb) sm. ཁ་བབ་ཙམ་.

ཐགས་སྤྲན་ (tāgdrɛn) va. to arrange the warp (threads) for weaving.

ཐགས་སྦྲན་ (tāgbɛn) sm. ཐགས་སྤྲན་.

ཐགས་མ་ (tāgma) female weaver.

ཐགས་བཟང་ (tāgsaŋ) well-arranged, well-set-up or laid out.

ཐགས་བཟང་རིས་ (tāg saŋrii) king of the demigods.

ཐགས་ར་ (tōgri) weaver's workshop, place where weaving is done.

ཐགས་རན་ (tāgrɛn) the lines in woven cloth (from the weaving).

ཐགས་ལ་བབ་ (tāgla bəb) sm. ཁ་བབ་ཙམ་.

ཐགས་ལྷོད་པ་ (tāà lhȫöba) a loose/ soft weave.

ཐང་ (tāŋ) 1. plain, steppe ། ཐང་འདིའི་སྟེང་ལ་འབྲོག་པ་མང་པོ་ཡོད་པ་རེད་ There are many nomads on this plain. 2. soup ། མོ་ཐང་འཐུང་གི་འདུག She is drinking soup. 3. liquid medicine that has been brewed. 4. T'ang Dynasty. 5. lightness ། ནམ་ལངས་ཐང་དཀར་པོ་ཆགས་བཞག The dawn rose and it has become light. 6. vi. to become clear (weather) ། ཆར་པ་བབས་རྗེས་གནམ་ཐང་བཞག After the rain the sky cleared. 7. sm. ཐེངས་. 8. abbr. of ཐང་ཡིག.

ཐང་ཀ་ (tāŋga) Tibetan scroll painting (thanka).

ཐང་དཀར་ (tāŋgar) 1. Tibetan white vulture. 2. white pine (a species of pine tree).

ཐང་དཀར་རྒོད་པོ་ (tāŋgar gȫöbo) sm. ཐང་དཀར་, 1.

ཐང་དཀར་པོ་ (tāŋ gārbo) light, clear, bright.

ཐང་རྒྱལ་ (tāŋgyɛɛ) sm. ཐང་ཁུག.

ཐང་སྐུ་ (tāŋgu) thanka.

ཐང་སྐུ་རྒས་པ་གྲལ་གཤམ་ (tāŋgu gɛɛ̀ba trɛɛsham) old people are shunted aside [Lit. the old thanka is put at the back of the row].

ཐང་ཁ་ (tāŋga) sm. ཐང་ཀ་.

ཐང་ཁུག (tōŋgu) skin bag in which Tibetan tsamba is mixed with tea and kneaded for eating; va.—གཡོག a) to mix tsamba in such a bag; b) to dupe/ trick/ deceive sb.; c) to cuckold sb.; vi.—གོན་ to be duped/ tricked/ deceived; vi. to be/ get cuckolded.

ཐང་ཁུལ་ (tāŋgüü) a flat area, a plain/ steppe area.

ཐང་ཁྲག (tāŋdraà) sap from a pine tree.

ཐང་ག (tāŋga) sm. ཐང་ཀ་.

ཐང་གལ་ (tāŋgɛɛ) eng. sm. ཐན་ཁེ་.

ཐང་གི་སྦྱོར་བ་ (tāŋgi jɔɔwa) process of brewing Tibetan liquid medicines.

ཐང་འགོ་ (tāŋgo) 1. the upper part of a thanka. 2. the upper part of a plain/ steppe.

ཐང་འགའ་ (tāŋga) a few times, several times ¶ ང་ལྷ་སར་ཐང་འགའ་འགྲོ་མྱོང་ I have gone to Lhasa several times.

ཐང་འགོ་ལ་ (tāŋgola) Thangola pass (in N. Tibet).

ཐང་ཀོད་ (tāŋgöö) a flat wasteland.

ཐང་རྒྱ་ཆེན་པོ་ (tāŋ gyacembo) vast field/ plain/ steppe.

ཐང་རྒྱལ་རབས་ (tāŋ gyɛɛrəb) the Tang Dynasty.

ཐང་སྒྲོན་ (tāŋdrön) pine lantern (made from pine wood which stays lit because of its sap).

ཐང་ངི་ཐུང་ངི་ (tāŋŋi tüŋŋi) short.

ཐང་ངེ་ཐིང་ངེ་ (tāŋŋe tiŋŋe) hesitating; va.—བྱེད་ to hesitate ¶ ཟིང་ཆ་ལངས་ཙང་ཁོ་བོད་ལ་འགྲོ་རྒྱུ་ཐང་ངེ་ཐིང་ངེ་བྱེད་ཀྱི་འདུག Because there was a disturbance he is hesitating about going to Tibet.

ཐང་ཅིག (tāŋjig) sm. ཐང་གཅིག.

ཐང་གཅིག (tāŋjig) one time, once ¶ ང་ཐང་གཅིག་འགྲོ་མྱོང་ I have experienced going once.

ཐང་གཅོད་ (tāŋ jöö) abbr. of ཐང་ཤ་གཅོད་.

ཐང་ཆད་ (tāŋ cɛ̀ɛ̀) vi. to be or get tired/ fatigued/ worn out ¶ ལས་ཀ་ཉིན་གང་བྱས་ཙང་ཐང་ཆད་བྱུང་ Because I worked all day, I got tired.

ཐང་ཆད་དེ་བ་ (tāŋ cɛ̀ɛ̀dewa) tired, fatigued, worn out ¶ ལས་ཀ་ཉིན་གང་བྱས་ཙང་ཐང་ཆད་དེ་བ་བྱུང་ Because I worked all day, I got tired.

ཐང་ཆུ་ (tāŋju) resin, gum, sap (of pine trees).

ཐང་ཆུ་དངས་མ་ (tāŋju taŋma) turpentine.

ཐང་ཆོད་ (tāŋ cöö) vi. to get stretched out.

ཐང་ཆེན་ (tāŋjen) 1. a large plain/ steppe. 2. a square, a plaza.

ཐང་ཆེན་བང་རྩལ་འགྲན་བསྡུར་ (tāŋjen paŋdzɛɛ drɛndur) cross-country race.

ཐང་ཆེན་གཡུལ་འགྱེད་དམག (tāŋjen yüügyeè māà) field army.

ཐང་འཇུག (tāŋjuù) the end/ edge of an open space or plain.

ཐང་སྟོང་ (tāŋdoŋ) wilderness, desert.

ཐང་སྟོང་རྒྱལ་པོ་ (tāŋdoŋ gyɛɛbo) name of a famous Tibetan lama.

ཐང་སྟོང་སོལ་ར་ (tāŋdoŋ sōōra) opencut coal mine.

ཐང་ཐང་ (tāŋdaŋ) 1. sm. ཐང་པོ་. 2. stretched out; va.—བཙོ་ to stretch sth. (usu. leather) ¶ ཀོ་བ་ཐང་བཙོས་བཞག (He) stretched out the leather.

ཐང་ཐུང་ (tāŋduŋ) abbr. of ཐང་ངི་ཐུང་ངི་.

ཐང་ཐེར་ (tāŋder) 1. virgin land, previously untouched/ uncultivated land. 2. open space. 3. a square, a plaza.

ཐང་འཐབ་དམག (tāŋdəb māg) sm. ཐང་འཐབ་དམག་སྡེ་.

ཐང་འཐབ་དམག་སྡེ་ (tāŋdəb māgde) field army ¶ ཐང་འཐབ་དམག་སྡེ་གཉིས་པ་ The 2nd Field Army.

ཐང་འཐེན་ (tāŋden) sm. ཐང་ངེ་ཐིང་ངེ.

ཐང་འཐོར་ (tāŋdɔɔ) shung. scattered on the floor/ ground ¶ ལུས་སྟེང་དུ་རྒྱུགས་པ་གྲངས་མེད་བཏང་བས་ཤ་ཁྲག་ཐང་འཐོར་མཆམས་ He was whipped innumerable times so his flesh and blood were scattered on the floor.

ཐང་དེབ་ (tāŋdeb) historical annals/ records of the Tang Dynasty.

ཐང་བདེ་མོ་ (tāŋ demo) an even or level plain/ open space.

ཐང་བདེ་མོའི་ཐོག་ཕོ་དང་ཕོ་འཛིང་རྒྱུ་ (tāŋ demö tɔ̄ɔ pōdaŋ pō dziŋgyu) two people/ forces competing with equal strength [Lit. two men fighting on a level open space].

ཐང་སྡེ་ (tāŋde) sm. ཐང་ཐེར་.

ཐང་སྡེར་ (tāŋder) sm. ཐང་ཐེར་.

ཐང་ནག (tāŋnag) black pine (a species of pine tree).

ཐང་སྣུམ་ (tāŋnum) sm. ཐང་ཆུ་.

ཐང་པོ་ (tāŋbo) 1. healthy, well, fit ¶ ཁོའི་གཟུགས་པོ་ཐང་པོ་འདུག He is healthy. 2. taut, tight, tense ¶ རྒྱུད་པ་དེ་ཐང་པོ་འཐེན་དགོས་ You have to pull the string taut.

ཐང་སྤུངས་རྒྱག (tāŋbuŋ gyaà) va. to pile sth. on the open ground.

ཐང་ཕྲོམ་དཀར་པོ་ (tāŋdrom gārbo) white henbane.

ཐང་ཕྲོམ་ནག་པོ་ (tāŋdrom nagbo) black henbane.

ཐང་བུ་ (tāŋbu) sm. ཐི་ཕྲུག.

ཐང་བྲང་ (tāŋdraŋ) an encampment on the steppes/ plains (where there are no people); va.—འདེབས་ to erect such an encampment.

ཐང་དབྱེ་ (tāŋye) a remote field/ plain.

ཐང་སྦྱོར་སྡེ་ཚན་ (tāŋjɔɔ dedzɛn) sm. ཐང་གི་སྦྱོར་བ་.

ཐང་མ་ (tāŋma) 1. healthy, well. 2. even, equal (usually pertains to grain) ¶ ས་སྟེང་འབྲུ་རིགས་ཐང་མར་བརྡལ་འདུག The grain is spread evenly on the ground.

ཐང་དམག (tāŋmaà) soldiers of the Tang dynasty.

ཐང་དམར་ (tāŋmar) red pine (a species of pine tree).

ཐང་མེད་ (tāŋmeè) unhealthy, unwell.

ཐང་སྨྱུལ་ (tāŋñüü) letting animals wander freely (untethered) to graze; va.—གཏོང་.

ཐང་སྨན་ (tāŋmɛn) liquid medicine.

ཐང་སྨུག (tāŋmug) 1. a kind of dark purple/ blackish vulture. 2. a type of pine tree.

ཐང་ཙམ་ནས་ (tāŋdzamnɛ) in a little while, soon ¶ ཐང་ཙམ་ནས་ང་ཁྲོམ་ལ་འགྲོ་གི་ཡིན་ I will go to the market in a little while.

ཐང་ཙམ་གནང་ (tāŋdzam nāŋ) wait for awhile/ for a moment ¶ བོད་ལ་ཟིང་ཡོད་ཙང་བོད་ལ་ཕེབས་རྒྱུ་ཐང་ཙམ་གནང་ན་ཡག་གི་རེད་ Because there are disturbances in Tibet, it will be better if you wait for awhile.

ཐང་ཙམ་སོང་ནས་ (tāŋdzam sōŋnɛ) sm. ཐང་ཙམ་ནས་.

ཐང་ཚི་ (tāŋdzi) pine tar/ sap/ resin.

ཐང་ཞྭ་ (tāŋshu) a hat worn by monks in the traditional Tibetan government.

ཐང་ཞིང་ (tāŋshiŋ) cultivated land on a plain or on flat/ level area.

ཐང་གཞལ་ (tāŋ shɛɛ) va. to set a price/ value.

ཐང་གཞི་ (tāŋshi) market rate/ price ¶ འབྲུ་ཁལ་གཅིག་ལ་དེ་དུས་ཐང་གཞི་ག་ཚོད་རེད་ What was the market price of one ཁལ་ of grain at that time?

ཐང་གཞིའི་གནས་ཚུལ་ (tāŋshi nɛ̀ɛ̀dzüü) market condition/ situation, market rate/ price.

ཐང་གཞུང་ (tāŋshuŋ) steppe, plain, flat area.

ཐང་ཡངས་པོ་ (tāŋ yaŋbo) sm. ཐང་ཆེན་.

ཐང་ཡིག (tāŋyii) 1. biography. 2. will, last testament. 3. history.

ཐང་ཡིག་སྡེ་ལྔ་ (tāŋyig deŋa) name of a historical text.

ཐང་གཡེར་ (tāŋyer) sm. ཐང་ཆེན་.

ཐང་རག (tāŋraà) cedar.

ཐང་རབས་ (tāŋrəb) Tang Dynasty.

ཐང་རིན་ (tāŋrin) sm. ཐང་གཞི་.

ཐང་ལི་ (tāŋli) squirrel.

ཐང་ཤ་གཅོད་ (tāŋsha jöö) va. to stretch leather.

ཐང་ཤ་དོད་པོ་ (tāŋsha tööbo) strong, healthy (in appearance).

ཐང་ཤིང་ (tāŋshin) pine tree.

ཐང་ཤིང་སྣུམ་ (tāŋshiŋ nūm) turpentine.

ཐང་ཤིང་ལོ་མ་ (tāŋshiŋ loma) pine needles.

ཐང་གསོང་ (tāŋshoŋ) sm. ཐང་ཆེན་.

ཐང་གསོངས་ (tāŋshoŋ) sm. ཐང་ཆེན་.

ཐང་ལྷ་ (tāŋlha) Tangla Mts.

ཐང་ལྷོད་ (tāŋlhöö) 1. tight and loose ¶ ཐང་རོལ་ཆའི་ལྒྱུགས་སྐྱུད་ཐང་ལྷོད་སྙོམས་པོ་ཞིག་སྒྲིག་དགོས་ One must twist the strings of the musical instrument so that they are evenly tight and loose. 2. (for work) hastily and slowly.

ཐད་ (tɛ̀ɛ̀) 1. (gen. + —) concerning, about ¶ གནས་ཚུལ་འདིའི་ཐད་ལ་ཁོས་འགྲེལ་བརྗོད་བྱས་ཡོད་པ་མ་རེད་ He hasn't made any comments about this news.

2. straight, direct ། ཁོང་གི་ཐད་དུ་གདང་ནས་ Facing directly towards him. 3. va. to go (h.). ། ཁོང་ལྷ་སར་ཐད་སོང་ He went to Lhasa.
ཐད་ཀ་ (tɛ̀ɛga) straight, direct.
ཐད་ཀར་ (tɛ̀ɛgar) straight, directly ། ཁོ་ལྷ་སར་ཐད་ཀར་ཕྱིན་པ་རེད་ He went straight to Lhasa.
ཐད་ཀར་འདེམས་བསྐོ་ (tɛ̀ɛgar demgo) direct election.
ཐད་ཀའི་རྒྱུ་རྐྱེན་ (tɛ̀ɛgɛ gyugyen) direct cause.
ཐད་ཀའི་ཉམས་མྱོང་ (tɛ̀ɛgɛ ñəmñuŋ) direct experience, firsthand experience.
ཐད་ཀའི་རི་བོ་ (tɛ̀ɛgɛ riwo) 1. the surrounding hills/ mountains. 2. hills and mountains in the front (rather than distant).
ཐད་ཀའི་འདེམས་བསྐོ་ (tɛ̀ɛgɛ demgo) sm. ཐད་ཀར་འདེམས་བསྐོ་.
ཐད་སྐྱོང་ (tɛ̀ɛgyoŋ) under direct jurisdiction ། ཀྲུང་དབྱང་གི་ཐད་སྐྱོང་གྲོང་ཁྱེར་ཁ་ཤས་ཡོད་པ་རེད་ There are several cities under the direct jurisdiction of the central government.
ཐད་བསྐོས་ (tɛ̀ɛgöö) appointed directly by the ruler/ chief/ head.
ཐད་ཁར་ (tɛ̀ɛgar) h. of འགྲོ་ཁར་.
ཐད་མཁན་ (tɛ̀ɛñɛn) h. of འགྲོ་མཁན་.
ཐད་ཁྲོན་ (tɛ̀ɛdrön) deep well, vertical shaft (in mine or well).
ཐད་འགྱེད་ (tɛ̀ɛgyeè) direct beaming (of rays).
ཐད་རྒྱ་གོད་པོ་ (tɛ̀ɛgya göbo) h. of འགྲོ་རྒྱ་གོད་པོ་.
ཐད་རྒྱུག་གློག་རྒྱུན་ (tɛ̀ɛgyuù lōggyün) direct current (DC).
ཐད་རྒྱུག་གློག་འདྲེན་འཕྲུལ་འཁོར་ (tɛ̀ɛgyuù lōgdren trũũgɔɔ) direct current generator.
ཐད་རྒྱུག་གློག་ལམ་ (tɛ̀ɛgyuù lōglam) direct current line.
ཐད་སྒྱུར་ (tɛ̀ɛgyur) literal translation, word-for-word translation; va.—བྱེད་.
ཐད་བརྗོད་ཚིག་གྲུབ་ (tɛ̀ɛjöö tsīgdrub) narrative sentence.
ཐད་གཏོགས་ (tɛ̀ɛdɔɔ̀) belonging to, affiliated with, part of ། རུ་ཁག་དང་པོའི་ཐད་གཏོགས་ Belonging to the first brigade.
ཐད་གཏོགས་གྲོང་ཁྱེར་ (tɛ̀ɛdɔɔ̀ troŋgyee) sm. དངོས་སྐྱོང་གྲོང་ཁྱེར་.
ཐད་གདོང་ཁ་པར་ (tɛ̀ɛdoŋ kābar) direct dial telephone.
ཐད་སྟངས་ (tɛ̀ɛdaŋ) h. of འགྲོ་སྟངས་.
ཐད་ཐད་སོ་སོ་ (tɛ̀ɛdɛɛ̀ sōso) shung. sm. ཁག་ཁག་སོ་སོ་.
ཐད་མཐོང་ (tɛ̀ɛdoŋ) 1. audio visual. 2. directly perceived through the senses.
ཐད་དང་བརྒྱུད་ (tɛ̀ɛ daŋ gyüü) directly and indirectly ། གནད་དོན་འདིའི་སྐོར་ངས་འགོ་ཁྲིད་ལ་ཐད་དང་བརྒྱུད་ནས་ཞུས་པ་ཡིན་ Concerning this issue, I asked the boss directly and (via) indirect (channels).
ཐད་དུ་ (tɛ̀ɛdu) sm. ཐད་.
ཐད་དུས་ (tɛ̀ɛdüù) h. of འགྲོ་དུས་.
ཐད་དོན་ (tɛ̀ɛdön) h. of འགྲོ་དོན་.
ཐད་དྲང་ (tɛ̀ɛdraŋ) straight, straight line ། གཞུང་ལམ་དེ་ཁྲོམ་གཞུང་ནས་ཐད་དྲང་དེ་བཟོས་བཞག (They) built that highway in a straight line from the market. ། ཁྱིམ་ཚང་གི་མདུན་ནས་ཐད་དྲང་དེ་ལམ་ཁ་བཟོས་པ་ They built the road right in front of the house.
ཐད་དྲངས་ (tɛ̀ɛdraŋ) sm. ཐད་དྲང་.
ཐད་ནས་ (tɛ̀ɛnɛ) sm. ཐད་, 1.
ཐད་དཔྱངས་ (tɛ̀ɛjaŋ) hanging vertically (usu. rope, thread).
ཐད་འཕུར་གནམ་གྲུ་ (tɛ̀ɛbur nəmdru) helicopter.
ཐད་བྲུས་གཏེར་ཁྲོན་ (tɛ̀ɛdrüù dērdrön) vertical shaft (in a mine).
ཐད་འབིགས་གཏེར་ཁྲོན་ (tɛ̀ɛbig dērdrön) sm. ཐད་བྲུས་གཏེར་ཁྲོན་.
ཐད་མཚམས་ (tɛ̄ndzam) at the time/ moment of ། ལས་འགན་རང་ཐོག་ཏུ་བབས་པའི་ཐད་མཚམས་ལ་འགན་ཡག་པོ་སྒྲུབ་དགོས་ At the time when the responsibility of a task falls on oneself, one must do it well.
ཐད་ཚོར་ (tɛ̀ɛtsɔɔ) seeing and feeling directly, perceiving directly.
ཐད་གཞུང་ (tɛ̀ɛshuŋ) vertical, lengthwise.
ཐད་ཟུར་ (tɛ̀ɛsur) at right angles.
ཐད་བཤད་ཐད་འབྲི་ (tɛ̀ɛshɛɛ̀ tɛ̀ɛ dri) va. to say and write right away.
ཐད་བཤར་ (tɛ̀ɛshar) straight, directly.
ཐད་ལ་ (tɛ̀ɛla) sm. ཐད་.
ཐད་སོ་ (tɛ̀ɛso) sm. ཐད་ཀ་.
ཐན་ (tɛ̄n) 1. abbr. of ཐན་པ་. 2. a disaster, sth. bad.
ཐན་ཀོར་ (tɛ̄ngɔɔ) near by, adjacent to, surrounding.
ཐན་སྐད་ (tɛ̄ngɛɛ) sounds that are considered bad omens.
ཐན་སྐོར་ (tɛ̄ngɔɔ) sm. ཐན་ཀོར་.
ཐན་སྐྱོན་ (tɛ̄ngyön) 1. drought. 2. drought damage.
ཐན་ཁི་ (tɛ̄nge) eng. tank.
ཐན་ཁི་འཁོར་ལོ་ (tɛ̄nge kɔ̄ɔlo) eng.tib. sm. ཐན་ཁི་.
ཐན་འགྱུར་དངོས་པོ་ (tɛ̄ngyüù ŋɔ̄ɔbo) carbonized material, carbide.
ཐན་འགྱེད་ (tɛ̄n gyeè) va. to send bad news.
ཐན་འགོག (tɛ̄ngɔɔ̀) drought prevention; va.—བྱེད་.
ཐན་འགོག་ཆུ་འགོག (tɛ̄ngɔɔ̀ shöngɔɔ̀) preventing drought and flood; va.— བྱེད་.
ཐན་ཆེན་ (tɛ̄njen) a great drought.
ཐན་ལྟས་ (tɛ̄ndɛɛ) a bad/ ill omen.
ཐན་ཐུབ་ (tɛ̄ndub) drought resistant ། ཐན་ཐུབ་ལོ་ཏོག Drought resistant crops.
ཐན་ཐུན་ (tɛ̄ndün) a few, a little.
ཐན་འདྲེ་ (tɛ̄ndre) 1. demons and spirits that convey bad omens. 2. demons that cause drought.
ཐན་ལྡན་འགྱུར་རྫས་ (tɛ̄ndɛn gyurdzɛɛ̀) sm. ཐན་འགྱུར་དངོས་པོ་.
ཐན་ནེ་ཐུན་ནེ་ (tɛ̄nne tũnne) small pieces.
ཐན་པ་ (tɛ̄mba) 1. drought; vi.—གཏོང་; —བསྐྱོན་ to be/ get drought ། ད་ལོ་ཐན་པ་ཞེ་དྲག་བཏང་སོང་ There was a lot of drought this year. 2. bad omen/ sign.
ཐན་པ་ཆེ་དུས་ཆར་པ་རྒྱ་བསམ་ (tɛ̄mba cēdüù cārba cūsam) sm. སྨོན་པ་རྒྱ་འདོད་ལྟར་.
ཐན་པ་ཐེག་ཐུབ་པ་ (tɛ̄mba tēgdubbə) sm. ཐན་ཐུབ་.
ཐན་པ་ཚ་པོ་ (tɛ̄mba tsābo) a severe drought.
ཐན་པའི་ས་ཁུལ་ (tɛ̄mbɛ sāgüü) drought prone region.
ཐན་སྤྲིན་ (tɛ̄ndrin) clouds that bare bad omens, clouds that indicate drought.
ཐན་ཕྱི་ནག་པོ་ (tɛ̄nje nagbo) carbon black.
ཐན་བྱ་ (tɛ̄nca) owl [Lit. a bird that portends bad omen].
ཐན་བྱུང་ (tɛ̄njuŋ) sm. ཐན་པ་བྱུང་.
ཐན་བྱུར་ (tɛ̄njur) drought disaster.
ཐན་རླུང་ (tɛ̄nluŋ) a dry wind that is a sign of drought.
ཐན་སོན་རླུང་ (tɛ̄nsönluŋ) ch.tib. carbonic acid gas.
ཐན་སྲོལ་ (tɛ̄nsöö) bad customs.
ཐན་ཧེ་ (tɛ̄nhe) ch. carbon black.
ཐབ་ (tə̄b) stove, fireplace ། མདང་དགོང་གི་ཐུག་ཐུག་དེ་ཐབ་ལ་བཀག་ (She) put last night's broth on the stove.
ཐབ་ཀ་ (tə̄bga) sm. ཐབ་.
ཐབ་ཀ་པ་ (tə̄bgəwə) cook.
ཐབ་ཀྱི་ས་ཚིག (tə̄bgi sə̄dzii) the earth from the middle opening of a stove (used in Tibetan medicine).
ཐབ་སྐམ་ (tə̄bgam) a type of pincer used to pick things out of the stove.
ཐབ་སྐྱེལ་ (tə̄bgyee) shung. seeing off people on a journey by accompanying them about a mile and then putting up a tent and cooking a meal.
ཐབ་སྐོར་ (tə̄bgyɔr) the area around a stove where ashes are kept.
ཐབ་ཁ་ (tə̄bga) sm. ཐབ་ཀ་.
ཐབ་ཁག (tə̄bgaà) a small group of people who cook together (usu. on a journey) ། ཚོང་པ་ཐབ་ཁག་ལྔ་ལྷ་སར་སླེབས་བཞག A group of traders who were divided into five groups who cook together, arrived in Lhasa.

ཐབ་ཁང་ (tābgaŋ) kitchen.

ཐབ་ཁུང་ (tābguŋ) hole on the side of the stove used for adding fuel (wood, etc.).

ཐབ་ཁེབ་ (tābgeb) tea cozy.

ཐབ་ཁོངས་ (tābgoŋ) people who eat together from the same kitchen/ canteen ¶ཁོ་ཚོ་ཐབ་ཁོངས་གཅིག་པ་རེད་ They eat together.

ཐབ་ཁྲོ་ (tābdro) iron pots and cauldrons.

ཐབ་གུར་ (tābgur) a tent which is used as a kitchen, cook tent.

ཐབ་གླ་ (tābla) shung. fee for using a stove ¶བཀའ་འགྱུར་གསུང་སྒྲོག་གིས་མཚོན་སྐྱབ་མཆོད་ཁག་གི་ཐབ་གླ་དང་ཆུ་གླ་མི་སེར་ནས་བསྡུ་མི་ཆོག (You) are not allowed to collect from the subjects stove and water fees when performing religious rites such as reading the Kangyur.

ཐབ་མགོ་ (tābgo) the side opening in a stove where the wood/ fuel is inserted.

ཐབ་འགྲམ་ (tābdram) around the stove.

ཐབ་རྒྱག (tāb gyaà) va. to build/ make a stove from stones or bricks.

ཐབ་སྒྱེད་ (tābgyeè) the raised part of a stove where the pots are placed.

ཐབ་སྒོ་ (tābgo) sm. ཐབ་མགོ་.

ཐབ་སྒྲོམ་ (tābdrom) 1. stove. 2. cupboard for keeping pots and pans.

ཐབ་ཆ་ (tābja) sm. ཐབ་ཆས་.

ཐབ་ཆ་སྒྲིག (tābja dri̲g) va. to prepare/ arrange a stove at night for lighting the next morning.

ཐབ་ཆང་ (tābjaŋ) ཆང་ given to a family when they build a new stove.

ཐབ་ཆས་ (tābjɛɛ̀) cooking/ kitchen utensils.

ཐབ་ཆི་ (tābji) button; vi.—གྲོལ་ to come unbuttoned; va.—འགྲོལ་ to unbutton; va.—རྒྱག to button ¶ཁོས་སྟོད་ཐུང་གི་ཐབ་ཆི་རྒྱག་གི་འདུག He is buttoning his shirt.

ཐབ་ཆུང་ (tābjuŋ) small mess/ canteen for high officials.

ཐབ་ཆུང་ཆུང་མེ་ཚ་པོ་ (tāb cūŋjuŋ me̲ tsābo) small but effective/ good, a few working but having a large effect [Lit. small stove, hot fire].

ཐབ་ཆུང་མེ་ཚ་ (tābjuŋ me̲dza) small but effective/ good, few working but having a large effect [Lit. small stove, hot fire].

ཐབ་ཆེན་ (tābjen) 1. great/ large furnace. 2. large mess/ canteen for common officials/ workers.

ཐབ་གཉེར་ (tābñer) shung. 1. steward/ manager of a kitchen. 2. person in charge of a furnace, furnace operator.

ཐབ་རྟེན་ (tābden) shung. salary estate (an estate held by a government official as a source of income).

ཐབ་སྡེགས་ (tābdeg) stand/ base for a stove.

ཐབ་ཐིབ (tābdib) 1. abbr. of ཐབ་པི་ཐིབ་པི་.

ཐབ་གདན་ཆ་ (tāb de̲nja) cooking/ kitchen utensils and rugs.

ཐབ་འདྲེན་ (tābdren) arc. chief of cooks.

ཐབ་རྡོ་ (tābdo) 1. a stove made from placing three (or four) stones around an open center (the pot is placed on top of the stones and the fire is lit between them and under the pot). 2. a stone for making a stone stove.

ཐབ་རྡོ་སུམ་ཛོམ་ (tābdo sūmdzom) sm. ཐབ་རྡོ་.

ཐབ་ནག (tābnaà) soot from a stove.

ཐབ་ནག་གི་མདུད་པ་འགྲོལ་ (tābnaàgi dü̲üba drö̲ö) differentiating what is right from wrong or good from bad [Lit. untying a sooty knot].

ཐབ་སྣོད་ (tābnöö) cooking pots and pans, cooking vessels.

ཐབ་ཕྱིས་ (tābcii) dustcloth, dust rug for cleaning/ wiping.

ཐབ་པི་ཐིབ་པི་ (tābbi ti̲bbi) 1. cloudy (weather). 2. dull, not sharp (mentally). 3. dizzy (for people).

ཐབ་སྦྱོར་ (tāb jo̲r) sm. ཐབ་རྒྱག.

ཐབ་མིག (tābmii) stove holes.

ཐབ་ཙ་ (tābdza) near the stove.

ཐབ་ཚགས་ (tābdzaà) ash sifter in a stove.

ཐབ་ཚང་ (tābdzaŋ) kitchen.

ཐབ་ཚུགས་ (tābdzuù) livelihood.

ཐབ་འཛིན་ (tāb dzi̲n) va. to maintain/ keep a household ¶ངའི་ཕྲུ་གུ་འདི་ཚོ་ད་ལྟ་ཐབ་འཛིན་ཐུབ་ཀྱི་མི་འདུག These children of mine are unable to keep (their own) a household now. ¶ཆབ་འབངས་མེད་པའི་དངུལ་ཀྲང་ཉུང་ངུས་བླ་བྲང་ཐབ་འཛིན་ཐུབ་མིན་ལ་ It is difficult to maintain the Labrang without subjects and with not much money.

ཐབ་གཞོབ་ (tābshob) sth. that has fallen into the fire and is causing a foul smell.

ཐབ་ཟངས་ (tābsaŋ) copper pot for use on a stove.

ཐབ་ཟིན་ (tābsin) sm. ཐབ་འཛིན་.

ཐབ་ཟུར་ (tābsur) corner of a stove.

ཐབ་ཟུར་དུ་སྐྱོལ་ (tābsur tu̲dröö) moving an official to a position with no power [Lit. moving to the corner of the stove].

ཐབ་བཟོའི་ས་ (tābsö sā) earth for building a stove.

ཐབ་གཡོག (tābyɔɔ̀) 1. kitchen helper/ assistant. 2. lower level position in a monastery. 3. shung. person who cooks food for travelers as a corvee tax.

ཐབ་རུང་ (tābruŋ) monastic kitchen.

ཐབ་ལས་ (tāblɛɛ̀) kitchen work; va.—བྱེད་.

ཐབ་ལུང་ (tābluŋ) button hole.

ཐབ་ཤིང་ (tābshiŋ) firewood (for cooking).

ཐབ་ཤོར་ (tābshɔɔ) 1. vi. to have a family cease to exist/ become extinct. 2. sm. ཐབ་གཞོབ་.

ཐབ་གསར་འཛུགས་ (tābsaa dzu̲ù) va. to start a new household.

ཐབ་བསང་ཐབ་ཁྲུས་ (tābsaŋ tābdrüü) cleaning a stove by burning incense to rid it of anything that is unclean.

ཐབ་བསུ་ (tābsu) shung. reception with food when sb. arrives for a visit (the traveler is received with a meal about a mile from the home).

ཐབ་བསུ་སྐྱེལ་ (tābsu gyēē) abbr. of ཐབ་སྐྱེལ་ and ཐབ་བསུ་.

ཐབ་གསུར་ (tābsur) sm. ཐབ་གཞོབ་.

ཐབ་གསོལ་ (tābsöö) sm. ཐབ་ཚང་.

ཐབ་ལྷ་ (tāblha) hearth deity.

ཐབས་ (tāb) 1. means, method, way. 2. (vb. + —) means of doing the verbal action ¶ལྕགས་བཟོ་ཐབས་གསར་པ་ A new means of making steel. ¶དེ་ལ་ཁས་ལེན་ནམ་ཡང་ཞུ་ཐབས་མེད་ There is no way at all (we) can recognize/ accept that. 3. (vb. + — བྱེད་) va. to try to do ¶ཁོ་ཚོ་ལྷ་སར་འགྲོ་ཐབས་བྱེད་ཀྱི་ཡོད་པ་རེད་ They are trying to go to Lhasa. 4. no choice but to do ¶ཁོ་ཚོ་ལྷ་སར་མ་འགྲོ་ཐབས་མེད་རེད་ They had no choice but to go to Lhasa.

ཐབས་ཀྱི་སྒོ་ (tābgi go̲) a way/ method/ means of doing ¶ན་ཚ་འདི་བཅོས་པའི་ཐབས་གང་ཡོད་དམ་ What methods are there for curing this illness? ¶ལས་ཀ་འདི་བསྒྲུབ་པར་ཐབས་ཀྱི་སྒོ་མང་པོ་བསམ་བློ་གཏོང་དགོས་ We must think of the many ways of doing things in order to complete this task.

ཐབས་ཀྱིས་བདུལ་ (tābgi dǖǖ) va. to conquer or subdue through techniques/ methods/ schemes rather than overt conflict.

ཐབས་ཀྱི་ཕྱོགས་ (tābgi cɔ̄ɔ̄) 1. sm. ཐབས་ཀྱི་སྒོ་. 2. period from the 1st to the 15th day of the month.

ཐབས་བཀོད་ (tābgöö) orders regarding methods of doing sth.

ཐབས་བཀོད་འཐེན་ (tābgöö tēn) sm. ཐབས་ཤེས་བྱེད་.

ཐབས་སྐྱོ་པོ་ (tāb gyōbo) pitiful ¶ཐབས་སྐྱོ་པོའི་གནས་སྟངས་ A pitiful condition.

ཐབས་མཁས་ (tābkɛ̄ɛ̄) skillful, ingenious, resourceful, clever ¶ཐབས་མཁས་ཀྱི་དབུ་ཁྲིད་ Skillful leadership. ¶ཐབས་མཁས་ཀྱི་ངང་ནས་དགྲ་བོས་མཐའ་བསྐོར་བའི་ནང་ནས་བྲོས་ཡོད་པ་རེད་ (They) cleverly escaped the enemy that surrounded them.

ཐབས་མཁས་པོ་ (tāb kɛ̄ɛ̄bo) skillful, clever,

ingenious.

ཐབས་གྲོས་ (tābdröö) a discussion about how to do sth; va.—བྱེད་ ¶ ཇེ་ལྟར་བྱས་ན་ལེགས་པའི་ཐབས་གྲོས་བྱས་སོང་ (They) had a discussion about what would be the best method to use.

ཐབས་སྒྲུབ་ (tābdrub) working ingeniously/ in a clever way; va.—བྱེད་.

ཐབས་བརྒྱ་ཇུས་སྟོང་ (tābgya jüüdoŋ) having many methods/ means/ ways [Lit. 100 methods and 1000 plans].

ཐབས་ངན་ (tābŋɛn) devious/ evil means.

ཐབས་ཅན་ (tābjɛn) sm. ཐབས་མཁས་པོ་.

ཐབས་ཅིག་ཏུ་ (tāb jīgdu) together.

ཐབས་ཆག (tābjaà) 1. mediocre, crude, poor in quality. 2. vi. to run out of means/ ways/ methods (to do sth.). 3. pitiful, pathetic.

ཐབས་མཆོག (tābjɔ̀ɔ) the best means/ method/ way.

ཐབས་གཅིག་ཏུ་ (tābjigdu) sm. ཐབས་གཅིག་ཏུ་.

ཐབས་ཇུས་ (tābjüü) strategy, tactics, plans, policy; va.—འགོད་; —གཏོང་; —འདོན་; —འདིང་ to make plans/ strategy/ tactics ¶ ཟམ་པ་གསར་པ་རྒྱག་རྒྱུའི་ཐབས་ཇུས་ལེགས་པོ་ཞིག་བཏིངས་བ་རེད་ (They) made a good plan to build a new bridge.

ཐབས་ཇུས་ཀྱི་གནས་བབ་ (tābjüügi nɛ̄ɛ̀bəb) strategic position.

ཐབས་ཇུས་མཁས་པོ་ (tābjüü kɛ̄ɛ̀bo) skilled at strategy, tactics and planning.

ཐབས་ཇུས་སྔོན་འགོད་ (tābjüü ŋōngöö) preplanning, planning in advance.

ཐབས་ཇུས་གཏན་འབེབས་ (tābjüü dēmbeb) deciding/ settling on a plan or strategy; va.—བྱེད་.

ཐབས་ཇུས་འདྲི་ཡུལ་ (tābjüü driyüü) adviser.

ཐབས་ཇུས་འཛོལ་ (tābjüü dzöö) vi. to miscalculate a plan/ strategy, to err in strategy, to use a wrong strategy ¶ ཐབས་ཇུས་འཛོལ་ནས་ཚོང་ལ་གྱོང་ཆེན་པོ་རག་པ་རེད་ (They) erred in the strategy and took a large loss in the business.

ཐབས་ཇུས་གང་གཟབ་ (tābjüü kaŋsəb) the best possible means/ method.

ཐབས་ཇུས་ཟབ་པོ་ (tābjüü səbbo) 1. sm. ཐབས་ཇུས་ཡག་པོ་. 2. sb. who has a lot of ways of getting things done.

ཐབས་ཇུས་ཡག་པོ་ (tābjüü yaggo) good plan/ strategy.

ཐབས་གཉིས་མཉམ་སྦྱོར་ (tābñii ñāmjöö) using two strategies at once.

ཐབས་རྙིང་ (tābñiŋ) old methods/ means/ ways.

ཐབས་གདོ་ (tābdo) shung. clever, ingenious means/ methods.

ཐབས་དང་བྲལ་ (tābdaŋ trɛɛ) sm. ཐབས་བྲལ་.

ཐབས་འདོན་ཇུས་འགོད་ (tābdün jüügöö) sm. ཐབས་འདོན་ཇུས་འདོན་.

ཐབས་འདོན་ཇུས་འདོན་ (tābdün jüüdön) coming forth with means/ methods/ strategies for doing sth.; va.—བྱེད་.

ཐབས་འདོན་ཇུས་འབུལ་ (tābdön jümbüü) sm. ཐབས་འདོན་ཇུས་འདོན་.

ཐབས་དུགས་ (tābduù) sm. ཐབས་ཆག.

ཐབས་སྡུག (tābduù) 1. terrible, bad ¶ རྒྱལ་ཁབ་འཚོང་བའི་བུ་ངན་དེ་དངོས་འབྲེལ་ཐབས་སྡུག་རེད་ Those people who are traitors to their country are terrible. 2. pitiful, pathetic ¶ ཐབས་སྡུག་གནས་ཚུལ་ A pathetic situation.

ཐབས་འཕྲུལ་ (tābdrüü) methods/ means to trick or deceive ¶ དགྲ་བོས་ཐབས་འཕྲུལ་སྣ་ཚོགས་ལ་བརྟེན་ནས་ང་ཚོར་མགོ་སྐོར་གཏོང་གི་ཡོད་པ་རེད་ The enemy was using many methods to trick and deceive us.

ཐབས་བྱུས་ (tābjüü) see ཐབས་ཇུས་.

ཐབས་བྱེད་ (tāb ceè) vi. to find sth., to look for sth. ¶ ངས་ཁང་པ་ཞིག་ཐབས་བྱེད་ཀྱི་ཡོད་ I am looking for a house.

ཐབས་བྲལ་ (tābdrɛɛ) 1. (vb. + —) no way to do the verbal action ¶ ཁོ་ཆུ་ཚོད་གཅིག་ནང་འབྱོར་ཐབས་བྲལ་བ་རེད་ There is no way for him to arrive in one hour. 2. (neg. + vb. + —) no choice but to do the verbal action ¶ ཁོ་འདི་རར་མ་ཡོང་ཐབས་བྲལ་རེད་ He has no choice but to come here.

ཐབས་བློ་ཞི་བསྐྱེད་ (tāblo shēgyeè) trying by every means/ ways/ methods ¶ ཁྱེད་ནས་ཐབས་བློ་ཞི་སྐྱེད་ཀྱིས་ལས་འགན་སྒྲུབ་དགོས་ You must complete your responsibility (work) using every means.

ཐབས་མེད་ (tābmeè) sm. ཐབས་བྲལ་, 2.

ཐབས་མེད་ཇུས་ཟད་ (tābmeè jüüsɛɛ̀) sm. ཐབས་བྲལ་, 2.

ཐབས་བཙན་པོ་ (tāb dzɛ̄mbo) 1. reliable means/ methods/ plans. 2. forcible/ forceful means or methods.

ཐབས་རྩལ་ (tābdzɛɛ) a skill, method.

ཐབས་བརྩོན་ (tābdzön) working hard for, striving for; va.—བྱེད་ ¶ ཡུལ་གྱི་དཔལ་འབྱོར་ཡར་རྒྱས་ལ་ཐབས་བརྩོན་བྱེད་ཀྱི་ཡོད་པ་རེད་ (They) are striving to improve (their) country's economy.

ཐབས་ཚུལ་ (tābdzüü) means, method, manner ¶ རྩ་མེད་བཏོང་ཡས་ཀྱི་ཐབས་ཚུལ་གཙོ་བོ་ The chief means for destroying.

ཐབས་ཚུལ་འདོར་མེད་ (tābdzüü dɔɔmeè) shung. a method that should not be discarded.

ཐབས་འཚོལ་ (tābdzöö) sm. ཐབས་བྱེད་.

ཐབས་གཞི་ (tābshi) plan, strategy, program.

ཐབས་ཟད་ (tābsɛɛ̀) vi. to have exhausted the means, to be helpless ¶ མོ་རང་ཐབས་ཟད་ནས་དུག་བཏུངས་པ་རེད་ Having exhausted all (other) means (to get out of difficulty), she drank poison.

ཐབས་ཟད་ཀ་མེད་ (tābsɛɛ̀ gāmeè) having no choice but to do sth. because one has exhausted all other means/ options/ alternatives.

ཐབས་ཟད་ཉེན་མཆོང་ (tābsɛɛ̀ ñencoŋ) taking risk or exposing oneself to danger out of desperation.

ཐབས་ཟད་ནུས་ཟད་ (tābsɛɛ̀ nüüsɛɛ̀) at the end of one's strength, having exhausted all one's means and power, helpless, having no alternatives/ options.

ཐབས་ཟད་ཝ་ཐུག (tābsɛɛ̀ wuduù) being desperate due to having exhausted all means, at the end of one's rope, desperate.

ཐབས་ཟབ་ (tābsɛɛ̀) sm. ཐབས་ཇུས་ཟབ་པོ་.

ཐབས་ཟབ་མོ་ (tāb səbmo) sm. ཐབས་ཇུས་ཟབ་པོ་.

ཐབས་བཟང་ཇུས་ལེགས་ (tābsaŋ jüüleg) good methods and good strategy.

ཐབས་གཟིགས་ (tābsii) h. of ཐབས་ཤེས་ལྟ་.

ཐབས་ཟླ་ (tāmda) wife.

ཐབས་གཡོ་ (tābyo) sm. ཐབས་འཕྲུལ.

ཐབས་ལམ་ (tāblam) sm. ཐབས་ཤེས་.

ཐབས་ཤེས་ (tābsheè) means, method, way, strategy; va.—བྱེད་ to do sth. (take measures/ means) so sth. can happen; va.—འདོན་; —སྒྲིག་; —ལྟ་; —འཚོལ་ to look for/ think of/ come up with a way or means or method; va.—རྒྱུད་བསྐུལ་བྱེད་ to encourage/ entreat/ appeal/ urge to make the means for doing sth. ¶ ང་སློབ་གྲྭ་ཆེན་མོ་ལ་འགྲོ་རྒྱུའི་ཐབས་ཤེས་བྱེད་ཀྱི་ཡོད་ I am taking measures in order to go to college. ¶ ལྷ་སར་འགྲོ་ཡས་ཀྱི་ཐབས་ཤེས་ཡོད་པ་མ་རེད་ There is no way to go to Lhasa. ¶ ངས་ཁྱེད་རང་ལ་ལས་རག་རྒྱུར་ཐབས་ཤེས་བལྟས་ཆོག I will look for a way to find you a job. ¶ འཐུས་མི་གཏོང་རྒྱུར་ཐབས་ཤེས་རྒྱུད་བསྐུལ་བྱས་པ་རེད་ (He) urged them to find a way to send delegates.

ཐབས་ཤེས་ཀྱིས་ (tābsheègi) doing sth. taking measures/ means (so sth. else can happen), using ways to do sth. ¶ ངས་རྒྱ་གར་ལ་འགྲོ་རྒྱུར་ཐབས་ཤེས་ཀྱིས་གནས་སྐོར་ལ་འགྲོ་རྩིས་ཡོད་ I plan to take measures to go to India to make a pilgrimage.

ཐབས་ཤེས་གཉིས་ (tābsheè ñii) 1. the two: wisdom and means/ methods. 2. a couple, husband and wife.

ཐབས་ཤེས་ཐུགས་འདུན་ (tābsheè tügdün) bride.

ཐབས་ཤེས་འཕྲོད་པ་ (tābsheè trööba) correct procedure/ means.

ཐབས་ཤེས་འབད་བརྩོན་ (tābsheè bɛɛ̀dzön) striving to find ways to do sth.

ཐབས་ཤེས་བཟང་པོ་ (tābsheè sa̲ŋbo) a resourceful person.

ཐབས་ཤེས་ཟུང་འབྲེལ་ (tābsheè su̲ŋdree) the combination/ union of method and wisdom.

ཐབས་ཤེས་ཡོད་རྒུ་རྩལ་སྒྲུགས་ (tābsheè yö̲ögu dzɛ̄ɛ̄druù) searching for all kinds of ways to do sth., sparing no effort to find means/ methods.

ཐབས་གསོམ་ (tābshom) preparing to do sth.; va.—བྱེད་ ། བཙན་འཛུལ་དམག་འཁྲུག་འགོག་རྒྱུའི་ཐབས་གསོམ་བྱེད་བཞིན་པ་རེད་ (They) are preparing to block the invasion.

ཐབས་གསར་ (tābsar) new method/ way/ means.

ཐམ་ཀ་ (tāmga) sm. ཐམ་ག.

ཐམ་ཁེབས་ (tāmgeb) shung. a piece of silk that covers a seal.

ཐམ་ག (tāmga) 1. a seal; va.—རྒྱག to affix a seal. 2. credentials.

ཐམ་ག་འཛིན་པ་ (tāmga dzi̲nba) one who holds a seal.

ཐམ་གའི་ཁ་ཡིག (tāmgɛ kāyig) the writing on a seal.

ཐམ་གའི་ཁ་རིས་ (tāmgɛ kārii) sm. ཐམ་གའི་ཁ་ཡིག.

ཐམ་གའི་སྣུམ་གཞོང་ (tāmgɛ nūmshoŋ) ink pad, stamp pad (for a seal).

ཐམ་སྒམ་ (tāmgam) a box in which seals are kept.

ཐམ་ཐག (tāmdaà) string handle on a seal.

ཐམ་ཐམ་ (tāmdam) 1. biting one's lower lip with the upper teeth to express anger and threat; va.—བྱེད་. 2. teeth chattering from cold; va.—བྱེད་.

ཐམ་ཐོམ་ (tāmdom) abbr. of ཐམ་མེ་ཐོམ་མེ་.

ཐམ་པ་ (tāmba) particle used with numbers that are multiples of ten ། བཅུ་ཐམ་པ་ Ten. ། བརྒྱད་ཅུ་ཐམ་པ་ Eighty.

ཐམ་སྣུམ་ (tāmnum) sm. ཐམ་གའི་སྣུམ་གཞོང་.

ཐམ་འབྱར་མ་ (tāmjarma) a letter or document affixed with a seal.

ཐམ་མེ་ཐོམ་མེ་ (tāmme tōmme) muddled, confused.

ཐམ་རྫི་ (tāmdzi) sm. ཐམ་གའི་སྣུམ་གཞོང་.

ཐམ་ཚོན་ (tāmdzön) ink for a stamp pad/ seal.

ཐམ་མཚལ་ (tāmdzɛɛ) the red ink/wax used with seals.

ཐམ་ཞུ་ (tām shu̲) va. to place a seal on a document.

ཐམ་ཡུ་ (tāmyu) handle of a seal.

ཐམ་གཡོག (tāmyoò) a secondary or duplicate seal attached to the main seal.

ཐམ་རིས་ (tāmrii) the designs on a seal.

ཐམ་ལག (tāmlaà) sm. ཐམ་ཐག.

ཐམས་ཅད་ (tāmjɛɛ̀) all, entire.

ཐམས་ཅད་ཀྱི་ཐམས་ཅད་ (tāmjɛɛ̀gi tāmjɛɛ̀) completely all.

ཐམས་ཅད་ཀྱི་ཐ་མ་ (tāmjɛɛ̀gi tāma) 1. the worst of all. 2. the last of all/ the lot.

ཐམས་ཅད་ཀྱི་དང་པོ་ (tāmjɛɛ̀gi ta̲ŋbo) the first/ best of all/ the lot.

ཐམས་ཅད་མཁྱེན་པ་ (tāmjɛɛ̀ kyēmba) all-knowing, omniscient (a title for high lamas and an epithet of the Buddha).

ཐམས་ཅད་འདུལ་ (tāmjɛɛ̀ dü̲ü̲) shung. 1. the fire pig year. 2. Buddha.

ཐམས་ཅད་བསྡོམས་ན་ (tāmjɛɛ̀ do̲mba) altogether.

ཐམས་ཅད་གཟིགས་ (tāmjɛɛ̀ si̲i̲) Buddha.

ཐའ་སི་གསར་འགྱུར་ཁང་ (tāsi sɔ̄ngyurgaŋ) TASS News Agency.

ཐའི་ཡུལ་ (tɛ̄yüü) Thailand.

ཐའི་ཀྲའོ་ (tɛ̄drao) ch. Giamda (town in Kongbo).

ཐའི་ཅི་ཆོན་ (tɛ̄ji cün) ch. Taichi: a system of Chinese physical exercise that emphasizes balance, coordination and effortlessness in movement.

ཐའི་ཇི་ (tɛ̄ji) mong. a third rank official in the tt. government.

ཐའི་དབན་ (tɛ̄wan) Taiwan.

ཐའི་ཝན་ (tɛ̄wan) Taiwan.

ཐའི་ཝན་མི་དམངས་དམངས་གཙོ་ཚོགས་པ་ (tɛ̄wan) Taiwan Democratic People's Party (DPP).

ཐའི་ལན་ཏ་ (tɛ̄lɛnda) Thailand.

ཐའི་གོ་ (tɛ̄go) Thailand.

ཐའི་ཆིའུ་ (tɛ̄ciwu) ch. 1. table tennis, ping pong. 2. billiards, pool.

ཐའི་ཆིའུ་སྦོ་ལོ་ (tɛ̄ci bōlo) ch.tib. sm. ཐའི་ཆིའུ་.

ཐའི་ཏིང་ (tɛ̄diŋ) ch. table lamp.

ཐའི་པེ་ (tāibe) Taipei.

ཐའི་ཕིང་ཐེན་གོ་ (tɛ̄piŋ tēngo) ch. T'aiping Rebellion (1851-1864).

ཐའི་ཝན་ (tɛ̄wan) Taiwan.

ཐའི་ཝན་མཚོ་འགག (tɛ̄wan tsōgaà) ch.tib. Taiwan Straits.

ཐར་ (tār) vi. to escape from, to get free of, to get out of ། རྙི་ལས་ཐར་བ་རེད་ (It) escaped from the trap.

ཐར་སྐང་ (tārgaŋ) not too old and not too young, just right.

ཐར་ཆགས་ (tārjaà) in order/ sequence.

ཐར་ཐར་ (tārdar) 1. sound made by sth. rolling on a hard surface. 2. inferior quality.

ཐར་ཐོ་ (tārdo) a square-headed hammer.

ཐར་ཐོར་ (tārdɔɔ) scattered, dispersed, in small numbers; va.—གཏོང་ to scatter/ disperse; vi.—དུ་ལྡང་; vi.—དུ་ཆགས་ to get dispersed/ scattered ། ལུང་པ་འདིའི་ནང་བོད་པ་ཐར་ཐོར་ཞིག་ལས་མེད་པ་རེད་ In this place Tibetans are only (found) scattered in small numbers.

ཐར་ཐོར་ཅུང་ཙག (tārdɔr cūŋdzaà) sm. ཐར་ཐོར་.

ཐར་ནད་ (tārnɛɛ̀) a disease from which one gets immunity after surviving the illness.

ཐར་པ་ (tārba) liberation, salvation, nirvana, breaking out of the wheel of life; vi.—ཐོབ་ to obtain nirvana.

ཐར་པར་གཏོང་ (tārba dōŋ) va. to let sb. go, to let sb. escape (punishment) ། ཁྱེད་ཀྱིས་ཡང་སྐྱར་ཁྲིམས་ལམ་དང་འགལ་ན་ཐར་པར་གཏོང་གི་མིན་ If you breech discipline again, I will not let you escape (without being punished).

ཐར་པ་དོན་གཉེར་ (tārba tö̲nñer) pursuing nirvana.

ཐར་པོ་ (tārbo) old, worn out, tattered.

ཐར་དཔག (tāābaà) plate.

ཐར་མ་ (tārma) immunity from a disease (as a consequence of surviving the disease) ། ལྷ་འབྲུམ་ཐར་མ་ Immunity from smallpox.

ཐར་ཞུན་སློལ་ (tārshün gȫȫ) sm. ཞུན་ཐར་སློལ་.

ཐར་བཞུན་སློལ་ (tārshün gȫȫ) sm. ཞུན་ཐར་སློལ་.

ཐར་གཟེང་ (tārsoŋ) a tool used by silversmiths.

ཐར་རེ་ཐོར་རེ་ (tāre tōre) sm. ཐར་ཐོར་.

ཐར་ལམ་ (tārlam) 1. path to liberation/ salvation (from the of the wheel of life). 2. escape route.

ཐར་ས་ (tārsa) sm. ཐར་ལམ་.

ཐར་ས་མེད་པའི་ལམ་ (tārsa me̲èbɛ la̲m) blind alley, dead end.

ཐལ་ (tɛ̄ɛ̄) 1. vi. to be excessive/ carried away, to overdo ། ཁོས་སྐད་ཆ་ཤོད་ཐལ་བ་རེད་ He talked excessively (implies let things slip that he should not have). ། འགོ་ཁྲིད་ཀྱིས་མ་མངགས་པའི་ལས་ཀ་ཁོས་བྱེད་ཐལ་བྱུང་བཞག He made a mistake by getting carried away and doing sth. that the boss didn't instruct him to do. ། ཐུགས་སྒྲོའི་ཁ་ལག་མང་པོ་ཞིག་བཟོ་ཐལ་བྱུང་བཞག (They) made too much food for the party. 3. va. to go ། སོ་པ་དེ་གར་ཐལ་ཆ་མེད་དུ་གྱུར་པ་རེད་ Where the spy went nobody knows. 4. sm. བཟང་ ཐལ་. 5. ash.

ཐལ་ཀར་ (tɛ̄ɛ̄gar) sm. ཐལ་དཀར་.

ཐལ་དཀར་ (tɛ̄ɛ̄gar) ash-colored, pale (usu. due to illness) [Lit. whitish ash color].

ཐལ་སྐད་ (tɛ̄ɛ̄gɛɛ̀) the first word uttered during debating.

ཐལ་སྐྱ་ (tɛ̄ɛ̄gya) sm. ཐལ་དཀར་.

ཐལ་སྐྱོད་ (tɛ̄ɛ̄gyöö) extremism; va.—བྱེད་.

ཐལ་སྐྱོར་ (tɛ̄ɛ̄gyɔr) a place where ashes are kept.

ཐལ་བསྐྱོད་ (tɛ̄ɛ̄gyöö) sm. ཐལ་སྐྱོད་.

ཐལ་སྐྱོད་པ་ (tɛ̄ɛ̄gyööba) extremist, radical.

ཐལ་སྐྱོན་ (tɛ̄ɛ̄gyön) the error/ mistake of doing things excessively ། ཚོགས་འདུའི་ཐོག་ཁོང་གིས་བཤད་

པའི་སྐད་ཆ་དེ་ཐལ་སྐྱོན་བྱུང་བཞག He said too much at the meeting.

ཐལ་འཁྲམས་ (tɛ̄ɛ̄gum) sm. ཐལ་ལུས་.

ཐལ་གོང་ (tɛ̄ɛ̄goŋ) part of the body from the tip of the shoulder to the neck joint.

ཐལ་གོག (tɛ̄ɛ̄gɔ̀ɔ) abbr. of ཐལ་བ་གོག་གོག.

ཐལ་གྱིས་ (tɛ̄ɛ̄gyii) (vb. + —) because of doing too much ¶ སྐྱོན་ཆ་འདི་སྐད་ཆ་ཤོད་ཐལ་གྱིས་བྱུང་བ་ཞིག་རེད་ The error was caused by talking too much.

ཐལ་རྒྱུགས་ (tɛ̄ɛ̄gyuù) 1. dashing/ darting around quickly (e.g., the movement of fish in the water). 2. doing sth. rashly without investigating it carefully; va.—བྱེད་.

ཐལ་སྒྲ་ (tɛ̄ɛ̄dra) applause, clapping; va.—རྡེབ་ to applaud, to clap.

ཐལ་ལྕག་གཞུ་ (tɛ̄ɛ̄jaà shu̱) va. to hit/ slap with the palm.

ཐལ་ཆ་ (tɛ̄ɛ̄ja) (usu. vb. + —) excessive, extreme, too much; va.—གཏོང to do to excess; vi.—ཤོར་ to have sth. inadvertently be done to excess ¶ རྒྱ་ནག་ལོ་ཉི་ཤུའི་རིང་འཕོ་འགྱུར་ཐལ་ཆ་དེ་ཙམ་ཕྱིན་ རུང་ Although China has undergone excessive changes in the past twenty years. ¶ ཕྲུ་གུ་དེ་གཉིས་རྒྱག་འདྲི་རྒྱག་སྐབས་ཕྲུ་གུ་གཅིག་ལ་སྲོག་སྐྱོན་ཐལ་ཆ་ཤོར་བཞག When the two children were fighting it inadvertently became excessive and one died.

ཐལ་ཆ་ཟིང་ཞིག (tɛ̄ɛ̄ja si̱ŋshig) shung. excessive disturbance ¶ སྔར་ཇུན་གར་གྱི་རྒྱུན་ལས་བོད་ཡུལ་ཐལ་ཆ་ཟིང་ཞིག་ཏུ་བཏང་ནས་གླ་སློབ་རྣམས་བསྒྲང་ཞིང་གཏོར་བའི་འཁྲུགས་ལོང་ལ་ Formerly, when the Dzungars caused excessive disturbanceas inTibet they murdered and dispersed the lamas.

ཐལ་ཆུ་ (tɛ̄ɛ̄ju) mixture of dust and water.

ཐལ་ཆེ་ན་ཕྱིན་ཅི་ལོག (tɛ̄ɛ̄cena cı̄njilɔɔ̀) if you do sth. too much it will come back and harm you.

ཐལ་ཆེ་བ་ (tɛ̄ɛ̄jewa) ultra, extreme ¶ ཐལ་ཆེ་བ་དམངས་གཙོ་ Ultrademocracy.

ཐལ་ཆེན་ (tɛ̄ɛ̄jen) human ashes (from a cremation).

ཐལ་ཉོར་ (tɛ̄ɛ̄ñɔr) accumulated dust (e.g., in the corner of a room).

ཐལ་སྙིགས་ (tɛ̄ɛ̄ñig) abbr. of ཐལ་བ་ and ་གད་སྙིགས་.

ཐལ་དུ་འགྱུར་ (tɛ̄ɛ̄du gyu̱r) vi. to die [Lit. to turn into dust].

ཐལ་དུ་སྒྱུར་ (tɛ̄ɛ̄du gyu̱r) va. to kill [Lit. to make into ash].

ཐལ་དོང་ (tɛ̄ɛ̄doŋ) a pit/ hole into which dust is thrown.

ཐལ་དྲགས་ (tɛ̄ɛ̄draà) (vb. + —) doing in excess of a limit/ standard ¶ སྐད་ཆ་ཤོད་ཐལ་དྲགས་བཞག (He) spoke excessively (said things he shouldn't have said). ¶ ལས་ཀ་བྱེད་ཐལ་དྲགས་ཙང་ན་པ་རེད་ Because (he) worked excessively he got sick.

ཐལ་དྲེག (tɛ̄ɛ̄dreg) dust and dirt.

ཐལ་མདོག (tɛ̄ndɔɔ̀) ash color.

ཐལ་མདོག་སྟོན་ (tɛ̄ɛ̄dɔɔ̀ tōn) vi. to look pale/ ashen/ unhealthy.

ཐལ་དུལ་ (tɛ̄ɛ̄düü) dust.

ཐལ་དུལ་རྩུབ་རྩུབ་ (tɛ̄ɛ̄düü tsündzub) dusty.

ཐལ་དུལ་སེལ་བྱེད་ཀྱི་འཁྲུལ་ཆས་ (tɛ̄ɛ̄düü sēljeègi lɔ̄gjɛɛ̀) vacuum cleaner.

ཐལ་བརྡབ་ (tɛ̄ɛ̄ də̱b) va. to clap, to applaud.

ཐལ་ཕྱགས་ (tɛ̄ɛ̄jaà) duster; va.—རྒྱག to dust.

ཐལ་ཕྱེ་ (tɛ̄ɛ̄je) sm. ཐལ་བ་.

ཐལ་འཕྱག་འཕྲུལ་ཆས་ (tɛ̄ɛ̄jaà trűűjɛɛ̀) vacuum cleaner.

ཐལ་བ་ (tɛ̄ɛ̄la) 1. dust; va.—རྡེབ་ to brush off dust; vi.—ལང་ to become/ get dusty. 2. error, fault, mistake; va.—འཛིན་ to blame sb. for making an error/ mistake.

ཐལ་བ་སྐྱ་ཆགས་ (tɛ̄ɛ̄la gyā cāà) 1. vi. to be white with dust.

ཐལ་བ་འཁོར་ (tɛ̄ɛ̄la kɔ̄ɔ) vi. to have dust accumulate.

ཐལ་བ་གོག་གོག (tɛ̄ɛ̄la gɔ̱ɔ̀gɔɔ̀) sm. ཐལ་བ་ཅིལ་ཅིལ་.

ཐལ་བ་ཅིལ་ཅིལ་ (tɛ̄ɛ̄la cı̄ijii) dusty.

ཐལ་བ་མདོག (tɛ̄ɛ̄la dɔ̱ɔ̀) gray, ash color.

ཐལ་བ་པ་ (tɛ̄ɛ̄waba) follower of a sect in India the cover themselves with dust.

ཐལ་བ་རྡེབ་ (tɛ̄ɛ̄la də̱b) va. to brush off dust.

ཐལ་བ་སྤར་གང་གནམ་ལ་བཤོས་ན་ ཕྱེད་ཀ་རང་དང་ཕྱེད་ཀ་མི་ (tɛ̄ɛ̄la ba̱rgaŋ nāmla shȫȍna cēèga ra̱ŋ da̱ŋ cēèga mi̱) wrongful deeds/ actions will not only effect others but also oneself [Lit. if one throws a handful of dust in the air half will fall on you and half on other people].

ཐལ་བ་བུན་བུན་ (tɛ̄ɛ̄la pü̱nbün) sm. ཐལ་བ་ཅིལ་ཅིལ་.

ཐལ་བ་འཚུབ་འཚུབ་ (tɛ̄ɛ̄la tsūbdzub) sm. ཐལ་བ་ཅིལ་ཅིལ་.

ཐལ་བ་ལང་ (tɛ̄ɛ̄la lāŋ) vi. to become/ get dusty.

ཐལ་བ་ལྷུང་བསྐུར་ (tɛ̄ɛ̄la lūŋgur). annihilate/ eradicate/ destroy completely [Lit. to throw dust into the wind].

ཐལ་བའི་རྡུལ་དུ་རློག (tɛ̄ɛ̄lɛ dü̱ü̱du lɔ̄ɔ̀) va. to destroy completely, to smash to dust.

ཐལ་བར་འགྱུར་ (tɛ̄ɛ̄lar gyu̱r) 1. vi. to become dust. 2. vi. to be at fault/ wrong.

ཐལ་བར་རློག (tɛ̄ɛ̄lar lɔ̄ɔ̀) va. to smash to bits, to crush/ pulverize.

ཐལ་བར་བརླགས་ (tɛ̄ɛ̄lar lāà) p. of ཐལ་བར་རློག.

ཐལ་བས་འགེངས་ (tɛ̄ɛ̄lɛɛ̀ ge̱n) vi. to be filled with dust.

ཐལ་བྱུང་ (tɛ̄ɛ̄juŋ) going right through sth., piercing sth. right through, doing sth. without thinking or without hesitation ¶ དཔའ་བོ་དེའི་མདའ་ཡིས་ལྷུགས་སླང་ཐལ་བྱུང་དུ་འབིག་ཐུབ་ཀྱི་ཡོད་ The hero's arrow can go right through the basin.

ཐལ་བྱུང་འགྲོ་ (tɛ̄ɛ̄juŋ dro̱) va. to go right ahead without hesitation.

ཐལ་སྦྱར་ (tɛ̄ɛ̄jar) va. to clasp the palms of the hands together as a sign of greeting or as a sign of respect for high lamas (or when praying).

ཐལ་མ་ (tɛ̄ɛ̄ma) sm. ཐད་ཀ་.

ཐལ་མོ་ (tɛ̄ɛ̄mo) palm (of hand), va.—བརྡབ་; —རྡེབ་ to clap, to applaud; va.—སྦྱར་ to clasp the palms of the hand together as a sign of greeting.

ཐལ་མོ་རྡེབ་སྒྲ་ (tɛ̄ɛ̄mo de̱bdra) sm. ཐལ་མོའི་རྡེབ་སྒྲ་.

ཐལ་མོ་སྤྱི་བོར་བཀོད་ (tɛ̄ɛ̄mo jı̄wor gȍȍ) va. to clasp the palms of the hand together on top of the head in a gesture of respect to deities.

ཐལ་མོ་རྡེབ་ (tɛ̄ɛ̄mo de̱b) va. to applause, to clap.

ཐལ་མོ་སྦྱོར་ (tɛ̄ɛ̄mo jɔ̄r) va. to clasp the palms of two hands together as a greeting or when paying as a sign of respect for high lamas or when praying.

ཐལ་མོའི་རྡེབ་སྒྲ་ (tɛ̄ɛ̄mö de̱bdra) sound of clapping/ applause.

ཐལ་མོའི་ཕྱག་རྒྱ་ (tɛ̄ɛ̄mö cāàgya) a mudra where the palms of the hands are placed together (usu. when paying respect to high lamas or praying).

ཐལ་སྨན་ (tɛ̄ɛ̄mɛn) medicine made from the ash of substances.

ཐལ་རྩེད་རྩེ་ (tɛ̄ɛ̄dze dzē) va. to play in the dust.

ཐལ་ཚང་ (tɛ̄ɛ̄dzaŋ) dust bin, place for throwing dust.

ཐལ་ཚལ་བད་ཚལ་ (tɛ̄ɛ̄dzɛɛ bɛ̱ɛ̀dzɛɛ) tearing/ ripping into shreds; va.—གཏོང་ ¶ མའོ་ཡི་པར་ཐལ་ཚལ་བད་ཚལ་བཏང་བཞག (They) tore the picture of Mao into shreds.

ཐལ་ཚན་ (tɛ̄ɛ̄dzɛn) hot ashes.

ཐལ་འཚུབ་ (tɛ̄ɛ̄ dzūb) vi. to get dusty.

ཐལ་ཞག (tɛ̄ɛ̄shaà) dusty; vi.—འཁོར་ to be dusty (air).

ཐལ་ཟིང་ཆེན་པོ་ (tɛ̄ɛ̄siŋ cēmbo) a great disturbance/ uprising.

ཐལ་རལ་འཛར་འཛར་ (tɛ̄ɛ̄rɛɛ dza̱rdzar) dusty (usu. for clothes).

ཐལ་རལ་ཡོག་ཡོག (tɛ̄ɛ̄rɛɛ yɔ̱ɔ̀yɔɔ̀) sm. ཐལ་རལ་འཛར་འཛར་.

ཐལ་ལྷུང་ (tɛ̄ɛ̄luŋ) dust storm; vi.—རྒྱག to have a dust storm; vi.—འཛགས་ to have a dust storm subside.

ཐལ་ལྡང་འཚུབ་འཚུབ་ (tɛ̄ɛluŋ tsūbdzub) highly dusty (from a dust storm).; vi.—བྱེད་.

ཐལ་ལ་ (tɛ̄ɛla) dust.

ཐལ་ལུས་ (tɛ̄ɛlüü) 1. too much and too little ¶ ཐལ་ལུས་མེད་པ་ Neither too much nor too little. 2. in error.

ཐལ་ལུས་ཧེ་བག་རིགས་མེད་པ་ (tɛ̄ɛlüü hēbaà rigmɛèba) shung. neither overstated nor understated ¶ གཏོང་ཡོང་རྩིས་ཁྲ་འདི་ར་ཐལ་ལུས་ཧེ་བག་རིགས་མེད་ངེས་ This income and expenditure account is neither overstated nor understated.

ཐལ་ལེ་བ་ (tɛ̄ɛlewa) 1. nothing to block one's view, straight (e.g., road, highway). 2. whitish in color.

ཐལ་ཤེལ་ (tɛ̄ɛshel) goggles/ glasses for use in dust storms.

ཐལ་ཤོག (tɛ̄ɛshɔ̄ɔ) an inferior Tibetan paper produced in སྐྱི་མོ་.

ཐལ་ཤོར་ (tɛ̄ɛ shɔ̄ɔ) vi. to be/ get overdone ¶ གཉིད་ཐལ་ཤོར་བཞག (He) overslept.

ཐལ་བསུབ་ལ་གཏོང་ (tɛ̄ɛsubla dōŋ) sm. ཐལ་བའི་དུལ་དུ་བརླག.

ཐི་གུ་ (tīgu) a kind of thin rope.

ཐི་གུ་ཁྲ་ཅུང་ (tīgu trājuŋ) a thin multicolored rope.

ཐི་ཅིན་ (tīcin) ch. violin.

ཐི་བ་ (tīwə) 1. pigeon. 2. swallow.

ཐི་བའི་མདོག (tīwɛ dɔ̄ɔ) pigeon colored.

ཐི་ར་ (tīra) 1. market, bazaar. 2. a place where people get together/ assemble/ gather.

ཐི་རི་པོ་ལི་ (tīri pōli) Tripoli.

ཐི་ཤོ་ལེགས་ (tīsholeg) the 12th in the line of ancient Tibetan kings.

ཐིག (tīg) 1. a line; va.—རྒྱག to line, to make/ draw lines ¶ ཤོག་བུའི་སྟེང་དུ་ཐིག་བརྒྱབ་འདུག (They) drew lines on the paper. 2. abbr. of ཐིག་པ་. 3. abbr. of ཐིག་སྐོར་. 4. a thin thread or rope ¶ བལ་ཐིག A woolen thread. 5. va. to estimate/ guess ¶ ཁོང་གིས་ཆར་པ་གཏོང་གི་རེད་ཟེར་བ་དེ་ཐིག་བརྒྱབ་སོང་ He guessed that it will rain. 6. vi. to be correct in one's divination.

ཐིག་ཀོར་ (tīggɔɔ) sm. ཐིག་སྐོར་.

ཐིག་ཀྲབ་ (tīgdrəb) sm. ཐིག་རལ་.

ཐིག་རྒྱལ་ (tīggyɛɛ) chalk pouch (usu. used by students to line their writing boards).

ཐིག་སྐུད་ (tīggüü) plumb line, carpenter's marking string, a string used for making lines (e.g., the string that children use to draw lines on their wooden writing boards).

ཐིག་སྐོར་ (tīggɔɔ) zero ¶ ཐིག་སྐོར་འོག་གི་དྲོད་ཚད་བཅུ་ཕྲག་ཡོད་ In the tens below zero (temperature). ¶ ཐིག་སྐོར་ཡན་གྱི་དྲོད་ཚད་ Above zero (temperature).

ཐིག་གི་མགྱོགས་ཚད་ (tīggi gyogdzɛɛ̀) linear velocity.

ཐིག་འགོད་ཅུའུ་ (tīggöö jū) tib.ch. surveying and mapping bureau.

ཐིག་རྒྱག (tīg gyaà) 1. va. to draw a line. 2. sm. ཐིག, 5.

ཐིག་སྒྱེ་ (tīggye) sm. ཐིག་རྒྱལ་.

ཐིག་སྒྲོམ་ (tīgdrom) square boxes on paper used for writing Chinese characters.

ཐིག་ལྔའི་ཕུའུ་ཙི་ (tīgŋɛ pūdzi) tib.ch. the five lined staff in music notation.

ཐིག་བཅད་ (tīgjɛɛ̀) demarcation, demarcating ¶ ས་མཚམས་ཐིག་བཅད་ཀྱི་ལྷན་ཚོགས་ Border demarcation commission.

ཐིག་མཉམ་གཤིབ་ཅན་ (tīg ñəmshibjɛn) parallel lines.

ཐིག་ཐིག (tīgdii) spots, dots.

ཐིག་གདབ་ (tīg dəb) f. of ཐིག་འདེབས་.

ཐིག་འདེབས་ (tīgdeb) measuring by means of a string/ plumb line/ ruler/ yardstick; va. ཐིག་འདེབས་; —བྱེད་.

ཐིག་དུམ་ (tīgdum) line segment.

ཐིག་ནག (tīgnaà) one of the realms in hell according to Tibetan Buddhism where bodies are marked with black lines and sawed with a burning saw.

ཐིག་སྣག (tīgnaà) a black ink used by carpenters for marking lines by plucking a string on the wood that is to be cut.

ཐིག་པོ་ (tīgbu) accurate, right on the mark, correct ¶ ངས་མོ་རྒྱག་པར་ཕྱིན་ནས་ཐིག་པོ་བྱུང་སོང་ I went for divination and it was accurate.

ཐིག་སྤྱད་ (tīgjɛɛ̀) utensils for marking things.

ཐིག་ཕོར་ (tīgbɔr) wooden ink bowl used by Tibetan carpenters to make lines.

ཐིག་བུམ་ (tīgbum) a marker used by carpenters.

ཐིག་དབྱིབས་ (tīgyib) linear shape.

ཐིག་མ་ (tīgmə) the pattern of crosses (used commonly on woolen materials).

ཐིག་དམར་ (tīgmar) the equator.

ཐིག་དམར་ས་ཁུལ་ (tīgmar səküü) equatorial region.

ཐིག་རྩ་ (tīgdza) drawing manual for making thankas.

ཐིག་རྩམ་ (tīgdzam) a white powder used for drawing lines.

ཐིག་རྩིས་ (tīgdzii) geometry.

ཐིག་ཚད་ (tīgdzɛɛ̀) sm. ཐིག་ལེན་.

ཐིག་ཚོན་ (tīgdzön) 1. colored powder for drawing lines. 2. abbr. of line and color.

ཐིག་རལ་ (tīgrɛɛ) a dangling rope skirt worn in the traditional Tibetan opera.

ཐིག་རིས་ (tīgrii) 1. the traditional Tibetan cross pattern used on woolen materials. 2. linear.

ཐིག་རིས་ཀྱི་ཆགས་ཚུལ་ (tīgriigi cəgdzüü) linear structure.

ཐིག་རིས་ཀྱི་འབྲེལ་བ་ (tīgriigi dreewa) linear relationship.

ཐིག་རིས་ཀྱི་རྩིས་ (tīgriigi dzii) geometry.

ཐིག་རིས་ཅུས་ (tīgrii jüü) tib.ch. mapping and survey office.

ཐིག་རིས་འབྲི་ (tīgrii drii) va. to map sth.

ཐིག་ལེ་ (tīgle) 1. sperm; va.—འཐེན་ to fertilize/ impregnate (with sperm); —འབྱིན་ to masturbate; vi.—ཐོན་ to ejaculate. 2. zero. 3. the essence.

ཐིག་ལེ་ལྔ་ཚོམ་ (tīgle ŋādzom) a type of dotted design characterized by a dot in middle surrounded by a dot in each corner.

ཐིག་ལེ་ཅན་ (tīglejɛn) one of the seven horses that pulls the sun according to Tibetan mythology.

ཐིག་ལེ་མདོག (tīgle dɔ̄ɔ) spots, dots (e.g., of a leopard).

ཐིག་ལེ་སྡེབ་སྦྱོར་ཁང་ (tīgle debjɔɔgaŋ) artificial insemination room.

ཐིག་ལེན་ (tīglen) surveying; va.—བྱེད་ to survey (land).

ཐིག་ལེན་དུས་འགོད་ (tīglen jüügöö) surveying; va.—བྱེད་.

ཐིག་ལེན་རུ་ཁག (tīglen rugaà) survey team.

ཐིག་ལེའི་མན་ (tīglɛ men) below zero degrees (temperature).

ཐིག་ལེའི་ཡན་ (tīglɛ yɛn) above zero degrees (temperature).

ཐིག་ཤར་ (tīgsshar) a line of letters.

ཐིག་ཤིང་ (tīgshiŋ) ruler, yardstick.

ཐིག་ཤོག (tīgshɔ̄ɔ) paper with lines, ruled paper.

ཐིག་ཤུབས་ (tīgshub) a pouch/ sack for wooden bowls that was carried by officials of the tt. government when the རྒྱ་ལུ་ཆས་ costume was worn.

ཐིག་གཤིས་ (tīgshii) linear.

ཐིག་གཤིས་ཚབ་རྩིས་ (tīgshii tsəbdzii) linear algebra.

ཐིག་གཤིས་མཉམ་བྱ་ (tīgshii ñāmca) linear equation (in math).

ཐིག་གཤིས་ཕྱིར་ལྡོག (tīgshii cīrdɔɔ) linear regression (in math).

ཐིག་ས་ (tīgsə) earth put on a roof to prevent leaking/ dripping.

ཐིགས་ (tīi) sm. ཐིག.

ཐིགས་གུ་ (tīigu) sm. ཐིག་པོ་.

ཐིགས་རྒྱུན་ (tīggyün) continuous drops/ dripping.

ཐིགས་ཆང་ (tīgjaŋ) a cup of ཆང་ served as a penalty when a drop of ཆང་ is left in the cup.

ཐིགས་པ་ (tīgbə) a drop; vi.—རྒྱག to drip ¶ ཆུ་ཐིགས་པ་རྒྱག་པའི་སྐབས་སུ་ When the water was dripping.

ཐིགས་པ་བསགས་ནས་རྒྱ་མཚོ་ (tīgbə sāànɛ gyadzo) saving/ collecting a little at a time leads to sth. big [Lit. saving drops of water makes an ocean].

ཐིགས་པོ་ (tīgbo) sm. ཐིག་པོ་.

ཐིགས་ཕྲེང་ (tīgdreŋ) a continuous dripping, a stream of drops.

ཐིགས་ཙམ་ (tīgdzam) a little ¶ ང་ལ་ཆུ་ཐིག་ཙམ་སྤྲེར་རོགས་གནང་ Please give me a little water.

ཐིགས་ཚགས་ (tīgdzaà) sm. ཐིག་ས་.

ཐིགས་བཟེད་ (tīgseè) a container that is put under sth. leaking (roof, pipe, etc.).

ཐིགས་རལ་འཕྲུག་འཕྲུག (tīgrɛɛ trūŋdrug) sm. ཐིགས་རལ་འཕྲུལ་འཕྲུལ་.

ཐིགས་རལ་འཕྲུལ་འཕྲུལ་ (tīgrɛɛ trūndrüü) torn, tattered (for clothes).

ཐིགས་ལིན་ (tīglin) sm. ཐིག་ལིན་.

ཐིགས་ས་ (tīgsə) sm. ཐིག་ས་.

ཐིགས་ས་ (tīgsə) earth used to patch a roof where there is a leak; va.—རྒྱག.

ཐིགས་ཧྲུལ་ (tīghrüü) extremely worn out/ torn/ tattered.

ཐིང་: p. ཐིངས་; f.; ཐིང་ (tīŋ) vi. to get/ obtain.

ཐིང་ (tīŋ) ch. 1. department, office 2. hall, room.

ཐིང་ཀྲང་ (tīŋdraŋ) ch. head of a ཐིང་.

ཐིང་སྒྲ་ (tīŋdra) the 'ting' sound of glass breaking/ banging.

ཐིང་ངེར་ (tīŋŋee) sm. ཐིང་ཐིང་.

ཐིང་ཐིང་ (tīŋdiŋ) an expression which adds the idea of "very" ¶ གསལ་ཐིང་ཐིང་ Very clear. ¶ ནག་ཐིང་ཐིང་ Very black.

ཐིང་ཤོག (tīŋshɔ̀ɔ̀) carbon paper.

ཐིང་རིལ་ (tīŋrii) sea gull.

ཐིང་རིལ་སྒྱུ་མོ་ (tīŋrii gyāmo) ཐིང་རིལ་.

ཐིངས་ (tīŋ) 1. f. of འདིངས་. 2. p. of ཐིང་.

ཐིན་ (tīn) ch. 1. a government department at the provincial level. 2. an office.

ཐིན་ཅིན་ (tīnjin) Tianjin.

ཐིབ་ (tīb) vi. to be overcast/ cloudy.

ཐིབ་ཙུ་ (tībju) button; va.—རྒྱག to button a button.

ཐིབ་ཐིབ་ (tībdib) 1. dense, dark, thick (e.g., clouds, fog). 2. drowsy, sleepy ¶ གཉིད་ཐིབ་ཐིབ་བྱེད་ཀྱི་འདུག Today I am sleepy.

ཐིབ་པོ་ (tībbu) sm. ཐིབ་ཐིབ་.

ཐིབས་ (tīb) p. of འཐིབས་.

ཐིབས་པོ་ (tībbu) 1. sm. ཐིབ་ཐིབ་. 2. overcast, cloudy.

ཐིབས་སེ་ (tībse) sm. ཐིབས་པོ་.

ཐིམ་ (tīm) 1. vi. to get absorbed (for liquids), to evaporate, to drain ¶ འདམ་རྫོག་ཐིམ་ཐབས་ Means for having the muddy swamp get drained. ¶ ཞིང་ཁའི་ཆུ་མགྱོགས་པོ་ཐིམ་བཞག The water on the field was absorbed quickly. 2. vi. to have one's money be/ get tied up (in business) ¶ ངའི་དངུལ་ཆང་མ་ཚོང་ཟོག་ལ་ཐིམ་བསྡད་ཡོད་ All my money is tied up in commodities.

ཐིམ་ཁུང་ (tīmguŋ) sm. ཐིམ་བུ་.

ཐིམ་ཕུག (tīmbuù) Thimphu (capital of Bhutan).

ཐིམ་བུ་ (tīmbu) a hole in a container through which liquid ཆང་ is drained off; va.—གློད་ to drain off liquid ཆང་ from a fermenting pot.

ཐིམ་རྩོལ་བསྟན་ (tīmdzüü dēn) vi. to die (with དགོངས་པ་ཆོས་དབྱིངས་སུ་).

ཐིམ་འཚང་ (tīmdzaŋ) cork (paper or flax) that is used to block the hole of a ཆང་ fermenting pot.

ཐིམ་རིམ་ (tīmrim) the five different stages of decomposition as a person dies.

ཐིའ་ན་ཅིན་ (tīnajin) sm. ཐིན་ཅིན་.

ཐིའུ་ (tīwu) 1. a flower bud; vi.—གཏོང་ to bud out, to flower.

ཐིའུ་རྒྱ་སྨུག (tīwu gyəmuù) a type of brocade with purplish red flower designs.

ཐིར་ (tīr) alarm; va.—སྒྲིག to set an alarm (on watch or clock); va.—གཏོང་ to ring a door bell, bicycle bell, school bell, etc.

ཐིར་ལྡན་ཆུ་ཚོད་ (tīrdɛn cūdzöö̀) sm. ཐིར་བརྡའི་ཆུ་ཚོད་.

ཐིར་བརྡའི་ཆུ་ཚོད་ (tīrdɛ cūdzöö̀) alarm clock/ watch.

ཐིར་པི་ལི་ (tīrbili) shung. a Mongolian hat worn by officials of the tt. government during certain ceremonies.

ཐུ་ཉི་སི་ (tūñisi) Tunisia.

ཐུ་སྣེ་ (tūne) the edge of a Tibetan dress/ gown.

ཐུ་པི་ལི་ (tūbili) shung. a type of hat worn by lay officials of the tt. government.

ཐུ་པོ་ (tūbo) sm. ཐུ་མོ་.

ཐུ་བ་ (tūwə) 1. front part of a dress (the inner and outer flaps of a Tibetan dress). 2. sm. ཐུ་མོ་.

ཐུ་བ་སྟེང་མ་ (tūwə gaŋma) the top/ outer part (flap) of a Tibetan dress.

ཐུ་བ་ཐོག་མ་ (tūwə tɔ̄gma) sm. ཐུ་བ་སྟེང་མ་.

ཐུ་བ་ནང་མ་ (tūwə naŋma) the inside (flap) of a Tibetan dress.

ཐུ་བ་ཕྱི་མ་ (tūwə cīmə) sm. ཐུ་བ་སྟེང་མ་.

ཐུ་བ་འོག་མ་ (tūwə wɔgma) sm. ཐུ་བ་ནང་མ་.

ཐུ་བོ་ (tūwo) 1. older brother. 2. the main one.

ཐུ་བོད་ (tūböö̀) ch. the Chinese name for the ancient Tibetan royal dynasty.

ཐུ་མི་ (tūmi) abbr. of ཐུ་མི་སམ་བྷོ་ཊ་.

ཐུ་མེད་ (tūmeè) (vb. + —) no choice but to do the verbal action ¶ ངས་ལས་ཀ་འདི་མ་བྱེད་ཐུ་མེད་བྱུང་ I had no choice but to do the work.

ཐུ་མི་སམ་བྷོ་ཊ་ (tūmisambhoda) the minister sent to India in the 7th century A.D. who created the Tibetan written alphabet.

ཐུ་མོ་ (tūmo) fierce, ferocious, mean ¶ ཁྱི་ཐུ་མོ་ A ferocious dog.

ཐུ་རུ (tūru) 1. wooden spoon. 2. a small weighing scale.

ཐུ་རེ་ (tūre) always, continuously.

ཐུ་ལ་ (tūla) sm. ཐུ་བ་.

ཐུ་ལུ་ (tūlu) sm. ཐུ་ལུད་.

ཐུ་ལུ་ལུ་ (tū lulu) a term used to describe the falling of snow or the rushing of water.

ཐུ་ལུད་ (tūlüù) spit; va.—རྒྱག; —འདེབས་ to spit.

ཐུ་ལུམ་ (tūlum) 1. hammer. 2. round.

ཐུ་ལེ་ (tūle) sm. ཐུ་བ་.

ཐུ་ཤུ་ (tūshu) ch. pension; va.—བྱེད་ to retire ¶ ཐུ་ཤུ་ཁང་པ་ Retirement house (usu. a house built to live in when one retires).

ཐུ་གཤམ་ (tūsham) the hem.

ཐུ་སི་ (dūsi) shung. ch. a title given by the Emperors of China to local chiefs.

ཐུག (tūù) 1. va. to meet ¶ ཁོ་ཐུག་ནས་འདིར་ཡོང་པ་ཡིན་ I came here after I met him. 2. (dat.-loc. + —) to rest on, to depend on ¶ རྒྱུ་རྐྱེན་གཙོ་བོ་ནི་ཀྲུང་གོའི་དམངས་ཚོགས་རྩ་འཛུགས་བྱས་མེད་པ་དེ་ལ་ཐུག་ཡོད་ The main cause rests on the fact that the Chinese masses are not organized. 3. va. to touch, to reach ¶ ཁོས་རྒྱལ་པོའི་ཞབས་ལ་ལག་པས་ཐུག་པ་རེད་ He touched the king's foot with his hand. ¶ མི་རྣམས་ཀྱི་སྙིང་ལ་ཐུག་པའི་གསར་བརྗེ་ A revolution that touches people's hearts. 4. vi. to get into (a fight/ clash) ¶ འཁྲུག་འཛིང་ཤུགས་ཆེ་ཐུག་སྟེ་ Having gotten into a big fight. 5. up to, until ¶ ཟླ་ ༢ ནས་ཟླ་ ༣ ཐུག་བསྡད་པ་རེད་ (He) stayed there from the second to the third month. 6. abbr. of ཐུག་པ་. 7. circular banner made from yak hair that is hung on the roof of large monasteries. 8. stud sheep or goat ¶ ར་ཐུག A stud ram.

ཐུག་སྐྱ་བ་ (tūù gyāwa) ladle for broth/ soup/ noodles.

ཐུག་སྐལ་ (tūggɛɛ) fate, fortune (of a meeting).

ཐུག་སྐྱོན་ (tūggyön) accident (caused by banging into sth./ sb.) ¶ མོ་ཊ་ཐུག་སྐྱོན་བྱུང་བཞག The cars crashed (had an accident).

ཐུག་ཁོག (tūùgɔ̀ɔ̀) pot for serving noodles/ soup/ stew/ porridge.

ཐུག་རྒྱུགས་ (tūggyuù) (in monasteries) share of porridge/ stew.

ཐུག་སྒྲ་ (tūgdra) 1. sound of sth. banging against another thing. 2. slurping sound made when eating noodles.

ཐུག་ཇ་ (tūgŋa) black banner made of yak hair that stands on the roof of monasteries.

ཐུག་ཆོམ་ (tūgjom) splashing sound of sth. hitting water.

ཐུག་མཆོད་ (tūgjöö) a prayer said before eating porridge/ soup/ stew.

ཐུག་ལྗང་ (tūgjaŋ) a green banner (that stands on the roof of monasteries).

ཐུག་བསྙལ་དུ་འཇོག (tūg ñɛ̃ɛ̃du jɔ̀ɔ) va. to set a pot of boiled soup/ stew aside on hot embers to simmer.

ཐུག་ཐལ་ (tūgtɛɛ) tsampa or flour that is used in soup/ stew.

ཐུག་ཐུག་གཏོང་ (tūgduù dōŋ) va. to poke/ pull/ tug at sb. or sth., to touch sb. or sth. ¶ འཕྲུལ་འཁོར་དེར་ཐུག་ཐུག་མ་གཏོང་ Don't touch the machine.

ཐུག་དར་ (tūgdar) abbr. of ཐུག and དར་ལྕོག.

ཐུག་དལ་ (tūgdɛɛ) sm. ཐུག་ཐལ་.

ཐུག་སྡོར་ (tūgdɔɔ) the meat and bones that go into a stew/ soup.

ཐུག་ནག (tūgnaà) black banner made of yak hair that stands on the roof of monasteries.

ཐུག་པ་ (tūgbə) 1. soup, broth, stew, gruel. 2. noodle dishes.

ཐུག་པ་འཐུང་བར་ཚྭས་ལག་ཐོགས་ (tūgbə tūŋwar tsɛ̃ɛ lagdɔɔ̀) sth. badly needed [Lit. salt is needed to eat soup].

ཐུག་པ་མན་ཚལ་ (tūgbə mendzi) tib.ch. flat noodle soup.

ཐུག་པ་བག་ཐུག (tūgbə bəduù) a soup with small dough dumplings.

ཐུག་པ་མིང་བདགས་ (tūgbə miŋdaà) a thick rice broth made with meat, fruit and butter.

ཐུག་པ་ར་བཟི་ (tūgbə rasi) sb. who is bizarre and doesn't know right from wrong or how to do things.

ཐུག་པ་ལྷེབ་གདུབ་ (tūgbə lhēmdub) a type of soup containing flat pieces of dough.

ཐུག་ཕུད་ (tūgbüü) sm. ཐུག་མཆོད་.

ཐུག་ཕྲུ་ (tūgdru) an earthenware pot for cooking broth/ soup/ stew.

ཐུག་འཕྲད་ (tūgdɛɛ) meeting, visiting; va.—བྱེད་ to visit/ meet ¶ ཐུག་འཕྲད་དུ་ཡོང་ Coming to meet.

ཐུག་འཕྲད་ཁང་ (tūgdrɛɛgaŋ) reception room, guest meeting room.

ཐུག་འཕྲད་ཚོགས་འདུ་ (tūgdrɛɛ tsōŋdu) a meeting to meet people, a mixer.

ཐུག་འབྲས་ (tūŋdrɛɛ) the scrotum / testicle of a castrated goat or sheep (used in Tibetan medicine).

ཐུག་སྦོད་ (tūgböö) a yak hair tassel used on banners erected on the roof of monasteries.

ཐུག་མེད་ (tūgmeè) 1. sm. ཐུག་ཡས་.

ཐུག་ཙམ་ཐུག་ཙམ་ (tūgdzam tūgdzam) 1. pulling, tugging, touching. 2. meeting occasionally.

ཐུག་རྩམ་ (tūgdzam) sm. ཐུག་ཐལ་.

ཐུག་མཚམས་ (tūgdzam) 1. at the time of our meeting. 2. the point where two lines meet.

ཐུག་གཟར་ (tūgsar) wooden ladle.

ཐུག་བཟོ་འཕྲུལ་འཁོར་ (tūgso trũũgɔɔ) noodle making machine.

ཐུག་བཟོའི་འཁོར་ལོ་ (tūgsö kɔɔ̄lo) sm. ཐུག་བཟོ་འཕྲུལ་འཁོར་.

ཐུག་ཡས་ (tūgyɛɛ) endless.

ཐུག་རལ་ (tūgrɛɛ) shung. ཐུག་སྦོད་.

ཐུག་རེས་ (tūgreè) 1. meeting each other; va.—བྱེད་. 2. the regular day scheduled for a meeting.

ཐུག་ཤན་ (tūgshɛn) shung. the metal bands used on the banners erected on the roof of monasteries.

ཐུགས་ (tūù) 1. h. of སེམས་ and སྙིང་. 2. a word that makes nonhonorific nouns honorific, e.g., the honorific of སེམས་ཁྲལ་ is ཐུགས་ཁྲལ་.

ཐུགས་ཀ་ (tūùga) h. of སྙིང་ག.

ཐུགས་དཀར་ (tūùgar) abbr. of ཐུགས་སྣང་དཀར་པོ་.

ཐུགས་དཀར་མི་མཉམ་ (tūùgar meñam) bile of bears (used in Tibetan medicine).

ཐུགས་ཀྱི་གེ་སར་ (tūùgi kesar) h. of ཡིད་ཀྱི་ཟེའུ་འབྲུ་.

ཐུགས་ཀྱི་ཟེའུ་འབྲུ་ (tūùgi sēwudru) sm. ཐུགས་ཀྱི་གེ་སར་.

ཐུགས་ཀྱི་སྲས་ (tūùgi sɛɛ̀) sm. ཐུགས་སྲས་.

ཐུགས་དཀྱིལ་ (tūùgyee) farsighted, having wide/ broad views.

ཐུགས་དགྲུགས་ (tūgdruù) h. of བསམ་དཀྲུག.

ཐུགས་སྐྱེད་ (tūggyeè) sm. ཐུགས་བསྐྱེད་.

ཐུགས་སྐྱོ་ (tūggyo) h. of སེམས་སྐྱོ་.

ཐུགས་སྐྱོང་ (tūggyoŋ) sm. གཟིགས་སྐྱོང་.

ཐུགས་བསྐང་ (tūggaŋ) sm. དགོངས་ཚོམ་.

ཐུགས་བསྐྱེད་ (tūggyeè) kindness, concern (h.). ¶ གོང་ས་སྐྱབས་མགོན་ཆེན་པོའི་བླ་ན་མེད་པའི་ཐུགས་བསྐྱེད་ལ་བརྟེན་ནས་ Based on the exceptional kindness of the Dalai Lama.

ཐུགས་ཁ་འགྱུར་ (tūù kā gyur) h. of ཡིད་ཆུས་.

ཐུགས་ཁ་འཆུས་ (tūù kā jüü) sm. ཐུགས་ཁ་འགྱུར་.

ཐུགས་ཁ་མ་མཐུན་ (tūù kā madün) vi. to be unfriendly.

ཐུགས་ཁག (tūùgaà) h. of ཁག.

ཐུགས་ཁག་མེད་ (tūùgaà meè) h. of ཁག་མེད་.

ཐུགས་ཁབ་གསང་ (tūù kəb sāŋ) a space/ gap in the chest area where acupuncture is applied.

ཐུགས་ཁུར་ (tūùgur) concern, care, dedication, interest (h.); va.—གནང་; —བཞེས་ to be concerned ¶ ཁོང་གིས་མི་དམངས་ཀྱི་འཚོ་བར་ཐུགས་ཁུར་གནང་གི་ཡོད་པ་རེད་ He is concerned about the livelihood of the people.

ཐུགས་ཁུར་ཆེ་བསྐྱེད་ (tūùgur cēgyeè) with great concern/ care/ dedication.

ཐུགས་ཁུར་སྣོམ་ (tūùgur nōm) h. of ཁུར་ལེན་.

ཐུགས་ཁུར་གཙོར་བཞེས་ (tūùgur dzōō sheè) taking the main responsibility; va.—གནང་ ¶ ཁོང་གིས་ལས་ཁུངས་ཀྱི་ཐུགས་ཁུར་གཙོར་བཞེས་གནང་གི་ཡོད་པ་རེད་ He is taking the main responsibility in the office.

ཐུགས་ཁུར་ཟབ་བཞེས་ (tūùgur səbsheè) deep/ profound concern.

ཐུགས་ཁོག (tūùgɔɔ) tolerant, magnanimous (h.); va.—གནང་ to be tolerant/ magnanimous.

ཐུགས་ཁོག་མེད་པ་ (tūùgɔɔ meèba) h. of མཁོམ་པ་.

ཐུགས་འཁོམ་ (tūùgom) necessities (h.).

ཐུགས་འཁུར་ (tūùgur) sm. ཐུགས་ཁུར་.

ཐུགས་ཁྱད་ (tūùgyɛɛ) h. of ཁྱད་པར་.

ཐུགས་མཁྱེན་ (tūùgyen) h. of མངོན་ཤེས་.

ཐུགས་ཁྲལ་ (tūùdrɛɛ) h. of སེམས་ཁྲལ་.

ཐུགས་ཁྲེལ་ (tūùdree) sm. ཐུགས་ཁྲལ་.

ཐུགས་ཁྲོ་ (tūùdro) h. of ཁོང་ཁྲོ་.

ཐུགས་འཁྲུགས་ (tūùdruù) 1. vi. to be angry/ agitated/ annoyed (h.). 2. vi. to be distressed/ disturbed (h.).

ཐུགས་གྲུ་ (tūgdra) h. of གྲུ་སྒྲིག.

ཐུགས་དགེ་ (tūùge) 1. h. of དགེ་བ་. 2. supporter, ally, friend (h.) ¶ རྭ་སྒྲེང་གི་ཐུགས་དགེ་ Supporters of Reting.

ཐུགས་དགོངས་ (tūùgoŋ) 1. h. of བསམ་བློ་. 2. wish/ desire/ hope (h.).

ཐུགས་འགན་ (tūùgɛn) h. of འགན་འཁུར་.

ཐུགས་འགན་བསྐྱེད་བཞེས་གནང་ (tūùgɛn gyēèsheè nāŋ) shung. va. to take responsibility ¶ ༧གོང་ས་མཆོག་སྐུ་གཞོན་ནུའི་དུས་ནས་ལུགས་གཉིས་ཆོས་སྲིད་ཀྱི་ཐུགས་འགན་བསྐྱེད་བཞེས་གནང་བ་ H.H. the Dalai Lama took the temporal and political responsibility of the government when he was young.

ཐུགས་འགན་བཙོལ་ (tūùgɛn shöö) va. to resign, to give up a responsibility/ duty.

ཐུགས་འགན་ལྷུར་བཞེས་ (tūùgɛn lhūrsheè) shung. va. to take full responsibility ¶ ལས་དོན་འདིའི་སྐོར་རིམ་པ་གོང་ནས་ཐུགས་འགན་ལྷུར་བཞེས་མཛད་པས་གསལ་རིམ་ཆམས་བྱེད་བདེ་བྱུང་བ་ Regarding this matter, the superiors took full responsibility and made it easy for the subordinates to work.

ཐུགས་དགྱེས་པོ་ (tūù gyeèbo) vi. liking sth., being glad; va.—གནང་ to like sth. ༈ ངས་ཁོང་ལ་ཕྱག་རྟགས་དེ་ཕུལ་བས་ཐུགས་དགྱེས་པོ་གནང་སོང་ I gave him a gift and he liked it.

ཐུགས་འགོར་ (tūùgɔɔ) h. of འགོར་འགྱངས་.

ཐུགས་འགོར་མེད་པ་ (tūùgɔɔ meèba) shung. without delaying ༈ ཕེབས་ལམ་དུ་ཐུགས་འགོར་མེད་པ་གང་མགྱོགས་ཞབས་སོར་འཁོད་པ་ They arrived without any delays on the way.

ཐུགས་འགྱུར་ (tūùgyur) sm. བློ་འགྱུར་.

ཐུགས་འགྱོད་ (tūùgyöö) h. of འགྱོད་པ་.

ཐུགས་འགྲུ་བ་ (tūù druwɔ) h. of བློ་གྲུ་བ་.

ཐུགས་རྒྱལ་ (tūggyɛɛ) 1. h. of ང་རྒྱལ་. 2. h. of ཁོང་ཁྲོ་.

ཐུགས་རྒྱུ་ (tūggyu) h. of རྒྱུ་དཔག.

ཐུགས་རྒྱུ་རིང་པོ་ (tūgyu riŋbu) tolerant (h.).

ཐུགས་རྒྱུད་ (tūggyüü) character, temperament, nature, personality (h.).

ཐུགས་རྒྱུད་ཁྲིད་ (tūggyüü trii) h. of རྒྱུད་ཁྲིད་.

ཐུགས་རྒྱུད་སྐྱོང་པོ་ (tūggyüü kyoŋbo) h. of གཤིས་ཀ་སྐྱོང་པོ་.

ཐུགས་རྒྱུད་གཏུམ་པོ་ (tūggyüü dūmbu) sb. who is quick tempered and volatile (h.).

ཐུགས་རྒྱུས་ (tūggyüü) h. of རྒྱུས་.

ཐུགས་སྒམ་པོ་ (tūù gambo) reserved, not open/ outgoing (h.).

ཐུགས་ངན་ (tūùŋɛn) grief, sorrow (h.).

ཐུགས་ངལ་ (tūùŋɛɛ) 1. discouraged, dissapointed, fed up; va.—གནང་. 2. being sad at sb.'s death, mourning/ grieving over sb.'s death (h.); va.—གནང་.

ཐུགས་ངོ་མཁྱེན་ (tūùŋo kyēn) va. to know sb. (h.).

ཐུགས་ངོ་ཚོད་ (tūùŋo cöö) h. of ངོ་དག་ཚོད་.

ཐུགས་མངའ་ལྟར་ (tūùŋadar) as (you) all know (h.).

ཐུགས་ཅ་ཟིང་པོ་ (tūùja siibu) a polite phrase used when asking for sth. that adds that your asking has inconvenienced/ troubled/ bothered/ annoyed the person asked; va.—བྱེད་; —བཟོ་ ༈ ངས་ཁྱེད་རང་ལ་རོགས་རམ་གནང་རོགས་གནང་ཞུས་པས་ཐུགས་ཅ་ཟིང་པོ་བཟོས་སོང་ My asking for help has caused you a lot of trouble.

ཐུགས་ཅག (tūùjaà) h. of ཅག་ག.

ཐུགས་ཅག་ཁྱོན་པོ་ (tūùjaà kyõmbo) sm. ཅག་ག་དག་པོ་ (h.).

ཐུགས་བཅད་ (tūùjɛɛ̀) 1. whatever you want or decide (h.) ༈ ཁོ་ལ་རྟེན་པ་ཁྱེད་རང་གིས་ཐུགས་བཅད་པ་ཞིག་གནང་ན་འགྲིག་གི་རེད་ You can give him whatever gift you want. 2. va. to annoy/ agitate/ anger.

ཐུགས་ལྕོགས་རྒྱ་གོད་པོ་ (tūùjoò gya gööbo) shung. a meddler, snooper (h.).

ཐུགས་ཆུང་ཆུང་ (tūù cūŋjuŋ) h. of སེམས་ཆུང་ཆུང་.

ཐུགས་ཆུང་ཆུང་ཐུགས་གཡེང་མ་གནང་ཞིག རྡོ་ཆུང་ཆུང་ལྷགས་པས་ཁྱེར་དོགས་མེད་ (tūù cūŋjuŋ tūùyeŋ manāŋshi do cūŋjuŋ lhāgbɛ kyērdɔɔmeè) there is nothing to worry about [Lit. don't worry you timid person, there is no fear that small stones will be blown away by the wind].

ཐུགས་ཆུད་ (tūù cüü) vi. to have kept in mind, to have memorized.

ཐུགས་ཆེ་ (tōje) thank you.

ཐུགས་ཆེས་ (tūù cēè) h. of ཡིད་ཆེས་.

ཐུགས་ཚོད་པོ་ (tūù cööbo) sb. who is able to make up his mind quickly, sb. who can come to a decision quickly (h.).

ཐུགས་འཆམ་པོ་ (tūù cāmbo) h. of འཆམ་པོ་.

ཐུགས་རྗེ་ (tōje) 1. thanks; va.—ཞུ་ to thank. 2. compassion, mercy (h.).

ཐུགས་རྗེ་བསྐུལ་ (tūùje gūū) shung. va. to make a request ༈ དེ་བཞིན་བོད་བཞུགས་ཨམ་བན་ནས་ཐུགས་རྗེ་བསྐུལ་བ་ལྟར་ བོད་ལྗོངས་འཚོ་ཆོས་བདེ་ཐབས་སུ་གསོལ་རས་བསྩལ་བ་ In accordance with the Amban's request, (the Emperor) granted (the land) for the welfare of the Tibetan people.

ཐུགས་རྗེ་ཆེ་ (tūùje cē) sm. ཐུགས་རྗེ་.

ཐུགས་རྗེ་ཆེ་གནང་ (tūùje cē nāŋ) thank you very much.

ཐུགས་རྗེ་ཆེན་པོ་ (tūùje cēmbo) 1. compassionate. 2. a name for Avaloketisvara.

ཐུགས་རྗེ་ཆེན་པོ་བཅུ་གཅིག་ཞལ་ (tūùje cēmbo jūgjii shɛɛ) a representation of Avaloketisvara with eleven heads (in statues or paintings).

ཐུགས་རྗེས་བྱམས་སྐྱོང་ (tuùje camgyoŋ) sm. ཐུགས་རྗེའི་གཟིགས་པས་འཛིན་པ་.

ཐུགས་རྗེ་མེད་པ་ (tūùje meèba) unmerciful, uncompassionate (h.).

ཐུགས་རྗེ་ལེགས་སྐྱེས་ (tūùje leggyeè) a 'thank you' gift; va.—ཞུ་ to reciprocate with a 'thank you' gift.

ཐུགས་རྗེ་ལེགས་འབུལ་ (tūùje lēŋbüü) sm. ཐུགས་རྗེ་ལེགས་སྐྱེས་.

ཐུགས་རྗེ་ལྷག་པར་སྐྱོང་ (tūùje lhāgbar gyõŋ) shung. sm. ཐུགས་རྗེའི་གཟིགས་པས་འཛིན་.

ཐུགས་རྗེའི་མཐུ་དཔུང་བཙན་པོ་ (tūùjee tūbuŋ dzēmbo) by the power and grace of ༈ བླ་མའི་ཐུགས་རྗེའི་མཐུ་དཔུང་བཙན་པོས་ལུང་པ་ཡར་རྒྱས་ཕྱིན་པ་རེད་ By the power and grace of the lama, the area improved.

ཐུགས་རྗེའི་བདག་ཉིད་ (tūùjee dagñii) sb. who is very compassionate.

ཐུགས་རྗེའི་གཟིགས་པས་འཛིན་ (tūùjee siibɛ dzin) shung. to treat with kindness (h.) ༈ ཆབ་འབངས་ངན་ཕྱུལ་གྱི་བདེ་ཕྱར་དགོངས་ནས་ཐུགས་རྗེའི་གཟིགས་པས་འཛིན་ Considering the welfare of the poor subjects, (they) treated them with kindness.

ཐུགས་རྗེས་འཛིན་ (tūùjee dzin) sm. ཐུགས་རྗེས་གཟིགས་.

ཐུགས་རྗེས་གཟིགས་ (tūùjee sii) please.

ཐུགས་རྗེས་བྱམས་སྐྱོང་ (tūùjee camgyoŋ) shung. sm. ཐུགས་རྗེའི་གཟིགས་པས་འཛིན་པ་.

ཐུགས་རྗེས་བཟུང་བ་ (tūùjee suŋwa) by the grace of ༈ བླ་མའི་ཐུགས་རྗེས་བཟུང་ནས་ང་ལ་བུ་ཡག་པོ་ཞིག་སྐྱེས་བྱུང་ By the grace of the lama, a good son was born to me.

ཐུགས་ལྗགས་སྤྱན་གསུམ་ (tūùjee jēnsum) heart, tongue and eyeballs.

ཐུགས་ཉམས་ཚོད་པོ་ (tūùñam cööbo) h. of ཉམས་ཚོད་པོ་.

ཐུགས་ཉར་གནང་ (tūùñar nāŋ) h. of ཉར་.

ཐུགས་ཉར་མཛད་ (tūùñar dzɛɛ̀) shung. h. of ཉར་.

ཐུགས་གཉེར་ (tūùñer) wish, aspiration, desire, hope (h.).

ཐུགས་མཉེས་ (tūùñeè) h. of མཉེས་པོ་.

ཐུགས་སྙིང་ (tūùñiŋ) h. of སྙིང་.

ཐུགས་བསྙེལ་ (tūùñee) h. of ང་བརྗེད་.

ཐུགས་གཏན་འཁེལ་ (tūù dēngee) h. of གཏན་འཁེལ་.

ཐུགས་རྟེན་ (tūgden) shung. stupa.

ཐུགས་བརྟག་ཞུ་ (tūùgaà shu) va. to request divination (usu. from a lama).

ཐུགས་ཐག་གཅོད་ (tūùdaà jöö) h. of ཐག་གཅོད་.

ཐུགས་ཐག་ཚོད་པོ་ (tūùdaà cööbo) decisive (h.).

ཐུགས་ཐུབ་ཏུ་སྤྱད་ (tūùtubdu jɛɛ̀) va. to use sth. freely as one wishes, to utilize as one desires (h.).

ཐུགས་མཐུན་ (tūùdün) h. of མོས་མཐུན་.

ཐུགས་མཐུན་ཁྲིམས་ཅན་ (tūgdün trimjaŋ) thinking alike and adhering to the law, being harmonious and adhering to the law.

ཐུགས་མཐུན་པོ་ (tūù tũmbo) sm. ཐུགས་འཆམ་པོ་.

ཐུགས་མཐུན་ཞལ་འཆམ་ (tūgdün sheenjam) of the same opinion/ attitude, thinking alike and getting along/ agreeing.

ཐུགས་མཐུན་འཐད་ (tūgdün tɛɛ̀) h. of ཡིད་འོང་.

ཐུགས་དག (tūùdaà) h. of བསམ་པ་རྣམ་དག.

ཐུགས་དམ་ (tūùdam) 1. divination (h.); va.—ཞུ་ to seek/ request divination; va.—གནང་ to do divination; vi.—ལ་ཕེབས་ to receive the answer from doing divination ༈ རྒྱ་གར་ལ་འགྲོ་ཡས་ཐུགས་དམ་བཟང་ཕེབས་བྱུང་ I received a favorable divination concerning going to India. 2. meditation; va.—འཕེལ་ to meditate. 3. va.—ལ་བཞུགས་ a term used for high lamas whose body lies in state without decomposing. 4. oath, promise. 5. tutelery deity.

ཐུགས་དམ་སྐོང་ (tūùdam gōŋ) va. to summon a tutelery deity.

ཐུགས་དམ་གོང་འཕེལ་ (tūùdam koŋbel) vi. to improve/ increase one's meditation.

ཐུགས་དམ་ཞུ་སོན་ (tūùdam shusön) sm. ཐུགས་དམ་ས་བོན་.

ཐུགས་དམ་ས་བོན་ (tūùdam sābön) the questions to be asked when asking a lama to do divination.

ཐུགས་དཔལ་ (tūù tɛɛ) h. of ཡིད་དཔལ་.

ཐུགས་དོགས་འཁྲུངས་ (tūùdɔɔ trūŋ) h. of དོགས་པ་ཟ་.

ཐུགས་དོགས་གནང་ (tūùdɔɔ nāŋ) h. of དོགས་པ་ཟ་.

ཐུགས་དོགས་ཟ་པ་གནང་ (tūùdɔɔ saba nāŋ) sm. ཐུགས་དོགས་འཁྲུངས་.

ཐུགས་དྭོགས་ (tūùdɔɔ) sm. ཐུགས་དོགས་.

ཐུགས་དྲན་ (tūùtrɛn) h. of དྲན་གསོ་.

ཐུགས་དྲན་སྐྱིན་པོ་ (tūùtrɛn gyēmbo) h. of དྲན་སྐྱིན་པོ་.

ཐུགས་དྲན་པ་གནང་ (tūù trɛmba nāŋ) shung. h. of དྲན་གསོས་.

ཐུགས་གདེངས་འཁེལ་ (tūùdeŋ kēē) shung. h. of གདེངས་འཁེལ་.

ཐུགས་བདེ་ (tūùde) h. of བློ་བདེ་.

ཐུགས་བདེན་ (tūùden) h. of དགོངས་དག.

ཐུགས་འདུན་ (tündün) 1. h. of རེ་འདུན་. 2. h. of བསམ་འདུན་.

ཐུགས་འདུན་སྲུས་མོ་ (tündün sɛɛmo) shung. bride.

ཐུགས་འདོགས་ (tūùdɔɔ) shung. h. of སེམས་ཁུར་.

ཐུགས་འདོགས་ཆེ་བ་ (tūùdɔɔ cēwa) sm. བརྩེ་མཐོང་ཆེ་བ་.

ཐུགས་འདོད་ (tündöö) h. of འདོད་པ་.

ཐུགས་འདོད་ཆེན་པོ་ (tündöö cēmbo) shung. h. of འདོད་པ་ཆེན་པོ་.

ཐུགས་འདྲིས་ (tündrii) h. of འདྲིས་པོ་.

ཐུགས་རྡོ་རྗེ་ (tūù dorje) the mind of Buddha.

ཐུགས་ནང་གཙང་མ་ (tūùnaŋ dzāŋmə) shung. close friend ༑ཞབས་དྲུང་གོང་མ་རྣམས་ནས་བཟུང་ངེད་རང་སྔ་ཕྱིར་ཐུགས་ནང་གཙང་མ་བྱུང་བ་ཡིན་པས་ From previous generations we were close friends.

ཐུགས་ནང་ཚགས་ (tūùnaŋ tsāà) h. of ནང་ཚགས་.

ཐུགས་ནད་འཁྱུག (tūùnɛɛ kyɔɔ) h. of ནད་འཁྱུག.

ཐུགས་ནུས་ (tūùnüü) the power of thinking, thinking energy/ power/ ability; va.—འདོན་ to think hard ༑མི་དམངས་ཀྱི་དོན་དུ་ཐུགས་ནུས་ཡོད་ཚད་བཏོན་གནང་བཞག (He) thought hard in all ways for the benefit of the people.

ཐུགས་གནག (tūùnaà) h. of སེམས་གནག.

ཐུགས་གནོང་ (tūùnoŋ) h. of གནོང་.

ཐུགས་རྣམ་པར་དག་པ་ (tūù nāmbar tagba) clear and generous mind.

ཐུགས་སྣང་ (tūùnaŋ) h. of དོ་སྣང་.

ཐུགས་སྣང་དཀར་པོ་ (tūùnaŋ gārbo) close relationship/ friendship, friendly.

ཐུགས་སྣང་དཀར་ཡུལ་ (tūùnaŋ gāryüü) sm. ཐུགས་དགེ་.

ཐུགས་སྣང་གང་དྲན་གནང་ (tūùnaŋ gandrɛn nāŋ) shung. va. to do whatever comes to mind (h.) ༑ཡབ་ཆེན་མ་བཞུགས་པའི་སྐབས་དང་བསྟུན་ནས་སྲས་སྐུས་ཐུགས་སྣང་གང་དྲན་གནང་ During the absence of his father, the son did whatever came to his mind (whatever he wanted).

ཐུགས་སྣང་དགེ་ཡུལ་ (tūùnaŋ geyüü) sm. ཐུགས་དགེ་.

ཐུགས་སྣང་གཤིན་པོ་ (tūùnaŋ shimbu) very friendly (h.).

ཐུགས་སྤྱང་པོ་ (tūù jāŋbo) smart.

ཐུགས་སྤྲོ་ (tɔɔdro) 1. party; va.—གཏོང་ to give a party (h.). 2. vi. to be happy/ elated.

ཐུགས་སྤྲོ་ཉིན་སྐྱོང་ (tɔɔdro ñingyoŋ) an all day party.

ཐུགས་ཕང་པོ་ (tūù pāŋbo) h. of ཕང་པོ་.

ཐུགས་ཕན་ (tūùbɛn) h. of ཕན་ཐོགས་.

ཐུགས་ཕན་གསོས་ (tūùbɛn sɔɔ) vi. to be useful/ beneficial.

ཐུགས་ཕན་གསོས་པོ་ (tūùbɛn sööbo) useful, beneficial ༑སྨན་དེ་ཐུགས་ཕན་གསོས་པོ་འདུག་གས་ Is this medicine beneficial?

ཐུགས་ཕམ་ (tūùbam) h. of བློ་ཕམ་.

ཐུགས་འཕྱང་ལ་འཁྱོག (tūùjaŋla kyɔɔ) h. of འཕྱང་མོ་ཁྱུག.

ཐུགས་འཕྲེང་ (tūùdreŋ) vi. to miss sb. (h.).

ཐུགས་འཕྲོག་པ་ (tūùdrɔɔ) h. of ཡིད་འཕྲོག.

ཐུགས་བག་ཕེབས་པོ་ (tūùbaà pēēbo) h. of བག་ཕེབས་པོ་.

ཐུགས་བག་ཡངས་པོ་ (tūùbaà yaŋbo) sm. ཐུགས་བག་ཕེབས་པོ་.

ཐུགས་བད་དྭངས་ (tūùbɛɛ taŋ) h. of བློ་བད་དྭངས་.

ཐུགས་བབ་ (tūùbəb) sm. ཐུགས་ལ་འབབ་.

ཐུགས་བྲེལ་ (tūgdree) h. of བྲེལ་བ་.

ཐུགས་བློ་ (tūùlo) h of བློ་.

ཐུགས་བློ་གཏད་ (tūùlo dɛɛ) h. of བློ་གཏད་.

ཐུགས་བློ་འཁུག (tūùlo guù) h. of བློ་འཁུག.

ཐུགས་བློས་ཁེལ་པོ་ (tūùlöö kēēbo) h. of བློས་འཁེལ་པོ་.

ཐུགས་བློས་གང་ལྕོགས་ (tūùlöö ganjɔɔ) sm. ཐུགས་བློས་གང་ཆོད་.

ཐུགས་བློས་གང་ཆོད་ (tūùlöö ganjöö) as much as one can ༑ཞལ་འདེབས་ཐུགས་བློས་གང་ཆོད་དེ་གནང་རོགས་གནང་ Please give as much as you can as a donation.

ཐུགས་བློས་ཁྱིངས་འགེལ་ (tūùlöö ciŋgee) h. of བློས་ཁྱིངས་འགེལ་.

ཐུགས་བློས་གཏོང་ (tūùlöö dōŋ) h. of བློས་གཏོང་.

ཐུགས་བློས་བཟོད་ (tūùlöö söö) h. of བློས་བཟོད་.

ཐུགས་མ་རང་ (tūù maraŋ) h. of ཡིད་མ་རང་.

ཐུགས་མད་ (tūùmɛɛ) sm. ཐུགས་བདེན་.

ཐུགས་མུག (tūùmug) h. of ཡིད་མུག.

ཐུགས་མོས་ (tūùmöö) 1. h. of མོས་མཐུན་. 2. wish, desire (h.).

ཐུགས་སྨོན་ (tūùmön) h. of སྨོན་ལམ་.

ཐུགས་སྨོན་བདེན་བདར་ (tūùmön dendar) shung. prayer for one's hopes coming to pass ༑རྟེན་མཆོག་སྤྱན་སྔར་ཐུགས་སྨོན་བདེན་བདར་དང་འབྲེལ་ In front of the sacred religious objects, (he) prayed that his hopes will come to pass.

ཐུགས་གཙིགས་ (tūù) h. of གཙིགས་.

ཐུགས་རྩིས་ (tūùdzii) h. of བརྩི་མཐོང་.

ཐུགས་རྩོལ་ (tūùdzöö) h. of རྩོལ་པོ་.

ཐུགས་རྩོམ་ (tūùdzom) h. of རྩོམ་.

ཐུགས་བརྩེ་ (tūùdze) h. of བརྩེ་གདུང་.

ཐུགས་བརྩོན་ (tūgdzön) h. of བརྩོན་འགྲུས་.

ཐུགས་ཚ་ (tūù tsā) h. of ངོ་ཚ་.

ཐུགས་ཚ་སྣང་གནང་ (tūù tsānaŋ nāŋ) shung. sm. ཐུགས་འཚེར་སྣང་གནང་.

ཐུགས་ཚ་པོ་ (tūù tsābo) h. of ངོ་ཚ་པོ་.

ཐུགས་ཚ་སྨིན་པོ་ (tūùdza mimbo) h. of ངོ་ཚ་སྨིན་པོ་.

ཐུགས་ཚབས་ (tūùdzəb) h. of སེམས་ཚབས་.

ཐུགས་ཚོད་མེད་པ་ (tūùdza meèba) having no idea of how things stand, having no plan.

ཐུགས་མཚར་པོ་ (tūù tsārbo) h. of མཚར་པོ་.

ཐུགས་འཚབས་ (tūùdzəb) h. of འཚབས་.

ཐུགས་འཚེར་ (tōŋdzer) h. of འཚེར་.

ཐུགས་འཚེར་སྣང་ (tūù tsērnaŋ) sm. ཐུགས་འཚེར་.

ཐུགས་འཚེར་མ་གནང་ (tōŋdzeè manaŋ) idiom. Don't be shy.

ཐུགས་མཛངས་ (tūùdzaŋ) sm. ཐུགས་འཚེར་.

ཐུགས་འཛིན་ (tündzin) h. of བློ་འཛིན་.

ཐུགས་རྫོགས་ (tūùdzɔɔ) shung. h. of བསྙེན་རྫོགས་.

ཐུགས་ཞིབ་གནང་ (tūùshib nāŋ) 1. va. to look (at) (h.). ༑ཁོང་མེ་ཏོག་ལ་ཐུགས་ཞིབ་གནང་བར་ཕེབས་འདུག He has come to look at the flowers. 2. va. to buy ༑ཙ་ལག་འདི་ཚོང་ཁང་ག་ནས་ཐུགས་ཞིབ་གནང་པ་ From which store did you buy this thing?

ཐུགས་ཞིབ་ཆུབ་པོ་ (tūùshib cūbbo) h. of ཞིབ་ཆུབ་པོ་.

ཐུགས་ཞུམ་ (tūùshum) h. of སེམས་ཞུམ་.

ཐུགས་ཞེན་ (tūùshen) h. of ཞེན་.

ཐུགས་བཞེད་ (tūùsheè) 1. thought, thinking (h.). 2. wanting, desiring (h.).

ཐུགས་ཟིན་ (tūùsön) h. of དོགས་ཟིན་.

ཐུགས་གཞོལ་ (tūù shöö) va. to concentrate. (h.).

ཐུགས་ཡི་རང་བ་ (tūù yi raŋwa) h. of ཡི་རང་བ་.

ཐུགས་ཡིད་ (tūùyii) mind, thinking (h.).

ཐུགས་ཡིད་གཅིག་འདྲིས་ (tūùyii jīgdrii) two persons who are so close that they think as one (h.).

ཐུགས་ཡིད་ཐང་ཆེད་ (tūùyii tāŋ cɛɛ) h. of ཡིད་ཐང་ཆེད་.

ཐུགས་ཡིད་ཆེས་ (tūùyii cēè) h. of ཡིད་ཆེས་.

ཐུགས་ཡེང་ (tūùyeŋ) sm. ཐུགས་གཡེང་.

ཐུགས་ཡིངས་པོ་ (tūù yiŋbo) h. of བག་ཡིངས་པོ་.

ཐུགས་གཡེང་ (tūùyeŋ) h. of གཡེང་.

ཐུགས་གཡེལ་ (tūùyee) sm. ཐུགས་གཡེང་.

ཐུགས་རབ་ (tūùrəb) h. of ཤེས་རབ་.

ཐུགས་རབ་གཞུངས་པ་ (tūùrəb shu̲ŋba) a great scholar.

ཐུགས་རིག (tūùriì) h. of རིག་པ་.

ཐུགས་རིག་ནོ་པོ་ (tūùriì nōbo) sm. ཐུགས་རིག་ཡག་པོ་.

ཐུགས་རིག་ཡག་པོ་ (tūùriì ya̲gbo) brainy, intelligent.

ཐུགས་རུ་ངར་པོ་ (tūùru ŋa̲rbo) 1. meticulous, fastidious in work (h.). 2. short-tempered, easy to anger (h.).

ཐུགས་རུ་གདུམ་པོ་ (tūùru dūmbu) short-tempered, easy to anger (h.).

ཐུགས་རུས་ (tūgrüù) sm. ཐུགས་བརྩོན་.

ཐུགས་རེ་ (tūùre) h. of རེ་བ་.

ཐུགས་ལ་མངའ་ (tūùlə ŋā) h. of སེམས་ལ་ངེས་.

ཐུགས་ལ་འཇོག (tūùlə jɔ̲ɔ̀) h. of སེམས་ལ་འཇོག.

ཐུགས་ལ་འདོགས་ (tūùlə dɔ̲ɔ̀) h. of སེམས་ལ་འཇོག.

ཐུགས་ལ་ཕོག (tūùlə pɔ̄ɔ̀) h. of སེམས་ལོག.

ཐུགས་ལ་འབབ་ (tūùlə bə̲b) sm. བློ་ལ་འབབ་.

ཐུགས་ལ་ཞུགས་ (tūùlə shu̲ù) h. of ཁོང་དུ་ཆུད་.

ཐུགས་ལས་ (tūùlɛɛ̀) virtue, virtuous acts. 2. worry, anxiety, distress, concern (h.).

ཐུགས་ལས་སྣ་པོ་ (tūùlɛɛ̀ lābo) h. of ལས་སྣ་པོ་.

ཐུགས་ལོག (tūùlɔɔ̀) h. of སེམས་ལོག.

ཐུགས་ལོན་ (tūùlön) h. of བློ་ཆོད་ལོན་.

ཐུགས་ཤོར་ (tūùshɔɔ) h. of སེམས་པ་ཤོར་.

ཐུགས་གཤིས་ (tūùshiì) h. of གཤིས་ཀ་.

ཐུགས་སང་ (tūùsaŋ) leisure time, free time.

ཐུགས་སར་ཆེན་པོ་ (tūùsar cēmbo) sb. who either gets up early in the morning or comes to work/ meetings/ etc. very early.

ཐུགས་སར་ཚ་པོ་ (tūùsar tsābo) sm. ཐུགས་ས་ཆེན་པོ་.

ཐུགས་སུ་ཕེབས་ (tūùsu pēè) h. of ཡིད་དུ་འོང་.

ཐུགས་སུ་ཆུད་ (tūùsu cǖǜ) h. vi. to comprehend/ understand/ grasp (h.).

ཐུགས་སུ་འཐད་ (tūùsu tɛ̄ɛ̀) h. of བློ་ལ་འབབ་.

ཐུགས་སུ་བྱོན་ (tūùsu jö̲n) sm. བློ་ལ་འབབ་.

ཐུགས་སུ་ཚུད་ (tūùsu tsǖǜ) sm. ཐུགས་སུ་མངའ་.

ཐུགས་སུན་ (tūùsün) 1. bothering, annoying; va.—བཟོ་; —གནང་ ¶ ང་གཉིས་ཀྱིས་ཁྱེད་ལ་དོན་མེད་ཐུགས་བསུན་བཟོས་སོང་ We two have bothered you without reason. 2. introverted, not outgoing.

ཐུགས་སེམས་ (tūùsem) h. of སེམས་.

ཐུགས་སེམས་དཀའ་པོ་ (tūùsem gābo) h. of སེམས་བཟང་པོ་.

ཐུགས་སེམས་སྐྱོ་སྣང་གནང་ (ūùsem gyōnaŋ nāā) h. of སེམས་སྐྱོ་.

ཐུགས་སེམས་བགྲུང་ (tūùsem dru̲ŋ) va. to pay attention (h.).

ཐུགས་སེམས་འགྱུར་ (tūùsem gyu̲r) va. to change one's mind (h.).

ཐུགས་སེམས་ཆགས་ (tūùsem cāà) h. of སེམས་ཆགས་.

ཐུགས་སེམས་ཆུང་ཆུང་ (tūùsem cūŋjuŋ) modest.

ཐུགས་སེམས་འཁྲུག (tūùsem drɔ̄ɔ̀) h. of ཡིད་འཁྲུག.

ཐུགས་སེམས་འཚབ་ (tūùsem tsə̄b) vi. to be nervous (h.).

ཐུགས་སེམས་བཟང་པོ་ (tūùsem sa̲ŋbo) generous, kind, unstinting (h.).

ཐུགས་སེམས་ལ་ངེས་ (tūùsemla ŋe̲è) va. to remember/ memorize (h.).

ཐུགས་སེམས་ཤི་ (tūùsem shī) h. of སེམས་ཤི་.

ཐུགས་སེམས་ཤོར་ (tūùsem shɔ̄ɔ) h. of སེམས་ཤོར་.

ཐུགས་སེམས་གསོ་ (tūùsem sō) h. of སེམས་གསོ་.

ཐུགས་སེར་སྣ་ཚ་པོ་ (tūù sērna tsābo) h. of སེར་སྣ་ཚ་པོ་.

ཐུགས་སྲས་ (tūùsɛɛ̀) a close disciple.

ཐུགས་སྙོང་ (tūùsoŋ) h. of དྭང་པོ་.

ཐུགས་གསལ་མེ་ལོང་ (tūùsɛɛ me̲loŋ) metal breast plate worn by oracles (h.).

ཐུགས་གསེང་ (tūùseŋ) sm. ཐུག་ལང་.

ཐུགས་གསོ་ (tūùso) h. of སེམས་གསོ་.

ཐུགས་གསོའི་མཇལ་དར་ (tūùsö jɛ̲ɛdar) h. of སེམས་གསོ་ཁ་བཏགས་.

ཐུགས་གསོས་ (tūùsöö̀) a condolence gift when sb. dies; va.—འབུལ་ to give such a gift.

ཐུགས་བསམ་ (tūùsam) h. of བསམ་བློ་.

ཐུགས་བསམ་བཞེད་ (tūùsam she̲è) h. of བསམ་བློ་གཏོང་.

ཐུགས་བསུན་ (tūùsün) sm. ཐུགས་སུན་.

ཐུགས་ལྷན་ནེ་ (tūù lhɛ̄nne) a clear mind.

ཐུགས་ལྷོད་པོ་ (tūù lhȫȍbo) relaxed, free from worry/ anxiety (h.) ¶ ཐུགས་ལྷོད་པོར་བཞུགས་རོགས་གནང་ Please relax (be at ease) (said to a guest).

ཐུགས་ལྷོད་ལྷོད་ (tūù lhȫȍlöö̀) sm. ཐུགས་ལྷོད་པོ་.

ཐུང་ (tūŋ) 1. sm. འཐུང་. 2. abbr. of ཐུང་ཐུང་.

ཐུང་སྐྱེལ་ (tūŋgyee) shung. 1. a corvee carrying tax that takes a day back and forth (so that one can return home the same day). 2. going a short distance to see a person off.

ཐུང་རྒྱུག (tūŋgyuù) sm. ཐུང་སྐྱེལ་.

ཐུང་ངུ་ (tūŋŋu) sm. ཐུང་ཐུང་.

ཐུང་རྟོད་བྱེད་ (tūŋdöö̀ ce̲è) sm. རྟོད་ཐག་རྒྱག.

ཐུང་ཐུང་ (tūŋduŋ) short ¶ ཐག་པ་འདི་ཐུང་ཐུང་རེད་ This rope is short.

ཐུང་དུ་ (tūŋdu) sm. ཐུང་རུ་.

ཐུང་མདའ་ (tūŋda) pistol, revolver.

ཐུང་མདའ་དཔལ་རྒྱག (tūŋda tɛ̲ɛ̲gyaà) free pistol shooting (a marksmanship event).

ཐུང་བ་ (tūŋwa) short.

ཐུང་ཝེ་སུའུ་ (tūŋwesu) ch. isotope.

ཐུང་རུ་ (tūŋru) shorten; va.—གཏོང་ to shorten; vi.—འགྲོ་ to get shorter.

ཐུང་ཤོས་ (tūŋsöö̀) shortest.

ཐུང་སི་ (tūŋsi) ch. interpreter.

ཐུད་ (tǖǜ) 1. a food made from cheese, tsamba and butter. 2. imp. of འདུད་.

ཐུད་སྒྲོམ་ (tǖǜdrom) a square frame/ hollow in which the food ཐུད་ is molded.

ཐུད་སྣེར་ (tǖǜ dēr) sm. ཐུད་རུལ་སྣེར་.

ཐུད་གདར་མ་ (tǖǜ da̲rma) a square shaped ཐུད་.

ཐུད་ཕོར་ (tǖǜbɔɔ) wooden bowl used to keep ཐུད་.

ཐུད་སྦུ་ (tǖǖ bu̲) va. to knead the ingredients in the process of making ཐུད་.

ཐུད་ཚོ་པོ་ (tǖǜ tsōbo) ཐུད་ that has a lot of butter and sugar.

ཐུད་འཚོ་བ་མར་གྱི་དྲིན་ (tǖǜ tsōwa ma̲rgi dri̲n) sm. ཛ་ཞིམ་པོ་མར་གྱི་དྲིན་.

ཐུད་རུལ་སྣེར་ (tǖǜrüü dēr) va. to not pay back sth. that is owed ¶ ཁོས་ཐོག་མར་ཁ་མཁས་པོའི་ངང་ནས་དངུལ་གཡར་དེ་རྗེས་སུ་ཐུད་རུལ་སྣེར་བྱུང་ At first he asked me for a loan using sweet talk and then he didn't pay me back. [Lit. giving rotten ཐུད་].

ཐུད་ལུད་ (tǖǜlüǜ) spittle; va.—རྒྱག to spit (at someone).

ཐུན་ (tǖn) 1. dosage, portion ¶ སྨན་ཐུན་རེར་རིལ་བུ་བཞི་བཞི་ Each dose of medicine consists of four pills. 2. a short retreat when one refrains from talking, va.—གཏོང་. 3. hour, time unit ¶ ནམ་གྱི་ཐུན་གསུམ་ The third hour of nighttime. 4. grain seeds that have been blessed through the recitation of mantras.

ཐུན་གྲོལ་ (tǖndröö) va. to finish a period of ཐུན་ retreat.

ཐུན་དངོས་གཞི་ (tǖnŋöö̀shi) (the time of) actual retreat.

ཐུན་བཅད་ (tǖnjɛɛ̀) a short retreat during which time one refrains from talking and meeting others.

ཐུན་ཐི་ (tǖndi) a kind of brocade.

ཐུན་ཐུན་ (tǖndün) in groups, in sections.

ཐུན་དོང་ (tǖndoŋ) a hole made in the ground when casting a spell.

ཐུན་དྲུག་རྣལ་འབྱོར་ (tǖndruù nɛ̄njɔɔ) yoga practitioner who makes short retreats during the six periods of the day (four times during the day and twice at night).

ཐུན་བརྡ་གཏོང་ (tǖnda dōŋ) va. to use a gong or a bell to signal the start of a period of prayer.

ཐུན་པ་ (tǖmbə) 1. a timekeeper (sb. who keeps track of time periods). 2. people who make short retreats during which they refrain from speaking. 3. a group of people.

ཐུན་ཕྱེད་ (tǖnceè) half a dose/ portion (of medicine).

2. half of a ཐུན་ time period.

ཐུན་བར་ (tũmbar) the time in between a ཐུན་ time period.

ཐུན་འབྲུ་ (tũndru) ears of grain that are leftover after harvesting.

ཐུན་སྦྱོར་ (tũnjɔɔ) night.

ཐུན་མ་ (tũnmə) sm. ཐུན་སྦྱོར་.

ཐུན་མོང་ (tũnmoŋ) common, communal, collective, joint, public.

ཐུན་མོང་སྐད་ལུགས་ (tũnmoŋ gɛ̃ɛ̀luù) common language.

ཐུན་མོང་གན་རྒྱ་ (tũnmoŋ kengya) collective agreement.

ཐུན་མོང་གི་ཁེ་ཕན་ (tũnmoŋgi kēbɛn) common interest/ welfare.

ཐུན་མོང་གི་ཐེག་པ་ (tũnmoŋgi tēgba) the common path for all the Yanas. (Mahayana, Hinayana, Vajrayana).

ཐུན་མོང་གི་དགྲ་བོ་ (tũnmoŋgi drawo) common enemy.

ཐུན་མོང་གི་འགོ་ཁྲིད་ (tũnmoŋgi gudri) collective leadership.

ཐུན་མོང་གི་འཐབ་རྩོད་ (tũnmoŋgi tə̄bdzöö̀) common struggle.

ཐུན་མོང་གི་འཕྲོད་སྦྱོར་ (tũnmoŋgi dröö̀jɔɔ) public health.

ཐུན་མོང་གི་འཚོ་བ་ (tũnmoŋgi tsōwa) collective life.

ཐུན་མོང་གི་ཞིང་གྲོང་ (tũnmoŋgi shiŋgə) collective farm.

ཐུན་མོང་གི་ཞིང་པ་ (tũnmoŋgi shiŋbə) collective farmer.

ཐུན་མོང་གི་རང་བཞིན་ (tũnmoŋgi rəŋshin) common/ collective nature.

ཐུན་མོང་གི་རེ་འདུན་ (tũnmoŋgi rendün) common hope/ desire.

ཐུན་མོང་གི་ལས་ (tũnmoŋgi lɛ̀ɛ̀) work that benefits this world in common.

ཐུན་མོང་གི་བསམ་ཚུལ་ (tũnmoŋgi sə̄mdzüü) common ideas/ attitudes/ views.

ཐུན་མོང་གིས་ (tũnmoŋgi) together, collectively, jointly ¶ ཚོང་ཁང་འདི་ཐུན་མོང་གིས་བདག་གཉེར་བྱེད་ཀྱི་ཡོད་པ་རེད་ (They) are collectively managing the store.

ཐུན་མོང་འགོག་སྲུང་ (tũnmoŋ gɔgsuŋ) joint/ common defense.

ཐུན་མོང་མཉམ་སྒྲུབ་ (tũnmoŋ ñə̃mdrub) achieving (sth.) together.

ཐུན་མོང་ཅན་དུ་འགྱུར་ (tũnmoŋjɛndu gyur) vi. to become collectivized.

ཐུན་མོང་ལྟ་ཚུལ་ (tũnmoŋ dədzüü) common/ collective point of view.

ཐུན་མོང་ཐོག་ནས་ (tũnmoŋ tɔ̃ɔ̀nɛ) sm. ཐུན་མོང་གིས་.

ཐུན་མོང་དུ་ (tũnmoŋdu) together, collectively, jointly, in common ¶ ཐུན་མོང་དུ་འགོ་ཁྲིད་བྱེད་ To lead collectively. ¶ ཐུན་མོང་དུ་ངལ་རྩོལ་བྱེད་ To labor collectively.

ཐུན་མོང་དུ་བསྒྱུར་ (tũnmoŋdu gyur) va. to collectivize.

ཐུན་མོང་དུ་སྤྱོད་ (tũnmoŋdu jöö̀) va. to be in use commonly/ everywhere.

ཐུན་མོང་སྡེ་ཁག (tũnmoŋ degaà) a collective unit.

ཐུན་མོང་ནས་ (tũnmoŋnɛ) sm. ཐུན་མོང་གིས་.

ཐུན་མོང་སྣང་ངོར་ (tũnmoŋ nāŋŋɔr) general/ common appearance ¶ ཐུན་མོང་སྣང་ངོར་མི་དཀྱུས་མ་ཞིག་ལས་དངོས་སུ་དེ་ལྟར་མིན་ In general appearance he is like any ordinary person but in reality he is not.

ཐུན་མོང་དཔལ་འབྱོར་ (tũnmoŋ bɛ̄njɔɔ) collectivized economy.

ཐུན་མོང་མ་ཡིན་པ་ (tũnmoŋ məyimbə) unique, extraordinary, uncommon ¶ བོད་པའི་གཞས་འདི་ནི་ཐུན་མོང་མ་ཡིན་པ་ཞིག་རེད་ This Tibetan song is unique.

ཐུན་མོང་མིན་པ་ (tũnmoŋ mimbə) sm. ཐུན་མོང་མ་ཡིན་པ་.

ཐུན་མོང་རྩ་ཚིག (tũnmoŋ dzədzii) the "common programme" of the People's Political Consultative Conference (promulgated in1949).

ཐུན་མོང་རྩ་འཛིན་ (tũnmoŋ dzəndzin) sm. ཐུན་མོང་རྩ་ཚིག.

ཐུན་མོང་ཚོང་ར་ (tũnmoŋ tsōŋra) the Common Market.

ཐུན་མོང་ཞིང་ར་ (tũnmoŋ shinrə) collective farm, kolkhoz.

ཐུན་མོང་རིང་ལུགས་ (tũnmoŋ riŋluù) collectivism.

ཐུན་མོང་རེ་སྨོན་ (tũnmoŋ remön) a wish/ desire/ want that is common to everyone.

ཐུན་མོང་ལ་དབང་བ་ (tũnmoŋla wāŋwa) collective ownership ¶ ཐུན་མོང་ལ་དབང་བའི་ལམ་ལུགས་ System of collective ownership.

ཐུན་མོང་ལས་དོན་ (tũnmoŋ lɛ̀ɛdön) common task/ work/ job.

ཐུན་མོང་ས་ (tũnmoŋsa) a commons area, a park.

ཐུན་ཚོད་ (tũndzöö̀) one of the six periods in which a day is divided.

ཐུན་མཚམས་ (tũndzam) 1. sm. དུས་མཚམས་. 2. night. 3. sm. ཐུན་བར་.

ཐུན་རྫས་ (tũndzɛ̀ɛ̀) shung. objects that have been blessed by mantras.

ཐུན་བཞིའི་རྣལ་འབྱོར་ (tũnshii nēnjɔɔ) yoga practioner who does four ཐུན་ a day: at dawn, morning, midday and late evening.

ཐུན་ཟོར་ (tũnsɔɔ) blessed grain that is put on torma.

ཐུན་བཟུང་ (tũn suŋ) va. to engage in a ཐུན་ retreat.

ཐུན་ཨན་མོན་ (tũnanmön) Tiananmen Square.

ཐུན་ཨན་མོན་ཐང་ཆེན་ (tũnanmön tāŋcen) ch.tib. sm. ཐུན་ཨན་མོན་.

ཐུན་རྭ་ (tũnra) a horn in which blessed ཐུན་རྫས་ are kept.

ཐུབ་ (tūb) vi. to be able (to) ¶ ང་ལྷ་སར་འགྲོ་ཐུབ་ཀྱི་རེད་ I am able to go to Lhasa. ¶ ལས་ཀ་ཡག་པོ་བྱེད་མ་ཐུབ་ན་ If (you) are unable to do good work.

ཐུབ་ཆི་ (tūbji) sm. ཐུབ་ཆུ་.

ཐུབ་ཆུ་ (tūbju) button; va.—རྒྱག to button.

ཐུབ་ཆེན་ (tūbjen) abbr. for ཐུབ་པ་ཆེན་པོ་.

ཐུབ་ཆེན་པོ་ (tūb cēmbo) durable, firm, enduring ¶ རས་འདི་ཐུབ་ཆེན་པོ་འདུག This cloth is durable.

ཐུབ་བསྟན་ (tūbdɛn) 1. Buddhist doctrine/ teachings. 2. person's name.

ཐུབ་བསྟན་རྒྱ་མཚོ་ (tūbdɛn gyatso) name of the 13th Dalai Lama.

ཐུབ་ཐབས་མེད་པ་ (tūbdəb meèba) unable to do/ accomplish ¶ ལས་ཀ་འདི་ཁྱེད་རང་གི་ཐུབ་ཐབས་ཡོད་པ་མ་རེད་ You will be unable to do this work.

ཐུབ་པ་ (tūbbə) 1. the Buddha. 2. resistant to sth. ¶ ཆུ་ཐུབ་པ་ Water resistant.

ཐུབ་པ་ཆེན་པོ་ (tūbə cēmbo) the Buddha.

ཐུབ་པ་སངས་རྒྱས་ (tūbbə sāŋgyɛɛ̀) the Buddha.

ཐུབ་པའི་དབང་པོ་ (tūbɛ wāŋbo) sm. ཐུབ་པ་ཆེན་པོ་.

ཐུབ་པའི་ཞལ་སྐྱིན་ (tūbbɛ shɛɛgyin) an image or statue of the Buddha.

ཐུབ་སྤྱད་ (tūbjɛɛ̀) sth. that can defeat/ subdue sb.

ཐུབ་དབང་ (tūbwaŋ) sm. ཐུབ་པའི་དབང་པོ་.

ཐུབ་དབང་རྡོ་རྗེ་འཆང་ (tūwaŋ dōjecaŋ) Vajradhara.

ཐུབ་དབང་གསུང་སྐྱེས་ (tūbwaŋ sūŋgyeè) the disciples/ followers of the Buddha.

ཐུབ་མེད་པ་ (tūb meèba) nondurable.

ཐུབ་ཙམ་ (tūbdzam) merely, just able ¶ བོད་ལ་འགྲོ་ཐུབ་ཙམ་བྱུང་སོང་ I was just able to go to Tibet (i.e., with difficulty).

ཐུབ་ཚད་ (tūbdzɛɛ̀) (vb. + —) capacity of the verbal action ¶ མདྲེལ་གྱིས་ཁལ་འཁྱེར་ཐུབ་ཚད་རྟ་ལས་ཆེ་བ་ཡོད་ The carrying capacity of a mule is greater than that of a horse.

ཐུབ་ཚོད་ (tūbdzöö̀) 1. bullying; va.—གཏོང་ to bully. 2. according to one's ability/ strength.

ཐུབ་ཚོད་ནུས་ཚོད་ (tūbdzöö̀ nuùdzöö̀) sm. ཐུབ་ཚོད་, 2.

ཐུབ་ཚོད་ཚ་པོ་ (tūbdzöö̀ tsābo) sb. who bullies a lot.

ཐུབ་བཟོད་ (tūbsöö̀) durable.

ཐུབ་ལུང་ (tūbluŋ) buttonhole.

ཐུམ་ (tūm) 1. case, sheath, wrapping; va.—རྒྱག to encase, to wrap. 2. package, parcel.

ཐུམ་ཀློག (tūm lɔ̄ɔ) va. to read a religious text not in order from the start of the text but by many monks each reading a part of the text at the same time (to save time).

ཐུམ་ཁྲིས་ (tūmdreè) a largish package/ bundle; va.—རྒྱག.

ཐུམ་རྒྱ་ཤོག་བུ་ (tūmgya shɔ̄gbu) wrapping paper.

ཐུམ་རྒྱག (tūmgya) a parcel/ package sealed with a seal.

ཐུམ་བསྒྲིལ་ (tūmdrii) sm. ཐུམ་ཁྲིས་.

ཐུམ་ཅན་ (tūmjɛn) wrapped up, encased.

ཐུམ་ཆུང་ (tūmjuŋ) a small package/ bundle; va.—རྒྱག.

ཐུམ་ཐུམ་ (tūmdum) sm. ཐུམ་ཆུང་.

ཐུམ་པ་ (tūmbə) momentarily, briefly, a short time.

ཐུམ་པོ་ (tūmbo) sm. ཐུམ་ཆུང་.

ཐུམ་བུ་ (tūmbu) sm. ཐུམ་ཆུང་.

ཐུམ་སྒྲོར་ (tūmjɔɔ) packing, packaging.

ཐུམ་སྒྲོར་རྒྱུ་ཆ་ཀུང་སི་ (tūmjɔɔ gyuja gūŋsi) packing material company.

ཐུམ་སྒྲོར་རྒྱན་སྤྲས་ (tūmjɔɔ gyɛndrɛɛ̀) packing/ packaging and decorations ། ཐུམ་སྒྲོར་རྒྱན་སྤྲས་ཀུང་སི་ A packaging and decorations company.

ཐུམ་སྒྲོར་འདྲེན་གཏོང་ཀུང་སི་ (tūmjɔɔ drendoŋ gūŋsi) a packing import and export company.

ཐུམ་སྒྲོར་འཕྲུལ་ཆས་ (tūmjɔɔ trūūjɛɛ̀) packing/ packaging machinery.

ཐུམ་སྒྲོར་ལས་ཚན་ (tūmjɔɔ lɛ̀ɛdzɛn) packing department.

ཐུམ་ལ་ (tūmla) together ། ཁོ་གཉིས་ཐུམ་ལ་ཤི་འདུག The two of them died together.

ཐུམས་ (tūm) sm. ཐུམ་.

ཐུའུ་མེ་སུའུ་ (tūmesu) ch. terramycin.

ཐུའུ་སི་ (tūūsi) ch. title given to native chief/ headman by the Emperors of China.

ཐུའོ་ལྷའ་ཅིའི་ (tūolaji) ch. sm. ཐུའོ་ལ་ཅི་.

ཐུའོ་ལ་ཅི་ (tūolaji) ch. tractor.

ཐུའོ་ལ་སི་ (tūolasi) ch. trust (company).

ཐུའོ་ལུའོ་ཚི་ (tūo luo tsī) Trotsky.

ཐུར་ (tūr) 1. down, downhill ། ཆུ་ཐུར་ལ་རྒྱུགས་འགྲོ་སྐབས་ When the water runs downhill. 2. spoon.

ཐུར་གྱེན་ (tūrgyen) downhill and uphill, the slope ། ལམ་ཁ་འདིར་ཐུར་གྱེན་མང་པོ་འདུག There are many uphill and downhill sections on this road.

ཐུར་ཁྲིབ་ (tūrdrib) divination done by means of a stick with seven notches (the calculation is done in relation to where the shadow falls on the notches on the stick).

ཐུར་མགོ་ (tūŋgo) spoon.

ཐུར་ངོས་ (tūrŋöö) down, downhill.

ཐུར་ཅི་ (tūji) Turkey.

ཐུར་ལྟ་ (tūr dā) looking downward; va.—བྱེད་ ། ཁོས་མིག་ཐུར་ལྟ་བྱས་ནས་སྐད་ཆ་བཤད་སོང་ He spoke with his eyes looking down.

ཐུར་ལྟའི་དཔེ་རིས་ (tūrdɛ bērii) sm. ཐུར་བལྟས་རི་མོ་.

ཐུར་བལྟས་རི་མོ་ (tūrdɛɛ̀ rimu) vertical view.

ཐུར་ཐག (tūrdaà) sm. ཐུར་མགོ་.

ཐུར་ཐུར་ (tūrdur) sm. ཐུར་དུ་.

ཐུར་དུ་ (tūrdu) downhill, down.

ཐུར་དུ་དཔྱང་ (tūrdu jāŋ) vi. to be hanging/ dangling down.

ཐུར་དུ་འཕྱང་ (tūrdu jāŋ) sm. ཐུར་དུ་དཔྱང་.

ཐུར་དུ་བསྣར་ (tūrdu nār) sm. ཐུར་དུ་དཔྱང་.

ཐུར་མདའ་ (tūnda) the stick on the steelyard hand scale that has the measure units.

ཐུར་རྡོ་ (tūrdo) the weight on the steelyard hand scale.

ཐུར་ནས་ཐུར་དུ་ (tūrnɛ tūrdu) down and down.

ཐུར་སྣོད་ (tūrnöö) a container for a spoon.

ཐུར་འཕྱར་ (tūrjar) vi. to dangle, to hang down.

ཐུར་འབབ་ (tūr bəb) va. to go down ། ང་ཐུར་བབས་ཡོང་དུས་རྐང་པ་རྨས་བྱུང་ When I was going downhill I injured my foot.

ཐུར་མ་ (tūrmə) 1. spoon. 2. sm. ཐུར་ཁྲིབ་. 3. general term for traditional Tibetan surgical tools.

ཐུར་མའི་རང་ཁྲིབ་བདུན་ (tūrmɛ randrib dün) the seven notches on a divination stick.

ཐུར་ཚད་ (tūrdzɛɛ̀) gradient, degree of a slope ། རི་འདི་ཐུར་ཚད་གཟར་པོ་ཡོད་པ་རེད་ This hill is steep (has a steep slope).

ཐུར་ཤོ་ (tūrsho) the units of measurement on a steelyard hand scale.

ཐུར་གཟར་ (tūrsar) a steep slope.

ཐུར་གཟར་པོ་ (tūrsar sarbo) a steep slope.

ཐུར་རེ་ (tūrre) arc. at once, right now.

ཐུར་ལམ་ (tūrlam) 1. a downhill road/ trail. 2. poet. anus.

ཐུར་ཤིང་ (tūrshiŋ) 1. wooden. spoon. 2. chopstick. 3. sm. ཐུར་མདའ་.

ཐུར་སེལ་རླུང་ (tūrsee lūŋ) one of the five main རླུང་ (of the body).

ཐུར་སོང་ (tūrsoŋ) shung. to become/ get worse ། ཕྱིར་ཞིང་བུ་བ་ངན་པས་ཁོ་རང་གི་ཇོ་ཇོ་བསད་ སླར་ཡང་ལྷག་པར་ཐུར་སོང་སྡིག་བསམ་པ་ངན་པ་འཆང་ Again he did evil and killed his brother, and furthermore, getting worst, he had additional evil thoughts.

ཐུར་སྲང་ (tūrsaŋ) a small scale/ steelyard.

ཐུར་གསེག (tūrseg) zigzag (on a steep hill) ། རིའི་སྟེང་གི་མོ་ཊའི་ལམ་ཐུར་གསེག་དུ་བཟོས་བཞག (They) made a zigzag road on the slope of the mountain.

ཐུལ་ (tūū) 1. imp. of འདུལ་. 2. arc. flock, herd.

ཐུལ་གྱིས་ (tūūgi) suddenly.

ཐུལ་ཆེན་པོ་ (tūū cēmbo) 1. big, large, vast. 2. loose (in reference to clothes).

ཐུལ་པ་ (tūūba) a kind of fleece cloak/ dress.

ཐུལ་པོ་ (tūūbo) sm. ཐོད་པོ་.

ཐུལ་རྩིས་ (tūūdzi) counting sheep and goats according to the amount needed to make a dress from their skins.

ཐུལ་ལེ་ (tūūle) a term used to describe sth. rising or drifting upwards (e.g., smoke).

ཐུས་ (tūū) imp. of འཐུ་.

ཐུས་ནི་སི་ (tūñisi) Tunisia.

ཐེ་: p. ཐེ་ or ཐེས་; f. ཐེ་ (tē) vi. to be included, to belong to ། ཕྲུ་གུ་ཐེ་བས་མི་བཞི་འདུག Including the children, there are four people.

ཐེ་ཁོངས་ (tēgoŋ) part of, belonging to.

ཐེ་མཁན་ (tēñɛn) a person who does not mind his own business, sb. who interferes with others.

ཐེ་གི་ (tēgi) sm. ཐེ་གེ་.

ཐེ་གེ་ (tēge) sm. ཨ་ཙུག.

ཐེ་སྒྲུབ་ (tēdrub) fulfilling or providing a tax/ obligation; va.—བྱེད་ ། ཁྲལ་རིགས་དྲུག་ཟུར་རེ་ཐེ་སྒྲུབ་བྱེད་དགོས་བྱུང་སོང་ They had to provide 1/6th of the taxes.

ཐེ་ཇུས་ (tējüü) sm. ཐེ་གཏོགས་.

ཐེ་གཏོགས་ (tēdɔɔ̀) intervention, interference; va.—བྱེད་ to interfere, to intervene ། ང་ཚོའི་ནང་སྲིད་ལ་ཐེ་གཏོགས་བྱས་པ་རེད་ (They) interfered in our internal affairs.

ཐེ་གཏོགས་ཚ་པོ་ (tēdɔɔ̀ tsābo) sb. who interferes or intervenes a lot in other's affairs.

ཐེ་གཏོར་བ་གཏོར་ (tēdɔɔ̀ badɔɔ̀) completely destroyed; va.—གཏོང་ ། འབོམ་འཕྱུགས་ནས་ཁང་པ་ཐེ་གཏོར་བ་གཏོར་བཏང་བཞག (They) threw the bomb and completely destroyed the house.

ཐེ་ཐོར་སྦར་ཐོར་ (tēdɔɔ̀ badɔɔ̀) sm. ཐེ་གཏོར་བ་གཏོར་.

ཐེ་པད་ (tēbɛɛ̀) a shuttlecock-like object (a feather that has a weight at the bottom) that is used in a game in which participants kick the shuttlecock into the air and see how long they can do so without it falling on the ground; va.—རྒྱག.

ཐེ་པེད་ (tēbeè) sm. ཐེ་པད་.

ཐེ་ཕིང་ཡང་ (tēpiŋyaŋ) ch. Pacific Ocean.

ཐེ་བ་ (tēwa) see ཐེ་.

ཐེ་བས་ (tēwɛ) including ། མཚོ་དམག་ཐེ་བས་དམག་མི་ཁྲི་གཅིག་ཡོད་པ་རེད་ Including the navy, there are ten thousand soldiers.

ཐེ་བན་ (tēbɛn) ch. the inside lining on the edge of clothing.

ཐེ་པེ་ (tēbe) sm. ཐེ་པད་.

ཐེ་བོང་ (tēboŋ) sm. མཐེ་བོང་.

ཐེ་བྱུས་ (tējüü) sm. ཐེ་གཏོགས་.

ཐེ་བྲང་ (tēdraŋ) a type of hungry ghost.

ཐེ་མི་ཐེ་ (tē mide) not certain whether sb. or sth. has been included or not ། ཚོགས་འདུའི་མཐུས་མིའི་ནང་བོད་པ་ཐེ་མི་ཐེ་དན་དན་མི་འདུག It isn't certain whether Tibetans have been included as delegates to the party.

ཐེ་མི་ཚོམ་ (tē mijom) without hesitation, with certainty.

ཐེ་བཙུགས་ (tēdzuù) p. of ཐེ་འཛུགས་.

ཐེ་རྩེ་ (tēdze) sm. ཐེལ་ཙེ་.

ཐེ་ཚོགས་ (tēdzɔ̀ɔ) sm. ཐེ་གཏོགས་.

ཐེ་ཚོགས་སླེང་མང་ (tēdzɔ̀ɔ lēŋmaŋ) shung. talking too much and getting involved unnecessarily in sb. else's business; va.—བྱེད་ ། ཐེ་ཚོགས་སླེང་མང་བྱེད་བབས་ཀྱི་ཉེས་པ་སྒང་༧ སོང་བ་སྤྲས་ Having talked too much and gotten involved unnecessarily, you are therefore fined one སྒང་.

ཐེ་ཚོམ་ (tēdzom) suspicion, doubt, hesitation; vi.—ཟ་; —སྐྱེ་ to have doubts/ suspicions/ apprehensions; va.—བྱེད་ ། ལས་ཀ་དེ་བྱ་རྒྱུ་ཁོང་གིས་ཐེ་ཚོམ་བྱེད་ཀྱི་ཡོད་པ་རེད་ He was hesitant whether to do that work. ། མི་འདི་སོ་པ་ཡིན་མིན་ང་ཐེ་ཚོམ་ཟ་གི་འདུག I have doubts about whether or not he is a spy.

ཐེ་ཚོམ་དྲ་བ་ (tēdzom trawa) a web of doubt/ hesitation.

ཐེ་ཚོམ་མེད་པ་ (tēdzom meèba) without doubt/ suspicion/ apprehension/ hesitation ། ངས་དམག་རྒྱག་པར་ཐེ་ཚོམ་མེད་པར་ཕྱིན་པ་ཡིན་ I went to battle without hesitation.

ཐེ་ཚོམ་ལ་འཇུག་པའི་སྒྲ་ (tēdzomla jugbɛ dra) grammatical particles that indicate "or."

ཐེ་ཚོམ་ལ་འཇུག་པའི་ན་ (tēdzomla jugbɛ na) grammatical particle indicating "if."

ཐེ་ཚོམ་ལོག་གེ་ (tēdzom lɔgge) hesitant, undecided ། ང་བོད་ལ་འགྲོ་མ་འགྲོ་ཐེ་ཚོམ་ལོག་གེ་བསྡད་ཡོད་ I am hesitant about whether I should go to Tibet or not.

ཐེ་ཚོམ་སེམས་ཉི་ (tēdzom sōmñi) doubt, suspicion, hesitation.

ཐེ་འཛུགས་ (tē dzuù) va. to give one's word, to promise.

ཐེ་ཞུགས་ (tēshuù) sm. ཐེ་གཏོགས་.

ཐེ་ཝན་ (tēwan) Taiwan.

ཐེ་རེ་ (tēre) smooth, unwrinkled.

ཐེ་ཧེ་རན་ (tēherɛn) Teheran.

ཐེ་ཧྲུག་དགུ་ཧྲུག་ (tēhruù guhruù) broken into small pieces.

ཐེ་ཨུ་ (tē ū) ch. special committee.

ཐེག (tēg) 1. vi. to be able to carry a load ། དོ་པོ་འདི་ངས་ཐེག་པ་མི་འདུག I can't carry this load. ། ཁྱེད་རང་གིས་འདི་ཐེག་གི་མ་རེད་ You will not be able to carry this. 2. imp. of འདེགས་. 3. sm. ཐེགས་. 4. vi. to tolerate, to bear, to block the impact of sth. ། འགྱུལ་སྣུགས་ཐེག་པའི་ལག་འདོགས་ཆུ་ཚོད་ A shock-proof wrist watch.

ཐེག་ཁུར་ (tēggur) abbr. of ཐེག་པ་ཁུར་ལེན་.

ཐེག་ཆུང་ (tēgjuŋ) sm. ཐེག་དམན་.

ཐེག་ཆུང་སྐྱེས་བུ་ (tēgjuŋ gyeèbu) sm. ཐེག་དམན་.

ཐེག་ཆེན་ (tēgjen) the Mahayana school of Buddhism (the Greater Vehicle).

ཐེག་ཆེན་གྱི་ལམ་ (tēgjengi lam) the path of Mahayana (the Greater Vehicle).

ཐེག་ཆེན་པ་ (tēgjemba) followers of the Mahayana school of Buddhism.

ཐེག་ཆེན་གསོ་སྦྱོང་ (tēgjen sōgyoŋ) a one day Boddhisattva vow taken both by monks and lay persons to increase their merit and repent their misdeeds/ sins.

ཐེག་ཐུབ་ (tēgdub) vi. to be able to carry, to be able to tolerate.

ཐེག་པ་ (tēgba) 1. vehicle (in a religious sense) ། ཐེག་པ་གསུམ་ The three vehicles (Mahayana, Hinayana, Vajrayana). 2. a transportation vehicle. 3. tolerant.

ཐེག་པ་ཁུར་ (tēgba kūr) vi. to carry sth. ། རང་ཉིད་ཀྱིས་གང་ཐེག་པ་ཁུར་ནས་འགྲོ་ཆོག You are permitted to go carrying as much as one can.

ཐེག་པ་ཁུར་ལེན་ (tēgba kūrlen) 1. abiding by, adhering to; va.—བྱེད་ ། མི་དམངས་རྣམས་ནས་རང་ཁྲིམས་ཐེག་པ་ཁུར་ལེན་བྱེད་དགོས་ The people should abide by their laws. 2. taking responsibility; va.—བྱེད་ ། རང་ཉིད་ལ་འཁྲི་བའི་ལས་འགན་ཐེག་པ་ཁུར་ལེན་བྱེད་དགོས་ One should take responsibility for one's duties.

ཐེག་པ་ཆུང་ངུ་ (tēgba cūŋŋu) sm. ཐེག་དམན་.

ཐེག་པ་ཆེ་ན་དགྲ་ཟླ་ཉུང་ (tēgba cēna drɛnda ñuŋ) one who is tolerant makes fewer enemies.

ཐེག་པ་ཆེན་པོ་ (tēgba cēmbo) 1. sm. ཐེག་ཆེན་. 2. tolerant.

ཐེག་པ་གཉིས་ (tēgba ñìi) Mahayana and Hinayana (the two vehicles).

ཐེག་པ་གསུམ་ (tēgba sūm) the three vehicles: Mahayana, Hinayana, Vajrayana.

ཐེག་དམན་ (tēgmɛn) the Hinayana school of Buddhism, the lessor vehicle.

ཐེག་དམན་པ་ (tēgmɛmba) followers of the Hinayana school of Buddhism.

ཐེག་ཙམ་ (tēgdzam) just able to carry ། དོ་པོ་དེ་ངས་ཐེག་ཙམ་བྱུང་སོང་ I was just barely able to carry that load.

ཐེག་ཚད་ (tēgdzɛɛ̀) load capacity/ weight; va.—བཀང་ to load fully, to load to capacity ། གྲུ་གཟིངས་དེ་ཐེག་ཚད་ལས་བརྒལ་བ་ The ship has exceeded its carrying capacity.

ཐེག་ཤུབས་ (tēgshub) shung. a small pouch for storing/ holding cups.

ཐེགས་ (teè) va. to go (h.) ། ལྷ་སར་ཐེགས་སྐབས་ When (he) went to Lhasa.

ཐེང་: p. ཐེངས་; f. ཐེང་ (tēŋ) vi. to reach a limit/ standard/ time ། སློབ་ཕྲུག་གི་གྲངས་ཚད་ཐེངས་བཞག (They) have reached the standard set for the number of students (in that school).

ཐེང་པོ་ (tēŋbo) a lung disease in Tibetan medicine.

ཐེང་བུ་ (tēŋbu) sm. ཐེང་པོ་.

ཐེངས་ (tēŋ) times, occurrences ། ད་རེས་ང་ཨ་མི་རི་ཀར་ཡོང་ཐེངས་གསུམ་པ་དེ་རེད་ This is the third time I've come to America. ། ཐེངས་འདིར་ On this occasion/ time.

ཐེངས་གྲངས་ (tēŋdraŋ) number of times.

ཐེངས་འགའ་ (tēŋga) several times.

ཐེངས་གཅིག (tēŋjig) one time.

ཐེངས་གཅིག་མིན་གཉིས་མིན་ (tēŋ jīgmin ñìimin) many times, repeatedly ། མི་དེ་ལ་ངས་ཐེངས་གཅིག་མིན་གཉིས་མིན་བཤད་པ་ཡིན་ཀྱང་ཁོས་ཉན་མ་བྱུང་ Even though I told him repeatedly, he didn't listen.

ཐེངས་གཅིག་སྨིན་འབྲས་ (tēŋjig mīndrɛɛ̀) rice that gets only one crop per year, single cropped rice.

ཐེངས་གཉིས་སྨིན་འབྲས་ (tēŋñìi mīndrɛɛ̀) rice that gets two crops per year, double cropped rice.

ཐེངས་དང་པོ་ (tēŋ taŋbo) first time.

ཐེངས་མ་ (tēŋma) sm. ཐེངས་.

ཐེངས་མང་ (tēŋmaŋ) many times.

ཐེད་ (teè) the leftover carcass of prey after being eaten by a carnivore/ scavenger.

ཐེད་པོ་ (teèbo) old and tattered.

ཐེད་བོར་ (teè bɔr) 1. va. to look down on. 2. va. to throw away leftovers.

ཐེད་ལ་བསྒྱུར་ (teèla gyūr) sm. ཐེད་བོར་.

ཐེན་ (tēn) sm. འཐེན་.

ཐེན་ཀའོ་ (tēngao) ch. a copper lid for covering the pot in which grain is distilled into alcohol.

ཐེན་ཅིན་ (tēndzin) Tianjin.

ཐེན་ཅེར་ (tēnjir) arc. permanently.

ཐེན་ཆེར་ (tēnjer) sm. ཐེན་ཅེར་.

ཐེན་ཕིང་ (tēnbiŋ) ch. scales.

ཐེན་ཧྲན་རི་བོ་ (tēnhrɛn riwo) T'ienshan Mountains.

ཐེན་ཨན་མུན་ (tēnanmün) ch. Tiananmen Square.

ཐེན་ཨན་མུན་ཐང་ཆེན་ (tēnanmün tāŋcen) ch.tib. sm. ཐེན་ཨན་མུན་.

ཐེན་ཨན་མོན་ (tēnanmün) ch. sm. ཐེན་ཨན་མུན་.

ཐེབ་ (tēb) sm. ཐེབས་.

ཐེབ་ཙེ་ (tēbdze) plate.

ཐེབ་རང་ (tēbraŋ) sm. ཐེའུ་རངས་.

ཐེབས་ (tēb) 1. vi. to undergo, to get/ fall into sth. (involuntarily), to get hit/ struck by, to reach/ arrive, to suffer ¶ ངར་མེ་མདའ་ཐེབས་བྱུང་ I was shot by a gun (hit by a bullet). ¶ ཁོ་ཚོ་ཇག་པའི་ལག་པར་ཐེབས་པ་རེད་ They fell into the hands of the bandits. ¶ ཁོ་ལྟོགས་ཤི་ཐེབས་བཞག He died of starvation. 2. abbr. of ཐེབས་རྩ་.

ཐེབས་རྒྱ་ (tēbgya) (with ཤུགས་རྐྱེན་) the area of influence ¶ ལུང་པ་འདིའི་ནང་ཆོས་ལུགས་ཀྱི་ཤུགས་རྐྱེན་ཐེབས་རྒྱ་ཆེན་པོ་ཡོད་པ་རེད་ In this place the area where there has been religious influence is large.

ཐེབས་གཅག (tēbjaà) f. of ཐེབས་གཅོག.

ཐེབས་གཅོག (tēbjoò) (vb. + —) vi. to have a negative effect (a loss, harm, damage), to get disturbed by sth. ¶ ལག་ཆ་དུས་ཐོག་མ་འབྱོར་ཙང་ཞིང་ལས་ལ་ཐེབས་བཅག་སོང་ The tools didn't come on time so the farm work was harmed. ¶ ཉི་མ་ལགས་ཀྱིས་ང་རར་དངུལ་མ་སྤྲད་ཙང་ཚོང་གི་ཐེབས་བཅག་བྱུང་ My business got harmed because Nyimala didn't give me the money (on time). ¶ གནས་ཚུལ་ངན་པ་དེ་གོ་ནས་ང་གཉིད་ཐེབས་བཅག་སོང་ Having heard the bad news, my sleep got disturbed. ¶ ངའི་སྨྱུ་གུ་ཡག་པོ་དེ་བརླགས་ནས་ཐེབས་བཅག་བྱུང་ I lost my good pen and it disturbed me.

ཐེབས་བཅག (tēnjaà) p. of ཐེབས་གཅོག.

ཐེབས་ཆག (tēbjaà) sm. ཐབས་ཆགས་, 1.

ཐེབས་ཅི་ (tēbji) button.

ཐེབས་ཇ་ (tēbja) tea given to workers after completion of planting seeds.

ཐེབས་པད་ (tēbbɛɛ̀) sm. ཐེ་པད་.

ཐེབས་སྤྲུར་ (tēbjaa) 1. leaving a trust fund. 2. sm. ཐེབས་རྩ་.

ཐེབས་སྤྲུར་ལས་ཁུངས་ (tēbjaa lɛ̀ɛ̀guŋ) shung. the office in the traditional Tibetan government that managed endowments used for Monlam.

ཐེབས་རྩ་ (tēbdza) fund, trust, endowment; va.—འཇོག; —སྤྲོར་ to give/ create an endowment ¶ ཚོང་པས་དགོན་པར་དངུལ་མང་པོ་ཐེབས་རྩ་བཞག་འདུག The trader left the monasteries a lot of money as an endowment fund.

ཐེབས་རྩ་ཚོགས་པ་ (tēbdza tsɔ̄gba) a foundation, a trust fund.

ཐེབས་རྩ་ལས་ཁུངས་ (tēbdza lɛ̀ɛ̀guŋ) shung. sm. ཐེབས་སྤྲུར་ལས་ཁུངས་.

ཐེབས་རྩའི་མ་རྐང་ (tēbdzɛ magaŋ) the capital/ principal of a trust.

ཐེབས་རྩིས་ལ་འགྲོ་ (tēbdziìla dro) vi. to go bankrupt and have one's possessions go to the creditors.

ཐེབས་ཡུལ་ (tēbyüü) sm. ཐེབས་རྒྱ་.

ཐེབས་རེ་ (tēbre) 1. once, sometimes, occasionally. 2. few, a little.

ཐེབས་ལུང་ (tēbluŋ) buttonhole.

ཐེབས་ལེ་ (tēble) sm. ཐེ་པད་.

ཐེམ་ (tēm) abbr. of ཐེམ་པ་.

ཐེམ་སྐས་ (tēmgɛɛ̀) 1. steps, stairs, rungs (of a ladder). 2. sm. ཐེམ་པ་.

ཐེམ་སྐས་རིམ་པ་ (tēmgɛɛ̀ rimbə) rungs of a ladder, steps on a staircase.

ཐེམ་ཁ་ (tēmga) top of a threshold.

ཐེམ་གྲངས་ (tēmdraŋ) the number of households ¶ ལུང་པ་དེ་ལ་ཐེམ་གྲངས་ག་ཚོད་ཡོད་པ་རེད་ How many households are there in that area?

ཐེམ་ཐོ་ (tēmdo) permanent residence (card) (used in PRC for the locality where one is officially registered as a resident) ¶ དགོན་པར་སྡོད་པའི་གྲྭ་པ་མང་པོའི་ཐེམ་ཐོ་གྲོང་གསེབ་ལ་ཡོད་པ་རེད་ Many monks in the monastery have their permanent residency card in villages (rather than the monastery).

ཐེམ་ཐོ་མིང་འགོད་ (tēmdo miŋ göö) va. to register one's name on the permanent residence card.

ཐེམ་དུད་ (tēmdüü) sm. ཐེམ་པ་, 2.

ཐེམ་དེབ་ (tēmdeb) 1. the ཐེམ་ཐོ་ document each household keeps. 2. sm. ཐེམ་ཐོ་.

ཐེམ་པ་ (tēmba) 1. threshold, door sill. 2. a household; va.—བཤེར་ to check on households (usu. the number and status).

ཐེམ་པ་སྐོར་ (tēmba gɔ̄ɔ) shung. va. to go on rounds of households.

ཐེམ་པ་སྔ་བརྒལ་ (tēmba ŋāgɛɛ) the early bird gets the worm [Lit. cross the threshold early].

ཐེམ་པ་མཐོ་པོ་ (tēmba tōbo) a stingy, ungenerous person who does not readily welcome others into his house [Lit. a high threshold].

ཐེམ་པ་དམའ་པོ་ (tēmba māābo) a generous person who is friendly with strangers and readily welcomes them into his house [Lit. a low threshold].

ཐེམ་པའི་སྒང་གི་བྱིའུ་ (tēmbɛ gaŋgi ciwu) a precarious situation, being in danger, being uncertain/ doubting/ suspicious [Lit. a bird on a threshold].

ཐེམ་པའི་སྒང་གི་རིལ་མ་ (tēmbɛ gaŋgi riimə) sm. ཐེམ་པའི་སྒང་གི་བྱིའུ་ [Lit. sheep/ goat's dung on the threshold].

ཐེམ་སྤང་ (tēmbaŋ) 1. precious items that a household doesn't let others see or use/ borrow. 2. secret teachings.

ཐེམ་ཕུག (tēmbuù) Thimphu (capital of Bhutan).

ཐེམ་བུ་ (tēmbu) 1. rung/ steps on a ladder. 2. sm. ཐེམ་བུ་.

ཐེམ་བུ་ཁ་ (tēmbuka) a slender spoon used for putting medicine down the throat.

ཐེམ་བྱང་ (tēmjaŋ) a sign by a door with a name or house number.

ཐེམ་འབེན་ (tēmben) carpenter's plane.

ཐེམ་སྨང་ (tēmmaŋ) base/ foundation of a threshold.

ཐེམ་རྩ་ (tēmdza) sm. ཐེམ་སྨང་.

ཐེམ་ཚང་ (tēmdzaŋ) shung. family, household.

ཐེམ་ཞིང་ (tēmshiŋ) terraced field.

ཐེམ་ཡིག (tēmyiì) sm. ཐེམ་བྱང་.

ཐེམ་རིམ་ (tēmrim) rungs of a ladder.

ཐེམ་བཤེར་ (tēmsher) shung. checking/ surveying on households (usu. the number and status); va.—གཏོང་.

ཐེམ་བཤེར་བདང་གཞུང་ (tēmsher dāŋshuŋ) shung. the list of households that results from a survey.

ཐེའུ་ (tēwu) 1. sm. ཐེལ་ཙེ་. 2. sm. ཐེའུ་. 3. a small hammer used by stone mason.

ཐེའུ་རངས་ (tēwuraŋ) a type of hungry ghost.

ཐེའུ་རངས་ལ་དབང་བྱུང་ན་གོ་ཁ་ཐལ་འཚུབ་གྱིས་རྒྱོང་ (tēwuraŋla wāŋcuŋnə koga tɛ̄ɛ̄dzubgi gyoŋ) if an evil person gets power he will cause lots of trouble [Lit. if a hungry ghost gets power there will be lots of dust around the stove].

ཐེའུ་རངས་ལག་པ་ (tēwuraŋ lagba) a type of traditional Tibetan medicine.

ཐེར་ཀ་ (tērga) sm. ཐེར་གེ་.

ཐེར་སྐུད་ (tērgüü) thin woolen thread.

ཐེར་གེ་ (tērge) two wheeled cart (usu. pulled by horse or mule); va.—གཏོང་.

ཐེར་གེ་པ་ (tērgewa) the driver of a ཐེར་གེ་.

ཐེར་སྒ་ (tērga) sm. ཐེར་གེ་.

ཐེར་ཆས་ (tērjɛɛ̀) things needed for a two wheeled cart.

ཐེར་ཆུང་ (tērjuŋ) a small ཐེར་གེ་.

ཐེར་བདོད་ (tērdöö) sm. ཐེར་འདོན་.

ཐེར་ཐག (tērdaà) rope used with a ཐེར་གེ.

ཐེར་ཐེར་ (tērder) flat, flattening; va.—བཟོ་; —བྱེད་ to make flat, to flatten.

ཐེར་འདོན་ (tērdön) exposing sth. or sb.; va.—བྱེད་ ¶ མི་གཞི་སྤྱོད་ངན་དེ་ལ་སྐྱོན་བརྗོད་དང་ཐེར་འདོན་བྱས་པ་

རེད་ They criticized and exposed the U.S. policy.

ཐེར་འདོན་སྒམ་ (tērdön gam) suggestion box, box for anonymous comments.

ཐེར་པོ་ (tērbo) 1. wide/ openmouthed bowls and vases. 2. sm. ཕྱི་ཐེར་.

ཐེར་ཕྲུག་འཇམ་གོས་ (tērdruù jamgöö) high quality Tibetan woolen serge.

ཐེར་བག (tērbaà) plate.

ཐེར་འབུམ་ (tērbum) one billion.

ཐེར་འབུམ་ཆེན་པོ་ (tērbum cēmbo) ten billion.

ཐེར་མ་ (tērma) wool cloth, serge.

ཐེར་མ་ཐ་ན་ (tērma tāna) bale of serge.

ཐེར་ཚལ་བར་ཚལ་ (tēēdzεε baadzεε) sm. ཐེར་ཚལ་སྦར་ཚལ་.

ཐེར་ཚལ་སྦར་ཚལ་ (tēēdzεε baadzεε) broken into pieces, completely destroyed/ smashed/ ripped to pieces; va.—བཟོ་; —གཏོང་ ། ལོ་ཏོག་ཡག་པོ་དེ་ཚོ་སྤྲེའུ་ཡིས་ ཐེར་ཚལ་སྦར་ཚལ་བཏོས་སོང་ The good harvest was completely ripped to pieces by the monkey.

ཐེར་རྫུན་ (tērdzün) fake/ artificial serge.

ཐེར་རྫོང་རྒྱག (tērdzoŋ gyaà) va. to load a cart.

ཐེར་ཟུག (tērsuù) unchanging, permanent, enduring.

ཐེར་ཟུག་ཐེར་ཟུག (tērsuù tērsuù) sm. ཐེར་ཟུག.

ཐེར་གཟན་ (tēr) serge shawl.

ཐེར་སྲབ་ (tērdrəb) thin/ light serge.

ཐེར་རུག་དགུ་རུག (tērhruù guhruù) breaking/ broken into small pieces.

ཐེལ་ (tēē) seal; va.—རྒྱག to affix/ put a seal (on sth).

ཐེལ་ཁ་ (tēēga) a spot/ point on the waist where acupuncture is done.

ཐེལ་གཏོང་ལུང་སྒྱུར་ (tēēdoŋ luŋgyur) shung. sealing an order and distributing (issuing) it; va.—བྱེད་.

ཐེལ་སྣོན་ (tēēnön) affixing/ putting on a seal; va.—རྒྱག.

ཐེལ་འབྱར་ (tēējar) shung. (sth.) sealed (with a seal).

ཐེལ་ཙེ་ (tēēdze) 1. seal, stamp; va.—རྒྱག; —མནན་ to affix a seal/ stamp; va.—འགོག; —བཤིག to break a seal (e.g., on a letter to open it).

ཐེལ་རྩེ་ལག་སྐོར་ (tēedze laggɔɔ) shung. a group of people agreeing to a written petition/ document and each affixing his seal to it; va.—བྱེད་.

ཐེལ་ཚེ་ (tēedze) sm. ཐེལ་ཙེ་.

ཐེལ་སེ་ (tēēse) sm.* ཐེལ་ཙེ་.

ཐེས་ (tēè) p. of ཐེ་.

ཐོ་ (tō) 1. list, note, register, record; va.—རྒྱག་; —འགོད་; —ཞེན་; —འབྲི་ to make a list, to take notes, to register, to enroll ། ཚོགས་འདུར་མི་སུ་སླེབས་ཡོད་མེད་ཐོ་རྒྱག་གི་འདུག (They) are taking notes of who is at the meeting. 2. abbr. ཐོ་བ་.

ཐོ་ཀོར་ (tōgɔɔ) near, nearby.

ཐོ་བཀོད་ (tōgöö) registered, noted ། ཐོ་བཀོད་ཏན་ གྲངས་ Registered tonnage.

ཐོ་བཀོད་མེད་པའི་མཇེད་པ་ (tōgöö meèbε dzεèba) unrecorded (not kept in a diary) reminiscences of sb.'s life.

ཐོ་འཁོར་ (tōgɔɔ) sm. ཐོ་ཀོར་.

ཐོ་ཁྲངས་ (tōguŋ) account (in a bank); va.—འཛུགས་ to open a bank account.

ཐོ་ཁྲངས་དངུལ་ཁང་ (tōguŋ ŋüügaŋ) savings bank.

ཐོ་འགོད་ (tōgöö) sm. ཐོ་བཀོད་.

ཐོ་འགོད་ཁང་ (tōgöögaŋ) registration office (e.g., of a hotel).

ཐོ་འགོད་སྙན་སེང་ (tōgöö ñεnseŋ) registration application.

ཐོ་འགོད་བཏང་ཡིག (tōgöö təŋyii) registered letter.

ཐོ་འགོད་རེའུ་མིག (tōgöö riumig) a form.

ཐོ་འགོད་ཨང་གྲངས་ (tōgöö āŋdraŋ) a place on an ordered list ། སྨན་ཁང་ལ་འགྲོ་དུས་ཐོ་འགོད་ཨང་གྲངས་ གཞིར་བཟུང་ལྟ་གི་ཡོད་པ་རེད་ When going to the hospital, they see you in accordance with your (place) in the list (of people waiting to be seen).

ཐོ་རྒྱག (tō gyaà) see ཐོ་.

ཐོ་སྒྲིགས་ (tō drig) shung. to arrange/ put together a list.

ཐོ་ཅོ་ (tōjo) nonsense, foolish talk; va.—བྱེད་ to talk nonsense/ foolishly.

ཐོ་ཆེན་ (tōjen) a big hammer (usu. used for breaking rocks).

ཐོ་ཚོ་ (tōjo) sm. ཐོ་ཅོ་.

ཐོ་ཐུག (tō tūù) 1. vi. to be in balance, to be correlated, to match/ coincide ། ངས་གོ་པ་དང་ཁོས་བཤད་པ་གཉིས་ཐོ་ཐུག་མ་སོང་ What I heard and what he said don't coincide ། རྩིས་ཁྲའི་ནང་གི་བྱུང་སོང་ཐོ་ ཐུག་གི་མི་འདུག The expenses and income on the account don't correlate. 2. vi. to meet suddenly/ unexpectedly.

ཐོ་ཐོ་ (tōdo) touching sth.; va.—གཏོང་ to touch ། འདིར་ཐོ་ཐོ་མ་གཏོང་ Don't touch this.

ཐོ་ཐོ་རི་གཉན་བཙན་ (tōdori ñεndzεn) the 28th king of Tibet.

ཐོ་ཐོ་རི་སྙན་ཤལ་ (tōdori ñεnshεε) sm. ཐོ་ཐོ་རི་གཉན་ བཙན་.

ཐོ་ཐོ་རེག་རེག (tōdo regreg) touching.

ཐོ་ཐོ་རེག་རེག་མེད་པ་ (tōdo regreg meèba) untouched, not touching.

ཐོ་དམ་པོ་ (tō tambo) strict.

ཐོ་དེབ་ (tōdeb) any book containing a list/ register/ accounts; va.—རྒྱག.

ཐོ་དོན་ (tōdön) shung. a phrase that appears at the beginning of an edict that coveys that the meaning/ content of the edict follows.

ཐོ་གདན་ (tōdεn) anvil.

ཐོ་རྡུང་ (tō duŋ) va. to hammer.

ཐོ་རྡོ་ (tōdo) sm. ཐོ་པོ་.

ཐོ་པོ་ (tōbo) stones piled one on top of the other (as a demarcation/ boundary line); va.—རྒྱག.

ཐོ་ཕུ་ཁོངས་ (tōbu kōŋ) topological field.

ཐོ་ཕུ་བར་སྣང་ (tōbu tārnaŋ) topological space.

ཐོ་ཕུ་ཕོག་འཕྲོ་ (tōpu pɔ̄ŋdro) topological mapping.

ཐོ་ཕུ་རང་བཞིན་ (tōpu rəŋshin) topological nature/ property.

ཐོ་ཕུ་རིག་པ་ (tōpu rigbə) topology.

ཐོ་ཕྱི་ (tōji) nearby, adjacent.

ཐོ་ཕྲུག (tōdruù) 1. a type of small hammer. 2. a type of small tractor.

ཐོ་འཕག (tōbaà) a type of hammer.

ཐོ་བ་ (tɔ̄ɔ) hammer; va.—བཞུ་; —རྡུང་ to hammer.

ཐོ་བ་ར་མགོ་ (tɔ̄ɔ rango) a hammer with one side having claws to pull out nails.

ཐོ་བས་རྡུང་ (tōwε duŋ) va. to strike/ hit with a hammer, to hammer.

ཐོ་པོ་ (tōwo) sm. ཐོ་བ་.

ཐོ་བྱང་ (tōjaŋ) a list ། ས་མིང་ཐོ་བྱང་ List of place names.

ཐོ་འབོག (tōmbɔɔ) a load.

ཐོ་མ་གོ་ (tō ma ko) vi. to not understand.

ཐོ་བཙམས་ (tōdzam) sm. མཐོ་འཚམས་.

ཐོ་འཚམ་ (tōdzam) sm. མཐོ་འཚམས་.

ཐོ་གཞུང་ (tōshuŋ) shung. a master/ main list of accounts, names, etc.

ཐོ་ཡིག (tōyii) list, catalogue, register.

ཐོ་ཡོར་ (tōyɔr) sm. ཐོ་པོ་.

ཐོ་རངས་ (tōraŋ) dawn, daybreak; vi.—ལངས་ to become dawn/ daybreak.

ཐོ་རངས་སྐར་ཆེན་ (tōraŋ gārjen) Venus, the morning star.

ཐོ་རི་སྙན་ཤལ་ (tōri ñεnshεε) sm. ཐོ་ཐོ་སྙན་ཤལ་.

ཐོ་རིལ་ (tōrii) hammer with one side being a round knob.

ཐོ་རུ་ (tōru) a two year old horse.

ཐོ་རེ་བ་ (tōrewa) a scattered few.

ཐོ་རེ་ལོང་ངེ་བ་ (tōre loŋŋewa) unclear, obscure (usu. about a past event).

ཐོ་རེངས་ (tōreŋ) sm. ཐོ་རངས་.

ཐོ་རེངས་སྐར་ཆེན་ (tōreŋ gārjen) sm. ཐོ་རངས་སྐར་ཆེན་.

ཐོ་ལ་ (tōla) ch. abbr. of ཐོ་ལ་ཅི་.

ཐོ་ལ་ཅི་ (tōlaji) ch. tractor.

ཐོ་ལ་ཐོ་ལ་ (tōlo tōla) sm. ཐོ་ལི་.

ཐོ་ལུམ་ (tōlim) sm. ཐུ་ལུམ་.

ཐོ་ལེ་ (tōle) suddenly, quite unexpectedly.

ཐོ་ལེ་གོར་ (tōlegɔr) talc.

ཐོ་ལོག (tōlɔɔ̀) a small mule that is a cross between a donkey and a horse.

ཐོ་ལོག་མོ་ལོག (tōlo kolo) having a large stomach due to pregnancy.

ཐོ་ལོང་མོ་ལོང་ (tōloŋ moloŋ) sm. ཏ་རེ་ཏུ་རེ་.

ཐོ་ཤོབ་མོ་ཤོབ་ (tōshob moshob) (for speech) not clear, indistinct; va.—ཤོད་. 2. whispering, talking secretly; va.—ཤོད་.

ཐོ་བཤེར་ (tō shēr) going over a list, checking a list; va.—གཏོང་; —བྱེད་.

ཐོ་སུབ་ (tō sūb) va. to erase, to write off, to delete (from a list).

ཐོ་སོ་ (tōso) mong. butter.

ཐོ་ཨང་ (tō āŋ) account number.

ཐོག (tɔ̄ɔ̀) 1. on, on top of ༑ ཆུ་ཐོག་ཏུ་སྡོད་པའི་མི་རྣམས་ People who live on the water (i.e., on houseboats). 2. via., through, by, by means of ༑ མོས་གནམ་ཐོག་ལ་ཡི་གེ་བཏང་བ་རེད་ She sent a letter by air. ༑ དེ་ནི་དངོས་དོན་གྱི་ཐོག་ནས་ར་སྤྲོད་བྱུང་བ་རེད་ It was proved by (means of) facts. 3. in, inside of ༑ གནམ་གྲུ་ཐང་གི་བསམ་ཚུལ་འབྲི་དེབ་ཀྱི་ཐོག་ཏུ་བསམ་འཆར་བྲིས་པ་རེད་ He wrote suggestions in the airport's suggestion book. 4. in addition to, on top of ༑ སྔོན་དུ་སྤྲད་པའི་དངུལ་ཐོག་སྒོར་ཁྲི་གཉིས་བསྐྱར་དུ་སྤྲད་པ་རེད་ On top of the money that was given previously, (they) again gave 20,000 dollars. 5. during, at the time of ༑ ཆུ་ཚོད་བཅུ་པའི་ཐོག At 10 o'clock. 6. concerning, with regard to, about ༑ འཆར་གཞི་འདིའི་ཐོག་གཞུང་གིས་བཀའ་བསྡུར་གནང་བ་རེད་ The government held discussions about this plan. ༑ ཁོ་ཚོའི་ཐོག་ལ་ཞིབ་གཅོད་བྱས་པའི་སྐབས་སུ་ At the time of conducting an investigation about them. 7. roof ༑ ཁང་པའི་ཐོག་ལ་བྱེའུ་བབ་བཞག A bird has landed on the roof of the house. 8. lightning; vi.—རྒྱག to have lightning flash/ strike.

ཐོག་དཀར་ (tɔ̄ɔ̀gar) sm. ཐོག་ཁུང་.

ཐོག་སྐོར་ (tɔ̄ɔ̀gɔɔ) going around the roof of a house; va.—བྱེད་; —ལ་འགྲོ་.

ཐོག་སྐྱིན་ (tɔ̄ɔ̀gyin) shung. compensation for damaging crops; va.—སྤྲོད་ ༑ ཐོག་སྐྱིན་བབས་མཚུངས་ཟླ་གཅིག་ཁོངས་སུ་སྤྲོད་རྒྱུ་ (You) must pay compensation for the damaged crops within one month.

ཐོག་ཁ་ (tɔ̄ɔ̀ga) 1. upstairs. 2. roof.

ཐོག་ཁང་ (tɔ̄ɔ̀gaŋ) a multistoried house or building, a building (with two or more floors).

ཐོག་ཁའི་དར་ལྕོག (tɔ̄ɔ̀gɛ tarjɔɔ̀) an unreliable/ undependable person [Lit. a prayer flag (that flutters) on the roof].

ཐོག་ཁུང་ (tɔ̄ɔ̀guŋ) 1. smoke hole, chimney. 2. skylight.

ཐོག་ཁེབས་ (tɔ̄ɔ̀geb) 1. roof. 2. cloth that covers the ceiling of a room.

ཐོག་གུ་ (tɔ̄ɔ̀gu) 1. arc. fruit. 2. point, tip, edge.

ཐོག་འགེལ་ (tɔ̄ɔ̀gee) sm. ཐོག་འབུབས་.

ཐོག་འགོག་ལྕགས་མདའ་ (tōŋgɔɔ̀ jāŋdaà) sm. ཐོག་འགོག་ཟངས་མདའ་.

ཐོག་འགོག་ཟངས་མདའ་ (tōŋgɔɔ̀ saŋda) lightning rod.

ཐོག་རྒོད་ (tɔ̄ɔ̀göö) powerful lightning.

ཐོག་རྒྱག (tɔ̄ɔ̀ gyaà) 1. see ཐོག, 8. 2. suddenly, unexpectedly.

ཐོག་རྒྱན་ (tɔ̄ɔ̀gyɛn) a roof ornament.

ཐོག་རྒྱུག (tɔ̄ɔ̀gyuù) 1. beam, rafter. 2. va. to run quickly/ swiftly/ fast.

ཐོག་སྒྲ་ (tɔ̄ɔ̀dra) 1. sound of lightning. 2. a noise upstairs/ above.

ཐོག་ཅག (tɔ̄ɔ̀jaà) a large verandah.

ཐོག་གཅིག་མ་ (tɔ̄ɔ̀ jīgmə) single-story house/ building.

ཐོག་ལྕུགས་ (tɔ̄ɔ̀jaà) sm. གནམ་ལྕུགས་.

ཐོག་ལྕོག (tɔ̄ɔ̀joò) sm. ལྕོག.

ཐོག་ཆས་ (tɔ̄ɔ̀jɛɛ̀) things/ items from meteors.

ཐོག་རྗེ་ཐོག་བཙན་ (tōgje tōgdzɛn) the 27th king of Tibet.

ཐོག་ཏུ་ (tōgdu) sm. ཐོག.

ཐོག་ཏུ་འཁེལ་ (tōgdu kēē) 1. vi. to come about exactly, to be done exactly on time, to be timely, to say or do sth. right on target ༑ ལྷའི་ལུང་བསྟན་ཐོག་ཏུ་འཁེལ་བ་རེད་ The god's prophecy came about exactly. ༑ ཁྱེད་རང་གི་ལས་ཀ་དེ་དུས་ཐོག་ཏུ་འཁེལ་སོང་ Your work was done exactly on time. 2. vi. to have sth. occur suddenly/ unintentionally.

ཐོག་ཏུ་བབ་ (tōgdu bəb) 1. vi. to come about exactly, to be done exactly on time, to be timely ༑ རྣམས་པར་སྨིན་པའི་ལས་ཀྱི་འབྲས་བུ་ཐོག་ཏུ་བབས་དེ་ To have the merits of one's karma bear fruit at the right time. 2. vi. to have sth. occur suddenly/ unintentionally.

ཐོག་ལྟར་དྲག་ལ་རླུང་ལྟར་མྱུར་བ་ (tɔ̄ɔ̀dar traàla lūŋdar ñurwə) speedily and vigorously [Lit. power of the lightning and the speed of the wind].

ཐོག་ཐག (tōgdaà) sm. ཐོག་མཐའ་.

ཐོག་ཐོག (tōgdɔg) sound of sth. like a hammer hitting against a hard object.

ཐོག་ཐོག་ན་ (tɔ̄ɔ̀ tɔ̄ɔ̀na) in the very beginning.

ཐོག་མཐའ་ (tɔ̄ɔ̀ tā) sm. ཐོག་མཐའ་གཉིས་.

ཐོག་མཐའ་གཉིས་ (tɔ̄ɔ̀ta ñii) at the beginning and the end ༑ ཚོགས་འདུའི་ཐོག་མཐའ་གཉིས་ལ་ཚོགས་ཆེན་ཡོད་པ་རེད་ There was a plenary session at the beginning and the end of the meeting. ༑ ལས་ཀའི་ཐོག་མཐའ་གཉིས་ཀར་ནོར་འཁྲུལ་བྱུང་མ་སོང་ There were no mistakes at the beginning and the end of the work.

ཐོག་མཐའ་བར་གསུམ་ (tɔ̄ɔ̀ tā parsum) at all times, from beginning to end, from first to last ༑ ཁོང་གིས་ཐོག་མཐའ་བར་གསུམ་ལས་ཀ་ཧུར་ཐག་བྱས་ཡོད་པ་རེད་ He worked enthusiastically all the time.

ཐོག་དང་དྲག་ཆར་ (tɔ̄ɔ̀daŋ tragjar) lightning and rainstorm.

ཐོག་དྲངས་ (པ་) (tɔ̄ɔ̀draŋ) 1. p. of ཐོག་འདྲེན་. 2. the main/ chief, the leading, led by ༑ བོད་པ་ཐོག་དྲངས་པའི་འཐུས་མི་མང་པོ་ཞིག་སླེབས་འདུག Many delegates came led by the Tibetans.

ཐོག་དྲུང་ (tɔ̄ɔ̀druŋ) recent times and long ago.

ཐོག་འདྲེན་ (tɔ̄ɔ̀ drēn) va. to lead, to direct, to govern.

ཐོག་མདའ་ (tōnda) 1. lightning. 2. shung. an archery competition on the 3rd day of the 1st Tibetan month.

ཐོག་མདེལ་ (tɔ̄ɔ̀del) sm. ཐོག་ལྕུགས་.

ཐོག་འདག (tōndaà) mud or cement used to cover a roof; va.—རྒྱག.

ཐོག་འདམ་ (tɔ̄ɔ̀dam) sm. ཐོག་འདག.

ཐོག་དིབ་ (tɔ̄ɔ̀ dib) vi. to have a roof collapse.

ཐོག་རྡོ་ (tɔ̄ɔ̀do) 1. meteorite stone. 2. stones placed on roofs.

ཐོག་གནོན་ (tɔ̄ɔ̀ nōn) va. to pressure from above.

ཐོག་ནས་ (tɔ̄ɔ̀nɛ) see ཐོག.

ཐོག་པང་ (tɔ̄ɔ̀baŋ) planks that make up a ceiling.

ཐོག་དཔངས་ (tɔ̄ɔ̀baŋ) the height of a room.

ཐོག་སྤང་ (tɔ̄ɔ̀baŋ) sm. ཐོག་པང་.

ཐོག་ཕིབས་ (tɔ̄ɔ̀bib) roof.

ཐོག་ཕུད་ (tɔ̄ɔ̀büù) shung. first offering of a crop ༑ ཞེལ་ཆོས་སུ་ཐོག་ཕུད་ཅེས་འབྲུ་ཁལ་༣ རེ་སྤྲོད་སྒྲོལ་ཡོད་ They had to pay the Shecho Monastery 3 ཁལ་ of grain as a first offering of the crop.

ཐོག་ཕེབས་ (tɔ̄ɔ̀peè) sm. ཐོགས་འཕེབས་.

ཐོག་ཕོག་གནོད་སྐྱོན་ (tɔ̄ɔ̀bɔɔ̀ nöögyön) a bad effect/ change.

ཐོག་འབབ་ (tɔ̄ɔ̀ bəb) vi. to be struck by lightning.

ཐོག་འབུབས་ (tɔ̄ɔ̀ bub) va. to put on roof.

ཐོག་མ་ (tɔ̄ɔ̀ma) first, beginning.

ཐོག་མ་ཉིད་ (tɔ̄ɔ̀mañii) sm. ཐོག་མ་.

ཐོག་མ་ཉིད་ནས་ (tɔ̄ɔ̀mañiinɛ) from the very beginning, from the very first.

ཐོག་མ་ཉིད་ནས་བཟུང་ (tɔ̄ɔ̀ma ñiinɛsuŋ) sm. ཐོག་མ་ཉིད་

ནས་.

ཐོག་མ་དང་ཐ་མ་མེད་པ་ (tɔ̄ɔma daŋ tāma meeba) having no beginning and no end.

ཐོག་མ་དང་མཐའ་མ་མེད་པ་ (tɔ̄ɔma daŋ tāmeèba) having no beginning and no end.

ཐོག་མ་ནས་ (tɔ̄ɔmanɛ) sm. ཐོག་མ་ཉིད་ནས་.

ཐོག་མ་མེད་པ་ (tɔ̄ɔma meèba) having no beginning.

ཐོག་མའི་སྐབས་ (tɔ̄ɔmɛ gəb) in the beginning, at first.

ཐོག་མའི་སྐར་མ་ (tɔ̄ɔmɛ gārma) the day a job or project is started.

ཐོག་མའི་གྲུབ་འབྲས་ (tɔ̄ɔmɛ drumdrɛɛ̀) first result/ achievement.

ཐོག་མའི་རྒྱུ་ཆ་ (tɔ̄ɔmɛ gyuja) raw materials.

ཐོག་མའི་ཚོར་ (tɔ̄ɔmɛ cɔ̄r) initially, at the beginning, at first.

ཐོག་མའི་མཐའ་མེད་པ་ (tɔ̄ɔmeè tā meèba) a long long time ago.

ཐོག་མའི་དུས་ (tɔ̄ɔmɛ düü) sm. ཐོག་མའི་སྐབས་.

ཐོག་མའི་དུས་རིམ་ (tɔ̄ɔmɛ düürim) first stage, beginning stage.

ཐོག་མའི་རྣམ་པ་ (tɔ̄ɔmɛ nāmba) the first/ beginning situation.

ཐོག་མའི་པར་མ་ (tɔ̄ɔmɛ bārma) first edition.

ཐོག་མའི་མ་ཟིན་ (tɔ̄ɔmɛ məsin) original record/ note.

ཐོག་མའི་མ་ཡིག (tɔ̄ɔmɛ məyii) first draft.

ཐོག་མའི་སྨན་བཅོས་ (tɔ̄ɔmɛ mēnjöö) first (medical) examination.

ཐོག་མའི་རྩོམ་ (tɔ̄ɔmɛ dzōm) one's first literary work.

ཐོག་མའི་ཟིན་ཐོ་ (tɔ̄ɔmɛ sindo) original record/ note.

ཐོག་མའི་ལོ་མ་ (tɔ̄ɔmɛ lōma) first/ new leaves.

ཐོག་མར་ (tɔ̄ɔmaa) at first, in the beginning ¶ ང་ལྷ་སར་ཐོག་མར་འགྲོ་དུས་ཁོང་མཇལ་བྱུང་ When I first went to Lhasa I met him.

ཐོག་མེད་ (tɔ̄ɔmeè) roofless, open-air ¶ ཐོག་མེད་གློས་གར་ཁང་ Open-air theater.

ཐོག་མེད་གློག་བརྙན་སྟོན་ས་ (tɔ̄ɔmeè lɔ̄ɔñɛn dōnsa) drive-in movie theater.

ཐོག་མེད་དུས་ (tɔ̄ɔmeèdüü) sm. ཐོག་མའི་མཐའ་མེད་པ་.

ཐོག་མེད་ཟློས་གར་འཁྲབ་ར་ (tɔ̄ɔmeè döögar trəbrə) open-air stage.

ཐོག་རྩེ་ (tɔ̄gdze) roof.

ཐོག་བརྩེགས་ (tɔ̄gdzeè) a story (for buildings) ¶ ཐོག་བརྩེགས་གསུམ་ཅན་གྱི་ཁང་པ་ A three story house.

ཐོག་བརྩེགས་ཁང་ཆེན་ (tɔ̄gdzeè kāŋjen) multistoried building.

ཐོག་བརྩེགས་ཅན་གྱི་ཁང་པ་ (tɔ̄gdzeèjɛngi kāŋba) multistoried building.

ཐོག་ཚད་ (tɔ̄ɔdzɛɛ̀) sm. ཐོག་ས་.

ཐོག་ཚད་མ་ (tɔ̄ɔdzɛɛ̀ma) a one story house.

ཐོག་བཙིར་ (tɔ̄ɔdzi) 1. bullying; va.—བྱེད་. 2. doing sth. in a rash manner; va.—བྱེད་.

ཐོག་བཞུ་ (tɔ̄ɔshu) lamp hung from a ceiling.

ཐོག་གློག (tɔ̄ɔdɔɔ) lightning rod.

ཐོག་ཡངས་ (tɔ̄ɔyaŋ) an opening on top of a Tibetan house.

ཐོག་ཡོལ་ (tɔ̄ɔyöö) cloth that covers a ceiling.

ཐོག་གཡབ་ (tɔ̄ɔyəb) verandah.

ཐོག་གཡོགས་ (tɔ̄ɔyɔɔ) roof.

ཐོག་རས་ (tɔ̄ɔrɛɛ̀) sm. ཐོག་ཡོལ་.

ཐོག་རིམ་ (tɔ̄ɔrim) stories (of a building/ house).

ཐོག་རུས་ (tɔ̄ɔrüü) bones of dead animals killed by lightning.

ཐོག་རླུང་ (tɔ̄ɔluŋ) lightning and wind.

ཐོག་ལ་ (tɔ̄ɔla) sm. ཐོག་དུ་.

ཐོག་ཤོག (tɔ̄ɔshɔɔ) paper that covers a ceiling.

ཐོག་ཤས་ (tɔ̄ɔshɛɛ̀) shung. a system of leasing wherein the lessee pays the lessor 1/2 of the yield.

ཐོག་བཤུས་ (tɔ̄ɔshüü) pulling down the roof of the house; va.—རྒྱག.

ཐོག་སེར་རྒོད་ (tɔ̄ɔ sērgöö) a storm. with hail and lightning.

ཐོག་ས་ (tɔ̄ɔsa) floor/ story of house or building ¶ ཐོག་ས་ཉིས་ཐོག The second floor/ story.

ཐོག་ས་ཉིས་རྩེག (tɔ̄ɔsa ñiidzeg) two floors, two stories.

ཐོག་ས་ཉིས་ (tɔ̄ɔsa ñii) sm. ཐོག་ས་ཉིས་རྩེག.

ཐོག་གསོལ་ (tɔ̄ɔsöö) ceremony held on a terrace/ roof to worship a ཐོག་ལྷ་.

ཐོག་ལྷ་ (tɔ̄ɔlha) roof diety; va.—གསོལ་ to hold a ritual to propitiate a ཐོག་ལྷ་.

ཐོགས་ (tɔ̄ɔ) 1. vi. to take time, to elapse (of time) ¶ དུས་ཡུན་རིང་པོ་ཐོགས་ཀྱི་མ་རེད་ It will not take a long time. 2. vi. to be delayed ¶ ང་ལམ་ཁར་ཞི་དྲག་ཐོགས་སོང་ I was delayed a lot on the road. 3. imp. of འདོགས་. 4. vi. to get stuck/ held up/ caught on sth. ¶ ངའི་རྐང་པ་རྡོ་ལ་ཐོག་ནས་རིལ་བྱུང་ I stubbed my foot on a stone and fell. 5. va. to take/ carry ¶ ཁོས་ལག་པར་གྲི་ཐོགས་ནས་རྒྱུགས་ཡོང་གི་འདུག He is running carrying a sword in his hand. 6. vi. to grow.

ཐོགས་འགག (tɔ̄ŋgaà) an obstacle/ barrier/ hindrance that causes a delay.

ཐོགས་ཐུག་མེད་པ་ (tɔ̄gduù meèba) 1. without hindrance/ obstruction/ difficulty. 2. continuously, perpetually.

ཐོགས་པ་ (tɔ̄gbə) sm. ཐོགས་འགག.

ཐོགས་པ་མེད་པ་ (tɔ̄gba meèba) 1. without hindrance/ obstruction/ difficulty. 2. continuously, perpetually.

ཐོགས་འབེབས་ (tɔ̄mbeb) 1. coming into trance spontaneously without a formal invocation of the deity; va.—རྒྱག. 2. all of a sudden.

ཐོགས་མེད་ (tɔ̄ɔmeè) 1. sm. ཐོགས་ཐུག་མེད་པ་. 2. Asanga.

ཐོགས་རྨས་ (tɔ̄ɔmɛɛ̀) injury caused by stubbing or scratching oneself.

ཐོང་ (tōŋ) 1. sm. ཐོང་གཤོལ་. 2. imp. of གཏོང་. 3. vi. of གཏོང་.

ཐོང་ཀ་ (tōŋga) sm. ཐོང་ག.

ཐོང་སྐལ་ (tōŋgɛɛ) lease fee for land.

ཐོང་མཁན་ (tōŋgɛn) plowman.

ཐོང་ག (tōŋga) 1. chest. 2. lease.

ཐོང་གུག (tōŋguù) a part of a plow.

ཐོང་ལྕགས་ (tōŋjaà) iron plow tip, iron plowshare.

ཐོང་མཆན་ (tōŋjɛn) visa.

ཐོང་ཐོང་ (tōŋdoŋ) a person at the prime of youth.

ཐོང་པ་ (tōŋba) sm. ཐོང་མཁན་.

ཐོང་རྩ་ (tōŋdza) a vein in the neck where blood is drawn for medical treatment in Tibetan medicine.

ཐོང་རྩེ་ (tōŋdza) upper part of the chest where the two clavicle bones meet.

ཐོང་ཚེར་ (tōŋdzer) three year old sheep or goat.

ཐོང་འཛིན་ (tōŋdzin) 1. plowman. 2. shung. a certificate of authorization for levying a corvee tax on animals.

ཐོང་འོག (tōŋwɔɔ) pit of the stomach.

ཐོང་གཤོལ་ (tōŋshöö) a plow.

ཐོང་གཤོལ་ལྕགས་གཉིས་འཁོར་གཉིས་མ་ (tōŋshöö jāàñii kɔ̄ɔñiibə) a two-wheeled two-bladed plowshare.

ཐོང་གཤོལ་ལྕགས་གཉིས་མ་ (tōŋshöö jāàñiibə) two-bladed plowshare.

ཐོང་སོ་ (tōŋso) sm. ཐོང་ལྕགས་.

ཐོངས་མཆན་ (tōŋjɛn) sm. ཐོང་མཆན་.

ཐོད་ (töö) above, over ¶ དེའི་ཐོད་དུ་སྤང་རི་གཅིག་འདུག There is a meadow above that.

ཐོད་ཀོར་ (töögɔɔ) 1. the circle used above certain letters to indicate nasal sounds. 2. a hat worn in Tibetan opera.

ཐོད་དཀར་ར་ (töögarra) 1. unlucky person. 2. stupid/ dull person.

ཐོད་དཀྲིས་ (töödrii) turban, scarf wrapped around the head.

ཐོད་སྐམ་ (töögam) human skull.

ཐོད་སྐམ་པ་ (töö gāmba) sm. ཐོད་དཀར་ར་.

ཐོད་སྐམ་རིགས་རྒྱན་ (töögam riggyɛn) the five skulls adorning the headdresses of wrathful deities.

ཐོད་སྒོམ་ (tōògom) sm. ཐོད་སྒམ་.

ཐོད་ཁྱིམ་ (tōògyim) hairline.

ཐོད་ཁྲག (tōòdraà) human skull-bowl with blood in it.

ཐོད་འཁུར་ (tōògur) va. to accept with utmost respect.

ཐོད་རྐལ་ (tōò gɛɛ) va. to be promoted suddenly ¶ ལས་ཁུངས་ཀྱི་དྲུང་ཡིག་དེ་ཐོད་རྐལ་གྱིས་འགོ་ཁྲིད་ལ་གནས་སྤར་བྱས་སོང་ The secretary was suddenly promoted to be head of the office.

ཐོད་རྒྱན་ (tōògyɛn) 1. head ornament. 2. cloth covering the ceiling of a room.

ཐོད་སྒོར་ (tōògɔɔ) head decoration made of stringed pearls that is worn by the wives of high ranking Tibetan government officials.

ཐོད་ང་ (tōòŋa) a small drum made from a human skull.

ཐོད་བཅིངས་ (tōòjiŋ) 1. turban. 2. sm. ཐོད་འཁུར་.

ཐོད་ཆ་ (tōòja) upper part/ level.

ཐོད་ཆིངས་ (tōòjiŋ) sm. ཐོད་དཀྲིས་.

ཐོད་མཆོངས་ (tōòjoŋ) jumping /leaping over; va.—རྒྱག.

ཐོད་གདུགས་ (tōòduù) 1. va. to meet face-to-face ¶ ང་གཉིས་ཐོད་གདུགས་ནས་སྐད་ཆ་བཤད་པ་ཡིན་ We met face-to-face and spoke. 2. counterbalanced, evened out, balanced ¶ རྩིས་ཁྲའི་ནང་ལ་གཏོང་ཡོང་ཐོད་གདུགས་བྱུང་སོང་ Expenditure and income in the account listing balanced out.

ཐོད་སྡིང་ (tōòdeŋ) upper part of the forehead.

ཐོད་ཐུག (tōò tūù) vi. to meet face-to-face.

ཐོད་མདའ་སྒྲོད་ (tōnda drōò) va. to shoot an arrow in sb.'s forehead.

ཐོད་སྡེམ་ (tōòdem) a bandanna/ ribbon tied on the forehead.

ཐོད་པ་ (tōòba) 1. skull. 2. merit, good karma, virtuous acts.

ཐོད་པ་དཀར་པོ་ (tōòba gārbo) bad karma.

ཐོད་པ་དོ་ཐུག (tōòba doduù) sm. ནུ་ཁུག་དབ་.

ཐོད་པ་རློན་པ་ (tōòba lōmba) a head that has just been cut off.

ཐོད་པང་ (tōòbaŋ) the surface boards of a table, box, etc.

ཐོད་པས་མ་འཆུན་ (tōòbɛ majün) ill-fated, unlucky (due to past karma) ¶ ང་རང་གི་ཐོད་པས་མ་འཆུན་པར་ཕྲུ་གུ་གྲོངས་སོང་ Because of my unfortunate past karma my child died.

ཐོད་སྦུ་ (tōòbu) forehead bangs.

ཐོད་ཕྲེང་ (tōòdreŋ) 1. rosary beads made from the bones of a human skull. 2. necklace with human skulls worn by wrathful deities.

ཐོད་ཕོར་ (tōòbɔɔ) skull-bowl.

ཐོད་རྩ་ (tōòdza) veins on the head.

ཐོད་ཚལ་ (tōòdzɛɛ) pieces of skull.

ཐོད་རས་ (tōòrɛɛ) sm. ཐོད་དཀྲིས་.

ཐོད་རུས་ (tōòrüü) skull bone.

ཐོད་ལེ་གོར་ (tōòlegɔr) sm. ཐ་ལེ་གོར་.

ཐོད་སོ་བྱེད་ (tōòso cee) va. to look at sth. by putting one's hand on one's forehead.

ཐོན་ (tōn) 1. ch. regiment, regimental headquarters ¶ ཐོན་ཨང་ ༡༥༤ པ་ The 154th regiment. 2. vi. to come out, to leave, to depart ¶ སློབ་གྲྭ་ཆེ་བ་ནས་ཐོན་དེ་ཨ་རིར་ཕྱིན་པ་རེད་ After leaving (graduating from) school, (he) went to the U.S. 3. vi. to become evident, to appear ¶ ཀློག་གཞོམ་དེ་གསལ་པོར་ཐོན་པ་རེད་ The conspiracy became evident. 4. vi. to be produced, to come forth ¶ ཕག་རིར་སྔར་ནས་འབྲུ་རིགས་ཐོན་གྱི་ཡོད་པ་མ་རེད་ Formerly no grain was produced in Phari. 5. imp. of འདོན་. 6. ch. youth league. 7. p. of འཐོན་.

ཐོན་ཀྲང་ (tōndraŋ) ch. regimental commander.

ཐོན་ཀྱི་ཕུའུ་ (tōn dribu) ch. youth league branch.

ཐོན་ཀྱི་ཧྲུའུ་ (tōn drihru) ch. secretary of a youth league branch.

ཐོན་སྐོར་ (tōngɔɔ) shung. the yield of a field as a proportion of the seed planted, e.g., 6 times the seed sown (this is a system for estimating agricultural field yields in terms of the number of times the seed planted) ¶ སོན་འགྲོ་ལ་གཞིགས་པའི་ལོ་གསུམ་ཐོན་སྐོར་ཡུལ་སྲོལ་འབྲིང་ཚད་བརྩི་རྒྱུ་ In accordance with the amount of seeds the land takes, the calculation of the number of times that the yield is greater than the seed shall be done at the medium level.

ཐོན་སྐྱེད་ (tōngyeè) production; va.—བྱེད་ to produce ¶ ལོ་འདིའི་ནང་བཟོ་གྲྭའི་ཐོན་སྐྱེད་ཡག་པོ་བྱུང་འདུག This year the factory's production was good.

ཐོན་སྐྱེད་ཀྱི་རྒྱུ་རྐྱེན་གཙོ་བོ་ (tōngyeègi gyugyen dzōwo) main factors in production.

ཐོན་སྐྱེད་ཀྱི་དངོས་པོ་ (tōngyeègi ŋōòbo) products.

ཐོན་སྐྱེད་ཀྱི་སྟོབས་ཤུགས་ (tōngyeègi dōbshuù) productive strength/ power, productive force.

ཐོན་སྐྱེད་ཀྱི་འཐབ་རྩོད་ (tōngyeègi tābdzöò) the struggle/ fight for production.

ཐོན་སྐྱེད་ཀྱི་ཐབས་ཚུལ་ (tōngyeègi tābdzüü) mode of production.

ཐོན་སྐྱེད་ཀྱི་འདོད་པ་ (tōngyeègi döòba) production morale/ desire/ motivation.

ཐོན་སྐྱེད་ཀྱི་ནུས་ཤུགས་ (tōngyeègi nüüshuù) productive forces.

ཐོན་སྐྱེད་ཀྱི་ནུས་ཚད་ (tōngyeègi nüüdzɛɛ) level of production.

ཐོན་སྐྱེད་ཀྱི་འབྲེལ་བ་ (tōngyeègi dreewa) relations of production.

ཐོན་སྐྱེད་ཀྱི་ཚོད་ (tōngyeègi tsōò) productivity.

ཐོན་སྐྱེད་ཀྱི་ལག་རྩལ་ (tōngyeègi lagdzɛɛ) production technique/ skill.

ཐོན་སྐྱེད་ཀྱི་ལས་འགན་ (tōngyeègi lɛngɛn) production quota/ obligation.

ཐོན་སྐྱེད་ཀྱི་ལས་ཚད་ (tōngyeègi lɛɛdzɛɛ) productivity, productive rate.

ཐོན་སྐྱེད་ཁྱབ་ཁོངས་ (tōngyeè kyəbgoŋ) production limit/ range.

ཐོན་སྐྱེད་ཁྲུའུ་ (tōngyeè trū) production section.

ཐོན་སྐྱེད་མཁས་པ་ (tōngyeègi kɛɛba) production expert.

ཐོན་སྐྱེད་གོང་འཕེལ་ (tōngyeè koŋbel) development/ improvement/ advance in production.

ཐོན་སྐྱེད་འགན་དགྲིའི་ལམ་ལུགས་ (tōngyeè gɛndrii ləmluù) production responsibility system.

ཐོན་སྐྱེད་འགྲན་བསྡུར་ (tōngyeè drɛnduu) labor emulation, production race/ competition.

ཐོན་སྐྱེད་རྒྱུ་ཆས་ (tōngyeè gyujɛɛ) means of production.

ཐོན་སྐྱེད་རྒྱུ་ཆས་སྒེར་ལ་དབང་བའི་ལམ་ལུགས་ (tōngyeè gyujɛɛ gerla wāŋwɛ ləmluù) the system of the private ownership of the means of production.

ཐོན་སྐྱེད་རྒྱུ་ཆས་སྤྱི་ལ་དབང་བའི་ལམ་ལུགས་ (tōngyeè gyujɛɛ jīlə wāŋwɛ ləmluù) the system of the collective ownership of the means of collective production.

ཐོན་སྐྱེད་རྒྱུ་ཆས་དབང་བའི་ལམ་ལུགས་ (tōngyeè gyujɛɛ wāŋwɛ ləmluù) the system of the ownership of the means of production.

ཐོན་སྐྱེད་རྒྱུན་མཐུད་སྒྲུབ་རིམ་ (tōngyeè gyüntüü drubrim) continuous production line.

ཐོན་སྐྱེད་སྒྲུབ་རིམ་ (tōngyeè drubrim) production line.

ཐོན་སྐྱེད་ངལ་རྩོལ་ (tōngyeè ŋɛɛdzöö) production labor.

ཐོན་སྐྱེད་སྔོན་ཐོན་མཁན་ (tōngyeè ŋōndönñɛn) outstanding worker/ producer.

ཐོན་སྐྱེད་སྔོན་ཐོན་པ་ (tōngyeè ŋōndömba) sm. ཐོན་སྐྱེད་སྔོན་ཐོན་མཁན་.

ཐོན་སྐྱེད་ཆག (tōngyeè cāà) vi. to decrease in output/ production.

ཐོན་སྐྱེད་ཆུང་ངུ་བ་ (tōngyeè cūŋŋuwa) small producer.

ཐོན་སྐྱེད་མཆོངས་བསྒྱོད་ཆེན་པོ་ (tōngyeè cōŋgyöò cēmbo) the great leap forward in production.

ཐོན་སྐྱེད་འཆར་འགོད་ཁྲུའུ་ (tōngyeè trū) tib.ch.

production planning section.

ཐོན་སྐྱེད་འཆར་གཞི་ (tõngyeè cārshi) production plan ¶ ད་ལོའི་ཐོན་སྐྱེད་འཆར་གཞི་ The production plan for this year.

ཐོན་སྐྱེད་མཉམ་ལས་ (tõngyeè ñāmlɛ̀ɛ̀) cooperative production ¶ ཐོན་སྐྱེད་མཉམ་ལས་ཁང་ Production/ producer's cooperative.

ཐོན་སྐྱེད་སྟོབས་ཤུགས་ (tõngyeè dōbshuù) sm. ཐོན་སྐྱེད་ཀྱི་སྟོབས་ཤུགས་.

ཐོན་སྐྱེད་འཐབ་རྩོད་ (tõngyeè tābdzöö) the fight/ struggle to produce.

ཐོན་སྐྱེད་དང་བྲལ་ (tõngyeèdaŋ trɛɛ) being released from production work (usu. to take on other duties).

ཐོན་སྐྱེད་དོ་དམ་ (tõngyeè todam) production control/ supervision.

ཐོན་སྐྱེད་བདེ་འཇགས་ (tõngyeè denjaà) production safety, safety in production.

ཐོན་སྐྱེད་བདག་གཉེར་ (tõngyeè dagñyer) production manager.

ཐོན་སྐྱེད་ནུས་ཤུགས་ (tõngyeè nüüshuù) sm. ཐོན་སྐྱེད་ཀྱི་ནུས་ཤུགས་.

ཐོན་སྐྱེད་སྤེལ་བ་དང་ མཁོ་སྤྲོད་འགན་ལེན་ (tõngyeè bēlwadaŋ kōdröö gɛnlen) develop production and guarantee supply (political slogan).

ཐོན་སྐྱེད་བྱ་རིམ་ (tõngyeè carim) production process, production steps.

ཐོན་སྐྱེད་བྱེད་སྟངས་སྲིད་གཞུང་མེད་པའི་རྣམ་པ་ (tõngyeè ceèdaŋ sīīshuŋ meèbɛ nāmba) anarchical production.

ཐོན་སྐྱེད་བྱེད་ཚུལ་ (tõngyeè ceèdzüü) sm. ཐོན་སྐྱེད་བྱེད་ལུགས་.

ཐོན་སྐྱེད་བྱ་ཡུལ་ (tõngyeè cəyüü) the place where production occurs, production site.

ཐོན་སྐྱེད་བྱེད་ལུགས་ (tõngyeè ceèluù) mode/ way of production.

ཐོན་སྐྱེད་འབྲེལ་བ་ (tõngyeè dreewa) relations of production.

ཐོན་སྐྱེད་མ་ཡིན་པ་ (tõngyeè məyimbə) nonproductive.

ཐོན་སྐྱེད་ཚོགས་ཆུང་ (tõngyeè tsōgjuŋ) work group (in communes these were under the ཐོན་སྐྱེད་རུ་ཁག).

ཐོན་སྐྱེད་འཛུགས་སྐྲུན་དཔུང་ཚོགས་ (tõngyeè dzugdrön būŋdzɔ̀ɔ̀) production and construction corps.

ཐོན་སྐྱེད་འཛུགས་སྐྲུན་བྱེད་མཁན་དཔུང་ཚོགས་ (tõngyeè dzugdrön ceèñɛn būŋdzɔ̀ɔ̀) production and construction corps.

ཐོན་སྐྱེད་ཡོ་བྱད་ (tõngyeè yobjɛ̀ɛ̀) sm. ཐོན་སྐྱེད་རྒྱུ་ཆས་.

ཐོན་སྐྱེད་རུ་ཁག (tõngyeè rugaà) production team (a unit that was under the brigade in communes).

ཐོན་སྐྱེད་རུ་ཆེན་ (tõngyeè rujen) production brigade (a unit above the production team in communes).

ཐོན་སྐྱེད་རུ་དཔུང་ (tõngyeè rubuŋ) sm. ཐོན་སྐྱེད་རུ་ཁག.

ཐོན་སྐྱེད་རོགས་རེས་ (tõngyeè rogreè) mutual assistance in production.

ཐོན་སྐྱེད་ལ་ཞུགས་ (tõngyeèla shuù) va. to begin production, to participate in production.

ཐོན་སྐྱེད་ལག་ཆ་ (tõngyeè lagja) tools of production.

ཐོན་སྐྱེད་ལག་རྩལ་ (tõngyeè lagdzɛɛ) production techniques/ skills.

ཐོན་སྐྱེད་ལུས་རྩལ་ (tõngyeè lüüdzɛɛ) sm. ཐོན་སྐྱེད་འགྲན་བསྡུར་.

ཐོན་སྐྱེས་ (tõngyeè) resources.

ཐོན་སྐྱེས་ཡོ་བྱད་ (tõngyeè yobjɛ̀ɛ̀) sm. ཐོན་སྐྱེད་རྒྱུ་ཆས་.

ཐོན་ཁུངས་ (tõnguŋ) resources ¶ ལུང་པ་འདི་ལ་འབྲུ་རིགས་ཐོན་ཁུངས་ཡག་པོ་ཡོད་པ་རེད་ This area has good resources for growing grain.

ཐོན་ཁུལ་ (tõngüü) area where a product or resources comes from.

ཐོན་ཁུལ་རྟེན་གཞི་ (tõngüü dēnshi) the main area where a product or resource comes from.

ཐོན་གྲངས་ (tõndraŋ) amount/ rate/ level of production, the yield, the output; va.—རྩི་ to count/ calculate output or yields ¶ བཟོ་གྲྭ་འདིའི་ཐོན་གྲངས་མཐོ་པོ་ཡོད་པ་རེད་ The production of this factory is high. ¶ རྒྱལ་ཁབ་འདིའི་ནང་འབྲུ་རིགས་ཐོན་གྲངས་མཐོ་པོ་ཡོད་པ་རེད་ In this country the production level of grain is high.

ཐོན་གྲངས་རྩི་བའི་བཟོ་གྲྭ་ (tõndraŋ dzīwɛ sodra) sm. ཐོན་གྲངས་བརྩི་པའི་ཕོགས་ཐོབ་.

ཐོན་གྲངས་བརྩི་བའི་ཕོགས་ཐོབ་ (tõndraŋ dzīwɛ pɔ̄ɔ̀dob) piecework wages.

ཐོན་གྲབས་ (tõndrəb) preparing to depart; va.—སྒྲིག to make preparations to depart.

ཐོན་འགན་ (tõngɛn) production quota, production responsibility.

ཐོན་འགན་གཙང་ལེན་ (tõngɛn dzāŋlen) 1. taking full responsibility for production quotas. 2. the "responsibility system" that was begun in the 1980s wherein households were given long-term use of farmland and in return had a responsibility to sell a quota of the production to the government at less than market price.

ཐོན་སྒོ་ (tõngo) 1. exit. 2. sm. ཐོན་ཁུངས་. 3. va.—འབྱེད་ to start utilize/ producing ¶ ཆུ་ཤུགས་ཀྱི་ཐོན་སྒོ་འབྱེད་པའི་འཆར་གཞི་ A plan for starting to utilize water power.

ཐོན་དངུལ་ (tõnŋüü) ch.tib. youth league membership dues.

ཐོན་དངོས་ (tõnŋöö) products, production goods ¶ ལག་ཤེས་སྒྱུ་རྩལ་གྱི་ཐོན་དངོས་ Handicraft products.

ཐོན་ལྔ་མ་ (tõn ŋāma) the earlier group(s) that departed or will depart.

ཐོན་ལྕག (tõnjaà) departing whipping: the whipping a prisoner in traditional Tibet got on the day he was released from prison.

ཐོན་ཆས་ (tõnjɛɛ̀) sm. ཐོན་དངོས་.

ཐོན་ཆེ་ (tõnje) high yield ¶ ཐོན་ཆེ་ལོ་ཏོག High yield crops.

ཐོན་ཇ་ (tõnja) tea given to all students when one's child graduates; va.—གཏོང་.

ཐོན་མཇལ་ (tõnjɛɛ) departure audience in tt. government (the audience just before one leaves for a trip/ provincial post) ¶ ངས་བློན་ཆེན་དེ་ར་ཐོན་མཇལ་ཞུ་རྒྱུ་མ་བྱུང་ I could not get a departure audience with the minister.

ཐོན་མཇུག་མ་ (tõn jüümə) the group that departs later.

ཐོན་ཉུང་ (tõnñuŋ) poor harvest, poor/ low production.

ཐོན་བརྟན་འབབ་ཆེ་ (tõndɛn bəbje) stable and high yielding (usu. crops).

ཐོན་ཐི་ (tõnti) sm. ཐུན་ཐི་.

ཐོན་མཐོ་ (tõnto) high production, high yield.

ཐོན་མཐོ་ཐོན་བརྟན་ (tõndo dõndɛn) high yield and steady yield.

ཐོན་མཐོ་སྡུད་ལེགས་ (tõnto düüleg) high production and effective collection of the harvest.

ཐོན་དང་གཉིས་ (tõndaŋ ñīī) leaving/ departing in staggered groups ¶ ང་ཚོ་འབྲུག་ཡུལ་ལ་འགྲོ་དུས་ཐོན་དང་གཉིས་བྱས་དེ་ཕྱིན་པ་རེད་ When we went to Bhutan, we went in staggered groups.

ཐོན་དཔུང་ (tõnbuŋ) ch.tib. regiment.

ཐོན་སྤེལ་ (tõnbel) increasing production/ output; va.—བྱེད་; —གཏོང་ to increase production.

ཐོན་སྤེལ་གྲོན་ཆུང་ (tõnbel drönjuŋ) increase production and economize (decrease expenses) (political slogan).

ཐོན་སྤེལ་གྲོན་བསྲི་ (tõnbel drönsi) sm. ཐོན་སྤེལ་གྲོན་ཆུང་.

ཐོན་སྤེལ་སྡུད་སྤེལ་ (tõnbel düübel) increase production and increase collection/ harvest (political slogan).

ཐོན་སྤེལ་སྐྱོད་མཁས་ (tõnbel jöökɛɛ̀) sm. ཐོན་སྤེལ་གྲོན་ཆུང་.

ཐོན་སྤེལ་ལས་འགུལ་ (tõnbel lɛngüü) the campaign to increase production.

ཐོན་ཕྱག (tõnjaà) 1. taking leave, saying goodbye; va.—ཞུ་ to say goodbye, to bid farewell, to take leave. 2. shung. official departure audience of tt.

government officials with the ruler ། ཐོན་ཕྱག་གནང་བས་བདེ་ The notice asking for an audience two days before the day of departure.

ཐོན་འཕར་ (tõmbar) increased/ increasing production ། ལོ་རྒྱུད་མར་ཐོན་འཕར་བྱུང་ They continuously increased production.

ཐོན་འཕེལ་ (tõmbel) sm. ཐོན་སྐྱེལ་.

ཐོན་བར་མ་ (tõn parma) the middle of several groups that departed or will depart.

ཐོན་བུ་ (tõmbu) sm. ཐོམ་བུ་.

ཐོན་འབབ་ (tõmbəb) yield, harvest ། ད་ལོ་འབྲུ་ཐོན་འབབ་ཡག་པོ་བྱུང་སོང་ This year the yield of grain was good.

ཐོན་འབོར་ (tõmbɔɔ) sm. ཐོན་གྲངས་.

ཐོན་འབྲས་ (tõndrɛɛ̀) 1. achievement, accomplishment, result. 2. sm. ཐོན་འབབ་.

ཐོན་འབྲུ་ (tõndru) shung. the yield (of a field) ། ཐོན་འབྲུའི་ཐོག་ནས་སོན་སྐྱིན་འབྲུ་ནུའི་ཁལ་ ༡༥ བཞག་པ་ They left 15 ཁལ་ of grain from the agricultural yield as a replacement for seed.

ཐོན་སྐྱེལ་འགན་འཁྲིའི་ལམ་ལུགས་ (tõndree gendrii ləmluù) a contract system wherein remuneration is linked to output.

ཐོན་སྐྱེལ་ཐོབ་རྩིས་ (tõndree tõbdziì) a system where income/ payment is linked to output.

ཐོན་མང་མགོ་ཉུང་ (tõnmaŋ kõñuŋ) produce much and use little (political slogan).

ཐོན་མི་སམ་བྷོ་ཊ་ (tõnmi sāmbhoda) 7th century historical figure who is said to have invented the Tibetan alphabet.

ཐོན་རྩིས་ (tõndziì) shung. to calculate the yield ། ད་བར་མུ་འབྲུམས་ལོ་ཇེ་སོང་གི་ཐོན་རྩིས་དགོས་གནས་ཙམ་འདུག་ཀྱང་ It is deemed appropriate to calculate the yearly yields but.

ཐོན་ཚད་ (tõndzɛɛ̀) sm. ཐོན་གྲངས་.

ཐོན་ཚད་ཀྱི་རིན་གོང་ (tõndzɛɛ̀gi rindaŋ) output/ production value.

ཐོན་ཚད་ཀྱི་རིན་ཐང་ (tõndzɛɛ̀gi rindaŋ) sm. ཐོན་ཚད་ཀྱི་རིན་གོང་.

ཐོན་ཚད་འགན་ལེན་ (tõndzɛɛ̀ genlen) taking responsibility for output/ yield.

ཐོན་ཚད་གཏན་འཁེལ་ (tõndzɛɛ̀ dēnkee) fixed/ set amount of production or output.

ཐོན་ཚད་མཐོ་པོ་ (tõndzɛɛ̀ tõbo) high yield/ output/ production.

ཐོན་ཚད་འཐོན་པོ་ (tõndzɛɛ̀ tõmbo) sm. ཐོན་ཚད་མཐོ་པོ་.

ཐོན་ཚད་བསྡོམས་གྲངས་ (tõndzɛɛ̀ domdraŋ) gross output, total output.

ཐོན་ཚད་མང་དྲགས་པ་ (tõndzɛɛ̀ maŋdragba) overproduction, excess production.

ཐོན་ཚད་དམའ་པོ་ (tõndzɛɛ̀ māābo) low yield/ output/ production.

ཐོན་ཚད་ལས་བརྒལ་ (tõndzɛɛ̀le gɛɛ) vi. to exceed a production quota, to overfulfill a production target ། ལྕགས་ཀྱི་བཟོ་གྲྭ་འདིའི་ལོ་རེའི་ཐོན་ཚད་ནས་བརྒལ་འདུག This iron factory has exceeded in its yearly production quota.

ཐོན་རྫོངས་ (tõndzoŋ) a farewell/ parting gift (by the person staying to the one going).

ཐོན་རྫས་ (tõndzɛɛ̀) products, produce ། ཕྱི་རྒྱལ་གྱི་ཐོན་རྫས་ Foreign products.

ཐོན་རྫས་ཀྱི་དཔྱ་ཁྲལ་ (tõndzɛɛ̀gi jādrɛɛ) tax on products.

ཐོན་རྫས་ཀྱི་ཚད་གཞི་ (tõndzɛɛ̀gi tsɛɛ̀shi) specifications/ standards for products.

ཐོན་རྫས་ཀྱི་རིན་ཐང་བསྡོམས་འབོར་ (tõndzɛɛ̀gi rindaŋ) total value of output.

ཐོན་རྫས་གྲུབ་མ་ (tõndzɛɛ̀ drubmə) finished products.

ཐོན་རྫས་བརྗེ་རེས་ (tõndzɛɛ̀ jereè) exchange of products.

ཐོན་རྫས་སྤུས་ཚད་ (tõndzɛɛ̀ bũũdzɛɛ̀) the quality of products.

ཐོན་རྫས་སྤུས་ཞེར་ (tõndzɛɛ̀ bũũsher) low quality/ inferior goods.

ཐོན་རྫས་མ་གནས་ (tõndzɛɛ̀ manɛɛ̀) cost of production/ goods.

ཐོན་རྫས་མང་དྲགས་པ་ (tõndzɛɛ̀ maŋdrawa) surplus of production, excess production, overproduction.

ཐོན་རྫས་རིན་ཐང་ (tõndzɛɛ̀ rindaŋ) price or value of goods/ products.

ཐོན་ཟོག (tõnsoò) sm. ཐོན་རྫས་.

ཐོན་ཟོང་ (tõnsoŋ) sm. ཐོན་རྫས་.

ཐོན་བཟང་ (tõnsaŋ) very productive, high / good productivity ། ཐོན་བཟང་ཞིང་ཁ་ A field with high productivity.

ཐོན་ཡུལ་ (tõnyüü) sm. ཐོན་ཁུལ་.

ཐོན་ཡོན་ (tõnyön) ch. 1. member of an organization. 2. a member of the communist Youth League in China.

ཐོན་ལས་ (tõnlɛɛ̀) 1. industry, industrial ། ཐོན་ལས་ཁག་གི་བཟོ་པ་ Workers of the (various) industries. 2. production work; va.—བྱེད་ to work producing, to produce.

ཐོན་ལས་རྗེས་གྲབས་དཔུང་སྡེ་ (tõnlɛɛ̀ jeèdrəb būŋde) industrial labor reserve.

ཐོན་ལས་དཔུང་སྡེ་ (tõnlɛɛ̀ būŋde) industrial workers, industrial labor force.

ཐོན་ལས་མ་རྩ་ (tõnlɛɛ̀ madza) industrial capital.

ཐོན་ལས་བཟོ་པ་ (tõnlɛɛ̀ soba) industrial worker.

ཐོན་ལས་བཟོ་ཚོགས་ (tõnlɛɛ̀ sodzoò) industrial labor union.

ཐོན་ལས་གསར་བརྗེ་ (tõnlɛɛ̀ sārje) industrial revolution.

ཐོན་ལས་གསུམ་ (tõnlɛɛ̀ sūm) the policy of taking unemployed workers and putting them into cooperative organizations to learn skills like haircutting and shoe repairing, etc.

ཐོན་ལེགས་ (tõnleg) abundant/ good production, bumper harvest.

ཐོན་ས་ (tõnsa) sm. ཐོན་ཡུལ་.

ཐོན་གསར་ (tõnsar) 1. new (invention or product) ། དེང་དུས་ཐོན་གསར་གྱི་གོ་ལག New modern weapons. 2. new fashion ། ཕྲུ་གུ་དེས་དུག་ལོག་ཐོན་གསར་ཞིག་གྱོན་བཞག That child is wearing clothes of the new fashion style.

ཐོན་གསལ་ (tõnsɛɛ) direct discourse. introducer: "as appeared" ། ཝ་ཤིང་ཀྲོན་ནས་ཕྱི་ཟླ་ ༡ ཚེས་ ༡༧ ཉིན་ཐོན་གསལ་ (As the story) appeared on the 17th of January in Washington.

ཐོན་ཨུ་ (tõn ū) abbr. committee of the communist youth league of China.

ཐོབ་ (tõb) 1. vi. to get, to obtain, to achieve, to gain ། གྲུབ་རྗེས་ཤིན་ཏུ་ཆེན་པོ་ཐོབ་པ་རེད་ (They) achieved a great result. 2. vi. to win ། རྒྱན་བཙགས་ནས་དངུལ་ཞི་དྲགས་ཐོབ་སོང་ (He) gambled and won a lot of money.

ཐོབ་ཀྱག (tõbgya) sm. ཐོབ་ཀྱག་གོ་ཀྱག.

ཐོབ་ཀྱག་གོ་ཀྱག (tõbgya kobgya) suddenly.

ཐོབ་སྐར་ (tõbgar) a work point that has been earned through labor in a commune/ collective.

ཐོབ་སྐལ་ (tõbgɛɛ) share, portion, allotment.

ཐོབ་ཁུངས་ (tõbguŋ) the place/ group/ section where one belongs ། སྤྱི་ཚོགས་ཐོབ་ཁུངས་དང་འབྲེལ་བ་ནི་བུ་ཕ་བདག་དང་བུ་མོ་མ་བདག་ཡིན་པ་རེད་ As for where they belong in society, the son belongs to the father's group and the daughter to the mother's. 2. shung. the geographic area that a ཁང་ཚན་ in a monastery has the right to recruit monks from.

ཐོབ་ཁོངས་ (tõngoŋ) sm. ཐོབ་ཁུངས་.

ཐོབ་ཁྲ་ (tõdra) bill.

ཐོབ་ཁྲལ་ (tõdrɛɛ) income tax.

ཐོབ་གོ་གནས་ (tõb konɛɛ̀) sm. གོ་གནས་.

ཐོབ་གྲངས་ (tõbdraŋ) quotient (in math).

ཐོབ་ཅི་ (tõbji) sm. ཐོབ་ཆི་.

ཐོབ་ཆ་ (tõbja) 1. sm. ཐོབ་སྐལ་. 2. term used for the share of the profit of a cooperative businesses or collective that is distributed to the workers.

ཐོབ་ཆི་ (tõbji) button; va.—རྒྱག to button.

ཐོབ་རྒྱུ་ (tõbju) sm. ཐོབ་ཆི་.

ཐོབ་དེ་ (tōbde) suddenly.

ཐོབ་དེ་ཁ་ལ་ (tōbde kāla) sm. ཐོབ་དེ་.

ཐོབ་ཐང་ (tōbdaŋ) 1. rights ¶ཡུལ་འགའ་ཞིག་ནང་བུད་མེད་ལ་འོས་བསྡུའི་ཐོབ་ཐང་མེད་ In some countries women do not have the right to vote. 2. qualification, status.

ཐོབ་ཐང་དང་རིམ་པ་ (tōbdaŋ daŋ rimbə) qualifications and rank.

ཐོབ་ཐང་དང་ལོ་རྒྱུས་ (tōbdaŋ daŋ lügyür) qualifications and background history.

ཐོབ་ཐང་འདྲ་མཉམ་ (tōbdaŋ drañam) equal rights.

ཐོབ་ཐོ་ (tōbto) receipt.

ཐོབ་དབང་ (tōbwaŋ) rights ¶བུད་མེད་ཀྱི་ཐོབ་དབང་ The rights of women.

ཐོབ་དོགས་ཤོར་དོགས་ (tōbdɔɔ̀ shɔ̄ɔdɔɔ̀) indecisive; va.—བྱེད་ [Lit. fearful of winning, fearful of losing].

ཐོབ་བསྡུ་བསྡད་ཕུད་ (tōbdu dɛ̀ɛbüü) shung. except for the amount yet to be collected ¶འདི་ལོའི་ཐོབ་བསྡུ་བསྡད་ཕུད་ ད་ལྟ་འབྲུའི་ཁལ་100ཡོད་པ་ Except for the amount yet to be collected for the year, now we have 100 ཁལ་ of grain.

ཐོབ་ནོར་ (tōbnɔɔ) 1. sm. ཐོབ་གྲངས་. 2. sm. ཐོབ་སྐལ་.

ཐོབ་བྱ་ (tōbja) extra perks/ benefits associated with a job.

ཐོབ་འབྲས་ (tōmdrɛɛ̀) results, achievements ¶སློབ་ཕྲུག་འདིའི་ཡིག་ཚད་ཐོབ་འབྲས་ཡག་པོ་བྱུང་བཞག The student got a good result on the exam.

ཐོབ་ཆིར་ (tōbdzir) sm. ཐོབ་སྐལ་.

ཐོབ་བཙོས་ (tōbsöö) an award, bonus ¶བཟོ་པ་ཚོར་ཟླ་རེ་ཐོབ་བཙོས་ཡག་པོ་རག་གི་ཡོད་པ་རེད་ The workers got a good bonus every month.

ཐོབ་ཡིག (tōbyii) 1. a list of religious initiations. 2. a list of awards/ bonuses/ distributions.

ཐོབ་རིམ་ (tōbrim) the sequence of religious initiations one has.

ཐོབ་རེ་ (tōbre) the hope of getting sth.

ཐོབ་ཤ་ (tōbsha) 1. scrambling to get sth.; va.—རྒྱག ¶སྤྲང་པོ་ཚོས་ལྟོ་ཆས་ལ་ཐོབ་ཤ་རྒྱག་གི་འདུག The beggars are scrambling to get food. 2. one's share of meat.

ཐོབ་ཤག་ཤག (tōb shāàshaà) certain/ sure/ confident about getting sth.; va.—བྱེད་ ¶ཁོས་ལས་ཀ་དེ་ཐོབ་ཤག་ཤག་བྱེད་ཀྱི་འདུག He is confident that he will get the job.

ཐོབ་གཤགས་ (tōbshaà) 1.sm. ཐོབ་ཤ་. 2. competing in verse/ song (usually between males and females).

ཐོབ་ཤོར་ (tōbshɔɔ) winning and losing.

ཐོབ་ཤོར་མེད་པ་ (tōbshɔɔ meèba) a draw, an event with no winners or losers.

ཐོབ་ཤོར་མཉམ་པ་ (tōbshɔɔ ñāmba) sm. ཐོབ་ཤོར་མེད་པ་.

ཐོབ་ས་ཐོབ་ཁུངས་ (tōbsa tōbguŋ) sm. ཐོབ་ཁུངས་.

ཐོབ་སེང་ (tōbseŋ) paid holiday.

ཐོམ་ཡོར་ (tōmyɔɔ) sm. འཐོམ་ཡོར་.

ཐོའི་སྒྲོ་ (tōdro) sm. ཐུགས་སྒྲོ་.

ཐོའི་ཕྲིལ་ (tōdree) sm. ཐུགས་ཕྲིལ་.

ཐོབས་ (tōb) imp. of འདེབས་.

ཐོམ་ (tōm) imp. of འདམ་.

ཐོམ་བུ་ (tōmbu) 1. wooden ladle. 2. utensils, pots, pans.

ཐོའན་ (tōan) sm. ཐོན་, 1.

ཐོའུ་ཀུན་ (tōu gen) sm. ཐུའུ་ཀུན་.

ཐོར་ (tɔ̄ɔ̄) p. of འཐོར་.

ཐོར་འབྱམས་དམག་མི་ (tɔ̄ɔ̄gyam mɔ̄ɔ̄mi) troops that have been scattered ¶ཐོར་འབྱམས་དམག་མི་ Troops that have been scattered (through defeat).

ཐོར་འགྲེམ་ (tɔ̄ndrem) scattering; va.—བྱེད་.

ཐོར་ཅོག (tɔ̄ɔ̄joò) hair worn in a bun; va.—རྒྱག.

ཐོར་ལྕོག (tɔ̄ɔ̄joò) sm. ཐོར་ཅོག.

ཐོར་ཆོས་ (tɔ̄ɔ̄jöö) 1. a short debating period in the morning in the monasteries. 2. a brief religious teaching.

ཐོར་དོ་ (tɔ̄rdo) sm. ཐོར་ཅོག.

ཐོར་ཐུན་ (tɔ̄rdün) dawn.

ཐོར་ཐོར་ (tɔ̄rdɔr) scattered, a few here and there ¶ས་ཆ་འདིར་བོད་པ་ཐར་ཐོར་ཞིག་ལས་མེད་པ་རེད་ In this area there are just a few scattered Tibetans.

ཐོར་སྡོད་ (tɔ̄ɔ̄ dö̀ö) va. to live scattered/ dispersed.

ཐོར་ནག (tɔ̄ɔ̄naà) black pimples.

ཐོར་ནད་ (tɔ̄ɔ̄nɛɛ̀) diseases characterized by pimples.

ཐོར་སྣམ་ (tɔ̄ɔ̄nam) Mongolian woolen cloth.

ཐོར་པ་ (tɔ̄ɔ̄ba) pimple; va.—སྐྱེས་ to get pimples; —ཡལ་ to have pimples disappear/ clear up.

ཐོར་པའི་སྨན་ (tɔ̄ɔ̄bɛ mɛ̄n) medicine for pimples.

ཐོར་འཕྲོ་ (tɔ̄ndro) the remains of sth. scattered/ destroyed, a remnant.

ཐོར་བུ་ (tɔ̄rbu) scattered, dispersed, a few here and there ¶ལུང་པ་འདིར་རྒྱ་མི་ཐོར་བུ་ཡོད་པ་རེད་ There are a few scattered Chinese in this area.

ཐོར་བུ་ཐོར་བུ་ (tɔ̄ɔ̄bu tɔ̄ɔ̄bu) sm. ཐ་རེ་ཐོ་རེ་.

ཐོར་འབུར་ (tɔ̄mbur) a skin disease characterized by pimples.

ཐོར་མ་ (tɔ̄ɔ̄ma) sm. ཐོར་བུ་.

ཐོར་མོ་ (tɔ̄ɔ̄mo) a two year old filly.

ཐོར་དམག (tɔ̄ɔ̄maà) troops that have been scattered.

ཐོར་ཙམ་ (tɔ̄ɔ̄dzam) sm. ཐ་རེ་ཐོ་རེ་.

ཐོར་ཙུགས་ (tɔ̄ɔ̄dzuù) sm. ཐོར་ཚུགས་.

ཐོར་རྩ་ (tɔ̄ɔ̄dza) hay fed to animals at dawn.

ཐོར་ཚུགས་ (tɔ̄ɔ̄dzuù) sm. ཐོར་ཅོག.

ཐོར་ཞིག (tɔ̄ɔ̄shiì) scattering, destroying; va.—གཏོང་.

ཐོར་ཡན་ (tɔ̄ɔ̄yɛn) a contagious disease that involves pimples.

ཐོར་བརླག (tɔ̄ɔ̄laà) sm. ཐོར་ཞིག.

ཐོར་ཞིག (tɔ̄ɔ̄shiì) failed, collapsed, crumbled, defeated ¶ང་ཚོའི་དམག་མིས་དགྲ་དམག་ཐོར་ཞིག་ཏུ་བཏང་བ་རེད་ Our soldiers destroyed the enemy troops.

ཐོར་ཟད་ (tɔ̄ɔ̄sɛɛ̀) exhausted, used up ¶ཕྲུ་གུ་འདིས་དངུལ་ཚང་མ་ཐོར་ཟད་དུ་བཏང་བཞག The child exhausted (spent) all the money.

ཐོར་རེ་གཏོང་ (tɔ̄ɔ̄re dōŋ) va. to scatter, to disperse.

ཐོར་རེ་བ་ (tōrewa) a few scattered.

ཐོལ་ (tȫȫ) suddenly.

ཐོལ་གྱིས་ (tȫȫgi) suddenly, all at once ¶ཁོ་ཐོལ་གྱིས་སླེབས་སོང་ He arrived suddenly.

ཐོལ་ཐོལ་ (tȫȫdöö) sm. ཐོལ་.

ཐོལ་བྱུང་ (tȫȫjuŋ) sudden.

ཐོལ་བྱུང་འགྱོད་བཤགས་ (tȫȫjuŋ gyȫȫshaà) sudden repentance.

ཐོས་ (tȫȫ) vi. to hear.

ཐོས་གྲོལ་ (tȫȫdröö) 1. being liberated from samsara when one hears a teaching. 2. name of a Ningma sect scripture.

ཐོས་རྒྱ་ཆེན་པོ་ (tȫȫgya cēmbo) 1. well read, learned, knowledgeable. 2. well informed.

ཐོས་རྒྱ་གོད་པོ་ (tȫȫgya gȫȫbo) sm. ཐོས་རྒྱ་ཆེན་པོ་.

ཐོས་རྒྱ་ཆུང་ཆུང་ (tȫȫgya cūŋjuŋ) 1. not well read, not learned. 2. not well informed.

ཐོས་དགའ་མཐོང་སྒྲོ་ (tȫȫga tōŋdro) being happy to see and hear; va.—བྱེད་.

ཐོས་ཆུང་ (tȫȫjuŋ) sm. ཐོས་རྒྱ་ཆུང་ཆུང་.

ཐོས་ལྡན་ (tōndɛn) sm. ཐོས་རྒྱ་ཆེན་པོ་.

ཐོས་ལྡན་པ་ (tȫȫdɛnba) scholar, pundit, learned person.

ཐོས་ལྡན་དབང་པོ་ (tȫȫdɛn wāŋbo) a great scholar or pundit.

ཐོས་ནོར་ (tȫȫnɔɔ) mishearing sth.

ཐོས་སྣང་ (tȫȫnaŋ) from what (I) heard ¶ངའི་ཐོས་སྣང་ལ་བོད་ནང་ཟིང་ཆ་ལངས་ཡོད་ཚོད་འདུག From what I heard, it seems that a disturbance has occurred in Tibet.

ཐོས་པ་དགའ་ (tȫȫbaga) Milarepa.

ཐོས་པ་བརྒྱ་ལས་མཐོང་བ་གཅིག་དགའ་ (tȫȫba gyalɛ tōŋba jīgga) a picture is worth a thousand words [Lit. one picture is better than a 100 things heard].

ཐོས་པ་ཅན་ (tȫȫbajɛn) sm. ཐོས་ལྡན་.

ཐོས་པ་ལས་བྱུང་བའི་ཤེས་རབ་ (tööbalɛ cu̱ŋwɛ shēèrəb) learned wisdom/ knowledge (in contrast to innate).

ཐོས་པའི་ཕ་རོལ་ཏུ་ཕྱིན་པ་ (tööbɛ pārööd̲u cīmbə) having reached the apex of religious studies.

ཐོས་པའི་ཤེས་རབ་ (tööbɛ shēèrəb) sm. ཐོས་པ་ལས་བྱུང་བའི་ཤེས་རབ་.

ཐོས་པའི་ཡོན་ཏན་ (tööbɛ yönd̲ɛn) sm. ཐོས་པ་ལས་བྱུང་བའི་ཤེས་རབ་.

ཐོས་པའི་ལམ་ (tööbɛ lām) a road/ path that one has heard of but not seen firsthand.

ཐོས་དབང་ (tööwaŋ) sm. ཐོས་ལྡན་དབང་པོ་.

ཐོས་བྱེད་ (tööjeè) poet. ears.

ཐོས་མང་ (tööma̱ŋ) sm. ཐོས་ལྡན་.

ཐོས་ཚད་ (töödzɛɛ̀) everything that (one) heard/ hears ། རང་གིས་ཐོས་ཚད་མི་གཞན་ལ་ཤོད་རྒྱུ་མེད་ One shouldn't tell others everything one hears.

ཐོས་ཚད་གཏམ་མིན་ མཐོང་ཚད་ཟས་མིན་ (töödzɛɛ̀ dāmmin tōŋdzɛɛ̀ sɛ̱ɛ̀min) don't take everything at face value [Lit. everything that (one) hears is not news, everything that one sees is not food].

ཐོས་ཚུལ་ (töödzüü) sm. ཐོས་སྣང་.

ཐོས་ཚོད་ (töödzöö) it's time to hear a reply/ response. ། ཡི་གེ་དེའི་སྐོར་གནས་ཚུལ་ཐོས་ཚོད་ཡིན་ནའང་ད་ལྟ་ཐོས་མ་བྱུང་ I should have heard sth. about that letter but as of now I have not heard anything.

ཐོས་ཚོར་ (töödzɔɔ) sense of hearing, auditory sense.

ཐོས་འཛིན་ (töndzin) the ear.

ཐོས་འཛིན་དབང་པོ་ (töndzin wāŋbo) the ear.

ཐོས་འཛིན་རྒྱབ་ཀྱི་ལྟུང་བུ་ (töndzin gya̱bgi lūŋbu) sm. རྣ་རྒྱབ་ཀྱི་ལྷག་པ་.

ཐོས་འཛིན་གསོས་ (töndzin söö) shung. pleasing to the ear.

ཐོས་ལོ་ (töölo) pretending to hear; va.—བྱེད་ to pretend to hear.

ཐོས་ཤུགས་ (tööshug) hearing ability.

ཐོས་བསམ་ (töösam) hearing and thinking.

ཐོས་བསམ་གྱི་གྲྭ་ (töösamgi tra̱) a dharma college/ center.

ཐོས་བསམ་གླིང་ (töösəmliŋ) a college in Tashilhunpo monastery.

ཐོས་བསམ་སྒོམ་གསུམ་ (töösam go̱msum) the three: hearing/ listening, thinking and meditating.

ཐོས་བསམ་སྒྲོ་འདོགས་ཆོད་པ་ (töösam drondɔɔ̀ cööba) hearing/ listening, thinking and clearing all doubts.

ཐོས་བསམ་ཕྱོགས་མེད་ (töösam cöömeè) hearing/ listening, thinking and making no distinctions (i.e., listening to all the doctrines).

ཐོས་བསམ་ཕྱོགས་རེ་བ་ (töösam cɔ̄ɔrewa) study (listening and thinking) in a partial fashion.

ཐོས་བསམ་སློབ་གཉེར་ (töösam lōbñer) hearing/ listening, thinking and studying (contemplating).

ཐོས་སོ་ཅོག (töösojoò) sm. ཐོས་ཚད་.

མཐག (tāà) shung. abbr. of ཉམ་ཐག.

མཐང་ (tāŋ) sm. མཐང་ག.

མཐང་ག (tāŋga) 1. the lower part. 2. female waistline.

མཐང་གོས་ (tāŋgöö) a skirt/ apron.

མཐང་སྦྲད་ (tāŋ drɛ̄ɛ̀) p. of མཐང་སྦྲོད་.

མཐང་སྦྲོད་ (tāŋ dröö) va. to have sexual intercourse.

མཐང་སྦྱར་ (tāŋ ja̱r) sm. མཐང་སྦྲོད་.

མཐང་ཤམ་ (tāŋsham) a skirt, a lower dress.

མཐའ་ (tā) limit, edge, end ། ས་ཞིང་གི་མཐའ་ The edge of the field.

མཐའ་ཀླས་ (tālɛɛ̀) sm. མཐའ་མེད་.

མཐའ་བཀག (tāgaà) insisting on one's opinion and not accepting other's opinions; va.—གཏོང་ ། རང་ཉིད་ཀྱིས་བཤད་པ་དེ་ར་མཐའ་བཀག་གཏོང་རྒྱུ་མེད་པར་གཞན་གྱི་བསམ་འཆར་ཉན་དགོས་ You should not insist on your own opinion but should listen to the opinions of others.

མཐའ་སྐྱུད་ (tāgüü) a hem on the edge.

མཐའ་སྐོར་ (tāgɔɔ) surrounding, encircling; va. མཐའ་སྐོར་; —བྱེད་ to surround; vi.—ཟིན་ to be/ get completely surrounded ། བྲོས་སའི་ལམ་མཐའ་སྐོར་གྱི་ནང་ནས་ཐད་དེ་བཅད་པ་རེད་ (They) completely cut off the escape route from all sides. ། དགྲ་ཚོས་མཐའ་བསྐོར་བ་རེད་ The enemy surrounded (them). 2. the outskirts of a place.

མཐའ་སྐོར་ནས་བཏེགས་པ་ (tāgɔɔne tēgba) helping from all sides/ in all ways [Lit. lifting from all around].

མཐའ་སྐོར་ཚར་གཅོད་ (tāgɔɔ tsārjöö) surrounding and then annihilating; va.—བྱེད་.

མཐའ་སྐོར་ལྡག་སྐོར་ (tāgɔɔ dāggɔɔ) sm. མཐའ་སྐོར་.

མཐའ་སྐོར་གཡུལ་ས་ (tāgɔɔ yüüsə) a battlefield that has been surrounded.

མཐའ་སྐོར་རི་སྐོར་ (tāgɔɔ rīgɔɔ) doing or getting sth. by all kinds of means/ methods/ strategies, to get by hook or by crook ། ཁོང་གིས་མཐའ་སྐོལ་རི་སྐོར་བཏང་ནས་ལས་ཀ་དེ་རག་པ་བྱུས་སོང་ He got that job using all kinds of means.

མཐའ་སྐྱེལ་ (tāgyeè) 1. completing, finishing, seeing to the end; va. མཐའ་སྐྱེལ་; —གཏོང་; —བྱེད་ ། ལས་ཀ་དེ་ཁག་པོ་ཡོད་ཀྱང་ཁོང་གིས་མཐའ་སྐྱེལ་བཏང་སོང་ Even though the work was difficult, he saw it through until the end. ། འདི་བྱེད་ཐབ་གྱི་མེད་ཅེས་མཐའ་སྐྱེལ་བཏང་བ་རེད་ (We) insisted until the end that we are unable to do this.

མཐའ་སྐྲོད་ (tādröö) driving out, expelling, evicting; va.—གཏོང་ ། བཙན་འཛུལ་པ་མཐའ་སྐྲོད་བཏང་བ་རེད་ (They) expelled the invaders.

མཐའ་བསྐོར་ (tāgɔɔ) sm. མཐའ་སྐོར་.

མཐའ་བསྐོར་རི་བསྐོར་ (tāgɔɔ ri̱gɔɔ) sm. མཐའ་སྐོར་.

མཐའ་བསྐྱལ་ (tāgyɛɛ) sm. མཐའ་སྐྱེལ་.

མཐའ་ཁུལ་ (tāgüü) frontier/ border region, boondocks.

མཐའ་འཁོབ་ (tāgob) 1. wilderness, boondocks. 2. uncivilized (place/country). 3. place where the dharma has not spread. 4. the borders of a (country, city, etc.).

མཐའ་འཁོབ་པ་ (tāgobbə) barbarian, hick.

མཐའ་འཁོར་ (tāgɔɔ) sm. མཐའ་སྐོར་.

མཐའ་འཁྱིར་ (tāgyir) around, surrounding.

མཐའ་འཁྱོངས་ (tāgyoŋ) sm. མཐའ་འཁྱོལ་.

མཐའ་འཁྱོལ་ (tāgyöö) seeing through to the end, carrying through to completion; vi. མཐའ་འཁྱོལ་; —བྱེད་ ། བར་ལམ་ང་ན་ནས་ལས་ཀ་དེ་མཐའ་འཁྱོལ་མ་སོང་ Recently I was ill and the work did not get finished.

མཐའ་གྲུ་ (tədru) outskirts, edge, fringe, border ། མཐའ་གྲུའི་ཞིང་ཡིན་ཕྱིན་སྟོན་ཐོག་ལེགས་པོ་མི་ཡོང་བ་ The fields that are on the fringe don't yield good crops.

མཐའ་གྲོགས་ (tādrɔɔ̀) lifelong partner/ spouse/ friend.

མཐའ་འགེགས་ (tāàgeg) deciding, settling; va.— བྱེད་.

མཐའ་འགྲིལ་ (tādrim) hem (of garments).

མཐའ་རྒྱན་ (tāgyɛn) the decorative border/ trim (of a Tibetan dress) that consist of valuable materials such as furs, brocade, etc.; va.—གཏོང་.

མཐའ་རྒྱལ་ཁམས་ (tā gyɛ̱ɛ̱gam) 1. adjacent/ neighboring/ surrounding countries. 2. nearby, surrounding places.

མཐའ་སྐོར་ (circumference) circumference ། འཛམ་གླིང་གི་མཐའ་སྐོར་ The circumference of the world.

མཐའ་སྒྲིལ་ (tā drii) va. to hem a garment.

མཐའ་ངན་ (tāŋɛn) treating badly, mistreating; va.—གཏོང་.

མཐའ་ངོས་ (tāŋöö) by the edge/ side of sth. (house, road, etc), outskirts.

མཐའ་ང་ (tā ŋā) sm. མཐའ་མཇུག.

མཐའ་ལྔ་དབྱིབས་ (tā ŋəyib) pentagonal (shape), a pentagon.

མཐའ་ཅན་ (tājɛn) 1. words with suffixed letters. 2. things that have endings/ an end ། མིའི་ཚེ་ནི་མཐའ་ཅན་ཞིག་རེད་ As for human life, it is sth. that has an end.

མཐའ་གཅིག (tājig) 1. one side. 2. sm. མཐའ་གཅིག་ཏུ་.

མཐའ་གཅིག་ཏུ་ (tā jīgdu) 1. consistently, always, continually ¶ དམར་པོའི་རིང་ལུགས་ལ་མཐའ་གཅིག་ཏུ་ངོ་རྒོལ་བྱེད་པའི་རྒྱལ་ཁབ་ Countries that consistently oppose communism. ¶ མི་དམངས་དང་མཐའ་གཅིག་ཏུ་མཛའ་བརྩེའི་འབྲེལ་བ་ཞིག་བཙུགས་ཡོད་པ་རེད་ (They) have always established friendly relations with the people. 2. completely, utterly, absolutely ¶ ང་ཚོའི་ཆོས་མཐའ་གཅིག་ཏུ་བསྐྱུར་ན་འགྲིགས་ཀྱི་རེད་དམ་ Is it right to completely cast aside our religion? 3. until the end, to the finish ¶ དམག་མ་ཐོབ་བར་མཐའ་གཅིག་ཏུ་རྒྱག་དགོས་ We must fight to the finish until we win the war.

མཐའ་གཅིག་པའི་རང་བཞིན་ (tā jībɛ ra̲ŋshin) absoluteness.

མཐའ་གཅོད་ (tā jö̀ö) sm. མཐའ་དཔྱོད་.

མཐའ་ཆགས་ (tā cāà) sm. མཐའ་འཁྱིལ་.

མཐའ་ཆུམས་ (tā cūm) va. to wind/ roll up from the end.

མཐའ་ཆོད་ (tāà cȫö) vi. to have doubts/ suspicions/ hesitations be cleared up.

མཐའ་འཇགས་ (tā ja̲à) sm. མཐའ་ཆགས་.

མཐའ་མཇུག (tə̄njuù) (in) the end, finally, in the future ¶ ཁྱེད་རང་གིས་ལས་ཀ་ངན་པ་དེ་འདྲ་བྱས་ན་མཐའ་མཇུག་ཡག་པོ་ཡོང་གི་མ་རེད་ If you do bad things like that in the end it will not turn out right.

མཐའ་མཇུག་ཏུ་ (tə̄njuùdu) in the end, finally, in the future.

མཐའ་མཇུག་བདེས་ (tə̄njuù d̲ɛ̀ɛ) va. to decide.

མཐའ་མཇུག་ཞུ་དག (tə̄njuù shu̲duù) the final proofreading.

མཐའ་གཉིས་ (tāñii) two extremes ¶ མཐའ་གཉིས་སྤངས་པའི་འཚོ་བ་སྐྱེལ་དགོས་པ་རེད་ One should seek one's livelihood in a manner that renounces extremes.

མཐའ་གཉིས་བྲལ་བ་ (tāñii tr̲ɛ̲ɛwa) separating from extremes, the middle path/ way.

མཐའ་གཉིས་སུ་གྱེས་ (tāñiisu gye̲è) va. to split into two extremes.

མཐའ་གཉིས་སྤང་བའི་སྤྱོད་པ་ (tāñiisu bāŋwɛ jö̀öba) behavior that has given up extremes.

མཐའ་གཉིས་སུ་ལྷུང་ (tāñiisu lhūŋ) vi. to fall into extremes.

མཐའ་མཉམ་པའི་དབྱིབས་ (tā ñāmbɛ yi̲b) having equal sides, equilateral shape (in math).

མཐའ་གདུགས་ (tāduù) in the end, in the long run ¶ ཚོང་འདི་གནས་སྐབས་ཁེ་བཟང་ཆེན་པོ་ཡོད་ན་ཡང་མཐའ་གདུགས་ནས་བཤད་ན་གྱོང་རག་གྱི་ཉེན་ཁ་ཡོད་པ་རེད་ Even though temporarily this sale will result in a big profit, in the long run, there is a danger it will create a loss.

མཐའ་རྟེན་ (tāden) suffixed (letters).

མཐའ་ལྷག (tādaà) second to last ¶ ཕྲུ་གུ་དེ་ཡིག་ཚད་གཏོང་མཁན་གྱི་དཀྱིལ་ནས་མཐའ་ལྷག་རེད་བཞག The child was second to last among those taking the exam.

མཐའ་བརྟེན་ (tāden) sm. མཐའ་སྐྱིལ་.

མཐའ་བརྟེན་པའི་ངང་ཚུལ་གཟི་ཅན་ (tādenbɛ ŋa̲ndzüü sij̲ɛn) shung. dignified in appearance ¶ རང་བཞིན་ཚུགས་སྦུབ་ཅིང་རྣམ་འགྱུར་མཐའ་བརྟེན་པའི་ངང་ཚུལ་གཟི་ཅན་ (He has) a dignified appearance and an easy manner.

མཐའ་ཐིག (tātig) the outer line.

མཐའ་ཐུམ་ (tādum) sm. མཐའ་འཁྱིལ་.

མཐའ་དག (tādaà) all, every ¶ གནམ་གྲུ་མཐའ་དག All the airplanes.

མཐའ་དག་པོ་ (tā da̲gbo) sm. ཁྲངས་དག་པོ་.

མཐའ་དོན་ (tādön) final point ¶ ཁོང་གི་གསུང་བཤད་ཀྱི་མཐའ་དོན་དུ་འགྲོ་བ་མིའི་ཐོབ་ཐང་སྐོར་གསུངས་སོང་ The final point of his speech was talking about human rights.

མཐའ་འདུམ་ (tāndum) the final arbitration/ mediation.

མཐའ་འདེད་ (tāndeè) 1. pursuing sth. in an insisting manner; va.—བྱེད་ ¶ ངས་ཁོང་ལ་བུ་ལོན་མཐའ་འདེད་བཏང་ནའང་སྤྲད་མ་བྱུང་ I pursued him insistently about atheloan but he didn't give me (payment).

མཐའ་འདུལ་གཙུག་ལག་ཁང་ (tādüü dzūglagaŋ) the four cathedrals built by King Songtsen Gampo.

མཐའ་སྡེམ་ (tādem) sm. མཐའ་བསྡོམས་.

མཐའ་འདོམས་ (tāndom) final conclusion/ decision ¶ དངོས་གནས་དག་འཛིར་གྱི་གནས་ཚུལ་རྫོང་སྡོད་དང་འདུ་ཤེའི་མཐའ་འདོམས་དང་འབྲེལ་བ་དགོས་རྒྱུ་ The Dzongpon and the people's representative should come to a final conclusion regarding the facts.

མཐའ་ལྡན་ (tādɛn) shung. sth. that has a border ¶ རྩིད་པའི་མཐའ་ལྡན་ཆེ་བ་གཉིས་ A skin rug with a border of red serge.

མཐའ་སྡོམ་ (tādom) sm. མཐའ་བསྡོམས་.

མཐའ་བསྡུས་ (tā dü̲ü) va. to complete, to wrap up ¶ ངའི་ལས་ཀའི་མཐའ་བསྡུས་ཚར་མ་སོང་ I have not completed my work.

མཐའ་བསྡོམས་ (tādom) final ¶ མཐའ་བསྡོམས་ཀྱི་གྲོས་ཆོད་ The final resolution.

མཐའ་བསྡོམས་གན་རྒྱ་ (tādom ke̲ngya) a final agreement.

མཐའ་ནན་ (tānɛn) doing sth. in an insisting manner ¶ ཁོས་ང་བྱེད་ཀྱི་མིན་ཞེར་མཐའ་ནན་སྨད་སོང་ He insisted, "I won't do it."

མཐའ་ནས་སྐོར་ (tānɛ gɔ̄ɔ) sm. མཐའ་སྐོར་.

མཐའ་སྣེ་ (tāne) edge/ end of sth. ¶ ཞིང་ཁའི་མཐའ་སྣེ་ The edge of the field.

མཐའ་པ་ (tāba) those who live on the outskirts of a place/ city/ town, etc.

མཐའ་དཔྱོད་ (tājöö) examining, inspecting; va.—བྱེད་ to examine, to inspect.

མཐའ་ཕུགས་ (tā pūù) in the end, finally, ultimately, in the long run.

མཐའ་ཕུད་ (tā būù) sm. མཐའ་འབུད་.

མཐའ་བེར་ (tāber) lassoing; va.—རྒྱག.

མཐའ་དབུས་ (tāwüü) the outskirts and the center of sth. (of a town, city, etc.).

མཐའ་འབུད་ (tābüü) banishing, exiling; va.—གཏོང་.

མཐའ་འབུད་ར་སྤྲུག (tābüü ra̲dröö) shung. bringing a matter to its final conclusion by a face-to-face confrontation (as in a court hearing).

མཐའ་འབྱམས་ (tājam) endless, boundless.

མཐའ་བྲལ་ (tātrɛɛ) sm. མཐའ་འབྱམས་.

མཐའ་འབྲས་ (tāndrɛɛ) final result, outcome.

མཐའ་མ་ (tāma) the end, the last, the final ¶ མཐའ་མའི་གནས་ཚུལ་ཐོན་པ་ཞིག་ནང་ In the final information that has come out.

མཐའ་མང་གི་དབྱིབས་ (tāmaŋgi yi̲b) many sided, polygonal, polygon.

མཐའ་མའི་རྒྱལ་ཁ་ (tāmɛ gye̲e̲ga) ultimate victory.

མཐའ་མའི་ཐ་ཚིག་བཅའ་ཡིག (tāmɛ tə̄dzii də̲yig) final ultimatum.

མཐའ་མའི་ཐག་གཅོད་བྱེད་ (tāmɛ tāgjö̀ö ce̲è) sm. ཐེང་ཐག་གཅོད་.

མཐའ་མའི་ནན་ཚིག་བཅའ་ཡིག (tāmɛ ne̲ndzig də̲yig) sm. མཐའ་མའི་ཐ་ཚིག་བཅའ་ཡིག.

མཐའ་མའི་འབྲས་བུ་ (tāmɛ dre̲ebu) final result.

མཐའ་མར་ (tāmaa) in the end, at last, finally ¶ ཁོང་ཚོས་ལོ་མང་འབད་བརྩོན་བྱས་ནས་མཐའ་མར་རྒྱལ་ཁ་ཐོབ་པ་རེད་ They persevered for many years and in the end they were victorious.

མཐའ་མི་ (tə̄mi) 1. people living on the border. 2. barbarian, hick.

མཐའ་མི་རྟོགས་ (tā mi̲dog) sm. མུ་མཐའ་མེད་པ་.

མཐའ་མེད་ (tāmeè) 1. sm. མཐའ་བྲལ་. 2. sm. ཡང་འཇུག་མེད་པ་.

མཐའ་མེད་མུ་མེད་ (tāmeè mu̲meè) endless and inexhaustible, infinite and boundless, without ends or borders.

མཐའ་བཙན་པོ་ (tā dzēmbo) stable, reliable, firmly based.

མཐའ་རྩ་བ་ (tādzwa) another name for ཕག་མོ་གྲུ་པ་.

མཐའ་ཚར་ (tādzar) a tassle.

མཐའ་མཚམས་ (tādzam) border, frontier, remote

area.

མཐའ་མཚམས་ས་ཐིག (tādzam sədig) border/ demarcation line between two countries/ areas.

མཐའ་གཞུག (tāshuŋ) in the end, at last, finally.

མཐའ་བཞི་ (tāshi) 1. the four ends, the four directions; everywhere ¶ མཐའ་བཞི་ལས་རྣམ་པར་རྒྱལ་བ་རེད་ (They) were victorious everywhere. 2. four year old horses (and mules).

མཐའ་རྫོགས་ (tā dzɔ̀ɔ) vi. to end, to be/ get worn out.

མཐའ་ཟད་ (tā sɛ̀ɛ) sm. མཐའ་རྫོགས་.

མཐའ་ཡུལ་ (tāyüü) a foreign country, a distant country.

མཐའ་ཡས་ (tāyɛ̀ɛ) sm. མཐའ་བྲལ་.

མཐའ་ཡས་རྒྱ་མཚོ་ (tāyɛɛ̀ gyadzo) the endless ocean.

མཐའ་ཡས་ཞིབ་ཕྲངས་ (tāyɛɛ̀ sīidraŋ) infinitely small, infinitesimal.

མཐའ་རུ་ (tāru) sm. མཐར་.

མཐའ་རིས་ (tārii) a line on the end/ edge.

མཐའ་ལ་ (tāla) sm. མཐར་.

མཐའ་ལ་བཀར་ (tāla gār) sm. སྣས་ལ་བཀར་.

མཐའ་ལ་ཐུག (tālə tūù) vi. to reach a limit, to come to the end (in the sense of a place) ¶ ཁོང་ཚོ་ཐེན་ཐེན་ནས་ས་མཚམས་ཀྱི་མཐའ་ལ་ཐུག་པ་རེད་ They went a long way and reached the end (the border). 2. vi. to reach the end of sth., to reach a limit ¶ དམག་མི་རྣམས་དམག་རྒྱགས་མཐའ་ལ་ཐུག་ནས་མགོ་བཏགས་ཞུས་པ་རེད་ The soldiers reached the limit of their supplies and surrendered.

མཐའ་ལ་མ་ཐུག་བར་ (tālə matugbar) to the end, until concluded ¶ ཁོ་ཚོས་མཐའ་ལ་མ་ཐུག་བར་དམག་བརྒྱབ་པ་རེད་ They fought the war until the end.

མཐའ་ལ་ཐུག་ཐུག་བར་ (tālə tūgduùbar) sm. མཐའ་ལ་མ་ཐུག་བར་.

མཐའ་ལ་རེག (tālə reg) vi. to touch the end/ edge of sth.

མཐའ་ལས་འདས་པ་ (tālɛɛ̀ dɛɛ̀ba) sm. མཐའ་ཡས་.

མཐའ་ཤ་ (tāsha) hem (of a garment).

མཐའ་ཤོག (tāshoò) back page.

མཐའ་སོ་ (tāso) molar tooth.

མཐའ་སྲུང་ (tāsuŋ) frontier/ border defence.

མཐའ་སྲུང་ཁྲུའུ་ (tāsuŋ trū) tib.ch. frontier department.

མཐའ་སྲུང་ནང་སྲུང་ (tāsuŋ naŋsuŋ) defending the frontier/ border, defending the heartland/ internal.

མཐའ་སྲུང་དམག་དཔུང་ (tāsuŋ məgbuŋ) frontier defense forces.

མཐའ་སྲུང་ནང་སྲུང་དམག་དཔུང་ (tāsuŋ məgbuŋ) frontier and internal defense/ defence forces.

མཐའ་སྲུང་ས་ཚིགས་ (tāsuŋ sədzii) frontier defense station.

མཐའ་གསལ་ (tāsɛɛ) (being) clear in the end; va.—གཏོང་ to make clear (in the end) ¶ བོད་དོན་བདེན་པ་མཐའ་གསལ་ཡོང་བའི་རེ་བ་ཡོད་ (I) hope the truth of the Tibetan cause will become clear in the end.

མཐའ་གསལ་རྒྱས་གཞོམས་ (tāsɛɛ gyɛɛ̀shom) shung. making sth. clear in the end.

མཐའ་གསལ་མཐིལ་མཐོང་ (tāsɛɛ tīidoŋ) 1. vi. to reveal/ expose sth. so that in the end it is clear ¶ ཁྱེད་རང་ལ་མ་ཉེས་ཁ་གཡོགས་ཡོག་པ་དེ་མཐའ་གསལ་མཐིལ་མཐོང་ཡོང་གི་རེད་ The false accusation of you will be exposed clearly in the end. 2. vi. to know completely and clearly.

མཐའ་གསེད་ནན་ཆགས་ (tāseè nenjaà) shung. giving a thorough explanation; va.—བྱེད་ ¶ ཁུར་ལེན་བྱེད་དགོས་ཚུལ་རྒྱ་མཚན་མཐའ་གསེད་ནན་ཆགས་བྱས་ཀྱང་ Even though I gave (him) a thorough explanation that he had to take the responsibility.

མཐའི་སོ་ཁ་སྲུང་ (tēsoka sūŋ) va. to guard/ protect the border/ frontiers.

མཐར་ (tār) in the end, finally, at last ¶ མཐར་ཁོ་ཚོ་དམག་བརྒྱབ་པ་རེད་ In the end, they went to war. ¶ མན་ཇུའི་དམག་ལ་འཐབ་རྒོལ་རིམ་བྱས་མཐར་ལྷོ་རྫོང་བར་ས་ལོན་ (They) fought a series of battles with the Manchu troops and in the end took the territory up to Lhozong.

མཐར་སྐྱེལ་ (tāā gyēē) 1. seeing through to the end/ completion, completing; va. མཐར་སྐྱེལ་; —གཏོང་ ¶ ཁོང་གིས་ལས་ཀ་དེ་མཐར་སྐྱེལ་བཏང་སོང་ He saw the work through to the end. 2. insisting; va.—གཏོང་ to insist on doing sth.; va.—ཤོད་ to speak in an insisting way.

མཐར་སྐྱོད་ (tāā drōò) sm. མཐའ་སྐྱོད་.

མཐར་སྐྱོད་གཏོང་བྱེད་གནམ་གྲུ་ (tāādröò dōŋjeè nəmdru) pursuit/ fighter plane.

མཐར་སྐྱོད་དམག་གྲུ་ (tāādröò məgdruù) destroyer (ship).

མཐར་འཁྱོལ་ (tāā kyōò) sm. མཐའ་འཁྱོལ་.

མཐར་འགྱུར་ (tā gyur) vi. to be or get finished/ completed.

མཐར་གྱིས་ (tārgi) gradually, by degrees/ stages, one after another ¶ མཐར་གྱིས་སློང་བའི་བསོད་སྙོམས་པ་ Monks who beg from house to house one after another.

མཐར་གྱིས་འཇོག (tārgi jɔ̀ɔ) va. to put in order, to put in sequence.

མཐར་ཆགས་ (tārjaà) sm. མཐར་གྱིས་.

མཐར་ཆགས་པར་ (tārjaàbar) sm. མཐར་གྱིས་.

མཐར་གདུགས་ (tārduù) sm. མཐའ་གདུགས་.

མཐར་ཐུག (tārduù) final, in the end, ultimate ¶ མཐར་ཐུག་གི་རྒྱལ་ཁ་ཡོང་གི་རེད་ The final victory will come.

མཐར་ཐུག་གི་ཐག་གཅོད་ (tārduùgi tāàjöò) final decision.

མཐར་ཐུག་གི་དམིགས་ཡུལ་ (tārduùgi mīgyüü) final end/ goal/ objective.

མཐར་ཐུག་རྙེད་དོན་ (tārdug ñēèdön) the final findings.

མཐར་ཐུག་ཏུ་ (tārdugdu) sm. མཐར་ཐུག.

མཐར་ཐུག་བསྡོམས་དོན་ (tārdug domdön) the future outcome/ conclusion.

མཐར་ཐུག་པ་ (tārdugba) the final/ ultimate one ¶ སློབ་ཕྲུག་ཚོའི་སློབ་སྦྱོང་ཡག་པོ་མེད་པའི་རྒྱུ་རྐྱེན་མཐར་ཐུག་པ་དེ་དགེ་རྒན་རེད་ The one finally responsible for the students not studying well is the teacher.

མཐར་ཐུག་ས་ (tārdugsə) terminal point, final place/ destination, finish.

མཐར་ཐོ་ (tārdo) a blacksmith's tool.

མཐར་ཐོན་ (tārdön) sm. མཐར་ཕྱིན་.

མཐར་འདེད་ཞི་བསྐྱེད་ (tāndeè shegyeè) shung. being always diligent ¶ སྐུ་ཡོན་གསན་བཞིན་ཐོག་མཐར་འདེད་ཞི་བསྐྱེད་གནང་བའི་འབྲས་བུ་མི་དམན་པ་བྱུང་ Concering his knowledge, he got a good result because he has been consistently diligent.

མཐར་ནན་ (tārnɛn) sm. མཐའ་ནན་.

མཐར་སྐྱུག (tārjuù) sm. མཐར་སྐྱོད་.

མཐར་ཕུར་ (tārbur) sm. མཐར་སྐོར་.

མཐར་ཕྱིན་ (tārjin) thoroughly, completely, exhaustively; va.—བྱེད་; —དུ་གཏོང་; —བསྒར་ to carry through or see to completion/ the end; va.—བསྒྱུར་ to change completely/ radically ¶ རིའི་རྩེར་མཐར་ཕྱིན་འཛེགས་ཐུབ་པ་རེད་ (They) were able to climb completely to the peak of the mountain. ¶ ཞིབ་འཇུག་མཐར་ཕྱིན་ན་ཡག་པོ་ཡོང་གི་རེད་ If the research is carried through to its completion, it will be good.

མཐར་ཕྱིན་པར་ (tār cīmbə) completely, thoroughly, exhaustively ¶ དགྲ་བོར་ཕམ་ཉེས་མཐར་ཕྱིན་པ་བྱུང་བ་རེད་ The enemy was completely defeated.

མཐར་ཕྱིན་སློབ་མ་ (tārjin lōbma) a graduate.

མཐར་བྱེད་ (tār ceè) 1. va. to kill. 2. poet. the lord of the dead.

མཐར་འབྱོལ་ (tār jöö) va. to flee /run away.

མཐར་སོན་ (tārsön) acme, pinnacle, the best; va.—བྱེད་ to do the best ¶ བྱམས་བརྩེ་མཐར་སོན་བྱེད་ Acting with the best love.

མཐར་སོན་པ་ (tārsömba) sm. མཐར་ཕྱིན་པ་.

མཐར་སླེབ་ས་ཚིགས་ (tārleb sədzii) station terminal, final station.

མཐར་ལྷུང་ (tār lhūŋ) vi. to fall into decay, to fall on bad times, to become the worst, to degenerate, to deteriorate.

མཐས་ཀླས་ (tɛ̄ɛ̀lɛɛ̀) without limits, boundless.

མཐས་གདུགས་ (tɛ̄ɛ̀dug) sm. མཐས་ཀླས་.

མཐིང་ (tīŋ) sky blue, azure.

མཐིང་སྐྱ་ (tīŋgya) light blue.

མཐིང་ཁ་ (tīŋgə) blue color.

མཐིང་ཁྲ་ (tīŋdrə) a blue design with white patterns.

མཐིང་ག (tīŋgə) sm. མཐིང་ཁ་.

མཐིང་གི་ཞལ་བཟང་མ་ (tīŋgi sheesaŋma) one of the female goddesses also known as ཚེ་རིང་མཆེད་ལྔ་.

མཐིང་རྒྱུས་ (tīŋgyüü) type of traditional medicine made from minerals.

མཐིང་སྔོན་ (tīŋŋön) indigo (blue).

མཐིང་ཆེན་ (tīŋjen) a blue mineral dye.

མཐིང་མདོག (tīŋdɔɔ̀) blue color.

མཐིང་རྡོ་ (tīŋdo) a stone that produces a blue dye.

མཐིང་ནག (tīŋnaà) dark blue.

མཐིང་ཞུན་ (tīŋshün) a liquid blue dye.

མཐིང་རིལ་ (tīŋrii) sm. ཐིང་རིལ་.

མཐིང་རིལ་རྒྱ་མོ་ (tīŋrii gyamo) sm. ཐིང་རིལ་.

མཐིང་རིལ་མཆུ་ (tīŋrii cū) a small, slender pincer/ tweezer used by Tibetan doctors to extract small items such as thorns, splinters.

མཐིང་ཤིང་ (tīŋshiŋ) a plant that produces blue dye.

མཐིང་ཤོག (tīŋshoò) blue paper on which scriptures are written in gold.

མཐིལ་ (tīī) 1. bottom, lowest part. 2. palm, sole ། ལག་མཐིལ་ Palm of the hand. 3. middle, center ། ང་གྲོང་ཁྱེར་མཐིལ་ལ་བསྡད་ཡོད་ I live in the center the city. 4. floor, ground ། ཁང་པའི་མཐིལ་ལ་པང་གཅལ་བཏིངས་བཞག (They) have laid wooden planks on the floor of the house.

མཐིལ་ཀོ་ (tīīgɔɔ) leather sole of shoes/ boots.

མཐིལ་རྟོགས་ (tīī dɔ̄ɔ̀) va. to completely know/ understand, to understand the real situation ། ང་ཚོས་ཁོ་ཚོའི་གནས་ཚུལ་རྣམས་མཐིལ་རྟོགས་པ་ཞིག་བྱུང་སོང་ We completely understood their circumstances [Lit. understanding the bottom].

མཐིལ་རྡོལ་ (tīī dȫȫ) 1. va. to expose, to lay bare, to poke a hole in ། ཁོ་ཚོའི་སྲིད་ཇུས་ཀྱི་མཐིལ་མཐར་ཕྱིན་པར་བརྡོལ་བ་རེད་ (They) completely exposed their strategy. 2. va. to make a hole in the bottom of sth.

མཐིལ་སྟོན་ (tīī dȫn) sm. མཐིལ་འདོན་.

མཐིལ་བརྡོལ་ (tīī dȫȫ) p. of མཐིལ་རྡོལ་.

མཐིལ་བདེ་ཁྲོ་ཐབ་ལས་ཚན་ (tīīde trōdəb lɛ̱ɛ̀dzɛn) open-hearth workshop.

མཐིལ་འདིང་ (tīī di̱ŋ) va. to spread/ lay out (a floor) ། ཁང་པའི་ནང་ཞལ་བའི་མཐིལ་བཏིངས་འདུག (They) have laid down a floor in the house.

མཐིལ་འདོན་ (tīīdön) exposing, revealing, laying bare; va. མཐིལ་འདོན་; —བྱེད་ to expose/ reveal, to lay bare.

མཐིལ་རྡོལ་ (tīī dö̱ö̱) vi. to be or get exposed/ revealed, to be or get laid bare ། གསང་བའི་རྩ་འཛུགས་མཐིལ་བརྡོལ་བ་རེད་ The secret association was exposed. 2. vi. to get ruptured/ punctured, to get a hole ། ཁོག་མའི་མཐིལ་རྡོལ་བཞག The bottom of the pot got a hole.

མཐིལ་བརྡོལ་ (tīī dö̱ö̱) 1. sm. མཐིལ་རྡོལ་. 2. p. of མཐིལ་རྡོལ་.

མཐིལ་མཐའ་ (tīīda) bottom and edge.

མཐིལ་དྲེག (tīīdreg) the dirt/ soot at the bottom of kettles, pots, pans.

མཐིལ་པང་ (tīībaŋ) the bottom part/ plank of a box.

མཐིལ་ཕྱིན་ (tīījin) sm.མཐར་ཕྱིན་པ་.

མཐིལ་ཕྱིན་རྟོགས་ (tīījin dɔ̄ɔ̀) va. to understand completely.

མཐིལ་ཕྱིན་པར་ (tīījinbar) sm. མཐར་ཕྱིན་པར་.

མཐིལ་མི་རེག་པ་ (tīī mi̱regba) sm. མཐིལ་མེད་.

མཐིལ་མེད་ (tīīmeè) bottomless, extremely deep.

མཐིལ་ཞལ་ (tīīshɛɛ) floor, floor coating (e.g., cement).

མཐིལ་ལེབ་ (tīīleb) flat bottom.

མཐིལ་ལོན་ (tīī lön) sm. མཐིལ་རྟོགས་.

མཐིལ་ཤིང་ (tīīshiŋ) sm. པང་གཅལ་.

མཐིལ་ལྷམ་ (tīīlham) slippers.

མཐིལ་ལྷན་ (tīīlhɛn) patch on the sole of a shoe/ boot.

མཐུ་ (tū) 1. power, strength, force. 2. curse, spell, sorcery, black magic; va.—རྒྱག to curse, to put a spell, to cast a spell or do sorcery ། དགྲ་བོར་མཐུ་བརྒྱབ་པ་རེད་ (He) cast a spell on the enemy.

མཐུ་རྒྱག་མཁན་ (tūgyaàñɛn) a person who casts spells or does sorcery.

མཐུ་ངན་ (tūŋɛn) sm. མཐུ་, 2.

མཐུ་སྔགས་ (tūŋaà) a mantric curse/ spell/ black magic; va.—རྒྱག.

མཐུ་ཆེན་ (tūjen) 1. very effective/ powerful. 2. a powerful curse/ spell.

མཐུ་གཏད་ (tūdɛɛ̀) sm. མཐུ་, 2.

མཐུ་སྟོབས་ (tūdob) 1. power, strength, force ། དེང་རབས་མཚོན་ཆའི་མཐུ་སྟོབས་ཀྱིས་དགྲ་བོ་གཏོར་ཕམ་བཏང་བ་རེད་ (They) defeated the enemy through the power of modern weapons. 2. the strength/ power/ force of a curse or spell or black magic.

མཐུ་ཐབས་ (tūdəb) methods of making curses/ doing black magic.

མཐུ་ཐོབ་ (tū tōb) 1. vi. to get energy/ power. 2. name of a Buddha.

མཐུ་དམ་པ་ (tū d̲amba) best energy/ power.

མཐུ་བསྡོངས་དཔུང་བསྡོངས་ (tūdoŋ būŋdoŋ) fighting in unison/ collectively.

མཐུ་ནུས་ (tūnüü) sm. མཐུ་སྟོབས་.

མཐུ་ལྡན་ (tūdɛn) powerful, strong.

མཐུ་པ་ (tūbə) sm. མཐུ་རྒྱག་མཁན་.

མཐུ་དཔལ་ (tūbɛɛ) 1. power and glory. 2. name of a Buddha.

མཐུ་སྤྱོད་ (tūjöö) the activities involved in making a curse/ black magic.

མཐུ་བྱད་ (tūjɛɛ̀) sm. མཐུ་, 3.

མཐུ་བྲི་ (tū tri̱) vi. to deteriorate/ decline/ decrease in energy or strength.

མཐུ་མེད་ (tūmeè) 1. powerless, feeble, weak 2. (neg. + vb. + —) no choice but to do sth. ། ངའི་གཞུང་གིས་གྲོས་མཐུན་དེ་ར་ཆ་འཛིན་མི་བྱེད་མཐུ་མེད་བྱུང་ My government had no choice but to abide by that agreement.

མཐུ་རྩལ་ (tūdzɛɛ) power, strength; va.—འགྲན་ to compete to see who is stronger; va.—འདོན་ to use one's power/ strength/ skill ། ལས་གྲྭ་དབུ་ཆེན་ཚོས་མཐུ་རྩལ་བཏོན་ནས་ཟམ་ཆེན་དེ་བརྒྱབ་པ་རེད་ The engineers used their skill to build a big bridge.

མཐུ་གཞུང་ (tūshuŋ) the text of a curse/ black magic spell.

མཐུ་ཡིས་ (tūyii) sm. མཐུས་.

མཐུ་ཡོད་པ་ (tū yö̱öba) effective, potent, efficacious.

མཐུག (tūg) abbr. of མཐུག་པོ་.

མཐུག་རྔམས་ (tūgŋam) the height of sth. ། ལྕགས་རི་འདི་མཐུག་རྔམས་ཆེན་པོ་འདུག The height of the wall is big.

མཐུག་འདེབས་ (tūgdeb) close/ thick sowing (of seed); va.—བྱེད་.

མཐུག་པ་ (tūgbə) sm. མཐུག་པོ་.

མཐུག་པོ་ (tūgbu) 1. thick ། པགས་པ་མཐུག་པོ་ Thick skin. 2. deep (usu. with sleep) ། གཉིད་མཐུག་པོ་ཁུག་པ་རེད་ (He) fell into a deep sleep. 3. thick, dense ། ཤིང་ནགས་མཐུག་པོའི་ནང་ལ་ In a dense forest.

མཐུག་འཕྲི་སྲབ་སྣོན་ (tūgdri drəbnön) equalizing, balancing; va.—བྱེད་ to equalize/ balance [Lit. reduce the thick and augment the thin].

མཐུག་སྨུག (tūgmug) thick/ dense fog.

མཐུག་ཚད་ (tūgdzɛɛ̀) thickness, density ། ཁོང་གིས་དབུ་ལོག་མཐུག་ཚད་རན་པོ་ཞིག་གྱོན་བཞག He is wearing clothes that are just the right thickness.

མཐུག་འཛུགས་ (tūgdzuù) sm. མཐུག་འདེབས་.

མཐུད་ (tüü) 1. va. to make up a shortage ། ངས་ལས་

ཀ་ཉིན་གྲངས་ཆད་པ་རྣམས་མཐུད་ཐུབ་པ་བྱུང་སོང་ I was able to make up the work days that I was short. 2. va. to join two ends, to piece together, to graft. 3. sm. མཐུད་ནས. 4. continued ། པར་ངོས་དང་པོར་མཐུད་ Continued from page one.

མཐུད་ཀ (tüügə) sm. མཐུད་ཁ.

མཐུད་སྐྱོན་ (tüü gyön) h. of མཐུད་རྒྱག.

མཐུད་ཁ (tüügə) 1. the point where two things join; va.—སྦྱོར་; —འགྲིག to join the ends of two things together (so there is no space between them) ། སྒམ་གྱི་པང་ལེབ་མཐུད་ཁ་འགྲིགས་པོ་བྱུང་མི་འདུག The planks of the box were not properly joined together. 2. alleviating a defect, making up or conveying that sth. is short; va.—རྒྱག. ། ངའི་ཕོགས་མ་རག་བར་ང་ལ་འགྲོ་སོང་མཐུད་ཁ་རྒྱག་ཡས་དངུལ་ཕྲན་བུ་གཡར་རོགས་གནང་ Please lend me a little money to cover my expenses until I get my salary.

མཐུད་རྒྱག (tüü gyaà) see མཐུད་.

མཐུད་རྒྱུག་དབྱུག་པ (tüügyuù yügbə) baton/ stick used in relay races.

མཐུད་རྒྱུག་རྩལ་འགྲན (tüügyuù dzεεdrεn) relay race; va.—བྱེད་.

མཐུད་བསྒྲིགས (tüüdrig) putting together, combining; va.—བྱེད་ ། ཁོང་གིས་སྒྲུང་ཐུང་མང་པོ་མཐུད་སྒྲིག་བྱས་ནས་དེབ་ཅིག་བཟོས་བཞག He put together many of his short stories and made a book.

མཐུད་རྟགས (tüüdaà) hyphen.

མཐུད་དམ (tüüdam) shung. the seal placed on official documents where a new page has been joined to an old one to extend the document; va.—རྒྱག.

མཐུད་ནས (tüünε) continuing, following ། རྩོམ་ཡིག་དེ་ཁ་སའི་ཚགས་པར་ལ་མཐུད་ནས་བཀོད་བཞག This article is a continuation from yesterday's newspaper.

མཐུད་པ (tüübə) joined, attached, connected ། ཐག་པ་མཐུད་པ་དེ་འཁྱེར་ཤོག Bring the ropes that were joined together.

མཐུད་བྱེད་འཕྲུལ་འཁོར (tüüjeè trüügɔɔ) machine for joining things together.

མཐུད་སྦྱོར (tüüjɔɔ) joining together, grafting; va.—བྱེད་ ། ཤོག་བུ་གཉིས་མཐུད་སྦྱོར་བརྒྱབ་བཞག (He) joined two pieces of paper together.

མཐུད་མ (tüümə) 1. replacement (items) ། འཕྲུལ་འཁོར་མཐུད་མ་ཞིག་དགོས (We) need a replacement machine. 2. patch (for a rip, hole); va.—རྒྱག to patch. 3. va. to lengthen pants, coats, etc.; va.—རྒྱག.

མཐུད་དམག (tüümaà) reinforcement/ replacement soldiers.

མཐུད་ཚབ (tüüdzəb) 1. sm. མཐུད་མ. 2. substitute, fill-in, replacement; va.—བྱེད་ ། ལས་བྱེད་རྣམ་ཡོལ་དུ་ཕྱིན་པའི་མཐུད་ཚབ་ཅིག་དགོས་ཀྱི་འདུག (We) need an official to replace the one that retired.

མཐུད་མཚམས (tüündzam) the point/ space where two things are joined/ connected/ attached.

མཐུད་འཛིན་ (tüü dzin) shung. va. to continue to hold a post or title.

མཐུད་འདུགས་གཉིས་སྨིན་འབྲས (tüü dzugñii mindrεε) rice that can be double cropped.

མཐུད་སྲུང་ (tüüsuŋ) relieving sb. on guard/ watch; va.—བྱེད་ to take over/ relieve sb. on guard duty.

མཐུན་ (tün) vi. to be in harmony, to be compatible, to be in accord/ agreement with ། འདི་ནི་འཛམ་གླིང་ཞི་བདེའི་ཁེ་ཕན་དང་ཡང་མཐུན་པ་རེད་ It is also in accord with the benefits of world peace.

མཐུན་རྐྱེན་ (tüngyen) 1. good/ harmonious conditions; vi.—འཛོམས་ to be in a state of having good conditions for sth.; va.—བཟོ་ to make conditions appropriate for doing sth. ། ཐོན་སྐྱེད་ཡར་རྒྱས་གཏོང་བར་ཞིང་ཆུ་སྦྱོར་ལུད་སོགས་ཀྱི་མཐུན་རྐྱེན་དགོས་ཀྱི་རེད་ One needs good conditions such as irrigation water and fertilizer in order to improve production. ། གནད་དོན་འདི་ཐག་གཅོད་བྱེད་པའི་མཐུན་རྐྱེན་བཟོས་པ་རེད་ (They) made the conditions (needed) for settling that question (issue). 2. helpful for doing sth. ། རྒྱ་ཡིག་ཤེས་ན་དབྱིན་ཇི་བོད་སྐད་དུ་སྒྱུར་རྒྱུའི་མཐུན་རྐྱེན་དུ་འགྱུར་གྱི་རེད་ If you know Chinese, it will be helpful for translating English to Tibetan.

མཐུན་རྐྱེན་གྲ་སྒྲིག (tüngyen trədrii) making necessary arrangements, preparing conditions for sth.; va.—བྱེད་ ། ཕྱི་རྒྱལ་གྱི་ཡུལ་སྐོར་བ་མ་ཡོང་གོང་མཐུན་རྐྱེན་གྲ་སྒྲིག་ཡག་པོ་བྱེད་དགོས་ (We) must create good conditions before the foreign tourists come.

མཐུན་རྐྱེན་ཕོགས་དངུལ (tüngyen pööŋüü) scholarship, fellowship.

མཐུན་རྐྱེན་ཞལ་འདེབས (tüngyen shendeb) donation.

མཐུན་རྐྱེན་འཛོམས (tüngyen dzom) see མཐུན་རྐྱེན་.

མཐུན་རྐྱེན་འཛོམས་པོ་ (tüngyen dzombo) a state in which conditions are good/ complete/ abundant ། ལུང་པ་འདི་རྩྭ་ཆུ་མཐུན་རྐྱེན་འཛོམས་པོ་འདུག This place is abundant in grass and water.

མཐུན་རྐྱེན་བཟོ་ (tüngyen so) see མཐུན་རྐྱེན་.

མཐུན་གྲུབ (tündrub) shung. an agreement ། ཚང་མས་མཐུན་གྲུབ་གན་རྒྱ་བཞག་པ་ All of them signed an agreement.

མཐུན་གྲོགས (tündrɔɔ) friend; va.—བྱེད་ to make friends, to act as a friend.

མཐུན་གྲོགས་རྒྱལ་ཁབ (tündrɔɔ gyεεgəb) an ally, a friendly nation.

མཐུན་གྲོགས་ཚོགས་པ (tündrɔɔ tsɔgbə) a club.

མཐུན་གྲོགས་བཟང་སྐྱོར (tündrɔɔ sanjɔɔ) friendly help/ support.

མཐུན་གྲོས (tündröö) 1. negotiating, consulting, deliberating, discussing; va.—བྱེད་. 2. an agreement; va.—འཛུགས to make an agreement ། རྒྱལ་ཁབ་གཉིས་དབར་ས་མཚམས་ཀྱི་སྐོར་མཐུན་གྲོས་བཞག་ཡོད་པ་རེད་ The two countries have made an agreement regarding the border. ། རྒྱལ་ཁབ་གཉིས་པོས་ས་མཚམས་སྐོར་མཐུན་གྲོས་བྱེད་བཞིན་པ་རེད་ The two countries are in the process of negotiating concerning the border.

མཐུན་གྲོས་ཆིངས་ཡིག (tündröö ciŋyii) treaty (mutually agreed upon).

མཐུན་གྲོས་ཆོད་ཡིག (tündröö cööyii) agreement, accord (mutually agreed upon).

མཐུན་འགྱུར (tüngyur) help, support.

མཐུན་འགྱུར་གང་ཆེ (tüngyur kaŋce) shung. helping/ supporting/ being in harmony as much as one can or as much as is possible ། ལས་བྱེད་ནང་ཁུལ་མཐུན་འགྱུར་གང་ཆེ་དགོས་གནས་ལ་བརྟེན་ The officials should help each other and live in harmony as much as is possible.

མཐུན་འགྱུར་ཡི་གེ (tüngyur yigi) letter of recommendation.

མཐུན་འགྲིག (tündrig) reconciling differences, becoming harmonious/ friendly; va.—བྱེད་ ། བཟའ་ཚང་ཁ་ལོག་གར་བྱས་པ་དེ་ཡང་སྐྱར་མཐུན་འགྲིག་བྱུང་བཞག The couple that was separated has reconciled (their differences and become harmonious again).

མཐུན་སྒྲིལ (tündrii) 1. unity; va.—བྱེད་ to act/ be unified, to unite ། མཐུན་སྒྲིལ་གྱིས་ཞི་བདེ་སྲུང་སྐྱོབ་བྱེད་དགོས་ We must defend peace through unity. ། འཛམ་གླིང་ཡོངས་ཀྱི་མི་དམངས་རྣམས་མཐུན་སྒྲིལ་བྱས་ནས་ All the people of the world, having united. 2. harmony, friendship, good relations, getting along well ། ཁོང་དང་ང་མཐུན་སྒྲིལ་ཡག་པོ་མེད་ He and I do not get along well.

མཐུན་སྒྲིལ་སྐྱོན་བརྗོད་མཐུན་སྒྲིལ (tündrii gyönjöö tündrii) unity-criticism-unity (for the purpose of unity, criticism; from out of criticism, unity) (political slogan).

མཐུན་སྒྲིལ་འཐབ་རྩོད (tündrii təbdzöö) united struggle.

མཐུན་སྒྲིལ་མེད་པ (tündrii meeba) disunified, discordant.

མཐུན་སྒྲིལ་ལས་སྐྱོང་ལྷན་ཚོགས (tündrii lεεgyoŋ

lhɛ̄ndzɔ̄ɔ) solidarity council.

མཐུན་སྒྲིལ་ལས་འཛིན་ཨུ་ཡོན་ལྷན་ཚོགས་ (tü̃ndrii lɛ̱̀ndzin ūyön lhɛ̄ndzɔ̄ɔ) sm. མཐུན་སྒྲིལ་ལས་སྐྱོང་ལྷན་ཚོགས་.

མཐུན་སྒྲིལ་ཤོག་ཁག (tü̃ndrii shɔ̄gaà) group of allies, alliance.

མཐུན་སྒྲིལ་ཤོག་ཁག་ཆེན་པོ་ (tü̃ndrii shɔ̄gaà cēmbo) the great alliance.

མཐུན་ཆ་ (tü̃nja) (དང་ + —) in agreement/ conformity/ harmony ¶ འདི་ནི་དེང་དུས་ཀྱི་སྤྱི་ཚོགས་དང་མཐུན་ཆ་རེད་ This is in conformity with modern society.

མཐུན་འཇུག (tü̃njuù) acting to have or make good / harmonious/ cordial relations with sb.; va.—བྱེད་ ¶ ངས་ལས་ཁུངས་ནང་གི་ལས་བྱེད་པ་ཚང་མ་དང་མཐུན་འཇུག་བྱེད་ཀྱི་ཡོད་ I am trying to have good relations with all the officials in the office. ¶ ལས་བྱེད་ནང་ཁུལ་མ་མཐུན་པ་རྣམས་ངས་མཐུན་འཇུག་བྱེད་ཀྱི་ཡོད་ (I am) trying to bring about good relations between the officials in the office who are not on friendly terms.

མཐུན་ཉེ་ (tü̃ñe) close/ friendly (in relations); va.—གཏོང་ to establish close/ friendly relations.

མཐུན་ཐབས་ (tü̃ndəb) reconciliation, making harmonious/ friendly; va.—བྱེད་ to reconcile, to bring about harmony/ agreement ¶ མེ་དང་སྤྲ་ལྟར་མཐུན་ཐབས་བྱེད་ཐུབ་ཀྱི་མ་རེད་ Like fire and hair, we are unable to make friendly relations (between them).

མཐུན་ཐབས་བྲལ་ (tü̃ndəb trɛ̱ɛ) sm. མཐུན་ཐབས་མེད་པ་.

མཐུན་ཐབས་མེད་པ་ (tü̃ndəb mèeba) irreconcilable, uncompromisable, withou a way to have friendly relations ¶ འགལ་བ་འདི་མཐུན་ཐབས་མེད་པ་ཞིག་རེད་ This is an irreconcilable contradiction.

མཐུན་ཐབས་ཡོད་པ་ (tü̃ndəb yööba) reconcilable, compromisable.

མཐུན་འཐབ་ (tü̃ndəb) friendly relations and hostile/ fighting relations.

མཐུན་འདུམ་ (tü̃ndum) mediation, mediating; va.—བྱེད་ ¶ ཁྱིམ་ཚང་དེ་གཉིས་དབར་ངས་མཐུན་འདུམ་བྱས་པ་ཡིན་ I mediated between those two families.

མཐུན་སྡེབ་ (tü̃ndeb) being friendly and hanging around together; va.—བྱེད་ ¶ ང་ཚོ་མི་ཚང་གཉིས་ཀྱི་ཕྲུ་གུ་ཚོ་རྟག་པར་མཐུན་སྡེབ་བྱེད་ཀྱི་ཡོད་པ་རེད་ The children of our two households are friendly and always hang around together.

མཐུན་སྣེ་གདུགས་ (tü̃nne dūù) 1. va. to bring discordant sides together ¶ ཁོང་གི་རྒྱལ་ཁབ་གཉིས་ཀྱི་རྩོད་རྙོག་ཐག་གཅོད་བྱ་རྒྱུའི་མཐུན་སྣེ་གདུགས་པ་རེད་ He is bringing the two countries who have a dispute together to settle their differences.

མཐུན་པ་ (tü̃mbə) 1. sm. མཐུན་ཆ་. 2. suitable, appropriate, proper ¶ ལས་ཀ་མཐུན་པ་ Suitable work.

མཐུན་པ་སྤུན་བཞི་ (tü̃mbə bü̃nshi) the four animals that symbolize friendship: elephant, monkey, hare and bird.

མཐུན་པ་འབྱེད་པར་བྱེད་ (tü̃mbə je̱ebar cɛ̱ɛ̀) va. to cause or instigate a break or disruption in sb's friendly relations.

མཐུན་པའི་ཆོས་ (tü̃mbɛ cö̀ö) things that are in harmony.

མཐུན་པའི་བུམ་པ་ (tü̃mbɛ pu̱mbə) cupping jar.

མཐུན་པའི་རང་བཞིན་ (tü̃mbɛ ra̱ŋshiŋ) compatibility, harmonious.

མཐུན་པའི་རླུང་ (tü̃mbɛ lūŋ) favorable wind.

མཐུན་པར་བྱེད་ (tü̃mbar ce̱è) 1. va. to act in harmony/ friendship ¶ བར་འདུམ་བྱས་རྗེས་ཕྱོགས་གཉིས་མཐུན་པར་བྱས་པ་རེད་ After the mediation, the two sides acted in a friendly manner. 2. sm. མཐུན་འཇུག་བྱེད་.

མཐུན་པོ་ (tü̃mbu) friendly, compatible, harmonious; va.—བྱེད་ ¶ ཁོ་ཚོ་མཐུན་པོ་ཡོད་པ་རེད་ They are friendly. ¶ ཚོས་གཞི་འདི་གཉིས་མཐུན་པོ་འདུག These two colors are compatible.

མཐུན་དཔུང་རྒྱལ་ཁབ་ (tü̃mbuŋ gyɛ̱ɛgəb) 1. allied countries. 2. the "Allies" (in WW II).

མཐུན་ཕྱོགས་ (tü̃njɔ̄ɔ) 1. friendly, amiable, getting along ¶ མི་ཚང་འདི་གཉིས་མཐུན་ཕྱོགས་རེད་ These two households are friendly. 2. having the same point of view or outlook, allies, pro- ¶ ཨ་རིའི་མཐུན་ཕྱོགས་རྒྱལ་ཁབ་ Pro-American countries.

མཐུན་ཕྱོགས་རྒྱལ་ཁབ་ (tü̃njɔ̄ɔ) the "Allies" (in WW II).

མཐུན་བྱེད་ (tü̃njeè) abbr. of མཐུན་པར་བྱེད་.

མཐུན་འབྲེལ་ (tü̃ndree) sm. མཐུན་ལམ་.

མཐུན་འབྲེལ་ཚོགས་འདུ་ (tü̃ndree tsōndu) a meeting convened so that people can establish friendly relations.

མཐུན་འབྲེལ་ལྷན་ཚོགས་ (tü̃ndree lhɛ̄ndzɔ̄ɔ) sm. མཐུན་འབྲེལ་ཚོགས་འདུ་.

མཐུན་སྦྱོར་ (tü̃njɔɔ) 1. coordinating; va.—བྱེད་ ¶ བཟོ་པ་དང་ཞིང་པ་དབར་མཐུན་སྦྱོར་ཡག་པོ་བྱེད་དགོས་ (We) have to make good coordination between the farmers and the workers. 2. friendly relations; va.—བྱེད་ ¶ མི་ངན་དང་མཐུན་སྦྱོར་བྱ་རྒྱུ་མེད་ (You) should not have friendly relations with evil people.

མཐུན་སྦྱོར་གཅིག་གྱུར་ (tü̃njɔɔ jiggyur) all in agreement, all unified.

མཐུན་སྒྲིལ་ (tü̃ndree) sm. མཐུན་ལམ་.

མཐུན་མིན་ (tü̃nmin) not in harmony/ agreement, disagreeing ¶ ལྟ་ཚུལ་མཐུན་མིན་ A disagreement in view.

མཐུན་མོང་ (tü̃nmoŋ) sm. ཐུན་མོང་.

མཐུན་མོང་གན་རྒྱ་ (tü̃nmoŋ kɛ̱ngya) a document that is certified/ accepted by most people.

མཐུན་ཚོགས་ (tü̃ndzɔ̄ɔ) council, society, association ¶ རི་པིན་རིག་རྩལ་པའི་མཐུན་ཚོགས་ The Japanese Artists and Writers Association.

མཐུན་ཟབ་ (tü̃nsəb) a good/ close friendship.

མཐུན་གཟུགས་ (tü̃nsuù) looking alike, similar in shape.

མཐུན་ཟླ་ (tü̃nda) comrades/ friends who share the same view.

མཐུན་གཤིབ་འགྲོགས་མཁས་ (tü̃nshib drɔ̄ɔkɛɛ̀) amiable, easy to get along with.

མཐུན་ལམ་ (tü̃nlam) friendship, friendly/ cordial relations, good will; va.—བྱེད་; —འཛིན་ to get along well ¶ ང་མི་དང་མཐུན་ལམ་ཡག་པོ་ཡོད་ I get along well with people.

མཐུན་ལམ་ཆེན་པོ་ (tü̃nlam cēmbo) friendly, accommodating.

མཐུན་ལམ་ཆེན་མོ་ (tü̃nlam cēmmo) sm. མཐུན་ལམ་ཆེན་པོ་.

མཐུན་ལམ་མཇལ་འཕྲད་ (tü̃nlam jɛ̱ndrɛɛ̀) 1. a courtesy call. 2. a friendly meeting.

མཐུན་ལམ་དམ་གཙང་ (tü̃nlam ta̱mdzaŋ) harmonious and close relationship.

མཐུན་ལམ་གཟེངས་བསྟོད་ (tü̃nlam sɛ̱ndöö) shung. to be in harmony and to praise.

མཐུན་གཤིབ་ (tü̃nshib) getting along well with others ¶ ཁོང་རྣམ་ཀུན་མི་དང་མཐུན་གཤིབ་ཡག་པོ་ཡོད་པ་རེད་ He always gets along well with others.

མཐུར་ (tūr) sm. མཐུར་མགོ་.

མཐུར་མགོ་ (tōŋgo) horse/ mule halter; va.—གཡོགས་ to put on a halter.

མཐུར་འགོ་ (tōŋgo) sm. མཐུར་མགོ་.

མཐུར་འགོ་སེར་པོ་གཡོགས་ (tōŋgo sērbo yɔ̄ɔ) shung. va. to give sb. a high position with no real power [Lit. to put on a yellow halter (the color used for the halter of a མཁན་ཆེན་ monk official in the tt. government who has a high rank but no power)].

མཐུར་ཐག (tūrdaà) rope that is attached to a halter.

མཐུར་ཐིག (tūrdig) sm. མཐུར་ཐག.

མཐུར་མདའ་ (tūnda) sm. མཐུར་ཐག.

མཐུར་འགོ་སྣ་ཐག (tūngo na̱daà) halter and nose rope.

མཐུར་མ་ (tūrmə) spoon.

མཐུས་ (tǖü) by the power of, because of ¶ རྐྱེན་དེར་

དེ་དག་གི་མཐུས་ By the power of these prayer flags. ༑འཆར་གཞི་དེ་དག་གི་མཐུས་ Because of these plans.

མཐུས་ཀུ་ (tűügu) robbing and stealing by force.

མཐུས་འཕྲོག (tűüdrɔɔ̀) sm. མཐུས་ཀུ་.

མཐེ་ (tē) abbr. མཐེ་བོ་.

མཐེ་ཆེན་ (tējen) sm. མཐེ་བོ་.

མཐེ་རྗེས་ (tējeè) thumbprint.

མཐེ་མཉེད་ (tẽñeè) kneading with one's thumb; va.—གཏོང་.

མཐེ་ཕྲ་ (tēdra) a type of divination in which thumbs are examined; va.—འབེབས་.

མཐེ་བོ་ (tēbo) thumb; big toe; va.—གེར་; —བསྒྲེང་ 1. to lift up one's thumb conveying "please" (usually when begging/ pleading); va.—སྟོན་. 2. va. to lift up one's thumb to convey victory.

མཐེ་བོང་ (tēboŋ) sm. མཐེ་བོ་.

མཐེ་བོང་སྡོ་གང་ (tēboŋ dōgaŋ) shung. a measurement unit equal to the length of a thumb.

མཐེ་བོང་ལག་སྐྱེས་ (tēboŋ laggyee) shung. corvee tax levied on everyone (with a thumb).

མཐེ་མོ་ (tēmo) sm. མཐེ་བོ་.

མཐེ་གཟེར་ (tēser) thumbtack; va.—རྒྱག to fasten with a thumbtack.

མཐེ་སེན་ (tēsen) thumbnail.

མཐེབ་གོར་ (tēbgɔr) a ring (usu. made of jade or ivory) worn by men on the thumb.

མཐེབ་རྒྱལ་ (tēbgyɛɛ) swollen.

མཐེབ་སྐྱུ་ (tēbgyu) a small, round, flat torma.

མཐེབ་འཁྲོལ་པོ་ (tēb drȫōbo) skilled at playing the Tibetan lute.

མཐེབ་གུང་རྡེབ་ (tēb kuŋdeb) va. to click/ snap one's fingers.

མཐེབ་གྲི་བ་ (tēbdriwə) a pickpocket.

མཐེབ་ཆུང་ (tēbjuŋ) little finger, pinkie.

མཐེབ་ཆེན་ (tēbjen) sm. མཐེ་བོ་.

མཐེབ་དྲས་ (tēbdrɛɛ̀) pickpocketing; va.—རྒྱག.

མཐེབ་དྲས་པ་ (tēbdɛɛ̀ba) pickpocket.

མཐེབ་དྲས་རྒྱག་མཁན་ (tēbdɛɛ̀ gyaàñɛn) sm. མཐེབ་དྲས་པ་.

མཐེབ་སྣུར་ (tēbnur) smashing/ crushing sth. between one's thumb and finger; va.—གཏོང་.

མཐེབ་ཕྲ་ (tēbdra) sm. མཐེ་ཕྲ་.

མཐེབ་ཕྲིག (tēbdreè) sm. མཐེབ་དྲས་.

མཐེབ་མོ་ (tēbmo) sm. མཐེ་བོ་.

མཐེབ་བཙིར་ (tēbdzir) squeezing/ pressing with the thumb; va.—གཏོང་.

མཐེབ་རྩེ་ (tēbdze) tip of the thumb.

མཐེབ་ཚིགས་ (tēbdzii) thumb joint.

མཐེབ་ཚིགས་དབུས་མ་ (tēbdzii űümə) the top joint of the thumb.

མཐེབ་རིལ་ (tēbrii) a short (deformed) thumb.

མཐེབ་སྲིན་ (tēbsin) abbr. of thumb and ring finger.

མཐེབ་ལྷེ་ (tēblhe) sm. ཐེ་ཡེད་.

མཐེའུ་ (tēwu) sm. མཐེའི་ཆུང་.

མཐེའུ་ཆུང་ (tējuŋ) pinkie, little finger.

མཐོ་ (tō) 1. abbr. of མཐོ་པོ་. 2. a measure equal to the span from the thumb to the middle finger when extended.

མཐོ་བཀའ་དམའ་བརྩི་ (tōga madzi) the lower level subordinates itself to the higher level, the upper level commands and the lower level accepts (political slogan).

མཐོ་ཁྱད་ (tōgyɛɛ̀) sm. མཐོ་ཚད་.

མཐོ་གང་ (tōgaŋ) the distance of one མཐོ་.

མཐོ་གང་གིས་སྣོབ་སར་འདོམ་གང་གིས་མ་སྣོབ་ (tōgaŋgi ñōbsar domgaŋgi mañob) one should have realistic goals [Lit. the distance of a མཐོ་ can be reached, the distance of an arm span can't be reached].

མཐོ་རྒྱག (tō gyaà) sm. མཐོ་འཇལ་.

མཐོ་ཁྲིམས་ཁང་ (tōtrimgaŋ) Supreme Court.

མཐོ་གྲང་ (tōdraŋ) high and cold ༑མཐོ་གྲང་ས་ཁུལ་ High and frigid zone/ area, arctic or tundra region.

མཐོ་གྲས་ (tōdrɛɛ̀) upper strata, high level ༑མཐོ་གྲས་སློབ་གྲྭ་ Higher level school/ college.

མཐོ་རྒྱག་མེ་མདའ་སྦག་སྦག (tōgyaà menda bagbaà) antiaircraft gun.

མཐོ་སྒང་ (tōgaŋ) plateau.

མཐོ་ལྕོག (tɔ̄ɔjɔɔ̀) a man-made hill/ protrudance/ watchtower on which a watchman sits to protect against theft.

མཐོ་མཆོང་ (tōjoŋ) high jump (in sports); va.—རྒྱག.

མཐོ་འཇལ་ (tō jɛɛ) va. to measure sth. by using the མཐོ་ measurement.

མཐོ་ཉོ་དམའ་འཚོང་ (tōño madzoŋ) doing things in a stupid manner [Lit. buying when the price is high and selling when it is low].

མཐོ་སྙེག (tōñeg) 1. pursuing/ seeking high status/ power. 2. sycophants who like to mix/ rub shoulders with people in high positions.

མཐོ་སྙེམས་ (tōñem) self-glorifying, vain, egoistic.

མཐོ་ཐབ་ (tōdəb) blast furnace, iron smelting furnace.

མཐོ་ཐུབ་དམའ་ཐུབ་ (tōdəb madəb) flexible [Lit. able to go up and come down].

མཐོ་གདུགས་ (tōdug) a brocade umbrella used by lamas.

མཐོ་འདོད་ (tōndöö) sm. མཐོ་སྙེག.

མཐོ་འདོད་ཆེན་པོ་ (tōndöö cēmbo) sb. who is very མཐོ་སྙེག.

མཐོ་འདོད་ཚ་པོ་ (tōndöö tsābo) sm. མཐོ་འདོད་ཆེན་པོ་.

མཐོ་ནོན་ཕྲག་དོག (tōnön trāgdɔɔ̀) jealousy.

མཐོ་གནོན་ (tōnön) high pressure, high tension, high voltage.

མཐོ་གནོན་གློག (tōnön lɔ̄ɔ̀) high-tension electricity, high-voltage electricity.

མཐོ་གནོན་གློག་སྐུད་ (tōnön lɔ̄ɔ̀güü) high-tension power line.

མཐོ་གནོན་གློག་སྐྱེལ་ (tōnön lɔ̄ɔ̀gyel) high-tension transmission.

མཐོ་གནོན་གློག་སྐྱེལ་སྐུད་ལམ་ (tōnön lɔ̄ɔ̀gyere gűübə) high-tension transmission line.

མཐོ་གནོན་གློག་སྒྱུར་འཁྱུལ་ཆས་ (tōnön lɔ̄ɔ̀gyur trűüjɛɛ̀) high-tension transformer.

མཐོ་གནོན་གློག་འདྲེན་ (tōnön lɔ̄gdren) sm. མཐོ་གནོན་གློག་སྐྱེལ་.

མཐོ་གནོན་གློག་འདྲེན་སྐུད་ལམ་ (tōnön lɔ̄gdren gűüləm) sm. མཐོ་གནོན་གློག་སྐྱེལ་སྐུད་ལམ་.

མཐོ་གནོན་གློག་ཤུགས་ (tōnön lɔ̄gshuù) high-tension electric power.

མཐོ་གནོན་སྡེམ་སྒོ་ (tōnön dēmgo) high-pressure value.

མཐོ་གནོན་ཏིམ་སྒམ་ (tōnön timgaŋ) high-pressure caisson.

མཐོ་གནོན་འདུལ་ཐབས་ (tōnön düüdəb) high-handed action, steamroller tactics.

མཐོ་གནོན་སྣུམ་འཐེན་འཁྱུལ་འཁོར་ (tōnön nümden trűügɔɔ) high-pressure oil pump.

མཐོ་གནོན་འབུར་ཁ་ (tōnön burga) ridge of high pressure.

མཐོ་གནོན་གཞིར་འཐེན་འཁྱུལ་འཁོར་ (tōnön shērden trűügɔɔ) high-pressure pump.

མཐོ་པོ་ (tōbo) high (physically and with respect to stature/ rank) ༑ཁང་པ་འདི་མཐོ་པོ་ཞི་དྲགས་འདུག This house is very tall.

མཐོ་དཔོག (tōbɔɔ̀) stone cairns or mounds that are used as boundary/ demarcation markers.

མཐོ་སྤྱོད་ (tōjöö) proud and arrogant/ obnoxious/ wild/ undisciplined.

མཐོ་སྤྲིན་ (tōdrin) high clouds.

མཐོ་འཕེན་མེ་སྒྲོགས་ (tōben mergyɔɔ̀) antiaircraft artillery.

མཐོ་བ་ (tōwa) high (physically and with respect to stature/ rank).

མཐོ་བའི་ཧྲགས་ (tōwɛ dāà) an imposing/ regal manner ༑དཔོན་རིགས་ཚེ་གྲས་ཤིག་གི་མཐོ་བའི་ཧྲགས་ཙམ་ཡང་མེད་ན་སྒོང་མི་ཕལ་པ་ཞིག་དང་ཁྱད་པར་ཅི་ཡོད་ If high officials do not look a little regal and imposing, then what difference is there between them and the common people.

མཐོ་འབྱར་དམའ་དུང་ (tōjar maduŋ) a kimd of person who flatters those above and abuses those below.

མཐོ་འབྲིང་ (tōdriŋ) high and medium/ middle.

མཐོ་དམན་ (tōmɛn) height, level, volume (of sound) [Lit. high low].

མཐོ་དམན་གཉིས་ཐུབ་ (tōmɛn ñīidub) a versatile/ flexible person who is able to perform duties of a high position as well as those of a low position.

མཐོ་དམན་མཉམ་ཚད་ (tōmɛn ñāmdzɛɛ̀) contour (line).

མཐོ་དམན་གནམ་ས་ལྟ་བུ་ཞིག་ཡོད་ཀྱང་ རྒྱུ་འབྲས་རྒྱ་ལམ་ལྟ་བུ་ཞིག་ཡོད་ (tōmɛn nāmsa dābushig yö̈ögyaŋ gyumdrɛɛ̀ gyalam dābushig yö̈ö) the law of karma is the same for all people whatever their status [Lit. even though there is high and low like the earth and sky, the law of karma is like a broad road].

མཐོ་དམན་བར་གསུམ་ (tōmɛn parsum) the three: high, low and middle.

མཐོ་དམན་འཚམ་པ་ (tōmɛn tsāmba) appropriate height.

མཐོ་དམའ་ (tōma) sm. མཐོ་དམན་.

མཐོ་དམའ་སྙོམས་ (tōma ñōm) va. to make things even.

མཐོ་ཚད་ (tōdzɛɛ̀) 1. height ¶ རྒྱ་མཚོ་ནས་མཐོ་ཚད་ Height/ altitude above sea level. 2. the size of a མཐོ་ span. 3. high level ¶ ཚན་རིག་ལག་རྩལ་གྱི་མཐོ་ཚད་དུ་སླེབས་ཡོད་པ་རེད་ (They) have reached a high level of scientific skill.

མཐོ་ཚད་འཇལ་ཆས་ (tōdzɛɛ̀ jɛɛjɛɛ̀) altimeter.

མཐོ་འཚམ་ (tō tsām) 1. va. to compete/ contest with sb. higher than oneself. 2. va. to look down on.

མཐོ་ཞིང་གྲོང་ངེ་རང་ལང་ (tōshiŋ drōŋŋee laŋ) va. to tower over, to be tall (e.g., a mountain, building).

མཐོ་ཡོར་ (tōyor) sm. ཐོ་ཡོར་.

མཐོ་རིགས་ (tōrig) sm. མཐོ་རིམ་.

མཐོ་རིམ་ (tōrim) 1. high level, high quality, advanced ¶ མཐོ་རིམ་ཉམས་ཞིབ་ཁང་ Advanced Research Institute. 2. upper stratum, upper class.

མཐོ་རིམ་རྒྱལ་གཅེས་མི་སྣ་ (tōrim gyɛɛjeè minə) upper strata patriotic personages.

མཐོ་རིམ་དབང་སྒྱུར་ (tōrim wāŋgyur) upper stratum ruling elite, the upper classes who hold power.

མཐོ་རིམ་མི་སྣ་ (tōrim minə) upper strata personages.

མཐོ་རིམ་མི་དམངས་ཁྲིམས་ཁང་ (tōrim mimaŋ trīmgaŋ) people's high court.

མཐོ་རིམ་རྩལ་འཁྲིད་པ་ (tōrim dzɛ̄ɛ̄tribə) senior coach, head coach.

མཐོ་རིམ་རྩིས་རིག (tōrim dziīrig) higher/ advanced math.

མཐོ་རིམ་ཞིང་ལས་ཐོན་སྐྱེད་མཉམ་ལས་ཁང་ (tōrim shiŋlɛɛ̀ tūŋgyeè ñāmlɛgaŋ) advanced agricultural cooperative.

མཐོ་རིམ་ཞིབ་ཕྲ་ (tōrim shibdra) high precision ¶ མཐོ་རིམ་ཞིབ་ཕྲའི་ཐོན་རྫས་ High precision products.

མཐོ་རིམ་བཟོ་བཀོད་པ་ (tōrim sogöòbə) higher level engineer.

མཐོ་རིམ་རུ་ཚོགས་ (tōrim rudzɔ̀ɔ̀) derogatory term for Tibetan government officials in the traditional society.

མཐོ་རིམ་ཤེས་ཡོན་ཅན་ (tōrim shēèyönjɛn) high level intellectuals.

མཐོ་རིམ་སེར་སྐྱ་དཔོན་རིགས་ (tōrim sērgya būnriì) high monk and lay officials.

མཐོ་རིམ་སློབ་གྲྭ (tōrim lōbdra) institution of higher learning, university, college.

མཐོ་རིམ་སློབ་གྲྭ་གི་དམག་ཞབས་སྦྱོར་བདར་སྡེ་ཚན་ (tōrim lōbdragi māgshəb jɔɔdar dedzɛn) Reserve Officers' Training Corps (ROTC).

མཐོ་རིམ་སློབ་གྲྭ་ཆུང་བ་ (tōrim lōbdra cūŋwa) a full six year primary school.

མཐོ་རིམ་སློབ་གྲྭ་འབྲིང་བ་ (tōrim lōbdra driŋwə) senior middle school (sth. like like high school in the U.S.A.).

མཐོ་རིམ་སློབ་ཆུང་ (tōrim lōbjuŋ) sm. མཐོ་རིམ་སློབ་གྲྭ་ཆུང་བ་.

མཐོ་རིམ་སློབ་ཞུགས་རྒྱུགས་ལེན་ (tōrim lōbshuù gyuùlen) college entrance examination.

མཐོ་རིམ་སློབ་གསོ་ (tōrim lōbso) higher education ¶ མཐོ་རིམ་སློབ་གསོ་ཁྲུའུ་ Office of higher education.

མཐོ་རིས་ (tōriì) sky, heavens, the upper realms/ worlds.

མཐོ་རིས་ཀྱི་འཇིག་རྟེན་ (tōriìgi jigden) the upper realms (the realms of gods and humans).

མཐོ་རིས་དགེ་བ་ (tōriì gewa) the virtues and merits of gods and humans.

མཐོ་རིས་གནས་ (tōriì nɛɛ̀) the realm of gods and humans.

མཐོ་རིས་བུ་མོ་ (tōriì pomo) goddess.

མཐོ་རིས་གསུམ་ (tōriì sūm) the three higher realms: gods, demigods and humans.

མཐོ་རུ་གཏོང་ (tōru dōŋ) va. to raise, to heighten, to elevate, to increase ¶ ཁང་པའི་མཐའ་སྐོར་གྱི་ལྕགས་རི་མཐོ་རུ་བཏང་བ་རེད་ (They) raised the fence that was around the house.

མཐོ་རླབས་ (tōlab) sth. moving high, an upsurge ¶ གསར་བརྗེའི་མཐོ་རླབས་ Revolutionary upsurge.

མཐོ་རླབས་སུ་བཏེགས་ (tōlabsu dēg) va. to raise sth. high, to hold sth. as important.

མཐོ་ལོས་ (tōlöö) how high/ tall ¶ ཁང་པ་འདི་མཐོ་ལོས་འདུག How tall is that house?

མཐོ་ཤོས་ (tōshöö) the highest, the tallest.

མཐོ་བཤད་དམའ་བཤད་ (tōshɛɛ̀ mashɛɛ̀) praising and insulting people; va.—བྱེད་ ¶ མི་ལ་མཐོ་བཤད་དམའ་བཤད་བྱེད་རྒྱུ་མེད་ (You) shouldn't praise some people and insult others.

མཐོ་ས་ (tōsa) a high place, a plateau.

མཐོ་སློབ་ (tōlob) an institution of high learning, a college.

མཐོ་ཧྲུལ་གཙོང་ཟོམ་ (tōhrüü jōŋsom) shung. a large dilapidated house that is ready to fall.

མཐོང་ (tōŋ) 1. esteem, status ¶ ཨ་རིའི་སྲིད་འཛིན་གྱི་མཐོང་ཉམས་དམས་སུ་ཕྱིན་པ་རེད་ The esteem of the U.S. president declined. 2. vi. to see ¶ ང་ཚོས་མཐོང་བྱུང་ We saw her. ¶ མོས་ཁོ་རིལ་བ་མཐོང་བ་རེད་ She saw him fall.

མཐོང་ཀ་ (tōŋga) sm. མཐོང་ག.

མཐོང་ཁ་ (tōŋga) sm. མཐོང་ག.

མཐོང་ག (tōŋga) chest (human).

མཐོང་གྲོལ་ (tōŋdrɛɛ) sth. that offers deliverance/ liberation by viewing it ¶ གོང་ས་མཆོག་གི་སྐུ་དཔར་མཐོང་གྲོལ་ The photograph of H.H. the Dalai Lama (which offers deliverance when one looks at it).

མཐོང་གྲོལ་མ་ (tōŋdrɛɛma) sm. མཐོང་གྲོལ་.

མཐོང་རྒྱ་ (tōŋgya) field of vision.

མཐོང་རྒྱ་ཆུང་བ་ (tōŋgya cūŋwə) 1. limited outlook, shortsighted. 2. sb. who has seen few places and things.

མཐོང་རྒྱ་ཆེ་བ་ (tōŋgya cēwa) 1. farsighted. 2. having seen many places and things.

མཐོང་རྒྱ་ཆེན་པོ་ (tōŋgya cēmbo) sm. མཐོང་རྒྱ་ཆེ་བ་.

མཐོང་རྒྱ་ཐོས་རྒྱ་ (tōŋgya tö̀ögya) sm. མཐོང་ཐོས་.

མཐོང་རྒྱ་མེད་པ་ (tōŋgya meèba) shortsighted, without vision.

མཐོང་རྒྱུ་ཆེ་བ་ (tōŋgyu cēwa) sb. who has seen a lot, sb. with great experience.

མཐོང་ཆུང་ (tōŋjuŋ) looking down on, viewing with contempt/ scorn/ disdain; va.—བྱེད་ ¶ མི་ཕྱུག་པོ་འདི་ཚོས་སྤྲང་པོར་མཐོང་ཆུང་བྱེད་ཀྱི་ཡོད་པ་རེད་ These rich people look down on beggars.

མཐོང་ཆུང་ཁྱད་གསོད་ (tōŋjuŋ kɛ̄ɛsöö) sm. མཐོང་ཆུང་.

མཐོང་ཆེན་ (tōŋjen) high regard/ esteem; va.—བྱེད་ ¶ གྲོང་གསེབ་ཚོས་བླ་མར་མཐོང་ཆེན་བྱེད་ཀྱི་ཡོད་པ་རེད་ The villagers regard lamas with high esteem.

མཐོང་ཆེན་པོ་ (tōŋ cēmbo) sm. མཐོང་ཆེན་.

མཐོང་ཆོས་ (tōŋjöö) things that can actually be seen ། གནས་ཚུལ་འདི་ཀུན་གྱི་མཐོང་ཆོས་སུ་འགྱུར་བ་ཞིག་རེད་ This situation has become sth. that can be seen by everyone.

མཐོང་ཆོས་མྱོང་འགྱུར་ (tōŋjöö ño̲ŋgyur) firsthand/ direct experience ། བཙོན་ཁང་ནང་བྱུང་བའི་གནས་ཚུལ་འདི་དག་ང་རང་གི་མཐོང་ཆོས་མྱོང་འགྱུར་ཞིག་ཡིན་ This information on what occurred in prison is based on my firsthand experience.

མཐོང་ཉིད་བྲོས་ (tōŋñii trö̲ö̲) va. to flee as soon as one sees sth.

མཐོང་ཉིད་མགོ་སྒུར་ (tōŋñii g̲ogur) va. to surrender as soon as one sees sth., to surrender at the sight (of the enemy).

མཐོང་ཐུབ་ཚད་ (tōŋ tūbdzɛɛ̀) as much as can be seen ། ཁྱེད་རང་ལུང་པ་དེར་འགྲོ་དུས་བཙོན་ཁང་གི་གནས་ཚུལ་མཐོང་ཐུབ་ཚད་རྣམས་པར་སྐྲུན་རོགས་གནང་ When you go to that place please photograph as much as you can see of the situation in prisons.

མཐོང་ཐོས་ (tōŋtöö) seeing and hearing, having knowledge/ experience ། བྱ་བ་ངོ་མཚར་ཅན་མང་པོ་མཐོང་ཐོས་བྱུང་བ་རེད་ (I) saw and heard many strange things.

མཐོང་ཐོས་རྙོག་བཟོ་ (tōŋtöö ñōgso) confusing what one sees and hears; va.—བྱེད་ ། ཁོ་ཚོས་དཀྲོག་གཏམ་བཟོས་ནས་མི་དམངས་ཀྱི་མཐོང་ཐོས་རྙོག་བཟོ་བྱས་པ་རེད་ They spread rumors and this confused what the public saw and heard.

མཐོང་ཐོས་དོགས་གསུམ་ (tōŋtöö d̲ɔg sūm) the three: seeing, hearing and doubting ། ཚོགས་འདུའི་ཐོག་མཐོང་ཐོས་དོགས་གསུམ་གྱི་གནས་ཚུལ་ཚང་མ་ཤོད་དགོས་མ་རེད་ At the meeting one does not have to say everything regarding what one has seen and heard and about one's doubts.

མཐོང་ཐོས་དྲན་རེག་ (tōŋtöö tr̲enreg) seeing, hearing, remembering and touching.

མཐོང་ཐོས་མེད་པ་ (tōŋtöö m̲eèba) neither seen nor heard ། སྤྱི་ལོ་ ༡༩༦༥ ནས་པཎ་ཆེན་རིན་པོ་ཆེ་མཆོག་མི་མང་མདུན་སར་མཐོང་ཐོས་མེད་པ་རེད་ Since 1965, the Panchen Lama has been neither seen nor heard by the people.

མཐོང་ཐོས་ཤེས་གསུམ་ (tōŋtöö shēè sūm) the three: seeing, hearing and knowing.

མཐོང་ཐོས་བསམ་ཚུལ་ (tōŋtöö sāmdzüü) sm. མཐོང་དྲན་.

མཐོང་མཐའ་ (tōŋta) sm. མཐོང་རྒྱ་.

མཐོང་མཐོང་བ་ (tōŋ tōŋwa) obvious ། གནས་ཚུལ་དེ་ཁྱེད་རང་གིས་མཐོང་མཐོང་བ་ཡིན་པས་ང་ལ་སྐད་ཆ་འདྲི་དགོས་དོན་མེད་ That issue is obvious so there is no reason to ask me.

མཐོང་མཐོང་ཐག་ཐག་ (tōŋdoŋ tāgdaà) experiences, things seen and done ། མི་དེས་མཐོང་མཐོང་ཐག་ཐག་མང་པོ་ཞིག་ཤོད་ཀྱི་འདུག་ཀྱང་བདེན་པ་ཡིན་མིན་མ་ཤེས་ That person is talking about the many things he has seen but I don't know whether it is true.

མཐོང་དགའ་ཐོས་དགའ་ (tōŋ g̲a tȫö g̲a) being happy at the sight and sound (of seeing a person or hearing good news).

མཐོང་དུག་ (tōŋduù) a type of poison that causes illness the moment a person sees it.

མཐོང་དོགས་མེད་ (tōŋdɔɔ̀ m̲eè) there is no reason to worry/ fear that sb. will see (sth.) ། ངས་ཅ་ལག་དེ་ཡག་པོ་སྦས་ཡོད་པས་གཞན་གྱིས་མཐོང་དོགས་མེད་ I have hid that thing well so that there is no need to worry that others will see it.

མཐོང་དོགས་ཀྱི་ཡོལ་བ་དང་མ་མཐོང་དོགས་ཀྱི་ཨོང་གུ (tōŋdɔɔ̀gi y̲ö̲ö̲wadaŋ m̲atoŋdoggi ōŋgu) hiding sth. because of the fear that others will see it and at the same time showing off [Lit. putting a curtain because one is afraid people will see and lighting a lamp because one is afraid people will not see].

མཐོང་དྲན་ (tōŋdrɛn) seeing and remembering ། འདི་ངའི་མཐོང་དྲན་གྱི་བསམ་འཆར་ཡིན་ This is my opinion based on what I have seen and remember.

མཐོང་འདོད་པོ་ (tōŋ t̲ö̲ö̲bo) 1. pleasant looking, appealing ། བུ་མོ་དེ་ཏོ་ཅང་མཛེས་པོ་མེད་ན་ཡང་མཐོང་འདོད་པོ་ཞིག་འདུག Even though that girl isn't very beautiful, she is pleasant looking. 2. appealing to sb. ། ལས་བྱེད་གསར་པ་དེར་བཅར་འདྲི་བྱེད་སྐབས་འགོ་ཁྲིད་ཀྱི་མཐོང་འདོད་པོ་བྱུང་འོང་ When the new official was interviewed, the boss found him appealing.

མཐོང་ནོར་ (tōŋnɔɔ) mistakenly seeing, seeing wrong; vi.—ཐེབས་ to see mistakenly ། སྦྱར་ཚིག་གི་ནང་དོན་ངས་མཐོང་ནོར་བྱུང་བཞག I mistakenly saw (read) the meaning of the poster.

མཐོང་སྣང་ (tōŋnaŋ) way/ manner of seeing.

མཐོང་སྣང་ལ་ཕྱིན་ (tōŋnaŋla c̄in) sm. མིག་སྣང་ལ་ཕྱིན་.

མཐོང་སྣང་འབྲི་དེབ་ (tōŋnaŋ tr̲ideb) notebook.

མཐོང་སྣང་མཛེས་པོ་ (tōŋnaŋ dz̲eèbo) beautiful.

མཐོང་ཕྱག་ (tōŋjaà) two people making the sign of greeting/ respect (ཕྱག་འབུལ་) when meeting.

མཐོང་ཕྱོགས་ (tōŋjɔɔ̀) 1. viewpoint, way of looking at sth., opinion ། མི་སོ་སོར་མཐོང་ཕྱོགས་འདྲ་མིན་རེ་ཡོད་པ་རེད་ Each person has his own different viewpoint. 2. prejudice, discrimination; va.—བྱེད་; —འཛིན་ to act with prejudice, to discriminate ། འགོ་ཁྲིད་དེས་ལས་བྱེད་པའི་ནང་མཐོང་ཕྱོགས་བྱེད་ཀྱི་ཡོད་པ་རེད་ That boss discriminates among the officials.

མཐོང་བ་ (tōŋwa) 1. seeing, perceiving. 2. having regard for someone.

མཐོང་བ་ཀུན་སྨོན་ (tōŋwa g̲ünmön) universal praise/ acclaim.

མཐོང་བ་གྲངས་མང་ཤེས་པ་རྒྱ་ཆེ་ (tōŋwa tr̲anmaŋ shēèba gy̲ace) one who has seen a lot and has vast knowledge.

མཐོང་བ་དོན་ལྡན་ (tōŋwa t̲öndɛn) one who benefits as soon as he sees sth. (like a great lama).

མཐོང་བ་ཞར་རྫུ་ (tōŋwa sh̲ardzu) pretending to be blind.

མཐོང་བའི་དངོས་པོ་ (tōŋwɛ ŋȫöbo) things that are visible.

མཐོང་བྱེད་ (tōŋ c̲eè) 1. va. to treat with respect. 2. poet. the eye.

མཐོང་མེད་དུ་བྱེད་ (tōŋmeèdu c̲eè) sm. མཐོང་ཆུང་བྱེད་.

མཐོང་མྱོང་མྱོང་ (tōŋ ñ̲oŋñoŋ) familiar looking ། མི་འདི་མཐོང་མྱོང་མྱོང་ཞིག་འདུག This man is familiar looking.

མཐོང་ཚད་ (tōŋdzɛɛ̀) whatever one sees ། ཕྲུ་གུ་འདིས་རྩེད་ཆས་མཐོང་ཚད་དགོས་ཡོད་ཟེར་གྱི་འདུག Whatever toys this child sees, he says (he) wants them.

མཐོང་ཚུལ་ (tōŋdzüü) viewpoint, opinion, way of seeing ། ཡུ་རོབ་རྒྱལ་ཁབ་ཀྱི་མཐོང་ཚུལ་ལ་རྒྱ་དམར་གྱི་ཕྱི་སྲིད་ལ་བསྒྱུར་བཅོས་ཕྱིན་ཡོད་པ་མ་རེད་ In the viewpoint of European nations, China's foreign policy hasn't changed. ། ཞི་དྲག་དབར་མཐོང་ཚུལ་མི་འདྲ་བ་ཡོད་པ་རེད་ The military and the civil offices have different viewpoints.

མཐོང་ཚོར་ (tōŋdzɔr) sense of sight.

མཐོང་འཛོལ་ (tōŋdzöö) 1. sm. མཐོང་ནོར་. 2. parallax.

མཐོང་བཟོས་ (tōŋsöö) award, citation.

མཐོང་བཟོས་བདག་རྐྱེན་ (tōŋsöö d̲aggyen) sm. མཐོང་བཟོས་.

མཐོང་ཡངས་ཆེ་བ་ (tōŋyaŋ cēwa) sm. མཐོང་རྒྱ་ཆེ་བ་.

མཐོང་ཡུལ་ (tōŋyüü) sm. མཐོང་རྒྱ་.

མཐོང་ལུགས་ (tōŋluù) sm. མཐོང་ཚུལ་.

མཐོང་ས་ (tōŋsa) field of vision/ sight ། ཁོ་མཐོང་སར་མ་སླེབས་སྐབས་ Because he hasn't arrived in sight.

མཐོང་གསལ་ (tōŋsɛɛ) seen clearly ། གནས་ཚུལ་དེ་ཚང་མས་མཐོང་གསལ་རེད་ That situation is clearly seen by all.

མཐོངས་ (tōŋ) opening, gap, hole (usu. in a roof).

མཐོངས་ཀ་ (tōŋga) silk/ brocade cloth used to cover the table of a lama.

མཐོངས་ཁུང་ (tōŋguŋ) 1. sm. མཐོངས་. 2. chimney. 3. skylight.

མཐོངས་སྒྲུག (tōŋgyuù) a pole used to open and close the lid/ flap over the smoke hole of a tent.

མཐོངས་རྒྱན་ (tōŋgyɛn) a square canopy of silk/ brocade put directly on the ceiling over where a lama or high official sits.

མཐོངས་ཐིག (tōŋtig) a strap to open and close the flap over the smoke hole of a tent.

མཐོངས་འཛུག (tōŋjuù) sm. ཐོང་གཡམ་.

མཐོངས་ཡངས་ (tōŋyaŋ) open, roofless.

མཐོངས་ཡངས་གཏེར་ཁ (tōŋyaŋ dērga) open-pit mine.

མཐོངས་ཡངས་རྡོ་སོལ་གཏེར་ཁ (tōŋyaŋ dosöö dērga) open-pit coal mine.

མཐོངས་གཡོགས་ (tōŋyɔɔ̀) the lid/ flap that is used to cover the smoke hole of a tent.

མཐོན་ཀ་ (tõnga) 1. azure blue, sky blue. 2. sapphire.

མཐོན་ཀ་ཆེན་པོ་ (tõnga cēmbo) sm. མཐོན་ཀ་.

མཐོན་ག (tõnga) sm. མཐོན་ཀ.

མཐོན་ཐི་ (tõndi) a type of brocade.

མཐོན་མཐིང་ (tõndiŋ) sm. མཐོན་ཀ་.

མཐོན་པོ་ (tõmbo) high, va.—བཀུག; —འདེགས་ to hold sth. high ༎ཁོས་དར་ཆ་མཐོན་པོར་བཀུག་པ་རེད་ He held the flag high.

མཐོན་མོ་ (tõmmo) sm. མཐོན་པོ་.

མཐོར་ (tɔ̃ɔ) overhead, above; va.—གཏོང་ to raise, to send up, to increase ༎ཐོན་ཚད་མཐོར་བཏང་བ་རེད་ (They) increased production.

མཐོར་འགྲན་དམན་སྣང་ (tɔ̃ɔdrɛn mendaŋ) competing with superiors and mistreating subordinates.

མཐོར་འདེགས་ (tɔ̃ɔdeg) raising, sending up, elevating; va.—བྱེད་ to raise, to send up, to elevate ༎རྒྱལ་དར་མཐོར་འདེགས་བྱས་པ་རེད་ (They) raised the country's flag.

མཐོར་འཕེན་མེ་སྒྱོགས་ (tɔ̃ɔben megyɔɔ̀) antiaircraft gun.

མཐོར་འཕེན་མེ་མདའ་ སྦག་སྦག (tɔ̃ɔben menda bagbaà) antiaircraft machine gun.

མཐོར་འཕྱུར་ (tõn jūr) vi. to flutter up (like smoke).

མཐོར་ཞུ་ (tɔ̃ɔshu) petitioning/ appealing to a superior; va.—བྱེད་.

མཐོལ་ (tɔ̃ɔ) va. to confess.

མཐོལ་ཚངས་ (tɔ̃ɔdzaŋ) sm. མཐོལ་བཤགས་.

མཐོལ་ལོ་བཤགས་ (tɔ̃ɔlo shāà) sm. མཐོལ་བཤགས་འབུལ་.

མཐོལ་བཤགས་ (tɔ̃ɔshaà) confessing, confession; va.—འབུལ་ to confess.

མཐོས་སློབ་སར་འཛུམ་གྱིས་མི་སློབས་ (tɔ̃ɔ dōbsaa domgi miñob) sm. མཐོ་གང་གིས་སློབ་སར་འཛུམ་གང་གིས་མ་སློབ་.

འཐག: p. བཏགས་; f. བཏག་; imp. འཐོག (tāà) va. 1. to grind ༎གྲོ་ཞིབ་འཐག་ཐུབ་ཀྱི་རེད་ (They) are able to grind (make) flour. 2. va. to weave ༎རས་སྣུས་ཞན་ཞིག་ལས་བཏགས་མ་ཐུབ་ན་ If (they) are able to weave only poor quality cloth.

འཐག་སྐོར་ (tāà gɔ̃ɔ) va. to turn a grinding stone.

འཐག་ཁ་མ་ (tāàgama) weaver.

འཐག་ཁྲི་ (tāgdri) loom.

འཐག་མཁན་ (tāàñɛn) weaver.

འཐག་མཁན་མ་ (tāà ñɛ̃nma) female weaver.

འཐག་འཁོར་ (tāàgɔɔ) spinning wheel, weaving machine.

འཐག་འཁྱུ་བལ་ལས་ (tāgju pe̲e̲lɛɛ̀) weaving and spinning (wool) work.

འཐག་ལྡན་ (tāàdɛn) sm. འཐག་ཁྲི་.

འཐག་འཐག (tāà tāà) va. to weave.

འཐག་རྡོ་ (tāàdo) millstone, grinding stone.

འཐག་འབྲུབ་མ་ (tāgdrumə) a woven picture.

འཐག་པ་པོ་ (tāgbabo) weaver.

འཐག་སྤྱད་ (tāgjɛɛ̀) weaving tools/ implements.

འཐག་མ་ (tāàma) a backstrap loom.

འཐག་ཤ་ (tāgsha) a weaving tool.

འཐག་སོ་ (tāgso) a comb-like tool used in weaving.

འཐད་ (tɛ̃ɛ̀) va. 1. to be willing/ agreeable 2. vi. to desire, to like ༎སྐད་ཆ་འདི་འདྲ་ཤོད་མི་འཐད་ It isn't okay to speak like that.

འཐད་མིན་ (tɛ̃ɛ̀min) whether it is okay/ correct (or not) ༎ལྷ་སར་འགྲོ་རྒྱུ་འཐད་མིན་གྲོས་སྡུར་བྱས་པ་རེད་ (They) discussed whether it is okay or not to go to Lhasa.

འཐན་ནེ་འཐེན་ནེ་ (tɛ̄nne tɛ̄nne) hesitant, doubtful, suspicious; va.—བྱེད་ ༎ཁོང་ལ་དྲི་བ་བྱེད་དུས་ལན་འཐན་ནེ་འཐེན་ནེ་ཞིག་བརྒྱབ་སོང་ He gave a hesitant answer when questioned.

འཐབ་ (tāb) 1. va. to fight, to struggle. 2. sm. ཁ་འཐབ་.

འཐབ་ཀྲོལ་ (tābdröö) sm. འཐབ་འཛིང་ས་.

འཐབ་ཀྲོལ་ཅན་ (tābdrööjɛn) troublemaker, sb. involved in a commotion/ fighting/ struggling.

འཐབ་འཁོར་ (tābgɔɔ) tank, armored vehicle.

འཐབ་འཁོར་ཐན་ཁ་ (tāgɔɔ tɛ̄nga) tib.eng. tank.

འཐབ་འཁྲུག (tābdruù) warfare, fighting, combat; va.—བྱེད་ to wage war, to fight, to engage in combat.

འཐབ་གོས་ (tābgöö) military uniform.

འཐབ་གྲུ་ (tābdru) sm. དམག་གྲུ་.

འཐབ་གྲོགས་ (tābdrɔɔ̀) comrade-in-arms; va.—བྱེད་ to be comrades-in-arms.

འཐབ་རྒོལ་ (tābgöö) an attack; va.—བྱེད་ to attack.

འཐབ་གྲ་སྒྲིག (tābdra drig) va. to prepare for war/ fighting.

འཐབ་རྔ་ (tābŋa) battle/ military drum.

འཐབ་ཆས་ (tābjɛɛ̀) war/ combat materials, war weapons.

འཐབ་ཇུས་ (tābjüü) policy/ strategy for warfare.

འཐབ་ཇུས་ཀྱི་གྲོང་སྡེ་ (tābjüügi tro̲nde) strategic hamlets.

འཐབ་ཇུས་ཀྱི་དགོངས་དོན་ (tābjüügi go̲ŋdön) strategic thought.

འཐབ་ཇུས་ཐོག་ནས་འགོག་སྲུང་ (tābjüü tɔ̃ɔnɛ go̲gsuŋ) strategic defense.

འཐབ་ཐིག (tābdig) battle line, front line ༎འཐབ་ཐིག་རིང་དྲགས་པ་ Overextended battle lines.

འཐབ་འཐབ་ཀྱིས་བགམས་ (tābdəbgi ga̲m) va. to eat grass/ vegetation/ hay with the lips (for horses).

འཐབ་ན་མི་རྒྱལ་བ་མེད་ (tābnə migyɛɛwa me̲è) invincible ༎འཐབ་ན་མི་རྒྱལ་བ་མེད་པའི་མཚོན་ཆ་ An invincible weapon.

འཐབ་ནུས་ (tābnüü) power/ strength to fight.

འཐབ་པོ་ (tābbo) sb. who is engaged in fighting/ struggling/ combat.

འཐབ་ཕྱོགས་ (tābjɔɔ̀) battle line, front ༎བཟོ་ལས་ཀྱི་འཐབ་ཕྱོགས་ Industrial front.

འཐབ་ཕྱོགས་གཅིག་འགྱུར་ (tābjɔɔ̀ ji̲ggyur) united front.

འཐབ་ཕྱོགས་གཅིག་འགྱུར་པུའུ་ (tābjɔɔ̀ ji̲ggyur bū) tib.ch. united front department.

འཐབ་ཕྱོགས་གཅིག་སྒྲིལ་ (tābjɔɔ̀ ji̲gdrii) sm. འཐབ་ཕྱོགས་གཅིག་འགྱུར་.

འཐབ་ཕྱོགས་མཉམ་འབྲེལ་ (tābjɔɔ̀ ñāmdree) sm. འཐབ་ཕྱོགས་གཅིག་འགྱུར་.

འཐབ་བྱུས་ (tābjüü) sm. འཐབ་ཇུས་.

འཐབ་བྱེད་གནམ་གྲུ་ (tābjeè nāmdru) fighter plane.

འཐབ་འབྲས་ (tāmdrɛɛ̀) 1. victory (in war/ battle). 2. result of a battle.

འཐབ་མི་ (tābmi) sm. འཐབ་འཛིང་པ་.

འཐབ་མོ་ (tābmo) fighting a war; va.—འགྱེད་ to fight/ engage in warfare ༎རྒྱལ་ཁབ་གཉིས་དབར་ས་མཚམས་ཀྱི་སྐོར་འཐབ་མོ་འགྱེད་པ་རེད་ The two countries fought a war over the border.

འཐབ་མོ་བ་ (tābmowa) combatant, fighter, soldier.

འཐབ་རྩལ་ (tābdzɛɛ) military tactics/ strategy.

འཐབ་རྩོད་ (tābdzöö) struggling, fighting, combating; va.—བྱེད་ ༎འཐབ་རྩོད་ཀྱི་གཞས་ Militant songs. ༎ཁོ་ཚོ་འཐབ་རྩོད་ཀྱི་མདུན་སར་ལངས་པ་རེད་ They rose to the front of the struggle.

འཐབ་བརྩོན་ (tābdzön) sm. འབད་བརྩོན་.

འཐབ་ཚད་ (tābdzɛɛ̀) everytime one fought/ struggled ༎དམག་འཐབ་ཚད་ལ་རྒྱལ་ཁ་ཐོབ་པ་རེད་ Everytime (they) fought they won.

འཐབ་འཛིང་ (tāmdzin) 1. combating, fighting,

battling; va.—བྱེད་. 2. public meetings ("struggle sessions") in China where criticism and beatings of "class enemies" took place; va.—གཏོང་ to do such a "struggle session" ། ཞིང་བདག་ལ་ཞིང་པ་ཚོས་འཐབ་འཛིང་བཏང་བ་རེད་ The farmers held a struggle session against the landlord.

འཐབ་འཛིང་གི་གླུ་ཞས་ (tāmdzingi lūshɛɛ̀) militant songs.

འཐབ་འཛིང་གི་སྟོབས་ཤུགས་ (tāmdzingi dōbshuù) fighting strength/ power, combat effectiveness.

འཐབ་འཛིང་གི་རྣམ་པ་ (tāmdzingi nāmba) militant appearance/ atmosphere.

འཐབ་འཛིང་གི་སྤྱོད་ཚུལ་ (tāmdzingi jöödzüü) fighting/ combat style.

འཐབ་འཛིང་གི་འབོད་ཚིག (tāmdzingi bö̱ödzii) battle cry/ slogan.

འཐབ་འཛིང་གི་བྱས་རྗེས་ (tāmdzingi cɛ̱ɛ̀jeè) sm. འཐབ་འཛིང་གི་བྱས་འབྲས་.

འཐབ་འཛིང་གི་བྱས་འབྲས་ (tāmdzingi cɛ̱ndrɛɛ̀) results/ fruits/ success of battle or struggle.

འཐབ་འཛིང་གི་རང་བཞིན་ (tāmdzingi ra̱ŋshin) combativeness, militancy ། འཐབ་འཛིང་གི་རང་བཞིན་ལྡན་པའི་འབོད་སྐུལ་ A militant appeal.

འཐབ་འཛིང་གྲུ་གཟིངས་ (tāmdzin tru̱siŋ) warship.

འཐབ་འཛིང་ཅན་ (tāmdzinjɛn) militant.

འཐབ་འཛིང་དྲག་པོ་ (tāmdzin tra̱gbo) militant.

འཐབ་འཛིང་ནུས་ཤུགས་ (tāmdzin nü̱üshuù) fighting power/ strength.

འཐབ་འཛིང་ནུས་པ་ (tāmdzin nü̱übə) sm. འཐབ་འཛིང་ནུས་ཤུགས་.

འཐབ་འཛིང་གནམ་གྲུ་ (tāmdzin nāmdru) fighter plane.

འཐབ་འཛིང་པ་ (tāmdzimbə) soldiers, combatants, fighters ། བཅིངས་འགྲོལ་དམག་གི་འཐབ་འཛིང་པ་ People's Liberation Army soldiers.

འཐབ་འཛིང་དཔའ་བོ་ (tāmdzin bāwo) combat hero.

འཐབ་འཛིང་བྱས་རྗེས་ (tāmdzin cɛ̱ɛ̀jeè) sm. འཐབ་འཛིང་གི་བྱས་འབྲས་.

འཐབ་འཛིང་དམག (tāmdzin māà) soldier.

འཐབ་འཛིང་རུ་ཁག (tāmdzin ru̱gaà) fighting unit, combat group.

འཐབ་ཞུགས་རྒྱལ་ཁབ་ (tābshuù gyɛ̱ɛ̱gəb) belligerent nation, a nation involved in a war.

འཐབ་ཟླ་ (tāmda) a rival, a competitor in fighting.

འཐབ་འོབས་ (tābwob) sm. འཐབ་ར་.

འཐབ་ཡ་ (tābya) antagonist, opponent in combat.

འཐབ་ཡུན་ (tābyün) duration of a battle.

འཐབ་ར་ (tābra) military entrenchment/ fortification, trench; va.—བྱེད་ to make/ use a འཐབ་ར་.

འཐབ་ར་འཕྲོད་ (tābra drö̀ö) vi. to have two sides engage in trench war/ battle, to wage trench warfare.

འཐབ་རགས་ (tābraà) sm. འཐབ་ར་.

འཐབ་རིང་དམག་ཉམས་ (tābriŋ māgñam) an army deteriorating in a long battle/ war.

འཐབ་རུ་བཀོད་གཤོམ་ (tābru gö̀öshom) preparing and arranging troops to wage war/ attack; va.—བྱེད་.

འཐབ་རུ་སྒྲིག (tābru dri̱g) va. to make arrangements for war/ attack, to preapre for waging war/ attacking.

འཐབ་རུ་གཤོམ་ (tābru shōm) va. to prepare to wage war/ attack.

འཐབ་རོལ་དུ་འགྲོ་ (tābröödu dro̱) vi. to get killed in battle incidentally (e.g., civilian casualties).

འཐབ་རེས་ (tābreè) taking turns to fight, fighting back and forth; va.—བྱེད་.

འཐབ་ཟླ་ (tāmda) enemy soldier.

འཐབ་ལན་ (tāblɛn) a military response, responding by fighting; va.—སྤྱོད་ to respond to sth. militarily, to launch a counterattack.

འཐབ་ལན་འཐབ་སྤྱོད་ (tāblɛn tābdrö̀ö) sm. འཐབ་ལན་ཡ་བཟུང་.

འཐབ་ལན་ཡ་བཟུང་ (tāblɛn ya̱suŋ) sm. འཐབ་ལན་ཐབ་སྤྱོད་.

འཐབ་ལམ་ (tāblam) battle route, the road one takes to battle.

འཐབ་ཤུགས་ (tābshuù) fighting strength/ power, combat efficiency/ capacity.

འཐབ་སེམས་ (tābsem) desire/ will to fight.

འཐབས་ (tāb) p. of འཐབ་.

འཐབས་སྤྱོས་ (tābjöö) a verbal as well as physical fight.

འཐམ་: p. **འཐམས་**, f. **འཐམ་**; imp. **འཐོམས་** (tām) va. to hug, to embrace ། ཨ་མས་ཕྲུ་གུར་འཐམ་པ་རེད་ The mother hugged the child.

འཐམ་འཁྱུད་ (tāmgyüü) hugging; va.—བྱེད་.

འཐམ་མེ་འཐོམས་མེ་ (tāmme tōmme) 1. lost, bewildered, muddled, dazed. 2. groggy.

འཐམ་རེས་ (tāmreè) mutual hugging, hugging each other; va.—བྱེད་.

འཐམ་ལག (tāmlaà) sm. ཐམ་ལག.

འཐམས་ (tām) p. of འཐམ་.

འཐར་ (tār) vi. to be/ get squashed/ crushed ། ལག་པ་འཕྲུལ་འཁོར་གྱི་བར་དུ་འཐར་ནས་རྨ་བཟོས་སོང་ (His) hand was crushed in the machine and injured.

འཐལ་ (tɛ̄ɛ) sm. ཐལ་.

འཐས་ཀན་ (tɛ̄ɛgɛn) hard palate.

འཐས་པ་ (tɛ̄ɛba) 1. hard, solid, unyielding. 2. insisting, stubborn.

འཐིག་པ་ (tīgbə) sm.* ཐིགས་པ་.

འཐིབ་ (tīb) sm. འཐིབས་.

འཐིབ་འཐིབ་ (tībdib) dark, gloomy, overcast.

འཐིབ་གནོན་ (tībnön) supressing; va.—བྱེད་.

འཐིབས་: p. **ཐིབས་**; f. **འཐིབས་** (tīb) 1. vi. to be cloudy/ overcast ། དེ་རིང་གནམ་ཐིབས་འདུག Its overcast today. 2. vi. to be enveloped, to be filled with, to be widespread ། མུན་པའི་ཡོལ་བ་དེ་རིམ་གྱིས་འཐིབས་པའི་སྐབས་སུ་ At the time when the curtain of darkness gradually became widespread 3. vi. to have diminished/ lessened ། ལོ་ན་རྒས་སྟབས་བློའི་དབང་པོ་འཐིབས་བཞག Because of old age, my mental faculties have diminished.

འཐིབས་པོ་ (tībbu) 1. dense, close. 2. dark, gloomy, overcast.

འཐིབས་སྤྱོད་ (tībjöö) depression, gloom.

འཐིམ་ (tīm) sm. ཐིམ་.

འཐུ་: p. **བཏུས་**; f. **བཏུ་**; imp. **ཐུས་** (tū) 1. va. to pick, to collect, to gather ། མེ་ཤིང་བཏུས་ནས་ནང་ལ་ཡོང་བ་རེད་ After collecting firewood (they) came home. 2. sm. འཐུ་ཆ་.

འཐུ་སྒྲུག (tūdruù) picking, collecting, gathering; va.—བྱེད་.

འཐུ་ཆ་ (tūja) pooling things together (e.g., money); va.—རྒྱག ། ང་ཚོ་དངུལ་འཐུ་ཆ་བརྒྱབ་ནས་གླིང་ཀ་བཏང་བ་ཡིན་ We pooled money together and had a picnic.

འཐུག (tūù) abbr. of འཐུག་པོ་.

འཐུག་གེ་བ་ (tūggewa) thick, dense.

འཐུག་འདེབས་ (tūgdeb) close/ thick planting; va.—བྱེད་.

འཐུག་པ་ (tūgbə) sm. མཐུག་པོ་.

འཐུག་པོ་ (tūgbu) 1. thick, dense, congested ། ནགས་ཚལ་མཐུག་པོ་ A dense forest. 2. deep ། གཉིད་མཐུག་པོ་ཞིག་ཁུག་བྱུང་ (I) fell into a deep sleep. 3. strong, intense ། འདོད་པ་མཐུག་པོ་ An intense desire. 4. sm. མཐུག་པོ་.

འཐུག་འཛིངས་ (tūgdziŋ) 1. tangled (for hair). 2. dense forest/ thicket.

འཐུག་འཛུགས་ (tūgdzuù) sm. མཐུག་འདེབས་.

འཐུང་: p. **བཏུངས་**; f. **བཏུང་**; imp. **འཐུངས་** (tūŋ) va. to drink ། ཁ་སྐོམ་ནས་ཆུ་བཏུངས་པ་ཡིན་ (I) was thirsty and drank water.

འཐུང་ཁ་བདེ་པོ་ (tūŋgə de̱bo) smooth/ easy to drink.

འཐུང་འཁོར་ (tūŋgɔɔ) a round of drinking/ drinks.

འཐུང་རྒྱུ་ (tūŋgyu) a drink ། ང་ལ་འཐུང་རྒྱུ་ཞིག་སྣེར་རོགས་གནང་ Please give me sth. to drink.

འཐུང་ཆུ་ (tūŋju) drinking water.

འཐུང་སྣོད་ (tūŋnöö) drinking utensil.

འཐུང་འཕྲོ་ (tūŋdro) leftover drinks.

འཐུང་སྨན་ (tūŋmɛn) liquid medicine.

འཐུང་ཆེན་ (tūŋdzɛn) sm. འཐུང་ཤེད་.

འཐུང་རིགས་ (tūŋrig) (kinds of) beverages.

འཐུང་ཡག་གི་སྨན་ (tūŋyaàgi mɛ̄n) sm. འཐུང་སྨན་.

འཐུང་ཤེད་ (tūŋsheè) the capacity to drink a lot (and not get drunk), holding one's liquor well ། མི་དེ་ཆང་འཐུང་ཤེད་ཆེན་པོ་ཡོད་པ་རེད་ That person can drink a lot and not get drunk.

འཐུང་ཧམ་ (tūŋham) ravenous /gluttonous regarding drinking alcohol.

འཐུངས་ (tūŋ) imp. of འཐུང་.

འཐུད་ (tūù) sm. འཐུད་རྒྱག.

འཐུད་རྒྱག (tūù gyaà) va. to splice, to join/ connect together (at the ends), to link, to make longer.

འཐུད་པ་ (tūùbə) sm. མཐུད་པ་.

འཐུད་མ་ (tūùmə) sm. མཐུད་མ་.

འཐུབ་པ་ (tūbbə) sm. གཏུབ་པ་.

འཐུམ་ (tūm) 1. a package, a bundle; va.—རྒྱག to wrap into a package ། རས་འཐུམ་ A package wrapped in cloth. 2. sm. གཏུམ་. 3. sm. འཐུམས་.

འཐུམ་སྒོང་ (tūmgoŋ) a preserved egg.

འཐུམ་སྒྲིལ་ (tūmdrii) 1. a bundle, sth. that is wrapped. 2. sm. འཐུམ་རྒྱག.

འཐུམ་ལ་མ་འཐུམ་ (tūmla madum) not completely covered/ wrapped.

འཐུམས་ (tūm) vi. to become suffocated, to choke.

འཐུལ་ (tūū) vi. to diffuse, to spread (for smell/ smoke) ། དྲི་བསུང་ཕྱོགས་ཀུན་དུ་འཐུལ་བ་རེད་ The smell of incense spread everywhere.

འཐུལ་འཐུལ་ (tūūdüü) a term conveying the way that smoke rises and smells diffuse; va.—བྱེད་ ། བསངས་ཀྱི་དུ་བ་འཐུལ་འཐུལ་བྱེད་ཀྱི་འདུག The smoke from the incense is rising up.

འཐུས་ (tūù) 1. vi. to be okay, to be satisfactory ། དེ་ར་ཁ་པར་བཏང་ན་འཐུས་ཀྱི་རེད་ If you telephone there it will be okay. 2. (vb. + —) va. to approve/ allow ། གཞུང་གི་ཞབས་ཞུར་སེར་དམག་དང་བླངས་འཇུགས་འཐུས་ཞུས་དེ་ (They) requested approval to enroll monk volunteer soldiers to serve the government. ། བསྐྱོད་འཐུས་ཤྭ་སི་ A ticket that gives permission to go somewhere. 3. representative, delegate ། གདན་འཐུས་ Representatives of the three གདན་ས་. 4. sm. གཅིག་འཐུས་. 5. imp. of འཐུ་.

འཐུས་ཁོངས་ (tūùgoŋ) a part of, a member of ། རྒྱལ་སྤྱིའི་འཐུས་ཁོངས་ཀྱི་ཡུལ་ཁག ། Those countries that are part of the UN.

འཐུས་སྒོ་ཚང་པོ་ (tūùgo tsāŋbo) complete, nothing missing, thorough ། ལས་ཀ་འཐུས་སྒོ་ཚང་པོ་བྱུང་བཞག The work was finished thoroughly. ། ལས་དོན་འཐུས་སྒོ་ཚང་སོང་ The work was done completely.

འཐུས་སྒོ་ཚང་དུ་ (tūùgo tsāŋdu) complete, perfect, nothing missing, completely effective; va.—གཏོང་ to make complete/ perfect; vi.—འགྲོ་ to get/ be done completely or perfectly.

འཐུས་སྒོ་ཚང་མིན་ (tūùgo tsāŋmin) shung. incomplete ། རང་འཁྲིའི་སྤྱི་ཞུ་སྒྲུབ་རྒྱུར་ཕྲུན་བུའི་འཐུས་སྒོ་ཚང་མིན་བྱུང་བ་ (He) could not complete his task.

འཐུས་མཆན་ (tūùjɛn) visa, written appeal; va.—འགོད ། བོད་ལ་ཡོང་རྒྱུའི་ལག་འཁྱེར་ལ་འཐུས་མཆན་འགོད་ (One) needs a visa on one's passport to come to Tibet.

འཐུས་འདོམས་ (tūndom) shung. well-ordered and comprehensible to all ། ས་གནས་རྫོང་སྡོད་ནས་བཀོད་ཁྱབ་འཐུས་འདོམས་དགོས་རྒྱུ་ The Dzongpon should give an order that is well-ordered and comprehensible to all.

འཐུས་མི་ (tūùmi) representative, delegate; va.—བྱེད་ to act as a representative/ delegate ། ཁོང་གིས་མི་དམངས་ཀྱི་འཐུས་མི་བྱས་ནས་ཚོགས་འདུའི་ཐོག་སྐད་ཆ་བཤད་པ་རེད་ He spoke at the meeting as a representative of the people.

འཐུས་མི་ཚོགས་པ་ (tūùmii tsɔ̄gba) sm. འཐུས་མིའི་ཚོགས་པ་.

འཐུས་མིའི་གྲོས་ཚོགས་ (tūùmii troöòdzɔɔ̀) sm. འཐུས་མི་ཚོགས་པ་.

འཐུས་མིའི་ཐོབ་ཐང་ཞིབ་བཤེར་ཨུ་ཡོན་ལྷན་ཁང་ (tūùmii tōbdaŋ shibsher ūyön lhɛ̄ngaŋ) (delegate's) credentials committee.

འཐུས་མིའི་སྣ་པོ་ (tūùmii nābo) the head of a group of representatives/ delegates.

འཐུས་མིའི་ཚོགས་ཆེན་ (tūùmii tsɔ̄gjen) a congress, a large meeting/ assembly of representatives.

འཐུས་མིའི་ཚོགས་པ་ (tūùmii tsɔ̄gba) 1. a meeting/ assembly of representatives. 2. a delegation.

འཐུས་གཙོ་ (tūùdzo) chief representative.

འཐུས་ཚང་ (tūùdzaŋ) thorough, careful, detailed, precise, complete, without anything amiss/ missing, perfect; va.—བྱེད་ ། ཟླ་བ་དགུ་པར་དཔུང་བསྐྱོད་ཀྱི་གྲ་སྒྲིག་འཐུས་ཚང་བྱེད་དགོས་ We have to thoroughly prepare to send the military in September.

འཐུས་ཚང་སྐྱོན་མེད་ (tūùdzaŋ gyȫnmeè) complete and without error.

འཐུས་ཚང་ལྡན་པ་ (tūùdzaŋ demba) sm. འཐུས་ཚང་.

འཐུས་ཚབ་ (tūùdzəb) sm. འཐུས་མི་.

འཐུས་ཚབ་ཚོགས་པ་ (tūùdzəb tsɔ̄gba) sm. འཐུས་མིའི་ཚོགས་པ་.

འཐུས་ཚོགས་ (tūùdzɔg) abbr. འཐུས་མིའི་ཚོགས་པ་.

འཐུས་ཚོགས་ཁང་ (tūùdzɔɔ̀gaŋ) parliament.

འཐུས་ཤོར་ (tūùshɔɔ) 1. hindrance, delay, holdup. 2. vi. འཐུས་ཤོར་; —འགྲོ་; va.—གཏོང་ ། ལས་བྱེད་པ་རྣམས་དུས་ཐོག་ཏུ་ལས་ཀར་མ་ཡོང་བར་བརྟེན་ལས་ཀར་འཐུས་ཤོར་བྱུང་བ་རེད་ Because the officials didn't come to work on time, the work was delayed ། ལག་ཆ་དུས་ཐོག་ལ་མ་འབྱོར་བ་ཡིན་ཙང་ལས་ཀར་འཐུས་ཤོར་བ་རེད་ Because the tools didn't arrive in time, the work was hindered. ། ཁོས་བཟོ་གྲྭའི་རྒྱུ་ཆ་དུས་ཐོག་མ་བཏང་བར་ལས་ཀར་འཐུས་ཤོར་བཏང་སོང་ He held up the work by not sending the factory the materials on time.

འཐུས་ཤོར་མེད་པ་ (tūùshɔɔ meèba) without slip up/ loss/ damage/ hindrance ། ལས་ཀ་འཐུས་ཤོར་མེད་པ་བྱེད་རྒྱུ་གལ་ཆེན་པོ་རེད་ It is very important to work in a manner that will result in no loses.

འཐུས་སུ་ (tūùsu) see འཐུས་.

འཐེང་ (tēŋ) vi. to walk with a limp.

འཐེང་འཐེང་ (tēŋdeŋ) lame/ crippled in the leg; va.—བྱེད་.

འཐེང་པོ་ (tēŋbo) lame/ crippled in the legs.

འཐེངས་ (tēŋ) p. of འཐེང་.

འཐེན་ (tēn) 1. va. to pull, to drag ། ཐག་པ་འདི་འཐེན་རོགས་ Please pull the rope. 2. va. to subtract, to deduct ། ཕོགས་ནས་བརྒྱ་ཆ་ ༡༠ ཁྲལ་ལ་འཐེན་གྱི་ཡོད་པ་རེད་ (They) deduct 10% from salary for taxes. 3. va. to withdraw (from a place) ། དམག་བརྒྱབ་ནས་ཕྱིར་འཐེན་བྱས་པ་རེད་ After (they) fought the war (they) withdrew. ། ལས་བྱེད་པ་ཁག་ཅིག་འཐེན་ནས་གྲོང་གསེབ་ཏུ་བཏང་བ་རེད་ A group of officials were withdrawn (from where they were) and sent to the villages. 4. va. to smoke ། ཐ་མག་མ་འཐེན་ན་ཡག་གི་རེད་ It is better if you don't smoke.

འཐེན་སྐུམ་མེད་པ་ (tēngum meèba) in full, complete.

འཐེན་བསྐོང་ (tēngoŋ) withdrawing and reassigning; va.—བྱེད་.

འཐེན་ཁྱེར་ (tēngyer) sm. འཐེན་འཁྱེར་.

འཐེན་ཁྲིད་ (tēndrii) pulling and dragging.

འཐེན་འཁྱེར་ (tēngyer) strained (relations), discord, disagreement, dissension; vi.—ཆགས་; —འགྱུར་ to come into discord/ disagreement/ dissension, to become strained (relations); va.—བྱེད་ to strain relations, to cause discord/ disagreement/ dissension ། ཁོས་ཆོས་ལུགས་གྲུབ་མཐའ་འདྲ་མིན་དབར་འཐེན་འཁྱེར་ཆེན་པོ་བྱེད་ཀྱི་ཡོད་པ་རེད་ He is causing discord between the different sects.

འཐེན་འཁྱེར་ཀར་ཀོར་ (tēngyer gārgor) dissension and delay/ procrastination.

འཐེན་འཁྲོལ་རོལ་ཆ་ (tēndröö rööja) stringed instruments played with a bow.

འཐེན་གྲུ། (tēndru) tugboat, towboat.

འཐེན་རྒྱག (tēngya) a style of building walls similar to that of a pyramid.

འཐེན་སྒམ། (tēngam) sm. ཤུག་སྒྲོག.

འཐེན་སྒོ། (tēngo) sliding door.

འཐེན་དངུལ། (tēnŋüü) money that is deducted ¶ ཟླ་རེའི་ཕོགས་ཐོབ་ནས་འཐེན་དངུལ་སྒོར་ ༡༠༠ རེ་འཐེན་གྱི་ཡོད་པ་རེད། (They) deduct 100 dollars each month from salary.

འཐེན་ཆ། (tēnja) sth. that is deducted from production or income.

འཐེན་བརྗེ། (tēnjeè) recalling and changing; va.—བྱེད། ¶ ཉེ་ཆར་ལས་བྱེད་པ་མང་པོ་འཐེན་རྗེས་བྱས་འདུག Recently many officials were recalled and new ones sent.

འཐེན་ཉར་གྱི་ཆ། (tēnñargi cā) automatic withdrawal (usu. from one's salary).

འཐེན་རྟགས། (tēndaà) subtraction sign, minus sign.

འཐེན་ཐག (tēndaà) a rope to pull things.

འཐེན་ཐབས། (tēndəb) subtraction.

འཐེན་ཐུག (tēnduù) a kind of soup containing flat pieces of dough.

འཐེན་འཐེན། (tēnden) stretching, pulling; va.—བྱེད།.

འཐེན་འཐོག (tēndɔɔ̀) abbr. pulling and plucking/ picking up.

འཐེན་སྤྱོད། (tēnjöö̀) misappropriating, embezzling; va.—བྱེད།.

འཐེན་འཕྲི། (tēndri) deduction ¶ ཟླ་ཕོགས་ཐོག་ནས་ཁང་གླ་འཐེན་འཕྲི་བྱུལ་བཞག (They) deducted rent from my salary.

འཐེན་ཙམ་འཐེན་ཙམ། (tēndzam tēndzam) tugging at sth. as a signal or to get attention (usu. at clothes); va.—བྱེད། ¶ ཚོགས་འདུ་ཚོགས་སྐབས་སྐད་ཆ་ཤོད་མི་ཆོག་པས་ཁོས་ངའི་དུབ་ལོག་ནས་འཐེན་ཙམ་འཐེན་ཙམ་བྱས་ནས་སྐད་བཏང་བྱུང་ Because one can not speak at the meeting hall, he tugged at my clothes to get my attention.

འཐེན་རྩིས། (tēndziì) subtracting; va.—རྒྱག to subtract.

འཐེན་རྩོད། (tēndzöö̀) shung. quarrelling, disputing ¶ དོ་བདག་ཕན་ཚུན་ གྲོ་མཐུན་གྱིས་འདེབས་རྩ་སྤྲོད་པ་ལས་འཐེན་རྩོད་དགོས་གྲས་མིན་རུང་ It would have been appropriate for both parties to hand over (the land) at the planting season without quarrel/ dispute, but.

འཐེན་ཞིབ། (tēnshib) taking sth. out for inspection/ examination.

འཐེན་རེས་གཏོང་། (tēnreè dōŋ) va. to pull at one another, to have a tug-of-war.

འཐེན་ཤར་རྒྱག (tēnshar gya̱à) sm. འཐེན་རེས་གཏོང་.

འཐེན་རོ། (tēnro) cigarette stub/ butt.

འཐེན་ཤུགས། (tēnshuù) 1. pulling force, tensile strength. 2. gravity, gravitational pull. 3. power of attraction.

འཐེན་ཤུགས་ཁྱབ་ཁོངས། (tēnshuù kyəbgoŋ) gravitational field.

འཐེན་ཤུགས་ར་བ། (tēnshuù ra̱wa) sm. འཐེན་ཤུགས་ཁྱབ་ཁོངས་.

འཐེན་བཤར། (tēnshar) tugging and pulling on sth. back and forth; va.—རྒྱག.

འཐེན་སྲུང་། (tēnsuŋ) withdrawing to defend sth.

འཐེབ་འཕྲོལ། (tēndröö) leftover, surplus, extra, residue, remainder.

འཐེབས། (tēb) sm. ཐེབས་.

འཐེམ་: p. ཐེམས་; f. འཐེམ། (tēm) vi. to be complete, to be not lacking, to be full.

འཐོག: p. བཏོགས་; f. བཏོག; imp. འཐོགས། (tɔ̄ɔ̀) va. to pick, to pluck ¶ ལྡུམ་རའི་ནང་ནས་མེ་ཏོག་ཞིག་བཏོགས་པ་རེད། (He) picked a flower from the garden.

འཐོགས། (tɔ̄ɔ̀) imp. of འཐོག.

འཐོན་: p. ཐོན་; f. འཐོན། (tȭn) 1. va. to leave/ go ¶ ཁོང་ཁ་སང་ལྷ་ས་ནས་ཐོན་བཞག He left Lhasa yesterday. 2. vi. to have occurred/ happened ¶ བོད་ནང་ཟིང་ཆའི་གནས་ཚུལ་ཐོན་བཞག A disturbance has occurred in Tibet. 3. vi. to have shoots sprout.

འཐོན་ཁ། (tȭnga) at the point sth. happens.

འཐོན་ཕྱག (tȭnjaà) shung. visit by lay officials to the Kashag (monks officials to the Yiktsang) to pay respects and to notify them that they are departing from Lhasa; va.—ཞུ་.

འཐོབ་: p. ཐོབ་; f. འཐོབ། (tōb) vi. to get/ obtain.

འཐོབ་དུ་ཆ་བ། (tōbdu cāwa) sm. འཐོབ་གྲབས་ཡོད་པ་.

འཐོབ་འོས། (tōbwöö̀) worthy of getting.

འཐོབས། (tōb) imp. of འཐབ་.

འཐོམ་: p. འཐོམས་; f. འཐོམ། (tōm) (usu. མགོ་ + —) vi. to be dazed/ lost/ confused/ puzzled/ bewildered/ dumbfounded ¶ ཕྱི་རྒྱལ་ལུང་པར་སླེབས་དུས་ང་འཐོམས་བྱུང་ When I went abroad I was bewildered (lost).

འཐོམ་རྒྱག (tōm gya̱à) doing things without fully knowing/ understanding.

འཐོམ་སྐྱེ། (tōmgye) dull-headed, witless, bewildered.

འཐོམ་སྐྱེ་འཐོམ་ནག (tōmgye tōmnaà) sm. འཐོམ་སྐྱེ་.

འཐོམ་སྟེར། (tōm dēr) sm. འཐོམ་ཞྭ་གཡོགས་.

འཐོམ་འཐོམ། (tōmdom) sm. འཐོམ་སྐྱེ་.

འཐོམ་མེ་བ། (tōmmewa) sm. འཐོམ་སྐྱེ་.

འཐོམ་ཞྭ་གོན། (tōmsha kö̱n) vi. to be/ get deceived/ tricked.

འཐོམ་ཞྭ་གཡོགས། (tōmsha yɔ̄ɔ̀) va. to deceive/ trick/ swindle.

འཐོམ་ཡོར། (tōmyɔɔ) sm. འཐོམ་སྐྱེ་.

འཐོམས། (tōm) 1. p. of འཐོམ་. 2. imp. of འཐམ་.

འཐོམས་ཀྱི། (tōmgye) sm. འཐོམ་སྐྱེ་.

འཐོམས་གཡོགས། (tōmyɔɔ̀) sm. འཐོམ་ཞྭ་གཡོགས་.

འཐོར། (tɔ̄ɔ) vi. 1. to become scattered/ dispersed ¶ ཁྱུ་འདི་འཐོར་ནས་ After the herd became scattered. 2. vi. to collapse, to disintegrate, to crumble, to break down ¶ ཁྱིམ་ཚང་འདི་འཐོར་བཞག This family has disintegrated. 3. vi. to be splattered/ splashed ¶ ཤོག་བུའི་སྟེང་ལ་ཆུ་འཐོར་བཞག Water got splattered on the paper.

འཐོར་རྐྱེན་ལ་འགྲོ། (tɔ̄ɔ̄gyenla dro̱) shung. vi. to be or become the cause of being scattered/ destroyed.

འཐོར་གོད། (tɔ̄ɔ̄göö̀) shung. to be scattered and destroyed ¶ ལོག་སྨོན་ཅན་གོར་དམག་གིས་ཟིང་སྐྱོན་ལ་བརྟེན་འཐོར་གོད་ཅི་ཆེ་བྱུང་རྗེས་ Because of the turbulence caused by the evil, heretical Nepalese troops, many (religious objects) were scattered and destroyed.

འཐོར་རྒྱར། (tɔ̄rgyaa) scattering, dispersing.

འཐོར་འགྱེད། (tɔ̄rgyeè) sparkling.

འཐོར་གྲུམ། (tɔ̄rdrum) things that are broken/ incomplete.

འཐོར་འཐུང་། (tɔ̄rduŋ) a water offering.

འཐོར་སྡོད། (tɔ̄rdöö̀) vi. to be scattered/ dispersed.

འཐོར་ནས། (tɔ̄rnɛ) barley offerings (that are tossed in the air) to deities.

འཐོར་སྦྱེད། (tɔ̄rjɛɛ̀) a sprinkler, a watering instrument.

འཐོར་བུ། (tɔ̄rbu) sm. ཐོར་བུ་.

འཐོར་བྱེད་ཡོ་བྱད། (tɔ̄rjɛɛ̀ yo̱bjɛɛ̀) atomizer, sprayer.

འཐོར་བྲོས། (tɔ̄rdröö̀) fleeing and getting scattered/ dispersed; va.—བྱེད། to flee/ run in a scattered manner.

འཐོར་འདྲུ། (tɔ̄ndru) sm. འཐོར་ནས་.

འཐོར་མ། (tɔ̄rma) scattered things.

འཐོར་མ་རག (tɔ̄r ma̱raà) just about to be scattered.

འཐོར་བརླག (tɔ̄ɔ̄laà) scattered and lost.

འཐོར་རླུང་། (tɔ̄ɔ̄luŋ) a wind that causes things to be scattered.

འཐོར་ཞིག (tɔ̄rshiì) sm. ཐོར་ཞིག.

འཐོར་འོད། (tɔ̄rwöö̀) astigmatism.

འཐོར་ལ་ཉེ་བ། (tɔ̄ɔ̄la ñe̱wa) tottering, shaky, crumbling, precarious.

འཐོར་བཤིག (tɔ̄rshiì) sm. ཐོར་བཤིག.

འཐོར་སོན་འདེབས། (tɔ̄rsön de̱b) va. to sow seeds by broadcasting.

འཐོལ་པ། (tȫö̀ba) extra ¶ མི་མདའ་འཐོལ་པ་ An extra

gun.

འཐོལ་བ་ (tȫȫwa) sm. འཐོལ་པ་.

འཐོལ་ཡོད་པ་ (tȫȫ yö̱ö̀ba) shung. having an extra of sth.

ད

ད་ (ta) 1. now ¶ ད་འགྲོ་དགོས་རེད་ (We) have to go now. 2. the present (in a temporal sense) ¶ ད་ལོ་ This year. ¶ ད་ཉིན་ Today (this day). 3. the letter ད་ (used in alphabetical ordering).

ད་ཀོ་ (tago) sm. ད་ཅི་.

ད་རྒྱ་ (tagya) sm. ད་རྒྱང་.

ད་བསྐུལ་ (tagüǜ) active service ¶ ད་བསྐུལ་དམག་མི་ Soldiers in active service.

ད་ཁ་ (taga) sm.* ད་ག.

ད་ག (taga) 1. (vb. + pa/ ba + —) as soon as, immediately ¶ ཁོས་དེ་བཤད་པ་ད་ག As soon as he said that. 2. that, just that, exactly that, specifically that ¶ ད་ག་བསྐྱར་དུ་གསུང་དང་ Please say that again. ¶ ད་ག་རེད་ That is exactly it. ¶ ད་གའི་ཉིན་མོ་ On that day specifically.

ད་ག་འདྲ་པོ་ (taga drabo) just like that, exactly like that, the same as that ¶ སྡུག་པོ་ད་ག་འདྲ་པོ་མྱོང་མ་མྱོང་ I have never experienced suffering like that.

ད་ག་ནང་བཞིན་ (taga nəŋshin) sm. ད་ག་འདྲ་པོ་.

ད་ག་ཙམ་ (tagadzam) like that.

ད་ག་རང་ (tagaraŋ) just that, exactly that, exactly right ¶ ཁྱེད་རང་གིས་གསུངས་པ་ད་ག་རང་རེད་ What you said is exactly right. ¶ ང་ལ་ད་ག་རང་དགོས་ I want just that.

ད་གྭ་ (taga) here.

ད་གྭ་སེ་ (tagas) just like that, without much thought, casually, not purposely ¶ ངས་ཁོང་ལ་ད་གྭ་སེ་ལབ་པ་ཡིན་ཀྱང་ཁོང་ནླུང་ལངས་སོང་ I said it casually (not purposely), but he got angry.

ད་གར་ (tagaa) sm. ད་ག, 1.

ད་གི་ (təgi) a while ago, some time ago.

ད་གིན་ (təgin) a while ago, some time ago.

ད་གིན་ནས་ (təginnɛ) (from) a while ago, (from) some time ago ¶ ཁོ་ད་གིན་ནས་ཕྱིན་སོང་ He left some time ago.

ད་འགྲིག་ག (ta driìga) idiom. that's enough!

ད་སྙོས་ (tagöö̀) shung. now (usu. used to introduce the conclusion in a request) ¶ ཞིབ་ཕྲའི་གནས་ཚུལ་གོང་ཞུས་ལྟར་དང་ད་སྙོས་ཞུ་དོན་རྙིང་པོར་ང་རང་ལྷ་སར་འགྲོ་རྒྱུའི་ཆོག་མཆན་གནང་སྐྱོང་ཡོད་པ་ཞུ་རྒྱུ་ In accordance with the detailed account presented above, now for the main point, as in my old request please give me permission to go to Lhasa.

ད་ཅི་ (təji) sm. ད་གི་.

ད་ཅི་ནས་ (təjinɛ) sm. ད་གིན་ནས་.

ད་ཆ་ (taja) now.

ད་ཆོག (ta cɔ̄ɔ̀) 1. it is okay. 2. a ritual done when the དགེ་སློང vow is taken.

ད་ཉིད་ (tañiì) sm. ད་ལྟ་ཉིད་དུ་.

ད་ཉིན་ (təñin) today, this day ¶ སང་ཉིན་ཕེབས་རྒྱུའི་ད་ཉིན་སྲིད་བློན་བསྐོ་གཞག་གནང་སོང་ Today, the day before leaving, (they) appointed two prime ministers.

ད་དིག (tadig) the fruit of the Chinese magnolia vine.

ད་ལྟ་ (tanda) now, at present.

ད་ལྟ་ཉིད་དུ་ (tanda ñiìdu) immediately, at once ¶ ད་ལྟ་ཉིད་དུ་སྨན་ཁང་དུ་སྐྱེལ་དགོས་ (You) must take (him) to the hospital at once.

ད་ལྟ་ནས་ (tandanɛ) 1. from now on ¶ ད་ལྟ་ནས་སློབ་སྦྱོང་ཡག་པོ་བྱེད་དགོས་ From now on you must study well. 2. already ¶ ཕྲུ་གུ་ལོ་ཆུང་ཆུང་དེས་ད་ལྟ་ནས་ཐ་མག་འཐེན་གྱི་འདུག That young child is already smoking cigarettes.

ད་ལྟ་མཇལ་ཡོང་ (tanda jɛɛyoŋ) phrase said when departing: see you later.

ད་ལྟ་ཕན་ (tandapɛn) sm. ད་ཕན་.

ད་ལྟ་ཕན་ཆད་ (tanda pɛ̄njɛɛ̀) sm. ད་ཕན་.

ད་ལྟ་ཕན་ལ་ (tanda pɛ̄nla) sm. ད་ཕན་.

ད་ལྟ་བ་ (tandawa) present tense (for verbs) ¶ ཕྱིན་གྱི་ད་ལྟ་བ་འགྲོ་རེད་ The present tense of ཕྱིན་ is འགྲོ་.

ད་ལྟ་བར་དུ་ (tanda pardu) until now, until today.

ད་ལྟ་རང་ (tandaraŋ) just now.

ད་ལྟ་ལམ་སེང་ (tanda lamsaŋ) at once, right now ¶ ད་ལྟ་ལམ་སེང་སྨན་ཁང་ལ་རྒྱུགས་ Go to the hospital at once.

ད་ལྟར་བར་དུ་ (tandar pərdu) until now, up to now ¶ ད་ལྟ་བར་དུ་ཁོ་སླེབས་མ་སོང་ Up to now, he hadn't arrived.

ད་ལྟའི་ཆར་ (tandɛ cār) for the present, for the time being, as it is now ¶ ད་ལྟའི་ཆར་འདིར་སྡོད་རྩིས་ཡིན་ For the present (we) plan to stay here. ¶ ད་ལྟའི་ཆར་ལས་ཀ་དེ་གཏན་འཁེལ་མི་འདུག For the time being the work hasn't been decided.

ད་ལྟའི་གནས་ཚུལ་ (tandɛ nɛɛ̀dzüü) present state of affairs, the present/ current situation.

ད་སྟེ་ (tade) from this time, henceforth.

ད་ཐུག (ta tūù) until now, up to now ¶ ཁོས་ད་ཐུག་རྒྱ་གར་ལ་བསྡད་པ་རེད་ He lived in India up to now.

ད་དར་ (tadar) Tartar.

ད་དུང་ (taduŋ) even now, still, furthermore, yet ¶ ཁོ་ད་དུང་ལས་ཀ་བྱེད་ཀྱི་འདུག He is still working. ¶ ང་ལས་ཀ་ད་དུང་ཚར་མ་སོང་ (I) still have not finished my work.

ད་དྲག (tadraà) the final "ད་" found in ancient Tibetan writings (e.g., བཙོལད་).

ད་ནང་ (tanaŋ) this morning.

ད་ནས་ (tanɛɛ̀) from now ¶ ད་ནས་དེ་འདྲ་བྱེད་མི་ཆོག From now (you) may not do such things.

ད་ནས་བཟུང་ (tanɛsuŋ) from now on, from this day forth.

ད་ནས་ཕྱིན་ཆད་ (tanɛ cīnjɛɛ̀) sm. ད་ནས་བཟུང་.

ད་ནུབ་ (tanub) this evening.

ད་ཕན་ (tabɛn) 1. until now, prior to this day, previously ¶ ད་ཕན་སྲིད་འཛིན་བྱས་ནས་ལོ་བཞིའི་ནང་ During the four years since (he) became president. ¶ ད་ཕན་གྱི་བྱས་ཉེས་ལ་བརྩད་གཅོད་བྱེད་ཀྱི་མིན་ (We) will not investigate the past crimes. 2. henceforth ¶ ད་ཕན་ཐ་མག་འཐེན་གྱི་མེད་ So far I have not smoked.

ད་ཕྱིན་ (tajin) from now on, henceforth ¶ ད་ཕྱིན་ངས་སློབ་སྦྱོང་ཡག་པོ་བྱེད་ཀྱི་ཡིན་ Henceforth, I will study hard.

ད་ཕྱིན་ཆད་ (ta cīnjɛɛ̀) sm. ད་ཕྱིན་.

ད་བར་ (tabar) until now, up to now.

ད་མུས་ (tamüǜ) continuing as is now or is at present ¶ ཁྱེད་རང་ཕྱག་ལས་ད་མུས་བཞིན་གནང་རོགས་གནང་ Please continue to work as you are doing now.

ད་མུས་བཞིན་ (tamüǜshin) see ད་མུས་.

ད་ཙམ་ (tadzam) (with དུས་) at this late date ¶ དུས་ད་ཙམ་ལ་སླེབས་སྐབས་འགྱོད་པ་སྐྱེས་ཀྱང་ཕན་ཐོགས་མེད་ At this late date, there is no point in having regrets.

ད་ཙུན་བར་དུ་ (tadzün pardu) until now, up to now.

ད་ཚོད་ (tadzöö̀) this time ¶ ན་ལོ་ད་ཚོད་ At this time last year.

ད་མཚམས་ (tadzam) now.

ད་གཟོད་ (tasöö̀) only now ¶ ཁོང་གུང་ཁྲན་ཏང་ཡོན་ཡིན་པ་ད་གཟོད་ཤེས་བྱུང་ Only now did I know that he is a communist party member.

ད་གཟོད་ནས་བཟུང་ (ta söönɛ suŋ) sm. ད་ནས་བཟུང་.

ད་ཡོད་ (tayöö̀) present, current, existing at present ¶ ད་ཡོད་གནས་ཚུལ་ Present situation/ conditions. ¶ ད་ཡོད་དཔེ་གཞི་ Existing model.

ད་ཡོད་མི་ (tayöö̀mi) all people in a rural area as opposed to just those who received a share at decollectivization.

ད་ར་ (tara) buttermilk.

ད་རང་ (taraŋ) this morning.

ད་རབས་ (tarəb) the present generation, contemporary, modern ¶ ད་རབས་ཀྱི་གཞོན་ནུ་ཚོ་

The youth of the present generation.

ད་རི་དི་རི་ (tari diri) the sound of a thunderstorm, etc.

ད་རིང་ (tariŋ) sm. དེ་རིང་.

ད་རུང་ (təruŋ) sm. ད་དུང་.

ད་རེས་ (tareè) this time, now, the present, at the time ། ད་རེས་ཁོ་འདིར་བདུན་ཕྲག་གཅིག་བསྡད་སོང་ This time he stayed here for a week.

ད་རེས་ཁ་སང་ (tareè kāsaŋ) nowadays.

ད་རེས་ནས་བཟུང་ (tareènɛsuŋ) sm. ད་ནས་བཟུང་.

ད་ལན་ (talɛn) sm. ད་རེས་.

ད་ལམ་ (talam) 1. at this time, now ། ད་ལམ་ངའི་ཚོང་ལས་ཀ་ཡག་པོ་བྱུང་མ་སོང་ At this time my business did not go well. 2. recently ། ད་ལམ་བོད་ནས་འབྱོར་བའི་སྐྱབས་བཅོལ་བ་ Refugees who arrived from Tibet recently.

ད་ལམ་རེས་ (talamreè) shung. sm. ད་རེས་.

ད་ལོ་ (talo) this year.

ད་ལའིན་ (talɛna) Darien.

ཌ་མ་རུ་ (damaru) 1. a small two-faced drum with attached strikers. 2. a two-faced/ duplicitous person.

ཌ་རུ་ (dəru) abbr. of ཌ་མ་རུ་.

ཌ་རུ་ངོ་གཉིས་ (dəru ŋoñii) two-faced [Lit. the two surfaces of a two sided drum].

དག (tag) pluralizing particle ། ཁང་པ་དེ་དག Those houses 2. vi. to be/ get clean ། གོས་ལོག་ལ་སྣུམ་རྩི་ཐོག་པ་བཀྲུས་ནས་དག་མི་འདུག Even though they washed the grease on the clothes it did not get clean. ། སྐོར་ར་བརྒྱབ་ན་སྡིག་པ་དག་གི་རེད་ ། If you do circumambulations it will cleanse your sins 3. vi. to be correct/ right (usu. for spelling) ། ཚིག་འདི་དག་འདུག This word is (spelled) correctly. 4. vi. to get void/ nullified/ cleared ། ཁྱོད་རང་གི་མོ་ཊ་ང་ལ་སྤྲད་ན་དེས་བུ་ལོན་དག་པ་བྱེད་ If you give me your car, I will nullify your loan.

དག་བཀྲུས་ (tagdrüü) shung. abbr. of མནའ་དག་གིས་བཀྲུས་པ་.

དག་སྐྱིད་ (taggee) sm. སྐྱིད་པ་.

དག་བསྐྱེལ་ (taggyee) proving sth., showing evidence of one's rightness/ innocence; va.—བྱེད་.

དག་འཁྱོལ་ (tag kyöö) shung. va. to wipe away/ eliminate, to wipe the slate clean ། དཔྱད་མཚམས་བསྒྲལ་བར་ཕན་ཚུན་གཉིས་ཕྱོགས་ནས་དག་འཁྱོལ་གྱི་ཁོན་མེད་ཉེ་མ་སྨིན་བྱལ་དགོས་རྒྱུ་ After the verdict, both parties should eliminate all their differences.

དག་འགྲེལ་ (tagdrel) explaining/ illustrating one's innocence or the correctness of sth.; va.—བྱེད་ ། ཁོང་མི་གསོད་གྱོད་གཞི་དང་འབྲེལ་བ་མེད་ཞེར་དག་འགྲེལ་བྱེད་ཀྱི་འདུག He is explaining that he is innocent of any relationship to the murder case.

དག་སྒྲོག (tagdrɔɔ̀) reading an entire (religious) text from start to finish; va.—བྱེད་.

དག་ཅི་ (təgji) mint (plant) ། དག་ཅི་སྣུམ་ Oil of mint.

དག་བཅོས་ (tagjöö) correction, correcting; va.—བྱེད་ to correct ། ནོར་འཁྲུལ་ཚང་མ་དག་བཅོས་བྱས་པ་རེད་ (They) corrected all the mistakes.

དག་ཆ་ (tagja) spelling ། ཚིག་དེ་དག་ཆ་ག་རེ་རེད་ What is the spelling of that word?

དག་མཆན་ (tagjɛn) a note indicating that an account is cleared.

དག་ཐེར་ (tagder) rectification, correcting/ cleaning up incorrect styles of thinking and working; va.—བྱེད་ ། ཏང་ནང་དག་ཐེར་མུ་མཐུད་བྱེད་ཀྱི་ཡོད་པ་རེད་ They are continuing to carry out rectification in the party.

དག་ཐེར་བསྐོར་ཞིབ་ (tagder gɔ̄ɔshib) inspecting/ making rounds to check standards.

དག་ཐེར་སྦྱོང་བརྡར་ (tagder joŋdar) rectification training.

དག་ཐེར་ལེགས་སྒྲིག (tagder legdrig) rectifying and reforming, reforming.

དག་ཐེར་ལེགས་བཅོས་ (tagder legjöö) rectifying and reforming, reforming; va.—གཏོང་.

དག་ཐེར་གསུམ་ (tagder sūm) "the three rectifications": (rectification of organization, ideology/ education, and style of work) (political slogan).

དག་དག་གང་ (tagdaà gaŋ) filling to the brim, full to the brim.

དག་སྣང་ (tagnaŋ) perceiving/ seeing sth. as good, seeing the good side; va.—བྱེད་ ། ཁོས་ཆོས་ལ་དག་སྣང་བྱེད་ཀྱི་ཡོད་པ་རེད་ He sees religion as good.

དག་པ་ (tagba) 1. pure, clean, honest, authentic ། བསམ་བློ་དག་པ་ Pure thoughts. 2. good, correct, well; va.—ཐེར་ to accept as correct.

དག་པོ་ (tagbo) 1. pure, clean ། སྟོད་ཐུང་འདི་དག་པོ་བྱུང་བཞག This shirt got washed clean (well). 2. good, correct, well (usu. in spelling) ། ང་ཡི་གེ་དག་པོ་མེད་ I am a poor speller. 3. honest, authentic.

དག་ཕུད་ (tagbüü) p. of དག་འབུད་.

དག་སྦྱི་ (tagce) laundry soap, detergent.

དག་འབུད་ (tagbüü) giving proof/ testimony; va.—བྱེད་ to give proof, to testify to the truth ། ཁོས་བཤད་པ་དེ་བདེན་པ་ཡིན་པའི་དག་ཕུད་པ་རེད་ (He) proved that what he said was true.

དག་འབྱེད་ (tagceè) correcting, revising; va.—བྱེད་.

དག་མི་དག (tag midag) correct or incorrect ། སྐད་ཆ་དེ་དག་མི་དག་ང་གོ་གི་མི་འདུག Whether his speech is correct or not I don't know.

དག་མོ་ (tagmo) sm. དག་པོ་.

དག་ཚར་ (tag dzār) shung. completely, to the end ། ལོ་ལྟར་ཟླ་འཕྲུལ་ཡར་ངོར་བཀའ་འགྱུར་དག་ཚར་རེ་གསུང་སྒྲོག་ཞུ་བ་ Every year, in the first lunar month, they completely read the Kangyur text aloud.

དག་རྫས་ (tagdzɛɛ̀) (washing) soap, detergent.

དག་ཞུས་ (tagshüü) shung. accounting for expenses; va.—བྱེད་ ། ངའི་ཕྱོགས་ལ་འགྲོ་ཡས་ཀྱི་རྩིས་ཁྲ་ཚང་མ་དག་ཞུས་ཟིན་པ་རེད་ I have accounted for all my expenses on the trips.

དག་ཞིང་ (tagshiŋ) pure land/ realm, pure Buddha field.

དག་ཞིང་དུ་གཤེགས་ (tagshiŋdu shēg) shung. going to a higher/ pure realm.

དག་ཞུས་དཔྱད་མཆན་ (tagshüü jɛ̀ɛ̀jɛn) an official signing that the expenses of a worker have all been accounted for.

དག་ཡིག (təgyii) 1. a book for learning to spell, spelling dictionary; va.—སློག; va.—འཚོལ་ to look up in a spelling dictionary. 2. shung. sm. གན་རྒྱ་.

དག་ཤིང་ (təgshiŋ) toothpick.

དག་སེལ་ (tagsel) redressing an abuse or conviction; va.—བྱེད་ ། བཙོན་ཁང་ལ་བཙུག་པའི་ལས་བྱེད་པ་ཁ་ཤས་གཞུང་གིས་དག་སེལ་བྱས་པ་རེད་ The government redressed the incarceration of several imprisoned officials.

དག་སེལ་དཀར་འདོན་ (tagsel gārdön) sm. དག་སེལ་.

དག་སེལ་བྱེད་པའི་དབང་ཆ་ (tagsel cɛ̀ebɛ wāŋja) the right to defend oneself in court.

དག་བསལ་ (tagsɛɛ) sm. དག་སེལ་.

དྭགས་ཀོང་ (taàgoŋ) the regions of དྭགས་པོ་ and ཀོང་པོ་.

དྭགས་པོ་ (tagbo) a traditional region in south central Tibet.

དྭགས་ཤིང་ (tagshiŋ) type of wood from དྭགས་པོ་ used in making Tibetan bowls.

དང་ (taŋ) 1. the conjunctive particle "and" ། བཀྲིས་དང་པད་མ་ཡོང་གི་རེད་ Tashi and Pema will come. 2. with, together with ། བཀྲིས་པད་མ་དང་མཐུན་པོ་འདུག Tashi gets along well with Pema. 3. (vb. + པ་/ བ་ + —) as soon as ། ལས་ཀ་ཚར་བ་དང་ནང་ལ་ལོག་པ་རེད་ (They) went home as soon as (they) finished work. 4. (vb. + —) polite imperative ། འདི་འདྲ་བྱེད་དང་ Do it like this. 5. certainly do (vb. + དང་ + vb.) ། ངས་ཞབས་ཕྱི་ཞུ་དང་ཞུ་ I will certainly work as your servant.

དང་ཁ་ (taŋga) 1. appetite; vi.—འབྱེད་ to have a good appetite; vi.—འགག to lose one's appetite. 2. chest.

དང་ཁ་མཐུན་པོ་ (taŋga tũmbu) appetizing.

དང་ཁ་བདེ་པོ་ (ta̱ŋga de̱bo) sm. དང་ཁ་མཐུན་པོ་.
དང་ཁར་འགྲོ་པོ་ (ta̱ŋgaa dro̱bo) sm. དང་ཁ་མཐུན་པོ་.
དང་ག (ta̱ŋga) sm. དང་ཁ་.
དང་ག་འབྱེད་སྨན་ (ta̱ŋga ce̱èmɛn) medicine for gaining one's appetite back.
དང་ག་འབྱེད་ཡག (ta̱ŋga ce̱èyaà) an appetizer (before the main meal).
དང་བཅས་ (ta̱njɛɛ̀) see བཅས་, 3.
དང་གཉིས་ (ta̱ŋñii) abbr. first and second ༎ འཛམ་གླིང་དམག་ཆེན་དང་གཉིས་ The First and Second World Wars.
དང་བསྟོད་ (ta̱ndöö) sm. དང་དོད་.
དང་བསྟོད་ཀུན་བླང་བྱེད་ (ta̱ndöö gũnlaŋ ce̱è) shung. va. to do sth. voluntarily ༎ གཞུང་སའི་ཞབས་འདེགས་ཞུ་སྒོ་གང་ སྒྲིའི་ཐད་དང་བསྟོད་ཀུན་བླང་བྱེད་པ་ They are voluntarily serving the government in all aspects.
དང་ཐོག (ta̱ndɔɔ̀) at very beginning, originally, at first ༎ ང་ཡུ་སི་རག་མཁན་དང་ཐོག་འཁྱིལ་སོང་ I was the first to get the ticket. ༎ དང་ཐོག་མི་མང་པོ་མི་འདུག At first there were not many people.
དང་ཐོག་གི་དཔྱད་གཞིའི་ཡིག་ཆ་ (ta̱ntɔɔ̀gi jɛ̄ɛ̀shi yi̱gja) original materials, primary data.
དང་ཐོག་ཤེས་པའི་སྐད་རིགས་ (ta̱ndɔɔ̀ shēèbɛ gɛ̄ɛ̀rig) mother tongue/ language.
དང་དུ་བླངས་ (ta̱ndu lāŋ) p. of དང་དུ་ལེན་.
དང་དུ་བཞེས་ (ta̱ndu she̱è) h. of དང་དུ་ལེན་.
དང་དུ་ལེན་ (ta̱ndu le̱n) 1. va. to assume/ bear/ undertake a task or responsibility voluntarily, to volunteer ༎ དམག་རྒྱག་པར་དང་དུ་བླངས་པ་རེད་ (They) volunteered to go to war. 2. va. to accept/ recognize ༎ ང་ཚོའི་སྐུ་ཚབ་དང་ལེན་བྱས་མི་འདུག They didn't accept our representative.
དང་དོད་ (ta̱ndöö) 1. style, fashion; va.—བྱེད་ to be fashionable/ stylish ༎ དེང་སང་བུད་མེད་ཚོས་སྨད་གཡོགས་སྐབ་ཐུང་ལ་དང་དོད་བྱེད་ཀྱི་འདུག Nowadays short skirts are fashionable for women. 2. showing concern for, being careful about, stressing ༎ ལས་ཁུངས་འདི་སྒྲིག་ལམ་ལ་དང་དོད་ཡོད་པ་རེད་ This office is very careful about discipline.
དང་དོད་ལྔ་དང་མཛེས་པོ་བཞི་ (ta̱ndöö nā ta̱ŋ dzeèbo shi̱) the five things to be careful about and the four points of beauty: (stresses on decorum, manners, hygiene, discipline and morals; beautifications of the mind, language, behavior and the environment).
དང་དོད་ཆེན་པོ་ (ta̱ndöö cēmbo) sm. very stylish/ fashionable.
དང་དོད་ཚ་པོ་ (ta̱ndö tsābo) sm. དང་དོད་ཆེན་པོ་.
དང་པོ་ (ta̱ŋbo) first ༎ ཟླ་བ་དང་པོ་ The first Tibetan month. ༎ གནམ་གྲུ་དང་པོ་དང་གཉིས་པ་སླེབས་སོང་ The first and second airplanes arrived.
དང་པོ་ཐོག་མར་ (ta̱ŋbo tɔ̄ɔ̀mor) at first, in the beginning.
དང་པོ་དང་རྒྱང་ (ta̱ŋbo ta̱ŋgyaŋ) the first one ༎ ང་ད་རང་སྨན་ཁང་དུ་འབྱོར་མཁན་དང་པོ་དང་རྒྱང་དེ་ཡིན་ I was the first person to arrive at the hospital this morning.
དང་པོ་དྭངས་ཐོག་ཁ་པོ་ པད་ཁ་སེར་པོའི་མེ་ཏོག གཉིས་པ་ལག་པར་ལེན་དུས་ སྦར་བ་གང་ལས་མི་འདུག (ta̱ŋbo ta̱ŋdɔɔ̀ kābo bɛ̄ɛ̀ga sērbö me̱dog ñīiba lagbar le̱ndüü ba̱rwa ka̱ŋlɛɛ̀ mi̱nduù) sth. that looks good in the beginning but has no substance [Lit. yellow mustard flowers look good at the beginning but when you take it in your hand it is only a handful].
དང་པོ་དང་པོ་ནས་ (ta̱ŋbo ta̱ŋbonɛ) in/ from the very beginning.
དང་པོ་འཕྲད་པ་གྲོགས་ཀྱི་མཆོག (ta̱ŋbo drɛ̄ɛ̀ba trɔ̱ggi cɔ̄ɔ̀) one's very first friend is the best friend.
དང་པོ་ཙ་ན་ (ta̱ŋbo dzāna) at first, in the beginning.
དང་པོའི་བཅོ་ལྔའི་དུས་ཆེན་ (ta̱ŋbö jɔ̃ŋɛ tü̱üjen) religious festival held on the 15th of the 1st Tibetan month (The Butter Sculpture Festival).
དང་པོར་ (ta̱ŋbor) at first.
དང་བ་ཆེན་པོ་ (ta̱ŋwa cēmbo) with great interest ༎ ལན་དུ་སྨྲས་པའི་ཚིག་རྣམས་དང་བ་ཆེན་པོས་ཉན་པ་རེད་ He listened to the answer with great interest.
དང་བ་འདྲེན་ (ta̱ŋwa dre̱n) vi. to be pleasant/ pleasing.
དང་བའི་ཡིད་ (ta̱ŋwɛ yi̱i) shung. honesty, sincerity.
དང་བའི་གཡའ་ཞག་འཁྱིལ་ (ta̱ŋwɛ yāshaà kyīl) vi. smoke to be circling/ curling over sth. ༎ ཁང་ཆུང་དཀར་པོ་དུ་བའི་གཡས་ཞག་འཁྱིལ་ Smoke circling over the roof of the white house.
དང་བས་ཀུན་ནས་ལེན་ (ta̱ŋwɛ gũnnɛ le̱n) sm. དང་བླངས་.
དང་བས་ལྷུར་ལེན་ (ta̱ŋwɛ lhūrlen) shung. sm. དང་བསྟོད་ཀུན་བླང་བྱེད་.
དང་བླངས་ (ta̱nlaŋ) volunteering to do sth.; va.—བྱེད་; —འདོན་ to volunteer (to do) ༎ ཁོང་དང་བླངས་དོན་ནས་དམག་རྒྱག་པར་ཕྱིན་པ་རེད་ He volunteered and went to war.
དང་བླངས་ཁྲག་འབུལ་རུ་ཁག (ta̱nlaŋ trāgbüü ru̱gaà) volunteer blood donation brigade.
དང་བླངས་དམག (ta̱nlaŋ māà) 1. volunteer army. 2. volunteer soldier.
དང་བླངས་དམག་སྒར་ (ta̱nlaŋ māàgar) volunteer batallion.
དང་སྦྲགས་ (ta̱ndraà) together with.
དང་འབྲེལ་ (ta̱ndree) in addition to, together with ༎ ཁོང་གིས་སློབ་སྦྱོང་ལག་པོ་བྱས་པ་དང་འབྲེལ་ཞོར་དུ་ལས་ཀ་ཡང་བྱེད་ཀྱི་ཡོད་པ་རེད་ In addition to studying, he also worked.
དང་དམག (ta̱nmaà) abbr. of དང་བླངས་དམག.
དང་རྩུགས་ (ta̱ndzuù) shung. right away.
དང་མཚུངས་ (ta̱ndzuŋ) sm. མཚུངས་.
དང་བཞེས་ (ta̱nsheè) sm. དང་ལེན་.
དང་ལེན་ (ta̱nlen) sm. དང་དུ་ལེན་.
དང་ལེན་བྱེད་ (ta̱nlen ce̱è) sm. དང་དུ་ལེན་.
དང་སློབ་ (ta̱nlob) primary school.
དང་སེམས་ (ta̱nsem) joy, happiness.
དད་ (tɛ̱ɛ̀) (with ཡོད་) vi. to have faith/ belief ༎ ང་བླ་མ་དེ་ལ་ཡིད་དད་སོང་ I have faith in that lama.
དད་བཀུར་ (tɛ̱ɛ̀gur) faith and respect; va.—བྱེད་; —ཞུ་.
དད་གུས་ (tɛ̱ɛ̀güü) sm. དད་བཀུར་.
དད་དགའ་ (tɛ̱ɛ̀ga) liking.
དད་དམ་འགྱུར་མེད་ (tɛ̱ɛ̀dam gyu̱rmeè) sm. དད་དམ་ལ་རྒྱ་འགྱུར་མེད་.
དད་དམ་ལ་རྒྱ་འགྱུར་མེད་ (tɛ̱ɛ̀dam lāgya gyu̱rmeè) unchanging faith/ belief and loyalty ༎ བོད་མི་ཚང་མ་དད་དམ་ལ་རྒྱ་འགྱུར་མེད་ཀྱིས་མཐུན་སྒྲིལ་བྱ་དགོས་ All Tibetans must be unified with unchanging faith and loyalty.
དད་དད་གུས་གུས་ (tɛ̱ɛ̀tɛɛ̀ gü̱ügüü) faith and respect.
དད་འདུན་ (tɛ̱ɛ̀ dü̱n) faith and hope; va. —བྱེད་; vi.—བསྐྱེད་.
དད་ལྡན་ (tɛ̱ndɛn) devout, having faith/ belief in sth. ༎ དད་ལྡན་གྱི་སློབ་མ་ Faithful disciple.
དད་ལྡན་པ་ (tɛ̱ndɛnma) a faithful follower/ disciple.
དད་པ་ (tɛ̱ɛ̀ba) faith; va.—བྱེད་ to have faith in, to believe in; va.—ལོག to lose one's faith in ༎ དད་པའི་རྟགས་མཚན་ A symbol of faith ༎ ཁོང་ཆོས་ལ་དད་པ་བྱེད་ཀྱི་ཡོད་པ་རེད་ He has faith in religion.
དད་པའི་ཆུ་གཏེར་ (tɛ̱ɛ̀bɛ cūder) shung. a stream of faith.
དད་པོ་ (tɛ̱ɛ̀bo) 1. faith/ belief in sth. ༎ ང་བླ་མ་དེ་ལ་དད་པོ་མེད་ I don't have faith in that lama. 2. liking sth. ༎ ཆང་ལ་དད་པོ་འདུག I like ཆང་.
དད་འབུལ་ (tɛ̱mbüü) a presentation or offering given out of faith; va.—ཞུ་ to give/ present a gift or offering out of faith.
དད་སྦྱིན་ (tɛ̱ɛ̀jin) shung. a patron/ sponsor who has faith ༎ དད་སྦྱིན་ཁག་ལ་དགེ་སླལ་ཞུ་འབྲས་ One can ask the patrons who have faith for donations.
དད་མོས་ (tɛ̱ɛ̀möö) sm. དད་པ་.
དད་རྫས་ (tɛ̱ɛ̀dzɛɛ̀) shung. things that are donated out of faith ༎ དད་རྫས་ཆུད་མི་འཛའ་བའི་ཆེད་མཚོད་རྒྱུན་ཐོག་སྦྱིན་གཏོང་དགོས་རྒྱུ་ In order not to waste the

things donated out of faith, one must make good use of it for religious offerings.

དད་ཞེན་ (tεὲshεn) faith and loyalty; va.—བྱེད་.

དད་ལོག (tεὲlɔ̀ɔ̀) losing one's faith; va.—བྱེད་; vi.—སྐྱེ་ to lose one's faith ། བླ་མས་ཆང་ས་བརྒྱབ་ཙང་སློབ་མ་ཚོས་དད་ལོག་བྱས་པ་རེད་ Because the lama got married, the disciples lost faith in him.

དད་ཤུགས་ (tεὲshug) strength of faith, the power of faith ། ཆོས་ལ་དད་ཤུགས་ཆེན་པོ་ཡོད་པ་རེད་ (They) have great faith in religion.

དད་སེམས་ (tεὲsem) sm. དད་མོས་.

དན་ (tεn) 1. agreement. 2. ch. telegram, wireless. 3. shung. a type of volume measure ། དམག་མི་རེ་ར་ལོ་ལྟར་འབྲུ་དན་གཉིས་རེ་དང་བརྟུལ་ལྔ་རེ་སྤྲོད་རྒྱུ་ Each soldier will be paid 2 དན་ and 5 བརྟུལ་ a year.

དན་ཁྲ་ (tεndra) castor beans.

དན་ཁྲ་སྣུམ་ (tεndra nūm) castor oil.

དན་གྲོགས་ (tεndrɔ̀ɔ̀) sb. who helps.

དན་དར་ (tεndar) ch. telegram, cable.

དན་རྟགས་ (tεndaà) proof, evidence (in logic).

དན་ཐེལ་ (tεntel) shung. a seal that conveys approval/ agreement ། འདུམ་གསལ་གང་ཡིན་ལ་དན་ཐེལ་ཕུལ་རིགས་མེད་པ་ We did not put the seal of approval on what was written in the mediation agreement.

དན་ད་ (tεnda) sm. དན་ཁྲ་.

དན་པའོ་ (tεmbao) ch. telegraph.

དན་དཔང་ (tεmbaŋ) sm. དཔང་པོ་.

དན་ཕེབས་གསལ་ (tεmpebsεl) shung. ch.tib. according to the telegraph.

དན་བག (tambaà) the village in below Drepung monastery.

དན་མིན་ (tεnmin) shung. not agreeing ། ཚོང་ལས་སྐོར་དན་མིན་དཔྱད་མཚམས་བཅུལ་བ་ A verdict was issued regarding the disagreement on trade.

དན་མྲག (tεnmag) Denmark.

དན་ཞེ་མེད་ཚེ་ (tεnshe meèdze) shung. if it is not likely to be agreed ། གལ་ཏེ་འདུམ་ཁྲ་འདིར་དན་ཞེ་མེད་ཚེ་ If (they) are not likely to agree to this verdict.

དན་རོགས་ (tεnrɔ̀ɔ̀) sm. དན་གྲོགས་.

དན་ཧྲི་ (tεnhri) ch. television.

དན་ཧྲི་གློག་བརྙན་ (tεnhri lɔ̄gñεn) ch.tib. television.

དབ་དིབ་ (tabdib) stuttering, stammering.

དམ་ (tam) 1. interrogative particle (used after final 'd') ། ཁོང་བཞུགས་ཡོད་དམ་ Is he living there? (Is he home?). 2. the 'or' particle (used after the final 'd'). ། བོད་དམ་རྒྱ་གར་ནང་ In Tibet or India. 3. abbr. of དམ་པོ་. 4. with verbs, conveys doing the verbal action strictly/ firmly/ carefully.

དམ་སྐྱོང་ (tamgyoŋ) administering strictly/ firmly/ carefully; va.—བྱེད་ ། སྲིད་འཛིན་གསར་པས་རྒྱལ་ཁབ་དམ་སྐྱོང་བྱེད་ཀྱི་ཡོད་པ་རེད་ The new president is administering the country firmly.

དམ་ཁ་ (tamga) seal, stamp; va.—རྒྱག to affix/ put on a seal, to stamp.

དམ་འགག (tamga) absolutely prohibited; va.—བྱེད་ ། འབར་རྫས་གནམ་གྲུའི་ནང་ལ་དམ་འགག་བྱེད་ཀྱི་ཡོད་པ་རེད་ Explosives are absolutely prohibited on airplanes.

དམ་རྒྱ་ (tamgya) 1. sm. དམ་ཁ་. 2. a network/ web. 3. an agreement.

དམ་བསྒྲགས་ (tamdraà) restriction, restricting; va.—བྱེད་ ། ཉོ་ཚོང་བྱེད་མི་ཆོག་པའི་དམ་བསྒྲགས་ཡོད་ There is a restriction against trading. ། གསང་བའི་བཀའ་མོལ་འདི་ཚོ་དམ་བསྒྲགས་བྱེད་དགོས་ (We) must restrict the secret talks.

དམ་བསྒྲགས་བཀོད་འདོམས་ (tamdraà gũũdom) shung. an order of restriction.

དམ་ཅན་ (tamjεn) sb. who has taken an oath/ pledge. 2. protective deity.

དམ་བཅག (tamjaà) careful, cautious; va.—བྱེད་ ། ལམ་བར་དམ་བཅག་བྱེད་རོགས་གནང་ Please be careful on the road.

དམ་བཅའ་ (tamja) oath, pledge, promise; va.—འཇོག; —འབུལ་ to take an oath, to pledge, to swear, to vow; vi.—འགལ་; —ཤོར་ to break an oath/ pledge/ promise; va.—སྲུང་ to keep one's oath/ pledge/ promise ། ཕ་ཡུལ་སྲུང་སྐྱོབ་བྱ་རྒྱུའི་དམ་བཅའ་བཞག་པ་རེད་ (They) took an oath to defend their motherland.

དམ་བཅའ་འཇོག (tamja jɔ̀ɔ̀) see དམ་བཅའ་.

དམ་བཅའ་རྡོ་རྗེའི་ཚིག (tamja dɔrjee tsi̋g) unshakable oath/ promise.

དམ་བཅའ་འབུལ་བཞེས་ (tamja bṹũshee) the act of taking an oath/ vow; va.—གནང་; —མཛད་ to take an oath, to give one's word, to be sworn in.

དམ་བཅའ་ཚོགས་འདུ་ (tamja tsōndu) a swearing in oath/ ceremony/ meeting.

དམ་བཅའ་བཞག (tamja shaà) p. of དམ་བཅའ་འཇོག.

དམ་བཅའ་བཞེས་ (tamja sheè) va. to accept an oath, to swear in sb., to administer an oath ། སྲིད་འཛིན་གྱི་ཁྲི་འདོན་མཛད་སྒོའི་སྐབས་ཁྲིམས་དཔོན་གཙོ་བོས་དམ་བཅའ་བཞེས་པ་རེད་ The head judge administered the oath at the inauguration of the President.

དམ་བཅའ་ལེན་ (tamja len) nh. of དམ་བཅའ་བཞེས་.

དམ་བཅའི་ཚིག (tamjε tsi̋g) oath, promise, vow, pledge.

དམ་བཅའི་ཡི་གེ་ (tamjε yigi) sm. དམ་བཅའི་ཚིག.

དམ་བཅའི་རི་མོ་སྙིང་ལ་བཀོད་ (tamjε rimu ñi̋ŋla gṹṹ) va. to take an unshakable oath [Lit. an oath drawn on the heart].

དམ་བཅས་ (tamjεὲ) sm. དམ་བཅའ་འཇོག.

དམ་བཅིངས་ (tamjiŋ) tying tightly, binding firmly; va.—བྱེད་ ། དེང་སང་སྒྲིག་ལམ་དམ་བཅིངས་བྱས་བཞག These days they have tightened discipline.

དམ་ཆས་ (tamjεὲ) sm. དམ་ཕྱུག.

དམ་ཆོས་ (tamjöö) the pure/ true dharma.

དམ་གཉེར་ (tamñer) the person/ steward who keeps a seal.

དམ་དུ་འགྲོ་ (tamdu dro) vi. to become tighter/ stricter.

དམ་དུ་གཏོང་ (tamdu dōŋ) va. to tighten, to make stricter ། སྐེ་རགས་དམ་དུ་བཏང་པ་རེད་ (He) tightened the belt. ། སློབ་གྲྭའི་ནང་སྒྲིག་ལམ་དམ་དུ་བཏང་ཡོད་པ་རེད་ (They) have made discipline stricter in school.

དམ་དུ་བཞེས་ (tamdu sheè) sm. དམ་བཅའ་བཞེས་.

དམ་དུམ་ (tamdum) short pieces ། ཤིང་དམ་དུམ་ Short pieces of wood. ། ལྕགས་སྐུད་དེ་དམ་དུམ་དུ་བཅད་སོང་ He cut the wire into small pieces.

དམ་དེམ་ (tamdem) sm. དམ་བཅའ་.

དམ་དོག (tamdɔɔ̀) sm. དང་དོག.

དམ་དོན་ (tamdön) sm. དམ་པ་དོན་གཉེར་.

དམ་དྲག (tamdraà) sm. དམ་བསྒྲགས་.

དམ་འདོགས་ (tamdɔɔ̀) sm. དམ་ལ་འདོགས་.

དམ་ལྡན་ (tamdεn) maintaining one's vow.

དམ་ནན་ (tamnεn) strict, rigorous, stern; va.—བྱེད་.

དམ་མནན་ (tamnεn) sm. དམ་ནན་.

དམ་སྣག (tamnaà) ink pad, stamp pad (for seals and stamps).

དམ་པ་ (tamba) 1. superior, excellent ། ཁོ་མི་དམ་པ་ཞིག་འདུག He is an excellent person. 2. pure, true, honest, holy ། དམ་པའི་ལས་ True, honest deeds. ། སྐྱེས་བུ་དམ་པ་ A holy person. 3. the late, the deceased ། ཁོང་གི་ཡབ་དམ་པ་ His late father. ། དམ་པ་དེ་ཉིད་ The deceased one. 3. sm. of དམ་པོ་.

དམ་པ་དོན་གཉེར་ (tamba tönñer) doing one's best; va.—བྱེད་ ། ཡི་གེ་འདི་དམ་པ་དོན་གཉེར་འཛམ་གླིང་རྒྱལ་སྤྱིར་འབུལ་རོགས་ Doing your best, you must help give this letter to the UN.

དམ་པའི་ཆོས་ (tambε cöö) sm. དམ་ཆོས་.

དམ་པའི་ཚིག (tambε tsi̋g) see དམ་ཚིག.

དམ་པའི་གསུང་རབ་ (tambε sūŋrəb) scriptures.

དམ་པོ་ (tambo) 1. tight, firm, close ། སྡོད་ཆས་དེའི་ཁ་དམ་པོ་བརྒྱབ་འདུག They have covered the pot tightly. ། མདུད་པ་དམ་པོ་ A tight knot. ། ཐག་པའི་སྣེ་ནས་དམ་པོར་བཟུང་ནས་མ་བཏང་བ་རེད་ They held on to the end of the rope firmly and did not let it go. 2. close, intimate ། ཁོ་ཚོའི་དབར་གྱི་མཛའ་འབྲེལ་དམ་པོ་ཡོད་ The relationship between them is close. 3. strict ། ཁྲིམས་ལམ་དམ་པོ་ Strict discipline. 4. (for shooting) accurate.

དམ་པོར་ (t̲ambor) firmly, tightly; va.—འཛིན་ to hold firmly; va.—སྲུང་ to protect resolutely.

དམ་པོས་དམ་བཅིངས་ (t̲amböö t̲amjiŋ) shung. strictly disciplining ། ལས་སྣེ་ཁག་ནས་ངོ་འཛིན་ཕྱོགས་ལྷུང་མེད་པར་དམ་པོས་དམ་བཅིངས་ཀྱིས་དགོན་པའི་འདུལ་ཁྲིམས་ཉམས་པ་སོར་ཆུད་ཡོང་བ་བྱ་རྒྱུ་ In order to maintain the pure monk's vows in the monastery, the person in charge should not be biased and should maintain strict discipline.

དམ་ཕྲུག (t̲əmdruù) sm. དམ་ཁ་.

དམ་བག (t̲ambaà) stamp pad.

དམ་བི་ (t̲ambi) jar for holding beer or liqueur.

དམ་བེ་ (t̲ambe) sm. དམ་བི་.

དམ་འབྱར་ (t̲amjar) 1. sealed/ stamped (with a seal). 2. anything that is sealed ། ཡིག་ཤོག་དམ་འབྱར་ཞིག A sealed envelope.

དམ་སྦྱར་ (t̲amjar) sm. དམ་འབྱར.

དམ་སྦྱར་ལྕགས་ཀྲིན་ (t̲amjar jəgdrin) sealed tin, airtight can.

དམ་མེ་དུམ་མེ་ (t̲amme t̲umme) in small pieces.

དམ་ཙམ་ (t̲amdzam) slightly tight, strict; va.—བྱེད་.

དམ་ཙམ་ལྷོད་ཙམ་ (t̲amdzam lhöödzam) sometimes strict and sometimes lenient.

དམ་གཙང་ (t̲amdzaŋ) 1. abbr. of དམ་ཚིག་གཙང་མ་. 2. pure vows.

དམ་གཙང་མཐའ་འཁྱོངས་ (t̲amdzaŋ tāgyoŋ) shung. to be continously faithful ། ཇི་སྲིད་བར་དམ་གཙང་མཐའ་འཁྱོངས་དགོས་རྒྱུ་ One must be continously faithful forever.

དམ་ཚགས་ (t̲amdzaà) taking care of, looking after sth. well; va.—བྱེད་ ། ཅ་ལག་འདི་གལ་ཆེན་པོ་ཡིན་པས་དམ་ཚགས་ཀྱིས་ཉར་དགོས་ These things are very important so you must look after them well.

དམ་ཚི་ (t̲əmdzi) a strong glue/ adhesive.

དམ་ཚིག (t̲əmdzig) 1. spiritual vow/ commitment/ pledge/ oath. 2. bitterness, ill feeling; va.—བཟོ་ to cause bitterness, ill feeling; vi.—ཆགས་; —ཤོར་ to have bitterness/ ill feelings occur. ། ཁྱེད་རང་སྐད་ཆ་འདི་འདྲ་བཤད་ན་མི་ཚང་གཉིས་བར་དམ་ཚིག་བཟོ་གི་རེད་ If you say that, it will cause bitterness between the two families. 3. to meet sb. unexpectedly with whom you are close; vi.—བྱུང་.

དམ་ཚིག་འགྱུར་མེད་ (t̲əmtsiì gyurmeè) sm. དམ་བཅའ་རྡོ་རྗེའི་ཚིག.

དམ་ཚིག་ཉམས་ཆགས་ (t̲əmtsiì ñamjaà) the deterioration of a commitment/ vow/ oath.

དམ་ཚིག་མེད་པ་ (t̲əmdzii meèba) having no bitterness/ ill feelings, having good relations ། ཐོག་མ་ནས་ཁ་དན་ཡག་པོ་བྱས་ན་ཕྱོགས་གཉིས་བར་དམ་ཚིག་མེད་པ་ཡོང་ཁི་རེད་ If you make a good agreement from the beginning, both sides will maintain a good relationship.

དམ་ཚིག་གཙང་མ་ (t̲əmdzii dzāŋma) faithful, close ། ང་གཉིས་དམ་ཚིག་གཙང་མའི་གྲོགས་པོ་ཡིན་ The two of us are close friends.

དམ་ཚིག་སེལ་ལྷད་ (t̲əmdzii sēlhεὲ) bad/ deteriorated relations ། ཁོང་གཉིས་གྲོགས་པོ་གཉིས་དབར་དམ་ཚིག་སེལ་ལྷད་བྱུང་བཞག Those two friends came to have bad relations.

དམ་ཚོན་ (t̲amdzön) sm. དར་ཚོན་.

དམ་མཚལ་ (t̲amdzεε) red stamp pad (used with seals).

དམ་འཛིན་ (t̲əmdzin) 1. make the best use of one's time; va.—བྱེད་ ། ལས་ཀའི་དུས་ཚོད་དམ་འཛིན་བྱེད་དགོས་ You must make the best use of your time when working. 2. working hard/ earnestly; va.—བྱེད་ ། སློབ་སྦྱོང་ལ་དམ་འཛིན་བྱེད་དགོས་ You must study hard. 3. holding on to sth. well; va.—བྱེད་ ། རང་གི་རིག་གནས་དམ་འཛིན་བྱེད་ཐབས་སུ་ In order to hold on to one's own culture. 4. keeping one's word, abiding by; va.—བྱེད་ ། རང་ཉིད་ཀྱི་བཤད་པའི་སྐད་ཆ་དམ་འཛིན་བྱེད་དགོས་ You should abide by what you say.

དམ་རྫི་ (t̲əmdzi) alertness to a situation, keeping a careful eye on a situation; va.—བྱེད་.

དམ་བཞག་པ་ (t̲amshagba) shung. sm. གཉེར་པ་.

དམ་ཟབ་ (t̲amsəb) firm and deep, close, intimate (relations, etc.) ། རྒྱལ་ཁབ་གཉིས་ཀྱི་མི་དམངས་ཀྱི་མཛའ་མཐུན་དམ་ཟབ་ཏུ་སོང་ཡོད་པ་རེད་ The friendship of the people of the two countries have become deeper (firmer).

དམ་བཟུང་ (t̲amsuŋ) p. of དམ་འཛིན་.

དམ་ལ་ (t̲amla) shung. vows and loyalty ། གཉིས་ཕྱོགས་ནས་མཆོད་ཡོན་དམ་ལར་བསམས་ལོ་རེའི་མར་འབབ་སྤྲོད་ལེན་སྒྲིང་མེད་དགོས་རྒྱུ་ Both parties, in considering the vows and loyalty between priest and the patron, should offer the yearly butter without delay.

དམ་ལ་འདོགས་ (t̲amla dɔɔ̀) va. to vanquish/ overcome ། བླ་མས་གདོན་འདྲེ་དམ་ལ་བཏགས་པ་རེད་ The lama vanquished the ghosts and demons.

དམ་ཤོས་ (t̲amshöö) closest, tightest, strictest.

དམ་སེལ་ (t̲amsel) shung. a bad/ deteriorated relationship ། མཆོད་ཡོན་དམ་གཙང་གི་འོ་མ་རྒྱན་དུ་གང་ལ་དམ་སེལ་ཁྲག་གི་ཐིགས་པ་ལྷུང་བ་ The relationship between the priest and the patron deteriorated just like a drop of blood fallen into a jar of milk.

དམ་སྲི་ (t̲amsi) demons that harm the dharma; vi.—ལང་ to rise up from dormancy (refers to demons and spirits that are normally under control).

དམ་སྲུང་ (t̲amsuŋ) protecting resolutely; va.—བྱེད་.

དའི་གོ་ (d̲ego) ch. Germany.

དའེ་ཡིའི་ཀྲོ་ (d̲eyidro) sm. དའི་གོ་.

དའོ་དན་ (t̲aodεn) ch. guided missile.

དར་ (tār) 1. silk. 2. ceremonial scarf. 3. the freezing of water; vi.—ཆགས་ to freeze, to become ice ། དགུན་དུས་གཙང་པོ་དར་ཆགས་པའི་སྐབས་ In the winter, when the rivers freezes. 4. vi. to become popular, to become widespread, to grow/ spread, to rise, to flourish ། འདས་ལོ་བརྒྱ་ཕྲག་བརྒྱད་པའི་ནང་བོད་ལ་ནང་ཆོས་རྒྱ་ཆེན་པོ་དར་བ་རེད་ In the eighth century Buddhism became widespread in Tibet. ། ཡུལ་གཞན་དག་འབྲེལ་བ་བྱུང་བར་བརྟེན་ནས་སྒྱུ་རྩལ་དང་ཆས་གོས་གསར་པ་མང་པོ་དར་བ་རེད་ Because there were relations with other countries, new arts and clothing became popular and widespread.

དར་དཀར་ (t̲argar) 1. white ceremonial scarf. 2. abbr. of དར་ཆ་དཀར་པོ་.

དར་སྐུད་ (t̲ərgüù) silk thread.

དར་སྐུད་བཙོས་འཐེན་ (t̲ərgüù jöödεn) silk reeling (the process of boiling the cocoons and reeling the thread).

དར་སྐུད་ཀྱི་གྲུ་གུ་ (t̲ərgüügi drugu) a ball made of strips of silk.

དར་ཁ་འཕྲིག (t̲arga drig) sm. དར་འཕྲིག.

དར་ཁྱབ་ (t̲argyəb) diffusion, dissemination, spreading; va.—གཏོང་ to disseminate, to spread; vi.—འགྱུར་ to get spread/ disseminated, to become widespread ། ཁོ་ཚོས་གུང་ཁྲན་རིང་ལུགས་དར་ཁྱབ་བཏང་བ་རེད་ They disseminated communism. ། ཕྱི་ལུགས་དར་ཁྱབ་འགྱུར་ན་ If foreign customs became widespread.

དར་ཁྱབ་ཆེ་བ་ (t̲argyəb cēwa) sm. དར་ཁྱབ་ཆེན་པོ་.

དར་ཁྱབ་ཆེན་པོ་ (t̲arkyəb cēmbo) widespread, flourishing, popular, fashionable.

དར་གོས་ (t̲argöö) 1. silk clothes/ garments. 2. silk, brocade.

དར་གོས་ཀྱི་དུག་ལོག (t̲argöögi t̲ugloò) silk clothing.

དར་གོས་ཆེན་ (t̲argöö cēn) silk brocade.

དར་གོས་འགྲོ་ལམ་ (t̲argöö drolam) the silk road.

དར་གོས་ཚོས་སྒྱུར་བཟོ་གྲྭ (t̲argöö tsöögyur s̲odra) silk dyeing mill.

དར་གྲི་ (t̲ardri) ice skates.

དར་གྲུ་ (t̲ardru) sailboat; va.—གཏོང་.

དར་སྒྲུའ་ (tardru) silk.

དར་འཁྱིག (tar drig) vi. to freeze over (usu. a lake, river, etc.) ¶ མཚོ་འདི་ཟླ་བ་གཉིས་པའི་ནང་ལ་དར་འཁྱིག་གི་རེད་ This lake will freeze in the 2nd lunar month.

དར་རྒུད་ (targüü) flourishing and declining, ups and downs, rich and poor, prosperity and adversity, rise and fall ¶ དུས་ཚོད་ཐུང་ཐུང་ཞིག་ནང་ཁོ་ཚོའི་དཔལ་འབྱོར་ལ་དར་རྒུད་མང་པོ་ཞིག་བྱུང་བ་རེད་ In a short period their economy has had many ups and downs.

དར་རྒུད་ཆགས་འཇིག (targüü cəgjii) flourishing and declining, surviving and becoming extinct/ destroyed.

དར་རྒྱས་ (targyɛɛ̀) development, progress; vi.—འགྲོ་ to get developed, to make progress; va.—བྱེད་ to develop, to make progress ¶ བཟོ་ལས་ཀྱི་དར་རྒྱས་ Industrial development.

དར་རྒྱས་མེད་པ་ (targyɛɛ̀ meèba) underdeveloped, backward, not developed ¶ དར་རྒྱས་མེད་པའི་རྒྱལ་ཁབ་ An underdeveloped nation.

དར་རྒྱུག (targyuù) flag pole.

དར་སྐྱང་ (targaŋ) fully grown person (sb. not too old or young, i.e., sb. around 30 to 40 years old.

དར་སྐྱིག (tar drig) sm. དར་འཁྱིག.

དར་ཅིག (tarjig) sm. ཡུད་ཙམ་.

དར་ལྕོག (tarjɔɔ̀) prayer flag.

དར་ལྕོག་རླུང་བསྐྱོད་ (tarjɔɔ̀ lūŋgyöö) sb. who follows whoever is in power [Lit. a prayer flag that goes in the wind].

དར་ཆ་ (tarja) flag, banner; va.—འཛུགས་; —སྒྲེངས་; —འགེལ་ to put up/ hoist/ raise a flag/ banner; vi.—གཡོ་ to flutter (in the wind); va.—གཡུག་ས་ to wave a flag; va.—འཕྱར་ to hold a flag on high.

དར་ཆ་དཀར་པོ་ (tarja gārbo) white flag (flag of truce/ surrender); va.—རྒྱག; —སྒྲེངས་ to raise a white flag (of truce/ surrender).

དར་ཆ་སྒྲེང་མཁན་ (tarja dreŋñɛn) flag bearer.

དར་ཆ་དམར་པོ་ (tarja mārbo) 1. a red flag. 2. the Communist flag. 3. Red Flag (a magazine).

དར་ཆ་དམར་པོའི་ཚོགས་པ་ (tarja mārbö tsɔ̄gbə) the Red Flag Party (a leftist party in China).

དར་ཆ་གསལ་སྒྲིང་ (tarja sɛ̄ɛ̄dreŋ) making a clear cut stand (about one's position); va.—བྱེད་ ¶ ཁོང་གིས་ཚོགས་འདུའི་ཐོག་དམག་འཁྲུག་ལ་ངོ་རྒོལ་བྱེད་པའི་དར་ཆ་གསལ་སྒྲིང་གི་གསུང་བཤད་གནང་བ་རེད་ At the meeting he made a clear stand of his opposition to war.

དར་ཆགས་ (tar cāā) vi. to freeze over, to turn to ice (for rivers and lakes) ¶ གཙང་པོ་དེ་ཚོར་དགུན་དུས་དར་ཆགས་ཀྱི་རེད་ Those rivers freeze over in the winter.

དར་ཆགས་པའི་གྲང་ཚད་ (tarjaàbɛ traŋdzɛɛ̀) the temperature at which water freezes, the freezing point.

དར་ཆགས་པའི་དུས་ (tarjaàbɛ tüü) the time/ period when rivers and lakes freeze.

དར་ཆགས་ཚད་ (tarjaà dzɛɛ̀) sm. དར་ཆགས་གྲང་ཚད་.

དར་ཆེན་ (tarjen) a tall prayer flag (usu. erected in front of a monastery or house).

དར་རྟགས་ (tardaà) a marker flag/ banner.

དར་ཐོད་ (tardöö) a silk bandanna tied around the head.

དར་འཐག་དངོས་རྫས་ (tardaà ŋöödzɛɛ̀) silk fabrics/ items.

དར་མདུད་ (tardüü) silk knot.

དར་མདུད་སྒྲུ་གུ་ (tardüü drugu) sm. དར་སྐུད་ཀྱི་སྒྲུ་གུ་.

དར་མདོ་ (tardo) abbr. of དར་རྩེ་མདོ་.

དར་མདོག་ཅན་ (tardɔjɛn) shung. colored silk/ satin.

དར་བརྡ་ (tarda) signal flag; va.—གཏོང་.

དར་ལྡིང་གཏོང་ (tardiŋ dōŋ) va. to put up prayer flags tied on a rope.

དར་སྣ་གོས་སྣ་ (tarna gööna) all sorts of cloth and clothing.

དར་སྣ་འདྲེན་ (tarna dren) va. to lead sb. by (holding) the end of a ceremonial scarf.

དར་སྣལ་ (tarnɛɛ) silk thread.

དར་པོ་ (tarbo) popular ¶ དེང་སང་དུག་ལོག་དེ་གྲས་དར་པོ་ཞེ་དྲག་འདུག These days this style of clothing is very popular.

དར་པོ་ཆེ་ (tarboce) sm. དར་ཆེན་.

དར་སྤེལ་ (tarbel) the act of spreading/ promoting/ popularizing (an idea, method, etc.), development, promotion; va.—(དུ་) གཏོང་ to spread, to popularize, to develop ¶ ཞིང་ལས་བྱེད་ཐབས་གསར་པ་དེ་ཚོ་དར་སྤེལ་དུ་གཏོང་གི་ཡོད་པ་རེད་ They are popularizing those new methods of agriculture.

དར་དཔྱང་ (tarjaŋ) 1. hanging or dangling steamers/ ribbons. 2. dangling silk ribbons/ scarves given by lamas as a blessing.

དར་དཔྱངས་ (tarjaŋ) sm. དར་དཔྱང་.

དར་ཕུང་ (tarbuŋ) a heap/ mass/ pile of prayer flags (e.g., on mountain passes).

དར་ཕོད་ (tarbüü) silk tassel.

དར་ཕྱར་རྔ་རྡུང་ (tarjaa ŋāduŋ) 1. banging drums and waving flags (in celebration). 2. conspicuously, openly, on a grand scale, with wide publicity ¶ དར་ཕྱར་རྔ་རྡུང་གི་ཐོག་ནས་སྲིད་ཇུས་གསར་པ་དེ་དྲིལ་བསྒྲགས་བྱས་པ་རེད་ They publicized the new policy on a grand scale.

དར་འཕན་ (tarbɛn) brocade decorative pieces that are hung from pillars (e.g., in temples).

དར་འཕེལ་ (tarbel) sm. དར་སྤེལ་.

དར་འཕྱར་ (tar cār) va. to brandish banners, to wave flags/ banners.

དར་འཕྲུ་ (tandru) silk banners attached to ancient flags.

དར་བ་ (tara) buttermilk.

དར་བབ་ (tarbəb) abbr. for དར་ལ་བབས་.

དར་བབ་མ་ (tarbəbma) a women in the prime of her life.

དར་བའི་དུས་སྐབས་ (tarwɛ tüügəb) time/ period when sth. is flourishing/ widespread/ in vogue/ popular ¶ དེང་སང་དམངས་གཙོའི་ལམ་ལུགས་དར་བའི་དུས་སྐབས་རེད་བཞག This is a period when democracy is flourishing.

དར་བུབས་ (tarbub) a roll of brocade.

དར་བྱང་ (tarjaŋ) a type of banner.

དར་བྱང་དཔོན་ (tarjaŋbön) an official who carries a banner.

དར་བྲིས་རི་མོ་ (tardrii rimu) a silk cloth painting.

དར་འབུ་ (tambu) silkworm.

དར་འབོག (tambɔɔ̀) a brocade roll symbolizing the rank of བཀའ་བློན་ that is carried by their aides when they go anywhere.

དར་མ་ (tarma) person in the prime of life, a person from about 30 to 40 years of age.

དར་མ་གླག (tarmalaà) an eagle.

དར་མ་ཡོལ་ (tarma yöö) vi. to be past the prime of life.

དར་མའི་སློབ་གསོ་ (tarmɛ lōbso) adult education.

དར་མི་ཆགས་པའི་གྲུ་ཁ་ (tar mijagbɛ drugə) ice free port.

དར་མོ་ཆེ་ (tarmoce) sm. དར་ཆེན་.

དར་མའི་སློབ་གསོ་ (tarmɛ lōbso) adult education.

དར་དམར་ (tārmar) abbr. of དར་ཆ་དམར་པོ་.

དར་དམར་འགྲན་བསྡུར་ (tarma drɛndur) red flag competition (competing to be best in production, etc. or most progressive - the most progressive is appraised as the Red Flag unit).

དར་དམར་འཛིན་མཁན་ (tarmar dzinñɛn) the red flag winner (in the Red Flag competition (see above)).

དར་སྨན་ (tarmɛn) alum.

དར་ཙམ་ (tardzam) sm. ཡུད་ཙམ་.

དར་རྩེ་མདོ་ (tardzedo) Tachienlu (town in Sichuan Province that formerly was capital of Xigang Province—also known as Kanding).

དར་ཚགས་ (tardzaà) sifter made from cloth; va.—

རྒྱུག to sift (with such a sifter).

དར་ཚིལ་ (tārdzii) cheese.

དར་ཚུར་ (tardzur) borax.

དར་ཚོན་ (tārdzön) colored flags/ ribbons; va.—འདྲེག to cut the ribbon (in inaugural ceremonies).

དར་ཚོན་སྣ་ལྔ་ (tartsön nāŋa) five-colored pieces of silk, five-colored ceremonial scarves ¶ དར་ཚོན་སྣ་ལྔ་བཏགས་པའི་མདའ་ A bow with five-colored pieces of silk attached.

དར་འཛར་ (tardzaa) silk ribbon/ scarf.

དར་རྫུས་ (tardzüü) fake silk, synthetic/ artificial silk.

དར་ཞིག (tarshii) vi. to thaw (for frozen lakes or rivers).

དར་ཞིང་རྒྱས་པ་ (tarshiŋ gyɛ̄ɛba) flourishing, prosperous ¶ རྒྱལ་ཁབ་ཀྱི་དཔལ་འབྱོར་དར་ཞིང་རྒྱས་པའི་དུས་སྐབས་ At the time when the nation's economy is prosperous.

དར་ཟབ་ (tārsəb) fine brocade.

དར་ཟམ་ (tarsam) a river that has frozen over so that it can be used (crossed) like a bridge.

དར་བཟོ་ (tarso) fashionable, in vogue, popular.

དར་བཟོ་ཆེན་པོ་ (tarso cēmbo) very popular/ fashionable.

དར་ཡ་ཀན་ (taryagɛn) ambrosia.

དར་ཡུག (taryuù) a roll of brocade.

དར་ཡུལ་ (taryüü) place where sth. diffused/ spread/ flourished ¶ ལུང་པ་འདི་ཆོས་དར་ཡུལ་རེད་ This area is a place where religion flourished.

དར་ཡོལ་ (taryöö) 1. a person past prime age, i.e., about 40 to 50 years of age. 2. a silk curtain.

དར་ར་ (tara) buttermilk.

དར་རགས་ (tarraà) ice dam.

དར་རས་ (tar rɛ̀ɛ) 1. silk and cotton. 2. cloth for making prayer flags or other kinds of banners/ flags.

དར་ལ་ (tarla) thin cloth.

དར་ལ་བབས་ (tarla bəb) vi. to be in the prime of life (i.e., about 30—40 years of age).

དར་ལམ་ (tarlam) a road covered by ice.

དར་ལིང་ (tarliŋ) a kind of thin silk/ brocade.

དར་ཤམ་ (tarsham) 1. a skirt made of brocade. 2. a window fringe made from silk.

དར་ཤིང་ (tərshiŋ) 1. flag pole. 2. mulberry tree ¶ དར་ཤིང་ཤུན་དཀར་ The white bark of a mulberry tree.

དར་ཤིང་རྡིང་དཀར་ (tərshiŋ dĩŋgar) flag pole from which the bark is peeled to create a white effect.

དར་གཤེག་གྲུ་གཟིང་ (tarsheg trusiŋ) ice cutter, icebreaker boat.

དར་བཞིག (tar shīi) vi. to have ice covering a lake or river melt/ thaw.

དར་སང་ (tarsaŋ) a screen made of silk.

དར་སི་ (tarsdi) silk.

དར་སེང་ (tarseŋ) gauze-like silk.

དར་སོ་ (tarso) sm. དར་སྲོལ་.

དར་སྲབ་ (tardrəb) thin silk.

དར་སྲིན་ (tarsin) sm. དར་འབུ་.

དར་སྲིན་གྱི་འབུ་སྲོབ་ (tarsingi busob) cocoon of silkworm.

དར་སྲིན་ཉལ་འབུ་ (tarsin ñɛ̃mbu) chrysalis of the silkworm.

དར་སྲོལ་ (tarsöö) popular, fashionable, in vogue.

དར་སྲོལ་ཆགས་ (tarsöö cāà) vi. to become common practice/ customary.

དར་སྲོལ་ཆེ་བ་ (tarsöö cēwa) fashionable, in vogue.

དར་སྲོལ་དང་མཐུན་པ་ (tarsöö daŋ tũmbə) modern, fashionable.

དར་གསོལ་ (tarsöö) putting up flag/ banner (usu. before going to war).

དར་བསླས་ (tarlɛ̀ɛ) woven from silk.

དར་ཧན་ (tarhan) mong. a high rank.

དར་ཧྲུག (tarhrug) 1. leftover pieces of silk/ brocade. 2. small flags.

དལ་ (tɛɛ) 1. abbr. of དལ་པོ་. 2. vi. to have leisure/ spare time ¶ ང་ལས་ཀ་དལ་སྐབས་ཡོང་གི་ཡིན་ I will come when I have spare time.

དལ་སྒྱོན་ (tɛɛgyön) doing sth. too slowly ¶ ཁྱེད་རང་གི་ལས་ཀ་དལ་སྒྱོན་འདུག་པས་མགྱོགས་ཙམ་བྱེད་དགོས་ Because you are working too slowly, you have to speed up somewhat.

དལ་སྒྱོན་འགོར་སྒྱོན་ (tɛɛgyön gɔɔgyön) sm. དལ་སྒྱོན་.

དལ་སྐྱེལ་དངོས་ཟོག (tɛɛgyee ŋöösɔɔ) goods shipped slowly.

དལ་ཁ་ (tɛɛga) 1. epidemic. 2. harm, disaster.

དལ་ཁོམ་ (tɛɛgom) leisure, free time ¶ དལ་ཁོམ་བྱུང་ན་བཅར་གྱི་ཡིན་ (I) will come over if (I) get the time.

དལ་གྱིས་ (tɛɛgi) slowly, leisurely ¶ ཆུ་ཆེན་པོ་དལ་གྱིས་བབ་པ་བཞིན་ Like a big river flowing slowly.

དལ་མགྱོགས་ (tɛɛgyɔɔ) speed ¶ མོ་ཊ་དལ་མགྱོགས་རན་པོ་གཏོང་ You must drive at the appropriate speed. [Lit. slowly and quickly].

དལ་འགོར་བྱེད་ (tɛɛgɔɔ cee) va. to make sb. late.

དལ་བགྲོད་ (tɛɛdröö) sm. དལ་འགྲོས་.

དལ་འགྲོ་ (tɛɛdro) 1. poet. river. 2. sm. དལ་འགྲོས་.

དལ་འགྲོ་འཁོར་ལོ་ (tɛɛdro kɔ̄ɔlo) a slow moving/ nonexpress vehicle.

དལ་བགྲོད་ (tɛɛdröö) sm. དལ་འགྲོས་.

དལ་འགྲོས་ (tɛɛdröö) 1. moving slowly, going at a slow pace, plodding along; va.—བྱེད་ ¶ དལ་འགྲོས་མེ་འཁོར་ Nonexpress train. 2. sm. དལ་འགྲོ་, 1.

དལ་བརྒྱད་ (tɛɛgyɛ̀ɛ) abbr. of དལ་བ་བརྒྱད་.

དལ་ཅག་གེར་ (tɛɛjagge) slowly.

དལ་ཅིག (tɛɛjig) a very short time.

དལ་འཇགས་ (tɛnjaà) sm. ཞིང་འཇགས་.

དལ་དལ་ཁོམ་ཁོམ་ (tɛɛdɛɛ kōmgom) sm. དལ་དལ་ལྷོད་ལྷོད་.

དལ་དལ་ལྷོད་ལྷོད་ (tɛɛdɛɛ lhöölhöö) slowly, leisurely, relaxed ¶ ང་གནས་ཡོལ་བྱས་ནས་དལ་དལ་ལྷོད་ལྷོད་ཡིན་ Since retiring, I have led a leisurely life.

དལ་སྡོད་ (tɛɛdöö) leisure, free time; va.—བྱེད་ to have leisure/ free time.

དལ་སྡོད་སྐྱིད་སྡོད་ (tɛɛdöö gyīdöö) living happily and leisurely.

དལ་ཕྱིར་འབྲུག་སྒྲ་ (tɛɛdir drugdra) the muffled sound of thunder.

དལ་འདོད་སྐྱིད་འདོད་ (tɛndöö gyīndöö) desiring leisure and happiness.

དལ་འདྲེན་འབོག་སྒྲིལ་ (tɛndren bɔgdrii) regular parcel delivery (as contrast to express).

དལ་པོ་ (tɛɛbo) 1. slow, slowly ¶ ཡར་རྒྱས་དལ་པོ་འདུག Progress is slow. ¶ ཁོང་ལྡུམ་རའི་ནང་དལ་པོར་འགྲོ་གི་འདུག He is walking slowly in the garden. 2. free time, leisure, not busy ¶ ཁོང་དེང་སང་དལ་པོ་འདུག He has free time these days.

དལ་བ་ (tɛɛwa) slower ¶ འདི་དལ་བ་འདུག This one is slower.

དལ་བབ་ (tɛɛ bəb) 1. vi. to have leisure/ free time ¶ རྗེས་སུ་ང་དལ་བབ་སོང་ན་ཁྱེད་རང་ལ་རོགས་རམ་བྱས་ཆོག Later if I have free time I will help you. 2. vi. to flow/ go slowly.

དལ་བུ་ (tɛɛbu) slow, low speed, leisurely ¶ འགྱུར་བ་དལ་བུ་ A slow change. ¶ དལ་བུར་ཕྱིན་པ་ཡིན་ (We) went slowly.

དལ་བུར་འཕྱོ་ (tɛɛbur cō) vi. to float in the air.

དལ་བྲེལ་ (tɛɛdree) 1. pace, speed ¶ ལས་ཀ་དལ་བྲེལ་སྙོམ་པོ་ཞིག་བྱེད་དགོས་ (You) should work steadily. 2. slow and fast, leisurely and hurriedly.

དལ་མ་ (tɛɛma) a female dancer.

དལ་མོ་ (tɛɛmo) sm. དལ་བུ་.

དལ་རྩ་ (tɛɛdza) low pulse.

དལ་བཟོད་མེད་པ་ (tɛɛso meèba) not calm, disturbed.

དལ་ཡམས་ (tɛɛyam) sm. རིམས་ནད་.

དལ་རླུང་ (tɛɛluŋ) a gentle wind.

དལ་ལངས་ནད་གཞི་ (tɛɛlaŋ nɛ̄ɛshi) a disease that develops slowly.

དལ་ཤིག་ཤིག (tɛɛ shīgshii) leisurely, slowly.

དལ་ལྷོད་ (tɛɛlhöö) sm. དལ་དལ་ལྷོད་ལྷོད་.

དལ་ལྷོད་ལྷོད་ (tɛɛ lhöölhöö) sm. དལ་ལྷོད་.

དས་ཕུད་ (tεεbüü) the prefix "ད".

ཌ་ཀ་ (taga) Dacca.

ཌག་ཌར་ (tagdar) eng. doctor.

དི་རི་རི་ (ti riri) a murmuring noise/ sound.

དི་དི་གུ་གུ་ (tidi gugu) turtledove.

དིག་སྐད་ (tiggεὲ) sm. དིག་པ་.

དིག་སྒྲ་ (tigdra) sm. དིག་པ་.

དིག་གདམ་ (tigdam) talking with a stutter.

དིག་དིག་ (tigdig) sm. དིག་པ་.

དིག་པ་ (tigbə) stammering, stuttering ། ཁོ་ཁ་དིག་པ་རེད་ He stutters.

དིང་ (tiŋ) today.

དིང་ཁྲི་བཙན་པོ་ (tiŋdri dzεmbo) the third ancient Tibetan king.

དིང་དིང་ (tiŋdiŋ) sound of drumming.

དིང་རི་ (tiŋri) Dingri district (in S.W. Tibet).

དིང་རི་རྫོང་མདའ་ (tiŋri döŋda) shung. sm. དིང་རི་བཞུགས་རིས་.

དིང་རི་བཞུགས་རིས་ (tiŋri shugreè) shung. the commander of a Tibetan army unit posted in Dingri.

དིང་སང་ (tiŋsaŋ) sm. དེང་སང་.

དིམ་ (tim) vi. to drown, to sink into/ under (mud, snow, water, etc.) ། གྲུ་དེ་ཆུའི་ནང་ལ་དིམ་པ་རེད་ The ship sank in the water.

དིམ་རྒྱལ་ (timgyεε) skin diving, swimming underwater.

དིམ་ཁྱུར་སློད་ (timgyur lööö) va. to dive.

དིམ་ཁྲོན་ (timdrön) a sunken well.

དིམ་གྲུ་ (timdru) 1. submarine. 2. a sunken boat.

དིམ་སྒམ་ (timgam) caisson box.

དིམ་བསགས་ (timsaà) sedimentary deposit; vi.—ཐེབས་ to be/ get deposited on (the bottom).

དིམ་བསགས་དངོས་པོ་ (timsaà ŋööbo) sth. that has been deposited, sediment.

དིམ་བསགས་བྲག་རྡོ་ (timsaà tragdo) sedimentary rock.

དིམ་ཆུ་རྒྱག་ (timju gyaà) va. to submerge, to put underwater.

དིར་ (tir) sm. ཐིར་.

དིས་གོ་ཀྲུའུ་ཡིས་ (tiigo drüyii) ch. imperialism.

དུ་ (tu) 1. (dat.-loc. particle used after final ང་, ད་, ན་, མ་, ར་ and ལ་) to, at, on, in ། ཁོ་ནང་དུ་ཕྱིན་སོང་ He went inside. ། ཀུབ་ཀྱིགས་སྟེང་དུ་བསྡད་འདུག He is sitting on the chair. ། མོ་དབྱིན་ཡུལ་དུ་འགྲོ་གི་རེད་ She will go to England. 2. (adj. + —) conveys comparative mood ། སྔར་ལས་མང་དུ་བཏང་བ་རེད་ They sent more than before. ། འགྲོ་སོང་ཆུང་དུ་ཕྱིན་ན་ If expenses become smaller. 3. how much, how many, how long ། ཁྱོད་ལ་ནང་མི་དུ་ཡོད་དམ་ How many people do you have in your family? 4. abbr. of དུ་བ་.

དུ་ཁ་ (tuga) skt. suffering, pain.

དུ་ཁུག (tuguù) sm. དུད་ཁུག.

དུ་ཁུང་ (tuguŋ) chimney, smokestack.

དུ་འགྲོ་ (tudro) sm. དུ་ཁུང་.

དུ་འགྲོའི་ཡོ་ཆས་ (tudro yojεὲ) equipment or devices for removing smoke (e.g., a chimney pipe).

དུ་མཆིས་ (tujii) sm. ཇི་ཙམ་ཡོད་.

དུ་ཐལ་ (tutεε) cigarette ash.

དུ་འཐེན་ (tu tēn) va. to smoke (cigarettes).

དུ་དག (tudaà) sm. ག་ཚོད་.

དུ་དུ་ (tudu) how many ། ཚོགས་འདུར་ཡོང་མཁན་མི་དུ་དུ་འདུག How many people came to the meeting?

དུ་དྲི་ (tudri) the smell of smoke.

དུ་དྲེག (tudreg) 1. smoke. 2. dirt, soot.

དུ་བདུག (tu dug) va. to inhale smoke.

དུ་མདེལ་ (tudel) smoke shell/ bomb.

དུ་མདོག (tudɔɔ) gray, smoke color.

དུ་ནག (tunaà) black soot from smoke.

དུ་སྤྲིན་ (tudrin) dark/ gray clouds; vi.—འཐིབ་ to be overcast with dark clouds.

དུ་བ་ (tuwə) smoke; vi.—འཕྱུར་ to have smoke come out/ rise up; va.—གཏོང་ to smoke sth. out ། ཐོག་ཁུང་ནས་དུ་བ་འཕྱུར་གྱི་འདུག Smoke is rising from the chimney. ། འཕྱི་ཁུང་ནང་དུ་བ་བཏང་ནས་འཕྱི་བ་བཟུང་བ་རེད་ (They) sent smoke into the hole and caught the marmot. 2. a cigarette; va.—འཐེན་ to smoke a cigarette ། དུ་བ་རྐང་གཅིག A single cigarette.

དུ་བ་འགྲོ་ཁུང་ (tuwə droguŋ) sm. དུ་ཁུང་.

དུ་བ་མཇུག་རིང་ (tuwə jugriŋ) comet.

དུ་བ་གནམ་གཏོང་ (tuwə nāmdoŋ) shung. every family ། གཞུང་ལམ་བཟོ་མཁན་དུ་བ་གནམ་གཏོང་བསྐུལ་བཞག (They) ordered every family to send someone to repair the road. [Lit. (everyone) who sends smoke to the sky].

དུ་བ་གནམ་གཏོང་གི་ཁྲལ་ (tuwə nāmdoŋgi trεε) a tax levied on every family.

དུ་བ་འབུད་ཆས་ (tuwə büüjεὲ) equipment for removing/ expelling smoke (e.g., chimney pipe).

དུ་བ་འཕྱུར་འཕྱུར་ (tuwə cūrjur) rising smoke.

དུ་བ་མེད་པ་ (tuwə meèba) no smoking ། དུ་བ་མེད་པའི་གཞུང་ལས་ཁང་ A no smoking office.

དུ་བ་རལ་བ་ (tuwə rεεwa) soot that is hanging down.

དུ་བ་རླངས་པ་གཉིས་ལ་འཛོལ་བཟོ་ཡོད་ (tuwə lāŋwa ñiilə dzöö soyöö) easy to misunderstand [Lit. smoke and steam are easy to mistake].

དུ་བ་ལོང་ལོང་ (tuwə loŋloŋ) sm. དུ་བ་འཕྱུར་འཕྱུར་.

དུ་འབུད་རླུང་གཡབ་ (tubüü lūŋyəb) exhaust fan.

དུ་མ་ (tumə) many ། དེབ་དུ་མ་ Many books.

དུ་མེད་ (tumeè) 1. smokeless. 2. no smoking (sign).

དུ་མེད་ཉི་མ་ (tumeè ñimə) nonsmoking day.

དུ་མེད་རྡོ་སོལ་ (dumeè dosöö) smokeless coal, anthracite.

དུ་སྨུག་འཁྲིགས་ (tumuù trig) vi. to become foggy/ misty.

དུ་ཚག (tudzaà) a container for taking out soot.

དུ་ཤག (tushaà) smoke.

དུ་ཡོད་ (tuyöö) 1. sm. ག་ཚོད་ཡོད་. 2. having smoke. 3. sm. ཡོད་ཚད་.

དུ་ཡོད་རྡོ་སོལ་ (tuyöö dosöö) coal that emits smoke.

དུ་རེ་བ་ (turewa) sm. རྒྱུན་ཆགས་པ་.

དུ་ལྡང་ (tuluŋ) smoke.

དུ་ལོ་ (tulo) tobacco ། དུ་ལོ་བཟོ་གྲྭ་ Tobacco factory.

དུ་ཤིང་ (tushiŋ) fuel for making smoke in a field to protect the crop from frost.

དུཿཁ་ (tūga) skt. suffering.

དུག (tuù) 1. poison; va.—གཏོང་; —རྒྱག; —སྦྱོར་; —སྣེར་ to poison; vi.—ཕོག to get poisoned. 2. drugs (like opium); va.—འཐེན་ to smoke/ take drugs.

དུག་ལྐོག་ཚོང་ (tuù gōgdzoŋ) illicitly selling drugs; va.—རྒྱག.

དུག་སྦྱོན་ (tuggyön) poisoning; va.—གཏོང་ to poison; vi.—ཕོག to get poisoned.

དུག་ཁ་ཚེག (tuùgā dzēg) outwardly nice but inwardly evil/ bad.

དུག་ཁྲུས་རྒྱག (tuù trüü gyaà) va. to wash poison out of a wound.

དུག་གི་མེ་ཏོག (tuùgi medog) black spots on the body of people who were poisoned to death.

དུག་འགོག (tuù gɔɔ) va. to stop/ prevent poison.

དུག་འགོག་མགོ་ཤུབས་ (tuùgɔɔ goshub) gas mask.

དུག་འགོག་ངོ་འབག (tuùgɔɔ ŋobaà) sm. དུག་འགོག་མགོ་ཤུབས་.

དུག་འགོག་འཐབ་རྩོད་ (tuùgɔɔ tābdzöö) the struggle/ fight to stop drugs; va.—བྱེད་.

དུག་འགོག་དངས་ཁྲག (tuùgɔɔ taŋdraà) antitoxin serum.

དུག་འགོག་སྨན་རྫས་ (tuùgɔɔ mendzεὲ) antitoxin.

དུག་འགོག་རྫས་ཆ་ (tuùgɔɔ dzεὲja) antitoxin.

དུག་རྒྱུན་ (tuùgyün) 1. poison. 2. bad acts/ work, wrong behavior ། གཡོན་གྱི་དུག་རྒྱུན་ཚང་མ་གཙང་སེལ་བྱེད་དགོས་ We must clean out the bad work of "leftism."

དུག་ལྔ་ (tuùŋa) 1. the five poisonous creatures: scorpion, snake, centipede, lizard and toad. 2. the five poisonous thoughts: desire-attachment, hatred-anger, closed-mindedness, pride, jealousy.

དུག་ལྔའི་འཇིགས་པ་ (tugŋɛ jigbə) shung. the disaster of the five poisonous thoughts ༎ འགྲོ་བ་སེམས་ཅན་དུག་ལྔའི་འཇིགས་པ་ལས་སྒྲོལ་ནས་ Liberating all sentient beings from the disaster of the five poisonous thoughts.

དུག་ཅན་ (tugjɛn) poisonous, having poison.

དུག་ལྕེ་ (tugje) poisonous tongue.

དུག་ཆང་ (tūgjaŋ) poisoned liquor/ beer.

དུག་ཆེན་ (tugjen) strong poison.

དུག་འཇིལ་ (tugjii) sterilizing; va.—བྱེད་ ༎ སྨན་ཁང་གི་སྨན་ཁབ་ཚང་མ་དུག་འཇིལ་བྱེད་དགོས་པ་རེད་ (They) have to sterilize all the hospital needles.

དུག་འཇོམས་ (tunjom) 1. medicine. 2. དུག་འཇིལ་.

དུག་གཉེན་ (tugñen) antidote.

དུག་གདོང་ (tugdoŋ) see དུག.

དུག་བཏང་བའི་མི་ཚད་དྲ་མའི་དར་ལྕོག (tūù dāŋwɛ midzɛɛ̀ ŋāmɛ darjoò) not only doing sth. bad, but gloating over it and showing off [Lit. not only poisoning sb. but erecting a yak tail flag].

དུག་ཐུབ་པ་ (tug tübbə) immunizing from poison.

དུག་གྲི་ (tugdri) a poisoned knife/ sword.

དུག་མདའ་ (tunda) poisonous arrow.

དུག་ལྡན་ལྟོ་ཆས་ (tugdɛn dōjɛɛ̀) poisoned food.

དུག་ནག (tugnaà) a strong poison, highly poisonous.

དུག་ནུས་ (tugnüù) the effect/ strength of poison.

དུག་པ་ (tugba) a person who poisons others.

དུག་པོ་ (tugbo) old clothes.

དུག་པོ་ཚེར་བེར་ (tugbo tsērber) worn out and patched old clothes.

དུག་ཕྱེ་ཐ་མག (tugce tāmaà) cocaine.

དུག་འཕྲོག (tundrɔɔ̀) birthwort (plant).

དུག་བོན་ (tuù pön) va. to give poison.

དུག་དབང་ (tuùwaŋ) power of poison.

དུག་འབུ་ (tumbu) poisonous insect.

དུག་འབུ་ཕྲ་མོ་ (tumbu tramo) pathogens.

དུག་འབུའི་འཁྲུག་འཐབ་ (tumbü trūgdəb) bacteriological warfare.

དུག་འབུའི་དམག (tumbü māà) sm. དུག་འབུའི་འཁྲུག་འཐབ་.

དུག་འབུལ་ (tuù büü) va. to give poison (h.).

དུག་སྦལ་ (tugbɛɛ) poisonous toad.

དུག་སྦྲང་ (tūgdraŋ) mosquito.

དུག་སྦྲང་བདུག་སྤོས་ (tugdraŋ dugböö̀) mosquito repellent incense.

དུག་སྦྲུལ་ (tugdrüü) poisonous snake.

དུག་མེད་བོང་གསུམ་ (tugmeè boŋsum) nonpoisonous yellow, white, and red rhizomes that are used for herbal medicine.

དུག་མོ་ (tugmo) a woman who poisons other people or animals to appease the "Poison God" or to get another person's good merit/ fortune.

དུག་མོ་ཉུང་ (tugmo ñuŋ) a type of medicine.

དུག་རྨ་ (tug mā) an infected sore/ wound that is difficult to cure.

དུག་སྨན་ (tugmɛn) 1. poisonous drug. 2. medication to counteract poison.

དུག་ཙེ་ (tugdze) rags, tatters.

དུག་རྩ་ (tugdza) poison.

དུག་རྩྭ་ (tugdza) poisonous weed/ grass.

དུག་ཚལ་ (tugdzɛɛ) sm. དུག་ཙེ་.

དུག་ཚེར་ (tugdzer) poison thorn.

དུག་ཚོང་ (tugdzoŋ) selling of narcotic drugs, narcotics trading; va.—རྒྱག.

དུག་མཚོན་ (tugdzön) poisonous weapons (i.e., a weapon to which poison has been applied).

དུག་འཚག་ཐ་མག (tugdzaà tāmaà) filter tip cigarette.

དུག་རྫས་ (tugdzɛɛ̀) 1. poison ༎ དུག་རྫས་ཉེན་བརྡ་ The symbol that warns of poison. 2. drugs, narcotics.

དུག་ཟོན་ (tugsön) precautions against poison; va.—བྱེད་ to take precautionary measures against poison.

དུག་གཟན་ (tugsɛn) poisoned bait.

དུག་རོ་ (tugro) 1. leftover/ residual poison. 2. an old, residual or chronic illness or behavior; vi.—ལང་ས་ to have a relapse of an old residual or chronic illness or behavior; va.—སློང་ to cause a relapse of an old residual or chronic illness or behavior.

དུག་རོ་གཏིང་འདོན་ (tugro dīŋdün) shung. eradicating completely (from the root) ༎ ད་ལམ་ཁྲིམས་ལམ་དགག་བཅོས་ཀྱི་ལས་རིམ་ནང་ལོ་མང་ལམ་ངན་མུ་འབྱམས་སུ་གྱུར་པའི་ཁྲིམས་སྲོལ་གྱི་དུག་རོ་གཏིང་འདོན་དགོས་རྒྱུ་ Many years of lawlessness should be eradicated from the root.

དུག་རླངས་ (tuglaŋ) poison gas.

དུག་རླངས་སྒྲོགས་མདེལ་ (tuglaŋ gyɔndel) poison gas cannon shell.

དུག་རླངས་འབར་མདེལ་ (tuglaŋ bandel) sm. དུག་རླངས་སྒྲོགས་མདེལ་.

དུག་ལ་འགྲོ་ (tugla dro) vi. to become poison/ poisonous ༎ ཟས་རིགས་བསྲེ་རྒྱུ་ནོར་ན་དུག་ལ་འགྲོ་ཉེན་ཡོད་ If you mix food mistakenly, there is a danger it will become poisonous.

དུག་ལོག (tugloò) clothes; va.—གྱོན་; —གོན་ to wear/ put on clothes, to dress; va.—བརྗེ་ to change clothes; va.—དྲ་ to cut out material/ cloth to make clothes; va.—ཕུད་; —ཕྱིད་ to take off clothes ༎ དུག་ལོག་གི་ནང་ཤ་ The lining of clothes.

དུག་ལོག་བརྗེ་ས་ (tugloò jesa) (clothes) changing room.

དུག་ཤིང་ (tugshiŋ) poison tree.

དུག་ཤུགས་ (tugshuù) sm. དུག་ནུས་.

དུག་ཤེད་ (tugsheè) degree/ strength of poison.

དུག་ཤེད་ཅན་གྱི་རྫས་རིགས་ (tugsheèjɛngi dzɛɛ̀rii) drugs, narcotics.

དུག་ཤེད་ཅན་གྱི་རྫས་རིགས་འགོག་འདོམས་ལས་ཁང་ (tugsheèjɛngi dzɛɛ̀rii gɔgdom lɛɛ̀gaŋ) Drug Enforcement Agency (U.S.A.).

དུག་ཤོར་ (tugshɔɔ) sm. དུག་ཡོག.

དུག་སེལ་ (tugsel) 1. removing/ countering a poison; disinfecting, detoxification, sterilizing; va.—བྱེད་. 2. a type of herb.

དུག་སེལ་ཁང་ (tugsel kāŋ) detoxification/ disinfection chamber.

དུག་སེལ་སེར་པོ་ (tugsel sērbo) a type of herb.

དུག་སེལ་གློག་ཞུན་ (tugsel lōgshün) heat lamp for disinfecting.

དུག་སེལ་སྨན་རྫས་ (tugsel mēndzɛɛ̀) disinfectants.

དུག་སྲིན་ (tugsin) sm. དུག་སྲིན་ཕྲ་མོ་.

དུག་སྲིན་འགོག་སྨན་ (tugsin gɔgmɛn) antibiotic medicine.

དུག་སྲིན་འགོག་རྫས་ (tugsin gɔgdzɛɛ̀) antibiotics, antibacterial materials.

དུག་སྲིན་ཕྲ་མོ་ (tugsin trāmo) germ, bacteria.

དུག་སྲིན་ཕྲ་མོའི་རྒྱུ་གསེར་ (tugsin trāmö gyuser) bacillary dysentery.

དུག་སྲིན་རྒྱམ་ཕྲེང་ཅན་ (tugsin dumdreŋjɛn) streptococcus.

དུག་གསུམ་ (tugsum) the three poisons: desire, hatred, ignorance.

དུག་སློག (tugloò) sm. དུག་ལོག.

དུག་ཧ་ལ་ཧ་ལ་ (tuù hāla hāla) black rhizome.

དུག་ལྷག (tuglhaà) sm. དུག་རོ་.

དུགས་ (tuù) a treatment for being hot/ (feverish) or cold ༎ དྲོད་དུགས་ Heat treatment.

དུང་ (tuŋ) 1. a horn (instrument); va.—འབུད་; —གཏོང་ to blow or play a horn/ trumpet/ bugle ༎ དམག་དུང་ Bugle. 2. conch shell.

དུང་: p. དུངས་; f. དུང་ (tuŋ) vi. to have love/ affection/ fondness.

དུང་དཀར་ (tuŋgar) white conch shell.

དུང་དཀར་འཁོར་ལོ་ (tuŋgar kɔ̄ɔlo) a vein between the eyebrows (in Tibetan medicine).

དུང་དཀར་དགོན་པ་ (tuŋgar gömbo) Dunggar monastery (in Yadung).

དུང་དཀར་སྤུ་ཁྲིད་ (tuŋgar pudrii) snail.

དུང་དཀར་གཡས་འཁྱིལ་ (tuŋgar yɛɛ̀gyii) sm. དུང་གཡས་འཁྱིལ་.

དུང་དཀར་གཡོན་འཁྱིལ་ (tuŋgar yõŋgyii) sm. དུང་གཡོན་འཁྱིལ་.

དུང་དཀར་རག་གཤོག་མ་ (tuŋgar ragshoma) a wing-shaped brass decorative piece attached to conch shells that monks use.

དུང་དཀར་གཤོག་པ་ཅན་ (tuŋgar shɔ̃gbajɛn) sm. དུང་དཀར་རག་གཤོག་མ་.

དུང་དཀར་སེར་སྣང་ (tuŋgar sẽrnaŋ) seeing sth. in accord with one's ideology/ views rather than what actually is [Lit. seeing a white conch shell as yellow].

དུང་སྐྱོང་ (tuŋgyoŋ) nāga king.

དུང་ཁང་ (tuŋgaŋ) the skull.

དུང་ཁྲག (tuŋdraà) 1. blood in the brain. 2. a skull filled with blood.

དུང་མཁན་ (tuŋñɛn) 1. people who decorate conch shells. 2. a trumpet/ horn maker. 3. a trumpet/ horn player.

དུང་འཁོར་ (tuŋgɔɔ) a white conch shell bracelet worn by women.

དུང་འཁྱིལ་ (tuŋgyii) spiral helix design.

དུང་འཁྱིལ་ཐིག (tuŋgyii tĩg) helix line.

དུང་ཁྱིལ་རི་མོ་ (tuŋgyii rimu) a whirling/ helix spiral pattern.

དུང་གི་ལྡེམ་ཤིང་དཀར་པོ་ (tuŋgi dēmshiŋ gārbo) a type of white tree.

དུང་གི་ཨ་ལོང་ (tuŋgi āloŋ) conch shell earring.

དུང་དགོན་ (tuŋgön) shung. abbr. of དུང་དཀར་དགོན་པ་.

དུང་རྒྱ་གླིང་ (tuŋ gyəliŋ) abbr. of དུང་དང་རྒྱ་གླིང་.

དུང་སྒོར་ (tuŋgɔɔ) sm. དུང་འཁོར་.

དུང་སྒྲ་ (tuŋdra) 1. the sound of a conch shell horn. 2. bugle call.

དུང་ངེ་བ་ (tuŋŋgewa) 1. sad ¶ གསར་འགྱུར་ངན་པ་དེ་གོ་ནས་སེམས་སྐྱོ་དུང་ངེ་བ་བྱུང་ When he heard the bad news he was sad. 2. with great love/ affection ¶ བཟའ་ཚང་གཉིས་སེམས་བརྩེ་དུང་ངེ་བའི་ངང་ནས་གནས་ཡོད་པ་རེད་ The couple lived together with love and affection.

དུང་ཆེན་ (tuŋjen) large musical horn/ trumpet used by monks.

དུང་ཆེན་མེ་ཏོག (tuŋjen medɔɔ̀) morning glory.

དུང་ཆོས་ (tuŋjöö) a small white conch shell.

དུང་མཆོག (tuŋjɔɔ̀) sm. དུང་དཀར་གཡས་འཁྱིལ་.

དུང་ཐག (tuŋdaà) the rope tied to a well bucket to pull up water.

དུང་ཐལ་ (tuŋdɛɛ) ash from conch shells (used for Tibetan medicine).

དུང་ཐིག (tuŋdig) spiral line.

དུང་དུང་ (tuŋduŋ) having a great deal of love/ affection.

དུང་རྡོ་ (tuŋdo) fossilized conch shell.

དུང་བརྡ་ (tuŋda) signal given by sounding a horn/ trumpet; va.—གཏོང་.

དུང་རྣ་ (tuŋna) an earring made of conch shell.

དུང་པ་ (tuŋbə) trumpeter, bugler.

དུང་པ་དམག་མི་ (tuŋbə mə̃əmi) army bugler.

དུང་པོ་ (tuŋbo) sm. དུང་དཀར་.

དུང་ཕན་ (tuŋbɛn) ch. wash basin.

དུང་ཕྱུར་ (tuŋcur) one hundred million ¶ དུང་ཕྱུར་དྲུག Six hundred million.

དུང་ཕྲེང་ (tuŋdreŋ) rosary made from conch shell.

དུང་འཕྱུར་ (tuŋcur) sm. དུང་ཕྱུར་.

དུང་ (tuŋ) p. of དུངས་.

དུང་བན་ (tuŋbɛn) sm. དུང་ཕན་.

དུང་འབུད་ (tuŋ büü) 1. one of the veins in Tibetan medicine. 2. va. to play the trumpet, to blow the conch shell.

དུང་འབྲས་ (tuŋdrɛɛ̀) type of mineral/ stone used in Tibetan medicine.

དུང་དམར་ (tuŋmar) 1. a reddish conch shell. 2. sm. དུང་ཁྲག, 2.

དུང་ཚེར་མ་ཅན་ (tuŋ tsẽrmajɛn) a type of conch shell.

དུང་ཞེན་ (tuŋshen) affection and loyalty.

དུང་ཡལ་ (tuŋ yɛɛ) vi. to vanish/ disappear.

དུང་གཡས་འཁྱིལ་ (tuŋ yɛɛ̀gyii) a conch shell that spirals toward the right.

དུང་གཡོན་འཁྱིལ་ (tuŋ yõŋgyii) a conch shell that spirals toward the left.

དུང་རིང་ (tuŋriŋ) long trumpet/ horn.

དུང་རྭ་ (tuŋra) deer horn/ antler.

དུང་རིས་སྐས་ (tuŋrigɛɛ̀) winding/ spiral staircase.

དུང་ལོང་ (tuŋloŋ) sm. དུང་རྣ་.

དུང་སེམས་ (tuŋsem) loving thoughts, love and affection.

དུང་སོ་ (tuŋso) teeth; vi.—འཁོར་ to have one's set of teeth fully appear.

དུངས་ (tuŋ) p. of དུང་.

དུད་ (tüü) 1. smoke. 2. vi. to hang/ bend over (for crops).

དུད་ཁ་ (tüügə) 1. household, family. 2. smoky color.

དུད་ཁུ་ (tüügu) moisture in smoke.

དུད་ཁུག (tüüguù) tobacco pouch.

དུད་ཁུང་ (tüüguŋ) chimney.

དུད་ཁྲལ་ (tüüdrɛɛ) shung. a tax performed by དུད་ཆུང་.

དུད་གྲངས་ (tüüdraŋ) shung. the number of households/ families.

དུད་འགྲོ་ (tündro) animals.

དུད་འགྲོའི་སྐྱེ་གནས་ (tündrö gyēnɛɛ̀) animal realm.

དུད་འགྲོའི་སྒྱུ་རྩལ་ཚོགས་པ་ (tündrö gyudzɛɛ tsõgba) circus troupe.

དུད་འགྲོའི་སྒྱུ་རྩལ་ (tündrö gyudzɛɛ) animal acts (e.g., in circus shows).

དུད་གན་ (tüügɛn) soot.

དུད་སྒོ་ (tüügo) chimney.

དུད་སྒོ་ཕྱུགས་ (tüü gojuù) household and domestic animals.

དུད་གཅིག་མ་ (tüü jigmə) a single/ lone household.

དུད་ཆུང་ (tüüjuŋ) shung. a type of lower status peasant (or peasant household) in tt. who belonged to a lord but normally had no land as a tax base so did not have to perform extensive corvee labor.

དུད་ཆུང་རྟེན་ཡོད་ (tüüjuŋ dēnyöö) a དུད་ཆུང་ with a small tax base in land.

དུད་སྟོངས་ (tüü dõŋ) a དུད་ཆུང་ household/ family that has become extinct or split up.

དུད་ཐོ་ (tüüdo) shung. a list/ record of families/ households.

དུད་ཐོར་ (tüütɔɔ) a family that has split up.

དུད་དྲི་ (tüüdrii) smell of smoke.

དུད་དྲེག (tüüdreg) sm. དུད་གན་.

དུད་མདེལ་ (tüüdel) smoke bomb.

དུད་ནག (tüünaà) opium.

དུད་པ་ (tüüba) sm. དུ་བ་.

དུད་པ་སྔོན་འཐུལ་ (tüüba ŋöndüü) a sign that sth. is going to happen [Lit. smoke before the fire].

དུད་སྤྱི་ (tüüji) shung. the དུད་ཆུང་ in general or as a whole ¶ དུད་སྤྱིས་རང་མཚམས་སྒོ་རྒྱ་བཤིག་ཐག The general public of དུད་ཆུང་ decided on their own and broke the seal of the door (without consulting the superior).

དུད་སྤྲིན་ཤ་མོའི་གཟུགས་ཅན་ (tüüdrin shāmö sugjɛn) mushroom cloud.

དུད་པ་བྱ་བལ་མ་ (tüüba capɛɛma) a type of seaweed that floats on water.

དུད་བལ་ (tüüpɛɛ) soot that is hanging down in strands.

དུད་རྩི་ (tüüdzi) sm. དུད་ཁུ་.

དུད་ཚང་ (tüüdzaŋ) family, household ¶ གྲོང་གསེབ་དེ་ར་དུད་ཚང་ག་ཚོད་འདུག How many households are there in that village?

དུད་ཚང་ཁ་ལས་ (tüüdzaŋ kēlɛɛ̀) a family/ household operated business.

དུད་ཚོ་ (tüüdzo) village.

དུད་འཚོ་ (tündzo) sm. དུད་ཚོ་.

དུད་ཡོད་རྡོ་སོལ་ (tüüyöö dosöö) bituminous (soft) coal.

དུད་ཡོལ་ (tüüyöö) smokescreen.
དུད་རླངས་ (tüülaŋ) abbr. smoke and steam.
དུད་ལམ་ (tüülam) sm. དུད་ཁུང་.
དུད་སའི་ལྷ་ཁང་ (tursɛ lhāgaŋ) burial place.
དུད་གསུམ་གྲོང་ཚོ་ (tüüsum troŋdzo) a three-family village (unit).
དུད་བསུང་ (tüüsuŋ) smell of smoke.
དུན་ལས་ (tünlɛɛ̀) amber.
དུབ་ (tub) vi. to be tired, to be fatigued ༈ ལུས་སེམས་གཉིས་ཀ་དུབ་སོང་ I am mentally and physically tired.
དུབ་ཅན་ (tubjɛn) tiring, fatiguing ༈ ལས་ཀ་དུབ་ཅན་ Tiring work.
དུབ་ལིན་ (tublen) Dublin.
དུམ་ (tum) abbr. for དུམ་བུ་.
དུམ་གྲུགས་ (tumdruù) broken into small pieces; vi.—དུ་སོང་ to be/ get broken into small pieces.
དུམ་རྒྱག (tum gyaà) va. to cut or break into small pieces/ chunks.
དུམ་གཅིག (tumjig) one piece/ section/ part.
དུམ་བཅད་ (tumjɛɛ̀) 1. cutting into pieces/ chunks; va.—རྒྱག; —གཏོང་. 2. making into sections/ groups; va.—བྱེད་.
དུམ་ཆུང་ (tumjuŋ) a small piece/ chunk.
དུམ་དུམ་ (tumdum) sm. དུམ་བུ་.
དུམ་པ་ (tumbə) a Tibetan-style book.
དུམ་བུ་ (tumbu) part, portion, chunk, section, piece; va.—གཅོད་; —བཟོ་ to cut/ break into chunks/ parts ༈ གྲོང་ཁྱེར་གྱི་དུམ་བུ་གཅིག་ལ་རྒྱ་རིགས་སྡོད་ཀྱི་ཡོད་པ་རེད་ The Chinese live in one part of the city. ༈ ཁོས་པང་ལེབ་དེ་དུམ་བུ་གསུམ་དུ་བཅད་སོང་ He cut the plank into three chunks.
དུམ་བུར་བགོ་ (tumbur go) va. to divide into parts/ sections, to dismember.
དུམ་སྦོམ་ (tumbom) fragment bomb/ grenade, cluster bomb.
དུམ་ཚན་ (tumdzɛn) a part, section, passage (of an essay or book).
དུམ་ཤིག (tumshig) a few ༈ མི་དུམ་ཤིག་སླེབས་བྱུང་ A few people came.
དུམ་རེ་ (tumre) 1. a bit or few at a time ༈ དམག་སར་དམག་མི་དུམ་རེ་བྱས་ནས་བཏང་སོང་ (They) sent the soldiers to battlefield a few at a time. 2. by groups/ sections.
དུམ་གཤག (tumshaà) profile.
དུམ་གཤག་རི་མོ་ (tumshaà rimu) sm. དུམ་གཤགས་རི་མོ་.
དུམ་གཤགས་རི་མོ་ (tumshaà rimu) sectional drawing, profile.
དུའུ་ (tuwu) 1. ch. kilowatt hour ༈ གློག་དུའུ་ kilowatt hours of electric power. 2. degree (temperature) ༈ ཐིག་སྒོར་འོག་གི་དུའུ་བཅུ་ཕྲག་ཡོད་པ་ In the ten degree below zero range.
དུའུ་ཕུག (tuwupu) ch. bean curd (tofu).
དུར་ (tur) sm. དུར་ཁང་.
དུར་ཀུན་ (turgün) a grave robber.
དུར་བསྐྱལ་ (turgyee) taking a corpse to the graveyard or sky burial site.
དུར་ཁང་ (turgaŋ) tomb, crypt.
དུར་ཁུང་ (turguŋ) grave hole; va.—ཀོ་; —འདུ་ to dig a grave.
དུར་ཁུང་ཀུ་མཁན་ (turguŋ gūñɛn) grave robber.
དུར་ཁྲོད་ (turdröö) graveyard, cemetery, tomb, sky burial site; va.—(དུ་) སྐྱེལ་ to take a corpse to the graveyard/ sky burial site.
དུར་ཁྲོད་ཀྱི་རས་ (turdröögi rɛɛ̀) cloth to cover the dead, burial shroud.
དུར་ཁྲོད་དུ་ཁྱེར་ (turdröödu kyēr) 1. va. to take a corpse to the graveyard/ cemetery/ sky burial site. 2. va. to take a secret to the grave.
དུར་ཁྲོད་བདག་པོ་ (turdröö dagbo) a ghost that appears as a skeleton.
དུར་ཁྲོད་པ་ (turdrööba) person who goes to a cemetery/ graveyard/ sky burial site to meditate.
དུར་ཁྲོད་མ་ (turdrööma) sm. དཔལ་ལྡན་ལྷ་མོ་.
དུར་གྱི་མཆོད་པ་ (turgi cööba) grave.
དུར་གླ་ (turla) a fee for the use of sky burial/ site.
དུར་རྒན་ (turgɛn) well experienced.
དུར་རྒྱགས་ (turgyaà) 1. food to be eaten at the site of a sky burial when a corpse is being dismembered. 2. bedding and clothing given to people who work at the sky burial site.
དུར་སྒམ་ (turgam) coffin.
དུར་སྒྲོམ་ (turgom) sm. དུར་སྒམ་.
དུར་མཆོད་ (turjöö) rituals performed during the day of a funeral/ sky burial.
དུར་འཇུག (turjuù) burying a corpse; va.—བྱེད་.
དུར་ཐོད་ (turdöö) skulls left around a sky burial site.
དུར་དོང་ (turdoŋ) tomb.
དུར་རྡོ་ (turdo) tombstone, gravestone.
དུར་གནས་ (turnɛɛ̀) sm. དུར་ཁྲོད་.
དུར་བ་ (turwə) cogan grass.
དུར་བོན་ (turbön) one of the Bon subsects.
དུར་བྱ་ (turja) birds that eat corpses at the sky burial site (usu. vultures).
དུར་བྱིད་ (turjii) a type of brewed Tibetan medicine.
དུར་བྱང་ (turjaŋ) gravestone, tomb inscription tablet.
དུར་བྱང་ཡི་གེ་ (turjaŋ yigi) tombstone or grave tablet inscription.
དུར་མཆེད་ (turdzeè) a grave and a funeral pyre/ crematorium.
དུར་རྫས་ (turdzɛɛ̀) funerary objects, burial objects.
དུར་ཝ་ (turwa) sm. དུར་བ་.
དུར་ལམ་ (turlam) the path leading to a grave/ cemetery.
དུར་གཤིན་མཚོན་ཆ་ཅན་ (turshen tsönjajɛn) one of the Bon subsects.
དུར་ལས་ (turlɛɛ̀) burial/ cemetery work.
དུར་ས་ (tursə) sm. དུར་ཁྲོད་.
དུར་སའི་རྡོ་རིང་ (turse doriŋ) tombstone.
དུར་སའི་ལྷ་ཁང་ (turse lhāgaŋ) temple at a grave site/ sky burial site.
དུར་སྲི་ (tursi) ghosts/ demons who inhabit sky burial sites or cemeteries.
དུར་སྲུང་པ་ (tursuŋwə) guard keeper of a graveyard.
དུལ་ (tüü) vi. to be tamed/ disciplined ༈ མི་དེ་བཙོན་ཁང་ལ་བཅུག་རྗེས་གཤིས་ཀ་དུལ་བཞག After being imprisoned that man's personality was tamed.
དུལ་པོ་ (tüübo) tame, peaceful, disciplined.
དུལ་མ་ (tüümə) 1. a tame person/ horse. 2. a young woman.
དུས་ (tüü) 1. time ༈ དུས་གཞན་ཞིག Another time. ༈ དབྱར་དུས་ Summertime. 2. (vb. + —) at the time of, while, when ༈ ང་ཚོ་རྩེད་མོ་རྩེ་དུས་ When we were playing.
དུས་ཀུན་དུ་ (tüügündu) sm. དུས་རྟག་ཏུ་.
དུས་ཀྱི་འཁོར་ཕྱོགས་ (tüügi gɔ̄ɔjɔɔ̀) the general situation, the general trend, the trend of the time ༈ དུས་ཀྱི་འཁོར་ཕྱོགས་ལ་བལྟས་ན་ཁོ་ཚོས་དབང་བསྒྱུར་བྱེད་ཐུབ་ཀྱི་མ་རེད་ Looking at the general situation, they will not be able to rule.
དུས་ཀྱི་འཁོར་ལོ་ (tüügi kɔ̄ɔlo) 1. Kalachakra. 2. the wheel of time ༈ དུས་ཀྱི་འཁོར་ལོ་ནི་ལྡོག་ཏུ་མེད་པར་ཞིག་ཡིན་ The wheel of time is unstoppable.
དུས་ཀྱི་འགྱུར་ལྡོག (tüügi gyundɔɔ̀) change, change of a whole situation ༈ ང་ཚོའི་རྒྱལ་ཁབ་ནང་དུས་ཀྱི་འགྱུར་ལྡོག་ཆེན་པོ་ཞིག་བྱུང་ཡོད་ There has been a great change in our country.
དུས་ཀྱི་ཆ་ཚད་ (tüügi cādzɛɛ̀) sundial.
དུས་ཀྱི་ཆ་ཤས་ (tüügi cāshɛɛ̀) different time periods that a day is divided into.
དུས་ཀྱི་ཚོ་ག (tüügi cōga) method of calculating time.
དུས་ཀྱི་ཆོས་ཉིད་ (tüügi cööñii) death, mortality.
དུས་ཀྱི་སྙིགས་མ་ (tüügi ñīgmə) the impurities of an eon/ period.
དུས་ཀྱི་ཐ་མ་ (tüügi tamə) 1. sm. དུས་ཀྱི་སྙིགས་མ་. 2. time just before dying/ death.
དུས་ཀྱི་ཐུང་མཐའ་ (tüügi tūŋda) split second, a very

short time, an instant.

དུས་ཀྱི་མཐར་འགྱུར་ (tüùgi tār gyur) vi. to die.

དུས་ཀྱི་འཕོ་འགྱུར་ (tüùgi pōgyur) changing times.

དུས་ཀྱི་ཕོ་ཉ་ (tüùgi pōña) the lord of death ། དུས་ཀྱི་ཕོ་ཉའི་ཞགས་པས་མ་བཅིངས་པར་ཐོས་བསམ་སྒོམ་ལ་སྒོ་གསུམ་གཞོལ་བར་གནས་ Not being tied by the rope of the lord of death, I am exerting my effort in studying, thinking, and meditating.

དུས་ཀྱི་ཟླ་བ་ (tüùgi dawa) a month.

དུས་བཀག་ (tüùgaà) set time, time limit, schedule, vi.—སླེབ་ to reach a time limit/ deadline/ scheduled time ། ལས་ཀ་དེ་དུས་བཀག་གི་སྔོན་དུ་གྲུབ་པ་རེད་ They completed the work ahead of schedule. ། དཔེ་དེབ་དང་ཚགས་པར་དུས་བཀག་ལྟར་སྐྱེལ་གྱི་ཡོད་པ་རེད་ They delivered the magazines and papers according to a schedule.

དུས་བཀག་བཙོན་འཇུག་ (tüùgaà dzōnjuù) prison term/ sentence.

དུས་བཀག་འབར་མདེལ་ (tüùgaà bandel) time bomb.

དུས་སྐབས་ (tüùgəb) 1. time, era, period ། དུས་སྐབས་གསར་པ་ཞིག་ལ་སླེབས་པ་རེད་ (We) have come to a new era. 2. chance, opportunity; vi.—རྙེད་; —ཐོབ་; —རག; —བྱུང་ to get an opportunity; vi.—ཤོར་ to lose an opportunity ། དུས་སྐབས་བཟང་པོ་ཞིག་ཐོབ་པ་རེད་ They got an excellent opportunity.

དུས་སྐབས་མཚམས་མེད་ (tüùgəb tsāmmeè) without a break, continuously, nonstop.

དུས་སྐབས་ཤོར་ (tüùgəb shɔ̄ɔ̄) vi. to lose an opportunity.

དུས་བསྐལ་ (tüùgɛɛ) the time of the end of the world, the end of an eon, doomsday.

དུས་བསྐལ་བར་ཐུག (tüùgɛɛ par tüù) shung. vi. to reach the end of an eon or world.

དུས་ཁྱད་ (tüùkyɛɛ̀) time difference.

དུས་ཁྲིམས་ (tüùdrim) a one day religious vow.

དུས་འཁོར་ (tüùgɔɔ) abbr. of Kalachakra (the wheel of time).

དུས་འཁོར་གྱི་རང་བཞིན་ (tüùgɔɔgi rəŋshin) periodic, cyclical.

དུས་འཁྲུགས་ (tüùdruù) sm. དུས་ཟིང་.

དུས་གང་ཞིག (tüù kaŋshi) 1. when ། དུས་གང་ཞིག་ལ་ཟ་ཁང་སྒོ་འབྱེད་ཀྱི་རེད་ When will the restaurant open? 2. one time.

དུས་འགའ་རེ་ (tüù gare) sometimes, at some times.

དུས་འགོ་ (tüngo) initial/ beginning stage or time ། རི་འགོག་དམག་འཁྲུག་གི་དུས་འགོར་ At the beginning of the "War of Resistance Against Japan."

དུས་འགྱངས་ (tüùgyaŋ) postponing, delaying; va.—གཏོང་ to postpone, to delay ། ཁོ་ཐོན་རྒྱུ་ཉིན་ཤས་དུས་འགྱངས་སུ་བཏང་བ་རེད་ They postponed his departure for a few days; vi.—འགྲོ་; —ཤོར་ to get delayed, postponed ། ཟླ་རེའི་རྩིས་ཁྲ་གཏོང་རྒྱུ་དུས་འགྱངས་ཤོར་བ་རེད་ The sending of the monthly account statement was delayed.

དུས་འགྱངས་ཆད་ལུས་ (tüùgyaŋ cɛ̄ɛ̀lüü) delayed payment, overdue payment.

དུས་འགྱུར་ (tüngyur) change in times/ period/ era/ circumstances ། ༡༩༣༧ ལོའི་ཟླ་ ༧ ཚེས་ ༧ གྱི་དུས་འགྱུར་རྗེས་ After the change of July 7, 1937.

དུས་འགྲིག (tüù drig) vi. to happen simultaneously, to occur at the same time ། ང་ལྷ་སར་འབྱོར་པ་དང་ཁོང་ཕེབས་པ་དུས་འགྲིགས་སོང་ My coming to Lhasa and his arrival there occurred at the same time.

དུས་རྒྱུན་ (tüùgyün) usually, regularly, always ། དུས་རྒྱུན་ཁོ་ལས་ཀར་སྔ་པོ་འགྲོ་བ་རེད་ He regularly goes to work early. ། དུས་རྒྱུན་དང་མི་འདྲ་བའི་དམིགས་བསལ་ཞིག་རེད་ This is not like usual. It is very special.

དུས་རྒྱུན་དུ་ (tüùgyündu) usually, regularly, always.

དུས་རྒྱུན་ལྟར་དུ་ (tüùgyün dārdu) in accordance with what is usually/ customarily done.

དུས་སྒོ་ (tüùgo) a time, a scheduled time; va.—འགོག to establish/ set a specific time to do sth., to make an appointment ། ང་ཚོ་སང་ཉིན་ཆུ་ཚོད་༧པར་འཛོམས་རྒྱུའི་དུས་སྒོ་བཀག་ཡོད་ We made an appointment to meet tomorrow at 7 o'clock.

དུས་སྒོ་སྔོན་བཀག (tüùgo ŋōngaà) establishing/ setting a time or schedule in advance.

དུས་སྒྲིག (tüù drig) va. to make an appointment ། ང་སང་ཉིན་སྨན་ཁང་ལ་འགྲོ་རྒྱུ་དུས་བསྒྲིགས་ཡོད་ I made an appointment to go to the hospital tomorrow.

དུས་སྒྲོག་ཆུ་ཚོད་འཁོར་ལོ་ (tüùdrɔɔ cūdzöö kɔ̄ɔ̄lo) alarm clock.

དུས་བརྒྱད་ (tüù gyɛɛ̀) the eight stages in a life of a person.

དུས་ངེས་ཅན་ (tüùŋeèjɛn) having a definite time ། དུས་ངེས་ཅན་གྱི་དཔེ་དེབ་ Periodical publication (a magazine having a definite time for publication).

དུས་ལྔ་ (tüù ŋā) the five seasons: winter, spring, autumn and two periods in between.

དུས་ལྔ་སྣུར་ (tüùŋa nūr) sm. དུས་སྣུར་.

དུས་ཅན་ཀྲ་དན་ (tüùjɛn drādɛn) time bomb.

དུས་ཅུང་ཟད་ (tüù jūŋsɛɛ̀) a short period of time.

དུས་གཅིག (tüùjig) at the same time.

དུས་བཅད་ (tüùjɛɛ̀) time limit, deadline; va.—བྱེད་ to set a time limit/ deadline ། ཚོང་ཁང་ཁག་ཆུ་ཚོད་བཅུ་པར་སྒོ་རྒྱག་དགོས་པ་དུས་བཅད་བྱས་ཡོད་པ་རེད་ They have set 10 o'clock as the time that shops must close.

དུས་བཅད་གླ་ཐོབ་ (tüùjɛɛ̀ lādob) a wage fixed by time (by the hour, day, month, etc.).

དུས་བཅད་ཚོང་ཟོག (tüùjɛɛ̀ tsōŋsɔɔ̀) 1. merchandise that has a delivery deadline. 2. merchandise that has to be used or sold before a set time.

དུས་བཅད་ཕྱིར་འགྱངས་ (tüùjɛɛ̀ cīrgyaŋ) extending a time/ deadline/ limit.

དུས་བཅར་ཞུ་ (tüùjaa shu) va. to come on time, to come at the proper time ། ཚོགས་འདུར་དུས་བཅར་མ་ཞུས་ན་སྐྱོན་བརྗོད་ཕོག་གི་རེད་ If you don't attend the meeting on time, you will be criticized.

དུས་ཆད་ (tüùjɛɛ̀) 1. interruption, break. 2. an appointment to meet sb.; va.—འདེབས་ to make an appointment.

དུས་ཆད་པ་མེད་པ་ (tüùjɛɛ̀ meèba) without interruption/ break, ceaseless, continuous.

དུས་ཆར་ (tüùjar) seasonal rain, timely rain.

དུས་ཆུང་ (tüùjuŋ) an unit of time (according to Chinese system of time calculation).

དུས་ཆེན་ (tüùjɛn) festival, holiday, occasion; va.—གཏོང་ to celebrate a festival/ holiday/ ceremony.

དུས་ཆེན་གསུམ་འཛོམས་ (tüùjɛn sūmdzom) Sagadawa —the festival on the 15th day of the 4th Tibetan lunar month celebrating the conception, enlightenment and death of the Buddha.

དུས་ཆོས་སུ་འགྱུར་ (tüù cöösu gyur) vi. to die, to pass away.

དུས་མཆོད་ (tüùjöö) prescribed religious service/ ceremony/ offering at a specific times.

དུས་ཇི་སྲིད་ (tüù jisii) 1. how much time. 2. at anytime, forever ། ཁྱེད་ཀྱི་བཀའ་དྲིན་དེ་ངས་དུས་ཇི་སྲིད་བརྗེད་ཐུབ་ཀྱི་མ་རེད་ I will never forget your kindness (I am not able to forget it at any time).

དུས་མཇུག (tünjuù) last stage, last phase.

དུས་མཇུག་ཏུ་ (tünjugdu) the end of sth. (an era/ time/ period) ། འདས་པའི་ལོ་བརྒྱ་ཕྲག་བཅོ་བརྒྱད་པའི་དུས་མཇུག་ཏུ་ At the end of the 18th century.

དུས་ཉེ་བར་ (tüù ñewar) until the end of sth. (an era/ period/ time).

དུས་ཉེ་བའི་ཆ་ (tüù ñewɛ cā) recently.

དུས་མཉམ་ (tüùñam) living/ occurring/ existing at the same time ། དམག་ཆེན་གཉིས་པ་དང་དུས་མཉམ་རྒྱ་ནག་ནང་གསར་བརྗེའི་ལས་འགུལ་དར་ཡོད་པ་རེད་ The revolutionary movement in China became widespread at the same time as World War II.

དུས་སྙིགས་ (tüùñii) abbr. of དུས་ཀྱི་སྙིགས་མ་.

དུས་གདན་ (tüùdɛn) always, all the time.

དུས་གདན་དུ་ (tüùdɛndu) always, all the time ། དུས་གདན་དུ་དཀའ་ངལ་ཡོང་གི་ཡོད་པ་རེད་ They always have problems.

དུས་གཏན་དུ་མི་འཇིག་པ་ (tüüdɛndu ma jigbə) immortal.

དུས་གདུགས་ (tüü düü) vi. to arrive at/ reach the time to do sth. ¶ ང་རྒྱ་གར་ལ་འགྲོ་རྒྱུའི་དུས་གདུགས་ནས་བྲེལ་བ་ཚ་པོ་ཞིག་དྲག་འདུག The time for me to go to India has arrived so I am very busy.

དུས་གཏོར་ (tüüdɔr) offering of torma done on particular or set occasions.

དུས་བདབ་ (tüü dəb) p. of དུས་འདེབས་.

དུས་རྟག་དུ་ (tüü dāgdu) sm. དུས་གཏན་དུ་.

དུས་རྟག་པར་ (tüü dāgbar) always, all the time.

དུས་སྟོང་ (tüüdoŋ) spare time.

དུས་སྟོན་ (tüüdön) sm. དུས་ཆེན་.

དུས་བསྟུན་ (tüüdün) in accordance with the time/ era ¶ དུས་བསྟུན་འགྱུར་བཅོས་ Changes/ reforms in accordance with the times.

དུས་ཐག (tüüdaà) sm. ཡུན་ཚད་.

དུས་ཐིམ་ (tüü tīm) vi. to expire (for a period/ time), to be finished (for a term of a contract, etc.) ¶ ཁོའི་ལས་ཀའི་དུས་ད་ལོ་ཐིམ་གྱི་ཡོད་པ་རེད་ His term of service expires this year.

དུས་ཐུག (tüü tüü) vi. to coincide ¶ ཁོ་སླེབས་པ་དང་མོ་ཕྱིན་པ་དུས་ཐུག་པ་རེད་ His arrival and her departure coincided.

དུས་ཐུང་ (tüüduŋ) short time ¶ དེ་དུས་ཐུང་ནང་ In a short time.

དུས་ཐུང་རེའུ་མིག (tüüduŋ riumig) short timetable, short schedule.

དུས་ཐུང་གླ་པ་ (tüüduŋ lāba) pieceworker, day wage laborer.

དུས་ཐུང་སྦྱོང་བརྡར་འཛིན་གྲྭ་ (tüüduŋ joŋdar dzindra) short-term training class.

དུས་ཐོག (tüüdɔɔ̀) 1. on time, according to schedule, punctually ¶ ཁོ་ལས་ཁུངས་ལ་དུས་ཐོག་ཡོང་གི་ཡོད་པ་རེད་ He comes to the office on time (according to the schedule, punctually). 2. opportunely, the right time; vi.—འཁེལ་ to be on time, to fall at the right time ¶ སྲིད་ཇུས་གསར་པ་དེ་དུས་ཐོག་ལ་དག་དག་འཁེལ་བ་ཞིག་རེད་ The new policy is one that falls exactly at the right time.

དུས་ཐོག་གི་ཁ་བ་ (tüüdɔɔ̀gi kāwa) 1. a seasonable snowfall. 2. a timely snowfall.

དུས་ཐོག་ཏུ་ (tüüdɔɔ̀du) sm. དུས་ཐོག.

དུས་ཐོག་གཏོང་བའི་གནམ་གྲུ་ (tüüdɔɔ̀ dōŋwɛ nāmdru) scheduled airplane/ flight.

དུས་ཐོག་འཕྲུལ་སྤྲོད་ (tüüdɔɔ̀ trɛ̄ɛ̄dröö) shung. delivering on time.

དུས་མཐའ་ (tüüda) 1. the end of an eon. 2. the shortest time. 3. a period of great calamities (associated with the end of an eon).

དུས་མཐའི་སྐད་ཅིག་མ་ (tüüdɛ gɛ̄ɛ̀jigmə) a very short time.

དུས་མཐའི་མེ་ (tüüdɛ me) destruction by fire when an eon comes to an end.

དུས་མཐའི་འཁོར་རླུང་ (tüüdɛ tɔ̄ɔ̄luŋ) sm. དུས་མཐའི་རླུང་.

དུས་མཐའི་རླུང་ (tüüdɛ lūŋ) destruction by wind when an eon comes to an end.

དུས་མཐུན་ (tüüdün) sm. དུས་བསྟུན་.

དུས་མཐུན་ལྭ་བ་ (tüüdün lawa) up-to-date style clothing.

དུས་དང་བསྟུན་ (tüüdaŋ dǖn) sm. དུས་བསྟུན་.

དུས་དང་མཐུན་པ་ (tüüdaŋ dǖmbə) sm. དུས་བསྟུན་.

དུས་དང་དུས་ལ་ (tüüdaŋ tüülə) from time to time ¶ དུས་དང་དུས་ལ་ཆོས་ལུགས་ཀྱི་དུས་ཆེན་གཏོང་གི་ཡོད་པ་རེད་ From time to time there are religious festivals.

དུས་དང་རྣམ་པ་ཀུན་ཏུ་ (tüüdaŋ nāmba gǖndu) always, all the time, constantly.

དུས་དང་མི་མཐུན་པ་ (tüüdaŋ midünbə) inopportune, unseasonable, untimely, out of date.

དུས་དང་མཚུངས་ (tüüdaŋ tsūŋ) at the same time.

དུས་དང་འཚམས་པ་ (tüüdaŋ tsūŋbə) sm. དུས་བསྟུན་.

དུས་དུས་ལ་ (tüüdüülə) sometimes, occasionally ¶ དུས་དུས་ལ་ཕ་མ་ཐུག་པར་འགྲོ་གི་ཡོད་པ་རེད་ Occasionally (they) go to see their parents.

དུས་དེ་སྲིད་བར་ (tüüde siilə) until such time as ¶ ལས་ཀ་དེ་མཇུག་འགྲིལ་བའི་དུས་དེ་སྲིད་བར་ང་འདིར་སྡོད་ཀྱི་ཡིན་ Until such time as the work is completed, I will stay here.

དུས་དེབ་ (tüüdeb) periodical, journal, magazine.

དུས་དེབ་བརྒྱུད་ཁྲིད་ (tüüdeb gyüüdrii) courses/ lessons/ instruction given through a journal or magazine or periodical.

དུས་དེབ་འཕར་མ་ (tüüdeb pārma) supplement (to a journal, magazine, or periodical).

དུས་དོན་ (tüüdün) current events/ affairs ¶ ཚགས་པར་ནང་དུས་དོན་ཁ་ཤས་བཀོད་བཞག The newspaper published several items on current events.

དུས་དྲན་ (tüüdrɛn) memorial, commemorative ¶ དུས་དྲན་དགའ་སྟོན་ A memorial cerebration.

དུས་དྲན་དཔྱད་གཏམ་ (tüüdrɛn jɛ̄ɛ̀dam) commentary, editorial.

དུས་དྲུག (tüüdruù) six parts of a day. 2. six seasons of two months each.

དུས་གདབ་ (tüü dəb) f. of དུས་འདེབས་.

དུས་བདེ་ (tüü de) peaceful/ quite/ calm time or era.

དུས་བདེ་པོ་ (tüü debo) peaceful/ quite/ calm time or era.

དུས་བདེ་ཞི་འཇགས་ (tüüdeè shijaà) a time of peace and happiness, a period of peace and calm/ tranquillity.

དུས་བདེ་ཞོད་འཇགས་ (tüüdeè shönjaà) sm. དུས་བདེ་ཞི་འཇགས་.

དུས་བདེ་ས་འཇམ་ (tüüdeè sānjam) sm. དུས་བདེ་ཞོད་འཇགས་.

དུས་མདའ་ (tünda) sm. དུས་ཚོད་.

དུས་འདའ་ (tüü da) vi. to elapse (time), to pass (of time) ¶ ཁོ་ཕྱིན་ནས་དུས་རིང་པོ་ཞིག་འདས་སོང་ A long time has passed since his departure.

དུས་འདའ་འབར་བྱེད་ (tüü daa bar ceè) va. to pass/ kill time.

དུས་འདས་ (tüü dɛ̄ɛ̀) 1. p. of དུས་འདའ་. 2. to expire (e.g., time on a visa) ¶ ངའི་ཐོངས་མཆན་གྱིས་དུས་འདས་སོང་ My visa has expired. 3. vi. to die ¶ ཁོང་ཁ་ས་མི་ཚེའི་དུས་འདས་པ་རེད་ Yesterday he died (his life expired).

དུས་འདེབས་ (tüü deb) va. to set a time, to make an appointment.

དུས་ལྡན་ (tüüdɛn) one of the sixteen arhats.

དུས་སྡུད་པ་ (tüü düübə) grammatical particles conveying "from" in a temporal sense.

དུས་བརྡ་ (tüüda) a signal or message that sth. is starting; va.—གཏོང་ to send such a signal/ message ¶ སང་ཉིན་ཚོགས་འདུ་འཚོག་རྒྱུའི་དུས་བརྡ་གཏོང་དགོས་ We have to send a message that there is a meeting tomorrow.

དུས་བརྡ་གཏོང་བའི་ཆུ་ཚོད་འཁོར་ལོ་ (tüüda dōŋwɛ cüdzöö kɔ̄ɔ̄lo) alarm clock.

དུས་ནམ་ཞིག་ན་ (tüü namshigna) whenever, all the time.

དུས་ནམ་ཡང་ (tüü namyaŋ) (with neg.) never ¶ ང་ཚོས་དུས་ནམ་ཡང་བརྗེད་ཀྱི་མ་རེད་ We will never forget it.

དུས་ནམ་ཡིན་ཡང་ (tüü nam yinyaŋ) sm. དུས་ནམ་ཡང་.

དུས་གནའ་རབས་ (tüü nərəb) ancient times, antiquity ¶ དུས་གནའ་རབས་ཀྱི་ཆས་གོས་ Ancient costumes.

དུས་གནས་ (tüü nɛ̄ɛ̀) sm. དུས་དོན་.

དུས་སྣ་ (tüünə) Tuna (a town on the route from Sikkim to Lhasa).

དུས་བསྔུར་ (tüü nūr) va. to make/ do at an earlier time/ date ¶ གཟའ་འཁོར་རྗེས་མར་འཚོག་རྒྱུའི་ཚོགས་འདུ་དེ་གཟའ་འཁོར་འདིའི་ནང་དུས་བསྔུར་ནས་ཚོགས་སོང་ The meeting that was to convene next week was moved earlier and met this week.

དུས་དཔགས་བབ་བསྟུན་ (tüübag bəbdün) sm. དུས་བསྟུན་.

དུས་སྤྲིན་ཕ་མོའི་གཟུགས་ཅན་ (tüüdrin sāmö sugjɛn) 1. clouds shaped like a mushroom. 2. mushroom cloud (as in a nuclear explosion).

དུས་ཕྱིར་ནུད་ (tü̱ü ci̅rnüü) delaying, postponing; va.—རྒྱག ། ཁོང་རྒྱ་གར་ལ་འགྲོ་རྒྱུའི་དུས་ཕྱིར་ནུད་སོང་ He postponed his going to India.

དུས་ཕྱིས་ (tü̱üji̅i) 1. nowadays, these days. 2. in the future ། ད་ལྟ་གྲ་སྒྲིག་ཡག་པོ་མ་བྱས་ན་དུས་ཕྱིས་ཡག་པོ་ཡོང་གི་མ་རེད་ If one does not prepare now, the future will not be good.

དུས་འཕྱུལ་ (tü̱ü pü̅ü) va. to waste time, to idle/ pass away time ། ཁོས་ལས་ཀ་ཡག་པོ་མ་བྱས་པར་དུས་འཕྱུལ་ཁི་འདུག He isn't working well but (instead) is wasting time. ། ཁོས་ལས་ཀ་འཚོལ་བར་མ་ཕྱིན་པར་ནང་དུ་དུས་འཕྱུལ་ནས་སྡོད་ཀྱི་འདུག He stays at home passing the time without looking for work.

དུས་འཕྱི་ (tü̱ü ci̅) sm. དུས་ཕྱིར་ནུར་.

དུས་བབ་ (tü̱übəb) 1. timely, opportune, seasonable ། དུས་བབ་ཀྱི་རྒྱབ་སྐྱོར་ Timely support. 2. on schedule. 3. situation, circumstance, condition, state ། གསར་བརྗེའི་དུས་བབ་དང་བསྟུན་ནས་ In accordance with the revolutionary situation.

དུས་བབ་ཀྱིས་དེད་ (tü̱übəbgi te̱è) vi. to be pushed by circumstances/ situation.

དུས་བབས་ (tü̱übəb) sm. དུས་བབ་.

དུས་བྱ་ (tü̱üca) 1. birds that migrate. 2. f. of དུས་བྱེད་.

དུས་བྱེད་ (tü̱ü ce̱è) 1. to die. 2. va. to set a time (to do sth.), to make an appointment, to set a time to do sth.

དུས་བྱས་ (tü̱ü cɛ̱è) p. of དུས་བྱེད་.

དུས་དབང་ (tü̱üwaŋ) shung. because of the changing times ། དུས་དབང་གིས་རྐྱེན་པས་མཆོད་ཡུལ་ལ་ཡོན་བདག་གིས་ཞུ་གཏུག་ཞུས་པ་ Because of the changing times the patron filed a law case against the priest.

དུས་འབྱོར་ (tü̱ü jɔ̱ɔ) arriving on time, coming exactly on a certain day/ date; va.—བྱེད་ ། སང་ཉིན་དུས་འབྱོར་བྱེད་དགོས་ (You) must come right on time tomorrow.

དུས་འབྲས་བུ་ཡོད་པ་ (tü̱ü drɛ̱èbu yo̱òbə) making good use of time, not wasting time; va.—བྱེད་ ། སློབ་སྦྱོང་བྱེད་སྐབས་དུས་འབྲས་བུ་ཡོད་པ་བྱེད་དགོས་ When you study, you must make good use of your time.

དུས་མ་ཡིན་པ་ (tü̱ü mə̱yimbə) wrong time, untimely ། དུས་མ་ཡིན་པར་ལྟོ་ཆས་བཟའ་ན་ན་གི་རེད་ If you eat at the wrong time you will get sick.

དུས་མིན་འཆི་ (tü̱ümin ci̅) vi. to die before one's time, to have an untimely death.

དུས་མིན་བཙའ་ (tü̱ümin dzā) vi. to be born prematurely, to have a premature birth.

དུས་སྨད་ (tü̱ü mɛ̄ɛ̀) the latter part of a century/ period/ era.

དུས་ཙ་ན་ (tü̱ü dzāna) sm. དུས་, 2.

དུས་བཙོན་ (tü̱üdzön) prison term ། ཁོང་ལ་ལོ་བཅུའི་དུས་བཙོན་གྱི་བཀའ་དཔྱད་བཏང་བ་རེད་ (They) sentenced him to a ten year prison term.

དུས་རྩིས་ཆུ་ཐིག (tü̱üdzii cūdii) a copper vase that drips water to tell time.

དུས་ཚང་ (tü̱üdzaŋ) sm. དུས་ཚོད་ཚང་.

དུས་ཚད་ (tü̱üdzɛɛ̀) sm. དུས་བཀག.

དུས་ཚད་ཀྱི་ཁྱད་པར་ (tü̱üdzɛɛ̀gi kyɛ̄ɛ̀bar) differences in time (zone).

དུས་ཚད་ཀྱི་སྔོན་དུ་ (tü̱üdzɛɛ̀gi ŋ̄öndu) ahead of schedule.

དུས་ཚད་ཀྱི་ཧེ་བག (tü̱üdzɛɛ̀gi hēbaà) sm. དུས་ཚད་ཀྱི་ཁྱད་པར་.

དུས་ཚད་ཐིམ་ (tü̱üdzɛɛ̀ ti̅m) sm. དུས་ཐིམ་.

དུས་ཚིགས་ (tü̱üdzii) a season, a quarter (of a year) ། ན་ནིང་དུས་ཚིགས་བཞི་པའི་ཐོན་ཚད་ལས་བརྒལ་བ་རེད་ They surpassed the production rate of the fourth quarter of last year.

དུས་ཚིགས་ཀྱི་རིན་ཁྱད་ (tü̱üdzii̱gi ri̱ngyɛɛ̀) seasonal fluctuation of prices.

དུས་ཚིགས་བཅུ་གཉིས་ (tü̱üdzii̱gi jū̱ñii) the 12 subdivisions of a year (i.e., four seasons each subdivided into three parts).

དུས་ཚིགས་ཉེར་བཞི་ (tü̱üdzii ñe̱rshi) a traditional way of dividing a year into 24 periods.

དུས་ཚིགས་དྲུག (tü̱üdzii tru̱ù) a traditional way of dividing a year into 6 periods.

དུས་ཚིགས་བཞི་ (tü̱üdzii shi̱) the 4 seasons.

དུས་ཚིགས་རེའི་དཔེ་དེབ་ (tü̱üdziiree bēdeb) quarterly magazine.

དུས་ཚིགས་གསུམ་ (tü̱üdzii sūm) a traditional way of dividing a year into three seasons: winter, spring and summer-fall.

དུས་ཚེས་ (tü̱üdzeè) date, time ། ཡི་གེའི་ནང་ཁོང་ཡོང་རྒྱུའི་དུས་ཚེས་གསལ་པོ་བཀོད་མི་འདུག The date he is coming was not stated clearly in his letter.

དུས་ཚོད་ (tü̱üdzöö) time; va.—བྱེད་; —བཀག; —བཟོ་ to fix/ set a time, to make an appointment; va.—སྐྱེལ་ to waste time; vi.—ཐིམ་ to expire (a time/ deadline); vi.—འགྱངས་ to be overdue, to be late/ delayed; vi.—ཐེབ་ to have arrived at the time specified for doing/ starting/ ending sth.; vi.—ཤར་ to have a time come/ arise/ begin ། ལས་ཀའི་དུས་ཚོད་ The time to work. ། ང་གཉིས་སང་ཉིན་འཛོམས་རྒྱུའི་དུས་ཚོད་བཟོས་པ་ཡིན་ We two made an appointment to meet tomorrow. ། ཁོས་ལས་ཀ་མ་བྱས་པར་དུས་ཚོད་སྐྱེལ་གྱི་འདུག He wastes time and doesn't do his work. ། གན་རྒྱའི་དུས་ཚོད་མ་ཐིམ་གོང་ Before the contract/ agreement expires. ། གནམ་གྲུ་འབྱོར་རྒྱུའི་དུས་ཚོད་འགྱངས་པ་རེད་ The arrival of the plane was delayed. ། ཉིན་དགུང་ཁ་ལག་གི་དུས་ཚོད་ཐེབ་བཞག The time for eating lunch has arrived. ། དེང་སང་ཆར་ཞོད་ཀྱི་དུས་ཚོད་ཤར་འདུག These days the time for the rainy season has begun.

དུས་ཚོད་ཀྱི་འགྲོ་སྟངས་ (tü̱üdzöögi dro̱daŋ) sm. དུས་ཀྱི་འཁོར་ཕྱོགས་.

དུས་ཚོད་འཁོར་ལོ་ (tü̱üdzöö kɔ̄ɔ̀lo) watch, clock.

དུས་ཚོད་འགྱངས་འཐེན་ (tü̱üdzöö gya̱nden) postponing, delaying; va.—བྱེད་ to postpone, to delay, to put off ། ཁོ་ཚོ་གཏོང་རྒྱུའི་དུས་ཚོད་འགྱངས་འཐེན་བྱས་པ་རེད་ They postponed sending them.

དུས་ཚོད་ངེས་ཅན་ (tü̱üdzöö ŋe̱èjɛn) scheduled, at regular intervals, at definite times.

དུས་ཚོད་སྔོན་བཀག (tü̱üdzöö ŋ̄öngaà) the time/ schedule that sth. has to be done or fulfilled ། ལྕགས་ཀྱི་བཟོ་གྲྭའི་ཏོན་ ༡༠༠༠ གི་ཐོན་སྐྱེད་ལས་འཆར་དུས་ཚོད་སྔོན་བཀག་གི་གོང་དུ་བསྒྲུབས་པ་རེད་ The iron factory's target quota of 1000 tons was fulfilled ahead of time.

དུས་ཚོད་བཅུ་གཉིས་ (tü̱üdzöö jū̱ñii) a traditional way of dividing a day into 12 parts.

དུས་ཚོད་གཏན་འཁེལ་ (tü̱üdzöö dēngee) sm. དུས་ཚོད་ངེས་ཅན་.

དུས་ཚོད་ཐིམ་ (tü̱üdzöö ti̅m) see དུས་ཚོད་.

དུས་ཚོད་དམ་འཛིན་ (tü̱üdzöö ta̱mdzin) doing work efficiently (not wasting time); va.—བྱེད་ ། ལས་ཀའི་དུས་ཚོད་དམ་འཛིན་བྱས་ན་མགྱོགས་པོ་ཚར་གྱི་རེད་ If you work efficiently you will finish quickly.

དུས་ཚོད་འདོམས་ (tü̱üdzöö do̱m) vi. to have a conflict in time ། ཐུགས་སྐྱོ་ལ་འགྲོ་ཡག་དང་ཚོགས་འདུའི་དུས་ཚོད་འདོམས་ཙང་ཐུགས་སྐྱོ་འགྲོ་ཐུབ་མ་སོང་ Because there was a time conflict between going to the party and the meeting, I wasn't able to go to the party.

དུས་ཚོད་ཕྱི་འགྱངས་ (tü̱üdzöö ci̅ngyaŋ) delaying, postponing; va.—བྱེད་ ། ཚོགས་འདུའི་དུས་ཚོད་ཕྱི་འགྱངས་བྱས་འདུག The time of the meeting was postponed.

དུས་ཚོད་འབུད་རྒྱག (tü̱üdzöö bü̱ügyaà) marking time, passing time; va.—གཏོང་.

དུས་ཚོད་གཙང་ (tü̱üdzöö dzāŋ) sm. དུས་ཚོད་ཚང་.

དུས་ཚོད་རྩི་ (tü̱üdzöö dzi̅) va. to count time, to keep a record of time/ hours ། དུས་ཚོད་རྩིས་པའི་གླ་ Hourly wages.

དུས་ཚོད་བརྩིས་པའི་ཕོགས་ཐོབ་ (tü̱üdzöö dzi̅ibɛ pɔ̄ɔ̀dob) hourly wages.

དུས་ཚོད་ཚང་ (tüüdzöö tsāŋ) vi. to complete a time specified contract/ sentence/ term ¶ བཙོན་འཛུག་གི་དུས་ཚོད་ཚང་ནས་གློད་བཀྲོལ་བཏང་བ་རེད་ After he completed his prison term he was released.

དུས་ཚོད་འཛིན་ (tüüdzöö dzin) sm. དུས་ཚོད་དམ་འཛིན་.

དུས་ཚོད་རྫོགས་ (tüüdzöö dzɔɔ̀) sm. དུས་ཚོད་ཚང་.

དུས་ཚོད་ཟིན་ (tüüdzöö sin) see. དུས་ཚོད་.

དུས་ཚོད་ཟུར་འདོན་ (tüüdzöö surdön) making time for sth.; va.—བྱེད་ ¶ དགེ་རྒན་གྱིས་དུས་ཚོད་ཟུར་འདོན་བྱས་ནས་སློབ་ཕྲུག་ལ་ཟུར་ཁྲིད་བྱེད་ཀྱི་ཡོད་པ་རེད་ The teacher made time and is tutoring the students on the side.

དུས་ཚོད་ཡོལ་ (tüüdzöö yüü) vi. to be passed/ finished/ expired (for time) ¶ ངའི་ཕྱི་སྐྱོད་ལག་ཁྱེར་གྱི་དུས་ཚོད་ཡོལ་བཞག My passport has expired.

དུས་ཚོད་རེའུ་མིག (tüüdzöö riumig) timetable, schedule.

དུས་ཚོད་ལ་བྱེད་ (tüüdzöö̀la cèè) va. to do sth. on time.

དུས་ཚོད་ལ་སླེབས་ (tüüdzöö̀la lēè) 1. va. to arrive/ come on time. 2. vi. to have a time come/ arrive ¶ ང་ཚོ་འགྲོ་ཡག་གི་དུས་ཚོད་ལ་སླེབས་བཞག The time has come for us to go.

དུས་མཚམས་ (tüüdzam) period, stage ¶ དུས་མཚམས་གསར་པ་ A new stage/ period.

དུས་མཚམས་རེས་འཁོར་ (tüüdzam reègɔɔ) a period that occurs in turns ¶ ང་ཚོ་དུས་མཚམས་རེས་འཁོར་གྱིས་ཁང་པ་གཙང་མ་བཟོ་གི་ཡོད་ We take turns periodically cleaning the house.

དུས་མཚུངས་ (tüüdzuŋ) at/ during the same time, contemporary with ¶ ན་ནིང་གི་དུས་མཚུངས་ At the same time last year.

དུས་འཛིངས་ (tüüdziŋ) sm. དུས་འདོམས་.

དུས་འཛིན་ཁང་ (tüüdzingaŋ) a room in which a time-telling copper vase (that drips water to tell time) was kept.

དུས་འཛིན་ཆུ་ཐིག (tüüdzin cūdii) a copper vase that drips water to tell time.

དུས་འཛོམས་འཁེལ་ (tüüdzom kēē) sm. དུས་འདོམས་.

དུས་བཞི་ (tüüshi) four seasons, all year.

དུས་བཞིའི་མེ་ཏོག (tüüshi medɔɔ̀) a pattern on Tibetan rugs and carpets which symbolizes the four seasons.

དུས་ཟིང་ (tünsiŋ) a time of disturbance/ chaos.

དུས་ཟླ་ (tünda) month.

དུས་གཟིར་ (tüüsir) shung. sm. དུས་ཟིང་.

དུས་བཟང་ (tüüsaŋ) 1. an auspicious day. 2. a good time.

དུས་ཡུན་ (tüüyün) duration, time; vi.—འགོར་ to take time, to elapse (of time) ¶ སློབ་མཚམས་གཅིག་གི་དུས་ཡུན་ The time of one class/ session. ¶ འདི་ནས་ནིའུ་ཡོག་བར་གནམ་གྲུའི་ནང་ཆུ་ཚོད་གཉིས་ཙམ་གྱི་དུས་ཡུན་འགོར་གྱི་འདུག It takes two hours by plane from here to New York.

དུས་ཡུན་རིང་པོ་ (tüüyün riŋbu) a long time.

དུས་ཡོལ་ (tüü yüü) sm. དུས་ཚོད་ཡོལ་.

དུས་ར་ (tüüra) 1. appointment time, time for a meeting; va.—བཟོ་ to make an appointment ¶ སང་ཉིན་ང་ཁོང་ཐུག་རྒྱུའི་དུས་ར་བཟོས་པ་ཡིན་ I made an appointment to meet him tomorrow. 2. a fixed period of time (usu. for receiving or paying out sth.) ¶ བུ་ལོན་དེ་ཟླ་བ་གཉིས་ཀྱི་ཐོག་སྤྲོད་རྒྱུའི་དུས་ར་བཟོས་པ་ཡིན་ I made a time period of two months to repay the loan.

དུས་རབས་ (tüürəb) 1. period, era ¶ རྡོ་ཆས་སྤྱོད་པའི་དུས་རབས་ The stone age. ¶ གསར་བརྗེའི་དུས་རབས་ཤིག་ཤར་ A revolutionary period emerged. 2. century ¶ དུས་རབས་བཅོ་བརྒྱད་པ་ The 18th century.

དུས་རབས་ཀྱི་མངོན་རྩལ་ (tüürəbgi ŋöndzüü) asense of the times.

དུས་རབས་ཀྱི་སྙིང་སྟོབས་ (tüürəbgi ñiŋdob) the spirit of the times.

དུས་རབས་ཀྱི་ཉམས་འགྱུར་ (tüürəbgi ñəmgyur) attributes of an era/ day/ period.

དུས་རབས་ཀྱི་རླབས་རྒྱུན་ (tüürəbgi lābgyün) the tendency of an era/ day/ period.

དུས་རབས་ཀྱི་དུས་མཚམས་དབྱེ་ (tüürəbgi tündzam ye) va. to open a new era/ age.

དུས་རབས་དཀྱིལ་མ་ (tüürəb gyiima) sm. དུས་རབས་བར་མ་.

དུས་རབས་སྔོན་མ་ (tüürəb ŋönma) ancient times/ era/ age.

དུས་རབས་ཉི་ཤུ་པ་ (tüürəb ñishubə) twentieth century.

དུས་རབས་བར་མ་ (tüürəb parma) the Middle Ages, medieval era.

དུས་རབས་འབྱེད་ (tüürəb cèè) va. to open a new era/ age.

དུས་རབས་རིམ་བྱུང་གི་ལོ་རྒྱུས་ (tüürəb rimjuŋgi lugyur) general history.

དུས་རབས་གསར་པ་ (tüürəb sārba) new period/ era.

དུས་རབས་གསར་འབྱེད་ (tüürəb sārjeè) the coming of a new era.

དུས་རབས་གསར་མ་ (tüürəb sārma) sm. དུས་རབས་གསར་པ་.

དུས་རིང་ (tüüriŋ) a long time.

དུས་རིམ་ (tüürim) stage, period, phase ¶ ལོ་རྒྱུས་ཀྱི་དུས་རིམ་ A historical stage. ¶ སློབ་སྦྱོང་གི་དུས་རིམ་ A period of study.

དུས་རིམ་ལས་བརྒལ་ (tüürim lɛ̀ɛ̀ gɛɛ) vi. to exceed/ go beyond a stage or period or phase ¶ ཕྲུ་གུ་དེ་དུས་རིམ་ལས་བརྒལ་ནས་འཛིན་གྲྭ་སྤར་བ་རེད་ That child was promoted in school in excess of the normal stage.

དུས་རེ་ཞིག (tüüreshig) at one time.

དུས་རེས་འགའ་ (tüü renga) sometimes.

དུས་རླུང་ (tüüluŋ) trade wind.

དུས་ལ་བབས་ (tüüla bəb) 1. vi. to be/ occur/ fall at the right time ¶ ད་ལོ་ཆར་པ་ཆུ་དུས་ལ་བབས་ནས་ལོ་ལེགས་བྱུང་ This year the rain came at the right time and we got a bumper harvest. ¶ ནུས་རྩལ་ཡོངས་རྫོགས་འདོན་པའི་དུས་ལ་བབས་པ་རེད་ The time has come for (us) to show all our talents. 2. vi. to occur because of universal fate/ karma ¶ ལུང་པའི་ནང་དམག་འཁྲུག་ཆེན་པོ་བྱུང་བ་དེ་དུས་ལ་བབ་པ་ཞིག་རེད་ The outbreak of a large war in that region occurred because of previous karma.

དུས་ལ་ལ་ (tüü lala) sm. དུས་རེས་འགའ་.

དུས་ལས་འགྱངས་ (tüülɛ gyaŋ) sm. དུས་འགྱངས་ཤོར་.

དུས་ལས་འདས་ (tüülɛ dɛ̀ɛ̀) 1. vi. to die. 2. vi. to be out of date.

དུས་ལས་སྔ་བ་ (tüülɛ ŋāwa) ahead of schedule.

དུས་ལས་ཡོལ་ (tüülɛ yöö) vi. to be out of season, to be out of date.

དུས་ལོག (tüü lɔɔ̀) a time of great change ¶ སྤྱི་ལོ་༡༩༥༩ དུས་ལོག་པའི་སྐབས་ཁྱེད་རང་ག་པར་བཞུགས་ཡོད་དམ་ At the time of great change in 1959, where were you living?

དུས་ལོག་པ་ཅན་ (tüü lɔgbajɛn) sm. དུས་ལོག.

དུས་ཤ་ (tüüsha) shung. the meat of an animal that was slaughtered at a specific/ set time.

དུས་ཤེས་པ་ (tüü shēèba) astrologer.

དུས་བཤོལ་ (tüü shöö) sm. དུས་འགྱངས་.

དུས་སང་ (tüüsaŋ) next year.

དུས་སུ་ (tüüsu) in/ on time; vi.—སྨིན་ to be the result of karma ¶ ཉིན་རེའི་ལས་ཀ་ཚང་མ་དུས་སུ་བྱེད་དགོས་ (You) have to do all (your) daily work on time. ¶ མི་ངན་དེ་ལ་ནད་གཞི་དྲག་པོ་ཐོག་པ་ནི་ལས་འབྲས་དུས་སུ་སྨིན་པ་ཞིག་རེད་ That evil person's serious illness is the result of karma.

དུས་སུ་འདྲི་ (tüüsu tri) va. to ask at the appropriate time.

དུས་སུ་བབས་ (tüüsu bəb) sm. དུས་ལ་བབས་.

དུས་སུ་འབྱོར་ (tüüsu jɔɔ) va. to arrive in/ on time.

དུས་སྲིང་ (tüüsiŋ) delaying, putting off; va.—བྱེད་.

དུས་སླེབས་སྐྱེད་ཀའི་ཐོབ་ཆ་ (tüüleb gyēègɛ tōbja) total interest obtained at the maturity of loan.

དུས་གསུམ་ (tüüsum) 1. the tenses (past, present and future). 2. all times, all the time (past, present and future).

དུས་གསུམ་མཁྱེན་པ་ (tüüsum kyēmba) the Buddha.

དུས་གསུམ་བརྟག་པ་ (tüüsum dāgba) name of a religious scripture on logic.

དུས་གསུམ་སངས་རྒྱས་ (tüüsum sāŋgyɛɛ̀) the Buddhas of the three eras: the past མར་མེ་མཛད་, the present ཤཱཀྱ་ཐུབ་པ་, the future བྱམས་པ་.

དུས་བསྲིང་ (tüüsiŋ) sm. དུས་སྲིང་.

དེ་ (te) 1. that ༑ མི་དེ་ That man. 2. (vb.+ —) sm. སྟེ་ (but used after final (ད་). 3. (vb.+ —) even though, but ༑ བཙོན་ཁང་འདྲ་མི་འདྲ་མང་པོ་ཡོད་པ་རེད་དེ་ Even though there are many different prisons.

དེ་ཀ་ (tega) 1. just that, no other than that ༑ ང་དེ་ཀ་བྱེད་ཀྱི་ཡིན་ I will do just that. 2. sm. དེ་ག.

དེ་ཀ་རང་ (tegaraŋ) sm. དེ་ཀ་.

དེ་སྐད་ (tegɛɛ̀) like that which was said before.

དེ་སྐད་ཁས་འཆེ་ (tegɛɛ̀ kɛ̄ɛ̄ chē) va. to take/ accept responsibility/ agree with sth. said before.

དེ་སྐད་ཅེས་ཞེར་ (tegɛɛ̀ jēè ser) va. to say/ tell like that said before.

དེ་སྐད་དེ་ལན་ (tegɛɛ̀ telɛn) retaliating/ answering to sth. that was said before; va.—འཇལ་ to retaliate verbally.

དེ་ཁུལ་ (tegüü) in that area, around that place, there.

དེ་ཁོ་ན་ཉིད་ (te kōnañiì) 1. that only, that itself. 2. emptiness.

དེ་ཁོ་ན་ཉིད་ཀྱི་དོན་ (te kōnañiìgi tön) the nature of emptiness/ the void.

དེ་ཁོ་ན་ཉིད་ཤེས་པ་ (te kōnañiì shēèba) the wisdom of realizing the nature of emptiness/ void.

དེ་ཁོ་ན་དེ་བཞིན་ཉིད་ (te kōna teshinñiì) emptiness, the void.

དེ་ཁོངས་ (tegoŋ) belonging to that ༑ ཚོགས་པ་དེ་ཁོངས་མི་སུམ་བརྒྱ་ཡོད་པ་རེད་ There are 300 people who belong to that association.

དེ་ག (tega) 1. there, over there ༑ དེ་ག་ས་གནས་ཀྱི་དཔོན་རིགས་ཁག The local officials there. 2. sm. དེ་ཀ་.

དེ་ག་ནང་བཞིན་ (tega naŋshin) just like that.

དེ་ག་ཙམ་ (tegadzam) about that much ༑ དེ་རིང་ཚོགས་འདུའི་ཐོག་ཞུ་རྒྱུ་དེ་ག་ཙམ་ཡིན་ Today, at the meeting, I am only going to say that much.

དེ་ག་རང་ (tegaraŋ) just as one says, correct ༑ ཁྱེད་རང་གིས་གསུངས་པ་དེ་ག་རང་རེད་ It is just as you said. 2. that's right!

དེ་གར་ (tegar) there ༑ གས་རང་དེ་གར་བཙར་རྩིས་ཡོད་ I am planning to go there myself.

དེ་གས་ཚོག (tegɛɛ̀jɔɔ̀) sm. དེ་ཆག.

དེ་གོང་ (tegoŋ) before that.

དེ་རྒྱུད་ (tegyɛɛ̀) those.

དེ་དགོང་ (tegoŋ) tonight, this evening.

དེ་སྒྲ་ (tedra) 1. that. 2. conjunction (in Tibetan grammar).

དེ་སྔ་ (teŋa) in the past, previously.

དེ་སྔོན་ (teŋön) sm. དེ་སྔ་.

དེ་མཇུག (tejuù) after that.

དེ་རྗེས་ (tejeè) after that.

དེ་རྗེས་གཞི་ནས་ (tejeè shinɛ) not till then, only after that.

དེ་ཉིད་ (teñiì) 1. that itself. 2. when used after a person's name it indicates the person is deceased.

དེ་ཉིད་ཀྱི་ཕྱིར་ (teñiìgi cīr) for the sake of.

དེ་ཉིད་ཀྱི་མོད་ (teñiìgi möö̀) as soon as, at once.

དེ་ཉིད་ཀྱི་ཚེ་ (teñiìgi tsē) during that time/ period.

དེ་ཉིན་ (teñin) that day.

དེ་སྙེད་ (teñeg) so many/ much, that much/ many.

དེ་རྟིང་ (tediŋ) after that.

དེ་ལྟ་ (teda) sm. དེ་ལྟ་བུ་.

དེ་ལྟ་ན་ (te dāna) if its like that, if that is the way ༑ གཞུང་གི་སྲིད་ཇུས་དེ་ལྟ་ན་ང་ལྟ་སྐོར་ལ་འགྲོ་གི་མིན་ If the government's policy is like that, I will not go on a tour there.

དེ་ལྟ་བས་ན་ (te dāwɛna) because of that ༑ ལོ་ན་གཞོན་དུས་སློབ་སྦྱོང་བྱ་རྒྱུ་གལ་ཆེན་པོ་ཡིན་ དེ་ལྟ་བས་ན་དུས་ཚོད་དམ་འཛིན་བྱེད་དགོས་ It is important to study when one is young. Because of that, one should use one's time well.

དེ་ལྟ་བུ་ (te dābu) like that, as much/ many as that ༑ གོ་སྐབས་བཟང་པོ་དེ་ལྟ་བུ་ A good opportunity like that. ༑ མི་མང་པོ་དེ་ལྟ་བུའི་དཀྱིལ་ལ་ Among as many people as that.

དེ་ལྟ་མོད་ཀྱི་ (te dāmöö̀gyi) however ༑ ད་ལྟ་ཚོགས་པ་དེ་མི་འཁོར་ཉུང་ཉུང་རེད་ དེ་ལྟ་མོད་ཀྱི་དུས་མི་རིང་བར་མི་འཁོར་མང་པོ་ཆགས་རྒྱུར་ངེས་ The association has few members now. However, soon the number will definitely become more.

དེ་ལྟར་ (tedar) like that, according to that, in accordance with that ༑ དེ་ལྟར་བྱས་ནས་ Having done it like that.

དེ་ལྟར་ལྟ་ (tedar dā) va. to regard/ think/ consider like that.

དེ་ལྟར་དེ་བཞིན་ (tedar teshin) like that, in that way, such and such ༑ དེ་ལྟར་དེ་བཞིན་ཐུགས་ལ་འཇོག་པར་མཛོད་ Please keep it mind in that manner.

དེ་ལྟར་ན་ (tedarna) sm. དེ་ལྟར་.

དེ་ལྟར་ན་ཡང་ (te dārnayaŋ) sm. དེ་ལྟར་ཡང་.

དེ་ལྟར་ཡང་ (te dāryaŋ) even though it is like that.

དེ་ལྟར་ཡིན་མོད་ཀྱི་ (tēdar yinmöö̀gyi) sm. དེ་ལྟ་མོད་ཀྱི་.

དེ་ལྟས་ (tedɛɛ̀) sm. དེ་ལྟ་བས་ན་.

དེ་ཐད་ (tetɛɛ̀) regarding that, concerning that ༑ གནད་དོན་དེ་ཐད་ Regarding that matter.

དེ་དག (tedag) those.

དེ་དང་དུས་མཚུངས་ (tedaŋ tüüdzuŋ) at the same time as that.

དེ་དང་དེ་ (tedaŋ te) so and so, such and such ༑ ལུང་པ་དེ་དང་དེ་ལ་གནས་ཚུལ་དེ་དང་དེ་བྱུང་སོང་ཞེར་གྱི་འདུག It is being said that in such and such a place such and such things happened.

དེ་དང་དེ་འདྲ་ (tēdaŋ tedra) indicates several things happening of the same type.

དེ་དང་འདྲ་བ་ (tedaŋ drawa) sm. དེ་དང་དེ་འདྲ་.

དེ་དང་འབྲེལ་ (tedaŋ drel) connected with that ༑ ལུང་པ་དེ་ལ་སྨན་ཁང་ཡོད་པ་མ་ཟད་དེ་དང་འབྲེལ་བའི་རྒན་གསོ་ཁང་ཡང་ཡོད་པ་རེད་ In that place not only is there a hospital but connected to that there is an old people's home.

དེ་དང་འཚམས་པ་ (tedaŋ tsāmba) according to that, appropriate with that ༑ ཁྱེད་རང་གིས་ཁོང་གི་སྐད་ཆ་དང་འཚམ་པའི་ལན་ཞིག་རྒྱག་དགོས་ You have to give an answer that is appropriate to his comments.

དེ་དུས་ (tedüü) at that time, then ༑ དེ་དུས་ང་སློབ་གྲྭར་ཡོད་ At that time I was at school.

དེ་དུས་དེ་མིན་ (tedüü temin) shung. at that time it was not like that ༑ རྗེས་སུ་ཕྱོགས་གཉིས་ཀས་དེ་དུས་དེ་མིན་གྱི་སྐད་ཆ་ཡོང་མི་ཆོག Later, both sides are not permitted to say "at that time it wasn't like that" (i.e., to go back on the terms of an agreement).

དེ་དེ་ (tede) abbr. of དེ་དང་དེ་.

དེ་དེ་བཞིན་ (te teshin) of course, just as you said.

དེ་དོན་ (tedön) the meaning/ content of that, the meaning/ content of what was said.

དེ་དོན་དགོངས་འཇགས་ཞུ་ (tedön gonjaà shu) shung. please bear in mind what I mentioned above.

དེ་དོན་ངེས་པ་གྱིས་ (tedön ŋeèba gyiì) shung. sm. དེ་དོན་དགོངས་འཇགས་ཞུ་.

དེ་དོན་སྙན་དུ་སྒྲོན་ (tedön ñɛ̄ndu drön) shung. va. to report what one has mentioned above ༑ བཀའ་ཤག་ནས་རྒྱལ་ཚབ་ལ་དེ་དོན་སྙན་དུ་སྒྲོན་པ་ The Kashak reported to the Regent what was mentioned above.

དེ་དོན་ཡིན་ཤག (tedön yinshaà) being sure sth. was like that.

དེ་དོན་ལས་མི་འགལ་ (tedönlɛ migɛɛ) shung. one shall not violate what was mentioned above ༑ ངོ་སྐྱིད་སྐྱུངས་ཚང་སྐྱིད་མེད་འབུལ་རྒྱུ་ཞུས་པར་དེ་དོན་ལས་མི་འགལ་ I promised not to violate what was mentioned above and will pay the principal and interest of the loan.

དེ་འདྲ་ (tendra) like that ། མཚོ་དེ་འདྲ་བོད་ལ་མང་པོ་ཡོད་ There are many lakes like that in Tibet.

དེ་འདྲ་སེ་ (te drase) sm. དེ་འདྲ་.

དེ་འདྲ་སོང་ཙང་ (tendra sōŋdzaŋ) because of that, because it was like that, therefore, consequently ། ལྷ་སར་རྡོ་རྗེ་ཟེར་བ་ཞིག་ཡོད་པ་རེད་ དེ་འདྲ་སོང་ཙང་ཁོ་ག་པར་བསྡད་ཡོད་མེད་ཚོད་ཞིབ་བྱས་ནས་དོ་དམ་གནང་དགོས་ The one called Dorje is in Lhasa. Because of that we have to find out where he is staying and arrest him.

དེ་འདྲོག (tendrɔɔ̀) shung. sm. དེ་མ་ཐག.

དེ་ལྡན་ (tendɛn) having that ། ང་ལ་ལག་རྩལ་དེ་ལྡན་གྱི་མི་ཞིག་དགོས་ཡོད་ I need a person who has that skill.

དེ་ན་ (tena) at that (place, location), there ། དེ་ན་ལོ་ཤས་བཞུགས་པ་རེད་ (He) stayed there for a few years.

དེ་ནས་ (tenɛ) 1. from there ། དེ་ནས་ཕྱག་བྲིས་གནང་དོན་བཞིན་ According to what you have written to me from there. 2. then, after that ། དེ་ནས་ཨ་རི་ར་བསྐྱོད་ཀྱི་རེད་ After that (they) will go to America.

དེ་ནས་བཟུང་ (tenɛsuŋ) from then/ that on.

དེ་ནི་ (teni) as for that.

དེ་ནུབ་ (tzēnub) 1. that night. 2. this evening.

དེ་པ་ (teba) he.

དེ་ཕན་ཆད་ (te pēnjɛɛ̀) before that ། དུས་ཚོད་དེ་ཕན་ཆད་ང་དབྱིན་ཇིའི་སྐད་ཤེས་ཀྱི་མེད་ Before that time I didn't know English. 2. excluding ། ཁང་པ་དེ་ཕན་ཆད་ངའི་རེད་ Excluding that house (the rest) are mine.

དེ་ཕར་བཞག (te pāāshaà) let alone ། ཨ་རི་ར་འགྲོ་རྒྱུ་དེ་ཕར་བཞག་རྒྱ་དཀར་ལ་ཡང་འགྲོ་ཐུབ་ཀྱི་མི་འདུག Let alone going to Tibet, (I) can't even go to India.

དེ་ཕུད་ (tebüü) except for that, with the exception of that ། ལས་ཁངས་འདིའི་ནང་མི་དེ་ཕུད་ཚང་མ་ཡག་པོ་ཡོད་ In this office everyone is good except for that person.

དེ་པོ་ (tepo) rooster, cock.

དེ་པོ་མཚལ་ལུ་ (tepo tsālu) red rooster.

དེ་ཕྱིན་ཆད་ (te cīnjɛɛ̀) since then, from then on.

དེ་ཕྱིར་ (tecir) sm. དེའི་དོན་དུ་.

དེ་འཕྲལ་ (te trɛ̄ɛ̀) at once, immediately ། ཁོས་དེ་འཕྲལ་བྲོས་པ་རེད་ He immediately escaped.

དེ་འཕྲོས་ (tedröö) the remainder, the remaining part, the rest.

དེ་བ་ (tewa) 1. white poplar. 2. a type of herbal medicine. 3. skt. deva.

དེ་བར་ (tewar) up to that (time, place) ། ལོ་དེ་བར་ང་རྒྱ་གར་ལ་བསྡད་པ་ཡིན་ Up to that year I lived in India.

དེ་བས་ (tewɛ) even more than that ། དེ་བས་གལ་ཆེ་ཞིག་རེད་ It is even more important than that.

དེ་བས་ཀྱང་ (tewɛgyaŋ) even more than that ། སྨན་དཀྱུས་མ་དཀོན་པོ་ཡོད་པ་སྨན་བཅོས་ཀྱི་ཡོ་ཆས་ནི་དེ་བས་ཀྱང་དཀོན་པོ་ཡོད་པ་རེད་ Common medicines were scarce and medical equipment was even more scarce (than that).

དེ་བས་ན་ (tewɛna) sm. དེས་ན་.

དེ་བྱིངས་ (tejiŋ) the rest, the remainder, the remaining part ། བུ་ཆུང་ཤོས་དེ་མ་གཏོགས་དེ་བྱིངས་བོད་ལ་སྐྱེས་པ་རེད་ Except for the youngest son the rest were born in Tibet.

དེ་བྱིངས་ཚང་མ་ (tejiŋ tsāŋma) sm. དེ་བྱིངས་.

དེ་དབང་དུ་གཞིགས་ན་ (tewaŋdu shignə) if we go according to that ། དེང་སང་གི་དཔལ་འབྱོར་གྱི་འགྲོ་སྟངས་དེ་དབང་དུ་གཞིགས་ན་ཁང་པ་ཉོ་ཐུབ་ཀྱི་མ་རེད་ If we go according to the way the economy is these days, (we) won't be able to buy a house.

དེ་འབྲེལ་ (tedrel) abbr. of དེ་དང་འབྲེལ་བ་.

དེ་མ་ཁད་ (temagɛɛ̀) sm. དེ་མ་ཐག.

དེ་མ་ཉིད་དུ་ (tema ñiidu) sm. དེ་མ་ཐག་ཏུ་.

དེ་མ་གཏོགས་ (te madɔɔ̀) only/ except that ། མི་དེ་མ་གཏོགས་ཚང་མ་ཡག་པོ་ཡོད་ Except for that person everyone is good.

དེ་མ་ཐག (te madaà) immediately, at once ། དེ་མ་ཐག་ཏུ་འགྲོ་དགོས་བྱུང་བ་རེད་ He had to go immediately.

དེ་མ་ཐག་ཏུ་ (te madagdu) sm. དེ་མ་ཐག.

དེ་མ་ཐག་པ་ (te madagba) sm. དེ་མ་ཐག.

དེ་མ་ཡིན་པ་ (te məyimbə) besides that.

དེ་མ་ལག་པས་ (te malagbɛ) sm. མ་ཚད་.

དེ་མན་ཆད་ (te mɛnjɛɛ̀) below, beyond that.

དེ་མར་ (temar) sm. དེ་མ་ཐག་ཏུ་.

དེ་མིན་ (temin) other than that, besides that ། དེ་མིན་ཞུ་རྒྱུ་མེད་ (I) have nothing other than that to say. ། དེ་མིན་པའི་རྒྱུ་མཚན་ཡོད་པ་རེད་ There are reasons other than that.

དེ་མིན་པ་ (te mimbə) sm. དེ་མིན་.

དེ་མུར་ (temur) in that way, as it is ། ཕར་རྒོལ་བྱ་རྒྱུའི་དོན་སྨིན་མ་སོན་པར་དེ་མུར་ལུས་ The idea of attacking (the enemy) did not come to pass and it was left as it is. ། ལས་ཀ་འདི་དེ་མུར་འཇོག་པ་ལས་འཕྲལ་དུ་བྱས་ན་དགའ་ It is better to do it immediately rather than to leave it as it is.

དེ་མུལ་ (temüü) sm. དེ་མུར་.

དེ་མོ་ (temo) 1. hen. 2. a place in Kongpo.

དེ་ཙ་ན་ (tedzana) that time ། དུས་དེ་ཙ་ན་ At that time.

དེ་ཙམ་ (ལ་) (tedzam) as much/ many as that, so much as that, that much, that many ། དུས་ཡུན་དེ་ཙམ་བསྒུགས་ཀྱང་མ་ཡོང་བ་རེད་ Even though they waited that long (he) did not come. ། ཇི་ཙམ་ཀློག་པ་དེ་ཙམ་ཤེས་ཀྱི་རེད་ As much as one reads, that much (one) will learn. ། ཅ་ལག་འདི་ལ་གོང་དེ་ཙམ་ལས་སྤྲོད་ཀྱི་མེད་ན་ང་འཚོང་གི་མིན་ If you will pay me (only) that much, I will not sell the thing.

དེ་ཙམ་དུ་མ་ཟད་ (tedzamdu masɛɛ̀) sm. དེས་མ་ཚད་.

དེ་ཙམ་མ་ཟད་ (tedzam masɛɛ̀) sm. དེས་མ་ཚད་.

དེ་ཙམ་ཞིག (tedzamshig) sm. དེ་ཙམ་.

དེ་རྗེས་ (tedzii) accordingly, in keeping with ། ཤེས་ཡོན་གྱི་ཆ་རྐྱེན་ལྡན་ངེས་ཚགས་ཡོད་སྐབས་དེ་རྗེས་ལས་ཀ་ཡག་པོ་ཞིག་ཐོབ་དགོས་ Because (they) have acquired adequate knowledge, accordingly, they should get a good job.

དེ་ཙུག (tedzug) like that.

དེ་ཚོ་ (tedzo) those ། གྲུའི་ནང་གི་མི་དེ་ཚོ་ Those people in the boat.

དེ་མཚམས་ (tedzam) at that time ། ལས་བྱེད་པ་གསར་པ་སླེབས་སོང་ན་དེ་མཚམས་ང་དགོངས་པ་ཞུ་གི་ཡིན་ When the new official arrives, at that time I will take leave.

དེ་མཚུངས་ (tedzuŋ) 1. in the same way, similarly, like that; va.—བྱེད་ to do in the same way/ manner ། རྒྱལ་ས་ར་དམག་འཁྲུག་ལ་ངོ་རྒོལ་གྱི་ཁྲོམ་སྐོར་བྱས་པ་དེ་མཚུངས་གྲོང་ཁྱེར་གཞན་དག་ལའང་བྱས་ཡོད་པ་རེད་ There were demonstrations against the war in the capital and similarly, demonstrations were also held in other cities.

དེ་ལྟ་ (tewa) sm. དེ་བ་.

དེ་ཤག (teshag) the past few days, the other day, recently ། ཁོ་དེ་ཤག་འབྱོར་བ་རེད་ He arrived recently.

དེ་བཞིན་ (teshin) 1. sm. དེ་ལྟར་. 2. that ། ཁང་པ་དེ་བཞིན་ཡག་པོ་འདུག That house is good.

དེ་བཞིན་གཤེགས་པ་ (teshin shēgba) Tathagata.

དེ་འོག (tēwɔɔ̀) below/ under that.

དེ་ཡང་ (teyaŋ) even that, even so, even though (refers to something done or said before) ། ཁོང་གི་བཤད་པ་དེ་ཡང་མ་རེད་ཟེར་ཡས་མི་འདུག Even what he said, no one can say it is wrong. ། ཁོས་མི་བསད་པ་དེ་ཡང་རང་སྲུང་གི་ཆེད་དུ་བསད་བཞག Even his killing of a person, he killed him in self-defense. ། བོད་ནང་ཟིང་ཆ་བྱུང་བཞག་དེ་ཡང་ཞིབ་ཏུ་བཤད་ན་ ལྷ་ས་དང་སྙེ་མོ་སོགས་ལ་བྱུང་འདུག A disturbance occurred in Tibet. If I talk about that in detail it occurred in Lhasa and Nyemo.

དེ་ཡན་ (teyɛn) above, over, prior, before.

དེ་ཡིན་ཙ་ན་ (teyin dzāna) because, therefore.

དེ་ཡོ་ (teyo) all (of that).

དེ་ཡོངས་ (teyoŋ) 1. completely, including all of sth.

¶ ཞིང་ཆེན་དེ་ཡོངས་ In all of that province. 2. over there.

དེ་རག (teraà) recently, lately.

དེ་རང་ (teraŋ) that itself, that one itself ¶ མ་དཔེ་ངོ་མ་དེ་རང་ནས་བཤུས་པ་རེད་ They copied it from the original itself.

དེ་རང་རེད་ (te raŋreè) that is it, that is right.

དེ་རིགས་ (terig) that type/ kind.

དེ་རིང་ (teriŋ) today.

དེ་རིང་ཁ་ས་ (teriŋ kāsa) these days, nowadays.

དེ་རིང་ཁ་སང་ (teriŋ kāsaŋ) sm. དེ་རིང་ཁ་ས་.

དེ་རིང་ཁར་ཙང་ (teriŋ kārdzaŋ) sm. དེ་རིང་ཁ་སང་.

དེ་རིང་ནས་བཟུང་ (teriŋēsuŋ) from today onwards.

དེ་རིང་བྱུང་ན་དེ་རིང་དང་སང་ཉིན་བྱུང་ན་སང་ཉིན་ (teriŋ cuŋna teriŋdaŋ sāŋñin cuŋna sāŋñin) consuming whatever one gets immediately/ that day [Lit. if one gets (sth.) today, today and if one gets (sth.) tomorrow, tomorrow].

དེ་རིང་སང་ (teriŋsaŋ) nowadays, these days.

དེ་རིང་སང་ཉིན་ (teriŋ sāŋñin) sm. དེ་རིང་སང་.

དེ་རིང་ཕན་ཆད་ (teriŋ pēnjɛɛ̀) until now/ today, up to now.

དེ་ལ་བརྟེན་ནས་ (tela dēnnɛ) because of that.

དེ་ལ་སོགས་པ་ (tela sōgba) etc.

དེ་ལན་དེ་འཇལ་ (telɛn tejɛɛ) repaying/ answering/ responding tit for tat; repaying good with good and bad with bad; va.—བྱེད་.

དེ་ལམ་ (telam) shung. in that way/ manner ¶ དེ་ལམ་སྡོད་ནུས་བཙོད་མིན་བྱུང་བ་ They did not dare to stay in that way.

དེ་ལས་ (telɛɛ̀) 1. than that; from that. 2. that only.

དེ་ལས་ལྡོག (telɛɛ̀ dɔg) contrary to that, opposite of that ¶ ཕོ་ཆོས་རེ་འདུན་བྱས་པ་དེ་ལས་ལྡོག་ནས་ Contrary to the hopes they had.

དེ་ལོ་ (telo) that year.

དེ་ཤག (teshaà) recently, these days.

དེ་སྲིད་ (tesiì) until then, till that time (usu. used with ཇི་སྲིད་) ¶ ཇི་སྲིད་རང་བཙན་མ་ཐོབ་བར་དེ་སྲིད་འཐབ་རྩོད་བྱེད་ཀྱི་རེད་ They will struggle until they gain their independence.

དེ་ལྷག (telhaà) more than that, better than that ¶ དེ་ལྷག་བྱེད་ཡག་ཡོད་པ་མ་རེད་ One can't do more than that.

དེང་ (teŋ) these days, nowadays, recently, lately.

དེང་སྐབས་ (teŋgəb) sm. དེང་དུས་.

དེང་གི་ཆ་ (teŋgi cā) these days, nowadays, recently, lately.

དེང་གི་ཆར་ (teŋgi cār) these days, nowadays, recently, lately.

དེང་བལྟས་སྔར་དྲན་ (teŋdɛɛ̀ ŋārdrɛn) seeing the present and remembering the past.

དེང་དུས་ (teŋdüü) 1. nowadays, these days, lately, recently ¶ དེང་དུས་ཀྱི་གནས་སྟངས་ The situation nowadays. 2. modern times ¶ དེང་དུས་ཀྱི་ཁང་པ་ A modern house.

དེང་དུས་ཅན་ (teŋdüüjɛn) sm. དེང་དུས་དང་མཐུན་པ་.

དེང་དུས་དང་མཐུན་པ་ (teŋdüü taŋdümbə) up-to-date, modern.

དེང་དོན་ (teŋdön) current affairs.

དེང་ནས་ (teŋnɛɛ̀) from now on, henceforth.

དེང་ཕན་ (teŋpɛn) sm. དེང་ཕན་ཆད་.

དེང་ཕན་ཆད་ (teŋ pēnjɛɛ̀) before, prior, in the past, henceforth.

དེང་ཕྱིན་ཆད་ (teŋ cīnjɛɛ̀) from now on, heretofore.

དེ་རྩེན་ (tedzen) above, on top.

དེང་ཡོད་ (teŋyöö) what exists now, current.

དེང་རབས་ (teŋrəb) modern times, the present era ¶ དེང་རབས་ཀྱི་རྒྱ་སྐད་ Modern Chinese language.

དེང་རབས་ཀྱི་རྒྱལ་ཁབ་ (teŋrəbgi gyɛɛgəb) modern state/ country.

དེང་རབས་ཀྱི་བཅོ་བཙོས་རིང་ལུགས་ (teŋrəbgi sobjöö riŋluù) modern revisionism.

དེང་རབས་ཅན་ (teŋrəbjɛn) modern; vi.—དུ་འགྱུར་ to get/ be modernized.

དེང་རབས་རྩོམ་རིག (teŋrəb tsōmrig) modern literature.

དེང་སང་ (teŋsaŋ) 1. nowadays, these days. 2. abbr. today and tomorrow.

དེངས་རྩེ་ (teŋdze) a traditional Tibetan coin that has a square hole in the center.

དེད་ (teè) p. and imp. of འདེད་.

དེད་བཅོམ་ (teèjom) pursuing and robbing; va.—གཏོང་; —བྱེད་.

དེད་དཔོན་ (teèbön) helmsman, pilot.

དེད་ཤར་ (teèshar) chasing after sth., pursuing; va.—གཏོང་ ¶ ཁོས་བུ་ལོན་དེད་ཤར་གཏོང་གི་འདུག He is pursuing (collection of) loans.

དེན་འདྲས་ (tendrɛɛ̀) sm. དེ་འདྲ་.

དེབ་ (teb) book; va.—ཀློག to read a book.

དེབ་དཀྱུས་མ་ (teb gyüümə) paperback books, common books.

དེབ་རྐྱང་པ་ (teb gyāŋma) books published singly (as opposed to those published in sets).

དེབ་སྐྱེལ་ (tebgyee) registration, recording; va.—བྱེད་ to register, to record ¶ ཅ་ལག་རྙིང་མ་ཚང་མ་གཞུང་ལ་དེབ་སྐྱེལ་བྱེད་དགོས་ (You) have to register all antiques with the government.

དེབ་སྐྱེལ་བཏང་ཡིག (tebgyee dāŋyiì) registered letter.

དེབ་སྐྱེལ་ཡིག་སྒྲམ (tebgyee yigdraà) sm. དེབ་སྐྱེལ་བཏང་ཡིག.

དེབ་འཁྱོལ་མ་ (teb kyöōma) things that are included/ mentioned/ listed in (a book).

དེབ་གྲངས་ (tebdraŋ) the number of books/ pamphlets printed in a run.

དེབ་འགོད་ (tebgöö) sm. དེབ་སྐྱོར་.

དེབ་སྒྲོམ་ (tebdrom) book shelf, bookcase.

དེབ་སྔོན་ (tebŋön) 1. blue book (book bound in a blue cover). 2. abbr. of དེབ་ཐེར་སྔོན་པོ་.

དེབ་གཅིག་མ་ (tebjigmə) sm. དེབ་རྐྱང་པ་.

དེབ་ཆུང་ (tebjuŋ) a small book such as a pamphlet, booklet, pocketbook.

དེབ་མཆན་ (tebjɛn) notes in a book.

དེབ་ལྟག (tebdaà) spine (of a book).

དེབ་གཏེར་ (tebder) sm. དེབ་ཐེར་.

དེབ་ཐེར་ (tebder) annals, chronicle, historical work.

དེབ་ཐེར་དཀར་པོ་ (tebdre gārbo) a historical text written by Gendun Chomphel.

དེབ་ཐེར་དངོས་གཞི་ (tebder ŋööshi) biography.

དེབ་ཐེར་སྔོན་པོ་ (tebder ŋömbo) a historical work written by འགོས་ལོ་ཙཱ་བ་ in the 15th century.

དེབ་ཐེར་གནད་བསྡུས་ (tebder nɛɛ̀düü) extracts from historical texts.

དེབ་ཐེར་དཔྱིད་ཀྱི་རྒྱལ་མོའི་གླུ་དབྱངས་ (tebder jīgi gyɛɛmö lūyaŋ) a historical text compiled by the 5th Dalai Lama.

དེབ་ཐེར་དམར་པོ་ (tebder mārbo) a historical text composed by ཚལ་པ་ཀུན་དགའ་རྡོ་རྗེ་ in the year 1346.

དེབ་ཐོད་ (tebdöö) top margin (of a book).

དེབ་སྤུས་ལེགས་ (teb būüleg) hardcovered book, deluxe edition.

དེབ་སྐྱོར་ (tebjɔr) recording/ listing in a book; va.—བྱེད་ ¶ ལས་ཁངས་ཀྱི་ཡོང་སྒོ་རྣམས་དེབ་སྐྱོར་བྱེད་དགོས One should record the office's income (in an account book).

དེབ་གཙོ་བོ་ (teb dzōwo) a registration book created during the Qing Dynasty.

དེབ་ཚད་ (tebdzɛɛ̀) size of a book.

དེབ་མཛོད་ཁང་ (teb dzöögaŋ) library.

དེབ་གཟེར་ (tebser) staple; va.—རྒྱག to staple together.

དེབ་བཟོ་སྐྱི་ཁྲིམས་ (tebso jīdrim) copyright (law) (for books).

དེབ་ཡིག (tebyiì) writings or letters compiled/ recorded/ bound into a book.

དེབ་རིན་ (tebrin) book price.

དེབ་ཤོག (tebshoò) pages (of a book).

དེབ་སིལ་ (tebsil) loose-leaf book.

དེབ་སེལ་ (tebsel) shung. va. to write/ record/ note in a book or register ¶ སྤྱང་བཙོ་བརྒྱུད་བྱུང་བ་དེབ་སེལ་

གྲུབ་ཅིང་ The the receipt of 18 སྲང་ was recorded (in a book).

དེབ་གསལ་ (tebsel) shung. documented/ recorded/ written in a book ༑ གཞིས་ཀའི་དེབ་གསལ་ཡོང་འབབ་ཚང་མ་བསྡུ་ལེན་བྱེད་དགོས་ One must collect all the income recorded in the books/ registers of manorial estates.

དེབ་གསལ་སྒྲིག་ཆུགས་ (tebsel drigdzuù) shung. customs/ rules/ traditions recorded in a book or register ༑ ལས་ཁུངས་ཀྱི་ལོ་རེའི་ཁྲལ་འབབ་བསྡུ་རྒྱུ་རྣམས་དེབ་གསལ་སྒྲིག་ཆུགས་ཡོང་བ་བྱ་དགོས་ The annual collection of this office's taxes should be done in accordance with what is recorded in the tax collection book.

དེམ་གང་ (temgaŋ) fully filled (container).

དེམ་ཙི་ (temdzi) sm. དེམ་ཙེ་.

དེམ་ཙེ་ (temdze) ch. stepping stones (in a stream).

དེའི་ (tee) of that (དེ་ + gen.).

དེའི་སྐབས་ (teegəb) at that time.

དེའི་སྐོར་ (tee gɔ̄ɔ) regarding/ concerning/ about that.

དེའི་རྐྱེན་གྱིས་ (tee gyēngi) sm. དེའི་ཕྱིར་.

དེའི་སྐབས་དང་དེའི་དུས་ (tee gəb dāŋ tee tüü) at that time.

དེའི་གོང་ཙམ་ལ་ (tee koŋdzamla) a bit before that.

དེའི་སྟེང་ལ་ (tee gaŋla) on top of that, in addition to that, besides ༑ ཁ་སང་སྨྱུ་གུ་ཉོས་པ་དེའི་སྟེང་ལ་ད་དུང་གསུམ་ཉོ་རོགས་ On top of the pen you bought yesterday, buy three more.

དེའི་ཐོག་ལ་ (tee tɔ̄ɔla) sm. དེའི་སྟེང་ལ་.

དེའི་དོན་དུ་ (tee töndu) for the purpose of that, in order to do that.

དེའི་ཕྱིར་ (tee cīr) sm. དེའི་དོན་དུ་.

དེའི་ཕྱིར་དུ་ (tee cīrdu) sm. དེའི་དོན་དུ་.

དེའི་མུར་ (tee mur) at the same time.

དེའི་མུས་ལ་ (tee müùlə) together with, at the same time ༑ ཁོང་གི་ཕ་མ་གྲོངས་པ་དེས་སེམས་ཁྲལ་ཆེན་པོ་བྱུང་བ་དེའི་མུས་ལ་འབྲས་སྣད་ཀྱི་ནད་གཞི་དེ་ཐོག་སོང་ Together with the sorrow caused by the death of his parents, he came down with cancer.

དེའི་ཚེ་ (tee tsē) sm. དེའི་སྐབས་.

དེའི་སང་ཉིན་ (tee sāŋñin) the next day.

དེའུ་ (tewu) small, little ༑ རི་དེའུ་ A small hill.

དེའུ་འབུར་ (tewubur) a mound, a hill.

དེའུ་མིན་ན་ (tewu minnə) almost, nearly ༑ ཁོ་དེའུ་མིན་ན་ཤི་སོང་ He almost died.

དེའུར་ (tewur) as soon as.

དེར་ (tee) there, to that.

དེར་བརྟེན་ (tzērden) therefore, because of that ༑ ཁོ་ལ་ལས་ཀ་གལ་ཆེ་ཞིག་ཡོད་པ་རེད་ དེར་བརྟེན་ཁོ་ཡོང་ཐུབ་མ་སོང་ Because he had important work he could not come.

དེར་བས་སོ་ (tewεso) sm. དེར་ཟད་དོ་.

དེར་མ་ཟད་ (tee masεὲ) not only that ༑ ཁོང་དབྱིན་སྐད་ཡག་པོ་ཡོད་པ་དེར་མ་ཟད་བོད་ཡིག་ཀྱང་ཡག་པོ་ཡོད་པ་རེད་ Not only is he good in English, he is also good in Tibetan.

དེར་ཟད་དོ་ (tee sεὲdo) only that ༑ བྱིའུས་ཁྲ་ལ་འཛིངས་པ་དེ་རང་ཚོད་མ་ཐེག་པའི་རྟགས་དེར་ཟད་དོ་ The bird having thoughts of attacking the hawk shows only that it doesn't know its capabilities.

དེས་ (teè) by that ༑ མི་དེས་བཟོས་པ་རེད་ That man made it. 2. because (of that) ༑ ཞིང་ལས་འཕྲུལ་འཁོར་ཅན་དུ་གྱུར་བ་དེས་ཐོན་སྐྱེད་ཡར་རྒྱས་འགྲོ་གི་ཡོད་པ་རེད་ Because agriculture has been mechanized, production is improving.

དེས་ཆོག (teèjɔɔ̀) that's okay, that's all right.

དེས་ན་ (teèna) sm. དེར་བརྟེན་.

དེས་པ་ (teèba) calm, tranquil, peaceful, gentle.

དེས་མ་ཚད་ (teè madzεὲ) not only that.

དེས་མ་ཟད་ (teè masεὲ) sm. དེས་མ་ཚད་.

དེས་མི་ཚད་ (teè midzεὲ) sm. དེས་མ་ཚད་.

དེས་མིན་ན་ (teè minnə) sm. དོག་ཙམ་མ་གཏོགས་.

དེས་མཛངས་ (teèdzaŋ) sm. མཁས་མཛངས་.

ཏེ་ར་ཌུན་ (teradün) Dehra Dun.

ཊེན་མཱར་ཀ་ (tenmarga) Denmark.

དོ་ (to) 1. sentence ending particle (used after final ད་) ༑ ཁོས་སྐྲ་བཅད་དོ་ He cut his hair. 2. two ༑ འོ་མ་དཀར་ཡོལ་དོ་ Two cups of milk. 3. match, counterpart, equal ༑ ཁོ་ལ་དོ་མེད་ He has no match. 4. let's ༑ ད་ལས་ཀ་དེ་བྱེད་དོ་ Lets do the work. 5. abbr. of དོ་པོ་. 6. va. to dare (to do) ༑ ཁྱེད་རང་འགྲོ་དོ་བ་འདུག་གས་ Do you dare to go?

དོ་ཀེར་ (toger) hair bun on top of the head.

དོ་སྐོར་ (togɔɔ) shung. a two for one exchange/ barter.

དོ་ཁག་ (togaà) abbr. of དོ་བདག་ and ཁག་ཐེག་པ་.

དོ་ཁང་ (togaŋ) warehouse, storehouse.

དོ་ཁུར་ (togur) concern; va.—བྱེད་ to show concern ༑ མི་དམངས་བདེ་དོན་ལ་དོ་ཁུར་ཆེན་པོ་བྱས་ཡོད་པ་རེད་ They have shown a great deal of concern for the public welfare.

དོ་འཁུར་ (togur) sm. དོ་ཁུར་.

དོ་འཁྱེར་གླ་མི་ (togyer lāmi) a person hired to carry a load, a coolie.

དོ་གལ་ (togεε) emphasis, stress, importance; va.—བྱེད་ to emphasize, to stress, to attach significance/ importance ༑ བཟོ་ལས་རྒྱ་སྐྱེད་ཀྱི་ཐད་ལ་དོ་གལ་ཆེན་པོ་བྱེད་ཀྱི་འདུག They are emphasizing the expansion of industry.

དོ་གལ་ནན་དན་ (tokεε nεndεn) doing sth. with great care and diligence; va.—བྱེད་ ༑ ལས་འགན་དེ་གལ་ཆེན་པོ་ཡིན་ཙང་དོ་གལ་ནན་དན་བྱེད་དགོས་ Because this responsibility is very important, (you) must do it with great care and diligence.

དོ་དགོང་ (togoŋ) this evening, tonight.

དོ་རྒྱག (to gyaà) va. to make up a load for carrying/ sending.

དོ་རྒྱག་པ་ (to gyagba) person who packs/ makes loads.

དོ་རྒྱབ་ (togyəb) a pack/ load to be carried by an animal (consisting of one load for each side of the animal).

དོ་ལྕགས་ (tojaà) a flat wire used to tie loads.

དོ་ཆས་རྒྱག (tojεὲ gyaà) va. to pack a suitcase/ load.

དོ་ཆས་བྱེད་ (tojεὲ cee) sm. དོ་ཆས་རྒྱག.

དོ་ཆོད་ (tojöö) sm. གོ་ཆོད་.

དོ་མཉམ་ (toñam) balanced, equal, even, in equilibrium ༑ གཏོང་ཡོང་དོ་མཉམ་ Equal income and expenditure.

དོ་མཉམ་ཙྲེད་ཤིང་ (toñam dzēesiŋ) balance beam (in gymnastics).

དོ་སྙོམས་ (to ñōm) 1. sm. དོ་མཉམ་. 2. va. to put in equilibrium.

དོ་སྙོམས་ཙྲེད་ཤིང་ (toñom dzēèshiŋ) sm. དོ་མཉམ་ཙྲེད་ཤིང་.

དོ་སྡོད་ (todöö) after awhile, a little later.

དོ་ཐབས་ (todəb) trying to compete against/ with; va.—བྱེད་ ༑ སྦྲེ་ག་འགྲན་སྡུར་ནང་རྒྱ་མི་དེས་ཨ་རི་བ་དང་དོ་ཐབས་བྱེད་ཀྱི་འདུག That Chinese is trying to compete with the American in wrestling.

དོ་དམ་ (todam) 1. in custody, arresting; va.—བྱེད་ to keep in custody, to arrest ༑ མི་དེ་སྐོར་སྲུང་བས་དོ་དམ་བྱས་པ་རེད་ The police arrested that man. 2. surveillance ༑ དོ་དམ་ས་ཁུལ་ Surveillance area. 3. managing, taking care of; va.—བྱེད་ to take care of, to manage, to administer, to act as trustee ༑ དམག་སྒར་ནང་གི་མཁོ་སྤྲོད་དང་ལྟོ་ཆས་དོ་དམ་བྱས་པ་རེད་ (They) managed the supplies and food of the regiment. 4. abbr. of དོ་དམ་པ་.

དོ་དམ་བསྐུལ་ལྕག (todam gǖǖjaà) shung. managing and speeding/ hurrying up, supervising and encouraging/ motivating; va.—བྱེད་.

དོ་དམ་གྲོན་དངུལ་ (todam drönŋüü) administrative/ management expenses (money).

དོ་དམ་གཅིག་གྱུར་ (todam jīggyur) unified management/ administration.

དོ་དམ་པ་ (todamba) commissioner, official in charge, supervisor, custodian.

དོ་དམ་བྱེད་རྒྱུར་བཅོལ་ (todam ceègyur jöö) placing/

putting under trusteeship/ guardianship.

དོ་དམ་སྤྱིལ་པོ་ཟུར་བསྐོས་ (todam dreebo surgöö) shung. specially appointed joint commissioners ¶ ད་ལམ་གྲོད་ཞིབ་དོ་དམ་སྤྱིལ་པོ་ཟུར་བསྐོས་ཀྱིས་ཆེད་ཐོང་སོང་དོན་ས་གནས་སུ་རྒྱུ་རྐྱེན་ཞིབ་ཞུ་དགོས་རྒྱུ་ This time we have sent specially appointed joint commissioners for settling the case, so you should report the matter in detail to them.

དོ་དམ་གཞན་བཅོལ་ (todam shenjöö) placing (one's affairs or business) with another to manage/ administer/ take care of.

དོ་དམ་བཙོན་བཅུག (todam dzõnjuù) arresting and imprisoning; va.—བྱེད་.

དོ་དམ་འཛིན་བཟུང་ (todam dzinsuŋ) 1. sm. དོ་དམ་བཙོན་བཅུག. 2. operating, running, managing.

དོ་དམ་ལམ་ལུགས་ (todam lamluù) system of management/ administration.

དོ་དམ་ས་ཚིགས་ (todam sədzii) management/ administration station.

དོ་དམ་སློབ་གསོ་ (todam lōbso) 1. management training/ education. 2. security training. 3. teaching sb. discipline, subjecting sb. to discipline.

དོ་དམ་ཨུ་ཡོན་ལྷན་ཁང་ (todam ūyön lhēngaŋ) control or security commission/ committee ¶ ལྷ་སའི་དམག་དོན་དོ་དམ་ཨུ་ཡོན་ལྷན་ཁང་ Lhasa military control commission.

དོ་དོ་དན་དན་ (todo dēndεn) sm. གཟབ་གཟབ་ནན་ནན་.

དོ་བདག (todaà) 1. protagonist, principal in an event, the proper person ¶ འཕྲིན་སྐྱེལ་བས་ཡི་གེ་ནོར་འཁྲུལ་མེད་པར་དོ་བདག་གི་ལག་ཏུ་རྩིས་སྤྲོད་བྱེད་ཀྱི་ཡོད་པ་རེད་ The postman delivers the mail without error to the proper person. 2. owner. ¶ དོ་བདག་དངོས་ The real owner.

དོ་བདག་ལེ་འབྲི་ (todaà ledri) the main people involved in sth., the principals ¶ མི་གསོད་གྲོད་གཞི་འདིའི་སྐོར་དོ་བདག་ལེ་འབྲི་ཁྲིམས་ཁང་ལ་བསྐོངས་བཞག The main people involved in the murder case were summoned.

དོ་བསྡུར་ (to dur) va. to compete.

དོ་བསྡོ་ (to do) sm. དོ་སྡུར་.

དོ་ནན་ (tonεn) sm. དོ་ནན་པོ་.

དོ་ནན་པོ་ (to nεmbo) careful, conscientious, exact, precise; va.—བྱེད་ ¶ ཁོ་ལས་ཀར་དོ་ནན་པོ་ཡོད་པ་རེད་ He is careful in his work.

དོ་ནུབ་ (tonub) tonight, this evening.

དོ་ནོན་པ་ (to nömbo) 1. two animal loads of equal weight. 2. responsible, able to take care of oneself.

དོ་སྣང་ (tonaŋ) 1. paying attention to, heeding, taking note of, having concern for; va.—བྱེད་ to be aware of, to pay attention to, to heed, to take note of, to have concern for ¶ ཁོ་ཚོས་རྒྱལ་ཕྱིའི་སྲིད་ཇུས་ལ་དམིགས་བསལ་དོ་སྣང་བྱེད་ཀྱི་ཡོད་པ་རེད་ (They) are paying special attention to their foreign policy. 2. being careful, cautious; va.—བྱེད་ ¶ རང་དོ་སྣང་མ་བྱས་ན་གཞུང་གིས་འཛིན་བཟུང་བྱེད་ཀྱི་རེད་ If you aren't careful the government will arrest you.

དོ་སྣང་ཆེན་པོ་བྱེད་གཞི་ (tonaŋ cēmbo ceèshi) a target of great attention, a central attraction.

དོ་སྣང་ལ་འགྲོ་ (tonaŋla dro) vi. to suit one's taste, to be to one's liking ¶ མནའ་མ་དེ་ཕ་མ་གཉིས་ཀྱི་དོ་སྣང་ལ་ཕྱིན་མ་སོང་ The parents did not take a liking to the new bride.

དོ་སྣང་ལ་འགྲོ་པོ་ (tonaŋla drobo) suiting one's tastes, being to one's liking ¶ མོ་ཊ་འདི་ངའི་དོ་སྣང་ལ་འགྲོ་པོ་བྱུང་མ་སོང་ This car was not to my liking.

དོ་པ་ (toba) a helper/ assistant to a muleteer.

དོ་པོ་ (tobo) load, bale, bundle, bag (usu. for animals), package; va.—འགེལ་; —རྒྱག to put on a load; va.—བཤིག to untie/ undo a load; va.—སིལ་ to take apart a load (and sell the contents by pieces).

དོ་པོ་རྒྱག་མཁན་ (tobo gyaàñεn) a person who loads and unloads transpoert animals.

དོ་པོའི་འཁོར་ལོ་ (tobö kɔ̄ɔlo) truck.

དོ་པོའི་ཕྱི་བཀོད་ (tobö cīgöö) a sign or mark on the outside of a box (e.g., "fragile").

དོ་ཕད་ (topεὲ) 1. bag for carrying things. 2. a backpack.

དོ་ཕོག (tobɔɔ̀) a bad effect/ change; vi.—བྱུང་ to have/ get a bad effect, to be changed negatively ¶ མུ་གེ་བྱུང་ཙང་མི་དམངས་ཀྱི་འཚོ་བར་དོ་ཕོག་ཆེན་པོ་བྱུང་བ་རེད་ Because there was a famine the livelihood of the people was negatively effected.

དོ་བ་ (towa) 1. see དོ་, 6. 2. an herbal medicine.

དོ་བོ་ (towo) sm. དོ་པོ་.

དོ་མ་ (toma) substitute.

དོ་མ་གལ་ (tōmagεε) unconcerned, unaware, oblivious.

དོ་མི་མཉམ་ (to miñam) vi. to be not matched/ equal/ balanced ¶ དོ་པོ་འདི་གཉིས་དོ་མཉམ་གྱི་མི་འདུག These two loads are unequal (in weight).

དོ་མི་བསྡོ་ (to mido) sm. དོ་མེད་.

དོ་མི་ཐུབ་ (to mitub) sm. དོ་མེད་.

དོ་མེད་ (tomeè) matchless, incomparable, unequaled ¶ ཨབ་དང་ཚད་མཁན་དེ་འགྲན་གྱི་དོ་མེད་རེད་འདུག That wrestler is unequaled.

དོ་མོད་ (tomöö) tonight.

དོ་རྩིས་སྤྲོད་ (to dzii dröö) shung. va. to hand over/ deliver a load ¶ མི་སྒྱེ་ནས་ལྷ་འདྲེན་གྱིས་སྐྱོན་མེད་དོ་རྩིས་སྤྲད་པ་ The loads were transported to Lhasa by the subjects and delivered without any damage.

དོ་བརྩོན་ (todzön) conscientiousness, seriousness; va.—བྱེད་ ¶ སློབ་སྦྱོང་ལ་དོ་བརྩོན་བྱ་རྒྱུ་དེ་གལ་ཆེན་པོ་རེད་ It is important to be conscientious in your work.

དོ་ཚད་ (todzεὲ) limit for a load.

དོ་འཚོང་ (todzoŋ) wholesale ¶ དེ་འཚོང་གི་རིན་ཐང་ Wholesale price.

དོ་རྫོངས་ (todzŋ) loading (carts/ trucks/ etc.); va.—བྱེད་.

དོ་ཞག (toshaà) these days.

དོ་ཞག་ལོ་དུས་ (toshaà lodüü) sm. དོ་ཞག.

དོ་ཟླ་ (tonda) sm. དོ་ཡ་.

དོ་ཟླ་བྲལ་བ་ (tonda treεwa) sm. དོ་ཡ་མེད་པ་.

དོ་ཟླ་དབེན་ (tondawen) sm. དོ་ཡ་མེད་པ་.

དོ་ཡ་ (toya) 1. matching, balanced; vi.—མཉམ་ to be balanced/ matched; va.—སྙོམ་; —བྱེད་ to balance, to match ¶ དམག་པོའི་སྟོབས་ཤུགས་ཀྱི་དོ་ཡ་སྙོམ་ཆེད་དུ་ In order to match (their) military power. ¶ ངས་ཁོང་དང་དཔལ་འབྱོར་གྱི་དོ་ཡ་བྱེད་ཐུབ་ཀྱི་མ་རེད་ I can not match him in wealth.

དོ་ཡ་མཉམ་པ་ (toya ñamba) equally matched/ balanced.

དོ་ཡ་མེད་པ་ (toya meèba) unmatched, unequal ¶ དོ་ཡ་མེད་པའི་སྟོབས་ཤུགས་ཡོད་པ་རེད་ (They) have unmatched power.

དོ་ཡ་ལོན་ (toya lön) equally matched/ balanced.

དོ་ར་ (tora) 1. area/ platform/ stage for dancing. 2. grasslands. 3. va. to pluck crops.

དོ་ར྄་ (tora) sm.* དོ་ར་.

དོ་ལི་ (toli) sedan chair, palanquin.

དོ་ལོ་ (tolo) a cheap stone resembling turquoise.

དོ་ལོག (tolɔɔ̀) 1. the 1st (best) brew in ཆང་. 2. sm. དོ་སྐོར་.

དོ་ཤལ་ (toshεε) necklace.

དོ་ཤི་ (to shī) close to death; vi.—འགྱུར་ to be close to death.

དོ་ཤི་དོ་ཚད་ (toshi todzεὲ) sm. དོ་ཤི་.

དོ་གསོད་ (to sōö) va. to be just about to kill (or get killed) ¶ ཁོ་དོ་གསོད་དུ་ངས་སྲོག་བསྐྱབས་པ་ཡིན་ Just when he was about to be killed, I saved his life.

དོག (tɔɔ̀) abbr. of དོག་པོ་.

དོག་དཀྲི་ (tɔɔ̀ drī) va. to wind yarn around the elbow and hand.

དོག་པ་ (togba) 1. pod (pea). 2. thread. 3. sm. དོག་པོ་. 4. stamen (of a flower). 5. sm. དོག་པོ་.

དོག་པོ་ (togbo) 1. ball of yarn. 2. narrow, closed in,

crowded together. 3. shung. sm. ངན་ཏོག.

ཏོག་པོར་ཁྱབ་ (togbor kyəb) vi. to be filled with sth.

ཏོག་མ་ (togma) 1. earth. 2. arc. front.

ཏོག་མི་བདེ་བ་ (tog midewa) sm. ཁ་སྐྱིངས་.

ཏོག་མོ་ (togmo) 1. sm. ཏོག་པ་. 2. sm. ཏོག་མ་.

ཏོག་མོན་ (togmön) sm. ཏོག་མོ་.

ཏོག་འཚང་བྱེད་ (togdzaŋ ceè) shung. va. to jostle/ push for sth. ། ཁོ་པས་བཀའ་བློན་ཏོག་འཚང་བྱས་རྐྱེན་ Because he jostled for the position of Council Minister.

ཏོག་རེ་ཏོག་རེ་ (togre togre) continuously.

ཏོག་ས་ (togsa) a bottleneck, a narrow place ། ས་འཁག་ཏོག་སར་འཛབ་དམག་བརྒྱབ་པ་རེད་ They ambushed them in a narrow place.

ཏོག་སྲིང་ (togsiŋ) under the earth, underground.

དོགས་ (tɔg) 1. (vb. + —) having suspicions/ doubts/ fears/ apprehensions ། ཁོ་རྗེས་ལུས་ཐེབས་དོགས་བྱུང་བ་རེད་ He was apprehensive that he might fall behind. ། ཁོ་མི་གཞན་གྱིས་གསོད་དོགས་ཀྱིས་བྲོས་ཤོར་པ་རེད་ He ran away because he suspected that others will kill him. ། ངང་ལ་བཙོན་ཞུར་བྱས་དོགས་མ་བྱུང་ I didn't have fear of being imprisoned.

དོགས་སྐྲག (tɔgdraà) doubt and fear.

དོགས་ཁ་པོ་ (tɔg kābo) sm. མདོག་ཁ་པོ་.

དོགས་ཅན་མི་ཡན་ (tɔgjɛn miyɛn) a person under suspicion.

དོགས་གཅོད་ (tɔgjöö) the act of removing or clearing up doubt/ suspicions/ uncertainty; va.—བྱེད་; —ཞུ་ to remove or clear up doubts/ fears/ suspicions ། འཆར་གཞི་གསར་པ་འདིའི་སྐོར་ངས་འགོ་ཁྲིད་ལ་དོགས་གཅོད་བྱས་པ་ཡིན་ I cleared up the doubts of the boss about the new plan.

དོགས་ཆགས་ (tɔgjaà) having suspicions; va.—བྱེད་ to have doubts about sb. ། ཁོང་སོ་པ་ཡིན་པའི་དོགས་ཆགས་བྱུང་བ་རེད་ (They) had suspicions about him being a spy.

དོགས་ཆོད་ (tɔgjöö) vi. to have a doubt/ suspicion removed or cleared up.

དོགས་འཆར་ (tɔg cār) 1. doubt, suspicion, fear; va.—ཤར་ to have a doubt arise; va.—སེལ་; —བསལ་ to clear up a doubt/ suspicion/ fear ། དོགས་འཆར་རྣམས་ Doubts. ། རྐུན་མ་ཐུག་ཡོང་བསམ་པའི་དོགས་འཆར་བྱུང་སོང་ He feared he would meet a thief.

དོགས་ཉེན་ (tɔgñen) suspicion of danger.

དོགས་མཐའ་ (tɔgta) the main reason/ cause for doubt or suspicion.

དོགས་འདྲི་ (tɔgdri) questioning or investigating with regard to doubts/ suspicions/ apprehensions; va.—བྱེད་.

དོགས་འདྲོག (tɔg drɔ̄ɔ) vi. to be frightened/ startled by doubt or fear.

དོགས་གནད་ (tɔgnɛɛ̀) sm. དོགས་མཐའ་.

དོགས་སྣང་ (tɔgnaŋ) feeling of doubt/ suspicion/ apprehension.

དོགས་པ་ (tɔgba) doubt, apprehension, misgiving, suspicion, fear; vi.—ཟ་; —སྐྱེ་; —འཆར་; —ལངས་ to get suspicious, to have doubts/ apprehensions/ fears/ misgivings; va.—བྱེད་ to suspect, to question, to doubt, to fear; va.—སློང་ to make a person suspicious, to raise doubts; va.—སེལ་ to clear up/ remove doubts/ suspicions/ apprehensions ། ཁོས་དོན་དངོས་ཤོད་ཀྱི་ཡི་ཡོད་བསམ་པའི་དོགས་པ་སྐྱེས་པ་རེད་ (They) got suspicious about whether he was telling the truth. ། ཁྱོད་ཚོ་སོ་པ་ཡིན་པའི་དོགས་པ་བྱེད་ཀྱི་མ་རེད་ (They) will not suspect that you are spies. ། གསང་བའི་ཚོགས་འདུ་དེས་མི་མང་པོར་དོགས་པ་བསླངས་པ་རེད་ The secret meeting made many people suspicious.

དོགས་པ་སྔོན་བསུ་ (tɔgba ŋõnsu) being doubtful/ suspicious from the beginning.

དོགས་པ་ཁོང་སློང་ (tɔgba kōŋloŋ) va. to cause sb. to be suspicious/ doubtful.

དོགས་པ་གཅོད་ (tɔgba jöö) sm. དོགས་གཅོད་.

དོགས་པ་ཆོད་ (tɔgba cöö) sm. དོགས་ཆོད་.

དོགས་པ་འདྲི་ (tɔgba dri) sm. དོགས་འདྲི་.

དོགས་པ་མང་ན་དོན་མི་འགྲུབ་ (tɔgba maŋna tönmi drub) if you are too suspicious you will not succeed/ accomplish anything.

དོགས་པ་མེད་པ་ (tɔgba meèba) without doubts/ suspicions/ apprehensions.

དོགས་པ་ཚ་པོ་ (tɔgba tsābo) suspicious, apprehensive, distrustful, having doubts.

དོགས་པ་ཟ་པོ་ (tɔgba sabo) sm. དོགས་པ་ཚ་པོ་.

དོགས་དཔྱོད་ (tɔjöö) sm. དོག་གཅོད་.

དོགས་དཔྱོད་པ་ (tɔjööba) a detective, secret agent.

དོགས་མེད་ (tɔgmeè) 1. having no doubts/ suspicions/ apprehensions. 2. (vb. + —) no need to fear/ worry regarding the verbal action. 3. (vb. + —) one should not do the verbal action ། ཁྱེད་རང་སྐྱག་རྫུན་འདི་འདྲ་ཤོད་དོགས་མེད་ You shouldn't lie like that.

དོགས་ཚོམ་ (tɔgdzom) abbr. of དོགས་པ་ and ཐེ་ཚོམ་.

དོགས་འཚབ་ (tɔgdzəb) suspicious/ doubtful and nervous.

དོགས་གཞི་ (tɔgshi) the basis for suspicion, doubt ། ལས་བྱེད་པ་གསར་པ་བའདི་སོ་པ་ཡིན་པའི་དོགས་གཞི་ཆེན་པོ་འདུག There is a great basis for suspecting the new official as a spy.

དོགས་ཟོན་ (tɔgsön) caution, vigilance, carefulness; va.—བྱེད་ to be cautious/ careful, to take precautionary measures, to be vigilant, to be on one's guard ། འཛབ་དྲང་གི་དོགས་ཟོན་ཆེན་པོ་བྱེད་ཀྱི་འདུག (They) are very cautious about ambushes.

དོགས་ཟོན་གྱི་རང་བཞིན་ (tɔgsöngi rəŋshin) vigilance, cautiousness.

དོགས་ཟོན་ཆེ་བསྐྱེད་ (tɔgsön cēgyeè) heightening one's vigilance, being extra cautious; va.—བྱེད་.

དོགས་ཟོན་པ་ (tɔgsömba) guard, watchman.

དོགས་ཟོན་གཡེལ་མེད་ (tɔgsön yēēmeè) extremely alert/ watchful/ vigilant.

དོགས་ཟོན་ཤོར་ (tɔgsön shɔ̄ɔ) vi. to lose one's caution/ vigilance, to have one's caution/ vigilance be breached.

དོགས་གཟབ་ (tɔgsəb) sm. དོགས་ཟོན་.

དོགས་ཡོད་ཉེས་ཅན་ (tɔgyöö ñeèjɛn) a criminal suspect; va.—བྱེད་.

དོགས་སློང་ (tɔgloŋ) causing sb. to be doubtful/ suspicious; va.—བྱེད་.

དོགས་གསལ་ (tɔgsɛl) sm. དོགས་གཅོད་.

དོང་ (toŋ) 1. deep hole, pit. 2. p. of འདོང་. 3. a hollow tube-like object ། ལྕགས་དོང་ Metal tube. 4. sm. དུར་དོང་.

དོང་ཀ་ (toŋga) sm. དོང་ག.

དོང་ཀོ་ (toŋga) underground waterway/ canal.

དོང་ཀོ་རུ་ཁག (toŋgo rugaà) drilling team.

དོང་ཁུང་ (toŋguŋ) a deep pit/ hole.

དོང་ག (toŋga) a type of Tibetan medicine.

དོང་སྒོ་ (toŋgo) the opening or mouth of a cave or pit.

དོང་ཆུ་ (toŋju) water that is standing in a hole/ pit.

དོང་རྙི་ (toŋñi) a pit trap; va.—ཀོ་ to dig a pit trap.

དོང་ཐབ་ (toŋdəb) the hearth section of a "kang" bed (i.e.,. a Chinese style bed with a built-in hearth underneath it).

དོང་དོང་ (toŋdoŋ) ch. bucket.

དོང་འདྲུ་རྩད་ཞིབ་ (toŋdru dzɛɛ̄shi) test well, test tunnel.

དོང་པ་ (toŋba) quiver, sheath (for arrows).

དོང་པོ་ (toŋbo) sm. དོང་, 3.

དོང་སྤྲུག (toŋdrug) eradicating/ pulling from the root; va.—བྱེད་.

དོང་མེད་ (toŋmeè) shallow.

དོང་ཙེ་ (toŋdze) ch. a traditional Chinese coin with a hole in the middle.

དོང་ཙེ་ཕྲང་ཤལ་ (toŋdze trāŋshɛɛ) a bunch of coins strung in a circle on a string.

དོང་ལམ་ (toŋlam) 1. tunnel ། དོང་ལམ་གྱི་འདེགས་ཤིང་ Braces for a tunnel. 2. subway.

དོང་ལམ་དམག་འཐབ་ (toŋlam məgdəb) tunnel/

underground warfare.

དོང་ས་ (toŋsa) tunnel.

དོངས་ (toŋ) imp. of འདོང་.

དོངས་རྩེ་ (toŋdze) sm.* དོང་ཙེ་.

དོད་ (töö) 1. an equivalent/ substitute for sth., sth. that makes up a deficit, sth. in place of sth. else ¶ ཁ་སའི་ལས་ཀའི་དོད་དེ་རིང་བྱེད་ཀྱི་ཡོད་པ་རེད་ He is working today to make up for yesterday's work. ¶ མཛལ་དར་གྱི་དོད་དུ་མེ་ཏོག་ཕུལ་བ་རེད་ He gave flowers as a substitute for a ceremonial scarf. 2. a payment in money in lieu of a tax in kind. 3. vi. to stand out/ protrude.

དོད་བསྐོས་ (töögöö) appointing a substitute/ replacement; va.—བྱེད་.

དོད་ཁང་ (töögaŋ) storage house.

དོད་སྐྱིན་ (töödrii) shung. money given in place of food that one has a responsibility to provide at ceremonies such as prayer rituals; va.—འབུལ་ ¶ དགོན་པར་ཞབས་བརྟན་གསང་རྒྱུའི་ཞལ་ལག་དོད་སྐྱིན་ཕུལ་བ་ཡིན་ (He) gave money in place of food at the monastery's prayer ceremony (in place of the required foodstuffs).

དོད་སྐྱིན་སྦོམ་སྒྲོད་ (töödrii bōmdröö) a large payment of cash in place of required foodstuffs.

དོད་དངུལ་ (tööŋüü) money paid as a substitute for foodstuffs or products that one has a responsibility to provide ¶ ངས་འབྲུ་ཁྲལ་འཇལ་རྒྱུ་དེ་དོད་དངུལ་སྤྲད་ན་འགྲིག་གི་རེད་པས་ Is it okay to give money in place of grain to meet the grain tax?

དོད་ཐུབ་ (töö tūb) vi. to be able to use as a substitute.

དོད་དུ་ (töödu) as an equivalent/ substitute, in place of.

དོད་དྲག (töödraà) emergency.

དོད་དྲག་ཁང་ (töödraàgaŋ) emergency room/ ward (in a hospital).

དོད་དྲག་པོ་ (töö dragbo) sm. དོད་དྲག.

དོད་པོ་ (tööbo) 1. a replacement, a substitute ¶ ཞལ་ལག་གི་དོད་པོར་དངུལ་ཕུལ་བ་རེད་ (He) gave money as substitute for food.

དོད་འཕེར་ (töö pēr) shung. vi. to replace ¶ དེང་གི་ཆར་སློབ་དཔོན་ལྷན་ཌིའི་དོད་འཕེར་བའི་སློབ་དཔོན་ཞིག་རྙེད་པར་དཀའ་ Nowadays it is difficult to find a leader to replace Gandhi.

དོད་འབབ་ (tömbəb) an amount of money used as substitute for sth. ¶ འབྲུ་ཁྲལ་གྱི་དོད་འབབ་དེ་འཁྱེར་ཡོད་པས་ Did you bring the amount of money needed to substitute for the grain tax?

དོད་ཡངས་གཏོང་ (tööyaŋ dōŋ) va. to let sb. go free without discipline ¶ ཕ་མས་ཕྲུ་གུ་དེ་དོད་ཡངས་སུ་བཏང་འདུག The parents have let that child go free without discipline.

དོད་ལོན་ (töölön) sm. དོད་ཐུབ་.

དོན་ (tön) 1. meaning, significance; vi.—གོ་; —རྟོགས་ to understand the meaning ¶ ཐ་སྙད་འདིའི་དོན་རྟོགས་ཁག་པོ་འདུག It is difficult to understand the meaning of this term. ¶ ཐ་སྙད་འགའ་ཞིག་གི་དོན་ The meaning of several terms. 2. (vb. + —) The reason for the preceding verbal act follows (will be explained) ¶ དམག་མི་བཏང་དོན་ The reason for sending troops (follows). 3. reason, purpose ¶ དེ་འདྲ་བྱེད་པའི་དོན་ག་རེ་རེད་ What is the reason for doing such a thing? ¶ དོན་ཡོད་པ་མ་རེད་ There is no purpose/ reason (for this). 4. welfare, interest ¶ ཚང་མའི་དོན་ The welfare/ interests of everyone. 5. affairs ¶ སྲིད་དོན་ Political affairs. 6. direct discourse introducer ¶ ཁོང་གིས་གསུངས་དོན་ He said, "—" ¶ ཌི་ལི་ནས་གནས་ཚུལ་འབྱོར་དོན་ According to information received from Delhi. 7. true, real, genuine ¶ དོན་གྱི་བདེ་བ་ Real happiness. 8 numerical particle for the seventies ¶ བདུན་ཅུ་དོན་གཅིག Seventy one. 9. (vb. + —) sense/ meaning of the verbal action ¶ ཁས་ལེན་བྱས་དོན་ལག་ལེན་བྱེད་དགོས་ (You) have to put into practice the meaning of what you have promised. 10. (vb. + — དོན་མི་འདུག) there is no sense in doing the verbal action ¶ ཨུ་ཚུགས་བྱེད་དོན་མི་འདུག There is no sense in insisting. 11. va. to come out ¶ ཁོང་ནང་ནས་དོན་ཡོང་གི་འདུག He is coming out of the house. 12. ch. a regiment. 13. sm. ཐོན་.

དོན་ཀྲང་ (töndraŋ) ch. regimental commander.

དོན་ཀུན་ (töngün) general welfare, public good.

དོན་ཀུན་གྲུབ་པ་ (töngün trubba) 1. accomplishing everything. 2. an epithet of the Buddha.

དོན་རྐྱེན་ (töngyen) incident, trouble, problem.

དོན་ཁང་ (töngaŋ) abbr. དོན་གཅོད་ཁང་.

དོན་མཁན་ (tönñɛn) actor, performer, player.

དོན་འཁེལ་ (tönkel) achieving one's purpose/ aim/ goal, realizing one's hopes ¶ ཁོ་ཚོའི་རེ་བ་དོན་འཁེལ་བྱུང་སོང་ (We) must act so that their hopes will be realized.

དོན་འཁྱོལ་ (tönkyöö) sm. དོན་འཁེལ་.

དོན་ག་ཚང་ (tönga tsāŋ) 1. va. to fulfill one's duty. 2. va. to do sth. meaningful.

དོན་གོ་ཆུང་ (tön gojuŋ) achieving a minor result ¶ དཀའ་ལས་ཆེ་ལ་དོན་གོ་ཆུང་བ་ Putting in a lot of effort, but getting minor results.

དོན་གོ་ཆོད་ (tön gojöö) vi. to achieve/ fulfill one's duty or task or purpose.

དོན་གྱི་ཁོག་ཕུབ་ (töngi kɔ̄gbub) arranging in order/ sequence.

དོན་གྱི་དམ་པ་ (töngi damba) the most important task ¶ རྒྱལ་ཁབ་ཀྱི་གསང་བ་མ་ཤོར་བ་བྱ་རྒྱུ་དེ་དོན་གྱི་དམ་པ་ཡིན་ The most important task is not to let secrets leak out of the country.

དོན་གྱི་བདག་པོ་ (töngi dagbo) the main owner, the head of sth. (a country, household, etc.). 2. the Dalai Lama.

དོན་གྱི་མདོ་ (töngi do) the main point/ aim/ object.

དོན་གྱི་འབྲས་བུ་དབེན་པའི་སྐད་ཆ་ (töngi drɛ̄ɛ̀bu bēnbɛ gɛ̄ɛ̀ja) speech with no substance.

དོན་འགྱུར་ (töngyur) 1. incident, event ¶ ཟ་ཁང་དེ་ལ་དོན་འགྱུར་ཞིག་བྱུང་སོང་ There was an incident at that restaurant. 2. translating the meaning.

དོན་འགྲེལ་ (töndrel) commentary on a scripture.

དོན་གྲུབ་ (töndrub) 1. person's name. 2. abbr. of དོན་དག་གྲུབ་.

དོན་སྒྲུབ་ (töndrub) shung. abbr. of དོན་གྲུབ་.

དོན་དགོས་ཚང་ (töngöö dzāŋ) va. to see to the end, to accomplish/ achieve one's objective ¶ ཕྲུ་གུ་དེ་སློབ་གྲྭར་བཏང་བའི་དོན་དགོས་ཚང་སོང་ ད་ཁོ་ལ་ལས་ཀ་ཡག་པོ་ཞིག་རག་སོང་ (We) achieved our objective in sending our son to school; now he got a good job.

དོན་དགོས་ཚང་པོ་ (töngöö dzāŋbo) accomplishing/ achieving one's objectives.

དོན་འགལ་ (töngɛɛ) incorrect, wrong ¶ རྩོམ་ཡིག་གི་ཚིག་དུམ་འདི་དོན་འགལ་རེད་འདུག This part of the article is wrong.

དོན་འགྲེལ་རི་མོ་ (töndrel rimu) illustration, illustrated explanation.

དོན་རྒྱས་པ་ (tön gyɛ̄ɛ̀ba) elaborate, in detail.

དོན་རྒྱུས་སྤྲད་ (töngyüü jɛ̄ɛ̀) shung. familiarizing/ filling in sb. about a situation ¶ དཔལ་མ་དོ་དམ་པ་དེ་ས་གནས་སུ་འབྱོར་བསྟུན་དོན་རྒྱུས་སྤྲད་དུ་དགོས་ When the official arrives you must familiarize him with the city.

དོན་སྒྱུར་ (töngyur) free translation, paraphrasing; va.—བྱེད་.

དོན་སྒྲུབ་ཁང་ (töndrubgaŋ) agency, office.

དོན་ངོ་མ་ (tön ŋoma) sm. དོན་དངོས་.

དོན་དངོས་ (tönŋöö) facts, reality, truth ¶ ཁོང་གི་གསུང་བཤད་དེ་དོན་དངོས་རེད་ His speech is true.

དོན་དངོས་ཁུངས་སྐྱེལ་ (tönŋöö kūŋgyel) real evidence/ proof.

དོན་དངོས་ཐོག (tön ŋöödɔɔ) in fact, in actuality, in reality ¶ དོན་དངོས་ཐོག་ཁོང་ཡོན་ཏན་ཆེན་པོ་ཞིག་མ་རེད་ In actuality, he isn't knowledgeable.

དོན་དངོས་དང་བྲལ་བ་ (tönŋöö taŋ trɛɛwa)

unrealistic, untrue, not accurate/ real.

དོན་དངོས་ཇུན་བཟོ་ (tönŋöö dzünso) lying/ falsifying the truth, fabricating.

དོན་དངོས་མཚོན་པའི་རིང་ལུགས་ (tönŋöö tsönbɛ riŋluù) realism.

དོན་ལྔ་ (tönŋa) the five viscera (heart, lungs, liver, kidneys, and stomach).

དོན་ལྔ་གཅིག་མཚུངས་ (tönŋa jigdzuŋ) same meaning, synonymous.

དོན་ཅན་ (tönjɛn) meaningful, having purpose/ significance.

དོན་གཅོད་ (tönjöö) an official (usu. sent to represent a government in another locality) ༶ དྲི་ལི་དོན་གཅོད་ The official (of the Dalai Lama's government-in-exile) in Delhi.

དོན་གཅོད་ཁང་ (tönjöögaŋ) sm. དོན་གཅོད་ལས་ཁུངས་.

དོན་གཅོད་ཁྲུའུ་ (tönjöö trū) tib.ch. bureau office.

དོན་གཅོད་པ་ (tönjööba) a person who makes decision regarding work, etc.

དོན་གཅོད་ལས་ཁུངས་ (tönjöö lɛ̀ɛguŋ) office, bureau.

དོན་གཅོད་དབང་ཆ་ (tönjöö wāŋja) decision-making power/ authority.

དོན་ཆུང་ (tönjuŋ) a minor matter/ affair.

དོན་ཆུང་སྒྲོ་འདོགས་ (tönjuŋ drondɔɔ̀) sm. དོན་ཆུང་ཆེ་སྒྲོག.

དོན་ཆུང་ཆེ་སྒྲོག (tönjuŋ cēdrɔɔ̀) making a big deal out of sth. small/ minor, exaggerating; va.—བྱེད་.

དོན་ཆུང་ཞིབ་བསྒྲང་ (tönjuŋ shibdraŋ) sm. དོན་ཕྲན་ཞིབ་བཤད་.

དོན་ཆེན་ (tönjen) an important matter/ affair.

དོན་ཆེན་སྒྲུབ་པར་ངང་རིང་ (tönjen drubbar ŋaŋriŋ) one should be patient when accomplishing important matters.

དོན་འཇལ་ (tön jɛɛ) va. to comprehend/ understand.

དོན་བརྗོད་སྙན་ངག (tönjöö ñēnŋaà) epic/ narrative poem.

དོན་ཉུང་ (tönñuŋ) little content/ meaning.

དོན་ཉུང་བ་བྱ་བ་ཉུང་བ་ (tönñuŋwa cawa ñuŋwa) a person who does not have much desire for things and lives a simple life.

དོན་ཉུང་ཚིག་མང་ (tönñuŋ tsïgmaŋ) having little content/ meaning but very wordy (for speeches, articles, etc.).

དོན་གཉིས་ (tönñii) 1. two meanings. 2. one's affairs and other's affairs.

དོན་གཉེར་ (tönñer) 1. working/ striving toward some goal; va.—བྱེད་ to strive for a purpose or cause, to endeavor, to work hard for ༶ གྲངས་ཉུང་མི་རིགས་ཀྱི་རང་དབང་ལ་དོན་གཉེར་རྒྱུ་མཐུད་བྱས་ཡོད་པ་རེད་ They have continuously worked for the freedom of the minority nationalities.

དོན་གཉེར་བ་ (tönñerwa) a person who is working / striving towards some goal ༶ དེབ་འདི་སློབ་སྦྱོང་དོན་གཉེར་བ་ཚོར་རིན་མེད་འབུལ་གྱི་ཡིན་ (I) will give the book free of charge to those people who are striving to study. ༶ ཞི་བདེ་དོན་གཉེར་བ་ Peace seekers.

དོན་སྙིང་ (tönñiŋ) 1. the main point, the heart of a matter ༶ དོན་སྙིང་ནི་རང་དོན་བློས་གཏོང་མི་ཐུབ་པ་དེ་རེད་ The heart of the matter is that (they) cannot give up their own interests. 2. significance, purpose ༶ རིག་པའི་གཞུང་ལུགས་ཀྱི་དོན་སྙིང་རླབས་ཆེན་ཞིག་རེད་ This is of great theoretical significance. 3. the heart. 4. internal organs. 5. entrails.

དོན་སྙིང་ལྔ་ (tönñiŋ ŋā) the five vital internal organs: heart, lung, liver, kidney and spleen.

དོན་སྙིང་མེད་པའི་རྩོམ་ཡིག (tönñiŋ meèbɛ dzōmyiì) an article/ essay without a significant point.

དོན་ལྟར་ (töndar) (vb. + —) as, like, as per ༶ ཁོས་གོ་དོན་ལྟར་བཤད་པ་རེད་ (He) told it as he had heard it.

དོན་ལྟར་ན་ (töndarna) a direct discourse introducer: according to ༶ ཁོང་གིས་གསར་འགོད་པ་ཚོར་གསུངས་དོན་ལྟར་ན་ According to the comments of the reporter.

དོན་རྟོགས་ (töndɔɔ̀) va. to understand/ comprehend ༶ རྩོམ་ཡིག་འདིའི་དོན་རྟོགས་ཁག་པོ་འདུག This article is hard to understand.

དོན་སྟོང་ (tondoŋ) devoid/ empty of meaning, meaningless, having no substance/ significance.

དོན་སྟོང་རིང་ལུགས་ (tondoŋ riŋluù) nihilism.

དོན་ཐག་གཅོད་ (tön tāà jöö) va. to decide/ settle a case, to pass judgment. ༶ གླ་ཡོགས་ཀྱི་སྐོར་དོན་ཐག་བཅད་མི་འདུག Concerning salary, they didn't settle it.

དོན་ཐོག་འཁེལ་ (töntɔɔ̀ kēē) sm. དོན་ཐོག་ཏུ་འཁེལ་.

དོན་ཐོག་འཁྱོལ་ (töntɔɔ̀ kyöö) sm. དོན་ཐོག་ཏུ་འཁེལ་.

དོན་ཐོག་ཏུ་འཁེལ་ (töntɔɔ̀du kēē) vi. to be put into practice, to be applied, to be carried out, to be implemented ༶ ཚོགས་འདུར་གྲོས་ཆོད་བཞག་པ་རྣམས་དོན་ཐོག་ཏུ་འཁེལ་བར་དཀའ་ངལ་ཡོང་གི་ཡོད་པ་རེད་ (They) are facing problems concerning putting the decisions made at the meeting into practice.

དོན་ཐོག་ཏུ་འཁྱོལ་ (töntɔɔ̀du kyöö) sm. དོན་ཐོག་ཏུ་འཁེལ་.

དོན་ཐོག་ཏུ་འབབ་ (töntɔɔ̀ bab) sm. དོན་ཐོག་ཏུ་འཁེལ་.

དོན་མཐུན་ (töntün) same in meaning; synonymous.

དོན་དག (töndaà) 1. meaning ༶ ཐ་སྙད་དེའི་དོན་དག་ག་རེ་རེད་ What does that term mean? 2. purpose, cause ༶ སྤྱི་པའི་དོན་དག Common purpose. 3. matter, affair ༶ དོན་དག་ཆུང་ཆུང་ཡིན་ན་ས་གནས་སུ་ཐག་གཅོད་ཀྱི་རེད་ If it is a small matter, (we) can decide it on the spot.

དོན་དག་གི་རྐྱེན་རྩ་ (töndaàgi gyēndza) cause of a trouble/ problem/ incident; va.—བཟོ་; —སློང་ to cause/ make trouble, to create an incident/ problem ༶ མོ་ཊ་བརྡབ་སྐྱོན་བྱུང་བའི་དོན་དག་གི་རྐྱེན་རྩ་བ་ནི་ལམ་ཀ་ཆུང་དྲགས་པ་རེད་ As for the cause of the car accident, it is that the road is too small. ༶ ཟིང་ཆ་སློང་རྒྱུའི་དོན་དག་གི་རྐྱེན་རྩ་བཟོ་མཁན་ཁོ་ཚོ་རེད་ They are the main cause of the disturbance.

དོན་དག་གྲུབ་ (töndaà drub) vi. to get one's aim/ goal accomplished.

དོན་དག་སྒྲུབ་ (töndaà drub) va. to accomplish one's goal / aim.

དོན་དག་ཆེན་པོ་ (töndaà cēmbo) important matter/ issue, having substance, meaning.

དོན་དག་དོག་དོག (töndaà dogdoò) heart of the matter, the main point.

དོན་དག་མེད་པ་ (töndaà meèba) 1. meaningless, senseless, aimless. 2. without reason.

དོན་དག་ཟབ་པོ་ (töndaà sɘbbo) deep/ profound meaning.

དོན་དང་ལྡན་པ་ (töndaŋ dɛmba) meaningful, significant ༶ བསམ་འཆར་དོན་དང་ལྡན་པ་ A meaningful suggestion.

དོན་དམ་ (tön dam) 1. the main issue/ item ༶ སྐུ་ཚབ་ཚོགས་པ་དེའི་དོན་དམ་གྱི་དམིགས་ཡུལ་ནི་ཞི་ཆིངས་རྒྱག་རྒྱུ་དེ་རེད་ The main aim of the delegation is a peace treaty. 2. real, true, genuine ༶ ཁ་ཙམ་མ་ཡིན་པའི་དོན་དམ་པའི་རོགས་རམ་བྱེད་དགོས་ You must give genuine help that isn't just in words only.

དོན་དམ་དུ་ (töndamdu) factually, actually, truly, genuinely.

དོན་དུ་ (töndu) 1. for the purpose of, in order to, for ༶ རྒྱལ་ཁབ་ཀྱི་དོན་དུ་ For the country. 2. in actuality, in reality ༶ ཞི་བདེ་ཟེར་བ་མ་གཏོགས་དོན་དུ་རྒྱ་སྐྱེད་རིང་ལུགས་ཀྱི་སྲིད་ཇུས་ལག་ལེན་བྱེད་ཀྱི་ཡོད་པ་རེད་ Though (they) talk of peace, actually (they) are carrying out an expansionist policy. 3. direct discourse introducer: see དོན་, 5.

དོན་དུ་གཉེར་ (töndu ñēr) sm. དོན་གཉེར་བྱེད་.

དོན་དོད་ (töndöö) later, after awhile.

དོན་དྲང་ཚིག་ནན་ (töndraŋ tsïgnɛn) true and emphatic ༶ ཁོང་གིས་དོན་དྲང་ཚིག་ནན་གྱི་བཀའ་སློབ་གནང་སོང་ He gave advice that was true and emphatic.

དོན་དྲང་ཚིག་རྣོ་ (töndraŋ tsïgno) sm. དོན་དྲང་ཚིག་ནན་.

དོན་དྲིལ་བ་ (tön triiwɘ) concise ༶ གོ་བདེ་ལ་དོན་དྲིལ་བ་ Easy to understand and concise.

དོན་མདོར་ (töndɔr) brief, abbreviated.

དོན་མདོར་བསྟན་ (töndɔr dēn) va. to say or write in an abbreviated/ condensed form.

དོན་མདོར་བསྡུས་ (töndɔr dǖü) va. to make brief, to abbreviate.

དོན་འདོད་པ་ (töndööba) a person who makes profit, a profiteer.

དོན་འདྲ་བའི་ཚིག (töndrawɛ tsīi) synonym.

དོན་ལྡན་ (töndɛn) sm. དོན་དང་ལྡན་པ་.

དོན་ལྡན་ཡི་གི་ (töndɛn yīgi) significant/ meaningful/ substantial letter.

དོན་ལྡོག (töndɔ̄ɔ) reverse/ opposite meaning.

དོན་ལྡོག་པའི་ཚིག (töndɔ̄ɔgi tsīg) antonym.

དོན་སྡོམ་ (töndom) shung. a combination of things/ issues ༎ དེའི་འཇའ་ས་སྐྱེལ་བ་དང་ མི་བརྩི་བ་དང་ སློབ་དཔོན་པ་གདན་འདྲེན་པའི་དོན་སྡོམ་ལ་མངགས་པ་ཡིན་ (You) are sent for the combined tasks: to take a census, to deliver a title, and to invite the teacher.

དོན་བསྡུས་ (töndüü) sm. དོན་མདོར་བསྡུས་.

དོན་བསྡུས་ཚིག་རྒྱས་ (töndüü tsīggyɛɛ) lacking in content but elaborate in language.

དོན་གནད་ (tönnɛɛ) 1. an important point. 2. issue, question, matter ༎ སྐྱབས་བཅོལ་བའི་དོན་གནད་ The refugee question.

དོན་གནད་ཆུང་ཆུང་ (tönnɛɛ cūŋjuŋ) a trifle, a small matter.

དོན་གནས་ (tönnɛɛ) affairs, business ༎ རང་རེའི་དོན་གནས་ Our own affairs.

དོན་སྣོད་ (toŋnöö) internal organs.

དོན་སྣོད་སྤྱི་གསང་ (toŋnöö) an area on the 15th vertebrae where moxabustion is applied.

དོན་པོ་ (tömbo) the main reason/ purpose.

དོན་དཔོག (tön bɔ̄ɔ) va. to know/ understand based on an example.

དོན་དཔྱོད་ (tön jöö) va. to analyze/ investigate/ inspect.

དོན་སྤྱི་ (tönji) a general concept/ notion/ idea.

དོན་སྤྱི་ཙམ་དུ་འགྱུར་ (tön jīdzamdu gyur) vi. to become generalized.

དོན་སྤྱོད་ (tön jöö) va. to do useful/ helpful things.

དོན་ཕན་ (tömbɛn) benefit, advantage, use ༎ དེ་ལ་དོན་ཕན་གང་ཡང་མཐོང་གི་མི་འདུག (I) do not see any benefit at all in that.

དོན་ཕིགས་ (tön pīi) 1. va. to know/ understand/ have knowledge of (sth.) completely. 2. vi. to hit the nail on the head, to be right on target.

དོན་ཕྲན་ཞིབ་བཤད་ (töndrɛn shībshɛɛ) enumeration of all details, counting all the little things.

དོན་བྱ་ (tönja) matters.

དོན་བྱེད་ (tönjeè) dealing with or working for the good of others, affairs ༎ མི་རིགས་དོན་བྱེད་ཨུ་ཡོན་ལྷན་ཁང་ The nationalities affairs commission.

དོན་བྱེད་ཁང་ (tönjeègaŋ) office, bureau, chancellery, commission.

དོན་བྱེད་ཁྲུའུ་ (tönjeè trū) tib.ch. sm. དོན་བྱེད་ཁང་.

དོན་བྱེད་ནུས་པ་ (tönjeè nǖübɔ) having the ability or being equipped to do or perform a duty.

དོན་བྱེད་ཨུ་ཡོན་ (tönjeè ūyün) executive officers, administrative officials.

དོན་འབུད་ (tönbüü) shung. being expelled/ thrown out ༎ དགྲ་ཕྱོགས་ལ་སློ་ཁ་ཕྱིར་གཏད་ཀྱིས་དོན་འབུད་དུ་སོང་བ་ Being a traitor, he was expelled (from the country).

དོན་འབྲས་ (töndrɛɛ) success, achievement, result, outcome ༎ ལོ་མང་དཀའ་བ་སྤྱད་པའི་དོན་འབྲས་ The results of many years of hardship.

དོན་འབྲེལ་ (töndrel) shung. according to what was said or written ༎ ས་ཞིང་རང་བདག་ཚོག་པའི་བཀའ་ཐམ་ལག་ཁྱེར་དོན་འབྲེལ་ཡང་ In accordance with the land tenure document that says he can own the field.

དོན་སྦྱོར་ (tönjɔɔ) sm. དོན་གྱི་འཇུག་ཚུལ་.

དོན་མ་གོ་ (tön mago) sb. who doesn't understand the meaning of things, sb. who speaks and acts blindly/ thoughtlessly.

དོན་མང་རྙོག་ཆེ་ (tönmaŋ ñogce) involving many thing and being very complicated.

དོན་མང་བའི་མིང་ (tönmaŋwɛ miŋ) a word with many different meanings.

དོན་མེད་ (tönmeè) 1. meaningless, useless, aimless, without purpose; vi.—དུ་འགྲོ་; —ཆགས་ to become meaningless, to go to waste, to become useless ༎ མ་ཉན་ན་སྐད་ཆ་བཤད་ཀྱང་དོན་མེད་རེད་ It's meaningless to talk if (one) doesn't listen. 2. without reason ༎ དོན་མེད་ཁོང་ཁྲོ་ཟ་ག་མ་རེད་ He is not angry without reason. ༎ ང་ཚོས་དཀའ་ལས་བརྒྱབ་པ་དོན་མེད་དུ་འགྲོ་གི་མ་རེད་ Our hard work will not go to waste. ༎ ལ་ལ་ཁ་བ་མེད་པར་ཀླུང་ལ་བ་མོ་ཡོང་དོན་མེད་ If there is no snow on the mountains there is no reason for frost to come in the valley.

དོན་མེད་ཁ་བདར་ (tönmeè kādar) talking aimlessly, talking without purpose/ reason.

དོན་མེད་གྲོས་སྣ་ (tönmeè trööna) a topic that has no substance.

དོན་མེད་དགོས་མེད་ (tönmeè gööomeè) without reason or need ༎ དོན་མེད་དགོས་མེད་ལ་རྙོག་དྲ་མ་ཤོད་ Don't make trouble for no reason.

དོན་མེད་སྣད་དཀྲིས་ (tönmeè ñɛ̄ndri) blaming sb. for no reason; va.—བྱེད་.

དོན་མེད་གཏམ་སྙིང་ (tönmeè dāmñiŋ) meaningless talk.

དོན་མེད་སྟོང་ཟད་ (tönmeè dōŋsɛɛ) spending (one's life) aimlessly, wasting (one's life).

དོན་མེད་དོན་འཚོལ་ (tönmeè töndzöö) seeking/ asking/ looking for trouble without reason.

དོན་མེད་དོགས་ཚོམ་ (tönmeè tɔgdzom) having doubts/ suspicions/ hesitation for no reason.

དོན་མེད་ནར་འགྱང་ (tönmeè nargyaŋ) dilly dallying/ delaying for no reason.

དོན་མེད་ཅི་མེད་ (tönmeè jīmeè) without any reason ༎ ཁོས་ང་ལ་དོན་མེད་ཅི་མེད་ལ་གཤེ་གཤེ་བཏང་བྱུང་ He scolded me without any reason.

དོན་མེད་འཕྱུང་གཡོ་ (tönmeè pūŋyo) shung. instigating and causing trouble without any reason.

དོན་མེད་རྩོད་གླེང་ (tönmeè dzöölɔŋ) unprovoked quarrel, quarreling for no reason.

དོན་མེད་ཚིག་སྐམ་ (tönmeè tsīggam) meaningless comment/ speech.

དོན་མེད་ཟད་པོ་ (tönmeè sɛ̄ɛbo) waste for no reason.

དོན་སྨིན་ (tönmin) sm. དོན་འབྲས་.

དོན་སྨིན་བདེ་རིགས་མི་འདུག (tönmin derii minduù) shung. it is not easy to fulfill your request ༎ འདི་སྐོར་གཞན་གྱི་མིག་འདྲེན་བྱ་ཡུལ་དུ་འགྱུར་གཞིས་ཆེན་པས་ དོན་སྨིན་བདེ་རིགས་མི་འདུག It is not easy to fulfill your request because it may cause other people to follow the example.

དོན་སྨྲ་ (tön mā) va. to give/ tell a reason.

དོན་གཙོ་བོ་ (tön dzōwo) sm. དོན་སྙིང་.

དོན་ཙ་ (töndza) point, meaning ༎ དོན་ཙ་ཆུང་ཚགས་ A small point.

དོན་ཙ་མེད་པ་ (töndza meèba) having no aim/ point/ purpose.

དོན་ཚང་ (töndzaŋ) shung. accomplishing (one's task).

དོན་ཚང་འཕྲུགས་མེད་ (töndzaŋ cūgmeè) shung. accomplishing (one's task) without mistakes.

དོན་ཚང་ཚུལ་བཞིན་སྤྱོད་ (töndzaŋ tsǖüshin jöö) shung. to accomplish (one's task) correctly.

དོན་ཚན་ (töndzɛn) article, clause, point, item ༎ ཆིངས་ཡིག་དོན་ཚན་བཅུ་བདུན་ The Seventeen Point Agreement (of 1951).

དོན་མཚོན་རི་མོ་ (töndzön) diagram, illustration.

དོན་ཞགས་ (tönshag) sm. དོན་ཡོད་ཞགས་པ་.

དོན་གཞན་ (tönshɛn) other matters.

དོན་ཟབ་གོ་སླ་ (tönsab kola) profound but easy to understand.

དོན་ཟབ་ཚིག་གསལ་ (tönsab tsīgsɛl) profound content with clear wording.

དོན་བཟང་ (tö̱nsaŋ) good news.

དོན་བཟང་ཚིག་བཟང་ (tö̱nsaŋ tsīgsaŋ) good content/ meaning and a good style of wording.

དོན་ཡོད་ (tönyöö) sm. དོན་དང་ལྡན་པ་.

དོན་ཡོད་འབྲས་བུ་ (tönyöö drɛ̱ɛ̀bu) 1. a good result, sth. that was achieved well. 2. a Tibetan herbal medicine.

དོན་ཡོད་ཞགས་པ་ (tö̱nyöö sha̱gba) a mythical precious gem.

དོན་གླིང་དང་རྫོགས་སླ་ (tönliŋdaŋ dɔ̄gla) sm. དོན་ཟབ་གོ་སླ་.

དོན་ལ་ (tö̱nla) sm. དོན་དུ་.

དོན་ལ་འཛུག་ (tö̱nla ju̱ù) va. to hit the nail on the head, to be right on target.

དོན་ལ་རྟོན་ (tö̱nla dōn) va. to trust/ believe in sth.

དོན་ལ་གནས་ (tö̱nla nɛ̄ɛ̀) 1. va. to fit in/ conform / be in accord with. 2. va. to do what sb. says.

དོན་ལ་ཕིགས་ (tö̱nla piì) sm. དོན་ཕིགས་.

དོན་སོན་ (tönsön) sm. དོན་སྨིན་.

དོན་གསལ་ (tö̱nsɛl) clear purpose/ aim; clear meaning/ content.

དོན་གསལ་ཚིག་བདེ་ (tönsɛl tsīgde) clear meaning and good wording.

དོན་གསལ་ཚིག་གསལ་ (tönsɛl tsīgsɛl) clear meaning or content and clear wording.

དོམ་ (to̱m) 1. bear. 2. loan.

དོམ་དཀར་པོ་ (to̱m gārbo) polar bear.

དོམ་ཁྲ་ (to̱mdra) panda bear.

དོམ་མཁྲིས་ (to̱m triì) bear's gallbladder.

དོམ་ཆགས་བུ་ལོན་ (to̱mjaà pu̱lön) 1. an old debt. 2. a debt, a loan.

དོམ་ཉོ་ (to̱mño) buying on credit.

དོམ་དོམ་ (to̱mdom) red tassel put on the neck of horses of high ranking tt. officials.

དོམ་དོམ་ཉིས་བརྩེགས་ (to̱mdom ñiìdzeg) the two red tassels put on the neck of horse's of tt. official of the 4th rank and higher.

དོམ་ནག་ (tomnaà) 1. brown bear. 2. black dog with a white patch on its chest.

དོམ་ཕྲུག་ (tomdruù) bear cub.

དོམ་ཚང་ (to̱mdzaŋ) bear den/ lair/ cave.

དོམ་ར་ (to̱mra) a bear skin band worn with the fur hanging over the eyes to prevent snow blindness.

དོམ་ལེན་ (to̱m le̱n) va. to take a loan, to borrow.

དོམ་སུག་ (to̱msug) bear's paw.

དོམ་གསོས་རྒྱག་ (to̱msöö gya̱à) va. to fatten an animal (usu. a pig) before slaughtering.

དོར་ (tɔ̱r) 1. p. of འདོར་. 2. a pair of plow animals ¶ གླང་དོར་གཉིས་ Two pairs of plowing bullocks. 3. pants, trousers.

དོར་ཁ་རྫི་ (tɔ̱rgə dzī) va. to measure land according to the amount of land a pair of plow animals can plow in one day.

དོར་ཁུག་ (tɔ̱rguù) a kind of leggings used to protect one's pants and knees.

དོར་གྲངས་ (tɔ̱rdraŋ) calculating the size of a field by the number of pairs of animals it takes to plow it.

དོར་སྐབ་ (tɔ̱rgəb) bottom of a pant leg.

དོར་རྟ་ (tɔ̱rda) the slit (crotch) part of Tibetan pants.

དོར་སྟབས་ (tɔ̱rdəb) manner/ style/ way of walking.

དོར་ཐག་ (tɔ̱rdaà) belt.

དོར་ཐུང་ (tɔ̱rduŋ) short pants, underpants.

དོར་སྡེ་ (tɔ̱rde) a group or unit of plowing animals.

དོར་བ་ (tɔ̱rwa) minus (in math).

དོར་མ་ (tɔ̱rma) pants, trousers.

དོར་མ་ཁ་ཕྱེ་མ་ (tɔ̱rma kācema) open seat/ crotch pants.

དོར་མ་སྤུ་མ་ (tɔ̱rma būmə) flannel sweatpants, flannel underwear.

དོར་མའི་སྐེད་ཁོར་ (tɔ̱rmɛ gēègɔɔ) waistband of pants.

དོར་མའི་ཁ་ཁོར་ (tɔ̱rmɛ kāgɔɔ) sm. དོར་མའི་སྐེད་ཁོར་.

དོར་མའི་སྐབ་ (tɔ̱rmɛ gə̱b) sm. དོར་སྐབ་.

དོར་མའི་སྐབ་ཆ་ (tɔ̱rmɛ gə̱bja) sm. དོར་སྐབ་.

དོར་མའི་རྟ་ (tɔ̱rmɛ dā) sm. དོར་རྟ་.

དོར་མའི་འཛབས་ (tɔ̱rmɛ dzə̱b) the length of trouser legs ¶ ངའི་དོར་མའི་འཛབས་ཐུང་དྲགས་བཞག My pants are too short.

དོར་རིང་ (tɔ̱rriŋ) long pants.

དོར་ལྷུག་མ་ (tɔ̱r lhūgmə) pants (not tucked in boots).

དོལ་ (tö̱ö) sm. དོལ་བུ་.

དོལ་རྒྱ་ (töögya) sm. དོལ་བུ་.

དོལ་གཅོད་ (tö̱ö jöö) va. to decide without doubt/ hesitation.

དོལ་ཆོད་ (tö̱ö cöö) vi. to do sth. with determination ¶ དོལ་ཆོད་དུ་སློབ་སྦྱོང་བྱེད་ཀྱི་ཡོད་པ་རེད་ (They) studied with determination.

དོལ་བུ་ (töö̱bu) fishing net, net used as a trap; va.—འགྲིགས་ to fling a net to catch sth. (e.g., when fishing).

དོལ་ཤོར་ཉ་མོ་ (töö̱shɔɔ ñamo) running quickly [Lit. a fish escaping from the net].

དོས་ (tö̱ö) a load; va.—རྒྱག to make up/ pack a load.

དོས་སྐྱེལ་ (töö̱gyee) transporting goods; va. དོས་སྐྱེལ་; —བྱེད་ ¶ དོས་སྐྱེལ་གནམ་གྲུ་ Transport plane.

དོས་ཁང་ (töö̱gaŋ) storehouse, warehouse.

དོས་ཁལ་ (töö̱gɛɛ) loading a pack animal; va.—བྱེད་ ¶ བལ་དོ་དོས་འགེལ་མགྱོགས་པོ་བྱས་པ་རེད་ The bale of wool was loaded on the animal quickly.

དོས་འཁོར་ (töö̱gɔɔ) abbr. of དོས་འདྲེན་རླངས་འཁོར་.

དོས་འགེལ་ (töö̱ ge̱e) va. to load, to fix a load on sb.

དོས་རྒྱག་ (töö̱ gya̱à) va. to make/ pack a load.

དོས་རྒྱབ་པ་ (töö̱ gyə̱bbə) muleteer, people who accompany transport animals.

དོས་ཆད་ (töö̱jɛɛ̀) alone, singly.

དོས་དྲག་པོ་ (töö̱ tra̱gbo) serious, severe (for illness).

དོས་འདེད་པ་ (töö̱ teèba) sm. དོས་རྒྱབ་པ་.

དོས་འདྲེན་ (töö̱ dre̱n) transporting/ trucking/ shipping goods; va.—བྱེད་ to transport/ ship goods.

དོས་འདྲེན་འཁོར་ལོ་ (tö̱ndren kɔ̄ɔlo) sm. དོས་འདྲེན་རླངས་འཁོར་.

དོས་འདྲེན་རླངས་འཁོར་ (tö̱ndren lāŋgɔɔ) truck, lorry.

དོས་པ་ (töö̱ba) coolie, sb. who carries loads.

དོས་པོ་ (töö̱bo) sm. དོ་པོ་.

དོས་པོ་འཁྱེར་མཁན་ (töö̱bo kyerñɛn) sm. དོས་པ་.

དོས་དཔོན་ (töö̱bön) caravan leader, person in charge of a caravan of transport animals.

དོས་ཚད་ (töö̱dzɛɛ̀) weight of a load/ pack/ bundle.

དོས་ར་ (töö̱ra) a loading or unloading place, a loading dock.

དོས་སིལ་ (töö̱sil) goods that have been taken from a load to sell individually.

དོས་སིལ་ཚོང་ཟོག་ (töö̱sil tsōŋsɔɔ̀) retail commodities/ items.

དྭ་གོད་ (ta̱göö) a type of Tibetan herbal medicine.

དྭ་ལྗགས་ (ta̱jaà) one of the 8 figures used in astrological divining.

དྭ་ཕྲུག་ (tə̱druù) orphan.

དྭ་ཕྲུག་ཁང་ (tə̱druùgaŋ) orphanage.

དྭ་ཕྲུག་ཁ་སེར་ (tə̱druù kāsee) young orphan.

དྭ་ཕྲུག་སློབ་གྲྭ་ (tə̱druù lōbdra) school for orphans.

དྭ་བ་ (ta̱wa) 1. a type of Tibetan liquid medicine. 2. sm. རྒྱ་སྒྲོ་བ་.

དྭ་ལིས་ (ta̱lii) a herbal medicine made from azaleas.

དྭགས་ཀོང་ (ta̱goŋ) shung. abbr. of དྭགས་པོ་ and ཀོང་པོ་.

དྭགས་ཀོང་སྤྱི་ཁྱབ་ (ta̱goŋ jīgyəb) shung. the governor general of དྭགས་ཀོང་ in tt.

དྭགས་པོ་ (ta̱gbo) a large region in SE Tibet.

དྭགས་པོ་གྲྭ་ཚང་ (tə̱druù tra̱dzaŋ) a Gelugpa monastery in དྭགས་པོ་.

དྭགས་ཕོར་ (ta̱gbɔɔ) wooden bowls made in དྭགས་པོ་.

དྭགས་ཤོག་ (ta̱gshog) paper made in དྭགས་པོ་.

དྭགས་སླེའུ་ (ta̱g le̱) a type of tightly woven wool from དྭགས་པོ་ that is used as a groundcloth/ blanket/ pancho.

དྭངས་ (ta̱ŋ) 1. vi. to become clear. ¶ ཆུ་དེ་མ་འཁྲུགས་

པར་ཡུད་ཙམ་བཞག་ན་དྭངས་ཀྱི་རེད་ If (you) leave the water without disturbing it for awhile it will become clear. 2. vi. to recover (from illness), to get well ¶ སྐུ་གཞི་ཡག་པོ་དྭངས་འདུག He has recovered well. 3. sm. འདང་.

དྭངས་ཀྲ་ (ta̱ŋdra) clear, bright, shinny.

དྭངས་ཁྲག (ta̱ŋdraà) serum.

དྭངས་ཁྲུང་ཁྲུང་ (ta̱ŋ trūŋdruŋ) clear, transparent.

དྭངས་སྒྲ་ (ta̱ŋdra) a voiceless sound (in linguistics).

དྭངས་ལྕགས་ (ta̱ŋjaà) tempered steel.

དྭངས་ཆུ་ (ta̱ŋju) clear water.

དྭངས་སྙིགས་འབྱེད་ (ta̱ŋñig cḛè) va. to let sediment settle so that the water will be clear.

དྭངས་དོད་ (ta̱ŋdöö) taking great care about one's food/ clothes/ appearance, fastidious; va.—བྱེད་.

དྭངས་དོད་ཚ་པོ་ (ta̱ŋdöö tsābo) someone who takes great care about his or her food/ clothes/ appearance, a fastidiously stylish person; va.—བྱེད་.

དྭངས་པོ་ (ta̱ŋbo) clear; va.—བཟོ་ to make clear.

དྭངས་ཐྲུམ་ཐྲུམ་ (ta̱ŋ trūmdrum) sm. དྭངས་ཁྲུམ་ཁྲུམ་.

དྭངས་བྱེད་སྨན་རྫས་ (ta̱ŋjeè mēndzɛɛ̀) a clarificant.

དྭངས་མ་ (ta̱ŋma) 1. sm. དྭངས་པོ་. 2. main, foremost, chief ¶ དགྲའི་དྭངས་མ་ The main enemy. 3. sperm.

དྭངས་གཙང་ (ta̱ŋdzaŋ) clean and pure ¶ ཆུ་དྭངས་གཙང་ Water that is clear and pure.

དྭངས་རྩེ་ (ta̱ŋdze) the best, the top ¶ དཔའ་བོ་དྭངས་རྩེ་ The best hero.

དྭངས་མ་ཟུང་སྦྱོར་ (ta̱ŋma su̱ŋjɔɔ) male sperm and female egg joining/ connecting.

དྭངས་སྨན་ (ta̱ŋmɛn) sm. དྭངས་རྫས་.

དྭངས་རྫས་ (ta̱ŋdzɛɛ̀) a clarificant.

དྭངས་རུ་འགྲོ་ (ta̱ŋru dro̱) sm.* དྭངས་སུ་འགྲོ་.

དྭངས་ཤིང་གཙང་བ་ (ta̱ŋsiŋ dzāŋwa) sm. དྭངས་གཙང་.

དྭངས་ཤེལ་ (ta̱ŋshel) clean/ clear glass window. 2. mirror, crystal.

དྭངས་ཤེལ་མེ་ལོང་ (ta̱ŋshel me̱loŋ) name of a penal code in the Tibetan judicial system.

དྭངས་ཤོས་ (ta̱ŋshöö) clearest.

དྭངས་སུ་འགྲོ་ (ta̱ŋsu dro̱) vi. to become clear. 2. vi. to become better (from an illness).

དྭངས་སང་ (ta̱ŋsaŋ) clever, smart, clearheaded ¶ བུ་མོའི་མག་པ་དེ་མི་དྭངས་སང་ཞིག་ཡིན་ཙང་ལས་ཀ་གང་ཡང་བྱེད་ཐུབ་ཀྱི་འདུག The girl's husband is very clever and can do all kinds of work.

དྭངས་སིང་ངེ་བ་ (ta̱ŋ sīŋŋewa) 1. clear and clean. 2. clear in thought.

དྭངས་སིངས་འབྱེད་ (tāŋsiŋ cḛè) sm. དྭངས་སྙིགས་འབྱེད་.

དྭངས་གསལ་ (ta̱ŋsel) clear and bright, clean, pure ¶ དྭངས་གསལ་ཆུ་ Water that is clear.

དྭངས་གསལ་གྱི་གཟུགས་ཅན་ (ta̱ŋselgi su̱gjɛn) transparent figure.

དྭངས་གསལ་དུས་ཚིགས་ (ta̱ŋsel dü̱üdzig) once a year occurrence (in China) when paper money is burnt for the deceased.

དྭངས་བསིལ་ (ta̱ŋsil) cool and refreshing, cool and clear.

ཌ་མ་རུ་ (da̱maru) a small (two-faced) hand drum.

ཌ་རུ་ (də̱ru) sm. ཌ་མ་རུ་.

ཌ་རུ་མགོ་ (də̱rugo) cunning, tricky, two-faced.

ཌབ་འཛིན་ (də̱mdzin) eng.tib. a draft (check) ¶ དངུལ་ཁང་ཌབ་འཛིན་ Bank draft.

ཌམ་འཛར་ (də̱mdzar) a silk tassle attached to a damaru drum.

ཌི་སི་ཀོ་ཞབས་བྲོ་འཁྲབ་ཁང་ (di̱sigo shə̱bdro drə̄bgaŋ) eng.tib. disco bar/ dance hall.

ཌོག་ཌར་ (do̱gdɔr) eng. doctor.

ཌོག་ལར་ (do̱glar) eng. dollar (U.S.).

དྲ་ (tra̱) 1. f. of འདྲ་. 2. net, network, grate, lattice.

དྲ་ཀང་ (traga̱ŋ) the smaller frames within a larger window frame.

དྲ་བསྐོར་ (tra̱gɔɔ) wire/ net fencing; va.—བཟོ་ to put wire/ net fencing around some area.

དྲ་ཁེབས་ (tra̱geb) net covering.

དྲ་གྲི་ (tra̱dri) a cutter, a blade/ knife.

དྲ་འགོ་ཉེན་མཁན་ (tra̱go dēññɛn) person who holds the end of paper, leather, etc. when it is being cut.

དྲ་རྒྱ་ (tra̱gya) trap made of net.

དྲ་སྒང་ (tra̱gaŋ) tennis ¶ དྲ་སྒང་ལྷན་ཚོགས་ Tennis Association.

དྲ་སྒྱེ་ (tra̱gye) a net or mesh pouch/ bag.

དྲ་དྲུབ་ (tra̱ tru̱b) cutting and sewing of clothing, tailoring; va.—བྱེད་ to cut and sew clothing, to tailor.

དྲ་གདན་ (tra̱dɛn) wooden board on which sth. is cut.

དྲ་པང་ (tra̱baŋ) sm. དྲ་གདན་.

དྲ་སྤྱད་ (tra̱jɛɛ̀) cutting implements, cutting tools.

དྲ་ཕད་ (tra̱pɛɛ̀) sm. དྲ་སྒྱེ་.

དྲ་ཕྱེད་ (tra̱ceè) 1. painting the design of fringes (ཤམ་བུ་) on walls just below the ceiling. 2. religious ornaments made of brocade and silk that are used to decorate beams.

དྲ་བ་ (tra̱wa) 1. a net, a trap. ¶ ཉ་དྲ་བ་གང་ A net full of fish. 2. network ¶ ཚོང་ལས་དྲ་བ་ Commercial/ trade network.

དྲ་བ་དྲ་ཕྱེད་ (tra̱wa tra̱ceè) sm. དྲ་ཕྱེད་.

དྲ་མ་ (tra̱ma) 1. good, excellent ¶ ཁོས་ལས་ཀ་དྲ་མ་ཞིག་བྱས་སོང་ He did an excellent job. 2. sm. ཁྲ་མ་.

དྲ་མིག (trə̱mii) the openings in net/ mesh. 2. window opening.

དྲ་མིག་པོ་ལོ་ (trə̱mii bōlo) tennis; va.—རྒྱག.

དྲ་ལྷུག་སྤོ་ལོ་ (trə̱luù bōlo) basketball; va.—རྒྱག.

དྲ་ཚགས་ (tra̱dzaà) sifter.

དྲ་ཡོལ་ (tra̱yöö) curtain made of net/ netting.

དྲག (tra̱à) 1. vi. to get well, to recover (from an illness) ¶ ཁོ་ནད་དྲག་པ་རེད་ He recovered from his illness. 2. abbr. of དྲག་པོ་. 3. better ¶ ད་ག་རེ་བྱས་ན་དྲག་གི་རེད་ What is better to do now?

དྲག་དཀྱུས་ (trə̱ggyüü) better and common, higher and lower ¶ སྡོད་འབངས་དྲག་དཀྱུས་ཚང་མས་ཤེས་ཀྱི་ཡོད་པ་རེད་ People from all strata (low and high) know it.

དྲག་སྐྱུགས་ (trə̱ggyuù) a medicine to induce vomiting.

དྲག་སྐྱེད་ (tra̱àgyeè) vi. to get better, to recover/ recuperate.

དྲག་སྐྱོད་ (tra̱àgyöö) radical ¶ དྲག་སྐྱོད་ཤོག་ཁག Radical groups.

དྲག་བསྐྱོད་ (tra̱àgyöö) sm. དྲག་སྐྱོད་.

དྲག་ག (tra̱ga) sm. དྲག་པ་, 1.

དྲག་གོས་ (tra̱àgöö) military uniform.

དྲག་གྲས་ (tra̱gdrɛɛ̀) better/ higher class ¶ གཡོག་པོ་དྲག་གྲས་ The better class of servants.

དྲག་རྒོལ་ (tra̱ggöö) violent uprising, militant or violent opposition; attacking violently; va.—བྱེད་.

དྲག་རྒོལ་གནམ་གྲུ་ (tra̱ggöö nəmdru) attack/ fighter plane.

དྲག་སྒྲུབ་ (tra̱gdrub) 1. working with great urgency; va.—བྱེད་ ¶ ནད་པ་རྨས་པ་ཚོར་ལྟ་སྐྱོང་གི་མཐུན་རྐྱེན་དྲག་སྒྲུབ་བྱས་པ་རེད་ (They) urgently sought means for taking care of the sick and the wounded. 2. casting a spell/ curse.

དྲག་བསྒྲུགས་ (tra̱gdruù) selecting/ picking out the best; va.—བྱེད་; —རྒྱག to select/ pick out the best ¶ ཞིང་པས་སོན་དྲག་བསྒྲུགས་བརྒྱབ་པ་རེད་ The farmers picked out the best seeds (for sowing).

དྲག་སྔགས་ (tra̱gŋaà) an evil spell/ curse; va.—རྒྱག.

དྲག་གཅོད་ (tra̱gjöö) torture, physical force in punishment/ trial/ interrogation; va. —བྱེད་ ¶ ཞུ་བ་ལེན་དུས་དྲག་གཅོད་མ་བྱས་ན་ཡག་གི་རེད་ When interrogating it is better not to use torture.

དྲག་བཅོས་ (tra̱gjöö) traditional Tibetan medical treatments that use harsh means such as moxabustion and blood draining; va.—བྱེད་.

དྲག་ཆར་ (tra̱gjar) thunderstorm, rainstorm; vi.—གཏོང to have/ get a thunderstorm/ rainstorm; va.—བྱེད་ to treat harshly, to use physical force.

དྲག་ཆར་ཀླུང་འཚུབ་ (tragjar lūŋdzəb) a violent/ raging thunderstorm.

དྲག་ཆས་ (tragjɛɛ̀) 1. arms, weapons; va.—སྤྲས་ to arm. 2. military uniform.

དྲག་ཆས་ཅན་ (tragjɛɛ̀jɛn) armed.

དྲག་ཆས་ཆ་ཚང་ (tragjɛɛ̀ cādzaŋ) fully armed.

དྲག་ཆས་ཕུའུ་ (tragjɛɛ̀ bū) tib.ch. department of the armed forces.

དྲག་ཆས་དཔུང་སྡེ་ (tragjɛɛ̀ būŋde) army, an armed force.

དྲག་ཆས་སྤྲས་ (tragjɛɛ̀ drɛɛ̀) va. to arm ¶ མའོ་ཙེ་ཏུང་གི་དགོངས་པས་དྲག་ཆས་སྤྲས་པའི་དཔའ་བོ་ Heroes armed with Mao's thoughts.

དྲག་ཆས་འབུལ་ (tragjɛɛ̀ büü) va. to hand over weapons, to lay down one's arms.

དྲག་ཆས་ལེན་ (tragjɛɛ̀ len) va. to disarm ¶ བཅིངས་བཀྲོལ་དམག་མིས་བོད་དམག་ཚོའི་དྲག་ཆས་བླངས་པ་རེད་ The People's Liberation Army disarmed the Tibetan army.

དྲག་མཆོང་ (tragjoŋ) a fierce charge/ attack; va.—བྱེད་.

དྲག་ཇུས་ (tragjüü) military strategy.

དྲག་འཇུན་ (tragjün) restricting/ controlling by force or strict discipline and rules; va.—བྱེད་.

དྲག་རྗེས་ནད་རོ་ (tragjeè nɛ̀ɛro) looking weak/ sickly after a prolonged illness.

དྲག་སྙེག་ (tragñeg) fierce pursuit; hot pursuit.

དྲག་ཏུ་ (tragdu) violently, militantly, fiercely ¶ དྲག་ཏུ་འབབ་པའི་ཆུ་བོ་ A violently flowing river. ¶ ཕྱོགས་གཉིས་དྲག་ཏུ་འཐབ་པའི་སྐབས་ When the two sides fought violently.

དྲག་ཏུ་རྒྱུག་ (tragdu gyuù) 1. va. gallop. 2. vi. to gush/ flow violently (for a river, stream).

དྲག་གཏུམ་ (tragdum) harsh/ fierce/ menacing in appearance.

དྲག་གཏོར་ (tragdɔɔ) smashing, breaking up, destroying (violently).

དྲག་འཐབ་ (tragtəb) fierce/ intense fighting, armed battle/ struggle; va.—བྱེད་.

དྲག་དལ་ (trag tɛɛ) abbr. of harsh/ fierce and gentle/ mild.

དྲག་འདེད་ (tragdeè) sm. དྲག་སྙེག.

དྲག་འདེམས་ (tragdem) sm. དྲག་བསྡུགས་.

དྲག་དེག་ (tragdeg) sm. དྲག་དུང་.

དྲག་དུག་ཅན་གྱི་སྨན་ (tragdugjɛngi mɛ̄n) strong drug/ medicine.

དྲག་དུང་ (trāgduŋ) hitting or striking a powerful/ telling blow; va.—བྱེད་.

དྲག་སྟེབས་ (tragdeb) associating with higher officials (has a negative connotation); va.—བྱེད་ ¶ Because that person likes to always associate with the higher officials, people don't like him.

དྲག་བདུང་ (tragduŋ) sm. དྲག་དུང་.

དྲག་ནད་ (tragnɛɛ̀) a severe/ serious illness.

དྲག་གནོན་ (tragnön) suppressing, repressing, oppressing; va.—བྱེད་ ¶ སེར་བྱེས་གྲྭ་ཚང་ནས་ལུགས་མཐུན་མ་ཞུས་ཚེ་དྲག་གནོན་བྱ་རྩིས་བྱས་སོང་ They plan to militarily suppress Sera Jey College if it doesn't abide by the law.

དྲག་པ་ (tragba) 1. better, nicer ¶ གཡོག་པོ་དྲག་པ་ཞིག་རྙེད་ཁག་པོ་འདུག It is hard to find a better servant. 2. powerful, severe.

དྲག་པ་ནི་མི་རག ཞན་པ་ནི་མི་དགའ་ (tragbani mirag shɛmbani miga) being thwarted/ unsuccessful in finding a spouse ¶ བུ་མོ་དེ་རང་མག་པ་དྲག་པ་ནི་མི་རག ཞན་པ་ནི་མི་དགའ་བ་བྱས་ནས་ད་ཆ་ལོ་སུམ་ཅུ་སོ་གྲངས་ལ་སླེབས་ཡོད་པ་རེད་ That girl has reached her thirties without finding a husband (couldn't get the better ones and didn't like the poorer ones). [Lit. not getting sth. better and not wanting sth. inferior].

དྲག་པོ་ (tragbo) 1. violent, fierce, militant; serious, severe ¶ རྣམ་པ་དྲག་པོ་ Violent appearance. ¶ ན་ཚ་དྲག་པོ་ Serious illness. ¶ ཉེས་ཆད་དྲག་པོ་ Severe punishment. 2. armed, military ¶ དྲག་པོའི་འཐབ་རྩོད་ Armed struggle. ¶ དྲག་པོའི་སྲིད་གཞུང་ Military goverment.

དྲག་པོ་མངོན་སྤྱོད་ (tragbo ŋönjöö) casting spells/ curses; va.—བྱེད་.

དྲག་པོའི་གོ་མཚོན་ (tragbö godzön) military arms/ weapons.

དྲག་པོའི་གྱེན་ལངས་ (tragbö gyenlaŋ) armed uprising/ rebellion.

དྲག་པོའི་སྟོབས་ཤུགས་ (tragbö dōbshuù) military power.

དྲག་པོའི་ཐེ་གཏོགས་ (tragbö tēdoò) armed intervention.

དྲག་པོའི་གནས་གཞི་ (tragbö nɛ̄ɛ̀shi) military base/ installation.

དྲག་པོའི་དཔོན་པོ་ (tragbö bõmbo) military leader.

དྲག་པོའིདཔོན་རིགས་ (tragbö bõnrig) military leaders.

དྲག་པོའི་དཔྱད་ (tragbö jɛɛ̀) va. to perform surgery.

དྲག་པོའི་སྤྱོད་པ་ (tragbö jööba) harsh/ brutal/ fierce behavior or personality.

དྲག་པོའི་སྦྱིན་སྲེག (tragbö jinseg) one of the ritual rites of exorcism.

དྲག་པོའི་གཞིར་ (tragbö sher) arc. severe punishment.

དྲག་པོའི་འོས་ལངས་ (tragbö wöölaŋ) armed uprising/ rebellion.

དྲག་པོའི་ལས་ (tragbö lɛɛ̀) 1. sm. དྲག་པོ་མངོན་སྤྱོད་. 2. violent acts.

དྲག་པོའི་ལས་དོན་ (tragbö lɛ̀ɛdön) military affairs.

དྲག་པོའི་སྲིད་གཞུང་ (tragbö sīishuŋ) military government.

དྲག་པོར་འགྱུར་ (tragbor gyur) vi. to become radical/ militant.

དྲག་པོར་སྦྱོང་ (tragbɔr joŋ) 1. va. to use a strong laxative. 2. va. to engage in military exercises. 3. va. to study studiously.

དྲག་པོས་གཞུང་འཛིན་ (tragböö shuŋdzin) military takeover of a government; va.—བྱེད་ ¶ ཐེངས་གཉིས་དྲག་པོས་གཞུང་འཛིན་བྱས་པ་རེད་ (They) have had military takeovers of the government two times.

དྲག་དཔུང་ (tragbuŋ) armed forces, army ¶ མི་དམངས་དྲག་དཔུང་ People's armed forces.

དྲག་དཔོན་ (tragbön) military officials/ officers.

དྲག་སྤྱོད་ (tragjöö) violent/ militant behavior; va.—བྱེད་ ¶ གཞུང་ལ་ངོ་རྒོལ་བྱ་རྒྱུར་དྲག་སྤྱོད་བྱས་ན་ཡག་པོ་ཡོང་གི་མ་རེད་ In opposing the government, it isn't good to use violent means.

དྲག་སྤྱོད་སྤོང་བ་ (tragjöö bōŋwa) nonviolent ¶ དྲག་སྤྱོད་སྤོང་བའི་སྤྱི་ཚོགས་རིང་ལུགས་ Nonviolent socialism.

དྲག་སྤྲས་ཕུའུ་ (tragjɛɛ̀ būŋde) sm. དྲག་ཆས་ཕུའུ་.

དྲག་འབབ་ཆུ་རྒྱུན་ (tragbəb cūgyün) rapids, fast flowing water.

དྲག་མོ་ (tragmo) 1. a fierce woman. 2. a fierce female deity.

དྲག་དམག་ (tragmaà) armed forces, troops, soldiers.

དྲག་བཙན་ (tragdzɛn) tyrannical, harsh, brutal.

དྲག་བཙན་ལྡུག་འཁུར་ (tragdzɛn dāggur) sm. ཆེ་བཙན་ཁ་འཁུར་.

དྲག་རྩལ་ (tragdzɛɛ) combat skills, martial skills or arts ¶ དྲག་རྩལ་སྦྱོང་བརྡར་ Training in the martial arts.

དྲག་རྩལ་པ་ (trəgdzɛɛba) sb. who does martial arts.

དྲག་རྩལ་སློབ་གྲྭ་ (trəgdzɛɛ lōbdra) martial arts school.

དྲག་རྩུབ་ (trəgdzub) harsh, brutal, cruel, ruthless; va.—བྱེད་ ¶ གཞིས་སྡོད་དེས་མི་སེར་ལ་དྲག་རྩུབ་བྱེད་ཀྱི་ཡོད་པ་རེད་ The estate steward is acting brutally toward the peasants.

དྲག་རྩོལ་ (tragdzöö) sm. ཉེར་བརྩོན་.

དྲག་ཚད་ (tragdzɛɛ̀) the speed/ degree/ rate of recovery (from an illness) ¶ ཁོང་གི་ན་ཚ་དྲག་ཚད་མགྱོགས་པོ་བྱུང་སོང་ His recovery from the illness was fast. ¶ སྨན་ཁང་འདིའི་དྲག་ཚད་མཐོ་པོ་ཡོད་པ་རེད་ This hospital has a high rate of a patient recovery.

དྲག་མཚོན་ (tragdzön) weapons.

དྲག་ཞན་ (tragshɛn) powerful and weak ¶ དྲག་ཞན་ཀུན་ All, the powerful and weak (i.e., everybody).

དྲག་ཞན་གར་བླ་ (tragshɛn karla) conveys everything is available: good, bad, strong, weak ¶ ཇ་ཁང་འདིའི་ནང་ཇ་དྲག་ཞན་གར་བླ་གང་དགོས་ཀྱང་འཚོང་རྒྱུ་ཡོད་པ་རེད་ In that tea shop they sell whatever you want (good, bad, strong or weak). [Lit. good, bad, strong and weak].

དྲག་ཞན་བར་གསུམ་ (tragshɛn parsum) the three: good, middle, and poor, the three: strong, middle and weak, the three: high, middle and low.

དྲག་གཞུང་ (trəgshuŋ) military government.

དྲག་གཟའ་བཞི་ (tragsa shi) the four inauspicious days of the week (Sunday, Tuesday, Thursday and Saturday).

དྲག་གཟའ་གསུམ་ (tragsa sūm) sm. དྲག་གསུམ་.

དྲག་ཡང་གོ་བཙན་ (tragyaŋ gōdzɛn) shung. the tyrannical powers of the aristocrats and monasteries.

དྲག་རིགས་ (trəgrig) better quality/ kind ¶ མི་ཚང་དྲག་རིགས་ The better families.

དྲག་རིམ་ (tragrim) sm. དྲག་གྲས་.

དྲག་རུ་འགྲོ་ (tragru dro) sm.* དྲག་ཏུ་འགྲོ་.

དྲག་རེས་ (tragreè) sending sb. because of their ability/ capability ¶ ལས་ཁུངས་ཀྱི་ལས་བྱེད་པའི་ནང་ནས་མི་གཉིས་དྲག་རེས་ཀྱིས་འཐུས་མི་ལ་བཏང་འདུག From among the officials in the office, the two better (more capable) ones were sent as representative.

དྲག་རླབས་ (tragləb) huge wave.

དྲག་རླུང་ (trəgluŋ) wind storm.

དྲག་ལས་ (traglɛɛ̀) abbr. of དྲག་པོའི་ལས་.

དྲག་ཤུགས་ (trəgshuù) military power/ strength ¶ དམག་ཆེན་གཉིས་པའི་དུས་ཀྱི་དྲག་ཤུགས་ Military strength at the time of the Second World War.

དྲག་ཤུལ་ (trəgshüü) sm. དྲག་རྩལ་.

དྲག་ཤུལ་ཅན་ (trəgshüüjɛn) sm. དྲག་ཤུལ་. 2. words and sounds of anger/ hatred. 3. strong and skilled in the martial arts.

དྲག་ཤུལ་ཆེ་བ་ (trəgshüü cēwa) sm. དྲག་ཤུལ་ཅན་.

དྲག་ཤུལ་གཟི་བརྗིད་ (trəgshüü siji) military might/ grandeur/ pomp.

དྲག་ཤུལ་འོད་འབར་ (trəgshüü wömbar) sm. དྲག་ཤུལ་གཟི་བརྗིད་.

དྲག་ཤོས་ (tragshöö) 1. the best, the most superior. 2. title for Bhutanese aristocrats.

དྲག་བཤལ་སྨན་ (tragshɛɛ mɛ̄n) strong laxative.

དྲག་སྲིད་ (trəgsii) military government.

དྲག་གསུམ་ (tragsum) three inauspicious days of the week (Tuesday, Thursday and Saturday).

དྲག་ལྷ་ (traglha) wrathful deity.

དྲག་ལྷགས་ (traglhaà) strong wind.

དྲག་ལྷམ་ (traglham) military boots.

དྲགས་ (traà) vi. to be in excess, to be too much, to be over the limit ¶ སྟོད་ཐུང་དེ་ཆེ་དྲགས་ཀྱི་རེད་ That shirt will be too big.

དྲང་ (traŋ) 1. abbr. of དྲང་པོ་. 2. f. of འདྲེན་.

དྲང་རྒྱང་ (traŋgyaŋ) perpendicular.

དྲང་མཁན་ (traŋñɛn) 1. arbitrator, mediator. 2. judge (in a court of law).

དྲང་གྲངས་ (traŋdraŋ) positive number (in math).

དྲང་འཁྱོག (traŋgyɔɔ̀) right and wrong, honest and dishonest, true and untrue.

དྲང་སྙོམས་ (traŋñom) fair, just, equitable, even.

དྲང་སྙོམས་འདུམ་འགྲིག (traŋñom dumdrig) mediation that is fair to both sides.

དྲང་ཏིག (traŋdig) sm. ཐད་ཀ་.

དྲང་གཏམ་ (traŋdam) true story.

དྲང་ཐད་ (traŋtɛɛ̀) sm. ཐད་ཀ་.

དྲང་ཐིག (traŋtig) straight line.

དྲང་དོན་ (traŋdön) truth, true meaning/ content.

དྲང་བདེན་ (traŋden) 1. just, honest, righteous ¶ ཁོ་ཚོའི་དྲང་བདེན་གྱི་འཐབ་རྩོད་ལ་རྒྱབ་སྐྱོར་བྱེད་དགོས་ (We) should support their just struggle. 2. true, real, genuine ¶ གུང་ཁྲན་རིང་ལུགས་པས་དྲང་བདེན་ཞིག་ཡིན་ན་ If (they) are true communists.

དྲང་བདེན་གྱི་འདུ་ཤེས་ (traŋdengi dusheè) sense of righteousness/ justice.

དྲང་བདེན་གྱི་བསམ་པ་ (traŋdengi sāmba) honesty, righteousness, uprightness.

དྲང་བདེན་ཟོལ་མེད་ (traŋden söömeè) honest, real, genuine.

དྲང་ལྡན་ (traŋdɛn) just, honest ¶ དྲང་ལྡན་གྱི་འཐབ་འཛིན་ A just struggle.

དྲང་ནན་ (traŋnɛn) emphatic and forceful and honest/ just; va.—བྱེད་ ¶ གོང་རིམ་ནས་ང་ལ་དྲང་ནན་གྱི་བཀའ་སློབ་གནང་བྱུང་ The higher authorities gave me forceful and honest advice.

དྲང་པོ་ (traŋbo) 1. honest, upright, frank, just, fair, equitable; va.—ཤོད་ to tell the truth, to speak honestly. 2. straight, not crooked.

དྲང་པོ་དྲང་ལྡན་ (traŋbo traŋdɛn) sm. དྲང་པོ་དྲང་གཞག.

དྲང་པོ་དྲང་གཞག (traŋbo traŋshaà) completely honest/ just/ truthful.

དྲང་པོ་བཤད་ན་མི་མི་དགའ་ རྒྱུག་པ་ཁྱེར་ན་ཁྱི་མི་དགའ་ (traŋbo shɛ̄ɛ̀na mi miga gyugba kērna kyī miga) people will not be glad if you tell the truth, dogs will not be glad if you beat them with a stick.

དྲང་པོ་ལུགས་མཐུན་ (traŋbo lugdün) sm. དྲང་པོ་.

དྲང་པོར་ (traŋbor) honestly, justly, fairly ¶ དྲང་པོར་བཤད་པ་རེད་ (They) spoke honestly.

དྲང་དཔོན་ (traŋbön) sm. ཁྲིམས་དཔོན་.

དྲང་ཕྱོགས་ (traŋjɔɔ̀) the proper/ upright/ honest/ side, the side of the truth.

དྲང་འབྲེལ་ (traŋdree) shung. true, truth; honest, just ¶ ལོ་རྒྱུས་དེ་དྲང་འབྲེལ་ཞིག་ཡིན་མིན་སུས་ཀྱང་ཤོད་དཀའ་ It's hard for anyone to say whether that story is true or not.

དྲང་འབྲེལ་ཁྲིམས་འདོམས་ (traŋdree trīmdom) shung. ruling/ controlling/ administrating justly; va.—བྱེད་ ¶ ས་གནས་རྫོང་སྡོད་ནས་ཆབ་འབངས་མི་སེར་ཐོག་དྲང་འབྲེལ་ཁྲིམས་འདོམས་བྱེད་དགོས་ The district head should rule the people justly.

དྲང་འབྲེལ་ཁྲུན་གཅོད་ (traŋdree trūnjöö̀) shung. settling justly ¶ གྱོད་དོན་དྲང་འབྲེལ་ཁྲུན་གཅོད་ཞུ་དགོས་ One must settle the case justly.

དྲང་བློའི་སྲང་ལ་འཇལ་བའི་ཆོད་འདོམས་ (traŋlö sāŋla jɛɛwɛ cōödom) shung. a verdict so just that it seems like it was weighed on a scale.

དྲང་བཙན་ (traŋdzɛn) stern, strict.

དྲང་ཚུགས་ལྡན་པ་ (traŋdzuù dɛmba) honest and unbiased ¶ དྲང་ཚུགས་ལྡན་པའི་འགོ་འཁྲིད་ An honest and unbiased leader.

དྲང་ཚུགས་ཟིན་པོ་ (traŋdzuù simbu) sm. དྲང་ཚུགས་ལྡན་པ་.

དྲང་ཞིང་འོས་པ་ (traŋshiŋ wööba) just and suitable/ appropriate.

དྲང་གཞག (traŋshaà) fair, just, equitable; va.—བྱེད་ ¶ to be fair/ just/ equitable; va.—སྒྲུབ་ to accomplish justly ¶ ཁོང་གི་ལས་འགན་དྲང་གཞག་སྒྲུབ་འདུག He accomplished the work justly.

དྲང་གཞག་ལུགས་མཐུན་ (traŋshaà lugdün) sm. དྲང་པོ་ལུགས་མཐུན་.

དྲང་གཞི་ (traŋshi) foundation of honesty.

དྲང་འོས་ (traŋwöö) sm. དྲང་ཞིང་འོས་པ་.

དྲང་ལམ་ (traŋlam) 1. path of truth. 2. a good custom/ tradition.

དྲང་ལམ་དུ་འདྲེན་ (traŋlamdu dren) va. to rectify/ correct.

དྲང་བཤད་ (traŋshɛɛ̀) true/ honest speech; va.—བྱེད་.

དྲང་སེམས་ (traŋsem) honesty, justness, fairness, truth; true, genuine, honesty, sincere.

དྲང་སྲོང་ (traŋsoŋ) 1. a religious hermit. 2. one of the seven traditional musical notes. 3. zinnia.

དྲང་སྲོང་མེ་ཏོག (traŋsoŋ medɔɔ̀) zinnia.

དྲང་གསོལ་ (traŋsöö) shung. telling the truth ¶ གང་སར་འགྲིགས་ཐབས་དྲང་གསོལ་ཁོ་ན་ཞུས་པ་ I have tried my best to reconcile in every aspect and tell the truth.

དྲངས་ (traŋ) 1. p. of འདྲེན་. 2. used in newspapers to convey "taken/ cited from" a source ‖ ཉིན་རེའི་ཚགས་པར་ནས་དྲངས་ Taken form the "People's Daily".

དྲངས་ཁྲི་ (traŋdri) sedan chair, palanquin.

དྲངས་རྟགས་ (traŋdaà) quotation mark.

དྲངས་ནས་ཚོང་ (traŋnɛ tsōŋ) va. to transport and sell.

དྲངས་ཚིག (traŋtsiì) a quote.

དྲངས་ཡིག (traŋyiì) sm. དྲངས་ཚིག.

དྲད་ (trɛ̀ɛ) sm. དྲད་དྲད་.

དྲད་ཆག (trɛ̀ɛjaà) fodder.

དྲད་དྲད་ (trɛ̀ɛdrɛ̀ɛ) 1. rubbing sth. to clean it; va.—གཏོང་ ‖ སྣོད་ཆས་དེ་ལག་པས་དྲད་དྲད་བཏང་ནས་གཙང་མ་བཀྲུས་པ་ཡིན་ I rubbed the pot with my hand and cleaned it. 2. vi. scratching or digging (e.g., a horse with its foot); va.—གཏོང་.

དྲན་ (trɛn) vi. to 1. to recollect, to remember, to recall ‖ཁོ་ལན་གཅིག་ཐུག་པ་དྲན་གྱི་འདུག (I) remember meeting him once. 2. vi. to miss ‖ མོ་ཕ་མ་དྲན་གྱི་འདུག She misses her parents.

དྲན་སྐུལ་ (trɛngüü) sm. དྲན་བསྐུལ་.

དྲན་སྐུལ་ཐ་ཚིག (trɛngüü tədzii) sm. དྲན་བསྐུལ་ཐ་ཡིག.

དྲན་སྐུལ་དྲིལ་བརྡ་ (trɛngüü triida) alarm bell.

དྲན་བསྐུལ་ (trɛngüü) reminding; va.—བྱེད་; —འདེབས་ to remind.

དྲན་བསྐུལ་ཐ་ཡིག (trɛngüü təyiì) a warning/ reminder/ notice; va.—གཏོང་ to send a warning/ reminder/ notice ‖ བཙོན་པ་དེས་བཙོན་ཁྲིམས་དང་འགལ་ཙང་དྲན་སྐུལ་ཐ་ཡིག་སྤྲད་པ་རེད་ That prisoner broke the prison rules and was sent a warning.

དྲན་སྐུལ་བེ་ཅོན་ (trɛngüü bejön) a wooden block used in China in the past by magistrates to call for attention or order.

དྲན་སྐྱེན་པོ་ (trɛn gyēnbo) sm. དྲན་རྒྱུ་གོད་པོ་.

དྲན་གོད་ཚ་པོ་ (trɛngöö tsābo) sm. དྲན་རྒྱུ་གོད་པོ་.

དྲན་རྒྱུ་གོད་པོ་ (trɛngyu gööbo) ingenious, clever, creative, smart.

དྲན་རྒྱུ་མང་པོ་ (trɛngyu məŋgu) sm. དྲན་རྒྱུ་གོད་པོ་.

དྲན་བརྒྱལ་ (trɛngyɛɛ) abbr. དྲན་པ་བརྒྱལ་.

དྲན་འཆར་ (trɛnjar) recollection/ reflection of sth. in the past. ‖ ཁྱེད་རང་བཙོན་ཁང་ནང་བཞུགས་པའི་སྐབས་ཀྱི་དྲན་འཆར་གསུང་རོགས་གནང་ Please tell us about your recollections of being in prison. 2. opinion ‖ ང་ཚོའི་མ་འོངས་པའི་འཆར་གཞི་འགོད་ཐུགས་སྐོར་སོ་སོའི་དྲན་འཆར་གང་ཡོད་གསུང་རོགས་གནང་ Each of you please say your opinion about our future plan.

དྲན་འཆར་འགོད་དེབ་ (trɛnjar göödeb) a book for writing comments/ opinions/ observations (usu. for visitors).

དྲན་འཆར་ཞན་པ་ (trɛnjar shɛmba) poor memory/ recollection.

དྲན་ཉམས་ (trɛnñam) sm. དྲན་འཆར་ཞན་པ་.

དྲན་གདམ་གསར་སྐྱེས་ (trɛndam sārgyeè) shung. not adhering to what was agreed upon and coming up with new thoughts/ ideas; va.—བྱེད་ ‖ རྩོད་དུ་འདི་ཐག་ཆོད་ཚར་ནས་དྲན་གདམ་གསར་སྐྱེས་བྱེད་མི་ཆོག After this dispute is settled you are not permitted to raise new issues/ thoughts regarding this matter.

དྲན་རྟགས་ (trɛndaà) sm. དྲན་གསོའི་རྟགས་མ་.

དྲན་རྟེན་ (trɛnden) remembrance, souvenir; va.—འཇོག to leave (sth.) in remembrance.

དྲན་རྟེན་ཉེས་པ་ (trɛnden ñeèba) imposing a small fine as a warning.

དྲན་རྟེན་རྡོ་རིང་ (trɛnden doriŋ) commemorative pillar.

དྲན་རྟེན་ས་ཡིག (trɛnden sāyiì) autograph; va.—རྒྱག.

དྲན་རྟོག (trɛndɔɔ̀) a thought that comes to mind after seeing or hearing sth.; vi.—འཆར་.

དྲན་ཐོ་ (trɛnto) 1. list, reminder note; va.—རྒྱག; —འགོད་; —འབྲི་. ‖ ཉོ་ཆ་མ་བརྒྱབ་གོང་དྲན་ཐོ་ཞིག་རྒྱག་དགོས་ Before going shopping one must make a list. 2. a memoir.

དྲན་འཐོར་བསྐྱར་གསོ་ (trɛndɔɔ gyārso) regaining consciousness, being revived.

དྲན་འཐོར་སོས་ (trɛndɔɔ sȫȫ) sm. དྲན་འཐོར་གསོ་.

དྲན་འཐོར་གསོ་ (trɛndɔɔ sō) vi. to regain consciousness, to got revived from a state of unconciousness.

དྲན་གདུང་ (trɛnduŋ) sorrow caused by missing someone.

དྲན་དུགས་ (trɛndug) forgetful.

དྲན་ནོ་པོ་ (trɛn nōbo) sm. དྲན་རྒྱུ་གོད་པོ་.

དྲན་སྣང་ (trɛnnaŋ) imaginary thought.

དྲན་པ་ (trɛmba) 1. memory, recollection ‖ དྲན་པ་གསལ་པོ་ A clear memory. 2. consciousness; vi.—འཐོར་; —བརྒྱལ་ to lose consciousness, to faint. vi.—གསོ་ to regain consciousness, to be/ get revived.

དྲན་པ་སྐྱེན་པོ་ (trɛmba gyēmbo) sm. དྲན་སྐྱེན་པོ་.

དྲན་པ་འཁྲུལ་ (trɛmba trǖǖ) vi. to hallucinate.

དྲན་པ་བརྒྱལ་ (trɛmba gyɛɛ) vi. to faint, lose consciousness.

དྲན་པ་སྒོམ་ (trɛmba gom) va. to meditate.

དྲན་པ་འཇོག (trɛmba jɔɔ̀) va. to focus the mind on one particular thing, to concentrate.

དྲན་པ་བརྗེད་ (trɛmba jeè) va. to forget sth.

དྲན་པ་ཉམས་ (trɛmba ñam) vi. to become forgetful.

དྲན་པ་རྙེད་ (trɛmba ñeè) sm. དྲན་པ་བསྐྱར་གསོ་.

དྲན་པ་མཐུ་ཆུང་བ་ (trɛmba tūjuŋwa) forgetful.

དྲན་པ་འཐོར་ (trɛmba tɔ̄ɔ) see དྲན་པ་.

དྲན་པ་གནས་ (trɛmba nɛɛ̀) vi. to concentrate on sth. ‖ ངའི་བཟའ་ཟླ་ན་གི་ཡོད་ཙང་ང་ལས་ཀའི་ཐོག་དྲན་པ་གནས་ཀྱི་མི་འདུག Because my spouse is ill, I cannot concentrate on my work.

དྲན་པ་མེད་པ་ (trɛmba meèba) sm. དྲན་མེད་.

དྲན་པ་རྩེ་གཅིག་པ་ (trɛmba dzējigbə) with good concentration, one's mind focused on sth. ‖ སློབ་ཕྲུག་དེས་སློབ་སྦྱོང་ཐོག་དྲན་པ་རྩེ་གཅིག་པར་གཏོད་ཀྱི་འདུག That student is completely focused on his studies.

དྲན་པ་བཞི་ (trɛmba shi) the four mental factors: mind, body, feeling/ sense and the dharma.

དྲན་པ་བརླག (trɛmba lāà) sm. དྲན་པ་འཐོར་.

དྲན་པ་གསལ་ (trɛmba sɛ̄ɛ) see དྲན་པ་.

དྲན་པ་གསལ་མི་གསལ་ (trɛmba sɛ̄ɛ misɛɛ) half conscious, one's thinking/ recollection being blurred and indistinct.

དྲན་པ་གསོ་ (trɛmba sō) 1. see དྲན་པ་. 2. va. to remind, to help sb. remember ‖ བཙོན་ཁང་ནང་བཙོན་པ་ཚོས་ཞུ་བ་འབྲི་དུས་ཕན་ཚུན་དྲན་པ་གསོ་རེས་བྱེད་ཀྱི་ཡོད་པ་རེད་ In prison when the prisoners were writing their confessions they helped each other to remember (events).

དྲན་པ་གསོ་སྨན་ (trɛmba sōmɛn) 1. truth serum. 2. smelling salts, medicine for reviving.

དྲན་པ་གསལ་པོ་ (trɛmba sɛ̄ɛbo) sharp/ clear memory.

དྲན་པར་མི་གདུབ་ (trɛmbar midub) inconceivable.

དྲན་པོ་ (trɛmbo) remembering, memory ‖ ང་གནས་ཚུལ་དེ་དྲན་པོ་མི་འདུག I don't remember that incident.

དྲན་འཕྲུལ་ (trɛndrüü) trickery.

དྲན་འཕྲུལ་ཚ་པོ་ (trɛndrüü tsābo) tricky, cunning.

དྲན་བྱང་ (trɛnjaŋ) a lable on which sth. to be remembered is written (and carried by officials).

དྲན་དབང་ (trɛnwaŋ) sm. དྲན་པའི་དབང་པོ་.

དྲན་མེད་ (trɛnmeè) unconscious; vi.—བརྒྱལ་ to faint, to become unconscious.

དྲན་མེད་དུ་བརྒྱལ་ (trɛnmeèdu gyɛɛ) sm. དྲན་མེད་.

དྲན་ཚོད་ (trɛndzɛ̀ɛ) what comes to mind, what one remembers/ recalls; va.—བྱེད་ to do whatever comes to mind; va.—ཤོད་ to say whatever comes to mind.

དྲན་རྒྱལ་ (trɛndzüü) impression, opinion.

དྲན་རྒྱལ་ཟིན་ཐོ་ (trɛndzüü sinto) a note of one's impression/ opinion.

དྲན་ཚོར་ (trendzɔɔ) impressions/ feelings about sth. remembered.

དྲན་འཛིན་ (trendzin) sm. དྲན་བསྐུལ་.

དྲན་བཞིན་ (trenshin) 1. in the processing of thinking/ remembering. 2. good memory.

དྲན་ཤེས་ (trensheè) memory ༑དྲན་ཤེས་བརྟན་པོ་ ༑ Good memory.

དྲན་ཤེས་ཀྱི་ནུས་པ་ (trensheègi nüübə) ability to memorize.

དྲན་ཤེས་ཉམས་ (trensheè ñam) vi. to experience a declining ability to remember.

དྲན་ཤེས་བག་ཡོད་ (trensheè pagyöö) a person who is clever and careful.

དྲན་སེམས་ (trensem) 1. དྲན་པ་. 2. the feeling that one misses sth. or sb.; vi.—སྐྱེ་ to miss sb. or sth. ༑ང་ཕ་མ་དྲན་སེམས་སྐྱེ་གི་འདུག I miss my parents.

དྲན་སོས་ (tren söö) 1. vi. to regain consciousness. 2. vi. to recollect/ remember.

དྲན་གསལ་ (trensɛl) clear/ sharp memory.

དྲན་གསོ་ (tren sō) vi. to remember, to recall ༑ང་གནས་ཚུལ་འདི་དྲན་གསོས་ཀྱི་མི་འདུག I don't remember this incident.

དྲན་གསོ་ (trenso) 1. commemoration, remembrance; va.—བྱེད་ to commemorate ༑དེ་རིང་ནི་དམག་འཁྲུག་ལས་རྒྱལ་ཁ་ཐོབ་པའི་དྲན་གསོའི་ཉིན་མོ་རེད་ Today is the commemoration day of the victory in the war. 2. reminding; va.—གཏོང་; —སྐུལ་ to remind ༑སང་ཉིན་ང་ཚོགས་འདུར་འགྲོ་རྒྱུ་དེ་དྲན་གསོ་སྐུལ་རོགས་བྱེད་ Please remind me about going to the meeting tomorrow. 3. recollecting, remembering, recalling; va.—བྱེད་ to recollect/ recall, to remember ༑ད་ཆ་དྲན་གསོ་བྱེད་དུས་སློབ་གྲྭར་ཐོག་མར་འགྲོ་དུས་རང་ལོ་ ༡༡ རེད་འདུག Now, when I recall, I started school when I was 11 years old.

དྲན་གསོ་སྐུལ་ (trenso gűű) see དྲན་གསོ་.

དྲན་གསོ་ཁང་ (trensogaŋ) memorial hall.

དྲན་གསོ་ཞིབ་བསྡུར་ (trenso shibdur) recalling and comparing; va.—བྱེད་.

དྲན་གསོའི་དངོས་རྫས་ (trensö ŋöödzɛὲ) souvenir, memento.

དྲན་གསོའི་མཆོད་རྟེན་ (trensö cööden) memorial stupa/ pagoda.

དྲན་གསོའི་ཉིན་ཆེན་ (trensö ñinjen) commemoration/ memorial day for some event.

དྲན་གསོའི་ཉིན་མོ་ (trensö ñimu) sm. དྲན་གསོའི་དུས་ཆེན་.

དྲན་གསོའི་རྟགས་མ་ (trensö dāŋma) memorial/ commemorative medal.

དྲན་གསོའི་དུས་ཆེན་ (trensö tüüjen) memorial/ commemoration day.

དྲན་གསོའི་རྡོ་རིང་ (trensö doriŋ) monument, memorial or commemorative pillar.

དྲན་གསོའི་ཚོགས་འདུ་ (trensö tsöndu) memorial/ commemorative meeting.

དྲན་གསོས་ (tren söö) p. of དྲན་གསོ་.

དྲན་གསོས་གཏོང་ (trensöö dōŋ) va. to remind.

དྲབ་ (trəb) 1. pieces of wood that are placed between ལྕམ་ on a roof. 2. wooden coracle frame.

དྲལ་ (trɛɛ) p. of འདྲལ་.

དྲལ་ལྕམ་ (trɛɛjam) abbr. of དྲབ་ and ལྕམ་.

དྲལ་པོ་ (trɛɛbo) older brother.

དྲལ་ཕྱམ་ (trɛɛjam) sm. དྲལ་ལྕམ་.

དྲལ་མ་ (trɛɛma sm. དྲབ་, 1.

དྲལ་ཇེ་ (trɛɛdze) ch. a report/ communique sent to the Emperor of China.

དྲལ་བཤགས་ (trɛɛshaà) sm. དྲབ་, 1.

དྲལ་ཧྲིལ་ (trɛɛhrii) sm. དྲབ་, 1.

དྲས་ (trɛὲ) 1. p. of འདྲ་. 2. writing a letter on a student's practice book/ slate to show or correct the shape; va.—རྒྱག to correct a student's handwriting by writing the correct shape; va.—སློག to write a Tibetan letter based on the shape of the teacher's handwriting of that letter. 3. the person who corrects the handwriting of a student. 4. va. to cut material for sewing sth.

དྲས་འཁོར་ (trɛὲgɔɔ) sewing machine.

དྲས་ཐག (trɛὲdaà) hesitation.

དྲས་མཐུད་ (trendüü) cutting and joining; va.—བྱེད་ to cut and join, to splice.

དྲས་དྲུབ་པ་ (trɛὲdrubbə) tailor.

དྲས་གདན་ (trɛὲdɛn) wooden board placed under sth. when it is being cut.

དྲས་པ་ (trɛὲba) 1. a cutter. 2. p. of འདྲ་.

དྲས་པང་ (trɛὲbaŋ) sm. དྲས་གདན་.

དྲས་སྤྱད་ (trɛὲjɛὲ) paraphernalia/ tools for cutting.

དྲས་སྦྱར་ (trɛὲjar) cutting and pasting; va.—རྒྱག to cut and paste.

དྲས་ཟུས་ (trɛὲsüü) tool used in Tibetan medicine.

དྲས་གཟོང་ (trɛὲsoŋ) a tool used by goldsmiths and silversmiths.

དྲས་ལེན་ (trɛὲ len) shung. va. to get the teacher's correction on one's practice penmanship.

དྲས་ཧྲུག (trɛὲhruù) sm. དྲས་ཧྲུལ་.

དྲས་ཧྲུལ་ (trɛὲhrüü) scraps of materials cut away in the process of manufacturing, waste pieces of cloth/ material left after the tailor makes sth.

དྲི་ (tri) 1. smell, odor, scent; vi.—ཁ་ to smell; va.—སྣོམ་ to smell, to sniff ༑སྟོད་ཐུང་འདི་དྲི་ཁ་གི་འདུག This shirt smells. ༑སྤོས་དྲི་ཞིམ་པོ་ Good smelling incense. ༑ཉ་དྲི་ Fish smell. ༑གཅིན་དྲི་ The smell of urine. 2. f. of འདྲི་.

དྲི་དཀྲ་ (trigu) abbr. of དྲི་མ་དཀྲ་.

དྲི་སྐོར་ (trigɔɔ) asking, questioning; va.—ཞུ་; —བྱེད་ ༑སློབ་གྲྭའི་གནས་སྟངས་སྐོར་དྲི་སྐོར་ཞུ་གི་འདུག (He) is asking about the conditions in the school.

དྲི་སྐྱོན་ (trigyön) contaminated, polluted; va.—གཏོང་ to contaminate/ pollute.

དྲི་གླུད་ (trilüü) kneaded tsampa dough that is spit upon and then thrown away so that it carries away all the ill-luck.

དྲི་ངབ་ (triŋawa) sm. དྲི་ངན་.

དྲི་ངད་ (triŋɛὲ) fragrant, aromatic, good smelling.

དྲི་ངན་ (triŋɛn) foul smelling.

དྲི་ངན་ཁ་བ་བཟོ་ (triŋɛn kāwa so) severely defeating/ vanquishing [Lit. making smell bad].

དྲི་ངན་ཐུལ་ཐུལ་ (triŋɛn tűűdüü) stinking, foul smelling.

དྲི་ངན་དབྱུང་རླུང་ (triŋɛn yəŋluŋ) ozone ༑དྲི་ངན་དབྱུང་རླུང་བར་རིམ་ Ozone layer.

དྲི་ངན་དབྱུང་རླུང་འགྱུར་རྫས་ (triŋɛn yāŋluŋ gyurdzɛὲ) ozonide.

དྲི་ངན་འཚུབ་འཚུབ་ (triŋɛn tsūbdzub) stinking, foul smelling.

དྲི་ངན་ས་འགེབས་ (triŋɛn sāgeb) hiding wrong doings/ misdeeds. [Lit. to cover sth. that smells with earth].

དྲི་ངན་ལ་སྣོམ་སྐྱོར་དང་ ལྟས་ངན་ལ་ལྟ་སྐྱོར་ (triŋɛnla nōmgyɔr daŋ dɛɛ̀ŋɛnla dāgyɔr) recalling or remembering bad events/ happenings [Lit. sniff sth. foul again, look at sth. terrible again].

དྲི་ངན་ས་གཡོགས་ (triŋɛn sāyɔɔ̀) sm. དྲི་ངན་ས་འགེབས་.

དྲི་ཅན་ (trijɛn) odoriferous, smelly.

དྲི་ཆབ་ (trijəb) scented water.

དྲི་ཆབ་མ་ (tri cābmə) name of a deity.

དྲི་ཆུ་ (triju) urine; va.—འདོར་; —བཤིལ་ to urinate.

དྲི་ཆེན་ (trijen) excrement, stool.

དྲི་ཆེན་ནྭང་མ་ (trijen ñāŋma) loose stool.

དྲི་མཆོག (drijɔɔ̀) 1. pleasant/ good smelling. 2. Tibetan beer.

དྲི་གཏུགས་ (triduù) getting to the bottom of some matter; va.—བྱེད་.

དྲི་ཐིག (tridig) a dirty spot/ stain.

དྲི་དང་བྲལ་བ་ (tridaŋ trɛɛwa) not a hint of sth. ༑འཛུམ་མདངས་ཀྱི་དྲི་དང་བྲལ་བའི་རྣམ་འགྱུར་ An expression without the hint of a smile.

དྲི་དུག (triduù) sm. དྲི་ངན་.

དྲི་དོན་ (tridön) question ༑ངས་ཁྱེད་རང་ལ་དྲི་དོན་གཉིས་ཡོད་ I have two questions to ask you.

དྲི་ལྡན་ (trindɛn) sm. དྲི་ཅན་.

དྲི་ལྡན་སྤོས་བསངས་ (trindɛn gūsaŋ) loose incense that is thrown on a fire as an offering.

དྲི་བསྡུར་ (triidur) discussion, asking and comparing; va.—བྱེད་; —ཞུ་ to discuss ། ཁོང་ཚོས་ལས་ཁུངས་ནང་དྲི་བསྡུར་བྱས་ན་མ་གཏོགས་ཐག་ཆོད་ཀྱི་མ་རེད་ Unless they have a discussion in the office they can't make a decision.

དྲི་ནོག (trinog) dirty and smelly; vi.—ཡོང་ to get dirty/ smelly ། ངའི་སྟོད་ཐུང་ལ་དྲི་ནོག་ཡོང་བཞག My shirt got dirty.

དྲི་མནམ་ (tri nām) 1. vi. to smell. 2. bad odor/ smell.

དྲི་སྣོམ་ (tri nōm) see དྲི་, 1.

དྲི་བསྣམས་ (tri nām) p. of དྲི་སྣོམ་.

དྲི་བ་ (triwə) a question; va.—གཏོང་; —འདོན་ to question, to ask questions; va.—ལེན་ to interrogate, to question ། ཁྲིམས་ཁང་ནས་བཙོན་པར་དྲི་བ་བླངས་པ་རེད་ The court interrogated the criminal.

དྲི་བ་དྲི་ལན་ (triwə trilɛn) sm. དྲི་བ་དྲིས་ལན་.

དྲི་བ་དྲིས་ལན་ (triwə trilɛn) questioning and answering ། མ་འོངས་པའི་སྐོར་ལ་དྲི་བ་དྲིས་ལན་དུ་ (They) engaged in questions and answers about the future.

དྲི་བ་བཞེས་ (triwə sheè) h. of དྲི་བ་ལེན་.

དྲི་བ་ལོག་པ་ (triwə lɔgba) an inappropriate question.

དྲི་བར་སླར་འདྲི་ (triwar lāndri) asking a question and getting a question in reply; va.—བྱེད་.

དྲི་བྲལ་ (tritrɛɛ) sm. དྲི་མ་མེད་པ་.

དྲི་བྲོ་ (tri tro) sm. དྲི་མ་ཁ་.

དྲི་འབུ་ (trimbu) sm. བསེ་ལེ་སྦྲུར་གོག.

དྲི་མ་ (trimə) smell, odor, scent; va.—སྣོམ་ to sniff/ smell sth.; va.—རྒྱག; —འཁོར་; —ཆགས་ to become smelly ། དྲི་མ་མངར་མོ་ Sweet smell. ། ཤ་དེ་ལ་དྲི་མ་འཁོར་བཞག That meat has become smelly.

དྲི་མ་དཀུ་བ་ (trimə gūwə) bad smell, foul smelling.

དྲི་མ་བཀྲུས་ (trimə drüü) va. to wash (to cleanse a smell).

དྲི་མ་ཁ་བ་བཟོ་ (trimə kāwa so) sm. དྲི་ངན་ཁ་བ་བཟོ་བ་.

དྲི་མ་འཁོར་ (trimə kɔ̄ɔ) vi. to become smelly, to get infused with a smell.

དྲི་མ་འགགས་པའི་ནད་ (trimə gagbɛ nɛɛ) constipation.

དྲི་མ་ངན་པ་ (trimə ŋamba) bad smell, foul odor.

དྲི་མ་མངའ་ (trimə ŋā) vi. to smell.

དྲི་མ་ཆགས་ (trimə cāā) 1. vi. to become smelly/ dirty. 2. vi. to have erred.

དྲི་མ་དྲུག (trimə truù) the 6 odoriferous objects: stool, urine, eye mucus, earwax, spittle, snot.

དྲི་མ་རྣམ་པར་དག་པ་ (trimə nāmbar tagba) 1. to be clean. 2. to be perfect.

དྲི་མ་རྣམ་གསུམ་ (trimə nāmsum) sm. དྲི་གསུམ་.

དྲི་མ་མེད་པ་ (trimə meèba) without any smell, pure, clean, perfect.

དྲི་མ་ཚ་པོ་ (trimə tsābo) stinking, foul smelling.

དྲི་མ་ས་གཡོགས་དྲི་ངན་ས་འགེབས་ (trimə sāyɔɔ triŋɛn sangeb) covering up one's own faults/ mistakes [Lit. throwing earth on sth. that smells bad].

དྲི་མ་གསུམ་ (trimə sūm) sm. དྲི་གསུམ་.

དྲི་མས་ནོགས་པ་ (trimɛ nōgba) dirty, unclean.

དྲི་མེད་ (trimeè) sm. དྲི་མ་མེད་པ་.

དྲི་མེད་དཀར་གཙང་ (trimɛ gārdzaŋ) pure/ clean/ white and without smell.

དྲི་མེད་དྭངས་གཙང་ (trimə taŋdzaŋ) sm. དྲི་མེད་དཀར་གཙང་.

དྲི་སྨྲེད་ (tri mēè) 1. va. to question. 2. to greet in a customary way (e.g. by saying, ' How are you? ').

དྲི་ཙམ་མེད་པ་ (tridzam meèba) without even a whiff, completely devoid ། སྙིང་རྗེ་དྲི་ཙམ་མེད་པར་ Without even the slightest compassion.

དྲི་ཙམ་མ་དགོས་པ་ (tridzam magööba) sm. དྲི་ཙམ་མེད་པ་.

དྲི་གཙང་ཁང་ (tridzaŋgaŋ) the main chapel in a temple.

དྲི་རྩད་ (tridzɛɛ) interrogating, questioning; va.—བྱེད་.

དྲི་ཚིག (tridzii) questions ། ཡིག་ཚད་ཀྱི་དྲི་ཚིག་ཁག་ཅིག་ལ་ངས་ལན་རྒྱག་ཐུབ་མ་སོང་ I wasn't able to answer some of the questions on the exam.

དྲི་འཛིན་ཁང་ (tridzingaŋ) sm. དྲི་གཙང་ཁང་.

དྲི་ཞིམ་ (trishim) sweet smelling, fragrant aroma; vi.—ཁ་; —འཐུས་; —བྲོ་ to smell good/ fragrant ། དྲི་ཞིམ་མེ་ཏོག A fragrant flower.

དྲི་ཞིམ་འདག་རྫས་ (trishim dagdzɛɛ) scented soap/ detergent.

དྲི་ཞིམ་ཟླ་ (trishim da) spring.

དྲི་བཞེས་གནང་ (trisheè nāŋ) h. of དྲི་བ་ལེན་.

དྲི་ཟའི་གྲོང་ཁྱེར་ (trisɛ troŋgyer) illusory phenomenon, mirage.

དྲི་ཟའི་གླུ་དབྱངས་ (trisɛ lūyaŋ) pleasant song, melody.

དྲི་བཟང་ (trisaŋ) fragrant aroma.

དྲི་བཟང་ན་གི་ (trisaŋ nəgi) scales (e.g., on a fish).

དྲི་ཡི་བཞོན་པ་ (triyi shōmba) poet. wind ། བདག་པོའི་བཀའ་ལུང་དྲི་ཡི་བཞོན་པ་ཡིས་ འབངས་ལུས་ལས་ཀྱི་བགོ་སྐལ་རིང་དུ་འཕྱངས་ The order from the master spread widely to the subjects just like wind.

དྲི་རོ་ (triro) abbr. smell and taste.

དྲི་ལན་ (trilɛn) answering, replying; va.—རྒྱག; —འདེབས་; —སློག to answer, to reply ། ཁོང་ལ་དྲི་བ་བཏོན་པ་ཚང་མར་དྲི་ལན་བརྒྱབ་སོང་ He answered all the questions.

དྲི་ཤོག (trishoò) 1. exam paper. 2. interview questionnaire.

དྲི་གསུམ་ (trisum) the three smells: excrement, urine, sweat.

དྲི་བསུང་ (trisuŋ) sm. དྲི་བསུང་ཞིམ་པོ་.

དྲི་བསུང་ཞིམ་པོ་ (trisuŋ shimbu) sweet smelling, fragrant, aromatic.

དྲིང་འཇོག (tri jɔɔ) va. rely/ depend on others.

དྲིད་ (trii) p. of འདྲིད་.

དྲིན་ (trin) kindness, gratefulness ། ཕ་མའི་དྲིན་ Parent's kindness.

དྲིན་སྐྱོང་ (trin gyōŋ) va. to look after with kindness, to act kind to.

དྲིན་གྱིས་སྐྱོང་ (tringi gyōŋ) sm. དྲིན་སྐྱོང་.

དྲིན་དངུལ་ (trinŋüü) monetary reward for doing sth. good; va.—སྤྲོད་ to give a monetary reward for doing sth. good.

དྲིན་ཅན་ (trinjɛn) grateful ། དྲིན་ཅན་ཕ་མ་ The parents to whom I am grateful. ། ཁྱེད་རང་ངའི་དྲིན་ཅན་ཡིན་ I am grateful to you.

དྲིན་ཅན་པོ་ (trinjɛnbo) sm. དྲིན་ཅན་.

དྲིན་ཆེན་ལ་དྲིན་ལོག གཡང་ཟེག་ལ་རྡོ་ཁ་ (trincenla trin lɔɔ yāŋsɔɔla do kā) sm. དྲིན་ལག་རྡོ་རྡུང་.

དྲིན་ཆུང་གཏོང་ (trinjuŋ dōŋ) va. to spoil/ pamper a child.

དྲིན་ཆུང་དུ་འགྱུར་ (trinjuŋdu gyur) vi. to become spoiled.

དྲིན་འཇགས་བྱེད་ (trinjaà ceè) va. to repay someone's kindness.

དྲིན་དུ་ཚོར་ (trindu tsōr) vi. to be grateful, to feel gratitude ། ཨ་ཞང་གིས་ཁྱེད་རང་ལ་རོགས་པ་ཞི་དྲག་བྱས་པ་དེའི་དྲིན་ཚོར་གྱི་མི་འདུག་གས་ Don't you feel gratitude to your uncle who helped you so much?.

དྲིན་དུ་ཤེས་ (trindu shēè) sm. དྲིན་དུ་ཚོར་.

དྲིན་དྲན་ (trintrɛn) vi. to recall/ remember kindness, to feel gratitude.

དྲིན་བྱེད་ (trin ceè) sm. དྲིན་སྐྱོང་.

དྲིན་གཟོ་ (trin so) sm. དྲིན་ལན་འཇལ་.

དྲིན་ཡུས་ཤོད་ (trinyüü shöö) va. to make a big deal of being kind to sb.

དྲིན་ལག་རྡོ་བརྡུང་ (trinlaà doduŋ) being ungrateful [Lit. to the hand of a person who is being kind, hit with a rock].

དྲིན་ལན་ (trinlɛn) repaying or returning kindness, showing gratitude; va.—འཇལ་; —གསོབ་; —གསོ་; —གསབ་ to return or repay a kindness/ favor.

དྲིན་ལན་འཁོར་དུ་མེད་པ་ (trinlɛn kɔ̄ɔdu meeba) shung. vi. to be unable to reciprocate kindness ¶ དྲིན་ལན་འཁོར་དུ་མེད་ཀྱང་བཟང་ལན་ཞན་འཇལ་བྱ་རྒྱུ་མེད་ Even if you are unable to reciprocate kindness, you should not be ungrateful.

དྲིན་ལན་ལོག་འཇལ་ (trinlɛn lɔgjɛɛ) ungratefulness; va.—བྱེད་ to be ungrateful.

དྲིན་ལན་སློག (trinlɛn lɔ̄ɔ) sm. དྲིན་ལན་ལོག.

དྲིན་ལན་གསོབ་ (trinlɛn sōb) va. to repay a kindness.

དྲིན་ལོག (trin lɔ̄ɔ) sm. དྲིན་ལན་ལོག་འཇལ་.

དྲིན་ཤེས་ (trinsheè) sm. དྲིན་དུ་ཤེས་.

དྲིན་གསོ་ (trin sō) sm. དྲིན་ལན་གསོབ་.

དྲིན་བསམ་ (trinsam) sm. དྲིན་དུ་ཤེས་.

དྲིན་གསབ་ (trinsəb) sm. དྲིན་ལན་འཇལ་.

དྲིའི་བག (trii paà) a tint/ hint of smell.

དྲིལ་ (trii) 1. abbr. of དྲིལ་བུ་. 2. p. and f. and imp. of འདྲིལ་. 3. sm. སྒྲིལ་. 4. combining, adding, including.

དྲིལ་སྒྲ་ (triidra) sound of a bell or alarm ringing.

དྲིལ་སྒྲུབ་ (triidrub) va. to gather together at one time.

དྲིལ་སྒྲོག (trii drɔ̄ɔ) va. to ring a bell.

དྲིལ་བསྒྲགས་ (triidraà) propaganda (can have either positive or negative connotation), publicity, advertisement; va.—བྱེད་ to propagandize, to publicize, to advertise.

དྲིལ་བསྒྲགས་ཁྱབ་ས་ (triidraà kyābsa) propaganda/ publicity/ advertisement network.

དྲིལ་བསྒྲགས་པ་ (triidragba) propagandist, publicist, advertising specialist.

དྲིལ་བསྒྲགས་ཕུའུ་ (triidraà janbu) tib.ch. propaganda/ publicity department.

དྲིལ་བསྒྲགས་བྱང་བུ་ (triidraà canbu) propaganda/ publicity poster or placard.

དྲིལ་བསྒྲགས་དམག་འཁྲུག (triidraà məgdruù) propaganda war.

དྲིལ་བསྒྲགས་ཟློས་གར་ (triidraà döögar) propaganda show/ play.

དྲིལ་བསྒྲགས་ཡིག་རིགས་ (triidraà yigrig) publicity/ propaganda materials.

དྲིལ་བསྒྲགས་རི་མོ་ (triidraà rimu) propaganda/ publicity/ advertisement poster or picture.

དྲིལ་བསྒྲགས་རུ་ཁག (triidraà rugaà) propaganda/ publicity team.

དྲིལ་བསྒྲགས་ལག་ཆ་ (triidraà lagja) propaganda/ publicity tool.

དྲིལ་ཅོང་ (triijoŋ) tib.ch. large bell.

དྲིལ་ལྕེ་ (triije) striker/ tongue of a bell.

དྲིལ་བཏགས་ཕུག་རོན་ (triidaà pūrön) pigeon on which a bell has been tied to give a signal.

དྲིལ་བརྡ་ (triida) alarm, warning bell, signal given with a bell; va.—གཏོང་ to signal with a bell.

དྲིལ་ཕྱིས་ (trii cīi) 1. va. to rub/ wipe off dirt from one's body. 2. va. to clean (clothes, etc.) by rubbing kneaded dough on it.

དྲིལ་བུ་ (triibu) bell; va.—དཀྲོག; —བརྡུང་; —གསིལ་ to ring a bell.

དྲིལ་བུ་ཙིང་ཙིང་ (triibu dzīŋdzīŋ) name of a prison in Shigatse in early times.

དྲིལ་བུ་སིང་སིང་ (triibu sīŋsīŋ) the sound of a bell ringing.

དྲིལ་ཡུགས་ (triiyug) shung. a roll (of silk).

དྲིལ་གཡེར་ (triiyer) abbr. of དྲིལ་བུ་ and གཡེར་ཁ་.

དྲིལ་གཡེར་གྱི་དྲ་བ་ (triiyergi trawa) net-like belts worn by dancers.

དྲིལ་ལོག (triilɔ̄ɔ) rolling upside down; vi.—རྒྱག.

དྲིས་ (trii) p. and imp. of འདྲི་.

དྲིས་ཐོ་ (triito) list of questions.

དྲིས་ལན་ (triilɛn) answer/ reply to a question; va.—རྒྱག; —འདེབས་; —སློག to answer a question, to reply ¶ ངས་དྲི་བ་བཏོན་པར་ཁོས་དྲིས་ལན་བརྒྱབ་མ་སོང་ He didn't answer the question I asked.

དྲུ་ (tru) sm.* འདྲུ་.

དྲུ་གུ་ (trugu) ball of yarn/ thread.

དྲུ་བུ་ (trubu) sm. དྲུ་གུ་.

དྲུ་མ་ (trumə) coral.

དྲུག (truù) six.

དྲུག་དཀར་ (truggar) a type of pale turquoise.

དྲུག་སྐྱེད་ (truggyeè) shung. 12 % interest.

དྲུག་སྐྱེས་ (truggyeè) one of the 7 Tibetan musical notes.

དྲུག་འགོ་ (truŋgo) an area near the elbow where blood is drained to treat illnesses.

དྲུག་སྒྲ་ (trugdra) a preposition in Tibetan grammar—"of."

དྲུག་བརྒྱ་ (truggya) six hundred.

དྲུག་ཅུ་ (trugju) sixty.

དྲུག་ཅུ་ཐམ་པ་ (trugju tāmba) sm. དྲུག་བཅུ་.

དྲུག་ཅུ་མ་ (trugjumə) 1. a type of torma. 2. a fast growing barley that ripens in 60 days. 2. a custom whereby water mill operators return 10 ཁལ་ of tsamba for each 6 ཁལ་ of grain they mill.

དྲུག་གཅིག་བྱིས་པའི་དུས་ཆེན་ (trug jīg ciibɛ tüüjen) Children's day (June 1st).

དྲུག་ཆ་ (trugjə) a sixth.

དྲུག་ཆ་གཅིག (trūgjə jīg) one sixth.

དྲུག་ལྡིར་ (trugdir) a pot that has the capacity to hold 6 སྲང་ worth of ཚང་.

དྲུག་སྟོང་ (trugdoŋ) six thousand.

དྲུག་ཐུལ་ (trugdüü) sm. དྲུག་ལྡིར་.

དྲུག་མཐའ་ (trugda) the six times table.

དྲུག་དྲུག་འཕར་ (trundraà pār) shung. abbr. of དྲུག་སྒྲ་, གྲོང་དྲུག, and འཕར་མ་ ¶ བསྟན་འཛིན་ཁང་གསུམ་ དྲུག་དྲུག་འཕར་བཅས་སྲང་བཞི་ཞོ་དོ་ The taxes for Tenzin's three kang and དྲུག་དྲུག་འཕར་ (of land) is 3 སྲང་ and 4 ཞོ་.

དྲུག་བདུན་ (trugdün) June 7: the day in 1968 when two groups of opposing Red Guards fought over control of the Tsuglagang Cathedral.

དྲུག་བདུན་འགྲོ་ (trugdün dro) 16% interest.

དྲུག་མདོ་ (trugdo) the end of the spinal cord.

དྲུག་པ་ (trugbə) sixth ¶ ཟླ་བ་དྲུག་པ་ The sixth month.

དྲུག་པ་ཚེས་བཞི་ (trugbə tsēshi) the Tibetan holiday on the 4th of the 6th Tibetan month commemorating the Buddha's first sermon on the Four Noble Truths.

དྲུག་པོ་ (trugbo) all six (together).

དྲུག་དམར་ (trugmar) turquoise with a reddish tint.

དྲུག་ཟུར་ (trugsur) a sixth.

དྲུག་ཤས་ (trugsheè) sm. དྲུག་ཆ་.

དྲུང་ (truŋ) 1. presence of, near to, before (usu. used with དུ་, ན་, ནས་). 2. shung. abbr. for དྲུང་འཁོར་ and/ or རྩེ་དྲུང་.

དྲུང་དཀྱུས་ (truŋgyüù) shung. abbr. of དྲུང་འཁོར་དཀྱུས་མ་.

དྲུང་དཀྱུས་འཕར་ (truŋ gyüù pār) shung. abbr. of དྲུང་འཁོར་དཀྱུས་མ་ and འཕར་མ་.

དྲུང་འཁོར་ (truŋgoo) shung. lay official in the tt. government.

དྲུང་འཁོར་དཀྱུས་མ་ (truŋgoo gyüümə) shung. lowest rank of དྲུང་འཁོར་ in the tt. government.

དྲུང་འཁོར་རྩལ་རྒྱུགས་ (truŋgoo dzɛ̄ɛgyuù) shung. a ceremonial test every 12 years (with bow, spear and gun) of all tt. lay officials who have not previously done this, i.e., who entered government service since the last ceremony.

དྲུང་མགྲོན་ཁང་ (truŋdröngaŋ) shung. a secretariat-like office under the Kashag consisting of བཀའ་དྲུང་ and བཀའ་མགྲོན་.

དྲུང་ཆེ་ (truŋce) shung. 1. secretary ¶ སྲུང་སྐྱོབ་དྲུང་ཆེ་ Secretary of Defense. 2. abbr. of དྲུང་ཡིག་ཆེ་མོ་.

དྲུང་ཆེ་དང་པོ་ (truŋce taābo) First Secretary.

དྲུང་ཆེན་ (truŋcen) shung. abbr. of དྲུང་ཡིག་ཆེན་མོ་.

དྲུང་ཇ་ (truŋja) shung. the required daily tea meeting attended by all monk officials; va.—ཚོགས་ to attend the tea meeting of the monk officials.

དྲུང་གདོགས་ (truŋdoò) shung. an honorary rank beneath that of government officials that is usually given to craftsmen.

དྲུང་དུ་ (tru̲ŋdu) 1. into/ to the presence of, near to, before ༈ཁོ་ཚོས་རྒྱལ་པོའི་དྲུང་དུ་བཅར་པ་རེད་ They went before the king. 2. phrase used in letters to end the heading ༈རྡོ་རྗེ་ལགས་ཀྱི་དྲུང་དུ་ To Mr. Dorje.

དྲུང་དྲག (tru̲ŋdraà) shung. the class of higher ranking officials/ aristocrats in the traditional Tibetan government.

དྲུང་དྲག་འབྲིང་དཀྱུས་གསུམ་ (tru̲ŋdraà dri̲ŋ gyǖü sūm) shung. all lay officials [Lit. the higher, middle, and lower ranking དྲུང་འཁོར་].

དྲུང་དྲུང་ (tru̲ŋdruŋ) real, true (in contrast to genealogically extended) ༈ཁོང་ངའི་ཨ་ཁུ་དྲུང་དྲུང་རེད་ He is my true paternal uncle (i.e., my father's brother).

དྲུང་ན་ (tru̲ŋnə) sm. དྲུང་དུ་.

དྲུང་ན་སྐྱོད་པ་ (tru̲ŋnə gyö̃ba) a kind of official/ attendant in ancient times.

དྲུང་ན་མོ་ (tru̲ŋ na̲mo) attendants.

དྲུང་ནས་ (tru̲ŋnɛɛ̀) from the presence, from in front of, from near.

དྲུང་ནས་ཕྱུང་ (tru̲ŋnɛ cūŋ) va. to get rid of, to give up completely.

དྲུང་ནས་འབྱིན་ (tru̲ŋnɛ ji̲n) va. to get rid of, to give up completely.

དྲུང་གནས་ (tru̲ŋnɛɛ̀) 1. sm. དྲུང་ན་མོ་. 2. shung. having the rank of official in the tt. government ༈དྲུང་གནས་ཡོད་པ་ཚང་མ་ཚོགས་འདུར་ཕྱིབས་པ་བཞག All those who hold the rank of official came to the meeting.

དྲུང་པ་ (tru̲ŋbə) 1. a geshe of the first rank. 2. brothers. 3. sm. སྐུ་ཞབས་.

དྲུང་པ་རིན་པོ་ཆེ་ (tru̲ŋbə ri̲mboce) shung. honorific term for sons of aristocratic families who have become monks.

དྲུང་པོ་ (tru̲ŋbu) sm. དྲུང་པ་.

དྲུང་སྤྱི་ (tru̲ŋji) shung. monk and lay officials in the tt. government.

དྲུང་སྤྱི་གླིང་ག (tru̲ŋji li̲ŋgə) shung. park in S.E. Lhasa for lay officials.

དྲུང་འབྱིན་ (tru̲ŋjin) shung. abbr. of དྲུང་ནས་འབྱིན་.

དྲུང་རྩིས་ (tru̲ŋdzii̇) shung. abbr. of དྲུང་ཡིག་ཆེ་མོ་ and རྩིས་དཔོན་.

དྲུང་རྩིས་བརྒྱད་ (tru̲ŋdzii̇ gyɛ̲ɛ̀) shung. 1. the four དྲུང་ཡིག་ཆེ་མོ་ and the four རྩིས་དཔོན་. 2. the occasional joint meetings of the four དྲུང་ཡིག་ཆེ་མོ་ and the four རྩིས་དཔོན་.

དྲུང་འཚོ (tru̲ŋdzo) doctor.

དྲུང་གཞོན་ (tru̲ŋshön) deputy secretary.

དྲུང་བཞེས་ (tru̲ŋsheè) h. of དྲུང་ཇ་.

དྲུང་ཡིག (tru̲ŋyii̇) secretary, clerk.

དྲུང་ཡིག་ཁང་ (tru̲ŋyii̇gaŋ) secretariat.

དྲུང་ཡིག་ཁྲུའུ་ (tru̲ŋyii̇ trūù) tib.ch. དྲུང་ཡིག་ཁང་.

དྲུང་ཡིག་ཆེ་མོ་ (tru̲ŋyii̇ cēmmo) 1. Secretary General. 2. shung. the four monk officials who headed the tt. government's ཡིག་ཚང་.

དྲུང་ཡིག་ཆེན་མོ་ (tru̲ŋyii̇ cēmmo) shung. sm. དྲུང་ཡིག་ཆེ་མོ་.

དྲུང་རིགས་སེར་སྐྱ་ (tru̲ŋrig sērgya) shung. monk and lay officials.

དྲུད་ (trü̲ǜ) p. and imp. of འདྲུད་.

དྲུད་དྲུད་ (trü̲ǜdrüǜ) pulling and dragging (back and forth); va.—བྱེད་; —གཏོང་.

དྲུད་འཐེན་འཁོར་ལོ་ (trü̲ǜden kɔ̄ɔlo) sm. འདྲུད་ཐེན་འཁོར་ལོ་.

དྲུད་འཐེན་འཕྲུལ་འཁོར་ (trü̲ǜten drǖǜgɔɔ) sm. འདྲུད་ཐེན་འཁོར་ལོ་.

དྲུད་ཤུལ་ (trü̲ǜshüü) the trace/ track of sth. that has been dragged.

དྲུབ་: p. དྲུབས་; f. དྲུབ་; imp. དྲུབས་ (tru̲b) va. to sew.

དྲུབས་ (tru̲b) p. and imp. of དྲུབ་.

དྲུམ་ (tru̲m) sm. གྲུམ་.

དྲུལ་ (trü̲ǜ) vi. to decay/ rot/ decompose.

དྲུས་རྒྱག (trü̲ǜ gya̲à) va. to stomp/ tramp on garins like barley to thresh/ husk it.

དྲུས་པོ་ (trü̲ǜbu) a four year old yak.

དྲུས་མ་ (trü̲ǜmə) 1. milch animals. 2. animals who are in heat. 3. roasted barley.

དྲུས་བཞག (trü̲ǜshaà) mating season (for animals).

དྲུས་ལོག་རྒྱག (trü̲ǜlɔ̀ɔ gya̲à) vi. to come into heat again after the mating season has ended.

དྲེ་ (dre̲) a type of spirit/ demon.

དྲེ་པོ་ (dre̲wo) 1. sm. དྲན་མ་. 2. male spirit/ demon.

དྲེ་མོ་ (drēmo) female spirit/ demon.

དྲེག (dre̲g) abbr. of དྲེག་པ་.

དྲེག་ཁུ་ (dre̲ggu) foul/ dirty water.

དྲེག་འཁྲུ་ (dre̲gdru) laundering, washing, cleaning; va.—རྒྱག.

དྲེག་གྲུམ་ (dre̲gdrum) sm. དྲེག་ནད་.

དྲེག་འགོས་སྐྱོན་ཤོར་ (dre̲ggöö̀ gyȫnshɔɔ) dirty and broken.

དྲེག་རྡོ་ (dre̲gdo) pumice stone.

དྲེག་ལྡན་ (dre̲gdɛn) dirty.

དྲེག་ནད་ (dre̲gnɛɛ̀) gout-like illness.

དྲེག་པ་ (dre̲gba) dirt, filth, soot; va.— འཁོར་; —ཆགས་ to collect dirt, to become dirty.

དྲེག་བལ་ (dre̲gpɛɛ) soot on rafters of kitchens that hang down looking like wool.

དྲེག་རིལ་ (dre̲grii) dirt on the body having become like pills.

དྲེགས་ (tre̲g) 1. vi. to be arrogant/ haughty/ insolently proud ༈ཡོན་ཏན་ཆུང་ངུས་དྲེགས་ནས་གཞན་ལ་མཐོང་ཆུང་བྱེད་པ་རེད་ Because of a little knowledge (he) was arrogant and looked down on others. 2. p. of འདྲེགས་.

དྲེགས་གྱོང་ (tre̲ggyoŋ) arrogant and tough/ headstrong.

དྲེགས་འགྱིང་ (tre̲ggyiŋ) sm. དྲེགས་ཉམས་.

དྲེགས་ཉམས་ (tre̲gñam) arrogant, proud, haughty.

དྲེགས་སྙེམས་ (tre̲gñem) arrogance, pride, haughtiness.

དྲེགས་པ་ (tre̲gba) sm. དྲེགས་.

དྲེགས་པས་ཡོན་ཏན་ཉམས་ (tre̲gbɛ yo̲ndɛn ña̲m) pride will diminish (one's) wisdom.

དྲེགས་སྤྱོད་ (tre̲gjö̀ö̀) arrogant, proud, haughty behavior.

དྲེགས་མེད་ཁེངས་བསྐྱུངས་ (tre̲gmeè kēŋgyuŋ) humble and modest.

དྲེགས་ཚིག (tre̲gdzii̇) words conveying pride and arrogance.

དྲེད་ (tre̲è) 1. sm. དྲེད་མོ་. 2. sm. ཞེད་.

དྲེད་ཁུང་ (tre̲ègun) sm. དྲེད་ཚང་.

དྲེད་དོ་ (tre̲èdo) sm. སྤྲལ་རལ་ཆེ་པོ་.

དྲེད་དེབ་ཤོར་ (tre̲èdeb shɔ̄ɔ) vi. to slip ༈ཁོང་ཁྱགས་པའི་སྟེང་ལ་འདྲེད་དེབ་ཤོར་སོང་ He slipped on the ice.

དྲེད་པོ་ (tre̲èbo) 1. tough, capable. 2. very ༈མི་དེ་ཡག་པོ་དྲེད་པོ་འདུག This man is very good. 3. sm. སྟོབས་ཉག.

དྲེད་ལྤགས་ (tre̲èbaà) skin of a brown bear.

དྲེད་ཕོ་ (tre̲èpo) male brown bear.

དྲེད་མ་ (tre̲èma) woman with a harsh/ tough/ rough character.

དྲེད་མོ་ (tre̲èmo) 1. female brown bear. 2. sm. དྲེད་མོང་.

དྲེད་མོང་ (tre̲èmoŋ) brown bear.

དྲེད་ཚང་ (tre̲èdzaŋ) bear's den/ lair.

དྲེད་ལམ་ (tre̲èlam) path/ trail on a mountain where bears pass.

དྲེབ་ཀྱི་ (tre̲bgye) sm. དྲེད་དོ་.

དྲེབ་དོ་ (tre̲bdo) sm. དྲེད་དོ་.

དྲེབ་ཚ་པོ་ (tre̲b tsābo) sm. དྲེད་དོ་.

དྲེབ་འཛོང་ (tre̲bdzoŋ) sm. སྤྲལ་རལ་བྱེད་.

དྲེའུ་ (tre̲wu) sm. དྲེལ་.

དྲེའུ་རྔོག (tre̲wu ŋōg) mule's mane.

དྲེའུ་ཐོ་ལོག (tre̲wu tōlɔ̀ɔ) a kind of mule that is a cross breed between a female donkey and a horse.

དྲེའུ་ལག (tre̲wu la̲à) sm. དྲེལ་ལག.

དྲེལ་ (tre̲e) mule.

དྲེལ་རྒྱ་མོ་ (tre̲e gya̲mo) black mule with white skin

around the eyes and mouth.
དྲེལ་རྒྱབ་ (treegyəb) mule load.
དྲེལ་ལྕགས་ (treejaà) iron horseshoe for mules.
དྲེལ་རྗེས་པ་ (tree jeèma) muleteer.
དྲེལ་གདང་ (treedaŋ) rope staked out to tether mules.
དྲེལ་པ་ (treeba) sm. དྲེལ་རྗེས་པ་.
དྲེལ་པ་ལག་དོ་ (treeba lagdo) assistant to a muleteer.
དྲེལ་པའི་སྒར་ཤོག (treebe garshɔɔ̀) group of muleteers traveling together.
དྲེལ་དཔོན་ (treebön) head muleteer.
དྲེལ་ཕྲུག (treedruù) baby mule.
དྲེལ་བྱམས་ (treejam) mule drawn palanquin.
དྲེལ་རྫི་ (treēdzi) mule herder.
དྲེལ་ར་ (treera) corral/ stable for mules.
དྲེལ་ལག (treelag) shung. one ལག unit of mules (=10 mules).
དྲེལ་སག (treesaà) leather/ hide from the back of a mule.
དྲེས་ཁྲལ་ (treèdrɛɛ) shung. a tax requiring provision of དྲེས་མ་.
དྲེས་མ་ (treèma) kind of grass used for making rope.
དྲེས་མ་མེ་ཏོག (treèma medoò) tulip.
དྲེས་མའི་གེ་སར་ (treèmɛ kesar) acanthaceous indigo.
དྲོ་ (tro) 1. abbr. of དྲོ་མོ་ or དྲོ་པོ་. 2. food taken to be eaten on a trip or while out herding or working.
དྲོ་སྐྱིད་ (trogyiì) good, happy ། དྲོ་སྐྱིད་ཀྱི་འཚོ་བ་ A good livelihood.
དྲོ་རྐྱལ་ (trogyɛɛ) leather pouch used for keeping food when traveling.
དྲོ་ཁ་ (troga) sm. དྲོ་, 1.
དྲོ་ཁང་ (trogaŋ) greenhouse, hot house.
དྲོ་ཁུལ་བྱང་མ་ (trogüü caŋma) north temperate zone.
དྲོ་ཁུལ་ལྷོ་མ་ (trogüü lhōma) south temperate zone.
དྲོ་གྲང་ (trodraŋ) warm and cold ། དེང་སང་གནམ་གཤིས་དྲོ་གྲང་སྙོམ་པོ་འདུག These days the temperature is not too hot and not too cold (it is balanced).
དྲོ་གྲང་ལྟ་ཆས་ (trodraŋ dājɛɛ̀) sm. དྲོ་གྲང་དཔྱད་ཆས་.
དྲོ་གྲང་བརྟག་ཆས་ (trodraŋ dājɛɛ̀) sm. དྲོ་གྲང་དཔྱད་ཆས་.
དྲོ་གྲང་དཔྱད་ཆས་ (trodraŋ jɛ̄ɛ̀jɛɛ̀) thermometer.
དྲོ་བཅོས་ (trojöö̀) keeping oneself warm; va.—བྱེད་.
དྲོ་ཆས་ (trojɛɛ̀) things to keep oneself warm.
དྲོ་ཅི་ལེ་བ་ (tro cīlewa) warm.
དྲོ་འཇམ་ (tronjam) 1. lukewarm. 2. abbr. warm and soft.
དྲོ་རྟེན་ (troden) shung. money for food expenses when traveling.
དྲོ་ཐིང་ཐིང་ (tro tīndiŋ) warm.

དྲོ་དོད་ (trodöö̀) shung. sm. དྲོ་རྟེན་.
དྲོ་འདེབས་ (tro deb) sm. ཚ་ཕོགས་རྒྱག.
དྲོ་པོ་ (trobo) warm ། དེ་རིང་གནམ་གཤིས་དྲོ་པོ་འདུག It is warm today.
དྲོ་བ་ (trowa) warm; warmer ། ས་དེ་ཚོ་དྲོ་བ་ཡོད་པ་རེད་ Those areas are warmer. ། ཡུལ་ལྗོངས་མཛེས་ལ་གནམ་གཤིས་དྲོ་བའི་གནས་ཤིག་རེད་ It is a place that has beautiful scenery and warm weather.
དྲོ་བའི་ཡི་གེ་བཞི་ (trowɛ yigi shi) the 4 Sanskrit letters: ཤ་ ཥ་ ས་ ཧ་.
དྲོ་སྔོར་ (trojɔɔ) morning.
དྲོ་མོ་ (tromo) sm. དྲོ་པོ་.
དྲོ་ཚད་ (trodzɛɛ̀) sm. དྲོད་ཚད་.
དྲོ་ཡ་ (troya) source of heat.
དྲོ་ཡོལ་ (troyɛɛ) afternoon.
དྲོ་ལུག (troluù) shung. a sheep brought to be slaughtered and used for food when traveling.
དྲོ་ལོ་མོ་ལོ་ (trolo molo) 1. lukewarm. 2. grayish color.
དྲོ་ཤ་ (trosha) shung. meat for eating when traveling.
དྲོ་ས་ (trosa) 1. warm weather place. 2. place where one eats lunch when traveling.
དྲོ་སོབ་སོབ་ (tro sōbsob) warm.
དྲོག (trɔɔ̀) sm. སྒྲོག.
དྲོག་སྐད་ (trɔggɛɛ̀) sm. སྒྲོག་སྐད་.
དྲོག་ལྷ་ (trɔgja) sm. སྒྲོག་ལྷ་.
དྲོངས་ (troŋ) imp. of འདྲེན་.
དྲོད་ (tröö̀) heat, warmth; va.—གཏོང་ to heat/ warm up sth. ། ཉི་མའི་དྲོད་ Heat from the sun.
དྲོད་བསྐུལ་གློག་ཁང་ (tröö̀güü lɔ̄ɔ̀gaŋ) thermal electric plant.
དྲོད་སྐྱེ་ (tröö̀gye) sm. དྲོད་སློབས་.
དྲོད་ཁང་ (tröö̀gaŋ) 1. hot house, greenhouse, incubator. 2. a heated house/ barn ། ཉི་འོད་ནུས་པའི་དྲོད་ཁང་ A solar heated house/ barn.
དྲོད་ཁུག (tröö̀guù) 1. vi. to get warm (usu. body) ། ཉལ་སའི་ནང་ལ་གཟུགས་པོ་དྲོད་ཁུག་བྱུང་ My body got warm in bed. 2. sm. དྲོད་སློབས་.
དྲོད་ཁྲིད་ནུས་པ་ (tröö̀drii nüǜbə) sm. དྲོད་ཁྲིད་བྱེད་ཀྱི་ནུས་པ་.
དྲོད་ཁྲིད་བྱེད་ཀྱི་ནུས་པ་ (tröö̀trii ceègi nüǜbə) heat conductivity.
དྲོད་གྲང་གཏོང་རྒྱུ་ (tröö̀draŋ dōŋgyu) heating and cooling system.
དྲོད་འགུགས་ (tröö̀ guù) va. to heat, to warm ། ཨ་མས་ཕྲུ་གུ་བྲང་ཁོག་ལ་སྦྲུར་ནས་དྲོད་བཀུག་པ་རེད་ The mother warmed the child by holding it to (her) chest.
དྲོད་རྒྱུན་ (tröö̀gyün) warm air current.

དྲོད་ཅན་ (tröö̀jɛn) warm.
དྲོད་ཆུང་ (tröö̀juŋ) 1. not warm, cool. 2. sb. who is not confident. 3. an inexperienced (person).
དྲོད་ཆེན་ (tröö̀jen) 1. warm. 2. sb. who is confident. 3. experienced.
དྲོད་བཅོས་ (tröö̀jöö̀) 1. heat therapy; va.—བྱེད་. 2. dressing/ keeping warm; va.—བྱེད་ ། དེང་སང་གནམ་གཤིས་འགྱུར་ལྡོག་ཆེན་པོ་འདུག ཁྱེད་རང་དུས་ཡོལ་དྲོད་བཅོས་བྱེད་དགོས་ These days the weather is changeable so dress warm.
དྲོད་མཉམ་འགྱུར་ལྡོག (tröö̀ñam gyundɔɔ̀) isothermal change/ transformation.
དྲོད་མཉམ་ཐིག་རིས་ (tröö̀ñam tīgrii̇̀) isotherm.
དྲོད་ཉུལ་ (tröö̀ ñül) va. to test sb.'s (feelings, thinking, etc.).
དྲོད་ཐུབ་ (tröö̀tub) heat resistant/ resisting.
དྲོད་དུགས་ (tröö̀duù) applying hot compress as a treatment.
དྲོད་མདོག (tröö̀dɔɔ̀) a warm color.
དྲོད་འདོན་ (tröö̀ dön) va. to bring out the heat/ warmth.
དྲོད་འདོན་ཚད་ (tröö̀ döndzɛɛ̀) amount of heat generated.
དྲོད་ལྡན་ (tröndɛn) warm ། དུག་ལོག་དྲོད་ལྡན་ Warm clothes.
དྲོད་སྡོབ་ཙམ་ (tröö̀ dobdzam) slightly warm.
དྲོད་མེད་པ་ (tröö̀ meèba) 1. without heat. 2. not content. 3. not confident.
དྲོད་སྨན་ (tröö̀mɛn) a Tibetan medicine that in said to bring heat to the body.
དྲོད་ཚད་ (tröö̀dzɛɛ̀) temperature; vi.—ཆག to get decreased/ diminished/ lessened in temperature; vi.—འཕར་ to get increased/ raised in temperature. ། ཆ་སྙོམས་ཀྱི་དྲོད་ཚད་ Mean temperature.
དྲོད་ཚད་ཀླད་ཀོར་སྟེང་ (tröö̀dzɛɛ̀ lɛ̄ɛ̀gɔɔ gaŋ) above zero.
དྲོད་ཚད་ཀླད་ཀོར་འོག (tröö̀dzɛɛ̀ lɛ̄ɛ̀gɔɔ wɔɔ̀) below zero.
དྲོད་ཚད་སྙོམ་སྒྲིག་ཁང་ (tröö̀dzɛɛ̀ ñōmdriggaŋ) air conditioned office.
དྲོད་ཚད་དཔྱད་ཆས་ (tröö̀dzɛɛ̀ jɛ̄ɛ̀jɛɛ̀) thermometer.
དྲོད་ཚད་ཉམས་པའི་རིམ་པ་ (tröö̀dzɛɛ̀ ñambɛ rimbə) stratosphere.
དྲོད་ཚད་བརྟག་ཆས་ (tröö̀dzɛɛ̀ dāgjɛɛ̀) sm. དྲོད་ཚད་དཔྱད་ཆས་.
དྲོད་ཚད་མཐོན་པོ་ལས་བརྒལ་བ་ (tröö̀dzɛɛ̀ tõmbolɛ gɛɛwa) super high temperature.
དྲོད་ཚད་དམའ་པོ་ (tröö̀dzɛɛ̀ maabo) low temperature.

དྲོད་ཚད་ཀླད་ཀོར་ (trö̲ö̲dzɛ̀ɛ̀ lɛ̀ɛ̀gɔɔ) zero temperature.

དྲོད་རྫོགས་ (trö̲ö̲ dzɔ̲ɔ̀) sm. དྲོད་ཡལ་.

དྲོད་འོངས་དུས་ (trö̲ö̲ o̲ŋdüü) spring.

དྲོད་ཡལ་ (trö̲ö̲ ye̲e̲) vi. to become cold, to lose heat ¶ཁ་ལག་གི་ཁོག་མ་ས་ལ་བཞག་ནས་དྲོད་ཡལ་བཞག The pot with food was left on the floor and got cold.

དྲོད་རླངས་ (trö̲ö̲laŋ) warm or hot air/ steam ¶དྲོད་རླངས་ཀྱི་ལུགས་མདོང་ A hot air pipe/ duct.

དྲོད་རླངས་ཀྱི་ཐབ་ (trö̲ö̲laŋgi tāb) forced air type furnace.

དྲོད་རླངས་ཚོམ་བུ་ (trö̲ö̲laŋ tsōmbu) warm air mass.

དྲོད་རླུང་ (trö̲ö̲luŋ) sm. དྲོད་ལྷགས་.

དྲོད་ལེན་ (trö̲ö̲ le̲n) va. to warm oneself (e.g., by a fire).

དྲོད་ལེན་ཁང་ (trö̲ö̲lengaŋ) heated house.

དྲོད་ཤུགས་ (trö̲ö̲shuù) the strength of heat.

དྲོད་ཤུགས་ཆེན་པོ་ (trö̲ö̲shuù cēmbo) hot.

དྲོད་ཤེས་ (trö̲ö̲ shēè) to get an understanding/ estimate/ evaluation of sth. or sb.

དྲོད་ཤོར་ (trö̲ö̲ shɔ̄ɔ̄) sm. དྲོད་ཡལ་.

དྲོད་གཤེར་ (trö̲ö̲ shēr) hot and humid.

དྲོད་སྲུང་འཕྲུལ་ཆས་ (trö̲ö̲ suŋ trüüjɛ̀ɛ̀) heat preserving machine.

དྲོད་སླེབས་ (trö̲ö̲ lēb) vi. to become warm, to have the warm time/ season arrive ¶དེང་སང་དྲོད་སླེབས་ནས་ཞིང་ཁ་འདེབས་རན་བཞག Nowadays, the warm season has arrived and it is time to plant.

དྲོད་ལྷགས་ (trö̲ö̲ lhāà) warm breeze, warm wind.

དྲོན་འཇམ་ (trö̲njam) sm. དྲོ་འཇམ་.

དྲོན་འཇུག (trö̲njuù) va. to falsify/ exaggerate/ lie.

དྲོན་པོ་ (trö̲nbo) sm. དྲོ་འཇམ་.

དྲོན་མ་ (trö̲nma) sm. དྲོ་འཇམ་.

དྲོན་མོ་ (trö̲nmo) sm. དྲོ་འཇམ་.

དྲོན་ཞོ་ (trö̲nsho) fresh yogurt that is still warm.

དྲོན་ཤ་ (trö̲nsha) meat of an animal that has just been killed (that is still warm).

དྲོལ་ (trö̲ö̲) imp. of འདྲུལ་.

དྲོས་ (trö̲ö̲) 1. vi. to warm/ heat up ¶ཁང་པ་འདི་དྲོས་ཁག་པོ་འདུག This house is hard to heat. 2. imp. of འདྲོ་.

དྲོས་ཆེན་ (trö̲ö̲jen) midday.

དྲྭ་མིག (tra̲mig) a cubby hole in a bookshelf (for keeping Tibetan books).

གདགས་ (dag) f. of འདོགས་.

གདགས་ཁྲི་བཙན་པོ་ (dagdri dze̲mbo) the 6th ancient king of Tibet.

གདགས་གཞི་ (dagshi) the basis for naming sth.

གདང་ (da̲ŋ) 1. a long piece of wood for hanging clothes on. 2. a long rope/ line pegged into the ground and used to tie/ tether several animals at once; va.—རྒྱག to tie animals to such a rope. 3. sm. རང་བུ་. 4. perch/ roost for fowl.

གདང་: p. གདངས་; f. གདང་; imp. གདོངས་ (da̲ŋ) 1. va. to open the mouth.

གདང་བཀག་མཆོངས་བརྒལ་ (da̲ŋgaà cōŋgɛɛ) jumping over hurdles, overcoming stumbling blocks.

གདང་སྐེ་ (da̲ŋgɛ̀ɛ̀) the middle of a long tether rope.

གདང་ག (da̲ŋga) sm. གདང་, 4.

གདང་འགོ་ (da̲ŋgo) the top/ upper section of a long tether rope.

གདང་ཐག (da̲ŋdaà) 1. rope for hanging clothes. 2. sm. གདང་, 2.

གདང་ཐག་འཕྲུལ་མིག (da̲ŋtaà drüümiì) the eye/ loop on a གདང་ཐག to which an animal is tied ¶གདང་ཐག་ཕྲུལ་མིག་བཅུ་འབྱར་པ་ A rope with ten loops.

གདང་ཕུར་ (da̲ŋbur) peg for tying animals or hanging clothes.

གདང་བུ་ (da̲ŋbu) rung of a ladder. 2. sm. གདང་, 1.

གདང་གཞུག (da̲ŋgɛ̀ɛ̀) the lower/ bottom of a long thether rope to which animals are tied.

གདང་ར་ (da̲ŋra) a place where animals are tied.

གདང་ཤིང་ (da̲ŋshiŋ) wooden clothing hanger.

གདངས་ (da̲ŋ) 1. tone, pitch ¶སྐད་གདངས་སྨྲོམ་ཕྲ་ Low and high tone. 2. tune, melody ¶གཞས་གདངས་སྙན་པོ་ A song with a pleasant melody. 3. p. of གདང་. 4. chanting in low tones.

གདངས་འགུགས་ (da̲ŋguù) pleasant melody/ tune.

གདངས་སྒྲིག (da̲ŋ dri̲g) va. to tune musical instruments.

གདངས་འདུར་ (da̲ŋdur) abbr. chanting and reciting prayers.

གདངས་དབྱངས་ (dāŋyaŋ) sm. གདངས་, 2.

གདངས་དབྱངས་མཚོན་བྱེད་ (da̲ŋyaŋ tsōnjeè) musical notation/ notes.

གདངས་མཐོ་ (da̲ŋto) soprano.

གདངས་བཙུམ་ (da̲ŋdzum) opening and closing (of eyes, mouth, etc.) ¶མིག་གདངས་བཙུམ་བྱེད་རྒྱུ་མེད་པ་ Unable to open or close the eyes.

གདངས་མཚམས་ (da̲ŋdzaŋ) a stopping point of a tune or prayer chant.

གདངས་རིང་པོ་ (da̲ŋ ri̲ŋbu) a long tone in a song.

གདན་ (de̲n) 1. low seat, mattress, mat, cushion. 2. rug. 3. throne.

གདན་བཀྱག (de̲ngyaà) a frame on which cushions/ mattresses are placed.

གདན་སྐྱོང་ (de̲ngyoŋ) sm. སྐྱོང་གདན་.

གདན་ཁང་ (de̲ngaŋ) place where rugs and cushions are stored.

གདན་ཁེབས་ (de̲nkeb) cushion/ mattress cover, bed sheet.

གདན་ཁྲི་ (de̲ntri) 1. sm. གདན་བཀྱག. 2. throne.

གདན་ཁྲི་སྟོང་པ་ (de̲ntri dōŋba) vacant throne.

གདན་ཁྲི་གཞན་ལ་སྤྲོད་ (de̲ntri shenla drȫȫ) va. to abdicate, to renounce (a throne).

གདན་གྲངས་ (de̲ndraŋ) a numbered seat.

གདན་གྲལ་ (de̲ndrɛɛ) rank, level.

གདན་སྒོར་ (de̲ngɔɔ) round rug/ cushion/ mattress.

གདན་ཅོག (de̲njɔɔ̀) sm. གདན་ལྕོག.

གདན་ལྕོག (de̲njɔɔ̀) rug/ cushion/ mattress and table.

གདན་ཆ་ (dēnja) 1. sm. གདན་ཆས་. 2. a pair of cushions/ mattresses/ rugs.

གདན་ཆས་ (de̲njɛ̀ɛ̀) things for sitting (e.g., rugs, cushions).

གདན་གཉེར་ (de̲nñer) shung. stewards in charge of cushions/ mattresses/ rugs at the Potala Palace and Norbulinga.

གདན་ཐོ་ (de̲ndo) seating list.

གདན་ཐོག་ལུས་རྩལ་ (de̲ntɔɔ̀ lü̲ü̲dzɛɛ) tumbling exercises.

གདན་ཐོབ་ (de̲ntob) 1. seat (in parliament/ congress/ organization) ¶རྒྱལ་ཚོགས་ནང་ལ་གདན་ཐོབ་ག་ཚོད་ཡོད་དམ་ How many seats are there in parliament? 2. position, status ¶ཁོང་ལ་རིམ་པ་ལྔ་པའི་གདན་ཐོབ་ཡོད་པ་རེད་ He has the position of fifth rank.

གདན་འཐུས་ (de̲ntüü) abbr. representatives of the three big monasteries around Lhasa (Drepung, Sera and Ganden).

གདན་དར་ (de̲ndar) a ceremonial scarf put on a carpet before leaving as a symbol of good luck.

གདན་དྲངས་ (de̲n dra̲ŋ) p. of གདན་འདྲེན་.

གདན་འདིང་ (de̲n di̲ŋ) va. to place/ put down a rug/ cushion/ mattress.

གདན་འདེགས་ (de̲n de̲g) va. to move/ change residence to a different place.

གདན་འདྲེན་ (de̲ndren) 1. inviting (h.); va.—ཞུ་ ¶ཁོང་གསོལ་ཚིགས་ལ་གདན་འདྲེན་ཞུས་པ་རེད་ (They) invited him to dinner. 2. taking (h.); va.—ཞུ་ to take ¶ཁོང་ལམ་སེང་སྨན་ཁང་ལ་གདན་འདྲེན་ཞུས་པ་རེད་ They took him to the hospital at once.

གདན་འདྲེན་ཞུ་ཡིག (de̲ndren shu̲yiì) letter of invitation.

གདན་འཕར་ (de̲mbar) shung. additional cushion/ mattress ¶ཕྱག་མཛོད་ལ་འང་གདན་འཕར་དང་འབྲེལ་བའི་རྟེན་འབྲུང་བསྐྱར་པ་ (They) honored the steward by putting out an additional cushion for him.

གདན་འཛོམས་ (de̲n dzo̲m) vi. to meet, to gather.

གདན་ཞུ་ (de̲nshu) 1. an invitation, inviting; va.—ཞུ་; —བྱེད་ to invite ¶གདན་ཞུའི་ཡི་གེ་ A letter of invitation. 2. the act of taking; va.—ཞུ་ to take.

གདན་ཞུ་ལྟར་ (densshudar) at the invitation of, according to the invitation.

གདན་ཞུའི་ཡི་གེ་ (denshü yigi) letter of invitation.

གདན་ཞྭ་ (densha) a type hat worn by the heads of Ham dong and Samlo Khamtsen (of Drepung monastery).

གདན་རབས་ (denrəb) the succession line of a monastery's lama/ abbot.

གདན་ལ་འདིངས་ (denla diŋ) va. to lay/ put down a cushion/ mattress/ rug for sitting.

གདན་ཤུབས་ (denshub) covering for a cushion/ mattress.

གདན་ས་ (densa) monastic seat, main monastery (that has branch monasteries).

གདན་ས་གསུམ་ (densa sūm) the three great monastic seats of the Gelugpa Sect (Drepung, Sera and Ganden).

གདན་གསུམ་ (den sūm) abbr. གདན་ས་གསུམ་.

གདབ་ (dəb) f. of འདེབས་.

གདམ་ (dam) f. of འདེམ་.

གདམ་ཀ་ (damga) choosing, selecting; va.—བྱེད་; —རྒྱག.

གདམ་ག (damga) sm. གདམ་ཀ་.

གདམ་ང་ (damŋa) optional, left to one's choice/ selection ¶ སློབ་ཚན་འདི་གཉིས་གདམ་ང་རེད་ These two lessons are optional.

གདམ་ང་ཅན་ (damŋajen) sm. གདམ་ང་.

གདམ་ངག (damŋaà) sm. གདམས་ངག.

གདམ་ (dam) f. of འདོམ་.

གདམ་བྱ་ (damja) nominee.

གདམ་བྱ་འདེམས་བྱེད་ (damja demjeè) the right to stand as a candidate and the right to vote.

གདམ་བྱའི་མི་སྣ་ (damje mina) candidate for selection/ election.

གདམ་བྱའི་དབང་ཆ་ (damje wāŋja) the right to be a candidate for election/ selection.

གདམ་ཚིག (damdzii) epigram, aphorism.

གདམ་གསེས་ (damseè) selecting, choosing; va.—རྒྱག;—བྱེད་ to select/ choose ¶ སློབ་ཕྲུག་དག་ཤོས་ཁ་ཤས་གདམ་གསེས་བྱས་པ་རེད་ They selected a few of the best students.

གདམས་ (dam) 1. sm. གདམ་. 2. p. of འདོམས་.

གདམས་ངག (damŋaà) essential instruction/ teachings; va.—ཤོར་; —སྟོན་.

གདའ་ (da) sm. གདའ་མོ་.

གདའ་མོ་ (damo) sm. འདུག.

གདར་མ་ (darma) a square/ rectangular piece of sth.

གདལ་ (dεε) vi. to be/ get spread.

གདལ་ཁ་ (dεεga) widespread.

གདལ་གདམ་ (dεεdam) a widespread rumor/ talk.

གདལ་པོ་ (dεεbo) shung. sm. གདལ་པོ་དུས་སྒྱུར་.

གདལ་པོ་དུས་སྒྱུར་ (dεεbo tüügyur) shung. sowing discord.

གདས་ (dεè) sm. ཤོད་.

གདིང་ (diŋ) f. of འདིང་.

གདིང་གྲགས་ (diŋdrag) a deep sound like the sound of deep thunder.

གདུ་: p. and imp. གདུས་; f. གདུ་ (du) 1. va. to brew sth. by cooking. 2. vi. to be attached to ¶ རྫས་ཅ་ལག་ལ་གདུ་བ་ To be attached to things.

གདུ་གུ་ (dugu) sm. གདུ་བུ་.

གདུ་བུ་ (dubu) bracelet, bangle.

གདུག (dug) 1. abbr. of གདུག་པ་. 2. sm. དུག.

གདུག་ཅན་ (dugjen) sm. གདུག་པ་ཅན་.

གདུག་དྲི་ (dugdri) 1. bad/ foul smelling. 2. flatus.

གདུག་འདྲེ་ (doŋdre) ghosts, demons.

གདུག་པ་ (dugba) cruel, evil ¶ གདུག་པའི་བསམ་པ་ Cruel ideas/ thoughts.

གདུག་པ་ཅན་ (dugbajen) cruel, wicked, vicious, savage.

གདུག་པ་གཉུག་མར་གནས་པ་ (dugba ñugmar nεèba) an evil spirit who is always with a person.

གདུག་སྤྱོད་ (dugjöö) cruel/ savage/ vicious behavior.

གདུག་རྩུབ་ (dugdzub) cruelty, ferocity, viciousness, savagery.

གདུག་རྩུབ་ཅན་ (dugdzubjεn) cruel, ferocious, vicious, savage.

གདུག་སེམས་ (dugsem) cruel/ savage/ vicious thoughts.

གདུག་གསོད་ (dugsöö) killing/ murdering cruelly; slaughtering; va.—གཏོང་.

གདུགས་ (dug) umbrella, parasol; va.—འབུབས་ to open an umbrella.

གདུགས་དཀར་ (duggar) 1. white umbrella. 2. a female goddess with a thousand hands and heads.

གདུགས་འཁོར་ (duggɔɔ) astrological drawing/ pattern.

གདུགས་མཆོང་ (dugcoŋ) parachuting; va.—བྱེད་ to parachute.

གདུགས་ཐོགས་ (dugtɔ̀) va. to hold/ carry an open umbrella.

གདུགས་ཕུབ་ (dugpub) p. of གདུགས་འབུབས་.

གདུགས་འཕན་ (dugpεn) shung. canopy and decorative hangings in monasteries.

གདུགས་འབུབས་ (dug) see གདུགས་.

གདུགས་དམག (dugmaà) paratrooper corps, paratrooper.

གདུགས་རྩིབས་ (dugdzib) umbrella spoke/ rib.

གདུགས་ཚོད་ (dugdzöö) 1. noon, midday. 2. lunch.

གདུགས་མཚན་ (dugdzεn) day and night.

གདུང་ (duŋ) 1. corpse. 2. lineage, descent line ¶ བོད་ཀྱི་རྒྱལ་པོའི་གདུང་ The lineage of the Kings of Tibet. 3. beam ¶ གདུང་དང་ཀ་བ་ Beams and pillars.

གདུང་: p. གདུངས་; f. གདུང་ (duŋ) 1. vi. to suffer from, to be tormented, to be in anguish ¶ བཀྲེས་པ་དང་ནད་ཀྱིས་གདུང་བའི་མི་ People tormented by hunger and disease. 2. vi. to have a great desire. ¶ ཕྱུག་པོ་ཆགས་རྒྱུར་གདུང་ནས་དཀའ་ལས་རྒྱག་གི་ཡོད་པ་རེད་ Having a great desire to get rich, he is working hard.

གདུང་སྐས་ (duŋgεὲ) a notched ladder made from a tree.

གདུང་སྐྱེལ་མཛད་སྒོ་ (duŋgyee dzεὲgo) coffin carrying ceremony.

གདུང་སྐྱེལ་འཁོར་ལོ་ (duŋgyee kɔ̄ɔlo) hearse.

གདུང་གོས་ (duŋgöö) grave clothes, shroud.

གདུང་ཁང་ (duŋgaŋ) sm. ཕུར་ཁང་.

གདུང་ཁྲི་ (duŋdri) bier.

གདུང་འཁོར་ (duŋgɔɔ) Tibetan architectural technique of forming a square with four beams.

གདུང་གྲུ་ (duŋdru) canoe, boat made from a hollowed out log.

གདུང་རྒྱུད་ (duŋgyüü) lineage, descent line (paternal).

གདུང་རྒྱུད་ཀྱི་འབྲེལ་བ་ (duŋgyüügi dreewa) paternal relatives.

གདུང་སྒམ་ (duŋgam) coffin.

གདུང་སྒྲིག (duŋdrig) sm. གདུང་ལྕགས་.

གདུང་སྒྲོམ་ (duŋdrom) sm. གདུང་སྒམ་.

གདུང་ལྕགས་ (duŋjaà) a type of leg shackles with a horizontal iron bar.

གདུང་ཆད་ (duŋjεὲ) vi. to have a descent line broken.

གདུང་ཆེན་ (duŋjen) a large beam.

གདུང་མཇལ་ (duŋjεε) visiting the corpse to pay one's respect (usu. to a lama).

གདུང་དལ་མ་ (duŋ tεεma) a room with no pillars because of long beams.

གདུང་རྟེན་ (duŋden) tomb/ stupa with a corpse inside.

གདུང་ཐལ་ (duŋtεε) cremation ashes.

གདུང་གདན་ (duŋdεn) bier.

གདུང་འདེགས་ (duŋdeg) 1. pillar. 2. va. to raise/ lift up a beam.

གདུང་བ་བརྒྱུས་གཟེར་ (duŋwa gyεὲser) experiencing suffering/ sorrow.

གདུང་བྱང་ (duŋjaŋ) inscribed gravestone/ grave board.

གདུང་འབོད་ (duŋböö) complaining/ exclaiming about suffering or grievances; va.—བྱེད་.

གདུང་འབོད་ཡི་གེ་ (duŋböö yigi) petition/ letter expressing one's sufferings or grievances.

གདུང་དབྱངས་ (duŋyaŋ) melancholy songs.

གདུང་དབྱངས་མཉམ་སྒྲོག (duŋyaŋ ñāmdrɔɔ̀) expressing grievances together [Lit. singing melancholy songs together].

གདུང་མ་ (duŋma) beam, girder.

གདུང་སྨྱུལ་རྒྱག (duŋñüü gyaà) va. to search/ poke around using a spear.

གདུང་ཚན་ (duŋdzɛn) relatives.

གདུང་ཚིག (duŋtsig) words of sorrow and sadness.

གདུང་འཛིན་ (duŋdzob) keeping/ maintaining/ preserving a lineage ¶ ས་སྐྱ་བདག་ཆེན་གྱི་གདུང་འཛིན་ཆེད་གདུང་སྲས་དེ་འཁྱུང་ས་བསྐྱོན་པ་རེད་ For the purpose of maintaining the lineage of the Sakya Dagchens, the Sakya (lama's) son got married. 2. descendant.

གདུང་འཛིན་ (duŋ dzin) sm. གདུང་འཛིན་.

གདུང་ཞུགས་ (duŋshug) cremating a corpse; va.—འབུལ་; —བྱེད་.

གདུང་ཟམ་ (duŋsam) a tree trunk used as a bridge.

གདུང་རབས་ (duŋrəb) a generation in a line of descent/ lineage ¶ གནས་ཚུལ་དེ་ས་སྐྱ་གདུང་རབས་བཅོ་ལྔ་པའི་སྐབས་སུ་བྱུང་བ་ཞིག་རེད་ This incident occurred at the time of 15th in the line of the Sakya (lamas).

གདུང་རབས་ཕྲེང་བ་ (duŋrəb dreŋwa) a lineage line.

གདུང་རིགས་ (duŋrig) sm. གདུང་རྒྱུད་.

གདུང་རིང་ (duŋriŋ) 1. long beam. 2. a long lineage line.

གདུང་རུས་ (duŋrüü) 1. bones of a deceased person (usu. lama). 2. lineage, descent line.

གདུང་ཤུགས་ (duŋshug) strong desire or wish for sth.

གདུང་ཤུགས་གཅིག་སྒྲིལ་ (duŋshug jīgdrii) a united effort, working together in full cooperation, a concerted effort; va.—བྱེད་.

གདུང་སེམས་ (duŋsem) sadness, sorrow.

གདུང་སེམས་མཉམ་སྐྱེ་ (duŋsem ñamgye) sympathizing or sharing with sadness/ sorrow; va.—བྱེད་ ¶ དམངས་གཙོའི་དབང་ཆ་བཙན་ལེན་གྱི་འཐབ་རྩོད་བྱེད་པ་དེ་ར་ང་ཚོས་གདུང་སེམས་མཉམ་སྐྱེ་བྱེད་ཀྱི་ཡོད་ We sympathize with their struggle for democratic rights.

གདུང་སེམས་གཏིང་སྐྱེས་ (duŋsem dīŋgyeè) having deep sympathy.

གདུང་སྲས་ (duŋsɛɛ̀) son of a lama with a lineage line (usu. the sons of the Sakya lama).

གདུང་བསབས་ (duŋsəb) sm. གདུང་འཛིན་.

གདུངས་ (duŋ) p. of གདུང་.

གདུད་ (düü) f. of འདུད་.

གདུབ་ (dub) bracelet, bangle ¶ ལག་གདུབ་ Wrist bangle/ bracelet.

གདུབ་ཀོར་ (dubgɔɔ) sm. གདུབ་.

གདུབ་བསྐོར་ (dubgɔɔ) sm. གདུབ་ཀོར་.

གདུབ་བུ་ (dubbu) sm. གདུབ་.

གདུབ་སིལ་ (dubsil) sound made by ornaments worn around the wrists and ankles (usu. by dancers).

གདུལ་ (düü) f. of འདུལ་.

གདུལ་བྱ་ (düülja) the object of religious teachings.

གདུས་ (düü) p. and imp. of གདུ་.

གདུས་ཁུ་ (düügu) juice that has been extracted by boiling sth.

གདེག (deg) f. of འདེགས་.

གདེང་ (deŋ) confidence, feeling of self assurance ¶ དེ་བྱེད་ཐུབ་པའི་གདེང་ཡོད་ (I) am confident that I can do that.

གདེང་: p. གདེངས་; f. གདེང་; imp. གདེངས་ (deŋ) va. to hoist/ raise/ fly (flags, banners, etc.), to brandish/ lift up.

གདེང་འཁེལ་ (deŋ kēē) vi. to be sure, to have confidence in ¶ ད་ལོ་ང་བོད་ལ་འགྲོ་ཐུབ་ཀྱི་ཡོད་མེད་གདེང་འཁེལ་གྱི་མི་འདུག This year it is not sure whether I will be able to go to Tibet or not.

གདེང་འཁྱོལ་ (deŋ kyöö) sm. གདེང་འཁེལ་.

གདེང་རྒྱག (deŋ gyaà) va. to have confidence ¶ རང་ངོས་ནས་ཨ་རེར་འགྲོ་ཐུབ་རྒྱུའི་གདེང་རྒྱག་གི་ཡོད་ From my point of view I am confident that I will be able to go to Tibet.

གདེང་ཆ་ (deŋja) stage, platform.

གདེང་འཇོག (deŋjɔɔ̀) appraisal, evaluation; va.—བྱེད་ ¶ ཁོའི་རྩོམ་ཡིག་དེ་གདེང་འཇོག་ཚད་མཐོ་པོ་ཞིག་བྱས་པ་རེད་ They gave his article a high appraisal.

གདེང་ཐུབ་ (deŋdub) sm. གདེན་འཁེལ་.

གདེང་དྲོད་ (deŋdröö) confidence.

གདེང་ལྡན་ (deŋdɛn) sm. གདེང་ཐོབ་.

གདེང་ཚད་ (deŋdzɛɛ̀) the degree of confidence.

གདེང་ཚོད་ (deŋdzöö) confidence, assurance ¶ གདེང་ཚོད་མེད་པའི་ལས་ཀ་ Work about which one is not confident.

གདེང་ཚོད་དོན་འཁྱོལ་ (deŋdzöö töŋgyöö) sm. གདེང་འཁྱོལ་.

གདེངས་ (deŋ) p. of གདེང་.

གདོང་ (doŋ) 1. the face ¶ ཁོའི་གདོང་ལ་རྨ་བཟོས་བཞག (He) got a cut on his face. 2. in front, before ¶ ང་ཚོའི་གདོང་ན་ཞབས་བྲོ་བརྒྱབ་སོང་ They danced in front of us. 3. by, through, with ¶ བཀྲ་ཤིས་ཀྱི་གདོང་ཡི་གེ་གཅིག་བསྐུར་ཡོད་ I have sent a letter through Tashi. 4. surface ¶ ཆུའི་གདོང་ལ་ On the surface of the water. 4. first, earlier ¶ ངས་གདོང་ལ་ཕྱིན་ཆོག ཁྱེད་རང་མཇུག་ལ་ཕེབས་ཤོག I will go first. You come later.

གདོང་དཀར་ (doŋgar) 1. white face. 2. smiling face. 3. name of a place located in the west of Lhasa.

གདོང་སྐམ་གཉེར་མང་ (doŋgam ñērmaŋ) sickly, in ill health [Lit. thin face and many wrinkles].

གདོང་བསྐུར་ (doŋgur) va. to send/ carry sth. through sb. ¶ ཚིག་ཐོ་དེ་མ་རྒྱ་གར་བརྒྱུད་གདོང་བསྐུར་མ་ནུས་པར་ Not daring to carry the memo through India on their person.

གདོང་བསྐྱོད་ (doŋgyöö) taking the lead, being the vanguard; va.—བྱེད་. to take the lead, to be the vanguard.

གདོང་བཀོས་ (doŋgöö) an abbreviated book title carved on the edge of each page a wooden printing block.

གདོང་ཁ་ (doŋga) face.

གདོང་ཁེབས་ (doŋgeb) 1. veil (facial). 2. piece of satin/ solk that hang from Tibetan manuscripts and serve as a label/ identifying marker. 3. face mask.

གདོང་ཁྲ་ (doŋdra) facial tattoo; va.—བཟོ་ to tattoo the face.

གདོང་གི་ཁྲག་མདོག་ཤོར་ (doŋgi trāà dɔɔ̀ shɔ̄ɔ) vi. to have one's face lose color/ become pale.

གདོང་གི་གཉེར་མ་ (doŋgi ñērma) face wrinkles.

གདོང་གི་ཚོན་རིས་ (doŋgi dzōnrìì) facial makeup (usu. for an actor).

གདོང་གུ་དུ་སྒྱུར་ (doŋ güüdu gyur) va. to turn (one's) face away in anger.

གདོང་གྲོགས་ (doŋdrɔɔ̀) sm. སྡོང་གྲོགས་.

གདོང་གློད་ (doŋ lōō) 1. vi. to put on a long face. 2. vi. to hold one's head down (in embarrassment/ shame).

གདོང་འགེབས་ལྕགས་རྨོག (doŋgeb jāgmɔɔ̀) helmet with an iron face mask attached to it.

གདོང་རྒོད་ཧར་འཛུལ་ (doŋgöö hāndzüü) shamelessly crashing a party, going to sb.'s house without invitation; va.—བྱེད་.

གདོང་སྒྱུར་ (doŋ gyur) va. to change one's facial expression ¶ ངས་ཁོང་ལ་གནས་ཚུལ་དེ་བཤད་མ་ཐག་ཁོང་གི་གདོང་བསྒྱུར་སོང་ As soon as I told him the news, his facial expression changed.

གདོང་ལྔའི་སྡེར་མོས་བཏགས་ (doŋ ŋɛ̄ dermö dig) sm. སྡེར་ལྔའི་ཁྲི་.

གདོང་སྔོ་མཆེ་རིང་ (doŋŋo cēriŋ) terrifying in appearance [Lit. face blue, canine teeth long].

གདོང་སྔོན་པོ་ (doŋŋön) a dark complexion [Lit. blue

face].

གདོང་ཆུང་ (do̲ŋjuŋ) 1. small face. 2. shy. 3. looking down on.

གདོང་ཆེན་ (do̲ŋjen) 1. big face. 2. shameless. 3. well-regarded.

གདོང་མཆོང་ (do̲ŋjoŋ) charging forward, attacking at the front; va.—བྱེད་.

གདོང་མཆོང་དུང་བརྡ་ (do̲ŋjoŋ tu̲ŋda) trumpet/ bugle signal for a charge or attack; va.—གཏོང་.

གདོང་མཆོང་པ་ (do̲ŋjoŋba) vanguard, pathbreaker.

གདོང་མཆོང་དཔུང་གཏོར་ (do̲ŋjoŋ būŋdɔɔ) charging and scattering/ destroying the enemy.

གདོང་གཏུག (do̲ŋduù) 1. meeting face-to-face; va.—བྱེད་. ། ཕྱོགས་གཉིས་ཀྱི་འཐུས་མི་རྣམས་གདོང་གཏུགས་ནས་གྲོས་མོལ་བྱས་འདུག The representatives of the two sides met face-to-face and held talks.

གདོང་གཏུགས་ཇུས་བསླབ་ (do̲ŋduù ju̲ùləb) teaching strategy/ planing face-to-face.

གདོང་སྟོན་ (do̲ŋ dõn) va. to make an appearance, to show one's face.

གདོང་རྟགས་ (do̲ŋdaà) sm. ཁྲིམས་ཆད་ཚགས་དམ་.

གདོང་བརྟན་པོ་ (do̲ŋ dēmbo) a steady/ reliable person.

གདོང་ཐུག (do̲ŋ tūù) meeting/ coming face-to-face, colliding; vi.—ཐེབས་; —རྒྱག to meet face-to-face, to collide ། རླངས་འཁོར་གདོང་ཐུག་ཐེབས་ནས་མི་ཁ་ཤས་ལ་སྲོག་སྐྱོན་བྱུང་འདུག The cars collided and a few people died.

གདོང་ཐུག་ཁུངས་སྐྱེལ་ (do̲ŋtuù kūŋgyee) proving sth. by meeting face-to-face.

གདོང་ཐུག་མཉམ་འཛོམས་ (do̲ŋtuù ñāmdzom) getting together in person.

གདོང་ཐུག་ཚོགས་འདུ་ (do̲ŋtuù tsōndu) an unplanned/ ad hoc conference or meeting.

གདོང་འཐབ་ (do̲ŋdəb) fighting face-to-face; va.—བྱེད་.

གདོང་དང་གདོང་གཏུགས་ནས་ (do̲ŋdaŋ do̲ŋ dūùnɛ) directly, face-to-face ། བཙན་འཛུལ་པ་གདོང་དང་གདོང་གཏུགས་ནས་འཐབ་རྩོད་བྱེད་ཀྱི་ཡོད་པ་རེད་ They are struggling face-to-face with the aggressors.

གདོང་དར་ (do̲ŋdar) loose piece of cloth hanging out from a manuscript indicating the title or the number of the volume.

.གདོང་དར་སུམ་བརྩེགས་ (do̲ŋdar sūmdzeg) shung. three layers of གདོང་དར་ fastened together.

གདོང་དྲུག་པ་ (do̲ŋ tru̲gbə) Shiva.

གདོང་མདོག (do̲ŋdɔɔ̀) 1. color of a person's face. 2. facial expression.

གདོང་མདོག་སྐྱ་ཐལ་ཆགས་ (do̲ŋdɔɔ̀ gyātɛɛ cāà) vi. to pale.

གདོང་མདོག་སེར་ཞིང་ཤ་རིད་ (do̲ŋdɔɔ̀ sērshiŋ shārii) (face) thin and pale.

གདོང་མདོག་ལོག (do̲ŋdɔɔ̀ lɔɔ̀) sm. གདོང་སྒྱུར་.

གདོང་ལྡོག (do̲ŋdɔɔ̀) 1. sm. གདོང་སྒྱུར་. 2. va. to suddenly turn back.

གདོང་བསྡུས་ (do̲ŋdüü) va. to show a look of anger.

གདོང་ནག་པོ་ (do̲ŋnaà) an angry/ sulking facial expression; va.—སྟོན་ to show an angry/ sulking expression.

གདོང་སྣ་གཏད་ (do̲ŋna dɛ̄ɛ̀) va. to turn towards sth., to face a direction (in empathy/ sympathy/ support) ། ལོ་ན་རྒས་རྗེས་པ་ཡུལ་ལ་གདོང་སྣ་གཏད་ནས་ལོག་ཕྱིན་པ་རེད་ After he became old, he turned towards his homeland and returned.

གདོང་པ་ (do̲ŋba) 1. sm. གདོང་, 1. 2. va.—དཔྱལ་ to expose, uncover. 3. vi.—སྐྱོད་ to show unhappiness by one's facial expressions.

གདོང་པ་དམད་ ཕྲག་པ་ལྷོད་ (do̲ŋba mɛ̄ɛ̀ pāgba lȫȍ) looking completely defeated/ dejected [Lit. hanging one's face down, drooping one's shoulders].

གདོང་པ་ཚ་ལམ་ཙམ་བྱེད་ (do̲ŋba tsālamdzam cɛ̲è) vi. to suddenly feel shy.

གདོང་ལྤགས་མཐུག་པོ་ (do̲ŋbaà tūgbu) shameless, not easily embarrassed [Lit. facial skin thick].

གདོང་ལྤགས་སྲབ་པོ་ (do̲ŋbaà drəbu) shy, bashful [Lit. facial skin thin].

གདོང་སྤྲོད་ (do̲ŋ drȫȍ) va. to cause sb. to meet sb. else ། ངས་ཡུན་རིང་མ་འཕྲད་པའི་གྲོགས་པོ་གཉིས་ངས་གདོང་སྤྲད་པ་ཡིན་ I made the two friends who have not met for a long time meet.

གདོང་ཕྱིས་ (do̲ŋ cīì) 1. va. to wash the face. 2. a face towel.

གདོང་ཕྱོགས་ (do̲ŋjɔɔ̀) 1. shung. standing on sb.'s side, supporting/ backing sb. ། གོར་བོད་སྡེ་གཟར་སྐབས་ཕ་རོལ་པར་གདོང་ཕྱོགས་ཀྱི་སྤྱོད་ངན་ལ་བརྟེན་འཛིན་བཟུང་བྱས་པ་ He was arrested because of standing on the enemy's side during the war between Tibetans and Nepalese. 2. facing towards sth.

གདོང་ཕྲད་ (do̲ŋ trɛ̄ɛ̀) vi. to meet face-to-face.

གདོང་འཕྲོག་རེས་བྱེད་ (do̲ŋ trɔ̄ɔreè cɛ̲ɛ̀) va. to push/ race to get in front of each other.

གདོང་བན་ (do̲ŋbɛn) tib.ch. wash basin.

གདོང་ཕྱུག་ཕྱེ་དཀར་ (do̲ŋcuù cēgar) facial (white) makeup or powder.

གདོང་དབྱིབས་ (do̲ŋyib) the form/ figure/ shape of a face.

གདོང་འབག (do̲ŋbaà) mask.

གདོང་འཕྱིད་ (do̲ŋjii) sm. གདོང་ཕྱིས་.

གདོང་དམར་ཅན་གྱི་ཡུལ་ (do̲ŋ mārjɛngi yü̲ü) Tibet [Lit. land of red faced people].

གདོང་དམར་པོ་ (do̲ŋ mārbo) 1. red face. 2. conveys a face exhibiting embarrassment or anger.

གདོང་དམར་བ་ (do̲ŋ mārwa) Tibetans.

གདོང་དམར་ཡུལ་ (do̲ŋ māryüü) sm. གདོང་དམར་ཅན་གྱི་ཡུལ་.

གདོང་སྨད་ (do̲ŋmɛɛ̀) hanging one's head down in shame/ embarrassment.

གདོང་རྩལ་ཆེན་པོ་ (do̲ŋdzɛɛ cēmbo) 1. bold, daring. 2. shameless (in a negative sense).

གདོང་སྨུག་ནག (do̲ŋ mūgnaà) a dark facial complexion.

གདོང་ཚན་ (do̲ŋdzɛn) thick skinned, not easily embarrassed/ ashamed ། ཁོ་གདོང་ཚན་ཆེན་པོ་འདུག He does not easily get embarrassed. ། ཁོ་གདོང་ཚན་མཐུག་པོ་མི་འདུག He is not thick-skinned (gets embarrassed easily). ། མོ་ལ་གདོང་ཚན་ཡོད་པ་མ་རེད་ She is not thick-skinned (gets embarrassed easily).

གདོང་ཚབ་ (do̲ŋdzəb) a substitute for sb. who is embarrassed or shy to go or do sth.; va.—དུ་གཏོང་ to send sb. as a substitute for sb. who feels shy or embarrassed to go or do sth.

གདོང་འཛར་ (do̲ŋdzar) piece of cloth hanging out from a manuscript indicating the title or the number of the volume.

གདོང་ཛ་རི་འདྲ་པོ་སྟོན་ (do̲ŋ dza̲ri dra̲bo dõn) va. to show an angry face.

གདོང་ཞུ་ (do̲ŋshu) shung. a request made directly (face-to-face) to a suerior person; va.—འབུལ་.

གདོང་བཞི་མིག་བརྒྱད་ (do̲ŋshi miggyɛɛ̀) a collective decision made by many people [Lit. four faces, eight eyes].

གདོང་ཡིག (do̲ŋyiì) the writing on a གདོང་འཛར་.

གདོང་ཡིག་གི་རྒྱ་ (do̲ŋyiìgi gya) sm. གདོང་འཛར་.

གདོང་གཡོགས་ (do̲ŋyɔɔ̀) a ribbon put over the eyes during certain Buddhist initiations; va.—རྒྱག་; —བྱེད་; —འཆིང་.

གདོང་ཡོལ་ (do̲ŋyöö) a kind of curtain put at the front of some statue' faces.

གདོང་རས་ (do̲ŋrɛɛ̀) 1. facial shape; vi.—འཁྱིལ་ to take after a close relative's facial looks. 2. true nature.

གདོང་རིས་ (do̲ŋriì) sm. གདོང་རས་.

གདོང་རིས་ངོ་མ་ (do̲ŋriì ŋo̲ma) real/ true nature; vi.—གསལ་ to show the real/ true nature ། བཙན་རྒྱལ་རིང་ལུགས་ཀྱི་གདོང་རིས་ངོ་མ་གསལ་རྗེན་དུ་ཐོན་པ་རེད་ The real nature of imperialism was exposed.

གདོང་ལ་ (do̲ŋla) 1. in the front, in advance, before

¶ཁོང་ཚོ་གདོང་ལ་ཕྱིན་སོང་ ང་མཇུག་ཙམ་ལ་འགྲོ་གི་ཡིན་ They went in advance. I will go later. 2. in/ at the face.

གདོང་ལ་ཁྲག་མེད་ཁོག་ལ་སྙིང་མེད་ (doŋla trāàmeè kōgla ñīŋmeè) extremely frightened [Lit. no blood in the face, no heart in the body].

གདོང་ལ་ལྟ་ (doŋla dā) 1. va. to look at a face. 2. sm. ངོ་ལ་ལྟ་.

གདོང་ལ་ཁྲེལ་པ་མེད་པ་ (doŋla bāgba meèba) shameless.

གདོང་ལ་གསེར་ཚབ་སྒྲོན་ (doŋla sērcəb drön) va. to flatter/ praise, to act sycophantic.

གདོང་ལ་གསེར་ཆུ་བྱུག (doŋla sērcu juù) sm. གདོང་ལ་གསེར་ཚབ་སྒྲོན་.

གདོང་ལེན་ (doŋlen) 1. being in the vanguard/ lead/ forefront; va.—བྱེད་. 2. sm. སྔོ་ལེན་.

གདོང་ལེན་པ་ (doŋlemba) person in the vanguard/ lead/ forefront, a pioneer ¶ཁོ་ཚོས་ངོ་རྒོལ་གསུམ་གྱི་ལས་འགུལ་གྱི་གདོང་ལེན་བྱས་པ་རེད་ They acted as the vanguard for the "Three Antis" campaign.

གདོང་ལེན་དཔུང་སྡེ་ (doŋlen būŋde) advance guard, military vanguard.

གདོང་ལེན་དཔུང་ཚོགས་ (doŋlen būŋdzɔɔ̀) sm. གདོང་ལེན་རུ་ཁག.

གདོང་ལེན་དམག་དཔུང་ (doŋlen māgbuŋ) military vanguard.

གདོང་ལེན་རུ་ཁག (doŋlen rugaà) "pioneer" group (the communist youth group).

གདོང་ལེན་རུ་མི་ (doŋlen rumi) member of a vanguard team, pioneer group member.

གདོང་ཤ་ལྷུག་ལྷུག (doŋsha lhūglhuù) flabby face.

གདོང་ཤེད་ (doŋsheè) sm. དྲམ་པ་.

གདོང་ཤེལ་ (doŋshee) mirror ¶གདོང་ཤེལ་ལ་བལྟ་ Looking into a mirror.

གདོང་གཤིས་ (doŋshii) facial expression; vi.—ལོག; —འགྱུར་ to have a sudden change in facial expression due to anger, sadness, etc.

གདོང་བཤལ་ (doŋshɛɛ) washing the face; va.—བྱེད་.

གདོང་བཤེར་ (doŋsher) confrontation, confronting.

གདོང་བཤེར་ར་སྤྲོད་ (doŋsher radröö) sm. གདོང་བཤེར་.

གདོང་སེམས་ (doŋsem) enthusiasm.

གདོང་བསུ་ (doŋsu) welcoming, receiving; va. གདོང་བསུ་; —བྱེད་.

གདོང་བསུས་ (doŋsüù) p. of གདོང་བསུ་.

གདོང་ལྷགས་ (doŋlhaà) wind blowing in one's face.

གདོངས་ (doŋ) imp. of གདང་.

གདོད་ (döö) abbr. of གདོད་མ་.

གདོད་སྐྱེས་ (döögyeè) the original (of sth.).

གདོད་སྐྱེས་སྲོག་ཆགས་ (döögyeè sōgjaà) protozoa.

གདོད་ནས་ (döönɛ) from the very beginning, from the first.

གདོད་མ་ (dööma) primitive, primeval, primordial ¶གདོད་མའི་དུས་སུ་ Primeval times.

གདོད་མ་ནས་ (döömanɛ) sm. གདོད་ནས་.

གདོད་མའི་ཀུང་ཧྲེ་ (döömɛ gūŋhri) tib.ch. primitive commune.

གདོད་མའི་བསྐལ་པ་ཡ་ཐོག (döömɛ gɛ̄ɛwa yatɔɔ̀) primitive period/ age.

གདོད་མའི་ཡུལ་མི་ (döömɛ yüümi) 1. primitive man. 2. autochtonous people, aboriginal inhabitants.

གདོད་མའི་ནགས་ཚལ་ (döömɛ nagdzɛɛ) primeval/ virgin forest.

གདོད་མའི་སྤྱི་ཚོགས་ (döömɛ jīdzoò) primitive society.

གདོད་མའི་མི་ (döömɛ mi) 1. primitive man. 2. autochtonous people, aboriginal inhabitants.

གདོད་གཟུགས་ (döösug) primitive forms/ shapes.

གདོན་ (dön) 1. f. of འདོན་. 2. a type of demon, evil spirit.

གདོན་གྱིས་བརླམས་ (döngi lām) vi. to be possessed by a demon ¶ཁོང་གི་ཐུགས་རྒྱུད་གདོན་གྱིས་བརླམས་ His mind was possessed by a demon.

གདོན་བགེགས་ (döngeg) sm. གདུག་འདྲེ་.

གདོན་འདྲེ་ (döndre) sm. གདུག་འདྲེ་.

གདོན་ནད་ (dönnɛɛ̀) sickness caused by evil spirits/ demons.

གདོན་གནོད་ (dönnöö) harm caused by demons and evil spirits.

གདོན་རྩ་ (dönca) method of divination in which the pulse is felt to see if any curse or spell has been cast by an evil spirit/ demon.

གདོན་མི་ཟ་ (dön misa) without doubt, certain, unquestionable ¶ཁྱེད་རང་གི་གསུངས་པར་ཚང་མས་མོས་མཐུན་བྱེད་རྒྱུ་གདོན་མི་ཟ་ Have no doubt. What you have said will be agreed to by everyone.

གདོན་ཞུགས་ (dön shuù) vi. to be possessed by an evil spirit/ demon.

གདོན་ཟོར་ (dön sɔɔ̀) things that have had a spell cast on them by witches and evil spirits (to bring harm/ bad luck).

གདོམས་ (dom) imp. of འདམ་.

གདོལ་པ་ (dööba) 1. butcher. 2. member of the lowest caste, an untouchable.

གདོལ་སྤྱོད་ (dööjöö) lowly/ base behavior.

གདོལ་རིགས་ (döörig) lowest caste, untouchables.

གདོས་ཆེ་བ་ (döö cēwa) abbr. of གདོས་སུ་ཆེ་བ་.

གདོས་ཆེན་པོ་ (döö cēmbo) abbr. of གདོས་སུ་ཆེ་བ་.

གདོས་ཐག (döötaà) rope (used for pulling boats ashore).

གདོས་པ་ (dööba) 1. oar. 2. boat. 3. banner on a boat. 4. boatsman.

གདོས་བུ་ (dööbu) 1. a small wooden clapper used to help a gelong monk stay awake. 2. sail of a boat.

གདོས་མེད་ (döömeè) short, small.

གདོས་ཚད་ (döödzɛɛ̀) size (of people or things).

གདོས་སུ་ཆེ་བ་ (döösu cēwa) 1. extremely heavy. 2. extremely large/ big.

བདག (daà) 1. I, me, myself ¶བདག་ཁྱིམ་ལ་ལོག་གི་ཡིན་ I am going home. 2. vi. to belong to, to own ¶ས་ཆ་འདི་ཁོང་ལ་བདག་གི་རེད་ This land will belong to him.

བདག་རྒྱེན་ (daggyen) 1. reward, award in recognition of one's service; va.—བྱེད་; —གནང་ ¶བདག་རྐྱེན་དུ་རྗེས་སུ་མདའ་དཔོན་བསྐོ་གཞག་གནང་འདུག In recognition of (his) service later (he) was appointed general.

བདག་རྐྱེན་གྱི་རྟགས་མ་ (daggyengi dāŋma) medal in recognition of service.

བདག་རྐྱེན་གནང་ (daggyen nāŋ) see བདག་རྐྱེན་.

བདག་སྐྱིད་གཞན་སྡོན་ (daàgyii shenmön) oneself happy, others envious.

བདག་སྐྱོང་ (dāàgyoŋ) caring for and protecting, looking after; va.—བྱེད་. ¶ཚོགས་པ་རེས་དྭ་ཕྲུག་ཚོར་བདག་སྐྱོང་བྱས་པ་རེད་ The organization took care of the orphans.

བདག་སྐྱོང་བཟོ་གྲྭ་ (dāàgyoŋ sodra) maintenance factory.

བདག་བསྐྱེད་ (daggyeè) 1. visualizing oneself as a deity; va.—ལེན་. 2. thinking of oneself well, priding oneself; va.—བྱེད་ ¶ཁོས་མཁས་པ་ཡིན་པའི་བདག་སྐྱེད་བྱེད་ཀྱི་འདུག He prides himself as an expert.

བདག་གི་ཕྱོགས་ (daàgi cɔɔ̀) 1. one's side. 2. the side of one's doctrine/ views/ beliefs/ ideology.

བདག་གིར་ལྟ་ (daàgir dā) va. to consider as belonging to oneself.

བདག་གིར་བྱེད་ (daàgir ceè) va. to take possession/ control of ¶སྤྱིས་བདག་གིར་བྱེད་མི་ཆོག One may not take possession of commonly held land.

བདག་གིར་འཛིན་ (daàgir dzin) taking possession/ control of things that one thinks one owns ¶སྤྱིས་བདག་གིར་འཛིན་མི་ཆོག One may not take possession of commonly held land.

བདག་གིར་བཞེས་ (daàgir sheè) sm. བདག་གིར་བྱེད་.

བདག་རྒྱུད་ (daàgyüù) mind and body.

བདག་སྒྲ་ (dagdra) in Tibetan grammar, the syllables པ་, བ་, མ་ which when added to a noun or verb conveys a person who does the action.

བདག་ངན་ཕྲད་པའི་རྟ་གཡག (dagŋɛn dreebɛ dāyaà)

making use of sb. and getting rid of them once their usefulness ends [Lit. horses and yaks who have met a bad owner].

བདག་ངལ་ (daà ŋεε) vi. to create one's own hardship.

བདག་དངོས་ (daàŋöö) one's possessions/ property.

བདག་ཅག (dagjaà) we, us, ourselves ༈ བདག་ཅག་གི་འགོ་ཁྲིད་ Our leader.

བདག་གཅེས་ (dagjeè) looking after/ maintaining with care, keeping up, taking care of; va.—བྱེད་. ༈ བཟོ་གྲྭའི་སྒྲིག་ཆས་ལ་བདག་གཅེས་བྱེད་ཀྱི་འདུག (They) are maintaining the factory's equipment.

བདག་གཅེས་ཉམས་གསོ་ (dagjeè ñamso) maintaining and repairing; va.—བྱེད་.

བདག་གཅེས་བཟོ་བཅོས་ (dagjeè sobjöö) sm. བདག་གཅེས་ཉམས་གསོ་.

བདག་ཆེན་ (dagjen) 1. title of the head lama of the Sakyapa sect. 2. abbr. of བདག་ཉིད་ཆེན་པོ་.

བདག་འཇུག (daŋjuù) before giving Buddhist initiationsentering of the teacher's consciousness into the mandala and his receiving blessings from the particular deity.

བདག་ཉར་ (dagñar) taking care of, looking after; va.—བྱེད་. ༈ ང་བོད་ལ་འགྲོ་ཤུལ་རྡོ་རྗེ་ལགས་ཀྱིས་ངའི་ཕྲུ་གུ་བདག་ཉར་བྱས་པ་རེད་ While I went to Tibet, Dorjela took care of my child.

བདག་ཉིད་ (dagñii) oneself, myself, himself, themselves ༈ འགའ་ཞིག་གིས་བདག་ཉིད་གཅིག་པུའི་བདེ་བར་བསམས་ཏེ་ Some (people), thinking only of happiness for themselves, ...

བདག་ཉིད་སྒྲོག (dagñii drɔɔ̀) va. to praise oneself.

བདག་ཉིད་གཅིག་པའི་འབྲེལ་བ་ (dagñii jigbε dreewa) one of the འབྲེལ་སྒྲ་ in Tibetan grammar— the particles ཀྱི་ གི་ གྱི་ འི་ ཡི་ which when used between two nouns conveys that one modifies the other (e.g., གསེར་གྱི་བུམ་པ་ = golden vase).

བདག་ཉིད་ཆེན་པོ་ (dagñii cēmbo) epithet for Buddhas. 2. title of address for great spiritual figures ༈ བདག་ཉིད་ཆེན་པོ་གཱན་དྷི་ Mahatma Gandhi.

བདག་གཉེར་ (dagñer) managing, supervising, taking charge; va.—བྱེད་ ༈ ཐུན་མོང་གིས་བདག་གཉེར་ Collective management. ༈ ཁེ་ལས་འདི་བདག་གཉེར་གཞུང་གིས་བྱེད་ཀྱི་ཡོད་པ་རེད་ The government manages this enterprise.

བདག་གཉེར་ཏོ་དམ་ (dagñer todam) sm. བདག་གཉེར་.

བདག་གཉེར་པ་ (dagñerba) manager, supervisor, administer.

བདག་གཉེར་བྱེད་ལུགས་ (dagñer ceèlug) method of management/ supervision/ administration.

བདག་གཉེར་མི་སྣ་ (dagñer mina) sm. བདག་གཉེར་པ་.

བདག་གཉེར་ས་ཁུལ་ (dagñer sɔküü) administrative district/ area.

བདག་ཏུ་འཛིན་ (dagdu dzin) sm. བདག་གིར་འཛིན་.

བདག་ཏུ་བཟུང་ (dagdu suŋ) p. of བདག་ཏུ་འཛིན་.

བདག་བསྟོད་གཞན་སྨོད་ (dagdöö shεnmöö) praising oneself and degrading others.

བདག་ཐོན་བདག་གཅེས་ (dagtön dagjeè) taking good care of one's possessions/ belongings; va.—བྱེད་.

བདག་ཐོབ་ (dagdob) individual ownership/ possession, right of ownership; va.—རྩོད་ to contest the right of ownership ༈ བདག་ཐོབ་ཀྱི་དབང་ཆ་ Right of individual ownership. ༈ ཁང་པ་དེའི་བདག་ཐོབ་མི་ཚང་གི་བུ་ལ་ཡོད་པ་རེད་ The right of ownership of the house is with the son of the family.

བདག་འཐུས་ (dagdüü) shung. giving permission to take possession of sth. ༈ ས་ཞིང་དེ་ཁྱོད་ཚོར་བདག་འཐུས་གོང་རིམ་ནས་བཀའ་ཕེབས་སོང་བ་ The order came from the superior giving permission for you to take possession of the land.

བདག་དམ་བྱེད་ (dagdam ceè) va. to agree to take a case, to accept a petition.

བདག་དོན་ (dagdön) one's affairs.

བདག་དོན་བདག་གཅེས་ (dagdön dagjeè) sm. རང་དོན་རང་གཅེས་.

བདག་བདེ་གཞན་སྨོད་ (dagde shεnmöö) making oneself happy and degrading others.

བདག་པས་གཞན་གཅེས་ (dagbε shεnjeè) putting the needs of others before oneself.

བདག་པོ་ (dagbo) owner, master, proprietor ༈ ས་ཞིང་གི་བདག་པོ་ Land owner.

བདག་པོ་རྒྱག (dagbo gyaà) sm. བདག་པོ་སྐྱོང་.

བདག་པོ་ངོ་མ་ (dagbo ŋoma) the original/ real owner.

བདག་པོ་སྐྱོང་ (dagbo drȫö) va. to keep, to take care of, to look after, to pay attention to ༈ ཁོས་ཁྱི་ཕྲུ་གུ་བདག་མེད་འདིར་བདག་པོ་སྐྱང་པ་རེད་ He took care of the stray puppy. ༈ དཀྲུག་གཏམ་དེ་ཚོར་ཁོ་ཚོས་བདག་པོ་རྩ་བ་ནས་མ་སྐྱང་པ་རེད་ They paid no attention to all those rumors. 2. va. to watch/ control (one's actions/ speech, etc.) ༈ ཁོས་ཁ་ལ་བདག་པོ་སྐྱོང་ཐུབ་ཀྱི་མ་རེད་ He cannot control what he says. 3. va. to own ༈ ཅ་ལག་འདིར་བདག་པོ་སྐྱོང་མཁན་མེད་ན་ངས་ཁྱེར་འགྲོ་གི་ཡིན་ If there is no owner of this thing I will take it.

བདག་པོ་མེད་པ་ (dagbo meèba) ownerless.

བདག་པོའི་བརྟུལ་ཞུགས་མ་ (dagbö dǖüshugmɔ) 1. bride. 2. ཁྱིམ་བདག.

བདག་པོའི་བློ་དང་མ་མཐུན་ན་ བཟོ་པ་མཁས་ཀྱང་དགོས་དོན་མེད་ (dagbö lōdaŋ mɔtünnɔ soba kεὲgyaŋ göödön meè) one should work to the satisfaction of the owner, master or boss [Lit. if the owner is unsatisfied with a craftsman's work, it does not matter how good the craftsman is).

བདག་པོའི་ས་ (dagbö sā) sm. བདག་སྒྲ་.

བདག་སྐྱོང་ (dagdröö) taking care of, looking after, keeping, paying attention to; va.—བྱེད་ to take care of, to look after, to keep, pay attention to ༈ ནང་དུ་ལོག་ས་མེད་པའི་མི་ཚོར་ཁོ་ཚོས་བདག་སྐྱོང་བྱེད་ཀྱི་ཡོད་པ་རེད་ They look after those who have no homes to return to. ༈ ཁོའི་སྐད་ཆར་སུས་ཀྱང་བདག་སྐྱོང་མ་བྱས་པ་རེད་ No one paid attention to what he said.

བདག་བེད་ (dagbeè) shung. taking possession and using sth. ༈ ད་བར་ཁང་པ་བདག་བེད་སྤྱད་པ་ (You) have been taking the possession and using the house up to now.

བདག་བྱེད་ (dagjeè) 1. sm. བདག་པོ་སྐྱོང་. 2. owner.

བདག་དབང་ (daàwaŋ) 1. sovereignty ༈ རང་རྒྱལ་གྱི་བདག་དབང་ The sovereignty of our country. 2. right of ownership ༈ སྒེར་གི་བདག་དབང་ Private ownership.

བདག་མི་དགའ་བ་གཞན་ལ་མི་བྱ་ (dag migawa shεnla mi ca) don't do to others what you would not like done to you.

བདག་མེད་ (dagmeè) 1. selflessness. 2. ownerless, unclaimed, not owned by anyone ༈ བདག་མེད་ཀྱི་ས་ཆ་ Unowned land.

བདག་མེད་ལ་འཇོག (dagmeèla jɔɔ̀) va. to leave sth. uncared for.

བདག་མེད་ལིང་སྐྱུར་ (dagmeè liŋgyur) leaving sth. uncared for.

བདག་མོ་ (daàmo) lady of the house. 2. title for wife of the head lama of the Sakya sect and for other married lama's wives.

བདག་དམན་པ་ (daàmεmba) sm. གུས་མ་.

བདག་ཚགས་ (dagdzaà) shung. sm. བདག་གཅེས་.

བདག་འཛིན་ (dəŋdzin) 1. egoism, selfishness. 2. ownership, possession; va.—བྱེད་ to own ༈ ཁང་པ་དེ་བདག་འཛིན་བྱེད་མཁན་སུ་རེད་ Who is the owner of the house?

བདག་གཞན་ (dagshεn) oneself and others.

བདག་གཞན་བརྗེ་བའི་བྱང་ཆུབ་ཀྱི་སེམས་ (dagshεn jewε caŋcubgi sēm) sm. བདག་གཞན་མཉམ་བརྗེ་.

བདག་གཞན་མཉམ་བརྗེ་ (dagshεn ñamje) a Boddhicitta act; an act bearing the pain/ suffering of others and giving one's happiness in exchange.

བདག་གཟུང་བྱེད་ (dagsuŋ ceè) sm. བདག་གིར་བྱེད་.

བདག་བཟུང་ (dagsuŋ) sm. བདག་གཟུང་.

བདག་སྲུང་ (dagsuŋ) self-defense, self-preservation; va.—བྱེད་.

བདག་སྲོག་གཅོད་ (dagsɔɔ̀ jöö) va. to kill oneself, to commit suicide.

བདག་བསླུས་གཞན་བསླུ་ (daglüü shenlu) tricking/ fooling/ deceiving not only oneself but others too; va.—བྱེད་.

བདམ་ (dam) sm. འདེམས་.

བདམ་བསྒོ་ (damgo) sm. འདེམ་བསྒོ་.

བདམ་རྟགས་ (damdaà) a mark indicating selection (of sth.); va.—རྒྱག.

བདམ་ཐོན་ (damtön) being selected/ elected ༑བདམ་ཐོན་ལག་ཁྱེར་ A certificate indicating sb. has been selected.

བདམ་ཐོན་པ་ (damtönba) contestant, sb. selected to compete ༑ལུས་རྩལ་འགྲན་སྡུར་གྱི་བདམ་ཐོན་པ་མང་པོ་འདུག There were many contestants in the gymnastic competition.

བདམ་ཐོན་འགྲན་བསྡུར་ (damtön drendur) election campaign/ contest; va.—བྱེད་.

བདམ་ཐོན་པ་ (damdömba) winner in an election.

བདམ་ཐོན་ལག་འཁྱེར་ (damdön laggyee) certification for an elected person.

བདམ་བདམ་སྒྲུག་སྒྲུག (damdam drugdrug) sm. selecting, choosing.

བདམ་གསེས་ (damseè) selecting, choosing; va.—བྱེད་ ༑དེ་རེས་ཀྱི་ཚོགས་འདུར་ལས་ཁུངས་ནས་འཐུས་མི་གསུམ་བདམ་གསེས་བྱས་སོང་ The officer selected three delegates for the conference.

བདམས་ (dam) p. of འདེམས་.

བདམས་བསྒྲིགས་ (damdrig) a collection of articles/ documents that have been selected from many.

བདམས་ཉོ་ (damño) picking/ choosing and buying; va.—བྱེད་.

བདམས་སྙིགས་ (damñig) goods left over after everything else has been bought/ picked through.

བདམས་བདུས་ (damdüü) sm. བདམས་བསྒྲིགས་.

བདམས་ཐོན་ (damdön) sm. བདམ་ཐོན་.

བདམས་ལུས་ (dam lüü) vi. to fail to be chosen, to lose an election.

བདའ་ (da) f. of འདེད་.

བདའ་གླ་ (dala) transportation fee/ fare; va.—གཏོང་ to rent out one's transportation vehicle ༑ལྷ་ས་ནས་ཕག་རིའི་བར་གྱི་བདའ་གླ་ཞི་དྲག་ཕར་བཞག The transportation fee between Phari and Lhasa has increased a lot.

བདའ་འདེད་ (dadeè) chasing after, going after (e.g., a loan, job, fact); va.—གཏོང་ ༑བུ་ལོན་རྙིང་པ་དེ་ཚོ་བདའ་འདེད་གཏོང་དགོས་ We have to go after (collecting) the old loans. ༑ཁ་རྩོད་འདིའི་རྩ་བ་ཐུག་ས་གང་ཡིན་བདའ་འདེད་གཏོང་དགོས་པ་རེད་ (We) have to go after finding out what is the root of the dispute.

བདར་ (dar) 1. va. to grind, to make into powder, to file down. 2. va. to arrange things (neatly or in formation). 3. va. to sharpen ༑ངས་གྲི་བདར་པ་ཡིན་ I sharpened the knife.

བདར་རྡོ་ (dārdo) whetstone.

བདར་སྤོས་ (darböö) powdered incense.

བདར་ཟད་ཀྱི་འཐབ་རྩལ་ (darsɛɛ̀gi tābdzöö) attrition strategy (in war).

བདར་ཟད་ཐེབས་ (darsɛɛ̀ tēb) vi. to get worn down/ worn off.

བདར་ཤ་ཚོད་ (dasha dzöö) sm. བརྡར་ཤ་ཚོད་.

བདལ་: p. བདལ་; f. བདལ་; imp. བདོལ་ (dɛɛ) vi. to spread, to lay out.

བདལ་གླ་ (dɛɛla) sm. བདའ་གླ་.

བདས་ (dɛɛ̀) p. of འདེད་.

བདས་བསགས་དངོས་རྫས་ (dɛɛ̀saà ŋöödzɛɛ̀) alluvial deposits.

བདས་བསགས་བདེ་ཐང་ (dɛɛ̀saà dedaŋ) alluvial plain.

བདས་བསགས་པང་རིམ་ (dɛɛ̀saà pəŋrim) alluvium.

བདུག: p. བདུགས་; f. བདུག་; imp. བདུགས་ (duù) va. to fill with scent/ odor (usu. by burning incense).

བདུག་པ་ (dugbə) sm. གདུག་སྤོས་.

བདུག་སྤོས་ (dugböö) incense.

བདུག་སྤོས་ཤིང་ (dugböö shiŋ) general term for shrubs and trees used for incense.

བདུག་སྤྱད་ (dugdzɛɛ̀) utensils used for burning incense.

བདུག་རྫས་ (dugdzɛɛ̀) things that are burned to cleanse pollution (e.g., a hair or piece of clothing from a high incarnate lama).

བདུག་ཤིང་ (dugshiŋ) abbr. of བདུག་སྤོས་ཤིང་.

བདུགས་ (duù) p. and imp. of བདུག.

བདུང་: p. བདུངས་; f. བདུང་; imp. བདུངས་ (duŋ) va. to pull the string of a bow, to shoot an arrow.

བདུངས་ (duŋ) p. and imp. of བདུང་.

བདུད་ (düü) devil, demon, monster.

བདུད་ཀྱི་བདག (düügi daà) a kind of demon.

བདུད་ཀྱི་བར་ཆད་ (düügi parjɛɛ̀) misfortune caused by a བདུད་.

བདུད་ཀྱིས་སྙིང་བརླམས་ (düügi ñiŋlam) sm. གདོན་གྱིས་བརླམས་.

བདུད་གདོན་ (düügɛn) sm. བདུད་.

བདུད་རྒྱལ་ (düügyɛɛ) king of the བདུད་.

བདུད་ཕོ་ (düüpo) male བདུད་.

བདུད་ཕྲུག (düüdruü) young བདུད་.

བདུད་བློན་ (düülön) evil minister.

བདུད་མོ་ (düümu) female བདུད་.

བདུད་རྩི་ (düüdzi) nectar.

བདུད་རྩི་ཤག (düüdzi shaà) a Tibetan medicine.

བདུད་རྩི་རིལ་བུ་ (düüdzi riibu) a pill that has been blessed by a lama.

བདུད་རྩིའི་སྙིང་པོ་ (düüdzii ñīŋbu) 1. the essence of sth. 2. fermenting yeast.

བདུད་ཞུགས་ (düü shuù) vi. to be possessed by a བདུད་ ༑ཁོ་ལ་བདུད་ཞུགས་བཞག He was possessed by a བདུད་.

བདུད་བཞི་ (düüshi) "gang of four" ༑བདུད་བཞི་བཙང་སྤྱོད་ཀྱི་གཏོར་བཤིག་ཚབས་ཆེན་ The serious destruction caused by the gang of four's cruel behavior.

བདུད་ལ་ལྷར་བསམ་ (düülə lhā sām) regarding an enemy as a friend.[Lit. thinking a demon is a god].

བདུད་ལུང་ (düüluŋ) the land of demons.

བདུད་སྲིན་ (düüsin) abbr. of བདུད་དང་སྲིན་པོ་.

བདུན་ (dün) 1. seven. 2. week ༑བདུན་གཉིས་ཀྱི་ལས་གསེང་ A vacation of two weeks.

བདུན་སྐྱེད་ (düngyeè) 14% interest.

བདུན་གྱི་བདུན་པ་ (düngi dümbə) Saturday.

བདུན་བརྒྱད་འགྲོ་ (düngyɛɛ̀ dro) sm. བདུན་སྐྱེད་.

བདུན་ཅུ་ (dünju) seventy ༑བདུན་ཅུ་དོན་གཅིག Seventy one.

བདུན་གཅིག (dünjig) a/ one week.

བདུན་མཐའ་ (dünta) the seven times table.

བདུན་པ་ (dümbə) 1. seventh. 2. the robe/ attire of a gelong.

བདུན་པོ་ (dümbo) the seven together ༑མི་བདུན་པོ་ཚང་མ་སླེབས་སོང་ Seven people arrived together.

བདུན་པའི་ཚེས་གཅིག (dümbɛ tsēèjig) July 1st.—the anniversary of the founding of the Communist Party of China in 1921.

བདུན་གཅིག་དང་གི་འཕྲུངས་སྐར་ (dünjig dāŋgi trūŋgar) བདུན་པའི་ཚེས་གཅིག.

བདུན་ཕྲག (dündraà) week ༑བདུན་ཕྲག་སྔོན་མའི་ནང་ During the previous week. ༑བདུན་ཕྲག་གཅིག One week.

བདུན་ཕྲག་བདུན་ (dündraà dün) 1. seven weeks. 2. the 49 days period of mourning.

བདུན་ཚར་གཅིག (dündzar jīg) a set of items that come in sevens (e. g., water offering bowls).

བདུན་ཚིག (dündzig) a poem with seven syllables/ characters per line.

བདུན་ཚིག་སྙན་ངག (düntsig ñɛ̃nŋaà) sm. བདུན་ཚིག.

བདུན་ཚིགས་ (dündzii) the 49 day period of mourning; va. འཛིན་ to adhere to/ maintain the 7 weeks of mourning.

བདུན་ཟུར་ (dünsur) 1. one seventh. 2. a seven year difference between the astrological signs of two people (this is considered unlucky for marriage).

བདུན་རེ་ (dünre) each/ every week, weekly.

བདུན་རེའི་གསར་ཤོག (dünre sārshɔɔ̀) weekly newspaper/ magazine.

བདུན་ཤོག (dünshɔɔ̀) a weekly letter given to authorities in China in which one had to express one's feelings and thoughts.

བདེ་ (de) 1. abbr. of བདེ་པོ་. 2. (— + vb.) easily, safely ¶ བདེ་འབྱོར་ Arrived safely.

བདེ་སྐབས་ (degəb) good/ peaceful times.

བདེ་སྐྱིད་ (dīgyiì) 1. happiness, joy, well-being. 2. girl's name.

བདེ་སྐྱིད་ཀྱི་གཤེད་མ་ (dīgyiìgi shēèma) shung. destroyer of happiness ¶ བདེ་སྐྱིད་ཀྱི་གཤེད་མ་ངན་པ་བྱས་རྒྱལ་དུ་མི་འགྲོ་བ་བཀག་ཞིབ་ནན་ཏན་ཡོང་བ་ One should not let a destroyer of happiness go unpunished.

བདེ་སྐྱིད་གྲངས་འབྱོར་ (dīgyiì traŋjɔɔ) fame, fortune and happiness.

བདེ་སྐྱིད་རྒྱལ་པོ་ (dīgyiì gyɛɛbo) the Qing Emperor Kangxi.

བདེ་སྐྱིད་དར་ (dīgyiì tar) vi. to have happiness or peace spread.

བདེ་སྐྱིད་གླིང་ཀ་ (dīgyiì līŋgə) 1. name of a park in Lhasa. 2. name of the British/ Indian political office in Lhasa.

བདེ་སྐྱིད་ཅན་ (dīgyiìjɛn) sm. བདེ་སྐྱིད་ལྡན་པ་.

བདེ་སྐྱིད་ལྡན་པ་ (dīgyiì dɛmba) happy, joyful ¶ བདེ་སྐྱིད་ལྡན་པའི་ཁྱིམ་ཚང་ A happy family.

བདེ་སྐྱིད་རྫོགས་ལྡན་ (dīgyiì dzɔŋdɛn) (an era) of happiness, tranquillity and prosperity.

བདེ་སྐྱོང་སྲོག་སྐྱོབ་ (degyoŋ sɔ̄ɔgyob) heal the sick and save the dying, protect happiness and save lives.

བདེ་ཁོད་ (degöò) arriving safely ¶ ཁོ་ཚོ་དེ་ར་ཕེབས་འབྱོར་བདེ་འཁོད་གནས་ཚུལ་འབྱོར་བྱུང་ (We) received information about their safe arrival.

བདེ་ཁོད་སྙོམས་ (degöò ñōm) va. to level/ even (ground) ¶ ཁྲོམ་ལམ་བདེ་འཁོད་བསྙོམས་པ་རེད་ They made the market road level.

བདེ་ཁོད་སྙོམས་པོ་ (degöò ñōmbo) level, even, flat.

བདེ་ཁོད་མི་སྙོམས་པ་ (degöò miñōmba) uneven, not level, bumpy.

བདེ་འཁོད་ (degöò) sm. བདེ་ཁོད་.

བདེ་འཁྱུག་གུ་འཁྱུག (degyuù gugyuù) moving around in a lively fashion.

བདེ་དགའ་ (dega) happy and healthy.

བདེ་དགེ་ (dege) happiness, joy.

བདེ་བགྲོད་ (dedröö) safe journey ¶ ལྷ་ས་ནས་ཨ་རི་བར་བདེ་འགྲོད་བྱུང་ (I) had a safe journey from Lhasa to America.

བདེ་འགྲོ་ (dendro) humans and gods.

བདེ་འགྲོ་གསུམ་ (dendro sūm) humans, gods, and demigods.

བདེ་ཅག་འཁྱུག་པོ་ (dejaà kyūgbu) sm. བདེ་ལྗག་དོད་པོ་.

བདེ་ལྗག་འཁྱུག་པོ་ (dejaà kyūgbu) sm. བདེ་ལྗག་དོད་པོ་.

བདེ་ལྗག་དོད་པོ་ (dejaà tööbo) 1. physically nimble, agile; deft, dexterous. 2. politically flexible ¶ གནས་ཚུལ་འགྱུར་ལྡོག་ཆེན་པོ་ཡོད་ཙང་བདེ་ལྗག་དོད་པོའི་སྲིད་བྱུས་ལག་ལེན་བསྟར་དགོས་ Because this is a changing situation, one should implement a flexible political policy.

བདེ་ཆམ་མེ་བ་ (de cāmmewa) a feeling of well-being and comfort.

བདེ་ཆེན་འཁོར་ལོ་ (dejen kɔ̄ɔlo) veins on the top of the head (in tt. medicine).

བདེ་ཆེན་ཞིང་ (decen shiŋ) heaven, paradise, Sukhavati.

བདེ་ཆས་ (dejɛɛ̀) convenient clothes (for work/ activity/ sports); va.—གྱོན་ to wear such clothes.

བདེ་ཆེན་ (decen) 1. name of a person. 2. great happiness. 3. a Tibetan region in Yunnan.

བདེ་ཆེན་ཕོ་བྲང་ (dejen podraŋ) palace of the Panchen Lama in Shigatse.

བདེ་ཆེན་བོད་རིགས་རང་སྐྱོང་ཁུལ་ (dejen pöörii raŋgyoŋ kūū) the Dechen Autonomous Area in Yunnan Province.

བདེ་འཇགས་ (denjaà) tranquillity, calmness, stability, peace ¶ བདེ་འཇགས་ཀྱི་སྤྱི་ཚོགས་ Stable society. 2. safety, security, law and order ¶ གནམ་གྲུལ་བདེ་འཇགས་ཀྱི་ངང་ནས་འཕུར་བསྐྱོད་ཆེད་ In order to have safe flights.

བདེ་འཇགས་ཆིངས་ཡིག (denjaà ciŋyiì) security treaty.

བདེ་འཇགས་ལྟ་རྟོག་ཁྲུའུ་ (denjaà dādoò trū) tib.ch. office of safety supervision.

བདེ་འཇགས་ལས་ཁུངས་ (denjaà lɛɛ̀guŋ) Security Bureau/ Office.

བདེ་འཇགས་ལས་འཛིན་ཚོགས་པ་ (denjaà lɛndzin tsɔ̄gba) Security Council (UN).

བདེ་འཇགས་ལས་འཛིན་ལྷན་ཚོགས་ (denjaà lɛndzin lhɛ̄ndzɔɔ̀) sm. བདེ་འཇགས་ལས་འཛིན་ཚོགས་པ་.

བདེ་འཇགས་སྲུང་སྐྱོབ་ (denjaà sūŋgyob) peace and security ¶ ལྷ་ས་གྲོང་ཁྱེར་གྱི་བདེ་འཇགས་སྲུང་སྐྱོབ་ལས་འགན་ Responsibility for the peace and security of Lhasa City.

བདེ་འཇགས་སྲུང་སྐྱོབ་ཁའོ་ (denjaà sūŋgyob kāwo) tib.ch. security section/ division.

བདེ་བརྗོད་ (dejöö) best wishes, greetings.

བདེ་ཉེན་ (deñen) danger to one's security/ well-being.

བདེ་སྙན་ (deñɛn) abbr. of བདེ་སྡུག་སྙན་ཞུ་.

བདེ་བརྟན་ (dedɛn) sm. བདེ་འཇགས་, 1.

བདེ་སྟན་ (dedɛn) a comfortable cushion.

བདེ་ཐང་ (detaŋ) health, well-being ¶ བཟོ་པའི་བདེ་ཐང་ལ་སྲུང་སྐྱོབ་ Protection of the worker's health. 2. abbr. of བདེ་བ་ཐང་. 3. plain, flatlands ¶ བདེ་ཐང་ཡངས་པོ་ A wide plain.

བདེ་ཐང་སྟོབས་ལྡན་ (dēdaŋ dōbdɛn) hale and hearty, strong and healthy.

བདེ་ཐང་ས་ཁུལ་ (dedaŋ sɔ̄güü) a plain.

བདེ་ཐར་ (dedar) vi. to escape safely.

བདེ་དོག (dedɔɔ̀) good and bad, happiness and suffering.

བདེ་དོན་ (dedön) well-being, welfare ¶ མི་དམངས་སྤྱིའི་བདེ་དོན་ལ་བསམ་བློ་གཏོང་དགོས་ One must think of the general welfare of the people.

བདེ་བདེ་ཐང་ཐང་ (dede taŋdaŋ) happy and healthy, safe and well.

བདེ་བདེ་ལྷོད་ལྷོད་ (dede lhöölhöö) safe and relaxed/ leisurely ¶ ཉེན་ཁ་དེ་དག་ལས་གྲོལ་ནས་བདེ་བདེ་ལྷོད་ལྷོད་དུ་འབྱོར་པ་རེད་ Coming through all that danger, they arrived (here) safe and relaxed.

བདེ་འདྲི་ (dendri) asking sb. about how they are; va.—བྱེད་.

བདེ་ལྡན་ (dendɛn) sm. ལྷ་ཡུལ་.

བདེ་སྡུག (deduù) 1. happiness and sadness. 2. well-being, welfare; va.—ལྟ་ To look after the well-being/ welfare ¶ རྒྱལ་ཁབ་ཀྱིས་མི་དམངས་ཀྱི་བདེ་སྡུག་ལ་ལྟ་གི་ཡོད་པ་རེད་ The state looks after the well-being of the people.

བདེ་སྡུག་གྲགས་དམས་ (deduù tragmɛɛ̀) praising and degrading (a brainwashing/ interrogating technique).

བདེ་སྡུག་མཉམ་འབྲེལ་ (deduù ñamdree) the linkage of happiness and suffering (one follows the other according to Buddhist philosophy).

བདེ་སྡུག་མཉམ་མྱོང་ (deduù ñamñoŋ) sharing/ experiencing the good and the bad times together.

བདེ་སྡུག་སྙན་ཞུ་ (deduù ñɛ̄nshu) a petition that tells one's story/ hardships/ sufferings.

བདེ་སྡུག་སྙོམས་ (deduù ñōm) va. to share the good and the bad together.

བདེ་སྡུག་ཞུ་ (deduù shu) va. to complain/ appeal to a superior of one's hardship/ suffering.

བདེ་སྡུག་གནས་སྟངས་ (deduù nɛɛ̀daŋ) condition of life/ livelihood.

བདེ་སྡུག་གསོལ་ཡུལ་མེད་པ་ (deduù sɔ̄ɔyüü meèba) a

situation where there is no one to complain/ appeal to.

བདེ་སྡོད་ལས་བརྩོན་ (dēdöö lɛ̱ɛ̀dzön) living happily and working diligently.

བདེ་ནང་ (de̱naŋ) abbr. for བདེ་འཇགས་ and ནང་སྲིད་.

བདེ་སྣང་ (de̱naŋ) feeling of comfort and happiness.

བདེ་པོ་ (de̱bo) 1. well, in good health ¶ ང་ཚོ་བདེ་པོ་ཡིན་ We are well. 2. comfortable ¶ ཀུབ་ཀྱག་འདི་བདེ་པོ་འདུག This chair is comfortable. 3. (vb. + —) easy/ convenient to do ¶ འདི་ཀློག་བདེ་པོ་འདུག This is easy to read. 4. level (ground) ¶ ཐང་བདེ་པོ་ཞིག་གི་ཐོག On a level ground.

བདེ་པོ་ཐང་པོ་ (de̱bo tāŋbo) well and healthy.

བདེ་སྤྱོད་ (dējöö) 1. pleasure, enjoyment. 2. toilet.

བདེ་ཕེབས་ (de̱peb) arriving or coming safely.

བདེ་བ་ (de̱wa) peace, tranquillity, calmness ¶ སེམས་ཀྱི་བདེ་བ་ Peace of mind. 2. pleasure ¶ ཆགས་པའི་བདེ་བ་ Sensual pleasure. 3. sm. བདེ་པོ་.

བདེ་བ་ཅན་ (de̱wajɛn) the sukhavati paradise of the Buddha Amitabha.

བདེ་བ་ཅན་གྱི་ཞིང་ཁམས་ (de̱wajɛngi shi̱ŋkam) sm. བདེ་བ་ཅན་.

བདེ་བ་ཐང་ (de̱wadaŋ) Deothang (Bhutan).

བདེ་བར་སྐྱོང་ (de̱war gyōŋ) va. to rule in a peaceful way ¶ རྒྱལ་པོ་དེའི་དུས་རྒྱལ་འབངས་བདེ་བར་སྐྱོང་ཐུབ་པ་བྱུང་བ་རེད་ During the time of that king, the subjects were ruled in a peaceful manner.

བདེ་བར་གཤེགས་པ་ (de̱war she̱gba) enlightened (Buddha).

བདེ་ཞིབ་ལས་ཁུངས་ (de̱shib lɛ̱ɛ̀guŋ) shung. an office in the traditional Tibetan government that saw to the situation of the peasantry/ countryside.

བདེ་ལག (de̱laà) easily, with little effort, without problem ¶ ལོ་མཇུག་ཡིག་ཚད་བདེ་ལག་ངང་ལོན་ཐུབ་པ་རེད་ He easily passed the final exam.

བདེ་ལག་ངང་ (de̱laàŋaŋ) sm. བདེ་ལག.

བདེ་ལག་ཐོགས་མེད་ (de̱laà tɔ̄ɔmeè) easy to accomplish/ complete.

བདེ་ལག་ཏུ་ (de̱lagdu) sm. བདེ་ལག.

བདེ་མིན་ (de̱min) 1. unwell, sick ¶ བར་ལམ་གཟུགས་པོ་བདེ་མིན་གྱིས་ལས་ཀར་འགྲོ་ཐུབ་མ་བྱུང་ Lately I couldn't go to work because I was sick. 2. shung. uneasy, uncomfortable, not happy ¶ ཁྲལ་འབབ་ཆག་ཡང་བདེ་མིན་ལ་ (I) am uncomfortable giving a tax exemption.

བདེ་མོ་ (de̱mo) 1. healthy. 2. an expression of greeting in Amdo dialect.

བདེ་མོ་གཏམ་ (de̱mo dām) asking after sb.'s health (i.e., How are you?).

བདེ་མོ་འཚམ་པོ་ (de̱mo tsāmbo) 1. healthy. 2. being complete.

བདེ་རྩ་ (de̱dza) basic/ fundamental welfare ¶ མི་དམངས་ཀྱི་བདེ་རྩར་ཕུག་པའི་ལས་ཀ་མང་པོ་བྱས་འདུག They have done a lot to improve the welfare of the people.

བདེ་རྩལ་ (de̱dzɛɛ) athletic capability/ talent, dexterousness, nimbleness.

བདེ་རྩལ་འཁྱུག་པོ་ (de̱dzɛɛ kyūgbu) nimble, dexterous (in athletics).

བདེ་རྩལ་དོད་པོ་ (de̱dzɛɛ töo̱bo) sm. བདེ་རྩལ་འཁྱུག་པོ་.

བདེ་རྩལ་ལྡན་པ་ (de̱dzɛɛ de̱mba) sm. བདེ་རྩལ་འཁྱུག་པོ་.

བདེ་འཚམས་འདྲི་ (de̱mo) sm. བདེ་མོ་གཏམ་.

བདེ་གཟར་ (de̱sar) sm. ཟིང་ཆ་.

བདེ་གཟར་ཡུལ་འཁྱོམས་ (de̱sar yüügyom) sm. ཟིང་ཆ་.

བདེ་ཡངས་ (de̱yaŋ) a college in Drepung monastery.

བདེ་རབ་ (de̱rəb) abbr. of the Delerapten aristocratic family.

བདེ་བསླིང་དུ་ (de̱liŋdu) sm. བདེ་ལྷིང་.

བདེ་ལ་འགོད་ (de̱la göo̱) va. to make happy.

བདེ་ལམ་ (de̱lam) a smooth or easy road.

བདེ་ལེགས་ (dēleè) well, fine.

བདེ་གཤེགས་སྙིང་པོ་ (de̱sheg ñi̱ŋbu) Buddha (Tathagata) nature or essence.

བདེ་སང་སང་ (de̱ sāŋsaŋ) physically fit/ healthy ¶ ཁ་སང་གཟུགས་པོ་ལྕི་ལྕི་ཡོད་ཀྱང་དེ་རིང་བདེ་སང་སང་བྱས་སོང་ Yesterday I felt heavy and dull, but today I feel fit.

བདེ་སིང་ངེ་བ་ (de̱ sāŋŋewa) sm. བདེ་ཆམ་མེ་བ་.

བདེ་སྲུང་ (de̱suŋ) security, protecting well-being; va.—བྱེད་ ¶ མི་དམངས་ཀྱི་བདེ་སྲུང་གི་ཆེད་དུ་སྨན་ཁང་མང་པོ་བཙུགས་པ་རེད་ They established many hospitals in order to protect the well-being of the people.

བདེ་སྲུང་སྐོར་བྱ་དམག་མི་ (de̱suŋ gɔ̄ɔja mɔ̄ɔmi) sm. སྐོར་བྱ་དམག་མི་.

བདེ་སྲུང་ཁང་ (de̱suŋgaŋ) security office.

བདེ་སྲུང་དམག་མི་ (de̱suŋ mɔ̄ɔmi) the National Guard (in the U.S.A.), security guard/ force.

བདེ་སྲུང་རུ་ཁག (de̱suŋ ru̱gaà) security unit/ brigade/ force.

བདེ་སྲུང་ལས་ཁུངས་ (de̱suŋ lɛ̱ɛ̀guŋ) Department of Defence (in the U.S.A.).

བདེ་སླེབས་ (de̱leb) vi. to arrive safely.

བདེ་ལྷིང་ (de̱lhiŋ) peaceful, quiet, tranquil.

བདེ་ལྷོད་ (de̱lhöö) sm. བདེ་ལྷིངས་.

བདེ་ལྷོད་ལྷོད་ (de̱ lhōōlhöö) sm. བདེ་ལྷོད་.

བདེན་ (de̱n) abbr. of བདེན་པོ་.

བདེན་སྐྱོང་ (de̱n kyōŋ) upholding/ supporting/ defending justice or truth; va. བདེན་སྐྱོང་; —བྱེད་.

བདེན་ཁ་སྒྲོད་ (de̱n kā dröo̱) sm. བདེན་ཁ་འཛིན་.

བདེན་ཁ་འཛིན་ (dēn kā ji̱n) va. to accept what sb. says as true ¶ ང་གཉིས་རྩོད་པ་རྒྱག་དགོས་དོན་མི་འདུག ངས་ཁྱེད་རང་ལ་བདེན་ཁ་འཛིན་ཆོག There is no point in arguing, I will accept what you say as true.

བདེན་རྒྱབ་ (de̱ngyəb) supporting the truth; va.—བྱེད་ ¶ ང་ཚོའི་རང་དབང་བཙན་ལེན་གྱི་འཐབ་རྩོད་ལ་བདེན་རྒྱབ་བྱེད་རོགས་གནང་ Please support the truth in our struggle for freedom.

བདེན་ཉོ་དྲང་འཚོང་ (de̱nño tra̱ndzoŋ) buying and selling at a fair price.

བདེན་ཅན་ (dēnjɛn) true.

བདེན་ཅན་སྤོབས་ཆེ་ (de̱njɛn bōbce) pride in having the truth.

བདེན་གཉིས་ (de̱nñii) relative and absolute truth.

བདེན་གཏམ་ (de̱ndam) true statement/ speech.

བདེན་རྟགས་ (de̱ndaà) sign/ evidence of truth.

བདེན་ཐུབ་ (de̱ndub) sm. བདེན་པ་བདེན་ཐུབ་.

བདེན་མཐའ་ (de̱nda) truth; vi.—གསལ་ to have the truth prevail ¶ ཁྱེད་རང་ལ་ཉེས་པ་མེད་ན་ནམ་ཞིག་བདེན་མཐའ་གསལ་གྱི་རེད་ If you are innocent, eventually the truth will prevail.

བདེན་དོན་ (de̱ndön) righteous/ truthful cause or principle, the truth; vi.—སྤེལ་ to spread the truth; va.—ལ་འཚོལ་ to seek the truth ¶ ཁོ་ཚོའི་རང་དབང་སླར་གསོའི་བདེན་དོན་ལ་རྒྱབ་སྐྱོར་བྱས་པ་རེད་ (He) supported the righteous cause of the restoration of their freedom.

བདེན་དོན་འགྱུར་མེད་ (de̱ndön gyu̱rmeè) unalterable truth.

བདེན་དོན་དུ་སྲོག་གཏོང་ (de̱ndöndu sɔ̄ɔ dōŋ) va. to die for a principle, to martyr oneself.

བདེན་དོན་འཚོལ་ (de̱ndön tsöö) va. to seek the truth.

བདེན་དོར་རྒྱུ་ཧམ་ (de̱ndɔɔ gyu̱ŋam) abandoning justice and greedily seeking wealth.

བདེན་མདོག་མེད་ (de̱ndɔɔɔ me̱è) it can't be true ¶ རྡོ་རྗེ་ལགས་བྲོས་བྱོལ་ཕྱིན་པ་རེད་ཟེར་བ་བདེན་མདོག་མེད ཁོང་མི་དེ་འདྲ་ཞིག་ཅ་བ་ནས་མ་རེད་ It can't be true that Dorjela fled to exile. He is definitely not someone like that.

བདེན་དྲང་ཟོལ་མེད་ (de̱ndraŋ söo̱mee) completely true/ honest, truthful.

བདེན་པ་ (de̱mba) righteous, true, just ¶ བདེན་པའི་འཐབ་རྩོད་ A just struggle. ¶ ཁོས་ཟེར་བ་དེ་བདེན་པ་རེད་ What he says is true.

བདེན་པ་ཐོབ (de̱mba tōb) just, true.

བདེན་པ་དག་སྐྱེལ་ (de̱mba taggyee) act of proving one's righteousness/ truth/ innocence; va.—བྱེད་.

བདེན་པ་བདར་ (de̱mba da̱r) va. to determine who is right or who is telling the truth.

བདེན་པ་བདེན་འཁྱོལ་ (de̱mba de̱ngyöö) sm. བདེན་པ་

བདེན་ཐོག.

བདེན་པ་བདེན་ཐུབ་ (demba dentub) honest, just, true.

བདེན་པ་བདེན་ཐོག (demba dendɔɔ) doing justice, supporting the truth; vi.—ལ་འགྲོལ་ ། ཁྲིམས་རྒྱུ་འདི་བདེན་ཐོག་ལ་འགྲོལ་པ་གནང་རོགས་གནང་ In this lawsuit, please support the truth.

བདེན་པ་མེད་པ་ (demba meèba) untrue, unjust, depraved, corrupt.

བདེན་པ་བཞི་ (demba shi) the four noble truths of the Buddha.

བདེན་པ་ར་སྤྲོད་ (demba radröö) proving the truth, proving sth. true.

བདེན་པ་ལུག་ལ་ཡོད་ཀྱང་ཤི་ཁྲལ་ལུག་ལ་འཁྱིལ་སོང་ (demba luùlə yöögyaŋ shīdreε luùlə kēesoŋ) suffering even though truth/ justice is on one's side [Lit. even though truth is on the side of the sheep, the death tax falls on the sheep].

བདེན་པའི་ངག (dembε ŋaà) sm. བདེན་གཏམ་.

བདེན་པའི་རང་བཞིན་ (dembε rɔŋshin) the nature of truth.

བདེན་པར་ (dembar) honestly, truthfully ། ཁོས་བདེན་པར་བཤད་པ་རེད་ He spoke truthfully.

བདེན་པར་འཛིན་ (dēmbar dzin) va. to take or hold as true/ factual, to believe in ། མི་དེའི་སྐད་ཆ་བདེན་པར་འཛིན་རྒྱུ་ཡོད་པ་མ་རེད་ ཁོས་རྣམ་ཀུན་རྫུན་མང་པོ་ཤོད་ཀྱི་ཡོད་པ་རེད་ You shouldn't take what that person says as the truth. He always says lots of lies.

བདེན་པས་མཐའ་འགྲོལ་ (dembε tāgyöö) 1. spending one's life doing what is right and just. 2. sm. བདེན་པ་བདེན་ཐོག.

བདེན་པས་བློ་བདེ་ (dembε lōde) having a clear conscience because sth. is true.

བདེན་པས་རྫུན་པམ་ (dembε dzünpam) truth overcoming falsehood/ lies.

བདེན་དཔང་ (dembaŋ) proof, evidence; va.—བྱེད་ ། ལྕགས་ལྟ་བུའི་བདེན་དཔང་ Ironclad proof.

བདེན་དཔང་ཁྲུའུ་ (dembaŋ trū) tib.ch. notary public office, notorial office.

བདེན་དཔང་ངོ་མ་ (dembaŋ ŋoma) true testimony/ evidence/ proof.

བདེན་དཔང་བྱེད་མཁན་ (dembaŋ ceèñεn) 1. person who gives evidence. 2. notary public.

བདེན་འདྲིལ་ (dendree) true, factual ། གནས་ཚུལ་དེ་བདེན་འདྲིལ་ཨ་ཡིན་ (I) wonder if that news is true?

བདེན་མེད་ (denmeè) untrue.

བདེན་མེད་གཏམ་ཟད་ (denmeè dāmsεὲ) running out of things to say because one's position is unjust/ untrue.

བདེན་མེད་དཔའ་འཁྲུམས་ (denmeè bāŋgum) afraid because one's cause or position is unjust/ untrue.

བདེན་མེད་དཔུང་འདྲེན་ (denmeè būŋdren) using force unjustly.

བདེན་མེད་རོགས་དཀོན་ (denmeè rɔ̄ɔgön) an unjust cause finds little support.

བདེན་མེད་ཧམ་བཤད་ (denmeè hāmshεὲ) shamelessly saying sth. that is untrue.

བདེན་གཙོའི་རིང་ལུགས་ (dendzö rinluù) realism.

བདེན་ཚིག (dentsiì) truth, true words; va.—ཤོད་; —བརྗོད་; —བཤད་ to speak the truth.

བདེན་འཛིན་ (dēndzin) abbr. of བདེན་པར་འཛིན་.

བདེན་རྫུན་ (dendzün) right and wrong, true and false/ lie; va.—དབྱེ་འབྱེད་ to discern truth from lies.

བདེན་རྫུན་དཀར་ནག (dendzün) sm. བདེན་རྫུན་.

བདེན་རྫུན་ཐང་མར་བདལ་ (dendzün tāŋmaa dεε) va. to display the true and false.

བདེན་རྫུན་དྲང་འཁྱོག (dendzün traŋgyɔɔ) sm. བདེན་རྫུན་.

བདེན་རྫུན་ཤན་དབྱེ་ (dendzün shöö yē) shung. va. to distinguish truth and falsehood by throwing dice ། ཞུ་ཚིག་ཁ་མ་དན་པ་བདེན་རྫུན་ཤན་དབྱེ་བ་ Because of the contradictory remarks of both sides, they distinguished truth and falsehood by throwing dice.

བདེན་ཞུ་ (den shu) shung. to speak the truth, to make true remarks/ statements ། ཁྲིམས་སར་གནས་ཚུལ་བདེན་ཞུ་དགོས་རྒྱུ་ (You) must make true remarks in court.

བདེན་ཞེན་ (denshen) having confidence/ belief in the truth (of sth.).

བདེན་བཞི་ (denshi) abbr. of བདེན་པ་བཞི་.

བདེན་ཡུས་ཤོད་ (denyüù shöö) va. to make a big deal about doing sth. good.

བདེན་ཡོད་དཔུང་འཇུག (denyöö būŋjuù) dispatching troops with just cause, a just war.

བདེན་ཡོད་དཔུང་འདྲེན་ (denyöö būŋdren) sm. བདེན་ཡོད་དཔུང་འཇུག.

བདེན་ཡོད་གཞུང་དྲང་ (denyöö shuŋdraŋ) just and honest.

བདེན་ལུགས་ (denluù) the system of justice/ truth.

བདེན་ཤགས་བདར་ (denshaà dar) sm. བདེན་ཡུས་ཤོད་.

བདེན་ཤན་དབྱེ་ (denshöö yē) shung. abbr. of བདེན་རྫུན་ཤན་དབྱེ་བ་.

བདེན་བཤེར་ (densher) explaining the truth of one's position; va.—རྒྱག.

བདེན་གསོལ་ (densöö) apology; va.—ཞུ་ to apologize.

བདེར་ (der) བདེ་ + dat.-loc. particle.

བདེར་བསྐྱོད་ (der dröö) sm. བདེ་བསྐྱོད་.

བདེར་ཆགས་ (der cāà) in peace ། ཇག་པས་མི་དམངས་བདེར་ཆགས་འདུག་གི་མེད་པ་རེད་ The bandits do not let people live in peace.

བདེར་གནས་ (dernεὲ) peaceful, tranquil, well, stable ། ང་ཚོ་ཚང་མ་བདེར་གནས་ཡོད་པས་སེམས་ཁྲལ་མ་དགོས་ We are all well here. There is no need to worry.

བདེར་འཚོ་ (derdzo) health, well-being, hygiene, sanitation.

བདེར་ བློམ་ (derlom) pretending to be happy.

བདོ་ (do) sm. དར་.

བདོག (dɔɔ) 1. va. to have, to possess, to keep ། དངུལ་ཇི་བདོག་པ་ཁོར་སྤྲད་པ་རེད་ (They) gave him all the money they had. 2. possessions.

བདོག་དངོས་ (dɔgŋöö) possessions.

བདོར་ (dɔɔ) imp. of བདར་.

བདོལ་ (döö) imp. of བདལ་.

མདག་པ་ (dagba) མདག་མ་.

མདག་མ་ (daŋma) a red hot ember (without flame).

མདག་མེ་ (daŋme) sm. མེ་མདག.

མདང་ (daŋ) abbr. of མདང་དགོང་.

མདང་སྐྱེས་བྱིས་པ་ (daŋgyeè ciibu) an infant born the previous night.

མདང་ཁ་ནུབ་ (daŋ kānub) the night before yesterday.

མདང་དགོང་ (daŋgoŋ) last night, last evening.

མདང་ནུབ་ (daŋnub) sm. མདང་དགོང་.

མདང་སང་ (daŋsaŋ) these days, nowadays.

མདང་སུམ་ (daŋsum) sm. མདང་དགོང་.

མདངས་ (daŋ) complexion, appearance ། གཞལ་མདངས་ Facial complexion. 2. radiance, brightness, luster, shine, glow; vi.—ཆགས་ to fade (colors/ luster/ complexion) ། འཛུམ་མདངས་ A radiant smile. ། ཉི་མའི་མདངས་ The glow of sunlight.

མདངས་སྐྱ་ལྷག་གེ་བ་ (daŋgya lhāggewa) pale white light.

མདངས་བཀྲ་ (daŋdra) sm. མདངས་བཀྲག.

མདངས་བཀྲག (daŋdraà) shining light.

མདངས་རྒྱས་ (daŋgyεὲ) having a healthy complexion.

མདངས་སྒྱུར་མཁྲིས་པ་ (daŋgyur triibə) a type of jaundice that discolors the complexion of the skin.

མདངས་ཅན་ (daŋjεn) having a good complexion.

མདངས་གཅོམ (daŋjoò) vi. to outshine, to make sth. look inferior/ shabby by contrast to oneself ། བུ་མོ་འདིའི་དར་སྤྱོལ་ཆེ་བའི་གྱོན་ཆས་དེས་བུ་མོ་གཞན་རྣམས་ཀྱི་མདངས་བཅོམ་སོང་ The fashionable clothes of that girl made the other girls look inferior.

མདངས་ཆེན་ (danjen) sm. མཐོང་ཆེན་.

མདངས་ཆེན་པོ་ (daŋ cēmbo) sm. མཛོང་ཆེན་པོ་.

མདངས་འདོན་ (daŋ dön) va. to make sth. shine.

མདངས་ལྡན་ (daŋdɛn) radiant, bright, shinning.

མདངས་ཕོག (daŋ pɔ̄ɔ̀) 1. vi. to be influenced/ effected. 2. vi. to have the sun's ray or light shine upon sth.

མདངས་ཕྱེ་ (daŋje) a drawing technique wherein one's lets the color of an outline of sth. (e.g., a flower) fade/ blend in with what is next to it.

མདངས་འཕྲོག (daŋ trɔ̄ɔ̀) va. to make a color fade/ blend in.

མདངས་མི་སྣུམ་པ་ (daŋ minumbə) pale looking (the face of a sick person).

མདངས་མེད་ (daŋmeè) dull, lackluster, not shining or glowing.

མདངས་རྫིས་ཆེན་པོ་ (daŋdzi cēmbo) sm. མཛོང་ཆེན་པོ་.

མདངས་འཚེར་ལྷག་གེ་བ་ (daŋdzee lhāgewa) shining brightly.

མདངས་འོད་ (daŋwöò) glow, shine, luster.

མདངས་རིས་ (daŋriì) glow/ shine/ luster of a drawing.

མདངས་གསོ་ (daŋ sō) va. to renovate/ restore a painting.

མདན་ཁོག (dɛngɔɔ̀) cheek; va.—ལ་གཞུ་ to slap/ hit on the cheek.

མདན་ལྕག་གཞུ་ (dɛnjaà shu) sm. མདན་ཁོག་ལ་གཞུ་.

མདན་པ་ (dɛmba) 1. cheeks. 2. door bolt.

མདའ་ (da) 1. arrow; va.—རྒྱག; —འཕེན་ to shoot an arrow. 2. axle, bar, shaft ¶ འཁོར་ལོ་གཉིས་བར་གྱི་མདའ་ The axle between two wheels. 3. lower part of a valley ¶ ལུང་པའི་མདའ་ The lower part of that area. 4. shung. abbr. of མདའ་དཔོན་.

མདའ་བཀང་ (dagaŋ) va. to pull back the bow string so that one is ready to shoot.

མདའ་དཀྲུག་ཕུ་དཀྲུག (dadrug pūdrug) sowing dissension, stirring up trouble; va.—བཟོ་ [Lit. stirring up the upper valley, stirring up the lower valley].

མདའ་སྐད་གླིང་བསྒྱུར་ (dagɛɛ̀ līŋgyur) lying about what one said in the past [Lit. change the sound of a whistling arrow into the sound of a flute].

མདའ་སྐྱེན་པོ་ (da gyēmbo) a good/ skilled archer.

མདའ་སྐྱེན་མོ་ (da gyēmmo) a good/ skilled female archer.

མདའ་ཁར་ཤི་ (daga shī) vi. to die by arrow/ gun wound.

མདའ་ཁུར་ཅན་ (dagurjɛn) archer, person carrying a bow and arrow.

མདའ་ཁོངས་ (dagoŋ) shung. subordinates/ underlings of a མདའ་དཔོན་.

མདའ་མཁན་ (dagɛn) 1. sm. མདའ་པ་. 2. maker of bows and arrows.

མདའ་འཁྱམས་ (dagyam) a stray arrow; vi.—ཕོག to be accidentally hit by a stray arrow.

མདའ་འཁྱར་ (dakyar) sm. མདའ་འཁྱམས་.

མདའ་གང་ (dagaŋ) a distance the length of an arrow.

མདའ་གླུ་ (dalu) archery song.

མདའ་གློ་ (dalo) the upper girth of a horse/ mule that is attached to a cart.

མདའ་གྲོང་ (dadroŋ) a village in the lower part of a valley.

མདའ་རྒྱང་ (dagyaŋ) the range an arrow can be shot.

མདའ་རྒྱན་ (dagyen) 1. a wager/ bet on an archery contest. 2. decoration for an arrow.

མདའ་རྒྱལ་ (da gyɛɛ) vi. to win an archery contest.

མདའ་རྒྱུས་ (dəgyüù) a type of herbal medicine.

མདའ་སྒྲོགས་འཕེན་ (dagyɔɔ̀ pēn) va. to open fire.

མདའ་སྒྲོ་ (dadro) feathers of an arrow.

མདའ་གཅིག་གིས་གླ་བ་གཉིས་གསོད་ (da jīggi lāwa ñiì sōò) va. to kill two birds with one stone [Lit. to kill two musk deer with one arrow].

མདའ་གཅིག་གིས་ཤྭ་བ་གཉིས་ (da jīggi shāwa ñiì) sm. མདའ་གཅིག་གིས་གླ་བ་གཉིས་གསོད་.

མདའ་ལྕགས་ (dajaà) iron arrow head/ point.

མདའ་ཆར་ (dajar) strafing; va.—རྒྱག; —འཕེན་ to strafe [Lit. arrow rain].

མདའ་ཆུ་ (dəju) a river in the lower part of a valley.

མདའ་ཆེན་ (dacen) a long arrow.

མདའ་ཉེ་འབེན་རྒྱང་ (dañe bɛngyaŋ) biased, discriminatory, prejudicial [Lit. arrow close, target far).

མདའ་སྙུག (dañug) shung. bamboo for making arrows.

མདའ་ལྟར་འདྲོངས་པོ་ (dadar droŋbo) straight (as an arrow).

མདའ་ལྟོང་ (dadoŋ) notch at the end of an arrow.

མདའ་སྟན་ (dadɛn) poet. bow (for shooting).

མདའ་ཐུང་ (daduŋ) the short/ hour hand (of a watch).

མདའ་དམ་འབྱར་མ་ (dadam jarma) shung. (sth.) on which the མདའ་དཔོན་'s seal has been affixed ¶ མདའ་དམ་འབྱར་མའི་རྩྭ་ཐོར་གསལ་པ་ It was mentioned in the list of grasslands with the མདའ་དཔོན་'s seal.

མདའ་དར་ (dadar) ceremonial arrow having ribbons of different colors fastened to it.

མདའ་དར་རྩེ་ལྔ་ (dadar dzēŋa) ceremonial arrow with ribbons of five different colors.

མདའ་མདེའུ་ (dadiwu) the point of an arrow.

མདའ་དོང་ (dadoŋ) quiver.

མདའ་རྡོ་ (dado) abbr. མདའ་ and རྡོ་.

མདའ་རྡོས་བསྡིགས་ (dadöò dig) va. to frighten with bows and arrows and stones.

མདའ་སྣོད་སྒམ་ (da nōògam) shung. box for keeping arrows.

མདའ་པ་ (daba) archer.

མདའ་དཔོན་ (dɛbön) shung. general in the traditional Tibetan army.

མདའ་འཕེན་ (da pɛ̄n) va. to shoot an arrow.

མདའ་པོ་ཆེ་ (daboce) sm. མདའ་ཆེན་.

མདའ་འབེན་ (dabɛn) archery target.

མདའ་མ་ (dama) the two long wooden cart poles that are attached to the horse/ mule that is pulling the cart.

མདའ་མང་གི་འབེན་ (damaŋgi bɛn) a common target [Lit. target for many arrows].

མདའ་མོ་ (damo) 1. sm. མདའ་. 2. a type of divination that uses arrows.

མདའ་མོ་ཆེ་ (damoce) sm. མདའ་པོ་ཆེ་.

མདའ་མོའི་རྩེ་ལ་རྣོ་མེད་ན་ གཞུ་མོ་བཀང་ནས་ཅི་ལ་ཕན་ (damö dzēla nā meèna shumo gāŋnɛ jīlə pān) there is no use doing things without having a good method [Lit. if the arrow is not sharp there is no use shooting it].

མདའ་རྨས་ (damɛɛ̀) arrow wound; vi.—ཕོག.

མདའ་རྩལ་ (dādzɛɛ) archery skill.

མདའ་རྩེ་ (dadze) arrow point, arrow head.

མདའ་རྩེད་ (dadzeè) archery (as a contest/ sport); va.—རྩེད་ to do archery, to compete in archery.

མདའ་ཚ་ཁ་ལྡ་ (dadza kāda) engaging in archery contest/ competition.

མདའ་ཚད་མ་ (da tsɛ̄ɛ̀ma) the length of an arrow.

མདའ་ཚན་ཆེན་པོ་ (dadzɛn cēmbo) a good/ skilled archer.

མདའ་རྫས་ (dadzɛɛ̀) ammunition.

མདའ་རྫོང་ (dadzoŋ) shung. abbr. of. མདའ་དཔོན་ and རྫོང་དཔོན་.

མདའ་ཞར་ (dashar) mounted archery competition.

མདའ་ཞར་ཕོག་གྲས་ (dashar pɔ̄gdrɛɛ̀) sb. who has hit the bullseye in the mounted archery competition.

མདའ་ཞིང་ (dashiŋ) shung. fields in the lower regions of the valley.

མདའ་གཞིས་ (dashiì) shung. 1. a military estate obligated to supply one or more corvee soldiers. 2. an estate granted to a མདའ་དཔོན་ to use while he is office.

མདའ་གཞུ་ (dəshu) bow and arrow.

མདའ་ཟོ་ (daso) a wooden container used to measure tsampa.

མདའ་བཟོ་པ་ (dasowa) maker of bows and arrows.

མདའ་འོག (dawɔɔ̀) sm. མདའ་ཁོངས་.

མདའ་ཡབ་ (dəyəb) eaves.

མདའ་ཡིག (dəyiì) 1. an "arrow letter." 2. a message tied to an arrow and send by shooting the arrow.

མདའ་གཡབ་ (dəyəb) sm. མདའ་ཡབ་.

མདའ་ར་ (dara) archery field.

མདའ་རམ་ (daram) abbr. General Ramba.

མདའ་རིང་ (dariŋ) minute hand of a watch.

མདའ་ཤུབས་ (dəshub) arrow case.

མདའ་ཤུལ་སྒྲོ་འཛིན་ (dashüü drondzin) succeeding, following up, continuing; va.—བྱེད་.

མདའ་ཤེས་གཞུ་ཉོས་ (dasheè shuñöö) confidence to do sth. [Lit. knowing how to shoot and buy a bow].

མདའ་ཤོག (dashɔɔ̀) a military unit/ regiment.

མདའ་གཤོག (dashɔɔ̀) sm. མདའ་སྒྲོ་.

མདའ་བཤད་ (dabshɛɛ̀) auspicious sayings recited to a new bride as a ceremonial arrow is placed behind her neck; va.—རྒྱག.

མདའ་གསང་ (dasaŋ) the open area inside the body where there are no organs, bones, or arteries.

མདའ་གསུམ་པ་ (da sūmbə) place where three roads/ paths intersect.

མདུང་ (duŋ) lance, spear; va.—རྒྱག; —འཛུགས་ to spear.

མདུང་མཁན་ (duŋñɛn) spearman.

མདུང་གི་རྩེ་རང་ནིག (duŋgi dzēraŋ nig) sm. མདུང་གི་རྩེ་ལ་འཛེར་.

མདུང་གི་རྩེ་ལ་འཛེར་ (duŋgi dzēla dzer) va. to poke sth. or sb. with a spear point.

མདུང་ལྕགས་ཀྱུ་མ་ (dunjaà gyūmə) a spear with a hook on it.

མདུང་ཐུང་ (duŋduŋ) a type of short spear.

མདུང་ཐོགས་དམག་མི་ (duŋdɔɔ̀ māɔ̄mi) spearman (in army).

མདུང་དར་ (duŋdar) banners tied on a spear.

མདུང་པ་ (duŋbə) sm. མདུང་མཁན་.

མདུང་མོ་རྩེ་གསུམ་ (duŋmo dzēsum) trident spear.

མདུང་རྩེ་ (duŋdze) spearhead, point of a spear/ lance.

མདུང་རྩེ་དཀར་པོ་ (duŋdze gārbo) a white medicine traditionally used for the eyes.

མདུང་རྩེ་ཁ་སྤྲོད་ (duŋdze kābdröö) battling tit for tat, blow-for-blow struggling, diametrically opposed (in struggle) ¶ སྤྱི་ཚོགས་རིང་ལུགས་དང་མ་རྩ་རིང་ལུགས་ཀྱི་བར་མདུང་རྩེ་ཁ་སྤྲོད་ཀྱི་འཐབ་རྩོད་བྱེད་ཀྱི་ཡོད་པ་རེད་ Capitalism and socialism are engaged in a tit for tat struggle.

མདུང་རྩེ་གར་གཏད་ (duŋdze kardɛɛ̀) wherever one considers the target of attack (the enemy) is, another does ¶ ཨ་རི་ར་མདུང་རྩེ་གར་གཏད་ལ་ཁ་ན་ཏས་མདུང་རྩེ་གར་གཏད་ཀྱི་ཡོད་པ་རེད་ Whoever America considers her enemy, Canada does likewise.

མདུང་རྩེ་གཏད་ས་ (duŋdze dɛɛ̀sa) the target of attack.

མདུང་རྩེ་ཕྱིར་སྣུན་ (duŋdze cīrnün) fighting back against one's own army/ group.

མདུང་རྩེ་སྨུག་པོ་ (duŋdze mūgbə) a traditional medicine for the eyes.

མདུང་རྩེ་གསུམ་པ་ (duŋdze sūmbə) a trident shaped spear.

མདུང་རྩེད་ (duŋdzeè) training with spears, bayonets, etc.

མདུང་རྩེའི་སོ་ (duŋdzɛ sō) a traditional medical tool for draining pus.

མདུང་འཛར་ (duŋdzar) a tassel attached to spears.

མདུང་ཞགས་ (duŋshaà) a short spear with rope attached at the end so that the enemy/ prey can be pulled or dragged back.

མདུང་ཟླ་ཚེས་མ་ (duŋda tsēèma) a crescent-shaped spear tip.

མདུང་ཡུ་ (duŋyu) the handle of a spear.

མདུང་ཤིང་ (duŋshiŋ) spear shaft.

མདུང་ཤུགས་གཅིག་སྒྲིལ་ (duŋshuù jīgdrii) unity, unanimously; va.—བྱེད་.

མདུད་ (düü) abbr. of མདུད་པ་.

མདུད་རྒྱ་ (düügyaà) knot.

མདུད་ནག (düünaà) a tight knot (that is not easily untied).

མདུད་པ་ (düübə) 1. knot; va.—རྒྱག; —བོར་ to tie a knot; vi.—ཐེབས་ to get all knotted up; vi.—ཞིག; —འགྲོལ་ to have a knot come untied. 2. bonds ¶ བརྩེ་བའི་མདུད་པ་ Bonds of love.

མདུད་འདྲ་ (düündra) a disease of the penis in Tibetan medicine.

མདུད་པ་ཤིག (düübə shig) see མདུད་པ་.

མདུད་འཛིན་ (düündzin) a large bead with a hole big enough to put the two ends of a rosary together.

མདུད་ལོག་རྒྱག (düülɔɔ̀ gyaà) va. to tie a knot that is difficult to untie.

མདུན་ (dün) front ¶ ཁང་པའི་མདུན་ལ་ཤིང་སྡོང་གཅིག་འདུག There is a tree in front of the house. 2. presence ¶ ཁོང་གི་མདུན་དུ་ཕྱིན་པ་ཡིན་ (I) went to him (his presence).

མདུན་ཀླད་ (dünlɛɛ̀) forebrain.

མདུན་བཀག (düngaà) sm. སྔོན་བཀག.

མདུན་བཀག་རྡོ་བཙད་ (düngaà dojɛɛ̀) shung. a stone wall erected in front of a main gate (to break the wind).

མདུན་སྐྱོད་ (düngyöö) going forward, advancing, progressing; va.—བྱེད་ to advance, to go forward, to progress, to improve ¶ མདུན་སྐྱོད་མི་སྣ་ Progressive people. ¶ ཞི་བདེ་ཡུན་བརྟན་གྱི་ཕྱོགས་སུ་མདུན་སྐྱོད་བྱས་པ་རེད་ (They) advanced towards a permanent peace.

མདུན་བསྐྱོད་ (düngyöö) sm. མདུན་སྐྱོད་.

མདུན་བསྐྱོད་གླུ་གཞས་ (düngyöö lūshɛɛ̀) marching songs.

མདུན་ཁག (düngaà) shung. ministers.

མདུན་ཁང་ (düngaŋ) the front house.

མདུན་གྱི་ས་སྐར་ (düngi sāgar) forward position.

མདུན་གྱི་སོ་པ་ (düngi sōba) reconnaissance soldier, point man, advance guard/ spy.

མདུན་གྱི་སྙིང་གསང་ (düngi ñīŋsaŋ) a point on the chest where moxibustion is applied to treat heart ailments.

མདུན་གྲལ་ (dündrɛɛ) front line/ row ¶ མདུན་གྲལ་གཡོན་གྱི་གསུམ་པ་ Third on the left in the front row.

མདུན་གྲོས་ (dündröö) face-to-face discussion/ meeting.

མདུན་བགྲོད་ (dündröö) sm. མདུན་སྐྱོད་.

མདུན་འགོག་རྗེས་སྙེག (düngɔɔ̀ jeèñeg) sm. མདུན་འགོག་རྗེས་འདེད་.

མདུན་འགོག་རྗེས་འདེད་ (düngɔɔ̀ jeèdeè) blocking the front and chasing from the rear.

མདུན་འགྱེལ་རྒྱབ་མཐུད་ (düngyee gyəbdüü) when frontline troops fall, continue with replacement (troops).

མདུན་འགྲོའི་དམག་མི་ (dündrö māɔ̄mi) vanguard troops/ scouts, advance or reconnaissance patrol.

མདུན་གོལ་བྱེད་ (düngöö cee) va. to attack frontally.

མདུན་རྒྱབ་ (düngyəb) front and back.

མདུན་སྒོ་ (düngo) front door.

མདུན་ངོས་ (dünŋöö) 1. in the front of sth. 2. front page/ cover.

མདུན་བཅར་ངོ་དགའ་ (dünjaa ŋoga) visiting in person and flattering.

མདུན་ཅོག (dünjɔɔ̀) a table set in front of a seat.

མདུན་ལྕོག (dünjɔɔ̀) sm. མདུན་ཅོག.

མདུན་ཆགས་མཉེན་རྩ་ (dünjaà mēndza) prostrate gland.

མདུན་མཆོང་ (dünjoŋ) leaping forward, advancing, progressing; va.—རྒྱག; —བྱེད་ to leap forward, to advance, to progress.

མདུན་མཆོང་པ་ (dünjoŋba) a person in the vanguard, a who leaps forward and advances.

མདུན་མཆོང་ཆེན་པོ་ (dünjoŋ cēmbo) the Great Leap Forward.

མདུན་མཆོང་དམག་མི་ (du̱njoŋ mɔ̄ɔmi) sm. མདུན་འགྲོའི་དམག་མི་.

མདུན་ཅབ་ (du̱ncəb) a satin/ brocade ornament that hangs down the front of some official's dresses.

མདུན་འཛོག (du̱njɔɔ̀) poet. present, gift.

མདུན་ལྗོངས་ (du̱njoŋ) scenery.

མདུན་ཐང་ (du̱ntaŋ) the flat area in front, the foreground ¶ པོ་བྲང་གི་མདུན་ཐང་དུ་ In the area in front of the palace.

མདུན་ཐད་ (du̱ndɛɛ̀) the front of sth.

མདུན་ཐབས་བསུ་བཞེས་ (du̱n tɔ̄bsu shee̱) va. to get married, to take a bride.

མདུན་དུ་ (du̱ndu) 1. in front of ¶ མི་དམངས་ཀྱི་མདུན་དུ་ In front of the public. 2. via, through, by ¶ ཡིག་ལན་ཞིག་ཁོའི་མདུན་དུ་གཏོང་རོགས་ Please send a reply (letter) through him. 3. in the presence of, in the face of ¶ ཁོང་གི་མདུན་དུ་ In his presence. ¶ གནས་ཚུལ་དེ་རིགས་ཀྱི་མདུན་དུ་ In the face of such a situation.

མདུན་དུ་སྐྱོད་ (du̱ndu gyöö) sm. མདུན་སྐྱོད་བྱེད་.

མདུན་དུ་འགྲོ་ (du̱ndu dro̱) sm. མདུན་སྐྱོད་བྱེད་.

མདུན་དུ་ལྷགས་ (du̱ndu lhāà) vi. to be confronted/ faced with ¶ གནད་དོན་ཁག་པོ་ཞིག་མདུན་དུ་ལྷགས་ཡོད་པ་རེད་ They are confronted with a difficult question.

མདུན་བདར་ (du̱ndar) lined up in front.

མདུན་བདར་དཔུང་དམག (du̱ndar būŋmaà) sm. མདུན་འགྲོའི་དམག་མི་.

མདུན་མདུན་གྱི་དམག་ས་ (du̱ndüngi māgsa) sm. མདུན་སའི་འཐབ་ར་.

མདུན་མདུན་དུ་ (du̱ndündu) the forefront, the very front.

མདུན་འདྲུད་རྒྱབ་འབུད་ (du̱ndrüù gyə̱mbüù) dragging from the front and pushing from the back; va.—བྱེད་.

མདུན་ན་འདོན་ (du̱nna du̱n) minister.

མདུན་ལྡབ་ (du̱ndəb) a stylistic dance step in Tibetan opera.

མདུན་དུ་སྡོད་ (du̱ndu dö̱ö) sm. མདུན་དུ་ལྷགས་.

མདུན་ན་མོ་ (du̱nna̱mo) attendants.

མདུན་ནས་ (du̱nnɛ) from the front.

མདུན་ནས་མདུན་དུ་ (du̱nnɛ du̱ndu) forward and forward, from one advanced state to a still more advanced state.

མདུན་སྣ་འདྲེན་ (du̱nna dre̱n) va. go in front and lead a group of people.

མདུན་སྣེ་ (du̱nne) front end, tip of the front (as in strings, etc).

མདུན་ཕྱོགས་ (du̱njɔɔ̀) front, front side.

མདུན་ཕྱོགས་དམག་ས་ (du̱njɔɔ̀ māgsa) the front, the battleground.

མདུན་ཕྱོགས་སོ་པ་ (dö̱njɔɔ̀ sōba) advance scout.

མདུན་མ་ (du̱nmə) 1. discussion, meeting, conference; va.—སྲིང་ to discuss. 2. methods, strategies.

མདུན་ཚེམ་ (du̱ndzeè) a type of single stitching where each new stitch goes in front of the last (opposite of ལྷག་ལོག).

མདུན་ཚེམས་ (du̱ndzem) h. of མདུན་སོ་.

མདུན་ཡིག (du̱nyii) shung. a clerk in the Tibetan traditional society.

མདུན་གཡོག (du̱nyɔɔ̀) servant who stays by the side of his master.

མདུན་རི་ (du̱nri) hills and mountains in the front of sth.

མདུན་རུ་ (du̱nru) front line troop units.

མདུན་རོལ་ (du̱nröö) in the front.

མདུན་ལུང་ (du̱nluŋ) sm. གདོང་ལྷག.

མདུན་ལ་ (du̱nla) sm. མདུན་དུ་.

མདུན་ལ་བཅར་ (du̱nla jāā) va. to meet, to go to the presence of sb.

མདུན་ལ་ཤོད་ (du̱nla shö̱ö) va. to say to sb.'s face.

མདུན་ལག (du̱nlaà) forehand (as in tennis/ ping pong); va.—རྒྱག to hit a forehand shot.

མདུན་ལོགས་ (du̱nlɔɔ) sm. མདུན་རོལ་.

མདུན་ལམ་ (du̱nlam) future prospects, future outlook ¶ གསར་བརྗེའི་མདུན་ལམ་ The future of the revolution.

མདུན་ལམ་ཆེན་པོ་ (du̱nlam cēmbo) a bright/ great future.

མདུན་ལམ་སྟོན་ (du̱nlam dȫn) 1. va. to show or reveal the future way/ a future opportunity ¶ ངའི་གྲོགས་པོས་ང་ལ་ལས་ཀ་གསར་པ་ཞིག་འཚོལ་རོགས་བྱས་ནས་མདུན་ལམ་བསྟན་བྱུང་ My friend revealed a future opportunity helping me to find a job. 2. va. to take care of the future ¶ སྲིད་གཞུང་ནས་དྲུག་ཆེད་དུ་སློབ་གྲྭ་བཙུགས་ནས་འཚོ་བའི་མདུན་ལམ་བསྟན་པ་རེད་ The government took care of the future livelihood of the orphans by establishing a school for them.

མདུན་ལམ་མེད་པ་ (du̱nlam mee̱ba) no future.

མདུན་ལམ་བཟང་པོ་ (du̱nlam sa̱ŋbo) having a good future.

མདུན་ཤིག་རྒྱག (du̱nshii gya̱à) va. to move forward (as to the front of a hall).

མདུན་ཤོག (du̱nshɔɔ̀) 1. cover, front page. 2. a political front ¶ བི་ཏི་ནམ་བཅིངས་འགྲོལ་མདུན་ཤོག Vietnam Liberation Front.

མདུན་ཤོག་ནང་མ་ (du̱nshɔɔ̀ na̱ŋma) the page behind the cover of a book.

མདུན་ས་ (du̱nsə) 1. front area, front part, front line, forefront. 2. a meeting, a conference.

མདུན་སོ་ (du̱nso) front teeth/ tooth.

མདུན་སའི་འཐབ་ར་ (du̱nsɛ tɔ̄bra) front line battlefield.

མདུན་གསལ་ (du̱nsɛɛ) shung. what is written above (at the top or front of a document) ¶ མདུན་གསལ་བཀའ་རྒྱ་རིན་པོ་ཆེའི་དགོངས་དོན་ The content of what is written above in the edict is as follows.

མདུན་བསུ་ (du̱nsu) reception, welcome; va.—བྱེད་; —ཞུ་ to receive/ meet (guests), to welcome.

མདུན་སྲུང་ (du̱nsuŋ) protecting the front; va.—བྱེད་.

མདེའུ་ (di̱wu) sm. མདེལ་.

མདེའུ་རྐྱང་ (di̱wugyaŋ) a single shot/ bullet; va.—རྒྱག to fire a single shot.

མདེའུ་ཁུག (di̱wuguù) pouch for bullets, cartridge belt.

མདེའུ་ཁུང་ (di̱wuguŋ) bullet hole.

མདེའུ་ཀྱུར་ (di̱wugyar) stray bullets; vi.—ཕོག to be hit by a stray bullet.

མདེའུ་ཆིང་དན་ (di̱wu ci̱ndɛn) tib.ch. hydrogen bomb.

མདེའུ་སྒམ་ (di̱wu ga̱m) ammunition box.

མདེའུ་ཆར་ (di̱wu cār) a rain of bullets, strafing.

མདེའུ་སྟོང་ (di̱wu dōŋ) an empty/ blank cartridge.

མདེའུ་དམ་ (di̱wu da̱m) cartridge case, gun belt.

མདེའུ་བླུག (di̱wu lūù) va. to put/ load bullets (in a gun).

མདེའུ་ཤུགས་ (di̱wu shūg) sm. མདེའུའི་འབིགས་ཤུགས་.

མདེའུ་ཤུབས་ (di̱wu shūb) sm. མདེའུ་ཁུག.

མདེའུ་གསོར་ (di̱wu sōr) a carpenter's tool.

མདེའུའི་འབིགས་ཤུགས་ (di̱wü bi̱gshuù) penetrating power of a bullet.

མདེའུའི་མེ་དྭ་ (di̱wü me̱da) detonating cap, detonator.

མདེལ་ (de̱l) 1. bullet; va.—འཕེན་; —རྒྱག to fire/ shoot bullets ¶ ཁོས་མདེལ་གསུམ་བརྒྱབ་པ་རེད་ (He) fired three bullets. 2. shell ¶ སྒྲོགས་མདེལ་ Cannon shells.

མདེལ་ཁུག (de̱lguù) sm. མདེའུ་ཁུག.

མདེལ་ཁུང་ (de̱lguŋ) 1. bullet hole. 2. chamber for loading bullets.

མདེལ་འཁྱུར་ (dēlkyar) sm. མདེའུ་ཀྱུར་.

མདེལ་འགོག་ས་དོང་ (de̱lgɔɔ̀ sa̱doŋ) bunker.

མདེལ་ཆག (de̱ljaà) 1. a clip (of bullets). 2. shrapnel.

མདེལ་ཆར་ (de̱ljar) sm. མདེའུ་ཆར་.

མདེལ་ཐུབ་ (de̱ldub) bulletproof ¶ མདེལ་ཐུབ་སྣུངས་འཁོར་ Bulletproof car.

མདེལ་དྲུག་མི་མདའ་ (de̱ldruù me̱nda) a gun that

holds six bullets.

མདེལ་པར་ (delbar) mold for making bullets.

མདེལ་ཚོགས་སྒྲོགས་མདེལ་ (deldzɔɔ gyɔndel) cluster artillery shell.

མདེལ་རྫོང་རྒྱག (deldzoŋ gyaà) va. to load (a gun) with bullets.

མདེལ་རིལ་ (delrii) pellet, musket ball (for gun).

མདེལ་རོ་ (delro) a spent cartridge or musket ball.

མདེལ་ལམ་ (dellam) trajectory/ path of a bullet.

མདེལ་ཤུགས་ (delshuù) sm. མདེའུ་ཤུགས་.

མདེལ་ཤུགས་དྲ་བ་ (delshuù trawa) a barrage of shooting.

མདེལ་ཤུགས་འཛོམས་ས་ (delshuù dzomsa) point at which firing is concentrated.

མདེལ་ཤུབས་ (delshub) sm. མདེའུ་ཤུབས་.

མདོ་ (do) 1. sutra. 2. lower part of a valley. 3. crossroads, juncture, crossing. 4. in summary, briefly ། སྐད་ཆ་མདོ་ལ་བསྡུས་ནས་བཤད་ན་ If I speak briefly.

མདོ་ཁ་ (doga) the point/ essence of sth.

མདོ་ཁང་ (dogaŋ) outer room.

མདོ་ཁམས་ (dokam) Eastern Tibet (Amdo and Kham).

མདོ་ཁམས་སྒང་དྲུག (dokam gaŋdruù) Eastern Tibet.

མདོ་ཁྱམས་ (dogyam) sm. ཁྱམས་ར་.

མདོ་མཁར་ (dogar) the name of an aristocratic family in Tibet (also known as Ragashar).

མདོ་འགག (dogaà) 1. waiting area. 2. place where roads or rivers intersect.

མདོ་རྒྱུད་ (dogyüü) sutra and tantra.

མདོ་སྒྲོག (do drɔɔ) va. to read sutras.

མདོ་སྔགས་ (do ŋää) sutra and mantra.

མདོ་ཆེན་ (dojen) director, head, chief ། ལས་ཁུངས་ཀྱི་མདོ་ཆེན་ Director of the office.

མདོ་སྙིང་ (doñiŋ) summary, main points, essence.

མདོ་སྟོད་ (dodöö) the Amdo region of Eastern Tibet.

མདོ་སྟོད་སྨད་ (do döömεὲ) abbr. of མདོ་སྟོད་ and མདོ་སྨད་.

མདོ་ཐག (dodaà) sm. རྡོ་ཐ་.

མདོ་དར་མ་ (do tarma) a type of music.

མདོ་དོན་ (dodön) the main issue/ point.

མདོ་སྡེ་ (dode) the collection of sutras in the Kangyur.

མདོ་སྤྱི་ (doji) shung. abbr. མདོ་སྨད་སྤྱི་ཁྱབ་.

མདོ་སྦུག (dobuù) inner and outer (e.g., room).

མདོ་མ་ (doma) 1. the outer room of a house. 2. straw consisting of the lower half of a stalk.

མདོ་སྨད་ (domεὲ) the Kham region of Eastern Tibet.

མདོ་སྨད་ཆོས་འབྱུང་ (domεὲ cöòjuŋ) an chronicle written in 1845 by Demba Rabgyal.

མདོ་སྨད་སྤྱི་ཁྱབ་ (domεὲ jigyəb) shung. the governor general of eastern Tibet headquartered at Chamdo.

མདོ་སྨད་མངའ་ཁུལ་ (domεὲ ŋəgüü) sm. མདོ་སྨད་.

མདོ་ཙམ་ (dodzam) in short, briefly ། དེའི་སྐོར་མདོ་ཙམ་ཞུས་ན་ If (I) speak briefly about that.

མདོ་འཛིན་ (dondzin) 1. sm. གཞུང་སྐྱོང་. 2. the larger (joint) beads on rosaries.

མདོ་ལས་ (doleὲ) shung. 1. abbr. officials on the staff of the Governor General of Eastern Tibet. 2. quotes from the sutra.

མདོ་ལི་ (doli) palanquin.

མདོ་གསུམ་པ་ (do sümmə) an intersection of three roads.

མདོ་ལྷ་བྱིན་དཀར་པོ་ (dola jiŋ gārbo) a kind of white cotton cloth (sth. like jeans).

མདོག (dɔɔ) 1. color ། དངུལ་གྱི་མདོག Silver colored. 2. appearance, looks ། དེ་འདྲའི་མདོག་ངན་པ་ལ་ཡང་ What a bad looking thing. 3. (vb. + — + vb.) to pretend, to act like ། ཧ་མ་གོ་ན་ཧ་གོ་མདོག་མ་བྱེད་ If you don't understand, don't act like you do. 4. (vb. + — + ཁ་པོ་ + vb.) seems like, appears to be (with regards to the verbal action) ། ཆར་པ་གཏོང་མདོག་ཁ་པོ་འདུག It seem as if it is going to rain.

མདོག་སྐྱ་ (dɔɔgya) sm. ཁ་ཐབས་.

མདོག་སྐྱོ་ (dɔɔgyo) sallow and thin.

མདོག་ཁ་ (dɔɔga) color.

མདོག་ཁ་པོ་ (dɔɔ kābo) see མདོག.

མདོག་ཁྲ་ཤིག་གེ་བ་ (dɔɔdra shiggewa) bright, shining, multicolored.

མདོག་གོག (dɔɔgɔɔ) 1. stupid, ignorant, ugly. 2. an inferior type of Chinese bowl.

མདོག་སྒྱུར་ (dɔɔ gyur) 1. va. to change color. 2. va. to change appearance.

མདོག་འགྱུར་ (dɔɔ gyur) 1. vi. to get changed in color. 2. vi. to have an appearance change.

མདོག་ངན་ (dɔɔŋεn) sm. མདོག་ཉེས་.

མདོག་ཅན་ (dɔɔjεn) 1. colored. 2. nonferrous (metals).

མདོག་ཅན་ལྕགས་བཞུ་ (dɔɔjεn jāgshu) nonferrous metallurgy.

མདོག་ཅན་ལྕགས་རིགས་ (dɔɔjεn jāgrig) nonferrous metals.

མདོག་ཅན་མིའི་རིགས་རྒྱུད་ (dɔɔjεn mii riggyüü) colored races, nonwhite races.

མདོག་གཅིག་པ་ (dɔɔ jigbə) same color.

མདོག་ཉམས་ (dɔɔñam) looking worn out/ weak/ pale.

མདོག་ཉེས་ (dɔɔñeè) ugly.

མདོག་ལྡན་ (dɔndεn) sm. མདོག་ཅན་, 1.

མདོག་དྲི་རོ་གསུམ་ (dɔɔ tri ro sūm) the three: color, smell and taste.

མདོག་མདོག (dɔndɔɔ) pretending; va.—བྱེད་ to act as if (can convey pretending) ། མི་དེས་མཁས་པ་ཡིན་མདོག་མདོག་བྱེད་ཀྱི་འདུག That person is acting as if he is a student. 2. showing/ giving a signal to do sth.; va.—བྱེད་ ། ཁོང་གིས་ང་ལ་སྐད་ཆ་ཤོད་མདོག་མདོག་བྱེད་ཀྱི་འདུག He is giving me a signal to speak.

མདོག་ལྡན་ལྕགས་རིགས་ (dɔŋdεn jārii) nonferrous metals.

མདོག་ནག་གི་མི་རྒྱུད་ (dɔɔnaggi migyüü) the dark-skinned races, people of color.

མདོག་ནག་ལྕགས་རིགས་ (dɔɔnag jāgrii) black metals.

མདོག་དྲོ་གཉིས་ལྡན་ (dɔɔ tro ñindεn) having both color and taste.

མདོག་མེད་ (dɔɔmeè) colorless.

མདོག་རྫི་ (dɔɔdzi) enamel.

མདོག་ཚོར་ (dɔɔdzɔr) the sensation of color.

མདོག་མཛེས་པོ་ (dɔɔ dzeèbo) pretty, beautiful in color.

མདོག་ཡལ་ (dɔɔ yεε) 1. vi. to fade/ lose color. 2. vi. to lose one's healthy complexion.

མདོག་རིམ་ (dɔɔrim) the color spectrum.

མདོག་ལེགས་ (dɔɔleg) sm. མདོག་མཛེས་པོ་.

མདོག་ཤོར་ (dɔɔ shɔɔ) sm. མདོག་ཉམས་.

མདོག་གསལ་འཁྲིས་པ་ (dɔɔsεε triibə) a type of jaundice.

མདོག་གསལ་ནད་ (dɔɔsεεnεὲ) sm. མདོག་གསལ་འཁྲིས་པ་.

མདོག་སེར་མི་རྒྱུད་ (dɔɔser migyüü) the mongoloid race, the yellow race.

མདོག་སེར་ཤ་སྐམ་ (dɔɔser shāgam) sallow and thin (conveys poor health).

མདོང་མོ་ (doŋmo) churn.

མདོང་མོ་ཅིག་ནང་ཤུགས་གཏོང་ (doŋmojig nəŋshuù dōŋ) va. to lend one's wife to a friend for sexual intercourse [Lit. lending a churn internally].

མདོངས་ (doŋ) 1. the white spot on the forehead of horses and other animals. 2. the pattern of colors on a peacock's feathers.

མདོངས་ཅན་ (doŋjεn) horses, mules, etc. that have a white patch on their foreheads.

མདོངས་མཐའ་ (doŋda) peacock.

མདོམས་ (dom) the crotch (of the body).

མདོམས་རས་ (domrεὲ) plain cloth.

མདོར་ (dɔr) abbr. of མདོར་བསྡུས་.

མདོར་བསྟན་ (dɔrdεn) a brief introduction/

explanation.

མདོར་སྡུད་ (dɔr düü) va. to abbreviate, to abridge ¶ དེབ་འདིའི་ནང་དོན་རྣམས་མདོར་སྡུད་ཀྱི་རེད་ They will abridge the contents of that book.

མདོར་བསྡུས་ (dɔrdüü) 1. brief, summary, abridgment ¶ གསར་འགྱུར་མདོར་བསྡུས་ A summary of the news. 2. p. of མདོར་སྡུད་.

མདོར་བསྡུས་དོན་གསལ་ (dɔrdüü tönsɛl) brief and clear in meaning.

མདོར་བསྡུས་ན་ (dɔrdüüna) in short, in summary, in brief.

མདོར་ན་ (dɔrna) sm. མདོར་བསྡུས་ན་. 2. even ¶ ཁོས་སློབ་སྦྱོང་ལ་ཧུར་བརྩོན་ཆེན་པོ་བྱེད་ཅིང་མདོར་ན་ལྟོ་ཟ་སྐབས་ཀྱང་དེབ་ཀློག་གི་ཡོད་པ་རེད་ He works hard in his studies. He reads even when eating.

མདོར་བསྡུས་པོ་ (dɔr düübu) very brief, abbreviated.

མདོར་བསྡུས་བཤད་ན་ (dɔrdüü shɛ̈ɛ̀na) to say in short/ in brief.

མདོར་བཤད་ (dɔrshɛɛ̀) sm. མདོར་བསྡུས་བཤད་ན་.

མདོས་ (döö) 1. sm. གླུད་. 2. sm. མདོས་ཀྱི་སྙུག་དྲ་.

མདོས་ཀྱི་སྙུག་དྲ་ (döögi ñügdra) a frame with colorful threads that is used to trap demons/ ghosts.

མདོས་རྒྱག (döö gyaà) va. to chant a tantric incantation.

མདོས་རྒྱག (döö gyaà) va. to trap a demon with a demon trap.

མདོས་བརྡ་སྦྱོད་ (dööda jöö) va. to communicate or say in brief.

མདོས་འཕངས་ (döö pāŋ) sm. མདོས་རྒྱག.

མདོས་ཟོར་ (döösɔr) abbr. གླུད་ and གཏོར་མ་.

མདོས་རིས་ (dööriì) the crisscrossing design on a demon trap.

འདག: p. དག; f. འདག (dag) 1. vi. to become clean. 2. abbr. of འདག་པ་.

འདག་གུ (daggu) 1. detergent. 2. sm. ལྷག་གུ་.

འདག་གུ་བཟོ་གྲྭ (daggu sodra) detergent factory.

འདག་རྒྱག (daà gyaà) va. to masturbate (men).

འདག་ཅལ་ (dagjɛɛ) sm. འདག་རྫས་.

འདག་ཆུ་ (dagju) muddy water.

འདག་དོང་ (dagdoŋ) mire, bog, marsh, swamp.

འདག་འདག (dagdaà) thick (like porridge consistency).

འདག་འདམ་ (dagdam) mud, mire.

འདག་པ་ (dāgba) mud, mire.

འདག་པ་གཡོ་ (dagba yō) va. to make a mud paste by mixing water and earth (for masonry construction).

འདག་པའི་ཞལ་ལྕགས་ (dagbɛ shɛɛjaà) trowel (for plastering walls, floors, ceilings).

འདག་བག (dagbaà) sm. འདམ་པ་.

འདག་བག་ཕར་འཁྱོལ་ (dagbaà pāägyöö) doing things in a slipshod/ casual/ offhand way.

འདག་བག་བྱུག (dagbaà cuù) va. to plaster with mud.

འདག་བྱིའུ་ (dagciwu) a swallow (the bird).

འདག་བྱིལ་ (dagcii) sm. འདག་བྱིའུ་.

འདག་འབྱར་ (dagjar) 1. plastering an opening. 2. sticking some things together with mud.

འདག་སྦྱར་ (dagjar) sm. འདག་འབྱར་.

འདག་རྩེད་ (dagdzeè) playing with mud; va.—རྩེ་.

འདག་ཚང་ (dagdzaŋ) swallow's nest.

འདག་རྫབ་ (dagdzɔb) muddy.

འདག་རྫས་ (dagdzɛɛ̀) cleansing agent, detergent, soap.

འདག་ཞལ་ (dagshɛɛ) sm. འདམ་ཞལ་.

འདག་ཞོ་ (dagsho) mud; vi.—ལང་ to be / get muddy.

འདག་རལ་ཡོག་ཡོག (dagrɛɛ yɔ̀ɔyɔɔ̀) muddy all over.

འདག་རལ་ལིང་ལིང་ (dagrɛɛ liŋliŋ) sm. འདག་རལ་ཡོག་ཡོག.

འདག་རིལ་ (dagrii) mud ball.

འདག་ལས་ (daglɛɛ̀) plastering work; va.—བྱེད་.

འདག་ལས་བྱེད་མཁན་ (daglɛɛ̀ ceèñɛn) plasterer.

འདང་: p. འདངས་; f. འདང་ (daŋ) vi. to be enough/ sufficient ¶ ཁ་ལག་འདི་མི་བཅུ་ལ་འདང་གི་རེད་ The food will be enough for ten people.

འདང་རྒྱག (daŋgyaà) thinking about sth. ¶ ཁོང་གིས་འདང་རྒྱག་ཅིག་བྱས་ནས་ལན་བརྒྱབ་སོང་ He thought about it for a while and then gave an answer.

འདང་ངེས་ (daŋŋeè) definitely enough ¶ ཁ་ལག་འདི་མི་བཅུ་ལ་འདང་ངེས་འདུག The food will definitely be enough for all ten of the people.

འདང་ངེས་ཐེངས་ངེས་ (daŋŋeè tēŋŋeè) sm. འདང་ངེས་.

འདང་ངེས་བཞིན་པ་ (daŋŋeè shimbɔ) sm. འདང་ངེས་.

འདང་ཅན་ (daŋjɛn) dear and cherished ¶ སློབ་མའི་འདང་ཅན་ A cherished disciple.

འདང་མ་འདངས་ (daŋ ma daŋ) whether sth. is enough or not, whether sth. suffices or not ¶ རས་འདིས་གོས་ཐུང་གཉིས་འདང་མ་འདངས་ལྟ་དགོས་ (We) have to see whether or not this cloth is enough for two pairs of trousers.

འདང་ཙམ་ (daŋdzam) just enough, just suffices.

འདངས་ (daŋ) p. of འདང་.

འདངས་ཙམ་ (daŋdzam) sm. འདང་ཙམ་.

འདན་པ་ (dɛmba) sm. འདན་བུ་.

འདན་བུ་ (dɛmbu) bolt or mechanism for locking a door.

འདན་ཤིང་ (dɛnshiŋ) sm. འདན་བུ་.

འདབ་ (dɔb) 1. near to. 2. sm.* ལྡབ་ ¶ འདབ་གསུམ་ Three times.

འདབ་དཀྲུག (dɔbdruù) tattling, telling on someone; va.—རྒྱག.

འདབ་དཀྲུག་ཚ་པོ་ (dɔbdruù tsābo) sb. who tattles a lot.

འདབ་ཁ་ (dɔbga) petal (of a flower).

འདབ་ཁྲ་ (dɔbdra) swallow (bird).

འདབ་འཁོར་ (dɔbgɔɔ) rotor of a turbine.

འདབ་ཆ་ (dɔbja) the lower part (of sth.).

འདབ་ཆགས་ (dɔbjaà) birds.

འདབ་སྟོང་ (dɔbdoŋ) lotus flower.

འདབ་སྟོང་ཅན་ (dɔbdoŋjɛn) sm. འདབ་སྟོང་.

འདབ་ལྡན་ (dɔbdɛn) 1. having petals. 2. having flaps (for hats).

འདབ་བེ་འདོབ་བེ་ (dɔbbe dobbe) mushy.

འདབ་བྱ་ (dɔbja) bird.

འདབ་མ་ (dɔbma) 1. leaf, petal. 2. flake (of snow). 3. wing of a bird.

འདབ་མ་བརྒྱད་པ་ (dɔbma gyɛɛ̀ba) eight petals (a lotus with eight petals).

འདབ་མ་འབུམ་བརྡལ་ (dɔbma bumdɛɛ) having many petals.

འདབ་བཟང་ (dɔbsaŋ) 1. good wings. 2. good leaf.

འདབ་ལོ་ (dɔblo) leaf.

འདབ་གསུམ་པ་ (dɔbsumba) poet. radish.

འདབ་སྲིན་ (dɔbsin) a leaf eating insect.

འདབ་ལྷེ་ (dɔblhe) flower, petal.

འདབས་ (dɔb) near, around, (the) foot of ¶ རི་ཡི་འདབས་ The foot of the hill.

འདབས་ཆགས་ (dɔbjaà) vi. to be situated/ located near.

འདབས་འབྲེལ་ (dɔbdrel) shung. neighboring, adjacent, sharing a border ¶ ང་གཉིས་ཁྱིམ་འདབས་འབྲེལ་ཡིན་ Our two houses are neighbors. ¶ ས་མཚམས་འདབས་འབྲེལ་གྱི་ཆབ་འབངས་བལ་པོར་ཕྱོགས་ཁ་གཏད་བྱེད་པ་ The people living on the joint border are turning (their allegiance) towards the Nepalese.

འདམ་ (dam) 1. swamp, marsh, bog; vi.—འཐེབས་ to get caught in a swamp/ bog. 2. a pastoral nomad area northwest of Lhasa. 3. clay.

འདམ་: p. བདམས་ or འདམས་; f. བདམ་ or འདམ་ imp. འདོམས་འདམ་ (dam) va. to choose/ select ¶ འཐུས་མི་གསར་པ་འདེམས་པ་རེད་ (They) chose new delegates.

འདམ་ཀ་ (damga) sm. འདམ་སྐྱག.

འདམ་ཁ་ (damga) sm. འདམ་སྐྱག.

འདམ་སྐྱེས་ (damgyeè) lotus.

འདམ་ཁུ་ (damgu) murky/ swampy/ muddy water.

འདམ་ཁྲོད་ (damdröö) in the middle of a swamp/ muddy area.

འདམ་ག (damga) sm. གདམ་ང་.

འདམ་རྒྱུག (dəmgyuù) a wooden stick used to knead clay.

འདམ་སྒྲུག (dəmdruù) 1. choosing, selecting, electing; va.—རྒྱག; —གཏོང་ to choose, to select, to elect. 2. tying; va.—རྒྱག to tie.

འདམ་བརྒྱད་ཤོག་པ་ (dəmgyɛɛ̀ shōgba) the eight traditional nomadic groups in the Dam area.

འདམ་སྒྲུག་པ་ (dam drugbə) a candidate (in an election).

འདམ་ང་ (damŋa) sm. འདམ་སྒྲུག.

འདམ་སྔོག་གྲུ་ (damŋɔ̀ɔ tru) dredging boat.

འདམ་ཆུ་ (dammju) swampy/ muddy water.

འདམ་ཉ་ (damña) leach.

འདམ་རྙོག (damñog) sm. འདམ་ཆུ་.

འདམ་འཐག (dam tāà) va. to dissolve a medicine or powder in water.

འདམ་དོང་ (damdoŋ) swamp, bog, muddy depression/ hole.

འདམ་སྡོང་ (damdoŋ) petal and stem of plants.

འདམ་པ་ (damba) mud, sludge; va.—སློག to dig out mud, to dredge.

འདམ་པ་ཕུར་བུ་བཏབ་པ་ལྟར་ (damba pūrbu dəbbədar) sth. unstable/ unreliable [Lit. like driving a stake in the mud].

འདམ་པག (dambaà) sm. འདམ་པ་.

འདམ་པད་ (dambɛɛ̀) lotus design.

འདམ་བག (dambaà) sm. འདམ་པ་.

འདམ་བུ་ (dambu) reeds and other similar plants that grow in swamps/ bogs.

འདམ་བུ་ག་ར་ (dambu gāra) a type of Tibetan herbal medicine.

འདམ་བུའི་མཆུ་རིང་ (dambü cūriŋ) a traditional Tibetan surgery tool.

འདམ་བུའི་རྩ་གདན་ (dambü dādɛn) reed mat.

འདམ་བུའི་ཚལ་ (dambü tsɛ̄ɛ) reed marsh.

འདམ་འབྱར་ (damjar) sm. འདག་འབྱར་.

འདམ་བྱིའུ་ (damciwu) swallow (the bird).

འདམ་སྦྱར་ (damjar) sm. འདག་འབྱར་.

འདམ་སྙགས་ (damñag) foul smelling mud/ mire.

འདམ་རྩྭ་ (damdza) tall grass/ reeds growing in a marsh or swamp.

འདམ་རྫིང་ (damdziŋ) a muddy pond.

འདམ་རྫབ་ (damdzəb) mud, mire, marsh; vi.—ལང་ to become muddy/ marshy/ swampy.

འདམ་རྫབ་ཉག་ཉིག (damdzəb ñagñii) murky/ foul smelling mud.

འདམ་བརྫིས་སྒྲ་ (damdzii dra) the sloshing sound of (sb.) walking/ stepping in the mud.

འདམ་ཞལ་ (damshɛɛ̀) mud for plastering; va.—གཏོང་ to plaster with mud.

འདམ་ཞལ་པ་ (damshɛwa) plasterer.

འདམ་ཞོ་ (damsho) sm. འདག་ཞོ་.

འདམ་གཞུང་ (damshuŋ) name of a nomad area northwest of Lhasa.

འདམ་གཞོང་ (damshoŋ) a large container in which mud for construction is kept.

འདམ་བཟོ་ལས་གྲྭ་ (damso lɛɛ̀dra) brickmaking group/ team.

འདམ་འོབས་ (damob) mud puddle.

འདམ་ར་ (damra) swampy/ marshy area, a bog.

འདམ་ལས་པ་ (damlɛba) plasterer.

འདམ་ལུད་ (damlüü) silt fertilizer.

འདམ་ལུམས་ (damlum) mud therapy.

འདམ་ས་ (damsa) sm. འདམ་, 1.

འདམ་སེང་ (damseŋ) lion.

འདམ་སོག (damsɔɔ̀) reeds.

འདམ་སོལ་ (damsöö) peat.

འདམ་ལྷ་ (damlha) a clay statue of a god.

འདམས་ (dam) p. of འདམ་.

འདམས་སྙིགས་ (damñig) sm. བདམས་སྙིགས་.

འདའ་: p. འདས་; f. འདའ་ (da) vi. to pass (time) ¶ ལས་ཀ་མེད་པར་དུས་ཡུན་རིང་འདས་སོང་ A lot of time has passed without having work. ¶ འདས་པའི་ལོ་རྒྱུས་ Past history. 2. vi. to pass away/ die ¶ ཁོང་གི་ཕ་མ་འདས་ནས་ཡུན་རིང་སོང་བ་རེད་ It has been a long time since his parents died. 3. va. to disobey, to violate/ break a promise ¶ རྒྱལ་པོའི་བཀའ་ལས་འདས་ནས་ Having disobeyed the king's order. 4. vi. to go beyond, to exceed, to surpass ¶ གྲངས་ལས་འདས་པ་ Innumerable [Lit. beyond number].

འདའ་ཁ་ (daka) the time/ point just before death.

འདའ་ག་མ་ (da gama) time/ point just before death.

འདའ་མ་ (dama) a piece of wool that has been carded and is ready to spin.

འདའ་རི་འདུར་རི་ (dari durri) mushy, pulpy.

འདར་ (dar) vi. to shiver, to tremble, to shake ¶ ཞེད་ནས་འདར་བྱུང་ (I) shook with fear. ¶ འཁྱག་ནས་འདར་གྱི་འདུག (They) are shivering from cold.

འདར་ཁྱོམ་ཁྱོམ་ (dar kyōmkyom) swaying back and forth (as in a drunken stupor).

འདར་འཁྱོམས་ (dar kyōm) vi. to sway/ shake.

འདར་ཁྲུག་ཁྲུག (dar trūdruù) shivering, trembling, shaking.

འདར་འཁྲུག་འཁྲུག (dar trūdruù) sm. འདར་ཁྲུག་ཁྲུག.

འདར་རྒྱག (dar gyaà) vi. to shiver, to shake, to tremble.

འདར་འདར་ (dardar) shivering, trembling, shaking; vi.—བྱེད་.

འདར་ནད་ (darnɛɛ̀) malaria [Lit. shivering disease].

འདར་ནད་འབུ་ཕྲ་ (darnɛɛ̀ budra) plasmodium/ malarial parasite.

འདར་ཕྲིལ་ཕྲིལ་ (dar triīdrii) sm. འདར་འདར་.

འདར་བུ་ (darbu) sm. འདར་ནད་.

འདར་རྩ་ (dardza) a pulsating vein.

འདར་ཚད་ (dardzɛɛ̀) the amount/ frequency of shivering or trembling.

འདར་ཞིང་འཁྱོ་བ་ (darshiŋ cowa) sm. འདར་འཁྱོམས་.

འདར་ཞུམ་ཞུམ་ (dar shumshum) shaking from fear or cold; vi.—བྱེད་.

འདར་ཡོམ་ (daryom) sm. འདར་འཁྱོམས་.

འདར་ཡོམ་མེ་ (dar yomme) shaking, swaying.

འདར་ཡོམ་མེ་བ་ (dar yomewa) sm. འདར་ཡོམ་མེ་.

འདར་ཤང་ཤང་ (dar shāŋshaŋ) sm. འདར་འདར་.

འདར་ཤིག་ཤིག (dar shīgshiì) sm. འདར་སིག་སིག.

འདར་ཤུམ་ཤུམ་ (dar shūmshum) sm. འདར་ཞུམ་ཞུམ་.

འདར་སིག (darsiì) 1. shivering; vi.—རྒྱག to shiver.

འདར་སིག་སིག (dar sīgsiì) shivering, trembling, shaking.

འདར་སིལ་སིལ་ (dar sīīsii) sm. འདར་སིག་སིག.

འདར་གསིག (darsiì) sm. འདར་སིག.

འདར་ཧད་དེ་བ་ (dar hɛ̄ɛ̀dewa) shivering/ shaking and panting.

འདར་ལྷིམ་ལྷིམ་ (dar lhēmlhem) sm. འདར་སིག་སིག.

འདལ་ (dɛɛ) 1. vi. to become absorbed/ dissolved ¶ ཆུའི་ནང་དུ་སྨན་འདལ་བ་རེད་ The medicine dissolved in the water. 2. vi. to bleed/ run (for ink) ¶ ཤོག་བུ་འདིའི་སྟེང་ལ་ཡི་གེ་འདལ་གྱི་འདུག The letters bled on the paper.

འདལ་ཀ་ཅེ་བ་ (dɛɛga cēwa) widespread, broad.

འདལ་འགྲོ་ (dɛndro) sm. འདལ་.

འདས་ (dɛɛ̀) 1. p. of འདའ་. 2. the past tense.

འདས་སྐར་ (dɛɛ̀gar) death day anniversary.

འདས་གྲོངས་ (dɛɛ̀droŋ) vi. to die.

འདས་བསྔོ་ (dɛɛ̀ŋo) prayers for the deceased/ dead.

འདས་མཆོད་ (dɛɛ̀jöö) religious service done when someone dies, funeral rite.

འདས་མཆོད་དངོས་པོ་ (dɛɛ̀jöö ŋöòbo) funerary objects, burial objects.

འདས་མཆོད་ཤོག་སྒོར་ (dɛɛ̀jöö shōggɔɔ) funerary paper money (Chinese custom).

འདས་མཆོད་ཨུ་ཡོན་ལྷན་ཁང་ (dɛɛ̀jöö ūyön lhēngaŋ) funeral commission.

འདས་འཇུག (dɛnjuù) burying a corpse; va.—བྱེད་.

འདས་རྗེས་ཁས་ལེན་ (dɛɛ̀jeè kɛ̄ɛ̀len) posthumous acknowledgment/ recognition/ acceptance; va.—བྱེད་.

འདས་དོན་ (dɛɛ̀dön) past events.

འདས་བརྡ་ (dɛɛ̀da) obituary notice; va.—གཏོང་ to

send an obituary notice.

འདས་པ་ (d̲ɛ̲ɛ̀ba) 1. past tense. 2. previous ¶ འདས་པའི་ལོ་དེའི་ནང་ In the previous year.

འདས་པའི་སངས་རྒྱས་ (d̲ɛ̲ɛ̀bɛ sa̲ŋgyɛɛ̀) the past Buddhas.

འདས་པོ་ (d̲ɛ̲ɛ̀bo) the one who is dead, the deceased one ¶ བཟའ་ཟླ་འདས་པོ་ The deceased spouse.

འདས་པོའི་ཆར་གྱུར་ (d̲ɛ̲ɛ̀bö cār gyu̲r) vi. (past tense only) to have a time for sth. pass.

འདས་མ་ཁད་ (d̲ɛ̲ɛ̀ ma̲kɛɛ̀) as soon as sth. passed or is over ¶ ཚོགས་འདུའི་དུས་ཚོད་འདས་མ་ཁད་མི་ཚང་མ་ལོག་སོང་ As soon as the time of the meeting ended, all the people left. 2. as soon as sb. died ¶ ཁོང་འདས་མ་ཁད་དུར་འཇུག་བྱས་སོང་ He was buried as soon as he died.

འདས་མ་ཐག (d̲ɛ̲ɛ̀ ma̲taà) sm. འདས་མ་ཁད་.

འདས་མཚན་ (d̲ɛ̲ɛ̀dzɛn) posthumous title.

འདས་ཚིག (d̲ɛ̲ɛ̀dzii) past tense.

འདས་ཟིན་པ་ (d̲ɛ̲ɛ̀sin) 1. past, finished ¶ འདས་ཟིན་པའི་ལོ་གསར་ The past New Year. 2. deceased.

འདས་ཟླ་ (d̲ɛ̲nda) previous months, past months.

འདས་ལོ་ (d̲ɛ̲ɛ̀lo) A.D. ¶ འདས་ལོ་བརྒྱ་ཕྲག་དྲུག་པ་ The 6th century A.D.

འདས་ལོག (d̲ɛ̲ɛ̀lɔɔ̀) 1. the dead coming back to life. 2. a person who returns from the dead.

འདས་ལོག་དུས་ཆེན་ (d̲ɛ̲ɛ̀lɔɔ̀ tüüjen) Easter.

འདས་གཤེགས་རྗེས་དྲན་ (d̲ɛ̲ɛ̀sheg jeèdrɛn) commemorative day for sb.'s death.

འདས་གསོན་ (d̲ɛ̲ɛ̀ sȫn) dead and living.

འདི་ (d̲i) this ¶ མི་འདི་ This man.

འདི་ཀོ་ (digo) this one.

འདི་སྐད་ (digɛɛ̀) talk like this, saying like this; va.—ཞེར་ to say like this; vi.—ཐོས་ to hear this talk ¶ ཁོང་གིས་ང་ལ་འདི་སྐད་ཞེར་གྱི་འདུག He is telling me like this.

འདི་སྐབས་ (digəb) at this time, during this period.

འདི་ཁོ་ན་ (di ko̲na) just this, only this ¶ འདི་ཁོ་ནར་བསམ་བློ་གཏོང་གི་ཡོད་ (I) think only about this.

འདི་ག (digə) here ¶ ང་འདི་ག་རང་ལ་བསྡད་ཡོད་ I am staying right here.

འདི་ག་ཙམ་ (digədzam) this much ¶ ཅ་ལག་འདི་ག་ཙམ་གྱིས་འགྲིག་གི་འདུག This much of things is enough.

འདི་གར་ (di̲gar) here, over here ¶ ང་འདི་གར་བསྡད་ཡོད་ I am staying here.

འདི་གྱུད་ (digyɛɛ̀) these.

འདི་གྲས་ (di̲drɛɛ̀) like this, this kind/ type ¶ ཅ་ལག་འདི་གྲས་ད་དུང་འཚོང་རྒྱུ་ཡོད་པས་ Do you have more of this kind of thing to sell.

འདི་ངོས་ (di̲ŋöö) this side.

འདི་ཉིད་ (di̲ñii) this itself, this (this particular one) ¶ དོན་དག་འདི་ཉིད་ད་ཙང་གལ་ཆེན་པོ་ཡིན་ This particular matter is very important.

འདི་གཉིས་ (di̲ñii) these two.

འདི་སྙེད་ཅིག (di̲ñeèjig) sm. འདི་ཙམ་.

འདི་ལྟ་སྡེ་ (di̲ dāde) vi. to be like this.

འདི་ལྟ་བུ་ (di̲ dəbu) like this, such as this ¶ དམག་འཁྲུག་འདི་ལྟ་བུ་སྔར་བྱུང་མ་མྱོང་བ་ཞིག་རེད་ A war like this has never occurred before.

འདི་ལྟར་ (di̲dar) sm. འདི་ལྟ་བུ་.

འདི་དག (di̲daà) sm. འདི་ཚོ་.

འདི་དང་འདི་ (di̲daŋ di̲) this and this, such and such ¶ འདི་དང་འདི་ཞིས་བྱེད་ཞེར་མཁན་མེད་པ་རེད་ There is no one to say 'do this and this'.

འདི་དུས་ (di̲düü) this time/ occasion.

འདི་འདྲ་ (di̲ndrɛ) like this.

འདི་འདྲ་སེ་ (di̲ndres) sm. འདི་འདྲ་.

འདི་ནས་ (di̲nɛ) from here.

འདི་ནས་འདི་བྱུང་ (di̲nɛ di̲juŋ) shung. received from so and so ¶ བུན་འདེད་པས་མི་ཚང་འདི་ནས་འདི་བྱུང་གི་བྱུང་ཐོ་གསལ་འགོད་བྱ་རྒྱུ་ The loan collectors should clearly have a record that they have received so much from so and so family.

འདི་ནས་པར་ (di̲nɛpāā) from here to there.

འདི་ནི་ (di̲ni) as for this, concerning this.

འདི་སྣང་གི་བྱ་བ་ (di̲naŋgi ca̲wa) worldly affairs.

འདི་པ་ (di̲bə) 1. this one (person) ¶ མི་འདི་པར་རོགས་རམ་གང་ཡོད་གནང་རོགས་ Please help this person as much as possible.

འདི་པར་ (di̲bar) 1. hereabouts, around here. 2. to this person.

འདི་ཕྱི་ (di̲ cī) this life and the next life.

འདི་ཕྱི་ཀུན་ཏུ་ (di̲ci gūndu) this life, the next life and always.

འདི་ཕྱི་གཉིས་ཀྱི་མཚམས་སུ་ (di̲ci ñiìgi tsāmsu) at the point of death.

འདི་ཕྱི་དཔང་འཕེར་ (di̲cii bāŋber) not violating the law of karma in this life and the next life.

འདི་ཕྱིའི་ལེགས་ཚོགས་ (di̲cii le̲gdzɔɔ̀) merit for this life and the next ¶ འདི་ཕྱིའི་ལེགས་ཚོགས་ཀུན་གྱི་འབྱུང་གནས་སངས་རྒྱས་ཀྱི་བསྟན་པ་ Buddhism, which is the merit for this life and the next.

འདི་ཕྱོགས་ (di̲cɔɔ̀) this side, this end, here ¶ ཁྱེད་རང་འདི་ཕྱོགས་ཕེབས་རྩིས་ཡོད་ན་ If you plan to come here.

འདི་ཕྱིའི་སོ་མཚམས་ (di̲cii sōdzam) sm. འདི་ཕྱི་གཉིས་ཀྱི་མཚམས་སུ་.

འདི་བྱ་འདི་བགྱིས་ (di̲ca di̲gyii) shung. what to do ¶ གནས་ཚུལ་འདི་སྐོར་འདི་བྱ་འདི་བགྱིས་ཀྱི་ལན་གསལ་འཕྲལ་སྟོལ་ཡོད་པ་ཞུ་ Regarding this matter, we request you to let us know what to do as soon as possible.

འདི་བྱ་འདི་བྱེད་ (di̲ca di̲jeè) shung. sm. འདི་བྱ་འདི་བགྱིས་.

འདི་བྱས་འདི་མིན་ (di̲jeè di̲min) what is or is not ¶ ལས་ཀ་གསར་པ་དེའི་སྐོར་འདི་བྱས་འདི་མིན་གང་ཡང་གོ་རྒྱུ་མི་འདུག Regarding the new job, (I) didn't hear anything about what it is (or is not).

འདི་བྱས་ཞུ་འཕེར་ཐུབ་པ་ (di̲jɛɛ̀ shu̲per tūbbə) shung. being able to justify what one has done ¶ གཙུག་ལག་ཁང་ལས་མས་ལ་བདག་ཚགས་སྐྱོད་མེད་ཞུས་ཐོག་ལོའི་བྱས་རྗེས་འདི་བྱས་ཞུ་འཕེར་ཐུབ་པ་དགོས་རྒྱུ་ (One) must be able to justify what one has done each year in maintaining the Tsuklakhang.

འདི་བྱེད་བསམ་པ་མེད་པ་ (di̲jeè sāmba me̲èba) not knowing what to do.

འདི་དབང་ལྟར་ན་ (di̲waŋ dārna) shung. from this viewpoint ¶ འདི་དབང་ལྟར་ན་ཞུ་ཚིག་སྔ་ཕྱི་གོ་ལྡོག་ཁར་ From this viewpoint there is a contradiction between what he said earlier and later.

འདི་འབའ་ཞིག (di̲ ba̲shig) only this.

འདི་མུར་ (di̲mur) like this, continuously, as it is now ¶ འདི་མུར་ཡུན་རིང་སྡོད་ཐུབ་ཀྱི་མ་རེད་ (He) will not be able to remain like this for long. ¶ རང་བཞིན་འདི་མུར་འཇོག་པ་མ་འོས་པ་ It is not appropriate to leave it like this.

འདི་མུས་ (di̲müü) sm. འདི་མུར་.

འདི་ཚུག (di̲dzug) sm. འདི་ལྟར་.

འདི་ཚོ་ (di̲ndzo) these ¶ མི་འདི་ཚོ་ང་ཚོའི་ཁྲོང་པ་རེད་ These people are our neighbors.

འདི་མཚམས་ (di̲dzam) at this time.

འདི་མཚུངས་ (di̲dzuŋ) just like this.

འདི་བཞིན་ (di̲shin) 1. sm. འདི་ལྟར་. 2. as for this, this ¶ དེབ་འདི་བཞིན་ཚང་མས་ཀློག་དགོས་པ་ཞིག་རེད་ This book is one that everyone should read.

འདི་ཟླ་ (di̲da) this month.

འདི་ཡིན་འདི་མིན་ (di̲yin di̲min) what something is or is not, answer, reply.

འདི་རིགས་ (di̲rig) this kind/ type.

འདི་རང་ (di̲raŋ) sm. དེ་ཉིད་.

འདི་རིང་ (di̲riŋ) sm.* དེ་རིང་.

འདི་རུ་ (di̲ru) sm. འདིར་.

འདི་ལ་འདི་བྱུང་ (di̲lə di̲juŋ) shung. this person has got this ¶ ཕྲན་དང་གཡོག་རིགས་ལ་དངོས་པོ་བྱུང་ཡོད་ཞེར་གྱི་ཡོད་ན་འདི་ལ་འདི་བྱུང་གི་ཁུངས་སྐྱེལ་བྱེད་དགོས་ If (they) say that I and my servant have got the things (they) must prove this.

འདི་ལས་ (di̲lɛɛ̀) abbr. the office here (as opposed to one somewhere else).

འདི་ལས་དེ་ (di̲lɛ de̲) this is ... than that ¶ འདི་ལས་དེ་ཡག་གི་རེད་ This is better than that.

འདི་ལོ་ (dilo) this year.

འདིག (dig) plug, stopper, cork.

འདིང་: p. **བཏིང་**; f. **གདིང་**; imp. **ཐིངས་** (diŋ) 1. va. to lay ¶ རྨང་གཞི་བརྟན་པོ་འདིང་གི་འདུག (They) are laying a firm foundation. 2. va. to formulate sth. ¶ ཁང་པ་རྒྱག་ཡས་འཆར་གཞི་འདིངས་ཀྱི་ཡོད་པ་རེད་ (They) are formulating plans to build a house.

འདིང་སྒྲོན་ (diŋdrön) sm. འདིང་.

འདིན་འདུས་ (diŋdrɛɛ̀) sm. འདི་འདུ་.

འདིར་ (dee) here ¶ ཁོ་འདིར་འདུག He is here.

འདིས་ (dii) by this.

འདིས་མ་ཚད་ (dii madzɛɛ̀) not only this but also ¶ འདིས་མ་ཚད་ ཁོང་གི་ཨུ་རུ་སུའི་སྐད་ཀྱང་ཤེས་ཀྱི་ཡོད་པ་རེད་ Not only this, he also knows Russian.

འདུ་: p. **འདུས་**; f. **འདུ་**; imp. **འདུས་** (du) 1. vi. to gather, to assemble, to accumulate, to collect ¶ ཁྲོམ་ར་དེར་མི་མང་པོ་འདུས་འདུག A lot of people have gathered at the marketplace. 2. vi. to be united, to be joined together ¶ རྒྱུ་མང་པོ་འདུས་པའི་དངོས་པོ་ Things composed of many materials. 3. vi. to be included ¶ དེའི་ནང་དུ་མི་རིགས་གཞན་དག་ཀྱང་འདུས་ཡོད་ There are other nationalities also included in this.

འདུ་བསྐུག (duguù) rounding up, recruiting, calling up (for a specific task); va.—བྱེད་ to round up, to recruit, to call up ¶ དམག་དོན་ཅ་ལག་འོར་འདྲེན་ལ་གཡག་མང་པོ་འདུ་བསྐུག་བྱས་པ་རེད་ They called up many yaks for the transportation of military goods (supplies).

འདུ་ཁང་ (dugaŋ) prayer assembly hall for monks (in monasteries).

འདུ་ཁོངས་ (dugoŋ) shung. 1. the area from which taxes and goods are collected. 2. individuals belonging to a district.

འདུ་ཁོངས་ཁྲལ་ཚོ་གཅིག་པ་ (dugoŋ trɛ̄ɛ̄dzo jīgbə) shung. taxpayers in the same tax collection area ¶ ཁྱོད་གཉིས་མི་སེར་འདུ་ཁོངས་ཁྲལ་འཚོ་གཅིག་པའི་གཅིག་ཕན་གཅིག་གྲོགས་དགོས་རྒྱུ་ Both of you being taxpayers in the same tax collection area should help each other.

འདུ་ཁོངས་ཀྱི་འཐུས་མི་ (dugoŋgi tū̄ümi) shung. representatives of the taxpayers in a tax collection area.

འདུ་འཁྲུག (dudruù) abbr. of འདུ་བ་འཁྲུགས་.

འདུ་བསྒོར་ (dugɔɔ) collecting and keeping nearby; va.—བྱེད་.

འདུ་འགག (duŋgaà) shung. main junctions (of roads/ trails) ¶ ཨམ་བན་ནས་ལམ་གྱི་འདུ་འགག་དུ་བཀྲམ་པའི་ཁྲིམས་འདོམས་ཡི་གེ Legal documents from the Amban that were distributed at the main junctions of the road.

འདུ་འགོད་ (duŋgöö) affairs, dealings ¶ དཔལ་འབྱོར་གྱི་འདུ་འགོད་ལ་དོ་སྣང་ཆེན་པོ་མ་བྱས་པ་རེད་ (They) did not pay a lot of attention to economic affairs.

འདུ་འགོད་ལས་ཁུངས་ (dugöö lɛ̄ɛ̄guŋ) 1. an office in the tt. government concerned with soldier's salaries. 2. an office in the Tibetan exile government that deals with economics.

འདུ་སྒོ་ (dugo) income.

འདུ་ཚོགས་ (dujaà) a gathering, a crowd ¶ མི་མང་འདུ་ཚོགས་ཧ་ཅང་ཆེ་བ་ A large gathering of people.

འདུ་འཐུས་ (dutüü) abbr. of འདུ་ཁོངས་ཀྱི་འཐུས་མི་.

འདུ་སྡོད་ (dudöö) living/ staying together ¶ རྒྱ་གར་ནང་བོད་མི་འདུ་སྡོད་ཀྱི་ས་གནས་ Local communities in India where Tibetans live together.

འདུ་གནས་ (dunɛɛ̀) sm. འདུ་སྡོད་.

འདུ་སྤྱི་ (duji) shung. an association of representatives from various places under the jurisdiction of a particular district.

འདུ་འབྲོད་ (du dröö) vi. to have two things come together.

འདུ་བ་འཁྲུགས་ (duwa drūg) vi. to be ill, to be not feeling well.

འདུ་བ་སྙོམས་ (duwa ñōm) physically well.

འདུ་བ་གཞིད་དུ་བབས་ (duwa shēēdu bəb) vi. to be cured of one illness and then get afflicted with another.

འདུ་ཚོགས་ (dudzɔɔ̀) mass rally, mass meeting; va.—བྱེད་ ¶ དམག་འཁྲུག་ལ་ངོ་རྒོལ་གྱི་འདུ་ཚོགས་ A mass rally to protest the war.

འདུ་འཛི་ (dudzi) noise, clamor, tumult.

འདུ་འཛོམས་ (dundzom) 1. sm. འདུ་ཚོགས་. 2. a gathering/ gettogether/ meeting; vi.—བྱེད་ ¶ ནང་མི་ཚང་མ་འདུ་འཛོམས་བྱས་པ་རེད་ All the family members gathered for a gettogether.

འདུ་ལོང་ (duloŋ) lively, bustling with noise.

འདུ་ལོང་ཆེན་པོ་ (duloŋ cēmbo) extremely lively/ active/ bustling.

འདུ་ཤེས་ (dusheè) concept, idea, ideology; va.—འཛུགས; —འཛིན་ to have or hold on to a concept/ idea/ ideology, to conceive of ¶ ཚང་མ་སྤུན་ཟླའི་འདུ་ཤེས་འཛིན་དགོས་ (You) should conceive of all as brothers. ¶ མི་དེས་འབྱོར་མེད་གྲལ་རིམ་གྱི་འདུ་ཤེས་འཛིན་སྟངས་ཐོག་ནས་གནད་དོན་ལ་དབྱེ་ཞིབ་བྱེད་ཀྱི་ཡོད་པ་རེད་ That person analyzed issues on the basis of the ideology of the proletariat.

འདུ་ཤེས་ཀྱི་རྣམ་པ་ (dusheègi nāmba) ideological form/ shape/ appearance.

འདུ་ཤེས་སྐྱེ་ཚུལ་ (dusheè gyēdzüü) sm. འདུ་ཤེས་ཀྱི་རྣམ་པ་.

འདུ་ཤེས་བསྒྱུར་ (dusheè gyur) va. to change (one's) way of thinking/ ideology.

འདུ་ཤེས་སྣང་པ་ (dusheè dōŋba) illusion, fantasy, hallucination.

འདུ་ཤེས་ཙམ་སྨྲ་བ་ (dusheèdzam māwa) idealism.

འདུ་ཤེས་འཛིན་སྟངས་ (dusheè dzindaŋ) ideology, ideological sphere ¶ འདུ་ཤེས་འཛིན་སྟང་ཐད་ཀྱི་གྲལ་རིམ་གྱི་འཐབ་རྩོད་ The class struggle in the ideological sphere.

འདུ་ས་ (dusə) focal point, place where people gather/ collect ¶ འགྲུལ་པ་མང་བའི་འདུ་ས་ The place where many travelers gather.

འདུ་གསོག (dusoò) sm. བསྡུ་གསོག.

འདུ་ལྷོང་ (dulhoŋ) coming together and dispersing.

འདུ་ལྷོང་ཆེ་བ་ (dūlhoŋ cēwa) sm. འདུ་ལྷོང་ཆེན་པོ་.

འདུག (duù) 1. existential verb (there is, there are) ¶ ནང་ལ་དེབ་ཅིག་འདུག There is a book at home. ¶ ཁོ་ནང་ལ་འདུག He is at home. ¶ ཁོ་ཤུགས་ཆེན་པོ་འདུག He is strong. ¶ ཁོར་དེབ་གཅིག་འདུག He has a book. 2. auxilliary verb in various verbal complements ¶ ཁོས་ལས་ཀ་བྱེད་ཀྱི་འདུག He is working. ¶ ཁོས་ལས་ཀ་བྱས་འདུག He has worked. 3. (linking vb. + —) found out/ confirmed/ certain about a statement ¶ ཁོ་སོ་པ་རེད་འདུག (It is certain that) he is a spy. 4. va. to stay/ live.

འདུག་ཁོམ་ (duùgom) sm. སྡོད་ཁོམ་.

འདུག་གམ་ (duùgam) interrogative form of འདུག.

འདུག་གས་ (duùgɛ) sm. འདུག་གམ་.

འདུག་གྲལ་ (dugdrɛɛ) a row/ line where people sit.

འདུག་སྟངས་ (dugdaŋ) 1. manner/ style/ way of sitting. 2. way of doing things.

འདུག་སྟེགས་ (dugdeg) chair, stool, seat.

འདུག་གནས་ (dugnɛɛ̀) sm. སྡོད་གནས་.

འདུག་རེས་ (dugrɛɛ̀) one's turn to be somewhere ¶ དེ་རིང་ང་ལས་ཁུངས་ལ་འདུག་རེས་ཡིན་ Today it's my turn to be at the office.

འདུག་རོགས་ (dugrɔɔ̀) 1. spouse. 2. roommate.

འདུག་ལུགས་ (dugluù) sm. འདུག་སྟངས་.

འདུག་ས་ (dugsə) sm. འདུག་སྟེགས་.

འདུག་སི་ (dugs) like this.

འདུད་: p. **བཏུད་**; f. **གདུད་**; imp. **ཐུད་** (düü) va. to bow, to show respect ¶ དགེ་རྒན་གྱི་ཞབས་ལ་བཏུད་པ་རེད་ (He) bowed in respect before the teacher's feet).

འདུད་སྟངས་ (düüdaŋ) way of showing respect.

འདུད་ཚུལ་ (düüdzüü) sm. འདུད་སྟངས་.

འདུན་ (dün) 1. va. to desire, to wish, to hope for ¶ རང་གི་གྲོགས་པོ་སླར་ཡང་ཐུག་འདུན་བྱུང་བ་རེད་ They hoped to see their friends again. 2. abbr. of འདུན་པ་ and འདུན་མ་.

འདུན་ཁང་ (düngaŋ) hall/ room for meetings and conferences.

འདུན་གྲོས་ (dugdröö) sm. གྲོས་མོལ་.

འདུན་པ་ (dümbə) hope, aspiration, wish; va.—བྱེད་; —ཞུ་; —སྐྱོང་ to aspire/ to long/ hope for, to desire, to wish for; va.—འཆང་ to hold on to a hope/ wish. ༑ ཕྱུགས་ཀྱི་འདུན་པ་ Future hopes. ༑ རང་ཡུལ་དུ་འགྲོ་ཐུབ་པའི་འདུན་པ་དྲག་པོ་བྱེད་ཀྱི་འདུག They have a great desire to go back to their own country.

འདུན་པ་ཆེན་པོ་ (dümbə cēmbo) great wish/ hope ༑ ང་བོད་ལ་འགྲོ་ཨག་གི་འདུན་པ་ཆེན་པོ་ཡོད་ I have a great wish to go to Tibet.

འདུན་པ་རྩེ་གཅིག (dümbə dzējig) sm. བློ་རྩེ་གཅིག་སྒྲིལ་.

འདུན་མ་ (dümmə) 1. ways and means, plans ༑ ཡུལ་ལུང་འཛུགས་སྐྲུན་གྱི་གནད་ཀྱི་འདུན་མ་ཞིག་དགོས་ (We) should have a long term plan for the construction of our country. 2. meeting, discussion; va.—བསྡུ་ to summon people for a meeting ༑ གནད་དོན་འདུན་མའི་ཐོག་ནས་ཐག་གཅོད་དགོས་ (We) should decide this matter through discussion.

འདུན་ཞུ་ (dünshu) asking for sth. one wishes/ desires; va.—བྱེད་.

འདུན་ལས་ (dünlɛɛ̀) sm. དུན་ལས.

འདུན་ས་ (dünsa) meeting/ assembly or meeting place, place for having a discussion.

འདུམ་: p. འདུམས་; f. འདུམ་ (dum) vi. to be or get reconciled/ settled ༑ ཁོང་ཚོའི་དབར་གྱི་འགལ་བ་འདུམས་པ་རེད་ The contradiction between them was reconciled.

འདུམ་ (dum) mediation, reconciliation, agreement; va.—གཏོང་; —བྱེད་ to mediate a dispute, to settle dispute by mediation ༑ ཁ་རྒྱ་དེའི་སྐོར་མི་གཞན་གྱིས་འདུམ་བཏང་བར་ཉན་མེད་པ་རེད་ Concerning this dispute, even though he mediated it (they) didn't listen.

འདུམ་ཁོངས་ (dumgoŋ) shung. included in a mediation agreement ༑ འདུམ་ཁོངས་ལ་མ་ཚུད་པའི་གནད་དོན་ Issues that were not included in the mediation.

འདུམ་ཁྲ་ (dumdra) written mediation decision/ agreement (in a dispute).

འདུམ་འགྲིག (dumdrig) mediating a dispute; va. འདུམ་འགྲིག; —བྱེད་ to mediate a dispute.

འདུམ་སྒྲིག (dumdrig) mediating a dispute; va.—བྱེད་.

འདུམ་སྒྲིག་ཨུ་ཡོན་ལྷན་ཁང་ (dumdrig ūyön lhɛ̄ngaŋ) tib.ch. mediation committee.

འདུམ་གཏོང་ (dum dōŋ) see འདུམ་.

འདུམ་མཐུན་ (dumdün) vi. to get settled/ mediated (for disputes).

འདུམ་དོན་ (dumdön) shung. the contents of a mediation agreement ༑ འདུམ་དོན་འདི་རེ་སོར་གནས་རྒྱུན་འཁྱོངས་ (You) must consistently adhere to the mediation agreement.

འདུམ་བདེ་པོ་ (dum debo) simple, easy.

འདུམ་གནས་ (dumnɛɛ̀) shung. able to be mediated ༑ ལས་རྙོགས་བྱིངས་རྣམས་འདུམ་གནས་པ་བདེན་ Because the other complicated matters can be mediated.

འདུམ་བསྟོན་འཛིན་ཐམ་ (dumnön dzindam) shung. a seal on a mediation agreement indicating acceptance ༑ གོང་གསལ་གཉིས་ནས་འདུམ་བསྟོན་འཛིན་ཐམ་བཏང་བར་ The two persons mentioned above put their acceptance seal on the written agreement.

འདུམ་པ་ (dumbə) mediator, go-between, arbitrator.

འདུམ་བྱེད་ (dum ceè) see འདུམ་.

འདུམ་འཛིན་ (dumdzin) shung. sm. འདུམ་ཁྲ་.

འདུམ་ཤོག (dumshɔɔ̀) shung. sm. འདུམ་ཁྲ་.

འདུམ་ས་ (dumsə) 1. a place to mediate a dispute. 2. a convenient path/ way.

འདུམ་གསལ་ (dumsɛl) shung. contents of a mediation agreement ༑ འདུམ་གསལ་གང་ཡིན་ལ་དན་ཐེལ་ཕྱུལ་རིགས་མེད་པ་ We did not put the seal indicating approval on what was written in the mediation agreement.

འདུམས་ (dum) p. of འདུམ་.

འདུར་ (dur) 1. va. to mash, to pulp (usu. by boiling). 2. vi. to crumble ༑ ལག་པའི་ནང་ལ་འདུར་སོང་ (It) crumbled in my hand. 3. va. to trot. 3. shung. vi. with no exemptions/ exceptions.

འདུར་འགྲོས་ (durdröö) a smooth trot (for horses) ༑ བཞོན་རྟས་འདུར་འགྲོ་བརྒྱབ་ནས་འགྲོ་དུས་ལུས་པོར་འཁྲུགས་མེད་པ་རེད་ When one rides a horse with a smooth trot, one's body does not shake much.

འདུར་རྒྱུགས་ (durgyuù) 1. shung. a tax that everyone has to fulfill equally, i.e., there are no exceptions ༑ རྟ་ཁལ་འདུར་རྒྱུགས་ཞུ་རེ་ཐུབ་ There is no way we can do the corvee carrying tax without having any exemption. 2. sm. འདུར་འགྲོས་.

འདུར་སྒྲུབ་ (durdrub) sm. འདུར་རྒྱུགས་, 1.

འདུར་མཆན་ (durjɛn) shung. a note stating that sth. should be done equally.

འདུར་འདུར་ (durduu) mashed, pulped.

འདུར་བོན་ (durbön) sm. དུར་བོན་.

འདུར་མ་རྒྱུགས་ (dur maguù) not running with a smooth gait/ trot, neither trotting not galloping.

འདུལ་: p. བཏུལ་; f. གདུལ་; imp. ཐུལ་ (düü) va. to overcome, to vanquish, to tame, to subdue ༑ རང་བྱུང་ཁམས་འདུལ་དགོས་ We must conquer nature. ༑ རྟ་རྒོད་བཟུང་ནས་བཏུལ་བ་རེད་ The wild horse was caught and tamed.

འདུལ་ (düü) abbr. of འདུལ་བ་.

འདུལ་སྐལ་ (düügɛl) one who is destined/ fated/ to be subdued or conquered.

འདུལ་སྐྱོང་བྱ་འོས་ (düügyoŋ cawöö) shung. appropriate to be subdued/ tamed ༑ དེའི་ཤར་འདུལ་སྐྱོང་བྱ་འོས་ས་ཞིང་ཁག་ཅིག་ཡོད་པ་ On the east side there are some fields that are appropriate to be cultivated (subdued).

འདུལ་ཁྲིམས་ (düüdrim) vinaya rules (for monks).

འདུལ་བཅོམ་ (düüjom) vanquishing, defeating.

འདུལ་ཆས་ (düüjɛɛ̀) monk's robes.

འདུལ་གདམ་ (düüdam) words that threaten/ intimidate/ condemn; va.—གཏོང་; —སློག་ to speak in a way that threatens/ intimidates.

འདུལ་བསྟན་ (düüdɛn) vinaya doctrine/ teachings.

འདུལ་ཐབས་ (düüdəb) sm. འདུལ་གསོ་.

འདུལ་བ་ (düüwa) vinaya section of the Kangyur (that lists monastic rules of conduct); va.—འཛིན་ to maintain the vinaya rules (one's vows).

འདུལ་སྦྱོང་ (düüjoŋ) 1. taming animals. 2. purifying sth.

འདུལ་འཛིན་ (düündzin) maintaining the vinaya rules (one's vows).

འདུལ་ཞིང་ (düüshiŋ) realms/ places where the Buddhas spread their teachings.

འདུལ་བཟོ་བྱ་འོས་ (düüso cawöö) shung. sm. འདུལ་སྐྱོང་བྱ་འོས་.

འདུལ་གསོ་ (düüso) taming, subduing; va.—བྱེད་ to tame, to subdue.

འདུས་ (düü) p. of འདུ་.

འདུས་འཁོད་ (düügöö) gathering/ assembling by many people.

འདུས་སྡོད་ (düüdöö) dwelling together, living in a community; va.—བྱེད་ to collect people together into a community.

འདུས་སྡོད་ས་ཁུལ་ (düüdöö səgüü) residential area.

འདུས་མདོ་ (düüdo) crossroads.

འདུས་སྡེ་ (düüde) gathering of monks; monastery.

འདུས་པ་རྒྱ་མཚོ་ (düüba gyadzo) an assembling/ gathering of many monks, e. g., during Monlam.

འདུས་པའི་ནད་ (düübɛ nɛɛ̀) sm. འདུས་ནད་.

འདུས་པའི་ཚ་བ་ (düübɛ tsāwa) a disease involving fever in traditional Tibetan medicine.

འདུས་པའི་ཚོགས་པ་ (düübɛ tsɔ̄gba) 1. a gathering of many people. 2. an assembly of monks.

འདུས་ཕྲད་ (düüdrɛɛ̀) converging/ meeting and becoming one (e.g., railway tracks).

འདུས་སྦྱོར་ (düüjɔɔ) gathering many ingredients to make a traditional Tibetan medicine.

འདུས་དམངས་ (düümaŋ) a gathering of people.

འདུས་ཚད་ (düüdzɛɛ̀) the amount of people or animals or things that are assembled or residing somewhere, residential/ population density.

འདུས་ཚོགས་ (düütsɔɔ̀) a gathering, assembly, collection ༎ མི་མང་འདུས་ཚོགས་སར་ At the place where there was a gathering of many people.

འདུས་ལ་ལྟ་ (düüla dā) shung. va. to look at a crowd of people, to look at a gathering/ assembly/ meeting ༎ རྒྱན་པོ་འགྱེད་དང་འདུས་ལ་ལྟ་བ་དང་ Gambling and looking at crowds of people.

འདུས་ས་ (düüsa) a gathering place, a meeting place.

འདུས་སོ་གསུམ་ (düüso sūm) three areas on top of the head used for acupuncture.

འདུས་སླེབས་ (düüleb) horses/ mules that are 8 to 9 years old.

འདི་ (de) sm. ལྡེ་.

འདི་གུ་ (degu) 1. sm. ལྡེ་གུ་. 2. sm. སྐྱོ་མ་.

འདི་བེ་ (debe) arc. a tool used by sculptors to smooth rough edges, etc.

འདི་བེ་ཁ་རིལ་ (dedbe kārii) sm. འདི་བེ་.

འདི་བེ་ཏ་ཀན་མ་ (debe dā gēmma) a sculptor's tool.

འདེགས་: p. བཏེགས་; f. གདེག; imp. ཐེག (deg) 1. va. to lift/ raise up ༎ སྒམ་ཆེན་པོ་དེ་མི་གཅིག་གིས་བཏེགས་མ་ཐུབ་པ་རེད་ One man was not able to lift the big box. 2. va. to support, to prop/ shore up ༎ ཀ་བས་གདུང་མ་འདེགས་པ་བཞིན་ Like a pillar supports the beams. 3. va. to weigh ༎ ཐུར་སྲང་ལ་གསེར་བཏེགས་པ་རེད་ They weighed the gold on a steelyard balance. 4. va. to serve (food) ༎ ཁོང་ལ་ཁོ་ཚོས་གསོལ་ཚིགས་བཏེགས་པ་རེད་ (They) served him food. 5. va. to go ༎ མོ་ཕྱིས་སུ་བཏེགས་སོང་ She left (for a different place).

འདེགས་སྐྱོར་ (deggyɔɔ) propping/ shoring up, supporting; va.—བྱེད་ to prop/ shore up, to support.

འདེགས་ཁལ་ (deggɛɛ) a ཁལ་ measured by weight rather than by volume.

འདེགས་འཁོར་ (deggɔɔ) sm. ལྡིད་འདེགས་འཕྲུལ་འཁོར་.

འདེགས་རྒྱ་ (deggya) 1. scale; va.—འགྲོགས་; —ལེན་ to weigh. 2. a jin ༎ མར་འདེགས་རྒྱ་གཅིག One jin of butter.

འདེགས་རྒྱག (deg gyaà) 1. va. to tighten the warp (when weaving). 2. va. to elevate/ hold up the beam (of a house that is being repaired).

འདེགས་རྒྱའི་བར་ཁྱད་ (deggyɛ pargyɛɛ̀) shung. the difference between weighings ༎ ཡོས་རྩམ་འདེགས་རྒྱའི་བར་ཁྱད་ The difference between weighing the roasted barley and the roasted barley flour (tsamba).

འདེགས་ཆས (degjɛɛ̀) a lifting machine/ implement, a machine jack.

འདེགས་རྟེན་ (degden) a gift that accompanies a petition/ request.

འདེགས་འཇལ་ (degjɛɛ) measuring, weighing; va.—བྱེད་ ༎ བཟའ་བཅའ་མང་པོ་འདེགས་འཇལ་བྱས་པ་རེད་ (They) weighed and measured many foodstuffs.

འདེགས་པང་ (degbaŋ) scaffolding; vi.—ཟགས་ to have a scaffolding collapse.

འདེགས་བྱ་ (degja) sm. འདེགས་རྟེན་.

འདེགས་འབུལ་ (deŋbüü) sm. འདེགས་, 4.

འདེགས་འབེབས་ (deŋbeb) 1. elevating/ lifting and lowering. 2. promotion and demotion.

འདེགས་འབེབས་འཕྲུལ་འཁོར་ (deŋbeb trüügɔɔ) elevator.

འདེགས་འབེབས་ཤིང་ནར་ (deŋbeb shīŋnar) seesaw.

འདེགས་ཚད་ (degdzɛɛ̀) 1. weight (general term). 2. the amount that can be lifted.

འདེགས་མཚོན་ (degdzön) things that are put in letters such as flowers, scarves, etc.

འདེགས་ཤུགས་ (degshuù) strength/ power to lift up.

འདེགས་ཤིང་ (degshiŋ) 1. stick/ pole used to carry a load across the shoulder. 2. supporting brace ༎ དོང་ལམ་གྱི་འདེགས་ཤིང་ A brace used to hold up a tunnel.

འདེགས་གཤོར་ (degshɔɔ̀) sm. འདེགས་འཇལ་.

འདེགས་སྲང་ (degsaŋ) weight of a སྲང་ ༎ གསེར་འདེགས་སྲང་གཅིག One སྲང་ of gold.

འདེང་ (deŋ) vi. to be enough/ sufficient, adequate, ample ༎ ཁང་པ་རྒྱག་ཡས་ཀྱི་ཤིང་ཆ་འདེང་གི་མི་འདུག This lumber is not enough to build a house. 2. va. to go.

འདེང་རྒྱག (deŋ gyaà) va. to think.

འདེང་འདེང་པ་ (deŋdeŋwa) while walking/ going.

འདེང་བརྡ་སྤྲོད་ (dēŋda drȫö) va. to send a note/ message indicating one is departing.

འདེང་ཚོད་ (dēŋdzȫö) estimate/ calculation of whether there is enough of sth.

འདེངས་ (deŋ) sm. འདེང་.

འདེད་: p. དེད་ and བདས་; f. བདའ་; imp. དེད་ (deè) 1. va. to follow ༎ ལམ་ཁ་དེ་རང་དེད་ནས་འགྲོ་དགོས་ (You) should go following that very road. 2. va. to drive/ herd (animals), to cause to move forward ༎ རྐུན་མས་ནོར་ཕྱུགས་མང་པོ་དེད་པ་རེད་ The thieves drove off many livestock. 3. va. to chase, to go after, to pursue ༎ ཁྱི་དེས་ཞི་མི་ཞིག་འདེད་ཀྱི་འདུག That dog is chasing a cat. 4. inference, reasoning.

འདེད་སྐུལ་ (deègüü) going after/ pursuing (usu. sb. who owes money); va.—བྱེད་.

འདེད་འགྲོ་ (dendro) shung. person who goes to collect debts ༎ འདེད་འགྲོ་འགའ་ཞིག་ནས་མི་སེར་གྱི་དངོས་ནོར་ཡང་སུ་ཐོབ་སྒྲར་ཤ་བྱེད་པ་ Some of the debt collectors even take the belongings of the people (debtors).

འདེད་སྒོ་ (deègo) sliding door.

འདེད་བཅོམ་ (deèjom) 1. pursuing and wiping out/ destroying; va.—བྱེད་ ༎ ཇག་པ་ལྷག་འཕྲོ་རྣམས་འདེད་བཅོམ་བཏང་བ་རེད་ (They) pursued and wiped out the remainder of the bandits. 2. pursuing and attacking; va.—བྱེད་ ༎ ཇག་པ་འདེད་བཅོམ་བྱེད་པར་ཕྱིན་ཀྱང་བྲོས་ཤོར་བ་རེད་ Even though (they) went to pursue and attack, the bandits got away.

འདེད་གཏོར་ (deèdɔɔ) pursuing and annihilating; va.—བྱེད་ to pursue and annihilate.

འདེད་དྲག་གཏོང་ (deèdraà dōŋ) va. to pursue (debts) harshly.

འདེད་རྡུང་ (deèduŋ) pursuing and attacking; va.—བྱེད་ to pursue and attack.

འདེད་པ་ (deèba) 1. pursuing/ chasing (for payment of a debt etc.). 2. a person who pursues debts. 3. a person who drives animals. 4. sm. འབུ་གཉེར་.

འདེད་འབབ་ (deèbɔb) shung. amount of debt that is to be pursued/ collected ༎ འདེད་འགྲོ་འགའ་ཞིག་ནས་སོ་སོའི་འདེད་འབབ་རྫིས་ལུས་ཀྱི་ཚད་འཛར་བྱུང་དོགས་མི་སེར་གྱི་དངོས་ནོར་ཡང་སུ་ཐོབ་སྒྲར་ཤ་བྱེད་པ་ Some of the people who collect loans, because they fear they will be unable to collect the amount owed, take the belongings of the people (debtors).

འདེད་སྐྱུང་ (deèjaŋ) sm. འདེད་སྐུལ་.

འདེད་སྐྱུང་རིམ་བྱེད་ (deèjaŋ rimjeè) shung. va. to go after/ pursue a loan many times.

འདེད་སྐྱུངས་ (deèjaŋ) sm. འདེད་སྐུལ་.

འདེད་མི་ (deèmi) sm. འདེད་པ་, 2.

འདེད་གཙེར་ (deèdzer) va. to pressure forcefully for payment of a loan (this term has a negative connotation).

འདེད་རྩིས་ (deèdzii) plan for pursuing collection of a loan/ debt.

འདེད་གཞུང་ (deèshuŋ) shung. sm. འདེད་ཁྲ་.

འདེད་བཟུང་ (deèsuŋ) pursuing and capturing; va.—བྱེད་.

འདེད་གཡོག (deèyɔɔ̀) a servant/ assistant of a monastic འབུ་གཉེར་ (who collects monastic debts/ loans).

འདེད་རེས་གཏོང་ (deèreè dōŋ) va. to play around chasing each other.

འདེད་རེས་ཡིབ་རེས་ (deèreè yibreè) child's game of hide and seek.

འདེད་ལེན་ (deèlen) pursuing and taking back/ collecting a loan, debt, etc.; va.—བྱེད་.

འདེད་སྲིད་ (deèsɛɛ̀) strong desire.

འདེད་གསོད་ (deèsöö) pursuing and killing.

འདེབས་: p. བཏབ་; f. གདབ་; imp. ཐོབས་ (deb) 1. va. to sow, to plant ¶ གྲོ་དང་སྲན་མ་བཏབ་རྗེས་ནས་འདེབས་ཀྱི་ཡོད་པ་རེད་ After planting wheat and lentils, (they) plant barley. 2. va. to do/ send ¶ མཆི་འདེབས་ To spit (to make sth. wet.). ¶ རྩིས་འདེབས་ To do accounting. ¶ གུར་འདེབས་ To pitch a tent. 3. va. to throw/ cast/ strike/ hit.

འདེབས་བཀོལ་ (debgöö) sm. འདེབས་འཛུགས་.

འདེབས་རྐོད་ (debgöö̀) sm. འདེབས་ཞིང་.

འདེབས་སྐྱོང་ (debgyoŋ) sm. འདེབས་འཛུགས་.

འདེབས་འཁོས་ (debgöö̀) shung. cultivating, planting; va.—བྱེད་ ¶ ས་ཞིང་འདེབས་འཁོས་དགེ་འདུན་གྲས་ནས་བྱེད་རྒྱུ་དགོན་པའི་ཁྲིམ་ལམ་ཕས་རྒྱན་དང་ Monks who engage in cultivating land will violate monastic law.

འདེབས་ཁྱོན་ (debgyön) area under cultivation, cultivated area.

འདེབས་ཆུ་ (debju) 1. irrigation when sowing seeds. 2. water added to fermented barley grain when it is ready to be served as beer.

འདེབས་ཇ་ (debja) tea for one's personal use.

འདེབས་འཇོག (debjɔɔ̀) leaving land fallow; va.—བྱེད་.

འདེབས་འཇོག་རེས་མོས་ (debjɔɔ̀ reèmöö̀) rotation of land in cultivation, leaving land fallow by turns.

འདེབས་བདག (debdaà) planting and taking care of fields; va.—བྱེད་.

འདེབས་མཚམས་འཇོག (debdzam jɔɔ̀) va. to leave land unplanted.

འདེབས་རྩ་ (debdza) shung. at the time of planting ¶ ལོ་ཉི་ཤུ་འདེབས་རྩར་བོགས་གཏོང་བྱས་པ་འདི་ལོ་ལོ་དུས་རྫོགས་པ་ The land was leased at the time of planting for twenty years and this year the leasing term is over.

འདེབས་རྩར་སྤྲོད་ (debdzaa drö̀ö) shung. va. to hand over fields at the time of planting ¶ བོགས་བདག་ནས་ས་ཞིང་འདེབས་རྩར་སྤྲད་པ་ The lessor handed over the land at the time of planting.

འདེབས་འཛུགས་ (debdzuù) planting by sticking in the ground (rather than by scattering); va.—བྱེད་.

འདེབས་འཛུགས་འཕྲུལ་འཁོར་ (debdzuù trüügɔɔ) sowing machine, seeder.

འདེབས་ཞིང་ (debshiŋ) arable land, farm land, land under cultivation.

འདེབས་རེས་ (debreè) crop rotation; va.—བྱེད་.

འདེབས་ལས་ (deblɛɛ̀) planting/ sowing work.

འདེབས་ལུད་ (deblüǜ) fertilizer applied at the time of planting seed.

འདེབས་ཤུལ་ (debshüü) planting one crop right after another; va.—བརྗེ་; —སྐོར་.

འདེབས་སོན་ (debsön) seeds; va.—གཤོ་ to broadcast seed.

འདེབས་གསོ་ (debso) planting and rearing/ raising; va.—བྱེད་.

འདེམ་ (dem) sm. འདེམས་.

འདེམ་སྒོ་ (demgo) sm. འདེམས་སྒོ་.

འདེམ་བསྒོ་ (demgo) sm. འདེམས་བསྒོ་.

འདེམ་བསྒོ་ས་ཁུལ་ (demgo sɔgüü) election district.

འདེམ་བསྒོ་ཨུ་ཡོན་ལྷན་ཁང་ (demgo ūyön lhɛ̄ngaŋ) election committee.

འདེམ་བསྒོའི་ཁྲིམས་ (demgö trīm) sm. འདེམས་བསྒོའི་ཁྲིམས་ལུགས་.

འདེམ་སྒུག་པ་ (dēmgugbə) sm. འདེམས་སྒུག་པ་.

འདེམ་སྒྲིག (demdrig) sm. འདེམས་སྒྲིག.

འདེམ་སྒྲུག (demdruù) sm. འདེམས་སྒྲུག.

འདེམ་ཉོ་ (demño) sm. འདེམས་ཉོ་.

འདེམ་འདེམ་ (demdem) sm. འདེམས་ག.

འདེམ་འདེམ་སྒྲུག་སྒྲུག (demdem drugdruù) sm. འདེམལ་འདེམལ་སྒྲུག་སྒྲུག.

འདེམ་སྣོན་ (demnön) sm. འདེམས་སྣོན་.

འདེམ་བྱེད་དབང་ཆ་ (demjeè wāŋja) sm. འདེམས་བྱེད་དབང་ཆ་.

འདེམ་འབངས་ (demban) sm. འདེམས་འབངས་.

འདེམ་དམངས་ (demmaŋ) sm. འདེམས་འབངས་.

འདེམ་ཤོག (demshɔɔ̀) sm. འདེམལ་ཤོག.

འདེམ་གསེས་ (demseè) sm. འདེམལ་གསེས་.

འདེམས་: p. བདམས་; f. གདམ་; imp. འདོམས་ or འདེམས་ (dem) va. to choose, to select, to elect ¶ ཁོ་སྔོན་ཐོན་དགེ་རྒན་དུ་བདམས་པ་རེད་ (They) selected him as an outstanding teacher.

འདེམས་ཀ་ (demga) choosing, selecting, electing; va.—བྱེད་; —གཏོང་; —བོར་.

འདེམས་བསྒོ་ (demgo) election, electing, voting; va.—བྱེད་ ¶ གཞི་རིམ་འདེམས་བསྒོ་ A primary election. ¶ ཁོ་ཚོའི་འཐུས་མི་འདེམས་བསྒོ་བྱས་པ་རེད་ (They) elected their representatives.

འདེམས་བསྒོ་འོས་སྒུག (demgo wöö̀guù) candidate for election.

འདེམ་བསྒོ་ལྷན་ཚོགས་ (demgo lhendzɔɔ̀) electoral commission/ committee.

འདེམས་བསྒོའི་ཁྲིམས་ལུགས་ (demgö trīmluù) electoral law.

འདེམ་བསྒོའི་ས་ཁུལ་ (demgö sɔgüü) a voting/ electoral district.

འདེམས་བསྒོར་ལྟ་ཞིབ་ (demgɔɔ dɔ̄shib) supervision and control of voting procedures ¶ འདེམས་སྒོར་ལྟ་ཞིབ་ལྷན་ཚོགས་ Board of elections.

འདེམས་བསྒོས་ (demgöö̀) elected/ chosen by voting ¶ འདེམས་བསྒོས་འཐུས་མི་ Elected representatives.

འདེམས་མཁན་ (demñɛn) a voter.

འདེམས་ག (demga) choosing, selecting, electing; va.—བྱེད་.

འདེམས་རྒྱུགས་ (demgyuù) exam taken before being recruited/ hired for a job.

འདེམས་སྒུག (demguù) candidacy, candidate ¶ འདེམས་སྒུག་མི་སྣ་ Candidates for an election.

འདེམས་སྒུག་པ་ (demguùbə) candidate for an election.

འདེམས་སྒྲིག (demdrig) choosing and arranging, editing; va.—བྱེད་.

འདེམས་སྒྲུག (demdruù) 1. selecting, choosing; va.—བྱེད་ to select, to choose ¶ བཟོ་པ་ཉམས་མྱོང་ཆེ་བ་རྣམས་འདེམས་སྒྲུག་བྱས་པ་རེད་ (They) selected the more experienced workers. 2. sm. འདེམས་བསྒོ་.

འདེམས་སྒྲུག་ས་ཁུལ་ (demdruù sɔ̄güü) sm. འདེམས་བསྒོའི་ས་ཁུལ་.

འདེམས་བསྒྲུགས་ (demdruù) sm. འདེམས་སྒྲུག.

འདེམས་མངག (demŋaà) selecting and sending a person to a position/ post; va.—བྱེད་ ¶ ལས་གནས་དེར་ལས་བྱེད་པ་ཁག་ཅིག་འདེམས་མངགས་བྱས་པ་རེད་ (They) selected and sent a group of officials to hold that position.

འདེམས་ཉོ་ (demño) selecting and buying; va.—བྱེད་.

འདེམས་བདོན་ (demdön) selecting, choosing, electing; va.—བྱེད་ to select, to choose, to elect.

འདེམས་ཐོན་ (demdön) sm. འདེམས་བསྒོས་.

འདེམས་སྣོན་ (demnön) choosing and adding, a supplementary/ extra selection (e.g., as a replacement); va.—བྱེད་ ¶ སྐབས་འཐུས་མི་གསར་པ་ཁ་ཤས་འདེམས་སྣོན་བྱས་པ་རེད་ (They) chose and added several delegates.

འདེམས་འདེམས་སྒྲུག་སྒྲུག (demdem drugdruù) sm. འདེམས་སྒྲུག.

འདེམས་བྱེད་དབང་ཆ་ (demjeè wāŋja) right to vote, voting franchise.

འདེམས་དབང་ (demwaŋ) sm. འདེམས་བྱེད་དབང་ཆ་.

འདེམས་འབངས་ (demban) the electorate, constituency in an election district.

འདེམས་འབངས་ཀྱི་ལག་འཁྱེར་ (dembaŋgi laggyer) voting eligibility certificate.

འདེམས་སྦྱོང་ (demjoŋ) elective course (of study), optional course.

འདེམས་དམངས་ (demmaŋ) sm. འདེམས་འབངས་.

འདེམས་ཤོག (demshɔɔ̀) a vote, va.—འཕེན་; —སྤྲུག to

cast a vote ། འདེམས་བསྐོ་དེའི་སྐབས་མི་འབོར་གྱི་བརྒྱ་ཆ་ 70 ཡིས་འདེམས་ཤོག་འཕངས་པ་རེད་ During that election 70% of the population voted.

འདེམས་ཤོག་གི་གྲངས་ཀ་ (demshɔɔgi traŋgə) election tally, vote count.

འདེམས་ཤོག་སྒམ་ (demshɔɔ gam) ballot box.

འདེམས་ཤོག་རྩིས་རྒྱག (demshɔɔ dziìgyaà) va. to count the votes/ ballots.

འདེམས་གསེས་ (demseè) choosing, selecting; va.—བྱེད་ ། ཅ་ལག་འདི་རྣམས་ཀྱི་ནང་ནས་ཕན་ཐོགས་པ་རྣམས་འདེམས་གསེས་བྱེད་དགོས་ From among these things you have to select the useful ones.

འདེམ་ལྷན་ (demlhen) abbr. of འདེམ་བསྐོ་ལྷན་ཚོགས་.

འདེལ་བ་ (delwa) Eucominia tree.

འདོ་ (do) 1. clever, bright. 2. sm. འདོ་བ་.

འདོ་པག (dobaa) around here ། ཁྱེད་རང་འདོ་པག་བཞུགས་ཀྱི་ཡོད་པས་ Do you live around here?

འདོ་བ་ (dowa) horse.

འདོ་མེད་ (domeè) not distinguishing/ knowing good from bad.

འདོ་མེད་ངང་རིང་ (domeè ŋaŋriŋ) a good-for-nothing person.

འདོ་ཟུངས་ (dosuŋ) sm. འདོ་མེད་.

འདོ་ཡོད་ (doyöö) understanding right from wrong.

འདོ་ལི་ (doli) sm. མདོ་ལི་.

འདོ་ལེ་ (dōle) sm. མདོ་ལེ་.

འདོགས་: p. **བཏགས་**; f. **གདག**; imp. **ཐོགས་** (dɔɔ) va. to tie, to fasten, to attach. ། ཁྱི་དེ་མི་བཏགས་ན་མི་ལ་སོ་རྒྱག་གི་རེད་ If you don't tie that dog it will bite people. 2. va. to put on, to wear (ornaments) ། རྒྱན་ཆ་བཏགས་ནས་ Having put on the jewelry/ ornaments. 3. (usu. མིང་ + —) va. to name.

འདོགས་ཁྱི་ (dɔɔgyi) 1. Tibetan mastiff. 2. a dog that is tied by a door to block entrance [Lit. tied dog].

འདོགས་རྒྱན་ (dɔɔgyɛn) ornament/ jewelry tied on the belt.

འདོགས་ཅན་ (dɔɔjɛn) sm. འདོགས་ཡིག.

འདོགས་ཆ་ལུས་རྒྱན་ (dɔgja lüügyɛn) shung. ornaments ། རྙིང་ཁྱངས་མནའ་མའི་འདོགས་ཆ་ལུས་རྒྱན་ The antique ornaments of the bride.

འདོགས་ཐག (dɔɔdaà) rope used for tying animals.

འདོགས་ཐག་ཆད་པའི་བཙང་ཁྱི་ (dɔɔdaà cɛ̄ɛbɛ saŋkyi) showing the appearance of wanting to fight when people are holding you back but then doing nothing when let go [Lit. a watch dog whose rope has broken].

འདོགས་ཐག་ཨ་ལོང་ནས་གྲོལ་ (dɔɔdaà āloŋnɛ tröö) settling/ deciding sth. by the main person or office [Lit. the rope that ties the animals was untied from the ring (to which it was tied)].

འདོགས་ཕུར་ (dɔgbur) shung. wooden peg for tying animals.

འདོགས་འཕྱུལ་ (dɔɔbüü) sm. འདོགས་ཡིག and འཕྱུལ་ཡིག.

འདོགས་བྱང་ (dɔgjaŋ) a signboard that is hung, a board that is hung on which other things are attached.

འདོགས་མིག (dɔgmii) a hole for hanging signs, labels, etc.

འདོགས་ཚིག (dɔgdzii) a name given to sth.

འདོགས་གཞི་ (dɔgshi) a place for hanging or tying.

འདོགས་ཟམ་ (dɔgsam) suspended/ hanging bridge.

འདོགས་ཡིག (dɔgyii) subfixed letters.

འདོགས་ལུང་ (dɔgluŋ) metal ring for hanging things.

འདོགས་ཤ་ (dɔgsha) meat dried in winter (by hanging).

འདོགས་ཤིང་ (dɔgshiŋ) wooden thethering pole for tying animals.

འདོང་: p. **དོང་**; f.**འདོང་**; imp. **དོངས་** (doŋ) va. to go.

འདོད་ (döö) 1. abbr. འདོད་པ་. 2. vi. to want, to desire ། བདེ་བ་འདོད་ནས་དངུལ་གསོག་སྒྲུབ་གི་ཡོད་པ་རེད་ Desiring a comfortable life, he is saving money. 3. (vb. + —) or (vb. + — + བྱེད་) desiring to do the verbal act ། ཁོ་ཚོས་ལས་ཀ་བྱེད་འདོད་ཡོད་པ་རེད་ They want to work. ། མོ་ཁྲོམ་ལ་འགྲོ་འདོད་བྱེད་ཀྱི་འདུག She wants to go to the market.

འདོད་ཁམས་ (döögam) the realm of desire.

འདོད་ཁམས་བདག་མོ་ (döögam daàmo) sm. དཔལ་ལྡན་ལྷ་མོ་.

འདོད་ཁྱེར་ (döögyer) selfish person.

འདོད་དགུ་ (döögu) all one's desires, every want/ wish; vi.—འཇོ་;—འཇོམས་ to obtain/ realize all one's wishes ། འདོད་དགུ་འཇོ་བའི་ནོར་བུ་ A wish fulfilling gem.

འདོད་སྒུ་ (döögu) sm. འདོད་དགུ་.

འདོད་སྒུ་ཀུང་སི་ (döögu gūŋsi) department store.

འདོད་རྒྱལ་ (döögyɛɛ) 1. doing whatever one desires ། བྱིས་པ་འདོད་རྒྱལ་དུ་མ་གཏོང་ Don't let children do whatever they desire. 2. root word.

འདོད་རྒྱལ་གྱི་སྒྲ་ (döögyɛɛgi dra) sm. འདོད་རྒྱལ་གྱི་མིང་.

འདོད་རྒྱལ་གྱི་མིང་ (döögyɛɛgi miŋ) the main or root term.

འདོད་རྒྱལ་སྨྲ་ (döögyɛɛ mā) va. to say whatever comes to mind.

འདོད་རྒྱུ་ (döögya) objects of desire/ wealth/ property.

འདོད་སྒྲིལ་ (döögdrii) sm. འཆམ་སྒྲིལ་.

འདོད་ཇམ་ (dooŋam) sm. འདོད་ཇམས་.

འདོད་ཇམས་ (dooŋam) greed, avarice, coveting, desiring; va.—བྱེད་ to be greedy/ avaricious, to covet.

འདོད་ཇམས་ཆེན་པོ་ (dooŋam cēmbo) sm. འདོད་ཇམས་ཚ་པོ་.

འདོད་ཇམས་ཚ་པོ་ (dooŋam tsābo) very greedy/ avaricious.

འདོད་ཅན་ (dööjɛn) sm. འདོད་ལྡན་.

འདོད་གཅིག (dööjig) shung. household (those living together).

འདོད་ཆ་ (dööja) one-thirteenth (1/13).

འདོད་ཆགས་ (dööjaà) lust, carnal desire, passion; vi.—སྐྱེད་ to have lust arise.

འདོད་ཆགས་དང་བྲལ་བ་ (dööjaà daŋ trɛɛ) 1. without lust. 2. an arahat.

འདོད་ཆགས་རིགས་བཞི་ (dööjaà rigshi) the four types of desire: desire to embrace; desire to touch; desire caused by sensual smile; desire after seeing.

འདོད་ཆུང་ཆོག་ཤེས་ (dööjuŋ cōgsheè) content with one's lot.

འདོད་མཆུ་སློང་བྲོ་ (dööju lōŋdro) shung. stirring up trouble ། སྐྱི་འཕྱུལ་དང་གདལ་པོ་སོགས་ལ་བསྐུལ་ནས་འདོད་མཆུ་སློང་བྲོ་མི་བྱེད་ No person is allowed to stir up trouble by demanding payment of loans or sowing discord.

འདོད་འཇོ་ (dönjo) giving whatever one wants.

འདོད་འཇོའི་བ་ (dönjö pa) 1. mythological cow that never stops giving milk. 2. the person wearing a cow's mask in the religious processions (སེར་བང་) that occurs on the 29/30th of the second Tibetan lunar month.

འདོད་འཇོའི་བ་མོ་ (dööjö pamo) sm. འདོད་འཇོའི་བ་.

འདོད་སྙིང་ (dooñiŋ) one's true desire/ wish.

འདོད་གཏམ་ (döödam) 1. sensual/ passionate/ sexual talk. 2. political propaganda in the sense of saying what one wants to convey to people.

འདོད་ཐང་ (döötaŋ) a thanka painting ordered to one's own wish/ desire.

འདོད་རྟེན་ (dööden) the object of desire.

འདོད་བསྟུན་ (döödün) in accordance with sb's wish/ desire ། ཁོའི་འདོད་བསྟུན་བྱེད་ཁག་པོ་རེད་ It's hard to act according to his wishes.

འདོད་ཐག་ཉེ་བ་ (döö tāàñewa) shortsighted, concerned only with the immediate.

འདོད་ཐོག་འདོད་བཞག (döödɔɔ dööshaà) having one's wishes fulfilled.

འདོད་ཐོག་སྨིན་ (döödɔɔ min) va. to realize, to get one's desires/ wishes fulfilled.

འདོད་ཐོག་ལ་ཏ་རྒྱུགས་པ་ (döödɔɔla dā gyuùbə)

realizing/ getting one's desire or wish completely fulfilled [Lit. riding a horse on one's wish].

འདོད་མཐུན་ཚོད་ལྟ་ (döödün tsööda) testing whether sb. is agreeable/ compatible.

འདོད་དོན་ (döödön) sm. འདོད་ཕྱོགས་.

འདོད་འདོད་ (döndöö) sm. འདོད་པ་.

འདོད་བདུངས་ (döö duŋ) shung. sm. འདོད་བརྣག.

འདོད་འདུན་ (döndün) desire and hope.

འདོད་ལྡན་ (dönden) 1. desirous, covetous, greedy. 2. lustful, passionate.

འདོད་ནག (döönaà) sm. འདོད་བརྣག.

འདོད་གནག (döönaà) sm. འདོད་བརྣག.

འདོད་རྣག་ཅན་ (döönagjen) greedy, avaricious.

འདོད་བརྣག (döönaà) greedy, avaricious.

འདོད་བརྣག་གི་སྐྱེ་ (döönaàgi jī) avaricious high interest.

འདོད་བརྣག་བརྡབ་གསིག (döönaà dəbsii) causing hardship due to one's greed/ avarice; va.—གཏོང་.

འདོད་པ་ (dööba) desire, want, wish; va.—བྱེད་ to desire/ wish; va.—སྐོང་ to satisfy/ fulfill one's desires/ wishes; vi.—ཁེངས་ to have one's desires be filled, to be content ། རྒྱུ་ནོར་གྱི་འདོད་པ་ Desire for wealth. ། མོས་ཟླ་བ་དང་ཆང་ས་རྒྱག་ཡས་ལ་འདོད་པ་བྱུས་པ་རེད་ She wanted to marry Dawa.

འདོད་པ་བཀང་ (dööba gāŋ) va. to satisfy one's desires.

འདོད་པ་སྐོང་ (dööba gōŋ) va. to satisfy one's desires.

འདོད་པ་ཁ་ཚང་ (dööba kādzaŋ) shung. sm. འདོད་བརྣག.

འདོད་པ་ཁེངས་ (dööba kēŋ) vi. to be satisfied, to be content ། ཁོང་ལ་འདོད་པ་ཁེངས་པའི་ཟླ་ཕོགས་རག་པ་རེད་ He got a salary that satisfied him.

འདོད་པ་གང་ (dööba gaŋ) sm. འདོད་པ་ཁེངས་.

འདོད་པ་གང་རྫོགས་བྱེད་ (dööba gaŋdzöö cee) shung. va. to do sth. until one is fully satisfied ། ཕ་མ་གཉིས་ནས་ཕྲུ་གུའི་འདོད་པ་གང་རྫོགས་བྱེད་བཅུག་པ་ The parents let their children do whatever they liked until they were fully satisfied.

འདོད་པ་སྒྲིལ་ (dööba dril) va. to join two families together.

འདོད་པ་ཆེན་པོ་ (dööba cēmbo) greedy, desirous, avaricious.

འདོད་པ་ལྟར་གྲུབ་ (döobadar drub) vi. to achieve one's goal/ desire/ ambition.

འདོད་པ་བསྟུན་ (dööba dün) in accord with sb.'s wish/ desire ། ཁོའི་འདོད་པ་དང་བསྟུན་ནས་ངས་མཉམ་དུ་ཕྱིན་པ་ཡིན་ In accord with his wish, I went with him.

འདོད་པ་མཐུན་ (dööba tün) vi. to share wishes/ desire, to be harmonious ། ང་གཉིས་འདོད་པ་མཐུན་ནས་ཆང་ས་བརྒྱབ་པ་ཡིན་ We two were harmonious in our desires and got married. ། ཁོང་གཉིས་འདོད་པ་མཐུན་ནས་ཚོང་གི་གན་རྒྱ་བཞག་པ་རེད་ They agreed about their wishes and signed a business contract.

འདོད་པ་ཕུན་སུམ་ཚོགས་པ་ (dööba pünsum tsögba) getting everything one desires.

འདོད་པ་བཙལ་ཀྱང་མི་རྙེད་པའི་སྡུག་བསྔལ་ (dööba dzēēgyaŋ miñeèbe duŋŋee) one of eight types of suffering: searching and never finding what one desires.

འདོད་པ་མ་བསྐངས་ (dööba magaŋ) shung. va. to not satisfy desires ། རྫོང་དཔོན་ནས་མི་སེར་གྱི་འདོད་པ་མ་བསྐངས་པ་རེད་ The Dzonpon did not satisfy the desires of the subjects.

འདོད་པ་ཚིམ་ (dööba tsīm) sm. འདོད་པ་ཁེངས་.

འདོད་པ་ལ་འདུན་པ་ (döobala dünba) sm. འདོད་འདུན་.

འདོད་པ་ལོངས་སུ་སྤྱོད་ (dööba loŋsu jöö) va. to have sexual intercourse.

འདོད་པ་བསོད་ཉམས་པ་ (dööba söönamba) not content regardless of what one has.

འདོད་པའི་འགྲོ་ཕྱོགས་ (dööbe drocöö) what one wants/ desires.

འདོད་པའི་བསྟན་བཅོས་ (dööbe dēnjöö) the Kama Sutra.

འདོད་པའི་ཐིག་ལེ་ (dööbe tīgle) one's main wish/ desire.

འདོད་པའི་དབང་གིས་ (dööbe wāŋgi) by one's own wish/ desire (i.e., not forced) ། ལས་ཀ་འདི་ཁོང་གིས་འདོད་པའི་དབང་གི་བྱས་པ་རེད་ He did the work because he wanted to.

འདོད་པའི་ཉོས་བུམ་ (dööbe ñööbum) female breast.

འདོད་པའི་ཡོན་ཏན་ (dööbe yönden) objects of sensual desire, sensory pleasures.

འདོད་པའི་ལོངས་སྤྱོད་ (dööbe loŋjöö) 1. things that one likes. 2. sexual intercourse.

འདོད་པར་བབས་མིན་ (döobar bəbmin) sth. one doesn't want/ like/ desire ། མི་གཞན་གྱིས་རང་གི་འདོད་པར་བབས་མིན་གྱི་སྐད་ཆ་བཤད་ཀྱང་ཁོང་ཁྲོ་བྱེད་རྒྱུ་མེད་ You shouldn't get angry even if somebody says sth. that you dislike.

འདོད་པར་མ་འཐད་ (döobar mateè) sm. འདོད་པར་མ་ཕྱིན་པ་.

འདོད་པར་མ་ཕྱིན་ (döobar macin) va. to not like sth.

འདོད་པར་མ་བབས་ (döobar məbəb) sm. འདོད་པར་བབས་མིན་.

འདོད་པས་ངོ་ཚ་སྒྲིབ་ (dööbe ŋodza drib) vi. to be/ act shameless because of strong desire.

འདོད་པས་བློ་མིག་སྒྲིབ་ (dööbe lōmig drib) vi. to have one's mind clouded/ blinded by desire.

འདོད་པས་ངོ་ཚ་ཉམས་ (dööbe ŋodza ñam) sm. འདོད་པས་ངོ་ཚ་སྒྲིབ་.

འདོད་དཔལ་ལས་ཁུངས་ (dööbee leègun) shung. an office created by the traditional Tibetan government that was composed of craftsmen of all kinds.

འདོད་སྤང་ (dööbaŋ) giving up sth. one wishes/ desire; va.—བྱེད་.

འདོད་ཕྱོགས་ (dööjöö) what one desires/ wishes/ likes; vi.—འཕྱད་ to achieve what one desires/ wishes/ likes; va.—སྒྲིལ་ to advance one's own purpose/ desire/ wishes/ likings; va.—ཤོད་ to say sth. according to one's desires/ wishes/ likes.

འདོད་བབས་ (dööbəb) desire, wish, liking; va.—བྱེད་ ། གྲོས་མོལ་མུ་འཕྱུད་བྱེད་རྒྱུར་འདོད་བབས་ཡོད་པ་རེད་ (They) desired to continue the talks. ། གཞུང་གི་དམག་དོན་སྲིད་ཇུས་ལ་ཁོ་ཚོས་འདོད་འབབ་མ་བྱུས་པ་རེད་ (They) did not like the government's military policy.

འདོད་བྲལ་ (döödree) without desire/ lust, without passion.

འདོད་བློ་ (döölo) wish, desire, liking; va.—སྟོན་ to show/ express one's desire or wishes; vi.—ཁེངས་; —ཚིམ་ to be satisfied ། མི་དམངས་ཀྱི་འདོད་བློ་དང་མི་མཐུན་པའི་སྲིད་ཇུས་ A policy contrary to the wishes of the people. ། མི་མང་བས་དམག་ཐག་ལམ་སེང་གཅོད་དགོས་པའི་འདོད་བློ་བསྟན་པ་རེད་ Most people expressed their wish that the war should be stopped right now. ། འདོད་བློ་ཁེངས་པའི་གྲུབ་འབྲས་ A result that satisfies one's desires.

འདོད་དབང་ (dööwaŋ) sm. འདོད་པའི་དབང་གིས་.

འདོད་སྦྱར་ (dööjar) shung. sm. འདོད་ཞུས་.

འདོད་མ་ (dööma) 1. a vein used in traditional Tibetan medicine. 2. a sensual female/ woman.

འདོད་མིན་ (döömin) disliking ། ཁྱིམ་ལ་ཕྲན་བུའི་འདོད་མིན་ཡོད་རུང་ Even though he dislikes his wife a little.

འདོད་མོས་ (döömöö) wish, choice, desire, preference; va.—བྱེད་ to do sth. based on one's own desire/ wish/ liking ། འགྲོ་དང་སྡོད་རང་གི་འདོད་མོས་རེད་ Its one's own wish whether to go or stay.

འདོད་མོས་ཞུ་ཡིག (döömöö shuyii) a letter volunteering sth.

འདོད་སྨོན་ (döömön) 1. prayers conveying a wish for (sth.). 2. abbr. desire and envy.

འདོད་ཙན་པ་ (döödzenba) prostitute.

འདོད་རྒྱལ་ (döödzüü) wish, desire; position,

attitude; va.—འཛིན་ to hold/ adhere to a wish/ desire/ position/ attitude ¶ མཛའ་མཐུན་མཉམ་ལས་ཀྱི་འབྲེལ་བ་གོང་འཕེལ་ཡོང་བ་བྱེད་དགོས་པའི་འདོད་རྒྱལ་འཛིན་གྱི་ཡོད་ We have the wish to develop friendly and cooperative relationships.

འདོད་ཞུས་ (dööshüü) shung. to ask/ request sth. one's desires/ wishes ¶ དམིགས་བསལ་ཁྲལ་ཆག་དེ་རིགས་བླ་བྲང་རང་ནས་འདོད་ཞུས་ཡིན་འདུག These special tax exemptions were requested by the Labrang itself (based on their own desires).

འདོད་ཞེན་ (dööshen) passion, lust, greed.

འདོད་ཞེན་ལོག་སྤྱོད་ (dööshen lɔgseè) corrupted by greed and desire; va.—བྱེད་.

འདོད་གཞས་ (dööshɛɛ̀) love song.

འདོད་གཟུགས་ (döösuù) 1. the object from which desire is born. 2. abbr. desire and form.

འདོད་ཡོན་ (dööyön) abbr. of འདོད་པའི་ཡོན་ཏན་.

འདོད་ཡོན་སྣ་ལྔ་ (dööyön nāŋa) the five sensual objects: form, sound, smell, taste, touch.

འདོད་རེ་ (dööre) wish, desire, hope.

འདོད་ལ་མ་འདོད་ (dööla mandöö) seeming or acting as if one doesn't want to do sth.; va.—བྱེད་ ¶ ངས་ལས་ཀ་བསྐྱལ་བར་ཁོས་འདོད་ལ་མ་འདོད་བྱེད་ཀྱི་འདུག I gave him a job to do but he is acting as if he doesn't want to do it.

འདོད་ལན་ (döölɛn) term used when debating in monasteries that conveys "yes".

འདོད་ལུགས་ (döölùù) sm. འདོད་རྒྱལ་.

འདོད་ལོག་ (döölɔɔ̀) 1. lust, passion; va.—སྤྱོད་ to commit adultery. 2. perverse sexual acts. 3. rape.

འདོད་སེམས་ (döösem) mind filled with desire; vi.—སྐྱེད་ to come to desire sth.

འདོད་གསོག་ཐེབས་པའི་ས་ (döösɔɔ̀ tēbbɛ sā) alluvial soil.

འདོད་གསོལ་ (döösöö) sm. འདོད་སྟོན་, 1.

འདོད་ཧམ་ (dööham) greedily/ avariciously desirous; va.—བྱེད་.

འདོན་: p. **བཏོན་**; f. **གདོན་**; imp. **ཐོན་** (dön) va. 1. to cause to come out, to put forth, to take/ bring out, to produce, to publish, to mine, to import ¶ ཁོའི་ཞྭ་མོའི་ནང་ནས་རི་བོང་ཞིག་བཏོན་སོང་ He took a rabbit out of his hat. ¶ ཁོ་ཚོས་བསམ་འཆར་མང་པོ་ཞིག་འདོན་གྱི་ཡོད་པ་རེད་ They are putting forth a lot of suggestions. ¶ རང་དབང་གསར་ཁང་ནས་དམིགས་བསལ་དེབ་ཆུང་ཞིག་བཏོན་འདུག The Freedom Press has published (put out) a special booklet. ¶ ས་གནས་དེ་ཚོ་ནས་རྡོ་སོལ་འདོན་གྱི་ཡོད་པ་རེད་ (They) mine coal from these regions. ¶ དེ་ལོ་ཁོ་ཚོས་རྒྱ་གར་ནས་འབྲས་ཁྲིན་ཆེ་བཏོན་པ་རེད་ That year (they) imported a lot of rice from India. 2. va. to say, to read (prayers), to intone ¶ ཆོས་འདོན་གྱི་འདུག (They) are intoning scriptures. 3. shung. a unit of land for aristocratic and monastic estates that is equal to two ཀང་. 4. va. to enthrone ¶ རྒྱལ་སྲས་ཁྲིར་འདོན་ To enthrone the prince.

འདོན་ཀློག (dönlɔɔ̀) va. to read aloud, to chant/ to intone.

འདོན་སྐྱལ་ (döngüü) money (alms) given to the monastic prayer leader (umdze) with a request that the monks intone a certain prayer; va.—འབུལ་.

འདོན་ཁྲལ་ (döndrɛɛ) sm. འདོན་ཁ་ཁྲལ་.

འདོན་ཁ་ཁྲལ་ (döng kādrɛɛ) an introductory text that new monks are required to memorize.

འདོན་འགྲེམས་ (döndrem) 1. publishing and distributing, producing and distributing; va.—བྱེད་ ¶ གློག་ཆས་དཔེ་གསར་མང་པོ་འདོན་འགྲེམས་བྱས་པ་རེད་ (They) produced and distributed many new model electrical appliances. ¶ དགོང་དྲོའི་ཚགས་པར་ཞིག་འདོན་འགྲེམས་བྱེད་རྒྱུ་ཡིན་པ་རེད་ (They) are going to publish (and distribute) an evening newspaper.

འདོན་སྒྲིལ་ (dön drii) shung. adding/ merging a འདོན་ tax unit of land to another འདོན་ tax unit ¶ སྐུ་དྲག་སྐྱིར་དྲག་ཡང་བཙན་རེ་གཉིས་ནས་འདོན་སྒྲིལ་དང་ཆག་ཡང་འགའ་རེ་གནང་བ་ Aristocrats and some of the well off persons are exempted from paying tax and are let to add it to another འདོན་.

འདོན་ཆ་བཟང་པོ་ (dönja saŋbo) shung. skilled in chanting prayers/ rituals ¶ དབུ་མཛད་འདོན་ཆ་བཟང་པོ་དགོས་པ་ The དབུ་མཛད་ should be one who is skilled in chanting prayers done when doing rituals.

འདོན་ཆོག (dönjɔɔ̀) prayers done when doing rituals.

འདོན་ཆོག་ག (dön cɔ̄gga) sm. འདོན་ཆོག.

འདོན་འཇུག (donjuù) loading and unloading, putting in and taking out; va.—བྱེད་ ¶ ཅ་ལག་འདོན་འཇུག་བྱས་པར་གླ་སྤྲོད་ཀྱི་རེད་ They will pay wages for loading and unloading things.

འདོན་འཇུག་ལས་ཁུལ་ (donjuù lɛɛ̀güü) a loading and unloading district, a stevedoring district.

འདོན་འཇུག་སྐོར་སྐྱེལ་ཀུང་སི་ (donjuù bōrgyee gūŋsi) a stevedoring and transporting company.

འདོན་ཐེངས་ (dönden) a printing or issue (in a series) ¶ འདོན་ཐེངས་གཉིས་པ་ The second printing.

འདོན་སྣ་འདྲེན་ (dönŋa dren) va. to lead prayers.

འདོན་པ་ (dömba) prayer; va.—འདོན་;—སྐྱོར་ to recite/ intone/ chant a prayer.

འདོན་པ་བསྐྱལ་ (dömba güü) va. to start/ initiate a prayer (chant).

འདོན་སྤེལ་ (dönbel) producing and distributing/ spreading; va.—བྱེད་; —གཏོང་ ¶ ཞིང་ལས་ཀྱི་ལག་ཆ་གསར་པ་མང་པོ་འདོན་སྤེལ་བྱས་པ་རེད་ (They) produced and distributed many new agricultural implements. ¶ ཁོང་ཚོའི་ལག་རྩལ་མང་པོ་འདོན་སྤེལ་བྱས་པ་རེད་ They developed and spread many new techniques.

འདོན་སྤྲོད་ (döndröö) taking out and giving, supplying, furnishing, providing; va.—བྱེད་ to provide, to supply, to furnish.

འདོན་བྱེད་གྲུ་ (dönjeè dru) dredging boat.

འདོན་དམག (dönmaà) shung. soldiers recruited as a tax from a འདོན་ of land ¶ ལྕགས་གླང་དུས་ཟིང་སྐབས་འདོན་དམག་མི་འབྱོར་ཤེལ་ཆོས་རང་ནས་གཏོང་དགོས་བྱུང་བ་ During the unrests in the Iron-Ox year, because the soldiers recruited from the འདོན་ did not arrive, the Shelcho Monastery had to send soldiers by themselves.

འདོན་འཚོང་ (dondzoŋ) producing and selling/ marketing; va.—བྱེད་.

འདོན་འཛུད་ (döndzüü) sm. འདོན་འཇུག.

འདོན་ལ་འདོན་སྒྲིལ་ (dönla döndrii) shung. sm. འདོན་སྒྲིལ་.

འདོན་ལེན་ (dönlen) taking out, unearthing, mining; va.—བྱེད་ ¶ ས་ཁུལ་དེ་ནས་གནའ་རྫས་འདོན་ལེན་བྱས་ཡོད་པ་རེད་ (They) have taken relics out from these areas.

འདོན་ཤ་སྡོན་མཇལ་ (dönsha dönjɛɛ) shung. a meat tax (in tt.).

འདོན་བཤུག (dönshuù) emptying sth. (a room, etc); va.—རྒྱག ¶ འགྲུལ་པ་ཡོང་གི་ཡོད་ཙང་ཁང་མིག་གཉིས་འདོན་བཤུག་བརྒྱབ་བཞག Because travelers are coming, they emptied two rooms.

འདོབ་ (dob) pretending to be stupid/ dumb.

འདོབ་ཚ་པོ་ (dob tsābo) sb. who frequently pretends to be stupid/ dumb.

འདོབ་ཟོ་ (dobso) a wooden strainer for ཆང་.

འདོབ་ཤོད་ (dob shöö) va. to pretend to be stupid/ dumb in speech.

འདོམ་ (dom) 1. a length measure defined as the span of a person's outstretched hands from fingertip to fingertip; va.—རྒྱག; —འཇལ་ to measure by means of a འདོམ་. 2. vi. to assemble, to gather, to come together ¶ ད་རེས་ལས་ཀ་མང་པོ་མཉམ་དུ་འདོམས་ཙང་བྲེལ་བ་ཆ་པོ་འདུག Because many work tasks have come together, (I) am very busy. ¶ ཐུགས་སྐྱོར་འགྲོ་རྒྱུ་དང་ཚོགས་འདུའི་དུས་ཚོད་འདོམ་ཙང་ཐུགས་སྐྱོར་འགྲོ་ཐུབ་མ་བྱུང་ Because going to the party and going to the meeting came at the same time, I wasn't able to go to the party.

འདོམ་གང་གྲུ་བཞི་ (domgaŋ trubshi) shung. a square prison room that is the size of the outstretched arms of a person.

འདོམ་ཐུག (dom tüù) vi. to meet/ come together.

འདོམ་པ་གང་ (domba kaŋ) one span of a person's outstretched hands from fingertip to fingertip.

འདོམས་: p. གདམས་; f. གདམ་; imp. འདོམས་ (dom) va. 1. to teach, to show, to explain ¶ དགེ་རྒན་གྱིས་སློབ་ཕྲུག་ཚོར་སློབ་ཚན་གྱི་དཀའ་གནད་རྣམས་གདམས་པ་རེད་ The teacher taught the students the difficult points in the lesson. 2. imp. of འདམ་. 3. p. of འདོམ་.

འདོམས་ (dom) 1. male and female sex organs. 2. imp. of འདོམས་.

འདོམས་ཀྱི་ཕྱོགས་ (domgi cɔ̈ɔ̀) the crotch area.

འདོམས་ཀྱི་སྦ་བ་ (domgi bawa) male genitals, penis.

འདོམས་དཀྲིས་ (domdriì) loincloth.

འདོམས་ཁྲིམས་སློད་ (domdrim lö̀ö) va. to lift a ban.

འདོམས་ལྤགས་ (dombaà) foreskin (of penis).

འདོམས་རས་ (domrɛɛ̀) sm. འདོམས་དཀྲིས་.

འདོམས་པོ་ (dombo) accurate, precise ¶ ཁོང་གིས་ལན་འདོམས་པོ་ཞིག་བརྒྱབ་སོང་ He gave an accurate/ precise answer.

འདོམས་སྤུ་ (dombu) genital/ pubic hair.

འདོར་: p., f. and imp. དོར་ (dɔɔ) va. 1. to cast away, to give up, to abandon, to discard ¶ ཁོ་ཐ་མག་འཐེན་རྒྱུ་རྩ་བ་ནས་དོར་བ་རེད་ He gave up smoking completely. ¶ དམ་བཅའ་འདོར་ To abandon an oath.

འདོར་བྱ་ (dɔɔja) 1. things that have to be given up or thrown away (e.g., cigarettes, old clothes, etc.). 2. excrement.

འདོར་བར་བྱེད་ (dɔɔwar cèe) va. to cast out/ abandon.

འདོར་མེད་ (dɔɔmeè) steadfast, firm, not abandoning/ giving up/ discarding ¶ ཀུན་པར་གང་ཅིའི་སྐྱབས་འཇུག་འདོར་མེད་ཡོང་བ་ཞུ་ Please help me in all ways and do not abandon me.

འདོར་ལེན་ (dɔɔ len) va. to decide what to do and what not to do, to decide what to discard and what to take.

འདོར་ལེན་འཛོལ་མེད་ (dɔɔlen dzöömeè) sm. བླང་འདོར་འཛོལ་མེད་.

འདོལ་ (döö) abbr. of འདོལ་བ་.

འདོལ་པོ་ (dööbo) sm. འདོལ་བ་.

འདོལ་བ་ (dööwa) soft (usu. for soil/ earth).

འདོལ་པོ་ (dööwo) soft (usu. for soil/ earth).

འདོལ་འདོལ་ (döödöö) 1. gentle in personality/ character. 2. soft (usu. for soil/ earth).

འདོལ་ཞིང་ (dööshiŋ) soft soil/ earth.

འདོལ་ས་ (döösa) sm. འདོལ་ཞིང་.

འདྲ་ (dra) 1. a copy, duplicate ¶ གན་རྒྱ་དེའི་འདྲ་གཅིག་ཁོ་ལ་ཡོད་པ་རེད་ He has one copy of the agreement. 2. vi. to be alike, to be the same ¶ དེ་དང་འདི་འདྲ་གི་མ་རེད་ This and that are not the same. 3. like, as according to, in accordance with ¶ འདི་འདྲ་བྱེད་དགོས་ One should do (it) like this. 4. (vb.+ པ་/བ་ + —) probably ¶ ཁོང་དགེ་རྒན་ཡིན་པ་འདྲ་ It seems he is a teacher. ¶ ཁོ་ལྷ་སར་ཕྱིན་པ་འདྲ་ He probably went to Lhasa.

འདྲ་: p. དྲས་; f. དྲ་; imp. དྲོས་ (dra) va. to cut.

འདྲ་སྐུ་ (drəgu) image, statue.

འདྲ་སྐུ་ལ་ཡིད་རྟོན་པ་ (drəgulə yiidömba) idolatry.

འདྲ་སྒྲིག (dra drig) 1. va. to put similar things together ¶ དངོས་པོ་རིགས་གཅིག་པ་རྣམས་འདྲ་བསྒྲིགས་ནས་བཞག་འདུག (They) put all the same things together. 2. va. to substitute sth. similar/ alike ¶ ཅ་ལག་ངོ་མ་དེ་བོར་བརླག་ཏུ་སོང་བར་བརྟེན་དེའི་ཚབ་ཅིག་འདྲ་བསྒྲིགས་འདུག Because the real item was lost, (they) substituted a similar item.

འདྲ་ཅོག (drajoò) sm. འདྲ་སྐུ་.

འདྲ་བཅོས་ (drajöö) making sth. similar ¶ ཅ་ལག་འདི་ངོ་མ་མིན་ན་འདྲ་བཅོས་ག་ཚོད་བྱས་ཀྱང་གཞན་གྱིས་ཡིད་ཆེས་ཀྱི་མ་རེད་ If the item isn't the original, however similar one makes another other people will not believe it.

འདྲ་ཆགས་ (drajaà) sm. འདྲ་ཆགས་པོ་.

འདྲ་ཆགས་པོ་ (dra cãgbo) 1. good looking, handsome, attractive ¶ ཁོང་འདྲ་ཆགས་པོ་འདུག He is handsome. 2. smooth, pleasant sounding (for lies) ¶ རྫུན་འདྲ་ཆགས་པོ་གང་འདྲ་ཞིག་བཤད་ཀྱང་ No matter how smooth a lie (they) tell ....

འདྲ་ཆོས་ (drajöö) similarity ¶ བོད་སྐད་དང་རྒྱ་སྐད་བར་འདྲ་ཆོས་གཏན་ནས་མེད་པ་རེད་ Tibetan and Chinese language have absolutely no similarity.

འདྲ་གཉིས་ (drañiì) two copies (of sth.).

འདྲ་གཉིས་སུ་གཤེག (drañiìsu shēg) va. to split/ divide into two parts.

འདྲ་མཉམ་ (drañam) equality; va.—བྱེད་ to treat/ act equally or with equally ¶ མི་རིགས་འདྲ་མཉམ་ Racial/ ethnic equality.

འདྲ་མཉམ་ཁ་གདང་ (drañam kābdeè) competing equally; va.—གཙོག to compete equally.

འདྲ་མཉམ་ཁེ་དབང་ (drañam kēwaŋ) equal rights.

འདྲ་མཉམ་གྲོས་མོལ་ (drañam trööməö) talks/ discussions held on the basis of equality.

འདྲ་མཉམ་གཉིས་ཕན་ (drañam ñiìbɛn) mutual benefit based on equality.

འདྲ་མཉམ་མེད་པ་ (drañam meèba) inequality, unequal.

འདྲ་བརྙན་ (drañɛn) image, statue.

འདྲ་དྲང་པོ་ (dra traŋbo) fair, just, equitable.

འདྲ་འདྲ་ (drandra) equal, alike, same ¶ ང་གཉིས་འདྲ་འདྲ་ཡིན་ We two are equal.

འདྲ་འདྲ་འགྲིག་འགྲིག (drandra drigdrig) making (sth.) look or sound good in a superficial or misleading way; va.—བཟོ་.

འདྲ་འདྲ་མཉམ་མཉམ་ (drandra ñamñam) 1. equal. 2. alike, similar.

འདྲ་འདྲ་ཐད་ཐད་ (drandra tɛɛ̀dɛɛ̀) sm. འདྲ་འདྲ་མཉམ་མཉམ་.

འདྲ་པར་ (drabar) photo, picture, portrait; va.—འདེབས་; —རྒྱག to photograph, to take a picture ¶ འདྲ་པར་ཚེམ་དྲུབས་མ་ An embroidered portrait.

འདྲ་པོ་ (drabo) alike, similar; vi.—ཆགས་ to become alike/ similar; va.—བཟོ་ to make alike/ similar ¶ ཁོ་རྡོ་རྗེ་འདྲ་པོ་འདུག He is like Dorje.

འདྲ་དཔར་ (drabar) sm. འདྲ་པར་.

འདྲ་དཔེ་ (drabe) model, specimen, sample.

འདྲ་དཔེ་རྒྱས་འགེབས་ (drabe gyɛɛ̀geb) applying one example/ model/ situation in an inappropriate manner, farfetched, distorted.

འདྲ་སྤྱད་ (drajɛɛ̀) sm. དྲས་སྤྱད་.

འདྲ་བ་ (drawa) similar, like, resembling ¶ རྡོ་རྗེ་ལགས་ཞལ་རས་ཁོང་འདྲ་པོ་འདུག Dorjela's face resembles his.

འདྲ་བར་ (drawar) similarly, like, as.

འདྲ་བྲིས་ (dradriì) sm. རི་མོ་རྗེན་བྲིས་.

འདྲ་འབག (drabaà) mask.

འདྲ་མ་ཆགས་པ་ (dra macagbə) unbecoming ¶ ཁོའི་སྤྱོད་ལམ་འདྲ་མ་ཆགས་པ་མི་འདུག His behavior is not unbecoming.

འདྲ་མི་འདྲ་ (dra mindra) sm. འདྲ་མིན་.

འདྲ་མིན་ (dramin) various, different ¶ ཁོ་ཚོ་ཚང་མར་བསམ་ཚུལ་འདྲ་མིན་བྱུང་ They all had different ideas.

འདྲ་མིན་ཅི་རིགས་ (dramin jiriì) sm. འདྲ་མིན་སྣ་ཚོགས་.

འདྲ་མིན་སྣ་ཚོགས་ (dramin nādzɔɔ̀) all sorts/ kinds of, many varieties ¶ ཆས་གོས་འདྲ་མིན་སྣ་ཚོགས་གྱོན་པའི་མི་རིགས་སྣ་ཚོགས་ཀྱི་མི་སྣ་ People of various nationalities in all kinds of costumes.

འདྲ་ཚད་ (dradzɛɛ̀) equivalent, similar.

འདྲ་ཚད་ཚད་ (dra tsɛɛ̀dzɛɛ̀) somewhat similar looking ¶ མི་འདི་གཉིས་གདོང་འདྲ་ཚད་ཚད་ཅིག་འདུག ཕལ་ཆེར་སྤུན་མཆེད་མིན་འགྲོ་ The two people have somewhat similar faces; probably they are related.

འདྲ་མཚུངས་ (drədzuŋ) equal, same ¶ ཚང་མར་གོ་

སྐབས་འདྲ་མཚུངས་སྤྲད་ཡོད་པ་རེད། (They) have given equal opportunities to all. ¶ 1999 ལོར་རྒྱ་གར་གྱི་མི་འབོར་རྒྱ་ནག་དང་འདྲ་མཚུངས་སུ་འགྱུར་གྱི་རེད། In 1999 India's population will equal that of China.

འདྲ་རྫུས། (drədzün) forgery.

འདྲ་གཟུགས། (drəsuù) effigy ¶ སྲིད་བློན་གྱི་འདྲ་གཟུགས་ཤིག་མེར་བསྲེགས་བཏང་བ་རེད། (They) burned an effigy of the Prime Minister.

འདྲ་གཟུགས་ཡི་གེ། (drəsuù yigi) hieroglyphics.

འདྲ་གཟོང་། (drasoŋ) a kind of chisel.

འདྲ་བཟོ། (dra so) va. to make similar/ alike (usu. in painting).

འདྲ་ཡ། (draya) 1. matching, copying (to make into a pair) ¶ ངའི་སྒམ་འདིའི་འདྲ་ཡ་གཅིག་བཟོ་དགོས་ཡོད། I have to make a matching box. 2. matching (in a competitive sense) ¶ མི་དེའི་ཤེད་ཤུགས་ཀྱི་འདྲ་ཡ་དོ་ཐུབ་པ་སུ་གཅིག་ཀྱང་མེད། There is no one who can match the strength of that person.

འདྲ་རིས། (drərii) a portrait (in drawing and painting).

འདྲ་ཤས་ཆེ། (dra shɛ̄ɛ̀je) almost alike/ similar.

འདྲ་གཤིབ། (drəshib) sm. འདྲ་མཉམ།.

འདྲ་བཤུས། (drəshüü) a copy, reprint, reproduction; va.—རྒྱག ¶ ཡིག་ཆ་འདིའི་འདྲ་བཤུས་ཤིག་བཟོས་དགོས། We have to make a copy of that document.

འདྲ་བཤུས་སྐུར་འཕྲིན། (drəshüü ñundrin) fax.

འདྲ་བཤུས་ནང་བཞིན། (drəshüü naŋshin) exactly alike.

འདྲ་བཤུས་དཔེ་དེབ། (drəshüü bēdeb) a book that is a copy.

འདྲ་ས། (drasa) (with neg.) dissimilar, different ¶ ཕྲུ་གུ་འདི་གཉིས་སློབ་སྦྱོང་ཐོག་འདྲ་ས་ཡོད་པ་མ་རེད། These two children are completely different with regards to studying (school).

འདྲ་སེ་འདྲེས་སེ། (drase dreèse) all mixed up ¶ ཅ་ལག་མང་པོ་ཞིག་འདྲ་སེ་འདྲེས་སེ་བྱས་ནས་བཞག་འདུག The things were put away all mixed up.

འདྲ་གསོབ། (drasob) 1. effigy. 2. taxidermy; va.—བཟོ།.

འདྲ་གསུམ་མ། (dra sūmmə) triplicate, sth. with three copies.

འདྲག་མཐིལ། (dragdil) arc. palm (of hand).

འདྲད། (drɛ̀ɛ̀) va. to eat meat from the bone without cutting off pieces, to eat a large piece of meat with one's teeth without cutting off pieces with a knife.

འདྲན། (drɛn) sm. འགྲན།.

འདྲལ།: p. and f. དྲལ།; imp. དྲོལ། (drɛɛ) va. to act shamelessly, to violate rules/ regulations.

འདྲི།: p. དྲིས།; f. འདྲི།; imp. དྲིས། (dri) va. to ask questions, to inquire, to question ¶ ཕྲུ་གུ་དེ་ག་པར་ཡོད་མེད་དྲིས་པ་རེད། (They) asked where the child was. ¶ སྐད་ཆ་ཞིག་དྲིས་པ་རེད། (They) asked a question.

འདྲི་མཁན། (driñɛn) sm. འདྲི་མི།.

འདྲི་གཅོད། (drijöö) judicial inquiry, trial, hearing; va.—བྱེད། to try, to have an inquiry/ hearing, to place on trial; va.—སྒུག to await trial ¶ ཉེས་ཅན་དེ་ལ་ཁྲིམས་ཁང་ནས་འདྲི་གཅོད་བྱེད་བཞིན་པ་རེད། The criminal is being tried by the court. [Lit. questioning and deciding].

འདྲི་གཅོད་ཀྱི་དབང་ཆ། (drijöö) judicial authority.

འདྲི་གཅོད་འཁུར། (drijöö kūr) vi. to be tried in court.

འདྲི་གཅོད་ཁྲིམས་སྟེགས། (drijöö trīmdeg) judge's desk/ platform.

འདྲི་གཅོད་ཁྲིམས་དཔོན། (drijöö trīmbön) a judge.

འདྲི་གཅོད་དང་པོ། (drijöö taŋbo) first hearing.

འདྲི་གཅོད་ཐ་མ། (drijöö tāma) sm. འདྲི་གཅོད་མཐའ་མ།.

འདྲི་གཅོད་མཐའ་མ། (drijöö tāma) final trial/ hearing.

འདྲི་གཅོད་པ། (drijööba) judge, magistrate.

འདྲི་གཅོད་བྱེད་དབང་། (drijöö ceèwaŋ) judicial authority, legal jurisdiction.

འདྲི་གཅོད་ལས་རོགས་ཚོགས་པ་ཆེན་པོ། (drijöö lɛ̀ɛ̀rɔɔ̀ tsōgba cēmbo) grand jury.

འདྲི་གཅོད་ལྷན་ཚོགས། (drijöö lhɛ̄ndzɔɔ̀) court room session/ hearing.

འདྲི་གཅོད་ཨུ་ཡོན་ལྷན་ཁང་། (drijöö ūyön lhɛ̄ngaŋ) tib.ch. judicial committee.

འདྲི་རྟགས། (dridaà) question mark.

འདྲི་རྟོག (dridɔɔ̀) examination, inquiry; va.—བྱེད། to examine, to make inquiries (into), to investigate, to interrogate ¶ འཕྲལ་བཅོས་ཁང་གི་སྨན་པས་འདྲི་རྟོག་ཞིབ་ཚགས་བྱེད་ཀྱི་ཡོད་པ་རེད། The doctors in the emergency ward make detailed examinations.

འདྲི་རྟོག་ཁང་། (dridɔɔ̀gaŋ) inquiry office, information counter/ desk.

འདྲི་རྟོག་ཞབས་ཞུ་ཁང་། (dridɔɔ̀ shəbjigaŋ) consultation/ consulting service.

འདྲི་དོན། (dridön) sm. དྲི་བ།.

འདྲི་དཔྱོད། (drijöö) sm. འདྲི་རྟོག.

འདྲི་བྱེད། (drijeè) sth. to ask ¶ ཁྱེད་རང་ལ་འདྲི་བྱེད་གང་ཡོད་དམ། What do you have to ask?

འདྲི་བྱེད་ཀྱི་ཚིག་གྲུབ། (drijeègi tsīgdrub) interrogative sentence.

འདྲི་མི་གཏོང་། (drimi dōŋ) va. to send sb. to inquire/ ask ¶ ངས་ཁོའི་སར་བོད་ཀྱི་སྐོར་སྐད་ཆ་འདྲི་མི་བཏང་བ་ཡིན། I sent sb. to him to ask about Tibet.

འདྲི་སྨེད། (dri mēè) 1. va. to ask about his/ her health or welfare. 2. va. to ask a question.

འདྲི་རྩད། (dridzɛɛ̀) sm. འདྲི་རྟོག.

འདྲི་རྩད་ཟིན་བྲིས། (dridzɛɛ̀ sindo) notes of investigation/ inquiry.

འདྲི་རྩད་ཞུ་ས། (dridzɛɛ̀ shusa) information desk/ counter.

འདྲི་བརྩད། (dridzɛɛ̀) sm. འདྲི་རྟོག.

འདྲི་ཚིག (dridzii) interrogative words/ particles.

འདྲི་ཞིབ། (drishib) investigating, cross-examining, inquiring; va.—བྱེད། to investigate/ cross examine/ hold an inquiry; vi.—འཁེལ། to be/ get cross-examined, to be the subject of an inquiry.

འདྲི་ཞིབ་འཇུག་སྒྲིལ། (drishib jugdrii) conclusion of an investigation/ cross-examination/ inquiry.

འདྲི་གཞུང་བྱེད། (drishuŋ ceè) va. to interrogate/ question in a harsh manner.

འདྲི་རོགས་པ། (drirɔgba) juror.

འདྲི་ལན། (dri lɛn) answering a question; va.—རྒྱག ¶ ཁོས་ང་ལ་འདྲི་ལན་བརྒྱབ་མ་བྱུང་། He didn't answer my question. ¶ ངས་ཁོ་ལ་འདྲི་ལན་བརྒྱབ་མེད། I didn't answer his question.

འདྲིད།: p., f. and imp. དྲིད། and བྲིད། (drii) va. to deceive, to delude.

འདྲིམ། (drim) sm. འགྲིམ།.

འདྲིལ།: p., f. and imp. དྲིལ། (drii) 1. sm. སྒྲིལ།. 2. vi. to roll/ tumble down.

འདྲིས། (drii) 1. vi. to be/ get used to, to get accustomed/ acclimated to ¶ ང་རྒྱ་གར་ལ་ལོ་གཉིས་བསྡད་ཀྱང་ལུང་པ་འདྲིས་མ་སོང་། Even though I lived in India for two years I am not used to living there.

འདྲིས་གྲོགས། (driidrɔɔ̀) close friends.

འདྲིས་ཆེན་པོ། (drii cēmbo) close relationship ¶ ཁོ་གཉིས་འདྲིས་ཆེན་པོ་རེད། The two of them are very close.

འདྲིས་གོམས། (driigom) used to, accustomed to ¶ ང་ཉ་ཟ་ལས་ཀྱི་འདྲིས་གོམས་ཆགས་མི་འདུག I am not used to eating fish.

འདྲིས་ཆ། (driija) experience.

འདྲིས་རྟག་པོ། (drii dāgbo) a person with whom one keeps in touch, sb. with whom one has close relations.

འདྲིས་སྟོབས། (driidob) the effect/ power of being accustomed to sth. or having experience/ acclimitization.

འདྲིས་བདེ་པོ། (drii debo) 1. easy to get used to/ accustomed to. 2. easy to get along with, makes friends easily.

འདྲིས་པོ། (driibu) close (in relations), knowing sb. well ¶ ཁྱེད་རང་གཉིས་འདྲིས་པོ་ཡོད་པས། Are the two of you close?

འདྲིས་ཟབ། (driisəb) good, close (friend or acquaintance).

འདྲིས་གཤིབ། (driishib) close contact/ association/

acquaintance/ relationship ། ང་ཁོ་ཚོ་དང་འདྲིས་བཤིབ་ཆེན་པོ་མེད I don't have close contact with them.

འདྲིས་གཤིབ་བདེ་བ (driishib dewa) sm. འདྲིས་བདེ་པོ.

འདྲུ: p. བྲུས; f. འདྲུ; imp. བྲུས (dru) va. to dig, to excavate ། ཁྲོན་པ་ཞིག་བྲུས་པ་རེད (They) dug a well.

འདྲུ་སྤྱད (drujɛɛ̀) digging/ excavating tools.

འདྲུད: p. བྲུད; f. འདྲུད; imp. བྲུད (drüü) va. to drag, to pull, to haul ། ཁོས་ཁྱི་རོ་དེ་ས་ལ་འདྲུད་འགྲོ་གི་འདུག He is dragging the corpse of the dog (on the ground).

འདྲུད་འཁོར (drüügɔɔ) 1. a vehicle to pull/ drag, tractor ། འདྲུད་འཁོར་བཟོ་གྲྭ Tractor factory. 2. a pulley, a winch.

འདྲུད་འཁོར་ཆུང་བ (drüügɔɔ jũŋwa) a small tractor.

འདྲུད་གྲུ (drüüdru) tug boat.

འདྲུད་འཐེན (dründen) dragging, pulling, hauling; va.—བྱེད.

འདྲུད་འཐེན་འཁོར་ལོ (dründen kɔ̃ɔlo) tractor.

འདྲུད་འཐེན་འཕྲུལ་འཁོར (dründen trüügɔɔ) sm. འདྲུད་འཐེན་འཁོར་ལོ.

འདྲུད་འཐེན་འཕྲུལ་འཁོར་ཁང (dründen trüügɔɔgaŋ) tractor station.

འདྲུད་འཐེན་རླངས་འཁོར (dründen lãŋgɔɔ) tractor.

འདྲུད་རྡོག་རྒྱག (drüüdɔ̀ɔ gyaà) sm. མདུད་རྡོག་རྒྱག.

འདྲུད་པ (drüübə) sm. མདུད་པ.

འདྲུད་ཤུགས (drüüshug) tractive force, dragging power/ force.

འདྲུད་བཤང (drüüsaŋ) clearing out, cleaning (a ditch, etc.); va.—བྱེད ། ཆུ་མ་བཏང་གོང་ཡུར་བ་འདྲུད་བཤང་བྱེད་དགོས Before irrigating we have to clean out the irrigation canal.

འདྲུད་ལྷམ (drüülham) slippers.

འདྲུབ: p. འདྲུབས; f. འདྲུབ (drub) 1. sm. འཚེམ. 2. vi. to heal (for sores, cuts) ། ངའི་རྨ་ཁ་འདྲུབས་བཞག My cut has healed.

འདྲུབ་སྤྱད (drubjɛɛ̀) needle.

འདྲུལ (drüü) arc. sm. རུལ.

འདྲེ (dre) demon, ghost, evil spirit.

འདྲེ: p. འདྲེས; f. འདྲེ (dre) vi. to get mixed up, to be/ get blended ། ཁོ་གཉིས་ཀྱི་གོས་ལོག་ཚང་མ་འདྲེས་འདུག All their clothes got mixed up.

འདྲེ་དཀར (dregaa) beggar wearing a mask who comes around on special occasions such as New Year reciting auspicious sayings (begging).

འདྲེ་སྐས (dregɛɛ̀) ladder made of a single log with deep notches.

འདྲེ་རྒྱོ་ཤོར (dregyo shɔ̃ɔ) vi. to have a wet dream.

འདྲེ་སྐར (dregar) sm. འདྲེ་མེ.

འདྲེ་ང་ཆུང (dreŋa jũŋ) sm. བྲེ་ག.

འདྲེ་གཏམ (dredam) a false/ untrue story or rumor.

འདྲེ་གདོན (drenöö) evil spirits, ghosts, demons.

འདྲེ་འདུལ (dre düü) va. to overcome/ conquer/ subdue demons, ghosts and evil spirits.

འདྲེ་རྡོ (dredo) petrified/ fossilized wood.

འདྲེ་ལྡོག (dredɔɔ̀) rolling over, rolling around; va.—བྱེད; —རྒྱག ། རྟ་ས་ཐང་ལ་འདྲེ་ལྡོག་རྒྱག་གི་འདུག The horse is rolling around on the ground.

འདྲེ་གནོན་རྒྱག (drenön gyaà) vi. to have a nightmare.

འདྲེ་དམག (dremaà) evil soldiers (term used for enemy soldiers).

འདྲེ་མེ (dreme) ghost light, jack-o'-lantern, will-o'-the-wisp.

འདྲེ་མོ (dremo) witch, female demon/ spirit/ ghost.

འདྲེ་མོ་རླུང་འཚུབ (dremo lũŋdzub) whirlwind; vi.—རྒྱག.

འདྲེ་ཚེར་མ (dre tsẽẽma) wolf berry.

འདྲེ་ཚོགས (drẽdzɔɔ̀) gathering of ghosts/ demons/ witches.

འདྲེ་ཞུགས (dre shuù) vi. to be possessed an by an evil spirits/ demon/ ghost ། ཁོ་ལ་འདྲེ་ཞུགས་བཞག He was possessed by a demon.

འདྲེ་ལོག (drelɔɔ̀) sm. འདྲེ་ལྡོག.

འདྲེ་རླུང (dreluŋ) evil wind, noxious trend (political).

འདྲེ་རླུང་རླབས་ངན (dreluŋ lãbŋɛn) evil wind, noxious trend (political).

འདྲེ་ལག (drelaà) invading, seizing; va.—རྐྱོང ། ཁོ་ཚོས་ངའི་ཕ་ཡུལ་འདྲེ་ལག་བརྐྱངས་པ་རེད They seized our homeland. [Lit. demon's hand].

འདྲེ་ཤར་སྒོ་ནང་སླུད་ནུབ་སྒོ (dre shããgo daŋ lũũ nubgo) doing the wrong or opposite thing [Lit. ghost (coming) from east door; exorcising from the west door].

འདྲི་ཤིག (drishii) bed bug.

འདྲི་སྲིན (drisin) sm. གདུག་འདྲི.

འདྲེག (dreè) sm. འབྲེག.

འདྲེག་མཁན (dreèñɛn) barber.

འདྲེགས་དྲི (dregtri) smell of sth. burning.

འདྲེད (dreè) vi. to slip ། ཁོ་འཁྱགས་སྟེང་དུ་འདྲེད་ནས་འགྱེལ་པ་རེད He slipped on the ice and fell.

འདྲེད་བརྡབ (dreè dəb) vi. to slip, to lose one's footing.

འདྲེད་བརྡབ་ཤོར (dreèda shɔ̃ɔ) vi. to slip, to lose one's footing.

འདྲེད་ཤུར (dreèshur) va. to slide down sth. (e.g., a tree).

འདྲེན: p. དྲངས; f. དྲང; imp. དྲོངས (dren) 1. va. to invite ། གྲོགས་པོ་རྣམས་རང་གི་ནང་ལ་དྲངས་ནས་གསོལ་ཇ་ཕུལ་བ་རེད (They) invited (their) friends home and offered them tea. 2. va. to pull/ drag ། ཐག་པས་ཤིང་སྡོང་ཞིག་འདྲེན་བཞིན་འདུག They are pulling a tree with a rope. 3. va. to transport, to ship, to convey ། འཕྲུལ་ཆས་མང་པོ་རླངས་འཁོར་ཐོག་འདྲེན་གྱི་ཡོད་པ་རེད They are shipping many machines by auto. 4. va. to irrigate, to bring (water) ། ཞིང་ཆུ་འདྲེན་པའི་སྐབས While (they) were irrigating (drawing water). 5. va. to quote/ cite ། ཚིག་བཅད་ཁ་ཤས་མི་ལའི་རྣམ་ཐར་ནས་དྲངས་ཡོད (I) have quoted a few verses from Mila's biography. 6. va. to serve ། སྐུ་མགྲོན་རྣམས་ལ་གསོལ་ཇ་དྲངས་པ་རེད They served the guests tea. 7. va. to liberate (religiously) ། སངས་རྒྱས་ཀྱིས་སེམས་ཅན་རྣམས་ལ་འཁོར་བའི་གནས་ལས་འདྲེན་གྱི་ཡོད་པ་རེད The Buddha is liberating sentient beings from samsara.

འདྲེནའི (dönbɛ) shung. abbr. of འདྲེན་པའི.

འདྲེན་ཁ་གཏོང (drenga dõŋ) va. to take the harvest to the mill to grind.

འདྲེན་འཁོར (drengɔɔ) cart.

འདྲེན་གླ (drenla) freight/ transport/ shipping charge or fee.

འདྲེན་གཏོང (drendoŋ) transporting, conveying, shipping, bringing; va.—བྱེད ། འཕོ་ཚོང་ནོར་མང་པོ་གྲུ་གཟིངས་ཐོག་ནས་འདྲེན་གཏོང་བྱས་པ་རེད They transported many goods by ship.

འདྲེན་གླ (drenla) freight/ transport/ shipping charge or fee.

འདྲེན་ཆས (drenjɛɛ̀) equipment or vehicles for bringing/ transporting/ shipping.

འདྲེན་ཐག (drendaà) conveyor belt.

འདྲེན་སྡུར (drendur) 1. checking, verifying; va.—བྱེད. 2. tug-of-war; va.—བྱེད.

འདྲེན་བྱེད (drenjeè) conveying, transporting ། རྡོ་སྣུམ་འདྲེན་བྱེད་ལུགས་མདོང Oil (conveying) pipeline.

འདྲེན་བྱེད་ཀྱི་ཡུལ་དུ (drenjeègi yüüdu) vision, eyesight.

འདྲེན་མ (drenma) sm. འདྲེས་མ.

འདྲེན་དམག (drenmaà) soldiers used as decoys/ bait.

འདྲེན་ཚད (drendzɛɛ̀) transport capacity/ limit.

འདྲེན་ཚད་བཅད་གྲངས (drendzɛɛ jɛɛdraŋ) fixed transport capacity.

འདྲེན་ཚོང (drendzoŋ) 1. importing; va.—བྱེད to import ། ངས་རྒྱ་གར་ནས་ཚོང་ཟོག་འདྲེན་ཚོང་བྱས་པ་ཡིན I imported goods from India. 2. transporting and selling, marketing.

འདྲེན་ཟམ (drensam) drawbridge.

འདྲེན་ལེན་ (dre̲nlen) transporting; va.—བྱེད་ ། འབྲུ་འབབ་རྣམས་འཕྲལ་དུ་བཏོན་ཏེ་འདྲེན་ལེན་བྱ་དགོས་ The grain yield should be transported as soon as possible.

འདྲེས་ (dre̲è) 1. p. of འདྲི་. 2. abbr. of འདྲེས་མ་.

འདྲེས་སྐྱོད་བྱེད་ (dre̲ègyöö ce̲è) va. t o have different people going together.

འདྲེས་འཁྱེར་ (dre̲è kyēr) 1. va. to be taken by a demon/ spirit/ ghost. 2. sleepwalking.

འདྲེས་རྙོག (dre̲èñɔɔ̀) confusion, turmoil, disorder, mix-up ། ཡིག་ཆ་མང་པོ་ཞིག་འདྲེས་རྙོག་བྱུང་བཞག Many documents got mixed-up.

འདྲེས་གཏོང་ (dre̲è dōŋ) va. to adulterate ། གསེར་ལ་རག་གིས་འདྲེས་བཏང་བཞག The gold was adulterated with brass.

འདྲེས་སྡོད་ (dre̲è dö̲ö̀) sm. འདྲེས་མར་སྡོད་.

འདྲེས་འདྲེས་ (dre̲ndreè) mixed, blended together, assimilated ། འབྲུ་དང་སྲན་མ་འདྲེས་འདྲེས་བཏང་ནས་རྩམ་པ་བཏགས་པ་རེད་ They mixed barley and peas and made tsamba.

འདྲེས་རྨོན་ (dre̲ènön) nightmare; vi.—རྒྱག to have a nightmare.

འདྲེས་གནས་ (dre̲ènεὲ) place where sth. is mixed/ blended.

འདྲེས་བརྡོས་ (dre̲ènöö̀) kneading different substances together.

འདྲེས་པ་ (dre̲èba) sm. འདྲེས་མ་.

འདྲེས་པའི་ཚལ་ (dre̲èbε tsεὲ) park/ garden with many different flowers, plants, and trees.

འདྲེས་སྦྱོར་ (dre̲èjɔɔ) 1. mixing, compounding, combining, synthesizing; va.—བྱེད་. 2. artificial insemination, crossbreeding.

འདྲེས་སྦྱོར་གྱི་འཁྱིག (dre̲èjɔɔgi gyig) synthetic rubber.

འདྲེས་སྦྱོར་དངོས་རྫས་ (dre̲èjɔɔ ŋö̀ödzεὲ) chemical compounds.

འདྲེས་སྦྱོར་ཚེ་སྐྲ་ (dre̲èjɔɔ tsi̲na) synthetic fibers.

འདྲེས་སྦྱོར་རྫས་འགྱུར་ (dre̲èjɔɔ dzε̲ègyur) synthetic chermicals.

འདྲེས་མ་ (dre̲èma) mixture, blend, compound ། མི་རིགས་མང་པོ་འདྲེས་མ་ A mixture of many races.

འདྲེས་མར་སྡོད་པ་ (dre̲èmaa dö̲öba) integrated (ethnically, racially).

འདྲེས་མེད་ (dre̲èmeè) unadulterated, pure, clean, genuine.

འདྲེས་ཚད་ (dre̲èdzεὲ) the amount of mixture, the percentage of components in a mixture ། ཆུའི་ནང་དུ་སྐྱེ་ལྡན་དངོས་པོའི་འདྲེས་ཚད་ The percent of organic matter in water.

འདྲེས་ཚལ་ (dre̲èdzεε) abbr. of འདྲེས་པའི་ཚལ་.

འདྲེས་མཚམས་ (dre̲èdzam) point at which two things join/ meet.

འདྲེས་བརླམས་ (dre̲èlam) sm. འདྲེ་ཞུགས་.

འདྲེས་ལྷད་ (dre̲èlhεὲ) 1. link, connection ། གསང་བའི་ལས་ཀ་དེ་ཚོའི་ནང་འདྲེས་ལྷད་མེད་ཟེར་བ་རེད་ (They) said (they) don't have any connection with the underground activities. 2. additives, alloys, dilutants; va.—གཏོང་ to mix/ alloy/ adulterate ། ནང་ཆོས་ལ་བོན་ཆོས་ཀྱི་འདྲེས་ལྷད་ཕྲན་བུ་བྱུང་ཡོད་པ་རེད་ Buddhism has gotten a little adulterated with Bon religion.

འདྲེས་ལྷད་མེད་པ་ (dre̲èlhεὲ me̲èba) clean, pure, unadulterated, genuine.

འདྲོག: p. **འདྲོགས་**; f. **འདྲོག** (drɔ̲ɔ̀) vi. to be/ get startled/ frightened/ scared, to shy (for horses) ། ཁོ་གློ་བུར་དུ་མཐོང་ནས་ང་འདྲོགས་བྱུང་ I was startled when I suddenly saw him.

འདྲོག་སྐད་ (drɔ̲ɔ̀gεὲ) sounds made when startled/ alarmed.

འདྲོག་མགོ་ (dro̲ŋgo) startled, shocked, scared, frightened; va.—སློང་ to startle/ frighten; vi.—ལང་; —བྱེད་ to get startled/ frightened/ scared ། འཛིན་གྲྭའི་ནང་དགེ་རྒན་གློ་བུར་དུ་ཡོང་ནས་སློབ་ཕྲུག་ཚོ་འདྲོག་མགོ་ལངས་པ་རེད་ The students were startled when the teacher suddenly came to the class. ། མེ་མདའི་སྒྲ་ཡིས་རྟ་འདྲོག་མགོ་ལངས་པ་རེད་ The horse was startled by the gunshot.

འདྲོག་མགོ་ཅན་ (dro̲ŋgojεn) skittish, easily alarmed/ startled.

འདྲོག་མགོ་ཚ་པོ་ (dro̲ŋgo tsābo) easily startled/ frightened (usu. pertaining to animals).

འདྲོག་འགོ་ (dro̲ŋgo) sm. འདྲོག་མགོ་.

འདྲོག་ཅན་ (dro̲gjεn) sm. འདྲོག་མགོ་ཅན་.

འདྲོག་ཉམས་ཅན་ (dro̲gñamjεn) sm. འདྲོག་མགོ་ཅན་.

འདྲོག་འདྲོག་པ་ (drɔ̲ŋdrɔɔ̀ba) sm. འདྲོག་མགོ་ཅན་.

འདྲོག་སློང་ (drɔ̲ɔ̀ lōŋ) sm. འདྲོག་མགོ་སློང་.

འདྲོགས་ (drɔ̲ɔ̀) p. of འདྲོག.

འདྲོགས་མགོ་ (dro̲ŋgo) sm. འདྲོག་མགོ.

འདྲོགས་རྒྱུགས་ (drɔ̲ggyuù) running/ fleeing due to being startled (usu. animals); va.—བྱེད་.

འདྲོགས་འཕུར་ (drɔ̲ɔ̀ pūr) taking off/ flying off due to being startled.

འདྲོང་ (dro̲ŋ) 1. abbr. of འདྲོང་པོ་. 2. vi. to arrive, to reach ། ཡི་གེ་དེ་འདྲོང་མི་འདུག That letter hasn't arrived.

འདྲོང་པོ་ (dro̲ŋbo) straight.

འདྲོང་པོ་རྐྱོང་ (dro̲ŋbo gyōŋ) va. to stretch ། ཁོང་རྐང་པ་འདྲོང་པོ་བརྐྱངས་ནས་ཉལ་བསྡད་འདུག He is sleeping with his feet outstretched.

འདྲོང་སྲོང་ (dro̲ŋ sōŋ) va. to straighten ། ཁོས་ལྕུག་མ་དེ་འདྲོང་བསྲངས་པ་རེད་ He straightened out the bamboo.

འདྲོངས་ (dro̲ŋ) 1. vi. to like/ approve ། ངའི་སྐད་ཆ་འདི་ཁོའི་སེམས་ལ་འདྲོངས་མ་སོང་ He didn't like what I said. 2. abbr. of འདྲོངས་པོ་. 3. p. of འདྲོང་, 2.

འདྲོངས་པོ་ (dro̲ŋbo) sm. འདྲོང་པོ་.

འདྲོད་ (drö̲ö̀) imp. of འདུད་.

ད་ཀ་ (da̲ga) a thick paste made from mixing tea with tsamba.

ད་དཀྲུག (da̲druù) tattling; va.—རྒྱག to tattle ། ཁོས་ངབ་དཀྲུག་བརྒྱབ་རྐྱེན་རྒན་ལགས་ཀྱིས་ང་ལ་གཤེ་གཤེ་བཏང་བྱུང་ Because he tattled on me, the teacher scolded me.

ད་ཁ་ཁྲས་དོ་ (da̲ga trεὲdo) stingy.

ད་གོང་ (da̲goŋ) ད་ཀ་.

ད་དཔན་ (da̲bεn) ch. large ceramic bowl.

ད་པེ་དོ་པེ་ (da̲be do̲be) sm. དབ་དོབ་.

ད་རམ་ས་ལ་ (da̲ram sāla) Dharamsala (residence of the Dalai Lama in India).

ད་ལབ་ཕྱི་ (da̲ləbje) a fur wrap worn on the shoulders of the traditional official's dress called ཁལ་ཁ་བྲག.

ད་ཡང་ (da̲yan) Chinese silver dollar.

ད་ས་ (da̲sa) abbr. of ད་རམ་ས་ལ་.

དྭ་ཀོ་ཚོན་ཁྲ་ (da̲go tsōndra) shung. ch.tib. a type of gown made from brocade/ silk.

དྭ་ཁུར་རལ་ (da̲gurε) Urga (today's Ulan Bator).

དྭ་ཁྲིའི་ (da̲dree) ch. truck.

དྭ་གོག (da̲gɔɔ̀) ch. big pot.

དྭ་པན་ (da̲bεn) ch. large ceramic bowl.

དྭ་ཡང་ (da̲yaŋ) ch. sm. ད་ཡང་.

དག་གེ་དོག་གེ་ (da̲ge do̲ge) small loads/ bundles of various sizes.

དག་སྒྲ་དིག་སྒྲ་ (da̲gdra di̲gdra) noises, noisy ། དེ་རིང་ཁང་པའི་ནང་དག་སྒྲ་དིག་སྒྲ་མང་པོ་འདུག Today there is a lot of noise in the house.

དག་དག (da̲gdaà) knocking (e.g., on door); va.—གཏོང་.

དང་ (da̲ŋ) sm. གདང་.

དང་ཐག (da̲ŋdaà) sm. གདང་ཐག.

དང་འཕེན་ (da̲ŋ pēn) va. to tie/ tether animals to a pegged rope or line.

དང་བུ་ (da̲ŋbur) 1. sm. གདང་ཕུར་. 2. rung of a ladder.

དབ་ (də̲b) sm.* རྡིབ་.

དབ་རྒྱལ་ (də̲bgyεὲ) chalk bag (used in traditional Tibetan schools to powder the wooden board on which students practice writing).

དབ་དཀྲུག (də̲bdruù) sm. ད་དཀྲུག.

དབ་སྐས་ (də̲bgεὲ) banging/ stomping when

climbing stairs; va.—བྱེད་.

རྡབ་སྒྲ་རྡིབ་སྒྲ་ (də̲bdra di̲bdra) sm. རྡག་སྒྲ་རྡིག་སྒྲ་.

རྡབ་སྒྲོ་ (də̲bdruù) banging on a door; va.—བྱེད་.

རྡབ་ཆག་ཤོར་ (də̲bjaà shɔ̄ɔ̄) vi. to break ¶ རྐང་པ་རྡབ་ཆག་ཤོར་བཞག (His) leg got broken.

རྡབ་འཆལ་ (də̲bjεε) arc. stumbling, tripping, falling.

རྡབ་རྡབ་ (də̲bdəb) dusting (by shaking); va.—བྱེད་; —གཏོང་ to dust.

རྡབ་རྡོབ་ (də̲bdoò) a type of deviant fighting monks found in the big monasteries such as Sera, Drepung and Ganden.

རྡབ་ཕོར་ (də̲bbɔɔ) ashtray.

རྡབ་བེ་རྡོབ་བེ་ (də̲bbe do̲bbe) boys and girls in their twenties.

རྡབ་ཙོག (də̲bdzog) stone; va.—གཞུ་ to hit with a stone.

རྡབ་ཞོགས་ (də̲bshɔɔ̀) commotion, disturbance, unrest.

རྡབ་ཤུགས་ (də̲bshuù) force of sth. hitting/ banging ¶ ཆུ་རགས་ལ་གཙང་ཆུའི་རྡབ་ཤུགས་ཆེན་པོ་ཡོད་པ་རེད་ The river is banging with great force on the dam.

རྡབ་ཤོག (də̲bshɔɔ̀) firecracker (which is thrown against wall or floor to explode).

རྡབ་གསིག (də̲bsii̇̀) hardship/ burden/ suffering; va.—གཏོང་ ¶ དམག་དཔུང་ཕྱོགས་ལ་འགྲོ་དུས་མི་སེར་ལ་ཁྲལ་རིགས་དང་ཟ་ཆས་རྡབ་གསིག་ཆེན་པོ་གཏོང་གི་ཡོད་པ་རེད་ When soldiers travel, they cause great hardship for the peasants regarding taxes and foodstuffs.

རྡབ་བསེ་ (də̲bse) sm. ཤོ་སྣན་.

རྡར་: p. and f. བརྡར་; imp. རྡོར་ (da̲r) va. to file/ grind (metals), to sharpen (knives etc.).

རྡར་འཁོར་ (da̲rgɔɔ) sharpening/ grinding wheel, sharpening machine.

རྡར་སྡེགས་ (da̲rdeg) grinder, grinding machine.

རྡར་རྡོ་ (da̲rdo) whetstone, grinding stone; va.—རྒྱག to sharpen with a whetstone.

རྡར་བྱེད་ (da̲rjeè) a substance used for sharpening things.

རྡར་ཚན་ (da̲rdzεn) eng. dozen.

རྡར་རྫས་ (da̲rdzεὲ) sm. རྡར་བྱེད་.

རྡར་ཟད་ (da̲rsεὲ) worn out by rubbing/ friction; vi.—ཐེབས་ to get worn out by rubbing/ friction ¶ འཕྲུལ་འཁོར་གྱི་ལྷུ་ལག་ཁག་ཅིག་རྡར་ཟད་ཐེབས་འདུག Some parts of the machine have worn out.

རྡར་བཟོ་ (da̲r so̲) va. to make things by grinding.

རྡར་རས་ (da̲rrεὲ) sandpaper.

རྡར་ལས་བཟོ་པ་ (da̲rlεὲ so̲ba) sb. who works as a grinder.

རྡར་ཤ་གཅོད་ (da̲rsha jȫȍ) va. to judge, to investigate, to determine ¶ གནས་ཚུལ་དེ་བདེན་པ་ཡིན་མིན་རྡར་ཤ་གཅོད་དགོས་ We have to investigate and decide whether this information is true or false.

རྡར་ཤུགས་ (də̲rshuù) force of friction.

རྡལ་: p. and f. བརྡལ་; imp. རྡོལ་ (dε̲ε̲) sm. འགྲེམས་.

རྡལ་གླ་ (da̲la) transportation fee (for truck, yak, etc.).

རྡལ་འདྲེན་ (da̲ndrεn) transporting for a fee; va.—བྱེད་.

རྡི་རྡི་གུ་གུ་ (di̲di gu̲gu) sm. དི་དི་གུ་གུ་.

རྡིག (di̲g) 1. precious things owned by a household. 2. cooking pot.

རྡིག་སྒྲ་ (di̲gdra) sound of a footstep, sound of sth. falling.

རྡིག་ར་ (di̲grə) pin/ clasp used by Tibetan women to hold together their apron or shawl.

རྡིབ་: p. བརྡིབས་; f. བརྡིབ་ (di̲b) vi. to fall down, to collapse, to crumble, to cave in (for house), to get dented (for cars, metals). ¶ ཆར་པ་ཆེན་པོ་བབས་ནས་ཁང་པ་རྙིང་པ་དེ་བརྡིབས་པ་རེད་ There was heavy rain and the old house collapsed.

རྡིབ་སྐྱོན་ (di̲bgyön) damage caused by sth. collapsing/ caving in or getting dented.

རྡུ་བ་ (du̲wa) setose thistle (used in Tibetan medicine).

རྡུ་ལུམ་ (du̲lum) the sound made by sth. falling in the water.

རྡུགས་ (du̲ù) 1. vi. to be worn out. 2. vi. to be boring. 3. immoral, unethical.

རྡུང་: p. བརྡུང་; f. བརྡུང་; imp. རྡུངས་ (du̲ŋ) 1. va. to beat, to strike, to hit ¶ ཁོས་ཕྲུ་གུ་དེ་བརྡུངས་སོང་ He beat the child. ¶ ཁོ་རྔ་རྡུང་གི་འདུག He plays (beats) the drum. 2. va. to forge, to make things from metal ¶ ཁོས་ཟངས་ཀྱི་བུམ་པ་ཡག་པོ་རྡུང་གི་ཡོད་པ་རེད་ He makes good copper vases. 3. va. to knock (on doors) ¶ སྒོ་ཐེངས་མང་བརྡུངས་ཀྱང་ Even though (they) knocked on the door many times.

རྡུང་ཁ་ (du̲ŋgə) sm. རྡུང་ག.

རྡུང་ག (du̲ŋga) colliding, banging into/ against; vi.—རྒྱག to collide/ bang together/ bang into/ against.

རྡུང་མགར་ (du̲ŋgar) blacksmith.

རྡུང་སྒྲ་ (du̲ŋdra) the sound of beating/ hitting ¶ འཁར་རྔའི་རྡུང་སྒྲ་ The sound of beating gongs.

རྡུང་གཏག (du̲ŋdaà) 1. beating up, giving a beating; va.—གཏོང་ to beat, to give a beating. 2. a diagnostic method in traditional Tibetan medicine involving hitting a patient with the hand or a small hammer.

རྡུང་བརྡག (du̲ŋdaà) sm. རྡུང་གཏག.

རྡུང་བརྡག་ཐོ་བ་ (du̲ŋdaà tōwa) a hammer used in making medical diagnosis.

རྡུང་འཐག (du̲ŋdaà) pounding to pulverize/ make into powder form.

རྡུང་མཐུད་ (du̲ŋdüǜ) forge welding.

རྡུང་འདེད་ (du̲ŋdeè) chasing/ pursuing and beating.

རྡུང་རྡེག (du̲ŋdeg) hitting a blow, beating, striking; va.—གཏོང་ to strike, to beat; vi.—རག to receive a beating ¶ དགྲ་བོར་རྡུང་རྡེག་དྲག་པོ་ལན་འགའ་བཏང་བ་རེད་ (They) struck the enemy a powerful blow several times.

རྡུང་རྡེག་ཚ་ནན་ (du̲ŋdeg tsānεn) strike hard (name of a political campaign); va.—གཏོང་.

རྡུང་གནོན་ (du̲ŋnün) forging (metals).

རྡུང་འབུད་ (du̲ŋbüǜ) beating and pushing.

རྡུང་འཚོག (du̲ŋdzɔɔ̀) sm. རྡུང་གཏག.

རྡུང་རྫོག (du̲ŋdzɔɔ̀) sm. རྡུང་གཏག.

རྡུང་གཟེར་ (du̲ŋser) rivet.

རྡུང་བཟོ་ (du̲ŋso) forging, smithy; va.—བྱེད་ to forge (metals).

རྡུང་རེས་ (du̲ŋreè) two sides coming to blows, hitting back and forth; va.—གཏོང་; —བྱེད་ to come to blows, to fight back and forth.

རྡུང་ལན་རང་སྒྲུད་ (du̲ŋlεn ra̲ŋdrεὲ) shung. retaliating by hitting back; va.—བྱེད་ ¶ རང་ཉིད་སྡུག་ཁུར་བྱ་ཐབས་བྲལ་བས་རྡུང་ལན་རང་སྒྲུད་བྱ་དགོས་བྱུང་བ་ The suffering was unbearable for me so I had to retaliate by hitting back.

རྡུང་ལས་ (du̲ŋlεὲ) forging work.

རྡུངས་ (du̲ŋ) imp. of རྡུང་.

རྡུམ་ (du̲m) 1. abbr. of རྡུམ་ རྡུམ་. 2. maimed, limbless, amputated ¶ ལག་རྡུམ་ Armless.

རྡུམ་རྡུམ་ (du̲mdum) 1. short (pieces); va.—བཟོ་ to cut into short/ small pieces ¶ མེ་ཤིང་རྡུམ་རྡུམ་བཟོས་བཞག (They) cut the firewood into short pieces. ¶ བསམ་བློ་རྡུམ་རྡུམ་ Shortsighted (in thinking). 2. short-tempered.

རྡུམ་པ་ (du̲mba) short.

རྡུམ་པོ་ (du̲mbo) sm. རྡུམ་རྡུམ་.

རྡུལ་ (dü̲ü̲) 1. small particles, dust; va.—སློང་ to raise dust; vi.—ལང་ to have dust get stirred/ raised up. 2. menstruation. 3. error.

རྡུལ་འཇིབ་འཕྲུལ་ཆས་ (dü̲ü̲jib trǖǖjεὲ) vacuum cleaner.

རྡུལ་དུ་རློག (dü̲ü̲du lɔ̄ɔ̀) va. to reduce to dust, to destroy, to annihilate, to crush.

རྡུལ་སྤྲིན་ (dü̲ü̲drin) dust cloud.

རྡུལ་སྤྲུགས་ (dü̲ü̲ drūù) sm. རྡབ་རྡབ་གཏོང་.

དུལ་ཕྲ་མོ་ (düü drāmo) small particles.
དུལ་ཕྲ་རགས་ (düü drāraà) small particles.
དུལ་ཕྲ་རབ་ (düü trārəb) atom, nuclear.
དུལ་ཕྲ་རབ་ཀྱི་ནུས་ཤུགས་ (düü trārəbgi nüüshug) atomic/ nuclear energy.
དུལ་ཕྲ་རབ་ཀྱི་མཚོན་ཆ་ (düü trārəbgi tsōnja) atomic/ nuclear weapon.
དུལ་ཕྲ་རབ་སྦུང་ན་རི་བོ་ (düü trārəb būŋna riwo) sm. ཐིག་པ་བསགས་པའི་རྒྱ་མཚོ་.
དུལ་ཕྲན་ (düüdrɛn) minute particle, an atom.
དུལ་ཕྲན་གོ་མཚོན་ (düüdrɛn kodzön) sm. དུལ་ཕྲ་རབ་ཀྱི་མཚོན་ཆ་.
དུལ་ཕྲན་གྱི་སྙིང་ (düüdrɛngi ñīŋ) atomic kernel/ nucleus.
དུལ་ཕྲན་འགས་མདེལ་ (düüdrɛn gɛ̀ɛdel) sm. དུལ་ཕྲན་འབར་མདེལ་.
དུལ་ཕྲན་དུས་རབས་ (düüdrɛn tüürəb) atomic age.
དུལ་ཕྲན་དོ་དམ་ལས་དོན་ཁང་ (düüdrɛn todam lɛ̀ɛdöngaŋ) Nuclear Regulatory Commission (in the U.S.A.).
དུལ་ཕྲན་མདེལ་ (düüdrɛn del) sm. དུལ་ཕྲན་འབར་མདེལ་.
དུལ་ཕྲན་ནུས་པ་ (düüdrɛn nüübə) sm. དུལ་ཕྲན་ནུས་ཤུགས་.
དུལ་ཕྲན་ནུས་པའི་གློག་འདོན་ས་ཚིགས་ (düüdrɛn nüübɛ lōgdön sādzii) nuclear power generating station.
དུལ་ཕྲན་ནུས་ཤུགས་ (düüdrɛn nüüshug) atomic/ nuclear energy.
དུལ་ཕྲན་ཕྲ་མོ་ (düüdrɛn drāmo) particles that cannot be seen with the naked eye; microbes.
དུལ་ཕྲན་ཕྱིར་འཕྲོའི་ཕུང་ (düüdrɛn cīrdrö pūŋ) atomic reactor.
དུལ་ཕྲན་འབར་མདེལ་ (düüdrɛn bardɛɛ̀) atom bomb.
དུལ་ཕྲན་མཚོན་ཆ་ (düüdrɛn tsōnja) atomic/ nuclear weapons.
དུལ་ཕྲན་མཚོན་ཆ་སྐྱེལ་འདྲེན་བྱེད་པའི་མཁའ་དམག་དཔུང་སྡེ་ (düüdrɛn tsōnja gyēndren cēbɛ kāmaà būŋde) Strategic Air Command (in the U.S.A.).
དུལ་འཕྱགས་ (düü cāà) va. to sweep up dust.
དུལ་ཕྱབ་ (düü cəb) sm. དུལ་འཕྱགས་.
དུལ་བྲལ་ (düüdrɛɛ) 1. clean, without dust. 2. Buddha. 3. nirvana, enlightenment.
དུལ་བྲལ་དྲི་མེད་ (düütrɛɛ trimeè) sm. དུལ་བྲལ་.
དུལ་ཙམ་ (düüdzam) a very small amount, as much as a minute particle.
དུལ་ཙམ་མེད་པ་ (düüdzam meèba) not even the least/ slightest amount.
དུལ་ཚུབ་འཕྱུར་ (düüdzub cūr) vi. dust rising after a vehicle passes on a dusty road.
དུལ་ཚོན་ (düüdzön) colored sand used in making mandalas.
དུལ་ཚོན་གྱི་དཀྱིལ་འཁོར་ (düüdzön gyīŋgɔɔ) sand mandala.
དུལ་མཚོན་ (düüdzön) abbr. of དུལ་ཕྲན་མཚོན་ཆ་.
དུལ་འཚུབ་ (düüdzub) sm. དུལ་ལང་.
དུལ་རྫས་ (düüdzɛɛ̀) sm. དུལ་ཕྲན་.
དུལ་ཞུན་བཀོལ་ (düüshün gōō) va. to inflict or cause hardship/ turmoil.
དུལ་ལིང་ལིང་ (düü liŋliŋ) sm. དུལ་ལོང་ལོང་.
དུལ་ལོང་ལོང་ (düü loŋloŋ) dusty, dust rising.
དེ་འགག (dengaà) a tumor in the bladder.
དེག: p. བརྡེགས་; f. བརྡེག; imp. དེགས་ (deg) va. to hit, to strike, to beat ¶ མི་དེ་ལ་མཚོན་གྱིས་དེགས་པ་རེད་ That person was struck with a weapon.
དེག་གསོད་ (degsöö) beating to death; va.—བྱེད་.
དེག་ཆ་མཁན་ (deg cañɛn) blacksmith.
དེག་འཆའ་ (deg cā) 1. vi. to totter, to stagger. 2. vi. to slip. 3. to fall forward.
དེག་འཆོས་ (deg cöö) sm. དེག་འཆའ་.
དེག་འཛོག (degdzɔɔ̀) sm. དེང་འཛོག.
དེགས་ (deg) imp. of དེག.
དེབ་: p. བརྡབས་; f. བརྡབ་; imp. དོབས་ or དེབས་ (deb) va. to beat against, to bang/ hit against, to collide with ¶ ཁང་གདན་འདི་རྩིག་པར་བརྡབས་པ་རེད་ He beat the doormat against the wall. ¶ ས་ནས་ཡར་ལང་དུས་ལྕོག་ཙེར་མགོ་བརྡབས་པ་རེད་ As he was getting up from the floor he banged his head against the table. 2. va. to clap/ applaud ¶ ལག་པ་དེབ་ཀྱི་འདུག They are applauding.
དེབ་དེབ་ (debdeb) dusting by flapping (e.g., blanket, sheets, etc).
དེབ་གནོན་ལས་ཚན་ (debnön lɛ̀ɛdzɛn) stamping/ punching workshop.
དེབས་ (deb) imp. of དེབ་.
དེའུ་ (diwu) 1. pebble, small stone. 2. traditional system of Tibetan calculation using small stones and other objects; va.—གཏོང་. 3. gallstone.
དེའུ་བཅུད་ལེན་ (diwu jüülen) a Tibetan ascetic practice whereby a practitioner can subsist through chewing stones that have been blessed with tantric mantras.
དེའུ་ཆང་སྦྲན་པ་ (diwu cāŋdrɛnma) a stone which has been blessed with mantras that is used for making ཆང་ when it is not fermenting quickly enough.
དེའུ་འབུར་དོན་ (diwu burdön) odd, outlandish, strange.
དེའུ་ཚུར་འགྲིལ་ (diwu tsūr dril) shung. this side (of the mountain) ¶ ས་མཚམས་སྐོར་རེ་དེའུ་ཚུར་འགྲིལ་གྱི་ཤར་ཕྱོགས་ནས་ཐད་དྲངས་ Regarding the border, it runs from the east part of this side of the mountain.
དེའུ་ཞོ་སྦྲན་པ་ (diwu shodrɛnma) a stone which has been blessed with mantras that is used for making yogurt when it is not fermenting quickly enough.
དེའུ་གསུམ་དོར་ (diwu sūm dor) an ancient way of divorcing (throwing three stones).
དེལ་ (del) sm. དེའུ་.
དེལ་དཀར་ (delgar) white pebbles/ stones.
དེལ་ཁྲ་ (deltra) exam sheet for a test on the traditional Tibetan system of arithmetic calculation.
དེལ་རྒྱུགས་ (delgyuù) test on the traditional Tibetan system of arithmetic calculation.
དེལ་མདའ་ (delda) stone used in a sling shot.
དེལ་བུ་ (delbu) small pebbles, stones.
དེལ་རྩིས་ (deldzii) the old method of Tibetan arithmetic calculation (using small stones and sticks).
དེལ་གཞོང་ (delshoŋ) container in which Tibetan arithmetic calculation is done.
རྡོ་ (do) stone, rock.
རྡོ་ཀ་མ་རུ་ (do gāmaru) marble ¶ རྡོ་ཀ་མ་རུའི་གྲུབ་རྫས་བཟོ་གྲྭ Marble products factory.
རྡོ་ཀ་མ་རུ་པ་ (do gāmaruba) sm. རྡོ་ཀ་མ་རུ་.
རྡོ་ཤུ་ཁ་ (doga shūgə) touchstone.
རྡོ་དཀར་གོང་ (do gārgoŋ) whitestone, cobblestone.
རྡོ་སྐྱག (dogyaà) stairs, steps.
རྡོ་བསྐྱག (dobgyaà) sm. རྡོ་སྐྱག.
རྡོ་རྐོ་ (do gō) va. to carve stone.
རྡོ་སྦྲན་ (dodrɛn) gallstone.
རྡོ་སྐས་ (dogɛɛ̀) sm. རྡོ་སྐྱག.
རྡོ་སྐུ་ (dogu) stone statue.
རྡོ་སྐྱེས་ (dogyeè) bitumen.
རྡོ་བརྐོས་ (dogöö) 1. stone carving/ engraving. 2. p. of རྡོ་རྐོ་.
རྡོ་བརྐོ་ར་བ་ (dogo rawa) stone pit/ quarry.
རྡོ་བརྐོས་པ་ (dogööba) person who carves stones.
རྡོ་བརྐོས་གཟུགས་བརྙན་ (dogöö sugñɛn) statue carved from stone.
རྡོ་ཀླད་ (dolɛɛ̀) naphtha (used in Tibetan medicine).
རྡོ་ཁ་ (doga) the main point/ essence/ topic; va.—ལེན་ to ask sb. to tell the essence/ main point ¶ ངས་མི་དེ་ལ་ལས་ཀ་གསར་པ་དེ་བྱེད་ཡིན་མིན་རྡོ་ཁ་བླངས་པ་ཡིན་ I asked that person the main question about whether or not he will do the new work.
རྡོ་ཁ་བྲིས་ (do kādrɛɛ̀) a hard person with a smiling countenance, sb. who is outwardly friendly but inwardly cruel.

རྡོ་ཁང་ (dogaŋ) stone house.

རྡོ་ཁབ་ལེན་ (do kāblen) magnet.

རྡོ་ཁབ་ལེན་གྱི་ནུས་པ་ (do kāblengi nüübə) magnetic force.

རྡོ་ཁབ་ལེན་གྱི་ནུས་ཤུགས་ཁྱབ་ཁོངས་ (do kāblengi nüüshug kyābgoŋ) magnet field.

རྡོ་ཁུང་ (dokuŋ) sm. བྲག་ཕུག.

རྡོ་ཁེབས་ (dokeb) stone lid/ cover.

རྡོ་ཁོག (dokɔɔ̀) stone pottery, stoneware.

རྡོ་ཁྲང་ཧྲེ་ (do trāŋhre) feldspan.

རྡོ་མཁན་ (doñɛn) stone cutter/ mason.

རྡོ་མཁར་ (dokar) stone castle.

རྡོ་མཁྲིས་ (dodrii) a type of mineral medicine.

རྡོ་འཁྱམས་ཕོག (dokyam pɔɔ̀) vi. to be accidentally hit by a falling stone.

རྡོ་གད་རྒྱག (dogɛɛ̀ gyaà) va. to pick/ sift out the stones from grain (before grinding or cooking).

རྡོ་གུ (dogu) small stones/ gravel.

རྡོ་འགྱོགས་ (dogyɔɔ̀) stones used in weight lifting competitions; va.—བྱེད་.

རྡོ་རྒོད (dogöö) hard stone.

རྡོ་རྒྱུས་ (dogyüü) actinolite (a substance used as an aphrodisiac).

རྡོ་རྒྱུས་པ་ (do gyüübə) asbestos.

རྡོ་རྒྱུས་བྱ་བལ་མ་ (dogyüü capɛɛma) sm. རྡོ་རྒྱུས་པ་.

རྡོ་སྒམ་ (dogam) box made of stone.

རྡོ་སྒྲོགས་ (do gyɔɔ̀) a strategy of warfare that involves rolling stones from a hill or mountain onto one's enemy.

རྡོ་སྒོང་ (dogoŋ) sm. རྡོ་རིལ་.

རྡོ་སྒོར་རྒྱག (dogɔɔ gyaà) va. to throw stones (as a competition).

རྡོ་སྔོན་པོའི་ལག་ཕྲེང་ (do ŋōmbö lagdreŋ) sapphire bead rosary.

རྡོ་གཅལ་ (dojɛɛ) stone floor/ pavement; va.—འདིང་ to lay a stone floor/ pavement.

རྡོ་ལྕོག (dojɔɔ̀) stone table.

རྡོ་ཆག་བཙན་སྒྲིག (docaà dzɛndrii) fixing sth. that is broken or has come apart [Lit. putting together broken stones].

རྡོ་ཆར་ (docar) sm. སེར་རྡོའི་ཆར་པ་.

རྡོ་ཆས་ (dojɛɛ̀) stone tools.

རྡོ་ཆས་ཀྱི་དུས་རབས་ (dojɛɛ̀gi tüürəb) sm. རྡོ་ཆས་སྤྱོད་པའི་དུས་རབས་.

རྡོ་ཆས་རྙིང་མའི་དུས་སྐབས་ (dojɛɛ̀ ñīŋmɛ tüügəb) sm. རྡོ་ཆས་སྤྱོད་པའི་དུས་རབས་རྙིང་པ་.

རྡོ་ཆས་སྤྱོད་པའི་དུས་རབས་ (dojɛɛ̀ jööbɛ tüürəb) stone age.

རྡོ་ཆས་སྤྱོད་པའི་དུས་རབས་རྙིང་པ་ (dojɛɛ̀ jööbɛ tüürəb ñīŋbə) old stone age, paleolithic.

རྡོ་ཆས་སྤྱོད་པའི་དུས་རབས་གསར་པ་ (dojɛɛ̀ jööbɛ tüürəb sārba) new stone age, neolithic.

རྡོ་ཆུ་ (docu) spring water.

རྡོ་ཆུང་ཆུང་ལྷག་པས་ཁྱེར་དོགས་མེད་ རི་ཆུང་ཆུང་པང་ལ་ཐེག་དོགས་མེད་ (do ccūŋjuŋ lhāgbɛ kyērdɔmeè ri cūŋjuŋ bāŋla tēgdɔmeè) no need to worry (about sth.) [Lit. there is no need to worry about tiny stones carried by the wind, there is no need to worry about a small mountain being lifted onto one's lap].

རྡོ་ཆོད་ (do cöö) sth. that can cut stone.

རྡོ་མཆོད་ (docöö) stone cairn.

རྡོ་ཛ་ (dosa) acacia catechu.

རྡོ་ཛེམ་ཙེ་ (do jemdze) sm. སོར་བཏད་.

རྡོ་རྗེ་ (dɔɔje) 1. vajra. 2. man's name.

རྡོ་རྗེ་སྐྱིལ་ཀྲུང་ (dɔɔje gyiidruŋ) a way of sitting cross-legged.

རྡོ་རྗེ་གླིང་ (dɔɔjeliŋ) Darjeeling.

རྡོ་རྗེ་རྒྱ་གྲམ་ (dɔɔje gyadram) crossed vajaras.

རྡོ་རྗེ་འཆང་ (dɔɔje cāŋ) Vajaradhara, vajra holder.

རྡོ་རྗེ་འཇིགས་བྱེད་ (dɔɔje jigjeè) Vajrabhairava (Yamantaka the wrathful manifestation of Manjushri).

རྡོ་རྗེ་ཐེག་པ་ (dɔɔje tēgba) vajarayana.

རྡོ་རྗེ་གདན་ (dɔɔjedɛn) Bodhgaya.

རྡོ་རྗེ་སྤུན་ (dɔɔje bün) abbr. of རྡོ་རྗེ་སྤུན་གྲོགས་.

རྡོ་རྗེ་སྤུན་གྲོགས་ (dɔɔje bündrɔɔ̀) individuals who have received initiation from the same root guru.

རྡོ་རྗེ་སྤུན་སྲིང་ (dɔɔje bünsiŋ) sm. རྡོ་རྗེ་སྤུན་གྲོགས་.

རྡོ་རྗེ་ཕ་ལམ་ (dɔɔje pālam) diamond.

རྡོ་རྗེ་ཕག་མོ་ (dɔɔje pāàmo) name of the highest female incarnation in Tibet.

རྡོ་རྗེ་ཕུར་པ་ (dɔɔje pūrbə) vajara dagger.

རྡོ་རྗེ་རྩེ་དགུ་པ་ (dɔɔje dzēgubə) vajara with nine heads.

རྡོ་རྗེ་རྩེ་ལྔ་པ་ (dɔɔje dzēŋaba) vajara with five heads.

རྡོ་རྗེ་རྩེ་གཅིག་པ་ (dɔɔje dzējigbə) vajara with one head.

རྡོ་རྗེ་གཞོན་ནུ་ (dɔɔje shōnnu) one of the meditation deities in the Nyigmapa tradition.

རྡོ་རྗེ་རིན་པོ་ཆེ་ (dɔɔje rimboce) diamond.

རྡོ་རྗེ་སེམས་པ་ (dɔɔje sēmba) Vajarasattva (a tantric diety).

རྡོ་རྗེ་སློབ་དཔོན་ (dɔɔje lōnbön) a lama who gives tantric initiations.

རྡོ་རྗེའི་དམ་ཚིག (dɔɔje tamtsig) a tantric vow.

རྡོ་རྗེའི་འདུག་སྟངས་ (dɔɔjee dugdaŋ) sm. རྡོ་རྗེ་སྐྱིལ་ཀྲུང་.

རྡོ་རྗེའི་སྨོན་ལམ་ (dɔɔjee mōnlam) tantric invocation/ prayer.

རྡོ་རྗེའི་ཚིག (dɔɔjee tsīg) tantric words.

རྡོ་སྙུག (doñug) sm. རྡོ་སྨྱུག.

རྡོ་ཏིང་ (dodiŋ) a stone bell used to summon/ call.

རྡོ་ཏེལ་ (dotel) a hammer used in masonry.

རྡོ་གཏུན་ (dodün) stone mortar.

རྡོ་རྟགས་ (dodaà) stones piled up as a boundary marker (usu. in agricultural fields).

རྡོ་སྟར་ (dodar) a stone axe.

རྡོ་སྟེགས་ (dodeg) a stone stand/ platform.

རྡོ་ཐ་ (doda) tobacco.

རྡོ་ཐག (dodaà) sm. རྡོ་ཐ་.

རྡོ་ཐབ་ (dodəb) stone stove.

རྡོ་ཐའི་བུལ་དོག (dodɛ büüdoò) nicotine.

རྡོ་ཐལ་ (dodɛɛ) 1. lime. 2. powder/ dust of rocks.

རྡོ་ཐལ་ཆུ་ (dodɛɛ cū) limewash.

རྡོ་ཐལ་རྡོ་ (dodɛɛ do) limestone.

རྡོ་ཐལ་བྲག་རྡོ་ (dodɛɛ tragdo) sm. རྡོ་ཐལ་རྡོ་.

རྡོ་ཐལ་རིགས་ལྔ་ (dodɛɛ rigŋa) five grayish colors.

རྡོ་ཐལ་སྲེག་ཐབ་ (dodɛɛ sēgdəb) lime kiln.

རྡོ་ཐེའུ་ (dotewu) 1. a small hammer used by stone masons. 2. stone seal.

རྡོ་ཐོ་ (dodo) 1. hammer used for breaking rocks. 2. pile of stones used as a marker.

རྡོ་ཐོག་ཆུ་བླུག (dodɔɔ cūluù) futility of advising sb. who won't listen [Lit. pouring water on stone].

རྡོ་ཐོག་ཕུར་བུ་ (dodɔɔ pūrbu) sm. རྡོ་ཐོག་ཆུ་བླུག.

རྡོ་དམ་ (dodam) sm. རྡོ་འདམ་.

རྡོ་དུགས་ (dodug) a traditional Tibetan medical treatment involving the application of hot stones.

རྡོ་དོན་དུ་ (dō döndu) the main meaning/ point/ result/ conclusion ། རྡོ་དོན་དུ་ཞོད་རྒྱུར་ང་ཚོས་ཚན་རིག་ཡར་རྒྱས་གཏོང་དགོས་ If we say the main point, it is that we have to improve science.

རྡོ་དྲེག་ཚོད་ལྟ་ཤོག་བུ་ (dodreg tsööda shōgbu) litmus paper.

རྡོ་དྲིལ་ (dodrii) abbr. of རྡོ་རྗེ་ and དྲིལ་བུ་.

རྡོ་འདམ་ (dodam) cement.

རྡོ་རྡོག (dōdɔɔ̀) stone, rock.

རྡོ་སྣག (donaà) graphite, slate ། རྡོ་སྣག་བཟོ་གྲྭ Graphite factory.

རྡོ་སྣོད་ (donöö) stone vessel.

རྡོ་སྣུམ་ (donum) 1. oil, petroleum, gasoline. 2. a trial involving having the accused pick a stone from hot oil to determine guilt.

རྡོ་སྣུམ་ཀུང་སི་ (donum gūŋsi) oil/ petroleum company.

རྡོ་སྣུམ་འཁེངས་པའི་འབར་མདེལ་ (donum kēŋbɛ bandee) napalm bomb.

རྡོ་སྣུམ་གྱི་བྲོན་པ་ (donum gi trōmba) oil well.

རྡོ་སྣུམ་གྱི་བྲོན་འདེགས་གྲུ་གཟིངས་ (donumgi trōnbig trudzin) oil drilling ship.

རྡོ་སྣུམ་གྱི་སྙིགས་མ་ (donumgi ñīgmə) pitch.

རྡོ་སྣུམ་ཚགས་རིམ་ (donum cəgrim) oil layer/ zone/ strata.

རྡོ་སྣུམ་རྗེན་པ་ (donum jemba) crude oil.

རྡོ་སྣུམ་སྙིགས་རོ་ (donum ñīgmə) sm. སྣུམ་སྙིགས་.

རྡོ་སྣུམ་གཏེར་ཁ་ (donum dērga) oil field.

རྡོ་སྣུམ་དོ་དམ་ཅུས་ (donum dodam jū) bureau of petroleum management/ administration.

རྡོ་སྣུམ་དྭངས་སྙིགས་དབྱེ་བའི་བཟོ་གྲྭ་ (donum taŋñig yēwɛ sodra) oil refinery.

རྡོ་སྣུམ་དྭངས་བྱེད་སྒྲིག་ཆས་ (donum taŋjeè drigjɛɛ̀) oil refining equipment.

རྡོ་སྣུམ་འདོན་ཁུལ་ (donum döngüü) oil producing area/ region.

རྡོ་སྣུམ་ཕྱིར་འཚོང་རྒྱལ་ཁབ་ (donum cīrdzoŋ gyɛɛgəb) oil exporting country.

རྡོ་སྣུམ་ཕྱིར་འཚོང་བྱེད་མཁན་ཡུལ་ཁག་གི་མཐུན་ཚོགས་ (donum cīrdzoŋ ceèñɛn yüügaàgi tūndzɔɔ̀) OPEC (Organization of Petroleum Exporting Countries).

རྡོ་སྣུམ་འཕྲུལ་འཁོར་ (donum trūūgɔɔ) gasoline motor/ engine.

རྡོ་སྣུམ་འཕྲུལ་ཆས་ (donum trūūjɛɛ̀) petroleum machinery.

རྡོ་སྣུམ་འབིགས་འདོན་སྒྲིག་ཆས་ (donum bigdön drigjɛɛ̀) oil drilling equipment.

རྡོ་སྣུམ་བཙོ་སྦྱང་ (donum dzōjaŋ) oil refining; va.—བྱེད་.

རྡོ་སྣུམ་རྫས་འགྱུར་བཟོ་ལས་ (donum dzɛɛ̀gyur solɛɛ̀) petrochemical works.

རྡོ་སྣུམ་རྫས་བཟོ་བཟོ་གྲྭ་ (donum dzɛɛ̀so sodra) petrochemical works, petroleum productions factory.

རྡོ་སྣུམ་བཞུ་འབྱེད་ (donum shujeè) sm. རྡོ་སྣུམ་བཙོ་སྦྱང་.

རྡོ་སྣུམ་བཟོ་གྲྭ་ (donum sodra) oil refinery.

རྡོ་སྣུམ་བཟོས་རྫས་ (donum sööddzɛɛ̀) petroleum products.

རྡོ་སྣུམ་བཟོ་ལས་ (donum solɛɛ̀) oil/ petroleum industry ¶ རྡོ་སྣུམ་བཟོ་ལས་པུའུ་ Ministry of Petroleum Industy.

རྡོ་སྣུམ་རླངས་པ་ (donum lāŋba) petroleum gas, natural gas.

རྡོ་སྣུམ་ས་ཚིགས་ (donum sədzii) petroleum station.

རྡོ་སྣུམ་གསོར་ཁྲོན་ (donum sɔ̄rdrön) oil drilling well.

རྡོ་པང་ (dobaŋ) shung. lifting stones.

རྡོ་པར་ (dobar) lithograph, stone plate printing, lithography; va.—རྒྱག.

རྡོ་པིར་ (dobir) lead pencil.

རྡོ་སྤུང་ (dobuŋ) pile of stones.

རྡོ་ཕ་བོང་ (do pāboŋ) huge rock/ boulder.

རྡོ་ཕུང་ (dobuŋ) pile of stones.

རྡོ་ཕུད་ (dobüü) the first stone that is offered to gods before building a temple, monastery, etc.

རྡོ་ཕུར་ (dobur) stone peg/ stake.

རྡོ་ཕྱུར་ར་ (do cūrrə) hardened/ dried cheese.

རྡོ་ཕྱེ་ (doce) pulverized stone.

རྡོ་ཕྲང་ (dodraŋ) a narrow, rocky path over a ravine.

རྡོ་བ་ (dowa) sm. རྡོ་.

རྡོ་བལ་ (dopɛɛ) asbestos ¶ རྡོ་བལ་གྲུབ་རྫས་བཟོ་གྲྭ Asbestos products factory.

རྡོ་བྱི་རིལ་ (do ciri) any type of hard sourball.

རྡོ་བྱུ་རུ་ (do curru) fake coral, poor quality coral.

རྡོ་བྲག (dodraà) boulder.

རྡོ་འབུམ་ (dobum) a hundred thousand stones with carved mantras.

རྡོ་སྤྱིན་སྦྱར་ (dō jīn jar) putting things together that don't belong/ fit together, putting together incompatibles [Lit. sticking stones together with glue].

རྡོ་སྦྲུལ་ (dōdrüü) serpentine design in stone carving.

རྡོ་མ་ན་ཧུ་ (doma nahu) agate.

རྡོ་སྨྱུག (doñuù) lead pencil.

རྡོ་རྩི་ (dodzi) sm. རྡོ་ཞོ་.

རྡོ་རྩིག (dodzig) stone wall; va.—རྒྱག to erect/ build a stone wall.

རྡོ་ཅོག (dojoò) sm. རྡོ་.

རྡོ་ཚད་ (dodzɛɛ̀) a unit in the traditional Tibetan currency equal to 50 སྐར་.

རྡོ་ཚིག (dodzii) shung. the main point, the crux of the matter ¶ གན་དོན་རྡོ་ཚིག་ཏུ་ The main point of the contract is.

རྡོ་ཚིག་ཟ་བརྣན་ (dodzii dzānɛn) shung. holding onto the crux of the matter. ¶

རྡོ་ཚིལ་ (dodzii) vaseline.

རྡོ་ཚོགས་ (dodzɔɔ̀) sm. རྡོ་ཚར་.

རྡོ་རྫུས་མ་ (do dzüümə) imitation stone.

རྡོ་ཞིབ་ (doshib) powered stone.

རྡོ་ཞུན་ (doshün) magma.

རྡོ་ཞོ་ (dōsho) limestone.

རྡོ་ཞོ་ཇུ་ (doshoju) lime, limewash.

རྡོ་ཞྭ་ (dōsha) "stone hat" (an instrument used with the punishment of plucking out the eyeballs in tt.).

རྡོ་གཞུ་ (do shu) va. to hit with a stone, to throw a stone at sb. or sth.

རྡོ་གཞོང་ (doshoŋ) stone trough, stone basin.

རྡོ་ཟན་ (dosɛn) sm. རྡོ་སྤལ་.

རྡོ་ཟམ་ (dosam) stone bridge.

རྡོ་གཟོང་ (dosoŋ) chisel (for use with stone).

རྡོ་བཟོ་ (doso) 1. masonry; va.—བྱེད་ to work at stone masonry. 2. sm. རྡོ་བཟོ་བ་.

རྡོ་བཟོ་བ་ (dosowa) stone mason.

རྡོ་ཡིང་ཧྲི་ (doyiŋhri) tib.ch. quartz.

རྡོ་གཡམ་ (doyam) slate, shale, slabstone, flagstone.

རྡོ་གཡམ་གྱི་སྣུམ་ (doyamgi nūm) shale oil.

རྡོ་གཡམ་གཏེར་ཁ་ (doyam dērga) shale/ slate mine.

རྡོ་རིང་ (doriŋ) 1. stone pillar, stele. 2. name of a Tibetan aristocratic family.

རྡོ་རིང་ནང་མ་ (doriŋ naŋma) name of the stone pillar in front of the Potala Palace (closer to the Potala Palace than རྡོ་རིང་ཕྱི་མ་).

རྡོ་རིང་ཕྱི་མ་ (doriŋ cīmə) name of a stone pillar in front of the Potala palace (further from the Potala Palace than རྡོ་རིང་ནང་མ་).

རྡོ་རིང་ཡི་གེ་ (doriŋ yigi) inscription carved on stone pillar.

རྡོ་རིལ་ (dorii) a round stone.

རྡོ་རིས་ (dirii) inscription/ carving on a stone.

རྡོ་རུབ་རྒྱག (dorub gyaà) shung. to stone sb. or sth. (by a group).

རྡོ་རོ་ (doro) stone rubble/ trash.

རྡོ་ལ་ (dola) paraffin wax.

རྡོ་ལ་སྤྱིན་སྦྱར་ (dola jīnjar) putting two things together that are totally impossible to join [Lit. sticking stones together with glue].

རྡོ་ལ་རི་མོ་བརྐོས་པ་ (dola rimə gööba) steady, unchangeable, reliable, firm [Lit. a design carved on a stone].

རྡོ་ལག་བཤུགས་ (dolaà shuù) passing sth. from one person to another, doing work like an assembly line [Lit. pass a stone from hand-to-hand].

རྡོ་ལེབ་ (doleb) stone slab, flat stone, flagstone.

རྡོ་ལས་ (dolɛɛ̀) stone work, masonry; va.—བྱེད.

རྡོ་ཤེལ་ (dōshee) crystal.

རྡོ་ཤེལ་སྨུག་པོ་ (doshee mūgbə) smoky quartz.

རྡོ་ཤོ་ (dōsho) 1. a small cubed stone. 2. a stone used in fortune-telling.

རྡོ་གཤག (dōshaà) breaking stones.

རྡོ་གཤག་བཟོ་པ་ (doshaà sōba) a person who breaks/ cuts stones.

རྡོ་གཤོལ་ (doshöö) stone plow.

རྡོ་སམ་ (dosam) slate.

རྡོ་སོལ་ (dosöö) coal.

རྡོ་སོལ་ཀོ་ཁུང་ (dosöö gōguŋ) coal pit.

རྡོ་སོལ་མཁྲེགས་པོ་ (dosöö trēgbo) hard/ anthracite coal.

རྡོ་སོལ་འཁྲུད་འདེམས་སྒྲིག་ཆས་ (dosöö trūndem drigjɛɛ̀) coal washing equipment.

རྡོ་སོལ་གི་སྣུམ་ (dosöögi nūm) coal oil.

རྡོ་སོལ་རོ་ཏོ་ (dosöö rodo) slag.

རྡོ་སོལ་སྔོག་འདོན་ (dosöö ŋɔ̄gdön) coal mining; va.—བྱེད་ to coal mine.

རྡོ་སོལ་སྔོག་འདོན་འཕྲུལ་འཁོར་ (dosöö ŋɔ̄gdön trũ̄ügɔɔ) coal mining machine/ equipment.

རྡོ་སོལ་ཆགས་རིམ་ (dosöö cāgrim) coal seam.

རྡོ་སོལ་གཏེར་ཁ་ (dosöö dērga) coal mine.

རྡོ་སོལ་གཏེར་ཁུལ་ (dosöö dērgüü) coalfield.

རྡོ་སོལ་གཏེར་ལས་ (dosöö dērlɛ̀ɛ̀) coal mining industry.

རྡོ་སོལ་དུས་རབས་ (dosöö tüürəb) the carboniferous period.

རྡོ་སོལ་ཚིག་མ་ (dosöö tsīgmə) coke; va.—བཟོ་ to make coke.

རྡོ་སོལ་ཚིག་མ་སྲེག་ཐབ་ (dosöö tsīgmə sēgtəb) coke oven.

རྡོ་སོལ་འཛད་ཚད་ (dosöö dzɛ̀ɛ̀dzɛɛ̀) coal consumption.

རྡོ་སོལ་ཡོད་ས་ (dosöö yȍosa) coal field.

རྡོ་སོལ་ཞིབ་བཟོ་འཕྲུལ་འཁོར་ (dosöö shibso trũ̄ügɔɔ) coal granulating/ pulverizing machinery.

རྡོ་སོལ་ཞན་པ་ (dosöö shünbə) low grade coal.

རྡོ་སོལ་ཟད་ཚད་ (dosöö sɛ̀ɛ̀dzɛɛ̀) coal consumption.

རྡོ་སོལ་སེར་ནག (dosöö sērnaà) brown coal.

རྡོ་སོལ་སྲེག་ཐབ་ (dosöö sēgtəb) coke oven.

རྡོ་སོལ་བསྲེགས་མ་ (dosöö sēgma) coke.

རྡོ་སོལ་ས་རིམ་ (dosöö sārim) coal vein/ layer.

རྡོ་སོལ་བསྲེགས་མ་བཟོ་གྲྭ་ (dosöö sēgma sodra) coking factory.

རྡོ་གསེག (doseg) gravel.

རྡོ་གསོབ་གསོབ་ (dō sōbsoò) soft stone.

རྡོ་ཧྲུག (dohruù) pebble, small rocks, gravel.

རྡོ་ཧྲུབ་ (dohrub) sm. རྡོ་ཧྲུག.

རྡོ་ཧྲོག (dohrog) small rocks/ pebbles, gravel.

རྡོ་ལྷང་ཚེར་ (do lhāŋdzer) sm. ལྷང་ཚེར་.

རྡོག (dɔ̀ɔ) single, individual piece ། འབྲས་རྡོག་ཁ་ཤས་ས་ལ་ལྷུང་བ་རེད་ A few grains of rice fell to the ground.

རྡོག་བརྒྱག་ཐེབས་ (dɔ̀ɔgyaà tēb) vi. to be kicked (accidentally).

རྡོག་བརྒྱག་གཞུ་ (dɔggyaà shu) va. to kick.

རྡོག་བཀྲོལ་ (dɔgdröö) p. of རྡོག་འགྲོལ་.

རྡོག་སྐོར་དབྱེ་འབྱེད་ (dɔggɔɔ yējeè) shung. investigating and distinguishing/ differentiating on the spot ། མདའ་རྫོང་ནས་གཞུང་རྒྱུག་གི་ས་ཞིང་རྡོག་སྐོར་དབྱེ་འབྱེད་བསྐྱངས་ཏེ་ The Depon and the Dzongpon investigated the fields of the government taxpayers.

རྡོག་ཁྲེས་ (dɔgdreè) load, pack, burden (mental or physical); va.—འཁུར་; —འཁྱེར་ to carry a burden; va.—དབོར་ to transport a load/ pack; va.—སྐྱུར་ to load a pack on sth. ། ཁོ་ལ་རྟ་དྲེལ་མེད་ཙང་རྡོག་ཁྲེས་ཁུར་ནས་འགྲོ་གི་འདུག Because (he) did not have horses and mules, he was carrying the load (himself). ། ཁོང་ལ་བུ་ལོན་ཆེན་པོ་ཡོད་ཙང་བསམ་བློའི་རྡོག་ཁྲེས་ཆེན་པོ་འཁུར་ཡོད་པ་རེད་ Because he has many debts, he carries a heavy mental burden. ། ཀུ་ལིའི་སྒལ་པར་རྡོག་ཁྲེས་སྐྱུར་ To put a load on the back of a coolie.

རྡོག་ཁྲེས་སྐྱུར་ (dɔgdreè gūr) 1. va. to load a pack/ load (on person) ། ཀུ་ལིའི་སྒལ་པར་རྡོག་ཁྲེས་སྐྱུར་ To put a load on the back of a coolie. 2. va. to be extremely infatuated ། མཛེས་མ་དེས་ང་ལ་རྡོག་ཁྲེས་བསྐྱུར་བྱུང་ This beautiful woman caused me to be infatuated with her. 3. va. to make sb. pregnant ། བུ་མོ་དེ་ལ་ཁོས་རྡོག་ཁྲེས་བསྐྱུར་བཞག He made that girl pregnant. 4. va. to cause sb. to be lose/ be in debt ། དེ་རིང་མ་ཙང་རྒྱག་སྐབས་ཁོ་ལ་རྡོག་ཁྲེས་ཡག་ཐག་ཆོད་བསྐྱུར་ཡོད་ When playing mahjong today I caused him to be in great debt (to me).

རྡོག་ཁྲེས་སྐྱུར་བཅོལ་ཁྲུའུ་ (dɔgdreè gūrjöö trū) tib.ch. baggage shipping counter.

རྡོག་ཁྲེས་ཁང་ (dɔgdreè kāŋ) sm. རྡོག་ཁྲེས་འཇོག་ས་.

རྡོག་ཁྲེས་འཇོག་ས་ (dɔgdreè jɔ̀ɔsa) a room to leave parcels/ baggage/ packages, left luggage room.

རྡོག་འགྲིལ་ (dɔgdrii) in brief, in short, in summary ། སྐད་ཆ་རྡོག་འགྲིལ་ནས་བཤད་ན་ If I speak briefly.

རྡོག་འགྲིལ་པོ་ (dɔg driibu) very brief, short but to the point, a summary ། ཁོང་གིས་ཚོགས་འདུའི་ཐོག་སྐད་ཆ་རྡོག་འགྲིལ་པོ་ཞིག་བཤད་སོང་ He spoke briefly and to the point at the meeting.

རྡོག་འགྲོལ་ (dɔg dröö) va. to clarify/ elucidate/ make clear ། ང་ཚོས་གནད་དོན་དེའི་སྐོར་འགོ་ཁྲིད་རང་གི་སར་རྡོག་བཀྲོལ་དགོས་ We need to clarify this matter in front of the leaders (themselves).

རྡོག་རྒྱག (dɔ̀gyaà) kicking; va.—གཞུ་ to kick.

རྡོག་སྒྲ་ (dɔgdraà) sm. ཀང་སྒྲ་.

རྡོག་ལྕག (dɔ̀jaà) sm. རྡོག་རྒྱག.

རྡོག་ཆས་ (dɔgjɛ̀ɛ) materials used for packing; va.—རྒྱག to pack in preparation for going/ leaving/ departing.

རྡོག་ཏུ་ཐོན་ (dɔgdu tȭn) outstanding, prominent ། བུ་མོ་དེ་བུ་མོ་མང་པོའི་དཀྱིལ་ནས་རྡོག་ཏུ་ཐོན་འདུག That girl is outstanding among many girls.

རྡོག་ཐོ་ (dɔgto) sm. རྡོག་རྒྱག.

རྡོག་ཐོན་ (dɔgdön) departing/ leaving a place; va.—བྱེད་ to leave/ depart from a place ། ཚེས་ 15 ཉིན་ལྷ་ས་ནས་རྡོག་ཐོན་བྱས་མེས་རྒྱལ་ནང་ཁུལ་དུ་ལྟ་སྐོར་བྱས་པ་ཡིན་ On the 15th (we) left Lhasa to tour in the motherland.

རྡོག་མཐིལ་ (dɔgdii) heel of a shoe/ boot.

རྡོག་དྲིལ་ (dɔgdrii) a summary.

རྡོག་དྲིལ་པོ་ (dɔg driibu) sm. རྡོག་འགྲིལ་པོ་.

རྡོག་དྲིས་ (dɔgdrii) asking a question in a straightforward/ to the point manner.

རྡོག་འདྲི་ (dɔgdri) shung. tenaciously/ persistently questioning.

རྡོག་དེག (dɔgdreè) sm. རྡོག་རྒྱག.

རྡོག་རྡོ་ (dɔgdo) sm. རྡོག་རྒྱག.

རྡོག་རྡོག (dɔgdɔg) 1. lump of sth. 2. straightforward, to the point (for statements/ speech).

རྡོག་སྣ་ (dɔgna) the tip/ toe of a shoe.

རྡོག་པ་ (dɔgba) 1. sole of a shoe; va.—རྒྱག to sole shoes. 2. a single/ individual piece.

རྡོག་པ་མཉམ་གཤིབ་ (dɔgba ñāmshib) shung. (to send sb.) together ། ཕྱོགས་ཡ་ཟུང་རྣམ་རྡོག་པ་མཉམ་གཤིབ་ཀྱི་རྫོང་བདུད་བྱ་རྒྱུར་ (We) are going to send both parties together.

རྡོག་པ་འདྲེད་ (dɔgba dreè) vi. to slip and fall.

རྡོག་པོ་ (dɔgbo) single, individual ། ལུང་པ་འདིའི་ནང་མི་དཀར་པོ་རྡོག་པོ་གཅིག་མེད་པ་རེད་ There is not a single white man in this place.

རྡོག་ཕྱིས་ (dɔgcii) cloth used to clean a floor by putting it under one's feet and sliding it back and forth over the floor; va.—རྒྱག.

རྡོག་འཕུལ་ (dɔgbüü) sm. རྡོག་རྒྱག.

རྡོག་མ་ (dɔgma) 1. a small stone used in Tibetan accounting that is equivalent to one unit. 2. a piece of sth.

རྡོག་སྙུག (dɔgñug) stalagmite.

རྡོག་སྙུ་གུ་ (dɔ̀ ñugu) sm. རྡོག་སྙུག.

རྡོག་རྩ་ (dɔgdza) the main idea/ point, the essence; va.—སྒྲིལ་ to unite together ། ཁོ་ཚོའི་སྐད་ཆའི་རྡོག་རྩ་དེ་དམག་མི་ལམ་སེང་ཕྱིར་འཐེན་བྱེད་དགོས་ཟེར་བ་དེ་རེད་ The main point of their talk is that the army must be withdrawn at once. ། མི་དམངས་ཚོས་རྡོག་རྩ་བསྒྲིལ་ནས་སྲིད་གཞུང་ལ་ངོ་རྒོལ་བྱས་པ་རེད་ The people united and opposed the government.

རྡོག་རྩ་གཅིག་སྒྲིལ་ (dɔgdza jīgdrii) united, consolidated, having solidarity ། གནད་དོན་དེའི་ཐད་ལ་ང་ཚོ་ཚང་མ་རྡོག་རྩ་གཅིག་སྒྲིལ་ཡིན་ On that issue we are all united.

རྡོག་རྩ་སྦུག་དཀྲོལ་ (dɔgdza bugdröö) seeking a decision/ permission from a higher authority.

རྡོག་ཙམ་ (dɔgdzam) sm. དོག་ཙམ་.

རྡོག་བརྩོས་ (dɔgdzöö) boiling chunks of meat; va.—རྒྱག.

རྡོག་ཚིག (dɔgdzii) sm. རྡོག་རྩ་.

རྡོག་རྫིས་ (dɔgdzii) sm. རྡོག་བརྫིས་.

རྡོག་བརྫིས་ (dɔgdzii) trampling/ stepping on/

stamping on; va.—གཏོང་ ། ཕྲུ་གུ་དེས་འབུ་རྡོག་བརྫིས་བཏང་ནས་བསད་སོང་ The child stepped on the bug and killed it.

རྡོག་གཟུགས་སྡོང་ཀང་ (dɔgsug dɔŋgaŋ) stem tuber.

རྡོག་རོལ་ (dɔgröö) 1. disregarding, not paying attention to; va.—གཏོང་ ། ཁོ་ཚོས་གོང་རིམ་གྱི་བཀའ་རྡོག་རོལ་བཏང་བ་རེད་ They disregarded the order of the authorities. 2. trampling on sth.

རྡོག་རོལ་དུ་གཏོང་ (dɔgröödu dōŋ) sm. རྡོག་རོལ་ (གཏོང་).

རྡོག་ལ་སྦྲིལ་ (dɔ̄la drii) va. to unite.

རྡོག་ལམ་ (dɔglam) sm. རྡོག་རོལ་.

རྡོག་ཤད་ (dɔgshɛ̀ɛ) sm. རྡོག་རྒྱག.

རྡོབ་རྡོབ་ (dobdob) sm. རྡབ་རྡོབ་.

རྡོབས་ (dōb) imp. of རྡེབ་.

རྡོའི་ཐུབ་པ་ (dö tūbbə) stone icon/ statue of the Buddha.

རྡོའི་རྩ་རིས་ (dö dzərii) vein on a rock (which is hit to split the rock).

རྡོའི་གསེག་མ་ (dö sēgma) gravel.

རྡོར་ (dɔɔ) 1. imp. of རྡར་. 2. sm. རྡར་. 3. abbr. of རྡོ་རྗེ་.

རྡོར་གོང་ (dɔɔgoŋ) a type of upper garment that is put on statues.

རྡོར་གྱུར་བ་ (dɔɔ gyurwə) fossilized.

རྡོར་འགྱུར་ (dɔɔ gyur) vi. to be/ get fossilized.

རྡོར་གླིང་ (dɔrliŋ) abbr. Darjeeling.

རྡོར་དྲིལ་ (dɔr drii) abbr. of རྡོར་རྗེ་ and དྲིལ་བུ་.

རྡོལ་: p. and f. བརྡོལ་ (döö) vi. to burst open, to break out, to get punctured ། ཀང་སྣ་རིལ་གྱི་ནང་ལྷུགས་བརྡོལ་བཞག The inner tube of the bicycle got a puncture.

རྡོལ་ཆོས་ (dööjöö) vulgar or coarse manners/ behavior.

རྡོལ་གཏམ་ (döödam) rumor, idle talk, gossip.

རྡོལ་ཐབས་སྨྲ་ (döödəb mā) 1. va. to talk without thinking; to blab/ chatter. 2. va. to talk incoherently.

རྡོལ་པ་ཕུག (dööba pūū) va. to poke a hole in sth.

རྡོལ་བུག (dööbug) a punctured/ pierced hole.

རྡོས་ (döö) 1. size, measurement, dimension ། མི་དེའི་ལུས་རྡོས་ཆུང་ཆུང་རེད་འདུག That person's body is small in size. 2. vi. to come out/ forth, to rise up.

ལྡ་མ་ལྡེབས་ (dāma deb) on the slope/ side of a hill.

ལྡག: p. བལྡགས་; f. བལྡག; imp. ལྡོག (daà) 1. va. to lick. 2. va. to eat yogurt.

ལྡག་གུ་ (daggu) 1. paste. 2. beans, lentils.

ལྡག་རྒྱག (daà gyaà) va. to masturbate (males).

ལྡག་མཛུབ་ (dagdzub) the second finger.

ལྡང་ (daŋ) 1. vi. to occur, to come to be, to arise ། དགུན་ལྷགས་རྒྱུན་ཆད་མེད་པ་ལྡང་བའི་དགུན་དུས་ཀྱི་མཚན་མོ་ཞིག A winter evening when continuous snowy winds occurred. 2. vi. to be sufficient/ enough, to suffice ། སྒོར་མོ་བརྒྱ་ལྡང་གི་མི་འདུག One hundred dollars (yuan) is not enough. 3. p. of ལྡིང་.

ལྡང་ངེ་ལྡང་ངེ་ (dəŋŋi dəŋŋi) work that nobody is taking responsibility for/ care of, work that is being left undone ། ལས་བྱེད་པའི་གླ་ཕོགས་སྤར་རྒྱུ་དེ་ལྡང་ངེ་ལྡང་ངེ་བྱས་ནས་ཐག་གཅོད་མ་བྱས་པ་རེད་ As for raising the salary of officials, nobody took responsibility for it and it wasn't decided.

ལྡང་ངེས་ (daŋŋeè) p. of ལྡིང་ངེས་.

ལྡང་མ་ལྡང་ (daŋ madaŋ) whether sth. is enough or not, whether sth. suffices or not ། རས་འདིས་གོས་ཐུང་གཉིས་ལྡང་མ་ལྡང་ལྟ་དགོས་ (We) have to see whether or not this cloth is enough for two pairs of trousers.

ལྡང་ཤེད་ཆེན་པོ་ (daŋsheè cēmbo) durable.

ལྡངས་ (daŋ) sm. ལྡང་.

ལྡད་: p. and f. བལྡད་; imp. ལྡོད་ (dɛ̀ɛ) va. to chew, to ruminate.

ལྡད་རྒྱག (dɛ̀ɛ gyaà) sm. ལྡད་.

ལྡན་ (dɛn) having, possessing ། ཡོན་ཏན་ལྡན་པའི་མི་ A person having knowledge. ། འབྱོར་པ་དང་ལྡན་པ་ Having wealth.

ལྡན་ཁོག (dɛngɔ̀ɔ) an area that traditionally was part of Derge.

ལྡན་ལྕག (dɛnjaà) a blow on the cheek (usu. with a piece of bamboo); va.—གཞུ་ to strike on the cheek.

ལྡན་པ་ (dɛmba) 1. cheek. 2. having, possessing.

ལྡན་པའི་ངང་ནས་ (dɛmbɛ ŋaŋnɛ) in the manner of ། དགའ་སྤྲོ་ལྡན་པའི་ངང་ནས་ In a joyful manner.

ལྡན་པོ་ (dɛmbo) fitting, proper, suitable.

ལྡབ་ (dəb) 1. double ། ཐོན་སྐྱེད་ལྡབ་གཅིག་གིས་འཕར་བ་རེད་ Production increased by double. 2. times ། ཁོ་ཚོ་མི་གྲངས་ལྡབ་གསུམ་གྱིས་མང་གི་རེད་ They are three times as many as we are.

ལྡབ་: p. བལྡབས་; f. ལྡབ་; f. ལྡོབས་ (dəb) va. to repeat ། མི་དེས་སྐད་ཆ་ཡང་ཡང་བལྡབས་ནས་ཤོད་ཀྱི་འདུག That person is repeating what he said again and again.

ལྡབ་ལྡོབ་ (dəbdob) sm.* རྡབ་རྡོབ་.

ལྡབ་སྐྱོར་ (dəbgyɔɔ) repeating; va.—བྱེད་; —གཏོང་ to repeat, to do/ say again ། དགེ་རྒན་དེས་སློབ་ཚན་ཁྲིད་དུས་ལྡབ་སྐྱོར་མང་པོ་གཏོང་གི་འདུག When the teacher teaches a lesson, he repeats things many times.

ལྡབ་གྲངས་ (dəbdraŋ) multiples of a number.

ལྡབ་གྲངས་མཉམ་པའི་རིམ་གྲངས་ (dəbdraŋ ñambɛ rimdraŋ) geometrical progression (in math).

ལྡབ་འགྱུར་ (dəbgyur) increasing by double.

ལྡབ་བརྒྱ་ (dəbgya) a hundred fold, a hundred times.

ལྡབ་གཅིག (dəbjii) double.

ལྡབ་གཉིས་ (dəbñii) quadruple.

ལྡབ་དང་ལྡབ་ (dəbdaŋ dəb) increasing by doubling.

ལྡབ་ལྡིབ་ (dəbdib) sm. ལྡབ་བེ་ལྡིབ་བེ་.

ལྡབ་ལྡོབ་ (dəbdob) sm. ལྡབ་བེ་ལྡོབ་བེ་.

ལྡབ་སྤར་ (dəbbar) va. to increase/ raise by double.

ལྡབ་འཕར་ (dəbpar) abbr. ལྡབ་ལོག་འཕར་.

ལྡབ་བེ་ལྡིབ་བེ་ (dəbi dibi) 1. stuttering. 2. unclear speech.

ལྡབ་ཚོང་རྒྱག (dəbdzoŋ gyaà) va. to do double the business.

ལྡབ་ལོག (dəblɔ̀ɔ) double, twice as much ། ཟ་ཆའི་གོང་ལྡབ་ལོག་འཕར་བ་རེད་ Food prices doubled.

ལྡབ་ལོག་ལྡབ་ལོག (dəblɔ̀ɔ dəblɔ̀ɔ) in or by doubles/ doubling.

ལྡབ་གསུམ་ (dəbsum) triple, three times as much.

ལྡམ་མེ་ལྡེམ་མེ་ (dəmme demme) malleable, supple.

ལྡར་ (dar) 1. sm. རྟོན་. 2. sm. གྲོན་པ་.

ལྡི་ལི་ (dili) Delhi.

ལྡིག (dig) sm. ཐིག.

ལྡིག་དོ་ (digdo) sm. ལྡིག་པ་.

ལྡིག་ལྡིག (didig) 1. best quality (usu. for food). 2. small but compact (for people).

ལྡིགས་ (dig) p. of ལྡིག.

ལྡིང་ (diŋ) vi. to hover, to circle.

ལྡིང་སྐོར་ (diŋgɔɔ) hovering, circling; va.—རྒྱག to circle/ hover in the air, to fly over ། གནམ་གྲུ་དེས་མ་བབས་གོང་ལ་ལྡིང་སྐོར་ཁ་ཤས་བརྒྱབ་སོང་ The plane circled (over the city) a few times before it landed.

ལྡིང་གུར་ (diŋgur) a large tent.

ལྡིང་གྲུ་ (diŋdru) glider, blimp, zeppelin; helicopter.

ལྡིང་སྒྲ་ (diŋdra) thundering/ roaring noise or sound.

ལྡིང་ཆུ་ (diŋju) still water.

ལྡིང་རྙིང་ (diŋñiŋ) shung. the older/ senior ལྡིང་དཔོན་.

ལྡིང་དཔོན་ (diŋbön) shung. traditional Tibetan army officer who was head of 25 troops.

ལྡིང་དམག (diŋmaà) shung. abbr. of ལྡིང་དཔོན་ and དམག་མི་.

ལྡིང་ཟམ་ (diŋsam) floating bridge.

ལྡིང་ཤུར་གནམ་གྲུ་ (diŋshur nəmdru) sm. ལྡིང་གྲུ་.

ལྡིང་ཤོག (diŋshɔ̀ɔ) shung. a unit in the traditional Tibetan army consisting of 25 soldiers (see དམག་སྒར་).

ལྡིབ་ (dib) sm. ལྡིག.

ལྡིར་ (dir) vi. to thunder, to roar ། གནམ་འཐིབས་ནས་འབྲུག་སྐད་ལྡིར་གྱི་འདུག It has become cloudy and is beginning to thunder. 2. vi. to bulge, to become distended/ inflated, to protrude ༶ མི་དེ་ཕོ་རྒྱགས་ལ་གྲོད་ཁོག་ལྡིར་བ་ཞིག་འདུག That person is fat and has a protruding stomach. 3. va. to aim (at) ༶ མི་མདའ་འབེན་ལ་ལྡིར་ནས་རྒྱག་གི་འདུག (He) aimed at the target and is shooting.

ལྡིར་སྐད་ (dirgɛɛ̀) talking noisily/ loudly (by many people); va.—རྒྱག ༶ ཁང་པ་དེའི་ནང་མི་མང་པོ་ཚོགས་ནས་ལྡིར་སྐད་རྒྱག་གི་འདུག Many people gathered in that house and talked noisily.

ལྡིར་སྒྲ་ (dirdra) a loud noise; vi.—སྒྲོག to have a loud/ thunderous noise come forth ༶ ཤོག་སྦག་གི་ལྡིར་སྒྲ་ The loud noise of firecrackers.

ལྡིར་ཅན་ (dirjɛn) sm. ལྡིར་ལྡིར་.

ལྡིར་ལྡིར་ (dirdir) bulgy, protruding, swollen; vi.—བྱེད་.

ལྡུག: p. ལྡུགས་; f. ལྡུག་; imp. ལྡུགས་ (dug) sm. བླུགས་.

ལྡུག་རྒྱག་བཟོ་གྲྭ (duggyaà sodra) foundry factory.

ལྡུགས་ (dug) p.and imp. of ལྡུག.

ལྡུད་ (dü̃ü) va. to give sth. to drink ༶ ཕྲུ་གུ་ར་འོ་མ་ལྡུད་པ་རེད་ (She) gave the child milk.

ལྡུམ་ (dum) vegetables, flowers, plants, greens.

ལྡུམ་འཇོམས་སྨན་མཆོག (dumjom mɛ̃njɔɔ̀) an herbal medicine.

ལྡུམ་བུ་ (dumbu) plants.

ལྡུམ་བུ་ཁྲག་གཅོད་ (dumbu trãgjöö) agrimonia pilosa.

ལྡུམ་ར་ (dumra) 1. garden, orchard. 2. name of region in Ladakh (Nupra).

ལྡུམ་ར་བ་ (dumrawa) gardener.

ལྡུམ་རའི་རིག་པ་ (dumrɛ rigbə) horticulture.

ལྡུམ་རའི་ལག་རྩལ་ (dumrɛ lagdzɛɛ) gardening, horticulture.

ལྡུམ་རའི་ལོ་ཏོག (dumrɛ lodoò) garden crops.

ལྡུར་ (dur) 1. vi. to get turned into pulp or mush (from too much boiling/ cooking). 2. abbr. of ལྡུར་ལྡུར་.

ལྡུར་ལྡུར་ (durdur) mashed, pulped, mushy, overly soft ༶ ཞོ་ཁོག་ལྡུར་ལྡུར་ Mashed potatoes. ༶ ཤ་བཙོས་དྲག་ནས་ལྡུར་བཞག The meat got cooked too much and became mushy.

ལྡུར་ཕིག (durbig) completely pulped/ mashed/ mushed (due to cooking).

ལྡུར་ཚགས་ (durdzaà) strainer.

ལྡེ་: p. ལྡེས་; f. ལྡེ་; imp. ལྡེས་ (de) va. to sit in the sun or by a fire (to warm oneself).

ལྡེ་ཁུ་ (degu) sm. ལྡེ་གུ་.

ལྡེ་ཁུང་ (deguŋ) the hole in a lock into which the key is inserted.

ལྡེ་གུ་ (degu) 1. a paste made by boiling a liquid mixture to thicken it. 2. water in which a scent is soaked to give a nice smell.

ལྡེ་རྒྱུང་ (dejuŋ) shung. a minor ལྡེ་འཆང་ official.

ལྡེ་མིག (dimii) key; va.—རྒྱག to wind a clock/ watch, toy, etc.; va.—ཕྱེ་ to open a can with a key.

ལྡེ་ཚབ་ (dedzəb) duplicate key.

ལྡེང་: p.and f. ལྡེངས་ (deŋ) vi. to suffice, to be sufficient ༶ དངོས་འདྲེན་འཁོར་ལོས་མ་ལྡེངས་པ་རེད་ There were not enough transport vehicles.

ལྡེང་མཁར་ (deŋga) area in Derge (in Sichuan).

ལྡེང་ངེས་ (deŋŋeè) sufficient, enough, ample, adequate ༶ ཁོ་ལ་ཚོང་གི་མ་རྩ་ལྡེང་ངེས་འདུག He has sufficient capital for business.

ལྡེང་འཆང་ (dejaŋ) shung. an official in a labrang.

ལྡེང་ཐབས་ (deŋtəb) sufficient/ enough to do sth.; va.—བྱེད་ to manage using sth. ༶ ཁོས་དངུལ་དེ་རང་གིས་ལྡེང་ཐབས་བྱེད་ཀྱི་འདུག He is managing with the money he has.

ལྡེང་མིན་ (deŋmin) insufficient, not enough.

ལྡེང་རེ་བྲལ་ (deŋre trɛɛ) vi. to have no hope of being sufficient or having enough.

ལྡེབ་ (deb) sm. བཞི་ལིང་.

ལྡེབས་ (deb) 1. the side/ surface of ༶ རྩིག་པའི་ལྡེབས་ལ་པར་མང་པོ་བཀལ་འདུག (They) have hung many pictures on the (surface of the) wall. 2. (— + ལ་) together ༶ ཁོ་གཉིས་ལྡེབས་ལ་ཕྱིན་པ་རེད་ They went together.

ལྡེབས་བྲིས་ (debrii) wall painting, mural, fresco.

ལྡེབས་ཞལ་ (debshɛɛ) mud plaster (used on walls); va.—རྒྱག; —གཏོང་.

ལྡེབས་རིས་ (debrii) sm. ལྡེབས་བྲིས་.

ལྡེམ་ (dem) abbr. of ལྡེམ་ལྡེམ་.

ལྡེམ་འགྲོ་.(demdro) va. to walk gracefully/ sensually (for women).

ལྡེམ་ཁྱུག་ཁྱུག (dem kyũùgyuù) 1. flexible, able to bend. 2. walking in a graceful swaying manner.

ལྡེམ་འགྱུར་ (demgyuu) walking with a graceful, swaying gait (for women); va.—བྱེད་ ༶ བུ་མོ་དེ་ལྡེམ་འགྱུར་བྱས་ནས་འགྲོ་གི་འདུག The girl is walking with a swaying gait.

ལྡེམ་རྒྱག (dem gyaà) va. to sway, to bend.

ལྡེམ་རྒྱུག.(demgyuù) pole vaulting pole.

ལྡེམ་རྒྱུག་མདོ་ (dem gyuù tõ) pole vaulting pole.

ལྡེམ་ལྡེམ་ཁྱུག་ཁྱུག (demdem kyũùgyuù) sm. ལྡེམ་ཁྱུག་ཁྱུག.

ལྡེམ་ལྡེམ་ལྕུག་ལྕུག (demdem jũgjuù) 1. flexible, able to bend. 2. walking with a graceful, swaying gait.

ལྡེམ་པའི་རང་བཞིན་ (dembɛ rəŋshin) elasticity, flexibility.

ལྡེམ་པོ་ (dembo) 1. sm. ལྡེམ་ཁྱུག་ཁྱུག. 2. unsteady, unstable, shaky, not trustworthy.

ལྡེམ་མེ་ལྡམ་མེ་ (demme damme) sm. ལྡེམ་ལྡེམ་ཁྱུག་ཁྱུག.

ལྡེམ་རྩིབ་ (demdzib) a spring (in a machine).

ལྡེམ་ཤུགས་ (demshuù) elastic power.

ལྡེའུ་མིག (dimii) key.

ལྡེའུའི་ངག (dewu ŋaà) enigmatic language, riddles.

ལྡེའུའི་ཚིག (dewu tsĩi) sm. ལྡེའུའི་ངག.

ལྡེར་ (der) 1. sm. ལྡེབས་. 2. clay.

ལྡེར་ཚོ་ (derso) clay statues.

ལྡེར་བཟོ་ (derso) statues/ figures made of clay; va.—སྐྲུན་ to make clay statues/ figures.

ལྡེར་བཟོ་མཁན་པོ་ (derso kɛ̃mbo) the chief of the clay statue makers.

ལྡེར་བཟོ་བ་ (dersowa) clay statue maker.

ལྡོག (dɔ̀ɔ) 1. va. to counteract ༶ ཆུ་ལོག་ལྡོག་པའི་ཆེད་དུ་རགས་བརྒྱབ་པ་རེད་ They built a dam to counteract the (danger) of flooding. 2. vi. to be opposite/ contrary to ༶ འདི་ང་ཚོའི་བསམ་ཚུལ་ལས་ལྡོག་པ་རེད་ This is contrary to our idea. ༶ དཀར་པོ་ནི་ནག་པོ་ལས་ལྡོག་པ་ཞིག་ཡིན་ White is opposite of black. ༶ འདི་ཁོས་བཤད་པ་ལས་དག་དག་ལྡོག་སྟེ་ This is completely opposite to what he said. ༶ ཁོ་འདི་མ་བཤད་པ་མ་ཟད་དེ་ལས་ལྡོག་སྟེ་ Not only didn't he say this, to the contrary. 3. vi. to have a color change/ fade ༶ རས་འདི་ཚོས་ལྡོག་བཞག The color of this cloth changed. 4. va. to give up/ abandon ༶ བཟང་ངན་འཇུག་ལྡོག་མ་ནོར་བ་བྱ་དགོས་ You must keep what is good and abandon what is bad without mistake.

ལྡོག་གྲངས་ (dɔgdraŋ) negative number (in math).

ལྡོག་དགག་རྗོད་གཞི་ (dɔggaà joõshi) rebuttal.

ལྡོག་འགྱུར་ (dɔggyur) changing, altering (to the opposite); va.—བྱེད་ ༶ གུང་ཁྲན་རིང་ལུགས་ནས་མ་རྩ་རིང་ལུགས་ལ་ལྡོག་འགྱུར་བྱུང་བ་རེད་ (There) has been a great change from communism to capitalism.

ལྡོག་རྒོལ་ (dɔɔ̀göö) counter attacking; va.—བྱེད་.

ལྡོག་ཏུ་མེད་པ་ (dɔgdu meèba) inevitable, certain, unalterable, irresistible.

ལྡོག་སྡེ་ (dɔgde) see ལྡོག, 4.

ལྡོག་ཐབས་མེད་པ་ (dɔgdəb meèba) irresistable, inevitable, unchangeable, certain, unalterable, unopposable.

ལྡོག་དྲོད་ (dɔgdröö) temperature inversion.

ལྡོག་དྲོད་བར་རིམ་ (dɔgdröö paŋrim) temperature inversion layer.

ལྡོག་སྡུར་ (dɔgdur) inverse proportion; inverse ratio.

ལྡོག་འདྲི་ (dɔgdri) asking a question, in reply to a question; va.—བྱེད་.

ལྡོག་ནས་རྩིས་ (dɔgnɛ dzĩ) va. to count backwards, to count from the bottom up.

ལྡོག་པའི་ལྟོས་ལྟ་ (dɔgbɛ dõnda) the opposite viewpoint.

ལྡོག་ཕྱོགས་ (dɔgjɔ̀ɔ) 1. negative or opposite aspect/ side ༑ ཐོག་མའི་ཐུགས་རེ་དེའི་ལྡོག་ཕྱོགས་སུ་འཕེལ་ The opposite of the original hope occurred. 2. (— + ལ་འགྲོ་); va. to go in the opposition direction.

ལྡོག་ཕྱོགས་ཀྱི་འགྱུར་བ་ (dɔgjɔ̀ɔgi gyuwa) a negative change.

ལྡོག་ཕྱོགས་འགྱུར་འབྱུང་ (dɔgjɔ̀ɔ gyüüjuŋ) a negative change.

ལྡོག་ཕྱོགས་སྡུར་ཚད་ (dɔgjɔ̀ɔ durdzɛɛ̀) inverse proportion/ ratio.

ལྡོག་མེད་ (dɔgmeè) sm. ལྡོག་ཏུ་མེད་པ་.

ལྡོག་མེད་ཀྱི་རང་བཞིན་ (dɔgmeègi rəŋshin) certainty, inevitability.

ལྡོག་མེད་ཆོས་ཉེར་ (dɔgmeè cööñer) inexorable/ certain/ unalterable law.

ལྡོག་རྩིས་ (dɔgdzii) 1. inverse operation/ calculation (in math). 2. counting backwards, counting from the bottom up; va.—རྒྱག.

ལྡོག་ལྟ་ (dɔŋda) sm. ལྡོག་ཕྱོགས་.

ལྡོག་འོད་ (dɔ̀wöò) reflective/ reflected light.

ལྡོག་ཤུགས་ (dɔgshuù) counter force.

ལྡོགས་ (dɔ̀ɔ) imp. of ལྡག.

ལྡོང་ (doŋ) (usu. མིག་ + —) blind.

ལྡོང་ (doŋ) vi. to be/ get blind.

ལྡོང་བར་ཉེན་ (doŋwar ñen) vi. to be/ get blind.

ལྡོང་མོ་ (doŋmo) sm. ལོང་མོ་.

ལྡོང་རོས་ (doŋröö) a medicine made from realgar.

ལྡོབ་ཀྱི་ (dobgye) person pretending to be a fool/ stupid.

ལྡོབ་ཤིག་ཤིག (dob shĩshiì) a feeling of well-being and comfort.

ལྡོབ་ཤོད་ (dob shö̃ò) va. to intentionally say sth. foolish/ stupid, to pretend to be foolish/ stupid in one's speech.

ལྡོབ་བཤད་ (dobshɛɛ̀) sm. ལྡོབ་ཤོད་.

ལྡོབས་ (dob) 1. imp. of ལྡབ་. 2. sm. ལྡོབ་ཤོད་.

ལྡོབ་ལྡོབ་ (dobdob) soft, mushy.

ལྡོམ་པ་ (dombo) sm. ལྡོམ་བུ་.

ལྡོམ་པོ་ (dombo) 1. wanderer. 2. a stray animal.

ལྡོམ་བུ་ (dombu) alms; va.—བྱེད་ to ask/ beg for alms.

སྡག་སྡག (dagdaà) 1. full, brimming; va.—རྫོང་; —བླུག to fill/ stuff to the brim. 2. a lot, many.

སྡག་སྡག་ཁེངས་ (dagdaà kẽŋ) vi. to be full to the top/ brim.

སྡག་སྡག་གང་ (dagdaà kaŋ) full to the brim ༑ ཁོས་ང་ལ་ཆང་སྡག་སྡག་གང་བླུགས་བྱུང་ He poured me a cup of ཆང་ filled to the brim.

སྡང་ (daŋ) va. to hate, to loathe ༑ ཁོང་ནི་མ་རྩ་རིང་ལུགས་ལ་སྡང་བའི་མི་ཞིག་རེད་ He is sb. who hates capitalism.

སྡང་ཁྲོ་ (daŋdro) hatred, enmity.

སྡང་དགྲ་ (daŋdra) hated/ bitter enemy.

སྡང་ཅན་ (daŋjɛn) hated, despised.

སྡང་སྡུག (daŋduù) sm. སྡང་པོ་.

སྡང་པོ་ (daŋbo) spiteful, vindictive, cruel (out of hatred); va.—བྱེད་ ༑ ཁོས་ང་ལ་དམིགས་བསལ་གྱི་སྡང་པོ་བྱེད་ཀྱི་འདུག Out of hatred, he is specially acting cruel to me. ༑ འདིར་བརྟེན་རྒྱལ་ཟུར་རྭ་སྒྲེང་ལ་སྡང་པོ་བྱེད་རྒྱུ་ Because of hatred, (he) will be cruel to the Ex-Regent Reting.

སྡང་མིག (dəŋmiĩ) angry look/ scowl, a look of hatred; va.—ལྟ་.

སྡང་ཟུག (daŋsug) sm. སྡང་པོ་.

སྡང་འཛིན་ (dəŋdzin) hatred, animosity; va.—བྱེད་ to hate; va.—འཆང་ to hold/ harbor hatred ༑ ཁོས་ཕྱི་རྒྱལ་ཚང་མར་སྡང་འཛིན་བྱེད་ཀྱི་ཡོད་པ་རེད་ He hates all foreigners.

སྡང་སེམས་ (daŋsem) sm. སྡང་འཛིན་.

སྡངས་ (daŋ) sm. སྡང་.

སྡམ་ (dam) p. of སྡོམ་, 2.

སྡམ་བཀྱིག (damgyiì) tying, bandaging; va.—བྱེད་.

སྡམ་ཁ་ (damga) a tied bundle, a wrapped bunch.

སྡར་མ་ (darma) coward.

སྡར་མ་ཝ་སྒྲོས་ (darma wadröö) cowardly, gutless.

སྡར་ཚན་ (dardzɛn) eng. dozen.

སྡི་ (di) sm. སྡི་ཁུང་སྒྲོད་.

སྡི་ཁུང་སྒྲོད་ (diguŋ drö̃ò) va. to aim (a gun).

སྡིག (dig) 1. type of cooking pot. 2. abbr. of སྡིག་པ་.

སྡིག: p. བསྡིགས་; f. བསྡིག; imp. སྡིགས་ (dig) va. to threaten, to menace, to intimidate.

སྡིག་གྲོགས་ (digdrɔ̀ɔ) a partner or cohort in crime/ murder/ evil.

སྡིག་གླ་ (digla) 1. wage/ money paid to a butcher for slaughtering animals. 2. wgae/ money paid to a murderer. [Lit. sin wage].

སྡིག་རྒྱལ་ (diggyɛɛ) an evil king, a king who destroys Buddhism.

སྡིག་སྒྲ་ (digdra) 1. thumping/ pounding noise; va.—བྱེད་ to thump/ pound.

སྡིག་ཅན་ (digjɛn) sinner, sinful ༑ མི་སྡིག་ཅན་ A sinful person.

སྡིག་ཉེས་ (digñeè) crime.

སྡིག་ཉེས་ཅན་ (digñeèjɛn) criminal.

སྡིག་སྡིག (digdig) pounding/ beating on sth. (e.g., a door); va.—གཏོང་.

སྡིག་སྡུག (digdug) sin and suffering.

སྡིག་པ་ (digbə) 1. sin; va.—གསོག to commit sins; va.—བཤགས་ to repent/ atone (for sins); vi.—དག to be cleansed of sin. 2. scorpion.

སྡིག་པ་མཐོང་ན་སྦལ་པ་ལྷ་རུ་མངོན་ (digbə tõŋna beeba lhāru ŋõn) encountering sth. exceptionally bad makes other things that are regularly bad appear good [Lit. when one sees a scorpion, a frog looks like a god].

སྡིག་པ་དུ་བ་ (digbə tuwə) sm. སྡིག་པ་ཆེ་བ་.

སྡིག་པ་མིག་བཙུམ་ (digbə migdzum) getting into sth. without thinking of the negative consequences, rushing headlong into sth.; va.—བྱེད་.

སྡིག་པ་རྭ་ཉག (digbə raña) scorpion.

སྡིག་པ་རྭ་ཙ་ (digbə radza) sm. སྡིག་པ་རྭ་ཉག.

སྡིག་པའི་སྐར་ཚོམ་ (digbə gārdzom) scorpius (the constellation).

སྡིག་སྤོང་དགེ་སྒྲུབ་ (digboŋ gedrub) renouncing bad deeds and achieving good deeds; va.—བྱེད་.

སྡིག་སྤྱོད་ (digjöö) sinful/ criminal behavior; va.—བྱེད་ to commit sins/ crimes.

སྡིག་སྤྱོད་པ་ (digjööba) a sinner, a criminal.

སྡིག་བྱས་རང་གནོད་ (digjɛɛ̀ raŋnöò) bad deeds come back to harm oneself.

སྡིག་སྦྱོང་དགེ་སྐྱེད་ (digjoŋ gegyeè) cleansing one's bad deeds and doing good deeds.

སྡིག་ར་ (digra) 1. sm. སྡིགས་ར་. 2. a pin for fastening belts. 3. a sifter used to take out leftovers/ food from deep frying oil.

སྡིག་རྭ་ (digra) 1. abbr. of སྡིག་པ་རྭ་ཙ་.

སྡིག་རྭ་བློ་ཕྲེང་ (digra lōdreŋ) an ornament worn by the women who serve ཆང་ to the Yasor.

སྡིག་བཤགས་བྱེད་ (digshaà ceè) va. to repent.

སྡིག་སོ་སྒྲོད་ (digso drö̃ò) va. to take aim.

སྡིག་སྲིན་ (digsin) crab.

སྡིག་བསགས་རང་འཁུར་ (digsaà raŋkur) reaping the negative fruits of one's sinful action.

སྡིགས་ (dig) imp. of སྡིག.

སྡིགས་བསྐུལ་ (diggüü) sm. སྡིགས་ར་.

སྡིགས་གཏམ་ (digdam) talk that threatens.

སྡིགས་སྡིགས་ (digdig) 1. thumping, pounding; va.—གཏོང་ to thump, to pound. 2. sm. སྡིགས་ར་.

སྡིགས་མོ་ (digmu) sm. སྡིགས་ར་.

སྡིགས་དམོད་ (digmüü) threatening and intimidating.

སྡིགས་མཛུབ་ (digdzub) a threatening sign made by extending the index finger and pinky fingers.

སྡིགས་ར་ (digrə) threatening, menacing, intimidating; va.—བསྐུལ་; —སྤྲོད་ to threaten, to menace, to intimidate ༑ དམག་གི་སྡིགས་ར་བསྐུལ་བ་རེད་ (They) threatened us with war.

སྡིང་ཆ་ (dinja) sm. སྡིངས་ཆ་.

སྡིང་སྒྲ་ (diŋdra) the sound made by banging.

སྡིངས་ (diŋ) 1. sm. དཀྱིལ་. 2. plateau, high area.

སྡིངས་ཆ་ (diŋja) rostrum, speaker's platform. 2. stage.

སྡིར་ (dir) va. to cook/ simmer for a long time.

སྡིས་ (dii) sm. སྡི་.

སྡུ་ (du) sm. སྡུད་.

སྡུ་གུ་ (dugu) sm. སྡུག་གུ་.

སྡུག་ (dug) 1. vi. to be depressed/ sad (usu. སེམས་ + —) ¶ མོ་སེམས་ཤི་དྲག་སྡུག་སོང་ She was very sad. 2. abbr. of སྡུག་པོ་. 3. pretty ¶ མཛེས་སྡུག Beautiful.

སྡུག་སྐད་ (duggɛ̀ɛ) 1. complaining, grumbling; va.—རྒྱག; —འདོན་; —ཤོར་ to complain, to grumble ¶ ལས་ཀ་བྱེད་མཁན་ཚོས་སྡུག་སྐད་རྒྱག་གི་འདུག The workers are complaining. ¶ སྤྱང་ཀིས་སྡུག་སྐད་རྒྱག་པ་བཞིན་ Like a howling wolf.

སྡུག་སྐད་ཚིག (dug gɛ̀ɛdzii) words of complaint/ discontent, grumblings.

སྡུག་སྐྲན་ (dugdrɛn) cancer.

སྡུག་དཀའ་ལས་ (dug gālɛɛ) hard work, hard labor/ toiling; va.—རྒྱག to work hard, to labor/ toil ¶ སྡུག་དཀའ་ལས་དེ་འདྲ་རྒྱག་གི་ཡོད་ན་ཡང་ངས་ལྟོ་ཆས་ལྡང་གི་ཡོད་པ་མ་རེད་ Even though (they) worked so hard (they) don't have enough food.

སྡུག་ཁུར་ (duggur) sm. སྡུག་འཁུར་.

སྡུག་ཁྲལ་ (dugdrɛɛ) a difficult/ hard tax.

སྡུག་འཁུར་ (duggur) putting up with/ bearing/ tolerating suffering or hardship ¶ ལས་ཀ་དཀའ་ལས་ཁག་པོ་འདུག་ཀྱང་སྡུག་ཁུར་རྒྱག་གི་ཡོད་ Even though the work involved hardship, (he) is bearing it.

སྡུག་གུ་ (duggu) pretty.

སྡུག་གོས་ (duggöö) mourning dress/ clothes.

སྡུག་གྱོང་ (duggyoŋ) 1. misfortune; va.—འཁྱེར་ to bear misfortune ¶ ང་རེས་ཚོང་རྒྱག་དུས་གྱོང་ཆེན་པོ་རག་བྱུང་ཡང་ངས་སྡུ་གྱོང་འཁྱེར་པ་ཡིན་ Even though I suffered a misfortune in business, I was able to bear it. 2. deserving misfortune, serves you right (slang) ¶ ཁྱེད་རང་གིས་གཟབ་གཟབ་མ་བྱས་ཙང་དངུལ་བརླག་པ་དེ་སྡུག་གྱོང་རེད་ Because you weren't careful, it serves you right that you lost the money.

སྡུག་གྱོང་འཁྱེར་ (duggyoŋ kyēr) va. to bear misfortune.

སྡུག་གྱོང་པུ་རུ་ (duggyoŋ puru) a type of pimple.

སྡུག་གྲོགས་ (dugdrɔɔ) friends who have shared suffering/ misfortune.

སྡུག་གླུ་ (duglu) melancholy song, blues; va.—ལེན་ to sing melancholy songs.

སྡུག་བགྲང་ (dugdraŋ) sm. སྡུག་བསྔལ་བགྲང་.

སྡུག་སྒོམ་ (duggom) tolerating misery/ suffering/ hardship; va.—རྒྱག to tolerate suffering/ misery/ hardship.

སྡུག་སྒོམ་དཀའ་སྤྱད་ (duggom gājɛɛ) tolerating misery and persevering in hardship; va.—བྱེད་.

སྡུག་སྒྲིག་འཇགས་ (dugdrig jaà) vi. to get into a bad habit.

སྡུག་ངུ་ (dugŋu) weeping, crying; vi.—ཤོར་ to weep/ cry.

སྡུག་བསྔལ་ (duùŋɛɛ) sadness, suffering, misery; vi.—མྱོང་ to suffer or undergo hardship/ misery; va.—བགྲང་ to recount one's miseries/ hardships; va.—བྱེད་ to be saddened/ miserable ¶ ཁོང་གི་ཕ་མ་གྲོངས་ཙང་སྡུག་བསྔལ་ཆེན་པོ་བྱེད་ཀྱི་འདུག Because his parents died, he is very miserable.

སྡུག་བསྔལ་གྱི་རྒྱུ་བོ་ཆེན་པོ་བཞི་ (duùŋɛɛgi cūwo cēmbo shi) the four main sources of suffering: birth, aging, sickness, death.

སྡུག་བསྔལ་གྱི་གནས་ (duùŋɛɛgi nɛ̀ɛ) the state of suffering.

སྡུག་བསྔལ་རྒྱ་མཚོ་ (duùŋɛɛ gyadzo) sea of bitterness/ misery/ sadness; va.—ཤོད་; —བགྲང་ to complain or recount or enumerate misery/ sadness.

སྡུག་ཅག (dugjaà) bad, evil, terrible, horrible; va.—རྩི་ to regard as bad/ evil.

སྡུག་ཅན་ (dugjɛn) terrible, bad, horrible.

སྡུག་གཅོད་གཏོང་ (dugjöö dōŋ) va. to torture.

སྡུག་ལྕོག་ཉོན་ (dugjoò ñön) a derogatory term that literally means "listen you damn ear."

སྡུག་ཆགས་ (dugjaà) sm. སྡུག་ཅག.

སྡུག་ཆེ་འཁོན་ཟབ་ (dugce kōnsəb) great suffering and deep animosity/ hatred ¶ སྡུག་ཆེ་འཁོན་ཟབ་ཀྱི་ངལ་རྩོལ་མི་དམངས་ The toiling masses who have experienced great suffering and deep hatred.

སྡུག་བརྗོད་ (dugjöö) sm. སྡུག་སྐད་.

སྡུག་ཉམས་ཤོར་ (dugñam shɔ̄ɔ) vi. to manifest/ show a sad look.

སྡུག་ཏུ་འགྲོ་ (dugdu dro) to worsen, to deteriorate ¶ ཡག་ཏུ་འགྲོ་རྒྱུའི་ཚབ་ལ་སྡུག་ཏུ་ཕྱིན་པ་རེད་ It got worse instead of getting better.

སྡུག་ཐང་བཙོལ་ (dugdaŋ jöö) va. to look down on ¶ མི་ཚང་མས་ཁོ་པར་སྡུག་ཐང་བཙོལ་གྱི་ཡོད་པ་རེད་ All the people look down on him.

སྡུག་ཐང་སྤྱོད་ (dugdaŋ jöö) va. to make suffer.

སྡུག་ཐུག (dug tūù) vi. to encounter suffering/ hardship/ difficulty.

སྡུག་ཐོག་སྡུག་བརྩེག (dugdɔɔ dugdzeg) one misfortune piled on top of another, one suffering on top of another; va.—བྱེད་.

སྡུག་ཐོག་མཚང་འདྲུ་ (dugtɔɔ tsāŋdru) digging up faults when a person is facing hardship/ difficulty/ suffering.

སྡུག་མཐའ་སྐྱིད་ཟིན་ (dugda gyiisin) finding/ getting happiness after a lifetime of hardship.

སྡུག་མཐའ་བདེ་ལ་འཁོད་པ་ (dugda dela kööba) after suffering comes happiness.

སྡུག་དྲན་སྐྱིད་བསམ་ (dugdrɛn gyiisam) recall the sorrow of the past and savor the joys; va.—བྱེད་.

སྡུག་འདྲེ་ (duŋdre) demon, evil spirit, ghost.

སྡུག་ནད་ (dugnɛɛ) 1. a bad/ severe illness. 2. hardship, suffering; vi.—ཐེག to tolerate/ bear hardship/ suffering ¶ ཁྱེད་རང་སྡུག་ནད་ཐེག་གི་མི་འདུག་ན་སྡུག་གྱོང་རེད་ If you cannot bear hardship, it serves you right.

སྡུག་གནས་ (dugnɛɛ) bad condition/ situation, difficult straits/ situation.

སྡུག་པ་ (dugbə) 1. pretty, lovely, attractive, pleasing ¶ ཤིན་ཏུ་མཛེས་ཤིང་སྡུག་པའི་ཡུལ་ལྗོངས་ Extremely beautiful scenery. 2. worse, inferior, poorer ¶ སྔོན་མ་ལས་གནས་སྟངས་སྡུག་པ་འདུག The conditions are worse than before.

སྡུག་པའི་སྣང་ལ་བབས་བརྗིས་ (dugbɛ ganla pɛɛ dzii)) sm. སྡུག་ཐོག་སྡུག་བརྩེག.

སྡུག་པོ་ (dugbu) suffering, misery; vi.—མྱོང་; —སྐྱེར་ to suffer/ undergo misery, to experience hardships; va.—གཏོང་ to make suffer, to cause misery, to mistreat, to torture ¶ མི་དེ་ཚོས་སྡུག་པོ་མྱོང་བའི་ལོ་རྒྱུས་ An account of the miseries those people suffered. 2. bad ¶ མི་དེ་སྡུག་པོ་མི་འདུག That man is not bad. 3. good-looking, attractive ¶ བཞིན་རས་སྡུག་པོ་ Pretty face.

སྡུག་སྤྱོད་ (dugjöö) bad behavior.

སྡུག་བོང་བུས་བརྒྱབ་ ཆག་ཏུ་རྟས་ཟས་ (dug poŋbü gyəb cāà dāpö sɛɛ) reward is not given to the one who deserves it [Lit. the donkey does the hard work but the horse gets to eat the fodder].

སྡུག་སྦྱོང་ (dugjoŋ) mistreatment, abuse, torture; va.—གཏོང་ to mistreat, to abuse ¶ བཙོན་པ་རྣམས་ལ་ལོ་མང་སྡུག་སྦྱོང་བཏང་བ་རེད་ (They) mistreated the prisoners for many years.

སྡུག་མོལ་ (dugmöö) sm. སྡུག་སྐད་.

སྡུག་བཙུན་མ་ (dugdzünma) a derogatory term used for berating nuns.

སྡུག་རྩུབ་ (dugdzub) ferocious, savage, cruel.

སྡུག་ཚང་ (dugdzaŋ) a derogatory term used for a household/ family.

སྡུག་ཚིགས་ (dugdzee) sm. དཀའ་སྡུག.

སྡུག་ཆོད་མ་ཟིན་ན་ (dugdzöö masinnə) slang. if you don't behave yourself, if you don't "cool it" ¶ སྡུག་ཆོད་མ་ཟིན་ན་གསོད་ཀྱི་ཡིན་ If (you) don't cool it I will kill you.

སྡུག་ཆོད་ཟེན་ (dugdzöö sin) va. to behave oneself.

སྡུག་ཛོགས་སྐྱིད་ཤར་ (dugdzɔ̀ɔ gyiishar) sm. སྡུག་ཟད་སྐྱིད་ཤར་.

སྡུག་ཟད་སྐྱིད་ཤར་ (dugsɛɛ̀ gyiishar) vi. to have the bad times wane and the good times begin.

སྡུག་ཡུས་ (dugyüü) making a great deal about one's suffering; va.—བགྲང་; —ཤོད་ to make a great deal of one's suffering/ hardship/ misery.

སྡུག་རུ་འགྲོ་ (dugru dro) vi. to worsen.

སྡུག་རུལ་ (dugrüü) depraved, rotten and bad.

སྡུག་རུས་ (dugrüü) enduring or tolerating hardship/ suffering/ misery; va.—བྱེད་; —རྒྱག to endure/ tolerate/ bear hardship or suffering or misery.

སྡུག་རུས་ཆེ་པོ་ (dugrüü tsäbo) very tolerant of hardship/ suffering/ misery.

སྡུག་རེ་གདངས་ན་ཧ་རེ་གོ་ (dugre dāgna hāre go) through hardship one gains knowledge, learning the hard way.

སྡུག་རོ་ (dugro) derogatory term for one's opponent/ enemy ༎སྡུག་རོ་དེ་ཚོ་ངས་ལས་སླ་པོར་གཏོར་ཐུབ་ I can easily defeat those enemies.

སྡུག་རོགས་ (dugrɔ̀ɔ) spouse.

སྡུག་ལྷུང་འཚུབ་འཚུབ་ (dugluŋ tsūbdzuù) rage, fury, anger; va.—བྱེད་ to be angry.

སྡུག་ལས་ (duglɛɛ̀) 1. hard work or labor. 2. term used to scold people who don't work well ༎ཁྱོད་རང་སྡུག་ལས་ཚར་མ་སོང་ངས་ Didn't you finish your god damn work?

སྡུག་ཤི་ (dugshi) dying miserably; vi.—རྒྱག; —ཐེབས་ to die miserably, to die a painful death.

སྡུག་ཤི་ཁ་ནག་རྒྱག་རྒྱུ་ (dugshi kānaà gyaàgyu) sm. སྡུག་ཤི་རྒྱག་རྒྱུ་.

སྡུག་ཤི་རྒྱག་རྒྱུ་ (dugshi gyaàgyu) term used in scolding/ cursing sb. [Lit. may you die a miserable death].

སྡུག་ཤུད་སྨུག་ཤུད་ (dugshüü mugshüü) sm. སྡུག་ཤོད་སྨུག་ཤོད་.

སྡུག་ཤོད་སྨུག་ཤོད་ (dugshöö mugshöö) complaining, grumbling; va.—གཏོང་.

སྡུག་ཤོས་ (dugshöö) the worst.

སྡུག་བཤད་སྨུག་བཤད་ (dugshɛɛ̀ mugshɛɛ̀) sm. སྡུག་ཤོད་སྨུག་ཤོད་.

སྡུག་སྡུད་སྨུ་སྡུད་ (dugsüü mugsüü) sm. སྡུག་ཤོད་སྨུག་ཤོད་.

སྡུག་སེམས་ (dugsem) evil mind.

སྡུག་སྣན་ (dugsɛn) sm. དུག་རུས་.

སྡུག་གསོད་ (dugsöö) killing/ murdering cruelly; va.—བྱེད་.

སྡུག་བསངས་ (dug sāŋ) vi. to have one's sadness/ sorrow cleared up.

སྡུག་བསལ་སྐྱིད་ཤར་ (dugsɛɛ gyiishar) sm. སྡུག་མཐའ་སྐྱིད་ཟེན་.

སྡུད་: p. བསྡུས་; f. བསྡུ་; imp. སྡུས་ (düü) 1. va. to collect/ assemble/ gather/ convene/ bring in sth. ༎རྒྱལ་ཡོངས་ནས་འབྲུ་རིགས་དཔེ་གཞི་དེ་ཚོ་བསྡུས་པ་རེད་ They collected specimens of grains from all over the nation. ༎ཁོ་ཚོ་ཚང་མ་ས་གནས་གཅིག་ཏུ་བསྡུས་པ་རེད་ They all gathered at one place. ༎ཞིང་པ་ཚོ་སྟོན་ཏོག་སྡུད་ཀྱི་འདུག The farmers are bringing in the harvest. 2. va. to abridge/ abbreviate/ condense ༎ཁོང་གིས་རྒྱལ་རབས་བསྡུས་པ་རེད་ (He) abridged the history.

སྡུད་བསྐུལ་ (düügüü) sm. བསྡུས་བསྐུལ་.

སྡུད་ཉར་ (düüñar) collecting and storing; va.—བྱེད་.

སྡུད་རྟགས་ (düüdaà) ellipsis.

སྡུད་དང་སྐུལ་བརྡ་བ་ (düüdaŋ gūū dawa) shung. a messenger in a district.

སྡུད་པ་ (düüba) abbreviated, condensed.

སྡུད་པའི་དཔག་པ་ (düübɛ bāgba) inductive reasoning.

སྡུད་ཚད་ (düüdzɛɛ̀) the amounted collected/ brought in.

སྡུད་འཚག (düüdzaà) collecting and storing; va.—བྱེད་ ༎ཞིང་པ་ཚོས་འབྲུ་རིགས་མང་པོ་སྡུད་འཚག་བྱས་པ་རེད་ The farmers collected and stored much grain.

སྡུད་འཚོང་ཁྲུའུ་ (düüdzoŋ trū) tib.ch. purchasing and selling division.

སྡུད་ཟུར་ (düüsur) hostile.

སྡུད་རུག (düüruù) gathering, congregating, collecting; va.—བྱེད་.

སྡུད་ལེན་ (düülen) sm. བསྡུ་ལེན་.

སྡུད་ལེན་དུས་སྐབས་ (düülen tüügəb) harvest time.

སྡུད་གསོ་ (düüso) collecting together and giving shelter/ harboring/ keeping.

སྡུད་གསོ་ཁང་ (düüsogaŋ) detention camp, reservation.

སྡུད་གསོག (düüsɔ̀ɔ) sm. སྡུད་འཚག.

སྡུམ་ (dum) arc. house.

སྡུམ་: p. བསྡུམས་; f. བསྡུམ་; imp. སྡུམས་ (dum) va. to mediate a dispute, to bring about a settlement (in a dispute, legal case, etc.) ༎ཁོ་ཚོའི་ས་ཞིང་གི་རྩོད་པ་དེ་བསྡུམ་རྒྱུ་ཁག་པོ་རེད་ It's hard to mediate and settle their land dispute.

སྡུམ་མཁན་ (dumñɛn) sm. སྡུམ་པ་པོ་.

སྡུམ་གཏོང་ (dumdoŋ) sm. སྡུམ་.

སྡུམ་པ་པོ་ (dumbabo) mediator, peace maker, conciliator.

སྡུམ་བྱེད་ (dumjeè) sm. སྡུམ་པ་པོ་.

སྡུམས་ (dum) imp. of སྡུམ་.

སྡུར་: p. and f. བསྡུར་; imp. སྡུར་ (dur) va. to compare ༎རྒྱུ་ཆ་འདི་གཉིས་མཉམ་དུ་བསྡུར་ན་ If (we) compare these two materials. ༎བསམ་ཚུལ་བསྡུར་ནས་འཆར་གཞི་བཟོས་པ་རེད་ (They) made the plan after comparing (their) ideas.

སྡུར་གྲངས་ (durdraŋ) proportionate number (in math).

སྡུར་སྡུར་ཚད་ཚད་ (durdur tsɛɛ̀dzɛɛ̀) comparing things (for size and quality); va.—བྱེད་ ༎ཞིང་པས་རྨོ་ཆས་མ་ཉོས་གོང་སྡུར་སྡུར་ཚད་ཚད་བྱེད་ཀྱི་ཡོད་པ་རེད་ The farmers are comparing plowing implements before buying them.

སྡུར་ཕྲེང་ (durdreŋ) sm. བསྡུར་ཕྲེང་.

སྡུར་ཚད་ (durdzɛɛ) sm. བསྡུར་ཚད་.

སྡུར་ཚད་ཁྲེ་ཙེ་ (durdzɛɛ̀ drēdze) ruler (for measuring).

སྡུར་ཚད་ལྟར་ (durdzɛɛ̀dar) according to the proportion ༎སློབ་ཕྲུག་བུ་དང་བུ་མོའི་སྡུར་ཚད་ལྟར་བསྡུས་པ་རེད་ (They) enrolled male and female students according to their proportion.

སྡུར་ཞིབ་ (durshib) comparing and investigating/ examining; va.—བྱེད་.

སྡུར་གཟིགས་ (dursii) looking at and comparing.

སྡུས་ (düü) imp. of སྡུད་.

སྡུས་རྒྱ་ (düügya) shung. a net used for holding hay.

སྡེ་ (de) community, tribe, enclave, section, village; va.—འཁྲུག to have communal disturbances/ disputes ༎འབྲོག་སྡེ་ Nomad group. ༎ཆོས་སྡེ་ Religious community. ༎སྡེ་དང་དགོན་པ་ The village community and monastery.

སྡེ་དཀྲུག་འཕྱུངས་སྦྱོར་ (dedruù pūŋjɔɔ) shung. instigating and causing trouble ༎མི་ནང་དཔོན་འབངས་སྡེ་དཀྲུག་འཕྱུངས་སྦྱོར་གྱི་བྱ་སྤྱོད་དངོས་ཤུགས་གང་གསུམ་ནས་མེད་པ་དགོས་རྒྱུ་ There shall not be any instigating and causing trouble between the lord and the subjects.

སྡེ་སྐོར་ (degɔɔ) traveling around villages/ towns.

སྡེ་ཁག (degaà) section, group, division, department, administrative unit in a country.

སྡེ་མཁར་ (degar) castle, citadel.

སྡེ་གླིང་གང་ (deliŋ kaŋ) whole village or small town.

སྡེ་དགེ་ (derge) Derge (traditional kingdom now located in Sichuan province).

སྡེ་དགེ་སྤྱི་ཁྱབ་ (derge jīgyəb) shung. sm. སྡེ་དགེ་ས་སྐྱོད་.

སྡེ་དགེ་ས་སྐྱོད་ (derge sājöö) shung. the governor general of Derge.

སྡེ་དགོན་ (degön) shung. civilian and monastic (communities), subjects and monasteries.

སྡེ་མགོ་སྐྱོང་ (dego gyōŋ) va. to head or govern a village/ town/ community.

སྡེ་རྒྱ་ (degya) the size of a village/ community.

སྡེ་ཐང་ (dedaŋ) fields, plains.

སྡེ་དུད་ (dedüü) shung. the subjects ¶ཁོངས་གཏོགས་གཡོག་རིགས་སྡེ་དུད་རང་འཇགས་བདག་རིགས་ཆོག་པ་ (You) are permitted to take possession of the servants and the subjects as before.

སྡེ་སྣོད་ (denöö) the pitakas ¶སྡེ་སྣོད་ཆེན་པོ་གསུམ་ The Tripitaka (vinaya, sutra, abhidharma).

སྡེ་སྣོད་གསུམ་ (denöö sūm) the Tripitaka (vinaya, sutra, abhidharma).

སྡེ་པ་ (deba) shung. 1. person in charge of an estate/ province. 2. chief of a territory. 3. group of letters in the Tibetan alphabet.

སྡེ་པ་གཞུང་ (dewashuŋ) shung. name of the traditional Tibetan Government.

སྡེ་དཔོན་ (debön) shung. 1. chief, head, leader. 2. the highest strata of the aristocracy.

སྡེ་དཔོན་མི་དྲག (debön midraà) shung. the highest strata of the aristocrats.

སྡེ་སྤྱི་ (deji) shung. abbr. of སྡེ་དགེ་སྤྱི་ཁྱབ་.

སྡེ་སྤྱི་ཁྱུང་སྐྱིད་ (deji kyüŋgyiì) shung. abbr. of སྡེ་དགེ་སྤྱི་ཁྱབ་ཁྱུང་རམ་ and སྐྱིད་སྨད་.

སྡེ་འབངས་ (debaŋ) 1. tribe. 2. lord/ chief and subject.

སྡེ་འབངས་མི་སེར་ (debaŋ miser) sm. སྡེ་འབངས་.

སྡེ་འབྱེད་ (de jeè) va. to separate or differentiate communities/ villages/ sections.

སྡེ་དམག (demaà) 1.the citizens/ subjects and the army. 2. militia.

སྡེ་ཚན་ (dedzɛn) unit, section, department ¶བཟོ་གྲྭ་འདིའི་སྡེ་ཚན་དང་པོ་ The first section of this factory.

སྡེ་ཚོ་ (dedzo) village.

སྡེ་ཚོགས་ (dedzɔɔ̀) 1. organization, association. 2. Youth League.

སྡེ་ཚོགས་ཀྲུང་དབྱང་ (dedzɔɔ̀ drūŋyaŋ) tib.ch. central committee of the Youth League.

སྡེ་ཞིབ་མཁན་མདའ་སྤྲེལ་པོ་ (dēshib kēnda dreebo) shung. abbr. of སྡེ་ཞིབ་མཁན་ཆུང་ and མདའ་དཔོན་.

སྡེ་ཞིབ་མཁན་པོ་ (dēshib kēmbo) shung. monk official of the 4th rank who is in charge of the Deshib office.

སྡེ་ཞིབ་ལས་ཁུངས་ (deshib lɛ̀ègun) shung. an office in charge of settling law cases in tt. government.

སྡེ་གཞུང་ (deshuŋ) local government.

སྡེ་གཟར་ (desar) 1. disturbance, trouble, war ¶གོར་བོད་སྡེ་གཟར་སྐབས་ At the time of the Nepalese-Tibetan disturbance.

སྡེ་ཟིང་དཀྲུག་ཟིང་ (desiŋ gusiŋ) disorderliness, disturbance.

སྡེ་ཡངས་ (deyaŋ) quadrangle.

སྡེ་ཤོག (deshɔɔ̀) tribe, group, unit, division.

སྡེ་སྲིད་ (desii) shung. regent.

སྡེ་སྲིད་ལྷན་ཚོགས་ (desiì lhɛndzɔɔ̀) shung. regent's council.

སྡེངས་ཆ་ (denja) sm. སྡིངས་ཆ་.

སྡེབ་: p. བསྡེབས་; f. བསྡེབ་; imp. བསྡེབས་ (deb) 1. va. to mix/ join together, to put all in one, to collect together ¶ཁོང་གིས་དཔྱད་གཞིའི་གནས་ཚུལ་མང་པོ་མཉམ་དུ་བསྡེབས་ནས་རྩོམ་ཞིག་བྲིས་པ་རེད་ He collected together much research information and wrote an article. 2. va. to compound/ mix (e.g., medicines) ¶ཁོས་སྨན་གསར་པ་ཞིག་སྡེབ་སྦྱོར་བྱས་པ་རེད་ He compounded a new medicine. 3. see སྡེབ་ལ་.

སྡེབ་སྐྱོད་ (debgyöö) going together.

སྡེབ་རྒྱ་ (debgya) kind, type ¶རས་འདིའི་སྡེབ་རྒྱ་མི་འདུག (We) don't have this type of cloth.

སྡེབ་སྒྲིག (debdrig) compiling, putting/ joining together, collecting together; va.—བྱེད་ ¶ལོ་རྒྱུས་ཀྱི་ཡིག་ཆ་ཁག་ཅིག་སྡེབ་སྒྲིག་བྱས་པ་རེད་ (They) collected together a group of documents on history.

སྡེབ་སྒྲིགས་ (debdrig) sm. སྡེབ་སྒྲིག.

སྡེབ་གཅིག (debjig) in one swoop, all at once ¶ཉ་མང་པོ་སྡེབ་གཅིག་ཏུ་འཛིན་ཐུབ་པ་རེད་ (They) were able to catch many fish all at once.

སྡེབ་བཙུར་ (debjur) laying siege to, besieging; va.—བྱེད་.

སྡེབ་མཆོང་བྱེད་ (debcoŋ ceè) va. to rush at/ for sth. all together.

སྡེབ་འཆམ་རྒྱག (debcam gyaà) va. to have many groups performing Tibetan operas at the same time.

སྡེབ་ཉོ་ (debño) wholesale buying/ purchasing, bulk purchasing; va.—རྒྱག; —བྱེད་ to purchase goods in bulk or wholesale.

སྡེབ་ཉོ་སྡེབ་ཚོང་ (debño debdzoŋ) wholesale buying and selling.

སྡེབ་སྦྱོར་ (debjɔɔ) 1. poetry, poetics, composition. 2. breeding animals. 3. constructing words from prefix/ suffix letters. 4. one of the five minor རིགས་གནས་. 5. sexual intercourse; va.—བྱེད་.

སྡེབ་སྦྱོར་ས་ཚིགས་ (debjɔɔ sədzii) breeding station.

སྡེབ་རྩིས་ (debdzii) accounting/ paying back for sth. all at once (in a lump sum); va.—རྒྱག ¶ངས་འགྲོ་སོང་རྣམས་ལོ་མཇུག་ལ་སྡེབ་རྩིས་རྒྱག་གི་ཡིན་ I will account for the expenses all at once at the end of the year.

སྡེབ་ཚོང་ (debdzoŋ) sm. སྡེབ་འཚོང་.

སྡེབ་ཚོང་ཁྲོམ་ར་ (debdzoŋ trōmra) wholesale market.

སྡེབ་ཚོང་ཚོང་ཁང་ (debdzoŋ tsōŋgaŋ) wholesale store.

སྡེབ་འཚོང་ (debdzoŋ) selling wholesale; va.—རྒྱག; —བྱེད་.

སྡེབ་འཚོང་ཁང་ (debdzoŋgaŋ) wholesale store.

སྡེབ་འཚོང་ཚོང་ར་ (debdzoŋ tsōŋra) wholesale market.

སྡེབ་འཚོང་རིན་གོང་ (debdzoŋ ringoŋ) wholesale price.

སྡེབ་འཚོང་ས་ཚིགས་ (debdzoŋ sədzii) wholesale station.

སྡེབས་འཛོམས་ (deb dzom) vi. to gather/ assemble many things all together.

སྡེབ་རྫོབ་ (debdzob) many things getting put/ piled/ loaded on together; va.—རྒྱག ¶དེང་སང་ལས་ཀ་མང་པོ་ཞིག་སྡེབ་རྫོབ་བརྒྱབ་ནས་བྲེལ་བ་ཆེན་པོ་ཡོད་ These days I am very busy because many different jobs have been piled on me.

སྡེབ་འུར་ (debwur) many people coming together and causing a disturbance; va.—རྒྱག.

སྡེབ་ཟིང་ (debsiŋ) many people causing a disturbance/ trouble all at once; va.—རྒྱག.

སྡེབ་གཟིགས་ (debsiì) h. of སྡེབ་ལེན་.

སྡེབ་བཞེས་ (debsheè) h. of སྡེབ་ཉོ་.

སྡེབ་རུབ་ (debrub) sm. རུབ་རྒྱག.

སྡེབ་ལ་ (debla) all together, in bulk, in mass ¶ངས་ཤ་སྡེབ་ལ་ཉོས་པ་ཡིན་ I bought meat in bulk.

སྡེབ་ལེན་ (deblen) va. to collect all at once.

སྡེབ་གསོད་ (debsöö) massacring/ killing many together; va.—གཏོང་; —བྱེད་.

སྡེབ་བསད་ (debsɛɛ̀) sm. སྡེབ་གསོད་.

སྡེབས་ (deb) imp. of སྡེབ་.

སྡེབས་གཅིག (debjig) sm. སྡེབ་གཅིག.

སྡེབས་འབུངས་ཐེབས་ (debuŋ tēè) sm. ཕུང་གསོག་ཐེབས.

སྡེབས་གསོད་ (debsöö) sm. སྡེབ་གསོད་.

སྡེམ་: p. བསྡམས་; f. བསྡམ་; imp. སྡོམས་ (dem) 1. va. to tie ¶ཁོས་བཙོན་པ་དེ་ཐག་པས་བསྡམས་བཞག He has tied up the prisoner with a rope. 2. va. to ban ¶དེང་སང་ཨ་རག་འཐུང་མི་ཆོག་པའི་ཁྲིམས་བསྡམས་བཞག These days they have banned the drinking of liquor.

སྡེམ་འཆིང་ (demjiŋ) tying up (usu. hair); va.—རྒྱག.

སྡེམ་ར་གནང་ (demra nāŋ) shung. va. (setting up land marks) where animals are not permitted to graze ¶རི་རྩྭ་ཕལ་ཆེར་རྩྭ་ཐོས་བཅད་དེ་སྡེམ་ར་གནང་བ་ (They) set up land marks on most of the grasses on the mountain where animals are not permitted to graze.

སྡེར་ (der) abbr. of སྡེར་མོ་ and སྡེར་མ་.

སྡེར་ཆགས་ (derjaà) animals with claws.

སྡེར་ཐང་ (derdaŋ) open space, open field.
སྡེར་ཐོགས་ (derdɔɔ̀) sm. སྡེར་ཆགས་.
སྡེར་སྙུད་ (derjɛɛ̀) plate, saucer.
སྡེར་མ་ (derma) plate, saucer.
སྡེར་མ་སྐྱུད་ཅན་ (derma gṻüjɛn) shung. cloisonné ware.
སྡེར་མོ་ (dermo) claws.
སྡེར་ཚེ་ (derdze) sm. སྡེར་མ་.
སྡེར་རྩལ་ (dērdzɛɛ) 1. skillful in climbing/ jumping. 2. powerful claws.
སྡེར་ཤད་ (dershɛɛ̀) clawing, scratching with claws; va.—རྒྱག ། ཞི་མིས་ས་ལ་སྡེར་ཤད་རྒྱག་གི་འདུག The cat is scratching the ground.
སྡོ་: p. **སྡོས་** or **བསྡོས་**; f. **བསྡོ་**; imp. **སྡོས་** (do) va. to risk, to endanger ། གཞན་གྱི་ལུས་སྲོག་ལ་སྡོ་ཡས་ལ་ Endangering the life of others.
སྡོག: p. **བསྡོགས་**; f. **བསྡོག**; imp. **སྡོགས་** (dɔɔ̀) 1. va. to pack/ get ready (for a trip) ། ལམ་དུ་དགོས་པ་དྲན་ཚད་བསྡོགས་ཡོད་ I've packed all the things for the road I could remember. 2. va. to wind up (thread, rope, etc.) ། སྐུད་པ་འདི་ཚང་མ་སྡོགས་དང་ Please wind the thread up completely. 3. va. to conclude/ finish ། ཁོ་ཚོ་ལས་འགན་ད་ལོ་བསྡུག་གི་རེད་ They are winding up their work this year. 4. va. to pull/ lift up one's pants or dress ། ཁོང་གིས་ཕྱུ་པ་ཡར་བསྡོགས་ནས་ཆུ་བརྒལ་སོང་ He pulled up his dress and crossed the river.
སྡོག་སྐྱོད་ (dɔggyöö) sm. སྡོག.
སྡོགས་ (dɔɔ̀) imp. of སྡོག.
སྡོང་ (doŋ) abbr. of སྡོང་པོ་.
སྡོང་: p. **བསྡོངས་**; f. **བསྡོང་**; imp. **སྡོངས་** (doŋ) va. to join, to accompany ། ཁོང་གྲོགས་པོ་དང་བསྡོངས་ཏེ་གནས་སྐོར་ལ་ཕྱིན་སོང་ He went on pilgrimage accompanied by his friends.
སྡོང་ཁང་ (doŋgaŋ) 1. tree trunk. 2. stem of a plant.
སྡོང་སྐམ་ (doŋgam) dried/ withered tree.
སྡོང་འཁྲིད་སྐྱེ་དངོས་ (doŋgyüü gyēŋöö) a climbing/ twining stem or plant.
སྡོང་གྲོགས་ (doŋdrɔɔ̀) helper; va.—བྱེད་ to help/ assist.
སྡོང་རྒན་ཁོག་རུལ་ (doŋgɛn kɔ̄grüü) a useless old person [Lit. old trunk, rotten inside].
སྡོང་གཅོད་ར་བ་ (doŋjöö rawa) lumbering area.
སྡོང་ཐུང་ཤིང་ (doŋduŋ shiŋ) shrubbery, shrubs.
སྡོང་དུམ་ (doŋdum) wood log.
སྡོང་པོ་ (doŋbo) 1. trunk (of tree), stalk/ stem (of plants). 2. a tree.
སྡོང་ཕུང་ (doŋbuŋ) a type of traditional medicine (tuber of gastrodia elata).
སྡོང་ཕྲུག (doŋdruù) sapling, young tree.
སྡོང་ཕྲུག་ར་བ་ (doŋdruù rawa) a fence to protect a young tree.
སྡོང་བུ་ (doŋbu) 1. small trunk/ stalk/ stem. 2. wick.
སྡོང་སྨྱུག་ར་བ་ (doŋñug rawa) seedling nursery.
སྡོང་རྩེ་ (doŋdze) the tip of a tree, tree top.
སྡོང་ཟླ་ (doŋda) sm. སྡོངས་གྲོགས་.
སྡོང་རས་ (doŋrɛɛ̀) a wick.
སྡོང་རིང་ཤིང་ (doŋriŋ shiŋ) tall/ majestic tree.
སྡོང་རུལ་ (doŋrüü) rotten/ rotted tree.
སྡོང་རུལ་སླར་སྐྱེས་ (doŋrüü lārgyeè) new lease on life [Lit. rotten tree again grow].
སྡོང་རོ་ (doŋro) a burnt-out wick.
སྡོང་རས་ (doŋrɛɛ̀) cotton wick.
སྡོང་ལོ་ (doŋlo) leaf.
སྡོང་སངས་རྒྱག (doŋsaŋ gyaà) va. to cut the tip of a butter lamp wick to make it burn brighter.
སྡོད་: p. and f. **བསྡད་** imp. **སྡོད་** (döö) va. to live, to reside, to stay, to remain, to sit ། ཁོ་ལྷ་སར་ཡུན་རིང་བསྡད་པ་རེད་ He lived in Lhasa a long time. ། ཀུབ་ཀྱག་སྟེང་ལ་སྡོད་དང་ Sit on the chair. ། ལུགས་སྲོལ་དེ་ཚོ་དེང་སང་ཡང་བསྡད་ཡོད་པ་རེད་ Those customs remain even these days. 2. (vb. + པར་/བར་ or ཏེ་ + — +) stay/ keep doing the verbal action ། རླུང་འཕྲིན་ཉན་ཏེ་བསྡད་པ་རེད་ (They) stayed listening to the radio.
སྡོད་ཁང་ (döögaŋ) residence/ living quarters, house, flat, apartment.
སྡོད་ཁང་གི་ཁུལ་ (döögaŋgi kṻü) sm. སྡོད་ཁུལ་.
སྡོད་ཁང་གི་ཆ་རྐྱེན་ (döögaŋgi cāgyen) housing conditions.
སྡོད་ཁུལ་ (döögüü) residential district/ neighborhood/ area.
སྡོད་ཁོམ་ (döögom) having time to stay.
སྡོད་ཁྱིམ་ (döögyim) sm. སྡོད་ཁང་.
སྡོད་མཁན་ (dööñɛn) 1. resident, dweller. 2. the one (who is) seated.
སྡོད་གྲལ་ (döötrɛɛ) row of seated people; va.—ལ་འཁོད་; —སྒྲིག; —ལ་གཏོང་ to seat/ arrange people in rows.
སྡོད་གྲོགས་ (dööroò) 1. spouse. 2. roommate.
སྡོད་སྒར་ (döögar) camp ། སྐྱབས་བཅོལ་བའི་སྡོད་སྒར་ Refugee camp.
སྡོད་སྒྲིག (döödrig) making accommodations for travelers; va.—བྱེད་; —བཙེ ། ཚོགས་འདུའི་འཐུས་མི་རྣམས་ལ་ང་ཚོས་སྡོད་སྒྲིག་བྱ་དགོས་ We have to arrange accommodations for the delegates to the meeting.
སྡོད་སྒྲོམ་ (döödrom) a wooden frame on which cushions are set for sitting.
སྡོད་ཆོག་དབང་ཆ་ (dööjɔɔ wāŋja) sm. སྡོད་དབང་.
སྡོད་སྟངས་ (döödaŋ) manner/ way of sitting or living ། ཁོའི་སྡོད་སྟངས་ཁ་བསྡུས་རེད་ His manner of living is simple.
སྡོད་སྟེགས་ (döödeg) chair, seat.
སྡོད་མདའ་ (dönda) shung. abbr. of བཅའ་སྡོད་མདའ་དཔོན་.
སྡོད་གནས་ (dööñɛɛ̀) place of residence, dwelling place.
སྡོད་བྱ་ (dööja) on duty; vi.—འཁོར་ to have one's turn to stay (on guard or on duty) come ། དེ་རིང་ང་ལས་ཁུངས་ཀྱི་སྡོད་བྱ་ཡིན་ Today I am the one on duty in the office.
སྡོད་བྱ་ཁང་ (dööjagaŋ) room/ office where the person on duty stays.
སྡོད་བྱ་རེས་མོས་ (dööja reèmöö) taking turns being on duty, working in shifts.
སྡོད་དབང་ (dööwaŋ) right of residence.
སྡོད་འབངས་ (dööbaŋ) residents, citizens, populace ། ལྷ་ས་གྲོང་ཁྱེར་གྱི་སྡོད་འབངས་ཁྲི་ལྔ་ The fifty thousand residents of Lhasa.
སྡོད་འབངས་ཨུ་ཡོན་ལྷན་ཁང་ (dööbaŋ ūyön lhēngaŋ) neighborhood committee.
སྡོད་མ་ཚུགས་ (döö madzuù) 1. promiscuous person, sb. who does not stick to one relationship. 2. a busybody, one who cannot sit still, one who interferes in other people's business.
སྡོད་མི་ (döömi) sm. སྡོད་མཁན་.
སྡོད་དམངས་ (dööman) sm. སྡོད་འབངས་.
སྡོད་ཚུགས་ (döödzuù) sm. སྡོད་ཚུགས་པོ་.
སྡོད་ཚུགས་པོ་ (döödzugbu) opposite of སྡོད་མ་ཚུགས་.
སྡོད་ཚུགས་མེད་པ་ (döödzuù meèba) sm. སྡོད་མ་ཚུགས་.
སྡོད་བཟོད་བདེ་པོ་ (döösöö dobo) safe and peaceful ། ཇག་པ་ཚང་མ་རྩ་མེད་བཟོས་ཙང་དེང་སང་ལུང་པའི་སྡོད་བཟོད་བདེ་པོ་འདུག Because they annihilated the bandits, these days the area is safe and peaceful.
སྡོད་བཟོད་མ་བདེ་བ་ (döösöö madewa) unsafe, in turmoil, dangerous.
སྡོད་བཟོད་པོ་ (döö sööbo) sm. སྡོད་བཟོད་བདེ་པོ་.
སྡོད་ཡུལ་ (dööyüü) place of residence.
སྡོད་རེས་ (dööreè) va. turns; va.—བྱེད་ to take turns staying, to alternate duty/ watch ། ཨེམ་ཆི་དེ་གཉིས་སྨན་ཁང་ནང་སྡོད་རེས་བྱེད་ཀྱི་ཡོད་པ་རེད་ The two doctors take turns being on duty in the hospital.
སྡོད་རོགས་ (dööroò) 1. roommate, companion. 2. spouse, common-law partner.
སྡོད་ལུགས་ (döölüù) 1. sitting posture. 2. way/ style of living.
སྡོད་ཤག (dööshaà) sm. སྡོད་ཁང་.
སྡོད་ས་ (döösa) 1. place of residence, place to stay or live; va.—སྤོས་ to move one's residence. 2. a

seat (in a congress, parliament, plane, etc.).

སྡོད་ས་སྟོང་པ་ (d̲ö̱ösa dōŋba) an empty seat.

སྡོད་སྲུང་ (d̲ö̱ösuŋ) occupying/ staying somewhere in order to defend it; va.—བྱེད་.

སྡོད་ས་ལེགས་གྲས་ (d̲ö̱ösa le̱gdrɛɛ̀) first class seat (in plane or train), the best seats in a section.

སྡོད་ས་ཨང་དང་པོ་ (d̲ö̱ösa āŋ ta̱ŋbo) first class seat.

སྡོམ་: p. བསྡམས་; f. བསྡམ་; imp. སྡོམས་ (do̱m) 1. va. to add, to total, to sum up ། ནང་གི་མི་ཚང་མ་བསྡོམས་ན་བཅུ་བདུན་ཙམ་ཡོད་ If (we) added up all the people at home, there are about seventeen. 2. va. to tie, to bind, to fasten ། མེ་ཏོག་མང་པོ་ཆག་པར་བསྡམས་འདུག Many flowers have been tied into a bunch.

སྡོམ་ (do̱m) 1. spider. 2. sm. སྡིམ་.

སྡོམ་དཀར་ (do̱mgar) sm. སྡོམ་སྐྱ་.

སྡོམ་སྐུད་ (do̱mgüü) spider web.

སྡོམ་སྐྱ་ (do̱mgya) a white spider.

སྡོམ་ཁྲིམས་ (do̱mtrim) covenant, vow, monk's vows.

སྡོམ་གྱི་དྲ་ཐག (do̱mgi tra̱daà) spider web.

སྡོམ་གྱི་དྲ་བ་ (do̱mgi tra̱wa) spider web.

སྡོམ་གྱི་དྲ་བ་ལྟ་བུ་ (do̱mgi tra̱wa də̱bu) extremely complicated/ involved/ intricate [Lit. like a spider's web].

སྡོམ་ཐག (do̱mdaà) 1. spider web; va.—གཏོང་ to spin a spider web. 2. cobweb.

སྡོམ་པ་ (do̱mba) vow; va.—སྲུང་ to keep one's vow/ oath/ promise; va.—ལེན་ to take a vow/ oath; vi.—དོར་ to lose or break one's vow/ oath; va.—འབུལ་ to give back one's vows (and stop being a monk/ nun).

སྡོམ་འབོར་ (do̱mbɔɔ) total.

སྡོམ་བྱེད་ཤ་གནད་ (do̱mjeè shānɛɛ̀) sphincter.

སྡོམ་གཙང་ (do̱mdzaŋ) a monk who is adhering to his vows/ celibacy.

སྡོམ་རྩིས་ (do̱mdzii̇) 1. statistics ། སྡོམ་རྩིས་ལྟར་ན་ According to statistics. 2. adding up, addition; va.—རྒྱག to do addition. 3. settling accounts; va.—རྒྱག to settle accounts, to calculate (totals).

སྡོམ་རྩིས་ཅུའུ་ (do̱mdzii̇ jū) tib.ch. statistical bureau.

སྡོམ་རྩིས་པ་ (do̱mdzii̇bə) statistician, accountant.

སྡོམ་རྩིས་དཔྱད་གཞི་ (do̱mdzii̇ jɛ̀ɛshi) statistical data.

སྡོམ་རྩིས་ཡིག་རིགས་ (do̱mdzii̇ yi̱grig) statistical figures/ data/ charts.

སྡོམ་རྩིས་རིག་པ་ (do̱mdzii̇ ri̱gbə) statistics (as a subject).

སྡོམ་རྩིས་རེའུ་མིག (do̱mdzii̇ ri̱umii̇) statistical form/ chart, a table of statistics.

སྡོམ་བརྩོན་ (do̱mdzön) monk.

སྡོམ་ཚིག (do̱mdzii̇) conclusion, decision, statement, summary statement, e.g., of a meeting.

སྡོམ་གཟེར་ (do̱mser) rivet; va.—རྒྱག to rivet sth.

སྡོམ་གཟེར་རྒྱག་མཁན་ (do̱mser gya̱àñɛn) riveter.

སྡོམ་གཟེར་རྒྱག་སྤྱད་ (do̱mser gya̱àjɛɛ̀) riveting gun/ equipment.

སྡོམ་ལ་ (do̱mla) sm. སྡོམ་ན་.

སྡོམ་ལུང་ (do̱mluŋ) religious initiation reading for taking vows.

སྡོམ་ཤ་ (do̱msha) sphincter.

སྡོམ་གསོས་ (do̱msöö) fattening an animal (before slaughtering); va.—རྒྱག.

སྡོམས་ (do̱m) imp. of སྡོམ་.

སྡོར་ (dɔ̱ɔ) meat or fat or butter put in soups/ noodles/ broths.

སྡོར་མར་ (dɔ̱rmar) shung. butter put in tea ། མང་ཇ་ཇེ་སྲིད་བར་བསྟུལ་རྒྱུའི་སྡོར་མར་དམིགས་ཐེབས་སུ་བསྟུལ་བ་ (They) set up a trust for tea butter that would be served in the monastery forever.

སྡོས་ (dö̱ö) p. of སྡོ་.

བརྡ་ (da̱) 1. signal, sign, gesture; va.—གཏོང་ to signal, to gesture, to give/ send a sign or signal ། གྲ་སྒྲིག་བྱེད་དགོས་པའི་བརྡ་བཏང་བ་རེད་ They gave the signal to get ready. 2. communicating; va.—སྤྲོད་ to communicate, to get a message across; vi.—འཕྲོད་ to be/ get communicated with. 3. term, terminology ། བརྡ་རྙིང་པ་ An old/ archaic term.

བརྡ་དཀྲོག (da̱drɔɔ̀) alarm, warning; va.—གཏོང་ to sound the alarm, to give warning.

བརྡ་སྐད་ (da̱gɛɛ) verbal signal.

བརྡ་སྐྱེལ་ (da̱ gyeē) va. to give or deliver a message/ notice ། མང་ཚོགས་རྣམས་ཚོགས་འདུར་ཡོང་དགོས་པའི་བརྡ་སྐྱེལ་དགོས་ (They) sent a message for the masses to come to a meeting.

བརྡ་ཁྱབ་ (də̱gyəb) notification, notice, announcement; va.—གཏོང་.

བརྡ་མཁན་ (da̱ñɛn) sb. who gives notices/ messages.

བརྡ་གྲོལ་བྱེད་ (da̱dröö ceè) sm. གསིག་འགྲོལ་བྱེད་.

བརྡ་རྒྱག་པ་ (da̱ gyaàba) message giver, messenger.

བརྡ་སྒྲོག (da̱ drɔɔ̀) va. to make an announcement.

བརྡ་ཆད་ (da̱jɛɛ̀) 1. special/ technical terms. 2. an equivalent term/ word.

བརྡ་མཇལ་ (da̱njɛɛ) greeting sb. of equal rank; va.—གཏོང་.

བརྡ་རྙིང་ (də̱ñiŋ) archaic term.

བརྡ་གཏོང་སྒྲོན་མེ་ (da̱doŋ drö̱nme) signal lamp/ light/ lantern.

བརྡ་གཏོང་གློག་ཤུ་ (da̱doŋ lōgshu) sm. བརྡ་གཏོང་སྒྲོན་མེ་.

བརྡ་གཏོང་དར་ཆ་ (da̱doŋ da̱rja) signal flag.

བརྡ་གཏོང་དྲིལ་བུ་ (da̱doŋ di̱ibu) signal bell.

བརྡ་གཏོང་མདེའུ་ (da̱doŋ di̱wu) signal flare/ bullet/ shot.

བརྡ་གཏོང་མེ་མདའ་ (da̱doŋ me̱nda) signal gun, flare gun.

བརྡ་ཏ་གཅིག (da̱daàjig) a little bit, a small amount.

བརྡ་རྟགས་ (da̱daà) symbol, sign, signal; va.—གཏོང་ ། དམག་མི་ཚོས་མགོ་སྒྲུར་རྒྱུའི་བརྡ་རྟགས་བཏང་བ་རེད་ The soldiers sent a signal that they will surrender.

བརྡ་སྟོན་འཕྲུལ་འཁོར་ (da̱dön trüügɔɔ) radar.

བརྡ་ཐོ་ (da̱do) a notice; va.—གཏོང་ ། ཞིབ་སར་བཅར་དགོས་པའི་བརྡ་ཐོ་བཏང་ (They) sent a notice saying that (they) had to come to the place of the investigation.

བརྡ་དག (da̱dag) sm. དག་ཆ་.

བརྡ་དྲིལ་ (da̱drii) signal/ alarm bell; va.—དཀྲོལ་ to sound a signal, to ring an alarm bell.

བརྡ་མདེལ་ (da̱del) signal flare/ shot/ bullet; va.—རྒྱག to fire a flare.

བརྡ་དཔྱད་ (da̱jɛɛ) sending/ giving a signal; va.—བྱེད་.

བརྡ་སྤྲོད་ (da̱dröö) 1. grammar ། བོད་ཡིག་བརྡ་སྤྲོད་ Tibetan grammar. 2. conveying, transmitting, communicating; va.—བྱེད་ ། གནས་ཚུལ་དེ་མང་ཚོགས་ལ་བརྡ་སྤྲོད་བྱ་དགོས་ They should communicate this information to the masses.

བརྡ་སྤྲོད་སྒམ་ (da̱dröö ga̱m) information box.

བརྡ་སྤྲོད་པ་ (da̱drööba) grammatical ། བརྡ་སྤྲོད་པའི་བསྟན་བཅོས་ Grammatical treatise.

བརྡ་སྤྲོད་རིག་པ་ (da̱dröö ri̱gbə) grammar.

བརྡ་ཕུལ་ (dābüü) h. of བརྡ་སྤྲོད་, 2.

བརྡ་འཕྲིན་ (da̱ndrin) message ། ང་ལ་བརྡ་འཕྲིན་འབྱོར་བྱུང་ I received a message.

བརྡ་འཕྲིན་བརྒྱུད་གཏོང་ས་ཚིགས་ (da̱ndrin gyü̱üdoŋ sə̱dzii) communication transfer station.

བརྡ་འཕྲོད་ (dā dröö) 1. vi. to have a message be received ། ངས་ལན་བསྐུར་བ་དེ་བརྡ་འཕྲོད་མི་འདུག The message I sent wasn't received. 2. vi. to understand (sth. said or written) ། ང་རྒྱ་སྐད་ཡག་པོ་མེད་ཙང་བརྡ་འཕྲོད་ཀྱི་མི་འདུག Because my Chinese is not good, it is not being understood.

བརྡ་བྱུང་ཀེར་རྟགས་ (da̱juŋ gērdaà) shung. a mark indicating that one has received a message ། རྩེ་ཚོམ་ཆེན་དུ་ཚང་འཛོམས་ཐུབ་པ་དགོས་རྒྱུ་བཅས་བརྡ་བྱུང་ཀེར་རྟགས་རེ་ངེས་འགོད་དང་འབྲིལ་ Everybody must assemble in the assembly hall in the Potala Palace and must put a mark indicating that one has received the message.

བརྡ་འབྱོར་ (da̱ jɔɔ) vi. to receive a message/ signal.

བརྡ་སྦྱོར་ (dajɔɔ) sending a message; va.—བྱེད་.

བརྡ་སྦྱོར་མཁན་པོ་ (dajɔɔ kēmbo) sb. expert in grammar.

བརྡ་སྦྱོར་དུང་སྦུབ་ (dajɔɔ tuŋbub) megaphone.

བརྡ་མ་ (dama) a type of drum played by the Dalai Lama's dance troupe (in tt.).

བརྡ་མེ་ (dame) a signal made from fire.

བརྡ་ཚིག (dədzii) term, word.

བརྡ་མཚོན་ (dandzön) sm. མཚོན་བྱེད་.

བརྡ་མཚོན་རྟགས་ཤད་ (dandzön dāgshɛɛ̀) punctuation marks.

བརྡ་མཛད་ (da dzɛɛ̀) va. to send/ give a sign or signal.

བརྡ་འཛིན་འཕྲུལ་འཁོར་ (dandzin trüügɔɔ) communications satellite.

བརྡ་ཡིག (dəyii) 1. written notice. 2. commentary (on grammar).

བརྡ་ལན་ (dalɛn) response, answer; va.—བྱེད་; —སྤྲོད་ ༖ངས་ཁོང་ལ་སྐད་ཆ་དྲིས་པ་དེ་ར་བརྡ་ལན་བྱས་མ་བྱུང་ He didn't answer the question I asked him.

བརྡ་ལེན་ (dalen) sm. བརྡ་ལན་.

བརྡ་ལེན་འཕྲུལ་འཁོར་ (dalen trüügɔɔ) sm. བརྡ་འཛིན་འཕྲུལ་འཁོར་.

བརྡ་ལོག (da lɔ̀ɔ) vi. to be misunderstood.

བརྡབ་ (dəb) f. of རྡེབ་.

བརྡབ་སྐྱོན་ (dəbgyön) damage from colliding/ crashing/ banging into sth. ༖མོ་ཊ་བརྡབ་སྐྱོན་བྱུང་ནས་མི་གཅིག་ཤི་བཞག The car crashed and one person died.

བརྡབ་དཀྲུག (dəbdruù) tattling on sb.; va.—རྒྱག.

བརྡབ་ཆག་ཤོར་ (dəbjaà shɔ̄ɔ) vi. to break from banging into sth. ༖ཁོང་སྐས་འཛེགས་སྐབས་ནས་རིལ་དེ་རྐང་པ་བརྡབ་ཆག་ཤོར་བཞག He fell from the ladder and broke his leg.

བརྡབ་འཆོས་དེ་འགྲོ་ (dəbjöòde dro) vi. to go staggering (from being drunk).

བརྡབ་གདན་ (dəbdɛn) small rug placed under the leather board that is used in a Tibetan dice game.

བརྡབ་བརྡབ་ (dəbdəb) dusting off (by banging/ hitting); va.—བྱེད་ ༖ཁོས་མལ་གཟན་བརྡབ་བརྡབ་བྱས་པ་རེད་ He dusted off his blanket (by banging it).

བརྡབ་བརྡབ་གསིག་གསིག (dəbdəb sīgsii) emptying one's pockets, wallets, etc. of everything ༖དངུལ་ཡོད་པ་ཚང་མ་སྦྲ་ཁུག་བརྡབ་བརྡབ་གསིག་གསིག་བཏང་ནས་སྤྲད་པ་ཡིན་ I emptied my wallet and gave him all the money I had.

བརྡབ་ཕོར་ (dəbbɔɔ) the cup in which dice are placed for throwing.

བརྡབ་རྨས་ (dəbmɛɛ̀) a sore/ bruise/ cut caused by banging against sth.

བརྡབ་ཞོགས་ (dəbshɔɔ̀) keeping up with friends/ neighbors in success or affluence; va.—ལང་.

བརྡབ་གཞུ་ (dəbshuù) beating and lashing.

བརྡབ་གཤོགས་ (dəbshɔɔ̀) sm. བརྡབ་ཞོགས་.

བརྡབ་གསིག (dəbsii) sm. བརྡབ་གསིགས་.

བརྡབ་བསིགས་ (dəbsii) 1. rough, harsh, severe ༖ཕྱག་ལས་བྱེད་ཡས་དེ་གཟུགས་པོར་བརྡབ་གསིགས་ཆེན་པོ་རེད་ Manual labor is rough on the body. 2. causing hardship, oppressing, exploiting; va.—བྱེད་ ༖དམག་པོའི་སྲིད་གཞུང་དེས་མི་དམངས་ལ་བརྡབ་གསིགས་ཆེ་བས་ Because the military government caused great hardship to the people.

བརྡབ་གསིགས་ཐེབས་ (dəbsii tēè) vi. to be/ get oppressed/ exploited.

བརྡབས་ (dəb) 1. p. of རྡེབ་. 2. sm. བརྡབ་.

བརྡབས་སྐྱོན་ (dəbgyön) sm. བརྡབ་སྐྱོན་.

བརྡབས་གདན་ (dəbdɛn) sm. བརྡབ་གདན་.

བརྡབས་ཕོར་ (dəbpɔɔ) sm. བརྡབ་ཕོར་.

བརྡབས་རྨས་ (dəbmɛɛ̀) sm. བརྡབ་རྨས་.

བརྡབས་བསེ་ (dəbse) sm. བརྡབ་གདན་.

བརྡར་ (dar) p. of རྡར་.

བརྡར་བཏགས་ (dar dāà) va. to give a name to sb. or sth.

བརྡར་སྡིགས་ (dārdeg) grinding sth.

བརྡར་རྡོ་ (dardo) sm. རྡར་རྡོ་.

བརྡར་སྦྱོང་ (darjoŋ) training.

བརྡར་གཙུབ་ (dardzub) scratching, rubbing; va.—བྱེད་.

བརྡར་ཟད་དུ་སོང་ (darsɛɛ̀du sōŋ) vi. to be worn out, to wear out.

བརྡར་ཤ་གཅོད་ (darsha jöò) va. to investigate and make a decision/ judgment/ conclusion ༖གནས་ཚུལ་དེ་བདེན་པ་ཡིན་མིན་བརྡར་ཤ་གཅོད་མི་འདུག (They) haven't investigated and decided whether that information is true or not.

བརྡར་ཤ་ཆོད་ (darsha cöò) vi. to arrive at a conclusion/ decision ༖གནས་ཚུལ་དེ་བདེན་པ་ཡིན་མིན་བརྡར་ཤ་ཆོད་མི་འདུག A conclusion hasn't been arrived at about whether that information is true or not.

བརྡལ་ (dɛɛ) p. and f. of རྡལ་.

བརྡལ་བཤིག (dɛɛshiì) tearing up, scrapping, not abiding by; va.—གཏོང་; —བྱེད་ ༖དོན་ཚན་ཚང་མར་ཁོ་རང་ཚོས་མ་གནས་པར་བརྡལ་བཤིག་བཏང་བ་རེད་ They did not abide by any of the articles (of the treaty).

བརྡས་ཐག་གཅོད་ (dɛɛ̀daà jöò) va. to decide by vote, to put to a vote.

བརྡས་ཐག་གཅོད་པའི་དབང་ཆ་ (dɛɛ̀daà jöòbɛ wāŋja) right to vote.

བརྡིབ་ (dib) f. of རྡིབ་.

བརྡིབས་ (dib) p. of རྡིབ་.

བརྡུགས་ (dug) p. of བརྡུག.

བརྡུང་ (duŋ) f. of རྡུང་.

བརྡུང་ལྕགས་ (duŋjaà) forged iron.

བརྡུང་བརྡེག (duŋdeg) sm. རྡུང་རྡེག.

བརྡུང་བརྫོགས་ (duŋdzɔɔ̀) sm. རྡུག་རྡེག.

བརྡུང་འཚོག་འཆིང་བརྒྱག (duŋdzɔɔ ciŋgyii) tying and beating; va.—བྱེད་.

བརྡུང་རུང་བའི་རང་བཞིན་ (duŋruŋde rəŋshin) forgeability; malleability.

བརྡུང་ཤུལ་ (duŋshüü) traces/ marks left from pounding on metal.

བརྡུངས་ (duŋ) p. of རྡུང་.

བརྡུངས་སྦྱར་ (duŋjar) joining metals by beating/ pounding.

བརྡུངས་གཟེར་ (duŋser) rivet.

བརྡུངས་ལོག (duŋlɔɔ̀) reworking/ refashioning/ reshaping (by pounding) a metal; va.—རྒྱག.

བརྡུལ་ (düü) 1. arc. to wave/ flourish. 2. va. to destroy.

བརྡེག (deg) f. of རྡེག.

བརྡེག་ཆ་ (degja) weapon.

བརྡེག་འཆལ་ (dēg cā) vi. to slip, to fall.

བརྡེག་འཆོས་ (deg cöò) sm. བརྡེག་འཆལ་.

བརྡེགས་ (deg) p. of རྡེགས་.

བརྡོལ་ (döö) 1. p. of རྡོལ་. 2. possessed by a demon.

བརྡོལ་སྒྲོག (döögyɔɔ̀) hole (caused through wear and tear).

བརྡོལ་གཏམ་ (döödam) vulgar speech.

བརྡོལ་པ་ (dööba) sm. བརྡོལ་སྒྲོག.

བལྡག (daà) f. of ལྡག.

བལྡགས་ (daà) p. of ལྡག.

བལྡད་ (dɛɛ̀) p. of ལྡད་.

བལྡབ་ (dəb) f. of ལྡབ་.

བལྡབས་ (dəb) p. of ལྡབ་.

བལྡི་ (di) sm. བལྡིར་.

བལྡིར་ (dir) sm. ལྡིར་.

བལྡེག (deg) f. of ལྡེག.

བལྡེགས་ (deg) p. of ལྡེག.

བསྡད་ (dɛɛ̀) 1. p. of སྡོད་. 2. (vb. + —) sth. remaining to be done ༖ལས་ཀ་བྱ་བསྡད་མང་པོ་ཡོད་ (I) have lots of work still to be done.

བསྡད་ཁང་ (dɛɛ̀gaŋ) shung. an existing ཁང་ (of land) ༖གཞུང་རྒྱུགས་པ་བུད་ཁང་དང་བསྡད་ཁང་གི་འབྲི་ཆག་སྤྲུལ་ཆག་སྐོར་ Regarding the payment and exemption of taxes of extinct and existing ཁང་ of the government taxpayers peasants.

བསྡད་གྲོང་ (dɛɛ̀droŋ) existing village/ town.

བསྡད་སྟངས་ (dɛɛ̀daŋ) 1. manner of sitting. 2. manner of life style.

བསྡད་དུད་ (dɛɛ̀düü) existing household.

བསྡད་ཤུལ་ (dɛɛ̀shüü) trace of having been sat on/ occupied/ lived in.

བསྡད་ས་ (dɛɛ̀sa) 1. place of residence. 2. place to sit.

བསྡམ་ (dam) f. of སྡོམ་.

བསྡམ་རྒྱ་ (damgya) a ban; va.—བྱེད་.

བསྡམ་རྒྱ་ཡུལ་གྲུ་ (damgya yüüdru) restricted/ prohibited area.

བསྡམ་བྱ་ (damja) sm. སྡང་བྱ་.

བསྡམ་ར་ (damra) sm. བསྡམ་རྒྱ་.

བསྡམས་ (dam) p. of སྡོམ་.

བསྡམས་འགོག་བསྒྲིས་ (damgɔɔ gyii) shung. va. to prohibit/ ban ། སྲོག་ཆགས་ཐམས་ཅད་ལ་རི་རྒྱ་ལུང་རྒྱ་བསྡམས་འགོག་བསྒྲིས་པ་ The (government) banned the killing of all wild animals.

བསྡམས་ཁྲིམས་ (damdrim) shung. regulations and laws.

བསྡམས་གཅོད་ (dam jöö) shung. to close ། རྒྱལ་སྒོ་རྣམས་བསྡམས་གཅོད་ཞིན་རྗེས་ After the main doors were closed.

བསྡམས་ཚོང་ (damdzoŋ) restricted sales (e.g., items that can be sold only to the government).

བསྡི་ (di) see སྡི་.

བསྡིས་ (dii) see སྡི་.

བསྡིགས་ (dig) p. of སྡིགས་.

བསྡིགས་ར་ (digrə) scaring, frightening; va.—སྐུལ་ to frighten/ scare.

བསྡུ་ (du) f. of སྡུད་.

བསྡུ་སྐོར་ (dugɔɔ) convening, summoning, calling together, assembling; va.—བྱེད་ ། སྐབས་འགར་ལྷ་སར་ཡོད་པའི་རོལ་ཆ་གཏོང་མི་རྣམས་བསྡུ་བཀོང་བྱས་ཏེ་མཉམ་གཏོང་བྱེད་ཀྱི་ཡོད་པ་རེད་ Sometimes he would assemble the musicians in Lhasa and play with them.

བསྡུ་བསྐྱལ་ (dugüü) recruiting, collecting, rounding up (as in troops for the military).

བསྡུ་ཁུལ་ (duküü) an area from which sth. is collected/ recruited.

བསྡུ་བགོད་ (dugöö) collecting and dividing; va.—བྱེད་.

བསྡུ་འགུགས་ (duguù) sm. བསྡུ་སྐོར་.

བསྡུ་འགུགས་བསྡི་ (duguù di) sm. བསྡུ་སྐོར་.

བསྡུ་འགྲེམས་ (dudrem) collecting and distributing.

བསྡུ་སྒྲིག་ (dudrig) putting in order, arranging, sorting out; va.—བྱེད་.

བསྡུ་ཆ་ (duja) pooling, collecting (money, etc.); va.—རྒྱག ། ང་ཚོ་བསྡུ་ཆ་བརྒྱབ་ནས་གླིང་ཀར་ཕྱིན་པ་ཡིན་ We pooled (money, food, etc.) and went on a picnic.

བསྡུ་འཇུག་ (dujuù) collecting and putting somewhere; va.—བྱེད་.

བསྡུ་ཉར་ (duñar) collecting and keeping/ storing; va.—བྱེད་.

བསྡུ་ཉོ་ (duño) collecting by purchasing (usu. by the government as a quota or monopoly); va.—བྱེད་.

བསྡུ་སྙིང་ (duñiŋ) abbr. of བསྡུ་དམ་སྙིང་པ་.

བསྡུ་དམ་ (dudam) shung. the person in charge of collecting taxes.

བསྡུ་དེབ་ (dudeb) shung. book listing what should be collected.

བསྡུ་ཚགས་ (dudzaà) sm. བསྡུ་ཉར་.

བསྡུ་ཚོགས་ (dudzɔɔ) convening, calling together, assembling.

བསྡུ་གཞུང་ལག་དེབ་ (dushuŋ lagdeb) shung. sm. བསྡུ་དེབ་.

བསྡུ་གཞུང་ལམ་ཡིག་ (dushuŋ lamyii) shung. abbr. corvee travel document and བསྡུ་གཞུང་ལག་དེབ་.

བསྡུ་རུབ་ (durub) sm. བསྡུ་སྐོང་.

བསྡུ་ལེན་ (delen) enrolling, admitting; va.—བྱེད་ ། ད་ལོ་སློབ་ཕྲུག་གསར་པ་ཁག་ཅིག་བསྡུ་ལེན་བྱེད་ཀྱི་ཡོད་པ་རེད་ They are enrolling a group of new students this year.

བསྡུ་སྒྲུབ་ (dusub) abbreviating and correcting (editing); va.—བྱེད་.

བསྡུ་སྒྲུབ་དག་བཅོས་ (dusub tāgjöö) editing.

བསྡུ་གསོག་ (dusɔɔ) 1. storing up, hoarding, accumulating; va.—བྱེད་ ། ཁོང་གིས་ཚོང་བརྒྱབ་ནས་རྒྱུ་ནོར་མང་པོ་བསྡུ་གསོག་བྱས་པ་རེད་ He did business and accumulated much wealth. 2. putting away in order; va.—རྒྱག ། ཁང་པའི་ནང་གི་ཅ་ལག་ཟ་རེ་ཟོར་རྣམས་བསྡུ་གསོག་ཡག་པོ་རྒྱག་དགོས་ (We) have to put away in good order the miscellaneous things in the house.

བསྡུར་ (dur) va. to compare ། ཅ་ལག་གསར་པ་དང་རྙིང་པ་བསྡུར་ན་གསར་པ་ཡག་གི་རེད་ If one compares old and the new things, new ones are better.

བསྡུར་གྲངས་ (durdraŋ) 1. proportion ། བསྡུར་གྲངས་བརྩིས་པའི་ཁྲལ་ Proportional taxes. 2. the score (e.g., in a sports event).

བསྡུར་གཅོད་ (durjöö) comparing and deciding/ judging, passing judgment on; va.—བྱེད་.

བསྡུར་འདེམ་ (durdem) selecting.

བསྡུར་ཕྲེང་ (durdreŋ) sm. བསྡུར་ཚད་.

བསྡུར་ཕྲེང་དཔེ་འདེམས་ (durdreŋ bēdem) proportional sampling.

བསྡུར་བའི་བརྟག་དཔྱད་ (durwɛ dāgjɛɛ̀) comparative research; va.—བྱེད་.

བསྡུར་མོལ་ (dūrmöö) discussing; va.—བྱེད་.

བསྡུར་ཚད་ (durdzɛɛ̀) 1. proportional, balanced, in proportion ། གསར་སྐྱེས་ཕྱུགས་ཕྲུག་གི་བསྡུར་ཚད་མཐོ་རུ་ཕྱིན་པ་རེད་ The proportion of new born calves increased.

བསྡུར་ཚད་ཁྲི་ཙེ་ (durdzɛɛ trēdze) tib.ch. surveying ruler.

བསྡུར་ཚད་ངེས་ཅན་ཞིག (durdzɛɛ ŋeèjɛnshig) a fixed proportion.

བསྡུར་ཚད་དངོས་ (durdzɛɛ ŋöö) ratio, proportion.

བསྡུར་ཚད་ལྟར་ (durdzɛɛ dār) in proportion to.

བསྡུར་ཚད་དང་བསྟུན་པ་ (durdzɛɛ̀daŋ dümbə) in proportion to.

བསྡུར་གཞི་ཡོད་པ་ (durshi yööbə) 1. comparable, competitive ། བསྡུར་གཞི་ཡོད་པའི་ཐོན་རྫས་ A competitive product. 2. constant, fixed, set ། བསྡུར་གཞི་ཡོད་པའི་རིན་གོང་ A fixed/ constant price.

བསྡུས་ (düü) p. of སྡུད་.

བསྡུས་ཀློག (düülɔɔ) pronouncing a Tibetan syllable as a unit (i.e., without spelling its various letters).

བསྡུས་གྲྭ་ (düüdra) an elementary class in logic in the monastic education curriculum.

བསྡུས་རྟགས་ (düüdaà) ellipsis.

བསྡུས་དེབ་ (düüdeb) abridged/ abbreviated book or edition of a book.

བསྡུས་དོན་ (düüdön) gist, essence, core meaning.

བསྡུས་བསྡུས་ (düüdüü) brief, short ། གཏམ་བཤད་བསྡུས་བསྡུས་ཤིག A brief speech.

བསྡུས་པོ་ (düübu) sm. བསྡུས་བསྡུས་.

བསྡུས་བྲིས་ (düüdrii) shorthand/ abbreviated writing, writing sth. in brief.

བསྡུས་མིང་ (düümiŋ) 1. abbreviation. 2. abbreviated name.

བསྡུས་ཚིག (düüdzii) abbreviated word.

བསྡུས་བཞག (düü shaà) va. to close down ། སྨན་ཁང་དེའང་བསྡུས་བཞག་རྒྱུ་ཡིན་ (We) will close down even that hospital.

བསྡུས་ཡིག (düüyii) 1. simplified Chinese character. 2. abbreviation.

བསྡུས་གཟུགས་ཡི་གེ་ (düüsuù yige) simplified Chinese characters.

བསྡེབ་ (deb) f. of སྡེབ་.

བསྡེབས་ (deb) p. of སྡེབ་.

བསྡེབས་བསྒྲིལ་ (debdrii) compiling, collecting; va.—བྱེད་ ། རྩོམ་ཡིག་མང་པོ་བསྡེབས་སྒྲིག་བྱས་ནས་དེབ་ཅིག་བཟོས་བཞག (They) collected many articles and made a book.

བསྡེབས་འཛོགས་ (debdzɔɔ) piled up, stuffed into (some space); va.—རྒྱག; vi.—ཐེབས་.

བསྡེབས་ལང་ (deblaŋ) action of many people together, rising of many people together །

བསྡེབས་ལང་གིས་སྤྱི་པའི་བརྩེ་ཁང་བརྒྱབ་པ་རེད་ Together (they) built the common recreation house.

བསྡེབས་གསོད་ (de̲bsöö̀) mass killing, massacre; va.—གཏོང་; —བྱེད་ to kill in mass, to massacre.

བསྡོ་ (do̲) f. of སྡོ་.

བསྡོག (dɔ̲ɔ̀) f. of སྡོག.

བསྡོགས་ (dɔ̲ɔ̀) p. of སྡོག.

བསྡོགས་ཆས་ (dɔ̲ɔ̀jɛɛ̀) see དོ་ཆས་.

བསྡོང་ (do̲ŋ) f. of སྡོང་.

བསྡོངས་ (do̲ŋ) p. of སྡོང་.

བསྡོམ་ (do̲m) see སྡོམ་.

བསྡོམས་ (do̲m) 1. sm. སྡོམ་. 2. together with ¶ བཟོ་བླ་དང་རྒྱུ་ཆ་བསྡོམས་སྒོར་མོ་བརྒྱ་གནས་སོང་ The making fee and the material together cost 100 dollars.

བསྡོམས་གྲངས་ (do̲mdraŋ) the total (amount) ¶ སྡོམས་གྲངས་ཀྱི་བརྒྱ་ཆ་བདུན་ Seven percent of the total.

བསྡོམས་ཐག་བྱེད་ (do̲mdaà ce̲è) va. to add a new loan on top of an old one.

བསྡོམས་ན་ (do̲mna) sm. བསྡོམས་ནས་.

བསྡོམས་ནས་ (do̲mnɛ) in sum, in total.

བསྡོམས་འབོར་ (do̲mbɔɔ) sm. བསྡོམས་གྲངས་.

བསྡོམས་རྩིས་ (do̲mdziì) sm. སྡོམ་རྩིས་.

བསྡོས་ (dö̲ö̀) 1. p. of སྡོ་. 2. arc. to attack.

ན་ (na) 1. the letter ན་ (used in alphabetical numbering). 2. (vb. (past stem) + —) if ། ཁོ་ལྷ་སར་ཕྱིན་ན་ If he goes to Lhasa. 3. (vb + pa / ba + —) when, as ། དེ་ནས་སྟག་ཅིག་དང་འཕྲད་པ་ན་ After that, when (he) met a tiger. 4. to, in, at (sm. ལ་) ། དབུས་ན་ In the center. 5. vi. to be sick/ ill ། ཁོས་ཤ་འདི་བཟས་ནས་ཞེ་དྲག་ན་པ་རེད་ (He) got very sick after eating the meat. 6. (vb. + ན་ + སྙམ་ or བསམ་) wishing/ hoping the verb will occur ། ཁོང་འདིར་ཕེབས་ན་སྙམ་ I wish he will come. ། ལས་འགན་འདི་ཚར་ན་བསམ་གྱི་འདུག I hope this work (responsibility) will end.

ན་ཀྲ་ (nadra) sm. ཆུ་སྐྱིན་.

ན་དཀྱིལ་ (nəgyii) middle aged.

ན་སྐད་ (nagɛɛ̀) cry of pain, groan, moan; va.—རྒྱག.

ན་ཁ་ (naga) meadow, pasture, lawn.

ན་ཁ་སྤོ་ཏོ་ (naga bōdo) grassy plain with tufts of earth growing all around.

ན་མཁན་ (nañɛn) a sick person.

ན་ག་གེ་སར་ (naga kesar) type of traditional medicine (a fruit from the Rangoon creeper).

ན་གི་ (nəgi) type of traditional medicine (pangolin scales).

ན་གླིང་ (naliŋ) shung. a type of grassland.

ན་གན་ (nagɛn) old.

ན་གས་ (nagɛɛ̀) old.

ན་གས་རྒྱུན་གཅོང་ (nagɛɛ gyünjoŋ) old and weak/ sickly.

ན་གས་རྫི་དྲིབ་ (nagɛɛ̀ dzidib) decrepit, old and used up, worn out due to old age [Lit. old with sagging eyelids].

ན་གས་གཟུགས་གཅོང་ (nagɛɛ̀ sugjoŋ) sm. ན་གས་རྒྱུན་གཅོང་.

ན་གས་ལུས་གཅོང་ (nagɛɛ̀ lüüjoŋ) sm. ན་གས་རྒྱུན་གཅོང་.

ན་རྒྱུ་ཆེན་པོ་ (nəgyu cēmbo) 1. deep dislike/ hatred/ enmity. 2. in a lot of pain ། མི་ཚང་དེ་གཉིས་དབར་ལ་ན་རྒྱུ་ཆེན་པོ་ཞིག་འདུག. There is deep hatred between the two families.

ན་རྒྱུ་ཚ་རྒྱུ་ (nəgyu tsəgyu) 1. sm. ན་ན་ཚ་ཚ་. 2. hurtful or offensive (speech) ། མི་ལ་སྐད་ཆ་ན་རྒྱུ་ཚ་རྒྱུ་དེ་འདྲ་མ་ཤོད་ ། Don't say hurtful things like that to people.

ན་སྒྲིང་སྒྲིང་ (na dreŋdreŋ) a twinge of pain, a dull pain; vi.—བྱེད་.

ན་གཅལ་ (najɛɛ) a lawn.

ན་གཅིག་ཤི་གཅིག (najig shījig) sb. who was never sick in his life but then got an illness and died.

ན་ཆུང་ (nəjuŋ) young person.

ན་ཆུང་ཉེས་ཅན་ (nəjuŋ ñeèjɛn) juvenile delinquent.

ན་ཆུང་གདོང་ལེན་རུ་ཁག (nəjuŋ doŋlen rugaà) Young Pioneers (organization).

ན་ཆུང་སྒྲོ་ཁྱིམ་ (nəjuŋ drōgyim) children's recreation center.

ན་ཆུང་ཕོ་བྲང་ (nəjuŋ pōdraŋ) children's palace (entertainment facility for children).

ན་ཆུང་བ་ (nəjuŋwə) a young (person or animal).

ན་ཆུང་མ་ (nəjuŋmə) young girl/ woman.

ན་མཉམ་ (nañam) person of the same age, age mate, peer.

ན་མཉམ་མ་ (nañamma) girls of same age. 2. girl friend.

ན་ད་མུ་དུས་ཆེན་ (nadamu tüüjen) mong.tib. nadam (the Mongolian traditional summer festival).

ན་སྡངས་ (nadaŋ) condition/ nature of illness, symptoms of illness ། ཁྱེད་རང་ན་སྡངས་ག་འདྲ་སི་ན་གི་འདུག་གམ་ What is the nature of your illness?

ན་ཐང་ (nadaŋ) field/ plain with clumps of earth/ vegetation.

ན་ཐིང་ཐིང་ (na tiŋdiŋ) sm. ན་སྒྲིང་སྒྲིང་.

ན་མདོ་ཁ་ཁྱེར་ (nado kāgyer) using old age as an excuse; va.—བྱེད་.

ན་དང་པོ་ (na taŋbo) five year old horse/ mule (first year of complete teeth).

ན་དྲན་དྲག་བརྗེད་ཤི་འཁོན་ (nadrɛn tragjeè shīgön) when sick one remembers the doctor, when one recovers one forgets the doctor, and when one dies one is angry at the doctor.

ན་འདམ་ (nadam) a marshy meadow.

ན་འདམ་ས་ཁུལ་ (nadam səgüü) a marshy meadow area.

ན་འདྲེད་སྤང་ཐོགས་ (nandreè bāŋdɔɔ̀) running into problems and difficulties one on top of another [Lit. slip on pasture, stub one's foot on the meadow].

ན་སྡེ་ (nade) a big meadow, a grassland area.

ན་ན་ཚ་ཚ་ (nana tsādza) illness, sickness ། ད་ལོ་ངར་ན་ན་ཚ་ཚ་གཞི་མ་བྱུང་ This year I haven't had any illnesses.

ན་ཉིང་ (nəniŋ) last year.

ན་སྤང་ (nabaŋ) meadow.

ན་ཕྲ་ (nadra) young.

ན་པ་ཅན་ (nawajɛn) sm. ནད་པ་.

ན་བའི་ཆུ་པོ་ (nawɛ cūwo) sm. ན་བའི་སྡུག་བསྔལ་.

ན་བའི་སྡུག་བསྔལ་ (nawɛ dugŋɛɛ) the suffering of sickness.

ན་བའི་བྱུང་རིམ་ (nawɛ juŋrim) the stages of a disease.

ན་བུན་ (nabün) fog, mist.

ན་བུན་པུ་མོ་ (nabün pomo) a type of snail used in Tibetan medicine.

ན་མ་ (nama) 1. a type of vegetation. 2. a type of sod used for fuel. 3. daytime.

ན་མ་གདོགས་ (na məndoò) (vb. + —) unless ། བུད་མེད་རྣམས་ཀྱིས་ཤེས་ཡོན་སློབ་སྦྱོང་བྱས་ན་མ་གདོགས་ Unless women get educated.

ན་མར་ (namar) doing sth. continuously.

ན་མ་སྤོ་ཏོ་ (nama bōdo) sm. ན་ཁ་སྤོ་ཏོ་.

ན་མོ་ (namo) sm. ན་ཁ་.

ན་དམར་གཞུང་ (na mārshuŋ) large grassy plain, grassland.

ན་སྨུག (nəmug) sm. ན་བུན་.

ན་ཙི་ (nadzi) eng. nazi.

ན་ཚ་ (nadza) illness, sickness, pain; vi.—གཏོང་; —ཐེབས་;—འདེབས་ to pain, to ache, to be sick; vi.—འཇགས་ to subside (pain or illness); va.—སྒོམ་ to tolerate/ bear pain or illness; vi.—དྲག to recover from sickness; vi.—ལང་ to have an illness recur, to have a relapse ། ཁྱེད་རང་ན་ཚ་ག་འདྲ་འདུག How is your illness? ། བསླབ་བྱ་ན་ཚ་ཅན་ཞིག A painful lesson.

ན་ཚ་མཉམ་བྱུང་ (nadza ñəmjuŋ) having several illnesses at once.

ན་ཚ་སྡེབ་ལྡངས་ (nadza deblaŋ) sm. ན་ཚ་མཉམ་བྱུང་.

ན་ཚ་ཚབས་ཆེན་ (nadza tsəbceb) a grave/ serious illness.

ན་ཚ་རོས་པ་ (nadza rööba) an old/ chronic sickness or disease.

ན་ཚའི་གཡའ་ (nadzɛ ya) a symptom of illness.

ན་རྫུལ་ (nədzüü) 1. sm. ན་སྡངས་. 2. feigning illness. va.—བྱེད་ ། ཁོས་ན་རྫུལ་བྱས་ནས་ལས་ཀར་མ་ཡོང་བ་རེད་ He feigned illness and didn't come to work.

ན་ཚོད་བགྲང་བྱ་ (nadzöò drāŋja) one's age, the number of years old one is.

ན་ཚོད་དར་མ་ (nadzöò tarma) a person in the prime of adult life (between the age of thirty and forty).

ན་ཚོད་ཡོལ་ (nadzöò yöö) vi. to become/ get old.

ན་ཚོད་འདར་བ་ (nadzöò tarma) sm. ན་ཚོད་དར་མ་.

ན་ཚོད་ལོངས་ (nadzöò loŋ) sm. ན་ཚོད་ལོན་.

ན་ཚོད་ལོན་ (nadzöò lön) vi. to be grown up, to reach adulthood.

ན་ཚོད་སོང་ (nadzöö sōŋ) sm. ན་ཚོད་ཡོལ་.

ན་རྫུ་ (nadzu) feigning/ shaming illness; va.—འདེབས་; —བྱེད་ to feign/ sham illness ༑ ཁྱོད་ཀྱིས་ཁྱིམ་དུ་ན་རྫུ་བཏབ་ནས་བསྡད་པ་རེད་ You feigning illness and stayed at home.

ན་གཞོང་ (nashöŋ) pastureland, grassland.

ན་གཞོན་ (nashön) youth, young ༑ ན་གཞོན་ཁ་ཤས་ Several youths.

ན་གཞོན་གླིང་ག་ (nashön lĩŋgə) youth park.

ན་གཞོན་གདོང་ལེན་རུ་ཁག (nashön doŋlen rugaà) Young Pioneers (organization).

ན་གཞོན་འབྲེལ་ཚོགས་ (nashön dreedzɔɔ̀) Youth Federation.

ན་ཟུག (nəsug) pain (from an illness/ injury); vi.—རྒྱག to pain, to hurt; vi. —འཛགས་ to have pain subside.

ན་ཟླ་ (nanda) persons of the same age.

ན་བཟའ་ (namsa) clothes, clothing (h.); va.—མཆོད་; —བཞེས་ to dress, to put on clothing; va.—སྒྲོན་ to dress a (person); —བསིལ་ to take off clothes, to undress.

ན་བཟའ་སྐུ་ཚར་ (namsa gūdzar) h. of པགས་ཚག.

ན་བཟའ་ཁང་ (namsagaŋ) shung. room where the robes of the Dalai Lama and other high ranking officials are kept.

ན་བཟའ་ཚར་པི་ (namsa cārbi) h. of ཚར་པི་.

ན་བཟའ་གདན་ཞུ་ (namsa dənshu) shung. an audience with a Lama when the Lama isn't present and the audience is with his clothes draped on a throne.

ན་བཟའ་ལྷང་པ་གཅིག (nāmsa daŋbajig) h. of གོན་ལྷེང་.

ན་བཟའི་རྒྱབ་སྲུལ་ (namsɛ gyəbsüü) h. of ཀྱག་སྲུལ་.

ན་ཡང་ (nayaŋ) (vb + —) 1. even though, even if ༑ ཁོ་སྨན་ཁང་ལ་ཕྱིན་ན་ཡང་ཤི་བ་རེད་ Even though he went to the hospital he died. 2. even though ill/ sick ༑ ཁོང་ན་ཡང་ལས་ཀར་ཡོང་བ་རེད་ Even though he was sick he came to work.

ན་ཡམ་ (nayam) guessing/ approximating when speaking; va.—ཤོད་. to say sth. with uncertainty, to say sth. as a guess/ approximation.

ན་ཡོལ་ (na yöö) 1. abbr. of ན་ཚོད་ཡོལ་. 2. an old person.

ན་གཡོག (nayɔɔ̀) sb. who looks after a sick person.

ན་གཡོག་ཤི་གཡོག (nayɔɔ̀ shĩyɔɔ̀) sb. who looks after/ takes care of a sick person until he/she dies.

ན་ར་ (nara) a field of ན་མ་ that has been set aside for making hay.

ན་ར་ར་ (narara) 1. loose and hanging out ༑ ཁྱི་དེ་ཚ་དྲག་འཚིག་ནས་ལྕེ་ན་ར་ར་བསྐྱངས་ནི་བསྡད་འདུག The dog was hot and his tongue was hanging out. 2. without a break, continuously.

ན་རམ་ (naram) 1. Asiatic plantain seed. 2. in sequence/ order.

ན་རིང་ (nariŋ) while ill/ sick.

ན་རིམ་ (narim) in series, serially, one after another, successively ༑ ཏཱ་ལའི་བླ་མ་སྐུ་ཕྲེང་ན་རིམ The succession series of Dalai Lamas.

ན་རེ་ནོ་རེ་ (nare nore) mistake, error ༑ ཚིག་ན་རེ་ནོ་རེ་ A mistaken word.

ན་རེ་ (nare) says, said (particle indicating the start of direct discourse) ༑ ཁོང་ན་རེ་ དོ་དགོང་གློག་བརྙན་ཡག་པོ་ཞིག་འདུག་ཟེར་ He said, "This evening there is a good movie."

ན་རེ་བ་ (narewa) continuously.

ན་རེ་རོ་རེ་ (nare rore) an error/ mistake.

ན་རོ་ (naro) the vowel "o."

ན་རོགས་ (naroò) useless, waste of time ༑ དོན་མེད་འཁྱམས་ཕྱིན་ན་ཀང་པ་ན་རོགས་རེད་ It is a waste of time to wander around for no reason.

ན་ལུགས་ (nəluù) sm. ན་སྣངས་.

ན་ལུགས་ན་སྣངས་ (nəluù nadaŋ) sm. ན་སྣངས་.

ན་ལུགས་ན་རྐྱེན་ (nəluù nagyen) cause of an illness/ disease.

ན་ལེ་ཤམ་ (nalesham) pepper.

ན་ལོ་ (nalo) last year.

ན་ལོངས་ (naloŋ) abbr. of ན་ཚོད་ལོངས་.

ན་ལོན་ (nalön) 1. a one year old animal ༑ ན་ལོན་ཕྱུགས་རིགས་ One year old cattle. 2. sm. ན་ཚོད་ལོན་.

ན་ཤུལ་ (nashüü) 1. while being ill/ sick ༑ ན་ཤུལ་རིང་ When (I) was ill. 2. trace or sign of an illness/ disease.

ན་ཤོ་ (nasho) a type of herbal medicine.

ན་གཤོངས་ (nashoŋ) pasture area, grassland, meadow.

ན་ས་ (nasa) 1. an area (where) pain is located. 2. the place where one got sick.

ན་སོ་ (naso) age (in years), stage of life ༑ ན་སོ་གཞོན་པ་ Youth.

ན་སོ་ཕྲ་བ་ (naso trāwa) childhood, youth.

ན་སོ་འཕེལ་ (naso pēl) vi. to become mature (for children).

ན་སོ་གཞོན་གཞོན་ (naso shönshön) young.

ན་སོ་ལོན་ (naso lön) vi. to become mature (for children).

ན་སོན་ (na sön) vi. to become an adult, to come of age.

ན་གསུམ་གླེབས་ (nāsum lēb) seven year old horses/ mules.

ན་བསྲན་ (nasɛn) tolerant of pain.

ན་ལྷང་ལྷང་ (na lhāŋlhaŋ) a slight/ dull pain, vi.—བྱེད་.

ནཱ་ག (naga) skt. nāga.

ནཱ་ག་གེ་སར་ (naga gesar) a medicine made from the cottonwood tree.

ནཱ་ག་རའི་ཡི་གེ་ (nagarɛ yige) an Indian script.

ནཱ་རོ་མཁའ་སྤྱོད་མ་ (naga kājöòma) vajara yogini.

ནཱ་རོ་པ་ (naroba) 11th century Indian master who was the teacher of Marpa.

ནག (nag) abbr. of ནག་པོ་.

ནག་རྒྱང་ (naggyaŋ) completely black.

ནག་སྐྱ་ (naggya) charcoal gray.

ནག་ཁང་ (naggaŋ) 1. sm. ནག་ཚང་, 2.

ནག་ཁུང་ (nəguŋ) dark, darkness.

ནག་ཁུང་ནག་རྒྱང་ (nəguŋ naggyaŋ) pitch black, completely dark.

ནག་ཁྲ་ (nāgdra) 1. sth. with black stripes. 2. crimes; va.—འཛུགས་ to accuse sb. of crimes.

ནག་ཁྲོམ་ (nāgdrom) black market.

ནག་གི་ནོ་གི་ (nagge noge) 1. dirty, stained. 2. murky, unclear, smudged.

ནག་གི་པ་ (nagewa) sm. ནག་གི་ནོ་གི་.

ནག་འགྲོས་ (naŋdröö) abbr. ནག་པོ་འགྲོ་ཤེས་.

ནག་རྒྱུ་ (nəggyu) small intestine.

ནག་ཅན་ (nagjɛn) criminal ༑ ནག་ཅན་ལ་ཁྲིམས་གཅོད་བྱས་པ་རེད་ They punished the criminal.

ནག་ཅན་པ་ (nagjɛnba) sm. ནག་ཅན་.

ནག་ཅན་དཔོན་པོས་མི་ཁེབ་ (nagjɛn bōmböö mikeb) a notorious criminal who cannot be brought to justice.

ནག་ཅིལ་ཅིལ་ (nag cĩijii) completely black in color.

ནག་ཅིལ་རི་ (nag cĩiri) sm. ནག་ཅིལ་ཅིལ་.

ནག་ཆུ་ (nəgju) abbr. ནག་ཆུ་ཁ་.

ནག་ཆུ་ཁ (nəgjugə) town and administrative center for the Nagchuka Prefecture (in Northern Tibet).

ནག་ཆུང་སྲན་མ་ (nəgjuŋ trɛ̀ɛma) type of black pea/ lentil.

ནག་ཆེ་ཆུང་ (nag cĩjuŋ) different levels/ seriousness of crimes ༑ ནག་ཆེ་ཆུང་ལ་གཞིགས་པའི་ཁྲིམས་གཅོད་བྱས་པ་རེད་ They punished (them) in a accordance with the level of their crimes.

ནག་ཆེན་ (nagjen) 1. great/ heinous crime. 2. a great criminal.

ནག་ཆེན་ཁྲག་སྐྱོར་གྱི་ཞལ་ལྕེ་ (nagjen trāgjɔɔgi shɛ̀ɛje) one of the sixteen laws laid down by Srongtsan Gampo for serious crimes punishable by amputations.

ནག་མཆན་ (nagjɛn) explanations/ comments written marginally in black ink on a religious text.

ནག་ཉིལ་ཉིལ་ (nag ñiiñii) blackish.

ནག་ཉེས་ (nag̲ñeè) crime, offence, violation, transgression; va.—བྱེད་ to commit a crime/ offence/ violation; va.—འཛུགས་ to accuse sb. of a crime; va.—བགྲང་ to enumerate/ list a person's crimes.

ནག་ཉེས་མཁྲེགས་བཟུང་ (nag̲ñeè trēgsuŋ) hardened/ incorrigible criminal.

ནག་ཉེས་དགུ་འཛོམས་ (nagñeè gundzom) extremely evil/ criminal [Lit. aggregation of nine crimes].

ནག་ཉེས་ཅན་ (nagñeèjɛn) evil, criminal ། དམིགས་ཡུལ་ནག་ཉེས་ཅན་ Evil aims.

ནག་ཉེས་ཆེ་ཆུང་ (nagñeè cījuŋ) the degree/ extent/ seriousness of a crime.

ནག་ཉེས་དྲང་ཞུ་ (nagñeè traŋshu) admitting one's crimes/ guilt; va.—བྱེད་.

ནག་ཉེས་མེད་པ (nagñeè meèba) innocent of a crime, guiltless.

ནག་ཉོག (nagñɔɔ̀) dirty, unclean.

ནག་དིང་དིང་ (nag dīŋdiŋ) completely black.

ནག་ཐིག (nɔgdig) 1. a black dot. 2. bull's eye (of a target); va.—རྒྱག་ to have what sb. said be exactly right/ correct ། ཁོང་གིས་བཤད་པའི་གནས་ཚུལ་དེ་ནག་ཐིག་བརྒྱབ་སོང་ The information that he said is exactly right. 3. va.—བཙས་ to unjustly/ blame accuse sb.

ནག་ཐིང་ངེ་ (nag tīŋŋe) sm. ནག་དིང་དིང་.

ནག་ཐིང་ཐིང་ (nag tīŋdiŋ) sm. ནག་དིང་དིང་.

ནག་ཐིབ་ཐིབ་ (nag tībdib) blackish, darkish.

ནག་ཐུམ་མེ་ (nag tūmme) 1. blacking out (as in fainting); vi.—འགྲོ་ to black out, to faint.

ནག་ཐོ་ (nagdo) a list of gifts/ money given at the time of a person's death.

ནག་ཐོམ་ (nagdom) 1. dark; vi.—བྱེད་. to become dark. 2. not intelligent, stupid.

ནག་ཐོམ་ཐོམ་ (nag tōmdom) dark.

ནག་ཐོམ་མེ་ (nag tōmme) dark; vi.—འགྲོ་ to become dark.

ནག་དྲེག (nagdreg) 1. soot, dirt. 2. black and dirty.

ནག་མདངས་ (nagdaŋ) blackish hue.

ནག་ཏོག་ཏོག (nag dɔgdɔɔ̀) black dots/ spots.

ནག་ནོག (nagnɔg) abbr. ནག་གི་ནོ་གི་.

ནག་ནོག་ཅན་ (nagnɔgjɛn) dirty, filthy.

ནག་པ་ཟླ་བ་ (nagbə dawa) name of the third Tibetan month.

ནག་པང་ (nagbaŋ) blackboard.

ནག་པང་ཚགས་པར་ (nagbaŋ tsāgbar) blackboard newspaper.

ནག་པའི་ཉ་ (nagbɛ ña) the 1st day of the 3rd Tibetan month.

ནག་པོ་ (nagbo) 1. black. 2. (with གཏོང་) unfriendly, hostile; gloomy. 2. very, extremely ། གནས་ཚུལ་དེ་གོ་ནས་ང་ནག་པོ་ཡ་མཚན་སོང་ I was extremely surprised when I heard that news.

ནག་པོ་འགྲོ་ཤེས་ (nagbo droshee) easy to understand; va.—འགོད་ to write in a manner that is easy to understand.

ནག་པོ་ཆེན་པོ་ (nāgbo cēmbo) Mahakala (a wrathful manifestation of Avaloketisvara).

ནག་པོ་བསྟན་པ་ (nagbo dēmba) an Indian doctrine/ philosophy which preaches the virtue of worldly existence.

ནག་པོ་ནག་རྐྱང་ (nagbo naggyaŋ) completely black.

ནག་པོ་སྣུམ་པོ་ (nagbo nūmbo) shiny black.

ནག་པོ་ཡོངས་འགེལ་ (nagbo yoŋgee) accusing/ blaming from generation to generation.

ནག་པོ་ཡོར་འགེལ་ (nagbo yɔrgee) unjustly accusing/ blaming; va.—བྱེད་.

ནག་པོའི་ཆ་ (nāgbö cā) 1. sins, nonvirtuous deeds. 2. the second half of the month.

ནག་སྤང་ (nagbaŋ) blackboard.

ནག་ཕྱུགས་ (nagcuù) cattle (mainly used for yaks).

ནག་ཕྱོགས་ (nagcɔɔ̀) 1. the enemy side/ direction. 2. ནག་པོའི་ཆ་.

ནག་བྲིས་ (nagdrii) black and white drawings (in contrast to color).

ནག་འབྱམས་ (naŋjam) getting blacked out/ blotted out (e.g., a word in a book); vi.—འགྲོ་. 2. becoming dark. 3. sth. bad becoming customary/ regular; vi.—འགྲོ་; —འགྱུར་.

ནག་མ་ (nagma) a traditional herbal medicine used for broken bones.

ནག་མེད་ (nagmeè) sm. ནག་ཉེས་མེད་པ་.

ནག་མེད་གྱོང་འཁེལ་ (nagmeè gyoŋkee) experiencing a loss due to the unjust blame or accusation of another.

ནག་མེད་ཉེས་འགེལ་ (nagmeè ñeè gee) unjustly accusing sb. of a crime; va.—བྱེད་.

ནག་མེད་ཉེས་འདོགས་ (nagmeè ñendɔɔ̀) sm. ནག་མེད་ཉེས་འགེལ་.

ནག་མེད་ཉེས་གཡོགས་ (nagmeè ñɛɛ̀yɔɔ̀) sm. ནག་མེད་ཉེས་འགེལ་.

ནག་མེད་ནག་བཙུགས་ (nagmeè nagdzuù) sm. ནག་མེད་ཉེས་འགེལ་.

ནག་མོ་ (nagmo) a female.

ནག་རྩི་ (nagdzi) black paint; va.—གཏོང་.

ནག་རྩིས་ (nɔgdzii) a kind of astrological calculation about one's fortune/ luck/ etc.

ནག་བཙུགས་ (nag dzuù) p. of ནག་འཛུགས་.

ནག་བཙོན་ (nagdzön) 1. prison. 2. a dark prison cell.

ནག་ཚང་ (nagdzaŋ) 1. the traditional name of Shendza county in Nagchuka Prefecture. 2. a den of criminals/ evil people ། ང་ལོག་ཐེང་འཕྲུག་གི་ནག་ཚང་བཙུགས་པ་རེད་ They established an evil den of rebels. 3. a nomad household who specializes in raising yaks. 4. a kind of squarish yak hair tent.

ནག་ཚུབ་ཚུབ་ (nag tsūbdzub) 1. dark, gloomy. 2. a feeling of darkness in one's mind, feeling moody/ gloomy.

ནག་ཚུབས་ཚུབས་ (nag tsūbdzub) sm. ནག་ཚུབ་ཚུབ་.

ནག་ཚུར་ (nagdzur) black vitriol.

ནག་ཚེག (nagdzeg) black dot/ spot.

ནག་ཚོང་ (nagdzoŋ) black market (trading); smuggling; va.—རྒྱག.

ནག་མཚུར་ (nagdzur) sm. ནག་ཚུར་.

ནག་འཛུགས་ (nag dzuù) sm. ནག་ཉེས་འཛུགས་.

ནག་ཟལ་ (nagsɛɛ) animals that are black and white.

ནག་ཟླ་ (naŋda) the 3rd month of the Tibetan lunar calendar.

ནག་ཡུལ་ཡུལ་ (nag yüüyüü) shadowy, blackish, darkish.

ནག་ཡོ་རེ་བ་ (nag yorewa) a obscure/ shadowy/ blackish figure.

ནག་རིས་ (nɔgrii) 1. ink sketch/ drawing (black and white). 2. black coloring put around the eyes.

ནག་རོག་གེ་བ་ (nag rogewa) sm. ནག་རོག་རོག.

ནག་རོག་རོག (nag rɔgrɔɔ̀) 1. sm. ནག་ཡུལ་ཡུལ་. 2. an angry/ hostile-looking face.

ནག་ཤིག་ཤིག (nag shīgshii) sm. ནག་ཡུལ་ཡུལ་.

ནག་ཤུར་ཤུར་ (nag sūrshur) sm. ནག་ཡུལ་ཡུལ་.

ནག་ལམ་ (naglam) path or course of evil/ crime.

ནག་ལས་ (naglɛɛ̀) evil/ criminal behavior, nonvirtuous deeds.

ནག་ཤ་ (nagsha) yak meat and beef.

ནག་ཤེད་ (nagsheè) shung. leasing out female yak and receiving butter as payment.

ནག་སུབ་ (nagsub) erasing completely; va.—གཏོང་.

ནག་སེང་ངེ་བ་ (nag sēŋŋewa) blackish.

ནག་སེར་ (nagser) dark brown (mixture of black and yellow).

ནག་སྔོ་ (nagse) greyish color.

ནག་སླེལ (nag lēē) a carrying basket in which the bark has not been removed so that it has a dark hue.

ནག་ཧུ་རེ་ (naghure) black, dark in appearance (as inside a cave).

ནག་ཧྲིལ་ཧྲིལ་ (nag hrīihrii) completely black.

ནག་ཧྲུལ་ལི་བ་ (nag hrūülewa) dirty and tattered (usu. clothes).

ནག་ལྷག་ལྷག (nag lhāglhaà) blackish.

ནག་ལྷད་ (naglhɛɛ̀) adulterated, impure.

ནགས་ (nag) forest.

ནགས་ལུང་ (nāgluŋ) sm. ནགས་ཚལ་.

ནགས་སྐྱོང་ཞིང་པ་ (naggyoŋ shiŋbə) a farmer who also has responsibility for protecting the forest.

ནགས་སྐྲུན་ཁྲུའུ་ (nagdrün trū) tib.ch. afforestration department.

ནགས་ཁུལ་ (nagüü) forest area, forest land, forest zone.

ནགས་ཁྲོད་ (nagdröö) in a forest.

ནགས་ཁྲོད་གནའ་སྤྲེ་ (nagdröö nadra) dryopithecus.

ནགས་སྟུག (nagdug) dense forest.

ནགས་ཐོན་དངོས་རྫས་ (nagdön ŋöödzɛɛ̀) forest products.

ནགས་མཐའ་ (nagda) the edge of a forest.

ནགས་དོན་གྱི་ཁྲིམས་ཁང་ (nagdöngi trīmgaŋ) court for forest issues, forestry court.

ནགས་དོན་ཉེན་རྟོག་པ་ (nagdön ñendɔgbə) forest ranger, forest guard.

ནགས་འདབས་ (nagdəb) outskirts/ border of a forest.

ནགས་བྱ་རོག་པོ་ (nagja rɔgba) raven.

ནགས་བྱི་ (nəgji) squirrel.

ནག་བྲིས་ (nagtrii) a black and white drawing.

ནགས་སྦྲང་ (nagdraŋ) bees/ flies that are found in forests.

ནགས་མེ་ (nagme) forest fire.

ནགས་ཚལ་ (nagdzɛɛ) forest.

ནགས་ཚལ་སྐོར་གྱི་བཅའ་ཁྲིམས་ (nagdzɛɛ gɔ̄ɔgi jədrim) forest laws.

ནགས་ཚལ་ཁེབས་ཚད་ (nagdzɛɛ kēbdzɛɛ̀) percentage of forest cover.

ནགས་ཚལ་བསྟར་ཕྲེང་ (nagdzɛɛ dārdreŋ) forest belt.

ནགས་ཚལ་ཐོན་ཁུངས་ (nagdzɛɛ tōnguŋ) forests resources.

ནགས་ཚལ་ཐོན་རྫས་ (nagdzɛɛ tōndzɛɛ̀) forest/ forestry products.

ནགས་ཚལ་དུ་འགྱུར་ (nagdzɛɛdu gyur) vi. to get afforested.

ནགས་ཚལ་མེ་སྐྱོན་འགོག་སྲུང་ (nagdzɛɛ megyön gɔgsuŋ) forest fire prevention.

ནགས་ཚལ་བཟོ་ལས་ (nagdzɛɛ solɛɛ̀) timber industry, forestry industry ¶ནགས་ཚལ་བཟོ་ལས་དོ་དམ་ཅུའུ་ Forest industry management bureau.

ནགས་ཚལ་རིག་པ་ (nagdzɛɛ rigbə) forestry, forestry science.

ནགས་ཚལ་ལས་ཀ་ (nagdzɛɛ lɛ̀ɛga) forestry work.

ནགས་ཚལ་ཤིང་གཅོད་ (nagdzɛɛ sīŋjöö) lumbering, cutting timber.

ནགས་ཚལ་ས་ཁུལ་ (nagdzɛɛ səgüü) forest area.

ནགས་ཚལ་སྲུང་སྐྱོང་གི་ཁྲིམས་སྲོལ་ (nagdzɛɛ sūŋgyoŋgi trīmsöö) forest protection laws.

ནགས་རྫོབ་ (nagdzob) thick forest.

ནགས་ཞོར་ཐོན་རྫས་ (nagshɔɔ tōndzɛɛ̀) minor or sideline forest products.

ནགས་བཟོ་ (nagso) afforestation; va.—བྱེད་ to afforest.

ནགས་ར་ (nagra) forestry center, tree farm.

ནགས་ར་དོ་དམ་ས་ཚིགས་ (nagra todam sādzii) tree farm management center.

ནགས་རི་ (nəgri) forest covered mountain.

ནགས་རིགས་སློབ་གྲྭ་ (nəgrii lōbdra) school of forestry.

ནགས་རོང་ (nagroŋ) sm. ནགས་ཁུལ་.

ནགས་ལས་ (naglɛɛ) forestry, forestry work; va.—བྱེད་.

ནགས་ལས་ཅུའུ་ (naglɛɛ̀ jū) tib.ch. forestry bureau, forestry service.

ནགས་ལས་སྤྱི་ཁྱབ་ཅུའུ་ (naglɛɛ̀ jīgyəb jū) general forestry bureau.

ནགས་ལས་འཕྲུལ་ཆས་བཟོ་གྲྭ་ (naglɛɛ̀ trūūjɛɛ̀ sodra) forestry machine plant/ factory.

ནགས་ལས་བྱེད་ས་ (naglɛɛ̀ ceesa) forestry center, forestry farm.

ནགས་ལས་ཚན་རིག་ཞིབ་འཇུག་ཁང་ (naglɛɛ̀ tsēnrii shimjuùgaŋ) forest sciences research institute.

ནགས་ལས་རིག་པ་ (naglɛɛ rigbə) the science of forestry.

ནགས་ལས་སློབ་གྲྭ་ (naglɛɛ̀ lōbdra) forestry school.

ནགས་ལས་སློབ་གྲྭ་ཆེན་མོ་ (naglɛɛ̀ lōbdra cēmmo) forestry college, institute of forestry.

ནགས་ལས་ས་ཁུལ་ (naglɛɛ̀ səgüü) forest work zone.

ནགས་སླེལ་ (naglee) wicker basket.

ནགས་ས་ (nagsa) forest land, forest.

ནགས་སྲིད་ཁྲུའུ་ (nagsii trū) tib.ch. forest administration office.

ནགས་སྲུང་ས་ཚིགས་ (nagsuŋ sādzii) forest protection station.

ནགས་གསེབ་ (nagseb) forest, jungle.

ནགས་གསོ་ (nagso) sm. ནགས་བཟོ་.

ནང་ (naŋ) 1. in, inside, within ¶ཁང་པའི་ནང་ལ་ Inside the house. 2. among ¶གཞོན་ནུ་དང་རྒན་པའི་ནང་ Among young people and adults. 3. home, house ¶མོའི་ནང་དུ་ཕྱིན་སོང་ (She) went home (to her house). 4. morning.

ནང་ཀར་ (naŋgar) poles used inside nomad tents as pillars.

ནང་དཀྲུག་ཀོ་བྱེད་ (naŋdruù gōjeè) a tool used to carve wood into bowls.

ནང་བཀྲ་མ་ཤིས་ན་ ཕྱི་དོན་མི་འགྲུབ་ (naŋ drā mashiinə cī tön midrub) if there is internal disorder/ quarreling, one can't accomplish one's external affairs.

ནང་རྐྱེན་ (naŋgyen) inner/ internal cause ¶ཕྱི་རྐྱེན་གྱི་ནུས་པ་དེ་ནང་རྐྱེན་ལ་བརྟེན་ནས་ཐོན་གྱི་ཡོད་ The external cause become operative due to the internal cause.

ནང་སྐོར་ (naŋgɔɔ) 1. close friends and relatives ¶དེ་རིང་ནང་སྐོར་ཚང་མ་ཐུགས་སྐྱིར་གདན་འདྲེན་ཞུས་པ་ཡིན་ I invited all my friends and relatives to a party today. 2. internal meaning. 3. inner circumambulation path. 4. clockwise; va.—རྒྱག to go/ do clockwise.

ནང་སྐྱོན་ (naŋgyön) 1. internal injury ¶ཁང་སྐས་འཛེགས་ནས་རིལ་དེ་ནང་སྐྱོན་བྱུང་བ་རེད་ He fell off the ladder and got internal injuries.

ནང་ཁ་མ་གཤིན་པོ་ (naŋ kā məshīmbu) not getting along well.

ནང་ཁ་ལོག (naŋ kā lɔɔ) clockwise.

ནང་ཁ་གཤིན་པོ་ (naŋ kā shīmbu) getting along well.

ནང་ཁ་གཤིན་མིན་ (naŋ kā shīnmin) not getting along well.

ནང་ཁག (naŋgaà) an internal guarantor, a guarantor with whom one has very close relations.

ནང་ཁུངས་ (nəŋguŋ) within, internal, inside ¶ལས་ཁུངས་ནང་ཁུལ་གྱི་གནས་ཚུལ་རྣམས་ལས་ཁུངས་ནང་ཁུལ་ནས་ཐག་གཅོད་དགོས་ Situations within the office should be settled within the office itself.

ནང་ཁུལ་ (nəŋgüü) internal, domestic, within ¶ནང་ཁུལ་ལ་དབང་འཛིན་ Internal control. ¶མི་དམངས་ནང་ཁུལ་གྱི་འགལ་བ་ A contradiction within the (ranks of the) people.

ནང་ཁུལ་གཙང་བོའི་སྐྱེལ་འདྲེན་ཅུའུ་ (nəŋgüü dzāŋwö gyēndren jūwu) tib.ch. bureau of internal waterway shipping.

ནང་ཁོངས་ (naŋgoŋ) internal, inland ¶ནང་ཁོངས་ཀྱི་ཆུ་བོ་ An inland river.

ནང་ཁོངས་དམག་འཁྲབ་ (naŋgoŋ māgdəb) internal war, civil war.

ནང་ཁོངས་དམག་རྒྱག (naŋgoŋ māàgyaà) sm. ནང་ཁོངས་དམག་འཁྲབ་.

ནང་ཁྱག (naŋgyaà) an internal guarantor.

ནང་ཁྱིམ་ (naŋgyim) 1. home. 2. family.

ནང་ཁྲལ་ (naŋdrɛɛ) shung. inner tax (tax paid to one's lord).

ནང་ཁྲིམས་ (nəŋdrim) internal discipline/ rules/ regulations ¶ལས་ཁུངས་སོ་སོར་ནང་ཁྲིམས་རེ་ཡོད་པ་རེད་ Each office has its own internal rules.

ནང་ཁྲོམ་ (naŋdrom) sale of used household items; va.—འཚོང་ to sell household items, to have a house sale.

ནང་གྲོལ་ (naŋdröö) internal organs, entrails.

ནང་གྲོལ་གྱི་དབང་པོ་ (naŋdröögi wāŋbo) internal organs.

ནང་འཁོར་ (naŋkɔɔ) 1. house servant/ serf, personal servants/ attendants. 2. clockwise.

ནང་འཁྲུག (nəŋdruù) civil war; va.—རྒྱག to fight internally, to wage civil war; vi.—ཤོར་ to have civil war break out ༑ བོད་ལ་ནང་འཁྲུག་མང་པོ་ཤོར་བ་རེད་ Many civil wars occurred in Tibet.

ནང་གང་ (naŋgaŋ) not hollow, solid.

ནང་གི་སྐྱེ་མཆེད་དྲུག (naŋgi gyējeè truù) the six "inner" sources of perception: eyes, nose, ears, tongue, body and mind.

ནང་གི་ཁམས་དྲུག (naŋgi kāmdruù) sm. ནང་གི་སྐྱེ་མཆེད་དྲུག.

ནང་གི་རྒྱུ་རྐྱེན་ (naŋgi gyugyen) sm. ནང་རྐྱེན་.

ནང་གི་བསྟན་བཅོས་ (naŋgi dɛ̄njöö) Buddhist commentaries.

ནང་གི་སྡུག་བསྔལ་ (naŋgi duŋŋɛɛ) 1. mental suffering. 2. suffering due to conflicts within a family.

ནང་གི་ཚིས་བྱེད་ (naŋgi tsī̀i jeè) va. to take the responsibility of running a family.

ནང་གི་ཚོར་བ་ (naŋgi tsōrwa) feelings/ sensations of the mind.

ནང་གི་མཚོ་དྲུག (naŋgi tsōdruù) the six items: honey, butter, yogurt, milk, water and ཆང་.

ནང་གི་ཡེ་ཤེས་དབྱུག་གུ་ (naŋgi yeshe yūggu) the central channel (that is used when meditating).

ནང་གི་རིག་པ་ (naŋgi rigbə) sm. ནང་རིག་པ་.

ནང་གི་རིགས་བཞི་ (naŋgi rigshi) the four original lineages of Tibet. (སེ་སྡེ་, རྨུ་སྡེ་, ལྡོང་སྡེ་, སྟོང་སྡེ་).

ནང་གི་ལུས་ (naŋgi lǖü) the physical body.

ནང་གི་ཁ་སོ་ (naŋgi kāso) internal affairs.

ནང་གོན་ (naŋgön) underwear, underpants, underclothes.

ནང་གོས་ (naŋgöö) sm. ནང་གོན་.

ནང་གྲུག (naŋgyaà) sm. ནང་རིག.

ནང་གྱོན་དོར་མ་ (naŋgyön tɔrmə) underpants.

ནང་གྲས་ (naŋdrɛɛ̀) 1. one of us, belonging to our group ༑ མི་དེ་ང་ཚོའི་ཚོགས་པའི་ནང་གྲས་རེད་ He is a member of our group.

ནང་གྲོས་ (naŋdröö) internal conversation/ discussion; va.—བྱེད་.

ནང་གྲོས་ཚོགས་འདུ་ (naŋdröö tsōŋdu) a meeting to discuss sth. internally; va.—བྱེད་.

ནང་གླེང་ (naŋleŋ) internal conversation/ talk.

ནང་དགྲ་ (naŋdra) the enemy within.

ནང་འགལ་ (naŋgɛɛ) internal contradiction.

ནང་འགྲིག (naŋdrig) internally settled/ agreed, settled through internal discussion; va.—བྱེད་ ༑ ཁོ་ཚོས་ཁ་མཆུ་དེ་ནང་འགྲིག་བྱས་འདུག They settled the dispute internally.

ནང་རྒྱ་ (naŋgya) the inner area/ space of a (house, room, etc.).

ནང་རྒྱུགས་ (naŋgyuù) rehearsal, trial, test; va.—ལོན་ to get familiar with the internal situation/ condition ༑ ལས་ཁུངས་ཀྱི་ནང་རྒྱུགས་ལོན་རྗེས་ལས་མྱུར་མགྱོགས་སུ་ཕྱིན་པ་རེད་ Having become familiar with the internal workings of the office, the speed of the work increased.

ནང་རྒྱུས་ (nəŋgyüü) 1. the internal situation/ conditions of sth.; va.—བྱེད་ to teach/ explain/ tell the internal workings of sth. ༑ མི་དེས་ནང་རྒྱུས་བྱས་ནས་ངས་ལས་ཁུངས་དེའི་གནས་ཚུལ་ཚང་མ་ཤེས་བྱུང་. He explained the inner workings of the office and through that I learned all about the office.

ནང་རྒྱུས་ཅན་ (nəŋgyüüjɛn) person familiar with the inner working of sth.

ནང་སྒང་ (nāŋgaŋ) inner tube ༑ རྐྱ་པོའི་ནང་སྒང་ The inner tube of the ball.

ནང་སྒང་ (naŋgaŋ) shung. abbr. of ནང་མ་སྒང་.

ནང་སྒོ་ (naŋgo) inner door.

ནང་སྒོས་ (naŋgöö) sm. ནང་ཁུལ་.

ནང་སྒྲིག (naŋdrig) sm. ནང་འགྲིག.

ནང་སྒྲིབ་ (nəŋdrib) cataract, glaucoma.

ནང་སྒྲིལ་ (nəŋdrii) internal unity; va.— བྱེད་ to act with internal unity.

ནང་ངོས་ (naŋŋöö) internally, inside ༑ ཁང་པའི་ནང་ངོས་ལ་ཚོན་རྩི་ཡག་པོ་བཏང་འདུག The inside of the house has been painted well.

ནང་བཅར་ (naŋjaa) shung. visiting/ meeting with an official at his home (rather than the office) to ask for sth. (this usually involves giving a gift so is something like a bribe); va.—ཞུ ༑ ཁྲིམས་དཔོན་ལ་ནང་བཅར་ཞུས་པ་རེད་ He went to judge's home to ask for favor.

ནང་བཅུད་ (naŋjüü) the essence.

ནང་ཆ་ (naŋja) sm. ནང་གྲོལ་.

ནང་ཆུ་ (nəŋju) inland water.

ནང་ཆོས་ (naŋ cōō) Buddhism.

ནང་ལྗོངས་ (nāŋjoŋ) the interior ༑ བཟོ་གྲྭ་གི་ནང་ལྗོངས་ The interior of factories.

ནང་ཆག (naŋjaà) shung. reducing a tax after an internal discussion (e.g., without changing the official documents).

ནང་ཆས་ (naŋjɛɛ̀) furniture.

ནང་ཆིངས་ (naŋjiŋ) 1. an internal belt (e.g., on underpants). 2. a secret/ internal treaty.

ནང་ཆེན་ (naŋjön) internal lining on the hem (of a dress).

ནང་མཆོད་ (naŋjöö) a type of tantric offering.

ནང་མཆོད་ཀ་པཱི་ (naŋjöö gəli) skull bowl (often made of metal) used for tantric offerings.

ནང་འཇམ་ (naŋjam) underwear.

ནང་ཉམས་ (naŋñam) acting excessively familiar (and thus disrespectful) with a superior; va.—བྱེད་ ༑ སློབ་ཕྲུག་དེས་དགེ་རྒན་ལ་ནང་ཉམས་བྱེད་ཀྱི་འདུག The student is acting excessively familiar with his teacher.

ནང་ཉེ་ (naŋñe) close relatives, close friends.

ནང་གཉེར་ (naŋñer) steward in charge of the internal affairs of a house/ household.

ནང་སྙན་ (naŋñɛn) shung. internal or inner petition/ request/ report.

ནང་སྙན་བཀའ་བཞེས་ (naŋñɛn gāsheè) shung. giving one's word in response to an inner petition ༑ གོང་རིམ་ནས་སྤྲུལ་སྐུ་རྣམ་གཉིས་ལ་གཞིས་ཀའི་ཁ་འཛིན་བསྐུལ་རྒྱུའི་ནང་སྙན་བཀའ་བཞེས་ཐོབ་པ་ The superiors gave their word to grant the possession of the estate to the two incarnate lamas in response to their inner petition.

ནང་སྙིང་ (naŋñiŋ) 1. kernel, core, pit, meat of a nut ༑ སྟར་ཀའི་ནང་སྙིང་ Walnut meat. 2. the main point ༑ ཁོང་གི་གསུང་བཤད་ཀྱི་ནང་སྙིང་དེ་དཔལ་འབྱོར་ཡར་རྒྱས་ཀྱི་སྐོར་རེད་འདུག The main point of his speech was economic development. 3. the stuffing of sth. (e.g., of dumplings).

ནང་སྙོམས་ (naŋñom) shung. equalizing internally; va.—བྱེད་ ༑ སྔར་ཆོས་ལ་ཆོད་རིགས་ཀྱི་གཞིས་ཀའི་ཁྲལ་འབབ་རྣམས་སེམས་ཅན་ཡོད་ཁངས་ལ་ནང་སྙོམས་བྱ་དགོས་ The taxes that originally were divided between the estates belonging to monasteries and aristocrats shall be equalized among the taxpayers who have animals.

ནང་གདད་ཟུར་ (naŋ dɛ̄ɛsur) diagonal angle.

ནང་གཏམ་ (naŋdam) internal/ confidential talk; va.—ཤོད་ ༑ མི་དེས་ལས་ཁུངས་ཀྱི་ནང་གཏམ་ཚང་མ་ཕྱི་ལ་བཤད་བཞག That person told all internal talk of the office to the outside.

ནང་གཏམ་ཕྱི་སྐྱེལ་ (naŋdam cīgyee) telling internal talk outside; va.—བྱེད་.

ནང་དག་ཏུ་ (naŋ dāgdu) inwardly, internally ༑ ཕྱི་དག་ཏུ་བོད་རང་བཙན་མ་རེད་ཟེར་གྱི་ཡོད་ཀྱང་ནང་དག་ཏུ་བོད་རང་བཙན་ཁས་ལེན་གྱི་ཡོད་པ་རེད་ Even though (he) externally (says) Tibet is not independent, inwardly he accepts that it was independent.

ནང་རྟེན་ (naŋden) religious items/ statues, sacred relics/ objects.

ནང་ལྟར་ (naŋdar) like, according to ༑ གནས་ཚུལ་དེ་

ནང་ལྟར་ According to that news (to what was in that news). ༑ང་ལ་སྨྱུ་གུ་དེ་ནང་ལྟར་ཞིག་དགོས་ I need a pen just like this one.

ནང་སྟག་ཕྱི་ཞིམ་ (naŋdaà cǐshim) externally mild/ meek but internally strong/ tough [Lit. inside tiger, outside cat].

ནང་སྟག་ཕྱི་ཞུམ་ (naŋdaà cǐshum)) sm. ནང་སྟག་ཕྱི་ཞིམ་.

ནང་སྡོངས་ (naŋdoŋ) a family that has become extinct.

ནང་བརྟག་ཕྱི་ཚོད་ (naŋdaà cǐdzɛɛ̀) investigating internally and externally; va.—བྱེད་ ༑གྲོད་གཞི་འདིའི་སྐོར་ཁྲིམས་ཁང་ནས་ནང་བརྟག་ཕྱི་ཚོད་བྱེད་བཞིན་པ་རེད་ Concerning this case, the court these days is investigating it internally and externally.

ནང་བསྟན་ (naŋdɛn) Buddhist teachings, Buddhism ༑ནང་བསྟན་རིག་གནས་ཀྱི་ལྟེ་གནས་ Buddhist cultural center.

ནང་བསྟན་མཐུན་ཚོགས་ (naŋdɛn tǚndzɔɔ̀) Buddhist Association (in China).

ནང་བསྟན་གཞུང་ལུགས་ (naŋdɛn shuŋluù) Buddhist scriptures.

ནང་བསྟན་རིག་པ་ (naŋdɛn rigbə) the study of Buddhist philosophy.

ནང་བསྟན་སློབ་གླིང་ (naŋdɛn lōbliŋ) Buddhist institute.

ནང་ཐུ་ (naŋtu) the part of a Tibetan dress that is folded/ wrapped under.

ནང་མཐུན་ (naŋdün) 1. internal accord/ agreement/ harmony. 2. sm. ནང་འགྲིག.

ནང་འཐབ་ (naŋdəb) sm. ནང་འཁྲུག.

ནང་དག་པོ་ (naŋ tagbo) friendly, getting along well, having the same point of view.

ནང་དན་ (naŋdɛn) shung. internal agreement ༑དོ་བདག་པན་ཚུན་ནང་དན་གྱི་གན་རྒྱ་སྒྲོལ་འཛིན་ཞུས་པ་རེད་ The two parties signed an internal agreement.

ནང་དུ་ (naŋdu) within, inside of, among ༑བོད་ནང་དུ་དགོན་པ་མང་པོ་ཡོད་པ་རེད་ There are many monasteries in Tibet.

ནང་དུ་ཆུད་ (naŋdu cǜü) vi. to fit in ༑ཅ་ལག་འདི་རྣམས་སྒམ་འདིའི་ནང་དུ་ཆུད་ཀྱི་མི་འདུག These things do not fit in this box. 2. vi. to understand/ comprehend/ know.

ནང་དུ་འདྲེན་ (naŋdu drɛn) sm. ནང་འདྲེན་.

ནང་དུ་བསྡུ་ (naŋdu du) 1. vi. to be included in, to be part of ༑ཁ་ཆེ་རྣམས་མི་གྲངས་འདིའི་ནང་དུ་བསྡུས་ཡོད་པ་མ་རེད་ The Muslims are not included in this population number. 2. va. to collect/ bring in ༑སྟོན་ཐོག་ཚང་མ་ནང་དུ་བསྡུས་ཟིན་པ་རེད་ All the harvest has been brought in.

ནང་དུ་ཚུད་ (naŋdu tsǜü) vi. to be included in, to be a part of ༑འགྲོ་སོང་འདི་ལོ་སྔོན་མའི་སྔོན་རྩིས་ནང་ཚུད་མི་འདུག These expenses were not included in last year's budget.

ནང་དུ་ཡོད་པ་ (naŋdu yööba) sm. ནང་ཡོད་.

ནང་དེག (naŋdeg) an internal guarantor (from one's group/ unit).

ནང་དོན་ (naŋdön) 1. inner / intrinsic meaning, inwardly, confidential ༑ཡི་གེ་འདིའི་ནང་དོན་མི་འགའ་ཞིག་གིས་མ་གཏོགས་རྟོགས་ཐུབ་ཀྱི་མ་རེད་ Only a few people will understand the inner meaning of this letter. ༑འདི་ནང་དོན་གྱི་སྐད་ཆ་རེད་ མི་ལ་མ་ཤོད་ This is confidential. Don't tell others. ༑ཕྱི་ལྟར་གྲོགས་པོའི་རྣམ་པ་བསྟན་ཀྱང་ནང་དོན་ཐད་དེ་འགལ་ཟླ་རེད་ Outwardly they acted like friends but inwardly they are completely the opposite. 2. the content/ meaning (of sth.) ༑འཐབ་འཛིང་གི་ནང་དོན་ལྡན་པའི་གླུ་གཞས་ Songs with militant content 3. sm. ནང་གསལ་.

ནང་དོན་བཀའ་མོལ་ (naŋdön gāmöö) secret/ inner talk or discussion.

ནང་དོན་གྱི་མཐིལ་ (naŋdöngi tĩĩ) the core meaning, the depth of the inner meaning; va.—རྟོགས་ to uncover the inner meaning, to get to the bottom of sth.

ནང་དོན་དངོས་གཞི་ (naŋdön ŋööshi) main meaning.

ནང་དོན་མདོར་བསྡུས་ (naŋdön dɔrdüü) abbreviated/ brief meaning.

ནང་དོན་ཕུའུ་ཁང་ (naŋdön būgaŋ) tib.ch. Ministry of the Interior.

ནང་དོན་མེད་པ་ (naŋdön meè) nonsensical, meaningless (content) ༑ནང་དོན་མེད་པའི་སྐད་ཆ་ Meaningless talk.

ནང་དོན་རིག་པ་ (naŋdön rigbə) Buddhist philosophy.

ནང་དོན་རྩོད་རྙོག (naŋdön dzööñog) internal dispute.

ནང་དོན་རང་དབང་རང་བཙན་ (naŋdön raŋwaŋ raŋdzɛn) internal autonomy/ freedom.

ནང་དོར་ (naŋdɔɔ) long johns, underpants.

ནང་འདུམ་ (naŋdum) internal mediation/ settlement/ reconciliation; va.—བྱེད་.

ནང་འདོམ་ (naŋdom) the coming together/ accumulation of many things ༑དེང་སང་ལས་ཀ་མང་པོ་ཞིག་ནང་འདོམ་བྱུང་ནས་བྲེལ་བ་ཆེ་པོ་འདུག I am very busy these days because many kinds of work have come together (for me).

ནང་འདྲེན་ (naŋdren) importing; va.—བྱེད་ to import.

ནང་འདྲེན་སྒོ་ཁྲལ་ (naŋdren gotrɛɛ) import duty.

ནང་འདྲེན་ཕྱིར་གཏོང་ (naŋdren cǐrdoŋ) importing and exporting; va.—བྱེད་.

ནང་འདྲེན་ཚོང་ཟོག (naŋdren tsōŋsɔɔ̀) import goods.

ནང་རྡུང་ (naŋduŋ) beating up sb. inside of sth. (e.g., a home); va.—གཏོང་.

ནང་སྡུར་ (naŋdur) comparing internally; va.—བྱེད་.

ནང་སྡོད་ཕྱི་མི་ (naŋdöö cǐmi) foreign settlers, alien residents.

ནང་ན་ (naŋna) sm. ནང་ལ་.

ནང་ནད་ (naŋnɛɛ̀) 1. internal illness. 2. internal medicine.

ནང་ནད་ཚན་ཁག (naŋnɛɛ̀ tsɛ̃ngaà) department of internal medicine.

ནང་ནས་ (naŋnɛɛ̀) 1. from within/ inside. 2. from. home.

ནང་ནུས་ (naŋnüü) internal energy; intrinsic energy.

ནང་ནོམ་ (naŋnom) inner wealth, wealth/ fortune of a family.

ནང་ནོར་ (naŋnɔɔ) sm. ནང་ནོམ་.

ནང་གནས་ (naŋnɛɛ̀) inner/ internal situation or information; vi.—འཁྱུར་; —ཐུར་ to have a confidence betrayed, to have the inner situation leak/ come out ༑དེང་སང་བོད་ཀྱི་ནང་གནས་གསལ་པོ་གོ་རྒྱུ་མི་འདུག These days we don't hear clearly about the internal situation in Tibet. ༑ཚོགས་པའི་ནང་གནས་ཚང་མ་ཕྱི་ལ་འཁྱུར་བཞག All the inner information of the group has leaked out.

ནང་གནས་འགལ་བ་ (naŋnɛɛ̀ gɛɛwa) internal contradiction.

ནང་གནས་གཏན་ཚིགས་ (naŋnɛɛ̀ dɛ̃ndzii) internal logic.

ནང་གནས་གསང་དོན་ (naŋnɛɛ̀ naŋdön) inner/ secret affairs; va.—བྱེད་.

ནང་གནོན་ (naŋnön) shung. inner part of a window.

ནང་གནོན་སྒོ་ཤག (naŋnön goshaà) shung. sm. ནང་གནོན་.

ནང་རྣ་ (naŋna) inner ear.

ནང་རྣམ་ (naŋnam) shung. a rank in the Tashilhunpo goverment equivalent to སྲས་རྣམ་པ་.

ནང་པ་ (naŋba) a Buddhist.

ནང་པ་སངས་རྒྱས་པ་ (naŋba sāŋgyɛɛba) a Buddhist.

ནང་པ་སངས་རྒྱས་པའི་ཆོས་ (naŋba sāŋgyɛɛ̀bɛ cöö) sm. ནང་པའི་ཆོས་.

ནང་པ་སངས་རྒྱས་པའི་ལྟ་བ་ (naŋba sāŋgyɛɛ̀bɛ dāwa) the Buddhist viewpoint/ ideology.

ནང་པའི་གྲུབ་མཐའ་ (naŋbɛ drubta) the Buddhist doctrine/ tenet.

ནང་པའི་ཆ་ལུགས་ (naŋbɛ cəluù) the attire of a Buddhist monk.

ནང་པའི་ཆོས་ (naŋbɛ cöö) Buddhism.

ནང་པའི་ཆོས་པ་ (naŋbɛ cööba) a Buddhist.

ནང་པའི་ལྟ་བ་ (naŋbɛ dāwa) Buddhist philosophy/ viewpoint.

ནང་པའི་སྟོན་པ་ (naŋbɛ dömba) the Buddha.

ནང་པའི་བསྟན་པ་ (naŋbɛ dẽmba) Buddhism.
ནང་པའི་རིང་ལུགས་ (naŋbɛ riŋluù) sm. ནང་པའི་ཆོས་.
ནང་པར་ (naŋbar) next year.
ནང་སྤུ་ (naŋbu) intestinal villi.
ནང་ཕུག (naŋbuù) the inner part/ inside of sth. ¶ཁང་པའི་ནང་ཕུག་ལ་འཛོམ་ཆས་མང་པོ་བཤམས་འདུག There are a lot of furniture inside the house.
ནང་ཕྱོགས་ (naŋjɔ̀ɔ) interior, inner part/ section.
ནང་ཕྲད་ (naŋdrɛɛ) informal meeting (usu. of close friends).
ནང་བུན་ (naŋbün) internal debt, domestic loan.
ནང་བོན་ (naŋbön) a Bon sect that is similar to Buddhism.
ནང་བྱན་ (naŋjɛn) 1. sm. བྲན་གཡོག. 2. sm. ནང་བྱན་ཆུད་.
ནང་བྱན་ཆུད་ (naŋjɛn cüü) va. to have mastered a subject ¶ཁོང་ནི་ཚན་རིག་ལག་རྩལ་ནང་བྱན་ཆུད་པ་ཞིག་རེད་ He is sb. who has mastered science and technology.
ནང་བྱན་ཚུད་ (naŋjɛn dzüü) sm. ནང་བྱན་ཆུད་.
ནང་བློན་ (naŋlön) Minister of Internal Affairs.
ནང་བློན་ཁང་ (naŋlöngaŋ) 1. Internal Affairs Ministry, Home Ministry. 2. council/ cabinet of ministers.
ནང་དབུགས་ (naŋyuù) the inner breath (according to Tibetan medicine).
ནང་འབར་ཅིས་ཁྲི་ (naŋbar jiitre) tib.ch. diesel locomotive.
ནང་འབར་འཁྲུལ་འཁོར་ (naŋbar trüügɔɔ) internal combustion engine.
ནང་འབར་མ་འཁོར་ (naŋbar magɔɔ) sm. ནང་འབར་འཁྲུལ་འཁོར་.
ནང་སྦུག (nəŋbuù) sm. ནང་ཕུག.
ནང་སྦུབས་ (naŋbub) inside of sth. like a pipe/ tube.
ནང་སྦྱོང་ (naŋjoŋ) rehearsal, practice, drill; va.—བྱེད་ to rehearse, to practice, to drill ¶ཁོང་ཚོས་ཟློས་གར་ནང་སྦྱོང་བྱེད་ཀྱི་འདུག They are rehearsing the show.
ནང་སྦྱོར་ (naŋjɔɔ) shung. internal pledge, agreement ¶ནང་སྦྱོར་གྱི་གན་རྒྱར་སེམས་ཅན་ཇི་ཡོད་རྩྭ་ཐར་གཏོང་རྒྱུ་གསལ་བ་ It was written clearly in the internal agreement that all of the animals can be grazed on the grasslands.
ནང་མ་ (naŋma) 1. inside, inner, private, not public. 2. a style of Tibetan lute music originated in Lhasa. 3. house servant/ serf. 4. a modern Tibetan music nightclub.
ནང་མ་མཁན་སྡེ་ཆེ་ཆུང་ (naŋma kẽnde cĩjuŋ) shung. the senior and junior fourth rank monk officials.
ནང་མའི་གྲོས་བསྡུར་ (naŋmɛ trö̀ödur) private/ inner discussion or talk. 2. sm. ནང་ཚགས་.
ནང་མ་ཁང་ (naŋmagaŋ) a place where attendants reside.
ནང་མ་སྒར་ (naŋmagaŋ) shung. 1. the highest office in the Panchen Lama's traditional government. 2. a place where attendants reside.
ནང་མ་ཚང་ (naŋmatsaŋ) the natal/ original home, the main home.
ནང་མའི་སྐྱིད་སྡུག (naŋmɛ gyĩiduù) an association that plays ནང་མ་ music.
ནང་མའི་འགྱིག་འཁོར་ (naŋmɛ gyiŋgɔɔ) inner tire, inner tube.
ནང་མའི་གསུང་མཆིད་ (naŋmɛ sũŋcĩi) inside/ inner talk or discussion.
ནང་མི་ (nəŋmi) family members ¶ངའི་ཁྱིམ་ལ་ནང་མི་ལྔ་ཡོད་ There are five people in my family.
ནང་མི་མོ་ (naŋmimo) female members of a family, female household members.
ནང་མིག (nəŋmii) sm. ཁང་མིག.
ནང་མོ་ (naŋmo) 1. female servant. 2. tomorrow.
ནང་མོལ་ (naŋmöö) private or internal conversation/ discussion/ talk, talk that is not for public dissemination; va.—བྱེད་ ¶ཆིངས་ཡིག་མ་བཞག་གོང་ནས་ནང་མོལ་ཐེངས་མང་བྱས་པ་རེད་ Before signing the treaty they held private discussions many times.
ནང་མོལ་གྲོས་བསྡུར་ (naŋmöö trö̀ödur) private/ internal discussion.
ནང་རྙགས་ (naŋ ñaà) vi. to be rotten at the core.
ནང་དམག (naŋmaà) an army that deals with internal affairs.
ནང་དམེ་ (naŋme) killing of relatives; va.—བྱེད་.
ནང་སྨུག (naŋmug) internal complaining/ grumbling.
ནང་གཙང་ (naŋdzaà) relatives and friends who are trustworthy/ dependable/ reliable.
ནང་རྩི་ (nəŋdzi) kernel, pit, meat (of nuts).
ནང་རྩོད་ (naŋdzöö) internal discord/ dispute/ argument; va.—རྒྱག; vi.—ཤོར་.
ནང་རྩོད་ཕྱི་འཁྲུག (naŋdzöö cĩdruù) internal and external discord/ dispute.
ནང་ཚ་འཛོག (naŋdzaà jɔ̀ɔ) va. to bet money on some event such as a game internally.
ནང་ཚགས་ (naŋdzaà) 1. close and informal; acting without shyness/ reserve (acting as an insider), making (oneself) at home ¶ང་ཚོ་ནང་ཚགས་ཡིན་ཙང་ཁ་ལག་སྐབས་བདེ་བྱུང་ན་འགྲིག་གི་རེད་ We are close so a simple meal will do. ¶དེ་རིང་ནང་ཚགས་གནང་རོགས་གནང་ Today act informal, don't be shy/ reserved. 2. a close/ old acquaintance.
ནང་ཚང་ (naŋdzaŋ) household, family, family members ¶ནང་ཚང་ཟ་གྱོན་བཏུང་གསུམ་གང་ཕྱིར་དགོས་གནད་ཆེ་བར་བརྟེན་ Because of the family members' great need of food, drink and clothing.
ནང་ཚང་གཉིས་ (naŋdzaŋ ñĩi) husband and wife.
ནང་ཚངས་ (naŋdzaŋ) the padded lining (of a jacket, etc.).
ནང་ཚངས་ཅན་ (naŋdzaŋjɛn) padded (for a jacket).
ནང་ཚན་ (naŋdzɛn) sm. ནང་གསེས་.
ནང་ཚི་བཙུག (nəŋdzi jũù) va. to stuff/ fill sth. ¶ནང་ཚི་བཙུག་པའི་ཆའོ་ཁི་ལི་ Chocolate that has a filling.
ནང་ཚིག (nəŋdzii) sm. ནང་རྩི་.
ནང་ཚིལ་ (nəŋdzii) internal fat (of animals).
ནང་ཚིས་ (nəŋdzii) livelihood of a family.
ནང་ཚུད་ (nəŋdzüü) within, in ¶ཟླ་བ་བརྒྱད་ཀྱི་ནང་ཚུད་ཚར་དགོས་རེད་ It has to be finished within eight months.
ནང་ཚུལ་ (nəŋdzüü) sm. ནང་ལོགས་ཀྱི་གནས་ཚུལ་.
ནང་ཚོག (naŋdzɔ̀ɔ) sm. ནང་ཚགས་.
ནང་ཚོང་ (naŋdzoŋ) internal trade/ commerce; va.—རྒྱག.
ནང་ཚོགས་ (naŋdzoò) sm. ནང་ཚགས་.
ནང་ཚོམས་ (naŋdzom) a large room in a Tibetan home (usu. where religious objects are displayed).
ནང་མཚང་ཕྱི་འབྱིན་ (naŋdzaŋ cĩnjin) domestic/ internal problems being exposed; va.—བྱེད་.
ནང་མཚོ་ (naŋdzo) inland sea.
ནང་འཚངས་ (naŋ dzaŋ) 1. va. to push and shove into sth. 2. sm. བར་བཙངས་.
ནང་འཚངས་ཅན་ (naŋdzaŋjɛn) sm. བར་བཙངས་.
ནང་འཚོང་ (naŋdzoŋ) sm. ནང་ཚོང་.
ནང་མཛོད་ (naŋdzöö) high quality traditional ceremonial scarf.
ནང་འཛིང་ (naŋdziŋ) internal quarrel/ fight; va.—བྱེད་; —རྒྱག ¶བུ་སྤུན་གཉིས་ནང་འཛིང་རྒྱག་གི་ཡོད་པ་རེད་ The two brothers are having an internal fight.
ནང་འཛིན་བོགས་མ་ (naŋdzin bɔɔma) shung. a type of internal lease ¶ཁང་ཞིང་དང་ལུག་ཁྱུ་གཅིག་བཅས་ཤེལ་ཆོས་པས་ནང་འཛིན་བོགས་མར་བཏང་སོང་ The Shecho (monastery) leased the house and the field and a herd of sheep as an internal lease.
ནང་འཛིན་མ་ (nəŋdzinma) the mother of a family, the head woman in a household.
ནང་འཛུལ་ (nəŋdzüü) intruding, entered; va.—བྱེད་ ¶ང་ཚོའི་རྒྱལ་ཁབ་ཀྱི་ས་མཚམས་སུ་ཕྱི་རྒྱལ་གྱི་དམག་མིས་ནང་འཛུལ་བྱས་འདུག Foreign soldiers have intruded into the border area of our country.
ནང་འཛུལ་ཉན་པ་ (nəŋdzüü ñɛmba) sb. who secretly listens/ eavesdrops.
ནང་འཛུལ་ཉུལ་མ་ (nəŋdzüü ñüümə) an enemy agent

planted within one's own ranks, an agent/ spy who infiltrates the enemy.

ནང་རྫས་ (naŋdzɛɛ̀) the filling/ stuffing of sth.

ནང་གཞིས་ (nəŋshiì) 1. home and manorial estate. 2. home.

ནང་བཞིན་ (nəŋshin) alike, identical, the same as ། ངས་མི་དེ་ནང་བཞིན་མཐོང་མ་མྱོང་ I've never seen a person like that.

ནང་བཞུགས་ (naŋshuù) 1. family member(s) who are at home ། ནང་བཞུགས་ཚང་མ་སྐུ་གཟུགས་བདེ་པོ་རེད་འདུག The family members at home are all well.

ནང་ཟིང་ (nəŋsiŋ) internal disorder/ trouble.

ནང་ཟད་ (naŋsɛɛ̀) worn out from/ on the inside; vi.—ཐེབས་.

ནང་ཟན་ (naŋsɛn) sm. ནང་བཟན་.

ནང་ཟུར་ (naŋsur) interior angle.

ནང་གཟན་ (naŋsɛn) 1. sm. ནང་བཟན་.

ནང་བཟན་ (naŋsɛn) 1. household servants who worked for room and board without wages (this was sometimes hereditary and sometimes voluntary). 2. clerks in the traditional Tibetan government.

ནང་བཟུང་ (naŋ suŋ) va. to establish a family/ household ། ཕུ་གུ་ཆེན་པ་ཆང་ས་བརྒྱབ་རྗེས་ནང་བཟུང་ནས་བསྡད་ཡོད་པ་རེད་ After the older child got married, (he) established a (separate) household.

ནང་འོབས་ (naŋob) inside pit (འོབས་དོང་).

ནང་ཡངས་པ་ (naŋ yaŋba) 1. carefree, light hearted. 2. spacious (for houses/ rooms).

ནང་ཡན་པ་ (naŋ yɛmba) 1. sm. ནང་ཡངས་པ་, 1. 2. vi. to have an internal secret leak out.

ནང་ཡིག (naŋyiì) 1. confidential letter. 2. letter to one's family.

ནང་ཡོང་ (naŋyoŋ) 1. importing, import goods ། ནང་ཡོང་དངོས་རྫས་ Import goods.

ནང་ཡོང་མང་བ་ (naŋyoŋ maŋwa) import surplus.

ནང་ཡོད་ (naŋyöö̀) internal, inner, inside.

ནང་ཡོད་འགལ་བ་ (naŋyöö̀ gɛɛwa) inner or internal contradiction.

ནང་ཡོད་རྒྱུ་རྐྱེན་ (naŋyöö̀ gyugyen) inner or internal factor/ cause.

ནང་ཡོད་འབྲེལ་བ་ (naŋyöö̀ dreewə) inner or internal relations/ connections.

ནང་གཡོག (naŋyɔɔ̀) servant in sb.'s home.

ནང་ར་ (naŋra) courtyard.

ནང་རས་ (naŋrɛɛ̀) sm. ནང་ཤ་.

ནང་རིམ་ (naŋrim) shung. an inner rank (in tt. government).

ནང་རིག་པ་ (naŋ rigbə) the study of Buddhist philosophy.

ནང་རུབ་ (naŋrub) morning and evening, dawn and dusk.

ནང་རུལ་ (naŋrüü) 1. disloyal, traitorous; va.—བྱེད་. 2. sm. ནང་རུལ་པ་.

ནང་རུལ་པ་ (naŋrüübə) traitor.

ནང་རོལ་ (naŋröö) sm. ནང་ལོགས་.

ནང་ལ་ (naŋla) sm. ནང་དུ་.

ནང་ལ་རྩམ་པ་མེད་པར་ སྒོ་ཁུང་རྩམ་རལ་ཡོག་ཡོག (naŋla) showing off even tough one is poor [Lit. having no tsamba inside but throwing tsamba on the window].

ནང་ལས་ (naŋlɛɛ̀) housework; va.—བྱེད་.

ནང་ལུགས་ (naŋluù) informal ways/ manners/ customs.

ནང་ལུགས་གསུང་མཆིད་ (naŋluù sūŋciì) sm. ནང་མའི་གསུང་མཆིད་.

ནང་ལོགས་ (naŋlɔɔ̀) inside, inner, internal ། ཁོ་ཁང་པའི་ནང་ལོགས་ལ་འདུག He is inside the house.

ནང་ལོགས་ཀྱི་སྐམ་ས་ (naŋlɔ̀ɔgi gāmsa) inland, hinterland.

ནང་ལོགས་ཀྱི་ཆུ་བོ་ (naŋlɔ̀ɔgi cūwo) inland river.

ནང་ལོགས་ཀྱི་གནས་ཚུལ་ (naŋlɔ̀ɔgi nɛ̄ɛ̀dzüü) inside story/ situation/ circumstance.

ནང་ལོགས་ཀྱི་མཚོ་ (naŋlɔ̀ɔgi tsō) inland sea.

ནང་ལོགས་ཀྱི་མཚོའུ་ (naŋlɔ̀ɔgi tsēwu) inland lake.

ནང་ལོང་ (naŋloŋ) internal organs.

ནང་ཤ་ (naŋsha) the lining of sth.

ནང་ཤངས་ (naŋshaŋ) 1. internally harmonious. 2. shung. internally settled/ agreed, settling through internal negotiation ། གྲྭ་ཚང་ཁང་ཚན་ནང་ཤངས་དང་ དགོན་འཐུས་ཕྱོགས་སོ་སོ་ནས་ཉེས་པ་གསེར་སྲང་ ༣ The (monastery's) College and the Kamtsen shall settle the matter through internal negotiation, and the representatives of the monastery shall be fined three srangs of gold.

ནང་ཤུགས་ (naŋshuù) internal/ inner force.

ནང་ཤུན་ (nəŋshün) inner rind/ peel/ skin.

ནང་བཤུག (nəŋshuù) trading/ selling internally (outside of the market place by sb. who is not a businessman/ trader); va.—གཏོང་ ། ཅ་ལག་འདི་དེ་རིང་ང་ལ་ནང་བཤུག་གཏོང་རོགས་ (Please) sell me this item today (internally).

ནང་བཤེར་ཕྱི་ཚད་ (naŋsher cīdzɛɛ̀) investigating internally and externally.

ནང་ས་ (naŋsa) 1. a territory that is within a larger unit. 2. inland China (a term used by Tibetans in China to refer to the rest of China outside of Tibet) ། ཁོ་ཚོ་ལྷ་ས་ནས་ནང་སར་ལོག་པ་རེད་ (They) returned from Lhasa to inland China.

ནང་སེམས་ (naŋsem) mind.

ནང་སེལ་ (naŋsel) on bad terms, not getting along; vi.—ཤོར་.

ནང་སོ་ (naŋso) border soldiers/ troops.

ནང་སོག (naŋsɔɔ̀) Inner Mongolia.

ནང་སོག་རང་སྐྱོང་ལྗོངས་ (naŋsɔɔ̀ raŋgyoŋjoŋ) the Inner Mongolia Autonomous Region.

ནང་སོབ་ (naŋsob) soft on the inside.

ནང་སྲིད་ (nəŋsiì) internal affairs, internal politics.

ནང་སྲིད་བཀའ་བློན་ (nəŋsiì gālön) Minister or the Interior, Home Minister, Internal Affairs Minister.

ནང་སྲིད་སྒང་ (nəŋsiìgaŋ) sm. ནང་སྲིད་ལས་ཁུངས་.

ནང་སྲིད་བློན་ཆེན་ (nəŋsiì lönjen) Minister or the Interior, Home Minister, Internal Affairs Minister.

ནང་སྲིད་ལས་ཁུངས་ (nəŋsiì lɛɛ̀guŋ) Ministry of Internal Affairs, Home Ministry.

ནང་སྲིན་ (nəŋsin) intestinal worms.

ནང་སྲུང་ (nəŋsuŋ) watchman (for a house, building); va.—བྱེད་.

ནང་གསལ་ (naŋsɛl) according to what is in sth., as written in ། ཆིངས་ཡིག་དེའི་དོན་ཚན་དང་པོ་ནང་གསལ་ According to the first article of the treaty.

ནང་གསེས་ (naŋseè) 1. part, category, heading, subtitle ། གནད་དོན་དེ་ཆིངས་ཡིག་གི་དོན་ཚན་དང་པོའི་ནང་གསེས་གསུམ་པའི་འགོད་ཡོད་ This point is written in part three of the first article of the treaty. 2. an internal/ local section or unit ། ལས་ཁུངས་འདིའི་ནང་ནང་གསེས་སྡེ་ཚན་མང་པོ་ཡོད་པ་རེད་ This office has many internal sections.

ནང་གསེས་ལེ་ཚན་ (naŋseè ledzɛn) subheading (in a book, chapter, etc.).

ནང་གསོད་ (naŋsöö̀) killing sb. within one's family/ group/ country; va.—གཏོང་.

ནང་བསངས་ (naŋ sāŋ) va. to explain clearly about a problem (to settle it) ། ཁྱེད་རང་ལ་གྲོགས་མོ་ཞིག་ཡོད་ལུགས་སྐོར་ཁྱེད་རང་གི་བཟའ་ཟླར་ནང་བསངས་ན་ཡག་པོ་ཡོད་པ་རེད་ It will be good if you explain clearly to your wife about (the talk) that you have a girlfriend.

ནང་ལྷོང་ (naŋlhoŋ) internal obstacle/ disaster/ impediment.

ནངས་ (naŋ) morning.

ནངས་སྔ་ལངས་དགོང་ཕྱི་ཉལ་ (naŋ ŋālaŋ goŋ cīñɛɛ) industrious, diligent, hard working [Lit. rising early, going to sleep late].

ནངས་ཇ་ (naŋca) morning tea.

ནངས་ཐུག་དགོང་ཐུག (naŋduù goŋdu') meeting in the morning and again in the evening; va.—བྱེད་.

ནངས་ནུབ་ (naŋnub) morning and night.

ནངས་པ་ (nāŋba) morning.

ནངས་མེ་ (na̲ŋme) fire lit in the morning (to make tea).

ནངས་མོ་ (na̲ŋmo) sm. ནངས་པ་.

ནངས་མོའི་སྐར་མ་ (na̲ŋmö gārma) sm. ཉིན་མོའི་སྐར་མ་.

ནངས་ཟས་ (na̲ŋsɛɛ̀) breakfast.

ནངས་རེ་དགོང་རེ་ (na̲ŋre go̲ŋre) every morning and night.

ནངས་རེ་ནུབ་རེ་ (na̲ŋre nu̲bre) sm. ནངས་རེ་དགོང་རེ་.

ནད་ (nɛ̲ɛ̀) disease, illness, sickness; vi.—ན་; —འཕོག་; —མནར་ to be/ get sick.

ནད་ཀྱི་རྒྱེན་རྫི་ (nɛ̲ɛ̀gi gyēndzi) medicine.

ནད་ཀྱི་ཁ་སྣོན་ (nɛ̲ɛ̀gi kānön) a disease that comes on top of another.

ནད་ཀྱི་འགྱུར་བ་ (nɛ̲ɛ̀gi gyu̲wə) sm. ནད་འགྱུར་.

ནད་ཀྱི་སྒོ་ནི་ཁ་ཡིན་ ཆུར་གྱི་སྒོ་ཡང་ཁ་ཡིན་ (nɛ̲ɛ̀gi go̲ni ḳāyin cu̲rgi go̲ni kāyin) the door of disease is the mouth, the cause of trouble is also the mouth.

ནད་ཀྱི་འཇིགས་པ་ (nɛ̲ɛ̀gi jigbə) disease.

ནད་ཀྱི་འཛུ་ས་ (nɛ̲ɛ̀gi ju̲sə) focus of disease.

ནད་ཀྱི་འབྱུང་རྐྱེན་ (nɛ̲ɛ̀gi ju̲ŋgyen) sm. ནད་ཀྱི་འབྱུང་གཞི་.

ནད་ཀྱི་འབྱུང་གཞི་ (nɛ̲ɛ̀gi ju̲ŋshi) 1. the cause/ origin of a disease. 2. pathogens, pathology.

ནད་ཀྱི་འབྱུང་རྩ་ (nɛ̲ɛ̀gi ju̲ŋdza) sm. ནད་ཀྱི་འབྱུང་གཞི་.

ནད་ཀྱི་ཡན་ལག་བརྒྱད་ (nɛ̲ɛ̀gi yɛ̲nlaà gyɛ̲ɛ̀) eight categories of disease in Tibetan medicine: 1. internal diseases. 2. infant diseases. 3. gynecological diseases. 4. disease caused by demons and spirits. 5. disease caused by wounds. 6. disease caused by poison. 7. diseases of old age. 8 venereal diseases.

ནད་ཀྱིས་འདས་ (nɛ̲ɛ̀gi dɛ̲ɛ̀) vi. to die of illness.

ནད་ཀྱིས་མནར་ (nɛ̲ɛ̀gi nār) vi. to be ill, to get sick.

ནད་རྒྱལ་ (nɛ̲ɛ̀gyɛɛ) chronic invalid.

ནད་རྐྱེན་ (nɛ̲ɛ̀gyen) cause of disease/ sickness.

ནད་རྐྱེན་ལས་འགྱུར་ (nɛ̲ɛ̀gyen lɛ̲ɛ̀ kyu̲r) 1. changing one's job due to illness. 2. being assigned back to the city from the village due to illness.

ནད་སྐྱེས་འབུ་ཕྲ་ (nɛ̲ɛ̀gyeè bu̲dra) bacteria.

ནད་སྐྱོང་པ་ (nɛ̲ɛ̀ gyōŋba) sm. ནད་གཡོག.

ནད་ཁང་ (nɛ̲ɛ̀gaŋ) ward in a hospital.

ནད་ཁང་གི་སྨན་འཛོག་ས་ (nɛ̲ɛ̀gaŋgi mɛ̲njɔ̀ɔ̀sa) dispensary for a ward (in a hospital).

ནད་ཁུངས་ (nɛ̲ɛ̀gu̲ŋ) sm. ནད་གཞི་.

ནད་ཁྱོག (nɛ̲ɛ̀kyɔ̀ɔ̀) sm. ནད་འཁྱོགས་.

ནད་ཁྲག (nɛ̲ɛ̀draà) diseased/ bad blood (that has to be drained to cure an illness/ sickness).

ནད་ཁྲི་ (nɛ̲ɛ̀dri) bed for patients, hospital bed.

ནད་འཁྱོག (nɛ̲ɛ̀ kyɔ̄ɔ̀) vi. to endure/ tolerate (illness or difficulty) ¶ སྲིད་གཞུང་གིས་དཀའ་སྡུག་ཚད་མེད་བཏང་བ་ནད་མ་འཁྱོགས་པར་མི་མང་པོ་རང་ཤི་བརྒྱབ་པ་རེད་ Many people committed suicide as they were unable to endure the sufferings inflicted by the goverment.

ནད་འགྲོལ་གདོན་འགྲོལ་ (nɛ̲ɛ̀dröö dö̲ndröö) having all one's difficulties and obstacles eliminated [Lit. released from sickness, released from demons].

ནད་གོག (nɛ̲ɛ̀gɔɔ̀) a derogatory term used for sick people.

ནད་གྲམ་ (nɛ̲ɛ̀ dra̲m) vi. to have a disease spread.

ནད་དགོངས་ (nɛ̲ɛ̀goŋ) sick leave; va.—ཞུ་ to ask for sick leave.

ནད་འགོ་ (nɛ̲ɛ̀ go̲) vi. to catch an illness/ disease.

ནད་འགོག (nɛ̲ngɔɔ̀) measures to prevent epidemics/ disease, preventive medicine.

ནད་འགོག་སྨན་ཁབ་ (nɛ̲ngɔɔ̀ mɛ̄ngəb) vaccination, innoculation.

ནད་འགོག་སྨན་སོན་ (nɛ̲ngɔɔ̀ mɛ̄nsön) sm. disease resistant seed.

ནད་འགོས་ (nɛ̲ngöö) p. of ནད་འགོ་.

ནད་འགྱུར་ (nɛ̲ɛ̀gyur) change in an illness.

ནད་འགྲེམས་ (nɛ̲ɛ̀ dre̲m) va. to spread disease.

ནད་རྒས་ (nɛ̲ɛ̀gɛɛ̀) an old or advanced illness/ sickness.

ནད་རྒྱུ་ (nɛ̲ɛ̀gyu) sm. ནད་གཞི་.

ནད་བརྒྱ་སྨན་གཅིག (nɛ̲ɛ̀gya mɛ̲njii) a panacea [Lit. one hundred illnesses, one medicine].

ནད་ངོ་ (nɛ̲ɛ̀ŋo) symptom.

ནད་ཅན་ (nɛ̲ɛ̀jɛn) ill, sick.

ནད་ཅན་གྱི་རྣམ་པ་ (nɛ̲ɛ̀jɛngi nāmba) morbid/ ill state.

ནད་ཅན་གྱི་བསམ་ཚུལ་ (nɛ̲ɛ̀jɛngi sɔ̄mdzüü) morbid psychology (or mentality).

ནད་ཅན་ཆུ་ (nɛ̲ɛ̀jɛn cū) a patient's urine.

ནད་གཅོང་ (nɛ̲ɛ̀joŋ) being sick over a long period of time, old/ chronic illness.

ནད་བཅོས་ (nɛ̲ɛ̀jöö) medical treatment; va.—བྱེད་.

ནད་བཅོས་མཁས་པ་ (nɛ̲ɛ̀jöö kɛ̄ɛ̀ba) medical specialist.

ནད་བཅོས་ནད་འགོག (nɛ̲ɛ̀jöö nɛ̲ngɔɔ̀) medical treatment and illness prevention; va.—བྱེད་.

ནད་བཅོས་སྲོག་སྐྱོབ་ (nɛ̲ɛ̀jöö sɔ̄ɔ̀gyob) treating illness and saving lives.

ནད་བཅོས་ཞབས་འདེགས་རུ་ཁག (nɛ̲ɛ̀jöö shɛ̲ndeb ru̲gaà) medical service team.

ནད་ལྕི་ (nɛ̲ɛ̀ji) serious illness/ sickness.

ནད་ལྗིད་པོ་ (nɛ̲ɛ̀ ji̲bu) severe/ serious illness.

ནད་གཉའ་ (nɛ̲ɛ̀ ña̲) the strength of an illness/ disease; vi.—ཆག to have the strength of an illness get reduced; va.—གཅོག to decrease/ reduce the strength of an illness.

ནད་རྙིང་ (nɛ̲ɛ̀ñiŋ) chronic illness/ ailment, old sickness/ disease.

ནད་བསྙད་ལས་གཡོལ་ (nɛ̲ɛ̀ñɛɛ̀lɛ yöö) vi. to pretend to be ill to avoid work.

ནད་རྟགས་ (nɛ̲ɛ̀daà) symptom of a disease, sign of illness.

ནད་བརྟ་ཉན་བྱེད་ (nɛ̲ɛ̀da ñɛ̲njeè) stethoscope.

ནད་བརྟག་ཁང་ (nɛ̲ɛ̀daàgaŋ) outpatient department/ clinic.

ནད་བརྟག་སྒུག་ཁང་ (nɛ̲ɛ̀daà gu̲ùgaŋ) waiting room in a hospital/ clinic.

ནད་བརྟག་སྨན་བཅོས་ (nɛ̲ɛ̀da mɛ̄njöö) medical, treatment/ care; va.—བྱེད་.

ནད་བསྟུན་སྨན་བཅོས་ (nɛ̲ɛ̀dün mɛ̄njöö) appropriate medical treatment.

ནད་བསྟུན་སྨན་གཏོང་ (nɛ̲ɛ̀dün mɛ̄ndoŋ) va. to do appropriate medical treatment.

ནད་ཐར་མ་ (nɛ̲ɛ̀ tārma) acquired immunity.

ནད་ཐུབ་ས་བོན་ (nɛ̲ɛ̀tub sābön) disease resistant seed.

ནད་ཐེག (nɛ̲ɛ̀deg) sm. ནད་འཁྱོག.

ནད་ཐོ་ (nɛ̲ɛ̀do) medical history/ record.

ནད་ཐོག (nɛ̲ɛ̀dɔɔ̀) clinical.

ནད་ཐོག་ངོས་འཛིན་ (nɛ̲ɛ̀dɔɔ̀ nö̲ndzin) clinical diagnosis of illness/ disease.

ནད་ཐོག་མངོན་ཚུལ་ (nɛ̲ɛ̀tɔɔ̀ nöndzüü) clinical symptom.

ནད་ཐོག་སྨན་འཁྱེལ་ (nɛ̲ɛ̀dɔɔ̀ mɛ̄ngee) an effective solution for a problem [Lit. for an illness bring medicine].

ནད་ཐོག་ཉམས་མྱོང་ (nɛ̲ɛ̀dɔɔ̀ ña̲mñoŋ) clinical experience.

ནད་ཐོག་ཉམས་ལེན་ (nɛ̲ɛ̀dɔɔ̀ ña̲mlem) clinical experience.

ནད་ཐོག་སྨན་བཅོས་ (nɛ̲ɛ̀dɔɔ̀ mɛ̄njöö) clinical treatment for a disease/ illness.

ནད་ཐོག་ཚན་རིག (nɛ̲ɛ̀dɔɔ̀ tsɛ̄nrii) clinical science.

ནད་ཐོག་གསོ་རིག (nɛ̲ɛ̀dɔɔ̀ sörii) clinical medicine.

ནད་ཐོག་ལག་ལེན་ (nɛ̲ɛ̀dɔɔ̀ la̲glen) clinical practice.

ནད་དང་འབུའི་གནོད་པ་ (nɛ̲ɛ̀ da̲ŋ bü̲ nööba) harm from disease and insects/ pests.

ནད་དྭངས་ (nɛ̲ɛ̀ ta̲ŋ) vi. to recover from an illness, to get cured.

ནད་དུག (nɛ̲ɛ̀dug) virus, germ.

ནད་དུག་འགོག་རྫས་ (nɛ̲ɛ̀dug gɔ̲gdzɛɛ̀) antibody.

ནད་དུག་ཅན་གྱི་མཆིན་ཚད་ (nɛ̲ɛ̀dugjɛngi cīndzɛɛ̀) viral hepatitis.

ནད་དུག་རིག་པ་ (nɛ̲ɛ̀dug ri̲gbə) virology.

ནད་དེབ་ (nɛɛ̀deb) patient records in a clinic/ hospital.

ནད་དྲག (nɛɛ̀ traà) vi. to recover/ get better (from an illness).

ནད་དྲག་པོ་ (nɛɛ̀ tragbo) a serious/ grave illness.

ནད་འདས་དགྲ་ཤོར་ (nɛɛ̀dɛɛ̀ drashɔɔ) killed or wounded in action (battle).

ནད་གདོང་ (nɛɛ̀doŋ) sickly appearance.

ནད་གདོན་ (nɛɛ̀dön) evil spirit/ demon that causes illness.

ནད་བདག (nɛɛ̀daà) evil spirit/ demon that causes illness.

ནད་བདག་ཨ་མ་ (nɛɛ̀daà āma) sm. ནད་བདག.

ནད་སྡུག་དུ་སོང་ (nɛɛ̀ dugdu sōŋ) vi. to have a relapse (from an illness), to have an illness get worse.

ནད་ན་ (nɛɛ̀ na) vi. to be sick, to suffer from illness.

ནད་མནར་ (nɛɛ̀ nār) sm. ནད་ན་.

ནད་པ་ (nɛɛ̀ba) patient, sick person.

ནད་པ་རྨས་པ་ (nɛɛ̀ba mɛɛ̀ba) sick and wounded.

ནད་པའི་སྡོད་ཁང་ (nɛɛ̀bɛ döögaŋ) hospital ward.

ནད་པའི་སྡོད་ཤག (nɛɛ̀bɛ dööshaà) sm. ནད་པའི་སྡོད་ཁང་.

ནད་ཕོག (nɛɛ̀ pɔ̄ɔ̀) vi. to catch/ come down with an illness.

ནད་བབ་ (nɛɛ̀bəb) condition of a patient/ illness ། ཁོང་གི་ནད་བབ་ག་འདྲ་འདུག How is his condition (regarding an illness)? ། ནད་བབ་ཕྱི་པོ་ A serious illness.

ནད་བབ་ཉེན་བཅར་ (nɛɛ̀bəb ñenjar) an illness that has reached a dangerous state.

ནད་བབས་ (nɛɛ̀bəb) sm. ནད་བབ་.

ནད་བུ་ (nɛɛ̀bu) minor disease/ sickness.

ནད་བྲང་ (nɛɛ̀draŋ) sm. ནད་པའི་སྡོད་ཁང་.

ནད་འབུ་ (nɛmbu) germs, bacteria, disease causing organisms, pathogens.

ནད་འབུ་ཕྲ་མོ་ (nɛmbu trāmo) microbe, bacteria (very minute pathogens).

ནད་འབྱམས་ (nɛnjam) sm. ནད་ཡམས་.

ནད་མུག་འཁྲུག་རྩོད་ (nɛɛ̀ mug drūg dzöö) abbr. sickness, famine, war and disputes.

ནད་མུག་འཁྲུག་གསུམ་ (nɛɛ̀ mug drūg sūm) the three: sickness, famine and war.

ནད་མེད་ (nɛɛ̀meè) well, healthy.

ནད་མེད་གཅོང་སྐྱེ་ (nɛɛ̀meè jōŋgye) a syndrome where one is chronically sickly/ feeble/ weak without having any identifiable sickness.

ནད་མེད་ཆུ་ (nɛɛ̀meè cū) urine (of a person who is not sick).

ནད་མེད་རྩ་ (nɛɛ̀meè dzā) a normal pulse beat.

ནད་མ་འཁྱོག (nɛɛ̀ ma kyɔ̄ɔ̀) vi. to be unable to bear/ endure/ tolerate (illness or difficulty).

ནད་མ་ཐེག (nɛɛ̀ ma tēg) sm. ནད་མ་འཁྱོག.

ནད་ཚ་ (nɛɛ̀tsa) fever.

ནད་ཚིག་ཟ་ (nɛɛ̀dziì sa) vi. to feel angry when sick.

ནད་རྒྱུལ་ (nɛɛ̀dzüü) nature/ character of an illness/ disease.

ནད་རྫུ་ (nɛɛ̀dzu) pretending/ feigning illness; va.—བྱེད་.

ནད་ཞབས་པ་ (nɛɛ̀shəbba) nurse.

ནད་ཞབས་པའི་སློབ་གྲྭ་ (nɛɛ̀shəbbɛ lōbdra) nursing school/ college.

ནད་ཞི་ (nɛɛ̀ shi) sm. ནད་དྲག.

ནད་གཞི་ (nɛɛ̀shi) 1. cause of disease/ illness ། ནད་གཞི་འགོག་བཅོས་ Disease prevention and eradication. 2. illness, sickness; va.—ཕོག to fall ill ། ཁོ་ནད་གཞི་ལྗིད་པོ་འདུག He has a serious illness.

ནད་གཞི་སྐྱེ་དངོས་ཕྲ་རབ་ (nɛɛ̀shi gyēŋöö trārəb) microorganisms that cause diseases.

ནད་གཞི་འགོག་བཅོས་ (nɛɛ̀shi gɔgjöö) disease prevention and eradication.

ནད་གཞི་ལྗིད་པོ་ (nɛɛ̀shi jiibu) grave/ serious illness.

ནད་གཞི་ཉན་ཆས་ (nɛɛ̀shi ñenjɛɛ̀) stethoscope.

ནད་གཞི་ཉན་བྱེད་ (nɛɛ̀shi ñenjeè) sm. ནད་གཞི་ཉན་ཆས་.

ནད་གཞི་ཐག་ཆོད་ (nɛɛ̀shi tāgjöö) diagnosing illnesses; vi.—བྱེད་.

ནད་གཞི་བརྟག་དཔྱད་ (nɛɛ̀shi tāgjɛɛ̀) examining for an illness, diagnosing; va.—བྱེད་.

ནད་གཞི་ཕོག (nɛɛ̀shi pɔ̄ɔ̀) see ནད་གཞི་.

ནད་ཟུག (nɛɛ̀sug) ache/ pain caused by illness.

ནད་ཡམས་ (nɛɛ̀yam) epidemic.

ནད་གཡོག (nɛɛ̀yɔɔ̀) nurse; va.—བྱེད་; —ཞུགས་. to nurse, to work as a nurse.

ནད་གཡོག་པའི་གཞུང་ལས་ཁང་ (nɛɛ̀yɔɔ̀bɛ shuŋlɛgaŋ) nurse's office.

ནད་གཡོག་པའི་སློབ་གྲྭ་ (nɛɛ̀yɔɔ̀bɛ lōbdra) sm. ནད་གཡོག་སློབ་གྲྭ.

ནད་གཡོག་མ་ (nɛɛ̀yɔɔ̀ma) sm. ནད་གཡོག.

ནད་གཡོག་སློབ་གྲྭ་ (nɛɛ̀yɔɔ̀ lōbdra) nursing school.

ནད་གཡོག་ཤི་གཡོག (nɛɛ̀yɔɔ̀ shīyɔɔ̀) serving elderly people until they die; va.—ཞུགས་.

ནད་ར་གཅོང་སྐྱེ་ (nɛɛ̀ra jōŋgye) sb. who is always sick.

ནད་རིགས་ (nɛɛ̀rig) diseases.

ནད་རིགས་སྔོན་འགོག (nɛɛ̀rig ŋöŋgɔɔ̀) inoculation/ prevention for a disease.

ནད་རིམས་ (nɛɛ̀rim) epidemic.

ནད་རོ་ (nɛɛ̀ro) 1. sm. ནད་རྙིང་. 2. an old or deep hatred/ animosity.

ནད་རོ་གཅོང་ཅན་ (nɛɛ̀ro jōŋjɛn) chronically ill.

ནད་ལས་གྲོལ་ (nɛɛ̀lɛ tröö) sm. ནད་དྲག.

ནད་ལུགས་ཚོད་ལྟ་ཁང་ (nɛɛ̀luù dzöödagaŋ) pathology laboratory.

ནད་ལུགས་ཞིབ་འཇུག་ཁང་ (nɛɛ̀luù shimjuùgaŋ) institute of pathology.

ནད་ལོག (nɛɛ̀lɔɔ̀) relapse (illness); vi.—རྒྱག; —ཐེབས་ to have a relapse ། མདང་དགོང་མོ་པའི་ནད་གཞི་ནད་ལོག་བརྒྱབ་སོང་ Last night (I) had a relapse of my stomach illness.

ནད་ཤི་ (nɛɛ̀shi) dying from an illness; vi.—ཐེབས་ to die from an illness.

ནད་སངས་ (nɛɛ̀ sāŋ) vi. to recover from illness, to be/ get well.

ནད་སེལ་ (nɛɛ̀ sēl) va. to cure an illness.

ནད་སོན་ (nɛɛ̀sön) sm. ནད་འབུ་.

ནད་སོན་ཕྲ་མོ་ (nɛɛ̀sön trāmo) sm. ནད་འབུ་ཕྲ་མོ་.

ནད་སོས་ (nɛɛ̀ söö) sm. ནད་དྲག.

ནད་སློང་རྐྱེན་གཉིས་ (nɛɛ̀loŋ gyēññiì) two causes of sickness (unsuitable food and inappropriate habits/ behavior).

ནད་གསེང་ (nɛɛ̀seŋ) the period without sickness (the time between getting well and being sick again).

ནད་གསོ་ (nɛɛ̀so) 1. convalescence, recuperation (from illness) va.—བྱེད་. 2. va. to treat illness.

ནད་གསོ་ཁང་ (nɛɛ̀sogaŋ) 1. sanitarium, rest home. 2. inpatient department.

ནད་གསོ་བའི་རིག་པ་ (nɛɛ̀sowɛ rigbə) medical science.

ནད་གསོ་སློབ་ཆོག (nɛɛ̀so lēbjɔɔ̀) ready/ able to decide sth. quickly [Lit. medicine ready to treat an illness].

ནད་གསོའི་སྨན་ཁང་ (nɛɛ̀sö mēngaŋ) sanitarium.

ནད་གསོས་བྱེད་ (nɛɛ̀söö ceè) va. to recuperate/ convalesce.

ནད་གསོས་སྨན་ཡོན་ (nɛɛ̀söö mēnyön) payment of medical costs for causing injury or illness to sb.

ནད་ལྷག (nɛɛ̀lhaà) sm. ནད་རོ་.

ནན་ (nɛn) abbr. of ནན་དན་.

ནན་ཀྭ་ (nɛnga) ch. pumpkin, squash.

ནན་བསྐུལ་ཆེན་པོ་ (nɛngüü cēmbo) emphatically, insistently ། ནན་བསྐུལ་ཆེན་པོས་བརྗོད་པ་རེད་ (He) said it emphatically.

ནན་ཁྲང་ (nɛndraŋ) Nanchang.

ནན་ཁྲང་འཁོས་ལངས་ (nɛndraŋ wöölaŋ) ch.tib. the Nanchang Uprising.

ནན་གྱིས་ (nɛngiì) sm. ནན་དན་གྱིས་.

ནན་འགུགས་ (nɛnguù) recalling sb. with insistence; va.—བྱེད་ ། གཞུང་གིས་ཕྱིར་སྡོད་སློབ་ཕྲུག་རྣམས་ནན་འགུགས་བྱས་པ་རེད་ The goverment insistently recalled the students studying overseas.

ནན་ཅིན་ (nɛnjiŋ) Nanjing.

ནན་དར་སེམས་པ་དགའ་ (nendar sēmba ga) shung. with great pleasure ། ངེད་ཀྱིས་ཁྱེད་ཀྱི་རྟ་བླངས་ནན་དར་སེམས་པ་དགའ་ I received your horse with great pleasure.

ནན་དན་ (nendεn) 1. emphatically, forcefully; va.—བྱེད་ to act emphatically/ forcefully ། ལན་ནན་དན་ཞིག་སྤྲོད་དགོས་ (We) have to answer (them) emphatically. 2. serious, severe ། ཐ་ཚིག་ནན་དན་ A serious warning. 3. careful ། ཁྱེད་རང་མོ་ཊ་གཏོང་དུས་ནན་དན་གནང་དགོས་ When you drive a car you have to be careful.

ནན་དན་གྱིས་ (nendεngi) emphatically, firmly, forcefully, earnestly ། ཁོས་གནས་ཚུལ་དེ་ནན་དན་གྱིས་བཤད་པ་རེད་ He spoke emphatically about the situation.

ནན་དུར་ (nendur) sm. ནན་དན་.

ནན་གདན་ (nendεn) sm. ནན་དན་.

ནན་རྟགས་ (nendaà) punctuation such as dots/ underlining/ italics that is used to indicate emphasis.

ནན་འདེད་ (nendeè) going after the collection of loans/ debts forcefully; va.—བྱེད་.

ནན་འདྲི་ (nendri) forceful questioning, interrogating; va.—བྱེད་.

ནན་ནན་ (nennεn) sm. ནན་དན་.

ནན་ནན་བཅག་བཅག (nennεn jààjaà) sm. ནན་དན་.

ནན་ནན་ལྕག་ལྕག (nennεn jààjaà) sm. ནན་དན་.

ནན་བནན་ (bennεn) sm. ནན་དན་.

ནན་པ་ (nemba) sm. ནན་དན་.

ནན་པོ་ (nembo) sm. ནན་དན་.

ནན་ཕེབས་ (nempeb) shung. saying/ ordering insistently ། སླར་ཡང་ལྷ་ཐོན་དགོས་ལུགས་ནན་ཕེབས་ Once again I received an insistent order to go to Lhasa.

ནན་དབྱང་གླིང་ཚོམ་ (nenyaŋ līŋdzom) Nanyang Island.

ནན་མ་ཐེག (nen madeg) vi. to be unable to ignore or go against someone's urgings/ insisting.

ནན་ཚིག་བརྡ་ཡིག (nendzii dəyii) urgent notice.

ནན་ཞུ་ (nenshu) reporting/ petitioning emphatically; va.—བྱེད་.

ནན་གཟབ་ (nensəb) sm. ནན་དན་.

ནན་ལ་གཏད་ (nenla dεὲ) 1. va. to order emphatically. 2. va. to impose forcefully.

ནན་བཤད་ (nenshεὲ) saying emphatically; va.—བྱེད་.

ནན་སི་ལ་ཕུ་འུ་ (nensila pūwu) Yugoslavia.

ནན་ཧའི་རྒྱ་མཚོ་ (nenhε gyatso) the South China Sea.

ནབ་: p. **མནབས་**; f. **མནབ་**; imp. **ནོབས་** (nəb) va. to wear, to put on ། ཁོང་ན་བཟའ་མནབས་ནས་ཕྱི་ལ་ཕེབས་སོང་ He put on his clothes and went out.

ནམ་ (nam) 1. question particle for words ending in 'n' ། ཁྱེད་ཀྱིས་ཆོས་སྟོན་ནམ་ Do you teach the dharma? 2. when, whenever ། ཁོང་བོད་ནས་ནམ་ཕེབས་སམ་ When did he come from Tibet? ། ཚོགས་འདུ་ནམ་ཚོགས་སྐབས་ Whenever there was a meeting. 3. "or" particle for word ending in 'n' ། ཤིང་ཚོན་ནམ་ས་ཚོན་ Vegetable dye or mineral dye. 4. abbr. for ནམ་མཁའ་. 5. a weighing unit used for gold and silver (7 ནམ་= 1 ཞོ་).

ནམ་སྐྱིལ་སྐར་མ་ (namgyee gārma) stars/ constellations that can be seen (remain visible) during the whole night.

ནམ་མཁའ་ (namka) sky.

ནམ་མཁའ་སྔོ་ལ་དྭངས་པ་ (namka ŋōla taŋba) blue and clear sky.

ནམ་མཁའ་སྔོ་སངས་ (namka ŋōsaŋ) blue and clear sky.

ནམ་མཁའ་དང་མཉམ་པ་ (namka daŋ ñamba) sm. ནམ་མཁའི་མཐའ་དང་མཉམ་པ་.

ནམ་མཁའ་དྭངས་གསལ་ (namka taŋsεl) sm. ནམ་མཁའ་སྔོ་སངས་.

ནམ་མཁའ་མདོག (namka dɔɔ̀) sky blue (color).

ནམ་མཁའ་འཇོམས་འཇལ་ (namka domjεε) sm. སངས་རྒྱས་ལ་ཀ་ཁ་ [Lit. measuring the sky with one's armspan].

ནམ་མཁའ་ཕོ་བྲང་ (namka pōdraŋ) heavenly palace.

ནམ་མཁའ་ཕྲ་སྦྲུག (namka drādruù) a way of drawing the sky in Tibetan thanka painting.

ནམ་མཁའ་དྲལ་བ་ (namka drεεwa) great strength/ power ། ཁོང་ཚོས་ནམ་མཁའ་དྲལ་བ་ལྟ་བུའི་ལས་ཀ་བྱས་དེ་ཟམ་པ་བརྒྱབ་པ་རེད་ They worked with great strength (like ripping the sky) and built a bridge. [Lit. ripping the sky].

ནམ་མཁའ་གཡའ་དག (namka yādaà) sm. ནམ་མཁའ་སྔོ་སངས་.

ནམ་མཁའ་གཡའ་དག་ས་གཞི་རྡུལ་དག (namka yādaà sɔ̄shi düüdaà) clearing up a dispute/ misunderstanding completely ། དེ་རིང་ནས་བཟུང་ནམ་མཁའ་གཡའ་དག་ས་གཞི་རྡུལ་དག་ཡིན་ From today, all our misunderstandings and disputed points are ended. Lit. the sky cleared of tarnish and the earth cleared of dust].

ནམ་མཁའི་ཁམས་ (namkε kām) celestial body.

ནམ་མཁའི་གླང་པོ་ (namkε lāŋbo) poet. cloud.

ནམ་མཁའི་འཇའ་ཚོན་ (namkε jadzön) vanishing/ disappearing quickly [Lit. rainbow in the sky].

ནམ་མཁའི་སྙིང་པོ་ (namkε ñīŋbu) name of one of the eight great disciples of the Buddha.

ནམ་མཁའི་མཐའ་དང་མཉམ་པ་ (namkε tādaŋ ñamba) innumerable ། ནམ་མཁའི་མཐའ་དང་མཉམ་པའི་སེམས་ཅན་ཐམས་ཅད་ All sentient beings who are innumerable. [Lit. endless sky].

ནམ་མཁའི་མཐོང་ས་ (namkε tōŋ) in the sky.

ནམ་མཁའི་མདངས་གསལ་ (namkε taŋsel) beginning of 3rd lunar month.

ནམ་མཁའི་གནས་ཚུལ་ (namkε nεὲdzüü) astrological/ celestial phenomena, the heavenly bodies, astronomical observation.

ནམ་མཁའི་གནས་ཚུལ་སྟོན་བྱེད་འཁྱུལ་ཆས་ (namkε nεὲdzüü dōnjeè trūūjεὲ) planetarium.

ནམ་མཁའི་པ་མཐའ་ (namkε pāta) horizon (edge of the sky).

ནམ་མཁའི་མེ་ཏོག (namkε medɔg) impossible [Lit. sky flower].

ནམ་མཁའི་ཟིལ་པ་ (namkε siibə) dew.

ནམ་མཁའི་གཡའ་དག ས་གཞིའི་རྡུལ་དག (namkε yādaà sɔ̄shi düüdaà) sm. ནམ་མཁའ་གཡའ་དག་ས་གཞི་རྡུལ་དག.

ནམ་མཁར་འཕུར་ (namkar cūr) vi. to rise/ swell upwards to the sky (e.g., smoke or enthusiasm).

ནམ་མཁར་མི་ཤོང་བའི་རྫུན་གཏམ་ (namkaa mishoŋwε dzündam) a tremendous/ gigantic lie [Lit. a lie that cannot fit in the sky].

ནམ་གང་ (namgan) sm. གནམ་གང་.

ནམ་གང་ལ་རྟ་གསོས་ (namgan dāsöö) sm. གནམ་གང་ལ་རྟ་གསོས་.

ནམ་གུང་ (nəmguŋ) midnight.

ནམ་གུང་ནམ་ནག (nəmguŋ namnaà) in the dead of night, in the middle of the night.

ནམ་གྱི་གུང་ཐུན་ (namgi guŋtün) midnight.

ནམ་གྱི་ཆ་སྟོད་ (namgi cādöö) first of the three parts of the night in traditional Tibetan time divisions.

ནམ་གྱི་ཆ་སྨད་ (namgi cāmεὲ) the third of the three parts of the night in traditional Tibetan time divisions.

ནམ་གྱི་སྟོད་ཆ་ (namgi dōōja) first half of the night in traditional Tibetan time divisions (evening before midnight).

ནམ་གྱི་ཐུན་ལྔ་ (namgi tūnŋa) 1. the five periods of the night in traditional Tibetan time divisions.

ནམ་གྱི་ཐོ་རངས་ཆ་ (namgi tōraŋja) last part of the night.

ནམ་གྱི་འཕྱི་དགུ་ (namgi cīgu) second half of the night (after midnight).

ནམ་གྱི་སྟོད་ཆ་ (namgi sōōja) sm. ནམ་གྱི་སྟོད་ཆ་.

ནམ་དགུང་ (nəmguŋ) midnight.

ནམ་རྒྱུ་ (nəmgyu) materials for making clothing.

ནམ་རྒྱུན་ (nəmgyün) usual, customary ། ཁོ་ཚོ་ནམ་རྒྱུན་སློབ་གྲྭར་འགྲོ་གི་ཡོད་པ་རེད་. They usually go to school.

ནམ་རྒྱུན་དང་མི་འདྲ་བ་ (namgyündaŋ mindrawa) unusual, abnormal.

ནམ་འཆི་ཆ་མེད་ (namci cāmeè) uncertainty of death.

ནམ་མཇུག (namjuù) end of autumn ¶ ནམ་མཇུག་རིང་པ་ The end of autumn lasted a long time.

ནམ་ཉིན་བསྐྱོད་མེད་ (namñin dōōmeè) (traveling or working) day and night.

ནམ་སྟོད་ (namdöö) first half of the night.

ནམ་ཐང་ (nam tāŋ) vi. to have the sky clear up.

ནམ་ཐོ་རེངས་ (nam tōreŋ) dawn.

ནམ་མཐོངས་ (nam doŋ) abbr. of ནམ་མཁའི་མཐོངས་.

ནམ་དུ་ཡང་ (nəmduyaŋ) sm. ནམ་ཡང་.

ནམ་དུས་ (nəmdüü) 1. season ¶ ལོ་གཅིག་ལ་ནམ་དུས་བཞི་ཡོད་. There are four seasons in a year. 2. time/ season when sth. is done ¶ དེང་སང་བུ་འཕུར་གཏོང་བའི་ནམ་དུས་རེད་ These days it is the time for flying kites.

ནམ་དུས་ཀྱི་ན་ཚ་ (nəmdüügi nadza) seasonal sickness/ disease.

ནམ་དུས་ཡལ་ (nəmdüü yɛɛ) vi. to pass (a season or the time to do sth.).

ནམ་ལྡེང་ (namdeŋ) material enough for one dress.

ནམ་བད་གཏོང་མཁན་ (namda dōŋñɛn) night watchman.

ནམ་ནག (namnaà) in the dark of the night, in the middle of the night.

ནམ་ནག་གུང་ (namnaà guŋ) sm. ནམ་ནག.

ནམ་ནམ་ཞ་ཞ་ (namnam shasha) all the time.

ནམ་པར་ (nambar) eng. number.

ནམ་ཕར་ཚུར་གྱི་ཞལ་ལྕེ་ (nambar tsūrgi shɛɛje) one of the 16 criminal codes laid down by King Srongtsan Gambo.

ནམ་ཕྱུགས་ (nambuù) in the future ¶ ཁྱེད་རང་ལས་ཀ་དེ་འདྲ་བྱས་ན་ནམ་ཕྱུགས་ཡག་པོ་ཡོང་གི་མ་རེད་ If you do work like this, it will not turn out well in the future.

ནམ་ཕྱེད་ (namceè) midnight.

ནམ་ཕྱེད་རྒྱལ་བའི་དཀྱིལ་འཁོར་ (namceè gyɛɛwɛ gyiŋgɔɔ) sm. ནམ་ཕྱེད་.

ནམ་ཕྱེད་ཕར་བསྐྱལ་ ཐོ་རེངས་ཚུར་བསུས་ (namceè pāāgyɛɛ tōreŋ tsūū sūū) working late in the evening and early in the morning [Lit. seeing off midnight and receiving dawn].

ནམ་ཕྱེད་ཡོལ་ (namceè yöö) vi. to have midnight pass.

ནམ་འཕང་གཅོད་ (nampaŋ jöö) sm. ནམ་འཕང་སྤྱོད་.

ནམ་འཕང་སྤྱོད་ (nampaŋ jöö) excelling ¶ དེ་རིང་ཚོགས་འདུའི་ཐོག་མཁས་དབང་དེས་གཏམ་བཤད་དེ་ཙང་ཡག་པོ་ཞིག་བྱས་ནས་ནམ་འཕང་སྤྱོད་སོང་ Today at the meeting, the scholar gave an excellent speech that excelled.

ནམ་དམུས་ (nam müü) sm. ནམ་རྨུས་.

ནམ་རྨུས་ (nam müü) 1. sm. གནམ་འཐིབས་. 2. ས་རུབ་.

ནམ་སྨད་ (nammɛè) second half of the night, the period from midnight to dawn.

ནམ་ཙམ་ (namdzam) about when, about whenever.

ནམ་ཚོད་བྱ་ཕོས་བཟུང་ དགེ་བ་བོང་བུས་ཁྱེར་ (namdzöö caböö suŋ gewa puŋbü kyēr) benefitting from sb. else's actions [Lit. the cock signals daybreak, the donkey carries away the benefits].

ནམ་ཚོད་བཟུང་ (namdzöö suŋ) va. to signal the coming of daybreak/ dawn.

ནམ་འཚོའི་བར་ (namdzö par) until one dies ¶ ངས་ཁྱེད་རང་ནམ་འཚོའི་བར་ཞབས་ཕྱི་ཞུ་ཆོག I will serve you until you die.

ནམ་ཞག་རྒྱུན་གཏན་ (namshaà gyündɛn) sm. ནམ་ཞག་རྒྱུན་དུ་.

ནམ་ཞག་རྒྱུན་དུ་ (namshaà gyündu) all the time, always, continously ¶ ཁོང་ནམ་ཞག་རྒྱུན་དུ་སློབ་སྦྱོང་ནར་བརྩོན་བྱེད་ཀྱི་ཡོད་པ་རེད་ He studies hard all the time.

ནམ་ཞག་རྒྱུན་པ་ (namshaà gyünbə) sm. ནམ་ཞག་རྒྱུན་དུ་.

ནམ་ཤར་ (namshar) arc. sm. ནམ་ཡང་.

ནམ་ཤར་ཀྱང་ (namshargyaŋ) arc. sm. ནམ་ཡང་.

ནམ་ཞིག (namshig) 1. once, one day, at one time. 2. eventually, one day ¶ རང་ཉིད་ལ་ཉེས་པ་མེད་ན་ནམ་ཞིག་བདེན་མཐའ་གསལ་གྱི་རེད་ If you are innocent, eventually the truth will prevail.

ནམ་ཞོད་ (namshöö) rainfall.

ནམ་གཞུག (namshug) 1. sm. ཕྱིན་ཆད་. 2. autumn.

ནམ་གཞུག་བསྡུ་ཁ་ (namshug duga) end of autumn, the start of the cold weather season.

ནམ་འོག (namwɔɔ̀) before dawn.

ནམ་ཟླ་ (namda) 1. climate, weather. 2. season; vi.—འགྱུར་ to change seasons ¶ ནམ་ཟླ་དུས་བཞི་ The four seasons of the year.

ནམ་ཟླ་བརྟག་དཔྱད་ས་ཚིགས་ (namda dāgjɛɛ̀ sədziì) climate/ weather station.

ནམ་བཟི་ (namsiì) early dawn.

ནམ་ཡང་ (namyaŋ) 1. (with negatives) never ¶ བོད་གཞུང་ནས་ཆིངས་ཡིག་འདི་ངོས་ལེན་ནམ་ཡང་གནང་མེད་ The Tibetan government has never accepted this treaty. 2. (with positives) always ¶ དུས་ནམ་ཡང་ངས་ཁྱེད་རང་དྲན་པ་བྱེད་ཀྱི་ཡིན་ I will always remember you.

ནམ་ཡང་མི་འཇིགས་པ་ (namyaŋ mijigbə) undying, immortal.

ནམ་ཡིན་ན་ཡང་ (nam yinnayaŋ) sm. ནམ་ཡང་.

ནམ་ཡིན་རུང་ (nam yinruŋ) ནམ་ཡང་.

ནམ་རིང་ (namriŋ) sm. ནམ་རིང་པོ་.

ནམ་རིང་པོ་ (nam riŋgu) long night.

ནམ་ལངས་ (namlaŋ) daybreak, dawn.

ནམ་ལངས་ (nam laŋ) 1. vi. to be daybreak/ dawn. 2. vi. to suddenly rise/ improve (usu. at the expense of sb. else's bad fortune) ¶ མ་ཡར་དེ་ཤི་ནས་ཕྲུ་གུ་དེ་ནམ་ལངས་པ་རེད་ After the stepmother died, the child's fortunes rose.

ནམ་ལངས་ཁའི་ཉལ་གཅིན་ (namlaŋgɛ ñɛɛjin) doing work well for a long time but erring/ screwing up at the very end when things are completed [Lit. to bed wet just before daybreak].

ནམ་ལངས་སྐར་མ་ (namlaŋ gārma) rare [Lit. stars at daybreak].

ནམ་ལངས་རི་གསལ་ (namlaŋ risɛl) sth. eventually will be cleared up [Lit. with daybreak the mountain is clear].

ནམ་ལངས་སྤར་མོས་མི་འགེབས་ (namlaŋ barmöö migeb) concealing/ blocking sth. that cannot be concealed, sth. that is unstoppable ¶ འཛམ་གླིང་ཐོག་དམངས་གཙོའི་ལམ་ལུགས་དར་ཁྱབ་རྒྱུ་དེ་ནམ་ལངས་སྤར་མོས་མི་འགེབས་པ་དང་བཞིན་རེད་ The spread of democracy is unstoppable in the world. [Lit. cover up dawn with one's palm].

ནམ་ལངས་མུན་རུབ་ (namlaŋ münrub) from daybreak to nightfall.

ནམ་ལེན་དངུལ་དེབ་ (namlen ŋüüdeb) savings account passbook.

ནམ་སེང་ཙམ་ (nam sēŋdzam) just before dawn.

ནམ་སྲོད་ (namsöö) sm. ནམ་གྱི་ཆ་སྟོད་.

ནམ་སྲོས་ (namsöö) nighttime.

ནམ་སྲོས་ (nam söö) vi. to become dark/ night.

ནམ་མོ་ (nammo) sm. ན་མོ་.

ནམ་གསལ་ (namsɛl) sm. ནམ་ལངས་.

ནམ་གསལ་ཆ་གཏོང་ (nam sɛɛca dōŋ) sm. ནམ་ལངས་.

ནམ་གསལ་ལ་མ་གསལ་ (namsɛɛla masɛɛ) dawn.

ནའང་ (naaŋ) sm. ཀྱང་.

ནའང་སི་ལ་བུ་ (naaŋ silabu) Yugoslavia.

ནཝུ་ག (nəwuga) lawn.

ནར་ (nar) 1. vi. to get stretched ¶ རས་འདི་ནར་བཞག The cloth got stretched. 2. vi. to get delayed/ extended in time, to slow down (work) ¶ འཛུགས་སྐྲུན་གྱི་ཅ་དངོས་དུས་ཐོག་མ་འབྱོར་ཙང་ལས་ཀ་ནར་འགྲོ་གི་འདུག Because the construction materials did not arrive on time, the work is being delayed. 3. see ནར་གཏོང་.

ནར་འགྱངས་ (nargyaŋ) postponing, delaying; va.—བྱེད་; —གཏོང་.

ནར་གཏོང་ (nar dōŋ) 1. free of charge; va.—བྱེད་ ¶

མོས་ཨར་པོ་བ་ཚོར་ཁ་ལག་ནར་གཏོང་བྱས་པ་རེད་ She provided the construction workers with free food. 2. provide sth. without a fixed limit ¶ འགྲོ་སོང་ཚང་མ་ལས་ཁུངས་ནས་ནར་གཏོང་བྱེད་ཀྱི་ཡོད་པ་རེད་ The office is providing all the expenses without any limit (as much as is needed).

ནར་འཐེན་ (nar tēn) 1. va. to extend, to stretch. 2. va. to put off (doing sth.).

ནར་ནར་ (narnar) 1. elongated/ cylindrical in shape. 2. hanging, dangling. 3. putting off (doing sth.); va.—བྱེད་.

ནར་ནར་ལྩེ་ལ་བདག་པོ་མ་བརྒྱབ་ན་ རིལ་རིལ་དབུ་ལ་འོ་བརྒྱལ་བཪོས་ཡོང་ངོ་ (narnar jēla dagbo məgyəbnə riirii ūlə ogyεε söōyoŋŋo) be careful what you say [Lit. if one does not take care of one's tongue, one can loose one's head].

ནར་ནར་པོ་ (nar narbo) 1. elongated/ cylindrical in shape. 2. hanging, dangling. 3. putting off (doing sth.); va.—བྱེད་ ¶ ལས་ཀ་ནར་ནར་པོ་བྱེད་རྒྱུ་ཡོད་པ་རེད་ (One) shouldn't put off doing one's work.

ནར་ནར་མོ་ (nar narmo) sm. ནར་ནར་པོ་.

ནར་ནོར་ (narnɔr) abbr. ན་རེ་ནོ་རེ་.

ནར་འབུལ་ (nambüü) giving sth. free of charge; va.—བྱེད་.

ནར་དབྱིབས་ (naryib) long narrow/ cylindrical/ elongated in shape.

ནར་མ་ (narma) continuous, without break.

ནར་མར་ (narmar) sm. ནར་མ་.

ནར་མོ་ (narmo) sm. ནར་དབྱིབས་.

ནར་གཟུགས་ (narsug) sm. ནར་དབྱིབས་.

ནར་རིང་ (narriŋ) long and narrow.

ནར་ལུས་ (narlüü) sm. ནར་འགྱངས་.

ནར་ལུས་ཤོར་ (narlüü shɔ̄ɔ) vi. to get/ be delayed.

ནར་ཤུགས་ལྡན་པ་ (narshuù dεmba) elastic, stretchable ¶ ནར་ཤུགས་ལྡན་པའི་ཨོ་མོ་སུ་ལུ་ Elastic socks.

ནར་གཤིས་ (narshii) elasticity, malleability, stretchability.

ནར་སོན་ (nar sōn) vi. to grow up, to reach adulthood.

ནལ་ (nεε) 1. a type of stone similar to a ruby. 2. sm. ནལ་མ་, 2.

ནལ་ཕྲུག་ (nεεdruù) sm. ནལ་བུ་.

ནལ་བུ་ (nεεbu) 1. sm. བྱི་ཕྲུག. 2. the offspring of a sexually inappropriate relationship, illegitimate child.

ནལ་མ་ (nεεma) 1. caragana brevifolia. 2. a woman in an inappropriate sexual relationship, adulterous woman.

ནལ་ཟེ་ (nεεse) a scratching instrument (usu. a long handle with a fork-like end to scratch the back).

ནལ་རིན་ཆེན་ (nεε rinjen) sm. ནལ་, 1.

ནལ་ལེ་ (nεεle) sm. ནལ་བུ་.

ནལ་བཤམས་ (nεε shām) va. to commit adultery.

ནས་ (nεὲ) 1. instrumental case particle, by ¶ བོད་གཞུང་ནས་གཞུང་འདི་ངོས་ལེན་མ་བྱས་པ་རེད་ The Tibetan government didn't recognize this government. 2. from ¶ ཁང་པའི་ནང་ནས་ From inside the house. 3. (vb. + —) having done/ after doing the verbal act ¶ ཁ་ལག་བཟས་ནས་འདིར་ཡོང་བ་རེད་ After (they) ate, (they) came here. 4. barley.

ནས་དཀར་པོ་ (nεὲ gārbo) white barley.

ནས་རྙིན་ (nεὲgεn) old barley.

ནས་ཆག་ (nεὲjaà) pounded/ flattened barley.

ནས་ཆང་ (nεὲjaŋ) barley beer.

ནས་ཇུ་ (nεὲcu) barley broth/.stew/ soup.

ནས་རྫིང་ (nεὲjaŋ) storage place for barley.

ནས་རྗེན་ (nεὲjen) 1. unroasted barley. 2. unroasted barley flour.

ནས་རྗེན་ཚ་བ་ (nεὲjen tsāwa) broth/ stew made from barley flour.

ནས་ལྗང་ (nεὲjaŋ) a barley shoot/ stalk.

ནས་སྙེ་ (nεὲñe) an ear of barley.

ནས་ནག་གྲ་གཉིས་མ་ (nεὲnaà tra ñiìmə) a type of barley.

ནས་ནག་པོ་ (nεὲ nagbo) black barley.

ནས་ཕུབ་ (nεὲpub) barley chaff/ husk/ stubble.

ནས་ཕྱེ་ (nεὲce) barley flour.

ནས་འབྲུ་ (nεὲdru) 1. barley. 2. barley kernels.

ནས་སྦྱང་ (nεὲjaŋ) sm. ནས་རྫིང་.

ནས་དམར་ (nεὲmar) reddish barley.

ནས་རྩམ་ (nεὲdzam) tsamba made from barley, roasted barley flour.

ནས་ཞིང་ (nεὲshiŋ) barley field.

ནས་ཟན་ (nεὲsεn) barley tsamba.

ནས་བཟུང་ (nεὲsuŋ) from then on, ever since ¶ 1965 ལོའི་དཔྱིད་ཀ་ནས་བཟུང་ From the spring of 1965 onwards.

ནས་ཡོས་ (nεὲyöö) popped barley.

ནས་སོ་བ་ (nεὲ sōwa) barley with the skin still on.

ནས་སོག་ (nεὲsɔɔ̀) barley hay/ straw.

ནས་སོན་ (nεὲsön) barley seed.

ནས་བསོད་ (nεὲsöö) barley given as alms (usu. to monks who come begging).

ནས་ཧྲལ་ (nεὲhrεε) roughly ground barley (used in soups).

ནི་ (ni) as for (indicates subject) ¶ འདི་ནི་ངའི་རེད་ As for this, it is mine.

ནི་ཀུའུ་ཀྲིང་ (nigudrin) eng. nicotine.

ནི་གུ་ (nigu) young girl.

ནི་རུ་ཧ་ (niruha) a traditional treatment for constipation.

ནིམ་པ་ (nimbə) sophora (an herbal medicine).

ནིམ་བུ་ (nimbu) lemon.

ནིའུ་ཌྀ་ལི་ (niwu dili) New Delhi.

ནིའུ་ཡོག་ (niwu yɔg) New York.

ནིའུ་ཡོག་མ་རྩའི་ཀང་གྲངས་ཉོ་ཚོང་ཁྲོམ་ར་ (niwu yɔg madzε gāŋdraŋ ñodzoŋ trōmra) New York Stock Exchange.

ནུ་ (nu) abbr. of ནུ་མ་.

ནུ་: p. ནུས་; f. ནུ་; imp. ནུས་ (nu) va. to suckle on a nipple or pacifier.

ནུ་སྤྲ་ (nudra) fetal hair.

ནུ་སྐྱེས་ (nugyeè) sm. ནུ་ཞོ་.

ནུ་ཁེབས་ (nugeb) brassiere, bra.

ནུ་མགོ་ (nungo) sm. ནུ་ཏོག.

ནུ་འགོ་ (nungo) sm. ནུ་ཏོག.

ནུ་ཏོག (nudɔɔ̀) nipple.

ནུ་ཏོག (nudɔɔ̀) sm. ནུ་ཏོག.

ནུ་འཐུང་ (nū tūŋ) va. to suckle.

ནུ་འཐུང་བྱིས་པ་ (nuduŋ ciibə) a child who is breast-feeding.

ནུ་འཐུང་སྨྱུག་ཆགས་ (nuduŋ sɔ̄gjaà) sm. འོ་འཐུང་སྨྱུག་ཆགས་.

ནུ་གདན་ (nudεn) aureole (area around the nipple).

ནུ་ཏོག (nudɔɔ̀) sm. ནུ་ཏོག.

ནུ་ལྡན་ (nūnden) woman.

ནུ་སྡུད་ཁང་ (nūdüügaŋ) sm. འོ་གསོ་ཁང་.

ནུ་བོ་ (nuwo) younger brother.

ནུ་འབུར་ (nubur) sm. ནུ་ཏོག.

ནུ་དབྲག (nudraà) the space between the breasts.

ནུབ་ཇོགས་ (nubjɔɔ̀) shung. abbr. of ནུབ་ཕྱོགས་.

ནུ་མ་ (numə) breasts; va.—སྟེར་; —སྣུན་ to nurse/ breast-feed a child; va.—ནུ་ to suck on a breast.

ནུ་མོ་ (numo) younger sister.

ནུ་མའི་འབྲས་ནད་ (numε drεὲdrεn) breast cancer.

ནུ་མའི་གཤེར་སྐྱིན་ (numε shērmen) mammary gland.

ནུ་རྩ་ (nudza) mammary gland.

ནུ་ཚབས་ (nudzəb) a disease of the breast.

ནུ་ཞོ་ (nusho) 1. mother's milk; va.—སྦུད་ to breast feed. 2. abbr. milk and yogurt.

ནུ་ཞོ་སྟེར་ཁང་ (nusho dērgaŋ) nursing room for mothers.

ནུ་རིན་ (nurin) dowry paid by the groom's family to the bride's family [Lit. suckling fee].

ནུ་ཤུབས་ (nushub) brassiere.

ནུ་སོ་ (nuso) baby teeth.

ནུ་སོར་ (nusɔr) nipple.

ནུད་ (nüù) va. to shift/ move ༎ ལྕོག་ཙེ་དེ་མདུན་དུ་ཕྲན་བུ་ནུད་དགོས་ (We) have to move the table a little forward.

ནུབ་ (nub) 1. west. 2. vi. to sink (in water) ༎ གྲུ་གཟིངས་ལ་སྐྱོན་ཤོར་ནས་རྒྱ་གཏིང་ལ་ནུབ་འདུག The ship had problems and sank beneath the ocean. 3. vi. to set (for sun) ༎ ཉི་མ་ནུབ་ནས་ཆུ་ཚོད་གཅིག་ཕྱིན་སོང་. One hour has passed since sunset. 4. vi. to decline ༎ གནའ་སྔ་མོའི་ལུགས་སྲོལ་ནུབ་བཞག The ancient customs have declined. 5. night, evening ༎ ནུབ་གཅིག One night.

ནུབ་ཁ་ (nubga) 1. at the time of sunset.

ནུབ་ཁའི་ཉི་མ་ (nubgɛ ñimə) setting sun.

ནུབ་ཁའི་ཉི་འོད་ (nubgɛ ñiwöö) the glow of the setting sun.

ནུབ་གླིང་ (nubliŋ) the Western World, the West.

ནུབ་རྒྱ་མཚོ་ (nub gyadzo) Atlantic Ocean.

ནུབ་རྒྱུད་ (nubgyüù) western, western side ༎ འབྲི་ཆུའི་ནུབ་རྒྱུད་ The western side of the Yangtse river.

ནུབ་སྒོ་ (nubgo) a door facing west.

ནུབ་ངོས་ (nubŋöö) sm. ནུབ་ཕྱོགས་.

ནུབ་ཆེན་རྒྱ་མཚོ་ (nubjen gyadzo) the Atlantic Ocean.

ནུབ་ཇ་ (nubja) sm. ཕྱི་ཇ་.

ནུབ་འཇར་མན་ (nun jarmɛn) tib. eng. West Germany.

ནུབ་བལྟ་ (nubda) facing west, west-facing ༎ ཁང་པ་དེ་ནུབ་བལྟ་རེད་བཞག This house faces west.

ནུབ་སྟོད་ (nubdöò) upper part of an area in the west.

ནུབ་མཐའ་ (nubda) western border/ frontier.

ནུབ་དེ་གོ་ (nubdego) tib.ch. sm. ནུབ་འཇར་མན་.

ནུབ་ནུབ་ (nubnub) sm. ནུབ་ནུབ་རྐྱང་.

ནུབ་ནུབ་རྐྱང་ (nun nubgyaŋ) due west, directly west.

ནུབ་སྤྲིན་ (nubdrin) westerly clouds.

ནུབ་ཕྱོགས་ (nubjɔɔ̀) the west, the western side/ direction ༎ ནུབ་ཕྱོགས་རྒྱལ་ཁབ་ The Western nations.

ནུབ་ཕྱོགས་པ་ (nub cɔ̄ɔ̀ba) westerner, Euro-American.

ནུབ་བ་གླང་སྤྱོད་ (nūb pālaŋjuoò) the western continent (one of the four continents that surround Mt. Meru).

ནུབ་བྱང་ (nubjaŋ) northwest.

ནུབ་མ་ (nubma) west.

ནུབ་མོ་ (nubmo) night.

ནུབ་སྨད་ (nubmɛɛ̀) lower section/ part of the west area.

ནུབ་ཟས་ (nubsɛɛ̀) dinner, evening meal.

ནུབ་ཡུལ་ (nubyüü) western countries.

ནུབ་ཡུལ་གྱི་མི་ (nubyüügi mi) westerner.

ནུབ་ལྷགས་ (nublhaà) westerly wind.

ནུབྱོགས་ (nunjɔɔ̀) shung. abbr. of ནུབ་ཕྱོགས་.

ནུར་ (nur) 1. vi. to be squashed/ pulverized/ crushed ༎ སྒམ་ཆག་ནས་ཤིང་ཏོག་ཁ་ཤས་ནུར་བཞག The box broke and some fruit got squashed.

ནུར་ནུར་ (nurnur) thick (for broth/ stew/ soup).

ནུར་ནུར་པོ་ (nur nurbo) the first week of the embryonic stage according to Tibetan medicine.

ནུར་བ་ (nurwa) sm. ནུར་ནུར་.

ནུས་ (nüù) 1. p. and imp. of ནུ་. 2. vi. to dare to ༎ ང་འདི་བྱེད་ནུས་ཀྱི་མི་འདུག I don't dare do this. 3. energy.

ནུས་ཁུངས་ (nüùguŋ) source of energy.

ནུས་ཁུངས་ཀྱི་སྐྱེ་དངོས་ (nüùguŋgi gyēŋöò) plants which are the source of energy.

ནུས་ཁུངས་ཉམས་ཉེན་ (nüùguŋ ñamñen) energy crisis, crisis of energy resources.

ནུས་ཁུངས་འདོན་སྤེལ་ (nüùguŋ dönbel) energy resource development.

ནུས་ཁུངས་ཟད་སྤྲོད་ (nüùguŋ sɛɛ̀drön) energy resource consumption.

ནུས་འགན་ (nüù gɛn) 1. ability and responsibility ༎ ནུས་འགན་མཐུན་པོ་ Abilities matching responsibility. 2. power/ strength and responsibility.

ནུས་ཆེའི་དངོས་ལུགས་རིག་པ་ (nüùcee ŋōòlug rigbə) high energy physics.

ནུས་ཆེའི་མྱུར་སྐྱོད་འཕྲུལ་ཆས་ (nüùcee ñurgüü trūūjɛɛ̀) high energy accelerator.

ནུས་ཆེན་དངོས་ཁམས་ཞིབ་འཇུག་ཁང་ (nüùjen ŋōògam shimjugaŋ) high energy physics research institute.

ནུས་སྟོབས་ (nüùdob) strength/ power and ability ༎ ང་ཚོའི་ནུས་སྟོབས་ལ་དཔགས་པ་ In proportion to our strength and ability.

ནུས་སྟོབས་ཞན་པ་ (nüùdob shɛmba) weak, feeble (in strength and ability).

ནུས་མཐུ་ (nüùdu) sm. ནུས་པ་.

ནུས་ལྡན་ (nündɛn) effective, powerful ༎ མཚོན་ཆ་ནུས་ལྡན་ A powerful weapon. ༎ ཁོང་ཚོས་ལས་ཀ་དེ་ནུས་ལྡན་གྱིས་བྱས་པ་རེད་ (They) did it effectively.

ནུས་པ་ (nüùbə) 1. effectiveness, efficacy, capableness, effective, efficacious ༎ སྨན་འདི་ནུས་པ་ཆེ་ཤོས་ཡིན་ This is the most effective medicine. 2. sm. ནུས་སྟོབས་. 3. see ནུས་པ་འདོན་; ནུས་པ་ཤོར་.

ནུས་པ་ཅན་ (nüùbəjɛn) capable, effective ༎ ཁོང་ནི་ངའི་ལས་རོགས་ནུས་པ་ཅན་ཞིག་ཡིན་ He is a capable helper of mine.

ནུས་པ་འདོན་ (nüùbə dön) va. to use one's ability/ power ༎ འགོ་ཁྲིད་དེས་ལས་ཁུངས་ནང་རང་གི་ནུས་པ་འདོན་ཐུབ་ཀྱི་མེད་པ་རེད་ The boss is unable to use his power in the office. ༎ ཁོང་ཚོས་ཚན་རིག་ལག་རྩལ་གྱི་ནུས་པ་འདོན་གྱི་ཡོད་པ་རེད་ They are using their technological ability.

ནུས་པ་བཏོན་ (nüùbə dōn) p. of ནུས་པ་འདོན་.

ནུས་པ་ཐོན་ (nüùbə tōn) vi. to be effective, to have an effect ༎ སྲིད་ཇུས་དེས་ནུས་པ་མ་ཐོན་པ་རེད་ That policy wasn't effective.

ནུས་པ་ཐོན་སའི་འཕེན་ཐག (nüùbə tōnsɛ pēndaà) effective range (of a gun).

ནུས་པ་འཕྲལ་ཐོན་ (nüùbə trɛ̄ɛdön) producing an immediate effect.

ནུས་པ་ཞན་པ་ (nüùbə shɛmba) low efficiency, inferior ability.

ནུས་པ་ཡོད་པ་ (nüùbə yöòba) having the ability to be effective/ capable/ efficacious.

ནུས་པ་ཤོར་ (nüùbə shɔ̄ɔ) vi. to lose effectiveness/ efficacy/ capability ༎ སྨན་དེ་རྙིང་པ་ཆགས་ནས་ནུས་པ་ཤོར་བཞག The medicine became old and lost it's effectiveness.

ནུས་པའི་ཟད་སྤྲོད་ (nüùbɛ sɛɛ̀dröm) the consumption of energy.

ནུས་པས་གང་ལྕོགས་ (nüùbɛ kaŋjoò) as effectively as one can do sth. ༎ རང་གི་ནུས་པས་གང་ལྕོགས་ཀྱི་ལས་ཀ་བྱེད་ཀྱི་ཡོད་ I am working as effectively as I am able.

ནུས་པས་ལྕིངས་ཚོད་ (nüùbɛ deŋdzöò) within the range/ scope of one's ability.

ནུས་པོ་ (nüùbo) sm. ནུས་ལྡན.

ནུས་སྤོབས་ (nüùbob) power and confidence.

ནུས་འབྲས་ (nündrɛɛ̀) the fruit/ result/ outcome of one's work ༎ འདི་ལོའི་ལས་ཀ་དེའི་ནུས་འབྲས་ཡག་པོ་ཐོན་བཞག This year we got good results from (our) work.

ནུས་མེད་ (nüùmeè) ineffective, weak, impotent, incapable.

ནུས་མེད་གཉོད་ཆུང་ (nüùmeè ñōòjuŋ) weak, incompetent.

ནུས་མེད་སྤོབས་མེད་ (nüùmeè bōbmeè) incompetent/ ineffective and not confident.

ནུས་མེད་འབྲས་མེད་ (nüùmeè drɛɛ̀meè) incompetent and unsuccessful, without effectiveness and without a good result/ success.

ནུས་གཙོ་སྨྲ་བ་ (nüùdzo māwa) energetic.

ནུས་རྩལ་ (nüùdzɛɛ) talent, ability, capability, skill; va.—སྦྱོང་ to train/ practice to improve one's skill ༎ ལོ་གཉིས་རིང་ཁོང་གིས་རྐང་རྩེད་སྒོ་ལོའི་ནུས་རྩལ་སྦྱངས་པ་རེད་ For two years he practiced his skills in soccer.

ནུས་རྩལ་མཁས་ཤོས་ (nṵ̈üdzɛɛ kɛ̄ɛshöö) 1. one's special skill, one's specialty ༑ངའི་ནུས་རྩལ་མཁས་ཤོས་དེ་ཚན་རིག་ཡིན་ My specialty is science. 2. the most skillful ༑ང་ཚོའི་ནང་གི་ནུས་རྩལ་མཁས་ཤོས་ཁོང་རེད་ He is the most skillful among us.

ནུས་ཚད་ (nṵ̈üdzɛ̀ɛ̀) 1. capacity or level of ability/ efficiency ༑ལོ་གཅིག་ལ་མེ་མདའ་འབུམ་གཉིས་བཟོ་ཐུབ་པའི་ནུས་ཚད་བྱུང་བ་རེད་ They achieved a capacity of being able to make 200,000 guns in one year. ༑རང་རྐང་འཛིན་རེས་ཀྱི་ནུས་ཚད་ཐོན་པ་ཞིག་མ་བྱུང་ན་ Unless (we) attain the capacity of being able to stand on our own two feet. 2. the number of able workers in a household.

ནུས་ཚད་ཀྱི་རིམ་པ་ (nṵ̈üdzɛɛgi ri̱mbə) different levels of capacity/ effectiveness ༑ནུས་ཚད་ཀྱི་རིམ་པ་མི་འདྲ་བའི་གློག་འདོན་འཕྲུལ་འཁོར་མང་པོ་ཞིག་བཟོས་པ་རེད་ They made many different levels of electric generators.

ནུས་རིམ་ (nṵ̈ürim) abbr. ནུས་ཚད་ཀྱི་རིམ་པ་.

ནུས་རླབས་ཤོག་པ་ (nṵ̈üləb pɔ̄ɔba) induction (electric).

ནུས་ཤུགས་ (nṵ̈üshuù) 1. strength, power; va.—འདོན་ to bring forth/ use (one's) power/ strength ༑ཐོན་སྐྱེད་ཀྱི་ནུས་ཤུགས་ Productive power. ༑ཨར་པོ་བ་ཚོས་ནུས་ཤུགས་ཆེན་པོ་བཏོན་ནས་ཟླ་བ་གཅིག་ནང་ཁང་པ་དེ་བརྐྱབ་ཚར་བ་རེད་ The construction workers used their strength (made a great effort) and finished building the house in one month. 2. sm. ནུས་ཚད་. 3. labor, people who have the ability to work.

ནུས་ཤུགས་གང་ཡོད་འདོན་ (nṵ̈üshuù ka̱ŋyöö dö̱n) va. to spare no effort, to make every endeavor, to go to all lengths.

ནུས་ཤུགས་ཆེ་རུ་གཏོང་ (nṵ̈üshuù cēru dō̱ŋ) 1. va. to intensify or increase the strength/ power of sth. 2. va. to intensify or increase the amount of labor one has available.

ནུས་ཤུགས་པའོ་ཀུང་ (nṵ̈üshuù bāwoguŋ) tib.ch. type of contract labor where the contractor provides the materials.

ནུས་ཤུགས་ཡོད་རྒྱུ་རྩལ་སྒྲུགས་འདོན་ (nṵ̈üshuù yöögyu dzɛ̄ɛdrug dö̱n) sm. ནུས་ཤུགས་གང་ཡོད་འདོན་.

ནུས་ཤུགས་རིན་ (nṵ̈üshuù ri̱n) the cost of labor.

ནུས་ཤུགས་ལས་ཁུངས་ (nṵ̈üshuù lɛ̱ɛguŋ) Department of Energy (DOE),

ནུས་ཤུགས་ལྷག་མ་ (nṵ̈üshuù lhāàma) 1. surplus energy/ strength. 2. surplus labor.

ནེ་ཀོ་ (jego) ch. the cabinet.

ནེ་སྒོར་ (negɔɔ) Nepalese rupee.

ནེ་ཐང་ (ne̱daŋ) small meadow/ grassland/ lawn.

ནེ་ནེ་ (ne̱ne) paternal aunt.

ནེ་ནེ་མོ་ (ne̱nemo) sm. ནེ་ནེ་.

ནེ་པ་ལ་ (ne̱pala) Nepal ༑ནེ་པ་ལའི་རྒྱལ་པོའི་རྒྱལ་ཁབ་ The Kingdom of Nepal.

ནེ་པ་ལི་ (ne̱pale) Nepalese.

ནེ་པཱལ་ (ne̱pala) Nepal; Nepalese.

ནེ་ཕ་ (ne̱pa) NEFA (Northeast Frontier Area) of India (today's Arunachal Pradesh).

ནེ་མོ་ (ne̱mo) sm. ནེ་ཐང་.

ནེ་ཙོ་ (ne̱dzo) parrot.

ནེ་ཙོའི་ཁ་དོན་ (ne̱dzö kādön) reading sth. without knowing the meaning [Lit. the praying of a parrot].

ནེ་ཙོའི་ཁ་འདོན་ (ne̱dzö kādön) sm. ནེ་ཙོའི་ཁ་དོན་.

ནེ་ཝ་ཅང་ (ne̱wajaŋ) plasterer.

ནེ་ལེ་ (ne̱le) sparrow hawk.

ནེ་གསེང་ (ne̱seŋ) sm. ནེ་ཐང་.

ནེག་སོན་ (negsön) Nixon.

ནེམ་ཐང་ (ne̱mdaŋ) a raw silk type of shawl that is woven in Bhutan.

ནེམ་ནུར་ (ne̱mnur) hesitation, uncertainity, doubt.

ནེམ་ནེམ་ (ne̱mnem) sm. ནེམ་ནེམ་པ་.

ནེམ་ནེམ་པ་ (ne̱mnemba) soft and springy. 2. doubt, hesitation, uncertainty.

ནེམ་ནེམ་ལིང་ལིང་ (ne̱mnem li̱nli̱ŋ) swaying unsteadily (e.g., a rope bridge).

ནེའུ་ཁ་ (ne̱wuka) lawn, grass, meadow.

ནེའུ་ལྡང་ (ne̱wudaŋ) sm. ནེ་ཐང་.

ནེའུ་ལྗང་ (ne̱wujaŋ) green lawn.

ནེའུ་ཐང་ (ne̱wudaŋ) sm. ནེ་ཐང་.

ནེའུ་ཟི་ལན་ཊ་ (ne̱wu si̱lɛnda) New Zealand.

ནེའུ་ཟླ་ (ne̱wuda) the same age.

ནེའུ་ལི་ (ne̱wuli) weasel.

ནེའུ་ལི་སེར་པོ་ (ne̱wuli sērbo) a kind of yellow weasel.

ནེའུ་ལེའི་རི་མོ་ (ne̱wule ri̱mu) the markings (loops and whorls) on the inner side of the tips of fingers.

ནེའུ་ལོ་པ་ (ne̱wulowa) sm. ནེའུ་ཟླ་.

ནེའུ་གསིང་ (ne̱wusiŋ) sm. ནེ་ཐང་.

ནེའུ་གསེང་ (ne̱wuseŋ) sm. ནེའུ་གསེང་.

ནེར་ (ne̱r) vi. to sink.

ནེཧ་རུ་ (ne̱ru) Nehru.

ནོ་ (no̱) a syllable that follows the final consonant ན་ to indicate the end of a sentence.

ནོ་ནོ་ (no̱no) older brother.

ནོ་བེར་བྱ་དགའ་ (no̱ber ca̱ga) eng.tib. Nobel Prize.

ནོ་ཝེ་ (no̱we) Norway.

ནོ་མོན་ཧན་ (no̱mönhɛn) mong. a Mongolian title used by the traditional Tibetan government.

ནོ་ཡོན་ (no̱yön) mong. noble, lord.

ནོ་ཡོན་ཧུ་ཐོག་ཐུ་ (no̱yön hūtugdu) mong. a Mongolian title given to high lamas.

ནོ་རོ་དོམ་སི་ཧ་ནོག (no̱rodom si̱hanog) Prince Sihanouk.

ནོག (no̱g) the hump (of camels and oxen).

ནོག་ཁ་ (no̱gga) dark brown.

ནོག་ཁ་སྐྱེན་པོ་ (no̱gga gyēmbo) things that are easy to get dirty.

ནོག་འབུར་ (no̱gbur) sm. ནོག.

ནོགས་ (nɔ̱ɔ) vi. to become dirty/ filthy.

ནོགས་བག (nɔ̱gbaà) dirt, filth.

ནོགས་མེད་ (nɔ̱gmeè) not dirty/ filthy.

ནོང་ (no̱ŋ) vi. to regret.

ནོངས་ (no̱ŋ) vi. to err, to make a mistake. ༑རང་ཉིད་ཀྱིས་ནོངས་ན་ངོས་ལེན་བྱ་དགོས་ If one makes a mistake, one should admit it.

ནོངས་འགྱུར་ (no̱ŋ gyu̱r) vi. to have a mistake occur.

ནོངས་པ་ (no̱ŋba) error, mistake ༑རང་ལ་ནོངས་པ་མེད་ན་གཞན་གྱིས་བསམ་འཆར་བཤད་པར་སྐྲག་མི་དགོས་ If one is not in error, one doesn't have to be afraid of receiving criticism from others.

ནོངས་སྤྱོད་ (no̱ŋjöö) 1. mistaken/ erroneous behavior, misdeed. 2. a crime.

ནོངས་བཤགས་ (no̱ŋshaà) apologizing, admitting an error; va.—འབུལ་; —བྱེད་ to apologize, to admit one's errors ༑ལམ་ནོར་དུ་ཕྱིན་པར་ནོངས་བཤགས་ཞུས་པ་རེད་ He apologized for going on the wrong path.

ནོད་ (nö̱ö) va. to receive/ obtain instruction or initiation (usu. religious).

ནོན་ (nö̱n) 1. vi. to be able to subdue/ suppress/ control/ handle ༑ཁོས་ཕྲུ་གུ་ནོན་ཐུབ་པ་བྱུང་བ་རེད་ He was able to control the children. 2. vi. to be attached to, to be fond of. 3. imp. of གནོན་.

ནོན་རྐྱང་ (nö̱njuŋ) 1. faded, lusterless (color). 2. not firm/ effective (in work).

ནོན་ཆེ་ (nö̱nce) sm. ནོན་པོ་.

ནོན་པོ་ (nö̱mbo) firm, aggressive, effective in work ༑འགོ་ཁྲིད་དེ་ནོན་པོ་ཡོད་པ་རེད་ That official is effective.

ནོབས་ (no̱b) imp. of ནབ་.

ནོམ་: p. **མནམས་**; f. **མནམ་**; imp. **ནོམས་** (no̱m) to hold ༑སྤུན་མཆེད་གཉིས་ཁ་བྲལ་སྐབས་ལག་པ་ནས་དམ་པོར་མནམས་པ་རེད་ When the two relatives separated, they held (each other's) hands tightly.

ནོམ་ཅི་ཐུ་ (no̱mcidu) mong. a Mongolian title.

ནོམ་ཆེན་ (no̱mjen) sm. ནོམ་པོ་.

ནོམ་སྡོབས་ (no̱mdob) sm. རྒྱུ་སྡོབས་.

ནོམ་ནོམ་ (no̱mnom) unable to not touch or leave

things alone (usu. is used for to children).

ནོམ་ནོམ་ལག་པ་ (nomnom lagba) a person who is about to die whose hands wander about touching things.

ནོམ་པ་ (nomba) wealth.

ནོམ་པོ་ (nombo) sm. གུ་ནོམ་པོ་.

ནོམ་ཕུད་ (nombüü) best of the lot that is firsty offered to a lama/ lord.

ནོམ་བུ་ (nombu) food given to a infant from one's mouth.

ནོམ་ཤེད་ (nomsheè) sm. རྒྱུ་སྟོབས་.

ནོམས་ (nom) imp. of ནོམ་.

ནོར་ (nɔɔ) 1. to err, to make a mistake ¶ཁོའི་སྐད་ཆ་དེ་ཡང་ནོར་པ་རེད་ This statement of his is also wrong. 2. wealth, things, possessions ¶ཁོ་ལ་ནོར་མང་པོ་འདུག He has a lot of wealth. 3. yak ¶འབྲོག་པ་དེར་ནོར་མང་པོ་འདུག That nomad has many yaks. 4. positive (in math).

ནོར་ཀོ་ (nɔɔgo) yak skin/ hide.

ནོར་ཀང་བྲི་ (nɔɔgaŋ tri) 1. vi. to have one's wealth or fortune depleted/ diminished ¶མི་ཚང་དེ་རང་ཤི་གོད་མང་པོ་བྱུང་བར་བརྟེན་ནོར་ཀང་བྲི་འདུག Because that household had many deaths, its wealth has been depleted. 2. vi. to have the number of yak diminish.

ནོར་སྐལ་ (nɔɔgɛɛ) an inheritance/ share/ portion of wealth.

ནོར་སྐྱོང་ (nɔɔgyoŋ) poet. steward.

ནོའུར་ (nur) mong. lake.

ནོར་སྐྱོན་ (nɔɔgyön) mistake, error ¶ཡིག་ཆ་དེའི་ནང་ནོར་སྐྱོན་མང་པོ་བྱུང་འདུག There are many mistakes in the document.

ནོར་ཁམ་པོ་ཆེ་ (nɔɔ kāmboce) precious items/ objects.

ནོར་ཁུང་ (nɔɔguŋ) sources of wealth.

ནོར་ཁྱུ་ (nɔɔgu) yak herd.

ནོར་ཁྲལ (nɔɔdrɛɛ) a tax on yaks or on wealth.

ནོར་འཁྲུལ་ (nɔndrüü) mistake; vi.—ཤོར་ to be mistaken, to unintentionally make a mistake; va.—གཏོང་ to purposely make a mistake ¶ཁོང་གིས་ཡི་གེ་བཤུ་དུས་ནོར་འཁྲུལ་མང་པོ་ཤོར་བཞག Many mistakes were made when he copied the document. ¶ཁོས་ལས་ཁུངས་ལ་གནོད་སྐྱོན་བའི་ཆེད་དུ་རྩིས་ཁྲའི་ནང་ནོར་འཁྲུལ་མང་པོ་བཏང་བཞག In order to harm the office, he purposely made many mistakes in the accounting.

ནོར་འཁྲུལ་གྱི་གྱོད་གཞི་ (nɔntrüügi gyööshi) a misjudged/ misdecided case.

ནོར་འཁྲུལ་ནོར་རྒྱང་ (nɔntrüü nɔɔgyaŋ) completely wrong, totally mistaken.

ནོར་གོམས་འགྲིག་བརྩི་ (nɔɔgom drigdzi) sm. ནོར་གོམས་བདེན་འཛིན་.

ནོར་གོམས་བདེན་འཛིན་ (nɔɔgom dendzin) growing accustomed to what is wrong and accepting it as right.

ནོར་གྲངས་ (nɔɔdraŋ) positive number (in math).

ནོར་གླིང་ (nɔɔliŋ) abbr. of ནོར་བུ་གླིང་ཁ་.

ནོར་རྒྱས་ (nɔɔgyɛɛ) abundance of wealth or yaks.

ནོར་ངེས་ལིང་ཚེ་ (nɔɔŋeè liŋdze) positive definite matrix (in math).

ནོར་དངོས་པོ་ (nɔɔ ŋööbo) wealth, goods, possessions, things.

ནོར་ཅན་ (nɔɔjɛn) wealthy, rich.

ནོར་བཅོས་ (nɔɔjöö) correction, correcting; va.—བྱེད་ ¶ཟིན་བྲིས་དེར་ནོར་བཅོས་བྱེད་དགོས་ (We) have to correct that draft.

ནོར་བཅོས་རེའུ་མིག (nɔɔjöö riwu mig) the errata (section of a book), corrigenda.

ནོར་ཆད་ (nɔɔjɛɛ) errors and things missing/ omissions ¶ཡིག་ཆ་འདི་བཤུ་དུས་ནོར་ཆད་མང་པོ་བྱུང་འདུག When copying this document many mistakes and omissions occurred.

ནོར་འཇལ་ (nɔɔ jɛɛ) va. to repay/ reimburse (a loan), to pay taxes ¶མི་སེར་གྱིས་གཞུང་ལ་ནོར་འཇལ་བ་རེད་ The subjects paid the taxes to the goverment.

ནོར་ཉན་པ་ (nɔɔ ñɛmba) 1. useful, helpful, good ¶མོ་ཊ་དེ་ནོར་ཉན་པ་ཨ་ཡོད་ Probably that isn't a good car. 2. (with neg.) useless, hopeless, bad, badly ¶མི་འདི་ནོར་ཉན་པ་ཡོད་པ་མ་རེད་ This man is useless. ¶ཁོས་ཡི་གེ་འདི་ནོར་ཉན་པ་བྲིས་མི་འདུག He did the writing badly.

ནོར་ཉན་པ་མེད་པ་ (nɔɔñɛmba meèba) useless, hopeless.

ནོར་གཉེར་ (nɔɔñɛr) steward, overseer, manager.

ནོར་གཉེར་པ་ (nɔɔñɛrba) sm. ནོར་གཉེར་.

ནོར་གཏེར་ (nɔɔder) hidden treasure.

ནོར་རྟགས་ (nɔɔdaà) sign/ symbol used to note or indicate an error (e.g., an X).

ནོར་སྟོབས་ (nɔɔdob) financial strength, wealth ¶རྒྱལ་ཁབ་དེ་ནོར་སྟོབས་ཆེན་པོ་ཡོད་པ་རེད་ That country is very wealthy.

ནོར་དང་བུ་ལོན་ (nɔɔdaŋ pulön) weath and debts, plus and minus, positive and negative.

ནོར་དད་ (nɔɔdɛɛ) greedy, avaricious ¶མི་དེ་ནོར་དད་ཆེན་པོ་ཡོད་པ་རེད་ That person is very avaricious.

ནོར་དོན་ (nɔɔdön) financial affairs.

ནོར་དོན་ཁང་ (nɔɔdöngaŋ) finance section/ department (of an office).

ནོར་དོན་གྱི་གཏོང་ཡོང་ (nɔɔdöngi dōŋyoŋ) financial expenditures and revenue.

ནོར་དོན་སྙན་ཞུ་ (nɔɔdön ñɛ̄nshu) financial statement/ report.

ནོར་དོན་དོ་དམ་ (nɔɔdön todam) financial management/ administration.

ནོར་དོན་རྩིས་གཉེར་ཁང་ (nɔɔdön dzīìñergaŋ) financial accounting office.

ནོར་དོན་རྩིས་གཉེར་པ་ (nɔɔdön dzīìñerba) financial accountant.

ནོར་བདག (nɔɔdaà) 1. wealthy man, capitalist. 2. owner (of sth.).

ནོར་བདུན་ (nɔɔdün) sm. འཕགས་པའི་ནོར་བདུན་.

ནོར་འདོད་ཆེ་བ་ (nɔndöö cēwa) sm. ནོར་དད་.

ནོར་འདྲེ་ (nɔndre) derogatory term used for greedy people [Lit. ghost of wealth].

ནོར་རྡོ་ (nɔɔdo) precious gems/ stones.

ནོར་ལྡན་ (nɔɔdɛn) sm. ནོར་ཅན་.

ནོར་གནག (nɔɔnaà) sm. ནོར་ཕྱུགས་.

ནོར་སྣ་ (nɔɔna) different kinds of goods/ items.

ནོར་པ་ (nɔɔba) mistake, error; vi.—ཤོར་; —ཐེབས་ to err, to make a mistake.

ནོར་དཔལ་ (nɔɔbɛl) abbr. of ནོར་སྲིད་ and དཔལ་འབྱོར་.

ནོར་དཔོན་ (nɔɔbön) the head of a group of herders.

ནོར་ཕྱུགས་ (nɔɔcuù) 1. cattle, livestock. 2. yak.

ནོར་ཕྱྭ་ (nɔɔca) luck in making money/ wealth.

ནོར་བ་ལམ་འགྲོ་ (nɔɔwa lamdro) the accidental production of a good result from a mistake.

ནོར་བེལ་ཞི་བདེའི་གཟེངས་རྟགས་ (nɔɔbel shidee seŋdaà) eng.tib. Nobel Peace Prize.

ནོར་བུ་ (nɔɔbu) 1. precious jewel. 2. magic weapon, talisman. 3. person's name.

ནོར་བུ་མཁན་ (nɔɔbugɛn) people who are experts at telling the quality of gems.

ནོར་བུ་གླིང་ཁ་ (nɔɔbu lïŋgə) summer palace of the Dalai Lama (in the Lhasa area).

ནོར་བུ་དགའ་འཁྱིལ་ (nɔɔbu gaŋgyii) 1. an ornament worn around the waist of Tibetan aristocratic women. 2. circular symbol (symbolizing yin and yang).

ནོར་བུ་དགའ་རིས་ (nɔɔbu gərii) circular symbol (symbolizing yin and yang).

ནོར་བུ་དགོས་འདོད་དཔུང་འཇོམས་ (nɔɔbu göödöö būŋjom) a mythical precious stone that fulfills everything that is asked.

ནོར་བུ་སྔོན་པོ་ (nɔɔbu ŋōmbo) sapphire.

ནོར་བུ་ལྗང་ཁུ་ (nɔɔbu jəŋgu) emerald.

ནོར་བུ་དབང་སྔོན་ (nɔɔbu wāŋŋön) sapphire.

ནོར་བུ་མེ་འབར་ (nɔɔbu membar) flaming precious stone symbol.

ནོར་བུ་རིན་པོ་ཆེ་ (nɔɔbu rimboce) one of the seven royal symbols.
ནོར་བུ་སེར་པོ་ (nɔɔbu sērbu) yellow topaz.
ནོར་བུ་བསམ་འཕེལ་ (nɔɔbu sāmbel) a type of traditional Tibetan medicine.
ནོར་བུན་ (nɔɔ bün) wealth and debts.
ནོར་བུའི་སྙིང་པོ་ (nɔɔbü ñīŋbu) the best of precious jewels.
ནོར་བུའི་ཕྲེང་བ་ (nɔɔbü trēŋwa) a string/ necklace of precious jewels.
ནོར་བུའི་བང་མཛོད་ (nɔɔbü paŋdzöö) sm. ནོར་མཛོད་.
ནོར་བྲན་ (nɔɔdrɛn) sm. སེར་སྣ་ཅན་.
ནོར་དབང་ (nɔɔwaŋ) financial power/ authority.
ནོར་སྦྱིན་ (nɔɔjin) 1. to give charity from one's wealth/ belongings. 2. god of wealth.
ནོར་མ་ཉན་ (nɔɔ mañɛn) a rascal-like person.
ནོར་མི་ཉན་པ་ (nɔɔ miñɛmba) 1. useless, not beneficial. 2. a rascal-like person.
ནོར་མེད་ (nɔɔmeè) 1. poor. 2. without errors/ mistakes.
ནོར་རྩིས་ (nɔɔdziì) 1. counting the number of yak/ livestock; va.—རྒྱག. 2. accounting.
ནོར་རྩིས་རྟུལ་ (nɔɔdziì düü) positive operator (in math).
ནོར་ཚད་ (nɔɔdzɛɛ̀) sm. ནོར་རྫས་.
ནོར་མཛོད་ (nɔɔdzöö) treasury, storehouse (for valuables).
ནོར་འཛིན་ (nɔndzin) the earth, the world.
ནོར་འཛོལ་ (nɔndzöö) mistake, error.
ནོར་རྫས་ (nɔɔdzɛɛ̀) property, wealth, possessions, goods.
ནོར་རྫི་ (nɔɔdzi) yak herder.
ནོར་ཝེ་ (nɔɔwe) Norway.
ནོར་ཝེ་བོད་ཀྱི་རང་དབང་ཀླུང་འཕྲིན་ (nɔɔwe pöögi raŋwaŋ lūŋdrin) Voice of Tibet broadcast (originating in Norway).
ནོར་ཟུར་ (nɔrsur) positive angle (in math).
ནོར་བཟང་ (nɔrsaŋ) 1. name of a Tibetan opera king. 2. person's name.
ནོར་གཞི་ (nɔrshi) basis/ danger for making a mistake or error ༈ རྩིས་འདི་ལ་ནོར་གཞི་ཡོད་པས་གཟབ་གཟབ་བྱེད་དགོས་ Because there is a danger of making a mistake in the calculations you must be careful.
ནོར་ཡ་ (nɔrya) sm. ནོར་གཞི་.
ནོར་གཡང་ (nɔryaŋ) sm. ནོར་ལྷ་.
ནོར་ར་ (nɔɔra) livestock corral, yak corral.
ནོར་ལོངས་སྤྱོད་ (nɔɔ lɔŋjöö) things, goods, wealth.
ནོར་ཤ་ (nɔɔsha) yak meat.
ནོར་ཤིང་ (nɔɔshiŋ) 1. legendary tree (in tales) from which money falls when shaken. 2. a ready source of money.
ནོར་ཤུགས་ (nɔɔshuù) 1. financial strength/ power/ force. 2. financial capacity.
ནོར་སིང་ཧོམ་ (nɔrsiŋhom) eng. nursing home.
ནོར་སྲིད་ (nɔrsiì) finance ༈ སྲིད་གཞུང་གི་ནོར་སྲིད་ Government finance.
ནོར་སྲིད་ཀྱི་ཁ་སྣོན་ (nɔrsiìgi kānön) financial subsidy, monetary grant.
ནོར་སྲིད་ཀྱི་འགན་གཙང་ (nɔrsiìgi gɛndzaŋ) financial responsibility system.
ནོར་སྲིད་ཀྱི་ཆད་གྲངས་ (nɔrsiìgi cɛ̄ɛ̀draŋ) financial deficit.
ནོར་སྲིད་ཀྱི་གཏོང་སྒོ་ (nɔrsiìgi dōŋgo) expenditures.
ནོར་སྲིད་ཀྱི་གཏོང་དངུལ་ (nɔrsiìgi dōŋŋüü) money that has been appropriated.
ནོར་སྲིད་ཀྱི་གཏོང་ལྷག (nɔrsiìgi dōŋlhaà) financial surplus.
ནོར་སྲིད་ཀྱི་གཏོང་ཡོང་དོ་མཉམ་ (nɔrsiìgi dōŋyoŋ toñam) balance of revenues and expenditures.
ནོར་སྲིད་ཀྱི་མཚལ་ཡིག (nɔrsiìgi tsɛ̄ɛ̀yiì) financial deficit, red ink.
ནོར་སྲིད་ཀྱི་ཡོང་ཁུངས་ (nɔrsiìgi yoŋguŋ) sm. ནོར་སྲིད་ཀྱི་འབྱུང་ཁུངས་.
ནོར་སྲིད་ཀྱི་ཡོངས་སྒོ་ (nɔrsiìgi yoŋgo) financial revenue.
ནོར་སྲིད་ཀྱི་ལས་ཁུངས་ (nɔrsiìgi lɛɛ̀guŋ) financial organ, financial administration, finance office.
ནོར་སྲིད་ཀྱི་ལོ་འཁོར་ (nɔrsiìgi logɔɔ) fiscal year.
ནོར་སྲིད་ཀྱི་སྲིད་ཇུས་ (nɔrsiìgi siìjüü) financial policy/ strategy.
ནོར་སྲིད་ཁུར་པོ་ (nɔrsiì kūrbu) financial burden.
ནོར་སྲིད་ཁྲུའུ་ (nɔrsiì trū) tib.ch. finance department/ office/ section.
ནོར་སྲིད་སྒེར་སྡེམ་ (nɔrsiì gerdem) financial monopoly.
ནོར་སྲིད་སྒྲིག་གཞི་ (nɔrsiì drigshi) financial structure.
ནོར་སྲིད་དངུལ་རྩ་ (nɔrsiì ŋüüdza) finance and banking.
ནོར་སྲིད་དངུལ་ལོར་འཆར་འགོད་ཁྲུའུ་ (nɔrsiì ŋüülɔɔ cārgöötru) tib.ch. financial and monetary planning office.
ནོར་སྲིད་ཉམས་ཉེན་ (nɔrsiì ñamñen) financial crisis.
ནོར་སྲིད་ཉོ་ཚོང་ (nɔrsiì ñodzoŋ) finance and trade/ commerce.
ནོར་སྲིད་ཉོ་ཚོང་གཞུང་ལས་ཁང་ (nɔrsiì ñodzoŋ shuŋlɛgaŋ) finance and trade/ commerce office.
ནོར་སྲིད་ཉོ་ཚོང་སློབ་གྲྭ་ (nɔrsiì ñodzoŋ lōbdra) finance and trade/ commerce school.
ནོར་སྲིད་གཏོང་ཡོང་ (nɔrsiì dōŋyoŋ) revenues and expenditures.
ནོར་སྲིད་ཐིང་ (nɔrsiì tīŋ) tib.ch. finance department.
ནོར་སྲིད་དང་ཡིད་རྟོན་དངུལ་ཁང་ (nɔrsiìdaŋ yiidön ŋüügaŋ) finance and credit bank.
ནོར་སྲིད་པུའུ་ (nɔrsiì bū) tib.ch. ministry of finance.
ནོར་སྲིད་དཔྱ་ཁྲལ་ (nɔrsiì jātrɛɛ) financial tax.
ནོར་སྲིད་བློན་ཆེན་ (nɔrsiì lōnjen) Finance Minister.
ནོར་སྲིད་འབྱུང་ཁུངས་ (nɔrsiì juŋguŋ) financial resources.
ནོར་སྲིད་མ་རྩ་ (nɔrsiì madza) financial capital.
ནོར་སྲིད་ཚོང་དོན་པུའུ་ (nɔrsiì tsōŋdönbu) / tib.ch. finance and commerce department/ office/ section.
ནོར་སྲིད་ལམ་ལུགས་ (nɔrsiì lɔmluù) financial system.
ནོར་སྲིད་ལས་ཁུངས་ (nɔrsiì lɛɛ̀guŋ) Department of the Treasury (U.S.A.).
ནོར་སྲུང་ (nɔrsuŋ) looking after,/ protecting/ guarding wealth; va.—བྱེད་.
ནོར་གསར་ (nɔrsar) newly rich.
ནོར་བསྲིས་ (nɔɔ siì) va. to live parsimoniously/ thriftily/ economically.
ནོར་ཧྲིལ་གྲངས་ (nɔr hrīīdraŋ) positive integer (in math).
ནོར་ལྷ་ (nɔrlha) god of wealth/ money.
ནོས་ (nöö) imp. of ནོད་.
གནག (nāg) cattle, livestock.
གནག་ཁྱུ་ (nāggyu) herd of cattle/ livestock.
གནག་རྗེས་ (nāgjɛɛ̀) footprint of cattle/ livestock.
གནག་རྟ་ (nāgda) cattle and horses.
གནག་ནད་ (nāgnɛɛ̀) cattle disease.
གནག་གནད་ (nāgnɛɛ̀) shung. mean, cruel ༈ མི་སེར་ལ་གནག་གནད་ཀྱི་བྱ་ཐབས་ལག་ལེན་ཇི་ཡོད་ཆ་མ་གཏོགས་པས་ It is uncertain what sort of mean and cruel method they will use on the subjects.
གནག་པ་ (nāgba) 1. black. 2. malicious, spiteful, vengeful.
གནག་པོ་ (nāgbo) sm. གནག་པ་.
གནག་ཕྱུགས་ (nāgjuù) cattle, livestock.
གནག་བག (nāgbaà) dirt, filth.
གནག་རྫི་ (nāgdzi) herdsman/ shepherd of cattle.
གནག་ལུག (nāglug) cattle and sheep.
གནག་སེམས་ (nāgsem) evil, wicked, cruel, sinister.
གནག་ལྷས་ (nāglhɛɛ̀) cattle shed/ barn.
གནང་ (nāŋ) 1. va. to give (h.) ༈ ཁོང་གིས་དངུལ་ཞེ་དྲག་གནང་སོང་ He gave a lot of money. 2. h. of བྱེད་. 3. verb used to make non honorific verbs honorific ༈ ཁོང་གིས་བསྟན་པ་གནང་སོང་ He showed it (h.).
གནང་སྐྱེས་ (nāŋgyeè) h. of ལག་རྟགས་.

གནང་བཀག (nāŋgaà) things that are permissible and not permissible.

གནང་སྒོ་ (nāŋgo) 1. h. of བྱེད་སྒོ་. 2. sm. མཛད་སྒོ་.

གནང་ཆ་ (nāŋja) sm. གནང་སྐྱིས་.

གནང་ཆེན་ (nāŋjen) reprieve from capital punishment.

གནང་གཏད་ (nāŋdɛɛ̀) sm. བྱེད་གཏད་.

གནང་གཏད་མཆིས་ (nāŋdɛɛ̀ cīì) shung. to be difficult to do/ handle/ decide ¶ རྩྭ་རིན་གསོལ་རས་བཀའ་འདོམས་ཐུགས་རྗེ་ཆེ་བ་དང་དེ་ཡང་གནང་གཏད་མཆིས་ཚེ་ཁྲལ་འབབ་གཟིགས་རྗེས་གྲིབ་འབྲངས་ཁོང་ཚོར་བཀའ་ཁྱབ་ཞུ་རྒྱུ་ We request (that the superiors) order them to pay the fee for grazing animals, and if it is difficult for you to give the order, please order them to pay the taxes for the pastureland.

གནང་རྟེན་ (nāŋden) 1. sm. གནང་སྐྱིས་. 2. flower/ scarf enclosed with a letter.

གནང་སྟངས་ (nāŋdaŋ) the manner in which sth. is given or done (h.).

གནང་ཕྱོགས་ (nāŋjɔ̀ɔ̀) h. of བྱེད་ཕྱོགས་.

གནང་བ་ (nāŋwa) approval, consent, permission; va.—ཞུ་ to ask for approval/ consent/ permission; vi.—ཐོབ་ to obtain approval/ consent/ permission; va.—གནང་ to give permission ¶ ང་ནང་ལ་འགྲོ་ཆོག་པའི་གནང་བ་ཐོབ་བྱུང་ I received permission to go home. ¶ འགོ་ཁྲིད་ཀྱིས་ང་ནང་ལ་འགྲོ་ཆོག་པའི་གནང་བ་གནང་བྱུང་ The boss gave me permission to go home.

གནང་འཕྱོར་ (nāŋjɔɔ) sent and received ¶ ཁོང་གིས་ཕྱག་བྲིས་གནང་འཕྱོར་བྱུང་ I received the letter he sent.

གནང་སྦྱིན་ (nəŋjin) a gift/ present given to performers.

གནང་མཛད་ (nāŋdzɛɛ̀) sm. གནང་.

གནངས་ (nāŋ) the day after tomorrow.

གནངས་ཆག (nāŋjaà) on alternating days ¶ ང་ལས་ཀ་གནངས་ཆག་བྱེད་ཀྱི་ཡོད་ I work on alternating days.

གནངས་ཆག་གནངས་ཆག (nāŋjaà nāŋjaà) sm. གནངས་ཆག.

གནངས་ཆེ་ས་ (nāŋ cēsa) important/ valuable/ precious things or events.

གནངས་ཆེན་པོ་ (nāŋ cēmbo) sm. གནངས་ཆེ་ས་.

གནངས་འཆར་ (nāŋcar) sm. གནངས་ཆག.

གནངས་ཉིན་ (nāŋñin) sm. གནངས་.

གནངས་ཉིན་ཀ་ (nāŋ ñinga) sm. གནངས་.

གནངས་བརྡ་ (nāŋda) notice given two days in advance ¶ བླ་མ་མཇལ་ཁ་ཞུ་དུས་གནངས་བརྡ་འབུལ་དགོས་ཀྱི་རེད་ When one requests an audience with a lama one should make it two days in advance.

གནངས་ཕོད་ (nāŋböö̀) two years hence, the year after next.

གནངས་གཞེས་ (nāŋ sheè) the day after tomorrow or three days from now ¶ ང་གནངས་གཞེས་ཤིག་ལ་ཐོན་གྱི་ཡིན་ I will depart the day after tomorrow or three days from now.

གནངས་ལོ་ (nāŋlo) sm. གནངས་ཕོད་.

གནངས་སླད་ (nāŋlɛɛ̀) sm. གནངས་ཕོད་.

གནད་ (nɛ̄ɛ̀) the key or main point/ significance, the importance, the essence ¶ འདིར་གནད་ག་རེ་ཡོད་པ་རེད་ What is the significance of this?

གནད་ཀ་ (nɛ̄ɛ̀ga) sm. གནད་འགག.

གནད་ཀྱི་དོན་པོ་ (nɛ̄ɛ̀gi tönbo) sm. གནད་སྙིང་པོ་.

གནད་འཁེལ་ (nɛ̄ngee) accurate, precise, exact, exactly to the point ¶ ཁོང་གིས་བསམ་འཆར་གནད་འཁེལ་ཞིག་བཤད་སོང་ He gave a suggestion that was exactly to the point.

གནད་འཁེལ་པོ་ (nɛ̄ɛ̀ kēēbo) sm. གནད་འཁེལ་.

གནད་གལ་ (nɛ̄ɛ̀gɛɛ) sm. གནད་འགག.

གནད་གོང་ (nɛ̄ɛ̀goŋ) price, worth.

གནད་འགག (nɛ̄ngaà) important, critical key to a situation ¶ འཆར་གཞི་འདི་གནད་འགག་ཆེན་པོ་ཞིག་རེད་འདུག This plan is very important.

གནད་འགག་ཅན་ (nɛ̄ngaàjɛn) sm. གནད་འགག་ཆེན་པོ་.

གནད་འགག་མེད་པ་ (nɛ̄ngaà meèba) unimportant, insignificant ¶ ལས་ཀ་འདི་མགྱོགས་པོ་མ་ཚར་ནའང་གནད་འགག་མེད་པ་རེད་ Even if you do not finish this work quickly, it is unimportant (doesn't matter).

གནད་འགངས་ (nɛ̄ngaŋ) sm. གནད་འགག.

གནད་འགྲོལ་ (nɛ̄ɛ̀ dröö) va. to clarify the important points/ significance of sth. ¶ ཁོང་གིས་ཡིག་ཆ་དེའི་གནད་བཀྲོལ་བ་རེད་ He clarified the significance of the document.

གནད་སྒྱུར་ (nɛ̄ɛ̀gyur) translating the essence/ main/ important points, va.—བྱེད་.

གནད་ཅན་ (nɛ̄ɛ̀jɛn) important, consequential, significant ¶ ཁོང་གསུམ་ལ་གནད་ཅན་གྱི་གོ་གནས་ཡོད་ཀྱང་ Even though those three had important positions.

གནད་གཅིག་རྡོལ་ (nɛ̄ɛ̀ jīg dȫö̀) va. to make/ affect a breakthrough in one place/ site ¶ སྲིད་ཇུས་གསར་པ་ཁྱོན་ཡོངས་ལ་ལག་ལེན་མ་བསྟར་གོང་གནད་གཅིག་བརྡོལ་ནས་ལག་བསྟར་བྱས་པ་རེད་ Before implementing a new policy everywhere, they made a breakthrough in one area. ¶ དམག་འཁྲུག་སྐབས་དགྲ་བོའི་ས་ཆའི་གནད་གཅིག་བརྡོལ་ནས་དམག་མི་རྣམས་འཛུལ་བ་རེད་ During the war, they made a breakthrough in one part of the enemy's area (allowing) their soldiers to enter.

གནད་གཅོད་ (nɛ̄ɛ̀ jö̀ö̀) va. to cut or sever the most important/ essential.

གནད་ཆུང་ཆེ་བཟོས་ (nɛ̄ɛ̀juŋ cēsöö̀) making a mountain out of a molehill.

གནད་ཆེ (nɛ̄ɛ̀je) important, consequential, significant, major ¶ གནད་ཆེའི་བཟོ་ལས་ཐོན་རྫས་ Major industrial products.

གནད་ཆེ་ས་ (nɛ̄ɛ̀ cēsa) important/ key point, main aspect.

གནད་ཆེན་པོ་ (nɛ̄ɛ̀ cēmbo) sm. གནད་ཆེ་.

གནད་ཆེའི་ས་བཅད་ (nɛ̄ɛ̀cee sābjɛɛ̀) important/ major/ consequential items or factors or sections.

གནད་ཆེའི་སློབ་གྲྭ་ཆེན་མོ་ (nɛ̄ɛ̀cee lōbdra cēmmo) key universities.

གནད་ཉིད་ཐིག་པ་ (nɛ̄ɛ̀ñiì tīgbə) sm. གནད་ཐིག་པ་.

གནད་སྙིང་པོ་ (nɛ̄ɛ̀ ñīŋbu) the main point/ issue/ significance/ subject.

གནད་བསྟུན་ (nɛ̄ɛ̀dün) according to the importance/ significance ¶ ལས་ཀ་འདི་སྐོར་ཁྱེད་རང་གིས་གནད་བསྟུན་ཐག་གཅོད་བྱས་ན་འགྲིགས་ Concerning this work, it is okay if you decide it in accordance with what is important.

གནད་ཐབས་ (nɛ̄ɛ̀dəb) important/ significant techniques or methods.

གནད་ཐིག་པ་ (nɛ̄ɛ̀ tīgbə) precise, accurate, just what is needed ¶ ཁོང་གིས་ང་ལ་གནད་ཐིག་པའི་སློབ་གསོ་བརྒྱབ་བྱུང་ He gave me exactly the advice I needed.

གནད་ཐོག་འཁེལ་ (nɛ̄ɛ̀dɔ̀ɔ̀ kēē) vi. to be just what is needed, to be exactly on the mark ¶ ད་རེས་ཁོང་གི་གསུང་བཤད་དེ་གནད་ཐོག་འཁེལ་སོང་ His speech today was exactly on the mark.

གནད་དུ་འཁེལ་ (nɛ̄ɛ̀du kēē) vi. to be accurate/ precise/ exact, to be just what is needed.

གནད་དུ་ཕོག (nɛ̄ɛ̀du pɔ̄ɔ̀) sm. གནད་དུ་འཁེལ་.

གནད་དོན་ (nɛ̄ɛ̀dön) question, problem, matter ¶ ཞིང་པའི་གནད་དོན་དེ་ The question concerning the peasants.

གནད་དོན་ངོ་མ་ (nɛ̄ɛ̀dön ŋoma) the essence/ true nature of sth. ¶ ཁོས་གནད་དོན་ངོ་མ་དེ་མགོ་ཚོད་མི་འདུག He did not understand the essence (of the matter).

གནད་སྡོད་ (nɛ̄ɛ̀döö̀) staying at a selected village unit to gain firsthand experience and help improve its work; va.—བྱེད་.

གནད་བསྡུས (nɛ̄ɛ̀düù) summary, abstract, synopsis, key points, essence, in brief ¶ གསར་འགྱུར་གནད་བསྡུས་ News in brief.

གནད་བསྡུས་གོ་བདེ་ (nɛ̄ɛ̀düù kode) easy to understand and concise.

གནད་བསྡུས་རྩ་ཚིག (nɛ̄ɛ̀düù dzədziì) outline, sketch, abstract, summary, synopsis.

གནད་འཕིགས་ (nɛ̄ɛbii) sm. གནད་དུ་འཁེལ་.

གནད་འཕྲོད་ (nɛ̄ɛ drȫö) sm. གནད་དུ་འཁེལ་.

གནད་མེད་གནད་བརྩི་ (nɛ̄ɛmeè nɛ̄ɛdzi) considering unimportant things important.

གནད་མེད་པ་ (nɛ̄ɛ m̲eèba) insignificant, unimportant, not to the point.

གནད་མེད་སྟོང་ཤོད་ (nɛ̄ɛmeè dōŋshöö) saying irrelevant/ pointless/ meaningless things.

གནད་སྨིན་པོ་ (nɛ̄ɛ mīmbu) effective ༈ སྨན་འདི་གནད་སྨིན་པོ་བྱུང་སོང་ This medicine was effective.

གནད་ཟིན་ (nɛ̄ɛsin) notes of the important points (of sth.); va.—འགོད་ to write down the important points (e.g., of a meeting).

གནད་ཡོད་ (nɛ̄ɛyöö) important ༈ གནད་ཡོད་མི་སྣ་ Important persons.

གནད་ལ་བཀར་ (nɛ̄ɛla gār) va. to focus on the critical point/ issue, to reach to the heart of a matter ༈ མི་དེས་དོན་དག་དེའི་ཐོག་གནད་ལ་བཀར་ནས་ཞུས་པ་རེད་ On that issue, he spoke right to the heart of the matter.

གནད་ལ་འཁེལ་ (nɛ̄ɛla kēē) sm. གནད་དུ་འཁེལ་.

གནད་ལ་བསྒྲེ་ (nɛ̄ɛla dre̲) 1. va. to harm through treacherous means. 2. untrue, unjust. 3. sm. རིགས་འགྲེ་.

གནད་ལ་འཕིགས་ (nɛ̄ɛla pīi) sm. གནད་དུ་འཁེལ་.

གནད་ལ་སྨིན་ (nɛ̄ɛla mīn) sm. གནད་སྨིན་.

གནད་བཤུ་ (nɛ̄ɛ shū) sm. གནད་བཤུས་.

གནད་བཤུས་ (nɛ̄ɛshüü) notes (on the main points); va.—བྱེད་ to make/ take notes on the main points of sth.

གནད་གསང་ (nɛ̄ɛsaŋ) points on the body for draining blood according to traditional Tibetan medicine.

གནན་ (nɛn) f. of གནོན་.

གནམ་ (nām) 1. sky. 2. atmosphere, air. 3. abbr. of གནམ་གཤིས་.

གནམ་ཀུ་ཉི་བརྗེ་ (nāmgu ñije) perpetrating a gigantic fraud [Lit. steal the sky and switch the sun].

གནམ་ཀུབ་བརྗེ་ (nāmgu je̲) vi. to have the weather begin to clear.

གནམ་སྐས་ (nāmgɛɛ) a long ladder used for scaling the walls of fortresses [Lit. sky ladder].

གནམ་སྐུད་ (nāmgüü) antenna.

གནམ་སྐེ་ལ་གོན་ སྤྲིན་པས་ཨོག་སྒྲོག་རྒྱག (nāmgela gö̲n drīnbɛ ōgdrɔɔ gyaà) extremely proud [Lit. wear sky on the neck, use cloud as a hat strap].

གནམ་སྐྱོད་ (nāmgyöö) 1. flying; va.—བྱེད་ ༈ ཁོ་ཨ་རི་ནས་གནམ་སྐྱོད་བྱས་བཞག He flew from America.

གནམ་སྐྱོན་ (nāmgyön) 1. a disaster caused by the weather (e.g., a storm, drought). 2. a stroke.

གནམ་བསྐོས་ (nāmgöö) 1. divinely selected (e.g., the selection of the emperor), mandate of heaven. 2. arc. positive karma/ merit.

གནམ་བསྐོས་གོང་མ་འཇམ་དབྱངས་བདག་པོ་ཆེན་པོ་ (nāmgöö go̲ŋma ja̲myaŋ da̲gbo cēmbo) title used for the Chinese Emperor.

གནམ་བསྐོས་དགའ་ལྡན་ཕོ་བྲང་ (nāmgöö ga̲ndɛn pōdraŋ) the traditional name of the Tibetan government.

གནམ་བསྐོས་གཉེན་སྒྲིག (nāmgöö ñēndrig) a marriage made in heaven.

གནམ་བསྐོས་གཙོ་བདག (nāmgöö dzōdaà) a divinely selected chief/ leader.

གནམ་བསྐོས་ལས་དབང་ (nāmgöö l̲ɛ̲ɛwaŋ) divine will, fate, destiny ༈ ཚེ་འདིར་སྡུག་པོ་མྱོང་བ་དེ་གནམ་བསྐོས་ལས་དབང་རེད་ His suffering in this lifetime is divine will.

གནམ་ཁ་སྔོན་ (nām kā ŋȫn) the blue sky, the blue heavens.

གནམ་ཁ་ཞེང་ (nām kā she̲ŋ) the expanse of the sky, the heavens.

གནམ་ཁུང་ (nəmguŋ) chimney opening.

གནམ་གང་ (nāmgaŋ) the thirtieth day of a Tibetan lunar month.

གནམ་གང་ལ་རྟ་གསོས་ (nāmgaŋla dāsöö) abbr. of གནམ་གང་ལ་རྟ་གསོས་ ཚེས་གཅིག་ལ་རྟ་རྒྱུག.

གནམ་གང་ལ་རྟ་གསོས་ ཚེས་གཅིག་ལ་རྟ་རྒྱུག (nāmgaŋla dāsöö tsējiglə dāgyuù) not ready/ prepared [Lit. to feed the horse on the 30th and race it on the 1st].

གནམ་གུང་ (nəmguŋ) sky, heavens.

གནམ་གྱི་སྐེ་རགས་ (nəmgi gēraà) the Milky Way.

གནམ་གྱི་ཁྲི་བདུན་ (nəmgi trīdün) the first seven kings of Tibet whose names bear the word ཁྲི་.

གནམ་གྱི་གོ་ལ་ (nəmgi k̲ola) the universe, the celestial sphere.

གནམ་གྱི་ཐང་རུབ་ (nəmgi tāŋrub) uncertain, changeable ༈ དེང་སང་གི་སྲིད་ཇུས་དེ་གནམ་གྱི་ཐང་རུབ་ནང་བཞིན་རེད་ Nowadays the political policy is uncertain. [Lit. weather clear and overcast].

གནམ་གྱི་ལུགས་ (nāmgi lu̲ù) shung. the will of heaven ༈ གནམ་གྱི་ལུགས་ལ་གུས་པ་དང་མཐུན་པ་གོང་ལ་སེམས་བཟང་པོ་བསམས་ནས་བཀུར་བསྐྱེ་བྱས་ Respect the will of heaven, honor the court and have a good sense of responsibility.

གནམ་གྱི་སྲས་ (nāmgi sɛ̄ɛ) title/ name used for the Emperor of China [Lit. son of heaven].

གནམ་གྲང་མོ་ (nəm tra̲ŋmo) cold (weather).

གནམ་གྲང་ས་འཁྱག (nāmdraŋ sāgyaà) extreme cold [Lit. the weather is cold and the ground is frozen].

གནམ་གྲུ་ (nəmdru) airplane, aircraft; va.—གཏོང་ to fly an airplane.

གནམ་གྲུ་སྒུག་ཁང་ (nəmdru gu̲ùgaŋ) airport lounge, airport waiting room.

གནམ་གྲུ་གཏོང་མཁན་ (nəmdru dōŋñɛn) pilot.

གནམ་གྲུ་ཐང་ (nəmdrutaŋ) airfield.

གནམ་གྲུ་ནས་དབྱུག (nəmdrunɛ yüù) va.to drop things/ people from an airplane, to parachute from a plane.

གནམ་གྲུ་འབབ་ཐང་ (nəmdru b̲əbtaŋ) sm. གནམ་གྲུ་ཐང་.

གནམ་གྲུ་འབབ་ས་ (nəmdru b̲əbsə) sm. གནམ་གྲུ་ཐང་.

གནམ་གྲུ་འབབ་སའི་གྲུ་གཟིངས་ (nəmdru b̲əbsɛ tru̲siŋ) aircraft carrier.

གནམ་གྲུ་འབབ་སའི་དམག་གྲུ་ (nəmdru b̲əbsɛ məgdru) sm. གནམ་གྲུ་འབབ་སའི་གྲུ་གཟིངས་.

གནམ་གྲུ་ལས་འཕེན་ (nəmdrulɛ pēn) sm. གནམ་གྲུ་ནས་དབྱུག.

གནམ་གྲུ་བཟོ་གྲྭ་ (nəmdru s̲odra) aircraft factory.

གནམ་གྲུམ་པ་ (nāmdrumba) a thunderous sound [Lit. when the sky breaks].

གནམ་གྲུའི་ཁ་ལོ་པ་ (nəmdrü kālowa) sm. གནམ་གྲུ་གཏོང་མཁན་.

གནམ་གྲུའི་འགྲོ་ལམ་ (nəmdrü dr̲olam) air route.

གནམ་གྲུའི་རྒྱུག་ལམ་ (nəmdrü gyu̲glam) runway (at airport).

གནམ་གྲུའི་གནོད་འགོག (nəmdrü nōngɔɔ) air defence.

གནམ་གྲུའི་ལམ་ཁག (nəmdrü l̲angaà) sm. གནམ་གྲུའི་འགྲོ་ལམ་.

གནམ་གྲུའི་ལམ་ཐིག (nəmdrü l̲amdig) sm. གནམ་གྲུའི་འགྲོ་ལམ་.

གནམ་གྲུའི་ཞབས་འདེགས་མ་ (nəmdrü sha̲mdegma) stewardess (on an airplane).

གནམ་གྲུར་ཡིབ་ཁུང་ (nəmdrur yi̲bguŋ) air raid shelter.

གནམ་གྲོ་ཐག་རྩེད་ (nāmdro tāgdzeè) an acrobatic exhibit performed at the Potala Palace in the 1st lunar month consisting of a person performing while holding a rope attached to a high pole.

གནམ་གློག (nāmlɔɔ) lightening; vi.—འཁྱུག to have a lightening flash.

གནམ་དགུང་ (nəmguŋ) midnight.

གནམ་འགུལ་ས་གཡོ་ (nəmgüü sāyo) sm. གནམ་གཡོ་ས་འགུལ་.

གནམ་རྒན་མ་ (nām ge̲mma) the sky.

གནམ་རྒྱ་ས་རྙི་ (nāmgya sāñi) surrounded by difficulties/ dangers ༈ གནམ་རྒྱ་ས་རྙི་ལས་ཐར་སོང་ (He) escaped from the dangers surrounding him. [Lit. nets in the sky and snares on the ground].

གནམ་རྒྱན་ (nāmgyɛn) a ceiling decorated with silk

and satin right above the throne where a high ranking lama or official is seated.

གནམ་སྒོ་ (nāmgo) 1. a skylight. 2. an entrance/ door on a roof (that has stairs going down inside the house).

གནམ་སྒྱུར་ས་བརྗེས་ (nāmgyur sājeè) changing completely/ totally, revolutionizing sth.; va.—བྱེད་ [Lit. change the sky, change the earth].

གནམ་སྒྲོགས་ (nāmgyɔɔ̀) antiaircraft gun; va.—འཕེན་.

གནམ་ངོ་ (nāmŋo) the look/ color of the sky (relating to the weather); vi.—འགྱུར་ to have a change of weather.

གནམ་ངན་ (nāmŋɛn) overcast sky.

གནམ་སྔོན་པོ་ (nām ŋombo) blue sky.

གནམ་གཅལ་ (nāmjɛɛ) ceiling.

གནམ་ལྕགས་ (nāmjaà) 1. meteoric iron. 2. a talisman believed to be naturally formed from meteorites.

གནམ་ལྕགས་སྐུད་ (nāmjaà gṻù) sm. གནམ་སྐུད་.

གནམ་ལྕགས་འགོག་མདའ་ (nāmjaà gɔgda) lightening rod.

གནམ་ལྕགས་ཐོག་འབབ་ (nāmjaà tōmbəb) an unexpected/ sudden occurrence, an event that occurs without warning [Lit. falling on top like lightening].

གནམ་ལྕགས་མེ་འབར་ (nāmjaà mebar) shooting star, comet.

གནམ་ལྕགས་འབར་བ་ (nāmjaà barwa) name of a mountain in southwest Tibet.

གནམ་ཆུ་ (nōmju) rainfall, rain water.

གནམ་ཆུ་སྒུག་པའི་ས་ཞིང་ (nōmju gugbɛ sōshiŋ) fields grown using rainfall only (i.e., no irrigation).

གནམ་ཆོད་ (nām cöö) vi. to stop raining ༑ད་གནམ་ཆོད་བཞག It has stopped raining now.

གནམ་འཇམ་ས་འཇམ་ (nāmjam sānjam) peace and tranquillity [Lit. calm sky, calm earth].

གནམ་བརྗེས་ས་སྒྱུར་ (nāmjeè sāgyur) sm. གནམ་སྒྱུར་ས་བརྗེས་.

གནམ་གདོང་ (nāmdoŋ) sm. གནམ་འབབ་.

གནམ་བདགས་ (nāmdaà) hanging sb. up (for punishing); va.—རྒྱག; —གཏོང་ ༑གནམ་བདགས་བརྒྱབ་ནས་ཉེས་དུང་བཏང་བ་རེད་ They hung him up and beat him.

གནམ་སྟོང་ (nāmdoŋ) sm. གནམ་གང་.

གནམ་བལྟས་ (nāmdɛɛ̀) looking up to the sky; va.—བྱེད་.

གནམ་ཐག (nāmdaà) a rope for hanging sth. up; va.—རྒྱག ༑ཁང་པའི་ནང་ཤ་གནམ་ཐག་བརྒྱབ་ནས་བཞག་འདུག (They) hang up the meat and left it.

གནམ་ཐག་ལ་ཕྱིབ་ (nāmdagla jēb) va. to commit suicide by hanging.

གནམ་ཐང་ (nāmdaŋ) 1. abbr. གནམ་གྲུ་འབབ་ཐང་. 2. clear sky, good weather.

གནམ་ཐིག་དམར་པོ་ (nāmdig mārbo) the equator.

གནམ་ཐོག (nāmdɔɔ̀) via/ by air.

གནམ་ཐོག་འཐབ་ཇོལ་ (nāmdɔɔ̀ tɔbgöö) air attack.

གནམ་ཐོག་འཕེན་ས་ (nāmdɔɔ̀ pēnsa) drop zone.

གནམ་ཐོག་སྲུང་སྐྱོབ་ (nāmdɔɔ̀ sūŋgyob) air defence.

གནམ་མཐའ་མཚོ་གཏིང་ (nāmda tsōdiŋ) the four corners of the earth, the ends of the earth [Lit. the edge of the sky, the depths of the ocean].

གནམ་མཐོངས་ (nāmtoŋ) a window on the ceiling, a skylight.

གནམ་འཐབ་ས་འཛིང་ (nāmdəb sōndziŋ) combating natural calamity [Lit. fighting the sky, fighting the earth].

གནམ་འཐིབ་ (nām ti̋b) vi. to be cloudy/ overcast.

གནམ་འཐིབས་ (nām ti̋b) sm. གནམ་འཐིབ་.

གནམ་འཐིབས་ས་རུབ་ (nāmtib sārub) a tragedy, a sad day [Lit. sky overcast, earth dark].

གནམ་དྭངས་ (nāmdaŋ) 1. a fine/ clear/ sunny day. 2. vi. to be clear (weather) ༑ད་གནམ་དྭངས་བཞག It is clear now (the weather).

གནམ་དྭངས་པོ་ (nām taŋbo) good/ clear weather.

གནམ་དུ་གཤེགས་ (nāmdu shēg) vi. to die (h.).

གནམ་གདུགས་ (nāmduù) parachuting, a parachute; va.—མཆོང་ to parachute.

གནམ་བདག (nāmdaà) God (Christian).

གནམ་བདག་གི་ཆོས་ལུགས་ (nāmdaàgi cȍȍluù) sm. གནམ་བདག་ཆོས་ལུགས་.

གནམ་བདག་ཆོས་གཞུང་ (nāmdaà cȍȍshuŋ) the roman catholic church.

གནམ་བདག་ཆོས་ལུགས་ (nāmdaà cȍȍluù). catholicism, the roman catholic religion.

གནམ་བདག་ཆོས་ལུགས་ཀྱི་ཆོས་པ་ (nāmdaàgi cȍȍluùgi cȍȍba) 1. Christian priest. 2. Christian religious practitioner.

གནམ་བདེ་ (nāmde) heavenly.

གནམ་བདེ་སྒོ་མོ་ཆེ་ (nāmde gomoce) Tiananmen gate (Beijing).

གནམ་བདེ་སྒོ་མོ་ཆེའི་ཐང་ཆེན་ (nāmde gomoce tāŋcen) Tiananmen square.

གནམ་བདེ་སྒོ་མོ་ཆེའི་ཡང་སྟེང་ (nāmde gomoce yaŋdeŋ) 1. rostrum. (of Tiananmen). 2. roof, penthouse.

གནམ་མདའ་ (nāmda) 1. shooting in the air, e.g., a warning shot; va.—རྒྱག. 2. a type of arrow shot in the air for sport; va.—རྒྱག.

གནམ་རྡིབ་ (nāmdib) sth. that is impossible [Lit. sky collapses].

གནམ་རྡིབ་ས་གས་ (nāmdib sāgɛɛ̀) sth. that is impossible [Lit. the sky collapses, the earth cracks].

གནམ་རྡོ་ (nāmdo) 1. a stone that has fallen from the sky, meteorite. 2. hail.

གནམ་ལྡིང་ས་མཆོང་ (nāmdiŋ sājoŋ) sm. ས་མཆོང་གནམ་མཆོང་.

གནམ་ལྡིང་ས་ལྡིང་ (nāmdiŋ sājoŋ) sm. ས་མཆོང་གནམ་མཆོང་.

གནམ་ལྡེ་འོད་སྲུང་ (nāmde wöösuŋ) son of King Langdarma's younger wife.

གནམ་པ་བ་ (nāmbawa) people who lived around the Lhasa area and worked breaking stones. 2. people who work breaking stones.

གནམ་པང་ (nāmbaŋ) ceiling.

གནམ་པོ་ (nāmbo) 1. honest, open, frank. 2. laughing. 3. a witness.

གནམ་ཕྲ་ (nāmdra) divining by the condition of the weather.

གནམ་དཔྱད་ (nāmjɛɛ̀) 1. meteorology. 2. astronomy.

གནམ་དཔྱད་ཀྱི་གྲངས་ཀ་ (nāmjɛɛ̀gi traŋga) astronomical figure/ number, an enormous figure.

གནམ་དཔྱད་ཁང་ (nāmjɛɛ̀gaŋ) planetarium.

གནམ་དཔྱད་རྒྱང་ཤེལ་ (nāmjɛɛ̀ gyaŋshɛɛ̀) astronomical telescope.

གནམ་དཔྱད་གཏམ་དཔེ་ (nāmjɛɛ̀ dāmbe) proverbs and allusions about the weather.

གནམ་དཔྱད་འཕྲུལ་ཆས་ (nāmjɛɛ̀ trṻṻjɛɛ̀) astronomical instruments, astroscope.

གནམ་དཔྱད་རྩིས་གཞི་ (nāmjɛɛ̀ dzi̋ishi) astronomical unit or formula.

གནམ་དཔྱད་རིག་པ་ (nāmjɛɛ̀ rigbə) astronomy.

གནམ་དཔྱད་རིག་པ་བ་ (nāmjɛɛ̀ rigbəwə) astronomer.

གནམ་དཔྱད་ཤེས་བྱ་སྐྱབ་གདལ་ཁང་ (nāmjɛɛ̀ shēèja kyəbdɛɛgaŋ) sm. གནམ་དཔྱད་ཁང་.

གནམ་འཕག་ས་མཆོངས་ (nāmpaà sācoŋ) hopping/ and skipping, jumping with joy; va.—བྱེད་.

གནམ་དབྱིངས་ (nāmyib) the sky, the heavens.

གནམ་འབབ་ (nām bəb) vi. to rain.

གནམ་འབྲུག་སྐར་ཚོམ་ (nāmdruù gārdzom) the constellation Draco.

གནམ་སྦྲག (nāmdraà) airmail ༑ངས་ཡི་གེ་གཉིས་གནམ་སྦྲག་ཐོག་བཏང་བ་རེད་ I sent two letters via airmail.

གནམ་དམག (nāmmaà) airforce.

གནམ་ཚོགས་ཁང་ (nāmdzii̋gaŋ) observatory.

གནམ་མཚན་ (nāmdzɛn) weather conditions, climate.

གནམ་མཚོ་ (nāmdzo) Namtso Lake in Tibet.

གནམ་ཟླ་ (nāmda) sm. ནམ་ཟླ་.
གནམ་གཟེར་ (nāmser) wooden poles used in tents/ yurts.
གནམ་འོག (nām wɔ̄ɔ̀) the world ༎ གནམ་འོག་ན་རྒྱལ་ཁབ་མང་པོ་འདུག There are many countries in the world. [Lit. under the sky].
གནམ་འོག་གཅིག་དུ་ (nāmwɔ̄ɔ̀ jīgdu) sm. གནམ་འོག་ཡོངས་སུ་.
གནམ་འོག་ཡོངས་སུ་ (nāmwɔ̄ɔ̀ yo̲ŋsu) to everyone, universal [Lit. to all under the sky].
གནམ་ཡངས་ཀ་བ་བཞི་ (nāmyaŋ gāwa shi̲) a shelter/ house with a roof held up by four pillars but with no sides.
གནམ་ཡིག (nəmyii̍) letters that fell from the sky.
གནམ་ཡེར་ (nāmyer) clear sky/ weather.
གནམ་ཡོལ་ (nāmyöö) material (e.g., cloth) that covers a ceiling.
གནམ་གཡེར་ (nāmyer) sm. གནམ་ཡེར་.
གནམ་གཡོ་ས་འགུལ་ (nāmyo sāngüü) a stupendous event/ achievement [Lit. sky move, earth move].
གནམ་རི་སྲོང་བཙན་ (nāmri sōŋdzɛn) the father of King Songtsen Gampo.
གནམ་རིག (nəmrii̍) astronomy.
གནམ་རིག་གི་ཉེ་མཐོང་རྒྱང་ཤེལ་ (nəmrii̍gi ñego gya̲ŋshee) astronomical telescope.
གནམ་རིག་བརྟག་དཔྱད་ཁང་ (nəmrii̍ dāgjɛ̀ɛ̀gaŋ) observatory.
གནམ་རིག་བརྟག་དཔྱད་འཕྲུལ་ཆས་ (nəmrii̍ dāgjɛ̀ɛ̀ trü̃üjɛ̀ɛ̀) astronomical instruments.
གནམ་རུ་ (nəmru) bow (the weapon).
གནམ་རློན་པ་ (nām lȭnba) humid.
གནམ་ལ་སྐས་ཀ་འཛུགས་ (nāmla gɛ̄ɛ̀ga dzu̲ù) sth. impossible [Lit. putting a ladder to the sky].
གནམ་ལ་སྐས་འགོས་མི་སླེབ (nāmla gɛ̄ngöö mi̲ñeg) sth. impossible [Lit. one cannot reach the sky by climbing a ladder].
གནམ་ལ་སླེབ་འདྲའི་ཁང་ཆེན་ (nāmla ñēgdɛ kā̲ŋjen) a skyscraper.
གནམ་ལ་སྟོན་ (nāmla dȭn) va. to face towards the sky.
གནམ་ལ་ཐུག་པའི་ས་ (nāmla tūgbɛ sā) a flat high place or plain with no mountains.
གནམ་ལ་བྱ་རྒྱ་ ས་ལ་བྱི་རྒྱ་ (nāmla ca̲gya sāla ci̲gya) sm. གནམ་རྒྱ་ས་རྡེ་.
གནམ་ལ་སྦར་འཛིན་དང་ས་ལ་རྡོག་རྡོ་ (nāmla ba̲ndzin da̲ŋ sāla də̲gdo) doing sth. that is extraordinary [Lit. grasping the sky and kicking the earth].
གནམ་ལངས་ (nāmlaŋ) sm.* ནམ་ལངས་.
གནམ་ལངས་རྒྱག (nāmlaŋ gya̲à) va. to rear (for horses).

གནམ་ལོ་ (nāmlo) year (used in reference to the New Year).
གནམ་ལོ་གསར་པ་ (nāmlo sārba) the New Year.
གནམ་ལོ་གསར་བཞད་ (nāmlo sārshɛ̀ɛ̀) arrival of new year ༎ གནམ་ལོ་གསར་བཞད་ཀྱི་སྔ་ནུབ་ New Year's eve.
གནམ་ལོ་གསར་ཚེས་ (nāmlo sārdzeè) sm. གནམ་ལོ་གསར་བཞད་.
གནམ་ལོ་གསར་དུ་བཞད་ (nāmlo sārdu shɛ̲̀ɛ̀) sm. གནམ་ལོ་གསར་བཞད་.
གནམ་གཤིས་ (nəmshii̍) 1. climate, weather. 2. meteorology.
གནམ་གཤིས་ཀྱི་སྔོན་བརྡ (nəmshii̍gi ŋ̄öndaà) weather forecasting.
གནམ་གཤིས་ཀྱི་སྔོན་བརྡ་ (nəmshii̍gi ŋ̄öndaà) weather forecasting; va.—གཏོང་.
གནམ་གཤིས་ཀྱི་ཆ་རྐྱེན་ (nəmshii̍gi cāgyen) weather/ climatic conditions.
གནམ་གཤིས་ཀྱི་རིག་པ་ (nəmshii̍gi rigbə) meteorology.
གནམ་གཤིས་འགྱུར་ལྡོག་གི་གནས་ཚུལ་ (nəmshii̍ gyu̲ndɔ̄ɔ̀gi nɛ̄ɛ̀dzüü) meteorological information.
གནམ་གཤིས་སྔོན་བསྙགས་ (nəmshii̍ ŋ̄öndraà) weather forecasting.
གནམ་གཤིས་སྔོན་བསྙགས་པ་ (nəmshii̍ ŋ̄öndraà) weather forecaster, meteorologist.
གནམ་གཤིས་སྔོན་བརྡ་བརྡ་ཚན་སྒར་ (nəmshii̍ ŋ̄öndaà da̲dzɛngɔ̄ɔ̀) weather forecast team.
གནམ་གཤིས་སྔོན་བརྡ་བརྡ་ཞབས་ཞུ་ཁྲུའུ་ (nəmshii̍ ŋ̄öndaàda sh̲əbji trū) tib.ch. weather forecast service office.
གནམ་གཤིས་སྔོན་བརྡ་ (nəmshii̍ ŋ̄önda) weather forecast; va.—གཏོང་.
གནམ་གཤིས་སྔོན་བརྡའི་འཕྲུལ་འཁོར་ (nəmshii̍ ŋ̄öndɛ trü̃ügɔ̀ɔ̀) weather forecasting machine/ equipment.
གནམ་གཤིས་བརྟག་དཔྱད་ཀྱི་ལེ་ད་ (nəmshii̍ dāgjɛ̀ɛ̀gi le̲da) tib.ch. meteorological radar.
གནམ་གཤིས་བརྟག་དཔྱད་ཁང་ (nəmshii̍ dāgjɛ̀ɛ̀gaŋ) weather station, meteorological station/ observatory.
གནམ་གཤིས་བརྟག་དཔྱད་འཁོར་སྐར་ (nəmshii̍ dāgjɛ̀ɛ̀ kɔ̄ɔ̀gar) meteorological satellite, weather forecasting satellite.
གནམ་གཤིས་བརྟག་དཔྱད་ཅུའུ་ (nəmshii̍ dāgjɛ̀ɛ̀ jū) tib.ch. bureau of meteorology.
གནམ་གཤིས་བརྟག་དཔྱད་བྱེད་མཁན་ (nəmshii̍ dāgjɛ̀ɛ̀ ce̲èñɛn) meteorologist.
གནམ་གཤིས་བརྟག་དཔྱད་ལས་ཁུངས་ (nəmshii̍ dāgjɛ̀ɛ̀ lɛ̲̀ɛ̀guŋ) meteorological observatory, weather analysis office.
གནམ་གཤིས་བརྟག་དཔྱད་ས་ཚིགས་ (nəmshii̍ dāgjɛ̀ɛ̀ sədzii̍) meteorological/ weather station.
གནམ་གཤིས་བརྟག་དཔྱད་སློབ་གྲྭ་ (nəmshii̍ dāgjɛ̀ɛ̀ lōbdra) school of meteorology.
གནམ་གཤིས་ལྟ་དཔྱོད་ཁང་ (nəmshii̍ dājöögaŋ) weather observatory, weather/ meteorological observation station.
གནམ་གཤིས་དྲོ་དྲང་གི་ཚད་ (nəmshii̍ tro̲draŋgi tsɛ̄ɛ̀) temperature (of the atmosphere).
གནམ་གཤིས་གནས་ཚུལ་ (nəmshii̍ nɛ̄ɛ̀dzüü) weather conditions.
གནམ་གཤིས་ཚན་རིག་ཞིབ་འཇུག་ཁང་ (nəmshii̍ tsɛ̄nrii̍ shi̲mjuùgaŋ) institute of meteorology.
གནམ་གཤིས་རིག་པ་ (nəmshii̍ ri̲gbə) meteorology.
གནམ་གཤིས་ལས་དོན་ (nəmshii̍ lɛ̲̀ɛ̀dön) meteorological work.
གནམ་གཤིས་ས་ཁྲ་ (nəmshii̍ sābdra) weather map, climatological map.
གནམ་གཤིས་ས་ཚིགས་ (nəmshii̍ sədzii̍) sm. གནམ་གཤིས་བརྟག་དཔྱད་ཁང་.
གནམ་གཤིས་སོ་ལྟ་ཁང་ (nəmshii̍ sōdagaŋ) weather post/ observatory.
གནམ་ས་ (nāmsa) 1. sky/ heaven and earth. 2. vi.—ཤོར་ to be a great or immense difference between sth. ༎ ཁང་པ་འདི་གཉིས་ཡག་ཉེས་གནམ་ས་ཤོར་བཞག The difference in quality between these two houses is immense.
གནམ་ས་ཁ་རྡེབ (nāmsa kādeb) a state of great turmoil/ shock/ disturbance [Lit. the sky and earth banging into each other].
གནམ་ས་ཁ་སྦྱར་ (nāmsa kājar) a great lie, confusing right and wrong, standing facts on their head [Lit. sky and earth joined together].
གནམ་ས་ཁ་འཛོལ་ (nāmsa kāndzöö) sm. གནམ་ས་ཤོར་.
གནམ་ས་ཁ་ལོ་བསྒྱུར་ (nāmsa kālo gyu̲r) vi. to change totally, to affect a drastic/ earthshaking change [Lit. change sky and earth).
གནམ་ས་འཁོར་ (nāmsa kɔ̄ɔ̀) vi. to feel dizzy/ giddy.
གནམ་ས་ག་འཛོལ་ (nāmsa ka̲ndzöö) sm. གནམ་ས་ཁ་འཛོལ་.
གནམ་ས་སྒྱུར་ (nāmsa gyu̲r) sm. གནམ་ས་ཁ་ལོ་བསྒྱུར་.
གནམ་ས་ལྟ་འོག་སྒྱུར་ (nāmsa lāwɔ̄ɔ̀ gyu̲r) sm. གནམ་ས་ཁ་ལོ་བསྒྱུར་.
གནམ་ས་མགོ་ཏིང་ལོག (nāmsa go̲diŋ lɔ̄ɔ̀) sm. གནམ་ས་གཡོ་བ་.
གནམ་ས་ལྟ་འོག་འགྱུར་ (nāmsa lāwɔ̄ɔ̀ gyu̲r) sm. གནམ་ས་གཡོ་.
གནམ་ས་གཡོ་ (nāmsa yō) shaking/ startling the universe, incredible, world shaking ༎ གནམ་ས་

གཡོ་བའི་ལི་དབར་ 25,000 གི་རྒྱང་བསྐྱོད་བྱས་ནས་ Having made the 25,000 li world shaking " Long March."

གནམ་ས་ཤོར་ (nāmsa shɔ̄ɔ) see གནམ་ས་.

གནམ་སའི་ཁྱད་པར་ (nāmsɛ kyɛ̀ɛbar) a great difference/ disparity [Lit. difference between sky and earth].

གནམ་སའི་དྲག་ཤུགས་ (nāmsɛ tragshuù) air and ground power.

གནམ་སའི་ཚུལ་དང་མཐུན་པ་ (nāmsɛ tsūūdaŋ tūmbə) shung. in compliance/ harmony with the will of heaven and earth ¶ ད་ལྟ་བདག་གིས་གནམ་སའི་ཚུལ་དང་མཐུན་པར་རྒྱལ་ཁྲིམས་དང་བྱ་དགའ་སྟོང་བ་ལ་ In compliance with the will of heaven and earth and demonstrating the magnanimity of my administration.

གནམ་བསིལ་པོ་ (nām sīibu) cold/ chilly weather.

གནམ་གསོར་ (nāmsɔɔ) a drill.

གནམ་ལྷ་ (nāmlha) god, deity.

གནམ་ཨ་སྔོན་ (nām āŋön) sky.

གནའ་ (nā) 1. sm. གནའ་སྔ་མོ་. 2. abbr. of གནའ་བ་.

གནའ་བཀུར་གནའ་ལད་ (nāgur nālɛɛ̀) highly traditional.

གནའ་ཁྱེར་དེང་སྨད་ (nākyee teŋmɛɛ̀) disparaging the present and extolling the past.

གནའ་གླུ་ད་ལེན་ (nālu talen) behaving in an old fashioned way [Lit. singing old songs in the present].

གནའ་གོད་ (nāgöö) sm. གནའ་བ་.

གནའ་སྔ་མོ་ (nālu ŋāmo) ancient times, antiquity.

གནའ་ཉམས་དོད་པོ་ (nāñam tööbo) classically beautiful, elegant.

གནའ་གཏམ་ (nādam) old/ ancient saying.

གནའ་བསྟོད་དེང་སྨད་ (nādöö teŋmɛɛ̀) praising old customs and degrading current customs; va.—བྱེད་.

གནའ་དུས་ (nədüü) ancient times, antiquity.

གནའ་དུས་ཀྱི་ཆ་ལུགས་ (nədüügi cəluù) ancient fashion/ style.

གནའ་དུས་ཀྱི་ལུགས་སྲོལ་ (nədüügi lugsöö) sm. གནའ་སྲོལ་.

གནའ་དེང་ (nādeŋ) ancient and contemporary ¶ གནའ་དེང་མི་སྣ་ Ancient and contemporary personages.

གནའ་དྲངས་དེང་དཔྱད་ (nādraŋ teŋjɛɛ̀) use the past to investigate the present.

གནའ་དྲངས་དེང་སྒྲུབ་ (nādraŋ teŋdrub) accomplishing today's work using ancient (methods).

གནའ་དཔེ་ (nābe) classical proverb/ saying.

གནའ་ཕྲུག་ (nədruù) baby blue sheep.

གནའ་བ་ (nāā) blue sheep (a type of wild mountain sheep).

གནའ་བོ་ (nāwo) primeval, ancient, classical ¶ གནའ་བོའི་གྲོང་ཁྱེར་ Ancient city.

གནའ་བོའི་གླང་གོད་ (nāwö lāŋgöö) mammoth (the extinct elephant-like animal).

གནའ་བོའི་སྙན་ངག་ (nāwö ñɛ̄nŋaà) old/ ancient poetry.

གནའ་བོའི་མི་བརྒྱུད་གནད་དོན་སྐོར་གྱི་ལས་ཁང་ (nāwö migyüù nɛ̄ɛ̀döngɔɔgi lɛɛgaŋ) Bureau of Indian Affairs (in U.S.A.).

གནའ་བོའི་རྩོམ་རིག་ (nāwö dzōmrii) classical/ ancient literature.

གནའ་བོའི་ཡིག་ཚགས་ཁང་ (nāwö yigdzaàgaŋ) archives ¶ རྒྱལ་ཡོངས་གནའ་བོའི་ཡིག་ཚགས་ཁང་ National Archives.

གནའ་བོའི་རིག་གཞུང་གཅེས་སྐྱོང་ཞིབ་འཇུག་ཁང་ (nāwö rigshuŋ jēegyoŋ shimjugaŋgaŋ) Cultural Survival (the organization). ¶

གནའ་བོའི་གསུང་རབ་ (nāwö sūŋrəb) classical/ ancient text.

གནའ་མི་ (nāmi) ancient people, primitive man.

གནའ་མོ་ (namo) ancient, classical ¶ གནའ་མོའི་གྲོང་ཁྱེར་ Ancient city.

གནའ་མོའི་རོལ་མོ་ (namö röömo) classical music.

གནའ་རྫས་ (nādzɛɛ̀) antiques, curios, ancient artifacts.

གནའ་རྫས་ཀོ་འཚོལ་ (nādzɛɛ̀ göndzöö) archaeological excavation.

གནའ་རྫས་འགྲེམས་སྟོན་ཁང་ (nādzɛɛ̀ dremdöngaŋ) sm. གནའ་རྫས་བཤམས་སྟོན་ཁང་.

གནའ་རྫས་རྟོག་ཞིབ་ (nādzɛɛ̀ dōgshib) archaeology.

གནའ་རྫས་རྟོག་ཞིབ་པ་ (nādzɛɛ̀ dōgshibə) archaeologist.

གནའ་རྫས་རྟོག་ཞིབ་རིག་པ་ (nādzɛɛ̀ dōgshib rigbə) archaeology.

གནའ་རྫས་བབ་ཆགས་ (nādzɛɛ̀ bəbjaà) primitive and crude.

གནའ་རྫས་རྙིང་ཤུལ་ (nādzɛɛ̀ ñīŋshüü) relics and artifacts.

གནའ་རྫས་ཞིབ་དཔྱོད་ (nādzɛɛ̀ shibjöö) sm. གནའ་རྫས་ལ་རྟོག་ཞིབ་.

གནའ་རྫས་ལ་རྟོག་ཞིབ་ (nādzɛɛ̀la dōgshib) archaeological investigation.

གནའ་རྫས་ལ་རྟོག་ཞིབ་མཁས་པ་ (nādzɛɛ̀la dōgshib kɛ̄ɛ̀ba) archaeologist.

གནའ་རྫས་རྟོག་ཞིབ་རིག་པ་ (nādzɛɛ̀la dōgshib rigbə) archaeology.

གནའ་རྫས་དཔྱད་ཞིབ་ (nādzɛɛ̀ jɛ̄ɛ̀shib) archaeological research.

གནའ་རྫས་བཤམས་སྟོན་ཁང་ (nādzɛɛ̀ shāmdöngaŋ) archaeological museum.

གནའ་གཞུང་ (nāshuŋ) ancient books.

གནའ་གཞུང་རྩོམ་རིག་ (nāshuŋ dzōmrig) classical literature.

གནའ་གཞུང་རིང་ལུགས་ (nāshuŋ riŋluù) classicism.

གནའ་ཟོག་ (nāsog) sm. གནའ་རྫས་.

གནའ་ཟོག་ཞིབ་དཔྱོད་ (nāsog shibjöö) sm. གནའ་རྫས་ལ་རྟོག་ཞིབ་.

གནའ་བཟང་དེང་སྤྱོད་ (nāsaŋ tenjöö) using the good traditions from the past for the present.

གནའ་ཡིག་ (nəyig) prose written in classical literary style.

གནའ་གཡག་ (nāyaà) sm. གནའ་བ་.

གནའ་རབས་ (nərəb) ancient, antique, paleo-, classical ¶ གནའ་རབས་མིའི་རིགས་རིག་པ་ Paleontology.

གནའ་རབས་སྐྱེ་དངོས་ (nərəb gyēŋöö) paleontological finds.

གནའ་རབས་ཀྱི་སྐྱེ་དངོས་རིག་པ་ (nərəbgi gyēŋoö rigbə) paleontology.

གནའ་རབས་ཀྱི་རྗེས་ཤུལ་ (nərəbgi jeeshüü) ancient remnants/ ruins/ site, an excavation of an ancient site.

གནའ་རབས་ཀྱི་གཏམ་དཔེ་ (nərəbgi dāmbe) old proverb/ saying.

གནའ་རབས་ཀྱི་བར་དུས་ (nərəbgi pardüü) medieval period, the Middle Ages.

གནའ་རབས་ཀྱི་སྨན་ཐོ་ (nərəbgi mɛ̄ndo) ancient medical prescription.

གནའ་རབས་ཀྱི་ལོ་རྒྱུས་ (nərəbgi lugyüù) ancient history.

གནའ་རབས་མིའི་རིགས་རིག་པ་ (nərəb miirig rigbə) paleoanthropology, paleontology.

གནའ་རབས་རྩོམ་རིག་ (nərəb dzōmrig) ancient literature.

གནའ་ལུགས་ (nəluù) ancient customs/ style ¶ གནའ་ལུགས་ཞབས་བྲོ་ Ancient style dance.

གནའ་ཤ་ (nəsha) meat of the blue sheep.

གནའ་ཤུལ་ (nəshüü) sm. གནའ་རབས་ཀྱི་རྗེས་ཤུལ་.

གནའ་ཤུལ་གནས་མཆོག་ (nəshüü nɛ̄ɛ̀jɔɔ) a famous ancient (archaeological) site.

གནའ་ཤུལ་འཛུགས་སྐྲུན་ (nəshüü dzugdrün) restoration of ancient sites.

གནའ་གཤིས་ (nəshii) ancient customs/ habits/ ways of behaving.

གནའ་སྲོལ་ (nāsöö) sm. གནའ་ལུགས་.

གནའ་གསོ་ (nāso) restoring ancient ways, returning to ancient customs; va.—བྱེད་.

གནའ་གསོ་ཕྱིར་ནུར་ (nāso cīrnur) restoring ancient

ways and going/ moving backwards.

གནའ་གསོ་ཕྱིར་བཤོལ་ (nāso cīrshöö) sm. གནའ་གསོ་ཕྱིར་ནུར་.

གནའ་གསོའི་རིང་ལུགས་ (nāsö rinluù) the doctrine of "restoring the ancient."

གནས་ (nɛ̄ɛ̀) 1. place, site; va.—གཏོང་; —སྦྱིན་ to give shelter, to give a place to live. 2. vi. to exist ། འབྲས་ལྗོངས་བོད་རྒྱལ་ཁབ་ཀྱི་ཆབ་འབངས་སུ་གནས་ཡོད་པ་རེད་ Sikkim existed as a subject of Tibet. 3. va. to live, to stay ། ང་འདིར་ལོ་གཉིས་གནས་པའི་རིང་ While I was staying here for two years. 4. vi. to cost ། དེབ་འདིར་སྒོར་མོ་གཉིས་གནས་ཀྱི་ཡོད་པ་རེད་ This book costs two dollars. 5. abbr. of གནས་ཚུལ་ ། བོད་གནས་ལྟ་རྟོག་བྱེད་ Looking at conditions in Tibet. 6. rank ། གནས་ལྔ་པ་ The fifth rank (in the traditional Tibetan government). 7. basis, cause ། ཁྱེད་རང་གི་སྐད་ཆ་དེ་གད་མོའི་གནས་རེད་ Your comment will cause people to laugh. 8. a part of a loom.

གནས་ཀྱི་དངོས་པོ་ (nɛ̄ɛ̀gi ŋȫòbo) household furniture/ things.

གནས་ཀྱི་སློབ་མ་ (nɛ̄ɛ̀gi lōbma) a disciple who remains close to his teacher.

གནས་སྐབས་ (nɛ̄ɛ̀gəb) temporary, for the time being, provisional ། གནས་སྐབས་ང་བོད་ལ་འགྲོ་གི་མིན་ For the time being I will not go to Tibet. ། གནས་སྐབས་ཀྱི་ཐག་གཅོད་ A temporary decision.

གནས་སྐབས་ཀྱི་ཐབས་ཚུལ་ (nɛ̄ɛ̀gəbgi tōbdzüü) a temporary arrangement/ measure.

གནས་སྐབས་ཀྱི་སྒྲོལ་ཡིག (nɛ̄ɛ̀gəbgi sȫòyig) provisional regulation/ measure/ rule.

གནས་སྐབས་ཆུ་རགས་ (nɛ̄ɛ̀gəb cūraà) temporary coffer dam.

གནས་སྐབས་བརྟན་ལྷིང་ (nɛ̄ɛ̀gəb dɛ̄nlhiŋ) temporary stability.

གནས་སྐབས་དམག་མཚམས་འཇོག (nɛ̄ɛ̀gəb māgdzam jɔ̄ɔ̀) va. a make a temporary truce/ armistice/ ceasefire.

གནས་སྐབས་རང་བཞིན་ (nɛ̄ɛ̀gəb rənshin) temporary situation ། ལུང་པའི་ནང་གི་ཞིང་ཆ་དེ་གནས་སྐབས་ཀྱི་རང་བཞིན་ཞིག་རེད་ The disturbances in this area are a temporary situation.

གནས་སྐབས་རིང་ (nɛ̄ɛ̀gəb riŋ) sm. གནས་སྐབས་.

གནས་སྐབས་ལམ་ཡིག (nɛ̄ɛ̀gəb ləmyig) shung. a permit that allows use of corvee transport services once only.

གནས་སྐབས་ལམ་སྲོལ་ (nɛ̄ɛ̀gəb ləmsöö) temporary rules and regulations.

གནས་སྐབས་སྲིད་གཞུང་ (nɛ̄ɛ̀gəb sīishuŋ) temporary government, caretaker goverment, provisional goverment.

གནས་སྐོར་ (nɛ̄ɛ̀gɔɔ) pilgrimage; va.—ལ་འགྲོ་ to go on a pilgrimage.

གནས་སྐོར་བ་ (nɛ̄ɛ̀gɔɔwa) pilgrims, people on pilgrimage.

གནས་ཁང་ (nɛ̄ɛ̀gaŋ̄) house, dwelling.

གནས་འཁོད་ (nɛ̄ɛ̀göö) residing, living, va.—བྱེད་ to live, to inhabit ། དེ་ར་དམག་མི་སུམ་སྟོང་ཙམ་གནས་འཁོད་བྱེད་བཞིན་ཡོད་ཀྱང་ Even though three thousand soldiers reside there.

གནས་འཁོད་པ་ (nɛ̄ɛ̀gööba) resident, settler, inhabitant ། ལྷ་སར་གནས་འཁོད་པ་ a resident of Lhasa.

གནས་འཁོད་བཞུགས་སྒར་ (nɛ̄ɛ̀göö shuùgar) settlement ། བོད་མི་གནས་འཁོད་བཞུགས་སྒར་སོ་སོར་ At each of the Tibetan settlements.

གནས་ཀྱི་ཐིག་ལེ་ (nɛ̄ɛ̀gi tīgle) the main characteristics/ essence of a location.

གནས་གོང་ (nɛ̄ɛ̀goŋ) price, value, worth ། གནས་གོང་ཆེ་བའི་ཅ་ལག Things that have high price/ value.

གནས་གླ་ (nɛ̄ɛ̀la) rent, lodging fee.

གནས་འགྱུར་ (nɛ̄ngyur) transformation, transmutation, changes in circumstances/ positions.

གནས་མགྲོན་ (nɛ̄ndrön) 1. inn on a road. 2. guest at an inn. 3. shung. abbr. of གནས་ཚང་ and མགྲོན་པོ་.

གནས་སྒོ་འབྱེད་ (nɛ̄ɛ̀ go jeè) va. to recognize/ accept/ confirm a holy (pilgrimage) site for the first time.

གནས་སྒོ་འགྲིམས་ (nɛ̄ɛ̀go drim) va. to leave one's home to go as a bride.

གནས་ངན་མ་ (nɛ̄ɛ̀ ŋɛnma) a girl who is still attached to her parent's house after she has gone to another house as a bride.

གནས་ངན་ལེན་ (nɛ̄ɛ̀ŋɛn len) 1. vi. to get a lower form of existence because of bad karma. 2. vi. to get born handicapped.

གནས་ངེས་མེད་ (nɛ̄ɛ̀ŋeè meè) not having a permanent residence.

གནས་ལྔ་ (nɛ̄ɛ̀ŋa) five points in the body (the middle of the head, the throat, the heart, navel and genitals).

གནས་བཅའ་ (nɛ̄ɛ̀ jāā) va. to settle (in terms of residence).

གནས་བཅའ་ས་ (nɛ̄ɛ̀ jāsa) place where one has permanent residence, place where one has settled permanently.

གནས་བཅས་ (nɛ̄ɛ̀ jɛ̄ɛ̀) p. of གནས་བཅའ་.

གནས་ཆ་ (nɛ̄ɛ̀ja) steadiness.

གནས་ཆགས་ (nɛ̄ɛ̀ cāà) vi. to get settled permanently.

གནས་ཆུང་ (nɛ̄ɛ̀juŋ) 1. sm. གནས་ཆུང་དགོན་. 2. sm. གནས་ཆུང་ཆོས་སྐྱོང་.

གནས་ཆུང་དགོན་ (nɛ̄ɛ̀juŋ gön) Nechung monastery (the residence of the Nechung oracle).

གནས་ཆུང་ཆོས་སྐྱོང་ (nɛ̄ɛ̀juŋ cȫògyoŋ) one of the main protector dieties and state oracles of Tibet and the Dalai Lama.

གནས་ཆུང་ཆོས་རྒྱལ་ (nɛ̄ɛ̀juŋ cȫògyɛɛ) sm. གནས་ཆུང་ཆོས་སྐྱོང་.

གནས་ཆུང་སྐུ་བླ་མ་ (nɛ̄ɛ̀juŋ dā lāma) the medium of གནས་ཆུང་ཆོས་སྐྱོང་ who holds the title of སྐུ་བླ་མ་.

གནས་ཆེན་ (nɛ̄ɛ̀jen) famous pilgrimage sites.

གནས་ཆེན་ལྔ་ (nɛ̄ɛ̀jen nā) the five important pilgrimage sites of Buddhism.

གནས་མཆོག (nɛ̄ɛ̀jɔɔ̀) 1. holy land/ place, place of pilgrimage. 2. an important/ significant site.

གནས་མཆོད་ (nɛ̄ɛ̀ cȫò) going on pilgrimage and giving offerings.

གནས་མཇལ་ (nɛ̄njɛɛ) sm. གནས་སྐོར་.

གནས་མཇལ་ཚོགས་པ་ (nɛ̄njɛɛ tsɔ̄gba) a group of people on a pilgrimage together.

གནས་འཇིག (nɛ̄njig) sm. ཆགས་འཇིག.

གནས་གཏོང་ (nɛ̄ɛ̀ dōŋ) see གནས་.

གནས་རྟེན་ (nɛ̄ɛ̀den) 1. base, station ། མཚོ་དམག་གི་གནས་རྟེན་ Naval base. 2. pilgrimage site, holy place.

གནས་རྟེན་པ་ (nɛ̄ɛ̀demba) sm. གནས་པོ་.

གནས་སྟངས་ (nɛ̄ɛ̀daŋ) status, situation, condition ། དེང་སང་བོད་ནང་གི་གནས་སྟངས་སྐོར་གོ་རྒྱུ་མི་འདུག These days we don't hear anything about the situation in Tibet.

གནས་བརྟན་ (nɛ̄ɛ̀dɛn) term of address (previously) used by a younger gelong to address an older gelong.

གནས་བརྟན་བཅུ་དྲུག (nɛ̄ɛ̀dɛn jūdruù) the 16 arhats.

གནས་བརྟན་པའི་སྡེ་པ་ (nɛ̄ɛ̀dɛnbɛ deba) one of the four main schools of Hinayana Buddhism.

གནས་ཐང་ (nɛ̄ɛ̀daŋ) value, worth ། དེང་སང་རའི་ཁུ་ལུ་གནས་ཐང་ཆེན་པོ་འདུག These days cashmere has great value.

གནས་ཐབས་བྱེད་ (nɛ̄ɛ̀dəb ceè) va. to preserve, to maintain ། བོད་ཀྱི་རིག་གཞུང་གནས་ཐབས་བྱེད་དགོས་ We have to preserve Tibetan culture.

གནས་ཐུབ་ (nɛ̄ɛ̀ tūb) vi. to be able stand on one's own two feet ། བོད་རིགས་གནས་ཐུབ་པ་བྱེད་དགོས་ Tibetans have to stand on their own two feet.

གནས་མཐོ་ (nɛ̄ɛ̀do) high rank/ position.

གནས་མཐོ་རྒྱུ་ཆེ་ (nɛ̄ɛ̀do gyuce) sm. གནས་མཐོ་འབྱོར་ཆེ་.

གནས་མཐོ་དབང་ཆེ་ (nɛ̀ɛdo wāŋce) powerful and influential, having high rank/ position and great power.

གནས་མཐོ་འབྱོར་ཆེ་ (nɛ̀ɛdo jɔ̄ɔce) having high rank/ position and wealth.

གནས་དུས་ (nɛ̀ɛdüü) times and circumstances, place and time ¶ གནས་དུས་ལ་དཔག་པའི་སྲིད་ཇུས་གཏན་འབེབས་བྱ་དགོས་ (We) must decide strategy in accordance with the time and circumstances.

གནས་དུས་ཚོད་རྩིས་ (nɛ̀ɛdüü tsōōdzii) tactics based on the times and circumstances, taking into account the time and circumstances ¶ ང་ཚོ་བོད་ཤོར་ནས་རྒྱ་གར་ས་ཐོག་ཏུ་ཡོང་དུས་གཞུང་ཞབས་ཚོས་གནས་དུས་ཚོད་རྩིས་ཀྱིས་སྣེ་ལེན་སྔར་བཞིན་བྱས་མ་བྱུང་ When we came to India after losing Tibet, the (Indian) government officials took into account the circumstances and didn't receive us as they had in the past.(since we now were powerless).

གནས་དུས་བཟང་བསྟུན་ (གྱིས་) (nɛ̀ɛdüü səŋdün) in accordance with appropriate times and circumstances.

གནས་བདག་ (nɛ̀ɛdaà) proprietor/ head of an inn or hotel.

གནས་བདེ་དུས་འཇགས་ (nɛ̀ɛde tüüjaà) good circumstances and peaceful times.

གནས་སྡོད་ (nɛ̀ɛdöö) living, residing; va.—བྱེད་ to live, to reside ¶ ཨ་རི་ར་གནས་སྡོད་བྱེད་མཁན་ཚོས་ By those living in America.

གནས་ནས་འཕྱུང་ (nɛ̀ɛnɛ cūŋ) sm. གནས་དབྱུང་གཏོང་.

གནས་པ་ཆེན་པོ་ (nɛ̀ɛba cēmbo) expensive.

གནས་པོ་ (nɛ̀ɛbo) innkeeper.

གནས་སྤར་ (nɛ̀ɛbar) promotion; va.—སྤེལ་; བྱེད་ to promote ¶ ཁོང་རིམ་པ་བཞི་པ་ནས་གསུམ་པར་གནས་སྤར་བྱས་པ་རེད་ (They) promoted him from the fourth to the third rank.

གནས་སྤོ་ (nɛ̀ɛbo) 1. emigrating, moving residence; va.—བྱེད་ ¶ ཁོང་གིས་ལྷ་ས་ནས་རྒྱལ་རྩེར་གནས་སྤོ་བྱས་པ་རེད་ He moved his residence from Lhasa to Gyantse. 2. transferring from a position/ office. ¶ ཁོང་ལས་ཁུངས་གཞན་ཞིག་ཏུ་གནས་སྤོ་བྱས་འདུག He was transferred to another office.

གནས་སྤོའི་གློག་རྒྱུན་ (nɛ̀ɛbö lōggyün) displacement current.

གནས་སྤོར་ (nɛ̀ɛbɔɔ) sm. གནས་སྤར་.

གནས་སྤོས་ (nɛ̀ɛböö) p. of གནས་སྤོ་.

གནས་སྤོས་གཏོང་ (nɛ̀ɛböö dōŋ) va. to transfer.

གནས་སྤོས་ཕྱོགས་མི་ (nɛ̀ɛböö cɔ̄ɔmi) sm. གནས་སྤོས་ཡུལ་མི་.

གནས་སྤོས་ཡུལ་མི་ (nɛ̀ɛböö yüümi) settler, immigrant, colonist.

གནས་ཕབ་ (nɛ̀ɛ pāb) va. to demote ¶ བཀའ་བློན་ཁེ་སྨད་པ་ཛ་སག་ཏུ་གནས་ཕབ་ (He) demoted Kalon Khemed to dzasa.

གནས་པོ་ (nɛ̀ɛbo) innkeeper.

གནས་ཕྱོགས་ (nɛ̀ɛjɔ̀ɔ) 1. position, point of view ¶ སྲིད་དོན་གྱི་གནས་ཕྱོགས་ Political point of view. 2. place where one lives.

གནས་འཕར་ (nɛ̀ɛ pār) vi. to get promoted.

གནས་འཕར་རྒྱུ་འཕེལ་ (nɛ̄mbar gyubel) winning promotion and getting rich.

གནས་འཕོ་ (nɛ̀ɛ pō) 1. vi. to transmigrate (the “སེམས་”). 2. vi. to change residence. 3. vi. to change one's job/ position.

གནས་འཕྱུགས་ (nɛ̀ɛ cūù) vi. to make a mistake/ error ¶ བླང་དོར་གྱི་གནས་འཕྱུགས་པ་ To make a mistake on what one ought to do and what one ought not to do.

གནས་འཕྲིན་ (nɛ̄ndrin) 1. letter ¶ ཐུགས་རྗེ་ཆེ་ཞུའི་གནས་འཕྲིན་ཡང་ཕུལ་འདུག (They) also sent a letter of thanks. 2. newsletter.

གནས་འཕྲིན་ཚགས་པར་ (nɛ̄ndrin tsāgbar) newsletter.

གནས་བབ་ (nɛ̀ɛbəb) position, situation, standing, status, condition, occasion ¶ འཐབ་ཇུས་ཀྱི་གནས་བབ་ Strategic position. ¶ སྤྱི་ཚོགས་ཀྱི་གནས་བབ་ Social status.

གནས་བབ་ངན་པ་ (nɛ̀ɛbəb ŋɛmba) inferior situation/ condition.

གནས་བླ་མ་ (nɛ̀ɛ lāma) the lama in charge of a sacred place.

གནས་དབྱུང་ (nɛ̀ɛyuŋ) 1. demoting, demotion; va.—གཏོང་ to demote ¶ ཁོང་རིམ་པ་གསུམ་པ་ནས་བཞི་པར་གནས་དབྱུང་བཏང་བ་རེད་ He was demoted from 3rd rank to the 4th rank. 2. expelling, expulsion; va.—བྱེད་ to expel/ banish ¶ རྐུན་མ་དེ་རྒྱལ་ས་ནས་མཐའ་མཚམས་ལ་གནས་དབྱུང་བཏང་བ་རེད་ The thief was banished from the capital to the border.

གནས་དབྱུངས་ (nɛ̀ɛyuŋ) sm. གནས་དབྱུང་.

གནས་འབུད་ (nɛ̄mbüü) banishing, expelling; va.—གཏོང་; —བྱེད་.

གནས་འབེབས་ (nɛ̄mbeb) 1. va. to settle down. 2. sm. གནས་དབྱུང་གཏོང་.

གནས་མ་ (nɛ̀ɛma) a married woman.

གནས་མ་ཡིན་ (nɛ̀ɛ ma yin) unsuitable, inappropriate.

གནས་མང་གྲངས་ཀ་ (nɛ̀ɛmaŋ traŋga) a many digit number.

གནས་མལ་ (nɛ̀ɛmɛɛ) residence, place to stay at, dwelling.

གནས་མལ་ཐང་དང་བཟའ་བཏུང་རླུང་གྲོད་སྐྱོད་ (nɛ̀ɛmɛɛ tāŋdaŋ səduŋ lūŋdröö jöö) the hardship of traveling [Lit. to eat in open air in the midst of the wind blowing and to sleep on the plain].

གནས་མིག་ (nɛ̀ɛmig) a part of a loom.

གནས་མིང་ (nɛ̀ɛmiŋ) 1. name of a place. 2. name of a pilgrimage site.

གནས་མིན་ (nɛ̀ɛmin) sm. གནས་མ་ཡིན་.

གནས་མེད་ (nɛ̀ɛmeè) homeless.

གནས་མེད་འཁྱམས་པོ་ (nɛ̀ɛmeè kyāmbo) destitute and homeless.

གནས་མེད་ཕྱོགས་འཁྱར་ (nɛ̀ɛmeè cɔ̄ɔgyar) sm. གནས་མེད་འཁྱམས་པོ་.

གནས་མེད་ཡུལ་འཁྱར་ (nɛ̀ɛmeè yüügyar) sm. གནས་མེད་འཁྱམས་པོ་.

གནས་མོ་ (nɛ̀ɛmo) 1. innkeeper (female). 2. woman of the house.

གནས་ཚང་ (nɛ̀ɛdzaŋ) hotel, inn; va.—གཡར་ to rent a room in an inn or hotel (either the person seeking the room or the inn owner); va.—གཏོང་ .to rent a room to sb. ¶ གནས་ཚང་གཡར་རོགས་གནང་ Please rent me a room. ¶ ཁོང་གིས་ང་ལ་གནས་ཚང་བཏང་བྱུང་ He rented me a room.

གནས་ཚད་ (nɛ̀ɛdzɛɛ) 1. level, standard ¶ ཁོང་གི་དབྱིན་ཇིའི་སྐད་ཡིག་གི་ གནས་ཚད་མཐོ་ལོས་ཡོད་དམ་ What is the level of his knowledge of English? 2. coordinate (in math).

གནས་ཚད་མཐོ་པོ་ (nɛ̀ɛdzɛɛ tōbo) high standard/ level.

གནས་ཚིག་ (nɛ̀ɛdzii) a noun indicating location.

གནས་ཚུགས་ (nɛ̀ɛdzuù) settling down somewhere.

གནས་ཚུལ་ (nɛ̀ɛdzüü) 1. conditions, circumstances, situation ¶ ཤན་ལྔའི་གནས་ཚུལ་རྟོག་ཞིབ་བྱས་པ་རེད་ (They) investigated the conditions in the five counties. 2. news, issues ¶ དེང་སྐབས་ཨ་མི་རི་ཀའི་ནང་གནས་ཚུལ་ཆེ་ཤོས་དམག་འཁྲུག་གསར་པ་དེ་རེད་ These days in America the biggest news is the new war.

གནས་ཚུལ་བསྒྲགས་ (nɛ̀ɛdzüü draà) p. of གནས་ཚུལ་སྒྲོག.

གནས་ཚུལ་སྒྲོག (nɛ̀ɛdzüü drɔ̄ɔ) va. to report/ publicize news ¶ རྩ་ཁྲིམས་གསར་པ་བཟོས་པའི་གནས་ཚུལ་བསྒྲགས་པ་རེད་ They publicized the making of a new constitution.

གནས་ཚུལ་ངོ་མ་ (nɛ̀ɛdzüü ŋoma) real facts, true situation ¶ གནས་ཚུལ་ངོ་མ་དེ་གསལ་པོ་ཤེས་མ་བྱུང་ I didn't know clearly the true situation.

གནས་ཚུལ་དངོས་ (nɛ̀ɛdzüü ŋöö) sm. གནས་ཚུལ་ངོ་མ་.

གནས་ཚུལ་དངོས་གཞི་ (nɛ̀ɛdzüü ŋööshi) sm. གནས་ཚུལ་ངོ་མ་.

གནས་ཚུལ་མདོར་བསྡུས་ (nɛ̀ɛdzüü dordüü) news summary.

གནས་ཚུལ་འདྲི་ (nɛ̄ɛ̀dzüü tri) va. to ask about the news/ situation/ events.

གནས་ཚུལ་ཞུ་ (nɛ̄ɛ̀dzüü shu) va. to report, to give an account.

གནས་ཚུལ་ཞུ་ཡིག (nɛ̄ɛ̀dzüü shuyig) message/ report about a situation.

གནས་ཚུལ་ལ་གཞིགས་ (nɛ̄ɛ̀dzüülə shig) according to the situation/ condition/ news.

གནས་ཚུལ་ལ་བལྟ་ (nɛ̄ɛ̀dzüülə dā) va. to look at/ observe a situation ¶ གནས་ཚུལ་ལ་བལྟས་ནས་སྲིད་ཇུས་བཟོས་པ་རེད་ (They) looked at the situation and made a policy.

གནས་ཚུལ་ལྷག (nɛ̄ɛ̀dzüü lāà) vi. to have a problem or difficulty ¶ འདི་འདྲ་བྱས་ན་གནས་ཚུལ་ལྷག་གི་རེད་ If you do that there will be a problem.

གནས་ཞུའི་རྩོམ་རིག (nɛ̄ɛ̀shü dzōmrig) reportage.

གནས་གཞི་ (nɛ̄ɛ̀shi) 1. base ¶ མཚོ་དམག་གནས་གཞི་ Naval base. 2. shung. foundation for a settlement/ residence ¶ ཧོ་ཐོག་ཐུའི་མཚན་བཟོས་དང་གནས་གཞི་ར་སྒྲེང་བསྐུལ་བ་ He was given the title of Hutuktu and the possession of Reting as a base for a settlement. 3. location.

གནས་གཞིའི་ས་ཁུལ་ (nɛ̄ɛ̀shii sāgüü) base area.

གནས་བཞུགས་ (nɛ̄ɛ̀shuù) residing in (h.) ¶ ཌི་ལིར་གནས་བཞུགས་སྐུ་ཚབ་ Representatives who reside in Delhi.

གནས་ཟོས་བདེ་པོ་ (nɛ̄ɛ̀söö debo) sm.* གནས་བཟོད་བདེ་པོ་.

གནས་གཟིགས་ (nɛ̄ɛ̀sii) pilgrimage to a holy site/ place (h.); va.—ལ་ཕེབས་ to go on a pilgrimage or visit to a holy place.

གནས་བཟང་པོ་ (nɛ̄ɛ̀ saŋbo) 1. pleasant place to live. 2. poet. abode of the gods, heaven.

གནས་བཟོད་བདེ་པོ་ (nɛ̄ɛ̀söö debo) peaceful, comfortable, easy ¶ དེང་སང་ལུང་པའི་ནང་ཟིང་ཆ་མེད་པ་གནས་ཟོས་བདེ་པོ་འདུག These days that place is peaceful without any disturbances.

གནས་ཡིག (nɛ̄ɛ̀yig) a traditional guidebook to a pilgrimage site or sites.

གནས་ཡུལ་ (nɛ̄ɛ̀yüü) location/ site/ place where one lives or stays; va.—བཅའ་ to live in, to reside ¶ བཀོད་འདོམས་ཁང་གི་གནས་ཡུལ་འདི་རེད་ This is the location of the command house.

གནས་ཡུལ་རྒྱལ་ཁབ (nɛ̄ɛ̀yüü gyɛɛgəb) country of one's residence.

གནས་ཡོད་ (nɛ̄ɛ̀yöö) those present or residing somewhere ¶ གནས་ཡོད་འགོ་བྱེད་རྣམས་ The headmen residing there.

གནས་གཡར་ (nɛ̄ɛ̀yar) 1. temporary residence. 2. borrowing a place to temporarily stay (e.g., on a overnight journey); va.—ཞུ་ to ask to borrow a place to stay.

གནས་རི་ (nɛ̄ɛ̀ri) holy/ sacred mountain.

གནས་རི་སྐོར་མཇལ་ (nɛ̄ɛ̀ri gɔ̄ɔ̄jɛɛ) circumambulating a holy/ sacred mountain.

གནས་རིམ་ (nɛ̄ɛ̀rim) rank (in a hierachy).

གནས་ལ་འགྲོ་ (nɛ̄ɛ̀la dro) va. to leave one's home to go as a bride.

གནས་ལ་ཕེབས་ (nɛ̄ɛ̀la pēè) h. of གནས་ལ་འགྲོ་.

གནས་ལ་སྦྱིན་ (nɛ̄ɛ̀la jin) va. to send one's daughter as a bride.

གནས་ལ་བསམ་ (nɛ̄ɛ̀la sām) shung. va. to consider ¶ ཁྲོད་དོན་དྲང་འབྲེལ་ཁྲིམས་ཐག་ཆོད་མིན་ཡོང་གནས་ལ་བསམ་ Considering that the case will not be settled justly.

གནས་ལན་ (nɛ̄ɛ̀lɛn) 1. reply/ response to a letter. 2. a return visit to a holy site/ pilgrimage location.

གནས་ལུགས་ (nɛ̄ɛ̀luù) situation, condition; va.—ཤོད་; —འདྲེན་ to elaborate/ talk about a situation or condition ¶ ནུབ་ཨེ་ཤེ་ཡའི་གནས་ལུགས་ The West Asian situation.

གནས་ལུགས་གོ་བསྡུར་ (nɛ̄ɛ̀luù kodur) discussion; va.—བྱེད་.

གནས་ལུགས་རྒྱུ་མཚན་ (nɛ̄ɛ̀luù gyumdzɛn) the reason for a situation.

གནས་ལུགས་རགས་བསྡུས་ (nɛ̄ɛ̀luù rəgdüü) a brief report.

གནས་ལུགས་རིག་པ་ (nɛ̄ɛ̀luù rigbə) a Confucian school of idealist philosophy.

གནས་ལུགས་གསེད་འགྲོལ་ (nɛ̄ɛ̀luù sēndröö) a detailed explanation of sth.

གནས་བཤད་ (nɛ̄ɛ̀shɛɛ̀) description/ explanation of a holy place; va.—རྒྱག ¶ དཀོན་གཉེར་གྱིས་ལྷ་ཁང་གི་གནས་བཤད་བརྒྱབ་པ་རེད་ The caretaker monk gave an explanation of the temple.

གནས་ས་ (nɛ̄ɛ̀sa) 1. sm. གནས་ཡུལ་. 2. a holy place where people go for pilgrimage.

གནས་ལ་བསམ་ (nɛ̄ɛ̀la sām) shung. va. to consider/ think ¶ ཁྲོད་དོན་དྲང་འབྲེལ་ཁྲིམས་ཐག་ཆོད་མིན་ཡོང་གནས་ལ་བསམ་ Considering that the case will not be settled justly.

གནས་སུ་གྱུར་ (nɛ̄ɛ̀su gyar) vi. to come to a state of, to come to be ¶ མུ་གེ་དང་ནད་ཀྱིས་མནར་བའི་གནས་སུ་གྱུར་པ་རེད་ (They) came to be oppressed by famine and disease.

གནས་སུ་འཇོག (nɛ̄ɛ̀su jɔ̄ɔ̀) va. to place/ put in a position or state ¶ ཁོང་ནི་མི་དམངས་ཀྱིས་གུས་བཀུར་ཞུ་ཡུལ་གྱི་གནས་སུ་འཇོག་གི་ཡོད་པ་རེད་ The people are putting him in a place of respect.

གནས་སུ་བཞག (nɛ̄ɛ̀su shaà) p. of གནས་སུ་འཇོག.

གནས་སུ་ལུས་ (nɛ̄ɛ̀su lüü) sm. གནས་སུ་གྱུར་.

གནུབས་མཚོ་ (nūbdzo) sm. ཡར་འབྲོག་གཡུ་མཚོ་.

གནོང་ (nōŋ) feelings of guilt ¶ གནོང་ངོས་ལེན་བྱེད་དུ་བཅུག་པ་རེད་ (They) made (them) confess their guilt.

གནོང་: p. གནོངས་; f. གནོང་ (nōŋ) vi. to feel remorse/ guilt ¶ རང་ཉིད་ཀྱིས་ལས་ཀ་སྡུག་པ་མ་བྱས་ན་གནོང་དགོས་དོན་མེད་ If you don't do bad deeds, you will not have to feel guilty.

གནོང་བཀུར་ (nōŋgur) sm. གནོང་ངོས་ལེན་བྱེད་.

གནོང་འཁུར་ (nōŋgur) sm. གནོང་བཀུར་.

གནོང་ངོས་ལེན་བྱེད་ (nōŋ ŋöölen cee) va. to admit one's guilt/ fault, etc.

གནོང་འགྱོད་ (nōŋgyöö) regretting one's fault/ crime; vi.—བྱེད་; —སྐྱེ་.

གནོང་བག (nōŋbaà) feeling of remorse, feeling of guilt/ shame.

གནོང་མེད་ (nōŋmeè) guiltless, remorseless.

གནོང་ལེན་ (nōŋ len) va. to show guilt/ remorse.

གནོངས་ (nōŋ) 1. imp. of གནང་. 2. p. of གནོང་.

གནོད་ (nöö) harm, injury, damage; va.—སྐྱེལ་; —བྱེད་ to harm/ injure/ damage, to cause trouble ¶ ཨ་རག་མང་པོ་བཏུངས་ན་གཟུགས་པོར་གནོད་ཀྱི་རེད་ If you drink a lot of alcohol, it will harm your body. ¶ ཁོས་གནོད་བསྐྱལ་ནས་ངའི་ཚོང་ལ་གྱོང་རག་སོང་ Because he caused me trouble, I sustained a loss in business.

གནོད་ (nöö) va. to harm/ injure/ damage.

གནོད་རྐྱེན་ (nöögyen) the cause of damage/ harm/ injury.

གནོད་སྐྱེལ་ (nöögyee) see གནོད་.

གནོད་སྐྱོན་ (nöögyön) 1. harm, injury, damage, misfortune, disaster; va.—བྱེད་; —གཏོང་ to harm/ injure/ hinder/ damage, to cause misfortune/ disaster; va.—སེལ་ to eliminate or overcome harm/ injury, misfortune ¶ དགོན་པའི་ནང་ལོགས་ལ་གནོད་སྐྱོན་བཏང་མེད་ (They) haven't damaged the inside of the monastery. ¶ ཞིང་སྨན་བསྒྲར་ནས་འབུའི་གནོད་སྐྱོན་སེལ་ཐུབ་པ་རེད་ They sprayed insecticide on the fields and eliminated the insect damage.

གནོད་སྐྱོན་ཁུལ་ (nöögyöngüü) disaster area.

གནོད་སྐྱོན་ཆེན་པོ་གསུམ་ (nöögyön cēmbo sūm) "the three great harms" (illiteracy, superstition, uncleanliness).

གནོད་སྐྱོན་བྱུང་མི་ (nöögyön cuŋmi) victims of a disaster/ calamity.

གནོད་སྐྱོན་བྱུང་ཡུལ་ (nöögyön cuŋyüü) sm. གནོད་སྐྱོན་ཁུལ་.

གནོད་བསྐྱལ་ (nöö gyɛɛ) p. of གནོད་སྐྱེལ་.

གནོད་འགལ་ (nöŋgɛɛ) sm. གནོད་པ་.

གནོད་འགོག (nõngɔɔ̀) prevention of harm/ injury/ disaster; va.—བྱེད་ །ཆུ་ལོག་སྔོན་འགོག་གི་ཆེད་དུ་རགས་བརྒྱབ་པ་རེད་ They built a dam to prevent flooding.

གནོད་འགོག་ཉེན་སེལ (nõngɔɔ̀ ñensel) preventing harm and eliminating danger.

གནོད་འགོག་ཕྱུགས་སྲུང་ (nõngɔɔ̀ cũgsuŋ) protecting livestock from harm/ disaster.

གནོད་འགོག་མྱུར་བསྡུ་ (nõngɔɔ̀ ñurdu) preventing calamity by harvesting quickly.

གནོད་འགྱེད་ (nöö gyeè) sm. གནོད་སྐྱེལ་.

གནོད་ཅན་ (nööjɛn) sm. གནོད་ལྡན་.

གནོད་ཉེན་ (nööñen) danger of harm.

གནོད་ལྟས་ (nöödɛɛ̀) an omen of harmful things to come.

གནོད་དོགས་ (nöö dɔɔ̀) suspicion of being harmful.

གནོད་ལྡན་ (nõndɛn) harmful །གནོད་ལྡན་དངོས་རིགས་ Harmful materials.

གནོད་པ་ (nööba) harm, injury; va.— སྐྱེལ་; —གཏོང་; —རྒྱགས་ to harm, to injure/ damage, to cause trouble །ཁོས་དཀྲིག་གཏམ་བཟོས་ནས་ང་ལ་གནོད་པ་བསྐྱལ་བྱུང་ He harmed me by making up rumors.

གནོད་པ་འཁྱོལ་པོ་ (nööba kyööbo) a person who causes trouble/ problems. harm.

གནོད་པ་གསོམ་ (nööba shõm) va. to prepare/ plan/ plot to do harm or damage.

གནོད་པའི་ནུས་པ་ (nööbɛ nṳṳbə) a harmful function/ force, a negative function/ force.

གནོད་པས་འཛག (nööbɛ dzaà) vi. to have a wet dream.

གནོད་བྱ་ (nööja) harmful/ injurious deeds །མི་དམངས་ལ་གནོད་བྱའི་ལས་ཀ་བྱེད་མི་ཆོག It is not permitted to do things that harm the people.

གནོད་བྱེད་གདོན་བགེགས་ (nööjeè dõngeg) harmful evil/ demons/ ghosts.

གནོད་འབུ་ (nõmbu) harmful/ injurious insects.

གནོད་འཛུལ་ཁང་ (nõnjöögaŋ) place of sanctuary/ asylum.

གནོད་འཛུལ་བ་ (nõnjööwa) a person seeking or under the protection of asylum.

གནོད་སྦྱིན་ (nööjin) a malevolent demon.

གནོད་མིག (nöömiì) an angry look/ glare; va.—ལྟ་ to look with an angry expression/ manner.

གནོད་ཚབས་ (nöödzəb) sm. གནོད་འཚེ་.

གནོད་ཚིག (nöödziì) harmful words.

གནོད་འཚེ་ (nöödze) harm, injury, damage; va.—བྱེད་; —གཏོང་; —སྐྱེལ་ to harm/ injure; va.—འགོག to stop or prevent harm/ injury/ damage; vi.—ཐོག to get injured/ harmed; vi.—མྱོང་ to suffer/ experience harm.

གནོད་འཚེ་སྔོན་འགོག (nöödze ŋõngaà) taking precautions against possible harm.

གནོད་གཞི་ (nööshi) causes of harm/ injury/ damage; va.—བྱེད་ །ཁོང་ལ་ན་ཚ་ཕོག་པའི་གནོད་གཞི་གསལ་པོ་ཤེས་ཀྱི་མེད་པ་རེད་ (They) do not know clearly the cause of the sickness.

གནོད་བཞི་ (nööshi) the four pests (rats, bedbugs, flies and mosquitoes) །གནོད་བཞི་གཙང་སེལ་ Eliminate the four pests.

གནོད་བཞི་རྩ་གཏོར་ (nööshi dzādɔr) eliminate/ annihilate the four pests (political slogan).

གནོད་ཟད་ (nöösɛɛ̀) one of the four noble truths: eliminating suffering.

གནོད་ཟས་ (nöösɛɛ̀) food that harms or doesn't agree with one.

གནོད་ཟློག (nõndɔɔ̀) avoiding or preventing harm/ injury/ damage །གནོད་ཟློག་གི་ཞབས་བརྟན་ཚུགས་པ་ (They) performed religious rites to prevent harm.

གནོད་བཟློག (nõndɔɔ̀) sm. གནོད་ཟློག.

གནོད་གཡོལ་ (nööyöö) avoiding harm/ injury/ damage; va.—བྱེད་ to do sth. to avoid harm.

གནོད་ལན་ (nöölɛn) revenging a harm/ injury; va.—འཇལ་ to revenge a harm/ injury.

གནོད་སེམས་ (nöösem) malevolent/ malicious/ injurious thoughts, ill will, rancor; va.—སྐྱེ་.

གནོད་སེལ་ཉེན་སེལ་ (nöösel ñensel) eliminating harm and danger.

གནོན་: p. and f. མནན་; imp. ནོན་ (nõn) va. to press down, to compress, to stamp on, to oppress, to subdue, to supress, to repress །མི་དམངས་ཀྱི་མཇེང་པ་གནོན་མཁན་ལ་འཐབ་འཛིང་བཏང་བ་རེད་ (They) had a struggle session against those who oppressed the people (those who pressed down on their shoulders). །ཀོ་བ་དེ་རྡོའི་ཐོག་ཏུ་མནན་ནས་བཞག་པ་རེད་ The leather was left pressed down under a rock.

གནོན་སྒྱུར་འཁྲུལ་ཆས་ (nõngyur trṻṻjɛɛ̀) transformer equipment.

གནོན་མཉམ་ཐིག་རིས་ (nõññam tīgriì) isobaric line.

གནོན་སྡེགས་ (nõndeg) compressor, press machine.

གནོན་ཐུབ་ (nõndub) compressive strength.

གནོན་སྡོམ་ (nõndom) strict vows/ discipline; va.—བྱེད་.

གནོན་བྱེད་འཁྲུལ་འཁོར་ (nõnjeè trṻṻgɔɔ) sm. གནོན་སྡེགས་.

གནོན་བཙིར་ (nõndzir) 1. pressing, compressing; va.—བྱེད་ །གནོན་བཙིར་བྱས་ལེབ་ལེབ་བཟོས་པ་རེད་ (They) flattened it by pressing on it. 2. oppression, oppressing; va.—བྱེད་; —གཏོང་ to oppress །ལོག་སྤྱོད་སྲིད་གཞུང་གིས་ང་ཚོར་གནོན་བཙིར་བྱས་པ་རེད་ The reactionary government oppressed us.

གནོན་ཚད་ཐོན་པོ་ལས་བརྒལ་བ་ (nõndzɛɛ tõmbolɛ gɛɛwa) superhigh pressure.

གནོན་གཟེར་ (nõnser) thumbtack; va.—རྒྱག.

གནོན་ཤིང་ (nõnshiŋ) 1. a large wooden bolt used to keep doors closed. 2. wooden pedals used for weaving.

གནོན་ཤུགས་ (nõnshuù) pressure; va.—སྤྲོད་; —རྒྱག to pressure sb. །ལས་ཀ་དེའི་སྐོར་གོང་རིམ་ནས་གནོན་ཤུགས་རྒྱག་གི་འདུག Concerning that work, the authorities are exerting pressure (to do it).

གནོན་ཤུགས་འཕྲུལ་ལོ་ (nõnshuù kɔɔ̄lo) pressing machine.

གནོན་ཤུགས་ཆུང་བ་ (nõnshuù cũŋwə) low pressure.

གནོན་ཤུགས་ཆེ་བ་ (nõnshuù cēwa) sm. གནོན་ཤུགས་ཆེན་པོ་.

གནོན་ཤུགས་ཆེན་པོ་ (nõnshuù cēmbo) high pressure; va.—རྒྱག to exert high pressure །སྲིད་གཞུང་གིས་མི་དམངས་ཚོགས་པ་ལ་དྲམ་སྟོན་ཁྲོམ་སྐོར་བྱེད་དགོས་པའི་གནོན་ཤུགས་ཆེན་པོ་རྒྱག་གི་ཡོད་པ་རེད་ The goverment is putting great pressure on the "people's party" to demonstrate.

གནོན་ཤུགས་འཁྲུལ་འཁོར་ (nõnshuù trṻṻgɔɔ) pressing machine.

གནོན་ཤུགས་མཚུངས་ཐིག (nõnshuù tsṻŋdig) isobaric line.

གནོན་གསོག (nõnsɔɔ̀) keeping (merchandise) in stock for too long; vi.—རྒྱག; —ཐེབས་ །ལྟ་སྐོར་བ་མང་པོ་མ་སླེབས་སྐབས་ཚོང་ཟོག་མང་པོ་གནོན་གསོག་ཐེབས་འདུག Because many tourists did not arrive, (the stores) ended up with much merchandise in stock.

མནག: p. མནགས་ (nāà) vi. to endure, to suffer, to tolerate/ bear.

མནག་དཀའ་ (nāgga) difficult to bear/ endure/ tolerate.

མནགས་ (nāà) p. of མནག.

མནངས་ཆུང་བ་ (nāŋ cũŋwə) of little worth/ value.

མནངས་ཆེ་བ་ (nāŋ cēwa) sm. མནངས་ཆེན་པོ་.

མནངས་ཆེན་པོ་ (nāŋ cēmbo) of high worth/ value.

མནན་ (nɛ̄n) p. of གནོན་.

མནན་གཏད་ (nɛ̄ndɛɛ̀) curse, spell; va.—བྱེད་.

མནན་རྡེབ་ (nɛ̄ndeb) smashing, breaking.

མནན་བཙིར་ (nɛ̄ndzir) sm. གནོན་བཙིར.

མནན་བཟོས་ལྟོ་ཆས་ (nɛ̄nsöö döjɛɛ̀) compressed foods, hardtack.

མནན་གསོག (nɛ̄nsɔɔ̀) sm. གནོན་གསོག.

མནབ་ (nāb) f. of ནབ་.

མནབ་རྒྱལ་ (nābdzεε) arc. food, snack.

མནབ་རུང་ (nābruŋ) wearable, fit to be worn.

མནབས་ (nāb) p. of ནབ་.

མནམ་ (nām) f. of ནོམ་.

མནམས་ (nām) p. of ནོམ་.

མནམས་བཟའ་ (nām) sm. ནམ་བཟའ་.

མནའ་ (nā) oath, pledge, vow; va.—སྐྱེལ་; —འཇོག to take an oath, to swear, to vow; va.—སྐྱོག to make/ force sb. to take an oath/ pledge/ vow; va.—ཟ་ to disregard/ renege on an oath / pledge/ vow ¶ ཁོང་གཉིས་གྲོགས་པོ་བྱ་རྒྱུའི་མནའ་བཞག་པ་རེད་ They took an oath to be friends.

མནའ་སྐྱེལ་ (nā gyeē) see མནའ་.

མནའ་སྐྱེལ་ཐོ་འཛུགས་ (nāgyeē tōndzuù) taking an oath/ vow, swearing to do sth.; va.—བྱེད་.

མནའ་སྐྱེལ་དམ་བཅའ་ (nāgyeē tamja) taking an oath/ vow, swearing to do sth.; va.—བྱེད་.

མནའ་བསྐྱལ་ (nā gyεε) p. of མནའ་སྐྱེལ་.

མནའ་གན་ (nagεn) written oath, treaty, agreement; va.—འཇོག to take a written oath, to sign a treaty, to make an agreement.

མནའ་གྲོགས་ (nādrɔɔ̀) ally, sworn friend, blood brother ¶ ནུབས་ཆེ་བའི་མནའ་གྲོགས་རྒྱ་གར་ Our great ally India.

མནའ་སྒྲོག (nādrɔɔ̀) see མནའ་.

མནའ་བཅད་ཐོ་བཅད་ (nājεὲ tōjεὲ) taking an oath/ vow, swearing to do sth.; va.—བྱེད་.

མནའ་བཅའ་ (nāja) sm. མནའ་སྐྱེལ་.

མནའ་ཆང་ (nājaŋ) ཆང་ drunk when taking an oath or swearing.

མནའ་ཆས་ (nājεὲ) special clothes worn in Tibet when taking an oath (an ancient custom).

མནའ་ཆིངས་ (nājiŋ) written agreement/ oath/ vow/ covenant.

མནའ་མཆིད་ (nājeè) sm. མནའ་ཤག.

མནའ་མཆིད་གྲོགས་པོ་ (nājeè trogbo) sworn friends, people who have taken an oath of friendship.

མནའ་འཇོག (nā jɔ̄ɔ̀) see མནའ་.

མནའ་ཐོ་གཅོད་ (nādo jȫö̀) va. to take an oath/ vow.

མནའ་ཐོ་བཅད་ (nādo jε̄ὲ) p. of མནའ་ཐོ་གཅོད་.

མནའ་མཐུན་ (nədün) alliance, league, union.

མནའ་མཐུན་འགོ་གཙོ་ (nədün) the leader of an alliance.

མནའ་མཐུན་རྒྱལ་ཁབ་ (nədün gyεεgəb) allied states/ countries.

མནའ་མཐུན་ཆིངས་ཡིག (nədün cīŋyiì) (treaty of) alliance ¶ རི་མི་དམག་དོན་མནའ་མཐུན་ཆིངས་ཡིག Japan-U.S. Military Alliance (treaty).

མནའ་མཐུན་པ་ (nədümbə) an ally.

གནའ་མཐུན་དཔུང་ཚོགས་ (nədün būŋdzɔɔ̀) sm. མནའ་མཐུན་དམག་དཔུང་.

མནའ་མཐུན་དམག་དཔུང་ (nədün məgbuŋ) allied forces/ troops/ armies.

མནའ་མཐུན་ཚོགས་པ་ (nədün tsɔ̄gba) the political party set up under the leadership of Sun Yatsen in 1905.

མནའ་དག་གིས་བཀྲུས་པ་ (nādaggi drǖùbə) shung. being cleared (of a crime) after swearing one's innocence ¶ གྲོད་ཡ་གཉིས་ཀའི་ཉེས་པ་རྣམས་མནའ་དག་གིས་བཀྲུས་པ་རེད་ Both parties were cleared (of a crime) after swearing their innocence.

མནའ་དམ་ (nādam) oath, promise, vow; va.—འབུལ་ to swear, to take an oath, to promise.

མནའ་འདོར་ (nā dɔɔ) sm. མནའ་སྐྱེལ་.

གནའ་སྤུན་ (nābün) sworn brothers, blood brothers.

མནའ་པོར་ (nā pɔɔ) sm. མནའ་སྐྱེལ་.

གནའ་འབྲེལ་ (nāndree) alliance, league, coalition, union, federation.

མནའ་འབྲེལ་གྱི་གཙོ་བོ་ (nāndreegi dzōwo) leader among allies/ federation.

མནའ་འབྲེལ་གྲོགས་པོ་ (nāndreegi trogbo) sworn friends, allies.

མནའ་འབྲེལ་རྒྱལ་ཁབ་ (nāndree gyεεgəb) allied states/ countries.

མནའ་འབྲེལ་དམག་དཔུང་ (nāndree məgbuŋ) allied forces/ troops.

མནའ་སྦྲེལ་ (nāndree) sm. གནའ་འབྲེལ་.

མནའ་མ་ (nāma) bride; va.—གཏོང་ to send a bride; va.—ལེན་ to take a bride; va.—སྟེར་ to give a bride; va.—ལོག to get divorced [Lit. bride returns].

མནའ་མ་སྐྱེལ་བསུ་ (nāma gyēēsu) accompanying a bride to her new family, bridal party.

མནའ་མ་ཆུང་གསོ་ (nāma cūŋso) child/ adoptive bride (girl sent as a child who lives with the family and becomes the wife of their son when she grows up).

མནའ་མ་སྟེར་ལེན་བྱེད་ (nāma dērlen ceè) va. to give and receive a bride (to exchange brides).

མནའ་མ་བཙན་ལེན་ (nāma dzε̄nlen) marriage by capture/ force/ kidnapping.

མནའ་མ་བཞེས་ (nāma sheè) h. of མནའ་མ་ལེན་.

མནའ་མ་ལེན་ (nāma len) see མནའ་མ་.

མནའ་མ་སློང་ (nāma lōŋ) va. to ask a woman's family for her as a bride.

མནའ་མའི་སྐལ་དངོས་ (nāmε gε̄εŋöö̀) dowry.

མནའ་མའི་སྐལ་བ་ (nāmε gε̄εwa) sm. མནའ་མའི་སྐལ་དངོས་.

མནའ་མའི་སྐྱོ་རོགས་ (nāmε gyōrɔɔ̀) bride's servant (a female servant who is sent with a bride to her new household) [Lit. one to help the bride's sorrow].

མནའ་མའི་སྟེར་སྒོ་ (nāmε dērgo) dowry.

མནའ་མའི་བར་གཡོག (nāmε paryɔɔ̀) temporary servant accompanying a new bride.

མནའ་མར་འགྲོ་ (nāmaa dro) va. to go as a bride.

མནའ་མར་གཏོང་ (nāmaa dōŋ) va. to send a bride.

མནའ་མར་སྟེར་ (nāmaa dēr) va. to give as a bride.

མནའ་མར་སླེབས་ (nāmaa lēb) va. to arrive as a bride.

མནའ་མི་ (nāmi) person who takes an oath.

མནའ་མེད་ཁྲེལ་མེད་ (nāmeè trēēmeè) sm. མནའ་མེད་དགེ་མེད་.

མནའ་མེད་དགེ་མེད་ (nāmeè gemeè) treacherous, deceitful, two-faced, unscrupulous.

མནའ་གཙིགས་ (nədziì) sm. མནའ་ཆིངས་.

མནའ་གཙིགས་ཆེན་པོ་ (nədziì cēmbo) sb. who adheres to his promises/ vows.

མནའ་ཚིག (nədziì) oath, covenant, vow.

མནའ་རྫུན་ (nədzün) a false promise/ oath; va.—སྐྱེལ་ to make a false promise/ oath.

མནའ་ཞུགས་ (nəshuù) allied, united.

མནའ་བཞག (nāshaà) p. of མནའ་འཇོག.

མནའ་ཟ་ (nā sa) see མནའ་.

མནའ་ཟ་དགེ་བསྒྱུར་ (nā sa ge gyūr) sm. མནའ་མེད་དགེ་མེད་.

མནའ་ཟན་ (nā sεn) going back on one's word/ vow/ oath.

མནའ་ཡིས་བསྐྱགས་ (nāyiì gyεε) sm. མནའ་བསྐྱལ་.

མནའ་ལ་བརྩི་ (nālə dzī) va. to maintain or adhere to one's promise/ oath/ vow.

མནའ་ཤག (nāshaà) sm. མནའ་གྲོགས་.

མནའ་བཤགས་ (nāshaà) swearing to repent; va.—བྱེད་.

མནར་ (nār) vi. to be oppressed (by/ with), to be afflicted, to be tortured/ tormented, to suffer ¶ བཀྲེས་ལྟོགས་དཀའ་སྡུག་གིས་མནར་བའི་སྐབས་ At the time when they were suffering from hunger and difficulties.

མནར་གཅོད་ (nārjöö̀) oppressing, torturing; va.—བྱེད་; —གཏོང་ to oppress, to torture; vi.—མྱོང་ to experience oppression/ torture; vi.—འཁེལ་; —གཟེད་ to get oppressed/ tortured ¶ ཁོང་ཚོས་བཙོན་ཁང་ནང་མནར་གཅོད་མང་པོ་མྱངས་པ་རེད་ In prison, they experienced much oppression (suffering).

མནར་གཅོད་འཇིགས་སྐྲག (nārjöö̀ jigdraà) oppression and fear.

མནར་བདུང་ (nārduŋ) sm. མནར་གཅོད་.

མནར་སྤྱོད་ (nārjöö̀) sm. མནར་གཅོད་.

མནར་སེམས་ (nārsem) oppressive, cruel (in

thoughts).

མནལ་: p. and f. མནལ་; imp. མནོལ་ (nɛ̄ɛ) va. to go to sleep (h.).

མནལ་ (nɛ̄ɛ) sleeping; vi.—ཁུག to fall asleep; va.—གཟིམས་ to got to sleep; vi.—སད་ to wake up; va.—དཀྲོག; —གསོད་ to wake sb. up.

མནལ་དཀྲོག (nɛ̄ɛdrɔ̀ɔ) va. to wake sb. up. ¶ཁོང་མནལ་དཀྲོག་ཀྱང་མནལ་ར་དྭངས་མི་འདུག Even though (they) woke him up, he isn't wide awake.

མནལ་སྒྲ་ (nɛ̄ɛdra) h. of. གཉིད་སྒྲ་.

མནལ་ཆོག་སྐྱོན་ (nɛ̄ɛjɔ̀ɔ gyȭn) vi. to doze off (h.).

མནལ་འཆོལ་འཁྱམས་ཉལ་ (nɛ̄ɛjöö kyāmñüü) sleepwalking; va.—བྱེད་.

མནལ་འཛམ་གནང་ (nɛ̄njam nāŋ) sm. གཟིམས་འཛམ་གནང་.

མནལ་ཕྱིད་པོ་ (nɛ̄ɛ jiibu) sound/ deep sleep (h.).

མནལ་གདམ་ (nɛ̄ɛdam) h. of.གཉིད་ལབ་.

མནལ་ལྷས་ (nɛ̄ɛdɛɛ̀) sm. མནལ་ལམ་.

མནལ་ཐལ་ཤོར་ (nɛ̄ɛtɛɛ shɔ̄ɔ) vi. to oversleep (h.).

མནལ་ཐུམ་ (nɛ̄ɛ tūm) sm. གཉིད་ཐུན་.

མནལ་དྭངས་ (nɛ̄ɛ taŋ) h. of གཉིད་དྭངས་.

མནལ་དུ་ཡུར་ (nɛ̄ɛdu yur) vi. to fall asleep, to go to sleep.

མནལ་འདྲོག (nɛ̄ɛ drɔ̀ɔ) vi. to be suddenly woken up by a disturbance/ nightmare/ etc. (h.).

མནལ་གདིང་མ་གཟིམས་ (nɛ̄ɛ diŋmə sim) vi. to be sound asleep, to be sleeping soundly (h.).

མནལ་ཕབ་ (nɛ̄ɛ pōb) va. to put sb. to sleep (h.).

མནལ་སྡོ་ (nɛ̄ɛ dro) vi. to feel sleepy (h.).

མནལ་གཟིམས་ (nɛ̄ɛ sim) see མནལ་.

མནལ་ར་དྭངས་ (nɛ̄ɛra taŋ) vi. to be wide awake (h.) ¶ཁོང་མནལ་དཀྲོག་ཀྱང་མནལ་ར་དྭངས་མི་འདུག Even though (they) woke him up, he isn't wide awake.

མནལ་ལབ་ (nɛ̄ɛ ləb) sleep talk; vi.—སྐྱོན་ to talk in one's sleep (h.).

མནལ་ལམ་ (nɛ̄ɛlam) dreaming; vi.—གཏོང་ to dream (h.).

མནལ་སད་ (nɛ̄ɛ sɛɛ̀) see མནལ་.

མནལ་ཧོབ་སད་སྐྱོན་ (nɛ̄ɛhob sɛ̀ɛgyön) vi. to wake up suddenly (h.).

མནུན་ (nǖn) va. to suckle, to nurse.

མནོ་: p. མནོས་ (nō) 1. va. to think, to consider. 2. f. of ནོད་.

མནོ་བསམ་ (nōsam) thoughts, thinking; va.—གཏོང་ to think, to consider; vi.—འཁོར་ to have a thought come to mind.

མནོག (nɔ̄ɔ) 1. profit, gain. 2. the essence, the core meaning.

མནོག་ཆུང་ (nɔ̄gjuŋ) 1. small profit/ gain. 2. insignificant, trifling.

མནོག་ཆེ་ (nɔ̄gce) 1. big profit/ gain. 2. important, significant.

མནོག་པ་ (nɔ̄gba) 1. tasty, delicious. 2. arc. many.

མནོག་མེད་ (nɔ̄gmeè) 1. profitless. 2. meaningless.

མནོག་ཟན་ (nɔ̄gsɛn) sm. ནོག་ཟན་.

མནོན་ (nȭn) sm. གནོན་.

མནོམས་ (nōm) sm. ནོམ་.

མནོལ་ (nȫȫ) 1. imp. of མནལ་. 2. dirt, filth.

མནོལ་སྒྲིབ་ (nȫȫdrib) dirt/ filth; va.—སེལ་ to cleanse.

མནོལ་བ་ (nȫȫwa) dirt, filth; va.—སེལ་ to cleanse.

མནོལ་བཙོག (nȫȫdzɔg) dirt, filth, contamination.

མནོལ་རིགས་ (nȫȫrig) a lower/ impure class or caste of people (e.g., blacksmiths, butchers).

མནོལ་ཤོར་ (nɛ̄ɛ shɔ̄ɔ) vi. to become dirty/ contaminated.

མནོལ་བསངས་ (nȫȫ sāŋ) vi. to cleanse by burning incense.

མནོས་ (nȫȫ) p. of ནོད་.

ན་ (nā) abbr. of ན་བ་.

ན་ཀོར་ (nāgɔɔ) earring.

ན་སྐྱག (nāgyaà) sm. ན་སྤབས་.

ན་ཁུང་ (nāguŋ) ear hole/ cavity.

ན་ཁེབས་ (nāgeb) the cap that covers the small saucer on the side of a Tibetan matchlock where gunpowder is placed to ignite the powder inside the barrel.

ན་རྒྱངས་ (nāgyaŋ) sm. ན་རྒྱན་.

ན་རྒྱན་ (nāgyɛn) earring, ear ornament.

ན་རྒྱན་ཨ་ལོང་ (nāgyɛn āloŋ) round/ hoop earring.

ན་རྒྱབ་ (nāgyəb) behind the ears.

ན་རྒྱབ་ཀྱི་ལྷགས་པ་ (nāgyəbgi lhāgbə) paying no attention to sth., brushing aside/ ignoring sth. ¶ངའི་བསླབ་བྱ་ནམས་ཕྲུ་གུ་དེས་ན་རྒྱབ་ཀྱི་ལྷགས་པ་ལར་བཏང་ནས་ཉན་གྱི་མི་འདུག The child, like wind behind the ear, didn't pay attention to my advice. [Lit. wind behind the ear].

ན་རྒྱུན་ (nāgyün) oral tradition.

ན་ཅོག (nājɔ̀ɔ) sm. ན་མཆོག.

ན་གཅོད་ (nā jȍȍ) va. to cut off an ear as a form of punishment.

ན་ལྕོག (nājɔ̀ɔ) sm. ན་མཆོག.

ན་ཆ་ (nāja) sm. ན་རྒྱན་.

ན་ཆ་གདུབ་ཀོར་ (nāja dubgɔɔ) sm. ན་རྒྱན་.

ན་ཆེན་ (nājen) big ears.

ན་མཆོག (nāmjɔ̀ɔ) ear.

ན་མཆོག་གི་ཚོར་བ་ (nāmjɔ̀ɔgi tsɔ̄rwa) the sense of hearing.

ན་མཆོག་འཇམ་པོ་ (nāmjɔ̀ɔ jambo) quiet.

ན་མཆོག་གཟེད་ (nāmjɔ̀ɔ sɛɛ̀) (with negative particles) va. to not listen ¶ཁོས་ན་མཆོག་གཟེད་ཀྱི་མི་འདུག He does not listen.

ན་མཆོག་གཙག་ཁབ་ (nāmjɔ̀ɔ dzāàgəb) acupuncture on the ears.

ན་མཆོག་ཚ་པོ་ (nāmjɔ̀ɔ tsābo) noisy.

ན་ཉན་པ་ (nā ñɛmba) spy.

ན་གདམ་ (nādam) talk that is passed on orally.

ན་ལྷག་གི་བསེར་བུ་ (nādaàgi sērbu) sm. ན་རྒྱབ་ཀྱི་ལྷག་པ་.

ན་ཐེག་ཅན་ (nā tēgjɛn) a person who is not moved or swayed by talk.

ན་ཐོད་ལ་ (nādöla) Natula Pass (the pass between Sikkim and Tibet).

ན་ཐོས་ (nādöö) hearing sth.

ན་ཐོས་ལ་ (nādöla) sm. ན་ཐོད་ལ་.

ན་འདབ་ (nādəb) flapping ears (usu. elephants); va.—བྱེད་.

ན་དྲེག (nādreg) sm. ན་སྤབས་.

ན་འདབ་ (nā dəb) the external part of the ear.

ན་གདུབ་ (nədub) earring.

ན་ནད་ (nānɛɛ̀) ear disease.

ན་ནད་སྡེ་ཚན་ (nānɛ dedzɛn) otology department.

ན་སྤབས་ (nābəb) earwax.

ན་འཕྱང་ (nājaŋ) ear lobe.

ན་བ་ (nāwa) ear; vi.—འོན་ to become deaf.

ན་བ་གྲོང་གྲོང་ (nāwa drōŋdroŋ) 1. erect/ upright ears (as with dogs when on the alert). 2. hoping/ wishing for sth.; va.—བྱེད་ to hope, to wish for ¶མི་དེས་ལས་གནས་གསར་པ་དེ་རག་རྒྱུར་ན་བ་གྲོང་གྲོང་བྱེད་ཀྱི་འདུག That person is hoping to get the new position.

ན་བ་མཁྲེགས་པོ་ (nāwa trēgbo) sm. ན་ཐེག་ཅན་.

ན་བ་ཕྱིད་པོ་ (nāwa jiibu) sm. ན་ཐེག་ཅན་.

ན་བ་གཏོད་ (nāwa dȍȍ) va. to listen.

ན་བ་ལྡེབ་རྩེག (nāwa dēbdzeg) 1. hopeless, without hope (of getting sth.) ¶ད་ལམ་ན་བ་ལྡེབ་རྩེག་རེད་བཞག ལས་ཀ་དེ་ཤོར་ཚར་འདུག Now it is hopeless. The job (I was hoping for) is lost. 2. va.—རྒྱག to not want to hear sth. ¶དེང་སང་སྲིད་དོན་སྐོར་ན་བ་ལྡེབ་རྩེག་བརྒྱབ་ནས་བསྡད་ཡོད་ Nowadays, I do not want to hear about politics.

ན་བ་དྲེགས་བྱེད་ (nāwa dregjeè) sm. ན་རྒྱན་.

ན་བ་བླགས་ (nāwa lāà) va. to listen.

ན་བ་མེད་པ་ (nāwa meèba) 1. not heeding advice. 2. deaf.

ན་བ་གཙེར་བ་ (nāwa dzērwa) sm. ན་བ་གཙེར་སྣུན་.

ན་བ་གཙེར་སྣུན་ (nāwa dzērsün) annoying, irritating (to the ears).

ན་བ་ཚ་པོ་ (nāwa tsābo) sm. ན་བ་གཙེར་སྣུན་.

ན་བ་ཚ་ལམ་ (nāwa tsālam) sm. ན་བ་གཙེར་སྣུན་.

ན་བ་འོན་ཁྲོག་ཁྲོག (nāwa wȍn trɔ̄gdrɔ̀ɔ) hard of

hearing.

ན་བ་འོན་འོན་ (nāwa wo̱nön) tired or fed up listening to sth.; va.—ཉན་.

ན་བ་སུན་འབྱིན་ (nāwa sūnjin) sm. ན་བ་གཅེར་སུན་.

ན་བ་སྲུ་བ་ (nāwa trɘ̄bɘ) 1. hard of hearing. 2. sm. ན་ཐེག་ཅན་.

ན་བ་སྲབ་པོ་ (nāwa trɘ̄bbu) gullible, a person who does or listens or believes whatever sb. says.

ན་བ་སླ་པོ་ (nāwa lābo) gullible, a person who does or listens or believes whatever sb. says.

ན་བ་གསང་པོ་ (nāwa sāŋbo) 1. good hearing. 2. sb. who knows what is going on, sb. who is up to date on the news, a well-informed person.

ན་བའི་སྐྱེ་མཆེད་ (nāwɛ gyējeè) hearing organs.

ན་བའི་ཁམས་ (nāwɛ kām) sm. ན་བའི་སྐྱེ་མཆེད་.

ན་བའི་ང་ལྤགས་ (nāwɛ ŋābaà) ear drums.

ན་བའི་བདུད་རྩི་ (nāwɛ dṳ̄üdzi) interesting, pleasing (talk, story, news, etc.) [Lit. ambrosia for the ears].

ན་བའི་རྣམ་ཤེས་ (nāwɛ nāmseè) sm. ན་ཤེས་.

ན་བའི་བུ་ག་འབིགས་པའི་གཏམ་ (nāwɛ pu̱ga bi̱gbɛ dām) talk that hurts people's feelings, talk that is painful to hear [Lit. talk that pokes a hole in the ear].

ན་བའི་བུ་རམ་ (nāwɛ pu̱rɘm) sm. ན་བའི་བདུད་རྩི་.

ན་བའི་དབང་པོ་ (nāwɛ wāŋbo) hearing organs.

ན་བའི་ཚེར་མ་ (nāwɛ tsērma) speech/ talk that is painful to hear, talk that hurts one's feelings [Lit. a thorn in the ear].

ན་བའི་མཛེས་རྒྱན་ (nāwɛ dze̱ègyɛn) sm. ན་བའི་བདུད་རྩི་.

ན་བའི་ཡུལ་ (nāwɛ yü̱ü) 1. sound, talk. 2. hearing.

ན་བའི་ཡོབ་རུས་ (nāwɛ yo̱brüü) stapes, stirrup bone.

ན་བར་འགྲོ་ (nāwar dro̱) vi. to be pleasing to the ears, to like (usually for sth. said) ¶ངས་བཤད་པའི་སྐད་ཆ་ཁོའི་ན་བར་ཕྱིན་མ་སོང་ He didn't like what I said.

ན་བར་འགྲོ་པོ་ (nāwar dro̱bo) 1. amiable, acceptable, likable, friendly ¶དགེ་རྒན་གྱི་བསླབ་བྱ་དེ་ན་བར་འགྲོ་པོ་ཞིག་བྱུང་ (I) found the teacher's advice acceptable/ likeable.

ན་བར་འཇེབས་ (nāwar je̱b) sm. ན་བར་འགྲོ་.

ན་བར་འཇོ་ (nāwar jo̱) sm. ན་བར་འགྲོ་.

ན་བར་འཇོག་ (nāwar jɔ̱ɔ̀) va. to listen.

ན་བར་འབབ་ (nāwar bɘ̱b) sm. ན་བར་འགྲོ་.

ན་བར་མི་འགྲོ་ (nāwar mi̱dro) 1. vi. to not like sth. said ¶ན་བར་མི་འགྲོ་བའི་སྐད་ཆ་ Talk talk that one doesn't like. 2. talking rubbish ¶ཚོང་པ་དེས་ན་བར་མི་འགྲོ་བའི་སྐད་ཆ་འདོད་ཀྱི་འདུག The trader talks a lot of rubbish.

ན་བར་གཟན་པ་ (nāwar se̱mba) an unpleasant sound, an irritating noise.

ན་བར་གཟོན་ (nāwar sö̱n) vi. to disregard advice, to not listen to suggestions.

ན་བར་ལྷུང་ (nāwar lhūŋ) vi. to hear.

ན་དབང་ (nāwaŋ) abbr. of ན་བའི་དབང་པོ་.

ན་བུག (nābuù) sm. ན་སྦུག.

ན་བོལ་ (nāböö) an ornament made from colored wool that is fastened to the ears of plowing animals.

ན་སྦབས་ (nābaà) sm. ན་སྐྲུག.

ན་སྦུག (nābuù) sm. ན་སྦུབས་.

ན་སྦུབས་ (nābub) the ear cavity.

ན་ཙ་ཕུས་འདེབས་ (nādza pǖndeb) parotitis (ear infection).

ན་ཙ་ (nādza) 1. vein in the ear. 2. near the ear.

ན་རྩེ་ (nādze) tip of the ear.

ན་ཚོར་ (nādzɔr) sense of hearing, auditory sense.

ན་རྫས་ (nādzɛɛ̀) the gunpowder used to ignite a Tibetan matchlock gun.

ན་ཞབས་ (nāshɘb) sm. ན་ཤལ་.

ན་འུར་ (nāwur) a ringing sound in the ears.

ན་གཡག (nāyaà) sm. གནའ་གཡག.

ན་གཡུ་ (nɘ̄yu) turquoise earring.

ན་གཡུ་ཅན་ (nɘ̄yujɛn) a person wearing a turquoise earring.

ན་རུ་ (nɘ̄ru) 1. the horn of a blue sheep. 2. sm. ན་རོ་. 3. arc. copulation, sexual intercourse.

ན་རོ་ (nāro) sm. ན་རོ་.

ན་རོས་ (nāröö̀) maroon color.

ན་ལམ་ (nālam) sm. ན་བའི་ཡུལ་.

ན་ལམ་འགོག (nālam go̱ɔ̀) va. to block sb. from hearing sth.

ན་ལམ་དུ་སོང་ (nālamdu sōŋ) vi. to hear.

ན་ལོང་ (nāloŋ) an earring, ear ornament.

ན་ཤལ་ (nāshɛɛ) ear lobe.

ན་ཤེས་ (nāsheè) the sense of hearing, auditory consciousness.

ན་གཤོག (nāshɔɔ̀) 1. outer part of the ear. 2. (with regard to fish) gills.

ན་སུན་པོ་ (nā sūmbu) noisy, irritating (to the ear).

ན་ལྷོང་སྒྲོག་སྒྲངས་ (nālhoŋ drɔ̱gjaŋ) shung. reading aloud so that everyone hears and understands (usu. refers to government edicts); va.—བྱེད་.

ནག (nāg) pus; vi.—གསོག; —ཁྱུག; —ཆགས་ to become pussy, to fester; va.—དོལ་; —གཙགས་; —འདྲེན་ to drain pus from a sore/ wound; va.—འཚིར་ to squeeze pus from a sore/ wound.

ནག་ཁྲག (nāgdraà) pus and blood.

ནག་རྒྱག (nāggyaà) sm. ནག་གསོག.

ནག་ཆུ་ (nɘ̄gju) pus.

ནག་ཅན་ (nāgjɛn) having pus, purulent.

ནག་གདོང་ (nāg dōŋ) va. to apply a paste of powdered glass, flour and glue on the line of a kite for use in kite fights.

ནག་དོལ་ (nāg dȫö) va. to drain pus from a sore/ wound.

ནག་ཐོག་གཙག་འཁེལ་ (nāgtɔɔ̀ dzāàgel) 1. hitting the nail on the head, being exactly right. [Lit. to pierce the pus with a knife]. 2. saying/ criticizing directly to the person involved.

ནག་དྲི་ (nɘ̄gdri) smell of pus.

ནག་འདོན་ (nāg dö̱n) vi. to have the pus come out of a sore/ wound.

ནག་འདོན་གཙག་བུ་ (nāgdön dzāgbu) a small knife used to drain pus.

ནག་བྲང་ (nāgdraŋ) pyothorax.

ནག་འབུར་ (nāgbur) abscess, a pus-filled boil/ pimple.

ནག་འབྱམས་ (nāg ja̱m) vi. to have pus spread.

ནག་འབྲུམ་ (nāŋdrum) sm. ནག་འབུར་.

ནག་སྦུག (nāgbuù) fistula.

ནག་སྨིན་ (na̱gmin) a sore ripe with pus (ready to be drained).

ནག་བཙིར་ (nāgdzir) p. of ནག་འཚིར་.

ནག་འཛག (nāg dza̱à) vi. to have a pus-filled sore/ wound drain.

ནག་ལུད་ (nāg lṳ̈ü) abbr. pus and phelgm.

ནག་སུངས་ (nāgsuŋ) sm. ནག་དྲི་.

ནག་གསོག (nāgsɔɔ̀) see ནག.

ནགས་ (nāà) vi. to get infected with pus.

ནང་ (nāŋ) abbr. of ནང་མ་.

ནང་ཀལ་ (nāŋgɛɛ) sm. ནང་མ་.

ནང་བཅད་ (nāŋjɛɛ̀) sm. ནང་མ་.

ནང་ཐོག་འདེབས་ལས་ (nāŋdɔɔ̀ de̱blɛɛ̀) planting a crop on a bund/ mound/ ridge.

ནང་མ་ (nāŋma) bunds on fields that differentiate subplots; va.—སྐོར་ to make such bunds on fields.

ནང་མའི་ས་ཤུར་ (nāŋmɛ sɘ̄shur) irrigation canal/ ditch on fields.

ནང་མར་ཆུ་འདྲེན་ (nāŋmar cūndren) irrigation by plots (that are surrounded by bunds/ mounds).

ནང་མིག (nɘ̄ŋmiì) the plot within a field that is surrounded by bunds.

ནང་རི་ (nāŋri) sm. ནང་ཀལ་.

ནབ་: p. བརྣབས་; f. བརྣབ་ (nɘ̄b) vi. to desire/ long for what belongs to others, to be greedy.

ནམ་ (nām) honorific term used for second and third person ¶འབྲུག་རྒྱལ་མཆོག་དང་ཕྱི་སྲིད་ནམ་གཉིས་

དབར་ Between the two, the King of Bhutan and the Foreign Minister.

རྣམ་ཀུན་ (nāmgün) usually, always, in all aspects ¶ རྣམ་ཀུན་ང་ལུས་རྩལ་བྱེད་ཀྱི་ཡོད་ I usually exercise.

རྣམ་དཀར་ (nāmgar) 1. virtuous work/ deeds/ activity. 2. completely white.

རྣམ་དཀར་དགེ་ལས་ (nāmgar gelεὲ) virtuous work/ deeds/ activities.

རྣམ་དཀར་འཕྲིན་ལས་ (nāmgar trinlεὲ) virtuous work/ deeds/ activity.

རྣམ་བཀྲ་ (nāmdra) abbr. of རྣམ་པར་བཀྲ་བ་.

རྣམ་མཁས་མ་ (nām kὲὲma) a learned woman.

རྣམ་མཁྱེན་ (nāmkyen) 1. all-knowing (skt. sarvajñā), omniscience, enlightened. 2. a name for the Buddha. 3. mind.

རྣམ་མཁྱེན་དྭངས་གནས་ (nāmgyen ta̱ŋnεὲ) shung. (you) will be fully aware ¶ ཁོ་པ་ཚོའི་བཀའ་གཏན་དུ་ཚུད་མེད་དེ་གས་རྣམ་མཁྱེན་དྭངས་གནས་ (You) will be fully aware that it (the land) is not included in their land tenure document.

རྣམ་འཁྲུལ་ (nām trüü) vi. to have an illusion.

རྣམ་གན་ (nāmgεn) sm. རྣམ་སྲུས་གན་མཛོད་.

རྣམ་གྲངས་ (nāmdraŋ) item, kind, type, category; va.—འགོད་ to enumerate, to display, to set out in order ¶ ཐོན་སྐྱེད་ཀྱི་རྣམ་གྲངས་དྲུག་བརྒྱ་བཅུ་མེད་གཉིས་ Six hundred and two kinds of products. ¶ ལྟད་མོའི་རྣམ་གྲངས་མང་པོ་ Many kinds of shows.

རྣམ་གྲངས་ཐ་དད་པ་ (nāmdraŋ tādεὲba) a term with many meanings/ synonyms.

རྣམ་གྲོལ་ (nām dröö) nirvana, enlightenment.

རྣམ་གྲྭ་ (nāmdra) abbr. of རྣམ་རྒྱལ་གྲྭ་ཚང་.

རྣམ་འགྱུར་ (nəmgyur) 1. appearance, attitude, countenance, look; vi.—ལོག, —འགྱུར་ to change one's attitude; va.—སྟོན་ to show one's appearance/ attitude/ feelings ¶ ཁོའི་རྣམ་འགྱུར་ཡག་པོ་མི་འདུག His attitude is not good. ¶ གནས་ཚུལ་དེ་གོ་མ་ཐག་ཁོའི་རྣམ་འགྱུར་ལོག་སོང་ As soon as he heard the news, his attitude (appearance) changed. ¶ ཁོའི་རྣམ་འགྱུར་གང་འདྲ་ཡོད་མེད་ལྟ་དགོས་ (You) have to look and see what his attitude is. 2. vi. to exhibit or show anger/ dislike ¶ ཁོས་ང་ལ་རྣམ་འགྱུར་སྟོན་གྱི་འདུག He is showing his dislike of me.

རྣམ་འགྱུར་སྒམ་པོ་ (nəmgyur ga̱mbo) reserved and proud.

རྣམ་འགྱུར་སྟོན་སྟངས་ (nəmgyur dōndaŋ) manner or style of appearance/ attitude/ countenance/ look.

རྣམ་འགྱུར་མཛེས་པ་ (nəmgyur dzeèba) 1. beautiful looking, attractive in appearance. 2. pleasant behavior.

རྣམ་འགྲེལ་ (nāmdrel) an explanation, an elucidation.

རྣམ་རྒྱལ་ (nāmgyεε) 1. complete victory. 2. name of the Sikkimese royal family. 3. name of a person.

རྣམ་རྒྱལ་གྲྭ་ཚང་ (nāmgyεε tra̱dzaŋ Namgyal monastery (in the Potala).

རྣམ་རྒྱལ་མཆོད་རྟེན་ (nāmgyεε cööden) name of a famous stupa.

རྣམ་རྒྱལ་བོད་ཀྱི་ཤེས་རིག་དཔེ་མཛོད་ཁང་ (nāmgyεε pöögi shēèrii bēndzomgaŋ) The Namgyal Institute of Tibetology (Gangtok, Sikkim).

རྣམ་རྒྱལ་མ་ (nāmgyεεma) name of a female diety.

རྣམ་རྒྱས་ (nāmgyεὲ) abundant.

རྣམ་སྙིག་མ་ (nām ge̱gma) a woman who is beautiful but proud/ conceited.

རྣམ་བཅུ་དབང་ལྡན་ (nāmju wāŋdεn) a form of Tibetan script that is written vertically.

རྣམ་འཇོམས་ (nām dzo̱m) 1. va. to eradicate/ annihilate/ exterminate. 2. a type of deity.

རྣམ་རྟོག (nāmdɔɔ̀) 1. superstitious beliefs, taboos; va.—བྱེད་ to act in a superstitious way, to adhere or act in conformity with a taboo; va.—ལ་བརྩི་ to consider things superstitiously, to believe in taboos; vi.—ཟ་; —ལངས་ to consider that sth. is taboo; vi.—སློང་ to deliberately do sth. inauspicious that brings bad luck ¶ བུད་མེད་ཚོས་ལུག་བསད་ན་ སྡུག་པ་ཡོང་གི་རེད་ ཟེར་ནས་འབྲོག་པས་རྣམ་རྟོག་བྱེད་ཀྱི་ཡོད་པ་རེད་ The nomads have a superstitious belief that if a woman kills a sheep sth. bad will come. 2. doubt, indecision, suspicion ¶ ཁྱེད་རང་གི་སེམས་ཀྱི་རྣམ་རྟོག་མ་གཏོགས་དོན་དངོས་དེ་འདྲ་ཡོད་པ་མ་རེད་ Except for the doubt in your mind, in reality there is nothing like that (no basis for it). ¶ ཕན་ཚུན་གཉིས་ཀར་མཐོང་ཕྱོགས་མི་བདེ་བའི་རྣམ་རྟོག་ཡོད་ They both suspected that the other didn't like them (and was doing some harm). 3. imagination, fantasy.

རྣམ་རྟོག་དགྲ་ལངས་ཁང་སྟོང་ཀུན་མ་སྣང་ (nāmdɔɔ̀ dra̱laŋ kāŋdoŋ gūnmə da̱ŋ) overly suspicious [Lit. to suspect a thief will come to an empty house].

རྣམ་རྟོག་དགྲ་ཁང་ (nāmdɔɔ̀ dra̱gaŋ) sm. རྣམ་རྟོག་དགྲ་ལངས་ཁང་སྟོང་ཀུན་མ་སྣང་.

རྣམ་རྟོག་ཅན་ (nāmdɔɔ̀jεn) superstitious.

རྣམ་རྟོག་རྩི་པ་ (nāmdɔɔ̀ dzi̱bə) sm. རྣམ་རྟོག་ཟ་པོ་.

རྣམ་རྟོག་ཚ་པོ་ (nāmdɔɔ̀ tsābo) sm. རྣམ་རྟོག་ཟ་པོ་.

རྣམ་རྟོག་ཟ་པོ་ (nāmdɔɔ̀ sa̱bo) 1. sb. who is very superstitious, sb. who believes in many taboos. 2. sb. who is very suspicious, a person who doubts everything.

རྣམ་རྟོག་སློང་ (nāmdɔɔ̀ lōŋ) see རྣམ་རྟོག.

རྣམ་ཐར་ (nāmdar) 1. biography, life story; va.—འཁྲབ་ to stage/ perform a story. 2. song/ aria from Tibetan operas; va.—གཏོང་ to sing an aria/ song from the traditional Tibetan opera.

རྣམ་ཐར་མདོར་བསྡུས་ (nāmdar dɔ̱rdüü) abridged biography.

རྣམ་ཐོས་ (nāmdöö) well read, well informed.

རྣམ་ཐོས་ཀྱི་བུ་ (nāmdöögi pu̱) sm. རྣམ་ཐོས་སྲས་.

རྣམ་དག (nāmdaà) 1. pure. 2. perfect, correct.

རྣམ་དག་སྒོ་གསུམ་ (nāmdaà go̱sum) window/ skylight on the ceiling area of the prayer assembly halls in some large monasteries.

རྣམ་འདུད་ (nām dü̱ü) 1. va. to show great respect.

རྣམ་འདྲེན་ (nām dre̱n) abbr. རྣམ་པར་འདྲེན་.

རྣམ་འདྲེན་བཞི་པ་ (nām dre̱n shi̱bə) the Buddha Sakyamuni.

རྣམ་གནོན་ (nāmnön) the iron dragon year.

རྣམ་སྣང་ཆོས་བདུན་ (nāmnaŋ cöödün) meditation in which the body has to be kept in seven different postures.

རྣམ་པ་ (nāmba) 1. type, kind, variety, form ¶ ཚོང་ཟོག་གི་རྣམ་པ་མི་འདྲ་བ་ Different kinds of merchandise. 2. situation, condition, circumstances ¶ དབུལ་ཞིང་རྗེས་སུ་ལུས་པའི་རྣམ་པ་བསྒྱུར་བ་རེད་ (They) transformed the conditions of poverty and backwardness. 3. face, look, appearance; va.—སྟོན་ to show the appearance of sth. ¶ དམག་དོན་གྲ་སྒྲིག་བྱས་པར་མ་དགའ་བའི་རྣམ་པ་བསྟན་པ་རེད་ (They) showed (the appearance of) dislike for the military preparations. 4. you (pl.), they ¶ གྲོགས་པོ་རྣམ་པ་ལྷན་རྒྱས་ལ་ཞུ་རྒྱུ་ To all you friends (of mine). 5. beauty, looks, attractiveness (for woman) ¶ བུད་མེད་འདི་རྣམ་པ་ཡག་པོ་ཞིག་དུག་འདུག The woman is very attractive (beautiful). 6. va.—སྟོན་ to apply make-up to look attractive; to show a sign.

རྣམ་པ་ཀུན་དུ་ (nāmba gündu) always, in every respect/ way ¶ དུས་དང་རྣམ་པ་ཀུན་དུ་མི་དམངས་ཀྱི་ཁེ་ཕན་ལ་བསམ་བློ་གཏོང་གི་ཡོད་པ་རེད་ (They) always think about the (interests) of the people.

རྣམ་པ་བཀྲ་བ་ (nāmba drāwa) beautiful, splendid.

རྣམ་པ་འགྱུར་ (nāmba gyu̱r) vi. to change appearance, to change form, to metamorphize, to become changed (of situation) ¶ དམངས་གཙོའི་ལམ་ལུགས་དར་ནས་ཡུལ་ལུང་གི་རྣམ་པ་འགྱུར་འདུག After democracy spread, the situation in that place has changed.

རྣམ་པ་རྒྱ་རྒྱུགས་བོད་རྒྱུགས་ (nāmba gyə̱gyuù

pöögyuù) ordinary looking, not so pretty and not so ugly.

རྣམ་པ་རྒྱ་ལོ་པོད་ལོ་ (nāmba gyalo pöölo) sm. རྣམ་པ་རྒྱ་ལོ་པོད་ལོ་.

རྣམ་པ་ངེས་ཅན་ (nāmba ŋeèjɛn) definite/ fixed form.

རྣམ་པ་ཉམས་ (nāmba ñam) vi. to have one's looks wane/ fade/ diminish/ deteriorate.

རྣམ་པ་རྙིང་པ་ (nāmba ñi̅ŋbə) old style.

རྣམ་པ་སྟོན་ (nāmba dö̃n) 1. va. to show a sign, to manifest the appearance (of) ༑མའོ་རར་ངོ་རྒོལ་བྱེད་རྒྱུའི་རྣམ་པ་སྟོན་གྱི་ཡོད་པ་རེད་ (They) are showing signs of opposing Mao. 2. sm. རྣམ་པ་འདོན་.

རྣམ་པ་བསྟན་ (nāmba dɛ̄n) p. of རྣམ་པ་སྟོན་.

རྣམ་པ་ཐམས་ཅད་ (nāmba tāmjɛɛ̀) all knowledge.

རྣམ་པ་ཐམས་ཅད་མཁྱེན་པ་ (nāmba tāmjɛɛ̀ kyēmba) the all-knowing one (i.e., the Buddha).

རྣམ་པ་དང་ནང་དོན་ (nāmba daŋ naŋdön) form and content.

རྣམ་པ་འདོན་ (nāmba dön) va. to make oneself look beautiful (by using cosmetics, etc.).

རྣམ་པ་སྣ་ཚོགས་ (nāmba nādzɔɔ̀) various kinds/ types, all sorts/ kinds.

རྣམ་པ་མེད་པ་ (nāmba meèba) not good looking, not beautiful.

རྣམ་པ་ཙམ་ (nāmbadzam) in name only ༑ཁོས་ངའི་བསམ་འཆར་ལ་མོས་མཐུན་ཡོད་པའི་རྣམ་པ་ཙམ་བསྟན་པ་ལས་དོན་དུ་ངོ་རྒོལ་བྱེད་ཀྱི་ཡོད་པ་རེད་ He agreed with my suggestion in name only but really he is opposing it.

རྣམ་པ་ཙམ་དུ་འགྱུར་ (nāmbadzamdu gyur) vi. to become a mere formality, to become sb. who does sth. in name only ༑ལས་ཁུངས་ཀྱི་འགོ་ཁྲིད་གཞོན་པ་དེ་སླེབས་རྗེས་འགོ་ཁྲིད་རྒན་པ་དེ་རྣམ་པ་ཙམ་དུ་འགྱུར་བ་རེད་ After the younger boss arrived, the older boss became a mere formality (i.e., became without power).

རྣམ་པ་ཙམ་དུ་ལུས་ (nāmbadzamdu lüù) sm. རྣམ་པ་ཙམ་དུ་འགྱུར་བ་.

རྣམ་པ་ཙམ་ལས་མེད་ (nāmbadzamlɛ meè) in name only.

རྣམ་པ་ཚོ་ (nāmbadzo) you (pl.) (h.).

རྣམ་པ་མཛེས་པོ་ (nāmba dzeèbo) beautiful, good-looking.

རྣམ་པ་མཛེས་བཟོ་ (nāmba dzeēso) cosmetology.

རྣམ་པ་མཛེས་བཟོ་ཁང་ (nāmba dzeēsogaŋ) beauty shop, beauty parlor.

རྣམ་པ་མཛེས་བཟོ་གཤགས་བཅོས་ (nāmba dzeēso shāgjöö̀) cosmetic surgery.

རྣམ་པ་འཛིན་ (nāmba dzin) va. to take the appearance/ form (of) ༑ངལ་རྩོལ་པ་དཀྱུས་མ་ཞིག་གི་རྣམ་པ་བཟུང་བ་རེད་ (They) took the appearance of common workers.

རྣམ་པ་ཇིག་པོ་ (nāmba dzigbu) handsome, good-looking.

རྣམ་པ་ཡག་པོ་ (nāmba yago) beautiful, good-looking.

རྣམ་པ་ཡལ་ (nāmba yɛɛ) vi. to have beauty fade.

རྣམ་པ་ཡོད་པ་ (nāmba yöö̀ba) beautiful, attractive, good-looking.

རྣམ་པར་ (nāmbar) completely, perfectly, in all/ every way, entirely ༑རྣམ་པར་རྒྱལ་ Completely victorious.

རྣམ་པར་བཀྲ་བ་ (nāmbar drāwa) 1. extremely pretty/ beautiful. 2. multicolored, brightly colored. 3. imaginative.

རྣམ་པར་གྲོལ་ (nāmbar dröö) vi. to be liberated/ freed from delusion.

རྣམ་པར་རྒྱལ་ (nāmbar gyɛɛ) 1. vi. to be completely victorious.

རྣམ་པར་དག་པ་ (nāmbar tagba) sm. རྣམ་དག.

རྣམ་པར་འདྲེན་ (nāmbar dren) 1. va. to lead, to pull. 2. a name for the Buddha.

རྣམ་པར་སྣང་མཛད་ (nāmbar nāŋdzɛɛ̀) the Buddha Vairocana.

རྣམ་པར་དཔྱོད་པ་ (nāmbar jȫö̀ba) understanding, knowledge, discrimination, discernment, judgement ༑རྣམ་པར་དཔྱོད་པའི་བློ་དང་ལྡན་པའི་རི་བོང་ A rabbit with a discerning mind.

རྣམ་པར་བྱང་བ་ (nāmbar caŋwa) 1. clean. 2. skilled. 3. liberated, enlightened.

རྣམ་པར་སྨིན་ (nāmbar mi̅n) vi. (with ལས་) to reap the fruit of one's karma, to get the effect of one's karma ༑ཁོ་ལ་ནད་ངན་ཕོག་པ་དེ་ལས་ཀྱི་རྣམ་པར་སྨིན་པ་ཞིག་རེད་ In his getting a bad illness he is reaping the fruit of his karma.

རྣམ་པར་སྨིན་པ་ (nāmbar mi̅mbə) ripe, mature.

རྣམ་པར་སྨིན་པའི་རྒྱུ་ (nāmbar mi̅mbɛ gyu) sm. རྣམ་སྨིན་གྱི་རྒྱུ་.

རྣམ་པར་སྨིན་པའི་འབྲས་བུ་ (nāmbar mi̅mbɛ drɛɛ̀bu) sm. རྣམ་སྨིན་གྱི་འབྲས་བུ་.

རྣམ་པར་གཞག (nāmbar shaà) sm. རྣམ་གཞག.

རྣམ་པར་རིག་པ་ (nāmbar rigbə) perceptible, consciousness.

རྣམ་པར་རིག་བྱེད་ (nāmbar rigjeè) sm. རྣམ་པར་རིག་པ་.

རྣམ་པར་ཤེས་པ་ (nāmbar shēèba) sm. རྣམ་ཤེས་.

རྣམ་པར་ཤེས་པའི་ཕུང་པོ་ (nāmbar shēèbɛ pūŋbu) one of the five aggregates: consciousness.

རྣམ་དཔྱོད་ (nāmjöö̀) abbr. རྣམ་པར་དཔྱོད་པ་.

རྣམ་དཔྱོད་ཅན་ (nāmjöö̀jɛn) knowledgeable, thoughtful.

རྣམ་ཕྱིང་ (nāmjiŋ) sm. སྣམ་ཕྱིང་.

རྣམ་ཕྱིས་ (nāmjii̇̀) sm. སྣམ་ཕྱིས་.

རྣམ་འཕྲུལ་ (nāmdrüü) emanation ༑སངས་རྒྱས་ཀྱི་རྣམ་འཕྲུལ་ An emanation of the Buddha.

རྣམ་བྱང་ (nāmjaŋ) nirvana.

རྣམ་དབྱེ་ (nāmje) 1. grammatical cases in the Tibetan system of grammar. 2. differences; va.—འབྱེད་ to differentiate; vi.—ཆོད་ to be differentiated ༑འདི་གཉིས་དབར་རྣམ་དབྱེ་ཆོད་ཀྱི་མི་འདུག These two aren't differentiated. 3. sb. who is very capable/ knowledgeable.

རྣམ་དབྱེར་བཞག (nāmyer shaà) va. to accomplish sth. especially well, to make a name for oneself ༑ཁོང་གིས་ཚོགས་འདུའི་ཐོག་གཏམ་བཤད་ཡག་པོ་ཞིག་བྱས་ནས་རྣམ་དབྱེར་བཞག་སོང་ He gave a good speech at the meeting and made a name for himself.

རྣམ་དབྱེར་སྟོན་ (nāmyer) vi. to look imposing/ grand.

རྣམ་འབྱེད་ (nāmjeè) discriminating intellect, wisdom.

རྣམ་འབྱེད་རིག་པ (nāmjeè rigbə) the system of deduction, deductive method.

རྣམ་སྦྱར་ (nāmjar) a yellow cloak worn by monks.

རྣམ་སྨིན་ (nāmmin) abbr. རྣམ་པར་སྨིན་.

རྣམ་སྨིན་འཁོར་ (nāmmin kɔ̄ɔ̀) vi. to have the effects of karma play themselves out, to reap the fruits (good or bad) of one's karma.

རྣམ་སྨིན་གྱི་རྒྱུ་ (nāmmingi gyu) the cause of karmic effects.

རྣམ་སྨིན་གྱི་འབྲས་བུ་ (nāmmingi drɛɛ̀bu) the result of karmic effect.

རྣམ་གཞག (nāmshaà) manner, system.

རྣམ་གཞག་རྙིང་པ་ (nāmshaà ñi̅ŋbə) old system.

རྣམ་གཡེང་ (nāmyeŋ) negligent, inattentive to tasks, not paying attention to doing sth., not conscientious/ serious/ diligent; va.—བྱེད་ ༑ཁོས་ལས་ཀ་བྱེད་དུས་རྣམ་གཡེང་བྱེད་ཀྱི་འདུག He is not conscientious when he is working.

རྣམ་གཡེང་ཆེན་པོ་ (nāmyeŋ cēmbo) negligent, inattentive to tasks, loafing, not conscientious/ serious/ diligent.

རྣམ་གཡེང་བག་མེད་ (nāmyeŋ pagmeè) sm. རྣམ་གཡེང་.

རྣམ་གཡེང་ཚ་པོ་ (nāmyeŋ tsābo) sm. རྣམ་གཡེང་ཆེན་པོ་.

རྣམ་རིག (nāmrig) mind, consciousness.

རྣམ་རིག་བཀྲ་བ་ (nāmrig drāwa) smart, intelligent.

རྣམ་རིག་གྲུང་པོ་ (nāmrig druŋbo) sm. རྣམ་རིག་བཀྲ་བ་.

རྣམ་རིག་སྒྲིམ་ (nāmrig drim) va. to concentrate.

རྣམ་ཤེས་ (nāmsheè) 1. consciousness, cognition, mind, ༑མི་ཤི་རྗེས་རྣམ་ཤེས་བར་དོར་འཁྱམས་ཀྱི་ཡོད་པ་རེད་ After one dies, one's "consciousness" wanders in Bardo (the stage between death and rebirth). 2. sense ་ ལྕེའི་རྣམ་ཤེས་ Sense of taste.

རྣམ་ཤེས་ཀྱི་ཁམས་བདུན་ (nāmsheègi kāmdün) the seven spheres of consciousness.

རྣམ་ཤེས་ཀྱི་ཕུང་པོ་ (nāmsheègi pūŋbu) sm. རྣམ་པར་ཤེས་པའི་ཕུང་པོ་.

རྣམ་ཤེས་ཙམ་པ་ (nāmsheè dzāmba) sm. སེམས་ཙམ་པ་.

རྣམ་ཤེས་ཙམ་སྨྲ་བ་ (nāmsheèdzam māwa) rationalism.

རྣམ་ཤེས་ཡལ་ (nāmsheè y̲ɛɛ) vi. to die.

རྣམ་བཤད་ (nāmshɛɛ̀) 1. speaking or writing in detail. 2. "on" (in titles) ་ ལག་ལེན་གྱི་རྣམ་བཤད་ "On practice."

རྣམ་སྲས་ (nāmsɛɛ̀) the guardian king of the north direction (Vaishravana).

རྣམ་སྲས་གན་མཛོད་ (nāmsɛɛ̀ k̲ɛndzöö) name of a treasury in the Potala Palace.

རྣམ་སྲས་བང་མཛོད་ལ་ཡི་དྭགས་ཀྱི་སྒྲ་གཉེར་ (nāmsɛɛ̀ p̲aŋdzööla y̲idaàgi gũñee) stingy, having a lot of possessions but not using them or giving them to others [Lit. in a treasury, a caretaker who is a "hungry ghost"].

རྣམ་སྒྲོལ་ (nāmsöö) sm. ལུགས་སྒྲོལ་.

རྣམ་གསལ་ཁྲིགས་ཆགས་ (nāmsɛl tr̲igjaà) shung. in a clear order ་ ཁྲད་དོན་ཁྲིམས་སུ་བཅའ་བའི་རིམ་པ་རྣམ་གསལ་ཁྲིགས་ཆགས་སུ་སྒྲིལ་བ་ལ་ They established the law in clear order which indicates what ought to be done and what ought not to be done.

རྣམས་ (nām) plural postposition ་ དམག་མི་རྣམས་ Soldiers.

རྣར་སྙན་ཡོད་འབབ་ (nārñɛn y̲imbəb) pleasant/ agreeable (to the ear).

རྣལ་དུ་ཕབ་པ་ (nɛ̄ɛdu pəb) vi. to be/ do in a calm/ tranquil state ་ ཁོང་ཡིད་རྣལ་དུ་ཕབ་ནས་སློབ་སྦྱོང་བྱེད་ཀྱི་འདུག He is studying in a calm state (not lettings things bother him). ་ ཁྱེད་རང་ཡིད་རྣལ་དུ་ཕབ་ནས་བསམ་བློ་ཡག་པོ་ཞིག་གཏོང་དང་ You should calm down and think (about this) well.

རྣལ་འབྱོར་ (nɛ̄njɔɔ) yoga.

རྣལ་འབྱོར་གྱི་རྒྱུད་ (nɛ̄njɔɔgi gyü̲ü) yogatantra.

རྣལ་འབྱོར་རྒྱུད་ (nɛ̄njɔɔ gyü̲ü) the yogatantra.

རྣལ་འབྱོར་ཆེན་པོ་ (nɛ̄njɔɔ cēmbo) mahāyoga (a type of trantra).

རྣལ་འབྱོར་པ་ (nɛ̄njɔɔba) yogin.

རྣལ་འབྱོར་ཆེན་པོའི་རྒྱུད་ (nɛ̄njɔɔ cēmbö gyü̲ü) sm. རྣལ་འབྱོར་བླ་མེད་རྒྱུད་.

རྣལ་འབྱོར་བླ་མེད་རྒྱུད་ (nɛ̄njɔɔ lāmeè gyü̲ü) abbr. of རྣལ་འབྱོར་བླ་ན་མེད་པའི་རྒྱུད་.

རྣལ་འབྱོར་སྤྱོད་པ་བ་ (nɛ̄njɔɔ jööbəwa) an adherent of the Yogacara school.

རྣལ་འབྱོར་བླ་ན་མེད་པའི་རྒྱུད་ (nɛ̄njɔɔ lāna m̲eèbɛ gyü̲ü) Anuttarayoga tantra.

རྣལ་འབྱོར་མ་ (nɛ̄njɔɔma) yogini.

རྣལ་མ་ (nɛ̄ɛma) truthful, righteous, correct, proper, real.

རྣལ་མའི་ལུས་ (nɛ̄ɛmɛ lü̲ü) primordial body.

རྣལ་མའི་སེམས་ (nɛ̄ɛmɛ sēm) primordial mind.

རྣལ་མིན་གྱི་བསམ་པ་ (nɛ̄ɛmin sāmba) unconventional thinking.

རྣལ་མོ་ (nɛ̄ɛmo) stable, at ease, calm.

རྣལ་ལམ་ (nɛ̄ɛlam) arc. ཉི་ལམ་.

རྣོ་ (nō) abbr. རྣོ་པོ་.

རྣོ་ངར་ (nāŋar) acute, sharp, powerful ་ འགལ་བ་དེ་ཉིན་བཞིན་རྣོ་ངར་ཆེ་རུ་འགྲོ་གི་ཡོད་པ་རེད་ The contradiction is becoming more acute daily.

རྣོ་བཅད་དྲས་གཅོང་ (nōjɛɛ̀ trɛɛ̀dzaŋ) shung. a decisive/ clear result or decision after an examination ་ བཀའ་ཞིབ་ས་གནས་སུ་ཆེད་མངགས་མཛད་པ་ལྟར་བཀའ་དཔྱད་རྣོ་བཅད་དྲས་གཅོང་ཞིག་རང་ཐུགས་རྗེ་ཆེ་བ་ We look forward to a clear result from the investigator you send.

རྣོ་ལྕགས་ (nōjaà) steel.

རྣོ་ལྕགས་ཀུང་སི་ (nōjaà gūŋsi) tib.ch. steel company/ corporation.

རྣོ་ཆས་ (nōjɛɛ̀) cutter, cutting instrument/ tool.

རྣོ་ཆེན་པོ་ (nō cēmbo) very sharp.

རྣོ་རྟུལ་ (nōdüü) abbr. of རྣོན་པོ་ and རྟུལ་པོ་.

རྣོ་བརྡོན་ (nōdön) p. of རྣོ་འདོན་.

རྣོ་ཐག (nōdaà) steel cable.

རྣོ་དྲག་ཏུ་འགྱུར་ (nōdragdu gyu̲r) vi. to become sharper, to become more acute.

རྣོ་མདའ་ (nōnda) sm. མི་མདའི་རུ་.

རྣོ་འདོན་ (nō d̲ön) va. to sharpen (a knife/ blade).

རྣོ་རྡུགས་ (nō d̲uù) vi. to become dull (knife/ blade).

རྣོ་པོ་ (nōbo) sharp, keen, acute ་ གྲི་རྣོ་པོ་ A sharp knife. ་ རིག་པ་རྣོ་པོ་ Keen intellect.

རྣོ་སྤུང་ (nō cūŋ) va. to sharpen (knife/ blade).

རྣོ་བའི་ཤེས་རབ་ (nōwɛ shēèrəb) sharp/ acute intelligence.

རྣོ་དཔལ་ (nōwɛɛ) the sharpness of a weapon.

རྣོ་སྦུག (nōbuù) steel pipe.

རྣོ་འབིགས་ (nōbig) 1. drill, borer. 2. firing pin.

རྣོ་མེད་ (nōmeè) dull, blunt.

རྣོ་ཟུར་ (nōsur) acute angle (in math).

རྣོ་ལས་བཟོ་གྲྭ (n̲olɛɛ̀ s̲odra) steel rolling mill.

རྣོ་ལེན་ (n̲olen) vi. to become sharp. ་ གྲི་བདར་རུང་རྣོ་ལེན་གྱི་མི་འདུག Even though (I) sharpened it, it did not get sharp.

རྣོ་ལོག (nō l̲ɔɔ̀) vi. to accidently make/ become dull ་ གྲི་བདར་མ་ཤེས་ཙང་རྣོ་ལོག་བཞག Because he didn't know how to sharpen knives, the knife (he sharpened) became dull.

རྣོག: p. བརྣགས་; f. བརྣག; imp. རྣོགས་ (nöò) 1. va. to bear/ hold/ keep (in mind) ་ ངས་ཡུན་རིང་ཡིད་ལ་བརྣགས་པའི་རེ་བ་དེ་འགྲུབ་སོང་ I achieved the hope I had kept in my mind for a long time. 2. vi. to tolerate/ bear.

རྣོག: p. བརྣོགས་; f. བརྣོག; imp. རྣོགས་ (nöò) va. to conceal/ hide.

རྣོག་ཟན་ (nōgsɛn) a type of fried Tibetan cookie (usually made during Tibetan New Year).

རྣོགས་ (nöò) imp. of རྣོག.

རྣོའོ་སེ་ (nōwose) yes, okay.

རྣོན་པོ་ (nōmbo) 1. sharp ་ གྲི་རྣོན་པོ་ A sharp knife. ་ རིག་པ་རྣོན་པོ་ Sharp intellect. 2. biting, sarcastic ་ སྐད་ཆ་རྣོན་པོ་ A biting comment.

སྣ་ (nā) 1. various kinds, varieties ་ ཟས་སྣ་ Varieties of food. 2. ahead of, in front of ་ ང་སྣ་ལ་འགྲོ་གི་ཡིན་ I will go ahead. 3. nose. 4. edge, rim. ་ གྲོང་གི་སྣ་ The edge of the village.

སྣ་དཀྱིལ་ (n̲agyii) middle of the nose.

སྣ་སྐད་ (n̲agɛɛ̀) nasal voice/ speech; va.—རྒྱག to speak nasally.

སྣ་སྐད་རྣོ་པོ་ (nāgɛɛ̀ nōbo) very strong nasal voice/ speech.

སྣ་ཁ་ (nāga) variety, kind, sort, type ་ དེབ་སྣ་ཁ་མང་པོ་འདུག (There) are many kinds of books.

སྣ་ཁ་འཛོམས་པོ་ (nāga dz̲ombo) many kinds/ items.

སྣ་ཁག (nāgaà) sm. སྣ་ཁ་.

སྣ་ཁུག (nāguù) nose; vi.—རྡབ་ to get disappointed, to be rebuffed/ thwarted in some endeavor ་ ང་ཕྱི་རྒྱལ་དུ་སློབ་སྦྱོང་ལ་འགྲོ་རྒྱུ་དེ་སྣ་ཁུག་བརྡབས་བྱུང་ I got thwarted in my going to study abroad. [Lit. to bang one's nose].

སྣ་ཁུག་ཁ་འཐེན་ (nāguù kāden) being obstinate/ inflexible/ stubborn (usu. regarding sth. that can't be achieved) ་ བྱང་ཐང་ལ་ཞིང་ག་འདེབས་རྒྱུ་ཟེར་བ་དེ་སྣ་ཁུག་ཁ་འཐེན་གྱི་ལས་ཀ་ཞིག་རེད་ Saying (we) will cultivate the Northern Plateau is sth. that is impossible. [Lit. the nose pulling the mouth].

སྣ་ཁུག་གི་ཨི་ཁུང་ (nāguùgi īguŋ) nostril openings.

སྣ་ཁུག་བགྲད་བགྲད་ (nāguù trɛɛ̀drɛɛ̀) a wide-shaped nose.

སྣ་ཁུག་འགག (nāguù g̲aà) vi. to have a stuffed nose (from a cold).

སྣ་ཁུག་ན་ཚ་གདོང་ (nāguù tsādoŋ) 1. vi. to have a pain in the nose, to have a nasal illness. 2. vi. to be very sad/ sorry ་ ཁོང་གིས་སྡུག་བསྔལ་གྱི་གནས་ཚུལ་བཤད་སྐབས་ང་སྣ་ཁུག་ན་ཚ་བཏང་བྱུང་ When he told the account of the suffering I got very sad.

སྣ་ཁུག་འཚིག (nəguù tsiì) 1. sm. སྣ་སྲུན་ཡོག. 2. sm. ཞེན་པ་སློག.

སྣ་ཁུག་ལེབ་ལེབ་ (nəguù le̲bleb) a flat nose.

སྣ་ཁུང་ (nəguŋ) nostril; va.—སྔོག to pick one's nose.

སྣ་ཁུང་གཅིག་ནས་དབུགས་གཏོང་ (nəguŋ jīgnɛ ūù dōŋ) holding identical opinions or point of view [Lit. breathing from one nostril].

སྣ་ཁུང་སངས་པོ་ (nəguŋ sāŋbo) sensitive nose, keen sense of smell.

སྣ་ཁོག (nāgɔɔ̀) nasal cavity, the inside of the nose.

སྣ་ཁྲག (nātraà) nose blood, nosebleed; vi.—རྒྱུག; —འཛག་ས་ to have or get a nosebleed; va.—གཅོད་ to stop a nosebleed.

སྣ་ཁྲིད་ (nā triì) sm. སྣ་འདྲེན་.

སྣ་འཁྲིད་པ་ (nā triìbə) sm. སྣ་འདྲེན་པ་.

སྣ་འཁྱོག (nākyɔɔ̀) 1. crooked nose. 2. owl.

སྣ་གུག (nāguù) aquiline nose, hooked nose.

སྣ་གོང་ (nāgoŋ) the area between the eyes (where the nose starts).

སྣ་གྲངས་ (nādraŋ) variety, items ¶ ཚོང་ཁང་དེ་ར་ཅ་ལག་སྣ་གྲངས་མང་པོ་འདུག There are many items in that store.

སྣ་དགུ་ (nəgu) sm. སྣ་ཚོགས་.

སྣ་དགོད་ (nāgöò) nasal sound made to show anger/ disapproval; va.—བྱེད.

སྣ་ཚོགས་ (nəgu) various kinds/ types/ items.

སྣ་ཚོགས་ཚོང་ཁང་ (nəgu tsōŋgaŋ) department store.

སྣ་རྒྱན་ (nāgyɛn) ornaments worn on the nose.

སྣ་རྒྱུག (nəgyuù) 1. striking a telling blow, blocking, halting; va.—སྤྲོད་; —གཞུ་ ¶ ཁོང་ཚོས་ཁུངས་མེད་ཀྱི་སྐྱོན་བརྗོད་ལ་སྣ་རྒྱུག་ཚ་ཐག་ཆོད་ཅིག་སྤྲད་པ་རེད་ (They) struck a telling blow to the baseless criticism. 2. vi.—ཡོག to be rebuffed/ blocked, to run into a stone wall ¶ དཀྲོག་གཏམ་བཟོ་མཁན་དེ་ར་ཚོགས་འདུའི་ཐོག་ལ་སྣ་རྒྱུག་ཡོག་བཞག The one who was spreading rumors got rebuffed at the meeting.

སྣ་སྒ་ (nāga) the bridge of the nose.

སྣ་སྒང་ (nāgaŋ) the bridge of the nose.

སྣ་སྒོ་ (nāgo) the nasal openings.

སྣ་སྒྲ་ (nādra) nasal sounds.

སྣ་གཅིག (nəjig) one kind.

སྣ་གཅིག་ཁོ་ན་གཉེར་ (nəjig kōna ñēr) va. to work for only one thing, to specialize in only one thing.

སྣ་གཅིག་དགེ་བསྙེན་ (nəjig ge̲ñen) a lay person who takes only one of the དགེ་བསྙེན་ vows.

སྣ་གཅིག་སྤྱོད་པའི་དགེ་བསྙེན་ (nəjig jööbɛ ge̲ñen) sm. སྣ་གཅིགས་དགེ་བསྙེན་.

སྣ་གཅིག་སྦྱོང་བརྩོན་ (nəjig jo̲ŋdzön) specializing in one area of study.

སྣ་གཙུ་ (nəju) wooden ring that is put on the nose of cattle.

སྣ་གཅོད་ (nā jöö) va. to cut off the nose (a form of punishment in Tibet).

སྣ་བཅག (nā jāà) 1. sm. སྣ་རྒྱུག, 1. 2. va. to break (someone's) nose. 3. va. to roll over and stitch the edge of a material.

སྣ་ཆམ་ (nācam) nose cold.

སྣ་ཆུ་ (nəju) nose mucus; vi.—འདོན་; —འཛག to have a runny nose.

སྣ་ཆེན་ (nājen) 1. big nose. 2. powerful minister. 3. the large colleges in Sera, Drepung and Ganden monasteries.

སྣ་ཆེན་ཡོ་དོག (nājen yo̲dɔɔ̀) a person who has an large nose.

སྣ་མཆུ་ (nā cū) abbr. nose and lips.

སྣ་འཇུ་ (nəju) 1. sm. སྣ་གཙུ་. 2. a part of a loom.

སྣ་འཇུག (nəjuù) sm. སྣ་གཙུ་.

སྣ་ཉག (nāñaà) a flat/ stubby nose.

སྣ་གཉེར་བྱེད་ (nāñer ce̲è) va. to twitch one's nose (conveys disapproval).

སྣ་བཏུས་ (nādüù) a collection/ anthology of various things ¶ སྙན་ངག་སྣ་བཏུས་ An anthology of poetry.

སྣ་རྟུག (nəduù) snot, mucus; va.—འཕྱིད་ to wipe one's nose; va.—དབུགས་ to blow out mucus from a nostril (a traditional form of cleaning mucus from one's nose); vi.—ལུག; —ལྷུག; —ཤོར་ to have snot/ mucus run from the nose.

སྣ་ཐ་ (nāda) snuff; va.—འཐེན་ to take snuff; va.—བརྡར་ to grind snuff.

སྣ་ཐག (nātag) the lead rope that is tied to the nose of animals; va.—སྣར་ to insert/ fasten a nose lead rope.

སྣ་ཐག་མགོར་དཀྲིས་ (nātag gɔ̲rdriì) carefree, free, free and independent [Lit. wrap the rope (that goes into the nose of cattle) on the head].

སྣ་ཐག་བསྡོགས་པ་ (nātag do̲mba) sm. སྣ་ཐག་མགོར་དཀྲིས་.

སྣ་ཐག་ཤོར་ (nātag shɔ̄ɔ) vi. to lose one's freedom to sb. else [Lit. to lose the nose lead rope].

སྣ་ཐིག (nədig) sm. སྣ་ཐག.

སྣ་ཐུག (nəduù) sm. སྣ་རྟུག.

སྣ་ཐུག་སྤུ་སུད་ (nəduù būsüù) short or quick tempered.

སྣ་ཐུང་ཐུང་ (nā tūŋduŋ) short or quick-tempered.

སྣ་ཐུང་བ་ (nātuŋwa) 1. wool with short fibers. 2. sm. སྣ་ཐུང་ཐུང་. 3. scarce, few, insufficient.

སྣ་ཐུང་མ་ (nātuŋma) sm. སྣ་ཐུང་ཐུང་.

སྣ་ཐོད་ལ་ (nādöòla) the main pass between Sikkim and Tibet.

སྣ་དྲངས་ (nā tra̲ŋ) p. of སྣ་འདྲེན་.

སྣ་དྲི་ (nədri) sm. སྣ་རྟུག.

སྣ་གདན་ (nādɛn) padding above the arch of a Tibetan woolen boot.

སྣ་གདོང་ (nādoŋ) the bridge of the nose.

སྣ་གདོང་མཐོ་བ་ (nādoŋ tōwa) European-style nose (high bridged nose).

སྣ་གདོང་བཟང་པོ་ (nādoŋ sa̲ŋbo) sm. སྣ་གདོང་མཐོ་བ་.

སྣ་འདེད་ (nāndeè) a person who goes with carrying animals.

སྣ་འདྲེན་ (nā drēn) va. to lead, guide ¶ ཁོས་སྣ་དྲངས་ནས་ཤིང་ནགས་ལ་སླེབས་སོང་ He leading them, they arrived in the forest.

སྣ་འདྲེན་གཅིག་གྱུར་ (nāndren jīgyur) united leadership.

སྣ་འདྲེན་པ་ (nāndrenba) leader, one who guides.

སྣ་ལྡན་ (nāndɛn) nasal sound.

སྣ་ལྡན་མཚོན་པ་ (nādɛn tsõmba) a written sign indicating a nasal sound/ nasality.

སྣ་ལྡོག (nā dɔ̲ɔ̀) vi. to change direction.

སྣ་བརྡབས་ (nā də̲b) sm. སྣ་ཁུག་བརྡབས་.

སྣ་ནག་མ་ (nā na̲gma) inauspicious.

སྣ་ནད་ (na̲nɛɛ̀) disease of the nose.

སྣ་ནད་ཤ་ལུ་ (nānɛɛ̀ shālu) a growth in the nose (a form of disease in Tibetan medicine).

སྣ་ནམ་ (nānam) a name of an ancient lineage.

སྣ་ནམ་བཟའ་ (nānamsa) name of Tride Tsukden's wife (queen).

སྣ་ན་གྲེ་བ་སྡེ་ཚན་ (nāna dre̲wa de̲dzɛn) ENT (ear, nose and throat) department.

སྣ་རྣོ་བ་ (nā nōwa) sharp/ acute sense of smell.

སྣ་རྣོན་པོ་ (nā nōbo) sm. སྣ་རྣོ་བ་.

སྣ་སྣབས་ (nānəb) snot.

སྣ་པ་ (nāba) guide.

སྣ་པུ་རྒྱག (nəbu gya̲à) va. to snort (usu. sign of displeasure).

སྣ་པུད་རྒྱག (nəbüù gya̲à) sm. སྣ་པུ་རྒྱག.

སྣ་ཕྱིས་ (nəbjiì) handkerchief.

སྣ་འཕྱིད་ (nəbjiì) sm. སྣ་ཕྱིས་.

སྣ་བ་ (nāwa) a handicapped person.

སྣ་བུག (nəbuù) sm. སྣ་ཁུང་.

སྣ་བོ་ (nāwo) leader, head, guide.

སྣ་བོ་ཆེ་ (nāwoce) minister, prime minister.

སྣ་དབང་ (nāwaŋ) organ of smell.

སྣ་དབྱུག་གཞུ་ (nəyuù shu̲) sm. སྣ་རྒྱུག་, 1.

སྣ་སྦྲང་ (nādraŋ) arc. arrowhead.

སྣ་སྦྲེལ་ (nādrel) the rope that joins plowing animals. 2. two animals tied together.

སྣ་མ་ (nāma) 1. nutmeg. 2. animals with nose ring holes.

སྣ་མ་མི་སྐྱལ་ (nāma mi̲gɛɛ) one ལག of transport

animals which are the responsibility of one person.

སྣ་མང་ (nāmaŋ) 1. many kinds. 2. complex, complicated, varied, diverse.

སྣ་མང་ངལ་རྩོལ་ (nāmaŋ ŋɛɛdzöö) complex/ diverse labor.

སྣ་མང་བདག་གཉེར་ (nāmaŋ da̲gñer) diversified economy/ ownership/ business.

སྣ་མང་ཕུན་ཚོགས་ (nāmaŋ pũndzoò) varied, diverse.

སྣ་མང་ཞབས་ཞུ་ (nāmaŋ sha̲bshu) many kinds of services, serving in many different ways.

སྣ་མའི་འབྲས་བུ་ (nāmɛ drɛ̀ɛbu) sm. སྣ་མ་.

སྣ་མའི་མེ་ཏོག (nāmɛ me̲dog) cymbidium; orchid.

སྣ་མིན་སྣ་ཚོགས་ (nāmin nādzɔɔ̀) assorted, various (kinds/ types/ sorts).

སྣ་མེད་ (nāmeè) 1. torn nose of cattle (where the ring goes through the nose for tying a lead rope). 2. an animal whose nose has not been pierced.

སྣ་སྨན་ (nāmɛn) nasal medicine.

སྣ་རྩེ་ (nədze) tip of the nose.

སྣ་ཚང་ (nādzaŋ) all kinds/ varieties, complete.

སྣ་ཚིག (nādziì) abbr. of སྣ་ཁྲག་ཚིག.

སྣ་ཚོགས་ (nādzɔɔ̀) various kinds/ types ¶ བཟའ་བཏུང་སྣ་ཚོགས་ Various things to eat and drink.

སྣ་ཚོགས་སྐྱོགས་བརྒྱ་ (nādzɔɔ̀ gyɔ̄ggya) various means/ ways/ methods.

སྣ་ཚོགས་ཐབས་ (nādzɔɔ̀ tāb) sm. སྣ་ཚོགས་སྐྱོགས་བརྒྱ་.

སྣ་ཚོགས་དེབ་གསལ་ (nādzɔɔ̀ te̲bsɛl) shung. written in a book that contains many different things ¶ སྣ་ཚོགས་དེབ་གསལ་འདི་ལོའི་གཞིས་འབྲུ་དངུལ་བསྒྱུར་གྱི་དངུལ་འབབ་ཐད་ Regarding the money obtained from selling the estate's grain that was written in the book that contains many different things.

སྣ་ཚོགས་པད་མ་ (nādzɔɔ̀ bɛ̀ɛma) lotus with different colored petals.

སྣ་ཚོགས་སྤྲུལ་སྐུ་ (nādzɔɔ̀ drũũgu) various icons and statues of the Buddha.

སྣ་ཚོགས་ལྷུ་སྒྲིག (nādzɔɔ̀ lhūdrig) assembling, putting together different things; va.—བྱེད་.

སྣ་མཚུལ་ (nādzüü) sm. སྣ་མཆུ་.

སྣ་འཚང་ (nā tsāŋ) sm. སྣ་ཁྲག་འགག.

སྣ་མཛུབ་སྒྲོད་ (nədzub drȭȍ) va. to point a finger at sb. to warn or threaten.

སྣ་འཛར་ (nādzar) tassle.

སྣ་འཛིན་ (nəndzin) person in charge, leader, guide.

སྣ་འཛོམ་ (nāndzom) sm. སྣ་འཛོམས་.

སྣ་འཛོམས་ (nāndzom) many kinds/ varieties.

སྣ་འཛོམས་དུས་དེབ་ (nāndzom tü̲üdeb) magazine, journal ¶ སྣ་འཛོམས་དུས་དེབ་ཁང་ Magazine office/ company.

སྣ་ཞག (nāshaà) grease from butter tea that is applied on the nose/ face; va.—རྒྱག to apply grease from butter tea on one's nose/ face.

སྣ་ཞགས་ (nāshaà) trunk of an elephant.

སྣ་ཞགས་ཅན་ (nāshaàjɛn) elephant.

སྣ་ཞོམ་ (nāshom) flatish nosed.

སྣ་གཞུང་ (na̲shuŋ) middle of the nose.

སྣ་གཞོང་ (nāshoŋ) stone bowl used to grind snuff.

སྣ་ཟིན་ཙམ་ (nā si̲ndzam) superficial, not in depth ¶ མྱོང་བ་སྣ་ཟིན་ཙམ་ A superficial experience.

སྣ་ཟུར་ (nāsur) corner.

སྣ་ཟོན་ (nāsön) sm. སྣ་སྲུན་.

སྣ་གཟེངས་མཐོ་བ་ (nāseŋ tōwo) high bridged nose.

སྣ་ཡོར་ (nāyɔr) nostril.

སྣ་རལ་ (nārɛɛ) torn nose.

སྣ་རིགས་ (nərig) kinds, variety.

སྣ་རིགས་སྤུ་ཚོགས་ (nərig būdzɔɔ̀) various kinds ¶ དེ་རིང་ཚོགས་འདུར་མི་སྣ་རིགས་སྤུ་ཚོགས་ཕྱིན་འདུག Today all sorts of people (from all walks of life) came to the meeting.

སྣ་རིང་ (nəriŋ) 1. cotton fluff that can be spun into pieces. 2. tolerant, patient. 3. abundant, plentiful. 4. a long nose. 5. a long planing tool.

སྣ་རིང་བ་ (nāriŋwə) sm. སྣ་རིང་.

སྣ་རིས་སྤུ་ཚོགས་ (nəriì būdzɔɔ̀) sm. སྣ་རིགས་སྤུ་ཚོགས་.

སྣ་རུ་ (nəru) snuff box.

སྣ་རུས་ (nārüü) nose bone.

སྣ་རེ་སྣ་གཉིས་ (nāre nəñiì) a few items.

སྣ་རེ་ཙམ་ (nāredzam) a few, some.

སྣ་རྭ་ (nāra) snuff box made from the horn of an animal.

སྣ་ལ་འགྲོ་ (nāla dro̲) see སྣ་.

སྣ་ལུང་ (nəluŋ) the rope that is put through the nose of an animal.

སྣ་ལུད་ (nəlüü) sm. སྣ་ཏུག.

སྣ་ལེབ་ (nāleb) a flat/ stubby nose.

སྣ་ལེན་ (nālen) sm. སྣེ་ལེན་.

སྣ་ལོ་ (nālo) 1. a riding yak. 2. a dehorned yak.

སྣ་ཤ་ (nāsha) the fleshy part of the nose. 2. sm. སྣ་ལུང་.

སྣ་ཤུ་ (nəshu) 1. a kind of nasal disease in Tibetan medicine. 2. hissing sound from the nose indicating anger/ disapproval; va.—རྒྱག.

སྣ་ཤེས་ (nāsheè) sense of smell.

སྣ་ཤོ་ (nāsho) sm. སྣ་རལ་.

སྣ་གཤོག (nāshɔɔ̀) alae of the nose (winged area on the sides of the nose).

སྣ་སྲུན་འཁེལ་ (nāsün kēē) sm. སྣ་སྲུན་ཕོག.

སྣ་སྲུན་འཁྱེར་ (nāsün kyēr) sm. སྣ་སྲུན་ཕོག.

སྣ་སྲུན་སྤྲོད་ (nāsün drȍȍ) va. to teach sb. a lesson.

སྣ་སྲུན་ཕོག (nāsün pɔ̄ɔ̀) vi. to be taught/ learn a lesson (as a result of sth.) ¶ ཕམ་ཉེས་ག་ཚོད་བྱུང་ཡང་སྣ་སྲུན་ཕོག་ཡས་མི་འདུག No matter how many defeats he experienced, he didn't learn his lesson.

སྣ་སྲུན་ཟབ་པོ་ (nāsün sa̲bbu) a profound lesson.

སྣ་སུབས་ (nəsub) an illness where breathing is difficult through the nose.

སྣ་སེལ་ (nā sēl) 1. overcoming difficulties. 2. clearing a path/ road.

སྣ་གསང་པོ་ (nā sāŋbo) keen sense of smell.

སྣ་བསྲུན་ (nā sŭn) sm. སྣ་སྲུན་ཕོག.

སྣ་ལྷགས་ (nālhaà) an animal sickness.

སྣག (nāà) 1. abbr. of སྣག་ཚ་. 2. relatives. 3. name of an ancient lineage in Tibet.

སྣག་གོང་ (nāggoŋ) sm. སྣག་བུམ་.

སྣག་སྐྱོགས་ (nāggyɔɔ̀) inkstone, inkslab (for grinding ink).

སྣག་གི་གཉེན་མཚམས་ (nāggi ñēndzam) 1. brothers and sisters. 2. cousins.

སྣག་གི་ཚ་པོ་ (nāggi tsāwo) maternal nephew/ niece.

སྣག་རྒྱུག (nəggyuù) pestle for blending/ making ink.

སྣག་སྙིགས་ (nəgñeg) ink dregs.

སྣག་ཐིག (nəgdig) ink blot/ stain.

སྣག་སྣུམ་ (nəgnum) black and shiny.

སྣག་བུམ་ (nəgbum) ink bottle/ holder, ink pot.

སྣག་བུམ་སྣག་ཤོག (nəgbum nāgshɔɔ̀) writing materials.

སྣག་བུམ་སྨྱུག་སྒྲོག (nəgbum ñu̲gdrɔɔ̀) pen holder and ink bottle.

སྣག་དཔོན་ (nāgbön) maternal cousins.

སྣག་མོ་ (nāgmo) tender (meat).

སྣག་སྨྱུག (nəgñuù) ink and pen.

སྣག་སྣོད་ (nāgnöö) ink pot.

སྣག་ཚ་ (nāgdza) ink; va.—མཉེད་; —དཀྲུར་ to blend solid ink with water to make liquid ink.

སྣག་རྫོབ་ (nāgdzob) a large blotch of ink.

སྣག་རིས་ (nəgriì) ink drawing, ink painting.

སྣག་ལེན་འགེབས་ (nāglen ge̲b) va. to blot ink.

སྣག་ལེན་ཤོག་བུ་ (nāglen shɔ̄gbu) blotting paper.

སྣག་ཤོག (nāgshɔɔ̀) 1. carbon paper. 2. abbr. ink and paper.

སྣགས་ (nāg) 1. arc. va. to rape. 2. va. to make dirty.

སྣང་ (nāŋ) 1. abbr. of སྣང་བ་. 2. name of a district in Lhoka.

སྣང་སྐྱིད་བློ་བདེ་ (nāŋgyiì lōde) happy and assured.

སྣང་ཁུང་ (nəŋguŋ) chimney, smoke hole.

སྣང་གྲགས་ (nāŋdraà) known and seen by all.

སྣང་གྲགས་རིག་གསུམ་ (nāŋdraà ri̲gsum) abbr. sight,

sound and knowing.

སྣང་ངོ་ (nāŋŋo) sm. སྣང་བ་.

སྣང་ངོར་ (nāŋŋor) sm. སྣང་བ་.

སྣང་ངོར་འཆར་ (nāŋŋɔr cār) vi. to visualize mentally, to imagine, to appear in one's mind.

སྣང་ངོར་མི་འཇུག་པ་ (nāŋɔr mijugbə) unbecoming in other's perception.

སྣང་ངོར་མཛེས་པ་ (nāŋŋɔr dzḛeba) becoming in other's perception.

སྣང་ངོས་ (nāŋŋöö) 1. front. 2. outlook.

སྣང་ཆུང་ (nāŋjuŋ) 1. holding in low esteem/ regard, looking down on; va.—བྱེད་; —གཏོང་ to hold in low esteem/ regard, to look down on ¶ཁོ་ཚོས་ཆོས་ལ་སྣང་ཆུང་བྱེད་ཀྱི་ཡོད་པ་རེད་ They have a low regard for religion. 2. not paying attention to sth., being negligent; vi.— ཤོར་; —ལུས་.

སྣང་ཆུང་ཁུར་མེད་ (nāŋjuŋ kūrmeè) looking down on and being irresponsible/ negligent.

སྣང་ཆུང་ལྷོད་གཡེང་ (nāŋjuŋ lhöòyeŋ) sm. སྣང་ཆུང་ཁུར་མེད་.

སྣང་ཆེན་ (nāŋjen) high esteem/ regard; va.—བྱེད་ to hold in high esteem/ regard.

སྣང་ཆེར་བརྩི་ (nāŋcer dzī) sm. སྣང་ཆེན་བྱེད་.

སྣང་འཆར་ (nāŋjar) feeling, impression, image, mental vision.

སྣང་འཆར་རིང་ལུགས་ (nāŋcar ri̱ŋluù) impressionism.

སྣང་འཇོག་ (nāŋjɔ̀ɔ) paying attention to, regarding well; va.—བྱེད་.

སྣང་བརྙན་ (nāŋñɛn) image.

སྣང་དག་ (nāŋdaà) (— + neg.) without fear/ worry, no problem ¶ཁོ་སློབ་གྲྭར་འགྲོ་ཡག་ལ་སྣང་དག་མི་འདུག There is no problem with him going to school. ¶ཁྱེད་རང་འདིའི་སྐོར་སྣང་དག་མི་དགོས་ You don't have to worry about this. ¶ཁྱེད་རང་བོད་ལ་འགྲོ་ཡག་འདི་སྣང་དག་གཏོང་དགོས་མ་རེད་ There is no need for you to worry about going to Tibet.

སྣང་དོགས་ (nāŋdɔ̀ɔ) feeling of suspicion ¶གནས་ཚུལ་སྡུག་པོ་འདི་འདྲ་ཡོང་གི་རེད་བསམ་པའི་སྣང་དོགས་མེད་ I had no suspicion that bad events like this would occur.

སྣང་བ་ (nāŋwa) 1. impression, feeling, sensation ¶གཞིས་ཆགས་མཐོང་དུས་བོད་ལ་སླེབས་པའི་སྣང་བ་བྱུང་ When I saw the settlement I had the feeling of being in Tibet. 2. attentiveness, interest; va.—བྱེད་ to take interest in ¶ཁོ་སློབ་སྦྱོང་ལ་སྣང་བ་མི་འདུག He has no interest in studying. 3. vi. to see ¶ཚེས་བཅོ་ལྔའི་དགོང་མོ་ནི་ཟླ་བ་ཧྲིལ་ཆང་སྣང་བའི་དུས་ཚོད་རེད་ The evening of the fifteenth is the time when you can see the whole (full) moon. 4. sm. ཡོད་པ་ (in some dialects). 5. awareness of sth. ¶ང་སླེབས་པ་ཁོ་ལ་སྣང་བ་བྱུང་མ་སོང་ He wasn't aware that I arrived.

སྣང་བ་སྐྱིད་པོ་ (nāŋwa gyiìbu) carefree, happy-go-lucky.

སྣང་བ་འཁྲུལ་ (nāŋwa trǖü) vi. to be/ act irrational ¶མི་དབུལ་པོ་དེ་སྣང་བ་འཁྲུལ་ནས་ཕྱུག་བདག་གི་བུ་མོ་མནའ་མར་སློང་འདུག The poor person acted irrational and asked for the hand of the rich man's daughter in marriage.

སྣང་བ་གང་དྲན་ (nāŋwa ka̱ŋdrɛn) doing whatever one wants or whatever comes to mind, acting without regard to rules, acting impulsively; va.—བྱེད་ ¶སྤྱི་ཁང་ཚང་མ་འགོ་ཁྲིད་ཀྱི་སྣང་བ་གང་དྲན་ལྟར་སྐྱོང་གི་ཡོད་པ་རེད་ The communes were run in accordance with whatever pleased the leaders.

སྣང་བ་གང་དྲན་བྱེད་ (nāŋwa ka̱ndraà cḛè) va. to do whatever one wants.

སྣང་བ་འགྱུར་ (nāwaŋ gyu̱r) vi. to have a change of mind.

སྣང་བ་འགྲོ་པོ་ (nāŋwa dro̱bo) amiable, likable, personable; vi.—བྱེད་ to find sth. to one's liking, to consider sth. likeable/ attractive ¶ཅ་ལག་དེ་ཁོང་གི་སྣང་བར་འགྲོ་པོ་བྱུང་སོང་ He found that thing to his liking. ¶མནའ་མོ་དེ་ཕ་མ་གཉིས་ཀྱི་སྣང་བ་འགྲོ་པོ་བྱེད་ཀྱི་འདུག The parents find the bride likable.

སྣང་བ་ཉིན་སྲིབ་ (nāŋwa ñi̱nsib) having a complete change of mind.

སྣང་བ་མཐོན་པོ་ (nāŋwa tõmbo) proud, arrogant.

སྣང་བ་མཐའ་ཡས་ (nāŋwa tāyɛɛ̀) 1. boundless light. 2. Amitabha.

སྣང་བ་དག་ (nāŋwa ta̱à) vi. to have a clear conscience ¶མི་གཞན་གྱིས་གང་བཤད་ཀྱང་རང་ཉིད་ཀྱི་སྣང་བ་དག་ན་འགྲིག་གི་རེད་ It doesn't matter what other say as long as you have a clear conscience.

སྣང་བ་དྲེད་ (nāŋwa trḛè) vi. to get spoiled doing bad things.

སྣང་བ་གདོང་འདེད་ (nāŋwa do̱ndeè) selfish.

སྣང་བ་བདེ་བ་ (nāŋwa de̱wa) happy.

སྣང་བ་འདོད་མེད་ (nāŋwa do̱meè) 1. apathetic, unfeeling, insensitive. 2. not knowing good from bad.

སྣང་བ་ནས་སྣང་བར་འགྲོ་ (nāŋwanɛ nāŋwar dro̱) happiness followed by happiness, continous good fortune.

སྣང་བ་ནུབ་ (nāŋwa nu̱b) vi. to die.

སྣང་བ་བན་བུན་ (nāŋwar pɛ̱nbün) confused, blurred, indistinct.

སྣང་བ་མུན་གྲོད་དུ་འགྲོ་ (nāŋwa mṵndröödu dro̱) vi. to get an inferior rebirth after a good rebirth.

སྣང་བ་མེད་པ་ (nāŋwa mḛeba) sm. སྣང་མེད་.

སྣང་བ་ཟ་ཟི་ (nāŋwa sa̱si) a vague impression ¶ང་རང་ཆུང་དུས་འགྲོ་སྡོད་སའི་ལུང་པ་དེའི་སྣང་བ་ཟ་ཟི་ཙམ་ལས་དྲན་གསལ་པོ་གསོས་ཀྱི་མི་འདུག I have only a vague impression of the place that I went to as a youngster and can't remember it very well.

སྣང་བ་ཟི་ (nāŋwa si̱) vi. to be in a daze. 2. to see a blurry image.

སྣང་བ་གཡེང་ (nāŋwa yēŋ) vi. to be diverted/ distracted in one's thoughts ¶རྩེ་མོར་སྣང་བ་གཡེང་ནས་ Being diverted by games.

སྣང་བ་ལ་འགྲོ་ (nāŋwala dro̱) sm. སྣང་བ་འགྲོ་པོ་བྱེད་.

སྣང་བ་ཤར་ཚུལ་ (nāŋwa shārdzüü) the impression a place or thing or incident leaves.

སྣང་བ་བསིལ་སང་དུ་འགྱུར་ (nāŋwa sīlsaŋdu gyu̱r) vi. to become relaxed.

སྣང་བར་འགྲོ་པོ་ (nāŋwar dro̱bo) sm. སྣང་བ་འགྲོ་པོ་.

སྣང་བར་འཆར་ (nāŋwar cār) vi. to get an impression/ feeling/ sensation ¶དཔྱིད་ཀ་ཡིན་པའི་སྣང་བ་འཆར་བྱུང་ I got the feeling of spring.

སྣང་བར་འཇོག་ (nāŋwar jɔ̀ɔ) see སྣང་བ་.

སྣང་མེད་ (nāŋmeè) 1. careless, indifferent, not paying attention to, unconcerned, neglectful; va.—བྱེད་; —གཏོང་; —དུ་འཇོག to disregard, to be indifferent, to overlook, to neglect, to be unconcerned ¶ཞུ་འབོད་དེ་དག་སྣང་མེད་དུ་བཞག་པ་རེད་ (They) were indifferent to those appeals. 2. casual, easygoing ¶མི་འདི་སྣང་མེད་ཅིག་འདུག He is a casual person.

སྣང་མེད་ཁུར་མེད་ (nāŋmeè kūrmeè) not paying attention to, not being concerned about.

སྣང་མེད་ཆད་ལུས་ (nāŋmeè cɛ̄ɛ̀lüü) a careless omission.

སྣང་མེད་དུ་སྒྱུར་ (nāŋmeèdu gyūr) va. to treat as unimportant, to treat coldly, to not to pay attention to.

སྣང་མེད་དུ་ཐལ་ (nāŋmeèdu tɛ̄ɛ) vi. to speak without thinking of the consequences.

སྣང་མེད་ནོར་འཁྲུལ་ (nāŋmeè no̱ndrüü) a careless mistake.

སྣང་མེད་ཚོར་མེད་ (nāŋmeè tsɔ̄ɔmeè) sm. སྣང་བ་འདོད་མེད་.

སྣང་མེད་གཡང་གཡེང་ (nāŋmeè yāŋyeŋ) not paying attention, being inattentive; va.—བྱེད་.

སྣང་མེད་ལིང་སྒྱུར་ (nāŋmeè li̱ŋgyur) sm. སྣང་མེད་དུ་སྒྱུར་.

སྣང་མེད་ལྷོད་གཡེང་ (nāŋmeè lhöòyeŋ) sm. སྣང་མེད་གཡང་གཡེང་.

སྣང་རྩེ་ཤག་ (nāŋdzeshar) sm. སྣང་རྩེ་ཤག་ལས་ཁུངས་.

སྣང་རྩེ་ཤག་ལས་ཁུངས་ (nāŋdzeshar lɛ̱ègun) shung. administrative headquarters of the Lhasa mayor in tt.

སྣང་ཚད་ (nāŋdzɛ̀ɛ̀) 1. degree of brightness. 2. whatever one sees ། ཕྲུ་གུ་འདིས་རྩེད་ཆས་སྣང་ཚད་ཉོ་དགོས་ཟེར་གྱི་འདུག Whatever toys the child sees he says he wants to buy it.

སྣང་ཚུལ་ (nāŋdzüü) 1. appearance, look; vi.—འཆར་ to appear/ look ། སྣང་ཚུལ་བཅོས་མ་ A false appearance. 2. form. phenomenon.

སྣང་ཞེན་ (nāŋshen) becoming attached to sth.

སྣང་འོད་ (nāŋwöö) brightness.

སྣང་ཡུལ་ (nāŋyüü) things that are visible.

སྣང་གཡེང་ (nāŋ yēŋ) vi. to be inattentive/ distracted, not paying attention.

སྣང་ལོག (nāŋ lɔ̀ɔ̀) being turned off by sth., coming to dislike; vi.—སྐྱེ་ ། ང་ན་བའི་རྗེས་སུ་ཨ་རག་འཐུང་རྒྱུར་སྣང་ལོག་སྐྱེས་བྱུང་ After I was sick, I came to dislike liqueur.

སྣང་ཤག (nāŋshaà) shung. abbr. of སྣང་ཅེ་ཤག.

སྣང་ཤག་མི་དཔོན་ (nāŋshar mibön) shung. the mayor of Lhasa in tt.

སྣང་ཤས་ (nāŋshɛ̀ɛ̀) temporary attachment.

སྣང་སྲིད་ (nāŋsii) all things in this world, all that appears and exists.

སྣང་གསལ་ (nāŋsɛɛ) 1. bright, airy ། ཁང་པ་འདི་སྣང་གསལ་ཡག་པོ་འདུག This house is very bright and airy. 2. butter lamp.

སྣང་གསལ་མར་མེ་ (nāŋsɛɛ marme) butter lamp.

སྣད་: p. and f. བསྣད་ (nɛ̀ɛ̀) vi. to get hurt/ injured.

སྣད་ཡར་ (nɛ̀ɛ̀yar) wounded, injured.

སྣབས་ (nɔ̄b) sm. སྣབས་རྡུག.

སྣབས་རྡུག (nɔ̄bduù) sm. སྣ་རྡུག.

སྣབས་ལྡུག (nɔ̄b duù) sm. སྣ་རྡུག་ལུག.

སྣབས་ཕྱི་ (nɔ̄b jii) va. to wipe one's nose.

སྣབས་ཕྱིས་ (nɔ̄bjii) handkerchief.

སྣབས་འབུ་ (nɔ̄mbu) a slug (the insect).

སྣབས་འབུད་ (nɔ̄b büü) sm. སྣབས་ལུད་འདོར་.

སྣབས་ལུད་ (nɔ̄blüü) nose mucus; va.—འདོར་ to blow one's nose.

སྣམ་ (nām) abbr. of སྣམ་བུ་.

སྣམ་དཀྲིས་ (nāmdrii) wooden roller on which finished woolen materials are rolled.

སྣམ་ཁྲུད་ (nāmgyɛ̀ɛ̀) sm. སྣམ་པ་.

སྣམ་གོས་ (nāmgöö) woolen clothes.

སྣམ་ཆས་ (nāmjɛ̀ɛ̀) woolen (woven) goods/ cloth ། སྣམ་ཆས་བཟོ་གྲྭ་ Woolen goods factory.

སྣམ་སྟོད་ (nāmdöö) woolen upper garment.

སྣམ་འཐག་པ་ (nām tāgba) weaver (of woolen materials).

སྣམ་པ་ (nāmba) a standard unit of width for woven wool materials ། ཕྱུ་པའི་མདུན་ཕྱི་ལ་སྣམ་བུ་སྣམ་པ་གསུམ་དགོས་ The front part of the dress requires three "namba".

སྣམ་ཕྱིང་ (nāmjiŋ) toilet, lavatory.

སྣམ་ཕྱིས་ (nāmjii) sm. སྣམ་ཕྱིང་.

སྣམ་ཕྲན་ (nāmdrɛn) sm. སྣམ་པ་.

སྣམ་ཕྲུག (nəmdruù) abbr. སྣམ་བུ་སྤུ་ཕྲུག.

སྣམ་བུ་ (nəmbu) woolen cloth, serge; va.—འཐག to weave woolen cloth.

སྣམ་བུ་རྒྱ་ཡ་མ་ (nəmbu gyāyama) woolen material woven with very thin yarn.

སྣམ་བུ་ཐིག་མ་ (nəmbu tīgmə) woolen cloth with a cross (++) design.

སྣམ་བུ་སྤུ་ཅན་ (nəmbu būjɛn) woolen material with a sof finish.

སྣམ་བུ་སྤུ་ཕྲུག (nəmbu būdruù) a high quality woven woolen cloth.

སྣམ་བུ་བལ་སྲིག་རྒྱག (nəmbu peeseg gyaà) va. to brush woolen material after it is woven to finish it and give it luster.

སྣམ་བུ་ཕྱིང་མ་ (nəmbu jiŋmə) medium quality woolen cloth.

སྣམ་བུའི་ལས་ཀ་ (nəmbü lɛ̀ɛ̀ga) work relating to making woolen cloth.

སྣམ་ཕྱིངས་ (nāmjiŋ) type of woolen material.

སྣམ་སྦྱར་ (nāmjaa) a type of monk's robe.

སྣམ་འཛར་ (nāmdzar) tassle of woolen material.

སྣམ་ཞིང་ (nāmsheŋ) sm. སྣམ་པ་.

སྣམ་གཞོགས་ (nāmshɔ̀ɔ̀) 1. nearby, close, adjacent. 2. behind.

སྣམ་ཡུག (nāmyuù) a roll of woolen material.

སྣམ་རས་ (nāmrɛ̀ɛ̀) abbr. woolen and cotton material.

སྣམ་ལོགས་ (nāmlɔ̀ɔ̀) sm. སྣམ་གཞོགས་.

སྣའི་ཀ་བ་ (nɛ̄ gāwa) nasal septum.

སྣའི་སྐྱེ་མཆེད་ (nɛ̄ gyējeè) organs of smell.

སྣའི་ཁམས་ (nɛ̄ kām) sphere/ realm of smell.

སྣའི་ཁྲུང་ཁྲུང་ (nɛ̄ trūndruŋ) nasal cartilage.

སྣའི་དྲི་མ་ (nɛ̄ trimə) snot, nose mucus.

སྣའི་དབང་པོ་ (nɛ̄ wāŋbo) sm. སྣའི་སྐྱེ་མཆེད་.

སྣར་: p. and f. བསྣར་; imp. སྣོར་ (nār) va. 1. to stretch, to extend, to stick out ། ཁ་གདངས་ལྕེ་སྣར་ To open one's mouth and to stick out one's tongue.

སྣར་ལྡུད་པའི་སྐྱུད་ (nārdüübɛ jɛ̀ɛ̀) a verterinarian's tool for putting medicine in the nose of animals.

སྣར་ཕོག (nār pɔ̄ɔ̄) sm. སྣ་སྣུན་ཕོག.

སྣལ་ (nɛ̄ɛ̄) abbr. of སྣལ་མ་.

སྣལ་འཕང་ (nɛ̄ɛ̄baŋ) sm. སྣལ་ཤིང་.

སྣལ་མ་ (nɛ̄ɛ̄ma) yarn.

སྣལ་མ་ཕྲ་བ་ (nɛ̄ɛ̄ma trāwa) thin or fine thread/ yarn.

སྣལ་མ་ཕྲ་བའི་འཁོར་ཁང་ (nɛ̄ɛ̄ma trɛ̄wɛ kɔ̄ɔ̄gaŋ) spinning/ textile shop or factory.

སྣལ་མའི་བཟོ་ཁང་ (nɛ̄ɛ̄mɛ sogaŋ) textile plant.

སྣལ་མའི་བཟོ་གྲྭ་ (nɛ̄ɛ̄mɛ sodra) sm. སྣལ་མའི་བཟོ་ཁང་.

སྣལ་ཚོས་རྒྱག་བྱེད་འཕྲུལ་འཁོར་ (nɛ̄ɛ̄dzöö gyaàjeè trüügɔɔ) machine for dyeing yarn.

སྣལ་ཤིང་ (nɛ̄ɛ̄shiŋ) spindle.

སྣས་ (nɛ̄ɛ̀) a part of a loom.

སྣས་འཁོར་ (nɛ̄ɛ̀gɔɔ) a part of a loom.

སྣུད་: p. བསྣུད་; f. བསྣུད་; imp. སྣུད་ (düü) va. to chase out, to throw out ། ཞིང་གཞི་ནང་ནས་བ་ལང་རྣམས་ཕྱིར་བསྣུད་པ་རེད་ They chased the cows and oxen from the field.

སྣུན་: p. and f. བསྣུན་; imp. སྣུན་ (nūm) 1. va. to stick in, to prick, to poke ། ཇེ་གྲི་དགྲ་ར་སྣུན་ To stick the enemy with bayonets. 2. va. to breastfeed, to suckle. 3. va. to beat/ hit.

སྣུབ་: p. བསྣུབས་; f. བསྣུབ་; imp. སྣུབས་ (nūb) 1. va. to destroy, to extinguish, to abolish, to annihilate. 2. va. to put/ hold under water. 3. va. to drown.

སྣུབས་ (nūb) imp. of སྣུབ་.

སྣུམ་ (nūm) 1. oil. 2. gasoline.

སྣུམ་ཀོང་ (nūmgoŋ) a small bowl for burning oil.

སྣུམ་རྐྱལ་ (nūmgyɛɛ) leather pouch for holding oil.

སྣུམ་སྐྱེལ་གྲུ་གཟིངས་ (nūmgyee trusiŋ) oil tanker.

སྣུམ་དཀྱུས་མ་ (nūm gyüüma) low grade oil.

སྣུམ་བཀྲག (nūmdraà) rich in color.

སྣུམ་ཁུལ་ (nūmgüü) oil field, oil-bearing area.

སྣུམ་ཁྲོན་ (nūmdrön) oil well.

སྣུམ་འཁུར་ (nūmgur) sm. སྣུམ་བཙོས་གོ་རེ་.

སྣུམ་འཁོར་ (nūmgɔɔ) automobile.

སྣུམ་འཁོར་ཀྲག (nūmgɔɔ drāg) tib.eng. truck.

སྣུམ་འཁོར་ཏྲིག་སི་ (nūmgɔɔ drīgsi) tib.eng. taxi.

སྣུམ་འཁོར་གྱི་འདྲེན་གཡོག་པ་ (nūmgɔɔgi deèyɔgba) motor driver (as distinct from owner), chauffeur.

སྣུམ་འཁོར་སྦ་སི་ (nūmgɔɔ bəse) tib.eng. bus.

སྣུམ་འཁོར་ཚོགས་སྡེ་ (nūmgɔɔ tsɔ̄gde) Motor Vehicle Board/ Bureau.

སྣུམ་འཁོར་ཚོགས་སྡེའི་ཞིབ་དཔྱོད་པ་ (nūmgɔɔ tsɔ̄gdee shibjööbə) motor vehicle inspector.

སྣུམ་འཁོར་ལམ་ཆེན་ (nūmgɔɔ lamjen) motor highway.

སྣུམ་འཁོལ་ (nūmgöö) boiling/ boiled oil.

སྣུམ་འཁོལ་ (nūm gȫö) vi. to be boiling (oil).

སྣུམ་འཁྱེར་གྲུ་གཟིངས་ (nūmgyer trusiŋ) oil tanker.

སྣུམ་གྱི་དུ་དྲེག (nūmgi tudreg) 1. oily soot. 2. lampblack.

སྣུམ་གྲུ་ (nūmdru) oil tanker.

སྣུམ་རྒྱུ་ (nūmgyu) oil materials/ resources.

སྣུམ་རྒྱུའི་སྐྱེ་དངོས་ (nūmgyü gyēŋuoȍ) sm. སྣུམ་རྒྱུའི་ལོ་ཏོག.

སྣུམ་རྒྱུའི་ལོ་ཏོག (nūmgyü lodoȍ) oil bearing crops.

སྣུམ་སྒམ་ (nūmgam) fuel tank, oil tank.

སྣུམ་སྣལ་འཕྲུལ་འཁོར་ (nūmgüü trűűgɔɔ) gasoline engine.

སྣུམ་སྣལ་སོག་ལེ་ (nūmgüü sɔ̀ɔle) gasoline operated chain saw.

སྣུམ་སྒོ་ (nūmgo) 1. throttle. 2. accelerator.

སྣུམ་བརྔོས་ (nūm ŋȍȍ) fried in oil.

སྣུམ་ཅན་ (nūmjɛn) oily, greasy.

སྣུམ་ཅིལ་ལི་བ་ (nūm ciĩliwə) oily.

སྣུམ་འཆོས་ (nūmjȍȍ) oil massage.

སྣུམ་ཇ་ (nūmja) Tibetan tea in which oil is mixed (rather than butter).

སྣུམ་རྗེན་པ་ (nūm jemba) crude oil.

སྣུམ་རྗེས་ (nūmjeè) 1. oil spot/ stain. 2. oily residue.

སྣུམ་ལྗང་ (nūmjaŋ) glossy dark green.

སྣུམ་སྙིགས་ (nūmñig) 1. sludge. 2. asphalt, tar, pitch ¶ སྣུམ་སྙིགས་ཀྱི་ཁྲོམ་ལམ་ Asphalt paved street.

སྣུམ་སྙིགས་བཟོ་གྲྭ་ (nūmñig sodra) asphalt factory.

སྣུམ་སྙིགས་ཨར་འདམ་བསྲེས་མ་ (nūmñig ārdam sēèma) asphalt concrete mixture.

སྣུམ་སྙིགས་ཨར་འདམ་བསྲེས་མ་བཟོ་གྲྭ་ (nūmñig ārdam sēèma sodra) asphalt concrete factory.

སྣུམ་སྙིགས་བཏིང་བའི་ལམ་ (nūmñig dīŋwɛ lam) a road paved with asphalt.

སྣུམ་སྙེད་ (nūmñeè) massaging with oil; va.—བྱེད་.

སྣུམ་གཏེར་ (nūmder) oil well.

སྣུམ་གཏེར་ཆགས་རྫུལ་ (nūmder cəgdzüü) oil bearing layer.

སྣུམ་ལྡང་བཙིར་ (nūmdaŋ dzīr) 1. va. to make a person have a hard time, to make a person experience hardship or difficulty ¶ སློབ་གྲྭ་བ་རྣམས་དེ་རིང་གི་ཡིག་ཚད་ཀྱིས་སྣུམ་ལྡང་བཙིར་འདུག The students had a difficult time with today's exam. 2. va. to question/ interrogate a person in a harsh, brutal manner ¶ ཁྲིམས་ཁང་ནས་མི་གསོད་ཉེས་ཅན་དེ་སྣུམ་ལྡང་བཙིར་འདུག The murderer was questioned in a harsh and brutal manner by the court.

སྣུམ་ཐབ་ (nūmdəb) kerosene stove.

སྣུམ་ཐིག (nūmdig) oily, having oil stains.

སྣུམ་ཐིང་ཐིང་ (nūm tīŋdiŋ) shinny clean, spick and span.

སྣུམ་ཐོན་ས་རིམ་ (nūmdön sərim) oil bearing layer.

སྣུམ་འཐེན་འཕྲུལ་འཁོར་ (nūmten trűűgɔɔ) oil pumping/ extracting machine.

སྣུམ་དམ་ (nūmdam) oil container.

སྣུམ་དྲག (nūmdraà) 1. tar. 2. oil residue.

སྣུམ་དྲི་ (nūmdri) oil smell; vi.—ཁ་ to smell of oil.

སྣུམ་དྲེག (nūmdreg) 1. tar. 2. oil residue.

སྣུམ་དྲེག་ལམ་ཁག (nūmdreg langaà) asphalt paved road.

སྣུམ་མདངས་ (nūmdaŋ) a rich color.

སྣུམ་མདོང་ (nūmdoŋ) oil pipe, oil pipeline.

སྣུམ་འདོན་ (nūm dön) va. to extract oil from a well, to take out oil.

སྣུམ་འདོན་བཟོ་པ་ (nūmdön soba) oil worker.

སྣུམ་འདྲེན་གྲུ་ཁ་ (nūmdren truga) oil jetty, oil tanker terminal.

སྣུམ་འདྲེན་ལྕགས་མདོང་ (nūmdren jāgdoŋ) sm. སྣུམ་མདོང་.

སྣུམ་རྡོ་སྦྲུག (nūmdo druù) an ancient method of deciding a dispute by letting the two parties pick white and black stones from boiling oil and whoever picks the white stone wins the case.

སྣུམ་ལྡན་ (nūmdɛn) a laxative made from melted butter.

སྣུམ་ལྡན་ཏ་ལ་ཤིང་ (nūmdɛn dāla shīŋ) oil palm tree.

སྣུམ་ལྡན་རྡོ་གཡམ་ (nūmdɛn doyam) oil shale.

སྣུམ་ལྡན་བྱུག་སྨན་ (nūmdɛn cūùmɛn) ointment, salve.

སྣུམ་ལྡན་ཤོག་ཁྱིང་ (nūmdɛn shɔ̄gjiŋ) 1. linoleum. 2. tar paper.

སྣུམ་ནག (nūmnaà) macadam; va.—འདིང་ to lay down macadam.

སྣུམ་ནག་ལམ་ཆེན་ (nūmnaà lamjen) macadam topped highway.

སྣུམ་ནག་གཞུང་ལམ་ (nūmnaà shunlam) macadam topped highway.

སྣུམ་གནོན་ལྦིད་འདེགས་ཡོ་བྱད་ (nūmnön jindeg yobjɛɛ̀) hydraulic jack, oil jack.

སྣུམ་སྣག (nūmnaà) oil ink, printing ink.

སྣུམ་སྣོད་ (nūmnöȍ) fuel tank, oil tank.

སྣུམ་སྣོན་ས་ཚིགས་ (nūmnön sədzii) gasoline station, filling station.

སྣུམ་པུ་ (nūmbu) sm. སྣུམ་པོ་.

སྣུམ་པར་ (nūmbar) mimeographing; va.—རྒྱག.

སྣུམ་པར་འཕྲུལ་ཆས་ (nūmbar trűűjɛɛ̀) mimeograph machine.

སྣུམ་པར་ཤོག་མ་ (nūmbar shɔ̄gma) master/ original for making mimeograph copies.

སྣུམ་པོ་ (nūmbu) 1. deep/ dark/ rich color, a conservative color ¶ མི་དེས་དུག་ལོག་སྣུམ་པོ་ཞིག་གྱོན་འདུག This man wore a rich, dark colored dress. 2. rich, healthy food (refers to oily foods) ¶ རྒྱུན་དུ་ཁ་ལག་སྣུམ་པོ་བཟས་ན་གཟུགས་པོ་ཐང་པོ་ཡོང་ (If you) always eat rich and healthy food, (you) will be healthy.

སྣུམ་སྤགས་ (nūmbaà) vegetable oil mixed into tsampa to make སྤགས་.

སྣུམ་བག་ཅན་ (nūmbaàjɛn) greasy, oily, glossy.

སྣུམ་བག་ལྡན་པ་ (nūmbaà dɛmba) sm. སྣུམ་བག་ཅན་.

སྣུམ་བག་འཚེར་བ་ (nūmbaà tsērwa) healthy looking.

སྣུམ་བག་འཚེར་འཚེར་ (nūmbaà tsērdzer) sm. སྣུམ་བག་འཚེར་བ་.

སྣུམ་བན་ (nūmbɛn) container for putting oil.

སྣུམ་བྲིས་རི་མོ་ (nūmdrii rimu) sm. སྣུམ་ཚོན་རི་མོ་.

སྣུམ་འབྱུག (nūm juù) va. to apply/ rub on oil.

སྣུམ་སྦུག (nūmbuù) sm. སྣུམ་མདོང་.

སྣུམ་སྦྱང་ (nūmjaŋ) oil refining/ processing ¶ སྣུམ་སྦྱང་བཟོ་གྲྭ་ Oil refinery.

སྣུམ་བཙག་འཁོར་ལོ་ (nūmdzaà kɔ̄ɔlo) oil mill (for extracting oil from seeds).

སྣུམ་བཙིར་ (nūm dzīr) va. to extract/ press oil.

སྣུམ་བཙིར་ཁང་ (nūmdzirgaŋ) oil extracting mill.

སྣུམ་བཙོས་ (nūmdzöȍ) fried/ cooked in oil ¶ སྣུམ་བཙོས་འཁུར་ར་ Cake/ pancake fried in oil.

སྣུམ་བཙོས་གོ་རེ་ (nūmdzöȍ kore) deep fried dough cake.

སྣུམ་བཙོས་ཡིའུ་ཐིའོ་ (nūmdzöȍ yiuti) tib.ch. deep fried twisted dough sticks.

སྣུམ་རྩམ་སྐྱོ་མ་ (nūmdzam gyōma) a gruel of sweetened, fried flour.

སྣུམ་རྩི་ (nūmdzi) oil, fat, grease.

སྣུམ་ཚག (nūmdzaà) oil pressing/ extracting.

སྣུམ་ཚིལ་ (nūmdzii) 1. oil and fat. 2. oily.

སྣུམ་ཚིལ་ཚིལ་ (nūm tsīīdzii) sm. སྣུམ་ཚིལ་ལི་བ་.

སྣུམ་ཚིལ་ལི་བ་ (nūm tsīīliwə) greasy, oily.

སྣུམ་ཚོན་རི་མོ་ (nūmdzön rimu) oil painting.

སྣུམ་ཚོས་མ་ (nūm dzȍȍma) deep fried in oil.

སྣུམ་འཚག་ཁང་ (nūmdzaàgaŋ) sm. སྣུམ་བཙིར་ཁང་.

སྣུམ་འཚག་བཟོ་གྲྭ་ (nūmdzaà sodra) oil/ gasoline refinery.

སྣུམ་མཛོད་ (nūmdzöȍ) oil storage tank.

སྣུམ་མཛོད་ཁང་ (nūmdzöògaŋ) gas station.

སྣུམ་ཞག (nūmshaà) 1. dark, rich in color. 2. abbr. oil and grease.

སྣུམ་ཞག་དོད་པོ་ (nūmshaà tȍȍbo) 1. dark, rich in color. 2. healthy looking. 3. shiny in an oily sense as after polishing.

སྣུམ་ཞིང་ (nūmshiŋ) oil field.

སྣུམ་བཞུ་ (nūmshu) oil lamp.

སྣུམ་ཟ་ (nūmsa) poet. lamp.

སྣུམ་ཟད་ཀྱི་མར་མེ་ (nūmsɛɛ̀gi marme) decrepit, old, weak (used for people and politics).[Lit. the flame of a butter lamp that is about to die].

སྣུམ་ཟད་མར་མེ་ (nūmsɛɛ̀ marme) sm. སྣུམ་ཟད་ཀྱི་མར་མེ་.

སྣུམ་ཟད་ཚད་ (nūm sɛɛ̀dzɛɛ̀) oil consumption.

སྣུམ་ཟན་མ་ (nūm sɛnmə) person who eats rich foods.

སྣུམ་ཟོ་ (nūmso) oil (storage) tank, oil drum.

སྣུམ་ཟོམ་ (nūmsom) sm. སྣུམ་ཟོ་.

སྣུམ་ཟོམ་འཁོར་ལོ་ (nūmsom kɔ̄ɔlo) oil transport truck.

སྣུམ་རས་ (nūmrɛɛ̀) oilcloth, oilskin, tarpaulin.

སྣུམ་རིགས་ (nūmrig) (different kinds of) oils.

སྣུམ་རིས་ (nūmriì) sm. སྣུམ་ཚོན་རི་མོ་.

སྣུམ་རོ་ (nūmro) oil residue/ dregs.

སྣུམ་རླུང་ (nūmlaŋ) natural gas.

སྣུམ་ལ་སྲེག (nūmla sēg) va. to fry in oil, to deep fry.

སྣུམ་ཤས་ཆེ་ཆུང་ (nūmshɛɛ̀ cījuŋ) oil content.

སྣུམ་ཤུར་ཤུར་ (nūm shūrshur) sm. སྣུམ་ཚིལ་ཚིལ་.

སྣུམ་ཤོག (nūmshoò) oil paper, wax paper.

སྣུམ་གསོག་ཁང་ (nūmsoògaŋ) oil storage building.

སྣུར་: p. and f. **བསྣུར་**; imp. **སྣུར་** (nūr) 1. va. to grind, to pulverize, to crush ¶ སྣག་ཚ་སྣུར་རྒྱུ་ Grinding ink. 2. va. to move ¶ ལྕོག་ཙེ་དེ་མདུན་ཕྱོགས་སུ་སྣུར་དགོས་ (You) must move the table to the front. 3. va. to make a time earlier/ sooner ¶ ཚོགས་འདུའི་དུས་ཚོད་བསྣུར་བཞག The time of the meeting was made sooner.

སྣེ་ (nē) 1. end, tip, extremity. 2. abbr. of སྣེ་ཁ་ ¶ སྣེ་གཅིག One kind.

སྣེ་ཁ་ (nēga) kind, type, part.

སྣེ་ཁ་འཛོམས་པོ་ (nēga dzombo) all kinds/ types.

སྣེ་ཁག (nēgaà) different kinds.

སྣེ་ཁྲིད་ (nēdriì) sm. སྣེ་འཁྲིད་.

སྣེ་ཁྲིད་རྟ་པ་ (nēdriì dāba) the rider who is leading/ heading a procession.

སྣེ་འཁྲིད་ (nē triì) 1. leading, heading; va.—བྱེད་ to lead, to head ¶ ཁོང་གིས་སྣེ་ཁྲིད་བྱས་ནས་ང་ཚོ་ལྟ་སྐོར་ལ་ཕྱིན་པ་རེད་ We went on a visit with him acting as leader. ¶ རྡོ་རྗེ་ལགས་ཀྱིས་སྐུ་ཚབ་ཚོགས་པའི་མི་སྣ་སྣེ་ཁྲིད་ཀྱིས་མཚོ་ཐོག་ནས་རྒྱ་གར་ལ་ཕྱིན་པ་རེད་ The group of representatives led by Dorje went to India by sea. 2. va. to set an example ¶ མི་ཚང་གཅིག་གིས་སྣེ་ཁྲིད་བྱས་ནས་ཚང་མས་བརྙན་འཁྱེར་ཉོས་སོང་ After one family set an example, all bought televisions.

སྣེ་འཁྲིད་གནམ་གྲུ་ (nētriì nāmdru) the lead/ front/ head aircraft.

སྣེ་གྲངས་ (nēdraŋ) the number of kinds/ items ¶ སྣེ་གྲངས་ཇེ་མང་དུ་སོང་བ་རེད་ The number of items increased.

སྣེ་མགྲོན་ (nēndrön) shung. 1. liason person/ official for visitors. 2. the lord chamberlain of the regent (in tt.).

སྣེ་འགུགས་ (nēguù) a short rope used to tie animals to the long main rope staked in the ground.

སྣེ་གོད་ (nēgöò) sm. སྣེའུ་གོད་.

སྣེ་རྒྱན་ (nēgyɛn) decorative materials (such as fur, brocades, etc.) used along the outer edge of a dress.

སྣེ་གཅིག (nējig) one kind/ unit, individual ¶ ཚོང་ཁང་དེ་ར་བཟའ་བཅའི་རིགས་སྣེ་གཅིག་མེད་སྐབས་ Because the store had not even one kind of food.

སྣེ་གཉིས་ (nēñiì) the two ends, the two poles (negative and positive).

སྣེ་རྙིད་ (nēñiì) sm.* སྣེ་རྙེད་.

སྣེ་རྙེད་ (nēñeè) 1. vi. to find the end (of a string). 2. vi. to find a clue for solving a case ¶ མི་གསོད་ཉེས་ཅན་དེའི་སྣེ་རྙེད་མི་འདུག They didn't find a clue regarding the murderer (who it is).

སྣེ་གདུགས་ (nēduù) 1. va. to join ends ¶ གློག་སྐུད་གཉིས་པོ་དེའི་སྣེ་གདུགས་བཞག (They) joined the ends of the two pieces of electric wire. 2. creating a connection/ relation; va.—བྱེད་ ¶ ལས་ཀ་དེའི་སྐོར་ངས་འབྲེལ་ཡོད་ལས་ཁུངས་ལ་སྣེ་གདུགས་བྱས་པ་ཡིན་ Concerning that work, I made relations with the relevant offices.

སྣེ་བདགས་ཙམ་ (nēdagdzam) shung. sm. སྣེ་སེལ་.

སྣེ་སྟོན་ (nēdön) 1. reminding; va.—བྱེད་ ¶ ལས་ཀ་དེའི་སྐོར་ཁོང་གིས་སྣེ་སྟོན་བྱས་རྗེས་ངས་དྲན་གསོ་བྱུང་ Concerning that work, after he reminded me I remembered it. 2. guiding, showing around; va.—བྱེད་ ¶ གྲོང་ཁྱེར་གསར་པ་ཞིག་ཏུ་སླེབས་སྐབས་སྣེ་སྟོན་བྱེད་མཁན་ཞིག་དགོས་ When one arrives in a new city one needs a guide.

སྣེ་ཐིག་གི་རྒྱ་ (nēdiggi gya) lines indicating the border of sth.

སྣེ་ཐུག (nēduù) vi. to meet by chance, to meet without prior plan.

སྣེ་ཐུང་ (nēduŋ) short.

སྣེ་མཐུད་ (nēdüü) va. to join together, to link, to coordinate.

སྣེ་གདོང་རྫོང་ (nēdoŋ dzoŋ) a district/ xian in Tibet.

སྣེ་འདོམས་ (nēdom) 1. many events/ things joined together ¶ ཕྱི་ནང་གི་རྒྱུ་རྐྱེན་སྣེ་འདོམས་ཀྱིས་ By many different inner and outer causes joined together.

སྣེ་འདྲེན་པ་ (nēdrɛmba) person who is the founder/ starter; the leader.

སྣེ་ནོར་ཤོར་ (nēnɔɔ shɔ̄ɔ) vi. to miss connections with sb. ¶ ང་གཉིས་ལམ་བར་དུ་སྣེ་ནོར་ཤོར་ནས་ཐུག་མ་བྱུང་ We two missed connbections and did not meet on the road.

སྣེ་སྦྲོད་ (nēdröò) introducing, recommending; va.—བྱེད་.

སྣེ་མ་ (nēma) 1. the beginning and end of sth., the front and the back ¶ སློབ་ཕྲུག་རྣམས་བསྒྲིགས་ནས་འགྲོ་དུས་སྣེ་མ་གཉིས་ལ་དགེ་རྒན་རེ་འགྲོ་གི་འདུག When students march in formation a teacher goes in front and back.

སྣེ་མང་ (nēmaŋ) many kinds/ types, numerous ¶ ཁོང་ལ་ཞིབ་འཇུག་གི་ལས་ཀ་སྣེ་མང་ཡོད་ཙང་དུས་ཚོད་ཡོད་པ་མ་རེད་ Because he has numerous research projects, he has no (spare) time.

སྣེ་མང་རྙོག་འཛིང་ (nēmaŋ ñōgdziŋ) many different and complicated jobs/ tasks.

སྣེ་མང་འདྲེས་འཛིང་ (nēmaŋ drendziŋ) sm. སྣེ་མང་རྙོག་འཛིང་.

སྣེ་མང་ཕྱོགས་བསྡུས་ (nēmaŋ cɔ̄ɔdüù) combining many different things/ kinds into one.

སྣེ་མོ་ (nēmo) end, tip ¶ ཁྲོམ་ལམ་གྱི་སྣེ་མོ་ The end of the street. ¶ ཐག་པའི་སྣེ་མོ་ Tip of a rope. 2. clue; va.—རྙེད་ to find a clue.

སྣེ་མོ་བ་ (nēmowa) chief, headman; person in charge.

སྣེ་མཚམས་ (nēdzam) demarcation line, boundary line.

སྣེ་འཛར་ (nēdzar) fringe, tassel.

སྣེ་འཛོམས་ (nēndzom) sm. སྣེ་འཛོམས་པོ་.

སྣེ་འཛོམས་པོ་ (nē dzombo) many different items/ things, a mixture of different things.

སྣེ་ཟིན་ (nē sin) vi. to reach one's border. 2. vi. to just start, to begin.

སྣེ་ཟུར་ (nēsur) edge, outskirts.

སྣེ་རིང་ (nēriŋ) long strand.

སྣེ་ལེན་ (nēlen) reception, hospitality, entertainment; va.—བྱེད་; —ཞུ་ to receive (people), to act as host/ liason, to entertain ¶ ཁོས་ཉིན་ལྟར་ཇ་ཆང་ཟས་རིགས་ཀྱི་སྣེ་ལེན་བྱས་པ་རེད་ He entertained with tea, food and ཆང་ every day.

སྣེ་ལེན་ཁང་ (nēlengaŋ) guest house, reception room / hall, house for travelers, hostel.

སྣེ་ལེན་ཁྲུའུ་ (nēlen trū) reception office.

སྣེ་ལེན་དགའ་ཚོགས་ (nēlen gadzɔɔ̀) sm. སྣེ་ལེན་འདུ་ཚོགས་.

སྣེ་ལེན་འདུ་ཚོགས་ (nēlen dudzɔɔ̀) 1. reception party/ banquet; va.—བྱེད་. 2. a press conference ¶ གསར་འགྱུར་འགོད་མཁན་གྱི་སྣེ་ལེན་འདུ་ཚོགས་ A press conference for reporters.

སྣེ་ལེན་པ་ (nēlemba) receptionist, host, liason person.

སྣེ་ལེན་མ་ (nēlemma) waitress, hostess.

སྣེ་ལེན་སྒྲོ་ཚོགས་ (nēlen drōdzɔɔ̀) sm. སྣེ་ལེན་འདུ་ཚོགས་.

སྣེ་ལེན་ཚོགས་འདུ་ (nēlen tsōndu) sm. སྣེ་ལེན་འདུ་ཚོགས་.

སྣེ་ལེན་ཚོགས་པ་ (nēlen tsɔ̄gba) sm. སྣེ་ལེན་འདུ་ཚོགས་.

སྣེ་ལེན་ཞིབ་རྒྱས་ (nēlen shibgyɛɛɛ̀) elaborate

reception/ liason.

སྣེ་ལེན་གཟབ་རྒྱས་ (nēlen sabgyɛɛ̀) sm. སྣེ་ལེན་ཞིབ་རྒྱས་.

སྣེ་ལེན་ས་ཚུགས་ (nēlen sədzuù) traveler's reception center.

སྣེ་ལེན་གསོལ་སྟོན་ (nēlen sȫȫdön) reception dinner/ banquet/ party.

སྣེ་ཤན་ (nēshɛn) a guide, liason officer; va.—བྱེད་ to guide, to act as guide ¶ ང་ཚོའི་སྣེ་ཤན་དང་སྐད་སྒྱུར་ཆབས་ཅིག Together with our guide and translator ¶ ཚེ་རིང་སྣེ་ཤན་དུ་བཏང་བྱུང་ (They) sent Tsering as our guide.

སྣེ་ཤན་པ་ (nēshɛmba) a guide, liason officer.

སྣེ་སེལ་ (nēsel) nominal, small, token ¶ རིན་འབབ་སྣེ་སེལ་ Nominal price.

སྣེ་སྲིན་ (nēsin) a little, a small amount/ number.

སྣེམ་: p. བསྣེམས་; f. བསྣེམ་; imp. སྣེམས་ (nēm) va. to press/ hold down.

སྣེམས་ (nēm) imp. སྣེམ་.

སྣེའུ་སྒོད་ (nēwugöö) a type of green vegetable.

སྣེའུ་སྔོན་ (nēwuŋön) sm. སྣེའུ་སྒོད་.

སྣེའུ་ཚོད་ (nēwudzöö) sm. སྣེའུ་སྔོན་.

སྣེའུ་གཡུང་ (nēwuyuŋ) a type of vegetable.

སྣོ་: p. བསྣོས་; f. བསྣོ་; imp. སྣོས་ (nō) to knead ¶ བག་ལེབ་བཟོ་དུས་གྱི་ཞིབ་ཡག་པོ་སྣོ་དགོས་ When one makes bread one must knead the dough well.

སྣོག (nōg) va. to mix up.

སྣོག་ཟན་ (nōgsɛn) sm. རྣོག་ཟན་.

སྣོད་ (nȫȫ) vessel, container, receptacle.

སྣོད་ཀོ་ (nȫȫgo) shung. leather vessel/ container.

སྣོད་ཀྱི་སྐྱོན་གསུམ་ (nȫȫgi gyȫnsum) the three shortcomings when listening to the teaching of the dharma: 1. being inattentive, 2. not keeping what is said in mind, 3. letting delusion overcome one during the teaching.

སྣོད་ཀྱི་འཇིག་རྟེན་ (nȫȫgi jigden) the material/ physical world.

སྣོད་ཀྱི་འཇིག་རྟེན་པའི་ཚན་རིག (nȫȫgi jigdenbɛ tsēnriì) natural science.

སྣོད་ཁོང་ཁོང་ (nȫȫ gōŋgoŋ) hollow containers such as cups/ mugs/ pots/ etc.

སྣོད་ཀྱི་མཁྲིས་སྐྲན་ (nȫȫgi triìdrɛn) tumor in the bladder.

སྣོད་ཁ་ (nȫȫga) the rim (of a cup, etc.).

སྣོད་མཁྲིས་ (nȫȫdriì) gallbladder.

སྣོད་བཅུད་ (nȫȫjüü) 1. a container and its contents. 2. the world and sentient beings.

སྣོད་ཆས་ (nȫȫjɛɛ̀) containers, pots, pans, utensils.

སྣོད་སྟོང་ (nȫȫdoŋ) 1. empty container/ vessel. 2. empty womb.

སྣོད་བསྟུན་སློབ་ཁྲིད་ (nȫȫdün lōbdriì) teaching in accordance with a student's capacity; va.—བྱེད་.

སྣོད་ཐེར་ཐེར་ (nȫȫ tērder) shallow utensils such as plates, saucers, etc.

སྣོད་ལྡན་སློབ་མ་ (nȫȫdɛn lōbma) a worthy student.

སྣོད་ནང་གི་རུས་སྦལ་ (nȫȫnaŋgi rubɛɛ̀) sth. that is very easy to catch [Lit. a turtle in a pot].

སྣོད་གནད་ (nȫȫnɛɛ̀) stomach.

སྣོད་སྤྱད་ (nȫȫjɛɛ̀) sm. སྣོད་ཆས་.

སྣོད་ཕད་ (nȫȫpɛɛ̀) container made of cloth.

སྣོད་མ་ཡིན་པ་ (nȫȫ məyimbə) 1. the unsuitable/ wrong container for sth. ¶ ཤེལ་དམ་དེ་ཆུ་ཚ་པོ་བླུག་སའི་སྣོད་མ་ཡིན་ That bottle is not suitable for hot liquids. 2. unsuitable for learning/ teaching/ etc.

སྣོད་མིན་ (nȫȫmin) sm. སྣོད་མ་ཡིན་པ་.

སྣོད་ཚད་ (nȫȫdzɛɛ̀) an infection in the digestive system.

སྣོད་ཞབས་ (nȫȫshəb) bottom of a cup, bowl, pot, etc.

སྣོད་ཞབས་བརྡོལ་ལ་ཆུ་བླུགས་པ་ (nȫȫshəb dȫȫla cūluùba) forgetful (person); futile activity [Lit. to pour water into a container that has burst].

སྣོད་རོ་ (nȫȫro) leftover food in a container.

སྣོན་: p. and f. བསྣན་; imp. སྣོན་ (nȫn) va. to add to, to augment ¶ ལས་ཁུངས་དེའི་ནང་ལས་བྱེད་པ་གསར་པ་འགའ་ཤས་བསྣན་འདུག They added several new officials to that office.

སྣོན་ཁ་ (nȫnga) supplementing, adding to; va.—རྒྱག.

སྣོན་གྲངས་ (nȫndraŋ) addend.

སྣོན་རྟགས་ (nȫndaà) addition sign, plus sign.

སྣོན་ཐབས་ (nȫȫdəb) addition (in math).

སྣོན་སྤལ་ (nȫnbɛl) sm. སྣོན་སྤེལ་.

སྣོན་སྤེལ་ (nȫnbel) 1. adding, augmenting; va.—རྒྱག; —སྤྲོད་ to add to, to augment 2. extra ¶ བྱེ་རིལ་སྣོན་སྤེལ་གཅིག་སྟེར་དང་ Please give me an extra candy.

སྣོན་འཕེལ་ (nȫnbel) sm. སྣོན་སྤེལ་.

སྣོན་འཕྲི་ (nȫndri) 1. adding and reducing/ subtracting; va.—བྱེད་. 2. fluctuating; vi.—བྱེད་.

སྣོན་འཕྲི་སྒྱུར་བགོ་ (nȫndri gyurgo) adding and subtracting, dividing and multiplying.

སྣོན་འཕྲི་སྤོར་གཅོག (nȫndri bɔ̄rjɔɔ̀) 1. balancing, equalling; va.—བྱེད་ ¶ ལས་ཁུངས་ཁག་གི་ལས་བྱེད་པ་སྣོན་འཕྲི་སྤོར་གཅོག་བྱས་འདུག The offices have equalized the (number) of officials they have. 2. correcting: making additions or deletions ¶ ངའི་རྩོམ་ཡིག་འདི་ར་སྣོན་འཕྲི་སྤོར་གཅོག་གནང་རོགས་གནང་ Please make additions or deletions to my article.

སྣོན་མ་ (nȫnma) additional, extra ¶ སྐྱུང་ངལ་སྣོན་མ་ Additional difficulties.

སྣོན་རྩིས་ (nȫndziì) addition; va.—རྒྱག to do addition (in math).

སྣོན་འཛུགས་ (nȫndzuù) establishing/ setting up an additional number of sth; va.—བྱེད་ ¶ ས་མཚམས་སུ་དམག་སྒར་འགའ་ཤས་སྣོན་འཛུགས་བྱས་འདུག They established several additional regiments on the border.

སྣོན་ལུད་ (nȫnlüǜ) top dressing (fertilizer); va.—རྒྱག.

སྣོམ་: p. བསྣམས་; f. བསྣམ་; imp. སྣོམ་ (nōm) 1.va. to smell. 2. h. of འཁྱེར་.

སྣོམ་བྱེད་ (nōmjeè) the nose.

སྣོམ་བྱེད་དབང་རྩ་ (nōmjeè wāŋdza) olfactory organ.

སྣོམ་ཚོར་ (nōmdzɔr) sense of smell.

སྣོམས་ (nōm) imp. of སྣོམ་.

སྣོར་: p. and f. བསྣོར་; imp. སྣོར་ (nɔ̄r) va. to stir up, to mix up.

སྣོར་མ་ (nɔ̄rma) lush grassy field. 2. remaining stalks after harvesting.

སྣོལ་: p. and f. བསྣོལ་; imp. སྣོལ (nȫȫ) 1. va. to overlap two items, e.g., when putting tiles on a roof ¶ ཐོག་ཁའི་ཇ་གཡམ་སྣོལ་ནས་བརྒྱིགས་པ་རེད་ The slates on the roof are arranged overlapping (each other). 2. va. to intertwine fingers to clasp hands. 3. va. to intersect.

སྣོལ་འཇོག་ཞུ་ (nȫnjɔɔ̀ shu̲) va. to sign an internal agreement/ pledge ¶ དོ་བདག་ཕན་ཚུན་ནང་དོན་གྱི་གན་རྒྱ་སྣོལ་འཇོག་ཞུས་པ་རེད་ The two parties signed an internal agreement.

སྣོལ་པར་ (nȫȫbar) chromatography.

སྣོལ་མར་ (nȫȫmar) combined, united, joined; va.—སྦྱོར་ to join/ combine/ unite together, to fold one's hand together.

སྣོལ་རེས་ (nȫȫreè) things that are intersecting one another.

སྣོལ་ས་ (nȫȫsa) the point of intersection.

སྣོས་ (nȫȫ) imp. of སྣོ་.

བནག (nāà) f. of ནོག.

བནག་མིན་གྱི་གཏམ་ (nāgmingi dām) intolerable/ unbearable talk.

བནགས་ (nāà) p. of ནོག.

བནངས་ (nāŋ) vi. to choke (on sth.).

བནན་ཚིག (nɛ̄ndziì) emphatic words/ speech.

བནབ་ (nəb) f. of ནབ་.

བནབ་སེམས་ (nəbsem) greedy, selfish, desirous of what others have.

བནབས་ (nəb) p. of ནབ་.

བནོག (nōg) f. of ནོག.

བནོགས་ (nōg) p. of ནོག.

བསྣད་ (nɛ̄ɛ̀) p. and f. of སྣད་.

བསྣན་ (nɛ̄n) p. and f. of སྣོན་.

བསྣན་གྲངས་ (nɛ̄ndraŋ) the sum.

བསྣན་ཚིག (nɛ̄ndziì) adverbials.

བསྣམ་ (nām) f. of སྣོམ་.

བསྣམས་ (nām) p. of སྣོམ་.

བསྣམས་ཕེབས་ (nām pēè) va. to go/ come bringing sth. (h.) ¶ ཁྱེད་རང་སྙུ་གུ་བསྣམས་ཕེབས་ཨང་ Please bring a pen.

བསྣར་ (nār) p. and f. of སྣར.

བསྣུད་ (nǖù) p. and f. of སྣུད་.

བསྣུན་ (nǖn) p. and f. of སྣུན་.

བསྣུབ་ (nūb) f. of སྣུབ་.

བསྣུབས་ (nūb) p. of སྣུབ་.

བསྣུར་ (nūr) p. and f. of སྣུར་.

བསྣེམ་ (nēm) f. of སྣེམ་.

བསྣེམས་ (nēm) p. of སྣེམ་.

བསྣོ་ (nō) f. of སྣོ་.

བསྣོག (nɔ̄ɔ̀) f. of སྣོག.

བསྣོགས་ (nɔ̄ɔ̀) p. of སྣོག.

བསྣོར་མ་ (nɔ̄rma) mixed up.

བསྣོན་མ་ (nȫnma) sm. སྣོན་མ་.

བསྣོལ་ (nȫȫ) p. and f. of སྣོལ་.

བསྣོལ་ཁ་ (nȫȫga) overlapping; va.—རྒྱག ¶ ཁང་པའི་ཐོག་ཁར་ཛ་གཡམ་བསྣོལ་ཁ་བརྒྱབ་ནས་བགྲིགས་འདུག They put down tiles on the roof in an overlapping fashion.

བསྣོལ་འཛོག (nȫnjɔɔ̀) signing/ exchanging (an agreement, treaty); va.—བྱེད་ ¶ གྲོས་མཐུན་བསྣོལ་འཛོག་བྱེད་རྒྱུའི་ཆེད་དུ་ For the purpose of exchanging (signing) the treaty.

བསྣོས་ (nȫò) p. of སྣོ་.

པ་ (bā) 1. the letter (used in alphabetical numbering). 2. agentive particle ༶བཟོ་པ་ A worker (One who does work). ༶བཙན་རྒྱལ་རིང་ལུགས་པ་ An imperialist. 3. a person from a country ༶བོད་པ་ A Tibetan. ༶འབྲུག་པ་ A Bhutanese. 4. nominalizing particle for verbs (used after all finals except: ང་, ཨ་, ར་, ལ་) ༶ཁོ་ཚོ་ཕྱིན་པ་ཁོས་མ་ཤེས་པ་རེད་ He wasn't aware of their going. 5. past tense particle (vb. + — + རེད་/ ཡིན་) ༶ཁོས་བྱས་པ་རེད་ He did it.

པ་ཀི་སི་ཏན་ (bāgisidɛn) Pakistan.

པ་ཀི་སི་ཐའན་ (bāgisitɛn) sm. པ་ཀི་སི་ཏན་.

པ་ཀིར་ (bāgir) eng. pocket.

པ་ཀིལ་ (bāgii) sm. པ་ཀིར་.

པ་ཁི་སི་ཐན་ (bāgesidɛn) sm. པ་ཀི་སི་ཏན་.

པ་ག་ཏ་ (bāgada) Baghdad.

པ་རྒྱལ་ (bāgyɛɛ) Pakistan.

པ་ཅི་སི་ཐན་ (bāji sĭdɛn) sm. པ་ཀི་སི་ཏན་.

པ་ལྩོག (bājɔɔ̀) the hair style worn by Tibetan lay officials in the tt. government in which their hair is tied up in two small bundles on top of the head; va.—རྒྱག.

པ་ཏ་ཡལ་ (bāda yɛɛ) vi. to disappear, to vanish ༶གླ་ཕོགས་སྤོར་རྒྱུ་དེ་པ་ཏ་ཡལ་བཞག The hope of increasing one's salary has vanished.

པ་ཏི་ (bədi) tea (Western style).

པ་ཏོ་ལ་ (bādalo) a herbal medicine.

པ་ཏྲ་ (bādra) a type of square design.

པ་ཊ་ (bāda) skt. rice.

པ་ཊ་ཧ་ (bādaha) skt. a type of drum.

པ་ཊུ་ (bādu) skt. learned scholar, expert.

པ་ཐ་ན་ (bātana) Patna.

པ་དག (bādaga) (vb. + —) as soon as ༶ཁོ་སླེབས་པ་དག་ང་རང་མཇལ་བྱུང་ As soon as he came I met him.

པ་དང་ (badaŋ) 1. sm. པ་དང་ག ༶ཁོས་ཁ་ལག་ཟས་པ་དང་འདིར་ཡོང་བ་རེད་ As soon as he ate he came here. 2. (vb. + —) and ༶ཁོས་ཁ་ལག་ཟས་པ་དང་ མོས་དེབ་ཉོས་པ་རེད་ He ate and she bought a book.

པ་སྡེ (bāde) the section of the Tibetan alphabet that contains words with the root letters: པ་ཕ་བ་མ་.

པ་ན་མ་ (bānama) Panama.

པ་རྣམ་མྱང་ཆུ་ (bānam ñaŋju) name of a river in Tsang.

པ་སྣམ་རྫོང་ (bānam dzoŋ) a district/ xian in Tibet.

པ་པ་ (bāba) father, dad.

པ་ཕ་ (bāba) sm. པ་པ་.

པ་བ་རི་སྒོན་ (bāwa regön) sm. པ་ཡག.

པ་བ་སངས་ (bāwasaŋ) sm. པ་སངས་.

པ་མེད་ (bāmeè) (vb. + —) would not have ༶དངུལ་འདི་བྱུང་ཡོད་ན་ལས་ཀ་བྱེད་བ་མེད་ If (he) had gotten the money he would not have worked.

པ་ལྷ་སངས་ (bāwasaŋ) sm. པ་སངས་.

པ་ཞི་ (bāshi) Brazil.

པ་གཞུ་ (bāshu) the Pakistan government.

པ་ཡག (bāya) the root of salvie.

པ་ཡན་ཧ་རི་ (bāyɛn hāri) Bayan Kara (Mt. Range).

པ་ཡིན་ (bəyin) first person past tense complement ༶ངས་ཕྱིན་པ་ཡིན་ I went.

པ་ཡོད་ (bəyöò) (vb. + —) would have ༶དངུལ་འདི་མ་བྱུང་ན་ལས་ཀ་བྱེད་བ་ཡོད་ If (he) had not gotten the money he would have worked.

པ་རི་པི་རི་ (bəri bĭri) unstable, unreliable, undependable.

པ་རི་པུ་རུ་ (bəri būri) sm. པ་རི་པི་རི་.

པ་རུ་ (bəru) 1. a container used for dyeing. 2. wooden bowl used for drinking tea and eating tsampa.

པ་རུའུ་ (bəru) in between.

པ་རུ་པ་རུ་ (bəru bəru) sometimes, occasionally.

པ་རུའུ་པ་རུའུ་ (bəru bəru) sometimes, occasionally.

པ་རེད་ (bəreè) 1. third person past tense complement ༶ཁོས་བྱས་པ་རེད་ He did it.

པ་ལ་ (bələ) follows an adj. conveying "what a" ༶བུད་མེད་འདི་མཛེས་པ་ལ་ What a beautiful woman.

པ་ལཱ་ཤ་ (bālasha) skt. a tree from which a yellow dye is made.

པ་ལ་ཀུའི་ (bālaguwi) Paraguay.

པ་ལགས་ (bālaà) father, dad (h.).

པ་ལི་ (bāli) Paris.

པ་ལ་ཀུང་ཧྲི་ (bāla gūŋhri) ch. the Paris Commune.

པ་ལུའུ་ཅུན་ (bālujün) ch. Eighth Route Army.

པ་ལེ་ (bāle) eng. ballet.

པ་ལེ་བྲོ་གར་ (bāle trogar) eng.tib. ballet dance.

པ་ལེ་རྒྱུ་རྩལ་ (bāle gyudzɛɛ) sm. པ་ལེ་.

པ་ལེ་ཞབས་བྲོ་ (bāle shəbdro) sm. པ་ལེ་བྲོ་གར་.

པ་ལེ་སི་ཐན་ (bālesedɛn) Palestine.

པ་ལེའི་ཞབས་བྲོ་ (bālee shəbdro) sm. པ་ལེ་བྲོ་གར་.

པ་ལོ་ (bālo) braids.

པ་ཤི་ (bāshi) sm. པ་ཞི་.

པ་སངས་ (bāsaŋ) 1. Venus. 2. friday (usu. གཟའ་ + —). 3. man's name.

པ་སུའུ་ཐུའོ་ལན་ (bāsuu tūlɛn) Basutoland.

པ་བསླས་ (bālɛɛ̀) a type of stitching used to sew the soles of Tibetan boots.

པཱ་ཐུར་ (bādur) mong. brave, courageous, fearless.

པཱ་སི་ (bāse) eng. ticket, stamp. pass; va.—གཙོད; —ཉོ་; —འཐོག to buy a ticket/ pass, to buy stamps.

པཱ་སི་གཙོང་མཁན་ (bāse dzōŋñɛn) conductor, ticket seller.

པཱ་ཁ་ལེབ་ (bāga leb) ch.tib. catfish.

པཱ་ཙམ་ (bādzam) sm. དཔག་ཙམ་.

པཱ་ལགས་ (bālaà) father, dad (h.).

པག (bāà) 1. sm.* སྤགས་. 2. sm.* ས་ཕག.

པག་མཁན་ (bāgñɛn) brick layer.

པག་རྩིག (bāgdzii) brick wall.

པག་ཚིར་ (bāgdzir) fired brick.

པག་ལཱ་ (bāgla) hind. wild, rascal-like; va.—བྱེད་; —འཁྲབ་ to act wild, to act like a rascal.

པག་ཤི་ (bāgshi) ch. Chinese storyteller.

པགས་ (bāà) abbr. of པགས་པ་.

པགས་རྐྱལ་ (bāggyɛɛ) skin or leather pouch/ bag.

པགས་གོས་ (bāggöò) skin or leather dress/ garment with fleece lining.

པགས་གྲི་ (bəgdri) a knife used to peel the residue from skins after skinning an animal.

པགས་ཆས་ (bāgjɛɛ̀) leather goods.

པགས་ཆེན་ (bāgjen) a sheep/ goat skin dress with thick fleece.

པགས་དོར་ (bāgdɔɔ) leather or skin trousers.

པགས་གདན་ (bāgdɛn) a rug made from a skin.

པགས་ནད་ (bāgnɛɛ̀) skin disease.

པགས་ནད་ཚན་ཁག (bāgnɛɛ̀ tsēngaà) dermatology department.

པགས་སྣུམ་ (bāgnum) oil used in tanning.

པགས་པ་ (bāgba) skin (of people, animals as well as of foods, fruits, etc.); va.—བཤུ་ to skin, to peel.

པགས་པ་དམར་བཤུ་ (bāgba mārshu) causing sb. to feel shame; va.—བྱེད་.

པགས་པ་བཤུ་ (bāgba shū) see པགས་པ་.

པགས་པའི་མགོ་ཤུབས་ (bāgbɛ goshub) sleeveless leather robe/ gown.

པགས་པའི་འདབ་ཆགས་ (bāgbɛ dəbjaà) bat (the animal).

པགས་པའི་འབྲས་སྐྲན་ (bāgbɛ drɛɛ̀drɛn) skin cancer.

པགས་པའི་གཉན་ཚད་ (bāgbɛ ñēndzɛɛ̀) skin infection/ inflamation.

པགས་བྱིའུ་ (bāg ciwu) bat (the animal).

པགས་པའི་སྤྲ (bāgbɛ tra) fur.

པགས་སྤྱིའི་བུ་ག (bāgbü pugə) skin pore.

པགས་འབྲུམ་ (bāgdrum) skin rash.

པགས་ཤུགས་ (bāgñaà) leprosy.

པགས་རྩུག (bāgdzaà) sm. པགས་ཚག.

པགས་མ་ཚར་ (bāgmatsar) a skin that is not as thick as an adult sheep and not as thin as a lamb.

པགས་ཚག (bāgdzaà) traditional dress made of sheep/goat skin worn with the fleece on the inside.

པགས་ཚག་དྲལ་ (bāgdzaà drɛ̄ɛ) spending money lavishly [Lit. tearing one's པགས་ཚག].

པགས་ཚར་ (bāgdzar) 1. abbr. of པགས་པ་དང་ཚ་རུ་. 2. sm. པགས་ཚག.

པགས་ཚིལ་ (bāgdzil) fat on the skin.

པགས་མཛེ་ (bāgdze) leprosy.

པགས་ཞྭ་ (bāgsha) skin/ fur cap.

པགས་བཟོས་ཐོན་རྫས་ (bāgsöö tōndzɛɛ̀) products made from animal skins.

པགས་རིགས་ (bəgriì) 1. skin, hide. 2. different kinds of skins/ hides.

པགས་རིགས་ཐོན་རྫས་ (bəgriì tōndzɛɛ̀) sm. པགས་བཟོས་ཐོན་རྫས་.

པགས་ཤུན་ (bāgshün) abbr. of པགས་པ་ and ཤུན་པ་.

པགས་ཤོག (bāgshɔɔ̀) parchment.

པགས་བཤུས་ (bāgshüù) skinned, shelled, peeled.

པགས་སྲིན་ (bəgdriin) a skin disease.

པགས་སློག (bāglɔɔ̀) a skin/ fur hat.

པགས་གསོབ་ (bāgsob) taxidermy, stuffed skin.

པང་ (bāŋ) 1. lap; va.—དུ་འཁྱེར་ to hold on the lap ¶ བུ་གུ་པང་དུ་འཁྱེར་མཁན་གྱི་བུད་མེད་རྣམས་ The women holding children on (their) laps. 2. a grassy field/ meadow. 3. abbr. of པང་ལེབ་.

པང་བཀག (bāŋgaà) room divider made of wooden planks.

པང་དཀྲིས་ (bāŋdriì) apron.

པང་ཁ་ (bāŋga) on the lap.

པང་ཁང་ (bāŋgaŋ) plank house.

པང་ཁེབས་ (bāŋgeb) sm. པང་དཀྲིས་.

པང་ཁྲག (bāŋdraà) blood from childbirth.

པང་ག་ལི་ (bāŋgali) short hair (men or women).

པང་འགྱོགས་ (bāŋ gyɔɔ̀) va. to lift sth. up to one's chest.

པང་སྒང་ (bāŋgaŋ) on the lap.

པང་གཅལ་ (bāŋjɛɛ) floor.

པང་སྟེང་ (bāŋdeŋ) sm. པང་སྒང་.

པང་ཐག (bāŋdaà) apron string.

པང་དུ་འདེབས་ (bāŋdu dəb) sm. པང་པར་ལེན་.

པང་གདན་ (bāŋdɛn) traditional Tibetan woman's apron; va.—རྡེབ་ to flap one's apron (an expression of anger or disapproval).

པང་གདན་འཇའ་ཆེན་ (bāŋdɛn jajen) a type of apron with multicolored design.

པང་པ་ (bāŋba) sm. པང་ཁ་.

པང་པ་གང་ (bāŋba kaŋ) an apron full of (sth.).

པང་པར་ཉར་ (bāŋba ñaa) va. to carry or hold in one's arms/ lap.

པང་པར་ལེན་ (bāŋba len) va. to take / hold on one's lap.

པང་ཚད་ (bāŋdzɛɛ̀) sm.• བང་ཚད་.

པང་རས་ (bāŋrɛɛ̀) sm. པང་དཀྲིས་.

པང་ལེབ་ (bāŋleè) plank, board.

པང་ལེབ་གསུམ་སྦྱར་ (bāŋleè sūmjar) three-ply board/ plank/ plywood.

པད་ (bɛ̄ɛ̀) 1. hind. paise (Indian monetary unit equal to one hundredth of a rupee). 2. abbr. of པད་མ་.

པད་ཀོར་ (bɛ̄ɛ̀gɔɔ) hand gestures made during prayers.

པད་དཀར་ (bɛ̄ɛ̀gar) abbr. white lotus.

པད་ཁ་ (bɛ̄ɛ̀gaŋ) rapeseed, mustard.

པད་ཁང་ (bɛ̄ɛ̀gaŋ) sm. པད་ཁ་.

པད་ཁང་སྣུམ་ (bɛ̄ɛ̀gaŋ nūm) rapeseed/ mustard oil.

པད་ཁུད་མཚོ་ (bɛ̄ɛ̀güù tsō) a lake in S.W. Tibet.

པད་ཁོག་བསྐྱོལ་ (bɛ̄ɛ̀gɔɔ̀ gōō) vi. to not make use of an opportunity, to blow an opportunity ¶ ཨ་རི་འགྲོ་ཡས་ཀྱི་པད་ཁོག་བསྐྱོལ་མ་སོང་ (I) did not make use of an opportunity to go to America.

པད་རྒྱུག (bɛ̄ɛ̀gyuù) 1. a tool used to make lotus designs on clay pots. 2. a stalk of a mustard plant.

པད་སྐོར་ (bɛ̄ɛ̀gɔɔ) sm. པད་ཀོར་.

པད་ཅིང་ (bɛ̄ɛ̀jiŋ) Beijing.

པད་ཆུང་ (bɛ̄ɛ̀juŋ) a type of small mustard seed.

པད་ཆེན་ (bɛ̄ɛ̀jen) a type of large mustard seed.

པད་ཏུང་ (bɛ̄ɛ̀duŋ) a metal made of a copper-nickel alloy.

པད་གདན་ (bɛ̄ɛ̀dɛn) lotus cushion.

པད་འདབ་ (bɛ̄ɛ̀dəb) lotus petal.

པད་སྡོང་ (bɛ̄ɛ̀doŋ) stalk of a lotus flower.

པད་སྡོང་ཁ་ (bɛ̄ɛ̀doŋga) the part of the beam that rests on the pillar.

པད་སྣུམ་ (bɛ̄ɛ̀num) mustard seed oil.

པད་པ་ (bɛ̄ɛ̀ba) leech.

པད་ཕྱེ་ (bɛ̄ɛ̀ce) starch extracted from the rhizomes of lotuses, lotus root starch.

པད་སྦུབས་ (bɛ̄ɛ̀bub) the capacity within a lotus flower when the petals fold together.

པད་མ་ (bɛ̄ɛ̀ma) 1. lotus. 2. person's name. 3. poet. vagina.

པད་མ་དཀར་པོ་ (bɛ̄ɛ̀ma gārbo) white lotus.

པད་མ་བཀའ་ཐང་ (bɛ̄ɛ̀ma gādaŋ) a biography of Padmasambava written in the 11th century by Ogyen Lingpa.

པད་མ་གེ་སར་ (bɛ̄ɛ̀ma keser) star anise.

པད་མ་རྒྱ་བྱ་ (bɛ̄ɛ̀ma gyaja) a design consisting of lotus and phoenix (used on rugs, brocades).

པད་མ་ཆོས་བརྩེགས་ (bɛ̄ɛ̀ma cōōdzeg) lotus design on the doors and beams of temples.

པད་མ་ཏ་མིག་མ་ (bɛ̄ɛ̀ma dāmigmə) common calla.

པད་མ་འདབ་བརྒྱ་ (bɛ̄ɛ̀ma dəbgya) a lotus flower with a hundred petals.

པད་མ་འདབ་བརྒྱད་ (bɛ̄ɛ̀ma dəbgyɛɛ̀) a lotus flower with eight petals.

པད་མ་འབྱུང་གནས་ (bɛ̄ɛ̀ma juŋnɛɛ̀) Padmasambhava.

པད་མ་དམར་པོ་ (bɛ̄ɛ̀ma mārbo) red lotus.

པད་མ་འོད་འབར་ (bɛ̄ɛ̀ma wömbar) name of a play and character in Tibetan opera.

པད་མ་ར་ག (bɛ̄ɛ̀ma raga) ruby.

པད་མ་སེར་པོ་ (bɛ̄ɛ̀ma sērbo) yellow peony.

པད་མ་ཧ་གོས་ (bɛ̄ɛ̀ma hāgöö) gown/ cloak with lotus design that monk's wear.

པད་མའི་འབྲུ་གུ་ (bɛ̄ɛ̀mɛ drugu) lotus seed.

པད་མའི་རྩ་བ་ (bɛ̄ɛ̀mɛ dzāwa) lotus root.

པད་མའི་སྐྱིལ་ཀྲུང་ (bɛ̄ɛ̀mɛ gyīīdruŋ) the lotus position of sitting (cross-legged).

པད་མའི་བར་ཤུན་ (bɛ̄ɛ̀mɛ parshün) a type of herbal medicine.

པད་མའི་ཟེའུ་འབྲུ་ (bɛ̄ɛ̀mɛ sewudru) the pistil or stamen of a lotus.

པད་མའི་སོན་ (bɛ̄ɛ̀mɛ sön) lotus seed.

པདྨ་ (bɛ̄ɛ̀ma) sm. པད་མ་.

པདྨ་རཱ་ག (bɛ̄ɛ̀ma raga) ruby.

པདྨ་ཀ་ར་ (bɛ̄ɛ̀ma gāra) sm. པད་མ་འབྱུང་གནས་.

པད་རྩ་ (bɛ̄ɛ̀dza) the root of a lotus.

པད་མཚོ་ (bɛ̄ɛ̀tso) a lake with lotus flowers.

པད་ཚལ་ (bɛ̄ɛ̀dzɛɛ) ch. Chinese cabbage.

པད་རྫིང་ (bɛ̄ɛ̀diŋ) lotus pond.

པད་རྫུས་ (bɛ̄ɛ̀dzüù) hind.tib. counterfeit money.

པད་ཞྭ་ (bɛ̄ɛ̀sha) hat worn by Padmasambava.

པད་ཞབས་ (bɛ̄ɛ̀shəb) the lotus base of statues.

པད་ཞུ་ (bɛ̄ɛ̀shu) a type of cap worn by Buddhist monks.

པད་རག (bɛ̄ɛ̀raà) ruby.

པད་ལད་ (bɛ̄ɛ̀lɛɛ̀) flattery, saying what another wants to hear; va.—ཤོད་; —བྱེད་ to flatter, to say what another wants to hear.

པད་ལད་འཕྲབ་ (bɛ̄ɛ̀lɛɛ̀ trāb) va. to flatter, to act as a sycophant.

པད་ལས་ (bɛ̄ɛ̀lɛɛ̀) sm. པད་ལད་.

པད་ལས་ཚ་པོ་ (bɛ̄ɛ̀lɛɛ̀ tsābo) flatterer, sycophant.

པད་ཤ་ (bɛ̄ɛ̀sha) sm. པད་ཤག.

པད་ཤག (bɛ̄ɛ̀shaà) hind. money.

པད་ཤག་ཆེན་པོ་ (bɛ̄ɛ̀shaà cēmbo) hind.tib. rich.
པན་ (bɛ̄n) ch. military squad.
པན་གོག (bɛ̄ngɔɔ̀) Bangkok.
པན་ཀྲང་ (bɛ̄ndraŋ) ch. squad leader.
པན་ཏོ་ཐེས་ (bɛ̄ndojɛɛ̀) ch. semiconductor ¶ པན་ཏོ་ཐེས་བཟོ་གྲྭ Semiconductor factory.
པན་དུངས་ (bɛ̄nduŋ) beggar.
པན་པ་ (bɛ̄mba) bisexual.
པན་ཙེ་ (bɛ̄ndze) ch. སྣན་ཙེ་.
པན་ཞེ་ (bɛ̄nsha) the tuber of pinellia.
པན་ཤོག (bɛ̄nshɔɔ̀) ch.tib. sm. པན་.
པན་ཧྲི་ (bɛ̄nhri) ch. dumplings (with meat and vegetable filling).
པཎ་གྲུབ་ (bɛ̄ndrub) abbr. པཎ་ཌི་ཏ་ and གྲུབ་ཐོབ་.
པཎ་ཆེན་ (bɛ̄njen) 1. pandit, scholar. 2. Panchen Lama.
པཎ་ཆེན་རིན་པོ་ཆེ་ (bɛ̄njen ri̲mboce) Panchen Lama.
པཎ་ཆེན་ཨེར་དེ་ནི་ (bɛ̄njen ērdini) Panchen Lama.
པཎ་ཇབ་ (bɛ̄njəb) Punjab.
པཎ་ཌི་ཏ་ (bɛ̄ndida) skt. pandit, scholar.
པཎ་ཏའོ་ཐི་ (bɛ̄ndaoti) ch. semiconductor, transistor.
པཎ་ཞྭ་ (bɛ̄nsha) type of hat worn by monks and lamas.
པཎ་ཡུས་ཆིའུ་ (bɛ̄n yüùci) ch. feather-ball game.
པའ་ཡི་ཁལ་ (bāyikɛl) Baikal.
པའ་ཞི་ (bāshi) Brazil.
པའ་ལི་ (bāli) Paris.
པའ་ལུའུ་ཙུན་ (bālujün) ch. the Eight Route Army.
པའ་ཤིས་ (bāshiì) sm. པའི་ཞི་.
པའན་ (bān) ch. sm. པན་.
པའི་ཆིའུ་ཨེན་ (bācien) Bethune (Norman).
པའི་ལན་གྭའུ་ (bālɛngwa) ch. melon.
པའི་ཧྭོ་ཀུང་སི་ (bāhhuo gūŋsi) ch. department store.
པའོ་ཅ་ལི་ཡ་ (bāwojaliyə) Bulgaria.
པའོ་ཅི་ (bāoji) Paochi.
པའོ་ཐོའུ་ (bāoto) Paotow.
པའོ་པང་ (bāobaŋ) S. Vietnam.
པའོ་ཧྲོའུ་ཏང་ (bāohro tāŋ) ch. Conservative Party (Britain).
པར་ (bār) 1. va. to print, to publish ¶ ཚད་གཞི་མཐོ་ཤོས་ཀྱིས་པར་གྱི་ཡོད་པ་རེད་ They are publishing it according to they highest standards. 2. picture, photograph; va.—རྒྱག to take a photograph ¶ ངས་པར་གཅིག་བརྒྱབ་པ་ཡིན་ I took a picture. 3. type, print; va.—རྒྱག་, —ལེན་ to print; va.—ཀོ་ to carve woodblocks (for printing).
པར་ཀོར་ (bārgɔɔ) a mold (for casting icons, etc.).
པར་ཀོ་ (bār gō) see པར་, 3.
པར་ཀོ་མཁན་ (bār gōñɛn) a woodblock carver.
པར་སྐྲུན་ (bārdrön) sm. པར་བསྐྲུན་.
པར་བསྐྲུན་ (bārdrön) 1. printing, publishing; va.—བྱེད་ to print, to publish. 2. Press and Publications Bureau (in TAR).
པར་བསྐྲུན་གྱི་དབང་ཆ་ (bārdröngi wāŋja) sm. པར་བསྐྲུན་བྱེད་དབང་.
པར་བསྐྲུན་བྱེད་དབང་ (bārdrön ce̲èwaŋ) copyright.
པར་བསྐྲུན་ཡིག་རིགས་ (bārdrön yigriì) printed materials, printed matter.
པར་བསྐྲུན་ལས་ཚན་ (bārdrön lɛ̲ɛ̀dzɛn) printing workshop.
པར་ཁ་ (bārka) a molded shape, a mold.
པར་ཁ་བདབ་ (bār kādəb) almost identical, very similar.
པར་ཁང་ (bārgaŋ) 1. a press, a printing house/ office. 2. photo studio/ store.
པར་མཁན་ (bārñɛn) sm. པར་པ་.
པར་གླ་ (bārla) price of printing sth.
པར་གྲངས་ (bārdraŋ) circulation (of a book/ edition).
པར་འགེབས་ (bāngeb) copying.
པར་འགོ་རྟེན་མཁན་ (bārgo dēnñɛn) the person who holds the carved wood block when printing.
པར་འགྲེམ་ (bārdrem) publishing, publication; va.—བྱེད་ to publish ¶ དེབ་འདི་ར་པར་འགྲེམས་བྱེད་ཐུབ་པ་བྱུང་བ་རེད་ (They) were able to publish the book.
པར་འགྲེམ་བྱེད་པོ་ (bārdrem cēèbo) publisher.
པར་རྒྱག་རྒྱུ་སྒྲོད་ (bārgyà gyu̲dröö) va. to put into print.
པར་རྒྱག (bār gya̲à) see པར་, 2-3.
པར་སྒྲིག (bār dri̲g) va. to set type.
པར་སྒྲིག་པར་འདེབས་ (bārdrig bārdeb) typesetting and printing.
པར་སྒྲིག་འཕྲུལ་འཁོར་ (bārdrig trüügɔɔ) typesetting machine/ equipment.
པར་སྒྲོམ་ (bārdrom) picture frame.
པར་ངོས་ (bārŋöö) 1. page (e.g., in a newspaper) ¶ པར་ངོས་དང་པོའི་འཕྲོས་ The continuation from page one. 2. surface of a printing plate.
པར་ཆང་ (bārjaŋ) the ཆང་ served when a person throws snake eyes (bāra) in Tibetan dice.
པར་ཆས་ (bārjɛɛ̀) camera.
པར་སྟེགས་ (bārdeg) the stand/ base on which the printing block is placed.
པར་བརྟེན་ (barden) (vb. + —) because ¶ ཁོས་ལས་ཀ་བྱས་པར་བརྟེན་ Because he worked.
པར་ཐབ་ (bār tāb) up to a date/ time ¶ 1959 པར་ཐབ་ Up to 1959.
པར་ཐུང་ (bārduŋ) a short wood block.
པར་ཐེངས་ (bārdeŋ) a printing, an edition ¶ པར་ཐེངས་དང་པོ་ The first printing/ edition.
པར་དང་བསྐྲུན་ (bārduŋ drön) va. to publish/ print.
པར་དུ་ལེན་ (bārdu le̲n) va. to photograph.
པར་དེབ་ (bārdeb) 1. photographic album. 2. book of photographs.
པར་དྲུང་ (bārdruŋ) the head printer. 2. the secretary of the printing office.
པར་འདེབས་ (bārdeb) printing, va.—བྱེད་ to print.
པར་འདེབས་འཕྲུལ་འཁོར་ (bāndeb trüügɔɔ) printing equipment, printing machine/ press.
པར་འདེབས་ཚོས་རྒྱག (bāndeb tsöögyaà) printing and dyeing.
པར་འདེབས་ལག་རྩལ་ (bāndeb la̲gdzɛɛ) the art/ skill of printing.
པར་སྣག (bārnag) printing ink.
པར་པ་ (bārba) a person who makes prints from woodblocks.
པར་པ་ཏ་ (bārbada) a type of herbal medicine.
པར་པར་ (bārbar) hopping.
པར་པར་བདབ་ (bārbar dāb) sm. པང་པར་ལེན་.
པར་པིར་ (bārbii) abbr. of པ་རི་པི་རི་.
པར་དཔོན་ (bārbön) the head of a printing operation.
པར་སྤྱི་ (bərji) the head of the association of printers prior to 1959 in Lhasa.
པར་ཕུད་ (bārbüü) the first print from a newly made printing block.
པར་བུ་ (bərbu) a small container.
པར་བྱང་ (bārjaŋ) postscript.
པར་བླངས་ (bār lāŋ) sm. པར་རྒྱག.
པར་དབང་ (bārwaŋ) copyright, publication rights.
པར་མ་ (bārma) 1. printed matter. 2. edition ¶ སྡེ་དགེ་པར་ཁང་གི་ཤིང་བཀོས་པར་མར་གཞི་བཟུང་ནས་ Based on the Derge printing house's wood block edition.
པར་རྩ་ (bārdza) the initial sketch written on paper before sketching on a wood block; va.—སྦྱར་ to stick the sketch on to the wood block.
པར་མཚོན་གསར་འགྱུར་ (bārdzön sāngyur) photojournalism.
པར་ཞུ་མཐའ་མ་ (bārshu tāma) the final print.
པར་ཞུས་ (bərshüü) proofreading; va.—བྱེད་ to proofread.
པར་ཞུས་ཤེན་དཔེ་ (bərshüü si̲mbe) proofs, galley sheet.
པར་གཞི་ (bərshi) 1. edition ¶ པར་གཞི་དང་པོ་ The first edition. 2. copy, film negative ¶ གཟུགས་མཐོང་སྐད་འཕྲིན་གྱི་པར་གཞི་ A copy of the television (show, e.g., on video).
པར་གཞི་སྐྱར་མ་ (bārshi gyārma) second edition.

པར་གཞི་རྒྱག (bārshi gya̲à) va. to arrange/ compose type, to typeset.

པར་གཞི་སྒྲིག (bārshi dri̲g) va. to arrange/ compose type, to typeset.

པར་གཞི་ཚོན་ཅན་ (bārshi tsönjɛn) color printing, color edition.

པར་ཡིག་ལྷུག་འཕྲུལ་འཁོར་ (bāryig lūgɔɔ) printing type founding/ casting machine.

པར་གཡོག (bparyɔɔ̀) apprentice printer, printer's assistant.

པར་རིགས་ (bārriì) photos.

པར་རིས་ (bārriì) 1. picture, portrait, photograph; va.—བྲི་ to draw a picture/ portrait ༎ པར་རིས་འགྲེམས་སྟོན་ A picture exhibition. 2. chart. 3. abbr. of པར་ and རིས་མོ་.

པར་ལེན་ (bār le̲n) sm. པར་རྒྱག.

པར་ལེན་ཁང་ (bārlengaŋ) photo studio, photo shop.

པར་ལེན་མཁན་ (bār le̲nñɛn) photographer.

པར་ལེན་སྒྱུ་རྩལ་ (bārlen gyu̲dzɛɛ) the art of photography.

པར་ལེན་པ་ (bārlemba) photographer.

པར་ལེན་འཕྲུལ་ཆས་ (bārlen trüüjɛè) sm. པར་ཆས་.

པར་ལེན་ཡིག་སྒྲིག་ལས་ཚན་ (bārlen trüüjɛè) photocomposing workshop.

པར་ལེན་ཞབས་ཞུ་ཁང་ (bārlen shəbjigaŋ) photoservice department.

པར་ལེན་ཤེལ་སྒོ་ (bārlen sheēgo) camera lens.

པར་ལེན་སློབ་ཚོགས་ (bārlen lōbdzɔɔ̀) photographic society/ organization/ association.

པར་ལེན་གསར་འགྱུར་བ་ (bārlen sə̄ngyurwa) photojournalist.

པར་ལོག (bārlɔɔ̀) photocopying, xeroxing; va.—རྒྱག.

པར་ཤིང་ (bə̄rshiŋ) woodblock (printing plate).

པར་ཤིང་ཁྲེས་པ་ (bə̄rshiŋ trēèba) type of hard wood from which printing wood blocks are made.

པར་ཤོག (bārshɔɔ̀) photographic paper, printing paper.

པར་བཤུས་ (bār shǖù) 1. va. to make prints/ copies. 2. identical.

པར་སྐྱོག་རྒྱག (bārlɔɔ̀ gya̲à) va. to reprint, republish.

པར་སིག (bārsiì) Iran.

པས་ (bɛ̄ɛ̀) (vb + —) question particle ༎ ཁྲོམ་ལ་ཕྱིན་པས་ Did (you) go to the market?

པས་ཁར་མཚོ་ (bēgar tsō) Lake Baikal.

པས་མ་ཚད་ (bē ma̲dzɛè) not only ... but also ༎ ལས་ཀ་བྱས་པས་མ་ཚད་སློབ་གྲྭར་ཕྱིན་པ་རེད་ (He) not only worked, (but he also) went to school.

པན་ (bēn) ch. a wooden board with writing in praise of a diety/ monastery/ person that is hung over a door.

པི་ཅིང་ (bījiŋ) Beijing.

པི་དོག (bīdoò) fried dough, usu. made for Tibetan New Year.

པི་པི་ (bībi) 1. small pipe; va.—བསྣར་ to insert the mouth of a pipe into sth. 2. funnel; va.—བསྣར་ to insert a funnel into a can/ jar. 3. the valve in a tire into which air is pumped.

པི་པི་ལིང་ (bībiliŋ) piper longum (used in Tibetan medicine).

པི་ཙི་ (bīdzi) small wine/ liquor glass; va.—བཀྱག to raise one's glass (as in a toast).

པི་ཙི་གདུག (bīdzi dǖù) va. to touch glasses in a toast.

པི་ཝང་ (bīwaŋ) ch. a Chinese string instrument.

པི་ཝང་སྐར་ཚོམ་ (bīwaŋ gārdzɔɔ̀) the constellation Lyra.

པི་ཝང་རྒྱུད་གཅིག་པ་ (bīwaŋ gyu̲ùjigbə) ch.tib. a one stringed པི་ཝང་.

པི་ཝང་རྒྱུད་མང་ (bīwaŋ gyu̲ùmaŋ) a many stringed པི་ཝང་.

པི་ཝང་རྒྱུད་བཞི་མ་ (bīwaŋ gyu̲ùshimə) a four stringed པི་ཝང་.

པི་ཝང་རྒྱུད་གསུམ་ (bvīwaŋ gyu̲ùsum) a three stringed པི་ཝང་.

པི་རི་ (bīri) a fine hair painting brush.

པི་ལི་སི་ (bīlisi) Belgium.

པི་ལི་སིལ་པོ་ (bīli sīibu) lively, active.

པི་ལི་ཧྲི་ (bīlihri) Belgium.

པི་ཤི་ (bīshi) 1. wanton. 2. a kind of meat dumpling.

པི་སིན་ (bīsin) pencil.

པིང་ཀན་ (bīŋgən) ch. biscuit.

པིང་ཀྱུ་མ་ (bīŋgyumə) eagle, kite.

པིང་ཁབ་ (bīŋgəb) eng.tib. pin, safety pin; va.—རྒྱག to pin, to fasten a pin.

པིང་ཆིའུ་ (bīŋciu) ch. ice hockey.

པིང་གདོང་བ་ (bīŋdoŋwa) a type of untouchable in Tibet subordinate to the རྒྱས་རྒྱལ་པ་.

པིང་ཐོན་ (bīŋdön) ch. an army.

པིང་པོང་ (bīŋboŋ) eng. table tennis, ping pong.

པིང་པོང་ཆིའུ་ (bīŋboŋciu) eng.ch. sm. པིང་པོང་.

པིང་པོང་སྤོ་ལོ་ (bīŋboŋ bōlo) eng.tib. sm. པིང་པོང་.

པིད་ (bīì) sm. འཕུད་, འབུད་ and འབིགས་.

པིན་ཁབ་ (bīngəb) sm. པིང་ཁབ་.

པིན་འགལ་མཚོ་ཁུག (bīngɛɛ tsōguù) ch.tib. Bay of Bengal.

པིན་ཆིའུ་ (bīciu) ch. ice hockey.

པིའི་ཙི་ (bīidzi) sm. པི་ཙི་.

པིར་ (bīr) Chinese pen/ brush made from felt or hair.

པིར་ཁ་ (bīrgə) the point of a pen/ brush.

པིར་གྱི་རུས་པ་ (bīrgi ru̲ùbə) mussel shell used in Tibetan medicine.

པིར་སྟེགས་ (bīrdeg) a stand for putting pens/ brushes.

པིར་དོང་ (bīrdoŋ) a pen or brush holder/ container.

པིར་སྤུ་ (bīrbu) the tip (hair) of a pen or small brush.

པིར་སྦུག (bīrbub) a long container for putting pens/ brushes.

པིར་ཙམ (bīrdzaà) very short ༎ མཇུག་མ་པིར་ཙམ A very short tail.

པིར་རྩེ་ (bīrdze) sm. པིར་ཁ་.

པིར་རྩལ་ (bīrdzɛɛ) skill in writing/ composing.

པིར་རྩེད་ (bīrdzeè) composing, writing.

པིར་རིས་ (bīrriì) a stroke (in writing a Chinese characters).

པིར་རིས་དང་པོ་ (bīrriì ta̲ŋgo) the first stroke of a Chinese character.

པིར་ལེབ་མོ་ (bīr le̲bmo) flat brush/ pen.

པིར་ཤུབས་ (bīrshub) a pen sheath/ case.

པིར་ཤད་ (bīrshɛɛ̀) a stroke (in writing or drawing).

པུ་ཁ་རེ་སིད་ (būga rēseè) Budapest.

པུ་གན་ (būgɛn) sm. ཕུ་གུ་.

པུ་ད་པེ་སིད་ (būda pēsiì) Budapest.

པུ་དི་ (būdi) a volume (book).

པུ་དེ་གུང་རྒྱལ་ (būde ku̲ŋgyɛɛ) the 9th ancient king of Tibet.

པུ་པུ་ཁྲ་ཤུད་ (būbu kūshüù) hoopoe (bird).

པུ་རངས་ (būraŋ) name of place in far W. Tibet.

པུ་རི་ (būri) skt. town.

པུ་རུ་ག་རི་ཡ་ (būru ga̲riya) Bulgaria.

པུ་རུ་ཟིལ་ (būrusii) Brazil.

པུ་ལ་ཁེ་ (būlege) Prague.

པུ་ལི་སི་ (būlisi) eng. police.

པུ་ལི་སི་ཚོགས་ཁང་ (būlisi tsɔ̄ɔ̀gaŋ) eng.tib. police station.

པུ་ལིས་ (būliì) sm. པུ་ལི་སི་.

པུ་ཤེལ་རྩེ་ (būsheedzi) the stem of dendrobium nobile (used in Tibetan medicine).

པུ་ཤུ་ (būshu) double-edged pick axe.

པུ་ཤུད་ (būshüù) sm. པུ་པུ་ཁྲ་ཤུད་.

པུ་ཤེལ་ (būshee) amber.

པུ་སུ་ལ་ (būsula) coriander.

པུ་ཨེ་ནེ་ས་ཨས་རི་སི་ (būüenesa ērisi) Buenos Aires.

པུ་ཨེར་ཧྲི་ཝེ་ཁེའི་རིང་ལུགས་ (būerhriweke ri̲ŋluù) ch.tib. bolshevism.

པུག་རིལ་ (būgrii) a ཚང་ container.

པུན་ཧྲེང་སྒྲོན་མེ་ (būnhreŋ drö̲nme) ch.tib. coleman-type gas lantern/ lamp.

པུའུ་ (bū) ch. ministry, bureau, department, unit ༎

ཉིལ་བསྒྲགས་པུའུ་ Propaganda bureau.
པུའུ་ཀྲང་ (būdraŋ) ch. head of a ministry/ bureau.
པུའུ་ཀྲང་གྲོས་ཚོགས་ (būdraŋ trö̱ödzɔɔ) ch.tib. meeting/ conference at the ministerial level.
པུའུ་ཀྲང་ལས་རོགས་ (būdraŋ lɛ̱ɛ̀rɔɔ) ch.tib. assistant minister.
པུའུ་ཁང་ (būgaŋ) ch.tib. 1. crematorium. 2. tomb.
པུའུ་དུའི་ (būdue) ch. the army.
པུའུ་ཡིས་རིགས་ (būyirig) Baoyei nationality.
པུའུ་ཤུལ་ (bushüü) double edged pickaxe.
པུར་ (būr) corpse.
པུར་ཁང་ (būrgaŋ) 1. tomb, crypt, funeral parlor. 2. undertaker's parlor, mortuary.
པུར་རྒྱལ་ (būrgyɛɛ) an ancient term for Tibet.
པུར་གོས་ (būrgöö) funeral clothes, shroud.
པུར་སྒམ་ (būrgam) coffin, casket.
པུར་སྒྲོམ་ (būrdrom) sm. པུར་སྒམ་.
པུར་ཅ་རི་ཡ་ (būrja riya) Bulgaria.
པུར་འཇུག (būr jùù) va. to set aside a corpse until the proper time for burial/ disposal.
པུར་འཇོག (būr jɔ̀ɔ) sm. པུར་འཇུག.
པུར་ཉར་ཁང་ (būrñargaŋ) 1. morgue. 2. mortuary.
པུར་རྡོལ་ (būrdöö) sm. བུར་རྡོལ་.
པུར་ཐལ་ (būrtɛɛ) ashes from a cremated corpse.
པུར་དར་ (būrdar) a white ceremonial scarf (khata) that is put on the deceased.
པུར་འདྲེན་ (būr dren) va. to carry a corpse.
པུར་སྦྱངས་ (būr jaŋ) sm. པུར་སྲེག.
པུར་མེ་འབུལ་ (būrme büü) shung. va. to cremate the dead.
པུར་ཚྭ་ (būrtsa) salt used to dry a corpse.
པུར་བཞུ་ (būr shüü) va. to cremate the dead/ deceased.
པུར་ལེན་ཁང་ (būrseggaŋ) crematory, crematorium.
པུར་སྲེག (būr sēg) va. to cremate.
པུར་སྲེག་ཐབ་ (būr sēgtəb) crematory.
པུར་ཧྲི་ཝ་ཁེ་ (būrhriwake) ch. bolshevik.
པུས་ (büü) sm. པུའུ་.
པུས་ཁེབས་ (büügeb) kneepad, knee cover.
པུས་འཁྱུད་ (büügyüü) a strap that goes from the shoulder to the knee (worn by people meditating).
པུས་གུག (büüguù) wooden plow tip.
པུས་ཁྱིབས་ (büüjib) sm. པུས་ཁེབས་.
པུས་དུད་ (büüdröö) walking/ crawling on one's knees; va.—རྒྱག.
པུས་མོ་ (büümo) knee; va.—གཅོད་ to amputate from the knee; va.—འཛུགས་ to kneel.
པུས་མོའི་ཚིགས་ (büümö tsiì) the knee joint.
པུས་མོའི་ལྷ་ང་ (büümö lhāŋa) kneecap.
པུས་བཙུགས་ཐལ་སྦྱར་ (büüdzuù tɛ̄ɛ̄jɔɔ) kneeling with one's hands clasped together in sign of respect.
པུས་ཚིགས་ (büüdzii) sm. པུས་མོའི་ཚིགས་.
པུས་ཚིགས་ཁྲི་ (büüdzii cī) an area around the knee for doing acupuncture.
པུས་ཤུབས་ (büüshub) knee pad.
པུས་ལྷང་ (büülhaŋ) kneecap.
པེ་ཀྲུན་ན་ (bēdrɛnna) Bechuanaland.
པེ་ཀྲོན་སྣུམ་ (bēdrön nūm) eng.tib. petrol.
པེ་ཅིན་ (bējin) Beijing.
པེ་ཅིན་ཁྲང་གཞི་ (bējin trāŋshi) the Beijing opera.
པེ་ཅིན་རླུང་འཕྲིན་ (bējin lūŋdrin) Radio Beijing.
པེ་ཅིན་གྱི་སྤྲ་མི་ (bējingi drāmi) Peking Man (the fossil).
པེ་ཅིན་ཛིབ་བཟོ་ལས་ཁང་ (bējin jib solɛ̀ɛgaŋ) Beijing Jeep factory.
པེ་ཅིན་བདུན་རེའི་གསར་དེབ་ (bējin dünree sārdeb) Beijing Weekly (magazine).
པེ་ཅིན་སློབ་གྲྭ་ཆེན་མོ་ (bējin lōbdra cēmmo) Beijing University.
པེ་དག་སློག (bēdaà lɔ̄ɔ) va. to roll back the foreskin (of the penis).
པེ་ཏྲོ་རོལ་ (bēdroröö) eng. petrol.
པེ་པིང་དབྱངས་རྒྱ་མཚོ་ཆེན་པོ་ (bēbiŋyaŋ gyadzo cēmbo) ch.tib. the Arctic Ocean.
པེ་པེ་ (bēbe) calf.
པེ་དབྱང་ (bēyaŋ) ch. northern.
པེ་དབྱང་དམག་ཤེད་ཅན་ (bēyaŋ māgshejɛn) ch.tib. the Northern Warlords (1912-27).
པེ་ཙམ་ (bēdzam) little, small.
པེ་ཅེ་ (bēdze) ch. small wine/ liquor cup or glass.
པེ་ཚལ་ (bētsɛɛ) ch. cabbage.
པེ་ཞི་ (bēshi) ch. a ravioli like Chinese food.
པེ་ཡང་ (bēyaŋ) sm. པེ་དབྱང་.
པེ་རི་སི་ (bērisi) Paris.
པེ་ལིང་ (bēliŋ) Berlin.
པེ་ལིས་ཐན་བཅིང་འགྲོལ་སྒྲིག་འཛུགས་ (bēliitɛn jīŋdrüü drigdzuù) Palestine Liberation Army (PLO).
པེ་ལུན་ཆུ་པོ་ (bēlün cūwo) Pelun River (in northern China).
པེ་ཧར་རྒྱལ་པོ་ (bēhar gyɛɛbo) one of the Tibetan guardian deities.
པེའི་དུའོ་ཕེན་ (bēdupen) Beethoven.
པེར་ཅིན་ (bērjin) Belgium.
པེར་ལིན་ (bērlen) sm. པེར་ལིང་.
པེལ་པེལ་ (beebee) calf.
པོ་ (bo) 1. agentive particle ¶ གནང་པ་པོ་ The one who does. 2. masculine particle ¶ རྒྱལ་པོ་ King. ¶ བློན་པོ་ Minister. 3. adjectival particle ¶ ཡག་པོ་ good. 4. (with numbers) a collectivizing particle ¶ ལྔ་པོ་ The five (together).
པོ་གོ་ཏ་ (bōgoda) Bogota.
པོ་ཏ་ལ་ (bōdala) Potala.
པོ་ཏ་ལའི་ཕོ་བྲང་དཀར་པོ་ (bōdalɛ pōdraŋ gāābo) the white section of the Potala Palace built in 1645 and completed in 1648.
པོ་ཏ་ལའི་ཕོ་བྲང་དམར་པོ་ (bōdalɛ pōdraŋ māābo) the red section of the Potala Palace built in 1690-1694.
པོ་ཏི་ (bōdi) sm. པུ་ཏི་.
པོ་ཏ་ལ་ (bōdrala) realm of Avaloketisvara; heaven, paradise.
པོ་ཏྲ་ (bōdra) eng. powder.
པོ་ཏྲི་ (bōdo) sm. པོ་ཏོ་.
པོ་བསྟོད་ (bōdöö) poems in which each line ends in པོ་.
པོ་ཏོ་ (bōdo) sm. པོ་ཏོ་.
པོ་མཐོ་ (bōdo) mound, knoll, hill.
པོ་པོ་ (bōbo) pocket.
པོ་པོ་རི་ཛ་ (bōbo rija) a type of herb.
པོ་པོ་ (bōō) 1. grandfather. 2. elderly man. 3. slang term of address for a good friend (used by a male) ¶ པོ་པོ་རང་ག་རེ་བྱེད་ཀྱི་ཡོད་ What are you doing "old man"?
པོ་པོ་ལགས་ (bōōlaà) grandfather (h.).
པོ་ཚལ་ (bōdzɛɛ) ch. spinach.
པོ་ཚི་ཐན་གྱི་སྒྲི་བསྒྲགས་ (bōdzitɛngi jīdraà) Potsdam Declaration.
པོ་ལན་ (bōlɛn) Poland.
པོ་ལའི་ཀུའུ་ (bōlɛgu) South Vietnam.
པོ་ལའི་མ་ (bōlɛma) Plei Me (Vietnam).
པོ་ལི་ཝི་ཡ་ (bōliwaya) Bolivia.
པོ་ལེ་སྐྱོ་པོ་ (bōle gyōbo) weak, frail.
པོ་ལོ་ (bōlo) ball, playing ball; va.—རྒྱག. to play ball (games such as soccer); vi.—འཐོབ་ to win a ball game; vi.—ཤོར་ to lose a ball game.
པོ་ལོ་འགྲན་བསྡུར་ (bōlo drɛndur) competition, contest (for ball games such as soccer).
པོ་ལོ་རྒྱག་ས་ (bōlo gyasa) place/ field where ball games are played.
པོ་ཤེལ་ (bōshee) amber.
པོ་ལོའི་ནང་ལྤགས་ (bōlö naŋbaà) bladder/ inner tube of a ball.
པོ་ལོའི་ཕྱི་ལྤགས་ (bōlö cībaà) the outer leather/ skin of a ball.
པོ་སོ་ཆ་ (bōsoja) Sesbania grandiflora (a plant used in Tibetan medicine).
པོ་སོན་འཆའ་ (bōsönja) sm. པོ་སོ་ཆ་.
པོ་ཧའི་རྒྱ་མཚོ་ (bōhe gyadzo) ch.tib. the North Sea.

པོ་ཧའི་སྣུམ་ (bōhe nūm) ch.tib. peppermint oil.
པོ་ཨིན་ (bōen) Bonn.
པོག (bɔ̄ɔ̀) a kind of incense.
པོག་ཕོར་ (bɔ̄ɔ̀bɔr) incense burner.
པོད་ (bȫȍ) sm. པོ་ཏི་.
པོན་ཊ་ (bōnda) eng. pound.
པོབ་ལིག (bōbliŋ) eng. public ¶ པོབ་ལིག་སློབ་གྲྭ་ Public school.
པོའོ་ལོ་ (bōlo) eng. ball.
པོའོ་ཧའི་ (bōhai) sm. པོ་ཧའི་.
པོའོ་ཧྲི་ (bōhri) ch. Ph.d.
པོར་སྐྱོག (bɔ̄rgyɔ̄ɔ̀) a twisted/ deformed mouth.
པོར་ནི་ (bɔrni) Bern.
སྤྱངས་ (jāŋ) imp. of དཔྱང་.
པྲ་ (drā) a type of divination using mirrors; va.—ཕབ་; —འདེབས་; —ཕབ་གཏང་ to do "mirror" divination.
པྲ་མཁན་ (drāñɛn) sb. who does པྲ་ divination.
པྲ་མིག (drəmig) eyes that can see the images brought about through the divining mirror.
པྲ་ངན་ (drāŋɛn) bad omen/ sign from པྲ་ divination.
པྲ་ཆལ་ (drājɛɛ) jesting, joking; va.—བྱེད་ to jest, to joke, to kid around.
པྲ་རྟགས་ (drādaà) signs or omens seen through the divining mirror.
པྲ་རྟེན་ (drāden) person who divines from the divining mirror.
པྲ་ཕབ་ (drā pəb) va. to do པྲ་ divination.
པྲ་མོ་ (drāmo) sm. པྲ་.
པྲ་རྩི་པོག (drādzibɔ) frankincense.
པྲ་ཚིལ་ (drādzii) beeswax.
པྲ་ཚིལ་གྱི་ཤིང་འབྲས་ (drədziigi shiŋdrɛɛ̀) wax fruit.
པྲ་ཚིལ་སྒྲོན་མེ་ (drədzii drönme) wax candle/ lamp.
པྲ་ཛྙཱ་ (brājña) skt. wisdom.
པྲ་ལི་ (drəli) type of rat.
པྲ་ལུང་ (drəluŋ) forecast/ prediction from པྲ་ divination.
པྲ་ལེགས་ (draleg) good omen/ sign from པྲ་ divination.
པྲ་སེ་ན་ (drāsena) sm. པྲ་.
པྲག་པྲིག (drəgdrig) a little, a few.
པྲི་ཡང་ཀུ་ (drīyaŋgu) dracocephalum tanguticum (used in Tibetan medicine).
པྲིག་རྒྱུམ་ (drīgjum) doubt, suspicion.
པྲེ་ཏ (drēda) skt. preta (hungry ghost: inhabitant of one of the Buddhist hells).
པྲེ་ཏ་པུ་རིའི་རྒྱལ་ཁམས་ (drēda būri gyɛɛgam) skt.tib. realm/ abode of the hungry ghosts.
པྲེ་ཏ་ལག་སྐམ་ (drēda laggam) skt.tib. a stingy person [Lit. hungry ghost with dry hands].

པྲོག (drōg) tip, stub, nip.
པྲོག་མ་ (drōgma) sm. ཕྲོག་མ་.
པྲོག་ཞུ་ (drōgshu) headdress.
དཔག (bāà) 1. sm. དཔོག. 2. f. of དཔོག.
དཔག་གྲངས་ (bāgdraŋ) number, amount, measure.
དཔག་ཆེན་ (bāgjen) 1. large number/ amount. 2. physically strong.
དཔག་འཇལ་ (bāg jɛɛ) va. to measure/ count.
དཔག་ཏུ་མེད་པ་ (bāgdu meèba) countless, immeasurable, boundless.
དཔག་ཏུ་རུང་བ་ (bāgdu ruŋwə) measurable, countable.
དཔག་ཐག (bāgdaà) measuring tape/ string.
དཔག་ཐབས་མེད་པ་ (bāgdəb meèba) sm. དཔག་ཏུ་མེད་པ་.
དཔག་བྱས་ (bāgjɛɛ̀) measurable.
དཔག་བྲལ་ (bāgdrɛɛ) sm. དཔག་མེད་.
དཔག་མི་ཐུབ་པ་ (bāg mi tübbə) unable to estimate (e.g., a man's mind or the depth of the water, etc).
དཔག་མེད་ (bāgmeè) immeasurable, inestimable, unimaginable ¶ དགའ་སྤྲོ་དཔག་མེད་ཀྱིས་ With immeasurable joy.
དཔག་ཙམ་ (bāgdzam) enormous, gigantic.
དཔག་ཚད་ (bāgdzɛɛ̀) a distance measure (about 6 miles).
དཔག་རྩལ་ (bāgdzüü) estimation, guess.
དཔག་ཚོད་ (bāgdzöö) 1. estimate, guess. 2. according to one's capabilities or to conditions ¶ སོ་སོའི་དཔག་ཚོད་ཀྱི་ལས་ཀ་ཞིག་བྱེད་ཀྱི་ཡོད་ I am working according to my own capability.
དཔག་ཡས་ (bāgyɛɛ̀) sm. དཔག་མེད.
དཔག་བསམ་ (bāgsam) estimating, guessing.
དཔགས་ (bāà) 1. vi. in proportion to, relative to, according to, in estimation ¶ མི་ལ་དཔགས་ནས་སློབ་ཁྲིད་བྱས་པ་རེད་ (They) taught according to a person's ability. ¶ ང་ཚོའི་ནུས་སྟོབས་ལ་དཔགས་པའི་གོམ་པ་རིམ་པ་སྤོད་ཀྱིས་ Moving along in proportion to our strength. ¶ གོང་གསལ་གནས་ཚུལ་ལ་དཔགས་ན་ According to the news above. 2. p. of དཔོག.
དཔང་ (bāŋ) evidence, proof.
དཔང་རྒྱ་ (bāŋgya) sm. གན་རྒྱ་.
དཔང་བརྒྱད་ (bāŋgyɛɛ̀) eight witnesses: four brought by each party when going to a law court during ancient times.
དཔང་དངོས་ (bāŋŋöö) material evidence.
དཔང་རྟགས་ (bāŋdaà) evidence, proof.
དཔང་རྟགས་ཁུངས་འཕེར་ (bāŋdaà kūŋber) confirming evidence/ proof.
དཔང་རྟགས་ཁུངས་བཙན་ (bāŋdaà kūŋdzɛn) evidence that has been confirmed.
དཔང་བསྟོད་ (bāŋdöö) praising/ complimenting highly; va.—བྱེད་.
དཔང་པོ་ (bāŋbo) witness, evidence, testimony; va.—བྱེད་ to act as a witness, to give evidence/ testimony.
དཔང་འཕེར་བ་ (bāŋ pērwa) person qualified to be a witness.
དཔང་བྱེད་ (bāŋ ceè) va. to be/ act as a witness.
དཔང་མེད་སྟོང་བཤད་ (bāŋmeè dōŋshɛɛ̀) empty talk without proof.
དཔང་ཚིག (bāŋdzii) testimony, an account of a witness.
དཔང་འཛུགས་ (bāŋdzuù) 1. va. to have someone serve/ act as a witness. 2. an exclamation of swearing ("I swear").
དཔང་རྫས་ (bāŋdzɛɛ̀) sm. དཔང་དངོས་.
དཔང་ཡིག (bəŋyig) 1. certificate, credentials, document, diploma. 2. notarized letter/ document. 3. an agreement.
དཔངས་ (bāŋ) height, altitude.
དཔངས་དཀྱུས་ (bāŋgyüü) height and length.
དཔངས་ཅན་ (bāŋjɛn) high.
དཔངས་བསྟོད་ (bāŋdöö) high/ lofty praise, commendation.
དཔངས་མཐོ་ (bāŋto) high, elevated.
དཔངས་དམའ་པོ་ (bāŋ mābo) low.
དཔངས་ཚད་ (baŋdzɛɛ̀) height.
དཔངས་ཞེང་ (bāŋshiŋ) height and width.
དཔད་ (bɛɛ̀) sm. དཔོད་.
དཔའ་ (bā) abbr. of དཔའ་བ་.
དཔའ་བཀོང་(ས་) (bā gōŋ) va. to intimidate, to frighten, to terrorize.
དཔའ་སྐད་ (bāgɛɛ̀) talking of being brave, bravado.
དཔའ་སྒོང་ (bāgoŋ) sm. དཔའ་བཀོང་.
དཔའ་སྐྱེད་ཚ་པོ་ (bāgyeè tsābo) braggart.
དཔའ་ཁ་ (bāga) victory.
དཔའ་ཁུག (bāguù) a type of ornament hung at the front of the body in Eastern Tibet.
དཔའ་ཁུམས་ (bāgum) cowardly.
དཔའ་འཁུམ་ནུས་མེད་ (bāgum nüümeè) weak and cowardly.
དཔའ་གོང་ (bā goŋ) vi. to lose enthusiasm/ spirit, to lose courage.
དཔའ་དགྱེ་དགྱེ་ (bā gyegye) brave, courageous.
དཔའ་རྒོད་ (bāgöö) masterful, powerful, fierce and courageous.
དཔའ་རྒྱས་ (bā gyɛɛ̀) vi. to become brave/ courageous, to have spirit/ enthusiasm.
དཔའ་ངར་ (bāŋar) bravery, courage, fearlessness,

valor, spirit, morale; va.—སྐྱེད་; —བསྐྱེད་ to be or get courage/ bravery/ valor/ spirit/ morale ¶ དཔའ་ང་ར་ཆེ་སྐྱེད་ཀྱིས་མདུན་དུ་སྐྱོད་ཀྱི་འདུག (They) are moving forward with great courage.

དཔའ་ང་ར་ཅན་ (bāŋarjɛn) brave, courageous.

དཔའ་ང་ར་ཆེན་པོ་ (bāŋar cēmbo) sm. དཔའ་ང་ར་.

དཔའ་ང་ར་ཆེར་སྐྱེད་ (bāŋar cēgyeè) vi. to be brave/ courageous.

དཔའ་ང་ར་བརྟུལ་ཕོད་ (bāŋar dūūböö) sm. དཔའ་ང་ར་ཅན་.

དཔའ་ང་ར་ལྡན་པ་ (bāŋar dembа) sm. དཔའ་ང་ར་ཅན་.

དཔའ་ང་ར་འབར་ (bāŋar bar) vi. to have one's spirits/ morale/ courage increase or burn brightly.

དཔའ་ང་ར་ཞུམ་མེད་ (bāŋar shummeè) dauntless, fearless, courageous, brave.

དཔའ་འཇོམས་ (bāŋom) brave, courageous; va.—བྱེད་ to show one's courage/ bravery.

དཔའ་འཇོམས་དཔུང་སྟོན་ (bāŋom būŋdön) saber rattling.

དཔའ་རྗམ་ (bāŋam) ferocious and brave.

དཔའ་རྗམ་ཆེ་ (bāŋam cē) extremely ferocious and brave.

དཔའ་ཆ་ཐང་པོ་ (bāca tāŋbo) 1. fit, healthy ¶ གཟུགས་པོ་དཔའ་ཆ་ཐང་པོ་ A healthy body. 2. sturdy ¶ ཁང་པ་དཔའ་ཆ་ཐང་པོ་ A sturdy house.

དཔའ་ཆེན་ (bājen) 1. brave, courageous. 2. a great hero.

དཔའ་ཉམས་ (bāñam) spirit, courage ¶ གསར་བརྗེའི་དཔའ་ཉམས་ Revolutionary spirit.

དཔའ་ཉམས་སྒྲུང་འགྱུག (bāñam truŋgyuù) agile and brave.

དཔའ་ཉམས་དང་ལྡན་པ་ (bāñam daŋ dembа) heroic, courageous, spirited.

དཔའ་ཉམས་ལྡན་པ་ (bāñam dembа) sm. དཔའ་ཉམས་དང་ལྡན་པ་.

དཔའ་སྙིང་ (bāñiŋ) sm. དཔའ་ང་ར་.

དཔའ་སྙེམས་ (bāñem) boasting of one's bravado.

དཔའ་གདམ་ཤོད་ (bādam shöö) va. to talk about one's own courage.

དཔའ་གདུམ་ (bādum) fierce and brave.

དཔའ་རྟགས་ (bādaà) sm. དཔའ་བོའི་རྟགས་མ་.

དཔའ་རྟུལ་ (bādüü) sm. དཔའ་ང་ར་.

དཔའ་སྟོབས་ (bādob) brave.

དཔའ་ཐལ་ (bādɛɛ) 1. shung. overbearing, brazen ¶ རང་མནོང་ངོས་ལེན་མེད་པར་སྤྱི་ཇུས་རྣམས་འཁྱེར་ཏེ་དཔའ་ཐལ་གྱིས་མི་སེར་སོགས་ནས་ཁྲིམས་འགལ་བྱས་རྩལ་ཨམ་བན་ཆེན་མོར་མི་བདེན་ཞུ་སྙིག་གི་ཞུ་ཡིག་ཕུལ་བ་ Instead of confessing the crime, he took away the publicly owned property and brazenly blamed the subjects while making a false report to the Ambans. 2. excessively/ overly brave.

དཔའ་ཐུལ་ (bādüü) hero.

དཔའ་དམ་ (bādam) a long Tibetan sword; va.—འདོགས་ to wear/ affix such a sword.

དཔའ་དར་ (bādar) gifts and ceremonial scarves awarded to heroes.

དཔའ་དྲེགས་ (bādreg) sm. དཔའ་སྙེམས་.

དཔའ་གདེངས་ (bādeŋ) sm. དཔའ་ང་ར་.

དཔའའི་སྡེ་ (bāde) army, military force.

དཔའའི་སྡེ་གསུམ་ (bāde sūm) the three armies of Srongtsen Gampo that guarded the left, right, and middle regions of Tibet.

དཔའ་པོ་ (bābo) heroic.

དཔའ་བ་ (bāwa) bravery, courage, valor.

དཔའ་བའི་ཕུལ་ཕྱིན་ (bāwɛ pūūjin) the best of the warriors.

དཔའ་བོ་ (bāwo) a hero.

དཔའ་བོ་དཀར་པོ་ (bāwo gārbo) phytolacca acinosa roxb. (a plant used in Tibetan medicine).

དཔའ་བོ་དགྲ་འདུལ་ (bāwo drandüü) fearless, brave.

དཔའ་བོ་ཅིག་ཐུབ་ (bāwo cīgdub) sm. དཔའ་བོ་ཆེན་པོ་.

དཔའ་བོ་ཆེན་པོ་ (bāwo cēmbo) panax ginseng (a plant used in Tibetan medicine).

དཔའ་བོ་ཕོ་གོད་པོ་ (bāwo pō gööba) a fierce male hero.

དཔའ་བོ་ཕོ་རབ་ (bāwo pōrəb) sm. དཔའ་བོ་ཕོ་གོད་པོ་.

དཔའ་བོ་གཙུག་ལག་ཕྲེང་བ་ (bāwo dzūglag tēŋwa) the 16th century author of the historical work titled ཆོས་འབྱུང་མཁས་པའི་དགའ་སྟོན་.

དཔའ་བོ་གཟུགས་ཉམས་ (bāwo sugñam) heroic image.

དཔའ་བོ་འདས་པ་ (bāwo dɛ̀ɛba) dead hero.

དཔའ་བོའི་རྟགས་མ་ (bāwö dāŋma) an award/ medal given to a hero.

དཔའ་བོའི་རིང་ལུགས་ (bāwö riŋluù) heroism.

དཔའ་བོ་སེར་པོ་ (bāwo sērbo) veratrilla baillonii Franch (a plant used in Tibetan medicine).

དཔའ་བོའི་དྲིལ་བུ་ (bāwö triibu) a type of bell.

དཔའ་བློ་ (bālo) brave, courageous.

དཔའ་བློ་ཁོག (bā lōgɔɔ) brave, courageous.

དཔའ་བློ་ཁོག་མེད་ (bā lōgɔɔ meè) cowardly.

དཔའ་མོ་ (bāmo) heroine.

དཔའ་མི་ཞུམ་ (bā mishum) sm. དཔའ་ང་ར་ཞུམ་མེད་.

དཔའ་རྩལ་ (bādzɛɛ) bravery, courage; va.—འགྲན་ to do combat, to duel.

དཔའ་རྩལ་ཆེན་པོ་ (bādzɛɛ cēmbo) brave and skillful.

དཔའ་རྩལ་མཉམ་སྟོན་ (bādzɛɛ ñamdön) skill and bravery equally matched.

དཔའ་རྩལ་འདོན་ (bādzɛɛ dön) va. to show/ exhibit/ manifest one's skill and bravery.

དཔའ་ཚུལ་ (bādzüü) appearance of a hero/ warrior.

དཔའ་མཛངས་ (bādzaŋ) heroism, bravery, courage, valor ¶ དཔའ་མཛངས་དང་ལྡན་པའི་ཡན་ཨན་མི་དམངས་ The heroic people of Yenan.

དཔའ་མཛངས་རྟུལ་ཕོད་ (bādzaŋ dūūböö) sm. དཔའ་མཛངས་.

དཔའ་མཛངས་དང་ལྡན་པ་ (bādzaŋdaŋ dembа) sm. དཔའ་མཛངས་རྟུལ་ཕོད་.

དཔའ་མཛངས་ལྡན་པ་ (bādzaŋ dembа) sm. དཔའ་མཛངས་རྟུལ་ཕོད་.

དཔའ་མཛངས་རིས་གསུམ་ (bādzaŋ teèsum) a hero who has the three characterisdtics: is brave, good in strategy and gentle in character.

དཔའ་ཞིང་འཁྲུལ་མཛངས་ལྡན་པ་ (bāshiŋ trūndzaŋ dembа) sm. དཔའ་མཛངས་ལྡན་པ་.

དཔའ་ཞུམ་ (bāshum) 1. cowardly, timid; vi.—བྱེད་ to act cowardly.

དཔའ་ཞུམ་ཉམས་ཤོར་ (bāshum ñamshɔɔ) sm. དཔའ་ཞུམ་.

དཔའ་ཟིལ་ (bāsii) sm. དཔའ་རྗམས་.

དཔའ་ཞུམ་མེད་པ་ (bāshum meèba) sm. དཔའ་ང་ར་ཞུམ་མེད་.

དཔའ་ཟླ་ (bānda) sm. རྗིང་གཉེན་.

དཔའ་ཡ་མེད་ (bā yameè) an unequaled brave hero/ warrior.

དཔའ་ཡང་དག (bā yaŋdaà) a true/ genuine hero.

དཔའ་རི་ (bāri) a mountain in Mili county in Sichuan Province.

དཔའ་རློམ་ (bālom) heroism, courage, bravery, valor.

དཔའ་རློམ་རིང་ལུགས་ (bālom riŋluù) heroism.

དཔའ་ལུགས་ (bāluù) the record/ accomplishments of heroes.

དཔའ་ལུང་ (bāluŋ) the rope attached to the handle of a sword.

དཔའ་ཤེད་འཕེལ་ (bāsheè pēl) sm. དཔའ་ང་ར་སྐྱེད་.

དཔའ་ཤོར་ (bā shɔɔ) vi. to lose one's courage.

དཔའ་སེམས་ (bāsem) sm. དཔའ་ང་ར་.

དཔར་ (bāā) sm. པར་.

དཔར་སྐྲུན་ (bārdrün) sm. པར་བསྐྲུན་.

དཔར་བསྐྲུན་ (bārdrün) sm. པར་བསྐྲུན་.

དཔར་ཁང་ (bārgaŋ) sm. པར་ཁང་.

དཔར་འགྲེམ་ (bārdrem) sm. པར་འགྲེམ་.

དཔར་ངོས་ (bārŋöö) sm. པར་ངོས་.

དཔར་དེབ་ (bādeb) sm. པར་དེབ་.

དཔར་འདེབས་ (bārdeb) sm. པར་འདེབས.

དཔར་པ་ (bārba) sm. པར་པ་.

དཔར་མ་ (bārma) sm. པར་མ་.

དཔར་ཤིང་ (bərshiŋ) sm. པར་ཤིང་.

དཔལ་ (bɛ̄ɛ̄) splendor, magnificence, glory.

དཔལ་ཀོ་ (bɛ̄ɛ̄gɔ̄ɔ̀) sm. དཔལ་ཁོག.

དཔལ་ཀོག (bɛ̄ɛ̄gɔ̄ɔ̀) sm. དཔལ་ཁོག.

དཔལ་ཀོའི་རི་མོ་ (bɛ̄ɛ̄gö ri̱mu) one's karmic fortune.

དཔལ་ཁང་ (bɛ̄ɛ̄gaŋ) an ancient lineage.

དཔལ་ཁོག (bɛ̄ɛ̄gɔ̄ɔ̀) forehead.

དཔལ་ཁོག་བསྐོས་ (bɛ̄ɛ̄gɔ̄ɔ̀ gȫö) slang. (— + neg.) va. to not make use an opportunity.

དཔལ་ཁེབས་ (bɛ̄ɛ̄geb) sm. དཔྲལ་ཁེབས་.

དཔལ་འཁོར་ཆོས་སྡེ་ (bɛ̄ngɔɔ cȫöde) a monastery in Gyantse.

དཔལ་གྱི་མགྲིན་ (bɛ̄ɛ̄gi dri̱n) shung. sm. དབང་ཕྱུག་ཆེན་པོ་.

དཔལ་གྱི་དུམ་བུ་ (bɛ̄ɛ̄gi du̱mbu) white sandalwood.

དཔལ་གྱི་དབང་ཕྱུག (bɛ̄ɛ̄gi wāŋjuù) shung. incomparably honorable ¶ དཔལ་གྱི་དབང་ཕྱུག་མི་ཡི་རྗེ་བོ་ You, the incomparably honorable leader.

དཔལ་མགོན་ (bɛ̄ngön) 1. a nomad district/ xian in Nagchuka prefecture. 2. savior.

དཔལ་སྡུག (bɛ̄ɛ̄dug) sm. དཔལ་དང་ལྡན་པ་.

དཔལ་དང་ལྡན་པ་ (bɛ̄ɛ̄daŋ de̱mba) glorious, splendid, magnificent, majestic, grand.

དཔལ་དང་གཟི་བརྗིད་ལྡན་པ་ (bɛ̄ɛ̄daŋ si̱ji de̱mba) sm. དཔལ་དང་ལྡན་པ་.

དཔལ་དུ་རྒྱས་ (bɛ̄ɛ̄du gyɛ̱ɛ̀) shung. vi. to flourish ¶ མཛད་འཕྲིན་མཐའ་དག་བསྟན་འགྲོའི་དཔལ་དུ་རྒྱས་པ་ May (his) glorious deeds for the promotion of Buddhism and the comforting of sentient beings flourish.

དཔལ་དུས་ཀྱི་འཁོར་ལོ་ (bɛ̄ɛ̄düügi kɔ̄ɔlo) Kalachakra.

དཔལ་ལྡན་ (bɛ̄ndɛn) 1. name of a person. 2. auspicious, glorious, splendid.

དཔལ་ལྡན་མ་ (bɛ̄ndɛnma) general term used for female deities.

དཔལ་ལྡན་ས་སྐྱོང་ (bɛ̄ndɛn sāgyoŋ) shung. honorific term used for the Prime Minister and Council Ministers in the traditional Tibetan goverment.

དཔལ་ལྡན་ལྷ་མོ་ (bɛ̄ndɛn lhāmo) the protective (female) diety of the Geluk sect.

དཔལ་ལྡན་ལྷ་མོའི་བླ་མཚོ་ (bɛ̄ndɛn lhāmo lādzo) lake in south Tibet where visions and prophecies can be seen.

དཔལ་ལྡན་ཨ་ཏི་ཤ་ (bɛ̄ndɛn ātisha) Atisha.

དཔལ་བེའུ་ (bɛ̄ɛ̄bewu) the auspicious knot design (one of the eight auspicious symbols).

དཔལ་འབར་ (bɛ̄mbar) 1. torch, torchlight ¶ རང་དབང་དང་དྲང་བདེན་གྱི་དཔལ་འབར་སྒྲེང་རྒྱུ་ཡིན་ (We) will raise the torch of freedom and justice. 2. district in Eastern Tibet.

དཔལ་འབྱོར་ (bɛ̄njɔɔ) 1. economy. 2. wealth ¶ དཔལ་འབྱོར་དང་ལྡན་པ་ Wealthy.

དཔལ་འབྱོར་གྱི་གྲུབ་ཆ་ (bɛ̄njɔɔgi tru̱bja) economic element.

དཔལ་འབྱོར་གྱི་ཉེན་ཁ་ (bɛ̄njɔɔgi ñe̱nga) economic crisis.

དཔལ་འབྱོར་གྱི་འཐབ་རྩོད་ (bɛ̄njɔɔgi tābdzȫö) economic struggle.

དཔལ་འབྱོར་གྱི་བཙན་འཛུལ་ (bɛ̄njɔɔgi dzɛ̄ndzüü) economic invasion.

དཔལ་འབྱོར་གྱི་འཚོ་བ་ (bɛ̄njɔɔgi tsōwa) economic conditions, standard of living.

དཔལ་འབྱོར་གྱི་ཞིབ་རྩིས་ (bɛ̄njɔɔgi shi̱bdziì) business accounting, cost accounting.

དཔལ་འབྱོར་གྱི་འཛུགས་སྐྲུན་ (bɛ̄njɔɔgi dzu̱gdrün) economic construction/ development.

དཔལ་འབྱོར་གྱི་རིག་པ་ (bɛ̄njɔɔgi ri̱gbə) economics.

དཔལ་འབྱོར་གྱི་སྲོག་རྩ་ (bɛ̄njɔɔgi sɔ̄ɔ̀gdza) economic lifeline, key points of the economy.

དཔལ་འབྱོར་འགན་གཙང་ལམ་ལུགས་ (bɛ̄njɔɔ ge̱ndzaŋ lə̱mluù) economic responsibility system.

དཔལ་འབྱོར་ཆགས་རྐྱུལ་ (bɛ̄njɔɔ cāgdzüü) the origin of the economic.

དཔལ་འབྱོར་འཆར་གཞི་ཁྲིང་ (bɛ̄njɔɔ cərshi tīŋ) tib.ch. Economic Planning Commission (in TAR).

དཔལ་འབྱོར་རྗེས་སུ་ལུས་པ་ (bɛ̄njɔɔ je̱ɛsu lṳ̄übə) economically backward.

དཔལ་འབྱོར་མཉམ་ལས་ (bɛ̄njɔɔ ñāmlɛɛ̀) economic cooperation.

དཔལ་འབྱོར་དོ་དམ་པ་ (bɛ̄njɔɔ to̱damba) officials in charge of economics, treasurer (in a club, etc.).

དཔལ་འབྱོར་དམངས་གཙོ་ (bɛ̄njɔɔ māŋdzo) economic democracy.

དཔལ་འབྱོར་འཛུགས་སྐྲུན་ (bɛ̄njɔɔ dzu̱gdrün) economic construction/ development.

དཔལ་འབྱོར་ཡར་རྒྱས་ (bɛ̄njɔɔ ya̱rgyɛɛ̀) economic growth/ development.

དཔལ་འབྱོར་རིག་གནས་ (bɛ̄njɔɔ ri̱gnɛɛ̀) economics.

དཔལ་འབྱོར་རིང་ལུགས་ (bɛ̄njɔɔ ri̱nluù) economism.

དཔལ་འབྱོར་ལོ་ཏོག (bɛ̄njɔɔ lo̱dɔɔ̀) economic crops, cash crops.

དཔལ་འབྱོར་ས་ཁུལ་ (bɛ̄njɔɔ səgüü) economic zone.

དཔལ་འབྱོར་གསར་པའི་སྲིད་ཇུས་ (bɛ̄njɔɔ sārbɛ siìjüü) new economic policy.

དཔལ་མར་མེ་མཛད་ཡེ་ཤེས་ (bɛ̄ɛ̄ ma̱rmedzɛɛ̀ ye̱sheè) Atisha.

དཔལ་མོ་ (bɛ̄ɛ̄mo) woman.

དཔལ་མཛེས་ (bɛ̄ɛ̄dzeè) grand and beautiful.

དཔལ་འཛོམས་པ་ (bɛ̄ɛ̀ dzo̱mba) all the good/ virtuous qualities joined together.

དཔལ་གཟི་འབར་བ་ (bɛ̄ɛ̄si ba̱rwa) sm. དཔལ་འབར་.

དཔལ་བཟང་པོ་ (bɛ̄ɛ̄ sa̱ŋbo) a title used after the names of lamas and teacher.

དཔལ་ཡིད་ལ་ (bɛ̄ɛ̄yila) name of a mountain pass in Gonjo in the Tibet Autonomous Region.

དཔལ་ཡུལ་ (bɛ̄ɛ̄yüü) name of a district/ xian in Ganze prefecture in Sichuan Province.

དཔལ་ཡོན་ (bɛ̄ɛ̄yön) 1. glorious, magnificent, splendid, majestic. 2. education ¶ དངོས་པོའི་དཔལ་ཡོན་ Material education. 3. civilization, prestige.

དཔལ་ཡོན་གཉིས་ (bɛ̄ɛ̄yön ñīì) material and spiritual civilization.

དཔལ་ཡོན་དར་བ་ (bɛ̄ɛ̄yön ta̱rwa) civilized.

དཔལ་ཡོན་རབ་དར་གཉིས་ (bɛ̄ɛ̄yön rəbdar ñīì) two highest stages of civilization (material and spiritual).

དཔལ་གཡང་ (bɛ̄ɛ̄yaŋ) good luck/ fortune.

དཔལ་ལད་ (bɛ̄ɛ̄lɛɛ̀) flattering, flattery; va.—བྱེད་.

དཔལ་ལད་ཚ་པོ་ (bɛ̄ɛ̄lɛɛ̀ tsābo) someone who flatters a lot, a sychophant.

དཔལ་གསོལ་མ་ (bɛ̄ɛ̄söoma) shung. well -dressed women who offer prayers to དཔལ་ལྡན་ལྷ་མོ་ during certain festivals.

དཔལ་ལས་ (bɛ̄ɛ̄lɛɛ̀) sm. དཔལ་ལད་.

དཔལ་ལྷ་ (bɛ̄ɛ̄lha) abbr. of དཔལ་ལྡན་ལྷ་མོ་.

དཔལ་ལྷའི་ཚོགས་འཁོར་ (bɛ̄ɛ̄lhɛ tsɔ̄ɔ̀gɔɔ) name of a park in eastern Lhasa.

དཔལ་ལྷའི་རི་གྲ་ (bɛ̄ɛ̄lhɛ ri̱dra) sm. དཔལ་ལྷའི་རི་རབ་.

དཔལ་ལྷའི་རི་རབ་ (bɛ̄ɛ̄lhɛ ri̱rəb) the festival on the 15th of the 10th month of the Tibetan calendar that celebrates the meeting of the goddess and god ("wife and husband") དཔལ་ལྷ་ and གྲིབ་རྫོང་བཙན་.

དཔུང་ (būŋ) 1. force (military), troops. 2. crowd, mass of people. 3. abbr. of དཔུང་པ་.

དཔུང་སྐྱོད་ (būŋgyȫö) army forces on the march; va.—བྱེད་.

དཔུང་ཁ་ (būŋga) sm. དཔུང་ཤུགས་.

དཔུང་ཁག (būŋgaà) 1. camp, team ¶ སྤྱི་ཚོགས་རིང་ལུགས་དཔུང་ཁག The socialist camp. 2. detachment, force, unit (military).

དཔུང་གི་སྦྱོར་བ་ (būŋgi jo̱owa) shung. using force ¶ ངས་དཔུང་གི་སྦྱོར་བ་དྲག་པོ་གཤམས་ན་སྐྱེ་འགྲོ་མང་པོ་མནར་བར་མི་འགྱུར་རམ་ If I used force wouldn't it cause great suffering for many human beings?

དཔུང་གི་སྒྲོན་ཐོ་ (būŋgi drö̱ndo) notice of conscription into the army.

དཔུང་གྲོགས་ (būŋdrɔ̄ɔ̀) sm. དཔུང་རོགས་.

དཔུང་བསྒོས་རུབ་འཛིང་ (būŋgȫö ru̱bdziŋ) attack by

converging columns.

དཔུང་མགོ་ (būŋgo) shoulder.

དཔུང་འགྱོགས་ (būŋgyɔ̀ɔ) carrying sth. on the shoulder; va.—བྱེད་; —རྒྱག.

དཔུང་རྒོལ་ (būŋgöö) military attack; va.—བྱེད་ to attack militarily.

དཔུང་རྒྱག (būŋ gyaà) sm. ཕྱག་རྒྱག.

དཔུང་རྒྱན་ (būŋgyɛn) decorations on the shoulders of military uniforms.

དཔུང་རྒྱུག (būŋ gyuù) sm. ཕྱག་རྒྱག.

དཔུང་སྒར་ (būŋgar) army camp.

དཔུང་སྒྲིག (būŋ drig) marching abreast, marching side-by-side.

དཔུང་སྒྲིག་རྩལ་ (būŋ drigdzüü) battle array, disposition of forces.

དཔུང་སྒྲིལ་ (būŋdrii) swarm/ throng/ gathering of people.

དཔུང་ངར་མ་ (būŋ ŋarma) fierce/ enraged troops.

དཔུང་ངོམ་ (būŋŋom) showing/ demonstrating military strength; va.—བྱེད་.

དཔུང་ངམ་ (būŋŋam) military/ troop demonstration.

དཔུང་བཅད་རས་ (būŋ jɛ̀ɛrɛɛ̀) sleeveless shirt, vest.

དཔུང་བཅུག་དབང་སྡུད་ (būŋjuù wāŋdüù) attacking and conquering; va.—བྱེད་.

དཔུང་ཆུང་ (būŋjuŋ) small force/ detachment/ unit (military).

དཔུང་ཆེན་ (būŋjen) huge army/ force.

དཔུང་འཇའ་ (būŋjaa) a type of traditional Tibetan wind disease.

དཔུང་འཇུག (būŋjuù) troops marching/ moving forward, ordering troops to advance, marching to battle, going on the attack; va.—བྱེད་.

དཔུང་འཇུག་གི་དུང་བད་ (būŋjuùgi tuŋda) a call for the march/ attack, a clarion call.

དཔུང་འཇུག་ (གི་) དམ་བཅའ་ (būŋjuùgi tamja) an oath/ pledge to fight or do battle.

དཔུང་གཉེན་ (būŋñen) comrade-in-arms, friend, pal.

དཔུང་གདོར་ལམ་གཤགས་ (būŋdɔɔ lamshaà) destroying the enemy [Lit. destroying the troops and breaking up the roads].

དཔུང་རྟགས་ (būŋdaà) insignia on soldiers' shoulder/ armband.

དཔུང་སྟར་སྒྲིག (būŋdar drig) va. to line up in formation/ lines.

དཔུང་སྟོབས་ (būŋdob) strength/ might of an army, military strength/ power.

དཔུང་སྟོབས་བཙན་པོ་ (būŋdob dzēmbo) sm. དཔུང་སྟོབས་.

དཔུང་དར་ (būŋdar) the flag or colors of a military company/ unit/ brigade.

དཔུང་དུ་འཁུར་ (būŋdu kūr) shung. va. to use the power/ position/ influence of sb. to get sth. ¶ གོར་རྒྱལ་དཔུང་དུ་འཁུར་ནས་འཕྲོག་པ་སོགས་ཡིན་ཚེ་ If it was stolen by using the power of the Nepalese king.

དཔུང་གདང་ཤིག་ཤིག (būŋdaŋ shīgshiì) standing shoulder to shoulder; va.—བྱེད་.

དཔུང་བདར་ཤིག་ཤིག (būŋdar shīgshiì) sm. དཔུང་གདང་ཤིག་ཤིག.

དཔུང་མདུན་མ་ (būŋ dünmə) frontline soldiers/ troops/ forces.

དཔུང་འདེགས་ (būŋ deg) va. to dispatch/ send an army or military force.

དཔུང་འདྲེན་ (būŋ dren) sm. དཔུང་འདེགས་.

དཔུང་རྡུལ་ (būŋdüü) dust raised by marching soldiers.

དཔུང་སྡེ་ (būŋde) 1. troops, military force/ unit ¶ དཔུང་སྡེ་ཁག་བཞི་ Four military units. 2. ranks ¶ དང་གི་དཔུང་སྡེའི་ནང་ལ་ In the party ranks.

དཔུང་སྡེབ་ (būŋdeb) sm. དཔུང་བསྡེབས་.

དཔུང་བསྡེབས་ (būŋdeb) joining/ combining forces; va.—བྱེད་.

དཔུང་གནོན་ (būŋnün) sm. དཔུང་སྣོན་.

དཔུང་སྣོན་ (būŋnün) reinforcements (military); va.—བྱེད་ to reinforce (troops); va.—ཞུ་ to ask for reinforcements ¶ དཔུང་སྣོན་དུ་འབྱོར་ (They) arrived as reinforcements.

དཔུང་པ་ (būŋbə) 1. shoulder; va.—དར་ to compete with/ against. 2. power, strength.

དཔུང་པ་གྲུ་བསྡེབས་ (būŋba tradeb) sm. དཔུང་བསྡེབས་.

དཔུང་པ་མཉམ་གཤིབ་ (būŋbə ñamshib) shoulder to shoulder.

དཔུང་པ་ཡང་དུ་འགྲོ་ (būŋbə yaŋdu dro) vi. to have one's work decrease, to get relief from hard work.

དཔུང་པ་གསིག་གསིག (būŋbə sīgsiì) lifting one's shoulder; va.—རྒྱག.

དཔུང་པའི་འོག་ཏུ་སྨན་བཙུག་པའི་བྱ་ཐབས་ (būŋbɛ wɔ̀ɔdu mɛ̄mjugbɛ cadəb) Norplant contraceptive method.

དཔུང་པར་འཁྱེར་ (būŋbar kyēr) va. to carry on one's shoulder.

དཔུང་པར་རྒྱག (būŋbar gyaà) sm. དཔུང་པར་འཁྱེར་.

དཔུང་ཕྱོགས་ (būŋjɔɔ̀) camp ¶ བཙན་རྒོལ་དཔུང་ཕྱོགས་ Antiimperialist camp.

དཔུང་འབྲིལ་ (būŋdree) sm. དཔུང་པ་མཉམ་གཤིབ་.

དཔུང་སྦྲེལ་ (būŋdree) sm. དཔུང་པ་མཉམ་གཤིབ་.

དཔུང་མེད་རྒྱབ་ཆད་ (būŋmeè gyəbcɛɛ̀) without reinforcements.

དཔུང་དམག (būŋmaà) troops, military forces.

དཔུང་དམག་རུ་སྒྲིག (būŋmaà rudrig) military review/ parade.

དཔུང་རྩ་ (būŋdza) 1. a vein around the shoulder used in traditional Tibetan medicine for draining blood. 2. the girth of the shoulders.

དཔུང་ཚིགས་ (būŋdzii) shoulder joint.

དཔུང་ཚོགས་ (būŋdzɔɔ̀) sm. དཔུང་སྡེ་.

དཔུང་ཚོགས་ཡན་ལག་བཞི་ (būŋdzɔɔ̀ yɛnlaà shi) 4 types of ancient warfare: cavalry, elephant, chariot, infantry.

དཔུང་འཚང་ (būŋdzaŋ) pushing/ shoving with one's shoulder; va.—རྒྱག་; —གཏོང་.

དཔུང་འཛུམ་ (būŋ dzum) a hollow part above the clavicle bone.

དཔུང་འཛུལ་ (būŋ dzüü) invading, invasion; va.—བྱེད་.

དཔུང་ཞང་ (būŋshaŋ) sm. དཔུང་ཞེང་.

དཔུང་ཞེང་ (būŋsheŋ) the width of the shoulder.

དཔུང་ཟུར་ (būŋsur) sm. དཔུང་འཚང་.

དཔུང་བཟང་ (būŋsaŋ) strong.

དཔུང་ཡ་ (būŋya) opponent, opposition, rival.

དཔུང་རུ་ (būŋru) troops.

དཔུང་རུབ་ (būŋrub) 1. military mass attack, attacking all at once; va.—རྒྱག. 2. mob attack; va.—རྒྱག.

དཔུང་རུས་ (būŋrüü) shoulder bone.

དཔུང་རོགས་ (būŋrɔɔ̀) relief troops, reinforcements, escort troops; va.—གཏོང་ to send reinforcements/ relief troops; va.—འཁྲིད་ to escort militarily; va.—ཞུ་ to ask for relief troops/ reinforcements.

དཔུང་རོགས་རྒྱབ་དམག (būŋrɔɔ̀ gyəbmaà) sm. དཔུང་རོགས་.

དཔུང་ཤུགས་ (būŋshuù) 1. the might/ power of an army. 2. having strong arms and shoulders.

དཔུང་ཤེད་ (būŋsheè) 1. physical strength. 2. military power.

དཔུང་ཤོག (būŋshoò) sm. དཔུང་གཤོག.

དཔུང་གཤིབ་ (būŋshib) shoulder to shoulder; va.—བྱེད་.

དཔུང་གཤིབ་ལག་སྦྲེལ་ (būŋshib lagdree) standing arm in arm/ shoulder to shoulder; va.—བྱེད.

དཔུང་གཤིག (būŋsheè) breaking through an encirclement; va.—བྱེད.

དཔུང་གཤོག (būŋshɔɔ̀) group, crowd.

དཔུང་གཤོང་ (būŋshoŋ) sm. དཔུང་འཛུམ་.

དཔུང་གཤོལ་ (būŋshöö) armistice.

དཔུང་གཤོལ་ཆིངས་ཡིག (būŋshöö cīŋyii) armistice agreement/ pact/ treaty.

དཔུང་ས་འོག་ལ་འཇུག (būŋ sāwɔɔ̀la juù) va. to work

doing hard/ manual labor.

དཔུང་ཤུ་བཙན་དང་དབང་ཤུ་ཆེ་ (būŋsu dzɛ̄n da̱ŋ wāŋsu cē) whoever is strong and powerful (benefits) ¶ ལུང་པ་འདིའི་ནང་དཔུང་ཤུ་བཙན་དང་དབང་ཤུ་ཆེ་ཡིན་པ་ལས་ཁྲིམས་ལ་བརྩི་མཁན་མེད་ In this area no one abides by the law and whoever is strong and powerful benefits.

དཔུང་སུག (būŋ suù) nudging/ shoving someone with the shoulder, to spoil for a fight, blaming/ accusing as a pretext for starting a fight; va.—གཏོང་.

དཔུང་གསར་སྣོན་ (būŋsar nōn) va. to reinforce.

དཔུང་གསིག (būŋsiì) lifting one's shoulder; va.—རྒྱག.

དཔུང་ཧྲག (būŋhraà) crack troops.

དཔེ་ (bē) 1. model, specimen, sample, representative. 2. proverb, metaphor. 3. book. 4. expression of shock and amazement (like the slang "something else") ¶ དགོན་པའི་ནང་ལ་མི་འདིའི་མགོ་ལག་བཀལ་དགོས་ཟེར་བ་དེ་དཔེ་རེད་ Saying that we must hang that person's head and hands up in the monastery is "something else."

དཔེ་ཀློག་འཛིན་གྲྭ་ (bēlɔ̀ɔ dzi̱ndra) reading class.

དཔེ་སྐྱོན་ཅན་ (bē gyō̃njɛn) a bad/ unsuitable example, a bad metaphor.

དཔེ་སྐྲུན་ (bēdrün) publishing, printing; va.—བྱེད་.

དཔེ་སྐྲུན་ཁང་ (bēdrüngaŋ) publishing house.

དཔེ་སྐྲུན་འགྲེམ་སྤེལ་ (bēdrün dre̱mbel) publication and circulation.

དཔེ་སྐྲུན་ཅུའུ་ (bēdrün jū) tib.ch. publishing bureau.

དཔེ་སྐྲུན་རང་དབང་ (bēdrün ra̱ŋwaŋ) freedom of the press.

དཔེ་སྐྲུན་ལས་རིགས་ (bēdrün lɛ̱ɛrig) publishing circles/ professions.

དཔེ་སྐྲུན་གསལ་བཤད་ (bēdrün sɛ̄ɛshɛɛ̀) publisher's note.

དཔེ་བསྐྲུན་ (bēdrün) sm. དཔེ་སྐྲུན་.

དཔེ་ཁང་ (bēgaŋ) 1. library. 2. bookstore.

དཔེ་ཁུག (bēguù) bag (for school books).

དཔེ་ཁྲི་ (bēdri) table for books, bookstand, bookshelf.

དཔེ་ཁྲིད་ (bēdriì) sm. དཔེ་འཁྲིད་.

དཔེ་མཁྱུད་ (bē kyǖü) va. to keep skills and certain knowledge to oneself.

དཔེ་འཁྲིད་ (bēdriì) teaching, lecturing, class with a teacher; va.—བྱེད་ to teach, to lecture, to explain (a text); va.—ལ་འགྲོ་ to go for teaching/ class with one's teacher ¶ ཉི་མ་རེ་རེ་དཔེ་འཁྲིད་ལ་འགྲོ་དགོས་ (I) must go everyday for teachings.

དཔེ་ག་ལ་སྲིད་ (bē ka̱la siì) it's impossible ¶ ང་ཚོས་ཁྱེད་ལ་གསོད་པ་དཔེ་ག་ལ་སྲིད་ཟེར་པ་ཡིན་ I said it was impossible for us to kill you.

དཔེ་མགོ་ (bēngo) beginning of a book.

དཔེ་འགྲེ་ (bēndre) example, analogy; va.—བྱེད་ to use an analogy/ example ¶ ད་ཆ་ས་ཞིང་རྣམས་ཕྱིར་ལོག་གིས་བུན་ཉིང་སྐོར་མཐའ་ཁུལ་དཔེ་འགྲེ་ཞུས་ཆོག་པ་ Now we will return the fields, and as for the question of the old debts, we can use the example of other subjects in that area.

དཔེ་རྒྱུགས་ (bēgyuù) demonstrating one's learning of a religious text by reciting it from memory; va.—སྤྲོད་ to demonstrate one's learning of a religious text by reciting it from memory.

དཔེ་སྒམ་ (bēgam) chest for books, bookcase.

དཔེ་སྒྲོག (bēdrɔ̀ɔ) writing desk.

དཔེ་སྒྲོམ་ (bēdrom) bookshelf, bookcase.

དཔེ་ངན་ཀུན་གནོད་ (bēŋɛn gǖnnöö) a bad example harms everyone.

དཔེ་ངན་པ་ (bē ŋe̱mba) sm. དཔེ་སྐྱོན་ཅན་.

དཔེ་ངོ་མ་ (bē ŋo̱ma) sm. དཔེ་དངོས་.

དཔེ་དངོས་ (bē ŋȫö) real example, real evidence/ proof.

དཔེ་ཆ་ (bēja) book (usu. traditional style); va.—འཁྲིད་ to teach a book; va.—ཀློག་; —ལྟ་ to read a text/ book, to study a text/ book; va.—བཟོ་ to write a book; va.—འགྲེམ་ to publish a book; va.—སྐྱོར་ to recite a religious text from memory; va.—རྩོམ་ to compose/ write a book; —ཟིན་ to memorize a text; va.—བརྩོན་ to study religious texts.

དཔེ་ཆ་ཁང་ (bējagaŋ) sm. དཔེ་ཁང་.

དཔེ་ཆ་ལྟ་ས་ (bēja dāsa) reading room.

དཔེ་ཆ་མདའ་ཚད་མ་ (bēja da̱dzɛɛ̀ma) a religious text whose length is the size of an arrow.

དཔེ་ཆ་པར་མ་ (bēja bārma) printed text/ book.

དཔེ་ཆ་བ་ (bējawa) 1. a category of monk who studies religious philosophy and debate. 2. a student.

དཔེ་ཆ་བཞག་ན་ (bē cā sha̱àna) for example, for instance.

དཔེ་ཆ་གཡོར་ས་ (bēja yɔ̄ɔsa) loan desk of a library.

དཔེ་ཆའི་རྒྱབ་ཤ་ (bējɛ gya̱bsha) book cover.

དཔེ་ཆའི་ཚོང་ཁང་ (bējɛ tsōŋgaŋ) bookstore.

དཔེ་ཆའི་ཨང་རྟགས་ (bējɛ āŋdaà) isbn number.

དཔེ་མཇུག (bēnjuù) the end or latter part of a book/ text.

དཔེ་འཛོག (bēnjɔɔ̀) sm. དཔེ་སྐྱོར་.

དཔེ་འཛོག་དངོས་པོ་ (bēnjɔɔ̀ ŋȫöbo) specimen, demonstration piece, showpiece, model.

དཔེ་འཛོག་ས་ (bē jɔ̱ɔ̀sa) model, example, sample, specimen, demonstration piece.

དཔེ་བརྗོད་ (bē jȫö) sm. དཔེ་སྟོན་.

དཔེ་ཉོག (bēñoò) a book or text that is useless/ incomplete/ disheveled, a book whose pages are out of order.

དཔེ་རྙིང་ (bēñiŋ) ancient texts, old books.

དཔེ་རྙིང་ཚོང་ཁང་ (bēñiŋ tsōŋgaŋ) bookstore that sells old books.

དཔེ་རྟགས་ (bēdaà) production number, edition number.

དཔེ་ལྟ་ (bē dā) va. to imitate, to follow an example.

དཔེ་ལྟ་ཁང་ (bēdagaŋ) reading room.

དཔེ་ལྟ་ས་ (bē dāsa) an example, sth. to emulate.

དཔེ་ལྟག (bēdaà) spine of a book.

དཔེ་སྟོན་ (bēdön) 1. example, sample, specimen, model ¶ ལོ་རྒྱུས་ཤུན་བུ་དཔེ་སྟོན་ཆེད་དུ་བྲིས་ན་ If I write a little history as an example. 2. taking the lead, setting an example, giving an example, demonstrating; va.—བྱེད་.

དཔེ་སྟོན་གྱི་དེབ་ (bēdöngi te̱b) sample, specimen, copy.

དཔེ་སྟོན་སྒྲིག་ཡིག (bēdön dri̱gyiì) model regulations.

དཔེ་སྟོན་དངོས་ཆས་ (bēdön ŋȫöjɛɛ̀) sample, specimen.

དཔེ་སྟོན་ཐོན་རྫས་ (bēdön tȭndzɛɛ̀) sample/ specimen product.

དཔེ་སྟོན་དུད་ཚང་ (bēdön tṳ̈üdzaŋ) exemplary household.

དཔེ་སྟོན་ནུས་པ་ (bēdön nṳ̈übə) model function.

དཔེ་སྟོན་ཚོད་ལྟ་ (bēdön dzȫöda) preliminary test/ trial, trial experiment.

དཔེ་བལྟ་ས་ (bē dāsa) sm. དཔེ་ལྟ་ས་.

དཔེ་བལྟས་ནས་ (bē dɛ̄ɛnɛ) using as an example/ model ¶ ཁང་པ་འདིར་དཔེ་བལྟས་ནས་གསར་པ་གཅིག་བརྒྱབས་པ་རེད་ Taking this house as a model, (he) built a new one.

དཔེ་ཐག (bēdaà) string for tying དཔེ་ཆ་.

དཔེ་ཐིག (bēdig) drawn lines on which text is written (in a book).

དཔེ་ཐུམ་ (bēdum) book cover.

དཔེ་ཐོ་ (bēdo) book list.

དཔེ་ཐོད་ (bēdöö) the top margin of a note pad or book page.

དཔེ་དང་སྦྲགས་ནས་ཤོད་ (bēdaŋ dra̱gnɛ shȫö) va. to say/ convey sth. using an example.

དཔེ་དར་ (bēdar) pennant, banner.

དཔེ་དར་ (bē ta̱r) vi. to become in vogue.

དཔེ་དེབ་ (bēdeb) book; va.—ལྟ་ to study.

དཔེ་དེབ་ཀྱི་མཛེས་ཆ་ (bēdebgi dzēèja) book illustration.

དཔེ་དེབ་ཀློག་ཁང་ (bēdeb lɔ̄ɔgaŋ) reading room.

དཔེ་དེབ་ཁང་ (bēdebgaŋ) bookstore.
དཔེ་དེབ་འགྲེམས་སྟོན་ (bēdeb dr̲emdön) book exhibition.
དཔེ་དེབ་བཏོན་རིགས་ (bēdeb dōnrig) publications.
དཔེ་དེབ་ལྟ་ཁང་ (bēdeb dāgaŋ) reading/ study room.
དཔེ་དེབ་དཔྱད་གཞི་ཁང་ (bēdeb jɛ̄ɛ̀shigaŋ) book and reference room.
དཔེ་དེབ་ཕྱོགས་བསྒྲིགས་ (bēdeb cɔ̄gdriì) encyclopedia.
དཔེ་དེབ་བྲིས་མ་ (bēdeb tr̲imə) handwritten book (in contrast to a printed book).
དཔེ་དེབ་འཚེམ་བྱེད་འཕྲུལ་ཆས་ (bēdeb tsēmjeè trűüjɛɛ̀) bookbinding machine.
དཔེ་དེབ་གཡར་ར་ (bēdeb yārŋa) circulation desk, circulation room in a library.
དཔེ་དེབ་རིང་ལུགས་ (bēdeb r̲iŋluù) book worshipism.
དཔེ་དོན་ (bēdön) example.
དཔེ་འདྲ་ (bēndra) emulation, example, specimen.
དཔེ་ནག་པོ་བསགས་ (bē n̲agbo sāà) sm. དཔེ་བསགས་.
དཔེ་པོད་ (bēböö) sm. པོ་ཏི་.
དཔེ་སྤྱིལ་ཁང་ (bējigaŋ) book kiosk, book stall.
དཔེ་བྱད་ (bējɛɛ̀) proportion, symmetry.
དཔེ་བྱད་བརྒྱད་ཅུ་ (bējɛɛ̀ gyɛɛ̀ju) the 80 minor marks of a Buddha.
དཔེ་བྱད་བཟང་པོ་ (bējɛɛ̀ s̲aŋbo) auspicious marks of a Buddha.
དཔེ་བྱས་ (bējɛɛ̀) p. of དཔེ་བྱེད་.
དཔེ་བྱེད་ (bē c̲eè) va. to take as a model/ example, to imitate/ emulate.
དཔེ་བླངས་ལས་སྟོན་ (bēlaŋ l̲ɛ̀nön) processing according to a model.
དཔེ་དབྱིབས་ (bēyib) 1. model ¶ གནམ་གྲུའི་དཔེ་དབྱིབས་ Model plane. 2. volume ¶ མའོའི་གསུང་རྩོམ་གཅེས་བསྡུས་ཀྱི་དཔེ་དབྱིབས་ A volume of the Selected Works of Mao.
དཔེ་འདྲི་ (bēdri) example, guide, module.
དཔེ་སྦྱར་ནས་ཤོད་ (bējarnɛ shȫö) sm. དཔེ་དང་སྦྲགས་ནས་བཤད་.
དཔེ་སྦྱར་ (bē j̲ar) p. of དཔེ་སྦྱོར་.
དཔེ་སྦྱོར་ (bē j̲ɔr) va. to give/ use examples ¶ དཔེ་སྦྱོར་བཞིན་དུ་འགྲེལ་བཤད་བརྒྱབ་སོང་ (He) explained by using examples.
དཔེ་མ་སྲིད་པས་ (bē m̲asiìbɛ) sm. དཔེ་མི་སྲིད་པ་.
དཔེ་མི་མཐུན་པ་ (bē m̲itümbə) sm. དཔེ་སྐྱོན་ཅན་.
དཔེ་མི་སྲིད་པ་ (bē m̲isiìbə) extraordinary, extraordinarily ¶ དཔེ་མི་སྲིད་པའི་ཡག་པོ་འདུག Extraordinarily good.
དཔེ་མེད་ (bēmeè) unequalled, incomparable, matchless, without precedent.
དཔེ་དམག (bēmaà) 1. exemplary/ model soldier. 2. model army.

དཔེ་ཙམ་ (bēdzam) just an example, not real.
དཔེ་རྩོམ་ (bē dzōm) va. to write/ compose a book.
དཔེ་ཚད་ (bēdzɛ̀ɛ̀) 1. model, example. 2. norm.
དཔེ་ཚིག (bēdziì) example, figure of speech.
དཔེ་ཚེམ་ (bēdzem) bookbinding; va.—བཟོ་ to bind books.
དཔེ་ཚོགས་ (bēdzɔ̀ɔ̀) collection of printed works, series of published books.
དཔེ་ཚོང་ཁང་ (bēdzoŋgaŋ) bookstore.
དཔེ་མཚམས་པ་ (bēdzamba) a scholar monk who lives with a patron family while studying religious philosophy.
དཔེ་མཚོན་ (bēdzön) example, model; va.—སྟོན་ to show/ give an example ¶ འདིའི་སྐོར་དཔེ་མཚོན་ཅིག་བརྗོད་ན་ If I give an example of this.
དཔེ་མཚོན་ལྟ་དེབ་ (bēdzön dādeb) 1. sample book. 2. book of samples.
དཔེ་མཚོན་དཔེ་དེབ་ (bēdzön bēdeb) sm. དཔེ་མཚོན་ལྟ་དེབ་.
དཔེ་མཚོན་ཞིང་ཁ་ (bēdzön sh̲iŋgə) demonstration/ sample/ model agricultural field.
དཔེ་མཚོན་ཞིབ་འཇུག (bēdzön sh̲imjuù) model/ demonstration/ trial investigation or survey or research.
དཔེ་མཚོན་རིས་མོ་ (bēdzön r̲iìmu) sample drawing, a drawing to illustrate sth.
དཔེ་མཚོན་ཤོག་ལྷེ་ (bēdzön shɔ̄glhe) sample page.
དཔེ་འཚེམ་ (bē tsēm) va. to bind books.
དཔེ་འཚོང་ཁང་ (bēdzoŋgaŋ) sm. དཔེ་ཚོང་ཁང་.
དཔེ་འཚོང་པ་ (bēdzoŋwa) people who sell books/ texts.
དཔེ་མཛོད་ (bēndzöö) sm. དཔེ་མཛོད་ཁང་.
དཔེ་མཛོད་ཁང་ (bēndzöögaŋ) library.
དཔེ་མཛོད་ཁང་སྐོར་གྱི་རིག་པ་ (bēndzöögaŋ gɔ̄ɔ̄gi r̲igbə) library science, librarianship.
དཔེ་འཛིན་པ་ (bē dz̲immbə) monks who learn the scriptures by heart.
དཔེ་གཞི་ (bēshi) model, specimen, sample.
དཔེ་གཞི་ཁང་ (bēshigaŋ) specimen hall.
དཔེ་བཞག (bē sh̲aà) va. to give an example, to use an example.
དཔེ་བཞག་ན་ (bē sh̲aàna) for example.
དཔེ་བཞག་ས་ (bē sh̲aàsa) using (sth.) as an example.
དཔེ་ཟླ་ (bēnda) comparison, match ¶ དཔེ་ཟླ་མེད་པ་ Matchless, unequalled.
དཔེ་ཟླ་མེད་པ་ (bēnda m̲eèba) sm. དཔེ་མེད་.
དཔེ་གཟིགས་ཁང་ (bēsiìgaŋ) h. of དཔེ་ལྟ་ཁང་.
དཔེ་གཟུགས་ (bēsuù) model.
དཔེ་བཟང་ (bēsaŋ) model, example, ideal, standard; va.—དུ་རྩི་ to hold up as a model.

དཔེ་བཟང་ཀུན་ཕན་ (bēsaŋ gűnbɛn) a good example benefits everyone.
དཔེ་བཟང་ཅན་ (bēsanjɛn) exemplary (person, group).
དཔེ་བཟང་ཡར་འགྲན་ (bēsaŋ y̲aadrɛn) following a good example.
དཔེ་བཟོ་ (bē s̲o) va. to make a model/ specimen.
དཔེ་འོས་ (bēwöö) sm. དཔེ་བཟང་.
དཔེ་ཡིག (bēyiì) letters used by students to copy when practicing their penmanship.
དཔེ་རང་ (bēraŋ) extremely ¶ དཔེ་རང་ཡག་པོ་ Extremely good.
དཔེ་རས་ (bērɛɛ̀) book cover/ wrapping (the cloth cover used to wrap traditional Tibetan books).
དཔེ་རིས་ (bēriì) pattern, design, illustration, chart, blueprint; va.—འབྲི་ to draw a pattern, to design ¶ རས་ཁྲ་གསར་པ་སྣ་ཁ་ 120 ལྷག་དཔེ་རིས་བྲིས་པ་རེད་ (They) designed over 120 kinds of new cotton prints. 2. a figure in a book ¶ དཔེ་རིས་ 2 Figure Two.
དཔེ་རིས་གྲུ་བཞི་མ་ (bēriì tr̲ubshimə) square picture frame.
དཔེ་རིས་འགྲེམས་སྟོན་ཁང་ (bēriì dr̲emdöngaŋ) photo exhibition hall.
དཔེ་རིས་པར་གཞི་ (bēriì bārshi) drawing board.
དཔེ་རིས་དཔྱད་ཆས་ (bēriì jɛ̀ɛ̀jɛɛ̀) drawing instruments.
དཔེ་རིས་འབྲི་ (bēriì tr̲i) va. to draw a pattern/ design/ blueprint/ illustration/ chart.
དཔེ་རིས་འབྲི་ཁང་ (bēriì tr̲igaŋ) drawing/ drafting room.
དཔེ་རིས་སྔོན་པོ་ (bēriì ŋȭmbo) blueprint.
དཔེ་རིས་རིའུ་མིག (bēriì r̲iwu m̲iì) 1. blueprint. 2. printed from.
དཔེ་རུལ་ (bērüü) a worthless/ useless book.
དཔེ་རེད་ (bēreè) very good!
དཔེ་ལགས་ (bēlaà) sm. དཔེ་བཟང་.
དཔེ་ལམ་ (bēlam) sm. དཔེ་སྟོན་.
དཔེ་ལེགས་ཀྱི་བྱས་རྗེས་ (bēleggi c̲ɛ̀ɛ̀dzɛɛ̀) exemplary deeds.
དཔེ་ལེགས་ཅན་ (bēlegjɛn) exemplary.
དཔེ་ལེགས་མི་སྣ་ (bēleg m̲inə) exemplary people.
དཔེ་ལེན་ (bē l̲en) sm. དཔེ་སྦྱོར་.
དཔེ་ཤུབས་ (bēshub) book cover, book container.
དཔེ་ཤུས་ (bē shǖü) sm.* དཔེ་བཤུས་.
དཔེ་བཤད་ (bēshɛɛ̀) proverb.
དཔེ་བཤུ་ (bē sh̲u) va. to copy a book.
དཔེ་བཤུས་ (bēshüü) 1. p. of དཔེ་བཤུ་. 2. copy of a book; va.—བྱེད་ to copy a book.
དཔེ་སྲིད་བཀའ་བཀྱོན་ (bēsiì gāgyön) a response used

to show modesty when you are given a compliment (something like "Oh. No").

དཔེ་སྲིད་པས་ (bēsiìbɛ) a phrase used to show modesty when you are given a compliment (something like "Oh. No").

དཔེ་སྲིད་དོགས་མེད་ (bēsiì dɔ̱ɔ̀meè) phrase conveying the impossibility of sth.

དཔེ་སློལ་ (bēsöö) example.

དཔེ་གསར་ (bēsar) 1. a new style/ type/ fashion ¶ ཞིང་ཆས་དཔེ་གསར་ New style farm implements. 2. modern.

དཔེ་གསར་ཡང་གསར་ (bēsar ya̱ŋsar) the most up-to-date/ new.

དཔེ་གསར་ལུགས་གསར་ (bēsar lu̱gsar) new, modern.

དཔེ་སློབ་དགེ་རྒན་ (bēlob ge̱gɛn) teacher, instructor.

དཔེ་བསམགས་ (bēsaà) slang exclamation conveying a lot of difficulties/ problems or sth. very bad ¶ དེ་རིང་དཔེ་བསམགས་སོང་ Today, my god (we had tremendous difficulties)!

དཔེན་པ་ (bēmba) 1. beautiful, pleasing. 2. useful, helpful.

དཔེའུ་ཆུང་ (bēwu cūŋ) small book.

དཔེའུ་རིག (bēwu ri̱g) sm. རིའུ་མིག.

དཔེའུ་རིས་ (bēwu ri̱ì) sm. དཔེ་རིས་.

དཔེར་བསྒྲུན་ (bēr drūn) va. to use sth. as an example.

དཔེར་བརྗོད་ (bēr jö̱ö) sm. དཔེ་སྟོན་.

དཔེར་བརྗོད་ (berjöö) an example, an illustration; va.—བྱེད་; va.—རྒྱག to use an example/ illustration.

དཔེར་བརྗོད་ཚིག་གྲུབ་ (bērjöö tsīgdrub) an exemplary sentence.

དཔེར་ལྟ་ (bēē dā) sm. དཔེ་ལྟ་.

དཔེར་སྟོན་ཞིང་ར་ (bērdön shi̱ŋrə) model farm.

དཔེར་འདྲེན་ (bēndren) giving/ using an example; va.—བྱེད་.

དཔེར་ན་ (bērna) for example.

དཔེར་ན་ཅ་བཞག་ན་ (bērna cāshaàna) sm. དཔེར་ན་.

དཔེར་བྱེད་ (bēr ce̱è) va. to give/ use an example.

དཔེར་བླངས་ (bēē lāŋ) sm. དཔེར་ལེན་.

དཔེར་མི་སྲིད་པ་ (bēē mi̱siìbə) sm. དཔེ་མི་སྲིད་པ་.

དཔེར་འོས་ (bērwöö) a worthy example.

དཔེར་ལེན་ (bēr le̱n) va. to copy/ follow an example.

དཔེར་སྲིད་དམ་ (bēē siìdam) sm. དཔེ་སྲིད་པས་.

དཔོག་: p. དཔགས་; f. དཔག; imp. དཔོགས་ (bɔ̄ɔ) va. to measure, to judge, to weigh.

དཔོག་དཀའ་ (bɔ̄ɔga) difficult to know/ measure.

དཔོག་རྩིས་ (bɔ̄gdziì) estimating; va.—རྒྱག.

དཔོགས་ (bɔ̄ɔ) imp. of དཔོག.

དཔོང་ཕྱིའི་རྒྱུག་འགྲན་ (bōŋci gyu̱ndren) crosscountry race.

དཔོད་ (bȫȫ) va. to dictate.

དཔོད་བྲིས་ (bȫȫdriì) dictating (a letter); va.—གཏོང་.

དཔོན་ (bȫn) chief, lord, master.

དཔོན་དཀྱུས་ (bȫngyüü) common/ ordinary official.

དཔོན་སྐད་ (bȫngɛɛ̀) the language used by officials.

དཔོན་སྐྱ་ (bȫngya) shung. lay officials ¶ བླ་མ་སློབ་དཔོན་མི་ཆེན་དཔོན་སྐྱ་ Lamas and teachers, important people and lay officials.

དཔོན་ཁག (bȫngaà) 1. different kinds of leaders/ masters / heads. 2. local chieftains.

དཔོན་ཁུངས་ (bȫnguŋ) the lord to whom one belongs.

དཔོན་འཁོར་ (bȫngɔɔ) master and servants, lord/ official and retinue.

དཔོན་འགོ་ (bȫngo) chief, lord, master.

དཔོན་རྒྱུད་ (bȫngyü̱ü̱) the lineage/ descent line of a lord.

དཔོན་བརྒྱུད་ (bȫngyü̱ü̱) succession of leaders.

དཔོན་སྒྲ་བསྒྲོགས་ (bȫndra gȫȫ) va. to talk or give an order in the manner of a superior/ leader.

དཔོན་ངན་ (bȫnŋɛn) bureaucracy, bureaucrat [Lit. bad/ evil lord].

དཔོན་ངན་རྒྱུ་གཟན་ (bȫnŋɛn gyu̱sɛn) corrupt/ profiteering officials.

དཔོན་ངན་འདོད་ཛམས་ཅན་ (bȫnŋɛn dö̱öŋamjɛn) corrupt officials.

དཔོན་ངན་འབྱོར་ལྡན་གྲལ་རིམ་ (bȫnŋɛn jɔ̱ndɛn tre̱e̱rim) bureaucratic-capitalist class.

དཔོན་ངན་མ་རྩ་ (bȫnŋɛn ma̱dza) bureaucratic capital.

དཔོན་ངན་མ་རྩའི་རིང་ལུགས་ (bȫnŋɛn ma̱dzɛ ri̱ŋluù) bureaucratic capitalism.

དཔོན་ངན་བཟའ་ཛམ་ཅན་ (bȫnŋɛn sa̱ŋamjɛn) corrupt officials/ bureaucrats.

དཔོན་ངན་རིང་ལུགས་ (bȫnŋɛn ri̱ŋluù) bureaucratism.

དཔོན་མངའ་ཐང་ཆེ་ན་ གཡོག་སྡུག་ཐང་ཆེ་བ་ (bȫn ŋadaŋ cēna yōg du̱gdaŋ cēwa) if the lord becomes powerful, the servants suffer more [due to more labor, etc.].

དཔོན་ཉམས་ (bȫnñam) grand/ regal manner.

དཔོན་ཉམས་དོད་པོ་ (bȫnñam tö̱öbo) sm. དཔོན་ཉམས་.

དཔོན་གདམ་ (bȫndam) certain words, phrases or sentences used by the aristrocracy or ruling class.

དཔོན་ཐག་གཡོག་གཅོད་ (bȫntaà yōgjöö) servants/ subordinates making decisions that should be made by the master/ chief.

དཔོན་དུ་སྐོ་ (bȫndu gō) va. to be appointed as a lord/ chief/ head.

དཔོན་གནས་ (bȫnnɛɛ̀) the position/ office of an official; va.—བྱེད་; vi.—ཤོར་ to lose one's position/ office.

དཔོན་པོ་ (bȫmbo) chief, lord, ruler, master, official; va.—བྱེད་ to be a chief/ lord/ master/ official.

དཔོན་པོ་ཕྱི་རྒྱལ་བ་ (bȫmbo cīgyɛɛwa) foreign envoy, person from one state serving in the court of another.

དཔོན་པོའི་ཐོབ་ཐང་ (bȫmbö tōbdaŋ) the rights of a chief/ lord/ master/ official.

དཔོན་སྤྱོད་ (bȫnjöö) lordly or bureaucratic behavior/ manners.

དཔོན་བློན་ (bȫnlön) chief/ king/ ruler and minister.

དཔོན་འབངས་ (bȫnbaŋ) chief/ lord/ ruler/ high officials and subjects.

དཔོན་མང་འབངས་ཉུང་ (bȫnmaŋ ba̱ŋñuŋ) the existence of too many officials/ leaders [Lit. many officials, few subjects].

དཔོན་མོ་ (bȫnmo) female chief/ ruler/ master/ official.

དཔོན་དམག (bȫnmaà) officers and soldiers.

དཔོན་དམག་ལྷན་རྒྱས་ (bȫnmaà lhēngyɛɛ̀) officers and solders (together).

དཔོན་བཙས་ (bȫndzɛɛ̀) shung. (subjects) harvesting a lord's agricultural fields.

དཔོན་རྩྭ་ (bȫndza) shung. pasture set aside for a chief/ lord.

དཔོན་ཚང་ (bȫndzaŋ) 1. residence of an official/ chief/ ruler. 2. family from which a chief/ ruler comes.

དཔོན་ཞྭ་ (bȫnsha) official's hat.

དཔོན་ཟུར་ (bȫnsur) ex-chief/ ruler/ king/ high official.

དཔོན་གཡོག (bȫnyoò) master/ chief/ ruler/ lord and servant.

དཔོན་རབས་ (bȫnrəb) sm. དཔོན་བརྒྱུད་.

དཔོན་རིགས་ (bȫnriì) officials, lords, authorities, bureaucrats.

དཔོན་རིམ་ (bȫnrim) the hierarchy of ranks of chief/ lord/ officials.

དཔོན་ལམ་ (bȫnlam) the way to get the status of chief/ official.

དཔོན་ཤག (bȫnshaà) lord's/ chief's/ official's quarters or dwelling.

དཔོན་སློབ་ (bȫnlob) 1. teacher and student/ disciple. 2. governor.

དཔོར་: p. དཔར་ (bɔ̄r) va. to dictate (a letter, etc.).

དཔོར་ཕྱོགས་ལོག (bɔ̄rjɔɔ lɔ̀ɔ) vi. to reverse, to go opposite/ contrary.

དཔོར་ཕྱོགས་སློག (bɔ̄rjɔɔ lɔ̄ɔ) va. to do the opposite/

contrary.

དཔྱ་ (jā) 1. tax. 2. a part.

དཔྱ་: p. དཔྱས་; f. དཔྱ་; imp. དཔྱོས་ (jā) va. to blame, accuse, criticize, denigrate.

དཔྱ་ཁྲལ་ (jātrɛɛ) taxes; va.—འཁུར་; va.—འཇལ་ to pay taxes; va.—སྡུད་ to collect taxes; va.—གཡོལ་ to evade paying taxes.

དཔྱ་ཁྲལ་གྱི་ཡོང་འབབ་ (jātrɛɛgi yoŋbəb) tax revenue.

དཔྱ་འགྲོས་ (jādröö) gradually, step by step.

དཔྱ་ཐང་ (jādaŋ) the amount of tax one has to pay.

དཔྱ་དང་སྐྱེས་ (jādaŋ gyēè) taxes and gifts.

དཔྱ་འབབ་ (jāmbəb) sm. དཔྱ་ཐང་.

དཔྱང་ (jāŋ) 1. va. to hang/ suspend/ dangle downwards. 2. f. of དཔྱོང་.

དཔྱང་བཀལ་ (jāŋ gɛ̄ɛ) va. to hang up.

དཔྱང་འཁོར་ (jāŋgɔɔ) crane (truck with crane).

དཔྱང་སྒོ་ (jāŋgo) swinging door/ gate.

དཔྱང་ད་ལིང་ད་ (jāŋda liŋda) sm. དཔྱང་དཔྱང་ཁྲོལ་ཁྲོལ་.

དཔྱང་བདགས་ (jāŋdaà) va. to hang, to suspend, to dangle.

དཔྱང་ཐག (jāŋdaà) 1.sm. དཔྱངས་ཐིག. 2. doubt, suspicion.

དཔྱང་ཐིག (jāŋdig) sm. དཔྱངས་ཐིག.

དཔྱངས་ཐིག (jāŋdig) 1. plumb line. 2. a rope by means of which sth. is suspended; va.—གཏོང་. 3. a perpendicular line.

དཔྱང་དར་ (jāŋdar) a dangling/ hanging silk ribbon.

དཔྱང་རྡོ་ (jāŋdo) the stone weight on a plumb line.

དཔྱང་དཔྱང་ཁྲོལ་ཁྲོལ་ (jāŋjaŋ trüüdrüü) dangling, hanging, suspended.

དཔྱང་ཞགས་ (jāŋshaà) hanging noose.

དཔྱང་ཟམ་ (jāŋsam) hanging/ suspended bridge.

དཔྱང་ཟོམ་ (jāŋsom) a water bucket suspended on a rope in a well.

དཔྱང་ལུང་ (jəŋluŋ) 1. a ring suspended on a rope. 2. the rings (in gymnastics).

དཔྱངས་ (jāŋ) p. of དཔྱོང་.

དཔྱངས་འཁོར་ (jāŋgɔɔ) sm. དཔྱང་འཁོར་.

དཔྱད་ (jɛ̄ɛ) 1. p. and f. of དཔྱོད་. 2. va. to analyze, examine, investigate.

དཔྱད་ཁྲ་ (jɛ̄ɛdra) decision, sentence, verdict.

དཔྱད་གླེང་ (jɛ̄ɛleŋ) appraising/ analyzing/ examining sth. through discussion.

དཔྱད་འགྲེལ་ (jɛ̄ndree) footnote.

དཔྱད་ལྔ་ (jɛ̄ɛŋa) five methods of Tibetan medical treatment (draining blood, moxibustion, inhalation of smoke, using medicated compresses, taking medicine).

དཔྱད་གཅོད་ (jɛ̄ɛjöö) examining/ investigating and deciding.

དཔྱད་ཆས་ (jɛ̄ɛjɛɛ) instrument or apparatus for appraising/ analyzing/ examining.

དཔྱད་མཆན་ (jɛ̄njɛn) sm. དཔྱད་བརྗོད་.

དཔྱད་འཆར་འབུལ་ (jɛ̄ncar büü) shung. va. to submit a verdict (to a higher authority, court) for their decision ¶ རྩ་ཞིབ་ཀྱི་ཞུ་བ་ཡིག་རིགས་དཔྱད་འཆར་ཕུལ་བ་ They submitted the documents regarding the investigation and verdict to the higher authorities for their decision.

དཔྱད་འཇོག (jɛ̄njöö) sm. དཔྱད་ཞིབ་.

དཔྱད་བརྗོད་ (jɛ̄ɛjöö) commentary, comments, notes, footnotes, remarks; va.—བྱེད་; —བརྗོད་; —འགོད to comment on, to critique, to footnote ¶ ཐོག་མའི་དཔྱད་བརྗོད་ A preliminary/ first commentary.

དཔྱད་བརྗོད་ཀྱི་རྩོམ་ཡིག (jɛ̄ɛjöögi dzōmyii) critical essay/ paper.

དཔྱད་གཏམ་ (jɛ̄ɛdam) sm. དཔྱད་བརྗོད་.

དཔྱད་གཏམ་བརྗོད་མཁན་ (jɛ̄ɛdam jööñɛn) commentator, analyst.

དཔྱད་གཏམ་ཐུང་ངུ་ (jɛ̄ɛdam tūŋŋu) short/ brief comment.

དཔྱད་གཏམ་པ་ (jɛ̄ɛdamba) sm. དཔྱད་གཏམ་བརྗོད་མཁན་.

དཔྱད་རྟོག (jɛ̄ɛdɔɔ) investigating, examining; va.—བྱེད་.

དཔྱད་ཐུང་ (jɛ̄ɛtuŋ) shung. a short/ brief verdict ¶ ནག་མེད་ཉེས་འགེལ་གྱི་དཔྱད་ཐུང་ཙམ་གནང་རིགས་མེད་བཞིན་དུ་ (They) did not issue even a short verdict that blamed an innocent person.

དཔྱད་དེབ་ (jɛ̄ɛdeb) abbr. of དཔྱད་གཞིའི་དཔེ་ཆ་.

དཔྱད་འདེམས་ (jɛ̄ndem) examining and choosing; va.—བྱེད་.

དཔྱད་བདར་ (jɛ̄ɛdar) detailed research.

དཔྱད་བསྡུར་ (jɛ̄ɛdur) 1. examining/ investigating and comparing; va.—བྱེད་. 2. grading (exams).

དཔྱད་བསྡུར་སྐར་འགོད་ (jɛ̄ɛdur gārgöö) grading exams and giving a score on the exam paper.

དཔྱད་པ་ (jɛ̄ɛba) outward appearance ¶ རྟ་དཔྱད་པ་ཡག་པོ་ A good looking horse.

དཔྱད་པ་བྱེད་ (jɛ̄ɛba cee) va. to examine/ investigate.

དཔྱད་སྒྲོད་ཀྱི་སྒྲོལ་ཡིག (jɛ̄ɛdröögi sööyii) a statement of rules that allows people to examine and compare whether they are eligible for sth.

དཔྱད་བྱད་ (jɛ̄ɛjɛɛ) medical tools.

དཔྱད་བྱེད་ (jɛ̄ɛjee) va. to examine, to research, to test, to analyze.

དཔྱད་འབྲས་ (jɛ̄ndrɛɛ) results of an examination/ investigation, diagnosis.

དཔྱད་རྩོམ་ (jɛ̄ɛdzom) a research paper/ article, commentary.

དཔྱད་རྩོམ་ཡི་གེ་ (jɛ̄ɛdzom yigi) thesis (for a degree in college).

དཔྱད་མཚམས་ (jɛ̄ɛdzam) judgement, decision, verdict; va.—གཏོང་.

དཔྱད་མཚམས་ཁྲ་མ་ (jɛ̄ɛdzam trāma) a written དཔྱད་མཚམས་.

དཔྱད་མཚམས་ལག་བསྟར་ (jɛ̄ɛdzam lagdar) implementing a judgement/ decision/ verdict.

དཔྱད་འཚོལ་ (jɛ̄ɛdzöö) investigating and researching.

དཔྱད་ཞིབ་ (jɛ̄ɛshib) examining, investigating; va.—བྱེད་.

དཔྱད་ཞིབ་བསྡུ་ལེན་ (jɛ̄ɛshib dulen) selecting or admitting sb. or sth. after examining/ investigating.

དཔྱད་ཞིབ་ཚད་བསྡུར་ (jɛ̄ɛshib tsɛ̄ɛdur) examining by comparing.

དཔྱད་གཞི་ (jɛ̄ɛshi) 1. reference data ¶ ཚན་རིགས་ཀྱི་དཔྱད་གཞི་ Scientific data. 2. question, problem, issue.

དཔྱད་གཞི་ཁང་ (jɛ̄ɛshigaŋ) reference room.

དཔྱད་གཞིའི་དེབ་ (jɛ̄ɛshii teb) sm. དཔྱད་གཞིའི་དཔེ་ཆ་.

དཔྱད་གཞིའི་དཔེ་ཆ་ (jɛ̄ɛshii bēja) reference book.

དཔྱད་གཞིའི་ཡིག་ཆ་ (jɛ̄ɛshii yigja) reference documents, reference materials ¶ དཔྱད་གཞིའི་ཡིག་རིགས་ཁང་ Reference room.

དཔྱད་གཞིའི་ཡིག་རིགས་ (jɛ̄ɛshii yigrii) sm. དཔྱད་གཞིའི་ཡིག་ཆ་.

དཔྱད་གཞིའི་གསར་འགྱུར་ (jɛ̄ɛshii sōngyur) an extract of world news circulated to high officials in China.

དཔྱད་གཟིགས་ (jɛ̄ɛsii) reviewing, examining; va.—བྱེད་.

དཔྱད་བཟོད་པ་ (jɛ̄ɛsööba) able to be examined/ investigated.

དཔྱད་ཡིག (jɛ̄ɛyii) reference works/ materials, documents, data.

དཔྱད་ཡིག་ཁང་ (jɛ̄ɛyigaŋ) 1. sm. དཔྱད་ཡིག་མཛོད་ཁང་. 2. a room within a library or archive where reference materials are kept/ read.

དཔྱད་ཡིག་མཛོད་ཁང་ (jɛ̄ɛyii dzöögaŋ) library or archive for reference materials/ documents.

དཔྱད་ཡིག་ཤོག་བྱང་ (jɛ̄ɛyii shōgjaŋ) index card with reference/ research data on it.

དཔྱད་ཡུལ་ (jɛ̄ɛyüü) main topic/ object of research or investigation.

དཔྱད་ཤོག (jɛ̄ɛshɔɔ) a judicial decision/ verdict.

དཔྱལ་ (jɛ̄ɛ) an ancient lineage of Tibet.

དཔྱས་ (jɛ̄ɛ) 1. p. of དཔྱ་. 2. va. to blame, to accuse.

དཔྱས་ཅན་ (jɛ̄ɛjɛn) blamable, criminal.

དཔྱས་བཏགས་ (jɛ̀ɛdaà) 1. blaming, accusing, criticizing, denigrating. 2. poking fun/ ridiculing.
དཔྱས་མདོགས་ (jɛ̀ɛdɔɔ̀) sm. དཔྱས་, 2.
དཔྱས་མེད་ (jɛ̀ɛmeè) faultless, blameless.
དཔྱི་ (jī) hip.
དཔྱི་དྲི་ (jīdri) the protuding knob on doors and windows that fit into a hole and acts as a hinge.
དཔྱི་མགོ་ (jīngo) hip.
དཔྱི་མགོ་རྡོལ་མ་ (jīngo dööma) bedsore.
དཔྱི་མིག (jīmig) hip bone socket.
དཔྱི་མ་ (jīma) sm. དཔྱི་མགོ་རྡོལ་མ་.
དཔྱི་ཚིགས་ (jīdzii) hip bone/ joint.
དཔྱི་ཟུར་ (jīsur) side of the hips.
དཔྱི་རུས་ (jīrüü) hip bone.
དཔྱིད་ (jīì) 1. spring. 2. prosperity. 3. semen or egg.
དཔྱིད་ཀ་ (jīìgə) sm. དཔྱིད་, 1.
དཔྱིད་ཀའི་ཉི་མ་ (jīìgɛ ñīmə) the spring sun.
དཔྱིད་ཀའི་དུས་ཆེན་ (jīìgɛ tüüjen) spring celebration/ festival (Chinese New Year).
དཔྱིད་ཀྱི་རྒྱལ་མོའི་གླུ་དབྱངས་ (jīìgi gyɛɛmö lūyaŋ) a historical work written by the 5th Dalai Lama.
དཔྱིད་ཀྱི་ཐིག་ལེ་ (jīìgi tīgle) sperm, semen.
དཔྱིད་ཀྱི་དཔལ་ཡོན་ (jīìgi bɛ̄ɛyön) sm. དཔྱིད་དཔལ་.
དཔྱིད་ཀྱི་དཔལ་ཡོན་རྒྱས་ (jīìgi bɛ̄ɛyön gyɛ̀ɛ) prosperously flourishing/ thriving.
དཔྱིད་ཀྱི་ཕོ་ཉ་ (jīìgi pōña) cuckoo bird.
དཔྱིད་འཁྱགས་ (jīìgyaà) a spell of cold spring weather.
དཔྱིད་གྲོ་ (jīìdro) spring wheat.
དཔྱིད་མགོའི་མེ་ཏོག (jīŋgö medoò) wintersweet (flower).
དཔྱིད་འགོ་ (jīŋgo) start of spring, early spring.
དཔྱིད་སྒང་ (jīngaŋ) middle of spring.
དཔྱིད་ཆར་ (jīìjar) spring rains.
དཔྱིད་ཆུ་ (jīìju) 1. rivers in spring; vi.—རྒྱས་ to flood in spring. 2. spring irrigation; va.—གཏོང་; —འདྲེན་ to water/ irrigate the fields in the spring.
དཔྱིད་ཆོས་ཆེན་མོ་ (jīìjöö cēmbo) the monastic study semester that occurs in spring.
དཔྱིད་ཉིན་མཚན་མཉམ་ (jīìñin tsɛ̄nñam) spring equinox.
དཔྱིད་མཉམ་ (jīìñam) abbr. དཔྱིད་ཉིན་མཚན་མཉམ་.
དཔྱིད་སྟོད་ (jīìdöö) first part of spring, early spring.
དཔྱིད་ཐ་མ་ (jīì tāma) the last month of spring (the 3rd month of the Tibetan calendar).
དཔྱིད་ཐན་ (jīìdɛn) spring drought.
དཔྱིད་ཐིག (jīìdig) abbr. of དཔྱིད་ཀྱི་ཐིག་ལེ་.
དཔྱིད་དུས་ (jīìdüü) springtime.
དཔྱིད་དྲོད་ (jīìdröö) the warm weather that comes with spring.
དཔྱིད་འདེབས་ (jīndeb) spring sowing/ planting; va.—བྱེད་.
དཔྱིད་འདེབས་དབྱར་ཡུར་ (jīndeb yāryur) plant in spring, weed in summer.
དཔྱིད་བསྡུའི་ལོ་ཏོག (jīìdü lōdoò) crops harvested in spring.
དཔྱིད་དཔལ་ (jīìbɛɛ) the beauty/ grandeur/ prosperity of spring; vi.—ཤར་ to become the season of spring.
དཔྱིད་སྤྲོད་ (jīìdröö) picnic/ banquet given in spring.
དཔྱིད་བལ་ (jīìpɛɛ) wool sheared during spring.
དཔྱིད་འབྲིང་ (jīìdriŋ) the 2th month of spring (the 2nd month of the Tibetan lunar calendar).
དཔྱིད་རྨོས་ (jīìmöö) spring cultivation/ plowing; va.—བྱེད་ to plow the land in the spring.
དཔྱིད་སྨིན་ལོ་ཏོག (jīìmin lōdoò) spring-ripening crops.
དཔྱིད་ཚུགས་ (jīìdzuù) start of spring.
དཔྱིད་མཚེར་ (jīìdzer) areas nomads inhabit during the spring.
དཔྱིད་ཞོད་ (jīìshöö) spring rains.
དཔྱིད་གཞུང་ (jīìshuŋ) middle of spring.
དཔྱིད་ཟུག (jīìsug) the start of spring (the 1st month of the Tibetan calendar).
དཔྱིད་ཟླ་ཐ་ཆུང་ (jīnda tājuŋ) final month of spring (the 3rd month of the Tibetan calendar).
དཔྱིད་ཟླ་འབྲིང་བ་ (jīnda driŋwə) middle month of spring (the 2nd month of the Tibetan lunar calendar).
དཔྱིད་ཟླ་གསུམ་ (jīnda sūm) the three months of spring.
དཔྱིད་ཟླ་ར་བ་ (jīnda rawa) beginning month of spring (the 1st month of the Tibetan calendar).
དཔྱིད་གཡོག (jīìyɔɔ̀) person hired during time of the spring plowing season.
དཔྱིད་རླུང་ (jīìluŋ) the winds of spring.
དཔྱིད་ཤར་ (jīìshar) sm. དཔྱིད་ཟུག.
དཔྱིད་གཤེར་ (jīìsher) spring humidity.
དཔྱིད་ས་ (jīìsə) land used for spring cultivation.
དཔྱིད་གསར་དུས་ཆེན་ (jīìsar tüüjen) spring festival (Chinese New Year).
དཔྱིད་བསུ་མེ་ཏོག (jīìsu medoò) primrose.
དཔྱིའི་འཁོར་མིག (jīì kɔ̄ɔmig) hip bone socket.
དཔྱིས་ (jīì) the end, last, conclusion.
དཔྱིས་འགྲོ་ (jīì dro) vi. to come to the end/ conclusion, to complete, to finish.
དཔྱ་ (jā) sm. དཔང་.
དཔྱོང་: p. དཔྱངས་, f. དཔྱང་; imp. དཔྱོངས་ (yāŋ) va. to hang/ suspend/ dangle downwards.
དཔྱོངས་ (yāŋ) imp. of དཔྱོང་.
དཔྱོད་: p. and f. དཔྱད་; imp. དཔྱོད་ (jöö) va. to examine, to investigate, to analyze.
དཔྱོད་ལྡན་ (jöndɛn) intelligent.
དཔྱོད་པ་པོ་ (jööbabo) examiner, investigator, analyst, researcher.
དཔྱོད་པ་བ་ (jööbawa) sm. དཔྱོད་པ་པོ་.
དཔྱོས་ (jöö) imp. of དཔྱ་.
དཔྱོར་ (jɔ̄ɔ) sm. དཔྱང་.
དཔྲ་ (drā) sm. དཔྱོར་.
དཔྲག (drāg) between.
དཔྲང་པོ་ (drāŋbo) beggar.
དཔྲལ་ (drɛ̄ɛ) abbr. of དཔྲལ་བ་.
དཔྲལ་ཀོ་ (drɛ̄ɛgo) forehead.
དཔྲལ་ཀོ་མཐུག་པོ་ (drɛ̄ɛgo tūgbu) 1. hardheaded, stubborn, obstinate. 2. courageous, brave.
དཔྲལ་ཀོ་སྐམ་པོ་ (drɛ̄ɛgo gāmbo) unlucky/ unfortunate person.
དཔྲལ་ཀོ་སྒམ་པོ་ (drɛ̄ɛgo gambo) sm. དཔྲལ་ཀོ་སྐམ་པོ་.
དཔྲལ་ཀོ་ཅན་ (drɛ̄ɛgojɛn) 1. hardheaded, stubborn, obstinate. 2. lucky, fortunate.
དཔྲལ་ཀོ་སྟུག་པོ་ (drɛ̄ɛgo dūgbu) sm. དཔྲལ་ཀོ་མཐུག་པོ་.
དཔྲལ་དཀྱིལ་ (drɛ̄ɛgyii) middle of the forehead.
དཔྲལ་ཁེབས་ (drɛ̄ɛgeb) piece of cloth/ material that covers the forehead of mules/ horses.
དཔྲལ་མགོ་ (drɛ̄ngo) sm. དཔྲལ་ཀོ་.
དཔྲལ་མགོ་སྟུག་པོ་ (drɛ̄ɛgo dūgbu) sm. དཔྲལ་ཀོ་མཐུག་པོ་.
དཔྲལ་རྒྱན་ (drɛ̄ɛgyɛn) ornament worn on the forehead of mules and horses.
དཔྲལ་སྒོ་ (drɛ̄ɛgo) space/ gap between the eyebrows.
དཔྲལ་སྒོར་ (drɛ̄ɛgɔr) thick ring worn on the thumb of men (usu. made of amber, ivory, jade).
དཔྲལ་གཉེར་ (drɛ̄ɛñer) wrinkles on forehead.
དཔྲལ་བ་ (drɛ̄ɛwa) forehead.
དཔྲལ་བ་གཏུག (drɛ̄ɛwa dūù) va. to touch foreheads (as a form of greeting).
དཔྲལ་བའི་མིག (drɛ̄ɛwɛ mii) sm. དཔྲལ་མིག.
དཔྲལ་བའི་མིག་དང་ཁོག་པའི་སྙིང་ (drɛ̄ɛwɛ mii taŋ kōgbɛ ñiŋ) sth. that is cherished/ loved deeply, precious [Lit. the eye on the forehead and the heart in the body cavity].
དཔྲལ་བར་བཀོད་ (drɛ̄ɛwar göö) having karmic good fortune ¶ང་ལ་ཕྲུ་གུ་ཡག་པོ་ཞིག་སྐྱེ་རྒྱུ་དེ་དཔྲལ་བར་བཀོད་མ་སོང་. I did not have the karmic fortune to give birth to a good child.
དཔྲལ་བར་རི་མོ་ཡོད་པ་ (drɛ̄ɛwar rimu yööba) very

lucky/ fortunate.

དཔྲལ་མིག (drɛ̄ɛmii) 1. wisdom eye (on forehead). 2. the smoke opening at the top/ center of a nomad's tent.

དཔྲལ་རྩ་སྒྲེང་ (drɛ̄ɛdza dre̱ŋ) vi. to show anger or fear.

དཔྲལ་རྩ་རེང་རེང་ (drɛ̄ɛdza dre̱ŋ) sm. དཔྲལ་རྩ་སྒྲེང་.

དཔྲལ་རྩ་ལངས་ (drɛ̄ɛdza la̱ŋ) sm. དཔྲལ་རྩ་སྒྲེང་.

དཔྲལ་གཡུ་ (drɛ̄ɛyu) women's turquoise ornament worn on the head.

དཔྲལ་རིས་ (drɛ̄ɛrii) 1. white painted lines on the forehead (usu. for Hindu ascetics). 2. lines/ wrinkles on the forehead.

དཔྲལ་རུས་ (drɛ̄ɛrüü) forehead bones.

དཔྲལ་ལག་འགེབས་ (drɛ̄ɛlaa ge̱b) va. to shade one's face from the sun by putting one's hand on the forehead.

དཔྲི་ལ་ཐ་ (drēlada) Beirut.

ལྤགས་ནད་ (bāgnɛɛ̀) skin disease.

ལྤགས་པ་ (bāgba) skin.

ལྤགས་སྨྱགས་ (bāgñaà) leprosy.

ལྤགས་མཛེ་ (bāgdze) leprosy.

ལྤགས་ཞྭ་ (bāgsha) sm. པགས་ཞྭ་.

སྤ་ (bā) 1. ornament, decoration. 2. bamboo.

སྤ་ཀི་སི་ཏན་ (bāgisidɛn) Pakistan.

སྤ་སྐོར་ (bāgɔɔ) round head ornament/ headdress worn by women of Tsang.

སྤ་བཀོང་ (bāgoŋ) sm. དཔའ་བཀོང་.

སྤ་ཁྲུམ་ (bā kūm) sm. སྤ་ཁུམ་.

སྤ་མཁན་ (bāñɛn) hairdresser.

སྤ་གྲོ་ (bādro) Paro (Bhutan).

སྤ་གླིང་ (bāliŋ) bamboo flute.

སྤ་ཙུ་གང་ (bājugaŋ) a parasitic fungus on bamboo.

སྤ་ཅོག (bājɔɔ̀) the two hair knots worn by traditional Tibetan government lay officials.

སྤ་ལྕོག (bājɔɔ̀) sm. སྤ་ཅོག.

སྤ་ལྕོག་གི་ག་འུ་ (bājɔɔgi ka̱wu) the small ག་འུ་ worn by traditional Tibetan government officials on their heads.

སྤ་ཆ་ (bāja) ornament.

སྤ་དི་ (bōdi) granulated/ loose tea.

སྤ་ཐག (bādaà) the string on which ornaments are strung.

སྤ་གདན་ (bādɛn) bamboo mat.

སྤ་ཕྲུག (bōdruù) woman's headdress; va.—གོན་ to wear a headdress.

སྤ་བ་ (bāwa) ornament, decoration.

སྤ་དབྱུག (bōyug) bamboo walking cane.

སྤ་འབྲུ་ (bāndru) sm. སྤ་འབྲུམ་.

སྤ་འབྲུམ་ (bāndrum) seeds of Sabina prezwalskii Kom and Juniperus formosana Hayata (used in Tibetan medicine).

སྤ་མ་ (bāma) 1. juniper shrub/ bush. 2. a type of incense made from juniper.

སྤ་ཡག་རྩ་བ་ (bāyaà dzāwa) lancea tibetica Hook (used in Tibetan medicine).

སྤ་ར་ (bāra) sm. སྤོ་ར་.

སྤ་རབ་ད་ (bārabda) Pravda.

སྤ་རབ་དྷ་ (bārabda) sm. སྤ་རབ་ད་.

སྤ་ལོ་ (bālo) braid (of hair).

སྤ་ཤུག (bōshuù) abbr. of སྤ་མ་ and ཤུག་པ་.

སྤ་སེ་ (bōse) eng. 1. pass, permit. 2. ticket.

སྤ་སེ་འཚོང་ས་ (bāse tsōŋsa) 1. ticket sale place. 2. place where people can buy items with ration coupons.

སྤ་ཧིན་ (bāhin) abbr. of Pakistan and India.

སྤག (bāà) 1. sm. སྤགས་. 2. f. of སྤོག.

སྤག་ཐང་ (bādaŋ) sm. སྤགས་ཐང་.

སྤགས་ (bāà) staple Tibetan food comprised of parched grain flour (tsamba) which is moistened with a liquid like tea and kneaded into balls; va.—གཡོ་ to knead tsamba into སྤགས་.

སྤགས་ཁུ་ (bōgu) tea/ liquid that is used to wet the tsampa flour so it can be kneaded into eatable dough.

སྤགས་སྐོང་ (bāà go̱ŋ) va. to make/ knead small balls of tsampa dough preparatory to eating.

སྤགས་སྒོང་ (bāàgoŋ) a small kneaded ball of tsamba dough.

སྤགས་བསྐོངས་ (bā go̱ŋ) sm. སྤགས་སྐོང་.

སྤགས་ཆང་ (bāàjaŋ) sm. ཟན་ཆང་.

སྤགས་ཐང་ (bādaŋ) leather pouch used for kneading སྤགས་; va.—གཡོ་ to knead སྤགས་ in a pouch.

སྤགས་འདེད་ (bāŋdeè) sm. སྤགས་འདྲེས་.

སྤགས་འདྲེས་ (bāŋdreè) food dishes that go with སྤགས་ (e.g., stew).

སྤགས་སྡ་ག་བཟོ་ (bāà da̱ga so̱) va. to knead tsamba flour into སྤགས་.

སྤགས་བོར་ (bāgbɔɔ) wooden bowl used to make/ eat སྤགས་.

སྤགས་ཕྱིས་ (bāgjii) cleaning a piece of clothing by rolling སྤགས་ on the clothing; va.—རྒྱག.

སྤགས་མ་ (bāŋma) things eaten with སྤགས་.

སྤགས་བརྫི་ (bāg dzi̱) va. to knead tsampa into སྤགས་.

སྤགས་བཙོས་ (bāgdzöö) tsampa broth made with tea and butter (commonly given to people who are sick).

སྤགས་ཟན་ (bāgsɛn) སྤགས་ eaters, people who eat སྤགས་ (refers to Tibetans).

སྤགས་ཟས་ (bāgsɛɛ̀) sm. སྤགས་ཟན་.

སྤགས་གཡོ་ (bāà yō) sm. སྤགས་བརྫི་.

སྤགས་རིལ་ (bāgrii) a ball of kneaded eatable dough.

སྤགས་ལུག (bāgluù) sheep reared for slaughtering by being fed སྤགས་.

སྤང་ (bāŋ) 1. p. of སྤོང་. 2. grassy field. 3. va. to renounce/ abandon/ discard/ abolish.

སྤང་བཀག (bāŋgaà) partition in a house.

སྤང་རྒྱང་ (bāŋgyaŋ) 1. a plain/ meadow/ pasture without trees. 2. a green paint.

སྤང་ཁ་ (bāŋga) grassland, pasture, plain, meadow.

སྤང་ཁེབས་ (bāŋgeb) sm. སྤང་གདན་.

སྤང་ཁྲུག (bāŋdruù) sm. སྤང་གདན་.

སྤང་འཁྱམས་ (bāŋgyam) wandering around, roaming homelessly; va.—རྒྱག.

སྤང་རྒྱ་ (bāŋgya) border, edging.

སྤང་རྒྱན་ (bāŋgyɛn) 1. gentiana plants. 2. plants that grow in meadows/ pasturelands.

སྤང་རྒྱན་དཀར་པོ་ (bāŋgyɛn gārbo) white gentian flower (Gentiana szechenyii Kaniez).

སྤང་རྒྱན་ཁྲ་བོ་ (bāŋgyɛn trāwo) gentiana flowers of mixed colors.

སྤང་རྒྱན་སྔོན་པོ་ (bāŋgyɛn ŋōmbo) blue gentiana (Gentiana stipitata Edgew).

སྤང་རྒྱན་ནག་པོ་ (bāŋgyɛn na̱gbo) dark blue gentiana (Gentiana veitchiorum Hemsl).

སྤང་རྒྱན་མེ་ཏོག (bāŋgyɛn me̱doò) 1. sm. སྤང་རྒྱན་. 2. name of a newspaper/ magazine in Tibet.

སྤང་རྒྱུས་ (bāŋgyüü) a type of actonolite.

སྤང་གཅལ་ (bāŋjɛɛ) wooden floor.

སྤང་ཆང་དོད་ (bāŋ cāŋdöö) shung. a money substitution fee for cutting sod ¶ མཐའ་སྐོར་སྤང་སློག་གི་སྤང་ཆང་དོད་ཆགས་ལུད་བླངས་མུས་ They were taking manure as a substitute for cutting sod.

སྤང་ལྗོངས་ (bāŋjoŋ) grassy plain/ field, meadow.

སྤང་ལྗོངས་སྲེག་པའི་མེ་ཆེན་ (bāŋjoŋ sēgbɛ me̱jen) conveys sth. that can't be stopped [Lit. a great prairie fire].

སྤང་རྟོགས་ཡོན་ཏན་ (bāŋdoò yö̱ndɛn) the knowledge of abandonment and insight (two of the qualities that the Buddha possesses).

སྤང་ཐང་ (bāŋdaŋ) plain, meadow, grassland.

སྤང་ཐིག (bāŋdig) a tie/ string/ belt attached to an apron.

སྤང་གདན་ (bāŋdɛn) apron.

སྤང་པོ་ (bāŋbo) sm. སྤྲང་པོ་.

སྤང་སྤོས་ (bāŋböö̀) nardostachys grandiflower (used in Tibetan medicine).

སྤང་ཕྲུག (bəŋdruù) beggar child.

སྤང་བ་བདེན་པ་གཉིས་ (bāŋwa de̱mba ñīì) the two truths that one should be rid of: suffering and the source of suffering.

སྤང་བྱ་ (bāŋja things that a person should abstain from/ renounce/ give up.

སྤང་བླང་ (bāŋlaŋ) renouncing/ giving up sth. and accepting or taking sth. ¶ སྤང་བླང་མ་འཛོལ་བ་ Deciding what to accept and reject without error.

སྤང་བླང་ཚུལ་གནས་ (bāŋlaŋ tsüünεὲ) keeping what is right/ important and discarding what is wrong/ not important; va.—བྱེད་ ¶ བསྟན་སྲིད་ཞབས་རིམ་ལ་ནག་འགྲུས་ཁུར་བཙོན་ཆེ་སྐྱིད་བཅས་ཚང་མས་སྤང་བླངས་ཚུལ་གནས་དགོས་རྒྱུ་ (You) must take good responsibility in performing the rites for religion and politics and discard what is wrong and keep what is right.

སྤང་བླངས་ (bāŋlaŋ) sm. སྤང་བླང་.

སྤང་འབུར་ (bāŋbur) bumps/ mounds of earth on a pasture/ meadow/ field.

སྤང་མ་ (bāŋma) green dye/ paint.

སྤང་མེ་ཆབས་ཅིག (bāŋme cəbjig) shung. all at once, everything together ¶ གཞིས་ཀའི་འབྲུ་རིགས་དང་སེམས་ཅན་ བུ་ལོན་བཅས་སྤང་མེ་ཆབས་ཅིག་རྩིས་འབུལ་ཞུ་འབུས་ཆོག་པ་ Please take possession of our grains, animals and also our debts all together.

སྤང་རྩྭ་ (bāŋdza) grass on meadows.

སྤང་རྩི་ (bāŋdzi) lichen.

སྤང་རྩི་དོ་བོ་ (bāŋdzi tobo) pterocephalus hookeri (used in Tibetan medicine).

སྤང་རྩི་འབྱར་བག (bəŋdzi jarbaà) teasel root (used in Tibetan medicine).

སྤང་ཚན་ (bāŋdzεn) sm. སྤང་ཚན་པུ་རུ་.

སྤང་ཚན་པུ་རུ་ (bāŋdzεn būru) eriophyton wallichii Benth (used in Tibetan medicine).

སྤང་ཚན་པུ་རུག (bāŋdzεn būru) sm. སྤང་ཚན་པུ་རུ་.

སྤང་ཚོན་ (bāŋdzön) sm. སྤང་མ་.

སྤང་མཚེ་ (bāŋdze) type of Chinese ephedra.

སྤང་ཞུན་ (bāŋshün) 1. liquid green dye/ paint. 2. skimia multinervia Huang (used in Tibetan medicine).

སྤང་རམ་ (bāŋram) polygonum macrophylum (used in Tibetan medicine).

སྤང་རས་ (bāŋrεὲ) sm. སྤང་གདན་.

སྤང་རི་ (bāŋri) hill/ mountain covered with meadows.

སྤང་ལ་མེ་ཤོར་ (bāŋla meshɔɔ) clever/ intelligent but not diligent [Lit. meadow catching fire].

སྤང་ལུམ་ (bāŋlum) adding water to rice before boiling; va.—རྒྱག.

སྤང་ལེབ་ (bāŋleè) plank, wooden board.

སྤང་ཤ་ (bāŋsha) 1. mushroom. 2. sm. ལ་མ་.

སྤང་གཤོངས་ (bāŋshoŋ) expanse of grassland/ meadow.

སྤང་གཤོངས་སྔོན་པོ་ (bāŋshoŋ ŋõmbo) expanse of green grassland/ meadow.

སྤང་གཤོངས་ཐང་ (bāŋshoŋ tāŋ) sm. སྤང་གཤོངས་.

སྤང་སེང་ (bāŋseŋ) light green, pale green.

སྤངས་ (bāŋ) sm. སྤང་, 2 and 3.

སྤད་ (bεὲ) son ¶ ཕ་སྤད་གཉིས་ The two of them—father and son.

སྤན་སྤུན་ (bεnbün) older and younger relatives.

སྤབས་ (bəb) 1. earwax. 2. dust.

སྤབས་དུལ་ (bəbdüü) dust.

སྤམ་ (bām) 1. attractive, good-looking. 2. height. 3. quantity.

སྤམ་ཆེ་བ་ (bām cēwa) 1. a large quantity. 2. putting on an act, giving a false impression. 3. very appropriate, suitable.

སྤམ་བསྟོད་ (bāmdöò) affectation; va.— བྱེད་ to act in an affected manner; va.—ཤོད་ to speak in an affected manner.

སྤམ་པ་ (bāmba) appropriate, suitable, well fitted, attractive, becoming.

སྤམ་པོ་ (bāmbo) sm. སྤམ་པ་.

སྤམ་སྤོམ་ (bāmbom) abbr. of སྤམ་མེ་སྤོམ་མེ་.

སྤམ་མེ་སྤོམ་མེ་ (bāmme bõmme) 1. acting/ behaving in an duplicitous manner manner. 2. unclear, inexact, imprecise ¶ མི་དབང་ཐོབ་ཁུངས་འདི་སུ་ཡིན་སྤམ་སྤོམ་ལས་མི་འདུག It is unclear who the lord (of the serf) is.

སྤམ་མེ་བ་ (bāmmewa) sm. སྤམ་པ་.

སྤམ་ཛུ་ (bāmdzu) giving a false appearance.

སྤམ་བཟོ་དོད་པོ་ (bāmso töòbo) sm. སྤམ་པ་.

སྤམ་ལ་མཛེས་པ་ (bāmla dzeèba) appropiate, suitable, fitting, becoming.

སྤའུ་ (bəwu) a brick.

སྤར་ (bār) 1. sm. སྤར་མོ་. 2. va. to increase, to raise ¶ གོང་ཚད་སྤར་པ་རེད་ (They) increased the price. 3. va. to light, to turn on a light ¶ ཞུ་མར་སྤར་རྗེས་ After turning on the light. 4. sm. པར་. 5. palm of the hand.

སྤར་ཁ་རྩིས་ (bārka dzĩi) va. to do a type of astrological calculation (e.g., to determine marriage compatibility).

སྤར་ཁྱིམ་ (bārgyim) palm (of the hand).

སྤར་གང་ (bārgaŋ) a handful.

སྤར་ཆ་བྱེད་ (bārja ceè) va. to increase, to raise.

སྤར་གཏོར་གཏོང་ (bārdɔr dõŋ) va. to explode sth., to ignite an explosion.

སྤར་མཐིལ་ (bārdii) palm (of the hand).

སྤར་འཐམ་ (bār tām) 1. va. to grasp/ grip with the palm/ hand. 2. vi. to have the hands shrivel up/ contract.

སྤར་འདེབས་ (bār deb) sm.* པར་འདེབས་.

སྤར་རྡོ་ (bārdo) 1. a stone that is thrown by hand; va.—འཕེན་ to throw a stone. 2. the stone that dragons hold in their paws in Tibetan art.

སྤར་པ་ (bārba) sm.* པར་པ་.

སྤར་བ་ (bārwa) a rake.

སྤར་འབྲད་ (bārdrεὲ) scratching with the hand; va.—རྒྱག. 2. digging up soil with the hand; va.—རྒྱག.

སྤར་མ་ (bārma) sm. པར་མ་.

སྤར་མོ་ (bārmo) 1. palm (of the hand); va.—རྒྱག to make a fist. 2. a handful.

སྤར་མོ་ཐེར་ཐེར་ (bārmo tērder) openhanded.

སྤར་མོ་ལྷོད་པ་ (bārmo lhõòba) generous, unsparing.

སྤར་བཙིར་རྒྱག (bārdzii gyaà) va. to squeeze with the hand.

སྤར་ཚད་ (bārdzεὲ) sm. སྤར་གང་.

སྤར་ཚོད་ (bārdzöò) a handful.

སྤར་འཛིན་ (bār dzin) sm. སྤར་འཐམ་, 1.

སྤར་ཤད་ (bārshεὲ) scratching; va.—རྒྱག to scratch.

སྤི་ (bī) sm. སྤྱི་.

སྤི་ཐག (bīdaà) a type of noodle made by rolling between the palms.

སྤི་མ་ (bīmə) sm. སྤྱི་མ་.

སྤིང་ (bīŋ) sm. སྤྱིན་.

སྤིང་ཤོག (bīŋshɔɔ) sm. སྤྱིན་ཤོག.

སྤིན་ཀྱག (bīngyaà) sm. སྤྱིན་སྐྱུ་.

སྤུ་ (bū) hair, fur; vi.—སྐྱེ་ to grow hair; to get rich (slang).

སྤུ་དཀར་ (būgaa) 1. white hair/ fur. 2. animals with white hair/ fur.

སྤུ་དཀྱིལ་ (būgyii) in the midst of hair/ fur.

སྤུ་ཀང་ (būgaŋ) a single hair.

སྤུ་སྐམ་བཙུད་ (būgam dzüü) va. to corner a prey (for hunting dogs).

སྤུ་སྐུད་ (būgüü) thread spun from hair/ fur.

སྤུ་སྒྱུར་ (bū gyūr) vi. to shed hair/ fur.

སྤུ་ཁ་ (būga) color of fur.

སྤུ་འཁྱིལ་ (būngyii) cowlick.

སྤུ་གུ་ (būgu) sm. ཕྲུ་གུ་.

སྤུ་གྲ་ (būdrə) quality (length) of hair/ fur.

སྤུ་གྲི་ (būdri) razor, sharp knife.

སྤུ་གྲིའི་སྦྲང་རྩི་ (būdrii drəŋdzi) sugarcoated bullet [Lit. a razor with honey].

སྤུ་ཅན་ (būjεn) hairy, shaggy.

སྤུ་ཆེན་ (būjen) coarse woolen material, woolen material with long fibers.

སྤུ་འཇམ་ (būnjam) 1. soft hair/ fur. 2. intestinal villi.

སྤུ་ཉལ་ (būñεε) flattened down hair/ fur.

སྤུ་ཉག (būñaà) one hair, a single hair.

སྤུ་ཉག་གི་གྲ་མ་ (būñaàgi trama) very detailed.

སྤུ་ཉག་གཅིག་གིས་ཕ་བོང་དཔྱངས་པ་ (būñaà jīggi pāboŋ yāŋba) imminent peril, very dangerous situation [Lit. suspended over a boulder by a single strand of hair].

སྤུ་སྨྱུག (būñuù) brush pen.

སྤུ་བསྙལ་ (būñεε) va. to supress/ stop anger.

སྤུ་ཐག (būdaà) rope made of hair.

སྤུ་ཐུལ་ (būdüü) thick blanket made of long strands of woven wool.

སྤུ་དེ་གུང་རྒྱལ་ (būde kuŋgyεε) sm. པུ་དེ་གུང་རྒྱལ་.

སྤུ་མདོག (būdɔɔ̀) color of fur/ hair.

སྤུ་འདྲག (bū draà) va. to shear/ cut (hair, fur).

སྤུ་རྡུལ་ (būdüü) tufts or strands of hair/ fur that fall off and get on clothing, etc.

སྤུ་ལྡང་ (bū daŋ) vi. to have one's hair stand on end (due to fright).

སྤུ་ལྡན་འཇུར་རྡ་ (būdεn jurda) suede shoes.

སྤུ་སྡུག་བཀྲ་བ་ (bū dügdrāwa) beautiful fur.

སྤུ་ནག (būnaà) 1. black hair/ fur. 2. nomad term for cattle/ yaks (in contrast to sheep and goats).

སྤུ་ནོར་ (būnɔɔ) cattle, yaks.

སྤུ་སྤྲོ་ (būdro) feather.

སྤུ་སྤྲུགས་ (būdruù) shaking one's fur (animals); va.—བྱེད་.

སྤུ་ཕྲུགས་ (būdruù) a type of woolen cloth/ serge.

སྤུ་འཕྱུག (bünjaà) the scraps of wool after sth. like a rug has been woven.

སྤུ་པག (bū paà) va. to shear, to cut, to crop hair.

སྤུ་ཕིད་ (bū pii) vi. to shed hair/ fur.

སྤུ་བུ་སྐྱོན་འཚོལ་ (būbu gyöndzöö) looking for faults (when there are none).

སྤུ་བྱད་ལེགས་པ་ (būjεὲ legba) 1. an animal with beautiful fur. 2. a beautiful woman.

སྤུ་འབུད་ (bū büü) vi. to shed hair/ fur.

སྤུ་འབྲེག (bū dreg) va. to shear/ cut/ crop hair.

སྤུ་མ་ (būmə) velvet.

སྤུ་མ་ཁྲ་རིང་ (būmə trəriŋ) long-pile velvet.

སྤུ་མ་ངོས་འཇམ་ (būmə ŋönjam) soft velvet.

སྤུ་མ་ཤུར་མ་ (būmə shürmə) corduroy.

སྤུ་མའི་ཁ་གདན་ (būmε kādεn) stuffed woolen mattress.

སྤུ་མེད་ (būmeè) hairless.

སྤུ་སྨྱུག (būñuù) brush pen.

སྤུ་ཙམ་ (būdzam) small, slight, little ¶ གནོད་འཚེ་སྤུ་ཙམ་བྱེད་ཐུབ་མེད་ (They) were not able to harm them even a little bit. [Lit. as much as a hair].

སྤུ་ཙམ་མེད་པ་ (būdzam mεὲba) not at all ¶ དབང་ཆ་སྤུ་ཙམ་མེད་པའི་མི་རྣམས་ People without the slightest power. [Lit. not as much as a hair].

སྤུ་རྩིད་ (būdzii) abbr. soft hair/ fur and yak hair.

སྤུ་རྩེ་ (būdze) the tip/ end of hair.

སྤུ་ཚོམ་ (būdzom) hair growing on a mole.

སྤུ་འཛིང་ (bū dziŋ) vi. to be tangled/ disheveled (hair).

སྤུ་ཛོབ་ཛོབ་ (bū dzobdzob) sm. སྤུ་སོབ་སོབ་.

སྤུ་མཛེས་ (būdzeè) beautiful fur.

སྤུ་ཞལ་ (būshεε) 1. a type of traditional Tibetan boot made of woolen cloth. 2. Chinese cloth shoes.

སྤུ་ཟལ་ (būsεὲ) variegated hair/ fur.

སྤུ་ཟིང་ཟིང་ (bū siŋsiŋ) hair standing on end.

སྤུ་གཟེངས་འབུ་ཕྲུག (būseŋ budruù) caterpillar.

སྤུ་ཡི་ལྕུག་ཕོན་ (būyi jūgbön) yak tail duster.

སྤུ་ཡོད་ཀོ་ལྷམ་ (būyöö gōlham) leather boots/ shoes lined with hair/ fur/ wool.

སྤུ་ཡོད་ཟླ་གམ་ (būyöö dagam) a cloak lined with wool/ hair/ fur.

སྤུ་རང་ (būraŋ) a district in far western Tibet.

སྤུ་རིང་ (būriŋ) long hair.

སྤུ་རིང་བསེ་རུ་ (būriŋ sēru) long-haired rhinoceros.

སྤུ་རིས་ (būrii) the color or design of an animal's hair/ fur.

སྤུ་རིས་གཅོད་ (būrii jöö) va. to distinguish/ differentiate.

སྤུ་རུགས་ (būruù) a type of woven woolen material.

སྤུ་རྭ་ (būra) horn like feather that sticks out from the ears of animals like owls.

སྤུ་ལངས་ (bū laŋ) sm. སྤུ་ལོང་.

སྤུ་ལོང་ (bū loŋ) vi. to have one's hair stand on end out of fear.

སྤུ་ལོང་གཡོ་ (būloŋ yō) sm. སྤུ་ལོང་.

སྤུ་ཤད་ (būshεὲ) 1. brush used for animals; va.—རྒྱག to brush the coat of animals. 2. carding comb/ brush.

སྤུ་བཤུར་གདོང་ (būshüü dōŋ) va. to singe hair/ fur.

སྤུ་བཤུར་ཐེབས་ (būshüü tēè) vi. to have hair/ fur get singed.

སྤུ་བཤུལ་གདོང་ (būshüü dōŋ) sm. སྤུ་བཤུར་གདོང་.

སྤུ་བཤུས་གདོང་ (būshüü dōŋ) va. to pluck out hair/ fur/ feathers.

སྤུ་སུ་ (būsu) a moment.

སྤུ་སུད་ (būsüü) 1. short-tempered, quick to anger. 2. changeable, unsteady.

སྤུ་སུད་པོ་ (bū süübu) 1. short-tempered/ quick to anger. 2. stingy, petty, small-minded.

སྤུ་སོབ་ (bū sōb) sm. སྤུ་སོབ་སོབ་.

སྤུ་སོབ་སོབ་ (bū sōbsob) hairy, having a lot of hair, shaggy.

སྤུ་སློང་ (bū lōŋ) va. to make hair stand on end.

སྤུ་གསར་ (būsar) a calf/ kid/ lamb born this year (still in its first year).

སྤུ་གསེད་ (bē sēè) va. to untangle hair/ fur.

སྤུ་ཧྲུག (būhruù) sm. སྤུ་རུགས་.

སྤུ་ཧྲེང་ (būhreŋ) district in far west Tibet.

སྤུག (būù) a precious stone.

སྤུག་སྤུག་གདོང་ (būgbuù dōŋ) va. to nudge.

སྤུག་སྤུག་བྱེད་ (būgbuù ceè) sm. སྤུག་སྤུག་གདོང་.

སྤུང་: p. སྤུངས་, f. སྤུང་, imp. སྤུངས་ (būŋ) va. to pile/ heap up, to store.

སྤུང་སྤུངས་ (būŋ būŋ) va. to pile up, to heap up.

སྤུང་ངེ་བ་ (būŋŋewa) a pile, heap.

སྤུང་ཐང་ (būŋdaŋ) Punakha (Bhutan).

སྤུང་པོ་ (būŋbo) pile, heap.

སྤུངས་ (būŋ) p. of སྤུང་.

སྤུངས་གསོག (būŋsɔɔ̀) storing up, piling/ heaping up; va.—བྱེད་ to store up, to pile/ heap up.

སྤུད་ (būü) va. to decorate, to adorn.

སྤུན་ (bün) 1. relative, kinsman, sibling ¶ བུ་མོ་སྤུན་ Sisters. 2. woof (in weaving); va.—འཁེལ་ to spin thread from wool.

སྤུན་ཀྱག (büngyaà) sm. སྤུན་སྐྱ་.

སྤུན་སྐྱ་ (büngyaà) relatives, kinsmen.

སྤུན་སྐྱ་ཆུང་བ་ (büngyaà cūŋwə) 1. younger relatives. 2. younger siblings.

སྤུན་སྐྱ་གཞོན་པ་ (büngyaà shömba) sm. སྤུན་སྐྱ་ཆུང་བ་.

སྤུན་སྐྱ་འོག་མ་ (büngyaà wɔɔ̀ma) younger sibling/ relative.

སྤུན་འཁེལ་ (bün kēē) va. to spin thread from wool.

སྤུན་རྒན་པ་ (bün gεmba) old sibling/ relative.

སྤུན་ཕ་ཚར་ (bün ŋādzar) stepbrothers/ sisters.

སྤུན་ཆ་ (bünja) thread for the warp.

སྤུན་མཆེད་ (bünjεὲ) sm. སྤུན་གཉེན་.

སྤུན་ཉེ་ (bünñe) sm. སྤུན་གཉེན་.

སྤུན་ཉེ་དུ་ (bün ñedu) sm. སྤུན་གཉེན་.

སྤུན་གཉེན་ (bünñen) relatives/ kinsmen, and friends.

སྤུན་གདོང་འཕྲུལ་འཁོར་ (bündoŋ trüügɔɔ) pirn winding machine.

སྤུན་དོག (bündɔɔ̀) yarn, thread.

སྤུན་དོག་གི་སྟོད་གོས་ (bündɔɔ̀gi dööɡöö) knitted sweater.

སྤུན་དོག་སླ་བྱེད་ལྕགས་མདའ་ (bündɔɔ̀ lājeè jāŋda) knitting needle.

སྤུན་དོག་ལྷས་ (bündɔɔ̀ lhεὲ) va. to knit.

སྤུན་དྲུང་ (bündruŋ) relatives, kinsmen.

སྤུན་པ་ (bümbə) falsehood, lie.

སྤུན་ཕྱི་ཚར་ (bün cīdzar) stepbrothers and sisters.

སྤུན་ཕྲུག (bündruù) cousins.

སྤུན་སྨྱུག (bünñuù) bamboo stick (used in weaving).

སྤུན་ཚ་ (bǖndza) brothers and sisters, cousins.

སྤུན་ཚ་རྒྱུད་བཅས་ (bǖndza gyǖǖjɛɛ̀) shung. immediate family and their close relatives (usu. siblings, cousins).

སྤུན་ཟླ་ (bǖnda) brother, compatriot, fraternal ¶ རྒྱ་མི་རྣམས་བོད་རིགས་སྤུན་ཟླ་རྣམས་དང་མཉམ་དུ་ Chinese together with (their) Tibetan brothers. ¶ སྤུན་ཟླའི་བཟོ་གྲྭའི་རོགས་རམ་འོག With the assistance of brother factories. ¶ སྤུན་ཟླའི་མཉམ་ལས་ Fraternal cooperation. ¶ སྤུན་ཟླའི་མནའའབྲེལ་ Fraternal alliance.

སྤུན་ཟླ་མི་རིགས་ (bǖnda mirii) brotherly nationalities.

སྤུན་ཤིང་ (bǖnshiŋ) stick on which the weaving yarn is rolled.

སྤུན་སེར་ (bǖnser) monks or nuns who are relatives.

སྤུབ་: p. སྤུབས་ (būb) (usu. ཁ་ + —) va. to turn upside down.

སྤུབས་ (būb) p. of སྤུབ་.

སྤུར་ (būr) 1. corpse; va.—བཞུས་ to cremate. 2. sm. འཕུར་. 3. va. to donate, to give charity.

སྤུར་ཁང་ (būrgaŋ) crematory, mortuary; cemetery.

སྤུར་རྒྱལ་ (būrgyɛɛ) an ancient name for Tibet.

སྤུར་སྒམ་ (būrgam) coffin.

སྤུར་སྒྲོམ་ (būrdrom) wooden frame/ bier on which the corpse is placed for cremation.

སྤུར་ཆས་ (būrjɛɛ̀) clothes that are put on a corpse.

སྤུར་སྦྱོང་ (būr joŋ) va. to cremate.

སྤུར་ཐལ་ (būrdɛɛ) ashes of cremated body.

སྤུར་བཞུས་ (būrshüü) cremating; va.—གཏོང་.

སྤུར་ལེན་ (būrlen) sm. གྲོས་ཤིང་.

སྤུར་ཤིང་ (būrshiŋ) wood for cremation.

སྤུས་ (bǖǖ) quality ¶ སྤུས་དག་པོ་ Good quality. ¶ ཁོ་ནི་སྤུས་ལ་ཞིབ་བཤེར་བྱེད་མཁན་རེད་ He is someone who checks quality.

སྤུས་ཀ་ (bǖǖgə) sm. སྤུས་ཁ་.

སྤུས་ཁ་ (bǖǖgə) 1. quality ¶ སྤུས་ཁ་དག་པོ་ Good quality. 2. buying, selling; va.—བྱེད་; —ཞུ་ to buy; va.—འབུལ་ to sell.

སྤུས་ཁ་དག་པོ་ (bǖǖgə tagbo) good/ fine quality.

སྤུས་འགྲེམས་ (bǖndrem) shung. selling and distributing ¶ སེམས་ཅན་རྣམས་ཁྲུངས་སོ་སོར་སྤུས་འགྲེམས་ཐོག They sold the animals and distributed them to each place.

སྤུས་སྒྱུར་ (bǖǖ gyur) va. to sell.

སྤུས་སྒྱུར་བ་ (bǖǖgyurwə) trader, merchant, businessman.

སྤུས་ཅན་ (bǖǖjɛn) high quality.

སྤུས་ཆ་ (bǖǖja) quality.

སྤུས་བརྗེ་ (bǖǖjee) bartering.

སྤུས་ལྟ་ (bǖǖ dā) va. to look at the quality of a thing.

སྤུས་བརྟག་ (bǖǖdaà) sm. སྤུས་ལྟ་.

སྤུས་དག་ (bǖǖdaà) high quality.

སྤུས་དག་པོ་ (bǖǖ tagbo) high quality.

སྤུས་ལྡན་ (bǖndɛn) high quality ¶ ཤ་སྤུས་ལྡན་ High quality meat.

སྤུས་གནང་ (bǖǖ nāŋ) va. to buy (h.).

སྤུས་བླངས་ (bǖǖ lāŋ) shung. va. to buy.

སྤུས་མ་ (bǖǖmə) sm. སྤུས་དག་པོ་.

སྤུས་མེད་ (bǖǖmeè) inferior/ poor quality.

སྤུས་གཙང་ (bǖǖdzaŋ) sm. སྤུས་དག་པོ་.

སྤུས་ཚད་ (bǖǖdzɛɛ̀) 1. quality. 2. a sample ¶ ཁོས་རས་དེའི་སྤུས་ཚད་ཅིག་ཁྱེར་སོང་ He took a sample of that material.

སྤུས་ཚད་འགན་ལེན་ (bǖǖdzɛɛ̀ gɛnlen) guarantee, warranty (of a product).

སྤུས་ཚད་ལྟ་ (bǖǖdzɛɛ̀ dā) va. to check the quality.

སྤུས་ཚད་ཡག་པོ་ (bǖǖdzɛɛ̀ yagbo) sm. སྤུས་དག་པོ་.

སྤུས་ཚོང་ (bǖǖdzoŋ) selling (h.); va.—གནང་ to sell; va.—ཞུ་ to buy (h.).

སྤུས་ཞན་ (bǖǖshɛn) low/ poor quality.

སྤུས་ཞན་གོང་ཆུང་ (bǖǖshɛn koŋjuŋ) poor quality and low price.

སྤུས་ཞན་གོང་མཐོ་ (bǖǖshɛn koŋto) poor quality and high price.

སྤུས་ཞུ་ (bǖǖ shu) shung. va. to buy ¶ སྔར་ལམ་ཚྭ་འབབ་སྤུས་ཞུས་ (We) bought salt in accordance with tradition.

སྤུས་ཟོང་ (bǖǖsoŋ) merchandise, goods.

སྤུས་གཟིགས་ (bǖǖ sii) va. to buy (h.).

སྤུས་གཡར་ (bǖǖ yāā) buying and borrowing.

སྤུས་རབ་ (bǖǖrəb) the best quality.

སྤུས་ལེགས་ (bǖǖleg) high/ superior quality.

སྤུས་ལེགས་གོང་ཆུང་ (bǖǖleg koŋjun) high quality and low price.

སྤེ་ (bē) house on top of a main door.

སྤེ་ཊྲོར་ (bēdrɔɔ) eng. gasoline, petrol.

སྤེན་ (bēn) abbr. of སྤེན་པ་.

སྤེན་དཀར་ (bēngar) a type of Chinese Tamarisk with white flowers.

སྤེན་སྐྱིད་ (bēngyii) Saturday picnic (Saturday was the day of the week that the traditional Tibetan government offices were closed); va.—གཏོང་.

སྤེན་རྒྱན་ (bēngyɛn) red top of walls of monasteries and temples that are made of Tasmarisk stalks.

སྤེན་བཅུ་འཁྲོད་ (bēnju trö̀ö̀) when the 10th day of the lunar month falls on Saturday.

སྤེན་དོག་ (bēndɔg) 1. small shrine made of Tamarisk stalks. 2. a type of woman's head ornament.

སྤེན་ཐོག་ (bēndɔg) sm. སྤེན་དོག.

སྤེན་ནག་ (bēnnaà) tamarisk with dark blue flowers.

སྤེན་པ་ (bēmba) 1. Saturn. 2. Saturday.

སྤེན་ཕོར་ (bēmbɔɔ) bowl made from tamarisk burl/ root.

སྤེན་ཕྱག་ (bēmjaà) sm. སྤེན་ཕྱགས་.

སྤེན་ཕྱགས་ (bēmjaà) broom made of tamarisk stalks.

སྤེན་བད་ (bēmbɛɛ̀) sm. སྤེན་རྒྱན་.

སྤེན་འབར་ (bēmbar) torch.

སྤེན་མ་ (bēmma) tamarisk.

སྤེན་མ་དཀར་པོ་ (bēmma gārbo) white tamarisk.

སྤེན་མ་སེར་པོ་ (bēmma sērbo) yellow tamarisk.

སྤེན་ཚོགས་ (bēndzɔɔ̀) Saturday meeting.

སྤེན་རྫབ་ (bēndzəb) burl of tamarisk used for making eating bowls.

སྤེའུ་ (bēu) 1. eaves. 2. small house. 3. tree trunk.

སྤེའུ་ཁང་ (bēugaŋ) small house.

སྤེའུ་ལྕོག་ (bēujɔɔ̀) watch tower.

སྤེའུ་ཞོལ་ (bēushöö) a small room/ apartment.

སྤེལ་ (bēl) 1. va. to spread/ disseminate. 2. va. to launch/ unfold ¶ སྤྱི་ཚོགས་རིང་ལུགས་ཀྱི་འགྲན་སྡུར་གྱི་ལས་འགུལ་ཞིག་སྤེལ་དགོས་ (They) have to launch a socialist emulation campaign. 3. va. to increase, to enlarge, to expand ¶ ནོར་ཕྱུགས་སྤེལ་ཆད་སློབ་གྲྭར་ཕྱིན་པ་རེད་ (He) went to school to (learn how to) increase (his) cattle. 4. va. to mix, to put together ¶ དམར་པོ་དང་སྔོན་པོ་སོགས་མཉམ་དུ་སྤེལ་ Mixing red and blue together. 5. sm. སྤེལ་སླལ་. 6. multiplication. 7. va. to do sth. in rotation ¶ ང་གཉིས་སྤེལ་ནས་བཏང་སོང་ (He) sent us in rotation. 8. va. to match colors to determine which ones go together or complement each other ¶ ཚོས་གཞི་འདི་གཉིས་ཡག་པོ་བྱས་སྤེལ་དགོས་ (You) have to match the two colors well.

སྤེལ་བསྐུལ་ (bēlgüü) encouraging, stimulating, urging; va.—གཏོང་ to encourage, to stimulate, to promote.

སྤེལ་རྒྱས་ (bēlgyɛɛ̀) sm. སྤེལ་, 1 and 2.

སྤེལ་རྒྱུག་གློག་རྒྱུན་ (bēlgyuù lɔ̄ggyɛn) alternating current.

སྤེལ་རྒྱུག་གློག་དོན་འཕྲུལ་འཁོར་ (bēlgyuù lɔ̄gdön trǖǖgɔɔ) alternating current generator.

སྤེལ་འདེབས་ (bēndeb) intercrop planting; va.—བྱེད་ to plant a crop between other crops.

སྤེལ་པར་ (bēlbar) printing plate for printing in two or more colors.

སྤེལ་འབྱོར་ (bēl jɔɔ) sent and received, sending and receiving.

སྤེལ་སྦྱོར་ (bēljɔɔ) increasing, expanding, augmenting; va.—བྱེད་ to increase, to expand, to augment.

སྤེལ་མ་ (bēlma) 1. mixed, intermingled, overlapped, intertwined; va.—བྱེད་ to mix, to intermingle, to overlap, to intertwine ¶ གྲོག་ཤུར་དང་བདེ་ཐང་སྤེལ་མ་བྱས་པའི་ས་ཁུལ་ An area with ravines and plains intermingled. 2. in rotation; va.—གཏོང་ to do sth. in rotation, to rotate ¶ ཁོས་ང་གཉིས་སྤེལ་མར་བཏང་བ་རེད་ (He) sent the two of us in rotation.

སྤེལ་ཚིགས་ (bēldzii) a Tibetan style of writing where verses and prose are written alternately.

སྤེལ་གཞི་ (bēlshi) origin, source.

སྤེལ་ཟླ་ (bēnda) colors matching/ complementing each other; va.—སྒྲིག to match colors so that they complement each other ¶ སྔོན་པོ་དམར་པོའི་སྤེལ་ཟླ་མི་འགྲོ་. Blue doesn't go with red.

སྤེལ་རེས་ (bēlreè) mutual exchange; va.—བྱེད་ to exchange (mutually).

སྤོ་ (bō) 1. grandfather. 2. old man. 3. term of address for a man's male friends. 4. tip, top, summit. 5. an area southeast of Kham.

སྤོ་: p. སྤོས་, f. སྤོ་; imp. སྤོས་ (bō) 1. va. to move, to shift residence ¶ ལྷ་ས་ནས་འདིར་སྤོས་རྗེས་ After moving here from Lhasa. 2. va. to change ¶ མིང་སྤོས་ནས་ Having changed names. 3. va. to transplant ¶ ལྗང་བུ་སྤོས་དགོས་ཡོད་ཙང་ Because (they) have to transplant the seedlings.

སྤོ་སྐྱེལ་ (bōgyee) transferring, transporting, transmitting; va.—གཏོང་ to transfer/ transport/ transmit.

སྤོ་སྐྱོད་ (bōgyöö) moving, shifting; va.—བྱེད་.

སྤོ་སྒྱུར་ (bōgyur) sm. སྤོ་.

སྤོ་སྐྱེལ་མོ་ལྡོང་ (bōgyee mōloŋ) supporting/ helping one side and subduing/ harming the other side.

སྤོ་དོ་ (bōdo) 1. a mound found on a grassland/ plain. 2. lumps of earth that are crested after ploughing and shoveling.

སྤོ་དོག (bōdoò) tip, top.

སྤོ་ཐུང་ (bōduŋ) sm. སྤྱི་ཐུང་.

སྤོ་ཐོ་ (bōdo) sm. སྤོ་དོ་.

སྤོ་ཐོ་ལ་བསྐོར་ནས་རི་བོང་ལ་འགྲམ་ལྕག (bōdola gɔ̄ɔ̄nɛ riboŋla dramjaà) sm. ཕ་བོང་ལ་བསྐོར་ནས་རི་བོང་ལ་འགྲམ་ལྕག.

སྤོ་སྡོད་ (bōdöö) moving residence; va.—བྱེད་.

སྤོ་པ་ (bōba) person from སྤོ་.

སྤོ་སྤོ་ (bōbo) sm. སྤོ་བོ་.

སྤོ་ཕོ་ (bōbo) sm. སྤོ་བོ་.

སྤོ་བོ་ (bōō) sm. སྤོ་, 1.

སྤོ་བོ་ལ་བི་སའི་རྣམ་ཐར་ (bōwola bisɛ nāmdar) sm. སངས་རྒྱས་ལ་ཀ་ཁ་.

སྤོ་བོ་ལ་ཕྲུ་གུའི་རྣམ་ཐར་ (bōwola bisɛ nāmdar) sm. སངས་རྒྱས་ལ་ཀ་ཁ་.

སྤོ་བོ་ལགས་ (bōōlaà) h. of སྤོ་བོ་.

སྤོ་འབག (bōmbaà) mask of an old man.

སྤོ་འབེབས་ (bō beb) va. to rely or depend on sb.'s support/ help.

སྤོ་མོ་ (bōmo) old man and old woman, grandfather and grandmother.

སྤོ་ཚལ་ (bōdzɛɛ) spinach.

སྤོ་འཛུགས་ (bōdzuù) transplanting; va.—བྱེད་.

སྤོ་ཡུལ་ (bōyüü) sm. སྤོ་, 3.

སྤོ་ཡོར་ (bōyor) a piled up mound in a field that is used as a scarecrow.

སྤོ་ལ་དར་འཕྱར་ (bōla tarjar) having great power/ strength [Lit. putting the flag on the summit].

སྤོ་ལགས་ (bōlaà) 1. grandfather (h.). 2. old man (h.). 3. term of address used between male friends.

སྤོ་ལོ་ (bōlo) sm. པོ་ལོ་.

སྤོ་ལོ་མཁས་མཆོག (bōlo kɛ̄ɛ̀cɔ̀ɔ) football star, sports star.

སྤོ་ལོ་འགྲན་བསྡུར་ (bōlo drɛndur) a ball game.

སྤོ་ལོ་རྒྱག་སྤྱད་ (bōlo gyagjɛɛ̀) implement for hitting a ball in a game (paddle, racket, etc).

སྤོ་ལོ་རྒྱག་ས་ (bōlo gyasa) athletic or sports field, ball field.

སྤོ་ལོ་ཚོད་འཛིན་ (bōlo tsōndzin) dribbling (a ball) in a game.

སྤོ་ལོའི་སྒོ་ (bōlö go) goal, goal post (in sports like soccer).

སྤོ་ལོའི་དྲ་བཅད་ (bōlö trajɛɛ̀) net for ball games.

སྤོ་ལོའི་རུ་ཁག (bōlö rugaà) ball team.

སྤོ་ལོར་དབྱིངས་ཞུགས་མཁན་ (bōlɔɔ yiŋshuùñɛn) fan (sports).

སྤོ་ཤུགས་ (bōshuù) sm. སྤོ་སྐྱོད་.

སྤོག (bɔ̄ɔ̀) 1. incense.

སྤོག: p. སྤགས་; f. སྤོག; imp. སྤོགས་ (bɔ̄ɔ̀) 1. va. to change/ move/ shift. 2. va. to mix/ blend together.

སྤོག་ཁེ་ (bɔ̄gge) incense.

སྤོག་ཐོ་ (bɔ̄gdo) a tool used by blacksmiths.

སྤོག་འདོན་ (bɔ̄ŋdön) moneylender.

སྤོག་མ་ (bɔ̄gma) a type of utensil/ container.

སྤོག་དོན་ (bɔ̄gdön) moneylender.

སྤོག་ར་ (bɔ̄gra) Pokhara.

སྤོགས་ (bɔ̄ɔ̀) 1. profit; va.—བྱེད་ to make a profit. 2. imp. of སྤོག.

སྤོགས་མ་ (bɔ̄ɔ̀ma) sm. ཕོགས་མ་.

སྤོང་: p. སྤངས་; f. སྤང་; imp. སྤོངས་ (bōŋ) va. to give up, to renounce, to abandon, to discard, to abolish, to revoke.

སྤོང་ཁང་ (bōŋgaŋ) hermitage, meditation retreat, meditation room.

སྤོང་ཐག (bōŋdaà) old custom whereby one gives away some of one's belongings as a donation to religion in order to help one get well from an illness.

སྤོང་བདུན་ (bōŋdün) va. to renounce/ give up the three nonvirtuous acts and the four nonvirtuous forms of speech.

སྤོང་བ་པ་ (bōŋwaba) hermit.

སྤོངས་ (bōŋ) imp. of སྤོང་.

སྤོད་ (bȫȫ) food spice.

སྤོད་ཅན་ (bȫȫjɛn) spicy (for food).

སྤོད་སྨན་ (bȫȫmɛn) sm. སྤོད་.

སྤོད་སྨན་སྣ་ལྔ་ (bȫȫmɛn nāŋa) the five spices (Sichuan peppercorn, star anise, cinnamon, clove, fennels).

སྤོད་ཚ་ (bȫȫdza) hot pepper, hot chili.

སྤོད་རྫས་ (bȫȫdzɛɛ̀) sm. སྤོད་.

སྤོད་ཡ་ (bȫȫya) sth. eaten incidental to the main food.

སྤོབ་ལིན་ (bōblɛn) eng. poplin.

སྤོབ་ལིག (bōblig) eng. public.

སྤོབས་ཉམས་ (bōbñam) brave and grand in stature.

སྤོབས་གདམ་ (bōbdam) talking proudly/ arrogantly; va.—ཤོད་.

སྤོབས་པ་ (bōbba) 1. bravery, courage, spirit. 2. pride, confidence; va.—བྱེད་ to act proud; vi.—སྐྱེད་ to become/ get proud.

སྤོབས་པ་སྐྱེད་ (bōbba gyēè) vi. to become proud/ confident.

སྤོབས་པ་རྒྱུན་མི་འཆད་པ་ (bōba gyünmi cɛ̄ɛ̀ba) 1. talk fluently, eloquently. 2. continuously proud.

སྤོབས་པ་ཆེ་བ་ (bōba cēwa) very proud/ (can convey boastful).

སྤོབས་པ་ཆེན་པོ་ (bōba cēmbo) sm. སྤོབས་པ་ཆེ་བ་.

སྤོབས་པ་ངམ་བརྗིད་ཆེ་བ་ (bōba ŋāmjiì cēwa) proud and fierce.

སྤོབས་པ་མི་ཟད་པ་ (bōba misɛɛ̀ba) limitless bravery/ courage/ fearlessness.

སྤོབས་མེད་སྙོམས་ཆུང་ (bōbmeè ñōmjuŋ) cowardly, timid, prideless.

སྤོབས་པ་མཐོ་པོ་ (bōba tōbo) conceited, smug, self-important.

སྤོབས་པ་བྱེད་ (bōba cee) va. to be proud/ arrogant.

སྤོབས་པ་ཞུམ་པ་ (bōba shumbɔ) 1. despondent, depressed, dejected. 2. not brave.

སྤོབས་སེམས་ (bōbsem) 1. pride, confidence. 2. feeling of self-importance.

སྤོབས་བསམ་ (bōbsam) sm. སྤོབས་སེམས་.

སྦོམ་ (bōm) 1. sm. སྦོམ་སྦོམ་. 2. bomb. 3. quantity, amount, magnitude.

སྦོམ་ཆེན་པོ་ (bōm cēmbo) a large quantity/ amount.

སྦོམ་ཐག (bōmdaà) sm. སྦོང་ཐག.

སྦོམ་སྦྲོད་ (bōm drȫȍ) va. to give an approximate amount.

སྦོམ་སྦོམ་ (bōmbom) in general, on the average, roughly.

སྦོམ་འབོར་ (bōmbɔɔ) sm. སྦོམ་, 3.

སྦོམ་རྩིས་ (bōmdziì) calculating roughly/ approximately.

སྦོམ་ཚིག (bōmdziì) a general/ rough statement.

སྦོམ་ཚོད་ (bōmdzöȍ) a rough estimate/ guess, a conjecture, a surmise.

སྦོམ་ཡོར་ (bōmyɔɔ) grandiose, pompous.

སྦོམ་གཡོར་ (bōmyɔɔ) shung. unclear, ambiguous.

སྦོམ་ཤོད་ (bōm shȫȍ) va. to conjecture/ surmise/ infer/ guess.

སྦོའི་ (bōō) sm. སྦོ་.

སྦོར་ (bōr) 1. a traditional weight measure equal to 1/4th of a nyaga. 2. jaw, mouth.

སྦོར་: p. སྦར་; f. སྦར་; imp. སྦོར་ (bōr) 1. va. to raise, to elevate, to make higher (price/ rank) ¶ ལས་བྱེད་པའི་གོ་གནས་སྦོར་སོང་ (They) elevated the official's position. 2. va. to light/ ignite ¶ མེ་སྦར་ནས་ Having lit the fire.

སྦོར་ཀྱོག (bōrgyɔ̀ɔ) distorted mouth/ jaw.

སྦོར་གང་ (bōrgaŋ) traditional measure equal to about one སྲང་.

སྦོར་གོར་ (bōrgɔr) wooden bowl for eating/ drinking.

སྦོར་དགྱེ་དགྱེ་ (bōr gyegye) lifting/ holding one's head high with pride.

སྦོར་སྒྲངས་ཁལ་སྒྲིལ་ (bōrdraŋ kɛ̄ɛdrii) converting སྦོར་ into ཁལ་.

སྦོར་གཅུ་ (bōr jū) va. to turn back.

སྦོར་གཅོག (bōr jɔ̀ɔ) va. to add and subtract to reach a specific number/ amount.

སྦོར་དོ་ (bōrdo) old, decrepit.

སྦོར་དོག (bōrdɔ̀ɔ) rifle bolt; va.—དཀྲུག་ to pull back the rifle bolt.

སྦོར་བསྣམས་ (bōr dam) va. to slaughter animals by tying their nostrils and suffocating them.

སྦོར་ཕྱོགས་ (bōrjɔ̀ɔ) direction.

སྦོར་ལ་གཞུ་ (bōrla shu) va. to hit on the jaw.

སྦོར་ཤིང་ (bōrshiŋ) tamarisk.

སྤོས་ (bȍȍ) 1. incense. 2. imp. of སྤོ་.

སྤོས་དཀར་ (bȍȍgar) 1. plastic. 2. frankincense.

སྤོས་ཀང་ (bȍȍgaŋ) single stick of incense.

སྤོས་བསྐོར་འགྲོ་ (bȍȍgɔɔ dro) va. to go around carrying sticks of burning incense (usu. used for the patron of a monks' prayer assembly goihng around while the monks are chanting).

སྤོས་ཁྲི་ (bȍȍtri) a table/ stand for an incense burner.

སྤོས་འཁོར་ (bȍȍgɔɔ) coiled incense.

སྤོས་གུར་ཀུམ་ (bȍȍ gurgum) shung. incense and saffron.

སྤོས་སྒམ་ (bȍȍgam) elongated box for holding/ carrying incense.

སྤོས་སྒོར་ (bȍȍgɔɔ) incense coil.

སྤོས་ངད་ (bȍȍŋɛɛ̀) sm. སྤོས་དུད་.

སྤོས་ཆག (bȍȍjaà) a bunch of incense.

སྤོས་མཆོད་མཇལ་ཕྱག (bȍȍjöȍ jɛɛjaà) burning incense and doing prayers and prostrations (as religious offerings).

སྤོས་གདུལ་ (bȍȍ dȕȕ) va. to burn incense.

སྤོས་སྟེགས་ (bȍȍdeg) a stand for placing sticks of incense.

སྤོས་ཐོལ་ (bȍȍdöö) sarcasm; va.—གཞུ་ to be sardonic/ cutting/ biting.

སྤོས་ཐོལ་ཚ་པོ་ (bȍȍdöö tsābo) person who is sarcastic/ biting/ sardonic (in his speech).

སྤོས་ཐལ་ (bȍȍdɛɛ) ashes of incense.

སྤོས་བདུག (bȍȍ duù) va. to burn incense.

སྤོས་བདུག་ཕྱག་མཆོད་ (bȍȍdug cānjöȍ) sm. སྤོས་མཆོད་མཇལ་ཕྱག.

སྤོས་དུད་ (bȍȍdüü) smoke from burning incense.

སྤོས་དྲི་ (bȍȍdri) smell of incense.

སྤོས་མདོང་ (bȍȍdoŋ) cylindrical incense container made from bamboo or tin.

སྤོས་འདམ་ (bȍndam) the paste from which incense is made.

སྤོས་དུང་པ་ (bȍȍdüŋbɔ) an incense maker.

སྤོས་སྣེས་སྣུན་བསུ་ (bȍȍneè ŋȕnsu) welcoming dignitaries such as high lamas with people carrying burning incense.

སྤོས་སྣོད་ (bȍȍnöȍ) sm. སྤོས་མདོང་.

སྤོས་སྦར་ (bȍȍ bār) va. to light incense.

སྤོས་སྦུག (bȍȍbɔɔ) sm. སྤོས་སྒམ་.

སྤོས་སྦྲུག (bȍȍdrɔ̀ɔ) sm. སྤོས་སྒམ་.

སྤོས་ཕོར་ (bȍȍbɔɔ) incense bowl/ burner.

སྤོས་བྲིས་ (bȍȍdrii) dictation, va.—བྱེད་ to take down dictation.

སྤོས་འབྱུག (bȍȍ juù) va. to rub/ apply pulverized incense.

སྤོས་སྦྱར་ (bȍȍ jar) va. to make incense.

སྤོས་སྨན་ (bȍȍmɛn) shung. materials used in making incense.

སྤོས་འཛིན་ (bȍndzin) incense holder.

སྤོས་འཛུགས་ (bȍndzuù) transplanting (seedlings) ¶ སྤོས་འཛུགས་འཕྲུལ་འཁོར་ A machine for transplanting seedlings.

སྤོས་ཞིམ་ལྡེ་གུ (bȍȍshim degu) water with sweet-smelling incense.

སྤོས་གཞོང་ (bȍȍshoŋ) an incense holder.

སྤོས་ཤེལ་ (bȍȍshee) amber.

སྤྱང་ཀི་ (jāŋgi) wolf.

སྤྱང་ཀིའི་ལྕེ་ (jāŋgii jē) wolf tongue (used in Tibetan medicine).

སྤྱང་ཀིའི་རྗེས་སུ་ཁྭ་ཏ་ (jāŋgii jeèsu kāda) evil people following one another [Lit. the raven follows the wolf].

སྤྱང་ཀིའི་ན་བར་ཆོས་ཤོད་པ་ (jāŋgii nāwaa cȍȍ shȍȍba) giving advice to evil people [Lit. teaching dharma to a wolf].

སྤྱང་ཀིའི་ཕོ་བ་ (jāŋgii pōwa) wolf stomach (used in Tibetan medicine).

སྤྱང་ཀིའི་བམ་རོར་ཧམ་པ་ (jāŋgii bamrɔɔ ŋāmba) being extremely greedy [Lit. a wolf greedily (eating) a corpse].

སྤྱང་ཀིའི་སེམས་ངན་ (jāŋgii sēmŋɛn) a nasty nature like a wolf.

སྤྱང་ཀིས་ལུག་རྫི་བྱེད་པ་ (jāŋgi lugdzi cēèba) limitless harm/ damage [Lit. a wolf acting as a shepherd].

སྤྱང་ཀུ་ (jāŋgu) sm. སྤྱང་ཀི་.

སྤྱང་ཁུ་ (jāŋgu) wolf.

སྤྱང་ཁྱི་ (jāŋgi) 1. sm. སྤྱང་ཀི་. 2. cross between a wolf and a dog.

སྤྱང་གྲུང་ (jāŋdruŋ) clever, intelligent; va.—ཊོམ་ to show one's cleverness; va.—བྱེད་ to be clever/ intelligent.

སྤྱང་གྲུང་བསྟུན་མཁས་ (jāŋdruŋ dȕŋgɛɛ̀) clever and bright.

སྤྱང་གྲུང་དོད་པོ་ (jāŋdruŋ tȍȍbo) sm. སྤྱང་གྲུང་.

སྤྱང་གྲུང་འཛོམས་པོ་ (jāŋdruŋ dzombo) sm. སྤྱང་གྲུང་.

སྤྱང་གྲུང་ཡིན་ལྟོམ་ (jāŋdruŋ yinlom) showing off one's smartness/ cleverness.

སྤྱང་གྲོས་ཕག་གྲོས་ (jāŋdrȍȍ pāgdrȍȍ) people who have large appetites [Lit. wolf's stomach and pig's stomach].

སྤྱང་གླེན་ (jāŋlen) abbr. of སྤྱང་པོ་ and གླེན་པ་.

སྤྱང་སྒམ་ (jāŋgam) wolf trap.

སྤྱང་བཅོས་ (jāŋjöȍ) pretending to be clever/ bright/ sharp.

སྤྱང་ལྡོགས་ཀྱི་ཧམ་ཟ་ (jāŋdɔ̀ɔgi hāmsa) wolfing down food, gobbling/ devouring ravenously.

སྤྱང་ཐག (jāŋdaà) sm. དཔྱང་ཐག.

སྤྱང་ཐུལ་ (jāŋdüü) a dress/ robe made from wolf fur.

སྤྱང་དོམ་ (jāŋdom) wolverine.

སྤྱང་པགས་ (jāŋbaà) wolf skin.

སྤྱང་ལྤགས་ (jāŋbaà) sm. སྤྱང་པགས་.

སྤྱང་པོ་ (jāŋbo) clever, intelligent ། རང་བཞིན་གྱི་སྤྱང་པོ་ Natural/ innate intelligence.

སྤྱང་པོ་གླད་མེད་ (jāŋbo lɛ̀ɛmeeè) clever but unstable/ unreliable.

སྤྱང་པོ་འདོད་མེད་ (jāŋbo domeè) clever but unreliable/ good-for-nothing.

སྤྱང་ཕྲུག (jāŋdruù) 1. wolf cub. 2. derogatory term for the children of landlords.

སྤྱང་ཕྲུག་གསོས་ཀྱང་སྒོ་ཁྱི་མི་ཉན་ (jāŋdruù sööogyaŋ gogyi miñɛn) it is futile to reform an evil person [Lit. one can not raise a wolf cub to become a watch dog].

སྤྱང་འཕར་འདུས་པ་ (jāŋpar düüba) a cross between a wolf and a jackal.

སྤྱང་མོ་ (jāŋmo) 1. wolf. 2. female wolf.

སྤྱང་མོ་མདེའུ་འཛིན་ (jāŋmo diujin) pterocephalus hookeri (used in Tibetan medicine.

སྤྱང་ཚང་ (jāŋdzaŋ) wolf den.

སྤྱང་ཚེར་ (jāŋdzer) setose thistle (used in Tibetan medicine).

སྤྱང་ཚོགས་ (jāŋdzoò) pack of wolves.

སྤྱང་ཞྭ་ (jāŋsha) hat made from wolf skin.

སྤྱང་རིག (jāŋrig) sm. སྤྱང་པོ་.

སྤྱང་རིག་འཛོམས་པོ་ (jāŋrig dzombo) intelligent.

སྤྱང་ལབ་བཤད་དུས་སྤྱང་ཀི་སླེབས་ (jāŋləb dāŋdüü jāŋgi lēè) sb. coming/ arriving when other people are just talking about them.

སྤྱང་ལུག་གོ་ནོར་ (jāŋluù konɔɔ) making a big mistake, mistaking sb. who is a danger [Lit. mistaking wolf and sheep].

སྤྱང་ཤ་དོད་པོ་ (jāŋsha töòbo) one who is clever/ witty/ smart.

སྤྱང་སློག (jāŋlɔɔ̀) gown/ robe/ dress made from wolf fur.

སྤྱང་ཨ་ཐང་ (jāŋ ātaŋ) a wolf in the prime of its life.

སྤྱད་ (jɛ̀ɛ) 1. va. to make use of ། སྒྲིག་ཆས་གསར་པ་མ་སྤྱད་གོང་ལ་ Before making use of the new equipment. 2. p. of སྤྱོད་.

སྤྱད་དངོས་ (jɛ̀ɛŋöö) things, materials.

སྤྱད་གདང་ (jɛ̀ɛdaŋ) clothing hanger, line for hanging clothes.

སྤྱད་པ་ (jɛ̀ɛba) utensils.

སྤྱད་ལག (jɛ̀ɛlaà) things.

སྤྱད་ལག་དངོས་པོ་ (jɛ̀ɛlaà ŋööbo) sm. སྤྱད་ལག.

སྤྱན་ (jɛ̄n) eye (h.).

སྤྱན་ཀྲུག (jɛ̄ngyuù) eyebrow (h.).

སྤྱན་དཀྱུས་མ་ (jɛ̄n gyūmə) the two regular eyes of Buddhist deities with three eyes.

སྤྱན་དཀྱུས་རིང་ (jɛ̄nhyüü riŋ) long eyes of Buddhist deities.

སྤྱན་སྐྱག (jɛ̄ngyaà) eye crud, eye mucus.

སྤྱན་བསྐྱངས་ཆེ་ (jɛ̄n gyāŋce) shung. looking upon with favor ། ཕོ་པར་སྲིད་འཛིན་རྒྱལ་ཐོག་ནས་སྤྱན་བསྐྱངས་ཆེའམ་ ཡང་ན་ཞུ་མོ་འཕྱེར་པ་ཇི་ལྟར་བཅས་ Maybe it is because the regent looked upon him with favor or because he himself is capable anyway.

སྤྱན་ཁྱེར་ (jɛ̄ngyer) sm. སྤྱན་ཁྱེར་གྱི་རྒྱ་.

སྤྱན་ཁྱེར་གྱི་རྒྱ་ (jɛ̄ngyergi gya) a label that hangs from the end of a religious book on which the name and volume are written.

སྤྱན་རྒྱ་སྤོས་འཛིན་ (jɛ̄ngya böndzin) playing the gyaling and holding incense (when a lama comes).

སྤྱན་སྔ་ (jɛ̄nŋa) 1. before, in the presence of (h.). 2. district governor.

སྤྱན་ལྤིབས་ (jɛ̄njib) eyelid (h.).

སྤྱན་ཆབ་ (jɛ̄njəb) tears (h.); vi.—ཤོར་; vi.—བསིལ་ to shed tears, to cry.

སྤྱན་ཆུ་ (jɛ̄nju) sm. སྤྱན་ཆབ་.

སྤྱན་འཆུས་ (jɛ̄n cüü) vi. to have tired looking eyes.

སྤྱན་ལྟོད་ (jɛ̄ndöö) imitation (h.).

སྤྱན་ལྟོས་ (jɛ̄ndöö) h. of མིག་ལྟོས་.

སྤྱན་བསྟར་ཞུ་ (jɛ̄ndar shu) va. to show/ present for inspection (h.).

སྤྱན་དྲངས་ (jɛ̄ndraŋ) sm. སྤྱན་འདྲེན་.

སྤྱན་བདར་ (jɛ̄ndar) showing; va.—ཞུ་ to show.

སྤྱན་འདན་ (jɛ̄ndɛn) 1. sculpturing tool. 2. a type of brocade.

སྤྱན་འདྲེན་ (jɛ̄ndren) invitation; va.—ཞུ་ to invite, to welcome (h.).

སྤྱན་ལྡན་ (jɛ̄ndɛn) 1. lotus design rug. 2. sm. སྤྱན་འདན་.

སྤྱན་ལྡན་སྐམ་པོ་ (jɛ̄ndɛn gambo) brocade with lotus and bat design.

སྤྱན་ལྡན་འབྲུག་འགྲོས་མ་ (jɛ̄ndɛn drugdrööma) brocade with lotus and dragon design.

སྤྱན་བརྡ་ (jɛ̄nda) an eye signal (such as winking); va.—གནང་ to send an eye signal (h.).

སྤྱན་རྣོན་པོ་ (jɛ̄n nömbo) keen/ sharp vision (h.).

སྤྱན་པ་ (jɛ̄mba) 1. supervisor, watchman. 2. steward. 3. sm. སྤྱན་བསལ་.

སྤྱན་ལྤགས་ (jɛ̄mbaà) eyelid (h.).

སྤྱན་སྤུ་ (jɛ̄mbu) eyelash (h.).

སྤྱན་སྤུས་ (jɛ̄mbüü) students showing their handwriting to the school prefect (in tt.).

སྤྱན་དབུས་མ་ (jɛ̄n üüma) the third eye (on the forehead of images of Buddhas).

སྤྱན་འབུལ་ (jɛ̄mbüü) showing sth.; va.—ཞུ་ to show.

སྤྱན་འབེབས་ (jɛ̄nbeb) in person inspection/ examination (h.).

སྤྱན་མ་བརྡུལ་ (jɛ̄n madüü) va. to look/ watch without losing concentration.

སྤྱན་མི་བཟང་ (jɛ̄n misaŋ) one of the 4 guardian kings.

སྤྱན་དམིགས་ (jɛ̄nmii) h. of དམིགས་པ་.

སྤྱན་སྨན་ (jɛ̄nmɛn) eye medicine (h.).

སྤྱན་བཙུམ་ (jɛ̄n dzūm) va. to close one's eyes ། ཁོང་གིས་སྤྱན་བཙུམ་ནས་བཞུགས་པ་རེད་ He sat with his eyes closed.

སྤྱན་བཙུམས་བཙུམས་ (jɛ̄n dzūmdzum) blinking.

སྤྱན་འཛུགས་ (jɛ̄ndzuù) picking, selecting, nominating; va.—གནང་ (h.).

སྤྱན་ཟིམ་མེ་ (jɛ̄n simme) half-closed eyes.

སྤྱན་ཟུར་གཡོ་རྟེན་ (jɛ̄nsur yōden) sm. གཟིགས་རྟེན་.

སྤྱན་གཟིགས་ (jɛ̄nsii) 1. zoo animals. 2. the offerings in the chapel of protective deities. 3. va. to look at (h.).

སྤྱན་གཟིགས་ཏག་ངུ་ (jɛ̄nsii dāgŋu) white flower sundew (used in Tibetan medicine).

སྤྱན་བཟོ་མགོ་སྐོན་ (jɛ̄nso gogön) a tool used by brasssmiths.

སྤྱན་རས་ (jɛ̄nrɛɛ̀) eyes (h.).

སྤྱན་རས་གཟིགས་ (jɛ̄nrɛsii) the Bodhisattva Avaloketisvara.

སྤྱན་རས་གཟིགས་བཅུ་གཅིག་ཞལ་ (jɛ̄nrɛsii jūgjii shɛɛ̀) Avaloketisvara image with eleven heads.

སྤྱན་རས་གཟིགས་ཕྱག་སྟོང་སྤྱན་སྟོང་ (jɛ̄nrɛsii cāgdoŋ jɛ̄ndoŋ) Avaloketisvara image with a thousand arms and eyes.

སྤྱན་རས་གཟིགས་ཕྱག་བཞི་པ་ (jɛ̄nrɛsii cāàshibə) Avaloketisvara image with four arms.

སྤྱན་རིལ་ (jɛ̄nrii) eyeball (h.).

སྤྱན་ལ་མཛེས་པ་ (jɛ̄nla dzeèba) beautiful, attractive to look at.

སྤྱན་ལ་གསལ་ (jɛ̄nla sɛɛ̀) vi. to like/ to be fond of.

སྤྱན་ལ་གཞུས་ (jɛ̄nla shüü) va. to like, to desire/ yearn for (h.) ། རྟ་ཡག་པོ་དེ་ས་དཔོན་པོའི་སྤྱན་ལ་གཞུས་སོང་ That horse came to be liked/ desired by the lord.

སྤྱན་ལམ་དུ་ (jɛ̄nlamdu) 1. before, near, in the presence of (h.). 2. in the eyes of, in the view of (h.).

སྤྱན་ལམ་དུ་འབུལ་ (jɛ̄nlamdu büü) va. to show (h.).

སྤྱན་ལོག (jɛ̄nlɔɔ̀) glancing/ looking backwards (h.); va.—གནང་ to look/ glance backward.

སྤྱན་ཤེལ་ (jɛ̄nshee) eyeglasses (h.); va.—སྐོན་ to put on one's eyeglasses, to wear eyeglasses.

སྤྱན་གསལ་ (jɛ̄nsɛɛ) shung. pleasing ། བོད་ཁམས་བདེ་

སྲིད་ཀྱི་ཆ་བར་སྤྱན་གསལ་ཆ་ཚོགས་རིན་པོ་ཆེ་སྤྱི་བསྒྲལ་ དགོངས་དོན་ In accordance with the proclamation which is issued for the fundamental welfare of the Tibetan people and is pleasing to the people.

སྤྱན་གསལ་སྐུ་འགྲིད་ (jɛ̄nsɛɛ gūgyeè) shung. alms given by the Dalai Lama to monks.

སྤྱན་བསལ་ (jɛ̄nsɛɛ) a favorite of sb. in power; vi.—ཆགས་ to become a favorite ¶ རྒྱལ་པོའི་སྤྱན་གསལ་ The king's favorite.

སྤྱན་བསལ་ཕོ་བྲང་ (jɛ̄nsɛɛ pōdraŋ) a palace of the Dalai Lama in Norbulinga.

སྤྱན་ཧུར་ (jɛ̄nhur) keen-sighted.

སྤྱར་མ་ (jārma) 1. a loose woman. 2. criminal.

སྤྱི་ (jī) 1. general ¶ ཏང་གི་སྤྱིའི་ལམ་ཕྱོགས་ General policy of the party. 2. public, common ¶ སྤྱི་སྒེར་ Public and private. ¶ མི་མང་སྤྱི་ནས་ From all the people. ¶ སྤྱིའི་ས་ཞིང་རྒྱ་ཁྱོན་སོན་ཁལ་ ༡༠༠ ཡོད་ The size of the agricultural fields held in common is 100 khal of seed. 3. the top of the head.

སྤྱི་བཀུར་ (jīgur) respecting; va.—ཞུ་. to show respect.

སྤྱི་སྐད་ (jīgɛɛ̀) common language.

སྤྱི་སྐར་ (jīgar) centimeter.

སྤྱི་སྐོར་ (jīgɔr) a revolution, a turn.

སྤྱི་སྐྲ་ (jīdra) hair on the crown of head.

སྤྱི་སྐྲ་བེད་བེད་ (jīdra be̱ɛ̀bɛɛ̀) close-cropped hair.

སྤྱི་ཁང་ (jīgaŋ) commune.

སྤྱི་ཁོག (jīgɔɔ̀) overall (plan/ scheme), the entire/ whole.

སྤྱི་ཁྱབ་ (jīgyəb) governor-general, viceroy, overall head of an area/ group; va.—བྱེད་ to act as governor-general/ viceroy/ head.

སྤྱི་ཁྱབ་ཀན་ཧྲི་ (jīgyəb gɛ̄nhri) tib.ch. general secretary, executive chief.

སྤྱི་ཁྱབ་ཀུང་སི་ (jīgyəb gūŋsi) tib.ch. chief company of a group of companies.

སྤྱི་ཁྱབ་ཀྲི་པུའུ་ (jīgyəb drību) tib.ch. general headquarters' branch office.

སྤྱི་ཁྱབ་ཀྲི་པུའུ་ཨུ་ཡོན་ལྷན་ཁང་ (jīgyəb drību ūyün lhɛ̄ngan) tib.ch. general headquarters' branch office committee.

སྤྱི་ཁྱབ་བཀོད་འདོམས་པ་ (jīgyəb gōōdomba) generalissimo, commander in chief, supreme commander.

སྤྱི་ཁྱབ་བཀོད་འདོམས་པུའུ་ (jīgyəb gōōdom bū) tib.ch. sm. སྤྱི་ཁྱབ་པུའུ་.

སྤྱི་ཁྱབ་ཁང་ (jīgyəbgaŋ) general headquarters, head office.

སྤྱི་ཁྱབ་མཁན་པོ་ (jīgyəb kɛ̄mbo) shung. highest official in monk official segment of the traditional Tibetan government.

སྤྱི་ཁྱབ་མགོ་སྒྲུབ་པུའུ་ (jīgyəb kōdrubbu) tib.ch. general logistics department.

སྤྱི་ཁྱབ་ཅིང་ལི་ (jīgyəb jīŋli) tib.ch. general manager, executive head.

སྤྱི་ཁྱབ་ཅུས་ (jīgyəb jǖü) tib.ch. general or chief office/ bureau.

སྤྱི་ཁྱབ་ཆབ་སྲིད་པུའུ་ (jīgyəb cābsiibu) tib.ch. general political bureau/ department.

སྤྱི་ཁྱབ་ཇེན་ཁྲ་ཀྲང་ (jīgyəb je̱ndra drāŋ) tib.ch. general chief procurator.

སྤྱི་ཁྱབ་ཇུས་འདོན་པུའུ་ (jīgyəb jü̱üdön bū) headquarters of the general staff.

སྤྱི་ཁྱབ་འཐུས་མི་ (jīgyəb tǖümi) chief representative.

སྤྱི་ཁྱབ་དྲུང་འཁོར་ (jīgyəb tru̱ŋgɔɔ) shung. lay official who was governor general of an area.

སྤྱི་ཁྱབ་དྲུང་ཆེ་ (jīgyəb tru̱nje) secretary general (of an organization).

སྤྱི་ཁྱབ་པུའུ་ (jīgyəb bū) tib.ch. general headquarters (usu. military).

སྤྱི་ཁྱབ་བློན་ཆེན་ (jīgyəb lōnjen) prime minister.

སྤྱི་ཁྱབ་དམག་སྤྱི་ (jīgyəb māgji) 1. commander in chief. 2. Joint Chiefs of Staff (U.S.A.).

སྤྱི་ཁྱབ་སྨན་ཁང་ (jīgyəb mɛ̄ngaŋ) a general hospital.

སྤྱི་ཁྱབ་རྩིས་པ་ (jīgyəb dzīibə) chief accountant.

སྤྱི་ཁྱབ་རྩིས་ཞིབ་ལས་ཁང་ (jīgyəb dzīishib le̱ɛ̀gaŋ) General Accountanting Office (GAO, U.S. Congress.).

སྤྱི་ཁྱབ་རྩོམ་སྒྲིག་པ་ (jīgyəb dzōmdrigbə) chief editor, editor in chief.

སྤྱི་ཁྱབ་ཚན་མོའུ་ཀྲང་ (jīgyəb tsɛ̄nmodraŋ) tib.ch. chief of staff.

སྤྱི་ཁྱབ་བཟོ་བཀོད་པ་ (jīgyəb so̱gööba) chief engineer.

སྤྱི་ཁྱབ་བཟོ་གྲྭ་ (jīgyəb so̱dra) the main/ chief factory of a group of factories.

སྤྱི་ཁྱབ་བཟོ་ཚོགས་ (jīgyəb so̱dzɔɔ̀) federation of trade unions.

སྤྱི་ཁྱབ་ཡན་ལག་ཁང་ (jīgyəb ye̱nlaàgaŋ) branch office of the general headquarters.

སྤྱི་ཁྱབ་རིམ་པ་ (jīgyəb ri̱mbə) prefectural level ¶ སྤྱི་ཁྱབ་རིམ་པའི་དོན་གཅོད་ཁང་ Prefecture level bureau.

སྤྱི་ཁྱབ་རུ་ཁག (jīgyəb ru̱gaà) general brigade.

སྤྱི་ཁྱབ་ལས་ཁུངས་ (jīgyən le̱ɛ̀guŋ) chief office.

སྤྱི་ཁྱབ་ལིང་ཧྲི་ (jīgyəb li̱ŋhri) tib.ch. consul general.

སྤྱི་ཁྱབ་ལིང་ཧྲི་ལས་ཁུངས་ (jīgyəb li̱ŋhri le̱ɛ̀guŋ) ch.tib. consulate general (office).

སྤྱི་ཁྱབ་ཤན་འབྱེད་པ་ (jīgyəb shɛ̄njeèba) chief umpire/ referee.

སྤྱི་ཁྱབ་སི་ལིང་ (jīgyəb sīliŋ) tib.ch. commander in chief.

སྤྱི་ཁྱབ་ཧྲུའུ་ཅི་ (jīgyəb hrūji) tib.ch. secretary general.

སྤྱི་ཁྱབ་ལྷན་ཚོགས་ (jīgyəb lhɛ̄ndzɔɔ̀) general office/ assembly/ headquarters (of an association or society).

སྤྱི་ཁྲལ་ (jītrɛɛ) public duty/ obligation, public service.

སྤྱི་ཁྲི་ (jīdri) tib.ch. meter ¶ སྤྱི་ཁྲི་གྲུ་བཞི་ Square meter.

སྤྱི་ཁྲིད་ (jīdrii) sm. སྤྱི་ཁྲི་.

སྤྱི་ཁྲིམས་ (jīdrim) the general law, pubic law.

སྤྱི་ཁྲེ་ (jīdre) sm. སྤྱི་ཁྲི་.

སྤྱི་ཁྲེ་གྲུ་བཞི་མ་ (jīdre tru̱bshimə) square meter.

སྤྱི་ཁྲིད་ (jīdrii) sm. སྤྱི་ཁྲི་.

སྤྱི་ཁྲིའི་ཚུན་ (jīdrii tsǖn) centimeter.

སྤྱི་ཁྲེ་ (jīdre) sm. སྤྱི་ཁྲི་.

སྤྱི་མཁན་ (jīgən) abbr. སྤྱི་ཁྱབ་མཁན་པོ་.

སྤྱི་གན་ (jīgən) an agreement which is agreed upon by all.

སྤྱི་གུ (jīgu) head ornament worn by the women of Tsang.

སྤྱི་གྱག (jīgyaà) a guarantor from outside of one's unit/ group.

སྤྱི་གྲི་གྲུ་བཞི་མ་ (jīdre tru̱bshimə) tib.ch. cubic meter.

སྤྱི་གྲོས་ (jīdröö) public discussion.

སྤྱི་གླིང་ (jīliŋ) public park.

སྤྱི་དགྲ་ (jīdra) public enemy, common enemy.

སྤྱི་མགྲིན་ནས་ (jīdrinnɛ) with one voice, unanimously.

སྤྱི་འགྲོས་ (jīdröö) formula.

སྤྱི་འགྲོས་ཀྱི་གཞུང་ཡིག (jīdröögi shu̱ŋyii) red tape.

སྤྱི་འགྲོས་ཅན་དུ་འགྱུར་ (jīdrööjɛndu gyu̱r) vi. to become formulaic/ stereotyped.

སྤྱི་འགྲོས་ཆ་སྲོལ་ (jīdröö dzāsöö) general rule.

སྤྱི་རྒན་ (jīgɛn) managerial official in a monastery.

སྤྱི་རྒྱ་ (jīgya) kilogram.

སྤྱི་སྒེར་ (jīger) private and public; everyone.

སྤྱི་སྒེར་གཉིས་མཐོང་ (jīger ñiidoŋ) sm. སྤྱི་སྒེར་གཉིས་ཕན་.

སྤྱི་སྒེར་གཉིས་ཕན་ (jīger ñiibɛn) benefiting both the private and public sectors.

སྤྱི་སྒོས་ (jīgöö) the particular and the general.

སྤྱི་སྒྲིག་གན་རྒྱ་ (jīdrig ge̱ngya) an agreement made through a collective decision within a group (rather than by an individual).

སྤྱི་སྒྲོས་སྤྱི་གན་ (jīdröö jīgɛn) sm. སྤྱི་སྒྲིག་གན་རྒྱ་.

སྤྱི་བརྒྱད་ (jīgyɛɛ̀) a money unit equal to 3 ཁ་གང་.

སྤྱི་བསྒྲགས་ (jīdraà) a general or public communique/ announcement/ proclamation/ bulletin/ notification.

སྤྱི་དངུལ་ (jīŋüü) public/ official funds; va.—ཟ་ to take graft from public funds.

སྤྱི་ཅེར་ (jījer) bald.

སྤྱི་གཅེར་ (jījer) sm. སྤྱི་ཅེར་.

སྤྱི་ཆིང་ (jījiŋ) tib.ch. hectare.

སྤྱི་ཆིངས་ (jījiŋ) pact, convention, treaty.

སྤྱི་ཆེ་སྒེར་མེད་ (jīce ge̱rmeè) thinking of the masses or the common good and not oneself.

སྤྱི་ཆོས་ (jījöö) public welfare, public matters.

སྤྱི་འཇག (jīnjaà) sm. ཐེབ་ཙ་.

སྤྱི་རྗེ་ (jīje) lord of all people.

སྤྱི་གཉེར་ (jīñer) 1. the person in charge of general affairs/ management, head manager. 2. shung. two of the 4 assistants to the heads of the རྩམ་བཞིས་ལས་ཁངས་ who were mainly in charge of transportation of supplies.

སྤྱི་གཉེར་ཁང་ (jīñergaŋ) sm. སྤྱི་གཉེར་ལས་ཁངས་.

སྤྱི་གཉེར་ཁྲུའུ་ (jīñerdru) tib.ch. general affairs/ management office.

སྤྱི་གཉེར་ལས་ཁངས་ (jīñer lɛ̱ɛ̀guŋ) an office/ department in charge of general management.

སྤྱི་མཉམ་ (jīñam) common, united, general.

སྤྱི་མཉམ་ཆེན་པོ་ (jīñam cēmbo) universal harmony.

སྤྱི་མཉམ་རྩ་ཚིག (jīñam dzādziì) the "general programme" (of the first Political Consultative Conference meeting).

སྤྱི་སྙན་ (jīñɛn) petition, request.

སྤྱི་སྙོམས་ (jīñom) equal, equality, general harmony.

སྤྱི་སྙོམས་ཆེན་པོ་ (jīñom cēmbo) great equality, great harmony.

སྤྱི་སྙོམས་འཇིག་རྟེན་ (jīñom ji̱gden) world of great harmony/ equality, utopia.

སྤྱི་བསྙད་སྒེར་ཕན་ (jīñɛɛ̀ ge̱rbɛn) sm. སྤྱི་བརྟེན་སྒེར་ཕན་.

སྤྱི་དན་ (jīdɛn) tib.ch. quintal.

སྤྱི་ཏོར་ (jīdɔr) hair bundled up in a knot on top of the head.

སྤྱི་གཏམ་ (jīdam) 1. writing or talking about sth. in general. 2. public opinion.

སྤྱི་གཏོར་ (jīdɔɔ) a type of torma offered to deities.

སྤྱི་བདང་ (jīdaŋ) sm. སྤྱིར་བཏང་.

སྤྱི་བརྟེན་སྒེར་ཕན་ (jīden ge̱rbɛn) promoting one's private interests under the guise of serving the public.

སྤྱི་བརྟོལ་ (jīdöö) shamelessness; va.—བྱེད་ to act shamelessly.

སྤྱི་བརྟོལ་ཅན་ (jīdööjɛn) shameless.

སྤྱི་བསྟབས་ (jīdəb) sm. སྤྱི་གཏོར་.

སྤྱི་ཐབ་ (jīdəb) commissary, mess, communal eating ¶ སློབ་གྲྭའི་སྤྱི་ཐབ་ The school commissary.

སྤྱི་ཐམ་ (jītam) shung. 1. seal (for monasteries it is the seal that represents the monastery as a whole). 2. the seal that represents the lay and monk officials that was used by national assembly in traditional Tibet.

སྤྱི་ཐམ་འབྱར་མ་ (jītam ja̱rma) shung. a document/ agreement sealed with the སྤྱི་ཐམ་.

སྤྱི་ཐམ་བཞི་འབྱར་ (jītam shi̱njar) shung. a document affixed with the seals of the Tibetan government and the three monastic seats: Drepung, Sera, and Ganden.

སྤྱི་ཐེར་ (jīdar) sm. སྤྱི་ཆེར་.

སྤྱི་ཐོག (jīdɔɔ) from or to the whole, in general ¶ ལས་བྱེད་སྤྱི་ཐོག་ནས་གཞུང་ལ་སྙན་སེང་ཞུས་པ་རེད་ The cadres as a whole made a report to the goverment.

སྤྱི་མཐུན་རྒྱལ་ཁབ་ (jītün) a country that is a republic.

སྤྱི་མཐུན་ཚོགས་པ་ (jīdün tsōgba) 1. union. 2. Republican Party (in U.S.A.).

སྤྱི་མཐུན་ཚོགས་པའི་རྒྱལ་ཡོངས་ཚོགས་ཆུང་ (jītün tsōgbɛ gyɛ̱ɛ̱yoŋ tsōgjuŋ) Republican National Committee (U.S.A.).

སྤྱི་མཐུན་དང་ (jītün dāŋ) tib.ch. republican party (in U.S.A.).

སྤྱི་མཐོང་སྦྱར་རིས་ (jīdoŋ ja̱rrii) poster/ placard/ handbill that is stuck on a wall.

སྤྱི་འཐུས་ (jīdüü) a representative, delegate.

སྤྱི་འཐུས་གྲོས་ཚོགས་ (jīdüü trö̱ödzɔɔ) the national assembly in Dharamsala (of the Tibetan exile community).

སྤྱི་འཐུས་ལྷན་ཚོགས་ (jīdüü lhɛndzɔɔ) sm. སྤྱི་འཐུས་གྲོས་ཚོགས་.

སྤྱི་དང་འདྲ་བ་ (jīdaŋ dra̱wa) as is common/ usually/ generally the case.

སྤྱི་དང་བྱེ་བྲག (jīdaŋ ce̱draà) shung. the general and the specific/ particular ¶ སྤྱི་དང་བྱེ་བྲག་གི་ཁྲལ་རིགས་ཐུར་འཁྱི་ཞ་ཆག་མེད་པ་དགོས་རྒྱུ་ One should perform the general and particular corvee taxes without delay.

སྤྱི་དམ་ (jīdam) sm. སྤྱི་ཐམ་.

སྤྱི་དམ་འབྱར་མ་ (jīdam ja̱rma) shung. sealed with a སྤྱི་ཐམ་.

སྤྱི་དོན་ (jīdön) 1. common good, public welfare, public work. 2. main point, basic principle, platform (in a political sense).

སྤྱི་དོན་ཁ་ཁྱེར་རང་དོན་ཁོག་བཙུག (jīdön kāgyer ra̱ndön kōgjuù) making a pretense of doing things for the general good but actually looking out for oneself; va.—བྱེད་.

སྤྱི་དོན་སྒེར་བརྗེད་ (jīdön ge̱rjeè) selflessness, working for the common good without concern for one's own interests.

སྤྱི་དྲོས་ན་སྒེར་འཁྱགས་པོར་མ་ལུས་ (jīdrööna ge̱r kyāgbor ma̱ lü̱ü̱) if society as a whole improves the individual will improve [Lit. If the public is warm the private (individual) will not remain cold].

སྤྱི་བདེ་ (jīde) public security.

སྤྱི་བདེ་ཁྲུའུ་ (jīde trū) tib.ch. public security office.

སྤྱི་བདེ་མངག་གཏོང་ཁང་ (jīde ŋāgdoŋgaŋ) lowest level (neighborhood) police station.

སྤྱི་བདེ་ཅུས་ (jīde jüü) tib.ch. public security bureau (PSB).

སྤྱི་བདེ་ཐིང་ (jīde tiŋ) tib.ch. public security administrative office.

སྤྱི་བདེ་པུའུ་ (jīde bū) tib.ch. ministry of public security.

སྤྱི་བདེ་ཞིབ་དཔྱོད་ཁྲིམས་ཁང་གསུམ་ (jīde shi̱bjöö trīmgan sūm) the three public security organs: the police, the procurator offices and the courts.

སྤྱི་བདེ་ལས་ཁངས་ (jīde lɛ̱ɛ̀guŋ) sm. སྤྱི་བདེ་ཅུས་.

སྤྱི་བདེ་ལས་བྱེད་པ་ (jīde lɛ̱ɛ̀jeba) public security officer, policeman.

སྤྱི་བདེའི་དཔུང་ཁག (jīdee būŋgaà) public security unit, home guard forces.

སྤྱི་བདེའི་དམག་དཔུང་ (jīdee məgbuŋ) sm. སྤྱི་བདེའི་དཔུང་ཁག.

སྤྱི་མདའ་ (jīnda) commander in chief.

སྤྱི་མདོ་ (jīdo) general principle.

སྤྱི་འདེམས་ (jīdem) general election.

སྤྱི་འདོམས་ (jīndom) head, chief, ruler; va.—བྱེད་ to lead, to control, to rule, to head ¶ སྤྱི་འདོམས་ཧྲུའུ་ཅི་ General secretary. ¶ མདོ་ཁམས་ཞི་དྲག་སྤྱི་བསྡོམས་ The head of military and civil affairs in Kham. ¶ སྒྲིག་འཛུགས་མང་པོར་སྤྱི་འདོམས་བྱ་རྒྱུ་དེ་ལས་དོན་རྙོག་འཛིངས་ཅན་ཞིག་རེད་ The task of heading many organizations is very complicated.

སྤྱི་འདོམས་ཚའན་མུ་ཀྲང་ (jīndom tsānmudraŋ) tib.ch. commander in chief.

སྤྱི་ལྡོག (jīdɔɔ) 1. the general and the particular. 2. in general. 3. concepts, ideas.

སྤྱི་བདོལ་སྨྲ་ (jīdöö mā) va. to talk haphazardly/ aimlessly.

སྤྱི་བསྡོམས་ (jīndom) sum, total, summary; va.—བྱེད་ to sum up, to total, to make a summary.

སྤྱི་ན་ (jīna) generally, in general, customarily.

སྤྱི་ནོར་ (jīnɔɔ) shung. 1. title used with the Dalai Lama's name ¶ སྤྱི་ནོར་གོང་ས་སྐྱབས་མགོན་ཆེན་པོ་ His Holiness the Dalai Lama. ¶ སྤྱི་ནོར་ཡང་སྲིད་ Incarnation of the Dalai Lama. 2. public wealth.

སྤྱི་གནོད་ (jīnöö) public nuisance, common harm.

སྤྱི་པ་ (jībə) 1. public. 2. chief, head.

སྤྱི་པའི་ཁེ་ཕན་ (jībɛ kēbɛn) public benefit.

སྤྱི་པའི་རྒྱ་མཚོ་ (jībɛ gyadzo) high seas, open sea.

སྤྱི་པའི་རྒྱུ་ནོར་ (jībɛ gyanɔɔ) public property.

སྤྱི་པའི་སྒྲིག་ལམ་ (jībɛ driglam) public order.

སྤྱི་པའི་བདེ་དོན་ (jībɛ dedön) public welfare/ benefit.

སྤྱི་པའི་འདས་མཆོད་ (jībɛ dɛ̀ɛ̀jöö) public sacrifice.

སྤྱི་པའི་སྤྱོད་བཟང་ (jībɛ jöösaŋ) public morality.

སྤྱི་པའི་ཕན་བདེ་ (jībɛ pɛ̄nde) public benefit/ welfare/ well-being.

སྤྱི་པའི་འཕྲོད་བསྟེན་ (jībɛ trööden) public health, public hygiene.

སྤྱི་པའི་འབྲེལ་བ་ (jībɛ dreewa) public relations.

སྤྱི་པའི་གཙང་སྦྲ་ (jībɛ dzāŋdra) sm. སྤྱི་པའི་འཕྲོད་བསྟེན་.

སྤྱི་པའི་ཟ་ཁང་ (jībɛ sagaŋ) community dining hall/ commissary, public canteen.

སྤྱི་པའི་བཟོ་སྐྲུན་ (jībɛ sodrön) public construction.

སྤྱི་པའི་ལས་དོན་ (jībɛ lɛ̀ɛ̀dön) public works.

སྤྱི་པའི་གསང་གཅོད་ (jībɛ sāŋjöö) public toilet.

སྤྱི་པའི་གསོག་འཇོག་ (jībɛ sōnjɔɔ) accumulated for the public/ the whole/ the entity in common.

སྤྱི་དཔོན་ (jībün) 1. sm. སྤྱི་པ་. 2. leader of an area.

སྤྱི་སྦམ་ (jī bām) va. to give an unclear/ obscure/ undetailed (answer, reply, report, etc.).

སྤྱི་སྦོམ་ (jībom) vague, ambiguous ¶ བཀའ་ལན་ཡང་སྤྱི་སྦོམ་ཞིག་ལས་མ་བྱུང་ (I) received only a vague reply.

སྤྱི་སྦོམ་སྦག་སྦུག་ (jībam bagbug) vague, ambiguous.

སྤྱི་སྤྱོད་ (jījüü) for public use, public.

སྤྱི་སྤྱོད་ཀྱི་བྱ་བ་ (jījüügi cāwa) sm. སྤྱི་སྤྱོད་ལས་དོན་.

སྤྱི་སྤྱོད་ཁ་པར་ (jījüü kābar) public telephone.

སྤྱི་སྤྱོད་གློག་སྐད་ཁང་ (jījüü lɔ̄ɔ̄gɛ̀ɛ̀gaŋ) public phone booth.

སྤྱི་སྤྱོད་ཆེའི་ཁྲིའི་ (jījüü cīdre) tib.ch. sm. སྤྱི་སྤྱོད་རླངས་འཁོར་.

སྤྱི་སྤྱོད་སྤྱོད་ཁང་ (jījüü jöögaŋ) public lavatory/ bathroom.

སྤྱི་སྤྱོད་རླངས་འཁོར་ (jījüü lāŋgɔɔ) bus.

སྤྱི་སྤྱོད་རླངས་འཁོར་ས་ཚིགས་ (jījüü lāŋgɔɔ sādzii) bus stop.

སྤྱི་སྤྱོད་ཟ་ཁང་ (jījüü sagaŋ) public dining hall/ canteen.

སྤྱི་སྤྱོད་ལས་དོན་ (jījüü lɛ̀ɛ̀dön) public utilities, public works.

སྤྱི་སྤྱོད་གསང་གཅོད་ (jījüü sāŋjöö) public bathroom / lavatory.

སྤྱི་སྤྱོད་སློབ་དཔྱད་ཁང་ (jījüü lōbjɛ̀ɛ̀gaŋ) a section of Tibet University that teaches Tibetan to students in other departments.

སྤྱི་ཕུད་ (jībüü) sm. སྤྱི་ཏེར་.

སྤྱི་ཕྱག་ (jījaà) the manager of a monastery.

སྤྱི་ཕན་ (jībɛn) public benefit/ good.

སྤྱི་ཕན་གྱི་ལས་དོན་ (jībɛngi lɛ̀ɛ̀dön) sm. སྤྱི་ཕན་ལས་དོན་.

སྤྱི་ཕན་འགྲོན་དངུལ་ (jībɛn drönŋüü) public funds.

སྤྱི་ཕན་མ་དངུལ་ (jībɛn maŋüü) public fund, fund or endowment for the benefit of the public.

སྤྱི་ཕན་ལས་དོན་ (jībɛn lɛ̀ɛ̀dön) activity/ work that benefits the public, public works.

སྤྱི་ཕིན་ (jībin) tib.ch. centimeter.

སྤྱི་ཕེབས་ (jīpeb) shung. receiving orders/ instructions from a supervisor or superior ¶ རྒྱལ་པོའི་བཀའ་སྤྱི་ཕེབས་བཞིན་ According to the King's order (that was received by me).

སྤྱི་ཕྱོགས་ལ་ (jījɔɔla) in general, to/ for all ¶ སྤྱི་ཕྱོགས་ལ་སྒོ་དབྱེ་བའི་སྲིད་ཇུས་ The open door policy for all.

སྤྱི་བུན་ (jībün) public debt, public bonds.

སྤྱི་བབ་ (jībəb) general situation/ circumstance.

སྤྱི་བོ་ (jīwo) top, apex, crown.

སྤྱི་བོ་ནས་དབང་བསྐུར་ (jīwonɛ wāŋkūr) baptizing/ initiating by pouring water on the top of head.

སྤྱི་བོ་གནམ་བསྟན་ (jīwo nāmdɛn) all humans.

སྤྱི་བོར་བཀུར་ (jīwo gūr) sm. སྤྱི་བོར་འཁུར་.

སྤྱི་བོར་འཁུར་ (jīwo kūr) va. to obey respectfully.

སྤྱི་བོར་གསོལ་སྐྱལ་ (jīwor söödzɛɛ) shung. a phrase conveying that the writer most respectfully entreats the recipient of the letter to instruct him about some issue (this is usually used for high officials in the traditional Tibetan goverment).

སྤྱི་བོས་ལེན་པ་ (jōwöö len) shung. a phrase conveying that the writer of the letter accepts most humbly the instructions of a high official.

སྤྱི་བོས་རི་ར་བདུང་ (jīwöö riidun) impossible, unattainable.

སྤྱི་བྱིངས་ (jījiŋ) overall, entire, whole.

སྤྱི་བྱེ་ (jīje) the general and the particular/ specific.

སྤྱི་བྱེ་བྲག (jī cedraà) sm. སྤྱི་བྱེ་.

སྤྱི་བྱེ་ཟུང་འབྲེལ་ (jīje sundree) merging or uniting the general and the specific/ particular.

སྤྱི་བླུག་བཞེད་ཞལ་ (jīluù sèèshɛɛ) shung. sm. ཞལ་བླུག.

སྤྱི་བླུགས་ (jīluù) a tiny vessel hanging from the front of the belt of monk officials and gelongs.

སྤྱི་དབང་ (jīwaŋ) sm. སྤྱི་འབངས་ཀྱི་དབང་ཆ་.

སྤྱི་འབངས་ (jībaŋ) citizen.

སྤྱི་འབངས་ཀྱི་དབང་ཆ་ (jībaŋgi wāŋja) civil rights, rights of citizenship.

སྤྱི་འབངས་ཀྱི་རང་དབང་ (jībaŋgi raŋwaŋ) sm. སྤྱི་འབངས་ཀྱི་དབང་ཆ་.

སྤྱི་འབོར་ (jīmbɔr) sum, grand total, overall, whole ¶ འཐོན་འབབས་སྤྱི་འབོར་གྱི་འཆར་གཞི་ The overall production plan.

སྤྱི་འབྱམས་ (jīnjam) universal, widespread, common.

སྤྱི་འབྲུ་ (jīndru) 1. public granary. 2. common/ public grain (grain given to the state with no payment).

སྤྱི་མ་ (jīmə) 1. association of workers (in traditional Tibet). 2. collective.

སྤྱི་མ་སྦོམ་ (jīmə bom) sm. སྤྱི་སྦོམ་.

སྤྱི་མང་ (jīmaŋ) sm. སྤྱི་དམངས་.

སྤྱི་མང་ཀློག་དེབ་ (jīmaŋ lōgdeb) popular literature/ books, books for the general public.

སྤྱི་མང་རྒྱན་རྒྱ་ (jīmaŋ gyɛngya) collective agreement.

སྤྱི་མང་ཞིང་ར་ (jīmaŋ shiŋrə) collective farm.

སྤྱི་མང་རིང་ལུགས་ (jīmaŋ riŋluù) collectivism.

སྤྱི་མི་ (jīmi) 1. member, delegate. 2. an elected group leader (in India).

སྤྱི་མིང་ (jīmiŋ) general term / name.

སྤྱི་མོས་ (jīmöö) liked/ approved by all.

སྤྱི་དམངས་ (jīmaŋ) the public, citizens.

སྤྱི་དམངས་ཀྱི་ཁེ་དབང་ (jīmaŋgi kēwaŋ) citizen's rights, civil rights.

སྤྱི་དམངས་རྒྱང་སྲིང་མཉམ་སྒྲིལ་ལས་ཁང་ (jīmaŋ gyəŋsiŋ ñamdree lɛ̀ɛ̀gaŋ) Corporation for Public Broadcasting (CPB).

སྤྱི་དམངས་བདེ་དོན་འཛིན་སྐྱོང་ཁང་ (jīmaŋ dedön dziŋgyoŋgaŋ) Social Security Administration (in U.S.A.).

སྤྱི་དམངས་ཕོ་མོ་ (jīmaŋ pōmo) all citizens male and female.

སྤྱི་དམངས་བུད་མེད་ (jīmaŋ büümeè) female citizens.

སྤྱི་གཙུག་ (jīdzuù) sm. སྤྱི་བོ་.

སྤྱི་གཙུག་སྤུ་འཁྱིལ་ (jīdzuù būgyii) cowlick (strand of hair).

སྤྱི་ཚབ་ (jītsəb) consul general.

སྤྱི་ཚིག་བསམ་པ་ (jīdzig sāmba) shung. public welfare ¶ སྔར་ཕན་སྤྱི་ཚིག་བསམ་པར་དགོན་སྡེར་ལུགས་གཉིས་གང་ཐད་ནས་ཕན་ཐབས་འཚོ་སྐྱོང་འདི་བྱས་མེད་པར་ In the past, they did not do anything that was beneficial to the public welfare of the monastery, both in terms of religion and politics.

སྤྱི་ཚིས་ (jīdzii) public affairs/ issues/ concern.

སྤྱི་ཚུགས་ (jī dzuù) va. to stand on one's head.

སྤྱི་ཚུགས་སུ་འགྲོ་ (jīdzugsu dro) va. to walk on one's hands.

སྤྱི་ཚེས་ (jīdzeè) the date according to the Western calendar.

སྤྱི་ཚོགས་ (jīdzoò) 1. society; social. 2. Tibetan National Assembly.

སྤྱི་ཚོགས་ཀྱི་ཀུན་སྤྱོད་ (jīdzoògi gūnjöö) sm. སྤྱི་ཚོགས་ཀྱི་སྤྱོད་བཟང་.

སྤྱི་ཚོགས་ཀྱི་ཁེ་ཕན་ (jīdzoògi kēbɛn) social welfare.

སྤྱི་ཚོགས་ཀྱི་ཁོངས་མི་ (jīdzoògi kōŋmi) member of society.

སྤྱི་ཚོགས་ཀྱི་ཁོར་ཡུག (jīdzoògi kɔ̄ɔ̄yuù) social environment, societal surroundings.

སྤྱི་ཚོགས་ཀྱི་གོམས་སྲོལ་ (jīdzoògi komsöö) social custom, societal customs.

སྤྱི་ཚོགས་ཀྱི་གྲུབ་ཆ་ (jīdzoògi drubja) elements/ ingredients of society.

སྤྱི་ཚོགས་ཀྱི་གྲལ་རིམ་ (jīdzoògi trɛɛrim) social strata/ class.

སྤྱི་ཚོགས་ཀྱི་གླེང་ཕྱོགས་ (jīdzoògi lēŋjɔɔ̀) public opinion.

སྤྱི་ཚོགས་ཀྱི་དགོས་ངེས་ངལ་རྩོལ་ (jīdzoògi gööŋeè ŋəədzöö) socially necessary labor.

སྤྱི་ཚོགས་ཀྱི་འགན་ལེན་ཐེབས་རྩ་ (jīdzoògi gɛnlen tēbdza) social security fund.

སྤྱི་ཚོགས་ཀྱི་རྒུད་སྐྱོབ་ (jīdzoògi gūügyəb) social relief.

སྤྱི་ཚོགས་ཀྱི་སྒྲིག་ལམ་ (jīdzoògi driglam) social order, public order.

སྤྱི་ཚོགས་ཀྱི་བསྒྱུར་བཅོས་ (jīdzoògi gyurgöö) social reforms.

སྤྱི་ཚོགས་ཀྱི་ངལ་རྩོལ་ (jīdzoògi ŋəədzöö) social labor.

སྤྱི་ཚོགས་ཀྱི་ངོ་བོ་ (jīdzoògi ŋowo) the nature/ character/ quality of society.

སྤྱི་ཚོགས་ཀྱི་ཆ་རྐྱེན་ (jīdzoògi cāgyen) social existence/ condition.

སྤྱི་ཚོགས་ཀྱི་སྟོབས་ཤུགས་ (jīdzoògi dōbshuù) social forces.

སྤྱི་ཚོགས་ཀྱི་ཐོན་སྐྱེད་ནུས་ཤུགས་ (jīdzoògi tōngyeè nüüshug) the productive force of society.

སྤྱི་ཚོགས་ཀྱི་ཐོན་སྐྱེད་རུ་ཁག (jīdzoògi tōngyeè rugaà) social production team.

སྤྱི་ཚོགས་ཀྱི་ཐོན་རྫས་བསྡོམས་གྲངས་ (jīdzoògi tōndzɛɛ̀ domdraŋ) total products of the society.

སྤྱི་ཚོགས་ཀྱི་ཐོན་རྫས་བསྡོམས་འབོར་ (jīdzoògi tōndzɛɛ̀ dombɔr) total products of the society.

སྤྱི་ཚོགས་ཀྱི་བདེ་སྐྱོང་ (jīdzoògi dedgyoŋ) societal security.

སྤྱི་ཚོགས་ཀྱི་བདེ་འཇགས་ (jīdzoògi denjaà) sm. སྤྱི་ཚོགས་ཀྱི་བདེ་སྐྱོང་.

སྤྱི་ཚོགས་ཀྱི་འདུ་ཤེས་ (jīdzoògi dusheè) social consciousness.

སྤྱི་ཚོགས་ཀྱི་གནད་དོན་ (jīdzoògi nɛɛ̀dön) social problem/ question.

སྤྱི་ཚོགས་ཀྱི་གནས་པ་ (jīdzoògi nɛɛ̀ba) social existence (in Marxist sense).

སྤྱི་ཚོགས་ཀྱི་གནས་བབ་ (jīdzoògi nɛɛ̀bəb) social status, social standing.

སྤྱི་ཚོགས་ཀྱི་རྣམ་པ་ (jīdzoògi nāmba) social type/ form.

སྤྱི་ཚོགས་ཀྱི་དཔལ་འབྱོར་གནས་སྟངས་ (jīdzoògi bɛnjɔɔ nɛɛ̀daŋ) socioeconomic position/ mode.

སྤྱི་ཚོགས་ཀྱི་དཔལ་འབྱོར་རྣམ་པ་ (jīdzoògi bɛnjɔɔ nāmba) sm. སྤྱི་ཚོགས་ཀྱི་དཔལ་འབྱོར་གནས་སྟངས་.

སྤྱི་ཚོགས་ཀྱི་སྤྱི་ཕན་ (jīdzoògi jībən) common benefit of society.

སྤྱི་ཚོགས་ཀྱི་སྤྱི་ལ་དབང་བའི་ལམ་ལུགས་ (jīdzoògi jīlə wāŋwɛ ləmluù) socialist system of public ownership.

སྤྱི་ཚོགས་ཀྱི་སྤྱིའི་དགོས་མཁོ་དང་སྤྱིའི་མཁོ་སྤྲོད་ (jīdzoògi jīī göögo daŋ jīī kōdröö) the total social supply and demand.

སྤྱི་ཚོགས་ཀྱི་སྤྱོད་བཟང་ (jīdzoògi jöösaŋ) social morals.

སྤྱི་ཚོགས་ཀྱི་ཕན་འབྲས་ (jīdzoògi pēndrɛɛ̀) social benefit.

སྤྱི་ཚོགས་ཀྱི་བྱེད་སྒོ་ (jīdzoògi ceègo) social activity.

སྤྱི་ཚོགས་ཀྱི་བྱེད་སྒོ་པ་ (jīdzoògi cēēgoba) social activist.

སྤྱི་ཚོགས་ཀྱི་འབྱུང་ཁུངས་ (jīdzoògi juŋguŋ) social origin.

སྤྱི་ཚོགས་ཀྱི་འབྲེལ་འདྲིས་ (jīdzoògi drendreè) social intercourse.

སྤྱི་ཚོགས་ཀྱི་འབྲེལ་བ་ (jīdzoògi dreewa) social relations.

སྤྱི་ཚོགས་ཀྱི་མི་སྣ་ (jīdzoògi minə) societal/ social celebrities.

སྤྱི་ཚོགས་ཀྱི་མྱོང་བྱ་ (jīdzoògi ñoŋja) social experience.

སྤྱི་ཚོགས་ཀྱི་དམངས་གཙོའི་རིང་ལུགས་ (jīdzoògi māŋdzö riŋluù) social democratism.

སྤྱི་ཚོགས་ཀྱི་རྨང་གཞི་ (jīdzoògi māŋshi) social base, social basis, social foundation.

སྤྱི་ཚོགས་ཀྱི་ཚན་རིག (jīdzoògi tsɛ̄nrii) social science.

སྤྱི་ཚོགས་ཀྱི་ཚོགས་ཁག (jīdzoògi tsɔɔ̀gaà) social groups.

སྤྱི་ཚོགས་ཀྱི་རང་བཞིན་ (jīdzoògi rəŋshin) social nature/ character, sociality.

སྤྱི་ཚོགས་ཀྱི་རིག་པ་ (jīdzoògi rigbə) sociology.

སྤྱི་ཚོགས་ཀྱི་ལག་ལེན་ (jīdzoògi laglen) social practice.

སྤྱི་ཚོགས་ཀྱི་ལམ་ལུགས་ (jīdzoògi ləmluù) social system.

སྤྱི་ཚོགས་ཀྱི་ལས་བགོས་ (jīdzoògi lɛɛ̀göö) social division of labor/ work.

སྤྱི་ཚོགས་ཀྱི་ས་ཁམས་ (jīdzoògi sāgam) social/ cultural geography, social dimensions of geography.

སྤྱི་ཚོགས་ཀྱི་ས་ཁམས་རིག་པ་ (jīdzoògi sāgam rigbə) social/ cultural geography.

སྤྱི་ཚོགས་ཀྱི་ས་རྒྱུས་ (jīdzoògi sāgyüù) social/ cultural geography.

སྤྱི་ཚོགས་ཀྱི་གསར་བརྗེ་ (jīdzoògi sārje) social revolution.

སྤྱི་ཚོགས་ཀྱི་བསམ་རྒྱལ་ (jīdzoògi sāmdzüü) social awareness, social thought.

སྤྱི་ཚོགས་སྐྱོན་ཆའི་རྣམ་པ་ (jīdzoò gyōnjɛ nāmba) social pathology.

སྤྱི་ཚོགས་ཁེ་ཕན་ (jīdzoò kēbɛn) social welfare.

སྤྱི་ཚོགས་གང་ལས་བྱུང་བ་ (jīdzoò kaŋlɛ cuŋwə) social origins.

སྤྱི་ཚོགས་སྒང་ (jīdzoò gaŋ) in society ། སྤྱི་ཚོགས་སྒང་ལ་དེང་སང་དངུལ་དཀོན་པོ་ཞེ་དྲགས་ཡོད་པ་རེད་ These days there is a great shortage of money in society.

སྤྱི་ཚོགས་ཅན་ (jīdzoòjɛn) 1. socialization. 2. vi.—དུ་འགྱུར་ to be socialized.

སྤྱི་ཚོགས་ཅན་དུ་སྒྱུར་ (jīdzoòjɛndu gyur) va. to socialize, to transform into a socialist society.

སྤྱི་ཚོགས་བཅོས་སྒྱུར་ (jīdzoò jöögyur) transformation/ change/ reform of society.

སྤྱི་ཚོགས་ཉེན་སྲུང་ (jīdzoò ñɛnsuŋ) social insurance.

སྤྱི་ཚོགས་རྙིང་པ་ (jīdzoò ñiŋbə) the old social system, the old society (conveys the society in pre 1959 Tibet).

སྤྱི་ཚོགས་དང་ (jīdzoò dāŋ) Socialist Party.

སྤྱི་ཚོགས་ཐོག་གི་སྤྱོད་བཟང་ཅན་ (jīdzoò tɔ̄ɔ̀gi jöösaŋjɛn) leading figures in a community.

སྤྱི་ཚོགས་ཐོག་གི་འབྲེལ་གཏུག (jīdzoò tɔ̄ɔ̀gi dreēdduù) social intercourse, social contact, social relations.

སྤྱི་ཚོགས་ཐོག་གི་འབྲེལ་བ་ (jīdzoò tɔ̄ɔ̀gi dreewa) sm. སྤྱི་ཚོགས་ཐོག་གི་འབྲེལ་གཏུག.

སྤྱི་ཚོགས་ཐོག་གི་མིང་གྲགས་ཅན་ (jīdzoò tɔ̄ɔ̀gi miŋdragjɛn) noted public figures.

སྤྱི་ཚོགས་མཐོ་གྲས་ (jīdzoò tōdrɛɛ̀) upper class society.

སྤྱི་ཚོགས་བདེ་དོན་ (jīdzoò dedön) social welfare.

སྤྱི་ཚོགས་ཕན་བདེ་ (jīdzoò pēnde) civil affairs, social welfare ། སྤྱི་ཚོགས་ཕན་བདེ་ཁང་ Civil Affairs Bureau.

སྤྱི་ཚོགས་ཕན་བདེ་ཁེ་ལས་ (jīdzoò pēnde kēlɛɛ̀) an enterprise/ business run by the Civil Affairs Bureau.

སྤྱི་ཚོགས་འཕེལ་རྒྱས་ (jīdzoò pēēgyɛɛ̀) social/ socialist development.

སྤྱི་ཚོགས་འཕེལ་རྒྱས་ཀྱི་ལོ་རྒྱུས་ (jīdzoò pēēgyɛɛ̀gi lugyur) history of social development.

སྤྱི་ཚོགས་དམངས་གཙོའི་དང་ (jīdzoò māŋdzö dāŋ)

social democratic party.

སྤྱི་ཚོགས་དམངས་གཙོའི་བཟོ་པའི་དང་ (jīdzoò māŋdzö sobɛ dāŋ) social democratic labor party.

སྤྱི་ཚོགས་དམངས་གཙོའི་རིང་ལུགས་ (jīdzoò māŋdzö riŋluù) social democratic system.

སྤྱི་ཚོགས་བཙན་རྒྱལ་རིང་ལུགས་ (jīdzoò dzɛngyɛɛ̀ riŋluù) social imperialism.

སྤྱི་ཚོགས་རྩ་འགྱུར་ (jīdzoò dzāngyur) the changing/ transforming of society.

སྤྱི་ཚོགས་ཚན་རིག (jīdzoò tsɛnrii) social science ¶ སྤྱི་ཚོགས་ཚན་རིག་ཁང་ Academy of Social Sciences.

སྤྱི་ཚོགས་ཚོགས་པ་ (jīdzoò tsōgba) social organization.

སྤྱི་ཚོགས་ཞིབ་འཇུག (jīdzoò shimjuù) social investigation/ research.

སྤྱི་ཚོགས་ཞབས་འདེགས་ (jīdzoò shəmdeg) social service.

སྤྱི་ཚོགས་ཡར་ཐོན་ (jīdzoò yardön) social progress.

སྤྱི་ཚོགས་རིག་པ་ (jīdzoò rigbə) sociology.

སྤྱི་ཚོགས་རིང་ལུགས་ (jīdzoò riŋluù) socialism ¶ སྤྱི་ཚོགས་རིང་ལུགས་རྒྱལ་ཁབ་ A socialist country.

སྤྱི་ཚོགས་རིང་ལུགས་ཀྱི་འགྲན་བསྡུར་ (jīdzoò riŋluùgi drɛndur) socialist emulation campaign/ movement.

སྤྱི་ཚོགས་རིང་ལུགས་ཀྱི་བསྒྱུར་བཀོད་ (jīdzoò riŋluùgi gyurgöö) socialist transformation.

སྤྱི་ཚོགས་རིང་ལུགས་ཀྱི་དངོས་ཡོད་རིང་ལུགས་ (jīdzoò riŋluùgi ŋööyöö riŋluù) socialist realism.

སྤྱི་ཚོགས་རིང་ལུགས་ཀྱི་དཔུང་ཁག (jīdzoò riŋluùgi būŋgaà) the socialist camp.

སྤྱི་ཚོགས་རིང་ལུགས་ཀྱི་སྤྱི་ཚོགས་ (jīdzoò riŋluùgi jīdzoò) socialist society.

སྤྱི་ཚོགས་རིང་ལུགས་ཀྱི་ཕྱོགས་ཁག (jīdzoò riŋluùgi cɔ̄ɔgaà) sm. སྤྱི་ཚོགས་རིང་ལུགས་ཀྱི་དཔུང་ཁག.

སྤྱི་ཚོགས་རིང་ལུགས་ཀྱི་མི་རིགས་ (jīdzoò riŋluùgi mirii) socialist nation/ nationality.

སྤྱི་ཚོགས་རིང་ལུགས་ཀྱི་འཛུགས་སྐྲུན་ (jīdzoò riŋluùgi dzugdrün) socialist construction.

སྤྱི་ཚོགས་རིང་ལུགས་ཀྱི་བཟོ་ལས་ཅན་དུ་འགྱུར་བ་ (jīdzoò riŋluùgi solɛɛ̀jɛndu gyurwə) socialist industrialization.

སྤྱི་ཚོགས་རིང་ལུགས་ཀྱི་གསར་བརྗེ་ (jīdzoò riŋluùgi sārje) socialist revolution.

སྤྱི་ཚོགས་རིང་ལུགས་ཀྱི་གསོག་འཇོག (jīdzoò riŋluùgi sōnjɔɔ̀) socialist accumulation.

སྤྱི་ཚོགས་རིང་ལུགས་ཀྱི་བསམ་པ་ (jīdzoò riŋluùgi sāmba) socialist thought.

སྤྱི་ཚོགས་རིང་ལུགས་ཚོགས་པ་ (jīdzoò riŋluù tsōgba) Socialist party.

སྤྱི་ཚོགས་རིང་ལུགས་བཟོ་ལས་ཅན་དུ་འགྱུར་བ་ (jīdzoò riŋluù solɛɛ̀jɛndu gyurwə) sm. སྤྱི་ཚོགས་རིང་ཀྱི་ལུགས་བཟོ་ལས་ཅན་དུ་འགྱུར་བ་.

སྤྱི་ཚོགས་རིང་ལུགས་ལ་ངོ་རྒོལ་ (jīdzoò riŋluùla ŋogöö) antisocialist.

སྤྱི་ཚོགས་རིང་ལུགས་ལ་དབང་བའི་ལམ་ལུགས་ (jīdzoò riŋluùla wāŋwɛ ləmluù) system of socialist ownership.

སྤྱི་ཚོགས་ལ་བརྟག་དཔྱད་ (jīdzoòla dāgjɛɛ̀) social investigation, social survey; va.—བྱེད་.

སྤྱི་ཚོགས་ལེགས་བཅོས་རིང་ལུགས་ (jīdzoò legjöö riŋluù) socialist reformism.

སྤྱི་ཚོགས་སུ་འགྱུར་ (jīdzoòsu gyur) vi. to become socialized, to become a socialist society.

སྤྱི་ཚོགས་སྲུང་སྐྱོབས་ཚོགས་འདུ་ (jīdzoò sūŋgyob tsōndu) UN Security Council.

སྤྱི་ཚོགས་གསར་བརྗེ་ (jīdzoò sārje) social revolution.

སྤྱི་མཚན་ (jīdzɛn) abstract, general character.

སྤྱི་མཚན་གྱི་རྟོག་པ་ (jīdzɛngi dōgba) abstract thought.

སྤྱི་མཚན་གྱི་བསམ་གཞིགས་ (jīdzɛngi sāmshig) abstract thinking.

སྤྱི་མཚན་དུ་འགྱུར་བའི་རང་བཞིན་ (jīdzɛndu gyurwɛ rənshin) abstract, abstraction.

སྤྱི་མཚུངས་ (jīdzuŋ) as is commonly done, like all others, as is common ¶ སྤྱི་མཚུངས་འགྲོ་སྡོད་ཀྱི་དབང་ཆ་ཡོད་པ་རེད་ As is common, (they) have freedom of movement.

སྤྱི་མཚོ་ (jītso) international waters, international waterway.

སྤྱི་འཛིན་ (jīndzin) leader, head, prefect ¶ དགོན་པའི་སྤྱི་འཛིན་སློབ་དཔོན་ The abbot who is the head of the monastery.

སྤྱི་རྫས་ (jīdzɛɛ̀) public property, property owned in common.

སྤྱི་རྫས་སྒེར་སྤྱོད་ (jīdzɛɛ̀ gerjöö) using public property for private ends.

སྤྱི་འཛར་ (jīndzar) women's head ornament.

སྤྱི་རྫོང་ (jīdzoŋ) shung. Shigatse district.

སྤྱི་རྫོང་གཉིས་ (jīdzoŋ ñīi) shung. the two heads of Shigatse district.

སྤྱི་ཞབས་པ་ (jīshəbbə) public servant.

སྤྱི་ཞིང་ (jīshiŋ) shung. public field, communally held field.

སྤྱི་ཞུ་རྒྱག (jīshüù gyaà) va. to report sth. unanimously from a group.

སྤྱི་གཞུང་ལྷན་རྒྱས་ (jīshuŋ lhɛngyɛɛ̀) parliament.

སྤྱི་གཞོལ་ (jīshöö) working for the common good, devoted to public work.

སྤྱི་བཞུར་ (jīshur) bark of eucommia (used in Tibetan medicine).

སྤྱི་ཟླ་ (jīnda) a month in the Western system.

སྤྱི་ཟུར་ (jīsur) an ex-representative (in the Tibetan exile government's assembly).

སྤྱི་ཟོམ་ (jīsom) shung. sm. སྤྱི་སྒོམ་.

སྤྱི་གཟུགས་ (jīsug) universal/ general form, amassed into one form.

སྤྱི་ཡོངས་ (jīyoŋ) the whole, the entire; general, common.

སྤྱི་ཡོད་ལམ་ལུགས་ (jīyöö ləmluù) communal system, common-ownership system.

སྤྱི་ར་ (jīrə) sm. སྤྱི་ལ་.

སྤྱི་ལ་ (jīlə) in general, in common, on the whole.

སྤྱི་ལ་དབང་བའི་ལམ་ལུགས་ (jīlə wāŋwɛ ləmluù) public ownership system.

སྤྱི་ལག་སྐོར་གྱི་རྟགས་ (jīlaggɔɔgi dāà) shung. a seal that is passed hand to hand to all of the concerned persons and put on a pledge/ agreement.

སྤྱི་ལམ་ (jīlam) general line.

སྤྱི་ལམ་ཕྱོགས་ (jī ləmjɔɔ̀) sm. སྤྱི་ལམ་.

སྤྱི་ལས་ (jīlɛɛ̀) work for the collectivity, public work.

སྤྱི་ལས་གཉེར་ཕྱག (jīlɛɛ̀ ñērjaà) shung. abbr. of སྤྱི་སོ་, ལས་སྤྱི་, གཉེར་པ་, ཕྱག་མཛོད་.

སྤྱི་ལི་ (jīli) millimeter.

སྤྱི་ལུགས་ (jīluù) 1. common right, universal principle, self evident truth, generally acknowledged truth. 2. axiom (in math).

སྤྱི་ལུགས་སྤྱི་སྲོལ་ (jīluù jīsöö) commonly acknowledged truth/ custom/ behavior.

སྤྱི་ལེ་ (jīle) kilometer.

སྤྱི་ལེབ་ (jīleb) flatheaded.

སྤྱི་ལེབ་འདུས་མགོ་ (jīleb düngo) sm. སྤྱི་ལེབ་.

སྤྱི་ལོ་ (jīlo) a year in the Western calendar.

སྤྱི་ལོ་གོང་ (jīlo koŋ) B.C. ¶ སྤྱི་ལོ་གོང་གི་དུས་རབས་བཅུ་བདུན་ནས་ From the seventeenth century B.C.

སྤྱི་ལོ་དང་པོ་ (jīlo taŋbo) the beginning of a reign/ era.

སྤྱི་ལོ་བྱུང་རྗེས་ (jīlo cuŋjeè) A.D.

སྤྱི་ལོའི་སྔོན་ (jīlö ŋōn) sm. སྤྱི་ལོ་གོང་.

སྤྱི་ལོའི་སྔོན་ཚད་ (jīlö ŋōndzɛɛ̀) sm. སྤྱི་ལོ་གོང་.

སྤྱི་བཤད་ (jīshɛɛ̀) sm. སྤྱི་གཏམ་.

སྤྱི་བཤལ་ (jīshɛɛ) a type of laxative.

སྤྱི་ས་ (jīsə) public land, jointly/ commonly owned land.

སྤྱི་སར་སྤུང་ (jīsar būŋ) va. to turn over to the community/ government.

སྤྱི་སེམས་ (jīsem) thinking of the common good/ interest, selfless; va.—འཆང་ to keep the public interest in mind.

སྤྱི་སེམས་ཆེན་པོ་ (jīsem cēmbo) just and selfless /

fair.

སྤྱི་སོ་ (jīso) sm. སྤྱི་བསོ་.

སྤྱི་སོན་ (jī sön) vi. to receive orders/ instructions (from higher authorities).

སྤྱི་སྲུང་ཉེན་རྟོག་པ་ (jīsuŋ ñɛndɔgba) security police.

སྤྱི་སྲོལ་ (jīsüü) general practice/ custom, common practice/ custom.

སྤྱི་སློབ་ (jīlob) abbr. of སྤྱི་ཚོགས་རིང་ལུགས་ཀྱི་སློབ་གསོ་.

སྤྱི་གསལ་ (jīsɛl) sm. སྤྱི་ཁྲི་.

སྤྱི་གསོག (jīsɔɔ̀) set aside for the public, public accumulation.

སྤྱི་གསོག་མ་དངུལ་ (jīsɔɔ̀ mə̱ŋüü) accumulated/ set aside public funds.

སྤྱི་བསགས་མ་དངུལ་ (jīsaà mə̱ŋüü) sm. སྤྱི་གསོག་མ་དངུལ་.

སྤྱི་བསམ་སྒེར་བརྗེད་ (jīsam ge̱rjeè) devotion to public service.

སྤྱི་བསོ་ (jīso) name of the highest economic officer/ manager for a monastery as a whole (as opposed to each college).

སྤྱི་ལྷན་ (jīlhɛn) abbr. of སྤྱི་འདུས་ལྷན་ཚོགས་.

སྤྱིང་ (jīŋ) sm. སྤྱིན་.

སྤྱིང་: p. སྤྱིངས་; f. སྤྱིང་; imp. སྤྱིངས་ (jīŋ) va. to sink, to immerse under water, to submerge.

སྤྱིངས་ (jīŋ) p.and imp. of སྤྱིང་.

སྤྱིན་ (jīn) glue.

སྤྱིན་ཀོང་ (jīngoŋ) glue container.

སྤྱིན་ཆུ་ (jīnju) liquid glue.

སྤྱིན་བག (jīnbaà) paste.

སྤྱིན་སྦྱར་ (jīnjar) gluing, pasting; va.— བྱེད་.

སྤྱིན་སྦྱར་སྤང་ལེབ་ (jīnjar bāŋleb) plywood.

སྤྱིན་ཚི་ (jīndzi) stickiness of glue.

སྤྱིན་རས་ (jīnrɛɛ̀) bandaid.

སྤྱིན་ཤོག (jīnshɔɔ̀) 1. negative (film). 2. film.

སྤྱིན་ཤོག་དཀར་ནག (jīnshɔɔ̀ gārnaà) black and white film.

སྤྱིན་ཤོག་ཚོན་ལྡན་ (jinshɔɔ̀ tsöndɛn) color film.

སྤྱིན་ཤོག་པར་འཁྲུ་ (jīnshɔɔ̀ bārtru) va. to develop film.

སྤྱིའི་སྐུལ་སློང་ (jīī gǖüloŋ) general mobilization; va.—བྱེད་.

སྤྱིའི་ཁ་ཕྱོགས་ (jīī kājɔɔ̀) general/ overall direction.

སྤྱིའི་གོ་དོན་ (jīī ko̱dön) general concept/ understanding.

སྤྱིའི་གྲུ་བཞི་ (jīī tru̱bshi) centimeter.

སྤྱིའི་བགོ་གྲངས་ (jīī go̱draŋ) common division (in math).

སྤྱིའི་རྒྱ་མ་ (jīī gya̱ma) kilogram.

སྤྱིའི་རྒྱ་མཚོ་ (jīī gya̱dzo) high seas, open seas.

སྤྱིའི་ངལ་རྩོལ་ (jīī ŋɛ̱ɛ̱dzöö) common/ public labor.

སྤྱིའི་ཐ་བ་ལ་སྣོས་ཀྱི་ག་ཤོལ་མི་གཅོག (jīī tāwala gö̱ö̀gi shöö mi̱jɔɔ̀) to not do anything that harms one's private affairs for the sake of public affairs [Lit. not to break one's private plow plowing the public field].

སྤྱིའི་ཐོན་ཚད་རིང་གོང་ (jīī töndzɛɛ̀ ri̱ngoŋ) the general price of productivity.

སྤྱིའི་དུར་ས་ (jīī tu̱rsə) public graveyard.

སྤྱིའི་དོན་ (jīīdön) affairs of the public.

སྤྱིའི་ལྡབ་གྲངས་ (jīī də̱bdraŋ) common multiple (in math).

སྤྱིའི་བསྡོམས་འབོར་ (jīī do̱mbɔr) sum, grand total.

སྤྱིའི་བསྡོམས་ཚིག (jīī do̱mdziì) general/ overall conclusion.

སྤྱིའི་འཕྲུལ་ཆས་བཟོ་གྲྭ་ (jīī trǖüjɛɛ̀ so̱dra) general machine/ shop.

སྤྱིའི་འབོད་ཚིག (jīī bö̱ö̀dziì) general slogan.

སྤྱིའི་མ་ཆ་ (jīī ma̱ja) common denominator (in math.).

སྤྱིའི་རྩ་དོན་ (jīī dzādön) general rules/ principles.

སྤྱིའི་རྩ་འཛིན་ (jīī dzəndzin) chief point/ principle, fundamental point/ principle, general principle.

སྤྱིའི་གཞུང་ (jīīshuŋ) central government, overall government.

སྤྱིའི་གཞུང་ལམ་ (jīī shu̱ŋlam) general line/ course/ policy.

སྤྱིའི་བཟའ་ཁང་ (jīī sa̱gaŋ) public canteen/ dining hall/ mess.

སྤྱིའི་བཟོ་ཚོགས་ (jīī so̱dzɔɔ̀) labor federation.

སྤྱིའི་ལམ་ཐིག (jīī la̱mdig) sm. སྤྱིའི་ལམ་ཕྱོགས་.

སྤྱིའི་ལམ་ཕྱོགས་ (jīī la̱mjɔɔ̀) general line/ direction.

སྤྱིའི་ལས་འགན་ (jīī lɛ̱ngɛn) general duty/ responsibility.

སྤྱིའི་ལེ་ (jīīle) kilometer.

སྤྱིའི་ལེ་ཐོ་ (jīī le̱do) Western calendar.

སྤྱིའི་ལེ་དབར་ (jīī le̱war) sm. སྤྱིའི་ལེ་.

སྤྱིའི་ལོ་བརྩི་རྩུལ་ (jīīlo dzīdzüü) a year according to the Christian calendar.

སྤྱིའི་གསོག་དངུལ་ (jīī sɔɔ̀ŋüü) public/ common reserve fund.

སྤྱིའི་ལྷན་ཁང་ (jīī lhɛ̄ngaŋ) general/ main meeting place.

སྤྱིའུ་ལྡུགས་ (jīwu lūù) sm. སྤྱི་ལྡུགས་.

སྤྱིའུ་རྩུགས་ (jīwu tsūù) sm. སྤྱི་རྩུགས་.

སྤྱིར་ (jīr) generally, in general.

སྤྱིར་གྲགས་ (jīrdraà) generally/ widely known ¶ གནས་ཚུལ་འདི་སྤྱིར་སྒྲགས་རེད་ This news is widely known.

སྤྱིར་བཏང་ (jīrdaŋ) 1. (at the beginning of a clause it conveys) in general, generally ¶ སྤྱིར་བཏང་གློག་ལས་བཟོ་པ་ཚོས་ཐོག་མར་ལག་རྩལ་སྦྱོང་དགོས་ In general, the electrical workers must first learn the technical skills. ¶ སྤྱིར་བཏང་བཤད་ན་ If I speak in general. 2. (— + gen.) general, common, usual ¶ སྤྱིར་བཏང་གི་ཁ་ལག Everyday/ common food.

སྤྱིར་བཏང་གི་རང་བཞིན་ (jīrdaŋgi rə̱ŋshin) generalization.

སྤྱིར་བཏང་ཅན་ (jīrdaŋjɛn) general, common, ordinary, usual.

སྤྱིར་བཏང་ནས་བཤད་ན་ (jīrdaŋnɛ shɛ̄ɛ̀na) sm. སྤྱིར་བཏང་བྱས་ནས་བཤད་ན་.

སྤྱིར་བཏང་པ་ (jīrdaŋba) sm. སྤྱིར་བཏང་ཅན་.

སྤྱིར་བཏང་སྤྱིར་བཏང་ (jīrdaŋ jīrdaŋ) very common/ ordinary/ usual/ simple.

སྤྱིར་བཏང་བྱས་ན་ (jīrdaŋ cɛ̱ɛ̀na) 1. as usual, as is commonly done. 2. in general.

སྤྱིར་བཏང་བྱས་ནས་བཤད་ན་ (jīrdaŋ cɛ̱ɛ̀nɛ shɛ̄ɛ̀na) generally speaking.

སྤྱིར་བཏང་མིན་པར་ (jīrdaŋ mi̱mbar) specially, special.

སྤྱིར་སྟངས་ (jīrdaŋ) sm. སྤྱིར་བཏང་.

སྤྱིར་བསྟན་ (jīr dɛ̄n) va. to give a summary, to speak in general.

སྤྱིར་དུ་ (jīrdu) sm. སྤྱིར་.

སྤྱིར་ཕྱིན་སློབ་གྲྭ་བ་ (jīrjin lōbdra) students studying abroad.

སྤྱིར་བཤད་ (jīrshɛɛ̀) sm. སྤྱིར་བསྟན་.

སྤྱིལ་པོ་ (jīību) sm. སྤྱིལ་བུ་.

སྤྱིལ་བུ་ (jīību) thatched or straw hut/ house.

སྤྱིལ་མོ་ (jīīmu) trowel (for plastering walls).

སྤྱུག: p. སྤྱུགས་; f. སྤྱུག; imp. སྤྱུགས་ (jūù) va. to expel, to drive out, to banish.

སྤྱུགས་ (jūù) p. and imp. of སྤྱུག.

སྤྱོ་: p. སྤྱོས་; f. སྤྱོ་; imp. སྤྱོས་ (jō) va. to criticize, to scold, to blame, to abuse.

སྤྱོ་སྡིགས་ (jōdig) scolding and threatening.

སྤྱོ་ཚིག (jōdziì) swear/ curse words.

སྤྱོད་: p. སྤྱད་; f. སྤྱད་; imp. སྤྱོད་ (jȫö̀) 1. va. to use, to make use of, to employ ¶ བཟོ་གྲྭ་འདི་གསུམ་གྱིས་ཆེས་ཡར་ཐོན་གྱི་ལག་རྩལ་སྤྱོད་ཀྱི་ཡོད་པ་རེད་ These three factors use the most advanced techniques. 2. va. to enjoy ¶ བདེ་དགེར་སྤྱོད་རྒྱུ་ཡོད་པ་རེད་ (They) are enjoying happiness.

སྤྱོད་ཁང་ (jȫö̀gaŋ) toilet, lavatory.

སྤྱོད་མཁན་ (jȫö̀ñɛn) user.

སྤྱོད་མཁས་ (jȫö̀kɛɛ̀) economical, thrifty, efficient; va.—བྱེད་ to be efficient, to be economical/ thrifty.

སྤྱོད་མཁོ་ (jȫö̀ko) sm. སྤྱོད་སྒོ་.

སྤྱོད་མགོ་ཆུང་ལ་ཁྲིམ་པོ་མེད་པ་ (jö̈ko jūŋla tri̲mbu me̲è̲ba) not useful and not selling well.

སྤྱོད་མགོ་ཙག་ཙིག (jö̈ko dzə̄gdzig) small incidental expenses.

སྤྱོད་འགྲོས་ (jö̈ndrö̈) behavior, manner.

སྤྱོད་རྒྱུད་ (jö̈gyüü) the second of the four classes of tantra stressing the importance of both external and internal mental activity.

སྤྱོད་སྒོ་ (jö̈go) usage, application, appropriation.

སྤྱོད་སྒོ་ཆེ་བ་ (jö̈go cēwa) practical, useful.

སྤྱོད་ངན་ (jö̈ŋɛn) bad behavior/ deportment; va.— བྱེད་; —སྤྱོལ་ to misbehave.

སྤྱོད་ངན་ནག་ཉེས་ (jö̈ŋɛn na̲ñeè) bad behavior and evil deeds.

སྤྱོད་ཆ་ (jö̈ja) sm. སྤྱོད་ཆས་.

སྤྱོད་ཆས་ (jö̈jɛɛ̀) materials, utensils ༑ཀོ་བའི་སྤྱོད་ཆས་ Leatherware.

སྤྱོད་འཇུག (jö̈juù) name of a famous Buddhist text by Shantideva.

སྤྱོད་ཉེས་ (jö̈ñeè) 1. bad/ evil/ wrong behavior. 2. for children, mischievous. 3. wrongly using, misusing.

སྤྱོད་སྟངས་ (jö̈daŋ) the way to use/ utilize.

སྤྱོད་ཐེར་ (jö̈der) reforming one's behavior.

སྤྱོད་དེབ་ (jö̈deb) reference book.

སྤྱོད་བདེ་ (jö̈de) easily usable/ applicable, convenient.

སྤྱོད་ལྡན་ (jö̈dɛn) well-behaved.

སྤྱོད་པ་ (jö̈bə) behavior ༑སྤྱོད་པ་ཁྱད་མཚར་པོ་ Strange/ wierd behavior.

སྤྱོད་པ་འཆལ་བ་ (jö̈bə cɛ̄ɛwa) uncontrolled behavior.

སྤྱོད་པ་ཉེས་པོ་ (jö̈bə ñēèbo) sm. སྤྱོད་ཉེས་.

སྤྱོད་པ་དྭངས་གཙང་ (jö̈bə ta̲ŋdzaŋ) well-behaved.

སྤྱོད་པ་དྲག་པོ་ (jö̈bə tra̲gba) belligerent/ warlike/ pugnacious behavior.

སྤྱོད་པ་རྣམ་དག (jö̈bə nāgdaà) noble/ magnanimous behavior.

སྤྱོད་པ་མ་སྡྲུང་མ་རྫིགས་ (jö̈bə mə̲druŋ mə̲dzii) untruthful/ bad behavior.

སྤྱོད་གཙང་ (jö̈dzaŋ) pure deeds/ acts.

སྤྱོད་གཙང་སྤྱི་གཞོལ་ (jö̈dzaŋ jīshöö) good work/ behavior, working for the common good.

སྤྱོད་གཙང་གཞུང་དྲང་ (jö̈daŋ shu̲ŋdraŋ) clear behavior.

སྤྱོད་པ་རྩིང་པོ་ (jö̈bə dzi̲ŋbu) rude, bad mannered.

སྤྱོད་ཚུལ་ངོ་གཉིས་མ་ (jö̈dzüü ŋo̲ñīimə) duplicitous, two-faced.

སྤྱོད་ཚུལ་ལྔ་ (jö̈dzüü ŋā) see ཀུན་སྤྱོད་གསུམ་དང་སྤྱོད་ཚུལ་ལྔ་.

སྤྱོད་ཚུལ་ཡང་དག་འཛིན་པའི་སྒྲིག་འཛུགས་ (jö̈dzüü ya̲ŋdag dzi̲nbɛ dri̲gdzuù) moral majority.

སྤྱོད་པ་ལོག (jö̈bə lɔ̀ɔ) vi. to be strange/ unruly/ disorderly in behavior.

སྤྱོད་པ་སློག (jö̈bə lɔ̄ɔ) va. to misbehave, to act unruly/ disorderly.

སྤྱོད་པ་ལྷིང་པོ་ (jö̈bə lhīŋbu) gentle behavior/ character.

སྤྱོད་པའི་རྒྱུད་ (jö̈bɛ gyü̲ü) sm. སྤྱོད་རྒྱུད་.

སྤྱོད་པབ་རྩེ་མཐུན་ (jö̈bəb dzēdün) 1. acting or behaving in a similar manner. 2. acting or behaving in a friendly/ harmonious manner.

སྤྱོད་དབང་ (jö̈waŋ) the right of use.

སྤྱོད་མིག (jö̈mig) toilet hole.

སྤྱོད་ཚད་ (jö̈dzɛɛ̀) rate of utilization.

སྤྱོད་ཚུལ་ (jö̈dzüü) 1. style, manner ༑གསར་བརྗེའི་སྤྱོད་ཚུལ་ Revolutionary style. 2. conduct, behavior, the way of acting ༑ཆོས་ཀྱི་སྤྱོད་ཚུལ་མང་པོ་བྱེད་ཀྱི་ཡོད་པ་རེད་ (They) do many religious acts.

སྤྱོད་ཚུལ་འཛིན་ (jö̈dzüü dzi̲n) va. to hold or adhere to an attitude/ opinion/ way of behaving ༑ནོར་འཁྲུལ་བྱུང་བའི་མི་རྣམས་ལ་བསླབ་བྱ་བྱེད་རྒྱུའི་སྤྱོད་ཚུལ་འཛིན་དགོས་ (We) should behave so that we advise those who have made mistakes.

སྤྱོད་ཚུལ་བཟང་པོ་ (jö̈dzüü sa̲ŋbo) sm. སྤྱོད་བཟང་.

སྤྱོད་ཚུལ་བཟུང་ (jö̈dzüü su̲ŋ) p. of སྤྱོད་ཚུལ་འཛིན་.

སྤྱོད་བཟང་ (jö̈saŋ) good behavior/ manners, well-behaved, upright, moral.

སྤྱོད་བཟང་འདུན་ཆེའི་མི་སྣ་ (jö̈saŋ dü̲ncee mi̲na) people with lofty ideals.

སྤྱོད་ཡུན་ (jö̈yün) the functional life of a machine or piece of equipment.

སྤྱོད་ཡུལ་ (jö̈yüü) sphere of activity ༑མཐོང་བའི་སྤྱོད་ཡུལ་ Range of vision.

སྤྱོད་ཡོན་གཉིས་ལྡན་ (jö̈yön ñīidɛn) knowledgeable and of good character.

སྤྱོད་ཡོན་གཉིས་ལེགས་ (jö̈yön ñīileg) sm. སྤྱོད་ཡོན་གཉིས་ལྡན་.

སྤྱོད་ལམ་ (jö̈lam) sm. སྤྱོད་པ་.

སྤྱོད་ལུགས་ (jö̈luù) behavior and customs.

སྤྱོད་ཤེད་ (jö̈sheè) durable, long lasting.

སྤྱོད་ཤེས་གཟུགས་གསུམ་ (jö̈sheè su̲gsum) the three: character, knowledge and physical body.

སྤྱོད་ཤེས་ལུས་གསུམ་ (jö̈sheè lü̲üsum) sm. སྤྱོད་ཤེས་གཟུགས་གསུམ་.

སྤྱོད་གཤིས་ (jö̈sheè) custom, way of doing things.

སྤྱོད་བསམ་ (jö̈sem) behavior and thought.

སྤྱོད་བསམ་གཉིས་འགལ་ (jö̈sem ñīŋgɛɛ) difference/ contradiction between behavior and thought.

སྤྱོན་ (jōn) va. to come.

སྤྱོམ་: p. སྤྱོམས་; f. སྤྱོམ་; imp. སྤྱོམས་ (jōm) sm. ང་རྒྱལ་.

སྤྱོམས་ (jōm) p. and imp. of སྤྱོམ་.

སྤྱོས་ (jö̈) p. of སྤྱོ་.

སྤྲ་ (drā) ape; baboon.

སྤྲ་འཆལ་ (drānjɛɛ) stupid, ignorant, silly.

སྤྲ་ཏོག (drādɔɔ̀) the seed of artimisa/ wormwood.

སྤྲ་དོ་ (drādo) tinder and flintstone.

སྤྲ་དཔུང་རིང་ (drā būŋriŋ) gibbon.

སྤྲ་བ་ (drāwa) a plant from which the tinder that is used with flintstones is made.

སྤྲ་བའི་ཏོག་གུ་ (drāwɛ tōggu) the seed of the སྤྲ་ཏོག་པ་.

སྤྲ་བའི་མེ་དོག (drāwɛ me̲dog) sm. སྤྲ་བ་.

སྤྲ་མི་ (drāmi) ape man, prehistoric man, fossil man, early hominid.

སྤྲ་མིའི་འགྱུར་རྡོ་ (drāmii gyu̲rdo) fossilized bones of early hominids.

སྤྲ་མེ་ (drāme) moxabustion.

སྤྲ་མོ་ (drāmo) a female ape/ baboon.

སྤྲ་ཚིལ་ (drədzii) beeswax.

སྤྲ་ཚིལ་དཀར་པོ་ (drədzii gārbo) white beeswax.

སྤྲ་ཚིལ་སྒྲོན་མེ་ (drədzii drö̲nme) torch/ lamp made of beeswax.

སྤྲ་ཚུགས་ (drədzuù) moxabustion.

སྤྲ་གཡུང་ (drəyuŋ) anaphilis hancockii Maxim (used in Tibetan medicine).

སྤྲ་རིགས་ (drərig) primates.

སྤྲ་ལག (drālaà) lying, cheating, tricking.

སྤྲ་ལག་མཁས་པོ་ (drālaà kɛ̄ɛbo) a person who is deceitful/ duplicitous/ cunning/ conniving/ scheming.

སྤྲ་ལག་དོད་པོ་ (drālaà tö̲öbo) sm. སྤྲ་ལག་མཁས་པོ་.

སྤྲ་ལག་ཚ་པོ་ (drālaà tsābo) sm. སྤྲ་ལག་མཁས་པོ་.

སྤྲ་ལག་ཤོད་ (drālaà shö̈) va. to trick/ con/ deceive.

སྤྲ་ལི་སྤྲུ་ལི་ (drəli drūli) doing sth. in a dillydallying manner.

སྤྲག (drāà) va. to fry.

སྤྲག་ཆགས་པ་ (drāà cāgba) hardened/ crusted dirt.

སྤྲང་ (drāŋ) 1. va. to beg. 2. abbr. of སྤྲང་པོ་.

སྤྲང་འཁྱམས་ (drāŋgyam) wandering like a beggar; va.—རྒྱག.

སྤྲང་འཁྱམས་པ་ (drāŋgyāmba) 1. wandering beggers. 2. term used to scold an idler/ loafer.

སྤྲང་འཁྱམས་ཡུལ་ཕུད་ (drāŋgyam yü̲übüü) leaving one's home and wandering as a beggar.

སྤྲང་ཁྱི་ (drōŋgyi) 1. term used to scold a dog. 2. beggar's dog.

སྤྲང་འཁྱིངས་ (drāŋgyiŋ) shung. a pompous/ arrogant beggar.

སྤྲང་རྒན་ (drāŋgɛn) 1. an old beggar. 2. a

derogatory exclamation: you old beggar.
སྤྲང་རྒྱུག (drāŋgyuù) a beggar's stick/ staff.
སྤྲང་སྒྱེ་ (drāŋgye) bag carried by beggars.
སྤྲང་རྣགས་ཚ་པོ་ (drāŋdaà tsābo) greedy, avaricious, like a beggar in character.
སྤྲང་གནམ་ (dāŋnam) a derogatory swear word for the weather.
སྤྲང་པོ་ (dāŋbo) beggar.
སྤྲང་པོ་ཀེར་ལངས་ (drāŋbo gērlaŋ) a poor person with nothing [Lit. a beggar standing alone].
སྤྲང་པོ་གཅེར་ལངས་ (drāŋbo jērlaŋ) a poor person with absolutely nothing [Lit. a begger standing naked].
སྤྲང་པོ་སྤྲང་རྒྱང་ (drāŋbo drāŋgyaŋ) absolutely impoverished, an absolute beggar.
སྤྲང་དབྱུག (drāŋyuù) beggar's staff/ stick.
སྤྲང་ཚང་ (drāŋdzaŋ) beggar's home.
སྤྲང་བན་ (drāŋbɛn) begging monks (a Hinayana Buddhist practice.
སྤྲང་མོ་ (drāŋmo) abusive word used for women (similar to "bitch") {Lit. female beggar].
སྤྲང་ཤས་ཚ་པོ་ (drāŋshɛɛ̀ tsābo) sm. སྤྲང་རྣགས་ཚ་པོ་.
སྤྲད་ (drɛ̄ɛ̀) 1. va. to give. 2. p. of སྤྲོད་.
སྤྲད་མཆན་ (drɛ̄ɛ̀jɛn) the notations a person makes when keeping a record of expenses.
སྤྲད་ལད་ (drɛ̄ɛ̀lɛɛ̀) sycophancy, flattery; va.—ཡོད་ to flatter.
སྤྲད་ལད་ཚ་པོ་ (drɛ̄ɛ̀lɛɛ̀ tsābo) sycophant, flatterer.
སྤྲས་ (drɛ̄ɛ̀) va. to adorn, to decorate, to embellish, to dress up ¶ བོད་པའི་ཆས་དགོས་སྤྲས་ཏེ་ Dressing up in Tibetan clothes.
སྤྲས་ཁོག (drɛ̄ɛ̀gɔɔ̀) ring worn on the thumb.
སྤྲི་ (drī) 1. cream ¶ འོ་མའི་སྤྲི་ The cream of milk. 2. protein.
སྤྲི་དཀར་ (drīgar) protein.
སྤྲི་དཀར་གྱི་རྒྱུ་མང་བ་ (drīgargi gyu̲maŋwa) high protein.
སྤྲི་དཀར་གྱི་རིགས་ (drīgargi ri̲g) albumin.
སྤྲི་བཏོན་པའི་འོ་མ་ (drīdönbɛ wo̲ma) nonfat milk.
སྤྲི་མ་ (drīmə) sm. སྤྲི་.
སྤྲི་གསར་ (drīsar) the thick cream of a cow that has just given birth.
སྤྲིང་: p. སྤྲིངས་; f. སྤྲིང་; imp. སྤྲིངས་ (driŋ) va. to send/ give.
སྤྲིང་ཡིག (driŋyii) sm. སྤྲིངས་ཡིག.
སྤྲིངས་ (driŋ) p. and imp. of སྤྲིང་.
སྤྲིངས་ཡིག (driŋyii) letter, note, communique ¶ གཞིགས་མཁྱེན་སྤྲིངས་ཡིག A government communique regarding a dispute.
སྤྲིངས་ལན་ (driŋlɛn) answer, reply.

སྤྲིན་ (drīn) cloud; vi.—to be cloudy/ overcast.
སྤྲིན་གློང་ (drīnloŋ) in the clouds, amidst the clouds.
སྤྲིན་དཀར་ (drīngar) white clouds.
སྤྲིན་ཁང་ (drīngaŋ) nimbus, rain cloud.
སྤྲིན་འཁྲིགས་ (drīndrig) cloudy.
སྤྲིན་གུག (drīnguù) cirrus clouds.
སྤྲིན་གྱི་ཁ་དོག (drīngi kādɔɔ̀) the color of clouds.
སྤྲིན་ཆར་ (drīnjar) 1. abbr. clouds and rain. 2. light rain.
སྤྲིན་ཆུ་ (drīnju) light rain.
སྤྲིན་འཇའ་ (drīnja) colored clouds (due to the reflection of the sun).
སྤྲིན་གཏོར་ཉི་ཤོན་ (drīndor ñi̲dön) settling/ solving/ overcoming a bad situation [Lit. disperse the clouds and the sun appears].
སྤྲིན་མཐོང་ས་ (drīndoŋ) the visible sky between the clouds.
སྤྲིན་འཐིབ་ཉི་སྒྲིབ་ (drīndib ñi̲drib) darkness [Lit. sky covered with clouds, sun hidden).
སྤྲིན་འཐིབས་ནམ་མཁའ་ (drīndib na̲mka) overcast sky.
སྤྲིན་དག་པ་ (drīn ta̲gba) white clouds.
སྤྲིན་བདུན་ (drīndün) a type of brocade with a cloud design.
སྤྲིན་ནག (drīnnaà) black clouds.
སྤྲིན་ནག་རླུང་གཏོར་ (drīnnaà lūŋdɔɔ) destroying enemies/ foes quickly [Lit. the wind scattering the black clouds].
སྤྲིན་ནག་ལང་ལོང་ (drīnnaà la̲ŋloŋ) billowing black clouds.
སྤྲིན་པ་ (drīmbə) sm. སྤྲིན་.
སྤྲིན་པ་འཁོར་ (drīmbə kɔ̄ɔ̀) vi. to have clouds appear.
སྤྲིན་པ་འཁྲིགས་པ་ (drīmbə trīgbə) cloudy.
སྤྲིན་པ་སྒམ་པོ་ (drīmbə ga̲mbo) a rug with the bat and cloud design.
སྤྲིན་པ་ཐར་ཐོར་ (drīmbə tārdɔɔ) sm. སྤྲིན་ཕྲེང་ཧྲལ་པོ་.
སྤྲིན་དཔངས་མཐུག་པོ་ (drīnbaŋ tūgbu) cumulus clouds.
སྤྲིན་ཕུང་ (drīnbuŋ) a mass of clouds, overcast with clouds.
སྤྲིན་ཕྲེང་ཧྲལ་པོ་ (drīndreŋ hrɛ̄ɛ̄bo) scattered clouds.
སྤྲིན་བུ་མགོ་ཙམ་མེད་ལ་ཐོག་སྟ་རེ་ཙམ་འཕངས་པ་ (drīnci go̲dzam me̲ela tɔ̄ɔ̀ dəridzam pāŋba) sth. suddenly/ unexpectedly frightening [Lit. on a cloud as small as the head of a bird, a thunderbolt as big as an axe].
སྤྲིན་བྲལ་གཡའ་དག (drīndrɛɛ yādag) clear, cloudless (weather).
སྤྲིན་འབོར་ (drīnbɔr) the amount of clouds.

སྤྲིན་དམར་ (drīnmar) red clouds.
སྤྲིན་སྨུག (drīnmug) clouds and mist/ fog; vi.—འཐིབ་ to be cloudy and foggy/ misty.
སྤྲིན་ཚོགས་ (drīndzɔɔ̀) a group/ mass of clouds, cloudy.
སྤྲིན་ཚོམ་ (drīndzom) a group/mass of clouds, cloudy.
སྤྲིན་མཚོ་ (drīntso) a sea of clouds.
སྤྲིན་ཟམ་ (drīnsam) a wooden passageway/ small bridge between two houses.
སྤྲིན་བཟང་ (drīnsaŋ) clouds that have auspicious significance.
སྤྲིན་བཟང་དཀར་པོ་ (drīnsaŋ gārbo) white clouds that have auspicious significance.
སྤྲིན་རིམ་ (drīnrim) cloud layers.
སྤྲིན་རིས་ (drīnrii) cloud pattern/ design (on brocade, paintings, rugs, etc.).
སྤྲིན་རིས་མ་ (drīn ri̲imə) brocade/ paintings/ rugs that have cloud designs.
སྤྲིན་རུམ་ (drīnrum) within the clouds.
སྤྲིན་སྲབ་རླུང་འཇམ་ (drīndrəb lūŋjam) weather without many clouds or heavy winds, mild and sunny weather.
སྤྲིན་གསར་ (drīnsar) newly formed clouds.
སྤྲིན་གསེང་ (drīnseŋ) the space between the clouds.
སྤྲིན་གསེབ་ (drīnseb) sm. སྤྲིན་གསེང་.
སྤྲིས་མ་ (drīimə) the cream (that forms on the top after boiling milk has been cooled).
སྤྲུ་དཀར་ (rūgar) herzcleum candicans Wall ex. (used in Tibetan medicine).
སྤྲུ་སྐྱ་ (drūgya) sm. སྤྲུ་དཀར་.
སྤྲུ་ནག (drūnaà) notopterygium forbensii Boiss (used in Tibetan medicine).
སྤྲུ་བ་ (drūwa) sm. སྤྲུ་བ་.
སྤྲུ་མ་ (drūmə) a general term that encompasses: སྤྲུ་དཀར་, སྤྲུ་ནག, སྤྲུ་སེར་.
སྤྲུ་ཙ་ (drūdza) notopterygium (used in Tibetan medicine).
སྤྲུ་སེར་ (drūser) notoptterygium incisum (used in Tibetan medicine).
སྤྲུག: p. སྤྲུགས་; f. སྤྲུག; imp. སྤྲུགས་ (drūù) va. to shake, to stir, to agitate.
སྤྲུག་བརྡབས་གཏོང་ (drūgdəb) dusting/ brushing off; va.—གཏོང་.
སྤྲུག་སྤྲུག (drūgdruù) agitating, shaking, stirring; va.—གཏོང་.
སྤྲུག་གསིག (drūgsii) agitating, shaking, stirring; va.—བྱེད་.
སྤྲུགས་ (drūù) p. and imp. of སྤྲུག.
སྤྲུལ་ (drūū) vi. to change/ transform one's state

(miraculously) ༑ཁོ་བྱིའུ་ཞིག་ཏུ་སྤྲུལ་ནས་ He transformed himself into a small bird and.

སྤྲུལ་སྐུ་ (drü̃ügu) incarnate lama, rimpoche.

སྤྲུལ་བསྒྱུར་ (drü̃ü gyu̱r) va. to manifest/ transform oneself into various forms.

སྤྲུལ་པ་སྐྱེ་ (drü̃übə gyē) va. to transform/ manifest oneself into a different form.

སྤྲུལ་པ་འགྱེད་ (drü̃übə gye̱è) va. to transform/ manifest oneself into a different form.

སྤྲུལ་པ་སྡུད་ (drü̃übə dü̱ü) va. to return to one's original form after manifesting oneself as sth. else.

སྤྲུལ་པ་སྟོན་ (drü̃übə dö̃n) va. to manifest/ transform oneself into a different form.

སྤྲུལ་པའི་སྐུ་ (drü̃übɛ gū) sm. སྤྲུལ་སྐུ་.

སྤྲུལ་པའི་རྫུ་འཕྲུལ་ (drü̃übɛ dzu̱drüü) sm. སྤྲུལ་བསྒྱུར་.

སྤྲེ་ (drē) sm. སྤྲེའུ་.

སྤྲེ་ད་ (drēda) grain that has spoiled and turned black.

སྤྲེ་མོ་ (drēmo) female monkey.

སྤྲེ་མོང་ (drēmoŋ) weasel.

སྤྲེ་རྩེད་ (drēdzeè) sm. སྤྲེའུ་རྩེད་.

སྤྲེའུ་ (drēwu) monkey.

སྤྲེའུ་དཔལ་འབྱུངས་ཅན་ (drēwu te̱e̱gyaŋjɛn) prosimian primate.

སྤྲེའུ་རྩེད་ (drēwudzēè) 1. monkeys playing. 2. pranks, jokes, kidding around.

སྤྲེའུ་རྫུ་འཕྲུལ་ཅན་ (drēwu dzu̱drüüjɛn) miraculous (fictional) monkey.

སྤྲེའུ་ལྷོད་ཡིངས་ཅན་ (drēwulhö̃ö ye̱njɛn) sm. སྤྲེའུ་དཔལ་འབྱུངས་ཅན་.

སྤྲེའུས་མི་ལ་ལད་མོ་བྱེད་པ་ལྟར་ (drēwüü mi̱lə le̱ɛ̃mo ce̱èbadar) mindlessly imitating [Lit. like a monkey imitating a man].

སྤྲེལ་ (drēē) monkey.

སྤྲེལ་གཞུག་དབྱུག་ (drēēshuù yũù) to abandon/ discard sb. after swindling or tricking them [Lit. the monkey waves his tail].

སྤྲེལ་ལ་ངོམ་རྒྱུ་རྐྱབ་ (drēēla ŋo̱mgyu gūb) boasting about something trivial.

སྤྲེལ་ལད་ (drēēlɛɛ̀) flattery, sycophancy; va.—འཁྲབ་; —ཤོད་ to flatter, to be a sycophant.

སྤྲོ་: p. སྤྲོས་; f. སྤྲོ་; imp. སྤྲོས་ (drō) 1. va. to disperse, to scatter. 2. vi. to be glad/ happy/ joyful.

སྤྲོ་སྐ་ (drōgu) short-tempered, impatient.

སྤྲོ་སྐྱིད་ (drōgyiì) 1. happy, glad, merry. 2. va.—བྱེད་; —གཏོང་ to have fun, to have a good time, to make merry.

སྤྲོ་སྐྱིད་ཁང་ (drōgyiìgaŋ) 1. club, recreation center. 2. summer cottage.

སྤྲོ་སྐྱིད་ལྟ་སྐོར་ (drōgyiì dāgɔɔ) tourism, tourist.

སྤྲོ་སྐྱིད་སྤོ་ལོ་ (drōgyiì bōlo) carom. (the game).

སྤྲོ་ཁང་ (drōgaŋ) sm. སྤྲོ་སྐྱིད་ཁང་.

སྤྲོ་གླུ་ (drōlu) sm. སྐྱིད་གླུ་.

སྤྲོ་ཆུང་ (drōjuŋ) shung. a picnic party given by the tt. government to its officials.

སྤྲོ་འཆམ་ (drõnjam) 1. going for a stroll; va.—བྱེད་. 2. going for a tour/ tourism.

སྤྲོ་འཆམ་པ་ (drõnjamba) tourist.

སྤྲོ་འཆམ་གྱི་ཡུལ་ལྗོངས་ཁུལ་ (drõnjamgi yü̱üjoŋgüü) tourist site.

སྤྲོ་ཉམས་ (drõñam) sm. སྤྲོ་སྣང་.

སྤྲོ་ཉམས་ཅན་ (drõñamjɛn) sm. སྤྲོ་སྣང་ལྡན་པ་.

སྤྲོ་མཉེས་ (drõñeè) happy, glad, liking something.

སྤྲོ་སྟོན་ (drōdön) party, banquet.

སྤྲོ་ཐུང་ (drōduŋ) sm. སྤྲོ་ཐུང་ཐུང་.

སྤྲོ་ཐུང་ཐུང་ (drō tūŋduŋ) impatient, hot tempered.

སྤྲོ་འདྲི་ (drō dri̱) shung. va. to ask a question ༑ཞིང་ནམས་སྤྲོ་འདྲི་ཙམ་མེད་པར་སྤྱི་བསོས་བཙན་ཤེད་ཀྱིས་འཕྲོག་པ་ The fields were seized by the Chiso monastic manager without asking as much as a question.

སྤྲོ་སྣང་ (drõnaŋ) 1. joy, pleasure, happiness; vi.—བསྐྱེད་; —རྒྱས་ to be happy / glad. 2. optimism.

སྤྲོ་སྣང་སྟོང་པ་ (drõnaŋ dõŋba) happy/ glad for no good reason.

སྤྲོ་སྣང་ལྡན་པ་ (drõnaŋ de̱mba) happy, gay, joyful, cheerful.

སྤྲོ་སྣང་རིང་ལུགས་ (drõnaŋ ri̱ŋluù) optimism.

སྤྲོ་སྣང་རིང་ལུགས་པ་ (drõnaŋ ri̱ŋluùbə) optimist.

སྤྲོ་པོ་ (drōbo) 1. h. of ཞིམ་པོ་. 2. happy, having a good/ enjoyable time; va.—བྱེད་ to have a good time, to enjoy, to have fun ༑ངས་བལྟས་ན་ཁྱེད་རང་འདི་གར་ཕར་མཚམས་སྤྲོ་པོ་བྱས་ནས་བཞུགས་ I think you should stay here enjoying yourself for awhile.

སྤྲོ་སྤྲོ་ (drōdro) happy, joyful, delightful, pleasurable.

སྤྲོ་བ་ (drōwa) joy, happiness; va.—བརྡ་; —བསྐྱིངས་ to be happy/ joyous.

སྤྲོ་བ་དཀྲུག (drōwa drūù) va. to spoil a happy occasion.

སྤྲོ་བ་ཆེ་བ་ (drōwa cēwa) extremely happy.

སྤྲོ་བག་ཕེབས་པ་ (drōbaà pēèba) happy and tranquil/ carefree/ peaceful/ calm.

སྤྲོ་བའི་ཟློས་གར་ (drōwɛ dö̱ögar) comedy.

སྤྲོ་མོ་ (drōmo) happy, joyful.

སྤྲོ་རྩེད་ (drōdze) concert, show, performance.

སྤྲོ་རྩེད་ཁང་ (drōdzegaŋ) sm. སྤྲོ་སྐྱིད་ཁང་.

སྤྲོ་ཚོགས་ (drōdzɔ̀) party ༑གླིང་ཁའི་སྤྲོ་ཚོགས་ Garden party.

སྤྲོ་ཞག་མེད་པ་ (drōshaà me̱èba) unreliable, of bad character, undependable.

སྤྲོ་ཞི་ (drō shi̱) vi. to have one's anger subside.

སྤྲོ་བཞུགས་གནང་ (drōshuù nāŋ) va. to stay enjoying oneself (h.).

སྤྲོ་རིང་པོ་ (drō ri̱ŋbu) tolerant, not quick to anger.

སྤྲོ་ལངས་ (drō la̱ŋ) vi. to become angry.

སྤྲོ་ཤི་ (drō shī) sm. སྤྲོ་ཞི་.

སྤྲོ་ཤུགས་ (drōshuù) the power of happiness.

སྤྲོ་ས་ (drōsa) 1. happy place. 2. a happier place.

སྤྲོ་སིང་ངེ་བ་ (drō sĩŋŋewa) in a happy/ joyful state.

སྤྲོ་སིང་སིང་ (drō sĩŋsiŋ) sm. སྤྲོ་སིང་ངེ་བ་.

སྤྲོ་སུད་པ་ (drō sü̃übə) easily angered/ agitated/ annoyed, hot-tempered.

སྤྲོ་སེམས་ (drōsem) 1. joy, gladness, happiness. 2. enthusiasm ༑པར་ཁང་གི་བཟོ་པས་སྤྲོ་སེམས་ཆེ་ཤོས་དང་ཚད་གཞི་མཐོ་ཤོས་ཀྱིས་པར་རྒྱག་གི་ཡོད་པ་རེད་ The workers at the publishing house are printing with the greatest enthusiasm and the highest standards.

སྤྲོ་སེམས་འཁོལ་བ་ (drōsem kõ̃õwɛ) warm/ happy feeling, bubbling over with joy/ happiness ༑ཁོ་སྤྲོ་སེམས་འཁོལ་བའི་ངང་ནས་བསྟོད་ནང་བྱས་པ་རེད་ (They) warmly praised him. ༑སྤྲོ་སེམས་འཁོལ་བའི་ངང་ནས་དགའ་བསུ་ཞུས་པ་རེད་ (They) warmly welcomed him.

སྤྲོ་སེམས་ཆེན་པོ་ (drōsem cēmbo) great warmth/ joy/ happiness/ enthusiasm ༑སྤྲོ་སེམས་ཆེན་པོའི་ངང་ནས་བསྟོད་བསྔགས་བྱས་པ་རེད་ (They) praised (him) with great warmth.

སྤྲོ་སེམས་དང་ལྡན་པ་ (drōsemdaŋ de̱mba) with great warmth/ enthusiasm.

སྤྲོ་གསང་ (drōsaŋ) sm. སྤྲོ་གསེང་.

སྤྲོ་གསེང་ (drōseŋ) vacation, tour, pleasure trip; va.—གཏོང་ to go on vacation, to take a trip.

སྤྲོ་གསེང་གཏོང་མཁན་ (drōseŋ dõŋñɛn) vacationer.

སྤྲོ་གསེང་ལྟ་སྐོར་ (drōseŋ dāgɔɔ) vacation tour/ holiday.

སྤྲོ་གསེང་ལ་ཕེབས་ (drōseŋla pēè) va. to go on a vacation/ holiday.

སྤྲོག་མ་ (drɔ̃gma) small bamboo woven box.

སྤྲོད་: p. སྤྲད་; f. སྤྲད་; imp. སྤྲོད་ (drö̃ö) va. to give ༑ངས་ཁོ་ལ་དངུལ་སྤྲད་པ་ཡིན་ I gave him some money.

སྤྲོད་ཁོངས་དཀར་ཆག (drö̃ögoŋ gārjaà) shung. list of payments that have to be made.

སྤྲོད་ཁོངས་ཡིག་རིགས་ (dö̃ögoŋ yi̱irig) shung. the documents and files of an office that have to be handed over by a departing official to his successor.

སྤྲོད་ཁྲ་ (drö̃ödra) shung. an order to hand over

documents, etc.

སྤྲོད་བྲ་འགྲིགས་ (dröödra drig) shung. vi. to be able to pay/ give ༑སྤྲོད་ནོར་ནད་གོད་ཐོག་ལོ་ཕྱུགས་ལམ་དུ་མ་ལྷོངས་ཀྱང་གཞན་གཡར་གྱིས་སྤྲོད་བྲ་འགྲིགས་པ་ Many animals that should be handed over died from the plague and the crop yield also was not good, but they were able to pay the animals by borrowing from other places.

སྤྲོད་འགྱངས་ (dröögyaŋ) shung. delaying handing over sth. ༑སྤྲོད་འགྱངས་ཟླ་ ༣ སོང་བ་ The handing over was delayed for 3 months.

སྤྲོད་རྒྱ་ (dröögya) shung. an edict issued ordering that sth. be handed over.

སྤྲོད་དངུལ་ (dööŋüü) money to be handed over.

སྤྲོས་ཆས་ (drööjɛɛ̀) things to be handed over.

སྤྲོད་འཇལ་ (drönjɛɛ) repaying, returning; va.—བྱེད་ to repay, to return.

སྤྲོད་ཐེབས་ (drööděb) shung. sm. སྤྲོད་དམིགས་.

སྤྲོད་དུས་འདེད་སྐྱང་ (drööduü teèjaŋ) shung. going after a debtor when the loan is due ༑སྤྲོད་དུས་འདེད་སྐྱང་ནམ་བྱུང་སྐབས་མ་སྐྱེད་སྒྲིགས་གཙང་འབུལ་རྒྱུ་ When you come after me to collect when the loan is due, I will pay the principal with interest.

སྤྲོད་དེབ་ (drööteb) shung. book listing payments.

སྤྲོད་ནོར་ (dröönɔɔ) shung. animals that should be handed over ༑ཁྱོད་ཚོས་ཞོར་སྐྱོང་བྱས་རྗེས་སྤྲོད་ནོར་ནད་གོད་ཐོག་ལོ་ཕྱུགས་ལམ་དུ་མ་ལྷོངས་ཀྱང་གཞན་གཡར་གྱིས་སྤྲོད་བྲ་འགྲིགས་པ་ Many animals that should be handed over died from the plague and the crop yield was also not good, but still they were able to hand over the animals by borrowing from other places.

སྤྲོད་པ་ (drööba) supply ༑མཁོ་བ་དང་སྤྲོད་པ་ supply and demand.

སྤྲོད་དཔང་ (drööbaŋ) shung. the person who witnesses the handing over of goverment documents etc., when there is a change of officials heading an office.

སྤྲོད་དཔང་ལྷན་རྒྱས་ (drööbaŋ lhɛ̃ngyɛɛ̀) shung. the committee of persons who witness the handing over of goverment documents, etc., when there is a change of officials heading an office.

སྤྲོད་བུན་ (drööbün) debts, loans.

སྤྲོད་དམིགས་ (dröömig) shung. the means of paying back a debt ༑མི་སེར་དབུལ་པོངས་བུ་ལོན་སྤྲོད་དམིགས་མེད་རིགས་མང་པོ་ཞིག་ཡོད་པ་ There are many poor subjects who do not have any means of paying back their debts.

སྤྲོད་ཡུལ་ (drööyüü) the address where sth. should be sent (on a letter, package, etc.).

སྤྲོད་འཛིན་ (dröndzin) 1. a check. 2. a note authorizing money/ goods to be collected (given).

སྤྲོད་ལེན་ (dröölen) 1. giving and receiving; va.—བྱེད་ ༑རྒྱ་གར་ལ་བོད་དངུལ་སྤྲོད་ལེན་བྱེད་ཀྱི་མེད་ (They) don't use (give and receive) Tibetan money in India. 2. supply and demand.

སྤྲོད་ལྷག (dröölhaà) shung. items leftover after giving the amount that was required (in a loan, tax).

སྤྲོད་ལྷན་ (dröölhɛn) shung. abbr. of སྤྲོད་དཔང་ལྷན་རྒྱས་.

སྤྲོས་ (dröö) 1. p. and imp. of སྤྲོ་. 2. sm. རྒྱས་སྤྲོས་.

སྤྲོས་ཀུན་ (dröögün) 1. all the things in the world. 2. luxury items/ things.

སྤྲོས་བཅས་ (drööjɛɛ̀) grand, imposing, large-scale.

སྤྲོས་ནས་བྲལ་བ་ (drööne dröowa) sm. སྤྲོས་བྲལ་.

སྤྲོས་བྲལ་ (drööďrɛɛ) impossible ༑ཁྱེད་རང་ལ་ལས་ཀ་དེ་རག་རྒྱུ་སྤྲོས་བྲལ་རེད་ It is impossible for you to get that job.

སྤྲོས་མེད་ (dröömeè) 1. medicore, unimposing. 2. concise, direct, to the point.

སྤྲོས་གཤོམ་ (drööshom) grand, imposing, large-scale.

ཕ

ཕ་ (pā) 1. father, paternal ། ཕ་ཡི་རྒྱུད་པ་ Paternal lineage. 2. male ། ཕ་གླང་ Bull. 3. the letter ཕ་ (used in alphabetical ordering).
ཕ་ཀུང་ (pāguŋ) sm. ཕུ་ཀོང་.
ཕ་སྐྱེས་ (pāgyeè) night.
ཕ་སྐྱེས་བུ་ (pāgyeè pu) father's son.
ཕ་ཁ་ (pāga) sm. ཕ་ག.
ཕ་ཁག་བུ་དྲི་ (pāgaà pudri) shung. va. to blame a junior/ inferior for the senior or superior's mistake [Lit. blaming the act/ mistake of the father on the son].
ཕ་ཁག་གཞོན་དྲིས་ (pākaà shöndri) shung. sm. ཕ་ཁག་བུ་དྲི་.
ཕ་ཁུ་ (pāgu) father and uncle.
ཕ་ཁོལ་ (pāgöö) obedient to one's father.
ཕ་ག (pāga) (on) the other side of sth.
ཕ་གི་ (pāgi) that one over there ། ཁང་པ་ཕ་གི་ཁོའི་རེད་ That house (over there) is his.
ཕ་གིར་ (pāgee) there, over there ། འདི་ནས་ཕ་གིར་ From here to there.
ཕ་གུ་ (pāgu) fired brick.
ཕ་གླང་ (pālaŋ) bull.
ཕ་རྒན་ (pāgɛn) 1. an aged/ old father. 2. derogatory term used for monks who have lost their vow of celibacy.
ཕ་རྒྱུད་ (pāgyüü) paternal lineage; vi.—ཕྱིད་; —འཕྲིར་ to inherit one's father's characteristics.
ཕ་རྒྱུད་སྤུན་མཆེད་ (pāgyüü bünjeè) paternal relatives.
ཕ་རྒྱུད་ཕྱོགས་མཐུན་ (pāgyüü cōgdün) paternal relatives, father's side of the family.
ཕ་རྒྱུད་བུ་རྒྱུད་ (pāgyüü pugyüü) paternal descendants from father to son, etc.
ཕ་རྒྱུད་བུས་འཛིན་ (pāgyüü pündzin) inheriting one's father's traits/ occupation.
ཕ་རྒྱུད་ཕ་ཉེ་ (pāgyüü shāñe) paternal relatives/ kinsmen.
ཕ་ཞང་འཕྲབ་ (pāshaŋ trəb) va. to act mischievous/ naughty.
ཕ་གཅིག་མ་གཅིག (pājii məjii) full siblings, children of the same father and mother.
ཕ་གཅིག་མ་གཉིས་ (pājii mañii) half siblings, children having the same father but different mothers.
ཕ་གཅིག་མ་གཡར་ (pājii mayaa) sm. ཕ་གཅིག་མ་གཉིས་.
ཕ་ཆོས་བུ་ཆོས་ (pājöö pujöö) name of the two main texts of the Kadampa sect.
ཕ་ཇོ་ (pājo) father.
ཕ་རྗེས་བུ་ (pājeè pu) son continuing in the footsteps of his deceased father.
ཕ་རྗེས་བུ་རབས་ (pājeè purəb) many generations patrilineally (from father to son).
ཕ་རྗེས་བུས་འཛིན་ (pājeè püü dzin) va. to follow in the footsteps of one's father after he dies.
ཕ་རྗེས་བུས་ཟིན་ (pājeè püü sin) following in one's father's footsteps after he dies.
ཕ་གཉིས་པ་ (pāñi¡ibə) stepfather.
ཕ་རྟ་ (pāda) stallion.
ཕ་གདམ་བུར་འཇགས་ (pādam pu jaà) 1. the words of the father imprinted/ internalized on the son. 2. saying what others have said before.
ཕ་ཐར་ཕྱིན་ (pādar cīn) shung. va. to go to the other side.
ཕ་ཐོག་བུ་ཐོག (pādɔ̄ɔ pudɔɔ) from generation to generation.
ཕ་མཐའ་ (pāta) the other end or side ། ཆུ་ཕ་མཐར་ On the other side of the river.
ཕ་མཐའ་སྐྱོལ་བྱེད་ (pāta dröőjeè) ship, boat.
ཕ་མཐའ་མེད་པ་ (pāta meèba) limitless, infinite, endless.
ཕ་མཐའ་ཡས་པ་ (pāta yɛ̄ɛba) sm. ཕ་མཐའ་མེད་པ་.
ཕ་མཐར་སྐྲོད་ (pāta drőő) to repel, to oust.
ཕ་དམ་པ་ (pā tāmba) (the/ my) late father.
ཕ་འདྲ་ (pāndra) like that.
ཕ་འདྲ་སེ་ (pāndrase) in that manner/ way.
ཕ་བདུན་པ་ (pā dümba) Thursday.
ཕ་ནས་ཚུར་ (pānɛ tsūū) from there to here.
ཕ་ནོར་ (pānɔɔ) inheritance from the father.
ཕ་པོ་ (pābo) sm. ཕུ་པོ་.
ཕ་སྤད་ (pābɛ̄ɛ) sm. ཕ་བུ་.
ཕ་སྤུན་ (pābün) shung. father and father's relatives, paternal relatives.
ཕ་སྤུན་རྒྱུད་ཁྲུངས་ (pābün gyüüguŋ) sm. ཕ་སྤུན་.
ཕ་ཕག (pābaà) boar.
ཕ་ཕྱུག་རར་བ་ (pājuù rawa) cattle breeding farm.
ཕ་ཕྱུགས་ (pājuù) bull, male livestock.
ཕ་ཕྱོགས་ (pājɔ̄ɔ) 1. the other side. 2. paternal relatives.
ཕ་ཕྱོགས་ངོགས་ (pājɔ̄ɔ ŋɔ̄ɔ) the other side.
ཕ་བ་དགོ་དགོ་ (pāwa gogo) calvatia cynthiformis (used in Tibetan medicine).
ཕ་བུ་ (pəbu) father and son.
ཕ་བུ་གཉིས་ (pəbu ñīi) the two: father and son.
ཕ་བོང་ (pāboŋ) rock, boulder.
ཕ་བོང་ཁ་ (pāboŋga) a retreat said to be built by Songtsen Gampo.
ཕ་བོང་གོལ་གོལ་ (pāboŋ göögöö) sm. ཕ་བ་དགོ་དགོ་.
ཕ་བོང་ལ་བསྐར་ནས་ རི་བོང་ལ་འགྲམ་ལྕགས (pāboŋla gārnɛ riboŋla dramjaà) beating about the bush, not getting to the point.
ཕ་དབང་ (pāwaŋ) patriatriachy.
ཕ་འབོད་མ་འབོད་ (pābuoö mabőö) crying out in despair [Lit. calling father, calling mother].
ཕ་འབབ་ (pābəb) gift, present.
ཕ་སྦྱོར་ (pājɔɔ) insemination.
ཕ་སྦྱོར་མངལ་ཆགས་ (pājɔɔ ŋɛɛjaà) insemination.
ཕ་སྦྱོར་ས་ཚིགས་ (pājɔɔ sədzii) breeding or insemination station.
ཕ་མ་ (pāma) 1. mother and father, parents. 2. wisdom and method. 3. male and female ། དགེ་སློང་ཕ་མ་ Male and female gelongs.
ཕ་མ་གཉིས་འཛོམས་ (pāma ñīndzom) having both parents alive.
ཕ་མ་གཉེན་བཤེས་ (pāma ñēnsheè) parents, relatives and friends.
ཕ་མ་སྤུན་ཀྱག (pāma būngyaà) parents and relatives.
ཕ་མ་སྤུན་མཆེད་ (pāma būnceè) sm. ཕ་མ་སྤུན་ཀྱག.
ཕ་མ་བུ་རྒྱུད་ (pāma pugyüü) parents and their children.
ཕ་མ་བུ་ཕྲུག (pāma pūdruù) parents and their children.
ཕ་མ་མེས་ཕྱི་ཚང་བ་ (pāma meèji tsāŋwa) people who have their parents and grandparents alive.
ཕ་མ་ཡ་བྲལ་ (pāma yadrɛɛ) children with only one parent ། ཕ་མ་ཡ་བྲལ་གྱི་ཕྲུ་གུ་ Children who have only one parent.
ཕ་མའི་དོད་པོ་ (pāmɛ töőbo) stepparents.
ཕ་མའི་འཚོ་རྟེན་ལ་བརྟེན་པའི་ཕྲུག་གུར་རོགས་དངུལ་ (pāmɛ tsōdenla dēnbɛ trūguu rəgnüü) Aid to Dependent Children (ADC, in U.S.A.).
ཕ་མིར་ས་མཐོ་ (pāmir sāto) the Pamir Mountains.
ཕ་མིང་ (pāmiŋ) 1. father's name. 2. father and older brothers.
ཕ་མེས་ (pāmeè) ancestors (paternal).
ཕ་མེས་ཀྱི་ཡིག་ཚང་ (pāmeègi yigdzaŋ) historical documents of prior generations.
ཕ་མེས་ཀྱི་ལག་རྒྱུན་ (pāmeègi laggyün) handed down from old, hereditary.
ཕ་མེས་གང་གསུང་ཆོས་དང་མཐུབ་མོ་གར་བསྟན་ཤར་ (pāmeè kaŋsuŋ cőő daŋ dzubmo kardɛn shār) taking whatever one's superiors say as correct [Lit. whatever the parents say is dharma and

wherever the finger points is east].

ཕ་མེས་རྒྱལ་ཁབ་ (pāmeè gyɛɛgəb) fatherland, motherland.

ཕ་མེས་པུ་རྒྱུད་སྨན་པ་ (pāmeè pugyüù mɛ̄mba) a Tibetan doctor from a lineage of doctors.

ཕ་མེས་ཡང་མེས་ (pāmeè yaŋmeè) forefathers, ancestors.

ཕ་སྨད་ (pāmeè) father and daughter.

ཕ་རྫ་མ་རྒྱུད་ (pādza magyüù) sm. ཕ་ས་མ་ཁུངས་.

ཕ་ཙན་དན་གྱི་སྡོང་པོ་ལ་ བུ་ཆུ་ཤུང་གི་ཨོམ་བུ་ (pādza dɛngi doŋbola pujushuŋgi ombu) a son who is very different in character/ behavior from his father [Lit. father like a sandalwood tree, son like a hollow tamarisk water container].

ཕ་ཚ་བུ་རྒྱུད་ (pādza pugyüù) sth. passed on patrilineally from father to son.

ཕ་ཚང་ (pādzaŋ) family of the father of the bride or bridegroom.

ཕ་ཚབ་ (pādzəb) stepfather.

ཕ་ཚབ་ཀྱི་བུ་དང་སོ་ཚབ་ཀྱི་སོ་ (pā dzəbgi pu daŋ sō tsəbgi sō) replacing/ substituting for sb. [Lit. the son replaces the father and (false) teeth replace the teeth].

ཕ་ཚད་ (pādzɛɛ̀) a little ways away, not far away.

ཕ་ཚན་ (pādzɛn) relatives on the father's side.

ཕ་ཚེ་ (pādze) gunny-bag.

ཕ་ཚེ་བུ་རབ་ (pādze purəb) generations.

ཕ་ཚོ་ (pātso) those (over there).

ཕ་འཛོམས་མ་འཛོམས་ (pādzom madzom) having both parents alive.

ཕ་ཝང་ (pāwaŋ) flying squirrel.

ཕ་ཝང་སྒོ་དི་ (pāwaŋ godi) sm. ཕ་བ་དགོ་དགོ་.

ཕ་ཝང་ལོང་བུ་ (pāwaŋ loŋbu) pyritum, pyrite (used in Tibetan medicine).

ཕ་ཞང་འཁྲབ་ (pāshaŋ trə̄b) va. to act mischievous/ naughty.

ཕ་ཞལ་ (pā shɛɛ) father's face.

ཕ་གཞིས་ (pəshiì) an estate that is transmitted patrilineally; va.—ཟིན་ to hold a patrilineal estate.

ཕ་ཟད་ (pāsɛɛ̀) 1. end, edge. 2. sm. ཕར་ཙམ་.

ཕ་བཟང་པོ་ (pā saŋbo) wise and benevolent father.

ཕ་ཡ་ (pāyaa) sm. ཕ་ཡར་.

ཕ་ཡག་རྩ་བ་ (pāyaà dzāwa) lancea tibetica Hook (used in Tibetan medicine).

ཕ་ཡར་ (pāyaa) stepfather.

ཕ་ཡིན་པ་དངོས་གསལ་ བུ་ཡིན་པ་ར་འཕྲོད་ (pāyinbə ŋȫòsɛɛ puyimbə rādröö) indisputable fact [Lit. it is evident he is the father; it is proved he is the son].

ཕ་ཡུལ་ (pəyüü) one's native place/ region/ country, one's homeland/ fatherland. ¶ ཕ་ཡུལ་དྲན་པའི་སྡུག་བསྔལ་ Homesick for one's country.

ཕ་ཡུལ་གཅིག་པ་ (pəyüü jīgbə) from the same place/ region/ country.

ཕ་གཡར་ (pāyaa) sm. ཕ་ཡར་.

ཕ་གཡར་མ་གཡར་ (pāyaa mayaa) stepfather and stepmother.

ཕ་རན་སི་ (pārɛnsi) France.

ཕ་རན་སི་གསར་སྤེལ་ལས་ཁང་ (pārɛnsi sērbel lɛ̀ɛgaŋ) Agence France Presse.

ཕ་རབས་ (pārəb) father's generation.

ཕ་རབས་ནས་མི་རབས་བར་ (pārəbnɛ mirəbbar) from generation to generation.

ཕ་རབས་བུ་རབས་ (pārəb purəb) generations.

ཕ་རས་རྒྱག་ (pārɛɛ̀ gyaà) va. to shout/ yell.

ཕ་རས་ཚ་པོ་ (pārɛɛ̀ tsābo) sb. who talks loudly.

ཕ་རི་ (pəri) 1. mountain/ hill on the opposite side. 2. on the other side of the river ¶ ཆུ་ཕ་རི་ On the other side of the river.

ཕ་རི་ལྕི་བ་མེད་པ་ ཚུ་རི་སླེ་པོ་མེད་པ་ (pəri jīwə meèbə tsüri lēbo meèbə) not having what is needed to do sth., incomplete [Lit. the hill on the other side has no dung and the hill on this side has no carrying basket].

ཕ་རི་ཕུ་རི་གཏོང་ (pəri pūri dōŋ) 1. va. to shake/ tug on a person (usu. by children when they want sth.). 2. va. to rub dice before throwing them.

ཕ་རིའི་སྤང་རྒྱན་ (pəri pāŋgyɛn) sth. that is unattainable or very difficult to obtain [Lit. the meadow on the hill on the other side].

ཕ་རུབ་བུ་རུབ་ (pārub purub) shung. father and son working together ¶ གྲོང་འགྲོས་རྒྱ་འཁྱོན་གང་མཚམས་ལ་རྟེན་ཕ་རུབ་བུ་རུབ་བྱེད་དགོས་པ་ Since the family is quite large the father and the son must work together.

ཕ་རུས་མ་ཁུངས་ (pārüù məguŋ) ancestry, parentage.

ཕ་རོལ་ (pārȫö) the other side, abroad, that beyond ¶ རྒྱ་མཚོའི་ཕ་རོལ་ན་ On the other side of the ocean. ¶ ཕ་རོལ་གྱི་དམག་མི་ཚོགས་ Troops from the other side (enemy troops).

ཕ་རོལ་གྱི་དོན་ (pārȫögi tōn) the other's affair/ issue.

ཕ་རོལ་གྱི་སྡེ་ (pārȫögi de) the other's area/ group/ force.

ཕ་རོལ་གྱི་སེམས་ (pārȫögi sēm) the other's mind.

ཕ་རོལ་འཇིག་རྟེན་ (pārȫö jigden) the next/ future life.

ཕ་རོལ་ཏུ་ (pārȫödu) on/ to the other side.

ཕ་རོལ་ཏུ་ཕྱིན་པ་ (pārȫödu cīmbə) paramita, perfection.

ཕ་རོལ་ཏུ་ཕྱིན་པ་དྲུག་ (pāroldu cīmbə truù) the six perfections: 1. giving. 2. morality. 3. patience. 4. effort/ vigor. 5. concentration. 6. wisdom.

ཕ་རོལ་གཏོང་ (pārȫö dōŋ) 1. va. to send/ drive to the other side. 2. va. to kill.

ཕ་རོལ་ན་ (pārȫöna) sm. ཕ་རོལ་ཏུ་.

ཕ་རོལ་གནོན་ (pārȫö nȭn) va. to subdue one's rivals/ opponents.

ཕ་རོལ་པ་ (pārȫöba) the others, outsiders, those from the other side ¶ ཁོ་ལ་ཕ་རོལ་པས་ཀྱང་དགའ་གུས་བྱེད་ཀྱི་ཡོད་པ་རེད་ Even the other side likes and respects him.

ཕ་རོལ་པོ་ (pārȫöbo) the other side/ party.

ཕ་རོལ་མི་མངོན་ (pārȫö miŋön) 1. endless, limitless. 2. poet. ocean.

ཕ་རོལ་ཚུར་རོལ་ (pārȫö tsūūrȫö) this side and the other side, ours and theirs, both sides.

ཕ་རོལ་གཤེགས་ (pārȫö shēg) 1. vi. to die. 2. va. to go to the other side.

ཕ་ལ་ (pāla) nutmeg.

ཕ་ལ་ཁག་པ་བུའི་མདུན་ཐབས་ བུ་ལ་ཁག་པ་ཕའི་རོ་འདོན་ (pāla kāgba püü dündəb püula kāgba pɛ̄ɛ ro dön) the son's marriage is most difficult for the father, the father's funeral is most difficult for the son].

ཕ་ལགས་ (pālaà) h. of ཕ་.

ཕ་ལམ་ (pālam) diamond.

ཕ་ལེ་བུ་དང་མ་ལེ་བུ་མོར་འཇོག་པ་ (pāle phu daŋ male pomo jɔgba) blaming other people [Lit. blaming the son for the father's fault and blaming the daughter for the mother's fault].

ཕ་ལོ་བུ་ལོ་ (pālo pulo) father and son taking one bride, bigenerational polyandry.

ཕ་ལོགས་ (pālɔɔ̀) sm. ཕ་ཕྱོགས་.

ཕ་ཤི་སི་ (pāshisi) eng. fascist, fascism.

ཕ་ཤི་སི་རིང་ལུགས་ (pāshisi riŋluù) fascism.

ཕ་ཤིད་ (pāshiì) meritorious work/ deeds for the deceased father.

ཕ་ཤུལ་རྒྱུ་རྫས་ (pəshüü gyundzin) inheritance (from father).

ཕ་ཤུལ་བུ་འཇགས་ (pəshüü pujaà) shung. patrilineal inheritance staying with the son.

ཕ་ཤུལ་བུས་འཛིན་ (pəshüü püü dzin) a son following in the footsteps of his late father with regard to inheritance ¶ ཕ་ཤུལ་བུས་འཛིན་གྱི་མི་ཚང་འདི་ This household which has continued over time from father to son.

ཕ་ས་མ་ཁུངས་ (pāsa maguŋ) family background.

ཕ་ལྷ་ (pālha) name of an aristocratic family.

ཕག (pāà) 1. pig, hog. 2. brick. 3. secret, hidden.

ཕག་ཀ་ (pāgga) a type of belt worn by Tibetan women.

ཕག་ཀོ་ (pāggɔɔ) pigskin.

ཕག་ཀྲིན་ (pə̄gdrin) tib.eng. canned pork.

ཕག་ཀྲུམ་ (pāgdrum) pork.

ཕག་སྐྱག་ (pāggyaà) pig's excrement.

ཕག་ཁྱུ་ (pə̄ggyu) a herd of pigs.

ཕག་ཁྲག་ (pāgdraà) pig's blood.

ཕག་གི་འགོ་ནད་ (pāggi gonɛɛ̀) pig cholera.

ཕག་གྲུ་ (pə̄gdru) abbr. of ཕག་མོ་གྲུ་པ་.

ཕག་གྲུ་བཀའ་བརྒྱུད་ (pə̄gdru gārgyüù) the Phagmodru subsect of the Kagyu sect.

ཕག་གྲུ་སྡེ་སྲིད་ (pə̄gdru desiì) a figure in Tibetan history who in the 14th century assumed power in Tibet.

ཕག་མགོ་ (pāŋgo) pig's head.

ཕག་རྒོད་ (pāgöö̀) wild boar.

ཕག་ལྕེ་ (pāgje) 1. tongue of a pig (used in Tibetan medicine). 2. va.—བྱེད་. to instigate/ incite.

ཕག་མཆུ་ (pə̄gju) pig's lips.

ཕག་མཆེ་ (pāgje) boar's tusks.

ཕག་ཉན་ (pāgñɛn) listening in secret, bugging; va.—རྒྱག; —བྱེད་ to listen in secret, to bug.

ཕག་ཏུ་ (pāgdu) secretly ། ཁོས་མཚམས་མོ་ཕག་ཏུ་ལན་སྐྱེལ་དུ་ཡོང་བ་རེད She came secretly at night to give the message.

ཕག་ལྟ་ (pāgda) looking secretly; va.—བྱེད་.

ཕག་ལྟོ་ (pāgdo) 1. feed for pigs, pig's food. 2. bad quality food.

ཕག་མདོ་ (pāŋdo) brush; va.—རྒྱག to brush.

ཕག་ནོར་ (pāgnɔɔ) hidden wealth.

ཕག་པ་ (pāgba) pig, hog.

ཕག་པ་སྡོམ་གསོས (pāgba domsöö) keeping pigs in a small shelter and feeding them heavily to fatten them prior to slaughtering.

ཕག་པ་གསོ་ (pāgba sō) va. to raise/ rear pigs.

ཕག་པའི་གསོ་ཐང་ (pāgbɛ sōdaŋ) pig farm.

ཕག་པའི་བྱ་གཅོད་ (pāgbɛ cajöö) castrating pigs.

ཕག་པས་གྲོ་མ་སྔོགས་པ་ལྟར་ (pāgbɛ troma ŋɔ̄ɔ̀badar) strewing things all over [Lit. like a pig digging up sweet potatoes].

ཕག་སྤུ་ (pə̄gbu) pig's hair.

ཕག་ཕྲུག (pə̄gdru) piglets.

ཕག་སྦྲུན་ (pə̄gdrün) pig's droppings.

ཕག་སྦྲུན་ནུས་བསྲེགས་ (pə̄gdrün nüǜseg) the ash of burned pig's droppings (used in Tibetan medicine).

ཕག་མོ་ (pāàmo) sow.

ཕག་མོ་གྲུ་པ་ (pāàmo drubə) 1. a subsect of the Kagyu sect. 2. the rulers of Tibet after the fall of the Sakyapa in 1354.

ཕག་ཚང་ (pāgdzaŋ) pig pen, pigsty.

ཕག་ཚིལ་ (pāgdzii) pork fat, lard.

ཕག་ཚོང་ (pāgdzoŋ) 1. smuggling, dealing in the black market. 2. trading/ dealing in pigs (business).

ཕག་རྫི་ (pə̄gdzi) swineherd.

ཕག་ཟན་ (pāgsɛn) 1. sm. ཕྱུག་ཟས་. 2. sm. ཕག་ལྟོ་.

ཕག་ཟེ་ (pāgse) 1. the standing hair on the shoulder and neck of pigs. 2. a brush; va.—རྒྱག to brush.

ཕག་ཟེར་རྒྱག (pāgser gyaà) va. to talk in secret, to talk behind sb.'s back.

ཕག་གཟན་ (pāgsɛn) sm. ཕག་ལྟོ་.

ཕག་ཟླ་ (pāgda) the 10th month of the Tibetan calendar.

ཕག་ར་ (pāgra) pig pen, pigsty.

ཕག་རི་ (pə̄ri) town in southern Tibet.

ཕག་རི་བ་ (pāriwa) person from Phari.

ཕག་རིལ་ (pāgrii) sm. ཕག་སྦྲུན་.

ཕག་རིལ་ཐལ་བ་ (pāgrii tɛ̄ɛla) sm. ཕག་སྦྲུན་ནུས་བསྲེགས་.

ཕག་ལབ་རྒྱག (pəgləb gyaà) va. to talking behind sb.'s back ། བསམ་འཆར་ཡོད་ན་མདུན་ལ་ཤོད་པ་ལས་ཕག་ལབ་རྒྱག་རྒྱུ་མི་ཉན་ If you have any criticism, you should say it openly rather than talk behind someone's back.

ཕག་ལ་སྣ་དགོས་མི་ལ་བློ་དགོས (pāgla nāgɔɔ̀ milə lōgöö) a saying used to convey that people should think and have ideas [Lit. pigs need snouts, people need ideas].

ཕག་ལོ་ (pāglo) year of the pig.

ཕག་ཤ་ (pāgsha) pork.

ཕག་སུག (pāgsug) pig's hoof.

ཕག་སྲེག (pāgseg) roast pig; va.—བཟོ་ to roast a whole pig.

ཕག་གསུག (pāgsug) bribery, bribe.

ཕག་གསེབ་ (pāgseb) stud pig.

ཕག་གསོ་ར་བ་ (pāgso rawa) pig farm.

ཕང་ (pāŋ) 1. va. to accumulate, to save up, to pile up. 2. a spindle.

ཕང་ཁེབས་ (pāŋgeb) apron worn by Tibetan women over their dress.

ཕང་ཁྲི་ (pə̄ŋdri) spindle.

ཕང་འགྲོ་ (pāŋdro) Tibetan lute.

ཕང་དོ་ (pāŋdo) brush (for hair); va.—རྒྱག to brush.

ཕང་པ་ (pāŋba) sm. ཕང་ཁ་.

ཕང་པོ་ (pāŋbo) shung. sm. མང་པོ་.

ཕང་ཕུང་ (pə̄ŋbuŋ) pile, heap; va.—བྱེད་ to pile/ heap up.

ཕང་ཕུང་ཅན་ (pə̄ŋbuŋjɛn) piled/ heaped up; va.—བྱེད་ to pile/ heap up.

ཕང་བུ་ (pāŋbu) sm. ཕང་.

ཕང་མ་ (pāŋma) thorny elacagnus (used in Tibetan medicine).

ཕང་ཞལ་ (pāŋshɛɛ) squares or lumps of dried cheese strung together.

ཕང་ཞལ་གཅིག (pāŋshɛɛ jig) one string of dried cheese strung together.

ཕང་ལོ་ (pāŋlo) sm. འཕང་ལོ་.

ཕང་ཤིང་ (pāŋshiŋ) sm. འཕང་ཤིང་.

ཕང་སེམས་ (pāŋsem) sm. ཕངས་སེམས་.

ཕངས་ (pāŋ) vi. to regret, to be sorry.

ཕངས་སྣང་ (pāŋnaŋ) a feeling of regret/ sorrow.

ཕངས་པ་མེད་པ་ (pāŋba meèba) sm. ཕངས་མེད་.

ཕངས་པོ་ (pāŋbo) regretful, unfortunate, shameful ། ཁོ་ཆུ་ཚོད་བརླགས་པ་འདི་ཕངས་པོ་རེད་ It is regretful that he lost his watch. ། ཁྱེད་རང་ཚོགས་འདུར་ཕེབས་མི་ཐུབ་པ་འདི་ཕངས་པོ་རེད་ It is a shame that you could not come to the meeting.

ཕངས་པོ་བྱེད་ (pāŋbo ceè) va. to regret.

ཕངས་མེད་ (pāŋmeè) without regret/ sorrow; va.—བྱེད་ to do sth. without regret/ care/ sorrow ། ཁོས་ཕྲུ་གུའི་སློབ་སྦྱོང་གི་དོན་ལ་འགྲོ་སོང་ཕངས་མེད་བཏང་བ་རེད་ He generously (without regrets) spent money for (his) children's education.

ཕངས་སེམས་ (pāŋsem) 1. regret, sorrow, repentance; vi.—སྐྱེ་; —བྱེད་ to feel regret, to feel repentance, to feel sorry. 2. stingy, greedy, avaricious.

ཕངས་སེམས་ཅན་ (pāŋsemjɛn) 1. regretful, sorrowful. 2. stingy, greedy.

ཕངས་སེམས་མེད་པ་ (pāŋsem meèba) sm. ཕངས་མེད་.

ཕད་ (pɛ̄ɛ̀) sm. ཕད་གོག.

ཕད་ཁུག (pɛ̄ɛ̀guù) a small gunny-bag.

ཕད་ཁོག (pɛ̄ɛ̀gɔɔ̀) sm. ཕད་གོག.

ཕད་གོག (pɛ̄ɛ̀gɔɔ̀) large bag/ sack.

ཕད་གང་ (pɛ̄ɛ̀gaŋ) full sack/ pack/ bag.

ཕད་སྣོད་ (pɛ̄ɛ̀nöö̀) sm. ཕད་གོག.

ཕད་བུ་ (pɛ̄ɛ̀bu) small bag.

ཕད་ཙེ་ (pɛ̄ɛ̀dze) large bag (usu. made of wool or yak hair).

ཕད་ཚེ་ (pɛ̄ɛ̀dze) sm. ཕད་ཙེ་.

ཕད་ཟོམ་ (pɛ̄ɛ̀som) a type of bucket.

ཕད་རས་ (pɛ̄ɛ̀rɛɛ̀) shouting, yelling; va.—རྒྱག.

ཕད་ལ་ཕུག (pɛ̄ɛ̀ ləbu) kohlrabi.

ཕད་ཤོག (pɛ̄ɛ̀shɔɔ̀) ch.tib. a platoon (directly under a ཡིང་).

ཕན་ (pēn) 1. sm. ཕན་ཆད་. 2. abbr. of ཕན་པོ་.

ཕན་སྐྱེས་ (pēngyeè) sm. ཕན་ཐོགས་.

ཕན་སྐྱོབ་ (pēngyob) helping/ benefiting and saving.

ཕན་བསྐྱེད་ (pēngyeè) sm. ཕན་ཐོགས་.

ཕན་ཁ་ (pɛ̄nga) sm. ཕན་པ་.

ཕན་ཁ་སྤྲོད་ (pɛ̄nga drȫö) sm. ཕན་པོ་དུང་.

ཕན་ཁེ་ (pɛ̄nge) benefit, reward.

ཕན་ཁྱད་ (pɛ̄ngyɛɛ̀) benefit, advantage, difference ༑ འདི་འདྲ་བྱས་ན་ཕན་ཁྱད་ག་རེ་ཡོད་པ་རེད་ If (one) does it this way, what is the advantage? ༑ ངར་ཕན་ཁྱད་ཆེན་པོ་འདུག (It) makes a lot of difference to me.

ཕན་གྲོགས་ (pɛ̄ndrɔ̄ɔ̀) 1. helpful friends. 2. help, benefit.

ཕན་གྲོགས་རོགས་རམ་ (pɛ̄ndrɔɔ̀ rɔ̄ɔ̀ram) help, benefit.

ཕན་མགྱོགས་སྨན་མཆོག (pɛ̄ngyɔ̄ɔ̀ mɛ̄ncɔɔ̀) a fast acting medicine.

ཕན་འགོ་ (pɛ̄ngo) the head/ top of a brocade/ silk tapestry that is used to cover pillars.

ཕན་ངེས་ (pɛ̄nŋeè) sm. ཕན་ཐོགས་ཅན་.

ཕན་ཅན་ (pɛ̄njɛn) sm. ཕན་ཐོགས་ཅན་.

ཕན་ཆ་ (pɛ̄nja) sm. ཕན་ཐོགས་.

ཕན་ཆད་ (pɛ̄njɛɛ̀) 1. up to, until ༑ དེ་རིང་ཕན་ཆད་ Up to today. ༑ ད་ཕན་ཆད་ཁོས་བོད་ལ་བསྡད་པ་རེད་ Until now he lived in Tibet. 2. from the far side of sth. onwards, beyond ༑ ཆུ་དེ་ཕན་ཆད་ From the far side of that river onwards. ༑ ཤིང་དོང་དེ་ཕན་ཆད་ཁོ་ཚོའི་ས་ཆ་རེད་ Beyond that tree the land is theirs.

ཕན་ཆར་ (pɛ̄njar) shung. helping, benefiting ༑ ཤེལ་ཆོས་པས་མི་སེར་ཐོག་ཕན་ཆར་དགོས་རིགས་བྱེད་དགོས་པ་རེད་ The Shelchö monastery should help the people in all ways.

ཕན་ཆུང་ (pɛ̄njuŋ) small benefit/ advantage.

ཕན་ཆུང་དྲིན་ཆུང་ (pɛ̄njuŋ dri̲njuŋ) if sth. has only small benefit it will bring only small gratitude.

ཕན་ཆེ་གནོད་ཆུང་ (pɛ̄nje nȫöjuŋ) great benefit and small harm.

ཕན་ཚོད་ (pɛ̄njȫö) sm. ཕན་ཆད་.

ཕན་འཆར་ (pɛ̄njar) a useful plan; va.—བྱེད་.

ཕན་ཉུང་གནོད་མང་ (pɛ̄nñuŋ nȫömaŋ) few benefits/ advantages and much harm.

ཕན་གཉེར་ཁྲུའུ་ (pɛ̄nñer trū) tib.ch. welfare office.

ཕན་གཉེར་གནོད་གཡོལ་ (pɛ̄nñer nȫöyöö) keeping the benefits and avoiding harm.

ཕན་བཏགས་ (pɛ̄ndaà) sm. ཕན་འདོགས་.

ཕན་ཐབས་ (pɛ̄ndəb) useful/ beneficial methods, ways to benefit.

ཕན་ཐབས་ལས་དོན་ (pɛ̄ntəb lɛ̀ɛ̀dön) working to find beneficial methods ༑ མི་སེར་གྱི་བདེ་བཙན་ཕན་ཐབས་ལས་དོན་སྒྲུབ་ཐུབ་པའི་རེ་བ་ The hope of being able to find methods beneficial for the welfare of the people.

ཕན་ཐོག (pɛ̄ndɔɔ̀) sm. ཕན་ཐོགས་.

ཕན་ཐོགས་ (pɛ̄ndɔɔ̀) 1. use, help, benefit ༑ ས་ཆ་དེ་ཚོར་ཤོག་དངུལ་གྱི་ཕན་ཐོགས་མིན་འདུག In those places there is no use for paper money. 2. vi. to be of help, to be of use ༑ ཡུལ་དེ་ར་རྒྱ་སྐད་ཀྱི་ཕན་ཐོགས་ཀྱི་མི་འདུག In that country Chinese language is of no use.

ཕན་ཐོགས་ཅན་ (pɛ̄ndɔɔ̀jɛn) useful, beneficial, helpful.

ཕན་ཐོགས་པོ་ (pɛ̄n tɔ̄gbo) useful.

ཕན་ཐོགས་མེད་པ་ (pɛ̄ntɔɔ̀ me̲èba) useless, of no benefit.

ཕན་དོན་ (pɛ̄ndön) beneficial, useful.

ཕན་གདགས་ (pɛ̄n da̲g) shung. va. to assist/ help ༑ རང་ལུགས་གྲུབ་མཐའི་ཕྱག་ལེན་ཇི་ཡོད་མི་ཉམས་དར་རྒྱས་འབྱུང་བའི་ཕན་གདགས་གང་འགྲོ་དགོས་རྒྱུ་ (You) must assist in seeing that the traditions of one's sect do not decline and are spread.

ཕན་བདེ་ (pɛ̄nde) well-being, common good, welfare ༑ འགྲོ་བ་མི་རིགས་ཀྱི་ཕན་བདེར་ For the well-being of all mankind.

ཕན་བདེ་པ་ (pɛ̄ndeba) a type of village worker in the QMP Nature Preserve.

ཕན་བདེ་ཟུ་ཤག (pɛ̄nde ca̲shaà) fringe benefit.

ཕན་བདེའི་འབྱུང་གནས་ (pɛ̄ndee ju̲ŋnɛɛ̀) shung. source of well-being ༑ ཕན་བདེའི་འབྱུང་གནས་ལུགས་གཉིས་གོང་མ་ཁྲིམས་བདག་རིན་པོ་ཆེ་ The source of the well-being of all. and the holder of both the spiritual and temporal power.

ཕན་འདོགས་ (pɛ̄n dɔ̄ɔ̀) va. to be useful/ helpful ༑ ཁོ་ཁག་པོ་ཡིན་དུས་ཁོ་ཚོས་ཕན་བཏགས་པ་རེད་ When he had problems they helped him.

ཕན་འདྲོང་ (pɛ̄ndroŋ) sm. ཕན་ཐོགས.

ཕན་ནི་ཕུན་ནི་ (pɛ̄nni pūnni) 1. dangling jewelry/ ornaments. 2. old/ ragged clothing, etc.

ཕན་ནུས་ (pɛ̄nnüü) efficacy, effectiveness, positive effect/ result ༑ སྨན་གྱི་ཕན་ནུས་ The effect of medicine.

ཕན་ནུས་ཐོན་ (pɛ̄nnüü tȫn) vi. to have an effect, to be beneficial.

ཕན་ནུས་ལྡན་པ་ (pɛ̄nnüü dɛ̲mba) effective, efficacious, beneficial.

ཕན་གནོད་ (pɛ̄nnöö) effects [Lit. benefit and harm].

ཕན་གནོད་རྒྱབ་འགལ་ (pɛ̄nnöö gyə̲mgɛɛ) one man's meat being another man's poison.

ཕན་པ་ (pɛ̄mba) advantage, benefit, use ༑ སྨན་འདི་ག་རེ་ལ་ཕན་པ་ཡོད་པ་རེད་ What is the benefit of this medicine?

ཕན་པ་ཆེན་པོ་ (pɛ̄mba cēmbo) great benefit/ advantage/ use.

ཕན་པའི་བཀྲོག་དགས་ (pɛ̄mbɛ dɔ̄gdaà) masquerading as sb. who can be of help.

ཕན་པོ་ (pɛ̄mbo) effective, beneficial, good for.

ཕན་པོ་དུང་ (pɛ̄mbo du̲ŋ) sm. ཕན་པོ་བྱུང་.

ཕན་པོ་བྱུང་ (pɛ̄mbo cu̲ŋ) phrase used to convey that sb. got what he deserved or that it serves sb. right.

ཕན་ཕུན་ (pɛ̄mbün) sm. ཕན་ནི་ཕུན་ནི་.

ཕན་ཕུན་དུ་འགྱུར་ (pɛ̄mbündu gyu̲r) vi. to be wasted/ spoiled/ ruined.

ཕན་ཕྱོགས་ (pɛ̄njɔɔ̀) positive/ beneficial side.

ཕན་འབོད་ (pɛ̄mböö) (idiom) serves you right.

ཕན་བྱ་ (pɛ̄nja) 1. useful/ helpful work ༑ ངས་ཁྱེད་ལ་ཕན་བྱ་གང་ཡང་འགྲུབ་ཐུབ་མ་སོང་ I have not been able to help you at all. 2. useful birds.

ཕན་འབུ་ (pɛ̄mbu) useful/ beneficial insects.

ཕན་འབྲས་ (pɛ̄ndrɛɛ̀) gain, profit, benefit, useful result.

ཕན་མ་ཐོགས་ (pɛ̄n ma̲tɔg) useless.

ཕན་མི་ཐོགས་ (pɛ̄n mi̲dɔg) sm. ཕན་མ་ཐོགས་.

ཕན་མེད་ (pɛ̄nmeè) sm. ཕན་མ་ཐོགས་.

ཕན་མེད་གནོད་སྐྱེན་ (pɛ̄nmeè nȫögyen) harmful, injurious.

ཕན་མེད་ཕན་སྒྱུར་ (pɛ̄nmeè pɛ̄ngyur) va. to change sth. that is useless into sth. that is useful/ valuable.

ཕན་མེད་གནོད་འགྱུར་ (pɛ̄nmeè nȫögyur) harming instead of helping/ benefiting.

ཕན་ཚུན་ (pɛ̄ndzün) each other, one another, here and there, back and forth, reciprocal, mutual ༑ ཁོ་ཚོ་ཕན་ཚུན་ཡི་གེ་གཏོང་སྐབས་ When they write back and forth to each other. ༑ ས་གནས་ཕན་ཚུན་ནས་འགྲོར་བའི་མི་ People who have come from here and there. ༑ གཙང་པོའི་ཕན་ཚུན་ན་ On either side of the river. ༑ ཕན་ཚུན་དགོངས་པ་དང་ས་ To forgive one another.

ཕན་ཚུན་གྱི་འབྲེལ་བ་ (pɛ̄ndzüngi dre̲ewa) mutual/ reciprocal relationship.

ཕན་ཚུན་འགེབས་བསྡུར་ (pɛ̄ndzün ge̲bdur) comparing quality (back and forth).

ཕན་ཚུན་འགྱུར་ལྡོག (pɛ̄ndzün gyu̲ndɔɔ̀) mutual transformation/ change.

ཕན་ཚུན་འགྲན་བསྡུར་ (pɛ̄ndzün drɛ̲ndur) competing back and forth.

ཕན་ཚུན་རྒྱབ་འགལ་ (pɛ̄ndzün gyə̲mgɛɛ) contradicting each other; va.—བྱེད་.

ཕན་ཚུན་གཅིག་ཕན་གཅིག་གྲོགས་ (pɛ̄ndzün ji̲gpɛn ji̲gdrɔɔ̀) sm. ཕན་ཚུན་རོགས་རམ་.

ཕན་ཚུན་གཅེས་སྐྱོང་ (pɛ̄ndzün jēègyoŋ) taking care of each other, mutual/ reciprocal care; va.—བྱེད་.

ཕན་ཚུན་གཅེས་འཛིན་ (pɛ̄ndzün jēndzin) loving/

cherishing each other; va.— བྱེད་.

ཕན་ཚུན་ཆགས་ས་རྟེན་ས་ (pēndzün cāgsa dēnsa) depending on each other.

ཕན་ཚུན་འཆམ་མཐུན་ (pēndzün cāmdün) getting along with each other.

ཕན་ཚུན་འཛུག (pēndzün ju̲ù) va. to exchange/ barter.

ཕན་ཚུན་རྫེས་སྙེག (pēndzün je̲èñeg) competing to go forward.

ཕན་ཚུན་བརྗེ་བའི་རིན་ཐང་ (pēndzün je̲wɛ ri̲ndaŋ) rate of exchange (financial).

ཕན་ཚུན་གཉིས་ཕན་ (pēndzün ñībɛn) mutual benefit/ advantage.

ཕན་ཚུན་གཉིས་མོས་ (pēndzün ñīimöö̀) mutually agreed on, agreeable to both sides.

ཕན་ཚུན་རྟེན་རེས་ (pēndzün dēnreè) depending on each other, mutual dependence.

ཕན་ཚུན་ལྟ་ཞིབ་ (pēndzün dəshib) mutual control/ supervision/ oversight.

ཕན་ཚུན་མཐུན་པ་ (pēndzün tũmbə) sm. ཕན་ཚུན་ལེགས་འབྲེལ་.

ཕན་ཚུན་ལྟོས་པ་ (pēndzün dõ̀ba) relative, comparative.

ཕན་ཚུན་དགའ་སྣང་ (pēndzün ta̲gnaŋ) mutual respect.

ཕན་ཚུན་དུ་འགྱུར་ (pēndzündu gyu̲r) 1. vi. to transform/ change back and forth. 2. metamorphosis.

ཕན་ཚུན་བསྡུར་ (pēndzün du̲r) va. to balance/ weigh/ compare back and forth.

ཕན་ཚུན་ནང་འགལ་ (pēndzün na̲ŋgɛɛ) mutually contradictory.

ཕན་ཚུན་བསྣོར་ (pēndzün nɔ̄r) va. to intermingle.

ཕན་ཚུན་སྤྲོད་ (pēndzün drõ̀) va. to exchange back and forth.

ཕན་ཚུན་བར་ (pēndzünwar) between one another.

ཕན་ཚུན་འབྲེལ་མཐུད་ (pēndzün dre̲edüù) sm. ཕན་ཚུན་ཟུང་འབྲེལ་.

ཕན་ཚུན་འབྲེལ་བ་ (pēndzün dre̲ewa) vi. to be connected/ joined.

ཕན་ཚུན་མི་གནོད་པའི་ཆིངས་ཡིག (pēndzün mi̲nöö̀bɛ ci̲ŋyig) mutual nonaggression pact.

ཕན་ཚུན་མཛའ་བརྩེ་ (pēndzün dza̲dze) mutual friendship/ love.

ཕན་ཚུན་གཞོགས་འདེགས་ (pēndzün shɔ̲ŋdeg) helping/ aiding/ assisting one another; va.—བྱེད་.

ཕན་ཚུན་ཟུང་འབྲེལ་ (pēndzün su̲ŋdree) mutual coordination/ relations/ connection.

ཕན་ཚུན་བཟོད་སྒོམ་ (pēndzün sö̲ö̀gom) mutually patient/ tolerant; va.—བྱེད་.

ཕན་ཚུན་ཡ་བཟུང་ (pēndzün ya̲suŋ) hostile against one another; va.— བྱེད་.

ཕན་ཚུན་ཡོད་མེད་བརྗེ་རེས་ (pēndzün yö̲ömeè je̲reè) mutual exchange of goods, products, etc. according to each other's needs.

ཕན་ཚུན་ར་སྤྲོད་ (pēndzün ra̲dröö̀) eyewitness/ firsthand evidence.

ཕན་ཚུན་རོགས་སྐྱོར་ (pēndzün rɔ̲̀ɔgyɔɔ) reciprocal aid/ help/ support; va.—བྱེད་.

ཕན་ཚུན་རོགས་རམ་ (pēndzün rɔ̲̀ɔram) sm. ཕན་ཚུན་རོགས་སྐྱོར་.

ཕན་ཚུན་ལེགས་འབྲེལ་ (pēndzün le̲ndrel) mutual friendship/ harmony.

ཕན་ཚུན་བློ་འགེལ་ (pēndzün lõ̲ŋgee) mutual belief/ trust/ confidence (in each other); va.—བྱེད་.

ཕན་ཚུན་སློག་མེད་པ་ (pēndzün lɔ̃ɔmeèba) sm. ཕ་སློག་ཚུར་སློག་མེད་པ་.

ཕན་ཚུན་སེམས་ཁུར་ (pēndzün sēmgur) mutual consideration/ concern.

ཕན་ཚུན་བསམ་ཤེས་ (pēndzün sāmsheè) mutual understanding/ knowledge.

ཕན་ཟས་ (pēnsɛɛ̀) nutritious/ beneficial food.

ཕན་ཟི་ལིང་ (pēnsiliŋ) paraffin.

ཕན་ཡོད་ (pēnyöö̀) sm. ཕན་ཐོགས་.

ཕན་ཡོན་ (pēnyön) sm. ཕན་ཐོགས་.

ཕན་ལབ་ (pēnləb) great benefit/ gain/ reward.

ཕན་སེམས་ (pēnsem) good intentions/ thoughts, helpful thoughts; va.—འཆང་ to have good intentions, to have thoughts of helping/ benefiting others.

ཕན་སྲུང་ (pēnsuŋ) sm. ཉེན་སྲུང་.

ཕན་སླེབས་ (pēnleb) sm. ཕན་ཐོགས་.

ཕབ་ (pəb) 1. p. of འབེབས་. 2. sm. ཕབས་.

ཕབ་རྒྱ (pəbgya) sm. ཕབ་རྒྱབ་.

ཕབ་རྒྱབ་ (pəbgyəb) affixing a seal; va.—བྱེད་ ¶ བཀའ་དམ་ཕབ་རྒྱབ་བྱེད་དུས་ When affixing the Kashag's seal.

ཕབ་བསྒྱུར་ (pəbgyur) transcribing, translating, changing, converting; va.—བྱེད་; —ཞུ་ to translate, to transcribe, to change, to convert ¶ ཁོང་གི་གསུང་བཤད་དེ་སྒྲ་འཛིན་འཁོར་ལོ་ནས་ཕབ་བསྒྱུར་ཞུས་འདུག (They) have transcribed the speech from the tape recording. ¶ བོད་ཡིག་ནས་དབྱིན་ཡིག་དུ་ཕབ་སྒྱུར་བྱས་པ་རེད་ (They) translated from Tibetan into English.

ཕབ་ཆ་ (pəbja) discounting, reducing the price; va.—གཏོང་ to discount.

ཕབ་ཏ་ (pəbda) sm. ཕབ་, 2.

ཕབ་ཕོབ་ (pəbbob) abbr. of ཕབ་བེ་ཕོབ་བེ.

ཕབ་བེ་ཕོབ་བེ་ (pəbbe pōbbe) bulky (for clothes).

ཕབ་ཙི་ (pəbdzi) fermenting agent, yeast.

ཕབ་ཙེ་ (pəbdze) ch. handkerchief.

ཕབ་ནས་རྩིས་ (pəbnɛ dzī) va. to convert/ calculate (usu. money).

ཕབ་རྩི་ (pəbdzi) sm. ཕབ་རྩིས་.

ཕབ་རྩིས་ (pəbdzii̇) conversion/ converting (usu. money), calculating (in math).

ཕབས་ (pəb) 1. yeast, starter for yogurt/ fermenting agent for ཆང་. 2. sm. ཕབ་, 1.

ཕབས་བསྒྱུར་ (pəbgyur) sm. ཕབ་བསྒྱུར་.

ཕབས་ཏ་ (pəbda) fermenting agent, yeast.

ཕབས་ཙི་ (pəbdzi) sm. ཕབ་རྫས.

ཕབ་རྫས་ (pəbdzɛɛ̀) sm. ཕབ་.

ཕབས་བཤུས་ (pəbshüù) sm. ཕབ་བསྒྱུར་.

ཕམ་ (pām) 1. a defeat, a loss; va.—འཁུར་; —འཁེལ་ to be/ get defeated, to get/ sustain a loss. 2. p. of འཕམ་.

ཕམ་ཁ་ (pāmga) sm. ཕམ་ཉེས་.

ཕམ་ཁ་འཁུར་ (pāmga kūr) 1. vi. to get/ sustain a loss, to be/ get defeated. 2. vi. to tolerate or accept a defeat/ loss.

ཕམ་འཁུར་ (pāmgur) a defeat, a loss.

ཕམ་འཁུར་རིང་ལུགས་ (pāmgur ri̲ŋluù) defeatism.

ཕམ་འཁུར་རིང་ལུགས་པ་ (pāmgur ri̲ŋluùbə) a defeatist.

ཕམ་འཁེལ་ (pām kēē) 1. sm. ཕམ་འཁུར་. 2. ཕམ་ཁ་འཁུར་.

ཕམ་འཁྱེར་ (pām kyēr) sm. ཕམ་འཁེལ་.

ཕམ་གྱོད་ (pāmgüù) sm. ཕམ་ཉེས་.

ཕམ་རྒྱལ་ (pāmgyɛɛ) loss and gain, defeat and victory; va.—གཏོང་ to put things at stake, to make a situation where one either wins or loses ¶ ཕམ་རྒྱལ་མཐའ་གསལ་གྱི་འཐབ་མོ་ A decisive fight. ¶ ཕམ་རྒྱལ་ཆེན་པོ་གཏོང་བའི་སྐུན་རྩེ་ High stake gambling (where one can win or lose).

ཕམ་རྗེས་སླར་ལོག (pāmjɛɛ̀ lārdɔɔ̀) a comeback/ recovery (after a defeat/ loss); va.—བྱེད་ to stage a comeback, to make recovery.

ཕམ་ཉེས་ (pāmñeè) a defeat; vi.—ཡོང་; —འགྱུར་ to be/ get defeated; va.—གཏོང་; —བཟོས་ to defeat/ vanquish.

ཕམ་ཉེས་འཁེལ་ (pāmñeè kēē) 1. vi. to get/ sustain a loss, to be/ get defeated. 2. vi. to concede or accept a defeat/ loss.

ཕམ་ཉེས་སུ་གཏོང་ (pāmñeèsu dõŋ) va. to defeat, to vanquish.

ཕམ་སྟེར་ (pām dēr) va. to cause sb. to sustain a loss (usu. to dupe/ deceive sb. into paying much more than what some item is actually worth).

ཕམ་ཐོར་ (pāmdɔɔ) sm. ཕམ་འཐོར་.

ཕམ་འཐོར་ (pāmdɔɔ) defeated and dispersed/

scattered.

ཕམ་པ་ (pāmba) sm. ཕམ་ཉེས་.

ཕམ་པ་བྱེད་ (pāmba cḛè) 1. sm. ཕམ་ཉེས་སུ་གཏོང་. 2. sm. ཕམ་ཉེས་འཁྱིལ་.

ཕམ་པ་ཁས་ལེན་ (pāmba kɛ̄ɛ̀len) admitting/ conceding defeat.

ཕམ་པ་བཞི་ (pāmba shi̱) the four root transgressions of an ordained monk: 1. killing. 2. stealing. 3. indulging in sexual acts. 4. lying about one's religious attainments.

ཕམ་པ་བཟོ་ (pāmba sö̱ö) va. to cause to lose or be defeated, to overturn/ topple.

ཕམ་པར་བྱེད་ (pāmbar cḛè) va. to defeat, to vanquish.

ཕམ་པར་རྒྱག (pāmbar gya̱à) sm. ཕམ་པར་བྱེད་.

ཕམ་པོ་ (pāmbo) sad.

ཕམ་བྱོལ་ (pāmjöö) withdrawal as a result of defeat; va.—བྱེད་.

ཕམ་བྲོས་ (pāmdröö) running away/ fleeing after a defeat ། ཕམ་བྲོས་དགྲ་བོ་ The defeated enemy who fled.

ཕམ་དམག (pāmmaà) 1. a defeated army/ troops. 2. a war that was lost.

ཕམ་ཆབས་ཆེ་བ་ (pāmdzəb cēwa) a great loss/ failure/ defeat.

ཕམ་ཚོང་ (pāmdzoŋ) selling at a loss, dumping goods at a loss; va.—རྒྱག; vi.—ཤོར་ to unintentionally sell at a loss.

ཕམ་འཚོང་ (pāmdzoŋ) sm. ཕམ་ཚོང་.

ཕམ་ཞིག (pāmshiì) losing and getting destroyed; vi.—འགྲོ་ to lose and get destroyed.

ཕམ་བཟོ་སྟོན་ (pāmso dö̱n) va. to pretend to lose.

ཕའི་ (pɛ̄) 1. of the father, paternal ། ཕའི་སྤུན་ Father's relatives. 2. ch. military platoon.

ཕའི་ཆིའུ་བོ་ལོ་ (pēciu bōlo) ch.tib. volleyball.

ཕའི་སྡེ་ (pēde) a community of monks.

ཕའི་ཕ་ (pɛ̄ pā) paternal grandfather.

ཕའི་དབང་ཆ་ (pɛ̄ wāŋja) paternal rights.

ཕའི་མ་ (pɛ̄ ma̱) paternal grandmother.

ཕའི་ (pɛ̄) ch. platoon.

ཕའི་ཀྲང་ (pɛ̄ drāŋ) ch. platoon leader.

ཕའི་ཆིའུ་ (pɛ̄ cīwu) volleyball.

ཕའི་ཆིའུ་པོ་ལོ་ (pēciwu bōlo) ch.tib. volleyball.

ཕར་ (pāā) 1. thither, away, over there ། ཁྱེད་རང་ཕར་ཐེབས་ནས་ After you went over there. ། ཕར་རྒྱུགས་ Go away! 2. (— + vb. + vb. + ཚུར་) this way and that, hither and thither ། ཕར་འགྲོ་ཚུར་འགྲོ་ Going hither and thither.

ཕར་ཀྱོག་ཚུར་ཀྱོག (pāāgyɔ̀ɔ tsūūgyɔ̀ɔ) in a zigzag/ curvy manner; va.—ལ་ཕྱིན་ to go in a zigzag manner.

ཕར་དཀྲུག་ཚུར་དཀྲུག (pāādruù tsūūdruù) creating chaos/ a mess/ dissension; va.—བྱེད་.

ཕར་སྐྱེལ་ (pāā kyēē) va. to take back.

ཕར་སྐྱོད་ཚུར་འཁོར་ (pāāgyöö tsūūkɔ̄ɔ) going out/ away and then returning.

ཕར་ཁ་ (pāāga) sm. ཕར་རོལ་.

ཕར་ཁག་ཚུར་དཀྲིས་ (pāāgaà tsūūdrii) blaming each other (back and forth); va.—བྱེད་ ། ཁོ་གཉིས་ཀྱིས་ཕར་ཁག་ཚུར་དཀྲིས་བྱས་ཙང་ལས་འགན་ཡག་པོ་བསྒྲུབ་མིན་འདུག Because they blamed each other, they were unable to perform their tasks well.

ཕར་འཁོར་ཚུར་འཁོར་ (pāāgɔ̀ɔ tsūūgɔ̀ɔ) going around and coming back to the same place (being lost).

ཕར་འཁོར་ཚུར་ལོག (pāāgɔ̀ɔ tsūūlɔ̀ɔ) turning one way and then turning back.

ཕར་འཁྱུད་ཚུར་འཁྱུད་ (pāāgyüü tsūūgyüü) hugging/ clinging to each other.

ཕར་འཁྱོག་ཚུར་འཁྱོག (pāāgyɔ̀ɔ tsūūgyɔ̀ɔ) sth. that goes in a zigzag/ curvy way.

ཕར་འཁྱོག་ཚུར་གུག (pāāgyɔ̀ɔ tsūūguù) sth. that goes in a zigzag/ curvy way.

ཕར་གབ་ཚུར་གབ་ (pāāgəb tsūūgəb) hiding here and there.

ཕར་དགྲ་ཚུར་འཐབ་ (pāādra tsūūdəb) fighting/ battling back and forth, mutual enmity and fighting; va.—བྱེད་.

ཕར་དགྲ་ཚུར་གཤེད་ (pāādra tsūūsheè) sm. ཕར་དགྲ་ཚུར་འཐབ་.

ཕར་བགྲོད་ཀྱི་དུས་སྐབས་ (pāādröögi tü̱ügəb) transition period.

ཕར་མགྲོན་ཚུར་འབོད་ (pāādrön tsūūböö) mutually inviting as guests, going as a guest and inviting as a guest back and forth; va.—བྱེད་.

ཕར་འགྱངས་ (pāā gya̱ŋ) postponing, putting off, delaying; va.—བྱེད་; —གཏོང་ to postpone, to put off, to delay; vi.—ཐེབས་ to get delayed/ postponed ། ལས་ཀ་འགོ་འཛུགས་རྒྱུ་རྗེས་ཟླའི་བར་ཕར་འགྱངས་བྱས་པ་རེད་ (They) postponed the start of work until next month.

ཕར་འགྲེ་ཚུར་འགྲེ་ (pāādre tsūūdre) 1. rolling over (usu. animals); va.—བྱེད་. 2. using analogies back and forth; va.—བྱེད་.

ཕར་འགྲོ་ཚུར་འགྲོ་ (pāādro tsūūdro) 1. coming and going, going here and there, going back forth; va.—བྱེད་ ། ཁོ་ཨ་རི་དང་ཡོ་རོབ་བར་ཕར་འགྲོ་ཚུར་འགྲོའི་སྐབས་ When he was going back forth between America and Europe. 2. reciprocally alternating/ exchanging visits.

ཕར་འགྲོ་ཚུར་འཆམ་ (pāādro tsūūjam) sm. ཕར་འགྲོ་ཚུར་འགྲོ་.

ཕར་འགྲོ་ཚུར་འོང་ (pāādro tsūūoŋ) sm. ཕར་འགྲོ་ཚུར་འགྲོ་.

ཕར་རྒོལ་ (pāāgöö) attacking, assaulting, going on the offense; va.—བྱེད་.

ཕར་རྒོལ་གནམ་གྲུ་ (pāāgöö nəmdru) attack aircraft, fighter plane.

ཕར་རྒོལ་དམག་འཐབ་ (pāāgöö məgdəb) offensive warfare.

ཕར་རྒོལ་རང་སྲུང་ (pāāgöö ra̱ŋsuŋ) attacking/ going on the offensive and defending oneself.

ཕར་རྒོལ་སྲིད་ཇུས་ (pāāgöö sīījüü) the policy of going on the offensive, offensive strategy.

ཕར་རྒྱུག་ཚུར་རྒྱུག (pāāgyuù tsūūgyuù) running back and forth, doing various/ miscellaneous things; va.—བྱེད་.

ཕར་རྒྱུགས་ (pāā gyu̱ù) sm. ཕར་རྒྱུགས་ཤིག.

ཕར་རྒྱུགས་ཤིག (pāā gyu̱ùsh) slang. get out! go away! ། ཕྲུ་གུ་ཚོ་ཕར་རྒྱུགས་ཤིག Children, go away!

ཕར་སྒྲོག་ཚུར་སྒྲོག (pāādrɔ̀ɔ tsūūdrɔ̀ɔ) sewing, stitching.

ཕར་ངོ་ཚུར་བལྟས་ (pāāŋo tsūūdɛɛ̀) staring at each other.

ཕར་ངོ་ཚུར་སྲུང་ (pāāŋo tsūūsuŋ) refraining from pointing out each other's faults, mutually allowing each other to keep face; va.—བྱེད་.

ཕར་ངོགས་ (pāāŋɔ̀ɔ) sm. ཕར་ཁ་.

ཕར་ངོས་ (pāāŋöö) the other side.

ཕར་ཅེར་ཚུར་ཅེར་ (pāājee tsūūjee) sm. ཕར་ཆེར་ཚུར་ཆེར.

ཕར་གཅོད་ (pāā jöö) va. to cross a river ། འབྲི་ཆུ་ཕར་བཅད་ནས་ Having crossed the Upper Yangtse River.

ཕར་ཆག (pārjaà) fluctuation (rising and falling); (— + verbs of motion) vi. to fluctuate.

ཕར་ཆམ་ཚུར་ཆམ་ (pāājam ysūūjam) sm. ཕར་འཆམ་ཚུར་འཆམ་.

ཕར་ཆིང་ (pārjiŋ) sm. ཕར་ཆིན་.

ཕར་ཆིན་ (pārjin) embroidery; va.—རྒྱག to embroider.

ཕར་ཆིན་མེ་ཏོག (pərjin me̱dɔ̀ɔ) an embroidered flower.

ཕར་ཆེར་ཚུར་ཆེར་ (pāācer tsūūcer) looking in an alert manner.

ཕར་མཆོངས་ཚུར་མཆོངས་ (pāācoŋ tsūūcoŋ) jumping hither and thither, jumping back and forth.

ཕར་འཆམ་ཚུར་འཆམ་ (pāācam tsūūcam) strolling back and forth.

ཕར་མཉེད་འཕུར་མཉེད་ (pāāñeè pūrñeè) sm. མཉེད་

འཕུར་.

ཕར་ལྟ་ཚུར་ལྟ་ (pāāda tsūūda) looking around, looking back and forth, looking everywhere.

ཕར་བསྟོད་ཚུར་བསྟོད་ (pāādöö tsūūdöö) praising each other (back and forth).

ཕར་ལྡོག (pāā dɔ̄ɔ) va. to go back, to return.

ཕར་ཐལ་ཚུར་ཐལ་ (pāātɛɛ tsūūtɛɛ) neither paying out too much or having too much coming in (usu. used in accounting).

ཕར་འཐབ་ཚུར་འཐབ་ (pāādəb tsūūdəb) fighting back and forth, fighting with one another; va.—བྱེད་.

ཕར་འཐམས་ཚུར་འཐམས་ (pāādam tsūūdam) hugging each other.

ཕར་འཐེན་ཚུར་འཐེན་ (pāāden tsūūden) pulling back and forth; va.—བྱེད་.

ཕར་འདེག་ཚུར་འདྲེན་ (pāādeg tsūūdren) serving ཆང་ to each other.

ཕར་དྲིལ་ཚུར་དྲིལ་ (pārdrii tsūūdrii) turning one's head back and forth from side to side.

ཕར་འདྲུད་ཚུར་འཐེན་ (pārdrüü tsūūdrüü) pulling and dragging back and forth.

ཕར་འདྲུད་ཚུར་འདྲུད་ (pārdrüü tsūūdrüü) dragging back and forth.

ཕར་སྡེབ་ཚུར་དཀྲུག (pādeb tsūūdrug) sowing discord all over.

ཕར་ནང་ (pārnaŋ) that side (over there).

ཕར་སྣུན་ཚུར་འཐེན་ (pāānün tsūūden) stabbing/ thrusting/ striking and withdrawing or pulling back (spear or sword).

ཕར་སྣུན་ཚུར་འཛུགས་ (pāānün tsūūdzuù) stabbing each other (in a fight).

ཕར་སྤྲད་ཚུར་ལེན་ (pāādrɛɛ̀ tsūūlen) giving and taking, crediting and debiting; va.—བྱེད་.

ཕར་སྤྲོད་ (pāā dröö) va. to return/ give back.

ཕར་སྤྲོད་ཚུར་ལེན་ (pāādrɛɛ̀ tsūūlen) giving and taking, crediting and debiting; va.—བྱེད་.

ཕར་ཕར་ (pārbār) farther and farther along, longer and longer along.

ཕར་ཕུད་ (pāā pǖü) 1. va. to expel. 2. va. to cast/ take off (clothes). 3. except for ¶ཁོ་ཕར་ཕུད་ མི་གཞན་དག་གིས་ངོ་རྒོལ་བྱས་པ་རེད་ With the exception of him, the other people opposed it.

ཕར་ཕྱིན་ (pārjin) 1. abbr. of ཕ་རོལ་ཏུ་ཕྱིན་པ་. 2. sm. ཕར་ཆེན་.

ཕར་ཕྱོགས་ (pāājɔ̀ɔ) sm. ཕ་རོལ་.

ཕར་ཕྱོགས་ཚུར་ཕྱོགས་ (pāājɔ̀ɔ tsūūjɔ̀ɔ) 1. that side and this side. 2. unstable, unsteady.

ཕར་འཕུར་ཚུར་འཕུར་ (pāābur tsūūbur) flying here and there, flying back and forth.

ཕར་འཕྱར་ཚུར་འཕྱར་ (pāājar tsūūjar) waving back and forth.

ཕར་བྲོས་ཚུར་བྲོལ་ (pāādröö tsūūdröö) running away hither and thither.

ཕར་འབུད་ཚུར་འབུད་ (pāābüü tsūūbüü) pushing back and forth, two people pushing each other.

ཕར་འབུལ་ཚུར་འབུལ་ (pāābüü tsūūbüü) exchanging giving gifts.

ཕར་འབྱར་ཚུར་འབྱར་ (pāājar tsūūjar) shifting loyalties [Lit. sticking hither, sticking thither].

ཕར་འབྱོན་ཚུར་འབྱོན་ (pāājön tsūūjön) going hither and thither.

ཕར་སྦྱར་ཚུར་སྦྱར་ (pāājar tsūūjar) making close relations here and there, siding here and there, sticking here and there.

ཕར་ཙམ་ (pāādzam) 1. awhile. 2. a short distance.

ཕར་ཙམ་ཞིག (pāādzamshig) sm. ཕར་ཙམ་.

ཕར་ཚད་ཚུར་ཚད་ (pāādzɛɛ̀ tsūūdzɛɛ̀) nearby.

ཕར་ཚུར་ (pāā tsūū) back and forth, here and there ¶ཡི་གེ་ཕར་ཚུར་བཏང་ནས་ Having sent letters back forth.

ཕར་ཚུར་འཁྱམས་ (pāā tsūū kyām) va. to wander around.

ཕར་ཚུར་འཁྱོར་ (pāā tsūū kyɔ̄r) vi. to sway (as when a person is drunk).

ཕར་མཚམས་ (pāndzam) for awhile.

ཕར་འཚོང་ (pāā tsōŋ) va. to sell.

ཕར་འཛིང་ཚུར་འཛིང་ (pāādziŋ tsūūdziŋ) fighting/ battling back and forth; va.—བྱེད་.

ཕར་ཞུ་ཚུར་ཉན་ (pāāshu tsūūñɛn) talking and listening to one another back and forth.

ཕར་ཞོག (pāāshɔ̀ɔ) sm. ཕར་བཞག.

ཕར་ཞོར་ (pāāshɔɔ) sm. ཕར་ལམ་.

ཕར་གཞུ་ཚུར་རྡེག (pāāshu tsūūdeg) hitting each other back and forth.

ཕར་བཞག (pāā sha̱à) leave alone, let alone (usu. vb. + རྒྱུ་ or ཡས་ + —) ¶ཁོས་བཤད་པར་ཉན་རྒྱུ་ཕར་བཞག Leave alone listening to what he said.

ཕར་གཟུར་ཚུར་གཡོལ་ (pāāsur tsūūyüü) attacking and avoiding the attack, thrusting and evading (in marital arts and war).

ཕར་ཡོན་ཚུར་ལོག (pāāyön tsūūlɔ̀ɔ) not standing still, twisting and turning.

ཕར་ཡོམ་ཚུར་ཡོམ་ (pāāyom tsūūyom) swaying back and forth.

ཕར་གཡོ་ཚུར་འགྱོམ་ (pāāyo tsūūgyom) sm. ཕར་ཡོམ་ཚུར་ཡོམ་.

ཕར་གཡོལ་ཚུར་གཡོལ་ (pāāyöö tsūūyöö) mutually avoiding each other.

ཕར་རི་ལྕི་བ་མ་རག ཚུར་རི་སླེ་པོ་མ་རག (pāāri jīwə ma̱raà tsūūri lēbo ma̱raà) sm. ཕ་རི་ལྕི་བ་མེད་པ་ ཚུ་རི་སླེ་པོ་མེད་པ་.

ཕར་རོལ་དྲུག (pāāröö tru̱ù) sm. ཕ་རོལ་ཏུ་ཕྱིན་པ་དྲུག.

ཕར་ལབ་ཚུར་ཤོད་ (pāāləb tsūūshöö) talking back and forth to each other.

ཕར་ལམ་ (pāālam) the road out on a trip, the part of a trip that is going somewhere in contrast to the return road.

ཕར་ལོག་ཚུར་ལོག (pāālɔ̀ɔ tsūūlɔ̀ɔ) returning back and forth; va.—བྱེད་.

ཕར་ལོགས་ (pāālɔ̀ɔ) the other side, that side.

ཕར་བཤད་ཚུར་བཤད་ (pāāshɛɛ̀ tsūūshɛɛ̀) conversing/ talking back and forth; va.—བྱེད་.

ཕར་བཤིག་ཚུར་བཤིག (pāāshiì tsūūshiì) people moving to both sides to make a space in between.

ཕར་སོང་ (pāasoŋ) go away! get lost!

ཕར་སློག (pāā lɔ̄ɔ) va. to return, to send/ give back.

ཕར་སློག་ཚུར་སློག་མེད་པ་ (pāālɔ̀ɔ tsūūlɔ̀ɔ me̱èba) two sides being even, two sides not owing each other anything.

ཕལ་ (pɛ̄ɛ̀) abbr. of ཕལ་པ་.

ཕལ་ཀ་ (pɛ̄ɛga) sm. འཕལ་ཀ་.

ཕལ་སྐད་ (pɛ̄ɛgɛɛ̀) colloquial/ vernacular language (speech).

ཕལ་སྐད་ཀྱི་རྩོམ་ཡིག (pɛ̄ɛgɛɛ̀gi dzōmyiì) vernacular or colloquial style of writing.

ཕལ་སྐད་མིན་པ་ (pɛ̄ɛgɛɛ̀ mi̱mbə) not colloquial/ informal speech, formal speech.

ཕལ་ཆེ་བ་ (pɛ̄ɛcewa) majority, most of ¶དེ་ར་སྡོད་མཁན་ཕལ་ཆེ་བ་ Most of the residents there.

ཕལ་ཆེར་ (pɛ̄ɛcee) 1. mainly, mostly, in the main, on the whole ¶མི་ཕལ་ཆེར་བོད་རིགས་རེད་ Most of the people are Tibetans. 2. almost ¶ཁོ་དེ་ར་ཕལ་ཆེར་ལོ་བཅུ་ཙམ་བསྡད་པ་རེད་ He lived there for almost ten years. 3. most probably, most likely ¶ཁོང་ཕལ་ཆེར་ཕེབས་ཚར་བ་རེད་ He most probably went.

ཕལ་གདམ་ (pɛ̄ɛdam) sm. ཁ་སྐད་.

ཕལ་པ་ (pɛ̄ɛba) common, ordinary ¶ཞིང་པ་ཕལ་པ་ཞིག A common farmer.

ཕལ་པ་ཕལ་རྒྱང་ (pɛ̄ɛba pɛ̄ɛgyaŋ) completely common/ ordinary/ mediocre.

ཕལ་སྤྱོད་ཉལ་མ་ (pɛ̄ɛjöö nɛ̄ɛma) arc. the conduct of ordinary people.

ཕལ་མིན་ (pɛ̄ɛmin) uncommon, not ordinary.

ཕལ་མོ་ཆེ་ (pɛ̄ɛmoce) sm. ཕལ་ཆེ་བ་.

ཕལ་ཚིག (pɛ̄ɛdziì) sm. ཕལ་སྐད་.

ཕལ་ཡིག (pɛ̄ɛyiì) informal letter, ordinary letter.

ཕས་ (pɛ̄ɛ̀) 1. by the father. 2. the other side.

ཕས་རྒོལ་ (pɛ̄ɛgöö) shung. the enemy ¶ ཕས་རྒོལ་མི་བཟུན་གདུག་པའི་ལྡི་གཉིས་པ་ Our enemy is like a wriggling poisonous snake.

ཕི་ (pī) sm. ཕྱི་.

ཕི་ཀྲི་ (pīdri) eng. foot.

ཕི་གླིང་པ་ (pīliŋwə) foreign, foreigner, European/ American.

ཕི་ཅིའུ་ (pīju) ch. sm. ཕི་ཇུ་.

ཕི་ཇུ་ (pīju) ch. beer.

ཕི་ཏ་ (pīdrə) eng. foot.

ཕི་ད་ (pīda) stripes on military uniform signifying rank.

ཕི་པ་ (pībə) sm. ཕྱི་པ་.

ཕི་རན་སི་ (pīrɛnsi) France.

ཕི་རན་སི་བོད་ཀྱི་སྐུ་ཚབ་དོན་གཅོད་ཁང་ (pīrɛnsi pööɡi gūdzəb lɛ̄ɛgaŋ) Bureau du Tibet, Paris.

ཕི་རན་སི་གསར་སྤེལ་ལས་ཁང་ (pīrɛnsi sārbel lɛ̄ɛgaŋ) Agence France Presse (AFP).

ཕི་རི་ཁྲུན་སི་ (pīri trūnsi) ch. radio frequency.

ཕི་རོལ་ (pīröö) sm. ཕྱི་རོལ་.

ཕི་ལིབ་པིན་ (pīlibin) Philippines.

ཕིག (pīi) vi. to have a hole open up.

ཕིག་ད་ (pīgda) a ribbon tied on the braids of women.

ཕིག་ཕིག (pīgpii) 1. coagulated meat broth. 2. jelly/ jello like substances.

ཕིགས་ (pīi) 1. sm. ཕིག. 2. p.of འབིགས་.

ཕིགས་བརྡོལ་ (pīgdöö) breaking through, penetrating.

ཕིགས་པར་སྨྲ་ (pīgbar mā) va. to give a thorough explanation.

ཕིང་ (pīŋ) ch. 1. vermicelli ¶ ཕིང་ཤའི་ཚལ་ A dish made of vermicelli and meat 2. Chinese currency unit equal to 1/100th of a Chinese yuan (dollar).

ཕིང་ཚག (pīŋjaà) ch.tib. a bunch of vermicelli.

ཕིང་ཕང་ཅིའུ་ (pīŋbaŋ cēwu) ch. Ping-Pong, table tennis.

ཕིང་ཕང་པོ་ལོ་ (pīŋbaŋ bōlo) sm. ཕིང་ཕང་ཅིའུ་.

ཕིང་ཕང་པོ་ལོ་རྒྱག་སྟེགས་ (pīŋbaŋ bōlo gyagdeg) ping pong table.

ཕིང་ཕང་པོ་ལོའི་སྟེགས་བུ་ (pīŋbaŋ bōlö dēgbu) sm. ཕིང་ཕང་པོ་ལོ་རྒྱག་སྟེགས་.

ཕིང་རྩམ་ (pīŋdzam) ground up lentils/ peas.

ཕིང་ཡང་ (pīŋyaŋ) Pyongyang.

ཕིང་ཧྥང་ (pīŋfaŋ) ch. square ¶ སྨི་ཁྲི་ཕིང་ཧྥང་ A square meter.

ཕིང་ཤ་ (pīŋsha) ch.tib. 1. vermicelli noodles and meat. 2. good friends/ buddies.

ཕིན་ (pīn) sm. ཕིང་, 2.

ཕིན་མགྱོགས་ (pīngyɔ̀ɔ) stone used in a water mill or stone grinder.

ཕིན་གཅིག (pīnjig) ch. 1. a unit of length. 2. sm. ཕིང་, 2.

ཕིན་འདྲས་ (pīndrɛɛ̀) sm. ཕ་འདྲ་.

ཕིན་ཕྱི་གོ་ལོག (pīnji koloò) sm. མན་ཕྱི་གོ་ལོག.

ཕིབས་ (pīb) roof, canopy.

ཕིབས་འོག་ཁང་ཆུང་ (pībwɔ̀ɔ kāŋjuŋ) attic.

ཕིའི་ལན་ (pīilɛn) ch. kohlrabi.

ཕིའོ་བཙོངས་ (pīudzoŋ) ch.tib. ticket sales, box office.

ཕིར་ (pīr) sm. ཕྱིར་.

ཕིས་ (pīi) sm. ཕིར་.

ཕིཊ་ (pīdrə) eng. foot.

ཕུ་ (pū) 1. the upper/ higher part of a valley ¶ ལུང་པའི་ཕུ་ The upland part of the region. 2. air, breath; va.—རྒྱག to blow air. 3. sleeve.

ཕུ་དཀྲུག་མདའ་དཀྲུག (pūdrɔ̀ɔ dadrɔ̀ɔ) causing disturbances/ agitation/ dissension everywhere, making trouble everywhere.

ཕུ་གུ་ (pūgu) sm. བུ་གུ.

ཕུ་སློད་ (pū lȫö) va. to let out the air (as in a tire), to extinguish a petromax lamp.

ཕུ་སྐང་ (pūgaŋ) sm. སྐང་བུ་, 2.

ཕུ་རྒྱག (pū gyaà) 1. va. to blow (in both literal and idiomatic senses) ¶ ཁོས་བཞུ་མར་ལ་ཕུ་བརྒྱབ་སོང་ He blew on the lamp (to extinguish it). ¶ ཁོས་གོ་སྐབས་བཟང་པོ་དེ་ཕུ་བརྒྱབ་སོང་ He blew that good opportunity. 2. va. to pump, to inflate ¶ མོ་ཊའི་འཁོར་ལོར་ཕུ་རྒྱག་དགོ་ཡོད་ (I) have to pump up the car tire. 3. va. to incite, to instigate ¶ ཁོས་ཟིང་ཆ་ཡོང་ལས་དེ་ཕུ་བརྒྱབ་པ་རེད་ He incited the disturbance.

ཕུ་རྒྱུགས་མདའ་རྒྱུགས་ (pūgyuù dagyuù) running around all over/ everywhere; va.—བྱེད་ [Lit. running to the upper part of valley, running to the lower part of valley].

ཕུ་ཕྱིབས་ (pūjib) sm. ཕུ་ཤུབས་.

ཕུ་ཆུ་ (pūju) a stream/ river flowing down from the upper part of a valley.

ཕུ་སྟོད་ (pūdöö) the outer garment worn over the traditional Tibetan dress by all lay government officials on New Years Day.

ཕུ་ཐག (pūdaà) the distance from the upper part of a valley to the lower part ¶ ཕུ་ཐག་རིང་པོ་ A long upland valley.

ཕུ་ཐག་གཅོད་ (pūdaà jȫö) va. to conclude/ settle decisively ¶ དཔུང་དམག་ཕྱིར་འཐེན་མ་བྱས་ན་ཞི་མོལ་ཡོང་གི་མ་རེད་ཅེས་ཕུ་ཐག་བཅད་པ་རེད་ (They) concluded decisively that there will be no peace talks without the withdrawal of troops.

ཕུ་ཐག་ཆོད་ (pūdaà cȫö) vi. to come to a decisive conclusion, to find a permanent solution ¶ ཕུ་ཐག་ཆོད་པའི་རྒྱལ་ཁ་ A decisive victory.

ཕུ་ཐག་ཐུང་ཐུང་ (pūdaà tūŋduŋ) shortsighted.

ཕུ་ཐུང་ (pūduŋ) sleeve; va.—རྗེ་ to roll up one's sleeve.

ཕུ་ཐུང་རྟ་རྨིག་གཟུགས་ (pūduŋ dāmigsuù) a sleeve made in the shape of horse's hoof.

ཕུ་ཐོ་ཡ་ (pūtoya) Portugal.

ཕུ་མཐའ་ (pūta) the edge/ end of the upper part of a valley.

ཕུ་དུང་ (pūduŋ) sm. ཕུ་ཐུང་.

ཕུ་དུང་ཐུང་ལ་ལག་པ་རིང་བ་ (pūduŋ tūŋla lagba riŋwa) sth. that doesn't suffice or is too small [Lit. short sleeves with a long arm].

ཕུ་དུང་རྩེ་ (pūduŋdze) the end of a sleeve.

ཕུ་དུད་ (pūdüù) sm. གུས་འདུད་.

ཕུ་མདའ་ (pūnda) 1. a pump (for air); va.—རྒྱག to pump (a tire, etc.). 2. the upper and lower part of a valley.

ཕུ་མདའ་བར་གསུམ་ (pūnda parsum) the upper, middle and lower (part of a valley), everywhere, all over an area.

ཕུ་མདའ་ལ་ཀླུངས་ (pūnda lāluŋ) everywhere, all over an area [Lit. the upper part of a valley, the lower part of a valley, the mountain pass, the valley].

ཕུ་མདོ་ (pūdo) the upper and lower part of a valley.

ཕུ་མདོ་བར་གསུམ་ (pūdo parsum) sm. ཕུ་མདའ་བར་གསུམ་.

ཕུ་འདེབས་སྨྱུག་མདོང་ (pūndeb mūgdoŋ) a bamboo pipe used to blow on a fire.

ཕུ་ནུ་ (pūnu) older and younger brothers ¶ ཕུ་ནུའི་བརྩེ་གདུང་ Brotherly love.

ཕུ་ནུ་མོ་ (pūnumo) older and younger sisters.

ཕུ་པ་ (pūbə) people who reside in the upper part of a valley.

ཕུ་པར་རྒྱག་གི་སྨ་ར་ཚུར་ཚིག (pū pāā gyəbbɛ āra tsūū tsīi) sm. ཕུ་པར་བརྒྱབ་པས་ཨ་ར་ཚུར་ཚིག.

ཕུ་པར་བརྒྱབ་པས་ཨ་ར་ཚུར་ཚིག (pū pāā gyəbbɛ āra tsūū tsīi) doing a good deed but being repaid with unkindness/ harm [Lit. to kindle the fire by blowing and burning one's moustache in the process].

ཕུ་བོ་ (pūwo) elder brother.

ཕུ་བྲོས་མདའ་བྲོས་ (pūdröö dadröö) fleeing to the upper and lower parts of the valley, fleeing all over/ everywhere.

ཕུ་དྲུག (pūdraà) the area between the upper and lower part of a valley.

ཕུ་འབྲོག (pūdrog) nomads who reside in the upper part of a valley.

ཕུ་མེད་ (pūmeè) sleeveless.

ཕུ་མོ་ (pūmo) older sister.

ཕུ་བརྗེས་དཔུང་སྒྲིང་ (pūjeè pūŋdreŋ) getting ready to fight [Lit. rolling up the sleeves and straightening the shoulders].

ཕུ་ཡོད་ (pūyöö) having sleeves.

ཕུ་ར་ག (pūraga) Prague.

ཕུ་རག (pūrag) the upper part of a valley where farming depends on rainfall.

ཕུ་རིང་ (pūriŋ) long sleeves.

ཕུ་རིང་སྟེང་གོས་ཆེན་ (pūriŋ dēŋgööjen) a long sleeve brocade overgarment.

ཕུ་རུང་ (pūruŋ) sm. ཕུ་དུང་.

ཕུ་རོན་ (pūrön) sm. ཕུག་རོན་.

ཕུ་ལག་བྱེད་ (pūlaà ce̱è) va. to put one's hands in one's sleeves (when cold).

ཕུ་ཤུབས་ (pūshub) sleeve cover, a protective sheath placed on the sleeve.

ཕུ་ཤོར་ (pū shɔ̄ɔ̄) 1. vi. to have the air leak out (from a tire, etc.). 2. vi. to lose one's determination or enthusiasm.

ཕུ་ཤོར་ཤོར་ (pū shɔ̄ɔ̄shɔɔ) angrily.

ཕུ་བཤད་མདའ་བཤད་ (pūshɛ̀ɛ̀ da̱shɛɛ̀) talking about sth. everywhere/ all over.

ཕུ་གསུམ་ཆུ་ (pūsūm cū) water (flowing) from three different upper valleys.

ཕུ་ལྷགས་ (pūlhaà) wind (blowing) from the upper region of a valley.

ཕུག (pūù) 1. cave, cavern, hermitage. 2. imp. of འབིགས་. 3. inside, in the inner part/ section ། ཁོ་ཁང་པའི་ཕུག་ལ་འདུག He is in the inner part of the house. 4. abbr. of ཕུག་རོན་.

ཕུག་སྐྱ་ (pūùgya) 1. white pigeon. 2. shades of white color like that of a pigeon.

ཕུག་གདུགས་ (pūg dūù) va. to trace to the source/ origin.

ཕུག་ཐག་ཆོད་ (pūgdaà cöö) sm. ཕུ་ཐག་ཆོད་.

ཕུག་པ་ (pūgbə) cave, cavern.

ཕུག་མ་ (pūgmə) 1. chaff, husk. 2. inner, interior.

ཕུག་མ་ལྟུང་ཁྱེར་ (pūgmə lūŋkyer) sm. ཕུབ་མ་ལྟུང་ཁྱེར་.

ཕུག་མའི་འོག་གི་ཆུ་དོང་ (pūgmɛ wɔ̀ɔ̀gi cūdoŋ) hidden danger [Lit. a pit with water under chaff].

ཕུག་རྩ་ (pūgdza) origin, roots, source; va.—རྩད་གཅོད་བྱེད་ to investigate the origin/ root/ source.

ཕུག་གཟིང་ (pūgsoŋ) a chisel used for in carving woodblocks.

ཕུག་རིང་ (pūgriŋ) sm. ཕུགས་རིང་.

ཕུག་རོན་ (pūgrün) pigeon.

ཕུག་རོན་སྐར་ཚོམ་ (pūgrön gārdzom) the constellation Columba.

ཕུག་ལམ་ (pūglam) tunnel.

ཕུག་ལུགས་ (pūglug) the system of astrological calculation created by ཕུག་པ་ལྷུན་གྲུབ་རྒྱ་མཚོ་.

ཕུག་སླེབ་ (pūgleb) long basket.

ཕུགས་ (pūù) future, long-term, long-range ། ཕུགས་ཀྱི་བསམ་བློ་ Future plan/ goal.

ཕུགས་སྐྱོན་ (pūggyön) long-term harm.

ཕུགས་འཁྱོངས་ (pūggyoŋ) sm. ཕུགས་འཁྱོལ་.

ཕུགས་འཁྱོལ་ (pūù kyöö) doing/ seeing sth. through to the end; va. ཕུགས་འཁྱོལ་; —བྱེད་ ། འཕྲལ་ཡུན་དྲིན་ཆུང་དུ་མི་འགྱུར་བའི་ཕུགས་འཁྱོལ་ཡུན་གནས་མཛད་རྒྱུ་དང་ You should not be ungrateful and should see (it) through to the end.

ཕུགས་རྒྱགས་ (pūùgyaà) sth. reserved/ saved/ stored up (e.g., food).

ཕུགས་གདད་ (pūgdɛɛ̀) hope, expectation.

ཕུགས་གདུག (pūù dūù) va. to investigate the future/ long-term.

ཕུགས་གཏོར་ (pūgdɔɔ) an everyday/ regular གཏོར་མ་ offering.

ཕུགས་བརྟན་ (pūgden) reliable, steady, dependable, durable.

ཕུགས་ཐག་ཆོད་ (pūgdaà cöö) vi. to be able to understand the root meaning of a text/ scripture.

ཕུགས་ཐུབ་ (pūgdub) sm. ཕུགས་བརྟན་.

ཕུགས་དོན་ (pūgdün) a long-term/ long-range hope or plan ། འདི་ནི་ཕུགས་དོན་ཡག་ཤོས་རེད་ This is the best long-range hope.

ཕུགས་བདེ་ (pūgde) future/ long-term/ long-range happiness or well-being.

ཕུགས་འདུན་ (pūŋdün) future/ long-term/ long-range hope or wish.

ཕུགས་འདོད་ (pūŋdöö) future/ long-term/ long-range desire or wish.

ཕུགས་དེག (pūgdig) (the main) wealth, capital or fortune (of a family).

ཕུགས་ན་ (pūgnə) sm. ཕུགས་སུ་.

ཕུགས་ནས་ཕུགས་སུ་ (pūgnɛ pūgsu) in the future/ long-term.

ཕུགས་ནོར་ (pūgnɔɔ) sm. ཕུགས་དེག.

ཕུགས་དཔྱོད་ (pūgjöö) foresight, investigating/ assessing for the long-term, a long-term view.

ཕུགས་ཕན་ (pūgpɛn) future or long-term benefit.

ཕུགས་འཕེར་ (pūŋbēr) reliable, durable, lasting.

ཕུགས་འབྲས་ (pūŋdrɛɛ̀) future or long-term outcome/ finale/ result ། ཕུགས་འབྲས་ངན་པ་ A bad future outcome.

ཕུགས་དམིགས་ (pūgmiì) (the person or fortune) that a family relies/ depends on for the future.

ཕུགས་རྩ་ (pūgdzə) root cause, fundamental issue/ concern/ cause ། ཕུགས་རྩ་རྩད་གཅོད་བྱེད་ To investigate the root cause.

ཕུགས་རྩད་གཅོད་ (pūgdzɛɛ̀ jöö) va. to look into the root cause, to get to the bottom of a matter.

ཕུགས་རྩ་འཚོལ་ (pūgdza tsöö) va. to get to the bottom/ root of a matter.

ཕུགས་ཟོག (pūgsɔɔ) sm. ཕུགས་དེག.

ཕུགས་ཡུན་ (pūgyön) the future, the long run.

ཕུགས་ཡུལ་ (pūgyüü) sm. ཕུགས་བསམ་གྱི་ཡུལ་.

ཕུགས་གཡེང་བྱེད་ (pūgyeŋ ce̱è) va. to search for sth. in an inner room.

ཕུགས་རིང་ (pūgriŋ) long-term, in the long run ། ཕུགས་རིང་གི་ཤུགས་རྐྱེན་བཟང་པོ་ཡོང་གི་རེད་ (This) will have a good effect in the long run.

ཕུགས་རེ་ (pūgre) sm. ཕུགས་བསམ་.

ཕུགས་རེའི་ཚོད་ལྟ་ (pūgree tsööda) sm. ཕུགས་བསམ་ཚོད་ལྟ་.

ཕུགས་རེའི་ཡུལ་ཁམས་ (pūgree yu̱ùgam) object of one's future hopes/ aspirations.

ཕུགས་ལ་ (pūùlə) sm. ཕུགས་སུ་.

ཕུགས་ལམ་ (pūglam) future path/ road.

ཕུགས་ལོན་ (pūg lö̱n) va. to know/ understand the gist/ essence (of a matter).

ཕུགས་སུ་ (pūgsu) in the future, in the end.

ཕུགས་སོ་ (pūgso) base, foundation.

ཕུགས་སོ་མེད་པ་ (pūgso me̱èba) baseless, without foundation.

ཕུགས་བསམ་ (pūgsam) ideals, hopes, thoughts of the future; va.—གཏོང་ to give careful thought about the future ། གསར་བརྗེའི་ཕུགས་བསམ་ Revolutionary ideals.

ཕུགས་བསམ་གྱི་ཡུལ་ (pūgsamgi yü̱ü) ideal society of the future.

ཕུང་ (pūŋ) 1. a heap, a pile ། རྡོ་ཕུང་ A pile of stone. 2. p. of འཕུང་. 3. abbr. of ཕུང་པོ་.

ཕུང་གྲོལ་རྒྱུད་སྐྱུལ་ (pūŋdröö gyṳ̈ṳ̈güü) causing disaster/ destruction.

ཕུང་དཀྲུག (pūŋdruù) stirring up/ inciting/ instigating disturbances or disorders or trouble; va.—སློང་ to stir/ incite/ instigate disturbances or disorder or trouble ། དགྲ་བོའི་སོ་ཉལ་དེ་ཚོས་ཡུལ་སྡེ་ཕུང་དཀྲུག་བྱེད་ཀྱི་རེད་ཟེར་ (They) say that those enemy agents will instigate disturbances.

ཕུང་དཀྲོལ་ (pūŋdröö) sm. ཕུང་དཀྲུག.

ཕུང་རྐྱེན་ (pūŋgyen) the cause of a disturbances/ disorder.

ཕུང་སྐྱེལ་ (pūŋgyee) taking a corpse to the graveyard/ sky burial site.

ཕུང་ཁ་ (pūŋgə) sm. ཕུང་དཀྲོལ་.

ཕུང་གྱོད་ (pūŋgyöö) law cases that lead a person to ruin/ penury/ bankruptcy.

ཕུང་གན་ (pūŋgɛn) black sheep, prodigal son, sb. who squanders away all the wealth of a family.

ཕུང་ངེ་བ་ (pūŋŋewa) piled up in a heap.

ཕུང་གཏོར་ (pūŋ dōr) disposing of a body by sky burial.

ཕུང་འདྲེ་ (pūŋdre) harmful demon/ spirits.

ཕུང་པ་ (pūŋbə) destruction, disturbance, disorder.

ཕུང་པོ་ (pūŋbo) 1. mass, form, substance, body, structure ༎ དངོས་ཡོད་ཀྱི་ཕུང་པོ་ Material substances. 2. a heap, pile. 3. corpse.

ཕུང་པོ་ལྔ་ (pūŋbo ŋā) the five aggregates: form; feeling; perception; compositional factors; consciousness.

ཕུང་པོ་དྲུག་ (pūŋbo truù) the six aggregates: form; feeling; perception; compositional factors; consciousness, wisdom.

ཕུང་པོ་སྲེག་ (pūŋbo sēg) va. to cremate.

ཕུང་ཕུང་འཕྲོ་བ་ (pūŋbuŋ drōwa) sparkling lights.

ཕུང་ཕྲུག་ (pūŋdruù) children who squander away all the wealth of a family.

ཕུང་སྦྱོར་ (pūŋjɔɔ) leading astray, bringing about a downfall; va.—གཏོང་ to lead astray, to bring about one's downfall.

ཕུང་རྩ་ (pūŋdza) the root or cause of trouble/ disturbance/ destruction; va.—སློང་ to create trouble, to cause destruction.

ཕུང་གཞི་ (pūŋshi) sm. ཕུང་རྩ་.

ཕུང་གཡོ་ (pūŋ yō) va. to cause trouble, to instigate dissension/ disturbance.

ཕུང་ལ་སྦྱར་ (pūŋla jar) sm. ཕུང་སྦྱོར་.

ཕུང་སེལ་ (pūŋsel) disaster, calamity.

ཕུང་སོ་ (pūŋso) pile, heap.

ཕུང་སྲི་ (pūŋsi) sm. ཕུང་འདྲེ་.

ཕུང་སྲི་སྡེ་དཀྲུག་ (pūŋsi dedruù) shung. instigating and causing trouble ༎ སླད་ནས་ཀྱང་ཕུང་སྲི་སྡེ་དཀྲུག་ཇི་བྱེད་མ་རྟོགས་ It is unknown what sort of instigating and troublemaking will happen in the future.

ཕུང་གསུམ་པ་ (pūŋ sūmbə) third party, neutral person, mediator.

ཕུང་གསོག་ (pūŋsɔɔ) sm. ཕུང་གསོགས་.

ཕུང་གསོགས་ (pūŋsɔɔ) accumulating, piling up; va.—རྒྱག་ to pile/ heap up, to store up, to accumulate; vi.—ཐེབས་ to get/ be piled/ heaped up/ accumulated ༎ ས་གནས་ཁ་ཤས་ལ་འབྲུ་རིགས་ཕུང་གསོགས་ཐེབས་པ་དང་ས་གནས་ཁ་ཤས་ལ་ཉོ་ས་མེད་པ་རེད་ In some localities grain has been accumulated (surplus) and in others there is no place to buy it.

ཕུད་ (pūū) 1. p. and imp. of འབུད་. 2. the first portion of food, crops, etc. offered to the gods ༎ ཟས་ཀྱི་ཕུད་ The first offering of food. 3. exclusive of, not including, with the exception of ༎ ཨ་ཞང་ཕུད་ན་མི་ལྔ་འདུག Not including the uncle, there are five. ༎ ཨ་རི་དང་དབྱིན་ཇི་ཕར་ཕུད་ང་ཚོ་ངར་ལྕགས་ཐོན་སྐྱེད་ཨང་གི་དང་པོ་རེད་ With the exception of the U.S. and Britain, we are first in steel production. 4. leave/ let alone, leave aside ༎ ཁོང་ལ་དངུལ་དགོས་ཡོད་ཟེར་བ་ཕུད་ད་དུང་གཟའ་ཆ་ཡང་དགོས་ཀྱི་འདུག Let alone asking him for money, he also needs food.

ཕུད་ཀོང་ (pūūgoŋ) cup/ glass for offering tea, etc. (to the gods).

ཕུད་སྒྲ་ (pūūdra) hissing sound that snakes make.

ཕུད་མཆོད་ (pūūjöö) the offering of a small portion of food and tea to the deities before one eats or drinks.

ཕུད་གཏོར་ (pūūdɔɔ) before drinking one's beer, dipping a finger into the beer cup and flicking some into the air as a first offering to the gods; va.—བྱེད་.

ཕུད་དམ་ (pūūdam) container in which the offerings such as tea and wine are kept, offering utensils for tea and beer.

ཕུད་འདེད་ (pūūdeè) pushing sb. away.

ཕུད་ཕོར་ (pūūbɔɔ) bowl in which the first offerings of food/ drink to the gods are kept.

ཕུད་ཕྱེ་ (pūūce) shung. the first offering of རྩམ་པ་ ༎ མཆོད་པ་ལྔ་ཚར་རེ་རྒྱ་ཕུད་ཕྱེ་རྩམ་ཁལ་གསུམ་ Three ཁལ་ of རྩམ་པ་ to be used for the five offerings.

ཕུད་བུ་ (pūūbu) hair tied in a bundle on top of head, hair tassle.

ཕུད་ཚོང་ (pūūdzoŋ) sales promotion, sample gift of a product.

ཕུན་ (pũn) 1. a measure unit roughly the size of a handful (6 ཕུན་ are equal to 1 ཁྱོར་). 2. ch. a measure equal to half the length of a finger.

ཕུན་ཁང་ (pũngaŋ) abbr. of ཕུན་ཚོགས་ཁང་གསར་.

ཕུན་གླིང་ (pũnliŋ) Phuntsholing (in Bhutan).

ཕུན་ཚོགས་ (pũndzoò) 1. abbr. of ཕུན་སུམ་ཚོགས་པ་. 2. a person's name.

ཕུན་ཚོགས་ཁང་གསར་ (pũndzoò kaŋsar) Phunkhang (name of an aristocratic family).

ཕུན་ཚོགས་རྒྱས་ (pũndzoò gyɛ̱ɛ̀) vi. to have/ get prosperity.

ཕུན་སུམ་ཚོགས་པ་ (pũndzoò tsōgba) complete, perfect, all good ༎ སློབ་སྦྱོང་བྱེད་ཡས་ཀྱི་མཐུན་རྐྱེན་ཕུན་སུམ་ཚོགས་པ་ཡོད་པ་རེད་ They have complete facilities for studies.

ཕུན་སུམ་ཚོགས་པར་བྱེད་ (pũndzoò tsōgbar ce̱è) sm. ཕུན་སུམ་ཚོགས་སུ་གཏོང་.

ཕུན་སུམ་ཚོགས་སུ་གཏོང་ (pũndzoò tsōgbar dōŋ) va. to make complete/ perfect/ best; to enrich, enhance.

ཕུབ་ (pūb) 1. a shield. 2. vi. to go bankrupt. 3. p. of འབུབས་.

ཕུབ་ཀར་ (pūbgar) pole erected at the center of a nomad's tent.

ཕུབ་ཀྱི་མེ་ལོང་ (pūbgi me̱loŋ) a metal (mirror-like) shield.

ཕུབ་པ་ (pūbbə) troops who carry shields.

ཕུབ་མ་ (pūbmə) chaff, husk, stubble.

ཕུབ་མ་རླུང་འཁྱེར་ (pūbmə lūŋgyer) a sudden/ unexpected misfortune, disaster, mishap; things getting scattered all over [Lit. chaff getting blown by the wind].

ཕུབ་དམག་ (pūbmaà) soldiers armed with shields.

ཕུབ་རྩེད་ (pūbdzeè) a display of martial skill using a shield.

ཕུབ་འཛིན་དམག་དཔུང་ (pūmdzin mə̄gbuŋ) soldiers armed with shields.

ཕུབ་སླེལ་ (pūbleè) basket woven from thin branches.

ཕུའུ་ (pū) ch. deputy, vice, assistant ༎ ཕུའུ་ཀྲུ་ཞི་ Deputy chairman.

ཕུའུ་ཐའོ་ཡ་ (pūtoya) Portugal.

ཕུའུ་བལ་ (pūpɛɛ) "wool" from the cattail plant that is used for stuffing pillows.

ཕུའུ་ཙི་ (pūdzi) ch. music notation, music score.

ཕུར་ (pūr) 1. va. to rub, to massage, to pet. 2. p. and imp. of འཕུར་.

ཕུར་ཁ་ (pūrgə) sm. མི་ཁ.

ཕུར་མཉེ་ (pūrñe) massaging, rubbing, petting, kneading, va.—གཏོང་.

ཕུར་གདང་ (pūrdaŋ) 1. wooden peg for tying animals. 2. wooden peg or stick for hanging coats, etc.

ཕུར་མདུད་ (pūrdüü) sm. སྤུང་མདུད་.

ཕུར་པ་ (pūrbə) peg, stake; va.—རྒྱག; —འདོགས་ to peg, to drive in a stake.

ཕུར་ཕུར་ (pūūbuu) rubbing, massaging, petting; va.—བྱེད; —གཏོང་.

ཕུར་བུ་ (pūrbu) 1. the planet Jupiter. 2. Thursday. 3. a religious/ ritual dagger. 4. a person's name.

ཕུར་བུ་རྒྱས་ཚོགས་ (pūrbu gyɛ̱ɛ̀dzoò) shung. the weekly meeting of the Kashag and the Silön.

ཕུ་བུ་འདྲ་བའི་རྒྱ་སྐར་ (pūrbu dra̱wɛ gyu̱gar) Jovian planets.

ཕུར་བུས་མཆོད་པའི་རྒྱུ་སྐར་ (pūrbuù cōnbɛ gyugar) Jovian planets.

ཕུར་མ་ (pūrmə) 1. a small pouch for keeping ground incense. 2. brocade hangings on the walls and pillars of temples and monasteries.

ཕུར་སྨུག (pūrmug) artemisia mattfeldii pamp (used in Tibetan medicine).

ཕུར་ཚེ་ (pūrdze) abbr. of ཕུར་བུ་ཚེ་རིང་.

ཕུར་ཚུགས་ (pūrdzuù) directly, concentrating, focused ¶ཁོང་གི་ཞལ་མིག་ཕུར་ཚུགས་སུ་ལྟས་ནས་ Looking with (his) eyes focused on his face.

ཕུར་འཛུགས་ (pūrdzuù) sm. ཕུར་ཚུགས་.

ཕུར་རག (pūrraà) fields in the upper part of a valley that exist on rainfall (without irrigation).

ཕུར་ལ་འདོགས་ (pūrla dɔ̄ɔ̀) sm. ཕུར་པ་ (འདོགས་).

ཕུར་ཤད་ (pūrshɛɛ̀) a type of punctuation "༑".

ཕུར་ཤིང་ (pūrshiŋ) wood for making wooden pegs.

ཕུར་སུག་གཞུ་ (pūrsuù shu) va. to hit sb. with an elbow to give a signal.

ཕུལ་ (pūū) 1. p. and imp. of འབུལ་. 2. a unit of measure equal to one sixth of a འབྲི་.

ཕུལ་གང་ (pūūgaŋ) one ཕུལ་.

ཕུལ་གྲངས་ཁལ་བསྒྲིལ་ (pūūdraŋ kɛ̄ɛ̄drill) converting lower/ smaller units to higher/ larger ones (e.g., ཕུལ་ into ཁལ་).

ཕུལ་ཆོག་བྱེད་ (pūūjɔ̄ɔ cēè) va. to be prepared to offer/ submit/ give sth.

ཕུལ་སྙན་ (pūūñɛn) a petition that has been given to a superior.

ཕུལ་དུ་གྱུར་ (pūūdu gyur) sm. ཕུལ་དུ་བྱུང་.

ཕུལ་དུ་ཕྱིན་ (pūūdu cīn) magnificent, the best, outstanding.

ཕུལ་དུ་བྱུང་ (pūūdu jīn) best, highest, outstanding ¶སློབ་ཕྲུག་ཕུལ་དུ་བྱུང་བ་ཞིག An outstanding student.

ཕུལ་ཕྱིན་ (pūūjin) sm. ཕུལ་དུ་ཕྱིན་.

ཕུལ་བྱུང་ (pūūjuŋ) abbr. of ཕུལ་དུ་བྱུང་ ¶ཕུལ་བྱུང་ཐོན་སྐྱེད་ཅན་ Outstanding producer/ stakhanovite.

ཕུལ་བྱུང་ཁྱད་འཕགས་ (pūūjuŋ kyɛ̄ɛ̄baà) excellent, outstanding, exceptional.

ཕུལ་བྱུང་གྲས་ (pūūjuŋdrɛɛ̀) the most excellent/ outstanding/ exceptional kind.

ཕུལ་ཡིག (pūūyiì) letter (correspondence).

ཕུལ་ལམ་འབྱམས་ (pūūlam jam) shung. vi. to have become a custom to pay sth. ¶དུས་ཀྱི་སོ་ནམ་ཡིགས་ཞིན་དང་བསྟུན་ནས་ལོ་རེ་འབྲུ་ཁལ་ ༡༠༠ རེ་ཕུལ་ལམ་འབྱམས་པ་ It has become a custom to pay 100 ཁལ་ of grain per year in accordance with the quality of the yield.

ཕུལ་ལུ་རེ་ཙམ་ (pūūlu redzam) about one ཕུལ་ (a unit in Tibetan measurement).

ཕུས་བཏབ་ (pūū dəb) p. of ཕུས་འདེབས་.

ཕུས་འདེད་གནམ་གྲུ་ (pūū dee nəmdru) jet plane.

ཕུས་འདེབས་ (pūū deb) va. to blow.

ཕེ་ཆེའུ་བོ་ལོ་ (pēce bōlo) ch.tib. volleyball; va.—རྒྱག to play volleyball.

ཕེ་ཡོ་ (pēyo) ch. ticket.

ཕེ་ལིའུ་པིན་ (pēlebin) Philippines.

ཕེག་རྡོབ་ (pēgdɔ̄ɔ̀) a type of small cymbal-like musical instrument.

ཕེང་སོན་ (pēŋsön) ch. boric acid.

ཕེད་ (pēè) 1. va. to bite, cut (with a knife). 2. to break ground/ plow.

ཕེན་ཙེ་ (pēndze) ch. 1. phonograph record. 2. film.

ཕེབ་རྡོབ་ (pēbdob) sm. ཕེག་རྡོབ་.

ཕེབས་ (pēb) 1. va. to go, to come, to arrive (h.) ¶ཁོང་ཕར་ཕེབས་ཀྱི་རེད་ He is going away. 2. with ages, coveys reaching an age ¶དགུང་ལོ་ཉི་ཤུ་ཕེབས་པའི་བླ་མ་འདི་ The lama who was twenty years old (the lama who has reached the age of twenty).

ཕེབས་ཀོ་ (pēbgɔ) h. of ཀོ་བ་.

ཕེབས་བཀག (pēbgaà) stopping sb. from going somewhere.

ཕེབས་སྐས་ (pēbgɛɛ̀) h. of སྐས་འཛེག.

ཕེབས་སྐྱེལ་ (pēbgyeè) sending/ seeing sb. off (h.); va.—ཞུ་ to see/ send sb. off ¶གནམ་ཐང་བར་ཕེབས་སྐྱེལ་ཞུས་པ་རེད་ (They) saw him off at the airport.

ཕེབས་ཁྲི་ (pēbdri) sm. ཕེབས་བྱམས་.

ཕེབས་འཁོར་ (pēbgɔɔ) car (h.).

ཕེབས་གྲ་ (pēbdra) preparing to go somewhere; va.—བྱེད་; —སྒྲིག to make preparations to go.

ཕེབས་འགོ་ (pēmgo) title of the people in charge of the Dalai Lama's palanquin.

ཕེབས་གྲུ་ (pēbdru) h. of གྲུ་.

ཕེབས་གྲོགས་ (pēbdroò) traveling companion (h.); va.—ཞུ་; —གནང་ to accompany on travel/ a trip.

ཕེབས་སྐུག (pēbguù) h. of སྐུག.

ཕེབས་སྒོ་ (pēbgo) shung. 1. a Tibetan Government tradition of giving fried cookies to government officials at New Year and other ceremonies. 2. an order/ edict.

ཕེབས་སྒོའི་གཞུང་ལམ་ (pēbgö shunlam) royal route.

ཕེབས་སྒྲིག (pēbdrig) preparing for sb.'s arrival (h.); va.—ཞུ་ to make preparations for sb.'s arrival.

ཕེབས་སྒྲིག་དོ་དམ་ (pēbdrig todam) shung. an official who is responsible for preparing for sb.'s arrival.

ཕེབས་སྒྲིག་སྤྱི་ཁྱབ་ (pēbdrig jīkyəb) shung. the chief official responsible for preparing for sb.'s arrival.

ཕེབས་དགོངས་ (pēbgoŋ) according to the order that arrived.

ཕེབས་ཆས་ (pēbjɛɛ̀) things for making a journey/ trip.

ཕེབས་རྗེས་ (pēbjeè) following sb. ¶ཁོང་གི་ཕེབས་རྗེས་སུ་མི་གསུམ་སླེབས་སོང་ Following his coming, three people arrived.

ཕེབས་སྟངས་ (pēbdaŋ) the manner/ way a person walks (h.).

ཕེབས་སྟོན་ (pēbdön) shung. farewell or welcoming party.

ཕེབས་སྟོན་བག་ར་སྒྲོ་ (pēbdön gārdro) a type of deep fried cookie given out at state ceremonies.

ཕེབས་བསྟུན་ (pēbdün) as one arrives/ leaves (h.) ¶སྲིད་འཛིན་མཆོག་ཕེབས་བསྟུན་རོལ་ཆ་བཏང་བ་རེད་ (They) played music as the president arrived.

ཕེབས་ཐོན་ (pēbdön) shung. departure, leaving (h.); va.—གནང་ to depart, to leave ¶ཁོང་ཚེས་ 2 ཉིན་རྒྱ་གར་ལ་ཕེབས་ཐོན་གནང་སོང་ He left for India on the 2nd.

ཕེབས་དོན་ (pēbdön) purpose of a journey/ trip (h.).

ཕེབས་གདོང་ (pēbdoŋ) 1. before one's departure (h.) ¶ཁོང་ཕེབས་གདོང་ང་ཚོའི་ནང་ལ་ཕེབས་བྱུང་ (He) came to our place before his departure. 2. shung. at the front of sb. walking or riding.

ཕེབས་དོག་ཐོན་ (pēbdog tōn) va. to leave/ depart.

ཕེབས་བརྡ་ (pēbda) 1. announcing a departure by drumbeat; va.—གཏོང་. 2. shung. the drumbeat made by the གར་ཕྲུག་པ་ signaling that the Dalai Lama is coming.

ཕེབས་པར་སྨྲ་ (pēbar mā) va. to talk in a calm and peaceful manner.

ཕེབས་དཔྱང་ (pēbjaŋ) sm. ཕེབས་བྱམ་.

ཕེབས་སྤྱི་ (pēbji) shung. abbr. of ཕེབས་སྒྲིག་སྤྱི་ཁྱབ་.

ཕེབས་སྤྱོད་བདེ་པོ་ (pēbjöö debo) convenient/ easy to travel or get to places.

ཕེབས་བྱམ་ (pēbjam) sedan chair, palanquin (h.).

ཕེབས་བྱམས་ (pēbjam) sm. ཕེབས་བྱམ་.

ཕེབས་བྱམས་པ་ (pēbjamba) people who carry a sedan chair/ palanquin.

ཕེབས་འབྱོར་ (pēbjɔɔ) arrival (h.); va.—གནང་ to arrive ¶ཁོང་ཕེབས་འབྱོར་སྐབས་ At the time of he arrived. ¶ཁོ་ཚོ་ཚང་མ་འདིར་ཕེབས་འབྱོར་བྱུང་ They all arrived here.

ཕེབས་ཚོགས་ (pēbdzɔ̄ɔ̀) a communication or letter about a situation or conditions.

ཕེབས་རྫོངས་ (pēbdzoŋ) going-away present/ gift; va.—འབུལ་ to give a going-away present/ gift.

ཕེབས་བཞུ་ (pēbshu) h. of བཞུ་མར་.

ཕེབས་བཞུགས་ (pēbshuù) going and staying ¶ཁོང་རྒྱ་གར་དུ་ཕེབས་བཞུགས་གནང་འདུག He went to India and stayed there.

ཕེབས་བཞིན་ (pēbsheè) having the thought of going ། ཁོང་རྒྱ་གར་དུ་ཕེབས་བཞིན་འདུག He is thinking of going to India.

ཕེབས་ཟམ་ (pēbsam) h. of ཟམ་པ་.

ཕེབས་རལ་ (pēbrεε) shung. cloth laid on the ground where the Dalai Lama is going to walk there.

ཕེབས་རིགས་ (pēbrii) va. to come, to go (h.) ། ཁོང་འདི་གར་ཕེབས་རིགས་མ་བྱུང་ He didn't come here.

ཕེབས་རེས་ (pēbreè) shung. the turn of a Council Minister (Kalon) to be on duty in the Potala.

ཕེབས་རོགས་ (pēbroò) sm. ཕེབས་གྲོགས་.

ཕེབས་ལམ་ (pēblam) 1. road, path, way journey (h.) ། ཁོང་གི་ཕེབས་ལམ་ལ་མ་བསྡད་ Do not stand in his way. ། ཕེབས་ལམ་ལ་ཐུགས་ཕྲུག་གནང་རོགས་ Please take care (of yourself) on the journey.

ཕེབས་ལམ་འཇམ་ (pēblamjam) nomad phrase said to a person leaving meaning "goodbye."

ཕེབས་ལུགས་ཕེབས་སྟངས་ (pēbluù pēndaŋ) describing how and by what route sb. came or went.

ཕེབས་གསལ་ (pēbsεε) shung. as per, according to, in accordance with, as it was stated (h.) ། བཀའ་བློན་ནས་བཀའ་ཡིག་ཕེབས་གསལ་ལ་ In accordance with the orders received from the Council Minister.

ཕེབས་གསོས་ (pēbsöö) welcoming gift when sb. arrives. va.—འབུལ་.

ཕེབས་བསུ་ (pēbsu) welcoming, welcoming reception (h.); va.—ཞུ་; —སྐྱེལ་ to welcome, to receive ། ཁོང་ལ་ཕེབས་བསུ་གཟབ་རྒྱས་ཤིག་ཞུས་པ་རེད་ They gave him an elaborate welcome.

ཕེབས་བསུ་སྐྱེལ་ཞུ་ (pēbsu gyēèshu) sm. ཕེབས་བསུ་.

ཕེའུ་ (pēwu) ch. fired brick.

ཕེའོ་ (pēwo) ch. ticket ། མེ་འཁོར་གྱི་ཕེའོ་ Train ticket.

ཕེར་པོ་ (pērbo) active.

ཕེར་བ་ (pērwɔ) suitable, fit, valid.

ཕེར་ཤ་ (pērsha) naughty and show-offish, smart-alecky; va.—བྱེད་ to be a smart aleck, to be naughty and show-offish.

ཕེར་ཤ་དོད་པོ་ (pēsha tööbo) naughty and show-offish, smart-alecky.

ཕེར་ཤ་ཚ་པོ་ (pērsha tsābo) sm. ཕེར་ཤ་དོད་པོ་.

ཕོ་ (pō) 1. male, masculine ། བྱ་ཕོ་ Male fowl. 2. positive ། ཕོ་གློག Positive electricity. 3. abbr. of ཕོ་བ་.

ཕོ་དཀར་ (pōgar) 1. animals or birds that have white breasts. 2. a man's cup (slightly larger than a woman's cup).

ཕོ་བཀྱག (pōgyaà) man's cup stand.

ཕོ་སྐད་ (pōgεὲ) male voice.

ཕོ་རྐྱང་ (pōgyaŋ) a single male, a bachelor.

ཕོ་སྐྱུར་ (pōgyur) a divorce initiated by the male.

ཕོ་སྐྱེས་ (pōgyeè) a man, male.

ཕོ་སྐྲན་ (pōdrεn) stomach tumor/ cancer.

ཕོ་ཁ་ (póga) sm. ཕོ་བ་.

ཕོ་ཁེབས་ (pōgeb) quilt.

ཕོ་ཁེབས་རྒྱབ་ཤ་ (pōgeb gyabsha) quilt cover.

ཕོ་ཁེབས་ནང་ཤ་ (pōgeb naŋsha) inside lining of a quilt.

ཕོ་ཁྱི་ (pūkyi) male dog.

ཕོ་ཁྱོག (pō kyōga) a real man, a he-man, a brave/ bold man.

ཕོ་ཁྱོ་གའི་བློ་ལ་མདའ་གཤོང་མདུང་གཤོང་ (pō kyōgε lōla dashoŋ duŋshoŋ) a real man should be both tolerant and magnanimous [Lit. arrow and spear will fit into the mind of a real man].

ཕོ་ཁྲག་འདོན་ (pōdraà dön) vi. to bleed from the stomach.

ཕོ་གུ་ (pōgu) the round silver/ brass studs put on the bridle of horses.

ཕོ་གོས་ཀྱི་ཞྭགས་ནག (pōgöögi jāànag) shung. a black brocade underskirt worn by male lay officials of the traditional Tibetan government during New Year.

ཕོ་གྲངས་ (pōdraŋ) positive number (in math).

ཕོ་གྲོད་ (pōdröö) stomach.

ཕོ་གླ་ (pōla) male musk deer.

ཕོ་གློག (pōlɔɔ̀) positive electricity.

ཕོ་གློག་རྡུལ་ (pōlɔɔ̀ düü) positive electron; positron.

ཕོ་གློག་ཅན་གྱི་དེན་ཙེ་ (pōlɔɔ̀jεngi dēndze) tib.ch. positive electron.

ཕོ་གོད་ (pōgöö) sm. ཕོ་ཁྱོ་ག.

ཕོ་གོད་པོ་ (pō gööbo) sm. ཕོ་ཁྱོ་ག.

ཕོ་གོད་པ་ལས་གཉིད་སྐྱིད་པ་དགའ་ (pō gööbalε ñīi gyiibə ga) it's better to live quietly than do dangerous/ risky things [Lit. it is better to sleep happily than be a brave/ bold man].

ཕོ་རྒྱུ་ (pōgyu) stomach and intestines.

ཕོ་རྒྱུད་ (pōgyüü) paternal relatives, patrilineal descent line.

ཕོ་རྒྱུད་རྨ་ལ་ནད་ (pōgyüü rüünεὲ) ulcer.

ཕོ་རྒྱུད་གཉན་ཚད་ (pōgyüü ñēndzεὲ) enterogastritis.

ཕོ་སྒོ་ (pōgo) strength and ability.

ཕོ་སྒྲོབ་ (pōdrob) bragging, boasting; va.—ཤོད་ to brag, to boast; va.—བྱེད་ to act boastful/ arrogant.

ཕོ་དགོན་ (pōgön) monastery.

ཕོ་བརྒྱའི་ཤེས་པ་ (pōgyε shēèba) collective wisdom/ knowledge.

ཕོ་ངན་ (pōŋεn) an evil man.

ཕོ་ངར་མ་ (pō ŋarma) a hot-blooded/ brave/ courageous man.

ཕོ་གཅུ་ (pōju) screw.

ཕོ་ལྕམ་ (pōjam) althea rosea (used in Tibetan medicine).

ཕོ་ཕྱིབས་ (pōjib) shawl wrapped around the waist.

ཕོ་ཆས་ (pōjεὲ) men's clothing.

ཕོ་ཆས་སྒམ་ (pōjεὲgam) chest for men's clothing, etc.

ཕོ་ཆུ་ (pōju) gastric juice.

ཕོ་ཆེན་ (pōjen) castrated male animals.

ཕོ་མཆོག་མོ་དམན་ (pōcɔɔ̀ momεn) male chauvinism.

ཕོ་ཉ་ (pōña) messenger; va.—རྫོང་; —བཀྱེ་ to send a messenger.

ཕོ་ཉ་མོ་ (pō ñamo) 1. female messenger. 2. maid servant, female servant. 3. pimp.

ཕོ་ཉའི་ཚོགས་པ་ (pōñε tsɔ̄gba) diplomatic corps.

ཕོ་ཏ་ (pōda) stallion.

ཕོ་རྟགས་ (pōdaà) penis.

ཕོ་རྟགས་པགས་ (pō dāgbaà) foreskin.

ཕོ་གཏམ་ (pōdam) men's talk (speaking boldly/ impetuously/ audaciously).

ཕོ་སྟོད་ (pōdöö) striped upper garment worn by opera performers.

ཕོ་ཐ་ (pōda) a coward.

ཕོ་ཐང་འབྲུག (pōtāŋdruù) dragon.

ཕོ་ཐེག (pōdeg) pride, self-esteem.

ཕོ་ཐོང་ (pōdoŋ) a young man.

ཕོ་འདོན་ (pōdön) sm. ཕོ་ཕུད་.

ཕོ་འདོམ་ (pōdom) the span of a man's outstretched arms.

ཕོ་དོར་ (pōdɔr) male pants.

ཕོ་དྲེལ་ (pōdree) male mule.

ཕོ་དྲོད་ (pōdröö) digestion.

ཕོ་དྲོད་ཉམས་ (pōdröö ñam) vi. to have one's digestive power decrease/ decline.

ཕོ་དྲོད་ཤོར་ (pōdröö shɔ̄ɔ) sm. ཕོ་དྲོད་ཉམས་.

ཕོ་གདོང་ (pōdoŋ) male countenance/ look/ appearance.

ཕོ་ནད་ (pōnεὲ) stomach illness, stomach disease.

ཕོ་ནད་གྲང་བ་ (pōnεὲ traŋwa) an disease of the digestive system.

ཕོ་ནོར་ (pōnɔɔ) male yak/ dzo.

ཕོ་སྣེ་ (pōne) anode, positive pole, electrode.

ཕོ་དཔའ་རྟ་མགྱོགས་ (pōba dāgyɔɔ̀) warrior on a swift horse.

ཕོ་ཕག (pōpaà) male pig.

ཕོ་ཕུད་ (pō püü) va. to castrate.

ཕོ་ཕྱག (pōcaà) a male way of doing the traditional greeting in Tibet.

ཕོ་ཕྱུ་ (pōcu) male robe-like dress.

ཕོ་ཕྱུགས་ (pōjuù) male domestic animals.
ཕོ་ཕྲུག་ (pōdrug) young crow.
ཕོ་བ་ (pōwa) stomach.
ཕོ་བ་བཀྲེས་ (pōwa drēè) vi. to be hungry.
ཕོ་བ་ངན་པ་ (pōwa ŋɛmba) a weak/ ill stomach.
ཕོ་བ་རྡོལ་ (pōwa döö) vi. to have a gastric perforation.
ཕོ་བ་ན་ (pōwa na) vi. to have a stomachache, to have a sick stomach.
ཕོ་བ་སྦོས་ (pōwa böö) vi. to have a bloated stomach.
ཕོ་བ་འཚང་བ་ (pōwa tsiŋwa) a digestive illness where a person feels full and loses appetite.
ཕོ་བ་བཟང་པོ་ (pōwa saŋbo) a strong/ good stomach.
ཕོ་བ་རི་ལུ་ (pōwa rilu) sm. ཕོ་བ་རིལ་བུ་.
ཕོ་བ་རིལ་བུ་ (pōwa riibu) piper nigrum (used in Tibetan medicine).
ཕོ་བ་རིས་ (pōwa rii) sm. ཕོ་བ་རིལ་བུ་.
ཕོ་བ་རྨུལ་ནད་ (pōwa rüünɛɛ̀) ulcer.
ཕོ་བའི་ནད་ (pōwɛ nɛè) stomach illness.
ཕོ་བའི་ཆུ་སྐྱུར་ (pōwɛ cūgyur) stomach acid.
ཕོ་བའི་བད་ཀན་ (pōwɛ bɛɛ̀gɛn) gastric juice.
ཕོ་བའི་རྨུལ་ནད་ (pōwɛ rüünɛɛ̀) sm. ཕོ་བ་རྨུལ་ནད་.
ཕོ་བའི་ལྷུང་ཚབས་ (pōwɛ lūŋdzəb) sm. ཕོ་བ་འཚང་བ་.
ཕོ་བའི་རྒྱ་རྩ་ (pōwɛ radza) a vein for draining blood.
ཕོ་བའི་གསང་ (pōwɛ sāŋ) moxabustion applied on the 12th vertebrae.
ཕོ་པོ་ (pōwo) older brother.
ཕོ་བོང་ (pōboŋ) male donkey.
ཕོ་བྱ་ (pōja) cock, rooster.
ཕོ་བྲང་ (pōdraŋ) 1. palace ¶ རྒྱལ་པོའི་ཕོ་བྲང་ King's palace. 2. barrel (of gun).
ཕོ་བྲང་སྐོར་གྱི་སྐད་ (pōdraŋ gɔ̄ɔ̄gi gēɛ̀) the King's English, court language.
ཕོ་བྲང་ཁེ་ལི་མུ་ལིན་ (pōdraŋ kēli mulin) the Kremlin.
ཕོ་བྲང་འཁོར་ (pōdraŋ kɔ̄ɔ̄) 1. queen. 2. court retinue/ attendants. 3. adjacent to the king's palace.
ཕོ་བྲང་ཐེག་ཆེན་ཆོས་གླིང་ (pōdraŋ tēgjen cɔ̄ɔ̄liŋ) Dalai Lama's residence in Dharamsala, India.
ཕོ་བྲང་ནང་འཁོར་ (pōdraŋ naŋgɔɔ) sm. ཕོ་བྲང་འཁོར་.
ཕོ་བྲང་ནང་མ་ (pōdraŋ naŋma) the inner part of the palace where the king resides.
ཕོ་བྲང་དམར་པོ་ (pōdraŋ māābo) the red section of the Potala Palace (the section where the Dalai Lama resides).
ཕོ་བྲང་གསར་པ་ (pōdraŋ sāāba) 14th Dalai Lama's new palace in Norbulingka.
ཕོ་དབང་ (pōwaŋ) 1. patriarchal rights. 2. penis.
ཕོ་འབྲིང་ (pōdriŋ) a man of average ability.
ཕོ་མིན་མོ་མིན་ (pōmin momin) hermaphrodite.
ཕོ་མོ་ (pōmo) male and female; man and woman; gender ¶ ཕོ་མོ་འདྲ་མཉམ་ Equality of the sexes.
ཕོ་མོ་ཁ་སློེལ་ (pōmo kādree) marrying.
ཕོ་མོ་གོ་བསྡེར་ (pōmo goder) shung. men and women going as grooms and brides ¶ ཕོ་མོ་གོ་བསྡེར་ཆོག་པའི་སྣན་སིང་ཞུ་རྟེན་དངུལ་ The money and gifts given when men and women seek permission (from their lords) to go as brides and grooms.
ཕོ་མོ་རྒན་གཞོན་ (pōmo gɛnshön) everybody [Lit. male, female, old, young].
ཕོ་མོ་གཉིས་ (pōmo ñīi) both sexes.
ཕོ་མོ་འདྲ་མཉམ་ (pōmo drañam) gender equality.
ཕོ་མོ་དབང་ཆ་འདྲ་མཉམ་ (pōmo wāŋja drañam) gender equality in power/ authority.
ཕོ་མོའི་སྐྱེ་འཕེལ་ (pōmö gyēpel) sexual reproduction.
ཕོ་མོའི་དབང་པོ་ (pōmö wāŋbo) sexual organs, genitals.
ཕོ་མོའི་དབྱེ་བ་ (pōmö yēwa) difference between men and women.
ཕོ་མོའི་མཚན་མ་ (pōmö tsɛ̄nma) sm. ཕོ་མོའི་དབང་པོ་.
ཕོ་རྫི་ (pōdzi) male hormone.
ཕོ་བཙོག (pōdzɔɔ̀) dauntless, unyielding.
ཕོ་ཚད་ (pōdzɛɛ̀) infection in the stomach.
ཕོ་ཚོད་ (pōdzöö) 1. boastful. 2. confident, assured.
ཕོ་ཚོས་ (pōdzöö) sm. རྒྱ་སྙིགས་.
ཕོ་མཚན་ (pōdzɛn) penis.
ཕོ་མཚན་སྐྱོན་ཅན་ (pōdzɛn gyönjɛn) penis unable to have an erection, impotent.
ཕོ་མཚན་སོས་ཟིན་ནད་ (pōdzɛn sōōsin nɛɛ̀) an infection of penis which causes excruciating pain.
ཕོ་ཞིམ་ (pōshim) male cat.
ཕོ་གཞུག (pōshuŋ) anus.
ཕོ་གཞོན་ (pōshön) young man.
ཕོ་བཞི་ (pōshi) males animals that are four years old.
ཕོ་ཟད་མོ་ཐུག (pōsɛɛ̀ moduù) fighting to the end; va.—བྱེད་ [Lit. the men have been killed, the women oppose].
ཕོ་ཟད་མོ་ལ་ཐུག་བར་ (pōsɛɛ̀ mola tūgbar) sm. ཕོ་ཟད་མོ་ཐུག.
ཕོ་ཟོམ་ (pōsom) Tibetan man's woolen boot.
ཕོ་གཟེར་ (pōser) a stomach disease.
ཕོ་བཟོ་ (pōso) 1. masculinity qualities/ characteristics. 2. va. to say things with uncertainty. 3. va. to concoct/ fabricate (a story).
ཕོ་བཟོ་དོད་པོ་ (pōso tööbo) masculine, manly.
ཕོ་ཡན་ (pōyɛn) sm. ཕོ་རེང་.
ཕོ་ཡིག (pōyii) five letters in the Tibetan alphabet that are considered male letters: ཀ་ཅ་ཏ་པ་ཙ་.
ཕོ་རབ་ (pōrəb) 1. real man, he-man. 2. a tolerant/ broad-minded man, a man of vision/ learning; va.—བྱེད་ to be the best among men.
ཕོ་རབ་ཁོག་པར་རྟ་བརྒྱ་རྒྱུག་ས་ཡོད་ (pōrəb kōgbar dāgya gyugsa yöö) sm. ཕོ་རྒྱ་གཞི་བློ་ལ་མདའ་གཞོང་མདུང་གཞོང་.
ཕོ་རབ་གཅིག་གི་བློ་རྩེ་ལས། ཕོ་འབྲིང་གསུམ་གྱི་གྲོས་བསྡུར་དགའ་ (pōrəbjiggi lödzelɛ pōdriŋsumgi trööödur ga) a decision made by three average persons is better than a decision made by one learned person.
ཕོ་རབ་བརྡ་ཡིས་ཆོག ཁྲུང་རྣན་བེར་ཀས་བཤད་ (pōrəb dayii cɔ̄ɔ̀ lāŋgɛn bergɛɛ̀ shɛ̄ɛ̀) the wise man needs only but a hint, fools need the stick (to get the message).
ཕོ་རབས་ཆད་པ་ (pōrəb cɛ̄ɛ̀ba) a sterile man.
ཕོ་རིགས་ (pōrii) males.
ཕོ་རེང་ (pōreŋ) bachelor.
ཕོ་རོག (pōrɔɔ̀) raven.
ཕོ་རོག་གིས་གཏོར་མ་སྒུག་པ་ལྟར་ (pōrɔɔ̀gi dɔ̄ɔ̄ma guùbadar) eagerly waiting for sth. [Lit. a raven waiting for གཏོར་མ་].
ཕོ་རོག་ནག་ཆུང་ (pōrɔɔ̀ nəgjuŋ) crow.
ཕོ་རོག་བརྗེད་སྐུང་ (pōrɔɔ̀ bɛ̄ègʊŋ) forgeting where sth. was put/ left [Lit. the crow forgets where sth. was hidden].
ཕོ་རོག་མིག (pōrɔɔ̀ mig) 1. crow's eye. 2. a riding gown worn by high ranking lamas.
ཕོ་ལྷུང་ (pōluŋ) a disease of the stomach.
ཕོ་ལྭ་ (pōla) a man's dress (ཕྱུ་པ་).
ཕོ་ལད་ (pōlɛɛ̀) a lazy person.
ཕོ་ལན་ (polɛn) Poland.
ཕོ་ལིང་མོ་ལིང་ (pōliŋ moliŋ) a person with both male and female organs, hermaphrodite.
ཕོ་ལུག (pōluù) male sheep.
ཕོ་ལུང་ (pōluŋ) a ribbon/ strap for tying.
ཕོ་ལོ་ (pōlo) males years (years in which the element is male).
ཕོ་ལོ་དྲུག (pōlo truù) six male years of the Tibetan calendar: rat, tiger, dragon, horse, monkey, dog.
ཕོ་ལོག (pōlɔɔ̀) 1. sm. གླང་ཐབས་. 2. name of dish which is made up of butter, tsampa and brown sugar.
ཕོ་ལོང་ (pōloŋ) ball of thread/ yarn.
ཕོ་ཤ་མོ་སྐྱོད་ (pōsha mogyöö) law cases involving murder or stealing of another person's wife.
ཕོ་ཤར་ (pōshar) a young male adult.
ཕོ་ཤའི་ཁུ་བ་ (pōshɛ kūwə) a broth made of rice with minced meat.

ཕོ་ཤལ་ (pōshɛɛ) the worst kind of man, a man who has no class.
ཕོ་ཤེད་ (pōsheè) brave.
ཕོ་ཤེལ་ (pōshee) gastroscope.
ཕོ་ཤོབ་ (pōshob) sm. ཕོ་སྒྲོབ་.
ཕོ་སུལ་ (pōsüü) stomach folds.
ཕོ་གསར་ (pōsar) young man.
ཕོ་ཧྲང་ (pōhraŋ) sm. ཕོ་ཧྲེང་.
ཕོ་ཧྲེང་ (pōhreŋ) bachelor.
ཕོ་ཧྲེངས་ (pōhreŋ) sm. ཕོ་ཧྲེང་.
ཕོག (pɔ̄ɔ) 1. vi. to be hit/ struck ། ཁོའི་མགོ་ལ་རྡོ་ཕོག་འདུག He was hit on the head by a stone. 2. vi. to be hurt (feelings) ། ཁོའི་སྐད་ཆ་འདི་མོའི་སེམས་ལ་ཕོག་སོང་ What he said hurt her feelings. 3. vi. to fall on ། ལས་འགན་དེ་ཁོ་ཕོག་གི་རེད་ The responsibility will fall on him. ། ཤོག་བུ་དེར་ཆུ་ཕོག Water fell on the paper. 4. sm. ཕྱུགས་. 5. imp. of འཕོག.
ཕོག་གུ་ (pɔ̄ɔgu) sm. ཕོ་གུ.
ཕོག་ཐུག (pɔ̄gduù) harming, offending, hurting; va.—གཏོང་ to offend, to hurt (feelings); vi.—འགྲོ་; —ཤོར་ to involuntarily offend/ hurt, to become offended/ hurt ། ཁོ་ཚོའི་སྤྱི་ཚོགས་ལམ་ལུགས་དེ་ལ་ཕོག་ཐུག་སོང་བར་སྐྲག་པ་རེད་ (They) feared (it) would offend their social system.
ཕོག་དུག (pɔ̄gduù) stimulation, excitement; va.—བྱེད་ to stimulate/ excite.
ཕོག་དུག་ཡོད་པའི་རྫས་ (pɔ̄gduù yö̱öbɛ dzɛ̱ɛ̀) a stimulant.
ཕོག་དུག་ཡོད་པའི་བཟའ་བཏུང་ (pɔ̄gduù yö̱öbɛ sa̱duŋ) foods that stimulate.
ཕོག་སླའི་ནད་རིགས་ (pɔ̄glɛ nɛ̱ɛ̀rig) a common malady/ illness.
ཕོགས་ (pɔ̄ɔ) wages, salary; va.—རྒྱག to pay salary.
ཕོགས་སྐལ་ (pɔ̄ɔgɛɛ) a share of a salary ། ཁོང་ལ་ཕོག་སྐལ་གཉིས་རག་པ་རེད་ He got two shares of salary.
ཕོགས་ཁང་ (pɔ̄ɔgaŋ) payroll office.
ཕོགས་ཁང་ལས་ཁུངས་ (pɔ̄ɔgaŋ lɛ̱ɛ̀guŋ) payroll office.
ཕོགས་དངུལ་ (pɔ̄ɔŋüü) salary, wage (in money).
ཕོགས་ཆ་ (pɔ̄ɔja) salary, wage.
ཕོགས་ཆག (pɔ̄ɔ cāà) vi. to have salary or wages reduced.
ཕོགས་གཉེར་ (pɔ̄ɔñer) abbr. of ཕོགས་ཁང་ and གཉེར་ཚང་.
ཕོགས་ཐེབས་ (pɔ̄gteb) an endowment fund for salary.
ཕོགས་ཐོབ་ (pɔ̄gdob) sm. ཕོགས་.
ཕོགས་ཐོབ་ཀྱི་འཚོ་སྐྱོང་ (pɔ̄gtobgi tsōgyoŋ) livelihood through wage earning.
ཕོགས་ཐོབ་ཀྱི་ལམ་ལུགས་ (pɔ̄gtobgi la̱mluù) wage/ salary system.
ཕོགས་ཐོབ་ལམ་ལུགས་ (pɔ̄gdob la̱mluù) sm. ཕོགས་ཐོབ་ཀྱི་ལམ་ལུགས་.
ཕོགས་མདའ་རྩིས་སྲུས་ (pɔ̄ɔ da̱ dzīì sɛ̄ɛ̀) shung. abbr. of ཕོགས་དཔོན་, མདའ་དཔོན་, རྩིས་དཔོན་ and སྲུས་རྣམ་པ་.
ཕོགས་ནས་རྒྱག་ཐེབས་ (pɔ̄ɔnɛɛ̀ gya̱gdeb) shung. grain meant to create an endowment to provide salary for sth. ། ཤེལ་ཆོས་དགེ་འདུན་གྱི་ཕོགས་ནས་རྒྱག་ཐེབས་སུ་མཐོང་སྨོན་གཞིས་ལྷེ་བ་མ་ལག་གི་ཁ་འཛིན་བསྐྱལ་བ་ The possession of the Tongmon estate was granted to the Shelcho Monastery as an endowment to provide salary for the monks.
ཕོགས་སྣོན་ (pɔ̄ɔnön) subsidy, allowance, additional/ supplementary salary.
ཕོགས་དཔོན་ (pɔ̄ɔbön) paymaster.
ཕོགས་སྤར་ (pɔ̄ɔ bār) va. to raise wages/ salary.
ཕོགས་སྤྲོད་ (pɔ̄ɔ drȫö) va. to pay salary/ wages.
ཕོགས་འཕར་ (pɔ̄ɔ pār) vi. to have wages/ salary get increased.
ཕོགས་འབབ་ (pɔ̄mbɔb) sm. ཕོགས་.
ཕོགས་དམིགས་ (pɔ̄ɔmig) shung. sth. meant for paying salary ། འབྲུ་ཁལ་ ༡༠༠ ཕོགས་དམིགས་སུ་བསྐྱལ་བ་ (They) gave 100 ཁལ་ of grain that was meant for salary.
ཕོགས་ཟན་ (pɔ̄gsɛn) salaried employees.
ཕོགས་ཟན་པ་ (pɔ̄gsɛmba) salaried workers.
ཕོགས་ལེན་ (pɔ̄ɔ le̱n) va. to get one's wage/ salary.
ཕོང་: p. ཕོངས་; f. ཕོང་ (pōŋ) 1. vi. to become destitute/ poor/ poverty-stricken ། ཟས་གོས་ཀྱིས་ཕོངས་ནས་ Being destitute with regards to food and clothing. 2. vi. to be incomplete, to be insufficient.
ཕོང་གན་ (pōŋgɛn) a huge boulder.
ཕོངས་ (pōŋ) p. of ཕོང་.
ཕོངས་གྲིར་ཤི་ (pōŋdri shī) vi. to starve to death.
ཕོངས་ངན་ (pōŋŋɛn) extremely poor/ destitute.
ཕོངས་རྟགས་ (pōŋdaà) 1. signs of poverty. 2. state of poverty.
ཕོངས་པ་ (pōŋba) poor/ destitute person.
ཕོངས་པར་འགྱུར་ (pōŋbar gyu̱r) vi. to become poor/ destitute.
ཕོངས་པར་བྱེད་ (pōŋbar ce̱è) va. to make poor/ destitute.
ཕོད་ (pȫö) 1. (vb.+ —) va. to dare or have the courage (to do) ། དགེ་རྒན་ལ་དྲི་བ་དེ་འདྲ་འདྲི་ཕོད་ཀྱི་མེད་ (They) did not dare ask the teacher such questions. ། ཁོ་སྡུག་པོ་འདི་འདྲ་གཏོང་ཕོད་ཀྱི་མ་རེད་ (They) will not dare to torture him like that. 2. revenge, rematch; va.—རྒྱག to get revenge, to have a rematch.
ཕོད་ཀ་ (pȫöga) a type of dress worn by the tantric practioneer and cham dancers.
ཕོད་དཀར་ (pȫögar) white spots (usu. refers to animals).
ཕོད་ཁ་ (pȫöga) sm. ཕོད་ཀ་.
ཕོད་རྒྱག (pȫö gya̱à) va. to challenge.
ཕོད་ཆུང་ (pȫöjuŋ) not courageous, cowardly.
ཕོད་ཆུང་ངེ་བ་ (pȫö cūŋŋewa) in a cowardly manner.
ཕོད་ཆུང་སེ་བ་ (pȫö cūŋsewa) sm. ཕོད་ཆུང་ངེ་བ.
ཕོད་པ་ཅན་ (pȫöbəjɛn) daring, brave.
ཕོད་པོ་ (pȫöbo) staunch, unshakable.
ཕོད་བཙུགས་ (pȫö dzūù) va. to throw the gauntlet, to challenge.
ཕོད་འཛར་ (pȫödzar) a kind of tassel.
ཕོན་ (pōn) quantity, amount, number ། ཉི་མ་གཅིག་ལ་ས་ཕག་བཟོས་པའི་ཕོན་ནི་ As for the number of bricks made in one day.
ཕོན་ཆུང་ (pōnjuŋ) small quantity/ amount/ number.
ཕོན་ཆེ་ (pōnje) sm. ཕོན་ཆེན་པོ་.
ཕོན་ཆེན་ (pōnjen) sm. ཕོན་ཆེན་པོ་.
ཕོན་ཆེན་པོ་ (pōn cēmbo) a large number/ amount/ quantity, many ། གཏེར་ཁ་ཕོན་ཆེན་པོ་གསར་དུ་རྙེད་ཡོད་པ་རེད་ (They) discovered many new mines.
ཕོན་པོ་ (pōmbo) 1. a bunch (of flowers, etc.). 2. a collection (of books).
ཕོན་བུ་ (pōnbu) sm. ཕོན་འཛར་.
ཕོན་འབོར་ (pōmbɔɔ) quantity, amount, number ། དངོས་ཟོག་བཙོང་བའི་ཕོན་འབོར་ The amount of goods sold.
ཕོན་འཛར་ (pōndzar) sm. ཕོད་འཛར་.
ཕོབ་ (pōb) imp. of འབེབས་.
ཕོམ་ (pōm) sm. ཕོམ་ཤོག.
ཕོམ་ཀྲིན་ (pōmdrin) eng. fountain pen.
ཕོམ་ཤོག (pōmshɔɔ) eng.tib. a form (to fill out).
ཕོའི་སྤྱོད་ཁང་ (pȫöjöögaŋ) men's toilet.
ཕོའི་རང་བཞིན་ (pȫö ra̱ŋshin) the male or positive element in nature.
ཕོའི་རང་བཞིན་གྱི་འགྱུར་ལྡོག (pȫö ra̱ŋshingi gyu̱ndo) positive reaction (in chemistry).
ཕོའོ་ (pōwo) ch. tickets.
ཕོར་ (pɔ̄ɔ) bowl, cup (abbr. of ཕོར་པ་) ། ཇ་ཕོར་ Tea cup.
ཕོར་དཀྲུག་འཁོར་ལོ་ (pɔ̄ɔdruù kɔ̄ɔlo) a lathe for making wooden bowls.
ཕོར་དཀྲུག་ལྕགས་ཀྱུ་ (pɔ̄ɔdruù jāggyu) a metal instrument for carving/ lathing wooden bowls.
ཕོར་ཁུག (pɔ̄ɔku) sm. ཕོར་པ་.
ཕོར་སྒྱེ་ (pɔ̄ɔgye) a bag for carrying bowls.
ཕོར་ཚས་ཚ་སྒམ་ (pɔ̄ɔjɛɛ̀ cāgam) a box/ case for wooden cups and related things.

ཕོར་རྙི་ (pɔ̄ɔ̄ñi) bird trap/ snare.

ཕོར་པ་ (pɔ̄ɔ̄bə) wooden bowl/ cup; va.—དཀྲུགས་ to lathe a wooden bowl.

ཕོར་ཕྱིས་ (pɔ̄ɔ̄cii) a cloth for wiping wooden bowls.

ཕོར་བུ་ (pɔ̄ɔ̄bu) a small wooden bowl.

ཕོར་དབྱིབས་ (pɔ̄ɔ̄yib) bowl shaped.

ཕོར་འཕྱིད་ (pɔ̄ɔ̄jii) sm. ཕོར་ཕྱིས་.

ཕོར་མོ་ས་ (pɔ̄rmosa) Formosa.

ཕོར་མར་ (pɔ̄ɔ̄mar) small pieces of butter that are put directly into cups containing black tea.

ཕོར་རྩི་ (pɔ̄ɔ̄dzi) the varnish used on Tibetan wooden bowls.

ཕོར་རས་ (pɔ̄ɔ̄rɛɛ̀) cloth used to wrap wooden bowls.

ཕོར་རུ་ (pɔ̄ɔ̄ru) sm. ཕོར་པ་.

ཕོར་རྭ་ (pɔ̄ɔ̄ra) horn in which gunpowder is kept for Tibetan rifles.

ཕོར་ཤུབས་ (pɔ̄ɔ̄shub) 1. a case for wooden bowls/ cups. 2. a traditional Tibetan pouch for wooden bowls/ cups which is worn at the back by tt. government officials.

ཕོལ་ (pȫȫ) boil, abscess, sore.

ཕོལ་འབྲས་ (pȫndrɛɛ̀) a type of cancerous sore.

ཕོལ་མིག་ (pȫö̀mig) a kind of infectious skin disease.

ཕོས་ (pȫö̀) p. of འཕོ་.

ཕོས་པོར་ (pȫö̀bɔɔ) a man who flees at the time of divorce because he is in the wrong.

ཕྱ་ (cā) luck, fortune, fate.

ཕྱ་མཁན་ (cāñɛn) fortune teller.

ཕྱ་ངན་ (cāŋɛn) bad luck/ fortune.

ཕྱ་པ་ (cāba) sm. ཕྱ་མཁན་.

ཕྱ་མ་ཕྱོ་ (cāma cō) vi. to be touched/ moved (emotionally).

ཕྱ་མ་ (cāma) fortune teller.

ཕྱ་མི་ (cāmi) sm. ཕྱ་མཁན་.

ཕྱ་རྩི་ (cā dzī) va. to tell fortunes.

ཕྱ་ཚན་ (cādzɛn) the first stool of a human infant, dog or horse before they have been breast feed that is used in Tibetan medicine.

ཕྱ་ཚན་གསུམ་ (cādzɛn sūm) sm. ཕྱ་ཚན་.

ཕྱ་ར་ (cāra) a tarpaulin-like blanket made of yak hair (usu. used for dying grain).

ཕྱ་ར་སྒྲུ་འདེགས་ (cāra trudeg) sm. ཕྱར་བ་སྒྲུ་འདེགས་.

ཕྱ་ལེ་བ་ (cālewa) sm. ལེབ་ལེབ་.

ཕྱག་ (cāà) 1. h. of ལག་པ་. 2. respect, honor; va.—བྱེད་; —འཚལ་ to pay one's respect, to prostrate as a sign of respect ¶ རྒྱལ་པོ་ཕྱག་བྱེད་པར་ཡོང་ (They) came to pay their respect to the king. 3. makes honorifics (e.g., ལས་ཀ་ becomes ཕྱག་ལས་).

ཕྱག་སྐྱིད་ (cāàgüü) h. of སྐྱིད་པ་.

ཕྱག་ཁང་ (cāàgaŋ) 1. mosque. 2. Buddhist temple where one does prostrations.

ཕྱག་ཁུག་ (cəguù) purse, handbag (h.).

ཕྱག་མཁར་ (cāàgar) staff, walking stick, cane (h.).

ཕྱག་འཁར་ (cāàgar) sm. ཕྱག་མཁར་.

ཕྱག་གོང་ (cāàgoŋ) back of the hand (h.).

ཕྱག་གྱང་འགྱེལ་ (cāàgyaŋ gyee) va. to prostrate putting one's body on the ground.

ཕྱག་སྒྲོན་ (cāàdrön) h. of སྒྲོན་.

ཕྱག་བགྱི་ (cāà gyi) va. to prostrate.

ཕྱག་འགྲོས་ (cāàdröö̀) giving out, distributing (h.); va.—གནང་ to give out/ distribute.

ཕྱག་རྒྱ་ (cāàgya) 1. mudra (a religious hand symbol); va.—བྱེད་. 2. clasping palms of hands together as a respectful greeting. 3. sm. གུས་ཚུལ་. 4. sm. ཕྱག་ཐེལ་.

ཕྱག་རྒྱ་མ་ (cāàgyama) consort of a lama.

ཕྱག་རྒྱུན་ (cāàgyün) method/ system/ manner of putting sth. into practice.

ཕྱག་རྒྱུས་ (cāàgyüǜ) h. of ཆགས་ཁེབས་.

ཕྱག་སྒམ་ (cāàgam) h. of སྒམ་.

ཕྱག་ངར་ (cāàŋar) h.of ལག་ངར་.

ཕྱག་དངུལ་ (cəŋüü) h. of དངུལ་.

ཕྱག་ལྕགས་ (cāàjaà) h. of སྒོ་ལྕགས་.

ཕྱག་བཅས་ (cāàjɛɛ̀) a honorific phrase usu. used when writing to the Dalai Lama or one's root lama that means: while prostrating (I say).

ཕྱག་ཆ་ (cāàja) h. of ལག་ཆ་.

ཕྱག་མཆོད་ (cāàjöö) prostrating and making offerings.

ཕྱག་ཇེམ་ (cāàjem) h. of ཇེམ་.

ཕྱག་འཇུག་ (cənjuù) h. of ཉེས་རྡུང་.

ཕྱག་རྗེས་ (cāàjeè) h. of ལག་རྗེས་.

ཕྱག་ཉ་ (cāàña) h. of ལག་ཉ་.

ཕྱག་སྙན་ (cāàñɛn) h. of སྒྲ་སྙན་.

ཕྱག་སྙུག་ (cāàñuù) h. of སྙུག་གུ་.

ཕྱག་བརྙན་ (cāàñɛn) h. of སྒྲ་བརྙན་.

ཕྱག་ཏག་གནང་ (cāgdaà nāŋ) va. to clap one's hands to summon a servant.

ཕྱག་ཏུ་ཐེངས་ (cāàdu tēŋ) vi. to get hold of (h.).

ཕྱག་ཏུ་བཞེས་ (cāàdu sheè) h. of ལག་ཏུ་ལེན་.

ཕྱག་ཏུ་སོན་ (cāàdu sōŋ) vi. to come into one's hand/ possession (h.).

ཕྱག་གདོང་བ་གནང་ (cāà dōŋwa nāŋ) va. to shake hands (h.).

ཕྱག་གདོང་རེས་ (cāà dōŋreè) shaking hands (h.); va.—མཛད་; —གནང་ to shake hands ¶ ཁོང་གཉིས་ཕྱག་གདོང་རེས་གནང་སོང་ They shook hands.

ཕྱག་བཏགས་ (cāàdaà) h. of ལག་བཏགས་.

ཕྱག་བཏབ་ (cāà dəb) p. of ཕྱག་འདེབས་.

ཕྱག་རྟགས་ (cāàdaà) h. of ལག་རྟགས་.

ཕྱག་རྟགས་དགོངས་དོན་ (cāàdaà goŋdön) shung. as per the approval/ order/ instructions (h.).

ཕྱག་རྟགས་ཕེབས་ (cāàdaà pēè) va. to receive approval (h.).

ཕྱག་རྟགས་ཕོག་ (cāàdaà pɔ̄ɔ̀) shung. vi. to get signed approval on a document from either the Dalai Lama or the regent.

ཕྱག་རྟེན་ (cāàden) a gift taken when going to meet sb.

ཕྱག་སྟོང་སྤྱན་སྟོང་ (cāàdoŋ jɛ̄ndoŋ) an image/ statue of Avaloketisvara with one thousand eyes and hands.

ཕྱག་བསྟར་ (cāàdar) sm. ཕྱག་བསྟར་མ་.

ཕྱག་བསྟར་མ་ (cāàdarma) made or written by (his or her) own hand (h.) ¶ སྲིད་འཛིན་ཕྱག་བྲིས་ཕྱག་བསྟར་མ་ A letter in the president's own handwriting.

ཕྱག་ཐམ་ (cāàdam) sm. ཕྱག་དམ་.

ཕྱག་ཐེལ་ (cāàdee) a seal; va.—སྤྲོན་ to affix a seal.

ཕྱག་མཐིལ་ (cāàdii) h. of སྣར་མཐིལ་.

ཕྱག་མཐིལ་ནང་སྒྲུག་འདྲ་ (cāàdii) h. of སྣར་མཐིལ་ནང་སྒྲུག་འདྲ་.

ཕྱག་མཐེ་ (cāàde) h. of མཐེ་བོང་.

ཕྱག་ཐོ་ (cāàdo) h. of ཐོ་.

ཕྱག་དམ་ (cāàdam) 1. a seal (h.); va.—རྒྱག་; —སྤྲོན་ to affix/ stamp a seal. 2. assistant to the monk ཚོགས་ཆེན་དགེ་བསྐོས་ at Monlam.

ཕྱག་དར་ (cāàdar) 1. sweeping, cleaning; va.—བྱེད་ to sweep, to clean up. 2. a hand-held flag/ banner. 3. waste, trash, garbage.

ཕྱག་དར་ཁྲོད་ཀྱི་ཆོས་གོས་ (cāàdar trö̀ögi cö̀ögö̀ö) a monk's vestment made of patched/ waste materials.

ཕྱག་དར་ཁྲོད་པ་ (cāàdar trö̀öbə) person who rummages through garbage looking for clothes.

ཕྱག་དར་གོས་ (cāàdar kö̀ö) clothes picked from the garbage.

ཕྱག་དེབ་ (cāàdeb) h. of དེབ་.

ཕྱག་དྲིལ་ (cədrii) h. of དྲིལ་བུ་.

ཕྱག་དྲུང་ (cāàdruŋ) shung. title of the head clerk of the ཕྱག་སྣང་.

ཕྱག་གདན་ (cāàdɛn) a wooden board used for prostrating.

ཕྱག་གདུབ་ (cəgdub) bangle, bracelet (h.).

ཕྱག་བདར་ (cāàdar) sweeping; va.—བྱེད་ to sweep.

ཕྱག་བདེ་པ་ (cāà dewa) 1. young monks who acts as tea servers at their monastery's prayer assemblies. 2. a person who is good with his hands (h.).

ཕྱག་མདའ་ (cānda) h. of མདའ་ and མེ་མདའ་.

ཕྱག་མདའ་སྐྱོན་ (cānda gyǒn) va. to fire a gun, to shoot an arrow (h.).

ཕྱག་མདའ་གནང་ (cānda nāŋ) sm. ཕྱག་མདའ་སྐྱོན་.

ཕྱག་མདུད་ (cāàdüü) protective ribbons blessed by a lama (h.).

ཕྱག་འདུད་ (cāndüü) h. of འདུད་པ་.

ཕྱག་འདེབས་ (cāà deb) va. to found (a monasteries, institutions, etc.) ¶ དགོན་པ་དེ་ཀརྨ་པ་སྐུ་ཕྲེང་བཞི་པས་ཕྱག་བཏབ་པ་རེད་ The Fourth Karma incarnation founded the monastery.

ཕྱག་འདེབས་པ་ (cāà debba) founder of a monastery/ temple.

ཕྱག་འདེབས་ཤས་བོགས་ (cāndeb shɛ̄ɛ̀bɔ̀ɔ) shung. (fields) that are planted by the estate and those that are leased a fee of 50% of the yield ¶ ཕྱག་འདེབས་ཤས་བོགས་སོགས་སྤྲོད་རིགས་ཆེ་ཕྲ་མཐའ་དག་འབྲེད་གདན་འབྲུ་དོན་བཞིན་དགོས་རྒྱུ་ Handing over (fields) such as those that are planted by the estate and those leased for 50% of the yield should be done in accordance with the land tenure document.

ཕྱག་འདྲེན་ (cāndren) helping someone stand and walk by holding their forearm or elbow; va.—ཞུ་.

ཕྱག་རྡོར་ (cāàdɔɔ) sm. ཕྱག་ན་རྡོ་རྗེ་.

ཕྱག་ལྡེ་ (cānde) h. of ལྡེ་མིག.

ཕྱག་སྡུད་ (cāndüü) h. of ལག་སྡུད་.

ཕྱག་བདར་ (cāàda) h. of ལག་བདར་.

ཕྱག་ན་རྡོ་རྗེ་ (cāàna dɔ̄ɔje) the Bodhisattva Vajrapani.

ཕྱག་ན་པདྨ་ (cāàna bɛ̀ɛma) the Bodhisattva Avaloketisvara.

ཕྱག་ནང་ (cāànaŋ) shung. 1. abbr. of ཕྱག་མཛོད་ and ནང་ཟན་. 2. clerk (jola) in the Tseja and Laja supply offices of the traditional Tibetan government.

ཕྱག་ནས་ (cāànɛɛ̀) barley that has been blessed by a high lama.

ཕྱག་ནས་དུག (cāànɛɛ̀ du̱ù) va. to burn barley (put barley on a fire) to ensure no bad/ evil occurs.

ཕྱག་ནས་མ་ (cāànɛɛ̀ma) statues that have been blessed by barley by a high lama.

ཕྱག་སྣག (cāànag) h. of སྣག་ཚ་.

ཕྱག་སྣམ་ (cāànam) h. of སྣམ་བུ་.

ཕྱག་སྣེ་ (cāàne) 1. h. of ལག་སྣེ་. 2. pocket money (h.).

ཕྱག་པ་ (cāgba) a bundle.

ཕྱག་དཔུང་ (cāàbuŋ) h. of དཔུང་པ་.

ཕྱག་དཔེ་ (cāàbe) h. of དཔེ་ཆ་.

ཕྱག་དཔེ་ཁང་ (cāàbegaŋ) the Dalai Lama's private library.

ཕྱག་ཕེབས་ (cāàpeè) 1. vi. to arrive (h.) ¶ ཁོང་ཚོས་ཐིམ་བུ་རུ་ཕྱག་ཕེབས་པ་ན་ When they arrived at Thimpu. 2. a phrase of greeting to an arriving person.

ཕྱག་ཕེབས་གནང་བྱུང་ (cāàpeè nāŋjuŋ) sm. ཕྱག་ཕེབས་, 2.

ཕྱག་ཕེབས་གནང་ (cāàpeè nāŋ) va. to arrive (h.).

ཕྱག་ཕྱི་ (cāgji) servant (h.).

ཕྱག་ཕྱི་ཞབས་ཏོག (cāgji shəbdoò) serving/ taking care of as a servant (usu. lamas).

ཕྱག་ཕྱིད་ (cāgjiì) servant, retinue; va.—ཞུ་ to serve, to be sb.'s servant or in sb.'s retinue ¶ ཉི་རིང་མེད་པར་ཕྱག་ཕྱིད་ཞུས་པ་རེད་ We have served impartially. ¶ རྒྱལ་པོའི་ཕྱག་ཕྱིད་ The king's retinue.

ཕྱག་ཕྲེང་ (cāàdreŋ) h. of ཕྲེང་བ་.

ཕྱག་འཕྲེང་ (cāàdreŋ) h. of ཕྲེང་བ་.

ཕྱག་བུན་ (cāàbün) h. of བུ་ལོན་.

ཕྱག་བྱ་ (cāgja) sm. ཕྱག་འཚལ་.

ཕྱག་བྲིས་ (cāgdriì) writing (h.); va.—གནང་.

ཕྱག་བྲིས་བཀའ་ལན་ (cāgdriì gālɛn) a reply/ answer (h.).

ཕྱག་དབང་ (cāàwaŋ) 1. type of blessing where lama puts his hands on the head of the supplicant; va.—ཞུ་ to request such a blessing; va.—གནང་ to give such a blessing. 2. paying respect to a superior ¶ བློན་པོ་གཉིས་ཀྱི་ཕྱག་དབང་དུ་བཅར་བ་རེད་ They came to call (pay respect) on the two ministers.

ཕྱག་འབབ་ (cāŋbəb) h. of ཡོང་འབབ་.

ཕྱག་འབུལ་ (cāmbüü) a type of respectful greeting made (to a superior or equal) by taking off one's hat and moving one's hands from the waist to the front of one's face while bowing the head down; va.—ཞུ་ to salute/ greet (superiors) (h.); va.—བཞེས་ to accept/ acknowledge such a greeting (h.).

ཕྱག་འབུལ་སྐྱབས་ཞུ་ (cāmbüü gyābshu) doing ཕྱག་འབུལ་ and asking for a favor.

ཕྱག་འབུལ་དཔྱལ་སྐོར་ (chāmbü drɛ̄ɛgɔɔ) greeting each other with ཕྱག་འབུལ་.

ཕྱག་འབེག (cāmbeg) h. of འབེག.

ཕྱག་འབེབས་ (cāmbeb) sm. ཕྱག་འཇུག.

ཕྱག་འབྱོར་ (cāmjɔɔ) sm. ཕྱག་སོན་.

ཕྱག་འབྲུ་ (cāndru) h. of འབྲུ་.

ཕྱག་སྦག (cāàbaà) h. of སྦག.

ཕྱག་སྦལ་ (cāàbəə) shung. sm. བཙོན་ཁང་.

ཕྱག་སྦུག (cəbuù) manager, steward (usu. of a monastery or a college within a monastery).

ཕྱག་འབྲེལ་ (cāndree) colleague, co-worker (h.).

ཕྱག་སྦྲེལ་ (cāàdree) sm. ཕྱག་འབྲེལ་.

ཕྱག་མ་ (cāàma) broom; va.—ཕྱག to sweep with a broom.

ཕྱག་མ་ཕྱག་རན་པའི་དུས་ལ་ (cāàma cāàrɛnbɛ tü̱ùla) (coneys the meaning that the time is right for sweeping out sth. bad. [Lit. it's time to sweep].

ཕྱག་མོ་ (cāàmo) h. of མོ་.

ཕྱག་སྨྱུག (cəñuù) h. of སྨྱུ་གུ.

ཕྱག་བཙལ་ (cāàdzɛɛ) p. of ཕྱག་འཚལ་.

ཕྱག་རྩ་ (cāàdza) 1. h. of མ་རྩ་. 2. h. of རྩ་.

ཕྱག་རྩིས་ (cədziì) 1. h. of རྩིས་. 2. shung. abbr. of རྩེ་ཕྱག and རྩིས་དཔོན་.

ཕྱག་རྩེ་སྡོད་ (cāàdze drɔ̃ɔ̀) va. to prostrate to one another simultaneously (usu. used for lamas).

ཕྱག་ཚང་ (cāàdzaŋ) kitchen (h.).

ཕྱག་ཚད་ (cāàdzɛɛ̀) the width of a line.

ཕྱག་ཚེམ་ (cāàdzem) h. of ཚེམ་བུ་.

ཕྱག་ཚོད་ (cāàdzöò) h. of ཆུ་ཚོད་.

ཕྱག་ཚོད་ཐག་པ་ (cāàdzöò tāgba) watchband.

ཕྱག་མཚན་ (cāàdzɛn) symbolic implement/ instrument.

ཕྱག་འཚལ་ (cāà tsɛ̄ɛ) 1. prostrating (h.); va. ཕྱག་འཚལ་; —རྒྱག to prostrate. 2. sm. གདོང་ཞུ་ཕུལ་.

ཕྱག་འཚལ་སྐོར་སྐྱོང་ (cāàdzɛɛ gɔ̄ɔjoŋ) doing religious activities like prostration or circumambulation.

ཕྱག་འཚལ་ཁང་ (cāàdzɛɛgaŋ) church, temple.

ཕྱག་འཚལ་ལོ་ (cāàdzɛɛlo) I pay homage (to).

ཕྱག་མཛུབ་ (cədzub) finger (h.).

ཕྱག་མཛོད་ (cāndzöò) 1. manager, steward, treasurer. 2. storeroom.

ཕྱག་མཛོད་ནང་ཟན་ (cāndzöò na̱ŋma) shung. low ranking officials of the རྩེ་ཕྱག and བླ་ཕྱག offices.

ཕྱག་མཛོད་ཟུར་པ་ (cāndzöò su̱rbə) shung. ex-manager, ex-treasurer.

ཕྱག་འཛངས་ (cāndzaŋ) sm. ལག་ཐོགས་པོ་.

ཕྱག་རྫས་ (cāgdzɛɛ̀) wealth, riches, fortune.

ཕྱག་ཞབས་ (cāàshəb) h. of ལག་རྐང་.

ཕྱག་ཞུ་ (cəgshu) accompanying, serving (h.).

ཕྱག་བཞི་པ་ (cāà shi̱bə) image/ statue of Avaloketisvara with four hands.

ཕྱག་བཞེས་ (cāà she̱è) 1. h. of ལག་ལེན་. 2. to accept the prostration (usu. of a devotee by a lama).

ཕྱག་ཟུར་ (cəsur) abbr. of ཕྱག་མཛོད་ཟུར་པ་.

ཕྱག་བཟོས་མ་ (cāà sö̱òma) things made by a lama's own hand (h.).

ཕྱག་འོས་ (cāà wö̱ò) worthy of prostrating to.

ཕྱག་གཡུག (cāà yüù) sm. ཕྱག་གཡུག་གཡུག.

ཕྱག་གཡུག་གཡུག (cāà yüùyuù) waving one's hand; va.—གནང་.

ཕྱག་རས་ (cāàrɛɛ̀) hand cloth (h.).

ཕྱག་རི་སིར་ (cəgri si̱r) va. to winnow.

ཕྱག་རིས་ (cārii) 1. drawing, painting (h.). 2. fingerprint (h.). 3. letter (h.). 4. handwriting (h.). 5. sm. བྱས་རྗེས་.

ཕྱག་རོགས་ (cāàroò) 1. h. of རོགས་. 2. colleague sharing work in an office.

ཕྱག་ལ་སོན་ (cāàla sōn) vi. to receive, to get into one's hands (h.).

ཕྱག་ལན་ (cāà len) va. to prostrate back to sb. who has just prostrated to you.

ཕྱག་ལས་ (cāàlɛɛ̀) h. of ལས་ཀ་.

ཕྱག་ལེན་ (cāàlen) 1. h. of ལག་ལེན་. 2. va. to accept sb. prostrating to oneself.

ཕྱག་ལེན་དུ་འཁེལ་ (cāàlendu kēē) sm. ལག་ལེན་བསྟར་.

ཕྱག་ལེན་དོན་འཁེལ་ (cāàlen tōngee) h. of ལག་ལེན་དོན་འཁེལ་.

ཕྱག་ལོར་ (cāàlɔɔ) h. of ལོར་ལ་.

ཕྱག་ཤན་ (cāàshɛn) h. of གྲི་.

ཕྱག་ཤད་ (cāàshɛɛ̀) h. of སྐྲ་ཤད་.

ཕྱག་ཤན་ལྡེབ་གྲི་ (cāàshɛn dābdri) folding knife (h.).

ཕྱག་ཤུབས་ (cəshub) h. of ལག་ཤུབས་.

ཕྱག་ཤོ་ (cāàsho) h. of ཤོ་.

ཕྱག་ཤོག (caàshɔ̀ɔ̀) h. of ཤོག་བུ་.

ཕྱག་ཤོར་ (cāà shɔ̄ɔ̄) vi. to accidentally drop sth. (h.).

ཕྱག་སམ་ (cāàsam) h. of སམ་ཁྲ་.

ཕྱག་སེན་ (cāàsen) h. of སེན་མོ་.

ཕྱག་སོན་ (cāàsön) receiving, getting hold of, obtaining (h.) ༈ འདིའི་གོང་ཕུལ་བའི་ཕྱག་བྲིས་དེ་ཕྱག་སོན་བྱུང་ཡོད་བཤགས་ (I) hope you have received the previous letter that (I) sent.

ཕྱག་སོར་ (cāàsɔɔ) finger (h.).

ཕྱག་སྲུང་ (cāgsuŋ) shung. sm. ལྟགས་མདུད་.

ཕྱག་སྲོལ་ (cāàsöö) customs, laws, traditions (h.).

ཕྱག་བསིལ་ (cāà sii) 1. washing the hands (h.); va. ཕྱག་བསིལ་; —གནང་. 2. the hands getting cold; vi. ཕྱག་བསིལ་; —གནང་.

ཕྱགས་ (cāà) 1. shoes, boots. 2. p. of འཕྱག.

ཕྱགས་སྙིགས་ (cāàñig) 1. dirt, rubbish, dust. 2. sm. ཕྱག་དར་, 1.

ཕྱགས་བཏེག་པ་ (cāà dēg) va. to leave/ depart.

ཕྱགས་དར་ (cāàdar) sm. ཕྱགས་སྙིགས་.

ཕྱགས་ཕེབས་ (cāàpeè) coming/ arriving; va. ཕྱགས་ཕེབས་; —གནང་ an expression of greeting said to sb. arriving (h.).

ཕྱགས་མ་ (cāàma) sm. ཕྱག་མ་.

ཕྱགས་ལྷམ་ (cāàlham) h. of ལྷམ་.

ཕྱང་ (cāŋ) sm. འཕྱང་.

ཕྱང་ངེ་བ་ (cāŋŋewa) long, lengthy (usu. with respect to dresses).

ཕྱང་ཆད་ (cāŋjɛɛ̀) certain, sure, definite.

ཕྱང་ཕྱང་བ་ (cāŋjaŋwa) sm. ཕྱང་ཕྱང་ཕྲུལ་ཕྲུལ.

ཕྱང་ཕྱང་ཕྲུལ་ཕྲུལ་ (cāŋjaŋ drūūdrüü) swinging, dangling.

ཕྱང་ཕྲུལ་ (cāŋdrüü) sm. ཕྱང་ཕྱང་ཕྲུལ་ཕྲུལ་.

ཕྱང་འཕྲུལ་ (cāŋdrüü) sm. ཕྱང་ཕྱང་ཕྲུལ་ཕྲུལ་.

ཕྱང་མ་ (cāŋma) sm. ཐེ་འཚོམ་.

ཕྱང་ཡར་ (cāŋyar) street talk, gossip.

ཕྱད་དེ་ཕྱོད་དེ་ (cɛ̄ɛ̀de cöòde) acting blindly/ without thinking.

ཕྱད་པར་ (cɛ̄ɛ̀du) sm. རྒྱུན་དུ་.

ཕྱད་ཕྱོད་ (cɛ̄ɛ̀jöò) abbr. of ཕྱད་དེ་ཕྱོད་དེ་.

ཕྱམ་ (cām) sm. ལྕམ་.

ཕྱམ་སྡེགས་ (cāmdeg) beams and walls on which rafters lie.

ཕྱམ་སྣ་ (cāmna) edge of a rafter (of a house).

ཕྱམ་པོ་ཆེ་ (cāmboce) river.

ཕྱམ་མེ་བ་ (cāmmewa) even, level.

ཕྱམ་ཤིང་ (cāmshiŋ) rafters, wood for rafters.

ཕྱར་ (cār) p. of འཕྱར་.

ཕྱར་ཀ་ (cārga) making fun of sth. or sb.; va.—རྒྱག་; —གཏོང་ to make fun of.

ཕྱར་ཁ་ (cārga) offending, insulting; va.—གཏོང་.

ཕྱར་གྲུ་རམ་འདེགས་ (cārdru ramdeg) sm. ཕྱར་བ་གྲུ་འདེགས་.

ཕྱར་པོ་ཆེ་ (cārboce) 1. a huge piece of material that is used for drying grains, etc. 2. a large tent made of yak hair.

ཕྱར་པ་ (cārwa) tarpaulin, groundsheet (usu. made from woven yak hair).

ཕྱར་པ་གྲུ་འདེགས་ (cārwa drundeg) common consent, cooperative effort [Lit. lifting the tarpaulin from all the corners].

ཕྱར་པ་ནག་པོ་ (cārwa nagbo) black yak hair cloth.

ཕྱར་གཡེང་ (cāryeŋ) fickle, vacillating.

ཕྱལ་ (cɛ̄ɛ) stomach, belly.

ཕྱལ་འཇོལ་ལེ་བ་ (cɛ̄njöö lewa) hanging paunch, potbelly.

ཕྱལ་མོ་ (cɛ̄ɛmo) sm. སྣུམ་མ་.

ཕྱི་ (cī) 1. outside ༈ ཁོ་ཕྱི་ལ་ཕྱིན་སོང་ He went outside. 2. abroad, foreign ༈ ཕྱིའི་རྒྱལ་ཁབ་ Foreign countries. 3. back, behind, rear ༈ ཕྱི་ལ་ཤིག་པ་དང་ As he stepped/ moved back. 4. physical, material, nonmental ༈ ཕྱི་དངོས་པོའི་ཆ་ནས་ From the physical/ material aspect. 5. abbr. of ཕྱི་པོ་. 6. abbr. of ཕྱི་མ་.

ཕྱི་ཀྱོག (cīgyɔɔ̀) deformity of leg where the leg is twisted outward.

ཕྱི་ཀླད་ (cīlɛɛ̀) cerebrum, cerebral.

ཕྱི་བཀན་ (cī gɛ̄n) va. to lay on one's back.

ཕྱི་བཀྲག་ནང་སྟོང་ (cīdraà naŋdoŋ) sth. that appears good externally but is actually not good [Lit. glittering on the outside, empty on the inside].

ཕྱི་རྐྱེན་ (cīgyen) external/ outside cause.

ཕྱི་སྐད་སྡེ་ཁག (cīgɛɛ̀ degaà) department of foreign languages.

ཕྱི་སྐད་ (cīgɛɛ̀) foreign language.

ཕྱི་སྐད་སློབ་གྲྭ་ཆེན་མོ་ (cīgɛɛ̀ lōbdra cēmmo) institute of foreign languages.

ཕྱི་སྐད་སློབ་ཚོགས་ (cīgɛɛ̀ lōbdzoò) foreign language association.

ཕྱི་སྐོགས་ (cīgɔɔ̀) shell, outer layer.

ཕྱི་སྐོར་ (cīgɔɔ) 1. turning/ going around anticlockwise. 2. rewinding; va.—རྒྱག to rewind.

ཕྱི་སྐོར་ནང་སྐོར་ (cīgɔɔ naŋgɔɔ) 1. clockwise and anticlockwise. 2. hanging around sb. ༈ བུ་མོ་མཛེས་པོ་ཡིན་ཙང་བུ་མང་པོས་ཕྱི་སྐོར་དང་སྐོར་བྱེད་ཀྱི་འདུག Because the girl is beautiful, many boys are hanging around her.

ཕྱི་སྐྱོར་ (cīgyɔɔ) external/ foreign aid or assistance.

ཕྱི་བསྐོར་ (cīgɔɔ) sm. ཕྱི་སྐོར་.

ཕྱི་སྐྱོར་ (cīgyɔɔ) external/ foreign aid or assistance.

ཕྱི་ཁ་ནང་ལོག (cīgə naŋlɔɔ̀) consorting with the enemy.

ཕྱི་ཁག (cīgaà) others, outsiders.

ཕྱི་ཁག་ནང་ཁག (cīgaà naŋgaà) shung. internal and external guarantors ༈ འཁྲུག་འཛིང་གཏན་ནས་མི་ཞུ་བའི་ཕྱི་ཁག་ནང་ཁག་དང་འབྲེལ་སྐྱེ་མིག་འབེན་གཙུགས་ཀྱི་དགོངས་དང་ཡོང་བ་ With internal and external guarantors, we swear upon our lives not to fight again and apologize for our past deeds.

ཕྱི་ཁམས་ (cīgam) the external world.

ཕྱི་ཁྱམས་ (cīgyam) outer yard, courtyard.

ཕྱི་འཁྱེར་ (cīgyer) taking away, taking out; va.—བྱེད་ to take away, to take out ༈ སྐུ་རྟེན་ཚང་མ་རྒྱ་ནག་ལ་ཕྱི་འཁྱེར་བྱས་པ་རེད་ (They) took all the statutes to China.

ཕྱི་ཁྲལ (cīdrɛɛ) tax paid to the government (rather than one's lord).

ཕྱི་ཁྲལ་ཉིན་ (cīdrɛɛ ñin) a day spent on government corvee tax.

ཕྱི་གོས་ (cīgöö) outerwear, coat.

ཕྱི་གོས་ཆེན་རྩམ་ཁུག ནང་སྤྱང་མའི་རྩམ་པ་ (cī gööjen dzāmguù naŋ baŋmɛ dzāmba) sth. that looks good but is not, sth. that is showy on the outside but has no substance [Lit. a brocade bag with the poorest quality tsampa inside].

ཕྱི་དགོང་ (cīgoŋ) tomorrow night.

ཕྱི་དགྲ་ནང་འཛིངས་ (cīdra naŋdziŋ) having trouble with one's enemy as well as having internal turmoil and unrest.

ཕྱི་གྱར་ (cīgyar) becoming known outside, being leaked/ dispersed to the public; vi.—འགྲོ་ to become known outside, to leak out ¶ རང་གཉིས་ཀྱི་ནང་གཏམ་ཕྱི་གྱར་བྱུང་བ་རེད་ Our private talks came to be public (leaked out) ¶ དམག་དོན་གསང་བ་ཕྱི་གྱར་ཕྱིན་པ་རེད་ Military secrets leaked out. ¶ ཕྱི་ལ་གྱར་པའི་བོད་རིགས་སྤུན་ཟླ་ Tibetan compatriots that have been dispersed outside (of China).

ཕྱི་གྱེད་ (cī gye̱è) va. to move back, to turn back.

ཕྱི་གླིང་ (cīliŋ) 1. foreign. 2. English, European, Western.

ཕྱི་གླིང་ཆེད་མཁས་ཅུའུ་ (cīliŋbə) tib.ch. bureau of foreign experts (affairs).

ཕྱི་གླིང་པ་ (cīliŋbə) foreigner, Englishman, European, Westerner ¶ ཕྱི་གླིང་པའི་ཁ་ལག Foreign/ Western food.

ཕྱི་གློ་ (cīlo) cinch strap.

ཕྱི་གྲོ་ཟ་ (cīdro sa̱) shung. to eat an evening meal.

ཕྱི་དགྲ་ (cīdra) foreign enemy.

ཕྱི་དགྲ་ནང་འདྲེན་ (cīdra na̱ŋdren) clandestinely bringing an enemy into one's midst; va.—བྱེད་.

ཕྱི་དགྲ་ནང་འཇུག (cīdra na̱ŋjuù) clandestinely bringing an enemy into one's midst; va.—བྱེད་.

ཕྱི་དགྲ་ནང་འཛིངས་ (cīdra nəŋdziŋ) the external enemy invading and internal disturbances breaking out; va.—བྱེད་.

ཕྱི་བསྒྲོད་ (cīdröö) stepping back, backing away; va.—རྒྱག to step back, to back away.

ཕྱི་མགྲོན་ (cīndrön) foreign guest/ visitor.

ཕྱི་མགྲོན་སྣེ་ལེན་ཁང་ (cīndrön nēlengaŋ) foreign guest/ visitor reception room.

ཕྱི་འགག (cīngaà) the area between the inner and outer doors of a house.

ཕྱི་འགྱངས་ (cīgyaŋ) delaying, postponing; va.— བྱེད་ to postpone/ delay/ put off; vi.—ཐེབས་; —ཤོར་ to be/ get delayed or postponed.

ཕྱི་འགྱུར་ (cīngyur) the later translated (Buddhist scriptures).

ཕྱི་འགྲིབ་ (cīndrib) cataract.

ཕྱི་འགྲོ་ (cīndro) 1. person who takes care of external/ outside affairs. 2. exports ¶ ཕྱི་འགྲོའི་ཐོན་སྐྱེད་ Export production. 3. going outside ¶ ཁང་པ་དེའི་ནང་ནས་ཕྱི་འགྲོ་ནང་ཡོང་གང་ཡང་མེད་པ་རེད་ There was no one going out and coming in from that house.

ཕྱི་འགྲོ་ནང་ཡོང་ (cīndro na̱ŋyoŋ) 1. going out and coming in. 2. expenditures and income.

ཕྱི་འགྲོ་ཟ་ (cīndro sa̱) va. to eat the evening meal (usu. for monks).

ཕྱི་འགྲོས་ (cīndröö) going backwards/ falling back; va.—རྒྱག.

ཕྱི་སྐས་ (cīgeè) dusk, at the point just before sunset.

ཕྱི་རྒོལ་ (cīgöö) 1. a war/ attack from the outside. 2. oppose the outside or the outsiders.

ཕྱི་རྒོལ་ནང་བཅོས་ (cīgöö na̱ŋjöö) oppose the outside/ outsiders and reform the inside.

ཕྱི་རྒྱ་ (cīgya) 1. outside ¶ ཕྱི་རྒྱར་གསང་བ་བྱས་པ་རེད་ (They) kept it secret outside. 2. external, overt.

ཕྱི་རྒྱལ་ (cīgyɛɛ) foreign country, abroad.

ཕྱི་རྒྱལ་སྐུ་ཚབ་ (cīgyɛɛ gūdzəb) foreign ambassador.

ཕྱི་རྒྱལ་གྱི་དངུལ་འགྱུལ་ (cīgyɛɛgi ŋǖǖdrüü) foreign exchange/ currency.

ཕྱི་རྒྱལ་དངུལ་བརྗེས་ (cīgyɛɛ ŋǖǖjeè) sm. ཕྱི་རྒྱལ་གྱི་དངུལ་འགྱུལ་.

ཕྱི་རྒྱལ་དོན་གཅོད་ལས་ཁུངས་ (cīgyɛɛ tö̱njöögaŋ) Foreign Affairs Office/ Bureau/ Ministry.

ཕྱི་རྒྱལ་ནང་དམག་འཐབ་བྱེད་སྐྱོང་བའི་དམག་ཞབས་ཟུར་པའི་སྒྲིག་འཛུགས་ (cīgyɛɛnaŋ māgdəb ce̱èñoŋwɛ māgshəb su̱rwɛ dri̱gdzuù) the Veterans of Foreign Wars (organization in the U.S.).

ཕྱི་རྒྱལ་སྐད་ཡིག་དཔེ་སྐྲུན་ཁང་ (cīgyɛɛ gɛ̄ɛyiì bēdrüngaŋ) Foreign Languages Press (in Beijing).

ཕྱི་རྒྱལ་པོ་ཉའི་ཚོགས་པ་ (cīgyɛɛ pōñɛ tsōgba) the diplomatic corps.

ཕྱི་རྒྱལ་བ་ (cīgyɛɛwa) foreigner.

ཕྱི་རྒྱལ་བློན་ཆེན་ (cīgyɛɛ lönjen) sm. ཕྱི་རྒྱལ་བློན་པོ་.

ཕྱི་རྒྱལ་བློན་པོ་ (cīgyɛɛ lōnbo) Foreign Minister.

ཕྱི་རྒྱལ་ཚོང་ཟོག (cīgyɛɛ tsōŋsɔɔ) foreign goods.

ཕྱི་རྒྱལ་ལས་ཁུངས་ (cīgyɛɛ lɛ̄ɛguŋ) Foreign Office/ Ministry.

ཕྱི་སྒོ་ (cīgo) outside door.

ཕྱི་སྒྲོབ་ (cīdrob) proud, arrogant.

ཕྱི་སྒྲོམ་ (cīdrom) frame (of a house).

ཕྱི་ངོས་ (cīŋöö) outside, outer surface, externally ¶ མོ་ཕྱི་ངོས་ནས་གཞུང་དྲང་ཡིན་ཡང་ Even though externally she was honest and truthful.

ཕྱི་ངོས་ཀྱི་དྲོད་ཚད་ (cīŋöögi trö̱ödzɛɛ̀) surface/ external/ outside temperature.

ཕྱི་ངོས་ཀྱི་རང་བཞིན་ (cīŋöögi rəŋshin) surface quality.

ཕྱི་ངོས་རྒྱ་ཁྱོན་ (cīŋöö gya̱gyön) surface area.

ཕྱི་ངོས་འཐེན་ཤུགས་ (cīŋöö tēnshuù) surface tension.

ཕྱི་དངུལ་དོ་དམ་ཅུའུ་ (cīŋüü to̱dam jū) foreign exchange (currency) control bureau.

ཕྱི་དངུལ་ཚབ་ལོར་ (cīŋüü tsəblɔɔ) foreign exchange certificate (FEC)—a type of paper money foreigners were required to use at one time in the PRC.

ཕྱི་བཅོས་སྨན་ཁང་ (jījöö mɛ̄ngaŋ) surgical hospital.

ཕྱི་བཅོས་ཁང་ (cījöögaŋ) surgical department/ clinic.

ཕྱི་བཅོས་ཚན་ཁག (cījöö tsɛ̄ngaŋ) surgical department.

ཕྱི་ལྕག་གཞུ་ (cījaà shu̱) va. to slap with the back of the hand.

ཕྱི་ལྕགས་རིལ་བསྐོར་ ནང་མཁར་བཙན་བསྲུང་ (cījaà ri̱igɔɔ na̱ŋgar dzɛ̄nsuŋ) being prepared/ ready [Lit. to surround the outer walls and to guard the castle].

ཕྱི་ཆ་ (cīja) the later part of a period or time.

ཕྱི་ཆབ་ (cījəb) shung. evening break (usu. in prayer assemblies) ¶ ཕྱི་ཆབ་མ་བཏང་བར་དཀོར་གཉེར་དང་ཕྱག་མཛོད་བདེ་མ་གཏོགས་ཚོགས་གྲལ་ནས་ཧར་ལངས་མི་བྱ་ Until the evening break no one is allowed to stand up from the (prayer) assembly rows except the stewards and the chapel overseers.

ཕྱི་ཆར་པའི་ཆར་ཐག་ཆོད་ཀྱང་ ནང་ཐིགས་པའི་ཐིགས་ཐག་མ་ཆོད་ (cī cārbɛ cārdaà cöögyaŋ na̱ŋ tīgbɛ tīdaà majöö) although the external conflict/ dispute/ quarrel is settled the inner dispute continues.

ཕྱི་ཆོད་ནང་ཆོད་ (cījöö na̱ŋjöö) making external and internal decisions.

ཕྱི་ཆོན་ (cījön) 1. hem (of a dress). 2. tent rope/ guyline.

ཕྱི་ཆོས་ (cīcöö) religions other than Buddhism.

ཕྱི་ཇ་ (cīja) 1. afternoon or evening tea. 2. the time when people are home (for tea) in the afternoon.

ཕྱི་འཇམ་ནང་རྩུབ་ (cījam na̱ŋdzub) a gentle appearance but really cruel/ ruthless and mean inside [Lit. outwardly soft and rough/ coarse on the inside].

ཕྱི་རྗེས་ (cījeè) 1. in the future. 2. a trace.

ཕྱི་ལྗོངས་ (cījoŋ) outdoor scene.

ཕྱི་ཉལ་ (cīñɛɛ) sleeping late; va.—བྱེད་.

ཕྱི་ཉིན་ (cīñin) the next day, the following day ¶ དེའི་ཕྱི་ཉིན་ང་ཚོ་འབྲས་ལྗོངས་ལ་ཐོན་པ་ཡིན་ The next day we left for Sikkim.

ཕྱི་གཉུལ་བ་པོ་ (cī ñü̱ü̱wabo) 1. begger. 2. a homeless wanderer.

ཕྱི་སྙིང་ (cīñiŋ) shung. an old ཕྱི་མཛོད་ ceremonial scarf.

ཕྱི་གཏོང་ (cīdoŋ) 1. an export, exporting ¶ ཕྱི་གཏོང་ནང་འདྲེན་གྱི་ངོ་ཚང་ Exporting and importing. 2. shung. to give sth. up ¶ མི་སེར་གཞན་གྱིས་གསེབ་འཚངས་བྱས་པ་ཡོད་ན་སྡོན་ཞི་སི་དང་ ཡུལ་དཔོན་སྲུང་པ་གིས་ཁ་ར་གྱིས་ལ་ཕྱིར་གཏོང་ Should anyone avail himself of loopholes to take possession of commoners in these places, the Pacification Commissioners and the local officials of the garrison are to persuade those involved to give them up.

ཕྱི་གཏོང་ནང་འདྲེན་ (cīdoŋ naŋdren) exporting and importing; va.—བྱེད་.

ཕྱི་བཏབ་ (cīndəb) late sowing of seed.

ཕྱི་ཏག་ཏུ་ (cīdagdu) externally, outwardly ¶ ཕྱི་ཏག་ཏུ་བཤད་ཡག་ལ་བོད་རང་བཙན་མ་རེད་ཟེར་གྱི་ཡོད་པ་རེད་ཀྱང་དོན་དངོས་ཐོག་བོད་རང་བཙན་རེད་ Outwardly they are saying Tibet is not independent, but in reality Tibet is independent.

ཕྱི་ཏིང་ (cīdiŋ) these days, nowadays.

ཕྱི་རྟེན་ (cīden) dependent on others/ outsiders.

ཕྱི་རྟེན་ཅན་དུ་འགྱུར་ (cīdenjɛndu gyur) vi. to come to be dependent on others/ outsiders.

ཕྱི་ལྟར་ (cīdar) outwardly, in outward appearance ¶ ཕྱི་ལྟར་ཁོ་ཚོ་ནང་ཁུལ་འཆམ་པོ་འདུག Outwardly they are friendly.

ཕྱི་བལྟས་ལྟ་ (cīdɛɛ dā) 1. va. to look back at sth. 2. va. to review/ reflect on the past, to look back in time.

ཕྱི་བལྟས་སློག (cīdɛɛ lɔ̄ɔ) va. to look back ¶ ཁོས་ཕྱི་བལྟས་སློག་དེ་མོ་ལ་མགྱོགས་པོ་ཤོག་ཅེས་ལབ་པ་རེད་ He looked back and told her to come quickly. 2. va. to review/ reflect on the past, to look back in time.

ཕྱི་ཐག (cīdaà) 1. enduring, lasting (usu. of friendship) ¶ ཕྱི་ཐག་རིང་བའི་གྲོགས་པོ་ A longtime friend.

ཕྱི་ཐང་སློག (cīdaŋ lɔ̄ɔ) va. to turn over.

ཕྱི་ཐན་ (cīdɛn) late summer drought.

ཕྱི་ཐབས་ (cīdəb) foreign/ western methods.

ཕྱི་ཐིག (cīdig) the outside/ outer line.

ཕྱི་ཐུམ་ (cīdum) the outside wrapper/ wrapping.

ཕྱི་ཐོ་ (cīto) wooden hammer used in weaving carpets.

ཕྱི་ཐོན་ལག་འཁྱེར་ (cīdön laggyer) passport.

ཕྱི་མཐའ་ (cīda) afterwards, eventually, later on, in the end, the final goal.

ཕྱི་མཐུན་ནང་འགལ་ (cīdün naŋgɛɛ) outwardly agreeable/ friendly but inwardly opposed.

ཕྱི་དར་ (cīdar) 1. dusting, wiping, cleaning; va.—རྒྱག་; —གཏོང་ ¶ ཕྱི་དར་གཙང་མ་བཏང་བའི་མཚོན་ཆ་ Weapons that have been wiped clean. 2. the later/ second spread of sth. 3. the later spreading of Buddhism into Tibet.

ཕྱི་དལ་ (cīdɛɛ) delaying, postponing, being late.

ཕྱི་དུས་ (cīdüü) later, afterwards.

ཕྱི་དོན་ (cīdön) foreign affairs, external affairs.

ཕྱི་དོན་དོན་གཅོད་ཁང་ (cīdön tönjöögaŋ) foreign affair's office/ ministry.

ཕྱི་དོན་གཅོད་ (cī tönjöö) overseas work/ duties.

ཕྱི་དོན་གཞུང་ལས་ཁང་ (cīdön shuŋlɛɛgaŋ) foreign affairs office.

ཕྱི་དྲགས་ (cīdraà) vi. to be too late ¶ ད་ཕྱི་དྲགས་པ་རེད་ Now (it) is too late.

ཕྱི་དྲིལ་ (cīdrii) abbr. of ཕྱི་སྲིད་དྲིལ་བསྒྲགས་.

ཕྱི་དྲོ་ (cīndro) afternoon, p.m. ¶ ཕྱི་དྲོ་ཆུ་ཚོད་དང་པོའི་ཐོག At 1:00 p.m. in the afternoon.

ཕྱི་བདར་ (cīdar) sm. ཕྱི་དར་.

ཕྱི་མདངས་ (cīndaŋ) external appearance/ complexion.

ཕྱི་མདའ་རྒྱག (cīnda gyaà) va. to shoot while turning back.

ཕྱི་འདེབས་ (cīndeb) late sowing of seed.

ཕྱི་འདོམས་ཀྱི་མེ་ལོང་ (cīdomgi meloŋ) learn from the past (a political slogan).

ཕྱི་འདྲེད་ཤོར་ (cīndreè shɔ̄ɔ) vi. to slip and land on one's back.

ཕྱི་འདྲེན་ (cīndren) exporting; va.—བྱེད་ to export.

ཕྱི་རྡོ་ (cīdo) 1. a stone used as toilet paper. 2. a stone that is thrown back (while being chased).

ཕྱི་ལྡིར་ནང་སྟོང་ (cīdir naŋdoŋ) 1. vessel with a broad midsection. 2. boastful person with no substance.

ཕྱི་སྡོད་ (cīdöö) living abroad.

ཕྱི་སྡོད་བོད་རིགས་སྤུན་ཟླ་ (cīdöö pöörii bünda) overseas Tibetan compatriots.

ཕྱི་སྡོད་མི་སེར་ (cīdöö miser) sm. ཕྱི་སྡོད་རང་མི་.

ཕྱི་སྡོད་རང་མི་ (cīdöö rəŋmi) overseas nationals, people of one country living in other countries ¶ ཀྲུང་གོའི་ཕྱི་སྡོད་རང་མི་ Overseas Chinese.

ཕྱི་སྡོད་རང་མིའི་འགྲུལ་དངུལ་ (cīdöö rəŋmii drüüŋüü) overseas remittances.

ཕྱི་སྡོད་རང་མིའི་དོན་བྱེད་ཨུ་ཡོན་ལྷན་ཁང་ (cīdöö rəŋmii tönjeè ūyön lhɛ̄ngaŋ) overseas Chinese affairs commission.

ཕྱི་སྡོད་རང་མིའི་ལས་དོན་ཁྲུའུ་ (cīdöö rəŋmii lɛɛdön trū) overseas Chinese department.

ཕྱི་བརྡ་ (cīda) warning shot/signal.

ཕྱི་ནང་ (cīnaŋ) 1. inside and outside, inner and outer, interior and exterior ¶ ཁང་པའི་ཕྱི་ནང་ཚང་མ་གཙང་མ་འདུག The inside and outside of the house is clean. 2. external and internal, national and international ¶ རྒྱལ་ཁབ་ཕྱི་ནང་གི་གསར་འགྱུར་ National and international news. 3. Buddhist and nonBuddhist.

ཕྱི་ནང་གང་སར་ (cīnaŋ kaŋsar) sm. ཕྱི་ནང་བར་གསུམ་.

ཕྱི་ནང་གི་གྲུབ་མཐའ་ (cīnaŋ drubda) Buddhism and the other religions.

ཕྱི་ནང་བསྒྱུར་ (cīnaŋ gyur) va. to turn inside out.

ཕྱི་ནང་གཉིས་རྡུགས་ (cīnaŋ ñīidug) bad both inside and outside.

ཕྱི་ནང་བར་བཙིར་ (cīnaŋ pardzir) attacking outside and inside, pincer attack from inside and outside.

ཕྱི་ནང་བར་གསུམ་ (cīnaŋ parsum) inside, outside and in between; everywhere, in all aspects.

ཕྱི་ནང་གཞོགས་འདེགས་ (cīnaŋ shɔŋdeg) acting from inside in coordination with forces attacking from outside, collaborate from within with forces from without.

ཕྱི་ནང་ཚོང་འགྲུལ་ (cīnaŋ sɔŋdrüü) internal and external circulation of commodities.

ཕྱི་ནང་ལྡོག (cīnaŋ dɔ̄ɔ) sm. ཕྱི་ནང་ལོག.

ཕྱི་ནང་ལག་འབྲེལ་ (cīnaŋ laŋdree) conspiring/ consorting with the enemy [Lit. insiders joining with outsiders].

ཕྱི་ནང་ལོག (cīnaŋ lɔ̄ɔ) vi. to get turned inside out.

ཕྱི་ནང་སློག (cīnaŋ lɔ̄ɔ) va. to turn inside out.

ཕྱི་ནང་གསང་གསུམ་ (cīnaŋ sāŋsum) sm. ཕྱི་ནང་བར་གསུམ་.

ཕྱི་ནད་སྡེ་ཚན་ (cīnɛɛ dedzɛn) department of surgery.

ཕྱི་ནད་སྡེ་ཚན་གྱི་ནད་ཁང་ (cīnɛɛ dedzɛngi nɛɛgaŋ) surgical ward.

ཕྱི་ནད་སྡེ་ཚན་གྱི་ནད་བརྟག་ཁང་ (cīnɛɛ dedzɛngi nɛɛdaàgaŋ) surgical observation room.

ཕྱི་ནད་ཚན་ཁག (cīnɛɛ tsɛ̄ngaà) department of surgery.

ཕྱི་ནད་གཤག་བཅོས་ (cīnɛɛ shāgjöö) surgery, operation.

ཕྱི་ནས་ (cīnɛɛ) from outside.

ཕྱི་ནས་ནང་ཤེས་ (cīnɛɛ naŋsheè) knowing the inside from the outside.

ཕྱི་ནུད་ (cīnüü) withdrawing, moving back; va.—རྒྱག.

ཕྱི་ནུར་ (cīnur) delaying, postponing; va.—བྱེད་.

ཕྱི་ནོར་ནང་རྫས་ (cīnɔɔ naŋdzɛɛ) external wealth (e.g., animals) and household goods.

ཕྱི་སྣང་ (cīnaŋ) things as they appear, external appearance.

ཕྱི་སྣེ་ནང་ཁྲིད་ (cīne naŋdrii) sm. ཕྱི་དགྲ་ནང་འདྲེན་.

ཕྱི་སྣུར་ (cīnur) sm. ཕྱི་ནུར་.

ཕྱི་སྣོད་འཇིག་རྟེན་ (cīnöö jigden) sm. སྣོད་ཀྱི་འཇིག་རྟེན་.

ཕྱི་པ་ (cībə) a nonBuddhist.

ཕྱི་པའི་ཆོས་ (cībɛ cöö) religions other than Buddhism, foreign religions.

ཕྱི་པོ་ (cībo) late ¶ མདང་དགོང་ཕྱི་པོ་བསྡད་པ་ཡིན་ (We) stayed late last night.

ཕྱི་ལྤགས་ (cībaà) outer layer, skin.

ཕྱི་ཕྱིད་ (cījɛɛ) wiping/ cleaning utensils.

ཕྱི་ཕྱིན་གཟིགས་ (cījɛn sii) h. of ཕྱི་མིག་བལྟ་.

ཕྱི་ཕྱག (cījaà) prostrating before a lama before

going (on journey, etc.); va.—འཚལ་ to prostrate before a lama before going somewhere.

ཕྱི་ཕྱིར་ (cĩjir) 1. later, afterwards, following, going after. 2. once again, once more.

ཕྱི་ཕྱོགས་ (cĩjɔɔ̀) outside, external ¶ཕྱི་ཕྱོགས་སུ་སྒོ་འབྱེད་ Opening the door to the outside.

ཕྱི་ཕྱོགས་ཀྱི་ཉོ་ཚོང་ (cĩjɔɔ̀gi ño̱dzoŋ) external trade.

ཕྱི་ཕྱོགས་ཉོ་ཚོང་ (cĩjɔɔ̀ ño̱dzoŋ) sm. ཕྱི་ཕྱོགས་ཀྱི་ཉོ་ཚོང་.

ཕྱི་ཕྱོགས་ཉོ་ཚོང་ཅུའུ་ (cĩjɔɔ̀ ño̱dzoŋ jū) tib.ch. bureau of foreign trade.

ཕྱི་ཕྱོགས་ཉོ་ཚོང་པུའུ་ (cĩjɔɔ̀ ño̱dzoŋ bū) tib.ch. ministry of foreign trade.

ཕྱི་ཕྱོགས་ཉོ་ཚོང་དཔལ་འབྱོར་ཐིན་ (cĩjɔɔ̀ ño̱dzoŋ bɛ̄njɔɔ tĩn) tib.ch. department of foreign trade and economic relations.

ཕྱི་ཕྱོགས་དཔལ་འབྱོར་འབྲེལ་གཏུག་པུའུ་ (cĩjɔɔ̀ bɛ̄njɔɔ dre̱ēduù bū) tib.ch. bureau for foreign economic relations.

ཕྱི་ཕྱོགས་དཔལ་འབྱོར་འབྲེལ་བ་དང་ཉོ་ཚོང་ཐིང་ (cĩjɔɔ̀ bɛ̄njɔɔ dre̱ewadaŋ ño̱dzoŋ tĩŋ) tib.ch. foreign economic relations and trade bureau.

ཕྱི་ཕྱོགས་ཚོང་དོན་ཀུང་སི་ (cĩjɔɔ̀ tsōŋdön gūŋsi) tib.ch. foreign trade company.

ཕྱི་ཕྱོགས་རིག་གནས་འབྲེལ་གཏུག་པུའུ་ (cĩjɔɔ̀ ri̱gnɛɛ̀ dre̱ēduù bū) tib.ch. bureau for cultural relations with foreign countries.

ཕྱི་འཕྲེད་ (cĩdreè) sm. ཕྱི་དྲོ་.

ཕྱི་བུན་ (cĩbün) external/ foreign loans.

ཕྱི་བྱད་ (cĩjɛɛ̀) outer garment, coat.

ཕྱི་བྲན་ (cĩdrɛn) slave of a foreign master; flunky of imperialism, worshipper of everything foreign.

ཕྱི་བློན་ (cĩlön) abbr. of ཕྱི་རྒྱལ་བློན་པོ་.

ཕྱི་དབུགས་ཆད་ (cĩwuù cɛɛ̀) outer breath/ external breathing; vi.—ཆད་ to stop breathing.

ཕྱི་དབྱིབས་ (cĩyib) external shape.

ཕྱི་འབབ་ཆུ་བོ་ (cĩbəb cūwo) river flowing outward (into the sea).

ཕྱི་འབུད་ (cĩmbüù) expelling, banishing; va.—བྱེད་ to expel/ banish/ eject.

ཕྱི་འབྱོར་ (cĩnjɔɔ) arriving late.

ཕྱི་འབྱོར་སྔ་ལོག (cĩnjɔɔ ŋālɔɔ̀) coming/ arriving late and leaving early.

ཕྱི་འབྲས་ (cĩndrɛɛ̀) late-ripening rice.

ཕྱི་འབྲེལ་ (cĩndree) pertaining/ related to external matters, external affairs, foreign relations, diplomacy; va.—བྱེད་ to conduct foreign affairs.

ཕྱི་འབྲེལ་སྐུ་ཚབ་ (cĩndree gūdzəb) diplomatic representative, ambassador.

ཕྱི་འབྲེལ་ཁྱད་དབང་ (cĩndree kyɛɛ̀waŋ) sm. ཕྱི་འབྲེལ་གྱི་དམིགས་བསལ་དབང་ཆ་.

ཕྱི་འབྲེལ་གྱི་འབྲེལ་བ་ (cĩndreegi dre̱ewa) external/ foreign relations.

ཕྱི་འབྲེལ་གྱི་དམིགས་བསལ་དབང་ཆ་ (cĩndreegi mĩgsɛɛ wā̱nja) diplomatic prerogative/ privileges; extraterritoriality.

ཕྱི་འབྲེལ་གྲོས་མོལ་ (cĩndree trö̱ömöö) diplomatic negotiation.

ཕྱི་འབྲེལ་ཉོ་ཚོང་ (cĩndree ño̱dzoŋ) external/ foreign trade.

ཕྱི་འབྲེལ་གནད་དོན་ (cĩndree nɛ̄ɛ̀dön) foreign affairs, foreign issue.

ཕྱི་འབྲེལ་པ་ (cĩndreeba) diplomat.

ཕྱི་འབྲེལ་པུའུ་ (cĩndree bū) tib.ch. Foreign Affairs Ministry.

ཕྱི་འབྲེལ་པུའུ་ཀྲང་ (cĩndree būdraŋ) tib.ch. Foreign Minister.

ཕྱི་འབྲེལ་པོ་ཉའི་ཚོགས་པ་ (cĩndree pōñɛ tsōgba) the diplomatic corps.

ཕྱི་འབྲེལ་མི་སྣ་ (cĩndree mi̱nə) diplomatic personnel.

ཕྱི་འབྲེལ་བློན་ཆེན་ (cĩndree lōnjen) Foreign Minister.

ཕྱི་འབྲེལ་ལས་ཁུངས་ (cĩndree lɛ̱ɛ̀guŋ) Foreign Office, Ministry of External Affairs.

ཕྱི་འབྲེལ་ལས་བྱེད་པ་ (cĩndree lɛ̱ɛ̀jeba) sm. ཕྱི་འབྲེལ་མི་སྣ་.

ཕྱི་འབྲེལ་སྲིད་ཇུས་ (cĩndree sĩijüù) foreign policy.

ཕྱི་འབྲེལ་སློབ་ཚོགས་ (cĩndree lōbdzoò) Foreign Affairs Institute.

ཕྱི་མ་ (cĩmə) 1. latter, following, subsequently, after. 2. outside, outer. 3. nonBuddhist.

ཕྱི་མ་ནང་ (cĩma na̱ŋ) one who consorts with the enemy, a spy ¶ཁོ་ཕྱི་མ་ནང་རེད་པག He is a spy.

ཕྱི་མ་ཕྱི་མ་ (cĩmə cĩmə) the very last.

ཕྱི་མའི་མཐའ་ (cĩmɛ tā) in the end.

ཕྱི་མི་ (cĩmi) aliens, foreigners ¶ཕྱི་མིའི་ཐོབ་ཐང་ The rights of aliens.

ཕྱི་མི་ཕར་ཕུར་ (cĩmi pārbur) antiforeign.

ཕྱི་མི་འབུད་འདེད་ (cĩmi bü̱ndeè) driving out/ expelling foreigners.

ཕྱི་མི་གཞིས་ཆགས་ལས་ཁུངས་ (cĩmi shi̱ijaà lɛ̱ɛ̀guŋ) Immigration and Naturalization Service (U.S.A.).

ཕྱི་མི་ཟུར་འབུད་ (cĩmi su̱rbüù) sm. ཕྱི་མི་ཕར་ཕུར་.

ཕྱི་མིག (cĩmiì) looking back; va.—བལྟ་ to look back (at the past) ¶ལོ་འདས་ཟིན་པའི་ཕྱི་མིག་བལྟ་དེ་ Looking back at the past year.

ཕྱི་མིག་དགུ་བསྒྲིགས་ (cĩmiìk gu̱drii) a slingshot with a woven desgn of nine eyes.

ཕྱི་མོ་ (cĩmu) 1. the original (versus the copy). 2. grandmother.

ཕྱི་སྨྱུལ་ (cĩ ñü̱ü) va. to search outside.

ཕྱི་སྨན་ (cĩmɛn) 1. yeast, fermenting agent. 2. Western medicines.

ཕྱི་སྨིན་ (cĩmɛn) late-ripening ¶ཕྱི་སྨིན་འབྲས་ Late-ripening rice.

ཕྱི་སྨིན་གནའ་གསོ་ (cĩmin nāso) embracing foreign customs/ ideas and maintaining one's ancient customs/ ideas.

ཕྱི་རྩེག་ནང་རྩེག (cĩdzeg na̱ŋdzeg) piled up in layers (usu. used for mountain ranges).

ཕྱི་རྩིས་ (cĩdzii) final tally.

ཕྱི་ཚད་ཙམ་ (cĩdzɛ) late ¶ཁོང་ཉིན་དགུང་ཕྱི་ཚད་ཙམ་དུ་སླེབས་སོང་ He arrived in late afternoon.

ཕྱི་ཚན་ (cĩdzɛn) sm. ཕྱི་ནད་ཚན་ཁག.

ཕྱི་ཚར་ (cĩdzar) children of the younger wife in a polgynous marriage.

ཕྱི་ཚིག (cĩdzig) (in) the following words/ sentence.

ཕྱི་ཚིགས་ (cĩdzii) late (time).

ཕྱི་ཚིལ་ (cĩdzii) the outer layer of fat on the body.

ཕྱི་ཚིས་ (cĩdzii) the future livelihood.

ཕྱི་ཚུལ་ (cĩdzüü) outward appearance/ shape/ form, exterior aspects, the surface, superficially ¶ཕྱི་ཚུལ་ཙམ་བརྗེས་པ་ A superficial change. ¶ཁོའི་བུ་འདི་ཡང་ཕྱི་ཚུལ་ལྐུགས་འདྲ་དུང་ Even though his son is like an idiot in outward appearance.

ཕྱི་ཚུལ་གྱི་གཏན་ཚིགས་རིག་པ་ (cĩdzüügi dɛ̄ndzig ri̱gbə) (the study of) formal logic.

ཕྱི་ཚུལ་སྒྱུར་ (cĩdzüü gyu̱r) 1. va. to change the outward appearance of sth. 2. va. to change sth. superficially.

ཕྱི་ཚུལ་ཙམ་ (cĩdzüüdzam) in name only.

ཕྱི་ཚུལ་རིང་ལུགས་ (cĩdzüü ri̱nluì) formalism.

ཕྱི་ཚོང་ (cĩdzoŋ) exporting, selling abroad; va.—བྱེད་.

ཕྱི་ཚོང་ལྟེ་གནས་ (cĩdzoŋ dēnɛɛ̀) foreign trade center.

ཕྱི་འཚོང་ (cĩdzoŋ) sm. ཕྱི་ཚོང་.

ཕྱི་མཛེས་ནང་སྟོང་ (cĩndzeè na̱ŋdoŋ) outwardly attractive but really worthless {lit. outside beautiful, inside empty].

ཕྱི་མཛོད་ (cĩndzöò) a type of ceremonial scarf.

ཕྱི་འཛིང་ནང་རྫོད་ (cĩdziŋ na̱ŋdzöö) sm. ཕྱི་དགྲ་ནང་འཛིངས་.

ཕྱི་རྫིག་ནང་སྟོང་ (cĩdzig na̱ŋdoŋ) sm. ཕྱི་བཀྲག་ནང་སྟོང་.

ཕྱི་བཞིན་ (cĩshin) 1. following after, following in the footsteps of sb.; va.—འབྲང་; —འགྲོ་. 2. shape, form.

ཕྱི་བཞིན་ཕྱི་བཞིན་ (cĩshin cĩshin) again and again, often.

ཕྱི་ཟུར་ (cĩsur) exterior angle.

ཕྱི་ཟོག (cĩsoò) imports.

ཕྱི་ཟོག་ཚོང་ཁང་ (cĩsoò tsōŋgaŋ) shop where foreign imports are sold.

ཕྱི་གཟུགས་ (cīsug) the outer form.

ཕྱི་བཟང་ནང་སྤྱོད་ (cīsaŋ na̲ŋjöȍ) use of foreign things for internal purposes.

ཕྱི་བཟོ་ (cīso) sm. ཕྱི་ཚུལ་.

ཕྱི་ཡིག་དཔེ་ཁང་ (cīyiì bēgaŋ) foreign languages bookstore.

ཕྱི་ཡིག་དཔེ་སྐྲུན་ལས་དོན་ཅུའུ་ (cīyiì bēdrün l̲ɛ̲ɛ̀döm jū) tib.ch. foreign languages publishing office.

ཕྱི་ཡུལ་ (cīyüü) 1. object, objective ¶ ཕྱི་ཡུལ་གྱི་གནས་ཚུལ་དངོས་དང་མི་མཐུན་པའི་བྱིས་བློ་ Infantile thoughts contradictory to objective reality.

ཕྱི་ཡུལ་གྱི་དངོས་པོ་ (cīyüügi ŋȫȍbo) things, objects.

ཕྱི་ཡུལ་གྱི་ཆ་རྐྱེན་ (cīyüügi cāgyɛn) objective conditions.

ཕྱི་ཡུལ་གྱི་ཆོས་ཉིད་ (cīyüügi cȫȍñiì) objective law.

ཕྱི་ཡུལ་གྱི་འཇིག་རྟེན་ (cīyüügi ji̲gden) objective world.

ཕྱི་ཡུལ་གྱི་བདེན་དོན་ (cīyüügi de̲ndön) objective truth.

ཕྱི་ཡུལ་གྱི་གནས་ཚུལ་ (cīyüügi nɛ̄ɛ̀dzüü) objective situation.

ཕྱི་ཡུལ་གྱི་རང་བཞིན་ (cīyüügi rə̲ŋshin) objectiveness, objectivity.

ཕྱི་ཡུལ་ཆོས་ཉིད་ (cīyüü cȫȍñiì) sm. ཕྱི་ཡུལ་གྱི་ཆོས་ཉིད་.

ཕྱི་ཡུལ་རིང་ལུགས་ (cīyüü ri̲ŋluù) objectivism.

ཕྱི་ར་ (cīrə) outer courtyard.

ཕྱི་རབས་ (cīrəb) 1. next/ future generation. 2. modern era ¶ ཕྱི་རབས་ཀྱི་མི་ Modern man.

ཕྱི་རབས་པ་ (cīrəbbə) sm. ཕྱི་རབས་.

ཕྱི་རས་ (cīrɛɛ̀) rag.

ཕྱི་རིག (cīrig) foreign/ alien system of thought.

ཕྱི་རིམ་ (cīrim) the outer layer/ wall/ fence.

ཕྱི་རིམ་ནང་རིམ་ (cīrim nə̲ŋrim) 1. outer and inner layers of sth. 2. layer upon layer.

ཕྱི་རིམ་པ་ (cīrimbə) an outsider/ alien.

ཕྱི་རེངས་ནང་འཁུམས་ (cīreŋ na̲ŋgum) sm. ཕྱི་རྗིག་ནང་སྐྱོང་.

ཕྱི་རུ་ (cīru) the back part of a saddle.

ཕྱི་རོ་ (cīro) sm. ཕྱི་དྲོ་.

ཕྱི་རོལ་ (cīröö) outside, outward, eternal ¶ གྲོང་ཁྱེར་གྱི་ཕྱི་རོལ་ Outside of the city.

ཕྱི་རོལ་གྱི་འགལ་བ་ (cīröögi gɛ̲ɛ̲wa) external contradiction.

ཕྱི་རོལ་གྱི་བདེན་དོན་ (cīröögi de̲ndön) external truth.

ཕྱི་རོལ་གྱི་སྣོད་ཀྱི་འཇིག་རྟེན་ (cīröögi nōngi ji̲gden) sm. ཕྱི་སྣོད་འཇིག་རྟེན་.

ཕྱི་རོལ་གྱི་འབྲེལ་བ་ (cīröögi dre̲e̲wa) external connections/ relations.

ཕྱི་རོལ་གྱི་ཡུལ་ (cīröögi yü̲ü̲) 1. the other side (of a place). 2. the outside world.

ཕྱི་རོལ་དུ་ (cīröödu) on the outside.

ཕྱི་རོལ་དུ་གཡེང་ (cīröödu yēŋ) vi. to have one's mind wander.

ཕྱི་རོལ་ན་ (cīrööna) sm. ཕྱི་རོལ་དུ་.

ཕྱི་རོལ་པ་ (cīrööba) 1. outsider, alien. 2. nonBuddhist.

ཕྱི་རོལ་པའི་གྲུབ་མཐའ་ (cīrööbɛ dru̲bda) those religions other than Buddhism.

ཕྱི་རོལ་ཡུལ་ (cīröö yü̲ü̲) sm. ཕྱི་ཡུལ་.

ཕྱི་རོལ་ཡུལ་གྱི་དངོས་པོ་ (cīröö yü̲ü̲gi ŋȫȍbo) object materials.

ཕྱི་རོལ་ཡུལ་གྱི་དོན་དངོས་ (cīröö yü̲ü̲gi tö̲nŋöȍ) objective reality.

ཕྱི་རོལ་ཡུལ་གྱི་ཆ་རྐྱེན་ (cīröö yü̲ü̲gi cāgyen) object condition.

ཕྱི་རོལ་ཡུལ་གྱི་ཆོས་ཉིད་ (cīröö yü̲ü̲gi cȫȍñiì) object law, object logic.

ཕྱི་རོལ་ཡུལ་གྱི་གཏན་ཚིགས་རིག་པ་ (cīröö yü̲ü̲gi dɛ̄ndzig ri̲gbə) objective logic.

ཕྱི་རོལ་ཡུལ་གྱི་གནས་ཚུལ་ (cīröö yü̲ü̲gi nɛ̄ɛ̀dzüü) outside/ external situation.

ཕྱི་རོལ་ཡུལ་གྱི་སྣང་ཚུལ་ (cīröö yü̲ü̲gi nāŋdzüü) objective phenomenon.

ཕྱི་རོལ་ཡུལ་གྱི་བྱ་དངོས་ (cīröö yü̲ü̲gi ca̲ŋöȍ) object things, objects.

ཕྱི་རོལ་ཡུལ་དང་མཐུན་པའི་ལྟ་ཚུལ་ (cīröö yü̲ü̲daŋ tǖnbɛ dədzüü) object view.

ཕྱི་ལ་གྱར་ (cīlə gya̲r) sm. ཕྱི་གྱར་.

ཕྱི་ལ་སྒྲོག (cīlə drɔ̲ɔ̀) va. to make public, to publicize.

ཕྱི་ལ་ཤིག (cīlə shīì) sm. ཕྱི་ཤིག.

ཕྱི་ལག (cīlaà) 1. backhand (as in tennis or ping pong). 2. outside/ external enemy.

ཕྱི་ལག་ནང་རུལ་ (cīlaà nə̲ŋrüü) external enemies and internal traitors.

ཕྱི་ལན་སྐུར་ (cīlɛn gūr) to send a message back/ home from outside (wherever one is at).

ཕྱི་ལས་ (cīlɛɛ̀) 1. outside/ outdoor work. 2. work outside (in another area/ place).

ཕྱི་ལེགས་ནང་བཙོག (cīleg na̲ŋdzɔɔ̀) looking good on the outside but dirty on the inside.

ཕྱི་ལུགས་ (cīluù) foreign custom/ tradition; western custom/ tradition ¶ ཕྱི་ལུགས་སྨན་བཅོས་ Western medicine.

ཕྱི་ལུགས་ཀྱི་འཆིང་རྒྱ་ (cīluùgi cīŋgya) foreign doctrines/ conventions.

ཕྱི་ལུགས་གྱོན་ཆས་ (cīluù kyö̲njɛɛ̀) foreign style clothes.

ཕྱི་ལུགས་སྨན་པ་ (cīluù mɛ̄mba) doctors of Western (foreign) medicine.

ཕྱི་ལུགས་ས་ཚད་མལ་ལི་ (cīluì sādzɛɛ̀ mɛ̲ɛ̲le) shung. (Western) mile.

ཕྱི་ལོ་མ་ (cī lo̲ma) the following/ next year ¶ དེའི་ཕྱི་ལོ་བོད་ལ་ཕྱིན་ (They) went to Tibet the following year.

ཕྱི་ལོག (cī lɔ̲ɔ̀) sm. ཕྱིར་ལོག.

ཕྱི་ལོགས་ (cīlɔɔ̀) outside ¶ ཁང་པའི་ཕྱི་ལོག་ལ་ Outside the house.

ཕྱི་ཤ་ (cīshə) 1. outer covering/ facing of a garment. 2. the outer skin (of the body).

ཕྱི་ཤ་གི་སྤྲ་རེ་ ནང་བཤིག་གི་སྤྲེའུ་ (cīshəgi dāre na̲ŋshiìgi dēwu) instigating discord and dissension.

ཕྱི་ཤུན་ (cīshün) outer skin/ layer.

ཕྱི་ཤོས་ (cīshöȍ) latest.

ཕྱི་བཤིག (cī shīì) shifting/ moving backwards, retreating, withdrawing; va.—རྒྱག་; —བྱེད་ to move backwards, to retreat, to withdraw, to backup.

ཕྱི་བཤོལ་ (cī shȫȍ) postponing; va.—བྱེད་; —རྒྱག to postpone, to put off ¶ མོ་ནང་ལ་འགྲོ་ཡག་གནས་སྐབས་ཕྱི་བཤོལ་བྱས་པ་རེད་ She temporarily put off going home.

ཕྱི་ས་ (cīsə) stool, excrement.

ཕྱི་ས་ཁང་ (cīsəgaŋ) toilet, lavatory.

ཕྱི་སད་ (cīsɛɛ̀) late frost.

ཕྱི་སོ་ (cīso) a watchman/ guard.

ཕྱི་སོག (cīsoò) Outer Mongolia.

ཕྱི་སྲིད་ (cīsiì) foreign policy.

ཕྱི་སྲིད་དྲིལ་བསྒྲགས་ (cīsiì tri̲i̲draà) international publicity.

ཕྱི་སྲིད་པུའུ་ (cīsiì bū) tib.ch. Ministry of Foreign Affairs (PRC).

ཕྱི་སྲིད་ལས་ཁུངས་ (cīsiì l̲ɛ̲ɛ̀guŋ) Foreign Office/ Bureau, Department of State (U.S.A.).

ཕྱི་སྲིད་ལས་དོན་ལྷན་ཚོགས་ (cīsiì l̲ɛ̲ɛ̀dön lhɛ̄ndzoò) Council on Foreign Relations.

ཕྱི་སྲོལ་ (cīsöö) current customs/ traditions.

ཕྱི་གསལ་ནང་གསལ་ (cīsɛɛ na̲ŋsɛɛ) 1. transparent, crystal clear. 2. sth. known to everyone, an open secret.

ཕྱི་ལྷོད་ནང་དམ་ (cīlhöȍ na̲ŋdam) loose/ easy-going for outsiders, tight/ strict for those inside.

ཕྱི་ཨ་ལོང་སྐོར་སྐོར་ ནང་ཁ་ཁ་སོ་སོ་ (cī āloŋ gɔ̄ɔ̄gɔɔ na̲ŋ kāga sōso) even though there is internal conflict when facing a common enemy they join forces.

ཕྱིང་སྐྱ་ (cīŋgya) white felt.

ཕྱིང་གུར་ (cīŋgur) felt tent, yurt.

ཕྱིང་གོས་ (cīŋgöȍ) felt garments/ clothes.

ཕྱིང་སྟན་ (cīŋdɛn) felt rug.

ཕྱིང་པོ་ (cīŋdo) roll/ ball of felt.

ཕྱིང་དྲིལ་ (cīŋdrii) rolled up felt.

ཕྱིང་གདན་ (cīŋden) felt rug.

ཕྱིང་པ་ (cīŋbə) felt.

ཕྱིང་པའི་ཆར་གོས་ (cīŋbɛ cārgöö) felt raincoat.

ཕྱིང་པའི་ནང་ལ་རྡོ་སྦྲིལ་ (cīŋbɛ naŋla dodrii) sth. that seems or sounds gentle and friendly but is really harmful and deadly [Lit. a stone wrapped in felt].

ཕྱིང་ཙེ་ (cīŋdzi) a type of Tibetan woolen material.

ཕྱིང་ཞྭ་ (cīŋsha) felt hat.

ཕྱིང་གཟར་ (cīŋsar) felt saddle pad.

ཕྱིང་སང་ (cīŋsaŋ) ch. minister.

ཕྱིང་ཧྲུལ་གནམ་འཕྱར་ (cīŋhrüü nāmjar) exposing everything negative.

ཕྱིང་ལྷམ་ (cīŋlham) felt shoes/ boots.

ཕྱིད་ (cīi) 1. vi. to be enough, to be adequate, to suffice ༑གླ་ཆས་འགྲོ་སོང་ཕྱིད་ཙམ་འདུག The wages are just enough for the expenses. 2. vi. to get frostbite ༑ཁོའི་ལག་པ་གངས་ཀྱིས་ཕྱིད་པ་རེད་ His hands got frostbitten. 3. after, following ༑ཕྱིད་ཉིན་ The day after tomorrow.

ཕྱིད་ཉིན་ (cīiñin) the day after tomorrow.

ཕྱིན་ (cīn) 1. p. of འགྲོ་. 2. sm. ཕྱིན་ཆད་. 3. (vb. + —) whenever, without exception ༑ཁོས་ཡི་གེ་བཏང་ཕྱིན་ཁོ་ཚོས་ལན་གཏོང་གི་རེད་ Whenever he sends a letter, they will reply. ༑ཞིང་བྲན་དབུལ་འཕོངས་དོ་མ་ཞིག་ཡིན་ཕྱིན་རང་བྱུང་ཁམས་ཀྱི་གནོད་འཚེ་ཐུང་བ་རེད་ All those poor serfs without exception were harmed by natural disaster.

ཕྱིན་ཅི་ལོག (cīnjilɔɔ̄) vi. to be opposite/ mistaken/ false/ distorted, to be backwards ༑གོ་བ་ཕྱིན་ཅི་ལོག་པ་རེད་ (They) had a distorted understanding. ༑བསམ་བློ་ཕྱིན་ཅི་ལོག་པ་ A distorted idea.

ཕྱིན་ཅི་ལོག་ཏུ་འགྲོ་ (cīnjilɔgdu dro) va. to run counter to, to go in the opposite way, to go backwards ༑བུ་འདི་གླང་ཐོག་ཕྱིན་ཅི་ལོག་ཏུ་འགྲོ་ནས་ཞོན་ The boy was riding the ox backward.

ཕྱིན་ཅི་ལོག་བཞི་ (cīnji m̀ɔ̄gshi) the four opposites: 1. considering dirty as clean. 2. considering selflessness as self. 3. considering suffering as happiness. 4. considering impermanence as being permanent.

ཕྱིན་ཅི་སློག (cīnji lɔ̄ɔ) va. to pervert, to do things in the opposite manner/ way, to distort (intentionlly), to make backwards.

ཕྱིན་ཆད་ (jīnjɛɛ̀) 1. henceforth, from here on ༑ད་ཕྱིན་ཆད་དེ་འདྲ་བྱེད་ཀྱི་མིན་ཟེར་བཤད་པ་རེད་ (He) said that from here on he would not do such things. 2. as long as, so long as, once ༑ལག་འཁྱེར་ཡོད་ཕྱིན་ཆད་ག་དུས་ཕྱིན་ཀྱང་ཆོག་གི་རེད་ As long as (you) have the passport you can leave any time. ༑མང་ཇ་ཡོད་པའི་ཕྱིན་ཆད་ཚང་མ་འགྲོ་གི་ཡོད་ As long as there is an early morning prayer meeting (manja), I go to all of them.

ཕྱིན་ཤུལ་ (jīnshüü) the trace of sth. that has passed by.

ཕྱིམ་འབྲེད་ (cīmdreè) sm. ཕྱི་དྲེ་.

ཕྱིའི་ (cīi) outside, foreign, external ༑ཕྱིའི་རོགས་རམ་ Foreign aid.

ཕྱིའི་དཀར་གསུམ་ (cīi gārsum) the three whites (diary products): milk, yogurt and butter.

ཕྱིའི་རྒྱ་མཚོ་ (cīi gyadzo) the oceans.

ཕྱིའི་རྒྱབ་སྐྱོར་ (cīi gyəbgyɔɔ) foreign/ outside support.

ཕྱིའི་མཆོད་པ་ (cīi cōōba) offerings made of flowers, incense, light, perfume and food.

ཕྱིའི་ལྟ་སྣང་ལ་ (cīi dānaŋla) the other's view, the outsider's view.

ཕྱིའི་རྣམ་འགྱུར་ (cīi nəmgyur) external appearance.

ཕྱིའི་བསྡམས་ (cīidum) sth. with the outside encased/ wrapped.

ཕྱིའི་དབང་བསྒྱུར་ཡུལ་ (cīi wāŋgyur yüü) a colony.

ཕྱིའི་རྨས་སྐྱོན་ (cīi mɛɛ̀gyön) external wounds.

ཕྱིའི་ཚོར་བ་ (cīi tɔ̄rwa) sensations of the body.

ཕྱིའི་གཟུགས་ (cīi sug) body, sound, smell, taste and touch.

ཕྱིའི་བཟོ་བལྟ་ (cīi sobda) sm. ཕྱིའི་རྣམ་འགྱུར་.

ཕྱིའི་རིག་པ་ (cīi rigbə) knowledge pertaining to mind and speech.

ཕྱིའི་ལས་འགན་ (cīi lɛngɛn) outside affairs, foreign affairs/ relations.

ཕྱིའི་ལྷོང་ (cīilhoŋ) obstacles caused by external forces.

ཕྱིར་ (cīr) 1. back, back to ༑དེ་ཕྱིར་ལམ་སེང་ཁྱེར་ཤོག Bring that back right away. ༑ཁོ་ཚོ་ཕྱིར་ལོག་སྐབས་ When they were going back. 2. outside, out ༑རྒྱལ་ཁབ་ཀྱི་ཕྱིར་འགྲོ་བ་ Going outside the country. 3. (vb. + —) for the purpose of, in order to ༑བོད་སྐད་ཤེས་པའི་ཕྱིར་བོད་པ་མཉམ་དུ་བསྡད་པ་རེད་ (He) stayed with Tibetans in order to learn Tibetan.

ཕྱིར་སྡུམ་ (cīr gūm) va. to withdraw/ recall.

ཕྱིར་སྐྱིལ་རྩོལ་ཚད་ (cīrgyee dzɔ̄ōdzɛɛ̀) extent of power/ energy.

ཕྱིར་བསྐོང་ (cīr gōŋ) va. to call back, to summon back.

ཕྱིར་སྐྱོད་ (cīrgyöö) going out/ outside/ abroad; va.—བྱེད་.

ཕྱིར་སྒྲོད་ (cīr dröö) kicking/ casting out, deporting, expelling; va.—གཏོང་ ༑ཁོ་སྒྲིག་སྡུད་ནས་ཕྱིར་བསྒྲད་པ་རེད་ (They) kicked him out of the organization.

ཕྱིར་སྒྲོད་སྦྱོང་བརྡར་ (cīrdröö joŋdar) sm. ཕྱིར་སྒྲོད་དམག་སྦྱོང་.

ཕྱིར་སྒྲོད་དམག་སྦྱོང་ (cīrdröö māgjoŋ) military field training.

ཕྱིར་བསྐྱོད་ (cīrgyöö) p. of ཕྱིར་སྐྱོད་.

ཕྱིར་བསྐྱོད་ལག་འཁྱེར་ (cīrgyöö laggyer) passport.

ཕྱིར་བསྒྲད་ (cīrdrɛɛ̀) p. of ཕྱིར་སྒྲོད་.

ཕྱིར་འཁོར་ (cīr kɔ̄ɔ) vi. to return, to come back.

ཕྱིར་གྲགས་མི་ཉན་ (cīrdrag miñɛn) confidential, secret.

ཕྱིར་འགུགས་ (cīrguù) calling back, recalling; va.—བྱེད་ to call back, to recall, to summon to return.

ཕྱིར་འགྱངས་ (cīrgyaŋ) sm. ཕར་འགྱངས་.

ཕྱིར་འགྱེད་ (cīngyeè) attacking back (externally/ outside); va.—བྱེད་.

ཕྱིར་འགྲོ་ (cīr dro) sm. ཕྱིར་སྐྱོད་.

ཕྱིར་འགྲོ་དངོས་ཟོག་ (cīrdro ŋüüdzɛɛ̀) goods for export.

ཕྱིར་འགྲོས་ (cīrdröö) stepping/ turning/ moving/ returning back; va.—རྒྱག.

ཕྱིར་རྒོལ་ (cīrgöö) counterattacking; va.—བྱེད་ to counterattack.

ཕྱིར་བསྒྲག (cīrdraà) publicizing/ making known to others; va.—བྱེད་.

ཕྱིར་བསྒྲལ་ (cīrdrɛɛ) driving out, expelling; va.—བྱེད་.

ཕྱིར་མངོན་ (cīrŋön) 1. vi. to be outwardly/ externally visible, to be translucent. 2. showing/ exposing externally (e.g., one's feelings through facial expression).

ཕྱིར་མངོན་གློག་སྐུད་ (cīrŋön lɔ̄ɔgüü) electric wire strung aboveground.

ཕྱིར་མངོན་མི་སྣ་ (cīrŋön minə) prominent figure, big shot, bigwig.

ཕྱིར་གཅུས་ (cīr jüü) va. to turn backwards at the waist ༑ཁོང་གིས་རྟ་ཐོག་ནས་གཟུགས་པོ་ཕྱིར་གཅུས་ནས་མདའ་འཕངས་པ་རེད་ He turned his body backwards on the horse and shot an arrow.

ཕྱིར་བཅིལ་ (cīr jīi) va. to pull out/ extract.

ཕྱིར་བཅོས་ (cīr jöö) va. to rectify/ repair, to cure (an illness), to take back the vows (of a monk).

ཕྱིར་ཆོད་ (cīr cōō) vi. to separate/ cut off from another.

ཕྱིར་མཆེད་ (cīr cēē) 1. va. to increase/ raise. 2. va. to make a secrets known externally.

ཕྱིར་འཆོས་ (cīr cōō) sm. ཕྱིར་བཅོས་.

ཕྱིར་བསྐྱིལ་ (cīr ñīl) 1. va. to throw out/ expel. 2. va. to pull down (a wall, building, etc.).

ཕྱིར་ལྟ་ (cīr dā) va. to look back, to look outside.

ཕྱིར་གཏོང་ (cīrdoŋ) sending out, exporting; va.—བྱེད་.

ཕྱིར་གཏོང་དངོས་ཟོག་ (cīrdoŋ ŋöödzɛɛ̀) export goods.

ཕྱིར་གཏོང་ཉུང་ལ་ནང་འདྲེན་མང་བ་ (cīrdoŋ ñu̱ŋla na̱ŋdren ma̱ŋwa) unfavorable balance of trade, importing more than exporting.

ཕྱིར་གཏོང་ནང་འདྲེན་ (cīrdoŋ na̱ŋdren) sending out and bringing in, exporting and importing.

ཕྱིར་གཏོང་ནང་འདྲེན་གྱི་ཉོ་ཚོང་ (cīrdoŋ na̱ŋdrengi ño̱dzoŋ) export and import trade/ sales.

ཕྱིར་གཏོང་ཚོང་པའི་གྲལ་རིམ་ (cīrdoŋ tsõŋbɛ trɛ̱ɛrim) comprador class.

ཕྱིར་གཏོང་ཚོང་པའི་འབྱོར་ལྡན་གྲལ་རིམ་ (cīrdoŋ tsõŋbɛ jɔ̱ndɛn trɛ̱ɛ̀rim) comprador bourgeois class.

ཕྱིར་གཏོང་ཚོང་པའི་མ་རྩ་ (cīrdoŋ tsõŋbɛ ma̱dza) comprador capital.

ཕྱིར་གཏོང་ཚོང་ཟོག (cīrdoŋ tsõŋsoò) goods for export.

ཕྱིར་བལྟས་ (cīrdɛɛ̀) sm. ཕྱི་བལྟས་.

ཕྱིར་བསྡམས་ (cīrdum) encased/ wrapped/ covered on the outside.

ཕྱིར་བལྟས་ཀློག (cīrdɛɛ̀ lɔ̄ɔ̀) sm. ཕྱི་བལྟས་ཀློག.

ཕྱིར་རྟེན་ཅན་ (cīrdenjɛn) one who relies or depends on things foreign (e.g., countries).

ཕྱིར་རྟེན་ཚོང་པ་ (cīrden tsõŋbə) comprador ། ཕྱིར་རྟེན་ཚོང་པའི་གྲལ་རིམ་ The comprador class.

ཕྱིར་རྟེན་ཚོང་པའི་མ་རྩ་ (cīrden tsõŋbɛ ma̱dza) comprador capital.

ཕྱིར་ཐོན་ (cīrdön) 1. leaving, departing, exiting. 2. showing/ exposing externally (e.g., one's feelings through facial expression).

ཕྱིར་ཐོན་ལག་ཁྱེར་ (cīrdön la̱ggyer) exit permit.

ཕྱིར་འཐག་འཕྲུལ་འཁོར་ (cīrdaà trũũgɔɔ) milling machine (e.g., for making flour).

ཕྱིར་འཐེན་ (cīrden) 1. withdrawing, retreating, pulling back, recalling; va.—བྱེད་; —རྒྱག to withdraw, to retreat, to recall, to pull back, to back off; vi.—ཐེར་ to have to withdraw/ retreat/ recall/ pull back ། བོད་ནང་གི་རྒྱ་རིགས་མང་པོ་ཕྱིར་འཐེན་བྱས་པ་རེད་ (They) recalled many Chinese. 2. va. to postpone ། གནམ་གཤིས་ཞན་པའི་རྐྱེན་གྱིས་འབྲས་ལྗོངས་སུ་ཕེབས་རྒྱུ་ཕྱིར་འཐེན་གནང་དགོས་བྱུང་བ་རེད་ The visit to Sikkim had to be postponed due to bad weather. 3. va. to dismiss from a job/ position ། དམག་སྤྱིའི་ལས་དོན་ནས་ཕྱིར་འཐེན་པ་རེད་ (They) dismissed (him) from the position of commander in chief.

ཕྱིར་དུ་ (cīrdu) sm. ཕྱིར་, 3.

ཕྱིར་དོང་ (cīr do̱ŋ) va. to go outside.

ཕྱིར་དོན་ (cīr dö̱n) 1. sm. ཕྱིར་དོང་. 2. va. to show/ expose (e.g., one's feelings through facial expression).

ཕྱིར་དྲན་ (cīrdrɛn) remembering the past.

ཕྱིར་མདའ་ (cīnda) shooting back at sb. when fleeing; va.—འཕེན་.

ཕྱིར་འདང་རྒྱག (cīndaŋ gyaà) sm. ཕྱི་མིག་ལྟ་.

ཕྱིར་འདེད་ (cīrdeè) expelling and pursuing; va.—བྱེད་.

ཕྱིར་འདྲེན་ (cīrdren) exporting; va.—བྱེད་ to export.

ཕྱིར་འདྲི་ (cīr dri̱) responding to a question with a question; va.—བྱེད་.

ཕྱིར་རྡེག (cīr de̱g) va. to hit back.

ཕྱིར་ལྡོག (cīr dɔ̱ɔ̀) 1. va. to return/ come back. 2. va. to counterattack, to strike back.

ཕྱིར་སྡོད་ (cīrdöö) sm. ཕྱི་སྡོད་.

ཕྱིར་སྡོད་ཀྲུང་གོའི་མི་ (cīrdöö drūŋgö mi̱) overseas Chinese.

ཕྱིར་སྡོད་སྤུན་ཟླ་ (cīrdöö bũnda) sm. ཕྱི་སྡོད་རང་མི་.

ཕྱིར་སྡོད་རང་མི་ (cīrdöö rə̱ŋmi) sm. ཕྱི་སྡོད་རང་མི་.

ཕྱིར་སྡོད་གཞུང་ཚབ་ (cīrdöö shu̱ndzəb) government officials living abroad.

ཕྱིར་སྡོད་སློབ་མ་ (cīrdöö lōbma) students studying abroad.

ཕྱིར་བསྡུ་ (cīrdu) recalling, calling back; va.—བྱེད་ to recall a product, official, etc.), to call back.

ཕྱིར་ནུད་ (cīrnüü) falling back, going backwards, retreating; va.—བྱེད་ to fall back, to go backwards, to retreat.

ཕྱིར་ནུར་ (cīr nu̱r) va. to yield, to give way, to cede.

ཕྱིར་སྣུར་ས་ (cīr nu̱rsə) a way out, an opening for retreat.

ཕྱིར་བསྣུར་ (cīr nu̱r) sm. ཕྱིར་ནུར་.

ཕྱིར་སྤྲོད་ (cīrdröö) returning, giving back; va.—བྱེད་.

ཕྱིར་ཕུ་འདེབས་ (cīrsu de̱b) va. to exhale (cigarette smoke).

ཕྱིར་ཕུད་ (cīr pũũ) p. of ཕྱིར་འབུད་.

ཕྱིར་ཕུལ་ (cīr pũũ) p. of ཕྱིར་འབུལ་.

ཕྱིར་ཕེབས་ (cīr pēè) returning, coming back; va. ཕྱིར་ཕེབས་; —གནང་; —མཛད་ to return, to come back ། ཁོང་ཕྱིར་ཕེབས་སྐབས་ On his way back.

ཕྱིར་ཕྱུང་ (cīrjuŋ) sm. ཕྱིར་སྤྲོད་.

ཕྱིར་ཕྱོགས་ (cīrjɔɔ̀) outside, exterior; va.—བྱེད་ ། སྒོའི་ཕྱིར་ཕྱོགས་ནས་ལང་ Standing outside the door.

ཕྱིར་འཕུད་ (cīrbüü) sm. ཕྱིར་འབུད་.

ཕྱིར་འཕྲོག (cīrdrɔɔ̀) stealing back, taking back by force; va.—བྱེད་.

ཕྱིར་འབུད་ (cīr büü) va. to oust/ expel/ drive out/ drive away.

ཕྱིར་བྲོས་ (cīrdröö) fleeing/ running away from; va.—བྱེད་ ། ན་གི་ཡོད་ན་ཡང་བོད་ནས་ཕྱིལ་བྲོས་བྱེད་ཐུབ་སོང་ Even though (he) was sick, he was able to flee from Tibet. ། ངས་དམག་འཐབ་བྱེད་དུས་ཕྱིར་བྲོས་བྱེད་མེད་ I didn't run away at the time of the fighting.

ཕྱིར་བྲོས་རིང་ལུགས་ (cīrdröö ri̱ŋluù) alarmism.

ཕྱིར་འབུད་ (cīmbüü) expelling, driving/ kicking out, deporting; va.—གཏོང་; —བྱེད་ to expel, to kick out, to deport.

ཕྱིར་འབུལ་ (cīmbüü) returning/ sending/ giving back; va.—བྱེད་; —གནང་ to return, to give back; to send back ། དངུལ་ཕྱིར་ཕུལ་པ་རེད་ (They) returned the money. ། ཆིང་གི་བོད་སྡོད་དཔོན་དམག་ཡོངས་རྫོགས་བོད་ནས་ཕྱིར་འབུལ་བྱས་པ་རེད་ (They) sent back (expelled) all the Qing (dynasty's) officers and troops living in Tibet.

ཕྱིར་འབྱིན་ (cīr ji̱n va. to sned out/ vent (anger, etc.).

ཕྱིར་འབྱོར་ (cīr jɔ̱ɔ) vi. to return, to arrive back.

ཕྱིར་འབྲང་ (cīr dra̱ŋ) vi. to follow, to imitate.

ཕྱིར་མི་མཐོང་བ་ (cīr mi̱nömbə) not visible from outside, opaque ། སྒེའུ་ཁུང་འདི་ལ་ཕྱིར་མི་མཐོང་བའི་ཤེལ་ཀོ་བསྒར་འདུག This window has opaque glass.

ཕྱིར་མི་ལྡོག (cīr mi̱dɔg) not returning, gone forever.

ཕྱིར་མི་འོང་ (cīr mi̱oŋ) sm. ཕྱིར་མི་ལྡོག་པ་.

ཕྱིར་མིག་ལྟ་ (cīrmiì dā) va. to look back.

ཕྱིར་ཚོང་ (cīrdzoŋ) 1. exporting, selling to the outside (can refer to goods or ideas); va.—བྱེད་ to export. 2. selling out, betraying; va.—བྱེད་ to sell out, to betray.

ཕྱིར་ཚོང་གོང་ཚད་ (cīrdzoŋ ko̱ŋdzɛɛ̀) sm. ཕྱིར་ཚོང་རིན་གོང་.

ཕྱིར་ཚོང་རིན་གོང་ (cīrdzoŋ ri̱ngoŋ) export price.

ཕྱིར་ཞིང་ (cīrshiŋ) sm. སླར་ཡང་.

ཕྱིར་ཞིང་ཕྱིར་ཞིང་ (cīrshiŋ cīrshiŋ) again and again.

ཕྱིར་བཞེས་གནང་ (cīrsheè) withdrawing, taking back.

ཕྱིར་ཟློག (cīrdɔɔ̀) va. to repel/ rebuff, to hit back.

ཕྱིར་འོང་ (cīr o̱ŋ) to return (back).

ཕྱིར་ཡང་ (cīryaŋ) sm. སླར་ཡང་.

ཕྱིར་རིམ་པ་ (cīi ri̱mbə) shung. an "outer" rank given to low provincial officials in the traditional Tibetan government (these did not have status of real officials).

ཕྱིར་རོགས་དངོས་ཟོག (cīīrɔɔ̀ ŋöödzɛɛ̀) foreign aid.

ཕྱིར་ལན་སྐྱལ་ (cīrlɛn dzɛ̃ɛ̃) va. to make a reply, to respond to.

ཕྱིར་ལམ་ (cīrlam) sm. ཚུར་ལམ་.

ཕྱིར་ལུས་ (cīrlüü) backward, left behind.

ཕྱིར་ལེན་ (cīrlen) taking back; va.—བྱེད་ ། རང་ས་དགྲ་ཤོར་རྣམས་ཕྱིར་ལེན་བྱ་རྒྱུ་ Taking back our territories that have been lost to the enemy.

ཕྱིར་ལོག (cīīlɔɔ̀) returning, going back; va. ཕྱིར་ལོག་;

—རྒྱག་; —བྱེད་; —འགྲོ་ to return, to go back ¶ མགྱོགས་པོར་ཕྱིར་ལོག་བརྒྱབས་པ་རེད་ (They) went back (home) quickly. ¶ གནང་སྐྱེས་རྣམས་ཕྱིར་སློག་པས་ (He) gave back the gifts. ¶ ཆུ་ཚོད་ ༩ ལ་ཕྱིར་ལོག་ཡོང་གི་ཡོད་ I return at 9 o'clock.

ཕྱིར་ལོག་དུ་ཕོག (cīīlɔ̀ɔdu pɔ̄ɔ̀) vi. to reflect, to bounce back on.

ཕྱིར་ལོག་གཏོང་ (cīīlɔ̀ɔ dōŋ) va. to send back, to return.

ཕྱིར་ལོག་གདོང་ (cīīlɔ̀ɔ do̲ŋ) to send (sth.) via/ through another.

ཕྱིར་ལོག་ཕྱིར་སྡོད་རང་མི་ (cīīlɔ̀ɔ cīīdöö rə̲ŋmi) overseas nationals who return to their own country.

ཕྱིར་ལོག་དམག་མི་ (cīīlɔ̀ɔ mɔ̄ɔ̀mi) demobilized soldiers.

ཕྱིར་ཤིག (cīīshiì) sm. ཕྱི་ཤིག.

ཕྱིར་ཤོག (cīī shɔ̄ɔ̀) va. to let/ leak out (secrets).

ཕྱིར་གཤེ་ (cīī shē) va. to scold back, to respond back with scolding.

ཕྱིར་བཤོལ་ (cīīshöö) retracting, withdrawing; va.—བྱེད་.

ཕྱིར་སོས་ (cīī söö) vi. to come back to life (usu. plants, etc.).

ཕྱིར་སློག (cīī lɔ̄ɔ̀) va. 1. to give back, to return, to make someone return ¶ ཡི་གེ་དེ་ཕྱིར་སློག་པ་རེད་ (They) sent back the letter. 2. va. to turn inside out, to reverse sides ¶ ཁོས་སྟོད་ཐུང་ཕྱིར་སློག་བྱས་ནི་གྱོན་འདུག He has put on the shirt inside out.

ཕྱིར་སློག་བྱེད་ (cīīlɔ̀ɔ ce̲è) sm. ཕྱིར་སློག.

ཕྱིར་ལྷོངས་ (cīī lhōŋ) sm. ཕྱིར་འབུད་.

ཕྱིས་ (cīī) 1. va. to erase, to wipe out. 2. later, in the future ¶ ཕྱིས་སྐྱོན་མེད་པར་ཡོང་ཆེད་ For the purpose of avoiding future harm/ injury.

ཕྱིས་སྐྱེས་ (cīīgyeè) younger brother.

ཕྱིས་འགྱངས་ (cīīgyaŋ) sm. ཕྱིར་འགྱངས་.

ཕྱིས་དྲགས་ (cīī tra̲à) vi. to be too late.

ཕྱིས་བདར་ (cīīdar) dusting, wiping; va.—གཏོང་ to dust, to wipe ¶ ལྕོག་ཙེ་དེར་ཕྱིས་བདར་གཏང་བས་ Did (you) wipe the table?

ཕྱིས་ན་ (cīīnə) in the future.

ཕྱིས་ནས་ (cīīnɛ) sm. ཕྱིས་སུ་.

ཕྱིས་པོ་ (cīību) late; vi.—ཆགས་ to become late ¶ ཕྱིས་པོ་ཆགས་སྐབས་ཁོ་ནང་ལ་ལོག་ཕྱིན་སོང་ Because it had become late he went home.

ཕྱིས་བུ་ (cīību) utensils, containers.

ཕྱིས་འབྱུང་ (cīījuŋ) in the future, afterwards, later ¶ ཕྱིས་འབྱུང་མི་འདྲ་ཞིག་ཡོང་གི་རེད་ It will be different in the future. ¶ ཕྱིས་འབྱུང་ང་འདི་འདྲ་བྱེད་ཀྱི་མིན་ In the future I will not do like this.

ཕྱིས་འབྲང་ (cīī dra̲ŋ) va. to follow after.

ཕྱིས་མ་ (cīīmə) sm. ཕྱིས་སུ་, 1.

ཕྱིས་ཚར་ (cīīdzar) remainder, remnant.

ཕྱིས་རས་ (cīīrɛɛ̀) dustcloth.

ཕྱིས་ལམ་ (cīīlam) the future path/ way/ road.

ཕྱིས་བཤིག (cīīshiì) backing up; va.—རྒྱག.

ཕྱིས་སུ་ (cīīsu) 1. afterwards, later. 2. lately, these days ¶ ཕྱིས་སུ་བུད་མེད་ཚོ་སློབ་སྦྱོང་ལ་དོ་སྣང་ཆེ་རུ་ཕྱིན་ཡོད་པ་རེད་ Lately, women have become more interested in education.

ཕྱུ་པ་ (cūbə) basic Tibetan dress (for men and woman).

ཕྱུ་པ་སྲམ་ཤན་མ་ (cūbə drām she̲mma) a dress embellished with otter skin around the hem.

ཕྱུ་ར་ (cūrə) sm. ཕྱུར་པ་.

ཕྱུ་རི་རི་ (cū ri̲ri) floating upwards (like smoke).

ཕྱུ་རིང་ (cūriŋ) long dress/ gown.

ཕྱུ་རུ་རུ་ (cū ru̲ru) sm. ཕྱུ་རི་རི་.

ཕྱུག (cūù) 1. vi. to be in possession of, to be rich ¶ ཉམས་མྱོང་གིས་ཕྱུག་པ་ (He) is rich in experience. 2. abbr. of ཕྱུག་པོ་.

ཕྱུག་ཁྱད་ (cūggyɛɛ̀) wealth, riches.

ཕྱུག་འགྱུར་སྲིད་ཇུས་ (cūggyur sīījüù) policy of people getting rich.

ཕྱུག་གན་ (cūggɛn) a rich person.

ཕྱུག་ཉམས་ (cūgñam) luxurious, sumptuous, extravagant.

ཕྱུག་བདག (cūgdaà) a rich/ wealthy person.

ཕྱུག་པོ་ (cūgbo) rich, wealthy; va.—བྱེད་ to get rich.

ཕྱུག་པོའི་རྒྱུ་ངོར་ལ་མི་ལྟ་ བཙན་པའི་ཚིག་རྗེས་ལ་མི་འབྲང་ (cūgbö gyu̲nola mi̲da dzɛ̄mbö tsīgjeèla mi̲draŋ) honest, just, independent in thinking [Lit. not looking at the wealth of rich people, not following the words of powerful people].

ཕྱུག་དབུལ་ (cūg üü) rich and poor.

ཕྱུགས་ (cūù) livestock, cattle.

ཕྱུགས་ཀྱི་རུ་མ་ (cūùgi ru̲mə) (cattle) breeding stock.

ཕྱུགས་སྐྱོང་ (cūùgyoŋ) sm. ཕྱུགས་འཚོ་.

ཕྱུགས་དཀར་ནག (cūù gārnaà) general term for all livestock: sheep, goats and large cattle (yak, cows, dzo).

ཕྱུགས་ཁྱུ་ (cūùgyu) cattle herd.

ཕྱུགས་ཁྲལ་ (cūgdrɛɛ) tax on livestock.

ཕྱུགས་རྒྱུད་ (cūggyüù) a breed of cattle/ livestock.

ཕྱུགས་རྒྱུད་ཕྱེལ་ར་ (cūggyüù bēēra) livestock breeding farm.

ཕྱུགས་རྒྱུད་ལེགས་བཅོས་ (cūggyüù le̲gjöö) livestock breed improvement.

ཕྱུགས་སྒྲོལ་ (cūgdröö) livestock crossing a river/ stream.

ཕྱུགས་བརྒྱུད་ (cūggyüù) sm. ཕྱུགས་རྒྱུད་.

ཕྱུགས་རྔོ་ (cūgŋo) livestock scabies.

ཕྱུགས་བཅག (cūgjaà) sm. ཕྱུགས་ཆགས་.

ཕྱུགས་བཅོས་ (cūgjöö) treating livestock illnesses.

ཕྱུགས་བཅོས་པ་ (cūgjööbə) veterinarian.

ཕྱུགས་ཆགས་ (cūgjaà) threshing by driving cattle over the grain stalks; va.—སྐོར་; —སྐོར་ to thresh by driving cattle over the grain stalks.

ཕྱུགས་ཆུང་ (cūgjuŋ) small livestock/ cattle.

ཕྱུགས་ཆེན་ (cūgjen) large livestock/ cattle.

ཕྱུགས་འཆག (cūgjaà) sm. ཕྱུགས་ཆགས་.

ཕྱུགས་གཉེར་ (cūgñer) person who looks after/ manages livestock and cattle.

ཕྱུགས་ལྡོ་ (cūgdo) livestock or cattle feed/ fodder.

ཕྱུགས་ཐོན་དངོས་ཟོག (cūgten ŋöösog) livesotck products.

ཕྱུགས་འཐེན་འཁོར་ལོ་ (cūgten kɔ̄ɔlo) animal drawn cart, bullock cart.

ཕྱུགས་དེབ་ (cūgdeb) a book keeping track of the death and birth of livestock/ cattle.

ཕྱུགས་བདག (cūgdaà) livestock owner.

ཕྱུགས་འདུལ་ (cūg du̲ü̲) va. to train livestock/ cattle.

ཕྱུགས་ནད་ (cūgnɛɛ̀) livestock or cattle sickness/ disease.

ཕྱུགས་ནད་སྨན་ཁང་ (cūgnɛɛ̀ mɛ̄ngaŋ) livestock/ cattle hospital.

ཕྱུགས་ནད་སྨན་པ་ (cūgnɛɛ̀ mɛ̄mba) veterinarian.

ཕྱུགས་ནད་སྨན་བཅོས་ས་ཚིགས་ (cūgnɛɛ̀ mɛ̄njöö sədzii) veterinary station.

ཕྱུགས་ནད་རིག་པ་ (cūgnɛɛ̀ rigbə) veterinary science.

ཕྱུགས་གནག (cūgnaà) yak.

ཕྱུགས་པ་ (cūgbə) one who looks after livestock/ cattle.

ཕྱུགས་ཕྱུང་མ་ (cūgjuŋmə) a young girl.

ཕྱུགས་ཕྲུག (cūgdruù) young livestock/ cattle.

ཕྱུགས་སྨན་ (cūgmɛn) medicine for livestock.

ཕྱུགས་སྨན་ཁང་ (cūgmɛngaŋ) veterinary/ livestock hospital.

ཕྱུགས་སྨན་བྱ་བའི་ས་ཚིགས་ (cūgmɛn ca̲wɛ sədzii) veterinary station.

ཕྱུགས་རྩྭ་ (cūgdza) pasture, fodder grass.

ཕྱུགས་རྩིས་ (cūgdzii) listing the births and deaths of livestock/ cattle; va.—རྒྱག.

ཕྱུགས་ཚང་ (cūgdzaŋ) cattle/ livestock shed or barn.

ཕྱུགས་འཚོ་ (cūg tsō) 1. va. to pasture / graze animals. 2. va. to raise/ rear animals.

ཕྱུགས་འཚོ་བ་ (cūgdzowa) sm. ཕྱུགས་རྫི་.

ཕྱུགས་འཚོ་ས་ (cūg tsōsa) grazing/ pasture area.

ཕྱུགས་རྫས་ཀུང་སི་ (cūgdzɛɛ̀ gūŋsi) livestock/ cattle products company.

ཕྱུགས་རྫས་ཁའོ་ (cūgdzɛɛ̀ kǝwu) tib.ch. animal products section.

ཕྱུགས་རྫས་ཉོ་སྒྲུབ་ས་ཚིགས་ (cūgdzɛɛ̀ ñodrub sǝdzii̇) animal products purchasing station.

ཕྱུགས་རྫི་ (cūgdzi) livestock/ cattle herder.

ཕྱུགས་ཟོག (cūgsoò) livestock, cattle.

ཕྱུགས་ཟོག་གི་སྦོད་ནད་ (cūgsoògi dȫȫnɛɛ̀) a lung disease of livestock/ cattle.

ཕྱུགས་ཟོག་གསོ་རིག་ཚན་རིག་ཞིབ་འཇུག་ཁང་ (cūgsoò sōrii̇ tsɛ̄nrii̇ shi̱mjuùgaŋ) institute of animal husbandry and veterinary sciences.

ཕྱུགས་ཟོག་གསོ་རིག་སློབ་གྲྭ་ཆེན་མོ་ (cūgsoò sōrii̇ lōbdra cēmbo) animal husbandry college.

ཕྱུགས་གཡང་མོ་ (cūg yāŋmo) sheep.

ཕྱུགས་ར་ (cūgra) 1. corral, fenced in area for livestock/ cattle. 2. livestock farm.

ཕྱུགས་ར་དོ་དམ་ཁྲུའུ་ (cūgra to̱dam trū) tib.ch. livestock farm management office.

ཕྱུགས་རིགས་ (cūgrii̇) livestock, cattle, domestic animals.

ཕྱུགས་རིགས་སྦོ་འཚོ་ (cūgrii̇ bōndzo) nomadic pastoralism, nomadic way of life.

ཕྱུགས་རིགས་སྦོ་འཚོའི་དཔལ་འབྱོར་ (cūgrii̇ bōndzö bɛ̄njɔɔ) nomadic economy.

ཕྱུགས་རིགས་སྦོ་འཚོའི་མི་རིགས་ (cūgrii̇ bōndzö mi̱rii̇) nomadic nationalities.

ཕྱུགས་རིགས་སྨན་པ་ (cūgrii̇ mɛ̄mba) veterinarian.

ཕྱུགས་རྭ་ (cūgra) livestock corral.

ཕྱུགས་ལས་ (cūglɛɛ̀) pastoral industry, animal husbandry.

ཕྱུགས་ལས་ཅུའུ་ (cūglɛɛ̀ jū) tib.ch. bureau of animal husbandry.

ཕྱུགས་ལས་ཐོན་སྐྱེད་མཉམ་ལས་ཁང་ (cūglɛɛ̀ tȫngyeè) livestock breeders production cooperative.

ཕྱུགས་ལས་ཐོན་རྫས་ (cūglɛɛ̀ tȫndzɛɛ̀) livestock/ animal products.

ཕྱུགས་ལས་སྡེ་ཁག (cūglɛɛ̀ de̱gaà) department of animal husbandry.

ཕྱུགས་ལས་དཔལ་འབྱོར་ (cūglɛɛ̀ bɛ̄njɔɔ) pastoral economy.

ཕྱུགས་ལས་དཔྱ་ཁྲལ་ (cūglɛɛ̀ jātrɛɛ) animal husbandry tax, animal tax.

ཕྱུགས་ལས་ཞིབ་འཇུག་ཁང་ (cūglɛɛ̀ shimjuùgaŋ) animal husbandry research institute.

ཕྱུགས་ལས་ཚན་རིག་ཞིབ་འཇུག་ཁང་ (cūglɛɛ̀ tsɛ̄nrii̇ shimjuùgaŋ) institute of animal husbandry.

ཕྱུགས་ལས་ས་ཁུལ་ (cūglɛɛ̀ sǝgüü) nomad/ pastoral area.

ཕྱུགས་ལས་སྨན་བཅོས་ས་ཚིགས་ (cūglɛɛ̀ mɛ̄njöö sǝdzii̇) veterinary station.

ཕྱུགས་ལུད་ (cūglüü) cattle/ livestock manure.

ཕྱུགས་ཤིག (cūgshi¡i) livestock/ cattle lice.

ཕྱུགས་ཤུགས་ (cūgshuù) livestock/ cattle power ¶ ཕྱུགས་ཤུགས་གྲོ་རྔ་འཕྲུལ་འཁོར་ Cattle powered wheat harvester.

ཕྱུགས་ས་ (cūgsǝ) livestock grazing area.

ཕྱུགས་སྲུང་ (cūgsuŋ) livestock protection.

ཕྱུགས་གསོ་ (cūgso) livestock/ cattle husbandry.

ཕྱུགས་གསོ་མཁན་ (cūg sōñɛn) person who raises livestock/ cattle.

ཕྱུགས་གསོ་ར་བ་ (cūgso ra̱wa) livestock farm, feed lot.

ཕྱུགས་གསོས་ (cūgsöö) fodder for livestock.

ཕྱུགས་ལྷ་ (cūglha) cattle deity.

ཕྱུགས་ལྷས་ (cūglɛɛ̀) sm. ཕྱུགས་ར་.

ཕྱུང་ (cūŋ) p. and imp. of འབྱིན་.

ཕྱུང་ (cūŋ) 1. va. to show/ exhibit ¶ ཁོང་གི་ཞལ་རས་ནས་འཛུམ་མདངས་ཕྱུང་བཞིན་དུ་ His face showed a smile.

ཕྱུར་ (cūr) p. of འཕྱུར་.

ཕྱུར་སྐམ་ (cūrgam) dried cheese.

ཕྱུར་སྐྱུམ་ (cūrgum) a kind of dried cheese.

ཕྱུར་ཁུ་ (cūrgu) whey liquid left after the cheese has been extracted from དར་བ་.

ཕྱུར་ཁུ་མདོག (cūrgudɔɔ̀) pale green (the color of ཕྱུར་ཁུ་).

ཕྱུར་ཁུ་སྨུག་རྩི་ (cūrgu mūgdzi) maroon color paste made from simmering ཕྱུར་ཁུ་ a long time.

ཕྱུར་རྒྱུ་ (cūrgyu) ingredients for making cheese.

ཕྱུར་པོ་ (cūrbu) full to the brim.

ཕྱུར་ཕྱུར་ (cūrjuu) rhubarb.

ཕྱུར་བ་ (cūrwǝ) cheese.

ཕྱུར་བ་སྐྱ་ཕྱུར་ (cūrwǝ gyājur) sour cheese.

ཕྱུར་བ་སྔོ་ཕྱུར་ (cūrwǝ ŋōjur) blue cheese.

ཕྱུར་བ་ཧྲོབ་ (cūrwǝ hrōb) dried/ rock cheese.

ཕྱུར་བ་ཧྲོག་པོ་ (cūrwǝ hrōgbo) dried cheese (the size of gravel stones).

ཕྱུར་བུ་ (cūrbu) sm. ཕྱུར་བུ་.

ཕྱུར་ཞིབ་ (cūrshib) powdered cheese.

ཕྱུར་ར་ (cūrrǝ) sm. ཕྱུར་བ་.

ཕྱུར་རེ་བ་ (cūrrewǝ) smoky, dusty.

ཕྱུར་རུལ་ (cūrrüü) "rotten" cheese (such as blue cheese).

ཕྱུར་ལེང་ (cūrleŋ) sm. ཕྱུར་ལེབ་.

ཕྱུར་ཧྲོབ་ (cūrhrob) abbr. of ཕྱུར་བ་ཧྲོག་ཧྲོག.

ཕྱེ་ (cē) 1. p. of འབྱེད་. 2. a ground/ powdered substance, flour ¶ གྲོ་ཕྱེ་ Wheat flour. 3. va. to grind.

ཕྱེ་རྐྱལ་ (cēgyɛɛ) leather pouch for keeping tsampa.

ཕྱེ་སྐྱོར་ (cēgyɔɔ) the part of a water mill grinding stone on which the ground grain comes down.

ཕྱེ་འགམས་ (cē ga̱m) va. to eat tsampa dry.

ཕྱེ་ཆག (cējaà) ground grains used as fodder for horses, mules, etc.

ཕྱེ་གཉེར་ (cēñer) person in charge of a grinding mill.

ཕྱེ་གདོར་ (cē dɔ̄ɔ) va. to overpraise, to flatter overly.

ཕྱེ་ཐུག (cēduù) soup made with barley flour.

ཕྱེ་འཐག (cēdaà) 1. milling/ grinding grain or tsamba. 2. va. to grind tsamba.

ཕྱེ་འཐག་ཁང་ (cēdaàgaŋ) grinding mill for grain/ tsamba.

ཕྱེ་འཐག་འཕྲུལ་འཁོར་ (cēdaà trǖǖgɔɔ) flour or tsamba grinding machine.

ཕྱེ་འཐག་བཟོ་གྲྭ་ (cēdaà so̱dra) flour/ tsamba grinding factory.

ཕྱེ་འདྲེས་མ་ (cēdreèma) flour made from a mixture of various grains.

ཕྱེ་སྦྲུལ་ (cēdrüü) crumbled tsamba ball.

ཕྱེ་འབོ་ (cēmbɔ) a wooden container with tsampa and grain offered at New Year.

ཕྱེ་མ་ (cēma) powder, any pulverized substance ¶ སྨན་ཕྱེ་མ་ Medicine in powdered form.

ཕྱེ་མ་ལེབ་ (cēmaleb) butterfly.

ཕྱེ་མར་ (cēmar) tsamba mixed with butter.

ཕྱེ་མར་བཏགས་ (cēmar dāà) p. of ཕྱེ་མར་འཐག.

ཕྱེ་མར་འཐག (cēmar dāà) va. to grind, to pulverize, to powder.

ཕྱེ་མར་དུང་ (cēmar dūŋ) sm. ཕྱེ་མར་འཐག.

ཕྱེ་མར་བརྡར་ (cēmar da̱r) sm. ཕྱེ་མར་འཐག.

ཕྱེ་མར་བྱེད་ (cēmar ce̱è) sm. ཕྱེ་མར་འཐག.

ཕྱེ་སྨན་ (cēmɛn) powdered medicine.

ཕྱེ་ལེབ་ (cēleb) sm. ཕྱེ་མ་ལེབ་.

ཕྱེ་ཧྲག (cēhag) medicine made from the foam of boiled brown sugar.

ཕྱེད་ (cēè) 1. abbr. of ཕྱེད་ཀ་. 2. when used before a number means half less than the number ¶ ཕྱེད་དང་བདུན་ Six and a half. 3. vi. to be separate/ differentiated.

ཕྱེད་ཀ་ (cēèga) half, semi- ¶ ཉི་མ་གཅིག་དང་ཕྱེད་ཀ་ A day and a half.

ཕྱེད་ཀྲུང་ (cēèdruŋ) sm. ཕྱེད་སྐྱིལ་.

ཕྱེད་སྐུང་ཕྱེད་བཤད་ (cēèguŋ cēèshɛɛ̀) hesitating to say/ tell the whole thing, telling bits and pieces, mincing words.

ཕྱེད་སྐྱིལ་ (cēègyee) crossing one leg only.

ཕྱེད་གང་ (cēègaŋ) half full.

ཕྱེད་གོང་མ་ (cēè ko̱ŋma) the first half.

ཕྱེད་གྲིབ་ཕོག (cēèdrib pɔ̄ɔ̀) vi. to become paralyzed on half the body.

ཕྱེད་གྲུབ་ཐོན་རྫས་ (cɛ̀ɛdrub tõndzɛɛ̀) semifinished product.

ཕྱེད་གླིང་ (cēèliŋ) peninsula.

ཕྱེད་བགོས་ (cēègöö) dividing in half; va.—རྒྱག་; —གཏོང་.

ཕྱེད་འགྲངས་ཕྱེད་ལྟོགས་ (cēndraŋ cēèdrɔɔ̀) half full and half hungry.

ཕྱེད་རྒྱགས་ཕྱེད་ལྟོགས་ (cēègyɛɛ̀ cēèdɔɔ̀) half full and half hungry.

ཕྱེད་རྒྱབ་ཕྱེད་ཕྱེ་ (cēègyəb cēèje) half open, half closed.

ཕྱེད་བརྒྱད་ (cēègyɛɛ̀) 1. a Tibetan coin worth one half of a tranga. 2. seven and a half.

ཕྱེད་བཅགས་ (cēèjaà) a concession of half; va.—གཏོང་ ། སྐར་གློག་ཕྱེད་བཅགས་བཏང་སོང་ (They) gave a concession of half on the price of a telegram.

ཕྱེད་ཆ་ (cɛ̀ɛja) half (of sth. that has been divided into two).

ཕྱེད་གཉིས་ (cēèñii) one and a half.

ཕྱེད་ཐང་ལྟོག (cēèdaŋ lɔɔ̀) sm. ཕབ་ཕྱི་ལྟོག.

ཕྱེད་ཕྱིར་ (cēèdir) a ཆང་ container that costs three kagang.

ཕྱེད་དྭ་ཕྲུག (cēè tədruù) half orphan (one parent dead).

ཕྱེད་དྲང་ཕྱེད་རྫུན་ (cēèdraŋ cēèdzün) half true and half false.

ཕྱེད་འདྲུད་ཕྱེད་འཁུར་ (cēèdrüü cēègur) half dragging half carrying; va.—བྱེད་.

ཕྱེད་བདེན་ཕྱེད་བགད་ (cēèden cēègɛɛ̀) half serious and half laughing.

ཕྱེད་འདྲེས་ (cēèdreè) half mixed, mixed half and half.

ཕྱེད་པ་ (cēèba) a part (in hair).

ཕྱེད་པོ་ (cēèbo) sm. ཕྱེད་མ་.

ཕྱེད་ཕྱེད་ (cēèjeè) half each.

ཕྱེད་བབས་ (cēèbəb) half of some amount due or owed.

ཕྱེད་མ་ (cɛ̀ɛma) half of (sth.).

ཕྱེད་མ་སྦྲུ་རུག (cēèma būruù) sm. ཐྲི་མ་སྦྲུ་རུག.

ཕྱེད་མི་སེར་སྐྱིལ་ཡུལ་ (cēè misee bēyüü) semicolonial.

ཕྱེད་སྨིན་པ་ (cēè mĩmbə) half ripe.

ཕྱེད་ཙམ་ (cēèdzam) about half, semi- ། ཕྱེད་ཙམ་གྲུབ་པའི་ཐོན་རྫས་ Semifinished products.

ཕྱེད་བཙོས་ (cēèdzöö) half done/ cooked.

ཕྱེད་ཚལ་ (cēèdzɛɛ) half of sth.

ཕྱེད་ཚིག (cēèdzii) half burned.

ཕྱེད་འཛིན་ (cēndzin) half an eclipse.

ཕྱེད་གཟན་འཕེབས་ (cēèsɛn beb) shung. va. to take one's upper shawl (for monks) down halfways as a sign of respect to higher officials or lamas.

ཕྱེད་གཟུགས་ (cēèsuù) figures of deities that have half their face colored differently from the other half.

ཕྱེད་འོག་མ་ (cēè wɔɔ̀ma) the bottom half.

ཕྱེད་ལས་ཕྱེད་སྦྱོང་ (cēèlɛɛ̀ cēèjoŋ) part time work and part time study.

ཕྱེད་ལུས་ (cēèlüü) half undone, half unfinished.

ཕྱེད་རིན་ (cēèrin) half price.

ཕྱེད་ཤས་ (cēèshɛɛ̀) shung. a lease system wherein half of the crop from the field goes to the owner.

ཕྱེད་གཤགས་ (cēèshaà) splitting in two, cutting in half; va.—གཏོང་.

ཕྱེད་བཤད་ཕྱེད་སྐུང་ (cēèshɛɛ̀ cēègum) not saying everything, speaking evasively [Lit. saying half and concealing half].

ཕྱེད་ལས་ལྷག (cēèlɛ lhāà) more than half, the majority.

ཕྱེད་གསལ་ (cēèsɛl) translucent.

ཕྱེད་ལྷག (cēèlhaà) more than half, the majority.

ཕྱེན་ (cēn) a fart; va.—གཏོང་ to intentionally fart; vi.—ཤོར་ to unintentionally fart.

ཕྱེན་དྲི་ (cēndri) smell of a fart.

ཕྱེས་ (cēè) 1. imp. of འབྱེད་. 2. sm. འབྱེད་.

ཕྱོ་ཕྱོ་ (cōjo) go get him! (said to urge on dogs).

ཕྱོགས་ (cɔ̄ɔ̀) 1. direction, side ། ཕྱོགས་མང་པོ་ནས་ From many directions. ། འདི་ཕྱོགས་སུ་ To this side. ། རང་ཕྱོགས་ One's own side. 2. (vb.+ —) conveys the means/ way/ method of doing the verbal action ། དཀའ་ངལ་དེ་ཚོར་གདོང་ལེན་བྱེད་ཕྱོགས་ཐད་ Concerning how to face those problems. ། ཁོང་གིས་གསུངས་ཕྱོགས་ལ་བལྟས་ན་ (If) we look at the way (he) said it. 3. va. to side with ། ཁོས་ང་ཚོའི་ཕྱོགས་བྱས་པ་རེད་ He sided with us. 4. va. to face towards (usu.+ —) ། ཚང་མས་ཁ་ཤར་དུ་ཕྱོགས་པ་རེད་ All (the people) faced to the east. 5. imp. of. འཕྱོགས་. 6. trips outside one's normal area ། ང་ཕྱོགས་ལ་འགྲོ་དུས་ When I go on a trip.

ཕྱོགས་ཀུན་ (cɔ̄ɔ̀gün) 1. all directions, everywhere, all over. 2. all ways, all aspects (see ཕྱོགས་ཀུན་ནས་).

ཕྱོགས་ཀུན་དུ་ (cɔ̄ɔ̀gündu) 1. in all directions, everywhere. 2. in all aspects (see ཕྱོགས་ཀུན་ནས་).

ཕྱོགས་ཀུན་ནས་ (cɔ̄ɔ̀günnɛ) from all directions, from everywhere ། དེར་ཕྱོགས་ཀུན་ནས་མི་སླེབས་ཡོད་པ་རེད་ People have come there from all directions. 2. from all points of view/ aspects, in all ways ། ཁོ་ཚོའི་གནས་སྟངས་ཕྱོགས་ཀུན་ནས་དྲག་ཏུ་ཕྱིན་ཡོད་པ་རེད་ Their condition has improved in all ways.

ཕྱོགས་ཀྱི་དངོས་པོ་ (cɔ̄ɔ̀gi ŋɔ̃ɔ̀bo) shung. local products/ goods.

ཕྱོགས་སྐྱོང་ (cɔ̄ɔ̀gyoŋ) the protective deities who guard the ten directions.

ཕྱོགས་བསྐྱོད་ (cɔ̄ɔ̀gyöö) sm. ཕྱོགས་འགྲོ་.

ཕྱོགས་ཁ་ (cɔ̄ɔ̀ga) sm. ཚལ་ཁ་.

ཕྱོགས་ཁག (cɔ̄ɔ̀gaà) section, group, clique, wing, party.

ཕྱོགས་འཁྱམས་ (cɔ̄ɔ̀gyam) person who wanders all over the place.

ཕྱོགས་འཁྱར་ (cɔ̄ɔ̀gyar) sm. ཕྱོགས་འཁྱམས་.

ཕྱོགས་ག་གེ་མོ་ (cɔ̄ɔ̀ gagemo) such and such place.

ཕྱོགས་གང་ཅིའི་ཐད་ (cɔ̄ɔ̀ kaŋjitɛɛ̀) sm. གང་ས་ཅི་ཐད་ནས་.

ཕྱོགས་གང་ཐད་ནས་ (cɔ̄ɔ̀ kaŋtɛɛ̀nɛ) 1. sm. ཕྱོགས་ཀུན་. 2. by all means/ methods.

ཕྱོགས་གོས་ (cɔ̄ɔ̀göö) traveling clothes.

ཕྱོགས་གྱུར་དུ་འགྲོ་ (cɔ̄ɔ̀ gyardu dro) va. to roam about, to lead a vagabond life.

ཕྱོགས་བགོས་ (cɔ̄ɔ̀göö) dividing, distributing, allocating; va.—བྱེད་.

ཕྱོགས་འགལ་ (cɔ̄ŋgɛɛ) counter to, opposed to; va.—བྱེད་ to oppose, to go counter to.

ཕྱོགས་འགལ་ཚོགས་སྡེ་ (cɔ̄ŋgɛɛ tsɔ̄gde) opposition group/ party.

ཕྱོགས་འགྲོ་ (cɔ̄gdro) travels, traveling; va.—བྱེད་ to travel.

ཕྱོགས་འགྲོའི་ཚོང་པ་ (cɔ̄gdrö tsɔ̄ŋba) traveling salesman.

ཕྱོགས་འགྲུལ་ (cɔ̄ŋdrüü) sm. ཕྱོགས་འགྲོ་.

ཕྱོགས་སྒྱུར་ (cɔ̄ggyur) changing one's course, striking out on a new path.

ཕྱོགས་སྒྱུར་ལམ་སྒྱུར་ (cɔ̄ggyur lamgyur) sm. ཕྱོགས་སྒྱུར་.

ཕྱོགས་སྒྲིག (cɔ̄ɔ̀drii) compiling (records, etc.); va.—བྱེད་.

ཕྱོགས་སྒྲིལ་ (cɔ̄gdrii) forming a group/ clique/ alliances/ confederation, allying; va.—བྱེད་.

ཕྱོགས་སྒྲིལ་སྤང་པའི་ཡུལ་ཁག (cɔ̄gdrii bāŋbɛ yüügaà) nonaligned countries.

ཕྱོགས་སྒྲིལ་སྤང་པའི་ཡུལ་ཁག་གི་ལས་འགུལ་ཚོགས་པ་ (cɔ̄gdrii bāŋbɛ yüügaàgi lɛngüü tsɔ̄gba) nonaligned movement.

ཕྱོགས་སྒྲོག (cɔ̄ɔ̀drog) ordering, regulating, adjusting; va.—བྱེད་.

ཕྱོགས་བསྒྲགས་ (cɔ̄ɔ̀drag) propagating, spreading information/ publicity; va.—བྱེད་ ། གསར་བརྗེའི་བདེན་དོན་ཕྱོགས་བྱེད་པ་ཙམ་ཅིག Along with spreading the revolutionary truth.

ཕྱོགས་བསྒྲིགས་ (cɔ̄ɔ̀drii) 1. sm. ཕྱོགས་སྒྲིག. 2. a compilation/ collection of essays.

ཕྱོགས་བསྒྲིལ་ (cɔ̄gdrii) sm. ཕྱོགས་སྒྲིལ་.

ཕྱོགས་བསྒྲིལ་སྤངས་པའི་ཡུལ་ཁག (cɔ̄gdrii bāŋbɛ yṳ̈ṳgaà) nonaligned/ neutral nations.

ཕྱོགས་བསྒྲིལ་སྤངས་པའི་སྲིད་ཇུས་ (cɔ̄gdrii bāŋbɛ sii̋jüü) policy of nonalignment.

ཕྱོགས་མགྲོན་ (cɔ̄gdrön) guests from a different place/ area.

ཕྱོགས་ཅན་ (cɔgjɛn) a 30 day month, a lunar month.

ཕྱོགས་གཅིག (cɔ̄ɔ̀jig) 1. one side. 2. unilateral, partial.

ཕྱོགས་གཅིག་ཁོ་ན་འཛིན་པ་ (cɔ̄ɔ̀jig kōna dzimbə) one-sidedness, partiality, prejudice.

ཕྱོགས་གཅིག་ཏུ་ (cɔ̄ɔ̀jigdu) to one side, in one direction, together, jointly; va.—སྡུད་ to concentrate, to collect together.

ཕྱོགས་གཅིག་ནས་ (cɔ̄ɔ̀jignɛ) 1. from one side/ direction. 2. on the one hand.

ཕྱོགས་བཅུ་ (cɔ̄gju) all sides/ places/ directions, everywhere ¶ ཕྱོགས་བཅུ་དང་དུས་གསུམ་གྱི་སངས་རྒྱས་ The Buddhas of all times and places. [Lit. the ten directions].

ཕྱོགས་ཆ་ (cɔ̄gja) one side, one part of (sth.), partial.

ཕྱོགས་ཆ་ཅན་ (cɔ̄gjajɛn) partial, biased, prejudiced.

ཕྱོགས་ཆས་ (cɔ̄gjɛ̀ɛ̀) traveling paraphernalia ¶ ཕྱོགས་ཆས་ན་བཟའ་ Traveling clothes.

ཕྱོགས་གཉིས་ (cɔ̄ɔ̀ñii̋) two sides, both sides, bilateral.

ཕྱོགས་གཉིས་ཀ་ (cɔ̄ɔ̀ ñii̋gə) sm. ཕྱོགས་གཉིས་.

ཕྱོགས་གཉིས་ཀྱི་གྲོས་མོལ་ (cɔ̄ɔ̀ñii̋gi trö̤ö̤mö̤ö) bilateral negotiations/ discussions.

ཕྱོགས་གཉིས་ཀྱི་ཆོད་དོན་ (cɔ̄ɔ̀ñii̋gi cö̀ödön) bilateral agreement.

ཕྱོགས་གཉིས་ཀའི་འབྲེལ་བའི་གནད་དོན་ (cɔ̄ɔ̀ñii̋gɛ dreewɛ nɛ̀ɛ̀dön) bilateral relations.

ཕྱོགས་གཉིས་སྨྲ་བ་ (cɔ̄ɔ̀ñii̋ māwa) the doctrine that everything has two aspects (in accordance with the Marxist view that "one divides into two").

ཕྱོགས་གཏོགས་ (cɔ̄gdoò) 1. an adherent, pro- ¶ མའོ་ཕྱོགས་གཏོགས་ ProMao. ¶ ཨུ་རུ་སུ་ཕྱོགས་གཏོགས་ཀྱི་རྒྱལ་ཁབ་ ProRussian nations. 2. members (of an organization or party) ¶ ཁོ་ཚོའི་ཚོགས་པའི་ཕྱོགས་གཏོགས་ཀྱི་མི་ A person who is a member of their party.

ཕྱོགས་གཏོགས་རྒྱལ་ཕྲན་ (cɔ̄gdoò gyɛɛdrɛn) satellite country.

ཕྱོགས་གཏོགས་པ་ (cɔ̄gdogba) sm. ཕྱོགས་གཏོགས་.

ཕྱོགས་རྟོག (cɔ̄gdoò) knowing only one side, lopsided/ one-sided (views, ideas, etc.).

ཕྱོགས་རྟོགས་ (cɔ̄gdoò) sm. ཕྱོགས་རྟོག.

ཕྱོགས་ལྟ་ (cɔ̄gda) abbr. of ཕྱོགས་རིས་ཀྱི་ལྟ་རྩལ་.

ཕྱོགས་ལྟ་འཁོར་ལོ་ (cɔ̄gda kɔ̄ɔ̀lo) sm. ཕྱོགས་བལྟ་འཁོར་ལོ་.

ཕྱོགས་བལྟ་འཁོར་ལོ་ (cɔ̄gda kɔ̄ɔ̀lo) compass.

ཕྱོགས་སྟོན་ (cɔ̄gdön) guiding, directing; va.—བྱེད་ ¶ ཁོང་གི་བཀའ་སློབ་རྣམས་ཕྱོགས་སྟོན་དུ་བཟུང་ནས་ Holding his advice as a guide. 2. a compass.

ཕྱོགས་སྟོན་དར་ཆ་ (cɔ̄gdön tarja) a banner/ flag that shows directions.

ཕྱོགས་སྟོན་མཛད་ཕྱོགས་ (cɔ̄gdön dzɛ̀ɛ̀jɔɔ̀) guiding policy.

ཕྱོགས་སྟོན་འཁོར་ལོ་ (cɔ̄gdön kɔ̄ɔ̀lo) a compass.

ཕྱོགས་སྟོན་དཔྱད་ཆས་ (cɔ̄gdön jɛ̀ɛ̀jeè) a compass.

ཕྱོགས་སྟོན་དབྱུ་གུ (cɔ̄gdön yūgu) 1. baton (used by a conductor). 2. a stick used to direct.

ཕྱོགས་སྟོན་དབྱུག་བད་ (cɔ̄gdön yūgda) conductor's baton.

ཕྱོགས་བསྟུན་ (cɔ̄gdön) in accordance with ¶ ད་ལྟའི་དུས་སྐབས་དང་ཕྱོགས་བསྟུན་ In accordance with the present time.

ཕྱོགས་ཐབས་ (cɔ̄gdəb) means, method.

ཕྱོགས་ཐོན་ (cɔ̄gdön) traveling; va.—བྱེད་ to go on a journey, to travel.

ཕྱོགས་མཐའ་ (cɔ̄gsa) far away places, distant places ¶ ཕྱོགས་མཐའ་ནས་ཡོང་བའི་འགྲུལ་པ་ Travelers from distant places.

ཕྱོགས་མཐའ་ཁ་བཞི་ (cɔ̄gta kāshi) sm. ཕྱོགས་ཀུན་.

ཕྱོགས་མཐའ་ཁག (cɔ̄gtakaà) different directions.

ཕྱོགས་མཐའ་དག (cɔ̄g tāda) all sides/ aspects ¶ ཕྱོགས་མཐའ་དག་དང་གོ་བསྡུར་བྱས་ནས་ཐག་གཅོད་བྱས་པ་རེད་ It was decided after consulting with all sides.

ཕྱོགས་མཐུན་ (cɔ̄gdün) 1. suitable, proper, fitting. 2. similar ¶ ཨ་རི་གཞུང་ནས་ཀྱང་ལན་འདེབས་ཕྱོགས་མཐུན་བྱེད་ The U.S. Government also made a similar reply.

ཕྱོགས་མཐོང་ (cɔ̄gdoŋ) seeing only one side, seeing only one point of view.

ཕྱོགས་འཐེན་ (cɔ̄gden) partiality towards sth., bias; va.—བྱེད་ to be partial, to take sides, to be biased ¶ ཕྱོགས་འཐེན་གྱི་འགྲེལ་བརྗོད་ Biased comments.

ཕྱོགས་དང་ཕྱོགས་མཚམས་ (cɔ̄ɔ̀daŋ cɔ̄gdzam) the four main directions and the eight subdirections.

ཕྱོགས་དུས་ (cɔ̄gdüü) in all times and directions ¶ བསྟན་པ་གསེར་སྦྱང་བཙོ་མ་ཕྱོགས་དུས་ཀུན་ཏུ་དར་རྒྱས་ཡུན་རིང་དུ་གནས་པ་དང་ May Buddhism, which is like pure gold, flourish in all times and directions and last forever.

ཕྱོགས་དུས་ཀུན་ཏུ་ (cɔ̄gdüü gūndu) all times and places, all times and everywhere.

ཕྱོགས་དྲུག (cɔ̄gdruù) the six directions: east, west, north, south, up, and down.

ཕྱོགས་སྡུད་ (cɔ̄gdüü) sm. ཕྱོགས་བསྡུས་.

ཕྱོགས་བསྡུས་ (cɔ̄gdüü) 1. collecting, gathering, uniting, combining; va.—བྱེད་ 2. complex, multipurpose, comprehensive. 3. summary ¶ གྲྭ་པ་བྱེད་སྐབས་ཀྱི་མཉམ་ཉང་ཕྱོགས་བསྡུས་ An summary account of the experience of monks. 4. an account/ book consisting of a variety of things from various sources.

ཕྱོགས་བསྡུས་ཀྱི་ལྟ་ཞིབ་ (cɔ̄gdüügi dəshib) a comprehensive survey/ inspection.

ཕྱོགས་བསྡུས་རྟོག་ཞིབ་ (cɔ̄gdüü dəshib) ཕྱོགས་བསྡུས་ཀྱི་ལྟ་ཞིབ་.

ཕྱོགས་བསྡུས་བདག་སྐྱོང་ (cɔ̄gdüü daàgyoŋ) comprehensive administration.

ཕྱོགས་བསྡུས་མཛོད་ཁང་ (cɔ̄gdüü dzö̤ö̤gaŋ) storehouse.

ཕྱོགས་བསྡུས་བེད་སྤྱོད་ (cɔ̄gdüü dejöö) multipurpose use/ utilization.

ཕྱོགས་བསྡུས་རིག་པ་ (cɔ̄gdüü rigbə) inductive method.

ཕྱོགས་བསྡུས་ཞབས་ཞུའི་ས་ཚིགས་ (cɔ̄gdüü shəbshü sədzii) a multipurpose service center.

ཕྱོགས་བསྡུས་གསར་འགྱུར་ (cɔ̄gdüü səŋgyur) comprehensive news/ news coverage.

ཕྱོགས་བསྡེབས་ (cɔ̄gdeb) a collection (of things).

ཕྱོགས་སྡོམ་ (cɔ̄gdom) summary, synthesis, conclusion; va.—བྱེད་ to sum up, to synthesize, to summarize.

ཕྱོགས་བསྡོམས་ (cɔ̄gdom) sm. ཕྱོགས་སྡོམ་.

ཕྱོགས་འདྲ་བ་ (cɔ̄ɔ̀ drawa) similar, alike.

ཕྱོགས་ན་མི་གནས་པ་ (cɔ̄ɔ̀na minɛɛ̀bə) unbiased, unprejudiced.

ཕྱོགས་ནོར་ (cɔ̄ɔ̀nɔɔ) deviation, error.

ཕྱོགས་སྤྲང་ (cɔ̄ɔ̀baŋ) a beggar who wanders from area to area.

ཕྱོགས་སྤང་ (cɔ̄ɔ̀baŋ) sm. ཕྱོགས་སྤྲང་.

ཕྱོགས་ཕེབས་ (cɔ̄ɔ̀peè) traveling (h.); va.—གནང་; —མཛད་ to travel, to take a trip.

ཕྱོགས་ཕེབས་གཟིགས་ཞིབ་ (cɔ̄ɔ̀peè sii̋shib) traveling for inspection.

ཕྱོགས་ཕྱི་མ་ (cɔ̄ɔ̀ cīmə) 1. rebutting, countering. 2. the period after the 15th of the month.

ཕྱོགས་ཕྱོགས་ (cɔ̄ɔ̀jɔɔ̀) various parts/ areas, different groups/ parties/ associations.

ཕྱོགས་ཕྱོགས་ནས་ (cɔ̄ɔ̀jɔɔ̀nɛ) shung. from each party ¶ བཀའ་ཁྲིམས་ཀྱི་ཆེ་འདེགས་ཕྱོགས་ཕྱོགས་ནས་ཁ་བཏགས་ཆེ་བ་ Each party shall offer a large ceremonial scarf in support of upholding the law.

ཕྱོགས་བྱེད་ (cɔ̄gjeè) sm. ཕྱོགས་ལང་.

ཕྱོགས་བྲལ་དྲང་ཐིག (cɔ̄gdrɛɛ traŋdii) honest, straight, just, unbiased ¶ ཕྱོགས་བྲལ་དྲང་ཐིག་གི་ཞལ་ལྟ་འདི་

བཅད་ཧྲིས་ After issuing this unbiased and just verdict.

ཕྱོགས་འབྲང་ (cōg dra̱ŋ) va. to follow one side/ group/ party.

ཕྱོགས་མང་གྲོས་མོལ་ (cɔ̄ɔ̀maŋ trö̱ömöö) multilateral negotiation/ discussion.

ཕྱོགས་མང་གྲོས་ཆོད་ (cɔ̄ɔ̀maŋ trö̱öjöö) multilateral treaty/ agreement.

ཕྱོགས་མི་ (cɔ̄ɔ̀mi) 1. an adherent of a side/ group/ clique/ party. 2. nonresident, outsider, migrant.

ཕྱོགས་མི་འདྲ་བ་ (cɔ̄ɔ̀ mi̱ndrawa) different sides/ perspectives/ aspects ། ཕྱོགས་མི་འདྲ་བའི་ཐོག་ནས་བོད་ཀྱི་ཞིང་ལས་སྐོར་བྲིས་ (He) wrote concerning different aspects of Tibetan agriculture.

ཕྱོགས་མིའི་འབོར་གྲངས་ (cɔ̄ɔ̀mi bo̱rdraŋ) size of floating population.

ཕྱོགས་མེད་ (cɔ̄ɔ̀meè) impartial, unbiased.

ཕྱོགས་མེད་རྒྱལ་ཁམས་ (cɔ̄ɔ̀meè gyɛ̱ɛ̀gam) everywhere.

ཕྱོགས་ཙམ་ (cōgdzam) rough, approximate ། གནས་ཚུལ་དེའི་སྐོར་ཕྱོགས་ཙམ་ལས་ཤེས་ཀྱི་མི་འདུག He has only a rough idea about the matter.

ཕྱོགས་གཙང་ (cōgdzaŋ) 1. astrological calculation which determines which direction the bride and groom or a new government appointee should face when seated at a ceremony. 2. astrological calculation which determines which direction a deceased body should be taken.

ཕྱོགས་ཚང་མ་ (cɔ̄ɔ̀ tsāŋma) 1. all directions. 2. all aspects/ parts.

ཕྱོགས་ཚད་ (cɔ̄ɔ̀dzɛɛ̀) vector (in physics).

ཕྱོགས་ཚོགས་ (cōgdzɔɔ̀) group, clique, party, bloc.

ཕྱོགས་མཚམས་ (cōgdzam) border, boundary, corner, end.

ཕྱོགས་མཚུངས་ (cōgdzuŋ) 1. likewise, similarly, accordingly ། ཕྱོགས་མཚུངས་ལུང་པ་གཞན་ལ་ཡར་རྒྱས་ཕྱིན་ཡོད་པ་རེད་ Similarly, other areas have progressed. 2. at the same time, concurrently (usu. དེ་དང་ + —) ། དེ་དང་ཕྱོགས་མཚུངས་རྒྱལ་ཁབ་མང་པོར་གསར་བརྗེའི་ལས་འགུལ་དར་ཡོད་པ་རེད་ At the same time revolutionary movements have spread to other countries.

ཕྱོགས་འཛིན་ (cōgdzin) sm. ཕྱོགས་འཐེན་.

ཕྱོགས་འཛོལ་ (cɔ̄ɔ̀ dzö̱ö̱) vi. to be going in the wrong direction.

ཕྱོགས་ཞྭ་ (cɔ̄ɔ̀sha) traveling hat.

ཕྱོགས་ཞེན་ (cōgshen) sm. ཕྱོགས་འཐེན་.

ཕྱོགས་ཞེན་ངོ་སྲུང་ (cōgshen ŋ̱osuŋ) biased, partial.

ཕྱོགས་ཞེན་མེད་པ་ (cōgshen me̱èba) unbiased, impartial.

ཕྱོགས་གཞན་ཞིག (cɔ̄ɔ̀ shēnjig) on the other hand.

ཕྱོགས་བཞི་ (cɔ̄ɔ̀shi) the four directions, all directions, everywhere.

ཕྱོགས་བཞི་འཁོར་ལོ་ (cɔ̄ɔ̀shi kɔ̄ɔ̀lo) compass.

ཕྱོགས་བཞི་མཚམས་བརྒྱད་ (cɔ̄ɔ̀shi tsāmgyüǜ) from all directions, from all over ། ལས་བྱེད་པ་དེ་ཚོ་ཕྱོགས་བཞི་མཚམས་བརྒྱད་ནས་ཡོང་བ་རེད་ Those officials came from all over. [Lit. the four directions; east, west, north, south and the eight intermediate directions, e.g., southeast, ...].

ཕྱོགས་བཟུང་ (cōgsuŋ) sm. ཕྱོགས་འཐེན་.

ཕྱོགས་ཡོངས་ (cɔ̄ɔ̀yoŋ) all around, everywhere, general ། ཕྱོགས་ཡོངས་ཀྱི་རྒྱལ་ཁ་ An all-round victory.

ཕྱོགས་ཡོངས་ཀྱི་བདམས་བསྐོ་ (cɔ̄ɔ̀yoŋgi de̱mgo) general election.

ཕྱོགས་རིས་ (cɔ̄ɔ̀riì) 1. sm. ཕྱོགས་འཐེན་. 2. faction, clique.

ཕྱོགས་རིས་ཀྱི་ལྟ་ཚུལ་ (cɔ̄ɔ̀riìgi dədzüü) a prejudiced/ biased view.

ཕྱོགས་རི་ཀི་རང་བཞིན་ (cɔ̄ɔ̀riìgi ra̱ŋshin) one sidedness.

ཕྱོགས་རིས་ཀྱིས་འདུ་ཤེས་ (cɔ̄ɔ̀riìgi du̱sheè) a biased/ partial view or tendency.

ཕྱོགས་རིས་བྱེད་ (cɔ̄ɔ̀riì ce̱è) va. to be partial/ biased.

ཕྱོགས་རིས་བྲལ་བ་ (cɔ̄ɔ̀riì drɛ̱ɛ̱wa) impartial, just.

ཕྱོགས་རིས་མེད་པ་ (cɔ̄ɔ̀riì me̱èba) sm. ཕྱོགས་རིས་བྲལ་བ་.

ཕྱོགས་རིས་རིང་ལུགས་ (cɔ̄ɔ̀riì me̱èba) sectarianism.

ཕྱོགས་རེ་བ་ (cɔ̄ɔ̀ re̱wa) bias, partiality. ། ཕྱོགས་རེ་བའི་བསམ་ཚུལ་ Biased thoughts.

ཕྱོགས་རེ་བའི་རང་བཞིན་ (cɔ̄ɔ̀ re̱wɛ ra̱ŋshin) factionalism, one-sidedness.

ཕྱོགས་རེ་ཙམ་གྱི་སྒོ་ནས་ (cɔ̄ɔ̀ re̱dzamgi go̱nɛ) unilaterally.

ཕྱོགས་རེ་ཙམ་གྱི་རང་བཞིན་ (cɔ̄ɔ̀ re̱dzamgi ra̱ŋshin) factionalism.

ཕྱོགས་རེས་ (cōgreè) one-sided, unilateral, partial, biased.

ཕྱོགས་ལ་འགྲོ་ (cɔ̄ɔ̀la dro̱) va. to go on a trip/ journey.

ཕྱོགས་ལ་འཐོན་ (cɔ̄ɔ̀la tön) sm. ཕྱོགས་ལ་འགྲོ་.

ཕྱོགས་ལང་ (cɔ̄ɔ̀ la̱ŋ) 1. vi. to divide up into sides, to become factionalized. 2. va. to side with sb., to take sb.'s side.

ཕྱོགས་སུ་ (cōgsu) toward, in the direction of a ཧུས་སྐྱོང་སྟངས་ American policy towards China. ། འབྲུ་རིགས་འཁྱེར་ནས་ཁག་བགོས་ནས་ཕྱོགས་སུ་ཐོན་ (They) divided into groups and left in (different) directions carrying grain.

ཕྱོགས་སུ་ལང་ (cōgsu la̱ŋ) sm. ཕྱོགས་ལང་.

ཕྱོགས་སོ་སོ་ (cɔ̄ɔ̀ sōso) each direction/ faction/ group/ part.

ཕྱོགས་སྡུ་ (cɔ̄ɔ̀ du̱) va. to collect/ combine from many sources.

ཕྱོགས་སློན་ (cɔ̄ɔ̀ lön) va. to gather/ collect.

ཕྱོགས་བསླད་ (cɔ̄ɔ̀ lɛ̄ɛ̀) va. to take the wrong path/ road.

ཕྱོགས་ལྷུང་ (cɔ̄ɔ̀ lūŋ) sm. ཕྱོགས་འཐེན་.

ཕྱོད་ (cȫö̀) output (of work) ། འཕྲུལ་འཁོར་ལེགས་བཅོས་བྱས་ནས་ལས་ཕྱོད་ཞི་དྲགས་ཆེ་རུ་ཕྱིན་པ་རེད་ After they innovated with the machine, the work output greatly increased.

ཕྱོར་ (cɔ̄r) imp. of འཕྱུར་.

ཕྱྭ་ (cā) 1. omen. 2. fortune, luck.

ཕྱྭ་གེན་ཙེ་ (cā gēndze) a diviner of the bon faith.

ཕྱྭ་མཁན་ (cāñen) sm. ཕྱྭ་འདེབས་པོ་.

ཕྱྭ་འགུགས་ (cā gu̱ù) va. to bring forth good luck/ fortune.

ཕྱྭ་འདེབས་པོ་ (cā de̱bbo) diviner, fortune-teller.

ཕྱྭ་པ་ (cāba) sm. ཕྱྭ་འདེབས་པོ་.

ཕྱྭ་བ་ (cāwa) sm. ཕྱྭ་འདེབས་པོ་.

ཕྱྭ་གཡང་ (cāyaŋ) fortune, luck.

ཕྲ་ (trā) 1. jewel, stone; va.—རྒྱག to inlay with jewels / stones ། ཕྲ་མང་པོ་ཡོད་པའི་ཚིགས་ཁེབས་ A ring with many stones. 2. abbr. of ཕྲ་པ་. 3. hawk, falcon.

ཕྲ་ཁུང་ (trāguŋ) a depression (on a piece of jewelry) where gems are stuck.

ཕྲ་རྒྱན་ (trāgyɛn) ornament of jewels/ stones; va.—རྒྱག.

ཕྲ་རྒྱས་བཟང་པོ་ (trāgyɛɛ̀ sa̱ŋbo) attractive, good looking.

ཕྲ་གཅོད་ (trā jȫö̀) va. to cut stones/ jewels.

ཕྲ་མཐོང་ཆེ་ཤོས་ (trātoŋ cēshö̀ö̀) microscope.

ཕྲ་མཐོང་ཆེ་ཤེལ་ (trātoŋ cēshel) sm. ཕྲ་མཐོང་ཆེ་ཤོས་.

ཕྲ་དོག (trādɔɔ̀) envy, jealousy; va.—བྱེད་ to envy, to be jealous of.

ཕྲ་ལྡེམ་ལྡེམ་ (trā de̱mdem) slender, gracefully.

ཕྲ་པོ་ (trābo) thin.

ཕྲ་པོ་རིང་པོ་ (trābo ri̱ŋbu) thin and long.

ཕྲ་ཕུང་ (trəbuŋ) cells.

ཕྲ་ཕུང་གི་ལྤགས་ (trəbuŋgi bāà) cell membrane.

ཕྲ་ཕུང་རྐྱང་མ་ (trəbuŋ gyāŋma) unicellular.

ཕྲ་ཕུང་གི་སྙིང་པོ་ (trəbuŋgi ñīŋbu) sm. ཕྲ་ཕུང་གི་ལྟེ་བ་.

ཕྲ་ཕུང་གི་ལྟེ་བ་ (trəbuŋgi dēwa) cell nucleus.

ཕྲ་ཕུང་གི་མདོག་རྒྱུ་ (trəbuŋgi dɔ̱ggyu) sm. ཕྲ་ཕུང་མདོག་རྫི་.

ཕྲ་ཕུང་གི་ཕྱི་ཤུན་ཕྲ་ཕུང་ (trəbuŋgi cīshün trəbuŋ) cell wall.

ཕྲ་ཕུང་གྲུབ་ཚུལ་ (trābuŋ trubdzüü) cell formation.

ཕྲ་ཕུང་ཆགས་ཚུལ་ (trābuŋ cāgdzüü) sm. ཕྲ་ཕུང་གྲུབ་ཚུལ་.

ཕྲ་ཕུང་མདོག་རྫི་ (trābuŋ dɔgdzi) cytochrome.

ཕྲ་ཕུང་གི་སྙིན་གཟུགས་ (trābuŋgi jīnsuù) cytoplasm.

ཕྲ་ཕུང་རིག་པ་ (trābuŋ rigbə) cytology.

ཕྲ་བ་ (trāwa) 1. sm. ཕྲ་མོ་. 2. young ། དགུང་ལོ་ཕྲ་བ་ A young age.

ཕྲ་སྦོམ་ (trābom) thickness [Lit. thickness and thinness].

ཕྲ་མ་ (trāma) 1. calumny, slander, malicious rumors; va.—འཛུག་; —བྱེད་ to calumniate, to spread malicious rumors. 2. edicts ། བཀའ་ཤག་གི་ཕྲ་མའི་འོག་ཏུ་ Under the edict of the council. 3. window ། ཁང་པའི་ཕྲ་མ་ A window of a house.

ཕྲ་མ་དབྱེན་སྦྱོར་ (trāma yēnjɔɔ) prompting/ inducing/ instigating trouble.

ཕྲ་མ་འཛོག་སྦྱོར་ (trāma dzɔgjɔɔ) instigating; va.—བྱེད་ ། ཕ་བུ་གཉན་གཞོན་དབར་ཕྲ་མ་འཛོག་སྦྱོར་དུ་འགྲོ་རིགས་བགྱིས་ན་མི་འཐུས་ No one is allowed to instigate between a father and son.

ཕྲ་མེན་ (trāmen) a supernatural spirit.

ཕྲ་མེན་མ་ (trā menma) a female ཕྲ་མེན་.

ཕྲ་མོ་ (trāmo) 1. small, minor ། རྒྱུ་རྐྱེན་ཕྲ་མོ་ Minor reason. 2. thin, fine, narrow ། རི་ལམ་ཕྲ་མོ་ Narrow mountain trail. 3. minute, detailed, complex.

ཕྲ་ཚུགས་ (trā tsūù) vi. to get firmly established, to be settled ། སྲིད་གཞུང་གསར་པ་དེ་ཕྲ་ཚུགས་ཐབས་ལ་ In order for the new government to be firmly established.

ཕྲ་ཚོང་ (trādzoŋ) selling of jewels/ gems; va.—རྒྱག.

ཕྲ་ཚོང་རྒྱག་མཁན་ (trādzoŋ gyaàñɛn) jeweler, person who sells gems.

ཕྲ་ཚོམ་ (trādzom) sm. ཕྲ་, 1.

ཕྲ་རྫུས་ (trādzüù) fake stone/ jewelry.

ཕྲ་ཞིང་ལྡེམ་པ་ (trāshiŋ demba) slender body (of a female).

ཕྲ་ཞིང་ཕྲ་བ་ (trəshiŋ trāwa) precise, detailed.

ཕྲ་ཞིབ་ (trəshib) detailed, minute.

ཕྲ་ཞིབ་འཐུས་འདོམས་ (trəshib tũndom) shung. detailed, containing all the useful points.

ཕྲ་ཞིབ་སྤུས་ལྡན་ (trəshib bũùdɛn) precision.

ཕྲ་གཟབ་ཆུང་ཟོན་ (trāsəb jūŋsön) cautious and meticulous.

ཕྲ་བཟུང་ (trāsuŋ) reluctant; va.—བྱེད་ ། ད་བར་གྱི་ཁྲལ་པ་འདྲ་མཚུངས་ལམ་བྱུང་ཇེ་ཡོད་ལ་ཕྲ་བཟུང་བྱེད་པ་ Being reluctant in performing the everyday corvee labors.

ཕྲ་བཟོ་བ་ (trā sowa) goldsmith.

ཕྲ་རགས་ (trāraà) detailed and cursory ། གསར་འགྱུར་དེ་གཉིས་དབར་ཕྲ་རགས་ཀྱི་ཁྱད་པར་འདུག These two news reports differ in terms of their detail and cursoriness.

ཕྲ་རབ་ (trārəb) extremely small, subatomic.

ཕྲ་རིང་ (trāriŋ) long and slender.

ཕྲ་ལ་ཕྲན་བུ་ (trāla trɛ̄mbu) a little bit.

ཕྲ་ལོས་ (trālöò) thinness.

ཕྲ་སིལ་སིལ་ (trā sīīsii) extremely fine/ minute/ detailed.

ཕྲག (trāà) 1. in between ། དེབ་ཀྱི་ཤོག་ལྷེའི་ཕྲག་ན་ In between the pages of the book. 2. shoulder ། སྤྲེའུ་དེ་ཁོའི་ཕྲག་ཏུ་སྡོད་བཅུག་པ་རེད་ (He) made the monkey sit on his shoulder. 3. term used to pluralize multiples of ten.

ཕྲག་ཁེབས་ (trāàgeb) shoulder padding (when carrying loads, etc.).

ཕྲག་འཁུར་ (trāgur) carrying on the shoulder; va.—བྱེད་ to carry on the shoulder.

ཕྲག་གོང་ (trāàgoŋ) sm. ཕྲག་པ་.

ཕྲག་གོང་དབྱུག་པ་ (traàgoŋ yūgbə) shoulder pole used for carrying loads.

ཕྲག་འགེལ་ (trāà gee) va. to carry (a load) on the shoulder.

ཕྲག་རྒྱུག (trəggyuù) pole used to carry loads on the shoulder; va.—ཁུར་ to carry by a shoulder pole.

ཕྲག་སྒོ་ (trāgo) shoulder.

ཕྲག་ཏུ་ལེན་ (trāgdu len) va. to shoulder (burden, responsibilities, etc.) ། ལས་འགན་ལྗིད་པོ་དེ་ཕྲག་ཏུ་བླངས་པ་རེད་ (They) shouldered the heavy responsibility.

ཕྲག་རྟགས་ (trāgdaà) epaulet.

ཕྲག་བརྟེགས་སྒྲོགས་མདའ་ (trāgdeg gyɔnda) bazooka.

ཕྲག་ཐོག (trāàtɔɔ̀) on the shoulder.

ཕྲག་དོག (trāàdɔɔ̀) jealousy, envy; va.—བྱེད་ to act jealously/ enviously; vi.—སྐྱེད་ to be jealous/ envious.

ཕྲག་དོག་འཁོན་འཛིན་ (trāàdɔɔ̀ kõndzin) being envious and angry.

ཕྲག་དོག་མཁྲིགས་བཟུང་ (trāàdɔɔ̀ trēgsuŋ) being envious of others.

ཕྲག་དོག་གི་ཁྱི་ཀན་རྒྱ་པོ་ (trāàdɔɔ̀gi kyīgɛn gyawo) derogatory term used for envious people.

ཕྲག་དོག་ཆ་པོ་ (trāàdɔɔ̀ tsābo) a very jealous/ envious person.

ཕྲག་རྡང་ (trāgdaŋ) sm. ཕྲག་གདང་.

ཕྲག་གདང་ (trāgdaŋ) sm. ཕྲག་རྒྱུག.

ཕྲག་གདན་ (trāgdɛn) shoulder pad.

ཕྲག་པ་ (trāgba) shoulder.

ཕྲག་པ་བཅུམ་ (trāgba jūm) va. to hunch one's shoulder forward towards the chest.

ཕྲག་པ་དབྱུག་པ་ (trāgba yūgbə) sm. ཕྲག་གོང་དབྱུག་པ་.

ཕྲག་པར་འཁུར་ (trāgbar kūr) sm. ཕྲག་འཁུར་.

ཕྲག་འབུར་བ་གླང་ (trāgbur palaŋ) cows and bulls that have a hump on their shoulder.

ཕྲག་མིག (trəgmii) a hole on the shoulder bone.

ཕྲག་ཚིགས་ (trəgdzii) shoulder joint.

ཕྲག་ཡོན་ (trāgyön) person with a lopsided/ crooked shoulder.

ཕྲག་ཤིང་ (trāgshiŋ) sm. ཕྲག་རྒྱུག.

ཕྲད་ (trɛ̄ɛ̀) 1. p. of འཕྲད་. 2. grammatical particles.

ཕྲད་ཀྱི་ཡི་གེ་ (trɛ̄ɛ̀gi yigi) sm. ཕྲད་, 2.

ཕྲད་གདང་ (trāgdaŋ) a banner tied on top of two long poles and carried by two people.

ཕྲད་ཕྲད་ (trɛ̄ɛ̀drɛɛ̀) meeting; va.—བྱེད་.

ཕྲན་ (trɛ̄n) 1. small, little, few ། འདིའི་སྐོར་ཕྲན་ཙམ་ཤེས་ཕྲན་ (I) know a little about this. 2. I ། ཕྲན་ཚོ་ We.

ཕྲག་ཆུང་ (trāgjuŋ) meek, humble, quiet, unassuming way of referring to oneself.

ཕྲན་གཉིས་ (trɛnñii) we two.

ཕྲན་བདག (trɛndaà) sm. ཕྲན་ཆུང་.

ཕྲན་བུ་ (trɛmbu) small, little, few ། མོས་བོད་སྐད་ཕྲན་བུ་ཤེས་པ་རེད་ She knows a little Tibetan.

ཕྲན་བུ་ཙམ་ (trɛ̄mbudzam) sm. ཕྲན་ཙམ་.

ཕྲན་བུའི་ནད་ (trɛmbü nɛɛ̀) minor illness/ sickness.

ཕྲན་ཙམ་ (trɛ̄ndzam) 1. a little ། དཀའ་ལས་ཕྲན་ཙམ་བརྒྱབ་དགོས་ན་ཡང་ Even if (they) have to struggle a little. 2. like me, like myself (humble reference to oneself) ། དེ་ལྟར་ཕྲན་ཙམ་གྱིས་ཡང་བྱེད་ཐུབ་ཀྱི་རེད་ Even a person like me can do that.

ཕྲན་ཙམ་ཞིག་ནས་ (trɛ̄ndzam shignɛ) after a little while, after a short while.

ཕྲན་ཙག (trɛ̄ndzà) details.

ཕྲན་ཚེགས་ (trɛ̄ndzeg) small, minute, insignificant, petty ། བྱ་བ་ཕྲན་ཚེགས་ A small matter.

ཕྲན་ཚེགས་ཀྱི་ཡོ་བྱད་ (tɛ̄ndzeggi yojɛɛ̀) those minor things that are used every day such as shoes, belts, cooking utensils bowls.

ཕྲན་ཚེགས་རིང་ལུགས་ (tɛ̄ndzeg riŋluù) routinism.

ཕྲན་ཚོ་ (trɛ̄ndzo) we.

ཕྲན་ཟུང་ (trɛ̄nsuŋ) we two.

ཕྲན་རང་ (trɛ̄nraŋ) I, myself.

ཕྲའུ་ (trəwu) very little/ few.

ཕྲལ་ (trɛ̄ɛ) 1. va. to part/ separate; to take apart. 2. p. of འཕྲལ་.

ཕྲལ་གྱིས་སྐྱེ་འཕེལ་འབུ་ཕྲ་ (trɛ̄ɛ̄gi gēmbel budrə) schizomycete.

ཕྲལ་དུ་ (trɛ̄ɛ̄du) sm. འཕྲལ་དུ་.

ཕྲལ་གསེད་ (trɛ̄ɛ̄seè) decomposing, breaking down.

ཕྲི་ (trī) f. of འཕྲི་.
ཕྲི་ལི་ལི་ (trīlili) term used to convey flowing water.
ཕྲིག་ཕྲིག (trīgdrig) chattering ། སོ་སྟེང་འོག་ཕྲིག་ཕྲིག་དུ་རེད་པ་ Upper and lower teeth were chattering.
ཕྲིགས་ (trīg) all, completely, thoroughly.
ཕྲིན་ (tīn) sm. འཕྲིན་.
ཕྲིན་འཁྱེར་པོ་ (trīn kyērbo) letter carrier, person who takes messages.
ཕྲིན་བཅོལ་ (trīn jöö) 1. va. to ask/ request sb. to do sth. 2. va. to ask protective deities for a favor.
ཕྲིན་པ་ (trīmbə) sm. ཕྲིན་འཁྱེར་པོ་.
ཕྲིན་ཡིག (trīnyii) sm. འཕྲིན་ཡིག.
ཕྲིན་ལས་ (trīnlɛɛ̀) sm. འཕྲིན་ལས་.
ཕྲིས་ (trīi) p. of འཕྲི་.
ཕྲིས་ལྷག (trīilhaà) leftover, remainder.
ཕྲུ་གུ (trūgu) child; va.—སྐྱེ་ to give birth.
ཕྲུ་གུ་སྐྱེ་ཡས་ཀྱི་འཆར་གཞི་ (trūgu gyēyɛɛ̀gi cārshi) family planning.
ཕྲུ་གུ་སྐྱེ་གསོག (trūgu gyēyɔɔ̀) midwifery.
ཕྲུ་གུ་སྐྱེ་གསོག་མ་ (trūgu gyēyɔɔ̀ma) midwife.
ཕྲུ་གུ་སྐྱེ་སའི་ཚན་ཁག (trūgu gyēsɛ tsēngaà) obstetrics (section, department).
ཕྲུ་གུ་སྐྱེ་བསུའི་སྨན་བཅོད་སྡེ་ཚན་ (trūgu gyēsü mēnjöö dedzɛn tsēngaà) maternity (section, department, division).
ཕྲུ་གུ་སྐྱེས་འབོར་ (trūgu gyēmbɔɔ) birthrate.
ཕྲུ་གུ་འཁོར་ (trugu kɔ̄ɔ̄) vi. to become/ get pregnant.
ཕྲུ་གུ་སྐྱིལ་གཟན་ (trūgu driisɛn) swaddling clothes.
ཕྲུ་གུ་མངལ་ཤོར་ (trūgu ŋɛ̄ɛ̄shɔɔ) sm. ཕྲུ་གུ་ཤོར་.
ཕྲུ་གུ་ཆགས་ (trūgu cāà) sm. ཕྲུ་གུ་འཁོར་.
ཕྲུ་གུ་ཉར་སྐྱོང་ཁང་ (trūgu ñaagyoŋgaŋ) nursery school.
ཕྲུ་གུ་ཉིན་བཅོལ་ (trūgu ñinjöö) day care center (for children).
ཕྲུ་གུ་བདེ་སྲུང་ཁང་ (trūgu desuŋgaŋ) sm. ཕྲུ་གུ་ཉར་སྐྱོང་ཁང་.
ཕྲུ་གུ་མ་འབྱར་ (trūgu manjar) infant, baby.
ཕྲུ་གུ་མ་ཆགས་པ་བྱེད་ (trūgu macagba cee) va. to use contraceptives, to practice birth control.
ཕྲུ་གུ་དམར་འབྱར (trūgu mānjar) infant, baby.
ཕྲུ་གུ་བཙའ་ཐབས་ (trūgu dzādəb) method/ way of delivering babies.
ཕྲུ་གུ་ཟླ་མག་ཙང་བ་ (trūgu dagu tsāŋwa) a month old baby.
ཕྲུ་གུ་ཤོར་ (trūgu shɔ̄ɔ̄) vi. to have a miscarriage.
ཕྲུ་གུ་ཤོལ་རུ་འཛུག (trūgu shɔ̄ɔ̄ru juù) va. to have an abortion.
ཕྲུ་གུ་སྲུང་སྐྱོབ་ཀྱི་ཐེབས་རྩ་ (trūgu sūŋgyobgi tēbdza) Children's Defense Fund.
ཕྲུ་གུ་སློང་རེས་ (trūgu lōŋreè) a game played by young children.
ཕྲུ་གུ་སློད་ (trūgu lȫȫ) va. to spoil a child.
ཕྲུ་གུ་གསོ་སྐྱོང་ཁང་ (tugu sōgyoŋgaŋ) sm. ཕྲུ་གུ་ཉར་སྐྱོང་ཁང་.
ཕྲུ་གུའི་ངུ་འབོད་ཨ་མ་ (trūgü ŋubȫȫ āma) the person on whom one depends/ relies [Lit. the mother to whom children cry].
ཕྲུ་གུའི་དུས་ (trūgü tüü) childhood.
ཕྲུ་གུའི་རྩེད་མོ་ (trūgü tzēèmo) children's games.
ཕྲུ་གུའི་བསམ་བློ་ (trūgü sāmlo) childish/ infantile ideas.
ཕྲུ་དིར་ (trūdir) ch. drawer.
ཕྲུ་དྲེག (trūdreg) soot on pots.
ཕྲུ་མདའ་ (trūnda) scrubber for cleaning utensils and pots (usu. made from plants).
ཕྲུ་འདེབས་ (trū deb) va. to spray/ sprinkle water from the mouth.
ཕྲུ་དོག་བཙུགས་ (trūdog dzūù) va. to put pots and pans on the stove.
ཕྲུ་སྣོད་ (trūnöö) clay pot.
ཕྲུ་དཔོན་ (trūbön) 1. general/ commander of an army. 2. a person in charge of livestock.
ཕྲུ་བ་ (trūwə) sm. ཕྲུ་སྣོད་.
ཕྲུ་བར་ཉེ་ན་ནག་གླ་ (trūwar ñena nagla) associating with (bad people) will rub off [Lit. if one touches a (black sooty) pot one will get dirty].
ཕྲུ་མ་ (trūmə) 1. womb. 2. placenta.
ཕྲུ་ཟངས་ (trūsaŋ) 1. a clay pot. 2. a brass pot.
ཕྲུ་ལོག (trū lɔɔ̀) va. to have a decision overturned.
ཕྲུ་སློག (trūlɔɔ̀) 1. turning/ plowing over the soil; va. ཕྲུ་སློག་;—བྱེད་ to plow/ turn over the soil. 2. subversive activities; va.—བྱེད་ to do subversive activities. 3. va. to overturn a decision.
ཕྲུ་སློག་འཕྲུལ་འཁོར་ (trūlɔɔ trūūgɔɔ) tractor, bulldozer.
ཕྲུག (trūù) 1. sm. ཕྲུ་གུ. 2. a kind of woven woolen cloth.
ཕྲུག་ཁྲ་ (trūgdra) woolen cloth with variegated colors.
ཕྲུག་གུ་ (trūggu) sm. ཕྲུ་གུ.
ཕྲུག་སྟན་ (trūgdɛn) wool mat.
ཕྲུག་ཐུལ་ (trūgdüü) wool cloak/ sleeveless gown worn in the house to keep warm.
ཕྲུག་ཕྲུག (trūgdruù) shaking, va.—གཏོང་.
ཕྲུག་ཚི་ (trūùdzi) silk.
ཕྲུག་ལོན་ (trūglön) an infant, a baby just born.
ཕྲུག་ཤད་ (trūshɛɛ̀) a bamboo brush for wool material to make it fluffy.
ཕྲུག་ལྷག (trūglhaà) cigarette butt.
ཕྲུགས་ (trūù) 1. imp. of འཕྲུག. 2. series, categories.
ཕྲུགས་སྡེབས་ (trūgdeb) series, categories.
ཕྲུགས་སྒྲུད་ (trūgjɛɛ̀) a scratcher (a gadget used for scratching).
ཕྲུམ་ (trūm) 1. a paste made with cheese and milk. 2. cartilage.
ཕྲུམ་ཕྲུམ་ (trūmdrum) 1. cartilage bone. 2. brimming with tears.
ཕྲུམ་ཚོད་ (trūmdzüü) yogurt container.
ཕྲུམ་རུས་ (trūmrüü) sm. ཕྲུམ་ཕྲུམ་.
ཕྲུལ་ (trūū) vi. to be hanging/ dangling.
ཕྲུལ་ཕྲུལ་ (trūūdrüü) 1. hanging, dangling. 2. ornament, jewelry.
ཕྲུལ་ཕྲུལ་འདོགས་ (trūūdrüü dɔ̀ɔ̀) va. to wear ornaments/ jewelry.
ཕྲེ་ཁ་རྒྱག (trēga gyaà) va. to level a ཕྲེ་ measuring box (so it is just full to the top but not piled high sp that it is more than the measure).
ཕྲེང་ (trēŋ) 1. series, line, row, string (of things); va.—སྒྲིག་; —འགོད་ to arrange in rows/ lines/ series. 2. a place on a road/ route. 3. a line on a page. 4. see སེམས་ཕྲེང་.
ཕྲེང་རྒྱུད་ (trēŋgyüü) rosary string.
ཕྲེང་རྒྱུད་ལྟར་ (trēŋgyüüdar) repeatedly, one after another. [Lit. like a rosary string].
ཕྲེང་རྒྱུད་ལྟ་བུ་ (trēŋgyüü dəbu) sm. ཕྲེང་རྒྱུད་ལྟར་.
ཕྲེང་སྒྲིག (trēŋdrig) see ཕྲེང་.
ཕྲེང་ལྕག་གཞུ་ (trēŋjaà shu) va. to hit sb. with a rosary.
ཕྲེང་བསྒར་ (trēŋ dār) va. to arrange in a line/ series.
ཕྲེང་ཐག (trēŋdaà) sm. ཕྲེང་རྒྱུད་.
ཕྲེང་ཐོགས་ (trēŋdɔɔ̀) a person carrying a rosary.
ཕྲེང་མདའ་ (trēŋda) machine gun.
ཕྲེང་དོག (trēŋdɔɔ̀) a bead used on rosaries to keep count of prayers.
ཕྲེང་བ་ (trēŋwa) rosary, string of beads/ jewels/ flowers; va.—རྒྱུ་ to string beads/ jewels/ etc.
ཕྲེང་བ་དོག་ཕུད་ (trēŋwa dɔgbüü) 1. subjecting to brutal questioning; va.—བྱེད་ ། བྱེད་གདེ་ཕྲེང་བ་དོག་ཕུད་མ་དགོས་པ་ཆོས་བྱེད་དགེ་འདུན་ལ་བསམ་ཡངས་པ་བྱས་ཤིང་ We shall not subject the ringleaders to brutal questioning one by one, and considering that they are monks, they shall be exempt from punishment. 2. relating (events) one by one.
ཕྲེང་བའི་གྲངས་འཛིན་ (trēŋwɛ traŋdzin) marker beads (usu. made of silver or brass) attached to the rosary to enable keeping track of the number of prayers.
ཕྲེང་མོ་རྒྱག (trēŋmo gyaà) va. to divine by counting beads on a rosary.
ཕྲེང་རྩིས་ (trēŋdzii) using beads/ rosary to do

calculations.

ཕྲེང་བ་རྡོག་འབུད་ (trēŋwa dɔŋbüü) singling someone out; va.—བྱེད་ [Lit. to move one bead on a rosary].

ཕྲེད་ (trēè) sm. འཕྲེད་.

ཕྲེད་གླིང་ (trēèliŋ) sm. འཕྲེད་གླིང་.

ཕྲེད་རྒྱུགས་ (trēègyuù) a pole carried on a shoulder and used to transport goods tied to each end.

ཕྲེད་གཅོད་ (trēèjöö) sm. འཕྲེད་གཅོད་.

ཕྲེད་བཅད་ (trēèjɛɛ̀) sm. འཕྲེད་བཅད་.

ཕྲེད་གདན་ (trēèdɛn) sm. འཕྲེད་གདན་.

ཕྲེད་སྟར་སྒྲིག (trēèdar drig) va. to line up sideways/ horizontally.

ཕྲེད་ཐིག (trēèdig) sm. འཕྲེད་ཐིག.

ཕྲེད་དུ་ (trēèdu) sm. འཕྲེད་དུ་.

ཕྲེད་གཞུང་ (trēèshuŋ) sm. འཕྲེད་གཞུང་.

ཕྲེད་ལ་ (trēèla) sm. འཕྲེད་ལ་.

ཕྲེད་ལམ་ (trēèlam) sm. འཕྲེད་ལམ་.

ཕྲེའུ་ (trēwu) belt.

ཕྲོགས་ (trɔ̄ɔ̀) va. to block ¶ ལམ་ཕྲོགས་ To block a road.

ཕྲོ་ཆེན་ (trōjen) drawing lots; va.—བྱེད་; va.—ཞུ་.

ཕྲོམ་ (trōm) Byzantium.

ཕྲོམ་ཕྲོམ་ (trōmdrom) shining, flickering, twinkling (of light).

ཕྲོམ་མེ་བ་ (trōmmewa) shining/ twinkling/ flickering brightly.

ཕྲོལ་ (trōō) imp. of འཕྲོལ་.

འཕག (pāg) sm. འཕགས་.

འཕག་འཕག (pāŋba) small jerky motions, bobbing; va.—བྱེད་.

འཕག་འཕག་སིག་སིག (pāgbag sīisiì) sm. འཕག་ཙག.

འཕག་མཆོང་ (pāgjoŋ) jumping around, jumping for joy; va.—བྱེད་ ¶ ཁོང་སྐྱིད་པོ་བྱུང་ཏེ་འཕག་མཆོང་བྱེད་ཀྱི་འདུག He is so happy that he is jumping around.

འཕག་མཆོང་ལུས་རྩལ་ (pāgjoŋ lṳ̈üdzɛɛ) jumping exercises; va.—བྱེད་.

འཕག་འཆོང་ (pāgjoŋ) sm. འཕག་མཆོང་.

འཕག་ཙག (pāgdzaà) jumping/ hopping around, moving around, not standing or sitting still; va.—རྒྱག.

འཕག་ཙག་ཤོར་ (pāgdzaà shɔ̄ɔ) vi. to be startled into jumping around.

འཕག་ཙམ་འཕག་ཙམ་ (pāgdzam pāgdzam) sm. འཕག་ཙག.

འཕག་འཚག (pāgdzaà) sm. འཕག་ཙག.

འཕག་མཚམས་ (pāgdam) 1. sm. འཕག་ཙག. 2. pulsating, beating.

འཕགས་ (pāg) 1. vi. to be elevated/ raised, to be exalted ¶ ཀུན་ལས་འཕགས་པའི་ཡོན་ཏན་ Knowledge that is elevated above all. 2. abbr. of འཕགས་ཡུལ་.

འཕགས་སྐད་ (pāggɛɛ̀) Sanskrit, Indian languages.

འཕགས་སྐྱེས་པོ་ (pāg gyēèbo) Virupaksha, one of the four guardian kings (the King of the West).

འཕགས་མཆོག (pāgjɔɔ̀) the most exalted, the Buddhas and the Bodhisattvas.

འཕགས་མཆོག་འཇིག་རྟེན་མགོན་པོ་ (pāgjɔɔ̀ jigden gömbo) sm. འཕགས་མཆོག་འཇིག་རྟེན་དབང་ཕྱུག.

འཕགས་མཆོག་འཇིག་རྟེན་དབང་ཕྱུག (pāgjɔɔ̀ jigden wāŋjuù) a title of the Dalai Lama.

འཕགས་མཆོག་འཇིག་རྟེན་གསུམ་མགོན་ (pāgjɔɔ̀ jigdensum gön) sm. འཕགས་མཆོག་སྙིང་རྗེའི་གཏེར་ཆེན་.

འཕགས་མཆོག་སྙིང་རྗེའི་གཏེར་ཆེན་ (pāgjɔɔ̀ ñiŋjee dērjen) Avaloketisvara ¶ འཕགས་མཆོག་སྙིང་རྗེའི་གཏེར་ཆེན་དཔང་བཙུགས་ཞུས་པེད་ (They) swore to Avaloketisvara.

འཕགས་པ་ (pāgba) exalted, sublime; a Boddhisattva ¶ འཕགས་པའི་ས་ The state of being a Boddhisattva.

འཕགས་པ་ཀླུ་སྒྲུབ་ (pāgba lūdrub) Nagarjuna, one of the India teachers of Buddhism.

འཕགས་པ་ལོ་ཀ་ཤྭ་ར་ (pāgba logashara) a famous statue of Avaloketisvara in the Potala.

འཕགས་པ་ལྷ་ (pāgbalha) a famous Indian Buddhist teacher who was a disciple of Nagarjuna.

འཕགས་པའི་ཡུལ་ (pāgbɛ yṳ̈ü) sm. འཕགས་ཡུལ་.

འཕགས་བོད་ (pāgpö̠ö) abbr. India and Tibet, Indo-Tibetan.

འཕགས་འབྲས་བོད་ (pāgdrɛɛ̀ pö̠ö) abbr. India, Sikkim and Tibet.

འཕགས་མ་ (pāgma) female འཕགས་པ་.

འཕགས་མ་སྒྲོལ་མ་ (pāgba drö̠öma) Tara.

འཕགས་ཡུལ་ (pāgyüü) holy land, land of the Bodhisattva, India.

འཕང་ (pāŋ) 1. f. of འཕེན་. 2. spindle (for thread). 3. height, elevation, glory, sublimity.

འཕང་འཁེལ་ (pāŋkel) spinning wool into thread.

འཕང་འཁོར་ (pāŋgɔɔ) spinning machine.

འཕང་ཁྲི་ (pāŋdri) spindle.

འཕང་མགོ་ (pāŋgo) spindle head.

འཕང་སྒྲིམ་ (pāŋdrim) clay sauce/ disc on which the spindle is rested to spin.

འཕང་མཐོ་བ་ (pāŋtowa) high, elevated.

འཕང་དུ་ (pāŋdu) in height/ elevation.

འཕང་གདན་ (pāŋdɛn) sm. འཕང་སྒྲིམ་.

འཕང་མདའ་ (pāŋda) the spine of a spindle.

འཕང་མདུང་ (pāŋduŋ) throwing spear, javelin, harpoon.

འཕང་བུ་ (pāŋbu) sm. འཕང་མདའ་.

འཕང་བུབ་ (pāŋbub) ups and downs, successes and failures, glory and decline.

འཕང་མ་ (pāŋma) sm. འཕང་, 2.

འཕང་སྨད་ (pāŋmɛɛ̀) va. to lower.

འཕང་དམའ་བ་ (pāŋ māwa) low.

འཕང་ལོ་ (pāŋlo) 1. spindle for spinning thread. 2. knee cap. 3. spindle wheel.

འཕང་ལོང་ (pāŋloŋ) sm. འཕང་ལོ་.

འཕང་ཤིང་ (pāŋshiŋ) sm. འཕང་མདའ་.

འཕངས་ (pāŋ) p. of འཕེན་.

འཕན་ (pɛ̄n) 1. banner, pillar decoration. 2. fractured, broken, damaged.

འཕན་མགོ་ (pɛ̄ngo) top of a pillar decoration.

འཕན་གདུགས་ (pɛ̄ndug) decorative umbrella that sits over a pillar decoration.

འཕན་པོ་ (pɛ̄mbo) name of an area north of Lhasa.

འཕན་མེད་ (pɛ̄nmeè) in sound condition, without damages/ faults.

འཕན་རྩེ་གསུམ་པ་ (pɛ̄ndze sūmbə) a three pointed banner/ flag.

འཕན་ཟེལ་ (pɛ̄nsel) broken, cracked.

འཕན་ལག (pɛ̄nlaà) the points of the brocade decorations that hang from pillars.

འཕམ་: p. ཕམ་; f. འཕམ་ (pām) vi. to be defeated, to lose, to suffer a loss (in business) ¶ རྐང་རྩེད་པོ་ལོའི་འགྲན་བསྡུར་ཁོ་ཚོ་ཕམ་པ་རེད་ They lost the soccer match.

འཕམ་ཉེས་ (pāmñeè) a loss, defeat, failure; va.—གཏོང་ to defeat, to cause to lose/ fail ¶ དགྲ་བོར་འཕམ་ངེས་བཏང་བ་རེད་ (They) defeated the enemy.

འཕམ་རྒྱལ་ (pāmgyɛɛ) defeat and victory.

འཕམ་པར་བྱེད་ (pāmbar ce̠e) va. to defeat, to cause to lose/ fail.

འཕར་ (pār) 1. vi. to increase, to rise ¶ ཐོན་སྐྱེད་བྱེད་ཀྱི་ཚད་བརྒྱ་ཆ་སུམ་ཅུ་འཕར་བ་རེད་ The production level rose by 30%. 2. vi. to be promoted ¶ ཁོ་ད་ལོ་གོ་གནས་འཕར་གྱི་ཡོད་པ་རེད་ He is being promoted this year. 3. extra, additional, on top of what is usual, special (usu. — + vb.) ¶ ཛ་དྲག་ལ་བརྟེན་ནས་ཚོགས་འདུ་འཕར་ཚོགས་གནང་དགོས་བྱུང་བ་རེད་ Because of the emergency, (they) had to have a special meeting. 4. vi. to bounce up, to fly up (e.g., sparks), to beat/ throb (e.g., pulse) ¶ པོ་ལོ་ས་ནས་འཕར་བ་ལྟར་ Like a bouncing ball.

འཕར་རྐང་གཞུ་ (pāŋgaŋ shu̠) va. to buck (horses).

འཕར་སྐྱལ་དངོས་དོད་ (pārgüü ŋöödöö) shung. substituting money for extra taxes in kind that have been imposed.

འཕར་སྐྱེད་ (pārgyeè) increasing.

འཕར་སྐྲུན་ (pārdrön) extra/ additional construction.

འཕར་དཀྲི་འགེལ་སྐྱབ་ (pārdri geedrub) shung. paying extra taxes that have imposed.

འཕར་ཁ་ (pārga) increasing.

འཕར་ཁྲལ་ (pārdrɛɛ) surtax, surcharge, extra tax.

འཕར་སྒོ་ (pārgo) the soft spot on top of the head of a baby.

འཕར་འགེལ་ (pārgee) imposing a tax; va.—བྱེད་.

འཕར་ཆ་ (pārja) an increase.

འཕར་ཆག (pār cāà) increase and decrease, rise and fall, fluctuation.

འཕར་ཆིངས་ (pərjiŋ) embroidering; va.—རྒྱག.

འཕར་ཉོ་ (pārño) purchases that are above an allocation or budget.

འཕར་ཐལ་ཤོར་ (pārdɛɛ shɔ̄ɔ̄) vi. to have increased too much.

འཕར་འདེམས་ (pāndem) an extra pick or selection.

འཕར་རྡོ་ (pārdo) a ricocheting stone.

འཕར་ལྡིང་ (pāndiŋ) beating (usu. of the heart).

འཕར་སྣོན་ (pārnön) increment, extra, additional, enlargement; va.—རྒྱག to increase, to expand/ enlarge, to add.

འཕར་སྤྱང་ (pārjaŋ) jackal and wolf.

འཕར་སྤྱང་ངན་འགྲིལ་ (pārjaŋ ŋɛndree) bad/ evil ones joining together; va.—བྱེད་.

འཕར་སྤྱང་དྲ་སྡེབ་ (pārjaŋ tradeb) bad, evil people getting together; va.—བྱེད་ [Lit. jackal and wolf getting together].

འཕར་སྤྱང་ལག་འགྲིལ་ (pārjaŋ laŋdree) sm. འཕར་སྤྱང་ལག་ངན་འགྲིལ་.

འཕར་འཕར་ (pārbar) pulsating, bouncing, throbbing, hopping.

འཕར་བ་ (pāra) jackal.

འཕར་མ་ (pārma) additional, extra ། ལས་འགན་འཕར་མ་ Additional responsibilities. 2. supplementary, special ། དུས་དེབ་འཕར་མ་ A supplementary issue (of a periodical).

འཕར་རྩ་ (pārdza) arteries.

འཕར་རྩ་ཆེན་པོ་ (pardza cēmbo) the aorta.

འཕར་ཚད་ (pārdzɛɛ̀) 1. rate of increase/ rise ། འདི་ལོའི་ཐོན་སྐྱེད་འཕར་ཚད་ This year's rate of increase in production. 2. the rate of pulsating/ beating.

འཕར་འཛུགས་ (pāndzuù) shung. an additional/ extra establishment; va.—བྱེད་ to establish an additional (part/ wing/ office/ etc.).

འཕར་རེ་འཕུར་རེ་ (pārre pūrre) rubbing, massaging.

འཕར་ཤུགས་ (pārshur) beating, pulsating (as in a heart beat).

འཕལ་ཀ་ (pɛ̄ɛ̄ga) drawing, sketch.

འཕལ་ཁ་ (pɛ̄ɛ̄ga) sm. འཕལ་ཀ་.

འཕིགས་ (pīi) sm. འབིགས་.

འཕིགས་པར་སྟོན་ (pīgbar dōn) va. to show exactly, to expose, to demonstrate right on target.

འཕིབས་ (pīb) sm. འབུབས་.

འཕིར་ (pīr) sm. འཕུར་.

འཕུག (pūg) sm. འབུགས་.

འཕུང་: p. ཕུང་; f. འཕུང་ (pūŋ) vi. to get destroyed, to come to ruin/ downfall ། ཁོ་གྲོགས་པོ་ངན་པས་འཕུང་བ་རེད་ His bad friends brought his downfall.

འཕུང་དཀྲུག (pūŋdruù) a disturbance/ uprising/ revolt; va.—སློང་ to stir up a disturbance.

འཕུང་གན་མ་ (pūŋgema) derogatory term for troublemaking women.

འཕུང་འདྲེ་ (pūŋdre) harmful demons/ spirits.

འཕུང་འདྲེ་མ་ (pūŋdrema) sm. འཕུང་གན་མ་.

འཕུང་སྦྱོར་ (pūŋjɔɔ) instigating/ inciting/ causing people to quarrel; va.—བྱེད་.

འཕུང་མོ་ (pūŋmo) sm. འཕུང་གན་མ་.

འཕུང་གཞི་ (pūŋshi) cause of downfall/ ruin.

འཕུང་ལ་གཏོང་ (pūŋla dōŋ) sm. འཕུང་ལམ་དུ་སྐྱེལ་.

འཕུང་ལ་སྦྱོར་ (pūŋla jɔr) sm. འཕུང་ལམ་དུ་སྐྱེལ་.

འཕུང་ལམ་སྐྱེལ་ (pūŋlam gyēē) sm. འཕུང་ལམ་དུ་སྐྱེལ་.

འཕུང་ལམ་དུ་སྐྱེལ་ (pūŋlamdu gyēē) va. to cause ruin, to cause destruction.

འཕུངས་ (pūŋ) sm. འཕུང་.

འཕུད་: p. ཕུད་; f. འཕུད་; imp. ཕུད་ (pūù) va. to move, to shift, to transfer ། ཁོས་སྡོད་ས་ཕུད་པ་རེད་ He moved his residence.

འཕུབ་ (pūb) va. to pitch, to erect (e.g., a tent).

འཕུར་: p. ཕུར་; f. འཕུར་; imp. ཕུར་ (pūr) 1. va. to fly. 2. va. to rub, to massage, to pet.

འཕུར་སྐྱོད་ (pūrgyöö) flying, flight; va.—བྱེད་ to fly ། གནམ་གྲུ་འཕུར་སྐྱོད་བདེ་འཇགས་ཡོང་ཆེད་ In order to have safe flight.

འཕུར་སྐྱོད་ཀྱི་ལས་དོན་ (pūrgyöögi lɛ̄ɛ̄dön) aviation ། འཕུར་སྐྱོད་ཀྱི་ལས་དོན་བྱེད་མཁན་ Pilot.

འཕུར་སྐྱོད་པ་ (pūrgyööba) pilot.

འཕུར་སྐྱོད་ཚོ་ཆུང་ (pūrgyöö tsōjuŋ) flight crew.

འཕུར་བསྐྱོད་ (pūrgyöö) sm. འཕུར་སྐྱོད་.

འཕུ་འཁྱེར་འཕུལ་མདེལ་ (pūrgyer trēndel) sm. འཕུར་མདའ་.

འཕུར་རྒྱང་མྱུར་ཚད་ (pūrgyaŋ ñurdzɛɛ̀) the range and speed of sth. flying (e.g., a rocket).

འཕུར་གྲི་ (pūrdri) a throwing knife, a knife that has been thrown.

འཕུར་གྲུ་ (pūrdru) airplane.

འཕུར་གྲོག (pūrdrɔ̀ɔ̀) flying ants.

འཕུར་འགྲུལ་ (pūndrüü) air travel; va.—བྱེད་ to travel by air.

འཕུར་འགྲོ་ (pūr dro) 1. va. to fly. 2. birds.

འཕུར་མཆོང་ (pūrjoŋ) by leaps and bounds, soaring forward ། དཔལ་འབྱོར་དེ་འཕུར་མཆོང་གིས་གོང་འཕེལ་འགྲོ་བཞིན་ཡོད་ The economy is increasing by leaps and bounds.

འཕུར་མཉེད་ (pūrñeè) massaging, rubbing; va.—གཏོང་.

འཕུར་གདོང་ (pūrdoŋ) flying; va.—བྱེད་ to fly.

འཕུར་མདའ་ (pūnda) missile, guided missile.

འཕུར་དང་འཕྲེན་ (pūrdaŋ tēn) (birds) flying in formation/ in a line.

འཕུར་ལྡིང་ (pūndiŋ) hovering (in the air); va.—བྱེད་ to hover (over).

འཕུར་འཕུར་ (pūrpur) rubbing, massaging; va.—གཏོང་; —བྱེད་ ། ན་དུས་མིག་འཕུར་འཕུར་མ་གཏོང་ When (you) are sick don't rub your eyes.

འཕུར་འབབ་ (pūnbəb) taking off and landing (of aircraft); va.—བྱེད་.

འཕུར་འབྲུག (pūrdrug) a flying dragon.

འཕུར་རྩལ་ (pūrdzɛɛ) a flying exhibition, flying stunts.

འཕུར་ལམ་ (pūrlam) airplane runway.

འཕུར་ལོག (pūrlɔ̀ɔ̀) return flight.

འཕུར་སུབ་ (pūrsub) 1. sm. འཕུར་མཉེད་. 2. rubbing out/ erasing; va.—གཏོང་.

འཕུལ་ (pǖǖ) 1. sm. འཕུད་. 2. prefixed letters.

འཕུལ་རྒྱག (pǖǖgyaà) shoving/ pushing; va.—གཏོང་.

འཕུལ་ཅན་ (pǖǖjɛn) words that have prefixed letters.

འཕུལ་རྗེས་གཉིས་ (pǖǖden ñīi) prefixed and suffixed letters.

འཕུལ་འདེད་ (pǖndeè) sm. ཕྱིར་འབུད་.

འཕུལ་འདྲེན་ (pǖndren) strife, struggle [Lit. pushing and pulling].

འཕུལ་རྡེག (pǖǖdeg) sm. འཕུལ་རྒྱག.

འཕུལ་སྤྱད་ (pǖǖjɛɛ̀) a wooden rake used to turn drying grain.

འཕུལ་མེད་ (pǖǖmeè) words without prefixed letters.

འཕུལ་ཡིག (pǖǖyii) prefixed letters (ག, ད, བ, མ, འ).

འཕུལ་ཡོད་ (pǖǖyöö) words with prefixed letters.

འཕེན་: p. འཕངས་; f. འཕང་; imp. འཕོངས་ (pēn) 1. va. to shoot, to fire ། མེ་མདའ་ཞིག་འཕངས་སོང་ He shot the gun. 2. va. to throw, to fling ། ཁོས་བྱིའུ་རེར་རྡོ་ཞིག་འཕངས་སོང་ He threw a stone at the bird.

འཕེན་རྒྱང་ (pēngyaŋ) abbr. འཕེན་པའི་རྒྱང་ཐག.

འཕེན་གཏོར་ (pēndɔɔ) torma used when performing a rites of exorcism.

འཕེན་ཐག (pēndaà) a sling.

འཕེན་མདུང་ (pēnduŋ) throwing spear.

འཕེན་མདོང་ (pēndoŋ) mortar.

འཕེན་རྡོ་ (pēndo) cannon ball.

འཕེན་པའི་རྒྱང་ཐག (pēnbɛ gyaŋdaà) the range of a rifle/ pistol/ cannon/ etc.

འཕེན་པའི་སྟོབས་ (pēmbɛ dōb) the initial motive.

འཕེན་བྱེད་ཀྱི་ལས་ (pēnjeègi lɛ̀ɛ̀) karmic law which determines rebirth.

འཕེན་དབྱུག (pēnyuù) throwing, flinging; va.—བྱེད་.

འཕེན་པའི་བར་ཐག (pēmbɛ pardaà) shooting range.

འཕེན་ཤོག (pēnshɔ̀ɔ̀) sm. འོས་ཤོག.

འཕེར་ (pēr) 1. vi. to be able, to be capable ། མོ་དགེ་རྒན་འཕེར་ངེས་འདུག She certainly is capable of teaching. ། རྒན་འཁོགས་ལས་ཀ་མི་འཕེར་བ་ Old people who are unable to work. 2. vi. to be able to meet a standard/ quality.

འཕེར་མདོག་འཛོན་མདོག (pēndɔ̀ɔ̀ jōndɔ̀ɔ̀) pretending to be able/ capable.

འཕེར་པོ་ (pērbo) capable, able, competent.

འཕེར་འབོར་ཆེ་བ་ (pērbɔr cēwa) large production.

འཕེར་ཙམ་ (pērdzam) just able to do.

འཕེར་ཤ་ (pērsha) sm. ཕེར་ཤ་.

འཕེལ་ (pēl) 1. vi. to increase, to multiply, to develop, to flourish ། ལོ་གཅིག་པོ་དེ་གའི་ནང་བཟོ་ལས་ཆུང་རིགས་སྟོང་ཕྲག་མང་པོ་འཕེལ་བ་རེ་ In that year alone small industries increased by the thousands. ། ཁ་ཚོའི་དམག་དོན་སྟོབས་ཤུགས་ནི་འཛམ་གླིང་ནང་ཆེ་ཤོས་ཞིག་ཏུ་འཕེལ་ཡོད་པ་རེད་ Their military power has developed into one of the biggest in the world. 2. vi. to rise.

འཕེལ་ཀ་ (pēlga) sm. འཕེལ་རྒྱས་.

འཕེལ་སྐྱེད་ (pēēgyeè) sm. འཕེལ་རྒྱས་.

འཕེལ་སྐྱེས་ (pēēgyeè) breeding, reproducing, propagating.

འཕེལ་ཁ་ (pēēga) sm. འཕེལ་ཀ་.

འཕེལ་འགྱུར་ (pēēgyur) evolving, evolution.

འཕེལ་འགྱུར་སྨྲ་བ་ (pēēgyur māwa) evolutionism, the theory of evolution.

འཕེལ་འགྲིབ་ (pēndrib) increasing and decreasing, rising and falling, growing and declining ། འཕེལ་འགྲིབ་ཀྱི་འབོར་ The amount of increase and decrease.

འཕེལ་རྒྱས་ (pēēgyɛɛ̀) development, growth, progress, expansion; va.—གཏོང་ to develop, to progress, to expand, to spread ། མའོ་ཙེ་ཏུང་གིས་མར་ལེ་ནིའི་རིང་ལུགས་འཕེལ་རྒྱས་སུ་བཏང་བ་རེད་ Mao Zedong spread Marxism-Leninism. ། གསར་བརྗེའི་དམག་འཁྲུག་འཕེལ་རྒྱས་བཏང་ན་ If (we) expand revolutionary war. ། སྤྱི་ཚོགས་ཀྱི་འཕེལ་རྒྱས་ད་ཅང་དལ་པོ་རེད་ Social progress is very slow.

འཕེལ་རྒྱས་ཀྱི་འགྲོ་ཕྱོགས་ (pēēgyɛɛgi drojɔ̀ɔ̀) sm. འཕེལ་ཕྱོགས་.

འཕེལ་རྒྱས་ཀྱི་ཆུ་ཚད་ (pēēgyɛɛ̀gi cūdzɛɛ̀) level of development/ progress.

འཕེལ་རྒྱས་ཀྱི་ཆོས་ཉིད་ (pēēgyɛɛ̀gi cö̀ö̀ñii) laws of development.

འཕེལ་རྒྱས་ཀྱི་གནས་སྐབས་ (pēēgyɛɛ̀gi nɛ̀ɛ̀gəb) stage of development.

འཕེལ་རྒྱས་སུ་གཏོང་ (pēēgyɛɛ̀su dōŋ) sm. འཕེལ་རྒྱས་གཏོང་ (see འཕེལ་རྒྱས་).

འཕེལ་སྟོབས་ (pēēdob) reproductive ability/ capacity.

འཕེལ་ཐབས་ (pēēdəb) ways or means to develop/ increase/ advance; va.—བྱེད་.

འཕེལ་སྣོན་ (pēēnön) 1. increasing, augmenting, enlarging; va.—བྱེད་. 2. adding, summing up.

འཕེལ་ཕྱོགས་ (pēējɔ̀ɔ̀) direction of development, tendency, trend, current ། ལོ་རྒྱུས་ཀྱི་འཕེལ་ཕྱོགས་ The trend of history.

འཕེལ་བ་བྱེད་ (pēēwa ceè) va. to develop, to cause to grow/ increase/ progress.

འཕེལ་བའི་ཟླ་བ་ (pēēwɛ dawa) 12th month of the Tibetan calendar.

འཕེལ་མེད་རང་འཇགས་ (pēēmeè ranjaà) sm. འཕེལ་མེད་སོར་གནས་.

འཕེལ་མེད་སོར་གནས་ (pēēmeè sōrnɛɛ̀) static, standing still, stagnating, without development/ progress.

འཕེལ་ཚད་ (pēēdzɛɛ̀) rate of development/ growth/ increase.

འཕེལ་ཚུལ་ (pēēdzüü) development, the way or manner in which something develops/ grows/ increases.

འཕེལ་རིམ་ (pēērim) successive changes/ stages, stages of progress/ development.

འཕེལ་ལམ་ (pēēlam) the path of development/ progress.

འཕེལ་ཤེད་ (pēēsheè) the degree in which sth. has risen (e.g., rice, dough).

འཕེལ་ཤུགས་ (pēēshug) the strength of development/ growth/ increase.

འཕོ་: p. འཕོས་; f. འཕོ་ (pō) vi. to be transferred, to be moved from one position/ place to another, to transmigrate ། གཞུང་ཞབས་རྙིང་པ་འཕོས་ནས་གསར་པ་ཕེབས་རྒྱུ་རེད་ The old official has been transferred and the new one is yet to come.

འཕོ་སྐར་ (pōgar) shooting star.

འཕོ་སྐྱས་ (pōgyɛɛ̀) moving from one place to another; va.—བྱེད་.

འཕོ་ཁེབས་ (pōgeb) breast cover.

འཕོ་འགྱུར་ (pōngyur) changing, altering; va.—གཏོང་ to change/ alter; vi.—འགྲོ་ to change naturally, to get altered ། ཞིང་པ་ཚོའི་འཚོ་བའི་འཕོ་འགྱུར་ Changes in the life of farmers.

འཕོ་ཉུལ་ (pōñül) moving from place to place.

འཕོ་ཉུལ་ངེ་མེད་ (pōñül ŋemeè) drifting about, wandering aimlessly.

འཕོ་བ་ (pōwa) transferring of consciousness; va.—རྒྱག to release consciousness (rite done when sb. dies).

འཕོ་བ་གྲོང་འཇུག (pōwa dronjuù) transferring consciousness into another person.

འཕོ་བ་འདེབས་ (pōwa deb) va. to release consciousness.

འཕོ་བ་སྦྱོང་ (pōwa joŋ) va. to train in the yogic practice of transference of consciousness.

འཕོ་མེད་ (pōmeè) immovable, permanent.

འཕོ་ལེན་ (pōlɛn) transfer of officials (new official taking over for the old one).

འཕོག: p. ཕོག; f. འཕོག (pɔ̄ɔ̀) 1. vi. to get hit/ struck ། མེ་མདའ་ཕོག་བྱུང་ (I) got shot. 2. vi. to be touched (emotionally), to be influenced ། འདི་ཁོའི་སེམས་ལ་ཕོག་སོང་ This touched him (emotionally).

འཕོག་ཏུ་མེད་པ་ (pōgdu meèba) language that doesn't offend/ hurt anyone.

འཕོག་ཐུག་ (pōgduù) harm, hurt, injury ། ལྷ་ལ་འཕོག་ཐུག་འགྲོ་ཡག་གི་ལས་ཀ་ག་བྱེད་མི་རུང་ Being involved in work harmful to the gods is not good. ། མི་ལ་འཕོག་ཐུག་འགྲོ་ཡག་གི་སྐད་ཆ་བཤད་རྒྱུ་ཡོད་པ་མེད་ One should not speak of things that will be hurtful to other people.

འཕོང་ (pōŋ) 1. archery. 2. sm. འཕོངས་.

འཕོང་སྐྱེན་པ་ (pōŋ gyēmba) skilled archer/ bowman.

འཕོང་རྒྱུག (pōŋgyuù) shooting an arrow while galloping on a horse; va.—བྱེད་.

འཕོང་སྤྱད་ (pōŋjɛɛ̀) paraphernalia that go with archery.

འཕོང་ཕྱི་ (pōŋjii) toilet paper.

འཕོང་ར་ (pōŋra) 1. archery field. 2. sm. འཕོངས་ར་.

འཕོང་ས་ (pōŋsa) archery field.

འཕོངས་ (pōŋ) 1. imp. of འཕེན་. 2. buttocks.

འཕོངས་ཀུབ་ (pōŋgub) sm. འཕོངས, 2.

འཕོངས་གྲལ་ (pōŋtrɛɛ) sitting in a row; va.—སྒྲིག to sit in rows.

འཕོངས་གིད་རྒྱག (pōŋgii gyaà) sm. ཀུབ་འཆག་རྒྱག.

འཕོངས་ལྕག (pōŋjaà) a whip.

འཕོངས་སྟེགས་ (pōŋdeg) folding chair, sofa.

འཕོངས་རྡུལ་ (pōŋdüü) dust clinging on the back of a dress (where one sits).

འཕོངས་པ་ (pōŋba) poor, indigent.

འཕོངས་ཚོས་ (pōŋdzöö) buttocks.

འཕོངས་ར་ (pōŋra) sitting in a circle.

འཕོངས་རུས་ (pōŋrüü) thighbone, femur.

འཕོངས་རུས་ཀྱི་དབང་རྩ་ (pōŋrüügi wāŋdza) sciatic nerve.

འཕོད་ (pöö) sm. ཕོད་.

འཕོན་པོ་ (pömbo) sm. ཕོན་པོ་.

འཕོས་ (pöö) p. of འཕོ་.

འཕོས་ཚབ་ (pöödzəb) a replacement.

འཕོས་ལེན་ (pöölen) taking over, replacing (sb.'s work or job); va.—བྱེད་ to take over, to replace.

འཕྱ་: p. **འཕྱས་**; f. **འཕྱ་**; imp. **འཕྱ་** (cā) va. to ridicule, to jeer, to deride ། བུད་མེད་མོ་རྐྱང་ཞིག་གིས་སྐྱེས་པ་ཞག་སྡོད་དུ་ཉར་ན་གཞན་གྱིས་འཕྱ་ངེས་རེད་ If a single woman keeps a man overnight (in her house) others will deride her.

འཕྱ་ཀ་ (cāga) ridicule, derision, mockery; va.—བྱེད་.

འཕྱ་སྐྱེན་པ་ (cā gyēmba) sb. who is quick to make fun of others.

འཕྱ་གླེང་ (cāleŋ) making fun (of others); va.—རྒྱག.

འཕྱ་དགོད་ (cāgöö) laughing/ sneering at.

འཕྱ་ཉམས་ (cāñam) making fun (of others).

འཕྱ་འཕྱོ་ (cāco) abbr. of འཕྱ་མི་འཕྱོ་མི་.

འཕྱ་མི་ཕྱོ་མི་ (cāmi cōmi) sm. འཕྱ་མི་འཕྱོ་མི་.

འཕྱ་མི་འཕྱོ་མི་ (cāme cōme) uncomfortable, in discomfort.

འཕྱ་སྨོད་ (cāmöö) sm. འཕྱ་ཀ་.

འཕྱ་དམོད་ (cāmöö) sm. འཕྱ་ཀ་.

འཕྱ་ཚིག (cādzii) sm. འཕྱ་ཀ་.

འཕྱ་ལད་ཀུ་རེ་ (cēlεε gūre) joking/ teasing/ making fun of.

འཕྱ་ལད་ (cēlεε) making fun of, disparaging, ridiculing; va.—རྒྱག.

འཕྱ་ལད་དམའ་འབེབས་ (cēlεε māmbeb) sm. འཕྱ་ལད་.

འཕྱག་: p. **འཕྱགས་**: p. **འཕྱག་**: p. **འཕྱོགས་** (cāà) va. to sweep.

འཕྱགས་ (cāà) 1. shung. a special collection of taxes. 2. p. of འཕྱག.

འཕྱང་: p. **འཕྱངས་**; f. **འཕྱང་** (cāŋ) 1. vi. to hang down, to be dangling/ suspended. 2. va. to cling to, to depend on.

འཕྱང་ངེ་བ་ (cāŋŋewa) hanging, dangling.

འཕྱང་ཐག (cāŋdaà) a hanging/ dangling rope.

འཕྱང་ཐིག (cāŋdig) perpendicular line.

འཕྱང་རྡོ་ (cāŋdo) the metal/ stone on a plumb line.

འཕྱང་འཕྲུལ་ (cāŋdrüü) suspended ornaments/ decorations.

འཕྱང་བའི་རྨ་ (cāŋwε mā) wounds that almost decapitate.

འཕྱང་མོ་ (cāŋmo) uncertain, hesitant, unsure, doubt.

འཕྱང་མོ་ཉག (cāŋmoñug) uncertainty, hesitancy ། དེ་དངོས་སུ་མ་མཐོང་བར་ཚང་མ་འཕྱང་མོ་ཉག་དུ་གནས་ Everybody was hesitant until they actually saw it.

འཕྱང་མོ་ཡུག (cāŋmo yu̱ù) sm. འཕྱང་མོ་ཉག.

འཕྱང་ཟམ་ (cāŋsam) a hanging/ suspension bridge.

འཕྱངས་ (cāŋ) p. of འཕྱང་.

འཕྱད་ (cεε) sm. ཕྱད་.

འཕྱན་ (cεn) 1. va. to wander/ roam around, to live the life of a vagabond. 2. in contrast to, opposite to ། དང་ཚུལ་དེ་ལས་འཕྱན་པས་ In contrast to that manner.

འཕྱན་མ་ (cāŋma) a loose female.

འཕྱམ་ (cāā) sm. ཕྱམ་.

འཕྱར་: p. **ཕྱར་**; f. **འཕྱར་**; imp. **ཕྱོར་** (cār) 1. va. to hoist/ raise/ fly (flags, banners, etc.), to brandish, to lift ། དར་ཆ་དེ་ཁང་ཐོག་ཏུ་ཕྱར་འདུག (They) have hoisted the flag on the roof. ། རལ་གྲི་འཕྱར་ནས་མདུན་དུ་མཆོང་གྲབས་བྱས་པ་རེད Brandishing (their) swords, they prepared to advance. 2. (ལྷག་པར་ + —) to winnow.

འཕྱར་ཀ་ (cārga) sm. འཕྱ་ཀ་.

འཕྱར་ཁ་ (cārga) sm. འཕྱ་ཀ་.

འཕྱར་རྒྱག (cār gya̱à) va. to do sth. just for show.

འཕྱར་དར་ (cārdar) a banner used during some religious rites.

འཕྱར་འཕྱར་ (cārjar) 1. exhibiting one's knowledge in a proud and arrogant way; va.—བྱེད་. 2. winnowing (grains); va.—བྱེད་. 3. making fun/ ridiculing others; va.—བྱེད་. 4. showing/ flaunting openly.

འཕྱར་གཡེང་ (cāryeŋ) 1. licentious, immoral, shameless. 2. glancing sideways.

འཕྱས་ (cεε) p. of འཕྱ་.

འཕྱས་གདགས་ (cεε da̱à) va. to poke fun at.

འཕྱི་: p. **འཕྱིས་**; f. **འཕྱི་** (cī) 1. vi. to be late ། ང་ཚོ་ལྟད་མོར་འཕྱིས་འདུག We were late for the show. 2. va. to wipe, to clean off.

འཕྱི་པོ་ (cību) late ། འཕྱི་པོ་འདི་འདྲ་ཡོང་ཡག་གང་ཡིན་ནམ་ Why did you come so late?

འཕྱི་བ་ (cīwə) marmot.

འཕྱི་ཕི་ (cībi) sm. འཕྱི་བ་.

འཕྱི་ཚིལ་ (cīdzii) the fat of marmots.

འཕྱིང་བ་ (cīŋwə) sm. ཕྱིང་བ་.

འཕྱིང་སང་ (cīŋsaŋ) ch. minister.

འཕྱིང་རུལ་གནམ་འཕྱར་ (cīŋhrüü nāmjar) shung. disgracing [Lit. displaying one's torn felt for everyone to see].

འཕྱིངས་ (cīŋ) vi. to become matted together (e.g., fur, hair, wool).

འཕྱིད་: p. **ཕྱིད་**; f. **འཕྱིད་** (cīi) 1. sm. འཕྱིད་. 2. vi. to have a sore occur due to rubbing.

འཕྱིད་བདར་ (cīidar) wiping; va.—གཏོང་.

འཕྱིད་རས་ (cīirεε) rag (for wiping).

འཕྱིས་ (cīi) p. of ཕྱིས་.

འཕྱུག་: p. **འཕྱུགས་**; f. **འཕྱུག** (cūù) vi. to fail, to make a mistake, to err, to blunder ། ཁོས་མ་འཕྱུགས་ན་ང་ཚོར་ཐོབ་པ་ཡོད་ If he had not blundered we would have won.

འཕྱུག་པ་མེད་པ་ (cūgbə me̱èba) correct, successful, without fail/ mistake.

འཕྱུག་མེད་ (cūgmeè) abbr. of འཕྱུག་པ་མེད་པ་.

འཕྱུགས་ (cūg) p. of འཕྱུག.

འཕྱུགས་སྐྱོན་ (cūggyön) mistake, error.

འཕྱུགས་མེད་ (cūgmeè) abbr. of འཕྱུག་པ་མེད་པ་.

འཕྱུགས་མེད་ཁུངས་ལྡན་ (cūgmeè kūŋdεn) correct, true, authentic.

འཕྱུགས་ལྷད་མེད་པ་ (cūglhεε me̱èba) unadulterated, true, correct, accurate.

འཕྱུར་: p. **ཕྱུར་**; f. **འཕྱུར་** (cūr) vi. to surge, to rise/ roll/ swell upwards (e.g., waves or smoke) ། རྒྱ་མཚོའི་ཆུ་རླབས་མཚོ་ཁར་འཕྱུར་བ་བཞིན་ Like the waves of the sea surging against the shore.

འཕྱུར་ཁ་མདོག (cūrgudɔɔ) cream-colored.

འཕྱུར་པོ་ (cūrbu) sm. འཕྱུར་བུ་.

འཕྱུར་འཕྱུར་ (cūrjur) curling upwards, billowing (as with smoke).

འཕྱུར་བུ་ (cūrbu) protruding.

འཕྱུལ་ཕྱགས་ (cūrjaà) vacuum cleaner.

འཕྱེ་: p. **འཕྱེས་**; f. **འཕྱེ་** (cē) va. to crawl, to creep.

འཕྱེ་བོ་ (cēbo) 1. creeping/ crawling animals. 2. crippled.

འཕྱེད་ཤིང་ (cēèshiŋ) wooden bar.

འཕྱེས་ (cēè) p. of འཕྱེ་.

འཕྱོ་ (cō) 1. vi. to float/ drift/ soar/ glide ། མི་རོ་ཞིག་ཆུ་ཁར་བཞིན་འདུག A dead body was floating on the water. ། བྱ་མང་པོ་ནམ་མཁར་འཕྱོ་བ་མཐོང་ (He) saw many birds soaring in the sky. 2. sm. འཕྱུར་.

འཕྱོ་དག (cōgu) a term used for birds and animals in the wild.

འཕྱོ་ལྡིང་ (cōdiŋ) circling around/ hovering in the air; va.—བྱེད་.

འཕྱོ་ཕུར་ (cōbur) floating corpse.

འཕྱོ་གཟུགས་ (cōsug) floating body.

འཕྱོ་ཟམ་ (cōsam) sm. འཕྱང་ཟམ་.

འཕྱོང་ (cōŋ) corner of a house.

འཕྱོངས་ (cōŋ) sm. འཕྱོང་.

འཕྱོན་ (cön) imp. of འཕྱན་.

འཕྱོན་པ་ (cömba) a womanizer/ playboy.

འཕྱོན་མ་ (cönma) prostitute.

འཕྱོར་ (cɔɔ) va. to dress up.

འཕྱོར་དགའ་ (cɔ̄rga) a fashionable/ stylish person.
འཕྱོར་འགྲོས་ (cɔ̄rdröö) walking with a swaying gait.
འཕྱོར་ཕྲེམ་ཅན་ (cɔ̄rdemjɛn) women who sway when they walk.
འཕྱོར་པོ་ (cɔ̄rbo) a person who is fashionable/ stylish.
འཕྱོར་འབྲི་ (cɔ̄rdri) writing about sth. in an adoring/ approving manner.
འཕྱོར་མོ་ (cɔ̄rmo) a stylish woman.
འཕྱོས་ (cōō) p.of འཕྱོ་.
འཕྲ་ (trā) kicking with the hind legs; va.—རྒྱག to kick with the hind legs, to buck.
འཕྲ་ཐོ་ (trādo) sm. འཕྲ་.
འཕྲ་འཛིངས་ (trādziŋ) horses and mules fighting by kicking/ bucking.
འཕྲ་ཤགས་ (trāshaà) sm. འཕྲ་འཛིངས་.
འཕྲང་ (trāŋ) narrow path along a gorge/ ravine.
འཕྲང་བཀག་རང་སྲུང་ (trāŋgaà ra̱ŋsuŋ) closed door policy.
འཕྲང་སྒུག (trāŋguù) waiting in ambush on a narrow path with mountain and river on either side; va.—རྒྱག.
འཕྲང་སྒོ་ (trāŋgo) the mouth of a narrow gorge/ ravine.
འཕྲང་འགག (trāŋgaà) a narrow and dangerous part of a path on a gorge/ ravine.
འཕྲང་དམ་པ་ (trāŋ da̱mba) a narrow gorge/ ravine.
འཕྲང་ལམ་ (trāŋlam) a narrow path through a gorge/ ravine.
འཕྲད་: p. ཕྲད་; f. འཕྲད་ (trɛ̀ɛ) vi. to meet ¶ ལམ་དུ་གྲོགས་པོ་ཞིག་འཕྲད་བྱུང་ I met a friend on the way.
འཕྲད་རྐྱེན་ (trɛ̀ɛgyen) coincidentally occurring ¶ ཁོ་སླེབས་པ་དང་རྙོག་ཆ་ལངས་པ་འཕྲད་རྐྱེན་བྱུང་པའོ་ The trouble coincidentally occurred when he came.
འཕྲད་ཁ་ (trɛ̀ɛga) sm. ཐུག་འཕྲད་.
འཕྲད་གནས་ (trɛ̀ɛnɛ̀ɛ) sm. འཕྲད་ས་.
འཕྲད་མཚམས་ (trɛ̀ɛdzam) tangent (in math).
འཕྲད་ཟུར་ (trɛ̀ɛsur) angle.
འཕྲད་ས་ (trɛ̀ɛsa) point where two things meet, point of contact.
འཕྲལ་ (trɛ̄ɛ) 1. immediate, present; immediately, at once ¶ འཕྲལ་གྱི་དགོས་མཁོ་ Immediate needs. ¶ དངུལ་ཕྲན་བུ་འཕྲལ་གཏོང་བྱེད་རོགས་ Please send some money at once. ¶ ཏར་འབྱོར་པ་དང་འཕྲལ་སྐྱོད་བྱས་པ་ཡིན་ (I) left immediately after (I) received the telegram. 2. temporarily, for the present ¶ འཕྲལ་དང་ཕུགས་གཉིས་ཀར་ཕན་པ་ Beneficial for both the past and the future. 3. (vb. + —) right after, as soon as ¶ ཁོང་ལས་ཁུངས་ལ་ཕེབས་འཕྲལ་ཁ་པར་འབྱོར་སོང་ The call came as soon as he went to the office.
འཕྲལ་: p. ཕྲལ་; f. དབྲལ་ (trɛ̄ɛ) va. to separate, to break apart, to split.
འཕྲལ་དཀའ་ཕུགས་བརླག (trɛ̄ɛga pūglaà) difficult current work that has no future.
འཕྲལ་རྐྱེན་ (trɛ̄ɛgyen) present problem / obstacle, immediate cause.
འཕྲལ་རྐྱེན་འཆི་གོད་ (trɛ̄ɛgyen cīgöö) accidental death.
འཕྲལ་སྐད་ (trɛ̄ɛgɛɛ̀) colloquial speech/ language.
འཕྲལ་སྐྱོབ་ (trɛ̄ɛgyob) first aid; va. to —བྱེད་ to give first aid.
འཕྲལ་སྐྱོབ་སྨན་བཅོས་ (trɛ̄ɛgyob mɛ̄njöö) emergency treatment, first aid treatment.
འཕྲལ་མཁོ་ (trɛ̄ɛgo) urgent necessities, immediate needs.
འཕྲལ་གང་ (trɛ̄ɛgaŋ) at present, for the time being, temporarily ¶ འཕྲལ་གང་སྡོད་ས་འདི་འགྲིགས་ཀྱི་རེད་ This place is fine to live in temporarily.
འཕྲལ་རྒོལ་ (trɛ̄ɛgöö) surprise attack, sudden onslaught.
འཕྲལ་རྒོལ་པ་ (trɛ̄ɛgööba) shock worker, shock trooper.
འཕྲལ་རྒོལ་རུ་ཁག (trɛ̄ɛgöö ru̱gaà) shock troops, shock brigade, commandos.
འཕྲལ་རྒྱགས་ (trɛ̄ɛgyaà) foodstuffs for temporary use.
འཕྲལ་སྐང་ (trɛ̄ɛgaŋ) sm. འཕྲལ་གང་.
འཕྲལ་སྒྲུབ་ (trɛ̄ɛdrub) sm. འཕྲལ་རྒོལ་.
འཕྲལ་སྒྲུབ་པ་ (trɛ̄ɛdrubba) sm. འཕྲལ་རྒོལ་པ་.
འཕྲལ་སྒྲུབ་རུ་ཁག (trɛ̄ɛdrub ru̱gaà) sm. འཕྲལ་རྒོལ་རུ་ཁག.
འཕྲལ་དགོས་ (trɛ̄ɛgöö) temporary needs.
འཕྲལ་མངོན་ལྷ་བཅོས་ (trɛ̄ɛŋön lājöö) doing things slipshod/ quickly; va.—བྱེད་.
འཕྲལ་གཅོད་དམག་འཐབ (trɛ̄ɛjöö məgdəb) quick decisive battle.
འཕྲལ་བཅོས་ (trɛ̄ɛjöö) sm. འཕྲལ་སྐྱོབ་.
འཕྲལ་བཅོས་ཁང་ (trɛ̄ɛjöögaŋ) emergency ward (in a hospital).
འཕྲལ་གཏོང་ (trɛ̄ɛdoŋ) sending at once/ urgently.
འཕྲལ་གཏོང་ཁ་པར་ (trɛ̄ɛdoŋ kābar) direct dial long distance phone.
འཕྲལ་ཐག་གཅོད་ (trɛ̄ɛdaà jöö) va. to make a quick decision.
འཕྲལ་ཐོན་ (trɛ̄ɛdön) leaving at once/ immediately; va.—བྱེད་ to leave at once/ immediately.
འཕྲལ་དུ་ (trɛ̄ɛdu) at once, immediately ¶ འདི་འཕྲལ་དུ་བྱེད་དགོས་ We must do this at once.
འཕྲལ་དོན་ (trɛ̄ɛdön) temporary affairs.
འཕྲལ་བདེ་ (trɛ̄ɛde) temporary happiness, happy for the time being.
འཕྲལ་བདེ་གླིང་ཀ་ (trɛ̄ɛde lĩŋgə) name of a park in Lhasa.
འཕྲལ་བདེ་ཕུགས་སྐྱིད་ (trɛ̄ɛde pūggyeè) good for the present and good for the long term.
འཕྲལ་བདེ་བ་ (trɛ̄ɛdewa) steward.
འཕྲལ་བདེ་ལས་ཁུངས་ (trɛ̄ɛde lɛ̄ɛguŋ) sm. རྩེ་ཕྱག་ལས་ཁུངས་.
འཕྲལ་འདོན་ཚགས་པར་ (trɛ̄ɛdön tsāgbar) special newspaper edition.
འཕྲལ་འདོན་ཡི་གེ་ (trɛ̄ɛdön yige) express letter.
འཕྲལ་སྣང་ (trɛ̄ɛnaŋ) sudden idea/ thought.
འཕྲལ་སྤྱོད་ (trɛ̄ɛjöö) for immediate use, instant ¶ འཕྲལ་སྤྱོད་བཟའ་བཅའ་ Instant food.
འཕྲལ་ཕུགས་ (trɛ̄ɛ pūù) present and future, temporary and ultimate, long and short term.
འཕྲལ་ཕུགས་རྒྱངས་གསུམ་ (trɛ̄ɛpuù gya̱ŋsum) long, middle and short term.
འཕྲལ་འཕྲལ་ (trɛ̄ɛdrɛɛ) 1. right then and there, immediately ¶ འདྲི་བ་དེ་ཚོར་འཕྲལ་འཕྲལ་ལན་འདེབས་བྱས་པ་རེད་ (He) answered those questions right then and there. 2. doing things on time, doing things quickly/ promptly.
འཕྲལ་བ་ (trɛ̄ɛwa) 1. minus. 2. forehead.
འཕྲལ་མ་ཉིད་དུ་ (trɛ̄ɛ ma̱ñiidu) right way, at that very moment, instantly.
འཕྲལ་མར་ (trɛ̄ɛmar) sm. འཕྲལ་མ་ཉིད་དུ་.
འཕྲལ་མྱུར་(དུ་) (trɛ̄ɛñur) quickly, rapidly, speedily; immediately, at once ¶ མི་འབོར་འཕྲལ་མྱུར་གྱིས་འཕར་བ་རེད་ The population increased rapidly.
འཕྲལ་མཚན་ (trɛ̄ɛdzɛn) (vb. + —) as soon as, immediately.
འཕྲལ་ཟུག་གཅོད་སྨན་ (trɛ̄ɛsuù jöömɛn) medicines for temporary relief of pain.
འཕྲལ་ཡུན་ (trɛɛyün) sm. འཕྲལ་ཕུགས་.
འཕྲལ་ཡུན་ལེགས་ཚོགས་ (trɛ̄ɛyün le̱gdzɔɔ̀) beneficial at present and in the future.
འཕྲལ་ཤར་བསམ་ཚུལ་ (trɛ̄ɛshar sāmdzüü) sudden idea/ thought/ opinion.
འཕྲལ་སེལ་ (trɛ̄ɛsel) temporary.
འཕྲལ་གསལ་ (trɛ̄ɛsɛl) a prompt/ quick reply.
འཕྲལ་བསྒྲིངས་ (trɛ̄ɛsiŋ) sending a reply quickly; va.—བྱེད་.
འཕྲས་ (trɛ̂ɛ) p.of འཕྲ་.
འཕྲས་པ་ (drɛ̀ɛba) sm. འཕྲིས་པ་.
འཕྲི་: p. ཕྲིས་; f. འཕྲི་ (trī) va. to subtract, to curtail, to diminish, to take away, to cut back ¶ ཁོ་བདུན་འདིའི་གླ་ཕོགས་ནས་བརྒྱ་ཟུར་གཉིས་ཕྲིས་འདུག They deducted 2% of this week's wages.

འཕྲི་ཆག (trījaà) reduction; va.—གཏོང་ to reduce། རང་གར་དཔོན་གྱིས་དམག་མིའི་ཕོགས་འཕྲི་ཆག་བཏང་སོང་ The generals on their own reduced the soldiers' salary.

འཕྲི་རྟགས་ (trīdaà) minus sign.

འཕྲི་ཐབས་ (trīdəb) subtraction.

འཕྲི་འཐེན་ (trīden) reduction, subtraction, curtailment; va.—བྱེད་ to cut back/ curtail, to reduce, to subtract.

འཕྲི་སྣོན་ (trīnün) reduction and/ or addition; va.—བྱེད་ to reduce or add། ཚོགས་པས་འཆར་གཞིའི་སྔོན་འགོར་འཕྲི་སྣོན་གང་ཡང་བྱས་མི་འདུག The committee neither reduced nor added to the budget.

འཕྲི་སྣོན་མེད་པ་ (trīnün me̱èba) without additions or subtractions.

འཕྲི་བྱ་ (trīja) subtrahend (in math).

འཕྲི་བྱེད་གྲངས་ཀ་ (trījeè tra̱ŋga) subtrahend (in math).

འཕྲི་རྩིས་ (tridzii) subtraction (in math).

འཕྲིག: p. འཕྲིགས་; f. འཕྲིག (trīg) 1. vi. to know indirectly/ implicitly; to know roughly. 2. vi. to doubt/ suspect.

འཕྲིག་ཚུད་ (trīg tsüü) sm. འཕྲིག.

འཕྲིག་ཟ་ (trīg sa̱) sm. འཕྲིག་, 2.

འཕྲིགས་ (trīg) p. of འཕྲིག.

འཕྲིན་ (trīn) message, signal, letter, correspondence; va.—གཏོང་; —བསྐུར་; —སྤྲོད་ to send a message/ signal/ letter; va.—སྐྱེལ་ to deliver a message/ letter; to communicate.

འཕྲིན་སྐྱེམས་ (trīngyem) sm. གསེར་སྐྱེམས་.

འཕྲིན་སྐྱེལ་ཁང་ (trīngyeegaŋ) post office.

འཕྲིན་སྐྱེལ་གློག་སྐུད་ (trīngyee lɔ̄ɔgyeè) communications cable factory.

འཕྲིན་སྐྱེལ་སྒྲིག་ཆས་ (trīngyee drigjɛɛ̀) communications equipment.

འཕྲིན་སྐྱེལ་བ་ (trīngyeeewa) postman.

འཕྲིན་སྐྱེལ་སྦྲག་རྟགས་ (trīngyee drāgdaà) postal cancellation mark (on letters).

འཕྲིན་སྐྱེལ་ཕུག་རོན་ (tringyee pūgrön) carrier pigeon.

འཕྲིན་སྐྱེལ་དམག་མི་ (trīngyee mɔ̄ɔmi) military signal corps.

འཕྲིན་སྐྱེལ་ཡོ་བྱད་ (trīngyee yo̱bjɛɛ̀) communications equipment.

འཕྲིན་བསྐུར་ (trīngur) sending a message/ communications.

འཕྲིན་འཁྲིད་སློབ་གྲྭ་ (trīndrii lōbdra) correspondence school.

འཕྲིན་གྲོགས་ (trīndrɔɔ̀) pen pal.

འཕྲིན་བཅོལ་ (trīnjöö) sm. ཕྲིན་བཅོལ་.

འཕྲིན་གཏོང་ (trīndoŋ) communications། འཕྲིན་གཏོང་གི་འགྲོ་སོང་ Expenses for communications.

འཕྲིན་གཏོང་སྒྲིག་ཆས་ (trīndoŋ drigjɛɛ̀) communication equipment/ facilities, communications system.

འཕྲིན་གཏོང་དྲ་བ་ (trindoŋ tra̱wa) communication net.

འཕྲིན་རྟགས་ (trīndaà) postage stamp.

འཕྲིན་རྟེན་སློབ་གྲྭ་ (trīnden lōbdra) sm. འཕྲིན་ཡིག་སློབ་གྲྭ་.

འཕྲིན་དེབ་ (trīnda) shung. a book containing official decress/ reports/ summaries.

འཕྲིན་བརྡ་ (trīnda) 1. signal. 2. notice (in a newspaper).

འཕྲིན་པ་ (trīmbə) messenger.

འཕྲིན་སྤྲིང་ (trīndriŋ) see འཕྲིན་.

འཕྲིན་བཟང་ (trīnsaŋ) good news/ tidings.

འཕྲིན་ཡིག (trīnyiì) correspondence, letters; va.—གཏོང་; —སྤྲིང་ to send letters, to correspond.

འཕྲིན་ཡིག་སྐྱེལ་གཏོང་ (trīnyiì gyēēdoŋ) postal and telegraphic communications.

འཕྲིན་ལན་ (trīnlɛn) reply, answer (to a letter or message); va.—གཏོང་; —སློག to reply/ answer (to a letter or message).

འཕྲིན་ལས་ (trīnlɛɛ̀) 1. deed, action, labor. 2. person's name.

འཕྲིན་ལས་རྒྱ་མཚོ་ (trīnlɛ̀ gya̱dzo) name of the 12th Dalai Lama (1856-1875).

འཕྲིན་བསྒྲིངས་ (trīnsiŋ) va. to send a message or letter.

འཕྲིས་ (grii) shung. abbr. of འཕྲིན་ལས་.

འཕྲུ་ (trū) sm. ཕྲུ་.

འཕྲུ་ཏོག (trūdoò) the top of official's hats in the traditional Tibetan government.

འཕྲུ་འདུལ་དོ་དམ་པ་ (trūndüü to̱damba) shung. a person in charge of breaking/ opening new land.

འཕྲུ་གསར་འདུལ་ཁོངས་ (trūsar dṳ̱ṳgoŋ) shung. the area/ expanse for breaking (opening) new land། ད་ནས་བཟུང་འཕྲུལ་གསར་འདུལ་ཁོངས་གསར་འཛུགས་བགྱིས་གཤིས་འཕྲུ་འདུལ་དོ་དམ་པས་ཉམས་ལེན་དང་ From now on because we have established the area for opening up new lands, the person in charge of opening up new land should take care of it.

འཕྲུག: p. འཕྲུགས་; f. འཕྲུག; imp. ཕྲུགས་ (trūù) 1. va. to scratch. 2. a unit, a complete entity། འཕྲུག་གཅིག One unit. །ཉིན་ཞག་འཕྲུག་གཅིག A day and night (24 hour period).

འཕྲུག་སྤྱད་ (trūgjɛɛ̀) a bamboo scratching stick used when itching.

འཕྲུགས་ (trūù) p. of འཕྲུག.

འཕྲུལ་ (trṳ̄ṳ̄) 1. vi. to change or transform form miraculously. 2. vi. to be perplexed/ dazed. 3. flirting; va.—ཤོད་.

འཕྲུལ་ཀོང་ (trṳ̄ṳ̄goŋ) a pot for smelting iron.

འཕྲུལ་བསྐུལ་ (trṳ̄ṳ̄güü) mechanical.

འཕྲུལ་བསྐུལ་འབྲུ་ལེན་འཕྲུལ་འཁོར་ (trṳ̄ṳ̄güü dru̱len trṳ̄ṳ̄gɔɔ) mechanical threshing machine.

འཕྲུལ་ཁང་ (trṳ̄ṳ̄gaŋ) sm. འཕྲུལ་བཟོ་ཁང་.

འཕྲུལ་འཁོར་ (trṳ̄ṳ̄gɔɔ) machine, machinery, mechanical equipment། ཤོག་བུ་གཏུབ་བྱེད་ཀྱི་འཕྲུལ་འཁོར་ Paper cutting machine.

འཕྲུལ་འཁོར་སྐོར་ (trṳ̄ṳ̄gɔɔ gɔ̄ɔ̄) va. to run/ operate a machine.

འཕྲུལ་འཁོར་འཁོར་ (trṳ̄ṳ̄gɔɔ kɔ̄ɔ̄) vi. to have a machine turn/ run.

འཕྲུལ་འཁོར་ལྗིད་རིགས་ (trṳ̄ṳ̄gɔɔ ji̱irig) heavy machinery.

འཕྲུལ་འཁོར་བདག་གཉེར་སྡེ་ཁག (trṳ̄ṳ̄gɔɔ da̱gñer de̱gaà) maintenance department (for machinery).

འཕྲུལ་འཁོར་མེད་པའི་གནམ་གྲུ་ (trṳ̄ṳ̄gɔɔ mɛ̄èbɛ nəmdru) glider (airplane).

འཕྲུལ་འཁོར་བརྩམས་ (trṳ̄ṳ̄gɔɔ tsām) shung. va. to plot། ཡུལ་གྲུ་འགའ་ཞིག་ཏུ་ངན་གཡོའི་འཕྲུལ་འཁོར་བརྩམས་པ་ Some evil people have plotted in various places.

འཕྲུལ་འཁོར་ཚོད་གཏོང་ (trṳ̄ṳ̄gɔɔ tsȫȫdoŋ) test or trial of a machine.

འཕྲུལ་འཁོར་བཟོ་པ་ (trṳ̄ṳ̄gɔɔ so̱ba) machine operator.

འཕྲུལ་འཁོར་བཟོ་བྱེད་བཟོ་ལས་ (trṳ̄ṳ̄gɔɔ so̱jeè so̱lɛɛ̀) sm. འཕྲུལ་འཁོར་བཟོ་ལས་.

འཕྲུལ་འཁོར་བཟོ་སྐྲུན་བཟོ་གྲྭ་ (trṳ̄ṳ̄gɔɔ so̱drün so̱dra) building machine factory.

འཕྲུལ་འཁོར་བཟོ་ལས་ (trṳ̄ṳ̄gɔɔ so̱lɛɛ̀) building machine industry.

འཕྲུལ་འཁོར་ཡོ་ཆས་ཉམས་གསོ་ལྷུ་སྒྲིག་བབས་ཚུགས་ (trṳ̄ṳ̄gɔɔ yo̱jɛɛ̀ ñamso lhūdrig bə̱bdzüü) machine repair and assembly station.

འཕྲུལ་འཁོར་ཨ་མ་ (trṳ̄ṳ̄gɔɔ āma) the main machine, the engine.

འཕྲུལ་གྲུ་ (trṳ̄ṳ̄dru) steamboat, steamer.

འཕྲུལ་གློག (trṳ̄ṳ̄lɔ̄ɔ̀) electrical, electronics.

འཕྲུལ་གློག་ཀུང་སི་ (trṳ̄ṳ̄lɔ̄ɔ̀ gūŋsi) electrical/ electronics company.

འཕྲུལ་གློག་བཟོ་པ་ (trṳ̄ṳ̄lɔ̄ɔ̀ so̱ba) electrician, electrical worker.

འཕྲུལ་གློག་ལྷུ་སྒྲིག་བཟོ་པ་ (trṳ̄ṳ̄lɔ̄ɔ̀ lhūdrig so̱ba) electricians and mechanics.

འཕྲུལ་འགྱུར་ཞིང་ར་ (trṳ̄ngyur shi̱ŋrə) mechanized farm.

འཕྲུལ་སྒུལ་ (trũũgüü) sm. འཕྲུལ་སྐུལ་.

འཕྲུལ་སྒུལ་འཁོར་ལོ་ (trũũgüü kɔ̄ɔ̄lo) motor car/ vehicle.

འཕྲུལ་ངན་ (trũũŋɛn) evil plot.

འཕྲུལ་ཆ་ (trũũja) 1. machinery. 2. weapons.

འཕྲུལ་ཆས་ (trũũjɛɛ̀) machines, machinery, mechanized ¶ འཕྲུལ་ཆས་ཀྱིས་རྩྭ་གསོ་བའི་ས་ཚུགས་ Mechanized grass-growing station.

འཕྲུལ་ཆས་ཀྱི་དཔུང་ཁག (trũũjɛɛ̀gi pūŋgaà) sm. འཕྲུལ་ཆས་ཅན་གྱི་དམག་དཔུང་.

འཕྲུལ་ཆས་ཀྱིས་ (trũũjɛɛ̀gi) mechanized ¶ འཕྲུལ་ཆས་ཀྱིས་མེ་འགོག་ས་ཚུགས་ Mechanized fire prevention station.

འཕྲུལ་ཆས་བཀོལ་སྤྱོད་ (trũũjɛɛ̀ gōòjöò) mechanical operation.

འཕྲུལ་ཆས་ཁང་ (trũũjɛɛ̀gaŋ) 1. generator or motor room, machine room. 2. engine room (of a ship). 3. instrument room.

འཕྲུལ་ཆས་ཅན་གྱི་དམག་དཔུང་ (trũũjɛɛ̀jɛngi māgbuŋ) mechanized troops, mechanized unit (in army).

འཕྲུལ་ཆས་ཅན་དུ་འགྱུར་ (trũũjɛɛ̀jɛndu gyur) vi. to be/ get mechanized.

འཕྲུལ་ཆས་ཅན་ཕྱེད་ཙམ་དུ་འགྱུར་ (trũũjɛɛ̀jɛn cēèdzamdu gyur) vi. to be/ get semimechanized.

འཕྲུལ་ཆས་ཆུ་གཏོང་ས་ཚིགས་ (trũũjɛɛ̀ cūdoŋ sādziì) mechanized water pumping station.

འཕྲུལ་ཆས་གླིང་རིགས་ (trũũjɛɛ̀ jiirig) sm. འཕྲུལ་འཁོར་གླིང་རིགས་.

འཕྲུལ་ཆས་མཚོན་ཆ་ (trũũjɛɛ̀ tsōnja) mechanized weapons.

འཕྲུལ་ཆས་བཟོ་བཀོད་ (trũũjɛɛ̀ sogöò) mechanical engineering.

འཕྲུལ་ཆས་བཟོ་སྐྲུན་སློབ་ཚོགས་ (trũũjɛɛ̀ sodrün lōbtsoò) Society of Mechanical Engineering.

འཕྲུལ་ཆས་བཟོ་གྲྭ་ (trũũjɛɛ̀ sodra) machine factory/ shop.

འཕྲུལ་ཆས་བཟོ་ལས་ (trũũjɛɛ̀ solɛɛ̀) machine/ mechanical machine industry.

འཕྲུལ་ཆས་ཡོ་བྱད་བཟོ་གྲྭ་ (trũũjɛɛ̀ yobjɛɛ̀ sodra) machine and tool factory.

འཕྲུལ་ཆས་རླུང་ཡོལ་ཅན་གྱི་གྲུ་ (trũũjɛɛ̀ lūŋyüüjɛngi tru) motorized sailboat.

འཕྲུལ་ཆས་ལས་ཀ་ (trũũjɛɛ̀ lɛɛga) work done by machinery (as opposed to hand labor).

འཕྲུལ་སྣེགས་ (trũũdeg) machine tools, lathe ¶ ལྕགས་རིགས་གཏུབ་གཞོག་འཕྲུལ་སྣེགས་ Metal cutting machine.

འཕྲུལ་སྣེགས་བཟོ་གྲྭ་ (trũũdeg sodra) machine tool/ lathe factory.

འཕྲུལ་སྟོབས་ (trũũdob) mechanical power, the energy/ strength/ power of a machine.

འཕྲུལ་ཐུར་ (trũũdur) a traditional Tibetan surgical catheter-like tool used to open a blocked urinary track.

འཕྲུལ་མདའ་ (trũnda) all modern guns (as opposed to matchlock guns).

འཕྲུལ་མདེའུ་ (trũndiwu) rocket.

འཕྲུལ་མདེལ་མེ་སྒྱོགས་ (trũndee mergyoò) modern (mechanized) artillery.

འཕྲུལ་འདེགས་སྲིན་ཟམ་ (trũndeè drĩnsam) a mechanical drawbridge.

འཕྲུལ་ནམ་གཞུང་བཙན་ལྡེ་ (trũũnam shuŋdzɛn de) the 17th ancient Tibetan King.

འཕྲུལ་སྣང་ (trũũnaŋ) 1. illusion, apparition, fantasy. 2. perplexed, bewildered, dazed; vi.—སྐྱེ་ to be perplexed/ bewildered/ dazed.

འཕྲུལ་སྣང་གི་ཇོ་བོ་ (trũũnaŋgi jowo) the statue of the Buddha in the Jokang brought by the wife of Srongtsen Gampo.

འཕྲུལ་སྣང་གཙུག་ལག་ཁང་ (trũũnaŋ tsūglagaŋ) the Lhasa cathedral which houses the Jokang chapel.

འཕྲུལ་སྣུམ་ (trũũnum) machine oil.

འཕྲུལ་ཕྱེད་ཅན་ (trũũjeèjɛn) semimechanized ¶ འཕྲུལ་ཕྱེད་ཅན་བྱ་གསོ་ར་བ་ Semimechanized chicken farm.

འཕྲུལ་འཕང་ (trũũpaŋ) spinning machine.

འཕྲུལ་འཕྱག (trũũjaà) vacuum cleaner.

འཕྲུལ་བག (trũũbaà) attitude/ appearance of flirting.

འཕྲུལ་བློན་ (trũũlön) wise/ learned minister.

འཕྲུལ་མ་ (trũũmə) 1. a screw. 2. a flirty/ coquettish woman.

འཕྲུལ་མིག་སྟོན་ (trũũmiì dõn) sm. འཕྲུལ་མིག་ལྟ་.

འཕྲུལ་མིག (trũũmiì) flirting (with the eyes); va.—ལྟ་.

འཕྲུལ་སྦུད་ (trũũbüù) mechanical blower.

འཕྲུལ་མེད་གནམ་གྲུ་ (trũũmeè nāmdru) sm. འཕྲུ་འཁོར་མེད་པའི་གནམ་གྲུ་.

འཕྲུལ་རྨོད་རུ་ཁག (trũũmöò rugaà) mechanized farm team.

འཕྲུལ་རྨོས་ (trũũmo) mechanized farming/ plowing; va.—རྒྱག to plow/ farm by machine.

འཕྲུལ་རྩལ་ཚོགས་པ་ (trũũdzɛɛ tsōgba) acrobatic troupe.

འཕྲུལ་ཚ་པོ་ (trũũ tsābo) a flirt.

འཕྲུལ་གཞུ་ (trũũshu) crossbow.

འཕྲུལ་བཟོ་ (trũũso) making/ producing machines.

འཕྲུལ་བཟོ་ཁང་ (trũũsogaŋ) machine workshop/ factory.

འཕྲུལ་བཟོའི་སྤྱི་ཁྱབ་ (trũũsö jĩgyəb) Minister of Industry.

འཕྲུལ་བཟོས་ (trũũsöò) machine-made ¶ འཕྲུལ་བཟོས་ཤོག་བུ་ Machine-made paper.

འཕྲུལ་གཡོར་གཉིས་ལྡན་གྱི་གྲུ་གཟིངས་ (trũũyɔɔñiìdɛngi trusiŋ) motorized sailboat.

འཕྲུལ་ལས་ (trũũlɛɛ̀) mechanical work, technology ¶ འཕྲུལ་ལས་ཀྱི་རོགས་རམ་ Technological assistance.

འཕྲུལ་ལས་བཟོ་པ་ (trũũlɛɛ̀ soba) machine worker.

འཕྲུལ་ལས་བཟོ་རིག (trũũlɛɛ̀ sorig) technology.

འཕྲུལ་ལས་སོ་ཕག་བཟོ་གྲྭ་ (trũũlɛɛ̀ sōbaà sodra) machine-made brick factory.

འཕྲུལ་ཤེས་ (trũũsheè) sense of being perplexed/ dazed.

འཕྲུལ་གཤེན་ (trũũshen) the founder of the Bon religion.

འཕྲུལ་བཤད་ (trũũshɛɛ̀) flirting (usu. refers to flirting in speech); va.—གཏོང་ to flirt.

འཕྲུལ་སློབ་ (trũũ lōb) va. to learn many methods/ ways/ means.

འཕྲེང་ (trēŋ) 1. sm. ཕྲེང་. 2. vi. to be attached/ fastened.

འཕྲེང་རྒྱུད་ (trēŋgyüü) sm. ཕྲེང་རྒྱུད་.

འཕྲེང་ཐག (trēŋdaà) sm. ཕྲེང་ཐག.

འཕྲེང་མདའ་ (trēŋda) sm. ཕྲེང་མདའ་.

འཕྲེང་དོག (trēŋdɔɔ̀) sm. ཕྲེང་དོག.

འཕྲེད་ (trēè) transverse, crosswise, across, horizontal, sideways.

འཕྲེད་ཀོ་ (trēègɔɔ) a coracle that crosses a river crosswise (rather than going downstream).

འཕྲེད་སྣད་ (trēègüü) 1. weft. 2. a thick string stitched along the edges of a thanka.

འཕྲེད་གླིང་ (trēèliŋ) transverse flute.

འཕྲེད་འགེལ་དར་ཆ་ (trēègee tarja) a horizontal flag/ banner (e.g., those carried at demonstrations).

འཕྲེད་རྒྱག (trēègyuù) sm. འཕྲེད་རྒྱུགས་, 1.

འཕྲེད་རྒྱུགས་ (trēègyuù) 1. a pole used to block a road. 2. sm. འཕྲེད་.

འཕྲེད་རྒྱུགས་རི་རྒྱུད་ (trēègyuù rigyüü) transverse mountain range.

འཕྲེད་ལྕམ་ (trēèjam) rafter.

འཕྲེད་གཅོད་ (trēèjöò) cutting transversely/ across; va.—བྱེད་.

འཕྲེད་གཅོད་ཆུ་རགས་ (trēèjöò cūraà) regulating dam.

འཕྲེད་གཅོད་ཆུ་སྒོ་ (trēèjöò cūgo) a gate for stopping or regulating the flow of water.

འཕྲེད་བཅད་ (trēèjɛɛ̀) sm. འཕྲེད་གཅོད་.

འཕྲེ་བཅད་ཀྱི་ངོས་ (trēèjɛɛ̀gi ŋöò) cross section, transverse section.

འཕྲེད་བཅད་གཏོང་ (trēèjɛɛ̀ dōŋ) va. to cut transversely, to cut across.

འཕྲེད་ཉལ་ (trēèñɛɛ) sleeping or lying sideways/

laterally on a bed; va.—བྱེད་.

འཕྲེད་བསྙལ་ (trēèñεε) sideways, laterally; va.—གཏོང་ to place or lay sideways/ laterally.

འཕྲེད་གདན་ (trēèdεn) bolt, bar (of door or gate); va.—རྒྱག to bolt, to lock.

འཕྲེད་ཐང་ (trēètaŋ) a horizontal tanka.

འཕྲེད་ཐིག (trēèdig) latitude, parallel ¶ ཕྲེད་ཐིག་ཉི་ཤུ་ The 20th parallel/ latitude.

འཕྲེད་ཐིག་ཀླད་སྐོར་ (trēèdig lε̄ὲgɔɔ) the equator.

འཕྲེད་ཐིག་གི་དུའུ་གྲངས་ (trēèdiggi dūraŋ) tib.ch. degrees of latitude.

འཕྲེད་ཐིག་སོ་བརྒྱད་པ་ (trēèdig sōbgyεὲ) the 38th Parallel (in Korea).

འཕྲེད་དར་ (trēèdar) sm. འཕྲེད་འགེལ་དར་ཆ་.

འཕྲེད་དུ་ (trēèdu) transversely, crossways, across.

འཕྲེད་གདུང་ (trēèduŋ) beams that are put laterally/ sideways.

འཕྲེད་སྤུན་ (trēèbün) weft.

འཕྲེད་བྱང་ (trēèjaŋ) sm. འཕྲེད་དར་.

འཕྲེད་བྲིས་ (trēèdrii) writing left to right or right to left (horizontally as opposed to vertically).

འཕྲེད་གཞུང་ (trēèshuŋ) vertically (front to back) and horizontally (top to botttom), width and length.

འཕྲེད་གཞུང་དཔྱད་ཆས་ (trēèshuŋ jε̄ὲjεὲ) theodolite (surveyor's instrument).

འཕྲེད་གཞུང་ལྡན་པ་ (trēèshuŋ m̱eèba) reasonable.

འཕྲེད་གཞུང་མེད་པ་ (trēèshuŋ m̱eèba) shameless.

འཕྲེད་གཟེར་ (trēèser) nails put in laterally/ sideways; va.—རྒྱག.

འཕྲེད་ལ་ (trēèla) sm. འཕྲེད་དུ་.

འཕྲེད་ལམ་ (trēèlam) side street, a path/ road that cuts across sth.

འཕྲེད་ཤིང་ (trēèshiŋ) wood used horizontally (usu. for doors and windows).

འཕྲེད་ཤོལ་ (trēèshöö) three by five/ six feet Tibetan rugs.

འཕྲེད་གཤག (trēèshaà) cutting in half (widthwise); va.—གཏོང་.

འཕྲེས་ (trēè) va. to lean back.

འཕྲོ་: p. འཕྲོས་; f. འཕྲོ་ (trō) vi. to radiate, to emanate, to shine, to give off/ emit light ¶ ཁང་པའི་གློག་བཞུ་འོད་ཆེམ་ཆེམ་དུ་འཕྲོ་གི་འདུག The electric lights of the house are shining.

འཕྲོ་ (trō) 1. leftover, remainder ¶ བཟས་འཕྲོ་ Leftover food. 2. (vb. + — + vb.) to leave/ stop doing the verbal action ¶ ཁོང་ཡོང་ཙང་ངས་དེབ་ཀློག་འཕྲོ་བཞག་པ་ཡིན་ I stopped reading the book (without completing it) because he came. ¶ ཁོ་སྐད་ཆ་ཤོད་འཕྲོ་ལང་ནས་འགྲོ་དགོས་བྱུང་སོང་ He had to get up and go in the middle of the discussion.

འཕྲོ་སྐྱོང་ (trōgyoŋ) continuing one's leftover work, completing the work one has left; va.—བྱེད་.

འཕྲོ་འགུམ་པར་ཆད་ (trō g̱umbar cε̄ὲ) sm. འཕྲོ་ཆད་.

འཕྲོ་གོད་ (trō g̱öò) vi. to be absentminded.

འཕྲོ་ཅན་ (trōjεn) leftover, remainder ¶ ལས་ཀ་འཕྲོ་ཅན་ནི་ As for the leftover work.

འཕྲོ་གཅོད་ (trō jȫò) va. to discontinue, to stop in the middle.

འཕྲོ་ཆ་ (trōja) leftover, remainder.

འཕྲོ་ཆགས་ (trō cāà) vi. to have sth. leftover, to have a remainder.

འཕྲོ་ཆད་ (trō cε̄ὲ) vi. to have sth. unfinished, to have sth. that has been left to complete.

འཕྲོ་ཐིག (trōdig) glittering rays/ spots, radiating/ shinning rays.

འཕྲོ་བསྡུད་ (trōdüü) sm. འཕྲོར་མཐུད་.

འཕྲོ་མཐུད་ (trōdüù) sm. འཕྲོར་མཐུད་.

འཕྲོ་བའི་རང་བཞིན་ (trōwε ṟəŋshin) radioactivity.

འཕྲོ་སླངས་ (trō lāŋ) va. to continue/ take up where sth. was left off.

འཕྲོ་མ་ (trōma) sm. འཕྲོ་ཆ་.

འཕྲོ་མ་བཅད་ (trō m̱ajεὲ) without break, continuously.

འཕྲོ་བཞག (trō sẖaà) va. to adjourn/ discontinue.

འཕྲོ་འོད་ (trōwöò) radiating, shining, glittering.

འཕྲོ་ལུས་ (trō ḻüù) vi. to have sth. leftover/ unfinished, to have an aftershock.

འཕྲོ་བརླག (trōlaà) 1. wasting; va.—གཏོང་ to waste; vi.—འགྲོ་ to go to waste, to become spoiled. 2. spoiling, leading astray; va.—གཏོང་.

འཕྲོ་བཤོལ་ (trō shȫȫ) va. to discontinue, to leave off doing sth.

འཕྲོ་ལྷག (trōlhaà) sm. འཕྲོ་ཆ་.

འཕྲོག: p. ཕྲོགས་; f. འཕྲོག; imp. ཕྲོགས་ (trɔ̄ɔ̀) va. to take away by force, to seize, to steal.

འཕྲོག་བཅོམ་ (trɔ̄gjom) robbing, plundering, looting; va.—བྱེད་ ¶ ཇག་པས་གྲོང་གསེབ་པར་འཕྲོག་བཅོམ་བྱས་འདུག The bandits robbed the villagers.

འཕྲོག་བྱེད་ (trɔ̄gjeè) 1. Vishnu. 2. lion ¶ འཕྲོག་བྱེད་སྡེར་མོ་བཏེགས་པའི་ཁྲི་འཕང་སྟོར་ On the high throne that is lifted by lions.

འཕྲོག་རེས་ (trɔ̄greè) stealing back and forth, plundering mutually.

འཕྲོག་བརླག (trōlaà) sm. འཕྲོ་བརླག.

འཕྲོག་ལེན་ (trɔ̄glen) sm. འཕྲོག.

འཕྲོད་ (tröò) 1. vi. to be suited for, to be good for, to be adapted to, to suit ¶ ལུང་པ་འདིའི་གནམ་གཤིས་འདི་ང་འཕྲོད་ཀྱི་མི་འདུག The climate of this country does not suit me. 2. vi. to receive, to get (letters, messages, etc.) ¶ ཁོང་ལ་ཡི་གེ་འདི་འཕྲོད་མི་འདུག He did not get the letter. 3. health, health treatment.

འཕྲོད་གོམས་ (trȫògom) getting acclimated/ accustomed/ used to ¶ ས་མཐོའི་ཐོག་ཐག་རིང་དཔུང་བསྐྱོད་བྱེད་རྒྱུར་འཕྲོད་གོམས་ཡོང་ཆེད་ In order to get acclimated to marching long distances at high altitude.

འཕྲོད་རྟགས་ (trȫòdaà) receipt.

འཕྲོད་བསྟེན་ (trȫòden) health care, hygiene, public health; va.—བྱེད་ ¶ ལུས་པའི་འཕྲོད་བསྟེན་ Personal hygiene.

འཕྲོད་བསྟེན་ཁང་ (trȫòdengaŋ) public health center, public health clinic.

འཕྲོད་བསྟེན་ཁྲུའུ་ (trȫòden drū) tib.ch. public health division.

འཕྲོད་བསྟེན་ཙུའུ་ (trȫòden jū) tib.ch. bureau of public health.

འཕྲོད་བསྟེན་ཐིན་ (trȫòden tīn) tib.ch. department of public health.

འཕྲོད་བསྟེན་སྡེ་ཚན་ (trȫòden ḏedzεn) public health office.

འཕྲོད་བསྟེན་པ་ (trȫòdenba) health worker, public health worker.

འཕྲོད་བསྟེན་པུའུ་ (trȫòden bū) tib.ch. ministry of public health.

འཕྲོད་བསྟེན་སྨན་ཁང་ (trȫòden mε̄ngaŋ) health care center, public health hospital.

འཕྲོད་བསྟེན་ཚགས་པར་ (trȫòden tsāgba) health/ hygiene newspaper.

འཕྲོད་བསྟེན་རིག་པ་ (trȫòden ṟigbə) the field of hygiene/ public health.

འཕྲོད་བསྟེན་རིམས་འགོག (trȫòden ṟimgɔɔ̀) public health and epidemic prevention.

འཕྲོད་བསྟེན་ལས་བྱེད་སྦྱོང་བརྡར་འཛིན་གྲྭ (trȫòden ḻεὲjeè j̱oŋdar dẕindra) public health training class for cadre.

འཕྲོད་བསྟེན་སློབ་གྲྭ (trȫòden lōbdra) public health school.

འཕྲོད་ཐབས་ (trȫòdəb) means, ways ¶ ས་མཐོའི་དམིགས་བསལ་གྱི་གནམ་གཤིས་འཕྲོད་ཐབས་སྐོར་གྱི་ཤེས་བྱ་ Knowledge regarding the means of adaptation to the special weather of high altitude places.

འཕྲོད་པ་ (trȫòba) suitable, proper, fit, agreeing with ¶ ས་བབས་དང་འཕྲོད་པའི་ཉ་ལས་ཐོན་སྐྱེད་ Fish production which is suitable to the landscape/ topography.

འཕྲོད་པའི་རང་བཞིན་ (trȫòbε ṟəŋshin) adaptability, suitability.

འཕྲོད་པོ་ (trȫòbo) suitable, suited, good for, agreeable ¶ ཚ་བར་ཡོད་པའི་ས་ཆར་ཤིང་ཏོག་འཕྲོད་པོ་ཡོད་པ་རེད་ In hot climates fruits are good for you.

འཕྲོད་སྦྱོར་ལེགས་འཛོམས་ (trööjɔɔ le̱ŋdzom) shung. auspicious (day).

འཕྲོད་འཛིན་ (tröndzin) receipt, written acknowledgment.

འཕྲོད་བཞེས་ (tröö she̱è) va. to take treatment ༖ ཆུ་ཚན་འཕྲོད་བཞེས་དུ་ཕེབས་ (He) came to take the hot springs treatment.

འཕྲོད་ལམ་ (tröölam) suitable, appropriate.

འཕྲོད་ཤུགས་ (trööshuù) suitability, fitness.

འཕྲོད་གཤིས་ (trööshiì) suitable/ appropriate weather/ climate.

འཕྲོར་མཐུད་ (trɔ̈r tǖǖ) vi. to continue/ take up where sth. was left off ༖ དུས་དེབ་གོང་མའི་འཕྲུར་མཐུད་རྒྱུ་ Continued from the previous magazine (issue).

འཕྲོས་ (trö̃ö) 1. p.of འཕྲོ་. 2. continuation (of articles in a newspaper/ magazine) ༖ གཟའ་འཁོར་སྔོན་མའི་འཕྲོས་ Continuation of last week's (article). 4. (vb. + —) while, during ༖ ལྟོ་ཟ་འཕྲོས་ While eating.

འཕྲོས་བསྒྲིགས་ (trööd rig) sm. འཕྲོས་སྒྲིག.

འཕྲོས་སྒྲིག (trööd rig) supplement, supplementary chapter.

འཕྲོས་ངན་ (trööŋɛn) shung. bad/ evil talks.

འཕྲོས་གཏམ་ (trööd am) 1. talk, conversation. 2. jumping from one subject/ topic to another when talking.

འཕྲོས་གཏམ་བན་བུན་ (trööd am be̱nbün) hearsay talk.

འཕྲོས་དོན་ (trööd ön) footnote, supplement, annotation.

འཕྲོས་པ་འདྲི་ཡུལ་ (trööba tri̱yüü) shung. someone to ask sth.

འཕྲོས་པ་བྱེད་ (trööba ce̱è) va. to discuss.

འཕྲོས་མོལ་ (trööm öö) a discussion/ talk that is leftover or not finished; va.—བྱེད་ ༖ ཁྱེད་རང་གཉིས་ཀྱི་འཕྲོས་མོལ་ཐག་གཅོད་བྱེད་རྩིས་ཡོད་པས་ Do you two plan to settle the unfinished talk? ༖ རྒྱ་བོད་ཀྱི་འཕྲོས་མོལ་བྱེད་དུ་སུ་ཕྱིན་པ་རེད་ Who went to conduct the remaining talks between China and India.

འཕྲོས་ཚབ་ (trööd zəb) replacement.

འཕྲོས་འཛར་ (tröndzar) sth. leftover, a remnant.

འཕྲོས་འོས་ (trööw öö) sth. that should be told/ said.

འཕྲོས་འོས་ཀྱང་འཚལ་ (trööw öögyaŋ tsɛɛ) shung. (manner of writing in official documents): If you have anything that should be told please write it.

འཕྲོས་ལས་ (dröölɛɛ̀) sm. འཕྲོས་ལུས་.

འཕྲོས་ལུས་ (dröölüü) remaining, leftover ༖ འཕྲོས་ལུས་གསུམ་ The remaining three.

འཕྲོས་བཤད་འཕྲོས་གཏམ་ (drööshɛɛ̀ drööd am) sm. འཕྲོས་གཏམ་.

འཕྲོས་སོང་ (drööso ŋ) sm. འཕྲོས་ལུས་.

འཕྲོད་ལྷག (dröölhaà) sm. འཕྲོས་འཛར་.

པ་ (pa) 1. cow. 2. particle used after final ང་, འ་, ར་, ལ་ and vowels indicating past tense ། ཁོས་ཡི་གེ་བཏང་པ་རེད་ He sent a letter. 3. agentive particle ། ཤིང་བཟོ་པ་ A carpenter. 4. nominalizing particle ། ཡི་གེ་གཏོང་པ་ཁག་པོ་རེད་ Sending letters is difficult. 5. the letter པ་ used in alphabetical order.

པ་ཀུ་ལ་ (pāgula) one of the 16 arhats.

པ་སྐྱ་ (pagya) dry nasal mucus/ snot.

པ་ཁྱུ་ (pəgyu) a herd of cows.

པ་འཁོར་ (pagɔɔ) a bib for babies that is square with a hole in the middle.

པ་གམ་ (pagam) a large house, a multistory house.

པ་གམ་མངོན་མཐོར་འཕགས་པ་ (pagam ŋōndɔr pāgba) shung. benevolent ། ཟབ་པ་དང་རྒྱ་ཆེའི་ཞབས་ཆེན་འཁྲིན་ལས་ཀྱི་པ་གམ་མངོན་མཐོར་འཕགས་བཞིན་པར་འཚོ་ཞིང་བཞེས་པ་ (We wish) your excellency good health and a long life and that you will continue your benevolent protection to us.

པ་གྲུས་མ་ (pa drüümə) sm. པ་དྲུས་མ་.

པ་གླང་ (palaŋ) sm. པ་ལང་.

པ་གླང་སྤྱོད་ (palaŋjöö) one of the four continents surrounding mount Meru.

པ་རྒན་གྱིས་བེའུ་ལྡག་པ་ (pagɛngi pewu dagba) parental love [Lit. an old cow licking a calf].

པ་རྒྱ་ (pagya) web, cobweb, spider's web.

པ་ལྕི་ (pəji) cow manure/ dung.

པ་ཆུ་ (pəju) cow urine (used in Tibetan medicine).

པ་འཇོ་ (pa jo) va. to milk a cow.

པ་ཉལ་མཛོ་གྲོད་ (pa ñɛɛ dzo tröö) derogatory term used for people who eat a lot and are lazy [Lit. sleeping cow, dzo's stomach].

པ་ཉལ་ཉལ་ཉལ་ (pañɛɛ ñɛɛñɛɛ) to sleep late [Lit. to sleep like a cow].

པ་སྙི་ (pañi) sm. པ་ལྕི་.

པ་ཏ་ (pada) a stack of barley straw (left in the field after harvest).

པ་ཐག་ (padaà) 1. sm. པ་རྒྱ་. 2. a web of tree roots.

པ་ད་ག་ (padaga) (vb.+ —) as soon as ། དཀའ་ལས་ཏོག་ཙམ་ཁ་པ་ད་ག་ As soon as he gets a little tired.

པ་དན་ (padɛn) banner, flag.

པ་དམ་ (paam) hind. peanut.

པ་དྲུས་མ་ (pa drüümə) milch cow.

པ་བདག་ (padag) shung. cow owner.

པ་ནུ་ (panu) cow udder.

པ་སྤུ་ (pabu) body hair; vi.—ལངས་; —གཡོ་ to have one's body hair stand on end out of fear/ fright.

པ་སྤུ་མེ་ཏོག་ (pabu medog) jasmine.

པ་སྤུ་ཙམ་ (pabudzam) a tiny bit ། ནོར་སྤུ་ཙམ་ཡོད་པ་མ་རེད་ There is not even a tiny mistake.

པ་སྤུ་ཟིང་དགོས་པ་ (pabu siŋ gööba) extremely frightened.

པ་སྤུ་གཡོ་ (pabu yō) vi. to have one's hair stand on end out of fear. 2. vi. to be deeply moved ། ཁོང་གི་གསུང་བཤད་ངེས་ངའི་ལུས་ཀྱི་པ་སྤུ་གཡོས་བྱུང་ I was deeply moved by his talk.

པ་སྤུ་ལངས་ (pabu laŋ) sm. པ་སྤུ་གཡོ་.

པ་སྤུའི་བུ་ག་ (pabu puga) skin pore.

པ་ཕྱུགས་ (pəjuù) cow.

པ་ཕྱེད་ (pajeè) sm. པ་ཟུར་.

པ་ཕྲུག་ (pədruù) calf.

པ་བེའུ་ཤི་དུ་ (pa piwu shī ŋu) shung. abbr. of པ་བེའུ་ཤི་དུས་ངུ་དགོས་.

པ་བེའུ་ཤི་དུས་ངུ་དགོས་ (pa piwu shīdüü ŋugɔɔ) shung. one should act or speak at the time when sth. takes place [Lit. when the calf dies the cow should cry].

པ་བླ་ (pala) auripimentum (used in Tibetan medicine).

པ་མ་ (pama) a kind of hand drill.

པ་མ་ཤི་ལྟོ་ཉོག་རྒྱུན་མི་འཆད་ (pa mashi jīñog gyün mijɛɛ̀) so long as the troublemaker is still around there will always be trouble [Lit. until the cow dies there will be cow dung].

པ་མར་ (pamar) butter made from cow's milk.

པ་མེན་ (pamen) wild ox.

པ་མོ་ (pamo) 1. hoarfrost, frost; vi.—འབབ་ to frost over, to get frost. 2. cow.

པ་མོ་དབྱར་བཞོ་དགུན་གསོ་གསོ་ (pamo yārsho günnɛɛ̀ sō) (one) must plan/ prepare for the future [Lit. if one wants cow milk in the summer then one must care for the cow in the winter].

པ་མོ་མེད་པའི་མར་དགྲོག (pamo meebɛ maadrɔɔ) income without a source [Lit. having butter without a cow].

པ་མོས་འཇོམས་ (pamöö jom) vi. to be destroyed by frost.

པ་རྨིག་ (pamig) cow hoof.

པ་ཚང་ (padzaŋ) cowshed.

པ་ཚྭ་ (padza) alkaline, saline.

པ་ཚྭ་ཅན་གྱི་ས་ (padzajɛngi sā) alkaline soil.

པ་ཚྭ་ཅན་གྱི་ས་ཞིང་ (padzajɛngi sɘshiŋ) alkaline land/ fields.

པ་ཚྭ་ཆུ་ (padza cū) brine. alkaline water.

པ་ཚྭའི་རང་བཞིན་ (padzɛ rəŋshin) alkalinity, salinity.

པ་མཛོ་ (padzo) cross between a cow and a yak.

པ་རྫི་ (padzi) cow herder.

པ་བཞོ་མ་ (pa shoma) milch cow.

པ་འོ་ (pawo) cow's milk.

པ་ཡར་ (payar) sm. པ་ཡར་མ་.

པ་ཡར་མ་ (pa yarma) a cow that gave birth the previous year.

པ་ར་ (para) sm. པ་ཚང་.

པ་ར་བོང་གསུམ་ (pa ra poŋsum) abbr. the three: cow, goat and donkey.

པ་རི་ (pari) a type of hat worn by ancient soldiers.

པ་རི་བུ་རི་ (pari buri) bumpy.

པ་རུ་ར་ (parura) chinoberry (used in Tibetan medicine).

པ་རུ་བཞི་སྦྱོར་ (paru shijɔɔ) a medicine made from chinoberry that is used to treat syphilis.

པ་རེ་བེ་རེ་ (pare bere) 1. uneasy, disturbed, bothered; va.—བྱེད་ ། གནས་ཚུལ་ངན་པ་དེ་གོ་ནས་སེམས་པ་པ་རེ་བེ་རེ་བྱེད་ཀྱི་འདུག་ After hearing the bad news, I feel uneasy. 2. tipsy, slightly drunk; vi.—བཟི་ to be tipsy/ slightly drunk ། ཁོ་ར་པ་རེ་བེ་རེ་བཟི་བཞག་ He was slightly drunk.

པ་རེ་བོ་རེ་ (pare bore) careless; va.—བྱེད་ to do carelessly ། ཁོས་ལས་ཀ་པ་རེ་བོ་རེ་བྱས་ནས་ནོར་འཁྲུལ་མང་པོ་ཤོར་བཞག་ He worked carelessly and made many mistakes.

པ་ལ་ཕྱར་བ་གཡོགས་པ་ (pala cārwa yɔ̄ɔba) wearing oversized clothes [Lit. putting a ground sheet on a cow].

པ་ལང་ (palaŋ) 1. abbr. cow and ox/ bull. 2. ox, cattle.

པ་ལང་ཀང་པ་ (palaŋ gāŋba) the 8th month of the Tibetan calendar.

པ་ལང་རྒྱལ་འདེད་ (palaŋ gyɛnjuù) shung. making sb. do sth. by force ། ལུགས་གཉིས་ཁྲིམས་སྲོལ་བཅང་པོར་ཧ་མི་སྐམ་པ་འགའ་ཞིག་ནས་པ་ལང་རྒྱལ་འདེད་ལྟ་བུའི་ཚུལ་མིན་བྱ་སྤྱོད་སྣ་ཚོགས་ལ་བརྟེན་ Some people who disregard the spiritual and the temporal law and drive people by force just like driving cows/ oxen into the water [Lit. to drive a cow/ ox into the water].

པ་ལང་སྐྱོང་བ་ (palaŋ gyōŋwa) 1. herder of cows and oxen. 2. owner of cows and oxen.

པ་ལང་ལྤྱི་པ་ (palaŋ jīwə) the root of dahurian angelica (used in Tibetan medicine).

པ་ལང་ལྤྱི་ (palaŋ jē) sm. ཁུར་མང་.

པ་ལང་སྤྱོད་ (palaŋ jȫȍ) sm. པ་གླང་སྤྱོད་.

པ་ལང་མི་གཟུགས་ (palaŋ misug) stupid, dumb, ignorant. [Lit. cow/ ox., human body].

པ་ལང་མིག་རྗེས་ (palaŋ mi̱gjeè) tracks made by cows and oxen.

པ་ལང་ཤིང་རྟ་ (palaŋ shi̱ŋdə) bullock cart.

པ་ལུ་ (pəlu) azalea.

པ་ལུད་ (pəlüü) cow/ cattle manure.

པ་ལེ་ཀ་ (palega) a type of birthwort (used in Tibetan medicine).

པ་ལེ་བོ་ལེ་ (pale bole) soft.

པ་ཤ་ (pasha) beef.

པ་ཤ་ཀ་ (pashaga) a type of figwort.

པ་ཤུ་ (pəshu) a severe boil/ sore.

པ་ཤེ་ (pashe) lease fee for a cow (paid in milk and cheese).

པ་ཤེ་གླང་འགེལ་ (pashe lāŋgee) shung. making sb. do work that sb. else should be doing ། ཁྲལ་གསལ་ཁྲལ་རིགས་མི་སྡེར་པ་ཤེ་གླང་འགེལ་མི་འབྱུང་བ་དགོས་རྒྱུ་ The taxes should be imposed on those who should pay them rather than on subjects in general. [Lit. the cow lease fee imposed on the ox/ bull].

པ་བཤའ་བ་ལས་བཞོ་བ་དགའ་ (pa shāwalɛ showa ga) a little bit of sth. every day is better than having sth. once [Lit. it is better to keep a cow for milking than to kill it].

པ་ས་ (pāsa) a type of yellow earth (used for painting walls).

པ་སོ་ (paso) ivory ། པ་སོའི་ཐུར་མ་ Ivory spoon.

པ་སོ་བརྐོས་མ་ (paso gȫȍma) carved ivory.

པ་སོ་མཁན་ (pasoñɛn) ivory carver.

པ་བསད་པ་ལས་བཞོས་པ་དགའ་ (pasɛɛbalɛ shöba ga) sm. པ་བཤའ་བ་ལས་བཞོ་བ་དགའ་.

པག (pag) 1. flour. 2. virtuous, moral ། པག་ཡོད་ཀྱི་སྤྱོད་པ་ Moral behavior. 3. a bit, a hint of, a trace of ། ཁོང་ལ་ནད་པག་ཙམ་མི་འདུག There is not even a hint of the illness left. 4. sm. བློ་ཉམས་. 5. abbr. of པག་མ་. 6. mahjong.

པག་སྐར་ (paggar) astrological calculations regarding sending/ taking a bride.

པག་རྐྱང་ (paggyaŋ) 1. sm. པག་ཡངས་པོ་. 2. not bashful.

པག་སྐྱོ་ (paggyo) a paste-like mixture (flour with a liquid mixed).

པག་ཁག (paàgaà) 1. a set of four bricks of tea. 2. a large brick of tea.

པག་ཁུ་ (pəggu) broth.

པག་ཁོག (paggɔ̀ɔ) sm. བྲང་ཁོག.

པག་ཁུམ་ཅན་ (paggumjɛn) cowardly, timid, conservative.

པག་འཁུམ་ (paà kūm) vi. to be timid/ intimidated, to be scared/ afraid ། ཁོའི་མདུན་དུ་པག་འཁུམ་དགོས་གང་ཡང་མེད་ There is no need to be scared in his presence.

པག་འཁུམ་སྙིང་ཞེན་ (paggum ñi̱ŋshen) conservatism, traditionalism; va.—བྱེད་.

པག་འཁུམས་རིང་ལུགས་ (paggum ri̱ŋluù) conservativism, traditionalism.

པག་གི་པུག་གི (paggi puggi) 1. speaking unclearly/ indistinctly. 2. small.

པག་གེ་པོག་གེ (pagge pogge) padded clothing, etc. that looks puffed up.

པག་གྲིབ་ (pagdrib) traditional belief that a bride brings pollution with her and this can cause illness.

པག་གྲོ་པ་ (pag trobo) sm. པག་དྲོ་.

པག་གྲོ་བྱིན་ཆེ་བ་ (pagdro jincewa) grand and imposing.

པག་གླུ་ (paglu) wedding song.

པག་རྒྱག (paà gyəaà) vi. to play mahjong.

པག་རྒྱུད་ (paggyüü) wife's relatives.

པག་སྒོ་ཀ་ལིང་ (paggo gəliŋ) sm. བྲག་སྒོ་ཀ་ལིང་.

པག་ཅན་ (pagjɛn) sm. པག་དྲོ་པོ་.

པག་ཆ་ (pagja) a bunch/ bundle/ package.

པག་ཆགས་ (pagjaà) effect, consequence, influence, impact, impression ། མོས་ཁྱིམ་ཚང་འཛིན་པ་ཡིན་ན་པག་ཆགས་གང་ཡང་འཇོག་ཐུབ་པ་མི་འདུག If she takes control of the house, it will not have a good effect. ། ཁོང་གི་བོད་ཀྱི་ཆེད་དུ་ལས་ཀ་ཡག་པོ་གནང་ཙང་མིའི་ཁྲོད་དུ་པག་ཆགས་ཡག་པོ་བྱུང་ཡོད་པ་རེད་ Because he did good work for the benefit of Tibet, he had good impression on people. 2. good luck/ fortune ། དེ་རིང་ང་པག་ཆགས་བཞག་སོང་ང་ལ་ལས་ཀ་གསར་པ་ཞིག་རག་བྱུང་ Today I had good fortune. I got a new job.

པག་ཆགས་ངན་པོ་ (pagjaà ŋəmba) bad influence/ impact/ fortune.

པག་ཆགས་འཇོག (pagjaà jɔ̀ɔ) va. to have/ get a good effect/ impact, to have good luck.

པག་ཆགས་སད་ (pagjaà sɛ̀ɛ) vi. to be affected/ impacted/ influenced (good or bad) by one's karma.

པག་ཆགས་གསུམ་ (pagjaà sūm) the three influences: body, mind and speech.

པག་ཆལ་ (pagjɛɛ) a type of round flat bread.

པག་ཆུང་ (pəgjuŋ) one brick of tea.

པག་ཆེན་ (pagjen) 1. sm. པག་ཁག. 2. a type of tile game something like mahjong.

པག་ཉལ་ (pagñɛɛ) latent tendency, predisposition.

པག་སྙོལ་ (pagñöö) arranging the bride and groom's first night's sleeping together; va.—གཏོང་.

པག་རྟ་ (pagda) bride's horse.

པག་སྟོན་ (pagdön) marriage party/ celebration.

པག་ཐུག (bəgduù) a type of soup/ stew containing small pieces of dough.

པག་དང་ལྡན་པ་ (pagdaŋ dəmba) sm. པག་ཡོད་.

པད་དྭངས་ (pagdaŋ) shung. sm. ཁམས་དྭངས་.

པག་དོག་པོ་ (pag tobo) narrow-minded.

པག་དྲོ་ (paàdro) personable, jolly, good-natured, pleasant.

པག་དྲོ་པོ་ (pag trobo) sm. པག་དྲོ་.

པག་དྲོ་བྱིན་ཆེ་ (paàdro jinje) grand and imposing.

པག་དྲོན་ (pagdrön) warm པག་ཐུག.

པག་ལྡན་ (paŋdɛn) sm. པག་ཅན་.

པག་སྦྱིན་ (pagjin) flour paste used as glue.

པག་པ་གྲོགས་ཆེ་ (pagba trəgje) 1. mahjong partner. 2. a person with whom one is in cahoots.

པག་ཕབ་ (pag pāb) vi. to be completely at ease, to be carefree.

པག་ཕུག (pagbuù) sm. ཐུག་ཕུག.

པག་ཕེབས་ (pagpeè) sm. པག་ཕབ་.

པག་ཕེབས་དལ་འགྲོད་ (pagpeè tɛɛdröö) taking a slow/ leisurely stroll.

པག་ཕེབས་སྣང་སྐྱིད་ (pagpeè nāŋgyii) carefree, happy.

པག་ཕེབས་པོ་ (pag pēèbo) carefree, at ease, without anxiety/ fear.

པག་ཕོར་བརྐོས་མ་ (pagbɔɔ gȫȍma) carved boxes.

པག་ཕེབས་ཞུམ་མེད་ (pagpeè shummeè) at ease without fear.

པག་ཕེབས་ཕྱིང་འཇགས་ (pagpeè lhi̱ŋjaà) sm. པག་ཕེབས་པོ་.

པག་ཕྱེ་ (pagje) flour; va.—རྗེ་; —སྦྱོ་ to knead flour dough.

པག་བུག (pagbuù) sm. པག་གི་བུག་གི་.

པག་བོག (pagbɔ̀ɔ) abbr. of པག་གེ་བོག་གེ་.

པག་མ་ (pagma) bride; va.—གཏོང་ to give/ send a bride; va.—ལེན་ to take a bride.

པག་མ་འབོག (pagma bɔ̀ɔ) to give and take a bride.

པག་མ་ལྷ་འཁྲོལ་ (pagma lhāndröö) asking a god (for permission to leave one's natal house and go as a bride or groom); va.—ཞུ་.

པག་མ་ལྷ་འདོགས་ (pagma lhāndɔɔ) a prayer flag which matches the birth sign of a new bride that is put on the roof of the house into which she marries.

པག་མེད་ (pagmeè) (acting) hedonistically, immorally, unrestrained, indulging in pleasures (drinking, smoking, womanizing), dissolute, wild, unconventional; va.— བྱེད་; —གཡེང་ to act in a hedonistic/ immoral way, to have concern only for one's pleasure, to be wild/ dissolute, to fool around and not do one's work.

བག་མེད་རྒྱས་སྤྲོས་ (pagmeè gyɛɛ̀dröö) acting without restraint in pursuit of hedonism/ immorality.

བག་མེད་ཆུད་ཟོས་ (pagmeè cüüsöö) acting hedonistically immoral and wasteful.

བག་མེད་རྣམ་གཡེང་ (pagmeè nämyeŋ) sm. བག་མེད་ལྷོད་གཡེང་.

བག་མེད་པ་ (pagmeèba) 1. hedonistic, immoral, dissolute. 2. cloth that is not stiff. 3. odorless, absence of an unclean smell.

བག་མེད་ཚུལ་མེད་ (pagmeè tsüümeè) immorally hedonistic, dissolute, wild.

བག་མེད་ཞུམ་མེད་ (pagmeè shummeè) without fear in the pursuit of hedonism/ pleasure.

བག་མེད་ལོང་སྤྱོད་ (pagmeè loŋjoö) hedonistic, immoral; va.—བྱེད་.

བག་མེད་ལྷོད་གཡེང་ (pagmeè) doing sth. carelessly/ negligently/ not conscientiously; va.—བྱེད་.

བག་ཙམ་ (pagdzam) a little, a slight/ small amount.

བག་རྩིས་ (pagdzii) astrological calculations for marriage.

བག་ཚ་ (pagdza) fear ༈ཁྱེད་རང་དཀའ་ངལ་ཅན་གྱི་ལས་ཀར་བག་ཚའདུག་གས་ Do you fear the difficult job?

བག་ཚ་བ་ (pagdzawa) sm. བག་ཚ་.

བག་ཚ་མར་ཁུ་ (pagdza maagu) a traditional paste-like food consisting of tsamba mixed with butter, raw sugar and cheese.

བག་ཚ་མེད་པ་ (padza meèba) not afraid, not shying away from, fearless.

བག་ཚ་ཞེད་པ་ (padza sheèba) sm. བག་ཚ་.

བག་ཚོས་ (pagdzöö) deep fried pastry.

བག་འཚེར་ (pagdzer) sm. བག་ཚ.

བག་རྫོངས་ (pagdzoŋ) dowry for a bride; va.—སྐྱེར་ to give a dowry for a bride.

བག་ཞ་ (pagsha) sm. བག་ཉལ་.

བག་ཞུམ་ (pagshum) sm. བག་མཆེར་.

བག་གཞག (pagshaà) splitting open; vi.—ཐེབས་ to get split open.

བག་ཟན་ (pagsɛn) traditional pancake-like bread.

བག་ཟོན་ (pagsön) caution, prudence, precautions, vigilance; va.—བྱེད་.

བག་ཡངས་ (pagyaŋ) sm. བག་ཡངས་པོ་.

བག་ཡངས་ཉམས་འཆལ་ (pagyaŋ ñamjɛɛ) undisciplined, dissolute, wild.

བག་ཡངས་པོ་ (pag yaŋbo) free (in thinking), open-minded (in thought and action), carefree, relaxed.

བག་ཡོད་ (pagyöö) upright, decent, conscientious, law-abiding.

བག་ཡོད་ཚུལ་མཐུན་ (pagyöö tsüüdün) sm. བག་ཡོད་ཚུལ་ལྡན་.

བག་ཡོད་ཚུལ་ལྡན་ (pagyöö tsüüdɛn) honest, upright, law-abiding, decent.

བག་ཡོད་ཚུལ་གནས་ (pagyöö tsüünɛɛ̀) sm. བག་ཡོད་ཚུལ་ལྡན་.

བག་གཡང་ (pagyaŋ) sm. བག་གཡེང་.

བག་གཡེང་ (pagyeŋ) not paying attention to things, not conscientious/ diligent, hedonistic, dissolute; va.—བྱེད་.

བག་གཡེང་ཚ་པོ་ (pagyeŋ tsäbo) a person who isn't conscientious, sb. who doesn't work diligently; sb. who is hedonistic/ dissolute.

བག་གཡོག (pagyɔ̀ɔ) a woman who accompanies the bride as servant to her new household.

བག་གཡོག་མ་ (pagyɔ̀ɔma) sm. བག་གཡོག.

བག་རེ་ (paàre) sm. བག་ཙམ་.

བག་རེ་བ་ (paàrewa) sm. བག་ཙམ་.

བག་རོགས་ (paàrɔ̀ɔ) sm. བག་གཡོག.

བག་ལྭ་ (pagla) dress worn by the bride.

བག་ལ་འགྲོ་ (pagla dro) va. to go as a bride.

བག་ལ་ཉལ་ (pagla ñɛɛ) sm. བག་ཉལ་.

བག་ལ་ཞ་ (pagla sha) sm. བག་ཉལ་.

བག་ལེབ་ (paàleè) bread; va.— བཟོ་; —སྲེག to make/ bake bread; va.—ཚོང་ to make a transaction at once (slang).

བག་ལེབ་སྦོམ་ (paàleè bom) tib. eng. bun, roll.

བག་ལོག (paglɔ̀ɔ) return of a new bride to her parent's home for her first visit.

བག་སླང་ (paàlaŋ) a pan for making fried bread.

བག་སློག (paglɔ̀ɔ) present taken by a bride when she returns home to visit her parents for the first time after her marriage.

བག་སློང་ (pagloŋ) asking parents for the hand of a bride; va.—བྱེད་.

བག་གསར་ (pagsar) new bride.

བག་ལྷོད་ (paglhöö) a military command: "at ease".

བགས་ (paà) step-by-step, gradually, by degrees.

བགས་ཀྱིས་ (paàgi) step-by-step, gradually, by degrees.

བང་ (paŋ) 1. running; va.—རྒྱུག to run; va.—འགྲན་ to race, to run a race. 2. pheasant. 3. child birth. 4. abbr. of བང་ཁང་.

བང་: p. བངས་; f. བང་ (paŋ) vi. to get soaked ༈ཆར་པས་དུག་ལོག་ཚང་མ་བངས་བཞག The rain soaked all my clothes.

བང་ཁ་ (paŋga) sm. བང་.

བང་ཁང་ (paŋgaŋ) storehouse, granary.

བང་ཁྲག (paŋdraà) afterbirth.

བང་ཁྲི་ (pəŋdri) shelf.

བང་གལ་ (paŋgɛl) Bengal.

བང་འགྲོས་ (paŋdröö) running; va. བང་འགྲོས་; —བྱེད་.

བང་རྒྱུག (paŋgyuù) sm. བང་འགྲོས་.

བང་སྒྲིག (paŋ drig) 1. va. to line up, to queue up. 2. va. to arrange or order in a line/ sequence.

བང་སྒྲོམ་ (paŋdrom) sm. བང་ཁྲི་.

བང་ངལ་གསོ་ (paŋ ŋɛɛso) a leave from work after giving birth, maternity leave.

བང་ཉལ་ (paŋñɛɛ) sm. བང་ངལ་གསོ་.

བང་ཆེན་ (paŋjen) messenger.

བང་ཆེན་པ་ (paŋjenba) sm. བང་ཆེན་.

བང་མཆོང་འགྲོས་ (paŋjoŋ drö̀ö) sm. བང་འགྲོས་.

བང་གཏོང་ (paŋ tõŋ) running.

བང་འཐོར་ (paŋ tɔ̄ɔ) vi. to have a line/ queue get scattered.

བང་འདུར་ (paŋdur) sm. བང་རྒྱུག.

བང་ཕུགས་ (pāŋbuù) able to run for a long time (animals).

བང་ཕུད་ (pāŋbüü) the first grain that is taken out of storage.

བང་ཕྱིན་པ་ (paŋjimbə) messenger.

བང་བ་ (paŋwa) storage cubicle for grain in a storehouse.

བང་བུ་ (paŋbu) 1. a small བང་བ་. 2. a bee.

བང་སྦྲང་ (paŋdraŋ) honey.

བང་མི་ (paŋmi) sm. བང་ཆེན་.

བང་རྩལ་ (paŋdzɛɛ) skill in running.

བང་རྩལ་འགྲན་བསྡུར་ (paŋdzɛɛ trɛndur) foot race, track meet.

བང་ཚད་ (paŋdzɛɛ̀) an infection to the mother resulting from childbirth.

བང་མཛོད་ (paŋdzöö) treasury, storehouse.

བང་མཛོད་པ་ (paŋdzööba) manager or steward in charge of a treasury/ storehouse.

བང་མཛོད་འཛིན་པོ་ (paŋdzöö dzimbu) sm. བང་མཛོད་པ་.

བང་གཞུག་བུད་མེད་ (paŋshuù pöömeè) pregnant woman.

བང་ཟད་ (pəŋsɛɛ̀) tired of running (horses, etc.).

བང་ཡ་ (pəŋya) rival/ opponent/ competitor in a race.

བང་རིམ་ (pəŋrim) steps, rungs, layers.

བང་རིམ་འོག་འོག (pəŋrim wɔ̀wɔɔ) the lowest steps/ rungs/ layer.

བང་བཤིག (paŋ shiì) va. to scatter/ breakup a line or queue.

བང་སངས་ (paŋ sāŋ) 1. vi. to regain one's health after childbirth. 2. purification of birth. 3. a "baby shower" (party after a baby is born when friends/ neighbors bring gifts).

བང་སེལ་ (paŋsee) sm. བང་སངས་.

བང་སོ་ (paŋso) tomb, burial site.

བང་སོ་ཁང་ (paŋsogaŋ) crypt. cemetery.

བང་སློང་ (paŋloŋ) sm. བང་སངས་.

བང་སོའི་རྡོ་རིང་ (paŋsö doriŋ) grave stone, tombstone.

བངས་ (paŋ) p. of བང་.

བད་ (pɛ̱ɛ̀) 1. vi. to be intoxicated/ drunk (h.). ¶ཁོང་ ཆང་རར་བད་འདུག He is drunk. 2. vi. to be satiated/ full/ satisfied.

བད་ཀ་ (pɛ̱ɛ̀ga) a low embankment built on the edge of the flat roof of a Tibetan house.

བད་ཀན་ (pɛ̱ɛ̀gɛn) a major disease category in the Tibetan medical system that often involves phlegm (includes T.B., pneumonia).

བད་ཀན་གྲི་ཐོགས་ (pɛ̱ɛ̀gɛn dre̱dɔɔ̀) a disease of the throat.

བད་ཁ་ (pɛ̱ɛ̀ga) sm. བད་ཀ་.

བད་ཁྲག་ (pɛ̱ɛ̀draà) phlegm with blood.

བད་མཆུ་ (pɛ̱ɛ̀ju) བད་ཀ་.

བད་ཐོར་ (pɛ̱ɛ̀tɔr) a type of pimple.

བད་དྭངས་ (pɛ̱ɛ̀daŋ) shung. sm. ཁམས་དྭངས་.

བད་ནག་ (pɛ̱ɛ̀naà) 9th month of the Tibetan calendar.

བད་ཕུར་ (pɛ̱ɛ̀bur) sm. བད་ཀ་.

བད་བད་གདོང་ (pɛ̱ɛ̀bɛɛ dōŋ) sm. བུད་བུད་གདོང་.

བད་གཡམ་ (pɛ̱ɛ̀yam) slate covering of a བད་ཀ་.

བད་རླུང་ (pɛ̱ɛ̀luŋ) vertigo, giddiness.

བད་རླུང་འཁོར་སྐོར་ (pɛ̱ɛ̀luŋ kɔ̄ɔ̄gɔɔ) motion sickness.

བད་རླུང་མགོ་འཁོར་ (pɛ̱ɛ̀luŋ gogɔɔ) sm. བད་རླུང་.

བད་སྲིན་ (pɛ̱ɛ̀sin) tapeworm.

བན་ (pɛ̱n) 1. Buddhist monk. 2. sm. པེན་.

བན་བརྒྱག (pɛ̱ngyaà) sm. བན་སྡེགས་.

བན་སྐལ་དཀོར་ཟ་ (pɛ̱ngɛɛ kɔ̄rsa) shung. the place where monks go to perform religious rites.

བན་སྐྱ་ (pɛ̱ngya) abbr. laymen and monks.

བན་རྒན་ (pɛ̱ngɛn) abbr. of བན་དེ་རྒན་པ་.

བན་ཅོག (pɛ̱njoò) bundles of crops made when harvesting.

བན་ཆུང་ (pɛ̱njuŋ) young monk.

བན་ཆེན་ (pɛ̱njen) high ranking monk.

བན་སྡེགས་ (pɛ̱ndeg) a stone stand on which the water bucket is rested.

བན་དང་ཛ་མ་ (pɛ̱ndaŋ dza̱ma) pots and pans.

བན་དེ་ (pɛ̱nde) monk.

བན་དེ་རྒན་པ་ (pɛ̱nde gɛ̱mba) older monk.

བན་དེ་བོན་དེ་ (pɛ̱nde pö̱nde) Buddhist monks and Bon monks.

བན་དེ་མོ་ (pɛ̱ndemo) sm. བན་མོ་.

བན་སྡེ་ (pɛ̱nde) a community of monks.

བན་ནི་བུན་ནི་ (pɛ̱nni pṵnni) unhappy, troubled, uneasy (mind); vi.—བྱེད་ ¶དེ་རིང་ང་སེམས་པ་བན་ནི་བུན་ནི་བྱེད་ཀྱི་འདུག་ཕལ་ཆེར་གསར་འགྱུར་ངན་པ་ཞིག་གོ་རྒྱུ་ཡིན་པ་འདྲ་ Today my mind is not at ease, probably I will hear some bad news.

བན་པོ་ (pɛ̱mbo) tattered/ patched clothes.

བན་སྤྲང་ (pɛ̱ndraŋ) monk who goes around begging.

བན་བུན་ (pɛ̱mbün) abbr. of བན་ནི་བུན་ནི་.

བན་བོན་ (pɛ̱nbön) abbr. of བན་དེ་བོན་དེ་.

བན་མོ་ (pɛ̱nmo) nun.

བན་བཙུན་ (pɛ̱ndzün) monks and nuns.

བན་ཙ་ (pɛ̱ndza) families that send young boys to become monks.

བན་གཟན་ (pɛ̱nsɛn) monk's shawl.

བན་གཟུགས་ (pɛ̱nsuù) monk's attire.

བན་རལ་ (pɛ̱nrɛɛ) a monk who has broken his vows.

བན་ལང་ (pɛ̱nlaŋ) arc. sm. པ་ལང་.

བན་ལོག (pɛ̱nlɔɔ̀) monks who have lost their celibacy and left the monastic order.

བབ་ (pə̱b) 1. sm. བབས་. 2. p. of འབབ་.

བབ་ཁེ་ (pə̱bke) middleman's profit; va.—ཟ་ to take profit as a middleman.

བབ་བགོད་ (pə̱bgöö) shung. sm. བགོད་སྒྲིག.

བབ་ཁེབས་ (pə̱bgee) long decorative panel above the door of a Tibetan home.

བབས་འགན་ (pə̱bgɛn) taking responsibility; va.—འཁུར་ to take on a responsibility.

བབ་ཅོལ་ (pə̱bjöö) 1. lacking in consideration, thoughtless, careless, hasty, rash, not serious; va.—བྱེད་ ¶ཁོས་བབ་ཅོལ་དུ་བཤད་པ་རེད་ He said it thoughtlessly.

བབ་ཅོལ་ཧོད་རྒྱུག (pə̱bjöö hȫögyuù) rash, hasty, careless.

བབ་ཕྱི་ (pə̱bji) shung. severe punishment.

བབ་ཆགས་ (pə̱bjaà) sm. བབ་ཆགས་པོ་.

བབ་ཆགས་པོ་ (pə̱b cāgbo) 1. just right (not too little or too much), appropriate ¶གསུང་བཤད་བབ་ཆགས་པོ་ཞིག་གནང་སོང་ (He) gave a most appropriate speech. ¶ཕྲུ་གུ་འདིའི་སྤྱོད་ལམ་བབ་ཆགས་པོ་ཞིག་འདུག This boy's behavior is just right. 2. attractive/ handsome in a simple and not ostentatious way ¶ཕྱུ་པ་བབ་ཆགས་པོ་ཞིག་གྱོན་བཞག (She) wore an attractive but simple dress.

བབ་ཆུ་ (pə̱bju) a shower (in a bathroom).

བབ་ཆོལ་ (pə̱bjöö) sm. བབ་ཅོལ་.

བབ་ལྟ་ (pə̱bda) looking at the conditions/ situations/ circumstances, using one's judgement; va.—བྱེད་ ¶གནད་དོན་ཆུང་ཙག་གོང་རིམ་ལ་སྙན་སེང་ཞུ་མ་དགོས་པར་ཁྱེད་རང་གིས་བབ་ལྟ་བྱས་ནས་ཐག་བཅད་ན་འགྲིགས་ You can use your judgement and settle small issues without petitioning the higher authorities.

བབ་ལྡན་ (pə̱bdɛn) sm. བབ་དང་བསྟུན་.

བབ་བསྟུན་ (pə̱bdün) sm. བབ་དང་བསྟུན་.

བབ་བསྟུན་མཁས་པ་ (pə̱bdün kɛ̄ɛ̄ba) sb. who is good at adapting to conditions.

བབ་བསྟུན་སྣེ་ཁྲིད་ (pə̱bdün nēdrii) leading in accordance with the conditions/ situation.

བབ་ཐང་ (pə̱bdaŋ) sm. བབས་ཐང་.

བབ་ཐོབ་ (pə̱bdob) 1. duty, responsibility, job. 2. appropiate, fitting ¶ཁོང་ལ་གཟིགས་བཙོས་དེ་འདྲ་རག་རྒྱུའི་བབ་ཐོབ་ཡོད་པ་མ་རེད་ It is not appropriate for him to receive such a prize. 3. right ¶ཁོང་ལ་ང་ཚོའི་ནང་སྲིད་ལ་ཕྱི་ཐོགས་བྱེད་པའི་བབ་ཐོབ་ཡོད་པ་མ་རེད་ He has no right to interfere in our internal affairs.

བབ་མཐུན་ (pə̱bdün) appropriate, fitting.

བབ་དང་བསྟུན་ (pə̱bdaŋ dṳ̄n) appropriate to conditions/ situations, in accordance with, in keeping with.

བབ་དང་མཚུངས་པ་ (pə̱bdaŋ tsṳ̄ŋba) sm. བབ་དང་བསྟུན་.

བབ་སྡོད་ (pə̱bdöö) perch, rest, roost (of birds).

བབ་བབ་ (pə̱bbəb) sm. བབ་ཅོལ་.

བབ་བླ་ (pə̱bla) sm. པ་བླ་.

བབ་འབྲེལ་ (pə̱mdree) sm. བབས་འབྲེལ་.

བབ་མལ་ (pə̱bmɛɛ) an overnight halting/ stopping place (on a journey).

བབ་སྨྱུག་བཞི་ཟུར་ (pə̱bñuù shi̱sur) 1/4 of the penalty of the fine goes to the clerk/ secretary of the court.

བབ་ཚུགས་ (pə̱bdzuù) sm. བབས་ཚུགས་.

བབ་ཚོད་ (pə̱bdzöö) sm. བབས་འབྲེལ་, 1.

བབ་མཚུངས་ (pə̱bdzuŋ) appropriate, fitting ¶ཁོའི་ཕྲོགས་བབ་མཚུངས་ཤིག་འཕར་བཞག His salary was increased appropriately.

བབ་གཟིགས་ (pə̱bsii) h. of བབ་ལྟ་.

བབ་འོས་ (pə̱bwöö) appropriate, fitting.

བབ་བརླིང་ (pə̱bliŋ) steady, stable, careful ¶ཁོས་བབ་བརླིང་དང་ནས་གནམ་གྲུ་བཏང་བ་རེད་ He flew the plane with great steadiness.

བབ་རླིང་ལྡན་པ་ (pə̱bliŋ de̱mba) steady, stable, careful.

བབ་ལ་ (pə̱bla) sm. པ་བླ་.

བབ་ལ་ལྟ་ (pə̱bla dā) va. to consider/ examine/ weigh a situation or circumstance ¶ཚོང་ལས་ཀྱི་བབ་ལ་བལྟས་ནས་ཁང་པ་འདི་ཉོས་པ་རེད་ (He) considered the business prospects and bought the house.

བབ་ལ་བསྟུན་ (pə̱bla dṳ̄n) sm. བབ་དང་བསྟུན་.

བབ་གཤོང་ (pəbshoŋ) sinking of the ground.

བབ་སེལ་ (pəbsel) explaining/ clearing up a misunderstanding; va.—བྱེད་.

བབ་གསེད་ (pəbseè) sm. བབ་སེལ་.

བབ་གསོལ་ (pəbsöö) sm. བབ་སེལ་.

བབ་ལྷིང་ (pəblhiŋ) sm. བབ་བརླིང་.

བབ་ལྷེ་ (pəblhe) the blue decorations sewn on picnic/ ceremonial tents.

བབས་ (pəb) 1. p. of འབབ་. 2. the manner of doing sth. ¶ཁོའི་ཤོད་བབས་ནི་ As for the manner of his talking. 3. in accordance with, considering ¶ས་གནས་ཉེ་འགྲངས་བབས་ཀྱིས་ In accordance with the distance.

བབས་བཀོད་གཅོད་ངེས་ (pəbgöö jööŋeè) a punishment will definitely be imposed ¶ཁྲལ་རིགས་དུས་ཐོག་དུ་མ་རྒྱུགས་ན་བབས་བཀོད་གཅོད་ངེས་ཡིན་ If you don't pay your corvee taxes on time, you will definitely be punished.

བབས་ཁུར་ (pəbgur) one's responsibility/ duty/ task.

བབས་ཆགས་ (pəbjaà) sm. བབ་ཆགས་.

བབས་དོག་དོག (pəb dɔ̃gdɔɔ̀) sm. བབ་ཆགས་པོ་.

བབས་བལྡ་ (pəbda) sm. བབ་ལྡ་.

བབས་སྡུན་ (pəbdün) sm. བབ་བསྡུན་.

བབས་སྡེགས་ (pəbdeg) a stand/ platform for landing or descending on.

བབས་བསྡུན་ (pəbdün) sm. བབ་དང་བསྡུན་.

བབས་ཐང་ (pəbdaŋ) airport ¶གནམ་གྲུའི་བབས་ཐང་ Airport.

བབས་ཐོབ་ (pəbdob) sm. བབ་ཐོབ་.

བབས་དང་བསྟུན་ (pəbdaŋ dũn) sm. བབ་དང་བསྟུན་.

བབས་འགྲིལ་ (pəmdree) 1. in accordance with, in conjunction with ¶ཡུལ་དུས་འབབ་འགྲིལ་ In accordance with time and place. 2. not so good ¶དེང་སང་ངའི་གཟུགས་པོ་བབས་འགྲིལ་ཞིག་འདུག Thesedays my health is not good. 3. appropriately ¶གྲོད་གཞི་དེ་ཐག་གཅོད་བབས་འགྲིལ་མ་བྱུང་བ་རེད་ That law case was not appropriately settled.

བབས་འགྲིལ་མ་ཆེ་བ་ (pəmdree macewa) shung. inappropriate ¶ད་བར་ལོ་མང་རིང་ལས་དོན་ཧུར་སྐྱེད་བྱ་ཤུས་ལ་ད་ཆ་ཕྱིར་སློག་བབས་འགྲིལ་མ་ཆེ་བ་ Since (he) has been working hard for many years it seems inappropriate to send him back.

བབས་ཚུགས་ (pəbdzuù) station, landing/ descending place ¶མེ་འཁོར་བབས་ཚུགས་ Railway station.

བབས་ཚུགས་སྡོད་སྒར་ (pəbdzuù döögar) barracks, quarters ¶དམག་མིའི་བབས་ཚུགས་སྡོད་སྒར་ Soldier's barracks.

བབས་ཚོད་ (pəbdzöö) sm. བབ་འགྲིལ, 1.

བབས་འོས་ (pəbwöö) sm. བབ་འོས་.

བབས་ལ་ལྡ་ (pəbla dā) sm. བབ་ལ་ལྡ་.

བབས་ལ་བསྟུན་ (pəbla dũn) sm. བབ་དང་བསྟུན་.

བབས་ལ་གཞིགས་ས་ (pəgla shigsa) sm. བབ་ལ་ལྡ་.

བབས་གཟིགས་ (pəbsii) sm. བབས་སེལ་.

བབས་སུ་འབྲིལ་མིན་ (pəbsu dreemin) shung. sm. བབས་འབྲིལ་མ་ཆེ་བ་.

བབས་སེལ་ (pəbsel) sm. བབ་སེལ་.

བབས་གསལ་ (pəbsεε) shung. giving a clear answer ¶གཞིས་གཉེར་སྐོར་སྔ་འཕྲོས་བབས་གསལ་མ་བདེ་བས་བླ་དཔོན་གོང་མར་སྙན་སེང་ཞུ་རྒྱུ་ Regarding the steward of the estate, it is inconvenient to give a clear answer so we will report this matter to the superiors.

བབས་གསེད་ (pəbseè) sm. བབ་གསེད་.

བབས་གསོལ་ (pəbsöö) sm. བབས་བསོལ་.

བབས་ལྷིང་ (pəblhiŋ) sm. བབ་ལྷིང་.

བམ་ (pam) 1. abbr. of བམ་པོ་. 2. question marker for 'b' finals ¶ཁོས་འདི་ལབ་བམ་ Did he say this? 3. 'or' particles for 'b' finals. 4. corpse. 5. vi. to rot/ to decay.

བམ་སྦྲངས་ (pamdraŋ) bloated (e.g., a corpse).

བམ་གྲངས་ཀྱི་རྒྱ་ (pamdraŋgi gya) a mark indicating a section/ chapter in a text.

བམ་སྒྲུབ་ (pamdrub) a meditation technique said to be able to bring the dead to life.

བམ་ཆག (pamjaà) sm. བམ་པོ་.

བམ་ཆེ་བ་ (pamcewa) large size.

བམ་དྲི་ (pamdri) 1. smell of a decaying corpse. 2. smell of sth. rotten.

བམ་པ་ (pāmba) vi. to rot/ decay.

བམ་པོ་ (pāmbo) 1. section/ chapter of a book. 2. a bunch/ load.

བམ་པོའི་གྲངས་ཀྱི་རྒྱ་ (pambö traŋgi gya) sm. བམ་གྲངས་ཀྱི་རྒྱ་.

བམ་པོའི་ཚད་ (pambö tsὲὲ) size of a chapter/ section.

བམ་བེ་ (pombe) Bombay.

བམ་རིལ་ (pamrii) a complete corpse.

བམ་རོ་ (pamro) corpse.

བའི་སྦུ་ (pεbu) sm. བ་སྤུ་.

བའོ་ (pawo) sm. བོང་གསེབ་.

བར་ (par) 1. in between, between ¶རྒྱལ་ཁབ་ཆེན་པོ་གཉིས་བར་ཡོད་པའི་རྒྱལ་ཕྲན་ The small countries that are between the big countries. 2. until, up to, to ¶ང་འདིར་ཚེས་ 20 བར་སྡོད་ཀྱི་ཡིན་ I am staying here until the 20th. ¶དེ་ནས་འདི་བར་ From there to here. 3. without ¶ཡུན་རིང་མ་སོང་བར་ Without a long time having passed.

བར་གྱི་རྡོ་རིལ་ (pargi dorii) instigator, person who causes trouble [Lit. a round stone in between].

བར་བཀུམས་ (pargum) shung. to reduce the amount ¶ཁྲལ་རྟེན་ས་ཞིང་ལ་མགོ་བདེ་དྲན་འཕྱུལ་གྱི་བར་བཀུམས་ཀུན་རྫོབ་དུ་མ་སོང་བ་དགོས་རྒྱུ་ One should not reduce the amount of taxable fields through cunning and deceit.

བར་དཀྱིལ་རྒྱལ་ཡོངས་འོས་བསྡུ་ (pargyii gyεεyoŋ wöödu) national off-year election in U.S.A.

བར་རྐྱེན་ (pargyen) impediment, obstacle, barrier, hindrance ¶ཨར་པོ་རྒྱག་སྐབས་བར་རྐྱེན་འགའ་ཤས་བྱུང་ཡོད་ཀྱང་ལས་ཀ་ལ་ཤུགས་རྐྱེན་བྱུང་མེད་ During construction, even though several obstacles occurred, they didn't have an effect on the result.

བར་སྐབས་ (pagəb) for a time, for a period of time, for the time being ¶བར་སྐབས་ཁོ་རྒྱ་དཀར་ལ་བསྡད་པ་རེད་ He lived in India for a time.

བར་སྐབས་ཀྱི་ཚིགས་སུ་བཅད་པ་ (pagəbgi tsĩgsu jεὲba) verses that are interspersed within prose.

བར་སྐབས་ཤིག (pagəbhig) at one point, at one period of time ¶བར་སྐབས་ཤིག་ལ་ང་རྒྱ་དཀར་ལ་བསྡད་པ་ཡིན་ At one point I lived in India.

བར་སྐོར་ (paagɔɔ) 1. the inner circular road in Lhasa which goes around Tsuglhakhang Cathedral and was the major market in the traditional era; va.—རྒྱག; —ལ་འགྲོ་ to go around the བར་སྐོར་, to circumambulate the Tsuglhakhang Cathedral. 2. a circular road/ path between two others.

བར་སྐོར་རྒྱག (paagɔɔ gyaà) va. to go around the inner ring road.

བར་སྒྱི་ (pərgyi) wood wedge used in splitting wood; va.—རྒྱག.

བར་སྐྱི་དུས་རབས་ (pargye tüürəb) Mesozoic Era.

བར་བསྐལ་ (pargεε) the middle eons.

བར་བསྐལ་ཉི་ཤུ་ (pargεε ñishu) the twenty middle eons.

བར་བསྐོར་ (pargɔɔ) sm. བར་སྐོར་.

བར་ཁང་ (pargaŋ) 1. the middle floor/ story. 2. the middle room.

བར་ཁེ་ (parke) profit as a middleman/ broker; va.—ཟ་ to take profit as a middleman/ broker.

བར་ཁེ་བ་ (parkewa) broker, agent, middleman, wholesaler.

བར་ཁྱད་ (parkεὲ) difference (between things) ¶རྒྱ་མིའི་རྒྱ་མ་དང་བོད་པའི་ཁལ་གྱི་དབར་ལ་བར་ཁྱད་ཆེན་པོ་ཡོད་པ་རེད་ There is a big difference between the Chinese "jin" and the Tibetan ཁལ་.

བར་ཁྱམས་ (parkyam) 1. a corridor. 2. an upstairs verandah without a roof.

བར་འཁྱམ་ (parkyam) sm. བར་ཁྱམས་.

བར་ཀུན་ (pargün) shung. suffering losses in

between ¶ གཞིས་ཀ་དེ་བར་བར་གུན་མེད་པ་ཁུངས་སྐྱེལ་ཡིག་ཆ་འདི་ཐོག་ནས་བྱ་ཆོག I can show documents to prove that the estate did not suffer losses in between (two different times).

བར་གོས་ (pargöö) clothes that are not too casual nor too dressy.

བར་གྲལ་ (pardrεε) middle row/ line.

བར་གྲས་ (pardrεὲ) sm. འདྲིང་གྲས་.

བར་འགག (paŋgaà) the middle/ intermediate corridor or waiting room.

བར་འགའ་ (panga) sometimes, occasionally.

བར་འགྲིབ་ (pardrib) cataract.

བར་བསྐལ་ (pargεε) transition, shift; vi.—བྱེད་ ¶ བར་བསྐལ་གྱི་དུས་སྐབས་ Transitional period.

བར་བསྐལ་གྱི་རྣམ་པ་ (pargεεgi nāmba) transitional form.

བར་བསྐལ་དུས་སྐབས་ (pargεε tüügəb) period of transition.

བར་རྒྱན་འཛུགས་ (pargεn dzuù) va. to make a side bet in a mahjong game when one is not one of the four players.

བར་རྒྱུག (pərgyuù) shung. a race on horseback after the Monlam.

བར་སྒོ་ (pargo) middle door.

བར་དངུལ་ (parŋüü) commission, brokerage fee, middleman's fee.

བར་རྔན་ (parŋεn) gift obtained for being a middleman; va.—ཟ་ to receive such a gift; va.—སྤྲོད་ to give such a gift.

བར་གཅོད་ (parjöö) interruption, obstruction, obstacle; va.—གཏོང་; —བྱེད་.

བར་བཅད་ (parjεὲ) shung. a divider.

བར་བཅུག་རི་མོ་ (parjuù rimo) illustration.

བར་བཅུག་རོལ་དབྱངས་ (parjuù rööyaŋ) intermittent music (e.g., in a film).

བར་ཆད་ (parjεὲ) 1. obstruction, obstacle, setback, misfortune, hindrance, interruption, obstacle, barrier; va.—གཏོང་ to hinder, to cause trouble/ misfortune/ obstructions/ setbacks; va.—སེལ་ to end or overcome misfortune/ obstruction/ etc. ¶ ད་ལོ་ཚོང་ལ་བར་ཆད་ཆེན་པོ་བྱུང་སོང་ This year we had a lot of obstacles in our business.

བར་ཆད་ཀྱི་ལྟོང་ (parjεὲgi lhōŋ) sign or omen of a pending disaster.

བར་ཆད་མེད་པ་ (parjεὲ meèba) uninterrupted, unimpeded, unobstructed.

བར་ཆིངས་ (parjiŋ) mediating dispute; va.—རྒྱག; —བྱེད་.

བར་ཆོད་ (parjöö) sm. བར་ཆད་.

བར་ཆོད་བྱེད་པའི་མི་དགེ་བ་ (parjöö ceèbε migewa) nonvirtuous deeds that obstruct/ hinder/ impede.

བར་ཆོད་ས་ཁུལ་ (parjöö səgüü) disaster/ obstacle zone.

བར་འཆད་ (par cεὲ) vi. to be interrupted/ obstructed/ hindered.

བར་བཏབ་ (pardəb) second planting ¶ བར་བཏབ་འབྲས་ The second rice crop.

བར་རྟ་ (parda) gelding.

བར་སྟོང་ (pardoŋ) space between things, gap ¶ བར་སྟོང་གི་རྒྱང་ཐག The distance between two things.

བར་སྟོན་ (pardön) a party given when a construction project is half complete.

བར་ཐག (pardaà) distance ¶ ལུང་པ་དེ་གཉིས་ཀྱི་དབར་བར་ཐག་རིང་པོ་ཡོད་པ་རེད་ The distance between the two areas is great.

བར་ཐག་མཉམ་པ་ (pardaà ñāmba) equidistant.

བར་ཐབ་ (pardəb) shung. the second (middle) kitchen of the Dalai Lama.

བར་ཐོ་ (pardo) a medium-sized hammer.

བར་ཐོག (pardɔɔ̀) second floor of a three story house.

བར་ཐོན་ (pārdön) sth. produced not recently and not a long time ago.

བར་ཐོན་དུས་རབས་ (pardön tüürəb) sm. བར་སྐྱེ་དུས་རབས་.

བར་མཐུད་ (pardüü) intermediate junction/ link.

བར་མཐོང་ (pardoŋ) sm. བར་འཁྱམས་.

བར་དུ་ (pardüü) 1. in between ¶ འདི་གཉིས་ཀྱི་བར་དུ་ Between these two. 2. up to, until ¶ ཁོ་ལོ་དགུ་བཅུ་བར་དུ་བསྡད་པ་རེད་ He lived until he was ninety. 3. on ¶ ཕྱི་དྲོ་ལོག་ཡོང་བའི་བར་དུ་ In the late afternoon on the return road.

བར་དུ་ལངས་ (pardu laŋ) sm. བར་སྡོད་.

བར་དོ་ (pardo) the intermediate stage, the stage between death and rebirth.

བར་དོ་ཐོས་གྲོལ་ (pardo tööhdröö) the Tibetan Book of the Dead.

བར་དོ་བ་ (pardowa) sentient beings in the stage between death and birth.

བར་དོའི་འཕྲེང་རིང་ (pardö trēŋriŋ) the long path of the intermediate stage between death and rebirth.

བར་གདང་ (pardaŋ) the horizontal stick on a weaving pole.

བར་གདོན་ (pardön) a type of spirit/ demon.

བར་འདུམ་ (pərdum) mediation, conciliation; va.—གཏོང་ to mediate, to conciliate, to reconcile.

བར་འདུམ་རིང་ལུགས་ (pərdum riŋluù) middle-of-the-roadism.

བར་རྡུལ་ (pərdüü) neutron.

བར་རྡུལ་མདེའུ་ (pərdüü dewu) neutron bomb.

བར་རྡུལ་མྱུར་མོ་ (pərdüü ñurmu) fast neutron.

བར་རྡུལ་ཚ་བ་ (pərdüü tsāwa) thermal neutron.

བར་ལྡིང་ (pərdiŋ) leaving sth. uncared for, leaving unsettled/ unfinished ¶ ལས་བྱེད་པའི་གླ་ཕོགས་སྤོར་རྒྱུའི་ལས་དོན་དེ་བར་ལྡིང་དུ་ལུས་བཞག The issue of increasing the salary of cadres has been left unfinished.

བར་ལྡིང་ཡ་ཡོལ་ (pərdiŋ yayöö) working poorly, wasting time at work, leaving work unfinished.

བར་སྡུམ་ (pərdum) sm. བར་འདུམ་.

བར་བསྡུ་ (pardu) shung. to collect (taxes/ debts) in between; va.—བྱེད་ ¶ ན་ལོའི་ཁྲལ་འབབ་ནམ་ཤེད་ཀྱིས་བར་བསྡུ་བྱས་འདུག They collected last year's tax in between (last year and now) by using force.

བར་སྡོད་ (pardöö) 1. middle reaches, midstream. 2. middle-of-the-road, neutral ¶ བར་སྡོད་རྒྱལ་ཁབ་ A neutral country. 3. mediating between two sides; va.—བྱེད་ to mediate between two sides ¶ སིམ་ལའི་གྲོས་མོལ་བྱེད་སྐབས་རྒྱ་བོད་གཉིས་དབར་དབྱིན་ཇིས་བར་སྡོད་བྱས་པ་རེད་ At the time of the Simla negotiation the British mediated between the Tibetan and the Chinese.

བར་སྡོད་རྒྱལ་ཁབ་ (pardöö gyεεgəb) neutral nation.

བར་སྡོད་ཆིངས་ཡིག (pardöö cīŋyii) neutrality agreement.

བར་སྡོད་པ་ (pardööba) middle-of-the-roader, neutral person (with regard to sth.).

བར་སྡོད་ལམ་ཕྱོགས་ (pardöö lamjɔɔ̀) middle-of-the-road position/ course.

བར་སྡོམ་ (pardom) sm. བར་སྐབས་ཀྱི་ཚོགས་སུ་བཅད་པ་.

བར་ན་ (parna) sm. བར་སྡོད་.

བར་གནས་ (parnεὲ) sm. བར་སྡོད་.

བར་གནས་ཀྱི་རྣམ་པ་ (parnεὲgi nāmba) intermediate state or form.

བར་གནས་ཀྱི་ལམ་ཕྱོགས་ (parnεὲgi lamjɔɔ̀) བར་སྡོད་ལམ་ཕྱོགས་.

བར་གནས་འགྲོ་ལམ་ (parnεὲ drolam) middle road.

བར་གནས་རྒྱལ་ཁབ་ (parnεὲ gyεεgəb) neutral country.

བར་གནས་པ་ (parnεὲba) sm. བར་སྡོད་པ་.

བར་གནས་རིང་ལུགས་ (parnεὲ riŋluù) neutralism.

བར་གནས་རིམ་གྲས་ (parnεὲ rimdrεὲ) intermediate state.

བར་གནས་སུ་སྡོད་ (parnεὲsu döö) va. to be in middle reaches/ midstream, to be middle-of-the-road/ neutral.

བར་གནས་སྲིད་ཇུས་ (parnεὲ sīijüü) neutralist policy.

བར་སྣང་ (parnaŋ) air space, atmosphere, sky ¶ མངའ་ཁོངས་ཀྱི་བར་སྣང་ Air space of a country (air territory).

བར་སྣང་ཁ་ལོ་སྒྱུར་དབང་ (parnaŋ kālo gyurwaŋ) right/ freedom to navigate space.

བར་སྣང་ཁང་ཆེན་ (parnaŋ kāŋjen) building castles in the air.

བར་སྣང་ཁམས་ (parnaŋ kām) outer space.

བར་སྣང་ཁྱབ་ཁོངས་ (parnaŋ kyəbgoŋ) airspace.

བར་སྣང་འཁོར་སྐྱོད་ (parnaŋ kōrgyöö) space travel.

བར་སྣང་གི་འདྲེད་འཁོར་ (parnaŋgi dreègɔɔ) ferris wheel.

བར་སྣང་གི་འབྲིང་འཁོར་ (parnaŋgi dreŋgɔɔ) sm. བར་སྣང་གི་འདྲེད་འཁོར་.

བར་སྣང་གི་ལག་རྩལ་ (parnaŋgi lagdzɛɛ) space technology.

བར་སྣང་ཆུ་རླབས་ (parnaŋ cūləb) mirage.

བར་སྣང་ཉམས་ཞིབ་ཁང་ (parnaŋ ñamshigaŋ) space laboratory.

བར་སྣང་མཐོང་ (parnaŋ tōŋ) the heavens, space.

བར་སྣང་དུ་ (parnaŋdu) in the sky; vi.—ཟུག to reach/ touch the sky.

བར་སྣང་ནས་ཐིག་ལེན་ (parnaŋnɛ tīglen) aerial photographic survey.

བར་སྣང་སྣུམ་ལྷུག (parnaŋ nūmluù) air refueling.

བར་སྣང་འཕུར་གྲུ་ (parnaŋ pūrdru) space ship.

བར་སྣང་ཚན་རིག (parnaŋ tsēnrii) space science.

བར་སྣང་ས་ཚིགས་ (parnaŋ sādzii) space station.

བར་བཙིར་ (pardzii) pincer attack, attack from outside and inside.

བར་ཚངས་ (pardzaŋ) padding in clothes/ shoes/ bedding.

བར་པ་ (parba) 1. the middle one. 2. a witness.

བར་དཔང་ (parbaŋ) witness; va.—བྱེད་ to testify/ serve as a witness.

བར་བར་དུ་ (parbardu) now and then, from time to time, at intervals.

བར་པོར་ (parbɔr) abbr. of པ་རི་པོ་རི་.

བར་བྱེད་ (par cēè) va. to arbitrate/ mediate.

བར་བློན་ (parlön) the middle minister.

བར་དབུས་གཙང་རུ་བཞི་ (par üdzaŋ rushi) the four divisions/ areas of Central Tibet (U and Tsang).

བར་དབྲག (pardraà) space between two objects ༎སྒོ་དང་རྩིགས་པའི་བར་དབྲག་ལ་ The space between the door and the wall.

བར་དབྲག་ས་ཁུལ་ (pardraà sāgüü) a space between, an intermediate area.

བར་མ་ (parma) the middle (in quality, size, age) ༎བུ་བར་མ་ The middle son. 2. female dancer.

བར་མ་ཆད་པར་ (parma cɛ̄ɛ̀ba) without break/ interval, continously, constantly ༎གླིང་སྐོར་འགྲོ་མཁན་བར་མ་ཆད་པ་ཡོད་པ་རེད་ People continously go on the Lingkor.

བར་མ་དོ་ (parma to) 1. sm. བར་ལྡིང་. 2. intermediate stage, in between ༎འབབ་ཁྲལ་ལས་ཀྱང་བར་མ་དོའི་འགྲོ་སྒོ་མང་བ་ (There are) more expenses in between than even the taxes (cost). 3. sm. བར་དོ་.

བར་མ་དོར་འཆི་ (par madɔɔ cī) vi. to die before one's time, to die an untimely death.

བར་མ་པ་ (parmaba) middlemen, mediator.

བར་མ་བཞག (par mashaà) doing sth. without pausing/ continuously.

བར་མི་ (pərmi) 1. witness. 2. mediator; va.—བྱེད་ to mediate.

བར་མི་ཚོད་ (parmijöö) sm. བར་མི་ཆད་པར་.

བར་མེད་ (parmeè) parmeè sm. བར་མི་ཆད་པར་.

བར་མོལ་ (parmöö) mediating (discussions); va.—བྱེད་ ༎ཁོ་གཉིས་རྩོད་པ་ཤོར་ཙང་ངས་བར་མོལ་བྱས་པ་ཡིན་ I held mediating discussions because the two of them had a disagreement.

བར་མོལ་ནང་འདུམ་ (parmöö naŋdum) shung. mediating བར་མོལ་ནང་འདུམ་ཞུས་འཁྲུས་ཞིབ་ས་བསྒྱུད་སྙོང་འབེབས་སྙན་ཞུ་ (We) submitted a petition to withdraw the lawsuit and settle out of court through mediation.

བར་སྨིན་ (parmin) mid-season, mid-ripening ༎བར་སྨིན་ཆུ་འབྲས་ Mid-ripening rice.

བར་ཙ་ལ་ (pardzala) among, between.

བར་བཙངས་ (pardzaŋ) stuffing, padding quilting.

བར་བརྩིགས་ (pərdzii) middle level/ layer.

བར་ཚགས་ (pardzaà) padding; va.—རྒྱག.

བར་ཚངས་ (pardzaŋ) sm. བར་བཙངས་.

བར་ཚུགས་ (pardzuù) transfer station.

བར་ཚེག (pardzeg) dot that separates syllables.

བར་ཚོང་ (pardzoŋ) brokering/ acting as a middleman in business; va.—རྒྱག.

བར་ཚོང་རྒྱག་མཁན་ (pardzoŋ gyaàñɛn) sm. བར་ཚོང་པ་.

བར་ཚོང་པ་ (pardzoŋba) broker/ middleman.

བར་མཚམས་ (pandzam) a break/ gap; va.—འཇོག to stop/ leave off for a while, to take a break; va.—ཞུ་ to mediate, to conciliate, to reconcile.

བར་མཚམས་ཀྱི་ངལ་གསོ་ (pandzamgi ŋɛɛso) rest break.

བར་མཚམས་ཀྱི་རོལ་དབྱངས་ (pandzamgi rööyaŋ) intermezzo.

བར་མཚམས་འགྲིགས་པོ་ (pandzam drigbu) tightly attached.

བར་མཚམས་གཅོད་ (pandzam jöö) va. to discontinue/ stop, to adjourn ༎སྦྱིན་བདག་གིས་རོགས་རམ་བྱ་རྒྱུ་བར་མཚམས་བཅད་བཞག The patron discontinued his aid.

བར་མཚམས་ཆད་ (pandzam cɛ̄ɛ) vi. to be discontinued, to come to a halt/ stop ༎རྒྱུ་ཆ་ཛོགས་ནས་ལས་ཀ་བར་མཚམས་ཆད་པ་རེད་ (They) ran out of materials and the work had to be stopped.

བར་མཚམས་འཆད་ (pandzam cɛ̄ɛ̀) sm. བར་མཚམས་ཆད་.

བར་མཚམས་མེད་པ་ (pandzam mɛɛ̀ba) sm. བར་མ་ཆད་པར་.

བར་མཚམས་ལ་ (pandzamla) in between, in the middle of, in the interim / interval ༎འཛིན་གྲྭའི་བར་མཚམས་ལ་ In between classes.

བར་འཚངས་ (pandzaŋ) stuffing, quilting, padding.

བར་ཞག (parshaà) an overnight stop on a journey.

བར་ཞིབ་ (parshib) middle quality tsampa.

བར་ཞུས་ལོ་ཙཱ་བ་ (parshüü lodzawa) the person who helps proofread a translator.

བར་ཞེང་ (parsheŋ) distance between two things.

བར་བཞུགས་ (pərshuù) sm. བར་གནས་.

བར་ཟ་ (parsa) middleman's profit.

བར་ཟས་ (parsɛɛ̀) snacks.

བར་ཟོས་ (parsöö) sm. བར་ཟ་.

བར་གཟབ་ (parsəb) sm. བར་གོས་.

བར་གཟུ་ (parsu) referee, mediator.

བར་གཡུ་ (paryu) middle quality turquoise.

བར་ལ་ (parla) sm. བར་དུ་.

བར་ལ་དོ་ (parla to) in between ༎ཁོ་ལས་ཁུངས་གཉིས་ཀྱི་བར་ལ་དོ་དེ་ར་ལུས་བཞག He is in between offices (jobs).

བར་ལག (parlaà) in between ༎ཁང་པ་དེ་གཉིས་ཀྱི་བར་ལག་ལ་ལམ་ཆུང་ཞིག་ཡོད་པ་རེད་ There is a small road going between the two houses.

བར་ལམ་ (parlam) recently, in recent times ༎བར་ལམ་གྱི་གནས་ཚུལ་ The recent situation.

བར་ལམ་ཞིག་ནས་ (parlam shignɛ) from recently, from recent times.

བར་ལམ་ཞིག་ལ་ (parlam shiglə) sm. བར་ལམ་.

བར་ཤ་ (parsha) webbed ༎རྐང་མཛུབ་བར་ཤ་ Webbed toes.

བར་ཤར་པ་ (parshawa) middle-aged monks.

བར་ཤུན་ (parshün) a layer underneath the skin.

བར་ཤུར་ (pərshu) corridor, passage.

བར་ས་ལག་ག་ (parsa lagga) sm. བར་ས་ལག་ལ་.

བར་ས་ལག་ལ་ (parsa lagla) in between; in the interim ༎ང་ལས་ཀར་འགྲོ་བའི་བར་ས་ལག་ལ་སློབ་སྦྱོང་བྱེད་ཀྱི་ཡོད་ In between going to work, I study.

བར་སེལ་ (parsel) discord, estrangement, alienation ༎བར་ལམ་གྲོགས་པོ་གཉིས་དབར་བར་སེལ་བྱུང་བཞག Recently, discord has risen between the two friends.

བར་སྲང་ (parsaŋ) narrow alley.

བར་སྲིད་ (pərsii) sm. བར་དོ་བ་.

བར་སྦུབས་ (pərsub) 1. space between sth. 2. sm.

བར་མཚམས་.

བར་སྐབས་ལ་ (parsubla) 1. opening, space, gap. 2. during free time.

བར་སྐབས་ལས་ (parsub lɛɛ̀) vi. to unintentionally miss/ leave out sth. ¶ སླ་འགྱིད་འབུལ་སྐབས་དགེ་འདུན་བསྟར་པ་གཅིག་བར་སྐབས་ལས་བཞག (We) missed a whole row of monks when giving alms.

བར་གསེང་ (parseŋ) 1. space between sth., crack, gap ¶ མི་དེས་སྒོའི་བར་གསེང་ནས་ལྟ་གི་འདུག That man is looking through the crack in the door. 2. off duty, interval/ time between ¶ ངས་ལས་ཀའི་བར་གསེང་སྐབས་ལ་ཁྱེད་རང་མཇལ་གྱི་ཡིན་ I will see you between work (when I am off duty).

བར་གསེང་བེད་སྤྱོད་ (parseŋ peèjöö) using spare time for sth.; va.—བྱེད་.

བར་གསེང་འཚོལ་ (parseŋ dzöö) va. to search/ look for time (to do sth.).

བར་ལྷུ་ (parlhu) in between the joints and parts (of a machine).

བར་ཕྲག་བར་ཕྲག (parhraà parhraà) in between other things, in spare time ¶ ང་བར་ཕྲག་བར་ཕྲག་ལ་ཁྱེད་ཀྱི་སར་ཡོང་གི་ཡིན་ I will come (to visit you) in my spare time.

བལ་ (pɛɛ) 1. wool; va.—འཁལ་ to spin woolen material; va.—འབྲེག to shear wool. 2. abbr. of བལ་པོ་ or བལ་ཡུལ་. 3. abbr. of བལ་ལུ་.

བལ་དཀར་ (pɛɛgar) white wool.

བལ་སྐད་ (pɛɛgɛɛ̀) Nepali. language.

བལ་སྐུད་ (pɛɛgüü) wool thread/ yarn ¶ བལ་སྐུད་སྤུ་རིང་ Long fiber wool thread.

བལ་སྐུད་ཁབ་འཐག་བཟོ་གྲྭ (pɛɛgüü kəbdaà sodra) woolen knitwear mill.

བལ་སྐུད་འཁལ་འཁོར་ (pɛɛgüü kēēgɔɔ) wool spinning machine.

བལ་ཁྲལ་ (pɛɛdrɛɛ) tax on wool.

བལ་འཁལ་ (pɛɛgee) see བལ་, 1.

བལ་འཁལ་འཐག་བཟོ་གྲྭ (pɛɛ kēēdaà sodra) woolen mill/ factory.

བལ་འཁྲུད་བཟོ་གྲྭ (pɛɛdrüü sodra) wool washing factory.

བལ་གུར་ (pɛɛgur) safflower.

བལ་གོང་ (pɛɛgoŋ) price of wool.

བལ་གོར་ (pɛɛgɔɔ) abbr. of བལ་པོ་ and གོར་ཁ་.

བལ་གོས་ (pɛɛgöö) 1. woolen clothes. 2. Nepalese clothes.

བལ་གྲི་ (pɛɛdri) shearing knife.

བལ་གླང་ (pɛɛlaŋ) elephant from Nepal.

བལ་རྒྱབ་ (pɛɛgyəb) 1. amount of wool sheared from one sheep. 2. one load of wool (for transport).

བལ་རྒྱུ་ (pɛɛgyu) the quality of wool.

བལ་སྒོར་ (pɛɛgɔɔ) 1. loads of twisted wool. 2. Nepalese coin/ dollar.

བལ་རྗེ་ (pɛɛje) Nepalese king.

བལ་སྙིགས་ (pɛɛñii) leftover wool (to be thrown away).

བལ་ཏམ་ (pɛɛdram) Nepalese tranka coin.

བལ་བཏག (pɛɛdaà) woven from wool.

བལ་བཏགས་ཐོན་རྫས་ (pɛɛdaà tőndzɛɛ̀) Woven wool products.

བལ་སྟན་ (pɛɛdɛn) woolen rug.

བལ་ཐག (pɛɛdaà) woolen rope.

བལ་ཐུལ་ (pɛɛdüü) sm. ཐེ་གམ་.

བལ་འཐག་བཟོ་གྲྭ (pɛɛdaà sodra) wool weaving mill, woolen mill.

བལ་དོ་ (pɛɛdo) a pack/ load of wool.

བལ་དོས་ (pɛɛdöö) bale of wool.

བལ་དྲིལ་ (pɛɛdrii) bell made in Nepal.

བལ་གདན་ (pɛɛden) woolen rug.

བལ་འདབ་ (pɛɛdəb) carded wool.

བལ་འདབ་རྡོ་བསྣུན་དུ་འཇོག (pɛɛdəb donɛndu jɔɔ̀) shung. putting/ leaving/ setting/ keeping aside ¶ ལས་རྙོག་བྱིངས་ནམས་འདུམ་གནས་ལ་བརྟེན་བལ་འདབ་རྡོ་བསྣུན་དུ་བཞག་ཅིང་ Leaving aside for the time being those problems that can be solved through a mediator. [Lit. putting the wool that has been carded under a stone].

བལ་སྣ་ (pɛɛna) stretchability/ elasticity of wool.

བལ་སྣམ་ (pɛɛnam) woolen woven materials.

བལ་པ་ཛ་ (pɛɛbadza) acanthaceous indigo.

བལ་པོ་ (pɛɛbo) a Nepalese, Nepalese.

བལ་པོ་མི་རེད་ ཁ་གང་དངུལ་རེད་ (bɛɛbo mireè kādaŋ ŋüü reè) one should not look down on others [Lit. Nepalese are humans and ཁ་གང་ (the smallest money unit) is money].

བལ་པོ་གུར་གུམ་ (pɛɛbo gurgum) sm. བལ་གུར་.

བལ་པོའི་སེའུ་ (pɛɛbö sīwu) pomegranate from Nepal.

བལ་པོའི་དོང་དོང་ (pɛɛbö dōŋdoŋ) large bell hung on the neck of animals that comes from Nepal.

བལ་སྤུ་ (pɛɛbu) wool and hair.

བར་སྤུ་འཁལ་འཐག (pɛɛbu kēēdaà) spinning wool and hair.

བལ་སྤུ་འཁལ་འཕང་ (pɛɛbu kēēbaŋ) spinning spindle.

བལ་སྤུ་ཞིབ་འཁལ་ (pɛɛbu shibgee) thin/ finely spun yarn.

བལ་པ་ཙ་ (pɛɛwadza) བལ་པ་ཛ་.

བལ་ཕྱར་ (pɛɛjar) woolen blanket.

བལ་བག (pɛɛbaà) sm.* བལ་འབྲེག.

བལ་བུ་ (pɛɛbu) shung. sm. བལ་པོ་.

བལ་བོད་ (pɛɛböö) Tibet and Nepal.

བལ་བྲིས་ (pɛɛdrii) Nepalese school of painting.

བལ་འབྲེག (pɛɛdreg) see བལ་, 1.

བལ་འབྲེག་རྗེམ་ཙེ་ (pɛɛdreg jemdze) shearing scissors.

བལ་ཕད་ཕོད་ (pɛɛ bɛɛ̀böö) matted wool.

བལ་སྦུབ་ (pɛɛbub) cymbal made in Nepal.

བལ་མ་ (pɛɛma) female wool spinner.

བལ་མི་ (pɛɛmi) wool spinner.

བལ་མོ་ (pɛɛmo) Nepalese woman.

བལ་མོ་བཟའ་ (pɛɛmo sa) the Nepalese wife of King Srongtsan Gampo (Bhrikuti Devi).

བལ་སྨིས་ (pɛɛ mēè) va. to card wool.

བལ་ཙེ་ (pɛɛdzi) sm. བལ་སྣ་.

བལ་ཚོང་ (pɛɛdzoŋ) wool trade; va.—རྒྱག to trade in wool.

བལ་ཚོན་ (pɛɛdzön) colored wool.

བལ་གཞུང་ (pɛɛshuŋ) government of Nepal.

བལ་ཟེ་ (pɛɛse) a tool to fluff woolen material.

བལ་ཟོམ་ (pɛɛsom) a Tibetan boot made of woolen material.

བལ་བཟའ་ (pɛɛsa) sm. བལ་མོ་བཟའ་.

བལ་བཟའ་ཁྲི་བཙུན་ (pɛɛsa trīdzön) sm. བལ་མོ་བཟའ་.

བལ་ཡིག (pɛɛyii) Nepalese script/ writing.

བལ་ཡུལ་ (pɛɛyüü) 1. Nepal. 2. the Kathmandu Valley.

བལ་ཡེ་ (pɛɛye) cotton swab.

བལ་གཡོག (pɛɛyɔɔ̀) sm. བལ་ལས་.

བལ་ལ་བལ་སྐྱེས་ (pɛɛla pɛɛgyeè) doing successful wool trading so that one ends up with more wool as profit.

བལ་ལས་ (pɛɛlɛɛ̀) wool work; va.—བྱེད་.

བལ་ལི་ (pɛɛli) bronze icons/ statues made in Nepal, Nepalese bronze.

བལ་ལུ་ (pɛɛlu) azalea, rhododendron.

བལ་ཤད་ (pɛɛshɛɛ̀) carding comb/ brush; va.—རྒྱག to card wool.

བལ་ཤད་འཕྲུལ་འཁོར་ (pɛɛshɛɛ̀ trǖǖgɔɔ) wool carding machine.

བལ་ཤོ་ (pɛɛsho) shung. tax collected on exports and imports of wool.

བལ་གསིད་ (pɛɛ̀ sēè) 1. va. to card wool. 2. sm. བལ་ཤད་.

བལ་གསིད་འཕྲུལ་འཁོར་ (pɛɛseè trǖǖgɔɔ) carding machine.

བལ་སླིའུ་ (pɛɛ liwu) blanket/ cloak made of tightly woven wool.

བལ་བསིད་ (pɛɛ sēè) p. of བལ་གསིད་.

བལ་བསླས་གྱོན་ཆས་ (pɛɛlɛɛ̀ kyönjɛɛ̀) woolen knitwear.

བས་ (pɛɛ̀) 1. than ¶ དེ་བས་ཀྱང་ Even more than that. 2. sm. འཇོད་.

བས་མཐའ་ (pɛɛda) 1. a remote area. 2. suburb of a town.

བས་བལྒགས་ (pɛɛŋaà) a type of skin disease.

བས་འཕུལ་ (pɛɛbüü) the prefixed letter བ་.

བི་ཅི་ལི་ (bijilii̇) hind. flashlight.

བི་ཅི་ལིའི་སྨན་ (bijilii̇ mɛ̄n) hind.tib. flashlight battery.

བི་ཅིའུ་ (piju) ch. beer.

བི་ཆུ་ (piju) sm. བི་ཅིའུ་.

བི་ཆུར་ཚ་པོ་ (piju tsābo) sm. པེར་ཤ་ཚ་པོ་.

བི་དི་ནམ་ (pidinam) Vietnam.

བི་དོར་ (pidɔɔ) ch. a cloth or wool bag used to carry clothes on horseback.

བི་ལ་བསིལ་པོ་ (pilə sīību) sm. སྦྲི་ལ་བསིལ་པོ་.

བི་ལ་བསིལ་བསིལ་ (pilə sīīsii) sm. བི་ལ་བསིལ་པོ་.

བི་ཤ་ཙེ་ (pishadze) a type of disease causing paralysis of the hand.

བི་ཤུ་ (pishu) wooden head put on the top of an arrow causing it to whistle when shot (i.e., whistling arrow).

བི་ས་ (pisə) child.

བི་སངས་པོ་ (pi sāŋbo) sm. སྦྲི་གསང་.

བི་སངས་དོད་པོ་ (pisaŋ töòbo) sm. སྦྲི་གསང་དོད་པོ་.

བི་ཧར་ (pihar) Bihar (in India).

བིག་པན་ (pigbɛn) chalconthite.

བིམ་ (pim) sm. སྦྲིན་.

བིམ་པ་ (pimbə) Chinese crabapple.

བིར་ཐིག (pirdig) fuse used to ignite Tibetan matchlock gun.

བིར་ཤུབས་ (pirshub) case/ pouch for a བིར་ཐིག.

བིལ་པ་ (piibə) aegle marmelos.

བིལ་བ་ (piibə) sm. བིལ་པ་.

བིལ་འབྲས་ (piidrɛɛ̀) the fruit/ seed of བིལ་པ་.

བིལྺ་ (piwu) sm. བིལ་པ་.

བུ་ (pu) 1. son, boy. 2. abbr. for བུ་ཕྲུག.

བུ་སྐལ་ (pugɛɛ) sm. བུ་ཆབ་.

བུ་སྐྱེ་ (pu gyēè) va. to give birth to a son ¶ མོ་ལ་བུ་སྐྱེས་པ་རེད་ She gave birth to a son.

བུ་སྐྱེ་ཁང་ (pugyeègaŋ) maternity home/ clinic, place where one goes to give birth.

བུ་སྐྱེ་ནད་བརྟག་ཁང་ (pugyeè nɛɛ̀dagaŋ) prenatal clinic. gynecology clinic.

བུ་སྐྱེད་ (pugyeè) interest on the interest of a loan.

བུ་སྐྱེའི་སྨན་ཁང་ (pugyee mɛ̄ngaŋ) obstetrical/ maternity hospital.

བུ་སྐྱེའི་ཚན་ཁག (pugyee tsɛ̄ngaà) obstetrical/ maternity department.

བུ་སྐྱེའི་ཚོད་འཛིན་ (pugyee tsõndzin) birth control, birth regulations/ limitations.

བུ་ཁ་ (puga) sm. བུ་ག.

བུ་ཁ་རླུང་འཚང་ (puga lūŋdzaŋ) weakness brings forth people to cause one harm [Lit. the wind rushes into a hole].

བུ་ཁྱིམ་ (pugyim) 1. a home for children. 2. the Children's Village (TCV) in Dharamsala.

བུ་ཁྱིམ་ཁང་ (pugyimgaŋ) sm. བུ་ཁྱིམ་.

བུ་འཁྲིད་ (pudrii̇) girl's name (typically used when a family has a lot of girls and this name is given in the hope that the next child may be a boy).

བུ་ག (pugə) 1. hole, opening, orifice; va.—འབུགས་; —འབིགས་ to pierce/ make a hole, to drill a hole/ opening. 2. folli.

བུ་ག་དགུ་ (pugə gu) sm. བུ་ག་སྒོ་དགུ་.

བུ་ག་སྒོ་དགུ་ (pugə gogu) the nine holes in the human body: two eyes, two nostrils, mouth, two ears, anus, vagina/ urethra.

བུ་ག་གཉིས་པ་ (pugə ñīibə) a medical tool used to examine hemorrhoids.

བུ་ག་བདུན་ (pugə dün) the seven openings in the human head: two eyes, two ears, two nostrils and mouth.

བུ་ག་བདུན་ནས་དུ་བ་འདོན་ (pugə dünnɛ tuwa dön) very angry [Lit. smoke coming from the seven openings of the head].

བུ་གུ (pugu) small hole/ opening.

བུ་རྒྱུད་ (pugyüù) children, offspring, descendants ¶ བུ་རྒྱུད་མེད་པའི་རྒས་པོ་རྒན་མོ་རྣམས་ Old men and women without children.

བུ་རྒྱུད་རྒན་གཞོན་ (pugyüù gɛnshön) old and young children/ descendents.

བུ་རྒྱུད་དམག (pugyüù māà) sm. བུ་ཕྲུག་དམག.

བུ་བཅོལ་ཁང་ (pujüügaŋ) nursery, creche, child care center.

བུ་ཆ་ (puja) numerator (in math).

བུ་ཆུང་ (pujuŋ) the younger son.

བུ་ཆེ་བ་ (pu cēwa) the elder son.

བུ་ད་པེ་སི་ (puda pēsi) Budapest.

བུ་དོག (pudɔɔ̀) sm. བུལ་དོག.

བུ་སྟོན་ཆོས་འབྱུང་ (pudön cõnjuŋ) a historical work by བུ་སྟོན་རིན་ཆེན་གྲུབ་.

བུ་ཐང་ (pudaŋ) sm. མག་པ་.

བུ་དོད་ (pudöò) adopted son.

བུ་དེབ་ (pudeb) copy of a n original manuscript/ master register.

བུ་དེབ་ངོ་བཤུས་ (pudeb ŋoshüù) shung. sm. བུ་དེབ་.

བུ་སྡུག (pudug) cute-looking boy.

བུ་ནད་ (punɛɛ̀) an illness assocaited with childbirth.

བུ་ནོར་ (punɔɔ) abbr. male heir and family fortune.

བུ་སྣོད་ (punöò) womb; vi.—ལུག to have a prolapse of the uterus.

བུ་དཔེ་ (pube) sm. བུ་དེབ་.

བུ་སྤུན་ (pubün) brother ¶ བུ་སྤུན་འབྲིང་བ་ Middle brother.

བུ་སྤུན་མཆེད་ (pu bũnjeè) sm. བུ་སྤུན་.

བུ་ཕ་བདག་བུ་མོ་མ་བདག (pu pādaà pomo madaà) custom in divorces where the son remains with the father and daughter goes with the mother [Lit. son owned by the father and the daughter owned by the mother].

བུ་ཕྲུག (pudruù) child, children.

བུ་ཕྲུག་ཐང་བསྐྱུར་ (pudruù tāŋgyur) shung. children left without care ¶ ཕ་རྟ་མགྲིན་དམ་པ་དེ་ཉིད་ཀྱི་བུ་ཕྲུག་ཐང་བསྐྱུར་ལུས་ཁར་ The children of the late father Tamdrin were left without anyone to care for them.

བུ་ཕྲུག་ལྡན་པའི་ཁྱིམ་ཚང་ལ་རོགས་དངུལ་ (pudruù dɛmbɛ kyīmdzaŋlə rɔɔ̀ŋüü) Aid to Families with Dependent Children (in U.S.A.).

བུ་ཕྲུག་དམག (pudruù maà) army made up of the children of the people.

བུ་མ་ཕྱིན་པའི་མོ་ནད་ (pumajinbɛ monɛɛ̀) a disease making delivery of a baby difficult.

བུ་མེད་ (pumeè) sm. བུད་མེད་.

བུ་མོ་ (pomo) 1. girl. 2. daughter.

བུ་མོ་སྤུན་ (pomo bũn) sisters ¶ བུ་མོ་སྤུན་བདུན་ Seven sisters.

བུ་མོ་སྐྲ་དཀར་ (pomo drāgar) "The White Haired Girl" (PRC ballet).

བུ་མོ་དགའ་སྟོབས་མ་ (pomo gadobma) the woman who offered milk to Buddha when he came out of fasting after six years.

བུ་མོ་བརྟན་མ་ (pomo dɛ̄nma) 1. a virgin. 2. a woman who hasn't had sexual relations with anyone other than her husband.

བུ་མོ་དར་མ་ (pomo tarma) an adult female in the prime of life (roughly between the ages of 20-35).

བུ་མོ་སྤུན་རྒན་ (pomo bũngɛn) older sister.

བུ་མོ་འཕང་བཟུང་ (pomo pāŋsuŋ) a coward [Lit. a female carrying a spindle].

བུ་མོ་གཙང་མ་ (pomo dzāŋma) sm. བུ་མོ་བརྟན་མ་.

བུ་ (pomo) abbr. བུ་མོ་.

བུའི་གདོང་ལེན་རུ་ཁག (pomö doŋlen rugaà) Girl Scouts.

བུ་མོའི་སྐར་ཚོམ་ (pomo gārdzom) the constellation Virgo.

བུ་མོའི་གདོང་ལེན་རུ་ཁག (pomo doŋlen rugaà) Girl Scouts.

བུ་མོའི་བདག་པོ་ (pomö dagbo) husband of a woman.

བུ་མོའི་འདུན་མ་ལན་གཅིག (pomö dünma len jig) a woman should marry only once.

བུ་སྨད་ (pumɛè) daughter and mother; females.

བུ་བཙའ་ (pu dzā) va. to give birth to a child ¶ མོ་ལ་བུ་ཞིག་བཙས་འདུག She gave birth to a son.

བུ་བཙའི་དུས་ཚེ་ (pudzɛ tüüdze) season of high births.

བུ་བཙའི་ན་ཚོད་ (pudzɛ nadzöö) the age of child bearing.

བུ་བཙའི་ནད་རིགས་ (pudzɛ nɛɛrig) obstetrical illness.

བུ་བཙའི་སྨན་ཁང་ (pudzɛ mɛngaŋ) maternity hospital.

བུ་བཙའི་ཚན་ཁག (pudzɛ tsɛngaà) obstetrical/ maternity department.

བུ་བཙའི་རིག་པ་ (pudzɛ rigbə) obstetrics.

བུ་བཙས་ཟླ་འཁོར་ (pudzɛ dagɔɔ) a one month old infant.

བུ་ཚ་ (pudza) 1. son and grandson. 2. son and nephew/ niece.

བུ་ཚ་བུ་རྒྱུད་ (pudza pugyüü) descendants, next generation.

བུ་ཚ་ཡང་ཚ་གསུམ་ཚ་ (pudza yaŋdza sūmdza) five generations of males: oneself, བུ་ (one's son), ཚ་བོ་ (grandson), ཡང་ཚ་ (great grandson), གསུམ་ཚ་ (great great grandson).

བུ་ཚབ་ (pudzəb) adopted son; adopted child.

བུ་འཛིན་མ་ (pundzimmə) woman with children.

བུ་ཛི་ (pudzi) babysitter; va.—བྱེད་ to babysit.

བུ་ཛི་མ་ (pudzimə) nurse in nursery/ creche.

བུ་ཡུག (puyuù) snowstorm, blizzard; va.—རྒྱག; —འཚུབ་ to have a snowstorm / blizzard.

བུ་གཡར་ (puyaa) sm. བུ་ཚབ་.

བུ་རབས་ (purəb) patrilineal descendants.

བུ་རབས་ཚ་རྒྱུད་ (purəb tsəgyüü) sm. བུ་རབས་.

བུ་རམ་ (puram) 1. congealed brown sugar.

བུ་རམ་གོང་བུ་ (puram koŋbu) brown sugar nuggets.

བུ་རམ་སྐར་མ་ (puram garma) brown sugar mixed with butter (kind of toffee).

བུ་རམ་སྒོང་ (puram goŋ) va. to make brown sugar nuggets.

བུ་རམ་ཆང་ (puram cāŋ) chang made with brown sugar.

བུ་རམ་ དིང་གོར་མ་ (puram diŋgɔrmə) brown sugar made into the shape of a water offering bowl.

བུ་རམ་དིང་པར་ (puram diŋbar) sm. བུ་རམ་དིང་གོར་མ་.

བུ་རམ་དྭངས་མ་ (puram taŋma) clear brown sugar (candy).

བུ་རམ་ཕར་ཁ་ (puram pārga) an inferior type of brown sugar.

བུ་རམ་མ་ལོ་ (puram malo) a high quality brown sugar.

བུ་རམ་མོག་མོག (puram momoò) a dumpling with brown sugar filling.

བུ་རམ་སྨུག་པོ་ (puram mūgbo) dark-colored brown sugar.

བུ་རམ་ཤིང་ (puramshiŋ) sugar cane.

བུ་རམ་ཤིང་པ་ (puram shiŋbə) name of the lineage of the family of Sakyamuni (Buddha).

བུ་རོ་ལུས་ (puro lüü) sm. བུ་རོགས་.

བུ་རོགས་ལུས་ (puro lüü) 1. vi. to have the placenta not come out. 2. vi. to have a dead baby remain in the womb.

བུ་རོགས་ (purɔɔ) placenta.

བུ་ལུག (pulu) a kind of Tibetan cookie.

བུ་ལོན་ (pulön) debt, loan; vi.—ཆགས་; — འཁྱེར་; — ཟུག to get into debt; va.—གཏོང་ to give a loan; va.—ལེན་ to borrow, to take a loan. ¶ སྐྱེད་ཆེའི་བུ་ལོན་ High interest loan.

བུ་ལོན་ཀྲབ་རྡུལ་ (pulön gūbrüü) sb. with a large number of debts.

བུ་ལོན་གྱི་འོབས་སུ་ཚུད་ (pulöngi obsu tsüü) sm. བུ་ལོན་ཀྲབ་རྡུལ་.

བུ་ལོན་འཇལ་ (pulön jɛɛ) va. to pay a debt, to repay a loan.

བུ་ལོན་འཇལ་དགོས་པའི་རྒྱལ་ཁབ་ (pulön jɛɛgööbɛ gyɛɛgəb) debtor nation.

བུ་ལོན་འཇོག (pulön jɔɔ) va. to leave a loan/ debt ¶ བཟའ་ཚང་ཁ་བྲལ་སྐབས་བུ་ལོན་ཚང་མ་སྐྱེ་དམན་ལ་བཞག་པ་རེད་ When the couple got divorced all the debts were left with the wife.

བུ་ལོན་གཏོང་ལེན་ (pulön dōŋlen) system of borrowing and lending, credit system.

བུ་ལོན་དག (pulön taà) vi. to have one's debt cleared up/ finished/ nullified.

བུ་ལོན་བདག་པོ་ (pulön dadbo) creditor.

བུ་ལོན་འདེད་ (pulön teè) va. to pursue collecting a debt/ loan, to go to ask for repayment of a loan.

བུ་ལོན་འདེད་མཁན་ (pulön teèñɛn) debt/ loan collector.

བུ་ལོན་སྡུད་ (pulön düü) va. to collect a loan/ debt.

བུ་ལོན་སྡུད་དབང་ (pulön düüwaŋ) right to collect debts/ loans.

བུ་ལོན་སྡུད་དབང་ཡོད་མཁན་ (pulön düüwaŋ yüüñɛn) creditors.

བུ་ལོན་སྡུད་དབང་ཡོད་པའི་རྒྱལ་ཁབ་ (pulön düüwaŋ yüübɛ gyɛɛgəb) creditor nation.

བུ་ལོན་པ་ (pulömba) a debtor.

བུ་ལོན་སྒྲོད་ (pulön dröö) va. to repay a loan/ debt.

བུ་ལོན་འཕྲོད་ (pulön tröö) sm. བུ་ལོན་དག.

བུ་ལོན་གཙང་སེལ་ (pulön dzāŋsel) repaying a loan.

བུ་ལོན་ཚ་འདེད་ (pulön tsādeè) aggressively chasing/ pursuing collection of loan.

བུ་ལོན་འཛིན་ཤོག (pulön dzinshoò) IOU letter.

བུ་ལོན་བཞག (pulön shaà) p. of བུ་ལོན་འཇོག.

བུ་ལོན་བཟོ་ (pulön so) va. to take a loan/ to go into debt.

བུ་ལོན་གཡར་ (pulön yāā) va. to lend out or take a loan.

བུ་ལོན་ལེན་ (pulön len) va. to borrow/ take a loan.

བུ་སྲིང་ (pusiŋ) brother and sister.

བུ་སློབ་ (pulob) disciple, pupil.

བུ་གསུམ་བར་པ་ (pusum parwa) sm. བུ་གསུམ་བར་པའི་བཙུན་ཁྲལ་.

བུ་གསུམ་བར་པའི་བཙུན་ཁྲལ་ (pusum parwɛ dzūntrɛɛ) shung. a type of tax obligation wherein the middle of three sons has to become a monk.

བུ་གསོ་ཁང་ (pusogaŋ) nursery for (children), creche.

བུག (puù) sm. བུ་ག.

བུག་ཀྲང་ (pugdraŋ) ch. minister.

བུག་སྒོ་ (puggo) door to a cave.

བུག་སྒོ་འདག་སྦྱར་ (puggo dagjar) a meditator who has the door to his cave closed.

བུག་རྡོལ་འཕྲུལ་འཁོར་ (pugdöö trüügɔɔ) a perforating/ hole punching machine.

བུག་རྡོལ་ (pug döö) vi. to get pierced/ punctured, to become torn, to get a hole torn.

བུག་པ་ (pugbə) a hole.

བུགས་ (puù) vi.to deteriorate.

བུང་ཀྱུག (punjaà) a stinger (of bee, wasp, etc.).

བུང་ཐལ་ (puŋtɛɛ) a fly.

བུང་བ་ (puŋwə) bee ¶ བུང་བའི་རྒྱལ་མོ་ Queen bee.

བུང་བ་ནག་པོ་ (puŋwa nagbo) black fly.

བུང་ཚང་ (pundzaŋ) beehive.

བུངས་ (puŋ) size ¶ འཕྲུལ་འཁོར་འདི་བུངས་ཆེན་པོ་འདུག This machine is very large.

བུངས་སྐྱེད་ (puŋgyeè) making bigger, enlarging; va.—གཏོང་.

བུངས་ཚན་ (pundzɛn) the space in sth. ¶ ཁང་པ་འདི་བུངས་ཚན་ཆེན་པོ་འདུག This house is very spacious.

བུད་ (püü) 1. imp. of འབུད་. 2. vi. to come off, to get unstrung, to lose (hair) ¶ ཁོང་ལོ་ཆུང་དུས་ནས་སྐྲ་ཚང་མ་བུད་བཞག He lost his hair from an early age. 3. va. to burn, to throw on a fire ¶ ཁོས་ཚགས་པར་རྙིང་པ་དེ་ཚོ་མེ་ལ་བུད་སོང་ He burned the old newspapers. 4. va. to go ¶ ཁོང་སྒོ་ཁར་བུད་སོང་ He went to the doorstep.

བུད་ཀྱིས་འཁྱེར་ (püügi kyēr) vi. to meet with

disaster.

བུད་ཀྱིས་འདེབས་ (pu̱ügi de̱b) sm. བུད་ཀྱིས་འཁྱེར་.

བུད་ཀང་ (pu̱ügaŋ) shung. an extinct/ deserted ཀང་ (a ཀང་ land unit on which the family has become extinct or has run away).

བུད་གྲོང་ (pu̱üdroŋ) deserted villages.

བུད་རྙིང་ (pu̱üñiŋ) fields and villages that have been deserted for a long time.

བུད་སྡོངས་ (pu̱üdoŋ) extinct for a lineage or family.

བུད་སྡོངས་ཡུལ་སྒྱུར་ (pu̱üdoŋ yu̱üɡyar) sb. whose family is extinct and has been forced to leave home and wander about.

བུད་མེད་ (pu̱ümeè) woman ¶ བུད་མེད་མཉམ་འབྲེལ་ལྷན་ཚོགས་ Women's association.

བུད་མེད་ཀྱི་ན་ཚ་ (pu̱ümeègi na̱dza) women's diseases.

བུད་མེད་ཀྱི་ན་ཚའི་ཚན་ཁག་ (pu̱ümeègi na̱dzɛ tsɛ̄ngaà) division of obstetrics and gynecology.

བུད་མེད་ཀྱི་དབང་ཆ་ (pu̱ümeègi wāŋja) women's rights.

བུད་མེད་རྐྱང་རྒྱག་ (pu̱ümeè gyāŋgyaà) women's singles (in sports).

བུད་མེད་དགེ་སྒྲུབ་ཁང་ (pu̱ümeè ge̱drubgaŋ) convent (for nuns).

བུད་མེད་མགོ་གཙང་ (pu̱ümeè go̱dzaŋ) a virgin.

བུད་མེད་མངལ་ལྡན་ (pu̱ümeè ŋɛ̱ndɛn) pregnant woman.

བུད་མེད་ལྕགས་མི་ (pu̱ümeè jɔ̄gmi) "iron woman" (nickname of Margaret Thatcher).

བུད་མེད་ཆ་རྒྱག་ (pu̱ümeè cāgyaà) women's doubles (sports).

བུད་མེད་མཆོག་ (pu̱ümeè cɔ̄ɔ̀) a beautiful woman.

བུད་མེད་མཉམ་སྦྲེལ་ཚོགས་པ་ (pu̱ümeè ñāmdree tsɔ̄gba) Women's Federation Committee (exists at all administrative levels such as xiang and deals with women's issues).

བུད་མེད་གདུམ་པོ་ (pu̱ümeè dūmmo) an intimidating/ fierce/ harsh woman.

བུད་མེད་མཐུན་སྒྲིགས་ཚོགས་པ་ (pu̱ümeè tũndrɔɔ̀ tsɔ̄gba) women's association/ union.

བུད་མེད་དར་མ་ (pu̱ümeè ta̱rma) adult woman in the prime of life (roughly between 20-35 years of age).

བུད་མེད་དུས་ཆེན་ (pu̱ümeè tu̱üjen) women's day.

བུད་མེད་འདོད་ལྡན་མ་ (pu̱ümeè dö̱ödɛmma) a desirable/ sexy woman.

བུད་མེད་ན་ཚ་ (pu̱ümeè na̱dza) women's diseases.

བུད་མེད་ནང་ཁུལ་འཁྲིག་སྦྱོར་ (pu̱ümeè nɔ̱ŋgüü trīgjɔɔ) lesbianism.

བུད་མེད་ནང་ཁུལ་འཁྲིག་སྦྱོར་བྱེད་མཁན་ (pu̱ümeè nɔ̱ŋgüü trīgjɔɔ ce̱èñɛn) a lesbian.

བུད་མེད་སྦྲུམ་མ་ (pu̱ümeè dru̱mma) pregnant woman.

བུད་མེད་དམག་དཔུང་ (pu̱ümeè māgbuŋ) detachment of women soldiers.

བུད་མེད་གཙང་མ་ (pu̱ümeè dzāŋma) virgin.

བུད་མེད་ཚོགས་པ་ (pu̱ümeè tsɔ̄gba) women's association/ club/ group.

བུད་མེད་བཞིན་བཟང་མ་ (pu̱ümeè shi̱nsaŋma) a pretty woman.

བུད་མེད་ཟླ་མཚན་ (pu̱ümeè dza̱dzɛn) women who are still menstruating (i.e., women who are postmenarche and premenopause).

བུད་མེད་བཟོ་པ་ (pu̱ümeè so̱ba) women workers.

བུད་མེད་འོས་འཕེན་པའི་སྒྲིག་འཛུགས་ (pu̱ümeè wö̱mbenbɛ dri̱gdzuù) League for Woman's Voters.

བུད་མེད་ཡུལ་དམག་ (pu̱ümeè yu̱ümaà) women's militia.

བུད་མེད་ལས་འགུལ་ (pu̱ümeè lɛ̱ngüü) woman's movement.

བུད་མེད་ཤེས་ལྡན་མ་ (pu̱ümeè shēè dɛ̱mma) learned/ intelligent woman.

བུད་མེད་སློབ་གྲྭ་ (pu̱ümeè lōbdra) woman's school.

བུད་རྫས་ (pu̱üdzɛ̀ɛ̀) sm. བུད་ཤིང་.

བུད་ཤིང་ (pu̱üshiŋ) firewood.

བུན་ (pu̱n) a loan; va.—གཏོང་ to give out a loan.

བུན་སྐྱེད་ (pu̱ngyeè) interest (on loans).

བུན་དངུལ་ (pu̱nŋüü) money given as a loan.

བུན་ཆད་ (pu̱njɛɛ̀) being short on a payment on a loan.

བུན་ཆད་གཙང་འཕྲོད་ (pu̱njɛɛ̀ dzāŋdröö̀) paying off a loan, clearing up debts.

བུན་རྙིང་ (pu̱nñiŋ) an old loan.

བུན་སྙན་ (pu̱nñɛn) a request for a loan; a report about a loan.

བུན་གཏོང་མ་རྩ་ (pu̱ndoŋ ma̱dza) capital used or set aside for loans.

བུན་གཏོང་ལས་ཁུངས་ (pu̱ndoŋ lɛ̱ɛ̀guŋ) an office that makes loans.

བུན་ཐོ་ (pu̱nto) list of outstanding loans.

བུན་བདག་ (pu̱ndaà) one who gives out loans, a creditor.

བུད་འདེད་ (pu̱ndeè) 1. going after/ pursuing the collection of a loan; va.—བྱེད་. 2. the person who goes to collect loans.

བྱེད་ (pu̱meè) abbr. of བུད་མེད་.

བྱེད་འོས་འཕེན་པའི་སྒྲིག་འཛུགས་ (pu̱meè wö̱mbembɛ dri̱gdzuù) League of Women Voters.

བུན་བུན་ (pu̱nbün) 1. bubbling/ boiling water. 2. feeling uneasy/ restless ¶ དེ་རིང་ང་སེམས་བུན་བུན་བྱེད་ཀྱི་འདུག Today I feel very uneasy.

བུན་འབབ་ངོ་སྐྱེད་ (pu̱nbəb ŋo̱gyeè) principal and interest (of loans).

བུན་འབྲེལ་ (pu̱ndree) the relation between the creditor and the debtor.

བུན་འཛིན་ (pu̱ndzin) promissory/ loan note.

བུན་ཞིབ་ (pu̱nshib) shung. investigating loans ¶ ལོ་རེ་ཞིང་རེན་ཡུལ་སྐྱོལ་ཐེ་ཐོབ་བརྩིས་དེ་བུན་ཞིབ་སྐབས་རྩིས་འགྲོ་གཏོང་རྒྱུ་མ་ཟད་ Not only to have the yearly payment of agricultural field fees calculated at the time of investigating loans.

བུན་ཡིག་ (pu̱nyiì) sm. བུན་འཛིན་.

བུན་གཡོར་ཆེ་ཟུག་ (pu̱nyɔɔ cēsug) shung. having lot of debts ¶ བུན་གཡོར་ཆེ་ཟུག་པའི་སྒྲོད་དམིགས་དང་བྲལ་ཁར་ Because of having a lot of debts (they) have no means to pay the debts.

བུན་རེ་ (bu̱nre) a little bit.

བུན་ལག་སྡེང་འོག་ (pu̱nlag dēŋwɔɔ̀) shung. the creditor and the debtor ¶ དེ་རྗེས་ཕྱིར་འཁོར་མཚམས་ཆེད་འབོད་ཀྱིས་བུན་འབབ་དགོས་ལུགས་བུན་ལག་སྡེང་འོག་གི་ལེན་རྒྱུ་མ་བྱུང་ན་ After they return, if the creditor can not collect the loan from the debtor.

བུན་ལས་ (pu̱nlɛɛ̀) shung. lending money ¶ གྲྭ་རྐྱང་སྣེར་ནས་ཚོང་ཁེ་བུན་ལས་སོགས་མི་ཆོག་པ་ Monks may not engage in lending money.

བུན་ལོན་པ་ (pu̱nlömba) debtor.

བུན་ལོང་ (pu̱nloŋ) seething, bubbling, swirling in turmoil.

བུབ་ (pu̱b) 1. p. of འབུབ་. 2. a roll of material/ cloth. 3. vi. to go bankrupt ¶ ཚོང་ཉེས་བྱུང་ནས་མི་ཚང་དེ་བུབ་པ་རེད་ After he had a loss in business his household went bankrupt.

བུབ་ཀ་ (pu̱bgə) sm. བུབ་ཁ་.

བུབ་ཁ་ (pu̱bgə) sm. ཕམ་ཁ་.

བུབ་འགྲིལ་ (pu̱bdrii) sm. བུབ་.

བུབ་ཐལ་ (pu̱bdɛɛ) bankrupt, bankruptcy.

བུབས་ (pu̱b) 1. imp. of འབུབ་. 2. a roll of cloth ¶ སྣམ་བུ་བུབས་གསུམ་ Three rolls of woolen cloth.

བུབས་ཚང་ (pu̱bdzaŋ) sm. བུབས་, 2.

བུབས་རིལ་ (pu̱brii) sm. བུབས་, 2.

བུབས་ལོང་ (pu̱bloŋ) sm. བུབས་, 2.

བུམ་ཁེབས་ (pu̱mgeb) lid/ cover of a vase.

བུམ་མཁན་ (pu̱mgɛn) potter.

བུམ་ཆུ་ (pu̱mju) water in vases that is used for/ as religious offerings.

བུམ་དར་ (pu̱mdar) ceremonial scarf tied on a vase.

བུམ་པ་ (pu̱mbə) vase.

བུམ་གདན་ (pu̱mdɛn) rug/ mat on which a vase is placed.

བུམ་ནང་མར་མེ་ (pumnaŋ marme) not to publicize one's knowledge/ skill/ etc. [Lit. butter lamp in a vase].

བུམ་པ་གང་བྱོ་ (pumba kaŋjo) a learned person teaching everything he knows to others [Lit. to pour out all the water from a vase].

བུམ་པ་ཅན་ (pumbajɛn) a type of meditational practice.

བུམ་པ་བཟང་པོ་ (pumba saŋbo) 1. one of the seven auspicious symbols (the vase). 2. a vase in which many elements are put so that good luck, good fortune and wealth may come to the household.

བུམ་རྫ་ (pumdzi) clay pot.

བུམ་རྫས་ (pumdzɛɛ̀) fragrant smelling things put in the water of a vase used as an offering.

བུའི་གདོང་ལེན་རུ་ཁག (püü donlen rugaà) Boy Scouts.

བུར་ཆང་ (purjaŋ) beer made from brown sugar.

བུར་ཐུད་ (purdüü) a Tibetan food made from brown sugar butter and cheese.

བུར་ཞིང་ (purshiŋ) sugar cane field/ farm.

བུར་ཤིང་ (purshiŋ) sugar cane.

བུལ་ (püü) 1. abbr. of བུལ་ཏོག. 2. slow, slowly.

བུལ་ཁུག (püüguù) bag for carrying baking soda.

བུལ་ཁྱི་ (püügyi) sm. འདོངས་ཁྱི་.

བུལ་འགྲོས་ (püü dröö) va. to walk/ go slowly.

བུལ་ཆུ་ (püüju) water in which baking soda has been added.

བུལ་ཏོག (püüdoò) baking soda.

བུལ་ཏོག་བསྲེགས་མ་ (püüdoò sēgma) caustic soda.

བུལ་ཐུག (püüduù) a type of Chinese square noodle made with baking soda.

བུལ་པོ་ (püübo) sm. དལ་པོ་.

བུལ་བུལ་ (püübüü) slow, slowly.

བུལ་གཙང་ (püüdzaŋ) soda ash.

བུལ་མཚོ་ (pumdzo) alkaline lake.

བུས་ (püü) p. and imp. of འབུད་.

བུས་པ་ (püübə) infant, small child.

བེ་ཁྱི་ (pegyi) squirrel.

བེ་ཁྲག (pedraà) sap from an oak tree that is used in Tibetan medicine.

བེ་ག་ (pege) measles.

བེ་ཅེ་ (peji) a young child, a kid.

བེ་ཅོན་ (pejön) stick.

བེ་ཆོན་ (pejön) sm. བེ་ཅོན་.

བེ་སྣབས་ (penəb) snot.

བེ་ཏ་ (peda) coconut ¶ བེ་ཏའི་ཤིང་ Coconut tree.

བེ་དར་གཡུལ་འགྱེད་ (pedar yüügyeè) the war between བེ་ར་ and དར་རྒྱས་དགོན་པ་པ་ in 1930.

བེ་དོ་ (pedo) sm. བེ་རྡོ་.

བེ་རྡོ་ (pedo) oak tree.

བེ་བེ་ (pebe) calf.

བེ་འབྲས་ (pedrɛɛ̀) acorn of an oak tree.

བེ་གཡམ་ (peyam) flagstone.

བེ་ར་ (pere) a disease which causes pimples and itching.

བེ་ལེ་ཁ་ (pelaga) a traditional Tibetan surgical tool used for head injuries.

བེ་ལོ་ (pelo) sm. བེ་རྡོ་.

བེ་ལོག (pelɔɔ̀) a piece of wood that is placed between the beam and pillar.

བཻཌཱུརྱ་དཀར་པོ་ (bēdurya gārbo) name of astrological book compiled in 1685 by Desi Sangye Gyatso.

བཻཌཱུརྱ་སྔོན་པོ་ (bedurya ŋōmbo) name of a medical book compiled by Desi Sangye Gyatso.

བཻཌཱུརྱ་སེར་པོ་ (bedurya sērbo) a history of famous Gelugpa monasteries and lamas compiled in 1698 by Desi Sangye Gyatso.

བེ་ཤ་ཁ་ (bēshaga) the fourth month of the Tibetan calendar.

བེ་ཤིང་ (peshiŋ) oak tree.

བེ་སེ་ཀོབ་ (pesegob) eng. motion picture.

བེག་གེ་ (pegge) sm. བེ་ག་.

བེད་ (peè) use, advantage, profit; va.—སྤྱོད་ to make use of, to use ¶ ང་མེད་ཤུལ་དུ་ཁོ་ཚོས་ངའི་འཛིན་ཆས་བེད་སྤྱོད་པ་རེད་ They used my furniture while I was gone.

བེད་གཅོད་ (peèjöö) sm. བེད་སྤྱོད་.

བེད་ཆོད་ (peè cöö) vi. to be able to use, to be of use ¶ ཁོའི་རྒྱ་སྐད་དེ་སྐད་ཆ་གལ་ཆེན་པོ་ཡོད་ཡག་ལ་བེད་ཆོད་ཀྱི་མི་འདུག His Chinese isn't of use in important conversations.

བེད་ཆོད་པོ་ (peè cööbo) useful.

བེད་སྤྱོད་ (peèjöö) using, utilizing; va.—བྱེད་; —གཏོང་ to use, to make use of, to utilize ¶ རང་གི་ཉམས་མྱོང་ལ་བེད་སྤྱོད་བྱེད་ཐུབ་པ་ Being able to use one's own experience.

བེད་སྤྱོད་པའི་རིན་ཐང་ (peèjööbɛ rintaŋ) value/ cost of using sth.

བེད་སྤྱོད་འཕེར་བ་ (peèjöö pērwa) worthy of using/ use.

བེད་སྤྱོད་བྱེད་ཚད་ (peèjöö ceèdzɛɛ̀) utilization rate.

བེད་སྤྱོད་རིན་ཐང་ (peèjöö rindaŋ) sm. བེད་སྤྱོད་པའི་རིན་ཐང་.

བེད་མེད་ (peèmeè) 1. useless, a waste ¶ བེད་མེད་ཀྱི་ཐོན་རྫས་ Useless products. 2. obsolete.

བེད་མེད་རྒྱུ་ཆ་ (peèmeè gyubja) waste materials.

བེད་མེད་རྙོག་རོ་ (peèmeè sɔgro) waste materials, scrap heap.

བེད་མེད་ས་སྟོང་ (peèmeè sādoŋ) a vacant lot/ open ground that is not useful for anything.

བེད་མེད་ས་ཞིང་ (peèmeè səshiŋ) empty/ unused/ useless field.

བེན་ (pen) ch. a jug/ pot (usu. for beer).

བེན་ཆང་ (penjaŋ) jug/ pot for beer.

བེན་ཐུལ་ (pendüü) sm. ཟླ་གམ་.

བེམ་ (pem) sm. བེན་.

བེམ་ཁུག (pem gūù) vi. to be/ get wet.

བེམ་ཆག (pemjaà) sm. དཀར་ཆག.

བེམ་དོལ་ (pemdöö) sm. བེལ་རྡོལ་.

བེམ་པ་ (pemba) sm. བེམ་པོ་.

བེམ་པོ་ (pembo) 1. an inanimate thing, a lifeless object, a corpse ¶ བེམ་པོ་བཞིན་རེལ་བསྡད་འདུག (He) was lying there as if lifeless. 2. patched up.

བེམ་པོ་ཞལ་གྲིལ་ (pembo shɛɛdrii) pretending to be knowledgeable when one is not.

བེམ་བེམ་ (pembem) slightly moist or damp.

བེམ་རྫེག (pemdzeg) (a type of) smallpox.

བེམ་རིག (pemrig) body and consciousness.

བེམ་རིག་གཉིས་ (pemrigñii) the two: body and consciousness.

བེམ་རིག་བྲལ་ (pemrig trɛɛ) vi. to die.

བེམ་ཤེས་ (pemsheè) consciousness and nonconsciousness.

བེམ་ཧྲུལ་ (pemhrüü) old/ tattered clothes.

བེའུ་ (piwu) calf.

བེའུ་ཁང་ (piwugaŋ) shed in which calves are kept.

བེའུ་གོག (piwugɔɔ̀) sm. བེའུ་.

བེའུ་ལྗང་འཁྲིད་ (piwu jaŋdrii) sm. བེའུ་ལྗང་འདྲིད་. [Lit. leading a calf with a barley shoot].

བེའུ་ལྗང་འདྲིད་ (piwu jaŋdrii) tricking/ conning sb. [Lit. deceiving a calf with a barley shoot].

བེའུ་ཏ་ (piwuta) calf of a dead cow, orphan calf.

བེའུ་གདང་ (piwudaŋ) sm. བེའུ་དང་.

བེའུ་དང་ (piwudaŋ) the staked out line to which calves are tied.

བེའུ་ཕྲུག (piwudruù) sm. བེའུ་.

བེར་ (per) cloak (usu.worn by monks).

བེར་ཀ་ (perga) club, stick, staff; va.— རྒྱག, —བརྡུ་ to hit with a club/ staff.

བེར་ཀན་ཤིང་ (pergɛn shīŋ) sm. བེར་རྡོ་.

བེར་རྒྱག (per gyaà) vi. to tremble/ shake.

བེར་རྒྱུག (pergyuù) sm. བེར་ཀ་.

བེར་ལྕག (perjaà) abbr. of བེར་མ་ལྕག.

བེར་ཆེན་ (perjen) a large gown or cloak worn in the house.

བེར་རྡོ་ (perdo) oak tree.

བེར་ནག (pernaà) black dress worn by tantric practitioners.

པེར་འབྲུ་ (perdru) acorn from an oak tree.
པེར་མ་ (perma) sm. པེར་ཀ་.
པེར་མ་ལྕག (perma jāà) a stick that can be used as a club and a whip.
པེར་ཟླུམ་ (perdam) sm. པེར་.
པེར་ལོ་ (perlo) leaf of an oak tree.
པེར་ཤ་ (persha) mushroom that grows on oak trees.
པེར་གཤོལ་ (pērshöö) plough made from the wood of an oak tree.
པེར་སོལ་ (persöö) charcoal made from oak trees.
པེལ་ (pee) sm. པེའུ་.
པེལ་ཏོལ་ (peēdöö) snapping/ clicking (one's) fingers; va.—གཏོགས་ to snap one's finger to make a noise.
པེལ་སྣབས་ (peenəb) 1. vomiting. 2. flintstone. 3. a type of mineral used in Tibetan medicine.
པེས་ (peè) sm. དྲེས་.
པོ་ (po) 1. sentence ending particle for words ending in པ་ ¶ཁོ་དང་འཐབ་པོ་ (He) fought with him. 2. vi. to unintentionally spill ¶ཐབ་ཁར་འོ་མ་ཏོག་ཙམ་པོ་སོང་ (I) spilled some milk on the stove.
པོ་སྐྱེལ་ (pogyee) falling and spilling.
པོ་དང་ (podaŋ) a place in གཙང་.
པོ་དེ་ཙེ་ (podedze) hind. a type of high quality rosary.
པོ་ཏོ་ (podo) lumps/ clods of earth.
པོ་ཏོག (podɔɔ̀) sm.* སྦོ་ཏོག.
པོ་ལོན་ (polön) sm. པུ་ལོན་.
པོག (pɔɔ̀) 1. p. of འབོག. 2. rifle.
པོག་དན་ (pɔgdɛn) a type of rifle.
པོག་ཕྲ་རིང་ (pɔg drāriŋ) a type of rifle.
པོག་ར་ (pɔgra) pilose antler.
པོགས་ (pɔɔ̀) 1. lease/ rent fee (usu. for arable land); va.—རྒྱག to pay a lease fee; va.—ལེན་ to lease sth. 2. benefit, beneficial; vi.—ཐོན་ to be beneficial.
པོགས་སྐྱེད་ (pɔɔ̀gyeè) lease payment/ fee and interest.
པོགས་ཁྲལ་ (pɔɔ̀trɛɛ) lease payment and tax.
པོགས་གན་ (pɔɔ̀gɛn) lease agreement.
པོགས་རྒྱག (pɔɔ̀gyaà) see པོགས་.
པོགས་དངུལ་ (pɔɔ̀ŋüü) money paid for a lease fee.
པོགས་ཆག (pɔɔ̀jaà) lease fee reduction; va.—གཏོང་.
པོགས་ཆག་སྐྱེད་ཆག (pɔɔ̀jaà gyēèjaà) reduction of lease fee and loan interest.
པོགས་འདོན་ (pɔɔ̀ dön) va. to make sth. beneficial/ useful.
པོགས་འཕར་ (pɔɔ̀ pār) vi. to be/ get increased (lease fee).
པོགས་གླངས་ (pɔɔ̀laŋ) leased ¶པོགས་གླངས་གནམ་གྲུ་ A leased airplane.
པོགས་འབོ་ (bɔŋbo) shung. a type of འབོ་ used for collecting the fee on agricultural fields that have been leased out.
པོགས་མ་ (pɔɔ̀ma) leasing, renting; va.—གཏོང་ to lease, to rent; va.—ལེན་ to take on a lease/ rental basis; va.—འཇལ་; —སྤྲོད་ to pay a lease fee; va.—སྡུད་ to collect a lease fee ¶ས་ཞིང་ཡོང་རྫོགས་པོགས་མར་བཏང་བ་རེད་ (They) leased all (their) land.
པོགས་མ་ཆག་ཡང་ (pɔɔ̀ma cāàyaŋ) reduction of a lease fee.
པོགས་མའི་གན་རྒྱ་ (pɔɔ̀mɛ kɛngya) lease contract/ agreement.
པོགས་མར་གཏོང་ (pɔɔ̀maa dōŋ) va. to lease, to rent.
པོགས་ཞིང་ (pɔɔ̀shiŋ) leased fields.
པོགས་ཞིང་འདེབས་མཁན་ (pɔɔ̀shiŋ debñɛn) tenant (farmer), person who plants a leased field.
པོགས་ཞིང་པ་ (pɔɔ̀ shiŋbə) sm. པོགས་ཞིང་འདེབས་མཁན་.
པོགས་གཡར་ས་ཆ་ (pɔɔ̀yaa sāja) sm. པོགས་ཞིང་.
པོགས་ལེན་དུད་ཚང་ (pɔɔ̀len tüüdzaŋ) དུད་ཚང་ families who hold leased land.
པོགས་ལེན་ཞིང་པ་ (pɔɔ̀len shiŋbə) sm. པོགས་ཞིང་འདེབས་མཁན་.
པོགས་ལེན་ས་ཞིང་ (pɔɔ̀len sāshiŋ) sm. པོགས་ཞིང་.
པོགས་ས་ (pɔɔ̀sa) sm. པོགས་ཞིང་.
པོང་ (poŋ) 1. size (of body) ¶ཁོ་མོ་ལས་གཟུགས་པོང་ཆེ་བ་འདུག He is taller/ bigger than she. 2. abbr. of པོང་བུ་.
པོང་དཀར་ (poŋgar) abbr. of པོང་ང་དཀར་པོ་.
པོང་སྐད་ (poŋgɛɛ̀) braying (of a donkey); va.—རྒྱག.
པོང་ཁྲོམ་ (poŋdrom) a market for selling donkeys.
པོང་གུ (puŋgu) sm. པོང་བུ་.
པོང་མགོ་ (puŋgo) 1. donkey's head. 2. derogatory term.
པོང་འགྲོས་ (poŋdröö) the speed of a donkey.
པོང་རྒྱ་ (poŋgya) a trap used to catch rabbits.
པོང་རྒྱབ་ (poŋgyəb) load carried by a donkey.
པོང་རྒྱུག (poŋgyuù) stick used to drive/ herd a donkey.
པོང་སྒ་ (poŋga) saddle used to hold donkey loads.
པོང་ང་ (poŋŋa) the rhizome of Chinese monkshood (aconitum carrmichaeli).
པོང་ང་དཀར་པོ་ (poŋŋa gārbo) rhizome of white Chinese monkshood.
པོང་ང་ནག་པོ་ (poŋŋa nagbo) rhizome of black Chinese monkshood.
པོང་ང་དམར་པོ་ (poŋŋa mārbo) rhizome red Chinese monkshood.
པོང་ང་སེར་པོ་ (poŋŋa sērbo) rhizome of yellow Chinese monkshood.
པོང་རྫིས་ (poŋjeè) a person who herds donkeys.
པོང་ཏི་ (poŋdi) young donkey.
པོང་ཐོར་ (poŋdɔɔ) two year old donkey.
པོང་འདན་ (poŋdɛn) a sculptor's tool.
པོང་ཏོག (poŋdɔɔ̀) a clod/ lump of earth.
པོང་ཏུང་ (poŋduŋ) breaking clods of earth after plowing; va.—རྒྱག.
པོང་ནག (poŋnaà) abbr. of པོང་ང་ནག་པོ་.
པོང་རྣ་ (poŋna) 1. donkey's ear. 2. a large fried dough which is made only during the Tibetan New Year.
པོང་ལྤགས་ (poŋbaà) donkey skin.
པོང་སྤྱིན་ (poŋjin) glue made from donkey skin.
པོང་ཕྲུག (poŋdruù) young donkey.
པོང་བ་ (poŋwa) lumps/ clods of earth.
པོང་བ་གསེར་གཟིགས་ (poŋwa sērsii) being given great responsibility or authority or honor despite one's low position/ rank/ station [Lit. seeing a lump of earth as a lump of gold].
པོང་བུ་ (puŋgu) donkey.
པོང་བུ་གུ་པ་ (puŋgu gubə) a type of donkey that has a white face.
པོང་བུ་གོམ་བགྲོད་ཆུག་ཡང་ ཞག་སར་ཡོ་དི་ལེག (puŋgu gomdröö cūùyaŋ shagsaa yodi lig) sb. who does work slowly but gets the same result as others [Lit. even though the stride of a donkey is small, it arrives at the evening halting place at the same time].
པོང་བུ་ཆུ་འཐུང་ (puŋgu cūduŋ) person who drinks (ཆང་) alone [Lit. a donkey drinking water].
པོང་བུ་སྔོན་དང་ས་ཐལ་རྫེས་ (puŋgu ŋōndaŋ sādɛɛ jeè) taking action too late, action after the fact [Lit. spreading dust (so as to not to slip) after the donkey has passed over (the ice)].
པོང་བུ་ཐོ་ལོག (puŋgu tōlɔɔ̀) a small donkey.
པོང་བུ་དོན་ (puŋgu tön) vi. to become bankrupt ¶ཁོ་ཚོང་ཉེས་བྱུང་ནས་པོང་བུ་དོན་བཞག He did badly in business and went bankrupt.
པོང་བུ་པ་ (puŋgoò) donkey driver/ herder.
པོང་བུ་ལག (puŋgu lag) a set of donkeys used for transport, donkey caravan.
པོང་བུ་ལན་ཚ་ (puŋgu lɛndza) buttercup.
པོང་བུ་ས་འཇམ་སར་བསྙལ་ན་དགའ་ (puŋgu sājamsaa ñɛ̄ɛna ga) its better to be peaceful and calm [Lit. it is better to let the donkey lie down on a smooth place].
པོང་བུའི་ཁྲག (puŋgü trāà) blood of a donkey (used in Tibetan medicine).
པོང་བུའི་རྣ་བར་ཆོས་སྒྲོག (puŋgü nāwar cōōdrɔɔ̀)

choosing the wrong audience [Lit. reciting dharma to the ears of a donkey].

བོང་བུའི་ཨམ་མཆོག (puŋgü āmjɔɔ̀) 1. donkey's ears. 2. a type of cookie made at New Year's celebrations that looks like a donkey's ear.

བོང་བུའི་ལོ་རིལ་ (puŋgü ōrii) donkey dung.

བོང་བུས་གཟིགས་ལྤགས་གྱོན་པ་ (puŋgüù sigbaà kõnba) pretending to be clever/ wise/ learned [Lit. donkey wearing a leopard skin].

བོང་བུས་གཡུགས་པས་ཡག་བྱུང་ རྟ་ཕོའི་སྒང་ལ་འགྱོལ་སོང་ (puŋgüù yūùbɛ yaàju dābö gaŋla kyɔ̃ɔ̀soŋ) coming into good luck because of some misfortune that befalls another [Lit. being thrown from a donkey's back was fortunate (because I) got a horse to ride].

བོང་ཁྲིས་ (puŋdreè) a feeding trough for donkeys.

བོང་འབོད་ཁྱི་ཟུག (puŋbòò kyĩsug) poor style/ quality of writing [Lit. donkey's braying and dog's barking].

བོང་སྦྲུམ་ (puŋdrum) a pregnant donkey.

བོང་མེ་ (poŋme) clods/ lumps of earth on fire.

བོང་དམར་ (poŋmar) abbr. of བོང་ང་དམར་པོ་.

བོང་སྨེད་ (poŋmeè) 1. saddle straps that go under the tail of donkeys. 2. a vein just above the navel in Tibetan medicine.

བོང་ཚང་ (poŋdzaŋ) donkey shed/ pen.

བོང་ཚད་ (poŋdzɛɛ̀) volume, size.

བོང་ཚིལ་ (poŋdzii) donkey's fat (used in Tibetan medicine).

བོང་འཚོ་བ་ (poŋtsowa) sm. བོང་རྫི་.

བོང་རྫི་ (puŋdzi) donkey keeper/ herder.

བོང་ཡར་ (poŋyar) a female donkey that is barren or has not given birth this year.

བོང་གཡོག (poŋyɔɔ̀) sm. བོང་རྫི་.

བོང་ར་ (poŋra) sm. བོང་ཚང་.

བོང་སེར་ (poŋser) abbr. of བོང་ང་སེར་པོ་.

བོང་ལུད་ (poŋlüù) fertilizer made from donkey dung.

བོང་གསེབ་ (poŋseb) stud/ breeding donkey.

བོངས་ (poŋ) size ¶ བོངས་ཆེ་ Large in size.

བོངས་སྙོམས་ (poŋñom) same/ equal size.

བོངས་ཚད་ (poŋdzɛɛ̀) sm. བོང་ཚད་.

བོངས་ཚོད་ (poŋdzöö) sm. བོང་ཚད་.

བོངས་རྫོགས་ (poŋ dzɔɔ̀) vi. to have reached the limit of size.

བོད་ (pöö) 1. Tibet. 2. farming areas.

བོད་ཀྱི་ཁང་པ་ (pöögi kāŋba) Tibet House (centers for Tibetan culture in New Delhi, New York, Barcelona, etc.).

བོད་ཀྱི་སྐུ་ཚབ་དོན་གཅོད་ཁང་ (pöögi gūdzəb tõnjöögaŋ) Office of Tibet ¶ བལ་ཡུལ་བོད་ཀྱི་སྐུ་ཚབ་དོན་གཅོད་ཁང་ The Office of Tibet in Nepal.

བོད་ཀྱི་ཁོད་དུམ (pöögi kõõdruù) a land division made during the time of Songtsen Gampo.

བོད་ཀྱི་དགེ་རྩ་ (pöögi gedza) Tibet Foundation (London).

བོད་ཀྱི་རྒྱལ་ཚོགས་སྐུ་ཚབ་དོན་གཅོད་ཁང་ (pöögi gyɛɛ̀dzɔɔ gūdzəb tõnjöögaŋ) Tibet Bureau, Geneva.

བོད་ཀྱི་ཐེབས་རྩ་ (pöögi tēbdza) Tibet Fund (New York).

བོད་ཀྱི་དུས་བབ་ (pöögi tüùbəb) Tibetan situation.

བོད་ཀྱི་ནང་བསྟན་ (pöögi naŋdɛn) Tibetan Buddhism.

བོད་ཀྱི་གནས་དོན་ (pöögi nɛɛ̀dön) the Tibet Question.

བོད་ཀྱི་དཔེ་མཛོད་ཁང་ (pöögi bēndzöögaŋ) Library of Tibetan Works and Archives.

བོད་ཀྱི་བུད་མེད་ལྷན་ཚོགས་ (pöögi püümeè lhɛ̃ndzɔɔ̀) Tibetan Women's Association.

བོད་ཀྱི་ཚོང་དོན་སྐུ་ཚབ་ (pöögi ledo) the Tibetan trade official/ mission (in India in tt.).

བོད་ཀྱི་གཞོན་ནུ་ལྷན་ཚོགས་ (pöögi shõnnu lhɛ̃ndzɔɔ̀) Tibetan Youth Congress.

བོད་ཀྱི་ཟློས་གར་ (pöögi dööḡar) Tibetan Institute of Performing Arts (in Dharamsala).

བོད་ཀྱི་རི་ཆེན་བཞི་ (pöögi rijen shi) the four great mountains of Tibet: ཡུགས་པོ་རི་; དྲས་པོ་རི་; ལྷགས་ཟམ་ཆུ་པོ་རི་; ཕུང་པོ་རི་བོ་ཆེ་.

བོད་ཀྱི་ལོ་ཐོ་ (pöögi ledo) Tibetan calendar.

བོད་ཀྱི་ལོ་གསར་ (pöögi losar) Tibetan New Year.

བོད་ཀྱི་ས་གནས་ (pöögi sānɛɛ̀) Tibetan area.

བོད་ཀྱི་སོ་བ་རིག་པ་ (pöögi sōwa rigbə) Tibetan traditional medicine.

བོད་དཀར་ (pöögar) Tibetan porcelain cups.

བོད་སྐད་ (pöögɛɛ̀) Tibetan language; va.—རྒྱག To speak Tibetan language.

བོད་སྐད་ཡིག་མཛུབ་འཁྲིད་ཨུ་ཡོན་ལྷན་ཁང་ (pöö gɛɛ̀yiì dzubdriì ūyün lhɛ̃ngaŋ) Tibetan Language Guidance Committee (in the PRC).

བོད་སྐས་ (pöögɛɛ̀) notches made on trees that are used as steps/ ladder.

བོད་སྐྱེས་ (pöögeè) born in Tibet.

བོད་སྐྱོད་དཔུང་སྡེ་ (pöögyöö būŋde) the Chinese army that entered Tibet in 1951.

བོད་སྐྱོབ་དགྲ་གོལ་ (pöögyob) save Tibet, oppose the enemy.

བོད་སྐྱོར་ (pöögyɔɔ) support for Tibet.

བོད་བསྐྱོད་ (pöögyöö) going to Tibet, Tibet bound ¶ ཀྲུང་གོའི་བོད་སྐྱོད་དམག་དཔུང་ The Chinese army that went to Tibet.

བོད་ཁ་བ་ཅན་ (pöö kāwajen) Tibet, the land of snow.

བོད་ཁང་ (pöögaŋ) sm. བོད་ཀྱི་ཁང་པ་.

བོད་གུར་གུམ་ (pöö guuguu) safflower.

བོད་གྲོ་ (püödro) Tibetan wheat.

བོད་དགེ (pööge) Tibetan language teacher.

བོད་རྒྱ་ (pöögya) 1. Sino-Tibetan, China and Tibet. 2. Indo-Tibetan, India and Tibet.

བོད་རྒྱལ་ཡོངས་ཀྱི་ཉི་མ་ (pöö gyɛɛyoŋgi ñimə) Tibetan National Day.

བོད་རྒྱལ་ཡོངས་དམངས་གཙོ་ཚོགས་པ་ (pöö gyɛɛyoŋ māŋdzo tsɔ̃gba) Tibetan National Democratic Party.

བོད་སྒྲ་ (pöödra) sm. འབོད་སྒྲ་.

བོད་བརྒྱུད་ནང་ཆོས་ (pöögyüù naŋjöö) Tibetan Buddhism.

བོད་བརྒྱུད་ནང་བསྟན་ (pöögyüù naŋdɛn) Tibetan Buddhism.

བོད་དངུལ་ (pööŋüü) Tibetan money/ currency.

བོད་ལྕགས་ (pööjaà) Tibetan lock.

བོད་ལྕང་ (pööjaŋ) Tibetan willow tree.

བོད་ཆས་ (pööjɛɛ̀) Tibetan clothes/ dress.

བོད་ཆེན་པོ་ (pöö cēmbo) Greater Tibet (political Tibet the plus ethnic Tibetans areas in Qinghai, Sichuan, Gansu and Yunnan).

བོད་ཆོལ་ཁ་གསུམ་ (pöö cõgasum) sm. ཆོལ་ཁ་གསུམ་.

བོད་ཇ་ (pööja) Tibetan tea.

བོད་རྗེ་ཆོས་རྒྱལ་ (pööje cöögyɛɛ) ancient Tibetan Kings.

བོད་རྗེ་རྒྱལ་ཚབ་ (pööje gyɛɛdzəb) regent of Tibet.

བོད་ལྗོངས་ (pönjoŋ) 1. Tibet. 2. abbr. Tibet Autonomous Region.

བོད་ལྗོངས་ཁྲིམས་འཛིན་ཅུས་ (pönjoŋ trĩmdzinjü) tib.ch. Justice Bureau (in TAR).

བོད་ལྗོངས་གློག་ཤུགས་འཛུགས་སྐྲུན་ཀུང་སི་ (pönjoŋ lɔ̃gshuù dzugdrün gūŋsi) tib.ch. Tibet Electric Construction Company.

བོད་ལྗོངས་ཉིན་རེའི་ཚགས་པར་ (pönjoŋ ñinree tsāgbar) sm. བོད་ལྗོངས་ཉིན་རེའི་གསར་འགྱུར་.

བོད་ལྗོངས་ཉིན་རེའི་ཚགས་དཔར་ (pönjoŋ ñinree tsāgbar) sm. བོད་ལྗོངས་ཉིན་རེའི་གསར་འགྱུར་.

བོད་ལྗོངས་ཉིན་རེའི་གསར་འགྱུར་ (pönjoŋ ñinree sāngyur) the Tibetan Daily Newspaper (the daily newspaper of the TAR).

བོད་ལྗོངས་བསྟན་སྲུང་དང་བླངས་དམག (pönjoŋ dɛ̃nsuŋ taŋlaŋ māà) Tibetan Buddhist Defence Voluntary Army (name of anticommunist guerrilla army).

བོད་ལྗོངས་ཐོན་སྒོ་གསར་སྤེལ་ཕྱི་ཕྱོགས་ཀུང་སི་ (pönjoŋ tõŋgo sārbel cĩjɔɔ gūŋsi) tib.ch. Tibet Foreign

Trade Development Company.

བོད་ལྗོངས་ནོར་སྲིད་ཐིང་ (pönjoŋ norsiì tiŋ) tib.ch. Finance Department (in TAR).

བོད་ལྗོངས་སྤྱི་ཚོགས་རྒྱས་པ་ (pönjoŋ jīdzoò gyɛ̀ɛba) shung. National Assembly of Tibet.

བོད་ལྗོངས་དཔལ་འབྱོར་འཆར་གཞི་ཐིང་ (pönjoŋ bɛ̄njɔɔ cārshi tiŋ) tib.ch. Economic Planning Commission (in TAR).

བོད་ལྗོངས་དཔར་སྐྲུན་ (pönjoŋ bārdrün) Press and Publications Bureau (in TAR).

བོད་ལྗོངས་སྤྱི་ཚོགས་ (pönjoŋ jīdzɔɔ̀) sm. བོད་ལྗོངས་སེར་སྐྱ་རྒྱས་ཚོགས་.

བོད་ལྗོངས་ཞིབ་འཇུག (pönjoŋ shimjuù) Tibetan Studies (name of a journal).

བོད་ལྗོངས་ཡིག་ཟམ་གློག་འཕྲིན་དོ་དམ་ཅུས་ (pönjoŋ yigsam lōŋdrin todam jū) tib.ch. Posts and Telecommunications Bureau (in TAR).

བོད་ལྗོངས་ཡུལ་བསྐོར་སྐྱོ་གསེང་ཅུས་ (pönjoŋ yüügɔɔ drōseŋ jū) Tourism Bureau (in TAR).

བོད་ལྗོངས་རི་འཛེགས་མཐུན་ཚོགས་ (pönjoŋ rindzeg tūndzɔɔ̀) Tibet Mountaineering Association.

བོད་ལྗོངས་རིག་གནས་ཐིང་ (pönjoŋ rignɛɛ̀ tiŋ) tib.ch. Department of Culture (in TAR).

བོད་ལྗོངས་རིག་རྩལ་ (pönjoŋ rigdzɛɛ) Tibet Literature.

བོད་ལྗོངས་རླུང་འཕྲིན་དང་བརྙན་འཕྲིན་ཐིང་ (pönjoŋ lūŋdrin taŋ ñɛ̄ndrin tiŋ) Radio and Television Department (in TAR).

བོད་ལྗོངས་ས་གཤིས་གཏེར་ཁ་ཅུས་ (pönjoŋ sāshiì dērga jū) Bureau of Geology and Mineral Resources (in TAR).

བོད་ལྗོངས་སེར་སྐྱ་རྒྱས་ཚོགས་ (pönjoŋ sērgya gyɛ̀ɛdzɔɔ̀) Tibet National Assembly (of tt. government).

བོད་ལྗོངས་སློབ་གྲྭ་ཆེན་མོ་ (pönjoŋ lōbdra cēmmo) Tibet University.

བོད་ལྗོངས་སློབ་གསོ་དང་ཚན་རིག་ཨུ་ཡོན་ལྷན་ཁང་ (pönjoŋ lōbso taŋ tsēnriì üyön lhēngaŋ) TAR Education and Science Commission.

བོད་སྟོན་ (pöötön) Tibetan scholars.

བོད་ཐབ་ (pöötəb) Tibetan style stove.

བོད་ཐུག (pööduù) Tibetan style noodles.

བོད་ཐོན་ཡུལ་ཟོག (pöödön yüüsoò) Tibetan local products.

བོད་མཐའ་ (pööda) border of Tibet.

བོད་དར་རྒྱས་རོགས་སྐྱོར་ཐེབས་རྩའི་ལྷན་ཚོགས་ (pöö targyɛɛ̀ rɔggɔɔ tēbdzɛ lhēndzoò) the China Tibet Development Fund.

བོད་དོན་ (pöödön) the Tibetan question/ issue (concerning the political status of Tibet).

བོད་དོན་རྒྱབ་སྐྱོར་ཚོགས་པ་ (pöödön gyəbgyɔɔ tsōgba) Tibet support group.

བོད་དོན་གནས་ཚུལ་ཁྱབ་སྤེལ་ལས་ཁང་ (pöödön nɛ̄ɛ̀dzüü kyəbbel lɛ̀ɛgaŋ) TIN (Tibet Information Network).

བོད་དོར་ (pöödɔɔ) Tibetan style trousers (with an open/ split seat).

བོད་མདའ་ (pöönda) Tibetan style matchlock.

བོད་སྡེ་ (pööde) a territory controlled politically by the traditional Tibetan government (this contrasts with རྒྱ་སྡེ་ or Chinese controlled territory).

བོད་སྡོད་དམག་དཔུང་ (pöödöö māgbuŋ) troops stationed in Tibet.

བོད་སྡོད་ཨམ་བན་ (pöödöö āmbɛn) Manchu China's Imperial Commissioner in Tibet (Amban).

བོད་བརྡ་ (pööda) sm. འབོད་བརྡ་.

བོད་གནས་སྐྱར་ཞིབ་ (pöönɛɛ̀ gyārshib) sm. བོད་གནས་བསྐྱར་ཞིབ་.

བོད་གནས་བསྐྱར་ཞིབ་ (pöönɛɛ̀ gyārshib) the magazine "Tibetan Review."

བོད་སྣུམ་ (pöönum) Tibetan oil.

བོད་པ་ (pööba) 1. a Tibetan. 2. a farmer (this is a term used by nomads in Central Tibet).

བོད་པ་གསལ་བྱེད་ཀྱི་སྒྲ་ (pööba sɛ̄ɛjeègi dra) sm. འབོད་སྒྲ་.

བོད་པའི་སྒྲ་ (pööbɛ dra) sm. འབོད་སྒྲ་.

བོད་པའི་རྣམ་དབྱེ་ (pööbɛ nāmje) sm. འབོད་སྒྲ་.

བོད་ཕག (pööbaà) Tibetan pig.

བོད་ཕྱི་ཟིང་བཤིག (pööji siŋshiì) shung. unrest outside Tibet ¶ བོད་ཕྱི་ཟིང་བཤིག་དང་དུས་མཚུངས་པར་བླ་བྲང་གི་ཁྲལ་འབབ་དངུལ་སྒྱུར་གྱིས་བསྡུས་པ་ At the time when there was unrest outside Tibet, they collected the taxes of Labrang by converting it into money.

བོད་ཕྲུག (pöödruù) Tibetan children.

བོད་ཕྲུག་ཁྱིམ་སྡེ་ (pöödruù kyīmde) Tibetan Children's Village (TCV in Dharamsala).

བོད་ཕྲུག་མཛངས་མི་བདུན་ (pöödruù dzaŋmi dün) the seven wise Tibetan ministers during the time of the ancient kings.

བོད་དབུས་ (pöö üü) Central Tibet.

བོད་འབངས་ (pööbaŋ) Tibetan subjects/ citizens ¶ བོད་འབངས་ཀྱི་འགོ་ཁྲིད་གཅིག་པོ་ The only leader of the Tibetan people.

བོད་འབར་ (pööbar) Tibet and Burma, Tibeto-Burman.

བོད་འབར་སྐད་རིགས་ (pööbar gɛ̀ɛrig) Tibeto-Burman language family.

བོད་འབྱོར་གསར་འགྱུར་ (pönjɔr sāngyur) news (arriving) from Tibet.

བོད་འབྲོག (pööndroò) 1. Tibetan nomads. 2. farmers and nomads ¶ བོད་འབྲོག་བརྗེ་ཚོང་ The bartering of goods between farmers and nomads.

བོད་འབྲོག་མི་སེར་ (pööndroò miser) shung. sm. ཞིང་འབྲོག་མི་སེར་.

བོད་སྦག (pööbaà) Tibetan type of mahjong.

བོད་མི་ (pöömi) a Tibetan, the Tibetan people.

བོད་མི་དམངས་སྤྱི་འཐུས་ལྷན་ཚོགས་ (pöö mimaŋ jītüü lhɛ̄ndzɔɔ̀) Assembly of Tibetan People's Deputies.

བོད་མིའི་རྩ་དོན་ (pöömii dzādön) Tibetan Affairs.

བོད་མིའི་རང་དབང་ (pöömii raŋwaŋ) Tibetan Freedom.

བོད་མིའི་རང་དབང་ལས་འགུལ་ལྷན་ཚོགས་ (pöömii raŋwaŋ lɛngüü lhɛ̄ndzɔɔ̀) Tibetan Rights Council.

བོད་མིར་རོགས་ཕན་གྱི་ལས་གཞི་ (pöömii rɔgbɛngi lɛ̀ɛshi) Tibetan Aid Project.

བོད་མོ་ (pöömo) a Tibetan woman.

བོད་དམག (pöömaà) Tibetan soldiers/ military, Tibetan army ¶ སྔ་དུས་བོད་དམག་ལ་སྟོབས་ཤུགས་ཆེན་པོ་བྱུང་ཡོད་ In the past, the Tibetan military was very powerful.

བོད་དམག་ཁྲུལ་ཁང་ (pöö māgüügaŋ) the Tibet Military Headquarters.

བོད་སྨན་ (pöömɛn) Tibetan medicine.

བོད་སྨྱུག (pööñuù) Tibetan pen.

བོད་རྩིས་ (pöödzii) Tibetan system of arithmetic/ calculation.

བོད་རྩོམ་ (pöödzom) Tibetan articles/ compositions.

བོད་ཚེམ་ (pöödzem) Tibetan style of stitching/ sewing.

བོད་ཚེས་ (pöödzeè) the date in the Tibetan calendar.

བོད་ཞི་བས་བཅིངས་འགྲོལ་འབྱུང་ཐབས་སྐོར་གྱི་གྲོས་མཐུན་དོན་ཚན་བཅུ་བདུན་ (pöö shiwɛ jīŋdrüü juŋtəbgɔɔgi tröödün töndzɛn jūbdün) the Seventeen Point Agreement for the Liberation of Tibet (agreement signed in Beijing in 1951).

བོད་ཞུགས་ (pööshuù) new entering monks who are from Tibet (བོད་).

བོད་གཞས་ (pööshɛɛ̀) Tibetan songs.

བོད་གཞུང་ (pööshuŋ) 1. Tibetan government. 2. Central Tibetan Administration (CTA) in Dharamsala.

བོད་གཞུང་ཆེས་མཐོའི་ཁྲིམས་ཞིབ་ཁང་ (pööshuŋ cēēdö trīmshibgaŋ) Tibetan Supreme Justice Commission (in Dharamsala).

བོད་གཞུང་ཆོས་རིག་ལས་ཁངས་ (pööshuŋ cöörig lɛ̀ɛguŋ) CTA Department of Religion and

Culture (in Dharamsala).

བོད་གཞུང་བདེ་སྲུང་ལས་ཁུངས་ (pöösuŋ desuŋ lɛɛguŋ) CTA Department of Security (in Dharamsala).

བོད་གཞུང་ནང་སྲིད་ལས་ཁུངས་ (pöösuŋ naŋsii lɛɛguŋ) CTA Department of Home (in Dharamsala).

བོད་གཞུང་དཔལ་འབྱོར་ལས་ཁུངས་ (pöösuŋ bɛnjɔɔ lɛɛguŋ) CTA Department of Finance (in Dharamsala).

བོད་གཞུང་ཕྱི་འབྲེལ་དྲིལ་བསྒྲགས་ལས་ཁུངས་ (pöösuŋ cindreedaŋ triidraà lɛɛguŋ) CTA Department of Information and International Relations (in Dharamsala).

བོད་གཞུང་འཕྲོད་བསྟེན་ལས་ཁུངས་ (pöösuŋ tröödɛn lɛɛguŋ) CTA Department of Health (in Dharamsala).

བོད་གཞུང་དབུས་ཀྱི་ཁྲབ་འདེམས་བསྡུ་ལས་ཁང་ (pöösuŋ üü jigyəb öödu lɛɛgaŋ) CTA Tibetan Central Election Commission (in Dharamsala).

བོད་གཞུང་དབུས་སྨན་རྩིས་ཁང་ (pöösuŋ üü mɛndzigaŋ) CTA Tibetan Medical and Astrological Institute (in Dharamsala).

བོད་གཞུང་གཞུང་ཞབས་འདེམས་བསྐོ་ལྷན་ཚོགས་ (pöösuŋ shuŋshəb demgo lhɛndzoò) CTA Tibetan Public Service Commission (in Dharamsala).

བོད་གཞུང་ཤེས་རིག་པར་ཁང་ (pöösuŋ shɛɛrii bärgaŋ) Tibetan Cultural Printing Press (in Dharamsala).

བོད་གཞུང་ཤེས་རིག་ལས་ཁུངས་ (pöösuŋ shɛɛrii lɛɛguŋ) CTA Department of Education (in Dharamsala).

བོད་གཞུང་གསར་འགྱུར་ (pöösuŋ särdrin) Tibetan Bulletin.

བོད་ཟས་ (pöösɛɛ) Tibetan food, Tibetan meal.

བོད་ཟས་ཟ་ཁང་ (pöösɛɛ sagaŋ) restaurant that serves Tibetan food.

བོད་ཐོན་ (pöö) products from Tibet.

བོད་ཟླ་ (pönda) a month in the Tibetan lunar system ¶ བོད་ཟླ་ 4 ཚེས་ 15 ཉིན་ On the 15th of the 4th Tibetan month.

བོད་ཡིག (pööyii) written Tibetan.

བོད་ཡུལ་ (pööyüü) Tibet.

བོད་གཡུ་ (pööyu) Tibetan turquoise.

བོད་རག (pööraà) Tibetan alcohol.

བོད་རང་སྐྱོང་ལྗོངས་ (pöö raŋgyoŋjoŋ) the Tibetan Autonomous Region (of the PRC) ¶ བོད་རང་སྐྱོང་ལྗོངས་གྲ་སྒྲིག་ཨུ་ཡོན་ལྷན་ཁང་ the Preparatory Committee for the Tibet Autonomous Region.

བོད་རང་སྐྱོང་ལྗོངས་ཆབ་སྲིད་གྲོས་ཚོགས་ཨུ་ཡོན་ལྷན་ཁང་ (pöö raŋgyoŋjoŋ cəbsii tröödzoò üyön lɛngaŋ) the Political Consultative Committee of the Tibet Autonomous Region.

བོད་རང་སྐྱོང་ལྗོངས་མི་དམངས་སྲིད་གཞུང་ (pöö raŋgyoŋjoŋ mimaŋ siishuŋ) the People's Government of the Tibetan Autonomous Region (of the PRC).

བོད་རང་བཙན་དོན་དུ་གཉེར་བའི་ཨ་རིའི་སློབ་ཕྲུག་ཚོགས་པ་ (pöö raŋdzɛndu ñërwɛ ärii lōbdruù tsɔ̄gba) Students for a Free Tibet.

བོད་རིག་པ་ (pöö rigba) Tibetology.

བོད་རིག་པར་བརྩོན་མཁས་ (pöö rigbar dzönkɛɛ) Tibetologist.

བོད་རིགས་ (pöörii) Tibetan people/ nationality, a Tibetan ¶ བོད་རིགས་གཞོན་ནུ་ Tibetan youth.

བོད་རིགས་སྤུན་ཟླ་ (pöörii bünda) Tibetan brothers.

བོད་རེ་བས་ཕུང་ རྒྱ་དོགས་པས་ཕུང་ (pöö rewɛ pūŋ gya tɔgbɛ pūŋ) Tibetans are hopeful and Chinese are suspicious (a traditional saying).

བོད་རོགས་སྐྱོར་ཐེབས་རྩ་ལྷན་ཁང་ (pöö rɔɔgyɔɔ tēbdza lhəngaŋ) Tibet Foundation (China).

བོད་རོགས་ཐེབས་རྩའི་ལྷན་ཚོགས་ (pöörɔɔ tēbdzɛ lhəndzɔɔ) sm. བོད་རོགས་སྐྱོར་ཐེབས་རྩ་ལྷན་ཁང་.

བོད་ལས་དོན་ཨུ་ཡོན་ལྷན་ཁང་ (pöö lɛɛdön üyön lhɛngaŋ) Tibetan Work Committee, (the main Chinese administrative office in Tibet in the 1950's).

བོད་ལུགས་ (pööluù) Tibetan type/ style, Tibetan custom ¶ བོད་ལུགས་གསོ་བ་རིག་པ་ Tibetan medicine.

བོད་ལྭ་ (pööla) Tibetan clothes/ costume.

བོད་ས་ (pöösa) Tibet, Tibetan territory.

བོད་ས་གནས་སྲིད་གཞུང་ (pöö sänɛɛ siishuŋ) the Tibet local government (the Chinese term for the Dalai Lama's government after 1951).

བོད་སིལ་བུའི་དུས་ (pöö siibü tüü) the period of decentralization in Tibet after the fall of the kingdom in the 9th century A.D.

བོད་ས་ཁུལ་ (pöö səgüü) the territory of Tibet.

བོད་སོག (pöösɔɔ) Tibeto-Mongolian, Tibet and Mongolia.

བོད་སོག་དོན་གཅོད་ལས་ཁུངས་ (pöösɔɔ tönjöö lɛɛguŋ) sm. བོད་སོག་ལས་ཁུངས་.

བོད་སོག་ལས་ཁུངས་ (pöösɔɔ lɛɛguŋ) the Tibetan-Mongolian Office (of the Chinese Nationalist government).

བོད་སྲན་ (pöösɛn) Tibetan lentils.

བོད་བཟོ་ (pööse) ཀོ་བཟོ་ made in Tibet.

བོན་ (pön) Bon, the preBuddhist religion of Tibet.

བོན་དཀར་ (pöngar) a Bon subsect.

བོན་སྐྱོང་ (pöngyoŋ) protective deities in the Bon sect.

བོན་ཆོས་ (pönjöö) the Bon religion.

བོན་སྟོན་ (pöndön) sm. བོན་གཤེན་.

བོན་བསྟན་ (pöndɛn) sm. བོན་ཆོས་.

བོན་མདོ་ (pöndo) the Bon scriptures.

བོན་ནག (pönnaà) a Bon subsect.

བོན་པོ་ (pömbo) followers of the Bon religion.

བོན་པོ་ཇ་ཁུར་ (pömbo ŋāgur) a type of herbal medicine.

བོན་པོ་ཇུ་ཐིག་ཅན་ (pömbo judigjɛn) Bon diviner.

བོན་སྤངས་ཆོས་ཞུགས་ (pömbaŋ cööshuù) abandoning the Bon religion and adopting Buddhism.

བོན་གཞུང་ (pönshuŋ) sm. བོན་མདོ་.

བོན་ཤོད་ (pönshöö) a Tibetan aristocratic family.

བོན་གཤེན་ (pönshen) the founder of the Bon religion.

བོབ་ (pob) imp. of འབབ་.

བོའུ་ (pɔwu) ch. gun.

བོའུ་མཆུ་ (pɔwu cū) ch.tib. muzzle of a gun.

བོར་ (pɔr) 1. vi. to lose ¶ ཉོ་ཆའི་ཐོ་དེ་བོར་འདུག (I) lost the shopping list. 2. p. and imp. of འབོར་.

བོར་དངོས་ (pɔrŋöö) lost item.

བོར་སྟོར་ (pɔrdɔr) sm. བོར་.

བོར་སྡོམས་ (pɔrdöö) sodomy, buggery; va.—གཏུ་ to sodomize.

བོར་ཐོ་ (pɔrdo) list of things lost or missing; va.—འགོད་ to make a list of things lost/ missing.

བོར་ཚོང་ (pɔrdzoŋ) sm. ཕམ་ཚོང་.

བོར་ཟེགས་ (pɔrseg) sm. བོར་བརླག.

བོར་བརླག (pɔrlaà) lost; vi.—ཤོར་ to lose ¶ ཁོང་གི་མེ་མདའ་བོར་བརླག་ཤོར་བཞག His gun was lost.

བོལ་ (pöö) the bottom part of a Tibetan woolen boot.

བོལ་དཀྲིས་ (pöödrii) a part of a Tibetan woolen boot.

བོལ་གོང་ (pöögoŋ) the upper part of the ankle.

བོལ་ནུབ་ (pöönub) the foot up to the ankle.

བོལ་རྩ་ (pöödza) ankle vein.

བོལ་ཚིགས་ (pöödzii) ankle joint.

བོས་ (pöö) p.and imp. of འབོད་.

བོས་རུ་ (pööra) rifle brace/ stand made of animal horns.

བྱ་ (ca) 1. f. of བྱེད་. 2. bird, fowl ¶ བྱ་འཕུར་བ་ལྟར་ Like the flight of a bird. 3. deeds, acts ¶ བྱ་མང་ Many deeds.

བྱ་ག་རུ་ར་ (cā gārura) swan.

བྱ་ཀྲུའུ་ཧོན་ (cadruhön) crested ibis.

བྱ་དཀའ་བྱེད་གདད་ (caga ceèdɛɛ) difficult to do ¶ ང་དེ་རིང་དགོང་པར་འགྲོ་ཡག་འདི་བྱ་དཀའ་བྱེད་གདད་ཆེན་པོ་འདུག It is extremely difficult for me to go to the monastery today.

བྱ་དཀར་ (cagar) pheasant.

བྱ་སྐད་ (cāgɛ̀ɛ) rooster's crow; va.—རྒྱག to crow.

བྱ་སྐད་དང་པོ་ (cagɛɛ̀ taŋbo) rooster's first crow; va.—རྒྱག.

བྱ་སྐད་བྱིའུ་སྒྱུར་ (cagɛɛ̀ cewu gyur) changing sth., going back on sth. ༄ཁ་ས་ཚོང་གི་སྐོར་སྐད་ཆ་བྱས་པ་དེ་དེ་རིང་བྱ་སྐད་བྱིའུ་སྒྱུར་བྱས་ནས་ཤོད་སྟངས་མི་འདྲ་བ་ཞིག་ཤོད་ཀྱི་འདུག The conversation we had yesterday on business, today, like changing the crow of a cock to that of a little bird's, (he) is saying sth. different. [Lit. change cock's crow into that of a little bird's].

བྱ་སྐས་ (cagɛɛ̀) sm. བོད་སྐས་.

བྱ་སྐོན་ (cagön) net/ trap for catching birds.

བྱ་སྐྱག (cagyaà) bird droppings.

བྱ་སྐྱིབས་ (cagyib) an overhanging rock.

བྱ་སྐྱིལ་ (cagyee) sm. གདོད་སྐྱིལ་.

བྱ་ཁག (cagaà) sm. བྱ་དཀའ་བྱེད་གདོད་.

བྱ་ཁང་ (cagaŋ) poultry/ chicken coop.

བྱ་ཁུ་དབྱུག (ca kuyuù) cuckoo bird.

བྱ་ཁྱུ་ (cəkyu) flock of birds.

བྱ་ཁྱུང་ (cəkyuŋ) garuda (a mythical bird).

བྱ་ཁྲ་ (cadra) falcon, hawk.

བྱ་ཁྲལ་བྱི་སོ་ (cadra ciso) sb. who sacrifices his principles to say/ do whatever benefits a situation [Lit. when the birds are taxed the (bat) shows his mouse's teeth].

བྱ་ཁྲི་བཙན་པོ་ (cadri dzɛmbo) sm. པུ་རི་གུང་རྒྱས་.

བྱ་ཁྲུང་ (cadruŋ) crane (the bird).

བྱ་ཁྲུང་ཁྲུང་ (ca drūndruŋ) sm. བྱ་ཁྲུང་.

བྱ་གག (cagaà) 1. chicken. 2. a kind of water fowl.

བྱ་གུ་གུ་ (ca gugu) cuckoo bird.

བྱ་གོང་མོ་ (ca koŋmo) sm. གོང་མོ་.

བྱ་གྲོགས་ (cadrɔɔ̀) a pair/ couple of birds.

བྱ་གླག (calaà) goshawk.

བྱ་གླག་གིས་ལུག་ཕྲུག་ཁྱེར་བ་བཞིན་ (calaàgi lugdruù kyērwashin) swift and decisive ༄ཇག་པལ་བུ་མོ་དེ་བྱ་གླག་གིས་ལུག་ཕྲུག་ཁྱེར་བ་བཞིན་བཙན་ཁྲིད་བྱས་པ་རེད་ The bandits swiftly and decisively kidnapped the girl. [Lit. like an eagle swooping down and carrying off a lamb].

བྱ་དགའ་ (caga) reward, prize, gift; va.—སྤྲོད་ to reward, to give a prize/ gift.

བྱ་དགའི་དངོས་རྫས་ (cagɛ ŋǘüdzɛɛ̀) goods given as a prize/ reward.

བྱ་དགའི་ཅ་ལག (cagɛ jalaà) sm. བྱ་དགའི་དངོས་རྫས་.

བྱ་དགའི་རྟགས་མ་ (cagɛ dāŋma) medal, decoration given as reward/ prize.

བྱ་དགའི་ཕོགས་ཐོབ་ (cagɛ pəgdob) bonus.

བྱ་འགུལ་ (cangüü) movement, campaign; va.—བྱེད་.

བྱ་འགོ་མ་གྲུགས་ (ca goma traà) sm. བྱ་སྐད་དང་པོ་.

བྱ་འགོས་ཚད་ནད་ (cagöö tsɛ̀ɛnɛɛ̀) parrot fever.

བྱ་འགྲོས་ (candröö) a style of walking like a bird (in the Tibetan opera).

བྱ་རྒན་ (cagɛn) an old bird.

བྱ་རྒན་སྒྲོ་ཟད་དུ་འགྱུར་ (cagɛn drosɛɛ̀du gyur) old and weak, worn out [Lit. old birds with worn out feathers].

བྱ་རྒས་སྒྲོ་ཟད་ (cagɛɛ̀ drosɛɛ̀) sm. བྱ་རྒན་སྒྲོ་ཟད་དུ་འགྱུར་.

བྱ་རྒོད་ (cagöö) vulture.

བྱ་རྒོད་སྐར་ཚོམ་ (cagöö gārdzom) the constellation Aquila.

བྱ་རྒོད་ཐང་ནག (cagöö tāŋnaà) a type of black vulture.

བྱ་རྒོད་ཐང་སྨུག (cagöö tāŋmuù) a type of brown vulture.

བྱ་རྒོད་ཕུང་པོའི་རི་ (cagöö pūŋböri) Vulture Peak Mountain, a sacred Buddhist place in India where Buddha gave teachings.

བྱ་རྒོད་ཤ་ (cagöö shā) vulture meat (used in Tibetan medicine).

བྱ་རྒོད་ཤ་ལ་རུབ་པ་ (cagöö shālə rubbə) surging/ pouncing (by a group of people) [Lit. vultures congregating on a piece of meat].

བྱ་རྒོད་སྤུག་པ་ (cagöö sūgbə) saussurea medusa maximum (used in Tibetan medicine).

བྱ་རྒྱ་ (cagya) sm. བྱ་སྐོན་.

བྱ་རྒྱུ་ (cəgyu) 1. work. 2. ways/ means/ methods of doing.

བྱ་རྒྱུགས་པོ་ (ca gyugbo) many vultures coming to eat a corpse.

བྱ་རྒྱུད་ (cəgyüü) the first of the four classes of tantra: the kriya or activity tantra.

བྱ་བརྒྱ་འུར་རྡོ་གཅིག་གིས་འདེད་ (cagya wurdo jiggi deè) one defeating many; one example explains many situations/ issues [Lit. chasing 100 birds with one sling shot].

བྱ་སྒབ་ (cagəb) muscles around the shoulders.

བྱ་སྒོ་བྱེད་སྒོ་ (cago ceègo) sm. བྱེད་སྒོ་.

བྱ་སྒོང་ (cagoŋ) bird egg, chicken egg; va.—སྒོལ་ to hatch an egg.

བྱ་སྒོང་སེར་ཐིག (cagoŋ sērdig) egg yolk.

བྱ་སྒྲུང་ (cadruŋ) name of a famous stories that has birds as the main characters.

བྱ་སྒྲོ་ (cadro) feather ༄ཕོ་རོག་གི་བྱ་སྒྲོ་ The feather of a crow.

བྱ་སྒྲོའི་པོ་ལོ་ (cadrö bōlo) badminton.

བྱ་ངན་ (caŋɛn) bad deeds/ actions; va.—བྱེད་ ༄ཁོས་མི་ལ་མགོ་སྐོར་གཏོང་བའི་བྱ་ངན་བྱས་པར་ཁྲིམས་གཅོད་ཕོག་པ་རེད་ He was punished for his bad deeds involving tricking people.

བྱ་ངན་མཉམ་བྱེད་ (caŋɛn ñamjeè) acting in collusion with, conspiring, colluding; va.—བྱེད་.

བྱ་ངན་སྤྱོད་ངན་ (caŋɛn jööŋɛn) bad deeds and bad behavior.

བྱ་དངོས་ (caŋoö) things, objects.

བྱ་དངོས་ཀྱི་རྩ་བ་ (caŋoögi dzāwa) the basis of things/ objects.

བྱ་གཅན་གཉིས་ (ca jɛ̄ñii) abbr. of བྱ་ and གཅན་གཟན་.

བྱ་གཅོད་ (ca jöö) va. to castrate.

བྱ་མཆུ་ (caju) beak/ bill of a bird.

བྱ་རྗེས་ (cajeè) footprint/ track of birds.

བྱ་ཉན་བྱེད་ཉན་མེད་པ་ (cañɛn ceèñɛn meèba) chaotic, disorderly.

བྱ་ཉལ་ཁྱི་ཉལ་ (canɛɛ kyīnɛɛ) very late at night [Lit. when birds and dogs are asleep].

བྱ་རྙི་ (cañi) trap/ snare for birds.

བྱ་རྙོང་ (cañoŋ) 1. sm. བྱ་རྙི་. 2. va. to stretch (after sitting for a long time).

བྱ་ལྟོ་ (cado) chicken feed, bird food.

བྱ་གཏོང་ (ca dōŋ) 1. va. to notify/ inform secretly. 2. sm. བྱ་བྲལ་.

བྱ་གཏོར་ (cadɔɔ) sky burial; va.—བྱེད་.

བྱ་བཏང་བ་ (ca dāŋwa) a religious practitioner who has given up secular life.

བྱ་ཐན་ (cadɛn) birds that give bad omens.

བྱ་ཐབས་ (cadəb) way/ means of doing sth. ༄དོན་དག་འདི་ཐག་གཅོད་བྱེད་པའི་བྱ་ཐབས་གསར་པ་ཞིག་འཚོལ་དགོས་ We have to come up with a new way to settle this issue. ༄ད་བྱ་ཐབས་ཡོད་པ་མ་རེད་ Now there is nothing (we) can do (no way to do it), va.—འཛིན་; —སྤྱོད་ to use a method, to put a method into practice; vi.—བྲལ་; —ཟད་ to be without the means of doing anything, to be unable to do anything ༄གནས་ཚུལ་ལ་གཞིགས་ནས་བྱ་ཐབས་འཛིན་རྒྱུ་རེད་ We will decide on using a method based on the situation. ༄དཔལ་འབྱོར་གྱི་དཀའ་ངལ་གྱིས་རྐྱེན་པས་བྱ་ཐབས་ཟད་ནས་ཕྲུ་གུ་སློབ་གྲྭ་ནས་འཐེན་དགོས་བྱུང་ Because of financial difficulties I could not avoid taking my child out of school.

བྱ་ཐབས་ཁག་པོ་ (catəb kāgbo) a method that is difficult to do.

བྱ་ཐལ་ (cadɛɛ) sm. བྱ་སྐྱག.

བྱ་ཐི་བ་ (ca tiwə) pigeon.

བྱ་དེ་ (cade) 1. chicken, fowl. 2. sb. who tells secrets; va.—སྐྱིལ་ to tell a secret (slang).

བྱ་དེ་པོ་ (cāde po) rooster, cock.

བྱ་དེ་མོ་ (cade mo) hen.

བྱ་དེ་གསོ་ར་ cāde sōra) poultry farm.

བྱ་དོད་ (cadöö) auspicious words sung by the hunter character at the start of Tibetan operas.

བྱ་དྲང་སྲོང་ (cā draŋsoŋ) vulture.

བྱ་གདང་ (cādaŋ) roosting/ nesting stand.

བྱ་གདང་བུ་ (cā daŋbu) a slender wooden stick used for weaving on a loom.

བྱ་གདང་མ་ (cā daŋma) two wooden sticks on the right and left of where the བྱ་གདང་བུ་ rests.

བྱ་གདོང་ཁྲ་མིག (cādoŋ trāmii) prov. sinister and fierce looking [Lit. hawk eyes and bird face.

བྱ་གདོན་ (cadön) an evil spirit that manifests itself as a bird and causes harm to children.

བྱ་མདའ་ (canda) a rifle for shooting birds.

བྱ་འདབ་ (candəb) 1. eaves. 2. wings of birds.

བྱ་འདྲེ་ (candre) sm. བྱ་གདོན་.

བྱ་རྡོ་ལམ་འཕྲད་ (cado lamdrɛɛ̀) spontaneously/ coincidentally meeting ། ངེད་གཉིས་བྱ་རྡོ་ལམ་འཕྲད་བྱུང་ནས་བཟའ་ཚང་འགྲིགས་སོང་ We met coincidentally and became husband and wife. [Lit. a bird meeting a stone on the road].

བྱ་ལྡེམ་ (cadem) sm. བྱ་སྙང་.

བྱ་སྡེར་ (cader) bird's talons.

བྱ་ན་ (cana) food.

བྱ་ནག (canaà) crow, raven.

བྱ་ན་པ་ (canaba) cook.

བྱ་ནོར་ (canɔɔ) mistake, error; vi.—འགྱུར་ to unintentionally err ། དགྲ་བོའི་སྟོབས་ཤུགས་ལ་ཚོད་དཔག་བྱ་ནོར་བྱུང་ནས་ང་ཚོར་ཕམ་ཉེས་བྱུང་བ་རེད་ Because (we) made a mistake in estimating the strength of the enemy we were defeated.

བྱ་པ་ (caba) 1. bird trapper. 2. man who cannot get an erection, impotent person.

བྱ་སྤུ་ (cəbu) feather.

བྱ་སྤུ་ནོན་ (cābu nõn) overlapping [Lit. like the feathers on a fowl].

བྱ་སྤུ་གནམ་གཏོར་ (cəbu nāmdɔɔ) scattered, dispersed [Lit. feathers scattered in the sky].

བྱ་སྤུ་གནམ་འཐོར་ (cəbu nāmdɔɔ) sm. བྱ་སྤུ་གནམ་གཏོར་.

བྱ་སྤུའི་ཉལ་ཆས་ (cəbü ñɛɛjɛɛ̀) down sleeping bag, down quilt.

བྱ་སྤུའི་སྟོད་ཐུང་ (cəbü dõödun) down jacket.

བྱ་སྤྱོད་ (cajöö) work, act, conduct; va.—སྤེལ་ to take action, to put into use ། བཀའ་ཤག་གྲོས་བསྡུར་གྱིས་ལམ་སང་བྱ་སྤྱོད་སྤེལ་ the Kashag discussed it and immediately took action.

བྱ་སྤྱོད་ཀྱི་ཙ་འཛིན་ (cajöö dzāndzin) program/ guide/ blueprint for action or conduct.

བྱ་སྤྱོད་ངན་པ་ (cajöö ŋɛmba) misconduct, evil/ bad action or conduct.

བྱ་སྤྱོད་དངོས་ (cajöö ŋöö) real behavior/ action ། ཁ་ནས་གང་བཤད་ལ་བལྟ་རྒྱུ་མིན་པར་བྱ་སྤྱོད་དངོས་ལ་ལྟ་གི་ཡིན་ We will look at what you really do and not what you say.

བྱ་སྤྱོད་གཅིག་གྱུར་ (cajöö jiggyur) united action.

བྱ་ཕེལ་ (cabee) bird.

བྱ་ཕོ་ (capo) rooster.

བྱ་ཕོ་རྩེ་ (cā pōdze) corydalis curvifora maxim (used in Tibetan medicine).

བྱ་ཕོའི་ཤ་ (cabösha) rooster meat.

བྱ་ཕྲུག (cədruù) baby chicken /bird.

བྱ་འཕིར་ (capir) sm. བྱ་འཕུར་.

བྱ་འཕུར་ (ca pūr) 1. va. to fly. 2. a kite; va.—སྐྱོད་; — གཏོང་ to fly a kite.

བྱ་འཕུར་འགོར་མཐའ་གཞུ་ (cabur gərda shu) va. to make a kite dive.

བྱ་འཕུར་ལེབ་ (capurleb) nut vormica (used In Tibetan medicine).

བྱ་བ་ (cawa) 1. a verb ། བྱ་བ་དང་མིང་ Verbs and nouns. 2. work, deeds, actions ། འཛུགས་སྐྲུན་གྱི་བྱ་བ་ Development work. 3. (ཅེས་/ཞེས་ + —) called, known as ། ཁོ་ལ་བཀྲ་ཤིས་ཞེས་བྱ་བ་རེད་ He is called Tashi. 4. effect.

བྱ་བ་གློ་བུར་འབབ་པའི་དཔུང་སྡེ་ (cawa lōbur bɛɛ̀bɛ bũŋde) shock brigade.

བྱ་བ་འགོ་དཀའ་ སྐད་ཆ་མཐའ་དཀའ་ (cawa goga gēēja tāga) it is difficult to start work and it is difficult to finish talk.

བྱ་བ་དངོས་ (cawa ŋöö) sm. བྱ་དངོས་.

བྱ་བ་མཉམ་སྒྲུབ་ (cawa ñamdrub) united action, working together; va.—བྱེད་.

བྱ་བ་བདུབ་པ་ (cawa dūbbə) easy work/ task/ chore.

བྱ་བ་སྤྱོད་ལམ་ (cawa jöölam) sm. བྱ་སྤྱོད་.

བྱ་བ་ཕྲན་ཚེགས་ (cawa trɛ̄ndzeg) small insignificant matter/ issue.

བྱ་བ་བྱེད་སྟངས་ (cawa ceèdaŋ) way/ method of working.

བྱ་བ་ལམ་འགྲོ་ (cawa lamdro) good fortune/ luck ། དེ་རིང་གི་ཚོང་ལ་བྱ་བ་ལམ་འགྲོ་ཆེན་པོ་བྱུང་ Today I was very lucky in business.

བྱ་བང་ (cabaŋ) sm. བྱ་བྲང་.

བྱ་བའི་རྒྱུད་ (cawɛ gyüü) sm. བྱ་རྒྱུད་.

བྱ་བའི་གཉེར་ (cawɛ ñēr) responsibility for work/ task, duty.

བྱ་བའི་ནུས་ཚད་ (cawɛ nüüdzɛɛ̀) work/ labor power (usu. the number of workers in a household).

བྱ་བའི་ཡུལ་ (cawɛ yüü) 1. the object (in grammar). 2. place of work/ labor/ activity.

བྱ་བར་མ་གྲགས་ (caparma traà) rooster's second/ middle crowing.

བྱ་བར་ཞུགས་ (cawar shuù) va. to start to do a task/ job/ work, to attend to a task/ job/ work.

བྱ་བལ་ (capɛɛ) high quality wool that grows around the testicles of sheep.

བྱ་བལ་མ་ (capɛma) 1. the softest feathers of a crane. 2. actinolite.

བྱ་བྱིའུ་ (caciwu) birds.

བྱ་བྱེད་ཐ་དད་པ་ (cajeè tādɛɛ̀ba) transitive verb.

བྱ་བྱེད་ཐ་མི་དད་པ་ (cajeè tā midɛɛ̀ba) intransitive verb.

བྱ་བྱེད་ (ca ceè) va. to castrate.

བྱ་བྱེད་སྤངས་ (cajeè pāŋ) va. to leave one's work, to give up one's work.

བྱ་བྱེད་ལས་གསུམ་ (cajeè lɛ̄ɛsum) verb, subject and object.

བྱ་བྲང་ (cadraŋ) 1. breast of a bird. 2. barrel chest (for humans).

བྱ་བྲལ་ (cadrɛɛ) separating oneself from wordly ways.

བྱ་བྲལ་བ་ (cadrɛɛwa) sb. who has separated himself from wordly ways.

བྱ་བྲུན་ (cadrün) bird droppings.

བྱ་བློ་བྱེད་བློ་ (calo ceèlo) thinking of doing sth.

བྱ་འབྲས་ (candrɛɛ̀) sm. བྱ་སྒོང་.

བྱ་མ་དྷ་ (camada) messenger, runner.

བྱ་མ་འདྲོགས་པར་སྒོང་ལོན་ཐབས་ (ca madrɔgbar goŋa löndəb) trying to do sth. without frightening people [Lit. trying to take the eggs without frightening the chicken].

བྱ་མ་བུམ་ (camabum) a small water container worn by monks.

བྱ་མ་བྱི་ (camaji) bat (animal).

བྱ་མ་བྱི་ཁོག་སྟོང་ (camaji kōgdoŋ) sm. བྱ་མ་བྱི་.

བྱ་མ་བྱིའུ་ (cama ciwu) sm. བྱ་མ་བྱི་.

བྱ་མལ་ (jamɛɛ) sm. བྱ་ཚང་.

བྱ་མེད་ན་བོང་བུས་ནམ་ཚོད་ཟིན་ (cameèna boŋbüü namdzöö sin) sm. བྱ་མེད་བོང་བུས་ནམ་ཚོད་བཟུང་.

བྱ་མེད་བོང་བུས་ནམ་ཚོད་བཟུང་ (cameè boŋbüü namdzöö suŋ) an imcompetent/ incapable person replacing sb. [Lit. if the cock is not there, the donkey crows (in the morning)].

བྱ་མོ་ (camo) hen.

བྱ་མོ་ལའི་ཧེང་ (cāmo leheŋ) tib.ch. leghorn chicken.

བྱ་སྙང་ (cañaŋ) stretching (one's body); va.—བྱེད་ to stretch.

བྱ་རྩོལ་ (cadzöö) working hard; va.—བྱེད་.

བྱ་ཚང་ (cadzaŋ) bird nest.

བྱ་ཚེ་རིང་ (ca tsēriŋ) crane (bird symbolizing long life).

བྱ་ཚིག (cədzii) a verb.

བྱ་ཚོགས་ (cadzɔɔ̀) flock of birds.

བྱ་མཚའ་ལུ་ (ca tsəlu) red cock.

བྱ་འཚོལ་ (ca tsǒǒ) va. to look/ search for daily livelihood by doing miscellaneous small tasks/ jobs; va.—བྱེད་.

བྱ་འཚོལ་བྱི་འཚོལ་ (candzöögi cidzöö) sm. བྱ་འཚོལ་.

བྱ་འཛིང་རྒྱག (cəndziŋ gyaà) a derogatory term used for women fighting.

བྱ་འཛིན་དབྱུག་པ་ (cəndzin yūgbə) a stick used to catch birds.

བྱ་རྫི་ (cədzi) sb. who looks after chickens, poultry keeper.

བྱ་རྫོགས་ (ca dzɔ̀ɔ̀) vi. to finished working.

བྱ་ཝང་ (cawaŋ) pheasant.

བྱ་ཝང་ཤ་ (cawaŋ shā) pheasant meat (used in Tibetan medicine).

བྱ་ཞྭ་ (casha) a type of hat worn in the Konpo region.

བྱ་གཞག (cashaà) affairs, work, cause ¶ཆབ་སྲིད་ཀྱི་བྱ་གཞག Political affairs.

བྱ་གཤུག (cəshuù) 1. tail of a bird. 2. rifle butt. 3. name of a star.

བྱ་ཟན་ (casɛn) bird food.

བྱ་ཟིན་ཉ་ཟིན་ (casin ñasin) catching indiscriminately, doing too many things at once, va.—བྱེད་ ¶ངས་དེང་སང་ལས་ཀ་བྱ་ཟིན་ཉ་ཟིན་བྱེད་ཀྱི་ཡོད་ These days I am doing too many things at once [Lit. catching birds, catching fish].

བྱ་ཟེ་ (case) cockscomb.

བྱ་ཟླ་ (canda) the 8th month of the Tibetan calendar.

བྱ་གཟུགས་མོ་ (ca sugmo) porcupine.

བྱ་གཟུངས་མོ་ (ca sunmo) sm. བྱ་གཟུགས་མོ་.

བྱ་བཟང་ (casaŋ) sm. ལས་བཟང་.

བྱ་ཡུལ་ (cəyüü) 1. object, target. 2. place of work.

བྱ་གཡབ་ (cayəb) canopy.

བྱ་ར་ (cara) watching over, standing guard; va.—བྱེད་; —ལྟ་ to watch, to stand guard.

བྱ་ར་བ་ (carawa) sentry, guard, watchman.

བྱ་རིགས་ (cərig) birds.

བྱ་རིགས་གདུམ་པོ་ (cərig dǖmmo) bird of prey.

བྱ་རིགས་རིག་པ་ (cərig rigbə) ornithology.

བྱ་རིམ་ (cərim) process, program, schedule, steps ¶འཕྲུལ་ཆས་བཟོ་གྲྭའི་ནང་དུ་བྱ་རིམ་མང་པོ་ཞིག་བརྒྱུད་དགོས་ཀྱི་རེད་ One has to follow many steps in a factory that makes machines.

བྱ་རིམ་འགག་རྩར་ཐུག་པ་ (cərim gagdzaa tūgbə) key process/ step.

བྱ་རུས་ (carüü) chicken bone.

བྱ་རོག (carɔɔ̀) raven, crow.

བྱ་རོག་སྐྲོད་ནུས་པ་ (carɔɔ̀ drǒǒ nüübə) a child about 8 years old [Lit. able to scare away crows].

བྱ་རོག་མཆུ་རིང་ (carɔɔ̀ cūriŋ) a traditional Tibetan surgical tool.

བྱ་རོག་མཐོ་གང་ (carɔɔ̀ tōgaŋ) a distance measure spanning from the thumb joint to the pinky joint when the hand is held in a fist.

བྱ་རོག་མཚལ་མཆུ་ (carɔɔ̀ tsɛ̄ɛnju) a type of raven/ crow with a red beak.

བྱ་ཀློམ་ཞུ་ (calom shu) sm. བྱས་ཡུས་ཕོད་.

བྱ་ལག (calaà) a naughty/ insubordinate/ michievous child.

བྱ་ལུང་ (cəluŋ) string or rope made of hide.

བྱ་ལུད་ (cəlüü) 1. sm. བྱ་བྲུན་. 2. the manner of doing sth.

བྱ་ལི་ (cale) clitoris.

བྱ་ལི་བྱོ་ལི་ (cale cole) doing things in an haphazard manner.

བྱ་ལོ་ (calo) the year of the bird.

བྱ་ལོག (ca lɔɔ̀) bad/ wrong work.

བྱ་ལོང་ (caloŋ) wild goose.

བྱ་ལོང་བྱེད་ལོང་ (caloŋ ceèloŋ) time to do a job/ task.

བྱ་ངན་སྤྱོད་ངན་ (caŋɛn jǒǒŋɛŋ) sm. བྱ་ལོག་སྤྱོད་ལོག.

བྱ་ལོག་སྤྱོད་ལོག (calɔɔ̀ jöölɔɔ̀) bad/ evil/ wicked work; va.—བྱེད་.

བྱ་ཤ་ (casha) chicken meat, meat of a bird.

བྱ་ཤ་སེན་བགོས་ (casha sēngöö) dividing equally; va.—བྱེད་.

བྱ་ཤང་ཤང་ (ca shāŋshaŋ) mythological being with the upper body of a man and the lower body of a bird.

བྱ་ཤང་ཤང་དེའུ་ (ca shāŋshaŋ dēwu) sm. བྱ་ཤང་ཤང་.

བྱ་ཤོར་ (ca shɔ̄ɔ) vi. to have a secret leak out.

བྱ་གཤོག་བྱི་སོ་ (cashɔɔ̀ ciso) sm. བྱ་བྲལ་བྱི་སོ་.

བྱ་གཤོར་ (ca shɔ̄ɔ) va. to hunt birds.

བྱ་གསོ་ (caso) poultry raising; va. བྱ་གསོ་; --བྱེད་.

བྱ་གསོའི་ར་བ་ (casö rawa) poultry farm.

བྱག་མཁན་ (cagñɛn) 1. archer. 2. bandit. 3. dancer.

བྱང་ (caŋ) 1. north. 2. p. of འབྱང་.

བྱང་བཀོད་རིན་གོང་ (caŋgöö riŋgoŋ) listed/ official price.

བྱང་སྐར་ (caŋgar) north star.

བྱང་སྐར་སྤུན་བདུན་ (caŋgar bǖndün) the Big Dipper.

བྱང་ཁུལ་ (caŋgüü) northern area/ region/ sector.

བྱང་ཁོག (caŋgɔ̀ɔ̀) chest area.

བྱང་ཁོག་སྟོད་སྨད་ (caŋgɔ̀ɔ̀ dǒǒmɛɛ̀) upper and lower part of the body.

བྱང་ཁོག་ཡུལ་ཐིག (caŋgɔ̀ɔ̀ yüüdig) drawing lines on the body to determine where to do treatments such as moxibustion.

བྱང་ཁྱི་ན་ལེབ་ (caŋgyi nāleb) a type of hunting dog from northern Tibet.

བྱང་ཁྲ་ (caŋdra) blister beetles (used in Tibetan medicine).

བྱང་ཁྲབ་ (caŋdrəb) shung. armor.

བྱང་ཁྲམ་ (caŋdram) small wooden placards.

བྱང་གི་འཕྲེད་ཐིག (caŋgi treèdig) northern latitude.

བྱང་གོམས་ (caŋgom) accomplishment, attainment.

བྱང་གོམས་ཐོན་པ་ (caŋgom tōmba) skillful, proficient.

བྱང་གྲོལ་ (caŋdröö) nirvana.

བྱང་དགུ་ (caŋgu) a small flat metal plate with nine holes that was used traditionally to make metal armor.

བྱང་རྒྱུད་ (caŋgyüü) north side, northern.

བྱང་སྒྲ་མི་སྙན་ (caŋdra miñɛn) one of the four continents surrounding mount Meru.

བྱང་ངེ་བྱིང་ངེ་ (caŋŋi ciŋŋi) on and off.

བྱང་ངོས་ (caŋŋöö) northern side.

བྱང་ཆ་ (caŋja) experience, training; vi.—ཡོད to get experienced/ trained.

བྱང་ཆ་ཆེན་པོ་ (caŋja cēmbo) very experienced/ skilled.

བྱང་ཆ་མེད་པ་ (caŋja meèba) unexperienced, unskilled, untrained.

བྱང་ཆིངས་སྒྲིག་འཛུགས་ (caŋjiŋ drigdzuù) sm. བྱང་ཨ་ཀྲི་ལན་ཏིག་དམག་དོན་ཆིངས་ཡིག་སྒྲིག་འཛུགས་.

བྱང་ཆིངས་རྩ་འཛུགས་ (caŋjiŋ dzəndzuù) sm. བྱང་ཨ་ཀྲི་ལན་ཏིག་དམག་དོན་ཆིངས་ཡིག་སྒྲིག་འཛུགས་.

བྱང་ཆུབ་ (caŋjub) 1. perfect, excellent, complete ¶བྱང་ཆུབ་སེམས་དཔའ་ A Bodhisattva. 2. skilled, experienced ¶བཟོ་བ་བྱང་ཆུབ་པ་ཞིག A skilled worker.

བྱང་ཆུབ་ཀྱི་སེམས་ (caŋjubgi sēm) bodhicitta, Buddha nature.

བྱང་ཆུབ་མཆོད་རྟེན་ (caŋjub cǒǒden) a type of stupa.

བྱང་ཆུབ་ལྗོན་ཤིང་ (caŋjub jönshiŋ) sm. བྱང་ཆུབ་ཤིང་.

བྱང་ཆུབ་སྙིང་པོ་ (caŋjub ñiŋbo) 1. Bodhgaya. 2. enlightenment, nirvana.

བྱང་ཆུབ་ལམ་གྱི་སྒྲོན་མེ་ (caŋjub lāmgi drönme) a text written by Atisha.

བྱང་ཆུབ་ལམ་གྱི་རིམ་པ་ (caŋjub lāmgi rimbə) a text written by Tsongapa.

བྱང་ཆུབ་ལམ་སྒྲོན་ (caŋjub lamdrön) abbr. of བྱང་ཆུབ་ལམ་གྱི་སྒྲོན་མེ་.

བྱང་ཆུབ་ཤིང་ (caŋcub shiŋ) the Bodhi tree (the tree under which the Buddha obtained enlightenment).

བྱང་ཆུབ་སེམས་དཔའ་ (caŋcub sēmba) Bodhisattva.

བྱང་ཆུབ་སེམས་པའི་སྡོམ་པ་ (caŋcub sēmbɛ domba)

the Bodhisattva vow.

བྱང་ཆུབ་སེམས་ཞྭ་ (caŋcub sēmsha) a type of hat worn by Gelug sect ascetics.

བྱང་ཉི་ལྡོག་ཐིག (caŋñi dɔ̀ɔdig) tropic of cancer.

བྱང་སྟོད་ (caŋdöö) sm. བྱང་ཤར་.

བྱང་བལྟ་ (caŋda) facing north ¶ ཁང་པ་ཁ་བྱང་བལྟ་ལ་ཉི་མ་ཡོག་གི་མ་རེད་ A house facing north will not get the sun.

བྱང་ཐང་ (caŋdaŋ) the vast upland nomad area known as the "northern plain."

བྱང་ཐང་རྒྱ་མོ་ (caŋdaŋ gyāmo) sm. བྱང་ཐང་.

བྱང་མཐའ་ (caŋda) North Pole.

བྱང་མཐའི་སྒོར་ཐིག (caŋdɛ gɔrdig) Arctic circle.

བྱང་དྲངས་ (caŋ draŋ) shung. va. to lead prayers ¶ སྐད་གསངས་ཤིང་འདོན་པ་ངེས་པ་ཞིག་གིས་བྱང་དྲངས་དེ་ The prayers shall be led by a monk who has a good voice and a good memory.

བྱང་འདུལ་དམག (caŋdüü māà) the war of 1924-26 waged by the Communists against the Northern Warlords in China.

བྱང་འདྲེན་པ་ (caŋdremba) the དབུ་མཛད་ of the two tantric colleges in Lhasa.

བྱང་སྡོམ་ (caŋdom) abbr. of བྱང་ཆུབ་སེམས་དཔའི་སྡོམ་པ་.

བྱང་ནུབ་ (caŋnub) northwest.

བྱང་གནམ་མཚོ་ (caŋ nāmdzo) Lake Namtso.

བྱང་སྣེ་ (caŋne) North Pole.

བྱང་པ་ (caŋba) 1. skilled, experienced ¶ བྱང་པའི་དམག་མི་ Skilled soldiers. 2. person from the north.

བྱང་པོ་ (caŋbo) skilled, well trained ¶ ད་ལྟ་རྐང་རྡེད་པོ་ལོ་བྱང་པོ་མེད་ Right now I am not skilled in soccer.

བྱང་སྤྱི་ (caŋji) governor general of the northern region in tt.

བྱང་ཕྱོགས་ (caŋjɔɔ) northern direction/ side ¶ བི་དི་ནམ་བྱང་ཕྱོགས་ North Vietnam.

བྱང་ཕྱོགས་པ་ (caŋjɔɔba) a northerner.

བྱང་བལ་ (caŋ pɛɛ) wool from northern Tibet.

བྱང་བི་དི་ནམ་ (caŋ bidinam) North Vietnam.

བྱང་བུ་ (caŋbu) 1. notice board, address board. 2. a strip of armor.

བྱང་བུ་ཐོན་པ་ (caŋgom tõmba) sm. བྱང་གོམས་ཐོན་པ་.

བྱང་བྱང་ (caŋjaŋ) the far north.

བྱང་བྱང་རྒྱང་ (caŋ caŋgyaŋ) sm. བྱང་བྱང་.

བྱང་བྱིང་ (caŋjiŋ) abbr. of བྱང་ངེ་བྱིང་ངེ་.

བྱང་འབྲོང་ (caŋdroŋ) wild yak (from the north of Tibet).

བྱང་མ་ (caŋma) 1. northern ¶ ཆུ་མགོ་བྱང་མ་ The northern source of a river. 2. skilled, experienced ¶ བཟོ་པ་བྱང་མ་ A skilled worker.

བྱང་མི་ (cəŋmi) sm. བྱང་པ་.

བྱང་མེ་གླིང་ (caŋ meliŋ) North America, North American continent.

བྱང་རྨོག་འཐོར་འགྲོས་ (caŋmɔg tɔ̄ndröö) shung. armor that is coming apart.

བྱང་རྩལ་ (caŋdzɛɛ) skills, talents.

བྱང་ཚད་ (caŋdzɛɛ̀) degree of accomplishment/ skills, expertise.

བྱང་ཚོང་ (caŋdzoŋ) trade products from northern Tibet.

བྱང་ཚྭ་དཀར་པོ་ (caŋdza gārbo) salt from northern Tibet.

བྱང་ཡིག (caŋyiì) 1. name of a deceased person written on a piece of paper that is ritually burnt. 2. business card.

བྱང་རིགས་སྡེ་བཞི་ (caŋrig deshi) four nomad administrative areas that were under the governor general of northern Tibet.

བྱང་རོང་ཁ་འཐབ་ (caŋroŋ kātəb) shung. nomads coming together with villagers and engaging in trade.

བྱང་ལམ་ (caŋlam) the northern highway running from Qinghai Province to Lhasa.

བྱང་ལུག (caŋluù) sheep from northern Tibet.

བྱང་ཤམ་བྷ་ལ་ (caŋ shāmbala) Shambala.

བྱང་ཤར་ (caŋshar) northeast.

བྱང་ཤར་མཐའ་མཚམས་ས་གནས་སྒྲིགས་བཙུགས་ (caŋshar tāndzam sānɛɛ̀ drigdzuù) NEFA (Northeast Frontier Agency).

བྱང་ཤིང་ (caŋshiŋ) sign board, notice placard.

བྱང་སེམས་ (caŋsem) 1. bodhicitta. 2. bodhisattva.

བྱང་སེག (caŋseg) name of a deceased person written on a piece of paper that is ritually burnt.

བྱང་གསུམ་ (jaŋsum) the three northern areas: north, northeast and northwest.

བྱང་ལྷགས་ (jaŋlhaà) northern wind.

བྱང་ཨ་ཀྲི་ལན་ཀྲིག་དམག་དོན་ཆིངས་ཡིག་སྒྲིག་འཛུགས་ (caŋ ādrelɛndreg māgdön ciŋyiì drigdzuù) NATO (North Atlantic Treaty Organization).

བྱང་ཨ་མེ་རི་ཀའི་རང་དབང་ཚོང་འབྲེལ་གྱི་གྲོས་མཐུན་ (caŋ āmerikɛ raŋwaŋ dreegi tröödün) North American Free Trade Agreement (NAFTA).

བྱང་ཨཊ་ལན་ཊིག་དམག་དོན་ཆིངས་ཡིག་སྒྲིག་འཛུགས་ (caŋ ādrelɛndreg māgdön ciŋyiì gyigdzuù) sm. བྱང་ཨ་ཀྲི་ལན་ཀྲིག་དམག་དོན་ཆིངས་ཡིག་སྒྲིག་འཛུགས་.

བྱང་ཨ་མེ་རི་ཀ་ (caŋ āmeriga) North America.

བྱད་ (cɛɛ̀) 1. face. 2. sm. སྤྱད་. 3. curse, spell.

བྱད་ཀ་ (cɛɛ̀ga) sm. བྱད་, 3.

བྱད་ཁ་ (cɛɛ̀ga) sm. བྱད་ཀ་.

བྱད་མཁན་ (cɛɛ̀ñɛn) person who casts an evil spell/ curse.

བྱད་འགྲོལ་ (cɛndröö) method of getting rid of an evil spell/ curse.

བྱད་གདད་ (cɛɛ̀dɛɛ̀) sm. བྱད་ཀ་.

བྱད་ལྟས་ (cɛɛ̀dɛɛ̀) sign/ symbol of a spell or curse.

བྱད་སྟེམས་ (cɛɛ̀dem) sm. བྱད་ཀ་.

བྱད་ཕུར་ (cɛɛ̀bur) a dagger used when performing the rite to cast a spell or curse.

བྱད་དབྱིབས་ (cɛɛ̀yib) facial appearance.

བྱད་མ་ (cɛɛ̀ma) sm. བྱད་ཀ་.

བྱད་བཙོག (cɛɛ̀dzɔɔ̀) ugly, unsightly, bad-looking.

བྱད་ཚུགས་ (cɛɛ̀dzuù) sm. བྱད་དབྱིབས་.

བྱད་བཞིན་ (cɛɛ̀shin) sm. བྱད་, 2.

བྱད་ཟློག་སྲི་ཟློག (cɛndɔɔ̀ sindɔɔ̀) sm. བྱད་འགྲོལ་.

བྱད་གཟུགས་ (cɛɛ̀suù) face and body.

བྱད་རིས་ (cɛɛ̀rii) sm. གདོང་རིས་.

བྱན་པོ་ (cɛmbo) male cook.

བྱན་མོ་ (cɛnmo) 1. female cook. 2. wife.

བྱབ་: p. བྱབས་; f. བྱབ་; imp.; ཕྱོབས་ (cəb) 1. va. to sweep away, to clean ¶ ཅོག་ཙེའི་སྟེང་གི་ཐལ་བ་ལག་པས་བྱབས་སོང་ (He) swept away the dust on the table with his hand. 2. making sense, having meaning ¶ སྐད་ཆ་བྱབས་མེད་པ་ Nonsensical talk.

བྱབ་བསྐྱལ་ (cəbgyɛɛ) 1. vi. to make a fool of oneself. 2. vi. to let an opportunity slip by.

བྱབ་ཆུང་བ་ (cəbjuŋwə) silly, foolish, childish.

བྱབ་མེད་པ་ (cəb meèba) 1. sm. བྱབས་ཆུང་བ་. 2. useless.

བྱབ་ཟེད་ (cəbseè) brush.

བྱབས་ (cəb) 1. p. of བྱབ་. 2. va. to rob completely.

བྱབས་ཁྲུས་ (cəbdrüü) baptism; va.—བྱེད་ to baptize.

བྱམ་ (cam) sm. བྱམས་, 2.

བྱམ་ཁྲི་ (camdri) sm. བྱམས་ཁྲི་.

བྱམ་པ་ (camba) a brush used to ink a printing block.

བྱམས་ (cam) 1. love, compassion, devotion, affection. 2. sedan chair, palanquin.

བྱམས་ཀློང་ (camloŋ) shung. compassionate thought ¶ ཕྱུན་ཆོ་འགོ་ཐོན་རེ་བྱུལ་བས་བྱམས་ཀློང་ནས་བརྩེ་བས་གཟིགས་པ་མཁྱེན་ Since (we) are unable to look after our affairs please look upon our problems with love and compassion.

བྱམས་སྐྱོང་ (camgyoŋ) loving care/ protection ¶ ཁོང་གི་བྱམས་སྐྱོང་འོག Under (his) loving care.

བྱམས་ཁང་ (camgaŋ) chapel/ temple whose main statue is the Maitreya Buddha.

བྱམས་ཁྲི་ (camdri) 1. stretcher. 2. sedan chair, palanquin.

བྱམས་ཁྲི་རུ་ཁག (camdri rugaà) 1. stretcher-bearer

unit. 2. palanquin bearer group.

བྱམས་མགོན་ (camgön) Maitreya Buddha.

བྱམས་འགྱོགས་རུ་ཁག (camgyɔɔ̀ rugaà) sm. བྱམས་ཁྲི་རུ་ཁག.

བྱམས་ཉམས་ (camñam) merciful, kind.

བྱམས་སྙིང་རྗེ་ (cam ñiŋji) sm. བྱམས་པ་ and སྙིང་རྗེ་.

བྱམས་ཐལ་གཅིག་ལང་ (camtɛɛ jèèlaŋ) spoiling a child, pampering a child excessively; va.—གཏོང་.

བྱམས་ཐལ་ཤོར་ (camtɛɛ shɔ̄ɔ) vi. to spoil a child, to pamper a child excessively.

བྱམས་དང་སྙིང་རྗེ་ (camdaŋ ñiŋje) love and compassion.

བྱམས་ལྡན་ (camdɛn) dear, beloved ¶ བྱམས་ལྡན་ཨ་མ་ལགས་སུ་ To my dear mother (a letter heading).

བྱམས་སྡང་ (camdaŋ) love/ kindness and hatred ¶ ཕོ་མོ་རྒན་གཞོན་ཚང་མར་བྱམས་སྡང་ཕྱོགས་རིས་མེད་པ་ཉེ་སྙོམས་ཚུལ་མཐུན་དགོས་རྒྱུ་ You should not make any distinction between the old and young of both sexes and (should not) treat them unfairly with regards to love and hate.

བྱམས་པ་ (camba) 1. love, compassion. 2. Maitreya Buddha.

བྱམས་པ་གོ་ལོག (camba kolɔɔ̀) being good to those who don't deserve it; va.—བྱེད་.

བྱམས་པ་མགོན་པོ་ (camba gömbo) sm. བྱམས་མགོན་.

བྱམས་པ་དང་ལྡན་པ་ (camba daŋdɛmba) love and compassion.

བྱམས་པ་གདན་འདྲེན་ (camba dɛndren) religious event that takes place on the 25th day of the 1st month of the Tibetan calendar when the statue of Maitreya is taken around Lhasa.

བྱམས་པ་ཚད་མེད་ (camba tsɛ̀ɛmeè) immeasurable love.

བྱམས་པའི་སེམས་ (cambɛ sēm) mind of a loving/ compassionate person.

བྱམས་པོ་ (cambo) affectionate, kind and loving; va.— བྱེད་ ¶ མོ་ཕྲུ་གུར་བྱམས་པོ་ཡོད་པ་རེད་ She is kind and loving to the children.

བྱམས་བརྩེ་ (camdze) loving and compassionate.

བྱམས་བརྩེ་ཤ་ཚ་ (camdze shādza) loving and compassionate.

བྱམས་བརྩེའི་མཐར་སོན་ (camdzee tārsön) loving and compassionate.

བྱམས་བརྩེས་སྐྱོང་ (camdzeè gyōŋ) va. to treat with love. 2. va. to protect out of love.

བྱམས་གཞས་ (camshɛɛ̀) a love song.

བྱམས་བཞུགས་ (camshuù) the sitting posture of Maitreya.

བྱམས་གཡོག (camyɔɔ̀) 1. covering for a sedan. 2. person who carries a sedan chair/ palanquin.

བྱམས་སེམས་ (camsem) kindness, compassion, love ¶ མའི་བྱམས་སེམས་ Maternal love.

བྱའོ་ཅོག (caojɔɔ̀) work.

བྱར་ (car) sm. བྱ་ར་.

བྱར་མི་བཏུབ་ (car midub) 1. བྱེད་མི་ཐུབ་. 2. བྱེད་མི་རུང་.

བྱར་མེད་ (carmeè) sth. that can not be undone, a thing that cannot be changed.

བྱར་རུང་ (caŋruŋ) things that are permitted/ allowed/ granted/ authorized.

བྱས་ (cɛ̀ɛ) 1. p. of བྱེད་. 2. va. to say, to tell ¶ ཁོས་ཤེས་མ་སོང་བྱས་པ་རེད་ He said that he did not know.

བྱས་འགལ་ (cɛ̀ɛgɛɛ) shung. criminal acts ¶ ཁོ་པས་ཇག་བཅོམ་བྱས་འགལ་དང་ཞྭ་ལོས་བཙོན་འཛུག་ཁྲིམས་གཅོད་བྱེད་བབས་བཅས་བཀའ་ཞིབ་ཡོང་བ་ Please look into the matter regarding the criminal act of banditry and the arrest made by Zhalo.

བྱས་རྒྱལ་ཁ་སྙོགས་ (cɛ̀ɛgyɛɛ kāñɔg) shung. showing insatiable greed ¶ ནུབ་ཕྱོགས་རྒྱལ་ཕྲན་རྣམས་རིམ་པར་བླངས་པས་བྱས་རྒྱལ་ཁ་སྙོགས་ཀྱིས་ Having successively invaded and occupied the principalities in the west in a show of insatiable greed.

བྱས་རྒྱལ་དུ་མ་སོང་བའི་ (cɛ̀ɛgyɛɛdu masoŋwɛ) shung. not to let sb. evade/ escape (punishment) ¶ ཕྱུན་ཚོའི་ཁ་ཐབས་ལ་བརྟེན་པའི་དབང་ཤེད་འདི་རིགས་བྱས་རྒྱལ་དུ་མ་སོང་བའི་བཀའ་ཁྲིམས་བརྡ་འདེད་རང་ཡོད་པ་མཁྱེན་ Please do not let those who use their power to oppress us escape punishment.

བྱས་ཅན་ (cɛ̀ɛjɛn) sm. བྱས་པ་ཅན་.

བྱས་རྗེས་ (cɛ̀ɛjeè) achievement, accomplishment, result, success; va.—འཛུགས་ to accomplish, to achieve, to succeed, to make/ leave a contribution; va.—འགོད་ to record meritorious acts/ achievements/ accomplishments ¶ ཚན་རིག་གི་བྱས་རྗེས་ Scientific accomplishments.

བྱས་རྗེས་ངོམ་ (cɛ̀ɛjeè ŋom) va. to brag about one's accomplishments.

བྱས་རྗེས་ཅན་ (cɛ̀ɛjeèjɛn) meritorious, successful.

བྱས་རྗེས་ཆེན་པོ་ (cɛ̀ɛjeè cēmbo) a person who has accomplished much.

བྱས་རྗེས་རྟགས་མ་ (cɛ̀ɛjeè dāŋma) medal or decoration that is given for achievement/ accomplishment.

བྱས་རྗེས་རྟོག་ཞིབ་ (cɛ̀ɛjeè dōgshib) investigation of achievements/ accomplishments.

བྱས་རྗེས་ཐོབ་རྟགས་ (cɛ̀ɛjeè tōbdaà) sm. བྱས་རྗེས་རྟགས་མ་.

བྱས་རྗེས་དྲུད་ཤུལ་ (cɛ̀ɛjeè drüüshüü) sm. བྱས་རྗེས་.

བྱས་རྗེས་བསྡུར་ (cɛ̀ɛjeè dur) va. to evaluate or compare merit/ achievement/ accomplishment.

བྱས་རྗེས་དཔྱད་ཞིབ་ (cɛ̀ɛjeè jɛ̀ɛshib) sm. བྱས་རྗེས་རྟོག་ཞིབ་.

བྱས་རྗེས་གཟེངས་རྟགས་ (cɛ̀ɛjeè seŋdaà) sm. བྱས་རྗེས་རྟགས་མ་.

བྱས་རྗེས་རང་བསྟོད་བྱེད་ (cɛ̀ɛjee raŋdöö cɛ̀e) sm. བྱས་རྗེས་ངོམ་.

བྱས་ཉེས་ (cɛ̀ɛñeè) crime, offense; va.—བཟོ་ to commit a crime/ offense ¶ ཁོ་རྐུ་མ་བརྐུས་ནས་བྱས་ཉེས་བཟོས་པ་རེད་ He committed the crime of stealing.

བྱས་ཉེས་རིམ་པར་གསོག་མཁན་ (cɛ̀ɛñeè rimbar sɔ̄ɔ̀ñɛn) recidivist, criminal who commits one crime after another.

བྱས་མཐའ་ (cɛ̀ɛda) the tail end of a job/ work/ task.

བྱས་དེབ་ (cɛ̀ɛdeb) book containing a list of work tasks.

བྱས་དྲིན་ (cɛ̀ɛdrin) gratitude, appreciation.

བྱས་དྲིན་ཅན་ (cɛ̀ɛdrinjɛn) grateful, appreciative.

བྱས་ན་ (cɛ̀ɛna) 1. if (you) do. 2. therefore, well then, if that is so ¶ བྱས་ན་ང་ཁྲོམ་ལ་འགྲོ་གི་མེད་ If that is so, I will not go to the market.

བྱས་པ་ (cɛ̀ɛba) 1. sm. བྱས་རྗེས་. 2. having, possessing ¶ ཁང་པ་རྫ་ཐོག་ལྗང་ཁུ་བྱས་པ་ཞིག A house having a turquoise tile roof. 3. made of/ from (usu. noun + ལས་ + —) ¶ སངས་རྒྱས་ཀྱི་སྐུ་གསེར་ལས་བྱས་པ་ཞིག A statue of the Buddha made from gold. 4. བྱས་དྲིན་.

བྱས་པ་ཅན་ (cɛ̀ɛbajɛn) 1. sm. བྱས་རྗེས་ཅན་. 2. sm. བྱས་དྲིན་ཅན་.

བྱས་པ་ཆུད་མི་ཟ་ (cɛ̀ɛba cǜü misa) one's deeds last forever (good or bad).

བྱས་པ་དྲིན་གཟོ་ (cɛ̀ɛba trinso) sm. བྱས་པ་གཟོ་.

བྱས་པ་མི་གཟོ་ (cɛ̀ɛba miso) shung. to not repay kindness/ favors, to be ungrateful ¶ བྱས་པ་མི་གཟོ་བའི་མི་ལ་ཕན་གྲོགས་བྱེད་མཁན་རྗེ་ཉུང་དུ་འགྲོ་ A person who does not show gratitude will have less people helping him.

བྱས་པ་གཟོ་ (cɛ̀ɛba so) va. to repay kindness/ favors.

བྱས་པ་ཤེས་ (cɛ̀ɛba shēè) va. to know that one ought to be grateful/ appreciative.

བྱས་བྱུང་ (cɛ̀ɛjuŋ) shung. sm. བྱས་རྗེས་.

བྱས་འབྲས་ (cɛndrɛɛ̀) result, outcome, achievement, accomplishment ¶ ཁོའི་ཞིབ་འཇུག་ལ་བྱས་འབྲས་ཆེན་པོ་བྱུང་བ་རེད་ His research got a great result.

བྱས་མ་བྱས་ (cɛ̀ɛma cɛ̀ɛ) whether one does or does not do sth. ¶ ཁོས་ལས་ཀ་བྱས་མ་བྱས་ང་ལ་ཁྱད་པར་མི་འདུག It make no difference to me whether he works or not.

བྱས་མྱོང་ལོ་རྒྱུས་ (cɛ̀ɛñoŋ lugyüü) historical

antecedents.

བྱས་ཙང་ (cɛ̀ɛdzaŋ) therefore ¶ཁོས་ལས་ཀ་བྱས་པ་རེད་ བྱས་ཙང་ངས་ནང་ལ་བསྡད་པ་ཡིན་ He worked, therefore I stayed at home.

བྱས་ཙང་ག (cɛ̀ɛdzaŋga) 1. idiomatic phrase: see, didn't I tell you ¶བྱས་ཙང་ག ངས་ཁྱོད་སྣ་རིལ་མ་བཞོན་ལབ་བྱུང་ང་ See. Didn't I tell you not to ride the bike? 2. is that so (a response to what sb. says).

བྱས་ཚད་ལམ་སོང་ (cɛ̀ɛdzɛɛ̀ lamsoŋ) shung. sm. བྱས་རྒྱལ་ཁ་སྐོགས་.

བྱས་ཡུས་ (cɛ̀ɛyüü) making a big deal out of sth.; va.—གཏོད་.

བྱས་རབས་ (cɛ̀ɛrəb) an account of work that one has done.

བྱས་རིམ་ (cɛ̀ɛrim) a list of (one's) past activities, a resume.

བྱས་རིམ་ལོ་རྒྱུས་ (cɛ̀ɛrim lugyüü) resume, curriculum vitae.

བྱས་ཤེས་ (cɛ̀ɛshee̖) abbr. of བྱས་པ་ཤེས་.

བྱས་སོ་ཅོག (cɛ̀ɛsojog) all/ anything/ whatever was or is done ¶ཁོས་ལས་ཀ་བྱས་སོ་ཅོག་ལ་སྐྱོན་མཐོང་གི་ཡོད་པ་རེད་ They see fault in everything he did.

བྱི་ (cī) vi. to lose hair, to get bald. 2. rat, mouse. 3. committing adultery; va.—བྱེད་ to commit adultery.

བྱི་ཀུ་ (cigu) ch. garlic.

བྱི་ཁུང་ (ciguŋ) rat/ mouse hole.

བྱི་ཆད་ (cijɛɛ̀) a punishment/ fine for adultery.

བྱི་འཇལ་ (cinjɛɛ) compensation paid for committing adultery.

བྱི་ཉི་ (ciñi) mouse trap.

བྱི་ཏའི་གཞུང་ཐིག (cidɛ shuŋdii) meridian line.

བྱི་ཐར་དུར་ (cidadur) porcupine, hedgehog.

བྱི་ཐུར་ (cidur) sm. བྱི་ཐར་དུར་.

བྱི་དོམ་ (cidom) panda bear.

བྱི་དོར་ (cidɔɔ) sweeping/ cleaning up; va.—བྱེད་.

བྱི་བདར་ (cidar) sm. བྱི་དོར་.

བྱི་མདའ་ (cida) arrow for killing mouse/ rat.

བྱི་ལྡེམ་ (cidem) mousetrap.

བྱི་དུར་ (cidur) sm. བྱི་ཐར་དུར་.

བྱི་ནག (cinaà) black mouse/ rat.

བྱི་ནད་ (cinɛɛ̀) plague.

བྱི་པོ་ (cibu) a womanizer.

བྱི་ཕོ་ (cibu) sm. བྱི་པོ་.

བྱི་ཕྲུག (cidruù) 1. illegitimate child. 2. baby mouse/ rat. 3. baby bird.

བྱི་ཕྲུག་སྐྱོལ་ (cidruù ñöö) chicken breeding/ incubating.

བྱི་ཕྲུག་ཐང་ལུས་ མི་ཤི་ཁྱི་ལུས་ (cidruù tāŋlüü mishi kyī lüü) discarding, throwing away, getting rid of [Lit. baby bird left on the plain, human corpse left for dogs].

བྱི་བ་ (ciwə) mouse, rat.

བྱི་བ་ལམ་རྒྱུག་ཀུན་གྱིས་བརྡུངས་ (ciwə ləmgyuù gũngi duŋ) the subject of everyone's hatred/ animosity/ attacks [Lit. a rat running across the street is hit by all].

བྱི་བའི་ཟས་ཅན་ (ciwɛ sɛɛ̀jɛn) cat.

བྱི་བོ་ (ciwo) 1. hairless, bald. 2. adultery; va.—བྱེད་ to commit adultery.

བྱི་བྱུད་ (cicɛɛ̀) sm. བྱི་བདར་.

བྱི་བྱས་བྱི་རིན་གྱི་ཞལ་ལྕེ་ (cicɛɛ̀ ciringi shɛɛje) one of the 16 laws laid down by Songtsan Gampo regarding adultery.

བྱི་བྲུན་ (cidrün) mouse/ rat droppings.

བྱི་མོ་ (cimo) 1. adulteress. 2. bald female.

བྱི་རྨ་ (cima) scrofula.

བྱི་འཛིན་ (cindzin) sm. བྱི་ལྡེམ་.

བྱི་རྫུས་ (cidzüü) man-made coral.

བྱི་ཟ་ (cisa) cat.

བྱི་ཟླ་ (cinda) the 11th month according to the Tibetan calendar.

བྱི་རིན་ (cirin) sm. བྱི་འཇལ་.

བྱི་རིམས་ (cirim) plague caused by rats/ mice.

བྱི་རིལ་ (cirii) candy, sweets.

བྱི་རུ་ (ciru) sm. བྱུ་རུ་.

བྱི་རུག (ciruù) 1. sm. བྱི་ཕྲུག. 2. peppila (used in Tibetan medicine).

བྱི་ལ་ (cilə) cat.

བྱི་ལ་དོམ་ (cilə tom) panda bear.

བྱི་ལ་དོམ་ཆེན་ (cilə tomcen) giant panda.

བྱི་ལ་དོམ་ཆུང་ (cilə tomjuŋ) small panda bear.

བྱི་ལ་དོམ་ཕྲུག (cilə tomdruù) baby panda.

བྱི་ལོ་ (cilo) year of the rat.

བྱི་ལོང་ (ciloŋ) a mole.

བྱི་ཤང་དཀར་མོ་ (cishaŋ gārbo) the root of the narrow leafed polygala.

བྱི་ཤོར་ (cishɔɔ) vi. to come to commit adultery.

བྱི་སྲན་དཀར་པོ་ (citrɛn gārbo) astragalus membranaceus (used in Tibetan medicine).

བྱིང་ (ciŋ) 1. p. of འབྱིང་. 2. vi. to lose consciousness, to faint. 3. not visible.

བྱིང་གྲུ་ (ciŋdru) sunken boat.

བྱིང་ཉོབ་ (ciŋñob) unclear/ dull mind.

བྱིང་འཐིབས་ (ciŋdib) sm. བྱིང་ཉོབ་.

བྱིང་པོ་ (ciŋbu) sm. བྱིང་ཉོབ་.

བྱིང་སྦུ་མ་ (ciŋ būmə) flannel.

བྱིང་བྱིང་ཐུ་ལུ་ (ciŋjiŋ tūlu) ground beetle.

བྱིང་མ་ (ciŋmə) thick flannel.

བྱིང་རྨུགས་ (cimug) sm. བྱིང་འཐིབས་.

བྱིང་རྫས་ (ciŋdzɛɛ̀) sediment at the bottom of water/ liquids.

བྱིངས་ (ciŋ) the remainder, what is/ was left over ¶ལས་བྱེད་བྱིངས་ནས་ཁ་བཏགས་རེ་ཕུལ་སོང་ The remainder of the officials were each given a ceremonial scarf.

བྱིངས་ཆེ་ (ciŋce) sm. བྱིངས་ཆེ་བ་.

བྱིངས་ཆེ་བ་ (ciŋ cēwa) most everyone, the majority ¶མི་བྱིངས་ཆེ་བས་ཁོ་ལ་དགའ་པོ་བྱས་པ་རེད་ Most of the people liked him.

བྱིངས་ན་གནས་པ་ (ciŋnə nɛɛ̀ba) living under water.

བྱིངས་པོ་ (ciŋbu) mostly, most.

བྱིངས་འཕྲོས་རྒྱག (ciŋdröö gyaà) va. to do spring replowing.

བྱིངས་མ་སྐྱོལ་ (ciŋma ñöö) va. to leave fields that have been plowed and watered in spring until they are ready to be planted.

བྱིངས་མང་ཆེ་བ་ (ciŋ maŋcewa) sm. བྱིང་ཆེ་བ་.

བྱིད་ (cii) p. of འབྱིད་.

བྱིན་ (cin) 1. p. of སྦྱིན་. 2. blessing. 3. splendor, magnificence.

བྱིན་ཀོག (cingyɔɔ̀) a vein in the ankle from which blood is drawn in Tibetan medicine.

བྱིན་དཀར་ (jingaa) shung. white jeans.

བྱིན་གྱིས་ཕྲ་བ་ (cingi trawa) becoming gradually thinner.

བྱིན་གྱིས་བརླབས་པ་ (cingi ləbbə) blessing, sanctifying; va.—བྱེད་.

བྱིན་གྱིས་བརླབས་པར་སྨོན་ (cingi ləbbar mõn) va. to pray for blessing/ sanctification.

བྱིན་ཅན་ (cinjɛn) holy, precious, sacred ¶རྟེན་བྱིན་ཅན་ A sacred relic.

བྱིན་ཆགས་པ་ (cin cāgba) magnificent, splendid.

བྱིན་ཆང་ (cinjaŋ) ཆང་ that has been blessed.

བྱིན་ཆེན་པོ་ (cin cēmbo) sm. བྱིན་ཅན་.

བྱིན་སྙིང་ (cinñiŋ) calf (of leg).

བྱིན་རྟེན་ (cinden) holy relic.

བྱིན་ལྟོ་བསྐུལ་ལས་ (cindo gũũlɛɛ̀) sb. who does what he is told [Lit. eat food, do work that is ordered].

བྱིན་མཐུ་ (cindu) sm. བྱིན་ནུས་.

བྱིན་ནུས་ (cinnüü) the effect of being blessed, the power of a blessing.

བྱིན་པ་ (cimbə) sm. བྱིན་སྙིང་.

བྱིན་པས་ལུས་མི་ཐེག (cimbɛ lüü mideg) aged and fragile (people).

བྱིན་པོ་ (jimbu) sm. བྱིངས་པོ་.

བྱིན་ཕྲུག (jimbuù) sm. ཉ་ཁྱིག.

བྱིན་འཕྲོག (cindrɔɔ̀) abbr. giving and stealing/

robbing.

བྱིན་བབ་ (cimbəb) receiving blessing/ sanctification.

བྱིན་ཚོང་ (cindzoŋ) peddling, street vending; va.—རྒྱག to peddle.

བྱིན་གཞུག (cinshuùjinsguù) vein around the heel that is used for draining blood in Tibetan medicine.

བྱིན་ཟ་ (cinsa) fire.

བྱིན་ཟའི་ཤིང་ (cinsɛè shiŋ) wood used for the fire when performing a rite of exorcism.

བྱིན་རླབས་ (cinləb) a blessing; va.—གནང་ to give a blessing; va.—ཞུ་ to request/ receive a blessing ༑ བླ་མས་མོ་ལ་བྱིན་རླབས་གནང་བ་རེད་ The lama blessed her.

བྱིན་ལག་རྒྱབ་རྩ་ (cinlaà gyəbdza) veins at the back of the hand in Tibetan medicine.

བྱིན་ལེན་ (cin len) taking whatever is given; va.—བྱེད་.

བྱིབ་དོག (cibdɔɔ̀) son, boy.

བྱིབས་ (cib) va. to hide, to cover up.

བྱིའུ་ (ciwu) small birds.

བྱིའུ་སྐད་ (ciwugɛɛ̀) sm. བྱ་སྐད་.

བྱིའུ་ཁྱུ་ (ciwu kyū) a flock of small birds.

བྱིའུ་མགོ་ (ciwu go) head of a bird.

བྱིའུ་ཐར་མ་ (ciwu tārma) 1. bird that is just old enough to fly. 2. a caged bird set free.

བྱིའུ་ཕུར་ (ciwu pūr) sty.

བྱིའུ་ཕྲུག (ciwudruù) fledgling, baby bird.

བྱིའུ་ཕྲུག་ཁ་དམར་ (ciwudruù kāmar) an orphan bird.

བྱིའུ་ཕྲུག་ཐང་གྱུར་ (ciwudruù tāŋgyar) left alone and helpless without anyone to help [Lit. baby bird left on the plain].

བྱིའུ་ཚང་ (ciwudzaŋ) bird nest; va.—གསོག to build a nest.

བྱིའུ་འཛུལ་བྱེད་ (ciwudzüü cèè) va. to enter a small hole/ opening [Lit. like a small bird entering].

བྱིའུ་ཞན་ཡང་འབུ་ཐུབ་ (ciwu shenyaŋ bu tūb) even though small/ weak can manage [Lit. even though the bird is weak it can still catch an insect].

བྱིའུ་ཝུར་བ་ (ciwu wurwə) locust.

བྱིའུ་ཡན་ཆུའི་ (ciwu yɛncu) bramble finch.

བྱིའུ་ལ་ཕུག (ciwu ləbu) torularia humilis (used in Tibetan medicine).

བྱིའུ་སྲེད་མ་ (ciwu sɛ̄ɛma) hedysarum multijugum (used in Tibetan medicine).

བྱིལ་ (cii)) sm. བྱིལ་བྱིལ་བྱེད་.

བྱིལ་ (cii) 1. imp. of འབྱིལ་. 2. p. and imp. of འབྱིལ་.

བྱིལ་བྱིལ་ (ciijii) caressing, stroking, patting; va.—བྱེད་ ༑ ཨ་མས་ཕྲུ་གུའི་མགོ་ལ་བྱིལ་བྱིལ་བྱས་པ་རེད་ The mother stroked the child's head.

བྱིལ་མོ་ (ciimu) bare, naked.

བྱིས་ (cii) abbr. of བྱིས་པ་.

བྱིས་གླེག་རྩོམ་རིག (ciilɔɔ̀ dzōmrig) children's literature.

བྱིས་ཀང་ (ciigaŋ) ch.tib. a type of revolver that holds seven bullets.

བྱིས་སྐད་ (ciigɛɛ̀) baby talk.

བྱིས་སྐད་ངག་ངོག (ciigɛɛ̀ ŋagŋɔg) sm. བྱིས་སྐད་.

བྱིས་གོས་ (ciigöö) children's garment/ clothes.

བྱིས་གླུ་ (ciilu) children's song.

བྱིས་འགྲོས་ (cii dröö) the way a child walks.

བྱིས་སྒྲུང་ (ciidruŋ) children's stories/ tales.

བྱིས་ཉམས་ (ciiñam) manner/ behavior/ attitude of a child.

བྱིས་གཉོར་ཁང་ (ciiñɔrgaŋ) kindergarden, nursery school.

བྱིས་དོག (ciidɔɔ̀) boy.

བྱིས་ནད་ (ciinɛɛ̀) children's diseases/ illnesses, pediatric diseases.

བྱིས་ནད་ཚན་ཁག (ciinɛɛ̀ tsɛ̄ngaà) pediatric section/ division/ department.

བྱིས་པ་ (ciibə) child.

བྱིས་པ་ཁང (ciibəgaŋ) nursery, kindergarten.

བྱིས་པ་ཉུང་ཁྲིད་ (ciibə ñuŋdrii) shung. using an inducement to lure sb. to do sth. [Lit. to lure children with turnips].

བྱིས་པ་མྱུར་སྐྱོབ་ལྟེ་བ་ (ciibə ñurgyob dēwa) children's first-aid center.

བྱིས་པ་བཟོ་པ་ (ciibə soba) child labor, child worker.

བྱིས་པ་རིག་མཆོག (ciibə rigjɔɔ̀) child prodigy.

བྱིས་པ་ཤེད་མ་བྱེ་བ་ (ciibə shēèma cewa) children that have not matured/ developed physically.

བྱིས་པའི་སྐྱེ་བོ་ (ciibɛ gyēwo) 1. a child. 2. retarded/ stupid person.

བྱིས་པའི་གོན་ཆས་ (ciibɛ könjɛɛ̀) children's clothing.

བྱིས་པའི་གླིང་ག (ciibɛ liŋgə) children's park.

བྱིས་པའི་ལྟ་བ་ (ciibɛ dāwa) children's viewpoint.

བྱིས་པའི་ལྟ་རྩལ་ (ciibɛ dədzüü) sm. བྱིས་པའི་ལྟ་བ་.

བྱིས་པའི་བརྟུལ་ཞུགས་ (ciibɛ dūūshuù) childish behavior.

བྱིས་པའི་དུས་ (ciibɛ tüü) childhood.

བྱིས་པའི་དུས་ཆེན་ (ciibɛ tüüjen) Children's Day.

བྱིས་པའི་བདེ་སྐྱོང་ཁང་ (ciibɛ degyoŋgaŋ) children's health care section.

བྱིས་པའི་སྣང་བ་ (ciibɛ nāŋwa) childish thought/ thinking.

བྱིས་པའི་ཕོ་བྲང་ (ciibɛ pōdraŋ) children's palace (a place where children are taken for amusement/ recreation).

བྱིས་པའི་སྨོངས་བསམ་ (ciibɛ mōŋsam) childish thinking.

བྱིས་པའི་སྨན་ཁང་ (ciibɛ mɛ̄ngaŋ) children's hospital.

བྱིས་པའི་ཚོགས་པ་ (ciibɛ tsɔ̄gba) children's corps.

བྱིས་པའི་རང་བཞིན་ (ciibɛ rəŋshin) immature, childish.

བྱིས་པའི་སློབ་གསོ་ (ciibɛ lōbso) children's education.

བྱིས་པའི་བསམ་སྤྱོད་ (ciibɛ sāmjöö) sm. བྱིས་བློ་.

བྱིས་པར་རོགས་སྐྱོར་ལྷན་ཚོགས་ (ciibar rɔ̀ɔgyɔɔ̀ lhɛ̄ndzɔɔ̀) Save the Children Fund.

བྱིས་པས་གྲི་ཁར་རྩེ་བ་ (cibɛ drigar dzēwa) shung. dangerous activities ༑ བྱིས་པས་གྲི་ཁར་རྩེ་བ་དང་མཚུངས་པའི་བྱ་སྤྱོད་བྱང་རྒྱལ་སྣ་ཚོགས་བྱེད་པ་ They were doing various reckless things just like children playing with a blade of a knife [Lit. children playing with the blade of a knife].

བྱིས་པས་གླུ་གཞས་མཉམ་གདོང་ (ciibɛ lūshɛɛ̀ ñamdoŋ) children's chorus/ choir.

བྱིས་བློ་ (ciilo) infantile/ childish/ naive thoughts or ideas; va.—སེལ་; — འབྱེད་ to eliminate infantile thoughts.

བྱིས་བློའི་སྐྱོན་ (ciilö gyön) infantile disorder.

བྱིས་མོ་ (ciimu) young girl.

བྱིས་སྨན་ལེན་ས་ (ciimɛn lensa) pharmacy/ dispensary for children.

བྱིས་རྩེད་ (ciidzeè) children's games; va.—རྩེ་ to play children's games.

བྱིས་རློན་ (ciilön) 1. new born baby who is still wet. 2. children's drinks (e.g., milk).

བྱིས་ལི་ (ciili) male child.

བྱིས་སོ་ (ciiso) baby teeth.

བྱིས་གསོ་ཁང་ (ciisogaŋ) nursery, kindergarten.

བྱུ་རུ་ (curu) coral (the gem).

བྱུ་རུ་མདོག (curu dɔɔ̀) the color of the coral.

བྱུ་རུའི་རྒྱ་མཚོ་ (curü gyadzo) the Coral Sea.

བྱུ་རུའི་མཆུ་ཅན་ (curü cüjɛn) poet. sm. སྨྱུ་ག་.

བྱུ་རུའི་སྡོང་པོ་ (curü doŋbo) coral reef.

བྱུ་རུའི་སྦ་ཕྲུག (curü bədruù) coral headdress worn by Tibetan women.

བྱུག (cuù) f. of འབྱུག.

བྱུག་སྣོན་ (cugnön) applying/ rubbing/ administer (e.g., medication on the skin); va.—བྱེད་.

བྱུག་པ་ (cugbə) oils, salves, etc. that are rubbed on/ massaged; va.—རྒྱག; —བྱུག.

བྱུག་པའི་བཅོས་ཀ་ (cugbɛ jööga) treating wounds/ sores by rubbing on an ointment or salve.

བྱུག་པིར་ (cugbir) a broad-tipped (in contrast to a pointed tip) brush.

བྱུག་སྤོས་ (cugböö) scented oils that are used for

treating wounds and sores.

བྱུག་མར་ (cugmaa) butter/ oil that is rubbed on the body/ face/ hair.

བྱུག་དམར་ (cugmar) a red facial make up worn by Tibetan women.

བྱུག་སྨན་ (cugmɛn) ointment/ salve/ lotion used as a medicine.

བྱུག་རྫས་ (cugdzɛɛ̀) ointment, salve, lotion.

བྱུག་བཞག་པ་ (cugshagba) 1. doing sth. well ¶ལས་ཀ་གང་ཡིན་ན་ཡང་ཁོང་གིས་བྱུག་བཞག་པ་ཞིག་བྱེད་ཀྱི་རེད་ Whatever the work, he will do it well. 2. well-fitting (for clothes).

བྱུག་རིས་ (cugrii) order, standing, sequence, arrangement.

བྱུག་གསེར་ (cugser) liquid gold used in painting.

བྱུགས་ (cuù) p. and imp. of འབྱུག.

བྱུགས་པ་རྒྱག (cugbə gyaà) sm. འབྱུག.

བྱུང་ (cuŋ) 1. p. of འབྱུང་. 2. first person past involuntary verb sentence final ¶ང་ན་བྱུང་ I got sick. 3. particle used with active verbs to indicate that the action went from a third person subject to a first person object ¶ཁོས་ང་ར་བཤད་བྱུང་ He said (that) to me. 4. vi. to take place, to happen (past tense only) ¶ལོ་དེའི་ནང་དམག་ཆེན་དང་པོ་བྱུང་བ་རེད་ The First World War took place in that year.

བྱུང་རྐྱེན་ (cuŋgyen) cause of sth. that happened.

བྱུང་རྒྱལ་ (cuŋgyɛɛ) doing sth. without thinking/ investigating; va.—དུ་སྨྲ་; —བརྗོད་ to say sth. without first thinking about it; va.—དུ་བྱེད་ to do sth. hastily without careful consideration ¶ཚོགས་འདུའི་ཐོག་སྐད་ཆ་བྱུང་རྒྱལ་དུ་ཤོད་རྒྱུ་མེད་ You shouldn't say things at the meeting without first thinking about it.

བྱུང་སྟངས་ (cuŋdaŋ) the manner in which sth. happened ¶དམག་ཕམ་ཉེས་བྱུང་སྟངས་ནི་ As for the manner in which they lost the war.

བྱུང་ཐོ་ (cuŋdo) receipt/ invoice/ list/ record of things received.

བྱུང་འབྲས་ (cuŋdrɛɛ̀) result, outcome.

བྱུང་མ་མྱོང་བ་ (cuŋ mañoŋwa) unprecedented, never happened before ¶འདི་ནི་སྔར་བྱུང་མ་མྱོང་བའི་གནས་ཚུལ་ཞིག་རེད་ This is an unprecedented situation.

བྱུང་མང་ (cuŋmaŋ) occurring frequently ¶བྱུང་མང་ནད་རིགས་ A frequently occurring disease.

བྱུང་ཚད་ (cuŋdzɛɛ̀) everything sb. has/ got ¶ཁོང་དངུལ་བྱུང་ཚད་ནང་ལ་བསྐུར་གྱི་ཡོད་པ་རེད་ He sends whatever money he got he sent to his home.

བྱུང་ཚུལ་ (cuŋdzüü) sm. བྱུང་སྟངས་.

བྱུང་འཛིན་ (cuŋdzin) receipt.

བྱུང་རབས་ (cuŋrəb) chronological narrative of past events/ history.

བྱུང་ལུགས་བྱུང་སྟངས་ (cuŋluù cuŋdaŋ) the way sth. happened/ occurred.

བྱུང་སོང་ (cuŋsoŋ) things received and things expended ¶བྱུང་སོང་རྩིས་ཁྲ་ An accounting of things received and expended.

བྱུང་སོང་ཁ་ཐུག་པ་བཟོ་ (cuŋsoŋ kāduùba so) va. to balance income and expenditure (in accounting).

བྱུང་སོང་མགོ་ཐུག (cuŋsoŋ goduù) income and expenditure in balance ¶འདི་ལོའི་དངུལ་འབབ་བྱུང་སོང་མགོ་ཐུག་རེད་བཞག This year income and expenditure balanced.

བྱུང་སོང་སྙོམས་ (cuŋsoŋ ñōm) vi. to have income and expenditure be in balance.

བྱུར་ (cur) disaster, calamity, misfortune.

བྱུར་རྐྱེན་ (curgyen) cause of a disaster/ calamity/ misfortune.

བྱུར་ཁ་ (curga) sm. བྱུར་རྐྱེན་.

བྱུར་གོད་ (curgöò) sm. བྱུར་.

བྱུར་གྱི་སྣ་འདྲེན་ (curgi nādren) sb. who brings about misfortune/ calamity/ disaster.

བྱུར་ཆག (curjaà) sm. བྱུར་ཆགས་.

བྱུར་ཆགས་ (curjaà) trouble, misfortune, disaster, calamity; va.—བཟོ་ to cause trouble/ misfortune/ disaster, calamity ¶ད་ལོ་ལུང་པ་དེར་བྱུར་ཆགས་མང་པོ་བྱུང་བ་རེད་ That area had many disasters this year.

བྱུར་ཆགས་རྐྱེན་ངན་ (curjaà gyēnŋɛn) sm. བྱུར་རྐྱེན་.

བྱུར་ཆགས་སྣེ་འདོམས་ (curjaà nēmdom) many disasters/ misfortunes occurring at the same time.

བྱུར་ཉེས་ (curñeè) sm. བྱུར་ཆགས་.

བྱུར་ལྟས་ (curdɛɛ̀) sign or omen of pending disaster/ misfortune/ calamity.

བྱུར་མདོག (cundɔɔ̀) coral color.

བྱུར་སྡུད་མ་ (curdüümə) derogative term used when scolding women: 'You disaster causing woman'.

བྱུར་ནག (curnaà) sm. བྱུར་ཅན་.

བྱུར་གནམ་དིབ་མ་ (curnɛɛ̀ dibmə) sudden disaster/ calamity.

བྱུར་པོ་ (curbu) 1. sm. བྱུར་ཆགས་. 2. full to the rim/ brim; vi.—ཁེངས་ to be full to the rim/ brim ¶ཁོས་འབྲུ་བླུག་ནས་ལྕགས་ཏིན་བྱུར་པོར་ཁེངས་སོང་ He poured grain in the tin filling it to the brim.

བྱུར་བུར་གང་ (curbu gaŋ) sm. བྱུར་བུར་.

བྱུར་བུ་ (curbu) sm. བྱུར་པོ་, 2.

བྱུར་བྱུར་ (curjur) piled/ heaped up, filled to the brim; vi.—ཁེངས་ to be filled to the rim/ brim.

བྱུལ་བྱུལ་ (cüüjüü) 1. wandering; va.— བྱེད་. 2. sm. བྱེལ་བྱེལ་.

བྱུས་ (cüù) strategy, tactics; va.— བྱེད་; —གཏོང་ to strategize, to make a strategy/ tactics ¶དམག་བྱུས་ Military strategy. 2. religious merit.

བྱུས་ཁག (cüùgaà) shung. sm. ཛུས་གཏོགས་.

བྱུས་འགོ་ནས་ཉེས་ (cüù gonɛ ñeè) vi. to start off with the wrong strategy.

བྱུས་འགྲོ་ (cündro) sm. ལམ་འགྲོ་.

བྱུས་ཉེས་ (cüùñeè) a catastrophe/ disaster/ misfortune caused by a bad or incorrect strategy.

བྱུས་ཉེས་དགྲ་ཤོར་ (cüùñeè drashɔɔ) a mishap/ defeat caused by a bad strategy or plan.

བྱུས་གཏོགས་ (cüùdoò) interference, meddling, butting into, minding other's affairs/ business; va.—བྱེད་.

བྱུས་གཏོགས་ཚ་པོ་ (cüùdoò tsābo) sb. who butts into or minds other people's affairs, sb. who is nosy and meddles/ interferes.

བྱུས་ཐེ་ (cüùde) shung. interfering in other's business or in inappropriate affairs ¶འཇིག་རྟེན་ལས་སྐོར་བྱུས་ཐེ་མི་ཆོག་ཅིང་ It is not permitted to interfere in secular affairs.

བྱུས་འདོན་ (cüù dön) va. to make a plan/ strategy.

བྱུས་མེད་ཐབས་རྡུགས་ (cüùmeè tābduù) coming to a dead end with no strategy to overcome the problem, falling on hard times with no alternatives.

བྱུས་མེད་བྱུས་འཁྲི་ (cüùmeè cüùdri) sm. བྱུས་གཏོགས་.

བྱུས་མེད་བྱུས་གཏོགས་ (cüùmeè cüùdɔɔ̀) sm. བྱུས་གཏོགས་.

བྱུས་ཚ་པོ་ (cüù tsābo) person who has the ability to come up with many plans/ means/ strategies/ methods/ techniques.

བྱུས་ལེགས་ (cüùleg) fortunate, lucky ¶བྱུས་ལེགས་ཤིག་ལ་ཨེམ་ཆི་ར་ཁ་པར་གཏོང་ཐུབ་འདུག Fortunately, (he) was able to call the doctor.

བྱེ་ (ce) 1. abbr. of བྱེ་མ་. 2. p. and f. of འབྱེ་.

བྱེ་ཀར་ (cegar) sugar.

བྱེ་དཀྱིལ་གསེར་སྒྲུག (cegyii sērdruù) working hard for a small gain [Lit. picking gold from sand].

བྱེ་དཀྲུག (cedruù) wooden utensil used to mix sand and grain when roasting grains in sand.

བྱེ་རྐྱལ་ (cegyɛɛ) sm. བྱེ་སྣོད་.

བྱེ་སྐྱེས་རྩི་ཤིང་ (cegyeè dzīshiŋ) plants growing in sand (or in the desert).

བྱེ་སྐྱོར་ཐལ་སྐྱོར་འཐེན་ (cegyɔɔ tɛ̄ɛgyɔɔ tēn) va. to put sand or dust near the door of a house to indicate they the inhabitants are in mourning.

བྱེ་ཁུག (ceguù) sm. བྱེ་སྣོད་.

བྱེ་འབྲུད་ (ce̱drüü) washing fur with sand (a traditional method); va.—རྒྱག.

བྱེ་འགོག (ce̱gɔɔ̀) protection against sand/ desertification.

བྱེ་འགོག་ཤིང་ནགས་ (ce̱gɔɔ̀ shiŋ̄naà) a forest created as an antierosion mechanism to prevent desertification.

བྱེ་རྒྱུན་ (ce̱gyün) the leather straps which join strips of armor.

བྱེ་སྒང་ (ce̱gaŋ) sand dune.

བྱེ་རྔོད་ (ce̱ŋöö) popping grain in heated sand; va.—རྒྱག.

བྱེ་སྔགས་ (ce̱ŋaà) a tantric practice where a spell is cast on sand.

བྱེ་བཙོས་ནགས་བཟོ་ (ce̱jöö na̱gso) forestation to prevent desertification.

བྱེ་བཙོས་རྩྭ་འདེབས་ (ce̱jöö dzāndeb) planting grass to prevent desertification.

བྱེ་འཛུགས་ཤིང་ནགས་ (ce̱njaà shiŋ̄naà) sm. བྱེ་འགོག་ཤིང་ནགས་.

བྱེ་སྡིག (ce̱daà) a small lizard.

བྱེ་བརྟན་རྩི་ཤིང་ (ce̱dεn dzi̱shiŋ) sm. བྱེ་འཛུགས་ཤིང་ནགས་.

བྱེ་སྡོང་ (ce̱doŋ) sm. བྱེ་འདམ་.

བྱེ་ཐང་ (ce̱daŋ) desert.

བྱེ་ཐང་དཀྱིལ་ནས་གསེར་རྙེད་པ་ལྟར་ (ce̱daŋ gyi̱inε sēē ñēèbadar) finding sth. valuable that is difficult to find [Lit. like finding gold in the desert].

བྱེ་ཐང་སྤང་ལྗོངས་ (ce̱daŋ bāŋjoŋ) oasis.

བྱེ་རྡོང་ (ce̱doŋ) quicksand.

བྱེ་འདམ་ (ce̱ndam) silt.

བྱེ་འདུལ་རྩྭ་འདེབས་ (ce̱düü dzāndeb) sm. བྱེ་བཙོས་རྩྭ་འདེབས་.

བྱེ་རྡིབ་ (ce̱dib) a sand slide (analagous to a mud slide).

བྱེ་རྡུལ་ (ce̱düü) sand and dust.

བྱེ་རྡོ་ (ce̱do) gravel.

བྱེ་སྣོད་ (ce̱nöö) a bag in which sand is put, a sandbag.

བྱེ་སྤུང་ (ce̱buŋ) pile of sand.

བྱེ་ཕད་ (ce̱bεὲ) sm. བྱེ་སྣོད་.

བྱེ་ཕུང་ (ce̱buŋ) sandpile, sand dune.

བྱེ་ཕུང་ལུང་སྟོང་ (ce̱buŋ lu̱ŋdoŋ) desert wilderness.

བྱེ་བ་ (ce̱wa) 1. ten million. 2. p. of འབྱེ་.

བྱེ་བྲག (ce̱draà) a special or particular kind/ class/ species; va.—(དུ་) འབྱེད་ to classify, to sort, differentiate ༑ངང་པ་ནི་ཆུ་བྱའི་བྱེ་བྲག་ཅིག་ཡིན་ The goose is a particular type of water bird.

བྱེ་བྲག་གི་ངལ་རྩོལ་ (ce̱draàgi ŋεə̱dzöö) specific/ particular type of labor.

བྱེ་བྲག་ཏུ་ (ce̱dragdu) in particular, specially specifically ༑སྤྱིར་མི་དམངས་ཡོངས་དང་བྱེ་བྲག་ཏུ་བྱིས་པའི་འཕྲོད་བསྟེན་ཡར་རྒྱས་ In general, the improvement of the hygiene of the public; in particular, that of the children.

བྱེ་བྲག་རྟོག་བྱེད་ (ce̱draà dōgjeè) name of a Tibetan-Sanskrit dictionary.

བྱེ་བྲག་པ་ (ce̱dragba) particular, specific.

བྱེ་འབུར་ (ce̱mbur) sand dune.

བྱེ་མ་ (ce̱ma) sand.

བྱེ་མ་ཀ་ར་ (ce̱ma gāra) granulated sugar.

བྱེ་མ་ཀ་རའི་ན་ཚ་ (ce̱ma gārε na̱dza) diabetes.

བྱེ་མ་ཉུ་གུ་ (ce̱ma ñugu) sm. བྱེ་སྙུག་གུ་.

བྱེ་མ་སྨྱུ་གུ་ (ce̱ma ñugu) sm. བྱེ་སྙུག.

བྱེ་མ་འདྲེས་ཚད་ (ce̱ma dre̱èdzεὲ) the sand content (of sth.).

བྱེ་མ་སྙུ་གུ་ (ce̱ma ñugu) sm. བྱེ་མ་སྨྱུ་གུ་.

བྱེ་མ་བཙིར་ན་སྣུམ་མི་ཐོན་ (ce̱ma dzi̱rnə nūm mi̱ tǖn) useless/ fruitless work or plans.[Lit. if one squeezes sand, oil does not come out].

བྱེ་མ་བཙིར་ན་མར་མི་ཐོན་ (ce̱ma dzi̱rnə ma̱r mi̱ tǖn) useless/ fruitless work or plans [Lit. if one squeezes sand, butter doers not come out].

བྱེ་མ་འཚག (ce̱ma dzāà) va. to shift sand (through a sieve).

བྱེ་མ་རེག་ཚོད་ (ce̱ma re̱gjöö) a type of whetstone.

བྱེ་མ་ས་ (ce̱masa) sandy soil.

བྱེ་མ་སྲེ་ (ce̱ma sē) va. to mix sand with sth.

བྱེ་མའི་ཚངས་བུ་ (ce̱mε cāŋbu) things that dont last or hold together. [Lit. sand that has been squeezed together].

བྱེ་མའི་སྙེ་མ་ (ce̱mε ñēma) rows of sand dunes.

བྱེ་མའི་ཐང་ (ce̱mε tāŋ) desert.

བྱེ་མའི་བྲག་རྡོ་ (ce̱mε tra̱gdo) sandstone.

བྱེ་མའི་སྨིགས་བུ་ (ce̱mε mi̱gbu) sand lizard.

བྱེ་མའི་ཞིང་ (ce̱mε shi̱ŋ) sandy field/ land.

བྱེ་མར་འགྱུར་ (ce̱mar gyu̱r) vi. to become desert, to get desertified.

བྱེ་སྨུག (ce̱ñuù) abbr. of བྱེ་མ་སྨྱུ་གུ་.

བྱེ་ཚན་ (ce̱dzεn) hot sand.

བྱེ་འཚུབ་ (ce̱dzub) sand storm; vi.—རྒྱག.

བྱེ་ཞིང་ (cēshiŋ) sandy field.

བྱེ་ཞིབ་ (ce̱shib) 1. finely sifted sand. 2. granulated sugar.

བྱེ་རགས་ (ce̱raà) 1. sand dam. 2. name of sandy area near Sera monastery.

བྱེ་རི་ (ce̱ri) sand dune.

བྱེ་རིལ་ (ce̱rii) candy, sweet.

བྱེ་རིལ་སྒྲིལ་ཤོག (ci̱rii dri̱ishoò) candy wrapper.

བྱེ་རིལ་བུ་དཀར་ (ci̱rii pu̱gar) a kind of white candy.

བྱེ་རིལ་སྣ་འདུས་ (ci̱rii nāndüü) an assortment/ mixture of candy.

བྱེ་རོ་ (ce̱ro) coarse sand.

བྱེ་རླུང་ (ce̱luŋ) sandstorm; va.—རྒྱག.

བྱེ་ལ་ (ce̱la) 1. sand dune. 2. mountain pass consisting of sand.

བྱེ་གཤོངས་ (ce̱shoŋ) a valley filled with sand.

བྱེ་ས་ (ce̱sa) sandy soil.

བྱེ་སླང་ (ce̱laŋ) a pan used for roasting barley in sand.

བྱེ་གསེར་ (cēser) gold dust; va.—སྤྱུག to pan/ sift for gold.

བྱེ་བསལ་གསེར་སྒྲུག (ce̱sεε sērdruù) choosing the best [Lit. clearing sand and picking up gold].

བྱེ་ལྷག (ce̱lhaà) sm. བྱེ་རླུང་.

བྱེག (ceg) shung. abbr. of བྱེ་བྲག.

བྱེད་: p. བྱས་; f. བྱ་; imp. བྱོས་ (ce̱è) 1. va. to do, to make, to act ༑ཁོས་འདི་འདྲ་བྱས་པ་རེད་ He did it like that. ༑མོས་སློབ་གྲྭའི་དགེ་རྒན་ཡུན་རིང་བྱས་པ་རེད་ She was a school teacher for a long time. 2. a verb that verbalizes nouns and nominals e.g., ལས་ཀ་ means "work" and ལས་ཀ་བྱེད་ means "to (do) work". 3. the instrument/ method/ means of doing sth. ༑གཅོད་བྱེད་ Cutting instrument. 4. vi. to become ༑ད་ཕྱི་པོ་བྱས་སོང་ Now it has become late. 5. va. to say ༑ངས་ཁོ་ཤོག་བྱས་པ་ཡིན་ I told him to come.

བྱེད་རྒྱུ་འབལ་པོ་ (ce̱ègyu be̱εbo) sm. བྱེད་རྒྱུ་འབེལ་པོ་.

བྱེད་རྒྱུ་འབེལ་པོ་ (ce̱ègyu be̱ebo) a person who does a lot of marginal/ dubious things.

བྱེད་རྒྱུ་རྫོགས་ (ce̱ègyu dzɔ̱ɔ̀) sm. བྱེད་རྒྱུ་ཟད་པ་.

བྱེད་རྒྱུ་ཟད་ (ce̱ègyu sεὲ) vi. to be bored ༑ཁོ་བྱེད་རྒྱུ་ཟད་ནས་ཉིན་ལྟར་ཨ་རག་འཐུང་ནས་སྡོད་ཀྱི་འདུག He got bored and stayed everyday drinking alcohol.

བྱེད་སྒོ་ (ce̱ègo) activities, affairs, work, duties, functions; va.—སྤེལ་ ༑རྟེན་འབྲེལ་གྱི་བྱེད་སྒོ་ལྟེ་བ་ཁག The main activities of the ceremony. ༑ལས་ཁུངས་སོ་སོའི་བྱེད་སྒོ་ The affairs of each office.

བྱེད་སྒོ་ཕུའུ་ (ce̱ègo bū) tib.ch. department that deals with activities/ business/ work.

བྱེད་སྒོའི་ནུས་པ་ (ce̱ègö nü̱übə) work or occupational skill/ ability.

བྱེད་སྒོའི་རྩ་ཚིག (ce̱ègö dzədzii) 1. a plan or guide to work. 2. shung. an order/ proclamation (of the traditional Tibetan government).

བྱེད་སྒྲ་ (ce̱dra) the instrumental case.

བྱེད་ངན་ (ce̱èŋεn) bad/ evil/ improper acts, crimes, misbehavior; va.—བྱེད་.

བྱེད་ངན་ཞོར་འགྲོགས་ (ce̱èŋεn sho̱ŋgyɔɔ̀) shung. getting involved with evil doers.

བྱེད་དཀའ་ (ce̱èdεὲ) difficult to do/ handle ༑ལས་དོན་

འདི་བྱེད་གཏད་བྱུང་ This matter became difficult (to handle).

བྱེད་གདེ་ (c<u>e</u>ède) ringleaders.

བྱེད་སྟངས་ (c<u>e</u>èdaŋ) way or manner of doing things, methods, techniques ¶ཁོང་གི་ལས་ཀ་བྱེད་སྟངས་ཡག་པོ་འདུག His way of working is good. ¶བྱེད་སྟངས་སྐྱུག་བྲོ་པོ་ A disgusting way of acting.

བྱེད་སྟངས་ངན་པོ་ (c<u>e</u>èdaŋ ŋ<u>e</u>mbo) malicious/ malevolent/ evil/ bad manner of doing sth.

བྱེད་སྟངས་ཉེས་པོ་ (c<u>e</u>èdaŋ ñ<u>e</u>èbo) sm. བྱེད་སྟངས་ངན་པོ་.

བྱེད་སྟངས་སྟོན་པའི་ཚིག (c<u>e</u>èdaa dõmbɛ tsiì) adverbial modifier.

བྱེད་ཐབས་ (c<u>e</u>èdəb) method, means, approach; vi.—ཐལ་ to exhaust ways to do/ accomplish sth. ¶བྱེད་ཐབས་རྙིང་པ་ Old ways of doing things.

བྱེད་ཐུབ་པའི་རང་བཞིན་ (c<u>e</u>ètubɛ rə̄ŋshin) possibility, potentiality.

བྱེད་བདེ་ཚགས་ཚུད་ (c<u>e</u>ède tsāgdzüü) work that is going well/ smoothly.

བྱེད་པ་རྒྱུ་མཐུན་ (c<u>e</u>èba gy<u>u</u>dün) the correspondence between action and effect.

བྱེད་པ་པོ་ (c<u>e</u>èbabo) 1. subject or actor (in grammar). 2. doer, the one who does ¶རང་དབང་ལ་རྩོད་ལེན་བྱེད་པ་པོ་ The ones who strive for freedom.

བྱེད་པ་པོའི་སྒྲ་ (c<u>e</u>èbabö dr<u>a</u>) sm. བྱེད་སྒྲ་.

བྱེད་པའི་སྒྲ་ (c<u>e</u>èbö dr<u>a</u>) sm. བྱེད་སྒྲ་.

བྱེད་པོ་ (c<u>e</u>èbo) sm. བྱེད་པ་པོ་.

བྱེད་པོ་གཙོ་བོ་ (c<u>e</u>èbo dzōwo) the subject (in grammar).

བྱེད་སྤྱོད་ (c<u>e</u>èjöö) behavior, style of behaving.

བྱེད་ཕྱོགས་ (c<u>e</u>èjɔɔ) policy, guiding principle, course of action ¶ཚན་རིག་གིས་ཐོན་སྐྱེད་ལ་ཞབས་འདེགས་ཞུ་དགོས་ཞེས་པའི་བྱེད་ཕྱོགས་ The policy that "science should serve production."

བྱེད་བྱེད་བྱེད་ (c<u>e</u>èjeè c<u>e</u>è) va. to pretend/ act as if one can do sth. one really can't.

བྱེད་དབྱིབས་ (c<u>e</u>èyib) shape, form.

བྱེད་མུས་ཉེས་ཅན་ (c<u>e</u>èmüù ñ<u>e</u>èjɛn) an active criminal.

བྱེད་མེད་ལས་ཚིག (c<u>e</u>èmeè l<u>ɛ</u>èdziì) involuntary verb.

བྱེད་མྱོང་ལོ་རྒྱུས་ (c<u>e</u>èñoŋ l<u>u</u>gyüù) resume, curriculum vitae.

བྱེད་རྩིས་ (c<u>e</u>èdziì) intending/ planning to do sth.; va.—བྱེད་.

བྱེད་རྩལ་ (c<u>e</u>èdzöö) strength or effectiveness of work/ activities.

བྱེད་ཚིག (c<u>e</u>èdziì) sm. བྱ་ཚིག.

བྱེད་ཚུལ་ (c<u>e</u>èdzüü) sm. བྱ་སྟངས་.

བྱེད་འཛོལ་ (c<u>e</u>ndzöö) making a mistake doing sth. ¶ངའི་ལས་ཀའི་ཐོག་ལ་བྱེད་འཛོལ་ཆེན་པོ་བྱུང་ I made a big mistake doing my work.

བྱེད་བཞིན་པ་ (c<u>e</u>èshimbə) being in the process of doing sth. ¶ང་སློབ་སྦྱོང་བྱེད་བཞིན་པ་ཡིན་ I am in the process of studying.

བྱེད་བཞིན་སྦྱོང་བཞིན་ (c<u>e</u>èshin j<u>o</u>ŋshin) on the job training, learning while working.

བྱེད་བཟོ་ (c<u>e</u>èso) 1. stylish; va.—བྱེད་; —སྟོན་ to be/ dress stylishly. 2. vi. to seems like doing ¶ཁོས་ལས་ཀ་དེ་ཁས་ལེན་བྱེད་བཟོ་མི་འདུག It doesn't seem like he will accept the job.

བྱེད་བཟོ་དོད་པོ་ (c<u>e</u>èso t<u>ö</u>ö̀bo) stylish.

བྱེད་བཟོ་ཆ་པོ་ (c<u>e</u>èso tsābo) sm. བྱེད་བཟོ་དོད་པོ་.

བྱེད་ཡག་མེད་པ་ (c<u>e</u>èyaà m<u>e</u>èba) there is nothing to do.

བྱེད་ཡུལ་ (c<u>e</u>èyüü) the one with whom one does sth. ¶ཞིང་པ་རྣམས་ང་ཚོའི་མཐུན་སྒྲིལ་བྱེད་ཡུལ་རེད་ The farmers are the ones with whom we are uniting.

བྱེད་རིན་ (c<u>e</u>èrin) worth doing, worthwhile ¶ལས་ཀ་དེ་བྱེད་རིན་མི་འདུག That job is not worth doing.

བྱེད་རིམ་ (c<u>e</u>èrim) stages of doing sth.

བྱེད་རོགས་ (c<u>e</u>èrɔɔ̀) a colleague in doing some task/ job.

བྱེད་ལུགས་ (c<u>e</u>èluù) sm. བྱེད་སྟོལ་.

བྱེད་ལུགས་བྱེད་སྟངས་ (c<u>e</u>èluù c<u>e</u>èdaŋ) manner and custom of doing things.

བྱེད་ལོག (c<u>e</u>èlɔɔ̀) bad/ wicked/ corrupt deeds.

བྱེད་ལོང་བྱ་ལོང་མེད་པ་ (c<u>e</u>èloŋ caloŋ m<u>e</u>èba) not having time to do sth.

བྱེད་སེམས་འཇུག་པའི་ཡིད་མཐུན་ (c<u>e</u>èsem j<u>u</u>gbɛ y<u>i</u>idün) to do everything according to sb.'s wish.

བྱེད་སྲོལ་ (c<u>e</u>èsöö) established ways of doing things, customs, traditions.

བྱིའུ་འབུར་ (c<u>e</u>mbur) a sty.

བྱིའུ་ལ་ཕུག (c<u>e</u>wu l<u>a</u>buù) sm. བྱིའུ་ལ་ཕུག.

བྱེར་ (c<u>e</u>r) p. and imp. of འབྱེར་.

བྱེར་འགྲམ་དུ་འགྲོ་ (c<u>e</u>ndramdu dr<u>o</u>) vi. to be/ get spread (usu. disease/ infection).

བྱེར་འགྲམས་ (c<u>e</u>ndram) sm. བྱེར་འགྲམ་.

བྱེར་ལྷེབས་ (c<u>e</u>eleb) toothless (for horses and mules).

བྱེལ་ (c<u>ee</u>) sm. བྱིའུ་.

བྱེལ་ཚང་ (c<u>ee</u>dzaŋ) sm. བྱིའུའི་ཚང་.

བྱེས་ c<u>e</u>è) shung. temporarily abroad, temporarily away from one's home base ¶གྲོ་མོར་བྱེས་བཀའ་ཤག་བཙུགས་པ་རེད་ The "away" Kashag was established in Yadong (when the Dalai Lama fled to Yadong in 1950/51).

བྱེས་སྐྱོད་ (c<u>e</u>ègyöö) temporarily going away from one's home; va.—བྱེད་.

བྱེས་འཁོད་ (c<u>e</u>ngöö) sm. བྱེས་འབྱོར་.

བྱེས་འཁོར་ (c<u>e</u>ngɔɔ) coming back/ returning from a trip.

བྱེས་མགྲོན་ (c<u>e</u>ndrön) out-of-town guest.

བྱེས་བགྲོད་ལྷངས་འཁོར་ (c<u>e</u>èdröö lāŋgɔɔ) crosscounty vehicle.

བྱེས་འགྲོ་ (c<u>e</u>è dr<u>o</u>) va. to go on a trip/ journey.

བྱེས་རྒུན་འབྲུམ་ (c<u>e</u>è g<u>u</u>ndrum) mountain grapes.

བྱེས་རྒྱུག་ཉེས་ཅན་ (c<u>e</u>ègyuù ñ<u>e</u>èjɛn) a criminal from another region.

བྱེས་སྔགས་ (c<u>e</u>ŋaà) abbr. the Che and Ngagpa Colleges of Sera Monastery.

བྱེས་སྡོད་ (c<u>e</u>èdöö) living/ residing/ staying abroad (in exile, etc.).

བྱེས་པ་ (c<u>e</u>èba) traveler.

བྱེས་ཕག (c<u>e</u>èpaà) wild boar.

བྱེས་འབྱོར་ (c<u>e</u>njɔɔ) 1. sm. བྱེས་འཁོར་. 2. people who come/ arrived in exile (abroad) ¶བྱེས་འབྱོར་བོད་མི་ Tibetans living in exile.

བྱེས་བཞུགས་ (c<u>e</u>èshuù) h. of བྱེས་སྡོད་.

བྱེས་ཞུགས་སྦྱོང་བརྡར་ (c<u>e</u>èshuù j<u>o</u>ŋdar) field training (outside of one's home area).

བྱེས་གཞུང་ (c<u>e</u>èshuŋ) shung. a government set up away from the permanent government location, e.g., when the Dalai Lama was in Yadong in 1950/51.

བྱེས་ལམ་ (c<u>e</u>èlam) route, road (of a trip).

བྱེས་སུ་འགྲོ་ (c<u>e</u>èsu dr<u>o</u>) va. to travel away from one's normal residence.

བྱེས་སུ་སྡོད་ (c<u>e</u>èsu döö) sm. བྱེས་སྡོད་.

བྱོ་ (c<u>o</u>) f. of འབྱོ་.

བྱོང་ (c<u>o</u>ŋ) vi. to be/ get skilled ¶ལྷངས་འཁོར་བཟོ་བཅོས་ཀྱི་ལག་རྩལ་བྱོང་བཞག He became skilled in repairing cars.

བྱོང་པོ་ (c<u>o</u>ŋbo) able, skilled.

བྱོན་ (c<u>ö</u>n) p. of འབྱོན་.

བྱོན་ལེགས་ (c<u>ö</u>nleg) attractive, beautiful, good-looking.

བྱོབས་ (c<u>o</u>b) imp. of བྱབ་.

བྱོལ་ (c<u>öö</u>) p. and. imp. of འབྱོལ་.

བྱོལ་འགྲོ་ (c<u>öö</u> dr<u>o</u>) va. to run away, to flee, to escape.

བྱོལ་ཐོག (c<u>öö</u>dɔɔ̀) running away, fleeing, deserting; va.—རྒྱག.

བྱོལ་ཐོག་པ་ (c<u>öö</u>dɔgba) deserter, runaway.

བྱོལ་ཐོག་ལ་འགྲོ་ (c<u>öö</u>dɔɔla dr<u>o</u>) va. to run away, to flee, to desert ¶དམག་སྒར་ནས་དམག་མི་ཁ་ཤས་བྱོལ་ཐོག་ལ་ཕྱིན་བཞག Several soldiers ran away from their regimental headquarters.

བྱོལ་པོ་ (c<u>öö</u>bo) sm. བྱོལ་མ་.

བྲོལ་ཕེབས་ (cööpeb) h. of བྲོལ་འགྲོ་.

བྲོལ་མ་ (cööma) deserter, runaway.

བྲོལ་སོང་ (cöösoŋ) 1. animal. 2. idiot, fool, imbecile, moron.

བྲོས་ (cöö) 1. p. and imp. of འབྲོ་ 2. imp. of བྲོད་.

བྲ་ (tra) 1. vi. to dare to ¶ཁོང་ནི་གཞན་ལ་སྐྱོན་བརྗོད་བྱེད་མི་བྲ་བའི་མི་ཞིག་རེད་ He is sb. who does not dare to criticize others. 2. abbr. of བྲ་བོ་.

བྲ་ཁུང་ (trəguŋ) a hole made by a mole/ mouse.

བྲ་འཁུར་ (trəgur) a pancake made from buckwheat.

བྲ་རྗེན་ (trajen) buckwheat flour.

བྲ་ནག (tranag) a buckwheat colored horse.

བྲ་ཕུགས་ (trabaà) buckwheat chaff.

བྲ་ཕྱེ་ (traje) buckwheat flour.

བྲ་བ་ (trawa) field mouse.

བྲ་བོ་ (trəwo) buckwheat.

བྲ་བོ་ཁ་ (trəwoga) a traditional Tibetan surgical tool.

བྲ་བོ་གསུམ་གཤགས་ (trəwo sūmshaà) dividing into three exactly equal parts.

བྲ་མ་ (trama) caragana franchetiana (used in Tibetan medicine).

བྲ་རྩམ་ (tradzam) buckwheat རྩམ་པ་.

བྲ་ཚང་ (tradzaŋ) field mouse nest.

བྲ་ཞིབ་ (trəshin) sm. བྲ་ཕྱེ་.

བྲ་རིལ་ (trərii) field mouse droppings.

བྲ་ཤུན་ (trəshün) buckwheat chaff.

བྲ་སོག (trasɔɔ̀) buckwheat straw.

བྲག (traà) a boulder.

བྲག་དཀན་ (draàgɛn) steep rocky mountain.

བྲག་དཀར་ (traàgar) white rocky mountain.

བྲག་སྐྱ་ཧ་བོ་ (traàgya hābo) corallodiscus kingianus Burtt (used in Tibetan medicine).

བྲག་སྐྱབས་ (traàgyəb) an overhanging rock/ cave.

བྲག་སྐྱིབས་ (traàgyib) sm. བྲག་སྐྱབས་.

བྲག་བརྐོས་སྐུ་འདྲ་ (traàgöö gūndra) religious images carved on rocks/ boulders.

བྲག་བརྐོས་ཡི་གེ (traàgöö yigi) prayers carved on rocks/ boulders.

བྲག་བརྐོས་ཡིག་རིས་ (traàgöö yigrii) sm. བྲག་བརྐོས་ཡི་གེ་.

བྲག་བརྐོས་རི་མོ་ (traàgöö rimu) designs/ pictures carved on rocks or boulders.

བྲག་ཁུག་རྟ་ (traà kūrda) a swallow that lives in rocky mountains.

བྲག་ཁུང་ (trəguŋ) cave.

བྲག་མཁན་ (traàgɛn) artemisa that grows on rocks.

བྲག་གི་ཆགས་རིམ་ (traàgi cāgrim) a rock layer.

བྲག་གོང་ (traàgoŋ) boulder, large rock.

བྲག་མགོ་ (traŋgo) the peak or top of a rocky hill/ mountain.

བྲག་འགག (traŋgaà) passage between two rocky hills/ mountains.

བྲག་སྒོ་ཀ་ལིང་ (traàgo gōliŋ) the stupa at the entrance to Lhasa.

བྲག་སྒོ་ཀ་རྣི་ (traàgo gārni) sm. བྲག་སྒོ་ཀ་ལིང་.

བྲག་ཅ་ (tragja) echo, echoing; vi.—འཁོར་; —འཕབ་ to echo.

བྲག་ཅའི་སྤུན་ཟླ་ (tragja bũnda) sb. who follows whatever others say [Lit. relative of an echo].

བྲག་ལྕམ་ (tragjam) primula littleidalei (used in Tibetan medicine).

བྲག་ཆ་ (tragja) sm. བྲག་ཅ་.

བྲག་ཆུ་ (trəgju) a stream descending from a rocky mountain.

བྲག་གཏོར་ (traà dɔ̄ɔ) va. to split/ break up/ blasting boulders.

བྲག་གཏོར་རྡོ་གཤག (traàdɔɔ doshaà) breaking/ splitting, blasting boulders; va.—བྱེད་.

བྲག་སྟོད་བྱ་རྒོད་ (traàdöö cagöö) a leader who is isolated from his people [Lit. mountain vulture in a high rocky mountain].

བྲག་དོང་ (tragdoŋ) sm. བྲག་ཕུག.

བྲག་དྲེད་ (tragdreè) brown bear that lives in rocky mountains.

བྲག་གདོང་ (tragdoŋ) the face of a rock/ boulder.

བྲག་རྡོ་ (tragdo) large rock/ boulder.

བྲག་རྡོ་ཞུན་མ་ (tragdo shümma) molten lava, igneous rock.

བྲག་རྡོ་ལེབ་མོ་ (tragdo lebmo) flat rock/ boulder.

བྲག་བརྡབས་ཆུ་བཤལ་ (tragdəb cūshɛɛ) 1. clarifying/ rectifying/ correcting (mistakes and wrong doing). 2. experiencing many disasters/ hardships/ troubles. [Lit. bang against the rock and rinse in water].

བྲག་ནག་བྱ་སྐྱིབས་ (tragnaà cəgyib) sm. བྲག་སྐྱིབས་.

བྲག་སྣ་ (traàna) sm. བྲག་གདོང་.

བྲག་སྤོ་མཐོ་ (traà bōto) high peaked rocky hill/ mountain.

བྲག་སྤྱིལ་ (tragjii) cave.

བྲག་ཕུག (trəbuù) cave.

བྲག་འཕྲང་ (traŋdraŋ) 1. sm. བྲག་དཀན་. 2. a dangerous narrow mountain road with a rocky mountain on one side and a canyon with a river on the other.

བྲག་བྲ་ (tragdra) a mouse that lives amongst the rocks.

བྲག་དམར་ (tragmar) reddish colored rock.

བྲག་དམར་འོམ་བུ་ཚལ་ (tragmar wombudzɛɛ) a palace of King Trisrong Detsan in southern Tibet.

བྲག་རྩངས་ (tragdzaŋ) rock lizard.

བྲག་རྩེ་ (tragdze) sm. བྲག་སྤོ་མཐོ་.

བྲག་ཚེ་རིང་ (trag tsēriŋ) one of the six symbols of longevity.

བྲག་ཚྭ་ (tragdza) a kind of rock salt.

བྲག་མཚེ་ (tragdze) a plant that grows amongst the rocks (ephedra).

བྲག་རྫོང་ (tragdzoŋ) a fortress/ fort built on rocky hill/ mountain.

བྲག་ཞུན་ (tragshun) 1. sm. བྲག་རྡོ་ཞུན་མ་. 2. trogopterus xanthipes milne (used in Tibetan medicine).

བྲག་ཟོམ་ (tragsom) space/ gap in rocky areas.

བྲག་གཟིག (tragsiì) steep and tall rocky mountain.

བྲག་གཟེངས་པ་ (tragseŋba) large narrow pointed rock.

བྲག་གཡང་ (traàyaŋ) rocky cliff, precipice, abyss.

བྲག་གཡབ་ (trəyəb) 1. shelter under an overhanging rock. 2. name of an area in Eastern Tibet.

བྲག་རི་ (trəgri) a rocky mountain.

བྲག་རིམ་ (trəgrim) strata/ layers of rocks.

བྲག་རོང་ (tragroŋ) precipice, steep gorge.

བྲག་ལ་ (tragla) a pass over a rocky mountain.

བྲག་ལ་ཡུག (traà layuù) sm. བྲག་ཁུག་རྟ་.

བྲག་ལེབ་ (tragleb) abbr. of བྲག་རྡོ་ལེབ་མོ་.

བྲག་ཤུར་ (trəgshur) 1. sm. བྲག་རོང་. 2. narrow path between houses.

བྲག་གཤགས་ (traà shāà) va. to split/ crack/ break boulders.

བྲག་སེར་ (tragser) a crack/ gap in a rock.

བྲག་སྲམ་ (tragdram) a type of otter that lives among rocks.

བྲག་སྲུབས་ (tragdrub) བྲག་གསེང་.

བྲག་སྲིན་མོ་ (trag sĩnmu) mountain female demon/ ogress.

བྲག་གསེང་ (tragseŋ) gap between rocks.

བྲག་ལྷ་ཀླུ་སྦུག (traglha lūguù) sm. བྲག་ལྷ་ཀླུ་ཕུག.

བྲག་ལྷ་ཀླུ་ཕུག (traglha lūbuù) a temple below the Jagpori in Lhasa.

བྲང་ (traŋ) 1. chest, breast. 2. house.

བྲང་རྒྱས་ (traŋgɛɛ̀) sm. བྲང་ཁོག.

བྲང་སྐྱི་ (traŋgyi) pleura.

བྲང་སྐྱིའི་གཟན་ཚད་ (traggyi jɛ̃ndzɛɛ̀) pleurisy.

བྲང་ཁ་ (traŋga) sm. བྲང་ཁོག.

བྲང་ཁང་ (traŋgaŋ) house.

བྲང་ཁའི་རླངས་ནད་ (traŋgɛ lāŋnɛɛ̀) pneumothorax.

བྲང་ཁུག (traŋguù) coat pocket.

བྲང་ཁེབས་ (traŋgeb) 1. breastplate (armor). 2. bib.

བྲང་ཁོག (traŋgɔɔ̀) chest, breast ¶བྲང་ཁོག་གི་ཕྱི་ནད་ཚན་

ཁག Department of thoracic surgery.

བྲང་ཁོག་རྡུང་ (traŋgɔɔ duŋ) va. to beat one's chest in anger or regret.

བྲང་མགོ་ (traŋgo) upper part of the chest.

བྲང་རྒྱན་ (traŋgyɛn) necklace.

བྲང་རྒྱབ་ (traŋgyəb) chest and back (of body).

བྲང་བཅར་ (traŋ jāā) va. to embrace.

བྲང་འཇུན་ (traŋjün) ch. kind of long shirt worn by men.

བྲང་སྟོན་ (traŋ dõn) va. to show one's chest (usu. in defiance).

བྲང་གདན་ (traŋdɛn) a type of apron worn over the chest.

བྲང་བདག (traŋdaà) landlord, owner of a house.

བྲང་འདོགས་རྟགས་མ་ (traŋdɔɔ dāŋma) a medal pinned on chest.

བྲང་རྡུང་ (traŋ duŋ) va. to beat one's chest in anger or regret.

བྲང་རྡུང་ངུ་འབོད་ (traŋduŋ ŋubö̀ö) extreme sadness; va.—བྱེད་ [Lit. beat one's chest and wail].

བྲང་པན་ཞུ་ (traŋbɛn shu) tib.ch. va. to line up to show respect at inspection ¶ མིང་ཐོ་ནང་གསལ་བསྟར་བསྒྲིགས་ཀྱིས་བྲང་པན་ཞུས་པ་རེད་ In accordance with the list of names, they lined up and made a show of respect.

བྲང་དཔོན་ (traŋbön) sm. བྲང་བདག.

བྲང་སྤན་ (traŋbɛn) sm. སྤྲང་སྤན་.

བྲང་བ་ཅན་ (traŋwajɛn) a traditional Tibetan surgical tool.

བྲང་བྲིང་ (traŋdreŋ) 1. mediocre. 2. a little bit.

བྲང་ཚ་ (traŋdza) heartburn; vi.—ལང་ to get heartburn.

བྲང་ཚིགས་ (traŋdzii) thoracic vertebra.

བྲང་མཚེས་ (traŋdzeè) neighbor.

བྲང་ཞེང་ (traŋsheŋ) chest size/ width ¶ བྲང་ཞེང་ཆེན་པོ་ A big chest.

བྲང་ཞོལ་ (traŋshöö) lower part of a chest.

བྲང་གཞུང་ (traŋshuŋ) the chest.

བྲང་གཞུང་དཀར་ནག་མཚམས་ (traŋshuŋ gārnaà tsām) an area on the chest between the nipples that is used as a point for moxabustion.

བྲང་ཟེ་ (traŋse) a bone located below the last rib.

བྲང་གྲྭ་ (traŋda) roommate.

བྲང་འོག་ལ་སྡོད་ (traŋ wɔɔla dö̀ö) a woman having sexual intercourse with a man [Lit. sitting under the chest].

བྲང་རུས་ (traŋrüü) breastbone.

བྲང་ཤ་ (traŋsha) breast meat, rib meat.

བྲང་གཤོགས་ (traŋshog) pectoral fin.

བྲང་ས་ (traŋsa) dwelling, house.

བྲང་གསེང་ (traŋseŋ) a gap or space in the chest.

བྲད་ (trɛɛ̀) p. of འབྲད་.

བྲད་འབྲུད་ (trɛɛ̀drüü) scraping or washing; va.—བྱེད་.

བྲད་སྒྲ་ (trɛɛ̀dra) sm. འབྲད་སྒྲ་.

བྲད་བྲད་ (trɛɛ̀dɛɛ̀) sm. འབྲད་འབྲད་.

བྲད་ཤད་ (trɛɛ̀shɛɛ̀) a rake used (for leveling fields).

བྲན་: p. and f. བྲན་; imp. བྲོན་ (trɛn) 1. va. to sprinkle water ¶ གད་མ་བརྒྱབ་གོང་ས་ལ་ཆུ་བྲན་དགོས་ Before sweeping one should sprinkle water. 2. va. to give, to supply ¶ སྲིད་གཞུང་ནས་རྒས་ཁོག་ཚོར་འཚོ་བ་བྲན་གྱི་ཡོད་པ་རེད་ The government is giving food and clothing to the elderly.

བྲན་ (trɛn) 1. servant, slave. 2. small, little, tiny ¶ ཆུ་བྲན་ A tiny stream.

བྲན་བཀོལ་ (trɛngöö) enslavement, slavery; va.—བྱེད་; —གཏོང་ to enslave, to make sb. a servant/ slave ¶ དམག་ཕམ་ནས་བཙན་འཛུལ་པས་ཡུལ་མི་ཚོར་བྲན་བཀོལ་བྱས་པ་རེད་ After losing the war, the invaders enslaved the people.

བྲན་སྐྱལ་ (trɛngüü) sm. བྲན་བཀོལ་.

བྲན་ཁྱིམ་ (trɛngyim) household of slaves.

བྲན་འཁོར་ (trɛngɔɔ) 1. servants and attendants. 2. vassals.

བྲན་འཁོར་རྒྱལ་ཁབ་ (trɛngɔɔ gyɛɛgəb) vassal state.

བྲན་གྱི་བདག་པོ་ (trɛngi dagbo) slave owner/ holder.

བྲན་འགྱུར་ (trɛngyur) becoming enslaved.

བྲན་འགྱུར་བསམ་པ་ (trɛngyur sāmba) servile thought/ thinking/ mentality.

བྲན་དུ་བཀོལ་ (trɛndu göö) va. to enslave.

བྲན་བདག (trɛndaà) slave owner/ holder.

བྲན་པོ་ (trɛmbo) servant.

བྲན་མི་ (trɛnmi) servant.

བྲན་མོ་ (trɛnmo) female servant.

བྲན་བཟའ་ (trɛnsa) 1. abbr. servant and spouse. 2. maidservant.

བྲན་གཡོག (trɛnyɔɔ) slave; va.—བཀོལ to enslave.

བྲན་གཡོག་བཀོལ་བའི་ལམ་ལུགས་ (trɛnyɔɔ göö̀bɛ ləmluù) the system of slavery/ serfdom.

བྲན་གཡོག་རྒྱལ་ཁབ་ (trɛnyɔɔ gyɛɛgəb) vassal country/ nation.

བྲན་གཡོག་ཏུ་བཀོལ་ (trɛnyɔɔdu göö) va. to enslave.

བྲན་གཡོག་ཏུ་འགྱུར་ (trɛnyɔɔdu gyur) vi. to become enslaved.

བྲན་གཡོག་ཏུ་བྱེད་ (trɛnyɔɔdu ceè) sm. བྲན་གཡོག་ཏུ་བཀོལ་.

བྲན་གཡོག་བདག་པོ་ (trɛnyɔɔ dagbo) sm. བྲན་བདག.

བྲན་གཡོག་སྤྱི་ཚོགས་ (trɛnyɔɔ jïtsoò) slave society.

བྲན་གཡོག་དབང་བའི་ལམ་ལུགས་ (trɛnyɔɔ wāŋbɛ ləmluù) sm. བྲན་གཡོག་ལམ་ལུགས་.

བྲན་གཡོག་ཞིང་པ་ (trɛnyɔɔ shiŋba) agricultural slave.

བྲན་གཡོག་ལམ་ལུགས་ (trɛnyɔɔ ləmluù) system of slavery.

བྲན་རབས་ (trɛnrəb) generation(s) of servants/ slaves/ serfs.

བྲན་རིགས་ (trɛnrii) kinds of slaves/ serfs/ servants.

བྲབ་ (trəb) f. of འབྲབ་.

བྲབས་ (trəb) p. of འབྲབ་.

བྲམ་ཟེ་ (tramse) brahmin ¶ བྲམ་ཟེའི་རིགས་ Brahmin caste.

བྲམ་ཟེ་མོ་ (tramsemo) female Brahmin.

བྲམ་ཟེའི་ཆོས་ལུགས་ (tramsee cöö̀luù) Bramanism, Hinduism.

བྲའུ་ (trəwu) buckwheat.

བྲའོ་ (trəwu) sm. བྲའུ་.

བྲལ་ (trɛɛ) 1. p. of འབྲལ་. 2. vi. to be separated from, to be divorced from, to be cut off from, to be disconnected, to come apart ¶ ནང་མི་ཚོ་དང་བྲལ་ནས་ལོ་མང་ཕྱིན་པ་རེད་ Many years have passed since (he) was separated from his family. ¶ མཐུད་མཚམས་ནས་བྲལ་གྱི་འདུག (It) is coming apart at the joint. 3. vi. to be without, to be devoid of, to be free from ¶ ད་ཆ་སྔོན་གྱི་དཀའ་ངལ་དེ་ཚོ་ལས་བྲལ་པ་རེད་ (We) are free now from the problems of the past.

བྲལ་ཐབས་མེད་པ་ (trɛɛrəb meèba) inseparable, indivisible.

བྲལ་བ་ (trɛɛwa) without ¶ འགྲན་ཟླ་བྲལ་བ་ Without match/ rival.

བྲལ་བྲལ་ (trɛɛdrɛɛ) 1. torn, tattered (clothes), worn out. 2. withered (for petals of flowers).

བྲལ་མཚམས་ཞུ་ (trɛndzam shu) va. to bid farewell.

བྲལ་ཧྲུལ་ (trɛɛhrüü) sm. བྲལ་བྲུལ་.

བྲི་ (tri) va. f. of འབྲི་. 2. p. and f. of འབྲི་.

བྲི་གང་ (trigaŋ) a cycle of increasing and declining.

བྲིང་ (triŋ) sm. བྲེང་.

བྲི་སྣངས་ (trïdaŋ) the manner of writing/ drawing.

བྲི་བ་གང་ (triwagaŋ) the 4th month of the Tibetan calendar.

བྲི་ཤོག (trïshoò) stationery, writing paper.

བྲིད་ (trii) p., f. and imp. of འབྲིད་.

བྲིད་གཏམ་ (triidam) deceiving talk.

བྲིན་ (trin) to sell, to be marketable ¶ ཐོན་ཟོག་གསར་པ་དེ་ཚོ་དྲིལ་བསྒྲགས་མ་བྱས་ན་ལམ་སེང་བྲིན་གྱི་མ་རེད་ If one doesn't advertise the new products they will not sell right away. ¶ བྲིན་དཀའ་པ་ Hard to sell.

བྲིན་སྐྱེན་པོ་ (trin gyēmbo) a fast/ quick selling item.

བྲིན་དཀའི་ཚོང་ཟོག (tringɛ tsõŋsoò) items that are difficult to sell, slow moving items.

བྲིན་ཁ་བདེ་བ་ (tringɛ dewa) sm. བྲིན་སྐྱེན་པོ་.

བྲིན་མགྱོགས་པའི་ཚོང་ཟོག (tringyɔɔ̀bɛ tsõŋsɔɔ̀) sm. བྲིན་སྐྱིན་པོ་.

བྲིན་རྒྱུག (tringyuù) sales demand, saleabilty ¶ དེང་སང་མོ་ཊ་བྲིན་པོ་འདུག These days the cars are selling well.

བྲིན་དུས་ (trindüü) the time/ period when goods sell.

བྲིན་བདེ་དངོས་རྫས་ (trinde ŋȫȍdzɛɛ̀) products that are easy to sell.

བྲིན་བདེ་དཔེ་ཆ་ (trinde bēja) a best selling book.

བྲིན་བདེ་པོ་ (trin debo) easy to sell, salable.

བྲིན་པོ་ (trinbu) sm. བྲིན་བདེ་པོ་.

བྲིན་འཚོང་ (trindzoŋ) marketing, selling ¶ ཐོན་སྐྱེད་དང་བྲིན་འཚོང་ Production and marketing.

བྲིན་ཡུལ་ (trinyüü) marketplace.

བྲིན་ས་ (trinsə) sm. བྲིན་ཡུལ་.

བྲིམ་ (trim) f. of འབྲིམ་.

བྲིམས་ (trim) p. and imp. of འབྲིམ་.

བྲིས་ (trii) va. p. and imp. of བྲི་, 1.

བྲིས་སྐུ་ (triigu) paintings of religious figures.

བྲིས་མཁན་ (triiñɛn) painter, writer.

བྲིས་གླ་ (triila) price for a drawing/ writing.

བྲིས་རྒྱུན་ (trigyün) style of painting or writing.

བྲིས་ཉེས་ (triiñeè) drawn or written incorrectly/ mistakenly; vi.—ཤོར་.

བྲིས་རྙིང་ (triiñiŋ) old writings/ paintings.

བྲིས་སྟངས་ (triidaŋ) style of writing or drawing.

བྲིས་ཐང་ (triidaŋ) tanka (Tibetan scroll painting).

བྲིས་དན་ (triidɛn) shung. a written agreement ¶ གཤམ་གསལ་གཉིས་མོས་བྲིས་དན་འདི་ར་སོར་གནས་རྒྱུན་འཁྱོངས་ཡོང་བ་གྱིས་ Both parties should keep the written agreement which was agreed to by both sides and is presented below.

བྲིས་དེབ་ (triideb) writing book, notepad.

བྲིས་ནོར་ (triinɔɔ tēb) making an error in. writing, making a clerical error. vi.—ཐེབས; —ཤོར་.

བྲིས་འབུར་ (trimbur) sm. འབུར་བྲིས་.

བྲིས་བྱ་ (triija) drawing, painting.

བྲིས་མ་ (triimə) sth. written, a manuscript.

བྲིས་ཞུས་ (triishüü) proofreading; va.—བྱེད་; —གཏོང་.

བྲིས་ལུགས་ (triiluù) sm. བྲིས་སྟངས་.

བྲིས་བཤུས་ (triishüü) copying by hand; va.—བྱེད་.

བྲིས་སུབ་ (triisub) erasing; va.—གཏོང་ to erase.

བྲུ་ (tru) 1. sm. དྲུ་. 2. f. of འབྲུ་.

བྲུག (truù) vi. to rise/ swell (for a river) ¶ ཆར་པ་ཉིན་བསྟུད་མར་བབ་ནས་གཙང་པོ་གློ་བུར་དུ་བྲུག་པ་རེད་ Because of continuous rainfall, the river rose suddenly.

བྲུག་ཆུ་ (tragju) river that has swollen/ risen.

བྲུངས་ཁུངས་ (truŋguŋ) sm. འབྲུང་ཁུངས་.

བྲུད་བྲུད་ (truŋdrüü) arc. ཆུང་ཆུང་.

བྲུན་ (trün) excrement, dung (of animals).

བྲུན་འཐྱིན་འཐྱིན་བཟོ་ (trün jinjin so) sm. སྐྱག་པ་ཤོར་ཤོར་བཟོ་.

བྲུན་རིལ་ (trünrii) the round (pellet-like) excrement/ droppings (of some animals like sheep and goats).

བྲུབ་ (trub) f. of འབྲུབ་.

བྲུབ་ཁུང་ (trubguŋ) hiding place.

བྲུབས་ (trub) p. and imp. of འབྲུབ་.

བྲུམ་འཛར་གའུ་ (trumdzr kəwu) an ornament worn by the རྒྱན་བཟང་མ་.

བྲུལ་ (trüü) 1. p. of འབྲུལ་. 2. bits, small pieces.

བྲུལ་ཆིན་ཆིན་བཟོ་ (trüüjin cīnso) va. to cause commotion ¶ མི་འདིའི་སར་བུ་ལོན་འདེད་མཁན་མང་པོ་ཡོང་ནས་བྲུལ་ཆིན་ཆིན་བཟོས་སོང་ Many loan collectors came to that person and caused a commotion.

བྲུལ་བྲུལ་ཆིན་ཆིན་བཟོ་ (trüüdrüü cīnjin so) sm. བྲུལ་ཆིན་ཆིན་བཟོ་.

བྲུལ་བྲུལ་བཟོ་ (trüüdrüü so) sm. བྲུལ་ཆིན་ཆིན་བཟོ་.

བྲུལ་ཐོར་ (trüüdɔr) scattered, in many small pieces.

བྲུས་ (trüü) p. and imp. of འབྲུ་ and འབྲུད་.

བྲུས་ཆུ་ (trüüju) well water.

བྲེ་: p. བྲེས་; f. བྲེ་; imp. བྲེས་ (tre) va. to put up, to hang (e.g., decorations).

བྲེ་ (tre) 1. a volume measure for solids (20 བྲེ་ = one ཁལ་) ¶ བྲེ་གང་ One བྲེ་. 2. a square piece of wood that is put on a pillar.

བྲེ་ཁ་ (trega) a large uncut piece of paper.

བྲེ་ཁྱད་ (tregyɛɛ̀) the difference in size between different བྲེ་.

བྲེ་ག (trega) thalaspi arvense (used in Tibetan medicine).

བྲེ་ཕུལ་ (tre pǖü) abbr. of བྲེ་ and ཕུལ་.

བྲེ་བོ་ (trewo) 1. a large བྲེ་. 2. a yak with a white face.

བྲེ་མོ་ (tremo) foolish/ nonsensical talk, blabber; va.—བྱེད་.

བྲེ་ལོག་སྲང་ལོག (trelɔɔ̀ sāŋlɔɔ̀) cheating by using a larger བྲེ་ and སྲང་ measure.

བྲེ་སེར་ (treser) a yak with a yellowish face.

བྲེ་སྲང་ (tresaŋ) abbr. of བྲེ་ and སྲང་.

བྲེག (treè) f. of འབྲེག.

བྲེགས་ (treè) p. and imp. of འབྲེག.

བྲེང་ (treŋ) a cable bridge over a gorge consisting of a rope on which one attaches a yoke and slides/ pull himself across.

བྲེང་བྲེང་པོ་ (treŋ treŋbo) (coming or going) in a line.

བྲེད་ (treè) vi. to be scared/ frightened.

བྲེད་སྐད་ (treègɛɛ̀) scream/ cry of fright; vi.—རྒྱག to scream/ cry out of fright.

བྲེད་འཁྲིམས་ (treè trīm) vi. to be extremely scared/ frightened.

བྲེད་དངངས་ (treèŋaŋ) frightened, scared; vi.—བྱེད་ to be frightened/ scared; va.—སྐྱོང་ va. to frighten/ scare.

བྲེད་འཐོམས་ (treè tōm) vi. to be frightened and confused/ bewildered.

བྲེད་གདངས་ (treèdaŋ) 1. a frightened scared voice. 2. mouth wide open with fright.

བྲེད་སྣང་ (treènaŋ) frightening, scary; vi.—བྱེད་ to get scared/ frightened; va.—སྐུལ་ to scare/ frighten.

བྲེད་ཕོངས་ (treèpoŋ) scared/ frightened and humble.

བྲེད་ཤ་ཐོན་ (treèsha tõn) sm. བྲེད་.

བྲེད་ཤ་དོད་པོ་ (treèsha tȍȍbo) scared, frightened.

བྲེའི་ཟླ་བ་ (tree dawa) the 6th month of the Tibetan calendar.

བྲེའུ་ཆུང་ (trejuŋ) a small བྲེ་.

བྲེལ་ (tree) busy.

བྲེལ་སྐུལ་ (treegüü) urging sb. to hurry up doing sth.; va.—བྱེད་.

བྲེལ་ཁོམ་མེད་པ་ (treegom meèba) busy.

བྲེལ་ཆེ་ (treeje) urgent, very busy.

བྲེལ་ཆེའི་ཡིག་ཆ་ (treejee yigi) urgent paper/ document.

བྲེལ་རྟབ་ (treedəb) hurrying, hastening, on the double ¶ ངའི་ཨ་མ་ལགས་སྨན་ཁང་དུ་ལུས་པའི་གནས་ཚུལ་གོ་རྗེས་ང་བྲེལ་རྟབ་ཀྱིས་ཡོང་བ་ཡིན་ After I heard that my mother was in the hospital I came on the double.

བྲེལ་རྟབ་ཚབ་ཚུབ་ (treedəb tsābdzub) sm. བྲེལ་རྟབ་.

བྲེལ་ཕོངས་ (treepoŋ) poor.

བྲེལ་བ་ (trɛɛwa) busy ¶ ཞིང་པ་ཚོ་དེང་སང་བྲེལ་བ་ཆེན་པོ་འདུག The farmers are very busy these days. ¶ ཆར་ཤོད་མ་ཚུགས་གོང་ཁང་པ་བཟོ་བཅོས་རྒྱག་རྒྱུའི་བྲེལ་བ་བྱེད་ཀྱི་འདུག They are hurrying to repair the house before the rain starts.

བྲེལ་ཆེ་ཟིང་མེད་ (treeje siŋmeè) busy and in a hurry but in an orderly way.

བྲེལ་བ་འཛགས་ (treewa jaà) vi. to have a busy/ hurried time or period die down or subside. ¶ ང་ཚོ་ལས་ཀ་བྲེལ་བ་འཛགས་སོང་ན་གླིང་ཀར་འགྲོ་དང་ Lets go for a picnic when our busy work schedule subsides.

བྲེལ་བ་དུར་དུར་ (treewa dūrdur) sm. བྲེལ་རྟབ་ཚབ་ཚུབ་.

བྲེལ་བ་མེད་པ་ (treewa meèba) not busy/ hurried.

བྲེལ་བ་ཚ་པོ་ (treēwa tsābo) very busy.

བྲེལ་བ་འཚུབ་འཚུབ་ (treēwa tsūbdzub) sm. ¶ བྲེལ་བྲེལ་ཚུབ་ཚུབ་.

བྲེལ་བ་ཡོད་ལ་མེད་ལ་ (treewa yöola meela) slightly busy.

བྲེལ་བ་ལང་ (treewa laŋ) vi. to start to get busy ¶ ནམ་དུས་དྲོད་སླེབས་ནས་ཞིང་ལས་ཀྱི་བྲེལ་བ་ལངས་བཞག The warm season has arrived and the farmer's busy time has started.

བྲེལ་བ་སླེབས་ (treewa lēb) sm. བྲེལ་བ་ལང་.

བྲེལ་བ་སློང་ (treewa lōŋ) va. to make sb. hurry, to rush sb.

བྲེལ་བྲེལ་ཚབས་ཚབས་ (tree tsəbdzəb) doing things in a hurried and nervous manner.

བྲེལ་བྲེལ་འཚུབ་འཚུབ་ (tree tsūbdzub) rushed, hurried, busy.

བྲེལ་དབང་ (treēwaŋ) busy ¶ བར་ལམ་ལས་ཀའི་བྲེལ་དབང་གིས་སྤུན་མཆེད་ཐུག་པར་འགྲོ་ཐུབ་མ་སོང་ Because of my busy work schedule these days I haven't been able to go to meet my relatives.

བྲེལ་མེད་ལས་རིགས་ (treemeè lɛèrii) slow/ unhurried work or business.

བྲེལ་བརྩོན་ (treedzön) doing sth. busily and intensely/ diligently ¶ ཡིག་ཚད་རན་ཐབས་ཡོད་སྐབས་སློབ་ཕྲུག་རྣམས་སློབ་སྦྱོང་ཐོག་བྲེལ་བརྩོན་བྱེད་ཀྱི་འདུག Because the exam time was nearing, the students are studying busily and intensely.

བྲེལ་ཚུབ་ (treedzub) sm. བྲེལ་བྲེལ་ཚུབ་ཚུབ་.

བྲེལ་འཚབ་ (treedzəb) restless, impatient ¶ ཁོས་བྲེལ་འཚབ་དང་གྲོགས་པོའི་སྐད་ཆ་བར་མཚམས་བཅད་སོང་ He was impatient and interrupted his friend's talking.

བྲེལ་འཚུབ་ (treedzub) sm. བྲེལ་བྲེལ་འཚུབ་འཚུབ་.

བྲེལ་ཟིང་ (treesiŋ) hectic, busy; va.—བྱེད་ to work hectically.

བྲེལ་ཟིང་འཁུར་ (treesiŋ aur) sm. བྲེལ་ཏབ་ཚབ་ཚུབ་.

བྲེལ་ལ་བྱེད་ (treela ceè) sm. བྲེལ་བ་བྱེད་.

བྲེལ་ལ་ཆེ་བ་ (treela ceewa) very busy.

བྲེས་ (treè) 1. p. and f. of བྲི་. 2. a livestock feeding trough.

བྲེས་སྒོར་ (treègɔɔ) sm. བྲེས་.

བྲེས་ར་ (treèra) 1. livestock feeding trough. 2. sm. བྲེས་.

བྲེས་ལུད་ (treèlüü) barnyard/ corral manure.

བྲོ་ (tro) 1. a type of dance from Eastern Tibet; va.—འཁྲབ་; —འཆམ་; —དུང་ to dance the བྲོ་. 2. vi. to taste ¶ དེ་ལ་བྲོ་བ་མི་འདྲ་བ་ཞིག་བྲོ་གི་འདུག That tastes different. 3. vi. to feel, to have a feeling ¶ ང་གཉིད་བྲོ་བྱུང་ I felt sleepy. ¶ ང་གཅིན་པ་བྲོ་བྱུང་ I felt like urinating. 5. oath.; va.—དོར་ to take an oath.

བྲོ་ཁ་ (troga) provisions for a trip/ journey.

བྲོ་མཁན་ (troñɛn) a dancer of བྲོ་.

བྲོ་འཁྲབ་ (tro trəb) va. to stage a བྲོ་ show.

བྲོ་གར་ (trogar) a dance show.

བྲོ་རྒྱགས་ལང་ (trogyaà laŋ) sm. བྲོད་རྒྱགས་ལང་.

བྲོ་རྒྱུ་ (trogyu) seasoning.

བྲོ་བཅུད་ (trojüü) 1. taste and nutritiousness. 2. seasoning, flavoring.

བྲོ་ཆས་ (trojɛè) sm. བྲོ་ཁ་.

བྲོ་དད་ཆེན་པོ་ (trodɛè cēmbo) sb. who likes spicy/ seasoned food.

བྲོ་དོར་ (tro dɔɔ) va. to swear/ promise/ take an oath.

བྲོ་ནད་ (tronɛè) disease, sickness.

བྲོ་ནད་ཅན་ (tronɛèjɛn) a patient, a sick person.

བྲོ་པ་ (troba) a dancer of བྲོ་ (usu. a wandering dancer).

བྲོ་པ་གཞས་མ་ (troba shɛ̄èma) dancing and singing, a dance and song group.

བྲོ་དཔོན་ (trobön) head of dancers, dance leader.

བྲོ་བ་ (trɔɔ) 1. taste, flavor; va.—ལྟ་; —མྱོང་ to taste ¶ ཁ་ལག་འདི་ལ་བྲོ་བ་མི་འདུག This food is tasteless. 2. meaningless, nonsensical, silly, (talk) ¶ མི་འདིའི་སྐད་ཆ་ལ་བྲོ་བ་མི་འདུག His conversation is meaningless.

བྲོ་བ་ཅང་ཅང་ (trɔɔ jāŋjaŋ) having very little taste.

བྲོ་བ་ཅི་ཡང་མེད་པ་ (trɔɔ jīyaŋ meèba) tasteless.

བྲོ་བ་ཆེན་པོ་ (trɔɔ cēmbo) tasty.

བྲོ་བ་སྙེད་ (trɔɔ ñēè) vi. to acquire a taste for a particular food.

བྲོ་བ་ལྟ་ (trɔɔ dā) va. to taste, to sample food.

བྲོ་བ་ལྡན་ (trɔɔdɛn) tasty.

བྲོ་བ་མྱོང་ (trɔɔ ñoŋ) vi. to taste sth.

བྲོ་བ་ཞིམ་པོ་ (trɔɔ shimbu) tasty, delicious.

བྲོ་བ་ཡལ་ (trɔɔ yɛɛ) vi. to lose flavor/ taste.

བྲོ་བ་བརླག (trɔɔ lāà) sm. བྲོ་བ་ཡལ་.

བྲོ་བ་ཤོར་ (trɔɔ shɔ̄ɔ) sm. བྲོ་བ་རླག.

བྲོ་བོར་ (tro bɔɔ) sm. བྲོ་དོར་.

བྲོ་སྦྱོར་སྤོད་སྨན་ (trojɔɔ bööměn) flavoring, seasoning.

བྲོ་མ་ (troma) female dancer of བྲོ་.

བྲོ་མེད་རོ་མེད་ (tromeè romeè) tasteless.

བྲོ་ཚིག (trodzii) sm. མནའ་ཚིག.

བྲོ་འཚལ་ (tro dzɛ̄ɛ) vi. to get sick, to become ill.

བྲོ་རྫས་ (trodzɛè) flavoring, seasoning, condiments.

བྲོ་ཞིམ་ (troshim) abbr. of བྲོ་བ་ཞིམ་པོ་.

བྲོ་གཞས་ (troshɛè) dancing and singing.

བྲོ་གཡོག (troyɔɔ̀) nurse, person who looks after the sick.

བྲོ་ར་ (trora) dance floor, dance area.

བྲོ་ཤ་ (trosha) meat taken as provisions for a trip.

བྲོ་ཤོན་ (troshön) a dance performed with the dancers carrying a drum.

བྲོད་ (tröö) abbr. of བྲོད་པོ་.

བྲོད་ (tröö) imp. of འབྲད་.

བྲོད་རྒྱགས་ལང་ (tröögyaà laŋ) vi. to have it too easy (negative connotation) ¶ ཁོ་བྲོད་རྒྱགས་ལངས་ནས་ཉིན་ལྟར་མ་ཅང་བརྒྱབ་ནས་སྡོད་ཀྱི་འདུག He has it too easy playing mahjong every day.

བྲོད་པོ་ (trööbo) sb. who is fun loving/ joyful/ amiable.

བྲོད་གསར་ལང་ (trööosaà laŋ) vi. to be exciting about doing or buying sth. new.

བྲོན་ (trön) imp. of བྲན་.

བྲོབས་ (trob) imp. of འབྲབ་.

བྲོའུ་ (trowu) sm. བྲ་བོ་.

བྲོའོ་ (trowo) sm. བྲ་བོ་.

བྲོས་ (tröö) p. of འབྲོས་.

བྲོས་བསྐྱོད་ (tröö) escaping, fleeing; va.—བྱེད་.

བྲོས་གབ་ (tröögəb) fleeing/ escaping and hiding; va.— བྱེད་.

བྲོས་འགྲོ་ (tröö dro) sm. བྲོས་བསྐྱོད་.

བྲོས་ཐར་ (tröö tār) vi. to be able to escape ¶ ཁོ་བཙོན་ཁང་ནས་བྲོས་ཐར་བཞག He escaped from prison.

བྲོས་ཐོར་དམག་མི་ (trööto mɔ̄ɔmi) stragglers/ deserters and scattered soldiers.

བྲོས་འདེད་ (tröndeè) chasing sb. who has escaped/ fled; va.—བྱེད་; —གཏོང་.

བྲོས་འདོན་ (tröö dön) va. to take an oath.

བྲོས་བྱོལ་ (trööjöö) escaping, fleeing; va.—(དུ་) འགྲོ་; — བྱེད་ to flee, to escape, to run away, to seek refuge ¶ བོད་པ་མང་པོ་རྒྱ་གར་དུ་བྲོས་བྱོལ་བྱས་པ་རེད་ Many Tibetans fled to India.

བྲོས་འབྱོར་ (trönjɔɔ) fleeing and reaching one's destination.

བྲོས་དམག (tröömaà) military deserter.

བྲོས་ཡོང་ (tröö yoŋ) va. to come fleeing.

བྲོས་ལམ་ (tröölam) escape route.

བྲོས་ཤོར་ (trööshɔɔ) vi. to successfully escape/ flee.

བླ་ (lā) 1. above, higher; superior. 2. see བླ་སྟོག. 3. abbr. of བླ་མ་. 4. abbr. of བླ་བྲང་.

བླ་སྐམ་ (lā gām) vi. to be petrified with fear.

བླ་སྐམ་པ་ (lāgamba) a coward.

བླ་སྐྱེས་ (lā gyeè) 1. present, gift, tribute. 2. tax. 3. boat/ ship fare.

བླ་བསྐྱལ་ (lāgyɛɛ) arc. inexhaustible, endless.

བླ་ཁོངས་ (lāgoŋ) 1. abbr. belonging to a Labrang. 2. belonging to Tashilunpo Labrang ¶ བླ་ཁོངས་མི་སེར་ Serfs of Tashilunpo Labrang.

བླ་ཁྱིམ་ (lāgyim) the place (e.g., a tree) where one's life essence lives/ dwells.

བླ་ཁྱེར་ (lā kyēr) vi. to be petrified with fright.

བླ་མཁྱེན་ (lāgyen) 1. queen's retinue. 2. astrologer. 3. tutor to a lama.

བླ་འཁར་ (lāgar) 1. one's life essence when still connected to one's body. 2. a walking stick on which one's life essence is attached.

བླ་འཁྱམས་ (lā kyām) vi. to have one's life essence leave one's body (through fear, etc.).

བླ་འཁྱར་ (lā kyār) sm. བླ་འཁྱམས་.

བླ་འཁྱར་ཧོན་ཐོར་ (lāgyar hõndɔɔ) extremely frightened/ scared.

བླ་འཁྱེར་ཧོན་ཐོར་ (lāgyer hõndɔɔ) sm. བླ་འཁྱར་ཧོན་ཐོར་.

བླ་གབ་ (lāgəb) any garment covering the upper part of the body.

བླ་གབ་ཅན་ (lāgəbjɛn) sm. ཁང་པ་.

བླ་གོས་ (lāgöö) sm. ཆོས་གོས་.

བླ་གྱུར་ (lāgyar) sm. བླ་འཁྱམས་.

བླ་གྲི་ (lādri) a dagger.

བླ་གྲྭ་ (lādra) 1. lama and his disciples. 2. lamas and monks.

བླ་དགོན་ (lāgön) shung. abbr. of བླ་མ་ and དགོན་པ་.

བླ་འགུག་ཚེ་འགུག (lāguù tsēguù) a ritual for restoring a life essence that has left a body; va.—བྱེད་.

བླ་རྒན་ (lāgɛn) old monk or old lama.

བླ་སྒྲོ་ (lādro) the feather on which the བླ་ spirit is attached.

བླ་བརྒྱུད་ (lāgyüü) lineage of incarnate lamas.

བླ་བརྒྱུད་པ་ (lāgyüüba) term for common monks.

བླ་ཅོལ་ (lājöö) sm. བབ་ཅོལ་.

བླ་བཅོལ་ (lājöö) sm. བབ་ཅོལ་.

བླ་ཆད་ (lā cɛ̃ɛ̀) 1. vi. to die of fright. 2. vi. to be extremely scared/ frightened.

བླ་ཆད་འཇིགས་ཞུམ་ (lājɛɛ̀ jigsum) extremely scared.

བླ་ཆད་ཧོན་ཐོར་ (lājɛɛ̀ hõndɔɔ) sm. བླ་ཆད་འཇིགས་ཞུམ་.

བླ་ཆས་ (lā cēè) clothes of lamas.

བླ་ཆུང་ (lājuŋ) lesser/ lower lama.

བླ་ཆེན་ (lājen) high lamas.

བླ་ཆེན་ (lājen mijen) high lamas and important people/ figures.

བླ་ཆོས་ (lājuöö) shung. abbr. of བླ་མ་ and ཆོས་སྡེ་.

བླ་མཆོད་ (lājöö) lama.

བླ་འཆོལ་ (lājöö) sm. བླ་ཅོལ་.

བླ་གཉེར་ (lāñer) shung. 1. steward (གཉེར་པ་) of a labrang. 2. title of a monk official who is in charge of a district.

བླ་སྟེང་ (lādeŋ) shung. abbr. of བླ་བྲང་སྟེང་.

བླ་ཐབས་ (lādab) sudden, suddenly.

བླ་ཐབས་སུ་ (lā tābsu) sudden, suddenly.

བླ་མཐང་ (lādaŋ) upper and lower, top and bottom.

བླ་འཐོར་ (lādɔɔ) sm. བླ་འཁྱམས་.

བླ་དྭགས་ (lādag) sm. བདགས་མིང་.

བླ་དར་ (lādar) prayer flags put on roof tops with particular colors to match the element in which the head of the family was born.

བླ་འདར་ (lā dar) vi. to be very scared.

བླ་འདར་བ་ (lā darwa) a coward.

བླ་རྡོ་ (lādo) a stone where the life essence has been attached.

བླ་བརྡོལ་ (lā döö) sm. བླ་འཆོལ་.

བླ་ན་ (lāna) above, over.

བླ་ན་འབར་བ་ (lāna barwa) sm. བླ་ན་མེད་པ་.

བླ་ན་མ་མཆིས་པ་ (lāna ma cĩiwə) sm. བླ་ན་མེད་པ་.

བླ་ན་མེད་པ་ (lāna meèba) incomparable, unequaled, unparalleled, supreme, excellent ། གྲུབ་རྗེས་བླ་ན་མེད་པ་བཞག་པ་རེད་ An incomparable accomplishment.

བླ་ནས་བླར་ (lānɛ lār) from better to best, from higher to higher.

བླ་ནས་བླར་འདེགས་ (lānɛ lār deg) sm. གོང་ནས་གོང་འཕེལ་.

བླ་ནས་སྐྱོར་ (lānɛ jɔɔ) supplied by the government.

བླ་གནས་ (lānɛɛ̀) the thing in which a བླ་ is attached.

བླ་དཔོན་ (lābön) abbr. of བླ་མ་དཔོན་པོ་.

བླ་དཔོན་གོང་ས་ (lābön koŋsa) shung. the highest lord (usu. refers to the Dalai Lama.).

བླ་སྤྱི་ (ləji) shung. sm. བླ་སྤྱི་ལྷན་རྒྱས་.

བླ་སྤྱི་དཔོན་རིགས་ (ləji bõnrii) shung. monastic officials and the Lachi (heads of large monasteries like Drepung and Sera.

བླ་སྤྱི་ལྷན་རྒྱས་ (ləji lhɛ̃ngyɛɛ̀) shung. a council in Sera, Drepung and Ganden monasteries composed of abbots, ཚོགས་ཆེན་དབུ་མཛད་, ཞལ་ངོ་, and སྤྱི་སོ་ that has the highest authority in the monastery.

བླ་སྤྲུལ་ (lādrüü) shung. lamas and trulkus.

བླ་དཔོན་ (lābön) abbr. of བླ་མ་དཔོན་པོ་.

བླ་ཕྱག (lājaà) shung. shung. 1. manager (abbr. བླ་བྲང་ཕྱག་མཛོད་) of a labrang. 2. sm. བླ་ཕྱག་ལས་ཁངས་.

བླ་ཕྱག་ལས་ཁུངས་ (lājaà lɛɛ̀guŋ) shung. a treasury office in the tt.

བླ་བོ་ (lāwo) talk, dialogue. speech; va.—བྱེད་.

བླ་བྲང་ (lābraŋ) 1. residence of a lama. 2. household corporation of a lama ། བླ་མ་འདིའི་བླ་བྲང་རྒྱ་སྐྱབས་ཆེན་པོ་ཡོད་པ་རེད་ This lama's labrang is very wealthy.

བླ་བྲང་བཀྲ་ཤིས་འཁྱིལ་ (lābraŋ trāshi kyĩi) Labrang monastery (in Gansu).

བླ་བྲང་སྟེང་ (lābraŝ dēŋ) shung. government offices in tt. that were located in the upper part of the Tsuglhakhang.

བླ་བྲང་ཕྱག་མཛོད་ (lābraŋ candzöö) shung. 1. treasury office that deals with income and expenditures, particularly those used during the Monlam festival. 2. a manager of a labrang. 3. head of a treasury/ storeroom.

བླ་བྲང་འོག་པ་ (lābraŋ wɔgba) shung. the Panchen Lama's territory/ domain.

བླ་བྲེ་ (lādre) a canopy with decorative silk and brocade that is placed above the throne or the seat of a lama or goverment official during ceremonies.

བླ་བྲེས་ (lādreè) sm. བླ་བྲེ་.

བླ་འབངས་ (lābaŋ) shung. abbr. of བླ་བྲང་ and འབངས་མི་སེར་.

བླ་འབོད་ (lāböö) 1. sm. བླ་འགུགས་. 2. abbr. of བླ་མ་འབོད་.

བླ་མ་ (lāma) lama, guru, teacher (spiritual/ religious).

བླ་མ་དཀོན་མཆོག (lāma gõnjoò) 1. the three jewels (Buddha, the dharma, sangha) and the lama. 2. trustworthy, upright, honest, kind.

བླ་མ་སྐྱེས་ཆེན་ (lāma gyēèjen) a lama who has reached a high level of spiritual realization.

བླ་མ་དགའ་སྟོན་ (lāma gadön) a party given by the government on the 16th, 17th and 18th of the first month that was headed by the Ganden Triba and the abbots of the three monastic seats together with other monastery officials.

བླ་མ་རྒྱུད་པ་ (lāma gyüübə) monks who are members of the two Tantric monasteries (colleges) in Lhasa.

བླ་མ་ཆེན་པོ་ (lāma cēmbo) a high lama.

བླ་མ་མཇལ་ཐོག་ལ་ཆོས་ (lāma jɛɛtɔɔ̀la cöö) doing sth. when an opportunity comes [Lit. receiving teachings when meeting a lama].

བླ་མ་གཉིས་ (lāma ñĩi) one's root lama and the lineage of one's root lama.

བླ་མ་དམ་པ་ (lāma tamba) 1. sm. བླ་མ་སྐྱེས་ཆེན་. 2. the late lama.

བླ་མ་དཔོན་པོ་ (lāma bõmbo) 1. abbr. of བླ་མ་ and དཔོན་པོ་. 2. monks who act as lords over peasants, monk administrators of estates, i.e. sb. who is both lama and lord. 3. h. lords.

བླ་མ་འབོད་ (lāma böö) va. to call out the word lama in time of trouble (sth. like "Oh God" in English).

བླ་མ་མ་ཎི་ (lāma mani) dragonfly.

བླ་མ་མ་ཎི་པ་ (lāma maniwa) people who narrate the religious story of a thanka painting in the marketplace.

བླ་མ་རིན་པོ་ཆེ་ (lāma ri̱mboce) term of respect used for a lama.

བླ་མ་ལོ་གསར་ (lāma lo̱sar) New Year receptionå for all government officials in the Potala on the 1st day of the 1st month.

བླ་མའི་སྐུ་སྐྱེ་ (lāmɛ gūgye) incarnation of a lama.

བླ་མའི་བརྒྱུད་པ་ (lāmɛ gyü̱übə) lineage line of a lama.

བླ་མའི་གདན་ས་ (lāmɛ de̱nsa) a lama's monastery/ monastic seat.

བླ་མའི་མར་བླ་མའི་ཁྱིས་བཟས་ (lāmɛ maa lāmɛ kyi̋i sɛ̱ɛ̀) things that are used by sb/'s subordinates [Lit. the lama's dog eats the lama's butter].

བླ་མས་བུམ་པ་གང་བཞག་མ་གཏོགས་བུམ་པས་བླ་མ་གང་བཞག་མེད་ (lāmɛ pu̱mba ka̱ŋshaà mə̱ndoò pu̱mbɛ lāma ga̱ŋshaà me̱è) things should be decided by the main person, not the underlings [Lit. the lama should decide where he wants to put the vase, the vase can not decide where the lama should be placed].

བླ་མེད་ (lāmɛɛ̀) abbr. of བླ་ན་མེད་པ་.

བླ་མེད་རྩོམ་རིག (lāmeè dzōmrig) masterpiece in literature.

བླ་མེད་རྩོམ་རིས་ (lāmeè) masterpiece in art.

བླ་སྨན་ཁང་ (lāmɛngaŋ) sm. སྨན་རྩིས་ཁང་.

བླ་སྨན་པ་ (lāmɛmba) Dalai Lama's personal physician.

བླ་རྩ་ (lādza) vein the pulse of which can be used to indicate long or short life.

བླ་རྩ་འཁུམ་ (lādza kūm) vi. to be frightened.

བླ་རྩིས་པ་ (lədziìbə) title given to a learned astrologist.

བླ་མཚོ་ (lātso) a lake to which a བླ་ is attached.

བླ་འཚོང་ (lā tsōŋ) va. to betray one's country for personal gains.

བླ་འཛིན་ (lāndzin) shung. held by Labrang (the Panchen Lama's government) ¶ བླ་འཛིན་རྩྭ་ར་གོང་འོག་ཏུ་མི་སེར་གྱི་བ་ཕྱུགས་བཏང་སྐོར་ Regarding the matter that the subjects grazed their cows in the grassland held by Labrang.

བླ་ཡལ་ (ləyüü) sm. བླ་འཁྱེར་.

བླ་གཡུ་ (ləyüü) a turquoise on which a བླ་ is attached.

བླ་འོག (lā wɔ̱ɔ̀) 1. high and low, up and down, above and beneath; va.—སྒྱུར་; va.—སློག to turn upside down. ¶ བླ་འོག་ཏུ་སྒྱུར་བའི་སྤྱོད་ངན་ Evil behavior of turning things upside down. 2. abbr. of བླ་བྲང་འོག་པ་.

བླ་རབས་ (lārəb) the lineage (generations) of a particular lama.

བླ་རབས་རྣམ་ཐར་ (lārəb nāmdar) the biography of a lineage/ line of lamas.

བླ་རི་ (ləri) a mountain on which a བླ་ is attached.

བླ་རེ་ (lāre) sm. བླ་བྲེ་.

བླ་ཤིང་ (ləshiŋ) tree on which a བླ་ is attached.

བླ་སྲོག (lāsɔ̄ɔ̀) life essence.

བླ་སྲོག་སྐྱེལ་ (lāsɔ̄ɔ̀ gyeē) vi. to let sb. take possession of one's བླ་.

བླ་སྲོག་གཅོད་ (lāsɔ̄ɔ̀ jöö̀) va. to kill by destroying sb.'s བླ་.

བླ་སློབ་ (lālob) a lama and his disciples.

བླ་ལྷ་ (lālha) lamas and dieties.

བླ་ལྷག (lālhaà) sm. ལྷག་པར་དུ་.

བླ་ལྷའི་ལུང་བསྟན (lālhɛ lu̱ŋdaà) divination by lamas and deities.

བླག: p. བླགས་; f. བླག; imp. བློགས་ (lāà) 1. va. to listen to, to pay attention. 2. va. to cast/ throw away.

བླགས་ (lāà) p. of བླག.

བླགས་ཆེ་ (lāgce) sm. ཕམ་ཉེས་ཆེན་པོ་.

བླང་ (lāŋ) f. of ལེན་.

བླང་དོར་ (lāŋdɔɔ) taking or discarding, accepting or refusing, doing and not doing, discriminating; va.—འབྱེད་ to separate/ differentiate that which should be accepted and that which should be refused/ discarded. ¶ ལས་འགུལ་འགོ་མ་བཙུགས་གོང་བླང་དོར་མ་ནོར་བའི་ཆེད་དུ་འགོ་ཁྲིད་ནས་སློབ་སྟོན་ཞིབ་ཕྲ་བྱས་པ་རེད་ In order not to differentiate things without making any mistakes, before the campaign started the leader gave detailed advice.

བླང་དོར་ཁྲིགས་ཆགས་ (lāŋdɔɔ tri̱gjaà) doing things in an orderly manner.

བླང་དོར་གྱི་གནས་ལ་མཁས་པ་ (lāŋdɔɔgi nɛ̄ɛ̀la kɛ̄ɛ̀ba) skilled in making choices/ decisions about what to accept/ take and what to discard.

བླང་དོར་དོན་ཚང་ (lāŋdɔɔ tö̱ndzaŋ) shung. making a correct choice in taking and discarding ¶ བརྙས་བསྙུན་བཟོད་མ་བདེ་ར་འགྲོ་རིགས་བགྱིས་ན་མི་འཐུས་པས་དེ་དོན་བླང་དོར་དོན་ཚང་ཡོང་བ་གྱིས་ You are not allowed to cause trouble and should make a correct choice in taking and discarding.

བླང་ནན་ (lāŋnɛn) requesting earnestly/ strongly/ forcefully; va.—འདོན་.

བླང་བྱ་ (lāŋja) 1. requirement, request, va.—འདོན་ to make a request. 2. things that ought to be done ¶ ལས་ཀའི་ནང་བླང་བྱ་རྣམས་ལེན་དགོས་ One should do all the things that should be done regarding the work.

བླངས་ (lāŋ) p. of ལེན་.

བླངས་ན་རྫོགས་མཐའ་མེད་པ་དང་ སྤྱད་ན་འཛད་མཐའ་མེད་པ་ (lāŋna dzɔ̄ɔta me̱èba ta̱ŋ jɛ̄ɛna dzɛ̱ɛta me̱èba) inexhaustible, endless ¶ ཚན་རིག་ཞིབ་འཇུག་ནི་བླངས་ན་རྫོགས་མཐའ་མེད་པ་དང་ སྤྱད་ན་འཛད་མཐའ་མེད་པ་ཞིག་རེད་ Scientific research is endless.

བླངས་མིན་གན་རྒྱ་ (lāŋmin ke̱ngya) shung. an involuntarily/ coercively signed agreement.

བླད་: p. and f. བླད་; imp. བློད་ (lɛ̀ɛ) to chew.

བླད་བླད་ (lɛ̀ɛlɛ̀ɛ) chewing; va.—བྱེད་ ¶ ཁ་ལག་ཟ་དུས་བླད་བླད་ཡག་པོ་བྱེད་དགོས་ When eating food (you) should chew well.

བླན་ (lɛ̄n) 1. va. to patch, to cover up ¶ མོས་གོས་ལོག་གི་བུག་དེ་ར་ལྷན་པ་བླན་པ་རེད་ She patched up the hole in the garment. 2. va. to reply/ answer ¶ ཁོས་ལམ་སེང་ལན་བླན་པ་རེད་ He answered at once. 3. va. to bring/ summon.

བླུ་: p. བླུས་; f. བླུ་; imp. བླུས་ (lū) 1. va. to ransom, to redeem ¶ ངས་བུ་ལོན་སྤྲོད་ནས་གཏའ་མ་ཚུར་བླུས་པ་ཡིན་ I repaid the loan and redeemed my pawn. 2. va. a euphemistic term used to buy a religious item such as a statue.

བླུ་དངུལ་ (lūŋüü) sm. བླུ་ཡག.

བླུ་ཉོ་ (lūño) 1. redeeming, ransoming; va.—བྱེད་ to redeem, to ransom. 2. a euphemistic term used when buying a religious item such as a statue.

བླུ་ཉོའི་སྲིད་ཇུས་ (lūñö sii̋jüü) the "redeeming policy" (the policy of gradually nationalizing the means of production while compensating the national bourgeoise for the loss of their resources [in PRC]).

བླུ་འབུལ་ (lūmbüü) selling statues/ scriptures/ etc.; va.—ཞུ་.

བླུ་ཡག (lūyaà) ransom money/ goods.

བླུ་ཡོན་ (lūyön) euphemistic term for the price of a religious object; va.—(དུ་) གཏོང་ to sell a religious object; va.—ཞུ་ to buy a religious item.

བླུ་རིན་ (lūrin) 1. the price or fee for redeeming/ ransoming sth. 2. sm. བླུ་ཡོན་.

བླུ་རིན་དངུལ་ (lūrin ŋü̋ü) sm. བླུ་རིན་.

བླུ་ལེན་ (lūlen) sm. བླུ་ཉོ་.

བླུག: p. བླུགས་; f. བླུག; imp. བླུགས་ (lūù) 1. va. to pour ¶ སྣོད་ཆས་དེའི་ནང་ཆུ་ཏོག་ཙམ་བླུགས་སོང་ (He) poured some water into that pot. 2. va. to cast (metals) ¶ ངར་ལྕགས་དུམ་པོ་བླུག་སྟངས་ The method of casting steel ingots. 3. va. to enclose/ put in a letter or package ¶ ཡི་གེ་ཡིག་སྐོགས་ནང་བླུགས་པ་རེད་ (He) put a letter in an envelope. 4. va. to have sexual intercourse ¶ ཁོས་མོ་ར་བླུགས་པ་རེད་ He had sexual intercourse with her.

བླུག་ཀོང་ (lūùgoŋ) iron bowl/ mould for casting.

བླུག་དབྱིན་ཅི་ (lūyinji) ch. tape recorder.

བླུགས་ (lūù) 1. p. of བླུག. 2. sth. made by a mould/ cast, sth. that has been casted. 3. vi. to make a profit at sb's expense ། ཁོས་ཚོང་འདིའི་ཐོག་ངའི་མགོ་ལ་བླུགས་བཞག Regarding this trade, he made a profit at my expense. 4. va. to hit.

བླུགས་སྐུ་ (lūùgu) casted icons/ statues.

བླུགས་སྐྱར་ (lūùgyɔɔ) repouring, refilling, recasting; va.—རྒྱག.

བླུགས་སྣོད་ (lūùnöö) container for casting.

བླུགས་པར་ (lūgbar) mould for casting.

བླུགས་མ་ (lūŋmə) things that have been cast.

བླུགས་གཟར་ (lūgsar) ladle used when performing exorcism rites.

བླུགས་ཤོག (lūgshoò) recycled paper.

བླུད་ (lūù) va. to give/ pour (a liquid) ། ང་ལ་ཇ་ཞིག་བླུད་ Give/ pour me some tea.

བླུན་སྒོམ་ (lūngom) meditating in a foolish manner.

བླུན་གཏམ་ (lūndam) stupid/ foolish talk.

བླུན་ཏགས་ (lūndaà) stupid, ridiculous.

བླུན་འཐོམས་ (lūndom) sb. who is stupid/ ridiculous/ out of it.

བླུན་དད་ (lūndɛɛ̀) superstitious.

བླུན་པ་ (lūnmbə) foolish, stupid.

བླུན་པོ་ (lūmbo) foolish, stupid.

བླུན་པོ་གྲགས་པའི་རྗེ་འབྲངས་ (lūmbo tra̱gbɛ je̱draŋ) shung. stupid people following gossip; va.—བྱེད་ ། བྱིངས་རྣམས་བླུན་པོ་གྲགས་པའི་རྗེ་འབྲངས་བྱེད་པ་ཆོས་ཉིད་བཞིན་ It is natural that the rest of the people will behave like stupid people following gossip.

བླུན་པོ་སྨྲ་བ་ཉུང་ན་མཛེས་ (lūmbo māwa ñuŋna dzeè) it is better for stupid people to say as little as possible.

བླུན་པོའི་གྲས་ཀྱི་མཁས་པ་ (lūnpēo trɛɛ̀gi kɛ̄ɛ̀ba) the best of the worst [Lit. the expert among the fools].

བླུན་མོངས་ (lūnmoŋ) ignorant, uneducated, stupid ། མང་ཚོགས་རྣམས་བླུན་མོངས་ཤིག་ཏུ་རྩི་གི་ཡོད་པ་རེད་ They consider the masses ignorant.

བླུན་མོངས་ནུས་མེད་ (lūnmoŋ nu̱ūmeè) stupid/ foolish and weak/ powerless.

བླུན་མོངས་ཤེས་དམན་ (lūnmoŋ shēèmɛn) stupid, unintelligent, ignorant.

བླུན་ཚིག (lūndzii) foolish remark/ comment/ statement.

བླུས་ (lūù) p. and imp. of བླུ་.

བླུས་མ་ (lūùmə) 1. items that have been purchased/ bought (usu. religious). 2. items that have been redeemed.

བློ་ (lō) 1. mind, thought, heart ། གནས་ཚུལ་དེ་བློ་ལ་ངེས་པ་བྱེད་རོགས་ Please keep that news in mind. ། བློ་དཀར་པོ་ Pure in mind/ heart. 2. intelligence, intellect ། བློ་དང་ལྡན་པ་ Intelligent. 3. wish, desire (usu. vb. + —) ། འདི་ནས་ཡུལ་གཞན་ཞིག་ལ་དམིགས་བསལ་འགྲོ་བློ་མི་འདུག (I) have no special desire to go to another country. 4. strategy, method, idea ། ཁྱེད་རང་གིས་ང་ལ་བློ་ཞིག་འདོན་རོགས་གནང་ Please give me an idea (method).

བློ་ཀྱོག (lōgyɔɔ̀) 1. doubts, uncertainty. 2. worried, uneasy, anxious.

བློ་དཀར་ (lōgar) 1. faithful, sincere, kind, pure in heart ། བློ་དཀར་གྱིས་སྐད་ཆ་བཤད་པ་རེད་ He spoke with sincerity. 2. close friend ། ངས་བློ་དཀར་ཚང་མ་ཐུགས་སྤྱིར་སྐྱིད་བཏང་བ་ཡིན་ I invited all my close friends for a party.

བློ་དཀར་ཁོང་ཡངས་ (lōgar kōŋyaŋ) kind and tolerant.

བློ་དཀར་དྲང་བདེན་ (lōgar tra̱nden) kind and honest.

བློ་དཀར་མོས་གུས་ (lōgar mo̱ògüù) kind and respectful.

བློ་དཀར་གཞུང་དྲང་ (lōgar shu̱ŋdraŋ) faithful, honest.

བློ་དཀར་སེམས་དཀར་ (lōgar sēmgar) sm. བློ་དཀར་, 1.

བློ་དཀར་སེམས་དྲང་ (lōgar sēmdraŋ) kind and truthful.

བློ་དཀྱིལ་ (lōgyee) sm. བློ་རྒྱ་.

བློ་དཀྲོགས་ (lō drɔ̄ɔ̀) va. to annoy/ agitate/ irritate.

བློ་བཀལ་ (lō gɛ̄ɛ̀) sm. བློས་བཀལ་.

བློ་བཀོད་ (lō gȫö) va. to guide, to direct.

བློ་བཀོད་པ་ (lō gȫöba) advisor, a person who gives guidance.

བློ་ཀུ་ (lō gū) sm. ཁོག་ཚོད་ལེན་.

བློ་སྐུལ་ (lōgüù) encouraging, inspiring; va.—བྱེད་.

བློ་སྐྱེ་ (lō gyē) vi. to have a thought come to mind.

བློ་སྐྱེད་ (lōgyeè) gaining understanding/ awareness; vi.—འཕེལ་; —འདོན་ to broaden understanding/ awareness.

བློ་སྐྱེད་ཐོན་ཤུགས་ (lōgyeè tōnshug) intelligence.

བློ་སྐྱེལ་ (lō gyēē) va. to have trust/ faith/ belief in others.

བློ་ཁ་ (lōga) 1. mind; vi.—ཁེངས་; — རྫོགས་ to be satisfied/ content ། ཁོས་བློ་ཁ་རྫོགས་པ་ཞིག་བཤད་འདུག He spoke all he wanted to say (until he was satisfied). 2. scope of mind, consciousness, outlook ། བློ་ཁ་ཡངས་པོ་ Broad in outlook.

བློ་ཁ་ཁྲིད་ (lōga trīi) sm. བློ་ཁྲིད་.

བློ་ཁ་སྒྲིལ་ (lōga dri̱i) va. to think with unity/ solidarity.

བློ་ཁ་མངོན་ཕྱོགས་ (lōga ŋōnjɔɔ̀) sm. བློ་ཁ་ཕྱོགས་.

བློ་ཁ་འཆོར་ (lōga cɔ̄ɔ̀) vi. to loose heart.

བློ་ཁ་གཏད་ཕྱོགས་ (lōga dɛ̄ɛ̀jɔɔ̀) sm. བློ་ཁ་ཕྱོགས་.

བློ་ཁ་ལྟ་ཕྱོགས་ (lōga dājɔɔ̀) sm. བློ་ཁ་ཕྱོགས་.

བློ་ཁ་མཐོན་པོ་ (lōga tōmbo) boundless enthusiasm, high spirits.

བློ་ཁ་ནང་འགུགས་ (lōga na̱ŋguù) winning over sb. (to one's side); va.—བྱེད་ ། སྲིད་ཇུས་གསར་པ་དེས་མི་མང་པོ་བློ་ཁ་ནང་འགུགས་བྱེད་ཐུབ་པ་བྱུང་བ་རེད་ The new policy was able to win over many people (to their side).

བློ་ཁ་ཕྱི་ལྟས་གྲོད་པ་ནང་བལྟས་ (lōga cīdɛɛ̀ tro̱òba na̱ndɛɛ̀) traitor; va.—བྱེད་ [Lit. mind faces outside, stomach faces inside].

བློ་ཁ་ཕྱོགས་ (lōga cɔ̄ɔ̀) va. to be in favor of sth., to be inclined towards, to be oriented towards ། མང་ཚོགས་རྣམས་དམངས་གཙོའི་ལམ་ལུགས་ལ་བློ་ཁ་ཕྱོགས་ཀྱི་ཡོད་པ་རེད་ The masses are inclined towards democracy.

བློ་ཁ་འབྱེད་ (lōga ce̱è) sm. བློ་སྒོ་འབྱེད་.

བློ་ཁ་མི་ཆགས་ (lōga mi̱caà) vi. to be unsettled, to not feel at home ། ཕ་ཡུལ་དང་བྲལ་ཕྱིན་ལུང་པ་གང་དུ་སླེབས་ཀྱང་བློ་ཁ་མི་ཆགས་པ་ཞིག་ཡོང་གི་འདུག After being separated from his homeland, wherever he went (he) didn't feel at home.

བློ་ཁ་རྩེ་གཅིག (lōga dzējig) single-minded, concentrated, focused.

བློ་ཁ་ཚིམ་ (lōga tsīm) vi. to be satisfied/ content.

བློ་ཁ་ཚུར་འཁོར་ (lōga tsūūgɔɔ) sm. བློ་ཁ་ནང་འགུགས་.

བློ་ཁ་རྫོགས་ (lōga dzɔ̱ɔ̀) vi. to be fulfilled/ satisfied/ content.

བློ་ཁ་ཡངས་པོ་ (lōga ya̱nbo) broad-minded.

བློ་ཁ་ཡང་པ་ (lōga ya̱ŋba) sm. བློ་ཁ་ཡངས་པོ་.

བློ་ཁམས་ཡང་བ་ (lōgam ya̱ŋba) sm. བློ་ཁ་ཡངས་པོ་.

བློ་ཁུག (lō kūù) vi. to come to (one's) senses, to be reformed/ changed ། མི་ངན་དེ་དེང་སང་བློ་ཁུག་བཞག These days that evil person has come to his senses. ། ཕྲུ་གུ་སྤྲིག་ཉེས་འདི་བློ་ཁུག་བཞག The naughty boy has reformed.

བློ་ཁེངས་ (lō kēŋ) vi. to be satisfied/ content. ། སྐུ་མགྲོན་ཚོ་བློ་ཁེངས་སོང་ The guests were satisfied.

བློ་ཁེངས་པོ་ (lō kēŋbo) satisfied, content.

བློ་ཁེངས་ཡིད་ཚིམ་ (lōkeŋ yi̱idzim) sm. བློ་ཁེངས་པོ་.

བློ་ཁེལ་ (lō kēē) va. to trust, to have confidence in, to rely on ། ང་ཁོ་ལ་བློ་ཁེལ་གྱི་འདུག I trust him completely.

བློ་ཁོག (lōgɔ̀ɔ̀) courage, bravery; va.—བྱེད་ to act courageous/ brave.

བློ་ཁོག་ཆེན་པོ་ (lōgɔɔ̀ cēmbo) courageous, brave.

བློ་ཁོག་དོག་པོ་ (lōgɔɔ̀ to̱gbo) narrow-minded.

བློ་ཁོག་འཚོང་ (lōgɔɔ̀ tsōŋ) va. to do sth. risky/ dangerous.

བློ་ཁོག་སློབ་ (lōgɔɔ̀ lōb) va. to teach/ encourage to be brave.

བློ་ཁྲིད་ (lō trii) va. to change a (person's) way of thinking, to help/ guide sb. to see what is right or sensible; va.—བྱེད་ ། དགེ་རྒན་གྱིས་སློབ་ཕྲུག་ཚོའི་བློ་ཁྲིད་བྱས་ནས་སློབ་སྦྱོང་ཐོག་ཡར་རྒྱས་ཆེན་པོ་བྱུང་འདུག The teacher helped the students to see what is right and their studies improved greatly.

བློ་འཁུམ་ (lō kūm) vi. to be afraid/ scared/ frightened.

བློ་འཁེལ་ས་ (lō kēesa) a trusted/ reliable person.

བློ་འཁྱོག་པོ་འཆང་ (lō kyōgbo cāŋ) va. to hesitate, to not be able to make up one's mind.

བློ་འཁྱོག་ལ་འཆང་ (lō kyōgla cāŋ) sm. བློ་འཁྱོག་པོ་འཆང་.

བློ་གུ་ཡངས་པ་ (lō guyaŋba) sm. བློ་ཁ་ཡངས་པ་.

བློ་གྲི་ (lōdri) dagger.

བློ་གྲོགས་ (lōdrɔ̄ɔ) trustworthy/ reliable friend.

བློ་གྲོས་ (lōdröö) wisdom, understanding, intellect.

བློ་གྲོས་ཀྱི་སྒོ་འབྱེད་ (lōdröögi gojeèd) opening the mind to wisdom/ understanding.

བློ་གྲོས་ངན་པ་ (lōdröö ŋɛmba) dull witted, stupid.

བློ་གྲོས་ཅན་ (lōdrööjɛn) wise, intelligent, knowledgeable.

བློ་གྲོས་ཆེན་པོ་ (lōdröö cēmbo) wise, broad-minded.

བློ་གྲོས་འདོན་ (lōdröö dön) va. to offer suggestions, to come up with ideas.

བློ་གྲོས་ལྡན་པ་ (lōdröö dɛmba) sm. བློ་གྲོས་ཅན་.

བློ་གྲོས་ལོག (lōdröö lɔɔ) va. to use one's skill/ knowledge in a wrong or negative way.

བློ་དགའ་ (lō ga) 1. vi. to like. 2. a person's name.

བློ་འགལ་སེམས་འགལ་ (lōgɛɛ sēmgɛɛ) opposing, disagreeing; va.—བྱེད་.

བློ་འགུག (lō guù) convincing, persuading, winning over (sb. to one's side); va.—བྱེད་.

བློ་འགུགས་ཐབས་བྱེད་ (lōguù tāb ceè) va. to try to convince, to try to persuade, to try to win over to one's side.

བློ་འགེལ་ (lōgee) sm. བློས་འགེལ་.

བློ་འགེལ་ཡིད་ཆེས་ (lōgee yijeè) trust, confidence; va.—བྱེད་ to trust, to have confidence in.

བློ་འགོང་ (lōgoŋ) regrets ། ལས་ཀ་གང་བྱས་ཀྱང་རྗེས་སུ་བློ་འགོང་མེད་པ་ཞིག་བྱེད་དགོས་ Whatever one does, one should do it so that later one does not have regrets.

བློ་འགྱུ་ (lōgyu) va. to be distracted ། སྤྱི་དོན་སྒྲུབ་སྐབས་སྒེར་དོན་ལ་བློ་མི་འགྱུར་བ་བྱེད་དགོས་ When performing sth. for the common benefit, one should not get distracted by personal ends.

བློ་འགྱུར་ (lō gyur) va. to change one's mind/ views ། ཁོང་ལ་འཐབ་འཛིང་ག་ཚོད་བཏང་ཡང་བློ་འགྱུར་མ་སོང་ No matter how many "struggle sessions" they had (against him), he did not change his mind.

བློ་འགྱོད་སྐྱེ་ (lōgyöö gyē) vi. to regret.

བློ་རྒོད་པོ་ (lō gööbo) creative, smart, quick thinking.

བློ་རྒྱ་ (lōgya) scope of mind, vision, mental capacity; va.—སྐྱེད་ to widen one's scope of mind/ vision.

བློ་རྒྱ་གྲོལ་ (lōgya tröö) vi. to have one's mind opened by sth.

བློ་རྒྱ་ཆུང་ཆུང་ (lōgya cūŋjuŋ) petty/ narrow-minded, not broad-minded.

བློ་རྒྱ་ཆུང་ངུ་ (lōgya cūŋŋu) sm. བློ་རྒྱ་ཆུང་ཆུང་.

བློ་རྒྱ་ཆེ་བསྐྱེད་ (lōgya cēgyeè) broad in vision/ outlook.

བློ་རྒྱ་ཆེན་པོ་ (lōgya cēmbo) able to think big, broad-minded, open-minded.

བློ་རྒྱ་ཡངས་པ་ (lōgya yaŋba) sm. བློ་རྒྱ་ཆེན་པོ་.

བློ་རྒྱང་དུ་སོང་ (lōgyaŋdu sōŋ) vi. to become estranged/ alienated.

བློ་རྒྱུ་རིང་པོ་ (lōgyu riŋbu) good-tempered, easygoing.

བློ་སྒོ་ཕྱེ་ (lō go cē) va. to open sb.'s mind to sth.

བློ་སྒོ་འབྱེད་ (lōgo ceè) p. of བློ་སྒོ་ཕྱེ་.

བློ་སྒོ་ཡངས་པ་ (lōgo yaŋba) sm. བློ་རྒྱ་ཆེན་པོ་.

བློ་སྒྱུར་ (lō gyur) va. to change sb.'s mind ། མོས་ཁོའི་བློ་བསྒྱུར་པ་རེད་ She changed his mind.

བློ་སྒྲིམས་ (lō drim) paying attention to sth., concentrating on sth.

བློ་བསྒྱུར་ (lō gyur) p. of བློ་སྒྱུར་.

བློ་ངན་ (lōŋɛn) evil-minded, evil thoughts.

བློ་ངོ་ (lōŋo) thought, thinking.

བློ་སྔོན་ལ་དྲན་ན་མཁས་པ་ (lōŋönla trɛnna kɛ̄ɛba) one who thinks beforehand is a wise man.

བློ་གཅིག་ལམ་མཐུན་ (lōjig lamdün) people engaged in the same pursuit, people united.

བློ་གཅིག་སེམས་གཅིག (lōjig sēmjig) wholeheartedly, with heart and soul, with one mind.

བློ་གཅིག་སེམས་གཉིས་ (lōjig sēmñii) halfheartedly.

བློ་བཅོལ་ (lō jöö) va. to believe/ trust in sb., to depend/ rely on sb. ། ངས་ཚོང་གི་ཐོག་ཁོང་ལ་བློ་བཅོལ་པ་ཡིན་ Concerning business, I depended on him.

བློ་ཆུང་ཉམས་ཅན་ (lōjuŋ ñamjɛn) humble/ plain appearance.

བློ་ཆུང་ (lōjuŋ) sm. བློ་ཆུང་བ་.

བློ་ཆུང་བ་ (lōjuŋwə) narrow-minded.

བློ་ཆེ་གཅོད་མཁས་ (lōce jöögɛɛ) broad-minded/ open-minded and decisive.

བློ་ཆེན་ (lōjen) sm. བློ་རྒྱ་ཆེན་པོ་.

བློ་ཆེན་པོ་ (lō cēmbo) sm. བློ་རྒྱ་ཆེན་པོ་.

བློ་འཆར་ (lōjar) thought, idea, conception.

བློ་ཇུས་ (lōjüü) strategy; va.—འདོན་ ། ད་རེས་ཚོང་འདི་རྒྱག་སྟངས་སྐོར་ང་ལ་བློ་ཇུས་འདོན་རོགས་ Please make a plan for me as to how to do (my) business.

བློ་འཇགས་ (lōnjaà) keeping in mind, remembering; va.—འཆལ་; —བྱེད་ ། ངས་ཁྱེད་རང་ལ་བཤད་པ་དེ་བློ་འཇགས་བྱེད་དགོས་ Please keep in mind what I said.

བློ་བརྗེད་འགྱུར་ (lōjeè gyur) vi. to forget.

བློ་ཉམས་ (lō ñam) vi. to decline in mental faculties.

བློ་ཉེ་བ་ (lō ñewa) intimate, close, dear, loved.

བློ་གཉིས་ཐེ་ཚོམ་ (lōñii tēdzom) having doubts/ hesitation, being of two minds about sth. ། ལྷ་སར་ཟིང་ཆ་ལངས་སྐབས་ཁོང་བོད་ལ་འགྲོ་རྒྱུར་བློ་གཉིས་ཐེ་ཚོམ་བྱེད་ཀྱི་འདུག Because there were disturbances in Lhasa, (he) is of two minds about going to Tibet.

བློ་སྙིང་འབིགས་པའི་བདའ་མོ་ (lōñiŋ bigbɛ damo) talk that hurts someone's feelings [Lit. an arrow that sticks into sb.'s heart].

བློ་སྙིང་སེམས་དཀར་ (lōñiŋ sēmgar) 1. sincere, faithful ། ཁོང་སྲིད་གཞུང་ལ་བློ་སྙིང་སེམས་དཀར་བྱེད་མཁན་ཞིག་རེད་ He is sb. who is faithful to the government. 2. close, trusted (friend) ། ཁོང་ངའི་བློ་སྙིང་སེམས་དཀར་གྱི་གྲོགས་པོ་ཡིན་ He is a close friend of mine.

བློ་གཏད་ (lōdɛɛ) va. to believe/ trust in sb., to depend/ rely on sb.

བློ་གཏད་ཆ་འཇོག (lōdɛɛ canjɔɔ) sm. བློ་བཅོལ་.

བློ་གཏད་ཚོག་པ་ (lōdɛɛ cōgba) reliable, dependable.

བློ་གཏད་ལིངས་བཅོལ་ (lōdɛɛ liŋjöö) reliable, dependable.

བློ་གཏད་ཤ་ཚ་ (lōdɛɛ shādza) sincere ། བློ་གཏད་ཤ་ཚའི་རེ་བསྐུལ་ A sincere request.

བློ་གཏམ་ (lōdam) intimate talk.

བློ་གཏིང་ཟབ་པོ་ (lō dīŋ sɘbbo) sb. who can think deeply.

བློ་གཏོད་ (lōdöö) sm. བློ་གཏད་.

བློ་རྟ་ (lōda) one's favorite horse.

བློ་རྟུལ་ (lō düü) abbr. of བློ་རྟུལ་པོ་.

བློ་རྟུལ་པོ་ (lō düübo) dull and obtuse, stupid.

བློ་རྟོགས་ (lōdɔɔ) knowledge, understanding.

བློ་སྟོབས་ (lōdob) 1. courage, spirit, bravery; vi.—སྐྱེད་; — རྒྱས་; —ཆེ་སྐྱེད་ to get courage/ spirit/ bravery ། དཀའ་ངལ་གང་འདྲ་བྱུང་ཡང་བློ་སྟོབས་མ་ཉམས་པར་ Not losing courage whatever the problem/ hardship encountered. 2. courageous, ambitious ། འཆར་གཞི་བློ་སྟོབས་ཅན་ཞིག An ambitious plan.

བློ་སྟོབས་ཆེན་པོ་ (lōdob cēmbo) brave, courageous.

བློ་བརྟན་འགྱུར་མེད་ (lōdɛn gyurmeè) resolute, determined, unchanging, steadfast.

བློ་བརྟན་པོ་ (lō dēmbo) stable, trustworthy, dependable.

བློ་བརྟན་གཞུང་དྲང་ (lōdɛn shuŋdraŋ) dependable and honest.

བློ་བལྟ་ས་ (lō dāsa) sb. on whom one relies/ depends/ places one's hope on ¶ བླ་མ་དེ་ལུང་པའི་མི་ནམས་ཀྱི་བློ་བལྟ་ས་རེད་ The lama is the person on whom the people of that area depend.

བློ་ཐག་གཅོད་ (lō tāàjöö) va. to make a decision ¶ ང་བོད་ལ་འགྲོ་རྒྱུའི་བློ་ཐག་བཅད་པ་ཡིན་ I decided to go to Tibet.

བློ་ཐག་ཆོད་པོ་ (lōtaà cööbo) decisive, firm, resolute.

བློ་ཐག་ཐད་བཅད་ (lōtaà bɛdjɛɛ̀) resolute, determined ¶ ཁོ་ཚོའི་དྲང་བདེན་གྱི་འཐབ་རྩོད་ལ་བློ་ཐག་ཐད་བཅད་ཀྱིས་རྒྱབ་སྐྱོར་བྱེད་ཀྱི་ཡོད་ (We) resolutely support their just struggle.

བློ་ཐག་གཅང་བཅད་ (lōtaà dzāŋjɛɛ̀) sm. བློ་ཐག་ཐད་བཅད་.

བློ་ཐབས་ (lōdəb) sm. བློ་ཐུས་.

བློ་ཐང་བ་ (lō tāŋwa) sm. བློ་ཁོག་ཆེན་པོ་.

བློ་ཐུག་པོ་ (lō tūgbo) trustful, trustworthy.

བློ་ཐུང་བ་ (lō tūŋwa) sm. བློ་སྣ་ཐུང་བ་.

བློ་ཐུབ་ (lōtub) sm. བློ་ཐུག་པོ་.

བློ་མཐུན་ (lōdün) comrade ¶ བློ་མཐུན་ཀྲང་ Comrade Zhang.

བློ་མཐུན་གྲོས་གཅིག (lōdün trööjig) speaking/ doing with one voice; va.—བྱེད་.

བློ་མཐུན་པ་ (lōdümbə) sm. བློ་མཐུན་.

བློ་མཐུན་སེམས་མཐུན་ (lōdün sēmdün) having the same opinion/ view; hitting it off perfectly.

བློ་འཐུམས་ (lōndum) dim, unclear, dull (in mind).

བློ་འཐོམས་ (lōndom) ignorant, dull.

བློ་དང་འཚམས་པ་ (lōdaŋ tsāmba) suitable, desirable, agreeable, compatible ¶ ང་རང་གི་བློ་དང་འཚམས་པའི་ལས་ཀ་ཞིག་རག་བྱུང་ I got a job that I desired.

བློ་དམ་པ་ (lōdamba) lover.

བློ་དོགས་ (lōdɔɔ̀) doubt, suspicion; vi.—སྐྱེ་ to have doubts/ suspicions arise; vi.—སེལ་ to have one's doubts/ suspicions cleared up ¶ བོད་གཞུང་ལ་བློ་དོགས་བྱུང་པ་རེད་ The Tibetan government was under suspicion.

བློ་དྲེད་པོ་ (lō treèbo) slick, sly.

བློ་གདེང་ (lōdeŋ) confidence, assurance; vi.—འཁེལ་ to be confident/ self-assured.

བློ་བདེ་ (lō de) vi. to feel at ease, to be relieved ¶ ནང་མི་བདེ་པོ་ཡིན་པའི་ཡི་གེ་འབྱོར་ནས་ང་བློ་བདེ་སོང་ I felt relieved after receiving the letter saying my family was well.

བློ་བདེ་པོ་ (lō debo) at ease, relaxed, relieved, without worries/ fears.

བློ་བདེ་པག་ཕེབས་ (lōde pagbeb) free and easy, easygoing, happy, carefree.

བློ་བདེ་ཞི་ལྷོད་ (lōde shelhöö) cool headed, unflustered, calmly without anger, dispassionately.

བློ་བདེ་སེམས་བདེ་ (lōde sēmde) happy, content; va.—བཟོ་ to make happy/ content.

བློ་འདས་ (lōdɛɛ̀) sm. བློ་ཡུལ་ལས་འདས་པ་.

བློ་འདས་བརྗོད་བྲལ་ (lōdɛɛ̀ jöödrɛɛ) sm. བློ་ཡུལ་ལས་འདས་པ་.

བློ་འདིང་ཅན་ (lō dinjɛn) a person of vision, farsighted.

བློ་འདུན་ (lōndün) sm. བློ་འདོད་.

བློ་འདོད་ (lōdöö) wish, desire; va.—བྱེད་ to wish, to desire ¶ བུ་མོ་དེ་ང་ཚོའི་བུས་བློ་འདོད་བྱེད་ཀྱི་མི་འདུག Our son doesn't desire that girl.

བློ་འདོད་ལྟར་འགྲུབ་ (lōdöödar drub) vi. to have one's wish/ desire come true.

བློ་འདོན་ (lō dön) 1. sm. བློ་གྲོས་འདོན་ 2. reading silently; va.—བྱེད་.

བློ་འདོན་ཚོགས་འདུ་ (lōdön tsōndu) a meeting to come up with ideas/ strategy/ means for doing sth.

བློ་འདུན་ཚོགས་པ་ (lōdün tsōgba) sm. བློ་འདོན་ཚོགས་འདུ་.

བློ་འདུན་ཞབས་འདེགས་ (lōdün shamdeg) consulting service.

བློ་འདྲི་ (lüdri) consulting, seeking advice; va.—བྱེད་ ¶ བགྲེས་སོང་དེ་ར་མི་ཚང་མས་བློ་འདྲི་བྱས་པ་རེད་ Everyone asked the elderly person for advice.

བློ་འདྲི་གྲོས་བསྡུར་ (lüdri troöduu) discussing and seeking advice; va.—བྱེད་.

བློ་འདྲི་བྱེད་ཡུལ་ (lüdri ceèyüü) adviser, consultant, counselor.

བློ་འདྲི་ས་ (lō drisə) sm. བློ་འདྲི་བྱེད་ཡུལ་.

བློ་འདྲིའི་ཞབས་འདེགས་ (lüdrii shamdeg) consultancy service.

བློ་འདྲོག (lō drɔɔ̀) vi. to become nervous/ scared.

བློ་ལྡན་ (lōdɛn) 1. wise, intelligent. 2. man's name.

བློ་ལྡན་སྲོག་ཆགས་རིགས་ (lōdɛn sōgjaà rig) primates.

བློ་ལྡོག (lōdɔɔ̀) 1. vi. to turn against, to revolt/ rebel against. 2. vi. to get sick of, to be/ get fed up with.

བློ་སྡུར་ (lōdur) exchange of ideas, discussion; va. བློ་སྡུར་; —བྱེད་ to exchange ideas, to discuss.

བློ་བསྡུར་དགེ་འཚོལ་ (lōdur gedzöö) collecting ideas and opinions from different sources and selecting the good ones.

བློ་བསྣོགས་ (lō ŋɔɔ̀) va. to keep in mind.

བློ་ནུས་ (lōnüü) mental/ intellectual capabilities or strength ¶ བློ་ནུས་གང་ཡོད་འདོན་ Doing to the best of one capabilities.

བློ་རྣོ་པོ་ (lō nōbo) clever, sharp witted.

བློ་སྣ་བསྡུངས་པ་ (lōna dūŋbə) sm. བློ་སྣ་ཐུང་བ་.

བློ་སྣ་ཐུང་བ་ (lōna tūŋwə) quick to anger, hot-tempered.

བློ་སྣ་མང་པོ་ (lōna maŋbo) undecided, having too many ideas (and thus unable to decide between them).

བློ་སྣ་རིང་པོ་ (lōna riŋbu) patient, tolerant, mild.

བློ་དཔོན་མཐོང་བ་དོན་ལྡན་ (lōbön tōŋwa döndɛn) the Dalai Lama.

བློ་སྤོབས་ (lōbob) 1. morale, confidence, courage; vi.—སྐྱེད་; vi.—རྙེད་ to get confidence/ courage.

བློ་ཕ་ལ་འདྲི་མི་དགོས་པ་ ཟས་མ་ལ་སློང་མི་དགོས་པ་ (lō pāla dri migööba tro mala lōŋ migööba) a mature/ grown up child, a child able to stand on his own two feet [Lit. doesn't need to seek his father's advice, doesn't need to beg food from his mother].

བློ་ཕམ་ (lōpam) sad, sorry ¶ ཡིད་སྐྱོའི་གནས་ཚུལ་དེ་ཐོས་ནས་བློ་ཕམ་ཆེན་པོ་བྱུང་ (I) was very sad when I heard the sad news.

བློ་ཕམ་ (lō pām) p. of བློ་འཕམ་.

བློ་ཕམ་ཡིད་སྐྱོ་ (lōpam yiigyo) sm. བློ་ཕམ་ཡིད་ཆད་.

བློ་ཕམ་ཡིད་ཆད་ (lōpam yiijɛɛ̀) sad/ sorry and hurt/ disappointed.

བློ་ཕམ་ཡིད་སྨུག (lōpam yiimuù) sm. བློ་ཕམ་ཡིད་ཆད་.

བློ་ཕུགས་ (lōpuù) final/ future goal ¶ ངའི་བློ་ཕུག་ཆོས་ལ་བཙོལ་ཡོད་ My final aim is religion.

བློ་ཕུགས་དོག་པོ་ (lōpuù togbo) narrow-minded, petty.

བློ་ཕུད་ (lō büü) 1. va. to come up with a way to do sth.; to advice ¶ བློ་ཕུད་མཁན་ Adviser.

བློ་ཕྱུང་ (lō cūŋ) va. to think.

བློ་ཕྱེད་སེམས་ཕྱེད་ (lōjeè sēmjeè) doing halfheartedly.

བློ་ཕྱོགས་ (lōjɔɔ̀) sm. བློ་ཁ་ཕྱོགས་.

བློ་ཕྱོགས་གཏད་མིན་ (lōjɔɔ̀ dɛ̀ɛmin) whether or not sb. supports a group or position.

བློ་འཕམ་ (lō pām) vi. to feel sad/ sorry.

བློ་འཕེལ་ (lō pēl) sm. བློ་འཁེལ་.

བློ་བ་ (lōwa) strategist.

བློ་བག་སྒྲོ་ (lōbaà dro) va. to comfort sb., to try to cheer up/ encourage sb.

བློ་བག་ཕེབས་པ་ (lōbaà pēèba) relaxed, calm, free from anxiety/ fear.

བློ་བག་ཕེབས་པོ་ (lōbaà pēèbo) 1. happy, jolly. 2. vi. to be relaxed/ at ease/ free from anxiety/ fear.

བློ་བག་ཡངས་པ་ (lōbaà yaŋba) sm. བློ་བག་ཕེབས་པོ་.

བློ་བག་ཡངས་པོ་ (lōbaà yaŋbo) sm. བློ་བག་ཕེབས་པ་.

བློ་བད་ (lōbɛɛ̀) hesitation, doubt; va.—དྲངས་ to

clear up one's doubts/ hesitation.

བློ་བབ་ཡིད་མཐུན་ (lōbəb yi̱idün) liking and trusting sb.

བློ་བབ་ཡིད་ཚིམ་ (lōbəb yi̱idzim) sm. བློ་བབ་སེམས་བབ་.

བློ་བབ་སེམས་བབ་ (lōbəb sēmbəb) satisfied, liking sth.

བློ་བབས་ (lōbəb) 1. interest; va.—བྱེད་ to show interest ¶ མོས་གསོ་རིག་གི་སློབ་སྦྱོང་ལ་བློ་བབ་བྱེད་ཀྱི་འདུག She shows interest in medicine. 2. va. to approve ¶ གནད་དོན་དེའི་ཐོག་མི་ནམས་ཀྱི་བློ་བབ་མ་བྱུང་བ་རེད་ Regarding that matter, the people did not agree.

བློ་བུར་ (lōbur) suddenly.

བློ་བུར་དུ་ (lōburdu) suddenly, quickly.

བློ་བྲིད་ (lūdrii̱) 1. deceit, guile; va.—བྱེད་ to deceive, to beguile, to delude. 2. p. of བློ་འབྲིད་.

བློ་བློང་ (lōloŋ) 1. feeling of unhappiness. 2. an unclear/ dull mind.

བློ་འབྱེད་འཇམ་ཁྲིད་ (lōjeè ja̱mdrii̱) inspiring/ opening the mind by leading in a gentle manner.

བློ་འབྲི་ (lōdrii̱) writing from memory; va.—བྱེད་.

བློ་འབྲིད་ (lōdrii̱) sm. བློ་བྲིད་བྱེད་.

བློ་སྦུག་འཐུམས་པ་ (lōbuù tūmbə) sm. བློ་སྦུག་དོག་པོ་.

བློ་སྦུག་དོག་པོ་ (lōbuù to̱gbo) a person whose thinking is stifling, suffocating, gloomy, stuffy; a person who is timid and worries about consequences so that he is unable to think big, a person who tends not to interact much with others.

བློ་སྦུབས་ (lōbub) sm. བློ་སྦུག.

བློ་སྦྱོང་ (lōjoŋ) improvement of the mind/ intellect through training, ideological cultivation.

བློ་སྦྱོང་ཁང་ (lōjŋgaŋ) shung. an office under the དམག་སྤྱི་ཁང་.

བློ་མ་བདེ་པ་ (lōma de̱wa) worried, uneasy, anxious; vi.—བྱེད་.

བློ་མ་གནས་ (lō ma̱nɛè) shung. va. to change one's mind.

བློ་མ་རྫོགས་ (lōma dzɔ̱ɔ̀) vi. to be not content/ satisfied.

བློ་མང་ (lōmaŋ) abbr. of བློ་སྣ་མང་པོ་.

བློ་མིག (lūmii̱) thinking, thought.

བློ་མིག་ཅན་ (lūmii̱jɛn) wise/ learned person.

བློ་མིག་ལྡོངས་ (lūmii̱ ŋōŋ) vi. to be blind in thinking.

བློ་མེད་ (lōmeè) senseless, foolish.

བློ་མོས་ (lōmöö̀) agreement, consent; va.—བྱེད་ to agree/ consent.

བློ་མོས་ཡིད་སྒྲོ་ (lōmöö̀ yi̱idro) coming to a happy agreement.

བློ་སྨྱོས་ (lō ñö̱ö̀) vi. to be crazy.

བློ་དམན་ཐབས་རྡུགས་ (lōmɛn tābduù) uneducated, ignorant, having no means to improve (oneself).

བློ་དམན་པ་ (lō mɛ̄mbə) a dumb/ stupid/ ignorant person.

བློ་རྨོངས་ (lōmoŋ) 1. vi. to be dejected/ dispirited/ disheartened. 2. vi. to be stupid.

བློ་རྨོངས་ཡིད་ཆད་ (lōmoŋ yi̱ijɛ̀ɛ̀) vi. to be dismayed/ disheartened.

བློ་གཙང་ (lōdzaŋ) wise, intelligent.

བློ་རྩ་ (lōdza) idea, thought, mind; va.—སྒྲིམ་ to concentrate one's mind/ thoughts/ attention.

བློ་རྩ་བརྟན་པོ་ (lōdza dɛ̄mbo) resolute, firm, steadfast, stable.

བློ་རྩལ་ (lōdzɛɛ) mental sharpness, keen perception/ wits.

བློ་རྩིང་ང་པོ་ (lōdziŋ ŋabo) crude or rough in thinking, unrefined.

བློ་རྩེ་ (lōdze) ideas, thoughts, mind.

བློ་རྩེ་གཅིག་སྒྲིམ་ (lōdze ji̱gdrim) mental concentration; va.— བྱེད་.

བློ་རྩེ་གཅིག་འགྱུར་ (lōdze ji̱ggyur) having only one idea or purpose in mind, united in purpose.

བློ་རྩེ་གཅིག་གཏོད་ (lōdze ji̱gdöö̀) sm. བློ་རྩེ་གཅིག་འགྱུར་.

བློ་རྩེ་གཅིག་མཐུན་ (lōdze ji̱gdün) sm. བློ་རྩེ་གཅིག་འགྱུར་.

བློ་རྩེ་གཉིས་ (lōdze ñi̱i̱) being of two minds.

བློ་རྩེ་གཉིས་སྐྱེས་ (lōdze ñi̱igyeè) hesitating to do, having second thoughts about doing sth.

བློ་རྩེ་གཉིས་ཀྱིས་དོན་མི་འགྲུབ་ ཁབ་རྩེ་གཉིས་ཀྱིས་འཚེམ་བུ་མི་འགྲུབ་ (lōdze ñi̱igi dö̱m mi̱drub kābdze ñi̱igi dzi̱mbu mi̱drub) it is difficult to do anything without concentrating/ focusing attention [Lit. one cannot accomplish anything with two minds, one cannot stitch with a needle with two points].

བློ་རྩེ་ཐུང་བ་ (lōdze tūŋwə) sm. བློ་སྣ་ཐུང་བ་.

བློ་རྩེ་གསར་རྙེད་ (lōdze sārñeè) thinking/ finding sth. new (a new idea).

བློ་བརྩོན་ཆེ་བ་ (lōdzön cēwa) shung. diligent ¶ མི་གཤིས་ལེགས་ཤིང་བློ་བརྩོན་ཆེ་བ་སོགས་ Good character and diligent.

བློ་ཚབས་ (lōdzəb) sm. བློ་འཚབ་.

བློ་ཚུབ་ (lōdzub) sm. བློ་འཚབ་.

བློ་ཚོད་ (lōdzöö̀) estimating/ getting the measure of sb; va.—བྱེད་ ¶ མི་དེའི་དྲག་ལོག་གྱོན་སྟངས་ལ་བལྟས་ན་ཁོང་ཞིང་པ་ཡིན་པར་བློ་ཚོད་བྱེད་ཐུབ་པ་འདུག Looking at the style of his clothing, one can estimate he is a farmer.

བློ་ཚོད་དང་བསྟུན་ (lōdzöö̀ da̱ŋ dǖm) 1. according to the mental ability/ standard of a person. 2. in accordance with an estimate.

བློ་ཚོད་ལོན་ (lōdzöö̀ lö̱n) va. to get the measure of a person.

བློ་འཚབ་ (lōdzəb) nervous, anxious; vi.—བློ་འཚབ་; —བྱེད་.

བློ་འཚེང་ (lō dzēŋ) sm. འདོད་བློ་ཁེངས་.

བློ་མཛོད་ (lōdzöö̀) brain trust.

བློ་མཛོད་ཚོགས་པ་ (lōdzöö̀ tsɔ̄gba) brain trust.

བློ་འཛིན་ (lōndzin) memorization; va.—བྱེད་ to memorize.

བློ་ཞུམས་ (lō shu̱m) vi. to be disheartened, to be demoralized ¶ ཡིག་ཚད་ཐེངས་གཅིག་མ་ཐོན་པར་བློ་ཞུམས་རྒྱུ་མེད་ You shouldn't lose heart due to not passing the exam once.

བློ་ཟིན་ (lō si̱n) sm. བློ་འཛིན་.

བློ་ཟློག (lōdɔ̀ɔ̀) va. to change sb.'s mind, to transform one's thinking (from bad to good).

བློ་བཟང་ (lōsaŋ) 1. kindhearted. 2. person's name. 3. sm. བློ་བཟང་པོ་.

བློ་བཟང་རྒྱ་མཚོ་ (lōsaŋ gya̱dzo) name of the 5th Dalai Lama.

བློ་བཟང་ཆོས་རྒྱན་ (lōsaŋ cöögyɛn) name of the 4th Panchen Lama.

བློ་བཟང་པོ་ (lō sa̱ŋbo) 1. brainy, smart. 2. kindhearted.

བློ་བཟང་ཡེ་ཤེས་ (lōsaŋ ye̱sheè) name of the 5th Panchen Lama.

བློ་བཟོ་ (lōso) creating/ fabricating in one's own mind/ imagination; va.—བྱེད་ ¶ ཁོ་རང་གིས་བློ་བཟོ་བྱས་པ་མ་གཏོགས་མི་དེས་ཁོང་ལ་གནོད་པ་སྐྱེལ་གྱི་མེད་པ་རེད་ That person didn't harming him, he created it all in his mind.

བློ་བཟོད་བདེ་པོ་ (lōsöö̀ de̱bo) sm. བློ་བདེ་པོ་.

བློ་ཡངས་པོ་ (lō ya̱ŋbo) sm. བློ་ཁ་ཡངས་པོ་.

བློ་ཡི་བག་ཕབ་ སེམས་ཀྱི་དཔའ་བསྐྱེད་ (lōyi ba̱gpəb sēmgi bāgyeè) heartened and encouraged.

བློ་ཡིད་ཚིམ་ (lōyii̱ tsi̱m) vi. to be satisfied/ content.

བློ་ཡུལ་ (lōyüü) mental faculties, imagination; vi. (དུ་)—འཆར་; —ཤར་ to imagine, to visualize in the mind, to conceive ¶ དེ་ནི་བློ་ཡུལ་དུ་འཆར་དཀའ་བ་ཞིག་རེད་ That is difficult to imagine.

བློ་ཡུལ་ལས་འདས་པ་ (lōyüülɛ de̱èba) beyond imagination, inconceivable, unbelievable, fantastic.

བློ་གཡེངས་ (lōyeŋ) worries, apprehension, anxiety, fears; vi.—བྱེད་; —སྐྱེས་ to be worried, to fear, to be apprehensive.

བློ་གཡོ་ (lō yō) mental wavering, mental fluctuating.

བློ་རིག (lūrii̱) intelligence, intellect; va.—ངོམ་ to show off one's smartness/ intelligence; vi.—འཆོལ་ to lose one's mental ability (e.g., when old).

བློ་རིག་མི་སྐྱེན་ (lūriì mi̱gyen) not intelligent.

བློ་རིག་གསལ་བ་ (lūriì sɛ̄ɛ̄wa) intelligent, bright, smart, clever.

བློ་རོགས་ (lōrɔ̀ɔ̀) advisor.

བློ་རོགས་གྲོས་རོགས་ (lōrɔ̀ɔ̀ tro̱òrɔ̀ɔ̀) sm. བློ་རོགས་.

བློ་ལ་འགྲོ་ (lōla dro̱) sm. བློ་ལ་བབ་.

བློ་ལ་ངེས་ (lōla ŋe̱è) vi. to remember, to remain/ stay/ stick in the mind ¶ཁོང་གསུངས་ཚང་མ་བློ་ལ་ངེས་མ་སོང་ Everything he said didn't stick in my mind.

བློ་ལ་འཇུག (lōla ju̱ù) sm. བློ་ལ་འབབ་.

བློ་ལ་བདགས་ (lōla dāà) 1. very close (to a person). 2. vi. to share similar ideas, views, thoughts.

བློ་ལ་འཐད་ (lōla tɛ̀ɛ̀) sm. བློ་ལ་འབབ་.

བློ་ལ་འཐད་པོ་ (lōla tɛ̀ɛ̀bo) fondness, liking ¶འདི་ཁོང་གི་བློ་ལ་ཐད་པོ་བྱུང་སོང་ He liked this.

བློ་ལ་བསྔོགས་ (lōla ŋɔ̄ɔ̀) to keep in one's mind.

བློ་ལ་འབབ་ (lōla bə̱b) 1. vi. to be appealing/ attractive/ agreeable. 2. to approve/ like sth.

བློ་ལ་མེད་པ་ (lōla me̱èba) disliking, not to one's liking ¶རང་གི་བློ་ལ་མེད་པའི་ལས་ཀ་བྱ་རྒྱུ་མེད་ You shouldn't do sth. that you don't like. 2. not having/ keeping/ retaining in one's mind.

བློ་ལ་ཚུད་ (lōla tsüü) sm. བློ་ངེས་.

བློ་ལ་ཟིན་ (lōla si̱n) va. to learn by heart, to memorize.

བློ་ལ་ཡོད་པ་ (lōla yo̱òba) 1. having/ keeping in mind. 2. liking, caring for.

བློ་ལས་ (lōlɛ̀ɛ̀) worry, worrying.

བློ་ལོག (lō lɔ̀ɔ̀) sm. བློ་ལྡོག.

བློ་ཤས་ (lōshɛ̀ɛ̀) regret; vi.—བྱེད་.

བློ་ཤེད་ (lōsheè) 1. courageous, bold. 2. sm. སེམས་ཤུགས་.

བློ་གཤོགས་ཆེ་བ་ (lōshgɔ̀ɔ̀ cēwa) courageous, bold, broad-minded.

བློ་གཤོགས་ཆེན་པོ་ (lōshgɔ̀ɔ̀ cēmbo) sm. བློ་གཤོགས་ཆེ་བ་.

བློ་གཤོམ་ (lō shōm) va. to make a plan.

བློ་གཤོམ་གྲོས་ཕུད་ (lōshom tro̱òbüü) making a plan; va.—བྱེད་.

བློ་སེམས་ (lōsem) mind, thoughts, heart, feelings, sentiments; vi.—ཁེངས་ to be satisfied/ content; va.—འགུག to attract/ bring sb. to one's position/ view/ group.

བློ་སེམས་དཀར་བ་ (lōsem gārwa) sincere, pure, noble.

བློ་སེམས་རྒྱབ་འགལ་ (lōsem gyə̱mgɛɛ) thinking negative/ contrary thoughts or views; va.—བྱེད་.

བློ་སེམས་གཅིག་སྒྲིམ་ (lōsem jīgdrim) mental concentration.

བློ་སེམས་གཅིག་སྒྲིལ་ (lōsem jīgdrii) 1. sm. བློ་སེམས་གཅིག་སྒྲིམ་. 2. unity, unified.

བློ་སེམས་ཉིས་འགལ་ (lōsem ñīngɛɛ) having contradictions in one's mind/ thoughts.

བློ་སེམས་དོག་པོ་ (lōsem tɔ̱gbo) narrow-minded.

བློ་སེམས་རྩེ་གཅིག (lōsem dzējig) having a single outlook/ view/ thought.

བློ་གསར་བུ་ (lō sārbu) a new student/ pupil.

བློ་གསལ་ (lōsɛɛ) intelligent, smart; va.—འདོན་ to give advice.

བློ་གསལ་གླིང་ (lōsɛɛliŋ) Loseling College of Drepung Monastery.

བློ་གསལ་མིག་གསལ་ (lōsɛɛ mi̱gsɛɛ) sm. བློ་གསལ་.

བློ་གསལ་ལག་བདེ་ (lōsɛɛ la̱gde) intelligent and skillful/ dexterous.

བློ་གསོ་ (lō sō) va. to console ¶ཁོང་གི་ཨ་མ་ལགས་གྲོངས་འདུག་པས་ང་ཚོས་ཁོང་གི་བློ་གསོ་དགོས་ We had to console him because his mother died.

བློ་གསོད་ (lō sȫȫ) va. to say hurtful things.

བློ་བསྐྱལ་ཆེ་ (lō sɛ̄ɛ̄je) sm. བློ་གཤོགས་ཆེ་བ་.

བློ་བསྲུན་པ་ (lō sūmbə) peaceful, gentle (mind).

བློ་ལྷད་ (lōlɛ̀ɛ̀) evil/ negative thoughts.

བློ་ལྷད་དྲན་འཁྱུལ་ (lōlhɛ̀ɛ̀ tre̱ndrüü) a person who has evil thoughts and is treacherous.

བློ་ལྷིང་པོ་ (lō lhīŋbu) calm, peaceful.

བློ་ལྷོད་བག་ཕེབས་ (lōlhöö ba̱gpeè) carefree, calm, peaceful.

བློ་ལྷོད་ཤིག་ཤིག (lōlhöö shīgshiì) sm. བློ་ལྷོད་བག་ཕེབས་.

བློ་ལྷོད་གྲོད་པ་འཇོལ་ (lōlhöö dro̱òba jö̱ö) sm. བློ་ལྷོད་ཡིད་འཇོམས་.

བློ་ལྷོད་ཡིད་འཇོམས་ (lōlhöö yi̱ijom) vi. to be completely at ease/ relaxed/ untroubled.

བློ་ལྷོད་ལྷོད་ (lō lhȫȫlhöö) sm. བློ་ལྷིང་པོ་.

བློགས་ (lɔ̄ɔ̀) imp. of བློག.

བློང་ (lōŋ) vi. to be dazed, to have an unclear/ dull mind.

བློད་ (lȫȫ) imp. of བློད་.

བློན་ (lȫn) abbr. of བློན་པོ་.

བློན་ཁམས་ (lȫngam) place/ area/ realm governed by a minister.

བློན་རྒྱུད་ (lȫngyüü) descent line of ministers, descendents of ministers.

བློན་ཆེན་ (lȫnjen) sm. བློན་པོ་.

བློན་པོ་མགར་སྟོང་བཙན་ (lȫnbo ga̱r dōŋdzɛn) sm. མགར་སྟོང་བཙན་.

བློན་སྟོང་བཙན་ (lȫn dōŋdzɛn) abbr. of བློན་པོ་མགར་སྟོང་བཙན་.

བློན་པོ་ (lȫmbo) minister.

བློན་ཚང་ (lȫndzaŋ) a minister's household.

བློན་ཚན་ (lȫndzɛn) a minister.

བློན་ཟུར་ (lȫnsur) an ex-minister.

བློན་རབས་ (lȫnrəb) a succession/ line of ministers.

བློའི་བྱེད་པ་ (lȫ cɛ̱ɛ̀ba) functioning of the mind.

བློའི་ཡུལ་ལས་འདས་པ་ (lȫyüülɛ dɛ̱ɛ̀ba) sm. བློ་ཡུལ་ལས་འདས་པ་.

བློར་ངེས་ (lōŋeè) sm. བློ་ལ་ངེས་.

བློར་བབ་ (lōbəb) sm. བློར་བབས་.

བློར་བབས་ (lōbəb) sm. བློ་ལ་.

བློས་བཀལ་ (lō gɛ̄ɛ̄) p. of བློས་འགེལ་.

བློས་བཀལ་ཆོག་པ་ (lō gɛ̄ɛ̄ cɔ̄gba) reliable.

བློས་ཁེལ་ (lȫȫkēē) sm. བློ་ཁེལ་.

བློས་ཁེལ་པོ་ (lȫȫ kēēbo) trustworthy.

བློས་འགྱུར་ (lȫȫgyur) sm. བློས་བཏོད་.

བློས་འགན་བཏོད་ (lȫȫ ge̱nsöö) sm. འགན་བློས་བཏོད་.

བློས་འགེལ་ (lȫȫgee) trust, reliance, confidence; va. བློས་འགེལ་; —བྱེད་ to trust in, to have confidence ¶ངས་ཁོང་ལ་བློ་འགེལ་གྱི་ཡོད་ I trust him.

བློས་འགེལ་མི་ཐུབ་པ་ (lȫȫgee mi̱tubbə) unreliable, undependable.

བློས་འགེལ་མི་ཉན་པ་ (lȫȫgee mi̱ñɛmba) sm. བློས་འགེལ་མི་ཐུབ་པ་.

བློས་ལྗོངས་ (lȫȫjɔ̀ɔ̀) sm. བློས་འཇལ་.

བློས་འཆུན་ (lȫȫjün) arc. sm. ཁོང་དུ་ཆུད་.

བློས་འཇལ་ (lȫȫ jɛ̱ɛ) va. to be conceivable/ comprehensible.

བློས་རྗེན་འགེལ་ (lȫȫjen ge̱e) vi. to have complete trust in sb.

བློས་གདད་ (lȫȫ dɛ̀ɛ̀) sm. བློ་གདད་.

བློས་གཏོང་ (lȫȫ dōŋ) 1. va. to give up, to abandon, to relinquish, to sacrifice ¶ཁོས་ནང་མི་རྒྱུ་དངོས་ཚང་མ་བློས་བཏང་ནས་ཕྱིན་པ་རེད་ He abandoned his family and possessions and went away. ¶རང་གི་བདེ་བ་གཞན་དོན་དུ་བློས་བཏང་པ་རེད་ (They) sacrificed their own welfare for that of the others.

བློས་བཏང་ (lȫȫ dāŋ) p. of བློས་གཏོང་.

བློས་ཐུག་པོ་ (lȫȫ tūgbo) sm. བློ་ཐུག་པོ་.

བློས་ཐུབ་པ་ (lȫȫ tūbbə) trusted, reliable (friend) ¶ཁོང་འདི་གྲོགས་པོ་བློས་ཐུབ་པ་ཅིག་ཡིན་ He is a trusted friend of mine.

བློས་བྱིངས་འགེལ་ (lȫȫjiŋ ge̱e) va. to trust sb. fully.

བློས་བླངས་ (lȫȫlaŋ) voluntarily accepting; va.—བྱེད་.

བློས་བླངས་མིན་པའི་གན་རྒྱ་ (lȫȫlaŋ mi̱mbe ke̱ngya) shung. involuntary contract/ agreement.

བློས་བླངས་དམག (lȫȫlaŋ māà) voluntary army/ troops.

བློས་བླངས་རང་བཙུགས་དམག (lȫȫlaŋ ra̱ndzuù māà) sm. བློས་བླངས་དམག.

བློས་མི་འཁྱུད་ (lȫȫ mi̱gyüü) sm. བློས་མི་བཏོད་.

བློས་མི་འདུམ་པ་ (lȫȫ mi̱dumbə) exceeding one's

expectations ། འདི་འདྲ་བྱས་ན་ཕུགས་འབྲས་ངན་པ་བློས་མི་འདས་པ་ཡོང་གི་རེད་ If you do that a bad result exceeding all expectations will occur.

བློས་མི་བཟོད་ (lȫö̀ mi̲sö̲ö̲) to not risk or handle a responsibility.

བློས་བཟོད་ (lȫö̀ sö̲ö̲) (vb. + —) va. to risk, to handle a responsibility ། ཕྲུ་གུ་དེ་གཅིག་པོ་གཏོང་བློས་བཟོད་ཀྱི་མ་རེད་ I cannot risk sending the child alone. ། འགན་བློས་བཟོད་མིན་ (I) can't handle taking the responsibility.

བློས་ལོང་བ་བྱེད་ (lȫö̀ lo̲ŋwa ce̲è) to not have any regrets ། རྒྱལ་ཁབ་ཀྱི་དོན་དུ་ཤི་ནའང་བློས་ལོང་བ་བྱེད་ I would not have regrets even if I die for my country.

བློས་སད་ (lȫö̀ sɛ̄ɛ̀) va. to estimate/ test.

བློས་གསོ་ (lȫö̀ sō) sm. བློས་གསོ་.

བློས་གསོས་པོ་ (lȫö̀ sȫö̀bo) sm. བློ་བདེ་པོ་.

བློས་བསླངས་ (lȫö̀ lāŋ) 1. a three dimensional mandala. 2. three dimensional.

བྷ་ཡིའི་ (bha̲yi) term used for Tibetan Muslims.

བྷན་གོལ་ (bhēngol) Bengal.

བྷན་ཛེ་ (bhe̲ndze) coral and turquoise head ornaments worn by the woman of northern Tibet.

བྷེ་རེ་ཛལ་ (bhe̲redzɛɛ) Brazil.

བྷོ་ཊ་ (bho̲da) Tibet.

དབགས་ (ba̲à) sm. འབག.

དབང་ (wāŋ) 1. power, authority ། སྲིད་དབང་ Political power. ། དབང་འདེབས་ Planting (fields) by force. 2. va. to own; to rule, to exercise power over ། ས་ཆ་དེ་ཁོ་ཚོས་དབང་གི་རེད་ They rule that land 3. (usu.: vb. + — + existential verb) the right to do ། རང་གི་བསམ་ཚུལ་ཤོད་དབང་ཡོད་པ་མ་རེད་ (They) do not have the right to express their own opinion. 4. abbr. of དབང་པོ་. 5. because ། གློག་ཆས་འཛོམས་པོ་མེད་པའི་དབང་གིས་བཟོ་གྲྭ་དེའི་སྐྱེད་ཕར་ཐུབ་ཀྱི་མེད་པ་རེད་ Because the equipment of the factory is incomplete, production cannot go up. 6. religious initiation/ empowerment (the empowerment by a lama to engage in a religious practice).

དབང་བསྐུར་ (wāŋ gūr) 1. va. to give authority/ power, to entrust with authority. 2. va. to give a religious initiation.

དབང་ཁ་ལག་ཇུས་ (wāŋ kālaàjüǜ) controlling, dominating, ruling; va.—བྱེད་.

དབང་ཁོངས་ (wāŋgoŋ) under the power/ jurisdiction/ authority/ rule ། གླིང་ཕྲན་དེ་ང་ཚོའི་རྒྱལ་ཁབ་ཀྱིདབང་ཁོངས་རེད་ That island is under the authority of our country.

དབང་ཁྱད་ (wāŋgyɛɛ̀) differences in power/ authority.

དབང་ཁྲིད་ (wāŋtrii) a religious empowerment/ initiation.

དབང་མཁན་ (wāŋgɛn) owner.

དབང་གི་ལྷ་ (wāŋgi lhā) meditational deity.

དབང་གིས་ (wāŋgi) because, as a result of ། དུས་ཚོད་རྫོགས་པའི་དབང་གིས་ Because they ran out of time.

དབང་གྲགས་ (wāŋdraà) power and fame.

དབང་གྲགས་ཆེ་བའི་མི་སྣ་ (wāŋdraà cēwɛ mi̲na) prominent figure, bigwig, big shot.

དབང་གྲལ་ (wāŋdrɛɛ) those who have received a religious initiation; va.—ལ་ཚུད་ to be included among those who are initiated; va.—(དུ་) ཞུ་ to attend an initiation.

དབང་རྒྱལ་ (wāŋgyɛɛ) name of a person.

དབང་རྒྱལ་གྲལ་རིམ་ (wāŋgyɛɛ tre̲e̲rim) sm. དབང་སྒྱུར་གྲལ་རིམ་.

དབང་སྒ་ (wāŋga) a type of saddle.

དབང་སྒྱུར་ (wāŋgyur) power, domination, rule; va.—བྱེད་ to dominate, to rule ། དབྱིན་ཇིའི་དབང་སྒྱུར་འོག Under British rule. ། དབྱིན་ཇི་ཚོས་ལོ་མང་རིང་ཧོང་ཀོང་ལ་དབང་སྒྱུར་བྱས་པ་རེད་ The English ruled Hong Kong for many years.

དབང་སྒྱུར་གོ་གནས་ (wāŋgyur ko̲nɛɛ̀) dominant position, ruling status/ class.

དབང་སྒྱུར་གྲལ་རིམ་ (wāŋgyur tre̲e̲rim) ruling class.

དབང་སྒྱུར་བ་ (wāŋgyurwa) ruler, the one in authority.

དབང་སྒྱུར་བྱེད་མཁན་ (wāŋgyur ce̲èñɛn) sm. དབང་སྒྱུར་བ་.

དབང་སྒྱུར་ཚོགས་ཁག (wāŋgyur tsɔ̄ɔ̀gaà) ruling clique.

དབང་བསྒྱུར་ (wāŋ gyu̲r) sm. དབང་སྒྱུར་.

དབང་ལྔ་ (wāŋŋa) sm. དབང་པོ་ལྔ་.

དབང་ལྔའི་ཚན་ཁག (wāŋŋɛ tsɛ̄ngaà) otolaryngological department.

དབང་སྔོན་ (wāŋŋön) sapphire.

དབང་ཅན་ (wāŋjɛn) powerful, mighty.

དབང་བཅོལ་ (wāŋjöö) empowering, authorizing.

དབང་ཆ་ (wāŋja) 1. power, authority ། ཆབ་སྲིད་ཀྱི་དབང་ཆ་ Political power. 2. rights ། གཏམ་བརྗོད་ཀྱི་དབང་ཆ་ The right of (free) speech.

དབང་ཆ་སྐྱུར་ (wāŋja gyūr) va. to relinquish/ give up power or authority.

དབང་ཆ་སྒེར་གཅོད་སྲིད་གཞུང་ (wāŋja ge̲rjöö sīīshuŋ) autocracy, despotic government, dictatorship.

དབང་ཆ་གཅིག་བདག (wāŋja jīgda̲à) monopolizing power.

དབང་ཆ་གཅིག་སྡུད་ (wāŋja jīdüü) centralization of authority/ power, monopolization of power/ authority.

དབང་ཆ་གཅིག་འཛིན་ (wāŋja jīgdzin) monopolizing power/ authority; va.—བྱེད་.

དབང་ཆ་འཕྲོག་རེས་ (wāŋja trɔ̄ɔ̀reè) seizing power back and forth; va.—བྱེད་.

དབང་ཆ་ཚང་མ་ (wāŋja tsāŋma) full/ complete power or authority.

དབང་ཆ་ཚང་མ་ཡོད་པའི་སྐུ་ཚབ་ (wāŋja tsāŋma yö̲ö̲bɛ gūdzəb) plenipotentiary.

དབང་ཆ་འཛིན་ (wāŋja dzi̲n) 1. va. to seize power. 2. va. to hold power/ authority.

དབང་ཆ་གཤམ་སྤྲོད་ (wāŋja shāmdröö) transfer of authority to lower levels.

དབང་ཆུ་ (wāŋju) blessed water given during initiations.

དབང་ཆེན་ (wāŋjen) 1. powerful. 2. person's name. 3. a great religious initiation.

དབང་ཆེན་དབང་མེད་ (wāŋjen wāŋmeè) using one's power to force sb. to do sth., bullying; va.—གཏོང་ ། ཁོས་ང་ལ་དབང་ཆེན་དབང་མེད་བཏང་ནས་དངུལ་འཕྲོག་སོང་ He bullied me and stole my money.

དབང་གདད་ (wāŋdɛɛ̀) sm. དབང་ཤྲད་.

དབང་རྟགས་ (wāŋdaà) a sign of power.

དབང་རྟུལ་ (wāŋdüü) sm. དབང་པོ་རྟུལ་པོ་.

དབང་རྟེན་ (wāŋden) 1. organs of the body. 2. an offering of money/ gift given when getting an initiation.

དབང་རྟེན་ལྔ་ (wāŋden ŋā) the five elements: sky, earth, water, fire, air.

དབང་བརྟེན་གཞན་བརྙས་ (wāŋden she̲nñɛɛ̀) using one's power to bully or abuse others; va.—བྱེད་.

དབང་ཐག་གཅོད་ (wāŋtaà jȫö̀) va. to make a decision based on power ། གནད་དོན་དེ་ཚོགས་འདུའི་སྲིད་འཛིན་གྱིས་དབང་ཐག་བཅད་འདུག The president decided that issue at the meeting based on his power.

དབང་ཐང་ (wāŋdaŋ) 1. power; vi.—ཆག to lose power. 2. sm. ཁམས་, 4.

དབང་ཐང་མེ་ཏོག (wāŋdaŋ me̲doò) name of a floral design on Tibetan rugs.

དབང་ཐང་ལ་བ་བསྒྲོལ་ཀྱང་བསོད་ནམས་ལ་བཞོན་སྐམ་པ་ (wāŋdaŋla pa̲ gȫö̀gyaŋ sȫö̀namla sho̲n gāmba) even though sb. gets a good position though power, it will turn out badly due to his bad karma/ merit [Lit. even though one gets a cow through power, it will not produce milk due to bad karma/ merit].

དབང་ཐུལ་ (wāŋdüü) calm/ peaceful manner.

དབང་ཐོབ་ (wāŋtob) vi. to obtain/ receive power or

authority from a superior ¶ གོང་རིམ་ནས་དབང་ཐོབ་པ་ལྟར་ང་ཚོའི་ལས་ཁངས་ནས་ཐག་བཅད་པ་ཡིན་ In accordance with receiving the authority from higher authorities, our office decided it. 2. vi. to receive a religious initiation.

དབང་དུ་འགྱུར་ (wāŋdu gyur) vi. to become dominated/ ruled by sb. ¶ ཡུལ་དེ་ཕྱི་རྒྱལ་བའི་དབང་དུ་འགྱུར་བ་རེད་ That area came under the rule of foreigners.

དབང་དུ་འགྲོ་ (wāŋdu dro) vi. to be influenced by sb.'s power ¶ གྲོས་ཆོད་དེ་དམངས་གཙོ་ཏང་གི་དབང་དུ་ཕྱིན་བཞག That resolution was influenced by the Democratic Party.

དབང་དུ་བསྒྱུར་ (wāŋdu gyur) va. to rule.

དབང་དུ་བཏང་ན་ (wāŋdu dāŋna) supposing, assuming, hypothetically ¶ ཁོ་ཚོར་བསམ་ཚུལ་མི་འདྲ་བ་ཞིག་ཡོད་པའི་དབང་དུ་བཏང་ན་ If (we) assume they have a different opinion.

དབང་དུ་གཏོང་ (wāŋdu dōŋ) sm. དབང་དུ་བཏང་ན་.

དབང་དུ་འདུ་ (wāŋdu du) sm. དབང་དུ་སྡུད་.

དབང་དུ་འདུས་ (wāŋdu düü) p. of དབང་དུ་འདུ་.

དབང་དུ་སྡུད་ (wāŋdu düü) va. to bring under control/ rule, to conquer ¶ ཁོ་ཚོས་ཡ་གླིང་དབང་དུ་སྡུད་པ་རེད་ They brought Asia under their rule.

དབང་དུ་བསྡུས་ (wāŋdu düü) p. of དབང་དུ་སྡུད་.

དབང་དུ་ཕྱིན་ (wāŋdu cīn) p. of དབང་དུ་འགྲོ་.

དབང་དུ་བྱེད་ (wāŋdu ceè) 1. va. to govern/ rule. 2. sm. དབང་དུ་གཏོང་.

དབང་དུ་མི་འགྲོ་བ་ (wāŋdu mindrowa) shung. not being influenced ¶ འགལ་རྐྱེན་གྱི་དབང་དུ་མི་འགྲོ་བ་བྱ་དགོས་ One should act so that one is not influenced by obstacles.

དབང་དུ་འཛིན་ (wāŋdu dzin) sm. དབང་འཛིན་.

དབང་དོན་ (wāŋdön) the five senses: sight, sound, taste, touch, smell.

དབང་བདག (wāŋdaà) shung. taking possession of ¶ ལུག་ཁག་གཅིག་གི་རིལ་མ་བཅས་གཞིས་ནས་དབང་བདག་དང་ The estate took possession of the dung of one sheep herd.

དབང་མདོག (wāŋdɔ̀ɔ) red color.

དབང་འདུས་ (wāŋdüü) 1. abbr. of དབང་དུ་འདུས་ 2. a man's name.

དབང་འདུས་ཕོ་བྲང་ (wāŋdüü pōdraŋ) a place in Bhutan.

དབང་ལྡན་ (wāŋdɛn) 1. sm. དབང་ཅན་. 2. a man's name.

དབང་སྡུད་ (wāŋdüü) centralization of authority.

དབང་སྡུད་རིང་ལུགས་ (wāŋdüü riŋluù) centralism.

དབང་སྒྲིམ་ (wāŋdem) control, domination, rule; va.—བྱེད་.

དབང་སྒྲིམ་རིང་ལུགས་ (wāŋdem riŋluù) totalitarianism.

དབང་གནང་ (wāŋ nāŋ) 1. va. to give authorization/ power. 2. va. to rule. 3. va. to give religious initiation.

དབང་གནོན་ (wāŋnön) sm. དབང་ཡོད་ཤོད་.

དབང་རྣོན་ (wāŋnön) clever, intelligent, brainy.

དབང་པོ་ (wāŋbo) 1. the senses. 2. the chief, the supreme.

དབང་པོ་སྐྱོན་ཅན་ (wāŋbo gyōnjɛn) disabled, crippled, handicapped.

དབང་པོ་སྐྱོན་ཅན་གྱི་མཉམ་འབྲེལ་ཚོགས་པ་ (wāŋbo gyōnjɛngi ñamdree) Association for the Disabled/ Handicapped.

དབང་པོ་ལྔ་ (wāŋbo ŋā) 1. the five senses. 2. the material elements producing the senses: eyes, ears, nose, tongue, body.

དབང་པོ་ཉམས་པ་ (wāŋbo ñamba) old, aged.

དབང་པོ་རྟུལ་པོ་ (wāŋbo dǖübo) dull, stupid.

དབང་པོ་དྲུག (wāŋbo truù) the six sense organs: eyes, ears, nose, tongue, body and the mind.

དབང་པོ་རྣོ་པོ་ (wāŋbo nōbo) intelligent, smart, sharp.

དབང་པོ་མ་ཚང་བ་ (wāŋbo madzaŋba) not having all the དབང་པོ་.

དབང་པོ་ཡར་སྐྱེས་ (wāŋbo yargyeè) the process of growing up.

དབང་པོ་ལག་པ་ (wāŋbo lagba) gymnadenia conopsea. 2. anise.

དབང་པོ་ཤོར་བ་ (wāŋbo shɔ̄ɔwa) defective organs.

དབང་པོའི་སྒོ་ (wāŋbö go) sm. དབང་པོ་ལྔ་.

དབང་པོར་གཅོད་བྲེགས་ (wāŋbor jȫȍdreg) shung. corporal punishment.

དབང་སྤྲོད་ (wāŋ drȫȍ) va. to empower, to turn over power/ authority.

དབང་ཕྱུག (wāŋjuù) 1. prosperity. 2. name of a deity. 3. fire-ox year. 4. person's name.

དབང་ཕྱོགས་ (wāŋjɔ̀ɔ) the days between the 16th and the 30th of the Tibetan month.

དབང་བའི་ལམ་ལུགས་ (wāŋwɛ lamluù) system of ownership.

དབང་བར་འགྱུར་ (wāŋwar gyur) sm. དབང་དུ་འགྱུར་.

དབང་བྱེད་ (wāŋjeè) sm. དབང་བསྒྱུར་.

དབང་བྱུས་ (wāŋjüü) the right to interfere ¶ ཕྱི་རྒྱལ་བ་ཚོར་ང་ཚོའི་ནང་སྲིད་སྐོར་ལ་དབང་བྱུས་མེད་པ་རེད་ The foreigners do not have the right to interfere in our internal affairs.

དབང་མང་ཚང་གི་དོན་མི་འགྲུབ་ (wāŋ mandzāŋgi tön midrub) too many cooks spoil the broth [Lit. (if there are) many with power the goal can't be achieved].

དབང་མེད་ (wāŋmeè) powerless, without control/ choice/ freedom ¶ མིག་ཆུ་དབང་མེད་དུ་ཤོར་བའི་ལོ་རྒྱུས་སྐྱོ་པོ་ A sad story which makes one shed tears uncontrollably. ¶ མིང་རྟགས་དབང་མེད་དུ་འགོད་བཅུག་པ་རེད་ (They) were made to sign without being given a choice.

དབང་མེད་རྗེས་འབྲང་པ་ (wāŋmeè jeèdraŋba) a person coerced to follow or join sth.

དབང་མེད་གཞན་འབྲང་པ་ (wāŋmeè shendraŋba) sm. དབང་མེད་རྗེས་འབྲང་པ་.

དབང་མེད་སྲིད་གཞུང་ (wāŋmeè sīisuŋ) puppet government/ regime.

དབང་མོ་ (wāŋmo) 1. woman's name.

དབང་བཙན་ (wāŋdzɛn) autocracy, absolute rule.

དབང་བཙན་པོ་ (wāŋ dzɛ̄nbo) autocratic, dictatorial.

དབང་རྩ་ (wāŋdza) nerves; vi.—ཁྲུག; —ཉམས་ to have a nervous breakdown.

དབང་རྩ་ལྟེ་བའི་སྡེ་ཁོངས་ (wāŋdza dēwɛ degoŋ) central nervous system.

དབང་རྩའི་ལྟེ་གནད་ (wāŋdzɛ dēnɛɛ̀) nerve center.

དབང་རྩའི་ནད་ (wāŋdzɛ nɛɛ̀) neurosis, neuropathy.

དབང་རྩའི་སྣེ་མོ་ (wāŋdzɛ nēmo) nerve endings.

དབང་རྩའི་ཕྲ་ཕུང་ (wāŋdzɛ trābuŋ) neuron.

དབང་རྩའི་མ་ལག (wāŋdzɛ malaà) nervous system.

དབང་ཚད་ (wāŋdzɛɛ̀) limit or scope of authority/ power, jurisdiction.

དབང་ཚོར་ (wāŋdzɔr) senses of the body.

དབང་མཚམས་ (wāŋdzam) sm. དབང་ཚད་.

དབང་འཛིན་ (wāŋdzin) control, rule, authority, in power; va.—བྱེད་ to be in control, to rule, to be in power, to wield authority over ¶ དབང་འཛིན་སྲིད་གཞུང་ The government in power.

དབང་འཛིན་མཁན་ (wāŋdzinñɛn) sm. དབང་འཛིན་པ་.

དབང་འཛིན་པ་ (wāŋdzinbə) person in authority/ power.

དབང་འཛིན་མི་སྣ་ (wāŋdzin mina) people in power/ authority.

དབང་འཛིན་ལས་ཁུངས་ (wāŋdzin lɛɛ̀guŋ) organs of power, offices in power.

དབང་འཛིན་ལོག་སྤྱོད་ (wāŋdzin lɔgjöö) reactionaries in power.

དབང་འཛིན་ཤོག་ཁག (wāŋdzin shɔ̄ɔgaà) clique that is in power, the people in power/ authority.

དབང་འཛིན་སྲིད་སྐྱོང་ (wāŋdzin sīigyoŋ) regent in power, ruling regent.

དབང་འཛུལ་ (wāŋ dzüü) sm. བཙན་འཛུལ་.

དབང་ཞུ་ (wāŋ shu) va. to ask for a religious initiation, to receive a religious initiation.

དབང་བཞི་ (wāŋshi) four types of initiations.

དབང་ཟ་ (wāŋ sa) va. to illegally use power, to use

power in unauthorized ways.

དབང་འོག་ཏུ་ (wāŋ wɔgdu) under the power/ control of.

དབང་ཡོད་ (wāŋyöö) 1. bullying; va.—གཏོང་; —ཤོད་ to bully. 2. rape; va.—གཏོང་ to rape.

དབང་ཡོད་འཁྱེར་ (wāŋyöö kyēr) vi. to let oneself be bullied.

དབང་ཡོད་ཤེད་འཁྱེར་ (wāŋyöö shēèkyer) abuse of power.

དབང་ཡོད་ཤོད་ (wāŋyöö shöö) va. to bully.

དབང་ཡོན་ (wāŋyön) a gift/ offering made to the lama who gives an initiation.

དབང་རིས་ (wāŋrii) 1. sphere of influence, jurisdiction. 2. one's possessions/ wealth.

དབང་ལ་འགྲོ་ (wāŋdu dro) sm. དབང་དུ་འགྲོ་.

དབང་ལག་ (wāŋlaà) abbr. of དབང་པོ་ལག་པ་.

དབང་ལུང་ (wāŋluŋ) the empowerment by a lama to engage in a religious practice and ལུང་.

དབང་ལུང་ཁྲིད་གསུམ་ (wāŋluŋ trii sūm) the three: དབང་, ལུང་ and explanation of a teaching.

དབང་ལེན་ (wāŋlen) shung. taking sth. by force; va.—བྱེད་.

དབང་ཤུགས་ (wāŋshuù) power, force.

དབང་ཤུགས་ཀྱིས་འཁྱེར་ (wāŋshuùgi kyēr) va. to be influenced by sb.'s power.

དབང་ཤུགས་ཆེན་པོ་ (wāŋshuù cēmbo) great force/ power.

དབང་ཤུལ་འཛིན་ (wāŋshu dzin) va. to succeed to sb.'s power/ authority.

དབང་ཤེད་ (wāŋsheè) force, power, influence; va.—བྱེད་ to use force/ power/ influence; —ཤོར་ to lose one's power.

དབང་ཤེད་ཀྱི་ངལ་རྩོལ་ (wāŋsheègi ŋɛɛdzöö) forced labor.

དབང་ཤེད་བསྙོན་ཧམ་ (wāŋsheè ñönham) bullying/ forcing without reason or justification.

དབང་ཤེད་བཙན་གདམ་ (wāŋsheè dzēndam) abusive language used by people in power.

དབང་བཤད་ (wāŋshɛɛ̀) religious initiations and explanations.

དབན་ལུང་ (bēnluŋ) Bandung.

དབབ་ (bāb) f. of འབེབས་.

དབའ་ (bā) 1. sm. ཐ་རླབས་. 2. sm. ལགས་སོ་.

དབའ་ཀློང་ (bāloŋ) sm. དབའ་རླབས་.

དབའ་རླབས་ (bāləb) sm. དབའ་རླབས་.

དབའ་སི་ (bāsi) ch. gas cylinder.

དབར་ (wār) sm. བར་.

དབར་མཆན་ (wārjɛn) notes between the lines.

དབལ་ (wɛɛ̄) 1. top, peak, summit. 2. heat wave.

དབལ་ལྷན་ (wēndɛn) a Tibetan medical knife with three points.

དབལ་ལྷན་ཤ་ཁབ་ (wēndɛn shāgəb) Tibetan medical needle used to stitch wounds.

དབལ་ཚ་བ་ (wɛɛ̄ tsāwa) hot, heat.

དབུ་ (ū) 1. head (h.). 2. leader, headman; va.—གནང་; — མཛད་ to head/ lead. 3. start, beginning (h.); va.—འཛུགས་ to start/ begin.

དབུ་ཀླད་ (ūlɛɛ̀) h. of ཀླད་པ་.

དབུ་དཀར་ (ūgar) white hair (h.).

དབུ་རྒྱང་རོ་གསུམ་ (ūgyaŋ rosum) the three channels of energy according to Tibetan medicine: central, left and right channels.

དབུ་སྐུ་གནང་ (ūgu nāŋ) va. to start a prayer.

དབུ་སྐྲས་གཙུག་ཕུད་ (ūgyeè dzūgbüü) hair cutting ceremony when a boy becomes a monk.

དབུ་སྐོར་ (ūgɔɔ) 1. entertaining, amusing (h.); va.—ཞུ་ to entertain/ amuse. 2. deceiving, cheating; va.—ཞུ་ to deceive/ cheat.

དབུ་སྐོར་གཡོ་ཞུས་ (ūgɔɔ yōshüü) lying, cheating, deceiving, tricking.

དབུ་སྐྲ་ (ūdra) h. of སྐྲ་.

དབུ་བསྐྱིངས་ (ūgyiŋ) h. of སྐྲ་བསྐྱིངས་.

དབུ་ཁེབས་ (ūgeb) h. of མགོ་ཁེབས་.

དབུ་འཁོར་ (ūŋgɔɔ) h. of མགོ་འཁོར་.

དབུ་འཁོར་གཡོ་ཞུ་ (ūŋgɔɔ yōshu) sm. དབུ་འཁོར་.

དབུ་འཁོར་ཞུ་མཁན་ (ūŋgɔɔ shuñɛn) sb. who accompanies aristocrats or rich people and helps them pass the time by amusing them with stories or playing games with them, etc.

དབུ་འཁྲིད་ (ū trii) h. of མགོ་འཁྲིད་.

དབུ་གུར་ (ūgur) h. of གུར་.

དབུ་གྲལ་ (ūtrɛɛ) h. of གྲལ་འགོ་.

དབུ་རྒྱན་ (ūgyɛn) h. of མགོ་རྒྱན་.

དབུ་རྒྱུད་ (ūgyüü) h. of མགོ་རྒྱུད་.

དབུ་སྒྲུར་སྒྲུར་གནང་ (ū guuguu nāŋ) h. of མགོ་སྒྲུར་སྒྲུར་.

དབུ་སྔས་ (ūŋɛɛ̀) h. of སྔས་མགོ་.

དབུ་ཅན་ (ūjɛn) the type of Tibetan script used in printed matter (as in this book).

དབུ་ལྕང་ (ūjaŋ) h. of ལྕང་ལོ་.

དབུ་ལྕོག (ūjɔɔ) 1. h. of ཐོ་ལྕོག. 2. h. of དར་ལྕོག.

དབུ་ལྕོག་ཁའུ་ (ūjɔɔ kawu) h. of ཐོ་ལྕོག་ཁའུ་.

དབུ་ལྕོག་ལྕོག (ū jɔgjɔɔ) va. nodding; va.—བྱེད་.

དབུ་ཆུང་ (ūjaŋ) title for craftsmen in tt.

དབུ་ཆེན་ (ūjen) 1. sm. དབུ་ཅན་. 2. chief, head ། ནད་གཡོག་དབུ་ཆེན་ Head nurse. 3. the senior monk (དབུ་མཛད་) who leads prayer assemblies in prayers. 4. title of master craftsman ། ལྷ་བྲིས་པ་དབུ་ཆེན་ A master icon painter.

དབུ་ཆེན་མོ་བ་ (ū cēmmowa) see. དབུ་ཆེན་, 3.

དབུ་ཆོས་ (ūjöö) abbr. of དབུ་མཛད་ and དགེ་སློས་.

དབུ་མཆན་ (ūjɛn) h. of མགོ་མཆན་.

དབུ་འཆིང་ (ūnjiŋ) h. of ལ་ཐོད་.

དབུ་འཇོག (ūnjɔɔ) h. of མགོ་འཇོག.

དབུ་རྗེ་ (ūje) titles for high lamas.

དབུ་ཉུང་གི་རྡོ་རིང་ (ūñuŋgi doriŋ) name of a stele in front of the Tsuglagang.

དབུ་ཉེས་ཕོག (ūñeè pɔ̄ɔ) 1. h. of ཉེས་པ་ཕོག. 2. vi. to get demoted.

དབུ་སྙུང་ (ūñuŋ) 1. h. of མགོ་སྙུང་. 2. oath, promise; va.—བཞེས་ to swear an oath; va.—མཆོད་ to break an oath/ promise.

དབུ་བརྙེས་ (ū ñēè) vi. to be founded, to come into existence/ being (h.) ། རྒྱལ་ཁབ་དབུ་བརྙེས་ནས་ལོ་བརྒྱ་ལྷག་ཕྱིན་པ་རེད་ More than a hundred years have passed since the nation was founded.

དབུ་གཏུག (ūduù) h. དཔྱལ་གཏུག.

དབུ་སྟོན་ (ūdön) banquet given when starting a religious project.

དབུ་ཐུག (ūduù) touching foreheads as a greeting; va.—བྱེད་.

དབུ་ཐོད་ (ūdöö) h. of ཀ་ལི་.

དབུ་ཐོམ་ (ū tōm) h. of མགོ་ཐོམ་.

དབུ་འཐོམས་ (ū tōm) h. of མགོ་འཐོམས་.

དབུ་གདུགས་ (ūduù) h. of ཉི་གདུགས་.

དབུ་འདོམ་ (ū dom) h. of མགོ་འདོམ་.

དབུ་བརྡ་ (ūda) a head signal/ sign (made by moving the head, nodding, etc.); va.—གཏོང་.

དབུ་ནན་ (ūnɛn) urging, insisting (h.) ། འགན་དབང་ལེན་དགོས་དབུ་ནན་གནང་ (He) urged that (he) accept the power and responsibility.

དབུ་གནས་ (ūnɛɛ̀) h. of གོ་གནས་.

དབུ་མནའ་ (ūna) h. of མནའ་.

དབུ་མནའ་རྒྱས་དབྱུད་ (ūnɛè gyɛɛ̀jɛɛ̀) h. of མནའ་སྐྱེལ་.

དབུ་སྣ་ཁྲིད་ (ūna trii) h. of སྣ་ཁྲིད་.

དབུ་སྣ་འདྲེན་ (ūna dren) h. of མནའ་འདྲེན་.

དབུ་སྣུམ་ (ūnum) h. of སྐྲ་སྣུམ་.

དབུ་པཙ་ (übɛn) shung. h. of པཙ་ཞུ་.

དབུ་དཔངས་དབེན་ (übaŋ wēn) sm. དབུ་འཕངས་.

དབུ་དཔྱལ་ (üdrɛɛ) h. of དཔྱལ་བ་.

དབུ་སྤྱི་ (üji) abbr. of དབུ་མཛད་དང་སྤྱི་སོ་.

དབུ་ཕོག་ཞབས་ཕོག (ū pɔ̄ɔ shəb pɔ̄ɔ) doing or saying sth. that offends one's leaders or superiors; va.—གཏོང་.

དབུ་ཕྲུག (üdruù) h. of ཐོ་ཕྲུག.

དབུ་ཕྲེང་ (üdreŋ) a string of water bubbles.

དབུ་འཕང་ (üpaŋ) h. of མགོ་འཕང་.

དབུ་བ་ (üwa) h. of ལྦུ་བ་.

དབུ་བྱིངས་ (ūjiŋ) 1. abbr. master craftsman and chief workers. 2. abbr. of དབུ་མཛད་ and ordinary monks.

དབུ་བླ་ (ūla) religious teacher, guru (h.).

དབུ་བྱེད་ (ūjeè) officer, leader, head, chief (h.).

དབུ་འབྱེད་ (ūjeè) h. of སྒོ་འབྱེད་.

དབུ་འབྱེད་རྟེན་འབྲེལ་ (ūjeè dēndree) inaugural ceremony (h.).

དབུ་མ་ (ūmə) 1. middle. 2. the Madhyamika school of Buddhism.

དབུ་མ་པ་ (ūməbə) a follower of the Madhyamika school.

དབུ་མའི་ལྟ་བ་ (ūmɛ dāwa) the idea of the middle way; the centrist view.

དབུ་མའི་ལམ་ (ūmɛ lam) the middle path.

དབུ་མེད་ (ūmeè) a type of Tibetan script that is intermediate between cursive and printed.

དབུ་རྨོག (ūmog) 1. h. མགོ་རྨོག. 2. sm. དབུ་འཕང་.

དབུ་དམར་པོ་ (ū māābo) h. of མགོ་དམར་པོ་.

དབུ་གཙོ་ (ūdzo) 1. top, peak. 2. the main leader.

དབུ་རྩེ་ (ūdze) top, peak (of a hill, mountain).

དབུ་རྩེའི་བྱ་འདབ་ (ūdzee cədəb) roof of a temple/ house/ palace.

དབུ་རྫོམ་ (ūdzom) h. of འགོ་རྫོམ་.

དབུ་རྫོམ་མཁན་ (ūdzomñɛn) h. of འགོ་རྫོམ་མཁན་.

དབུ་བཙུགས་ (ūdzuù) h. of འགོ་འཛུགས་.

དབུ་ཚད་ (ūdzɛɛ̀) abbr. of དབུ་མ་ and ཚད་མ་.

དབུ་ཚུགས་ (ūdzuù) h. of འགོ་ཚུགས་.

དབུ་ཚོགས་མཐུག་པོ་ (ūdzɔɔ̀ tūgbu) h. of སྐྲ་ཚོགས་མཐུག་པོ་.

དབུ་མཚམས་ (ūndzam) h. of སྐྲ་མཚམས་.

དབུ་འཚོས་པོ་ (ū tsȫȫbo) h. of མགོ་འཚོས་པོ་.

དབུ་མཛད་ (ūmdzɛɛ̀) 1. monk official who leads the prayer assembly sessions. 2. sm. དབུ་འཛིན་.

དབུ་འཛིན་ (ūndzin) leading officer.

དབུ་འཛུགས་ (ū dzuù) h. འགོ་འཛུགས་.

དབུ་ཛི་ (ūdzi) nanny, babysitter (h.).

དབུ་ཞུར་ (ūshur) bald head.

དབུ་ཞྭ་ (ūsha) h. of ཞྭ་མོ་.

དབུ་ཞྭ་ཏྭ་ཞྭ་ (ūsha dāsha) a type of hat worn by lamas and monk officials when riding.

དབུ་ཞྭ་པགས་ཞྭ་ (ūsha bāgsha) leather hat.

དབུ་ཞྭ་ཚེ་རིང་དཀྱིལ་འཁོར་ (ūsha tsēriŋ gyīŋgɔɔ) a type of ladies brocade hat with two flaps.

དབུ་གཞུག (ū shuù) 1. h. of སྐྲ་གཞུག 2. h. of མགོ་མཇུག.

དབུ་བཞུགས་ (ūshuù) chairman, head (h.).

དབུ་བཞུགས་སྐུ་ཚབ་ (ūshuù gūdzəb) the head delegate/ representative.

དབུ་བཞུགས་ཁྲིམས་དཔོན་ (ūshuù trimbön) chief judge.

དབུ་བཞུགས་བློན་ཆེན་ (ūshuù lönjen) chief minister, senior ranking minister, prime minister.

དབུ་འོག (ūwɔɔ̀) the rank below the head/ chief/ leader.

དབུ་འོག་དཔུང་འདེགས་ (ūwɔɔ̀ būŋdeg) the main supporters/ helpers of the head/ chief/ leader.

དབུ་ཡ་ (ūya) h. of ཡ་མ་.

དབུ་ཡིག (ūyii) the main or head entry in a dictionary.

དབུ་ཡུ་ (ūyu) hornless cattle.

དབུ་གཡང་ (ūyaŋ) h. of མགོ་གཡིང་.

དབུ་གཡབ་ (ūyəb) canopy.

དབུ་གཡིང་ (ūyeŋ) h. མགོ་གཡིང་.

དབུ་གཡོར་འཁྲུགས་ཟིང་ (ūyɔɔ trūgsiŋ) sm. དབུ་གཡོར་འཁྲུགས་སློང་.

དབུ་གཡོར་འཁྲུགས་སློང་ (ūyɔɔ trūgloŋ) the civil war that occurred between the two sons of Langdarma.

དབུ་རིལ་ (ūrii) h. of མགོ་རིལ་.

དབུ་རུ་ (ūru) central Tibet.

དབུ་རུ་སྟོད་ (ūru dȫȍ) the eastern part of central Tibet in the upper Lhasa river area.

དབུ་རུ་ཤོད་ཆེན་ (ūru shȫȍjen) Central Tibet around Lhasa.

དབུ་རེག (ūreg) h. of མགོ་རིལ་.

དབུ་ལོ་ (ūlo) h. of སྐྲ་.

དབུ་ཤད་ (ūshɛɛ̀) h. of རྒྱུག་ཤད་.

དབུ་ཤུབ་ (ūshub) h. of སྐྲ་ཤུབས་.

དབུ་ཤོག (ūshoò) first page of a book (h.).

དབུ་ཤོག་མཐའ་གཤམ་ (ūshoò tāsham) shung. the top, edge and the bottom (of a document).

དབུ་ཤོག་ནང་མ་ (ūshoò naŋma) title page of a text (h.).

དབུ་བསིལ་ (ūsii) h. of སྐྲ་འཁྲུད་.

དབུག (ūù) f. of འདབུགས་.

དབུགས་ (ūù) 1. breathing, respiration; air; va.—གཏོང་ to breathe; va.—རྔུབ་; —འཐེན་ to breathe in, to inhale; vi.— ཧལ་; —འཁུན་ to be short of breath, to pant. 2. slang. money.

དབུགས་བཀང་ (ūùgaŋ) aerated.

དབུགས་སྐྱེས་ (ūùgyeè) a thirty day month.

དབུགས་སྐྱོ་པོ་ (ūù gyōbo) weak, frail །ཁོ་རྒྱུན་རིང་ན་ཙང་དབུགས་སྐྱོ་པོ་ཆགས་བཞག Because he was sick for a long time, he became weak.

དབུགས་ཁ་འཇགས་ (ūù kā jaà) vi. to stop panting after taking a rest.

དབུགས་ཁྲག (ūùdraà) breath and blood.

དབུགས་ཁྲག་གཉིས་ཞན་ (ūùdraà ñīishɛn) weak, in poor physical shape [Lit. weak in blood and breathing].

དབུགས་འཁར་ (ūù kār) vi. to have difficulty in breathing because of blockage in one's breathing passage.

དབུགས་འཁུན་ (ūù kūn) vi. to pant (usu. accompanying dying).

དབུགས་འགག (ūù gaà) choking, suffocating; va.—གཏོང་ to choke/ suffocate sb.; vi.—ཐེབས་ to suffocate/ choke.

དབུགས་འགྲོ (ūù dro) sm. དབུ་ཆད་.

དབུགས་གོད་ (ūù gȫȍ) vi. to be gasping/ panting.

དབུགས་ཕྱང་ (ūùgaŋ) balloon.

དབུགས་སྐང་ (ūùgaŋ) the first half of a month.

དབུགས་སྒོ་ (ūùgo) 1. windpipe. 2. air vent, air hole, air passage.

དབུགས་སྒོམ་ (ūù gom) va. to hold one's breath.

དབུགས་བརྒྱངས་ (ūù gyaŋ) vi. to be short of breath due to anger.

དབུགས་ངར་ (ūù ŋar) vi. to be breathing hand due to anger.

དབུགས་ངལ་གསོ་ (ūù ŋɛɛso) va. to relax/ slow down one's heavy breathing.

དབུགས་རྔུབ་ (ūùŋub) breathing in and out, exhaling and inhaling; va.—བྱེད་; —གཏོང་.

དབུགས་སྔུར་ (ūùŋur) snoring; vi.—རྒྱག.

དབུགས་ཆ་ (ūgja) 1. the period in between breathing. 2. the second hand of a watch.

དབུགས་ཆགས་ (ūgjaà) all things that breathe, living beings.

དབུགས་ཆད་ (ūù cɛɛ̀) vi. to die, to stop breathing.

དབུགས་འཆག (ūùjaà) walking a horse to give it a chance to catch its breath/ slow down its breathing; va.—བྱེད་.

དབུགས་གཏོང་ (ūù dōŋ) see དབུགས་.

དབུག་གཏོང་འཐེན་ (ūù dōŋten) sm. དབུགས་གཏོང་ལེན་.

དབུགས་གཏོང་ལེན་ (ūù dōŋlen) va. to breath in and out.

དབུགས་རྟ་ང་འདྲ་པོ་ (ūù dāŋa drabo) the last breath at the time of death [Lit. breath like a horse's tail].

དབུགས་ཐག (ūgtaà) the length of a breath.

དབུགས་ཐག་རིང་པོ་ (ūùtaà riŋbu) great endurance (breathing).

དབུགས་ཐེངས་གཅིག (ūù tēŋjig) one breath.

དབུགས་ཐེབ་རེ་ (ūù tēbre) sm. དབུགས་ཐེངས་གཅིག.

དབུགས་འཐུམས་ (ūù tūm) vi. to be unable to breathe, to be suffocating.

དབུགས་འཐེན་ (ūù tēn) va. to breath in.

དབུགས་ཐོབ་ (ūù tōb) 1. vi. to be revived after fainting. 2. sm. དབུགས་འཆག.

དབུགས་འདྲེན་ (ūù dren) va. to breathe in/ to inhale.

དབུགས་དེབ་ (ūù deb) sm. དབུགས་དད་.

དབུགས་བསྡུ་ (ūù du) va. to take a person's life supernaturally (by a demon, ghost, etc.).

དབུགས་ནད་ (üünɛɛ̀) respiratory disease/ illness.
དབུགས་སྔོན་ (üünön) sm. དབུགས་བཀག་.
དབུགས་པད་ (üübɛɛ̀) money.
དབུགས་ཕྱིན་ (üü cīn) 1. vi. to stop breathing and die. 2. vi. to decrease/ diminish suffering.
དབུགས་ཕྱུང་ (üü cūŋ) 1. va. to exhale. 2. va. to liberate from suffering.
དབུགས་བྲལ་ (üü trɛɛ) sm. དབུགས་མེད་.
དབུགས་བླུག (üü lüü) administering/ giving oxygen (as therapy).
དབུགས་དབྱུང་ (üü yūŋ) sm. དབུགས་འབྱིན་.
དབུགས་འབྱིན་ (üü jin) 1. sm. སེམས་གསོ་གཏོང་. 2. sm. དབུགས་ཕྱུང་.
དབུགས་འབྱིན་རྔུབ་ (üü jīnŋub) sm. དབུགས་གཏོང་ལེན་.
དབུགས་འབྱིན་རྔུབ་ཀྱི་དབང་པོ་ (üü jinŋubgi wāŋbo) the respiratory organs.
དབུགས་མི་བདེ་བའི་ནད་ (üü midewɛ nɛɛ̀) disease which causes problems in breathing/ respiration.
དབུགས་མི་བདེ་བ་ཆེན་པོ་ (üü midewa cēmbo) a serious disease which is characterized by difficulty in breathing.
དབུགས་མེད་ (üü mee̱) 1. breathless, out of breath. 2. weak.
དབུགས་བརྩེགས་ (üü dzēg) sm. དབུགས་འཁུན་.
དབུགས་འཚང་བའི་ནད་ (üü tsāŋbɛ nɛɛ̀) asthma.
དབུགས་འཚངས་ (üü tsāŋ) vi. to pant (for breath).
དབུགས་ཡན་གཏོང་ (üüyɛn dōŋ) vi. to gasp (in pain).
དབུགས་རིང་ (üü riŋ) sighing; va.—གཏོང་ to sigh.
དབུགས་རིང་ནར་ནར་ (üüriŋ narnar) sm. དབུགས་རིང་.
དབུགས་རླངས་ (üü lāŋ) breath from mouth and nose which is visible when the weather is extremely cold.
དབུགས་རླུང་ (üü lūŋ) breath.
དབུགས་ལམ་ (üülam) respiratory path.
དབུགས་ལམ་གཅིག་གི་འབྲེལ་བ་ (üülam jīggi dree̱wa) a very close relationship.
དབུགས་ལམ་གཅིག་སྒྱུར་ (üülam jīggyur) sm. དབུགས་ལམ་གཅིག་གི་འབྲེལ་བ་.
དབུགས་ལམ་སྟོད་མ་ (üülam dööma) the upper respiratory tract.
དབུགས་ལམ་སྟོད་མའི་གཉན་ཚད་ (üülam döömɛ ñɛndzɛɛ̀) upper respiratory inflamation/ infection.
དབུགས་ལེན་ (üü le̱n) sm. དབུགས་བསྔུ་.
དབུགས་ཤོར་ (üü shɔ̄ɔ) 1. vi. to loose strength, to get weak. 2. vi. to lose heart, to get deflated.
དབུགས་སུབ་ (üü sūb) suffocating; va.—གཏོང་ to suffocate, to choke; vi.—ཤི་; —ཐིབས་ to die from suffocation, to choke to death.
དབུགས་གསོ་ (üü sō) repairing/ restoring correct breathing.
དབུགས་གསོག (üü sɔ̄ɔ) va. to breath, to pant.
དབུགས་ཧད་ (üü hɛ̄ɛ̀) va. to pant.
དབུགས་ཧལ་ (üü hɛ̄ɛ) sm. དབུགས་ཧད་.
དབུགས་ཧད་ཤོར་ (üühɛɛ shɔ̄ɔ) sm. དབུགས་ཤོར་.
དབུགས་ལྷེབ་ལྷེབ་ (üü lhēblheb) the slow/ labored breathing of a person or animal near to death.
དབུགས་ལྷེམ་མེ་ (üü lhēmme) sm. དབུགས་ལྷེབ་ལྷེབ་.
དབུགས་ལྷེམ་ལྷེམ་ (üü lhēmlhem) sm. དབུགས་ལྷེབ་ལྷེབ་.
དབུབ་ (üb) f. of འདུབས་.
དབུར་ (ür) va. to pulverize, to make into powder.
དབུར་ཆག (üüjaà) rubbing/ polishing to make smooth; va.—རྒྱག.
དབུར་དི་ (üüti) an iron (for pressing); va.—རྒྱག to iron.
དབུར་དོ་ (üdɔɔ̀) sm. ཏོག་རིལ་.
དབུར་སྡོད་ (üüdöö) sm. དབུ་རུ་སྡོད་.
དབུར་འདན་ (üüdɛn) a sculptor's tool.
དབུར་དེལ་ (üüdee) 1. a piece of flat iron with a long handle that is heated and used for ironing things. 2. a stone used to smooth walls, floors etc.
དབུར་རྡོ་ (ürdo) a stone used for grinding.
དབུར་བརྡར་ (ürdar) 1. rubbing two things against each other; va.—བྱེད་. 2. a stone used to mix ink.
དབུར་བརྡར་གློག་སྒྲོན་ (ürdar lōgdrön) dynamo-powered lamp (e.g., on a bicycle).
དབུར་པང་ (üübaŋ) ironing board.
དབུར་ཞལ་རྒྱག་བྱེད་ (ürshɛɛ gyagjeè) trowel (for plastering).
དབུར་རིས་ (üürii) lines/ creases caused by poor ironing.
དབུར་ཤིང་ (ürshiŋ) wooden implements used for smoothing walls, etc.
དབུར་ཤོག (ürshɔɔ) sandpaper.
དབུལ་ (üü) 1. f. of འབུལ་. 2. abbr. of དབུལ་པོ་.
དབུལ་རྐྱང་ (üügyaŋ) completely poverty stricken, extremely poor.
དབུལ་རྐྱང་མཉམ་ལས་ཁང་ (üügyaŋ ñamlɛgaŋ) a cooperative unit/ association for poor people.
དབུལ་སྐྱོང་ (üügyɔŋ) sm. དབུལ་སྐྱོབ་.
དབུལ་སྐྱོབ་ (üügyob) helping/ supporting/ assisting/ saving the poor; va.—བྱེད་.
དབུལ་སྐྱོབ་དབུལ་བཅོས་ (üügyob üüjöö) support/ help the poor and correct poverty (political slogan).
དབུལ་སྐྱོར་ (üügyɔɔ) sm. དབུལ་སྐྱོབ་.
དབུལ་ཁུལ་ (üügüü) pretending to be poor; va.—བྱེད་.
དབུལ་ཁྱིམ་ (üügyim) poor household.
དབུལ་བཅོས་ (üüjüü cüggyur) alleviating poverty; va.—བྱེད་.
དབུལ་བཅོས་ཕྱུག་སྒྱུར་ (üüjüü cüggyur) improve the poor and make them wealthy, alleviate poverty (political slogan).
དབུལ་བཅོས་ཕྱུག་འགྱུར་ (üüjüü cüggyur) improve the poor and have them become wealthy, alleviate poverty (political slogan).
དབུལ་ཐ་ (üüda) abject poverty.
དབུལ་ཐར་ཕྱུག་འགྱུར་ (üütar cüggyur) escape poverty and become wealthy (political slogan).
དབུལ་པོ་ (üübu) poor.
དབུལ་པོ་སྡོད་ཡུལ་ (üübu dööyüü) slum, ghetto.
དབུལ་པོའི་གནས་ཡུལ་ (üübü nɛɛ̀yüü) sm. དབུལ་པོ་སྡོད་ཡུལ་.
དབུལ་ཕོངས་ (üübuŋ) poor ༖ མང་ཚོགས་དབུལ་ཕོངས་རེད་ The masses are poor.
དབུལ་ཕོངས་ཅན་ (üübuŋjɛn) poor, impoverished.
དབུལ་ཕྱུག་ (üücüü) poor and rich, poverty and wealth.
དབུལ་རྩ་ (üüdza) the root of being poor/ poverty.
དབུལ་ཞྭ་ (üüsha) poverty [Lit. the hat of poverty].
དབུལ་ཞིང་ཕོངས་པ་ (üüshiŋ pōŋba) poor.
དབུས་ (üü) 1. center, middle ༖ གྲོང་ཁྱེར་གྱི་དབུས་ན་ In the middle of the city. ༖ དབུས་གཞུང་ The central government. 2. the central region of Tibet. 3. led/ headed by ༖ བློན་ཆེན་མཆོག་གིས་དབུས་འཛུས་མི་རྣམས་ The representatives, headed by the minister.
དབུས་ཀྱི་འདུན་ས་ (üü) shung. a meeting/ session of the Tibetan Council of Ministers (བཀའ་ཤག་) and the Dalai Lama, a meeting of a king and his ministers.
དབུས་སྐད་ (üügɛɛ̀) the dialect used in the region of དབུས་ (Central Tibet).
དབུས་ཁུལ་ (üügüü) the area of དབུས་ (Central Tibet).
དབུས་ཁང་ (üügaŋ) middle room.
དབུས་གུར་ (üügur) the leader's tent, the main tent, the headquarters' tent.
དབུས་གྲོས་ཚོགས་ (üü trö̱ödzɔɔ̀) national parliament (usu. used for India).
དབུས་གྲོས་ཚོགས་བོད་དོན་ཚོགས་པ་ (üü trö̱ödzɔɔ̀ pö̱ödön tsɔ̄gba) sm. དབུས་འཐུས་ཚོགས་བོད་དོན་ཚོགས་པ་.
དབུས་འགྱུར་ (üü gyu̱r) main centers where Buddhism has spread.
དབུས་འགྱུར་འཚལ་ (üügyurdzɛɛ cāŋ) Magadha.
དབུས་རྒྱུད་ (üügyüü) central area.
དབུས་སྒར་ (üügar) central camp.
དབུས་ཐིག (üüdig) middle line.
དབུས་མཐའ་ཀུན་ (üü tā gün) everywhere.
དབུས་འཐུས་ཚོགས་ཁང་ (üü tüüdzɔɔ̀gaŋ) house of

representatives, parliament, congress.

དབུས་འཐུས་ཚོགས་གོང་མ་ (ǖǜ tǖǜdzɔ̄ɔ̀ koŋma) the upper house in parliament.

དབུས་འཐུས་ཚོགས་བོད་དོན་ལྷན་ཚོགས་ (ǖǜ tǖǜtsɔg pö̱ödön lhēndzɔ̄ɔ̀) the parliamentary committee for Tibetan affairs.

དབུས་མདའ་ (ǖǜnda) the generals of the Trabchi regiment in the tt.

དབུས་འདྲེན་ (ǖǜndren) shung. to transport to the center/ central area/ Central Tibet ¶ ཉེ་མཁོ་དབུས་འདྲེན་བཅས་ཀྱི་ཏ་ཁལ་ Carrying animals for transporting necessary supplies to Central Tibet.

དབུས་གནས་ (ǖǜ nɛ̄ɛ̀) central/ middle part of an area.

དབུས་པ་ (ǖǜba) a person from Central Tibet.

དབུས་པར་ (ǖǜbār) woodblock print/ manuscript from Lhasa/ Central Tibet.

དབུས་ཕྱོགས་ (ǖǜ cɔ̄ɔ̀) 1. central Tibet. 2. the middle/ center.

དབུས་ཕྲུག (ǖǜ trūù) woolen products from Central Tibet.

དབུས་འཕྲིན་གཏོང་ལས་ཁང་ (ǖǜ drīndoŋlɛɛ̀gaŋ) FCC (Federal Communications Commission, in U.S.A.).

དབུས་འཕྲོད་བསྟེན་དང་སྤྱི་དམངས་བདེ་དོན་ལས་ཁུངས་ (ǖǜ trȫödendaŋ jīmaŋ de̱dön le̱ɛ̀guŋ) Department of Health and Human Services, in U.S.A. (HHS).

དབུས་བྲིས་ (ǖǜ tri̱i̱) Central Tibet style of painting thankas.

དབུས་དབུས་རྒྱང་ (ǖǜ ǖǜgyaŋ) due center, dead center.

དབུས་འབུན་སྐྱོར་གཅིག (ǖǜ bu̱n bōrjɔ̄ɔ̀) an increase by half of the principal.

དབུས་མོ་ (ǖǜmo) girl from central Tibet.

དབུས་མ་ (ǖǜmə) middle, center.

དབུས་གཙང་ (ǖǜdzaŋ) the regions of དབུས་ and གཙང་.

དབུས་གཙང་ཁམས་གསུམ་ (ǖǜdzaŋ kāmsum) the three regions of དབུས་, གཙང་ and ཁམས་.

དབུས་གཙང་གི་མི་བཅུ་ (ǖǜdzaŋgi mi̱ju) the first ten monks who were ordained in Kham during the revival of Buddhism after Langdharma had wiped out Buddhism in Central Tibet.

དབུས་གཙང་ཆོས་ཀྱི་ཆོལ་ཁ་ (ǖǜdzaŋ cȫögi cȫöga) the area of Central Tibet in the traditional tripartite division of Tibet.

དབུས་གཙང་རུ་བཞི་ (ǖǜdzaŋ ru̱shi) the four ancient divisions of Central Tibet.

དབུས་གཙང་མངའ་རིས་སྐོར་གསུམ་ (ǖǜdzaŋ ŋə̱rii̱ gɔ̄ɔ̀sum) the three regions of དབུས་, གཙང་, and མངའ་རིས་.

དབུས་གཙང་མདོ་གསུམ་ (ǖǜdzaŋ do̱sum) sm. དབུས་གཙང་ཁམས་གསུམ་.

དབུས་ཞིབ་དཔྱོད་ལས་ཁང་ (ǖǜ shi̱bjȫö le̱ɛ̀gaŋ) FBI (Federal Bureau of Investigation).

དབུས་གཞུང་ (ǖǜshuŋ) the central government, the federal government.

དབུས་གཞུང་གི་བཀར་འཇུག་གན་འཛིན་ལྷན་ཚོགས་ (ǖǜshuŋgi gānjuù ge̱ndzin lhēndzɔ̄ɔ̀) Federal Reserve Board (U.S.A.).

དབུས་གཞུང་གི་མཁའ་འགྲུལ་ལས་ཁང་ (ǖǜshuŋgi kāndrüü le̱ɛ̀gaŋ) FAA (Federal Aviation Agency).

དབུས་གཞུང་གི་ཚོང་དོན་ལྷན་ཚོགས་ (ǖǜshuŋgi tsōŋdön lhēndzɔ̄ɔ̀) FTC (Federal Trade Commission).

དབུས་གཞུང་གི་ཛ་དྲག་གནད་དོན་ལས་ཁང་ (ǖǜshuŋgi dza̱draà nɛ̄ɛ̀dön le̱ɛ̀gaŋ) FEMA (Federal Emergency Management Agency).

དབུས་གཞུང་གི་འཛིན་ཆས་ཉོ་སྒྲུབ་དང་བདག་འཛིན་ལས་ཁང་ (ǖǜshuŋgi dzi̱njɛɛ̀ ño̱drubdaŋ dāŋdzin le̱ɛ̀gaŋ) General Services Administration (GSA).

དབུས་གཞུང་གི་ས་ཁང་བདག་གཉེར་ལས་ཁང་ (ǖǜshuŋgi sāgaŋ dagñer le̱ɛ̀gaŋ) FHA (Federal Housing Administration.

དབུས་འོས་བསྡུ་ལས་ཁང་ (ǖǜshuŋ ö̱ödu le̱ɛ̀gaŋ) Federal Election Commission (FEC).

དབུས་ཡེ་ཤར་ (ǖǜ ye̱shar) Central Asia.

དབུས་རི་ (ǖǜri) the middle mountain.

དབུས་རིས་ (ǖǜrii) Central Tibet.painting style.

དབུས་རུ་ (ǖǜru) sm. དབུ་རུ་.

དབུས་རྭ་ (ǖǜra) the middle point of a vajra.

དབུས་ལམ་ (ǖǜlam) middle road/ route/ line.

དབུས་ཤར་ (ǖǜshaa) Middle East.

དབུས་གསང་བའི་ལས་ཁང་ (ǖǜsaŋwɛ le̱ɛ̀gaŋ) Central Intelligence Agency (CIA).

དབུས་གསལ་འདེབས་ཚོགས་པ་ (ǖǜsɛɛ de̱bdzɔgbə) central advisory board.

དབུས་ལྷོ་ (ǖǜlho) middle south.

དབེན་ (ēn) 1. abbr. of དབེན་པོ་. 2. vi. to be without, to be devoid of ¶ དེ་དག་སྙིང་པོ་དབེན་པར་མངོན་ It is obvious they are without substance.

དབེན་ཁང་ (ēngaŋ) hermitage.

དབེན་ཁུག (ēnguù) a remote place.

དབེན་འཁྲིམས་ (ēndrim) sm. དབེན་བཞུགས་.

དབེན་ཆུང་ (ēnjuŋ) young monk, child monk.

དབེན་ཐིང་ངེར་ (ēn ti̱ŋŋee) extremely quiet/ silent.

དབེན་གནས་ (ēnnɛɛ̀) 1. a desolate/ deserted/ remote/ secluded place. 2. a retreat.

དབེན་པ་ (ēmba) remote, desolate, deserted, secluded.

དབེན་པ་ཅན་ (ēmbajɛn) sm. དབེན་པ་.

དབེན་པའི་གནས་ (ēmbɛ nɛ̄ɛ̀) sm. དབེན་གནས་.

དབེན་པོ་ (ēmbo) remote, desolated, deserted.

དབེན་ཕུག (ēmbuù) cave in a remote/ deserted/ secluded place.

དབེན་ཚམ་ (ēndzam) sm. ཁྲུག་ཚམ་.

དབེན་བཞུགས་ (ēnshuù) staying in a remote place.

དབེན་ལམ་ (ēnlam) a road in a remote/ deserted/ area.

དབེན་ས་ (ēnsa) sm. དབེན་གནས་.

དབེན་ས་པ་ (ēnsaba) a person who lives in remote/ deserted/ secluded place.

དབོ་ (ō) f. of འབོ་.

དབོ་ཁ་ཐིག་ཚགས་ (ōga ti̱gdzaà) shung. putting mud on the roof and drain pipe to prevent dripping.

དབོ་ཅན་ (ōjɛn) sm. དབོ་ཟླ་.

དབོ་ཟླ་ (ōnda) the 2nd month of the Tibetan calendar.

དབོ་ཡིས་ཉ་བ་ (ōyiì ña̱wa) the 15th day of the 2nd Tibetan month.

དབོག (ɔ̄ɔ̀) f. of འབོགས་.

དབོན་རྒྱུད་ (ōngyüù) paternal relatives.

དབོན་མོ་ (ōnmo) 1. queen. 2. niece.

དབོན་ཞང་ (ōnshaŋ) maternal uncle and nephew (sister's son).

དབོན་པོ་ (ōmbo) 1. sm. དབོན་སེར་གཟུགས་ 2. nephew. 3. sm. དབོན་རྒྱུད་.

དབོན་ཞང་དབུ་སྣང་རྡོ་རིང་ (ōnshaŋ ǖñuŋ do̱riŋ) an ancient stone pillar located in front of the Cathedral in Lhasa.

དབོན་སེར་གཟུགས་ (ōn sēsug) a married person dressing as a monk, married monks.

དབོན་སྲས་ (ōnsɛɛ̀) 1. nephew. 2. name of a Bon lama.

དབོར་ (ɔ̄ɔ̀) va. to transport, to move from one location to another.

དབོར་སྐྱེལ་ (ɔ̄ɔ̀gyee) transporting; va.—རྒྱག to transport, to move.

དབོར་གླ་ (ɔ̄ɔ̀la) transportation fee/ charge.

དབོར་ཆུ་ (ɔ̄ɔ̀ju) roof drain pipe.

དབོར་འདྲེན་ (ɔ̄ndren) sm. དབོར་སྐྱེལ་.

དབོར་འདྲེན་ཀུང་སི་ (ɔ̄ndren gūŋsi) tib.ch. transport company.

དབོར་འདྲེན་འཁོར་ལོ་ (ɔ̄ndren kɔ̄ɔ̀lo) transportation vehicles.

དབོར་འདྲེན་ལམ་ཐིག (ɔ̄ndren lə̱mtig) transportation line.

དབོར་པ་ (ɔ̄ɔ̀ba) sm. དབོར་ཆུ་.

དབོར་པོ་ (ɔ̄ɔ̀bo) sm. དབོར་ཆུ་.

དབོལ་ (ȫö̀) arc. vi. to throw out.

དཔོས་ (ȫȫ) arc. va. to swell.
དབྱག་པ་ (yāgba) wooden rake.
དབྱང་ (yāŋ) abbr. of དབྱང་རླུང་.
དབྱང་འགྱུར་ (yəŋgyur) oxidizing, oxidate.
དབྱང་འགྱུར་སྐྱེལ་རྫས་ (yəŋgyur gũũdzɛɛ̀) oxidizer, oxidant.
དབྱང་འགྱུར་དངོས་པོ་ (yəŋgyur ŋȫȫbo) materials that oxidize, materials that have oxidized.
དབྱང་འགྱུར་རྫས་ (yəŋgyur dzɛɛ̀) sm. དབྱང་འགྱུར་དངོས་པོ་.
དབྱང་བརྟེན་ལྕགས་གཅོད་ (yāŋden jāgjöö) acetylene torch.
དབྱང་གཅིག་ཐན་འགྱུར་རྫས་ (yāŋjig tɛ̃ngyur dzɛɛ̀) carbon monoxide.
དབྱང་རླུང་ (yəŋluŋ) oxygen.
དབྱང་རླུང་དཀུ་བ་ (yəŋluŋ gūwə) ozone.
དབྱང་རླུང་བླུག (yəŋluŋ lūù) va. to give oxygen (as therapy).
དབྱངས་ (yāŋ) 1. vowel. 2. melody, tune. 3. va. to sing.
དབྱངས་ཀྱི་མཚམས་ཚིགས་ (yāŋgi tsāmdziì) musical rhythm.
དབྱངས་སྙན་ (yāŋñɛn) melodious voice/ sound.
དབྱངས་ཅན་ (yāŋjɛn) 1. melodious. 2. girl's name.
དབྱངས་ཅན་མ་ (yāŋjɛnma) the goddess Sarasvati.
དབྱངས་ཅན་ལྷ་མོ་ (yāŋjɛn lhāmo) sm. དབྱངས་ཅན་མ་.
དབྱངས་བཅུ་དྲུག (yāŋ jūdruù) the sixteen vowels in Sanskrit.
དབྱངས་འཆར་ (yāŋjar) a kind of divination/ astrological calculation done through the vowels.
དབྱངས་འཆར་གྱི་རྩིས་ (yāŋjargi dzīì) sm. དབྱངས་འཆར་.
དབྱངས་ཉམས་ (yāŋñam) 1. vi. to have a sound become lower. 2. vowelless words.
དབྱངས་ཏ་ (yāŋda) intonation in songs and prayers.
དབྱངས་ཏགས་ཐིག་ལྔ་ (yāŋdaà tĩgŋa) the musical staff/ stave.
དབྱངས་མཐུན་ཚིག་མཇུག (yāŋdün tsĩŋjuù) ending a line with a rhyming vowel.
དབྱངས་མཐུན་ཡི་གེ་ (yāŋdün yigi) the rhyming word that ends a line of verse.
དབྱངས་དང་རྗེས་འཇུག (yāŋdaŋ jenjuù) vowels and suffix.
དབྱངས་པ་ (yāŋba) 1. chant/ prayer leader. 2. singer.
དབྱངས་བྲལ་ (yāŋdrɛɛ) sm. དབྱངས་ཉམས་པ་.
དབྱངས་དབུགས་བཟོ་གྲྭ (yāŋuù sodra) oxygen factory.
དབྱངས་མེད་ (yāŋmeè) sm. དབྱངས་བྲལ་.
དབྱངས་རྩོམ་པ་ (yāŋdzomba) composer (musical).
དབྱངས་ཚིགས་ (yəŋdziì) music score/ notation.
དབྱངས་འཛོམས་ (yāŋdzom) person's name.
དབྱངས་གཞུང་ (yāŋshuŋ) music score.
དབྱངས་བཞི་ (yāŋshi) the four vowels in the Tibetan alphabet.
དབྱངས་ཡིག (yəŋyiì) vowel.
དབྱངས་གསལ་ (yāŋsɛl) vowels and consonants.
དབྱངས་གསལ་བརྡ་ཏགས་ (yāŋsɛl dadaà) phonetic alphabet.
དབྱར་ཀ་ (yāāga) sm. དབྱར་ཁ་.
དབྱར་སྐྱིད་ (yərgyiì) summer outing.
དབྱར་སྐྱེས་སྤྲིན་ང་ (yārgyeè drĩnŋa) shung. sm. འབྲུག་སྐད་.
དབྱར་དཀྱིལ་ (yərgyii) midsummer.
དབྱར་ཁ་ (yāāga) summer, summertime.
དབྱར་ཁ་སྤེན་མའི་མེ་ཏོག (yāāga bēnme medoò) a flower design used in Tibetan rugs.
དབྱར་ཁས་བླངས་ (yāā kēlaŋ) sm. དབྱར་གནས་.
དབྱར་ཁང་ (yāāgaŋ) summer home/ cottage.
དབྱར་ཁའི་གུང་སེང་ (yāākɛ kuŋsaŋ) summer vacation.
དབྱར་ཁའི་རྩྭ་ར་ (yāāke dzāra) summer pasture.
དབྱར་ཁྲལ་ (yāādrɛɛ) shung. taxes that are collected in the summer.
དབྱར་ཁྲིམས་ (yəədrim) summer rules in villages involving prohibitions against such things as fighting that will bring bad luck for the crops.
དབྱར་གོས་ (yāāgöö) summer clothing.
དབྱར་གྱི་དུས་ (yārgi tüü) 1. summertime. 2. the time of དབྱར་གནས་.
དབྱར་དགུན་ (yārgün) summer and winter.
དབྱར་དགུན་ཆད་མེད་ (yārgün cɛ̀ɛmeè) the whole year, throughout the year.
དབྱར་དགུན་སྟོན་དཔྱིད་ (yārgün dõn jīì) summer, winter, autumn and spring.
དབྱར་རྔ་མ་ (yār ŋāma) the day དབྱར་གནས་ starts (16th day of the 6th month of the Tibetan calendar).
དབྱར་ང་ (yārŋa) poet. thunder.
དབྱར་གཅིག་མ་ (yərjigmə) a year old calf.
དབྱར་ཆས་ (yārjɛɛ̀) summer clothes.
དབྱར་ཆུ་ (yārcu) summer rain; vi.—ལོག; —རྒྱས་ to have river/ streams swell due to summer rains.
དབྱར་ཆོས་ (yārjöö) gathering of monks in summer for Buddhist philosophical debating, summer monastic semester.
དབྱར་མཆོད་ (yārjöö) summer religious ritual.
དབྱར་མཇལ་ (yār jɛɛ) shung. an audience given to the student monk officials by the Dalai Lama during the summer.
དབྱར་ཉམས་ལྡན་པ་ (yārñam dəmba) tropical areas where things are green all year round.
དབྱར་ཉལ་ཞིང་ (yārñɛɛ shiŋ) fields that are left fallow every alternate year (summer).
དབྱར་ཉལ་ལངས་ (yārñɛɛ laŋ) va. to leave fields fallow for one year (summer).
དབྱར་ཉི་ལྡོག (yār ñindɔɔ̀) the summer solstice.
དབྱར་ཉི་ལོག (yār ñilɔɔ̀) sm. དབྱར་ཉི་ལྡོག.
དབྱར་གཉིས་མ་ (yərñiìmə) a 2 year old calf.
དབྱར་སྙོལ་ (yār ñȫȫ) va. to leave fallow (in the summer).
དབྱར་བསྙལ་བསླངས་ (yārñɛɛ lāŋ) sm. དབྱར་ཉལ་ལངས་.
དབྱར་སྟོད་ (yārdöö) first part of summer.
དབྱར་སྟོན་ (yārdön) summer festival.
དབྱར་ཐ་སྟོན་མགོ་ (yārta dõngo) the end of summer and the beginning of fall.
དབྱར་ཐ་མ་ (yār tāma) the last month of summer, the 6th month of the Tibetan calendar.
དབྱར་ཐའི་སྐང་ཚད་ (yārdɛ gaŋdzɛɛ̀) the middle of the 6th month of the Tibetan calendar.
དབྱར་ཐའི་དབུགས་ཐོབ་ (yārdɛ ūgdob) the start of the 6th month of the Tibetan calendar.
དབྱར་དུས་ (yārdüü) summer, summertime.
དབྱར་དུས་བྱ་རིགས་ (yārdüü cərii) birds that migrate in summer.
དབྱར་འདབ་ (yāndəb) a stand for a gelong's begging bowl.
དབྱར་འདེབས་ (yārdeb) summer crops; va.—བྱེད་ to plant a summer crop.
དབྱར་སྡུད་ (yārdüü) 1. summer harvest. 2. va. to harvest the summer crop.
དབྱར་སྡུད་ལོ་ཏོག (yārdüü lodɔɔ̀) summer harvested crops.
དབྱར་བསྡུ་ (yārdu) harvested in summer; va. དབྱར་བསྡུ་; —བྱེད་ to harvest the summer crop.
དབྱར་གནས་ (yārnɛɛ̀) summer retreat for monks.
དབྱར་པ་ (yārba) sm. སྦུར་པ་.
དབྱར་ཕྱི་མ་ (yār cĩmə) the last day of དབྱར་གནས་ (the 16th day of the 7th month of the Tibetan calendar).
དབྱར་འབུལ་ (yāmbüü) giving/ transferring things from an estate to the lord's residence in summer.
དབྱར་འབྲིང་སྐང་ཚད་ (yārdriŋ gaŋdzɛɛ̀) the middle of middle month of summer (the middle of the 5th month of the Tibetan calendar).
དབྱར་འབྲིང་དབུགས་ཐོབ་ (yārdriŋ ūgdob) the beginning of the middle month of summer (the beginning of the 5th month of the Tibetan calendar).
དབྱར་མ་ (yārma) fallow land, a field left fallow for

the summer.

དབྱར་མར་ (yārmaa) 1. summer butter. 2. butter paid by nomads in summer in exchange for grain and other products.

དབྱར་མོ་ཁང་ (yārmogaŋ) nunnery for female gelong.

དབྱར་རྨོ་ (yārmo) summer plowing; va.—རྒྱག.

དབྱར་སྨད་ (yārmɛɛ̀) the later part of summer.

དབྱར་སྨིན་ལོ་ཏོག (yārmin l̲o̲dɔɔ̀) summer ripening crops.

དབྱར་རྩམ་ (yārdzam) རྩམ་པ་ boored or lent in summer.

དབྱར་རྩྭ་དགུན་འབུ་ (yārdza gü̲mbu) caterpillar fungus.

དབྱར་ཚད་ (yārdzɛɛ̀) the hot season.

དབྱར་ཚུགས་ (yārdzuù) the beginning of summer.

དབྱར་མཚེར་ (yārdzer) nomad's summer camps.

དབྱར་མཚོ་རྒྱས་པ་ (yārdzo gyɛ̲̀ba) vigorous, energetic [Lit. swollen like a lake in the summer].

དབྱར་ཞལ་བཞེས་ (yārshɛɛ sh̲e̲è) sm. དབྱར་གནས་.

དབྱར་ཞྭ་ (yārsha) summer hat.

དབྱར་ཞྭ་བསེ་ཐེབས་ (yārsha sēdeb) a kind of hat worn by monk officials in summer.

དབྱར་ཞོ་ (yārsho) summer yogurt.

དབྱར་གཞུག (yārshug) late summer, end of summer.

དབྱར་གཞུང་ (yārshuŋ) midsummer.

དབྱར་ཟུག (yārsug) sm. དབྱར་ཚུགས་.

དབྱར་ཟླ་ (yānda) the three summer months (the 4th, 5th and 6th months of the Tibetan calendar).

དབྱར་ཟླ་ཐ་ཆུང་ (yānda tājuŋ) late summer (the 6th. month of the Tibetan calendar).

དབྱར་ཟླ་འབྲིང་པ་ (yānda driŋwɔ) midsummer (the 5th. month of the Tibetan calendar).

དབྱར་ཟླ་ར་བ་ (yānda r̲a̲wa) early summer (the 4th. month of the Tibetan calendar).

དབྱར་གཟིགས་ (yərsii) summer tours/ trips/ picnics.

དབྱར་ཡུར་ (yəryuu) summer weeding; va.—རྒྱག.

དབྱར་རའི་སྒང་ཚད་ (yārre ga̲ŋdzɛɛ̀) middle of the 4th month of the Tibetan calendar.

དབྱར་རའི་དབུགས་ཐོབ་ (yārre ūgdob) the start of the 4th month of the Tibetan calendar.

དབྱར་ལམ་ (yārlam) 1. a narrow precipitous road/ path. 2. strict.

དབྱར་ལུག (yərluù) summer born lamb.

དབྱར་ལྭ་ (yārla) sm. དབྱར་ཆས་.

དབྱར་ས་ (yārsa) summer dwelling place.

དབྱར་སངས་ (yārsaŋ) sm. དབྱར་གཟིགས་.

དབྱར་སོས་མཚམས་ (yārsö tsām) the juncture between spring and summer.

དབྱར་གསུམ་ (yārsum) 1. three year old cattle. 2. the three summer months.

དབྱི་ (yī) 1. f. of འབྱེད་. 2. lynx.

དབྱི་ཀྲང་ (yīdraŋ) ch. president of parliament, speaker of a representatives body (e.g., the House of Representative in the U.S.A.).

དབྱི་དཀར་ (yīgar) 1. white lynx. 2. clematis brevieaudata.

དབྱི་གུ་ (yīgu) sm. དབྱུག་གུ་.

དབྱི་ཏ་ལི་ (yīdali) Italy.

དབྱི་ནག (yīnaà) 1. black lynx. 2. clematis tangutica.

དབྱི་ལྤགས་ (yībaà) lynx skin.

དབྱི་མོ་ (yōmu) female lynx.

དབྱི་མོང་ (yīmuŋ) clematis.

དབྱི་དམར་ (yīmar) red lynx.

དབྱི་སྨི་སྒྲིབ་སྨན་ (yīmi dri̲i̲mɛn) ch.tib. ether.

དབྱི་ཙེ་ (yīdzi) ch. soap.

དབྱི་ཚང་ (yīdzaŋ) lynx den/ lair/ hole.

དབྱི་ཡོན་ (yīyün) ch. member of parliament, congressman, senator.

དབྱི་ཡོན་གྲོས་མི་ (yīyün trö̲ö̲mi) ch.tib. sm. དབྱི་ཡོན་.

དབྱི་ལ་ཁེ་ (yīlake) Iraq.

དབྱི་སི་ལན་ (yīselɛn) Islamic, Moslem.

དབྱི་སི་ལན་གྱི་ཕྱག་འཚལ་ཁང་ (yīselɛngi cāàdzɛɛgaŋ) Mosque.

དབྱི་སི་ལན་ཆོས་ལུགས་ (yīselɛn cööluù) Islam, Moslem religion.

དབྱི་སུའོ་ (yīso) Aesop.

དབྱི་སི་ལི་ (yīsele) Israel.

དབྱི་ཧུའི་གྲོས་ཚོགས་ (yīhue trö̲ö̲dzɔɔ̀) ch.tib. parliament ¶ དབྱི་ཧུའི་གྲོས་ཚོགས་ཀྱི་ལམ་ལུགས་ Parliamentary system.

དབྱི་ཧོ་ཐོན་གྱི་ལས་འགུལ་ (yīhodöngi l̲ɛ̲ngüü) ch.tib. the Boxer Rebellion.

དབྱིག (yīi) precious stones/ materials/ gems.

དབྱིག་གི་ཁུ་བ་ (yīigi kūwɔ) sun.

དབྱིག་གི་སྙིང་ (yīigi ñiŋ) 1. precious stones/ gems. 2. Brahma.

དབྱིག་གི་གདངས་ཅན་ (yīigi d̲a̲ŋjɛn) a clear sound made by a ringing bell.

དབྱིག་གུ་ (yīigu) thin stick.

དབྱིག་དངོས་ (yīiŋöö) wealth.

དབྱིག་དུག (yīidug) poison made from precious stones.

དབྱིག་དར་ (yīgdar) a type of whetstone.

དབྱིག་པ་ (yīgbɔ) a stick.

དབྱིག་བུ་ (yīgbu) 1. a whetstone. 2. a stick for leveling earth.

དབྱིག་དབྱིག (yīgyii) sound made by grinding.

དབྱིག་མོ་ (yīgmu) 1. powdered dye. 2. soft.

དབྱིག་འཛིན་གྱི་ཐིག་ལེ་ (yīŋdzingi tīgle) shung. sm. ས་གཞི་.

དབྱིངས་ (yīŋ) 1. midst, middle of, mid. ¶ ནམ་མཁའི་དབྱིངས་སུ་ In mid air. ¶ དགོངས་པའི་དབྱིངས་སུ་འཇགས་རོགས་གནང་ Please keep (it) in (the middle of your) mind. 2. interest, liking, fascination, enchantment ¶ ཁོ་བོད་གཞས་ལ་དབྱིངས་འདུག He has a deep interest in Tibetan music. 3. source, origin. 4. acting stylish/ grand; va.—བྱེད་ to act stylish/ grand. 5. addiction; vi.—ཞུགས་; —འཇགས་ to be addicted ¶ ཁོང་ཉལ་ཐའི་དབྱིངས་ཞུགས་བཞག He is addicted to opium. 6. amorous; va.—བྱེད་ to act amorous ¶ ན་གཞོན་དེ་གཉིས་དབྱིངས་བྱེད་ཀྱི་འདུག The two youths are acting amorous toward each other.

དབྱིངས་འཁོར་ (yīŋ kɔ̄ɔ̀) vi. to be high/ intoxicated on drugs.

དབྱིངས་གོག (yīŋ g̲ɔɔ̀) vi. to be satiated when using drugs.

དབྱིངས་ཅང་དོད་ (yīŋjaŋ tö̲ö̲) stylish, attractive, pretty.

དབྱིངས་ཅང་བྱེད་ (yīŋjaŋ c̲e̲è) va. to act stylish, attractive (in dressing, etc.).

དབྱིངས་ཅན་ (yīŋjɛn) addict, addicted ¶ ཉལ་ཐ་དབྱིངས་ཅན་ Opium addict.

དབྱིངས་ཆག (yīŋ cāà) ch.tib. vi. to lose interest/ fascination/ appeal/ attraction.

དབྱིངས་ཆོད་ (yīŋjöö) shung. fully aware.

དབྱིངས་འཇགས་པའི་ཚད་ (yīŋjagbɛ tsɛ̄ɛ̀) degree of addiction.

དབྱིངས་འདོན་ (yīŋ d̲ö̲n) va. to act stylish/ chic/ attractive.

དབྱིངས་དཔྱད་ (yīŋjɛɛ̀) a phrase used in letter writting to convey please "think over and decide the matter" ¶ གནད་དོན་དེའི་སྐོར་ཁྱེད་རང་གིས་དབྱིངས་དཔྱད་གནང་རོགས་གནང་ Concerning this issue, please think over and decide it.

དབྱིངས་འཕར་ (yīŋ pār) 1. vi. to be greatly fascinated and engrossed in ¶ ཁོ་གཉིས་ཞིབ་འཇུག་བྱེད་ཡག་གི་སྐོར་ལ་དབྱིངས་འཕར་བཤད་ཤག The two of them are engrossed in (talking) about research. 2. vi. to have a craving for a drug, to be addicted to a drug ¶ ཁོ་ཉལ་ཐག་གི་དབྱིངས་འཕར་ཡོད་པ་རེད་ He is addicted to opium. 3. sm. དབྱིངས་, 6.

དབྱིངས་བྱེད་ (yīŋ cɛ̀ɛ) sm. དབྱིངས་, 4. and 6.

དབྱིངས་འབྱར་ (yīŋjar) sm. དབྱིངས་ལ་ཚུད་.

དབྱིངས་ལ་ཚུད་ (yīŋlə tsüù) 1. sm. དབྱིངས་, 5. 2. sm. དབྱིངས་འཕར་.

དབྱིངས་ཞུགས་ (yīŋ shu̲ù) sm. དབྱིངས་ལ་ཚུད་.

དབྱིངས་ཞུགས་པའི་ཚད་ (yi̊ŋshuùbɛ tsɛ̀ɛ) sm. དབྱིངས་འཛུགས་པའི་ཚད་.

དབྱིངས་གཞུག (yi̊ŋ shu̱ù) sm. དབྱིངས་ཞུགས་.

དབྱིངས་བཟོ་དོད་པོ་ (yi̊ŋso to̱òbo) sm. དབྱིངས་ཅང་དོད་པོ་.

དབྱིངས་ལ་འབྱར་ (yi̊ŋla ja̱r) sm. དབྱིངས་ལ་ཚུད་.

དབྱིངས་ལ་འཚུད་ (yi̊ŋlə tsu̍ù) sm. དབྱིངས་ལ་ཚུད་.

དབྱིངས་ཤོད་ (yi̊ŋ shö̍ö) va. to show an interest in the opposite sex, to flirt (verbally).

དབྱིངས་ས་ (yi̊ŋsə) a term used in ancient times to refer to regents and ministers.

དབྱིན་ (yi̊n) eng. abbr. of དབྱིན་ཇི་.

དབྱིན་སྐད་ (yi̊ngɛɛ̀) English language, the spoken English language.

དབྱིན་སྐད་དེ་ཕྱི་རྒྱལ་གྱི་སྐད་ཡིག་གི་ཆ་ནས་ཡིག་རྒྱུགས་ལེན་པ་ (yi̊ngɛɛ̀de ci̊gyɛɛgi gɛ̀ɛyii̊gi cänɛ yi̱ggyuù le̱mba) TOEFL (Test of English as a Foreign Language).

དབྱིན་ཁོངས་ (yi̊ngoŋ) eng.tib. British, belonging to the British ¶ དབྱིན་ཁོངས་རྒྱ་གར་གཞུང་ The IndianGovernment of Britain.

དབྱིན་ཁྲེ་ (yi̊ndre) eng.tib. foot (the linear measure).

དབྱིན་གོ་ (yi̊ngo) eng.ch. England, Britain.

དབྱིན་གོ་བ་ (yi̊ngowa) eng.ch. Englishman.

དབྱིན་དགེ་ (yi̊nge) eng.tib. abbr. English teacher.

དབྱིན་ཇི་ (yi̊nji) eng. England, English, Englishman.

དབྱིན་ཇི་ཁ་ཐུང་ (yi̊nji kədu̱ŋ) eng.tib. the English 303 carbine.

དབྱིན་ཇི་ཁ་རིང་ (yi̊nji kəri̱ŋ) eng. English rifle.

དབྱིན་ཇི་གོང་མ་ (yi̊nji ko̱ŋma) the king/ queen of Great Britain.

དབྱིན་ཇི་གོང་མས་བཙུགས་པའི་རིག་གནས་ཀྱི་ལྟེ་གནས་ཁང་ (yi̊nji ko̱ŋmɛ dzu̱gbɛ ri̱gnɛɛ̀ dēnɛɛ̀gaŋ) Royal Academy of Britain.

དབྱིན་ཇིའི་སྐད་ (yi̊njii gɛ̀ɛ) eng.tib. English language.

དབྱིན་ཇིའི་རླུང་འཕྲིན་ལས་ཁང་ (yi̊njii lūŋdrin lɛ̱ɛ̀gaŋ) British Broadcast Company (BBC).

དབྱིན་ཇིའི་ཚོང་དོན་སྐུ་ཚབ་ (yi̊njii tsōŋdön gūdzəb) British Trade Officer/ Office.

དབྱིན་ཇིའི་ཡི་གེ་ (yi̊jii yigi) eng.tib. English letters/ writing.

དབྱིན་ཇི་ཨན་པ་ (yi̊nji ēmba) eng.ch. American Indians; native Americans.

དབྱིན་དྲུང་ (yi̊ndruŋ) eng.tib. English language secretary/ clerk.

དབྱིན་མདའ་ (yi̊nda) eng.tib. a British made rifle ¶ དབྱིན་མདའ་ཁ་ཐུང་ The British 303 carbine.

དབྱིན་མདའ་ཁ་ཐུང་ (yi̊nda kəndum) sm. དབྱིན་མདའ་ཁ་འདུམ་.

དབྱིན་མདའ་ཁ་འདུམ་ (yi̊nda kəndum) shung. the British 303 cabine (rifle).

དབྱིན་པང་ (yi̊nbaŋ) eng. the English pound.

དབྱིན་བོད་ (yi̊npöö) eng.tib. Anglo-Tibetan.

དབྱིན་མུའུ་ (yi̊nmu) eng.ch. acre.

དབྱིན་ཚུན་ (yi̊ndzün) eng.ch. inch.

དབྱིན་གཞུང་ (yi̊nshuŋ) eng.tib. the British government.

དབྱིན་ཟླ་ (yi̊nda) eng.tib. a Western month.

དབྱིན་གཟུགས་བོད་ཡིག (yi̊nsug pö̱öyii) romanization of the Tibetan alphabet.

དབྱིན་ཡུལ་ (yi̊nyüü) eng.tib. the British Isles, England.

དབྱིན་ཡུལ་གྱི་རྒྱ་གར་ཚོང་ལས་ཁང་ (yi̊nyüügi gya̱gar tsōŋlɛgaŋ) eng.tib. the British East India Company.

དབྱིན་ཡུལ་གྱི་ཡི་ཤུའི་ཆོས་བརྒྱུད་ (yi̊nyüügi yi̱shü cōögyü̍ü) eng.tib. the Anglican Church of England.

དབྱིན་ཡུལ་གྲོས་ཚོགས་གོང་མ་ (yi̊nyüü trö̱ödzɔɔ̀ ko̱ŋma) eng.tib. the British House of Lords.

དབྱིན་ཡུལ་གྲོས་ཚོགས་འོག་མ་ (yi̊nyüü trö̱ödzɔɔ̀ wɔgma) eng.tib. the British House of Commons.

དབྱིན་ཡུལ་ཞིབ་བཤེར་ལས་ཁུངས་ (yi̊nyüü shi̱bser lɛ̱ɛ̀guŋ) Scotland Yard.

དབྱིན་ལུགས་ (yi̊nluù) eng.tib. English custom, English style.

དབྱིན་ལེ་ (yi̊nle) eng.tib. mile.

དབྱིན་ལོ་ (yi̊nlo) eng.tib. a Western year.

དབྱིན་སྲང་ (yi̊nsaŋ) eng.tib. ounce.

དབྱིན་ཧྲན་རི་རྒྱུད་ (yi̊nhrɛn ri̱gyüü) Yinshan mountain range.

དབྱིབས་ (yi̊b) shape, form, figure.

དབྱིབས་གྲུ་བཞི་མ་ (yi̊b tru̱shimə) square.

དབྱིབས་ཅན་ངར་ལྕགས་ (yi̊bjɛn ŋa̱rjaà) shaped/ fashioned steel.

དབྱིབས་ཆགས་ཚུལ་ (yi̊b cə̄gdzüü) formation process.

དབྱིབས་ཆུང་ (yi̊bjuŋ) small size, small ¶ དབྱིབས་ཆུང་ཁེ་ལས་ Small enterprise.

དབྱིབས་ཆུང་བཀོད་ལེགས་ (yi̊bjuŋ gö̍öleg) small but well designed.

དབྱིབས་ཆུང་སྤུས་དག (yi̊bjun bü̍üdaà) small but high in quality.

དབྱིབས་ཆུང་ལ་སྤུས་དག་པོ་ (yi̊bjuŋla bü̍ü ta̱gbo) sm. དབྱིབས་ཆུང་སྤུས་དག.

དབྱིབས་ཆེན་ (yi̊bjen) large size, large, heavy.

དབྱིབས་ཆེན་ཁེ་ལས་ (yi̊bjen kēlɛɛ̀) large enterprise.

དབྱིབས་འཆོ་ (yi̊b cō) va. to shape, to make into a shape.

དབྱིབས་རྙིང་ (yi̊bñi̱ŋ) old shape, old style.

དབྱིབས་རྟགས་ཡི་གེ་ (yi̊bdaà yigi) sm. དབྱིབས་མཚོན་ཡི་གེ་.

དབྱིབས་ཐོན་ (yi̊b tȫn) vi. to take shape.

དབྱིབས་མཐའ་བཞི་མ་ (yi̊bta shi̱mə) quadrilateral.

དབྱིབས་འདོན་འཕྲུལ་འཁོར་ (yi̊bdön trü̍ügɔɔ) modeling equipment.

དབྱིབས་སྡུག (yi̊bduù) beautiful.

དབྱིབས་བྱད་ (yi̊bjɛɛ̀) sm. གཟུགས་བྱད་.

དབྱིབས་འབྲིང་ (yi̊bdriŋ) middle-sized, medium.

དབྱིབས་རྩིས་ (yi̊bdzii) sm. དབྱིབས་ཚད་རྩིས་རིག.

དབྱིབས་ཚད་རྩིས་རིག (yi̊bdzɛɛ̀ dzi̊irii) geometry ¶ ངོས་མཉམས་དབྱིབས་ཚད་རྩིས་རིག Plane geometry.

དབྱིབས་མཚུངས་ (yi̊bdzuŋ) similar in shape/ form.

དབྱིབས་མཚོན་ཡི་གེ་ (yi̊bdzön yi̱gi) pictograph, hieroglyph.

དབྱིབས་ཟུར་གསུམ་ (yi̊b su̱rsum) triangle.

དབྱིབས་གཟུགས་ (yi̊bsuù) shape, structure, form.

དབྱིབས་བཟོ་ (yi̊bso) molding, sculpturing; va.—བྱེད་. 2. situation, circumstance ¶ དེང་སང་དཔལ་འབྱོར་གོང་འཕེལ་འགྲོ་སྟངས་ཀྱི་དབྱིབས་བཟོ་ཡག་པོ་མི་འདུག Thesedays the situation regarding economic development is not good.

དབྱིབས་བཟོའི་སྒྱུ་རྩལ་ (yi̊bsö gyu̱dzɛɛ) plastic arts, sculpturing.

དབྱིབས་རིས་ (yi̊brii) drawing of a shape/ design.

དབྱིབས་གསར་ (yi̊bsar) new model ¶ ད་ལོའི་མོ་ཊ་དབྱིབས་གསར་ This year's new car model.

དབྱིས་ (yi̊i) the Yi nationality (a minority group in Sichuan and Yunnan Provinces).

དབྱིས་ (yi̊i) 1. va. to wipe off, to clean off. 2. va. to apply.

དབྱིས་རིགས་ (yi̊irig) the Yi nationality.

དབྱུ་གུ་ (yūgu) stick.

དབྱུ་གུ་ཟླ་བ་ (yūgu da̱wa) the 9th month of the Tibetan calendar.

དབྱུག: p. དབྱུགས་; f. དབྱུག; imp. དབྱུགས་ (yūù) 1. va. to throw, to cast away, to fling ¶ ང་ལག་ཐན་མ་ གོགས་དེ་ཚོ་གད་སྙིགས་ནང་དབྱུགས་པ་ཡིན་ (I) threw away all the useless thing in the garbage. 2. va. to strike/ hit ¶ ཁོས་མི་དབྱུགས་ནས་མི་བསད་བཞག He stuck a man with a sword and killed him. 3. sm. དབྱུག་འཇོག. 3. abbr. of དབྱུག་པ་.

དབྱུག་ཀྱོག་བོ་ལོ་ (yūggyɔɔ̀ bōlo) 1. cricket. 2. cricket ball.

དབྱུག་རྒྱབ་ (yūggüü) shung. beating (a drum) with a stick ¶ ང་བོ་ཆེ་དབྱུག་བརྡུང་བྱུང་བསྟུན་རྒྱལ་སྒོ་སྒྲིམས་རྒྱག་གིས་ When the big drum was beaten the main gate was closed at once.

དབྱུག་སྐོར་ (yūùgɔɔ) flail (for threshing grain).

དབྱུག་གུ་ (yūùgu) a wooden stick.
དབྱུག་གུ་སྐམ་ཁ་ (yūùgu gāmga) a wooden key.
དབྱུག་གུ་ཕོག་པའི་སྐྱང་མདའི་ཁྱི་ལྟར་ (yūùgu pɔ̄gbɛ sāŋdɛ kyi̊dar) grumbling/ complaining loudly [Lit. like a dog beaten with a stick].
དབྱུག་གུའི་པོ་ལོ་ (yūùgü bōlo) field hockey.
དབྱུག་རྒྱུག་མཆོང་གསུམ་ (yūùgyuù cōŋsum) the three sports: throwing, running and jumping.
དབྱུག་བཅོས་ (yūgjöò) a method of Tibetan medical treatment wherein a patient is tapped with a small stick.
དབྱུག་འཇལ་ (yūg jɛɛ) va. to pay compensation in a divorce—paid by the person who initiated the divorce to his/ her spouse.
དབྱུག་འཇོག (yūg jɔ̀ɔ̀) leaving/ setting aside, forsaking, abandoning; va. དབྱུག་འཇོག; —བྱེད་ to leave/ set aside ། ཁོས་བཟའ་ཚང་དབྱུག་བཞག་ནས་ཕྱིན་པ་རེད་ He left his wife and went away.
དབྱུག་ད་ (yūgda) prostitute, a loose woman; va.—བྱེད་ to be a prostitute, to be a loose woman.
དབྱུག་དོ་ (yūgdo) sm. དབྱུག་པ་.
དབྱུག་གདོང་ (yūgdoŋ) parachuting; va.—བྱེད་ to parachute.
དབྱུག་ཐོ་ (yūgdo) sm. དབྱུག་དོ་.
དབྱུག་རྡོ་ (yūgdo) a throwing stone.
དབྱུག་བད་ (yūgda) 1. a staff indicating rank. 2. baton.
དབྱུག་བསྡམས་ (yūgdam) keeping silent, not talking to one another.
དབྱུག་པ་ (yūgbə) club, stick; va.—རྒྱག to beat or hit with a stick/ club.
དབྱུག་དབྱུག (yūùyuù) waving; va.—བྱེད་ ། ང་ཚོ་ཁ་བྲལ་དུས་ཁོང་གིས་ལག་པ་དབྱུག་དབྱུག་བྱས་པ་རེད་ When we were separating he waved his hand.
དབྱུག་མ་ (yūgmə) sm. དབྱུག་སྐོར་.
དབྱུག་རྩལ་ (yūgdzɛɛ) Chinese martial art that use sticks/ poles.
དབྱུག་འཛེག་ལུས་རྩལ་ (yūgdzeè lüüdzɛɛ) pole vault.
དབྱུག་ཞོག (yūg shòò) forget about it, drop it, leave it at that (slang).
དབྱུག་བཞག (yūg shaà) 1. sm. དབྱུག་ཞོག. 2. p. of དབྱུག་འཇོག.
དབྱུག་ཟོར་ (yūgsɔɔ) a long-handled sickle.
དབྱུག་ཟླ་ (yūgda) the 9th month of the Tibetan calendar.
དབྱུགས་ (yūù) p. and imp. of དབྱུག.
དབྱུགས་འཇོག (yūg jɔ̀ɔ̀) sm. དབྱུག་བཞག.
དབྱུགས་ཞོག (yūg shòò) sm. དབྱུག་ཞོག.
དབྱུགས་བཞག (yūg shaà) p. of དབྱུགས་འཇོག.
དབྱུང་ (yūŋ) f. of འབྱིན་.

དབྱེ་ (yē) 1. f. of འབྱེད་. 2. sm. དབྱེ་བ་འབྱེད་.
དབྱེ་ཁྱད་ (yēgyɛɛ̀) different, difference ། ད་ཚ་གྲང་དབྱེ་ཁྱད་ཆེ་ལ་ A great difference in the temperature.
དབྱེ་ཐང་ (yēdaŋ) sm. གཡེ་ཐང་.
དབྱེ་ཐང་ག (yē tāŋga) sm. གཡེ་ཐང་.
དབྱེ་ཞྲལ་ (yēdrɛɛ) decomposing, breaking down.
དབྱེ་ཞྲལ་འགྱུར་འབྱུང་ (yēdrɛɛ gyunjuŋ) decomposition reaction, the process of decomposition.
དབྱེ་བ་ (yēwa) distinctions, differences; va.—འབྱེད་; —གཅོད་ to differentiate, to distinguish, to classify, to sort by class or type ། འབུ་རིགས་ཀྱི་དབྱེ་བ་འབྱེད་ཀྱི་ཡོད་པ་རེད་ (They) are classifying the kinds of insects. ། དམངས་གཙོའི་བཅོས་སྒྱུར་སྐབས་གྲལ་རིམ་གྱི་དབྱེ་བ་ཕྱེ་བ་རེད་ At the time of (the implementation of) democratic reforms, they differentiated (people) into classes.
དབྱེ་བ་ཆོད་ (yēwa cöò) 1. vi. to be differentiated/ distinguished/ classified ། གྲོང་གསེབ་འདིའི་ནང་གྲལ་རིམ་གྱི་དབྱེ་བ་ཆོད་མ་སོང་ Differentiation into classes hasn't been done in that village. 2. vi. to be judged/ decided ། སྐད་ཆ་དེ་བདེན་རྫུན་གྱི་དབྱེ་བ་ཆོད་མ་སོང་ It hasn't been decided whether that comment is true or false.
དབྱེ་བ་ཕྱེ་ (yēwa cē) p. of དབྱེ་བ་འབྱེད་.
དབྱེ་བ་མེད་པ་ (yēwa meèba) without distinction/ difference/ regard to ། ཕོ་མོར་དབྱེ་བ་མེད་པ་ Without regards to gender.
དབྱེ་བའི་གསང་ (yēwɛ sāŋ) spaces/ gaps within the body where there are no bones, arteries or vital organs.
དབྱེ་བྲལ་ (yēdrɛɛ) sm. དབྱེ་བ་མེད་པ་.
དབྱེ་འབྱེད་ (yēnjeè) differentiation, discrimination, classification, analysis; va.—བྱེད་ to differentiate, to discriminate, to classify, to sort, to analyze ། ཚོང་པ་རྣམས་ཀྱིས་ཁྱེར་བའི་ཅ་ལག་དབྱེ་འབྱེད་བྱས་པ་རེད་ They sorted and differentiated the things brought by the (various) traders.
དབྱེ་འབྱེད་བསྡོམས་རྩིས་ (yēnjeè domdzii) statistical facts/ figures ། དབྱེ་འབྱེད་བསྡོམས་རྩིས་ཅུས་ Bureau of Statistics.
དབྱེ་འབྱེད་གྲོས་མོལ་ (yējeè tröömöö) holding negotiations/ talks to settle disputes; va.—བྱེད་.
དབྱེ་འབྱེད་ངོས་འཛིན་ (yējeè ŋöndzin) picking out/ identifying one's own things from a group of mixed things va.—བྱེད་.
དབྱེ་མཚམས་ (yēndzam) demarcating/ differentiating/ bounding line; va.—བྱེད་; —གཅོད་ to draw a dividing line, to make a boundary/ limit, to demarcate ། ཁོ་ཚོས་མཚམས་དབྱེ་མཚམས་བྱས་པ་རེད་ They demarcated the boundary.
དབྱེ་མཚམས་ས་ཐིག (yēndzam sādig) demarcation/ boundary line ། གནས་སྐབས་ཀྱི་དམག་དོན་དབྱེ་མཚམས་ས་ཐིག Provisional military boundary.
དབྱེ་ཞིབ་ (yēshib) analyzing; va.—བྱེད་ to analyze.
དབྱེ་ཞིབ་འཕྲུལ་ཆས་ (yēshib trüüjɛɛ̀) analyzing instruments.
དབྱེ་ཞིབ་རིག་པ་ (yēshib rigbə) the study of analytical methods, analytics.
དབྱེ་གཞི་ (yēshi) subject matter, subjects to be analyzed.
དབྱེ་ཤིང་ (yēshiŋ) door bolt/ latch.
དབྱེ་གསེས་ (yēseè) sm. དབྱེ་འབྱེད་.
དབྱེ་བསལ་ (yēsɛɛ) sm. དབྱེ་བ་འབྱེད་.
དབྱེན་ (yēn) discord, dissension, disagreement; va.—འབྱེད་; —བྱེད་ to cause discord, to instigate dissension/ disagreement.
དབྱེན་དཀྲུག (yēndruù) sm. དབྱེན་སྦྱོར་.
དབྱེན་འཁྲུན་ཆོད་མིན་ (yēndrün cöömin) shung. to be unable to settle a case/ dispute.
དབྱེན་འདུམ་ (yēndum) vi. to have people in conflict get back together through mediation.
དབྱེན་བསྡུམས་ (yēndum) va. to mediate between people in conflict/ dissension/ discord.
དབྱེན་པ་ (yēmba) troublemaker, troublemaking; va.—བྱེད་.
དབྱེན་སྤྱོད་ (yēnjöò) troublemaking, instigating disorder/ dissension.
དབྱེན་འབྱེད་ (yēn jeè) va. to make trouble, to instigate dissension/ discord.
དབྱེན་འབྱེད་དཀྲུག་ཤིང་ (yēnjeè drūgshiŋ) sm. དབྱེན་སྦྱོར་དཀྲུག་ཤིང་.
དབྱེན་འབྱོར་ (yēnjɔɔ) sm. དབྱེན་སྤྱོད་.
དབྱེན་སྦྱོར་ (yēnjɔɔ) causing or fomenting discord/ dissension/ disagreement; va.—བྱེད་.
དབྱེན་སྦྱོར་དཀྲུག་ཤིང་ (yēnjɔɔ drūgshiŋ) causing or fomenting or instigating dissension/ discord; va.—བྱེད་.
དབྱེན་སྦྱོར་རྩོད་གླེང་ (yēnjɔɔ dzxöölɔŋ) causing or fomenting or instigating dissension/ discord; va.—བྱེད་.
དབྱེན་སྦྱོར་སེལ་འཇུག (yēnjɔɔ sēljuù) sm. དབྱེན་བསྡུམས་.
དབྱེན་བསྡུམས་ (yēn dum) sm. དབྱེན་བསྡུམས་.
དབྱེར་ (yēē) sm. དབྱེ་བ་.
དབྱེར་ཐོན་ (yēēdön) sm. གཟེངས་ཐོན་.
དབྱེར་ཕུད་ (yēēbüù) best ། དབྱེར་ཕུད་ཐོན་རྫས་ The best products.
དབྱེར་མི་ཕྱེད་པ་ (yēē mi cēèba) sm. དབྱེ་བྲལ་.

དབྱེར་མེད་ (yēēmɛɛ̀) sm. དབྱེ་བ་མེད་པ་.

དབྱེས་ (yēè) 1. size, magnitude. 2. chance, opportunity.

དྲ་ (drā) one of the six lineages of ancient Tibet.

དྲ་གོག (drāgɔ̄ɔ̀) sm. རྡ་ཅོ་.

དྲ་ཉག (drāñaà) sm. རྡ་ཉག.

དབྲག (drāà) in between, a space/ gap between. ¶ ཁང་པ་དེའི་དབྲག་ལམ་ཆུང་ཞིག་འདུག There is a small lane between the houses. 2. an interval ¶ ཚོགས་འདུའི་དབྲག་ལ་ཇ་ལྷུགས་པ་རེད་ In the interval between the meetings (or sessions of the meeting) they served tea.

དབྲག་དབྲག (drāgdraà) sm. དབྲག, 2.

དབྲད་ (drɛ̄ɛ̀) f. of འབྲད་.

དབྲལ་ (drɛ̄ɛ̄) 1. va. to tear, to rip. 2. p. and f. of དབྲལ་.

དབྲལ་བཤིག (drɛ̄ɛ̄shiì) destroying by tearing/ ripping; va.— གཏོང་; —བྱེད་.

དབྲི་ (drī) f. of འབྲི་.

དབྲིལ་ (drīī) va. to push/ knock down ¶ ཁོས་ཕྲུ་གུ་དེ་ས་ར་དབྲིལ་བ་རེད་ He knocked the boy down. ¶ རི་སྟེང་ནས་ཤིང་སྡོང་དབྲིལ་བ་རེད་ (They) rolled the trees down the hill.

དབྲིལ་དབྲིལ་ (drīīdrīī) 1. round. 2. small and stout (for people). 3. rolled into a ball; va.—བཟོ་.

དབྲིལ་མ་ (drīīmə) sheep and goat dung.

དྲེ་ (drē) sm. སྦྲེ་.

དྲེ་གདམ་ (drēdam) dirty/ foul/ coarse language.

དྲེ་པོ་ (drēbo) dirty/ foul/ coarse ¶ མི་དེས་སྐད་ཆ་དྲེ་པོ་ཞིག་ཤོད་ཀྱི་འདུག This man is talking dirty.

དྲེ་བོ་ (drēwo) sm. དྲེ་བཙོག.

དྲེ་བེ་ (drēbe) baby goat.

དྲེ་བཙོག (drēdzɔ̄ɔ̀) dirt, filth, dirty, filthy.

དབྲོག (drɔ̄ɔ̀) f. of འཕྲོག.

དབྲོལ་: p. **དབྲལ་**; f. **དབྲལ་**; imp. **དབྲོལ་** (drōō) va. to tear/ rip.

འབག (baà) mask; va.—གྱོན་; —གོན་ to wear a mask, to use sth. as a pretext ¶ ཁོ་ཚོས་དམངས་གཙོ་འབག་ལ་གོན་ནས་མི་དམངས་ལ་གཉའ་གནོན་བྱེད་ཀྱི་ཡོད་པ་རེད་ Using democracy as a pretext, they oppressed the people.

འབག: p. **འབགས་**; f. **དབག** (baà) vi. to be defiled/ polluted/ desecrated.

འབག་སྐུ (baàgu) 1. clay statue. 2. an effigy on which a mask has been placed.

འབག་གི་འབུག་གི (baàge buùge) unclear/ ambiguous (response or statement); va.—ཤོད་ ¶ ཁོང་གིས་གསར་འགོད་པའི་དྲི་བ་ལ་ལན་འབག་གི་འབུག་གི་ཞིག་བརྒྱབ་སོང་ He answered the reporter's questions ambiguously.

འབག་འཆམ་ (bagjam) religious dance in which the dancers wear masks; va.—རྒྱག.

འབག་པོ་ (baàbo) male witch.

འབག་པར་གཡར་ འཇིགས་ཚུར་ངོམ་ (baà pāā yāā jig tsūū ŋom) doing sb. a favor and being paid back with harm/ unkindness [Lit. to lend a mask (of a wrathful deity) and be frightened by it].

འབག་པར་གཡོག འཇིགས་རལ་ཚུར་སྐྱུལ་ (baà pāā yɔ̄ɔ̀ jigrɛɛ tsūū gǖū) sm. འབག་པར་གཡར་འཇིགས་ཚུར་ངོམ་.

འབག་པར་གཡོགས་ ཇིག་རལ་ཚུར་སྐྱུལ་ (baà pāā yɔ̄ɔ̀ jigrɛɛ tsūū gǖū) འབག་པར་གཡོགས་ འཇིགས་ཚུར་ངོམ་.

འབག་འབག (bagbaà) 1. machine gun. 2. motorcycle.

འབག་འབུག (bagbug) sm. འབག་གི་འབུག་གི་.

འབག་མོ་ (baàmo) witch (female).

འབག་བཙོག (bagdzɔ̄ɔ̀) pollution; va.—བཟོ་ to pollute.

འབག་བཙོག་གཙང་བཅོས་ (bagdzɔ̄ɔ̀ dzāŋjöö) cleaning up pollution.

འབག་བཙོག་བཅོས་སེལ་ (bagdzɔ̄ɔ̀ jöösel) sm. འབག་བཙོག་གཙང་བཅོས་.

འབག་བཟོ་བ་ (bagsowa) person who makes masks.

འབགས་ (baà) p. of འབག.

འབགས་གོད་ (baàgöö) wear and tear ¶ འགྲུལ་པ་དེ་ཚོ་བསྡད་ནས་ཁང་པར་འབག་གོད་ཆེན་པོ་བྱུང་བཞག Because travelers were staying in the house it got lots of wear and tear. 2. waste; va.—གཏོང་ to waste.

འབགས་ལྷག (baglhaà) leftover (food).

འབང་: p. **བངས་**; f. **འབང་** (baŋ) vi. to be or get dipped/ soaked in water.

འབངས་ (baŋ) subject, dependent ¶ དཔོན་འབངས་ Lords and subjects.

འབངས་ཁྱིམ་ (baŋgyim) household of subjects.

འབངས་མཁོའི་གནམ་གྲུ (baŋkö nəmdru) civilian airplane.

འབངས་འཁོར་ (baŋgɔɔ) attendants and servants.

འབངས་འཁོར་གཡོག་རིགས་ (baŋgɔɔ yɔ̄ɔ̀rii) sm. འབངས་འཁོར་.

འབངས་གྱེན་ལོག (baŋgyen lɔ̄ɔ̀) va. to revolt/ rebel (made by subjects).

འབངས་གཉུག་མ་ (baŋñugba) permanent attendants/ servant.

འབངས་རྣལ་མར་བཀུག (baŋ nɛ̄ɛmar gūù) sm. འབངས་སུ་བྱེད་.

འབངས་མི་ (baŋmi) sm. འབངས་.

འབངས་མི་སེར་ (baŋ miser) sm. འབངས་.

འབངས་མོ་ (baŋmo) 1. female servant/ attendant. 2. female subject.

འབངས་དམངས་ (baŋmaŋ) the people, the masses.

འབངས་རིགས་ (baŋrii) servant/ attendant class or stratum.

འབངས་ལ་གདོགས་ (baŋla dɔ̄ɔ̀) sm. འབངས་སུ་བྱེད་.

འབངས་སུ་བཀུག (baŋsu gūù) va. to make into a servant/ subject, to subjugate.

འབངས་སུ་འཁོལ་ (baŋsu kȫȫ) vi. to be made into a servant/ subject, to be subjugated.

འབངས་སུ་གདོགས་ (baŋsu dɔ̄ɔ̀) sm. འབངས་སུ་བྱེད་.

འབངས་སུ་བྱེད་ (baŋsu ceè) va. to make into a servant/ subject, to subjugate.

འབད་ (bɛɛ̀) va. to endeavor, to make an effort, to strive for ¶ མོས་ཕྲུ་གུ་ཚོའི་སློབ་གསོ་བྱེད་རྒྱུ་འབད་ཡོད་པ་རེད་ She has endeavored to educate the children.

འབད་འཐབ་ (bɛɛ̀dəb) struggling, endeavoring; va.—བྱེད་.

འབད་པ་ (bɛɛ̀ba) sm. འབད་རྩོལ་.

འབད་པ་བརྒྱ་ཕྲག (bɛɛ̀ba gyadraà) a tremendous effort [Lit. hundreds of attempts].

འབད་པ་སྟོང་ཟད་ (bɛɛ̀ba dōŋsɛè) wasting one's efforts.

འབད་པ་སྟོན་ (bɛɛ̀ba tön) shung. vi. to be diligent ¶ བྱ་བ་ལ་འབད་པ་སྟོན་ To work diligently.

འབད་པ་དོན་མེད་ (bɛɛ̀ba tönmeè) endeavoring without benefit/ gain/ result.

འབད་པས་སྲུང་ (bɛɛ̀bɛ sūŋ) to guard/ protect with great effort.

འབད་འབད་དུང་དུང་ (bɛɛ̀bɛɛ̀ tuŋduŋ) diligently and enthusiastically, with great effort.

འབད་འབད་འབུངས་འབུངས་ (bɛɛ̀bɛɛ̀ buŋbuŋ) sm. འབད་རྩོལ་.

འབད་འབུངས་ (bɛɛ̀buŋ) abbr. of འབད་འབད་འབུངས་འབུངས་.

འབད་འབུངས་ཆེར་སྐྱེད་ (bɛɛ̀buŋ cērgyeè) with great diligence/ enthusiasm; va.—བྱེད་.

འབད་འབུངས་སྟོབས་བརྩོན་ (bɛɛ̀buŋ dōbdzön) going all out, making a great effort; va.—བྱེད་.

འབད་མེད་ (bɛɛ̀meè) without making an effort, without hard work ¶ འབད་མེད་ལ་ཕྱུག་པོ་ཡོང་མི་སྲིད་ It isn't possible to become rich without hard work.

འབད་མེད་ངང་འབྱུང་ (bɛɛ̀meè naŋjuŋ) vi. to get/ accomplish sth. without hard work.

འབད་མེད་ལྷུན་གྲུབ་ (bɛɛ̀meè lhündrub) sm. འབད་མེད་ངང་འབྱུང་.

འབད་རྩོལ་ (bɛɛ̀dzöö) striving, endeavoring, struggling, making an effort; va.—བྱེད་.

འབད་བརྩོན་ (bɛɛ̀dzön) sm. འབད་རྩོལ་.

འབད་བརྩོན་ཆེ་སྐྱིད་ (bɛɛ̀dzön cēgyeè) sm. འབད་འབུད་ཆེ་སྐྱིད་.

འབད་བརྩོན་ལྷོད་མེད་ (bɛ̱èdzön lhöömeè) constant effort/ endeavor/ struggle [Lit. endeavoring without relaxing].

འབད་སེམས་ (bɛ̱èsem) sm. ནུར་སེམས་.

འབབ་: p. **བབ་**; f. **འབབ་** (ba̱b) 1. vi. to fall (rain, snow, water, etc.), to descend ¶ ད་ཆ་ཆར་པ་འབབ་གྱི་འདུག (It) is raining now. ¶ གནམ་གྲུ་དེ་འབབ་གྱི་འདུག The plane is landing. 2. yield, harvest ¶ ད་ལོ་ཁྱེད་རང་གི་གཞིས་ཀའི་འབབ་ག་འདྲ་འདུག How is your estate's yield this year? 3. vi. to be attractive to, to appeal to ¶ ཁོས་བཤད་པ་དེ་ཁོ་ཚོའི་སེམས་ལ་བབས་སོང་ What he said appealed to them. 4. vi. to become time to do ¶ ད་ཚང་མ་གཅིག་སྒྲིལ་བྱེད་ཡས་ཀྱི་དུས་ལ་བབས་པ་རེད་ The time has now come for all the people to unite. 5. in accordance, considering ¶ ས་གནས་ཉེ་འབྱུངས་བབས་ཀྱིས་ In accordance with distance. 6. what is owed on a loan/ tax. 7. income.

འབབ་: p. **བབ་** or **བབས་**; f. **འབབ་**; imp. **བོབ་** (ba̱b) va. to dismount, to get off, to descend ¶ ཁོ་རྟ་ནས་བབ་པ་རེད་ He dismounted from the horse. ¶ ཁོ་སྐས་འཛེགས་བབ་དུས་རིལ་བ་རེད་ He fell as he was climbing down the stairs.

འབབ་ཁ་ (ba̱bga) sm. འབབ་ཁུངས་.

འབབ་ཁུངས་ (ba̱bguŋ) source, origin.

འབབ་ཁོངས་ (ba̱bgoŋ) 1. belonging to or part of a source/ origin. 2. family background, class background ¶ ངའི་འབབ་ཁོངས་ཞིང་པ་ཡིན་ My family background is farmer.

འབབ་འགྲོས་ (ba̱bgöö) standard of living.

འབབ་འཁྲི་ (ba̱btri) tax obligation.

འབབ་རྒྱུད་ (ba̱bgyüü) river or stream basin/ valley.

འབབ་སྒོ་ (ba̱bgo) income.

འབབ་ཆག (ba̱bjaà) exemption on a tax/ loan; va.—གཏོང་.

འབབ་ཆུ་ (ba̱bju) a stream/ river that flows (usu. rapidly) downhill.

འབབ་རྟེན་ (ba̱bden) the box/ bag (etc.) on which a newly arrived bride dismounts from her horse.

འབབ་སྟེགས་ (ba̱bdeg) a platform used for landing/ descending/ dismounting ¶ མེ་འཁོར་གྱི་འབབ་སྟེགས་ Train (station) platform.

འབབ་ཐང་ (ba̱bdaŋ) sm. བབས་ཐང་.

འབབ་ཐོ་ (ba̱bdo) shung. a list of income/ yields.

འབབ་དེབ་ (ba̱bdeb) book for keeping a record of income.

འབབ་འདེད་ (ba̱bdeè) shung. person who goes to collect taxes/ loans that are in arrears.

འབབ་རྡོ་ (ba̱bdo) a falling stone (from a mountain or hill); vi.—རིལ་ to have a stone roll down from a mountain/ hill; va.—སྒྲིལ་ to roll a stone intentionally down a mountain/ hill.

འབབ་སྒྲོད་ (ba̱b droö) va. to pay sth. owed ¶ ཁོས་བུ་ལོན་གྱི་འབབ་ཚང་མ་སྤྲོད་པ་རེད་ He paid off the full loan.

འབབ་ཕྱོགས་ (ba̱bjɔɔ̀) 1. the direction a river/ stream flows. 2. income.

འབབ་དབྱུག (ba̱byuù) dropping from an airplane, parachuting.

འབབ་མ་ (ba̱bma) handle of a plow.

འབབ་སྨྱུག (ba̱bñuù) fee given to court clerk for writing the verdict.

འབབ་ཚུགས་ (ba̱bdzuù) station (railway/ bus).

འབབ་འཛེགས་སྡིངས་ཆ་ (ba̱bdzeg di̱nja) sm. འབབ་སྟེགས་.

འབབ་ཡོང་ (ba̱byoŋ) income.

འབབ་ཞིབ་ལས་ཁུངས་ (ba̱bshib lɛ̱ɛ̀guŋ) name of an office in the tt. government that was in charge of newly opened fields and taxes newly levied as a result of Lungshar's investigations.

འབབ་གཞི་ (ba̱bshi) source of income ¶ བཟོ་གྲྭ་བཙུགས་ནས་འབབ་གཞི་གསར་པ་བཟོས་པ་རེད་ They built a factory and created a new source of income.

འབབ་གཞོངས་ (ba̱bshoŋ) a plate put under a cup being used to offer sth. like tea to deities.

འབབ་བཟོ་ (ba̱bso) making/ establishing a source of revenue; va.—བྱེད་ ¶ ས་ཞིང་གསར་པ་སྤྱིལ་བུ་པ་རྣམས་ལ་གཞུང་ནས་འབབ་བཟོ་བྱས་པ་རེད་ The government made the new estates a source of income.

འབབ་ཤུགས་ (ba̱bshuù) the force or amount of sth. falling.

འབབ་ས་ (ba̱bsa) station, port ¶ གྲུ་གཟིངས་འབབ་ས་ Seaport.

འབམ་ (ba̱m) rheumatism.

འབམ་གྲུམ་ (ba̱mdrum) sm. འབམ་.

འབམ་ནད་ (ba̱mnɛɛ̀) rheumatism.

འབམ་པོ་ (ba̱mbo) ligusticum pteridophyllum franch ex oliv (used in Tibetan medicine).

འབམ་རྫོང་ (ba̱mdzoŋ) sm. འབམ་རྫོང་ཉོས་བསྒྱུར་.

འབམ་རྫོང་ཉོས་བསྒྱུར་ (ba̱mdzoŋ ñüügyur) forcing or bullying sb. into buying.(at a high price); va.—གཏོང་.

འབའ་ (ba̱) 1. a fine for violating an agreement/ pledge. 2. abbr. of འབའ་ཐང་. 3. va. to bleat.

འབའ་སྐད་ (ba̱gɛɛ̀) bleating cry of sheep.

འབའ་ཁུག (ba̱guù) purse, wallet.

འབའ་ཁུག་ཁབ་ཤུབས་ (ba̱guù kābshub) go!d ornament worn around the waist by the ladies (of the upper aristocracy).

འབའ་ཁྱལ་ (ba̱bgüü) sm. འབའ་ཐང་.

འབའ་ག་ཤ་ག (ba̱ga shāga) 1. frank, straightforward. 2. easy to get along with, compatible, amiable.

འབའ་གན་ (ba̱gɛn) shung. an agreement with a clause including a fine/ punishment for breaking/ violating the contract.

འབའ་འགལ་ (ba̱gɛɛ) shung. fine for breaking or violating a contract ¶ ཁྲ་དོན་བརྟལ་བཞིག་ཏུ་འགྲོ་རིགས་ཕྲ་མོ་ཙམ་ཞུས་སྲིད་ཚེ་མདུན་གསལ་འབའ་འགལ་སྤྲོ་ཕྱི་རིམ་འགྲོས་ཀྱིས་སྒྲུབ་འབུལ་ཐོག If there are any violations against this verdict you must pay the fine for the violation as mentioned in the verdict.

འབའ་རྒུན་ (ba̱gün) grapes from the འབའ་ཐང་ area.

འབའ་རྒྱ་ (ba̱gya) sm. འབའ་གན་.

འབའ་སྒྲ་ (ba̱dra) sm. འབའ་སྐད་.

འབའ་དངུལ་ (ba̱ŋüü) a fine for breaking/ violating a contract.

འབའ་ཅན་ (ba̱jɛn) shung. having a clause (in an agreement) to pay a fine if terms are violated).

འབའ་ཅེ་ (ba̱je) sm. འབའ་ཆ་.

འབའ་ཆ་ (ba̱ja) 1. seeds that have been pressed to extract their oil (i.e., the residue from oil making). 2. musical instrument; va.—གཏོང་ to play a musical instrument.

འབའ་ཆ་བ་ (ba̱jawa) musicians.

འབའ་ཆ་རུ་ཁག (ba̱ja ru̱gaà) band.

འབའ་ཆའི་ལུད་ (ba̱jɛ lü̱ü) a type of fertilizer made from འབའ་ཆ་.

འབའ་ཆི་ (bə̱ji) hind. a pounded and flattened rice.

འབའ་ཇི་ (bə̱ji) sm. འབའ་ཆི་.

འབའ་བརྗོད་གོང་ཞུར་ (ba̱jöö̀ ko̱ŋshur) shung. as stipulated above in the contract/ agreement ¶ འབའ་བརྗོད་གོང་ཞུར་གུས་འབངས་ནས་ངོ་བོ་ཊམ་དཀར་༡༠༠ ལ་སྐྱིད་ As stipulated above in the contract, I have borrowed 100 ཊམ་དཀར་.

འབའ་ཉེས་ (ba̱ñeè) shung. sm. འབའ་.

འབའ་ཐང་ (ba̱daŋ) Batang (an important area in Eastern Tibet (in today's Sichuan Province).

འབའ་དམ་ (ba̱dam) peanut, groundnut.

འབའ་དམ་སྣུམ་ (ba̱dam nūm) peanut oil.

འབའ་དིར་ (ba̱ di̱r) va. to bleat.

འབའ་འདེད་གཙང་སྒྲུབ་ (ba̱deè dzāŋdrub) meeting/ paying the fine for breaking a contract; va.—བྱེད་.

འབའ་འདེད་ཡན་སོང་མེད་པ་ (ba̱ndeè yɛ̱nsoŋ me̱èba) shung. not letting sb. evade paying a fine ¶ ཁྲིམས་ཁུངས་སུ་གན་འགལ་སྙན་ཞུ་ཕུལ་བར་གནང་རྒྱུའི་འབའ་འདེད་ཡན་སོང་མེད་པ་ Please do not let them evade paying the fine for submitting the petition and violating the agreement.

འབའ་ལྡིར་ (badir) bleating cry of sheep.
འབའ་པ་ (baba) person from འབའ་ཐང་.
འབའ་ཕྱི་ (bəji) sm. འབའ་ཆེ་.
འབའ་ཞིག (bashig) exclusively, solely, purely, only ¶ རང་དོན་འབའ་ཞིག Purely for one's own purpose.
འབའ་གཞས་ (bashɛɛ̀) folk song from Batang.
འབའ་བཞག (ba shaà) va. to make a bet.
འབའ་བཞུ་ (bashu) a torch.
འབའ་ཡིག (bəyiì) sm. འབའ་འགན་.
འབའ་ཡུལ་ (bəyüü) sm. འབའ་ཐང་.
འབའ་ལི་ཐང་ (ba lidaŋ) two adjacent areas in Eastern Tibet: Batang and Litang (in today's Sichuan Province).
འབའ་ལི་འབོལ་ལི་ (bale böle) soft.
འབའ་ལེན་ (balen) sm. རྐང་འབའ་ལེན་.
འབའ་ཤ་ (basha) a type of large black grape.
འབའ་ཤི་ཧོར་ལང་ (bashi hɔ̄ɔlaŋ) a saying describing satirically the following historical shift: in the early years after 1951 the leading Tibetan cadre came from Batang in Kham but in recent years there has been a shift and the leading cadre such as Ragdi and Tenzin come from northern Tibet (the Horpa area) [Lit. people from Batang have died and people from Northern Tibet have risen up].
འབའ་སེལ་ (basel) paying a fine for breaking a contract.
འབར་ (bar) vi. to burn, to catch fire, to explode ¶ ཤིང་རློན་པ་དེ་ལ་མེ་འབར་གྱི་མི་འདུག The wet wood is not catching fire. ¶ འབར་མདེལ་དེ་ལམ་སེང་འབར་མ་སོང་ The bomb didn't explode at once.
འབར་སྐད་ (bargɛɛ̀) sound of an explosion.
འབར་ཁ་ (barga) galloping; va.—གཏོང་; —རྒྱོད་ to gallop.
འབར་དངོས་ (barŋöö) 1. combustible/ flammable materials. 2. explosive materials.
འབར་གདག (bardaà) scolding; —གཏོང་; —བཀོལ་ to scold.
འབར་འབར་ (barbar) 1. an expression conveying extreme anger. 2. always burning (e.g., having a light on all the time).
འབར་འབུར་ (barbur) 1. abbr. of འབར་རེ་ and འབུར་རེ་. 2. a type of skin disease.
འབར་ཁ་ (barga) kindling materials.
འབར་ཁོག (bargɔɔ̀) derogatory name for monks.
འབར་གས་ (bargɛɛ̀) an explosion.
འབར་གོག (bargɔɔ̀) sm. འབར་ཁོག.
འབར་རྒྱ་ (bargya) combustible/ flammable materials.
འབར་དག་བཀོལ་ (bardaà gɔ̄ɔ) va. to scold.
འབར་གཏོར་ (bardɔɔ) exploding, blowing up; va.—གཏོང་; —བྱེད་ to explode, to blow up, to demolish.
འབར་ཐུབ་པའི་དངོས་པོ་ (bartubbɛ ŋööbo) combustible/ flammable matter or agents.
འབར་ཐུབ་པའི་རླངས་པ་ (bartubbɛ lāŋba) combustible/ flammable gases.
འབར་དུ་འཇུག (bardu juù) 1. va. to ignite, to set on fire. 2. va. to detonate.
འབར་བྱེད་དངོས་རྫས་ (barjeè ŋöödzɛɛ̀) flammable/ combustible/ incendiary materials or agents.
འབར་མདེལ་ (bandee) an explosive, bomb, mine, dynamite.
འབར་འབུར་ (barbur) bumpy/ uneven in surface.
འབར་མ་ (barma) Burma.
འབར་མེ་ (barme) flame; vi.—འབར་ to be burning (a flame).
འབར་མེད་མེ་རི་ (barme meri) extinct volcano.
འབར་མོ་ (baamo witch (female).
འབར་ཚག (bardza) pockmarked (from smallpox); vi.—ཚགས་; —བྱེད་ to get/ be pockmarked.
འབར་ཚད་ (bardzɛɛ̀) ignition point.
འབར་རྫས་ (bardzɛɛ̀) 1. explosives, dynamite. 2. fuel. 3. combustible/ flammable substances.
འབར་རྫས་སྣུམ་རིགས་ (bardzɛɛ̀ nūmriì) fuel oils.
འབར་ཤུན་ (barshün) 1. a kindling stick, match; va.—སྦྱིན་ to light a kindling stick to start a fire. 2. an oil lamp.
འབར་ཤུན་བཟོ་གྲྭ་ (barshün sodra) match factory.
འབར་གཡུག་གནམ་གྲུ་ (baryuù nəmdru) bomber (plane).
འབར་རེ་འབུར་རེ་ (bare bure) sm. འབར་རི་འབུར་རི་.
འབར་རི་འབུར་རི་ (bari buri) sm. འབར་འབུར་.
འབར་རོ་ཁ་གྱོག (baro kāgyɔɔ̀) very rich.
འབར་རླུང་ (bərluŋ) oxygen.
འབར་ཤ་ (barsha) sm. འབར་གཏོར་.
འབར་གཤག (barshaà) an explosion that splits rocks, etc.; va.—གཏོང་.
འབར་སླའི་དངོས་རྫས་ (barlɛ ŋöödzɛɛ̀) combustible/ inflammable goods or substances.
འབལ་: p. འབལ་; f. འབལ་; imp. འབོལ་ (bɛɛ) 1. va. to pluck/ pull out hair. 2. abbr. of འབལ་པོ་.
འབལ་གྲོ་ (bɛɛdro) mixture of wheat and peas.
འབལ་ཉོས་དཀོན་ཚོང་ (bɛɛ ñöö göndzoŋ) hoarding, profiteering [Lit. buy when abundant, sell when scarce].
འབལ་པོ་ (bɛɛbo) abundant, plentiful.
འབལ་སྲན་ (bɛɛdrɛn) mixture of barley and peas.
འབལ་འབལ་ལྷུག་ལྷུག (bɛɛbɛɛ lhūgluù) sm. འབལ་པོ་.
འབལ་འབོལ་ (bɛɛböö) 1. sm. འབལ་པོ་. 2. soft, spongy.
འབལ་ལེའི་དགུ་ལེའི་ (bɛɛlɛ gulɛ) sm. འབལ་པོ་.
འབལ་ལེ་བ་ (bɛɛlɛwa) the thick hair of animals that hangs down loosely.
འབལ་ལེ་འབོལ་ལེ་ (bɛɛle böölɛ) soft, spongy.
འབི་འབི་ (bimbi) 1. round. 2. term used for the penis of young boys.
འབི་ལཱ་ས་ (bilasə) hind. cement.
འབི་ལར་ (bilaa) hind. England.
འབིགས་: p. ཕུག; f. དབུག; imp. ཕུག (bii) va. to bore/ drill a hole, to pierce.
འབིགས་རྒྱག (bii gyaà) va. to bore/ make a hole in a wall in order to break into a home and rob it.
འབིགས་ལྕགས་འཁོར་སྒྲོམ་ (bigjaà kɔ̄ɔdrom) drilling frame (for oil wells).
འབིགས་ལྕགས་ལྕགས་གདུང་ (bigjaà jɔ̄gduŋ) drill pipe.
འབིགས་ཆས་ (bigjɛɛ̀) drilling equipment.
འབིགས་གདུང་ (bigduŋ) drill pipe.
འབིགས་མདའ་ (binda) sm. འབིགས་གདུང་.
འབིགས་བྱེད་འཕྲུལ་འཁོར་ (bigjeè trüügɔɔ) sm. འབིགས་གསོར་འཕྲུལ་འཁོར་.
འབིགས་ཚད་ (bigdzɛɛ̀) drilling rate; drilling level.
འབིགས་གཟོང་ (bigsoŋ) drill.
འབིགས་གསོར་ (bigsɔr) the bit/ point of a drill.
འབིགས་གསོར་འཕྲུལ་འཁོར་ (bigsɔr trüügɔɔ) drilling/ boring machine.
འབིབས་: p. ཕིབས་; f. ཕིབས་ (bib) sm. འབུབས་.
འབུ་ (bu) insect, bug.
འབུ་ཀྲང་ལང་ (bu drāŋlaŋ) tib.ch. cockroach.
འབུ་དཀར་ (bugar) 1. white raw silk. 2. a type of cookie fried in butter. 3. white insects.
འབུ་རྐང་བརྒྱ་པ་ (bu gāŋgyaba) centipede.
འབུ་རྐང་བརྒྱ་ལག་བརྒྱ་ (bu gāŋgya laggya) sm. འབུ་རྐང་བརྒྱ་པ་.
འབུ་སྐོག་ཅན་ (bu gɔ̄gjɛn) beetle.
འབུ་སྐྱོགས་ (bugyɔɔ̀) sm. འབུ་སྐྱོགས་དུང་.
འབུ་སྐྱོགས་དུང་ (bu gyɔ̄gduŋ) snail.
འབུ་སྐྱོག་དུང་འཁྱིལ་ (bugyɔɔ̀ duŋgyii) snail shell.
འབུ་སྐྱོན་ (bugyön) damage done by insects.
འབུ་ཁུང་ (buguŋ) hole caused by an insect.
འབུ་ཁྲུ་ (budru) shung. a type of hat worn by aristocrats of the traditional Tibetan goverment.
འབུ་མགོ་སེ་ (bu gose) sm. འབུ་འབུ་.
འབུ་རྒྱག (bu gyaà) vi. to be infested/ damaged by insects ¶ ཤ་ལ་འབུ་བརྒྱབ་བཞག The meat has gotten infested by insects.
འབུ་སྒོང་ (bugoŋ) egg of an insect.
འབུ་ལྕགས་ཀྱུ་མ་ (bu jɔ̄gyumə) hookworm.
འབུ་ཆ་ག་པ་ (bu cāgaba) locust.
འབུ་ཆེ་ (buje) an adult insect.

འབུ་ཆེས་ཆུང་ཟོས་ (bujeè cūŋ söö) the powerful/ big/ strong taking advantage of the weak, exploitation, imperialism [Lit. the big insect eats the small].

འབུ་ཆེས་ཆུང་བཟོས་ (bujeè cūŋ söö) sm. འབུ་ཆེས་ཆུང་ཟོས་.

འབུ་འཇོང་ (bujoŋ) a kind of worm.

འབུ་སྡུག (buduù) sm. སྡི་ཐག.

འབུ་དུང་དཀར་ (bu tuŋgar) insects/ animals with shells.

འབུ་དོང་ (budoŋ) pit for punishing criminals (that contains many insects).

འབུ་སྡོམ་ (budom) spider.

འབུ་ནད་ (bunɛɛ̀) diseases involving intestinal worms.

འབུ་ནར་ (bunar) sm. འབུ་ཆེ་.

འབུ་གནོད་ (bunöö) sm. འབུ་སྐྱོན་.

འབུ་གནོད་འགོག་བཅོས་ (bunöö gɔgjöö) preventing and treating insect damage.

འབུ་ཕྲ་ (budra) bacteria, germs, microbes.

འབུ་ཕྲ་འགོག་སྨན་ (budra gɔgmɛn) antibiotic medicines.

འབུ་ཕྲ་ཚོད་ལྟ་ཁང་ (budra tsöödagaŋ) bacteriology laboratory.

འབུ་ཕྲ་མོ་ (bu drāmo) 1. tiny insects. 2. sm. འབུ་ཕྲ་.

འབུ་ཕྲ་ཞུན་རྫས་ (budra shündzɛɛ̀) bacteriolisin.

འབུ་ཕྲན་ལྗང་མདོག (budrɛn jaŋdɔɔ̀) corn earworm.

འབུ་ཕྲའི་དམག་འཐབ་ (budrɛ mɔ̄gdəb) bacteriological/ germ/ warfare, biological warfare.

འབུ་ཕྲའི་མཚོན་ཆ་ (budrɛ tsɔ̃nja) biological weapon, germ warfare weapon.

འབུ་ཕྲའི་རིག་པ་ (budrɛ rigbə) bacteriology.

འབུ་ཕྲུག (budruù) larva of insects.

འབུ་བལ་ (bupɛɛ) 1. silk wadding. 2. cotton.

འབུ་བྱང་པ་ (bu jaŋba) Chinese blister beetle (cantharides).

འབུ་བླ་མ་མ་ཎི་ (bu lāma mani) dragon fly.

འབུ་སྦྲང་ (budraŋ) insects.

འབུ་སྦྲང་གི་རིག་པ་ (budraŋgi rigbə) entomology.

འབུ་མ་ (buma) moth.

འབུ་མེ་ཁྱེར་ (bu megyer) firefly.

འབུ་དམར་ (bumar) red worm.

འབུ་སྨུག (bumug) cookie that is fried in melted butter until its darkish in color.

འབུ་སྨིན་ (buñɛn) pollination by insects.

འབུ་ཚགས་ (budzaà) sm. འབུ་ཁྲང་.

འབུ་ཚང་ (budzaŋ) insect nest/ den.

འབུ་འཛིང་འཛིང་ (bu dziŋdziŋ) cicada.

འབུ་འཛེར་ (budzer) an abnormal excrescence on plants caused by insects.

འབུ་ཡིས་སྨིན་བྱེད་མེ་ཏོག (buyiì ñɛnjeè medɔɔ̀) flower pollinated by insects.

འབུ་རས་ (burɛɛ̀) raw silk fabric/ cloth.

འབུ་རིགས་མཁས་པ་ (buriì kɛ̄ɛ̀ba) entomologist.

འབུ་རིགས་ (buriì) a species of insect.

འབུ་ལང་ (bulaŋ) sm. ཙྭ་ལང་.

འབུ་སི་ (busi) silk thread.

འབུ་སུ་ཧང་ (bu sūhaŋ) tib.ch. lucerne, alfalfa.

འབུ་སེར་སྐྱེ་རིང་ (buser gēriŋ) mole cricket.

འབུ་སྲིན་ (busin) sm. འབུ་སྦྲང་.

འབུ་སྲིན་རིག་པ་ (busin rigbə) entomology.

འབུ་སླུ་སྒྲོན་མེ་ (bulu drönme) insect-killing lamp.

འབུ་གསོད་སྨན་ཕྱེ་ (busöö mɛ̄nje) powder insecticide.

འབུ་གསོད་སྨན་རྫས་ (busöö mɛ̄ndzɛɛ̀) insecticide.

འབུ་བསེ་བོས་འབྲོང་ལ་རྭ་གཡུག (bu sēböö droŋla ra yūù) overly optimistic. [Lit. a beetle shaking its horns when confronting a wild yak].

འབུ་གསོད་སྨན་ (bu sɔ̃ömɛn) sm. འབུ་གསོད་སྨན་རྫས་.

འབུ་ཨ་ར་ར་ (bu ārrara) sm. འབུ་སྐྱོགས་.

འབུག (buù) 1. sm. འབིགས་. 2. awl.

འབུག་པའི་ཟླ་བ་ (bugbɛ dawa) the 8th month of the Tibetan calendar.

འབུག་མ་ (bugmə) moth.

འབུག་ཨ་ལོང་ཅན་ (bug āloŋjɛn) a type of awl with a round metal handle.

འབུགས་ (buù) sm. འབུག.

འབུང་: p. འབུངས་; f. འབུང་; imp. འབུངས་ (buŋ) va. to work diligently/ hard, to strive.

འབུང་ཤ་ (buŋsha) pumpkin seeds.

འབུང་གསུམ་འདོན་པ་ (buŋsum dönba) doing everything possible, doing one's utmost.

འབུངས་ (buŋ) p. and imp. of འབུང་.

འབུད་: p. བུད་; f. འབུད་; imp. བུད་ (böö) 1. va. to expel, to drive out ¶ཁོ་ཚོས་ཁོ་སྐྱིད་སྡུག་ནང་ནས་ཕུད་པ་རེད་ (They) expelled him from their organization. 2. va. to push, to shove ¶འཁོར་ལོ་རྒྱབ་ནས་འབུད་ནས་བཟོ་བཅོས་པའི་སར་འཁྱོལ་ཐབས་བྱས་པ་རེད་ They pushed the vehicle from behind and tried to get to the service area. 3. va. to pass time ¶ལས་ཀ་མེད་སྐབས་དུས་ཚོད་འབུད་དཀའ་པ་འདུག Because (I) dont have any work, it is difficult to pass the time. 4. va. to take off ¶ཞྭ་མོ་འབུད་མ་ཐུབ་ཙང་ Because (he) couldn't take off (his) hat. 5. sm. བུད་. 6. va. to put firewood/ dung on a fire.

འབུད་: p. བུས་; f. འབུད་; imp. བུས་ (büü) 1. va. to play/ blow (usu. horns) ¶དུང་བུས་སོང་ (He) played the horn. 2. va. to burn.

འབུད་ཀྱག (büügyaà) 1. pushing, shoving; va.—གཏོང་; —རྒྱག to push/ shove; vi.—ཐེབས་ to get pushed/ shoved. 2. sm. འབུད་, 3.

འབུད་དཀྲོལ་ (büüdröö) wind and string instruments.

འབུད་དཀྲོལ་རོལ་ཆ་ (büüdröö rööja) orchestral music.

འབུད་དཀྲོལ་རོལ་མོའི་རུ་ཁག (büüdröömö rugaà) orchestra.

འབུད་གྲི་ (büüdri) a type of chisel.

འབུད་རྒྱག (büügyaà) sm. འབུད་ཀྱག.

འབུད་གདོང་རོལ་ཆ་ (büüdoŋ rööja) wind instrument.

འབུད་འཐེན་ (bünden) pushing and pulling; va.—བྱེད་.

འབུད་དུང་ (büüduŋ) white conch shell used as a wind instrument during religious ceremonies.

འབུད་འདེད་ (bündeè) pushing, shoving (in sense of directing/ herding); va.—བྱེད་; —གཏོང་.

འབུད་སྡེ་ (bündeè) sm. སྡི་ཐེ་.

འབུད་པ་ (büübə) bellows; va.—རྒྱག to use/ pump a bellows.

འབུད་འབུད་དུང་དུང་ (büübüü duŋduŋ) blowing horns and drumming/ beating on drums.

འབུད་ཤིང་ (büüshiŋ) fuel, firewood.

འབུན་ (bün) 50% interest.

འབུན་སྐྱེད་ (büngyeè) 50% interest.

འབུན་ཙམ་ (bündzam) shung. one and a half ཁལ་ of tsampa that was made from one ཁལ་ of grain.

འབུན་རྩིས་ (bündzii) calculating in a way that increases sth. by 50%.

འབུན་ཚོང་ (bündzoŋ) trade that yields a profit of 50%.

འབུབས་: p. ཕུབ་; f. དབུབ་; imp. ཕུབ་ (bub) 1. va. to put up, to pitch ¶གུར་ཕུབ་པ་རེད་ (They) put up a tent.

འབུམ་ (bum) a hundred thousand.

འབུམ་ཐེར་ (bumder) sm. འབུམ་.

འབུམ་པ་ (bumba) stupa.

འབུམ་ཕྲག (bumdra) multiple units of hundred thousands.

འབུམ་ཚོ་ (bumdzo) sm. འབུམ་ཕྲག.

འབུམ་ཟུར་ (bumsur) one hundred thousandth.

འབུའི་མཇུག་མས་འབུས་ཟ་བ་ (büü jugmɛɛ̀ büü sawa) always being short of money or food and having to borrow but then when this must be paid having to borrow again so being continuously in debt [Lit. an insect eating its own tail].

འབུར་ (bur) 1. any protuberance. 2. vi. to bulge out, to swell up, to protrude. 3. bas relief carving. 4. see མགོ་འབུར་.

འབུར་ཀ་ (burgə) sm. འབུར་, 1.

འབུར་གོང་ (burgoŋ) abbr. of འབུར་འབུར་གོང་གོང་.

འབུར་འབུར་ཀོང་ཀོང་ (burbur gōŋgoŋ) a place that has a lot of bumps and holes/ depressions.

འབུར་ཀྱོང་ (burgyoŋ) sm. འབུར་ཀོང་.

འབུར་སྐུ་ (burgu) bas-relief statue.

འབུར་སྐྱེ་ (bur gyē) vi. to have a pimple grow.

འབུར་བརྐོས་ (burgöö) carving in relief; va.—རྒྱག.

འབུར་འཇོམས་ (burjom) stifling, suppressing, inhibiting; va.—གཏོང་ ¶ སྤྱོད་ཚུལ་ངན་པ་ཐོན་མ་ཐག་འབུར་འཇོམས་གཏོང་དགོས་ As soon as (one) starts to behaves badly, one should supress it.

འབུར་ཐིག (burdig) a raised line.

འབུར་ཐོན་ (burdön) 1. vi. to protrude. 2. vi. to be conspicuous.

འབུར་ཐོན་ས་ཁྲ་ (burdön sābdra) a relief map.

འབུར་དུ་གཏོད་ (burdu tȫȫ) va. to make sth. protrude/ bulge out.

འབུར་དུ་དོད་ (burdu töö) vi. to protrude, to bulge out.

འབུར་དོད་ (burdöö) sm. འབུར་.

འབུར་དུང་ (burduŋ) sm. འབུར་འཇོམས་.

འབུར་པོ་ (burbu) sm. འབུར་འབུར་.

འབུར་གྲིས་ (burdrii) relief carving.

འབུར་འབུར་ (būrbur) protuberant, bulging.

འབུར་མ་ (burmə) sm. འབུར་འབུར་.

འབུར་ཚག (burdzaà) relief engraving.

འབུར་ཚུགས་ (burdzuù) glaring at; va.—སུ་ལྟ་ to glare at ¶ དགེ་རྒན་གྱིས་སློབ་ཕྲུག་ཚོར་མིག་འབུར་ཚུགས་བལྟས་འདུག The teacher glared at the students.

འབུར་ཚུགས་སུ་འཕྱུངས་ (burdzuùsu cūŋ) sm. འབུར་དུ་གཏོད་.

འབུར་ཤུན་ (burshün) wood shavings.

འབུར་ཟུར་ (bursur) a protruding edge/ point/ side.

འབུར་གཟུགས་ (bursuù) three dimensional.

འབུར་གཟུགས་གློག་བརྙན་ (bursuù lɔ̄ɔ̀ñɛn) three-dimensional film.

འབུར་རིས་ (burriì) three-dimensional drawings or paintings.

འབུར་ལེན་ (burlen) a carpenter's plane; va.—རྒྱག to plane sth.

འབུར་ལེན་ཁ་རིལ་ (burlen kārii) a type of carpenter's plane.

འབུར་ལེན་ཐེ་འབེ་ (burlen tēmbe) a type of plane.

འབུར་ལེན་སྣ་རིང་ (burlen nərіŋ) a type of long-nosed plane.

འབུར་ལེན་འཕྲུལ་སྡེགས་ (burlen trǖǖdeg) a planning machine.

འབུར་ལེན་བཟོ་རིགས་ (burlen sorig) planning work.

འབུར་ཤེལ་ (burshee) convex lens.

འབུར་ཤོག (burshɔ̀ɔ) wood shavings.

འབུར་གཤོང་ (burshoŋ) sm. འབུར་ཀོང་.

འབུར་གསལ་གློག་བརྙན་ (bursɛɛ lɔ̄ɔ̀ñɛn) sm. འབུར་གཟུགས་གློག་བརྙན་.

འབུར་གསལ་ལྟ་ཤེལ་ (bursɛɛ dāshee) sm. འབུར་གསལ་མིག་ཤེལ་.

འབུར་གསལ་པར་ལེན་ (būrsɛɛ bārlen) 3-D photography.

འབུར་གསལ་དཔེ་རིས་ (bursɛɛ bēriì) stereopicture, three dimensional picture.

འབུར་གསལ་མིག་གསལ་ (bursɛɛ migsɛɛ) 3-D glasses.

འབུར་གསལ་ཡུལ་ལྗོངས་ (bursɛɛ yünjoŋ). 3 dimensional scenery.

འབུལ་: p. ཕུལ་; f. དབུལ་; imp. ཕུལ་ (büü) va. to give, to present, to offer (h.) ¶ ཁོང་ལ་ཕྱག་རྟགས་ཞིག་འབུལ་གྱི་རེད་ (They) will give him a present.

འབུལ་སྐྱེས་ (büügyeè) gift, present (h.).

འབུལ་རྒྱ་ (büügya) a letter to superiors (with a seal).

འབུལ་སྒྲུབ་ཚོད་ཡིག (büüdrub cōōyii) shung. sm. སྒྲུབ་སྤྱོད་ཚད་ཡིག.

འབུལ་ཆས་ (büüjɛɛ̀) sm. འབུལ་སྐྱེས་.

འབུལ་ཆེན་ (büüjɛn) a large offering.

འབུལ་འཛོག་བྱེད་ (bünjɔɔ̀ ceè) va. to agree to, to sign ¶ གན་རྒྱ་འབུལ་འཛོག་བྱས་སོང་ They signed an agreement.

འབུལ་གཏོར་ (büüdɔɔ) torma for giving as an offering to deities.

འབུལ་རྟ་ (büüda) shung. horse given as a present.

འབུལ་རྟེན་ (büüden) 1. འབུལ་སྐྱེས་. 2. a gift given to get sth. in return.

འབུལ་རྟེན་དངུལ་ (büüden ŋüü) money given as gift (or bribe).

འབུལ་ཐོ་ (büüdo) list of presents received (e.g., at a marriage); va.—རྒྱག to record gifts on a list.

འབུལ་དུས་ (büüdüü) shung. time when a payment should be made ¶ འབུལ་དུས་གོང་མཚུངས་ཞུ་རྒྱུ་ The time when the payment will be made shall be the same as mentioned above.

འབུལ་དེབ་ (büüdeb) a book in which a list of presents received is kept.

འབུལ་སྡུད་པ་ (büü düübə) monks sent to various remote places by their monastery to preach and conduct rites so that they can collect gifts and offerings for the monastery (or monastic subunit).

འབུལ་གནང་མཛད་ (büünaŋ dzɛ̄ɛ̀) h. of འབུལ་.

འབུལ་སྤམ་ (büübam) the quantity of a gift/ present.

འབུལ་སྤྲོད་ (büüdrüǜ) va. to give and to receive.

འབུལ་འཕང་མཛད་ (büübaŋ dzɛ̄ɛ̀) h. of འཕེན་.

འབུལ་བ་ (büüwə) gift, offering, present (h.); va.—འབུལ་; —ཀྱག; —རྒྱག to give a gift/ offerin/ present.

འབུལ་འབབ་ (büübəb) shung. the amount of payment ¶ མེ་ཕག་ནས་འབུལ་འབབ་གསར་ཐོན་ Since (the year of the) fire boar, a new amount of payment was established.

འབུལ་བྱ་ (büüja) sth. to be given, gift.

འབུལ་སྦྱོར་ (büüjɔɔ) shung. handing over; va.—བྱེད་ ¶ མི་ཚ་ཤི་སྡོང་གི་རྗེས་ཤུལ་དངོས་རིགས་ལིགས་ཉིས་རྗེ་འདྲ་ཡིན་རུང་གཞུང་ཁོངས་སུ་འབུལ་སྦྱོར་བྱེད་དགོས་ (One) must hand over to the government all the belongings of the deceased serf.

འབུལ་དམིགས་ས་ཞིང་ (büümig sə̄shiŋ) shung. fields that can be used as a collateral on a loan.

འབུལ་ཚན་ (büüdzɛɛ̀) sm. འབུལ་སྐྱེས་.

འབུལ་ཚིག (büüdziì) a card or letter that accompanies a gift.

འབུལ་མཚོན་ (büüdzün) a token gift, a modest gift.

འབུལ་རྫས་ (büüdzɛɛ̀) sm. འབུལ་སྐྱེས་.

འབུལ་རྫོངས་ (büüdzoŋ) a parting/ farewell present, a gift to a person leaving.

འབུལ་བཞེས་གནང་ (büüsheè nāŋ) h. of སྤྲོད་ལེན་བྱེད་.

འབུལ་ཡིག (büüyiì) h. of གཏོང་ཡིག.

འབུལ་ཡུལ་ (büüyüü) the one to whom sth. is given, the recipient.

འབུལ་ལན་ (büülɛn) return gift (usu. given to a subordinate).

འབུལ་བཤམས་གནང་ (büüsham nāŋ) 1. va. to give food. 2. va. to make an offering to a deity.

འབུལ་ལོག (büülɔɔ̀) returning/ giving back sth. (usu. when a lama returns the scarf one has just given him).

འབུས་ (büǜ) vi. to sprout/ blossom (for plants, flowers).

འབུས་སྨྲན་མེ་ཏོག (büǜñɛn medɔɔ̀) pollinated flowers.

འབུས་བཟས་ (büǜ sɛɛ̀) worm-eaten, eaten/ nibbled on by insects.

འབེ་ལོག (belɔɔ̀) the middle brace between the beam and pillar.

འབེག (beg) eng. bag.

འབེན་ (ben) target.

འབེན་དངོས་ (benŋüü) live target.

འབེན་ཕོག་ཚད་ (ben pɔ̄ɔ̀dzɛɛ̀) percentage of hits (on a target).

འབེན་མིག (benmiì) the bull's-eye (on a target).

འབེན་མེད་མདའ་འཕེན་ (benmeè damben) aimless behavior [Lit. shooting when there is no target].

འབེན་ཡོད་སར་མདའ་རྒྱག (ben yȫȫ sāā dagyaà) behaving with purpose [Lit. shooting at a target].

འབེན་ར་ (benra) shooting range, target range.

འབེན་ལ་གཏོང་ (benla dõõ̀) va. to aim at a target.

འབེན་ས་ (bensa) a target.

འབེབ་ (beb) sm. འབེབས་.

འབེབས་: p. ཕབ་; f. དབབ་; imp. ཕོབ་ (beb) 1. va. to make/ cause to descend, to bring down, to demote ¶ གོ་གནས་འབེབས་ To demote in rank. ¶ རིན་གོང་ཕབ་ནས་བཙོངས་པ་རེད་ (They) lowered the price (gave a discount) and sold it. ¶ པ་ཕས་ཕྲུ་གུ་རྟ་ནས་ཕབ་པ་རེད་ The father brought down the child from the horse. 2. (with གཏན་) va. to settle, to decide. 3. va. to lay down one's arms/ weapons. ¶ གོ་ལག་ཕབ་པ་རེད་ (They) laid down (surrendered) their weapons. 4. va. to transcribe ¶ སྒྲ་འཇུག་འཕྲུལ་འཁོར་ནས་ཡིག་ཐོག་ལ་ཕབ་པ་རེད་ (He) transcribed the speech/ words from the tape recorder. 5. va. to convert currency/ money ¶ རུ་པི་ནས་ཨ་སྒོར་ལ་འབེབས་དགོས་ (You) have to convert rupees into U.S. dollars.

འབེབས་རྟེན་ (bebden) small gifts such as flower petals put in letters.

འབེབས་གདན་ (bebdɛn) sacks of grain put out for the bride to dismount from her horse.

འབེབས་མཚོན་ (bebdzön) sm. འབེབས་རྟེན་.

འབེབས་བཤད་ (bebshɛɛ̀) auspicious sayings that are repeated when the bride arrives and dismounts from her horse.

འབེམ་ (bem) sm. འབེན་.

འབེལ་ (bee) abbr. of འབེལ་པོ་.

འབེལ་དཀོན་ (beegön) abundance and scarcity, availability ¶ ལུང་པ་ཚང་མར་འབྲུ་རིགས་འབེལ་དཀོན་སྙོམ་པོ་འདུག The availability of grains in all the areas is equal.

འབེལ་མཆིད་ (beejiì) 1. talking freely and frankly. 2. a letter.

འབེལ་ཉོ་དཀོན་འཚོང་ (beeño göndzoŋ) buying when abundant and selling when scarce; va.—བྱེད་; —རྒྱག.

འབེལ་གཏམ་ (beedam) frank/ free discussion.

འབེལ་དུས་ (beēdüü) the abundant season (the time when certain items are in abundant supply).

འབེལ་པོ་ (beebo) abundant, plentiful.

འབེལ་འབེལ་ལྷུག་ལྷུག (beebee lhūglhuù) abundant, plentiful.

འབེལ་འཚོང་ལྷུག་འདོན་ (beedzoŋ lhūgdön) plenty to sell, much available for sale.

འབོ་ (bo) shung. a volume measure (in the form of a box) that is used to measure grains (one bo is equal to one ཁལ་ or about 28-31 pounds).

འབོ་: p. ཕོས་; f. དབོ་; imp. ཕོས་ (bo) vi. to get/ be spilled ¶ ཤོག་བུའི་སྟེང་ལ་སྣག་ཚ་ཕོས་སོང་ Ink spilled on the paper.

འབོ་ཁ་པ་ (bokawa) shung. a person who measures འབོ་.

འབོ་ཁ་རྒྱག (boga gyaà) va. to level the amount grain in the measuring box with a stick when measuring འབོ་.

འབོ་ཁ་འཇོག (boga jɔɔ̀) sm. འབོ་ཁ་རྒྱག.

འབོ་རྒྱུག (bogyaà) shung. a stick used to measure barley (to level the amount in the box).

འབོ་གང་ (bogaŋ) one འབོ་ of sth. like barley/ wheat.

འབོ་བྲེ་ (bodre) abbr. འབོ་ and བྲེ་ (one འབོ་ consists of 20 བྲེ་).

འབོ་བྲེ་ལ་ (bodrela) a mountain pass in Sichuan's Ngaba Prefecture.

འབོ་ལ་ཤར་ (bōla shār) va. to level the top of a འབོ་ measuring box (eliminating the excess).

འབོ་ལོ་ (bolo) a type of pine tree.

འབོ་ལོག་བྲེ་ལོག (bolɔɔ̀ drelɔɔ̀) shung. illegal འབོ་ and བྲེ་ that are larger than the official size.

འབོ་ཤར་གཏོང (boshar dōŋ) sm. འབོ་ལ་ཤར་.

འབོ་བཤེར་ (bosher) investigating/ examining/ checking whether a འབོ་ is accurate; va.—གཏོང་.

འབོག (bɔɔ̀) a square cloth used for wrapping clothes/ bedding, etc.

འབོག: p. ཕོག; f. དབོག; imp. བོག (bɔɔ̀) va. to give ¶ སྡོམ་པ་འབོག་པ་ To give vows.

འབོག: p. འབོགས་; f. འབོག; imp. འབོགས་ (bɔɔ̀) vi. to cross a river ¶ གཙང་ཆུ་འབོགས་ནས་ཕྱིན་སོང་ He crossed the river.

འབོག: p. བོག; f. འབོག (bɔɔ̀) vi. to faint. 2. vi. to fall down.

འབོག་སྒྲིལ་ (bɔgdrii) wrapped bundle.

འབོག་ལྕུག (bɔgjaà) shung. tiger or leopard skin patterned rug that is stuffed and hung on each side of the door of the palace of the Dalai Lama and a select few top Tibetan government officials (these were also used as symbolic whips when these officials traveled).

འབོག་ཆེན་ (bɔgjen) shung. a type of hat worn by officials of the traditional Tibetan goverment.

འབོག་འཇོལ་ (bɔgjöö) a bag/ container for bedding when traveling.

འབོག་ཏོ་ (bɔgdo) sm. འབོག་ཐོ་.

འབོག་གཏོང་རྒྱག (bɔgdoŋ gyaà) va. to lease out.

འབོག་ཐོ་ (bɔgto) 1. a flat stone used to even a floor that is under construction; va.—རྒྱག 2. shung. a lay official hat of the tt. government.

འབོག་རྡོ་ (bɔgdo) sm. འབོག་ཐོ་.

འབོག་སྡིག (bɔgdig) a clasp that fastens shawls (on the chest); va.—རྒྱག.

འབོག་རྭ་ (bɔgra) the newly grown sections of a deer's antler.

འབོག་རས་ (bɔgrɛɛ̀) 1. cloth for wrapping a bundle. 2. gunny sack.

འབོགས་ (bɔɔ̀) p. and imp. of འབོག.

འབོགས་ཆོག (bɔgjɔɔ̀) a vow taking ritual for monks.

འབོང་ (boŋ) vi. to get soaked/ wet.

འབོད་: p. བོས་; f. བོད་; imp. བོས་ (böö̀) 1. va. to call out, to shout out (to come) ¶ ཁང་པའི་ཕྱི་ནས་མི་གཅིག་གིས་ཁྱེད་རང་འབོད་ཀྱི་འདུག Outside the house someone is shouting for you (to come). 2. va. to call/ summon ¶ ང་རང་བཀའ་ཤག་སྣུག་དུ་བོས་བྱུང་ I was summoned to the inner room of the Kashag.

འབོད་བཀུག (bööguù) sm. འབོད་འགུགས་.

འབོད་སྐད་ (böögɛɛ̀) the sound of calling/ shouting/ summoning.

འབོད་སྐུལ་ (böögüü) sm. འབོད་བསྐུལ་.

འབོད་བསྐུལ་ (böögüü) an appeal, a call (for action); va.—བྱེད་; —གནང་ to appeal, to issue a call ¶ སློབ་གྲྭ་འཛུགས་རྒྱུའི་རྒྱབ་སྐྱོར་ཡོང་བའི་འབོད་བསྐུལ་བྱས་པ་རེད་ (They) issued an appeal for supporting the establishment of a school.

འབོད་བསྐུལ་གདན་ཞུ་ (böögüü dɛnshu) invitation; va.— འབུལ་; —བྱེད་.

འབོད་འགུག (bööguù) sm. འབོད་འགུགས་.

འབོད་འགུགས་ (bööguù) summoning, calling, convening; va.—བྱེད་ to summon, to call, to convene ¶ འདྲི་ཙད་ཆེད་འབོད་འགུགས་བྱས་པ་རེད་ (They) summoned (him) for questioning.

འབོད་སྒྲ་ (böödra) 1. a shout, cry. 2. an interjection.

འབོད་སྟངས་ (böödaŋ) the manner of summoning/ calling/ convening.

འབོད་བརྡ་ (bööda) 1. calling, announcing; va.—གཏོང་ ¶ ཚོགས་འདུར་ཤོག་ཟེར་འགོ་ཁྲིད་ཀྱིས་འབོད་བརྡ་བཏང་བ་རེད་ The leader announced, "come to the meeting". 2. commands used in military marching ¶ དམག་རྩེ་ད་འབོད་བརྡ་ Military drill commands.

འབོད་དབྱངས་ (bööyaŋ) shouting, hailing; va.—སྒྲོག to shout, to hail.

འབོད་མི་ (böömi) a person sent to call sb.

འབོད་མིང་ (böömiŋ) a term of address, title.

འབོད་ཚིག (böödziì) 1. slogan; va.—སྒྲོག; —འདོན་ to shout slogans. 2. interjection ¶ ཛམ་སྟོན་བྱེད་མཁན་ཚོས་འབོད་ཚིག་བཏོན་པ་རེད་ The demonstrators shouted slogans.

འབོད་རྩུལ་ (böödzüü) title, name.

འབོད་ལན་ (böölɛn) responding to a call/ appeal; va.—སློག; —བྱེད་ to respond to a call/ appeal ¶ ཟེང་ཆ་སློང་ཕྱོགས་སྐོར་ཁོ་ཚོས་འབོད་ལན་བྱེད་ཀྱི་ཡོད་པ་

རེད་ They are responding to an appeal to incite a disturbance.

འབོད་ལུགས་ (bööluù) sm. འབོད་སྟངས་.

འབོད་ལེན་ (böölen) sm. འབོད་ལན་.

འབོད་སློང་ (bööloŋ) va. to instigating/ inciting/ arousing through appeals/ calls; va.—བྱེད་ ¶ མང་ཚོགས་འབོད་སློང་བྱས་ཙང་ཏུ་སྟོན་ཁྲོམ་སྐོར་བྱས་པ་རེད་ Because (they) instigated the masses, (the masses) held a demonstration.

འབོབ་ (bob) 1. socks. 2. sth. thick put on the shoulders when carrying a load there.

འབོབ་ཤུབས་ (bobshub) sm. འབོབ་.

འབོམ་ (bom) eng. bomb; va.—དབྱུགས་; —རྒྱག; —འཕེན་ to drop bombs, to bomb.

འབོམ་རྒྱག་གནམ་གྲུ་ (bomyuù nəmdru) bomber (plane).

འབོར་ (bɔɔ) quantity, amount, number ¶ བོད་རིགས་འབོར་ཆེན་པོ་རྒྱ་གར་ནང་འབྱོར་ཡོད་པ་རེད་ A large number of Tibetans have come to India.

འབོར་: p. **བོར་**; f. **འབོར་**; imp. **བོར་** (bɔɔ) va. throw, fling, discard; divorce ¶ ཅ་ལག་ཕན་མི་ཐོགས་རྣམས་བོར་བ་རེད་ (He) threw out the useless things. ¶ ཁོས་ལོ་མང་སོང་བའི་བཟའ་ཟླ་བོར་བ་རེད་ He divorced his spouse of many years.

འབོར་གྲངས་ (bɔɔdraŋ) sm. འབོར་.

འབོར་ཆེ་ (bɔɔje) sm. འབོར་ཆེན་.

འབོར་ཚུང་ (bɔɔ cījuŋ) quantity, amount, number.

འབོར་ཆེན་ (bɔɔjen) large quantity/ amount/ number.

འབོར་ཆེན་པོ་ (bɔɔ cēmbo) sm. འབོར་ཆེན་.

འབོར་བསྡོམས་ (bɔɔdom) total quantity/ amount/ number.

འབོར་སྦོམ་ (bɔɔbom) sm. འབོར་.

འབོར་ཚད་ (bɔɔdzɛɛ̀) amount, number, quantity.

འབོར་ཚོང་ (bɔɔdzoŋ) wholesale trade.

འབོར་བརླག (bɔɔlaà) sm. བོར་བརླག.

འབོར་ཤོབ་ (bɔɔshob) boasting, bragging; va.—ཤོད་ to boast, to brag.

འབོར་ཤོབ་ཚ་པོ་ (bɔɔshob tsābo) boastful (person).

འབོར་སིལ་ཚོང་ཁང་ (bɔɔsii tsōŋgaŋ) wholesale and retail store.

འབོལ་ (böö) 1. imp. of འབབ་. 2. abbr. of འབོལ་པོ་.

འབོལ་སྐྱིད་ (böögyii) having a good livelihood and being happy.

འབོལ་ཁྲི་ (böödri) a soft seat/ berth, a cushioned seat/ berth.

འབོལ་མཁྲེགས་ (böödreg) 1. soft and hard. 2. flexibility.

འབོལ་གྲུམ་ (böödrum) a cushion with a rug on top of it.

འབོལ་སྙས་ (bööŋɛɛ̀) sm. སྙས་འབོལ་.

འབོལ་ཉོ་དཀོན་ཚོང་ (bööño gōndzoŋ) buying when the price is low and selling when there is scarcity.

འབོལ་སྟན་ (böödɛn) sm. འབོལ་གདན་.

འབོལ་སྟན་རྒྱབ་བརྙེས་ (böödɛn gyəbñeè) seat back cushion.

འབོལ་གདན་ (böödɛn) cushion, mattress.

འབོལ་ལྡན་ (böödɛn) soft, pliable.

འབོལ་པོ་ (bööbo) soft, pliable.

འབོལ་བ་ (bööwa) sm. འབོལ་པོ་.

འབོལ་འབོལ་ (bööböö) soft.

འབོལ་འབོལ་ལྷུག་ལྷུག (bööböö lhūluù) abundant, plentiful.

འབོལ་རྩོམ་ (böödzom) popular literature (an essay/ article written so that it can be easily understood).

འབོལ་རྩོམ་ཀློག་དེབ་ (böödzom popular literature.

འབོལ་རྩོམ་སྙན་ངག (böödzom ñɛ̄ŋaà) prose poem.

འབོལ་ལེ་ (bööle) at ease/ relaxed ¶ ཁོང་ཕྱོགས་འཁེལ་ལེ་བསྡད་འདུག He is staying there relaxed.

འབོལ་ལོག (bööløɔ̀) 1. stacked/ piled up; va.—རྒྱག to pile up/ stack up. 2. a thick cushion.

འབོལ་ས་ (böösa) 1. ground that is soft. 2. a place/ area that has an abundance of resources/ products.

འབོལ་ལྷུག (böölhuù) abbr. of འབོལ་འབོལ་ལྷུག་ལྷུག.

འབོས་ (böö) p. of འབོ་.

འབྱང་: p. **བྱང་**, f. **འབྱང་** (jaŋ) 1. vi. to be/ get cleansed ¶ ཕྱག་འཚལ་སྐོར་སྐྱོར་བྱས་ནས་སྡིག་པ་འབྱང་གི་ཡོད་པ་རེད་ (He) is cleansing his sins by doing prostations and circumambulations. 2. va. to be knowledgeable/ skillful (usu. in crafts), to master a craft ¶ ལག་ཤེས་དེ་ཚོ་ལམ་སེང་འབྱང་ཁག་པོ་རེད་ It is hard to master those crafts at once. 3. va. to cleanse or purge the bowels.

འབྱམ་: p. **འབྱམས་**; f. **འབྱམ་** (jam) sm. ཁྱབ་.

འབྱམ་པོ་ (jambo) a cushon with padding/ wadding.

འབྱམས་ (jam) p. of འབྱམ་.

འབྱམས་ཀླས་ (jamlɛɛ̀) sm. མཐའ་ཡས་པ་.

འབྱར་ (jar) 1. va. to be stuck on/ to, to be glued/ pasted ¶ ཤོག་བུ་གཉིས་མཉམ་དུ་འབྱར་བསྡད་བཞག The two pages are stuck together. 2. va. to get close to sb. in power.

འབྱར་ཁ་ (jarga) a gift, bribe; va.—རྒྱག.

འབྱར་ཀོ་ (jərgu) glue, adhesive.

འབྱར་བཅོས་ (jarjöö) medication that is applied to the skin.

འབྱར་ལྡན་ཆེ་སྣ་ (jardɛn tsīnə) substances that have a sticky/ adhesive quality.

འབྱར་བག (jarbaà) sm. འབྱར་རྫི་.

འབྱར་བག་དཀར་པོ་ (jarbaà karbo) a thick glue.

འབྱར་བག་ཅན་ (jarbaàjɛn) sth. that sticks or is adhesive.

འབྱར་བའི་རང་བཞིན་ (jarbɛ rəŋshin) the nature of stickiness.

འབྱར་བྱེད་ (jarjeè) glues, adhesives.

འབྱར་འབྱར་བྱེད་ (jarjar ceè) sm. འབྱར་, 2.

འབྱར་མ་ (jarma) things that are stuck/ attached to sth.

འབྱར་རྫི་ (jərdzi) sm. འབྱར་ཚེ་.

འབྱར་རྫིའི་རང་བཞིན་ (jərdzi rəŋshin) stickiness.

འབྱར་ཚེ་ (jərdzi) stickiness, sticky ¶ སྤྱིན་འདི་འབྱར་འཚེ་ཡག་པོ་མི་འདུག This glue's stickiness is not good.

འབྱར་ཚད་ (jardzɛɛ̀) sticky quality, stickiness, adhesiveness.

འབྱར་ཤུགས་ (jərshuù) stickiness, adhesiveness.

འབྱར་ས་ (jarsa) 1. clay. 2. backing, protection.

འབྱི་ (ji) f. of འབྱིད་.

འབྱིང་: p. **བྱིང་**; f. **འབྱིང་** (jiŋ) 1. vi. to sink, to drown ¶ ཁོ་ཆུའི་ནང་དུ་བྱིང་བཞག He drowned in the water. 2. vi. to feel dazed or befuddled.

འབྱིང་རྡོ་ (jiŋdo) anchor.

འབྱིངས་ (jiŋ) sm. འབྱིང་.

འབྱིད་: p. **ཕྱིད་**; f. **འབྱིད་** (jii) vi. to be able to earn a living/ livelihood.

འབྱིད་: p. **ཕྱིས་**; f. **དབྱི་** or **འབྱི་**; imp. **ཕྱིས་** (jii) 1. va. to wipe.

འབྱིད་: p. **བྱིད་**; f. **འབྱིད་** (jii) 1. vi. to slip/ slide and fall. 2. vi. to get blinded (e.g., from smoke). 3. vi. to get erased.

འབྱིན་: p. **ཕྱུང་**; f. **དབྱུང་**; imp. **ཕྱུང་** (jin) va. to cast/ throw out, to get rid of ¶ དབུགས་འབྱིན་ To breathe out ¶ སྲིད་ཇུས་གསར་པ་དེས་དབུལ་ཕོངས་ཀྱི་རྩ་བ་ཕྱུང་བ་རེད་ The new policy got rid of the root of poverty. ¶ ཁོ་ཚོགས་འདུའི་ཁྲོད་ནས་ཕྱུང་འདུག They threw him out of the meeting.

འབྱིན་རྔུབ་ (jinŋub) respiring, breathing.

འབྱིན་མཐུ་ (jindu) the power to cast/ throw out/ get rid of.

འབྱིལ་: p. **བྱིལ་**; f. **འབྱིལ་**; imp. **འབྱིལ་** (jii) 1. sm. འབྱུག. 2. va. to stroke sb.'s head/ beard. 3. arc. sm. ལྷུང་.

འབྱུག: p. **བྱུགས་**; f. **བྱུག**; imp. **བྱུགས་** (juù) va. to apply, to put/ rub on ¶ རྨ་ལ་སྨན་བྱུགས་པ་ཡིན་ (I) rubbed some medicine on the wound.

འབྱུང་: p. **བྱུང་**; f. **འབྱུང་** (juŋ) vi. to come about, to get, to come to be, to take place ¶ འཕོ་འགྱུར་སྔར་ལས་ཆེ་བ་འབྱུང་རྒྱུར་ཡིད་ཆེས་ཡོད་ (We) believe that changes greater than before will come about.

འབྱུང་རྐྱེན་ (juŋgyen) cause of sth. ¶ འབར་གཏོར་གྱི་འབྱུང་རྐྱེན་དེ་ད་ལྟ་རྩད་ཆོད་བྱེད་བཞིན་པ་རེད་ The cause of the explosion is being investigated now.

འབྱུང་ཁམས་ (juŋgam) the elements.

འབྱུང་ཁུངས་ (juŋguŋ) origin, source.

འབྱུང་ཁུངས་ཀྱི་ཁྱིམ་ཚང་ (juŋguŋgi kyīmdzaŋ) family origin.

འབྱུང་འཁྲུགས་ (juŋdruù) abbr. of འབྱུང་བ་འཁྲུགས་པ་.

འབྱུང་འགྱུར་ (juŋgyur) in the future, in times to come ¶ འབྱུང་འགྱུར་གྱི་འཆར་གཞི་ Future plans.

འབྱུང་འགྱུར་གྱི་རེག་བྱ་བདུན་ (juŋgyurgi regja dün) the seven types of physical sensation: smooth, rough, heavy, light, cold, hunger, thirst.

འབྱུང་འགྱུར་མི་རིང་བ་ (juŋgyur miruŋbə) the near future.

འབྱུང་ངེས་རང་བཞིན་ (juŋŋeè rəŋshin) objective necessity, objective inevitability.

འབྱུང་སྟངས་ (juŋdaŋ) sm. འབྱུང་ཚུལ་.

འབྱུང་ཐབས་ (juŋdəb) the way or means for sth. to come about ¶ ཞི་བདེ་འབྱུང་ཐབས་ཀྱི་གྲོས་མོལ་བྱེད་ཀྱི་ཡོད་པ་རེད་ They are discussing the way to achieve peace.

འབྱུང་གནས་ (juŋnɛɛ̀) sm. འབྱུང་ཁུངས་.

འབྱུང་པོ་ (juŋbu) 1. living beings. 2. demons.

འབྱུང་པོའི་གདོན་ (juŋbö dön) sm. འབྱུང་པོ་, 2.

འབྱུང་པོའི་གནས་ (juŋbö nɛ̄ɛ̀) chinoberry (used in Tibetan medicine).

འབྱུང་པོའི་བྱ་ (juŋbɛ ca) owl.

འབྱུང་བ་འཁྲུགས་པ་ (juŋwa trūgba) ill/ poor health.

འབྱུང་བ་ལྔ་ (juŋwa ŋā) 1. the 5 elements: fire, water, wind/ air, earth and sky. 2. the 5 elements used in Tibetan astrology: fire, water, wood, earth and iron.

འབྱུང་བ་ཆེན་པོ་ (juŋwa cēmbo) the basic elements: air, water, earth and fire.

འབྱུང་བ་སྙོམས་པ་ (juŋwa ñōmba) physical well-being.

འབྱུང་བ་ཐིམ་རིམ་ (juŋwa tīmrim) the five elements gradually merging into each other prior to death.

འབྱུང་བ་བཞི་ (juŋwa shi) the four elements: earth, fire, water and wind.

འབྱུང་བའི་གནོད་འཚེ་ (juŋwɛ nōȍdze) natural disaster.

འབྱུང་བའི་གཙུག་ལག (juŋwɛ dzūglaà) astrological calculation when people die.

འབྱུང་འབྲས་ (juŋdrɛɛ̀) outcome, result ¶ ཁྱེད་རང་ལས་ཀ་འདི་འདྲ་བྱས་ན་འབྱུང་འབྲས་ཡག་པོ་ཡོང་གི་མ་རེད་ If you work like that, the result will not be good.

འབྱུང་མོ་ (juŋmu) female demon/ spirit.

འབྱུང་རྩ་ (juŋdza) sm. འབྱུང་ཁུངས་.

འབྱུང་རྩ་རྩད་གཅོད་ (juŋdza dzɛ̄ɛ̀jöȍ) searching for the root/ origin, finding out the root of a matter; va.—བྱེད་.

འབྱུང་རྩ་རྩད་ཆོད་ (juŋdza dzɛ̄ɛ̀cöȍ) sm. འབྱུང་རྩ་རྩད་གཅོད་.

འབྱུང་རྩ་ར་འགྱུར་བའི་སྐད་རིགས་ (juŋdzar gyurwɛ gɛ̄ɛ̀riì) the parent language (of a language family).

འབྱུང་རྩིས་ (juŋdziì) sm. འབྱུང་བའི་གཙུག་ལག.

འབྱུང་རྩིས་ཀྱི་གབ་རྩེ་ཐང་ག (juŋdziìgi kəbdze tāŋga) thanka used with astrological calculations.

འབྱུང་ཚད་ (juŋdzɛɛ̀) frequency of sth. occurring.

འབྱུང་ཚུལ་ (juŋdzüü) manner of origination, way sth. came about ¶ ཟིང་འཁྲུག་དེའི་ཐོག་མའི་འབྱུང་ཚུལ་ང་ཚོས་ཤེས་ཀྱི་མི་འདུག We don't know the way the disturbance originally came about.

འབྱུང་གཞི་ (juŋshi) origin, source.

འབྱུང་གཞི་བདེ་པོ་ (juŋshi debo) good health.

འབྱུང་གཞིར་རྟོག་ཞིབ་ (juŋshi dōgshib) investigating the origins/ sources; va.—བྱེད་.

འབྱུང་བཞི་ (juŋshi) sm. འབྱུང་བ་བཞི་.

འབྱུང་བཞི་སྙོམས་པ་ (juŋshi ñōmba) sm. འབྱུང་བ་སྙོམས་པ་.

འབྱུང་ལུགས་འབྱུང་སྟངས་ (juŋluù juŋdaŋ) sm. འབྱུང་ཚུལ་.

འབྱུང་ས་ (juŋsə) sm. འབྱུང་རྩ་.

འབྱེ་: p. **བྱེ་**; f. **འབྱེ་** (je) vi. to open, to come apart, to separate ¶ སྒོ་དེ་རང་བཞིན་གྱིས་བྱེ་སོང་ The door opened by itself.

འབྱེད་: p. **ཕྱེ་**; f. **དབྱེ་**; imp. **ཕྱེས་** (jeè) 1. va. to open, to unlock, to uncover ¶ མོས་སྒོ་ཕྱེ་སོང་ She opened the door. 2. va. to classify, to separate, to differentiate, to divide ¶ ཁོ་ཚོ་ཚོགས་ཁག་གསུམ་ལ་ཕྱེ་བ་རེད་ (They) separated them into three groups.

འབྱེད་བཀོད་ (jeègöȍ) shung. abbr. of འབྱེད་དེབ་གསར་བཀོད་.

འབྱེད་ཁྲ་ (jeèdra) shung. land-tenure document.

འབྱེད་གདན་ (jeèdɛn) abbr. of འབྱེད་ཁྲ་ and བཀའ་གདན་.

འབྱེད་རྟགས་ (jeèdaà) semicolon.

འབྱེད་མཐུད་ (jeèdüù) the clutch in a car/ motorcycle); va.—རྒྱག to engage the clutch.

འབྱེད་མཐུད་ཡོ་བྱད་ (jeèdüù yobjɛɛ̀) sm. འབྱེད་མཐུད་.

འབྱེད་དེབ་གསར་བཀོད་ (jɛɛ̀deb sārgöȍ) shung. writing a new land tenure document.

འབྱེད་སྡུར་ (jeèdur) comparing and differentiating; va.—བྱེད་ ¶ བཟང་ངན་འབྱེད་སྡུར་བྱས་ནས་ Having differentiated between good and bad.

འབྱེད་དཔྱད་ (jeèjɛɛ̀) analysis and classification; va.—བྱེད་.

འབྱེད་བཙུམས་ (jēèdzum) opening and closing sth.

འབྱེད་གསལ་ (jēèdra) shung. the contents of a འབྱེད་ཁྲ་.

འབྱེར་: p. **བྱེར་**; f. **འབྱེར་**; imp. **བྱེར་** (jer) 1. va. to escape, to flee. 2. va. to disperse, to scatter.

འབྱོ་: p. **བྱོས་**; f. **བྱོ་**; imp. **བྱོས་** (jo) va. to pour liquid from one container to another.

འབྱོག: p. **འབྱོགས་**; f. **འབྱོག**; imp. **འབྱོགས་** (jɔ̄ɔ̀) sm. ལྡུག.

འབྱོགས་ (jɔ̄ɔ̀) p. and imp. of འབྱོག.

འབྱོང་: p. **འབྱོངས་**; f. **འབྱོང་** (joŋ) sm. འབྱང་.

འབྱོང་པོ་ (joŋbo) skilled, expert.

འབྱོངས་ (joŋ) p. of འབྱོང་.

འབྱོན་: p. **བྱོན་**; f. **འབྱོན་**; imp. **བྱོན་** (jön) va. to come (h.).

འབྱོན་ཐང་ (jöndaŋ) sm. འཇོན་ཐང་.

འབྱོན་པོ་ (jömbo) capable, able ¶ མི་འདི་ལས་ཀ་འབྱོན་པོ་ཡོད་པ་རེད་ That person is a capable worker.

འབྱོན་ཚོད་དཔག་ཚོད་ (jöndzöȍ bāgdzöȍ) evaluating the kind of work sb. can do based on his capabilities.

འབྱོན་བཤུད་ (jönshüù) sm. འགྲོ་འོང་.

འབྱོར་ (jɔɔ) 1. vi. to arrive/ come, to receive/ get ¶ འབབ་ཚུགས་སུ་ཆུ་ཚོད་བཞི་པར་འབྱོར་བྱུང་ (We) arrived at the station at four o'clock. ¶ ཁོང་གི་ས་ནས་ཕྱག་བྲིས་ཁ་ཤས་འབྱོར་འདུག (They) have received several letters from him. 2. wealth.

འབྱོར་འཁོད་ (jɔɔgöȍ) sm. འབྱོར་, 1.

འབྱོར་འཁོས་ (jɔɔgöȍ) financial status/ situation ¶ སོ་སོའི་འབྱོར་འཁོས་ལ་གཞིགས་པའི་འགྲོ་སོང་གཏོང་དགོས་ (One) should spend according to (one's) financial situation.

འབྱོར་སྐྱུད་ (jɔɔ güù) rich and poor.

འབྱོར་སྐྱུད་འདུ་འབྲལ་ (jɔɔ güù du drɛɛ) being rich and poor and coming together and separating.

འབྱོར་ལྕག (jɔɔjaà) shung. whipping of criminals when they are brought to jail; va.—གཞུ་ [Lit. arrival whipping].

འབྱོར་ཆུང་གྲལ་རིམ་ (jɔɔjuŋ trɛɛrim) petty-bourgeoisie class.

འབྱོར་ཆུང་པ་ (jɔɔ cūŋbə) petty bourgeois.

འབྱོར་ཆེན་གྲལ་རིམ་ (jɔɔjen trɛɛrim) big bourgeoisie class.

འབྱོར་ཆེན་ཚོགས་ཁག (jɔɔjen tsɔ̄ɔ̀gaà) financial group.

འབྱོར་འཇགས་པ་ (jɔɔjagba) a gift in money or in kind given by major monastic officials at the end of their term of office.

འབྱོར་མཇལ་ (jɔɔjɛɛ) sm. འབྱོར་ལྕག.

འབྱོར་ཉིན་ (jɔɔñin) the day sb. arrived.

འབྱོར་སྙན་ (jɔɔñɛn) shung. a report made when one arrives; va.—ཞུ་.

འབྱོར་ཐོ་ (jɔɔdo) signing or registering one's arrival or attendance; va.—འགོད་; —རྒྱག to sign/ report one's arrival, to register at a meeting.

འབྱོར་ཐོ་འགོད་ས་ (jɔɔdo göösa) registration desk/ place.

འབྱོར་ཐོན་ (jɔɔdön) arrival and departure.

འབྱོར་དུས་བཟོ་ (jɔndüü so) va. to make an appointment/ arrangement for arrival.

འབྱོར་ལྡན་ (jɔndɛn) wealthy, rich.

འབྱོར་ལྡན་གྲལ་རིམ་ (jɔndɛn trɛɛrim) bourgeoisie.

འབྱོར་ལྡན་གྲལ་རིམ་གྱི་མཁས་དབང་ (jɔndɛn trɛɛrimgi kɛ̄ɛ̀waŋ) bourgeois authority.

འབྱོར་ལྡན་གྲལ་རིམ་གྱི་ཁྲིམས་དབང་ (jɔndɛn trɛɛrimgi trīmwaŋ) bourgeois rights.

འབྱོར་ལྡན་གྲལ་རིམ་གྱི་གོང་མ་སྲུང་མཁན་ (jɔndɛn trɛɛrimgi kɔŋma sūŋgɛn) bourgeois royalists (term used during the Cultural Revolution).

འབྱོར་ལྡན་གྲལ་རིམ་གྱི་ལྟ་ཚུལ་ (jɔndɛn trɛɛrimgi dədzüü) bourgeois view.

འབྱོར་ལྡན་གྲལ་རིམ་གྱི་ལོག་སྤྱོད་ལམ་ཕྱོགས་ (jɔndɛn trɛɛrimgi lɔgjöö lamjɔ̄ɔ̀) bourgeois reactionary line (name given by the Jing Qing faction during the Cultural Revolution to the policies advocated by Liu Shaoqi).

འབྱོར་ལྡན་གྲལ་རིམ་གྱི་ཕྱོགས་གཤིས་ (jɔndɛn trɛɛrimgi jɔ̄ɔ̀shiì) bourgeois faction.

འབྱོར་ལྡན་གྲལ་རིམ་གྱི་དམག་སྤྱི་ཁང་ (jɔndɛn trɛɛrimgi məgjigaŋ) bourgeois military command headquarters (term used during Cultural Revolution attacking the Liu Shaoqi-Deng Xoping faction).

འབྱོར་ལྡན་གྲལ་རིམ་གྱི་དམངས་གཙོ་ (jɔndɛn trɛɛrimgi māŋdzo) bourgeois democrats/ democracy ¶ འབྱོར་ལྡན་གྲལ་རིམ་གྱི་དམངས་གཙོའི་གསར་བརྗེ་ Bourgeois democratic revolution.

འབྱོར་ལྡན་གྲལ་རིམ་གྱི་གཡས་ཕྱོགས་ (jɔndɛn trɛɛrimgi yɛ̄ɛ̀jɔɔ̀) bourgeois rightists.

འབྱོར་ལྡན་གྲལ་རིམ་གྱི་རང་དབང་ཅན་ (jɔndɛn trɛɛrimgi raŋwaŋjɛn) bourgeois liberalization (a term coined in 1981).

འབྱོར་ལྡན་གྲལ་རིམ་གྱི་ལངས་ཕྱོགས་ (jɔndɛn trɛɛrimgi laŋjɔɔ̀) bourgeois standpoint/ position.

འབྱོར་ལྡན་གྲལ་རིམ་གྱི་སྲིད་ཏང་ (jɔndɛn trɛɛrimgi siìdaŋ) bourgeois political party.

འབྱོར་ལྡན་གྲལ་རིམ་གྱི་སྲིད་དབང་སྒེར་འཛིན་ (jɔndɛn trɛɛrimgi siìwaŋ gerdzin) the dictatorship of the bourgeoisie.

འབྱོར་ལྡན་གྲལ་རིམ་གྱི་གསར་བརྗེ་ (jɔndɛn trɛɛrimgi sārje) bourgeois revolution.

འབྱོར་ལྡན་གྲལ་རིམ་གྱི་བསམ་བློ་ (jɔndɛn trɛɛrimgi sāmlo) bourgeois ideology/ ideas/ thoughts.

འབྱོར་ལྡན་ཆེ་ཁག (jɔndɛn cēgaà) the richer strata.

འབྱོར་ལྡན་པ་ (jɔndɛmba) wealthy/ rich person.

འབྱོར་ལྡན་ཧྲུལ་པོ་ (jɔndɛn hrūūbu) a rich person who dresses poorly.

འབྱོར་བསྡད་ (jɔɔdɛɛ̀) sm. འབྱོར་འཁོད་.

འབྱོར་ནད་ (jɔɔnɛɛ̀) infectious/ contagious disease.

འབྱོར་གནང་ (jɔɔnaŋ) h. of འབྱོར་.

འབྱོར་པ་ (jɔɔba) wealth, fortune, prosperity.

འབྱོར་པ་རྒྱ་ཆེ་བ་ (jɔɔba gyacewa) having great wealth/ fortune, very prosperous.

འབྱོར་པ་ཅན་ (jɔɔbajɛn) sm. འབྱོར་ལྡན་པ་.

འབྱོར་པོ་ (jɔɔbu) 1. fat, chubby. 2. wealthy, opulent.

འབྱོར་ཕྱག (jɔɔjaà) shung. calling on or reporting in person to one's superior after one's arrival from a trip; va.—ཞུ་.

འབྱོར་ཕྱུག (jɔɔjuù) rich, wealthy.

འབྱོར་བའི་ཡི་གེ་ (jɔɔwɛ yigi) letters to the editor.

འབྱོར་འབྲིང་གྲལ་རིམ་ (jɔɔdriŋ trɛɛrim) the middle bourgeoisie, the middle class.

འབྱོར་མེད་ (jɔɔmeè) poor.

འབྱོར་མེད་པ་ (jɔɔmeèba) proletariat, proletarian.

འབྱོར་མེད་གྲལ་རིམ་ (jɔɔmeè trɛɛrim) the proletariat/ proletarian class.

འབྱོར་མེད་གྲལ་རིམ་གྱི་རྒྱལ་སྤྱིའི་རིང་ལུགས་ (jɔɔmeè trɛɛrimgi gyɛɛjii riŋluù) proletarian internationalism.

འབྱོར་མེད་གྲལ་རིམ་གྱི་རིག་གནས་གསར་བརྗེ་ཆེན་པོ་ (jɔɔmeè trɛɛrimgi rignɛɛ̀ sārje cēmbo) the Great Cultural Proletarian Cultural Revolution.

འབྱོར་མེད་གྲལ་རིམ་གྱི་སྲིད་ཏང་ (jɔɔmeè trɛɛrimgi siìdaŋ) the Proletarian Party.

འབྱོར་མེད་གྲལ་རིམ་གྱི་སྲིད་དབང་སྒེར་འཛིན་ (jɔɔmeè trɛɛrimgi siìwaŋ) dictatorship of the proletariat.

འབྱོར་མེད་གྲལ་རིམ་གྱི་བསམ་པ་ (jɔɔmeè trɛɛrimgi sāmba) proletarian thought/ ideology.

འབྱོར་མེད་གྲལ་རིམ་གྱི་གསར་བརྗེ་ (jɔɔmeè trɛɛrimgi sārje) proletarian revolution.

འབྱོར་མེད་གྲལ་རིམ་ཕྱེད་ཙམ་ (jɔɔmeè trɛɛrim cēèdzam) semiproletariat, semiproletarian.

འབྱོར་མེད་པ་ (jɔɔmeèba) proletarian.

འབྱོར་དམན་ (jɔɔmɛn) poor.

འབྱོར་ཚེས་ཞུ་ (jɔɔdzeè shu) va. to report the time of one's arrival.

འབྱོར་ཚོགས་ (jɔɔdzɔɔ̀) wealth, riches.

འབྱོར་འཛིན་ (jɔndzin) receipt (that sth. arrived).

འབྱོར་ཡིག (jɔɔyiì) a letter one has received.

འབྱོར་ཡོན་ (jɔɔyön) sm. འབྱོར་པ་.

འབྱོར་ལན་ (jɔɔlɛn) 1. reply, answer (to a letter); va.—གཏོང་. 2. a receipt.

འབྱོར་ཤེད་ཅན་ (jɔɔsheèjɛn) financial magnate, plutocrat.

འབྱོལ་: p. བྱོལ་; f. འབྱོལ་; imp. བྱོལ་ (jöö) va. to avoid, to step aside, to give way to ¶ ལམ་ཉེན་ཁ་ཅན་བྱོལ་བ་རེད་ They avoided the dangerous trail. ¶ ཁོས་རང་གི་ལས་འགན་ལས་བྱོལ་བ་རེད་ He avoided his work responsibility.

འབྲ་གོ་ (drago) persimmon.

འབྲག (draà) a butter and oil container.

འབྲང་: p. འབྲངས་; f. འབྲང་; imp. འབྲོངས་ (draŋ) va. to follow after, to pursue to catch up with.

འབྲང་ (draŋ) line (of people or things), queue; va.—སྒྲིག to line up, to make into a line, to put in lines ¶ གློག་བརྙན་ལག་ཁྱེར་ཉོ་སར་འབྲང་གསུམ་བསྒྲིགས་བཞག (They) put people in three lines to buy movie tickets. 2. nomad's tent.

འབྲང་རྒྱས་ (draŋgyɛɛ̀) a kind of torma.

འབྲང་བཏབ་ (draŋ dəb) 1. va. to pitch/ put up a tent. 2. va. to stop for a meal when traveling.

འབྲངས་ (draŋ) p. of འབྲང་.

འབྲད་: p. བྲད་; f. དབྲད་; imp. བྲོད་ (drɛɛ̀) va. to scratch, to scrape, to rub.

འབྲད་འབྲད་ (drɛɛ̀drɛɛ̀) scratching, gnawing (on piece of bone); va.—རྒྱག.

འབྲབ་: p. བྲབས་; f. བྲབ་; imp. བྲབས་ (drəb) 1. va. to cast/ throw/ scatter. 2. va. to strike, to hit.

འབྲབ་ལྕག (drəbjaà) a whip.

འབྲབ་རྡུང་ (drəbduŋ) hitting, beating; va.—བྱེད་.

འབྲབ་རྡུང་ནན་འདྲི་ (drəbduŋ nɛndri) interrogating/ questioning through beating; va.—བྱེད་.

འབྲལ་: p. བྲལ་; f. འབྲལ་ (drɛɛ) 1. vi. to be separated, to be cut off/ disconnected from, to come apart. 2. vi. to be without, to be devoid of.

འབྲལ་ཐབས་མེད་པ་ (drɛɛdəb meèba) sm. འབྲལ་མེད་.

འབྲལ་སྦང་ (drɛɛbaŋ) inseparable, always together.

འབྲལ་སྦང་སྐུ་ (drɛɛbaŋ gū) a small statue of the Buddha that gelong monks must keep with them at all times.

འབྲལ་མེད་ (drɛɛmeè) inseparable, always together ¶ མཛའ་གྲོགས་འབྲལ་མེད་ Inseparable friends.

འབྲལ་མེད་མཉམ་གཤིབ་ (drɛɛmeè ñəmshib) staying together without separating.

འབྲས་ (drɛɛ̀) 1. rice ¶ འབྲས་ཞིང་ Rice field. 2. result, outcome, fruit (usu. vb.+ —) ¶ སློབ་སྦྱོང་བྱས་འབྲས་ The result of studying. 3. fruit ¶ འབྲས་ལྡན་རྩི་ཤིང་སྣ་ཚོགས་ཀྱིས་ཁེངས་ It was filled with various different fruit bearing plants. 4. abbr. of

འབྲས་སྤུངས་.

འབྲས་དཀར་ (drɛ̱ɛ̀gar) 1. white rice. 2. a type of beggar who during Tibetan new year goes around visiting homes chanting auspicious sayings.

འབྲས་སྐོགས་ (drɛ̱ɛ̀gɔɔ̀) burned rice at the bottom of a pot.

འབྲས་བཀྲུས་ཆུ་སྙིགས་ (drɛ̱ɛ̀drüǜ cũñig) leftover water after rice has been washed.

འབྲས་སྐྲན་ (drɛ̱ɛ̀drɛn) cancer.

འབྲས་ཁང་ (drɛ̱ɛ̀gaŋ) 1. storage room for rice. 2. shung. an official in the Tibetan government who's duty was to acquire rice for the goverment.

འབྲས་ཁུ་ (drɛ̱ɛ̀gu) the water in which rice has been boiled.

འབྲས་ཁོག (drɛ̱ɛ̀gɔɔ̀) rice steamer, pot in which rice is cooked.

འབྲས་གྱི་ (drɛ̱ɛ̀gyi) name of a place just outside of Shol.

འབྲས་གྲྭ་ (drɛ̱ɛ̀dra) a monk from Drepung monastery.

འབྲས་གྲུགས་ (drɛ̱ɛ̀druù) broken pieces of rice/ grain.

འབྲས་བགྲུ་འཕྲུལ་འཁོར་ (drɛ̱ɛ̀dru trũũgɔɔ) rice husking machine.

འབྲས་བགྲུད་འཕྲུལ་འཁོར་ (drɛ̱ɛ̀drüǜ trũũgɔɔ) sm. འབྲས་བགྲུ་འཕྲུལ་འཁོར་.

འབྲས་བགྲུས་ (drɛ̱ɛ̀drüǜ) husking rice; va.—རྒྱག to husk rice.

འབྲས་བགྲུས་རྡོ་རིང་ (drɛ̱ɛ̀drüǜ do̱riŋ) stone roller for husking rice.

འབྲས་འགྱེད་ (drɛ̱ɛ̀gyeè) rice given as alms to monks.

འབྲས་རྒྱུག (drɛ̱ɛ̀gyuù) staff carried by འབྲས་དཀར་ beggar (to ward away dogs).

འབྲས་སྒོ་མང་ (drɛ̱ɛ̀ go̱maŋ) Drepung monastery's Gomang College.

འབྲས་སྒྲུབ་པ་ (drɛ̱ɛ̀ dru̱bba) sm. འབྲས་ཁང་, 2.

འབྲས་ངན་ (drɛ̱ɛ̀ŋɛn) abbr. of འབྲས་བུ་ངན་པ་.

འབྲས་སྔགས་པ་ (drɛ̱ɛ̀ ŋāgba) Drepung monastery's Ngagpa College.

འབྲས་བརྔོས་ (drɛ̱ɛ̀ŋöö̀) 1. puffed/ popped rice. 2. fried rice.

འབྲས་ཆག (drɛ̱ɛ̀caà) pounded rice.

འབྲས་ཆང་ (drɛ̱ɛ̀jaŋ) 1. rice wine. 2. a kind of rice candy.

འབྲས་ཆན་ (drɛ̱ɛ̀jɛn) steamed rice.

འབྲས་རྗེན་པ་ (drɛ̱ɛ̀ je̱mba) uncooked rice.

འབྲས་ལྗང་ (drɛ̱njaŋ) rice seedlings; va.—འཛུགས་ to plant rice seedlings.

འབྲས་ལྗང་ཞིང་ཁ་ (drɛ̱njaŋ shi̱ŋgə) rice seedling bed.

འབྲས་ལྗོངས་ (drɛ̱njoŋ) Sikkim.

འབྲས་ལྗོངས་པ་ (drɛ̱njoŋba) Sikkimese.

འབྲས་ལྗོངས་ཆོས་རྒྱལ་ (drɛ̱njoŋ cõõgyɛɛ̀) shung. Maharaja of Sikkim.

འབྲས་ལྗོངས་ས་སྐྱོད་ (drɛ̱njoŋ sājöö̀) shung. sm. འབྲས་ལྗོངས་ཆོས་རྒྱལ་.

འབྲས་ཉག (drɛ̃ɛ̀ñaà) rice kernel.

འབྲས་སྙིགས་ (drɛ̱ɛ̀ñii̇) rice husk.

འབྲས་ལྟང་ (drɛ̱ɛ̀daŋ) a skin bag/ load of rice.

འབྲས་སྟོང་ (drɛ̱ɛ̀doŋ) 1. an empty ear of rice. 2. a work or task that bears no results/ fruits.

འབྲས་བརྟོལ་ (drɛ̱ɛ̀ dõõ̀) va. to drain a boil/ puss that is ripe.

འབྲས་ཐུག (drɛ̱ɛ̀duù) rice gruel/ porridge.

འབྲས་ཐུད་ (drɛ̱ɛ̀düǜ) rice cake.

འབྲས་དུས་ (drɛ̱ɛ̀düǜ) season or time when crops ripen.

འབྲས་དོར་མ་ (drɛ̱ɛ̀dɔrma) Chinese ilex.

འབྲས་དོས་ (drɛ̱ɛ̀döö̀) a load of rice (for shipping).

འབྲས་ལྡན་ (drɛ̱ndɛn) 1. autumn, fall. 2. the second month of the Tibetan calendar.

འབྲས་ལྡན་ཤིང་ (drɛ̱ndɛn shĩŋ) fruit tree.

འབྲས་ལྡུར་ (drɛ̱ɛ̀duu) sm. འབྲས་ཐུག.

འབྲས་རྡུང་འཕྲུལ་འཁོར་ (drɛ̱ɛ̀duŋ trũũgɔɔ) rice threshing machine.

འབྲས་རྡོག (drɛ̱ɛ̀dog) grain of rice.

འབྲས་ནད་ (drɛ̀ɛnɛɛ̀) 1. a type of cancer. 2. ulcer.

འབྲས་ཕུགས་ (drɛ̀ɛ̀baà) rice skin/ husk.

འབྲས་སྤུངས་ (drɛ̱ɛ̀buŋ) sm. འབྲས་སྤུངས་དགོན་པ་.

འབྲས་སྤུངས་ཀླུ་འབུམ (drɛ̱ɛ̀buŋ lũmbum) a religious festival celebrated by Drepung monastery on the 8th day of the 7th month of the Tibetan calendar.

འབྲས་སྤུངས་དགོན་པ་ (drɛ̱ɛ̀buŋ gö̱mba) Drepung Monastery.

འབྲས་སྤུངས་རྡོ་ཁང་སྔོན་མོ་ (drɛ̱ɛ̀buŋ do̱gaŋ ŋõmba) an ancient name for འབྲས་སྤུངས་དགའ་ལྡན་ཕོ་བྲང་.

འབྲས་སྤུངས་སྤྱི་སོ་ (drɛ̱ɛ̀buŋ ci̇so) the chief economic managers of Drepung Monastery (as a whole).

འབྲས་སྤྱི་ (drɛ̱ɛ̀ji) 1. abbr. of འབྲས་སྤྱི་བློན་ཆེན་. 2. abbr. of འབྲས་སྤུངས་སྤྱི་སོ་.

འབྲས་སྤྱི་བློན་ཆེན་ (drɛ̱ɛ̀ji lõnjen) shung. the representative of the Indian government in Sikkim (known as the "Political Officer").

འབྲས་སྤྱིའི་ལམ་རོགས་ (drɛ̱ɛ̀ji la̱mrɔɔ̀) shung. Assistant Political Officer.

འབྲས་འཕགས་བོད་གསུམ་ (drɛ̱ɛ̀ pāg pö̱ö̀ sūm) the three: Sikkim, India and Tibet.

འབྲས་ཕུབ་ (drɛ̱ɛ̀pub) sm. འབྲས་ཕུགས་.

འབྲས་ཕྱེ་ (drɛ̱ɛ̀je) rice flour.

འབྲས་བུ་ (drɛ̱ɛ̀bu) 1. fruit. 2. result, outcome, effects; vi.—སྨིན་; —ཐོན་; —འབྱིན་ to have/ get a result ¶ ཁོས་དཀའ་ལས་བརྒྱབ་ཀྱང་འབྲས་བུ་ཐོན་མེད་པ་རེད་ Even though he worked hard, he didn't get any result. 3. scrotum, testicle. 4. a type of abscess/ boil.

འབྲས་བུ་ངན་པ་ (drɛ̱ɛ̀bu ŋɛ̱mba) evil or bad result/ outcome/ effect; vi.—འཁོར་ to have bad result fall on sb. ¶ ལས་ཀ་ངན་པ་བྱས་ན་འབྲས་བུ་ངན་པ་རང་ལ་འཁོར་གྱི་རེད་ If you do bad things, bad results will occur to you.

འབྲས་བུ་སྟོང་པ་ (drɛ̱ɛ̀bu dōŋba) work or task that bears no fruits/ results.

འབྲས་བུ་ཅན་གྱི་ཤིང་ (drɛ̱ɛ̀bujɛngi shĩŋ) fruit tree.

འབྲས་བུ་དུད་ (drɛ̱ɛ̀bu tü̱ǜ) vi. to hang down (for ripe fruits/ grains).

འབྲས་བུ་ནག (drɛ̱ɛ̀bu na̱à) poet. jute/ flax.

འབྲས་བུ་རྣམ་པར་སྨིན་ (drɛ̱ɛ̀bu nāmbar mĩn) vi. to have one's past actions bear fruit (have a result).

འབྲས་བུ་འབྱིན་ (drɛ̱ɛ̀bu ji̱n) vi. to get a result from an action. 2. va. to castrate.

འབྲས་བུ་འབྱུང་ (drɛ̱ɛ̀bu ju̱ŋ) eunuch.

འབྲས་བུ་སྨིན་ (drɛ̱ɛ̀bu mĩn) vi. to ripen (for fruits). 2. vi. to achieve the result of one's work. 3. sm. འབྲས་བུ་རྣམ་པར་སྨིན་.

འབྲས་བུ་གཡུར་དུ་ཟ་བ་ (drɛ̱ɛ̀bu yūrdu sa̱wa) having/ getting great results [Lit. ripe fruits falling to the ground].

འབྲས་བུ་ལ་རྒྱུ་མིང་བཏགས་ (drɛ̱ɛ̀bula gyu̱ mi̱ŋ dāà) va. to give a product or thing a name for what it does (e.g., race horse).

འབྲས་བུ་ལ་ཉེ་བར་སྤྱོད་ (drɛ̱ɛ̀bula ñe̱war jö̃ö̀) va. to make use of sb.'s result/ outcome.

འབྲས་བུ་ལོ་མས་བསྒྲིབ་ (drɛ̱ɛ̀bu lo̱mɛ dri̱b) usu. refers to speeches, articles, papers where the main point/ issue is not made clear because of useless rhetoric or words [Lit. fruit shaded by leaves].

འབྲས་བུ་གསུམ་ (drɛ̱ɛ̀bu sūm) three types of Tibetan medicine ཨ་རུ་ར་, བ་རུ་ར་, སྐྱུ་རུ་ར་.

འབྲས་བུའི་ཕུང་པོ་ (drɛ̱ɛ̀bü pūŋbo) poet. coconut tree.

འབྲས་བུའི་ཤིང་ (drɛ̱ɛ̀bü shĩŋ) fruit tree.

འབྲས་འབུ་ (drɛ̱mbu̱) rice borer (insect).

འབྲས་འབྲུ་ (drɛ̱ɛ̀ dru̱) grain of rice.

འབྲས་སྦྱར་སྡོང་པོ་ (drɛ̱ɛ̀jar do̱ŋbo) a general term for fruit bearing trees.

འབྲས་མེད་ (drɛ̱ɛ̀meè) in vain, without good result/ outcome ¶ ངལ་བ་འབྲས་མེད་ Undergoing hardship without achieving a result (success).

འབྲས་མེད་སོ་མ་ (drɛ̱ɛ̀meè sōma) seedless jute.

འབྲས་མོ་ལྗོངས་ (dr<u>ɛ</u>̀mojoŋ) sm. འབྲས་ལྗོངས་.

འབྲས་མོ་གཞོངས་ (dr<u>ɛ</u>̀mshoŋ) sm. འབྲས་ལྗོངས་.

འབྲས་མོ་གཤོངས་ (dr<u>ɛ</u>̀mshoŋ) sm. འབྲས་ལྗོངས་.

འབྲས་དམར་ (dr<u>ɛ</u>̀mar) red rice.

འབྲས་སྨིན་ (dr<u>ɛ</u>̀men) scar.

འབྲས་སྨིན་སར་ལྷུང་ (dr<u>ɛ</u>̀min sār lhūŋ) person who dies after having led a full life (words of condolence) [Lit. ripened fruits fallen to ground].

འབྲས་རྩམ་ (dr<u>ɛ</u>̀dzam) 1. rice tsamba. 2. abbr. rice and tsamba.

འབྲས་ཚ་ (dr<u>ɛ</u>̀dza) sm. འབྲས་ཐུག.

འབྲས་ཚིགས་རོ་ (dr<u>ɛ</u>̀ tsīgro) the burnt rice leftover in a pot.

འབྲས་ཚོད་ (dr<u>ɛ</u>̀dzöö) shung. sm. འབྲས་ཐུག.

འབྲས་ཞིང་ (dr<u>ɛ</u>̀shiŋ) rice/ paddy field.

འབྲས་ཟ་མཁན་ (dr<u>ɛ</u>̀ s<u>a</u>ñɛn) sm. འབྲས་ཟན་, 2.

འབྲས་ཟན་ (dr<u>ɛ</u>̀sɛn) 1. steamed rice. 2. a rice eater (term used to convey ethnic Chinese). 3. ཐུགས་ made from rice རྩམ་པ་.

འབྲས་ཟན་ཐུགས་བཙོས་མ་ (dr<u>ɛ</u>̀sɛn bāgdzööma) a thick rice porridge made with meat and fruits.

འབྲས་ཟས་ (dr<u>ɛ</u>̀s<u>ɛ</u>̀) food made form rice.

འབྲས་ཟླ་ (dr<u>ɛ</u>̀nda) the 2nd month of the Tibetan calendar.

འབྲས་བཟང་ (dr<u>ɛ</u>̀saŋ) a good result/ outcome.

འབྲས་བཟོས་ཁ་ཏོག (dr<u>ɛ</u>̀söö kādoò) snacks/ cookies made from rice.

འབྲས་ཡུལ་ (dr<u>ɛ</u>̀yüü) 1. rice producing country. 2. sm. འབྲས་ལྗོངས་.

འབྲས་ཡོས་ (dr<u>ɛ</u>̀yüü) popped/ roasted rice.

འབྲས་རིལ་ (dr<u>ɛ</u>̀rii) sm. འབྲས་འབྲུ་.

འབྲས་ཤིང་ (dr<u>ɛ</u>̀shiŋ) fruit tree.

འབྲས་ཤིང་གནོད་འབུ་ (dr<u>ɛ</u>̀shiŋ nōmbu) an insect that attacks fruit trees.

འབྲས་ཤུན་ (dr<u>ɛ</u>̀shün) rice husk.

འབྲས་ཤུན་པ་ཅན་ (dr<u>ɛ</u>̀ shūnbajɛn) unhusked rice.

འབྲས་ས་ལུ་ (dr<u>ɛ</u>̀ sālu) unplanted rice (found in Tibetan mythological stories).

འབྲས་སོ་བ་ (dr<u>ɛ</u>̀ sōwa) sm. འབྲས་ཤུན་པ་ཅན་.

འབྲས་སོག (dr<u>ɛ</u>̀sɔɔ̀) rice straw/ hay.

འབྲས་སོན་ (dr<u>ɛ</u>̀sön) rice seed.

འབྲས་སོབ་ (dr<u>ɛ</u>̀sob) sm. འབྲས་སོ་བ་.

འབྲས་སིལ་ (dr<u>ɛ</u>̀sii) ceremonial rice pudding (rice mixed with butter, sugar and raisin).

འབྲས་སྲུས་ (dr<u>ɛ</u>̀süü) unripened rice eaten as snacks.

འབྲི་ (dr<u>i</u>) female yak.

འབྲི་: p. བྲིས་; f. བྲི་; imp. བྲིས་ (dr<u>i</u>) va. to write, to draw, to paint ¶ཁོས་དེབ་གཅིག་འབྲི་གི་ཡོད་པ་རེད་ He is writing a book.

འབྲི་: p. བྲི་; f. འབྲི་ (dr<u>i</u>) vi. to decrease in price.

འབྲི་ཀོ་ (dr<u>i</u>gɔɔ) a female yak skin.

འབྲི་ཀློག (dr<u>i</u>lɔɔ̀) reading and writing.

འབྲི་ཀློག་འཆད་གསུམ་ (dr<u>i</u>lɔɔ̀ c<u>ɛ</u>̀ɛsum) the three: reading, writing, verbal explanation.

འབྲི་སྐམ་མ་ (dr<u>i</u> gāmma) female yak that is not producing milk.

འབྲི་སྐྱར་བྱེད་ (dr<u>i</u>gyɔɔ c<u>e</u>è) va. to rewrite.

འབྲི་བརྐོས་ (dr<u>i</u>göö) carving words (usu. on stones); va.—བྱེད་.

འབྲི་མཁན་ (dr<u>i</u>ñɛn) writer, painter.

འབྲི་གུང་བཀའ་བརྒྱུད་ (dr<u>i</u>guŋ kāgyüü) one of the 4 བཀའ་བརྒྱུད་ sects.

འབྲི་གུང་མཐིལ་དགོན་པ་ (dr<u>i</u>guŋtii g<u>ö</u>mba) a monastery in the Drikung area built in 1179 by Rinchen Pal.

འབྲི་ཆུ་ (dr<u>i</u>ju) Yangtse River.

འབྲི་ཆུའི་རྒྱུད་ (dr<u>i</u>jü gy<u>ü</u>ü) the Yangtse River.

འབྲི་ཉེས་ཤོར་ (dr<u>i</u>ñeè shɔɔ̄) vi. to make a mistake in writing.

འབྲི་ཏ་ (dr<u>i</u>da) abbr. of འབྲི་ཏ་ས་འཛིན་.

འབྲི་ཏ་ས་འཛིན་ (dr<u>i</u>da sāndzin) strawberry.

འབྲི་སྟངས་ (dr<u>i</u>daŋ) sm. འབྲི་ལུགས་.

འབྲི་དེབ་ (dr<u>i</u>deb) notebook, writing pad.

འབྲི་བ་གནང་ (dr<u>i</u>wə nāŋ) h. of འབྲི་.

འབྲི་མ་བེའུ་འབྱར་མ་ (dr<u>i</u>ma p<u>ee</u> j<u>a</u>rma) a female yak with its calf.

འབྲི་མར་ (dr<u>i</u>mar) yak butter.

འབྲི་མོ་ (dr<u>i</u>mo) female yak.

འབྲི་མོག (dr<u>i</u>mog) Asian puccoon, Chinese gromwell.

འབྲི་སྨྱུག (dr<u>i</u>ñuù) pen.

འབྲི་རྩོམ་ (dr<u>i</u>dzom) composing sth. written; va.—བྱེད་.

འབྲི་ཚུལ་ (dr<u>i</u>dzüü) the style of writing.

འབྲི་ཚེར་མ་ (dr<u>i</u> tsērma) the fruit of Chinese wolfberry.

འབྲི་ཞོ་ (dr<u>i</u>sho) yogurt make from yak (dri) milk.

འབྲི་འོ་ (dr<u>i</u>wo) yak (dri) milk.

འབྲི་གཡག (dr<u>i</u>yaà) yaks (female and male).

འབྲི་ལུགས་ (dr<u>i</u>luù) sm. འབྲི་ཚུལ་.

འབྲི་ཤུག (dr<u>i</u>shuù) a kind of large ཤུག་པ་.

འབྲི་ཤོག (dr<u>i</u>shoò) stationery, paper for writing.

འབྲི་བཤུ་ཁང་ (dr<u>i</u>shugaŋ) mimeograph service office, copying office.

འབྲིང་ (dr<u>i</u>ŋ) medium, middle.

འབྲིང་ཀ་ (dr<u>i</u>ŋgə) middle size, medium (quality and size).

འབྲིང་གྲས་ (dr<u>i</u>ŋdr<u>ɛ</u>̀) intermediate, middle, medium (quality or size).

འབྲིང་ངེ་བ་ (dr<u>i</u>ŋŋewa) sm. འབྲིང་ཙམ་.

འབྲིང་ཆུང་ (dr<u>i</u>ŋjuŋ) medium / middle and small.

འབྲིང་དེ་སྡོད་ (dr<u>i</u>ŋde d<u>ö</u>ö) staying firm/ steady ¶མི་ས་གང་བཤད་ཀྱང་རང་ཉིད་འབྲིང་དེ་སྡོད་དགོས་ Whatever people say, you must stay firm (i.e., not be swayed).

འབྲིང་པོ་ (dr<u>i</u>ŋbu) sm. འབྲིང་བ་.

འབྲིང་སྤྲིན་ (dr<u>i</u>ŋdrin) medium sized clouds.

འབྲིང་འཕེན་འཕུར་མདའ་ (dr<u>i</u>ŋpen pūnda) intermediate ballistic missile.

འབྲིང་འཕེན་མི་ཤུགས་འཕུར་མདའ་ (dr<u>i</u>ŋpen m<u>e</u>shug pūnda) sm. འབྲིང་འཕེན་འཕུར་མདའ་.

འབྲིང་བ་ (dr<u>i</u>ŋwə) intermediate, medium, middle ¶སློབ་གྲྭ་འབྲིང་བ་ Middle school.

འབྲིང་ཙམ་ (dr<u>i</u>ŋdzam) middle in size or quality.

འབྲིང་འོག་མ་ (dr<u>i</u>ŋ w<u>ɔ</u>̀ma) lower middle ¶ཞིང་འབྲིང་འོག་མ་ Lower middle peasants.

འབྲིང་རིགས་ (dr<u>i</u>ŋrii) medium size.

འབྲིང་རིམ་ (dr<u>i</u>ŋrim) medium/ intermediate level.

འབྲིང་རིམ་མི་དམངས་ཁྲིམས་ཁང་ (dr<u>i</u>ŋrim m<u>i</u>maŋ tr<u>i</u>mgaŋ) intermediate people's court.

འབྲིང་རིམ་དགེ་ཐོན་སློབ་གྲྭ་ (dr<u>i</u>ŋrim gēdön lōbdra) secondary teachers' training school.

འབྲིང་རིམ་ཆེད་སྦྱོང་སློབ་གྲྭ་ (dr<u>i</u>ŋrim c<u>ɛ</u>̀ɛjoŋ lōbdra) secondary specialize training school.

འབྲིང་རིམ་སློབ་གྲྭ་ (dr<u>i</u>ŋrim lōbdra) secondary school, middle school.

འབྲིང་རིམ་སློབ་གསོ་ (dr<u>i</u>ŋrim lōbso) secondary education.

འབྲིང་སོན་ (dr<u>i</u>ŋsön) seed that is used on medium quality fields.

འབྲིད་: p. ཕྲིས་; f. དབྲི་; imp. ཕྲིས་ (dr<u>i</u>i) 1. va. to deceive, to delude, to trick ¶ཉ་མོ་ཟས་ཀྱིས་ཕྲི་ནས་བཟུང་བ་རེད་ He caught the fish tricking it with food. 2. minus (in math). 3. va. to cut/ take away/ deduct a small portion or amount ¶གླ་ཕོགས་ནས་བརྒྱ་ཆ་ཁ་ཤས་སྨན་བཅོས་ལ་འབྲིད་ཀྱི་ཡོད་པ་རེད་ (They) take a few percent off the salary for medical care.

འབྲིད་ཟས་ (dr<u>i</u>isɛɛ̀) bait.

འབྲིམ་: p. བྲིམས་, f. བྲིམ་, imp. བྲིམས་ (dr<u>i</u>m) va. to distribute, to hand out.

འབྲུ་ (dr<u>u</u>) 1. grains ¶འབྲུ་རིགས་འདྲ་མིན་ Various types of grain. 2. barley. 3. a small piece of grain. 4. a letter ¶ཡིག་འབྲུ་རེ་རེ་བཞིན་ Letter by letter. 5. a design ¶འབྲུ་ཞིབ་པ་ A fine/ detailed design.

འབྲུ་: p. བྲུས་; f. འབྲུ་; imp. བྲུས་ (dr<u>u</u>) va. to dig out, to carve, to chisel ¶ཁྲོན་པ་འབྲུས་ནས་ Digging a well.

འབྲུ་དཀར་ནག་ཁྲ་གསུམ་ (drugar nagtra sūm) three grains: barley, peas/lentils and a mixture of barley and lentils (describes grains harvested from fields).

འབྲུ་དཀར་པོ་ (dru gārbo) white barley.

འབྲུ་སྒྱེ་ (drugye) a grain bag.

འབྲུ་སྐྱེད་ (drugyeè) interest paid in grain.

འབྲུ་སྐྱེད་ལས་ཁུངས་ (drugyeè lɛ̀ɛ̀guŋ) an office that lends out grain.

འབྲུ་སྐྱེད་ཕོགས་སྤྲེལ་ (drugyeè pɔ̄ɔ̀dree) shung. the two officials in charge of interest on grain loans.

འབྲུ་ཁང་ (drugaŋ) granary.

འབྲུ་ཁང་ལས་ཁུངས་ (drugaŋ lɛ̀ɛ̀guŋ) shung. office that lends out grain and pays salaries from this (begun in the early 1950's).

འབྲུ་ཁྲལ་ (drudrɛɛ) shung. barley or grain tax.

འབྲུ་ཁྲུ་ (drudru) shung. a hat worn by low level tt. goverment officials.

འབྲུ་ཁྲེ་ (drudre) millet.

འབྲུ་གད་ (drugɛɛ̀) winnowing grains, winnowing barley; va.—རྒྱག.

འབྲུ་གད་གཙང་ (dru kɛ̀ɛ̀dzaŋ) winnowed grain/ barley.

འབྲུ་གུ་ (drugu) pits, kernels, seed (of fruit) ¶ ཀུ་ཤུའི་ནང་ལ་འབྲུ་གུ་འདུག There are pits in the apple.

འབྲུ་གྲུ་ (drudru) a boat that transports grain.

འབྲུ་འགྲེལ་ (drudree) an explanation of a text.

འབྲུ་སྒྲུག (drudruù) shung. collecting/ picking fallen kernels of grains after the crop has been harvested and removed from the field; va.—རྒྱག.

འབྲུ་སྒྱེ་ (drugye) grain bag.

འབྲུ་དངུལ་ (druŋüü) 1. abbr. money and grain; va.—བསྒྱུར་; —བརྗེས་ to convert grain into money.

འབྲུ་དངུལ་སྒྱུར་གཏོང་ (druŋüü gyurdoŋ) va. to convert grain into money.

འབྲུ་ལྔ་ (druŋa) the five grains: barley, rice, wheat, lentils and millet.

འབྲུ་ལྕིབ་ (drujib) a type of barley.

འབྲུ་ཆང་ (drujaŋ) barley ཆང་.

འབྲུ་ཆན་ (drujɛn) cooked barley.

འབྲུ་ཆར་ (drujar) start of the rainy season for barley (the 3rd month of the Tibetan calendar).

འབྲུ་ཆེན་ (drudzen) the large Tibetan script that is written with a thick bamboo pen.

འབྲུ་གཉིས་ (druñii) a better quality tea.

འབྲུ་གཉེར་ (druñer) grain keeper/ steward.

འབྲུ་སྙིགས་ (druñii) residue of poor quality barley that is left after winnowing (usu. used for animals).

འབྲུ་སྙེ་ (druñe) ear/ head of unhusked grain.

འབྲུ་དང་ (drudaŋ) the best quality of Tibetan tea.

འབྲུ་དོ་པོ་ (dru tobo) a load of barley.

འབྲུ་དོན་ (drudön) meaning of each word/ point/ provision ¶ གན་རྒྱའི་འབྲུ་དོན་ The meaning of the items in a contract.

འབྲུ་དོན་རས་བོར་ (drudön rɛ̀ɛ̀bɔɔ) showing indifference/ contempt for the wordings of sth. or for the points/ items in an agreement.

འབྲུ་དོས་ (drudöö) 1. a load of barley/ grain. 2. shung. a corvee tax on animals for carrying loads of barley; va.—སྐྱེལ་.

འབྲུ་འདེད་ (drudeè) 1. reading words by spelling out each letter. 2. shung. going to collect loans of barley that have not been paid; va.—བྱེད་; —གཏོང་.

འབྲུ་འདེབས་སྐར་མ་ (drudeb gārma) the 2nd month of the Tibetan calendar when barley is planted.

འབྲུ་འདོན་འཕྲུལ་འཁོར་ (drudön trũ̃ũgɔɔ) sm. འབྲུ་དོག་འདོན་བྱེད་འཁོར་ལོ་.

འབྲུ་འདྲེན་ཨར་དོའི་ནང་གཉེར་ (drundren ārdö naŋñer) shung. the steward in charge of grain transportation and construction.

འབྲུ་དོག (drudɔɔ̀) a single grain of grain.

འབྲུ་དོག་ཆགས་མི་ཐུབ་པ་ (drudɔɔ̀ cāà mi tūbbə) grain that doesn't form into kernals.

འབྲུ་དོག་འདོན་བྱེད་འཁོར་ལོ་ (drudɔɔ̀ dönjeè kɔ̄ɔ̀lo) grain husking machine.

འབྲུ་ལྡན་སྲིང་བལ་ (drundɛn sĩŋbɛɛ) raw/ unginned cotton.

འབྲུ་སྡུད་མཁན་ (dru düũñɛn) grain collector.

འབྲུ་ནག (drunaà) black barley.

འབྲུ་ནག་པོ་ (dru nagbo) sm. འབྲུ་ནག.

འབྲུ་གནོད་སྲིན་བུ་ (drunöö sĩŋbu) an insect that harms grain.

འབྲུ་གནོན་ (drunön) reading thoroughly/ carefully (word by word); va.—བྱེད་.

འབྲུ་སྣ་ (druna) different varieties of grain.

འབྲུ་སྣ་ལྔ་ (dru naŋa) sm. འབྲུ་ལྔ་.

འབྲུ་སྣུམ་ (drunum) oil made from grains, vegetable oil.

འབྲུ་སྣོན་ (drunön) 1. additional words; va.—རྒྱག. 2. extra/ supplementary grain.

འབྲུ་དཔྱ་ (druja) shung. grain tax.

འབྲུ་ཕྱགས་ (drubaà) husk of grain.

འབྲུ་ཕུང་ (drubuŋ) pile of barley/ grain.

འབྲུ་ཕུད་ (drubüü) barley/ grain given as first religious offering.

འབྲུ་ཕོགས་ (drubɔɔ̀) wages/ salary that is paid in grain.

འབྲུ་ཕོགས་སྐྱེད་འབྲུ་ (drupɔɔ̀ gyēndru) shung. grain salary and grain interest.

འབྲུ་ཕོགས་ལས་ཁུངས་ (drubɔɔ̀ lɛ̀ɛ̀guŋ) shung. sm. འབྲུ་ཁང་ལས་ཁུངས་.

འབྲུ་འཕྱར་ (dru jār) va. to winnow grain.

འབྲུ་འཕྱར་འཕྲུལ་འཁོར་ (drujar trũ̃ũgɔɔ) winnowing machine.

འབྲུ་བང་ (drubaŋ) grain storage room in a house (where the grain is taken out from the bottom through a hole).

འབྲུ་བུན་ (drubün) a loan in grain; va.—གཏོང་ to give out a loan in grain.

འབྲུ་བོགས་ (drubɔɔ̀) lease payment in grain; va.—སྤྲོད་.

འབྲུ་འབབ་ (drumbəb) 1. grain/ barley yield. 2. the amount of grain or barley.

འབྲུ་འབུ་ (drumbu) an insect that eats grain.

འབྲུ་འབྲེལ་ (drundree) shung. the contents (of a verdict, etc.) ¶ ད་ཆ་དཔྱད་མཚམས་བཀའ་ཁྲའི་འབྲུ་འབྲེལ་སྐྱ་གཅིག་ཀྱང་མ་གནས་པ་ They did not comply with any of the contents of the verdict.

འབྲུ་མ་ (druma) 1. a single grain of barley/ grain. 2. sm. དབུ་ཆེན་.

འབྲུ་མར་ (drumar) 1. abbr. grain and butter. 2. mustard seed oil.

འབྲུ་སྨར་ (drumar) a fine quality grain.

འབྲུ་ཙ་ (drudza) a type of Tibetan script.

འབྲུ་རྩམ་ (drudzam) 1. abbr. barley/ grain and tsamba. 2. tsamba made from grain.

འབྲུ་གཙང་གད་རྒྱག (drudzaŋ gɛ̀ɛ̀ gyaà) sm. འབྲུ་གད་རྒྱག.

འབྲུ་ཚ་ (drudza) sm. འབྲུ་ཙ་.

འབྲུ་ཚད་ (drudzɛɛ̀) the quality of grain.

འབྲུ་ཚུགས་ (drudzuù) straight, directly (in terms of looking).

འབྲུ་འཚག་འཕྲུལ་འཁོར་ (drudzaà trũ̃ũgɔɔ) grain filtering machine.

འབྲུ་མཛོད་ (drudzöö) sm. འབྲུ་ཁང་.

འབྲུ་འཛིན་ (drundzin) grain or food coupon (used after 1959 for buying grain and other foodstuffs).

འབྲུ་ཟན་ (drusɛn) 1. abbr. grain and hay. 2. ཐུག་ཆ་ made from any kind of ground grain.

འབྲུ་གཟན་ (drusɛn) sm. འབྲུ་ཟན་.

འབྲུ་ཞ་ (drusha) ancient area located in today's Pakistan.

འབྲུ་ཞིང་ (drushiŋ) 1. a field on which barley is cultivated. 2. any grain field.

འབྲུ་རིགས་ (drurii) grains.

འབྲུ་རིགས་མཁོ་སྒྲོད་དོ་དམ་ཅུའུ་ (drurii kōdröö todam jüü) tib.ch. bureau of staple grain supplies.

འབྲུ་རིགས་ཅུའུ་ (drurii jüü) tib.ch. grain office/ bureau.

འབྲུ་རིགས་ཅུས་ (drurii jüü) tib.ch. grain office/ bureau.

འབྲུ་རིགས་འདེབས་ཞིང་ (drurii debshiŋ) sm. འབྲུ་ཞིང་.

འབྲུ་རིགས་པུའུ་ (drurii būù) tib.ch. grain ministry.

འབྲུ་རིགས་པུ་སེ་ (drurii bāse) tib.eng. sm. འབྲུ་འཛིན་.

འབྲུ་རིགས་འབང་མཛོད་ (drurii baŋdzöö) sm. འབྲུ་ཁང་.

འབྲུ་རིགས་བཟོ་ལས་ (drurii solɛɛ̀) grain industry.

འབྲུ་རིགས་ལས་ཁུངས་ (drurii lɛɛ̀guŋ) an office in tt. government dealing with grains (after 1959).

འབྲུ་རིགས་ལས་སྣོན་ཅུའུ་ (drurii lɛ̀ɛnön jū) tib.ch. grain processing bureau.

འབྲུ་རིགས་ལོ་ཏོག (drurii lodoò) grain crops.

འབྲུ་ལེན་འཁྲུལ་འཁོར་ (drulen trǖügɔɔ) threshing machine.

འབྲུ་ཤ་གང་ (drushagaŋ) full-bodied (of grains).

འབྲུ་ཤས་ (drushɛɛ̀) shung. leasing one's land for payment of half of the yield; va.—གཏོང་.

འབྲུ་ལྷག་སྤུས་ཚོང་ (drulhaa bǖüdzoŋ) grain that one has to sell at less than market price.

འབྲུ་ས་ (drusa) field on which grains are cultivated.

འབྲུ་སོན་ (drusön) grain/ barley seeds.

འབྲུ་ལྷག (drulhaà) 1. surplus grain/ barley. 2. grain reserves.

འབྲུ་ལྷག་སྤུས་ཚོང་ (drulhaà bǖüdzoŋ) selling surplus grain at the government (lower than market) price.

འབྲུག (druù) 1. dragon. 2. Bhutan.

འབྲུག་ཀེར་ལངས་ (druù gērlaŋ) a design of standing dragons.

འབྲུག་སྐད་ (druùgɛɛ̀) 1. thunder; vi.—རྒྱག to thunder. 2. Bhutanese (language).

འབྲུག་སྐད་ཆེ་ལ་ཆར་པ་ཆུང་བ་ (druùgɛɛ̀ cēla cārbə cūŋwə) big noise but small result [Lit. loud thunder and small rain].

འབྲུག་གབ་ཁྱུང་ཡིབ་ (druùgəb kyūŋyib) having talent but no opportunity to use it [Lit. dragon hiding, mythical garuda hiding].

འབྲུག་གོས་ (druùgöö̀) brocade with dragon design pattern.

འབྲུག་གྲགས་ (drugdraà) sound of thunder.

འབྲུག་གྲི་ (drugdri) Bhutanese knife.

འབྲུག་གློག (druglɔ̀ɔ) thunder and lightning.

འབྲུག་མགོ་སྦྲུལ་འཇུག (druŋgo drūnjuù) great at the beginning and poor at the end [Lit. a dragon's head, snake's tail].

འབྲུག་འགྲོས་མ་ (druù gööma) brocade with a design of flying dragons.

འབྲུག་རྒྱལ་ (druggyɛɛ) the king of Bhutan.

འབྲུག་རྒྱལ་སྐུ་འཁོར་ (druggyɛɛ gūgɔɔ) the royal family of Bhutan.

འབྲུག་རྒྱལ་མངའ་བདག་མཆོག (druggyɛɛ ŋadaà cɔ̀ɔ) title of the King of Bhutan.

འབྲུག་རྒྱལ་མངའ་བདག་རིན་པོ་ཆེ་ (druggyɛɛ ŋadaà rimboce) the king of Bhutan.

འབྲུག་སྒྲ་ (drugdra) thunder; vi.—ཞིར་; —སྒྲོག to thunder.

འབྲུག་སྒྲའི་གར་ (drugdɛ kar) poet. peacock.

འབྲུག་བརྒྱབ་ཆུང་ (druù gyəbjuŋ) brocade with small designs of dragons.

འབྲུག་བརྒྱབ་ཆེན་པོ་ (druùgyəb cēmbo) brocade with large designs of dragons.

འབྲུག་ལྕེ་ (drugje) lightning [Lit. dragon's tongue].

འབྲུག་ཆར་ (drugjar) 1. thunder storm. 2. thunder and rain.

འབྲུག་མཆིན་གཟིག་མངལ་ (drugjin siiŋɛɛ) great or rare, delicacies [Lit. dragon's liver and leopard's womb].

འབྲུག་པ་ (drugbə) Bhutanese (person) ¶ འབྲུག་པའི་དམག་མི་ Bhutanese soldiers.

འབྲུག་པ་བཀའ་བརྒྱུད་ (drugbə gāgyüü) one of the four sects of the བཀའ་བརྒྱུད་ tradition.

འབྲུག་པ་ལོ་ཕྱག (drugba lojaà) shung. originally the Bhutanese trader/ official who brought an annual tribute of goods to Lhasa; later a Bhutanese who lived in Lhasa and looked after trade and other affairs dealing with Bhutanese and Bhutan for the Butanese government.

འབྲུག་ཕྲུག (drugdruù) woolen materials from Bhutan.

འབྲུག་འཕྱོའི་ཞབས་བྲོ་ (drucö shabdro) dragon dance.

འབྲུག་དབྱངས་ (druùyaŋ) sm. འབྲུག་སྐད་.

འབྲུག་དབྱིབས་གྲུ་གཟིངས་ (druùyib trusiŋ) dragon boat.

འབྲུག་འབྲས་ (druŋdrɛɛ̀) rice from Bhutan.

འབྲུག་མེ་ཏོག (drug medoò) dragon flower.

འབྲུག་མེ་རིས་མ་ (drugme riimə) brocade with the design of dragon and flame.

འབྲུག་ཚ་ (drugdza) sm.* འབྲུ་ཚ་.

འབྲུག་ཚང་འཁོར་མ་ (drugdzaŋ kɔ̄ɔma) brocade with design of circles with coiled dragons within it.

འབྲུག་ཞུ་ (drugshu) lantern with a dragon design.

འབྲུག་གཞུང་ (drugshuŋ) the government of Bhutan.

འབྲུག་གཟུགས་ (druŋsug) dragon shaped.

འབྲུག་ཟླ་བ་ (druŋ dawa) the 3rd month of the Tibetan calendar.

འབྲུག་ཡུལ་ (drugyüü) Bhutan.

འབྲུག་གཤོག་ལག་ཅན་ (drugshɔɔ̀ lagjɛn) pterodactyl.

འབྲུག་རང་མདངས་མ་ (drugraŋ daŋma) brocade with the design of a shining dragon.

འབྲུག་རིས་མ་ (druùrimə) dragon design.

འབྲུག་རུས་ (druùrüü) dragon bone.

འབྲུག་ལོ་ (drūglo) the year of the Dragon.

འབྲུག་ཤིང་ (drugshiŋ) a type of Tibetan traditional medicine.

འབྲུག་ཤོག (drūgshɔɔ̀) paper made in Bhutan.

འབྲུད་: p. བྲུས་; f. བྲུ་; imp. འབྲུ་ (drüü) sm. འབྲུ་.

འབྲུབ་: p. བྲུབས་; f. འབྲུབ་; imp. བྲུབས་ (drub) va. to hide/ bury ¶ མི་གསོན་པོར་བྲུབས་པ་རེད་ They buried the man alive.

འབྲུབ་: p. བྲུབས་; f. འབྲུབ་ (drub) vi. to flood/ overflow, to rise (for rivers) ¶ དབྱར་ཁ་གཙང་པོ་འབྲུབ་ཀྱི་རེད་ In the summer the river will flood.

འབྲུབ་ཆུ་ (drubju) a river that has risen/ flooded, flood water; va.—འགོག to prevent floods.

འབྲུམ་ (drum) smallpox.

འབྲུམ་སྐོགས་ (drubgɔɔ̀) smallpox scab.

འབྲུམ་འགོག་སྨན་སོན་ (drumgɔɔ̀ mɛnsön) sm. འབྲུམ་སོན་.

འབྲུམ་ངོ་ (drumŋo) smallpox symptoms.

འབྲུམ་དུག (drumduù) sm. གྲུ་ཅི་རི་དུག.

འབྲུམ་ཐོར་ (drumtɔr) smallpox pimples.

འབྲུམ་ནག (drumnaà) a serious type of smallpox.

འབྲུམ་ནད་ (drumnɛɛ̀) smallpox.

འབྲུམ་པ་ (drumbə) sm. འབྲུམ་ནད་.

འབྲུམ་བུ་ (drumbu) sm. འབྲུམ་ནད་.

འབྲུམ་བུ་རྩེལ་དེ་ (drumbu dzēēde) a type of smallpox.

འབྲུམ་སྨན་ (drummɛn) smallpox medicine.

འབྲུམ་འཛུགས་གཙག་བུ་ (drumdzuù dzəgbu) vaccination knife for smallpox.

འབྲུམ་ཡང་ (drumyaŋ) sm. འབྲུམ་དཀར་.

འབྲུམ་ཤུལ་ (drumshüü) pockmarks (from smallpox).

འབྲུམ་སོན་ (drumsön) smallpox vaccination.

འབྲུམ་སྲབ་ (drumdrəb) a mild form of smallpox.

འབྲུའི་ཆན་ (drüüjɛn) cooked barley/ grain.

འབྲུལ་: p. བྲུལ་; f. འབྲུལ་ (drüü) vi. to fall (fruits, leaves, etc.), to come off, to come out (e.g., teeth) ¶ སྟོན་དུས་ཤིང་ལོ་རྣམས་འབྲུལ་བའི་སྐབས་ In the autumn when the leaves are falling.

འབྲུས་འགོགས་ (drüŋgɔɔ̀) sm. བཙོན་འབྲུས་.

འབྲེག: p. བྲེགས་; f. འབྲེག; imp. བྲེགས་ (dreè) va. to cut, to shave off, to shear ¶ སྐྲ་དང་ཁ་སྤུ་རྣམས་གཙང་མ་བྲེགས་འདུག He has completely shaved off his hair and moustache. ¶ བལ་འབྲེག་པའི་དུས་ལ་སླེབས་པ་རེད་ The shearing time has come. ¶ སྐྲ་འབྲེག To cut off the nose.

འབྲིག་གཅོད་ (dregjöö) sm. འབྲིག.

འབྲིག་གདུབ་ (dregduù) sm. འབྲིག.

འབྲིག་སྤྱད་ (dregjɛɛ̀) shaving kit/ materials.

འབྲིང་ (dreŋ) 1. sm. འབྲང་. 2. sm. འབྲིང་པ་. 3. sm. བྲིང་.

འབྲིང་འཁོར་ (dreŋgɔɔ) cable car.

འབྲིང་ལྕག (dreŋjaà) leather whip.

འབྲིང་ཐག (dreŋdaà) sm. འབྲིང་པ་.

འབྲིང་འདྲུད་ (dreŋdrüù) see ཞིར་འབྲིང་འདྲུད་.

འབྲིང་པ་ (dreŋbə) leather or rawhide rope/ strap.

འབྲིང་བུ་ (dreŋbu) sm. འབྲིང་པ་.

འབྲིང་འབྲིང་ (dreŋdreŋ) in a line, continuous, unbroken.

འབྲིང་ཞགས་ (dreŋshaà) leather lasso.

འབྲིང་ཟམ་ (dreŋsam) sm. བྲིང་.

འབྲིང་རིལ་ (dreŋrii) round leather/ rawhide rope.

འབྲེལ་ (dree) 1. vi. to be connected/joined, to be linked ༈ ས་གནས་དེ་རྣམས་གཅིག་ལ་གཅིག་འབྲེལ་གྱི་ཡོད་ Those regions are connected to each other. 2. along with, together with, at the same time (དང་ + —) ༈ གཟིགས་སྐོར་དང་འབྲེལ་ལས་ཁུངས་ཁག་གི་དཔོན་རིགས་མཇལ་འཕྲད་གནང་གི་ཡོད་པ་རེད་ (He) will go for a tour (of the) place and at same time (he) will meet the heads of the departments. 3. in accordance with ༈ ཡུལ་དུས་བབས་འབྲེལ་ In accordance with time and place.

འབྲེལ་ཆགས་ (dreejaà) vi. to become joined, to continue one after the other.

འབྲེལ་ཆགས་ཆེ་བ་ (dreejaà cēwa) having a close relationship.

འབྲེལ་ཆགས་པ་ (dree cāgba) joined, linked.

འབྲེལ་ཆགས་པའི་རང་བཞིན་ (dreejagbɛ rəŋshin) continuity, coherence.

འབྲེལ་ཆགས་པོ་ (dree cāgbo) proper, suitable, appropriate ༈ ཁོང་གིས་ལན་འབྲེལ་ཆགས་པོ་ཞིག་བརྒྱབ་སོང་ He gave an appropriate answer.

འབྲེལ་ཆགས་རང་བཞིན་ (dreecaà rəŋshin) sm. འབྲེལ་ཆགས་པའི་རང་བཞིན་.

འབྲེལ་གཏམ་ (dreedam) talking about the old times/ historical events.

འབྲེལ་གཏུག (dreēduù) contact, communication, liaison; va.—བྱེད་ to get in touch with, to contact, to liaison with ༈ ལས་ཀ་འདིའི་སྐོར་ངས་ལས་ཁུངས་མང་པོར་འབྲེལ་གཏུག་བྱས་པ་ཡིན་ Concerning this work, I contacted many offices.

འབྲེལ་གཏུག་ཁྲུའུ་ (dreeduù trū) tib.ch. liaison office.

འབྲེལ་གཏུག་གླེང་མོལ་ (dreeduù lēŋmöö) discussions to develop contact/ liaison; va.—བྱེད་.

འབྲེལ་ཐག (dreedaà) relations, connections, associations, links, contacts; va.—གཅོད་ to break/ cut off relations/ contact/ connections.

འབྲེལ་ཐག་ཕད་བཅད་ (dreedaà bɛɛ̀jɛɛ̀) severing/ cutting off relations completely, making a clean break of relations.

འབྲེལ་ཐག་གཙང་བཅད་ (dreedaà dzāŋjɛɛ̀) sm. འབྲེལ་ཐག་ཕད་བཅད་.

འབྲེལ་ཐག་ས་ཚིགས་ (dreedaà sədzii) connecting station.

འབྲེལ་ཐུག (dreeduù) sm. འབྲེལ་གཏུག.

འབྲེལ་ཐོགས་པ་ (dreedɔgba) sb. who is involved/ connected with sth. ༈ ཁ་མཆུ་འདིའི་ནང་ལ་འབྲེལ་ཐོགས་པ་མང་པོ་ཡོད་པ་རེད་ There are many people having connections with the case.

འབྲེལ་འདུད་ (dreedüü) sm. འབྲེལ་མདུད་.

འབྲེལ་མདུད་ (dreedüü) connected/ joined; va.—བྱེད་ to make a connection ༈ ཚོགས་ཁ་དེ་གཉིས་དབར་འབྲེལ་མདུད་བྱེད་མཁན་ང་ཡིན་ I am the one who made the connection between the two groups.

འབྲེལ་འདྲིས་ (drendrii) connection/ relationship that is close.

འབྲེལ་བ་ (dreewa) relationship, connection, link, tie; va.—བྱེད་ to have relations; va.—གཏོད་; —འཛུགས་ to start a relationship ༈ ཁོས་བྲིས་པའི་དེབ་གཉིས་པོ་དེའི་དབར་འབྲེལ་བ་ག་རེ་ཡོད་པ་རེད་ What is the relationship between the two books he wrote? ༈ ང་ཚོས་ཚོགས་པ་དེ་དང་འབྲེལ་བ་གཏོད་པ་ཡིན་ We started a relationship with the association.

འབྲེལ་འདྲེས་ (drendreè) merging with, becoming one with; va.—བྱེད་ ༈ ཁོང་ཚོ་མང་ཚོགས་དང་འབྲེལ་འདྲེས་བྱུང་ཡོད་པ་རེད་ They became one with the masses.

འབྲེལ་བ་ (dreewa) a relationship, connection; va.—བྱེད་.

འབྲེལ་བ་སྒྱུར་ (dreewa gyur) va. to change/ alter a relationship.

འབྲེལ་བ་ཆད་ (dreewa cɛ̄ɛ̀) vi. to have a relationship/ link/ connection be broken.

འབྲེལ་བ་སྦྱོར་ (dreewa jɔɔ) va. to make a relationship/ link/ connection.

འབྲེལ་བ་འཛུགས་ (dreewa dzuù) va. to establish relations.

འབྲེལ་བ་བཟོ་ (dreewa so) va. to make a relationship/ link/ connection.

འབྲེལ་བ་ཡོད་པ་ (dreewa yööba) having a relationship/ link/ tie/ connection.

འབྲེལ་བའི་སྒྲ་ (dreewɛ dra) sm. འབྲེལ་སྒྲ་.

འབྲེལ་སྦྱོར་ (dreejɔɔ) making a relationship/ link/ tie/ connection between others; va.— བྱེད་ ༈ ཁོང་གིས་ལས་ཁུངས་དེ་གཉིས་འབྲེལ་སྦྱོར་བྱས་པ་རེད་ He made a connection between those two offices.

འབྲེལ་མ་ཆགས་ (dree ma cāà) sm. འབྲེལ་མ་མཚུངས་.

འབྲེལ་མ་མཚུངས་ (dree ma tsūŋ) unrelated, unconnected ༈ ཁོས་ཚོགས་འདུའི་ཐོག་སྐད་ཆ་འབྲེལ་མ་མཚུངས་པ་ཞིག་བཤད་སོང་ He said things at the meeting that were unconnected.

འབྲེལ་མེད་ (dreemeè) unrelated, unconnected, without a relationship.

འབྲེལ་མེད་ཁེར་སྡོད་ (dreemeè kērdöö) sm. འབྲེལ་མེད་ཟུར་སྡོད་.

འབྲེལ་མེད་ཟུར་སྡོད་ (dreemeè surdöö) staying isolated without any relations with others.

འབྲེལ་དམག (dreemaà) allied troops/ soldiers.

འབྲེལ་ཚུལ་ (dreedzüü) the way or manner that sth. is connected/ related.

འབྲེལ་ཚོགས་ (dreedzɔɔ̀) federation.

འབྲེལ་མཚམས་ (drendzam) junction, place where two things meet, border line.

འབྲེལ་མཚུངས་ (dreedzuŋ) 1. related ༈ གནད་དོན་དེ་དང་འབྲེལ་མཚུངས་ཀྱི་དྲི་བ་ A question related to that issue. 2. attached, connected ༈ ཁང་མིག་འབྲེལ་མཚུངས་གཉིས་ Two connected rooms (in a house).

འབྲེལ་འཛིན་ (dree dzin) va. to make/ have a relationship (usu. refers to marriage) ༈ ང་ཚོ་ཁྱིམ་ཚང་གཉིས་དབར་གཉེན་གྱི་འབྲེལ་བཟུང་བ་རེད་ We two families are related through marriage.

འབྲེལ་འཛུགས་ (drendzuù) establishing relations; va.—བྱེད་.

འབྲེལ་ཟམ་ (dreesam) link or bridge between people or organizations.

འབྲེལ་བཟང་ (dreesaŋ) a good relationship.

འབྲེལ་ཡོད་ (dreeyöö) related, concerned, connected ༈ འབྲེལ་ཡོད་ལས་ཁུངས་ (The) concerned offices.

འབྲེལ་ཡོད་སྡེ་ཁག (dreeyöö degaà) concerned/ related offices.

འབྲེལ་ཡོད་ཚན་ཁག (dreeyöö tsɛ̄ngaà) concerned/ related departments.

འབྲེལ་ལམ་ (dreelam) sm. འབྲེལ་བ་.

འབྲོ་ (dro) 1. name of a place. 2. name of an ancient lineage.

འབྲོག (drog) abbr. of འབྲོག་པ་.

འབྲོག་སྐད་ (droggɛɛ̀) dialect spoken by nomads.

འབྲོག་ཁུལ་ (droggüü) nomadic or pastoral area/ region.

འབྲོག་ཁྱི་ (drɔggyi) nomad dog.

འབྲོག་ཁྲལ་ (drɔgkɛɛ) taxes on nomads.

འབྲོག་གླུ་ (drɔglu) nomad song; va.—ལེན་; —གཏོང་ to sing a nomad song.

འབྲོག་དགོན་པ་ (drɔg gömbo) a remote/ isolated

place.
འབྲོག་གཡོག (drɔgyɔɔ̀) nomad servant.
འབྲོག་ཆས་ (drɔgjɛɛ̀) nomad clothing/ dress.
འབྲོག་རྟ་ (drɔgda) horse from nomads areas.
འབྲོག་སྟོང་ (drɔgdoŋ) a remote/ isolated area.
འབྲོག་ཐང་ (drɔgdaŋ) 1. sm. འབྲོག་ཁུལ་. 2. pastureland.
འབྲོག་དུད་ (drɔgdüù) nomad family/ household.
འབྲོག་བདག (drɔgdaà) nomad lord, very rich nomad.
འབྲོག་སྡེ་ (drɔgde) nomad group/ tribe/ unit.
འབྲོག་སྣམ་ (drɔgnam) woolen materials woven by nomads.
འབྲོག་པ་ (drɔgba) herdsman, nomad.
འབྲོག་པ་ཁྱིས་དེད་པའི་གྲལ་འགོ་ (drɔgba kyiì teèbɛ trɛngo) to come to first place/ success by accident [Lit. the nomad got to the head of the row because he was chased by a dog].
འབྲོག་ཕྱུགས་ (drɔgjɔɔ̀) sm. འབྲོག་ཁུལ་.
འབྲོག་ཕྲུག (drɔgdruù) nomad children.
འབྲོག་དབུལ་ (drɔgwüü) poor strata nomads.
འབྲོག་འབངས་ (drɔŋbaŋ) sm. འབྲོག་དམངས་.
འབྲོག་འབྲིང་ (drɔŋdriŋ) middle strata nomads (in socialist class system).
འབྲོག་འབྲིང་འོག་མ་ (drɔŋdriŋ wɔɔ̀ma) nomads just below the middle stratum (in the socialist class system), lower-middle stratum nomads.
འབྲོག་མོ་ (droŋmo) female nomad.
འབྲོག་མོའི་སྐྲ་ཞྭ (droŋmö drāsha) hair style with many braids that is worn by nomad women.
འབྲོག་དམངས་ (dröŋmaŋ) the common/ ordinary nomads, the nomad masses.
འབྲོག་ཡུལ་ (drɔgyüü) grazing/ pasture area.
འབྲོག་རུ་ (drɔgru) nomadic group/ tribe/ unit.
འབྲོག་ར་ (drɔgra) grazing/ pasture area.
འབྲོག་ལས་ (drɔglɛɛ̀) dairy work, pastoral/ herding work, animal husbandry.
འབྲོག་ལས་ཁང་ (drɔglɛɛ̀gaŋ) dairy plant.
འབྲོག་ས་ (drɔgsa) sm. འབྲོག་ཁུལ་.
འབྲོག་ལྷས་ (drɔglhɛɛ̀) nomad animal shelter/ corral.
འབྲོང་ (droŋ) wild yak.
འབྲོང་ཁྲག (droŋdraà) blood of wild yak (used for Tibetan medicine).
འབྲོང་མགོ་ (droŋgo) 1. head of a wild yak. 2. mask of a wild yak (used in religious dances).
འབྲོང་རྔ་ (droŋŋa) tail of a wild yak.
འབྲོང་སྙིང་ (droŋñiŋ) heart of a wild yak.
འབྲོང་གཉན་ལྡེ་རུ་ (droŋñɛn deru) name of the 30th ancient king of Tibet.
འབྲོང་ལྤགས་ (droŋbaà) wild yak skin.
འབྲོང་འབྲི་ (droŋdri) female wild yak.
འབྲོང་རྩེའི་བེ་བུམ་ (droŋdzee pebum) a medical commentary composed by Drongtse Gyatso.
འབྲོང་རྩེད་ (droŋdzeè) masked dance of the wild yak.
འབྲོང་ཞོར་ལེགས (droŋ shɔrleg) name of the 14th ancient King of Tibet.
འབྲོང་རྭ་ (droŋra) horn of a wild yak.
འབྲོང་ཤ་ (droŋsha) meat of wild yak.
འབྲོང་གསོབ་ (droŋsob) stuffed skin of a wild yak.
འབྲོང་བསད་པས་མི་ཆོག་རྔ་མའི་དར་ལྕོག (droŋsɛɛ̀bɛ mijɔɔ̀ ŋāmɛ tarjɔɔ̀) not only doing sth. but showing it off / flaunting it [Lit. not only killing the wild yak but hoisting its tail as a banner].
འབྲོངས་ (droŋ) imp. of འབྲང་.
འབྲོབ་པ་ (drobba) sm. འབྲབ་.
འབྲོམ་སྟོན་པ་ (drom dõmba) the name of the founder of the Kadampa Sect (1005-1064).
འབྲོས་: p. བྲོས་; f. འབྲོས་; imp. བྲོས་ (dröö) va. to escape, to run away, to flee ¶ བཙོན་ཁང་ནས་བྲོས་པ་རེད་ (They) escaped from prison.
འབྲོས་འདེད་ (dröndeè) giving chase, running after those who have fled; va.—བྱེད་.
འབྲོས་འགྱོལ་ (drönjöö) sm. བྲོས་འགྱོལ་.
འབྲོས་ཤ་ (dröösha) a muscle under the shoulder blade.
འབྲོས་ཤ་ཁྲ་བོ་ (dröösha trāwo) muscle on the shoulder blade.
བ་ (ba) abbr. of. བ་རླབས་.
བ་གློང་ (baloŋ) 1. sm. བ་རླབས་. 2. whirlpool.
བ་ཆུ་ (bəju) a sea/ ocean/ lake with waves.
བ་བཞེད་ (basheè) sm. སྦ་བཞེད་.
བ་ཡི་འི་ (ba yi i) sm. ཟླ་ཡིའི་.
བ་རླབས་ (bələb) wave (of water); vi.—འཕྱུར་ to rise/ surge/ swell up (for waves).
བ་རླབས་ཀྱི་ཟེགས་མ་ (bələbgi segma) spray, spindrift.
བ་རླབས་གྱེན་ལྡོག (bələb gyendɔɔ̀) backward flow, reverse flow of water.
བ་རླབས་ལང་ལོང་དུ་འཕྱུར་ (bələb laŋloŋdu cūr) vi. to rise/ surge/ swell up (of waves).
བ་ལེན་ (bə len) va. to take the main responsibility.
བག་བག (bagbaà) 1. motorcycle. 2. machine gun ¶ མེ་མདའ་བག་བག A machine gun.
བང་ག་ལི་ (baŋgali) 1. Bengali. 2. Western-style short hair (as opposed to the traditional style of Tibetan hair that is kept long).
བད་ (bɛɛ̀) 1. p. and f. of བོད་. 2. sm. བད་དེ་. 3. (with ཁ་ —) boasting, bragging.
བད་ཁམ་ (bɛɛ̀gam) 1. sm. བད་, 3.
བད་མགོ་ (bɛngo) bangs (hair).
བད་མགོ་ལིང་ལིང་ (bɛngo liŋliŋ) sm. བད་མགོ་.
བད་བཅད་ (bɛɛ̀jɛɛ̀) absolutely determinedly, resolutely; va.—བྱེད་ ¶ ང་ལས་ཀ་འདི་བྱ་རྒྱུ་སེམས་ཐག་བད་བཅད་ཡིན་ I am determined to do this work.
བད་ཆོད་ (bɛɛ̀jöö) absolutely determined, resolute ¶ ཁོ་བོད་ལ་འགྲོ་རྒྱུ་སེམས་ཐག་བད་ཆོད་རེད་འདུག He is determined to go to Tibet.
བད་དེ་ (bed) absolutely, completely, entirely, all ¶ བད་དེ་ཁས་མ་བླངས་པ་རེད་ (They) didn't accept it completely. ¶ ངའི་བསམ་འདུན་དང་བད་དེ་མཐུན་སོང་ It has come about completely as I wished. ¶ བད་དེ་རང་སྐྱོང་ Complete autonomy.
བད་དེ་ཁ་ལ་ (bedda kāla) sm. བད་དེ་.
བད་བད་ (bɛɛ̀bɛɛ̀) close-cropped, short ¶ སྐྲ་བད་བད་ Close-cropped hair.
བད་བོད་ (bɛɛ̀böö) tangled/ matted hair.
བད་ལིང་ (bɛɛ̀liŋ) abbr. བད་མགོ་ལིང་ལིང་.
བབ་ (bəb) a steep slope. 2. sm. བབ་རྡོ་.
བབ་གྲི་ (bəbdri) sm. བབ་འདྲིལ་.
བབ་སྒྲིལ་ (bəbdrii) rolling, tumbling (downhill); vi.—གཏོང་ to intentionally roll sth. down a mountain slope.
བབ་ཆུ་ (bəbju) waterfall, river that is flowing down a steep slope.
བབ་དུ་བསྒྲིལ་ (bəbdu drii) va. to intentionally roll sth. downhill ¶ རྡོ་ཆེན་མང་པོ་བབ་དུ་བསྒྲིལ་བ་རེད་ (They) rolled many rocks down the mountain slope.
བབ་གདུང་སྒྲིལ་ (bəbduŋ drii) va. to roll timber down a mountain slope (to get the wood).
བབ་འདྲིལ་ (bəbdrii) rolling/ tumbling down a mountain slope.
བབ་རྡོ་ (bəbdo) a stone rolling downhill; vi.—ཐེབས་; —སྒྲིལ་; —འདྲིལ་ to unintentionally roll downhill (for a stone).
བབ་གཞུག (bəbshuù) the final section of the canal that brings water to a water mill.
བབ་རིལ་ (bəbrii) sm. བབ་དྲིལ་.
བབ་ཤུར་ (bəbshur) the canal that brings water to a water mill.
བིག་དོ་ (bigdo) sm. བིག་བིག.
བིག་བིག (bigbig) short.
བིག་ཙམ་ (bigdzam) a short bit ¶ སྐུད་པ་བིག་ཙམ་ A short bit of string.
བིད་རྒྱུག (biìgyaà) pushing, shoving; va.—གཏོང་.
བུད་རྒྱུག (büùgyaà) sm. བིད་རྒྱུག.
བོད་: p. and f. བད་; imp. བོད་ (böö) va. to set loose/ sic (one's dog on sb.) ¶ ཀུ་མ་ཡོང་དུས་འབྲོག་པས་ཁྱི་བད་པ་རེད་ When the thief came the nomad sicced the dogs on him.

རྦོད་གཏོང་ (böö dōŋ) va. to curse, to cast a spell.

རྦོད་མ་ (bööma) 1. a curse, spell; va.—གཏོང་ —སྐྱེལ་ to curse, to cast a spell. 2. tax.

ལྦ་སྒོར་ (bagɔɔ) bib.

ལྦ་བ་ (baa) goiter; vi.—སྐྱེ་ to have a goiter; vi.—ཡལ་ to have a goiter disappear.

ལྦ་ནད་ (banɛɛ̀) goiter (as illness).

ལྦ་རྫ་ (badza) sm. ལྦ་བ་འཛོམས་.

ལྦ་བ་འཛོམས་ (bawadzom) a type of salt that contains iodine.

ལྦ་ལེ་སྦོ་ལེ་ (bale bole) soft.

ལྦར་འཆང་ང་ (baajaŋŋa) food made by squeezing it in one's hand.

ལྦུ་བ་ (buwə) bubble, foam, froth.

ལྦུ་བ་ཅན་གྱི་ཨར་འདམ་ (buwəjɛngi ārdam) foam concrete.

ལྦུ་བ་ལྡན་པའི་རྒྱུ་ཆ་ (buwə dɛmbɛ gyuja) foam materials.

ལྦུ་བ་ཡལ་བ་ལྟར་ (buwə yɛɛwadar) vanishing/ disappearing immediately [Lit. vanishing like a bubble].

ལྦུར་བརྡེན་མེ་གསོད་ཆས་ (burden mesööjɛɛ̀) foam fire extinguisher.

སྦ་ (ba) 1. cane (kind of wood), rattan. 2. f. of སྦེད་. 3. སྦྲ་.

སྦ་ (ba) f. སྦེད་.

སྦ་ཀ་སི་ (bagasi) eng. packet. box ༡ ང་ཐག་མ་སྦ་ཀ་སི་གཅིག་ཉོ་གི་ཡིན་ I am going to buy a pack of cigarettes.

སྦ་ཀོ་ (bago) anise.

སྦ་གླད་ (balɛɛ̀) the center of a yak hair tent.

སྦ་དཀར་ (bagar) a type of cane/ rattan that is white.

སྦ་སྒང་ (bəguŋ) sm. སྦས་སྒང་.

སྦ་ཁང་ (bəgaŋ) secret treasure room.

སྦ་ཁུག་ (bəguù) purse.

སྦ་ཁུག་ཁབ་ཤུབས་ (bəguù kəbshub) an ornament worn by the རྒྱན་བཟང་མ་.

སྦ་ཁྲའི་སློ་མ་ (badrɛ loma) cane/ rattan basket.

སྦ་ཁྲི་བཞེར་ (ba trisher) one of the first seven Tibetan monks in the 8th century.

སྦ་འཁར་ (bakar) a cane walking stick.

སྦ་འགུགས་ (bəguù) a carpenter's tool.

སྦ་འགེབས་ (bageb) sm. སྦས་སྒང་.

སྦ་སྒོད་ (bagöö) cane growing wild on hills.

སྦ་རྒྱུག་ (bəgyuù) sm. སྦ་འཁར་.

སྦ་སྒམ་ (bagam) cane/ rattan box.

སྦ་སྒོ་ (bago) the door of a yak hair tent.

སྦ་སྒྲོམ་ (badrom) Chinese wisteria (Wisteria sinensis).

སྦ་ལྕུག་ (bajaà) whip (made of cane).

སྦཱ་ཆ་ (baja) hind. musical instrument; va.—གཏོང་ to play musical instruments.

སྦ་ཆས་ (bajɛɛ̀) things made from cane/ rattan.

སྦ་ཆིངས་ (bəjiŋ) cane that is wrapped/ tied around a churn/ barrel.

སྦ་སྟེགས་ (baseg) a stand made of cane/ rattan.

སྦ་ཐག་ (badaà) cane rope.

སྦ་ཐག་ཟམ་པ་ (badaà samba) sm. སྦ་ཟམ་.

སྦ་དམ་ (badam) hind. peanut.

སྦ་ཕུབ་ (babub) cane/ rattan (military) shield.

སྦ་ཕོར་ (babɔɔ) wooden eating bowl made from cane/ rattan.

སྦ་བ་ (bawa) 1. female and male genitals. 2. confidential, secret.

སྦ་བེར་ (baber) sm. སྦ་རྒྱུག་.

སྦ་བླངས་ (ba lāŋ) 1. va. to take the main/ full responsibility ༡ ཁོང་གིས་ལས་ཁུངས་ནང་གི་ལས་ཀ་སྦ་བླངས་ནས་བྱེད་ཀྱི་ཡོད་པ་རེད་ He is taking the full responsibility for the work in the office. 2. va. to take the full responsibility for a crime so that one's accomplices go free ༡ གྱོད་དོན་འདི་སྐོར་ཁྲིམས་ཁང་ནང་ཁོང་གིས་སྦ་བླངས་ནས་རོགས་པ་རྣམས་ལ་ཉེས་སྐྱོན་ཐོག་མེད་པ་རེད་ Concerning the case, because he took full responsibility, his accomplices did not get punished.

སྦ་དབྱུག་ (bəyuù) sm. སྦ་རྒྱུག་.

སྦ་དམར་ (bamar) 1. Chinese wisteria. 2. red colored earth used for plastering walls.

སྦ་རྩ་ (badza) roots of climbing palm trees (Calamus, Daemonorops, or Plectomia).

སྦ་ར་ཛིལ་ (baradzii) Brazil.

སྦ་བཞེད་ (basheè) a famous historical book on Samye written by སྦ་གསལ་སྣང་.

སྦ་ཟམ་ (basam) a cane/ rattan bridge.

སྦ་ཡག་པ་ (ba yagba) the root of red salvia (used in Tibetan medicine).

སྦ་ཡི་ག་ག་ (bayi gāga) type of inferior paper (used to practice calligraphy).

སྦ་ར་གང་ (baragaŋ) a handful ༡ རྩམ་པ་སྦ་ར་གང་ A handful of རྩམ་པ་.

སྦ་རི་སྦི་རི་ (bəri biri) 1. slightly numb; vi.—བྱེད་ ༡ ངའི་ལག་པ་སྦ་རི་སྦི་རི་ཆགས་ནས་ཁབ་རྒྱག་དུས་ཚ་མ་བྱུང་ My hand was slightly numb so when I got an injection it didn't sting a lot. 2. slightly dizzy/ tipsy.

སྦ་ལ་ (bala) an important pass between the Lhasa area and Kongpo.

སྦ་ལན་ (balɛn) sweater.

སྦ་ལེབ་ (baleb) a pot for beer.

སྦ་ཤན་ (bashɛn) sm. སྦ་ཆིངས་.

སྦ་ཤིང་ (bashiŋ) cane, rattan.

སྦ་ཤིང་ཀུབ་བཀྱག་ (bashiŋ gūbgyaà) cane/ rattan chair.

སྦ་ས་ (basa) a place where nomads put up their tents, tent site.

སྦ་སེ་སྦོ་སེ་ (base bose) careless, casual.

སྦ་སྲི་ (basi) keeping one's skill and knowledge to oneself.

སྦ་སློམ་ (balom) abbr. of སྦ་ཁྲའི་སློ་མ་.

སྦ་གསང་ (basaŋ) sm. སྦས་སྒང་.

སྦ་གསང་མེད་པ་ (basaŋ mɛɛ̀ba) candid, frank, open.

སྦ་གསལ་སྣང་ (ba sɛ̄ɛnaŋ) the author of the སྦ་བཞེད་.

སྦ་ཧྲལ་ཧྲལ་ (ba hrɛ̄ɛhrɛɛ) va. to stand with one's legs apart; va.—བྱེད་.

སྦག་ (baà) mahjong; va.—རྒྱག་ to play mahjong.

སྦག་: p. སྦགས་; f. སྦག་; imp. སྦོགས་ (baà) 1. va. to stain/ soil/ make dirty, to pollute, to contaminate ༡ ཁོས་དྲེག་པས་སྦགས་པའི་དུག་ལོག་ཅིག་གྱོན་འདུག He wore clothes that were soiled with dirt. 2. va. to spoil/ ruin (behaviorally) ༡ ཕྲུ་གུ་དེ་རོགས་པའི་གོམས་གཤིས་ངན་པས་སྦགས་ནས་ཀུ་མ་བརྐུས་པ་རེད་ The child was ruined by the bad habits of his friends and stole things.

སྦག་དཀྲུགས་ (bagdruù) shuffling a deck of cards, stirring/ shaking mahjong tiles; va.—རྒྱག.

སྦག་དཀྲུགས་གཏིང་ནས་རྒྱག (bəgdruù diŋnɛ gyaà) va. to cause a major shake up [Lit. stir the mahjong tiles from the bottom rather than cursorily from the top].

སྦག་ཁག (baàgaà) 1. a package which contains four pieces of brick tea. 2. a table of four mahjong players.

སྦག་ཁང་ (baàgaŋ) a mahjong parlor.

སྦག་ཁྲིམས་ (bagdrim) the rules of mahjong.

སྦག་འཁོར་ (bag kɔ̄ɔ) vi. to have a hot hand in mahjong, to win in mahjong.

སྦག་འཁོར་ (baggɔɔ) motorcycle.

སྦག་འཁོར་གསོ་སྒྲིག་བཟོ་གྲྭ (baggɔɔ sōdrig sodra) motorcycle repair shop/ factory.

སྦག་ལྕོག (bagjɔɔ̀) 1. a square table for playing mahjong. 2. a square table.

སྦག་ཆས་ (bagjɛɛ̀) mahjong paraphernalia.

སྦག་ཆུང་ (bəgjuŋ) a small size brick of tea.

སྦག་ཆེན་ (bagjen) 1. sm. སྦག་ཁག. 2. a large package of brick tea. 3. a type of tile game/ mahjong similar to hearts in that each player plays the hand he is dealt without drawing new tiles; va.—རྒྱག.

སྦག་གདན་ (bagdɛn) blanket, cloth, etc. put on a table when playing mahjong.

སྦག་འདྲེས་ (bagdreè) mixed with dirt/ pollution;

vi.—བྱེད་.

སྦག་པ་ (bagba) gambler, mahjong player.

སྦག་པ་གྲོགས་མཆེད་ (bagba drɔgjeè) a mahjong buddy.

སྦག་སྦག (bagbaà) 1. motorcycle. 2. machine gun; vi.—རྒྱག to shoot a machine gun.

སྦག་སྦག་ཁ་ (bagbaàga) sb. who scolds/ criticizes a lot (like a machine gun) ¶ བུ་མོ་དེ་སྦག་སྦག་ཁ་ཡིན་ཙང་ཁྱོ་ག་མ་རག་པ་རེད་ Because that girl is sb. who scolds a lot (she) didn't get a husband.

སྦག་སྦག་གསིག་གསིག (bagbaà sīgsiì) shaking with anger; va.—བྱེད་.

སྦག་རྩེས་ (bagshaà) the strategies of playing mahjong.

སྦག་ཤག (bagshaà) breaking into two; vi.—ཐེབས་ to get split into two; va.—གཏོང་ to break into/ split into two.

སྦག་གཞུག་སྐྱིད་པར་གཟེར་ (bagshuù gēèbar ser) va. to win the final round of the mahjong game.

སྦག་གཡོག (bagyɔ̀ɔ) people who serve food/ drinks where people are playing mahjong.

སྦག་རོགས་ (bagrɔ̀ɔ) mahjong partners, people with whom one regularly plays mahjong.

སྦག་ལྷུང་ལང་ (bagluŋ laŋ) vi. to get angry when losing in mahjong.

སྦགས་ (baà) f. of སྦག.

སྦང་ (baŋ) p. of སྦོང་.

སྦང་ཀ་ལི་ (baŋgali) 1. Bengali. 2. Western style haircut (as opposed to the traditional Tibetan style).

སྦང་སྐམ་ (baŋgam) abbr. of སྦང་མ་སྐམ་པོ་.

སྦང་བུ་ (bəŋgu) fly.

སྦང་གླུམ་ (bəŋlum) fermented grain to which water has been added but not yet drained as beer.

སྦང་ཇ་ (baŋja) Chinese style tea where tea is added to boiled water in a cup/ jar where it soaks.

སྦང་མ་ (baŋma) the leftover grain after beer has been made (after the water has been drained).

སྦང་རྩམ་ (baŋdzam) རྩམ་པ་ made from སྦང་མ་.

སྦང་ཟན་ (baŋsɛn) food made from སྦང་མ་.

སྦང་ཟན་མ་ (baŋsɛnma) a derogatory term used for people from སྟོ་མོ་ people who eat སྦང་རྩམ་.

སྦང་ལུམས་ (baŋlum) སྦང་གླུམ་ to which medicine has been added, heated, and when hot, applied on the body.

སྦངས་ (baŋ) 1. dung (of horses and mules) ¶ རྟ་སྦངས་ Horse dung. 2. p. of སྦོང་.

སྦངས་འབུད་སྨན་རྫས་ (baŋduŋ mɛ̄ndzɛɛ̀) medicine to be taken after being dissolved and soaked in liquid.

སྦངས་དུགས་ (bəŋduù) fresh dung applied to the body as medical treatment while still warm.

སྦངས་འཛིན་ (bəndzin) shung. permission to keeping horses and mules in Lhasa during Monlam.

སྦངས་ལུད་ (bəŋlüü) fertilizer made from horse and mule dung (སྦངས་).

སྦངས་ཕུང་ (baŋbuŋ) pile of སྦངས་.

སྦབ་ཙ་ (bəbja) sm. སྦབ་ཆ་.

སྦབ་ཆ་ (bəbja) a package/ box ¶ མུ་ཟེ་སྦབ་ཆ་གཅིག One package of matches.

སྦམ་ (bam) f. of སྦོམ་.

སྦམ་རྫུ་ (bamdzu) sm. སྦམ་རྫུ་.

སྦམས་ (bam) p. of སྦོམ་.

སྦའོ་ཙ་ལི་ཡ་ (baja liya) Bulgaria.

སྦར་ (bar) 1. a handful. 2. p. and f. of སྦོར་.

སྦར་ཀ་བློད་ (barga lö̀ö) va. to gallop. 2. va. to run.

སྦར་ཁེབ་རྒྱག (bargeb gyaà) va. to cover sth. with one's palms.

སྦར་ཁྱིམ་ (bargyim) sm. སྦར་མོ་.

སྦར་ཆ་ (barja) hind. musical instrument; va.—གཏོང་ to play a musical instrument.

སྦར་ཆ་པ་ (barjawa) a musician.

སྦར་ཆ་ཚོགས་པ་ (barja tsɔ̄gba) an orchestra.

སྦར་འཇུ་ (banju) shung. sm. ལག་འཇུ་.

སྦར་ཉུལ་ (bərñüü) groping around (in the dark); va.—རྒྱག.

སྦར་སྙོག་རྒྱག (barñɔ̀ɔ gyaà) 1. sm. སྦར་ཉུལ་. 2. va. to grasp/ take by handfuls.

སྦར་ཐུད་སྡེར་ (bartüü dēr) sm. ཐུད་རུལ་སྡེར་.

སྦར་མཐིལ་ (bardii) palm (of the hand).

སྦར་མཐིལ་དུ་ལྷུགས་འདྲ་ (bardiidu lūndra) sm. སྦར་མཐིལ་ནང་དུ་ལྷུགས་འདྲ་.

སྦར་མཐིལ་ནང་དུ་ལྷུགས་འདྲ་ (bardii naŋdu lūndra) knowing sth. very well, knowing sth. like the back of one's hand ¶ ལུང་པ་དེ་སྦར་མཐིལ་ནང་དུ་ལྷུགས་འདྲ་ཤེས་ཀྱི་ཡོད་ I know this place like the back of my hand [Lit. like having sth. poured in the palm of one's hand].

སྦར་རྡོ་གཞུ་ (bardo shü) va. to hit with a rock held in one's hand.

སྦར་འཕུར་རྒྱག (barpur gyaà) va. to rub with the hand.

སྦར་བ་ (barwa) palm of the hand, handful; va.—གདངས་ to open the hand; —འཛུམ་ to close the hand, to clench one's fist; va.—གཟེད་ to hold out one's open hands for sth. to be poured in ¶ ཚྭ་སྦར་བ་གང་ A handful of salt.

སྦར་མ་ (barma) Burma.

སྦར་མིག་འགེབས་ (barmiì geb) va. to shade the sun by holding one's hand over the forehead.

སྦར་མིག་སྒྲོས་ (barmiì drö̀ö) sm. སྦར་མིག་འགེབས་.

སྦར་མོ་ (barmo) 1. a winnowing rake; va.—རྒྱག to winnow with a rake. 2. palm of the hand, sole of the foot. 3. scratching with claws; va.—རྒྱག.

སྦར་མོའི་ཕྱི་ནང་ངོ་ཤེས་དགོས་ (barmö̀ö cīnaŋ ŋosheè gö̀ö) one should know clearly what is right and wrong [Lit. one should recognize the outside and inside of one's palm].

སྦར་མོས་རུབ་ (barmö̀ö rub) va. to gather or collect with the hand.

སྦར་སྨྱུལ་ (bərñüü) sm. སྦར་ཉུལ་.

སྦར་བ་གཟེད་ (barwa seè) va. to wait with open hands (palms) for sth. to be poured in.

སྦར་སྦྲད་ (barrɛɛ̀) 1. scratching —རྒྱག to scratch ¶ ཁོས་ལག་པའི་རྨ་ལ་སྦར་སྦྲད་བརྒྱབ་སོང་ He scratched the sore on his hand. 2. clawing; va.—རྒྱག to claw.

སྦར་སྦྲད་ཚ་པོ་ (barrɛɛ̀ tsābo) sb. who scratches a lot when they fight.

སྦར་བཙིར་ (bərdzir) squeezing in one's hand; va.—གཏོང་; —རྒྱག.

སྦར་འཛིང་ (bərdziŋ) sm. ལག་འཛིང་.

སྦར་འཛིན་ (bəndzin) seizing/ grabbing in one's hand; va.—བྱེད་ ¶ ཆུ་ཡུར་ནང་ནས་ཉ་སྦར་འཛིན་རྒྱག་གི་འདུག (He) is grabbing in the irrigation canal to catch a fish in his hand.

སྦར་རྫོགས་ (bardzɔ̀ɔ) grabbing/ taking with the hand; va.—གཏོང་; —རྒྱག ¶ འབྲས་སྦར་རྫོགས་བརྒྱབ་ནས་ཟ་གི་འདུག (He) is eating rice by grabbing handfuls (in his hand).

སྦར་ཟིན་ (bar sin) sm. སྦར་འཛིན་.

སྦར་ཡུལ་ (baryüü) sm. སྦར་མ་.

སྦར་ཤད་ (barshɛɛ̀) sm. སྦར་སྦྲད་.

སྦར་ཤད་བརྒྱབ་ཤུལ་ (barshɛɛ̀ gyəbshüü) a scar/ mark caused by scratching.

སྦར་ཤུགས་ (barshuù) hand grip/ strength.

སྦར་བསིལ་ལྟ་ (barsii dā) va. to put a little ཆང་ in one's palm and taste it.

སྦལ་རྒྱལ་ (bɛɛgyɛɛ) breaststroke (in swimming); va.—རྒྱག.

སྦལ་ (bɛɛ) abbr. of སྦལ་པ་.

སྦལ་མགོ་ (bɛngo) 1. a Tibetan traditional surgical tool. 2. frog's head.

སྦལ་འགྲོས་ (bɛɛdrö̀ö) 1. the way a frog moves/ jumps; va.— བྱེད་; —རྒྱག. 2. leapfrogging; va.—བྱེད་; —རྒྱག to leapfrog.

སྦལ་རྒྱབ་ (bɛɛgyəb) type of mineral medicine (iron hydroxide and hematitum).

སྦལ་སྒ་ (bɛɛga) a type of saddle that is covered with frog skin.

སྦལ་ལྕོང་ (bεεjoŋ) 1. abbr. frog and tadpole. 2. tadpole.

སྦལ་ཆེན་ (bεεjen) toad.

སྦལ་དུག (bεεduù) 1. poisonous toad/ frog. 2. a traditional Tibetan medicine.

སྦལ་སྣབས་ (bεεnəb) spirogyra varians kutzing (used in Tibetan medicine).

སྦལ་པ་ (bεεba) frog.

སྦལ་པ་ཀང་མང་ (bεεba gāŋmaŋ) crab.

སྦལ་པ་རྒྱ་མཚོའི་གཏིང་ནས་ངུས་པ། ལྷའི་དབང་པོ་བརྒྱ་བྱིན་གྱི་སྙན་ལ་མ་འགྱོལ་ (bεεba gyadzö dīŋnε ŋüü ba lhē wāŋbo gyajingi ñēnla magöö) the ruler doesn't hear the complaints of his poor/ humble subjects [Lit. the crying of the frog from the bottom of the ocean does reach the ear of the king of the gods].

སྦལ་པ་རྡོ་ཟན་ (bεεba dosεn) a forest frog that is used in Tibetan medicine.

སྦལ་པ་འཕུར་དུ་རེ་ (bεεba pūrdu re) aspiring to do sth. impossible [Lit. a frog trying to fly].

སྦལ་པ་རྨ་ཅན་ (bεεba mājεn) bad things/ habits spread quickly [Lit. a frog having a sore].

སྦལ་པའི་ཤ་ (bεεbε shā) frog meat.

སྦལ་བངས་ (bεεbaŋ) sm. སྦལ་པ་.

སྦལ་མིག (bεεmii) bud of a flower.

སྦལ་ཚང་ (bεεdzaŋ) frog nest.

སྦལ་རྫིང་ (bεεdziŋ) frog pond.

སྦལ་ལག (b εεlaà) 1. type of traditional Tibetan medicine. 2. a kind of celery.

སྦལ་ལེབ་ (bεεleb) a flatish container with two handles and a round bottom.

སྦས་ (bεὲ) p. of སྦེད་.

སྦས་སྐུང་ (bεὲguŋ) keeping secret, concealing, hiding; va.—བྱེད་ ¶ མི་མདའ་སྦས་སྐུང་བྱས་པའི་རྙོག་དྲ་ནི་ As for the problem caused by secretly keeping the gun.

སྦས་སྐུང་མེད་པ་ (bεὲguŋ meèba) candid, frank, open.

སྦས་སྐུངས་ (bεὲguŋ) sm. སྦས་སྐུང་.

སྦས་བསྐུངས་ (bεὲguŋ) sm. སྦས་སྐུང་.

སྦས་ཉོ་ཁློག་ཚོང་ (bεὲño kōgdzoŋ) buying and selling secretly; va.—བྱེད་; —རྒྱག.

སྦས་དངོས་ (bεὲŋöö) hidden things/ objects.

སྦས་གནས་ (bεὲnεὲ) sm. སྦས་ལུང་.

སྦས་པའི་རྩ་ཆེན་བརྒྱད་ (bεὲbε dzājen gyεὲ) name of the eight main veins of the human body in Tibetan medicine.

སྦས་ལུང་ (bεὲluŋ) 1. a secret/ hidden area or valley. 2. a remote region.

སྦས་ཤུགས་ (bεὲshuù) potential; va.—འདོན་ to uncover/ expose/ bring forth potential.

སྦས་སྲུང་ (bεὲsuŋ) being straightforward, not concealing/ hiding; va.—བྱེད་.

སྦས་གསང་ (bεὲsaŋ) concealing, hiding; va.—བྱེད་.

སྦས་གསང་མེད་པ་ (bεὲsaŋ meèba) not concealing/ hiding.

སྦི་ཅི་ལི་ (bijili) hind. flashlight.

སྦི་ཅི་ལིའི་སྨན་ (bijili mēn) hind.tib. battery (for a flashlight).

སྦི་དི་ (bidi) 1. fuse/ wick on a matchlock gun. 2. Spiti region.

སྦི་སྡི་ (bidi) sm. སྦི་དི་.

སྦི་ཐི་ (bidi) sm. སྦི་དི་.

སྦི་སྟི་ (bidi) sm. སྦི་དི་.

སྦི་སྦི་སི་ (bibisi) eng. BBC.

སྦི་རག (biraà) eng.tib. beer.

སྦི་རིལ་ (birii) hind. a type of cigarette rolled in leaf.

སྦི་ལ་བསིལ་པོ་ (bila siību) spirited, active, lively.

སྦི་ལྭ་ས་ (bilasa) hind.tib. cement.

སྦི་གསང་ (bisaŋ) watchful, cautious, on guard, careful, alert; va.—བྱེད་.

སྦི་གསང་དོད་པོ་ (bisaŋ töòbo) a very cautious/ careful, watchful/ alert person.

སྦིད་ (bii) sm. སྦྱིད་.

སྦིད་པ་ (biibə) sm. སྦུད་པ་.

སྦིན་བུ་ (bimbu) chaff, husk.

སྦིར་ (bir) 1. sm.* སྦྱིད་. 2. vi. to vibrate/ tremble/ shake ¶ ཉེ་འགྲམ་དུ་སྒྲོགས་ཤོག་ནས་ཁང་པ་ཡང་སྦིར་སོང་ Nearby an artillery shell fell and the house shook.

སྦིར་གྲགས་ (birdraà) sm. སྦིར་གཏམ་.

སྦིར་སྒྲ་ (birdra) 1. noise of a gun firing or bomb exploding. 2. sm. སྦིར་གཏམ་.

སྦིར་གཏམ་ (birdam) negative rumor/ talk; vi.—གྲགས་ to have a rumor exist; va.—བཟོ་ to make/ start a rumor ¶ དེང་སང་གྲོང་ཁྱེར་ནང་དམག་འཁྲུག་ཡོང་རྒྱུའི་སྦིར་གཏམ་གྲགས་ཀྱི་ཡོད་པ་རེད་ Thesedays it is being rumored that war will come to the city.

སྦིར་ཐོས་ (birtöö) shung. gossip, rumor.

སྦིར་སྨན་ (birmεn) anesthesia.

སྦུ་གུ (bugu) 1. hollow, cavity. 2. tube, pipe. 3. bushings.

སྦུ་གུའི་སྒྲོ་འདྲ་ (bugü drondra) a small knife used in Tibetan medicine.

སྦུ་ལུ་ (buluù) shung. a kind of hat worn by the ཡ་སོར་. 2. sm. ཞུ་ཐུང་.

སྦུ་ལུག (buluù) a kind of cookie made from flour mixed with milk.

སྦུག (buù) 1. the interior/ inner part. 2. the inside.

སྦུག་ཁངས་ཕྱག་མཛོད་ (bùugoŋ cāndzöö) shung. sm. མཛོད་སྦུག.

སྦུག་ཆལ་ (bugjεε) cymbals; va.—དཀྲོལ་ to play the cymbals.

སྦུག་ཆུང་ (bugjuŋ) small cymbals.

སྦུག་ཆོད་ (bugjöö) shung. included in ¶ ཞིང་ཁ་བཞི་བཅུ་དེ་ཁོངས་སྦུག་ཆོད་མེད་ངེས་ Forty fields were not included in that part.

སྦུག་ཆོལ་ (bugjöö) sm. སྦུག་ཆལ་.

སྦུག་འཛོག (buŋjɔɔ) depositing, storing ¶ དངུལ་ཁང་གི་སྦུག་འཛོག Safe deposit box (in a bank).

སྦུག་གདམ་འབྱར་མ་ (bugdam jarma) shung. a document that is sealed with the seal of the Dalai Lama.

སྦུག་སྟོང་ (bugdoŋ) 1. vacuum. 2. hollow.

སྦུག་ཐང་ (bugdaŋ) a pouch used for making སྦུ་ལུག cookies.

སྦུག་ཐག་རིང་པོ་ (bugdaà riŋbu) deep and long (e.g., for a room, cavern).

སྦུག་ཐམ་ (bugdam) sm. སྦུག་དམ་.

སྦུག་ཐམ་བཀའ་རྒྱ་ (bugdam gāgya) shung. an order from the Dalai Lama (with the Dalai Lama's seal).

སྦུག་ཐམ་རྩ་ཚིག (bugdam dzōdzii) shung. a general proclamation issued by the Dalai Lama (with the Dalai Lama's seal).

སྦུག་མཐུན་བསྡུ་སྒྲིལ་ (bugdün sūgyee) collaborating in evil/ duplicitous acts; va.—བྱེད་.

སྦུག་འཐུམ་ (bugdum) shung. included in sth.

སྦུག་དམ་ (bugdam) shung. the personal seal of the Dalai Lama.

སྦུག་དམ་ལག་རྩ་རིན་པོ་ཆེ་ (bugdam lagdza rimboce) shung. a document with the Dalai Lama's seal.

སྦུག་དོང་ (bugdoŋ) 1. pipe, tube. 2. tunnel.

སྦུག་དོག་པོ་ (buù tɔgbo) narrow, constricted, not spacious.

སྦུག་དྲུས་ (bugdrüü) hollowing the inside of sth; va.—རྒྱག.

སྦུག་འདྲེན་ཐལ་ལུས་ (bugdren tεεlüü) shung. overstating and understating expenses/ income (a term used in tt. accounting) ¶ ལས་ཁུངས་ཀྱི་བྱུང་སོང་རྩིས་རྒྱག་སྦུག་འདྲེན་ཐལ་ལུས་མེད་པ་བྱེད་དགོས་ One must do the accounting of the office's accounts (income and expenses) without overstating or understating.

སྦུག་པ་ (bugbə) a person who manages a storehouse/ treasury.

སྦུག་པོ་ (bugbo) 1. a room that is long and narrow. 2. taciturn.

སྦུག་ཕྲན་ (bugdrεn) capillaries.

སྦུག་དབྱིབས་མེ་ཏོག (bugyib medoò) tubular flower.

སྦུག་འབྱར་ (bunjar) abbr. of སྦུག་གདམ་འབྱར་མ་.

སྦུག་སྦུག (bugbuù) ambiguous, not open/ clear (in speech); implicit, veiled ¶ སྐྱོན་བརྗོད་སྦུག་སྦུག Veiled criticism.

སྦུག་མ་ (bugmə) the inner ¶ ཁང་པ་སྦུག་མ་ An inner room in a house.

སྦུག་རྩ་ (bugdza) root/ bottom of sth.; vi.—གཙོད་ to get to the bottom/ root of sth.; vi.—ཚོད་ to get to the root/ bottom of sth.

སྦུག་ཚིག (bugdzìì) 1. unclear, ambiguous words/ language ¶ ཡིག་ཆ་འདིའི་ནང་སྦུག་ཚིག་མང་པོ་ཞིག་བཀོད་པ་དེ་ཚོ་གསལ་པོ་རྟོགས་ཀྱི་མི་འདུག I don't understand clearly many words (phrases) that are written in this document. 2. inner/ confidential/ secret talk ¶ གནད་དོན་འདི་བཀའ་ཤག་གི་སྦུག་ཚིག་རེད་ཕྱི་ལ་སྒྲུར་ན་ཡོང་གི་མ་རེད་ This issue is the inner talk of the Kashag and should not be spread outside.

སྦུག་ཚེམས་ (bugdzem) h. of སྦུག་སོ་.

སྦུག་མཛོད་ (buŋdzöö) shung. the managers of Drepung College's estates (appointed by the colleges).

སྦུག་ཞུགས་ (bugshuù) shung. sm. ཁོག་ཞུགས་.

སྦུག་ཟོས་ (bugsöö) embezzlement, fraud, misappropriation; va.—བྱེད་.

སྦུག་གཟོང་ (bugsoŋ) a type of chisel used for carving letters on wood blocks (for printing).

སྦུག་ལམ་ (buglam) a road/ path going through a stupa, a road going through a tunnel.

སྦུག་སུབ་ (bugsub) suffocating stifling; vi.—ཐེབས་ to feel suffocated/ stifling due to a crowded space/ atmosphere. 2. sm. དབུགས་འགག, 2.

སྦུག་སུབ་དོག་པོ་ (bugsub togbo) 1. a stifling/ suffocating atmosphere, a small/ crowded space. 2. a withdrawn/ unsociable person, person who does not go out and interact much with people.

སྦུག་སོ་ (bugso) molar teeth.

སྦུག་སོ་མདུན་མ་ (bugso dünmə) premolar teeth.

སྦུག་སོ་སྦུག་མ་ (bugso bugmə) wisdom teeth.

སྦུག་གསང་ (bugsaŋ) shung. concealing/ keeping in the dark.

སྦུག་གསོག་ཐེབས་ (bugsoò tēè) vi. to get accumulated over a long time.

སྦུངས་ (buŋ) arc. 1. strength, power. 2. diligent, hardworking; va.—སྐྱེད་ to work diligently, to exert effort. 3. oath/ pledge; va.—སྐྱེད་ to give one's oath.

སྦུད་སྒམ་ (büügam) a wooden (box-like) bellows.

སྦུད་མཆུ་ (bünju) the nose/ tip a bellow.

སྦུད་དེ་ (büüdi) sm. སྦི་ཐི་.

སྦུད་ལྡན་ཐབ་ཀ་ (bündɛn tābga) blast furnace.

སྦུད་པ་ (büübə) bellows, blowers; va.—འབུད་; —རྒྱག to use bellows.

སྦུད་པ་དབུགས་མངགས་ (büübə üùŋaà) acting according to what one is expected to do with respect to one's station in life [Lit. the bellow is meant for blowing].

སྦུད་སྦུད་ (büübüü) 1. sm. སྦུད་ཙམ་. 2. pulsating.

སྦུད་ཙམ་ (büüdzam) short, small ¶ བདེ་པོ་ཡིན་ཞེར་བ་ཡི་གེ་སྦུད་ཙམ་ཞིག་གཏོང་རོགས་ Please send a short letter saying that (you) are well. ¶ དུས་ཚོད་སྦུད་ཙམ་ཞིག་རིང་ For a short time.

སྦུད་ཤན་ (büüshɛn) sm. སྦུད་པ་.

སྦུན་གོག (büngɔɔ̀) 1. tree bark. 2. grain chaff.

སྦུན་སྙིགས་ (bünñig) sm. སྦུན་གོག, 2.

སྦུན་གདེར་ (bünder) things that have quantity but are not useful [Lit. pile of chaff].

སྦུན་པ་ (bümbə) 1. sm. སྦུན་གོག. 2. alloyed, impure.

སྦུན་ཕུབ་ (bünpub) sm. སྦུན་གོག, 2.

སྦུན་མ་ (bünmə) sm. སྦུན་གོག, 2.

སྦུབ་: p. སྦུབས་; f. སྦུབ་; imp. སྦུབས་ (bub) va. to turn over, to turn upside down (usu. ཁ་ + —) ¶ ཁོས་སྣོད་ཆས་ཁ་སྦུབས་སོང་ He turned the vessel upside down.

སྦུབ་ཆོལ་ (bubjöö) sm. སྦུག་ཆལ་.

སྦུབ་རིལ་ཉིས་གོ་ (bubrii ñigo) a type of container for ཆང་.

སྦུབས་ཁོང་ (bubgoŋ) the inner part, the inside of sth. ¶ སྒམ་གྱི་སྦུབས་ཁོང་ཆེན་པོ་མི་འདུག The inside of the box is not big.

སྦུབས་གྲོལ་ (bub dröö) vi. to open (for flowers).

སྦུབས་ཅན་མོ་ (bubjɛnmo) a traditional Tibetan tool for treating hemorrhoids.

སྦུབས་ཅོག (bubjɔɔ̀) a table without drawers.

སྦུབས་ཆུང་ (bubjuŋ) 1. things with a small capacity. 2. a thin pipe/ tube.

སྦུབས་སྟོང་ (bubdoŋ) hollow.

སྦུབས་བརྡོལ་ (bub döö) 1. va. to clear sth. that is blocking the inside of sth. (e.g., a pipe). 2. vi. to have an egg hatch.

སྦུབས་ཐུར་ (bubdur) a small pipe/ tube.

སྦུབས་ཐུར་སྨྱུ་གུ་ཁ་ (bubdur ñugu kā) a traditional Tibetan medical tool for drawing out blood and pus.

སྦུབས་ཐོ་ (bubdo) a hammer used for working on metals.

སྦུབས་དོང་ (bubdoŋ) tunnel.

སྦུབས་དྲུས་ (bubdrüü) making sth. hollow or semihollow (e.g., carving out a wooden bowl, etc.); va.—རྒྱག.

སྦུ་འབྱར་ (bunjar) a traditional Tibetan disease that blocks the urinary track.

སྦུབས་མ་ (bubmə) a pipe/ tube.

སྦུབས་ཡུར་ (bubyur) an underground/ covered irrigation canal.

སྦུབས་བཤངས་ (bubshaŋ) enlarging the inside/ opening of sth; va.—རྒྱག.

སྦུབས་བཤད་ (bubshɛɛ̀) whispering into sb.'s ears.

སྦུར་ནག (burnaà) dung beetle.

སྦུར་པ་ (burbə) crustacean.

སྦུར་བ་ (burwə) sm. སྦུར་མ་.

སྦུར་མ་ (burmə) 1. chaff, husks. 2. a pile of hay and straw left for later use as fertilizer.

སྦུར་མེ་ (burme) a small bush fire.

སྦུར་ལེན་ (burlen) sm. སྤོས་ཤེལ་.

སྦུར་ལོང་ (burloŋ) a kind of gold and silver earring (worn in Eastern Tibet).

སྦུས་རུ་ (büüru) one of the four traditional units (རུ་) of Central Tibet.

སྦེ་ (be) sm. སྦེ་ག.

སྦེ་ཀ་ (bega) sm. སྦེ་ག.

སྦེ་ཁ་ (bega) sm. སྦེ་ག.

སྦེ་ག (bega) wrestling; va.—རྒྱག; —འཆང་; —སྦྱར་; —འགྱེད་; —ཚད་ to wrestle.

སྦེ་ག་འགྱེད་མཁན་ (bega gyeèñɛn) wrestler.

སྦེ་ག་འགྲན་བསྡུར་ (bega drɛndur) wrestling match/ competition.

སྦེ་ག་རྡོ་འགྱོགས་ (bēga dogyɔɔ̀) traditional Tibetan athletic competitions of stone lifting and wrestling.

སྦེ་ག་ཤེད་རྡོ་ (bēga shēèdo) sm. སྦེ་ག་རྡོ་འགྱོགས་.

སྦེ་གའི་ལུས་རྩལ་པ་ (begɛ lüüdzɛɛba) a wrestler.

སྦེ་རེག (bereg) eng. brake; va.—རྒྱག to put the brakes; va.—གློད་ to release the brake.

སྦེ་སི་ཀུ་ཏི་ (besi gūdi) eng. biscuit.

སྦེ་སི་གོ་པི་ (besigobi) hind. movie.

སྦེག་སྦེག (begbeg) short and stout.

སྦེད་: p. སྦས་; f. སྦས་; imp. སྦོས་ (beè) va. to conceal, to hide, to cover up, to bury ¶ ཁོས་དངུལ་དེ་གདན་གྱི་འོག་དུ་སྦས་པ་རེད་ He hid the money under the mattress.

སྦེད་བྱེད་པ་ (beèjeèba) one of the 16 arahats.

སྦེད་ཡུལ་ (beèyüü) hidden/ secret land/ place/ area.

སྦེབ་ (beb) vi. to swell/ puff up.

སྦེར་རྒྱག (ber gyaà) va. to quiver/ shake/ tremble/ vibrate.

སྦེར་པོ་ (berbo) active, lively.

སྦེར་ལང་ (ber laŋ) vi. to be in turmoil, to be agitated ¶ དཀྲོག་གཏམ་དེ་གོ་ནས་མི་ཚང་མ་སྦེར་ལངས་པ་རེད་ After hearing the rumor, all the people were in turmoil.

སྦོ་ (bo) 1. stomach/ chest area ¶ སྦོ་ཉལ་རྒྱལ་ To lie

on one's stomach/ chest. 2. sm. དབོ་.

སྦོ་དཀར་ (bogar) a lump of earth.

སྦོ་སྐྱེར་སྐྱེར་ (bo gyērgyer) 1. standing with one's chest out; va.—བྱེད་. 2. arrogant, conceited.

སྦོ་འཁྲོག (bo trōg) vi. to have one's stomach grumble.

སྦོ་སྒྲོ་ (bodro) stomach feathers of large birds like vultures.

སྦོ་གྱིད་གྱིད་ཁེད་ (bo gyeègyeè kēè) sm. སྦོ་སྐྱེར་སྐྱེར་.

སྦོ་དགྱེར་དགྱེར་ (bo gyeegyee) sm. སྦོ་སྐྱེར་སྐྱེར་.

སྦོ་ཇོ་ (bojo) sm. འབོག་འཛོལ་.

སྦོ་ཉལ་བྱེད་ (boñεε ceè) va. to lay down on one's belly.

སྦོ་སྙེ་རྒྱག (boñe gyaà) va. to sit with one's elbows resting on sth.

སྦོ་ཏོ་ར་ (bodora) eng. bottle.

སྦོ་གདོར་ (bodɔɔ) tool that is used to flatten soil.

སྦོ་འདོག (bodɔɔ̀) sm. སྦོ་བལ་.

སྦོ་དོག (bodɔɔ̀) sole for the front part of a shoe.

སྦོ་བལ་ (bopεε) the wool of sheep from the chest to the abdomen.

སྦོ་མ་ (boma) a type of cataract.

སྦོ་ཚིལ་ (bodzii) fat in the stomach of animals.

སྦོ་ཟླ་ (bonda) the 2nd month of the Tibetan calendar.

སྦོ་འུར་ (bo wur) sm. སྦོ་འཁྲོག.

སྦོ་རིལ་ (borii) sm. སྦུག་རིལ་.

སྦོ་ལུག་མ་ (bo luŋmə) Tibetan robe/ gown without the belt tied.

སྦོ་ལུག (boluù) 1. vi. to get wrecked/ ruined, to come to be in disarray ། དམག་འཁྲུག་བྱུང་ཙང་ཁོང་ལྟ་སྐོར་དུ་གདན་ཞུའི་འཆར་གཞི་སྦོ་ལུག་པ་རེད་ Because a war broke out, his plan to bring tourists was ruined.

སྦོ་ལི་ (bole) a child's game in which coins are thrown into holes.

སྦོ་ལོགས་ (boloò) one side of the body.

སྦོ་ཤོབ་ (bɔshoò) boasting, bragging, boasting/ showing-off; va.—ཤོད་.

སྦོ་ཤོབ་ཚ་པོ་ (boshoò tsābo) one who brags/ boasts/ exaggerates/ shows off a lot.

སྦོ་ལྷུག་མ་ (bo lhūgma) sm. སྦོ་ལུག་མ་.

སྦོ་ལྷུག་ལྷུག (bo lhūgluù) sm. སྦོ་ལུག་མ་.

སྦོག་ཀྱི་ (bɔggye) snobbish; va.—བྱེད་; —ཤོད་ to be/ act snobbish.

སྦོག་སྦོག (bɔgbɔɔ̀) bulging, protruding.

སྦོག་ཤོད་ (bɔɔ̀ shöö) va. to talk or act in a snobbish manner.

སྦོགས་ (bɔɔ̀) imp. of སྦག.

སྦོང་: p. སྦངས་; f. སྦང་; imp. སྦོངས་ (boŋ) va. to soak, to wet ། ཁོའི་ལག་པ་ཆུ་ཚ་པོའི་ནང་ལ་སྦངས་པ་རེད་ He soaked his hand in hot water.

སྦོངས་ (boŋ) imp. of སྦོང་.

སྦོད་ (böö) a tassle.

སྦོམ་: p. སྦོམས་; f. སྦོམ་; imp. སྦོམས་ (bom) 1. sm. སྦོམ་. 2. va. to mix. 3. va. to collect. 4. abbr. of སྦོམ་པོ་.

སྦོམ་ལྡིར་ (bomdir) a fat/ rotund/ potbellied person.

སྦོམ་པོ་ (bombo) 1. thick (in circumference), broad, large, bulky ། ཐག་པ་སྦོམ་པོ་ A thick rope. 2. low or deep (in voice) ། སྐད་སྦོམ་པོ་ A low/ deep voice. 3. (with ཉམ་འགྱུར་) arrogant, proud and tough/ harsh (this has a negative connotation).

སྦོམ་ཕྲ་ (bomdra) 1. thickness ། སྦོམ་ཕྲ་ཆུ་ཟོམ་ལྟར་ As thick as a wooden water bucket. 2. thick and thin.

སྦོམ་སྦེ་ (bombe) Bombay.

སྦོམ་ལོས་ (bomlöö) the degree of thickness.

སྦོམས་ (bom) 1. imp. of སྦོམ་. 2. circumference.

སྦོར་ (bɔɔ) sm. སྦོར་.

སྦོར་ཤོབ་ (bɔɔshob) sm. སྦོ་ཤོབ་.

སྦོལ་ (böö) 1. va. to cultivate/ open virgin land. 2. va. to mix.

སྦོལ་འདེབས་ (böö deb) sm. གསར་སྦོལ་འདེབས་འཛུགས་.

སྦོས་ (böö) 1. vi. to swell up, to become inflated/ distended/ bloated ། ཁ་ལག་གྲང་མོ་བཟས་ཙང་གྲོད་ཁོག་སྦོས་བྱུང་ Because (I) ate cold food (my) stomach got bloated. 2. imp. of སྦེད་.

སྦོས་སྐྲངས་ (böödraŋ) bloated and swollen.

སྦོས་འཁུམ་ (böögum) swelling and contracting.

སྦོས་འཚང་ (böödzaŋ) (stomach) bloated and rumbling.

སྦྱག: p. སྦྱགས་; f. སྦྱག (jaà) vi. to lose weight ། ངའི་གཟུགས་པོའི་ཤ་སྦྱགས་བཞག I have lost weight.

སྦྱག་ཐག་འཕེན་ (jagtaà tēn) sm. ཁྱིམ་ཐག་འཕེན་.

སྦྱག་སྦྱག་གཏོང་ (jagjaà dōŋ) sm. བཅག་བཅག་གཏོང་.

སྦྱག་མ་ (jaàma) shovel; va.—རྒྱག.

སྦྱག་ཚེ་ (jaàdze) becoming thin, losing weight; vi.—ཆགས་; —འགྱུར་.

སྦྱག་གཞས་ (jaàshεὲ) work song sung when shoveling; va.—གཏོང་.

སྦྱག་ཡུ་ (jagyu) shovel handle.

སྦྱག་སློག (jaàlɔɔ̀) turning over the earth with a shovel; va.—རྒྱག.

སྦྱགས་ (jaà) p. of སྦྱག.

སྦྱང་ (jaŋ) 1. f. of སྦྱོང་. 2. sm. ཇང་.

སྦྱང་ཆོག (jaŋjɔɔ̀) prayer/ ritual performed for the deceased.

སྦྱང་དེབ་ (jaŋdeb) exercise book, practice book.

སྦྱང་འབྲས་ (jaŋdrεὲ) the result/ fruit of studying.

སྦྱང་རྩོམ་ (jaŋdzom) practice composition.

སྦྱང་བརྩོན་ (jaŋdzön) studious/ hardworking/ diligent/ in one's studies.

སྦྱང་གཞི་ (jaŋshi) 1. birth, death and the intermediate state. 2. the Buddha nature that all sentient beings have. 3. exercises for study (in a textbook).

སྦྱང་ཤིང་ (jəŋshiŋ) a wooden board used in Tibet for practicing writing.

སྦྱང་ཤིང་པ་ (jəŋshiŋbə) students who are at the level of practicing writing on wooden boards.

སྦྱངས་ (jaŋ) p. of སྦྱོང་.

སྦྱངས་གོམས་ (jaŋgom) studying/ learning and getting familiar with, studying and getting proficient; va.—བྱེད་; —འཐོན་ ། ཁོ་ཚོས་ཅབ་སྲིད་སློབ་སྦྱོང་སྦྱངས་གོམས་བྱེད་པའི་ཐབས་ཤེས་བྱས་པ་རེད་ They tried to find ways to study and get proficient.

སྦྱངས་སྟོབས་ (jaŋdob) learning ability/ skill ། སྦྱངས་སྟོབས་ཀྱི་ཡོན་ཏན་ Acquired knowledge.

སྦྱངས་བདུངས་ (jaŋ duŋ) va. to purify/ eliminate impurities.

སྦྱངས་བདུངས་མ་ (jaŋduŋmə) pure, unadulterated.

སྦྱངས་ན་རྒན་མོས་མ་ཧེ་ཐེག (jaŋna gεnmöö mahe tēg) with practice one can achieve anything [Lit. even an old woman can lift a buffalo if she practices].

སྦྱངས་པ་ (jaŋba) knowledge ། ཕྱི་རྒྱལ་སྐད་ཡིག་ལ་སྦྱངས་པ་ཆེ་བ་ཞིག་རེད་ He has great knowledge of foreign languages.

སྦྱངས་པའི་ཡོན་ཏན་ (jaŋbε yöndεn) learned or acquired knowledge (as opposed to innate knowledge).

སྦྱངས་འབྲས་ (jaŋdrεὲ) the result/ fruit of one's studies.

སྦྱངས་མ་ (jaŋma) pure ། དངུལ་སྦྱངས་མ་ Pure silver.

སྦྱངས་རྩལ་ (jaŋdzεε) skill acquired through practice.

སྦྱངས་བརྩོན་ (jaŋdzön) sm. སྦྱང་བརྩོན་.

སྦྱངས་ཡིག (jəŋyii) notes a teacher uses for teaching, teaching/ lesson materials.

སྦྱངས་ཤ་སྟོན་ (jaŋsha tōn) va. to show that sth. was practiced/ studied ། ཁོང་གི་ཡིག་གཟུགས་སྦྱང་ཤ་སྟོན་པ་ཞིག་འདུག His penmanship shows that he has practiced a lot (i.e., it shows skill).

སྦྱངས་སོན་ (jaŋsön) skilled, experienced.

སྦྱར་ (jar) p. and f. of སྦྱོར་.

སྦྱར་ཀ་ (jargə) 1. joined/ linked/ stuck/ fit together well; va.—རྒྱག ། སྒམ་བཟོ་དུས་པང་ལེབ་སྦྱར་ཀ་རྒྱག་དགོས་ When making a box, the planks have to be fitted together well. 2. a bribe; va.—རྒྱག to give a bribe ¶ ཁྱེད་རང་གིས་དཔོན་པོ་དེ་ར་སྦྱར་ཀ་ཞིག་མ་བརྒྱབ་ན་དོན་དག་བསྒྲུབ་ཀྱི་མ་རེད་ Unless you bribe that official, you will not succeed.

སྦྱར་དཀར་ (jaŋgar) white poplar.

སྦྱར་ཁ་ (jaŋga) sm. སྦྱར་ཀ་, 2.

སྦྱར་ཁ་ལེབ་པོ་ (jaŋga lebbo) a person who can be bribed easily.

སྦྱར་འགྲེམ་ (jandrem) putting/ sticking up sth.(e.g., a poster); va.—བྱེད་.

སྦྱར་འགྲེམས་ཚགས་པར་ (jandrem tsāgbar) poster newspaper.

སྦྱར་ཅར་ (jarjaa) a type of sleeveless dress.

སྦྱར་བཅོས་ (jārjöö) plaster cast (for a broken leg, etc.); va.—བྱེད་.

སྦྱར་ཆགས་ (jarjaà) a potter's tool.

སྦྱར་ཆང་ (jarcaŋ) mixed alcoholic beverages.

སྦྱར་སྟངས་ (jardaŋ) the way things are joined/ fit together.

སྦྱར་མཐུད་ (jardüü) sticking together; va.—བྱེད་.

སྦྱར་དུག (jarduù) poison composed of many elements.

སྦྱར་དྲི་ (jərdri) the smell of many ingredients mixed together.

སྦྱར་སྡོང་ཁང་གཅིག (jardoŋ gāŋjii) a person who keeps to himself.

སྦྱར་པ་ (jarba) poplar tree, aspen tree.

སྦྱར་པང་ (jarbaŋ) two wooden boards used by cobblers when sewing the heel of shoes/ boots.

སྦྱར་འཕུར་ (jarbur) touching and stroking;va.—བྱེད་.

སྦྱར་བྱང་ (jarjaŋ) name of the author or publisher that is cited at the end of a book, the colophon.

སྦྱར་བྱུང་གི་དྲི་ (jarjuŋgi dri) sm. སྦྱར་དྲི་.

སྦྱར་བྱེད་དྲི་མ་ (jarjeè drimə) perfume.

སྦྱར་མ་ (jarma) joined, connected, stuck together.

སྦྱར་སྨན་ (jarmɛn) adhesive tape (used as medicine in Tibet on the face or temple to relieve pain).

སྦྱར་རྫི་ (jərdzi) glue, adhesive.

སྦྱར་རྫི་ཚི་སྣ་ (jərdzi tsīnə) adhesive substance, fibers with adhesive quality.

སྦྱར་ཚིག (jərdzii) sm. སྦྱར་ཡིག.

སྦྱར་ཟས་ (jarsɛɛ̀) foods that consist of different ingredients.

སྦྱར་ཡིག (jəryii) a poster (that is stuck up on a wall) ¶ ངོ་རྒོལ་གྱི་སྦྱར་ཡིག A protest poster.

སྦྱར་རིས་ (jərrii) a poster.

སྦྱར་གསར་ (jarsön) a new poplar tree.

སྦྱར་སོན་ (jarsön) poplar seed.

སྦྱིག (joii) 1. vi. to slip. 2. heat season for female animals. 3. arc. va. to press clothes.

སྦྱིག་མོ་ (jigmu) bare, naked, unclothed.

སྦྱིན་: p. བྱིན་; f. and imp. སྦྱིན་ (jin) 1. va. to give ¶ ཁོ་ལ་གོས་གསར་བྱིན་པ་རེད་ (They) gave him new clothes. 2. abbr. of སྦྱིན་བདག.

སྦྱིན་ (jin) alms, charity; va.—གཏོང་.

སྦྱིན་གྲོགས་ (jindrɔɔ̀) sm. སྦྱིན་བདག.

སྦྱིན་མགྲོན་ (jindrön) host and guest.

སྦྱིན་བདག (jindaà) 1. patron, donor, sponsor, dispenser of gifts ¶ སློབ་གྲྭའི་སྦྱིན་བདག་རྣམས་ The patrons of the school. 2. master, boss, employer ¶ སྦྱིན་བདག་དང་གཡོག་པོ་ Master and servants.

སྦྱིན་བདག་མ་ (jindaàma) a female སྦྱིན་བདག.

སྦྱིན་གནས་ (jinnɛɛ̀) an object worthy of being worshipped or given a gift.

སྦྱིན་པ་ (jimbə) charity, alms; va.—གཏོང་ to give charity/ alms ¶ ཁོང་གིས་དབུལ་ཕོངས་ལ་སྦྱིན་པ་བཏང་བ་རེད་ He gave charity to the poor.

སྦྱིན་པའི་དངོས་པོ་ (jimbɛ ŋööbo) things that are given as charity/ alms.

སྦྱིན་པའི་ཞིང་ (jimbɛ shiŋ) the object of charity/ alms (e.g., the dharma, the clergy, beggars).

སྦྱིན་གཡོག (jinyɔɔ̀) 1. the servant of a boss/ master/ employer. 2. master/ boss/ employer and servant.

སྦྱིན་རླབས་ཅན་ (jinləbjɛn) generous, charitable.

སྦྱིན་ལེན་ (jinlen) giving and taking.

སྦྱིན་སྲེག (jinseg) fire exorcism rite; va.—སྲེག; —སྲུག to perform a fire exorcism rite.

སྦྱིན་སྲེག་ཆོ་ག (jinseg cōga) ritual of fire exorcism.

སྦྱིན་སྲེག་རྫས་ཆ་ (jinseg dzɛɛ̀ja) material used in the སྦྱིན་སྲེག rite.

སྦྱིལ་མོ་ (jiimu) a tool used for smoothing plaster on walls.

སྦྱོང་: p. སྦྱངས་; f. སྦྱང་; imp. སྦྱོངས་ (joŋ) 1. va. to practice, to study, to undergo training ¶ མོས་ཞབས་བྲོ་སྦྱངས་པ་རེད་ She practiced dancing. 2. va. to clean, to wash off ¶ ཁོང་གིས་ལྷ་ཁང་ལ་སྐོར་བ་བརྒྱབ་ནས་སྡིག་པ་སྦྱངས་པ་རེད་ He cleansed his sins by circumambulating the temple. 3. va. to supply/ furnish/ give ¶ ཕྲུ་གུས་ཕ་མའི་ལྟོ་གོས་སྦྱོང་གི་ཡོད་པ་རེད་ The child is furnishing the livelihood for his parents.

སྦྱོང་སྒྲིག (joŋdrig) training and organizing/ arranging; va.—བྱེད་.

སྦྱོང་ཐར་ (joŋdar) sm. སྦྱོང་བརྡར་.

སྦྱོང་དེབ་ (joŋdeb) exercise book.

སྦྱོང་བརྡར་ (joŋdar) training, practicing; va.—བྱེད་ to train, to practice; va.—སྤྲོད་ to give training ¶ ཁ་སང་གི་སློབ་ཚན་རྣམས་དེ་རིང་སྦྱོང་བརྡར་བྱས་པ་རེད་ (They) practiced yesterday's lesson today. ¶ ཁོ་ཚོར་ཀང་རྩེད་པོ་ལོའི་སྦྱོང་བརྡར་སྤྲད་པ་རེད་ (They) gave them soccer training.

སྦྱོང་བརྡར་འཛིན་གྲྭ་ (joŋdar dzindrə) training class.

སྦྱོང་པོ་ (jaŋbo) fatigued, tired, weary.

སྦྱོང་སྤྱོད་སྤེལ་གསུམ་ (joŋ jöö bēl sūm) the three: studying, using, spreading/ disseminating.

སྦྱོང་སྨན་ (joŋmɛn) laxative.

སྦྱོང་སྨན་སྣུམ་རིགས་ (joŋmɛn nūmrii) laxatives.

སྦྱོང་རྩོམ་ (joŋdzom) practice writing/ composing and essay, a composition (in school).

སྦྱོང་ཚན་ (joŋdzɛn) homework; va.—བཟོ་ to make up exercises/ homework (by a teacher).

སྦྱོང་གཞི་ (joŋshi) an assignment for studying.

སྦྱོང་རིམས་ (joŋrim) an epidemic that causes diarrhea.

སྦྱོངས་ (joŋ) imp. of སྦྱོང་.

སྦྱོར་: p. and f. སྦྱར་, imp. སྦྱོར་ (jor) 1. va. to attach, to stick on, to affix, to paste on, to put/stick up ¶ ཡིག་ཤོགས་ཐོག་ཀྱི་སི་སྦྱར་པ་ཡིན་ (I) stuck the stamp on the envelope. 2. va. to compound, to mix ¶ རྫས་རིགས་དེ་སྦྱར་སྟངས་མང་པོ་ཡོད་པ་རེད་ There are many ways to mix that chemical. 3. va. to compose ¶ ཚིག་བཅད་འདི་དག་བཀྲ་ཤིས་ཀྱིས་སྦྱར་པ་རེད་ Tashi composed these verses. 4. va. to put into practice, to use.

སྦྱོར་ཀློག (jɔrlɔɔ̀) saying a word by spelling out its letters; va.—རྒྱག.

སྦྱོར་ཁ་ (jɔrga) sm. སྦྱར་ཁ་.

སྦྱོར་སྒྲོལ་ (jɔɔdröö) sexual intercourse.

སྦྱོར་དངོས་མཇུག་གསུམ་ (jɔɔŋöö jugsum) sm. སྦྱོར་དངོས་རྗེས་གསུམ་.

སྦྱོར་དངོས་རྗེས་གསུམ་ (jɔɔŋöö jeèsum) the three stages of action: preparation, doing and the outcome/ result ¶ འཛུགས་སྐྲུན་གྱིས་ལས་ཀ་དེ་སྦྱོར་དངོས་རྗེས་གསུམ་ཚང་མ་ཡག་པོ་བྱུང་སོང་ The construction was good in all three: preparing, doing, and result.

སྦྱོར་འཇགས་ (jɔnjaà) 1. gifts in kind or money made by monastic officials to the monastery at the end of their term of office (commonly for a trust fund/ endowment); va.—བྱེད་; —འཇོག. 2. putting down by force; va.—རྒྱག.

སྦྱོར་སྡེ་ (jɔɔde) a mixed, compound ¶ སྦྱོར་སྡེ་བྱེད་པའི་སྨན་ A medicine that has been mixed.

སྦྱོར་སྡེབ་ (jɔɔdeb) 1. sexual intercourse; va.—བྱེད་. 2. artificial inseminating ¶ སྦྱོར་སྡེབ་ཀྱི་དུས་ཚིགས་ Insemination station.

སྦྱོར་སྤྱོད་ (jɔɔdröö) sm. སྦྱོར་སྡེབ་.

སྦྱོར་བ་ (jɔɔwa) conduct, behavior.

སྦྱོར་བ་བརྒྱ་པ་ (jɔɔwa gyaba) name of a medical

treatise written by Nagarjuna.
སྦྱོར་བྱེད་ (jɔɔjeè) 1. woman. 2. prostitute.
སྦྱོར་འབུལ་ (jɔɔbüü) sth. donated by a patron.
སྦྱོར་ཚིག (jɔɔdzii) preposition.
སྦྱོར་ཚུལ་ (jɔɔdzüü) manner of joining or putting things together.
སྦྱོར་རྫས་ (jɔɔdzɛɛ̀) adhesive materials, glue.
སྦྱོར་ཞུགས་ (jɔɔshuù) candidate for sth. (e.g., for party membership).
སྦྱོར་ཞུགས་དུས་ཚོད་ (jɔɔshuù tüüdzöö) the period of candidacy.
སྦྱོར་ལུད་ (jɔɔlüü) fertilizer.
སྦྱོར་བསྲེས་ (jɔɔseè) mixed/ blended together.
སྦྲ་ (dra) 1. thick material woven from yak hair. 2. sm. སྦྲ་གུར་.
སྦྲ་ཁག (dragaà) nomadic tribes/ groups.
སྦྲ་ཁྱིམ་ (drəgyim) sm. སྦྲ་གུར་.
སྦྲ་གུར་ (drəgur) black yak hair tent.
སྦྲ་གུར་སློབ་ཆུང་ (drəgur lōbjuŋ) primary school held in a tent (used in nomad areas).
སྦྲ་ཐག (dradaà) tent rope, tent guy line.
སྦྲ་དུད་ (drədüü) nomadic household.
སྦྲ་དུད་སོལ་ཁྲལ་ (drədüü sōōdrɛɛ) shung. a type of charcoal tax on nomad households.
སྦྲ་ནག (dranaà) black yak hair tent.
སྦྲ་ནག་ཞོལ་ (banagshöö) the Banagshol area in Lhasa.
སྦྲ་ནག་ཤོག་པ་ (dranaà shōgba) nomadic tribe/ group.
སྦྲ་སྣམ་ (dranam) shung. a fabric/ material woven from yak hair.
སྦྲ་པ་ (draba) people who live in tents, nomads.
སྦྲ་ཞོལ་ (bashöö) abbr. of སྦྲ་ནག་ཞོལ་.
སྦྲ་འཛིན་རི་ཕྱུག (drəndzin rijuù) nomads and their animals.
སྦྲ་འཛུགས་ (drandzuù) shung. establishing a herd of cattle; va.—བྱེད་.
སྦྲ་ར་ (drara) a low fence surrounding a nomad tent.
སྦྲ་རེ་ (drare) material for making a nomad tent.
སྦྲ་ཤིང་ (drəshiŋ) tent pole.
སྦྲ་ས་ (drasa) a place for putting up a tent, camp/ tent site.
སྦྲ་སོལ་ལས་ཁུངས་ (drasöö lɛ̀ɛguŋ) shung. an office in charge of the charcoal tax.
སྦྲག: p. སྦྲགས་; f. སྦྲག་; imp. སྦྲོགས་ (draà) 1. together with, along with ¶ ཕྲུ་གུ་དེ་གཉིས་མཉམ་དུ་སྦྲགས་ནས་བཏང་བ་རེད་ (They) sent the two children together. ¶ གནང་སྐྱེས་དང་སྦྲགས་ཕྱག་བྲིས་ཤིག་གནང་འདུག (He) has sent a letter along with the present. 2. hind. post, mail ¶ ཁོས་ཡི་གེ་སྦྲག་ལ་བཏང་བ་རེད་ He sent the letter by mail.
སྦྲག་སྒྲོག (draàgɔɔ) hind.tib. an envelope, postcard.
སྦྲག་ཁང་ (draàgaŋ) hind.tib. post office, postal relay station.
སྦྲག་ཁྲིད་སློབ་གྲྭ (draàdrii lōbdra) hind.tib. correspondence school.
སྦྲག་འཁོར་ (draàgɔɔ) hind.tib. postal car/ vehicle.
སྦྲག་གླ་ (draàla) hind.tib. postage fee.
སྦྲག་གློག་པུའུ་ (dragloɔ̀ bū) hind.tib.ch. ministry of post and telecommunications.
སྦྲག་གློག་ཡན་ལག་ཀྲུའུ་ (dragloɔ̀ yɛnlaà jū) hind.tib.ch. branch post and telecommunications office.
སྦྲག་གློག་སློབ་གྲྭ (dragloɔ̀ lōbdra) hind.tib. school of post and telecommunications.
སྦྲག་དར་ (dragdar) hind.tib. post and telegraph. ¶ སྦྲག་དར་ཁང་ Post and telegraph office.
སྦྲག་རྟགས་ (dragdaà) hind.tib. postage stamp.
སྦྲག་ཐེལ་ (dragdee) hind.tib. post mark, stamp cancellation.
སྦྲག་ཐོག (dragdɔɔ̀) hind.tib. by or via post/ mail; va.—སྐུར་; —གཏོང་ to send by post/ mail.
སྦྲག་ཐོག་བསྐུར་བྱ་ (dragdɔɔ̀ gūrja) hind.tib. things to be mailed.
སྦྲག་དམ་ (dragdam) hind.tib. sm. སྦྲག་ཐེལ་.
སྦྲག་དམ་ཀྲི་ཀ་སི་ (dragdam drīgisi) hind.tib. postage stamp.
སྦྲག་དོན་ (dragdön) hind.tib. postal affairs.
སྦྲག་པ་ (dragba) hind.tib. postman, postrunner, mailman.
སྦྲག་ཕིག་ལྷས་མལ་ (draàpig lhɛ̃ɛ̀mɛɛ) shung. yak hair tent and corral.
སྦྲག་བང་ (dragbaŋ) sm. སྦྲག་པ་.
སྦྲག་འབོག (draŋbɔɔ̀ hind.tib. a parcel sent by mail/ parcel post.
སྦྲག་བྱང་ (dragjaŋ) hind.tib. stamp.
སྦྲག་མ་ (dragma) pair of sth. together (e.g., cup and saucer, rider and horse) ¶ མི་རྟ་སྦྲག་མ་ ༡༠༠ སླེབས་སོང་ One hundred men and horses arrived together.
སྦྲག་འཛིན་ (drəgdzin) hind.tib. postage stamp.
སྦྲག་ལས་ཀྲུའུ་ (draglɛɛ̀jū) tib.ch. post office.
སྦྲག་ཤོག (dragshoò) hind.tib. postage stamp.
སྦྲག་ས་ (drəgsa) shung. postal station.
སྦྲག་སྲིད་ (drəgsii) hind.tib. postal administration.
སྦྲག་སྲིད་ཀྲུའུ་ (drəgsii jüü) hind.tib.ch. post office.
སྦྲག་སྲིད་སྦྲག་རྟགས་ (drəgsii dragdaà) hind.tib. postal system.
སྦྲག་ཨང་ (dragaŋ) hind.tib. postal code, zip code.
སྦྲགས་ (draà) 1. p. of སྦྲག. 2. sm. སྦྲག.
སྦྲགས་གཅིག (dragjii) together (with) ¶ ཁོང་གིས་ཡི་གེ་དང་ཅ་ལག་སྦྲགས་གཅིག་བཏང་བ་རེད་ He sent a letter together with the goods.
སྦྲགས་མཆན་ (dragjɛn) comments ¶ རྩོམ་པ་པོའི་སྦྲགས་མཆན་ The author's comments.
སྦྲགས་དར་ (dragdar) sm. སྦྲག་དར་.
སྦྲགས་དམ་ (dragdam) sm. སྦྲག་དམ་.
སྦྲགས་པ་ (dragba) sm. སྦྲག་པ་.
སྦྲགས་མ་ (dragma) sm. སྦྲག་མ་.
སྦྲགས་འཛིན་ (drəndzin) sm. སྦྲག་འཛིན་.
སྦྲགས་ཡིག (drəgyii) sm. སྦྲག་ཡིག.
སྦྲགས་ཤོག (dragshoò) sm. སྦྲག་ཤོག.
སྦྲགས་སྲིད་ཀྲུའུ་ (drəgsii jüü) sm. སྦྲག་སྲིད་ཀྲུའུ་.
སྦྲང་ (draŋ) 1. abbr. of སྦྲང་བུ་. 2. sm. སྦྲང་རྩི་.
སྦྲང་དཀར་ (draŋgar) white honey.
སྦྲང་སྐད་ (draŋgɛɛ̀) humming, buzzing (usu. of flies, bees, etc.).
སྦྲང་སྐྱབས་ (draŋgyəb) protective devices used against flies or insects, mosquito net.
སྦྲང་སྐྱོབ་ (draŋgyob) sm. སྦྲང་སྐྱབས་.
སྦྲང་རྒོད་ (draŋgöö) 1. raw honey. 2. mosquito.
སྦྲང་ཕྱག (dranjaà) fly swatter.
སྦྲང་ཆང་ (dranjaŋ) ཆང་ made from honey.
སྦྲང་ཆར་ (dranjar) 1. a beneficial/ timely rain (usu. for crops). 2. a light drizzle.
སྦྲང་ཆར་སིལ་མ་ (dranjar siīmə) sm. སྦྲང་ཆར་.
སྦྲང་སྙིགས་ (drəŋñig) beeswax.
སྦྲང་ནག (dragnaà) a fly.
སྦྲང་ནོར་བུ་ (draŋ nɔɔbu) bee.
སྦྲང་ཕྲུག (drəŋdruù) baby fly.
སྦྲང་བུ་ (drəŋbu) 1. fly; vi.—འཁོར་ to have flies swarm. 2. bee.
སྦྲང་བུ་མཆུ་རིང་ (drəŋbu cūriŋ) a type of mosquito.
སྦྲང་བུའི་སྐྱུགས་པ་ (drəŋbü gyūgba) poet. honey.
སྦྲང་མ་ (draŋma) sm. སྦྲང་བུ་.
སྦྲང་མ་རྒྱལ་མོ་ (draŋma gyɛɛmo) queen bee.
སྦྲང་མོ་ཆེ་ (draŋmoje) bumblebee.
སྦྲང་རྩི་ (drəŋdzi) honey; va.—གསོག to accumulate honey.
སྦྲང་རྩིའི་བློ་གྲོས་ (drəŋdzii lōdröö) Mohammed—the founder of Islam.
སྦྲང་རྩིའི་ཚིགས་མ་ (drəŋdzii tsiŋmə) residue of purified honey.
སྦྲང་ཚང་ (drandzaŋ) beehive.
སྦྲང་ཚང་གི་བུ་ག (drandzaŋgi buga) honeycomb.
སྦྲང་ཡབ་ (draŋyəb) sm. སྦྲང་གཡབ་.
སྦྲང་གཡབ་ (draŋyəb) fly swatter, a fan to shoo away flies.
སྦྲང་རོ་ (draŋro) 1. the taste of honey. 2. corpse of a bee/ fly/ mosquito.
སྦྲང་གཤོག (dranshoò) bee or fly wings.
སྦྲང་གསོ་ར་བ་ (dranso rawa) apiary.

སྦྲང་གསོད་ལས་འགུལ་ (draŋsöö lɛŋgüü) fly eradication campaign.

སྦྲང་ལྷག (draŋlhaà) sm. སྦྲང་ལྷད་.

སྦྲང་ལྷད་ (draŋlhɛɛ̀) sm. སྦྲང་སྙིགས་.

སྦྲན་ (drɛn) p. of སྦྲོན་.

སྦྲམ་ (dram) 1. largeness, bulk. 2. poisonous snakes.

སྦྲམ་ཆེན་ (dramdzen) sm. སྦྲམ་.

སྦྲམ་པོ་ (drambo) 1. a steady/ reliable/ dependable person. 2. large size.

སྦྲམ་བུ་ (drɔmbu) a small flat ingot (gold or silver).

སྦྲིད་ (drii) 1. vi. to sneeze. 2. vi. to become/ get numb ¶ ལི་དབར་ཁ་ཤས་སོང་རྗེས་རྐང་པ་ན་ཞིང་སྐེད་པ་སྦྲིད་ After going for several miles (his) foot hurt and his waist got numb. 3. vi. to be/ get numb in a political sense ¶ རྨོངས་དད་ཀྱིས་མི་རྣམས་བསམ་བློ་སྦྲིད་དུ་བཅུག་པ་རེད་ Superstition made people's thinking numb. 3. སྦྲིད་པ་.

སྦྲིད་གདམ་ (driidam) deceiving talk, talk that numbs one's ability to think/ reason; va.—ཤོད་.

སྦྲིད་པ་ (driba) sneeze, sneezing; vi.—རྒྱག to sneeze.

སྦྲིད་པར་བྱེད་ (driibar cɛɛ̀) va. to anesthetize, to numb.

སྦྲིད་སྨན་ (driimɛn) anesthetic medicine, va.—རྒྱག.

སྦྲིད་སྨན་སྡེ་ཚན་ (driimɛn dedzɛn) anesthesiology department.

སྦྲིད་བཟི་ (driisi) numb, anesthetized; va.—བྱེད་.

སྦྲིད་ཤུར་ཤུར་ (drii shūūshuu) feeling numb.

སྦྲུ་: p. སྦྲུས་; f. སྦྲུ་; imp. སྦྲུས་ (dru) va. to make/ knead dough.

སྦྲུམ་ (drum) 1. vi. to get pregnant ¶ མོ་ཆང་ས་བརྒྱབ་འཕྲལ་ལུས་པོ་སྦྲུམ་པ་རེད་ As soon as she got married she became pregnant. 2. fetus, fetal.

སྦྲུམ་སྐྱ་ (drumgya) fetal membrane.

སྦྲུམ་གྱི་གནས་སྟངས་ (drumgi nɛɛ̀daŋ) position of a fetus.

སྦྲུམ་འགུལ་ (drumgüü) movement of the fetus.

སྦྲུམ་འགོག་སྐྱེའུ་ (drumgɔɔ̀ gyēwu) condom.

སྦྲུམ་འགོག་སྦྲེའུ་ (drumgɔɔ̀ drewu) sm. སྦྲུམ་འགོག་སྐྱེའུ་.

སྦྲུམ་འགོག་སྨན་ (drumgɔɔ̀ mɛ̄n) birth control medicine.

སྦྲུམ་ལྡན་མ་ (drumdɛnma) pregnant woman.

སྦྲུམ་ཕྱུགས་ (drumjuù) pregnant livestock.

སྦྲུམ་མ་ (drumma) pregnant woman.

སྦྲུམ་མ་སྐྱུག་ལོག (drumma gyūglɔɔ̀) morning sickness during pregnancy.

སྦྲུམ་མ་སྨན་ཁང་ (drumma mēngaŋ) maternity hospital.

སྦྲུམ་ཡོལ་སྨན་ (drumyöö mɛ̄n) sm. སྦྲུམ་འགོག་སྨན་.

སྦྲུམ་སྲིང་ (drumsiŋ) embryo.

སྦྲུམ་སྲིང་རིག་པ་ (drumsiŋ rigbə) embryology.

སྦྲུལ་ (drüü) snake.

སྦྲུལ་སྐོགས་ (drüügɔɔ̀) snake skin.

སྦྲུལ་མཁྲིས་ (drüüdrii) snake gallbladder.

སྦྲུལ་གྱི་མགོ་བོ་བྲལ་ན་བགྲོད་ཐབས་མེད་ (drüügi gowo drɛɛna dröödəb meè) people can not go ahead without a leader [Lit. snake can not go if its head is cut off].

སྦྲུལ་གྱི་སྙིང་པོ་ (drüügi ñiŋbu) a type of sandalwood.

སྦྲུལ་གྱི་གདེངས་ཀ་ (drüügi deŋga) snake head ornaments worn by deities.

སྦྲུལ་གྱི་པགས་པ་ (drüügi bāgba) snake skin.

སྦྲུལ་གྱི་སྒྲོག་མ་ (drüügi drɔ̄gma) baskets in which snakes are kept by snake charmers.

སྦྲུལ་མགོ་ (drüngo) 1. snakehead. 2. a Tibetan surgical knife shaped like a snake head that is said to be used for extracting tumors from the bladder.

སྦྲུལ་མགོ་ལོག (drüü golɔɔ̀) two-headed snake.

སྦྲུལ་ལྕེ་ (drüüje) the forked tongue of a snake.

སྦྲུལ་ཆེན་ (drüüjen) boa; python.

སྦྲུལ་ཉ་ (drüüña) eel, loach.

སྦྲུལ་དུག (drüüduù) snake poison.

སྦྲུལ་གདུག་པ་ (drüü dugbə) 1. poisonous snake. 2. a term used to describe a bad, evil person.

སྦྲུལ་གདུབ་ (drüüdub) snake bangle/ bracelet worn by deities.

སྦྲུལ་གདོང་གཉིས་མ་ (drüüdoŋ ñiimə) sm. སྦྲུལ་མགོ་ལོག.

སྦྲུལ་མདུད་ (drüüdüü) coiled snake.

སྦྲུལ་མདུད་སྦྲུལ་བཤིག (drüüdüü drüüshii) one must undo problems caused by oneself [Lit. a snake has to untie its own knots (coils)].

སྦྲུལ་ལྤགས་ (drüübaà) snake skin.

སྦྲུལ་མིག (drüümii) a Tibetan surgical tool used for extracting bullets from the body.

སྦྲུལ་མེ་ (drüüme) breath of a snake.

སྦྲུལ་རྫངས་ (drüüdzaŋ) lizard.

སྦྲུལ་ཚིལ་ (drüüdzii) snake fat (used for Tibetan medicine).

སྦྲུལ་ཞགས་ (drüüshaà) the seed of Chinese dodder (used in Tibetan medicine).

སྦྲུལ་རིས་ལ་རྐང་སྣོན་ (drüüriila gāŋnön) sth. superfluous, an unnecessary addition [Lit. feet added to a snake by an artist].

སྦྲུལ་ལོ་ (drüülo) year of the snake.

སྦྲུལ་ཤ་ (drüüsha) 1. snake meat. 2. a Tibetan traditional medical ingredient.

སྦྲུལ་ཤད་ (drüūshɛɛ̀) a symbol used to head a Tibetan letter.

སྦྲུལ་ཤུན་ (drüüshün) snake skin.

སྦྲུས་ (drüü) p. of སྦྲུ་.

སྦྲུས་བརྡིས་ (drüü dzii) va. to knead.

སྦྲེ་ (dre) 1. a type of small fox. 2. urine.

སྦྲེ་དྲི་ (dredri) smell of urine.

སྦྲེང་: p. སྦྲེངས་; f. སྦྲེང་; imp. སྦྲེངས་ (dreŋ) 1. va. to line up, to stand in line, to queue. 2. va. to raise up. 3. va. to play an instrument with a bow.

སྦྲེང་ཚར་ (dreŋdzar) sm. སྦྲེངས་ཚར་.

སྦྲེང་ཟམ་ (dreŋsam) a cable bridge.

སྦྲེངས་ (dreŋ) 1. p. and imp. of སྦྲེང་ 2. line, queue.

སྦྲེངས་ཚར་ (dreŋdzar) a line, a row, a queue.

སྦྲེབ་: p. སྦྲེབས་; f. སྦྲེབ་ (dreb) 1. vi. to be hungry/ thirsty. 2. vi. to be cold.

སྦྲེབས་ (dreb) p. of སྦྲེབ་.

སྦྲེལ་ (dree) va. to join together, to link, to hold together ¶ ཁོ་ཚོ་དང་ལག་པ་སྦྲེལ་བསྐྱོད་པ་རེད་ (They) went holding hands.

སྦྲེལ་སྒྲིག་མཉམ་བྱ་ (dreedrig ñamja) simultaneous equations (in math).

སྦྲེལ་ཐག (dreedaà) rope for tying things together.

སྦྲེལ་མཐུད་ (dreedüü) joining, connecting; va.— བྱེད་.

སྦྲེལ་གདུང་ (dreeduŋ) beams that are joined together.

སྦྲེལ་མདའ་ (drenda) a connecting bar, a connecting lever.

སྦྲེལ་པོ་ (dreēbo) a pair, together, joint.

སྦྲེལ་བྱེད་གཅུས་གཟེར་ (dreējeè jüüser) bolt, nut.

སྦྲེལ་མ་ (dreema) joined/ connected together ¶ ཡིག་ཆ་ཤོག་ལྷེ་གསུམ་སྦྲེལ་མ་ཞིག་སྤྲད་འདུག They distributed a document with three pages joined together.

སྦྲེལ་ཚིག (dreedzii) conjunction.

སྦྲེལ་ཟླ་ (drenda) colleague with whom one's shares responsibility.

སྦྲེལ་གཟེར་ (dreesee) rivet; va.—རྒྱག to rivet.

སྦྲེལ་གཟེར་རྒྱག་མཁན་ (dreesee gyaàñɛn) riveter.

སྦྲེལ་གཟེར་རྒྱག་སྒྱུད་ (dreesee gyagjeè) riveting gun.

སྦྲེལ་གཟེར་རྒྱག་བྱེད་འཕྲུལ་ཆས་ (dreesee gyagjeè trǖūjɛɛ̀) riveting machine.

སྦྲེས་ (dreè) 1. frozen, stiff. 2. hungry, thirsty. 3. to combine/ collect/ make one.

སྦྲོགས་ (drɔɔ̀) imp. of སྦྲོག.

སྦྲོན་ (drön) sm. འདོན་.

མ

མ་ (ma̱) 1. mother. 2. the main one ¶ ལྷ་སའི་སློབ་གྲྭ་འདི་མ་སློབ་རེད་ The school in Lhasa is the main school (i.e., it has branches elsewhere). 3. principal ¶ བུ་ལོན་གྱི་མ་སྐྱེད་ The principal and interest of the loan. 4. (— + vb.) verbal negative particle ¶ ཁོས་མ་བྱས་པ་རེད་ He didn't do it. ¶ འདི་དེབ་མ་རེད་ This is not a book. 5. (— + vb. + པར་/ བར་) so as not to, without ¶ ལས་བྱེད་པ་བོད་ནས་གསར་གཏོང་མ་དགོས་པར་ Without needing to send an official newly from Tibet. ¶ སློབ་གྲྭར་མ་ཕྱིན་པར་ཡི་གེ་ཤེས་ཀྱི་མ་རེད་ Without going to school you will not be literate. 6. (— + vb.+ ཀ་/ བཀའ་མེད་ or — + vb. + མཐུ་མེད་ or — + vb. + རང་ + vb. or — + vb. + ཐབས་མེད་ or — + vb. + ཚད་བྲལ་) no choice but to do the verbal act ¶ མི་གཞན་པ་འགྲོ་མཁན་མེད་སྟབས་ང་མ་འགྲོ་ཀ་མེད་བྱུང་ Because no one else was going I had no choice but to go. 7. (— + vb. + བར་/ པར་) until the verbal action ¶ བོད་ལ་མ་ལོག་བར་དུ་འདིར་སྡོད་ཀྱི་ཡིན་ I am going to stay here until I return to Tibet. 8. feminine particle. 9. (vb. + — + vb.) whether one does or does not ¶ ཁོས་ལས་ཀ་བྱས་མ་བྱས་ང་ལ་ཁྱད་པར་མི་འདུག It makes no difference to me whether to work or not. 10. (vb. + མ་ + ཅིག/ ཞིག་ལ་) just when one is about to do sth. ¶ ང་ཚོ་ཁ་ལག་བཟས་མ་ཅིག་ལ་ཁོ་སླེབས་བྱུང་ Just as when we were about to eat, he came. 11. (— + vb. + གོང་ལ་) before ¶ ང་རྒྱ་གར་ལ་མ་ཕྱིན་གོང་ལ་བོད་ལ་ཕྱིན་པ་ཡིན་ Before I went to India I went to Tibet. 12. (— + vb. དགུ་ + vb.) doing (many) things you are not supposed to do ¶ མ་བྱེད་དགུ་བྱེད་བྱས་ན་ལས་ཀ་ཤོར་གྱི་རེད་ If you do all sorts of things you aren't supposed to do you will lose your job.

མ་ཀི་ (g) sm. མ་གི་.

མ་ཀི་ལིས་པོ་ (ma̱gilibu) Morocco.

མ་ཀྭ་ཙེ་ (ma̱gadze) ch. jacket, coat (usu. made of Chinese brocade).

མ་ཀླས་པ་ (ma̱ lɛ̈ɛ̀ba) arc. sm. མ་གུས་པ་.

མ་རྐང་ (ma̱gaŋ) 1. stock, share; va.—འཛོག; —ཉོ་ to buy shares/ stocks, to become a shareholder/ stockholder ¶ མཉམ་ འབྲེལ་ཚོགས་པའི་མ་ རྐང་ཉོས་པ་ཡིན་ (I) bought shares in the Co-operative Society. 2. root, base, cause.

མ་རྐང་ཀུང་སི་ (ma̱gaŋ gūŋsi) tib.ch. joint stock company/ corporation.

མ་རྐང་གི་སྐྱེད་ཀ་ (ma̱gaŋgi gyēèga) stock dividend.

མ་རྐང་གི་ཐེབས་རྩ་ (ma̱gaŋgi tēbdza) stock fund/ trust.

མ་རྐང་འཛོག (ma̱gaŋ jɔ̱ɔ̀) see མ་རྐང་.

མ་རྐང་འཛོག་མཁན་ (ma̱gaŋ jɔ̱ɔ̀ñɛn) shareholder, stockholder.

མ་རྐང་མཉམ་བསྡུས་ (ma̱gaŋ ña̱mdüù) partnership, joint ownership; va.—བྱེད་.

མ་རྐང་ཚད་ཡོད་ (ma̱gaŋ tsɛ̄ɛ̀yöò) limited liability ¶ མ་རྐང་ཚད་ཡོད་ཁེ་ལས་ Limited liability enterprise.

མ་རྐང་ཚོད་འཛིན་ (ma̱gaŋ tsȫndzin) controlling/ regulating capital.

མ་རྐང་བཞག (ma̱gaŋ sha̱à) p. of མ་རྐང་འཛོག.

མ་རྐང་ལམ་ལུགས་ (ma̱gaŋ lə̱mluù) system of shares ownership, system of stocks.

མ་རྐང་སློག་དངུལ་ (ma̱gaŋ lɔ̄ɔ̀ŋüü) commune fund used to pay back members who put more into the commune initially than the value of the average share.

མ་རྐན་ (ma̱gɛn) lower jaw.

མ་སྐད་ (ma̱gɛɛ̀) mother tongue/ language.

མ་སྐྱེད་ (ma̱gyeè) principal and interest, capital and interest.

མ་སྐྱེད་གཉིས་བསྡོམས་ (ma̱gyeè ñīìdom) principal and interest together.

མ་སྐྱེད་རྩིས་ཁྲ་ (ma̱gyeè dzīdrə) shung. accounting of principal and interest.

མ་བསྐུལ་ (mə̱güü) without coercion/ compulsion.

མ་བསྐུལ་དང་བླངས་ (mə̱güü ta̱ŋlaŋ) sm. བསྐུལ་དང་ལེན་.

མ་བསྐུལ་དང་ལེན་ (mə̱güü ta̱ŋlen) doing voluntarily, doing on one's own initiative, doing without compulsion/ coercion; va.—བྱེད་ ¶ ཆུ་ལོག་འགོག་པར་ཡུལ་མི་ཚང་མས་མ་བསྐུལ་དང་བླངས་བྱས་པ་རེད་ All the local people volunteered without coercion to fight the flood.

མ་བསྐུལ་རང་མོས་ (mə̱güü ra̱ŋmöò) sm. མ་བསྐུལ་དང་ལེན་.

མ་ཁ་ (ma̱ga) 1. chin. 2. capital.

མ་ཁང་ (ma̱gaŋ) main house.

མ་ཁེ་སྒོར་ (ma̱ke gɔ̱r) mark (the German currency unit).

མ་ཁོངས་ (ma̱goŋ) maternal side, matrilateral.

མ་ཁོམ་ (ma̱kom) without leisure and relaxation, no time to do things.

མ་མཁལ་ (ma̱gɛɛ) chin.

མ་མཁྱེན་མཁྱེན་མདོག (ma̱gyen kyēndɔɔ̀) h. of མ་ཤེས་ཤེས་མདོག.

མ་མཁྱེན་དགུ་མཁྱེན་ (ma̱kyen gu̱kyen) h. of མ་ཤེས་དགུ་ཤེས་.

མ་འཁྲུལ་བ་ (mə̱trüüwə) having no illusion ¶ མ་འཁྲུལ་བའི་ཤེས་པ་ Unmistaken knowledge.

མ་གི་ (mə̱gi) (that) down there ¶ དེབ་མ་གི་ངའི་རེད་ That book down there is mine.

མ་གིར་ (mə̱gii) down there ¶ མ་གིར་ངའི་དེབ་ཡོད་པ་རེད་ My book is down there.

མ་གུས་པ་ (ma̱ gü̱ùbə) disrespectful ¶ རང་ཉིད་ཀྱི་ཕ་མར་མ་གུས་པའི་རྣམ་འགྱུར་སྟོན་རྒྱུ་མེད་ One shouldn't act disrespectful to one's parents.

མ་གོ་མ་ཐོས་མེད་པ་ (ma̱go ma̱töò me̱èba) common knowledge, known to all ¶ སྲིད་ཇུས་རྣམས་མང་ཚོགས་ལ་མ་གོ་མ་ཐོས་མེད་པ་ཁྱབ་བསྒྲགས་བྱས་པ་རེད་ The policies were publicized to the masses so that they would be known to all.

མ་གོང་ (ma̱goŋ) cost price, original or base cost.

མ་གྲོས་གཅིག་མཐུན་ (ma̱dröò jīgdün) sm. མ་གྲོས་རང་མཐུན་.

མ་གྲོས་མོས་མཐུན་ (ma̱dröò mö̱òdün) sm. མ་གྲོས་རང་མཐུན་.

མ་གྲོས་རང་མཐུན་ (ma̱dröò ra̱ŋdün) an agreement/ consensus without discussion, a spontaneous agreement ¶ མ་གྲོས་རང་མཐུན་གྱིས་ཁོའི་བྱ་སྤྱོད་ལ་སྐྱོན་བརྗོད་བྱས་པ་རེད་ (They) criticized his behavior spontaneously.

མ་གྲོས་བསམ་པ་གཅིག་མཐུན་ (ma̱dröò sāmba jīgdün) sm. མ་གྲོས་རང་མཐུན་.

མ་གྲོས་སེམས་མཐུན་ (ma̱dröò sēmdün) sm. མ་གྲོས་རང་མཐུན་.

མ་དགའ་ཞེ་འཛིན་ (ma̱ga she̱ndzin) harboring hatred/ ill thoughts/ grudges/ resentment; va.—བྱེད་ ¶ ལ་རྒྱ་གཅིག་གྱུར་བུ་རྒྱུ་ལྟ་བཞག་ཁོ་པ་མགོ་མཐོ་བ་འགའ་ཞིག་ནས་མ་དགའ་ཞེ་འཛིན་རང་འདོད་སྦུགས་སུ་བཅུག་པ་ Leave alone having similar loyalty, some powerful people harbored hatred in the minds.

མ་དགའ་ལྷ་གསོལ་ (ma̱ga lhāsöö) treating sb. extremely well (like a god) even though you do not like them.

མ་དགོན་ (ma̱gön) the main monastery, a monastic seat (with subordinate monasteries).

མ་བགྲོས་རང་མཐུན་ (ma̱dröò ra̱ŋdün) sm. མ་གྲོས་རང་མཐུན་.

མ་མགལ་ (ma̱gɛɛ) sm. མ་མཁལ་.

མ་མགུ་མ་རག (ma̱gu ma̱raà) not getting the good/ high one and not wanting the bad/ ordinary, being unable to achieve one's heart's desire but unwilling to accept less; va.—བྱེད་ ¶ བུ་མོ་དེ་ཁྲོ་ག་མ་མགུ་མ་རག་བྱས་ནས་ལོ་མང་སོང་སྐྱིད་མོ་རྫིང་བྱས་ནས་

བསྡད་ཡོད་པ་རེད་ For many years that girl didn't get the good man she wanted and didn't accept the ordinary ones, and (now) she lives alone as a spinister.

མ་འགྲོ་རང་འགྲོ་ (mandro randro) no choice but to go.

མ་མགལ་རུས་པ་ (magεε rüübə) chinbone, lower jawbone, mandible.

མ་འགབ་ཞི་འཛིན་ (magəb shendzin) shung. sm. མ་དགའ་ཞི་འཛིན་.

མ་འགྲིགས་ (məndrii) not okay.

མ་འགྲིགས་མ་འདུས་ (məndrii məduü) sm. མ་འགྲིགས་.

མ་རྒད་ (magεè) emerald.

མ་རྒན་ (magεn) 1. old woman/ mother. 2. the best jumper in the dobdo monk's competition.

མ་རྒན་མ་ (magεnma) the term used for best jumper in the དབ་དོབ་ athletic competition.

མ་རྒོལ་རང་ཐོར་ (magöö randɔɔ) self-destruction.

མ་རྒྱན་ (magyεn) stake in gambling, capital for gambling.

མ་རྒྱུ་ (məgyu) element (in physics).

མ་རྒྱུ་ལྗིད་རིགས་ (məgyu jirii) heavy element (in physics).

མ་རྒྱུད་ (məgyüü) 1. maternal relatives, maternal descent line. 2. mother's characteristics.

མ་རྒྱུད་འཁྱེར་ (məgyüü kyēr) sm. མ་རྒྱུད་འཁྲིད་.

མ་རྒྱུད་འཁྲིད་ (məgyüü trii) vi. to inherit one's mother's characteristics.

མ་རྒྱུད་སྤྱི་ཚོགས་ (məgyüü jidzɔɔ) matriarchal/ matrilineal society.

མ་རྒྱུད་རུས་རྒྱུད་ (məgyüü rüügyüü) matrilineal descent group, matrilineage.

མ་རྒྱུན་ (məgyün) the main stream. ¶ ཨ་རིའི་ཕྱི་འབྲེལ་སྲིད་ཇུས་ཀྱི་མ་རྒྱུན་ནི་ The main stream of American foreign policy.

མ་རྒྱུའི་དུས་འཁོར་རེའུ་མིག (məgyü tüügɔɔ rewumig) periodic table of elements.

མ་རྒྱུའི་མཚོན་རྟགས་ (məgyü tsöndaà) sign/ symbol of an element in the periodic table of elements.

མ་སྒོ་ (mago) main gate, main entrance.

མ་བསྒྲིགས་རང་འགྲིག (mədrig rəndrig) happening or occurring coincidentally/ spontaneously/ at the same time ¶ ང་བོད་ལ་ཕྱིན་པ་དང་བསོད་ནམས་སླེབས་པ་དུས་ཚོད་མ་བསྒྲིགས་རང་འགྲིག་བྱུང་སོང་ My going to Tibet coincided with Sonam's arrival.

མ་སྒྲིག་ལྷུན་གྲུབ་ (mədrig lhündrub) sm. མ་བསྒྲིགས་རང་འགྲིག.

མ་ངེས་པ་ (maneèba) uncertain, not sure, indefinite ¶ ཁོ་ནམ་འབྱོར་མ་ངེས་པ་ཞིག་ཡིན་ཙང་ Because it is not certain when he is arriving.

མ་དངུལ་ (məŋüü) capital, money, principal (as in a loan); va.—འཛུག to invest money, to contribute capital.

མ་དངུལ་འཁོར་སྐྱུག (məŋüü kɔ̄ɔgyuù) capital turnover ¶ ལོ་རེའི་མ་དངུལ་འཁོར་སྐྱུག་གི་གྲངས་ཚད་ The limit of capital turnover.

མ་དངུལ་འགུག་ཐབས་ (məŋüü gugdəb) strategy for soliciting investment/ capital.

མ་དངུལ་འཛུགས་གྲངས་ (məŋüü jɔgdraŋ) amount of investment.

མ་དངུལ་གསོག་འཇོག (məŋüü sɔ̄njɔɔ) savings (money), capital accumulation.

མ་དངུལ་གསོག་འཇོག་འགན་སྲུང་ (məŋüü sɔ̄njɔɔ gεnsuŋ) savings insurance.

མ་མངོན་པ་ (maŋömba) anything not outwardly visible or evident, covert, latent ¶ མ་མངོན་པའི་ནུས་ཤུགས་ A latent force (or hidden strength).

མ་སྣུན་བུ་བཤའ་ (maŋum pusha) proofreading by sb. reading a handwritten copy while another compares it against the original; va.—བྱེད་.

མ་གཅིག་པ་ (məjigbə) different, unlike ¶ ལུང་པ་མ་གཅིག་པའི་མི་མང་པོ་འཛོམས་འདུག Many people from different areas have assembled.

མ་གཅིག་བུ་གཅིག (məjig pujig) an only son.

མ་བཅོལ་སློ་ལེན་ (majöö nelen) shung. sm. མ་བསྐུལ་རང་མོས་.

མ་བཅོས་ (majöö) natural, not artificial, unprocessed, raw, crude ¶ མ་བཅོས་རྒྱུ་ཆ་ Raw materials. ¶ མ་བཅོས་རྡོ་སྣུམ་ Crude oil. ¶ མ་བཅོས་རྡོ་སོལ་ Natural coal.

མ་བཅོས་རྣམ་འགྱུར་ (majöö nəmgyur) natural expression.

མ་བཅོས་ཤིང་ཆ་ (majöö shiŋja) unprocessed timber.

མ་བཅོས་ཤིང་ཏོག་གི་ཁུ་བ་ (majöö siŋdoògi koo) natural fruit juice.

མ་བཅོས་སྲིན་བལ་ (majöö siŋbεε) natural cotton.

མ་ཆ་ (maca) denominator (in math).

མ་ཆེན་ (majen) cook.

མ་མཆུ་ (məju) lower lip.

མ་མཆོག (majɔɔ) the lower part of a bow (weapon).

མ་འཆམས་པ་ (macamba) not getting along, disliking, disagreeing ¶ ཁོང་ཚོ་ནང་ལོག་ལ་མ་འཆམས་པས་ཁག་ཁག་བྱེད་དགོས་བྱུང་བ་རེད་ They had to separate since they didn't get along together.

མ་འཆུས་པ་ (majüübə) straight, not crooked/ twisted, honest ¶ ཐིག་འཆུས་པ་རྒྱབས་རོགས་ Please draw straight lines.

མ་འཛེམ་འཛེམ་མདོག (majem jem dɔɔ) pretending to be skillful.

མ་བརྗེད་སྙིང་བཅངས་ (majeè ñiŋjaŋ) not forgetting and holding dear or keeping in mind ¶ ཁྱེད་རང་གི་བཀྲིན་ངས་མ་བརྗེད་སྙིང་བཅངས་ཞུ་གི་ཡིན་ I will hold dear and not forget your kindness.

མ་ཉམས་པ་ (mañamba) undeteriorated, unimpaired ¶ རྒྱལ་ཁབ་ཀྱི་དཔལ་འབྱོར་མ་ཉམས་པར་གནས་ཡོད་པ་རེད་ The nation's economy stands unimpaired.

མ་ཉར་སྐྱེད་འཇལ་ (mañar gyeènjεε) keeping the principal and paying the interest.

མ་ཉལ་རྨི་ལམ་ (mañεε ñīləm) daydream.

མ་ཉི་ལ་ (manila) Manila.

མ་ཉིད་ (mañii) sm. ཐག.

མ་ཉིད་དུ་ (məñiidu) sm. ཐག་ཏུ་.

མ་ཉུང་དགུ་ཐུག (məñuŋ guduù) many experiences.

མ་ཉུང་བ་ (məñuŋwə) sufficient, enough, not short ¶ ཚང་མ་ཉུང་བ་ཞིག་བཟོས་པ་རེད་ (They) made enough ཚང་.

མ་ཉེས་ཁ་ཡོག (mañeè kāyɔɔ) sm. མ་ཉེས་ཁག་གཡོགས་.

མ་ཉེས་ཁག་གཡོགས་ (mañeè kāyɔɔ) wrongfully/ unjustly accusing or blaming; va.—བྱེད་ ¶ བཙན་འཛུལ་སྐྱོང་མཁན་ལ་མ་ཉེས་ཁག་གཡོགས་བྱས་པ་རེད་ (They) unjustly accused the one's who were invaded.

མ་ཉེས་ནག་གཡོགས་ (mañeè nagyɔɔ) sm. མ་ཉེས་ཁག་གཡོགས་.

མ་ཉེས་པ་ (mañeèba) without crimes/ offenses/ faults/ illegal acts.

མ་གཉིས་པ་ (mə ñiibə) poet. a nanny.

མ་ཏ་ (mada) ch. a generator.

མ་ཏོ་ (mado) ch. screwdriver; va.—སྐྱུག to screw in.

མ་གཏོགས་ (məndoò) 1. only, except for; unless ¶ མི་གསུམ་མ་ཏོགས་མི་འདུག There are only three people. ¶ ཁོས་མ་ཤེས་པ་མ་གཏོགས་ཤེས་ཚད་མི་ལ་སློབ་ཀྱི་རེད་ Except for his not knowing the subject, he would teach it. 2. unless (vb. + —) ¶ རང་ལ་ལག་འཁྱེར་ཡོད་ན་མ་གཏོགས་ཤེབས་ཆོག་གི་མ་རེད་ Unless you have a pass (travel document) you are not allowed to go. 3. or else (vb. + —) ¶ ཁ་ལག་གྲང་མོ་མ་ཟ་མ་གཏོགས་གྲོད་ཁོག་བཤལ་ཀྱི་རེད་ Don't eat the cold food or else you will get diarrhea.

མ་གཏོར་ན་མི་ཚུགས་ (madɔɔna midzug) there is no construction without destruction; there is no making progress without first breaking things up (political slogan).

མ་བདབ་བྲ་བོ་ (mədəb trawo) wild wormwood (used in Tibetan medicine).

མ་རྟ་ (mada) mare.

མ་རྟོགས་ལོག་འགྲེལ་ (madoò ləndrel) not knowing/ understanding so giving wrong explanations.

མ་བརྟགས་ཁྱུར་མིད་ (madaà kyūrmii) accepting sth.

at face value/ superficially, doing sth. without thoroughly investigating it first ¶ མ་བརྟགས་ཁྲུར་མེད་ཀྱིས་ཁྲིམས་བཅད་ནོར་པ་འདི་བཏང་བ་རེད་ (They) issued this wrong sentence because he didn't thoroughly investigate (the case) first.

མ་བརྟགས་མ་དཔྱད་ (madaà majɛ̀ɛ̀) not looking into/ investigating/ researching sth.; va.—བྱེད་.

མ་ལྟོས་པར་ (madööbar) regardless of, notwithstanding, irrespective of ¶ མི་ཚང་མཐོ་དམན་ལ་མ་ལྟོས་པར་ Regardless of the family's class (high or low). ¶ རྒྱུ་ཆེ་ཆུང་ལ་མ་ལྟོས་པར་ Regardless of wealth.

མ་བལྟོས་པར་ (madööbar) sm. མ་ལྟོས་པ་.

མ་ཐ་ན་ (matana) sm. མ་མཐར་.

མ་ཐག (madaà) (vb + —) as soon as ¶ ལན་འབྱོར་མ་ཐག་ཡོང་བ་ཡིན་ (I) came as soon as the message arrived.

མ་ཐག་ཏུ་ (madagdu) sm. མ་ཐག.

མ་ཐག་པ་ (madagba) 1. (vb.+ —) just ¶ འབྱོར་མ་ཐག་པའི་འགྲུལ་པ་ A traveler who just arrived. ¶ བཟོས་མ་མ་ཐག་པའི་བག་ལེབ་ཚ་པོ་ Hot bread which has just been made. 2. as soon as ¶ ཁོ་འབྱོར་མ་ཐག་པར་ཁ་ལག་བཟས་སོང་ As soon as he arrived he ate.

མ་ཐེ་ (made) sm. མ་སྣེ་ཐེ་.

མ་ཐེ་ (made) sm. མ་ཐེབས་པས་.

མ་ཐེབས་ (mateb) endowment, trust fund.

མ་ཐེབས་པས་ (matebbɛɛ̀) not including, excluding ¶ ཁོང་མ་ཐེབས་པས་ང་ཚོ་མི་བཅུ་ཡོད་ Excluding him, we are ten people.

མ་ཐོག་སྐྱེད་རྒྱག (ma tɔ̄ɔ̀ gyēè gyaà) both the principal and the interest ¶ མ་ཐོག་སྐྱེད་རྒྱག་གི་བུ་ལོན་སྒོར་ ༡༠༠༠ ཡོད་ I have a loan that is 1000 dollars including the principal and the interest.

མ་ཐོགས་པར་ (madɔgbar) 1. without delay ¶ ཁོང་ལམ་བར་ཡུན་རིང་མ་ཐོགས་པར་ལོག་སླེབས་བྱུང་ He returned without delaying a long time on the road. 2. without tripping/ stumbling ¶ ལམ་དུ་འགྲོ་དུས་རྐང་པ་རྡོ་ལ་མ་ཐོགས་པ་བྱེད་དགོས་ When going on the road you should (be careful) not to trip on rocks.

མ་མཐའ་ (ma tā) the minimum, the least ¶ ལོ་རེའི་དངུལ་འཁོར་རྒྱུག་མ་མཐའ་སྒོར་ཆིག་འབུམ་རེད་ The minimum annual capital turnover is about one hundred thousand dollars.

མ་མཐའ་མཐར་ (ma tā tār) at the very least ¶ འདིའི་རིན་ཐང་མ་མཐའ་མཐར་ཨ་སྒོར་ ༡༠༠༠ རེད་ The value of this at the very least is 1000 U.S. dollars.

མ་མཐར་ (matar) at least, at minimum ¶ ཁོ་དབུགས་ཆད་ནས་མ་མཐར་སྐར་བཅུ་དྲུག་ལྷག་ཕྱིན་ཡོད་པ་ར་སྤྲོད་བྱུང་ It was proved that at the least over sixteen minutes passed since he stopped breathing.

མ་མཐར་ཡང་ (mataryaŋ) even at the least ¶ དཔུང་དམག་གསོག་འཇོག་བྱས་པའི་གྲངས་འབོར་ནི་མ་མཐར་ཡང་ས་ཡ་བརྒལ་ཡོད་པ་རེད་ The number of reserve troops, even at the least, exceeds one million.

མ་མཐོང་དགུ་མཐོང་ (mātoŋ gutoŋ) 1. seeing/ experiencing inconceivable misfortune; va.—མཐོང་. 2. seeing many unusual things; va.—མཐོང་.

མ་མཐོང་མཐོང་མདོག (matoŋ tōŋdɔɔ̀) pretending to see sth. even if it isn't there.

མ་མཐོང་ལུས་ཚུལ་ (matoŋ lüüdzüü) pretending not to see sth. (and leaving it alone).

མ་དག་རྒྱུན་འཇགས་ (mādaà gyünjaà) sth. (usu. a word) that is incorrect but has come to be accepted and is widely used/ practiced.

མ་དག་རྒྱུན་འབྱམས་ (madaà gyünjam) sm. མ་དག་རྒྱུན་འཇག.

མ་དག་པ་ (madagba) incorrect ¶ ཁོས་བོད་ཀྱི་སྐོར་མ་དག་པ་མང་པོ་ཤོད་ཀྱི་འདུག He is saying a lot of incorrect things about Tibet.

མ་དག་མུག་བཟོས་ (madag mugsöö) shung. intruding/ grabbing illegally ¶ ཆོས་སྡེས་མ་དག་མུག་བཟོས་བགྱིས་པར་ལོ་སོང་ཐོན་འབབ་སློས་ཅི་ཉེས་པ་ཙམ་ཐོབ་གྲས་ཀྱང་ཡང་པ་བྱས་ As for the illegal intrusion by the monastery, not only do they have to pay back the year's crop yield, but they also deserve punishment although this time they will be exempted from punishment.

མ་དག་འུད་ཆེ་ (madaà wööce) shung. sm. མ་དག་ཡུས་ཆེ་.

མ་དག་ཡུས་ཆེ་ (madaà yüüce) making a big deal or taking credit for sth. that one has not really done.

མ་དད་པ་ (madɛɛ̀ba) without faith ¶ སངས་རྒྱས་ལ་མ་དད་པ་རྣམས་ལ་ཕྱི་པ་ཞེས་ཟེར་བ་རེད་ (Those) who don't have faith in the Buddha are called "outsiders."

མ་དེབ་ (madeb) 1. a master (copy/ book), the main book.

མ་དྲང་མ་འཐུས་ (madraŋ madüü) unjust and not acceptable/ not satisfactory.

མ་དྲངས་ (madraŋ) crude, wild, rough (in behavior).

མ་དྲངས་དྲོལ་བ་ཅན་ (madraŋ dröövajɛn) shung. to loiter and spend one's time in playing/ fooling around ¶ གང་ལྟར་མ་དྲངས་དྲོལ་བ་ཅན་གྱི་གང་ཟག་འགའ་ཞིག་ནས་བསྟན་འགྲོའི་ཕན་བདེ་དང་འདི་ཕྱིའི་བདེ་འབྲས་གང་ལའང་བསམ་གཞིགས་མེད་པར་ Some people who spend their time fooling around do not take into consideration the promotion of Buddhism, the welfare of the sentient beings, and the cause and effect of this life and the future life.

མ་དྲོས་མཚོ་ (madröö tsō) sm. མཚོ་མ་ཕམ་.

མ་གདན་ (madɛn) foundation, basis.

མ་བདག (madaà) 1. owned by the mother. 2. not owned.

མ་བདག་བདག་བཟུང་ (madaà dagsuŋ) keeping sth. that doesn't belong to you; va.—བྱེད་ to keep sth. that doesn't belong to you ¶ མ་བདག་བདག་བཟུང་བྱེད་མཁན་ Ones who keep things that don't belong to them.

མ་འདང་བ་ (madaŋwa) not enough, insufficient.

མ་འདོད་ (mandöö) not liking/ wanting.

མ་འདོད་འོན་གོག (mandöö wöngɔɔ̀) pretending to be deaf because one doesn't want to do sth.; va.—བྱེད་.

མ་འདོད་འོན་པ་ (mandöö wömba) sm. མ་འདོད་འོན་གོག.

མ་འདྲིས་པ་ (məndriibə) unfamiliar, unacquainted ¶ ལམ་ཁ་མ་འདྲིས་པ་ཡིན་སྟབས་ Because the road is unfamiliar.

མ་འདྲེས་པ་ (mandreèba) unmixed, pure, unadulterated.

མ་རྡོ་ (mado) the bottom stone.

མ་ལྡངས་བ་ (madaŋwa) insufficient, deficient ¶ ཁོས་ཇ་མ་ལྡངས་བ་ཞིག་བཟོས་འདུག He has made insufficient tea.

མ་ན་ཧོ་ (manaho) ch. agate.

མ་ནག་ནག་ལ་བུ་དཀར་དཀར་སྐྱེས་ (ma nagnagla pu gārgar gyēè) a saying used to convey an evil or nonvirtuous mother having an excellent and virtuous son [Lit. a black mother gives birth to a white son].

མ་ནས་ (manɛ) in any case, anyway, basically ¶ མ་ནས་ཁྱེད་རང་ལ་དངུལ་དེ་ག་ནས་བྱུང་ངམ་ In any case, where did you get the money? ¶ གནད་དོན་དེའི་སྐོར་དེ་འདྲ་མ་ནས་མ་རེད་ Concerning this issue, it is basically not like that.

མ་ནིང་ (məniŋ) 1. hermaphrodite, neuter. 2. neutral letters in Tibetan grammar.

མ་ནུ་ (mənu) 1. a kind of incense. 2. an herbal medicine.

མ་ནུ་ཁྲག་ཅན་ (mənu tragjɛn) senecarpus anacardius (used in Tibetan medicine).

མ་ནུ་ཧུ་ (mənuhu) ch. agate.

མ་ནུ་སྦོས་དཀར་ (mənu bööɡar) camphor.

མ་ནུ་བསེ་ཤིང་ (mənu sēshiŋ) senecarpus anacardius (used in Tibetan medicine).

མ་ནུས་མ་ལྩོག (mənüü majɔɔ̀) not able and having no time to do sth.

མ་ནེ་ (mane) sm. མ་ལེ་.

མ་ཎི་ (mani) the prayer: 'o mani padme hum'; va.—བགྲང་; —འདྲེན་ to recite the mani prayer either orally or counting on a rosary or both; va.—འདོན་ to recite mani prayer (this verb is usually not used when sb. is counting on a rosary).

མ་ཎི་བཀའ་འབུམ་ (māni gāmbum) a historical book written by Srongtsen Gampo.

མ་ཎི་འཁོར་ལོ་ (mani kɔ̄ɔlo) prayer wheel; va.—སྐོར་ to turn a prayer wheel.

མ་ཎི་བགྲང་བགྲང་ (mani draŋdraŋ) continuously, endlessly, repititiously; va.—བྱེད་; —སྐོད་ [Lit. like doing the o mani padme hum prayer over and over again].

མ་ཎི་ཆུ་འཁོར་ (mani cūgɔɔ) a water-powered pray wheel.

མ་ཎི་མཆེད་གྲོགས་ (mani cēèdrɔɔ̀) partners in a group praying the o mani prayer together.

མ་ཎི་དར་ལྕོག (māni tarjoò) prayer flag on which the omani prayer is printed.

མ་ཎི་དུང་འཁོར་ (mani duŋgɔɔ) a large prayer wheel which contains a 100 million mani prayers.

མ་ཎི་འདོན་འདོན་ (mani döndön) sm. མ་ཎི་འདྲེན་འདྲེན་.

མ་ཎི་རྡོ་བཀོས་ (mani dogöö) a stone on which the mani prayer is carved.

མ་ཎི་རྡོ་སྤུང་ (mani dobuŋ) heaps of rocks with mani prayers carved on them.

མ་ཎི་ནག་པོ་ (mani nagbo) a person who is outwardly religious but has a bad heart (a religious hypocrite) [Lit. black mani].

མ་ཎི་བྲག (mani traà) rocks on which mani prayers are carved.

མ་ཎི་མ་ (manima) 1. a type of cymbal. 2. a brocade that has mani woven into its design. 3. a woman who chants the mani prayer.

མ་ཎི་ཡིག་དྲུག (mani yiŋdru) the six-syllable mantra—o ma ni padme hum.

མ་ཎི་རླུང་འཁོར་ (mani lūŋgɔɔ) a prayer wheel that is turned by the wind.

མ་ཎི་ལག་བསྐོར་ (mani laggɔɔ) a hand-operated prayer wheel.

མ་ཎི་ལྷ་ཁང་ (mani lhāgaŋ) a temple in which a huge prayer wheel is set.

མ་གནང་དགོས་གནང་ (mani gööǹaŋ) h. of མ་བྱེད་དགུ་བྱེད་.

མ་གནས་ (manɛɛ̀) cost price ། མ་གནས་ནས་བཅག་ནས་བཙོང་སོང་ They sold it below cost.

མ་གནས་ཀྱི་རྩིས་ (manɛɛ̀gi dzīì) cost accounting, calculating the cost price; va.—རྒྱག.

མ་གནས་སྐོར་ཐང་རྩིས་པ་ (manɛɛ̀ gɔ̄ɔdaŋ dzīìwə) cost accounting.

མ་གནས་གཅོག (manɛɛ̀ jɔ̄ɔ̀) va. to reduce/ lower production costs.

མ་པང་བུ་དོར་མེད་པ་ (mabaŋ pudɔɔ meèba) shung. cherishing, taking good care of ། དེ་དོན་ཁྲིམས་བདག་ཁྲིམས་གཅེས་ཀྱིས་བཀའ་འདོམས་སྐྱབས་འདུག་མ་པང་བུ་དོར་མེད་པ་མཁྱེན་ We request the law-holders to treasure the law like a mother holding her infant with care.

མ་པད་ (mabɛɛ̀) the lotus cushion on which deities sit (on statues) [Lit. shung. like a mother holding her infant with her on her lap].

མ་དཔེ་ (mabe) the original manuscript/ model, the master copy ། ཁོང་གི་མ་དཔེ་བརླག་ཀྱང་ངོ་བཤུས་ཁ་ཤས་ཡོད་པ་འདུག Even though the original is lost there are several copies.

མ་སྤུན་ (mabön) maternal relatives.

མ་སྤུན་གྱི་མཆེད་ཟླ་ (maböngi cēnda) maternal cousins.

མ་ཕམ་མཚོ་ (mapam tsō) Lake Manasarowa.

མ་ཕམ་གཡུ་མཚོ་ (mapam yūmdzo) Lake Manasarowa.

མཕྱི་ (məji) 1. sm. མ་དཔེ་. 2. maternal grandmother.

མ་ཧྥེ་ (mafe) ch. morphine.

མ་ཕྱི་མ་ (ma cīmə) stepmother.

མ་ཕྱོགས་ (majɔɔ̀) 1. below, down there. 2. maternal side, maternal relatives.

མ་ཕྲད་གྲོགས་པོ་ (madrɛɛ̀ trogbo) a friend one doesn't meet (e.g., a pen pal).

མ་ཕྲུག (madruù) children of capitalist-roaders/ capitalists.

མ་འཕྲོག་མ་འཐེན་ཆུག (madrɔɔ̀ manden cūù) shung. not letting (anyone) take sth. away ། ལྷ་ཁང་ལ་གཏོགས་པའི་ས་ཆ་དང་ཆུ་དང་ཆུ་ཐགས་ལ་སོགས་ཅི་ཡིན་པ་ཐམས་ཅད་མ་འཕྲོག་མ་འཐེན་ཆུག Do not let (anyone) take away the property of the temple, such as the land, houses, the water mills, etc.

མ་འཕྲོས་ (ma trȫò) shung. abbr. of མ་རྩ་ལྷག་འཕྲོ་.

མ་ཕིན་ (məbin) lying, cheating; va.—བྱེད་; —ཤོད་ to lie, to cheat; va.—བཟོ་ to make sb. into a liar/ cheat.

མ་བུ་ (mīəbu) 1. mother and child. 2. mother and son. 3. original and the copy. 4. principal and interest.

མ་བུ་འཁོར་སྒུག་ཁང་ (məbu kɔ̄ɔguùgaŋ) waiting room for mothers with children.

མ་བུ་གོ་ལྟོག་གི་ཕྱ་ (məbu kodɔɔ̀gi cā) a method of divining through feeling the pulse of mother and child.

མ་བུ་དགྲ་གྲོགས་ (məbu dradrɔɔ̀) sm. མ་བུ་གོ་ལྟོག་གི་ཕྱ་.

མ་བུ་གཉིས་ (məbu ñīì) mother and child.

མ་བུ་བདེ་སྐྱོང་ས་ཚིགས་ (məbu degyoŋ sədziì) health center for maternal and child health care.

མ་བུ་བདེ་གྲོལ་ (məbu dedröö) both mother and newborn child doing well.

མ་བུ་བདེ་སྲུང་ (məbu desuŋ) sm. མ་བུའི་བདེ་སྲུང་.

མ་བུ་འཕྲོད་བསྟེན་ (məbu trȫöden) maternal and child hygiene/ health.

མ་བུ་འཕྲོད་བསྟེན་ཁྲུའུ་ (məbu trȫöden trū) tib.ch. office of maternal and child hygiene/ health.

མ་བུ་འཕྲོད་བསྟེན་བྱ་བའི་རུ་ཁག (məbu trȫöden cawɛ rugaà) maternal and child health work team.

མ་བུ་མེ་སྒྱོགས་ (məbu mergyɔɔ̀) a large artillery piece surrounded by smaller ones.

མ་བུན་ (mabüb) principal (in a loan).

མ་བུན་གྱི་ཆ་ཤས་ (mabüngi cāshɛɛ̀) an installment (of a loan).

མ་བུན་གཏོང་ཐེབས་ (mabün dōŋdeb) principal for a trust fund/ endowment.

མ་བུའི་སྒུག་ཁང་ (məbü guùgaŋ) mother and children's waiting room.

མ་བུའི་བདེ་སྲུང་ (məbü desuŋ) maternal and child/ infant health care or hygiene.

མ་བུའི་འཕྲོད་བསྟེན་ (məbü trȫöden) maternal and child/ infant hygiene or hygiene.

མ་བོས་མགྲོན་པོ་ (maböö drömbo) uninvited guest.

མ་ཇོང་ (majaŋ) mahjong; va.—རྒྱག to play mahjong.

མ་ཇན་ (majɛn) sm. མ་ཆེན་.

མ་ཇན་ཁང་ (majɛngaŋ) kitchen staff room.

མ་ཇན་ལས་རིགས་ (majɛn lɛ̀ɛrig) the occupation of cook/ chef.

མ་བྱིན་པར་ལེན་ (majinbar len) va. to take without being given, to steal/ rob.

མ་བྱིན་ལེན་ (majin len) sm. མ་བྱིན་པར་ལེན་པ་.

མ་བྱུང་སྔོན་དཔག (məjuŋ ŋōnbaà) prophetic vision, foresight.

མ་བྱེད་དགུ་བྱེད་ (majeè gujeè) doing all sorts of (improper) things; va.—བྱེད་ ། མ་བྱེད་དགུ་བྱེད་བྱས་ན་ཁྲིམས་ལ་ཐུག་རྒྱུའི་ཉེན་ཁ་ཡོད་པ་རེད་ If you do all sorts of things there is a danger you will come afoul of the law.

མ་བྱེད་སྒུ་བྱེད་ (majeè gujeè) sm. མ་བྱེད་དགུ་བྱེད་.

མ་བྱེད་མ་བལྟ་ (majeè mada) telling not to do and not to look.

མ་བྱུང་སྔོན་འགོག (məjuŋ ŋȫngɔɔ̀) preventive measures, preventing/ blocking in advance; va.—བྱེད་ ། ཞིང་པ་ཚོས་དགུན་ཀ་ཆུ་རག་བརྒྱབ་དེ་ཆུ་ལོག་མ་བྱུང་སྔོན་འགོག་བྱས་པ་རེད་ The farmers built a dike in the winter as a preventive measure against floods.

མ་འབོད་ (ma böȍ) sound of a child crying/ wailing, a child calling "ama" (mother) ¶ མ་འབོད་འུར་སྒྲ་ A child wailing "ama" (mother).

མའབོད་རང་ཐོབ་ (maböȍ raŋdob) getting sth. that one has not worked for, profiting by another person's work.

མ་འབྱར་ (manjaa) baby, infant.

མ་འབྲུ་ (mandru) capital/ endowment that consists of grain.

མ་དྲིན་ (mədrin) sm. མ་པེན་.

མ་དབང་ལམ་ལུགས་ (mawaŋ ləmluù) matriarchy.

མ་དབྱིབས་ (məyib) model, prototype.

མམ (mama) sm. བུ་རྫེ་.

མ་མད་ (mamɛɛ̀) mother and daughter.

མ་མིང་ (mamiŋ) mother's name.

མ་མེད་ (mameè) 1. motherless ¶ ཕྲུག་གུ་མ་མེད་དེ་ The motherless child. 2. without the main part ¶ འཕྲུལ་འཁོར་མ་མེད་ A machine without the main part.

མམེད་ཉོ་ཚོང་ (mameè ñudzoŋ) selling or buying without capital; va.—བྱེད་.

མམེད་ལྷན་རྩེག (mameè lhɛ̄ndzeg) clothing that has so many patches that it difficult to see the main part.

མམེད་ལྷན་པ་དགུ་རྩེག (mameè lhɛ̄mba gudzeg) sm. མམེད་ལྷན་རྩེག.

མ་མེས་ (mameè) maternal grandfather.

མ་མོ་ (mamo) 1. adult female sheep. 2. sm. མ་གཞི་.

མམོག (mamɔg) cotton.

མམྱོང་དགུ་ཐུག (mañoŋ guduù) experiencing all sorts of troubles/ events.

མམྱོང་དགུ་མྱོང་ (mañoŋ guñoŋ) experiencing all sorts of troubles/ events.

མམྱོང་གུ་མྱོང་ (mañoŋ guñoŋ) sm. མམྱོང་དགུ་མྱོང་.

མམྱོང་རང་མྱོང་ (mañoŋ raŋñoŋ) no choice but to bear some trouble/ difficulty.

མ་རྨོས་ (ལོ་ཏོག) (mamöö) maize, corn.

མརྨོས་ལོ་ཏོག (mamö lodoò) sm. མརྨོས་.

མ་སྨད་ (mamɛɛ̀) 1. sm. མ་མད་. 2. sm. ཁྱད་དུ་འཕགས་པ་.

མ་སྨིན་ཚ་བ་ (mamin tsāwa) fever that is not ready to break.

མ་སྨོས་རྟོགས་གསལ་ (mamöö dɔ̄gsɛɛ) sth. being clear without having to say anything.

མ་ཙང་ (madzaŋ) sm. མ་གཞི་.

མ་རྩ་ (madza) capital ¶ ཁོས་ཚོང་རྒྱག་ཡས་ཀྱི་མ་རྩ་གཡར་པ་རེད་ He borrowed capital for trading.

མ་རྩ་ཁུག (madza kūù) sm. མ་རྩ་ཕྱུག.

མ་རྩ་སྒེར་འཛིམ་ (madza gerdem) monopoly of capital.

མ་རྩ་ཅན་ (madzajɛn) 1. capitalist. 2. wealthy person.

མ་རྩ་ཆག (madza cāà) va. to lose one's capital, to lose a great sum of money.

མརྩ་ཆག་གྲངས་ (madza cāgdraŋ) the amount of capital lost.

མརྩ་ཅན་ཕྱུག་ཆེན་ (madzajɛn cūgjen) capitalist bigwig, capitalist rich person.

མརྩ་ཆག་པའི་ཁེ་ལས་ (madza cāgbɛ kēlɛɛ̀) an enterprise that loses capital.

མརྩ་ཆག་པའི་དངུལ་གྲངས་ (madza cāgbɛ ŋũũdraŋ) amount of capital loss.

མ་རྩ་འཛུགས (madza jɔɔ̀) va. to invest capital.

མ་རྩ་རྙིང་པ་ (madza ñīŋbə) original capital, old capital.

མ་རྩ་སྟོང་ (madza dōŋ) vi. to be/ go bankrupt, to lose one's capital.

མ་རྩ་སྟོང་པ་ (madza dōŋba) bankruptcy.

མ་རྩ་འཐེན་ (madza tēn) va. to withdraw/ draw down on capital.

མ་རྩ་དྲིབ་ (madza dib) vi. to be unable to make a profit, to lose money/ capital.

མརྩ་དྲིབ་པའི་ཚོང་ (madza dibbɛ tsōŋ) a business running at a loss, a losing business venture.

མ་རྩ་ནས་གཙོང (madzanɛjɔ̄ɔ̀) va. to sell below cost.

མ་རྩ་ནས་ཆག (madzanɛ cāà) vi. to sell below cost.

མརྩ་ཕངས་མེད་ (madza pāŋmeè) sparing neither labor nor money, sparing no expenses at any cost.

མ་རྩ་ཕྱིར་གཏོང་ (madza cīrdoŋ) capital exportation; va.—བྱེད་ to export capital.

མ་རྩ་ཕྱིར་འདྲེན་ (madza cīrdren) sm. རྩ་ཕྱིར་གཏོང་.

མ་རྩ་སྦྱོར་འཇགས་ (madza jɔnjaà) an endowment, a trust fund.

མ་རྩ་འཛུགས་ (madza dzuù) sm. མ་རྩ་འཛུགས.

མ་རྩ་བཞག (madza shaà) p. of མ་རྩ་འཛུགས.

མ་རྩ་ཟིན་ (madza sin) sm. མ་རྩ་ལྷོག.

མ་རྩ་བཟོ་ (madza so) va. to raise money/ capital, to create capital.

མ་རྩ་སློག་ (madza lɔ̄ɔ̀) va. to return capital (that was invested) ¶ ངའི་མ་རྩ་ཚང་མ་སློག་རོགས་བྱེད་ Please return all my capital (that was invested).

མ་རྩ་ལྷག་འདྲོ་ (madza lhāgdro) shung. remaining, leftover principal (of a loan).

མ་རྩ་ལྷོག (madza lhɔ̄ɔ̀) vi. to just get back one's initial capital investment.

མ་རྩའི་ཀང་གྲངས་ (madzɛ gāŋdraŋ) sm. མ་ཀང་.

མ་རྩའི་རྣམ་བཤད་ (madzɛɛ nāmshɛɛ̀) "Das Kapital" (by Karl Marx).

མརྩའི་བཙན་རྒྱལ་རིང་ལུགས་ (madzɛ dzɛ̄ngyɛɛ riŋluù) capitalist-imperialism.

མ་རྩའི་རིང་ལུགས་ (madzɛ riŋluù) capitalism, capitalist ¶ མ་རྩའི་རིང་ལུགས་རྒྱལ་ཁབ་ Capitalist countries.

མ་རྩའི་རིང་ལུགས་ཀྱི་རང་འཕེལ་སྟོབས་ཤུགས་ (madzɛ riŋluùgi raŋpel dōbshuù) spontaneous capitalist forces.

མ་རྩའི་རིང་ལུགས་ཁྱོན་ཡོངས་ཀྱི་ཉམས་ཉེན་ (madzɛ riŋluù kyōnyoŋgi ñamñen) general crisis of capitalism.

མ་རྩའི་རིང་ལུགས་ཀྱི་སྒྲུབ་ཆ་ (madzɛ riŋluùgi trubja) capitalist sector, capitalist element.

མ་རྩའི་རིང་ལུགས་ཀྱི་ཐོན་སྐྱེད་བྱེད་ལུགས་ (madzɛ riŋluùgi tōngyeè ceèluù) capitalist mode of production.

མ་རྩའི་རིང་ལུགས་ཀྱི་ཐོན་སྐྱེད་འབྲེལ་བ་ (madzɛ riŋluùgi tōngyeè dreewa) capitalist relations of production.

མ་རྩའི་རིང་ལུགས་ཀྱི་སྤྱི་ཚོགས་ (madzɛ riŋluùgi jīdzɔɔ̀) capitalist society.

མ་རྩའི་རིང་ལུགས་ཀྱི་ཕྱོགས་ལྷུང་ (madzɛ riŋluùgi cɔ̄ɔlhuŋ) tendency towards capitalism.

མ་རྩའི་རིང་ལུགས་ཀྱི་བཟོ་ཚོང་ལས་རིགས་ (madzɛ riŋluùgi sodzoŋ lɛ̄rii) capitalist industry and commerce.

མ་རྩའི་རིང་ལུགས་ཀྱི་ལམ་ལུགས་ (madzɛ riŋluùgi ləmluù) capitalist system.

མ་རྩའི་རིང་ལུགས་རོ་ལངས་རྒྱག་པ་ (madzɛ riŋluù rolaŋ gyagba) the restoration of capitalism.

མ་རྩའི་རིང་ལུགས་ཀྱི་ལམ་ལ་འགྲོ་མཁན་ (madzɛ riŋluùgi lamla droñɛn) capitalist roader.

མརྩའི་རིན་ཐང་ (madzɛ rindaŋ) capital value.

མ་རྩའི་རོགས་རམ་ (madzɛ rɔ̄ɔram) helping with capital.

མ་རྩོམ་ (madzom) the main/ original composition or essay or writing.

མ་ཚང་ (madzaŋ) 1. basically ¶ མ་ཚང་མི་འདི་ཡག་པོ་ཡོད་ན་ཡང་ཉོབ་པོ་ཞིག་འདུག This man is good basically but he is lethargic. 2. the main family (if there are branches they would be called ཟུར་པ་). 3. maternal side of families.

མ་ཚང་བ་ (madzaŋwa) short of, missing, lacking, incomplete ¶ འཕྲུལ་འཁོར་མ་ཚང་བ་དེ་ཉོ་གི་མ་རེད་ (They) will not buy the incomplete machine.

མ་ཚང་བ་མེད་པ་ (madzaŋwa meèba) complete, whole, nothing missing ¶ ཁོ་ཚོར་ཞིང་ལས་ཀྱི་འཕྲུལ་འཁོར་མ་ཚང་བ་མེད་པ་སྤྲད་པ་རེད་ (They) gave them a complete set of agricultural machinery.

མ་ཚད་ (madzɛɛ̀) not only ¶ དེས་མ་ཚད་རྗེས་སུ་སླར་

ཡང་དམག་བྱུང་བ་རེད་ Not only that, later once again there was war. ༎ ལས་ཀ་བྱས་པས་མ་ཚད་སློབ་གྲྭར་ཕྱིན་པ་རེད་ (He) not only worked, (he also) went to school.

མཚན་ (madzɛn) maternal relatives.

མཚབ་ (mədzəb) 1. stepmother. 2. nursery teacher.

མཚོས་ (madzöö) primary colors.

མའཚལ་ (ma dzɛ̄ɛ) to not comprehend/ understand/ know.

མ་འཚོས་པ་ (madzööba) uncooked, raw.

མ་མཛད་མཛད་ (ma dzɛ̄ɛdzɛɛ̀) sm. མ་མཛེས་མཛེས་.

མ་མཛེས་མཛེས་ (ma dzeèdzeè) sarcastic; va.—བྱེད་ to be sarcastic.

མ་འཛུགས་བྱེད་ (mandzuù cèè) sm. མ་རྒྱ་འཛུགས་.

མ་འཛེམས་ (mandzem) sm. མ་འཛེམས་པར་.

མ་འཛེམས་པར་ (mandzembar) 1. without shirking, not fearing, without shying away from ༎ དཀའ་ངལ་ལ་མ་འཛེམས་པར་མི་དམངས་ཀྱི་ཞབས་འདེགས་ཞུས་པ་རེད་ Not fearing hardship, (they) served the people. 2. (with ཁ་) not refraining from eating things that are bad for one's health when sick.

མཞང་ (mashaŋ) abbr. mother and maternal uncle.

མ་ཞིང་ (məshiŋ) shung. the main field.

མཞུ་སྐྲན་ (məshu drɛ̄n) tumor caused by digestive problems.

མ་གཞི་ (məshi) 1. actually, really, of course ༎ མ་གཞི་ད་ལོ་ཁོང་ལོ་བརྒྱད་བཅུ་ཐམ་པར་སླེབས་ཡོད་པ་རེད་ Actually he is eighty years old this year. 2. foundation, basis ༎ ཁང་པའི་མ་གཞི་ The foundation of the house.

མ་གཞི་དངོས་གནས་བྱས་ན་ (məshi ŋöönɛ cɛ̄ɛna) sm. མ་གཞི་ནས་.

མ་གཞི་ནས་ (məshinɛ) actually, really, of course ༎ ཁོ་ཚོ་མི་རིགས་དང་སྐད་ཡིག་མ་གཞི་ནས་ཁག་ཁག་རེད་ Actually, they are ethnically and linguistically different.

མ་གཞི་བྱས་ན་ (məshi cɛ̄ɛna) sm. མ་གཞི་ནས་.

མགཞིའི་རིན་གོང་ (məshii ringoŋ) basic price.

མགཞིན་ (məshin) sm. མ་གདོགས་.

མ་ཟིན་ (məsin) a draft.

མ་ཟིན་ཙམ་ (məsindzam) just before ༎ ཉིན་དགུང་མ་ཟིན་ཙམ་ལ་ཁ་ལག་ཟ་བར་འགྲོ་གི་ཡོད་ I go to eat lunch just before noon.

མ་ཟུར་ (məsur) abbr. of མ་ཚང་ and མ་ཟུར་.

མ་ཟོག་ (məsog) shung. the principal goods (used for exchange/ barter).

མ་གཟིགས་གཟིགས་མདོག་ (məsii sindɔɔ̀) h. of མ་མཐོང་མཐོང་མདོག.

མ་གཟུགས་ (məsuù) 1. prototype, model. 2. female body.

མ་བཟོ་དགོས་བཟོ་ (maso gööso) sb. who causes difficulty or problems between others; va.—བཟོ་ ༎ སློབ་གྲྭར་མ་བཟོ་དགོས་བཟོ་བཟོ་མཁན་སློབ་ཕྲུག་ཁྲིག་ཉིས་པ་འགའ་ཤས་རེད་ It is only a few students who are the ones causing problems in school.

མ་འོག (mawɔɔ̀) arc. sm. འོག་རོལ་.

མ་འོངས་ (maoŋ) future ༎ མ་འོངས་ཀྱི་འཆར་གཞི་ A plan for the future.

མ་འོངས་འགྲོ་ཡུལ་ (maoŋ droyüü) future course.

མ་འོངས་སྔོན་མཐོང་ (maoŋ ŋōndoŋ) anticipating sth. in the future, predicting or seeing the future, foresight ༎ ད་ལྟའི་གནས་སྟངས་འདི་ཕལ་ཆེར་དེ་སྐབས་ནས་མ་འོངས་སྔོན་མཐོང་བྱུང་ཡོད་ (They) probably anticipated the current situation from that time (in the past) ༎ མ་འོངས་སྔོན་མཐོང་དཀའ་བའི་ཆགས་སྟངས་ A situation difficult to predict.

མ་འོངས་སྔོན་དཔག (maoŋ ŋōnbaà) sm. མ་འོངས་སྔོན་མཐོང་.

མ་འོངས་སྔོན་གཟིགས་ (maoŋ ŋōnbaà) sm. མ་འོངས་སྔོན་མཐོང་.

མའོངས་སྔོན་ཤེས་ (maoŋ ŋōnsheè) sm. མ་འོངས་སྔོན་མཐོང་.

མ་འོངས་སྔོན་བཤད་ (maoŋ ŋōnshɛɛ̀) sm. མ་འོངས་ལུང་བསྟན་རྒྱག.

མ་འོངས་སྔོན་གསུང་ (maoŋ ŋōnsuŋ) sm. མ་འོངས་ལུང་བསྟན་རྒྱག.

མ་འོངས་མཐོང་ཡུལ་ (maoŋ tōŋyüü) farsighted goal/ aim.

མ་འོངས་པ་ (maoŋba) in the future.

མའོངས་པའི་དུས་ (maoŋbɛ tüü) the future (time).

མའོངས་པའི་དཔེ་ (maoŋbɛ bē) an example for the future.

མ་འོངས་པར་ (maoŋbar) in the future.

མ་འོངས་ལུང་བསྟན་ (maoŋ lundɛn) prophecy, future prediction; va.—རྒྱག to prophesize.

མ་ཡར་ (mayaa) stepmother.

མ་ཡིག (məyii̇) the original of a text/ manuscript.

མཡིག་དངོས་ (məyii ŋöö) sm. མཡིག.

མཡིག་འབྲི་ཤོག (məyii drishoò) sm. མཡིག.

མ་ཡིག་ཞུ་དག (məyii shudaà) proofreading; va.—གཏོང་.

མ་ཡིན་གོ་ཡིན་ (məyin koyin) letting sb. off with only a warning; va.—བྱེད་ ༎ དེ་རིང་མ་ཡིན་གོ་ཡིན་བྱེད་ཨ་ མཇུག་མ་དེ་འདྲ་བྱས་ན་གཏོར་གྱི་ཡིན་ནྭ་ I will overlook it this time, but if you do it in the future I will destroy you.

མ་ཡིན་ཀུ་ཡིན་ (məyin kuyin) sm. མ་ཡིན་གོ་ཡིན་.

མ་ཡིན་པ་ (məyimbə) is not, not being ༎ ཁོ་ཀུ་མ་མ་ཡིན་པར་ཀུ་མ་རེད་ཟེར་གྱི་འདུག (They) are saying he is a thief although he is not.

མཡིན་ཡིན་ཁུལ་ (məyin yingüü) pretending it is when it is not, pretending to be what you are not; va.—བྱེད་ ༎ ཁོས་བོད་པ་མ་ཡིན་ཁུལ་བྱེད་ཀྱི་འདུག He is pretending he is a Tibetan.

མ་ཡིན་ཡིན་མདོག (məyin yindɔɔ̀) sm. མཡིན་ཡིན་ཁུལ་.

མཡིན་ཡིན་རྩུལ་ (məyin yindzüü) sm. མཡིན་ཡིན་ཁུལ་.

མཡུམ་ (məyum) mother (h.).

མ་ཡུར་ (məyur) main canal/ drain.

མ་ཡོང་ཀུ་ཡོང་ (mayoŋ guyoŋ) many bad events happening/ occurring.

མ་གཡར་ (mayaa) sm. མ་ཡར་.

མ་གཡོག (mayɔɔ̀) cook's assistant/ helper.

མ་རངས་ (maraŋ) disapproving, displeased, disliking ༎ མ་རངས་པའི་གད་མོ་ Laughter that showed dislike.

མརངས་ཁྲེལ་གད་ (maraŋ trēēgɛɛ̀) a sneering laugh.

མ་རབས་ (mərəb) unprincipled, vulgar, immoral, contemptible.

མ་རབས་ཐ་ཤལ་ (mərəb tāshɛɛ) extremely unprincipled/ immodest/ crude/ base/ contemptible.

མརབས་ཐབས་སྡུག (mərəb tābduù) sm. མརབས་ཐ་ཤལ་.

མ་རབས་ཚ་པོ་ (mərəb tsābo) unprincipled, immoral, base, contemptible.

མ་རབས་རུལ་ལྷུང་ (mərəb rüülhuŋ) sm. མ་རབས་སུ་ལྷུང་.

མ་རབས་སུ་ལྷུང་ (mərəbsu lhūŋ) vi. to become degenerate/ depraved/ immoral.

མ་རི་མུ་རི་ (məri muri) munching/ chewing by toothless people.

མ་རིག་པ་ (mərigbə) ignorant, ignorance.

མ་རུང་ (məruŋ) malevolent, ill intentioned, spiteful.

མ་རུང་ཁོག་བཙུག (məruŋ kōgjuù) malevolent, ill intentioned, spiteful; va.—བྱེད་.

མ་རུངས་ (məruŋ) sm. མ་རུང་.

མ་རུལ་མ་ (mərüümə) a woman who sleeps until late in the morning.

མ་རེད་ (mareè) it is not ༎ འདི་ཁྱི་མ་རེད་ This is not a dog.

མལ་ (mala) an expression of sorrow/ sadness.

མལ་དི་ (maladi) a kind of cardamom.

མ་ལ་ཡ་ (malaya) Malaya.

མལ་སུང་ (malasuŋ) marathon.

མ་ལག (malaà) the main and the branch ༎ ལས་ཁུངས་མ་ལག The main and branch offices.

མ་ལག་རྒྱོབ་ (malaà gyob) va. to do quickly.

མ་ལག་ཆ་ཚང་བ་ (malaà cādzaŋwa) the whole set, a complete set.

མ་ལག་དོད་པོ་ (malaà tööbo) dexterous, agile, having quick hands ༎ ཁོ་ཀུན་ཀུ་དུས་མ་ལག་དོད་པོ་

ཡོད་པ་རེད་ He is quick with his hands when he steals.

མ་ལག་བདེ་པོ་ (malaà debo) sm. མ་ལག་དོད་པོ་.

མལག་ཚང་སྒྲིག (malaà tsāŋdrig) linking up the parts to form the whole (including filling in gaps).

མལག་བཤངས་ (malaà shāŋ) sm. མ་ལག་རྐྱབ་.

མལགས་ (malaà) it is not.

མལན་ (malɛn) with no faults/ errors/ mistakes ¶ རང་གིས་མ་ལན་པ་ཞིག་བྱས་ན་གཞན་གྱིས་གང་བཤད་ཀྱང་སྐྱོན་མེད་པ་རེད་ If you work without making errors, it doesn't matter what others say.

མལན་མའགྱོད་ (ma lɛn magyöö) no mistakes and no regrets ¶ ལས་གང་བྱས་ཀྱང་མ་ལན་མ་འགྱོད་པ་ཞིག་བྱ་དགོས་ Whatever work (you) do you should do it without making mistakes so that you will have no regrets (later).

མ་ལམ་ (malam) main line, main route/ road.

མ་ལུས་ཀུན་མཐོང་ (malüü gündoŋ) seeing everything.

མ་ལུས་ཀུན་འདུས་ (malüü gündüü) all-embracing, all-inclusive, comprehensive.

མལུས་ཀུན་ཚང་ (malüü gündzaŋ) all-complete, nothing left out.

མལུས་ཀུན་ཤེས་ (malüü günsheè) all-knowing.

མ་ལུས་པ་ (məlüübə) without remainder, all, completely ¶ ཁོས་ཆང་མ་ལུས་པ་བཏུངས་སོང་ He drank the ཆང་ completely (there was none remaining).

མ་ལེ་ (male) chin.

མ་ལེའི་ཕྱེད་གླིང་ (malee cēèliŋ) Malayan Peninsula.

མ་ལེགས་པ་ (malegba) bad, not good.

མལོ་ (malo) a kind of brown sugar.

མལོངས་རྒན་འཁོགས (maloŋ gɛngɔɔ̀) a young person who seems or acts old.

མལོངས་རྒས་པོ་ (maloŋ gɛɛ̀bo) sm. མལོངས་རྒན་འཁོགས.

མ་ཤི་ཀ་ (mashigə) Jesus Christ.

མ་ཤི་དམྱལ་བ་ (mashi ñɛɛ̄wa) sm. མི་ཡུལ་དམྱལ་བ་.

མ་ཤུ་ (mashu) sm. སྨམ་པ་, 2.

མ་ཤེས་བཀའ་སློབ་ (masheè gālob) advice, instruction; va.—གནང་ to give advice; va.—ཞུ་; —གནང་སྐྱོང་ཞུ་; —གནང་སྐྱོང་ཡོད་པ་ཞུ་; —གནང་སྐྱོང་ཐུགས་རྗེ་ཆེ་ to ask for advice (h.).

མ་ཤེས་དགུ་ཤེས་ (masheè gusheè) having a lot of diverse knowledge/ skill (can be used in either a negative or positive sense).

མ་ཤེས་དགུ་ཤེས་ཚ་པོ་ (masheè gusheè tsābo) sb. who has diverse knowledge/ skills (depending on context can have either negative or positive connotation).

མ་ཤེས་ཤེས་ཁུལ་ (masheè shēègüü) pretending to know; va.—བྱེད་.

མ་ཤེས་ཤེས་མདོག (masheè shēndɔɔ̀) sm. མ་ཤེས་ཤེས་ཁུལ་.

མ་ཤོད་དགུ་ཤོད་ (mashöö gushöö) sm. མི་ཤོད་དགུ་ཤོད་.

མ་གཤིས་ (məshiì) 1. maternal instinct. 2. sm. རང་གཤིས་.

མ་སན་ཚོགས་པ་ (məsɛn tsɔ̄gba) eng.tib. Masons.

མ་སི་གྱི་དི་ (məsigidi) eng. mosque.

མ་སུ་རི་པུ་ཁྱིམ་ (məsuri pugyim) Tibetan Homes Foundation.

མསོ་ (maso) the lower teeth.

མ་སྲིད་པ་ (məsiìbə) impossible, not possible.

མ་སྲུ་ (məsu) abbr. mother and maternal aunt.

མ་གསང་ (masaŋ) openly, without keeping sth. a secret.

མ་གསང་དྲང་གཏམ་ (masaŋ traŋdam) true/ open/ frank talk.

མ་བསམ་དགུ་བསམ་ (masam gusam) having all sorts of thoughts, imagining all sorts of things; va.—བསམ་.

མ་བསུས་མགྲོན་པོ་ (məsüü raŋjɔɔ) sm. མ་བོས་མགྲོན་པོ་.

མ་བསུས་རང་འབྱོར་ (məsüü raŋjɔɔ) sb. coming without invitation.

མཧཱ་ཀཱ་ལ་ (maha gāla) skt. Mahakala (a protective deity).

མཧཱ་ར་ཛ་ (maha radza) Maharaja.

མཱ་ཅང་ (majaŋ) mahjong; va.—རྒྱག va. to play mahjong.

མག་གི་མུག་གི་ (maggi muge) unclear/ indistinct speech, mumbling speech.

མག་རྒན་ (maggɛn) the bridegroom of the oldest daughter.

མག་པ་ (maggba) bridegroom who resides at marriage matrilocally, adopted bridegroom; va.—སློང་ to request sb. as an adopted bridegroom; va.—གཏོང་; —སྐྱེར་ to give/ send as an adoptive bridegroom; va.—ལེན་ to take a bridegroom into one's family.

མག་པ་བསུ་མཁན་ (magba sūñɛn) person who goes to receive the bridegroom. moving matrilocally.

མག་པར་འགྲོ་ (magbar dro) va. to go as a matrilocally residing bridegroom.

མག་མུག (magmug) abbr. of མག་གི་མུག་གི.

མག་མོག (magmog) blurry, unclear.

མག་གཡོག (magyɔɔ̀) 1. a person who goes with a matrilocal residing bridegroom as a servant. 2. sb. who assists a matrilocal residing bridegroom during the marriage.

མང་ (maŋ) abbr. of མང་པོ་.

མང་བཀུར་རྒྱལ་པོ་ (maŋgur gyɛɛbo) shung. king of universal respect (a term of praise).

མང་སྐོལ་ (maŋgöö) tea and food given as offerings/ alms to monks during their collective prayers.

མང་ཁ་ཉུང་ཉན་ (maŋka ñuŋñɛn) the minority is subordinate to the majority, the minority must obey the majority.

མག་ག་བུར་ (mag gəbur) camphor (used in Tibetan medicine).

མང་གེ་མོ་ (maŋ gemo) so and so, this and that.

མང་འགྱེད་ (maŋgyeè) shung. abbr. of མང་ཇ་ and འགྱེད་.

མང་འགྱེད་ཐོ་སྒྲིག་ཆེན་མོ་ (maŋgyeè tōdrig cēmbo) shung. the list compiled before the start of Monlam in which all the donations/ alms are listed.

མང་ཆེ་བ་ (maŋcewa) the majority, the most part, the greatest part ¶ མང་ཆེ་བ་གཞུང་ཞབས་རེད་ The majority are government officials.

མང་ཇ་ (manja) 1. tea offered as alms to the monks in a monastery during collective prayer assemblies. 2. the first morning prayer assembly in some monasteries, e.g., Sera and Drepung.

མང་ཉུང་ (məŋñuŋ) quantity, amount, number; va.—གཏོང་ to do sth. unequally or disproportionately ¶ མི་མང་ཉུང་ལ་གཞིགས་ཏེ་ According to the number of people. ¶ ཕ་མས་ཕྲུ་གུར་རྫན་པ་མང་ཉུང་གཏོང་གི་ཡོད་པ་རེད་ The parents are giving gifts to the children unequally. [Lit. many and few].

མང་ཉུང་སྙོམས་པོ་ (məŋñuŋ ñōmbo) equal, even, proportionate.

མང་མཐར་ (maŋtar) at most ¶ ལས་ཀ་བྱེད་མཁན་མང་མཐར་མི་བརྒྱད་ལས་དགོས་ཀྱི་མི་འདུག At most, not more than eight people are needed as workers.

མང་མཐར་ཡང་ (maŋtaryaŋ) sm. མང་མཐར་.

མང་འཐེན་ཉུང་སྣོན་ (maŋten ñuŋnön) equalizing, taking from where there is a lot to compensate where there is little; va.—བྱེད་.

མང་དག (maŋdaà) very many.

མང་འདེབས་ཉུང་སྡུད་ (maŋdeb ñuŋdüü) uneconomical [Lit. plant a lot but harvest a little].

མང་དྲགས་ (maŋdraà) too much ¶ སློབ་གྲྭ་འདིར་སློབ་ཕྲུག་མང་དྲགས་བཞག There are too many students in this school.

མང་སྣ་ (maŋna) many, various kinds.

མང་སྣེ་ཉུང་གིས་མི་བཏན་ (maŋne ñuŋgi miden) being overpowered by superior numbers ¶ མང་སྣེ་ཉུང་གིས་མི་བཏན་པར་ང་ཚོ་དམག་ཕམ་པ་རེད་ We were overpowered by superior numbers and lost the war.

མང་པོ་ (maŋbo) many, a lot.

མང་པོ་སྣ་ཚོགས་ (maŋbo nādzɔ̀ɔ) many various things.

མང་པོས་བཀྱག་ན་མདུང་མ་ཡང་ (maŋböö gyāàna duŋmayaŋ) if many cooperate even the difficult tasks can be accomplished, many hands make light work [Lit. if many lift, even the beam becomes light].

མང་པོས་བཀྱག་པའི་ཡང་པོ་ (maŋböö gyāgbɛ yaŋbo) sm. མང་པོས་བཀྱག་ན་མདུང་མ་ཡང་.

མང་ཕྱོགས་ (maŋjɔ̀ɔ) the majority, the most ༑ མང་ཕྱོགས་ཀྱི་འདོད་པ་ལྟར་ According to the wishes of the majority.

མང་ཕྱོགས་ཀྱི་ཁ་ལ་ཉན་པ་ (maŋjɔ̀ɔgi kāla ñemba) following the wishes of the majority.

མང་ཕྱོགས་ལ་བསྟུན་པ་ (maŋjɔ̀ɔla dūmbə) sm. མང་ཕྱོགས་ཀྱི་ཁ་ལ་ཉན་པ་.

མང་འབྲི་ཉུང་སྣོན་ (maŋdri ñuŋnön) equalizing, balancing; va.—བྱེད་ [Lit. taking from that which has a lot and adding to that which has little].

མང་འབྲི་ཉུང་གསབ་ (maŋdri ñuŋsəb) sm. མང་འབྲི་ཉུང་སྣོན་.

མང་བ་ (maŋwa) more, majority ༑ བོད་པ་ལས་རྒྱ་མི་མང་བ་ཡོད་པ་རེད་ There are more Chinese than Tibetans.

མང་བའི་གྲོས་འཆམས་ (maŋwɛ trönjam) majority agreement.

མང་མིན་ཉུང་མིན་ (maŋmin ñuŋmin) neither too much nor too little.

མང་མོས་ (maŋmöö) agreeable to the majority, majority preference ༑ མང་མོས་ཀྱི་རྒྱལ་ཁ་ཆེན་པོ་ཐོབ་ They won a great majority victory.

མང་མོས་འདེམས་བསྒོ་ (maŋmöö demgo) sm. མང་མོས་འོས་འདེམས་.

མང་མོས་འོས་འདེམས་ (maŋmöö wööndem) majority election, majority selection, majority approval, elected by the majority ༑ མི་དྲུག་ལ་མང་མོས་འོས་འདེམས་ཀྱིས་བསྐོ་གཞག་བྱུང་བ་རེད་ The six people were appointed with majority approval.

མང་མྱོང་དགུ་ཐུག་ (maŋñoŋ guduù) experienced and able to differentiate between good and bad.

མང་མྱུར་ལེགས་བསྲི་ (maŋñur legsi) greater, faster, better and more economical (political slogan).

མང་ཙམ་ (maŋdzam) a little more ༑ དཀའ་ལས་མང་ཙམ་རྒྱག་རྒྱུ་ལས་འོས་གཞན་དག་མེད་ There is nothing else (to do) but to undergo a little more hardship.

མང་གཙོ་ (maŋdzo) sm. དམངས་གཙོ་.

མང་རྩིས་ཉུང་གཏོང་ (maŋdzii ñuŋdoŋ) budget liberally and spend sparingly (political slogan).

མང་རྩིས་མང་གཏོང་ (maŋdzii maŋdoŋ) budget and spend liberally.

མང་ཚིག (maŋdzii) plural words.

མང་ཚོགས་ (maŋdzɔ̀ɔ) the masses, the people.

མང་ཚོགས་ཀྱི་ཁེ་ཕན་ལ་དམིགས་པའི་ཚན་རིག་ཞིབ་འཇུག་ཁང་ (maŋdzɔ̀ɔgi kēbenla mīgbɛ tsɛ̄nrii shimjugaŋ) Center for Science in the Public Interest.

མང་ཚོགས་ཀྱི་ཁྲོད་ནས་བླངས་ཏེ་མང་ཚོགས་ཀྱི་ཁྲོད་དུ་སྤེལ་ (maŋdzɔ̀ɔgi trööne lāŋde maŋdzɔ̀ɔgi tröödu bēl) take from the masses and give back to the masses (political slogan).

མང་ཚོགས་ཀྱི་སྒྱུ་རྩལ་ཁང་ (maŋdzɔ̀ɔgi gyudzɛɛgaŋ) fine arts building of the masses.

མང་ཚོགས་ཀྱི་བདང་ཡིག (maŋdzɔ̀ɔgi dōŋyii) letters from the masses.

མང་ཚོགས་ཅན་ (maŋdzɔ̀ɔjɛn) the majority.

མང་ཚོགས་ལྟ་ཕྱོགས་ (maŋdzɔ̀ɔ dājɔ̀ɔ) the viewpoint of the masses.

མང་ཚོགས་དང་ཁ་བྲལ་ (maŋdzɔ̀ɔdaŋ kā trɛ̀ɛ) vi. to be alienated from the majority/ masses.

མང་ཚོགས་དང་བྲལ་ (maŋdzɔ̀ɔdaŋ trɛɛ) sm. མང་ཚོགས་དང་ཁ་བྲལ་.

མང་ཚོགས་དང་འབྲེལ་འདྲིས་ (maŋdzɔ̀ɔdaŋ drendrii) maintenance of close contact with the masses, mingling with the masses; va.—བྱེད་.

མང་ཚོགས་དང་འབྲེལ་བ་ (maŋdzɔ̀ɔdaŋ dreewa) connected with the masses, having a relationship with the masses.

མང་ཚོགས་སྣེ་ལེན་ས་ཚུགས་ (maŋdzɔ̀ɔ nēlen sədzuù) reception center for the masses.

མང་ཚོགས་ལམ་ཕྱོགས་ (maŋdzɔ̀ɔ lamjɔ̀ɔ) line/ policy made according to the masses, policy of the masses.

མང་ཚོགས་ལས་འགུལ་ (maŋdzɔ̀ɔ lɛngüü) a mass movement/ campaign, a campaign of the masses.

མང་ལེན་ཉུང་གསབ་ (maŋlen ñuŋsəb) to take from those who have a surplus and give to those who have a shortage (political slogan).

མང་རབས་ (maŋrəb) many, much.

མང་དུ་འགྲོ་ (maŋru dro) vi. to become more.

མང་དུ་གཏོང་ (maŋru dōŋ) va. to increase, to make more.

མང་ལས་མང་ཐོབ་ (maŋlɛɛ̀ maŋ tōb) more work, more pay/ wages (political slogan).

མང་ལོས་ (maŋlöö) how many, how much ༑ ཚོགས་འདུར་མི་མང་ལོས་སླེབས་འདུག་གམ་ How many people came to the meeting?

མང་སེམས་མཐུན་པ་ལྕགས་རི་ཡིན་ (maŋsem tūmbə jāāri yin) if people are united they are strong [Lit. unanimity of purpose is like an iron wall].

མང་སྲོང་མང་བཙན་ (maŋsoŋ maŋdzɛn) an ancient King of Tibet.

མངས་ (maŋ) vi. to be too much ༑ ཇ་འདི་ལ་ཅི་ནི་མངས་བཞག There is too much sugar in the tea.

མད་ (mɛɛ̀) sm. བདེན་.

མད་པ་ (mɛɛ̀ba) shung. sm. བདེན་པ་.

མད་པོ་ (mɛɛ̀bo) sm. བདེན་པོ་.

མན་ (mɛn) 1. sm. མན་ཆད་. 2. ch. noodles. 3. sm. མིན་.

མན་ཁན་ (mɛngɛn) a small drill.

མན་ངག (mɛnŋaà) oral religious teaching/ instruction; va.—གནང་.

མན་ངག་རྒྱུད་ (mɛnŋaà gyüü) one of the four basic Tibetan medical texts.

མན་ཅད་ (དུ་) (mɛnjɛɛ̀) sm. མན་ཆད་.

མན་ཆད་ (དུ་) (mɛnjɛɛ̀) 1. below, under, lower, before ༑ ལོ་ ༢༡ མན་ཆད་ Below 21 years (of age). ༑ རི་མཚམས་མན་ཆད་དུ་འབྲས་བཏབ་པ་རེད་ (They) planted rice below the mountain. ༑ བློན་པོ་མན་ཆད་ཀྱི་གཞུང་ཞབས་ Officials lower than the minister (in rank). 2. from this time on ༑ ཟླ་བ་འདི་མན་ཆད་ From this month on.

མན་ཅིལ་ (mɛncii) sm. མན་ཅིལ་ཙེ་.

མན་ཅིལ་ཙེ་ (mɛnciidzi) ch. a type of slender flat noodle.

མན་ཆོད་ (mɛnjöö) sm. མན་ཆད་.

མན་ཇུ་ (mɛnju) Manchu ༑ མན་ཇུ་གོང་མ་ The Manchu Emperors.

མན་དུ་ (mɛndu) sm. མན་ཆད་.

མན་ནེ་མུན་ནེ་ (mɛnne münne) mumbling; —ཤོད་ To speak in a mumbling manner.

མན་ཕྱི་ཀོ་ལོག (mɛnji kolɔ̀ɔ) sm. མིན་ཕྱི་ཀོ་ལོག.

མན་མུན་ (mɛnmün) abbr. of མན་ནེ་མུན་ནེ་.

མན་ཊ་ལ་ (mɛndala) a type of religious offering (mandala).

མན་ཊ་ལ་རྟེན་གསུམ་ (mɛndala) a type of religious offering (mandala) representing the body, speech and the mind.

མན་པའོ་ (mɛnbao) ch. bread.

མན་ཙི་ (mɛndzi) ch. a thin silk covering hanging over a thanka.

མན་ཞལ་ (mɛnshɛɛ) ch. padded winter shoes.

མན་ཡན་ (mɛnyɛn) abbr. of མན་ཆད་ and ཡན་ཆད་.

མན་ཡི་འི་ (men yii) ch. cotton-padded jacket/ overcoat.

མན་ལ་ (mɛnla) sm. མན་ཆད་.

མན་ཤེལ་ (mɛnshee) crystal, glass.

མན་ཤེལ་དཀར་པོ་ (mɛnshee gārbo) crystal.

མཎ་ཐང་ (mantaŋ) a temple in which a huge prayer

wheel is set.

མམ་ (mam) 1. interrogative particle for verbs ending in 'm' ¶ ཁོ་ག་རེ་བསམ་མམ་ What did he think? 2. "or" particle for words ending in 'm' ¶ ཤིང་སྒམ་མམ་ལྕགས་སྒམ་ Wooden box or iron box.

མའ་ཇང་ (majaŋ) mahjong.

མའ་ཧ་ (maha) ch. salmon.

མའ་ཧ་ཉ་ཆེན་པོ་ (maha ña cēmbo) ch.tib. Siberian Salmon.

མའི་བྱམས་སེམས་ (mɛ camsem) mother's maternal love.

མའོ་ (mao) 1. Mao. 2. the མའོ་ཙེ་ coin denomination.

མའོ་ཀྲུའུ་ཞི་ (mao trūshi) ch. Chairman Mao.

མའོ་ཀྲུའུ་ཞིའི་དྲན་གསོ་ཁང་ (mao trūshii trɛnsogaŋ) ch.tib. Chairman Mao's Memorial Hall.

མའོ་གུང་ (maoguŋ) Maoist communist.

མའོ་གོལ་ (maogöö) antiMao.

མའོ་དབྱི་ཀུང་སི་ (maoyi gūŋsi) ch. trade company.

མའོ་ཙག་ཕིང་ཙག་ (maodzaà piŋdzaà) ch.tib. loose change.

མའོ་ཙེ་ (maodze) ch. Chinese currency unit equal to one 10th of a yuan.

མའོ་ཙེ་དུང་ (maodzeduŋ) Mao Zedong.

མའོ་ཙེ་ཏུང་ (maodzeduŋ) sm. མའོ་ཙེ་དུང་.

མར་ (maa) 1. butter. 2. down, downward ¶ ང་ཚོ་རི་ནས་མར་བབས་དུས་ When we were descending from the mountain. 3. facing toward the main door (inside a house).

མར་ཀག་ (maagaà) a butter container made of bamboo/ wood.

མར་ཀོ་ (margo) sm. མར་ཀོག.

མར་ཀོག་ (margɔɔ̀) sm.* མར་སྐོགས་.

མར་ཀྲིན་ (mədrin) vegetable oil, crisco.

མར་དཀར་ (margar) white butter (made from the milk of sheep and goats).

མར་དཀྱིལ་ནས་སྤུ་འདོན་ (mar gyīinɛ bū dön) selecting sth. carefully, singling sth. out [Lit. plucking a hair from the middle of butter].

མར་སྐོགས་ (maagɔɔ̀) leather hide (usu. stomach skin) into which butter is packed and sewn tightly for storage or transport.

མར་སྐོགས་བརྡུང་མཁན་ (maagɔɔ̀ duŋñɛn) the worse student on an exam (the one who because he/she scored worst has no one lower to hit on the cheek so must hit an empty butter hide container [Lit. the one who hits the butter hide container].

མར་སྐྱུང་ (maagyuŋ) a knife-like tool that is poked into a large sewn skin bag of butter to pull out a sample of the butter's quality.

མར་སྒྲོག (maadrɔɔ̀) a lump of butter (e.g., those that appear from churning yogurt).

མར་སྒྲོག་ག (maadrɔɔ̀ga) sm. མར་སྒྲོག.

མར་སྒྲོག་ཕུལ་ (maadrɔɔ̀ pūū) va. to do sth. politely and skillfully to get out of a situation ¶ མི་དེ་ལ་ལས་ཀ་གསར་པ་ཞིག་ལས་ཁུངས་རྙིང་པ་སྤྲིང་པ་དེར་མར་སྒྲོག་ཕུལ་ནས་ཐོན་ཕྱིན་པ་རེད་ After getting a new job, that person very politely and skillfully make arrangements with his old office and departed. [Lit. to give a lump of butter].

མར་ཁུ་ (mərgu) melted butter; va.—བཞུ་ to melt butter; vi.—ཞུང་ས་; —ཁྱང་ས་ to coagulate (melted butter).

མར་ཁུ་མདོག (mərgu dɔɔ̀) color of melted butter.

མར་ཁུ་བྲུ་རིལ་ (mərgu cirii) a type of caramel candy.

མར་ཁུག (mərguù) leather pouch for keeping butter.

མར་ཁེ་སི་ (markese) Marx.

མར་ཁེ་སི་ལེ་ཉིན་རིང་ལུགས་ (margese lenñin riŋluù) Marxism-Leninism.

མར་ཁེ་སིའི་རིང་ལུགས་ (margese riŋluù) Marxism.

མར་གད་ (margɛɛ̀) emerald.

མར་གྱི་ཉིང་ཁུ་ (margi ñiŋgu) pure melted butter.

མར་གྱི་ཡས་བཞེད་ (margi yɛɛ̀seè) a swab of butter put on the rim of a tea or ཆང་ cup/ container.

མར་སྒོད་རིལ་ (mar dröörill) a lump/ ball of butter sewn tightly into the stomach skin of a sheep or goat for storage or transporting.

མར་འགྲིབ་ (mandrib) the waning/ declining phase of the moon.

མར་འགྲོ་ (maa dro) vi. to decline/ deteriorate/ degenerate ¶ དེང་སང་ལུང་པ་འདི་མར་འགྲོ་གི་ཡོད་པ་རེད་ These days this country is on the decline.

མཀད་ (margɛɛ̀) sm. མར་གད་.

མཀད་ (margɛɛ̀) sm. མར་གད་.

མར་སྒྱེད་ (margyeè) the back stone or the back iron leg of a tripod hearth/ stove.

མར་རྒྱན་ (margyen) butter decorations on torma.

མར་རྒྱུགས་ (maa gyuù) get out! go away! leave!

མར་སྒམ་ (marga) wooden or bamboo boxes used for keeping butter.

མར་ངོ་ (marŋo) the second half of the lunar month (the 16th to the 30th).

མར་ངོའི་བཅོ་ལྔ་ (marŋö jōŋa) the 30th day of a Tibetan month [Lit. the 15th day of the second half of the month].

མར་ངོའི་ཚེས་གཅིག (marŋö tsēējig) the 16th day of the Tibetan calendar [Lit. the first day of the second half of the month].

མར་ངོའི་ཟླ་བ་ (marŋö dawa) the 15 day period of the moon after the full moon.

མར་གཅོག (maa jōò) va. to reduce, to bring down ¶ ཚོང་ཟོག་གི་གོང་ཚད་མར་བཅག་ནས་བཙོང་པ་རེད་ (They) reduced the price of the commodities and sold them.

མར་ཆག (maa cāà) vi. to be/ get decreased, to go down ¶ ཡུལ་དེའི་མི་འབོར་མར་ཆག་གི་ཡོད་པ་རེད་ That country's population is decreasing.

མར་རྙིང་ (maañiŋ) old butter.

མར་སྙིགས་ (maañig) the residue/ leftover from melted butter.

མར་གཏུབ་ (mardub) a square implement used for cutting butter.

མར་གཏོར་ (mardɔɔ) torma made of butter.

མར་བཏོན་འོ་ཕྱེ་ (mardön woce) lowfat dry or powdered milk.

མར་ལྟང་ (maadaŋ) skin bag into which butter has been tightly sewn.

མར་ཐུར་ (maatur) sm. མར་གཏུབ་.

མར་དོ་ (mar to) a load of butter.

མར་གདར་མ་ (maa darma) brick-shaped square of fresh butter.

མར་འདོན་འཁྲུལ་ཆས་ (mardön trūūjɛɛ̀) machine for separating butter from milk.

མར་འདོན་ (mar dön) va. to extract/ separate butter from milk (by churning yogurt).

མར་འདྲ་ (mandra) artificial butter, crisco.

མར་དོག (mardɔɔ̀) a piece/ lump of butter.

མར་ལྡན་འོ་ཕྱེ་ (mardɛn woce) whole fat dry or powdered milk.

མར་ནག (marnaà) vegetable oil.

མར་ནང་ (maanaŋ) lower part of a place/ area/ village.

མར་ནས་ཡར་ (mənɛ yaa) from down there upwards/ up.

མར་སྣེ་ (maane) the edge, the end of sth. ¶ ཁོང་བཞུགས་གྲལ་མར་སྣེ་དེར་བསྡད་འདུག He is sitting at the very end of the row.

མར་པ་ (marba) a famous lama.

མར་པ་ལོ་ཙཱ་ཆོས་ཀྱི་བློ་གྲོས་ (marba lodza cōògi lōdröö) the famous lama Marpa.

མར་སྤགས་ (maabaà) a food dish consisting of tsamba mixed with butter.

མར་ཕབ་ (maa pāb) p. of མར་འབེབས་.

མར་ཕུད་ (maa būù) sm. the first symbolic offering of butter from newly made butter.

མར་ཕུད་འོ་ཛམ་ (maabūù wodzam) sm. མར་བཏོན་འོ་ཕྱེ་.

མར་ཕོགས་ (maajɔɔ̀) a salary/ wage/ payment made in butter.

མར་ཕྱུར་ (maacuu) butter and cheese, dairy products.

མར་བབས་ (maa bəb) p. of མར་འབབ་.

མར་བུར་ (maabur) abbr. of མར་ and བུ་རམ་.

མར་འབབ་ (maa bəb) sm. མར་འགྲོ་.

མར་འབེབས་ (maa beb) va. to lower, to demote, to degrade ¶ དར་ཅ་དེ་མར་ཕབ་པ་རེད་ They lowered the flag. ¶ ཁོའི་གོ་གནས་མར་ཕབ་པ་རེད་ (They) demoted him.

མར་མི་དྭགས་གསུ (mar mi tag sūm) abbr. Marpa, Milarepa and Dakpo Lhache.

མར་མུར་ (marmur) abbr. of མ་རི་མུ་རི་.

མར་མེ་ (marme) butter lamp (a religious offering); va.—འབུལ་ to make an offering of a butter lamp; va.—སྤར་ to light a butter lamp.

མར་མེ་སྡོང་འཁོལ་ (marme doŋköö) doing things on one's own initiative [Lit. wick of a butter lamp burning to the end).

མར་མེ་སྣུམ་ཟད་ བྱ་རྒན་སྒྲོ་ཟད་ (marme dzɛɛ̀) old, exhausted, used up [Lit. a butter lamp with the oil finished, an old bird with worn out feathers].

མར་མེ་མཛད་ (marme dzɛɛ̀) Dipamkara, a past Buddha.

མར་ཙམ་ (maadzam) a little below, a little ways back.

མར་ཙམ་ (mardzam) a little below/ away, a little way from here.

མར་ཙམ་དག (maadzam taga) a little way from here, a little way away.

མར་གཙག (mar dzāà) a traditional Tibetan medical treatment consisting of dipping a wool swab in melted butter and applying it on the body; va.—རྒྱག.

མར་བཙོས་ (mardzöö) dough cookie fried in melted butter.

མར་ཚིལ་ (mar tsīī) abbr. butter and fat.

མར་ཚེས་ (mardzeè) the second half of the month.

མར་འཛིན་ (maa dzin) va. to recognize/ regard as one's own mother.

མར་བརྫིས་ (mardzii) kneading butter.

མར་ཞག་གཅིག (marshaà jīì) enough butter for one bowl of Tsampa.

མར་ཞུན་ (marsün) melted butter.

མར་ཟན་ (marsɛn) a type of food consisting of tsampa, butter and brown sugar mixed together.

མར་ཟེའུ་ (marseu) a butter container.

མར་ཡས་ (maryɛɛ̀) sm. མར་གྱི་ཡས་བཟེད་.

མར་ལུགས་ (marluù) 1. the doctrine of མར་པ་. 2. the doctrine of Marx.

མར་ལེ་ (marle) abbr. Marx and Lenin.

མར་ལེ་རིང་ལུགས་ (marle riŋluù) Marxism and Leninism.

མར་ལེ་རིང་ལུགས་ཁྲིད་དཔྱོད་ཁང་ (marle riŋluù trīijüügaŋ) Marxism and Leninism. teaching and research/ study room.

མར་ལས་སྐྲ་ཕྱུང་ (μārlɛ būjuŋ) selecting sth. carefully, singling out [Lit. throwing out a strand of hair from (a piece of) butter].

མར་ཤེད་ (marsheè) leasing out animals in return for payment in butter.

མར་ཤེས་ (maasheè) maternal understanding/ instinct.

མར་སིལ་ (mārsii) small bits of butter.

མར་སོར་ (marso) a tool for making screws.

མར་སོས་པ་ (mār sööba) fresh butter.

མར་གསར་ (marsar) sm. མར་སོས་པ་.

མར་གསུར་ (marsur) the smell/ odor of burnt butter.

མལ་ (mɛɛ) bed ¶ མལ་དུ་ཉལ་ To sleep in bed. ¶ མལ་དུ་ལུས་ To be bedridden.

མལ་ཁང་ (mɛɛgaŋ) bedroom.

མལ་ཁྲི་ (mɛɛdri) a bed.

མལ་གུར་ (mɛɛgur) mosquito net (for a bed).

མལ་གོས་ (mɛɛgöö) 1. bedding. 2. bed clothes, sleepwear.

མལ་གྲོ་གུང་དཀར་ (mɛɛdro guŋgar) a district/ xian northeast of Lhasa.

མལ་སྒྲོམ་ (mɛɛdrom) bed frame.

མལ་ཅོ་ (mɛɛjo) sm. མལ་འཆའ་.

མལ་ཆ་ (mɛɛja) sm. མལ་གོས་.

མལ་ཆས་ (mɛɛjɛɛ̀) bedding.

མལ་འཆའ་ (mɛɛ cā) va. to make up a bed (e.g., to put down bedding).

མལ་སྟན་ (mɛɛ dɛ̄n) sm. མལ་གདན་.

མལ་གདན་ (mɛɛdɛn) mattress.

མལ་གདིང་ (mɛɛdiŋ) bed sheet.

མལ་འབུར་ (manjaa) infant.

མལ་མུལ་ (mɛɛmüü) tender, delicate.

མལ་རྩེ་ (mɛɛdze) sm. མེལ་ཚེ་.

མལ་གཞུག (mɛɛ shuù) at the end/ foot of a bed ¶ ཁོ་ངའི་མལ་གཞུག་ལ་ལངས་བསྡད་འདུག He is standing at the foot of my bed.

མལ་གཟན་ (mɛɛsɛn) bedding.

མལ་ཡོལ་ (mɛɛyöö) curtain dividing a bedroom.

མལ་གཡོག (mɛɛyoò) helping to prepare a bed; va.—བྱེད་.

མལ་ལུས་ (mɛɛlüü) bedridden.

མལ་ལེ་ (mɛɛle) eng. mile.

མལ་ཤག (mɛɛshaà) sm. ཉལ་ཁང་.

མལ་གཤོམ་ (mɛɛshom) making/ preparing a bed; va.—བྱེད་.

མལ་ས་ (mɛɛsa) bedroom, sleeping quarters.

མས་ (mɛɛ̀) the lower part, below, downward.

མས་ཀན་ (mɛɛ̀gɛn) lower jaw, mandible.

མས་ཁོད་ (mɛɛ̀göö) the bottom grindstone.

མས་འགེབས་ (mɛɛ̀geb) the way birds close their eyes where the bottom part of the eyelid covers the eye.

མས་འགེམས་ (mɛɛ̀gem) a protuding jaw/ bottom part of the mouth.

མས་འགྲམ་ (mɛɛ̀dram) lower jaw bone.

མས་སྒྲིལ་ (mɛɛ̀drii) a strip of thin round leather used for stitching the sole to the shoe.

མས་ཀྱིབས་ (mɛɛ̀jib) lower eyelid.

མས་མཆིག (mɛɛ̀jig) 1. the bottom wheel of a grindstone. 2. a mortar.

མས་མཆུ་ (mɛɛ̀ju) lower lip.

མས་ཉིན་ཀ་ (mɛɛ̀ ñiŋgə) three days ago.

མས་གདུན་ (mɛɛ̀dün) a mortar (for pulverizing).

མས་ཐིག (mɛɛ̀tig) a rope with a weight tied to it that is used on a fishing net to keep the net under water.

མས་མཐའ་ (mɛɛ̀ta) hem.

མས་གདན་ (mɛɛ̀dɛn) anvil.

མས་རྡོ་ (mɛɛ̀do) sm. མས་མཆིག.

མས་འཕུལ་ (mɛɛ̀büü) the prefix "མ་".

མས་མུལ་ (mɛɛ̀müü) soft, delicate.

མས་ཚེམས་ (mɛɛ̀dzem) h. of འོག་སོ་.

མས་འཛེགས་ (mɛɛ̀ dzeg) va. to climb from the bottom.

མས་རལ་ཚ་པོ་ (mɛɛ̀rɛɛ tsābo) sm. མ་རབས་.

མས་ལ་ (mɛɛ̀la) downward.

མས་ལེ་ (mɛɛ̀le) chin.

མས་སོ་ (mɛɛ̀so) lower teeth.

མཧཱ་ (maha) skt. great.

མཧཱ་ཀཱ་ལ་ (maha gāla) skt. Mahakala (a protective deity).

མི་ (mi) 1. person, human, man. 2. negative particle ¶ ཁོས་རྒྱ་སྐད་མི་ཤེས་ཤིང་ He does not know Chinese. 3. sm. མ་, 6. 4. agentive particle ¶ སློབ་གྲྭར་འགྲོ་མི་ཚོ་ The ones going to school. 5. (མི་ + vb. + དགུ་ or རྒྱུ་+ vb. + vb.) to overdo, to do to extreme (with active verbs this has a negative connotation) ¶ ངོ་ལོག་པས་མི་བྱེད་དགུ་བྱེད་བྱས་ཙང་མི་དམངས་ཀྱིས་ངོ་རྒོལ་བྱས་པ་རེད་ Because the rebels acted wantonly, the people opposed them.

མི་ཀི་རི་ (migiri) the 6th month of the Tibetan calendar.

མི་དཀར་ (migar) a white man, a caucasian.

མི་དཀར་ཞྭ་ནག (migar shanaà) accusing sb. who is innocent [Lit. white person black hat].

མི་དཀར་ལ་ཞྭ་ནག་དང་ཧ་དཀར་ལ་གདོང་ནག (migarla shanaà daŋ dāgarla doŋ naà) sm. མི་དཀར་ཞྭ་ནག.

མི་དཀར་ལ་ཞྭ་ནག་དང་ཧ་དཀར་ལ་སྦྲུབ་ནག (migarla shanaà daŋ dāgarla drəbnaà cuùbə) sm. མི་དཀར་ཞྭ་ནག.

མི་དཀར་སྲིད་གཞུང་ (migar sīishuŋ) apartheid government (in South Africa).

མི་ཀང་ (migaŋ) thigh bones (of humans).

མི་ཀང་གླིང་བུ་ (migaŋ liŋbu) human thigh bone trumpet.

མི་རྐྱང་ (migyaŋ) 1. a single person, a person alone ¶ མི་རྐྱང་ཉལ་ཁྲི་ A single bed. 2. slave.

མི་རྐྱང་ཧ་རྐྱང་ (migyaŋ dāgyaŋ) alone, a single person, a person alone ¶ ཁོས་བོད་ནས་མི་རྐྱང་ཧ་རྐྱང་བྱས་ནས་ཡོང་པ་རེད་ He came alone from Tibet.

མི་སྐད་ (migɛɛ̀) human speech/ language.

མི་སྐྱ་ (migya) layman.

མི་སྐྱིད་སར་མི་ཁྱུག ར་བདེ་སར་མི་སྡོད་ (mi gyiisaa migyaà ra desaa midöö) to be unsatisfied/ discontented [Lit. a person who does not stay put in a pleasurable place, goats not staying in a good place].

མི་བསྐྱོད་རྡོ་རྗེ་ (migyöö dɔɔje) 1. the statue of Akshobaya Buddha brought by Srongtsan Gampo's Nepalese Queen (in Ramoche). 2. the 8th Karmapa incarnation. 3. Akshobaya Buddha.

མི་བསྐྱོད་པ་ (migyööba) 1. sm. མི་བསྐྱོད་རྡོ་རྗེ་. 2. constant, unchanging, unshakable.

མི་ཁ་ (migə) gossip, rumors; va.—འཁྱེར་ to endure rumors/ gossip; va.—འགྲེམ་ to spread rumors/ gossip; vi.—ཐོག; —ཟུག to be talked of in a ill manner by others.

མི་ཁ་གདམ་ངན་ (migə dāmŋɛn) people gossiping and saying bad things (about one).

མི་ཁ་སྡང་པོ་ (migə daŋbo) sb. who is being negatively talked about a lot by people.

མི་ཁལ་ (mi kɛ̄ɛ) shung. abbr. people and carrying/ transport animals.

མི་ཁག (migaà) group of people ¶ ཚོགས་འདུའི་ཐོག་མི་ཁག་གཅིག་གིས་ During the meeting, one group of people.

མི་ཁུངས་ (miguŋ) shung. sm. མི་རྩ་མི་ཁུངས་.

མི་ཁུར་ (migur) a load that a person can carry.

མི་ཁེར་རྐྱང་ (mi kērgyaŋ) a person alone.

མི་ཁོག་འདྲེ་ཞུགས་ (mikɔɔ̀ dreshuù) inciting others to perform one's evil/ dirty work [Lit. a person possessed by a spirit].

མི་ཁོག་མིས་མི་ལོན་ རྡོ་ཁོག་ཆུས་མི་ལོན་ (mii kɔ̄gba mii mi lön do kōg cüü mi lön) sm. མིའི་ཁོག་པ་མིས་མི་ལོན་.

མི་ཁོག་མིས་མི་ལོན་ ཁྱི་ཁོག་རྒྱུག་པས་མི་ལོན་ (mii kɔ̄gba mii mi lön kyī kōg gyugbɛ mi lön) sm. མིའི་ཁོག་པ་མིས་མི་ལོན་.

མི་ཁོངས་ (migoŋ) one's lord, the person to whom one belongs ¶ ཁྱོད་སུའི་མི་ཁོངས་རེད་ Who is your lord?

མི་ཁོངས་བདག་ཡུལ་ (migoŋ dagyüü) one's lord, the person to whom one belongs.

མི་ཁོམ་ (migom) without leisure/ free time.

མི་ཁོམ་མི་ལྕོགས་ (migom mijɔɔ̀) having not enough time, having no time to do sth. ¶ ཁོང་ལ་ལས་ཀ་མང་པོ་ཡོད་ན་ཙང་མི་ཁོམ་མི་ལྕོགས་པ་ཆགས་པ་འདུག Because he had many tasks, he came to have no free time.

མི་ཁྱིམ་ (migyim) household, family.

མི་ཁྱུ་ (mikyu) a crowd of people.

མི་ཁྲག (midraà) human blood.

མི་ཁྲལ་ (midrɛɛ) sm. མི་ཐོགས་.

མི་འཁུར་ (migur) sm. མི་ཁུར་.

མི་འཁྱམ་ (migyam) sm. མི་འཁྱར་.

མི་འཁྱར་ (migyar) wanderer, vagrant, homeless person.

མི་འཁྱར་འཁྱོར་མེད་ (migyar jɔɔmeè) lumpen proletariat.

མི་ཁྱིམ་འགྲིམ་ (migo drim) sm. མི་མགོ་འགྲིམ་.

མི་འཁྲུགས་པ་ (midrugba) sm. མི་བསྐྱོད་པ་.

མི་འཁྲོལ་ (midröö) shung. release/ manumission from one's hereditary status as serf of a lord; va.—ཞུ་ to request release from serf status; va.—གནང་ to give release from serf status ¶ མོས་དཔོན་ཁོངས་གཞན་གྱི་མི་དང་ཆང་ས་མ་བརྒྱབ་གོང་དཔོན་ཁོངས་དེ་ར་མི་འཁྲོལ་ཞུས་པ་རེད་ Before she married a boy under another lord, she asked her lord for manumission of her serf status.

མི་གང་ (migaŋ) 1. a measurement unit running from the tip of the finger of one outstretched arms to the tip of the finger of the other outstretched arm. 2. who ¶ བསམ་འཆར་དེ་མི་གང་ཞིག་གིས་བཤད་པ་རེད་དམ་ Who made that criticism?

མི་མགོ་འགྲིམ་ (migo drim) va. to go as a bride or bridegroom.

མི་མགོ་གཅོད་ (migo jöö) va. to fulfill one's duty.

མི་མགོ་ཆོད་ (migo cöö) vi. to have one's duty get fulfilled.

མི་ཁྲ་ (midrə) shung. head tax in tt.

མི་གྲགས་ཅན་ (mi tragjɛn) famous/ eminent/ distinguished person.

མི་གྲངས་ (midraŋ) number of people, population size ¶ མི་གྲངས་ ༣༠༠༠ ཡོད་པ་རེད་ There are three thousand people.

མི་གྲངས་ཁྱབ་བཤེར་གཞུང་ལས་ཁང་ (midraŋ kyəsher shuŋlɛɛ̀gaŋ) census bureau.

མི་གྲངས་འདུ་ཚད་ (midraŋ dudzɛɛ̀) sm. མི་གྲངས་.

མི་གྲངས་འདུས་ཚད་ (midraŋ düüdzɛɛ̀) sm. མི་གྲངས་.

མི་གྲངས་ཞིབ་བཤེར་ལས་ཁང་ (midraŋ shibsher lɛɛ̀gaŋ) census bureau.

མི་གྲངས་ཡོངས་ཁྱབ་ཞིབ་བཤེར་ (midraŋ yoŋkyəb shibsher) sm. མི་གྲངས་ཡོངས་ཞིབ་.

མི་གྲངས་ཡོངས་ཞིབ་ (midraŋ yoŋshib) census.

མི་གྲངས་ལོང་ (midraŋ loŋ) vi. to reach a quota/ limit of people ¶ བཟོ་པའི་མི་གྲངས་ལོང་ཙང་མི་དགོས་ཀྱི་མི་འདུག Because they reached the limit of workers (they needed to hire) now they don't need people.

མི་གྲངས་ལོན་ (midraŋ lön) sm. མི་གྲངས་ལོང་.

མི་གྲིབ་ཤོར་ (midrib shɔɔ̄) vi. to become ill because of other's uncleanliness/ pollution.

མི་གྲོང་ (midroŋ) village.

མི་གླ་ (milə) a hired hand; va.—སྒྲིག to arrange to hire sb.; va.—རྒྱུག to go to work as a hired hand, to hire out for wages.

མི་གླ་བ་ (milaà) sm. མི་གླ་.

མི་དགའ་བ་ (migawə) not liking, disliking, averse, repugnant ¶ མི་དགའ་བའི་སྒྱུར་བཅོས་ A disliked reform.

མི་དགའ་རང་སྐྱིད་ (miga raŋgyii) oneself and others both happy.

མི་དགེ་བ་ (migewa) sinful, nonvirtuous ¶ མི་དགེ་བའི་སྲིད་བྱུས་ལག་ལེན་བསྟར་གྱི་ཡོད་པ་རེད་ (They) are implementing a sinful policy.

མི་དགེ་བ་བཅུ་ (migewa jū) ten nonvirtuous deeds (in Tibetan Buddhism).

མི་དགའ་ཞེ་འཛིན་ (miga shendzin) unhappy and hating, holding a grudge.

མི་དགའ་རང་སྐྱིད་ (miga raŋgyii) making others and onself happy.

མི་དགོས་ (migöö) not needing, being unnecessary.

མི་དགོས་དགུ་དགོས་ (migöö gugöö) wanting everything whether useful or not.

མི་དགོས་པ་བཟོ་ (migööba so) va. to eliminate a need or necessity ¶ ཉིན་ལྟར་ཆུ་ཚོད་བཅུའི་རིང་ལས་ཀ་བྱེད་མི་དགོས་པ་བཟོ་གི་རེད་ (They) will eliminate the need to work ten hours everyday.

མི་བགྲད་བགྲད་ (mi drɛ̄ɛdrɛɛ̀) a short, squat person.

མི་མགོ་ (mingo) 1. human head. 2. number of people.

མི་མགོ་ཆ་སྙོམས་ (mingo cāñom) equal number of people; va.—བྱེད་; —སྒོ་བགོ་ to divide into an equal number of people.

མི་མགོ་ཆ་ཤས་ (mingo cāshɛɛ̀) sm. མི་མགོ་ཆ་སྙོམས་.

མི་འགབ་ (migəb) unsuitable, inappropriate, unbecoming, not good ¶ ལས་ཀ་བྱེད་སྟངས་དེ་རིགས་མི་འགབ་པས་བྱེད་སྟངས་ལ་སྒྱུར་བཅོས་གཏོང་དགོས་ Because this kind of behavior is not good, you must reform that way of acting.

མི་འགལ་བར་ (migεεwar) not in opposition or contradiction to, not contrary to, not violating ¶ ཁོའི་བསམ་བློ་མི་འགལ་བར་བཤད་པ་རེད་ (They) spoke without contradicting his ideas.

མི་འགོ་ (mingo) leader, headman.

མི་གྱོད་ (migyöö) personal lawsuit/ law case.

མི་འགྱུ་དགུ་འགྱུ་ (migyu gugyu) sm. མི་དྲན་དགུ་དྲན་.

མི་འགྱུར་བ་ (mingyurwə) steady, constant, dependable, unchanging, consistent.

མི་འགྲིག་པ་ (mindrigbə) not right, not okay.

མི་འགྲིག་གཙོ་བཟུང་ (midrig dzōsuŋ) shung. making trouble; va.—བྱེད་.

མི་འགྲུལ་ (midrüü) human traffic ¶ འདི་ནས་ལྷ་ས་བར་མི་འགྲུལ་ཆེན་པོ་ཡོད་པ་རེད་ There is heavy human traffic between Lhasa and here.

མི་འགྲུལ་བཀག་བསྡོམས་ (midrüü gāgdom) travel restriction/ prohibition; va.—བྱེད་ ¶ རྒྱ་ནག་ནང་མི་འགྲུལ་བཀག་བསྡོམས་ཡོད་ཙང་ Because there are travel restrictions in China.

མི་འགྲོ་ (midro) 1. ones who are officially sent to go somewhere, a delegation ¶ རྒྱ་ནག་ཏུ་བོད་གཞུང་དོན་གཅོད་སྐུ་ཚབ་མི་འགྲོ་ཐེངས་གཉིས་པ་ The second group of the Tibetan Government's representatives going to China.

མི་འགྲོ་འོས་བབས་ (midro wööbəb) worthy, suitable, appropiate (for performing a task) ¶ ད་ལམ་གྲོས་མོལ་བྱེད་པར་མི་འགྲོ་འོས་བབ་ཚོད་པ་འགའ་ཤས་གཏོང་དགོས་ We have to send several suitable people to hold talks.

མི་རྒན་ (migεn) an old person.

མི་རྒས་ (migεὲ) sm. མི་རྒན་.

མི་རྒས་ན་ཡུལ་དང་ བྱ་རྒས་ན་ཤིང་དྲན་ (migεὲna yüüdaŋ cagεὲna sīŋ trεn) missing one's home, feeling homesick [Lit. when people grow old they miss their home and when birds grow old they miss their tree].

མི་རྒོད་ (migöö) 1. ape, gorilla. 2. yeti, abominable snowman. 3. strong, brave, courageous, tough.

མི་རྒོད་པོ་ (mi gööbo) 1. able, capable. 2. domineering. 3. strong, brave, courageous, tough. 4. surly, gruff (usu. for old men).

མི་རྒོད་ཁ་དྲག་ཅན་ (migöö kādraàjεn) sm. ཁ་དྲག་དང་ཤེད་ཅན་.

མི་རྒོད་ཁེར་འགྲོ་ རྟ་རྒོད་ཁེར་རྒྱུག (migöö kēr dro dāgöö kēr gyuù) brave [Lit. a brave man will go alone, a strong horse will run alone].

མི་རྒྱལ་བ་མེད་པ་ (mi gyεεwa meèba) invincible, undefeatable, ever victorious ¶ མི་རྒྱལ་བ་མེད་པའི་སྟོབས་ཤུགས་ལ་བརྟེན་ནས་ Based on invincible strength.

མི་རྒྱུ་ (migyu) people and wealth.

མི་རྒྱུ་གཉིས་སྟོངས་ (migyu ñiìdoŋ) exhausted/ empty of both people and wealth.

མི་རྒྱུ་གཉིས་ཞན་ (migyu ñiìshεn) short/ weak in both people/ manpower and wealth.

མི་རྒྱུ་མཉམ་ཆད་ (migyu ñamcεὲ) people and wealth simultaneously or jointly declining/ deteriorating.

མི་རྒྱུ་ཟ་བར་ལྕགས་ཀྱི་འགྲམ་པ་དགོས་ (migyu ñamcεὲ) it is extremely difficult to exploit or take from others [Lit. one needs an iron cheek to eat other's property/ wealth].

མི་རྒྱུག (migyuù) a foot race; va.—སློད་; —རྒྱུག to race (on foot).

མི་རྒྱུག་པ་ (migyuùbə) 1. a runner. 2. things that sell slowly ¶ མི་རྒྱུག་པའི་དུས Slack season (for sales).

མི་རྒྱུག་པའི་དུས་ (migyuùbə tüü) slack season, off-season.

མི་རྒྱུགས་ (migyuù) sm. མི་རྒྱུག.

མི་རྒྱུད་ (migyüù) 1. lineage, descendants ¶ རྒྱ་ནག་གོང་མའི་མི་རྒྱུད་ The lineage of the Emperors of China. 2. character or nature of a person ¶ ཁོ་མི་རྒྱུད་བཟང་པོ་འདུག He has a good character. 3. race.

མི་རྒྱུད་དཀར་པོ་ (migyüù gāābo) the caucasian/ white race.

མི་རྒྱུད་ཆད་ (migyüù cεὲ) sm. མི་རྒྱུད་བརླག.

མི་རྒྱུད་སྟོངས་ (migyüù dōŋ) vi. to die out (family) because of no offspring.

མི་རྒྱུད་ནག་པོ་ (migyüù nagbo) negro race.

མི་རྒྱུད་སྤེལ་ (migyüù bēl) vi. to reproduce/ increase one's descendants/ race (to have lots of children).

མི་རྒྱུད་བརླག (migyüù lāà) vi. to have one's family/ lineage disappear.

མི་རྒྱུད་ལེགས་སྒྱུར་རིག་པ་ (migyüù leggyur rigbə) eugenics.

མི་རྒྱུད་སེར་པོ་ (migyüù sērbo) the yellow/ mongoloid race.

མི་རྒྱུས་མེད་ (migyüü meè) 1. sm. མི་ཆ་ཞན་པ་. 2. a stranger, sb. one doesn't know.

མི་བརྒྱ་ཁ་གཅིག (migya kājig) everyone expressing the same view, united as one man, unanimous [Lit. a hundred people with one mouth].

མི་བརྒྱ་སེམས་གཅིག (migya sēmjig) united as one man [Lit. a hundred people with one mind].

མི་བརྒྱ་སེམས་གཅིག རྟ་བརྒྱ་འགྲོས་གཅིག (migya sēmjig dāgya dröòjig) unity, solidarity, oneness. [Lit. A hundred people with one mind, a hundred horses with the same gait].

མི་སྒེར་ (miger) private persons/ individuals ¶ ཚོགས་པ་དང་མི་སྒེར་ Organizations and private individuals.

མི་སྒེར་ལ་རྨོངས་དད་ (migerla mōŋdεὲ) cult of the individual, personality cult.

མི་སྒོ་སྒྲིམ་ (migo drim) va. to go to another family as bride or groom.

མི་སྒྱིད་ལ་ངན་པོ་ (mi gyiìlə ŋεmbo) a lazy person.

མི་སྒྲ་ (midra) 1. sm. མི་སྐད་. 2. the sound of people talking.

མི་ངན་ (miŋεn) evil or bad person.

མི་ངན་ཁ་མཐུན་ (miŋεn kātün) evil people collaborating together.

མི་ངན་ཁྲ་ཀུན་ (miŋεn trāgün) scoundrel, rogue.

མི་ངན་འཁྱམས་ཀྱི་ (miŋεn kāmgye) evil tramp, vagrant, wanderer.

མི་ངན་མཉམ་འགྲོགས་ (miŋεn ñamdrɔɔ̀) associating with/ assisting evil doers.

མི་ངན་མཉམ་ཚོགས་ (miŋεn ñamdzɔɔ̀) sm. ཁྲི་སྐྱོང་ངན་འབྲེལ་.

མི་ངན་བསྟེན་སྐོར་ (miŋεn tēngɔɔ) under the influence of evil persons, relying on evil people.

མི་ངན་དོན་ངན་ (miŋεn tönŋεn) evil people and evil deeds/ intentions.

མི་ངན་ནག་ཅན་ (miŋεn nagjεn) incorrigible criminal.

མི་ངན་པའི་གྲིབ་མ་ ཤིང་རློན་པའི་དུ་བ་ (miŋεnbε tribmə shīŋ lōmbε tuwə) the bad influence/ impact of bad people [Lit. shadow of evil people, smoke of wet wood].

མི་ངན་ཡོངས་གྲགས་ (miŋεn yondraà) infamous, notorious.

མི་ངན་རིགས་བཞི་ (miŋεŋ rigshi) the four types of bad people (landlords, rich peasants, counterrevolutionaries and bad elements).

མི་ངན་ལ་དབང་སྤྲད་ བསྟན་པ་འགོ་བཞིག (miŋεnla wāŋdrεὲ dēmba goshiì) giving authority to evil people will cause problems from the top.

མི་ངན་ལ་ཡ་བྱས་ན་ སྐྱག་པར་འཇུས་པ་དང་འདྲ་ (miŋεnla ya cεὲna gyāgbaa jüüba daŋ dra) if you deal with/ pay attention to evil people it will cause you trouble [Lit. if you deal with evil persons it is like touching shit].

མི་ངན་ལག་བྲེལ་ (miŋεn laŋdree) sm. ཁྲི་སྐྱོང་ངན་འབྲེལ་.

མི་ངན་ལང་ཤོར་གཏོང་ (miŋεn laŋshɔɔ) spoiling evil

people; va.—གཏོང་ to let sb. evil become spoiled in his evil ways.

མི་ངན་ལས་ངན་ (miŋɛn lɛ̀ɛŋɛn) evil people and evil deeds.

མི་ངལ་ (miŋɛɛ) a tired person.

མི་ངས་ (miŋɛ̀ɛ) 1. epidemic (among humans). 2. a sign/ omen of war.

མི་ངོ་ (miŋo) 1. sm. མི་ངོ་མ་. 2. number of persons.

མི་ངོ་མ་ (mi ŋoma) in person, the actual person ¶ མི་ངོ་མ་འགྲོ་དགོས་རེད་ The actual person has to go.

མི་ངོ་མ་རང་ (mi ŋoma raŋ) sm. མི་ངོ་མ་.

མི་ངོ་ཚ་མེད་ན་ཁྱི་རེད་ ཁྱི་ཐུང་མ་མེད་ན་འདྲེ་ཡིན་ (mi ŋodza meèna kyī reè kyī ŋāma meèna dre yin) outrageously incorrect behavior (or that one should act correctly/ properly) [Lit. a person without shame is like a dog, a dog without a tail is like a ghost].

མི་དངོས་དོན་དངོས་ (miŋuoò tönŋoò) the actual person and the actual/ true events.

མི་མངོན་ནུས་ཤུགས་ (miŋön nüùshuù) sm. མི་མངོན་པའི་ཤུགས་.

མི་མངོན་པ་ (miŋömba) covert, hidden, latent, invisible.

མི་མངོན་པའི་དུས་ (miŋömbɛ tüù) latent period/ stage ¶ ན་ཚ་འདི་མི་མངོན་པའི་དུས་ལ་ In the latent stage of this illness.

མི་མངོན་པའི་ནུས་ཤུགས་ (miŋömbɛ nüùshuù) unseen force, potentiality, latent capacity.

མི་མངོན་པའི་ཤུགས་ (miŋömbɛ shūg) latent/ potential strength.

མི་མངོན་དབྱིངས་ (miŋön yiŋ) poet. the sky.

མི་ཅལ་ཅལ་ (mi jɛ̄ɛjɛɛ) an easygoing/ hedonistic person.

མི་གཅིག་སྙིང་གཅིག (mijig ñīŋjig) best of friends.

མི་གཅིག་པ་ (mijigbə) different ¶ སྣ་མི་གཅིག་པ་ Different kinds.

མི་གཅིག་ལག་གཅིག (mijig lagjig) shung. alone, single handed ¶ ཁོ་པ་མི་གཅིག་ལག་གཅིག་ཏུ་ཐུག་གཞིས་གཞན་དག་ནས་རོ་ཡུལ་འགྱུར་དམིགས་མེད་པ་ Because I am alone, there is no hope of receiving help from others. [Lit. one person, one hand].

མི་གཅིག་སེམས་གཅིག (mijig sēmjig) best of friends.

མི་ལྩོག་མི་ཁ་ (mijoò miga) not having time (to do) ¶ མི་ལྩོག་མི་ཁ་བཞིན་དུ་ལས་ཀ་མང་པོ་ཁས་ལེན་རྒྱུ་མེད་ (If you) don't have time, (you) shouldn't take on many jobs.

མི་ལྩོགས་པ་ (mijogba) 1. sm. མི་ལྩོག་མི་ཁ་. 2. unable to do sth., inability.

མི་ཆ་ (mija) the amount of people ¶ མི་ཆ་མི་ལྡང་བའི་ཁ་སྐོན་བྱེད་དགོས་ (We) need to add more people because of the inadequate number of people.

མི་ཆ་མེད་ (mija meè) sm. མི་ཆ་ཞན་པ་.

མི་ཆ་ཞན་པ་ (mija shəmba) poor in people and resources.

མི་ཆད་རྟ་ཆད་ (mijɛɛ̀ dā jɛ̄ɛ̀) tired, exhausted [Lit. an exhausted man and an exhausted horse].

མི་ཆད་རྟ་དུབ་ (mijɛɛ̀ dādub) sm. མི་ཆད་རྟ་ཆད་.

མི་ཆུ་ལ་དབྱུགས་པར་ རང་ཆུའི་ཕྱེད་ཀ་ (mi cūlə yūùbar raŋ cūū cēēga) accusing sb. means you have to get involved and risk getting harmed [Lit. to throw a person in the water one must also get half wet].

མི་ཆུ་ལ་གཡུགས་པར་རང་ཆུའི་ཕྱེད་ཀ་ (mi cūlə yūùbar raŋ cūū cēēga) sm. མི་ཆུ་ལ་དབྱུགས་པར་རང་ཆུའི་ཕྱེད་ཀ་.

མི་ཆུང་ (mijuŋ) a very short person, a dwarf.

མི་ཆུང་བ་ (mi cūŋwa) 1. not a little. 2. a younger person. 3. a short person, a dwarf.

མི་ཆུང་ཡང་གློ་སྙིང་ཚང་ (mi cūŋyaŋ lō ñīŋdzaŋ) even though small it is complete [Lit. even though small, the heart and lungs are complete].

མི་ཆུང་སེམས་སྐྱིད་ (mijuŋ sēmgyeè) a small person having big ideas.

མི་ཆུང་བསམ་བཟང་ (mijuŋ sāmsaŋ) sm. མི་ཆུང་སེམས་སྐྱིད་.

མི་ཆུང་བསམ་ཤེས་ (mijuŋ sāmsheè) sm. མི་ཆུང་སེམས་སྐྱིད་.

མི་ཆེན་ (mijen) 1. important people, people with high rank/ status ¶ ཡུལ་གྱི་མི་ཆེན་ The important people of the area. 2. a tall person.

མི་ཆེན་པོ་ (mi cēmbo) sm. མི་ཆེན་.

མི་ཆོས་ (mijöö) 1. worldly affairs, secular etiquette/ ethics/ morals. 2. marriage arrangements.

མི་ཆོས་ཀྱི་ཀུན་སྤྱོད་ (mijöögi gūnjöö) secular ethics, secular moral principles.

མི་ཆོས་འཕེར་པོ་ (mijöö pērbo) a person who is capable in worldly affairs.

མི་ཆོས་མ་མཁས་པོ་ (mijööma kɛ̄ɛbo) sm. མི་ཆོས་འཕེར་པོ་.

མི་ཆོས་གཙང་བཅུ་དྲུག (mi cōōdzaŋ jūdruù) the 16 virtuous ethical principles laid down by King Songtsan Gampo.

མི་ཆོས་རིག་པ་ (mijöö rigbə) ethics.

མི་ཆོས་རིང་ལུགས་ (mijöö riŋluù) humanitarianism.

མི་མཆོག (mijɔ̀ɔ) 1. king. 2. Buddha. 3. person of the highest quality.

མི་འཆད་པ་ (micɛɛ̀ba) 1. continuously. 2. va. to not talk, to remain silent.

མི་འཆོལ་པོ་འདོད་མེད་ (mijööbo wöömeè) stupid, ignorant, idiotic.

མི་ཇག (mijaà) kidnapping (a person); va.—རྒྱག.

མི་ཇགས་ (mijaà) sm. མི་འཕྲོགས་.

མི་འཇིད་ (mijeè) unafraid, unfrightened.

མི་མཇེད་འཇིགས་རྟེན་ (mijeè jigden) the world.

མི་མཇེད་བདག་པོ་ (mijeè dagbo) 1. Sakyamuni. 2. Brahma.

མི་འཇམ་ཁྱི་འཇམ་ (mijam kyījam) late evening [Lit. men and dogs are quiet/ silent].

མི་འཇམ་པོས་བདུལ་ རང་རྩུབ་མོས་བདུལ་ (mi jamböö dūū raŋ dzūbböö dūū) sm. མི་འཇམ་པོས་འདུལ་རང་རྩུབ་པོས་འདུལ་.

མི་འཇམ་པོས་འདུལ་ རང་རྩུབ་པོས་འདུལ་ (mi jamböö düü raŋ dzūbböö düü) one should use gentle/ mild means to achieve one's ends [Lit. one should treat others with gentleness and oneself with harshness].

མི་འཇིག་ཡུན་གནས་ (mijig yünnɛɛ̀) existing through the ages for all times, everlasting, eternal.

མི་འཛོན་འཛོན་མདོག (mijön jöndɔɔ̀) pretending to be able to do sth. when one is not.

མི་འཛོན་འཛོན་མདོག སྡོང་ལོ་ལང་འཕྱར་ (mijön jöndɔɔ̀ doŋlo laŋjar) disgracing oneself by trying to do sth. beyond one's ability; va.—བྱེད་.

མི་འཛོན་གསུམ་རྒྱུག (mijön sūmgyaà) sm. མི་འཛོན་འཛོན་མདོག.

མི་རྗེ་ (mije) 1. title for a person of high position. e.g., His Excellency. 2. མི་མཆོག.

མི་རྗེ་མངའ་བདག་རིན་པོ་ཆེ་ (mije ŋadaà rimboce) shung. H.M. the King of Bhutan.

མི་བརྗེ་ (mije) sm. མི་བརྗེས་.

མི་བརྗེས་ (mijeè) shung. exchanging serfs/ servants between two lords; va.—རྒྱག.

མི་ཉག (miñaà) name of an area in Kham.

མི་ཉན་པ་ལ་ཁ་ཏ་བྱེད་པ་ལས་ ཀོ་བ་སྐམ་པོ་ལག་པས་མཉེད་པ་དགའ་ (miñɛnbala kāda cēēbalɛ gɔ̄ɔ gāmbo lagbɛ ñeba ga) it is useless to give advice to people with a closed mind [Lit. it is better to tan dry leather by hand than to give advice to sb. who doesn't listen].

མི་ཉམས་ (miñam) sm. མ་ཉམས་པ་.

མི་ཉམས་གོང་འཕེལ་ (miñing) developing, improving and not letting decline.

མི་ཉམས་རྒྱུན་འཛིན་ (miñam gyündzin) maintaining sth. without decline, keeping sth. up, preserving; va.—བྱེད་.

མི་ཉམས་ཆུང་ཅན་ (miñam cūnjɛn) sm. མི་གཉོམ་ཆུང་.

མི་ཉམས་ཚོད་ (miñam cöö) vi. to know the character of a person.

མི་ཉམས་ཡུན་གནས་ (miñam yünnɛɛ̀) preserving for

a long time, everlasting, eternal ¶ མི་ཉམས་ཡུན་གནས་ཀྱི་བདེ་སྐྱིད་ Everlasting happiness.

མི་ཉལ་ཁྱི་ཉལ་ (mi ñɛɛ kyi ñɛɛ) late in the evening [Lit. when people and dogs go to sleep].

མི་ཉུང་སྟོབས་ཞན་ (miñuŋ dōnshɛn) few people strong and weak.

མི་ཉུང་བ་ (miñuŋwɔ) more than a few, some, quite a few ¶ ཞིང་པ་ཕོ་གཞོན་མོ་གཞོན་མི་ཉུང་བ་ཞིག Quite a few young male and female farmers.

མི་ཉེ་མི་རྒྱང་ (miñe migyaŋ) neither too close nor too distant (usu. of relationships).

མི་ཉོབ་དོ་ (mi ñobdo) lazy, indolent (person).

མི་གཉིས་དབར་ལ་རྫ་ཆག (miñambarla dza cāà) too many cooks spoil the broth [Lit. between two people the pot breaks].

མི་གཉོམ་ཆུང་ (mi ñomjuŋ) a humble person.

མི་མཉམ་མཉམ་པ་མེད་པ་ (miñam ñamba meèba) unparalleled.

མི་མཉམ་པ་ (mi ñamba) 1. different, not the same. 2. the Buddha.

མི་མཉམ་པའི་རྟགས་ (miñambɛ dāà) unequal sign.

མི་རྙིང་པ་ཡག གོས་གསར་པ་ཡག (mi ñiŋbə yaà göö sārba yaà) a saying conveying the value of old friends [Lit. old friends are better, new clothes are better.

མི་གཏའ་ (mida) hostage; va.—ཉར་ to hold/ keep as a hostage; va.—གློད་ to release a hostage.

མི་གཏེ་ (mide) sm. མི་གཏའ་.

མི་རྟག་གྱ་གྱུ་ (midaà gyagyu) impermanent.

མི་རྟག་པ་ (midagba) impermanent.

མི་ལྟད་ (midɛɛ̀) looking at people (congregated or returning from a ceremony) as a form of entertainment (to see what they are wearing; etc.); va.—ལྟ་.

མི་ལྟོགས་ཁོག་པར་མེ་འབར་ན་ རྒྱལ་པོའི་ཁྲིམས་ལ་ཡ་མི་ང་ (midɔg kɔ̄ɔbar mebarna gyɛɛbö trimla ya miŋa) when one is desperate one will do anything [Lit. when the fire of hunger burns in the stomach there is no fear in disobeying the king].

མི་ལྟོགས་པར་ཁྱིས་སྐྱུག་པའི་རེ་བ་ (mi dɔ̄ɔbar kyii gyūgbɛ rewa) looking for sth. from the wrong source, hoping for the wrong thing [Lit. a hungry man hoping for a dog's vomit].

མི་སྟོ་ (mido) it doesn't matter, its okay, never mind.

མི་སྟོང་ (midoŋ) shung. indemnity/ compensation for killing sb.; va.—འཇལ་ to pay murder compensation.

མི་སྟོབས་ཅན་ (mi dōbjen) a strong/ well-built person.

མི་བརྟན་པ་ (midɛmba) unstable, unsteady ¶ མི་བརྟན་པའི་འཚོ་བ་ Unstable livelihood.

མི་བརྟེན་ཐབས་མེད་ (miden tābmeè) no choice but to rely/ depend on ¶ཁོང་ལ་མི་བརྟེན་ཐབས་མེད་བྱུང་བ་རེད་ (We) had no choice but to rely on him.

མི་བསྟུན་ལས་བཀོད་ (midün lɛɛ̀göö) creating a job to accommodate a person; va.—བྱེད་; —རྒྱག.

མི་བསྟོད་དགུ་བསྟོད་ (midöö gudöö) extreme flattery, praising too much.

མི་ཐ་སྙད་གསུམ་ལྡན་ (mi tāñɛɛ̀ sūmdɛn) the 3 qualities of a normal person: 1. ability to talk. 2. ability to comprehend/ understand. 3. sanity.

མི་ཐ་གསུམ་བགྲོས་ན་མི་རབ་ཡིན་ (mi tāsum drööna mirəb yin) more of less quantity is equivalent to less of higher quality [Lit. if three poorer people go it is (like) one superior person].

མི་ཐབས་སྡུག (mi tābduù) an inferior person.

མི་ཐེར་ (miter) a man-drawn cart.

མི་ཐོག (midɔɔ̀) generation ¶ མི་ཐོག་ལྔ་པ་ The 5th generation.

མི་ཐོག་གཅིག་པ་ (midɔɔ̀ jigbə) the same generation.

མི་ཐོག་ཆུང་གྲས་ (midɔɔ̀ cūŋdrɛɛ̀) the younger generation.

མི་ཐོག་རྗེས་ (midɔɔ̀ jeè) the next generation, the future generation.

མི་ཐོག་ན་རིམ་ (midɔɔ̀ nərim) from generation to generation, one generation after another.

མི་ཐོག་ནས་མི་ཐོག (midɔɔ̀nɛ midɔɔ̀) sm. མི་ཐོག་ན་རིམ་.

མི་ཐོག་ནས་མི་ཐོག་བར་ (midɔɔ̀nɛ midɔɔ̀bar) sm. མི་ཐོག་ན་རིམ་.

མི་ཐོམ་ཀྱེ་ (mi tōmgye) a bewildered/ confused person.

མི་མཐུན་ཀྱུད་ཚོགས་ (midün güüdzɔɔ̀) shung. decline ¶ རྒྱལ་ཁམས་རྣམས་སུ་མི་མཐུན་ཀྱུད་ཚོགས་ཞི་བ་ Overcoming the decline in the areas in the county.

མི་མཐུན་རྟ་གཡག་མགོ་སྦྲེལ་ (midün dāyaà godree) shung. putting two opposite things together ¶ ཚང་མའི་ཡིད་ཡུལ་དུ་ཡང་མི་མཐུན་རྟ་གཡག་མགོ་སྦྲེལ་དུ་བཞག་འདུའི་བློ་འཁག་མི་བཟོད་པ་ All of the people are afraid of putting two opposite things together like tying the head of a horse together with that of a yak. [Lit. tying the head of a horse and yak together].

མི་མཐུན་ནང་འཐབ་ (midün naŋdəb) disharmony and internal conflict/ strife.

མི་མཐུན་པ་ (midünbə) not in harmony, incompatible, contrary to, contradictory, in disagreement/ conflict ¶ ལས་ཀ་འདི་མི་དམངས་ཀྱི་བློ་དང་མི་མཐུན་པ་ཞིག་རེད་ This action is contrary to the people's wishes. ¶ ཚོགས་མི་ཚོ་གནད་དོན་འདིའི་སྐོར་མི་མཐུན་པ་བྱུང་བ་རེད་ The members had a disagreement on this issue. ¶ ཡུལ་དེའི་ཤར་ནུབ་ཀྱི་མི་རིགས་དབར་མི་མཐུན་པ་ཡོང་གི་ཡོད་པ་རེད་ The ethnic groups of the eastern and western parts of that country are in conflict.

མི་མཐུན་པའི་ཕྱོགས་ (midünbɛ cɔɔ̀) the reverse/ opposite ¶ སློབ་ཕྲུག་ཚོས་དགེ་རྒན་གྱི་སློབ་བྱ་བཀྱབ་པར་མི་མཐུན་པའི་ཕྱོགས་ཀྱི་གོ་བ་བླངས་པ་རེད་ The students understood the reverse of what the teacher advised.

མི་མཐུན་པའི་རླུང་ (midümbɛ lūŋ) adverse wind.

མི་མཐོང་རྒུ་མཐོང་ (midoŋ gutoŋ) seeing many bad events/ disasters/ etc.

མི་མཐོང་ཆ་འཛོག (midoŋ cānjoò) sm. མཐོང་ཆེན་.

མི་འཐུས་ (mi tüü) vi. to be forbidden, to be not permitted/ allowed.

མི་འཐེང་ (mideŋ) crippled in the leg (for people).

མི་མཐོ་ (mito) low.

མི་འཐད་པ་ (mi tɛɛ̀ba) not good ¶ ལས་ཀ་འདི་འདྲ་བྱས་ན་མི་ཐད་པར་སྒྱུར་བཅོས་གཏོང་དགོས་ It is not good if you do like that so you should make changes.

མི་འཐེན་འཁོར་ལོ་ (miden kɔ̄ɔlo) a person-drawn cart/ rickshaw.

མི་དང་མི་འདྲ་ན་མི་གཡོག་སུ་ཡིས་རྒྱུགས་ (midaŋ mindrana mi yɔɔ̀ sū yii gyuù) because of different capabilities some people become leaders and others servants [Lit. if there is no difference between people, who would go as servants].

མི་དང་རང་ (midaŋ raŋ) oneself and others.

མི་དར་ (midar) a person in the prime of his life, a young adult.

མི་དལ་པོ་ (mi dɛɛbo) 1. a person who has a leisurely life style (i.e., who doesn't work hard). 2. a tolerant/ easygoing person.

མི་དུག (miduù) "people sickness" caused by being among too many people (usu. involves a headache); vi.—རྒྱག ¶ འབྲོག་པ་མི་མང་པོའི་དཀྱིལ་ལ་སླེབས་དུས་མི་དུག་རྒྱག་གི་ཡོད་པ་རེད་ When nomads arrive among many people they get ill.

མི་དུད་ (midüü) sm. དུད་ཚང་.

མི་དོ་ (mido) unable to compete/ handle/ challenge/ contest, unrivaled, unequaled ¶ རང་གིས་མི་དོ་བའི་མི་དང་ཤུགས་ཚད་རྒྱ་མེད་ One shouldn't compete in strength with sb. with whom one can't handle.

མི་དོ་བ་ (midowa) unrivaled, unequaled. ¶ མི་དོ་བ་རྒྱལ་ཁ་ Unrivaled victory.

མི་དོན་ (midön) human affairs, personnel affairs ¶

མི་དོན་ལས་ཁུངས་ Personnel office.
མི་དོན་ཀུའུ་ (midön kūwu) tib.ch. personnel section.
མི་དོན་ཁའོ་ (midön kāwo) tib.ch. personnel section.
མི་དོན་ཁང་ (midöngaŋ) personnel office.
མི་དོན་ཁྲུའུ་ (midöngaŋ) tib.ch. personnel division.
མི་དོན་གྱི་འབྲེལ་བ་ (midöngi dreewa) personnel relations.
མི་དོན་ཅུའུ་ (midön jū) tib.ch. personnel bureau.
མི་དོན་སྡེ་ཚན་ (midön dedzɛn) personnel office.
མི་དོན་ཡིག་ཚག (midön yigdzaà) personal file/ dossier.
མི་དོན་ལམ་ལུགས་ (midön lamluù) system of human affairs.
མི་དོན་ལས་ཁུངས་ (midön lɛègun) sm. མི་དོན་སྡེ་ཚན་.
མི་དྲག (midraà) 1. shung. the highest stratum within the aristocracy. 2. the gentry. 3. an excellent person.
མི་དྲག་གྲལ་རིམ་ (midraà trɛɛrim) the aristrocracy, the gentry, the noble class.
མི་དྲག་ངན་པ་ (midraà ŋɛmba) the bad gentry, the exploiting aristocracy.
མི་དྲག་གཤེད་མ་ (midraà shēēba) exploitative landlord, despotic gentry.
མི་དྲག་བསམ་ཤེས་ཅན་ (midraà sāmsheèjɛn) enlightened gentry.
མི་དྲན་དགུ་དྲན་ (midrɛn gudrɛn) sm. མི་བསམ་དགུ་བསམ་.
མི་དྲན་དགུ་དྲན་ཚ་པོ་ (midrɛn gudrɛn tsābo) sm. མི་བསམ་དགུ་བསམ་.
མི་དྲེད་ (midrɛɛ̀) a type of brown bear.
མི་གདོང་སྤྱང་སེམས་ (midoŋ jaŋsem) person who appears nice on the surface but is really is cruel/ evil [Lit. human face, wolf's mind].
མི་བདག (midaà) 1. shung. lord, serf owner ། ངའི་མི་བདག་རྡོ་རིང་རེད་ My lord is Doring (the Doring family). 2. king.
མི་བདག་བདག་བཟུང་ (midaà dagsuŋ) shung. taking possession of things that do not belong to oneself.
མི་བདེ་བ་ (midewa) 1. uncomfortable, uneasy ། ཁྱེད་རང་གི་ཞབས་ལྷམ་ང་ལ་མི་བདེ་བ་མི་འདུག Your shoes are not uncomfortable for me. 2. ill, unhealthy ། ང་རྒྱ་གར་ནས་འབྱོར་ནས་མི་བདེ་བ་མ་བྱུང་ I didn't get ill after arriving from India.
མི་བདེན་ (miden) untrue, false.
མི་བདེན་བདེན་ཚུལ་ (miden dendzüü) pretending sth. is true when it is not.
མི་བདེན་བརྫུན་སྒྲིག (miden dzündrig) lying, deceiving.
མི་འདང་ས་ (midaŋsa) not enough of sth. 2. shortcomings, deficiencies ། ལས་ཀའི་ཐོག་མི་འདང་ས་གང་ཡོད་ཕན་ཚུན་གོད་རེས་བྱེད་དགོས་ You must discuss back and forth the shortcomings regarding the work.
མི་གདའ་ (mida) sm. མི་འདུག.
མི་འདའ་ (minda) not to exceed/ transcend/ surpass.
མི་འདུག (minduù) does not exist, is not there, does not have.
མི་འདོད་ (mindöö) not desiring sth.
མི་འདོད་པ་བྱེད་ (mindööba cee) va. to not like/ desire ། ཁོས་སློབ་སྦྱོང་ལ་མི་འདོད་པ་བྱེད་ཀྱི་འདུག He doesn't like to study.
མི་འདོད་པའི་རྣམ་འགྱུར་ (mindööbɛ nāmgyur) an expression or appearance of disliking/ unwillingness/ reluctance; va.—སྟོན་ to show reluctance/ unwillingness/ disliking.
མི་འདོད་བཞིན་དུ་ (mindöö shindu) not desiring sth., unwilling, against one's will, reluctant ། མི་འདོད་བཞིན་དུ་དམག་མིར་བཙུགས་པ་རེད་ (They) conscripted (him) into the army against his will.
མི་འདྲ་ (mindra) sm. མི་འདྲ་བ་.
མི་འདྲ་བ་ (mindrawa) different, unlike, unusual ། ཡུལ་དེའི་ནང་མི་རིགས་མི་འདྲ་བ་མང་པོ་ཡོད་ There are many different nationalities in this country.
མི་འདྲོག་ཁྱི་འདྲོག (mi drɔɔ̀ kyī drɔɔ̀) all people getting frightened [Lit. people getting frightened, dogs getting frightened].
མི་ལྡད་ཁྱུར་མིད་ (midɛɛ̀ kyūrmeè) lapping up information without digesting it; doing sth. without investigating it carefully [Lit. swallowing without chewing].
མི་རྡུང་རང་ངུས་ (miduŋ raŋŋüü) stupid behavior [Lit. hit sb. and cry oneself].
མི་སྡར་ (midar) a coward.
མི་སྡེ་ (mide) 1. laymen. 2. village.
མི་སྡེའི་འཇའ་མོ་ཆེ་ (midee jamoce) shung. official in charge of postal station.
མི་སྡོད་འཇིག་རྟེན་འཕུར་གྲུ་ (midöö jigdɛn pūrdru) manned spaceship.
མི་སྡོད་སར་རང་བཞག (midöösar raŋshaà) sm. མི་སར་རང་བཞག.
མི་ནག (minaà) 1. layman. 2. negro.
མི་ནག་སྐྱ་བོ་ (minaà gyāwo) layman.
མི་ནག་ཅན་ (minagjɛn) a criminal.
མི་ནག་པོ་ (mi nagbo) negro [Lit. black person], negroid race.
མི་ནག་པོའི་སྲིད་དབང་ (mi nagbö siiwaŋ) black power.
མི་ནག་མེད་ལ་ནག རྡོ་ཟུར་མེད་ལ་ཟུར་ (mi nag meèla nag do sur meèla sur) accusing unjustly, blaming the innocent [Lit. (saying) a person who is not black is black and a stone that has no corner has a corner].
མི་ནུབ་ཡུན་གནས་ (minub yünnɛɛ̀) sm. མི་ཉམས་ཡུན་གནས་.
མི་ནོར་ཕྱུགས་གསུམ་ (minɔɔ cūgsum) the three: people, wealth and livestock.
མི་ནོར་བ་ (minɔɔwa) unerring, unmistaken.
མི་གནས་པ་ (minɛɛ̀ba) changeable, unstable, unsettled.
མི་གནོད་པ་ (minööba) harmless, innocuous.
མི་སྣ་ (minə) person, people, personnel, members ། ཀྲུང་གོ་གསར་པའི་སྨན་བཅོས་མི་སྣ་ The medical personnel of the new China.
མི་སྣ་ཀྲུང་གྲས་ (minə cūŋdrɛɛ) common people.
མི་སྣ་སྣེ་ཁྲིད་ (minə nēdrii) leader or guide of people/ group.
མི་སྣ་འཛོམས་པོ་ (minə dzombo) diverse kinds of people.
མི་སྣ་ཉུང་འཕྲི་ (minə ñuŋdri) reducing/ cutting personnel; va.—བྱེད་.
མི་སྣང་བ་ (minaŋwa) invisible.
མི་སྣེ་ (mine) shung. sm. མི་སྣ་.
མི་དཔང་ (mibaŋ) witness.
མི་དཔུང་ (mibuŋ) a group/ mass/ force of people.
མི་དཔུང་གྲ་རྒྱས་ (mibuŋ dragyɛɛ̀) shung. increased manpower.
མི་དཔུང་དགྲ་སློབས་ (mibuŋ dradeb) mass riot, turmoil/ turbulence involving many people.
མི་དཔོན་ (mibön) shung. traditional "mayor" of Lhasa (head of སྣང་རྩེ་ཤག).
མི་ལྤགས་ (mibaà) human skin.
མི་ལྤགས་དྲི་བདུམས་ (mibaà dredum) a dangerous person, a wolf in sheep's skin [Lit. a ghost wearing human skin].
མི་ལྤགས་བཤུ་ཁྲིགས་ (mibaà shūdeg) a stand on which human skin is skinned.
མི་སྤུས་ (mibüü) the quality of people.
མི་སྤུས་སྤུན་ཞུ་ (mibüü jɛ̄nshu) shung. sm. མི་བབ་སྤུན་ཞུ་.
མི་སྤུས་དག་པོ་ (mi büü tagbo) a well-groomed/ good-looking/ excellent person.
མི་སྤྱང་ (mijaŋ) a killer, a murdered [Lit. man wolf].
མི་སྤྱི་ (miji) shung. abbr. of མི་སེར་སྤྱི་.
མི་སྤྱོད་ (mijöö) human behavior.
མི་སྤྱོད་ལས་འདས་པ་ (mijööle dɛ̄ɛ̀ba) inhuman ། ཁྲིམས་མི་སྤྱོད་ལས་འདས་པ་བཅད་པ་རེད་ Inhuman sentences were meted out.
མི་སྤྲེ་ (midrə) 1. anthropoids. 2. ape man.
མི་ཕན་མི་ཐོགས་དེ་སྟོན་ཁ་ན་ ཕྱུགས་ཕན་མི་ཐོགས་དེ་

དཔྱིད་ཀ་ཤི་ (mi̲ pɛ̄nmitɔɔ̀de dōŋga na̲ cūg pɛ̄nmitɔɔ̀de jīīgə shī) a saying used to convey uselessness [Lit. useless people get sick in autumn (harvest time), useless livestock die in spring (plowing time)].

མི་ཕམ་མགོན་པོ་ (mi̲bam gö̲mbo) Maitreya (the Buddha of the future).

མི་ཕར་བསད་སྟོང་ཚུར་ལོན་ (mi̲ pāāsɛ̄ɛ̄ tōŋ tsūūlö̲n) a saying used for sb. whose evil knows no limits [Lit. killing sb. and then taking murder compensation].

མི་ཕལ་པ་ (mi̲ pɛ̄ɛ̄wa) common people.

མི་ཕུགས་ (mi̲buù) 1. sm. རྒྱུ་དག. 2. origin, background.

མི་ཕུང་ (mi̲buŋ) crowd, throng, swarm, vi.—འཁྲིལ་ to have a crowd or throng form/ arise.

མི་ཕུང་རང་བརླགས་ (mi̲buŋ ra̲ŋlaà) destroying/ harming others will bring ruin to oneself [Lit. people get destroyed, oneself gets ruined].

མི་ཕོད་པ་ (mi̲pɛ̀ɛ̀ba) unable to chew ༑ རྒན་འཁོག་ལ་སོས་མི་ཕོད་པའི་ལྟོ་ཆས་སྟེར་རྒྱུ་མེད་ One should not serve food that the elderly are unable to chew.

མི་ཕོ་ (mi̲po) sm. ཕོ་གྲོ་ག.

མི་ཕྱུགས་ (mi̲ cūù) people and cattle.

མི་ཕྱུགས་གཉིས་འཕེལ་ (mi̲cuù ñīī bēl) man and livestock both increasing.

མི་ཕྱེད་པ་ (mi̲ cēèba) unchanging, constant, stable, unvarying ༑ ཁོང་ནང་ཆོས་ལ་མི་ཕྱེད་པའི་དད་པ་ཡོད་པ་རེད་ He has a unchanging faith in Buddhism.

མི་འཕེར་བ་ (mi̲ pērwa) unable/ unqualified to do sth. ༑ ལས་ཀ་མི་འཕེར་བའི་རྐྱེན་གྱིས་ཁོང་ལས་ཀ་དེ་རག་མི་འདུག He did get the job because he was unqualified.

མི་འཕྱུགས་ (mi̲ cāà) conscripting people for a special task; va.—རྒྱག ༑ གཞུང་ལམ་བཟོ་བར་ས་གནས་ཁག་ནས་མི་འཕྱུགས་བརྒྱབ་པ་རེད་ (They) conscripted people from various places to build a highway.

མི་འཕྲོད་པ་ (mi̲ trö̀öba) 1. unsuitable, incompatible, inappropriate, unfitting ༑ ས་གནས་འདིའི་གནམ་གཤིས་ནི་གཟུགས་པོར་མི་འཕྲོད་པ་ཞིག་ཡིན་ཙང་ Because the climate of this place is unsuitable (for my health). 2. not understanding/ comprehending ༑ ལན་མི་འཕྲོད་པ་ Not understanding the reply message.

མི་བག་བྲོ་པོ་ (mi̲ pa̲g tro̲bo) handsome, good-looking.

མི་བབ་ (mi̲bəb) appearance ༑ ཁོ་མི་བབ་ཡག་པོ་རེད་ He has a good appearance (He is good-looking).

མི་བབ་འགྲོ་བསྙད་ (mi̲bəb dro̲nɛɛ̀) shung. taking advantage of, bullying.

མི་བབ་སྤྱན་ཞུ་ (mi̲bəb jɛ̄nshu) shung. going in person before authorities in tt. to show what one looks like when being considered for sth. (there is no formal interview per se, just visual inspection).

མི་བབ་སྤྱན་ལམ་ (mi̲bəb jɛ̄nlam) shung. sm. མི་བབ་སྤྱན་ཞུ་.

མི་བབ་ཆགས་པོ་ (mi̲bəb cāàgo) elegant, well-dressed, well-mannered.

མི་བབ་ཚོད་རྩིས་ (mi̲bəb tsȫödzii) taking advantage of, bullying; va.—བྱེད་.

མི་བབས་ (mi̲bəb) sm. མི་བབ་.

མི་བུ་རིགས་དྲུག (mi̲bu ri̲gdruù) sm. མིའུ་གདུང་དྲུག.

མི་བུ་རུས་དྲུག (mi̲bu rü̲ü̲druù) sm. མིའུ་གདུང་དྲུག.

མི་བུད་ཁྱིམ་སྟོངས་ (mi̲büü kyīmdoŋ) shung. a family that is ruined— their house is destroyed and the members had to leave/ flee.

མི་བོགས་ (mi̲bɔɔ̀) shung. "human lease" (the annual fee paid by a serf to his lord or owner for exemption from having to live on the estate and provide corvee labor).

མི་བྱིངས་ (mijiŋ) the rest/ remainder of the people.

མི་བྱེད་དགུ་བྱེད་ (mijeè gu̲jeè) acting wantonly/ recklessly/ unconventionally (pejorative connotation); va.—བྱེད་.

མི་བྱེད་ཀུ་བྱེད་ (mi̲jeè gu̲jeè) sm. མི་བྱེད་དགུ་བྱེད་.

མི་འབྲུ་དྭངས་པོ་ (mi̲dru ta̲ŋbo) good-looking, pretty.

མི་བྲེལ་ཧ་འཆེར་ (mi̲dree dādzer) the turmoil and chaos of war.

མི་བླ་ (mi̲la) 1. owner, chief, head. 2. the བླ་ of a person.

མི་བློ་གདད་ཕྱོགས་ (mi̲lo dɛɛ̀jɔɔ̀) inclination/ tendency of a person.

མི་བློ་ནང་འགུགས་ (mi̲lo naŋguù) winning over a person; va.—བྱེད་.

མི་བློ་བསལ་ཅན་ (mi̲lo sɛ̄ɛ̄jɛn) bright, clever, sharp, astute.

མི་དབང་ (mi̲waŋ) 1. lord, king. 2. human ༑ མི་དབང་ཐོབ་ཐང་ Human rights.

མི་དབང་ཆེན་པོ་ (mi̲waŋ cēmbo) 1. sm. མི་དབང་. 2. a bossy person.

མི་དབང་ཚོགས་ཆུང་ (mi̲waŋ tsōgjuŋ) human rights subcommittee (of U.S. Congress).

མི་དབང་རྟོགས་བརྗོད་ (mi̲waŋ dōgjöö) the biography of Miwang Sonam Topgyal (Pholhanas).

མི་དབང་ཐོབ་ཐང་ (mi̲waŋ tōbdaŋ) human rights.

མི་འབག (mi̲baà) mask of a human (as opposed to animal).

མི་འབངས་ (mi̲baŋ) sm. མི་དམངས་.

མི་འབོགས་ (mi̲bɔɔ̀) sm. མི་བོགས་.

མི་འབོར་ (mi̲mbɔɔ) population ༑ འཛམ་གླིང་གི་མི་འབོར་ The population of the world.

མི་འབོར་དངོས་འཕར་བྱུང་ཚད་ (mi̲mbɔɔ ŋȫö̀bar ju̲ŋdzɛɛ̀) population net growth.

མི་འབོར་སྡོམ་རྩིས་ (mi̲mbɔɔ do̲mdzii̍) vital statistics, population statistics.

མི་འབོར་འཕེལ་རྒྱས་ཚོད་འཛིན་བྱེད་པའི་སྒྲིག་འཛུགས་ (mi̲mbɔɔ pēēgyɛɛ̀ tsȫ̀ndzin ce̲èbɛ dri̲gdzuù) zero population growth.

མི་འབོར་འབར་གས་ (mi̲mbɔɔ ba̲rgɛɛ̀) population explosion.

མི་འབོར་ཆེ་ས་ (mi̲mbɔɔ cēsa) an area that has a large population.

མི་འབོར་ཆེན་པོ་ (mi̲mbɔɔ cēmbo) a large population.

མི་འབོར་འདུས་ཚད་ (mi̲mbɔɔ dü̲ü̲dzɛɛ̀) population density.

མི་འབོར་སྤོ་འཛུལ་ (mi̲mbɔɔ pōndzüü) in migration, immigration.

མི་འབོར་རང་བཞིན་འཕར་ཚད་ (mi̲mbɔɔ ra̲ŋshin pārdzɛɛ̀) the rate of natural population growth.

མི་འབྱར་རྡོལ་སྦྱིན་སྦྱར་ (mi̲njar dö̲ö̲jin ja̲r) trying to get two unlikely persons to form a relationship or fall in love [Lit. trying to stick stones together with glue].

མི་འབྲལ་ལུས་ཀྱི་ཁྲིབ་མ་ (mi̲drɛɛ lü̲ü̲gi tri̲bmə) unbreakable/ indestructible relationship.

མི་འབྲུ་དྭངས་པོ་ (mi̲dru ta̲ŋbo) handsome, beautiful.

མི་མ་ཤི་ན་བློ་མི་ཟད་ (mi̲ mə̲shinə lō mi̲sɛɛ̀) as long as there is life there is hope.

མི་མ་ཡིན་ (mi̲məyin) one of the realms inhabited by creatures that are neither men nor demons.

མི་མང་ (mi̲maŋ) 1. sm. མི་དམངས་. 2. many people.

མི་མང་གི་བཤད་རྫུལ་ (mi̲maŋgi shɛ̄ɛ̄dzüü) public opinion.

མི་མང་འགྲུབ་སླ་ (mi̲maŋ dru̲bla) having many people makes accomplishing a task easy.

མི་མང་ལྕེ་མང་ (mi̲maŋ jēmaŋ) the more people the more criticism/ talk.

མི་མང་བདེ་སྲུང་ཛུའུ་ (mi̲maŋ de̲suŋ dzu̲) tib.ch. the office in charge of police and security work under the revolutionary committee.

མི་མང་འདུ་ཚོགས་ (mi̲maŋ du̲dzɔɔ̀) a gathering of many people, a public gathering.

མི་མང་སྡོད་ཁང་དང་གྲོང་ཁྱེར་ཡར་རྒྱས་ལས་དོན་ལས་ཁུངས་ (mi̲maŋ dö̲ö̲gaŋ da̲ŋ tro̲ŋgyee lɛɛ̀dön lɛɛ̀guŋ) HUD (Department of Housing and Urban Development).

མི་མང་དཔུང་ལྡེབས་ (mi̲maŋ būŋdeb) shung. sm. མི་དཔུང་དག་ལྡེབས་.

མི་མང་སྤྱི་ཁང་ (m̲imaŋ jīgaŋ) people's commune.

མི་མང་སྤྱི་འཐུས་ (m̲imaŋ jītüü) people's representative; congressman (U.S.).

མི་མང་སྤྱི་ཕན་ (m̲imaŋ jībɛn) benefit/ welfare for the general public.

མི་མང་དབང་གཙོ་ (m̲imaŋ wāŋdzo) democracy.

མི་མང་ཚོགས་པ་ (m̲imaŋ tsɔ̄gba) people's party.

མི་མང་ལག་མང་ (m̲imaŋ l̲agmaŋ) many people together doing sth.

མི་མང་སེམས་གཅིག (m̲imaŋ sēmjii) being of a single mind/ united.

མི་མང་ལས་ཉུང་ (m̲imaŋ l̲ɛ̀ɛñuŋ) many people with little work, overstaffed.

མི་མང་ཤུགས་ཆེ་ (m̲imaŋ shūgce) the more people the stronger.

མི་མིང་གི་ཚབ་ཚིག (m̲imaŋgi tsəbdzii) personal pronoun.

མི་མིན་ (m̲imin) sm. མི་མ་ཡིན་.

མི་མུས་བཅས་བརྒྱུད་ (m̲imüü jɛ̀ɛgyüü) continuous across generations (as in a family/ lineage) ¶ ཁང་པ་འདི་མི་ཚང་དེའི་མི་མུས་རྒྱུད་བཅས་ལ་བདག་པ་རེད་ This house has been owned by that family in the past and will be so in the future.

མི་མེད་ (m̲imeè) wilderness, a deserted place (place with no people).

མི་མེད་རི་སྟོང་ (m̲imeè r̲idoŋ) an isolated/ deserted mountain, wilderness.

མི་མེད་ལུང་སྟོང་ (m̲imeè l̲uŋdoŋ) a deserted place, a wilderness.

མི་མེད་ས་སྟོང་ (m̲imeè sādoŋ) sm. མི་མེད་ལུང་སྟོང་.

མི་མོ་ (m̲imo) woman.

མི་མྱོང་དགུ་མྱོང་ (m̲iñoŋ g̲uñoŋ) experiencing all kinds of things.

མི་དམངས་ (m̲imaŋ) the people, the masses.

མི་དམངས་ཀུང་ཧྲི་ (m̲imaŋ gūŋhri) sm. མི་དམངས་ཀུང་ཧྲེ་.

མི་དམངས་ཀུང་ཧྲེ་ (m̲imaŋ gūŋhre) people's commune.

མི་དམངས་ཀུན་ཁྱབ་རླུང་འཕྲིན་ལས་ཁང་ (m̲imaŋ gūŋgyəb lūŋdrin l̲ɛ̀ɛguŋ) people's broadcasting bureau.

མི་དམངས་ཀྱི་སྤྱི་དགྲ་ (m̲imaŋgi jīdra) people's enemy, public enemy.

མི་དམངས་ཀྱི་དམག་དཔུང་ (m̲imaŋgi məgbuŋ) people's army.

མི་དམངས་ཀྱི་ཚོགས་པ་ (m̲imaŋgi tsɔ̄gba) people's organization, people's party.

མི་དམངས་ཀྱི་རང་བཞིན་ (m̲imaŋgi r̲əŋshin) the nature/ character of the people.

མི་དམངས་ཀྱི་ཤོག་ཁག (m̲imaŋgi shɔ̄ɔgaà) mass organization, people's party/ clique.

མི་དམངས་ཀྱི་ཁྲིམས་ཁང་ (m̲imaŋgi trīmgaŋ) people's court.

མི་དམངས་ཀྱི་དྲག་ཆས་ (m̲imaŋgi tr̲agjɛ̀ɛ) people's arms/ weapons.

མི་དམངས་ཀྱི་དྲག་དཔུང་ (m̲imaŋgi tr̲əgbuŋ) people's armed forces.

མི་དམངས་ཀྱི་འདུམ་འགྲིག (m̲imaŋgi d̲umdrii) people's mediation.

མི་དམངས་ཀྱི་འདོད་བློ་ (m̲imaŋgi d̲ȫölo) feelings of the people.

མི་དམངས་ཀྱི་འདྲི་གཅོད་ (m̲imaŋgi dr̲ijöö) people's prosecution.

མི་དམངས་ཀྱི་ནོར་སྟོབས་ (m̲imaŋgi nɔ̄ɔdob) financial resources/ power of the people.

མི་དམངས་ཀྱི་གནས་ཚུལ་ (m̲imaŋgi nɛ̄ɛdzüü) condition/ situation of the people.

མི་དམངས་ཀྱི་སྤྱི་ཞབས་པ་ (m̲imaŋgi jīzhəbbə) servant of the people.

མི་དམངས་ཀྱི་བར་འདུམ་ཨུ་ཡོན་ལྷན་ཁང་ (m̲imaŋgi p̲ərdum ūyün lhɛ̄ngaŋ) people's mediation committee.

མི་དམངས་ཀྱི་བློ་སྟོབས་ (m̲imaŋgi lōdob) people's morale, popular morale.

མི་དམངས་ཀྱི་ཤ་ཁྲག (m̲imaŋgi shādraà) flesh and blood of the people.

མི་དམངས་ཀྱི་ཤེས་རིག (m̲imaŋgi sheèrii) wisdom of the masses.

མི་དམངས་ཁྲིམས་ཁང་ (m̲imaŋ trīmgaŋ) people's court.

མི་དམངས་མཁའ་སྲུང་གཞུང་ལས་ཁང་ (m̲imaŋ kəsuŋ shuŋlɛ̀ɛgaŋ) civil air defense office.

མི་དམངས་གྲོས་ཚོགས་ (m̲imaŋ tr̲ȫödzɔ̄ɔ) people's assembly, people's council.

མི་དམངས་གླིང་ག (m̲imaŋ līŋgə) people's park.

མི་དམངས་གློག་བརྙན་ཁང་ (m̲imaŋ lɔ̄gñɛngaŋ) people's movie theater.

མི་དམངས་དངུལ་ཁང་ (m̲imaŋ ŋüügaŋ) people's bank.

མི་དམངས་ཅིང་ཁྲ་ (m̲imaŋ jīŋdra) tib.ch. people's police.

མི་དམངས་བཅིངས་འགྲོལ་དམག (m̲imaŋ jīŋdrööö māà) People's Liberation Army.

མི་དམངས་བཅིངས་འགྲོལ་དམག་འཁྲུག (m̲imaŋ jīŋdröö məgdruù) people's war of liberation.

མི་དམངས་བཅིངས་འགྲོལ་ཨུ་ཡོན་ལྷན་ཁང (m̲imaŋ jīŋdrüü ūyün lhɛ̄ngaŋ) people's liberation committee.

མི་དམངས་ཆབ་སྲིད་གྲོས་མཐུན་ཚོགས་འདུ་ (m̲imaŋ cəbsii tr̲ȫödön tsɔ̄ŋdu) People's Political Consultative Conference.

མི་དམངས་ཉིན་རེ་ཚགས་པར་ (m̲imaŋ ñ̲inre tsāgbar) People's Daily (newspaper).

མི་དམངས་ཉིན་རེའི་ཚགས་པར་ (m̲imaŋ ñ̲inree tsāgbar) People's Daily (Renmin Ribao newspaper).

མི་དམངས་ཉིན་རེའི་ཚགས་པར་ཁང་ (m̲imaŋ ñ̲inree tsāgbar) People's Daily newspaper office.

མི་དམངས་ཉེན་རྟོག་དྲག་དཔུང་ (m̲imaŋ ñ̲endoò tr̲əgbuŋ) the people's armed police.

མི་དམངས་ཉེན་རྟོག་པ་ (m̲imaŋ ñ̲endogba) people's police/ policemen.

མི་དམངས་འཐུས་མི་ (m̲imaŋ tǖümi) people's representative/ delegate.

མི་དམངས་འཐུས་མི་ཚོགས་ཆེན་ (m̲imaŋ tǖümi tsɔ̄gjen) sm. མི་དམངས་འཐུས་མིའི་གྲོས་ཚོགས་.

མི་དམངས་འཐུས་མིའི་ཚོགས་ཆེན་མི་རིགས་ཨུ་ཡོན་ལྷན་ཁང་ (m̲imaŋ tǖümii tsɔ̄gjen m̲irig ūyön lhɛ̄ngaŋ) Nationalities Committee of the People's Assembly.

མི་དམངས་འཐུས་མིའི་གྲོས་ཚོགས་ (m̲imaŋ tǖümii tr̲ȫödzɔ̄ɔ) people's congress, people's representative assembly/ council.

མི་དམངས་འཐུས་མིའི་ཚོགས་ཆེན་ (m̲imaŋ tǖümii tsɔ̄gjen) sm. མི་དམངས་འཐུས་མིའི་གྲོས་ཚོགས་.

མི་དམངས་འཐུས་མིའི་ཚོགས་ཆེན་རྒྱུན་ཨུ་ (m̲imaŋ tǖümii tsɔ̄gjen gyü̲n ū) the Standing Committee of the People's Congress.

མི་དམངས་འཐུས་ཚོགས་ (m̲imaŋ tǖüdzɔ̄ɔ) abbr. of མི་དམངས་འཐུས་མིའི་གྲོས་ཚོགས་.

མི་དམངས་དང་བླངས་དམག (m̲imaŋ t̲anlaŋ māà) People's Volunteer Army.

མི་དམངས་དྲག་སྒྲུབ་པུའུ་ (m̲imaŋ tr̲əgdrub pū) tib.ch. department/ bureau of the people's armed forces.

མི་དམངས་དྲག་ཆས་པུའུ་ (m̲imaŋ tr̲agjɛɛ pū) tib.ch. department of the people's armed forces (usu. concerned with militias).

མི་དམངས་དྲག་པོའི་ཉེན་རྟོག (m̲imaŋ tr̲agbö ñ̲endog) people's armed police.

མི་དམངས་དྲག་པོའི་ཉེན་རྟོག་པ་ (m̲imaŋ tr̲agbö ñ̲endogba) people's armed policeman.

མི་དམངས་དྲག་དཔུང་ (m̲imaŋ tr̲əgbuŋ) people's armed forces, people's army.

མི་དམངས་དྲག་སྲུང་ཉེན་རྟོག་པ་ (m̲imaŋ tr̲əgdrɛ̀ɛ ñ̲endogba) people's armed police.

མི་དམངས་འདུམ་འགྲིག་ཨུ་ཡོན་ལྷན་ཁང་ (m̲imaŋ d̲umdrig ūyün lhɛ̄ngaŋ) people's mediation committees.

མི་དམངས་པར་ལེན་ཁང་ (m̲imaŋ bārlengaŋ) people's photo studio.

མི་དམངས་དཔའ་བོ་དྲན་གསོའི་རྡོ་རིང་ (miman bāwo trensö dorin) stone pillar monument to people's heroes.

མི་དམངས་དཔར་ཁང་ (miman bārgan) people's printing house.

མི་དམངས་དཔེ་སྐྲུན་ཁང་ (miman bēdrüngan) people's printing/ publishing house.

མི་དམངས་སྤྱི་ཁང་ (miman jīgan) people's commune.

མི་དམངས་སྤྱི་མཐུན་རྒྱལ་ཁབ་ (miman jīdün gyεεgəb) people's republic.

མི་དམངས་སྤྱི་ལ་དབང་བའི་ལམ་ལུགས་ (miman jīlə wāŋwε ləmluù) system of common/ joint ownership of property by the people, system of public property.

མི་དམངས་དབང་གཙོ་ (miman wāndzo) democracy.

མི་དམངས་མང་ཚོགས་ (miman mandzo) the people, the masses.

མི་དམངས་དམངས་གཙོ་ (miman māndzo) people's democracy.

མི་དམངས་དམངས་གཙོའི་འཐབ་ཕྱོགས་གཅིག་གྱུར་ (miman mandzö tābjoò jīggyur) people's democratic united front.

མི་དམངས་དམངས་གཙོའི་འཐབ་ཕྱོགས་གཅིག་སྒྲིལ་ (miman mandzö tābjoò jīdrii) people's democratic united front.

མི་དམངས་དམངས་གཙོའི་སྲིད་དབང་ (miman mandzö sīiwan) people's democratic authority/ political power.

མི་དམངས་དམངས་གཙོའི་སྲིད་དབང་སྒེར་གཅོད་ (miman mandzö sīiwan gerjöö) sm. མི་དམངས་དམངས་གཙོའི་སྲིད་དབང་སྒེར་འཛིན་.

མི་དམངས་དམངས་གཙོའི་སྲིད་དབང་སྒེར་འཛིན་ (miman mandzö sīiwan gendzin) people's democratic dictatorship.

མི་དམངས་སྨན་ཁང་ (miman mēngan) people's hospital.

མི་དམངས་ཚོགས་ཁང་ཆེ་མོ་ (miman tsōggan cēmo) The Great Hall of the People" (in Beijing).

མི་དམངས་ཚོགས་པ་ (miman tsōgba) people's congress/ assembly/ council.

མི་དམངས་ཚོམས་ཁང་ཆེན་མོ་ (miman tsōmgan cēmmo) he Great Hall of the People.

མི་དམངས་ཞིབ་དཔྱོད་ཁང་ (miman shibjöögan) people's procuratorate.

མི་དམངས་ཞིབ་དཔྱོད་ཨུ་ཡོན་ལྷན་ཁང་ (miman shibjöö ūyön lhēngan) people's procuratoratorial committee, people's control commission.

མི་དམངས་ཞུ་གཏུག་ཁྲུའུ་ (miman shuduù trū) tib.ch. people's complaint/ suggestion office.

མི་དམངས་ཞུ་གཏུག་གཞུང་ལས་ཁང་ (miman shuduù shunlεεgan) sm. མི་དམངས་ཞུ་གཏུག་ཁྲུའུ་.

མི་དམངས་ཟློས་གར་ཁང་ (miman döògargan) people's theater.

མི་དམངས་ཡོངས་ལ་དབང་བའི་ལམ་ལུགས་ (miman yonla wāŋwε ləmluù) sm. མི་དམངས་སྤྱི་ལ་དབང་བའི་ལམ་ལུགས་.

མི་དམངས་ལུས་རྩལ་ར་བ་ (miman lüüdzεε rawa) people's stadium.

མི་དམངས་ཤོག་དངུལ་ (miman shɔ̄ɔŋüü) people's currency (in China).

མི་དམངས་བཤེར་ཁང་ (miman shērgan) people's procuratorate.

མི་དམངས་སྲིད་དབང་ (miman sīiwan) people's political power.

མི་དམངས་སྲིད་གཞུང་ (miman sīishun) people's government.

མི་དམངས་ཨུ་ཡོན་ལྷན་ཁང་ (miman ūyün lhēngan) people's council/ committee.

མི་དམན་པ་ (mimεmba) not bad, good, well ། ད་བར་ཞིང་ལས་ཡར་རྒྱས་མི་དམན་པ་བྱུང་ཡོད་པ་རེད་ Until now there has been good progress in agricultural development.

མི་དམའ་བར་ (mimaawar) not less than, not lower than ། མི་འབོར་ 200 ལས་མི་དམའ་བར་ཉིན་ལྟར་འགྲོར་གྱི་ཡོད་པ་རེད་ Not less than 200 people arrive every day.

མི་སྨན་ (mimεn) doctor, physician.

མི་སྨོན་རང་སྐྱིད་ (mimön rangyiì) doing sth. well so that you are happy and others will admire your work ། ཁྱེད་རང་གིས་མི་སྨོན་རང་སྐྱིད་ཡོང་བའི་ལས་ཀ་བྱེད་དགོས་ You should work so that you are happy and others will admire it. [Lit. people admire, oneself happy].

མི་གཙང་བ་ (midzaŋwa) 1. dirty, unclean. 2. excrement.

མི་གཙོའི་རིང་ལུགས་ (midzö rinluù) humanism.

མི་གཙོའི་རིང་ལུགས་ཀྱི་མཚན་ཉིད་རིག་པ་ (midzö rinluùgi tsēnñiì rigbə) philosophy of humanism.

མི་བཙོངས་ནས་རང་ཕྲོ་བ་ (midzoŋnε raŋñöòwa) betraying people for one's own gain.

མི་རྫ་ (midzə) shung. a person who belongs to a lord, a serf ། ཁོ་ཕུན་ཁང་གི་མི་རྫ་རེད་ He is a serf of the Phunkhang (family).

མི་རྫ་མི་ཁུངས་ (midzə migun) shung. one's lord, the lord to whom one belongs.

མི་རྫ་མགོ་བདགས་ཞུ་ (midzə godaà shu) shung. offering oneself to a lord to become his serf (done when one flees from one's original lord and needs a new one).

མི་རྫ་མགོ་ལེན་ (midzə golen) shung. accepting a serf who is offering himself to you (i.e., running from his/ her original lord).

མི་རྫ་ཕྱིར་འཁྱར་ (midzə cīi kyār) shung. serfs who run away from their lord.

མི་རྫ་ཡན་སྡོད་ (midza yendöö) shung. runaway serfs who have not placed themselves under another lord.

མི་རྫ་ཡུལ་སྐོང་ (midzə yüügon) shung. the right of lords to retrieve runaway serfs.

མི་རྩུབ་པོ་ (mi dzūbbu) a crude/ harsh/ caustic person.

མི་རྩིས་དུད་བགྲང་ (mi dzūbbu) vital statistics, population statistics.

མི་ཚང་ (midzan) family, household; vi.—སྡོངས་ to become extinct (for a household) ། ལུང་པ་འདིར་མི་ཚང་ ༡༠ ཡོད་པ་རེད་ There are ten households in that place.

མི་ཚང་སྡོངས་ (midzan dōn) vi. to become extinct (a family/ household).

མི་ཚང་བཅའ་བསྡུས་ (midzan jāādüù) family planning.

མི་ཚང་ཐེམ་པ་ (midzan tēmba) family, household.

མི་ཚང་བ་ (mi tsāŋwa) sm. མ་ཚང་བ་.

མི་ཚང་བ་མེད་པ་ (midzaŋwa meèba) sm. མ་ཚང་བ་མེད་པ་.

མི་ཚངས་སྤྱོད་ (midzan jöò) to have intercourse/ sex.

མི་ཚད་ (midzεὲ) 1. not only, in addition to ། བོད་སྐད་ཀྱིས་མི་ཚད་བོད་ཡིག་ཀྱང་ཤེས་ཀྱི་ཡོད་པ་རེད་ (He) not only knows spoken Tibetan but also literary Tibetan. 2. the size of a human, man-size ། འདྲ་པར་མི་ཚད་ལས་ཆེ་བ་ The photograph is bigger than the size of a (real) person. 3. a reliable/ trustworthy person.

མི་ཚན་ (midzεn) the smallest residential administrative subunit beneath a monastic residence unit (ཁང་ཚན་).

མི་ཚན་སྤྱི་འཐུས་ (midzεn jīdüù) representative of a མི་ཚན་.

མི་ཚབ་ (midzəb) shung. a substitute person ། ངའི་མི་རྫ་བུ་མོ་ཞིག་ཁྱེད་རང་གི་མི་རྫ་དང་ཚང་ས་བརྒྱབ་པའི་མི་ཚབ་ཅིག་གནང་རོགས་བྱེད་ A female serf of mine is marrying one of your serfs so please give me a substitute person (for her).

མི་ཚུགས་པ་ (midzugbə) cant be harmed ། ཆུས་མི་ཚུགས་པའི་ཆུ་ཚོད་ A waterproof watch [Lit. a watch that can't be harmed by water].

མི་ཚུལ་རིང་ལུགས་ལ་ (midzüü rinluù) Humanism.

མི་ཚེ་ (midze) human lifespan; vi.—སྐྱེལ་ to live one's life; vi.—རྒས་ to grow old, to age ། མི་ཚེ་གང་ One lifetime. ། ཁོ་མི་ཚེ་ཧྲིད་ཀ་ཕྱི་རྒྱལ་ལ་བསྐྱལ་བ་

རེད་ He lived half his life abroad.

མི་ཚེ་འཁྱོལ་ (midze kyöö) vi. to live one's life ། འཚོ་བ་དཀའ་ངལ་ཆེན་པོ་ཡོད་སྟབས་མི་ཚེ་འཁྱོལ་ཁག་པོ་འདུག Because he has difficulty earning his livelihood, it is difficult for him to live.

མི་ཚེ་འཁྱོལ་ཙམ་ཡོད་པ་ (midze kyöödzam yööba) having just enough things to live/ subsist.

མི་ཚེ་གང་ (midze kaŋ) a lifetime, one's whole life.

མི་ཚེ་སྐང་ཚང་ (midze gaŋdzaŋ) sm. མི་ཚེ་གང་.

མི་ཚེ་གཅིག (midze jii) one lifetime ། མི་ཚེ་གཅིག་རིང་ During one lifetime.

མི་ཚེར་ལྟ་ཚུལ་ (midze dədzüü) view of life, philosophy of life.

མི་ཚེ་སྟོང་སྐྱེལ་ (midze dõŋgyee) wasting one's life; leading an empty life; vi.—འགྲོ་ to lead an empty life, to waste one's life.

མི་ཚེ་སྟོང་ཟད་ (midze dõŋsɛɛ̀) sm. མི་ཚེ་སྟོང་སྐྱེལ་འགྲོ་.

མི་ཚེ་དར་དཀར་ཡུག་གཅིག (midze targar yugjig) a life of accomplishments/ positive achievements ། ཁོང་ནི་རང་ཉིད་ཀྱི་རྒྱལ་ཁབ་ཀྱི་དོན་དུ་ལས་བྱས་ན་མི་ཚེ་དར་དཀར་ཡུག་གཅིག་ཏུ་འཁྱོལ་བ་རེད་ Working for his country, he has compiled a life of accomplishments.

མི་ཚེ་དོན་ལྡན་ (midze töndɛn) a purposeful/ meaningful life.

མི་ཚེ་རིང་ (mi tsēriŋ) the old man depicted in paintings as a symbol of long life.

མི་ཚེ་རིང་དྲགས་ན་ལྷ་ཤི་བའི་རོ་མཐོང་ (mi tsēriŋ traàna lhā shĩwɛ ro tõŋ) its not good to live too long, when people live too long they will see many bad things [Lit. if one lives too long one will see the corpse of gods].

མི་ཚེའི་འདུ་བྱེད་ (midzee dujeè) sm. མི་ཚེའི་འདུ་བྱེད་སྟོངས་.

མི་ཚེའི་འདུ་བྱེད་སྟོངས་ (midzee dujeè dõŋ) vi. to die.

མི་ཚེའི་མཚན་ཉིད་རིག་པ་ (midzee tsɛ̃nñii rigbə) philosophy of life.

མི་ཚེ་ལས་གཏམ་ཚེ་རིང་ (midzelɛ dām tsē riŋ) the reputation of a person is longer than his life.

མི་ཚེ་ཧྲིལ་པོ་ (midze hrĩibu) a life span.

མི་ཚོ་ (midzo) people ། བྱེད་རང་གིས་ལས་ཀ་དེ་འདྲ་བྱས་ན་མི་ཚོས་སྐྱོན་བརྗོད་བྱེད་ཀྱི་རེད་ If you work in this way, people will criticize you.

མི་ཚོགས་ (midzɔ̃ɔ) a crowd, a gathering/ mass of people.

མི་ཚོགས་ཆེ་བའི་ས་ཁུལ་ (midzɔ̃ɔ cēwɛ sāgüü) a densely populated area.

མི་ཚོགས་ཆེན་པོ་ (midzɔ̃ɔ cēmbo) a huge crowd of people.

མི་ཚོགས་འཐུག་ཚད་ (midzɔ̃ɔ tūgdzɛɛ̀) population density ། གྲོང་ཁྱེར་འདིའི་མི་ཚོགས་འཐུག་ཚད་ཆུང་ཆུང་རེད་ The population density of this city is small.

མི་ཚོགས་མང་ཉུང་ (mitsɔ̃ɔ məŋñuŋ) the size of a population.

མི་ཚོགས་མང་ས་ (mitsɔ̃ɔ maŋsa) a large crowed, a big gathering.

མི་འཚམས་པ་ (mi tsāmba) unfitting, improper, inappropriate ། དེང་དུས་ཀྱི་སྤྱི་ཚོགས་ནང་མི་འཚམས་པའི་འགྲོལ་ལུགས་ A system that is inappropriate in modern society.

མི་འཛད་རིམ་འབྱུང་ (mi dzɛ̱ɛ̀ rimjuŋ) emerging in an endless stream.

མི་འཛོམས་དགུ་འཛོམས་ (midzom guzom) gathering of many (people) from different places; va.—བྱེད་.

མི་འཛོམས་རྒུ་འཛོམས་ (midzom guzom) sm. མི་འཛོམས་དགུ་འཛོམས་.

མི་འཛོམས་རྟ་འཛོམས་ (midzom dādzom) to have gathered everything [Lit. soldiers gathered, horses gathered].

མི་འཛོམས་པ་ (mi dzomba) incomplete, not full.

མི་ཞར་བ་ (mi shara) a blind person.

མི་ཞིམ་སྣ་གཉེར་ (mishim nāñer) making a face because the food tastes bad; va.—སྟོད་ to make such a face.

མི་ཞུན་ (mishün) boiled human bone marrow (used in Tibetan medicine).

མི་གཞན་དག (mi shɛndaà) other people, another person.

མི་གཞི་ (mishi) sm. མི་ཤུགས་, 1.

མི་བཞི་ཤོག་ཁག (mishi shɔ̃ɔga) the "Gang of Four."

མི་ཟ་གནོད་འབུ་ (misa nõmbu) pests, harmful bugs ། མི་ཟ་གནོད་འབུ་ཡོད་ཚད་གཙང་འཕྱགས་བྱེད་དགོས་ (We) must sweep away all pests.

མི་ཟད་པ་ (misɛɛ̀ba) inexhaustible, ceaseless, endless ། ཐབས་ཤེས་མི་ཟད་པ་བཏང་བའི་མཐར་ At the end of (their) ceaseless trying.

མི་ཟན་ (misɛn) sth. that eats people ། སྟག་མི་ཟན་ Man eating tiger.

མི་ཟས་ (misɛɛ̀) 1. foods eaten by human beings. 2. foods served by other people ། རང་ཟས་ཟོ་ལ་མི་ཟས་སྤོང་ Eat your own food and give up food served by other people.

མི་ཟླ་ (minda) people ། ཁོང་ལ་སྐུ་སྲུང་བ་མི་ཟླ་བརྒྱད་འདུག He has eight people as bodyguards.

མི་ཟེར་རའི་མི་ (miserrɛ mi) good man/ person.

མི་གཟུགས་ (misug) 1. human figure, body ། མི་གཟུགས་ཡག་པོ་འབྲི་གི་འདུག (He) draws the human body well. 2. scarecrow.

མི་གཟུགས་དུར་རྫས་ (misug turdzɛɛ̀) wooden or clay human figurines buried with the dead.

མི་བཟང་ (misaŋ) 1. not good, bad. 2. a good/ generous person.

མི་བཟང་དོན་བཟང་ (misaŋ tönsaŋ) sm. མི་བཟང་ལས་བཟང་.

མི་བཟང་ལས་བཟང་ (misaŋ lɛ̱ɛ̀saŋ) good people and good deeds/ work ། ང་ཚོས་མི་བཟང་ལས་བཟང་ལ་བསྔོད་བསྔགས་བྱེད་དགོས་ We must praise good deeds and good people.

མི་བཟད་པ་ (miaɛ̱ɛ̀ba) frightful, horrifying.

མི་བཟོད་པ་ (misööba) intolerable, unbearable ། མི་བཟོད་པའི་བཙན་གནོན་ Unbearable oppression.

མི་བཟོས་ (misöö) artificial, man-made.

མི་བཟོས་སྐོར་སྐར་ (misöö gɔ̃ɔgar) man-made (space) satellite.

མི་བཟོས་འཁོར་སྐར་ (misöö gɔ̃ɔgar) sm. མི་བཟོས་སྐོར་སྐར་.

མི་བཟོས་གཙང་པོ་ (misöö dzāŋbo) man-made canal.

མི་བཟོས་ཚེ་སྣ་ (misöö tsēna) artificial fibers.

མི་བཟོས་སྲུང་སྐར་ (misöö sūŋgar) sm. མི་བཟོས་སྐོར་སྐར་.

མི་འོས་བསྙད་འཚོལ་ (miöö ñɛ̃ɛ̀ndzöö) finding fault without any cause/ reason; va.—བྱེད་.

མི་འོས་པ་ (miööba) unsuitable, unfit, not deserving.

མི་འོས་མི་འཚམས་ (miööba) sm. མི་འོས་པ་.

མི་ཡན་ (miyɛn) 1. sm. མི་འབྱམས་. 2. extra people.

མི་ཡི་གར་མཛད་ (miyi gəardzɛɛ̀) taking human form ། འཇམ་དབྱངས་མི་ཡི་གར་མཛད་ལྷ་སྐྱོང་ཆེན་པོ་ The great king who is the human form of Manjushri.

མི་ཡི་འཇིག་རྟེན་ (miyi jigden) the human world.

མི་ཡུལ་ (miyüü) 1. foreign land. 2. human world, the planet earth.

མི་ཡུལ་གྱི་བདེ་བ་ཅན་ (miyüügi dewajɛn) heaven on earth.

མི་ཡུལ་གྱི་དམྱལ་བ་ (miyüügi ñɛ̱ɛla) hell on earth ། མི་དམངས་རྣམས་མི་ཡུལ་གྱི་དམྱལ་བ་ལྟ་བུའི་སྡུག་བསྔལ་མྱོང་ས་པ་རེད་ People have suffered hardships like hell on earth.

མི་ཡུལ་དང་གདན་སྤྲལ་ (miyüüdaŋ dɛ̃ndrɛɛ) dying; vi.—བྱེད་ to die.

མི་ཡོང་དགུ་ཡོང་ (miyoŋ guyoŋ) all sorts of things coming (in a negative sense) ། ཁྱེད་རང་མི་བྱེད་དགུ་བྱས་ན་མི་ཡོང་དགུ་ཡོང་ཡོང་གི་རེད་ If you act recklessly, all sorts of bad things will come.

མི་ཡོང་བ་བྱེད་ (miyoŋwa cɛ̱ɛ̀) va. to prevent/ avoid sth. coming or occurring ། མང་ཚོགས་ཀྱི་བདེ་སྐྱིད་ལ་གནོད་སྐྱོན་ཡོང་བ་བྱེད་ཀྱི་ཡོད་ (We) are doing things to prevent harm coming to the happiness of the masses.

མི་གཡེང་བ་ (miyeŋwa) not letting one's mind

wander, being attentive, concentrating.

མི་གཡོ་བ་ (miyowa) not wavering, stable, firm.

མི་གཡོ་བའི་ས་ (miyo wɛ sā) the 8th stage of a Boddhisatva.

མི་རང་ (miraŋ) 1. he, she. 2. abbr. མི་དང་རང་. 3. a lone / single person.

མི་རང་རང་ (mi raŋraŋ) herself or himself ༑ ལས་ཀ་དི་མི་རང་རང་གིས་བྱེད་དགོས་ཡོད་ཟེར་གྱི་འདུག (He) said that he wants to do this work himself.

མི་རང་རང་སོ་སོ་ (mi raŋraŋ sōso) each person himself/ herself ༑ མི་རང་རང་སོ་སོའི་བསམ་ཚུལ་གང་ཡོད་ཤོད་དགོས་ Each person should say whatever opinion he himself/ herself has.

མི་རབས་ (mirəb) generation ༑ མི་རབས་གསར་པ་ The new generation ༑ མི་རབས་རྗེས་མ་ The next/ future generation.

མི་རབས་གོང་མ་ (mirəb koŋma) the previous generation.

མི་རབས་གོང་མའི་མི་ (mirəb koŋmɛ mi) people of the previous generation.

མི་རབས་རྒན་པ་ (mirəb gɛmba) the older generation.

མི་རབས་བརྒྱུད་འཛགས་ (mirəb gyüünjaà) possessions that have been passed down from generation to generation.

མི་རབས་བརྒྱུད་སྒྲོད་ (mirəb gyüüdröö) handing/ passing down from one generation to the next generation.

མི་རབས་རྗེས་མ་ (mirəb jeèma) future generation.

མི་རབས་མཉམ་པ་ (mirəb ñamba) same generation.

མི་རབས་བསྡུད་མ་ (mirəb dǖüma) from generation to generation, successive generations.

མི་རབས་ནས་མི་རབས་བར་ (mirəbnɛ mirəbbar) from generation to generation.

མི་རབས་གཞོན་པ་ (mirəb shömba) the younger generation.

མི་རི་ (mi ri) not worth its price.

མི་རི་བོང་གི་ཚོད་ཀྱིས་ཟས་སྦོ་དོག (mi riboŋgi tsöögi sɛ̄ɛbodoò) acting inappropriately [Lit. people acting like rabbits and eating (grass) on mounds of earth].

མི་རིགས་ (mirii) 1. race, nationality, ethnic group. 2. vi. to be not okay/ appropriate/ worthy ༑ དུད་འགྲོ་དང་མཚུངས་པའི་སྤྱོད་ཚུལ་ཇི་ལྟར་ནའང་འཛིན་པར་མི་རིགས་ Whatever one does, one shouldn't act like an animal.

མི་རིགས་ཀྱི་སྐད་ (miriigi gɛ̄ɛ) national/ nationality/ ethnic group's language.

མི་རིགས་ཀྱི་སྐད་ཡིག (miriigi gɛ̄ɛyii) nationality/ ethnic group's language.

མི་རིགས་ཀྱི་ཁེ་དབང་ (miriigi kēwaŋ) nationality/ ethnic rights.

མི་རིགས་ཀྱི་ཁྱད་ཆོས་ (miriigi kyɛ̄ɛjöö) nationality/ racial/ ethnic characteristics.

མི་རིགས་ཀྱི་གོམས་གཤིས་ (miriigi komshii) ethnic or nationality customs/ habits.

མི་རིགས་ཀྱི་ཆ་ལུགས་ (miriigi cəluù) national style of dress.

མི་རིགས་ཀྱི་གཉའ་གནོན་ (miriigi ñanön) nationality/ racial/ ethnic oppression.

མི་རིགས་ཀྱི་སྙིང་སྟོབས་ (miriigi ñiŋdob) nationality/ racial/ ethnic spirit.

མི་རིགས་ཀྱི་འཐབ་རྩོད་ (miriigi təbdzöö) nationality/ racial/ ethnic struggle.

མི་རིགས་ཀྱི་འདུ་ཤེས་ (miriigi dusheè) nationality consciousness.

མི་རིགས་ཀྱི་གནད་དོན་ (miriigi nɛ̄ɛdön) nationality/ racial/ ethnic problem or issue or question.

མི་རིགས་ཀྱི་རྣམ་པ་ཅན་དུ་འགྱུར་ (miriigi nāmbajɛndu gyur) vi. to become assimilated to a nationality, race, or ethnic group's cultural style.

མི་རིགས་ཀྱི་རྣམ་པ་ (miriigi nāmba) nationality or race or ethnic group's cultural style/ form/ appearance.

མི་རིགས་ཀྱི་དཔའ་བོ་ (miriigi bāwo) nationality/ racial/ ethnic hero.

མི་རིགས་ཀྱི་འབྲེལ་བ་ (miriigi dreewa) a relationship between nationalities/ races/ ethnic groups.

མི་རིགས་ཀྱི་བརྩེ་དུང་ (miriigi dzēduŋ) nationality/ racial/ ethnic love.

མི་རིགས་ཀྱི་ཚུལ་ལུགས་ (miriigi tsǖüluù) sm. མི་རིགས་ཀྱི་གཤིས་ལུགས་.

མི་རིགས་ཀྱི་རིག་གནས་ (miriigi rignɛɛ) nationality/ ethnic group/ racial culture.

མི་རིགས་ཀྱི་རིག་གནས་ཕོ་བྲང་ (miriigi rignɛɛ pōdraŋ) Nationalities Cultural Palace.

མི་རིགས་ཀྱི་རིག་པ་ (mīriigi rigbə) anthropology, ethnology.

མི་རིགས་ཀྱི་རིག་རྫས་ (mīriigi rigdzɛɛ) cultural relics or artifacts of a nationality/ ethnic group/ race.

མི་རིགས་ཀྱི་ཞབས་འདྲེན་ (mīriigi shamdren) disgrace to a nationality/ ethnic group/ race.

མི་རིགས་ཀྱི་ལ་རྒྱ་ (mīriigi lagya) nationality/ racial/ ethnic loyalty.

མི་རིགས་ཀྱི་ལས་དོན་ (mīriigi lɛɛdön) nationality/ ethnic/ racial affairs.

མི་རིགས་ཀྱི་ལོ་རྒྱུས་ (mīriigi lugyüü) nationality/ ethnic/ racial/ history.

མི་རིགས་ཀྱི་གཤིས་ལུགས་ (mīriigi shiiluù) nationality/ racial/ ethnic character.

མི་རིགས་ཀྱི་སྲོལ་རྒྱུན་ (mīriigi sööɡyön) nationality/ racial/ ethnic traditions.

མི་རིགས་ཀྱི་གསར་བརྗེ་ (mīriigi sārje) nationality/ racial/ ethnic revolution.

མི་རིགས་སྐད་ཡིག (mīrii gɛ̄ɛyii) nationality/ racial/ ethnic language.

མི་རིགས་སྐད་ཡིག་མཛུབ་འཁྲིད་ཨུ་ཡོན་ལྷན་ཁང་ (mīrii gɛ̄ɛyii dzubdrii ūyün lhɛ̄ngaŋ) Minority Language Commission (China), ethnic/ nationality/ racial language commission.

མི་རིགས་སྐད་ཡིག་སློབ་ཚོགས་ (mirii gɛ̄ɛyii lōbdzɔɔ) nationality language association.

མི་རིགས་སྐད་ཡིག་དོན་བྱེད་གཞུང་ལས་ཁང་ (mirii gɛ̄ɛyii tönjeè shuŋlɛgaŋ) office of nationalities language work/ affairs.

མི་རིགས་སྐད་ཡིག་དོན་བྱེད་ཨུ་ཡོན་ལྷན་ཁང་ (mirii gɛ̄ɛyii tönjeè ūyön lhɛ̄ngaŋ) nationalities language affairs committee.

མི་རིགས་སྐྱར་དར་ (mirii gyārdar) revival of nationality/ ethnicity, nationality/ ethnic rejuvenation.

མི་རིགས་ཁྱད་འཛིན་ (mirii kyɛ̄ndzin) nationality/ ethnic/ racial discrimination.

མི་རིགས་ཁྱིམ་ཚང་ཆེན་པོ་ (mirii kyīmdzaŋ cēmbo) the great family of nationalities.

མི་རིགས་འཁྲུག་སློང་ (mirii trūgloŋ) racial/ nationality/ ethnic disturbances or unrest.

མི་རིགས་གྲངས་ཉུང་ (mirii trəŋñuŋ) minority nationality/ race/ ethnic group.

མི་རིགས་གླུ་གར་ཚོགས་པ་ (mirii lūgar tsōgba) nationalities song and dance ensemble.

མི་རིགས་དགེ་ཐོན་སློབ་གྲྭ (mirii gedön lōbdra) teacher's training school for nationalities.

མི་རིགས་མགོ་འདོགས་རིང་ལུགས་ (mirii godog riŋluù) nationality/ ethnic/ racial capitulism.

མི་རིགས་ལྔ་ (mirii ŋā) the five main nationalities in China.

མི་རིགས་བཅིངས་འགྲོལ་ (mirii jiŋdröö) nationality/ ethnic/ racial liberation.

མི་རིགས་བཅིངས་འགྲོལ་གྱི་ལས་འགུལ་ (mirii jiŋdrüügi lɛngüü) nationality/ ethnic group liberation movement.

མི་རིགས་བཅིངས་འགྲོལ་འཐབ་ཕྱོགས་ (mirii jiŋdrüü təbjɔɔ) national liberation front.

མི་རིགས་ཆས་གོས་ (mirii cɛ̄ɛgöö) the dress/ costume of a nationality/ ethnic group/ race.

མི་རིགས་ཆེན་པོའི་རིང་ལུགས་ (mirii cēmbö riŋluù) 1. big nationality chauvinism (the majority ethnic group dominates the over smaller ones). 2. in China, Great Han chauvinism.

མི་རིགས་ཆོས་དོན་ལྷན་ཁང་ (mirii cöödön lhɛ̄ngaŋ)

nationalities and religious affairs commission.

མི་རིགས་ཆོས་ལུགས་ལས་དོན་ཨུ་ཡོན་ལྷན་ཁང་ (mirii cööluù lɛɛ̀dön ūyön lhēngaŋ) nationalities and religious affairs commission.

མི་རིགས་ཆོས་ལུགས་ཞིབ་འཇུག་ཁང་ (mirii cööluù shimjuìgaŋ) nationalities and religion research office.

མི་རིགས་ཉོ་ཚོང་ཀུང་སི་ (mirii ñodzoŋ gūŋsi) nationalities trading company.

མི་རིགས་མཉམ་འདྲེས་ (mirii ñamdreè) nationality/ racial/ ethnic integration.

མི་རིགས་བརྙན་པར་ཁང་ (mirii ñɛmbargaŋ) nationality pictorial publishing house.

མི་རིགས་ལྟ་རྒྱལ་ (mirii dədzüü) nationality/ ethnic group/ racial viewpoint.

མི་རིགས་ཐུན་མོང་གི་སྐད་ (mirii tũnmuŋgi gɛ̀ɛ) common national language (the common language of all nationalities).

མི་རིགས་ཐུན་མོང་གི་སྐད་ཆ་ (mirii tũnmuŋgi gɛ̀ɛja) sm. མི་རིགས་ཐུན་མོང་གི་སྐད་.

མི་རིགས་མཐུན་སྒྲིལ་ (mirii tũndrii) national/ racial/ ethnic unity or solidarity.

མི་རིགས་མཐོང་ཆུང་ (mirii tōŋjuŋ) looking down on a nationality/ racial/ ethnic group.

མི་རིགས་འཐབ་ཕྱོགས་གཅིག་གྱུར་ (mirii təbjɔɔ̀ jiggyur) united front of nationalities (in a country).

མི་རིགས་དང་དམངས་གཙོའི་ལས་འགུལ་ (miriìdaŋ māŋdzö lɛngüü) national democratic movement.

མི་རིགས་དོན་གཅོད་ཨུ་ཡོན་ལྷན་ཁང་ (mirii tönjöö ūyün lhēngaŋ) nationality affairs bureau/ commission.

མི་རིགས་དོན་སྟོང་རིང་ལུགས་ (mirii töndoŋ riŋluù) nationality nihilism.

མི་རིགས་འདྲེས་སྡོད་ས་ཁུལ་ (mirii dreèdöö səgüü) a multinationality area/ region.

མི་རིགས་པ་ (mirigbə) inappropriate, unsuitable.

མི་རིགས་བར་གྱི་འགལ་ཆ་ (mirii pargi gɛɛja) national estrangement, contradictions between nationalities.

མི་རིགས་འབྱོར་ལྡན་གྲལ་རིམ་ (mirii jɔndɛn trɛɛrim) nationality bourgeoise/ bourgeoisie.

མི་རིགས་དམངས་གཙོའི་འཐབ་ཕྱོགས་གཅིག་གྱུར་ (mirii māŋdzö təbjɔɔ̀ jiggyur) nationality democratic united front.

མི་རིགས་དམངས་གཙོའི་གསར་བརྗེ་ (mirii māŋdzö sārje) nationality democratic revolution.

མི་རིགས་དོན་གཅོད་ཨུ་ཡོན་ལྷན་ཁང་ (mirii tönjöö ūyün lhēngaŋ) sm. མི་རིགས་དོན་བྱེད་ཨུ་ཡོན་ལྷན་ཁང་.

མི་རིགས་དོན་བྱེད་ཨུ་ཡོན་ལྷན་ཁང་ (mirii tönjeè ūyün lhēngaŋ) Nationalities Affairs Commission (China).

མི་རིགས་འདུས་སྡོད་ས་ཁུལ་ (mirii düüdöö səgüü) a region or area with mixed nationalities/ ethnic groups/ races.

མི་རིགས་འདྲ་མཉམ་ (mirii drañam) nationality/ racial/ ethnic equality.

མི་རིགས་འདྲེས་སྡོད་ས་ཁུལ་ (mirii drɛɛ̀döö səgüü) mixed nationality/ ethnic/ racial region or area.

མི་རིགས་དཔར་ཁང་ (mirii bārgaŋ) nationalities printing/ publishing house.

མི་རིགས་དཔེ་སྐྲུན་ཁང་ (mirii bēdröngaŋ) nationalities printing/ publishing house.

མི་རིགས་དབྱེ་འབྱེད་ (mirii yējeè) racial/ nationality/ ethnic discrimination; va.—བྱེད་ to discriminate on a racial/ national/ ethnic basis.

མི་རིགས་འབྱོར་ལྡན་གྲལ་རིམ་ (mirii jɔndɛn trɛɛrim) nationality bourgeoisie.

མི་རིགས་མང་པོ་ཡོད་པ་ (mirii maŋbo yööba) multinationality, multiethnic, multiracial ¶ མི་རིགས་མང་པོ་ཡོད་པའི་རྒྱལ་ཁབ་ A multinationality state.

མི་རིགས་གཞུང་ལུགས་ཞིབ་འཇུག་ཁང་ (mirii shuŋluù shimjuùgaŋ) institute of nationality theory.

མི་རིགས་བཞི་ (mirii shi) the four varna (castes) of India: Brahmin, Kshatriya, Vaishya, Shudra.

མི་རིགས་ཡུལ་ཚོ་ (mirii yüüdzo) nationality/ ethnic/ racial region or area.

མི་རིགས་རང་སྐྱོང་ (mirii raŋgyoŋ) nationality/ ethnic/ racial autonomy.

མི་རིགས་རང་སྐྱོང་ས་གནས་ (mirii raŋgyoŋ sānɛɛ̀) autonomous nationality/ ethnic/ racial region.

མི་རིགས་རང་ཁོངས་ཀྱི་ལས་བྱེད་ (mirii raŋgoŋgi lɛɛ̀jeè) nationality/ ethnic/ racial cadre.

མི་རིགས་རང་ཐག་རང་གཅོད་ (mirii raŋdaà raŋjöö) nationality/ ethnic/ racial self-determination.

མི་རིགས་རང་འདྲར་སྒྱུར་ (mirii raŋdraa gyur) va. to assimilate nationalities.

མི་རིགས་རང་ཕན་རིང་ལུགས་ (mirii raŋbɛn riŋluù) a nationality/ ethnic group/ race that thinks of its own benefits (instead of the nation's).

མི་རིགས་རང་བློ་རང་འཁེལ་བསམ་པ་ (mirii raŋlo raŋkee sāmba) nationality/ ethnic/ racial self-confidence.

མི་རིགས་རང་དབང་ (mirii raŋwaŋ) nationality/ ethnic group/ racial freedom.

མི་རིགས་རང་བཙན་ (mirii raŋdzɛn) nationality/ ethnic group/ racial independence.

མི་རིགས་རང་བརྩིའི་བསམ་པ་ (mirii raŋdzii sāmba) nationality/ racial/ ethnic self respect or pride.

མི་རིགས་རིག་གནས་ཕོ་བྲང་ (mirii rignɛɛ̀ pōdraŋ) Cultural Palace of the Nationalities.

མི་རིགས་རིག་པ་ (mirii rigbə) anthropology.

མི་རིགས་རིང་ལུགས་ (mirii riŋluù) nationalism.

མི་རིགས་རིང་ལུགས་གུ་དོག་པོ་ (mirii riŋluù ko togbo) narrow/ local nationalism (the kind of nationalism where the interests of one's own nationality take precedence over that of the nation).

མི་རིགས་རིང་ལུགས་པ་ (mirii riŋluù) a nationalist.

མི་རིགས་རོལ་ཆས་ (mirii yüüröòjɛɛ̀) nationalities/ ethnic groups/ racial musical instruments.

མི་རིགས་ལས་དོན་ (mirii lɛɛ̀dön) nationality/ ethnic group/ race affairs.

མི་རིགས་ལས་དོན་ཅུའུ་ (mirii lɛɛ̀dön jūwu) tib.ch. nationality affairs bureau.

མི་རིགས་ལས་དོན་ཨུ་ཡོན་ལྷན་ཁང་ (mirii lɛɛ̀dön) nationality affairs commission.

མི་རིགས་ལས་བྱེད་སློབ་གྲྭ་ (mirii lɛɛ̀jeè lōbdra) school for nationality cadre.

མི་རིགས་ས་ཁོངས་རང་སྐྱོང་ (mirii sāgoŋ raŋgyoŋ) regional autonomy for nationalities.

མི་རིགས་སྲིད་ཇུས་ (mirii sīijüü) nationality/ racial/ ethnic policy.

མི་རིགས་སློབ་གྲྭ་ (mirii lōbdra) nationalities school (a school attended by nationality students).

མི་རིགས་སློབ་གྲྭ་ཆེན་མོ་ (mirii lōbdra cēmbo) a nationality university, a nationalities institute.

མི་རིགས་སློབ་འབྲིང་ (mirii lōbdriŋ) a nationality middle school.

མི་རིགས་སློབ་ཚོགས་ (mirii lōbdzoò) nationalities society/ association.

མི་རིགས་སློབ་གསོ་ཁྲུའུ་ (mirii lobso trū) tib.ch. nationalities education bureau/ division.

མི་རིགས་ཨུ་ཡོན་ལྷན་ཁང་ (mirii ūyön lhēngaŋ) nationalities committee.

མི་རིན་ (mirin) shung. price/ payment for buying and selling serfs.

མི་རིང་ (miriŋ) sm. མི་རིང་བར་.

མི་རིང་བར་ (miriŋwar) soon, before long ¶ མི་རིང་བར་མཇལ་རྒྱུ་ཡིན་སྟབས་ Because (we) will meet soon.

མི་རིང་བའི་སྔོན་ལ་ (miriŋwɛ ŋōnla) not long ago.

མི་རིས་ (mirii) mankind, humanity.

མི་རུ་དགུ་འཁོན་བྱེད་དུ་བཅུག (miru gugön cɛɛ̀du jūù) va. to instigate trouble between people.

མི་རུང་བ་ (miruŋwə) 1. unsuitable, inappropriate. 2. improper.

མི་རུང་ཧམ་རྩོད་ (miruŋ hāmdzöö) an inappropriate/ improper and shameless argument.

མི་རུས་ (miruù) human bone.

མི་རུས་ཀང་གླིང་ (miruù gāŋliŋ) sm. ཀང་གླིང་.

མི་རེ་ངོ་རེ་ (mire ŋore) each and every one ¶ཁོ་ཚོ་མི་རེ་ངོ་རེ་ངོ་སྤྲོད་གནང་བྱུང་ (They) introduced me to each and every one of them.

མི་རེ་ཟུང་ (miresuŋ) sm. མི་ཉུང་ཤས་.

མི་རེང་ (mireŋ) sm. མི་རྡིང་.

མི་རེངས་ (mireŋ) sm. མི་རྡིང་.

མི་རེའི་ཚ་སྙོམས་ (miree cāñom) average per capita ¶མི་རེའི་ཚ་སྙོམས་ཀྱི་ས་ཞིང་ Per capita fields. ¶མི་རེའི་ཚ་སྙོམས་ཡོང་བབས་ Per capita income.

མི་རོ་ (miro) human corpse.

མི་ལྷོམ་ (milom) modest, humble.

མི་ལ་ (milə) Milarepa.

མི་ལ་ངོ་ཚ་མེད་ན་ཁྱི་ ཁྱི་ལ་རྔ་མ་མེད་ན་འདྲེ་ (milə ŋodza meèna kyī kyīlə ŋāma meèna dre) shameless people are not human [Lit. a person without shame is a dog, a dog without a tail is a ghost].

མི་ལ་རྙིང་པ་གོས་ལ་གསར་པ་ (milə ñīŋbə köòla sāāba) conveys characteristics that are valued/ admired [Lit. old people are good, new clothes are good].

མི་ལ་མི་དགོས་ཁ་མཆུ་དང་ ཤིང་ལ་མི་དགོས་འཛེར་པ་ (milə migöò kāmjudaŋ shīŋlə mgöò dzerba) one should avoid disputes/ law cases [Lit. people don't need disputes, wood doesn't need knots].

མི་ལ་འཛིན་པའི་སྲིད་ཇུས་ (milə dzimbε sīījüü) policy of looking at individuals in politics.

མི་ལ་རས་པ་ (milə rεèba) Milarepa.

མི་ལ་རས་པའི་རྣམ་ཐར་ (milə rεèbε nāmdar) the biography of Milarepa written by Sangye Gyaltsen in 1488.

མི་ལ་རེ་དགོས་བྱུང་ན་ ཁྱིས་སྤྲགས་ཟ་གི་མ་རེད་ (milə regöò juŋnə kyīī bāà səgimareè) a saying used when sb. you ask for help refuses—conveys there will be a time when he needs help and will get paid back in kind [Lit. if one has to ask a person a favor, (it is like) the dog will not eat སྤྲགས་ (i.e., we all will have to do this just as the dog never does not eat bag)].

མི་ལ་རེ་དགོས་མ་གཏོང་ དཔོན་ལ་ཞུ་དགོས་མ་གཏོང་ (milə regöò madoŋ bõnla shugöò madoŋ) conveys the desirability of independence/ self-sufficiency [Lit. don't depend on others, don't ask things from one's lord].

མི་ལག (milaà) hired hand, hired laborer; va.—གླ་ to hire a laborer; va.—རྒྱུགས་ to go to work as wage laborer. 2. a human hand.

མི་ལང་ (milaŋ) sm. མི་ཟླ་.

མི་ལས་དགུ་ལས་ (milεè gulεè) doing all sorts of different work/ tasks.

མི་ལུས་ (milüù) human body, human being; vi.—ལེན་ to be born as a human ¶ཞིང་བྲན་ཚོར་མི་ལུས་ཀྱི་རང་དབང་མེད་ Serfs have no control over their bodies (person).

མི་ལུས་ཀྱི་ཁེ་དབང་ (milüùgi kēwaŋ) human rights.

མི་ལུས་ཀྱི་ཆག་སྒོ་ (milüùgi cāàgo) personal problems.

མི་ལུས་ཀྱི་རང་དབང་ (milüùgi raŋwaŋ) personal freedom, freedom over one's body/ person.

མི་ལུས་བདུད་སེམས་ (milüù düùsem) an evil person pretending to be good [Lit. body of a human and the mind of a demon].

མི་ལུས་རིན་ཆེན་ (milüù rinjen) the preciousness of being human.

མི་ལུས་རིན་ཆེན་གསེར་ལས་དཀོན་པས་སྙིང་པོ་ཡོད་པ་བྱ་དགོས་ (milüù rinjen sērlε gõnbε ñīŋbo yööba cagöò) to be born as a human is dearer than gold, therefore one should lead a meaningful (religious) life.

མི་ལེགས་པ་ (milegba) improper, bad, ugly.

མི་ལོ་ (milo) 1. a year ¶མི་ལོ་བཅུ་ཕྲག་གཅིག A decade (a set of ten years). 2. sm. མི་བབ་.

མི་ལོ་ལོན་ (milo lön) vi. to be grown up (person).

མི་ཤ་ (misha) 1. human flesh. 2. vengeance, revenge; va.—ལེན་ to take vengeance, to take revenge.

མི་ཤ་འཕྲང་ཕྲད་ (misha trāŋ trεὲ) no choice but to fight for revenge [Lit. meeting the person against whom one seeks revenge in a narrow gorge].

མི་ཤན་འབྱེད་ (mishεn jeè) va. to distinguish people's character (good and bad).

མི་ཤི་སྐྱོན་ཆག (mishi kyõnjaà) deaths as a result of an accident ¶མོ་ཊ་བརྡབས་ནས་མི་ཤི་སྐྱོན་ཆག་བྱུང་བཞག Some people died in a car accident.

མི་ཤི་ཁྱི་ལུས་ (mishi kyīlüù) sm. དུ་ཕྱུག་ཐང་ལུས་.

མི་ཤི་ཁྱིམ་སྟོངས་ (mishi kyīmdoŋ) people in a family die and the family becomes extinct, total extinction of a family.

མི་ཤི་ཁྱིམ་འཐོར་ (mishi kyīmdɔɔ) sm. མི་ཤི་ཁྱིམ་སྟོངས་.

མི་ཤི་རྒྱུ་བརླག (mishi gyulaà) people in a family die and the family loses its wealth.

མི་ཤི་རྟ་འགྱེལ་ (mishi dāgyee) suffering all kinds of problems and setbacks [Lit. the rider dies, the horse falls].

མི་ཤི་ཟོག་ཤོར་ (mishi sɔgshɔɔ) sm. མི་ཤི་རྒྱུ་བརླག.

མི་ཤི་ནའང་སེམས་མི་ཤི་ བྱ་ཤི་ནའང་མིག་མི་འཛུམ་ (mi shīnayaŋ sēm mishi ca shīnayaŋ miì midzum) defeated people will never forget their hatred/ loss [Lit. even if people die their "soul" will not die, even if a bird dies its eyes will not close].

མི་ཤིགས་རྟག་པའི་ཁམས་སུ་བརྟན་པ་ཤོག (mishiì dāgbε kāmsu dεmba shōò) shung. may sth. live forever.

མི་ཤིགས་པ་ (mishigbə) undefeatable, unbeatable, unconquerable.

མི་ཤིས་ལྟས་ངན་ (mishiì dεὲŋεn) inauspicious.

མི་ཤུགས་ (mishuù) manpower ¶མི་ཤུགས་ཀྱིས་རང་བྱུང་ཁམས་བསྒྱུར་བཀོད་བྱས་པ་རེད་ Through manpower (they) transformed nature.

མི་ཤུགས་རྒྱུ་སྟོབས་ (mishuù gyudob) manpower and material wealth, human and material strength/ resources.

མི་ཤུགས་རྒྱུ་ཤུགས་ (mishuù gyushuù) sm. མི་ཤུགས་རྒྱུ་སྟོབས་.

མི་ཤུགས་ཆར་ཕབ་འཕྲུལ་འཁོར་ (mishuù cārbəb trũũgɔɔ) a person operated water sprinkler/ sprayer.

མི་ཤེས་དགུ་ཤེས་ (misheè gusheè) knowing a lot.

མི་ཤེས་ (misheè) ignorant, not knowing.

མི་ཤེས་ཤེས་ཁུལ་ (misheè shēègüü) pretending to know.

མི་ཤེས་ཤེས་མདོག (misheè shēndɔɔ̀) sm. མི་ཤེས་ཤེས་ཁུལ་.

མི་ཤོད་དགུ་ཤོད་ (mishöò gushöò) unnecessary/ reckless/ excessive comments or talk; va.—ཤོད་ to talk too much, to talk recklessly.

མི་གཤའ་བ་ (mishawa) unreasonable, unwise.

མི་གཤིས་ (mishiì) 1. human nature ¶མི་གཤིས་ལས་འདས་པའི་གདུག་རྩུབ་ Inhuman cruelty (cruelty beyond human nature). ¶མི་གཤིས་དང་འགལ་བའི་དམག་འཁྲུག An inhuman war. 2. an individual's character or nature ¶ཁོ་མི་གཤིས་བཟང་པོ་ཞིག་རེད་ He is a good-natured person. ¶མི་གཤིས་འཇམ་པོ་ A person with a gentle nature.

མི་གཤིས་གཉིས་ལྡན་ (mishiì ñīìdεn) dual personality.

མི་གཤིས་སྨྲ་བ་ (mishiì māwa) the theory of human nature.

མི་གཤིས་བརླག (mishiì lāà) vi. to lose one's humanity.

མི་གཤིས་ལས་འདས་པ་ (mishiìlε dεèba) inhuman [Lit. beyond human nature].

མི་བཤད་དགུ་བཤད་ (mishεὲ gushεὲ) sm. མི་ཤོད་དགུ་ཤོད་.

མི་ས་འོག་གཏམ་སྟེང་ (mi sāwɔɔ̀ dāmdeŋ) the deeds a person does will be talked about after one dies [Lit. the person is under the ground the talks is on top of the ground].

མི་སར་རང་སྡོད་ (misaa raŋdöò) sb. who is quick to volunteer to do things.

མི་སར་རང་བཞག (misaa raŋshaà) putting oneself in another's shoes/ place, seeing things from another's point of view.

མི་སི་ (misi) eng. Miss.

མི་སི་སྒྲར་ (misidrar) eng. Mr.

མི་སི་ཏར་ (misidrar) eng. sm. མི་སི་སྒྲར་.

མི་སེམས་ (misem) the mind's of people; va.— འདུལ་ to capture the minds of the people; va.— འགུལ་ to move people's minds.

མི་སེམས་འཁོར་ཕྱོགས་ (misem kɔ̄ɔ̄jɔɔ̀) sm. མི་སེམས་གཏད་ཕྱོགས་.

མི་སེམས་གཏད་ཕྱོགས་ (misem dɛ̄ɛ̀jɔɔ̀) 1. the way or direction people are thinking ¶ མི་སེམས་གཏད་ཕྱོགས་ལ་བལྟས་ན་ལྷ་སར་མུ་མཐུད་ཐེང་ཆ་ལང་གི་རེད་ Considering the way people are thinking, there will be continuing demonstrations in Lhasa. 2. the one to whom one looks/ trusts/ depends/ relies on ¶ བོད་མི་དམངས་ཀྱི་མི་སེམས་གཏད་ཕྱོགས་ནང་པའི་ཆོས་རེད་ The Tibetan people depend on Buddhism.

མི་སེམས་མཐུན་པ་ (misem tũmbə) having the same thoughts or opinions.

མི་སེམས་ཕྱོགས་ས་ (misem cōgsa) sm. མི་སེམས་གཏད་ཕྱོགས་.

མི་སེམས་མ་ཟིན་ (misem masin) doing things against people's will/ wish.

མི་སེམས་མི་གཅིག་སོ་སོའི་གདོང་དང་འདྲ་ (misem mijig sōsö dondaŋ dra) different people have their own way of thinking about things [Lit. people's thinking is different just like their faces are different].

མི་སེམས་འཚབ་འཚུབ་ (misem tsābdzub) anxious, nervous, jittery.

མི་སེམས་ལོག (misem lɔɔ̀) vi. to have a change of mind.

མི་སེམས་བསླུ་བྲིད་ (misem lūdriì) sm. བསླུ་བྲིད་.

མི་སེམས་ལྷིང་འཇགས་ (misem lhĩŋjaà) the minds of people being at ease.

མི་སེར་ (misee) 1. serf, subject of a lord ¶ སྐུ་དྲག་དེ་ར་མི་སེར་མང་པོ་ཡོད་པ་རེད་ That aristocrat has many serfs. 2. citizens, subjects ¶ མི་སེར་དཀྱུས་ The common subjects. ¶ རྒྱལ་ཁབ་ཀྱི་མི་སེར་ཚོར་འདེམས་ཤོག་འཐེན་པའི་དབང་ཆ་ཡོད་པ་རེད་ The citizens of the country have the right to vote.

མི་སེར་རྒྱལ་ཁབ་ (misee gyɛɛgəb) a republic.

མི་སེར་དོན་གསུམ་རིང་ལུགས་ (misee tõnsum riŋluù) the "Three Principles of the People" (written by Sun Yatsen).

མི་སེར་གླིང་ (misee bēl) va. to colonize.

མི་སེར་གླིང་མཁན་རྒྱལ་ཁབ་ (misee bēēñɛn gyɛɛgəb) a colonial nation (a country with colonies).

མི་སེར་གླིང་མཁན་བཙན་རྒྱལ་ (misee bēēñɛn dzɛ̄ngyɛɛ) colonial imperialist nation/ country.

མི་སེར་གླིང་བའི་ (mīsee bēēwɛ) colonial ¶ མི་སེར་གླིང་བའི་དབང་བསྒྱུར་ ¶ Colonial rule. ¶ མི་སེར་གླིང་བའི་དམག་དཔུང་ Colonial troops.

མི་སེར་གླིང་བའི་རིང་ལུགས་ (mīsee bēēwɛ riŋluù) colonialism.

མི་སེར་གླིང་བྱེད་རིང་ལུགས་ (mīsee bēējeè riŋluù) sm. མི་སེར་གླིང་བའི་རིང་ལུགས་.

མི་སེར་གླིང་ཡུལ་ (mīsee bēēyüü) a colony, colonial.

མི་སེར་གླིང་ཡུལ་ཕྱེད་ཙམ་ (mīsee bēēyüü cēēdzam) a semicolony, semicolonial.

མི་སེར་སྤྱི་ (misee jī) shung. the subjects/ citizens/ serfs in general or in common.

མི་སེར་དབང་གཙོའི་ལམ་སྲོལ་ (misee wāŋdzö lamsöö) democratic system (of government).

མི་སེར་དབང་འཛིན་རིང་ལུགས་ (misee wāŋdzin riŋluù) democracy (one of the three principles of Sun Yatsen).

མི་སེར་རྨོངས་བྱེད་ཀྱི་སྲིད་ཇུས་ (misee mōŋjeègi sīījüü) policy of duping the people.

མི་སེར་འཚོ་གནས་རིང་ལུགས་ (misee tsōnɛɛ̀ riŋluù) people's livelihoodism (one of the three principles of Sun Yatsen).

མི་སེར་སྲིད་གཞུང་ (misee sīīsuŋ) shung. sm. མི་དམངས་སྲིད་གཞུང་.

མི་སོའི་བརྡ་ཆོག་བསྒྲགས་རྒྱ་ (misöö dõnjɔɔ̀ dzɛ̄ɛ̄gya) shung. an edict issued by the Agriculture Department (སོ་ནམས་ལས་ཁུངས་) of tt. government giving permission to take grain from storage in its granaries.

མི་སྲིད་པ་ (misiìbə) impossible, impossibility ¶ འདི་བདེན་མི་སྲིད་པ་ཞིག་རེད་ It is impossible that this is true.

མི་སྲིད་སྲིད་པ་ (misiì sīībə) unbelievable, impossible ¶ ཕྲུ་གུ་སློབ་སྦྱོང་ཡག་པོ་མེད་པ་འདིས་ཡིག་ཚད་ལོན་པ་མི་སྲིད་སྲིད་པ་ཞིག་རེད་ It is unbelievable that the bad student passed the exam.

མི་སྲོག (misɔɔ̀) human life; va.—གཅོད་ to kill a person; vi.—ཆད་ to die.

མི་སྲོག་གི་ཉེན་སྲུང་ (misɔɔ̀gi ñensuŋ) life insurance.

མི་སྲོལ་ (misöö) humanness, humanity.

མི་སྲོལ་རིང་ལུགས་ (misöö riŋluù) humanism.

མི་གསལ་བ་ (misɛɛwa) unclear, dim, indistinct.

མི་གསར་དོན་གསར་ (misaa tõnsaa) new people and new things/ events/ work ¶ ཡུལ་དེའི་ནང་མི་གསར་དོན་གསར་མང་པོ་ཐོན་བཞག In this place many new people and things have appeared.

མི་གསར་པ་ (mi sāāba) newcomer, stranger.

མི་གསར་ལས་གསར་ (misaa lɛ̄ɛ̀saa) sm. མི་གསར་དོན་གསར་.

མི་གསུམ་ཁ་འཆམ་ན་བྲམ་ཟེའི་ར་མ་ཁྱི་རུ་འགྱུར་ (mi sūm kā cāmna dramsee rama kyīru gyur) if a group of people jointly agree to do sth. there is nothing they cannot accomplish [Lit. if three people agree to sth. they can change a Brahman's goat into a dog].

མི་གསོང་པོ་ (mi sāŋbo) an honest person.

མི་གསོད་ (mi sȫȫ) va. to kill a person.

མི་གསོད་ཁྲག་སྐྱོར་ (misöö trāàjɔɔ) killing and bloodshed; va.—བྱེད་ to kill and cause bloodshed.

མི་གསོད་ཉེས་ཅན་ (misöö ñeèjɛn) a murderer.

མི་གསོད་མ་ (misööma) a female murderess.

མི་གསོད་མཚང་བཀག་ (misöö tsāŋgəb) sm. མི་བསད་ཁ་བཀག.

མི་གསོད་མཚོན་ཆ་ (misöö tsōnja) lethal weapons.

མི་གསོད་ལག་དམར་བ་ (misöö lagmarwa) murderer.

མི་གསོན་པ་ཟ་ (mi sōmba sa) va. to lie shamelessly [Lit. to eat a person alive].

མི་གསོབ་ (misob) effigy of a person.

མི་བསད་ཀྱང་ཁྲག་མི་མཐོང་བ་ (misɛɛ̀gyaŋ trāà mitoŋwa) killing without spilling blood, killing/ destroying by subtle means.

མི་བསད་ཀྱི་གྱོད་དོན་ (misɛɛ̀gi gyȫȫdön) murder case.

མི་བསད་ཁ་བཀག (misɛɛ̀ kāgaà) murdering sb. to prevent them divulging one's secrets.

མི་བསད་ཁྲག་སྐྱོར་ (misɛɛ̀ trāgjɔɔ) killing and shedding blood.

མི་བསད་གྱོད་གཞི་ (misɛɛ̀ gyȫȫshi) sm. མི་བསད་ཀྱི་གྱོད་གཞི་.

མི་བསད་རྒྱ་འཕྲོག (misɛɛ̀ gyundrɔɔ̀) killing and plundering; va.—བྱེད་ to kill and plunder.

མི་བསད་རྟ་ཁྱེར་ (misɛɛ̀ dāgyer) heinous/ abominable crime [Lit. kill a person steal the horse].

མི་བསད་མེ་བརྒྱབ་ (misɛɛ̀ megyəb) murder and arson.

མི་བསམ་དྲག་བསམ་ (misam gusam) wild/ fantastic thoughts and ideas, thinking all sorts of things, thinking too much ¶ ད་ལྟ་ཆུ་ལོག་ཡོང་གི་ས་ཟེར་གོ་པ་དང་མི་བསམ་དྲག་བསམ་བསམ་བྱུང་ As soon as I heard the flood was coming I had all sorts of wild thoughts.

མི་བསམ་རྒྱ་བསམ་ (misam gusam) sm. མི་བསམ་དྲག་བསམ་.

མི་བསམ་ཤེས་ཅན་ (misam shēējɛn) an enlightened/ broadminded/ understanding person.

མི་བརྣུན་ (midrün) malevolent, evil, ill-intentioned, harsh, brutal.

མི་བརྣུན་སྐྱེ་བོ་ (midrün gyēwo) wicked/ evil person.

མི་བསྡུན་བརླང་སྤྱོད་ (midrün lāŋjöö) evil/ wicked acts.

མི་ཧ་རི་ཧུ་རི་ (mi hāri hūri) sb. who does things in a hasty manner.

མི་ཧ་ལེ་ཧོ་ལེ་ (mi hāle hōle) sm. མི་ཧ་རི་ཧུ་རི་.

མི་ཧྲག་ཏ་ཧྲག (mihraà dāhraà) well-equipped [Lit. good men and good horses].

མི་ཧྲག་པོ་ (mi hrāgbo) a well-built/ physically fit person.

མི་ཧྲང་ (mi hrāŋ) sm. མི་ཧྲང་ཧྲང་.

མི་ཧྲང་ཧྲང་ (mi hrāŋhraŋ) a single individual (with no family), an individual who is alone.

མི་ཧྲེང་ (mihreŋ) sm. མི་ཧྲང་ཧྲང་.

མི་ཧྲེངས་ (mihreŋ) sm. མི་ཧྲང་ཧྲང་.

མི་ཧྲེངས་ (mi hrēŋ) vi. to become incorrigible/ spoiled/ uncontrollable.

མི་ཧྲེངས་རྒན་འཁོགས་ (mihraŋ gɛŋgɔɔ) an old man who is alone (with no family).

མི་ཧྲེངས་ཧྲེངས་ (mi hrēŋhreŋ) sm. མི་ཧྲང་ཧྲང་.

མི་ལྷིང་པོ་ (mi lhīŋbu) a calm/ gentle person.

མིག (mii) 1. eye; va.—ལྟ་ to look at; vi.—མཐོང་ to see. 2. hole ❘ པང་ལེབ་དེ་ར་མིག་ཁ་ཤས་འབུགས་དགོས་ (We) have to make several holes in that plank.

མིག་གོང་ (miggoŋ) a hollow/ sunken-eyed person.

མིག་ཀྲང་ཏོག་ལ་ཁྲ་མཚུར་གཞུ་བ་ (migdraŋ tōɔla kūdzuu shuwə) sm. འགྲེལ་ཐོག་ཏོག་བརྗེས་.

མིག་ཀྲབ་ཀྲབ་ (mii drābdrəb) blinking; vi.—བྱེད་.

མིག་དཀྱུས་བཟང་བ་ (miggyüü saŋwə) sm. མིག་དཀྱུས་རིང་བ་.

མིག་དཀྱུས་རིང་བ་ (miggyüü riŋwə) long, narrow eyes (a sign of beauty).

མིག་སྐྱ་ལོག་ལོག (miigya lɔglɔɔ) eyes showing white when someone is about to die.

མིག་སྐྱག (miigyaà) eye crud.

མིག་སྐྱི་ (miigyi) cornea.

མིག་སྐྱེལ་བྱེད་ (miigyee cèè) va. to look for a long time at people walking away/ departing.

མིག་སྐོར་ (miigɔɔ) glancing/ looking around; va.—རྒྱག.

མིག་སྐྱོ་ (miigyo) sm. མིག་སྐྱག.

མིག་ཁུང་ (miggun) 1. eye socket. 2. a hole ❘ སྣོད་ཆས་འདི་ལ་མིག་ཁུང་ཞིག་འདུག This pot has a hole.

མིག་ཁྱིམ་ (miggyim) eye socket.

མིག་ཁྲམ་ (mindrm) sm. མིག.

མིག་འཁྱུག (mig kyüù) va. to move one's eye from side to side to look at sth. without moving one's head.

མིག་འཁྲུལ་ (mindrüü) magic; va.—བསྟན་ to do sth. magically.

མིག་གི་སྐྱ་རིབ་ (miigi gyərib) sm. མིག་གི་སྐྱ་སྒྲིབ་.

མིག་གི་སྐྱ་སྒྲིབ་ (miigi gyədrib) cataract.

མིག་གི་རྒྱལ་མོ་ (miigi gyɛɛmo) pupil of the eyes.

མིག་གི་མཐའ་འཁོར་ (miigi tāgɔɔ) the orbit of the eye.

མིག་གི་དྲུང་ (miigi trun) in front of, before one's eyes.

མིག་གི་བདུད་རྩི་ (miigi düüdzi) sth. that is pleasing to the eyes, beautiful, good-looking.

མིག་གི་མདུན་ (miigi dün) sm. མིག་གི་དྲུང་.

མིག་གི་ནང་གི་འཛེར་བུ་ (miigi naŋgi dzərbu) sm. མིག་ནང་གི་གྲུ་མ་.

མིག་གི་ནུས་པ་ (miigi nüübə) power of eyesight/ vision.

མིག་གི་རྣམ་འགྱུར་ (miigi nāmgyur) expression of the eyes.

མིག་གི་རྣམ་ཤེས་ (miigi nāmsheè) sm. མིག་ཤེས་.

མིག་གི་ནོ་ (miigi nō) sm. མིག་གི་ནུས་པ་.

མིག་གི་ནོ་ཤུགས་ (miigi nōshuù) sm. མིག་གི་ནུས་པ་.

མིག་གི་པུ་ཆུང་ (miigi pujuŋ) sm. མིག་གི་རྒྱལ་མོ་.

མིག་གི་དབང་པོ་ (miigi wāŋbo) sm. མིག་གི་སྐྱེ་མཆེད་.

མིག་གི་རྫི་མ་ (miigi dzimə) eyelash.

མིག་གི་ཟེའུ་འབྲུ་ (miigi sendru) sm. མིག་གི་རྒྱལ་མོ་.

མིག་གི་ཟེར་ཕྲེང་གཡོ་ (miiigi sərdreŋ yō) way of looking at sth. ❘ ཁོང་ཁྲོའི་མིག་གི་ཟེར་ཕྲེང་གཡོ་གི་འདུག (He) is looking angrily.

མིག་གིས་སྐྱེལ་ (miigi gyēē) va. to follow sb. with one's eyes, to watch sb. going, to gaze after sb.

མིག་གིས་ཚོད་འཛལ་ (miigi tsɛnjɛɛ) sm. མིག་འཛལ་.

མིག་གིས་མཐོང་གིན་མཐོང་གིན་ (miigi tōŋgin tōŋgin) doing sth. right in front of one's eyes ❘ ངའི་མིག་གིས་མཐོང་གིན་མཐོང་གིན་ཁོས་རྐུན་མ་བརྒྱབས་སོང་ He stole right in front of my eyes.

མིག་གིས་མཐོང་མཐོང་བ་ (miigi tōŋtoŋwa) obvious/ apparent to one's eyes ❘ སྦྱར་ཚག་སྦྱར་བ་ཁྱེད་རང་གི་མིག་གིས་མཐོང་མཐོང་བར་ང་ལ་སྐད་ཆ་འདྲི་དགོས་དོན་གང་ཡིན་ནམ་ When the poster is so obvious, why do you have to ask me?

མིག་གིས་མཐོང་ས་ (miigi tōŋsa) 1. the place where sth. is visible or can be seen. 2. (with negatives) sth. can not be or is not seen ❘ དེང་སང་ཡུལ་དེ་ར་གྲྭ་པ་མིག་གིས་མཐོང་ས་ཡོད་པ་མ་རེད་ These days there are no monks to be seen in that place.

མིག་གྲུང་པོ་ (mii trunbo) a person who watches carefully/ accurately.

མིག་འགྲན་བྱེད་ (migdrɛn cèè) sm. གཞན་གྲུན་ནད་ཡངས་.

མིག་འགྲམ་ (mindram) just before one's eyes, right in front of one's eyes.

མིག་འགྲིབ་ (mindrib) cataract.

མིག་རྒྱ་ (miggya) perspective, foresight, vision ❘ ཆབ་སྲིད་ཀྱི་མིག་རྒྱ་ Political foresight.

མིག་རྒྱ་ཁབ་ལས་ཆུང་བ་ (miggya kəblɛ cūŋwa) lack of foresight, shortsighted; vi.—བྱེད་ to be shortsighted/ narrow-minded.

མིག་རྒྱག (mii gyaà) 1. va. to drill a hole. 2. vi. to just become ripe (for grains).

མིག་རྒྱང་ (miigyaŋ) 1. sight, vision. 2. outlook, foresight. 3. the distance one can see with the naked eye.

མིག་རྒྱང་གང་ (miigyaŋ kaŋ) as far as the eye can see, in the distance ❘ མིག་རྒྱང་གང་གི་ས་ནས་ངས་མི་དེ་ངོ་ཤེས་བྱུང་ I recognized that person from a distance.

མིག་རྒྱང་ཐུང་ (miigyaŋ tūŋ) sm. མིག་རྒྱང་ཐུང་ཐུང་.

མིག་རྒྱང་ཐུང་ཐུང་ (miigyaŋ tūŋduŋ) 1. shortsighted (with regards to thinking). 2. nearsighted (visually).

མིག་རྒྱང་ཐུང་བ་ (miigyaŋ tūŋwa) sm. མིག་རྒྱང་ཐུང་ཐུང་.

མིག་རྒྱང་རིང་པོ་ (miigyaŋ riŋgu) sm. མིག་རྒྱང་རིང་བ་.

མིག་རྒྱང་རིང་བ་ (miigyaŋ riŋwə) farsighted (with regard to thinking or vision).

མིག་རྒྱན་ (miggyɛn) shung. sth. important, a treasure.

མིག་རྒྱུན་ (miggyün) an example (behavioral); va.—སྟོན་ to set an example ❘ ཁོ་ཚོས་མིག་རྒྱུན་ངན་པ་བསྟན་ཙང་ Because they set a bad example.

མིག་སྒྲིབ་ (mii drib) va. to blindfold, to put sth. over sb.'s eyes.

མིག་སྒྲིམ་པོ་ (mii drimbu) looking at sth. with concentration/ focus.

མིག་འགྲན་ (miədrɛn) imitating; va.—བྱེད་ to imitate.

མིག་ངན་བལྟ་ (mignɛn dā) va. to give an angry look.

མིག་ངོར་ (mignor) sm. མིག་སྔར་.

མིག་སྔར་ (minnar) 1. before one's eyes, in one's field of vision ❘ མཚོ་ཆེན་པོ་ཞིག་མིག་སྔར་འཆར་བྱུང་ A big lake appeared before my eyes. 2. at present ❘ མིག་སྔར་ཟམ་པ་དེ་རང་རྒྱལ་གྱི་ཟམ་པ་ཆེ་ཤོས་རེད་ At present, that is the biggest bridge in our country.

མིག་ཅན་གཡང་མཚོང་ (migjɛn yāŋcoŋ) shung. sm. མིག་ལྡན་གཡང་མཚོང་.

མིག་ཅེ་རེ་ (mig jēre) wide-eyed, staring; va.—ལྟ་ to stare wide-eyed.

མིག་ཅེར་བ་ (mig jērwa) sm. མིག་ཅེ་རེ་.

མིག་བཅར་ (mii jāā) va. to extract/ take out sb.'s eyeballs (as a form of corporal punishment).

མིག་བཅོས་མཁས་པ་ (migjöö kɛɛba) eye specialist, eye doctor.

མིག་ལྕིབས་ (migjib) eyelid.

མིག་ཆབ་མ་བདེ་བ་ (migjəb madewa) poor vision.

མིག་ཆུ་ (migju) tears; vi.—ཤོར་; —ཐོན་; —དོན་ to cry, to weep; va.—གཏོང་ to shed tears; vi.—འཁོར་ to have one's eyes tear up/ water.

མིག་ཆུ་ཉིལ་ཉིལ་ (migju ñiiñii) eyes full of tears, eyes brimming with tears.

མིག་ཆུ་ཉིལ་ལེ་ (migju ñiile) sm. མིག་ཆུ་ཉིལ་ཉིལ་.

མིག་ཆུ་ལོང་ལོང་ (migju loŋloŋ) sm. མིག་ཆུ་ཉིལ་ཉིལ་.

མིག་ཆུ་ལྷུང་ལྷུང་ (migju lhūŋlhuŋ) sm. མིག་ཆུ་ཉིལ་ཉིལ་.

མིག་ཆུ་ཤོར་ (migju shɔ̄ɔ) vi. to shed tears, to cry.

མིག་ཆུའི་ཐིགས་ཕྲེང་ (migjü tigdreŋ) sm. མིག་ཆུའི་ཕྲེང་དོག.

མིག་ཆུའི་ཕྲེང་དོག (migjü trēŋdɔɔ) a teardrop.

མིག་ཆེ་བ་ (migjewa) 1. a large hole. 2. great desire/ want.

མིག་འཚུས་ (mii cüü) vi. to have one's eyes strained or tired.

མིག་འཆོལ་ (mii cöö) vi. to see sth. wrongly, to see sth. illusory.

མིག་འཇལ་ (migjɛɛ) estimating visually (rather than actually measuring), eyeballing; va.—བྱེད་.

མིག་ཉལ་ (mìgñüü) searching with one's eyes; va.—རྒྱག to look/ search with one's eyes.

མིག་གཏོད་ (mig dȫȫ) va. to stare.

མིག་བཏོན་ (mig dōn) p. of མིག་འདོན་.

མིག་རྟགས་ (migdaà) 1. a landmark to find one's way; va.—རྒྱག to use sth. as a landmark ¶གྲོང་ཁྱེར་ནང་ལམ་མ་ནོར་བའི་ཆེད་དུ་ཆོས་ཁང་དེ་རང་ངས་མིག་རྟགས་བརྒྱབ་པ་ཡིན་ In order not to lose my way in the city, I used that church as a landmark. 2. looking at sth. carefully and making a mental note of it ¶ངས་ཚོང་ཁང་ནང་གི་ཅ་ལག་ཁ་ཤས་ལ་མིག་རྟགས་བརྒྱབ་ནས་རྗེས་སུ་ཉོ་བར་ཕྱིན་པ་ཡིན་ I looked at several things carefully in the store and later went (back) to buy them.

མིག་ལྟ་ (mig dā) 1. va. to look at ¶ངས་པར་འདི་ཚོར་མིག་ལྟས་པ་ཡིན་ I looked at the photos. 2. looking after, watching over; va.—བྱེད་ ¶ངའི་ཕྲུ་གུ་འདི་ལ་མིག་ལྟ་བྱེད་རོགས་ (Please) look after my child. ¶སློབ་གྲྭ་བ་དེ་ཚོར་མིག་ལྟ་བྱེད་མཁན་དགོས་ཀྱི་ཡོད་པ་རེད་ These students need sb. to look after them. 3. va. to look at in the sense of forming a serious/ love relationship with ¶མི་ཕྱུག་པོ་དེས་བུ་མོ་དབུལ་པོ་ལ་མིག་ལྟ་གི་མ་རེད་ The rich man will not look at a poor girl to form a serious relationship.

མིག་ལྟ་ས་ (mii dāsa) sm. མིག་བལྟ་ས་.

མིག་ལྟས་ངན་པ་ (miidɛɛ ŋəmba) a bad omen/ sign.

མིག་ལྟོས་ (mii dȫȫ) 1. sm. མིག་ལྟ་. 2. sm. མིག་དཔེ་.

མིག་ལྟོས་འགོ་ (migdöö go) vi. to be influenced by sb.'s example.

མིག་ལྟོས་ངན་འབྲན་ (migdöö ŋɛndrɛn) following the example of a wrongdoer, imitating bad examples; va.—བྱེད་.

མིག་ལྟོས་འཇགས་ (migdöö jaà) sm. མིག་ལྟོས་འགོ.

མིག་ལྟོས་དཔེ་སྟོན་ (migdöö bēdön) 1. demonstrating; va.—བྱེད་ to demonstrate. 2. sm. མིག་དཔེ་སྟོན་.

མིག་ལྟོས་མར་ལྟ་ (miidöö maa dā) following a bad example/ standard/ model.

མིག་ལྟོས་བཟང་པོ་ (migdöö saŋbo) a good example/ model/ standard.

མིག་ལྟོས་ཡར་ལྟ་ (migdöö yaa dā) following or imitating a good example/ standard/ model.

མིག་ལྟོས་ཡར་འབྲན་ (migdöö yaa drɛn) following or imitating a good example/ standard.

མིག་ལྟོས་རིམ་ལྡད་ (migdöö rimlɛɛ) gradually imitating/ copying/ following sth. ¶ཉེ་ལམ་ལས་ཁངས་ནང་མིག་ལྟོས་རིམ་ལྡད་བྱུང་ནས་སྒྲིག་ལམ་སྲུང་མཁན་མེད་པ་ཆགས་བཞག Recently, there were a series of bad examples in the office and (now) nobody follows discipline.

མིག་ལྟོས་ཤས་རྒྱན་ (migdöö shɛ̄ɛgyen) a bad example.

མིག་ལྟོས་ལ་ཕན་པ་ (migdööla pɛmba) a good example.

མིག་ལྟོས་སུ་འདོམས་པ་ (migdöösu domba) shung. sm. མིག་ལྟོས་ལ་ཕན་པ་.

མིག་སྟོན་ (mig dōn) showing, demonstrating; va.—བྱེད་ ¶འཕྲུལ་འཁོར་གསར་པ་དེ་ཚོ་མི་དམངས་ལ་མིག་སྟོན་བྱེད་དགོས་ (We) must demonstrate these new machines to the people.

མིག་བལྟ་ས་ (mig dāsa) 1. model, example; va.—བྱེད་ to use as an example, to look up to, to hold up as an example. 2. the object of one's hope ¶ཁོ་ཚོའི་མིག་བལྟ་ས་ཡིད་བཞིན་ནོར་བུ་རེད་ The Dalai Lama is the one they put all (their) hopes in.

མིག་བལྟས་ལག་སྦྱོང་ (migdɛɛ lagjoŋ) putting an example into practice; va.—བྱེད་.

མིག་བལྟས་བློས་འཛིན་ (migdɛɛ lōndzin) bearing/ keeping in mind what one sees.

མིག་བསྟར་ (mig dār) shung. va. to show.

མིག་ཐུང་ (migduŋ) abbr. of མིག་རྒྱང་ཐུང་ཐུང་.

མིག་ཐུར་ (migdur) a traditional Tibetan medical tool used for operating on cataracts.

མིག་མཐའ་ (migda) the rim of the eyes.

མིག་མཐོང་ (mii tōŋ) vi. to see.

མིག་མཐོང་རྣ་ཐོས་ (mii tōŋ na tȫȫ) seeing with the eyes and hearing with the ears, experiencing firsthand, real, true.

མིག་མཐོང་གཟུགས་གྲུབ་ (migtoŋ sugdrub) visible, obvious.

མིག་མཐོང་ལག་ཞེན་ (mii tōŋ lag sin) firsthand knowledge, firsthand account ¶རྒྱ་ནག་ནང་གི་གནས་ཚུལ་མིག་མཐོང་ལག་ཞེན་མང་པོ་བྱུང་འདུག There are many firsthand accounts of events inside China.

མིག་མཐོང་གསལ་གྲུབ་ (migtoŋ sɛ̄ɛdrub) sm. མིག་མཐོང་ལག་ཞེན་.

མིག་དར་ (migdar) a blindfold.

མིག་དྭངས་ (miidaŋ) bright eyes.

མིག་དྲ་ (migdrə) a net-like eye covering that is made from yak hair that is worn to protect the eyes from snow blindness.

མིག་གདངས་ (mii daŋ) va. to open one's eyes.

མིག་མདའ་ (migda) a signal with one's eyes; va.—འཕེན་ to give/ send a signal with one's eyes.

མིག་འདག (miŋdaà) filling in the cracks of a wall; va.—རྒྱག.

མིག་འདོན་ (mig dön) sm. མིག་བཙིར་.

མིག་འདྲིས་ (miŋdrii) 1. familiar, accustomed ¶བཟོ་ལས་ལ་མིག་འདྲིས་མེད་ཙང་ཐོག་མར་ཁག་པོ་བྱུང་ Because I wasn't accustomed to factory work, I had difficulty at first. 2. vi. to be/ get familiar with, to be accustomed to.

མིག་འདྲིས་ནར་འཇགས་ (miŋdrii nanjaà) familiar/ accustomed to ¶སྲིད་དོན་གྱི་ཚིག་གསར་པ་འདི་ཚོ་མིག་འདྲིས་ནར་འཇགས་ཆགས་པ་རེད་ The new political words have become familiar.

མིག་འདྲེན་ (miŋdren) sm. མིག་འབྲན་.

མིག་ནིབ་ (mii dib) vi. to have one's eyes be/ get sunken (due to loss of weight, illness, etc.).

མིག་ནིབ་ཡུད་ཙམ་ (migdeb yüüdzam) in a twinkling of the eyes, in a flash of the eyes.

མིག་ལྡན་ (miŋdɛn) 1. a learned person. 2. having eyes.

མིག་ལྡན་ཀུན་གྱིས་ཤེས་གསལ་ (miŋdɛn güngi shēèsɛɛ) known by all/ everyone.

མིག་ལྡན་གཡང་མཆོངས་ (miŋdɛn yāŋjoŋ) knowingly taking risks [Lit. having eyes and jumping over the abyss].

མིག་ཕྱིར་ (mii dir) va. to glare ¶ཁོས་ངར་མིག་ཕྱིར་ནས་བལྟས་བྱུང་ He glared at me.

མིག་ཕྱིར་ཕྱིར་བྱེད་ (mii dirdir cèè) sm. མིག་ཕྱིར་.

མིག་ལྡོག (mii dɔɔ) vi. to have the eyeballs roll back (e.g., when a person dies).

མིག་ལོངས་ (mii doŋ) vi. to become blind.

མིག་ལྡང་བསྒྲད་ (migdaŋ drɛɛ) sm. མིག་ལོག་ལྟ་.

མིག་ལྡེབ་ (miideb) sm. མིག་ཟིམ་ཟིམ་.

མིག་བརྡ་ (migda) an eye signal, a wink; va.—བྱེད་; —གཏོང་ to give an eye signal.

མིག་བརྡ་བརྗེ་རེས་ (migda jereè) exchanging eye signals.

མིག་ན་ལག་བཟོས་ (mignə lagsöö) creating problems

for oneself, bringing harm to oneself [Lit. eye sickness caused by the hand (rubbing)].

མིག་ནག་སེང་ངེ་བ་ (mignaà sẽŋŋewa) dark black eyes.

མིག་ནག་ཧྲིག་ཧྲིག (mignaà hrighrii) darting/ moving eyes; va.—བྱེད་, —ལྟ་.

མིག་ནང་གི་གྲ་མ་ (miinaŋgi trama) sth. that irritates, a thorn in one's side [Lit. awl in one's eye].

མིག་ནང་གི་ཚེར་མ་ (miinaŋgi tsēēma) sm. མིག་ནང་གི་གྲ་མ་ [Lit. a thorn in one's eye].

མིག་ནང་ལ་མ་འགྲོ་བ་ (miinaŋla mandrowa) not favoring or liking sth.

མིག་ནད་ (mignɛɛ̀) eye sickness/ disease/ injury.

མིག་ནད་སྡེ་ཚན་ (mignɛɛ̀ dedzɛn) department of opthalmology.

མིག་ནད་ནང་སྒྲིབ་ (mignɛɛ̀ naŋdrib) a type of cataract (in Tibetan medicine).

མིག་ནད་ཕྱི་སྒྲིབ་ (mignɛɛ̀ cīdrib) a type of cataract (in Tibetan medicine).

མིག་ནད་བར་སྒྲིབ་ (mignɛɛ̀ pardrib) a type of cataract (in Tibetan medicine).

མིག་ནད་སྨན་ཆུ་ (mignɛɛ̀ mẽnju) eyedrops.

མིག་ནད་ཚན་ཁག (mignɛɛ̀ tsẽngaà) department of ophthalmology.

མིག་ནད་རབ་རིབ་ (mignɛɛ̀ rəbrib) a type of eye disease that causes blurred vision.

མིག་ནད་ཤ་འཛེར་ (mignɛɛ̀ shāndzer) a sty.

མིག་ནུས་ (mignüü) vision ¶ མིག་ནུས་དམའ་བ་ Poor vision. [Lit. power of eyes].

མིག་གནོན་འདེབས་སྦུར་ (mignün debdur) a traditional Tibetan medical tool used on the eyes.

མིག་རྣ་ (migna) ears and eyes.

མིག་རྣག (mignaà) sm. མིག་སྐྱག.

མིག་རྣོ་པོ་ (mii nōbo) sharp eyes, acute vision.

མིག་སྣང་ (mignaŋ) the way sb. sees/ perceives things ¶ མི་དེ་འགོ་ཁྲིད་ཀྱི་མིག་སྣང་ལ་འགྲོ་གི་ཡོད་པ་མ་རེད་ That person is not seen favorably by the leaders. ¶ མི་གཞན་གྱི་མིག་སྣང་ལ་མ་མཛེས་པའི་ལས་ཀ་བྱ་རྒྱུ་མེད་ One shouldn't do things (work) that other people do not perceive well.

མིག་པོ་ཆེ་ (migboje) a covetous/ greedy person.

མིག་དཔངས་ (migbaŋ) aspiration, aims, goals ¶ མིག་དཔངས་མཐོ་པོ་ High aspirations/ aims/ goals.

མིག་དཔངས་མཐོ་ལ་འཇོན་ཐང་ཆུང་བ་ (migbaŋ tōla jöndaŋ cūŋwə) high aspirations but low ability, inability to live up to one's aspirations/ goals/ aims.

མིག་དཔེ་ (migbe) example, model; va.—བྱེད་ to set/ be an example, to take/ use as an example; va.—སྟོན་ to show/ demonstrate as an example; va.—ལེན་; —རྩི་; —ལྟ་ to imitate, to use as an example ¶ མིག་དཔེ་བཟང་པོ་ A good example. ¶ ཁྱེད་ཚོས་མིག་དཔེ་ཡག་པོ་ཞིག་བྱེད་དགོས་ You should set a good example. ¶ མིག་དཔེ་སྟོན་མཁན་མེད་ན་ཤེས་ཁག་པོ་རེད་ Without sb. to demonstrate it, it will be difficult to understand it.

མིག་དཔེ་ལྟ་ས་ (migbe dāsa) sth. or sb. to emulate/ follow/ imitate.

མིག་དཔེ་འཛུགས་ (migbe dzuù) va. to select sth./ sb. and use it as an example.

མིག་དཔེའི་རུ་ཁག (migbee rugaà) a model or exemplary team/ unit.

མིག་ལྤགས་ (migbaà) eyelids.

མིག་ལྤགས་གོང་མ་ (migbaà koŋma) the upper eyelid.

མིག་ལྤགས་འོག་མ་ (migbaà wɔɔma) the lower eye lid.

མིག་ལྤགས་ལས་མ་ (migbaà lɛɛma) sm. མིག་ལྤགས་གོང་མ་.

མིག་སྤུ་ (migbu) eyebrow; va.—འབྲི་ to use an eyebrow pencil (for makeup).

མིག་སྤུ་བཟང་པོ་ (migby saŋbo) thick eyebrows.

མིག་སྤྲིན་ (migdrin) cornea.

མིག་ཕུག (mig pūù) va. to make a hole in sth.

མིག་ཕོར་ (migbɔɔ) a circular metal template used by blacksmiths to punch holes in metal.

མིག་ཕྱིད་ (migjɛɛ̀) sm. མིག་འཕྱིད་.

མིག་ཕྱེ་ (migje) sm. མིག་འབྱེད་.

མིག་ཕྲ་པོ་ (mii drəwo) stingy, miserly.

མིག་འཕང་བྲལ་ (migpaŋ trɛɛ) vi. to have no hope of winning (in a fight, etc.).

མིག་འཕར་ (mii pār) vi. to have one's eye twitch (involuntarily).

མིག་འཕེན་ (mii pēn) 1. va. to watch, to stand guard. 2. sm. མིག་མདའ་འཕེན་.

མིག་འཕྱིད་ (migjii) snow blindness; vi.—རྒྱག to be/ get snowblind.

མིག་འཕྲད་ལྟ་ཤེལ་ (migdrɛɛ̀ dāshee) contact lens.

མིག་འཕྲུལ་ (mindrüü) 1. magic, conjuring, performing tricks; va.—སྟོན་ to do magic/ conjuring/ tricks ¶ ཁོས་མིག་འཕྲུལ་བསྟན་ཏེ་སྒམ་སྟོང་པ་ནས་ངང་པ་ཞིག་བཏོན་སོང་ He performed magic and pulled out a duck from an empty box. 2. vi. to hallucinate, to see illusions. ¶ ང་མིག་འཕྲུལ་ནས་གང་བྱུང་མ་བྱུང་མཐོང་བྱུང་ I was hallucinated and saw many strange things.

མིག་འཕྲུལ་སྒྱུ་རྩལ་ (mindrüü gyudzɛɛ) magic, conjuring; va.—སྟོན་.

མིག་བུ་ (migbu) a guide helping the blind.

མིག་བློ་ (miglo) sm. མིག་དབང་.

མིག་དབང་ (migwaŋ) 1. the sense of sight. 2. visually, through sight.

མིག་འབུད་ལུང་རྒྱུད་ (minbüü luŋgyüü) shung. sm. མིག་མཐོང་ལག་ཆེན་.

མིག་དབྲག་རུས་པ་ (migdraà rüübə) brow ridge.

མིག་འབུར་ (minbur) bulging eyes.

མིག་འབུར་ཚུགས་ (minbur tsūù) va. to look in a glaring/ staring/ angry manner.

མིག་འབེན་ (minben) target or subject of vision/ sight.

མིག་འབྱེད་ (mii jeè) va. to restore eyesight, to remove a cataract.

མིག་འབྱེད་ཐུར་མ་ (migjeè tūrmə) a surgical tool in Tibetan medicine for removing cataracts.

མིག་འབྱེད་ཐུར་གཙག (migjeè tūrdzaà) sm. མིག་འབྱེད་ཐུར་མ་.

མིག་འབྲས་ (mindrɛɛ̀) eyeball.

མིག་འབྲས་སྐྱི་མོ་ (mindrɛɛ̀ gyīŋmu) conjunctiva.

མིག་འབྲས་སྐྱི་མོའི་ཚད་ནད་ (mindrɛɛ̀ gyīŋmü tsɛɛ̀nɛɛ̀) conjunctivitis.

མིག་འབྲས་ལྟར་གཅེས་ (mindrɛɛ̀dar jēè) loving deeply [Lit. love like one's eyeball].

མིག་འབྲས་རྩ་སྐྱི་ (mindrɛɛ̀ dzāgyi) membrane of the eyeball, choroid membrane.

མིག་སྦྱར་ལྟ་ཤེལ་ (migjar dāshee) contact lens.

མིག་སྦྲིད་ (mii drii) vi. to see unclearly.

མིག་འབྲུ་ (mindru) trachoma.

མིག་མང་ (minmaŋ) sm. མིག་མངས་.

མིག་མངས་ (minmaŋ) the game of "go"; va.—རྒྱག.

མིག་མངས་ཀྱི་འཁྲབ་གཞི་ (minmaŋ gyəgrii) the board for playing "go."

མིག་མངས་རྒྱག་རིས་ (minmaŋ gyəgrii) the board for playing "go."

མིག་མངས་རྡེའུ་ (minmaŋ diwu) the black and white stones used for playing "go".

མིག་མངས་རྡོ་ (minmaŋ do) sm. མིག་མངས་རྡེའུ་.

མིག་མི་བཟང་ (migmisaŋ) one of the four guardian deities (the guardian of the west).

མིག་སྨུལ་ (miiñüü) searching by means of the eyes; va.—རྒྱག.

མིག་དམག (miimaà) sm. མིག་མངས་.

མིག་དམན་ (mii mɛn) looking down with the eyes (conveys with guilt/ embarrassment).

མིག་དམར་ (minmar) 1. tuesday. 2. Mars. 3. a person's name.

མིག་སྨན་ (migmɛn) eye medicine.

མིག་སྨན་འདེབས་བྱེད་ (migmɛn debjeè) eye drop applicator.

མིག་སྨན་མིག་ཕན་ (migmɛn migbɛn) allocating (a fund) where it was initially planned/ intended ¶ བསྟན་སྲིད་ཞབས་བརྟན་སྨྲུབ་རྒྱུའི་མཚོན་རྒྱུན་དུ་མིག་སྨན་

མིག་ཕན་ཞུ་དང་ཞུ་བཞིན་ལགས་ན་ We are allocating the fund for performing religious rites and for the promotion of the dharma and political development as it was initially planned [Lit. eye medicine benefits the eyes].

མིག་བཙའ་ (mii dzā) va. to look at ༑ཁོ་ཚོས་པར་འདི་ཚོར་ཁ་ས་མིག་བཙས་པ་རེད་ They looked at the photos yesterday.

མིག་བཙུམས་ནས་བྱིའུ་འཛིན་པ་ (miidzumnɛ ciwu dzimbə) acting blindly [Lit. catching a bird with one's eyes closed].

མིག་རྩ་ (migdzə) optical nerve, blood vessels in the eye.

མིག་རྩ་སྦྲུང་པོ་ (migdzə trunbo) sm. མིག་སྦྲུང་པོ་

མིག་རྩ་ཅན་ (migdzəjɛn) sm. མིག་ཕྲ་པོ་.

མིག་ཚ་ (mig tsā) 1. vi. to be envious/ jealous ༑གཞན་གྱི་གྲུབ་འབྲས་ལ་མིག་ཚ་ནས་ Being envious of another's success. 2. vi. to have a burning sensation in the eye ༑བཙོང་མིག་ནང་ལ་འཛུལ་ནས་མིག་ཚ་པ་རེད་ (His) eyes burned when the onion got into (his) eyes.

མིག་ཚག (migdzaà) blinking of the eyes (usu. due to illness); va.—བྱེད་.

མིག་ཚག་ཚག (mig dzāàdzaà) blinking of the eyes; va.—བྱེད་.

མིག་ཚད་ (migdzɛɛ̀) eye infection.

མིག་མཚམས་ (migdzam) around the eyes/ eyebrows.

མིག་འཚུམ་འཚུམ་ (mig tsūmdzum) sm. མིག་ཚག་ཚག.

མིག་མཛེར་ (mīgdzer) sm. མིག་ནད་ཤ་འཛེར་.

མིག་རྫི་ (migdzi) eyelash.

མིག་འཛུགས་ (mig dzuù) va. to place sth. as pawn for a loan.

མིག་འཛུམ་: p. མིག་བཙེམ་; f. མིག་བཙེམས་; imp. མིག་འཚུམས་ (mig dzum) va. to close one's eyes.

མིག་ཞག་འཁོར་ (migshaà kɔ̄ɔ) sm. མིག་རྒྱ་འཁོར་.

མིག་ཞར་གོག (mig shaagɔɔ) sm. མིག་ཞར་བ་.

མིག་ཞར་བ་ (mii shara) blind.

མིག་བཞུར་ (migshuu) looking/ glancing at sth.; va.—རྒྱག ༑དམག་མིའི་གྲལ་བསྒར་ལ་མིག་བཞུར་ཞིག་བརྒྱབ་ནས་ཕྱིན་སོང་ He took a look at the lined up troops and then left.

མིག་ཟིམ་མི་བ་ (mig simmewa) sm. མིག་ཟིམ་ཟིམ་.

མིག་ཟིམ་ཟིམ་ (mii simsim) eyes squinting; va.—བྱེད་.

མིག་ཟུམ་ཟུམ་ (mig sumsum) sm. མིག་ཟིམ་ཟིམ་.

མིག་ཟུར་ (migsur) 1. the corner of the eye. 2. looking at sth. from the corner of the eye; va.—ལྟ་ to look at from the corner of the eye.

མིག་གཟི་ལོག (mii siloò) cockeyed, cross-eyed; vi.—ལྟ་ to look with eyes crossed.

མིག་གཟེ་ (migse) eyelash.

མིག་གཟེར་ (migsee) jealous; vi.—རྒྱག to be/ feel jealous.

མིག་གཟོང་ (migsoŋ) a tool for making horseshoes.

མིག་འོག་ལ་ཐོགས (migwɔɔ̀la tɔ̄ɔ̀) sm. མིག་ལྟ་, 3.

མིག་འོད་ (migwöö) sight, vision.

མིག་ཡ་གཅིག (mig yəjii) one eye.

མིག་ཡངས་པ་ (mig yanba) knowledgeable.

མིག་ཡངས་མ་ (mig yanma) a young woman.

མིག་ཡར་ (migyaa) an eye covering used to prevent snow blindness (usu. made of the black tail of horses or yaks).

མིག་ཡུད་ཙམ་ (mig yüüdzam) in a twinkling of the eyes, in a flash of the eyes, in an instant.

མིག་ཡུལ་ (migyüü) tthe object of one's looking; va.—རྒྱག to look all around ཁོས་རང་འཁོར་གི་མི་ཚོར་མིག་ཡུལ་ཞིག་བརྒྱབ་པ་རེད་ He looked at all of the people around him.

མིག་ཡོ་ (migyo) cross-eyed.

མིག་ཡོད་པ་ (mii yööba) Thursday.

མིག་ཡོད་བཞིན་དུ་གཡང་ལ་མཆོངས་ (mii yööshindu yāŋla cōŋ) sm. མིག་ལྡན་གཡང་མཆོངས་.

མིག་ཡོན་ (migyün) sm. མིག་ཡོ་.

མིག་ཡོར་ (mig yɔɔ) vi. to see double images.

མིག་གཡས་ཞར་བ་དང་རྣ་གཡས་འོན་པ་བྱེད་ (mig yɛɛ̀ shara daŋ nā yɛɛ̀ wömba cee) pretending not to hear or see sth. [Lit. right eye blind, right ear deaf].

མིག་གཡོར་ (mig yɔɔ) sm. མིག་ཡོར་.

མིག་ར་ (migrə) sm. མིག་དྲ་.

མིག་རས་ (migrɛɛ̀) eyes; va.—བཙའ་ to look at sth.

མིག་རིག་རིག (mig riirii) sm. མིག་ཧྲིག་ཧྲིག.

མིག་རིན་ (migrin) shung. a token payment.

མིག་རིམས་ (migrim) infectious eye disease.

མིག་རིམས་ཐོར་པ་ (migrim tōrba) trachoma.

མིག་རིལ་ (migrii) eyeball.

མིག་རིལ་ཁྲག་རྩ་རྒྱས་པ་ (migrii trāgdza gyɛɛ̀ba) bloodshot eyes.

མིག་རོགས་ (migroò) a partner or helper just for appearance (not in actuality); va.—བྱེད་.

མིག་ལ་གྲི་ལོང་ཡོད་པ་ (miilə drīloŋ yööba) a blind person with eyes wide open.

མིག་ལ་སྐར་ཤར་ (miglə gār shār) vi. to see stars (after being struck on the head).

མིག་ལ་འཁྱུག (miglə kyūg) vi. to be pleasing to sb., to find sth. suitable/ becoming/ attractive.

མིག་ལ་འཁྱུག་པོ་ (miglə kyūgbu) someone who is pleasing.

མིག་ལ་འགྲོ་ (miglə dro) sm. sm. མིག་ལ་འཁྱུག.

མིག་ལ་རྒྱུག་པོ་ (miglə gyugbo) sm. མིག་ལ་འཁྱུག་པོ་.

མིག་ལ་མངར་བ་ (miglə ŋarwa) beautiful, attractive.

མིག་ལ་མིག་ལེན་དང་སོ་ལ་སོ་ལེན་ (mīgla miglɛn daŋ sōla sōlɛn) taking revenge in kind [Lit. an eye for an eye and a tooth for a tooth].

མིག་ལ་ཚ་འཐོར་ཤར་ (miglə tsātɔɔ shār) vi. to get cataracts.

མིག་ལ་མཛེས་པོ་ (miglə dzeèbo) pretty, beautiful.

མིག་ལ་ཟུག (miglə sug) vi. to like sth., to see sth. as attractive.

མིག་ལ་གཟན་པོ་ (miglə sɛmbo) 1. bad for the eyes ༑བརྙན་འཕྲིན་མང་པོ་བལྟས་ན་མིག་ལ་གཟན་པོ་ཡོང་ If (you) watch a lot of TV it will be bad for the eyes. 2. behavior that others will look at unfavorably or dislike ༑ཁྱེད་རང་རྟག་པར་ལས་ཁུངས་ལ་ཕྱི་དགོས་ན་འགོ་ཁྲིད་ཀྱི་མིག་ལ་ཟན་པོ་ཡོང་གི་རེད་ If you always come late to the office, the boss will look unfavorably.

མིག་ལམ་ (miglam) before the eyes, in the field of vision ༑དེ་ཁོའི་མིག་ལམ་དུ་འཆར་བ་རེད་ It appeared before his eyes.

མིག་ལམ་ཆད་ (miglam cɛɛ̀) 1. vi. to become dark ༑ལམ་འགྲོ་དུས་མིག་ལམ་ཆད་ཙང་གནས་ཚང་ཅིག་ལ་བསྡད་པ་རེད་ Because it became dark while (they) were traveling, (they) stayed at an inn.

མིག་ལམ་དུ་འགྱུར་ (miglamdu gyur) vi. to come into one's field of vision (in the real world and in dreams).

མིག་ལམ་དུ་མང་ཚོགས་མེད་པ་ (miglamdu mandzɔɔ̀ meèba) being conceited, arrogant [Lit. not considering the interests of the masses].

མིག་ལམ་དུ་མི་འཇོག (miglamdu minjɔɔ̀) va. to look down on.

མིག་ལར་འདོམས་ (miglar dom) va. to set an example by imposing strict/ harsh punishment ༑ལྐོག་ཚོང་རྒྱག་མཁན་རྣམས་ལ་མིག་ལར་འདོམས་པའི་ཁྲིམས་གཅོད་བཏང་བ་རེད་ They punished the smugglers harshly in order to set an example.

མིག་ལུག (migluù) a type of kite design which looks like two eyes hanging down.

མིག་ལོག (miglɔɔ̀) looking in anger/ hatred/ dislike; va.—ལྟ་; va.—སྒྲོག to look at angrily/ with hatred.

མིག་ལོང་ (mig loŋ) vi. to go blind, to lose one's eyesight ༑ཁོ་ཆུང་དུས་མིག་ལོང་བ་རེད་ He lost his eyesight when he was young.

མིག་ལོང་ (migloŋ) blind.

མིག་ལོག་ངན་པ་ (miglob ŋɛmba) a bad example.

མིག་ཤར་རྒྱག (migshaa gyaà) va. to take a quick look, to glance to ༑ཡིག་ཆ་འདི་ལ་མིག་ཤར་ཞིག་རྒྱག་རོགས་བྱེད་ Please have a quick look at this document.

མིག་ཤུགས་ (migshuù) 1. strength of vision/ sight ༑

མིག་ཤུགས་ཞན་པ་ Poor vision. 2. perception, shrewdness.

མིག་ཤུགས་དཔྱད་རིས་ (migshuù jèɛrii) eye chart (for eye exams).

མིག་ཤུར་རྒྱག (migshuu) sm. མིག་ཤར་རྒྱག.

མིག་ཤེད་ (migsheè) sm. མིག་ཤུགས་.

མིག་ཤེད་ཞོར་ (migsheè shɔ̄ɔ) vi. to have one's eyes get weaker.

མིག་ཤེལ་ (migshee) eyeglasses; va.—རྒྱག to wear eyeglasses.

མིག་ཤེལ་དུག་སྦྲུལ་ (migshee tugdruù) cobra (snake).

མིག་ཤེལ་ནག་པོ་ (migshee nagbo) sunglasses.

མིག་ཤེལ་སྦྲུལ་རྒྱལ་ (migshee drüügyɛɛ) sm. མིག་ཤེལ་དུག་སྦྲུལ་.

མིག་ཤེལ་ཚོས་ལྡན་ (migshee tsōndɛn) sm. མིག་ཤེལ་ནག་པོ་.

མིག་ཤེས་ (mīgsheè) vision, sight.

མིག་སེར་ (migsee) jealousy; va.—རྒྱག; —ལང་, —སྐྱེ་ to feel jealous.

མིག་སེར་པོ་ (mii sēēbo) yellow/ jaundiced eyes.

མིག་སེར་ཚ་པོ་ (migsee tsābo) jealous (person).

མིག་སྲུང་མིག་ཤེལ་ (migsuŋ migshee) protective glasses/ goggles.

མིག་སླུ་ (miglu) 1. sm. མིག་འཁྲུལ་. 2. va. to be confused/ puzzled/ perplexed.

མིག་སླེ་པོ་ (mig lēbo) cross-eyed.

མིག་གསུམ་པ་ (mii sūmbə) the Hindu god Vishnu.

མིག་བསྲིངས་ (mii sīŋ) va. to look at from a distance.

མིག་བསླེ་པོ་ (mii lēbo) sm. མིག་སླེ་པོ་.

མིག་ཧར་པོ་ (mig hārbo) clear/ bright eyes.

མིག་ཧུ་རེར་ལྟ་ (mii hūree dā) sm. མིག་ཧྲིག་གེར་ལྟ་.

མིག་ཧུར་ (mighur) a look of amazement/ astonishment.

མིག་ཧྲིག་གེར་ལྟ་ (mig hrīggee dā) va. to stare at.

མིག་ཧྲིག་ཧྲིག་ལྟ་ (mig hrīhrig dā) va. to stare at.

མིང་ (miŋ) name.

མིང་བཀྲ་ལེགས་པ་ (miŋ drā legba) auspicious name.

མིང་ཀུ་ (miŋ gū) va. to impersonate, to pose as, to represent oneself to be, to pass for ¶ བོད་ཀྱི་མི་དམངས་འཐུས་མིའི་མིང་བཀུས་ནས་ས་ཡིག་བརྒྱབ་པ་རེད་ Passing himself off as the representative of the Tibetan people, (he) signed (it).

མིང་རྐྱང་ (miŋgyaŋ) 1. the name of sth. 2. a noun.

མིང་ཁུངས་ (miŋguŋ) the origin of a name.

མིང་ཁུར་ (miŋgur) sm. མིང་འཁྱེར་.

མིང་འཁྱེར་ (miŋ kyēr) vi. to use sb.'s name, to do sth. in the name of another ¶ བྱམས་པའི་མིང་འཁྱེར་ནས་ཅ་ལག་གཡར་པ་རེད་ (He) borrowed things using Chamba's name.

མིང་གི་གོ་རི་ (miŋgi gori) position in a list of names, place in a competition.

མིང་གི་རྣམ་གྲངས་ (miŋgi nāmdraŋ) synonym.

མིང་གི་དབྱེ་བ་ (miŋgi yēwa) parts of speech.

མིང་གི་ཚོགས་པ་ (miŋgi tsɔ̄gba) dictionary, glossary of words.

མིང་གི་མཛོད་ (miŋgi dzȫȍ) sm. མིང་གི་ཚོགས་པ་.

མིང་གོ་ (miŋgo) ch. republic ¶ ཀྲུང་ཧྭ་མིང་གོ་ The Republic of China.

མིང་གྲགས་ (miŋdraà) reputation, fame.

མིང་གྲགས་ཆེ་བ་ (miŋdraà cēwa) famous, well-known.

མིང་གྲགས་ཐོབ་དབང་ (miŋdraà tōbwaŋ) the privileges of name/ reputation/ fame.

མིང་གྲོགས་ (miŋdroò) a person with the same name, namesake.

མིང་འགོ་ (miŋgo) prefix.

མིང་འགོད་ (miŋ gȫȍ) va. to sign.

མིང་འགྲེལ་ (miŋdree) definition/ explanation of a word; va.—རྒྱག.

མིང་རྒྱབ་ཁུར་ (miŋ gyəb kūr) sm. མིང་འཁྱེར་.

མིང་སྒྲ་ (miŋdra) noun.

མིང་སྒྱུར་ (miŋgyur) change of name, change of title, title transfer; va.—བྱེད་ to change names, to transfer title.

མིང་བསྒྱུར་ (miŋgyur) 1. p. of མིང་སྒྱུར་. 2. sm. མིང་སྒྱུར་.

མིང་ངན་ (miŋŋɛn) bad reputation, bad name.

མིང་ངན་ཀུན་གྲགས་ (miŋŋɛn gūndraà) infamous, a bad name known to all.

མིང་ངན་དབྱིར་ཕུད་ (miŋŋɛn yērbüü) sm. མིང་ངན་ཀུན་གྲགས་.

མིང་ངན་ཡོངས་གྲགས་ (miŋŋɛn yoŋdraà) sm. མིང་ངན་ཀུན་གྲགས་.

མིང་སྔོན་འགོད་ (miŋŋön gȫȍ) va. to sign a document first, to head a list of signers/ signatures (of a document).

མིང་ཅན་ (miŋjɛn) well-known, having a reputation.

མིང་བཅོས་ (miŋ jȫö) sm. མིང་སྒྱུར་.

མིང་ཆེ་བ་ (miŋcewa) sm. མིང་ཅན་.

མིང་ཆེན་ (miŋjen) sm. མིང་ཅན་.

མིང་བརྗེ་ (miŋ je) sm. མིང་སྒྱུར་.

མིང་བརྗེས་ (miŋ je) 1. sm. མིང་བརྗེ་. 2. p. of མིང་བརྗེ་.

མིང་བཏགས་ (miŋ dāà) p. of མིང་འདོགས་.

མིང་བཏགས་ཐུག་པ་ (miŋdaà tūgbə) rice gruel offered when a monk passes his geshe degree examination.

མིང་བཏགས་ལག་ཁྱེར་ (miŋdaà laggyer) diploma, certificate.

མིང་བཏོན་ (miŋ dȫn) p. of མིང་འདོན་.

མིང་རྟགས་ (miŋdaà) signature; va.—འགོད་ to affix a signature, to sign ¶ ཁོ་ཚོས་ཆིངས་ཡིག་ལ་མིང་རྟགས་བཀོད་པ་རེད་ They signed the treaty.

མིང་སྟོང་པ་ (miŋ dōŋba) having the name/ title but not the associated authority, an empty title/ rank.

མིང་སྟོང་ཙམ་ (miŋ dōŋdzam) sm. མིང་སྟོང་པ་.

མིང་སྟོན་ (miŋdön) 1. party given in honor of sb. passing a test/ degree, etc., va.—གསོམས་. 2. va. to say the name of sth.

མིང་ཐོ་ (miŋdo) list of names, roll, register; va.—འགོད་; —རྒྱག to compile/ make a list of names; va.—འདོན་ to write/ produce/ issue/ publish a list of names; va.—སུབ་ to erase a name from a list; to eliminate sb. from a position. ¶ ཚོགས་པ་འདི་ནང་གི་མི་ཚང་མའི་མིང་ཐོ་བཏོན་པ་རེད་ The names of all the party members were published.

མིང་ཐོ་སྒྲོག་སྦྱངས་ (miŋto drəgjaŋ) calling roll, taking attendance.

མིང་ཐོ་མཉམ་འགོད་ (miŋto ñamgȫȍ) jointly signed; va.—བྱེད་ to sign jointly.

མིང་ཐོག (miŋdɔ̄ɔ) 1. by means of or through one's name. 2. in name only, token.

མིང་ཐོག་གླ་ཕོགས་ (miŋtɔ̄ɔ lābɔ̄ɔ) nominal wages.

མིང་ཐོབ་ (miŋdob) a title.

མིང་མཐའ་ (miŋda) 1. suffix. 2. the second word of a Tibetan compound noun.

མིང་དང་བརྗོད་པ་ (miŋdaŋ jȫöba) word and sentence.

མིང་དུ་འདོགས་ (miŋdu dɔ̄ɔ) va. to name, to call ¶ བཀྲ་ཤིས་ཞེར་མིང་བཏགས་ (They) named (him) Tashi.

མིང་དེབ་ (miŋdeb) a register/ book of names.

མིང་གཞི་ (miŋshi) the root letter of a Tibetan syllable.

མིང་གཞུང་ (miŋshuŋ) a list of names.

མིང་དོན་ (miŋdön) name and deed/ actions/ behavior, what is said and what is done.

མིང་དོན་གཉིས་མཐུན་ (miŋdön ñīidün) sm. མིང་དོན་མཚུངས་པ་.

མིང་དོན་མཚུངས་པ་ (miŋdön tsūŋbə) proper accord between name and deed/ actions/ behavior, genuine, true, authentic ¶ བཙན་རྒྱལ་རིང་ལུགས་པའི་རྒྱུག་ཁྱི་མིང་དོན་མཚུངས་པ་ཞིག་རེད་ (He) is a true running dog of the imperialists.

མིང་འདེམས་ཤོག (miŋ demshoò) ballot; va.—འཕེན་ to cast a ballot, to vote.

མིང་འདོག (miŋ dɔ̄ɔ) sm. མིང་དུ་འདོགས་.

མིང་འདོག (miŋdoò) 1. nickname ¶ ཁོའི་མིང་འདོགས་ལ་སྤྲེའུ་ཞེར་གྱི་ཡོད་པ་རེད་ His nickname is monkey. 2. sm. མིང་དུ་འདོགས་.

མིང་འདོགས་སྣ་ཚོགས་ (miŋdoò nadzɔ̄ɔ) calling sth. by various names.

མིང་ལྡན་གྲངས་ (mi̲ŋdɛn tra̲ŋ) concrete number (in math).

མིང་འདོན་ (mi̲ŋdön) mentioning sb.'s name (e.g., in a speech); va.—འདོན་; —བྱེད་; —རྒྱག.

མིང་བརྡ་ (mi̲ŋda) 1. name of sth. 2. terms, words.

མིང་གནས་ (mi̲ŋnɛɛ̀) status, position, rank.

མིང་པས་ (mi̲ŋbɛ) a term used when concluding a Tibetan letter (to show humility) ། དགེ་མིང་པས་ From your humble teacher.

མིང་པོ་ (mi̲ŋbo) elder brother.

མིང་དཔྱས་ (mi̲ŋjɛɛ̀) sm. མིང་བྱད་.

མིང་འཕྲོག (mi̲ŋ drɔ̄ɔ̀) va. to take away sb.'s position/ rank.

མིང་བྱང་ (mi̲ŋjaŋ) 1. label, tag, title (books). 2. sm. མིང་ཐོ་.

མིང་བྱང་མཉམ་འགོད་ (mi̲ŋjaŋ ña̲mgöö̀) jointly signed.

མིང་བྱད་བཟོ་ (mi̲ŋjɛɛ̀ so̲) va. to give sb. a bad name/ reputation ། ངས་ཀུན་མ་བརྐུས་བཞག་ཟེར་མིང་བྱད་བཟོས་བཞག He gave me a bad name saying that I stole.

མིང་བྲིས་རྟགས་བཞག (mi̲ŋdriì dāgshaà) letters/ documents that have been signed and also have had a seal affixed.

མིང་འབུར་ (mi̲ŋ bu̲r) vi. to become increasingly well-known/ famous ། དེང་སང་གློག་བརྙན་འཁྲབ་མཁན་དེ་མིང་འབུར་ཡོང་གི་འདུག These days the movie star is becoming increasingly famous.

མིང་འབག (mi̲ŋbaà) mask, false front; va.—གྱོན་ to put on a false front.

མིང་འབོད་ (mi̲ŋ böö̀) va. to call a name.

མིང་འབྲེལ་ (mi̲ŋdree) jointly signed or agreed to ། མིང་འབྲེལ་གློག་འཕྲིན་ A telegram jointly signed.

མིང་སྦྱོར་ (mi̲ŋjɔɔ) word building, word formation.

མིང་སྦྲེལ་ (mi̲ŋ dre̲e) va. to put together words to form a phrase/ sentence.

མིང་མེད་ (mi̲ŋmeè) nameless, anonymous.

མིང་མེད་པོ་ (mi̲ŋ me̲èbo) sm. མིང་མེད་.

མིང་ཙམ་ (mi̲ŋdzam) nominal, token, in name only, figurehead ། མིང་ཙམ་གྱི་རང་སྐྱོང་སྤྲད་པ་རེད་ (They) gave them token autonomy.

མིང་ཙམ་གྱི་ཆབ་སྲིད་པ་ (mi̲ŋdzamgi cābsiìbə) armchair politician.

མིང་ཙམ་མེད་པ་བཟོ་ (mi̲ŋdzam mɛ̲ɛ̀ba so̲) va. to destroy completely, to annihilate.

མིང་ཙམ་བཟུང་བའི་སྲིད་གཞུང་ (mi̲ŋdzam su̲ŋwɛ siìshuŋ) token government, figurehead government.

མིང་ཙམ་ཡང་མེད་པ་བཟོ་ (mi̲ŋdzamyaŋ me̲èba so̲) sm. མིང་ཙམ་མེད་པ་བཟོ་.

མིང་གཙོ་སྨྲ་བ་ (mi̲ŋdzo māwa) nominalism, tokenism.

མིང་ཚབ་ (mi̲ŋdzəb) pronoun.

མིང་ཚིག (mi̲ŋdzii) 1. name and word. 2. noun, name of sth.

མིང་ཚོགས་ (mi̲ŋdzɔɔ̀) compound word.

མིང་ཚོགས་གསར་པ་ (mi̲ŋdzɔɔ̀ sāāba) new term/ word.

མིང་མཛོད་ (mi̲ŋdzöö̀) dictionary, glossary.

མིང་རྫས་ (mi̲ŋ dzɛ̲ɛ̀) va. to disgrace ། ཁོ་ཚོས་བོད་པའི་མིང་རྫས་པ་རེད་ They disgraced the name of Tibetans.

མིང་རྫུ་ (mi̲ŋ dzu̲) va. to pretend to be sb. else, to assume another's name.

མིང་རྫུས་ (mi̲ŋdzüù) false name.

མིང་རྫུས་ཁ་བསླུས་ (mi̲ŋdzüù kālüù) impersonating, assuming a false name/ identity; va.—བྱེད་.

མིང་གཞན་ (mi̲ŋshɛn) a different name, another name; va.—འདོགས་ to give a different name, to use another's name, to do sth. in another person's name, to use as a pretext.

མིང་གཞི་ (mi̲ŋshi) the root letter (consonant) of a syllable.

མིང་གཞི་རྐྱང་པ་ (mi̲ŋshi gyaŋba) a single letter syllable with no vowels, prefixes and suffixes.

མིང་གཞི་ཉི་ཤུ་ (mi̲ŋshi ñi̲shu) the twenty main "root" letters in the Tibetan alphabet that cannot be used either as suffix or prefix.

མིང་གཞི་གཙོ་ཕལ་ (mi̲ŋshi dzōbɛɛ) the main letter and the super and subsuffixed letters.

མིང་གཞི་སུམ་ཅུ་ (mi̲ŋshi sūmju) the thirty letters of the Tibetan alphabet.

མིང་གཞི་སུམ་ཅུ་སོ་བཞི་ (mi̲ŋshi sūmju sōbshi) the thirty consonants and four vowels of the Tibetan written language.

མིང་གཞི་གསུམ་སྦྲེལ་ (mi̲ŋshi sūmdree) the main letter of a syllable with the super and subsuffixed letters.

མིང་གཞི་གཙོ་བོ་ (mi̲ŋshi dzōwo) sm. མིང་གཞི་.

མིང་གཞིའི་ཕོ་ཡིག (mi̲ŋshi pōyiì) the male consonants of the Tibetan alphabet: ཀ་ཅ་ཏ་པ་ཙ་.

མིང་གཞིའི་མ་ནིང་ (mi̲ŋshi mə̲niŋ) the hermaphrodite letters of the Tibetan alphabet: ཁ་ཆ་ཐ་ཕ་ཚ་.

མིང་གཞིའི་མོ་ཡིག (mi̲ŋshi mo̲yiì) the female letters of the Tibetan alphabet: ག་ཇ་ད་བ་ཛ་ཞ་ཟ་འ་ཡ་ཤ་ས་.

མིང་གཞིའི་མོ་གཤམ་ (mi̲ŋshi mo̲sham) the barren letters of the Tibetan alphabet: ར་ལ་ཧ་ཨ་.

མིང་གཞིའི་མཚན་མེད་ (mi̲ŋshi tsɛ̄nmeè) the nongender barren letter of the Tibetan alphabet: ཨ་.

མིང་གཞིའི་ཤིན་ཏུ་མོ་ (mi̲ŋshi shīndu mo̲) the super female letters of the Tibetan alphabet: ང་ཉ་ན་.

མིང་གཞུང་ (mi̲ŋshuŋ) a directory, a list of names.

མིང་ཟླ་ (mi̲ŋda) 1. having the same name, namesake. 2. the second noun in a compound.

མིང་གཟུགས་ཟླ་བ་ (mi̲ŋsuù da̲wa) the 3rd month of the Tibetan calendar.

མིང་ཡིག (mi̲ŋyiì) signature; va.—འགོད་ to sign one's name.

མིང་ཡན་འདོགས་ (mi̲ŋyɛn dɔ̲ɔ̀) va. to give a nickname.

མིང་ཡོད་དོན་མེད་ (mi̲ŋyöö̀ tö̲nmeè) having name/ reputation and a goal/ purpose.

མིང་གཡར་ (mi̲ŋ yāā) va. to use as a pretext ། བུ་ལོན་འདེད་པའི་མིང་གཡར་ནས་སོ་པ་བྱས་པ་རེད་ Using the collection of debts as a pretext he spied on them.

མིང་རིམ་ (mi̲ŋrim) level, standing (as in a contest or listing).

མིང་ལེན་དམ་བཅའ་ (mi̲ŋlen ta̲mja) oath of office; va.—འཇོག; —ལེན་ to take an oath of office ། བཀའ་བློན་གྱི་མིང་ལེན་དམ་བཅའ་བཞག་པ་རེད་ (He) took the oath of office of Council Minister.

མིང་བཤེར་ (mi̲ŋsher) roll call; va.—བྱེད་; —གཏོང་ to call roll.

མིང་སྲིང་ (mi̲ŋsiŋ) brothers and sister.

མིང་སྲིང་གདུགས་ (mi̲ŋsin dūù) va. to marry a cross-cousin.

མིང་གསང་བའི་ཡི་གེ་ (mi̲ŋsaŋwɛ yi̲ge) unsigned letter/ document.

མིང་གསོལ་ (mi̲ŋ sōō) va. to give sth. a name.

མིད་ (mi̲i) va. to swallow.

མིད་འགྱུར་ (mi̲igyur) swallowing; va.—གཏོང་; vi.—ཤོར་ to involuntarily/ unintentionally swallow.

མིད་ནད་ཚན་ཁག (mi̲inɛɛ̀ tsɛ̄ngaà) department of throat diseases.

མིད་པ་ (mi̲ibə) throat, gullet; vi.—འཆུས་ to be deeply moved (emotionally), to be choked with emotion; vi.—འགག to choke (on sth.); vi.—འཛེར་ to become hoarse.

མིད་པའི་གློ་ཡུ་ (mi̲ibɛ lōyu) larynx.

མིད་པར་གཏོང་ (mi̲ibar dōŋ) va. to swallow.

མིད་པར་སྤུ་སྐྱེ་ (mi̲ibar būgye) taking sth. one isn't entitled to [Lit. hair growing in the throat].

མིད་སྦུབས་ (mi̲ibub) throat cavity.

མིད་ལ་ (mi̲ila) sm. མི་ལ་.

མིན་ (mi̲n) 1. negative linking verb ། ང་འགྲོ་གི་མིན་ I will not go. ། ཁོ་རྒྱ་རིགས་མིན་ཙང་. Because he is not Chinese. ། མོ་གཟུགས་པོ་བདེ་མིན་གྱིས་ཡོང་ཐུབ་མ་སོང་ Because she isn't well she couldn't come.

2. (vb. + —) whether or not, whatever, whenever ¶ འདི་བྱེད་དགོས་མིན་ཐག་གཅོད་མ་ཐུབ་པས་ Because they couldn't decide whether they should do it (or not). ¶ ཡིག་བསྐྱར་འདི་སུས་བྲིས་མིན་ཤེས་རྟོགས་མ་བྱུང་ (I) didn't know who wrote the protest poster.

སྨིན་ (min) manganese ¶ སྨིན་གཏེར་ Manganese mine.

མིན་གྲང་ (mindraŋ) isn't it so?

མིན་འགྲོ་ (mindro) probably ¶ ཕལ་ཆེར་རྡོ་རྗེ་མིན་འགྲོ་ Probably it is Dorje.

མིན་ད་ (minda) no.

མིན་འདྲ་ (mindrə) probably not.

མིན་ནམ་ (minnam) maybe ¶ ཁོ་ཨུ་རུ་སུའི་སོ་པ་མིན་ནམ་བསམ་པས་ Because (they) thought maybe he was a Russian spy.

མིན་པ་ (mimbə) 1. is/ was not, non ¶ རྒྱུ་མཚན་དེ་ལྟར་མིན་པ་ཁུངས་སྐྱེལ་བྱས་པ་རེད་ (They) proved that this was not the reason. ¶ རྒྱལ་ཁབ་དམར་ཤོག་མིན་པ་ཚོ་ The noncommunist countries.

མིན་པ་ཉིད་ (mimbəñii) absolutely not.

མིན་པ་འདྲ་ (mimbədra) does not seem to be, probably not, probably isn't.

མིན་པ་ཡིན་ན་ (mimbə yinnə) if it is not.

མིན་པ་ལོག་པ་ (mimbə ləgba) wrong/ opposite acts.

མིན་ཕྱི་གོ་ལོག (minji koləə) doing or saying sth. inappropriate/ unsuitable; va.—བྱེད་; —ཤོད་.

མིན་ཕྱི་གོ་སློག (minji koləə) sm. མིན་ཕྱི་གོ་ལོག.

མིན་ལས་ཆེ་ (minlεje) probably is not.

མིན་ལོག (minləə) it is.

མིན་ཤག (minshaà) most probably is not.

མིའི་ (mii) (of) humans.

མིའི་ཀུན་སྤྱོད་ (mii gũnjöö) human behavior/ conduct.

མིའི་ཁོག་པ་མིས་མི་ལོན་ (mii kõgba mii mi lön) a person can not guess another person's thoughts.

མིའི་ཁོག་པ་མིས་མི་ལོན་ དོའི་ཁོག་པ་ཆུས་མི་ལོན་ (mii kõgba mii mi lön do kõg cũũ mi lön) sm. མིའི་ཁོག་པ་མིས་མི་ལོན་.

མིའི་གྲིབ་མ་ (mii tribmə) a person's shadow.

མིའི་གྲིབ་གཟུགས་ (mii tribsuù) sm. མིའི་གྲིབ་མ་.

མིའི་བགྲོད་ལམ་ (mii dröölam) sidewalk, pavement.

མིའི་ཆོལ་ཁ་ (mii cõõga) one of the three traditional divisions/ provinces of Tibetan (མདོ་སྟོད་).

མིའི་ཐབས་ཀྱིས་ (mii tãbgi) man-made, artificial.

མིའི་ཐབས་ཀྱིས་ཐིག་ལེ་འཇུག་པ་ (mii tãbgi tĩgle juùbə) artificial insemination; va.—སྣུག to do artificial insemination.

མིའི་ཐབས་ཀྱིས་སྡེབ་སྦྱོར་ (mii tãbgi debjɔɔ) artificial insemination/ breeding; va.—བྱེད་.

མིའི་ཐེངས་གྲངས་ (mii tẽŋdraŋ) number of times (e.g., a person goes somewhere).

མིའི་ཐོབ་ཐང་ (mii tõbdaŋ) human rights.

མིའི་ཐོབ་ཐང་འགན་སྲུང་ (mii) human rights guarantee.

མིའི་དུལ་ (miidüü) sm. ཁམས་དམར་.

མིའི་ནད་ (mii nεὲ) human disease/ illness.

མིའི་ནུས་པ་གནམ་ལས་རྒྱལ་ (mii nüübə nãmlε gyεε) man can conquer nature.

མིའི་གནས་སྐབས་ལྔ་ (mii nεὲgəb ŋã) the five stages of a man's life.

མིའི་སྤུས་ཚད་ (mii bũüdzεὲ) sm. མི་སྤུས་.

མིའི་བབ་དང་བསྟུན་ (mii bəbdaŋ dũn) in accordance with what is suitable/ appropriate given an individual's capability ¶ མིའི་བབ་དང་བསྟུན་ཏེ་ལས་ཀ་སྤྲོད་པ་རེད་ (They) gave jobs in accordance with each person's characteristics.

མིའི་བར་གྱི་འབྲེལ་བ་ (mii pargi dreewa) the relations between people.

མིའི་དབང་ཆ་ (mii wãŋja) human rights.

མིའི་བཙད་པོ་ (mii dzεὲbo) sm. མིའི་བཙན་པོ་.

མིའི་བཙན་པོ་ (mii dzẽnbo) king, monarch.

མིའི་རྩ་བའི་དབང་ཆ་ (mii dzãwε wãŋja) fundamental human rights.

མིའི་མཚན་ཉིད་ (mii tsẽnñii) human character, human nature.

མིའི་རི་མོ་ནང་སྟག་གི་རི་མོ་ཕྱི་ (mii rimu naŋ dããgi rimu cĩ) the real nature/ motives of a person can not be see externally [Lit. the stripes of a person are inside, the stripes of a tiger are outside].

མིའི་རིགས་ (mii rig) mankind, humanity ¶ མིའི་རིགས་ཀྱི་འབྱུང་འགྱུར་ The future of mankind.

མིའི་རིགས་ཀྱི་རིག་པ་ (mii riggi rigbə) anthropology.

མིའི་རིགས་གོང་འཕེལ་ (mii rig koŋbee) human evolution/ development.

མིའི་རིགས་རྒྱུད་ (mii riggyüü) human race.

མིའི་ལུང་པར་ཁྱིའི་རྒྱུ་མ་ (mii luŋbar kyĩĩ gyumə) showing one's dirty laundry outside [Lit. showing the dog's intestines outside].

མིའི་ལུས་ (mii lüü) human form/ body.

མིའི་ལོ་རྒྱུས་མདོར་བསྡུས་ (mii lugyüü dɔrdüü) resume, biographical sketch.

མིའི་གཤིས་ལུགས་ (mii shĩĩluù) human nature.

མིའི་བསམ་བློ་རྟ་རྒྱུག (mii sãmlɔɔ dəgyuù) people thinking about all sorts of things [Lit. people think about riding horses in their minds].

མིའི་ཧྲུའུ་ཀྲང་ (mii hrũdraŋ) ch. secretary general (of a government office).

མིའུ་ (miwu) dwarf, pigmy.

མིའུ་ཆུང་ (miwu cũŋ) sm. མིའུ་.

མིའུ་ཐུང་ (miwu tũŋ) sm. མིའུ་.

མིའུ་གདུང་དྲུག (miwu duŋdruù) the six ancient lineages that arose from the mating of a monkey and demoness (according to Tibetan mythology).

མིའུ་ལྡོང་དྲུག (miwu doŋdruù) sm. མིའུ་གདུང་དྲུག.

མིའུ་རིན་ཆེན་ (miwu rinjen) person, human.

མིའོ་ (miwo) ch. a second (of time).

མིའོ་རིགས་ (miwo rig) Miao nationality.

མིས་ (mii) ch. meter ¶ མིས་གཉིས་ Two meters.

མིས་འཕྱ་རང་སྡུག (mii cã raŋ duù) being saddened by others making fun of oneself.

མིས་བཅོས་པ་ (mijööbə) artificial.

མིས་ཆེད་དུ་བཟོས་པ་ (miiceèdu söòbə) sm. མིས་བཟོས་.

མིས་སྟོངས་ཁང་རོ་ (miidoŋ kãŋro) deserted/ empty/ ruined house.

མིས་ཏར་ (miidar) sm. མིས་.

མིས་འཐེན་འཁོར་ལོ་ (miiten kɔ̃ɔ̃lo) a rickshaw pulled by a person.

མིས་འབོད་རྟས་འཚེར་ (miibòò dεὲdzer) crying of men and neighing of horses (phrase used to describe the heat of the battle).

མིས་བྲེལ་རྟ་བྲེལ་ (miidree dãdree) busy, prosperous [Lit. people busy, horse busy].

མིས་བཟོས་ (miisöö) man-made, artificial.

མིས་བཟོས་ཀོ་བ་ (miisöö gɔ̃ɔ̃) artificial leather, leatherette, vinyl.

མིས་བཟོས་སྐོར་སྐར་ (miisöö kɔ̃ɔ̃gar) sm. མིས་བཟོས་འཁོར་སྐར་.

མིས་བཟོས་འཁོར་སྐར་ (miisöö kɔ̃ɔ̃gar) satellite.

མིས་བཟོས་འཁྱག་པ་ (miisöö kyãgba) artificial ice.

མིས་བཟོས་འཁྱགས་རོམ་ (miisöö kyãgrom) man-made glacier.

མིས་བཟོས་འགྱིག (miisöö gyig) synthetic rubber.

མིས་བཟོས་རྒྱུ་སྐར་ (miisöö gyugar) man-made planet.

མིས་བཟོས་ཆར་འབེབས་ (miisöö cãrbeb) artificial rain.

མིས་བཟོས་བལ་ (miisöö pεε) synthetic wool.

མིས་བཟོས་གཙང་པོ་ (miisöö dzãŋbo) man-made canal.

མིས་བཟོས་རྩྭ་ར་ (miisöö dzãra) artificially sown pasture.

མིས་བཟོས་ཚི་སྣ་ (miisöö tsĩnə) synthetic fibre.

མིས་བཟོས་མཚེའུ་ (miisöö tsẽwu) artificial lake.

མིས་བཟོས་རྫིང་བུ་ (miisöö dziŋbu) artificial reservoir.

མིས་བཟོས་རིག་སྟོབས་ (miisöö rigdob) artificial intelligence.

མིས་བཟོས་སི་ཤན་ (miisöö sĩshεn) artificial silk.

མིས་བཟོས་སྤྱིང་བལ་ (miisöö sĩŋbεε) synthetic

cotton.

མིས་བཟོས་སྐུད་སྐར་ (miisöö sūŋgar) sm. མིས་བཟོས་འཁོར་སྐར་.

མིས་གསོ་སྐྱོང་ (mii sōgyoŋ) cultivated by humans, artificially raised; va.—བྱེད་.

མིས་ཧྲུའུ་ (miihru) ch. secretary (in office).

མུ་ (mu) edge, border, boundary ◆ཞིང་གི་མུ་ལ་རྩྭ་མང་པོ་སྐྱེས་འདུག A lot of grass has grown on the edge of the field.

མུ་ཁ་ (mugə) 1. mouth. 2. sm. མུ་.

མུ་ཁྱུད་ (mugyüü) circumference, rim; surrounded, bounded ◆ལུང་པ་འདི་ནི་གངས་རི་མུ་ཁྱུད་དུ་སྐོར་པ་ཞིག་རེད་ This region is one that is surrounded by snow mountains.

མུ་ཁྲི་བཙན་པོ་ (mudri dzɛ̄mbo) one of the ancient kings of Tibet.

མུ་གེ་ (muge) famine; vi.—ཐེབས་; —བྱུང་ to have a famine/ drought.

མུ་གེའི་ཁ་ལ་ཟླ་ལྷག (muge kāla dalhaà) sm. མུ་གེའི་སྟེང་ལ་ཟླ་ལྷག.

མུ་གེའི་སྒང་ལ་ཟླ་བསྒོལ་ (muge gaŋla dashöö) sm. མུ་གེའི་སྟེང་ལ་ཟླ་ལྷག.

མུ་གེའི་སྟེང་ལ་ཟླ་ལྷག (muge dēŋla dalhaà) "when it rains it pours", one problem occurring on top of another [Lit. on top of famine, an extra month].

མུ་འགྲམ་ (mudram) 1. around the edge/ circumference. 2. slandering, talking negatively about sb.; va.—སྨྲ་ to slander, to talk negatively about sb.

མུ་ཅོར་ (mujɔɔ) nonsensical talk; va.—སྨྲ་ to talk nonsense.

མུ་ཆུ་སྒོང་ (muju goŋ) va. to fold and sew the hem of a piece of material.

མུ་གཅིག (mujig) 1. one side ◆ཅ་ལག་དེ་ཚོ་མུ་གཅིག་ལ་ཞོག་དགོས་ We must put these things on one side. 2. kind, type ◆ཅ་ལག་དེ་ཚོ་མུ་གཅིག་རེད་ These things are of one type.

མུ་ཏིག (mudiì) pearl.

མུ་ཏིག་སྐྱེ་གནས་ (mudiì gyēnɛɛ̀) oyster.

མུ་ཏིག་མགུལ་ཕྲེང་ (mudiì güüdreŋ) necklace of pearls.

མུ་ཏིག་ཐུག་ཁོག (mudiì tūggɔɔ̀) pearl adorned headdress of high ranking Tibetan ladies.

མུ་ཏིག་ཕྲེང་བ་ (mudiì trēŋwa) a strand of pearls, a rosary made of pearls.

མུ་ཏིག་འབྲུ་ (mudiì dru) a single pearl.

མུ་ཏིག་བཙན་པོ་ (mudiì dzɛ̄mbo) one of the ancient kings of Tibet.

མུ་ཏིག་ཙེམ་བུ་ (mudiì dzēmbu) a type of even stitching which looks like pearls on a string.

མུ་ཏིག་རྫུས་མ་ (mudiì dzüümə) cultured pearl, artificial pearl.

མུ་དོ་བ་ (mudowa) beggar.

མུ་ལྟར་ (mudar) just as before, like before.

མུ་ལྡོ་བ་ (mudowa) sm. མུ་དོ་བ་.

མུ་སྟེགས་ཅན་ (mudegjɛn) religions other than Buddhism.

མུ་སྟེགས་པ་ (mudegba) a heretic; a brahmin, a Hindu.

མུ་ཐི་ལ་ (mudilə) sm. མུ་ཏིག.

མུ་ཐི་ལི་ (mudili) sm. མུ་ཐི་ལ་.

མུ་མཐའ་ (muta) edge, border, boundary, limit.

མུ་མཐའ་བྲལ་བ་ (muta drɛɛwa) limitless, endless, boundless, vast ◆མུ་མཐའ་བྲལ་བའི་རྩྭ་ཐང་ A vast grassland plain.

མུ་མཐའ་མི་མངོན་པ་ (muta minömba) sm. མུ་མཐའ་བྲལ་བ་.

མུ་མཐའ་མེད་པ་ (muta meèba) sm. མུ་མཐའ་བྲལ་བ་.

མུ་མཐུད་ (mutüü) continuously, continually, without interruption/ break, steadily; va. མུ་མཐུད་; —བྱེད་ to do continuously/ continually ◆བཙན་རྒྱལ་རིང་ལུགས་ལ་འཛམ་གླིང་མི་དམངས་ཀྱིས་ངོ་རྒོལ་མུ་མཐུད་བྱེད་བཞིན་པ་རེད་ The people of the world are continuously opposing imperialism. ◆ཁོ་རྒྱ་གར་ནས་ལོག་ནས་སློབ་སྦྱོང་མུ་མཐུད་ཀྱི་རེད་ He will continue (his) studies after returning from India.

མུ་མཐུད་ཀྱིས་ (mutüügi) continuously, continually, without interruption/ break ◆ཁོ་ཚོས་ཀུང་ཧྲེ་ཡར་རྒྱས་མུ་མཐུད་ཀྱིས་བཏང་བ་རེད་ They improved the commune continually.

མུ་མཐུད་རྒྱུན་འཁྱོངས་ (mutüü gyüngyoŋ) sm. མུ་མཐུད་རྒྱུན་ཆགས་.

མུ་མཐུད་རྒྱུན་ཆགས་ (mutüü gyünjaà) continuously, continually, without interruption/ break.

མུ་མཐུད་དེ་ (mutüüde) sm. མུ་མཐུད་ཀྱིས་.

མུ་མཐུད་ནས་ (mutüünɛ) sm. མུ་མཐུད་ཀྱིས་.

མུ་འདྲེས་ལྕགས་གཏེར་ (mudreè jāgder) a mine with both phosphorus/ sulphur and iron.

མུ་རྡོ་ (mudo) piles of stone at the edge of fields.

མུ་ནེ་བཙན་པོ་ (muge dzɛ̄mbo) the 39th ancient king of Tibet.

མུ་འབྱམས་ (mujam) shung. in perpetuation, continuously from long ago ◆སྙན་ཞུས་འགོ་མཆན་འབྱར་མར་གཞིགས་ཚེ་ས་དེ་ནས་ཆོས་ཁོངས་སུ་མུ་འབྱམས་སོང་བ་མིན་ནམ་སྙམ་ཁར་ According to the marginal notes on the petition, we think that the (land) belonged to the monastery from long age.

མུ་འབྲེལ་ (mudree) 1. joined side by side, together. ◆རྒྱ་གར་དང་བོད་གཉིས་ས་མཚམས་མུ་འབྲེལ་རེད་ The border of Tibet and India are joined. 2. sm. མུ་མཐུད་.

མུ་འབྲེལ་ཆ་གྲངས་ (mudree cādraŋ) 1. the series of even numbers. (e.g., 2, 4, 6, etc.). 2. continuous fraction (in math).

མུ་འབྲེལ་ཡ་གྲངས་ (mudree yadraŋ) the series of odd numbers (e.g., 1, 3, etc.).

མུ་འབྲེལ་སྐྱེལ་འདྲེན་ (mudree gyēndren) a line of transport.

མུ་འབྲེལ་བསྒར་ སྒྲིག (mūdree dārdrig) lined up one after another.

མུ་འབྲེལ་རི་བོ་ (mudree riwo) mountain range.

མུ་འབྲེལ་རི་མོ་ (mudree rimu) comic book series, comic strip series.

མུ་འབྲེལ་ལས་སྒྲུབ་ (mudree lɛɛ̀drub) production assembly line.

མུ་འབྲེལ་ལས་རིམ་ (mudree lɛɛ̀rim) sm. མུ་འབྲེལ་ལས་སྒྲུབ་.

མུ་འབྲེལ་ས་ཁུལ་ (mudree səgüü) contiguous/ adjacent area, areas sharing a border/ frontier.

མུ་མེད་ (mumeè) boundless, endless, limitless, vast.

མུ་མེན་ (mumen) 1. lapis lazuli. 2. dark purple.

མུ་ཚིགས་ (mudzii) the outer edge of a field.

མུ་རྫུས་ (mudzüü) artificial pearl.

མུ་ཟི་ (musi) 1. sulphur. 2. match; va.—སྦར་ to light a match; va.—གསོད་ to put out a match.

མུ་ཟི་འགྱུར་འགྱིག (musi gyurgyig) vulcanized rubber.

མུ་ཟི་ཅན་དུ་འགྱུར་བ་ (musijɛndu gyurwə) vulcanized.

མུ་ཟི་ལྕགས་གཏེར་ (musi jāgder) a mine of both phosphorus/ sulphur and iron.

མུ་ཟི་གཏེར་ཁ་ (musi dērga) sulphur mine.

མུ་ཟི་རྡོ་ (musi do) sulphur ore.

མུ་ཟི་ནག་པོ་ (musi nagbo) a type of sulphur.

མུ་ཟི་ལིམ་ (musilim) Muslim.

མུ་ཟི་སེར་པོ་ (musi sērbo) sulphur.

མུ་ཟིའི་སྐྱུར་ (musii gyūr) sulphuric acid.

མུ་ཟིའི་སྒམ་ཆུང་ (musii gəmjuŋ) match box.

མུ་ཟིའི་ཆུ་ཚན་ (musii cūdzɛn) sm. མུ་ཟིའི་ཚ་ཆུ་.

མུ་ཟིའི་ཚ་ཆུ (musii tsəju) sulfur spring.

མུ་ར་ (murə) acorus calamus (used in Tibetan medicine).

མུ་རུ་ (muru) sm. མུ་ར་.

མུ་རན་ (murɛn) edge, side.

མུ་རུག་བཙན་པོ་ (murug dzɛ̄mbo) sm. མུ་ཏིག་བཙན་པོ་.

མུ་ལ་ (mulə) 1. along with, together with, while, at the same time ◆བོད་སྐད་ཀྱི་མུ་ལ་བོད་ཡིག་ཀྱང་སློབ་སྦྱོང་བྱས་པ་རེད་ Along with studing spoken Tibetan, (he) also studied written Tibetan. 2. sm. ཁོངས་སུ་.

མུ་ལ་ཕྱིང་ (muləjiŋ) cotton flannel.

མུ་སལ་མན་ (musɛlmɛn) a Muslim.

མུག (mug) 1. famine ། ནད་མུག་འཁྲུག་གསུམ་འགོག་ཐབས་སུ་ For the purpose of preventing sickness, famine and war. 2. despondent, desperation, despair ། ཁོ་ལས་ཀ་ཤོར་ནས་ཡིད་མུག་བྱས་བསྡད་བཞག He was despondent after losing his job.

མུག་ཀུན་ (muggön) sm. ལང་ཀུ་.

མུག་སྐྱོན་ (muggyön) famine disaster.

མུག་སྐྱོབ་ (muggyob) famine disaster relief.

མུག་སྐྱོབ་གྲབས་གསོམ་གྱི་འབྲུ་ཁང་ (muggyob trəbshomgi drugaŋ) famine reserve granary.

མུག་གུ་ (muggu) sm. ལང་ཀུ་.

མུག་དིར་དིར་ (mug dirdir) talking in a low voice.

མུག་པ་ (mugbə) 1. moth; vi.—རྒྱག; —ཟ་ to be eaten by a moth. 2. despondent, desperation, despair ། ཁོ་ལས་ཀ་ཤོར་ནས་ཡིད་མུག་བྱས་བསྡད་བཞག He was despondent after losing his job.

མུག་བྱོལ་ (mugjöö) a refugee from a famine area.

མུག་མ་ (mugmə) sm. མུག་པ་.

མུག་ཟ་ (mugsə) sm. མུག་ཟོས་.

མུག་ཟོས་ (mugsöö) eaten by a moth.

མུག་ཟོས་སྲིད་ཇུས་ (mugsöö siijüü) policy of "nibbling," tt. policy of slowly eating away at sb.'s strength so as to finally overcome them, the policy of attrition. [Lit. eaten by a moth].

མུག་ཟོས་དམག་འཐབ་ (mugsöö məgdəb) war of attrition.

མུག་རི་ (mugri) a bare hill.

མུག་ཤ་ (mugsha) meat of animals killed by famine.

མུག་ཤི་ (mugshi) death caused by famine; vi.—ཐེབས་.

མུག་ཤོད་འདྲེན་ (mugshöö dren) sm. ལྷག་ཤོད་མུག་ཤོད་.

མུག་སེང་ (mugseŋ) airing out one's clothes in summer and adding mothballs; va.—རྒྱག.

མུང་ (muŋ) sm. མུག་པ་.

མུན་ (mün) dark, darkness.

མུན་བསྐལ་ (müngɛɛ) an eon when there was no Buddha.

མུན་ཁང་ (müngaŋ) a dark room.

མུན་ཁུག (münguù) a dark corner of a hall/ room.

མུན་ཁུང་ (münguŋ) dungeon.

མུན་གྲོད་ (mündröö) in the midst of darkness.

མུན་འཁྲིགས་ (mündrig) sm. མུན་ནག.

མུན་གླིང་ (münliŋ) 1. shady side of a mountain or hill. 2. places where the dharma has not spread.

མུན་ཅན་ (m,ünjɛn) a respiratory illness.

མུན་གདིབས་ (mündib) overcast, dark due to heavy cloud cover.

མུན་འཐོམས་ (müntom) blind action, action without reflection/ consideration, ignorant action/ behavior; va.—བྱེད་ ། མུན་འཐོམས་ཀྱིས་བྱས་པ་རེད་ (They) acted blindly.

མུན་འཐོམས་ཀྱིས་སྒྲུབ་ (müntomgi drub) sm. མྱོངས་ཚོད་ཀྱིས་སྒྲུབ་.

མུན་འཐོམས་ཀྱིས་བྱེད་ (müntomgi cee) sm. མུན་འཐོམས་བྱེད་.

མུན་འཐོམས་ཐལ་བསྐྱོད་ (müntom tɛɛgyöö) leaping to act without reflection/ consideration, blind/ rash action, following blindly; va.—བྱེད་ ། བརྟག་དཔྱད་མེད་པར་མུན་འཐོམས་ཐལ་བསྐྱོད་བྱས་ཏེ་ཟིང་ཆ་བསླངས་པ་རེད་ Without investigating (the matter) (they) acted rashly causing a disturbance.

མུན་མདངས་ (mündaŋ) twilight.

མུན་འདོར་གསལ་ལེན་ (mündɔɔ sɛɛlen) reforming one's views/ ideas/ behavior [Lit. cast away darkness and take in the light].

མུན་རྡོ་འཕེན་ (mün do pēn) doing sth. aimlessly, doing without thought/ plan/ guidelines [Lit. to throw a stone in the dark].

མུན་ནག (münnaà) 1. the dark. 2. dim, gloomy, somber, dismal.

མུན་ནག་གུག་གྱོག (münnaà kuggyɔɔ) a dark corner.

མུན་ནག་མདའ་འཕེན་ (münnaà daben) sm. མུན་རྡོ་འཕེན་ [Lit. to shoot an arrow in the dark.].

མུན་ནག་འདོམ་འཛལ་ (münnaà domjɛɛ) sm. མུན་ནག་སྦར་ཉུལ་.

མུན་ནག་སྦར་ཉུལ་ (münnaà baañüü) acting without specific guidelines/ plan/ goal, acting aimlessly/ blindly [Lit. groping in the dark with one's hand].

མུན་ནག་སྦར་རྙོབ་ (münnaà barñob) sm. མུན་ནག་སྦར་ཉུལ་.

མུན་ནག་སྦར་སྙུལ་ (münnaà barñüü) sm. མུན་ནག་སྦར་ཉུལ་.

མུན་ནག་སྦར་ཡུར་ (münnaà baayur) sm. མུན་ནག་སྦར་ཉུལ་.

མུན་པ་ (mümbə) 1. dark. 2. ignorant.

མུན་པ་ནག་པོ་ (mümbə nagbo) dark ། ཁང་པ་འདི་མུན་པ་ནག་པོ་འདུག This house is dark.

མུན་པ་མུན་ནག (mümbə münnaà) pitch dark.

མུན་པ་རུབ་ (mümbə rub) vi. to become dark (as at nightfall).

མུན་པ་སེལ་ (mümbə sēl) va. to illuminate darkness.

མུན་པ་སྲོད་འདྲ་ (mümbə dröndra) extremely dark [Lit. like late at night when it is dark].

མུན་པ་གསལ་ (mümbə sɛɛ) 1. vi. to become clear/ light, to illuminate darkness/ ignorance ། ཁོང་གི་བཀའ་སློབ་དེས་ངའི་བློ་ཡི་མུན་པ་གསལ་སོང་ His advice cleared the darkness in my mind (my ignorance). 2. vi. to become dawn.

མུན་པོ་ (mümbo) sm. མུན་པ་.

མུན་མུན་ཐོམ་ཐོམ་ (münmün tōmdom) dull, dazed.

མུན་མཚན་ (mündzɛn) night.

མུན་རུབ་ (münrub) sm. མུན་པ་རུབ་.

མུན་རུབ་རུབ་ (mün rubrub) the time just prior to darkness.

མུན་སྲིབ་ (münsib) sm. མུན་པ་རུབ་.

མུན་སེལ་ (münsee) sm. མུན་པ་སེལ་.

མུན་སེག (münseg) sm. མུན་མཚན་.

མུན་སོས་ (münsöö) sm. མུན་པ་རུབ་.

མུའུ་ (muu) ch. Chinese area measurement equaling 0.1647 acres ། མུའུ་རེའི་ཐོན་ཚད་ The yield per unit of མུའུ་.

མུའུ་སི་ལིན་ (muusilin) Moslem.

མུའུ་ཧན་མོ་ཏེ་ (muu hɛnmode) Mohammed.

མུར་ (muu) 1. along with, together with, while ། གདན་ཞུའི་སྐོར་བཀའ་མོལ་གནང་མུར་ While talking about the invitation. 2. va. to suck on ། ཁོས་བྱི་རིལ་མུར་གྱི་འདུག He is sucking on a candy. 3. in that/ this way, like that ། དེ་མུར་འཇོག་འདོད་མེད་ (We) don't want to leave it like that.

མུར་གོང་ (murgoŋ) 1. cheeks. 2. temple (of head).

མུར་གོང་རུས་པ་ (murgoŋ rüübə) 1. cheek bone. 2. temple bone.

མུར་ཐུག (mur tūù) finally, in the end, in the long run.

མུར་མུར་ (muumuu) 1. sucking (on sth.); va.—བྱེད་ ། སོ་མེད་པའི་རྒན་འཁོགས་ཚོས་ཤ་མུར་མུར་བྱེད་ཀྱི་འདུག The elderly without teeth are sucking on the meat. 2. the upper lip of a horse/ mule.

མུར་ཟས་ (mursɛɛ) eating slyly, eating so that others can't see; va.—རྒྱག.

མུར་མཛུག (murdzɔɔ) a fist; va.—ཞུ་ to hit with the fist; va.—སྒྲིང་ to make a fist.

མུར་གསང་ (mursaŋ) temple.

མུལ་ལྡོ་བ་ (muüdowa) sm. མུ་ཏོ་པ་.

མུས་ (müü) 1. verbal particle indicating present action in process ། ཁོ་གཉིས་སྐད་ཆ་བྱེད་མུས་རེད The two of them are talking (are in the process of talking).

མེ་ (me) 1. fire; va.—སྦར་ to light a fire; va.—གཏོང་ to make a fire; va.—རྒྱག to set fire to, to burn; vi.—འབར་ to catch fire; to burn; vi.—ཤོར་ to catch fire; va.—གསོད་ to put out/ a extinguish a fire. 2. abbr. of མེ་གོ་.

མེ་གྲྭའུ་གླིང་ (medrawu liŋ) ch.tib. Americas, the American continent.

མེ་བཀྲ་ (medra) the flame of a fire as seen from a distance.

མེ་ཀུན་ (megün) fire and theft.

མེ་སྒ་ (mega) 1. iron prongs (used in making fire); va.—རྒྱག to use iron prongs. 2. trigger (of a gun).

མེ་སྒར་ (megar) 1. sparkle of a flame. 2. name of a star.

མེ་སྒོང་ (megoŋ) sm. མེ་བསྒོང་.

མེ་སྒོར་འདུ་ཚོགས་ (megɔɔ dudzɔɔ̀) campfire party.

མེ་སྒྱོགས་ (megyɔɔ̀) a utensil for taking coal/ embers out of fire.

མེ་སྒྱོན་འགོག་གསོད་རུ་ཁག (megyön gɔgsöö rugaà) sm. མེ་གསོད་རུ་ཁག.

མེ་དཀྲུག (medruù) iron poker; va.—རྒྱག to turn/ stir a fire (to keep it going).

མེ་བསྒོང་ (megoŋ) 1. a heaped up bonfire; bonfire; va.—རྒྱག; —གཏོང་ ། མེ་བསྒོང་གི་ཁྱོན་དུ་མཚན་གང་བསྡད་པ་རེད་ (They) sat around the bonfire all night.

མེ་སྒྱོན་ (megyön) 1. conflagration, a wild fire ། དགས་ཚལ་གྱི་མེ་སྒྱོན་ Forest fire. 2. fire damage.

མེ་སྒྱོན་ཤོར་བརྡ་ (megyön shɔɔ̄da) fire alarm.

མེ་ཁ་ཁ་དང་དུ་བ་སོ་སོ་ (me kāga daŋ tuwə sōso) close but not the same, linked/ related but distinct or different [Lit. fire and smoke different].

མེ་ཁ་བཟུང་ (mega suŋ) sm. མེ་ཁ་གསོ་.

མེ་ཁ་གསོ་ (mega sō) va. to light a fire.

མེ་ཁང་ (megaŋ) kitchen.

མེ་ཁབ་རྩེ་ཙམ་གྱིས་རི་བོ་སྲེག (me kəbdzedzamgi riwo sēg) a flame the size of the tip of a needle can burn a mountain.

མེ་ཁམས་ (megam) the element fire.

མེ་ཁུག (meguù) a pouch for carrying flint and tinder.

མེ་ཁེ་ཧུང་ས་ཐིག (megehuŋ sādig) eng.tib. McMahon Line.

མེ་ཁེབས་ (megeb) a lid for covering a stove/ fire pot, etc.

མེ་ཁོག (megɔɔ̀) a pot in which red hot dung or charcoal is put to keep a tea pot that is set on top of it warm.

མེ་ཁོང་ (megoŋ) Mekong River.

མེ་ཁྱི་ (megyi) fire-dog year.

མེ་ཁྱིམ་ (megyem) flatheaded iron poker.

མེ་ཁྱེར་ (megyer) firefly.

མེ་འཁོར་ (megɔɔ) a train.

མེ་འཁོར་སྐྱེ་འདྲེན་འཁན་ལེན་ཚན་སྒོར་ (megɔɔ gyēdreŋ gɛnlen tsɛ̄ngɔɔ) locomotive crew.

མེ་འཁོར་ཁང་ཕྲེང་ (megɔɔ kāŋdreŋ) assembling and despatching trains, marshaling trains.

མེ་འཁོར་འཁོར་སྒྲོམ་ (megɔɔ kɔɔ̄drom) train compartment.

མེ་འཁོར་འཁོར་གཉེར་ཁྲུའུ་ (megɔɔ kɔɔ̄ñeetru) tib.ch. rolling stock (railway cars) division.

མེ་འཁོར་འཁོར་གཉེར་འཕྲུལ་ཆས་བཟོ་གྲྭ་ (megɔɔ kɔɔ̄ñee trūūjɛɛ̀ sodra) rolling stock (railway cars) parts plant.

མེ་འཁོར་འཁོར་ལོ་བཟོ་གྲྭ་ (megɔɔ kɔɔ̄lo sodra) rolling stock factory.

མེ་འཁོར་གྱི་ཁ་ལོ་པ་ (megɔɔgi kālowa) engine/ locomotive driver.

མེ་འཁོར་གྱི་ཁང་མིག (megɔɔgi kəŋmiì) train compartment.

མེ་འཁོར་གི་མགོ་ (megɔɔgi go) locomotive.

མེ་འཁོར་གྱི་སྒྲོམ་ (megɔɔgi drom) railway carriage/ compartment.

མེ་འཁོར་གྱི་མཇུག་ཁང་ (megɔɔgi juggaŋ) caboose (in train).

མེ་འཁོར་གྱི་ཨ་མ་ (megɔɔgi āma) sm. མེ་འཁོར་གི་མགོ་.

མེ་འཁོར་གཏོང་མཁན་ (megɔɔ dōŋñɛn) sm. མེ་འཁོར་གྱི་ཁ་ལོ་པ་.

མེ་འཁོར་བསྟར་འཕྲེང་ (megɔɔ dārdreŋ) a train with a string of railway coaches/ cars.

མེ་འཁོར་འབབ་ཚུགས་ (megɔɔ bəbdzuù) railway station.

མེ་འཁོར་འབབ་ཚོགས་ (megɔɔ bəbdziì) railway station.

མེ་འཁོར་འབབ་ཚོགས་ཐང་ཆེན་ (megɔɔ bəbdziì tāŋjen) railway station square.

མེ་འཁོར་ཞབས་ཕྱི་ཁང་ (megɔɔ shibjigaŋ) attendant's room on a train.

མེ་འཁོར་ཞིག་གསོ་བཟོ་གྲྭ་ (megɔɔ shigso sodra) rolling stock repair plant.

མེ་འཁོར་ཟ་ཁང་ (megɔɔ sagaŋ) dining car on a train.

མེ་འཁོར་བཟོ་གྲྭ་ (megɔɔ sodra) rolling stock plant.

མེ་འཁོར་བཤེར་གསོ་བཟོ་གྲྭ་ (megɔɔ shērso sodra) rolling stock examination and repair plant.

མེ་འཁོར་ས་ཚོགས་ (megɔɔ sədziì) sm. མེ་འཁོར་འབབ་ཚུགས་.

མེ་འཁོར་ཨ་མ་ (megɔɔ āma) locomotive.

མེ་འཁྱུད་ (megyüù) flame, blaze.

མེ་འཁྱེར་ (megyer) sm. མེ་ཁྱེར་.

མེ་འཁྲིད་སྐུད་པ་ (medriì gūūbə) fuse, detonator.

མེ་ག་ཝཌ་ (megawad) eng. megawatt.

མེ་གོ་ (mego) ch. America, U.S.A. ། མེ་གོ་བཙན་རྒྱལ་རིང་ལུགས་ U.S. imperialism.

མེ་གོའི་སྒོར་མོ་ (megö gɔɔmo) U.S. dollar.

མེ་གོའི་སྔོན་ཐོན་ངལ་རྩོལ་བཟོ་པའི་དང་ (megö ŋōndön ŋɛɛdzöö sobɛ dāŋ) U.S. Progressive Labor Party.

མེ་གྲུང་པོ་ (me druŋbu) a smokeless fire.

མེ་གྲུབ་བྲག་རྡོ་ (medrub tragdo) magmatic rock.

མེ་གླང་ (melaŋ) fire-ox year.

མེ་གླིང་ (meliŋ) ch.tib. America; American continent ། ལ་ཏིང་མེ་གླིང་ Latin America.

མེ་གླིང་བྱང་ (meliŋ) ch.tib. North America.

མེ་གླིང་ལྷོ་ (meliŋ) ch.tib. South America.

མེ་གློག་བཟོ་སྐྲུན་ཁྲུའུ་ (melɔɔ̀ sodrün trūwu) tib.ch. department of thermoelectric power construction.

མེ་དགྲ་འདུལ་འགོག་རུ་ཁག (medra düŋgɔɔ̀ rugaà) fire brigade.

མེ་མགལ་ (megɛɛ) firebrand.

མེ་འགག་ས་ཚོགས་ (megɛɛ sədziì) fire prevention station.

མེ་འགག་ས་ཚུགས་ (megɛɛ sədzuù) fire prevention station.

མེ་འགོག་བཀོད་འདོམས་པུའུ་ (megɔɔ̀ tra rɔɔ̀) tib.ch. fire prevention command post.

མེ་འགོག་ཁྲའོ་རོགས་ (megɔɔ̀ tra rɔɔ̀) ch.tib. resist/ block America and aid Korea (a political slogan during the Korean War).

མེ་འགོག་རྒྱལ་སྐྱོབ་ (megɔɔ̀ gyɛɛgyob) tib. ch. resist/ block America and defend the nation (political slogan during the Korean War).

མེ་ཀློལ་ (megöö) anti-U.S., oppose the U.S.

མེ་ཀློལ་འཐབ་ཕྱོགས་གཅིག་སྒྲིལ་ (megöö təbjɔɔ jïgdrii) anti-U.S. united front.

མེ་རྒྱག་གཏོར་ (megyaà dɔɔ̄) va. to destroy sth. by setting fire to it. ། གོ་མཛོད་ལ་མེ་རྒྱག་གཏོར་བ་རེད་ They destroyed the armory by setting fire to it.

མེ་སྒོང་ (megoŋ) sm. མེ་བསྒོང་.

མེ་སྒོར་ (megɔɔ) U.S. dollar.

མེ་སྒྱོགས་ (megyɔɔ̀) cannon, artillery; va.—རྒྱག; —འཕེན་; —འཕངས་ to shell, to bombard, to fire artillery.

མེ་སྒྱོགས་ཀྱི་ཐལ་བ་ (megyɔɔ̀gi tɛ̄ɛwa) cannon fodder.

མེ་སྒྱོགས་ཁ་ (megyɔɔ̀ kā) outspoken, utterly frank (usu. for sb. who is critical) [Lit. cannon mouth].

མེ་སྒྱོགས་རྒྱ་གླིང་ཁ་ (megyɔɔ̀ gyaliŋgə) bazooka.

མེ་སྒྱོགས་ཆེ་རིགས་ (megyɔɔ̀ cērig) heavy artillery.

མེ་སྒྱོགས་གནམ་ལྕུག (megyɔɔ̀ nəmluù) mortar.

མེ་སྒྱོགས་པའི་ཅི་པའོ་ (megyɔɔ̀ pējipao) tib.ch. sm. མེ་སྒྱོགས་གནམ་ལྕུག.

མེ་སྒྱོགས་འཕེན་མཁན་ (megyɔɔ̀ pēnñɛn) gunner, artillery man.

མེ་སྒྱོགས་དམག (mergyɔɔ̀ māà) artillery troops, artillery unit/ regiment.

མེ་སྒྱོགས་དམག་དཔུང་ (mergyɔɔ̀ māgbuŋ) artillery unit/ regiment/ group.

མེ་སྒྱོགས་དམག་མི་ (mergyɔɔ̀ māāmi) artilleryman, artillery soldier.

མེ་སྒྱོགས་ཞའོ་ཀང་པའོ་ (mergyɔɔ̀ shao gāŋpao) tib.ch.

light artillery.
མོ་སྒྲོགས་ལིའུ་དན་ (mergyɔɔ̀ liudɛn) tib.ch. howitzer.
མེ་སྒྲོགས་ཧྲན་པའོ་ (mergyɔɔ̀ hrɛ̄npao) tib.ch. howitzer, mountain gun.
མེ་བསྒོས་ (mer göö) va. to light a fire.
མེ་སྒྲོན་ (medrön) 1. lamp, torch. 2. va. to light a fire.
མེ་ངར་ (meŋar) a big/ hot fire.
མེ་ངར་པོ་ (me ŋarbo) conflagration.
མེ་ཅན་ (mejɛn) fiery.
མེ་ལྕགས་ (mejaà) flint striker; va.—བྱེད་; —སྤོར་ to light a fire with a flint striker.
མེ་ལྕེ་ (meje) a flame; vi.—འབར་; —མཆེད་ to flame, to burn ༎ཁོང་ཁྲོའི་མེ་ལྕེ་འབར་རེ་ Burning with anger.
མེ་ལྕེ་འཁོར་ལོ་ (meje kɔ̄ɔ̀lo) ringworm, tinea.
མེ་ལྕེ་གཏོར་ཆས་ (meje dɔ̄ɔ̀jɛɛ̀) flame thrower.
མེ་ལྕེ་དྲག་པོ་ (meje tragbo) raging fire.
མེ་ལྕེ་ནམ་འབར་ (meje nāmbar) sth. increasing/ growing rapidly [Lit. a fire flaring up into the sky].
མེ་ལྕེའི་སྒྲོགས་མདའ་ (mejee gyɔŋda) rocket launcher.
མེ་ཆ་ (meja) the set of things used to make fire: flint striker, tinder and flint stone.
མེ་ཆུ་གཉིས་ཀྱིས་ཤ་མི་ཆ་ (meju ñiigi shāmidza) sm. མེ་དང་ཆུ་ལ་སྙིང་རྗེ་མེད་.
མེ་ཆུ་མཐུན་ཐབས་མེད་པ་ (meju dūndəb meèba) incompatible ༎སྤྱི་ཚོགས་རིང་ལུགས་དང་མ་རྩའི་རིང་ལུགས་མེ་ཆུ་མཐུན་ཐབས་མེད་པ་རེད་ Communism and capitalism are incompatible. [Lit. incompatible like fire and wood].
མེ་ཆུང་ཐོག་ནས་གསོད་ (mejuŋ tɔ̄ɔ̀nɛ sɔ̄ɔ̀) addressing a problem while its small [Lit. stop a fire while its still small].
མེ་ཆུའི་ཁྲོད་ནས་སྐྱོབ་ (mejü trɔ̄ɔ̀nɛ gyōb) saved from great danger [Lit. saved from fire and water].
མེ་ཆུར་འཛེམས་མེད་ (mejuu dzemmeè) fearless, undaunted [Lit. unafraid of fire and water].
མེ་མཆེད་ (me cēè) vi. to have fire spread.
མེ་མཆོད་ (mecöö) sm. སྦྱིན་སྲེག.
མེ་ཉེན་སྔོན་འགོག (meñen ŋōngɔɔ̀) stopping a fire before it starts, fire prevention.
མེ་མཉམ་གསང་ (meñam sāŋ) a point around the stomach for applying moxabustion.
མེ་སྙིང་ (meñiŋ) the embers kept during the night and used to reignite the fire in the morning.
མེ་སྙོལ་ (meñöö) va. to cover the embers at the night with ashes so that they will remain alive during the night and can be used to reignite a fire in the morning.
མེ་ཏེ་ཐེ་རེ་ཨན་རྒྱ་མཚོ་ (mede tērean gyadzo) Mediterranean Sea.
མེ་ཏེལ་ (medee) branding iron.
མེ་ཏོག (medoò) flower.
མེ་ཏོག་ཀ་ར་བི་ར་ (medoò gāra birə) the flower of the winter daphne (used for making paper).
མེ་ཏོག་ཀུན་བཟང་ (medoò gūnsaŋ) 1. passion flower. 2. dahlia.
མེ་ཏོག་ཀུའི་ཧྭ་ (medoò gūweha) sweet-scented osmanthus.
མེ་ཏོག་བཀྲམ་ (medoò drām) va. to sprinkle/ shower with flowers.
མེ་ཏོག་ཁ་ལེན་ (medoò kālɛn) a type of riding skill wherein a rider picks up a flower off the ground with his mouth.
མེ་ཏོག་ཁོག་མ་ (medoò kɔ̄ɔ̀ma) flower pot.
མེ་ཏོག་གངས་ལྷ་ (medoò gaŋlha) snow lotus.
མེ་ཏོག་གི་ཕྲེང་བ་ (medoògi trēŋwa) floral wreath.
མེ་ཏོག་ཅིའུ་ཧའི་ཐང་ (medoò ciu hētaŋ) tib.ch. begonia.
མེ་ཏོག་ཆུང་ཡང་ལྷ་རྫས་ (medoò cūnyaŋ lhādzɛɛ̀) its the thought behind a gift offering that counts [Lit. even if the flower is small, it is a offering to the gods].
མེ་ཏོག་ཆུན་པོ་ (medoò cūnbo) bouquet.
མེ་ཏོག་མཉམ་བཞད་ རྙིང་འབུད་གསར་འདོན་ (medoò ñamshɛɛ̀ ñiŋbüü sārdön) let a hundred flowers blossom and weed through the old to let the new emerge (political slogan).
མེ་ཏོག་མཉམ་བཞད་ མཁས་བརྒྱ་འགྲན་གླེང་ (medoò ñamshɛɛ̀ kɛɛ̀gya drɛnleŋ) let a hundred flowers blossom and a hundred school of thoughts contend (political slogan).
མེ་ཏོག་ཐག་འཁྱུད་ (medoò tāàgyüü) flowers that climb/ creep.
མེ་ཏོག་ཐོད་ (medoò tüü) ornaments made with flowers.
མེ་ཏོག་མཐུད་སྦྱོར་ (medoò tüüjɔɔ) grafting flowers/ plants.
མེ་ཏོག་འདབ་མ་ (medoò dəbma) flower petal.
མེ་ཏོག་དུལ་ (medoò düü) 1. pollen. 2. menstruation period.
མེ་ཏོག་ལྡན་པའི་ཟླ་བ་ (medoò dɛmbɛ dawa) the 4th month of the Tibetan calendar.
མེ་ཏོག་ལྡུམ་ར་ (medoò dumra) flower garden.
མེ་ཏོག་ནས་ (medoò nɛɛ̀) barley put in bowls to hold flowers (as offerings).
མེ་ཏོག་ཕོན་པོ་ (medoò pōmbo) a bunch of flowers.
མེ་ཏོག་ཕྱེ་ལེབ་ (medoò cēleb) pansy (flower).
མེ་ཏོག་འཕྲེང་བརྒྱུད་ (medoò trēŋgyüü) wreath of flowers.
མེ་ཏོག་འཕྲེང་བ་ (medoò trēŋwa) wreath of flowers.
མེ་ཏོག་བུམ་པ་ (medoò pumbə) flower vase.
མེ་ཏོག་བྱ་ཟེ་ (medoò case) cockscomb.
མེ་ཏོག་མོ་ལི་ (medoò moli) jasmine.
མེ་ཏོག་ཚོམ་བུ་ (medoò tsōmbu) bunch/ pile of flowers.
མེ་ཏོག་ཡལ་ (medoò yɛɛ) vi. to wither/ die (flowers or blooms).
མེ་ཏོག་ཡིང་ཧྭ་ (medoò yiŋha) oriental cherry.
མེ་ཏོག་ཡུས་ཅིན་ཞང་ (medoò yüüjinshaŋ) tib.ch. tulip.
མེ་ཏོག་ཡུས་ལན་ཧྭ་ (medoò yüülɛnha) tib.ch. magnolia.
མེ་ཏོག་སིལ་མ་ (medoò sīlmə) flowers that hand down.
མེ་ཏོག་གསར་པ་ (medoò sāāba) new flowers, fresh flowers.
མེ་ཏོག་སོས་པ་ (medoò sōōba) fresh flowers.
མེ་ཏོག་ཧ་ལོ་ (medoò hālo) high mellow (used in Tibetan medicine).
མེ་ཏོག་ཧྲན་ཁྲ་ (medoò hrēndra) tib.ch. camellia.
མེ་གཏོང་ (me dōŋ) va. to make a fire.
མེ་རྟ་ (meda) 1. fire-horse year. 2. sm. སྦྱི་སྦྱི་.
མེ་ལྟར་ཚ་བ་ (medar tsāwa) fiery, intense ༎འཐབ་རྩོད་མེ་ལྟར་ཚ་བ་ཞིག An intense struggle.
མེ་སྟག (medaà) 1. spark ༎མེ་སྟག་གིས་ཐང་ལྷོངས་སྲེག་ཐུབ་ A (single) spark can start a prairie fire. 2. fire-tiger year.
མེ་ཐག་གཙོད་ (medaà jöö) va. to put out a cooking fire.
མེ་ཐལ་ (medɛɛ) ashes from a fire.
མེ་ཐལ་ཕུང་དོང་ (medɛɛ pūŋdoŋ) a hole/ depression into which ashes from a fire are thrown.
མེ་ཐབ་ (medəb) stove, furnace.
མེ་ཐབ་སོ་ཕག (medəb sōbaà) firebrick, refractory brick.
མེ་ཐུབ་ (medub) heat resistant.
མེ་ཐུབ་རྒྱུ་ཆ་ (medub gyuja) fireproof materials.
མེ་ཐུབ་རང་བཞིན་ (medub rəŋshin) the nature of being resistant to fire.
མེ་ཐུབ་སོ་ཕག (medub sōbaà) fireproof bricks.
མེ་ཐུབ་ཨར་འདམ་ (medub ārdam) fireproof cement.
མེ་ཐུར་ (medur) 1. spark. 2. spoon made from metal.
མེ་ཐུར་སྒམ་ཆུང་ (medur gəmjuŋ) match box.
མེ་ཐེལ་ (medee) sm. མེ་ཏེལ་.
མེ་དང་ཆུ་ལ་སྙིང་རྗེ་མེད་ (medaŋ cūla ñiŋje meè) heartless, cruel [Lit. fire and water do not have compassion].

མེ་དང་ཆུ་ལ་ཞུ་བ་མེད་ (medaŋ cūlə shuwa mee̱) sm. མེ་དང་ཆུ་ལ་སྙིང་རྗེ་མེད་.

མེ་དང་སྐྲ་ལྟར་ (medaŋ būdar) things that can't be put/ kept together, incompatible things [Lit. like fire and hair].

མེ་དང་སྐྲ་ཐུག་པ་ (medaŋ bū tūgbə) an irreconcilable difference [Lit. fire and hair meeting].

མེ་དམ་ (medam) flower pot.

མེ་དུགས་ (meduù) heating a pouch containing various herbal medicines and applying it to the part of the body where there is pain (used in Tibetan medicine).

མེ་དོང་ (medoŋ) firepit.

མེ་དྲོད་ (medröö) the heat from fire.

མེ་ཊིག་ཊོན་ (medigdön) eng. metric ton.

མེ་མདག (medaà) ember, hot ash from a fire.

མེ་མདངས་ (mendaŋ) light/ glow of a fire.

མེ་མདའ་ (menda) gun, rifle; va.—རྒྱག to shoot (a gun).

མེ་མདའ་སྐྱེན་པོ་ (menda gyēmbo) expert marksman, sharpshooter.

མེ་མདའ་ཁ་ཤོར་ (menda kāshɔɔ) vi. to have a gun go off accidentally.

མེ་མདའ་ཁྲུང་ཧྥིང་ཅང་ (menda drūŋfeŋjaŋ) tib.ch. submachine gun, tommy gun.

མེ་མདའ་ཅན་ (mendajan) person carrying a gun, gun-toting.

མེ་མདའ་ཅི་ཀོན་ཅང་ (menda jīgönjaŋ) tib.ch. machine gun.

མེ་མདའ་ལྕགས་ཚགས་ (menda jāgdzaà) submachine gun, tommy gun.

མེ་མདའ་སྟོང་སྤག (menda dōŋbaà) firing a gun in the air; va.—རྒྱག.

མེ་མདའ་ཐུང་མདའ་ (menda tūŋda) hand gun, pistol; va.—རྒྱག.

མེ་མདའ་ཐེབས་ (menda tēb) vi. to be hit/ shot (by a bullet).

མེ་མདའ་ཕྱིར་ (menda dīr) va. to aim a gun/ rifle.

མེ་མདའ་སྦག་སྦག (menda bagbaà) machine gun; va.—རྒྱག.

མེ་མདའ་ཚ་པོ་ (menda tsābo) a crack shot. a marksman.

མེ་མདའི་སྐམ་པ་ (mendɛ gāmba) trigger of a gun.

མེ་མདའི་ཁ་ (mendɛ kā) muzzle of a gun.

མེ་མདའི་ཁ་ནས་སྲིད་དབང་ཐོན་ (mendɛ kāne sīiwaŋ tõn) political power comes from the muzzle of a gun (a quote from Mao).

མེ་མདའི་ཁོག་རིས་ (mendɛ kɔ̄ɔgrii) the rifling of the barrel of a gun.

མེ་མདའི་སྐུམ་ཤིང་ (mendɛ gumshiŋ) gunstock, rifle butt.

མེ་མདའི་སྒྲ་ (mendɛ dra) the sound of a gunshot.

མེ་མདའི་ལྡིའུ་མིག (mendɛ diu mii) sm. མེ་མདའི་པོར་དོག.

མེ་མདའི་པོར་དོག (mendɛ bɔ̄rdoò) rifle bolt.

མེ་མདའི་སྦོར་དོག (mendɛ bɔ̄rdoò) sm. མེ་མདའི་པོར་དོག.

མེ་མདའི་ཕོ་བྲང་ (mendɛ pōdraŋ) the chamber of gun.

མེ་མདའི་བྱ་གཞུག (mendɛ cashuù) gun handle.

མེ་མདའི་ཚ་ཁ་ (mendɛ tsāga) gunsight.

མེ་མདའི་རུ་ (mendɛ ru) gun brace/ rest/ stand.

མེ་མདའི་རྭ་ཅོ་ (mendɛ rajo) rifle brace/ stand/ rest made of horns.

མེ་མདས་གསོད་ (mendɛɛ sȍȍ) va. to execute by shooting/ firing squad.

མེ་མདེལ་ (medee) guns and ammunition/ bullets.

མེ་འདག (mendaà) glowing embers.

མེ་འདྲེན་སྦུ་གུ་ (mendren bugu) detonator.

མེ་དེལ་ (medee) bullet, cartridge, shell.

མེ་རྡོ་ (medo) flint.

མེ་རྡོ་བཟོ་གྲྭ་ (medo sodra) flint factory.

མེ་དོག (medoò) a burning/ glowing ember.

མེ་ལྡན་མདའ་མོ་ (medɛn damo) a fire arrow (used in warfare).

མེ་པོ་ཆེ་ (meboce) a big fire.

མེ་པྲ་ (medra) a type of divination done by reading the flames of a fire.

མེ་དཔུང་ (mebuŋ) a large fire.

མེ་སྦར་ (me bār) 1. va. to light a fire. 2. p. of མེ་སྦོར་.

མེ་སྦོར་: p. and f. སྦར་; imp. སྦོར་ (me bɔ̄r) va. to light a fire.

མེ་སྦོར་རླུང་སླུལ་ (mebar lūŋgüü) sm. མེ་སྦོར་རླུང་གཡབ་.

མེ་སྦོར་རླུང་གཡབ་ (mebar lūŋyəb) instigating [Lit. fanning a flame].

མེ་སྤུ་ (mebu) things that can't be put together, incompatible things [Lit. fire and hair].

མེ་སྤུ་ལྟར་ (mebu dār) sm. མེ་དང་སྤུ་ལྟར་.

མེ་སྤྲིན་ (medrin) cloud of smoke.

མེ་སྤྲེ་ (medre) fire-monkey year.

མེ་སྤྲེལ་ (medree) sm. མེ་སྤྲེ་.

མེ་ཕག (mebaà) fire-pig year.

མེ་ཕུང་ (mebuŋ) any heaped up fire, bonfire, campfire; va.—རྒྱག.

མེ་ཕུང་གཅིག་ལ་ཆུ་ཕོར་གང་ (mebuŋ jīglə cūbɔr kaŋ) utterly inadequate [Lit. a bowl of water to put out a bonfire].

མེ་ཕུང་མཚན་ཚོགས་ (mebuŋ tsɛ̄ndzɔɔ̀) people dancing and singing around a bonfire at night.

མེ་ཕོ་ (mepo) male fire year.

མེ་ཕོར་ (mebɔɔ) 1. brazier, pot in which coals are heated to keep a teapot warm. 2. sm. མེ་བུམ་, 2.

མེ་ཕོར་ཁོག་ལྡིར་ (mebɔɔ kɔ̄ɔ̀dii) Tibetan tea kettle and brazier.

མེ་འཕེན་ (meben) shooting (guns); va.—བྱེད་.

མེ་འཕེན་མཚམས་འཛོག (meben tsāmjɔɔ̀) cease-fire; va.—བྱེད་ ¶ མེ་འཕེན་མཚམས་འཛོག་ས་ཐིག Cease-fire line.

མེ་བུམ་ (mebum) 1. flower vase. 2. moxibustion cupping; va.—རྒྱག.

མེ་བྱ་ (meja) fire-bird year.

མེ་བྱི་ (meji) fire-mouse year.

མེ་བྲག (medraà) igneous rock.

མེ་དབལ་ (mewɛɛ) heat from a fire.

མེ་དབྱིན་ (mejin) ch.eng. America and Britain, American and British ¶ མེ་དབྱིན་བཙན་རྒྱལ་རིང་ལུགས་ American and British imperialism.

མེ་འབར་ (me bar) vi. to catch fire, to burn ¶ ཤོག་བུ་དེ་ལ་མེ་འབར་གྱི་མ་རེད་ That paper will not catch fire. ¶ ཁང་པ་འདི་རུ་མེ་འབར་གྱི་འདུག This house here is burning.

མེ་འབར་སྟེང་དུ་གཡོས་ལྷུག (me bar dēŋdu yīiduù) sm. མེ་འབར་བའི་སྐང་ལ་ཤིང་གཤགས་པ་.

མེ་འབར་མདའ་མོ་ (mebar damo) a fire arrow (in warfare).

མེ་འབར་བའི་སྐང་ལ་ཤིང་གཤགས་པ་ (me barwɛ gaŋla shīŋ shāgba) making a bad situation worse, exacerbating a situation [Lit. adding firewood to a burning fire].

མེ་འབར་རླུང་བསྐྱོད་ (mebar lūŋgyöö) sm. མེ་སྦར་རླུང་སླུལ་.

མེ་འབུད་ (me büü) 1. va. to start a fire. 2. to blow on/ fan a fire.

མེ་འབེན་ (meben) target (for shooting).

མེ་འབྱར་ (mejar) eng. a low level noncommissioned officer in the traditional Tibetan army.

མེ་འབྲུག (medruù) fire-dragon year.

མེ་སྦྲུལ་ (medrüü) fire-snake year.

མེ་མ་ཐལ་ (mematɛɛ) a fire that just about to die and become ash.

མེ་མ་མུར་ (mema mur) sm. མེ་མདག.

མེ་མ་མུར་གྱི་འོབས་ (mema murgi wob) a fire pit.

མེ་མུར་ (memur) sm. མེ་མདག.

མེ་མོ་ཡོས་ (memo yöö) female fire-hare year.

མེ་དམག (memaà) ch.tib. U.S. army, U.S. soldiers.

མེ་དམིགས་ (memii) the points or areas on the human body where moxabustion can be applied.

མེ་བཙག (medzaà) spark, ember.

མེ་བཙན་ (medzɛn) ch.tib. U.S. imperialism/

imperialists.

མེ་བཙའ་ (me̱dzaa) 1. spark, ember. 2. cauterization; va.—རྒྱག to cauterize.

མེ་རྩེད་ (me̱dzeè) acrobatic feats using fire, playing with fire.

མེ་རྩེད་བརྩེས་ན་རང་བསྲེག (me̱dzeè dzēèna ra̱ŋ sēg) if you play with fire you will get burned.

མེ་ཚག (me̱dzaà) sm. མེ་སྟག.

མེ་ཚང་ (me̱dzaŋ) kitchen.

མེ་ཙུགས་ (me̱ dzu̱ù) applying moxabustion.

མེ་མཚོན་ (me̱dzöö) firearms, weapons.

མེ་མཚམས་ (me̱ndzam) 1. cease-fire; va.—གཅོད་. 2. stopping/ putting out a fire; va.—གཅོད་.

མེ་ཛ་ (me̱dza) brazier made of clay. 2. flower pot.

མེ་རྫས་ (me̱dzɛɛ̀) gunpowder, va.—ཀྱིས་གཏོར་ to destroy by exploding a bomb/ explosives; va.—སྦོར་ to light/ ignite a bomb/ explosives.

མེ་རྫས་ཐི་ཨེན་ཐི་ (me̱dzɛɛ̀ tiendi) tib.eng. TNT (the explosive).

མེ་རྫས་མེ་ཏོག (me̱dzɛɛ̀ me̱doò) fireworks.

མེ་ཞར་ (me̱shar) shooting a rifle from horseback (in a special sports competitions); va.—རྒྱག.

མེ་ཞར་ཕོག་གྲས་ (me̱shar pɔ̄ɔ̄drɛɛ̀) one who has hit the bullseye in the competition of shooting a rifle from horseback.

མེ་གཞི་ (me̱shi) anvil.

མེ་ཟོན་ (me̱sön) fire prevention; va.—བྱེད་ to be careful with fire, to practice fire prevention ¶ ཤིང་ཁང་ནང་ལ་བསྡད་ན་མེ་ཟོན་བྱེད་དགོས་ You have to be careful with fire if you live in a wooden house.

མེ་འོད་ (me̱wöö) light/ glow of a fire.

མེ་འོབས་ (me̱wob) sm. མེ་དོང་.

མེ་ཡིས་མེ་གསོད་ (me̱yiì me̱söö) making matters worse [Lit. using fire to extinguish a fire].

མེ་ཡོག (me̱yɔɔ̀) firepoker.

མེ་ཡོན་ (me̱yön) ch. American dollar.

མེ་ཡོས་ (me̱yöö) fire-hare year.

མེ་རང་ཤི་དང་ དུ་བ་རང་ཡལ་ (me̱raŋ shīdaŋ tu̱wa ra̱ŋyɛɛ) 1. if the primary cause is eliminated the secondary will not occur. 2. letting sth. quiet down on its own. [Lit. the fire goes out and smoke disappears].

མེ་རི་ (me̱ri) 1. volcano. 2. abbr. U.S. and Japan.

མེ་རིས་ (me̱riì) paintings or drawing of fire/ flames.

མེ་རོ་ (me̱ro) ashes, cinders, embers.

མེ་རླབས་ (me̱ləb) blazing flames, wall of fire [Lit. a wave of fire].

མེ་ལ་ལྡེ་ (me̱la de̱) sm. མེར་བསྲོ་.

མེ་ལ་བསྲོ་ (me̱la sō) sm. མེར་བསྲོ་.

མེ་ལན་ (me̱lɛn) return fire; va.—སློག་; —སྤྲོད་ to return fire, to shoot back.

མེ་ལི་ (me̱li) eng. mile.

མེ་ལུག (me̱luù) fire-sheep year.

མེ་ལེ་ (me̱le) eng. mile.

མེ་ལེ་གྲུ་བཞི་ (me̱le tru̱bshi) tib.eng. square mile.

མེ་ལེན་ (me̱len) 1. fire tongs. 2. a type of branding iron.

མེ་ལེན་སྒྲུད་པ་ (me̱len gū̀ùbə) the wick used to ignite a Tibet matchlock rifle.

མེ་ལེན་གྱི་རྫས་ (me̱lengi dzɛɛ̀) gunpowder used to ignite a Tibet matchlock rifle.

མེ་ལོང་ (me̱loŋ) mirror.

མེ་ལོང་སྤུ་གྲི་ (me̱lon būdri) a traditional Tibetan medical instrument for shaving hair.

མེ་རོ་བསྐྱར་འབར་ (me̱ro gyāmbar) resurgence, revival [Lit. dying ember lighting again].

མེ་ཤིང་ (me̱shiŋ) firewood, fuel, dung; va.—བྱེད་ to use as firewood/ fuel; va.—རྒྱག to add firewood/ fuel to the fire ¶ ཀུབ་ཀྱག་རྙིང་པ་དེ་མེ་ཤིང་བྱས་པ་རེད་ (They) used the old chair as firewood.

མེ་ཤུགས་ (me̱shuù) 1. heat from a fire, thermo. 2. firepower (as in war) ¶ མེ་ཤུགས་གཅིག་ཏུ་བསྒྲིལ་ (They) concentrated their firepower.

མེ་ཤུགས་གློག་སྐྱེད་ས་ཚིགས་ (me̱shuù lɔ̄ɔ̄gyeè sōdziì) thermoelectric power plant/ station.

མེ་ཤུགས་གློག་འདོན་ (me̱shuù lɔ̄gdön) thermoelectric power.

མེ་ཤུགས་གློག་འདོན་བཟོ་གྲྭ་ (me̱shuù lɔ̄gdön) thermoelectric power plant.

མེ་ཤུགས་གློག་འདོན་འཕྲུལ་འཁོར་ (me̱shuù lɔ̄gdön trū̀ūgɔɔ) thermoelectric power generator.

མེ་ཤུགས་འཕུར་མདའ་ (me̱shuù pūnda) missile, rocket ¶ ཡོན་ཚེ་རྡུལ་ལྡན་མེ་ཤུགས་འཕུར་མདའི་རྟེན་གཞི་ Atomic missile base.

མེ་ཤུགས་འཕུར་མདའ་འཕེན་གནས་ (me̱shuù pūnda pēnnɛɛ̀) rocket launching site.

མེ་ཤུགས་འཕུར་མདའི་མེ་སྒྱོགས་ (me̱shuù pūndɛ me̱rgyɔɔ̀) rocket/ mortar launcher, bazooka.

མེ་ཤུགས་འཕུར་མདེལ་ (me̱shuù pūndee) missile, rocket.

མེ་ཤུགས་འབར་མདེལ་ (me̱shuù ba̱ndee) rocket/ mortar launcher, bazooka.

མེ་ཤུགས་འཛོམས་ས་ (me̱shuù dzo̱msa) the target of firing/ bombing/ shooting, firing range for a target ¶ མེ་ཤུགས་འཛོམས་སར་སླེབས་མ་ཐག As soon as they got into firing range for that target.

མེ་ཤུལ་ (me̱süü) remains of a fire.

མེ་ཤེད་ (me̱sheè) 1. མེ་ཤུགས་. 2. the amount of time a substance burns.

མེ་ཤེལ་ (me̱shee) magnifying glass.

མེ་ཤོར་ (me̱ shɔ̄ɔ̄) vi. to catch fire ¶ ཁང་པ་དེར་མེ་ཤོར་བ་དང་ཚང་མས་བྲོས་ཐབས་བྱས་པ་རེད་ As soon as the house caught fire everybody tried to escape.

མེ་སངས་རྒྱག (me̱saŋ gya̱à) va. to poke/ stir a fire.

མེ་སུའུ་ (me̱suu) abbr. U.S.A. and USSR.

མེ་སོན་ (me̱sön) starter fire (to ignite a large fire).

མེ་སྲུབ་ཤིང་ (me̱sub shiŋ) 1. piece of kindling wood. 2. white sandalwood.

མེ་སྲེག (me̱seg) burning; va.—གཏོང་ to burn/ roast; vi.—ཐེབས་ to get burned ¶ ཁོས་ཡི་གེ་མེ་སྲེག་བཏང་བ་རེད་ He burned the letter.

མེ་སྲེག་གྲིས་རྨོས་ (me̱seg dri̱imöö) swidden agriculture, slash-and-burn agriculture.

མེ་སྲོས་ (me̱ sōō) va. to keep warm by sitting close to a fire.

མེ་སླང་ (me̱laŋ) sm. མེ་ཕོར་.

མེ་གསོད་ (me̱ sōō) va. to put out/ extinguish a fire.

མེ་གསོད་འཁོར་ལོ་ (me̱söö kɔ̄ɔ̄lo) fire engine.

མེ་གསོད་རྒྱུ་རྫས་ (me̱söö gyu̱dzɛɛ̀) fire extinguishing materials.

མེ་གསོད་སྒྲིག་ཆས་ (me̱söö dri̱gjɛɛ̀) fire fighting equipment.

མེ་གསོད་ཆུ་སྒོ་ (me̱söö cūgo) fire hydrant.

མེ་གསོད་འཕྲུལ་འཁོར་ (me̱söö trū̀ūgɔɔ) sm. མེ་གསོད་འཁོར་ལོ་.

མེ་གསོད་འཕྲུལ་ཆས་ (me̱söö trū̀ūjɛɛ̀) fire extinguisher.

མེ་གསོད་མི་སྐྱོབ་ (me̱söö mi̱gyob) putting out fires and protecting the people.

མེ་གསོད་མོ་ཊ་ (me̱söö mo̱dra) sm. མེ་གསོད་འཁོར་ལོ་.

མེ་གསོད་ཡོ་བྱད་ (me̱söö yo̱bjɛɛ̀) sm. མེ་གསོད་སྒྲིག་ཆས་.

མེ་གསོད་རུ་ཁག (me̱söö ru̱gaà) fire brigade.

མེ་གསོད་རུ་མི་ (me̱söö ru̱mi) fireman.

མེ་གསོད་གླང་འཁོར་ (me̱söö lāŋgɔɔ) fire engine.

མེ་གསོས་ (me̱söö) paper or tinder used to start a fire.

མེ་བསངས་ (me̱saŋ) incense; va.—གཏོང་ to burn incense.

མེ་བསྲེག (me̱ sēg) sm. མེ་སྲེག.

མེ་ལྷ་ (me̱lha) 1. fire deity. 2. stove.

མེ་ལྷོག (me̱lhog) a type of disease/ illness.

མེག་སི་ཀོ་ (me̱gsigo) sm. མེག་སི་ཁོ་.

མེག་སི་ཁོ་ (me̱gsigo) Mexico.

མེང་ལྕགས་ (me̱njaà) manganese steel.

མེང་ཧྲེ་ཝེ་ཁེ་ (me̱heweke) ch. Menshevik.

མེད་ (me̱è) negative existential verb (there is not, there was not, does not exist/ have) ¶ ཁོ་ལ་རྟ་མེད་ཙང་རྐང་ཐང་དུ་ཡོང་བ་རེད་ Because he doesn't have a horse, he came on foot ¶ ང་ལ་མི་མདའ་མེད་ I don't have a gun.

མེད་འགྲོ་ (meèndro) probably there is ༑ཁོ་ལ་དངུལ་མེད་འགྲོ་སྙམས་པ་རེད་ (They) thought he probably has money.

མེད་ཐབས་མེད་པ་ (meèdəb meèba) sth./ sb. that one cannot do without, a necessity ༑མི་འདི་ལས་ཁུངས་ལ་མེད་ཐབས་མེད་པ་རེད་ The office cannot do without that person.

མེད་དུ་འགྱུར་ (meèdu gyur) vi. to vanish, to disappear ༑དེ་དགོས་མེད་དུ་འགྱུར་པ་རེད་ The need disappeared.

མེད་དུ་མི་རུང་བ་ (meèdu miruŋwə) indispensable, essential ༑ང་ཚོའི་ལས་དོན་ལ་ཁྱེད་རྣམས་པའི་རྒྱབ་སྐྱོར་ནི་མེད་དུ་མི་རུང་བ་ཞིག་ཡིན་ Your support is indispensable to our cause.

མེད་པ་ཆགས་ (meèba cāà) sm. མེད་པ་འགྱུར་.

མེད་པ་བ་ (meèbawa) a nihilist.

མེད་པ་བྱས་ནས་ (meèba cɛ̄ɛ̀nɛ) sm. མེད་པར་.

མེད་པ་བཟོ་ (mɛ̄ɛ̀ba so) va. to annihilate, to completely destroy, to wipe out ༑ཨ་མི་རིའི་དམག་དཔུང་ནི་ང་ཚོས་མེད་པ་བཟོས་དགོས་རེད་ We have to annihilate the American troops.

མེད་པར་ (mɛ̄ɛ̀bar) without ༑དངུལ་མེད་པར་ཁང་པ་རྒྱག་ཐུབ་ཀྱི་མ་རེད་ Without money (you) can not build a house.

མེད་པར་འགྱུར་ (meèbar gyur) vi. to disappear, to vanish ༑ཁྲུས་བྱས་ནས་དྲི་ངན་མེད་པར་གྱུར་པ་རེད་ After he washed, the bad smell disappeared.

མེད་པར་གཏོང་ (mɛ̄ɛ̀bar dōŋ) sm. མེད་པ་བཟོ་.

མེད་པར་བྱེད་ (meèbar cɛ̄ɛ̀) sm. མེད་པ་བཟོ་.

མེད་པར་བཟོ་ (mɛ̄ɛ̀bar so) sm. མེད་པ་བཟོ་.

མེད་པོ་ (mɛ̄ɛ̀bo) a poor man, a have not, a beggar.

མེད་མི་རུང་ (meè miruŋ) shung. sm. མེད་དུ་མི་རུང་བ་.

མེད་སར་ཁ་གསབ་ (meèsaa kāsəb) filling in the blanks, filling in the gaps; va.—བྱེད་.

མེདར་ (meèbar) shung. abbr. of མེད་པར་.

མེན་ (men) ch. manganese.

མེན་པའོ་ (membao) ch. bread.

མེའི་མཆོད་པ་ (mee cōòba) 1. a butter lamp offering. 2. exorcism.

མེའི་ཐལ་བ་ (mee tɛ̄ɛ̀wa) ashes.

མེའི་ཚ་ཚ་ (mee tsādza) a sparkling fire.

མེའི་ཧྭ་ (meeha) ch. plum tree.

མྲེའི་ (mee) ch. magnesium.

མེའོ་རིགས་ (meo rig) Miao nationality.

མེར་ (mee) 1. vi. to be filled to the brim. 2. sm. སྐྱུགས་. 3. flexible, malleable. 4. thin (for broths/ soups).

མེར་གྲོ་ (meedro) sm.* མེར་བསྲོ་.

མེར་སྐམ་ (meegam) drying by fire; va.—གཏོང་.

མེར་གྱིས་ཁེངས་ (mergi kēŋ) full of, filled to the brim ༑ཚང་གིས་མེར་གྱིས་ཁེངས་པའི་དཀར་ཡོལ་ A bowl filled to the brim with ཚང་.

མེར་གྱིས་གང་ (mergi kaŋ) sm. མེར་གྱི་ཁེངས་.

མེར་འདེབས་ (mee deb) va. to put sth. into a fire.

མེར་པུན་ (merbün) Melbourne.

མེར་མེར་ (mee mee) rolling/ flowing (of rivers, streams).

མེར་མེར་ཤིག་ཤིག (meemee shīgshiì) 1. vibrating, trembling (sound or shaking of the earth). 2. rolling, flowing. 3. the collective movement of insects which creates a wave-like movement.

མེར་སྲེག (mee sēg) burning; va. མེ་སྲེག; va.—གཏོང་ to burn.

མེར་བསྲེགས་ (meēseg) sm. མེ་སྲེག.

མེར་བསྲོ་ (mee sō) va. to keep warm by sitting close to a fire.

མེལ་གེ་ (meege) sm. སེབ་ཏུ་.

མེལ་ཚེ་ (meedze) a watch at night; va.—བྱེད་ to stand night watch.

མེལ་ཚེ་བ་ (meedzewa) night watchman.

མེལ་ལི་ (meeli) eng. mile.

མེལ་ལི་གྲུབ་བཞི་ (meeli trubshi) eng.tib. square mile.

མེལ་ལི་ (meele) sm. མེལ་ལི་.

མེས་ (meè) abbr. of མེས་པོ་.

མེས་རྒྱལ་ (meègyɛɛ) motherland, fatherland.

མེས་རྒྱལ་ཁྱིམ་ཚང་ཆེན་པོ་ (meègyɛɛ kyīmdzaŋ cēmmo) the big family of the motherland/ fatherland.

མེས་རྒྱལ་ཅན་བཞི་ (meègyɛɛ jēnshi) the four modernizations program of the Motherland.

མེས་རྒྱུད་ (meègyüù) ancestral lineage.

མེས་པོ་ (meèbo) 1. grandfather (paternal). 2. forefather, ancestor.

མེས་དབོན་ (meèbön) abbr. of grandfather and grandson.

མེས་དབོན་རྣམ་གསུམ་ (meèbön nāmsum) abbr. of the three great kings: Srongtsan Gampo, Trisrong Detsan, Tritsug Detsan.

མེས་འཚིག (meè tsiì) vi. to get burned ༑ཁོའི་ཁང་པ་མེས་ཚིག་པ་རེད་ His house got burned.

མེས་ཚིག་རྨ་ (meèdziì mā) burn wound.

མེས་ཚིག་མེར་གདུགས་ (meèdziì meeduù) doing sth. even though it is painful or difficult (e.g., losing a war then having to negotiate with the victors) [Lit. burned by the fire, touching the fire].

མེས་རབས་ (meèrəb) ancestral generation, previous generation.

མེས་སྲེག (meè sēg) va. to burn.

མེས་བསྲེགས་ (meè sēg) p. of མེས་སྲེག.

མེས་ཨག་ཚོམ་ (meè āgdzo) the 37th Tibetan king.

མོ་ (mo) 1. particle indicating female gender ༑བྱ་མོ་ Hen. 2. she ༑མོ་སློབ་ཕྲུག་མ་རེད་ She is not a student. ༑མོས་བྱས་པ་རེད་ She did it. 3. divination; va.—རྒྱག; —འདེབས་; —སྐོར་ to divine, to do divination. ༑ཁོང་གིས་ཚོང་ལ་ལམ་འགྲོ་ཡོང་མིན་མོ་བརྒྱབ་པ་རེད་ He did divination to see whether business will be good or not. 4. linking verb (in some dialects) ༑དོན་ག་ཅི་མོ་ what is the meaning (of this)?

མོ་ཀོར་ (mogɔɔ) sm. མོ་སྐོར་.

མོ་དཀར་ (mokar) a woman's cup (it is smaller than a man's cup).

མོ་ཀྲ་ (modra) sm. མོ་ཏར་.

མོ་བཀུག (mogyaà) a stand for a Tibetan woman's cup.

མོ་སྐད་ (mogɛɛ̀) sound of woman's voice.

མོ་སྐོར་ (mo gɔ̄ɔ̀) see མོ་.

མོ་སྐྱུར་ (mogyur) a divorce that was forced/ precipitated by the wife.

མོ་སྐྱེས་ (mogyeè) woman.

མོ་རྐྱང་ (mogyaŋ) 1. spinster, a single woman. 2. female wild ass.

མོ་ཁབ་ (mogəb) small needle.

མོ་ཁྱི་ (mugyi) bitch, a female dog.

མོ་མཁན་ (mogɛn) sm. མོ་པ་.

མོ་འཁོར་ (mogɔɔ) woman's bicycle (the type made without the center bar).

མོ་འཁྲབ་ (modrəb) male actors who play a female role.

མོ་གུམ་མ་ (mo gummə) sm. མོ་རྐྱང་.

མོ་གོས་ (mogöò) woman's clothes.

མོ་གློག (molɔ̄ɔ̀) negative electricity.

མོ་གློག་ཅན་གྱི་རྡེན་ཙི་ (molɔ̄ɔ̀jɛngi dēndzi) negative electron.

མོ་རྒྱག (mo gyaà) see མོ་.

མོ་རྒྱག་དཔེ་དེབ་ (mogyaà bēdeb) divination book/ text.

མོ་རྒྱུད་ (mogyüù) maternal descendants.

མོ་སྒོ་ (mogo) female, woman.

མོ་སྒོར་ (mogɔɔ) ch.tib. badge (usually made of gold) that military officers and aristocrats wear on their hat or cap.

མོ་དགོན་ (mogön) nunnery.

མོ་གཅུས་ (mojüù) nut (that goes with a screw).

མོ་ཆས་ (mojɛɛ̀) sm. མོ་གོས་.

མོ་ཉམས་དོད་པོ་ (moñam tȫòbo) a female who is very feminine.

མོ་བརྙན་ (moñɛn) female statue.

མོ་ཉེ་ (moñe) maternal relatives.

མོ་རྟ་ (moda) mare.

མོ་རྟགས་ (modaà) vagina.

མོ་བརྟག (modaà) divination.

མོ་ཊ་ (modra) 1. automobile, car; va.—གཏོང་ to drive car. 2. mortar (the weapon).

མོ་ཊར་ (modrar) sm. མོ་ཊ་.

མོ་ཊ་འཇིབ་ (modra jib) eng. jeep.

མོ་ཊོར་ (modor) sm. མོ་ཊ་.

མོ་སྟོན་ (modön) sm. མོ་པ་.

མོ་ཐིག (motig) a string used for divining/ divination.

མོ་ཐིག་པོ་ (mo tĩgbu) accurate divination ¶ གྲྭ་པ་དེ་མོ་ཐིག་པོ་ཡོད་པ་རེད་ That monk is accurate when divining.

མོ་ཐུའོ་གྲུ་གཟིངས་ (motu trusiŋ) ch.tib. motor boat.

མོ་ཐུའོ་ཅན་གྱི་དཔུང་སྡེ་ (motujɛngi bũŋde) ch.tib. motorized force/ army.

མོ་ཐོ་ (moto) a list for divination.

མོ་དོང་ (modoŋ) a coin used in divination.

མོ་དོར་ (modɔɔ) female petticoat/ underwear.

མོ་དྲེལ་ (modree) female mule.

མོ་མདོང་ (modoŋ) the container in which the coins used in divination are shaken.

མོ་འདེབས་ (modeb) see མོ་.

མོ་འདེབས་མཁན་ (mo debñen) sm. མོ་འདེབས་པ་.

མོ་འདེབས་པ་ (mo debba) a diviner.

མོ་ནག (monaà) divination that gives a bad sign/ answer.

མོ་ནད་ (monɛɛ̀) female illness/ disease, gynecological problems.

མོ་ནད་མཁྲིས་ཚབས་ (monɛɛ̀ triìdzəb) a type of female illness in Tibetan medicine.

མོ་ནད་ཐོར་བུ་ (monɛɛ̀ tɔ̄rbu) leukorrhea.

མོ་ནད་སྡེ་ཚན་ (monɛɛ̀ dedzɛn) department of gynecology.

མོ་ནད་བུ་སྐྱེས་སྨན་ཁང་ (monɛɛ̀ pugyeè mẽngaŋ) gynecology and obsetrics hospital, maternal and child health hospital.

མོ་ནད་སྨན་བཅོས་ཁང་ (monɛɛ̀ mẽnjöögaŋ) gynecology department/ clinic.

མོ་ནད་རྩ་སྐྲན་ (monɛɛ̀ dzādren) growth of tumor after childbirth.

མོ་ནད་འོ་ཚབས་ (monɛɛ̀ wodzəb) menstrual problems.

མོ་ནད་རླུང་ཚབས་ (monɛɛ̀ lũŋdzəb) female disease caused by རླུང་.

མོ་ནོར་ (monɔɔ) female yaks.

མོ་སྣ་གཅོད་ (mona jöö) va. to cut off the nose of a woman.

མོ་སྣེ་ (mone) the negative pole, cathode.

མོ་པ་ (moba) diviner.

མོ་སྤྲ་ (modra) abbr. of མོ་ and སྤྲ་.

མོ་དཔེ་ (modeb) book for divination.

མོ་ཕག (mopaà) female pig.

མོ་ཕྱུ་ (mocuù) female dress.

མོ་ཕྱུགས་ (mojuù) female livestock/ cattle.

མོ་ཕྱོགས་ (mojɔɔ̀) woman's side.

མོ་ཕྱྭ་ (moja) divination.

མོ་བ་ (mowa) sm. མོ་པ་.

མོ་བེའུ་ (mobiu) female calf.

མོ་བོང་ (mopoŋ) female donkey.

མོ་བོན་ (mobön) abbr. divination and Bon.

མོ་བྱ་ (moja) female birds.

མོ་བྱིས་ (mojiì) young girl.

མོ་བྲན་ (modrɛn) female servant, maidservant.

མོ་དབང་ (mowaŋ) vagina.

མོ་འབྲས་ (mondrɛɛ̀) the result of divination.

མོ་མ་ (moma) sm. མོ་པ་.

མོ་མ་ཉིང་ (mo məniŋ) woman with a nonfunctional vagina.

མོ་དམན་ (momɛn) sm. མོ་སྣེ་.

མོ་མོག (momɔɔ̀) sm. མོག་མོག.

མོ་རྩ་ (modza) a type of pulse characteristic of females in Tibetan medicine.

མོ་རྩིས་ (modziì) abbr. of མོ་ and རྩིས་.

མོ་རྩེ་ (mōdze) jiao (a Chinese money unit worth 1/ 10 of a yuan).

མོ་ཚིག (modziì) words used in divination.

མོ་མཚན་ (modzɛn) vagina.

མོ་མཚན་གྱི་ཁ་ (modzɛngi kā) vaginal orifice.

མོ་ཞི་གོ་ (moshigo) Mexico.

མོ་ཞི་ (moshi) female cat.

མོ་གཞུང་ (moshuŋ) sm. མོ་དཔེ་.

མོ་གཞོན་ (moshön) a young woman.

མོ་ཟོམ་ (mosom) women's Tibetan woolen boot.

མོ་ཟོམ་མཐིལ་གཉིས་མ་ (mosom tĩĩñiimə) a type of woman's woolen boot with two soles.

མོ་ཡན་ (moyɛn) tenant, lessee, renter; va.—གཏོང་ to lease/ rent a house or apartment; va.—བྱེད་ to be a renter, to rent a house/ apartment ¶ ཁང་མིག་མང་པོ་མོ་ཡན་ལ་གཏོང་གི་ཡོད་པ་རེད་ (He) is renting many apartments to tenants. ¶ ང་མི་ཚང་དེའི་མོ་ཡན་བྱས་ནས་བསྡད་ཡོད་ I am living as that family's tenants.

མོ་ཡིག (moyiì) feminine letters (in the Tibetan alphabet).

མོ་ཡོན་ (moyön) fee for divination.

མོ་ར་ (mora) 1. sm. མོ་རང་. 2. female goat.

མོ་རང་ (moraŋ) 1. she herself ¶ མོ་རང་ཚོགས་འདུ་རུ་མ་ཡོང་བར་ཚབ་ཅིག་བཏང་འདུག She didn't come to the meeting herself (but) sent a substitute. 2. slang in Lhasa: he, him ¶ ངས་མོ་རང་ལ་བཤད་པ་ཡིན་ I told him.

མོ་རབས་ཆད་ (mo rəbjɛɛ̀) a barren woman.

མོ་རེ་ (more) term used for calling women: " hey woman".

མོ་རིགས་ (morii̇) female sex/ gender, women.

མོ་རིགས་མེ་ཏོག (morii̇ medoò) female flower.

མོ་རེངས་ (moreŋ) unmarried woman, spinster. 2. widow.

མོ་རོ་ (moro) ch. an edible fungus.

མོ་ལ་འཇིང་ (moləjiŋ) tib.hind. flannel, cotton cloth.

མོ་ལས་ (molɛɛ̀) women's work.

མོ་ལུག (moluù) female sheep.

མོ་ལུང་ (moluŋ) 1. ring (on which a hook is fastened). 2. abbr. of divination (མོ་) and prophesy (ལུང་).

མོ་ལུང་བརྟག་ཞུ་ (moluŋ dāàshu) asking advice from diviners, lamas and oracles; va.—བྱེད་.

མོ་ལུས་ (molüù) female body/ form; vi.—ལེན་ to be born as a female.

མོ་ལོ་ཀོ་ (mologo) Morocco.

མོ་ལོ་དྲུག (molo truù) the six female years of the Tibetan Zodiac.

མོ་ཤར་ (moshar) young girls.

མོ་ཤིང་ (moshiŋ) female tree.

མོ་ཤེལ་ (moshee) female mirror.

མོ་ཤོ་ (mosho) dice used for divining.

མོ་གཤམ་ (mosham) barren woman.

མོ་གཤམ་ཡི་གེ་ (msham yigi) the four barren letters in the Tibetan alphabet: ར་ལ་ད་ཨ་.

མོ་སི་ཁའི་ (mosigo) sm. མོ་སི་ཁོ་.

མོ་སི་ཁོ་ (mosigo) Moscow.

མོ་སློག (molɔɔ̀) woman's fleece dress.

མོ་གསར་ (mosar) virgin; va.—འཕེབས་ to have the first intercourse with a virgin.

མོ་གསར་སྐྱི་པགས་ (mosar gyībaà) hymen.

མོ་ལྷ་ (molha) gods and deities used in divination. 2. goddess.

མོ་ལྷམ་ (molham) woman's shoes.

མོ་ཧྲེངས་ (mohreŋ) sm. མོ་རེངས་.

མོག (mɔg) eng. mug.

མོག་པོ་ (mɔgbo) sm. མོག་མོག་པོ་.

མོག་ཕྲུ་ (mogdru) a steamer (pot).

མོག་མོག (mɔɔ̀mɔɔ̀) Tibetan stuffed dumpling.

མོག་མོག་པོ་ (mɔɔmɔgbo) lackluster, faded (of color).

མོག་མོག་སི་ཀའོ་ (mɔɔmɔɔ̀ sĩgəo) tib.ch. steamed corn cake.

མོག་དམར་ (mɔgmar) dark purplish (usu. for

horses).

མོག་ཟངས་ (mogsaŋ) a steamer.

མོག་རོ་ (moro) 1. a kind of black fungus used for cooking. 2. dark purplish (usu. for horses).

མོག་རོ་དཀར་པོ་ (moro gārbo) a white fungus (tremella) used in cooking.

མོག་རོ་སེར་པོ་ (moro sēēbo) yellow fungus (used in cooking).

མོག་ཤ་ (mogsha) a fungus that grows in wet/ marshy areas.

མོག་ཤད་ (mogshɛɛ̀) a potter's tool for making the snout of kettles.

མོང་གོལ་ (moŋgöö) Mongols, Mongolia ¶ མོང་གོལ་མི་དམངས་སྤྱི་མཐུན་རྒྱལ་ཁབ་ Mongolian People's Republic.

མོང་ཅ་ལ་རྒྱལ་ཁབ་ (moŋjala gyɛɛgəb) ch.tib. Bangladesh.

མོང་ཏེ་ཝི་དེ་ཨོ་ (moŋde wideo) Montevideo.

མོང་རྟུལ་ (moŋdüü) foolish, stupid.

མོང་བརྟུལ་ (moŋdüü) sm. མོང་རྟུལ་.

མོང་བཟའ་ཁྲི་ལྕམ་ (moŋsa trīja) the Tibetan wife of King Srongtsan Gampo.

མོད་ (möö̀) 1. although, even though ¶ ཁོ་བོད་ནས་ཡོང་མོད་འོན་ཀྱང་གནས་ཚུལ་གང་ཡང་ཤོད་རྒྱུ་མི་འདུག Even though he came from Tibet, he has nothing to say about the situation there. 2. as soon as ¶ བོད་ལ་སླེབས་མོད་ལ་ཁོང་དང་མཇལ་བྱུང་ As soon as I arrived in Tibet, I met him. 3. plentiful, abundant.

མོད་ཆིལ་ལི་བ་ (möö̀ cēēlewa) sm. འཐིལ་འཐིལ་ལྡུག་ལྡུག.

མོད་ཉོ་དཀོན་ཚོང་ (möö̀ño gōndzoŋ) buying when things are plentiful and selling when they are scarce.

མོད་སྙོམས་ (möö̀ñom) equalizing, balancing; va.—བྱེད་.

མོད་སྙོམས་པོ་ (möö̀ ñōmbo) equal.

མོད་པ་ (möö̀ba) sm. མོད་པོ་.

མོད་པོ་ (möö̀bo) abundant, plentiful.

མོད་མི་དམའ་བ་ (möö̀ mimawa) not worse than, not inferior to ¶ གཟབ་མཆོར་དཔོན་རིགས་ལས་མོད་མི་དམའ་བ་སྒྲད་འདུག (He) wore clothes that were not worse than the officials.

མོད་ཚོང་ (möö̀dzoŋ) flooding the market, selling when things are plentiful; va.—བྱེད་.

མོད་ལ་ (möö̀la) as soon as, immediately ¶ བོད་ལ་སླེབས་མོད་ལ་ཁོང་དང་མཇལ་བྱུང་ As soon as I arrived in Tibet I met him.

མོན་ (mön) a place in southeast Tibet (that is now part of Arunachal Pradesh in India).

མོན་ཀ་ (mönga) sm. མོན་ཡུལ་.

མོན་ཁྲེ་ (möndre) sm. མོན་སྲན་.

མོན་གྱི་རས་ཟན་ (möngi rɛɛ̀sɛn) cotton shawl from མོན་.

མོན་ཆ་ར་ (mönchara) oak tree.

མོན་ཆག (mönjaà) millet.

མོན་རྟ་དབང་ (mön dāwaŋ) Tawang, main monastery and town in མོན་.

མོན་དར་ (möndar) 1. gunny, burlap. 2. raw silk.

མོན་དར་གྱི་གོས་ (möndargi köö̀) clothes/ garments made from gunny, burlap or raw silk.

མོན་དོ་ (möndo) eng. a unit of weight measurement (mound).

མོན་པ་ (mömba) name of the tribal people living in མོན་.

མོན་ཕྲུག་ཡུལ་བོར་ (möndruù yüübɔɔ) a person who is lost in strange land. [Lit. mömba child lost in an (outside) area].

མོན་ཡུལ་ (mönyüü) a place in southeast Tibet (now part of Arunachal Pradesh in India).

མོན་ཤོག (mönshɔɔ̀) paper from མོན་.

མོན་སྲན་ (mönsɛn) a kind of pea/ lentil from མོན་.

མོན་སྲན་དཀར་པོ་ (mönsɛn gārbo) a type of white pea/ lentil from མོན་.

མོན་སྲན་སྔེའུ་ (mönsɛn ŋēwu) a type of pea/ lentil from མོན་.

མོན་སྲན་ལེབ་མོ་ (mönsɛn lebmo) a kind of flat bean from མོན་.

མོན་སླེའུ་ (mönlewu) woolen blanket from མོན་.

མོའི་རྐང་འཁོར་ (mö gāŋgɔɔ) woman's bike, bike made for females without the center bar.

མོའི་ལྕགས་རྟ་ (mö jāgda) sm. མོའི་རྐང་འཁོར་.

མོའི་ཆུ་ཚོད་འཁོར་ལོ་ (mö cūdzöö̀ kɔ̄ɔlo) women's watch.

མོའི་རང་བཞིན་ (mö rəŋshin) negative nature ¶ མོའི་རང་བཞིན་གྱི་འགྱུར་ལྡོག Negative reaction (e.g., in medicine).

མོའུ་འགལ་གྱི་བུ་ (moŋgɛɛgi pu) name of one of the main disciples of the Buddha.

མོའུ་ཙེ་ (modze) currency unit in PRC =1/10 of a yuan.

མོལ་ (möö) va. to speak, to say, to talk ¶ ངས་ཁོང་ལ་གནས་ཚུལ་དེའི་སྐོར་ཞིབ་ཕྲ་མོལ་བ་ཡིན་ I told him about the situation in detail.

མོལ་ཁྱབ་ (möögyəb) disseminating/ information by speech; va.—བྱེད་ ¶ སྲིད་ཇུས་གསར་པའི་སྐོར་མི་སེར་ལ་མོལ་ཁྱབ་བྱེད་དགོས་ (We) have to disseminate (by speech) the new policy to the subjects.

མོལ་བགྲོས་ (mööŋaà) discussion, talk.

མོལ་མངགས་ (mööŋaà) saying/ telling/ instructing via speech; va.—བྱེད་ ¶ གཞམ་རིམ་ལས་བྱེད་པར་ལས་ཀའི་སྐོར་མོལ་མངགས་ཡག་པོ་བྱེད་དགོས་ (You) have to instruct the subordinate officials well about the work.

མོལ་ཅེན་ (mööjen) sm. མོལ་ཆེན་.

མོལ་ཆེན་ (mööjen) a big meeting in ancient Tibet.

མོལ་མཆིད་ (mööjii) sm. མོལ་གླུར་.

མོལ་བསྡུན་ (möödün) consultation; va.—བྱེད་ to consult ¶ ཐག་གཅོད་གང་བྱས་ཀྱང་ཁོང་ལ་མོལ་བསྡུན་བྱེད་དགོས་རེད་ Whatever decisions you make, first you must consult with him.

མོལ་གླུར་ (möödur) discussion, talk; va.—བྱེད་ to discuss, to have a talk.

མོལ་བགླུར་ (möödur) sm. མོལ་གླུར་.

མོལ་ཞིབ་ (mööshib) discussing/ talking in detail; va.—བྱེད་.

མོས་ (möö̀) 1. vi. to agree, to be in accord with ¶ ཁོའི་བསམ་འཆར་ལ་ཚང་མས་མོས་སོང་ Everyone agreed with his suggestion. 2. (vb. + —) to want to or to wish to do ¶ ཁོ་ཚོ་ཚོང་ཁང་ལ་འགྲོ་མོས་ཡོད་པ་རེད་ They want to go to the store. ¶ ཁོ་ཚོ་ལྷ་སར་འགྲོ་མོས་བྱས་པ་རེད་ They wanted to go to Lhasa. ¶ ཚོགས་ཆེན་དེར་ཡོང་མོས་བྱས་པར་དགའ་པོ་བྱུང་ I am happy that you want to come to the meeting. ¶ ང་བོད་ལ་འགྲོ་རྒྱུ་མོས་ནས་ཕྱིན་པ་ཡིན་ I went to Tibet because I wanted to. 3. by her ¶ ལས་ཀ་འདི་མོས་བྱས་པ་རེད་ This work was done by her.

མོས་བཀུར་ (möö̀gur) liking and respecting; va.—བྱེད་ to admire/ like and respect. ¶ བླ་འདི་ལ་མི་དམངས་རྣམས་ཀྱིས་མོས་བཀུར་བྱེད་ཀྱི་འདུག Many people like and respect that lama.

མོས་གུས་ (möö̀güù) admiration, respect; vi.—བྱེད་ to look up to with admiration and respect.

མོས་སྙོམས་ (möö̀ñom) even, balanced, equal.

མོས་བསྟོད་ (möö̀döö̀) praising, commending; va.—བྱེད་.

མོས་ཐག་གཅོད་ (möö̀ tāàjöö̀) va. to agree (to) ¶ སྙན་ཞུ་འབུལ་རྒྱུར་མོས་ཐག་བཅད་སོང་ (They) agreed to send a petition.

མོས་མཐུན་ (möö̀dün) 1. agreement; va.—བྱེད་ to agree (to) ¶ གྲོས་མོལ་བྱེད་རྒྱུར་མོས་མཐུན་བྱས་པ་རེད་ (They) agreed to have talks.

མོས་མཐུན་ཐག་གཅོད་ (möö̀dün tāgjöö̀) deciding to agree/ accept.

མོས་མཐུན་ཞལ་བཞེས་ (möö̀dün shɛɛsheè) agreeing, accepting; va.—བྱེད་ ¶ ང་ཚོར་རྒྱབ་སྐྱོར་གནང་རྒྱུར་མོས་མཐུན་ཞལ་བཞེས་གནང་བ་རེད་ (They) agreed to support us.

མོས་ལྡན་ (möndɛn) likable, agreeable.

མོས་པོ་ (möö̀bo) 1. liking, admiring; va.—བྱེད་ ¶

ཁོང་ལ་མི་ཚང་མས་མོས་པོ་བྱེད་ཀྱི་འདུག Everyone likes him. 2. wishing, desiring, wanting ¶ ང་གྲོགས་མོ་ཡག་པོ་ཞིག་རག་པའི་མོས་པོ་ཡོད་ I want to get a good girlfriend.

མོས་ཕྱོགས་ (mö̱öjɔɔ) 1. liking, admiring. 2. wishing, desiring, wanting ¶ ཁོང་གིས་མི་དམངས་ཀྱི་མོས་ཕྱོགས་དང་མཐུན་པའི་ལས་ཀ་གནང་བ་རེད་ He has done the work in accordance with the wishes of the people.

མོས་བོར་ (mö̱öbɔɔ) divorces in which the woman leaves her husband.

མོས་བློ་ (mö̱ölo) agreeing, liking.

མོས་ཤོག (mö̱öshoò) vote, ballot; va.—བླུགས་; —བསྒྱུ་; —བྱེད་ to vote, to cast a vote.

མྱ་ངན་ (ña̱ŋɛn) mourning, suffering; va.—བྱེད་; —ཞུ་ to grieve, to mourn; va.—སེལ་ to console mourners.

མྱ་ངན་འཁུར་ཞྭ་ (ña̱ŋɛn kūrsha) mourning cap/ hat.

མྱ་ངན་སྒྲོན་བདར་ (ña̱ŋɛn drö̱nda) sm. མྱ་ངན་སྒྲོན་ཡིག.

མྱ་ངན་སྒྲོན་ཡིག (ña̱ŋɛn drö̱nyii) a letter or notice informing about the death of sb. (usu. for the leader of a country or high officials).

མྱ་ངན་ཚོགས་འདུ་ (ña̱ŋɛn tsōndu) memorial meeting.

མྱ་ངན་ཞུ་ཚིག (ña̱ŋɛn shu̱dzii) memorial or condolence speech, eulogy.

མྱ་ངན་ཞུ་ཡིག (ña̱ŋɛn shu̱yii) note of condolence.

མྱ་ངན་ལས་འདས་ (ña̱ŋɛnlɛ dɛ̱ɛ) 1. vi. to die. 2. vi. to obtain nirvana/ enlightenment.

མྱ་ངན་སེམས་གསོ་ (ña̱ŋɛn sēmso) consoling, condolence; va.—བྱེད་; —གཏོང་ to console.

མྱ་ངན་བསང་ (ña̱ŋɛn sāŋ) vi. to get over grief/ sorrow ¶ ཕ་མ་གྲོངས་ནས་ཡུན་རིང་ཕྱིན་ཙང་མྱ་ངན་བསངས་བཞག Because a long time has passed since his parents died, (he) has gotten over the grief.

མྱ་ངམ་ཐང་ (ña̱ŋɛn tāŋ) a deserted place, a poor/ difficult area.

མྱ་ངམ་གྱི་འབྲོག་ཆེན་ (ña̱ŋɛngi drɔ̱gjen) a vast deserted area/ place.

མྱ་ངམ་བཤུལ་རིང་ (ña̱ŋɛn shü̱ü̱riŋ) sm. མྱ་ངམ་ཐང་.

མྱ་ངམ་ས་ཐང་ (ña̱ŋɛn sādaŋ) sm. མྱ་ངམ་ཐང་.

རྙག: p. རྙགས་; f. of **རྙག** (ña̱à) vi. to decompose, to rot.

རྙག་པ་ (ña̱gba) sm. རྙག་རྙོག.

རྙག་ཕྲན་ (ña̱gdrɛn) sm. ཉག་ཕྲན་.

རྙག་བྱེད་ (ña̱gjeè) a decomposing agent.

རྙག་རྙོག (ña̱gñog) 1. muddy. 2. unclear in intellect.

རྙགས་ (ña̱g) 1. clay, mud. 2. p. of རྙག. 3. abbr. of རྙགས་པ་.

རྙགས་དྲི་ (ña̱gdri) smell of rotten/ decomposing flesh.

རྙགས་པ་ (ña̱gba) sm. རྙགས་རུལ་.

རྙགས་རུལ་ (ña̱grüü) rotten, putrid, decomposing.

སྙུང་ (ña̱ŋ) f. of སྙོང་.

སྙུང་གོས་ (ña̱ŋgöö) mourning dress/ clothes.

སྙུང་ཆས་ (ña̱ŋjɛɛ) sm. སྙུང་གོས་.

སྙུང་འདས་ (ña̱ŋdɛɛ) nirvana.

སྙུང་སྙུང་སྙུག་སྙུག (ña̱ŋñaŋ ñu̱gñuù) sm. སྙུང་སྙུང་.

སྙུང་སྙུང་ ((ña̱ŋñaŋ) 1. stretching one's neck to look; va.—བྱེད་ ¶ ཁོང་གིས་འཚང་གཞི་དཀྱིལ་ནས་སྐེ་སྙུང་སྙུང་བྱས་ནས་ལྟད་མོ་ལྟ་གི་འདུག From inside the crowd, he stretched his neck to see the show. 2. testing the taste of food; va.—བྱེད་.

སྙུང་རྩི་སྣས་ (ña̱ŋdzidɛɛ) the rhizome of Chinese goldthread (coptis chineasis—used in Tibetan medicine).

སྙུང་ཞིབ་ (ña̱ŋshib) examining/ investigating/ inspecting firsthand; va.—བྱེད་ ¶ སྲིད་གཞུང་ནས་ཞིང་ལས་སྙུང་ཞིབ་བྱེད་མཁན་བཏང་ཡོད་པ་རེད་ The government sent people to investigate agriculture.

སྙུང་ཞྭ་ (ña̱ŋsha) 1. a mourning hat. 2. a new style hat without an outer brocade covering (in the 1950s).

སྙུངས་ (ña̱ŋ) p. of སྙོང་.

སྙུངས་སྙོང་ (ña̱ŋñoŋ) experience ¶ དབུལ་ཕོངས་ཀྱི་འཚོ་བ་སྙུངས་སྙོང་མེད་པར་ Without having experienced the life of the poor.

སྙུངས་ཞིབ་ (ña̱ŋshib) sm. སྙུང་ཞིབ་.

སྙི་ (ñi̱) arc. sm. མི་.

སྙི་རིགས་ (ñi̱rig) arc. sm. མི་རིགས་.

སྙི་ཧུད་ཧུད་ (ñi̱ hrü̱ührüü) showing off in front of a stranger.

སྙིག (ñi̱g) sm. མིག.

སྙིང་ (ñi̱ŋ) arc. sm. མིང་.

མྱུ་གུ་ (ñu̱gu) seedling, shoot, sprout; vi.—སྐྱེ་; —རྒྱས་; —ཐོན་; —གཏོང་; —འབུས་ to have a seedling or shoot first come out/ sprout/ germinate ¶ འབྲས་ཀྱི་མྱུ་གུ Rice seedling.

མྱུ་གུ་འཚོ་སྐྱོང་ཁང་ (ñu̱gu tsōgyoŋgaŋ) horticultural nursery (for raising seedlings).

མྱུ་གུ་གསོ་ (ñu̱gu sō) va. to raise seedlings.

མྱུ་གུའི་ཁ་འབུས་ཚད་ (ñu̱gü kəmbüü tsɛ̱ɛ) rate of germination.

སྙུག: p. **སྙུགས་**; f. **སྙུག**; imp. **སྙུགས་** (ñu̱g) 1. sm. སྙུང་སྙུང་. 2. va. to search ¶ ཤིང་ནགས་དཀྱིལ་འགྲོ་ལམ་སྙུགས་པ་རེད་ He searched in the forest for the road. 3. sm. མྱུ་གུ.

སྙུག་སྐྱོང་ས་ཚིགས་ (ñu̱ggyoŋ sādzii) nursery (seedlings) station.

སྙུག་སྙུག (ñu̱gñuù) sm. སྙུག.

སྙུག་ཙམ་ (ñu̱gdzam) sm. སྙུག་པ་.

སྙུག་རྩེ་ (ñu̱gdze) a sprout.

སྙུག་གཟན་འབུ་ (ñu̱g sɛ̱mbu) caterpillar.

སྙུག་སོན་ (ñu̱gsön) a sprout, seedling.

སྙུག་གསོ་ (ñu̱gso) raising seedlings; va.—བྱེད་.

སྙུགས་ (ñu̱g) imp. of སྙུག.

མྱུར་ (ñu̱r) abbr. of མྱུར་པོ་.

མྱུར་སྐྱེལ་འཕྲིན་ཆ་ (ñu̱rgyee tri̱njə) express mail.

མྱུར་སྐྱོད་ (ñu̱rgyöö) going quickly/ fast, advancing quickly; va.—བྱེད་.

མྱུར་སྐྱོབ་ (ñu̱rgyob) emergency aid, first aid, va.—བྱེད་.

མྱུར་སྐྱོབ་ཁང་ (ñu̱rgyobgaŋ) rescue ward.

མྱུར་སྐྱོབ་མལ་ཁྲི་ (ñu̱rgyob mɛ̱ɛdri) emergency bed.

མྱུར་སྐྱོབ་སྨན་སྒམ་ (ñu̱rgyob mēndum) first aid box/ kit.

མྱུར་བསྐྱོད་ (ñu̱rgyo̱ö̱) sm. མྱུར་སྐྱོད་.

མྱུར་གྲུ་ (ñu̱rdru) motor boat, speed boat.

མྱུར་འགྲོད་ལྕགས་ལམ་ (ñu̱rdröö jāglam) express railway/ rail line.

མྱུར་འགྲོད་གཞུང་ལམ་ (ñu̱rdröö shu̱nlam) express highway, freeway.

མྱུར་མགྱོགས་ (ñu̱rgyɔɔ) quick, fast, high speed, rapid, express ¶ མྱུར་མགྱོགས་རྟ་པོ་ A fast horse.

མྱུར་མགྱོགས་གོང་འཕེལ་ (ñu̱rgyɔɔ ko̱nbel) rapid progress.

མྱུར་མགྱོགས་ཚད་བཀལ་ (ñu̱rgyɔɔ tsɛ̱ɛgɛɛ) high speed, supersonic ¶ མྱུར་མགྱོགས་ཚད་བཀལ་གྱི་ལྕགས་ལམ་ High speed train.

མྱུར་འགྲུབ་ (ñu̱rdrub) quick accomplishment, quick success, intensive ¶ མྱུར་འགྲུབ་སློབ་གྲྭ་ Intensive school.

མྱུར་འགྲོས་ (ñu̱rdröö) moving/ going at a fast pace.

མྱུར་སྒྲུབ་རུ་ཁག (ñu̱rdrub ru̱gaà) shock brigade.

མྱུར་བཅོས་ (ñu̱rjöö) repairing quickly, emergency aid; va.—བྱེད་ to repair quickly.

མྱུར་ཉིད་ལེགས་གྲུབ་ (ñu̱rñii le̱gdub) shung. accomplishing as soon as possible ¶ གསེར་ཁྲིར་མངའ་གསོལ་མྱུར་ཉིད་ལེགས་གྲུབ་ཡོང་བ་ To be able to accomplish the work of enthronement as soon as possible.

མྱུར་བརྡག་སྨན་བཅོས་ཁང་ (ñu̱rdaà mēnjöögaŋ) emergency room (in a hospital or medical facility).

མྱུར་སྟབས་ (ñu̱rdəb) quickly, speedily ¶ རྟ་བཀའ་མྱུར་སྟབས་སུ་བཏང་བ་རེད་ He quickly sent a mounted messenger.

མྱུར་སྟབས་ཀྱི་སྒོ་ནས་ (ñu̱rdəbgi go̱nɛɛ) sm. མྱུར་སྟབས་.

མྱུར་འཐབ་མྱུར་གཅོད་ (ñurdəb ñurjöö̀) doing sth. quickly, making a rapid decision/ settlement [Lit. fight a quick battle, make a quick decision].

མྱུར་དུ་ (ñurdu) quickly, fast, rapidly; va.—གཏོང་ to speed up, to accelerate ¶ ང་ཚོས་ཡུལ་དེ་མྱུར་དུ་བཅིངས་འགྲོལ་གཏོང་དགོས་ We must quickly liberate that country.

མྱུར་བདེ་ (ñurde) quick and comfortable ¶ གནམ་གྲུའི་ཐོག་འགྲུལ་རྒྱག་པ་དེ་མྱུར་བདེ་ཡོད་པ་རེད་ Traveling by plane is quick and comfortable.

མྱུར་འདྲེན་ (ñurdren) quick transportation, express transport; va.—བྱེད་ to transport quickly, to transport by express.

མྱུར་སྡུད་ (ñurdüǜ) quick/ rapid collection, quick harvest; va.—བྱེད་.

མྱུར་པོ་ (ñurbu) quick, fast, rapid.

མྱུར་ཕན་ལུད་རྫས་ (ñurbɛn lüǜdzɛè) rapid action fertilizer.

མྱུར་སྐྱོད་འདྲུ་སྔོག (ñurjöö̀ druŋɔɔ̀) high-speed or rapid digging/ excavation.

མྱུར་སྐྱོད་ཨར་ལས་ (ñurjöö̀ ārlɛɛ̀) fast/ rapid construction.

མྱུར་བ་ (ñurwə) swift, fast, rapid, quick.

མྱུར་བྱོན་ (ñurjön) a prayer written when a lama dies asking for his speedy reincarnation.

མྱུར་མོ་ (ñurmo) sm. མྱུར་པོ་.

མྱུར་མྱུར་བ་ (ñurñurwa) extremely fast/ quick.

མྱུར་མྱུར་ཐྲིལ་སྒྲུབ་ (ñurñur dreedrub) finishing sth. in a hurry.

མྱུར་ཙམ་ (ñurdzam) sm. མགྱོགས་ཙམ་.

མྱུར་ཚད་ (ñurdzɛɛ̀) rate, speed, velocity ¶ ཐོན་སྐྱེད་མྱུར་ཚད་ལོ་རེ་བཞིན་མཐོ་རུ་འགྲོ་གི་ཡོད་པ་རེད་ The rate of production is going higher each year.

མྱུར་ཚད་སྙོམས་སྒྲིག་འཕྲུལ་ཆས་ (ñurdzɛɛ̀ ñōmdrig trǖǖjɛɛ̀) regulator, speed governor.

མྱུར་ལམ་ (ñurlam) short cut (path).

མྱུར་གསོ་རུ་ཁག (ñurso rugaà) emergency crew/ team.

མྱུར་གསོལ་ཟ་ཁང་ (ñursöö sagaŋ) snack counter, quick-lunch counter.

མྱུར་ཨར་འདམ་ (ñur ārdam) fast-drying cement.

མྱུལ་ (ñüü) 1. va. to wander, to roam. 2. va. to reconnoiter, to spy, to explore.

མྱུལ་པོ་ (ñüübo) tramp, vagabond.

མྱུལ་དཔྱད་ (ñüüjɛɛ̀) exploration; va.— བྱེད་.

མྱུལ་དཔྱད་པ་ (ñüüjɛɛ̀ba) explorer.

མྱུལ་དཔྱད་རུ་ཁག (ñüüjɛɛ̀ rugaà) exploration party, expedition.

མྱུལ་མ་ (ñüümə) secret agent, spy, intelligence agent.

མྱུལ་འཛུགས་ (ñüü dzuù) va. to plant a secret agent/ spy/ intelligence agent.

མྱུལ་མི་ (ñüümi) 1. a loafer/ wanderer/ idler. 2. a spy. 3. a womanizer.

མྱུལ་ཞིབ་ (ñüüshib) reconnaissance, spying, secret investigation; va.—བྱེད་.

མྱུལ་ཞིབ་འཁོར་སྐར་ (ñüüshib kɔ̄ɔgar) reconnaissance satellite.

མྱུལ་ཞིབ་འདྲི་གཅོད་ (ñüüshib drijöö̀) secret inquiry/ probe.

མྱུལ་ཞིབ་གནམ་གྲུ་ (ñüüshib nəmdru) reconnaissance/ spy plane.

མྱུལ་ཞིབ་པ་ (ñüüshibbə) sm. མྱུལ་མ་.

མྱུལ་ཞིབ་དབུགས་ལྒང་ (ñüüshib üggaŋ) reconnaissance/ spy balloon.

མྱུལ་ཞིབ་དམག (ñüüshib māà) scout/ reconnaissance/ troops.

མྱུལ་ཞིབ་དམག་མི་ (ñüüshib məəmi) sm. མྱུལ་ཞིབ་དམག.

མྱེ་ (ñe) arc. sm. མེ་.

མྱེན་ (ñen) abbr. of མཁྱེན་.

མྱེས་ (ñeè) arc. sm. མེད་.

མྱེས་ (ñeè) arc. sm. མེས་.

མྱོག (ñɔɔ̀) sm. བྱིས་པ་.

མྱོང་: p. མྱངས་; f. མྱང་; imp. མྱོངས་ (ñoŋ) 1. vi. to experience, to undergo ¶ ཁོ་ཚོ་དཀའ་ངལ་ཆེན་པོ་མྱོང་གི་ཡོད་པ་རེད་ They are experiencing great hardship. 2. (vb. + —) experience ¶ ང་ལྷ་སར་འགྲོ་མྱོང་ I have experienced going to Lhasa. 3. va. to taste ¶ ངས་འདི་བྲོ་བ་མྱངས་པ་ཡིན་ I tasted this.

མྱོང་ཁྲིད་ (ñoŋdriì) teaching others through one's own experience; va.—བྱེད་.

མྱོང་གོམས་ (ñoŋgom) experience ¶ ཁོང་གཉིས་རྒྱལ་ཚོགས་ནང་མྱོང་གོམས་འབྱུང་ཆེད་དུ་བཏང་གནང་བ་རེད་ The two of them were sent to the UN to get experience.

མྱོང་གྲུབ་ (ñoŋdrub) sm. མྱོང་གོམས་.

མྱོང་ཅན་ (ñoŋjɛn) experienced.

མྱོང་ཆ་ (ñoŋja) sm. མྱོང་གོམས་.

མྱོང་ཆེ་ཡོད་པ་ (ñoŋce yööba) experienced.

མྱོང་སྟོབས་ (ñoŋdob) the strength of one's experience.

མྱོང་ཐོག (ñoŋtɔɔ̀) through (one's) experience ¶ སྐད་ཆ་དེ་ཁོང་གིས་མྱོང་ཐོག་ནས་བཤད་པ་རེད་ He said that from his own experience.

མྱོང་ཐོག་ཤེས་རྟོགས་ (ñoŋtɔɔ̀ shēèdɔg) learning through experience.

མྱོང་མཐའ་ (ñoŋta) the end of experiencing sth. ¶ སྡུག་བསྔལ་གྱི་མྱོང་མཐའ་ The end of experiencing suffering.

མྱོང་འདྲིས་ (ñoŋdriì) experienced, accustomed, familiar.

མྱོང་བ་ (ñoŋwa) experience ¶ མྱོང་བ་ཟབ་མོ་ Profound experience.

མྱོང་བ་སྔ་ཟིན་ (ñoŋwa nāsin) preliminary experience.

མྱོང་བ་སྤྱོད་ (ñoŋwa jōö̀) va. to experience oneself/ firsthand.

མྱོང་བྱང་ (ñoŋjaŋ) 1. a list of (one's) experiences. 2. experienced.

མྱོང་བྱང་ཆེ་ (ñoŋjaŋ cē) shung. having great stores of experience.

མྱོང་ཚོར་ (ñoŋdzɔr) experience ¶ མྱོང་ཚོར་གཏིང་ཟབ་ A profound experience.

མྱོང་ཚོར་བསམ་འཆར་ (ñoŋtsɔr sāmjar) giving one's impression/ experience/ opinions; va.—ཞུ་.

མྱོངས་ (ñoŋ) imp. of མྱོང་.

མྱོས་ (ñöö̀) vi. to be drunk.

མྱོས་ཁུ་ (ñöö̀gu) sm. མྱོས་ཆུ་.

མྱོས་ཆུ་ (ñöö̀ju) 1. a liquid that is said to make people mad. 2. alcoholic drinks.

མྱོས་འགྱུར་ (ñöngyur) alcoholic beverages.

མྱོས་འཐོམས་ (ñöndom) 1. drunk; vi.—ལང་ to get drunk. 2. dazed, stunned; vi.—ལང་.

མྱོས་པའི་ཅ་ཅོ་ (ñöö̀bɛ jājo) talk of a drunk person.

མྱོས་བྱེད་ཀྱི་བཏུང་བ་ (ñöö̀jeègi dūŋwə) sm. ཆང་རག.

མྱོས་མ་ (ñöö̀ma) a young woman.

མྱོས་མྱོས་པོ་ (ñöö̀ñöö̀bo) having unclear thinking.

དམག (māà) troops, soldiers, army; va.—གཏོང་ to send troops ¶ གནམ་དམག Airforce. 2. war; va.—རྒྱག to wage war; vi.—ཤོར་ to have war breakout ¶ ཁོ་ཚོས་ལུང་པ་གཞན་ལ་དམག་བརྒྱབ་པ་རེད་ They waged war on the other area.

དམག་ཀྲང་ (māgdraŋ) tib.ch. a military rank in the Chinese army similar to Lt. Colonel.

དམག་དཀྱུས་ (məgdrüǜ) ordinary/ regular soldiers.

དམག་བཀའ་ (māà gā) military order.

དམག་བཀའ་ལྟར་སྒྲུབ་རྒྱུའི་ཁག་ཐེག་ཞུ་ཡིག (maà gādar drubgyü kāgdeg shuyiì) a military pledge (usu. an agreement made between an army officer and his superior that the officer will carry out his special mission).

དམག་བཀུར་ཁྱིམ་སྐྱོང་ (māggur kyīgyoŋ) support the army and give preferential treatment (support) to the families of the soldiers.

དམག་བཀུར་དམངས་གཅེས་ (māàgur māŋjeè) support the army and love the masses (political slogan).

དམག་བཀོད་བརྡ་བྱང་ (māàgöö̀ dajaŋ) a notice board on which military orders are posted.

དམག་རྐང་ (māàgaŋ) a military རྐང་ (i.e., a tax unit

of land requiring the holder to provide a corvee soldier to the army).

དམག་སྐྱལ་ (mɘggüü) sm. དམག་བསྐྱལ་.

དམག་སྐྱོད་ (mäàgyöö) the marching (of troops); va.—བྱེད་ to march, to go to war ༊ དགྲ་བོས་བཙན་འཛུལ་བྱས་པའི་ས་ཁུལ་དུ་དམག་སྐྱོད་བྱས་པ་རེད་ (They) marched to the area where the enemy had invaded.

དམག་བསྐྱལ་ (mɘggüü) military conscription/ drafting; va.—རྒྱག to recruit, to conscript, to draft (into the army).

དམག་བསྐྱལ་དང་ལེན་ (mɘggüü tanlen) voluntary military recruitment/ draft.

དམག་བསྐྱལ་དུས་བསྲིང་ (mɘggüü tüüsiŋ) military draft deferment.

དམག་བསྐྱལ་ལམ་ལུགས་ (mɘggüü lɘmluù) system of military conscription.

དམག་བསྐྱོད་ (mäàgyöö) sm. དམག་སྐྱོད་.

དམག་ཁག (mäàgaà) military unit/ group/ detachment.

དམག་ཁང་ (mäàgaŋ) military barracks.

དམག་ཁུངས་ (mɘguŋ) military, pertaining to the military ༊ མི་བཅུའི་ནང་ནས་ཕྱེད་ཀ་དམག་ཁུངས་རེད་ Half of the ten men are from the military.

དམག་ཁུལ་ (mɘgüü) military district/ area.

དམག་ཁུལ་ཁང་ (mɘgüügaŋ) military area headquarters ༊ བོད་དམག་ཁུལ་ཁང་ The Tibetan Military Area Headquarters.

དམག་ཁུལ་ཟི་ལིན་པུའུ་ (mɘgüü silinbu) tib.ch. headquarters of a military area/ command.

དམག་ཁོངས་ (mäàgoŋ) belonging to the military, military section ༊ ཁོས་དམག་ཁོངས་སུ་ཞུགས་པ་རེད་ He joined the army. ༊ དམག་ཁོངས་ནས་ཕྱིར་ལོག་པའི་དམག་མི་ Demobilized soldiers.

དམག་ཁོངས་སྐྱེལ་འདྲེན་ (mäàgoŋ gyēndren) military transportation.

དམག་ཁོངས་སྨན་པ་ (mäàgoŋ mɛ̄mba) military doctor/ surgeon.

དམག་ཁོངས་ཡིག་ཟམ་ (mäàgoŋ yigsam) army postal service.

དམག་ཁྱི་ (mɘggyi) military police dog.

དམག་ཁྲལ་ (mägdrɛɛ) military tax.

དམག་ཁྲི་རྟ་སྟོང་ (mäà krī dā dōŋ) a large/ huge army [Lit. ten thousand troops, a thousand horses].

དམག་ཁྲིམས་ (mɘgdrim) military law, martial law.

དམག་མཁོ་ (mäàgo) military needs/ supplies.

དམག་མཁོའི་སྒྲིག་ཆས་ (mäàgö drigjɛɛ̀) military equipment.

དམག་མཁོའི་སྒྲིག་ཆས་ཉུང་འཕྲི་ (mäàgö drigjɛɛ̀ ñuŋdri) military disarmament.

དམག་མཁོའི་སྒྲུབ་འདྲེན་ (mäàgö drumdren) military supply service.

དམག་མཁོའི་དངོས་རྫས་ (mäàgö ŋöödzɛɛ̀) military stores/ provisions/ supplies.

དམག་འཁོར་ (mäàgɔɔ) military trucks/ vehicles.

དམག་འཁྱམས་ (mäàgyam) soldier of fortune, mercenary.

དམག་ཁྱེར་ (mäàgyee) sm. དམག་འཁྲུག.

དམག་འཁྲི་ (mɘgdri) 1. the obligation (of certain families) to send/ provide a soldier. 2. military service.

དམག་འཁྲིད་ (mäà trīi) va. to lead (soldiers) to war.

དམག་འཁྲུག (mɘgdruù) war, warfare; va. དམག་འཁྲུག; —བྱེད་; —རྒྱག to fight a war, to wage a war; va.—སློང་ to provoke/ start/ incite a war; vi.—ལངས་ to have a war breakout/ start.

དམག་འཁྲུག་གི་གྲ་སྒྲིག (mɘgdruùgi trɘdrii) preparations for war; va.—བྱེད་.

དམག་འཁྲུག་གི་སྒྲིག་ཁྲིམས་ (mɘgdruùgi drigdrim) military discipline.

དམག་འཁྲུག་གི་འཇིགས་སྣང་ (mɘgdruùgi jignaŋ) war intimidation/ threats; va.—སྐུལ་ to threaten / intimidate with war.

དམག་འཁྲུག་གི་ཉེས་ཅན་ (mɘgdruùgi ñɛ̀ɛjɛn) war criminal.

དམག་འཁྲུག་གི་གནས་ཚུལ་ (mɘgdruùgi nɛ̄ɛdzüü) 1. state of war, war situation/ condition. 2. war news.

དམག་འཁྲུག་གི་མེ་ལྕེ་ (mɘgdruùgi meje) flames of war ༊ དམག་ཆེན་གཉིས་པར་དམག་འཁྲུག་གི་མེ་ལྕེ་ག་ས་ག་ལ་འབར་གྱི་ཡོད་པ་རེད་ The flames of war were burning everywhere during the Second World War.

དམག་འཁྲུག་གི་མཚམས་སུ་སྐྱོལ་བའི་སྲིད་ཇུས་ (mɘgdruùgi tsāmsu gyēēwɛ siìjüü) brink-of-war policy, brinkmanship.

དམག་འཁྲུག་ཉེས་ཅན་ (mɘgduù ñɛ̀ɛjɛn) war criminal.

དམག་འཁྲུག་ལྷོམ་པ་ (mɘgdruù lōmba) warlike, martial, militant.

དམག་འཁྲུག་སློང་མཁན་ (mɘgduù lōŋñɛn) warmonger, one who starts a war.

དམག་གི་ (mäàgi) military, army ༊ དམག་གི་སྨན་པ་ Army doctor.

དམག་གི་སྒྲིག་ལམ་ (mäàgi driglam) military discipline.

དམག་གི་འདྲེན་པ་ (mäàgi dremba) military commander.

དམག་གི་དཔའ་ངར་ (mäàgi pāŋar) military morale.

དམག་གི་དཔུང་ཚོགས་ཡན་ལག་བཞི་ (mäàgi būŋdzɔɔ̀ yenlaà shi) four branches of the military: infantry, cavalry, chariots and elephants.

དམག་གི་སྨན་པ་ (mäàgi mɛ̄mba) military doctor.

དམག་གི་ས་རྟེན་ (mäàgi säden) land given to families as the tax basis for providing a soldier.

དམག་གི་ས་གཞི་ (mäàgi sɘshi) battlefield.

དམག་གུར་ (maagur) army tent.

དམག་གོས་ (mäàgöö) military uniform.

དམག་གྲ་ (mägdra) war preparations; va.—སྒྲིག to make war preparations.

དམག་གྲངས་ (mägdraŋ) number of soldiers ༊ དམག་གྲངས་ 1000 One thousand soldiers.

དམག་གྲབས་ (mägdrɘb) sm. དམག་གྲ་.

དམག་གྲབས་མེད་པའི་གྲོང་ཁྱེར་ (mägdrɘb meèbɛ troŋgyer) undefended city, open city.

དམག་གྲབས་ཡོད་པའི་གྲོང་ཁྱེར་ (mägdrɘb yööbɛ troŋgyer) fortified city.

དམག་གྲབས་ཟོག་ཁག (mägdrɘb sɔgaà) a fund set aside by communes for war preparations.

དམག་གྲལ་ (mägdrɛɛ) soldiers in formation/ line, a line of soldiers.

དམག་གྲི་ (mɘgdri) military sword.

དམག་གྲུ་ (mɘgdru) naval vessel, warship.

དམག་གྲུ་རུ་ཁག (mɘgdrü rugaà) sm. དམག་གྲུའི་རུ་ཁག.

དམག་གྲུའི་རུ་ཁག (mɘgdrü rugaà) naval fleet, armada ༊ རྡོ་མཚོན་ཆ་ཡོད་པའི་དམག་གྲུའི་རུ་ཁག A nuclear fleet.

དམག་གྲོགས་ (mägdrɔɔ̀) 1. allies, allied forces/ troop. 2. friend in or from the army.

དམག་གྲོགས་ཀྱི་མཛའ་བཤེས་ (mägdrɔɔ̀gi dzāsheè) comrade-in-arms.

དམག་གྲོན་ (mägdrön) military expenses.

དམག་གླ་ (mägla) salary or wage paid to soldiers.

དམག་གླུ་ (mɘglu) battle song, military song.

དམག་དགེ་ (mägge) military instructor.

དམག་མགོ་ (mäàgo) front line.

དམག་འགན་ཅུའུ་ (mäàgɛn jū) tib.ch. military service bureau.

དམག་འགན་ཆག (mäàgɛn cāà) vi. to get exempt from military obligation/ service.

དམག་འགུལ་ (mɘgüü) militant movement; va.—བྱེད་ to make a militant movement ༊ མི་མང་གིས་རང་བཙན་གྱི་དམག་འགུལ་བྱེད་བཞིན་ཡོད་པ་རེད་ The people are making a militant movement for independence.

དམག་འགུགས་ (mäà guù) va. to conscript soldiers.

དམག་འགོ་ (mängo) military leader/ officer.

དམག་འགྱེད་ (mäàgyeè) sm. དམག་འཁྲུག.

དམག་རྒྱགས་ (mäggyaà) military provisions/ supplies; va.—སྤྲོད་ to give military provisions/ supplies.

དམག་རྒྱགས་གྲ་སྒྲིག (māggyaà trədriì) the part of production that was set aside by communes for use as military preparation.

དམག་རྒྱལ་རིང་ལུགས་ (māàgyɛɛ riŋluù) militarism.

དམག་སྒར་ (māàgar) military barrack, military camp, military regiment; va.—རྒྱག to station/ billet troops, to build barracks.

དམག་སྒར་གནས་ས་ (māàgar nɛ̄ɛ̀sa) military residential area, military compound.

དམག་སྒྲིག (məgdriì) 1. military line/ formation. 2. preparation for war; va.—བྱེད་.

དམག་རྔ་ (māgŋa) war drum.

དམག་ཆག (māgjaà) shung. the tax reduction given to families that have to provide corvee soldiers.

དམག་ཆག་ལག་འཁྱེར་ (māgjaà laggyer) shung. military tax exemption document for a family that has to provide a soldier as a corvee tax.

དམག་ཆས་ (māgjɛè) 1. military equipment/ weapons/ ordnance. 2. military uniform; va.—སྲུས་ to wear a military uniform.

དམག་ཆས་ཁོའི་ (māgjɛè kō) tib.ch. ordnance section.

དམག་ཆས་གྲན་བསྡུར་ (māgjɛè trɛnduu) arms race.

དམག་ཆས་འཕྲི་ (māgjɛè trī) va. to reduce arms/ armaments.

དམག་ཆས་བཟོ་གྲྭ་ (māgjɛè sodra) 1. ordnance factory. 2. military uniform factory.

དམག་ཆས་བཟོ་ལས་ (māgjɛè solɛɛ̀) war industry.

དམག་ཆེན་ (māgjen) 1. full-scale war, great war, world war ¶ འཛམ་གླིང་དམག་ཆེན་གཉིས་པའི་སྐབས་ During World War II. 2. a large/ major battle.

དམག་ཇུས་ (məgjüù) military strategy.

དམག་འཇམས་ (māŋjam) shung. abbr. military affairs and postal stations.

དམག་ཉིན་ (məgñin) days of warfare ¶ ང་ཚོའི་དམག་དཔུང་གིས་དམག་ཉིན་བཅུ་བརྒྱབ་སོང་ Our forces fought for ten days.

དམག་གཉེར་ཞིང་ར་ (məgñer shiŋrə) army reclamation farm.

དམག་གཏོང་ (māà dōŋ) va. to send troops ¶ རྒྱལ་ཁབ་དེར་དམག་བཏང་ནས་དབང་དུ་འདུས་པ་རེད་ (They) sent troops to that country and brought it under their control.

དམག་གྲངས་ (māgdöò) the number of soldiers.

དམག་རྟ་ (māgda) army horse.

དམག་རྟགས་ (māgdaà) military insignia/ emblem.

དམག་རྟེན་ (māgden) shung. land held as tax basis for providing a soldier ¶ དམག་རྟེན་ས་ཞིང་ Field held as tax basis for sending soldiers.

དམག་སྟོང་རྟ་ཁྲི་ (māgdoŋ dədri) shung. powerful army, an unstoppable army [Lit. thousands of men and tens of thousands of horses].

དམག་སྟོན་ (māgdön) military banquet; va.—གཞོམ་ to give/ have a military banquet.

དམག་སྟོབས་ (māgdob) the strength/ size of an army.

དམག་སྟོབས་ཆེ་ཞིང་རྟ་ཤེད་བཟང་བ་ (māgdob cēshiŋ dāsheè saŋbo) militarily powerful [Lit. great military strength, fine horses].

དམག་ཐག་གཅོད་ (māgdaà jȫò) va. to make an armistice/ truce.

དམག་ཐག་ཆོད་ (māgdaà cȫò) vi. to have an armistice/ truce come about.

དམག་ཐང་ (māgdaŋ) military parade/ drill ground.

དམག་ཐུག (māà tūù) vi. to be engaged in battle/ war.

དམག་ཐོབ་ (māà tōb) vi. to win a war/ battle.

དམག་ཐོབ་དངོས་ཛས་ (māgdob ŋȫòdzɛɛ̀) war spoils, war booty.

དམག་འཐབ་ (məgdəb) warfare, battle, war, fight; va.—བྱེད་ ¶ དམག་འཐབ་ཀྱི་དགོས་པ་ལྟར་ According to the needs of war. ¶ མི་ལོ་བཅུ་ཕྲག་རིང་དམག་འཐབ་བྱས་ཡོད་པ་རེད་ They have fought for decades.

དམག་འཐབ་ཀྱི་འཚོ་བ་ (māgdəbgi tsōwa) army life, military life, life at war.

དམག་འཐབ་དྲག་པོ་ (māgdəb tragbo) fierce war.

དམག་འཐབ་བྱས་རྗེས་ (māgdəb cɛɛ̀jeè) military accomplishment/ achievement.

དམག་འཐེན་ (māà tēn) va. to withdraw troops, to retreat.

དམག་དར་ (māgdar) military flag/ banner.

དམག་དུང་ (məgduŋ) military bugle/ trumpet; va. གཏོང་.

དམག་དུས་ (məgdüù) wartime, time of the war/ battle.

དམག་དུས་ཛ་དྲག (məgdüù dzadraà) time of military emergency.

དམག་དོད་ལག་འཛིན་ (māgdöò ləŋdzin) shung. a document issued by the traditional Tibetan government accepting money in place of a corvee soldier.

དམག་དོན་ (magdön) military, military affairs ¶ དམག་དོན་ཁོ་ནའི་ལྟ་ཚུལ་ Purely military viewpoint.

དམག་དོན་གྱི་བཀའ་བཅད་ (magdöngi gājɛɛ̀) military manuals.

དམག་དོན་བཀག་རྒྱ་ (magdön gāggya) martial law.

དམག་དོན་རྐྱང་པའི་མཐོང་ཚུལ་ (magdön gyāŋbɛ tōŋdzüü) purely military viewpoint.

དམག་དོན་ཁོ་ནའི་ལྟ་ཚུལ་ (magdön kōnɛ dədzüü) sm. དམག་དོན་རྐྱང་པའི་མཐོང་ཚུལ་.

དམག་དོན་ཁྲིམས་ཁང་ (magdön trīmgaŋ) sm. དམག་དོན་ཁྲིམས་ར་.

དམག་དོན་ཁྲིམས་ར་ (magdön trīmrə) military court.

དམག་དོན་མཁས་པ་ (magdön kɛ̄ɛ̀ba) military expert.

དམག་དོན་འཁྲུག་རྐྱེན་ (magdön trūggyen) military provocation.

དམག་དོན་གྱི་རོགས་སྐྱོང་ (magdöngi rɔ̄ɔ̀gyoŋ) military aid/ assistance.

དམག་དོན་གྱི་གློ་འདྲི་ས་ (magdöngi lōdrisə) military adviser.

དམག་དོན་གྲུ་ཁ་ (magdön trugə) military dock/ harbor/ port.

དམག་དོན་འགྲན་བསྡུར་ (magdön drɛnduu) military competition (in skills regarding the military); va.—བྱེད་.

དམག་དོན་དངོས་མངའ་བཤམས་སྟོན་ཁང་ (magdön ŋȫòŋa shāmdöngaŋ) military museum.

དམག་དོན་ཅན་གྱི་སྒྲིག་ཁྲིམས་ (magdönjɛngi drigdrim) rules of discipline in war.

དམག་དོན་ཉེས་ཅན་ (māgdön ñeèjen) war criminal.

དམག་དོན་རྟེན་གཞི་ (māgdön dēnshi) military base.

དམག་དོན་དུ་འགྱུར་ (māgdöndu gyur) vi. to become militarized, to become a military affair ¶ ས་མཚམས་ཀྱི་རྩོད་གཞི་དེ་དམག་དོན་དུ་གྱུར་པ་རེད་ The dispute over the boundary became a military affair.

དམག་དོན་དོ་དམ་ཨུ་ཡོན་ལྷན་ཁང་ (māgdön todam ūyön lhɛ̄ngaŋ) military control commission ¶ བོད་རང་སྐྱོང་ལྗོངས་ཀྱི་ལྷ་སའི་དམག་དོན་དོ་དམ་ཨུ་ཡོན་ལྷན་ཁང་ The Lhasa Military Control Commission of the Tibet Autonomous Region.

དམག་དོན་ནག་ཉེས་ (māgdön nagñeè) war crimes.

དམག་དོན་ནག་ཉེས་ཞིབ་དཔྱོད་བྱེད་པའི་རྒྱལ་སྤྱིའི་ཁྲིམས་ཁང་ (māgdön nagñeè shibjöò cɛɛ̀bɛ gyɛɛjii trīmgaŋ) International War Crimes Tribunal.

དམག་དོན་ནང་སྦྱོང་ (māgdön naŋjoŋ) military exercise/ practice.

དམག་དོན་མནའ་མཐུན་ (māgdön natün) military alliance.

དམག་དོན་གནས་གཞི་ (māgdön nɛ̄ɛ̀shi) sm. དམག་དོན་རྟེན་གཞི་.

དམག་དོན་པ་ (māgdönba) military strategist.

དམག་དོན་ཚན་རིག (māgdön tsɛ̄nriì) military science.

དམག་དོན་ཚོགས་ཁག (māgdön tsɔ̄ɔ̀gaà) military bloc/ alliance.

དམག་དོན་ཞིབ་བཤེར་ཁང་ (māgdön shibshergaŋ) military procuratorate.

དམག་དོན་བཟོ་ལས་ (māgdön solɛɛ̀) war/ military industry.

དམག་དོན་རིག་པ་ (māgdön rigbə) military science.

དམག་དོན་ལས་ཁངས་ (māgdön lɛ̄ɛguŋ) military administration.

དམག་དོན་ལས་འགན་ (māgdön lɛngɛn) military tasks/ responsibilities.

དམག་དོན་ལུས་རྩལ་པུའུ་ (māgdön lüüdzɛɛ būū) tib.ch. military sports department.

དམག་དོན་ལུས་རྩལ་སློབ་གྲྭ་ (māgdön lüüdzɛɛ lōbdra) military sports school.

དམག་དོན་སློབ་གྲྭ་ (māgdön lōbdra) military school/ academy.

དམག་དོན་སློབ་སྦྱོང་ (māgdön lōbjoŋ) sm. དམག་ལུགས་སློབ་སྦྱོང་.

དམག་དོན་གསང་བ་ (māgdön sāŋwa) military secret.

དམག་དོན་ཨུ་ཡོན་ལྷན་ཁང་ (māgdön ūyön lhɛ̄ngaŋ) military commission.

དམག་དོས་ (māgdöö) military loads/ supplies/ bales (of supplies).

དམག་བདག (māgdaà) shung. the owner of a serf who is serving as a corvee soldier (or of the person hired to serve in his place in the army).

དམག་དྲངས་ (māgdraŋ) p. of དམག་འདྲེན་.

དམག་དྲུང་ (məgdruŋ) shung. a military secretary (in the དམག་སྤྱི་ཁང་ in the traditional Tibetan army).

དམག་འདེད་ (māg deè) shung. va. to recruit soldiers.

དམག་འདྲེན་ (māg dren) va. to wage war, to send troops, to send a military expedition.

དམག་རྡོལ་ (māg dɔ̄ɔ) vi. to have a war occur/ break out.

དམག་ལྡོག (māg dɔ̄ɔ) va. to pull back/ retreat (militarily).

དམག་ལྡོམ་ (māgdom) soldiers who are shirkers.

དམག་སྡུད་ (māgdüü) sm. དམག་བསྐུལ་.

དམག་སྡེ་ (māgde) army, military division, corps ¶ དམག་སྡེ་བརྒྱད་པ་ The Eight Route Army (in PRC). ¶ དམག་སྡེ་བཞི་པ་གསར་པ་ The New Fourth Army (in PRC). ¶ དམག་སྡེ་བཅོ་བརྒྱད་ The Eighteenth Corps.

དམག་སྡོད་ས་སློག (māgdöö sālɔ̄ɔ) cultivation of land by resident military troops.

དམག་བརྡ་ (māgda) 1. declaration of war; va.—གཏོང་ to declare war. 2. message to conscript troops for war. 3. orders given to troops when marching (e.g., left turn).

དམག་བསྡུ་རྟ་ཉོ་ (māgdu dāño) increasing one's military strength [Lit. conscript troops, buy horses].

དམག་བསྡུའི་ལམ་ལུགས་ (māgdü ləmluù) system of military conscription.

དམག་ནང་ཞུགས་ལོ་ (māgnaŋ shuglo) the number of years spent in the military.

དམག་སྣེ་མཁན་ (māgneñɛ̄n) military scout/ guide.

དམག་སྣོན་ (māgnön) reinforcing troops; va.—རྒྱག; —གཏོང་.

དམག་དཔུང་ (məgbuŋ) military force, troops, army; va.—གཏོང་ to send troops/ army ¶ དམག་སྡེ་བརྒྱད་པའི་དམག་དཔུང་ Troops of the Eight Route Army.

དམག་དཔུང་གི་འཐུས་ཚབ་ (məgbuŋgi tűüdzəb) representatives from the military.

དམག་དཔུང་གི་ཟིང་སློང་ (məgbuŋgi siŋloŋ) army mutiny, disturbance in the army.

དམག་དཔུང་གི་རོལ་ཆ་ (məgbuŋgi rööja) martial music.

དམག་དཔུང་མཉམ་འཛོམས་ (məgbuŋ ñamdzom) combined forces/ troops; va.—བྱེད་ to combine troops/ forces.

དམག་དཔུང་གི་གཟི་རྔམ་ (məgbuŋgi siŋam) military might.

དམག་དཔུང་ཕྱིར་འཐེན་ (məgbuŋ cīnden) retreating, withdrawing troops; va.—བྱེད་.

དམག་དཔུང་འཛུགས་ (məgbuŋ dzuù) sm. དམག་འཛུགས་.

དམག་དཔུང་ཞིན་སི་ཇུན་ (məgbuŋ shinsijün) tib.ch. the New Fourth Army.

དམག་དཔུང་རིགས་གསུམ་ (məgbuŋ rigsum) the three branches of the armed forces.

དམག་དཔུང་དྲག་སྒྲུབ་དང་ལས་ཁངས་ཁ་བསྡུ་ (məgbuŋ hrāgdrub daŋ lɛ̄ɛguŋ kūdu) recruit better troops and simplify administration (political slogan).

དམག་དཔུང་ལྷན་འཛོམས་ (məgbuŋ lhɛ̄ndzom) vi. to assemble/ gather military troops.

དམག་དཔོན་ (māgbön) military officer.

དམག་དཔོན་གྱི་ལས་གནས་ (māgböngi lɛ̄ɛnɛɛ̀) the rank of officer in the army.

དམག་དཔོན་ངན་པ་ (māgbön ŋɛmba) warlord.

དམག་དཔོན་ཆེན་པོ་ (māgbön cēmbo) high ranking military officer.

དམག་དཔོན་རིན་པོ་ཆེ་ (māgbön rimboce) one of the seven royal symbols.

དམག་སྤོ་ (māg bō) va. to change the battlefield.

དམག་སྤྱི་ (māgji) generalissimo, commander in chief; va.—བྱེད་ to be commander in chief.

དམག་སྤྱི་ཁང་ (məgjigaŋ) shung. 1. military headquarters, headquarters of commander in chief. 2. office in traditional Tibetan government in charge of military affairs.

དམག་སྤྱི་ལས་ཁངས་ (məgji lɛ̄ɛguŋ) sm. དམག་སྤྱི་ཁང་.

དམག་སྤྱོད་ (māgjöö) military, pertaining to military needs or use ¶ དམག་སྤྱོད་གནམ་གྲུ་ Military planes.

དམག་སྤྱོད་འཁོར་ལོ་ (māgjöö kɔ̄ɔlo) military vehicles.

དམག་ཕམ་ (māà pām) vi. to lose a war/ battle, to be defeated.

དམག་ཕེབས་ (māà pēb) (soldiers) going off to war ¶ དཔའ་བོ་རྣམས་དམག་ཕེབས་སྐབས་ When the heroes went off to war.

དམག་ཕོགས་ (māgbɔ̄ɔ̀) military salary/ pay.

དམག་འཕྱུགས་ (māgjaà) shung. military conscription (tax).

དམག་འཕྲིན་ (məgdrin) military postal service, military mail.

དམག་ཇུས་ (məgjüü) war tactics, military strategy.

དམག་ཇུས་པ་ (məgjüüba) military advisor, military counselor.

དམག་ཇུས་ལས་ཁངས་ (məgjüü lɛ̄ɛguŋ) general staff headquarters.

དམག་བྲང་ (māgdraŋ) sm. དམག་སྒར་.

དམག་བློན་ (māglön) military minister.

དམག་དབང་ (māàwaŋ) military authority.

དམག་དབང་བཀའ་བྱང་ (māàwaŋ gājaŋ) shung. an insignia bestowing military authority.

དམག་དབང་མཚན་རྟགས་ (māàwaŋ tsɛ̄ndaà) an insignia/ certificate bestowing military authority.

དམག་འབངས་ (magbaŋ) civil and military, army and people.

དམག་འབངས་གཅིག་མཐུན་ (māgbaŋ jīgdün) army and people united.

དམག་འབྲུ་ (məgdru) sm. དམག་རྒྱགས་.

དམག་སྦྲོས་ཞིང་ར་ (māgböö shinrə) army reclamation farm, army farm made from reclaimed land.

དམག་སྦྱོང་ (māgjoŋ) military training, military drill; va.—བྱེད་.

དམག་སྦྲོན་ (māà drön) sm. དམག་འགུགས་.

དམག་མི་ (məəmi) soldier; va.—བྱེད་ to be a soldier, to act as a soldier; va.—གཏོང་ to send troops/ soldiers.

དམག་མི་བཀྲམ་ (məəmi drām) vi. to deploy troops.

དམག་མི་བཀྲམ་ཐིག (məəmi drāmtig) front line, picket line.

དམག་མི་གླས་པའི་ལམ་ལུགས་ (məəmi lɛ̄ɛbɛ ləmluù) the system of military recruitment/ enlistment.

དམག་མི་སྡུད་ (məəmi düü) va. to draft/ conscript (soldiers).

དམག་མིའི་ཁྱིམ་ཚང་ (məəmii kyīmdzaŋ) army dependents, families of soldiers.

དམག་མིའི་གུལ་ལུགས་ (məəmii güülüù) military salute.

དམག་མིའི་ཉམས་འགྱུར་ (məəmii ñamgyur) soldier's appearance.

དམག་མིའི་གོ་རྟགས་ (māāmii kodaà) military rank.
དམག་མིའི་གོ་རྟགས་རིམ་པ་ (māāmii kodaà rimbə) the hierarchy of military ranks/ grades.
དམག་མིའི་ནང་མི་ (māāmii nəŋmi) sm. དམག་མིའི་ཁྲིམས་ཚང་.
དམག་མིའི་ནང་ལ་ཚུད་ (māāmii nəŋla tsüü) vi. to become enlisted (as a soldier).
དམག་མིའི་སྤྱི་ཁྱབ་ (māāmii jīgyəb) army general, commander in chief.
དམག་མིའི་བྲང་བསྟན་ (māāmii draŋbɛn) tib.ch. military salute, military guard of honor.
དམག་མིའི་རོལ་མོ་རུ་ཁག (māāmii röömo rugaà) military band.
དམག་མིའི་ཨེམ་ཆི་ (māāmii ēmji) military doctor.
དམག་མིར་འཛུལ་ (māāmii dzüü) va. to become a soldier, to join the army.
དམག་མིར་ཞུགས་ (māāmii shuù) va. to join the army, to serve as a soldier.
དམག་སྙི་ (māāñi) sm. དམག་མི་.
དམག་དམངས་ (māāmaŋ) the army and the people, military and civilian.
དམག་དམངས་མཐུན་སྒྲིལ་ (māāmaŋ tǖndrii) unity between the military and the people.
དམག་རྩལ་ (māgdzɛɛ) military exercises, military sports; va.—སྦྱོང་ to do/ practice military exercises.
དམག་རྩལ་དགེ་རྒན་ (māgdzɛɛ gegɛn) military teacher, army drill instructor.
དམག་རྩལ་བཅའ་ཡིག (māgdzɛɛ jāəyii) military training code.
དམག་རྩལ་ཐང་ (māgdzɛɛ tāŋ) military training ground, military drill ground.
དམག་རྩལ་སྦྱོང་བརྡར་ (māgdzɛɛ joŋdar) military training.
དམག་རྩལ་སྦྱོང་སྲོལ་ (māgdzɛɛ joŋsöö) style of military training.
དམག་རྩེད་ (māgdzeè) military drill/ parade; va.—རྩེད་ to parade, to march.
དམག་རྩེད་ཀྱི་སྐད་བརྡ་ (māgdzeègi gɛ̄ɛ̀da) military drill commands.
དམག་རྩེད་སྐད་བརྡ་གཏོང་མཁན་ (māgdzeè gɛ̄ɛ̀da dōŋñɛn) one who is in charge of military drills and signals, drill instructor.
དམག་ཚིགས་ (māgdzii) sm. དམག་ཚུགས་.
དམག་ཚིགས་སྨན་ཁང་ (māgdzuù) military station hospital.
དམག་ཚུགས་ (māgdzuù) military station/ depot.
དམག་ཚོགས་ (māgdzɔ̀ɔ) a large military unit.
དམག་མཚམས་ (māgdzam) armistice, ceasefire; va.—འཛུགས to make/ sign an armistice or ceasefire.
དམག་འཛུགས་ (māà dzuù) va. to build up the army ¶ འབྱོར་མེད་གྲལ་རིམ་གྱི་ཆབ་སྲིད་གཙོར་གཟུང་བྱས་པའི་དམག་འཛུགས་ཀྱི་འགྲོ་ལམ་དེད་ནས་ Following the path of building up the army by placing proletarian politics in command.
དམག་འཛུགས་དུས་ཆེན་ (māgdzuù tüüjen) army day (August 1st.).
དམག་འཛོམས་ (māgdzom) army mobilization; va.—བྱེད་ to mobilize (the army), to call up troops.
དམག་རྫས་ (māgdzɛɛ̀) military supplies.
དམག་རྫས་མཁོ་སྤྲོད་ཁང་ (māgdzɛɛ̀ kōdröö kāwo) military supply section.
དམག་ཞྭ་ (māgsha) military hat/ cap/ helmet.
དམག་ཞབས་བཅའ་ཁྲིམས་ (māgshəb jādrim) military service law.
དམག་ཞབས་ཐོན་པའི་དམག་མི་ (māgshəb tõmbɛ māāmi) retired soldiers, veterans.
དམག་ཞབས་ནང་འདེམས་སྒྲུག་གི་ལམ་ལུགས་ (māgshəbnaŋ demdruùgi ləmluù) selective service system, military recruitment system.
དམག་ཞབས་ཟུར་པ་ (māgshəb surba) veteran, retired soldier.
དམག་ཞབས་ཟུར་པའི་བདེ་དོན་ལས་ཁང་ (māgshəb surbɛ dedön lɛ̀ɛgaŋ) veterans' administration (VA).
དམག་ཞབས་ལོ་གྲངས་ (māgshəb lodraŋ) sm. དམག་ཞུགས་ལོ་གྲངས་.
དམག་ཞབས་ལོ་བཅད་ (māgshəb lojɛɛ̀) time limit/ term of military service.
དམག་ཞབས་ཞུ་ཡུན་ (māgshəb shuyün) sm. དམག་ཞབས་ལོ་བཅད་.
དམག་ཞུགས་ (māgshuù) service in the military ¶ དམག་ཞུགས་ལོ་ཚད་ Number of year in military service.
དམག་ཞུགས་དུས་བསྒྱིང་ (māgshuù tüüsiŋ) military service deferment.
དམག་ཞུགས་ལོ་གྲངས་ (māgshuù lodraŋ) age for military service, enlistment age.
དམག་ཞེན་རིང་ལུགས་ (magshen riŋluù) militarism.
དམག་གཞུང་ (magshuŋ) military theory.
དམག་ཟིང་ (māgsiŋ) war; vi.—ལངས་ to be/ get in a state of war; va.—སློང་ to cause/ incite war.
དམག་ཟོར་ (māgsɔr) religious offering made to prevent war; va.—འཕེན་ to make such an offering.
དམག་ཟློག (mag dɔ̀ɔ) va. to counter attack (in war).
དམག་གཟིགས་ (māgsii) military review, troop review; va.—བསྐྱངས་ to review troops.
དམག་གཟིགས་མཛད་སྒོ་ (māgsiì dzɛ̄ɛ̀go) sm. དམག་གཟིགས་.
དམག་ཡོངས་ (māgyoŋ) the whole (or entire) army.
དམག་ར་ (māgra) battlefield.
དམག་རྭ་ (māgra) trench, bunker (in warfare).
དམག་རིགས་ (māgrii) types of military forces, military branches.
དམག་རུ་ (māgru) military unit/ section.
དམག་རུབ་ (māgrub) two-sided attack, pincer attack; va.—རྒྱག to attack from two sides.
དམག་རོགས་ (magroò) relief troops, reinforcements.
དམག་ལྡོག (mag lɔ̄ɔ) sm.དམག་ཟློག.
དམག་ལ་ཞུགས་ (māgla shuù) va. to join the army, to serve as a soldier.
དམག་ལན་ (māglɛn) counter attack, counteroffensive; va.—འཛལ་; —ལྡོག to counter attack.
དམག་ལས་ (māglɛɛ̀) sm. དམག་དོན་.
དམག་ལས་ཝུར་ཆེ་ (māglɛ wurce) exaggeration that is larger than the real event [exaggeration bigger than the war].
དམག་ལུགས་ (māgluù) military system.
དམག་ལུགས་སློབ་སྦྱོང་ (māgluù lōbjoŋ) system of military training ¶ རུ་སུའི་དམག་ལུགས་སློབ་སྦྱོང་ The Russian system of military training.
དམག་ལོག (māglɔ̀ɔ) 1. fighting back, counter attacking, making a counter offensive; va.—རྒྱག to fight back, to counterattack, to go on the offensive ¶ རྒྱ་དམར་ལ་དམག་ལོག་བརྒྱབ་ནས་རྒྱལ་ཁབ་སླར་གསོ་མྱུར་དུ་ཡོང་གི་རེད་ Fighting back against the Red Chinese, (we) will quickly have (our) nation restored. 2. vi. to get discharged from the army.
དམག་ཤུགས་ (māgshuù) military force/ strength.
དམག་ཤུགས་རྒྱ་སྐྱེད་ (māgshuù gyagyen) increasing military strength.
དམག་ཤུགས་ཉུང་འཕྲི་ (māgshuù ñuŋdri) reduction of military strength/ force, military disarmament.
དམག་ཤེད་ཅན་ (māgsheèjɛn) warlord, militarist.
དམག་ཤེད་རིང་ལུགས་ (māgsheè riŋluù) warlordism; militarism.
དམག་ཤེས་ཅན་ (māgsheèjɛn) military expert.
དམག་ཤོག (māgshɔ̀ɔ) a group/ unit of soldiers.
དམག་ཤོར་ (māà shɔ̄ɔ) vi. to lose a war/ battle.
དམག་ཤོར་རྒྱལ་ཁབ་ (māgshɔɔ gyɛɛgəb) the defeated country (in a war).
དམག་ས་ (māgsa) battle position, front line, battleground ¶ དམག་ས་ལྟེ་བ་ The main battleground.
དམག་ས་དང་པོ་ (māgsa taŋbo) front line.

དམག་སའི་བར་དུ་ཆོད་པའི་རྒྱལ་ཁབ་ (māgsɛ pardu cööbɛ gyɛɛgəb) buffer state.

དམག་སའི་དམག་འཐབ་ (māgsɛ məgdəb) positional warfare.

དམག་སེམས་ (māgsem) military mind/ will, soldiers' morale.

དམག་སྲིད་ (məgsii) military and political, civil and military ¶ དམག་སྲིད་འགོ་པ་ Military and civil leaders.

དམག་སྲིད་ཉེན་རྟོག་པ་ (məgsii ñendɔgbə) military police.

དམག་སྲིད་ཉེན་རྟོག་མ་ (məgsii ñendogmaà) sm. དམག་སྲིད་ཉེན་རྟོག་པ་.

དམག་སྲིད་སློབ་གྲྭ་ཆེན་མོ་ (məgsii lōbdra cēmmo) military and political university.

དམག་སྲིད་ལྷན་ཚོགས་ (məgsii lhɛndzɔɔ) joint military and political commission/ office.

དམག་སྲིད་ཨུ་ཡོན་ལྷན་ཁང་ (məgsii ūyön lhɛ̄ngaŋ) tib.ch. military and civil committee (system of transitional administrative offices in China in the early 1950s that functioned until full civilian governments were created).

དམག་དྲག་ (māghraà) top troops/ soldiers.

དམག་དྲག་དཔོན་ངར་ (māghraà bōŋar) top troops and brave officers, troops with high morale.

དམག་ཨུད་ (māg ūü) tib.ch. military committee.

དམངས་ (māŋ) 1. the people, the masses, the public ¶ དམངས་ཀྱི་འདོད་པ་དང་བསྟུན་ནས་ In accordance with the wishes of the people. 2. popular, folk ¶ དམངས་ཀྱི་སྒྲུང་ A folk story.

དམངས་ཀྱི་འཁོན་སྡང་ (māŋgi kōndaŋ) sm. དམངས་འཁོན་.

དམངས་ཀྱི་སྙིང་ནད་ (māŋgi ñīŋnɛè) popular enmity/ indignation.

དམངས་བཀོལ་མཁའ་སྐྱོད་དོ་དམ་ཅུའུ་ (māŋgöö kājöö todam jūwu) tib.ch. Civil Aviation Administration.

དམངས་དཀྱིལ་ (māŋgyii) among the masses.

དམངས་དཀྱུས་ (māŋgyuù) the ordinary/ common people.

དམངས་ཁྲིམས་ (məŋdrim) civil law.

དམངས་ཁྲོད་ (māŋdröö) among the common people, the folk.

དམངས་ཁྲོད་ཀྱི་སྒྱུ་རྩལ་ (māŋdröögi gyudzɛɛ) folk art.

དམངས་ཁྲོད་ཀྱི་རོལ་རྩེད་ (māŋdröögi röödzeè) folk entertainment.

དམངས་ཁྲོད་ཀྱི་གཏམ་རྒྱུད་ (māŋdröögi dāmgyüü) popular/ folk legend.

དམངས་ཁྲོད་ཀྱི་རོལ་མོ་ (māŋdröögi röömo) folk music.

དམངས་ཁྲོད་ཀྱི་རིག་རྩལ་ (māŋdröögi rigdzɛɛ) folk art and literature.

དམངས་ཁྲོད་ཀྱི་རིག་རྩལ་པ་ (māŋdröögi rigdzɛɛbə) folk/ people artist.

དམངས་ཁྲོད་སྒྱུ་རྩལ་ (māŋdröö gyudzɛɛ) sm. དམངས་ཁྲོད་ཀྱི་རིག་རྩལ་.

དམངས་ཁྲོད་སྒྱུ་རྩལ་རུ་ཁག (māŋdröö gyudzɛɛ rugaà) folk arts group/ troupe.

དམངས་ཁྲོད་རྩོམ་རིག (māŋdröö dzūmrii) folk literature.

དམངས་ཁྲོད་རྩོད་དོན་ (māŋdröö dzöödön) civil dispute, dispute relating to civil law.

དམངས་ཁྲོད་རིག་རྩལ་ (māŋdröö rigdzɛɛ) sm. དམངས་ཁྲོད་ཀྱི་རིག་རྩལ་.

དམངས་ཁྲོད་རོལ་མོ་མཉམ་དཀྲོལ་ (māŋdröö röömo ñamdröö) folk ensemble of traditional instruments.

དམངས་མཁོའི་དངོས་ཟོས་ཀྱི་སྐྱེལ་འདྲེན་ (māŋkö ŋöödzɛègi gyēndren) civil transport.

དམངས་འཁོན་ (māŋgön) mass hatred/ anger, popular indignation, the people's wrath.

དམངས་འཁོན་གཉེན་བྲལ་ (māŋgön ñēndrɛɛ) hated by the masses and separated from one's family.

དམངས་གླུ་ (māŋlu) folk song/ ballad.

དམངས་རྒྱལ་ (māŋgyɛɛ) the republic instituted in China in 1912.

དམངས་རྒྱལ་སྲིད་གཞུང་ (māŋgyɛɛ sīishuŋ) the republican government instituted in China in 1912.

དམངས་རྒྱལ་སྲིད་ལོ་ (māŋgyɛɛ sīilo) a year in the reign of the republican government in China.

དམངས་སྒྲུབ་ (məŋdrub) run by the local people (schools, business enterprises, etc.) ¶ དམངས་སྒྲུབ་སློབ་ཆུང་ Locally run primary school.

དམངས་སྒྲུབ་གཞུང་རོགས་ (məŋdrub shuŋrɔɔ) run by the local people and subsidized by the government (schools, business enterprises, etc.).

དམངས་གཅེས་ (māŋjeè) cherishing the people.

དམངས་གཅོད་ (māŋjöö) shung. toilet to be used by servants/ the masses.

དམངས་ཆེན་རྒྱུན་ཨུ་ལྷན་ཁང་ (māŋjen gyün ū lhɛ̄ngaŋ) the standing committee of the National People's Congress.

དམངས་མཆོག་རྗེ་དམན་ (māŋjɔɔ jemɛn) the masses are more important than the ruler.

དམངས་གཉེར་གཞུང་རོགས་ (māŋñer shuŋrɔɔ) sm. དམངས་སྒྲུབ་གཞུང་རོགས་.

དམངས་གཏམ་གླེང་ཕྱོགས་ (māŋdam lēŋjɔɔ) public opinion.

དམངས་དོན་ (māŋdön) civil affairs.

དམངས་དོན་སྐོར་གྱི་ཁྲིམས་གཞུང་ (māŋdön gɔɔgi trīmshuŋ) civil law code.

དམངས་དོན་སྐོར་གྱི་གྱོད་གཞི་ (māŋdön gɔɔgi gyööshib) civil case.

དམངས་དོན་གྱི་ཁྲིམས་འཛུགས་ (māŋdöngi trīmdzuù) civil legislation.

དམངས་དོན་བཅའ་ཁྲིམས་ (māŋdön jədrim) sm. དམངས་ཁྲིམས་.

དམངས་དོན་འདྲི་གཅོད་ཁྲིང་ (māŋdön drijöö tīŋ) the civil division of a people's court, civil court.

དམངས་དོན་རྩོད་གཞི་ (māŋdön dzööshib) civil dispute.

དམངས་བདེ་འབྱོར་ཚོགས་ (māŋde jɔɔdzɔɔ) abundant goods and happy people, people living in peace with goods in abundance.

དམངས་འདེམས་ (māŋdem) democratic election., electing by the people.

དམངས་འདོད་ (māŋdöö) wishes/ will of the people, popular opinion.

དམངས་འདོད་ཚོད་ལེན་ (māŋdöö tsōŋlen) public opinion poll.

དམངས་སྡུག་རྒྱུ་བརླག (məŋduù gyulaà) masses suffering by losing wealth.

དམངས་གནོད་ཆོམ་རྐུན་ (māŋnöö cōmgün) 1. traitor to the people. 2. thief who harms the people.

དམངས་སྤྱོད་ (māŋjöö) 1. civil, civilian. 2. public.

དམངས་སྤྱོད་ཁང་པ་ (māŋjöö kāŋba) public owned house.

དམངས་སྤྱོད་མཁའ་འགྲུལ་ (māŋjöö kəndrüü) civil aviation, civil airlines.

དམངས་སྤྱོད་གྲུ་གཟིངས་ (māŋjöö trusiŋ) passenger ship.

དམངས་སྤྱོད་གློག་ཆས་བཟོ་གྲྭ་ (māŋjöö lɔ̄gjɛɛ̀ sodra) civil electrical appliance factory.

དམངས་སྤྱོད་གནམ་གྲུ་ (māŋjöö nəmdru) civilian/ passenger plane.

དམངས་སྤྱོད་ཚོང་ཟོག (māŋjöö tsōŋsɔɔ) civilian goods/ products.

དམངས་ཕན་ (māŋpɛn) beneficial to the masses.

དམངས་ཕལ་པ་ (māŋpɛɛwa) sm. དམངས་དཀྱུས་.

དམངས་ཕྱུག་སྲིད་ཇུས་ (māŋjuù sīijüü) policy for making the people rich.

དམངས་བྱིང་ (māŋjiŋ) sm. དམངས་དཀྱུས་.

དམངས་དབང་ (māŋwaŋ) the rights of the people.

དམངས་དབང་རིང་ལུགས་ (māŋwaŋ riŋluù) system in which the people have rights.

དམངས་དབུལ་རྒྱུ་ཟད་ (məŋüü gyusɛɛ̀) poverty [Lit. people poor, materials/ resources exhausted].

དམངས་མ་ (māŋma) sm. དམངས་.

དམངས་མོ་ (māŋmo) female servant.

དམངས་གཙོ་ (māŋdzo) democracy, democratic ¶ སྤྱི་ཚོགས་རིང་ལུགས་ཀྱི་དམངས་གཙོ་ Socialist democracy.

དམངས་གཙོ་སྐྱེལ་སྤེལ་ཚོགས་པ་ (māŋdzo gǖübel tsōgba) association for promoting democracy.

དམངས་གཙོ་ཁོ་ན་ (māŋdzo kōna) absolute (pure) democracy.

དམངས་གཙོ་ཁོ་ནས་འཛིན་པའི་སྲིད་དབང་ (māŋdzo kōnɛɛ̀ dzimbɛ sīiwaŋ) democratic dictatorship, dictatorship of the people.

དམངས་གཙོ་རྒྱལ་འཛུགས་ཚོགས་པ་ (māŋdzo gyɛɛdzuù tsōgba) democratic national construction association (name of political party at the time the Communists took power in China).

དམངས་གཙོ་གཅིག་སྡུད་ (māŋdzö jīdüù) democratic centralism.

དམངས་གཙོ་གཅིག་སྡུད་ཀྱི་ལམ་ལུགས་ (māŋdzo jīgdüügi ləmluù) democratic centralism.

དམངས་གཙོ་བཅོས་བསྒྱུར་ (māŋdzo jöögyur) democratic reforms (in China, the socialist reforms that replaced the traditional politico-economic system); va.—བྱེད་; —གཏོང་ to implement democratic reforms.

དམངས་གཙོ་ཆེན་པོ་གསུམ་ (māŋdzo cēmbo sūm) democracy in three main fields: political, economic and military.

དམངས་གཙོ་དང་ (māŋdzo dāŋ) Democratic Party (in U.S.A.).

དམངས་གཙོ་ཐལ་ཆེ་བ་ (māŋdzo tɛ̄ɛ̄cewa) ultrademocracy, placing people as the main entity with no organization or structure above them.

དམངས་གཙོ་བདག་གཉེར་ཨུ་ཡོན་ལྷན་ཁང་ (māŋdzo dag̃ñer ūyün lhēngaŋ) democratic management committee (the post 1959 office in charge of a monastery).

དམངས་གཙོ་མནའ་མཐུན་ (māŋdzo nādün) democratic alliance.

དམངས་གཙོ་མནའ་མཐུན་ཚོགས་པ་ (māŋdzo nādün tsōgba) democratic league.

དམངས་གཙོ་པ་ (māŋdzoba) a democrat.

དམངས་གཙོ་སྤྱི་མཐུན་ (māŋdzo jīdün) democratic republic.

དམངས་གཙོ་སྤྱི་མཐུན་རྒྱལ་ཁབ་ (māŋdzo jīdün gyɛɛgəb) a country that is a democratic republic.

དམངས་གཙོ་སྤྱི་ཚོགས་དང་ (māŋdzo jīdzɔ̄ɔ dāŋ) democratic socialist party.

དམངས་གཙོ་ཕྱོགས་ཁག (māŋdzo cɔ̄ɔ̀gaà) democratic group/ faction, democratic party (in U.S.A.).

དམངས་གཙོ་ཚོགས་སྡེ་ (maŋdzo tsōgde) sm. དམངས་གཙོ་ཕྱོགས་ཁག.

དམངས་གཙོ་ཚོགས་པ་ (maŋdzo tsōgba) sm. དམངས་གཙོ་ཕྱོགས་ཁག.

དམངས་གཙོ་ཚོགས་པའི་འགོ་ཁྲིད་ལྷན་ཚོགས་ (maŋdzo tsōgbɛ gəudrii lhēndzɔɔ̀) Democratic Leadership Council.

དམངས་གཙོ་ཚོགས་པའི་རྒྱལ་ཡོངས་ཚོགས་ཆུང་ (maŋdzo tsōgbɛ gyɛɛyoŋ tsōgjuŋ) democratic national committee (in U.S.A.).

དམངས་གཙོ་རང་སྐྱོང་མནའ་མཐུན་ (māŋdzo raŋgyoŋ nədün) Democratic Self-Rule League.

དམངས་གཙོ་རབ་ཏུ་དར་བ་ (māŋdzo rəbdu tarwa) a highly developed democracy.

དམངས་གཙོའི་ཁེ་དབང་ (maŋdzö kēwaŋ) democratic rights.

དམངས་གཙོའི་གྲོས་མོལ་ (māŋdzö trȫömöö) democratic consultation/ discussion/ negotiation; va.—བྱེད་ to hold democratic discussions/ negotiations.

དམངས་གཙོའི་བཅོས་བསྒྱུར་ (māŋdzö jöögyur) sm. དམངས་གཙོ་བཅོས་བསྒྱུར་.

དམངས་གཙོའི་དང་ (māŋdzö dāŋ) the Democratic League (a party in post war China), the Democratic Party (in the U.S.A.).

དམངས་གཙོའི་དང་པའི་ (māŋdzö dāŋpe) tib.ch. democratic party.

དམངས་གཙོའི་དང་ཤོག (māŋdzö dāŋshoò) sm. དམངས་གཙོའི་དང་པའི་.

དམངས་གཙོའི་དོ་དམ་ (māŋdzö todam) democratic management.

དམངས་གཙོའི་དོ་དམ་ཨུ་ཡོན་ལྷན་ཁང་ (māŋdzö todam ūyün lhēngaŋ) sm. དམངས་གཙོ་དོ་དམ་ཨུ་ཡོན་ལྷན་ཁང་.

དམངས་གཙོའི་འདེམས་སྒོ་ (māŋdzö demgo) democratic election.

དམངས་གཙོའི་མནའ་འབྲེལ་ (māŋdzö nāndree) democratic alliance.

དམངས་གཙོའི་སྤྱི་མཐུན་ (māŋdzö jīdün) sm. དམངས་གཙོའི་སྤྱི་མཐུན་.

དམངས་གཙོའི་སྤྱོད་ཚུལ་ (māŋdzö jöödzüü) democratic way of doing things.

དམངས་གཙོའི་སྤྱི་ཚོགས་དོན་གཉེར་ཅན་གྱི་སློབ་ཕྲུག་སྒྲིག་འཛུགས་ (māŋdzö jīdzɔɔ̀ tönñerjɛngi lōbdruù drigdzuù) Students for a Democratic Society (SDS).

དམངས་གཙོའི་ཕྱོགས་ཁག (māŋdzö cɔ̄ɔ̀gaà) sm. དམངས་གཙོ་ཕྱོགས་ཁག.

དམངས་གཙོའི་མི་སྣ་ (māŋdzö minə) democrats, democratic elements, democratic personages.

དམངས་གཙོའི་རིང་ལུགས་ (māŋdzö riŋluù) democracy ¶ དམངས་གཙོའི་རིང་ལུགས་གསར་པའི་གསར་བརྗེ་ The new democratic revolution.

དམངས་གཙོའི་སྲིད་འཛུགས་ (māŋdzö sīndzuù) the development/ build up of democracy.

དམངས་གཙོའི་སྲིད་གཞུང་ (māŋdzö sīnshuŋ) democratic goverment.

དམངས་གཙོའི་གསར་བརྗེ་ (māŋdzö sārje) democratic revolution.

དམངས་བཙུགས་ (māŋdzuù) established/ organized/ started by the people (as opposed to the government) ¶ དམངས་བཙུགས་སློབ་གྲྭ་ A school organized by the people.

དམངས་བཙུགས་གཞུང་རོགས་ (māŋdzuù shuŋrɔɔ̀) sm. དམངས་སྐྱབ་གཞུང་རོགས་.

དམངས་བཙུགས་སློབ་གྲྭ (māŋdzuù sōbdra) community established school (usu. a primary school with grades 1 to 3).

དམངས་བཙུགས་སློབ་ཆུང་ (māŋdzö lōbjuŋ) a primary school run by the local community.

དམངས་རྩམ་ (māŋdzam) an ordinary/ inferior type of tsampa.

དམངས་རྩོད་གཏུག་བཤེར་ (māŋdzöö dūgser) civil lawsuit, civil action.

དམངས་རྩོད་འདྲི་གཅོད་ཁང་ (māŋdzöö drijöögaŋ) the civil division of a people's court, civil court.

དམངས་ཚོགས་ (māŋdzɔɔ̀) the masses.

དམངས་ཚོགས་ཀྱི་དམག་དཔུང་ (māŋdzɔɔ̀gi drəgbuŋ) the masses' armed forces.

དམངས་ཚོགས་ཀྱི་ཚོགས་པ་ (māŋdzɔɔ̀gi tsōgba) people's organization, mass organization.

དམངས་ཚོགས་ཀྱི་ལས་འགུལ་ (māŋdzɔɔ̀gi lɛngüü) mass movement.

དམངས་ཚོགས་ཀྱི་ཤོད་ཚུལ་ (māŋdzɔɔ̀gi shöödzüü) public opinion.

དམངས་ཚོགས་ཀྱི་འདུ་འཛོམས་ (māŋdzɔɔ̀gi dudzom) mass rally.

དམངས་ཚོགས་ཀྱི་ལམ་ཕྱོགས་ (māŋdzɔɔ̀gi ləmjɔɔ̀) the mass-line ¶ དམངས་ཚོགས་ཀྱི་ལམ་ཕྱོགས་ལག་ལེན་བྱེད་དགོས་ (We) have to implement the mass-line.

དམངས་ཚོགས་ཅན་དུ་འགྱུར་ (māŋdzɔɔ̀jɛndu gyur) vi. to become a mass movement/ mass campaign.

དམངས་ཚོགས་ལྟ་ཚུལ་ (māŋdzɔɔ̀ dədzüü) the point of view of the masses, public opinion.

དམངས་ཚོགས་དང་ཐ་དད་དུ་འགྱུར་ (māŋdzɔɔ̀ daŋ tādɛɛ̀du gyur) vi. to become isolated/ alienated/ separated from the masses, to lose touch with the masses.

དམངས་ཚོགས་དང་མཐུན་པ་ (māŋdzɔɔ̀daŋ tümbə) in harmony with the masses, popular with the masses.

དམངས་འཚོ་ (māŋtso) the standard of living of the

people/ masses.
དམངས་འཚོའི་རིང་ལུགས་ (māŋdzö ri̱ŋluù) the principle of the people's/ masses' livelihood.
དམངས་འཛུགས་ (māŋdzuù) sm. དམངས་བཙུགས.
དམངས་ཞབས་པ་ (māŋshəbbə) name of a village level development worker.
དམངས་གཞས་ (māŋshɛɛ̀) folk song, ballad.
དམངས་བཟོ་ (māŋso) masses and workers.
དམངས་ཡོངས་ (māŋyoŋ) all the people, the masses.
དམངས་ཡོངས་དམག་མི་ (māŋyoŋ māāmi) the entire populace bearing arms, every citizen is a soldier; va.—བྱེད་.
དམངས་རིགས་ (māŋrii) the people.
དམངས་རིགས་མ་ (māŋ ri̱gmə) the female masses/ populace.
དམངས་སེམས་ (māŋsem) people's feelings/ aspirations.
དམངས་སེམས་འཁོར་ཕྱོགས་ (māŋsem kɔ̄ɔ̄jɔɔ̀) the will/ aspirations of the populace.
དམངས་སྲིད་ (māŋsiì) civil administration.
དམངས་སྲིད་ཁྲུའུ་ (māŋsiì trū) tib.ch. office of civil affairs.
དམངས་སྲིད་ཅུའུ་ (māŋsiì jū) tib.ch. sm. དམངས་སྲིད་ཅུས་.
དམངས་སྲིད་ཅུས་ (māŋsiì jūù) tib.ch. Civil Affairs Bureau.
དམངས་སྲིད་པུའུ་ (māŋsiì būwu) tib.ch. Ministry of Civil Affairs.
དམངས་སྲོལ་ (māŋsöö) folk custom, habits/ customs of the masses.
དམངས་སྲོལ་རིག་པ་ (māŋsöö ri̱gbə) folklore studies.
དམན་ (mɛ̄n) abbr. of དམན་པ་. 2. abbr. of སྐྱེས་དམན་.
དམན་ཆ་བཟུང་ (mɛ̄nja su̱ŋ) sm. དམའ་ས་བཟུང་.
དམན་ཆུང་ (mɛ̄njuŋ) young girl.
དམན་ཆུང་བུ་མོ་ (mɛ̄njuŋ po̱mo) sm. དམན་ཆུང་.
དམན་པ་ (mɛ̄mba) poor, low ¶ རིག་གནས་གཞན་གྱི་ཤེས་ཡོན་དམན་པ་ (My) poor knowledge of other cultures.
དམན་པོ་ (mɛ̄mbo) sm. དམན་པ་.
དམན་མ་ (mɛ̄nma) old and leftover.
དམན་མོ་ (mɛ̄mmo) sm. དམན་པ་.
དམན་ཤར་ (mɛ̄nshar) young woman.
དམན་ས་བཟུང་བས་རྒྱལ་ས་ཟིན་ (mɛ̄nsa su̱ŋwɛ gyɛ̱ɛ̱sa si̱n) if one is meek and humble, one will reach one's goal.
དམའ་ (mā) low, inferior; vi.—འགྲོ་ to become/ go lower, to go/ become infoerior; va.—གཏོང་ to lower, to make inferior ¶ སྒོ་དམའ་ཞིང་ཆུང་བ་ཞིག A low and small door. ¶ གོ་གནས་དམའ་ཞིང་ལས་འགན་ཆུང་བ་ Low rank and little responsibility. ¶ མི་རྒོལ་གྱི་རྦ་རླབས་བས་དེ་དམའ་རུ་ཕྱིན་པ་རེད་ The anti-U.S. wave receded (went lower). ¶ ཀྱག་དེ་དམའ་རུ་བཏང་པ་རེད་ (They) lowered the stand.
དམའ་གྲས་ (mādrɛɛ̀) lower level, subordinate level.
དམའ་ཐབ་ (mādəb) open-hearth furnace.
དམའ་མཐའ་ (māta) at the minimum, at least ¶ དེབ་དེ་དམའ་མཐའ་སྒོར་ 30 རེད་ This book costs at least 30 dollars.
དམའ་མཐའ་ལ་ (mātala) sm. དམའ་མཐའ་.
དམའ་གནོན་ (mānön) 1. low pressure. 2. low tension/ voltage.
དམའ་པོ་ (māābo) low, inferior ¶ དེ་སྔ་ཁོ་ཚོའི་འཚོ་བའི་གནས་སྟངས་དམའ་པོ་ཞིག་ཡིན་ཡང་ Even though their living conditions were very low before. ¶ ཀུབ་སྐྱིགས་དམའ་པོ་ A low chair.
དམའ་ཕབ་ (mā pəb) sm. དམའ་འབེབས་.
དམའ་བ་ (māwa) low.
དམའ་འབེབས་ (māmbeb) 1. insulting, humiliating, disgracing, degrading; va.—བྱེད་; —གཏོང་ to insult/ humiliate/ degrade/ disgrace ¶ ཚོགས་འདུའི་སར་ཁོང་ལ་དམའ་འབེབས་བཏང་བ་རེད་ (They) humiliated him at the meeting. 2. reproaching, censuring, condemning; va.—བྱེད་; —གཏོང་ to reproach, to condemn, to censure.
དམའ་འབེབས་བརྙས་བཅོས་ (māmbeb ñɛ̄ɛ̄jöö) insulting, deriding, defaming, humiliating.
དམའ་མོ་ (māāmo) sm. དམའ་པོ་.
དམའ་འབྱིན་ (mānjin) blame, censure, reproach, reprimand; va.—བྱེད་.
དམའ་རྩིས་རྒྱག་ (mādziì gya̱à) 1. va. to consider or estimate at the lowest rate/ number. 2. va. to have low esteem.
དམའ་རིམ་ (mərim) lower, low-grade, low-level ¶ དམའ་རིམ་འབྲིང་བའི་སློབ་གྲྭ་ Lower middle school, Jr. high school.
དམའ་རིམ་དུས་སྐབས་ (mərim tü̱ügəb) elementary stage, initial stage.
དམའ་རིམ་སློབ་གྲྭ་ (mərim lōbdra) primary and secondary schools.
དམའ་རིམ་སློབ་གྲྭ་ཆུང་བ་ (mərim lōbdra cūŋwa) primary school.
དམའ་རིམ་སློབ་ཆུང་ (mərim lōbjuŋ) sm. དམའ་རིམ་སློབ་གྲྭ་ཆུང་བ་.
དམའ་རིམ་སློབ་གྲྭ་འབྲིང་བ་ (mərim lōbdra dri̱ŋwə) middle school (Jr. and Sr. High School).
དམའ་རིམ་སློབ་འབྲིང་ (mərim lōmdri̱ŋ) sm. དམའ་རིམ་སློབ་གྲྭ་འབྲིང་བ་.
དམའ་རིམ་སློབ་གསོ་ (mərim lōbso) elementary and secondary education.
དམའ་རིམ་སྲོག་ཆགས་ (mərim sōgjaà) invertebrate animals.
དམའ་རུ་འགྲོ་ (məru dro̱) vi. to become lower, to become inferior.
དམའ་རུ་གཏོང་ (məru dōŋ) va. to lower, to make inferior.
དམའ་རླབས་ (mələb) low ebb, low tide.
དམའ་ཤོས་ (māshöö̀) lowest.
དམའ་ས་ (māsa) low-lying area/ region/ place ¶ ས་དམའ་ས་དེ་ཚོར་འབྲས་འདེབས་པ་རེད་ (They) planted rice in the low-lying areas.
དམའ་ས་ཟིན་ (māsa si̱n) va. to act humble, to be modest.
དམའ་ས་བཟུང་ (māsa su̱ŋ) sm. དམའ་ས་ཟིན་.
དམར་ (māā) abbr. of དམར་པོ་.
དམར་ཀོ་ (māāgɔɔ) untanned hide, rawhide.
དམར་ཀིན་ (māāgin) a kind of cloth from India.
དམར་རྐྱང་ (mārgyaŋ) 1. bright red, completely red ¶ དར་ཆ་དམར་རྐྱང་ཞིག་ཡོད་ (I) have a bright red flag. 2. in cash (with respect to payments) ¶ རིན་འབབ་དམར་རྐྱང་དགོས་ (I) need payment in cash. 3. pure, only ¶ མར་དམར་རྐྱང་ཁལ་བཅུ་བཀུགས་སོང་ He weighed ten ཁལ་ of butter itself.
དམར་སྐྱ་ (mārgya) light red, pink.
དམར་བསྐྱངས་འཚུད་ (mārgaŋ tsüǜ) vi. to gain weight/ become fat (usu. for fattening livestock).
དམར་ཁ་དྭངས་པ་ (mārka ta̱ŋba) bright red color.
དམར་ཁེ་ (mārke) butchering business (buying and butchering animals and selling the meat) [Lit. profit from butchering].
དམར་ཁེ་བ་ (mārkewa) a person who butchers animals and sells the meat.
དམར་ཁོག་ཁོག (māā kɔ̄ɔ̀gɔɔ̀) reddish ¶ བུ་མོ་ཆུང་ཆུང་འདི་མཁུར་ཚོས་དམར་ཁོག་ཁོག་ཞིག་འདུག This young girl has red cheeks.
དམར་ཁྲ་ (mārdra) sth. with a red base, sth. mostly red.
དམར་ཁྲིད་ (mārdriì) teaching through practice/ practicum/ firsthand experience; va.—རྒྱག; —བྱེད་ to teach through practice.
དམར་ཁྲིད་ཁང་ (mārdriìgaŋ) demonstration room.
དམར་མཁས་ (mārkɛɛ̀) both red and expert, both socialist and proficient.
དམར་མཁས་སློབ་གྲྭ་ (mārkɛɛ̀ lōbdra) a red and expert school (a school to train experts in the communist manner, usually by sending them to work in the rural areas).
དམར་གྱིས་གསོལ་ (mārgyi sȫȫ) sm. དམར་མཆོད་འབུལ་.
དམར་རྒྱ་ (mārgya) scarlet red.
དམར་ངོ་ (mārŋo) 1. red color. 2. a bad omen.
དམར་ཆ་ (mārja) 1. part of sth. that is red. 2. the

latter half of the month.

དམར་ཆག་ཆག (mār cājaà) reddish ¶ གྲྭ་པ་མང་པོ་དམར་ཆག་ཆག་མཐོང་བྱུང་ (I) saw many reddish (robed) monks.

དམར་ཅིལ་ཅིལ་ (mār cīījii) sm. དམར་ཆག་ཆག.

དམར་ཆུང་དམག (mārjuŋ māà) sm. ན་གཞོན་གདོང་ལེན་དུ་ཁག.

དམར་ཅེམ་ཅེམ་ (mār cēmjem) blinking/ glittering red.

དམར་ཅེམ་མེ་བ་ (mār cēmmewa) sm. དམར་ཅེམ་ཅེམ་.

དམར་ཅེམ་སེ་བ་ (mār cēmsewa) དམར་ཅེམ་མེ་བ་.

དམར་མཆན་ (mārjɛn) document/ letter/ note written with red ink.

དམར་མཆོད་ (mārjöö) a rite of blood sacrifice (animals or human); va.—བྱེད་; —འབུལ་.

དམར་མཆོད་དུས་ཆེན་ (mārjöö tüüjen) a rite/ ritual with blood sacrifice.

དམར་འཇབ་ (mārjəb) communist guerrilla.

དམར་འཇལ་ (mārjɛɛ) compensation made for killing or injuring somebody else's animal.

དམར་རྗེན་ (mārjen) raw, naked; va.—འདོན་ to expose, to show the true nature ¶ བཙན་རྒྱལ་རིང་ལུགས་ཀྱི་ཉེས་སྤྱོད་ཁྲེལ་མེད་དམར་རྗེན་དུ་བཏོན་པ་རེད་ They exposed the outrageous crimes of the imperialists.

དམར་ལྗང་ (mārjaŋ) sth. that is reddish and green.

དམར་གཉིད་ (mārñii) a dream with bad omens/ signs; vi.—གཏོང་.

དམར་གཏོར་ (mārtɔɔ) a type of red torma (offering).

དམར་སྟོན་ (mārdön) banquet where the main courses are meat.

དམར་ཐག་ཆོད་དུས་ (mārdaà cöödüü) at the time of sunset.

དམར་ཐབ (mārdəb) sm. ཐབ་གཞོབ་.

དམར་ཐིག (mərdii) 1. the "bull's eye" of a target. 2. red dots.

དམར་ཐིང་ཐིང་ (mār tīŋdiŋ) sm. དམར་ཅིལ་ཅིལ་.

དམར་ཐོར་ (mārdɔɔ) red pimples.

དམར་དོད་ (mārdɛɛ̀) liking/ desiring meat and blood; vi.—ལང་ to have a desire to eat meat and blood.

དམར་དྲི་ (mərdri) smell of meat/ blood.

དམར་གདུང་ (mārduŋ) tomb with the corpse of a lama.

དམར་མདངས་ (mārdaŋ) 1. a healthy/ ruddy complexion; vi.—རྒྱག; vi.—བཀྲ་; vi.—རྒྱས་; vi. to have a healthy red glow. 2. a reddish glow.

དམར་འདུར་ (mənduu) powdered hot pepper made into a paste (with water).

དམར་འདོན་ (mārdön) 1. shamelessly/ brazenly/ flagrantly doing bad things; va.—བྱེད་. 2. a traditional Tibetan treatment for wind disease.

དམར་སྡོར་ (mārdɔɔ) soup with meat and fat.

དམར་ནག (mārnaà) 1. dark red. 2. shung. the two official guardian deities of the state: Pandenlhamo and Nechung.

དམར་པོ་ (māābo) 1. red ¶ དེབ་འདི་དམར་པོ་རེད་ This book is red. 2. communist ¶ དམར་པོས་བཅིངས་བཀྲོལ་བཏང་བ་རེད་ The communists liberated (it). ¶ དམར་པོའི་རྒྱལ་ཁབ་ A communist country.

དམར་པོ་བྱུག (mārbo cuù) va. to wear/ apply cosmetics (e.g., lipsticks, rouge).

དམར་པོ་དམར་རྒྱང་ (māābo māāgyaŋ) completely red.

དམར་པོ་རི་ (māābori) name of the hill on which the Potala is built.

དམར་པོའི་ཀྲོན་ཙ་ (māābö drönja) tib.ch. red expert.

དམར་པོའི་རིང་ལུགས་ (mārbö riŋluù) communism.

དམར་པོའི་སྲིད་དབང་ (mārbö sīīwaŋ) red political power.

དམར་དཔེ་ (mārbe) exemplary specimen, showpiece, demonstration piece.

དམར་སྤྲད་སྤྲེར་ (mārdrɛɛ̀ dēē) va. to give a soul kiss/ French kiss/ tongue kiss.

དམར་ཕིག་ཕིག (mār pīgbiì) red and quivering (like jelly).

དམར་ཕྱིའི་འོད་ཟེར་ (mārjii wööser) heat ray.

དམར་ཕྱུར་ཕྱུར་ (mār cūūjuu) reddish looking.

དམར་ཕྱོགས་ (mārjɔɔ̀) second half of the month.

དམར་ཕྲུག (mərdruù) a type of red woolen material.

དམར་བ་ (mārwa) red.

དམར་འབོལ་ (mārböö) a red mattress or cushion for sitting.

དམར་འབྱུར་ (mānjaa) infant, baby.

དམར་སྦོས་སུ་འགྱུར་ (māböösu gyur) vi. to become red and swollen (usu. eyes).

དམར་སྦྱར་ (mānjar) sm. དམར་འབྱུར་.

དམར་མེད་པའི་ཚལ་ (mār meebɛ tsɛɛ̀) vegetarian dish.

དམར་མོ་ (māāmo) red.

དམར་མོག (māāmɔɔ̀) dark red.

དམར་དམག (māāmaà) the Red Army.

དམར་དམག་རྒྱང་སྐྱོད་ (māāmaà gyaŋgyöö̀) The Long March of the Red Army.

དམར་དམར་རྗེན་རྗེན་ (mārmar jenjen) obviously, plainly, openly, clearly, evidently ¶ ཁོང་གིས་ཚོགས་འདུའི་ཐོག་འགོ་ཁྲིད་ཀྱི་སྐྱོན་རྣམས་དམར་དམར་རྗེན་རྗེན་དུ་བརྗོད་སོང་ He criticized the leader openly at the meeting.

དམར་དམར་ཐིང་ཐིང་ (mārmar tīŋdiŋ) sm. དམར་རྒྱང་.

དམར་དམར་དིག་དིག (mārmar digdiì) 1. high quality ¶ མི་ཚང་དེ་ལྟོ་ཆས་དམར་དམར་དིག་དིག་ཟ་མཁན་ཞིག་རེད་ That family is one that eats high quality food. 2. the real issue, the essence of sth.

དམར་དམར་སྡིག་སྡི་ (mārmar digdiì) sm. དམར་དམར་དིག་དིག.

དམར་སྨུག (mərmuù) deep red, maroon.

དམར་ཙ་རེ་བ་ (mārdza rewa) bloody.

དམར་བཙོད་ (mādzöö̀) sm. དམར་ཚོས་.

དམར་བཙོས་ (mār dzöö̀) va. to boil meat.

དམར་ཚལ་དགུ་ཚལ་ (mārdzɛɛ gudzɛɛ) bloody, covered with blood ¶ གྲི་མང་པོ་བརྒྱབ་ནས་དམར་ཚལ་གོ་ཚལ་ཅགས་བཟོས་པ་རེད་ (He) was made bloody after being stabbed many times.

དམར་ཚོས་ (mārdzöö̀) red dye.

དམར་མཚུར་ (māndzur) a substance used to make to red vegetable dye.

དམར་འཛིང་ (mərdziŋ) hand-to-hand combat; va.—རྒྱག.

དམར་འཛིང་ཁྲག་འཛིང་ (mārdziŋ trəgdziŋ) a bloody battle, bloody hand-to-hand combat.

དམར་ཞིང་མཁས་པ་ (mārshiŋ kɛ̄ɛba) both red and expert.

དམར་གཞུང་ (mārshuŋ) communist government.

དམར་ཟལ་ (mārsɛɛ) things with a red background.

དམར་ཟས་ (mārsɛɛ̀) meat dishes; va.—སྤོང་ to give up eating meat.

དམར་ཟས་ཀུང་སི་ (mārsɛɛ̀ gūŋsi) tib.ch. meat products company.

དམར་ཟས་གྲང་མོ་ (mārsɛɛ̀ traŋmo) cold meat dish.

དམར་ཟས་ལས་སྣོན་བཟོ་གྲྭ་ (mārsɛɛ̀ lɛɛ̀nön sodra) meat processing factory.

དམར་གཟོང་ (mārsoŋ) tool for cutting red hot iron.

དམར་འོད་ (mārwöö) shining red light; vi.—འཕྲོ་ to be shining red.

དམར་ཡག་སྟག (māryaà dāà) a ferocious tiger.

དམར་རང་བ་ (mārraŋwa) sm. དམར་རྡང་བ་.

དམར་རུ་ (mərru) a kind of red.

དམར་རུ་མགོ་ནག (mərru gonaà) a type of red bean.

དམར་རེངས་ (māāreŋ) day break, dawn.

དམར་ལམ་པ་ (mārlamba) sm. དམར་ལམ་ལམ་.

དམར་ལམ་མེ་བ་ (mār lammewa) sm. དམར་ལམ་ལམ་.

དམར་ལམ་ལམ་ (mār lamlam) reddish light/ glow.

དམར་ལུགས་ (mərluù) communism; va.—འཛིན་ to hold/ adhere to communism.

དམར་ལུགས་འཛིན་པ་ (mərluù dzimbə) a communist.

དམར་ལུད་ (mərlüü) dung, natural fertilizers.

དམར་ཤར་ཤར་ (mār shāāshae) reddish gleam/ glimmer.

དམར་ཤོད་ཚ་པོ་ (mārsheè tsābo) sb. who speaks

shamelessly/ bluntly/ harshly without any regard for others' feelings.

དམར་ཤོག (mārshoò) communist block, coimmunist group ¶ དམར་ཤོག་མིན་པའི་ཡུལ་ཁག Noncommunist block countries.

དམར་ཤོག་ཚོགས་པ་ (mārshoò tsōgba) communist party.

དམར་ཤོག་རིང་ལུགས་ (mārshoò ri̱ŋluù) communism.

དམར་གཤོག (mārshoò) sm. དམར་ཤོག.

དམར་བཤལ་ (mārshεε) dysentery.

དམར་སི་ (mārsi) dry dung of animals.

དམར་སེང་ (mārseŋ) light red (color).

དམར་སེར་ (mārser) sm. དམར་སེར་མཚོན་.

དམར་སེར་མཚོན་ (mārser tsö̃n) reddish yellow/ orange color.

དམར་སྲིད་ (mərsii) communist political system, communism.

དམར་སྲིད་རིང་ལུགས་ (mərsii ri̱ŋluù) communism.

དམར་སྲུང་དམག (mərsuŋ māà) sm. དམར་སྲུང་དམག་མི་.

དམར་སྲུང་དམག་མི་ (mərsuŋ mə̄əmi) Red Guards (during Cultural Revolution).

དམར་སྲུང་རུ་ཁག (mərsuŋ ru̱gaà) sm. དམར་སྲུང་དམག་མི་.

དམར་གསུར་ (mārsur) a religious offering to deities consisting of smoke from burnt meat and fat.

དམར་གསོད་ (mārsöò) murder, slaughter, massacre; va.—གཏོང་.

དམར་ཧུར་ཧུར་ (mār hūrhur) glowing red.

དམར་ཧྲང་ (mārhraŋ) naked; va.—ཕུད་ to undress, to be naked.

དམར་ཧྲང་བ་ (mārhraŋwa) naked.

དམར་ཧྲང་ཧྲང་ (mār hrāŋhraŋ) naked.

དམར་ཧྲེང་ (mārhreŋ) sm. དམར་ཧྲང་.

དམར་ལྷང་ལྷང་ (mār lhāŋlaŋ) glowing red.

དམར་ལྷབ་ལྷབ་ (mār lhəbləb) flickering red, flickering flames.

དམར་ལྷེམ་ལྷེམ་ (mār lhemlem) blinking red, blinking flames.

དམས་ (mεὲ) vi. to go down, to deteriorate ¶ ལུས་སྟོབས་དམས་པས་ Because (his) health deteriorated.

དམས་ཉམས་ (mεὲñam) 1. deteriorated, declining ¶ ལུས་སྟོབས་དམས་ཉམས་བྱུང་བ་རེད་ (His) health has deteriorated. 2. modest, humble, meek.

དམིག (mīg) hole.

དམིག་སྨྱུག་གཏོང་ (mīggyaà dōŋ) vi. to be fully ripened (for crops).

དམིག་ཁུང་ (mīgguŋ) hole.

དམིག་གུ་ (mīggu) sm. དམིག་བུ་, 1.

དམིག་གཏོང་ (mīg dōŋ) vi. to be fully ripened (for crops).

དམིག་པ་ (mīgbə) sm. དམིག་བུ་.

དམིག་བུ་ (mībbu) 1. hole. 2. a type of sand lizard.

དམིག་གསང་ (mīgsaŋ) a space or gap within the body where there are no vital organs.

དམིགས་ (mīì) 1. (dat. + —) vi. to be aimed at, to be meant for ¶ གོང་འཕེལ་དུ་གཏོང་རྒྱུར་དམིགས་པ་རེད་ (It) was meant for development. 2. vi. to consider, to see ¶ ཚན་རིག་ལག་རྩལ་གྱི་དགེ་མཚན་དམིགས་པ་རེད་ (They) saw the advantages of science. 3. ones marked or stated to be sth. ¶ སློབ་དམིགས་ Those stated/ considered to be students. 4. means, source ¶ ཁོ་ལ་བུ་ལོན་སྤྲོད་དམིགས་མེད་པ་རེད་ He doesn't have the means to pay the loan. 5. vi. to obtain ¶ ཁོང་གིས་སློབ་སྦྱོང་ཐོག་གྲུབ་འབྲས་ཡག་པོ་དམིགས་པ་རེད་ He obtained great achievement in his studies. 6. specially (— + vb.) ¶ ལས་བྱེད་པ་གསར་པ་གཅིག་དམིགས་བསྐོས་བྱེད་དགོས་ (We) have to specially appoint/ select some new officers.

དམིགས་བཀར་ (mīggar) 1. specially, exclusively, for the purpose of; va.—བྱེད་ to do sth. specially ¶ རྡོ་རྗེ་ལགས་མཇལ་བར་དམིགས་བཀར་གྱིས་དགོངས་པ་ཞུས་པ་རེད་ (He) took leave specially to meet Dorje. 2. special ¶ སོ་སོའི་དམིགས་བཀར་གྱི་ལས་འགན་ The special responsibility of each person.

དམིགས་བཀར་ཚོད་འཛིན་ཚོང་རྫས་ (mīggar tsöndzin tsōŋdzεὲ) specially controlled commodities/ goods.

དམིགས་བཀར་གསོ་ཆགས་ (mīggar sōdzaà) specially raising/ bringing up.

དམིགས་སྐོ་ (mīggo) source, means, resources ¶ ཚོང་རྒྱག་ཡས་ཀྱི་དམིགས་སྐོ་ག་རེ་ཡོད་པ་རེད་ What kind of means do you have for trading? ¶ དངུལ་དེ་ཁང་པ་རྒྱག་ཡས་ཀྱི་དམིགས་སྐོ་རེད་ This money is the means for building a house.

དམིགས་རྟེན་ (mīgden) 1. meditative object/ support. 2. sm. དམིགས་སྐོ་. 3. source of hope ¶ རྒན་གོན་གཉིས་ཀྱི་དམིགས་རྟེན་ཕྲུ་གུ་དེ་རེད་ The source of hope of the elderly is that child.

དམིགས་དོན་ (mīgdön) aim, objective, purpose ¶ ལས་ཀ་འདིའི་དམིགས་དོན་ག་རེ་རེད་ What is the aim of this work?

དམིགས་ནས་ (mīgnε) for the purpose of, aimed at, directed towards ¶ སློབ་གྲྭ་འཛུགས་རྒྱུར་དམིགས་ནས་ཞལ་འདེབས་བསྡུས་པ་རེད་ (They) collected donations for the purpose of building schools.

དམིགས་རྣམ་ (mīgnam) impression.

དམིགས་པ་ (mīgbə) 1. visualization (of one's deities). 2. sm. དམིགས་ཡུལ་.

དམིགས་པ་མེད་པ་ (mīgbə me̱èba) shung. sm. བསམ་ཡུལ་ལས་འདས་པ་.

དམིགས་བུ་ (mīgbu) sb. who guides the blind.

དམིགས་བྱ་ (mīgja) aim, goal, purpose.

དམིགས་འབེན་ (mīgben) goal, target.

དམིགས་འབྲས་ (mīŋdrεὲ) sm. དམིགས་ཡུལ་.

དམིགས་མེད་ (mīgmeè) 1. the void, emptiness. 2. aimless, purposeless, goalless.

དམིགས་ཚད་ (mīgdzεὲ) 1. quota, objective, goal, target ¶ འཆར་གཞིའི་དམིགས་ཚད་དུས་བཀག་གི་སྔོན་དུ་བསྒྲུབས་པ་རེད་ (They) achieved the goal of the plan ahead of schedule. 2. target range ¶ མེ་མདའ་རྒྱག་སའི་དམིགས་ཚད་ A target range for shooting guns.

དམིགས་འཛུགས་བྱེད་ (mīgdzuù ce̱è) va. to assign, to specify, to designate ¶ ཏང་གི་དམིགས་འཛུགས་བྱས་པའི་ས་ཁུལ་ The areas designated by the party.

དམིགས་ཡུལ་ (mīgyüü) 1. aim, goal, objective; va.—འཆང་ to hold one's aim/ goal/ objective; va.—སྒྲུབ་ to fulfill/ achieve/ obtain a goal or aim; vi.—འགྲུབ་ to have an aim/ purpose/ aspiration achieved ¶ དམིགས་ཡུལ་གཙོ་བོ་ The main objective/ aim/ goal.

དམིགས་ཡུལ་མེད་པ་ (mīgyüü me̱èba) having no purpose/ aim/ goal.

དམིགས་ཡུལ་གཙོ་བཟུང་ (mīgyüü dzōsuŋ) focusing/ aiming primarily on a goal.

དམིགས་ཡུལ་ཡོད་པ་སྨྲ་བ་ (mīgyüü yo̱òbə māwa) teleology.

དམིགས་ཤ་ (mīgsha) meat of an animal slaughtered at one's request.

དམིགས་སུ་བཀར་ (mīgsu gār) va. to emphasize ¶ གནད་དོན་དེ་དམིགས་སུ་བཀར་བ་རེད་ (They) emphasized the matter. ¶ ཁོང་གིས་དམིགས་སུ་བཀར་ནས་གསུངས་པ་རེད་ He said it specially with emphasis.

དམིགས་སུ་རེ་བ་ (mīgsu re̱wa) the hope for (obtaining) one's objective/ aim/ goal ¶ ང་ལ་རྗེས་འཛིན་གྱི་དམིགས་སུ་རེ་བའི་བུ་ཞིག་ཡོད་ I have a son who is the hope of my aim of continuing the family.

དམིགས་བསལ་ (mīgsεε) special, specially; va.—བྱེད་ to do/ treat specially ¶ ངས་དམིགས་བསལ་གྱིས་དགའ་བསུ་ཞུ་བར་ཕྱིན་པ་ཡིན་ I went specially to welcome (him).

དམིགས་བསལ་གོང་ཕུད་ (mīgsεε ko̱ŋbüü) special exception/ exemption ¶ རྒན་འཁོགས་རྣམས་དམིགས་བསལ་གོང་ཕུད་ཀྱིས་དེ་བྱིངས་ལས་བྱེད་ཚང་མ་ངལ་རྩོལ་ལ་འགྲོ་དགོས་ With the exception of the elderly people, all officials have to go for manual labor.

དམིགས་བསལ་གྱི་དབང་ཆ་ (mīgsɛɛgi wāŋja) privilege, special rights or authority.

དམིགས་བསལ་གྱི་བཙོན་གྲོལ་ (mīgsɛɛgi dzōndröö) amnesty, pardon (from prison).

དམིགས་བསལ་ཐོན་རྐྱེན་ (mīgsɛɛ tōngyen) special facilities/ materials.

དམིགས་བསལ་ཐོན་རྫས་ (mīgsɛɛ tōndzɛɛ̀) special products.

དམིགས་བསལ་ཕོགས་གསབ་ (mīgsɛɛ pɔ̄ɔsəb) special allowance (with salary), special supplement to salary.

དམིགས་བསལ་དབང་ཆ་ (mīgsɛɛ wāŋja) sm. དམིགས་བསལ་གྱི་དབང་ཆ་.

དམིགས་བསལ་སྡོང་བདར་ཅན་གྱི་ཉེན་སྐྱོབ་རུ་ཁག (mīgsɛɛ jo̱ŋdarjɛngi ñe̱ngyob ru̱gaà) SWAT team.

དམིགས་བསལ་གཞེན་སྐུལ་ (mīgsɛɛ shēngüü) special appeal/ request.

དམིགས་བསལ་ཤེས་ཡོན་ (mīgsɛɛ shēèyön) special skill/ knowledge.

དམིགས་བསལ་སྦྲགས་འགོད་ (mīgsɛɛ dra̱àgöö̀) special delivery mail.

དམུ་ (mū) 1. mean, nasty; va.—བྱེད་ to act mean/ nasty, to cause trouble. 2. one of the ancient lineages. 3. a type of spirit/ ghost.

དམུ་གོད་ (mūgöö̀) mean, nasty, cruel; va.—བྱེད་ to act mean, nasty cruel. 2. sb. who gets angry/ irritable, sb. who is hot-tempered.

དམུ་གོད་པོ་ (mū gö̱öbo) sm. དམུ་གོད་.

དམུ་ཆུ་འཁྱིམས་ཆུ་ (mūju kyīmju) a type of dropsy caused by རླུང་ disease.

དམུ་ཆུ་བྱེར་ཆུ་ (mūju cērju) a type of dropsy caused by poor digestion.

དམུ་ཆུ་ཟགས་ཆུ་ (mūju sa̱gju) sm. དམུ་ཆུ་བྱེར་ཆུ་.

དམུ་བྱེད་ (mū ce̱è) see. དམུ་.

དམུ་བློ་ (mūlo) black hearted, evil, cruel, mean, nasty; va.—འཆང་ to be black hearted/ evil/ cruel/ mean/ nasty.

དམུ་རྫིང་ (mūdziŋ) a type of dropsy that causes the body to swell.

དམུ་ཤུས་རྒྱག (mūshüǜ gya̱à) va. to complain (in a whining fashion).

དམུན་པ་ (mū̃mbə) a fool, an idiot.

དམུར་ (mūr) sm. སྨུར་.

དམུལ་ (mū̃ū̃) va. to smile.

དམུས་ (mū̃ǜ) vi. to feel sorrow/ sadness. 2. vi. to be annoyed/ bothered.

དམུས་དེ་ལོང་བ་ (mū̃ǜde lo̱ŋwa) a blind person.

དམུས་ལོང་ (mū̃ǜloŋ) a blind person.

དམུས་ལོང་གླང་བཤེར་ (mū̃ǜloŋ lāŋsher) groping in the dark blindly.[Lit. a blind man investigating what an elephant is like].

དམུས་ལོང་ལྟར་ (mū̃ǜloŋ dār) lacking definite aim [Lit. like a blind person].

དམུས་ལོང་ལྷན་ཚོགས་ (mū̃ǜloŋ lhɛ̱ndzoò) Association for the Blind.

དམེ་ (mē) pollution, polluted (e.g., due to incest).

དམེ་གྲིབ་ (mēdrib) sm. དམེ་.

དམེ་པོ་ (mēbo) a polluted man (a man who has who has committed incest or killed his relatives).

དམེ་མོ་ (mēmo) a polluted female (a woman who has committed incest or killed her relatives).

དམེ་ཚང་བ་ (mēdzaŋwa) a polluted household, a low caste person/ family.

དམོད་ (mō̃ȍ) 1. va. to curse. 2. va. scold/ rebuke. 3. va. to invoke a deity to harm sb.

དམོད་ངན་ (mō̃ȍŋɛn) a curse; va.—རྒྱག.

དམོད་སྔགས་ (mō̃ȍŋaà) invocation curse.

དམོད་དོར་ (mō̃ȍdɔɔ) sm. དམོད་.

དམོད་པ་འདོར་ (mō̃ȍba dɔ̱ɔ̱) sm. དམོད་.

དམོད་པ་བཙུགས་ (mō̃ȍba dzūù) sm. དམོད་.

དམོད་པོར་ (mō̃ȍbɔɔ) sm. དམོད་.

དམོད་མོ་ (mō̃ȍmo) cursing; va.—རྒྱག; —འདེབས་.

དམོད་ཚིག (mō̃ȍdzii) words of a curse.

དམོད་འཛུགས་ (mō̃ȍdzuù) sm. དམོད་མོ་རྒྱག.

དམོད་ཟོར་ (mō̃ȍsɔr) a curse.

དམྱལ་ (ñɛ̄l) abbr. of དམྱལ་བ་.

དམྱལ་ཁམས་ (ñɛ̄ɛ̄gam) sm. དམྱལ་བ་.

དམྱལ་ཁམས་བཅོ་བརྒྱད་ (ñɛ̄ɛ̄kam jōbgyɛɛ̀) the eighteen realms of hell.

དམྱལ་བ་ (nɛ̄ɛ̄la) hell.

དམྱལ་བ་མྱོང་ (ñɛ̄ɛ̄la ño̱ŋ) vi. to go through hell, to suffer/ experience hell.

དམྱུག (ñūù) va. to go.

དམྱུགས་ (ñūù) p. of དམྱུག.

རྨ་ (mā) wound, sore, cut; vi.—བཟོ་ to get a wound/ sore/ cut.

རྨ་: p. རྨས་ (mā) vi. to get wounded/ injured.

རྨ་དཀྲིས་ (mādrìì) bandage.

རྨ་སྐོགས་ (māgɔɔ̀) sm. རྨ་ཁོག.

རྨ་སྐྱེས་ (māgyeè) blood.

རྨ་སྐྱེས་ནད་མནར་ (māgyeè nɛ̱ɛ̀nar) injured and sick.

རྨ་སྐྱོན་ (māgyön) sm. རྨ་.

རྨ་སྐྱོབ་ (māgyob) bandages or medication to treat sores/ cuts/ wounds.

རྨ་ཁ་ (māga) the surface/ orifice of a wound; va.—གཏུམ་ to dress/ bandage a wound, va.—གསོ་ to treat a wound, vi.—བྱེ་ to have a wound open; vi.—ཟུམ་; —རུབ་ to have a cut/ sore/ heal; vi.—འབར་; —ཁྲོས་ to have a cut/ sore get worse (infected); va.—འཚེམ་ to stitch/ sew up a wound.

རྨ་ཁ་མཐེབ་གནོན་ (māga tēbnön) covering up one's errors or faults. [Lit. to cover a sore or cut with the thumb].

རྨ་ཁ་སྨན་གྱིས་གསོ་ གྱོད་ཁ་གཉེན་གྱིས་གསོ་ (māga mɛ̄ngi sō gyö̱ȍga ñēngi sō) sores can be cured by medicine, law cases can be solved by kinsmen.

རྨ་ཁ་ཟུམ་ (māga su̱m) see རྨ་ཁ་.

རྨ་ཁ་རུབ་ (māga ru̱b) see རྨ་ཁ་.

རྨ་ཁོག (māgɔɔ̀) scab.

རྨ་ཁྲག་སྨིན་ (mādraà mīn) vi. to have a sore get infected with pus.

རྨ་ཁྲོས་ (mādröö̀) sm. རྨ་འབར་.

རྨ་གོས་ (māgöö̀) a gift consisting of a full set of clothing—an ancient custom in Tibet whereby a person injured in a fight is compensated by his rival with clothing.

རྨ་རྒན་ (māgɛn) an old wound/ sore.

རྨ་གོད་ (māgöö̀) a bad wound/ cut/ sore.

རྨ་སྒོ་ (māgo) the orifices/ openings of the body ¶ རྨ་སྒོ་དགུ་ The nine openings in a human body: two eyes, two ears, two nostrils, mouth, urethra and anus.

རྨ་སྒོ་གསུམ་ (māga sūm) the three openings of a female body: mouth, vagina and anus.

རྨ་སྒྲོས་ (mādröö̀) sm. རྨ་རྗེས་.

རྨ་བརྒྱ་བུག་སྟོང་ (māgya pu̱gdoŋ) corrupt, decrepit ¶ སྲིད་གཞུང་དེ་རྨ་བརྒྱ་བུག་སྟོང་ལྟ་བུར་གྱུར་ཡོད་པ་རེད་ That government has become decrepit (like sth. with one hundred sores and one thousand holes) [Lit. one hundred sores, one thousand holes].

རྨ་ངན་དུག་མཆེད་ (māŋɛn gu̱jeè) tetanus.

རྨ་བཅོས་ (mājöö̀) 1. treatment for a wound/ sore/ cut; va.—བྱེད་ to treat a wound/ sore/ cut. 2. རྨ་བཟོས་.

རྨ་ཆས་ (mājɛɛ̀) sm. རྨ་རས་.

རྨ་ཆུ་ (māju) Yellow River.

རྨ་ཆུ་སེར་ཅན་ (māju sērjɛn) sores or wounds with pus.

རྨ་འཇལ་ (mānjɛɛ) injury payment—an ancient Tibetan custom whereby an injured person is compensated by the person who caused the injury.

རྨ་རྗེས་ (mājeè) scar.

རྨ་བཏོད་ (mādöö̀) sm. རྨ་བཟོ་.

རྨ་བརྡོན་ (mādön) sm. རྨ་བཟོ་.

རྨ་འཐུམ་ (māndum) binding a wound; va.—རྒྱག.

རྨ་འཐུམ་སིང་རས་ (māndum sēŋrɛɛ̀) gauze for binding wounds.

རྨ་ཐོ་སྐོར་ཞིབ་ (māto gɔ̄ɔ̄shib) shung. (government officials in tt.) going around to investigate and make a list of the wounds in the case of a fight/ beating ¶ རྡུང་མཛོག་རྨ་ཐོ་སྐོར་ཞིབ་བསྐྱངས་པ་རེད་ They investigated the wounds of the person who was beaten and made a list of them.

རྨ་ཐོན་ (mā tȍn) vi. to have a sore grow/ appear.

རྨ་དོན་ (mā dō̱n) sm. རྨ་ཐོན་.

རྨ་དྲུབ་ (mā dru̱b) va. to stitch or sew up a cut/ wound/ sore.

རྨ་འདྲུབ་ (mā dru̱b) sm. རྨ་དྲུབ་.

རྨ་ནད་ (mānɛɛ̀) a sore/ wound/ cut that has become infected and swelled up.

རྨ་བྱ་ (mābja) peacock.

རྨ་བྱ་ཁ་འབབ་ (mābja kābəb) of the four rivers that flow from Mount Kaliash (becomes the Karnali River in Nepal and part of the Ganges in India).

རྨ་བྱ་ཅན་ (mābjajɛn) peacock green color.

རྨ་བྱའི་སྒྲོ་ (mābjɛ dro̱) peacock feather.

རྨ་བྱའི་སྒྲོ་མདོངས་ (mābjɛ dro̱m) sm. རྨ་བྱའི་མདོངས་.

རྨ་བྱའི་མདོངས་ (mābjɛ do̱ŋ) the circular patterns on the feathers of a peacock.

རྨ་བྱའི་ཞྭས་གར་ (mābjɛ dö̱ögar) peacock dance.

རྨ་བྱའི་ཤ་ (mābjɛ shā) peacock meat (used in Tibetan medicine).

རྨ་བྱས་སྒྲོ་གུར་ཕུབ་ (mābjɛɛ̀ dro̱gur pūb) va. to display/ spread one's tail feathers (for peacocks).

རྨ་བྱས་དབྱར་རྔ་ཐོས་པ་ (mābjɛɛ̀ yārŋa tȍȍbə) hearing good news [Lit. a peacock hearing summer thunder].

རྨ་འབར་ (mā ba̱r) vi. to have a wound or sore get infected.

རྨ་འབྱིན་ (mā ji̱n) 1. sm. རྨ་བཟོ་. 2. va. to offend/ displease/ irritate.

རྨ་འབྲས་ (māndrɛɛ̀) an infected wound or sore that is difficult to cure.

རྨ་མ་ཐུག་གོང་ལ་སྨན་བསྐུས་ (mā ma̱nagoŋla mɛ̄n gǘü) preparing for a problem before it occurs [Lit. apply medicine before the wound gets pussy].

རྨ་མེད་ (mā me̱è) sm. རྨ་མེད་པ་.

རྨ་མེད་པ་ (mā me̱èba) without deceit/ distortion, straightforward, sincere.

རྨ་སྨུག་ (māmug) wounds and bites; wounds and bruises.

རྨ་སྨན་ (māmɛn) medicine for cuts/ sores/ wounds, salve, ointment.

རྨ་སྨན་ཨའུ་ཙི་ (māmɛn āudzi) a type of salve/ ointment (purslane).

རྨ་ཙི་ (mādzi) sm. རྨ་སྨན་.

རྨ་ཚད་ (mādzɛɛ̀) infected wound/ cut.

རྨ་མཚན་ (mādzɛn) sm. སོ་རྗེས་.

རྨ་བཟོ་ (mā so̱) vi. to get a wound/ sore/ cut.

རྨ་འོག་གཞགས་ཞི་ (māwɔ̀ɔ shāgshi) ending a dispute or feud by compensating the injured party.

རྨ་ཡི་རུས་ཟན་ (māyi rü̱üsɛn) a deeply infected wound/ sore that has reached the bone.

རྨ་ར་ (māra) sm. རྨ་ཁྲག.

རྨ་རལ་སྐྱེ་རལ་ (mārɛɛ gyērɛɛ) having many rashes/ sores.

རྨ་རལ་ཛ་རལ་ (mārɛɛ dzarɛɛ) having many cuts and wounds ¶ གདོང་རྨ་རལ་ཛ་རལ་བྱས་བཞག (His) face is (covered) with cuts.

རྨ་རས་ (mārɛɛ) bandage; va.—འཆིང་; —དཀྲི་ to bandage.

རྨ་རོ་ (māro) 1. a wound or sore that has healed only on the surface. 2. a scar.

རྨ་ལིང་ (māliŋ) sm. རྨ་རས་.

རྨ་ཤུ་ (māshu) a festering/ suppurating wound.

རྨ་ཤུལ་ (māshüü) sm. རྨ་རྗེས་.

རྨ་སོས་ (māsö̀ö) vi. to have a wound/ cut/ sore heal.

རྨ་གསོ་ (mā sō) vi. to heal ¶ རྨ་དེ་མགྱོགས་པོ་གསོས་བྱུང་ The wound healed fast.

རྨ་གསོས་ (mā sö̀ö) p. of རྨ་གསོ་.

རྨ་ལྷོ་བོད་རིགས་རང་སྐྱོང་ཁུལ་ (mālho pö̱ȍriì ra̱ŋgyoŋ kǘü) the Malho Tibetan Autonomous Area (in Qinghai Province south of the Yellow River).

རྨང་ (māŋ) abbr. of རྨང་གཞི་.

རྨང་འདིང་ (māŋ di̱ŋ) va. to lay the foundation stone.

རྨང་རྡོ་ (māŋdo) foundation stone; va.—འདིང་ to a lay a foundation stone.

རྨང་གཞི་ (māŋshi) foundation, base; va.—འདིང་; —འཛུགས་; —བྱེད་ to lay a foundation, to lay the groundwork for, to use as a basis ¶ སྤྱི་ཚོགས་རིང་ལུགས་ཀྱི་རྨང་གཞི་ The foundation of socialism. ¶ བཟོ་ལས་རྨང་གཞི་བྱས་ཏེ་དཔལ་འབྱོར་འཛུགས་སྐྲུན་བྱས་པ་རེད་ Using industry as the foundation, (they) built up the economy. ¶ རྨང་གཞི་སྐྱོ་པོ་ A poor base/ foundation.

རྨང་གཞི་འདིང་མཁན་ (māŋshi di̱ŋñɛn) founder, creator, originator.

རྨང་གཞི་མེད་པར་ཁང་ཆེན་སྐྲུན་པ་ (māŋshi me̱èbar kāŋjen drǘnbə) building on sand [Lit. build a large house without a foundation].

རྨང་གཞིའི་ (māŋshii) basic ¶ རྨང་གཞིའི་ཡུལ་སྐད་ Basic dialect.

རྨང་གཞིའི་དཔལ་འབྱོར་ (māŋshii bɛ̄njɔɔ) basic economy.

རྨང་ལམ་ (māŋlam) sm. རྨི་ལམ་.

རྨངས་འཐེབ་ (māŋjəb) a tweezer for pulling facial hair.

རྨད་ (mɛ̄ɛ̀) outstanding, wonderful, marvellous, great.

རྨད་དུ་བྱུང་བ་ (mɛ̄ɛ̀du ju̱ŋwa) sm. རྨད་བྱུང་.

རྨད་པ་ (mɛ̄ɛ̀ba) sm. རྨད་བྱུང་.

རྨད་པོ་ (mɛ̄ɛ̀bo) sm. རྨད་བྱུང་.

རྨད་བྱུང་ (mɛ̄ɛ̀juŋ) outstanding, excellent, marvelous, wonderful, admirable, great ¶ ངང་ཚོའི་དབུ་ཁྲིད་ཀྱི་དགོངས་པ་རྨད་བྱུང་ནི་ As for the outstanding thoughts of our leader.

རྨད་བྱུང་གོ་ན་མེད་པ་ (mɛ̄ɛ̀juŋ gö̱öna me̱èba) sm. རྨད་བྱུང་.

རྨད་བྱུང་བུ་མོ་ (mɛ̄ɛ̀juŋ po̱mo) a pretty/ beautiful female.

རྨད་རྨད་ (mɛ̄ɛ̀mɛɛ̀) nanny.

རྨད་མཚར་ (mɛ̄ɛ̀dzar) sm. རྨད་བྱུང་.

རྨད་འོག (mɛ̄ɛ̀wɔ̀ɔ) sm. གཟན་, 2.

རྨད་ཤམ་ (mɛ̄ɛ̀sham) sm. ཤམ་ཐབས་.

རྨན་ (mɛ̄n) a small cut/ wound.

རྨའི་ངོས་ (mɛ̄ɛŋö̀ö) sm. རྨ་ཁ་.

རྨའུ་ (ma̱u) ch. measurement equal to 1/16 of an acre.

རྨར་ཁམས་ (mārkam) Markham (an area in Sichuan Province).

རྨ་རར་ཕན་ཁྱི་ཚིལ་ཡིན་ཡང་དྲུག (mārbɛn kyīdzii yi̱nyaŋ cu̱ù) doing whatever it takes to solve a problem or rectify a situation [Lit. if it heals a sore, it is okay to use dog fat].

རྨར་ལུད་ (mārlüù) natural fertilizers.

རྨས་ (mɛ̄ɛ̀) vi. to get injured/ wounded ¶ དམག་རྒྱག་སྐབས་མི་མང་པོ་རྨས་པ་རེད་ Many people were wounded at the time of the battle.

རྨས་སྐྱོན་ (mɛ̄ɛ̀gyön) 1. injury; va.—གཏོང་ to injure, to wound. 2. casualties.

རྨས་སྐྱོན་དམག་མི་ (mɛ̄ɛ̀gyön mɔ̄ɔmi) sm. རྨས་དམག.

རྨས་འགྲམས་ (mɛ̄ɛ̀ dra̱m) vi. to have a sore spread.

རྨས་རྟགས་མཚོན་བྱེད་རྩོམ་རིག (mɛ̄ɛ̀daà tsōnjeè tsōmriì) literary works reflecting the wounds inflicted by the Cultural Revolution.

རྨས་ནོར་ (mɛ̄ɛ̀nɔɔ) accidental injury.

རྨས་ཕོག (mɛ̄ɛ̀ pɔ̄ɔ) vi. to get injured/ wounded/ hurt.

རྨས་ཁྱམས་ (mɛ̄ɛ̀jam) a stretcher; va.—འཁུར་ to carry on a stretcher.

རྨས་མ་ (mɛ̄ɛ̀ma) sm. རྨས་པ་.

རྨས་དམག (mɛ̄ɛ̀maà) wounded soldier, military casualty.

རྨས་དམག་དང་བཙུང་དམག (mɛ̄ɛ̀maàtaŋ su̱ŋmaà) wounded soldiers and prisoners of war.

རྨས་རྨས་ཤུལ་ཤུལ་ (mɛ̄ɛ̀mɛɛ̀ shǘüshüü) many small wounds and cuts.

རྨས་ཚུལ་ (mɛ̄ɛ̀dzüü) the manner/ condition of being wounded or injured.

རྨི་: p. རྨིས་; f. རྨི་ (mī) vi. to dream.

རྨི་ (mī) meter ༎ཁོ་རྨི་སུམ་སྟོང་ཕྱིན་པ་རེད་ He went three thousand meters.

རྨི་གྲུ་བཞི་ (mi̱ tru̱bshi) square meter.

རྨི་ལྟས་ (mi̱dɛɛ̀) omens/ signs in a dream.

རྨི་ལམ་ (ñīləm) dream; vi.—གཏོང་; —རྨི་ to dream; vi.—ཤོར་ to dream; va.—བརྟག to interpret a dream; vi.—འཁྲུག to have a nightmare; va.—ཤོད་ to narrate/ talk about one's dream ༎ངས་མདང་དགོང་རྨི་ལམ་འཚུབ་པོ་རྨིས་བྱུང་ Last night I had a bad dream (nightmare).

རྨི་ལམ་གྱི་ཟླ་བ་ (ñīlamgi da̱wa) the 10th month of the Tibetan calendar.

རྨི་ལམ་ངན་པ་ (ñīlam ŋɛmba) a bad dream/ nightmare.

རྨི་ལམ་འཇམ་པོ་ (ñīlam ja̱mbo) a pleasant dream.

རྨི་ལམ་བརྟགས་པ་ (ñīlam dāgba) the interpretation of dreams.

རྨི་ལམ་བན་བུན་ (ñīlam pe̱nbün) unclear dreams.

རྨི་ལམ་འཚུབ་པོ་ (ñīlam tsūbbu) nightmare.

རྨི་ལམ་ཟ་ཟི་ (ñīlam sə̱si) sm. རྨི་ལམ་བན་བུན་.

རྨི་ལམ་ཟས་སུ་ཟ་བ་ (ñīlam sɛ̱ɛ̀su sa̱wa) sb. who earns his livelihood by interpreting dreams.

རྨི་ལམ་བཟང་པོ་ (ñīlam sa̱ŋbo) auspicious dream.

རྨིག་སྒ་ (mīgga) a type of saddle that looks like a horse's hoof.

རྨིག་སྒྲ་ (mīgdra) sound of horse hoofs/ hoofbeats.

རྨིག་གཅིག་མ་ (mīgjiimə) noncloven hoofed animals.

རྨིག་ལྕགས་ (mīgjaà) horseshoe; va.—རྒྱག to shoe a horse.

རྨིག་ཆགས་ (mīgjaà) animals with hooves.

རྨིག་གཉིས་ (mīgñii) sm. རྨིག་པ་ཁ་དྲལ.

རྨིག་མཐིལ་ (mīgtii) the center of a horse's hoof.

རྨིག་འདྲ་ (mīŋdra) a knife used for cutting the hoof when putting on horseshoes.

རྨིག་རྡུལ་ (mīgdüü) dust raised by hoofs.

རྨིག་པ་ (mīgbə) hoof.

རྨིག་པ་ཁ་དྲལ (mīgbə kādraà) cloven hoof.

རྨིག་པ་བརྩེ་ (mīgbə dzē) vi. to injure a hoof so that it is difficult walking.

རྨིག་ཚ་ (mīgdza) a contagious disease that infects hooves.

རྨིག་ལྡུམ་ (mīgdum) sm. རྨིག་གཅིག.

རྨིག་གཟེར་ (mīgser) nails for putting on horseshoes.

རྨིག་རལ་ (mīgrɛɛ) 1. a disease that causes hooves to tear. 2. cloven hoof.

རྨིག་ཤ་ (mīgsha) the fleshy part of a horse's hoof.

རྨིགས་པ་ (mīgbə) lizard, gecko.

རྨིགས་བུ་ (mīgbə) sm. རྨིགས་པ་.

རྨིན་ཅིང་ (mīnjiŋ) ch. policeman, militia guard.

རྨིའི་ (mīī) meter.

རྨིས་ (mīì) p. of རྨི་.

རྨུ་གབ་ (mūgəb) ignorance; vi.—གྱིས་སྒྲིབ་. to be ignorant.

རྨུ་ངན་སེམས་བཙངས་ (mū ŋɛn sēm ja̱ŋ) sm. ངན་སེམས་ཁོག་བཙངས་.

རྨུ་དར་ (mūdar) prayer flags erected on the top of mountain passes.

རྨུ་སུ་ (mūsu) female pubic hair.

རྨུག : p. རྨུགས་; f. རྨུག; imp. རྨུགས་ (mūū) va. to bite ༎ཁྱི་འདིས་ཁོ་ལ་རྨུགས་པ་རེད་ The dog bit him.

རྨུག་ཐིག (mūgdig) a bruise; vi.—ཆགས་ to get bruised.

རྨུགས་ (mūg) p. of རྨུག.

རྨུགས་པ་ (mūgbə) 1. sluggish, inert, languid. 2. gloomy ༎སེམས་རྨུགས་པ་ Gloomy.

རྨུགས་ཚིག (mūgdzii) things said when mentally sluggish.

རྨུགས་སེ་བ་ (mūgsewa) sluggish, muddy-headed.

རྨུན་པ་ (mūmbə) sm. རྨུན་པོ་.

རྨུན་པོ་ (mūmbo) a fool.

རྨུར་ (mūr) sm. རྨུག.

རྨུར་རྡུང་ (mūrduŋ) beating, torturing; va.—གཏོང་.

རྨུས་ (mūù) 1. sm. སྐྱོ་བ་ཡི་ཆད་. 2. sm. འཐིབས་.

རྨེ་ (mē) 1. mole, birthmark. 2. va. to ask, to say. 3. sm. བསྒོ་ཚགས་བྱེད་.

རྨེ་ངན་ (mēŋɛn) sm. ལྟས་ངན་.

རྨེ་བའི་ཟླ་བ་ (mēwɛ da̱wa) the 7th month of the Tibetan calendar.

རྨེ་བོ་ (mēwo) sm. དམེ་བོ་.

རྨེ་བཞི་ (mēshi) shung. abbr. རྨེ་རུ་ monastery and བཞི་སྡེ་ monastery (in Lhasa).

རྨེ་ཤ་ཅན་ (mēshajɛn) cannibal.

རྨེག (mēè) sm. གཏན་ནས་.

རྨེག་ངན་ (mēèŋɛn) bad omen, inauspicious vision.

རྨེག་མེད་ (mēèmeè) sm. རྨེག་མེད་ཙ་བརླག.

རྨེག་མེད་དུ་གཏོང་ (mēèmeèdu dōŋ) va. to wipe out/ destroy/ annihilate, to root out, to purge, to liquidate.

རྨེག་མེད་དུ་འགྱུར་ (mēèmeèdu gyu̱r) vi. to become destroyed/ annihilated/ wiped out/ purged.

རྨེག་མེད་ཙ་བརླག (mēèmeè dzālaà) destroying/ uprooting completely.

རྨེད་ (mēè) 1. va. to ask. 2. a strap that goes under the tail of a horse to keep the saddle from moving forward.

རྨེད་སྒྲོགས་ (mēèdrɔg) sm. རྨེད་, 2.

རྨེད་ཆད་གོང་ཕུད་ (mēèjɛɛ̀ ko̱ŋbüü) everything goinging wrong [Lit. tail strap breaks, strap under horse's neck comes off].

རྨེད་གདན་ (mēèdɛn) sm. རྨེད་.

རྨེད་ཕྱིང་ (mēèjiŋ) sm. རྨེད་.

རྨེད་འཛར་ (mēnjar) piece of red cloth attached to the རྨེད་.

རྨེད་ཧྲིལ་ (mēèhrii) a soft felt or leather band that is attached to the རྨེད་ and that goes under the horse's tail.

རྨེན་ (mēn) mole, birthmark.

རྨེན་སྐྲན་ (mēndrɛn) tumor in the womb of a young girl caused by premature sex (according to Tibetan medicine).

རྨེན་ངན་ (mēnŋɛn) bad omen.

རྨེན་པ་ (mēnba) type of cancerous black growth in the flesh and fat of animals such as sheep and pigs.

རྨེན་བུ་ (mēmbu) lymph nodes.

རྨེན་བུ་སྐྲང་ (mēmbu drāŋ) vi. to have a swelling of the lymph nodes.

རྨེན་བུའི་ནད་ (mēnbü nɛ̱ɛ̀) infection of the lymph nodes.

རྨེན་འབྲས་ (mēndrɛɛ̀) sm. རྨེན་བུ་.

རྨེན་སྦུབས་ (mēnbub) lymph node.

རྨེན་རྨེན་ (mēnmem) ripe (for fruits).

རྨེན་ཙ་ (mēndza) a vein in the neck.

རྨེལ་ (mēē) sm. གསེད་ and འཁལ་.

རྨོ་ (mōō) 1. grandmother. 2. old woman.

རྨོ་: p. རྨོས་: p. རྨོ་; p. རྨོས་ (mō) va. to plow.

རྨོ་ཀོ་ (mō gō) abbr. plowing and digging.

རྨོ་ཀོ་མཁན་ (mōgoñɛn) farmer, plowman.

རྨོ་བསྒྱུར་ཕྱུགས་སྐྱོང་ (mōgyur cūggyoŋ) giving up farming for animal husbandry.

རྨོ་རྒན་ (mōgɛn) derogatory term used when scolding an old woman.

རྨོ་འདེབས་ (mōndeb) plowing, cultivation; va.—བྱེད་ to plow, to cultivate.

རྨོ་ཕྱུགས་ (mōjuù) draft/ plowing animals.

རྨོ་པོ་ (mōō) sm. རྨོ་.

རྨོ་པོ་སྤྲ་ཕྱུག་བརླག་པའི་གདོང་འདྲ་པོ་ (mōō bādruù lāàbɛ do̱ŋ dra̱bo) showing a sad/ sullen/ morose face [Lit. face like an old woman who has lost her headdress].

རྨོ་པོ་སྦྲི་སེར་ (mōō bi̱sii) a vain old woman.

རྨོ་མོ་ (mōmo) grandmother.

རྨོ་མོད་ (mōmöö) plowing; va.—བྱེད་ to plow.

རྨོ་རྨོད་ (mōmöö) plowing; va.—བྱེད་ to plow.

རྨོ་རྨོད་པ་ (mōmööba) plowman.

རྨོ་རྨོན་ (mōmön) sm. རྨོ་རྨོད་.

རྨོ་རྨོན་པ་ (mōmönba) sm. རྨོ་རྨོད་པ་.

རྨོ་ཞིང་ (mōshiŋ) cultivated land, farmland, agricultural fields.

རྨོ་གཡག (mōyaà) plowing yaks.

རྨོ་ཡུར་འཕྲུལ་འཁོར་ (mōyur trǖǖgɔɔ) a machine that plows and weeds.

རྨོ་ཡུས་ (mōyüü) ch. cuttle fish.

རྨོ་ལས་ས་རིམ་ (mōlɛ̀ɛ̀ sārim) layer of soil that is cultivated/ plowed.

རྨོ་རུང་བའི་ས་ཞིང་ (mō ruŋbɛ sāshiŋ) arable land.

རྨོ་ལས་ (mōlɛ̀ɛ̀) plowing.

རྨོ་ས་ (mōsa) field, arable land, farmland.

རྨོ་སློག (mōlɔ̀ɔ̀) plowing; va.—རྒྱག.

རྨོ་སློག་ཕྲུ་གསུམ་ (mō lɔ̄ɔ̀ trū sūm) plowing, turning over and leveling.

རྨོ་སློབ་གཉིས་བྱེད་སློབ་གྲྭ་ (mōlob ñīījeè lōbdra) a school where one studies while doing plowing (agriculture labor).

རྨོག (mɔ̄ɔ̀) 1. helmet. 2. a type of gambling game that uses dice.

རྨོག་མགོ་སྦྱི་བྲུམ་ (mɔ̄ggo jīndum) a type of smallpox.

རྨོག་རྒྱན་ (mɔ̄ggyɛn) banner/ standard attached to a Tibetan helmet.

རྨོག་སྟན་ (mɔ̄gdɛn) a cap worn under a helmet.

རྨོག་ཕུར་ (mɔ̄gdur) the tip on a helmet on which the banner/ standard is attached.

རྨོག་ཐོད་ (mɔ̄gdöö) front of the helmet.

རྨོག་དར་ (mɔ̄gdar) banner attached to a helmet.

རྨོག་ཞྭ་ (mɔ̄gsha) sm. རྨོག.

རྨོག་ཞུ་ (mɔ̄gshu) sm. རྨོག.

རྨོག་གཞོལ་ (mɔ̄gshöö) ear protective flaps on a helmet.

རྨོག་རིལ་ (mɔ̄grii) 1. a round helmet-like hat (worn in traditional Tibetan society). 2. helmet.

རྨོག་རིལ་ཨམ་ཅོག་ཅན་ (mɔ̄grii āmjoòjɛn) a round satin hat with ear flaps.

རྨོང་འཇབ་ (mōŋjəb) sm. རྨོངས་འཇབ་.

རྨོངས་ (mōŋ) 1. vi. to be confused, to be puzzled. 2. vi. to be ignorant of.

རྨོངས་ཁ་ (mōŋga) urethra.

རྨོངས་འགྱུར་ནུས་མེད་ (mōŋgyur nǖǖmeè) ignorant and ineffective/ useless.

རྨོངས་རྒན་ (mōŋgɛn) ignorant, imbecilic ¶ རྨོངས་རྒན་བདག་ལྟ་བུ་ An ignorant person such as myself.

རྨོངས་རྒྱུགས་ (mōŋgyuù) following blindly; va.—བྱེད་ to follow blindly.

རྨོངས་ཅན་ (mōŋjɛn) ignorant.

རྨོངས་བཅོས་ (mōŋjöö) revising/ correcting ignorance; va.—བྱེད་.

རྨོངས་འཆར་ (mōŋjar) a phrase used to convey humbleness (e.g., ignorant me).

རྨོངས་གཉིད་ (mōŋñīì) state of ignorance; vi.—སད་ to remove a state of ignorance.

རྨོངས་གཉིད་ལས་སད་ (mōŋñīìlɛ sɛ̀ɛ̀) va. to awaken from ignorance/ unawareness ¶ རྨོངས་གཉིད་ལས་སད་པའི་མི་དམངས་ནི་འཛམ་གླིང་ཐོག་སྟོབས་ཤུགས་ཆེ་ཤོས་རེད་ The greatest force in the world is the awakened masses.

རྨོངས་གཏམ་ (mōŋdam) stupid/ ignorant talk.

རྨོངས་རྟགས་ (mōŋdaà) shung. ignorant, stupid.

རྨོངས་རྟུལ་ (mōŋdüü) sm. རྨོངས་པ་.

རྨོངས་བརྟུལ་ (mōŋdüü) sm. རྨོངས་རྟུལ་.

རྨོངས་དད་ (mōŋdeè) blind faith, superstition; va.—བྱེད་ to have blind faith, to be superstitious ¶ སྔོན་མའི་རྨོངས་དད་དག་ནི་ང་ཚོས་རྩ་མེད་བཟོ་དགོས་ We must eradicate the old superstitions.

རྨོངས་དད་སེལ་ (mōŋdeè sēl) va. to eradicate blind faith/ superstition.

རྨོངས་འདོད་ (mōŋdöö) wishing for sth. that is unattainable, blind hope.

རྨོངས་ནོར་ཐེབས་ (mōŋnɔɔ tēè) vi. to make an ignorant mistake.

རྨོངས་པ་ (mōŋba) stupid, ignorant ¶ རྨོངས་པའི་བསམ་བློ་ A stupid idea/ thought.

རྨོངས་སྤུ་ (mōŋbu) pubic hair.

རྨོངས་པར་བྱེད་ (mōŋbar ceè) va. to make sb. believe in superstition, to keep ignorant.

རྨོངས་བྱེད་སྒྲིད་སྨན་ (mōŋjeè driimɛn) 1. medicine that makes one numb. 2. an ideology that deceives.

རྨོངས་བྱེད་འཕྲུལ་འཁོར་ (mōŋjeè trǖǖgɔɔ) deceiving, duping.

རྨོངས་བློ་ (mōŋlo) ignorance, delusion; va.—བྱེད་ to enlighten, to remove ignorance/ delusion.

རྨོངས་འབྱེད་སློབ་གྲྭ་ (mōŋjeè lōbdra) sm. རྨོངས་སེལ་སློབ་གྲྭ་.

རྨོངས་མུན་སེལ་བ་ (mōŋmun sēlwa) va. to overcome the darkness of ignorance.

རྨོངས་དྲི་ (mōŋdre) genital smell/ odor.

རྨོངས་རྨོངས་ཚོད་ཚོད་ (mōŋmoŋ dzȫȍdzöö) sm. རྨོངས་ཚོད་.

རྨོངས་ཚོད་ (mōŋdzöö) blind guess; va.—བྱེད་; —རྒྱབ་ to do blindly, to do without a clear plan.

རྨོངས་མཚམས་ (mōŋdzam) 1. area around the genitals. 2. a point on the body used for moxabustion or accupuncture.

རྨོངས་ཞེན་ (mōŋshen) blind loyalty/ faith; va.—བྱེད་.

རྨོངས་ཞེན་ཕྱོགས་ལྷུང་ (mōŋshen cɔ̄ɔlaŋ) blindly taking sides; va.—བྱེད་.

རྨོངས་ཞེན་ལྡན་དད་ (mōŋshen lǖndɛ̀ɛ̀) blind faith.

རྨོངས་སེལ་སློབ་གྲྭ་ (mōŋsel lōbdra) school for illiterates.

རྨོངས་བསམ་ (mōŋsam) ignorant or stupid thought/ idea.

རྨོད་: p. རྨོས་; f. རྨོ་; imp. རྨོས་ (mȫȍ) va. to plow.

རྨོད་རྒྱག (mȫȍ gyaà) va. to plow.

རྨོད་རྒྱག་ཡོ་བྱད་ (mȫȍgyaà yobjɛ̀ɛ̀) plowing equipment/ implements.

རྨོད་གཉའ་གཅོག (mȫȍñaà jōò) va. to start the plowing of the fields (on an auspicious day).

རྨོད་གཏིང་རིང་པོ་ (mȫȍdīŋ riŋbu) deep plowing.

རྨོད་འདེབས་ (mȫȍ deb) va. to plow.

རྨོད་ཕྱུགས་ (mȫȍjuù) draft animals.

རྨོད་ཞིབ་ཚགས་པོ་ (mȫȍshib tsāgbar) plowing fastidiously.

རྨོད་ལམ་ (mȫȍman) furrow (made by a plow).

རྨོད་སློག (mȫȍlɔ̀ɔ̀) plowing; va.—རྒྱག.

རྨོན་ (mȫn) va. to plow.

རྨོན་གླང་ (mȫnlaŋ) bullock used for plowing.

རྨོན་ལྕགས་ (mȫnjaà) plowshare.

རྨོན་ཆས་ (mȫnjɛ̀ɛ̀) plowing utensils.

རྨོན་རྟ་ (mȫnda) a plow horse.

རྨོན་དོར་ (mȫndɔɔ) 1. a pair of plowing animals; va.—སྡེབ་ to tie a pair of animals together for plowing ¶ ཁོ་ཚོས་རྨོན་དོར་བཅུས་ཞིང་རྨོས་པ་རེད་ They plowed the field with ten pairs of animals. 2. a unit of land equal to what a pair of plowing animals can plow in one day.

རྨོན་དོར་གཅིག་གི་ས་ (mȫndɔɔ jiggi sā) an area that can be plowed by a pair of animals in one day.

རྨོན་དོར་སྡེབ་ (mȫndɔɔ deb) va. to tie a pair of animals together for plowing.

རྨོན་འདེབས་ (mȫndeb) the 5th month of the Tibetan calendar (when it is time for plowing and planting).

རྨོན་པ་ (mȫmba) plowing; va.—རྒྱག; —རྨོ་ to plow.

རྨོན་པ་དོར་སྡེབ་ (mȫmba tɔɔdeb) sm. རྨོན་དོར་སྡེབ་.

རྨོན་ཕྱུགས་ (mȫnjuù) plowing/ draft animals.

རྨོན་མཛོ་ (mȫndzo) a plowing མཛོ་.

རྨོན་མཛོ་དོར་སྦྲེལ་ (mȫndzo dɔɔdrel) sm. རྨོན་དོར་བསྡེབས་.

རྨོན་མཛོའི་རྔ་དམར་ (mȫndzö ŋāmar) the red yak tail adorning the head of plowing animals.

རྨོན་གཡག (mȫnyaà) plowing/ draft yaks.

རྨོན་གཡོག (mȫnyɔ̀ɔ̀) sb. who assists during plowing.

རྨོའ་ (mōō) 1. grandmother. 2. old woman.

རྨོར་དོ་ (mɔ̄rdo) old woman (used in derogatory sense).

རྨོས་ (mȫȍ) p. and imp. of རྨོ་.

རྨོས་འཁོར་ (mȫȍgɔɔ) tractor.

རྨོས་གླང་ (mõõlaŋ) plowing/ draft oxen.
རྨོས་ཉིན་ (mõõñin) shung. the area that a pair of plowing yak can plow in one day.
རྨོས་དོར་ (mõõdɔɔ) a team of two plowing animals.
རྨོས་མཛོ་ (mõõndzo) plowing/ draft མཛོ་.
སྙ་ (ñã) arc. vi. to feel lazy.
སྙང་ (ñãŋ) va. to stretch, to extend ། ཁོ་རྐང་ལག་སྙངས་ནས་ཉལ་བསྡད་འདུག He is sleeping with his arms and legs stretched out.
སྙང་ཤད་ (ñãŋshɛɛ̀) stretching (hands and feet); va.—བྱེད་.
སྙངས་ (ñãŋ) p. of སྙང་.
སྙི་ལམ་ (ñĩləm) arc. sm. རྨི་ལམ་.
སྙིས་ལྟས་ (ñĩdɛɛ̀) arc. sm. རྨི་ལྟས་.
སྙོང་ (ñõŋ) sm. སྙང་.
སྙོང་ཤད་ (ñõŋshɛɛ̀) sm. སྙང་ཤད་.
སྙོངས་ (ñõŋ) imp. of སྙོང་བ་.
སྨ་ (mã) low, inferior.
སྨ་སྙན་ (mãdrɛn) the rug put under a saddle.
སྨ་འཇབ་ (mãnjəb) tweezer (used for plucking facial hair).
སྨ་ཕབ་ (mãpəb) sm. དམའ་འབེབས་.
སྨ་ར་ (mãra) moustache, beard.
སྨ་ར་རྫུས་མ་ (mãra dzṳ̈ṳ̀mə) sm. ཨར་རྫུས་.
སྨག་ཁྲུན་ (məgdrün) sm. སྨ་སྙན་.
སྨག་རྒྱུ་ (məggyu) black pepper.
སྨག་ནག་ (mãgnaà) darkness, dark.
སྨག་ནག་གི་མཚན་མོ་ (mãgnaàgi tsɛ̃nmo) a dark night, a moonless night.
སྨག་སྟན་ (mãgdrɛn) sm. སྨག་སྙན་.
སྨག་རུམ་ (məgrum) absolute darkness, pitch blackness.
སྨག་ཤོག་ (mãgshoò) the rug that is put over a saddle.
སྨད་ (mɛɛ̀) 1. lower part, lower region ། རི་སྨད་ལ་ཤིང་ནགས་ཡོད་པ་རེད་ There are forests in the lower part of the mountain. 2. p. of སྨོད་.
སྨད་དཀྲི་ལྗང་ཁྲ་ (mɛɛ̀dri jaŋdra) shung. a type of skirt.
སྨད་དཀྲིས་ (mɛɛ̀drii) sm. སྨད་གཡོགས་.
སྨད་ཁམས་ (mɛɛ̀kam) Kham.
སྨད་ཁེབས་ (mɛɛ̀keb) tampon, sanitary napkin.
སྨད་ཁོག་ (mɛɛ̀gɔɔ̀) the hind part of an animal.
སྨད་གོས་ (mɛɛ̀göö) petticoat, lower skirt.
སྨད་འགོ་ (mɛ̃ngo) a contagious animal disease that infects the lower part of the body.
སྨད་རྒྱས་ (mɛɛ̀gyɛɛ̀) sm. སྨད་ཆེན་.
སྨད་རྒྱུད་ (mɛɛ̀gyüü) lower part ། ཆུ་བོ་ཞིན་ཨང་ཅང་གི་སྨད་རྒྱུད་ཀྱི་མཛེས་ལྗོངས་ནི་ As for the beautiful scenery of the lower reaches of the Hsinan River.
སྨད་རྒྱུད་པ་ (mɛɛ̀gyüüba) the lower tantric school founded in the 15th century by Sherab Senge (a disciple of Tsongapa).
སྨད་ཆ་ (mɛɛ̀ja) the second of two parts in a book or in a two volume set of book.
སྨད་ཆར་ (,ɛɛ̀jaa) latter part (of a life); lower part ། སྐུ་ཚེའི་སྨད་ཆར་སླེབས་པའི་སྐབས་ During the latter part of (his) life.
སྨད་ཆད་ (mɛɛ̀jɛɛ̀) arc. sm. མ་སྨད་པ་.
སྨད་ཆེན་མ་ (mɛɛ̀jenma) poet. a beautiful/ attractive woman.
སྨད་འཆལ་ (mɛ̃ncɛɛ) licentiousness, dissoluteness.
སྨད་འཇལ་ (mɛ̃njɛɛ) penalty for committing adultery.
སྨད་ཐུང་ (mɛɛ̀ndüü) sm. ཀ་ཐུང་.
སྨད་མདོ་ཁམས་སྒང་དྲུག (mɛɛ̀ dogam gaŋdruù) the six mountain ranges of eastern Tibet (Kham).
སྨད་འདུལ་ (mɛ̃ndüü) the resurgence of Buddhism from eastern Tibet after King Langdarma had obliterated the religion in Central Tibet.
སྨད་འདོགས་ (mɛɛ̀dɔɔ̀) suffixed letters (in the Tibet alphabet system).
སྨད་ནག་ (mɛɛ̀naà) the second half of a month that is inauspicious (in Tibetan astrology).
སྨད་ཕྱོགས་ (mɛɛ̀jɔɔ̀) 1. lower area. 2. Eastern Tibet or Kham.
སྨད་མ་ (mɛɛ̀ma) the lower part.
སྨད་ཚིག་ (mɛɛ̀dzii) insult, verbal abuse, invective, curse.
སྨད་ཚོང་ཁང་ (mɛɛ̀dzoŋgaŋ) brothel.
སྨད་ཚོང་མ་ (mɛɛ̀dzoŋma) prostitute.
སྨད་འཚོང་ (mɛɛ̀ tsõŋ) va. to prostitute, to work as a prostitute.
སྨད་འཚོང་མ་ (mɛɛ̀dzoŋma) prostitute.
སྨད་འཚོང་གནས་ (mɛɛ̀dzõŋnɛɛ̀) sm. སྨད་ཚོང་ཁང་.
སྨད་གཟུག་ (mɛɛ̀sug) the hind part of a carcass.
སྨད་གཡོགས་ (mɛɛ̀yɔɔ̀) petticoat, skirt.
སྨད་གཡོགས་གོང་བ་ (mɛɛ̀yɔɔ̀ koŋma) piece of material added to the waist of a woman's petticoat/ underskirt.
སྨད་ར་ (mɛɛ̀ra) sm. དམའ་འབེབས་.
སྨད་རུས་ (mɛɛ̀rüü) bones of the lower part of the body.
སྨད་ལིང་ (mɛɛ̀liŋ) back half of a carcass.
སྨད་ཤམ་ (mɛɛ̀sham) sm. སྨད་གཡོགས་.
སྨན་ (mɛ̃n) 1. medicine. 2. any chemical disinfectant or pesticide; va.—རྒྱག; —གཏོར་ to spray/ apply a disinfectant or pesticide. 3. vi. to be beneficial/ helpful ། སེམས་ལ་སྨན་པའི་བཀའ་སློབ་གནང་བྱུང་ (He) gave me helpful advice. ། སྨན་པའི་དཔལ་འབྱོར་ A beneficial economy.
སྨན་དཀར་ (mɛ̃ngar) boiled radish broth (used in Tibetan medicine).
སྨན་བཀུ་ (mɛ̃ngu) extracting medicine (from herbs, etc.) by boiling/ brewing.
སྨན་སྐུ་ (mɛ̃ngu) icons and statues made of clay mixed with sweet smelling herbs/ medicines.
སྨན་སྐུད་ (mɛ̃n gṹü) va. to put on/ apply medicine.
སྨན་སྐོལ་ (mɛ̃n gõõ) va. to boil/ brew medicines.
སྨན་ཁང་ (mɛ̃ngaŋ) hospital.
སྨན་ཁང་ཆུང་བ་ (mɛ̃ngaŋ cũŋwa) dispensary, clinic.
སྨན་ཁབ་ (mɛ̃ngəb) injection; va.—རྒྱག to give an injection, to inoculate.
སྨན་ཁབ་རྒྱག་ས་ (mɛ̃nkəb gya̤asa) injection room.
སྨན་ཁབ་བཟོ་གྲྭ་ (mɛ̃nkəb so̤dra) syringe factory.
སྨན་ཁུ་ (mɛ̃ngu) liquid medicine.
སྨན་ཁུག་ (mɛ̃nguù) bags used by Tibetan doctors for keeping medicines.
སྨན་ཁྱིམ་ (mɛ̃ngyim) cup with handle for measuring medicines.
སྨན་ཁྲོག་ (mɛ̃ndrɔɔ̀) unprocessed medicinal materials.
སྨན་གོས་ (mɛ̃ngöö) the uniforms worn by doctors and nurses.
སྨན་གྱི་རྒྱུད་བཞི་ (mɛ̃ngyi gyṳ̈ṳ̀shi) the four basic texts of Tibetan medicine.
སྨན་གྱི་ཐུན་ཚད་ (mɛ̃ngi tṹndzɛɛ̀) the amount of medication that should be taken in one dose.
སྨན་གྱི་མཐུ་ (mɛ̃ngi tũ) the effect of a medicine.
སྨན་གྱི་ལྡེ་གུ་ (mɛ̃ngi di̤gu) medicine brewed into a paste.
སྨན་གྱི་ཕབས་ཏ་ (mɛ̃ngi pə̃bda) an agent used to bring out the power of the ingredients of medicines.
སྨན་གྱི་སྦྱོར་བཅད་ (mɛ̃ngi jo̤o̤da) the components of a medicine.
སྨན་འགོག་ (mɛ̃n go̤ɔ̀) va. to pick medicinal herbs.
སྨན་རྒྱུ་ (mɛ̃ngyu) materials for making medicine.
སྨན་སྒ་ (mɛ̃nga) ginger.
སྨན་སྒམ་ (mɛ̃ngam) medicine chest.
སྨན་གཅིའུ་ (mɛ̃njiwu) a type of pipe used for treating a patient through the anus.
སྨན་བཅོས་ (mɛ̃njöö) medical care, medical treatment; va.—བྱེད་ to treat (medically) ། སྐོར་བསྐྱོད་སྨན་བཅོས་ Mobile health/ medical care. ། སྨན་པ་རྣམས་ཀྱིས་ནད་པ་ཚོར་སྨན་བཅོས་བྱས་པ་རེད་ The doctors treated the patients.
སྨན་བཅོས་ཁང་ (mɛ̃njöögaŋ) clinic, doctor's consulting room.
སྨན་བཅོས་འཕྲུལ་ཆས་ (mɛ̃njöö trṻüjɛɛ̀) medical

apparatus.

སྨན་བཅོས་འཕྲོད་བསྟེན་ (mɛ̄njöö trö̀öden) public health care, medical care and public health.

སྨན་བཅོས་འཕྲོད་བསྟེན་སྡེ་ཁག (mɛ̄njöö trö̀öden degaà) public health units/ clinics.

སྨན་བཅོས་མི་སྣ་ (mɛ̄njöö minə) medical personnel.

སྨན་བཅོས་མྱུར་སྐྱོབ་ས་ཚིགས་ (mɛ̄njöö ñurgyob sədzii) first-aid station.

སྨན་བཅོས་ཡོ་བྱད་ (mɛ̄njöö yobjɛɛ̀) medical instruments/ equipment.

སྨན་བཅོས་རུ་ཁག (mɛ̄njöö rugaà) medical team/ group/ unit.

སྨན་བཅོས་ལག་འཁྱེར་ (mɛ̄njöö laggyee) certificate showing eligibility for medical care.

སྨན་བཅོས་ལས་ཁུངས་ (mɛ̄njöö lɛ̀ɛguŋ) medical office, medical institution.

སྨན་བཅོས་ལས་དོན་ (mɛ̄njöö lɛ̀ɛdön) medical affairs/ work.

སྨན་བཅོས་ལས་བྱེད་པ་ (mɛ̄njöö lɛ̀ɛjeèba) medical staff, medical-aid workers.

སྨན་བཅོས་སྲིང་བལ་ (mɛ̄njöö sīŋbɛɛ) absorbent cotton.

སྨན་བཅོས་སྲུང་སྐྱོབ་ཁང་ (mɛ̄njöö sūŋgyobgaŋ) medical aid station.

སྨན་ཆང་ (mɛ̄njaŋ) medicinal alcohol.

སྨན་ཆབ་ (mɛ̄njəb) h. of སྨན་ཆུ་.

སྨན་ཆས་ (mɛ̄njɛɛ̀) medical equipment.

སྨན་ཆུ་ (mɛ̄nju) 1. liquid medicine. 2. liquid disinfectant, pesticide; va.—རྒྱག; —གཏོར་ to spray/ apply a disinfectant or pesticide.

སྨན་ཆུ་གཏོར་ཆས་ (mɛ̄nju dɔ̄rjɛɛ̀) disinfectant/ pesticide spraying equipment.

སྨན་ཆུང་གཏོར་བྱེད་འཕྲུལ་ཆས་ (mɛ̄nju dɔ̄rjɛɛ trǖǖjɛɛ̀) sm. སྨན་ཆུ་གཏོར་ཆས་.

སྨན་ཆུ་སྨུག་པོ་ (mɛ̄nju mūgbu) gentian violet.

སྨན་ཆེན་ (mɛ̄njen) a plant used in Tibetan medicine—the rhizome of Chinese monkshood (Aconitum Carmichaeli).

སྨན་མཆོག (mɛ̄njɔ̀ɔ) extremely effective medicines.

སྨན་འཇིམ་ (mɛ̄njim) clay mixed with different kinds of herbs/ medicines and used for making statues.

སྨན་འཛོག་ས་ (mɛ̄njɔgsa) dispensary, pharmacy.

སྨན་ལྗོངས་ (mɛ̄njoŋ) an area rich in medicinal materials.

སྨན་བརྗེ་ཁང་ (mɛ̄njegaŋ) changing/ dressing room in a hospital or clinic.

སྨན་ཉར་སྒྲོད་ཁང་ (mɛ̄n ñardröögaŋ) pharmacy, drugstore.

སྨན་ཉར་ཚོང་ཁང་ (mɛ̄nñar tsōŋgaŋ) sm. སྨན་ཉར་སྒྲོད་ཁང་.

སྨན་གཉེར་ (mɛ̄nñer) pharmacist.

སྨན་སྙིང་ (mɛ̄nñiŋ) a thin silk that is usu. hung over the front of thankas.

སྨན་སྙིགས་ (mɛ̄nñii) the residue of brewed medicine.

སྨན་གཏོང་ (mɛ̄n dōŋ) va. to take medicines.

སྨན་གཏོང་ལུགས་ (mɛ̄n dōŋluù) directions on how to take medicines.

སྨན་གཏོར་ (mɛ̄n dɔ̄ɔ) va. to spray insecticide/ pesticides.

སྨན་གཏོར་ཡོ་བྱད་ (mɛ̄ndɔɔ yobjɛɛ̀) sm. སྨན་འཐོར་འཕྲུལ་ཆས་.

སྨན་བདགས་ (mɛ̄n dāà) 1. va. to grind medicines. 2. va. to be of use/ helpful.

སྨན་སྡོབས་ (mɛ̄ndob) sm. སྨན་གྱི་མཐུ་.

སྨན་བསྟེན་ (mɛ̄n dēn) va. to take medicine.

སྨན་ཐ་ (mɛ̄nda) the liquid taken together with a medicine (in Tibetan medicine); vi.—བྱེད་ ¶ སྨན་འདི་སྨན་ཐ་ཆུ་འཁོལ་གྱིས་གཏོང་དགོས་ This medicine has to be taken with boiled water.

སྨན་ཐང་ (mɛ̄ndaŋ) liquid medicine.

སྨན་ཐབས་བྱེད་ (mɛ̄ndəb ceè) 1. va. to treat medically. 2. va. to try to benefit, to do things to benefit ¶ སྤྱི་པའི་བདེ་དོན་ལ་སྨན་ཐབས་བྱས་པ་རེད་ (They) tried to benefit the welfare of the society.

སྨན་ཐུན་ (mɛ̄ndün) a dosage, dose ¶ སྨན་ཐུན་གཅིག One dosage/ dose of a medicine.

སྨན་ཐུར་ (mɛ̄ndur) a small spoon used for measuring medicine.

སྨན་ཐོ་ (mɛ̄ndo) a prescription.

སྨན་མཐུ་ (mɛ̄ndu) sm. སྨན་གྱི་མཐུ་.

སྨན་འཐུང་སྟངས་ (mɛ̄n tūŋdaŋ) sm. སྨན་གཏོང་སྟངས་.

སྨན་འཐོར་འཕྲུལ་ཆས་ (mɛ̄ndön trǖǖjɛɛ̀) sprayer for pesticides/ insecticides.

སྨན་དང་ས་བོན་མཉམ་བསྲེས་ (mɛ̄ndaŋ sābön ñāmseè) pesticide-treated seeds.

སྨན་དུ་འགྲོ་ (mɛ̄ndu dro) va. to use as medicine.

སྨན་དུ་རུང་ (mɛ̄ndu ruŋ) sm. སྨན་དུ་འགྲོ་.

སྨན་དེབ་ (mɛ̄ndeb) medical book.

སྨན་དོན་མི་སྣ་ (mɛ̄ndön minə) medical personnel.

སྨན་འདམ་ (mɛ̄ndam) sm. སྨན་འཇིམ་.

སྨན་འདམ་གྱི་སྐུ་ (mɛ̄ndamgi gū) shung. a statue made from སྨན་འཇིམ་.

སྨན་ལྡེ་ (mɛ̄nde) medicinal syrup.

སྨན་ལྡེ་གུ་ (mɛ̄n digu sm. སྨན་ལྡེ་.

སྨན་སྡེབ་ (mɛ̄ndeb) compounding medicines.

སྨན་བདུང་སྦྱོར་ཁང་ (mɛ̄nduŋ jɔɔgaŋ) pharmacy, dispensary.

སྨན་ནད་ (mɛ̄nnɛɛ̀) an allergic reaction to a medicine; vi.—རྒྱག; —ཐེབས་ to get an allergic reaction to a medicine.

སྨན་ནུས་ (m¯ɛnnüü) effect/ strength of a medicine.

སྨན་ནུས་ལྡོག (mɛ̄nnüü dɔ̀ɔ) vi. to be resistant to the effect of a drug.

སྨན་ནོར་བུ་བདུན་ཐང་ (mɛ̄n nɔɔbu dündaŋ) a liquid medicine made up of seven different ingredients.

སྨན་སྣ་ (mɛ̄nna) 1. medicines. 2. spices; va.—རྒྱག to spice (food).

སྨན་པ་ (mɛ̄mba) 1. doctor, physician; va.—བསྟེན་ to see/ consult a doctor.

སྨན་པ་ཀང་རྗེན་ (mɛ̄mba gāŋjen) barefoot doctor.

སྨན་པ་ཀང་རྗེན་མ་ (mɛ̄mba gāŋjemma) sm. སྨན་པ་ཀང་རྗེན་.

སྨན་པ་གྲྭ་ཚང་ (mɛ̄mba tradzaŋ) 1. a (གྲྭ་ཚང་) college in a large monastery that specializes in teaching medicine. 2. name of the Cogpori Medical College.

སྨན་པའི་རྒྱལ་པོ་ (mɛ̄mbɛ gyɛɛbo) the medicine Buddha.

སྨན་པོ་ (mɛ̄mbo) sm. ཕན་པོ་.

སྨན་དཔྱད་ (mɛ̄njɛɛ̀) medical examination, medical checkup; va.—བྱེད་ to do a medical checkup/ examination.

སྨན་དཔྱད་ཁང་ (mɛ̄njɛɛ̀gaŋ) medical clinic.

སྨན་དཔྱད་མཁས་པ་ (mɛ̄njɛɛ̀ kɛ̄ɛba) doctor, expert in medical diagnosis.

སྨན་སྤྱོད་པ་ (mɛ̄njööba) doctor.

སྨན་སྤོས་ (mɛ̄mböö) sm. སྨན་བསངས་.

སྨན་ཕོར་ (mɛ̄nbɔɔ) cup/ bowl for keeping medicines.

སྨན་ཕྱེ་ (mɛ̄nje) 1. powdered medicine. 2. powdered chemicals/ pesticides.

སྨན་ཕྱེ་གཏོར་ཆས་ (mɛ̄nje dɔ̄ɔjɛɛ̀) equipment for spraying powdered insecticides/ fungicides.

སྨན་ཕྱེ་གཏོར་བྱེད་འཕྲུལ་ཆས་ (mɛ̄nje dɔ̄ɔjeè trǖǖjɛɛ̀) sprayer for powdered insecticides/ fungicides.

སྨན་ཕྱེ་དྲི་བཟང་ (mɛ̄nje trisaŋ) a red powdered incense.

སྨན་ཕྲུག (mɛ̄ntruù) medical student.

སྨན་འཕྱག་ཕག་ཟེ་ (mɛ̄njaà pāgse) brush for cleaning out medicine from a mortar.

སྨན་འཕྲོད་ (mɛ̄n trö̀ö) vi. to be cured by a medicine ¶ སྨན་དེ་ང་ལ་འཕྲོད་མ་བྱུང་ That medicine didn't cure me. 2. (in negative constructions) vi. to have a side effect/ allergic reaction (to a medicine).

སྨན་བར་ (mɛ̄nbar) a type of yellow silk with red and blue flowers designs.

སྨན་བྱེད་ (mɛ̄n ceè) va. to use as a medicine.

སྨན་བླ་ (mɛ̄nla) the medicine Buddha.

སྨན་འབྱུག (mɛ̄n cu̱ù) va. to apply a medication.

སྨན་འབྲས་ (mɛ̄ndrɛɛ̀) a type of rice from Nepal.

སྨན་སྦྱིན་ཁང་ (mɛ̄njingaŋ) pharmacy.

སྨན་སྦྱོར་ (mɛ̄njɔɔ) making/ mixing/ compounding medicines; va.—བྱེད་.

སྨན་སྦྱོར་ཁང་ (mɛ̄njɔɔgaŋ) sm. སྨན་སྣུར་སྦྱོར་ཁང་.

སྨན་སྦྱོར་པ་ (mɛ̄njɔɔwa) compounder of medicines, pharmacist.

སྨན་སྦྱོར་བྱེད་མཁན་ (mɛ̄njɔɔ ce̱èñɛn) sm. སྨན་སྦྱོར་པ་.

སྨན་མར་ (mɛ̄nmar) butter mixed with various medicines to gain strength.

སྨན་མོ་ (mɛ̄nmo) female doctor.

སྨན་རྩ་ (mɛ̄ndza) herbal medicine.

སྨན་རྩིས་ཁང་ (mɛ̄ndzigaŋ) college of traditional Tibetan medicine and astrology in Lhasa.

སྨན་རྩེ་ (mɛ̄ndze) a yellow brocade with red and blue flower design.

སྨན་ཚགས་ (mɛ̄ndzaà) a sifter for powdered medicines.

སྨན་ཚད་ (mɛ̄ndzɛɛ̀) 1. quantity of different medical ingredients. 2. the amount of dosage to be taken.

སྨན་ཚོང་ཁང་ (mɛ̄ndzoŋgaŋ) pharmacy, drug store.

སྨན་ཚོང་པ་ (mɛ̄ndzoŋwa) pharmacist, one who sells medicine.

སྨན་འཛིན་ (mɛ̄ndzin) a prescription; va.—གཏོང་ to give a prescription.

སྨན་འཛུགས་ (mɛ̄n dzu̱ù) va. to vaccinate.

སྨན་མཛོད་ (mɛ̄ndzöö̀) medicine storehouse.

སྨན་རྫས་ (mɛ̄ndzɛɛ̀) 1. things that medicine are made from, medicinal ingredients/ materials. 2. flashlight battery.

སྨན་རྫས་ཅུའུ་ (mɛ̄ndzɛɛ̀ jū) tib.ch. medical service.

སྨན་རྫས་རྟོག་བཤེར་ཁང་ (mɛ̄ndzɛɛ̀ dōgshergaŋ) medicine testing office.

སྨན་རྫས་ཚོང་ཁང་ (mɛ̄ndzɛɛ̀ tsōŋgaŋ) pharmacy.

སྨན་རྫས་ཞིབ་འཇུག་ཁང་ (mɛ̄ndzɛɛ̀ shi̱mjuùgaŋ) institute of pharmacology.

སྨན་རྫུས་ (mɛ̄ndzüù) fake medicine.

སྨན་ཞིབ་ཞིབ་ (mɛ̄n shi̱bshiì) powdered medicine.

སྨན་གཞུང་ (mɛ̄nshuŋ) medical texts. 2. medical records.

སྨན་གཞུང་རིག་པ་ (mɛ̄nshuŋ ri̱gbə) science of medicine.

སྨན་གཞོང་ (mɛ̄nshoŋ) large stone bowl used for grinding medicines.

སྨན་ཟབ་ (mɛ̄nsəb) an effective medicine.

སྨན་ཟུག (mɛ̄n su̱g) sm. སྨན་འཕྱོད་.

སྨན་ཟོག (mɛ̄nsog) 1. medical products/ items. 2. pesticide products/ items.

སྨན་བཟང་ (mɛ̄nsaŋ) a good medicine.

སྨན་བཟང་རོ་ཁ་ (mɛ̄nsaŋ ro̱ga) good advice that isn't pleasant to hear [Lit. good medicine with a bitter taste].

སྨན་བཟི་ (mɛ̄nsi) sm. སྨན་ནད་.

སྨན་བཟོ་ཁང་ (me̱nsogaŋ) pharmacy, dispensary.

སྨན་བཟོའི་བཟོ་གྲྭ་ (me̱nsö so̱dra) pharmaceutical factory.

སྨན་བཟོས་བཟོས་ (mɛ̄n so̱ösöö̀) ready-made medicines.

སྨན་ཡིག (mɛ̄nyiì) 1. prescription. 2. sm. སྨན་གཞུང་.

སྨན་ཡོན་ (mɛ̄nyön) 1. medical fee, doctor's fee, prescription fee. 2. the effectiveness of a medicine.

སྨན་གཡོག (mɛ̄nyɔɔ̀) nurse; va.—རྒྱག་; —བྱེད་ to nurse, to work as a nurse.

སྨན་གཡོག་རྒྱག་མཁན་ (mɛ̄nyɔɔ gyu̱ùñɛn) nurse.

སྨན་ར་ (mɛ̄nra) a plant used in Tibetan medicine (the tuber of hyacinth bletilla—Bletilla Striata).

སྨན་རག (mɛ̄nraà) medicinal wine/ liquor.

སྨན་རམས་པ་ (mɛ̄nramba) title for a learned Tibetan doctor.

སྨན་རས་ (mɛ̄nrɛɛ̀) bandage; va.—འཆིང་ to bandage.

སྨན་རིག (mɛ̄nriì) the science of medicine, medical ¶ སྨན་རིག་སློབ་གྲྭ་ཆེན་པོ་ Medical school.

སྨན་རིགས་ (mɛ̄nriì) medicines, kinds of medicines.

སྨན་རིགས་ཚོང་ཁང་ (mɛ̄nriì tsōŋgaŋ) drug store, pharmacy.

སྨན་རིགས་བཟོ་གྲྭ་ (mɛ̄nriì so̱dra) pharmaceutical factory.

སྨན་རིན་ (mɛ̄nrin) medicine fee/ price.

སྨན་རིལ་ (mɛ̄nrii) pill.

སྨན་རིལ་བུ་ (mɛ̄n ri̱ibu) sm. སྨན་རིལ་.

སྨན་རེ་ (mɛ̄nre) wish/ hope that sth. will be beneficial ¶ མི་དམངས་ཀྱི་བདེ་ཐང་ལ་སྨན་རེས་ས་གནས་མང་པོར་སྨན་ཁང་བཙུགས་པ་རེད་ Hoping to be beneficial to the people, (they) established hospitals in many places.

སྨན་རོ་ (mɛ̄nro) the taste of medicine.

སྨན་རོ་ཁ་རུང་ནད་ལ་ཕན་ སྙིང་གཏམ་རྩུབ་རུང་མི་ལ་ཕན་ (mɛ̄nro kāruŋ nɛ̱èla pɛ̄n ñīŋādam dzūbruŋ mi̱lə pɛ̄n) telling people the truth will help them even if it is painful [Lit. even though the medicine taste's bitter it helps the illness, even though one's innermost feelings (opinions) are harsh it helps the other person].

སྨན་ལྷབས་ཅན་ (mɛ̄n lābjɛn) very effective, very beneficial ¶ ཕྱག་ལས་འདི་སྨན་ལྷབས་ཅན་ཞིག་རེད་ This work is very beneficial.

སྨན་ལན་དུག་འཇལ་ (mɛ̄nlɛn tu̱njɛɛ) repaying a good deed by doing sth. evil; va.—བྱེད་ [Lit. in response to medicine pay back with poison].

སྨན་ལུགས་ (mɛ̄nluù) pharmacology.

སྨན་ལེན་ཁང་ (mɛ̄nlengaŋ) pharmacy, dispensary.

སྨན་ལེན་ས་ (mɛ̄nlensa) sm. སྨན་ལེན་ཁང་.

སྨན་ལེབ་ (mɛ̄nleb) flat tablet (medicine).

སྨན་ལོག (mɛ̄nlɔɔ̀) bad reaction (from medicine); vi.—རྒྱག to get a bad reaction from medicine ¶ སྨན་གསར་པ་དེ་བཟས་སྟེ་སྨན་ལོག་བརྒྱབ་ནས་སྡུག་པོ་ན་བྱུང་ I had a bad reaction to the new medicine and got very ill.

སྨན་ཤར་ (mɛ̄nshaa) sm. དམན་ཤར་.

སྨན་ཤིང་ (mɛ̄nshiŋ) a tree that is used for medicines.

སྨན་ཤེལ་ (mɛ̄nshee) a type of quartz/ mineral used in medicines.

སྨན་གཤིས་ (mɛ̄nshiì) content/ make-up/ property of a medicine.

སྨན་གཤོངས་ (mɛ̄nshoŋ) sm. སྨན་ལྗོངས་.

སྨན་སག (mɛ̄nsaà) a tool for sharpening/ polishing bones.

སྨན་སེམས་ (mɛ̄nsem) sm. ཕན་སེམས་.

སྨན་སོན་ (mɛ̄nsöm) inoculation, vaccination; va.—རྒྱག.

སྨན་སྲིད་ཁྲུའུ་ (mɛ̄nsiì trū) tib.ch. medicine policy office.

སྨན་གསོ་ (mɛ̄n sō) va. to treat medically.

སྨན་གསོའི་སྐོར་ཁག (mɛ̄nsö gɔ̄ɔgaà) mobile medical or health unit.

སྨན་བསང་ (mɛ̄nsaŋ) medicated incense.

སྨན་བསྲེས་པ་ (mɛ̄nsēēba) sm. སྨན་སྦྱོར་པ་.

སྨན་ལྷད་ (mɛ̄nlhɛɛ̀) adulterating a medicine; va.—གཏོང་.

སྨན་ཧྲོབ་ (mɛ̄nhrob) medicine in small pieces before they are ground into powder.

སྨར་རྒྱང་ (mārgyaŋ) sm. དམར་རྒྱང་.

སྨར་ཐོག (mārdɔɔ̀) in cash.

སྨར་འདེགས་ (mārdeg) net weight.

སྨར་པོ་ (mārbo) 1. clean, pure. 2. net (profit, income). 2. useful.

སྨར་སྨར་ཁྲིག་ཁྲིག (mārmar di̱gdig) top quality.

སྨར་ཟོང་ (mārsoŋ) money and goods/ commodities.

སྨར་རིན་ (mārrin) value of precious things.

སྨར་ལུད་ (mārlüù) high quality fertilizer.

སྨལ་ཟླ་ (māndа) the 11th month of the Tibetan calendar.

སྨི་ (mī) eng. meter (distance measure).

སྨི་གྲུ་བཞི་ (mī trūbshi) eng.tib. square meter.

སྨི་གྲུ་བཞི་ལྷམ་པ་ (mī trūbshi lhāmba) sm. སྨི་གྲུ་བཞི་.

སྨི་རྒྱ་དཔངས་གྲུ་བཞི་ (mī gya̱baŋ trūbshi) eng.tib.

cubic meter.

སྨི་རང་སུམ་སྒྱུར་ (mīraŋ sūmgyur) eng.tib. cubic meter.

སྨི་ལྷམ་པ་ (mī lhāmba) sm. སྨི་སྨྲ་བཞི་.

སྨི་ཧྲུའུ་ཀྲང་ (mī hrūdraŋ) ch. Secretary General.

སྨི་ཧྲུའུ་ཁྲུའུ་ (mī hrūdru) ch. office of the Secretary General.

སྨིག (mīì) arc. bamboo.

སྨིག་རྒྱུ་ (mīggyu) a mirage.

སྨིན་ (mīn) 1. vi. to mature, to ripen ¶ འབྲུ་རིགས་འདི་ཉིན་ 60 ནང་སྨིན་གྱི་ཡོད་པ་རེད་ This variety of barley ripens in 60 days. ¶ ལོ་ན་སྨིན་ to age/ grow old. 2. va. to achieve, accomplish ¶ དོན་དུ་སྨིན་ To achieve one's idea. 3. eyebrow. 4. abbr. of སྨིན་མ་.

སྨིན་དཀྱུས་ (mīngyüù) eyebrows ¶ སྨིན་དཀྱུས་རིང་བ་ Long eyebrows (considered beautiful).

སྨིན་གྲོལ་ (mīndröö) liberation (from samsara) ¶ སེམས་ཅན་རྣམས་སྨིན་གྲོལ་གྱི་ལམ་བཟང་པོར་དཀྲི་བར་མཛད་ (They) led sentient beings onto the glorious path of liberation from samara.

སྨིན་རྒྱས་ (mīngyɛɛ̀) sm. སྨིན་སྒྲུབ་.

སྨིན་སྣང་ (mīngaŋ) in a state of being ripe ¶ དེང་སང་འབྲུ་རིགས་སྨིན་གང་རེད་ Nowadays that grain is ripe.

སྨིན་སྒྲུབ་ (mīndrub) shung. achieving, accomplishing.

སྨིན་ཐེབས་ (mīnteb) shung. a trust fund, an endowment ¶ མཆོད་ཁང་ཉམས་གསོར་སྨིན་ཐེབས་སུ་དངུལ་སྒང་བཅོ་ལྔ་རེ་གཞུང་དུ་འབུལ་ལམ་ཞུ་རྒྱུ་ Each person will donate 15 སྒང་ of money to set up the trust for the renovation of the temple.

སྨིན་བདུན་ (mīndün) the Big Dipper.

སྨིན་བརྡའ་ (mīnda) sm. མིག་མདའ་.

སྨིན་པོ་ (mīmbu) 1. ripe ¶ འདི་སྨིན་པོ་མི་འདུག This is not ripe. 2. old (in age) ¶ དགུང་ན་སྨིན་པོ་ Old in years.

སྨིན་ཕྲག (mīndraà) the space between the eyebrows.

སྨིན་དཔྲག (mīndraà) sm. སྨིན་ཕྲག.

སྨིན་འབུ་ (mīmbu) an adult insect.

སྨིན་མ་ (mīnmə) eyebrow.

སྨིན་མའི་མཐའ་སྣེ་ (mīmmɛ tāne) the tip of the eyebrow.

སྨིན་མའི་རུས་འབུར་ (mīmmɛ rü̱ümbur) brow, brow ridge.

སྨིན་དམར་འོས་ལངས་ (mīnmar wö̱ölaŋ) the Red Eyebrows Uprising in A.D. 18 (in China).

སྨིན་མཚམས་ (mīndzam) space between the eyebrows.

སྨིན་པའི་དུས་ (mīmbɛ tü̱ü) the ripening season.

སྨིན་ཕྲག (mīmdraà) the space between the eyebrows.

སྨིན་དཔྲག (mi̱ndraà) sm. སྨིན་ཕྲག.

སྨིན་མ་ (mīnmə) eyebrow; va.—སྡུད་ to frown, to show angry countenance, to show displeasure (by contracting one's eyebrows).

སྨིན་མ་སྡུད་ (mīnmə dṳ̈ü) see སྨིན་མ་.

སྨིན་མ་འཁྱོག་པོར་སྡུས་ (mīnmə) sm. སྨིན་མ་སྡུད་.

སྨིན་ཤིང་ཤིང་ (mīn si̱ŋsiŋ) sm. སྨིན་མ་གཤིང་.

སྨིན་མཚམས་ (mīndzam) sm. སྨིན་ཕྲག.

སྨིན་མཚམས་སུ་མདུད་ལོག་རྒྱག (mīndzamsu dṳ̈ülɔ̀ gya̱à) sm. སྨིན་མ་སྡུད་.

སྨིན་རུས་ (mīmrüü) brow, brow ridge.

སྨིན་ལ་སྨིན་ (mīnla mīn) semiripe (fruits, etc.).

སྨིན་ལེགས་ (mīnleg) pretty/ beautiful face.

སྨིན་ལེགས་མ་ (mīnlegma) pretty/ beautiful woman.

སྨིས་ཧྲུའུ་ཀྲང་ (mīì hrūdraŋ) ch. སྨི་ཧྲུའུ་ཀྲང་.

སྨུ་སྐས་ (mūggɛɛ̀) a ladder used by ancient kings to climb to heaven after they die.

སྨུ་ཐག (mūgdaà) a rope used by ancient kings to climb to heaven after they die.

སྨུག་དཀར་ (mūggaa) pale purple.

སྨུག་སྐྱ་ (mūggya) pale purple.

སྨུག་ཁུ་ (mūggu) red/ purplish paint used on torma.

སྨུག་རྒྱ་ (mūggya) dark maroon.

སྨུག་ཅུང་ (mūgjuŋ) 1. mule color, brown.

སྨུག་ཐུང་ (mūgduŋ) a kind of fried dough.

སྨུག་ཐིག (mūgdiì) bruise; vi.—ཆགས་; —བྱེད་ to get bruised.

སྨུག་དྲི་ (mūgdri) stale or musty smell/ odor; vi.—ཁ་ to smell a stale/ musty odor.

སྨུག་འདུས་འོད་གསལ་ (mūgdüü wö̱ösɛɛ) ultraviolet.

སྨུག་ནག (mūgnaà) maroon.

སྨུག་པ་ (mūgbə) fog, mist; vi.—འཁོར་ to get/ be foggy or misty.

སྨུག་པ་འཁོར་ (mūgbə kɔ̄ɔ) see སྨུག་པ་.

སྨུག་པ་འཁྲིམས་ (mūgbə trīm) sm. སྨུག་པ་འཁོར་.

སྨུག་པ་འཐིབ་ (mūgbə tīb) sm. སྨུག་པ་འཁོར་.

སྨུག་པ་དྭངས་ (mūgbə tu̱ŋ) vi. to have fog clear up.

སྨུག་པ་ལང་ (mūgbə la̱ŋ) sm. སྨུག་པ་འཁོར་.

སྨུག་པོ་ (mūgbu) any dark color (usu. purplish) ¶ པགས་པ་སྨུག་པོར་གྱུར་ The skin turned purplish.

སྨུག་པོའི་ནད་ (mūgbö nɛ̱ɛ̀) a kind of ulcer.

སྨུག་པོའི་འབྲས་སྐྲན་ (mūgbö drɛ̱ɛ̀drɛn) cancerous ulcer.

སྨུག་སྤྲིན་ (mūgdrin) clouds and fog.

སྨུག་ཕུང་ངེ་ (mūgbuŋŋe) a pile of sth. purplish/ maroonish/ dark red.

སྨུག་མན་ (mūgmɛn) purple.

སྨུག་རྩི་ (mūgdzi) a plant used in Tibetan medicine (Asian puccoon—Chinese gromwell).

སྨུག་ཚོས་ (mūgdzüü) darkish colored paints.

སྨུག་ཞག (mūgshaà) fog.

སྨུག་ཡོམ་ (mūgyom) sth. that is darkish/ blackish and moving.

སྨུག་ལོང་ (mūgloŋ) sm. སྨུག་ཞག.

སྨུག་ཤིག་གེ་བ་ (mūg shīgewa) maroonish in color.

སྨུག་སེར་ (mūgsee) yellowish maroon.

སྨུག་བསླངས་སྤྲིན་བསྡུམས་ (mūglaŋ drīndum) causing fog and clouds to arise (through magic).

སྨུགས་པ་ (mūgbə) sm. སྨུག་པ་.

སྨེ་ཐིག (mēdiì) mole, freckle, birth mark.

སྨེ་བདུན་ (mēdün) the Big Dipper constellation.

སྨེ་བ་ (mēwa) mole, freckle birthmark.

སྨེ་བ་ནག་པོ་ (mē na̱gbo) a black mole/ wart/ freckle.

སྨེ་གཙང་ (mēdzaŋ) dirty and clean.

སྨེ་བརྩེགས་ (mēdzeg) a wrathful guardian deity.

སྨེ་ཤ་ཅན་ (mē shājɛn) 1. person who has a mole on his body. 2. scorpion. 3. a low caste in India.

སྨེད་ (mēè) sm. རྨེད་.

སྨོ་ལུགས་ (mōluù) Mohism (doctrines and beliefs of Mo-Tse who believed in universal love and absolute monarchy).

སྨོ་ལུགས་པ་ (mōlugbə) a Mohist.

སྨོག (mɔ̄ɔ̀) va. to dip ¶ སྨྱུ་གུ་སྣག་ཚ་ལ་སྨོག་པ་རེད་ (He) dipped the pen in the ink.

སྨོད་ : p. སྨད་; f. སྨད་; imp. སྨོད་ (mȫö̀) 1. va. to insult, to revile, to abuse, to scold, to criticize ¶ མི་དེ་ཚང་མས་སྨད་པ་རེད་ Everyone reviled that man. 2. va. to hang one's head in shame/ embarrassment ¶ གདོང་སྨོད་པ་རེད་ (He) hung his head.

སྨོད་ (mȫö̀) imp. of སྨོད་.

སྨོད་བྱེད་ (mȫö̀jeè) people who revile/ insult/ scold/ criticize.

སྨོད་ཚིག (mȫö̀dziì) words of criticism or derision.

སྨོན་ (mȫn) 1. va. to envy, to desire, to wish for ¶ མི་རྣམས་ཁོའི་འགྲུབ་འབྲས་ལ་སྨོན་ནས་ The people, having envied his accomplishments. 2. va. to admire ¶ ཁྱེད་རང་གིས་མི་སྨོན་རང་སྐྱིད་ཡོང་བའི་ལས་ཀ་བྱེད་དགོས་ You should work so that you are happy and others will admire you.

སྨོན་དཀར་ལས་ཤོག (mȫngar lɛ̱ɛ̀shoò) a high quality paper from ཉི་མོ་.

སྨོན་འགྲིན་ (mȫndrin) a close/ dear friend.

སྨོན་ངན་ (mȫŋɛn) sm. དམོད་མོ་.

སྨོན་རྔོད་ (mȫŋoò) shung. a tax that involves roasting the barley used by the monks during Monlam.

སྨོན་རྡ་ (mȫnda) the ceremony of soldiers on

horseback dressed in ancient costumes (that is performed during Monlam).

སྨོན་འདུན་ (mǖndün) 1. hope, wish, desire; va.—བྱེད་; —ཞུ་ to hope for, to pray for ༎ཁོང་ལ་ལམ་འགྲོ་ཡག་པོ་ཡོང་བའི་སྨོན་འདུན་ཞུས་པ་རེད་ (They) prayed that he would have good luck. ༎གྲོགས་པོ་ཚོས་ཁོང་མགྱོགས་པོ་མཇལ་བའི་སྨོན་འདུན་ཞུས་པ་རེད་ His friends expressed the hope they would see him again soon. 2. (— + རྟེན་འབྲེལ་) greetings of good wishes (usu. used on cards).

སྨོན་འདྲིན་ (mǖndrin) a good friend.

སྨོན་ཚིག་ (mǖndzii) good wishes, congratulatory wishes; va.—ཞུ་ va. to offer congratulatory words, to offer good wishes.

སྨོན་ཚོགས་ (mǒndzɔ̀ɔ) shung. 1. the assembly of monks at the prayer sessions of the Monlam Chemo Prayer Festival in Lhasa. 2. abbr. of Monlam Chemo and ཚོགས་མཆོད་.

སྨོན་ཚོགས་གཉིས་ (mǒndzɔ̀ ñii) shung.abbr. the སྨོན་ལམ་ཆེན་མོ་ (Monlam) and ཚོགས་མཆོད་ Prayer Festivals.

སྨོན་བཟང་ (mǒnsaŋ) sm. སྨོན་ཚིག.

སྨོན་ལམ་ (mǒnlam) a prayer for sth.; va.—རྒྱག་; —འདེབས་ to pray for sth. ༎ངས་ཁོང་ལ་ལམ་འགྲོ་ཡོང་བའི་སྨོན་ལམ་བརྒྱབ་པ་ཡིན་ I prayed that he would have good luck.

སྨོན་ལམ་ངན་པ་ (mǒnlam ŋɛmba) praying for sth. bad to happen; va.—རྒྱག་; —འདེབས་.

སྨོན་ལམ་ཆེན་མོ་ (mǒnlam cēmmo) the annual religious prayer festival in Lhasa in the first 1st Tibetan month ("The Great Prayer Festival").

སྨོན་ལམ་གཏོར་རྒྱག་ (mǒnlam dɔ̄ɔgyaà) the great exorcism to drive away evil forces that takes place after the Monlam festival on the 24th of the first Tibetan month.

སྨོན་ལམ་འདེབས་ (mǒnlam) see སྨོན་ལམ་.

སྨོན་ལམ་ཚོགས་ཤིང་ (mǒnlam tsɔ̄gshiŋ) fuel/ firewood for the Monlam Prayer Festival.

སྨོན་ལམ་ཞུ་ (mǒnlam shu̱) sm. སྨོན་ལམ་འདེབས་.

སྨོན་སེམས་ (mǒnsem) 1. admiring; vi.—སྐྱེ་ to admire/ envy. 2. hoping, desiring, wanting; vi.—སྐྱེད་ ༎ལས་ཀ་ཡག་པོ་ཞིག་རག་པའི་སྨོན་སེམས་སྐྱེ་གི་འདུག I am hoping to get a good job.

སྨོས་ (mǒ̀ö) va. to say, to mention ༎གོང་དུ་སྨོས་པ་བཞིན་ As said before. 2. vi. to be called a name ༎བོད་ཀྱི་དོན་གཅོད་ཁང་ཞེས་མིང་སྨོས་དགོས་ It has to be called the Tibetan Bureau Office.

སྨོས་ཅི་དགོས་ (mǒ̀öjigöö) 1. leave alone, let alone, not only ༎ཁོ་རང་ལ་ཁྲིམས་གཅོད་བཏང་བ་སྨོས་ཅི་དགོས་ཁོའི་ནང་མི་བཙོན་ལ་བཙུགས་པ་རེད་ Leave alone punishing him, (they) put his whole family in jail. ༎མགྲོན་ཁང་འདི་ཆ་རྐྱེན་མཐོ་པོ་ཡོད་པ་འདི་སྨོས་ཅི་དགོས་དང་ཞབས་ཞུ་ཐལ་འབྱུར་ཡང་ཡག་པོ་ཡོད་པ་རེད་ Not only are the facilities of this hotel good, but they also give good service.

སྨོས་མི་དགོས་ (mǒ̀omigöö) sm. སྨོས་ཅི་དགོས་.

སྨོས་མེད་ (mǒ̀omeè) 1. undoubtedly, without question, certainly ༎ཁོང་ནི་མི་དམངས་ཀྱི་འགོ་ཁྲིད་སྨོས་མེད་ཅིག་རེད་ He is unquestionably the leader of the people. ༎ང་ཚོར་རྒྱལ་ཁ་ཐོབ་རྒྱུ་སྨོས་མེད་པ་རེད་ There is no doubt but that we will win a victory. 2. natural ༎སྨོས་མེད་འཐུས་མི་ Natural representative. ༎མི་དམངས་ཀྱི་ཁ་ལོ་སྒྱུར་མཁན་སྨོས་མེད་ཅིག་ཏུ་བརྩི་གི་ཡོད་པ་རེད་ They consider (themselves) as the natural rulers of the people.

སྨྱང་ (ñāŋ) sm. སྙང་.

སྨྱན་ (ñɛ̄n) va. to pollinate.

སྨྱན་ཀ་ (ñɛ̄nga) matchmaking; va.—བྱེད་, —སྒྲོར་ to arrange marriages.

སྨྱན་ཁ་ (ñɛ̄nga) sm. སྨྱན་ཀ་.

སྨྱི་གུ་ (ñīgu) sm. སྨྱུ་གུ་.

སྨྱིག (ñīi) abbr. of སྨྱི་གུ་.

སྨྱིག (ñīi) bamboo, cane, reed.

སྨྱུ་ཁ་ (ñūgə) nib (of a pen).

སྨྱུ་ཁང་ (ñūgaŋ) bamboo house.

སྨྱུ་ཁྲོད་ (ñūdröö) sm. སྨྱུག་ཁྲོག.

སྨྱུ་གུ་ (ñūgu) pen.

སྨྱུ་གུ་འཛིན་པ་ (ñūgu dzi̱mbə) sb. who writes letters for others.

སྨྱུ་གུའི་ཁ་ (ñūgü kā) nib (of pen).

སྨྱུག (ñūù) 1. bamboo. 2. sm. སྨྱུ་གུ་.

སྨྱུག་བརྐོས་ (ñūggöö) carved bamboo.

སྨྱུག་ཁ་ (ñūgka) point/ nib of a pen.

སྨྱུག་ཁ་གསེག་ཅན་ (ñūgka sēgjen) a Tibetan bamboo pen where the nib is cut at an angle going down from right to left.

སྨྱུག་ཁ་གསེག་ལོག (ñūgka sēglɔ̀ɔ) a Tibetan bamboo pen where the tip of the pen is cut at a slight angle going down from left to right (opposite of usual).

སྨྱུག་ཁམ་ (ñūggam) the strokes that make up a Chinese character.

སྨྱུག་ཁའི་གསེག (ñūggɛ sēg) the tip/ nib of a pen.

སྨྱུག་ཁྱིམ་ (ñūgkyim) bamboo hut.

སྨྱུག་ཁྱོགས་ (ñūggyɔ̀ɔ) bamboo sedan chair/ palanquin.

སྨྱུག་ཁྲོག (ñūgdrɔ̀ɔ) metal container for bamboo pen.

སྨྱུག་མཁན་ (ñūgñɛn) person who works with bamboo.

སྨྱུག་གྲི་ (ñūdri) penknife.

སྨྱུག་གླིང་ (ñūgliŋ) 1. a bamboo forest. 2. bamboo flute.

སྨྱུག་སྒམ་ (ñūggam) bamboo box.

སྨྱུག་སྒྲོག (ñūdrɔ̀ɔ) sm. སྨྱུག་ཁྲོག.

སྨྱུག་ཅུ་གང་ (ñūgjugaŋ) a parasitic fungus that attacks bamboo.

སྨྱུག་ལྕུག (ñūgjaà) 1. bamboo cane. 2. sm. སྨྱུག་གཤག.

སྨྱུག་ཆས་ (ñūgjɛɛ̀) things made of bamboo.

སྨྱུག་ལྗང་ (ñūgjaŋ) yellowish-green color.

སྨྱུག་ཐག་ཟམ་པ་ (ñūgdaà sa̱mba) sm. སྨྱུག་ཟམ་.

སྨྱུག་ཐོགས་ (ñūgdɔ̀ɔ) sm. སྨྱུག་འཛིན་.

སྨྱུག་གདན་ (ñūgdɛn) a rug/ mat made of bamboo.

སྨྱུག་གདུགས་ (ñūgduù) bamboo umbrella.

སྨྱུག་མདའ་ (ñūgda) 1. a slender pointed piece of bamboo. 2. an arrow made from bamboo.

སྨྱུག་མདོང་ (ñūgdoŋ) bamboo pole.

སྨྱུག་འདབ་སྔོ་ཆང་ (ñūgdəb ŋōjaŋ) wine made from bamboo.

སྨྱུག་སྡེར་ (ñūgder) bamboo plate.

སྨྱུག་སྡོང་ (ñūgdoŋ) bamboo tree.

སྨྱུག་ནག (ñūgnaà) black bamboo.

སྨྱུག་ནགས་ (ñūgnaà) bamboo forest.

སྨྱུག་སྣོད་ (ñūgnöö) bamboo pen holder/ container.

སྨྱུག་དཔེ་ (ñūgbe) bamboo book (used in the ancient times).

སྨྱུག་སྤར་ (ñūgbar) bamboo rake.

སྨྱུག་ཕྱར་ (ñūgjar) bamboo mat.

སྨྱུག་ཕྱིའི་འོད་ཟེར་ (ñūgjii wö̱ösee) ultraviolet light, ultraviolet rays.

སྨྱུག་ཕྲན་ (ñūgdrɛn) thin bamboo.

སྨྱུག་བུ་ (ñūgbu) 1. pen. 2. bamboo.

སྨྱུག་བྱ་ (ñūgja) a type of partridge.

སྨྱུག་སྦུབས་ (ñūgbub) the cavity/ hollow part of bamboo.

སྨྱུག་མ་ (ñūŋmə) bamboo.

སྨྱུག་མ་མཁན་ (ñūŋməgɛn) person who works with bamboo.

སྨྱུག་མ་མདའ་རྒྱུ་ (ñūgmə da̱gyu) bamboo used for making arrows.

སྨྱུག་མེ་ཏོག (ñūg me̱dog) name of a flower (the stem of which looks very much like a bamboo).

སྨྱུག་མའི་ནགས་ཚལ་ (ñūŋmɛ na̱gdzɛɛ) bamboo grove/ forest.

སྨྱུག་མའི་པར་བུ་ (ñūŋmɛ bərbu) small basket woven from bamboo.

སྨྱུག་མའི་ཝ་ཤུ་ (ñūŋmɛ wəshu) a short bamboo drain which extends from the roof.

སྨྱུག་རྩ་ (ñūŋdzə) bamboo shoot.

སྨྱུག་རྩྭ་ (ñūgdza) sm. སྨྱུག་རྩ་.

སྨྱུག་རྩལ་ (ñūŋdzɛɛ) skill of writing.

སྨྱུག་ཙི་ཙུ་གང་ (ñūgdzi jūgaŋ) sm. སྨྱུག་ཙུ་གང་.

སྨྱུག་ཙིར་ (ñūgdzir) bamboo cage.

སྨྱུག་ཙེ་ (ñūgdze) sm. སྨྱུག་ཁ་.

སྨྱུག་ཙེན་ (ñūgdzen) sm. སྨྱུག་འཛིན་.

སྨྱུག་ཚགས་ (ñūgdzaà) bamboo strainer/ sieve.

སྨྱུག་ཚད་ (ñūgdzɛɛ̀) bamboo ruler.

སྨྱུག་ཚལ་ (ñūgdzɛɛ) sm. སྨྱུག་སྦྲིང་.

སྨྱུག་ཚིགས་ (ñūgdziì) knot in bamboo.

སྨྱུག་འཛིན་ (ñūgdzin) a person who writes letters for others.

སྨྱུག་ཞུ་ (ñūgshu) sm. སྨྱུག་ཞྭ་.

སྨྱུག་ཞྭ་ (ñūgsha) bamboo hat.

སྨྱུག་གཞོན་ (ñūgshön) young/ new bamboo.

སྨྱུག་ཟམ་ (ñūgsam) bridge made from bamboo.

སྨྱུག་ཟེབ་ (ñūgseb) small bamboo basket.

སྨྱུག་གཟེབ་ (ñūgseb) sm. སྨྱུག་ཟེབ་.

སྨྱུག་གཟེར་ (ñūgsee) 1. bamboo nails. 2. type of punishment in which a bamboo nail/ sliver is pushed under a fingernail; va.—རྒྱག.

སྨྱུག་བཟོ་བ་ (ñūgsowa) a craftsman who makes things from bamboo.

སྨྱུག་བཟོས་ཤོག་བུ་ (ñūgsöö̀ shōgbu) paper made from bamboo.

སྨྱུག་ཡོལ་ (ñūgyöö) bamboo curtain.

སྨྱུག་ར་ (ñūgra) bamboo fence.

སྨྱུག་རིལ་ (ñūrii) bamboo stick.

སྨྱུག་རིས་ (ñūgriì) bamboo designs/ patterns/ figures.

སྨྱུག་རོལ་མགྱོགས་གཏམ་ (ñūgröö gyɔgdam) a style of Chinese comic talk/ story said to the accompaniment of a bamboo clapper.

སྨྱུག་ཤ་ (ñūgsha) the inner pulp of the bamboo stem.

སྨྱུག་ཤད་ (ñūgshɛɛ̀) bamboo comb; va.—རྒྱག to comb with a bamboo comb.

སྨྱུག་ཤིང་ (ñūgshiŋ) bamboo tree.

སྨྱུག་ཤུན་ (ñūgshün) bamboo bark.

སྨྱུག་ཤུབས་ (ñūgshub) bamboo pen container/ holder.

སྨྱུག་ཤོག (ñūgshɔ̀ɔ) paper made from bamboo.

སྨྱུག་གཤག (ñūgshaà) flat bamboo stick (like a ruler) used in school to punish the students by either hitting on the cheeks in the case of boys or on the hands for girls; va.—གཞུ་ to hit with a bamboo stick.

སྨྱུག་སླས་ (ñūlɛɛ̀) woven bamboo (usu. refers to containers).

སྨྱུག་སླེ་ (ñūgle) bamboo basket (usu. for carrying on back).

སྨྱུག་སློམ་ (ñūglom) small flat bamboo basket.

སྨྱུང་: p. སྨྱུངས་; f. སྨྱུང་; imp. སྨྱུངས་ (ñūŋ) 1. va. to lessen, to reduce, to minimize ¶ མི་འབོར་སྨྱུང་ནས་ Having reduced the population. 2. va. to starve oneself, to go on a hunger strike ¶ བཙོན་པ་ཚོས་ལྟོ་ཆས་སྨྱུངས་ནས་ངོ་རྒོལ་བྱས་པ་རེད་ The prisoners protested by going on a hunger strike.

སྨྱུང་གྲོལ་དུས་ཆེན་ (ñūŋdröö tü̱üjen) the festival celebrating the end of the period of fasting.

སྨྱུང་གནས་ (ñūŋnɛɛ̀) a fast, fasting; va.—ལ་སྡོད་; —གཏོང་ to fast.

སྨྱུང་གནས་གྲོལ་ (ñūŋnɛɛ̀ trö̱ö) vi. to finish/ conclude a fast.

སྨྱུང་གནས་སྡོམ་པ་ (ñūŋnɛɛ̀ do̱mba) the vow to fast.

སྨྱུང་བར་གནས་ (ñūŋwar nɛɛ̀) sm. སྨྱུང་གནས་.

སྨྱུང་བུ་ (ñu̱ŋbu) awl.

སྨྱུང་སྨྱུང་ (ñūŋñūŋ) elongated in shape.

སྨྱུང་སྲུང་ཟླ་བ་ (ñūŋsuŋ da̱wa) the month of fasting.

སྨྱུངས་ (ñūŋ) f. and imp. of སྨྱུང་.

སྨྱུར་ (ñūr) va. to quicken, to make sooner.

སྨྱོ་: p. སྨྱོས་; f. སྨྱོ་ (ñō) vi. to be insane/ crazy/ mad ¶ མོའི་ཕྲུ་གུ་ཚོ་ཤི་ནས་མོ་སྨྱོས་པ་རེད་ She went crazy after her children died.

སྨྱོ་སྐད་ (ñōgɛɛ̀) wild/ crazy/ mad talk; va.—རྒྱག.

སྨྱོ་མཁན་ (ñōngɛn) mad/ crazy person.

སྨྱོ་ཅོལ་བབ་ཅོལ་ (ñōjöö bə̱bjüü) acting wild/ slightly crazy/ eccentric (but does not convey mental illness); va.—བྱེད་.

སྨྱོ་ཅོལ་ཁང་ (ñōjüügaŋ) sm. སྨྱོ་བཅོལ་ཁང་.

སྨྱོ་ཅོར་ (ñōjɔɔ) sm. སྨྱོ་སྐད་.

སྨྱོ་བཅོལ་ཁང་ (ñōjöögaŋ) asylum for the insane, mental hospital.

སྨྱོ་བཅོས་བབ་བཅོས་ (ñōjöö̀ bə̱bjüǜ) sm. སྨྱོ་ཅོལ་བབ་ཅོལ་.

སྨྱོ་ཆུ་ (ñōju) a potion that causes madness.

སྨྱོ་མཆོང་རྒྱག (ñōjoŋ gya̱à) va. to behave like a mad person, to act crazy.

སྨྱོ་འཆོལ་དགུ་འཆོལ་ (ñōjöö gu̱jöö) mad, crazy, insane.

སྨྱོ་གཏམ་ (ñōdam) sm. སྨྱོ་སྐད་.

སྨྱོ་གཏམ་ཁུངས་མེད་ (ñōdam kūŋmeè) crazy or insane talk that is without substance/ foundation.

སྨྱོ་ནད་ (ño̱nɛɛ̀) mental illness, insanity, psychosis; vi.—ན་ to be insane/ mad/ psychotic.

སྨྱོ་ནད་སྨན་ཁང་ (ño̱nɛɛ̀ mɛ̃ngaŋ) mental hospital.

སྨྱོ་སྤྱོད་ (ñōjöö̀) insane/ mad behavior, wanton/ wild/ savage behavior ¶ ཁོའི་སྨྱོ་སྤྱོད་དེ་ར་སུ་གང་གིས་དོ་སྣང་བྱས་མ་སོང་ No one paid attention to his mad behavior. ¶ དམག་མི་ཚོས་སྨྱོ་སྤྱོད་ཀྱི་སྒོ་ནས་མི་མང་པོ་དམར་གསོད་བཏང་བ་རེད་ The soldiers wantonly massacred many people.

སྨྱོ་བྱེད་ནད་ (ñōjeè nɛ̱ɛ̀) sm. སྨྱོ་ནད་.

སྨྱོ་འབོག (ñō bɔ̱ɔ) vi. to faint while going mad/ crazy ¶ སྐྲག་པ་དང་དངངས་ནས་སྨྱོ་འབོག་པར་གྱུར་བ་རེད་ (He) got so frightened that he fainted (as if he had gotten mad).

སྨྱོ་ཙ་ (ñōdza) mad, crazy; vi.—ཡོང་ to become mad/ crazy.

སྨྱོ་འཚུབ་ (ñōdzub) half-mad/ crazy.

སྨྱོ་འཚུབ་འཚུབ་ (ñō tsūbdzub) half-mad/ insane/ crazy; vi.—ཆགས་ to become half-mad/ insane/ crazy.

སྨྱོ་རྫུན་ (ñōdzün) pretending to be mad/ insane/ crazy; va.—འདེབས་.

སྨྱོ་བཟྲུ་ (ñōdzu) sm. སྨྱོ་རྫུན་.

སྨྱོ་རོས་འཚོང་ (ñōröö̀ tsōŋ) va. to misbehave (especially children).

སྨྱོ་རོས་ཤོད་ (ñōröö̀ shö̃ö̀) sm. སྨྱོ་རོས་འཚོང་.

སྨྱོ་ལབ་ (ñōləb) sm. སྨྱོ་སྐད་.

སྨྱོ་བཤད་ (ñōshɛɛ̀) sm. སྨྱོ་སྐད་.

སྨྱོ་ཧམ་ (ñōham) 1. a crazy or preposterous claim/ statement ¶ དགྲ་བོའི་སྨྱོ་ཧམ་ལ་འཛམ་གླིང་མི་མང་གིས་ཆ་འཇོག་བྱེད་ཀྱི་རེད་ The people of the world will not trust the preposterous claims of the enemy. 2. ferocious, unbridled, rampant ¶ ཨ་ཕྲིའི་མི་དམངས་ལ་སྨྱོ་ཧམ་གྱིས་ཚུར་རྒོལ་བྱེད་ཀྱི་ཡོད་པ་རེད་ (They) are ferociously attacking the people of Africa and Asia.

སྨྱོ་ཧམ་ཆེན་པོ་ (ñōham cēmbo) sm. སྨྱོ་ཧམ་.

སྨྱོན་གཏམ་ (ñōndam) sm. སྨྱོ་སྐད་.

སྨྱོན་ནད་ (ñōnnɛɛ̀) mental illness.

སྨྱོན་པ་ (ñōmba) an insane/ mad/ deranged person.

སྨྱོན་པའི་སྐད་ཆ་ (ñōmbɛ gɛ̃ɛ̀ja) sm. སྨྱོ་སྐད་.

སྨྱོན་པའི་སྨན་ཁང་ (ñōmbɛ mɛ̃ngaŋ) mental hospital, psychiatric ward, insane asylum.

སྨྱོན་སྤྱོད་ (ñōmjöö̀) sm. སྨྱོ་སྤྱོད་.

སྨྱོན་མ་ (ñōmma) an insane/ mad/ deranged woman.

སྨྱོན་སེམས་ཅན་ (ñōnsemjɛn) insane/ mad/ deranged.

སྨྱོས་ (ñöö̀) p. of སྨྱོ་.

སྨྲ་ (mā) : p. སྨྲས་; f. སྨྲ་; imp. སྨྲོས་ (mā) va. to say, to tell ¶ ཁོས་མོ་ལ་སྨྲས་སོང་ He told her.

སྨྲ་མཁན་ནེ་ཙོ་ (māgɛn ne̱dzo) talking parrot.

སྨྲ་མཁས་ (mākɛɛ̀) 1. a good at speaking, eloquent, articulate. 2. Thursday.

སྨྲ་རྒྱུ་ (mə̄gyu) sm. ལབ་རྒྱུ་.

སྨྲ་སྒོ་ (māgo) mouth.

སྨྲ་སྒོ་མཚོན་ཆ་ (māgo tsõnja) name of a Tibetan grammar book.

སྨྲ་གཅོད་ (mā jöö̀) va. to stop sb. talking.

སྨྲ་བཅད་ (mā jɛ̃ɛ̀) p. of སྨྲ་གཅོད་.

སྨྲ་ལྕེ་ (māje) tongue.

སྨྲ་ལྕེ་བདེ་པོ་ (māje de̱bo) verbal, articulate.

སྨྲ་མཆུ་ (māju) lips, mouth.

སྨྲ་འཆལ་ (mājɛɛ) empty/ idle/ useless talk.

སྨྲ་བརྗོད་ (mājöö) speech, talking; va.—སྒྲོག ¶ སྨྲ་བརྗོད་ཀྱི་རང་དབང་ The right to speak.

སྨྲ་བརྗོད་ཉུང་བ་ (mājöö ñūŋwə) a taciturn person, a person who says little.

སྨྲ་བརྗོད་ཀྱི་ཡུལ་ལས་འདས་པ་ (mājöögi yüülɛ dɛ̀ɛ̀ba) beyond words, inexpressible ¶ ཡུལ་ལྗོངས་དེའི་མཛེས་སྡུག་ནི་སྨྲ་བརྗོད་ཀྱི་ཡུལ་ལས་འདས་པ་ཞིག་རེད་ The beauty of the scenery was beyond words.

སྨྲ་གདམ་ (mādam) sm. སྨྲ་བརྗོད་.

སྨྲ་བདེ་ (māde) sm. སྨྲ་མཁས་.

སྨྲ་ལྡིབ་ (mādib) unclear or incoherent speech due to lisp/ stuttering/ speech defect.

སྨྲ་བ་ (māwa) talk.

སྨྲ་བ་ངན་པ་ (māwa ŋɛɱba) fallacious/ misleading/ evil talk.

སྨྲ་བ་གཅོད་ (māwa jöö) 1. va. to pause while talking. 2. va. to cease talking.

སྨྲ་བ་ལྡིབ་པ་ (māwa dibbə) sm. སྨྲ་ལྡིབ་.

སྨྲ་བ་ཡངས་པ་ (māwa yaŋba) loose-lipped, overly talkative, sb. who can't keep secrets.

སྨྲ་བའི་གཞི་ (māwɛ shi) the basis for talk.

སྨྲ་བའི་ཟླ་ (māwɛ da) one's counterpart when debating or talking.

སྨྲ་འོར་ (māwɔɔ) sm. ཁུར་སྐད་.

སྨྲ་ཤེས་དོན་གོ་ (māsheè töngo) ability to comprehend/ understand talk.

སྨྲ་བསམ་བརྗོད་ལས་འདས་པ་ (mā sāmjöölɛ dɛ̀ɛ̀ba) sm. བསམ་བརྗོད་ལས་འདས་པ་.

སྨྲས་ (mɛ̄ɛ̀) p. of སྨྲ་.

སྨྲེ་ངག (mēŋaà) sm. སྨྲེ་སྔགས་.

སྨྲེ་སྔགས་ (mēŋaà) wailing, moaning, lamenting; va.—འདོན་ to wail, to moan, to lament.

སྨྲེ་སྔགས་དིར་དིར་ (mēŋaà tirdir) many wailing and lamenting all at once; va. va.—འདོན་.

སྨྲེ་བ་ (mēwa) sm. སྨྲེ་སྔགས་.

སྨྲོས་ (mõö) imp. of སྨྲ་.

ཙ་ (dzā) the letter ཙ་ (used in alphabetical numbering).

ཙ་གོ་ར་ (dzāgora) partridge.

ཙ་གི་ཙི་གི་ (dzəgi dzīgi) sm. ཙག་ཙིག.

ཙ་གེ་ཙོ་གེ་ (dzāge dzōge) sm. ཙག་ཙིག.

ཙ་རྟགས་ (dzādaà) the mark on the right hand head of the letter ཅ that makes it ཙ་.

ཙ་དར་ (dzādaa) hind. shawl.

ཙ་སྡེ་ (dzāde) the four letters ཙ་ཚ་ཛ་ཝ་.

ཙ་ན་ (dzāna) 1. when, at the time of ། ང་ལྷ་སར་སྡོད་ཙ་ན་ན་པ་རེད་ I got sick when I lived in Lhasa. 2. because, since ། ཁ་སང་ང་ཞེ་དྲག་ན་ཙ་ན་འདིར་ཡོང་ཐུབ་མ་བྱུང་ I was unable to come here yesterday because I was very sick.

ཙ་ན་ཀ་ (dzānaga) a type of small bean.

ཙ་འདྲུ་ (dzəndru) sm. ཙ་ལག.

ཙ་བྱ་ (dzāja) a kind of clematis.

ཙ་སྨུན་ཛ་ (dzāmündza) a kind of jute.

ཙ་ཙར་ཙ་བྱུས་ (dzādzaa dzājɛɛ̀) continuously, without break ། དམག་མི་ཙ་ཙར་ཙ་བྱུས་སླེབས་པ་རེད་ The soldiers arrived one after another without break.

ཙ་ཙར་ཙ་ལ་ (dzādzaa dzāla) sm. ཙ་ཙར་ཙ་བྱུས་.

ཙ་ར་ (dzāra) 1. corporal punishment (usu. whipping); va.—གཏོང་ to inflict corporal punishment, to whip. 2. sm. རྡུང་.

ཙ་ར་ཁུང་ (dzāraguŋ) a point in the body used for acupuncture.

ཙ་རི་ (dzəri) a sacred mountain in what had been S.E. Tibet and is now a part of India.

ཙ་རི་རོང་སྐོར་ (dzəri roŋgɔɔ) 1. the lower and longer route for circumambulating ཙ་རི་. 2. duping, tricking; va.—འཁྱིད་ to trick/ dupe.

ཙ་རུ་ (dzəru) sm. གམ་དུ་.

ཙ་རེ་བ་ (dzārewa) sm. ཙ་ཙར་ཙ་བྱུས་.

ཙ་ལག (dzālaà) sm. ཙ་རྟགས་.

ཙ་ལྷག (dzālhaà) sm. ཙ་རྟགས་.

ཙཱ་རུ་ (dzāru) abbr. of ཙཱ་རུའི་བཟའ་བ་.

ཙཱ་རུའི་བཟའ་བ་ (dzārü sawa) an offering given at a consecration of a religious building.

ཙག་ཀྲ་ (dzāgdra) sm. ཙག་སྒྲ་.

ཙག་གི་ཙིག་གི (dzəgi dzīgi) sm. ཙག་ཙིག.

ཙག་གེ་ཙོག་གེ (dzāge dzōge) of different heights.

ཙག་སྒྲ་ (dzāgdra) 1. a match ། ཐ་མ་སྦར་ཡས་ཀྱི་ཙག་སྒྲ་ཡོད་པས་ Do you have a match to light a cigarette? 2. a sound.

ཙག་སྒྲའི་སྒམ་ཆུང་ (dzāgdrɛ gəmjuŋ) match box.

ཙག་གཙོད་ (dzāg jöö) va. to boil butter to eliminate the water and leave the solids.

ཙག་བཙད་མར་ (dzāgjɛɛ̀ maa) butter that has been boiled to eliminate the water.

ཙག་ཙག (dzāgdzaà) 1. skinny (in negative sense). 2. bad and cramped (for handwriting).

ཙག་ཙིག (dzəgdzig) various small things, odds and ends, small (scale), petty ། ཙག་ཙིག་འཚོང་མཁན་ A peddler (street vendor).

ཙག་ཙིག་ཉོ་དངུལ་ (dzəgdzii ñoŋüü) petty expenditure fund.

ཙག་ཙོག (dzāgdzog) abbr. of ཙག་གི་ཙོག་གི་.

ཙག་བཤགས་ (dzāgshaà) 1. cutting sth. in half; va.—གཏོང་. 2. half of an animal carcass (that has been cut). 3. slang. refuting/ countering sth.; va.—གཏོང་.

ཙང་ (dzāŋ) (vb. + —) because, since ། ཁོ་ལྷ་སར་ཕྱིན་ཙང་ Because he went to Lhasa.

ཙང་ཀུན་ (dzəŋgün) a type of spirit/ ghost.

ཙན་དན་ (dzɛ̄ndɛn) sandalwood.

ཙན་དན་དཀར་པོ་ (dzɛ̄ndɛn gāābo) white sandalwood.

ཙན་དན་གུ་ཡོག (dzɛ̄ndɛn kuyɔɔ̀) sm. ཙན་དན་གྱིས་གུ་ཡོག་དང་གོས་ཆེན་གྱིས་ཐབ་ཕྱིས་.

ཙན་དན་གྱིས་གུ་ཡོག་དང་ གོས་ཆེན་གྱིས་ཐབ་ཕྱིས་ (dzɛ̄ndɛngi kuyɔɔ̀ daŋ kööjengi təbjiì ciì) using inappropriately [Lit. using sandalwood as a fire iron and brocade as a kitchen cleaning cloth].

ཙན་དན་སྦྲུལ་གྱི་སྙིང་པོ་ (dzɛ̄ndɛn drüügi ñiŋbu) a rare type of sandalwood.

ཙན་དན་དམར་པོ་ (dzɛ̄ndɛn māābo) red sandalwood.

ཙན་དན་སྨུག་པོ་ (dzɛ̄ndɛn mūgbo) dark red sandalwood.

ཙན་དན་ས་མཆོག (dzɛ̄ndɛn sājɔɔ̀) sm. ཙན་དན་དཀར་པོ་.

ཙནྡན་ (dzɛ̄ndɛn) sm. ཙན་དན་.

ཙན་སྡོང་ (dzɛ̄ndoŋ) sandalwood tree.

ཙབ་ (dzəb) 1. a thing for putting under sth. to balance it or make it even; va.—རྒྱག ། ལྕོག་ཙེ་འདི་ལ་ཙབ་ཅིག་རྒྱག་དགོས་ཀྱི་འདུག (We) have to put sth. under the (legs of the table) to make it even. 2. see ཙབ་ལངས་.

ཙབ་ད་ཙུབ་ད་ (dzəbdə dzūbda) sm. ཙབ་ཙུབ་.

ཙབ་བེ་ཙུབ་བེ་ (dzəbbe dzūbe) sm. ཙབ་ཙུབ་.

ཙབ་ཙབ་ (dzəbdzəb) sm. ཙབ་ཙུབ་.

ཙབ་ཙུབ་ (dzəbdzub) rushed, hurried; va.—བྱེད་ to rush, to hurry ། ཁོས་ལས་ཀ་འདི་ཙབ་ཙུབ་བྱས་ནི་བྱས་པ་རེད་ He did the work hurriedly. ། ཙབ་ཙུབ་མ་བྱེད་ Don't rush.

ཙབ་ཙུབ་ཅན་ (dzəbdzubjɛn) hasty, hurried.

ཙབ་ཙོབ་ (dzəbdzob) sm. ཙབ་ཙུབ་.

ཙབ་རལ་ (dzəbrɛɛ) torn, tattered; va.—བཟོ་ to tatter, to tear into pieces, to wreck ། མི་དེ་ཚོས་གཞུང་ཙབ་རལ་བཟོས་པ་རེད་ These people wrecked the government.

ཙབ་ལངས་ (dzəb laŋ) vi. to feel nervous/ jittery.

ཙབ་ལིང་ (dzəbliŋ) sm. ཙབ་ཙུབ་.

ཙབ་རུལ་ (dzəbrɛɛ) torn, tattered.

ཙབས་རུ་ཚྭ་ (dzəbru tsā) a kind of salt.

ཙམ་ (dzām) 1. about, approximately ། མི་ཉི་ཤུ་ཙམ་ཡོད་པ་རེད་ There are about twenty people. ། ཆུ་བུམ་པ་ཕྱེད་ཙམ་འདུག The vase is about half full of water. 2. (adj. + —) quite ། ཁོ་ཚོར་རོགས་དངུལ་མང་ཙམ་སྤྲོད་དགོས་ You have to give them quite a lot of aid. 3. (ཇི་ + —) however much, however many ། དམག་མི་ཇི་ཙམ་བཏང་ཡང་ However many soldiers were sent. ། རིན་འབབ་ཇི་ཙམ་སྤར་ཀྱང་ཁེ་ཆེན་པོ་མ་བྱུང་བ་རེད་ However much the price was raised the profit was not big. 4. (with དེ་ or འདི་) that/ this many, that/ this much, as much/ many as that/ this, so much/ many ། དམག་མི་ག་ཚོད་བཏང་ཡང་དེ་ཙམ་ཆ་མེད་དུ་གཏོང་རྒྱུ་ཡིན་ However many soldiers they send, that many we will destroy. ། ཁོས་དངུལ་དེ་ཙམ་བརྐུས་པ་ཡོད་ཆེས་ཁག་པོ་རེད་ It's hard to believe he stole so much money. 5. (vb. + —) just barely managing to do sth. ། མཐར་རྒྱ་གར་དུ་སླེབས་ཙམ་བྱུང་ Finally (I) just barely made it to India. ། ལོ་མང་པོ་དངུལ་བསགས་ནི་ཁང་པ་ཉོ་ཐུབ་ཙམ་བྱུང་ Having saved money for many years, (I) was barely able to buy a house. ། ཁོ་བཙོན་ལ་འགྲོ་མི་དགོས་ཙམ་བྱུང་བ་རེད་ He barely managed not to go to prison. ། མ་ཤི་ཙམ་བྱུང་ (I) barely stayed alive. ། ཁོ་མ་ཤི་ཙམ་བརྡུངས་པ་རེད་ He was beaten till (he) was almost dead. 6. only, just, merely ། དེ་ནི་ཁ་ནས་བཤད་པ་ཙམ་མ་གཏོགས་དོན་དངོས་ལག་ལེན་བསྟར་ཀྱི་མ་རེད་ As for this, (they) are only saying it. (They) won't actually carry it out. ། ཚོགས་འདུར་ཞུགས་པ་ཙམ་ལས་གྲོས་ཆོད་ཁག་ལ་འོས་ཤོག་མ་སྤྲུགས་ Only attend the meeting, don't vote on motions.

ཙམ་དུ་ (dzāmdu) at about, in about, to about ། ཉི་མ་བཞི་ཙམ་ལ་ལྷ་སར་འབྱོར་གྱི་རེད་ In about four days (they) will reach Lhasa. ། འདི་ནས་མེ་ལི་བཞི་ཙམ་དུ་མེ་འཁོར་བབས་ཚུགས་ཤིག་ཡོད་པ་རེད་ About four miles from here there is a railway station. ། རི་

རིའི་ཕྱེད་ཙམ་དུ་འཛེགས་དུས་ When they climbed about halfway up the mountain. 2. just at (sight or hearing) ¶ཁོ་མཐོང་བ་ཙམ་དུ་དགའ་པོ་བྱུང་ Just seeing him made me glad.

ཙམ་དུ་མ་ཟད་ (dzāmdu ma̲sɛɛ) not only, just ¶གཏེར་ཁ་གསར་པ་འཚོལ་བ་ཙམ་དུ་མ་ཟད་སྔོག་འདོན་ཡང་བྱ་དགོས་ Not only do we just search for new mines, we have to excavate them.

ཙམ་ན་ (dāmna) sm. ཙམ་དུ་.

ཙམ་ནས་ (dzāmbɛɛ) from about (usu. with numbers) ¶ལོ་ཉི་ཤུ་ཙམ་ནས་ From about twenty years.

ཙམ་པ་ཀ་ (dzāmbaga) lily magnolias.

ཙམ་པོ་བ་ (dzāmbowa) ordinary, common, so so, medium, not standard.

ཙམ་ཤིག་ (dzāmshig) about, approximately ¶ཁོ་ཨ་རི་ལོ་བཞི་ཙམ་ཤིག་བསྡད་པ་རེད་ He stayed in America about four years.

ཙམ་ཡང་ (dzāmya) even, so much as ¶གོས་སྣེ་གཅིག་ཙམ་ཡང་མ་སྤྲེར་བ་རེད་ (They) didn't give even one piece of clothing. ¶དབྱིན་སྐད་ཚིག་གཅིག་ཙམ་ཡང་ཤེས་ཀྱི་མེད་ I don't know even a word of English.

ཙམ་ལ་ (dzāmla) sm. ཙམ་དུ་.

ཙར་ཙར་ (dzārdzar) 1. falling out unintentionally; vi.—ཐེབས ¶སྒྲ་ཁུག་ནང་ནས་དངུལ་ཙར་ཙར་ཐེབས་ཀྱི་འདུག Money is falling out of the purse. 2. odds and ends. 3. sm. ཙ་ཙར་ཙ་བྱུས་.

ཙར་རེར་འཇོག (dzārre jɔ̱ɔ̀) va. to leave without completing/ finishing it ¶ཁོང་ན་ནས་ལས་མཇུག་ཙར་རེར་འཇོག་དགོས་བྱུང་སོང་ He got sick and had to leave the work unfinished.

ཙི་ (dzī) abbr. of ཙི་ཙི་.

ཙི་ཁུང་ (dzīguŋ) mouse hole.

ཙི་གི་ (dzīgi) mouse, rat.

ཙི་གུ་ (dzīgu) pit (of a fruit).

ཙི་ཏྲ་མ་ཎི་ (dzīnda ma̲ni) another way of writing.ཙིན་ད་མ་ཎི་.

ཙི་ན་ (dzīni) China.

ཙི་པ་ཏ་ (dzībada) a mythological animal—drawings and carving of the head of this animal that are found on the pillars of monasteries and aristrocratic homes.

ཙི་ཙི་ (dzīdzi) mouse, rat.

ཙི་ཙི་གླ་ཙི་ཅན་ (dzīdzi lādzimə) muskrat.

ཙི་ཙི་སྣམ་པོ་ (dzīdzi ga̲mbo) 1. bat. 2. sb. who is two-faced.

ཙི་ཙི་གསོད་སྨན་ (dzīdzi sȫö̀mɛn) mouse/ rat poison.

ཙི་ཙི་ (dzīdze) ch. sm. ཙི་ཚེ་.

ཙི་ཚེ་ (dzīdze) ch. millet.

ཙི་ཝའི་ཤེན་ (dzīwɛshɛn) ch. ultraviolet rays.

ཙིག་ཙིག (dzīidzii) sm. ཙི་ཙི་.

ཙིན་ད་མ་ཎི་ (dzīnda ma̲ni) a precious gem, a wish-fulfilling gem.

ཙིའུ་ (dzi̲wu) sm. ཙི་གུ་.

ཙིར་སྒྲ་ཝུར་སྒྲ་ (dzīrdra wu̲rdra) noisy, boisterous.

ཙིར་ཙིར་ཝུར་ཝུར་ (dzīrdzir wu̲rwur) crowded and noisy/ boisterous.

ཙིར་སིང་ (dzīrsiŋ) extremely afraid; vi.—རྒྱག.

ཙུ་མ་དི་ (dzūmadi) a traditional Tibetan surgical tool.

ཙུ་མོ་དི་ (dzūmodi) sm. ཙུ་མ་དི་.

ཙུ་ད་ (dzūda) 1. a mythological land where people have one leg only. 2. a name of a precious stone/ gem.

ཙུག (dzūg) 1. how ¶ང་ཚོ་ཙི་ཙུག་བྱེད་ How should we do it? 2. ch. sm. ཙུའུ་.

ཙུག་ཀྲང་ (dzūgdraŋ) ch. sm. ཙུའུ་ཀྲང་.

ཙུག་གུལ་སྡོད་ (dzūùgüü dö̱ö̱) vi. to sit/ be still ¶པར་རྒྱག་དུས་གཟུགས་པོ་ཙུག་གུལ་སྡོད་དགོས་ When having a picture taken one must sit still.

ཙུག་གུལ་འཇོག (dzūùgüü sha̲à) vi. to leave sth. alone ¶འཕྲུལ་འཁོར་དེ་ཙུག་གུལ་ཞོགས་ Leave the machine alone (don't touch it).

ཙུག་ཙུག (dzūgdzuù) the sound of chewing.

ཙུང་ཀྲི་ (dzūŋdri) ch. general branch.

ཙུང་ཏུའུ་ (dzūŋdu) ch. governor, general.

ཙུང་ཏུའི་ (dzūŋduwe) ch. column (military) ¶ཙུག་ཏུའི་ལྔ་པ་ The 5th column.

ཙུང་ཐུང་ (dzūŋduŋ) ch. president of a republic.

ཙུང་ཐུང་གཞོན་པ་ (dzūŋduŋ shö̱mba) ch.tib. vice president.

ཙུང་ཙི་ (dzūŋdzi) ch. a triangular shaped rice dumpling that is wrapped in bamboo leaves and steamed.

ཙུང་ལི་ (dzūŋli) ch. premier, prime minister, chancellor.

ཙུང་ལི་གཞོན་པ་ (dzūŋli shö̱mba) ch.tib. vice or deputy premier/ prime minister/ chancellor.

ཙུང་སི་ལིང་ (dzūŋ sīliŋ) ch. commander in chief.

ཙུང་ཧྲུའུ་ཅི་ (dzūŋ hrūūji) ch. secretary general.

ཙུབ་འཁྱིལ་ (dzūbgyii) curly hair.

ཙུམ་ (dzūm) arc. va. to kiss.

ཙུའུ་ (dzūū) ch. small group, team.

ཙུའུ་ཀྲང་ (dzūūdraŋ) ch. leader/ head of a ཙུའུ་.

ཙུའུ་ཆིའུ་ (dzūū cīwu) ch. soccer ¶ཙུའུ་ཆིའུ་རུ་ཁག Soccer team.

ཙུའུ་ཨན་ (dzūūan) ch. histamine.

ཙུའོ་ཐེང་ (dzūwo tēŋ) ch. Sato (former Prime Minister of Japan).

ཙུའོ་ཐེང་སྲིད་གཞུང་ (dzūwo tēŋ sīishuŋ) ch.tib. the Sato government (Japan).

ཙུའོ་དབྱི་ (dzūwo yī) ch. custom of showing greeting/ respect when giving sth. by placing the palm under the elbow of one's arm at right angles; va.—ཞུ་.

ཙུའོ་ཆན་དར་འབུ་ (dzūdzɛn ta̲rbu) ch.tib. tussah, tussore.

ཙུའོ་ཆན་དར་སྐུད་ (dzūdzɛn ta̲rgüü) ch.tib. tussah silk.

ཙེ་ནེ་ (dzēne) 1. firm, unwavering. 2. all, entire.

ཙེ་པོ་ (dzēbo) a small basket carried on the back.

ཙེ་རེ་ (dzēre) squeaking sound (e.g., made by creaking doors).

ཙེག་ཙེག (dzēgdzeg) rustling sound.

ཙེབ་ཙེབ་ (dzēbdzeb) sharp pointed.

ཙེམ་སྐྱི་ (dzēmgye) vi. to worry and fear sth. bad will occur ¶གྲོང་ཁྱེར་བཙོག་པ་དེར་སླེབས་དུས་ན་མི་ཡོང་ངམ་བསམས་པའི་ཙེམ་སྐྱིས་བྱུང་ I worried and feared for my health when I came to the unhygienic (dirty) town.

ཙེམ་ཙེ་ (dzēmdze) sm. ཛམ་ཙེ་.

ཙེམ་ཚ་པོ་ (dzēm tsābo) squeamish.

ཙེམ་ཟ་ (dzēm sa̲) sm. ཙེམ་སྐྱི་.

ཙེར་ (dzēr) a squeaking noise.

ཙེར་ཙེར་ (dzērdzer) sm. ཙེ་རེ་.

ཙེལ་པོ་ (dzēēbo) basket for carrying things on the back.

ཙོ་ལོ་ (dzōlo) sm. སོག་སོག.

ཙོག (dzōò) sm. ཙོག་པུར་སྡོད་.

ཙོག་གེ་ (dzōòge) erect; va.—ལངས་ to stand erect; va.—སྡོད་ to sit erect.

ཙོག་སྒྲོམ་ (drōgdrom) a square wooden frame with a cushion inside.

ཙོག་ཐུམ་ (dzōgdum) coins wrapped in a cloth (usu. 1 dotse).

ཙོག་པ་ (dzōgba) sm. ཙོག་པུ་.

ཙོག་པུ་ (dzōgbu) upright.

ཙོག་པུར་ (dzōgbur) squatting; vi.—སྡོད་ to squat, to sit on one's haunches/ heels.

ཙོག་པུར་སྡོད་ (dzōgbur dö̱ö̱) see ཙོག་པུར་.

ཙོག་པོ་ (dzōgbo) 1. pestle. 2. stone.

ཙོག་མི་ཚུགས་ (dzōg mi̲ tsūù) vi. to be unable to stand erect (usu. toddlers).

ཙོག་ཙོག (dzōgdzog) 1. upright, erect; va.—བྱེད་. 2. squatting down on one's heels; va.—བྱེད་. 3. sth. piled up (e.g., dirt/ sand); va.—བཟོ་.

ཙོག་ཙོག་ཆགས་ (dzōgdzoò cāà) vi. to be upright, to be piled up.

ཙོག་ཙོག་པུ་ (dzōg dzōgbu) sm. ཙོག་ཙོག.

ཙོག་ཙོག་པུར་ (dzōg dzōgbur) sm. ཙོག་ཙོག.

ཙོག་ཙོག་བྱེད་ (dōgdzoò ce̲e) 1. va. to sit upright

(e.g., in a bed). 2. va. to squat on one's haunches/ heels.

ཙོག་ཙོག་བཟོ་ (dōgdzoò so̲) va. to make sth. into a pile.

ཙོང་ (dōŋ) onion.

ཙོང་ཁ་པ་ (dzōŋgaba) Tsongkhapa.

ཙོང་མདོག (dzōŋdɔɔ̀) light green.

ཙོང་ཙོང་ (dzōŋdzoŋ) long/ tall objects like hats.

ཙོབ་རླུབ་ཆགས་ (dzōbgyεε cāà) vi. to become completely wet.

ཙོབ་རླུབ་བཟོ་ (dzōbgyεε so̲) va. to make completely wet.

ཙོས་ཙི་ (dzȫòdzi) cigarette holder.

གཙག: p. གཙགས་; f. གཙོགས་; imp. གཙོགས་ (dzāà) va. to draw out/ extract blood ¶ ཁྲག་གཙག་གི་འདུག (He) is drawing blood (as a medical treatment).

གཙག་ཁབ་ (dzāàgəb) needle used in acupuncture, lancet used for drawing blood; va.—རྒྱག to do acupuncture, to draw blood.

གཙག་གདན་ (dzāàdεn) a Tibetan medical clasp for holding the tongue still when draining blood from it.

གཙག་བུ་ (dzāgbu) sm. གཙག་ཁབ་.

གཙག་བུ་སྣ་རེ་ཁ་ (dzāgbu dārega) a traditional Tibetan medical tool for draining blood.

གཙག་བུ་འབྲི་ལྕེ་ (dzāgbu drije) a traditional Tibetan medical tool.

གཙག་བྲིས་ (dzāgdriì) tattooing; va.—རྒྱག.

གཙང་ (dzāŋ) 1. clean ¶ ཁང་པ་འདི་གཙང་ཞིང་ཆེ་བ་ཞིག་འདུག This house is big and clean. 2. the Tsang area (the southwest part of Central Tibet). 3. va. to clear up a debt, to reimburse sb. ¶ ངའི་བུ་ལོན་ཚང་མ་གཙང་སོང་ I have cleared all my debts. 4. vi. to be ended/ finished ¶ ཁ་སང་ནས་ངའི་གུང་སེང་གཙང་སོང་ My vacation ended yesterday. 5. (— + vb.) doing completely ¶ གཙང་སྤྲོད་ Delivering completely.

གཙང་སྐད་ (dzāŋgεὲ) the dialect used in Tsang.

གཙང་ཁང་ (dzāŋgaŋ) rooms inside temples where statues are kept.

གཙང་ཁུལ་ (dzəŋgüü) the Tsang area.

གཙང་ཁེ་ (dzāŋke) net profit.

གཙང་ཁྲུས་ (dzāŋdrüù) washing; va.—བྱེད་.

གཙང་འཁྱེར་ (dzāŋgyer) taking everything out (cleaning); va.—བྱེད་ to take everything out, to clean out.

གཙང་འཁྲུད་ཁང་ (dzāŋdrugaŋ) 1. laundry/ washing room. 2. laundering/ cleaning shop.

གཙང་འཁྲུད་ཚོས་སྒྱུར་ཁང་ (dzāŋdru tsȫògyurgaŋ) laundry/ cleaning and dyeing shop.

གཙང་གད་ (dzāŋgεὲ) 1. sweeping to clean up; va.—རྒྱག. 2. removing spoiled parts of vegetables; va.—རྒྱག.

གཙང་དགོན་ (dzāŋgön) shung. a monastery in which the monks are adhering to their vows.

གཙང་སྒྲིག (dzəŋdrig) clearing away, rearranging, clearing up, reorganizing, putting in order; va.—བྱེད་.

གཙང་སྒྲིག་ལེགས་བསྡུ་ (dzəŋdrig le̲gdu) putting in order and simplifying/ streamlining; va.—བྱེད་.

གཙང་བསྒྲིགས་ (dzəŋdrig) sm. གཙང་སྒྲིག.

གཙང་བཅོམ་ (dzāŋ jōm) robbing completely; va.—བྱེད་.

གཙང་བཅོས་ (dzāŋjöò) completely changing/ reforming/ transforming; va.—བྱེད་.

གཙང་ཆག (dzāŋcaà) complete elimination/ exemption (from taxes/ debts).

གཙང་ཆབ་ (dzāŋjəb) sm. གཙང་ཆུ་.

གཙང་ཆུ་ (dzāŋju) 1. clean water. 2. river, stream. 3. rivers flowing from the Tsang area of Tibet.

གཙང་མཆོད་ (dzāŋjöò) an offering made to gods before using/ consuming sth.

གཙང་འཇལ་ (dzāŋjεε) completely paying off a debt or a tax obligation; va.—བྱེད་.

གཙང་ཉ་ (dzāŋña) river fish.

གཙང་ཐག་ཆོད་ (dzāŋda cȫò) vi. to be settled completely.

གཙང་དག (dzāŋña)1. clean; va.—བཟོ་ to clean. 2. wiping out, eradicating, purging; va.—བཟོ་ ¶ གསར་བརྗེ་ར་ངོ་རྒོལ་པ་གཙང་དག་བཟོ་དགོས་ (We) must eradicate the counterrevolutionaries.

གཙང་དག་འཐུང་ (dzāŋdaà tūŋ) va. to drink to the bottom in one sip, to drink bottoms up.

གཙང་དག་བཟོ་ (dzāŋdaà so̲) 1. va. to clean. 2. va. to wipe out, to eradicate.

གཙང་དག་ཤུལ་མེད་བཟོ་ (dzāŋdaà shǖümeè so̲) 1. va. to clean so that there is no trace (of dirt). 2. va. to wipe out/ eradicate totally.

གཙང་དུས་ (dzāŋdüù) 1. a period of expiration. 2. a period of time to clear debts ¶ བུ་ལོན་འདིའི་གཙང་དུས་ལོ་གསུམ་གྱི་ནང་ཚུད་ཡིན་ This debt must be cleared within three years. 3. the time when a vacation is over ¶ གུང་སེང་གཙང་དུས་ཕྱིར་ལོག་ཡོང་དགོས་ (You) have to come back when your vacation is over.

གཙང་དྲས་རྒྱག (dzāŋdrεὲ gya̲à) va. to cut in a straight line.

གཙང་མདའ་ (dzāŋda) shung. commander/ general of the Tsang Regiment in tt.

གཙང་དོག་དོག (dzāŋ do̲gdog) tidy, neat, clean.

གཙང་སྣམ་ (dzāŋnam) woolen material woven in གཙང་.

གཙང་པ་ (dzāŋba) a person from གཙང.

གཙང་པོ་ (dzāŋbo) 1. a river. 2. the main river that bisects Tibet and then turns south to flow into India as the Brahmaputra River.

གཙང་པོ་འཕྲེད་བཅད་ (dzāŋbo trēèjεὲ) crossing a river transversely; va.—གཏོང་.

གཙང་སྤྱི་ (dzāŋji) shung. governor-general of Tsang in tt.

གཙང་སྤྱོད་ (dzāŋjöò) 1. principled behavior. 2. toilet, lavatory.

གཙང་སྤྲོད་ (dzāŋdröò) sm. གཙང་འཇལ་.

གཙང་ཕུད་ (dzāŋbüù) sm. གཙང་འབུད་.

གཙང་ཕྱགས་ (dzāŋjaà) annihilating, eradicating, exterminating; va.—རྒྱག; —བྱེད་ ¶ དགྲ་དམག་གཙང་ཕྱགས་མཐར་ཕྱིན་བྱས་ཡོད་ (We) completely annihilated the enemy [Lit. sweeping clean].

གཙང་འཕྱག (dzāŋjaà) sm. གཙང་ཕྱགས་.

གཙང་འཕྱར་ (dzāŋjaa) winnowing grain; va.—གཏོང་.

གཙང་འཕྲོག (dzāŋdrɔɔ̀) cleaning out sb. by robbing; robbing everything a person has; va.—བྱེད་ ¶ ཇག་པས་རྒྱུ་ནོར་ཡོད་ཚད་གཙང་འཕྲོག་བྱས་པ་རེད་ The bandits robbed (them) of everything.

གཙང་འཕྲོད་ (dzāŋdröò) sm. འཕྲོད་བསྟེན་.

གཙང་བ་ (dzāŋwa) clean, pure; va.—བྱེད་ to clean, purify ¶ མི་གཙང་བའི་ཅ་ལག Impure/ unclean things.

གཙང་བྲིས་ (dzāŋdri) 1. making a final copy, writing a copy neatly; va.—རྒྱག. 2. thankas painted in the Tsang style.

གཙང་དྲི་ (dzāŋdre) sm. གཙང་མ་ and བཙོག་པ་.

གཙང་འབུད་ (dzāŋbüù) eliminating, expelling, firing from a job; va.—བྱེད་.

གཙང་འབུལ་ (dzāŋbüü) h. of གཙང་སྤྲོད་.

གཙང་སྦྲ་ (dzāŋdra) cleanliness, sanitation, hygiene; va.—བྱེད་ ¶ མི་སྒེར་གྱི་གཙང་སྦྲ་ Personal hygiene.

གཙང་སྦྲ་དོད་པོ་ (dzāŋdra tö̲òbo) clean, hygienic.

གཙང་སྦྲ་འཕྲོད་བསྟེན་ (dzāŋdra trȫòden) sanitation and hygiene.

གཙང་སྦྲ་རུ་ཁག (dzāŋdra ru̲gaà) hygiene/ sanitation unit.

གཙང་སྦྲ་ཁང་ (dzāŋdragaŋ) toilet.

གཙང་མ་ (dzāŋma) 1. clean; va.—བཟོ་ to clean ¶ སྟོད་ཐུང་གཙང་མ་ཞིག་ཡོད་ I have a clean shirt. ¶ ང་ཚོས་ཁང་པ་འདི་གཙང་མ་བཟོ་དགོས་ We have to clean the house. 2. cleaning up, mopping up (an enemy) ¶ དགྲ་བོ་ལྷག་འཕྲོས་རྣམས་གཙང་མ་བཟོས་པ་རེད་ (They) cleaned up the remnants of the enemy soldiers. 3. full, complete ¶ རང་བཙན་

གཙང་མ་ Complete or full independence. 4. pure ། ཁོས་དབུས་སྐད་གཙང་མ་རྒྱག་གི་འདུག He speaks pure Central Tibetan (dialect).

གཙང་མའི་ཟླ་བ་ (dzāŋmɛ dawa) the 5th month of the Tibetan calendar.

གཙང་མོ་ (dzāŋmo) a woman from གཙང་ province.

གཙང་དམག (dzāŋmaà) soldiers from གཙང་ province.

གཙང་དམི་ (dzāŋme) sm. གཙང་རྨི་.

གཙང་གཙང་ (dzāŋdzaŋ) only, entirely, wholly, one hundred percent ། ང་བོད་པ་གཙང་གཙང་ཡིན་ I am wholly Tibetan (both parents Tibetan).

གཙང་བཙན་ (dzāŋdzɛn) a clear/ authentic order.

གཙང་བཙོག (dzāŋdzɔ̀ɔ) clean and dirty.

གཙང་རྩིས་ (dzə̄ŋdzii) full settlement of an account; va.—རྒྱག ། བུ་ལོན་ཚང་མ་གཙང་རྩིས་བརྒྱབ་པ་ཡིན་ I fully settled the entire loan (paid it back fully).

གཙང་ཚད་ (dzāŋdzɛɛ̀) degree of cleanliness/ sanitation.

གཙང་འཛིན་ (dzāŋdzin) shung. receipt for completely paying sth. such as a lease/ loan ། ལོ་ལོའི་ཐོབས་འབབ་དགོན་སྡེའི་གཙང་འཛིན་རིམ་པ་བཅས་ར་སྤྲོད་བྱུང་བ་འདུས་མེད་ They had receipts to prove that they had paid the yearly lease to the monastery.

གཙང་རྫོང་ (dzāŋdzoŋ) districts in Tsang province.

གཙང་ཞིང་གྲ་འགྲིག་པོ་ (dzāŋshiŋ tra drigbu) clean and neat.

གཙང་ཞིབ་ (dzə̄ŋshib) investigation, examination, check, audit; va.—བྱེད་.

གཙང་བཞི་ (dzə̄ŋshi) abbr. of གཙང་བཤེར་བཞི་.

གཙང་བཞེས་གནང་ (dzāŋsheè nāŋ) h. of ཞབས་དག་རྒྱག.

གཙང་ཟོན་ (dzāŋsön) woolen boot from Tsang.

གཙང་རགས་ (dzāŋraà) a dam on a river.

གཙང་རིས་ (dzə̄ŋrii) 1. sm. གཙང་བྲིས་. 2. abode of the gods.

གཙང་རུམ་ (dzāŋrum) a carpet from Tsang.

གཙང་ལེགས་གྲུབ་ (dzāŋlegdrub) name of one of the first seven monks during the time of King Trisong Detsan.

གཙང་ཤོག (dzāŋshoò) 1. paper from Tsang. 2. clean paper.

གཙང་བཤང་ (dzāŋshaŋ) completely clearing sth. (a path, a canal, etc.); va.—བྱེད་.

གཙང་བཤལ་ (dzāŋshɛɛ) rinsing; va.—གཏོང་ to rinse.

གཙང་བཤུས་ (dzāŋshüü) a clean copy of sth.; va.—རྒྱག; —བྱེད་ to prepare a clean copy of sth., to copy neatly.

གཙང་བཤེར་ (dzāŋshee) taking inventory, cleaning up; va.—བྱེད་ ། དེང་སང་མཛོད་ཁང་གཙང་བཤེར་བྱེད་པའི་སྐབས་རེད་ These days they are in the midst of taking inventory of the contents of the warehouse.

གཙང་བཤེར་བཞི་ (dzāŋshee shi) the four cleanups (ཆབ་སྲིད་གཙང་བཤེར་དང་བསམ་བློ་གཙང་བཤེར་ རྩ་འཛུགས་གཙང་བཤེར་ དཔལ་འབྱོར་གཙང་བཤེར་) clean up politics, clean up ideology, clean up organization and clean up economy) (political slogan).

གཙང་སིང་ངེ་བ་ (dzāŋ siŋŋewa) very clean.

གཙང་སིང་སིང་ (dzāŋ siŋsiŋ) sm. གཙང་སིང་ངེ་བ་.

གཙང་སེལ་ (dzāŋsee) 1. eradicating, exterminating, liquidating, completely destroying, purging; va.—བྱེད་ ། རྨོངས་དད་ཀྱི་བསམ་བློ་གཙང་སེལ་བྱ་དགོས་ (We) have to eradicate superstitious thinking. 2. pasteurization; va.—བྱེད་ ། འབྲོག་ལས་ཁང་དེས་འོ་མ་དེ་དག་འཕྲུལ་འཁོར་གྱིས་གཙང་སེལ་བྱས་པ་རེད་ The animal husbandry office pasteurized the milk by machine.

གཙང་གསུམ་ (dzāŋsum) the three atrocities: burn all, kill all, loot all (གཙང་སྲེག གཙང་གསོད་ གཙང་འཕྲོག) (political term relating to the Japanese occupation of China).

གཙབ་: p. **བཙབས་**; f. **བཙབ་**; imp. **གཙོབས་** (dzə̄b) va. to mince/ chop ། ཤ་ཞིབ་མོ་ར་གཙོབས་རོགས་ (Please) chop the meat finely.

གཙབ་གྲི་ (dzə̄bdri) chopping/ mincing knife, cleaver.

གཙབ་གཅོད་ (dzə̄bjöö) chopping, mincing.

གཙབ་སྟན་ (dzə̄bdɛn) sm. གཙབ་གདན་.

གཙབ་གདན་ (dābdɛn) chopping block/ board.

གཙབ་ཤིང་ (dzə̄bshiŋ) wooden wedge put under the leg of a table, chair, etc. to steady it; va.—རྒྱག.

གཙའ་ (dzā) rust, tarnish; vi.—རྒྱག to rust, to tarnish.

གཙའ་ཐུབ་ངར་ལྕགས་ (dzātub ŋarjaà) stainless steel.

གཙའ་ནད་ (dzānɛè) blight, rust (of crops).

གཙའ་མི་ཆགས་པའི་ངར་ལྕགས་ (dzāmi cāgbɛ ŋarjaà) stainless steel.

གཙིགས་ (dzii) 1. va. to bare one's teeth, to snarl. 2. important, valued.

གཙིགས་ཀྱི་ཡི་གེ (dzīg jēèba) sm. གཙིགས་ཡིག.

གཙིགས་ཁ་ (dzīigə) sm. དམ་བཅའ་.

གཙིགས་བཅས་པ་ (dzīg jēèba) shung. sm. གཏན་ལ་འབེབས་པ་

གཙིགས་ཆེ་བ་ (dzīi cēwa) of great value, high regard/ esteem; va.—བྱེད་ to value greatly.

གཙིགས་ཆེན་ (dzīijen) high esteem, regard/ value; va.—བྱེད་; —འཛིན་ to value/ esteem/ regard highly.

གཙིགས་ཆེན་པོ་ (dzīi cēmbo) sm. གཙིགས་ཆེན་.

གཙིགས་མཐོང་ (dzīgdoŋ) respect, esteem; va.—བྱེད་.

གཙིགས་སྣང་ (dzīinaŋ) sm. གཙིགས་མཐོང་.

གཙིགས་བློ་ (dzīilo) feeling of great respect/ regard.

གཙིགས་གཙིགས་ (dzīgdzii) treasuring/ valuing/ cherishing, holding in esteem; va.—བྱེད་.

གཙིགས་འཛིན་ (dzīŋdzin) sm. གཙིགས་བཟུང་.

གཙིགས་བཟུང་ (dzīi suŋ) va. to consider important, to hold in esteem, to cherish/ value.

གཙིགས་ཡིག (dzīiyii) arc. letters carved on stone pillars.

གཙིགས་སུ་ཆེ་བ་ (dzīgsu cēwa) sm. གཙིགས་ཆེ་བ་.

གཙིགས་སུ་འཛིན་ (dzīgsu dzin) sm. གཙིགས་བཟུང་.

གཙིར་སྒྲ་ (dzīrdra) squeaking sound.

གཙིར་རིལ་ཝུ་རིལ་ (dzīrrii wurii) crowded, packed, jammed in.

གཙུག (dzūg) 1. the top/ crown of the head. 2. arc. palace.

གཙུག་མཁན་ (dzūggɛn) abbr. of གཙུག་ལག་མཁན་པོ་.

གཙུག་འཁྱིལ་ (dzūggyii) cowlick.

གཙུག་རྒྱན་ (dzūggyɛn) head ornament.

གཙུག་སྒྲོ་ (dzūgdro) feather on the head of a fowl.

གཙུག་ཏུ་བཀུར་ (dzūgdu gūr) sm. སྤྱི་བོར་བཀུར་.

གཙུག་ཏོར་ (dzūgdɔɔ) 1. a growth on the head of very holy people (e.g., Buddha). 2. hair tied in a bundle on top of head.

གཙུག་ཏོར་འཁྱོགས་ (dzūgdɔɔ kyɔ̄ɔ) vi. to be drunk/ tipsy/ intoxicated.

གཙུག་ན་རིན་ཆེན་ (dzūgna rinjen) king of the Nagas.

གཙུག་ནོར་ (dzūgnɔɔ) 1. supreme, consummate, highest. 2. a jewel worn on top of the head.

གཙུག་སྤུ་ (dzūgbu) hair on the top of the head.

གཙུག་ཕུད་ (dzūgbüü) 1. the best, the most outstanding. 2. the strands of hair ceremonially cut when becoming a monk.

གཙུག་ཕུད་འཁྱིལ་བ་ (dzūgbüü kyīiwə) braided hair tied in a circle behind the head.

གཙུག་འཕྲུ་ (dzūŋdru) comb. of a rooster.

གཙུག་ཞྭ་ (dzūùsha) a small cap.

གཙུག་གཡུ་ (dzūùyu) turquoise ornament worn on the top of the head.

གཙུག་གཡུ་ཐག་པ་ (dzūùyu tāgba) a turquoise head ornament worn by wives of high ranking officials of the traditional Tibetan government.

གཙུག་ལག་ཁང་ (dzūglagaŋ) 1. temple. 2. the Lhasa Cathedral (that houses the Jokang).

གཙུག་ལག་མཁན་པོ་ (dzūglaà kɛ̄mbo) someone knowledgeable in cultural studies.

གཙུབ་: p. **གཙུབས་**; f. **གཙུབ་**; imp. **གཙུབས་** (dzūb) va. to rub.

གཙུབ་གདན་ (dzūbdɛn) sm. གཙུབ་སྟན་.

གཙུབ་སྟན་ (dzūbdɛn) wooden base used for making fire by a rubbing a stick on it.

གཙུབ་ཤིང་ (dzūbshiŋ) a wooden rubbing stick used for making fire.

གཙུབས་ (dzūb) p. and imp. of གཙུབ་.

གཙེ་: p. གཙེས་; f. གཙེ་; imp. གཙེས་ (dzē) 1. vi. to be hurt/ damaged/ injured/ sick ། ནད་ཀྱིས་གཙེས་ནས་ཤི་བ་རེད་ (He) got sick with an illness and died. 2. f. of འཚེ་.

གཙེའུ་ (dzēwu) a traditional Tibetan surgical tool.

གཙེར་ (dzēr) va. to annoy/ bother (usu. by making noise).

གཙེར་སུན་ (dzērsün) bothering, annoying; va.—བྱེད་.

གཙེས་ (dzēè) p. of གཙེ་ or འཚེ་.

གཙོ་ (dzō) abbr. of གཙོ་བོ་.

གཙོ་སྐུ་ (dzōgu) the main statue in a temple or shrine.

གཙོ་སྐྱོང་ (dzōgyoŋ) 1. leading/ chief/ dominant; va.—བྱེད་ to lead, to dominate, to act as chief (at a meeting or event this could convey chairman).

གཙོ་སྐྱོང་པ་ (dzōgyoŋ) leader, chief, chairman, head.

གཙོ་ཁྲིད་ (dzōdrii) 1. leading, dominanting; va.—བྱེད་ to dominate, to lead ། གཙོ་ཁྲིད་ཀྱི་བསམ་པ་ Dominant ideas. 2. the main teacher/ lecturer; va.—བྱེད་.

གཙོ་འཁུར་ (dzōgur) carrying the main responsibility/ initiative; va.—བྱེད་ to take the main responsibility.

གཙོ་འཁོར་ (dzōgɔɔ) the head and the servants/ retinue.

གཙོ་གལ་ཅན་ (dzō kɛ̄ɛ̄jɛn) sm. གཙོ་གལ་ཆེ་བ་.

གཙོ་གལ་ཆེ་བ་ (dzōkɛɛ cēwa) important, essential.

གཙོ་གལ་ཆེན་པོ་ (dzōkɛɛ cēmbo) sm. གཙོ་གལ་ཆེ་བ.

གཙོ་གྱུར་ (dzōgyur) the main, the chief, the most important ། ཚོགས་འདུ་འདིའི་ནང་སྲིད་འཛིན་འདེམས་རྒྱུ་དེ་གཙོ་གྱུར་གྱི་ལས་དོན་ཞིག་རེད་ The most important (task) of this meeting is selecting a president.

གཙོ་གྱུར་དབང་རྩ་ (dzōgyur wāŋdza) nerve center.

གཙོ་གྲས་ (dzōdrɛɛ̀) the main person, the main superior.

གཙོ་འགན་ (dzōngɛn) the main responsibility; va.—ལེན་; —ཁུར་; —བཞེས་ to take the main responsibility, to head, to lead.

གཙོ་འགན་བཞེས་མི་ (dzōngɛn sh̲eèmi) h. of གཙོ་འགན་ལེན་མི་.

གཙོ་འགན་ལེན་མི་ (dzōngɛn l̲enmi) the person who is responsible, the person in charge.

གཙོ་འགན་ཁྱེར་མཁན་ (dzōngɛn kyērñɛn) sm. གཙོ་འགན་ལེན་མི་.

གཙོ་རྒན་ (dzōgɛn) abbr. of གཙོ་དྲག་དང་རྒན་པོ་.

གཙོ་རྒོལ་ (dzōgöö) the main/ chief battle; va.—བྱེད་ to fight the main/ chief battle.

གཙོ་རྒོལ་དམིགས་འབེན་ (dzōgöö mīŋben) main target of an attack.

གཙོ་སྒྲུབ་ (dzōdrub) main responsibility, main charge; va.—བྱེད་ to be the main one responsible for, to be the main one in charge of, to direct, to manage.

གཙོ་བཅོས་ (dzōjöö) main treatment.

གཙོ་ཆུང་བ་ (dzō cūŋwə) subordinate, secondary, less important.

གཙོ་ཆེ་ (dzōce) important, essential, chief, major.

གཙོ་ཆེ་བ་ (dzō cēwa) sm. གཙོ་ཆེ་.

གཙོ་ཆེན་ (dzōjen) sm. གཙོ་ཆེ་.

གཙོ་གཉེར་ (dzōñer) the main person in charge, the general head/ manager; va.—བྱེད་ to head, to manage, to administer, to lead.

གཙོ་གཉེར་སྡེ་ཁག (dzōñer d̲egaà) a directly controlled section/ office/ department/ division.

གཙོ་མཉམ་ (dzōñam) of equal importance ། ཚང་མའི་ལས་དོན་གཙོ་མཉམ་རེད་ Everybody's work is equally important.

གཙོ་རྟེན་ (dzōden) sm. རྟེན་གཙོ་.

གཙོ་དོན་ (dzōdön) the main idea/ issue.

གཙོ་དྲག (dzōdraà) shung. a custom begun by the 13th Dalai Lama wherein important families in a district were appointed to represent the peasants.

གཙོ་བདག (dzōdaà) leader, chief, ruler.

གཙོ་འདེབས་ལོ་ཏོག (dzōden l̲odoò) staple crop, main crop.

གཙོ་འདོན་ (dzōdön) the chief or most important task; va.—བྱེད་ to hold/ take as the chief or most important task ། ཚང་མས་ཞི་འཇགས་ཡོང་བ་གཙོ་འདོན་བྱེད་དགོས་ (We) must hold the coming of peace and order as the most important task.

གཙོ་གནད་ (dzōnɛɛ̀) main point/ issue, crux of the matter.

གཙོ་སྤེལ་ཕལ་གནོན་ (dzōbel pɛ̄ɛ̄nön) increase the main and suppress the ordinary/ common/ secondary (political slogan).

གཙོ་ཕལ་ (dzōbɛɛ) the main and secondary ། ལས་ཀ་ག་རེ་བྱེད་ཀྱང་གཙོ་ཕལ་དབྱེ་བ་ཡོད་པ་བྱེད་དགོས་ Whatever work one does, one must always differentiate between the main and the secondary.

གཙོ་ཕལ་གོ་ལྡོག (dzōbɛɛ k̲odɔɔ̀) reversing/ inverting the main and secondary, reversing/ inverting the important and the unimportant; va.—བྱེད་.

གཙོ་བོ་ (dzōō) chief, principal, foremost, main, most important ། འགལ་བ་གཙོ་བོ་ The principal contradiction. ། མགྲོན་གྱི་གཙོ་བོ་ The guest of honor. ། གཙོ་བོ་ཞིང་ལས་ངལ་རྩོལ་བྱེད་མཁན་ཡིན་ལ་ཚེ་གཡོག་ཀྱང་རེད་ Most important, they are laborers and also lifetime servants.

གཙོ་བོ་གྲོས་ལ་དབང་བ་ (dzōō tr̲ööla wāŋwa) person with the main power in a discussion.

གཙོ་བོར་ (dzōō) chief, principal, foremost, main, most important; va.—བཟུང་; —འཛིན་; —འདོན་; —ཐེན་ to hold as the most important/ main/ chief/ principal ། ཞི་བདེ་འབྱུང་ཐབས་ཀྱི་ལས་དོན་གཙོ་བོར་བཟུང་ནས་ Holding the cause of peace as the most important.

གཙོ་བོར་ལྟ་བ་ (dzōwor dāwa) shung. revered ། སྐྱེ་བོ་སེར་སྐྱ་ཐམས་ཅད་ཀྱིས་གཙོ་བོར་ལྟ་བ་ Revered by all monks and lay people.

གཙོ་བོར་བཟུང་ (dzōwor s̲un̲) see གཙོ་བོར་.

གཙོ་མོ་ (dzōmo) lady/ woman of high birth or status.

གཙོ་ཚིག (dzōdzii) subject, actor (in grammar).

གཙོ་མཛད་ (dzōdzɛɛ̀) leader, person in charge, director.

གཙོ་འཛིན་ (dzōmdzin) leader, person in charge; va.—བྱེད་ to lead, to be in charge ། གསར་བརྗེའི་གཙོ་འཛིན་ཚོ་ Revolutionary leaders.

གཙོ་འཛིན་མི་སྣ་ (dzōndzin m̲inə) leading personnel, persons in leading positions.

གཙོ་བཞུགས་ (dzōshuù) president, chairman, chief.

གཙོ་ཟས་ (dzōsɛɛ̀) staple food, main food.

གཙོ་བཟུང་ (dzō s̲un̲) sm. གཙོ་བོར་བཟུང་.

གཙོ་བཟུང་བྱེད་ (dzōsuŋ c̲eè) sm. གཙོ་གཟུང་བྱེད་.

གཙོ་ཤུགས་ (dzōshuù) the main force ། གཙོ་ཤུགས་དམག་དཔུང་ཚན་ཁག The main military force.

གཙོ་ཤུགས་དམག་དཔུང་ (dzōshuù māgbuŋ) the main military force.

གཙོ་ཤུགས་དམག་མི་ (dzōshuù māāmi) soldiers in the main military force.

གཙོགས་ (dzɔɔ̀) imp. of གཙོག.

གཙོད་ (dzöö) Tibetan antelope.

གཙོད་ཁྲག (dzöödraà) Tibetan antelope blood (used in Tibetan medicine).

གཙོད་མ་ (dzööma) female Tibetan antelope.

གཙོད་གཞུ་ (dzööshu) bow made from the horn of a Tibetan antelope.

གཙོད་རུ་ (dzööru) Tibetan antelope horn.

གཙོད་རྭ་ (dzööra) sm. གཙོད་རུ་.

གཙོབས་ (dzōb) imp. of གཙབ་.

གཙོར་འདོན་ (dzōrd̲ön) sm. གཙོ་འདོན་.

གཙོར་བཟུང་བྱེད་ (dzōōsuŋ c̲ɛ̄è) sm. གཙོ་བོར་བཟུང་.

གཙོས་ (dzöö) conveys that a group is headed by

(the most important thing or person) ¶ ཡུལ་དེའི་སྲིད་འཛིན་གྱིས་གཙོས་དབུ་ཁྲིད་མང་པོ་ཕེབས་པ་རེད་ Headed by the president, many leaders of the country came. ¶ མི་གོས་གཙོས་པའི་བཙན་རྒྱལ་རིང་ལུགས་པ་ The imperialists, headed by the U.S.

གཙོས་པ་ (dzööba) as the main/ chief one.

བཙག (dzāà) 1. f. of འཙག. 2. red ochre.

བཙག་སྙིགས་ (dzāgñii) oil/ butter sediment.

བཙག་དང་བསྡེབས་ན་དམར་ རམས་དང་བསྡེབས་ན་སྔོ་ (dzāàdaŋ d̲ebna māā r̲amdaŋ dēbna ŋō) people will be affected by the company they keep [Lit. (he who) comes in contact with ochre will turn red, and (he who) comes into contact with indigo will turn blue].

བཙག་གདན་ (dzāgdɛn) a red base (in painting).

བཙག་རྡོ་ (dzāgdo) a stone from which red dye is made.

བཙག་སྦུག (dzəgbug) funnel (for pouring oil).

བཙག་དམར་ (dzāgmaa) red dye/ ochre.

བཙགས་ (dzāà) p. of འཙག.

བཙགས་ཁུ་ (dzāàgu) a filtered liquid.

བཙགས་དངོས་ (dzāàŋöö) the material that is filtered.

བཙགས་འདེམས་ (dzāgdem) selecting the best.

བཙགས་མ་ (dzāgma) sm. བཙགས་དངོས་.

བཙང་ (dzāŋ) f. of འཚང་.

བཙང་རྒྱག (dzāŋ gya̲à) va. to put padding in a box to prevent the objects from breaking.

བཙངས་ (dzāŋ) p. of འཚང་.

བཙངས་རྒྱག (dzāŋ gya̲à) sm. བཙང་རྒྱག.

བཙན་ (dzɛn) 1. power, force, strength. 2. (— + vb.) doing a verbal action by force ¶ བཙན་བཟུང་ Seizing by force. 3. a type of spirit/ demon. 4. abbr. of བཙན་པོ་. 5. abbr. of བཙན་རྒྱལ་.

བཙན་བཀག (dzɛ̄ngaà) (forcible) detention, (forcible) blockage/ obstruction/ prevention; va.—བྱེད་ to (forcibly) detain/ block/ obstruct/ prevent ¶ ཁོ་ཚོས་ཆོས་དང་རིག་གཞུང་བཙན་བཀག་བྱས་པ་རེད་ They prevented (the practice of) religion and culture.

བཙན་བཀའ་ (dzɛ̄nga) an order/ command (backed by the threat of force); va.—གཏོང་; —འབེབས་.

བཙན་བཀུག (dzɛ̄nguù) conscripting, summoning by force; va.—བྱེད་ ¶ གཞུང་གིས་ཡུལ་མི་མང་པོ་ལམ་ལས་བྱེད་པར་བཙན་བཀུག་བྱས་པ་རེད་ The government conscripted many local people to do road work.

བཙན་བཀོལ་ (dzɛ̄ngüü) sm. བཙན་བསྐུལ་.

བཙན་སྐུལ་ (dzɛ̄ngüü) sm. བཙན་བསྐུལ་.

བཙན་བསྐུལ་ (dzɛ̄ngüü) coercing, forcing, intimidating; va.—བྱེད་ to coerce, to force, to compel ¶ བཙོན་པ་རྣམས་ལ་ངལ་རྩོལ་བཙན་བསྐུལ་བྱེད་ཀྱི་ཡོད་པ་རེད་ (They) are forcing the prisoners to do manual labor.

བཙན་བསྐུལ་བཀའ་འབེབས་ (dzɛ̄ngüü gāmbeb) coercive commanding, ordering forcibly.

བཙན་ཁང་ (dzɛ̄ngaŋ) 1. temple where local spirits/ gods reside and are propitiated. 2. a fortress, stronghold.

བཙན་ཁྲིད་ (dzɛ̄ndrii) taking away by force, abducting, hijacking; va.—བྱེད་.

བཙན་མཁར་ (dzɛ̄ngar) fortress, stronghold, citadel.

བཙན་འཁྱེར་ (dzɛ̄ngyer) forcibly carrying away, robbing, stealing; va.—བྱེད་.

བཙན་གོས་ (dzɛ̄ngöö) robes worn by oracles.

བཙན་གླ་ (dzɛ̄nla) lease/ rent obtained through coercion or force.

བཙན་གླའི་ས་ཆ་ (dzɛ̄nlɛ sāja) a concession (foreign) settlement ¶ སྔོན་མ་རྒྱ་ནག་ནང་དུ་བཙན་གླའི་ས་ཆ་མང་པོ་འདུག Formerly there were many (foreign) concessions in China.

བཙན་འགག (dzɛ̄ngaà) a defensive position ¶ རང་བྱུང་གི་བཙན་འགག A natural defensive position.

བཙན་འགེལ་ (dzɛ̄ngee) imposing/ forcing sb.; va.—བྱེད་ ¶ དམག་འཁྲུག་དེ་ཀྲུང་གོའི་མི་དམངས་ཀྱི་མགོ་ཐོག་ཏུ་བཙན་འགེལ་བྱེད་རྩིས་ཡོད་པ་རེད་ (They) plan to impose war on the Chinese people.

བཙན་འགོག (dzɛ̄ngɔɔ) anti-imperialist.

བཙན་འགོག་རྒྱལ་སྐྱོབ་ (dzɛ̄ngɔɔ gyɛ̲ɛ̲gyob) oppose imperialism and defend the nation; va.—བྱེད་ (political slogan).

བཙན་གོད་ (dzɛ̄ngöö) a type of spirit/ demon.

བཙན་རྒོལ་ (dzɛ̄ngöö) 1. committing aggression, attacking; va.—བྱེད་ to commit aggression, to attack by force; va.—བྱེད་. 2. oppose imperialism; va.—བྱེད ¶ བཙན་རྒོལ་དང་ཞི་བདེ་སྲུང་སྐྱོང་བྱེད་དགོས་ (We) must combat imperialism and defend peace.

བཙན་རྒོལ་རྒྱལ་གཅེས་ (dzɛ̄ngöö gyɛ̲ɛ̲jeè) attack imperialists/ imperialism and be patriotic (love the nation); va.—བྱེད་ (political slogan).

བཙན་རྒོལ་དཔུང་ཕྱོགས་ (dzɛ̄ngöö būŋjɔɔ) anti-imperialist camp.

བཙན་རྒོལ་གསར་བརྗེ་ (dzɛ̄ngöö sārje) anti-imperialist revolution.

བཙན་རྒྱལ་ (dzɛ̄ngyɛɛ) an imperialist country.

བཙན་རྒྱལ་རིང་ལུགས་ (dzɛ̄ngyɛɛ ri̲ŋluù) imperialism.

བཙན་རྒྱལ་རིང་ལུགས་ཀྱི་དཔུང་ཁག (dzɛ̄ngyɛɛ ri̲ŋluùgi būŋgaà) the imperialist camp.

བཙན་རྒྱལ་རིང་ལུགས་ཀྱི་དམག་འཁྲུག (dzɛ̄ngyɛɛ ri̲ŋluùgi mōgdruù) an imperialist war.

བཙན་རྒྱལ་རིང་ལུགས་དགའ་ཉེར་བསྙེན་མཁན་ (dzɛ̄ngyɛɛ ri̲ŋluù ga̲ñee dēnñɛn) pro-imperialists (people/ forces).

བཙན་བརྒལ་ (dzɛ̄ngɛɛ) crossing a river or border by force; va.—བྱེད་.

བཙན་སྒྲིག (dzɛ̄ndrii) forcible marriage; va.—བྱེད་.

བཙན་སྒྲིལ་ (dzɛ̄ndrii) forcible acquisition/ annexation; va.—བྱེད་ to forcibly take over, to annex ¶ དམག་ཐོབ་ཙང་ཁོ་ཚོས་ས་ཆ་མང་པོ་བཙན་སྒྲིལ་བྱས་པ་རེད་ Because they won the war they annexed much land.

བཙན་ངག (dzɛ̄nŋaà) a strict order.

བཙན་ངམ་ཆེ་བ་ (dzɛ̄nŋam cēwa) powerful and fierce.

བཙན་གཅོད་ (dzɛ̄njöö) deciding by force, arbitrarily deciding; va.—བྱེད་.

བཙན་འཇོག (dzɛ̄njöö) making sb. sign an agreement/ treaty by force; va.—བྱེད་.

བཙན་བརྗིད་ (dzɛ̄njii) forceful and imposing/ grand ¶ བཙན་བརྗིད་ལྡན་པའི་རྒྱལ་སྤྱིའི་གྲོས་མཐུན་ A forceful and imposing international agreement.

བཙན་ཉམས་ (dzɛ̄nñam) an overbearing attitude; va.—བྱེད་; —སྟོན་ to act in an overbearing fashion.

བཙན་ཉར་ (dzɛ̄nñar) sm. བཀག་ཉར་.

བཙན་ཉེ་ (dzɛ̄nñe) abbr. of བཙན་རྒྱལ་རིང་ལུགས་དགའ་ཉེར་བསྙེན་མཁན་.

བཙན་ཉེ་མཁན་ (dzɛ̄nñeñɛn) pro-imperialists.

བཙན་ཉོ་ (dzɛ̄nño) buying through coercion/ force; va.—བྱེད་.

བཙན་ཉོ་བཙན་ཚོང་ (dzɛ̄nño dzɛ̄ndzoŋ) forcing to buy and sell, buying and selling through coercion; va.—བྱེད་.

བཙན་སྙིག (dzɛ̄nñeg) extorting; va.—བྱེད་ to extort.

བཙན་བཉས་ (dzɛ̄nñɛɛ̀) raping; va.—བྱེད་.

བཙན་གདམ་ (dzɛ̄ndam) sm. བཙན་ངག.

བཙན་ཐབས་ (dzɛ̄ntəb) forcing, coercing, compulsive methods; va.—བྱེད་ to compel, to intimidate, to force, to coerce ¶ གྲོང་གསེབ་པ་འདི་ཚོར་བཙན་ཐབས་ཀྱིས་ལས་ཀ་བསྐུལ་པ་རེད་ (They) coerced the villagers to work.

བཙན་ཐར་ (dzɛ̄ndar) escaping from coercion/ compulsion/ oppression; va.—བྱེད་.

བཙན་དུག (dzɛ̄ndug) sm. བོང་ང་ནག་པོ་.

བཙན་དེད་ (dzɛ̄ndeè) sm. བཙན་འདེད་.

བཙན་མདོས་ (dzɛ̄ndöö) a type of offering made to spirits/ local demon.

བཙན་འདྲི་ (dzɛ̄ndri) questioning by torture; va.—བྱེད་ to question by torture.

བཙན་བདག (dzɛ̄ndaà) tyrant, despot; va.—བྱེད་ to be

a tyrant/ despot, to act tyrannical/ despotic.

བཙན་འདུལ་ (dzɛ̄ndüü) coercion, intimidation; va.—བྱེད་.

བཙན་འདེད་ (dzɛ̄ndeè) forcibly driving/ herding ¶ དམག་མི་ཚོས་མི་མང་པོ་ཁང་པ་ཆུང་ཆུང་ནང་དུ་བཙན་འདེད་བྱས་པ་རེད་ The soldiers drove many people into a small house.

བཙན་སྡིགས་ (dzɛ̄ndig) threatening to use force; va.—སྐྱོད་; —གཏོང་ to threaten to use force.

བཙན་སྡུད་ (dzɛ̄ndüü) taking/ collecting by force; va.—བྱེད་.

བཙན་སྡོད་ (dzɛ̄ndöö) forcible occupation; va.—བྱེད་ to occupy (forcibly) ¶ བཙན་སྡོད་དམག་མི་ Occupation army/ troops.

བཙན་ནན་ (dzɛ̄nnɛn) strict ¶ བཙན་ནན་ཆེ་བའི་ཁྲིམས་ལུགས་ Strict laws.

བཙན་གནོད་ (dzɛ̄nnöö) harming through force; va.—བྱེད་.

བཙན་གནོན་ (dzɛ̄nnön) oppression, suppression; va.—བྱེད་ to oppress.

བཙན་པོ་ (dzɛ̄mbo) 1. power, force ¶ བཙན་པོ་ཨུ་བཙུགས་ Insistence backed by force. 2. strict, stern ¶ ཁྲིམས་བཙན་པོ་ཞེ་དྲག་འདུག The law is very strict. 3. secure, safe ¶ དངུལ་ཁང་འདི་བཙན་པོ་ཞེ་དྲག་འདུག This bank is very secure (well guarded). 4. king ¶ བཙན་པོ་སྲོང་བཙན་སྒམ་པོ་ King Srongtsen Gampo.

བཙན་པོ་དབང་ཡོད་ (dzɛ̄mbo wāŋyöö) acting as a tyrant/ despot, using one's power to force people to do things; va.—བྱེད་. 2. raping; va.—བྱེད་.

བཙན་པོ་ཨུ་ཚུགས་ (dzɛ̄mbo ūdzuù) insisting through force.

བཙན་པོའི་རྒྱལ་ཁབ་ (dzɛ̄mböö gyɛ̱ɛ̱gəb) imperialist countries.

བཙན་པོའི་གཉའ་གནོན་ གཉོམ་པོའི་རྒྱབ་རྟེན་ (dzɛ̄mböö ña̱nön ñōmböö gya̱bden) subdue those who are tyrannical and support those who are humble.

བཙན་དཔྱག་ཐེབས་ (dzɛ̄ndraà tēb) vi. to put sth. in a safe/ secure place and then forget where you put it.

བཙན་སྤེལ་ (dzɛ̄nbel) forcibly spreading/ disseminating; va.—བྱེད་ ¶ ཁོ་ཚོས་ཡིག་ཆ་དེ་བཙན་སྤེལ་བྱས་སོང་ They forcibly spread that document.

བཙན་ཕྱུག་ (dzɛ̄njuù) powerful and wealthy.

བཙན་ཕྱུག་འཛོམས་པ་ (dzɛ̄njuù dzo̱mba) power and wealth combined.

བཙན་འཕྲོག་ (dzɛ̄ndrɔɔ̀) forcible seizure/ annexation/ capture; va.—བྱེད་ to seize/ take/ capture by force ¶ 1947 ལོར་གོ་མིན་ཏང་གིས་ཡན་ཨན་བཙན་འཕྲོག་བྱས་པ་རེད་ In 1947 the Kuomintang took Yenan by force.

བཙན་བྱོལ་ (dzɛ̄njüü) refuge [Lit. escaping from oppression/ coercion]; va.—བྱེད་; va.—དུ་འགྲོ་; —དུ་ཡོང་; —དུ་ཐེབས་ to go/ come as a refugee ¶ བཙན་བྱོལ་བོད་མི་ Tibetan refugees. ¶ 1959 ལོར་ཁོང་རྒྱ་གར་ལ་བཙན་བྱོལ་དུ་ཐེབས་པ་རེད་ In 1959 he came as a refugee to India.

བཙན་བྱོལ་པ་ (dzɛ̄njüübə) refugee.

བཙན་བྱོལ་བོད་མི་ (dzɛ̄njüü pö̱ömi) Tibetan refugees.

བཙན་བྱོལ་བོད་གཞུང་གི་སྒྲིག་འཛུགས་ (dzɛ̄njüü pö̱öshuŋgi dri̱gdzuù) Central Tibetan Administration (Dharamsala).

བཙན་དབང་ (dzɛ̄nwaŋ) oppression; va.—བྱེད་ ¶ ང་ཚོ་གུང་ཁྲན་གྱི་བཙན་དབང་འོག་ནས་ཐར་པ་རེད་ We escaped from under communist oppression.

བཙན་དབང་ཁྲལ་འགེལ་ (dzɛ̄nwaŋ trɛ̄ngee) imposing taxes through coercion/ force; va.—བྱེད་.

བཙན་དབང་གིས་ (dzɛ̄nwaŋgi) forcibly, coercively ¶ ང་ཚོར་བཙན་དབང་གིས་ལས་ཀ་བྱེད་བཅུག་པ་རེད་ (They) forced us to work.

བཙན་དབང་རྒྱལ་ཁབ་ (dzɛ̄nwaŋ gyɛ̄ɛ̄gəb) powerful country, a coercive/ imperialist country.

བཙན་དབང་ཆབ་སྲིད་ (dzɛ̄nwaŋ cəbsiī) power politics.

བཙན་སྦྲེལ་ (dzɛ̄ndree) forcing or coercing a merger/ connection/ relationship; va.—བྱེད་.

བཙན་མོ་ (dzɛ̄nmo) wife of a lord/ leader/ high official.

བཙན་དམག་ (dzɛ̄nmaà) 1. mythological army of spirits and local gods. 2. abbr. imperialist army.

བཙན་དམར་ (dzɛ̄nmar) a local spirit/ local demon who is red and rides a red horse.

བཙན་རྫུབ་ (dzɛ̄ndzub) cruelty and oppression; va.—བྱེད་ to act with cruelty and oppression.

བཙན་ཚུགས་ (dzɛ̄ndzuù) sm. བཙན་ཤེད་.

བཙན་འཛུལ་ (dzɛ̄ndzüü) aggression, invasion; va.—བྱེད་ to invade, to commit aggression ¶ ཁོ་ཚོས་བཙན་འཛུལ་གྱི་དམག་ཅིག་རྒྱག་གི་ཡོད་པ་རེད་ They are waging a war of aggression.

བཙན་འཛུལ་མཁན་ (dzɛ̄ndzüüñen) invaders, aggressors.

བཙན་འཛུལ་པ་ (dzɛ̄ndzüüba) sm. བཙན་འཛུལ་མཁན་.

བཙན་འཛུལ་དམག་འཁྲུག་ (dzɛ̄ndzüü nə̄gdruù) war of aggression.

བཙན་འཛུལ་ཟིང་སློང་ (dzɛ̄ndzüü si̱ŋloŋ) invading and causing a disturbance/ uprising; va.—བྱེད་.

བཙན་འཛུལ་ལ་ངོ་རྒོལ་གྱི་དམག་འཁྲུག་ (dzɛ̄ndzüüla ŋo̱göögi māgdruù) anti-aggression war.

བཙན་རྫོང་ (dzɛ̄ndzoŋ) fortress, citadel, bulwark.

བཙན་ཞན་ (dzɛ̄nshɛn) strong and weak.

བཙན་ཞྭ་ (dzɛ̄nsha) hat worn by oracles.

བཙན་ཟོས་ (dzɛ̄nsöö) sm. བཙན་བཟུང་.

བཙན་བཟུང་ (dzɛ̄nsuŋ) forcible seizure/ occupation; va.—བྱེད་ ¶ བཙན་བཟུང་དམག་དཔུང་ Occupation army/ troops.

བཙན་བཟུང་བྱེད་མཁན་རྒྱལ་ཁབ་ (dzɛ̄nsuŋ ce̱èñɛn gyɛ̱ɛ̱gəb) aggressor countries, countries that invade and occupy.

བཙན་བཟོ་ལོག་གསུམ་ (dzɛ̄n so̱ lɔ̱g sūm) abbr. the three: imperialists, revisionists, and reactionaries.

བཙན་གཡར་ (dzɛ̄nyaa) coercing/ forcing sb. to lease or rent or lend; va.—བྱེད་.

བཙན་གཡར་ས་ཆ་ (dzɛ̄nyaa sāja) sm. བཙན་གླའི་ས་ཆ་.

བཙན་གཡེམ་ (dzɛ̄nyem) rape; va.—བྱེད་ to rape.

བཙན་གཡེམ་ཉེས་ཅན་ (dzɛ̄nyem ñe̱èjɛn) rapist.

བཙན་གཡོག་ (dzɛ̄nyɔɔ̀) forcibly imposing; va.—བྱེད་ to force on, to impose on ¶ མི་དམངས་ཀྱི་མགོ་ལ་ནང་འཁྲུག་བཙན་གཡོག་བྱས་པ་རེད་ (They) forcibly imposed a civil war on the people.

བཙན་གཡོགས་ (dzɛ̄nyɔɔ̀) sm. བཙན་གཡོག.

བཙན་ལ་ངོ་དགའ་ གཉོམ་ལ་ཐུབ་ཚོད་ (dzɛ̄nla ŋo̱ga ñōmla tūbdzöö) sycophantic with those in power and bullying the meek and the humble.

བཙན་ལེན་ (dzɛ̄nlen) taking by force; va.—བྱེད་ ¶ མ་སྐྱེད་སྤྲོད་ཐུབ་མིན་བྱུང་ན་སྒོ་ཟོག་སེམས་ཅན་བཙན་ལེན་བྱེད་ཀྱི་ཡོད་པ་རེད་ If (a debtor) was unable to pay the principal and interest, they forcibly took (their) livestock.

བཙན་ཤུགས་ (dzɛ̄nshuù) power, force, coercion ¶ ཁོ་ཚོས་བཙན་ཤུགས་ཀྱིས་ང་ཚོ་ཆིངས་ཡིག་དེ་འཛེག་དུ་བཅུག་པ་རེད་ They coerced us into signing this treaty.

བཙན་ཤུགས་རྒྱ་བསྐྱེད་རིང་ལུགས་ (dzɛ̄nshuù gya̱gyeè ri̱ŋluù) expansionism.

བཙན་ཤུགས་སྲིད་ཇུས་ (dzɛ̄nshuù sīijüü) the policy or politics of power/ force/ coercion.

བཙན་ཤེད་ (dzɛnsheè) force, coercion, compulsion, intimidation; va.—བྱེད་ ¶ ཁོས་བཙན་ཤེད་ཀྱི་སྒོ་ནས་ང་ཚོ་ཁང་པ་རྒྱག་དུ་བཅུག་པ་ཅིག་རེད་ He made us build the house through force.

བཙན་ཤེད་བཀའ་འཕེབས་ (dzɛnsheè gāmbeb) an order imposed by force.

བཙན་ཤེད་ལོག་གཡེམ་ (dzɛnsheè lɔ̱gyem) rape; va.—བྱེད་ to rape.

བཙན་བཤད་ (dzɛ̄nshɛɛ̀) a forced/ coerced statement; va.—བྱེད་.

བཙན་ས་ (dzɛ̄nsa) a safe/ secure place, a fortified place.

བཙན་དམ་ (dzɛ̄nham) excessive force/ intimidation/ coercion; va.—བྱེད་ to intimidate, to coerce.

བཙབ་ (dzəb) f. of གཙབ་.

བཙབ་གྲི་ (dzəbdri) chopping knife.

བཙབ་སྡན་ (dzəbdɛn) cutting/ chopping block.

བཙབས་ (dzəb) p. of གཙབ་.

བཙབས་རལ་ (dzəbrɛɛ) sm. ཙབ་རལ་.

བཙབས་ཤ་ (dzəbsha) minced/ ground meat.

བཙམ་ (dzām) f. of འཚམ་.

བཙམས་ (dzām) p. of འཚམ་.

བཙའ་ (dzā) 1. rust, tarnish; vi.—རྒྱག; —ཆགས་ to rust, to tarnish ¶ཁོའི་མོ་ཊ་ལ་བཙའ་བརྒྱབ་བཞག His car got rusted. 2. rust (plant disease), blight. 3. sm. བཙངས་.

བཙའ་: p. བཙས་; f. བཙའ་ (dzā) 1. vi. to give birth, to bear a child ¶མོ་ལ་བུ་ཞིག་བཙས་སོང་ She gave birth to a son. 2. va. to look at ¶ཁོས་བུ་མོ་དེར་མིག་བཙས་སོང་ He looked at the girl. 3. va. to love and protect, to cherish ¶སློབ་ཕྲུག་རྣམས་ཀྱིས་དཔེ་དེབ་མིག་ལྟར་བཙའ་བ་རེད་ The students loved and protected the book like their own eyes.

བཙའ་སྐྱོན་ (dzāgyön) damage or harm caused by blight/ rust/ tarnish.

བཙའ་འགོག (dzāgɔɔ̀) rust resistant ¶བཙའ་འགོག་གྲོ་སོན་ Rust resistant wheat seed.

བཙའ་སྡེ་ (dzāde) obstetrical/ maternity department.

བཙའ་ཐན་ (dzādɛn) abbr. of བཙའ་ and ཐན་པ་.

བཙའ་ནད་ (dzānɛɛ̀) crop disease (blight/ rust).

བཙའ་མ་ (dzāma) sth. that has become rusted.

བཙའ་ཟུག (dzāsug) labor/ birth pains.

བཙའ་ལོ་ (dzālo) age of giving birth.

བཙའ་ཧམ་བཞའ་ལྷད་མེད་པ་ (dzāham sha̲lhɛɛ̀ me̲èba) shung. without rust, mildew, moisture, and impurities ¶སྐྱིན་འབྲུས་བསྐྱུ་མཚམས་བཙའ་ཧམ་བཞའ་ལྷད་མེད་པ་འབད་གཙང་འབུལ་རྒྱུ་ We will pay the grain for the loan without rust, mildew, moisture, and impurities.

བཙལ་ (dzɛ̄ɛ) 1. p. and f. of འཚོལ་ and འཚལ་.

བཙལ་འཚོལ་ (dzɛ̄ɛ̲dzöö) searching, looking for; va.—བྱེད་ ¶བརྙགས་པའི་མེ་མདའ་ཡུན་རིང་བཙལ་འཚོལ་བྱས་པ་རེད་ (They) searched for the lost gun for a long time.

བཙལ་འཚོལ་ཚོགས་ཆུང་ (dzɛ̄ɛ̄dzöö tsɔ̄gjuŋ) a search committee (e.g., one that goes to search out a new incarnation).

བཙལ་རྙེད་ (dzɛ̄ɛ̄ñeè) searching/ looking for and finding.

བཙས་ (dzɛ̄ɛ̀) 1. p. and f. of བཙའ་. 2. wage/ salary. 3. a fare.

བཙས་སྐར་ (dzɛ̄ɛ̀gar) birthday.

བཙས་ཁྱེར་ (dzɛ̄ɛ̀ kyēr) vi. to be attacked by blight/ rust ¶སྟོན་ཏོག་བཙས་ཁྱེར་བ་རེད་ The crop was attacked by blight.

བཙས་ཆེན་ (dzɛ̄ɛ̀jen) the day when the harvesting begins.

བཙས་སྟོན་ (dzɛ̄ɛ̀dön) 1. birth ceremony. 2. party given after the harvest.

བཙས་པའི་དུས་ (dzɛ̄ɛ̀bɛ tü̲ǜ) the first of the eight stages in human life: birth.

བཙས་མ་ dzɛ̄ɛ̀ma) harvesting; va.—བཟང་ to harvest; vi.—ལང་ to have the time of harvesting arrive.

བཙས་ཟླ་ (dzɛ̄nda) the month when the baby is to be born.

བཙིར་ (dzīr) p. of འཚིར་.

བཙིར་རྒོལ་ (dzīrgöö) attacking from both sides, a pincer attack; va.—བྱེད་.

བཙིར་སྒྲ་ (dzīrdra) sound of sth. being squeezed.

བཙིར་རྡུང་ (dzīrduŋ) beating while interrogating; va.—གཏོང་.

བཙིར་གནོན་ (dzīrnün) 1. compressing, crushing; va.—བྱེད་ to compress, to crush. 2. oppressing, suppressing; va.—བྱེད་ to oppress/ suppress.

བཙིར་སྒྱུད་ (dzīrjüǜ) a clamping/ compressing apparatus.

བཙིར་བྱེད་ཤིང་ལེབ་ (dzīrjeè shīŋleb) two blocks of wood used for squeezing things.

བཙིར་བཙིར་ (dzīrdzir) squeezing pressing; va.—བྱེད་.

བཙིར་རི་ཀུ་རི་ (dzīrri gu̲ri) crowded/ huddled together; vi. and va.—བྱེད་ to crowd/ huddle together ¶ཤིང་གྲུ་ཆུང་ཆུང་ཞིག་ནང་མི་མང་པོ་ཞིག་བཙིར་རི་ཀུ་རི་བྱས་ནས་བསྡད་འདུག There were many people crowded together in a small wooden boat.

བཙིར་རིལ་ཝུ་རིལ་ (dzīrrii wu̲rii) sm. བཙིར་རི་ཀུ་རི་.

བཙིར་ལེན་ (dzīrlen) pressing out, extracting, squeezing out; va.—བྱེད་.

བཙིར་ཤུགས་ (dzīrshuù) the power/ pressure to squeeze sth.

བཙིར་གསོད་ (dzīrsöǒ) killing by strangling; va.—གཏོང་.

བཙུགས་ (dzūù) p. of འཛུགས་.

བཙུགས་ནོར་ (dzūùnɔɔ) prone to error; vi.—ཐེབས་ to make a mistake as soon as one starts sth.

བཙུགས་ཕྲུག (dzu̲gdruù) a type of shaggy woolen bedding/ blanket.

བཙུགས་ཕྲུག་མཛུབ་བཅད་ (dzu̲gdruù dzu̲bjɛɛ̀) woolen bedding/ blanket with very long strands.

བཙུགས་ལེགས་ (dzūgleg) sm. ཉམས་དགའ་བ་.

བཙུགས་ཤིང་ (dzūgshiŋ) trees that are to be or have been planted.

བཙུད་ (dzṻǜ) p. of འཛུད་.

བཙུན་ (dzṻn) abbr. of བཙུན་པ་; བཙུན་མ་ and བཙུན་མོ་.

བཙུན་སྐལ་ (dzṻngɛɛ) sm. གྲྭ་སྐལ་.

བཙུན་ཁྲལ་ (dzṻndrɛɛ) shung. a tax in which a family has to send a son to a monastery to become a monk.

བཙུན་གོས་ (dzṻngöǒ) monk's clothing/ robes.

བཙུན་གྲངས་ (dzṻndraŋ) sm. གྲྭ་གྲངས་.

བཙུན་དགོན་ (dzṻngün) nunnery.

བཙུན་བགྲེས་ (dzṻndreè) sm. གྲྭ་རྒན་.

བཙུན་རྒན་ (dzṻngɛn) old/ elderly monk.

བཙུན་ཆས་ (dzṻnjɛɛ̀) monk's clothing/ robes.

བཙུན་ཆུང་ (dzṻnjuŋ) a young monk.

བཙུན་པ་ (dzṻmbə) monk.

བཙུན་པ་ཁྲིམས་མེད་ (dzṻmbə trīmmeè) monks who have broken their vows.

བཙུན་པ་བུད་མེད་ (dzṻmbə pṳ̈ǜmeè) nun.

བཙུན་པ་བསླབ་པ་རྒན་པ་ (dzṻmbə lābbə gɛ̲mba) senior monks, monks with seniority.

བཙུན་པ་བསླབ་པ་གཞོན་པ་ (dzṻmbə lābbə shö̲mba) junior/ novice monks.

བཙུན་པོ་ (dzṻmbo) diligent, hardworking; va.—བྱེད་.

བཙུན་མ་ (dzṻmmə) nun; va.—ཕབ་; —སློག to defrock a nun; vi.—ལོག to have a nun to lose her vows.

བཙུན་མ་བཀའ་ཕབ་ (dzṻmmə gābəb) see བཙུན་མ་ (ཕབ་).

བཙུན་མོ་ (dzǜnmo) queen.

བཙུན་མོ་རིན་པོ་ཆེ་ (dzṻnmo ri̲mboce) one of the seven royal symbols.

བཙུན་མོ་རོལ་སྟབས་ (dzṻnmo rö̲ö̲dəb) sitting position of statues where the left leg is stretched and the right leg is crossed.

བཙུན་མོའི་སླས་ (dzṻnmü lɛɛ̀) queen's attendants.

བཙུན་གཟུགས་ (dzṻnsug) dressing to look like monks/ nuns.

བཙུན་གཡོག (dzṻnyɔg) servant of monks/ nuns.

བཙུམ་ (dzūm) f. of. འཛུམ་.

བཙུམ་པ་སྦྱོར་ (dzūmba jɔ̲ɔ̲) sm. ཁ་སྐྱེལ་.

བཙུམས་ (dzūm) p. of. འཛུམ་.

བཙུམས་མ་ཕྱེ་ (dzūm ma̲ cē) half open and half closed (e.g., eyes).

བཙེམ་ (dzēm) f. of འཚེམ་.

བཙེམས་ (dz!em) p. of འཚེམ་.

བཙོ་ (dzō) 1. f. of. འཚོད་. 2. undigested remains in the stomach of a slaughtered animal. 3. a traditional method of treating disease/ illness.

བཙོ་ཁང་ (dzōgaŋ) a dye workshop.

བཙོ་འགྱུར་ (dzōgyur) splitting (of atoms).

བཙོ་རྒྱག (dzōgyaà) a traditional Tibetan medical treatment wherein precious metals and gems are placed in the center of a clay plate and burned for several days before being taken out and used as medicine.

བཙོ་ཐལ་ (dzōdɛɛ) the ash resulting from བཙོ་རྒྱག.

བཙོ་ལྡག (dzōlaà) a dye; va.—རྒྱག to dye sth.

བཙོ་ལྡག་མཁན་ (dzōlaàñɛn) dyer.

བཙོ་སྦྱང་ (dzōjaŋ) smelting, refining, tempering, forging; va.—བྱེད་ ༈ གཞའ་དཀར་བཙོ་སྦྱང་བྱེད་རྒྱུ་ The smelting of tin.

བཙོ་སྦྱང་སྒྲིག་ཆས་ (dzōjaŋ drigjɛɛ̀) metallurgical equipment, smelting/ refining equipment.

བཙོ་མ་ (dzōma) 1. pure, unadulterated. 2. orange (color).

བཙོ་ཛ་ (dzodza) a clay pot for cooking meat, etc.

བཙོ་ལུད་ (dzōlüù) sm. བཙོ་, 2.

བཙོ་ལུམས་ (dzōlum) a traditional method of medical treatment involving steam.

བཙོག (dzɔ̄ɔ̀) f. of འཚོག.

བཙོག་གྲིབ་ (dzɔ̄gdrib) pollution from contact with a polluted object or a defiling act.

བཙོག་གཅིན་ (dzɔ̄gjin) excrement and urine; va.—གཏོང་.

བཙོག་ཆུ་ (dzɔ̄gju) foul/ dirty water, cesspool.

བཙོག་ཆུ་འདྲེན་གཏོང་ (dzɔ̄gju drendoŋ) drawing off of foul/ dirty water.

བཙོག་སྙིགས་ (dzɔ̄gñig) dirt, filth, pollutants.

བཙོག་གཏམ་ (dzɔ̄gdam) dirty words/ stories.

བཙོག་ལྟ་ (dzɔ̄gda) sm. བཙོག་སྣང་.

བཙོག་འཐུམ་ (dzɔ̄gdum) a package of one dotse in coins wrapped in cloth.

བཙོག་དྲིག (dzɔ̄gdreè) sm. བཙོག་པ་.

བཙོག་སྣང་ (dzɔ̄gnaŋ) looking on sth. as dirty; va.—བྱེད་.

བཙོག་པ་ (dzɔ̄gba) 1. dirty, filthy, polluted; va.—བཟོ་ to make dirty, to pollute; vi.—བྱེད་; —ཆགས་ to have sth. become dirty ༈ ཁང་པ་དེ་བཙོག་པ་བཟོས་འདུག They made the house dirty. ༈ སྟོད་ཐུང་བཙོག་པ་ཆགས་བཞག The shirt has become dirty. 2. excrement; va.—གཏོང་ to defecate.

བཙོག་པ་འགག (dzɔ̄gba gaà) vi. to be/ get constipated.

བཙོག་པ་འགོ་ (dzɔ̄gba go) vi. to get sth. dirty on (oneself).

བཙོག་པ་ཤོར་ (dzɔ̄gba shɔ̄ɔ) 1. vi. to pass stool unintentionally/ involuntarily. 2. vi. to be/ get contaminated/ polluted.

བཙོག་པོ་ (dzɔ̄gbo) 1. sm. རྒོད་པོ་ (in a positive sense). 2. stubborn. 3. dirty, filthy.

བཙོག་འཕྱར་ (dzɔ̄gjar) winnowing grain roughly; va.—གཏོང་.

བཙོག་དམེ་ (dzɔ̄gme) sm. བཙོག་པ་.

བཙོག་དམེའི་རིགས་ (dzɔ̄gmee rig) unclean/ untouchable castes (in India).

བཙོག་རིགས་ (dzɔ̄rig) dirt, filth, pollutants.

བཙོག་སིང་ (dzɔ̄gsiŋ) sm. བཙོག་པོ་, 2.

བཙོག་ལས་ (dzɔ̄glɛɛ̀) dirty work, polluted jobs/ tasks.

བཙོག་ཤུལ་ (dzɔ̄gshüü) stain, smear of dirt.

བཙོགས་ (dzɔ̄ɔ̀) p. of འཚོག.

བཙོང་ (dzōŋ) 1. onion, leek. 2. f. of འཚོང་.

བཙོང་ཇ་ (dzōŋ ca) tea for sale.

བཙོང་ནག (dzōŋnaà) a type of onion.

བཙོང་རྩ་དཀར་པོ་ (dōŋdza gārbo) root of a type of onion used in traditional Tibetan medicine.

བཙོངས་ (dzōŋ) p. of འཚོང་.

བཙོངས་འབོར་ (dzōŋbɔɔ) amount of sales/ trade, trade volume.

བཙོངས་འཛིན་ (dzōŋdzin) sales receipt, invoice.

བཙོངས་ཡིག (dzūŋyiì) sm. བཙོངས་འཛིན་.

བཙོད་ (dzȫȫ) a reddish vegetable dye.

བཙོད་མདོག (dzōndɔɔ̀) a reddish color.

བཙོན་ (dzȫn) prison, jail; va.—དུ་འཇུག to imprison ༈ ངོ་ལོག་པ་ཚོ་བཙོན་དུ་བཅུག་པ་རེད་ The rebels were imprisoned.

བཙོན་བཀྲོལ་ཆེན་མོ་ (dzȫndröö cēmbo) shung. general amnesty.

བཙོན་སྒྲིལ་འཁོར་སྒྲོམ་ (dzȫngyee kɔ̄ɔdrom) a wooden cage with wheels in which prisoners are taken around.

བཙོན་ཁང་ (dzȫngaŋ) prison.

བཙོན་ཁྲིམས་ (dzȫndrim) prison regulations/ rules.

བཙོན་གྲོགས་ (dzȫndrɔɔ̀) prison mate.

བཙོན་གྲོལ་ (dzȫndröö) pardon, amnesty; va.—གཏོང་ to pardon, to grant amnesty.

བཙོན་གྲོལ་ཆེན་མོ་ (dzȫndröö cēmbo) sm. བཙོན་བཀྲོལ་ཆེན་མོ་.

བཙོན་འགྲོལ་ (dzȫndröö) sm. བཙོན་གྲོལ་.

བཙོན་འགྲོལ་ཆེན་པོ་ (dzȫndröö cēmbo) sm. བཙོན་གྲོལ་ཆེན་མོ་.

བཙོན་སྒར་ (dzȫngar) prison camp.

བཙོན་སྒྲོམ་ (dzȫndrom) prisoner's cage.

བཙོན་ཆས་ (dzȫnjɛɛ̀) prisoner's uniform, prison dress.

བཙོན་འཇུག (dzȫnjuù) imprisoning; va.—བྱེད་ ༈ ཤར་ཆེན་ལྕོག་ཏུ་བཙོན་འཇུག་བྱས་པ་རེད་ (They) imprisoned (him) in the Sharchenchog prison.

བཙོན་ཉར་ (dzȫñar) imprisoning, putting/ keeping in jail; va.—བྱེད་.

བཙོན་ལྟོ་ (dzȫndo) food for a prisoner; prison food.

བཙོན་ཐངས་ (dzȫndaŋ) arc. an order to release prisoners.

བཙོན་དུ་འཇུག (dzȫndu juù) va. to imprison, to jail.

བཙོན་དུ་བཟུང་ (dzȫndu suŋ) sm. བཙོན་དུ་འཇུག.

བཙོན་དུས་ (dzȫndüù) the length of a prison term/ sentence.

བཙོན་དོང་ (dzȫndoŋ) underground prison, pit prison.

བཙོན་སྡོད་ལོ་ཚད་ (dzȫndȫȫ lodzɛɛ̀) prison term.

བཙོན་ནས་སྔོན་བཏང་ (dȫnnɛ ŋȫndaŋ) parole; va.—བྱེད་ to parole.

བཙོན་པ་ (dzȫnba) prisoner, convict.

བཙོན་པ་གློད་བཀྲོལ་ (dzȫnba lȫȫdröö) releasing prisoners; va.—གཏོང་.

བཙོན་པ་འདྲེན་འཁོར་ (dzȫnba drengɔɔ) prison van.

བཙོན་དཔོན་ (dzȫnbön) head of a prison, warden.

བཙོན་མ་ (dzȫnma) sm. བཙོན་མོ་.

བཙོན་མོ་ (dzȫnmo) female prisoner.

བཙོན་རྫི་ (dzȫndzi) prison guard.

བཙོན་ཞག (dzȫnshaà) prison/ jail term, imprisonment.

བཙོན་ཟུར་ (dzȫnsur) ex-convict.

བཙོན་ར་ (dzȫnra) prison, jail.

བཙོན་ལ་འཇུག (dzȫnla juù) sm. བཙོན་དུ་འཇུག.

བཙོན་ལ་སྡོད་ (dzȫnla dȫȫ) vi. to be in jail/ prison.

བཙོན་ཤུ་ (dzȫnshu) a whistle blown when prisoners' work starts and stops.

བཙོན་སྲུང་ཁང་ (dzȫnsuŋgaŋ) detention house, jail for prisoners awaiting trail.

བཙོན་སྲུང་པ་ (dzȫnsuŋwə) prison guard, jailer.

བཙོས་ (dzȫȫ) p. of བཙོ་.

བཙོས་ཟན་ (dzȫȫsɛn) sm. ཟན་བཙོས་.

བཙོས་ཤ་ (dzȫȫsha) cooked/ boiled meat.

བཙོས་ཤ་རྗེན་ལོག (dzȫȫsha jenlɔɔ̀) shung. to not keep one's word, to reverse a decision [Lit. cooked meat becoming raw again].

རྩ་ (dzā) 1. blood vessel, vein, artery, nerve, pulse; va.—ལྟ་ to take/ feel pulse ༈ ཁོ་ན་དུས་ཨེམ་ཆིས་རྩ་བལྟས་པ་རེད་ The doctor took his pulse when he was sick. 2. root ༈ ཤིང་རྩ་ The root of a tree. 3. foot, base (of hills/ mountains) ༈ རི་བོའི་རྩ་ The foot of a hill. 4. the presence of ༈ ཞིང་བདག་ཅིག་གི་རྩ་ལ་ཕྱིན་པ་ཡིན་ I went to (the presence of) a landlord. 5. connecting particle for numbers in the twenties ༈ ཉི་ཤུ་རྩ་གསུམ་ Twenty three. 6. stool, excrement; vi.—བབ་ to defecate; vi.—འགག to have constipation.

རྩ་སྐྲན་ (dzādrɛn) cancer of the blood vessels.

རྩ་དཀར་ (dzāgar) nerve ༈ རྩ་དཀར་ནད་ A disease of nerves.

རྩ་བཀོག (dzāgɔɔ̀) digging out from the root; va.—གཏོང་.

རྩ་ཀང་ (dzāgaŋ) stem of a plant.

རྩ་ཀང་མཐོ་བའི་ལོ་ཏོག (dzāgaŋ tōwɛ lodoò) high-stemmed plants.

རྩ་རྒྱང་མ་ (dzā gyaŋma) the left energy channel (in Buddhist meditation).

རྩ་རྐྱེན་ (dzāgyen) reason, cause ¶ཁོ་ཚོའི་དམག་འཁྲུག་གི་རྩ་རྐྱེན་ནི་ As for the cause of their war.

རྩ་ཁབ་ (dzōgəb) 1. acupuncture; va.—རྒྱག to do acupuncture. 2. acupuncture needle. 3. needle for drawing blood from a vein.

རྩ་ཁམས་ (dzāgam) nerve system.

རྩ་ཁུངས་ (dzəguŋ) proof, verification ¶གྱོད་དོན་འདི་ཐག་གཅོད་བྱེད་པའི་རྩ་ཁུངས་ངོ་མ་ཞིག་རྙེད་མེད་པ་རེད་ (They) have been unable to find real proof to settle the case.

རྩ་ཁུར་ (dzāgur) taking full responsibility; va.—བྱེད་ ¶ཁོང་གིས་ལས་ཁུངས་ཀྱི་ལས་འགན་རྩ་ཁུར་བྱས་ནས་ལོ་གསུམ་ཕྱིན་པ་རེད་ It has been three years since he took the full responsibility for the office.

རྩ་ཁོག (dzāgɔɔ̀) the cavity within the veins.

རྩ་ཁྲག་འདྲེན་ (dzādraà) va. to transfuse blood, to give a blood transfusion.

རྩ་ཁྲག་སྡོམ་ (dzādraà dom) va. to stop the flow of the blood (e.g., by tying the arm).

རྩ་ཁྲིད་ (dzədrii) 1. explaining/ commenting on a main text; va.—རྒྱག. 2. teaching how to diagnose by feeling the pulse.

རྩ་ཁྲིམས་ (dzədrim) constitution.

རྩ་ཁྲིམས་དང་མཐུན་པའི་གཞུང་ (dzədrim daŋ tümbɛ shuŋ) constitutional government.

རྩ་འཁུམ་ (dzā gūm) vi. to get a cramp, to cramp up.

རྩ་འཁུམས་ (dzā gūm) p. of རྩ་འཁུམ་.

རྩ་འཁྱུད་ཡལ་སྦྲེལ་ (dzəgyüü yɛɛdree) complicated and difficult to deal with [Lit. roots twisted together, branches joined].

རྩ་འགུད་ (dzā güü) vi. to have one's pulse get weaker.

རྩ་གྲངས་ (dzādraŋ) cardinal numbers.

རྩ་གྲུམ་ (dzədrum) arthritis.

རྩ་འགག (dzā gaà) vi. to be constipated.

རྩ་འགངས་ (dzāŋgaŋ) important, significant, valued ¶འདི་ནི་རྩ་འགངས་ཆེ་བའི་འཕྲུལ་འཁོར་ཞིག་རེད་ (This) is a very valuable machine.

རྩ་འགལ་ dzāngɛɛ) fundamental contradiction/ difference.

རྩ་འགོག (dzāngɔɔ̀) complete prohibition, total ban; va.—བྱེད་ to completely prohibit, to totally ban ¶ལས་འགུལ་དེ་ཚོ་རྩ་འགོག་བྱེད་ཆེད་ For the purpose of completely prohibiting those campaigns.

རྩ་དགོངས་ཞུ་ (dzāgoŋ shu) va. to resign completely.

རྩ་དགོན་ (dzāgön) sm. མ་དགོན་.

རྩ་འགྱུར་ (dzōngyur) fundamental/ complete reform; va.—གཏོང་ to reform completely, to make fundamental reforms.

རྩ་འགྲེལ་ (dzāndree) the main text and its explanation/ commentary.

རྩ་རྒོད་པོ་ (dzā gööbo) women who like to have (and seeks) intercourse, hot/ sluttish women.

རྩ་རྒྱུ་ (dzōgyu) element (in chemistry).

རྩ་རྒྱུད་ (dzəgyüü) 1. one of the four basic Tibetan medical texts. 2. a tantric text. 3. lineage, ancestry.

རྩ་རྒྱུད་འདུ་ཤེས་ (dzəgyüü dushee) orthodox ideas.

རྩ་རྒྱུད་ཕྱོགས་ཁག (dzəgyüü cɔ̄ɔgaà) orthodox party/ sect.

རྩ་རྒྱུས་ (dzəgyüü) veins and ligaments; vi.—འཁུམས་ to get a cramp, to have veins and ligaments shrivel up.

རྩ་སྒོ་ (dzāgo) anus.

རྩ་སྒོ་སྡེམ་ (dzāgo dem) va. to stop a medium or person from being possessed by deities.

རྩ་སྒོ་འབྱེད་ (dzāgo jeè) va. to make a person capable of being possessed by deities.

རྩ་སྔགས་ (dzāŋaà) a mantra.

རྩ་སྔོག་མཐིལ་འདྲི་ (dzāŋɔ̄ɔ tīīndri) getting to the bottom of a matter [Lit. search the root, question the bottom].

རྩ་གཅོད་ (dzā jöö) va. to stop sth. completely. 2. deciding sth. completely; va.—བྱེད་. 3. va. to cut a root, to cut a vein.

རྩ་གཅོད་པགས་ཤུ་ (dzājöö bāgshu) brutal and inhuman treatment [Lit. peeing the skin, cutting the vein/ root].

རྩ་བཅད་ཙད་སྐོར་ (dzājɛɛ̀ tsɛ̄ɛ̀gɔɔ) investigating thoroughly.

རྩ་བཅོས་ (dzājöö) a basic/ fundamental/ complete cure or correction; va.—བྱེད་.

རྩ་ཆག (dzājaà) shung. exemption, exempting; va.—གཏོང་ to exempt, to free from (taxes, etc.) ¶བུན་རྙིང་ངོ་སྐྱེད་རྩ་ཆག་གཏོང་རྒྱུ་ Exempting from principal and interest on old loans.

རྩ་ཆབ་ (dzājəb) h. of རྩ་ཆུ་.

རྩ་ཆུ་ (dzāju) 1. urine and feces; vi.—འགག to be/ get constipated. 2. pulse and urine ¶རྩ་ཆུ་བརྟག་དཔྱད་ Examination of pulse and urine.

རྩ་ཆུང་ (dzājuŋ) small nerves.

རྩ་ཆེ་ (dzāce) sacred, rare, invaluable, precious ¶བོད་མིའི་རྩ་ཆེའི་རིག་གནས་ The invaluable culture of the Tibetans.

རྩ་ཆེ་ས་ (dzā cēsa) sth. or some place that is precious/ important/ valuable.

རྩ་ཆེན་ (dzājen) sm. རྩ་ཆེ་.

རྩ་ཆེན་པོ་ (dzā cēmbo) sm. རྩ་ཆེ་.

རྩ་འཆུས་ (dzā cöö) vi. to sprain a muscle/ tendon.

རྩ་འཇགས་ (dzānjaà) restraining/ calming/ soothing completely; va.—གཏོང་ to restrain, to calm, to soothe ¶སྲིད་གཞུང་གིས་ཟིང་ཆ་རྩ་འཇགས་བཏང་བ་རེད་ The government completely calmed the disturbance.

རྩ་འཛིང་ (dzājiŋ) relatives and close friends.

རྩ་འཛིང་ཆེན་པོ་ (dzājiŋ cēmbo) very close relatives and friends.

རྩ་འཛིང་སྡུག་པ་ཕུན་ཚོགས་ (dzājiŋ dugbə pündzɔɔ) having many relatives and friends.

རྩ་ཉོན་དྲུག (dzāñön truù) the six causes of delusion: ignorance, desire, anger, hatred, hesitation, ideology.

རྩ་དྲེམ་ (dzādrem) a type of arthritis in traditional Tibetan medicine.

རྩ་གཏོར་ (dzādɔɔ) completely rooting out/ destroying/ annihilating; va. རྩ་གཏོར་; —གཏོང་; —བྱེད་.

རྩ་ལྟ་ (dzā dā) va. to check the pulse.

རྩ་བལྟས་ (dzā dɛ̄ɛ̀) p. of རྩ་ལྟ་.

རྩ་སྟོངས་ (dzādoŋ) total ruin, destruction, downfall; vi.—(དུ་) འགྲོ་ to go or come to ruin/ downfall/ destruction ¶གྲོང་ཁྱེར་རྩ་སྟོང་དུ་ཕྱིན་པ་དེ་ཚོ་ The cities that were totally ruined.

རྩ་སྟོར་ (dzādɔɔ) sm. རྩ་གཏོར་.

རྩ་བརྟག་པ་ (dzā dāgba) sm. རྩ་ལྟ་.

རྩ་བསྟོར་ (dzādɔɔ) sm. རྩ་གཏོར་.

རྩ་ཐིག (dzōdig) the initial sketch (of a painting).

རྩ་ཐོར་ (dzādɔɔ) destruction, breakdown, collapse, disintegration; vi.—(དུ་) འགྲོ་ to go/ come to destruction, to collapse/ breakdown/ disintegrate.

རྩ་དང་རྩེ་མོ་ (dzā daŋ dzēmo) the root/ base and the apex. 2. beginning/ origin and the peak.

རྩ་དོན་ (dzādön) 1. main cause, basic reason, main factor, main point ¶ཕྱི་རྒྱལ་ལ་ཡོང་དགོས་པའི་རྩ་དོན་ནི་ As for the main reason for having to come to foreign countries. 2. principle, tenet ¶ཞི་བདེ་མཉམ་གནས་ཀྱི་རྩ་དོན་ལྔ་པོ་ The Five Principles of Peaceful Coexistence.

རྩ་དོན་གྱི་རང་བཞིན་ (dāsöngi rəŋshin) the nature of principles/ tenets.

རྩ་དོན་མེད་པ་ (dzādön mɛɛ̀ba) unprincipled.

རྩ་དོར་ཡལ་ལེན་ (dzādɔɔ yɛɛlen) doing things backwards, discarding what is important and keeping the unimportant [Lit. discard the root and keep the branch].

རྩ་དྲ་ (dzādra) a disease of the eyes which causes blurriness (in Tibetan medicine).

རྩ་བདག (dzādag) shung. to own sth. completely ¶ གོང་གསལ་ཁང་ཁྱིམ་རྩ་བདག་ཏུ་སྤྲད་པ་ The possession of the house mentioned above was given to him with complete ownership.

རྩ་མདུད་ (dzādüù) a blood clot in the vein.

རྩ་འདར་ (dādar) involuntary shaking/ trembling/ twitching; vi.—བྱེད་.

རྩ་དོག (dzādɔɔ̀) root nodule/ burl.

རྩ་དོག་འབུ་ཕྲ་ (dzādɔɔ̀) nodule of bacteria.

རྩ་དོལ་ (dzādöö) vi. to have a blood vessel break.

རྩ་སྡེམ་ (dzādem) a ribbon tied around the arm by dobdo monks; va.—རྒྱག.

རྩ་སྡོང་ (dzādoŋ) 1. a date/ jujube tree. 2. abbr. of རྩ་བའི་སྡོང་པོ་.

རྩ་བདར་གཅོད་ (dzādar jöö) va. to inquire/ investigate ¶ མི་དེ་སྡོད་ས་གང་དུ་ཡིན་མིན་རྩ་བདར་གཅོད་དགོས་ (You) must investigate where that person lives.

རྩ་ནས་ (dzānε) 1. (— + vb. + neg.) not in the least, not at all, never ¶ གནས་རྒྱལ་དེ་རྩ་ནས་གོ་མ་བྱུང་ I never heard that news. ¶ ང་ཚོའི་གྲོང་གསེབ་ལ་དམག་མི་རྩ་ནས་མི་འདུག There are no soldiers at all in our village. 2. from the presence of ¶ ང་ཁོའི་རྩ་ནས་ཡོང་བ་ཡིན་ I came from his presence.

རྩ་གནད་ (dzānεὲ) 1. chief or main point/ question/ thesis ¶ གྲོས་ཆོད་ཀྱི་རྩ་གནད་ནི་ As for the main point of the resolution. 2. main outline/ sketch/ plan.

རྩ་གནད་གོལ་ (dzānεὲ gεε) vi. to go beyond the main point or thesis or the main outline/ plan.

རྩ་བསྣན་ (dzānεn) shung. to add on the main amount ¶ དེ་སྔའི་ཆོད་གན་ནང་གསལ་རྩ་བསྣན་ཞུས་ཐོག One must add it to the main amount in accordance with the previous contract.

རྩ་བསྣུབས་ (dzā nūm) shung. sm. རྩ་མེད་གཏོང་.

རྩ་དཔོན་ (dzābön) the principal landlord/ lord.

རྩ་དཔྱད་རིག་པ་ (dzājεὲ rigbə) neurology.

རྩ་སྤོས་ (dzāböö) transplanting; va.—རྒྱག to transplant.

རྩ་ཕོགས་ (dzābɔɔ̀) base salary.

རྩ་ཕྲན་ (dzādrεn) small blood vessels, arteries, capillaries.

རྩ་འཕར་ (dzā pār) vi. to palpitate/ pulsate/ throb.

རྩ་འཕར་གློག་རྒྱུན་ (dzābar lɔ̀ɔgyün) pulsating current.

རྩ་འཕར་རྒྱུ་སྐར་ (dzābar gyugar) pulsating star.

རྩ་འཕར་རྩལ་ (dzāpar tsεε) degree of palpitation/ pulsation/ throbbing.

རྩ་འཕྲོག (dzādrɔ̀ɔ) robbing completely, stealing everything.

རྩ་བ་ (dzāwa) root, basis, foundation ¶ རྩ་བའི་ཁེ་དབང་ Basic rights. ¶ ཕྱེ་རླུང་ནི་ང་ཚོ་དབུལ་པོ་ཆགས་པའི་རྩ་བ་རེད་ Dust storms are the basis of our becoming poor. 2. main, chief leading.

རྩ་བ་འགོག (dzāwa gɔ̀ɔ) va. to pull out from the root.

རྩ་བ་ཆད་པའི་སྡོང་རྒན་བཞིན་ (dzāwa cεὲbε doŋgεn shin) coming crashing down [Lit. like an old tree that has its roots cut].

རྩ་བ་ཆེན་པོ་ (dzāwa cēmbo) valuable; va.—བྱེད་ to hold as valuable/ precious.

རྩ་བ་ཉིད་ནས་ (dzāwa ñiinε) sm. རྩ་བ་ནས་.

རྩ་བ་འཐུད་ཐབས་ (dzāwa tūūdəb) root grafting method.

རྩ་བ་དང་ཡུ་བ་དྲི་ (dzāwa taŋ yuwə tri) va. to ask everything in great detail [Lit. to ask the roots and the stem].

རྩ་བ་དོག་པོ་ (dzāwa dɔgbo) root tuber.

རྩ་བ་ནས་ (dzāwanε) completely, totally, never, at all ¶ གྲོང་སྡེ་དེ་རྩ་བ་ནས་མེད་པ་བཟོས་པ་རེད་ (They) completely destroyed that town. ¶ འདི་རྩ་བ་ནས་བྱེད་ཆོག་གི་མ་རེད་ (You) are not allowed to do this at all.

རྩ་བ་ནས་ལྡོག (dzāwanε dɔ̀ɔ) in complete contrast, completely opposite/ contradictory to ¶ ཁ་ནས་གང་བཤད་དང་རྩ་བ་ནས་ལྡོག་སྟེ་བྱས་པ་རེད་ (They) acted completely opposite to what they said.

རྩ་བ་ནས་བྲལ་ (dzāwanε trεε) vi. to be completely severed/ cut, to be out of the question ¶ ལས་ཀ་འདི་དུས་ཐོག་ཏུ་ཚར་བའི་རེ་བ་རྩ་བ་ནས་བྲལ་བ་རེད་ (They) had no hope of finishing the work on time (their hope was severed).

རྩ་བ་ཚུགས་ (dzāwa tsūù) vi. to have taken root ¶ ཤིང་གསར་པ་བཙུགས་པ་རྣམས་རྩ་བ་ཚུགས་བཞག The new trees we planted have taken root.

རྩ་བ་འཛུགས་ (dzāwa dzuù) va. to establish, to found ¶ རྒྱལ་པོ་དེའི་དུས་ལ་ནང་ཆོས་ཀྱི་རྩ་བ་བཙུགས་པ་རེད་ During the time of that king (he/ they) established Buddhism.

རྩ་བ་བཞི་ (dzāwa shi) the four basic principles of monks: not to kill, steal, commit sex/adultery and tell lies.

རྩ་བ་རང་ནས་ (dzāwa raŋnε) totally, completely ¶ ང་མི་དེ་ལ་རྩ་བ་རང་ནས་དགའ་གི་མེད་ I totally dislike that man.

རྩ་བ་གསུམ་ (dzāwa sūm) the three sources or roots of devotion: root guru/ teacher, one's meditational deities, and dakinis and dakas.

རྩ་བའི་དཀར་ཆག (dzāwε gārjaà) table of contents, general index, general catalogue.

རྩ་བའི་ཁ་དོག་བཞི་ (dzāwε kādɔɔ̀ shi) the four main colors in Tibetan culture: white, blue, yellow, red.

རྩ་བའི་ཁག་ཐེག (dzāwε kagdeg) main guarantor.

རྩ་བའི་ཁེ་དབང་ (dzāwε kēwaŋ) basic rights.

རྩ་བའི་ཁྲིམས་ལུགས་ (dzāwε trimluù) basic/ fundamental laws.

རྩ་བའི་གོ་དོན་ (dzāwε kodön) basic conception.

རྩ་བའི་གྲངས་ཀ་ (dzāwε tranga) sm. རྩ་གྲངས་.

རྩ་བའི་དགོངས་དོན་ (dzāwε goŋdön) essential/ fundamental spirit, fundamental sense/ essence.

རྩ་བའི་འགན་ལེན་ (dzāwε genlen) the main guarantor.

རྩ་བའི་འགུལ་ཤུགས་ (dzāwε güüshuù) sm. རྩ་བའི་སྐུལ་ཤུགས་.

རྩ་བའི་འགྱུར་ལྡོག (dzāwε gyundɔɔ̀) primary change.

རྩ་བའི་སྐུལ་ཤུགས་ (dzāwε güüsguù) prime power/ impetus, the moving/ originating/ driving force ¶ ཨ་རི་བ་ཚོས་ལས་ཀ་ནན་པོ་བྱེད་ཡག་ནི་ཕོགས་ཆེན་པོ་ཡོད་པ་དེས་རྩ་བའི་སྐུལ་ཤུགས་སུ་བྱས་པ་རེད་ As for the Americans working hard, the primary impetus is because they get high salary.

རྩ་བའི་ཆ་ནས་ (dzāwε cānε) in principle ¶ ཁོ་མི་རྩ་བའི་ཆ་ནས་ཡག་པོ་འདུག He is a person who in principle is good (i.e., he has some faults but basically is good).

རྩ་བའི་ཐ་སྙད་ (dzāwε tāñεὲ) basic vocabulary.

རྩ་བའི་དོན་སྙིང་ (dzāwε tönñiŋ) basic concept.

རྩ་བའི་སྡོང་པོ་ (dzāwε doŋbo) the main trunk of a tree.

རྩ་བའི་ནད་དྲུག (dzāwε nεὲdruù) the six causes of disease in Tibetan medicine: bile, wind, phlegm, lymph, blood and germs.

རྩ་བའི་ཕ་མ་ (dāwε pāma) one's real parents.

རྩ་བའི་བླ་མ་ (dzāwε lāma) root guru.

རྩ་བའི་དབྱངས་དགུ་ (dzāwε yāŋgu) the nine main vowels in Sanskrit.

རྩ་བའི་མ་ (dzāwε ma) one's real mother.

རྩ་བའི་རྩ་དོན་ (dzāwε dzādön) fundamental principle, basic principle, general rules/ provisions.

རྩ་བའི་འཛུགས་སྐྲུན་ (dzāwε dzugdrün) capital construction.

རྩ་བའི་རིག་པ་ (dzāwε rigbə) basic principle/ theory/ axiom ¶ མར་ལེ་རིང་ལུགས་ཀྱི་རྩ་བའི་རིག་པ་ Basic principles of Marxist-Lenninism.

རྩ་བའི་རིགས་ལམ་ (dzāwε riglam) the main reasoning/ logic.

རྩ་བའི་རིན་གོང་ (dzāwɛ ri̲ngoŋ) basic/ capital costs.

རྩ་བའི་རོ་དྲུག (dzāwɛ ro̲druù) the six main tastes: sweet, bitter, sour, light, spicy hot, salty.

རྩ་བའི་ལས་འགན་ (dzāwɛ lɛ̲ngɛn) main/ basic/ fundamental task or mission.

རྩ་བར་འགྱུར་ (dzawar gyu̲r) vi. to become fundamental/ basic ། གསར་བརྗེའི་གནད་དོན་རྩ་བར་གྱུར་བ་དེ་ནི་ As for that which has become the basic question of the revolution.

རྩ་བྲལ་ (dzādrɛɛ) abbr. of རྩ་བ་ནས་བྲལ་.

རྩ་དབུ་མ་ (dzā ūmə) the central energy channel.

རྩ་འབོར་ (dzābɔɔ) basic amount/ principal ། རྩ་འབོར་སྟོང་ཕྲག་གསུམ་དང་སྐྱེད་ཀ་བདུན་བཅུ་ The principal is 3,000 and the interest is 70.

རྩ་སྦིར་ (dzābir) sm.* རྩ་སྦྲིད་.

རྩ་སྦུག (dzābug) sm. རྩ་སྦུབས་.

རྩ་སྦུབས་ (dzabub) the cavities/ inner opening of the veins.

རྩ་སྦོམ་ (dzābom) tap root.

རྩ་སྦྱོང་ (dzājoŋ) emptying the stomach by inducing diarrhea.

རྩ་སྦྲིད་ (dzā drii̇) vi. to become numb.

རྩ་མིག (dzəmii̇) vein.

རྩ་མེད་ (dzāmeè) annihilation, complete/ total destruction, extermination, eradication; va.—བཟོ་; —གཏོང་ to annihilate, to exterminate, to destroy completely; vi.—དུ་འགྱུར་ to be or gets annihilated/ exterminated/ totally destroyed ། གྲོང་གསེབ་དེ་རྩ་མེད་བཟོས་པ་རེད་ (They) annihilated the village. ། གྲོང་གསེབ་དེ་རྩ་མེད་དུ་གྱུར་པ་རེད་ The village got annihilated.

རྩ་མེད་ཤུལ་མེད་ (dzāmeè shũũmeè) destroying/ annihilating so completely that there is no trace; va.—གཏོང་.

རྩ་མེད་ཤུལ་བརླགས་ (dzāmeè shüülaà) sm. རྩ་མེད་ཤུལ་མེད་.

རྩ་སྨྱོ་ (dzāño) obsessed/ mad/ crazy about sex; vi.—ཐེབས་.

རྩ་རྩ་ལུང་ལུང་ (dzādza lu̲ŋluŋ) origin, beginning; va.—ཤེས་ to know the origin/ beginning; va.—འདྲི་ to ask about the origin/ beginning of sth.

རྩ་རྩེ་ (dzādze) abbr. of རྩ་ and རྩེ་མོ་.

རྩ་ཚིག (dzədzii̇) 1. shung. a public notice, proclamation, ordinance; va.—འགྲེམས་ to issue a notice/ proclamation, ordinance; va.—སྦྱར་ to put up a notice/ proclamation, ordinance. 2. principle, idea.

རྩ་ཚིག་འགྲེམ་བྱང་ (dzədzii̇ dre̲mjaŋ) shung. a board on which a proclamation is stuck.

རྩ་ཚེམ་གནོན་ཚེམ་ (dzādzem nõndzem) sewing stitches a second time on a piece of material that has been joined together by stitching; va.—རྒྱག.

རྩ་འཚོང་ (dzādzoŋ) shung. va. to sell ། གཞུང་རྒྱུགས་ས་རིགས་རྩ་འཚོང་མི་ཆོག་པ་སོགས་འཆར་འཕར་རྩ་ཚིག་ཏུ་ཞལ་གསལ་འཁོད་པ་ It was clearly mentioned in the regular and addition proclamations, that the lands of government taxpayer serfs are not allowed to be sold.

རྩ་འཛིན་ (dzəndzin) platform, program ། ཆབ་སྲིད་ཀྱི་རྩ་འཛིན་ Political platform. 2. va. to maintain/ follow (a policy) ། དབྱིན་ཇིའི་དུས་སྐབས་ཀྱི་སྲིད་ཇུས་ལ་རྩ་འཛིན་གནང་ (They) maintained the policy of the British period. 3. shung. whipping (as punishment); va.—བྱེད་; va.—གཅོད་ ། དོན་རྩ་ཆུང་ངུར་བརྟེན་ལུས་སྟེང་རྩ་འཛིན་བྱེད་པ་བཀའ་ཁྲིམས་དང་རྒྱུ་འབྲས་ཁྲད་སོང་ཡིན་པ་ Whipping people for some small reasons is against the law and karmic cause and effect.

རྩ་འཛིན་རྒྱུན་འཁྱོངས་ (dzəndzin gyü̲ngyoŋ) maintaining/ following/ pursuing continuously (e.g., a policy); va.—བྱེད་.

རྩ་འཛིན་ཇེའུའི་ཆོས་བརྒྱུད་ (dzəndzin ji̲wu cõõgyüü) orthodox Judaism.

རྩ་འཛིན་བབ་བླ་ (dzəndzin bə̲bda) maintaining basic principles but acting according to circumstances.

རྩ་འཛིན་གཡོ་མེད་ (dzəndzin yõmeè) maintaining/ following/ pursuing a course or principle without making any changes.

རྩ་འཛིན་རླུང་ནད་ (dzəndzin lũŋnɛè) one type of traditional Tibetan wind disease.

རྩ་འཛུགས་ (dzəndzuù) organizing, organization; va.—བྱེད་ to organize, to establish ། ཏང་གི་རྩ་འཛུགས་ Party organization. ། སྐྱིད་སྡུག་བརྒྱ་ལྷག་རྩ་འཛུགས་བྱས་པ་རེད་ (They) organized over one hundred clubs.

རྩ་འཛུགས་ཀྱི་འབྲེལ་བ་ (dzəndzuù) organizational relations.

རྩ་འཛུགས་ཀྱི་འཚོ་བ་ (dzəndzuùgi tsõwa) organizational life.

རྩ་འཛུགས་ཀྱི་རང་བཞིན་ (dzəndzuùgi rə̲ŋshin) the nature of organizations.

རྩ་འཛུགས་ཀྱི་སྲོལ་ཡིག (dzəndzuùgi sũũyii̇) sm. རྩ་འཛུགས་ཁྲིམས་ལུགས་.

རྩ་འཛུགས་ཁྲིམས་ལུགས་ (dzəndzuù trĩmluù) rules/ regulations/ constitution of an organization.

རྩ་འཛུགས་པུའུ་ (dzəndzuù bū) tib. ch. office in charge of personnel.

རྩ་འཛུགས་རྩ་དོན་ (dzəndzuù dzādön) organizational principles.

རྩ་འཛུགས་རྫུས་མ་ (dzəndzuù dzü̲ümə) false/ fake organization.

རྩ་རྫོགས་ (dzəndzɔɔ̀) sm. རྩ་མེད་.

རྩ་ཞིབ་ (dzəshib) investigating thoroughly; va.—བྱེད་.

རྩ་གཞི་ (dzəshib) root, base, foundation; va.—འཛུགས to use or make as the basis/ foundation, to base on ། དཔལ་འབྱོར་གྱི་རྩ་གཞི་ The foundation of the economy. ། ཁོང་གི་དགོངས་པ་རྩ་གཞིར་བཞག་ནས་ Based on his thoughts.

རྩ་གཞུང་ (dzāshu) main text.

རྩ་བཞི་ (dzəshi) shung. abbr. of རྩ་ལྷུང་བཞི་.

རྩ་ཟབ་སྡོང་བརྟན་ (dzāsəb do̲ŋdɛn) deep-seated, well-ingrained, firm. ། ནང་ཆོས་ནི་བོད་པའི་ནང་རྩ་ཟབ་སྡོང་བརྟན་ཞིག་རེད་ Buddhism among Tibetans is deep-rooted and well established.

རྩ་ཟབ་ལོ་རྒྱས་ (dzāsəb lo̲gyɛɛ̀) well established and fast developing. [Lit. deep roots and many leaves].

རྩ་གཟིགས་ (dzā si̲i̲) h. of རྩ་ལྟ་.

རྩ་ཡང་ (dzāyaŋ) shung. complete elimination (usu. of a debt or fine); va.—གཏོང་ ། གཞུང་གིས་བུ་ལོན་རྙིང་པ་ཚང་མ་རྩ་ཡང་བཏང་བ་རེད་ The goverment eliminated all old loans.

རྩ་གཡོག (dzāyɔɔ̀) shung. 1. hereditary servant. 2. servant given permanently to a bride or bridegroom when they move to their new home.

རྩ་ར་བགྱིས་ (dzāra gyi̲i̲) shung. sm. རྩ་འཛིན་, 4.

རྩ་ར་གཅོད་ (dzāra jöö) sm. རྩད་གཅོད་.

རྩ་རེག (dzāreg) sm. རྩ་ལྟ་.

རྩ་རོ་མ་ (dzāroma) the right energy channel (in tradition Tibetan medicine).

རྩ་བརླགས་ (dzālaà) 1. destruction, ruin; va.—གཏོང་ to destroy/ ruin; vi.—འགྲོ་ to be destroyed/ ruined ། རྩ་བརླགས་གཏོང་བའི་མཚོན་ཆ་ Weapons of destruction.

རྩ་ལ་ (dzāla) sm. རྩར་.

རྩ་ལག (dzālaà) 1. relatives, family. 2. branches and roots (of plants).

རྩ་ལག་གྲོལ་བ་ (dzālaà drö̲öwa) skillful in doing things.

རྩ་ལངས་ (dzā la̲ŋ) vi. to be horny, to get/ be aroused (sexually).

རྩ་ལམ་ (dzālam) 1. vein, blood vessel. 2. buttock.

རྩ་ལུགས་ (dzəluù) main or fundamental rule/ principle.

རྩ་ལུགས་མེད་པ་ (dzəluù me̲èba) unprincipled.

རྩ་ཤོར་ (dzā shɔ̃ɔ̃) vi. to unintentionally defecate (e.g., in one's pants).

རྩ་གཤགས་ (dzāshaà) sm. ཙག་བཤགས་.

རྩ་བཤད་ (dzāshɛɛ̀) 1. explanation of a text. 2.

abbr. original text and commentary/ explanation.

ཙ་བཞིག (dzəshiì) sm. ཙ་གདོར་

ཙ་ལྡོག (dzālɔɔ̀) overthrowing, upsetting, subverting, undermining; va.—གཏོང་ to overthrow, to subvert, to upset, to undermine ¶ སྲིད་གཞུང་རྙིང་པ་ཙ་ལྡོག་བཏང་བ་རེད་ (They) overthrew the old goverment.

ཙ་ལྡོག་ལས་འགུལ་ (dzālɔɔ̀ lɛngüü) a campaign/ movent to overthrow, an uprising, putsch; va.—སྤེལ་ to make an uprising/ putsch.

ཙ་གསུམ་ (dzāsum) 1. the three channels that are used for meditation. 2. the three: root guru, meditational deity, dakas and dakinis.

ཙ་གསུམ་ཀུན་འདུས་ (dzāsum gǖndüü) root guru.

ཙ་གསུམ་གནས་ (dzāsum nɛ̄ɛ) realm of the gods.

ཙ་ཧྲལ་ (dzāhrɛɛ) lawless behavior.

ཙ་ཧྲེང་བ་ (dzā hrēŋwa) vascular sclerosis.

ཙ་ལྟུང་བཞི་ (dzā lhūŋshi) shung. four downfalls: 1. taking life. 2. taking what is not given. 3. indulging in sexual misconduct. 4. lying.

ཙག (dzāà) 1. va. to bargain over a price. 2. sm. ཙེག.

ཙག་གེ་ཙིག་གེ་ (dzāgge dzīgge) sm. ཙག་ཙིག.

ཙག་པ་ (dzāgba) dress made from the skins of goats or sheep (worn with the fleece inside).

ཙག་ཙག་ (dzāgdzag) sm. ཙེག་ཙེག.

ཙག་ཙིག (dzəgdzig) sundry, miscellaneous, odds and ends ¶ འགྲོ་སོང་ཙག་ཙིག Miscellaneous expenses.

ཙག་ཙིག་ཚོང་ཁང་ (dzəgdzig tsōŋgaŋ) a shop that sells miscellaneous items.

ཙག་ཙིག་ཐོ་འགོད་ (dzəgdzig tōgöö) miscellaneous notes.

ཙངས་པ་ (dzāŋba) lizard, gecko.

ཙངས་པ་ཁ་རལ་ (dzāŋba kārɛɛ) lizard, gecko.

ཙངས་པ་སྐལ་རལ་ (dzāŋba gɛɛrɛɛ) sm. ཙངས་པ་ཁ་རལ་.

ཙད་ (dzɛ̄ɛ) sm. ཙ་བ་.

ཙད་ཁུངས་ (dzɛ̄ɛguŋ) proof, evidence; va.—གཅོད་ to investigate for proof/ evidence.

ཙད་གཅོད་ (dzɛ̄ɛjöö) investigating, probing, inquiring, exploring; va.—བྱེད་ to investigate, to probe, to explore, to inquire, to search into, to prospect ¶ མི་དེའི་སྡོད་ས་གང་དུ་ཡིན་མིན་ཙད་གཅོད་བྱེད་དགོས་ (You) must investigate where he lives.

ཙད་གཅོད་ཁྲིན་བཀོ་རུ་ཁག (dzɛ̄ɛjöö trōngo rugaà) exploration borehole team.

ཙད་གཅོད་ཐིག་ལེན་ (dzɛ̄ɛjöö tiglen) surveying; va.—བྱེད་ to survey, to prospect.

ཙད་གཅོད་ཞིབ་དཔྱད་ (dzɛ̄ɛjöö shibjɛɛ) making a thorough/ detailed inquiry or probe; va.—བྱེད་.

ཙད་བཅད་ (dzɛ̄ɛjɛɛ) p. of ཙད་གཅོད་.

ཙད་བཅད་གསལ་ལོན་ (dzɛ̄ɛjɛɛ sɛ̄ɛlön) understanding sth. after investigating it; va.—བྱེད་.

ཙད་ཆོད་ (dzɛ̄ɛ cöö) 1. vi. to find out about sth., to get information on sth. ¶ ཁོ་སོ་པ་ཡིན་པ་ཙད་ཆོད་པ་རེད་ (They) found out that he was a spy.

ཙད་འདྲི་ (dzɛ̄ndri) sm. ཙད་གཅོད་.

ཙད་དཔྱོད་ (dzɛ̄ɛjöö) ཙད་གཅོད་.

ཙད་མེད་ནང་མི་ (dzɛ̄ɛmeè nəŋmi) the wives/ family members of men who fled to exile in 1959.

ཙད་འཚོལ་ (dzɛ̄ɛ tsöö) searching, investigating; va.—བྱེད་ to search, to investigate.

ཙ་འཛིན་ (dzəndzin) shung. whipping; va.—བྱེད་; —གཅད་ ¶ དོན་ཙ་ཆུང་ངུ་ར་བསྙད་ལུས་སྟེང་ཙ་འཛིན་བྱེད་པ་བཀའ་ཁྲིམས་དང་རྒྱུ་འབྲས་ཁྲུད་སོད་ཡིན་པ་ Whipping people for minor infractions is against the law and karmic cause and effect.

ཙད་ཞིབ་ (dzɛ̄ɛshib) investigation, inquiry, probe, survey; va.—བྱེད་ to investigate, to make an inquiry/ probe/ survey.

ཙད་ཞིབ་ཇུས་འགོད་ (dzɛ̄ɛshib jüügöö) surveying and making a plan.

ཙད་ཞིབ་ཐིག་ལེན་ (dzɛ̄ɛshib tiglen) survey; va.—བྱེད་.

ཙད་ཡིག (dzɛ̄ɛyiì) a letter inquiring about sth.

ཙད་གཡུང་ (dzɛ̄ɛyuŋ) a plant used in Tibetan medicine (Notopterygium incisium).

ཙབ་ (dzəb) a wedge; va.—རྒྱག; —འཛུག to put a wedge somewhere to make sth. even.

ཙབ་རྒྱུ་ (dzəbgyu) fermenting agent for yogurt or beer.

ཙབ་གཅོད་ (dzəbjüü) va. to spend/ exhaust all one's money.

ཙབ་དོ་ (dzəbdo) tattered, torn.

ཙབ་ཙུབ་ (dzəbdzub) sm. ཙབ་ཙུབ་.

ཙབ་རལ་ཙབ་ནག (dzəbrɛɛ dzəbnaà) completely torn, in tatters.

ཙབ་ཧྲལ་ (dzəbhrɛɛ) sm. ཙབ་རལ་.

ཙབ་ཧྲུལ་ (dzəbhrü) sm. ཙབ་རལ་.

ཙབས་ (dzəb) 1. sm. ཕབས་. 2. sm. ཙབ་.

ཙམ་ (dzām) 1. abbr. of ཙམ་པ་. 2. powder ¶ འོ་ཙམ་ Powdered milk.

ཙམ་སྐྱ་ (dzāmgya) plain tsamba.

ཙམ་ཁལ་ (dzāmgɛɛ) one ཁལ་ of tsampa.

ཙམ་ཁུ་ (dzāmgu) sm. ཇ་ཐུར་.

ཙམ་ཁུག (dzāmguù) bag for holding ཙམ་པ་.

ཙམ་ཁུག་སྟོང་པ་དབ་དབ་བྱེད་པ་ (dzāmguù dōŋba dəbdəb ceèba) arguing about sth. that is far fetched/ remote/ hypothetical, trying to get sth. from nothing [Lit. shaking an empty ཙམ་པ་ bag].

ཙམ་རྒྱུ་ (dzāmgyu) grain for making tsampa.

ཙམ་སྒམ་ (dzāmgam) bowl/ box for putting ཙམ་པ་.

ཙམ་སྒྱེ་ (dzāmgye) large bag in which ཙམ་པ་ is put.

ཙམ་གཉེར་ (dzāmñer) 1. sm. ཙམ་བཞེས་པ་. 2. shung. sm. ཙམ་བཞེས་ལས་ཁུངས་.

ཙམ་སྟེགས་ (dzāmdeg) shung. a shelf/ platform for keeping ཙམ་པ་.

ཙམ་ཐུག (dzāmtuù) broth made with ཙམ་པ་.

ཙམ་ཐུར་ (dzāmduu) spoon kept in a bag of ཙམ་པ་.

ཙམ་པ་ (dzāmba) parched/ roasted barley that has been ground into flour.

ཙམ་པ་སྐམ་གསོབ་ (dzāmba gāmsob) inferior quality ཙམ་པ་.

ཙམ་པ་རང་གིས་ཟས་ ཙམ་ཁུག་མིའི་མགོ་ལ་གཡོགས་ (dzāmba rəŋgi sɛɛ dzāmguù miigola yɔ̄ɔ) putting the blame for one's own acts on another [Lit. eat the ཙམ་པ་ oneself; put the ཙམ་པ་ bag on a person's head].

ཙམ་པ་གཤོ་ (dzāmb shō) 1. va. to toss barley into the air (during certain religious festivals). 2. va. to flatter.

ཙམ་པའི་ཁག་ཐེག་བུལ་ཏོག་གི་བྱས་ ལྷག་པས་ཁྱེར་ན་མཉམ་ཁྱེར་ཡིན་ (dzāmbɛ kāgdeg püüdoògi cɛɛ lhāgbɛ kyērna ñāmkyer yin) a guarantor to a loan who is no more stable than the person taking the loan [Lit. (when) baking soda acts as a guarantor to ཙམ་པ་, if the wind blows, both will be blown away].

ཙམ་ཕོགས་ (dzāmbɔɔ̀) wages paid in ཙམ་པ་.

ཙམ་ཕོར་ (dzāmbɔɔ) wooden bowl used to keep/ hold ཙམ་པ་.

ཙམ་ཕྱེ་ (dzāmce) sm. ཙམ་པ་.

ཙམ་བང་ (dzāmbaŋ) place for keeping ཙམ་པ་.

ཙམ་རྩི་ (dzāmdzi) 1. tsampa for putting in broth. 2. a little bit of tsampa.

ཙམ་བཞེས་པ་ (dzāmsheèba) shung. person in charge of ཙམ་བཞེས་ལས་ཁུངས་.

ཙམ་བཞེས་ལས་ཁུངས་ (dzāmsheè lɛɛguŋ) shung. an treasury of the traditional Tibetan Government that collected certain agricultural products that were mainly used for ceremonial and ritual purposes.

ཙམ་ཟན་ (dzāmsɛn) 1. people whose staple diet is ཙམ་པ་ (ཙམ་པ་ eaters, i.e., Tibetans). 2. food made from ཙམ་པ་.

ཙམ་ཟོམ་ (dzāmsom) wooden bucket for keeping ཙམ་པ་.

ཙམ་གཟར་ (dzāmsaa) wooden ཙམ་པ་ ladle.

ཙམ་རུ་ (dzāmru) wooden stick used for stirring ཙམ་པ་ broth.

ཙམ་ལས་ (dzāmlɛɛ) abbr. ཙམ་བཞེས་ལས་ཁུངས་.

རྩམ་ལེན་ཏོ་དམ་ (dzāmlen todam) sm. རྩམ་བཞིས་པ་.

རྩམ་བཤོས་ (dzāmshöö) throwing རྩམ་པ་ in the air as offering at certain holidays and religious ceremonies such as the birthday of the Dalai Lama; va.—གཏོང་.

རྩམ་གསུར་ (dzāmsur) burning རྩམ་པ་ as an offering to gods.

རྩམ་གསོག (dzāmsɔɔ̀) barley roasted without first soaking it in water (considered inferior).

རྩམ་ལྷག (dzāmlhaà) leftover རྩམ་པ་.

རྩའི་འགྲོས་མཐང་ (dzɛ̄ɛ drö̱ödraŋ) རྩ་རྫིང་པ་.

རྩར་ (dzāā) to, near, in/ to the presence of ¶ཁོ་དགེ་རྒན་གྱི་རྩར་ལ་ཕྱིན་པ་རེད་ (He) went to the presence of the teacher.

རྩར་གཅོད་ (dzār jōò) abbr. of རྩ་ར་གཅོད་.

རྩར་རྩར་ (dzārdzar) sm. ཙར་ཙར་, 2.

རྩལ་ (dzɛ̄ɛ) skill, mastery, dexterity, adroitness.

རྩལ་མཁས་འགྲན་ཟླ་ (dzɛ̄ɛ kɛ̄ɛ̀ drɛndrɛɛ) skilled without parallel/ equal.

རྩལ་འཁྲིད་པ་ (dzɛ̄ɛdribə) coach (in sports).

རྩལ་འགྲན་ (dzɛ̄ɛdrɛn) gymnastics/ acrobatics/ sports competition.

རྩལ་འགྲན་ཚོགས་འདུ་ (dzɛ̄ɛdrɛn tsōŋdu) gymnastics/ acrobatics/ sports meet.

རྩལ་ཅན་ (dzɛ̄ɛjɛn) sm. རྩལ་ལྡན་.

རྩལ་ཆེན་པོ་ (dzɛ̄ɛ cēmbo) sm. རྩལ་ལྡན་.

རྩལ་ཉམས་སྟོན་ (dzɛ̄ɛñam tō̃n) va. to show one's skill/ mastery at sports/ games/ competition.

རྩལ་ཉམས་དོད་པོ་ (dzɛ̄ɛñam tö̱öbo) skilled or good at sports/ games/ competition ¶མི་འདི་ཀང་རྩེད་པོ་ལོ་རྒྱག་དུས་རྩལ་ཉམས་དོད་པོ་ཡོད་པ་རེད་ When playing soccer, this man is very skillful.

རྩལ་བཏོན་ (dzɛ̄ɛ dō̃n) p. of རྩལ་འདོན་.

རྩལ་སྟོབས་ (dzɛ̄ɛdob) 1. capability. 2. athletic ability, martial arts skill.

རྩལ་ཐང་ (dzɛ̄daŋ) field for sports, athletic playing field.

རྩལ་ཐབས་ (dzɛ̄dəb) sm. རྩལ་སྟོབས་, 2.

རྩལ་འདོན་ (dzɛ̄ɛ dö̱n) va. to manifest/ reveal one's skill.

རྩལ་བདེ་བ་ (dzɛ̄ɛ de̱wa) skillful, adroit, dexterous.

རྩལ་ལྡན་ (dzɛ̄ndɛn) skillful, adroit, dexterous.

རྩལ་པོ་ཆེ་ (dzɛ̄ɛboje) person who is very skillful/ adroit/ dexterous.

རྩལ་སྤྲུགས་ (dzɛ̄ɛdruù) using one's skill/ abilities; va.—བྱེད་ ¶ཐབས་ཤེས་ཡོད་ཚུ་རྩལ་སྤྲུགས་བྱས་ཀྱང་ལས་དོན་དེ་བསྒྲུབས་མ་སོང་ Even after using all of (his) skills, (he) was not able to achieve his task.

རྩལ་འཕྲུལ་ (dzɛ̄ɛdrüü) acrobatics, juggling, circus performances.

རྩལ་འབུལ་ (dzɛ̄ɛmbüü) shung. participating in the དུང་འཁོར་རྩལ་རྒྱུགས་.

རྩལ་སྦྱོང་ (dzɛ̄ɛjoŋ) exercise, drill, practice (games, gymnastics, sports, etc); va.—བྱེད་.

རྩལ་སྦྱོང་ཐང་ (dzɛ̄ɛjoŋdaŋ) sm. རྩལ་སྦྱོང་ར་བ་.

རྩལ་སྦྱོང་བྱ་བ་ (dɛ̄ɛjoŋ ca̱wa) physical culture/ activity.

རྩལ་སྦྱོང་ར་བ་ (dzɛ̄ɛjoŋ ra̱wa) drill ground, athletic field, stadium.

རྩལ་རྩེ་བའི་འཁྱུགས་ཤུད་ (dzɛ̄ɛ dzēwɛ kyə̄gsüü) figure (ice) skating.

རྩལ་རྩེད་ (dzɛ̄ɛdzeè) acrobatic stunts, acrobatic sports, gymnastics.

རྩལ་རྩེད་སྟོན་མཁན་ (dzɛ̄ɛdzeè dō̃ngɛn) acrobatic performer, acrobat, gymnast.

རྩལ་རྩེད་སྣ་ཚོགས་ (dzɛ̄ɛdzeè nādzoò) (various) acrobatics, gymnastics.

རྩལ་རྩེད་པ་ (dzɛ̄ɛdzeèba) sm. རྩལ་རྩེད་སྟོན་མཁན་.

རྩལ་རྩེད་ཚོགས་པ་ (dzɛ̄ɛdzeè dzɔ̄gba) acrobatic troupe/ team.

རྩལ་གཟིགས་སྟེགས་ཆ་ (dzɛ̄ɛsiì di̱nja) a stage, rostrum for seeing a martial arts/ gymnastic displays.

རྩལ་ཡིག (dzɛ̄ɛyiì) writing style of an uneducated person.

རྩལ་ཡོན་ (dzɛ̄ɛyön) physical skills and scholarly attainment, physical talents and academic knowledge.

རྩལ་ཡོན་གཉིས་མེད་ (dzɛ̄ɛyön ñīimeè) without scholarly and physical skills.

རྩལ་རིགས་ (dzɛ̄ɛriì) kinds/ types of skills.

རྩལ་ལྷོམ་ (dzɛ̄ɛlom) proud of one's skills.

རྩལ་ལག (dzɛ̄ɛlaà) skill, adroitness.

རྩལ་ལག་དོད་པོ་ (dzɛ̄ɛlaà tö̱öbo) very skillful/ adroit.

རྩལ་ལག་བདེ་པོ་ (dzɛ̄ɛlaà de̱bo) sm. རྩལ་ལག་དོད་པོ་.

རྩལ་ཤིང་ཆ་ཅན་ (dzɛ̄ɛshiŋ cājɛn) parallel bars (in gymnastics).

རྩལ་ཤིང་ཧྲོང་གང་ (dzɛ̄ɛshiŋ hrōŋgaŋ) sm. རྩལ་ཤིང་ཆ་ཅན་.

རྩལ་ཤུགས་ (dzɛ̄ɛshuù) skill and strength.

རྩལ་སློབ་དགེ་རྒན་ (dzɛ̄ɛlob ge̱gɛn) coach, trainer.

རྩི་: p. བརྩིས་; f. བརྩི་; imp. རྩིས་ (dzī) va. 1. to calculate/ count ¶རྩིས་ནོར་ཡོད་མེད་སྐྱར་དུ་རྩི་རོགས་གནང་ Please calculate again whether the calculation is correct or not. 2. va. to consider ¶ཁོང་མཁས་པ་ཞིག་ཏུ་རྩི་གི་ཡོད་པ་རེད་ They consider him to be a scholar. 3. sap, juice, extract ¶སྦྲང་རྩི་ Honey. ¶ཚང་རྩི་ Yeast.

རྩི་བཀུར་ (dzīgur) sm. བརྩི་བཀུར་.

རྩི་སྐྱི་ (dzīgyi) adhesive.

རྩི་ཁོག (dzīgɔɔ̀) baby goat.

རྩི་སྒམ་ (dzīgan) neatly tied woodblock printed book ready for painting the sides.

རྩི་སྒམ་པང་ལེབ་ (dzīgam bāŋleb) the two wooden boards between which a woodblock printed text is placed to be painted.

རྩི་བཅུད་ (dzījüü) nutritious substance, nutrient.

རྩི་ཆས་ (dzījɛɛ̀) a meter (an instrument).

རྩི་ཆུ་ (dzīju) liquid paint/ lacquer.

རྩི་འཇོག (dzīnjoò) sm. བརྩི་འཇོག.

རྩི་དོག (dzīdoò) sm. རྩི་ཐོག.

རྩི་གཏོང་ (dzī dōŋ) va. to paint.

རྩི་གཏོར་ (dzī dɔ̄ɔ) va. to spray paint, to spray lacquer.

རྩི་སྟག་མོ་ (dzī dāgmo) rheum pumilum (a type of traditional Tibetan medicine).

རྩི་ཐོག་ཟླ་བ་ (dzīdɔɔ da̱wa) the 9th month of the Tibetan calendar.

རྩི་མཐོང་ (dzīdoŋ) great regard/ respect; va.—བྱེད་ to have great regard for.

རྩི་དྲུད་ (dzīdrüü) musk deer rubbing its tail against tree because of being in heat (a sign used in hunting).

རྩི་གདན་ (dzīdɛn) the base coat of paint.

རྩི་འཕྱིད་ (dzījiì) polishing; va.—རྒྱག ¶ཁོའི་ལྷམ་དེ་རྩི་འཕྱིད་བརྒྱབ་མི་འདུག His shoes were unpolished.

རྩི་སྦྲང་ (dzīdraŋ) honeybee.

རྩི་མ་ (dzīmə) painted/ lacquered materials.

རྩི་མར་ (dzīmar) butter.

རྩི་དམར་ (dzīmaa) 1. red paint/ lacquer. 2. coral.

རྩི་སྨན་ (dzīmin) vitamins, medicines that builds strength.

རྩི་རྩི་ (dzīdzi) sm.* ཙི་ཙི་.

རྩི་ཞྭོའི་ཞེན་ (dzīwö she̱n) ch. ultraviolet.

རྩི་རས་ (dzīrɛɛ̀) cloth used in varnishing.

རྩི་རིང་པོ་ (dzī ri̱ŋgu) sm. ཚི་རིང་པོ་.

རྩི་རེངས་ (dzīreŋ) hard soil, uncultivated fields; vi.—སུ་ལུས་ to leave fields uncultivated for many years.

རྩི་ལོག་གཏོང་ (dzīlɔɔ̀ dōŋ) va. to repaint/ relacquer.

རྩི་ཤིང་ (dzīshiŋ) plants ¶ཟླ་བའི་ནང་སྲོག་ཆགས་དང་རྩི་ཤིང་སོགས་གང་ཡང་མེད་ There are no plants or animal life on the moon.

རྩི་ཤིང་སྐྱེས་མེད་རི་པོ་ (dzīshiŋ gyēèmeè ri̱wo) bare hills.

རྩི་ཤིང་གི་ཐལ་བ་ (dzīshiŋgi tɛ̄ɛwa) wood ash (the ash of plants).

རྩི་ཤིང་གི་ནད་རིགས་ (dzīshiŋgi ŋe̱ɛ̀rig) a disease that withers trees and vegetation.

རྩི་ཤིང་གི་ནད་ལུགས་རིག་པ་ (dzīshiŋgi ŋe̱ɛ̀luù ri̱gbə) phytopathology.

རྩི་ཤིང་གི་སྣུམ་ (dzīshiŋgi nūm) vegetable oil.

རྩི་ཤིང་གི་བུལ་རྡོག (dzīshiŋgi büüdoò) plant alkaloid.

རྩི་ཤིང་གི་ཚི་སྣ་ (dzīshiŋgi tsīnə) vegetable/ plant/ fibre.

རྩི་ཤིང་གི་བཟའ་སྣུམ་ (dzīshiŋgi sənum) vegetable oil.

རྩི་ཤིང་གི་ར་བ་ (dzīshiŋgi rawa) hedgerow, hedge.

རྩི་ཤིང་སྙིད་ནད་ (dzīshiŋgi ñīìnεὲ) a disease that causes plants to wilt.

རྩི་ཤིང་འདེབས་གསོ་ (dzīshiŋ debso) plant cultivation.

རྩི་ཤིང་བཟའ་སྣུམ་ (dzīshiŋ sənum) sm. རྩི་ཤིང་གི་བཟའ་སྣུམ་.

རྩི་ཤིང་སྣུམ་རིགས (dzīshiŋ rigbə) vegetable oils.

རྩི་ཤིང་ར་བ་ (dzīshiŋ rawa) botanical garden.

རྩི་ཤིང་རིག་པ་ (dzīshiŋ rigbə) botany.

རྩི་ཤིང་རིགས་འབྱེད་རིག་པ་ (dzīshiŋ rigjeè rigbə) systematic botany.

རྩི་ཤིང་རུལ་བ་ (dzīshiŋ rüüwə) humus.

རྩི་ཤིང་ལོ་ཏོག (dzīshiŋ lodoò) plant crop ¶ བཟོ་ལས་རྒྱུ་ཆས་རྩི་ཤིང་ལོ་ཏོག Industrial crops.

རྩི་ཤིང་སྲུང་སྐྱོང་ (dzīshiŋ sūŋgyoŋ) sm. རྩི་ཤིང་སྲུང་སྐྱོབ་.

རྩི་ཤིང་སྲུང་སྐྱོབ་ (dzīshiŋ sūŋgyob) plant protection.

རྩི་ཤུན་ (dzīshün) varnish, shellac, lacquer.

རྩི་ལྷེབ་ (dzīlheb) color chips.

རྩིག: p. བརྩིགས་; f. བརྩིག; imp. རྩིགས་ (dzīì) va. to pile up, to stack up, to build/ erect (by piling up) ¶ ཁོ་ཚོས་རྩིག་པ་བརྩིགས་པ་རེད་ They built a wall.

རྩིག་བཀལ་ལོ་ཐོ་ (dzīigεε ledo) wall calendar.

རྩིག་སྐྱོར་ (dzīigyɔɔ) a brace/ support for a wall.

རྩིག་ཁུག (dzīiguù) corner of a wall.

རྩིག་ཁྱོག (dzīggyɔɔ̀) sm. རྩིག་ཁུག.

རྩིག་མཁན་ (dzīìñεn) རྩིག་བཟོ་.

རྩིག་འཁྱུད་ (dzīg kyüǜ) 1. clinging to a wall, along a wall ¶ ནུབ་ཀྱི་རྩིག་འཁྱུད་དུ་ཚོམ་ཆེན་དུ་སྐྱོད་བྱེད་གསང་སྒོ་ཞིག་ཡོད་པ་ There was a secret door along the west wall leading to the hall. 2. walking by leaning/ balancing on a wall.(for infants); va.—རྒྱག.

རྩིག་འགྲམ་ (dzīndram) near/ by the side of a wall.

རྩིག་རྒྱན་ (dzīigyεn) wall decoration.

རྩིག་ངོས་ (dzīiŋöö) the side/ face of a wall.

རྩིག་ངོས་ཚགས་པར་ (dzīiŋöö tsāgbaa) wall newspaper (news posted on walls).

རྩིག་ཆུ་ (dzīgju) water seeping through a wall.

རྩིག་རྟེན་ (dzīiden) sm. རྩིག་རྨང་.

རྩིག་བརྡོལ་འཕུར་ཕྱིན་ (dzīidöö pūrjin) suddenly becoming famous/ eminent [Lit. breaking through the wall and fly away].

རྩིག་ཐབ་ (dzīgtəb) fireplace (in a wall).

རྩིག་ཐོ་ (dzīgdo) bribe, bribery; va.—རྒྱག to bribe.

རྩིག་གདན་ (dzīgdεn) sm. རྩིག་རྨང་.

རྩིག་གདན་རྡོ་ (dzīgdεn do) foundation stone.

རྩིག་གདོང་ (dzīgdoŋ) (outside) face of a wall/ fence.

རྩིག་རྡོ་ (dzīgdo) construction/ building stones.

རྩིག་ལྡེབས་ (dzīgdeb) sm. རྩིག་ངོས་.

རྩིག་ལྡེབས་ཚགས་པར་ (dzīgdeb tsāgbaa) sm. རྩིག་ངོས་ཚགས་པར་.

རྩིག་པ་ (dzīgbə) wall; va.—རྒྱག to build/ erect a wall.

རྩིག་པ་མཁན་པོ་ (dzīgbə kε̄mbo) sm. རྩིག་དཔོན་.

རྩིག་པའི་རྒྱ་ (dzīgbε gyā) wall.

རྩིག་པའི་ལྡེབས་རིས་ (dzīgbε debrii) wall painting/ mural.

རྩིག་པའི་ར་སྐོར་ (dzīgbε ragɔɔ) wall, fence.

རྩིག་པོ་ (dzīgbo) sm. གར་པོ་.

རྩིག་དཔོན་ (dzīgbön) master mason, master bricklayer.

རྩིག་ཕག (dzīgbaà) brick.

རྩིག་བུག (dzīgbuù) hole in a wall.

རྩིག་འབྲིལ་ (dzīgbuù) sm. སྐྱེ་འབྲིལ་.

རྩིག་རྨང་ (dzīgmaŋ) foundation of a wall; va.—འདིང་; —གཙུག to lay the foundation of a wall.

རྩིག་ཞལ་ (dzīgshεε) plaster (for a wall); va.—རྒྱག to plaster a wall.

རྩིག་གཞི་ (dzīgshi) sm. རྩིག་རྨང་.

རྩིག་ཟུར་ (dzīgsur) the corner (of a wall) ¶ ཁང་པའི་རྩིག་ཟུར་ The corner of a house.

རྩིག་ཟུར་འདྲུ་ (dzīgsur dru) 1. va. to dig up a corner of a wall (to undermine the foundation to demolish a house). 2. va. to undermine, to undercut (politically) ¶ མི་དེ་ཚོས་སྤྱི་ཚོགས་རིང་ལུགས་ཀྱི་རྩིག་ཟུར་འདྲུ་གི་ཡོད་པ་རེད་ These people are undermining the foundation of socialism.

རྩིག་བཟོ་ (dzīgso) building/ constructing a wall; va.—བྱེད་.

རྩིག་བཟོ་བ་ (dzīgsowa) mason, bricklayer.

རྩིག་ཡོལ་ (dzīìyöö) curtain hung on wall, wall hanging.

རྩིག་ར (dzīgrə) courtyard wall.

རྩིག་ལས་ (dzīglεὲ) architecture, building ¶ རྩིག་ལས་སློབ་གྲྭ Engineering school.

རྩིག་ལས་རྒྱུ་ཆ་མཐོ་ལས་ (dzīglεὲ gyuja solεὲ) building material industry.

རྩིག་ལུགས་ (dzīgluù) architecture.

རྩིག་ཤོག (dzīgshoò) wallpaper.

རྩིག་སུབ་ (dzīgsub) a crack in a wall.

རྩིགས་ (dzīì) imp. of རྩིག.

རྩིང་ (dzīŋ) abbr. of རྩིང་པོ་.

རྩིང་ཆོས་ (dzīŋjöö) those ideas and behaviors that do not adhere to the dharma.

རྩིང་པོ་ (dzīŋbu) coarse, rough, crude ¶ རྩམ་པ་རྩིང་པོ་ཞིག་བཏགས་འདུག (They) ground the རྩམ་པ་ coarsely.

རྩིང་སྤྱོད་ (dzīŋjöö) coarse/ crude/ unprincipled/ wild in behavior; va.—སྟོན་ va. to behave appallingly, wildly/ crudely.

རྩིང་ཕྱེ་ (dzīŋce) coarse flour.

རྩིང་ཤད་ (dzīŋshεὲ) sm. རྩིང་སྤྱོད་.

རྩིང་ཤིབ་ (dzīŋshib) big and small pieces of sth.

རྩིང་བཟོ་ (dzīŋso) embryonic form.

རྩིང་ལོས་ (dzīŋlöö) degree of roughness/ coarseness.

རྩིང་ཤོག (dzīŋshoò) rough/ inferior quality paper.

རྩིད་ (dzīì) abbr. of རྩིད་པ་.

རྩིད་སྐུད་ (dzīìgüü) yak hair thread.

རྩིད་སྐུད་ཀྱིས་གཡག་རོ་འདྲུད་པ་ (dzīìgüügi yāgro drüüba) giving a small gift in the hope of getting a big return [Lit. dragging the carcass of a yak by a thread of yak hair].

རྩིད་གུར་ (dzīìgur) yak-hair tent.

རྩིད་གོག (dzīìgɔɔ̀) two year goat.

རྩིད་གྲི་ (dzīìdri) knife for shearing/ cutting yak hair.

རྩིད་སྟན་ (dzīìdεn) sm. རྩིད་གདན་.

རྩིད་ཐག (dzīìdaà) yak-hair rope.

རྩིད་གདན་ (dzīìdεn) cushion/ mattress made from yak hair.

རྩིད་པ་ (dzīìbə) the belly hair of yaks.

རྩིད་པོ་ (dzīìbu) sm. རྩུབ་པོ.

རྩིད་ཕྱར་ (dzīìjar) yak-hair blanket.

རྩིད་ཕྱིང་ (dzīìjiŋ) felt made from yak hair.

རྩིད་བུ་ (dzīìbu) two year old goat.

རྩིད་མོ་ (dzīìmu) two year old female goat.

རྩིད་ཤང་འཐག་མ་ (dzīìshaŋ tāgma) shung. woven yak hair ¶ རྨོག་གི་མཐའ་ལྷུགས་རྩིད་ཤང་འཐག་མ་འཇའ་སྦྲག Helmet lining made from woven yak hair.

རྩིབ་ (dzīb) abbr. of རྩིབ་མ་.

རྩིབ་སྐྱི་ (dzībgyi) pleura.

རྩིབ་སྐྱིའི་གཉན་ཚད་ (dzībgyii ñε̄ndzεὲ) pleurisy.

རྩིབ་སྐྱིའི་ཚ་ནད་ (dzībgyii tsānεὲ) sm. རྩིབ་སྐྱིའི་གཉན་ཚད་.

རྩིབ་ཆུང་ (dzībjuŋ) short ribs.

རྩིབ་ལྡུང་ (dzībduŋ) 1. short ribs. 2. a point in the body for acupuncture.

རྩིབ་རྡོ་གཞུ་ (dzībdo shu) sm. རྩིབ་མ་གཙོག.

རྩིབ་དབྲག་དབང་རྩ་ (dzībdraà wāŋdza) intercostal nerves.

རྩིབ་མ་ (dzībmə) sm. རྩིབས་མ་.

རྩིབ་མ་ (dzībmə) 1. rib; va.—གཙོག to break (a person's rib). 2. va. to bribe (slang).

རྩིབ་མ་བཤེར་ (dzībmə shēr) va. to talk about other's faults [Lit. counting/ checking ribs].

རྩིབ་མ་ཧྲང་ཧྲང་ (dzībmə hra̱ŋhraŋ) skinny with protruding ribs.

རྩིབ་མའི་གོ་བར་ (dzībmɛ ko̱war) the space/ gap between the left and right ribs.

རྩིབ་གཟེར་ (dzībser) pain in the ribs; vi.—རྒྱག.

རྩིབ་རུས་ (dzībrüü) ribs, rib bone.

རྩིབ་ལོགས་ (dzīnlɔ̀ɔ) on the ribs.

རྩིབ་ཤ་ (dzībsha) meat on the ribs, spareribs.

རྩིབ་གསེང་ (dzībseŋ) space in between the ribs.

རྩིབས་ (dzīb) abbr. of རྩིབས་མ་.

རྩིབས་ཀྱི་མུ་ཁྱུད་ (dzīngi mu̱gyüü) rim of a wheel.

རྩིབས་སྒོ་ (dzībgo) 1. a small side door attached to a house. 2. spoke (of a wheel).

རྩིབས་སྟོང་འཁོར་ལོ་ (dzībdoŋ kɔ̄ɔlo) a wheel with one thousand spokes.

རྩིབས་ལྡན་ (dzībdɛn) Tuesday.

རྩིབས་མ་ (dzībmə) spoke (of wheel).

རྩིའུ་ཐག་མ་ (dzīwu tāgmə) a kind of ornament worn by the རྒྱན་བཟང་མ་.

རྩིས་ (dzīi) 1. calculation, computation, accounting, mathematics, arithmetic; va.—རྒྱག; —འདེབས་ to calculate, to count, to compute, to do accounts, to do mathematics/ arithmetic. 2. (vb. + རྩིས་) to plan to do ¶ ཁོ་ཚོས་སང་ཉིན་ལས་ཀ་བྱ་རྩིས་ཡོད་པ་རེད་ They plan to work tomorrow.

རྩིས་ཀྱི་ཡི་གེའི་ལས་ལྔ་ (dzīigi yigii lɛ̄ɛŋa) five types of calculating: numbers, addition, subtraction, multiplication, division. 3. astrology.

རྩིས་ཀྱི་རིག་བྱེད་ (dzīigi rigjeè) astrology.

རྩིས་སྐོར་ (dzīigɔɔ) va. to calculate in advance about what sth. will cost ¶ ཁང་པ་ཞིག་རྒྱག་པར་འགྲོ་སོང་ག་ཚོད་འགྲོ་མིན་རྩིས་བསྐོར་དགོས་ You have to calculate beforehand how much building a house will cost.

རྩིས་སྐྱོར་ (dzīigyɔr) calculating/ computing again; va.—རྒྱག.

རྩིས་བསྐོར་ (dzīigɔɔ) p. of རྩིས་སྐོར་.

རྩིས་ཁང་ (dzīigaŋ) shung. the Revenue Office in the traditional Tibetan government (this office deals with taxes, revenues/ expenses and training of new lay officials).

རྩིས་ཁམས་དྭངས་ (dzīigam da̱ŋ) a complete and clear accounting; va.—སྤྲོད་ to hand over a complete and clear accounting.

རྩིས་ཁོག་ (dzīigɔ̀ɔ) the result of an astrological calculation.

རྩིས་ཁྲ་ (dzīidrə) 1. account book/ ledger, statement of accounts; va.—བཟོ་; —སྒྲིག་ to make/ compile an account statement/ book/ ledger; va.—འབུལ་ to submit an accounting; va.—གཏོང་ to send a bill/ statement. 2. account number ¶ ཁོང་གི་དངུལ་ཁང་རྩིས་ཁྲ་ཨང་གྲངས་གཉིས་པ་རེད་ His bank account number is two.

རྩིས་ཁྲ་སྒྱུར་ (dzīidra gyu̱r) va. to transfer an account (between banks).

རྩིས་མཁན་ (dzīiñɛn) sm. རྩིས་པ་.

རྩིས་འཁོར་ (dzīigɔɔ) 1. calculating machine ¶ གློག་རྡུལ་རྩིས་འཁོར་ Electronic calculator. 2. computer.

རྩིས་འཁོར་ལྟེ་བ་ (dzīigɔɔ dēwa) computer center.

རྩིས་འཁོར་ལག་རྩལ་ཞིབ་འཇུག་ཁང་ (dzīigɔɔ la̱gdzɛɛ shi̱mjuùgaŋ) institute of computer technology.

རྩིས་འཁྲི་སྤྲོད་ (dzīidrii drȫö) shung. va. to be given responsibility over sth. (that later will have to be accounted for) ¶ རྫོང་གཞིས་དེ་ར་སེམས་ཅན་སྒོ་ནག་བརྒྱ་ཐམ་པ་རྩིས་འཁྲི་སྤྲད་པ་རེད་ That district estate was given responsibility for 100 yak (and would have to account for them when the district head changed).

རྩིས་གྲངས་ལོངས་ (dzīidraŋ lo̱ŋ) vi. to reach the correct amount/ figure (for an account/ plan/ schedule) ¶ དམག་ཕོགས་བསྡུ་རྒྱུའི་འབྲུའི་རྩིས་གྲངས་ལོངས་བཞག The grain specified for the military salary (tax) has been collected (reached in full).

རྩིས་མགོ་ཐོན་པ་ (dzīigo tōmbo) sb. who is capable in accounting.

རྩིས་འགྲོ་ (dzīndro) 1. paying attention to, heeding, relying, depending; va.—གཏོང་ to pay attention to, to heed (sm. ཆ་བཞག་) ¶ ཕ་ཚོས་ཐེངས་མང་པོ་བསྒྲགས་ཀྱང་རྩིས་འགྲོ་མ་བཏང་བ་རེད་ Even though we warned them many times, they didn't heed it. 2. shung. a receipt that can be accepted as part of an expense account; va.—གཏོང་ to submit a receipt for expenses ¶ གཞུང་དོན་དུ་སྐུ་མགྲོན་བདག་འདྲེན་ཞུས་པའི་འགྲོ་སོང་རྩིས་འགྲོར་གཏོང་ཆོག You can submit receipts for entertaining guests for goverment business.

རྩིས་འགྲོ་མེད་པ་ (dzīndro me̱èba) 1. not paying attention to, not heeding. 2. expenses or expenses account not cleared/ accounted for.

རྩིས་འགྲོ་སེལ་དག (dzīndro sēēdaà) shung. clearing/ accounting for (expenses) ¶ བྱུང་སོང་རྩིས་ཁྲ་འདི་ཐོག་ནས་རྩིས་འགྲོ་སེལ་དག་ཞུ་རྒྱུ The expenditures and incomes will be cleared through this account.

རྩིས་འགྲོའི་འཛིན་ (dzīndro dzīndrö dzi̱n) shung. a document that clears/ accounts for expenses.

རྩིས་རྒྱག (dzīi gyə̱b) va. to compute/ account/ calculate ¶ འགྲོ་སོང་ག་ཚོད་ཕྱིན་མིན་རྩིས་རྒྱག་དགོས་ You must calculate how much has been spent in expenses.

རྩིས་རྒྱག་ཁྲི་ཙེ་ (dzīigyaà trēdzi) tib. ch. slide rule.

རྩིས་རྒྱག་འཁོར་ལོ་ (dzīigyaà kɔ̄ɔlo) calculator.

རྩིས་རྒྱག་ཐོ་འགོད་ (dzīigyaà tōgöö) accounting; va.—བྱེད་.

རྩིས་རྒྱག་འཕྲུལ་འཁོར་ (dzīigyaà trüügɔɔ) calculating machine.

རྩིས་རྒྱག་ལོ་དུས་ (dzīigyaà lo̱düü) financial statement for the fiscal year, annual balance sheet.

རྩིས་སྒོ་ (dzīigo) 1. closing/ settling an account at the end of a year; va.—རྒྱག; —གཏོང་. 2. sm. རྩིས་འགྲོ་.

རྩིས་སྒྲོམ་ (dzīidrom) abacus; va.—རྒྱག; —གཏོང་ to calculate with an abacus.

རྩིས་ངན་ (dzīiŋɛn) a bad/ evil/ wicked/ intention or plan; va.—རྒྱག.

རྩིས་དངོས་རྫས་གསུམ་ (dzīi ŋȫö dzɛ̱̀ sūm) the three: mathematics, physics and chemistry.

རྩིས་ཆེན་ (dzīijen) valuable, dear, esteemed; va.—བྱེད་ to treasure, to value, to cherish, to hold dear.

རྩིས་ཆེན་པོ་ (dzīi cēmbo) regarded as valuable, dear, esteemed; va.— བྱེད་.

རྩིས་འཛིན་ (dzīnjoò) respect, adherence (e.g., to opinions, laws); va.—བྱེད་ to respect, to adhere to, to regard, to pay attention to, to listen to, to obey ¶ རྒྱ་ནག་གི་བསམ་འཆར་འདི་ཚོར་རྩིས་འཛིན་མ་བྱས་པ་རེད་ (They) disregarded the opinions of China. ¶ ཆིངས་ཡིག་འདི་ལ་རྩིས་འཛིན་བྱས་པ་རེད་ (They) respected (adhered to) the treaty.

རྩིས་གཉེར་ (dzīiñer) bookkeeping, accounting, bookkeeper, accountant.

རྩིས་གཉེར་ཁང་ (dzīiñergaŋ) accounting office.

རྩིས་གཉེར་དངུལ་གཉེར་ཁའུ་ (dzīiñer ŋüüñwe kəwu) tib. ch. accounting and cashier department.

རྩིས་གཉེར་དེབ་གཞུང་ (dzīiñer te̱bshuŋ) account book, accounting ledger.

རྩིས་གཉེར་པ་ (dzīiñerba) sm. རྩིས་པ་.

རྩིས་གཉེར་མི་སྣ་ (dzīiñer mi̱nə) bookkeepers, accountants.

རྩིས་གཉེར་ཚན་པ་ (dzīiñer tsɛ̄mba) accounting office.

རྩིས་གཉེར་ལོ་དུས་ (dzīiñer lo̱düü) sm. རྩིས་རྒྱག་ལོ་དུས་.

རྩིས་ཏ་ (dzīida) a horse that should be handed over to sb.

རྩིས་ཐབས་ (dzīitəb) method of accounting/ calculating/ computing.

རྩིས་ཐེབས་ (dzīiteb) 1. vi. to be able to calculate ¶ རྩིས་ཁྲ་འདི་རྙོག་དྲ་ཆ་པོ་ཡིན་ཙང་རྩིས་ཐེབས་ཀྱི་མི་འདུག Because the account was complicated, (we) were unable to calculate it. 2. vi. to be able to plan/ estimate ¶ མ་འོངས་པའི་ལས་ཀ་གང་བྱེད་རྩིས་ཐེབས་ཀྱི་མི་འདུག (We) are unable to plan our future work.

རྩིས་ཐོ་ (dzīìto) 1. account book/ ledger/ list. 2. records, notes, accounts ¶ མི་དམངས་ཀྱི་སྡུག་བསྔལ་བཀོད་པའི་རྩིས་ཐོ་ཡོད་པ་རེད་ There are records which note the sufferings of the people.

རྩིས་ཐོར་འགོད་ (dzīìtɔɔ gö̱ö̀) va. to make an entry in an account book.

རྩིས་མཐོང་ (dzīìdoŋ) esteem, deference, reverence, importance; va.—བྱེད་ to think highly of, to revere, to esteem, to attach importance to ¶ ཁོ་ལ་རྒྱ་དམར་གཞུང་གིས་རྩིས་མཐོང་མེད་པ་ཆགས་པ་རེད་ He became unimportant to the Red Chinese Government.

རྩིས་འཐབ་ (dzīìtəb) shung. balancing (of an account) ¶ མ་དངུལ་གན་ཐོག་རྩིས་འཐབ་སྤྲོད་ལེན་ཟིན་ཅིང་ The finances of the contract were balanced.

རྩིས་དག (dzīìdaà) settling accounts completely (e.g., at the completion of a trip or work); va.—ཞུ་; —འབུད་.

རྩིས་དེབ་ (dzīìdeb) bookkeeping ledger, account book.

རྩིས་གདབ་གཏོང་ (dzīìdəb dōŋ) va. to choose/ pick (what is beneficial/ profitable) and to discard (what is not profitable).

རྩིས་འདེབས་ (dzīìdeb) va. to estimate/ guess/ approximate.

རྩིས་དེལ་ (dzīìdee) shung. the traditional Tibetan way of accounting by means of stones and sticks and beans.

རྩིས་ལྡན་ (dzīìdɛn) planned, calculated ¶ རྩིས་ལྡན་དཔལ་འབྱོར་ Planned economy.

རྩིས་བསྡོམས་ (dzīìdom) totaling, adding up, calculating (an amount); va.—བྱེད་.

རྩིས་ནོར་ (dzīìnɔɔ) miscalculating, making a mistake/ error in a calculation; va.—ཐེབས་ to unintentionally miscalculate.

རྩིས་པ་ (dzīìbə) 1. bookkeeper, accountant, cashier. 2. astrologer. 3. shung. junior officer in the traditional Tibetan government's རྩིས་ཁང་.

རྩིས་པོ་ཆེ་ (dzīìboje) precious, valuable, dear.

རྩིས་དཔེ་ (dzīìbe) sm. རྩིས་དེབ་.

རྩིས་དཔོན་ (dzīìbön) shung. title of the four heads of the Revenue Bureau (རྩིས་ཁང་) of the tt. goverment.

རྩིས་སྤྲད་ (dzīì drɛ̄ɛ̀) p. of རྩིས་སྤྲོད་.

རྩིས་སྤྲོད་ (dzīìdrö̀ö̀) handing over, transferring (e.g., authority, wealth, suspected criminals etc.); va.—བྱེད་; —རྒྱག ¶ ཁོའི་ལས་འགན་ལས་བྱེད་གསར་པར་རྩིས་སྤྲོད་བྱས་པ་རེད་ (He) handed over his responsibilities to the new officer. ¶ ཁོས་ཁོ་ཚོར་རྒྱུ་ནོར་ཚང་མ་རྩིས་སྤྲད་པ་རེད་ He handed over all his wealth to them.

རྩིས་སྤྲོད་རྩིས་ལེན་ (dzīìdrö̀ö̀ dzīìlen) shung. handing over and taking responsibility ¶ རྫོང་སྡོད་གསར་རྙིང་རྩིས་སྤྲོད་རྩིས་ལེན་བྱས་ཟིན་པ་རེད་ The exchange of the old district officer handing over accounts, things, etc.) and the new one taking the responsibilities for these has been completed.

རྩིས་ཕུལ་ (dzīìbüü) p. of རྩིས་འབུལ་.

རྩིས་ཕྲུག (dzīìdruù) shung. a lay official who is a student in the Revenue Bureau (རྩིས་ཁང་).

རྩིས་ཕྲུག་པ་ (dzīìdrugbə) sm. རྩིས་ཕྲུག.

རྩིས་ཕྲེང་ (dzīìdreŋ) formula (in math).

རྩིས་བྱེད་ (dzīì je̱è) see རྩིས་.

རྩིས་འབུལ་ (dzīìbüü) h. of རྩིས་སྤྲོད་.

རྩིས་འབྲས་ (dzīndrɛɛ̀) 1. the answer to a calculation, the product/ sum. 2. an astrological answer/ result/ calculation; va.—སྐོར་ to calculate sth. through astrology (astrological divination).

རྩིས་མེད་ (dzīìmeè) disrespect, contempt, disregard; va.—བྱེད་; —གཏོང་; —དུ་སྐྱུར་ to disregard, to disrespect, to show contempt for ¶ ཁོ་ཚོས་ཆིངས་ཡིག་ལ་རྩིས་མེད་བྱས་པ་རེད་ They disregarded the treaty.

རྩིས་གཙང་དག་རྒྱག (dzīìdzaŋ ta̱ggyaà) sm. རྩིས་དག་ཞུ་.

རྩིས་ཞིབ་ (dzīìshib) sm. རྩིས་བཤེར་.

རྩིས་ཞིབ་ལས་ཁུངས་ (dzīìshib lɛ̱ɛ̀guŋ) Auditing Office (in Dharamsala).

རྩིས་ཞུ་ (dzīìshu) shung. settling accounts, doing an accounting, repaying/ clearing a debt or account; va.—བྱེད་; —ཞུ ¶ རྫོང་གི་འགྲོ་སོང་ཚང་མ་རྩིས་ཞུ་ཞུས་འདུག (He) settled the accounting on all the district expenses.

རྩིས་ཞུའི་རིགས་ (dzīìshü ri̱g) shung. accounting materials such as receipts, invoices, etc.

རྩིས་ཞུགས་ (dzīìshuù) shung. enrolling in the རྩིས་ཁང་ as a student; va.—བྱེད་.

རྩིས་གཞི (dzīìshi) 1. a plan; va.—འདིང་; —སྒྲིར་ to plan ¶ གྲོས་མོལ་བྱེད་རྒྱུའི་རྩིས་གཞི་མེད་པ་རེད་ There is no plan for having discussions. 2. sm. རྩིས་སྒྲིར་.

རྩིས་གཞི་རེའི་རྒྱ་ཁྱོན་ (dzīìshi re̱e gya̱gyön) unit of area ¶ རྩིས་གཞི་རེའི་རྒྱ་ཁྱོན་གྱི་ཐོན་ཚད་ Yield per unit of area.

རྩིས་གཞི་རེའི་དུས་ཚོད་ (dzīìshi re̱e tü̱üdzöö) unit of time.

རྩིས་གཞི་རེའི་ཤོང་ཚད་ (dzīìshi re̱e shōŋdzɛɛ̀) unit of volume.

རྩིས་གཞིའི་རྒྱ་ཁྱོན་ (dzīìshii gya̱gyön) sm. རྩིས་གཞི་རེའི་རྒྱ་ཁྱོན་.

རྩིས་གཞུང་ (dzī¡ishuŋ) 1. account/ record book. 2. astrology text.

རྩིས་གཞོང་ (dzī¡ishoŋ) astrological chart for making calculations.

རྩིས་བཞུགས་བྱེད་ (dzīìshuù ce̱è) shung. va. to be studying as a student in the Finance Office in tt.

རྩིས་བཞེས་ (dzīì she̱è) h. of རྩིས་ལེན་.

རྩིས་རིག (dzīìrig) mathematics; arithmetic. 2. astrology.

རྩིས་རིག་མཁས་པ་ (dzīìrig kɛ̄ɛ̀ba) 1. mathematician. 2. sb. expert in astrology.

རྩིས་རིག་གི་སྤྱི་འགྲོས་ (dzīìriìgi jīndröö̀) mathematical formula.

རྩིས་རིག་སྡེ་ཁག (dzīìriì de̱gaà) department of mathematics.

རྩིས་རིག་པ་ (dzīìrigbə)1. sm. རྩིས་པ་. 2. mathematician.

རྩིས་རིག་ཞིབ་འཇུག་ཁང་ (dzīìrig shi̱mjugaŋ) institute of mathematics.

རྩིས་རིན་ (dzīìrin) worthwhile, valuable, worth considering ¶ འགྲོ་སོང་ཙག་ཙིག་རྩིས་རིན་མེད་པ་རེད་ These small expenses are not worth considering.

རྩིས་ལས་ (dzīìlɛɛ̀) accounting, bookingkeeping; va.—བྱེད་.

རྩིས་ལན་ (dzīìlɛnn) a solution (in math); va.—འཚོལ་ to find the solution or solve a problem (in math).

རྩིས་ལེན་ (dzīìlen) 1. taking over possession, assuming control over; va.—བྱེད་ ¶ དཔོན་ཁག་གི་ཞིང་ཁ་ཚང་མ་རྩིས་ལེན་བྱས་པ་རེད་ They took possession of all the fields of the lords. ¶ ཁོང་གིས་འགོ་ཁྲིད་ཀྱི་ལས་འཁུར་རྩིས་ལེན་བྱས་པ་རེད་ He assumed the responsibility of boss.

རྩིས་ལེན་བསྒྱུར་སྒྲིག (dzīìlen gyārdrig) taking over and reorganizing.

རྩིས་ལེན་བདག་སྤྲོད་ (dzīìlen da̱gdröö̀) taking over the management of sth., taking charge of a situation; va.—བྱེད་.

རྩིས་ལོག (dzīìlɔɔ̀) 1. checking sth. one has calculated by recalculating from the opposite side (so if one added a list of numbers from top to bottom one would check the total by adding from the bottom to the top); va.—རྒྱག. 2. a wrong calculation/ estimation, a miscalculation; vi.—ཐེབས་ ¶ ཁོང་ལ་ལས་ཀ་གསར་པ་ཞིག་རག་གི་རེད་བསམས་པ་དེ་རྩིས་ལོག་ཐེབས་པ་རེད་ He miscalculated, thinking he would get a new job.

རྩིས་བཤར་ (dzīìshar) a type of astrological divine

done after a person's death.

རྩིས་བཤེར་ (dzīīsher) inspecting, examining, auditing; va.—གཏོང་; —བྱེད་.

རྩིས་བཤེར་ལས་ཁུངས་ (dzīīsher lɛ̱ɛ̀guŋ) auditing office.

རྩུག་དུ་སྡོད་ (dzūgdu dö̱ö) va. to stay somewhere permanently ། ཁོང་ས་ཆ་འདིར་རྩུག་དུ་སྡོད་ཀྱི་ཡོད་པ་རེད་ He is staying here permanently.

རྩུབ་ (dzūb) abbr. of རྩུབ་པོ་.

རྩུབ་ཆགས་ (dzūbjaà) calamity, disaster.

རྩུབ་གདམ་ (dzūbdam) harsh talk/ words.

རྩུབ་དར་ (dzūbdar) sharpening sth. against a coarse stone; va.—རྒྱག.

རྩུབ་དར་ཤེལ་སྒོ་ (dzūbdar shēēgo) frosted glass.

རྩུབ་པོ་ (dzūbbu) 1. rough, coarse, crude ། རས་འདི་རྩུབ་པོ་འདུག This cloth is rough. 2. harsh, severe, rough, crude ། ཁོའི་སྤྱོད་པ་རྩུབ་པོ་འདུག His behavior is rough.

རྩུབ་པོ་བལ་ལ་མི་འགྲོ་ འཇམ་པོ་ཤིང་ལ་མི་འགྲོ་ (dzūbbu pɛ̱ɛla mi̱ndro ja̱mbo shiŋla mi̱ndro) one can't use gentle tactics/ methods with tough people (have to be strict and tough in applying the law) [Lit. coarse things don't go with wool, soft things don't go with wood].

རྩུབ་པས་རྩུབ་ཐུལ་ (dzūbɛɛ̀ dzūbdüü) harshness is needed to vanquish harshness (in people/ behavior).

རྩུབ་པོས་འཇམ་འདུལ་ (dzūböö ja̱mdüü) harshness vanquishes/ overcomes gentleness; va.—བྱེད་.

རྩུབ་སྤྱོད་ (dzūbjöö) 1. violent/ outrageous/ harsh/ severe behavior ། དབྱིན་གོའི་དམག་གྲུའི་རྩུབ་སྤྱོད་སྐོར་ Concerning the outrageous behavior of the British warships. 2. coarse/ crude behavior.

རྩུབ་མོ་ (dzūbmu) sm. རྩུབ་པོ་.

རྩུབ་ཚིག (dzūbdzii) sm. ཚིག་རྩུབ་.

རྩུབ་ཞན་ (dzūbshɛn) mediocre/ inferior in quality.

རྩུབ་ལོས་ (dzūblöö) degree of coarseness/ crudness/ roughness.

རྩུབ་ལན་རྩུབ་འཇལ་ (dzūblɛn dzūmjɛɛ) retaliating to harshness in kind; va.—བྱེད་.

རྩུབ་ལོས་ (dzūblöö) degree of coarseness/ crudeness/ roughness.

རྩུབ་ཤས་ཆེན་པོ་ (dzūbshɛɛ̀ cēmbo) coarse, crude, rough.

རྩུབ་སྲིད་ (dzūbsii) harsh/ rough policy.

རྩེ་ (dzē) 1. top. tip, peak ། རིའི་རྩེ་ལ་དར་ཆ་ཞིག་འདུག There is flag on the top of the mountain. ། གྲི་རྩེ་ The tip of a knife. 2. abbr. of རྩེ་པོ་བྲང་. 3. shung. abbr. of རྩེ་དྲུང་.

རྩེ་: p. བརྩེས་; f. བརྩེ་; imp. རྩེས་ (dzē) va. to play, to amuse oneself ། ཁོ་ཚོས་པོ་ལོ་བརྩེས་པ་རེད་ They played ball.

རྩེ་སྒོར་ (dzēgɔɔ) shung. the monk official segment in the traditional Tibetan Government, monk officials in the traditional Tibetan government.

རྩེ་མཁན་མགྲོན་ཆེ་བ་ (dzēgɛn dro̱n cēwa) shung. sm. མགྲོན་གཉེར་ཆེ་མོ་.

རྩེ་གྲ་ (dzēdra) the best, the most excellent ། ཁོས་བོད་སྐད་རྩེ་གྲ་ཤེས་ཀྱི་འདུག He knows Tibetan excellently.

རྩེ་གྲས་ (dzēdrɛɛ̀) sm. རྩེ་གྲ.

རྩེ་གྲི་ (dzēdri) bayonet; va.—སྣུན་; —རྒྱག to bayonet.

རྩེ་གྲོགས་ (dzēdrɔɔ̀) playmate.

རྩེ་དགའ་ (dzēga) activities that entertain/ amuse; va.—ལ་རོལ་ to be engaged in entertaining/ amusing activities.

རྩེ་དགའ་མ་ (dzē ga̱ma) female in the prime of her life.

རྩེ་དགུ་གཏོར་ (dzē gu̱dɔɔ) religious exorcism festival which takes place on the 29th day of 12th month of the Tibetan calendar.

རྩེ་མགྲོན་ (dzēndrön) shung. monk official aide-de-camp in རྩེ་འགག.

རྩེ་འགག (dzē ga̱à) shung. the secretariat office of the Dalai Lama headed by the མགྲོན་ཆེ་.

རྩེ་འགོ་ (dzē go̱) apex, top.

རྩེ་རྒོད་ (dzēgöö) playing pranks, amusing; va.—ལ་རོལ་.

རྩེ་སྒྲུང་ (dzēdruŋ) humorous tale/ story.

རྩེ་སྒྲོ་ (dzēdro) wooden slab with butter decorations that are put on an offering plate (at the New Year celebration).

རྩེ་གཅིག (dzējig) sm. རྩེ་གཅིག་ཏུ.

རྩེ་གཅིག་ཏུ་ (dzējigdu) 1. one thing alone, a single thing/ idea ། རིག་པ་རྩེ་གཅིག་ཏུ་བསྒོམས་ནས་ Having concentrated on that one thing alone. 2. complete ། བླ་མ་དེ་ར་དད་པ་རྩེ་གཅིག་ཏུ་ཡོད་པ་རེད་ (He) has complete faith in that lama.

རྩེ་གཅིག་ཏུ་གཞོལ་ (dzējigdu shö̱ö) va. to put all one's effort (into a particular endeavor).

རྩེ་གཅིག་དད་མོས་ (dzējig tɛ̱ɛ̀möö) complete faith va.—ཞུ་ to have complete faith ། བོད་མི་ཚོས་ཏ་ལའི་བླ་མར་རྩེ་གཅིག་དད་མོས་ཞུ་གི་ཡོད་པ་རེད་ Tibetans have complete faith in the Dalai Lama.

རྩེ་ལྕགས་ (dzējaà) 1. iron arrow head. 2. sm. ཐོང་ལྕགས་.

རྩེ་ཆུང་ (dzējuŋ) back of the neck.

རྩེ་འཇིལ་ (dzēnjii) va. to make the (tip of a knife) blunt.

རྩེ་འཛོ་ (dzēnjo) sm. རྩེད་འཛོ་.

རྩེ་གཉེར་ཚང་བ་ (dzē ñēēdzaŋwa) shung. an officer in the treasury department in the Potala.

རྩེ་གཉེར་ཚང་ལས་ཁུངས་ (dzē ñēēdzaŋ lɛ̱ɛ̀guŋ) shung. Treasury Office in the Potala that deals with offerings.

རྩེ་དོག (dzēdɔɔ̀) the tip/ top.

རྩེ་ཐང་ (dzēdaŋ) the prefectural capital of Lhoka (Shannan) in the TAR.

རྩེ་ཐེར་ (dzēder) a serge that is made in རྩེ་ཐང་.

རྩེ་ཐོག (dzēdɔɔ̀) top floor/ story.

རྩེ་མཐུན་ (dzēdün) in agreement, of one opinion, unanimous ། གནད་དོན་འདིའི་ཐོག་ང་གཉིས་བསམ་འཆར་གཅིག་མཐུན་རེད་བཞག On this issue we are in full agreement.

རྩེ་མཐོ་ (dzēdo) top, highest, peak.

རྩེ་དྲ་ (dzēdra) sm.* རྩེ་གྲ་.

རྩེ་དྲུང་ (dzēdruŋ) shung. monk official (in the traditional Tibetan government).

རྩེ་དྲུང་དཀྱུས་མ་ (dzēdruŋ gyüümə) shung. an ordinary status monk official (in the traditional Tibetan government).

རྩེ་དྲུང་གླིང་ཁ་ (dzēdruŋ liŋgə) a park in the south of Lhasa.

རྩེ་དྲུང་དབྱར་སྐྱིད་ (dzēdruŋ yərgyii) shung. holiday in summer when monk officials go for a picnic.

རྩེ་དྲུང་མི་དྲག (dzēdruŋ mi̱draà) shung. a monk official who comes from an aristocratic family.

རྩེ་མདུང་ (dzēnduŋ) spear.

རྩེ་འདོད་ (dzēndöö) 1. passion, lust. 2. liking games and amusement.

རྩེ་གནས་ (dzēnɛɛ̀) a place for sports/ games/ amusement/ recreation.

རྩེ་རྣམ་གན་ལས་ཁུངས་ (dzē nāmgɛn lɛ̱ɛ̀guŋ) shung. a treasury office in the Potala.

རྩེ་རྣམ་རྒྱལ་གྲྭ་ཚང་ (dzē nāmgyɛɛ tra̱daŋ) Namgyal Monastery (in the Potala).

རྩེ་རྣམ་སྲས་གན་མཛོད་ (dzē nāmsɛɛ̀ gɛ̱ndzöö) shung. the large storehouse in the Potala that is under the རྩེ་རྣམ་གན་ལས་ཁུངས་.

རྩེ་རྣམ་སྲས་བང་མཛོད་ (dzē nāmsɛɛ̀ pa̱ndzöö) shung. sm. རྩེ་རྣམ་སྲས་གན་མཛོད་.

རྩེ་པོ་ཏ་ལ་ (dzē bōdala) sm. རྩེ་པོ་བྲང་.

རྩེ་སྤྲོད་ (dzēdröö) 1. face-to-face fight/ combat. 2. exchanging ceremonial scarves.

རྩེ་ཕུད་ (dzēbüü) the best offering, the first offering (that is made to the gods).

རྩེ་པོ་བྲང་ (dzē pōdraŋ) Potala (the winter palace of the Dalai Lama in Lhasa).

རྩེ་ཕྱག (dzējaà) shung. 1. supply office for the Dalai Lama's personal needs. 2. the 4th rank officer who heads this office.

རྩེ་ཕྱག་ཇོ་ལགས་ (dzējaà colaà) sm. རྩེ་ཕྱག་ནང་.

རྩེ་ཕྱག་དྲུང་ (dzējaà truŋ) shung. the chief of clerks in the རྩེ་ཕྱག་ལས་ཁུངས་.

རྩེ་ཕྱག་ནང་ (dzē cāànaŋ) shung. low ranking clerks in the རྩེ་ཕྱག office.

རྩེ་ཕྱག་ཞའུ་ལི་ (dzējaà shawoli) shung. a candidate for the position of རྩེ་ཕྱག་ནང་ who is working in the རྩེ་ཕྱག office until an official slot becomes available.

རྩེ་ཕྱག་ལས་ཁུངས་ (dzējaà lɛ̀ɛguŋ) shung. sm. རྩེ་ཕྱག.

རྩེ་ཕྲན་ (dzēdrɛn) head ornament.

རྩེ་བྲོ་ (dzēdro) singing and dancing; va.—རོལ་; —འཁྲབ་.

རྩེ་མ་ (dzēma) sm. རྩེ་ད་.

རྩེ་མོ་ (dzēmo) pinnacle, peak, summit, top.

རྩེ་མོར་འགྲོ་ (dzēmɔr dro) vi. to reach or attain the highest level/ acme/ pinnacle, to become the best ¶ ཚན་རིག་ཡར་ཐོན་གྱི་རྩེ་མོར་ཕྱིན་པས་ Because of reaching the highest level of scientific development.

རྩེ་མོར་འཕགས་ (dzēmɔɔ pāg) sm. རྩེ་མོར་འགྲོ་.

རྩེ་མོར་སོན་ (dzēmɔɔ sön) sm. རྩེ་མོར་འགྲོ་.

རྩེ་གཙུག (dzēdzuù) a top knot of hair.

རྩེ་རྫམ་གཉེར་ཁང་ (dzēdzam ñēēgaŋ) shung. a storeroom/ warehouse in the Potala where རྫམ་པ་ is stored.

རྩེ་ཚོགས་པ་ (dzēdzɔgba) name of an 11th century monastery in Nethong (this is one of the monasteries that is required to send monk candidates to the རྩེ་སློབ་གྲྭ་).

རྩེ་མཚར་ (dzēndzaa) a joke, joking; va.—ཤོད་ to joke.

རྩེ་ཡིག་ཚང་ (dzē yidzaŋ) shung. sm. ཡིག་ཚང་.

རྩེ་ཡིག་ཚང་ལས་ཁུངས་ (dzē yigdzaŋ lɛ̀ɛguŋ) shung. sm. རྩེ་ཡིག་ཚང་.

རྩེ་ཞབས་ (dzēshəb) shung. རྩེ་ཤོད་.

རྩེ་ཞྭ་ (dzēsha) the yellow hat worn by the monks of the Gelugpa sect.

རྩེ་ཞོལ་ (dzē shöö) shung. the Potala and the ཞོལ་ town/ area beneath the Potala.

རྩེ་གཞུང་ (dzēshuŋ) hill and valley.

རྩེ་གཟིམ་འགག (dzē simgaà) shung. sm. རྩེ་འགག.

རྩེ་ཟླ་ (dzēnda) arc. 1. sexual partner. 2. girlfriend, boyfriend.

རྩེ་འོག (dzēwɔɔ̀) next to best, second best.

རྩེ་རི་ (dzēri) top of a mountain/ hill.

རྩེ་རིག་གནས་སློབ་གྲྭ་ཆེན་མོ་ (dzē rignɛɛ̀ lōndra cēmmo) shung. the name of the government school for training monk officials (in the Potala).

རྩེ་རིང་ (dzēriŋ) sth. that is long with a pointed tip/ edge.

རྩེ་ལེགས་ (dzēleg) sm. རྩེ་གྲུས་.

རྩེ་ཤོད་ (dzēshöò) 1. top and bottom, upper and lower. 2. shung. monk and lay officials in the traditional Tibetan government. 3. shung. the Dalai Lama (རྩེ་) and the Regent (ཤོད་) (or their aide de camps).

རྩེ་ཤོད་དྲུང་འཁོར་ (dzēshöò truŋgɔɔ) shung. monk and lay officials of the traditional Tibetan goverment.

རྩེ་ཤོད་ཕྱག་ནང་ (dzēshöò cāànaŋ) shung. abbr. of རྩེ་ཕྱག་ནང་ and ཤོད་ཕྱག་ནང་.

རྩེ་ཤོད་ལས་ཁུངས་ (dzēshöò lɛ̀ɛguŋ) shung. all of the offices of the traditional Tibetan government.

རྩེ་སེམས་ཅན་ (dzē sēmjɛn) gay, lighthearted, fun loving.

རྩེ་སོར་ལྔ་ (dzēsɔŋa) a length unit equal to a fist and the extended thumb.

རྩེ་གསུམ་ (dzēsum) trident shaped tip/ apex (usu. for weapons).

རྩེ་གསོལ་ཐབ་ཁང་ (dzē sōōdəbgaŋ) shung. kitchen of the Dalai Lama in the Potala.

རྩེ་སློབ་གྲྭ་ (dzē lōbdra) shung. sm. རྩེ་རིག་གནས་སློབ་གྲྭ་ཆེན་མོ་.

རྩིག: p. བརྩིགས་; f. བརྩིག; imp. རྩིགས་ (dzēè) 1. va. to pile up, to stack up, to build up ¶ ཁང་པའི་ཐོག་ས་གཅིག་བརྩིགས་ཚར་འདུག (They) have finished building up one story of the house. 2. (quantity/ number + བརྩིགས་ + རྒྱག) va. to stack/ pile up ¶ དེབ་སུམ་བརྩིགས་བརྒྱབ་ནས་འཇོག་དགོས། (You) have to put the books in stacks of three. 3. va. to think about, to be concerned about ¶ ཁོང་གིས་དངུལ་ལ་མ་རྩིག་པར་ཅ་ལག་དེ་ཉོས་སོང་ He did not think about money and bought the thing. 4. va. to bargain ¶ ཁོང་གིས་ཅ་ལག་དེ་ཉོ་དུས་གོང་རྩིག་མ་སོང་ When he bought that thing he did not bargain.

རྩིག་བྱེད་རྩེད་ཤིང་ (dzēèjeè dzēèshiŋ) wooden stacking blocks (toys).

རྩིག་རྩིག (dzēgdzeè) bargaining over a price; va.—བྱེད་.

རྩིགས་ (dzēè) imp. of རྩིག.

རྩེང་: p. བརྩེངས་; f. བརྩེང་; imp. རྩེངས་ (dzēŋ) va. to raise up (usu. clothes) ¶ ན་བཟའ་ཏོག་ཙམ་རྩེངས་དང་ Please raise your dress a little.

རྩེང་པོ་ (dzēŋbo) short.

རྩེང་རྩེང་ (dzēŋdzeŋ) raising up (usu. for clothes); va.—བྱེད་.

རྩེད་ (dzēè) abbr. of རྩེད་མོ་.

རྩེད་ཁང་ (dzēègaŋ) recreation/ amusement center.

རྩེད་གད་སློང་ (dzēgɛɛ̀ lōŋ) va. to cause to make laugh, to joke.

རྩེད་སྒྲོགས་ (dzēèdrɔɔ̀) sm. རྩེ་སྒྲོགས་.

རྩེད་དགར་རོལ་ (dzēèga röö) 1. va. to enjoy playing games. 2. va. to have sexual intercourse.

རྩེད་འགྲན་ (dzēèdrɛn) a sports event/ competition; va.—བྱེད་ to take part in a sports event/ competition.

རྩེད་འགྲོས་ (dzēndröò) the way children hop and jump when playing.

རྩེད་སྒོད་ (dzēègöò) laughing; va.—དགོད་ to laugh.

རྩེད་རྒྱན་ (dzēègyɛn) betting, wagering (in a game); va.—འཛུགས་ to maker a bet/ wager.

རྩེད་རྒྱན་ཆེ་རིགས་ (dzēègyɛn cērìì) high-stakes gambling.

རྩེད་རྒྱུགས་ (dzēègyuù) playing and running.

རྩེད་ཆས་ (dzēèjɛɛ̀) 1. toy ¶ རྩེད་ཆས་བཟོ་གྲྭ་ Toy factory. 2. game/ sports equipment ¶ པོ་ལོ་དང་མ་ཇོང་སོགས་ཀྱི་རྩེད་ཆས་འཚོང་ལས་འདུག They sell recreational equipment for such things as soccer and mahjong.

རྩེད་ཆས་ཚོང་ཁང་ (dzēèjɛɛ̀ tsōŋgaŋ) toy store.

རྩེད་འཇོ་ (dzēnjo) entertainment, recreation, amusement; va.—བྱེད་ to engage in entertainment/ recreation.

རྩེད་འཇོ་ཁང་ (dzēnjo kāŋ) club, recreation hall/ room.

རྩེད་འཇོའི་བྱེད་སྒོ་ (dzēnjö ceègo) recreational activities.

རྩེད་གཏམ་ (dzēèdam) humor, humorous talk, jokes.

རྩེད་སྟོན་ (dzēèdön) sports day, sports competition.

རྩེད་ཐང་ (dzēèdaŋ) sm. རྩེ་ཐང་.

རྩེད་ཐེར་ (dzēèder) sm. རྩེ་ཐེར་.

རྩེད་མདའ་ (dzēnda) playing with guns or arrows; va.—རྒྱག.

རྩེད་འདུན་པ་ (dzēè dümbə) sb. who loves to play games.

རྩེད་སྤྱད་ (dzēèjɛɛ̀) sm. རྩེད་ཆས་.

རྩེད་སྣ་ (dzēèna) various kinds of sports/ games.

རྩེད་སྦྱོང་ར་བ་ (dzēèjoŋ rawa) sports practice field.

རྩེད་མོ་ (dzēèmo) game, play, recreation; va.—རྩེ་ to play a game, to play around.

རྩེད་མོ་མཁན་ (dzēèmogɛn) player in a game.

རྩེད་མོ་རྒྱགས་ཚད་རྩེ་ (dzēèmo gyagdzɛɛ̀ dzē) va. to play till one has had enough/ is completely satiated.

རྩེད་མོའི་འགྲན་བསྡུར་ (dzēèmö drɛndur) sports competition.

རྩེད་མོའི་ཡོ་བྱད་ (dzēèmö yobjɛɛ̀) 1. toys. 2. paraphernalia for various sports.

རྩེད་མོར་ཤོར་ (dzēèmɔ shɔ̄ɔ) vi. 1. to become hooked on a game/ sport or on games/ sports in general. 2. vi. to lose a game.

རྩེད་ཚོགས་རུ་ཁག (dzēèdzɔɔ̀ r̲ugaà) sports team ¶ཨ་མི་རི་ཀའི་ཀྱི་བོལ་ཀྲུས་ནི་སི་རྩེད་ཚོགས་རུ་ཁག The American table tennis team.

རྩེད་ཞོར་དགོད་ཞོར་ (dzēèshɔɔ g̲öòshɔɔ) playing/ fooling/ joking around and laughing.

རྩེད་ཞོར་རྒོད་ཞོར་ (dzēèshɔɔ g̲öòshɔɔ) sm. རྩེད་ཞོར་དགོད་ཞོར་.

རྩེད་ཟླ་ (dzēnda) sm. རྩེ་གྲོགས་.

རྩེད་ཡ་ (dzēèya) sm. རྩེ་གྲོགས་.

རྩེད་ཡུལ་ (dzēèyöö) the partner/ object of sex ¶ང་ཁྱེད་རང་གི་རྩེད་ཡུལ་མ་ཡིན་ I will not be your sexual partner.

རྩེད་ར་ (dzēèra) playground, playing field.

རྩེད་རོགས་ (dzēèrɔɔ̀) sm. རྩེ་གྲོགས་.

རྩེད་ཤིང་ (dzēèshiŋ) wooden toys.

རྩེན་ (dzēn) 1. va. to play. 2. va. to live. 3. vi. to rise/ surge (for waves).

རྩེན་འདོད་ (dzēndöò) sm. རྩེ་འདོད་.

རྩེན་གནས་ (dzēnnεὲ) 1. sm. རྩེད་ར་. 2. a stage (for theater). 3. sky.

རྩེན་སྦྱོར་ (dzēnjɔɔ) touching in a sexual/ sensual manner; va.—བྱེད་.

རྩེབས་ཡོང་ (dzēb y̲oŋ) va. to come.

རྩེའུ་ (dzēwu) tiny veins.

རྩེར་ (dzēē) 1. neck. 2. arguing; va.—རྒྱག to argue; vi.—ཤོར་ to get into an argument.

རྩེར་ཀྱོག་ག (dzēr gyɔɔ̀ga) person whose neck is bent towards one side.

རྩེར་སྒྲེང་ (dzērdreŋ) 1. va. to be stubborn. 2. va. to refuse to yield/ budge, to act tough.

རྩེར་རངས་ (dzēēraŋ) arguing; va.—རྒྱག.

རྩེར་ཤོར་ (dzēē shɔ̄ɔ) see རྩེར་.

རྩེར་སོན་ (dzēēsön) acme, epitome. 2. top, peak ¶ཁོས་རྩེར་སོན་གྱི་ལག་རྩལ་བསྟན་པ་རེད་ He exhibited the epitome of that handicraft skill.

རྩེར་སོན་ཚན་རིག (dzēēsön tsε̄nriì) the acme or pinnacle of science.

རྩེར་སོན་ལུས་རྩལ་པ་ (dzēēsön lṳ̈ùdzεεba) star athletes/ players.

རྩེར་སློང་ (dzēēloŋ) va. to intentionally cause an argument.

རྩེས་ (dzēè) p. of རྩེ་.

རྩོད་: p. and f. བརྩད་; imp. རྩོད་ (dzȫò) va. to argue, to dispute, to quarrel, to debate ¶ནོར་འཁྲུལ་དེ་སུའི་ཡིན་མིན་ལ་རྩོད་ཅིང་ Arguing about whose mistake that was.

རྩོད་མཁས་ (dzȫòkεὲ) skilled in debate/ argument.

རྩོད་རྒྱར་ (dzȫògyar) shung. vi. to fall into a state of quarrel/ legal dispute/ disagreement.

རྩོད་གྲྭ་ (dzȫòdra) a class in a monastery that studies debate.

རྩོད་གླེང་ (dzȫòleŋ) dispute, quarrel, contention, argument, debate; va.—བྱེད་ ¶མཐའ་མཚམས་རྩོད་གླེང་ A frontier dispute.

རྩོད་སྒྲུབ་ (dzȫòdrub) dialectic.

རྩོད་སྒྲུབ་ཀྱི་དངོས་གཙོའི་རིང་ལུགས་ (dzȫòdrubgi ŋȫòdzö r̲iŋluù) dialectical materialism.

རྩོད་སྒྲུབ་ཀྱི་དངོས་གཙོ་སྨྲ་བ་ (dzȫòdrubgi ŋȫòdzo māwa) sm. རྩོད་སྒྲུབ་ཀྱི་དངོས་གཙོའི་རིང་ལུགས་.

རྩོད་སྒྲུབ་ཀྱི་གཅིག་གྱུར་ (dzȫòdrubgi jīggyur) dialectical unity.

རྩོད་སྒྲུབ་ཀྱི་ཆོས་ཉིད་ (dzȫòdrubgi cȫòñiì) dialectical law.

རྩོད་སྒྲུབ་ཀྱི་གཏན་ཚིགས་རིག་པ་ (dzȫòdrubgi dε̄ndziì r̲igbə) dialectical logic, dialectics.

རྩོད་སྒྲུབ་ཀྱི་རིག་པ་ (dzȫòdrubgi r̲igbə) dialectics.

རྩོད་སྒྲུབ་ཀྱིས་དངོས་པོ་ཙམ་སྨྲ་བ་ (dzȫòdrubgi ŋȫòbodzam māwa) sm. རྩོད་སྒྲུབ་ཀྱི་དངོས་གཙོའི་རིང་ལུགས་.

རྩོད་སྒྲུབ་ཀྱི་ལྟ་ཚུལ་ (dzȫòdrubgi dədzüü) dialectical views.

རྩོད་སྒྲུབ་ཀྱི་བསམ་གཞིགས་ (dzȫòdrubgi sāmshiì) dialectical thought/ thinking.

རྩོད་ཅན་ (dzȫòjεn) shung. controversial, disputed, in conflict.

རྩོད་བརྙད་ (dzȫòñεὲ) shung. dispute, controversy argument ¶ན་ལོ་རྩོད་བརྙད་སྐབས་ས་ཆ་དེ་དགུས་ཆོའི་དེབ་ཐོག་ཏུ་གསལ་གཞིས་ཤིལ་ཆོས་སུ་རང་འཛུགས་ཀྱི་རྩོད་མེད་བྱ་རྒྱུ་ Last year when there was a dispute, (it was found that) the land was listed in the monastery's book therefore the monastery shall take the possession of the land as before.

རྩོད་རྙོག (dzȫòñog) dispute, argument, controversy ¶ས་མཚམས་རྩོད་རྙོག A border dispute.

རྩོད་ཐུག (dzȫò tūù) vi. to be in conflict/ dispute, to get into a conflict/ dispute.

རྩོད་འཐེན་ (dzȫò tēn) sm. རྩོད་ལེན་.

རྩོད་དུས་ (dzȫòdüù) shung. abbr. of རྩོད་ལྡན་གྱི་དུས་.

རྩོད་དོན་ (dzȫòdön) civil lawsuit/ case/ dispute.

རྩོད་དོན་སྐོར་གྱི་ཁྲིམས་ལུགས་ (dzȫòdön gɔ̄rgi trīmluù) civil law.

རྩོད་དོན་རྒྱུད་གཞི་ (dzȫòdön gyö̲òshi) civil law case.

རྩོད་དོན་གདུག་བཤེར་ (dzȫòdön dūgsher) a hearing (of a case/ lawsuit/ dispute); va.—བྱེད་; —གཏོང་ to hear or try a case/ lawsuit/ dispute.

རྩོད་དོན་ལབ་གླེང་ (dzȫòdön l̲əbleŋ) civil dispute, quarrel.

རྩོད་ལྡན་གྱི་དུས་ (dzȫòdεngi tṳ̈ù) 1. the time of a quarrel/ conflict/ dispute. 2. shung. a time/ era of conflict/ dispute, a quarrelsome period, a degenerate era/ age.

རྩོད་ལྡན་ (dzȫòdεn) quarrelsome, disputatious, in conflict.

རྩོད་གནས་ (dzȫònεὲ) an era when quarrels/ disputes abound.

རྩོད་པ་ (dzȫòba) dispute, quarrel, argument, debate; va.—བྱེད་; —རྒྱག to dispute, to argue, to quarrel, to debate; vi.—ཤོར་; —ཐུག to unintentionally get into a dispute/ quarrel.

རྩོད་པ་ཇི་ཟད་ཟད་ (dzȫòba jē sε̲ὲsεὲ) endless verbal quarrel.

རྩོད་པ་ལྷུར་ལེན་ (dzȫòba lhūrlen) liking and enthusiastic about arguing/ disputing; va.—བྱེད་.

རྩོད་དཔང་ (dzȫòbaŋ) judge in a debate competition.

རྩོད་དཔྱོད་ (dzȫòjöò) examining/ investigating a dispute or quarrel.

རྩོད་འཁྲུག་བརྐུས་གཙེར་ (dzȫòdrɔɔ̀ ñε̄ὲdzee) arguing, stealing, abusing/ insulting and bothering (political slogan).

རྩོད་བྲལ་ (dzȫòdεε) sm. རྩོད་མི་དགོས་པ་.

རྩོད་མི་དགོས་པ་ (dzȫò m̲igööòbə) indisputable, beyond dispute, without dispute ¶ཁོང་ནུས་པ་ཆེན་ཡིན་པ་རྩོད་མི་དགོས་པ་ཞིག་རེད་ It is indisputable that he is great.

རྩོད་མེད་ (dzȫòmeè) sm. རྩོད་མི་དགོས་པ་.

རྩོད་མེད་འཆམ་མཐུན་ (dzȫòmeè cāmdün) friendly, harmonious.

རྩོད་མེད་བདེ་སྡོད་ (dzȫòmeè d̲edöò) living in peace with others.

རྩོད་མེད་ཡོངས་གྲགས་ (dzȫòmeè y̲oŋdraà) unquestionable known by all.

རྩོད་འཛིང་ (dzȫndziŋ) sm. འཐབ་འཛིང་.

རྩོད་ཞུ་ཞིབ་ཉན་ (dzȫòshu sh̲ibñεn) a hearing of a lawsuit; va.—བྱེད་.

རྩོད་གཞི་ (dzȫòshi) subject of a debate, basis/ root or a dispute or quarrel or controversy; va.—བཟོ་; —སློང་ to cause a dispute/ quarrel.

རྩོད་གཞི་སློང་ (dzȫòshi lōŋ) va. to raise a subject for debate.

རྩོད་གཞི་བསླང་ (dzȫòshi lāŋ) p. of རྩོད་གཞི་སློང་.

རྩོད་ཟིང་ (dzȫòsiŋ) unruly/ rowdy (people) arguing and causing a disturbance.

རྩོད་ཟླ་ (dzȫnda) sm. རྩོད་ཡ་.

རྩོད་བཟློས་ (dzȫndöò) shung. filing a lawsuit ¶ངང་ཚུལ་དེ་ལས་ལྡོག་སྟེ་ རྩོད་བཟློས་ཀྱིས་འདི་ག་ཁྲིམས་ཁྲངས་སུ་ཞུ་འཛུར་བྱུང་དོན་ On the contrary, they have filed a lawsuit.

རྩོད་ཡ་ (dzööya) one's opponent in a debate.

རྩོད་ཡིག (dzööyiì) 1. a letter arguing sth. 2. texts on logic.

རྩོད་རིགས་ (dzöörii) science of debating.

རྩོད་རེས་འགྲོག་རེས་ (dzööreè trɔ̄ɔreè) competing with each other, vying to obtain sth., grappling for sth.; va.—བྱེད་.

རྩོད་ལན་ (dzöölɛn) replying/ retorting when debating; va.—རྒྱག; va.—འདེབས་.

རྩོད་ལེན་ (dzöölen) winning over (usu. by discussions, propaganda, etc.); va.—བྱེད་ ¶ ང་ཚོ་ དྲིལ་བསྒྲགས་དང་གྲོས་མོལ་གྱི་སྒོ་ནས་མཐོ་རིམ་མི་སྣ་རྩོད་ལེན་བྱེད་དགོས་ We must win over the upper circles through propaganda and negotiation.

རྩོད་ཤགས་ (dzööshaà) arguing, disagreeing (verbally); va.—རྒྱག.

རྩོད་བཤེར་ (dzöösher) hearing a dispute/ case in court; va.—རྒྱག; —བྱེད་.

རྩོམ་: p. བརྩམས་; f. བརྩམ་; imp. རྩོམས་ (dzōm) 1. va. to compose, to write ¶ ཁོས་དེབ་ཅིག་བརྩམས་ཡོད་པ་རེད He has written a book. 2. va. to start/ begin ¶ ལས་ཀ་འདི་སུས་བརྩམས་པ་རེད་དམ་ Who started this work?

རྩོམ་ (dzōm) a composition, an essay, a literary work.

རྩོམ་མཁན་ (dzōmñɛn) author, writer.

རྩོམ་མཁན་མཐུན་ཚོགས་ (dzōmñɛn tǖndzɔ̀ɔ) writer's union/ association.

རྩོམ་འགན་རང་ཁུར་ (dzōmgɛn ra̲ŋgur) taking responsibility oneself for composing sth.

རྩོམ་འགན་ལྷན་ཚོགས་ (dzōmgɛn lhēndzoò) writer's union.

རྩོམ་རྒྱུགས་ (dzōm gyu̲ù) the final composition/ essay written by the students before completing a course or graduating; va.—ལེན་ to give such an exam; va.—སྤྲོད་ to take such an exam.

རྩོམ་སྒྱུར་ (dzōmgyur) 1. composing and translating; va.—བྱེད་ to compose and translate ¶ ཁོང་གིས་དཔེ་དེབ་མང་པོ་རྩོམ་སྒྱུར་བྱས་ཡོད་ He composed and translated many books. 2. translating and editing.

རྩོམ་བསྒྱུར་ (dzōmgyur) sm. རྩོམ་སྒྱུར་.

རྩོམ་སྒྲིག (dzōmdrig) editing; va.—བྱེད་ to edit.

རྩོམ་སྒྲིག་ཁང་ (dzōmdriggaŋ) editorial office/ department.

རྩོམ་སྒྲིག་ཐད་ཀྱི་གསལ་བཤད་ (dzōmdrigtɛɛgi sēēshɛɛ̀) editor's/ author's foreward (of a book).

རྩོམ་སྒྲིག་པ་ (dzōmdrigbə) editor, compiler ¶ རྩོམ་སྒྲིག་པའི་མཆན་ Editor's note(s).

རྩོམ་སྒྲིག་པུའུ་ (dzōmdrigbu) tib. ch. editorial office.

རྩོམ་སྒྲིག་རམ་འདེགས་པ་ (dzōmdrig ra̲mdegba) assistant editor.

རྩོམ་སྒྲིག་ཨུ་ཡོན་ལྷན་ཁང་ (dzōmdrig ūyön lhēngaŋ) editorial board.

རྩོམ་བཅོས་ (dzōmjöö) sm. རྩོམ་སྒྲིག.

རྩོམ་མཇུག་བསྡུ་ (dzōmjuù du̲) va. to finish writting a book/ article.

རྩོམ་རྙིང་ (dzōmñiŋ) classical/ ancient literature.

རྩོམ་བདམས་ (dzōmdüü) selected works ¶ མའོའི་རྩོམ་བདམས་ Selected Works of Mao.

རྩོམ་སྟངས་ (dzōmdaŋ) style of writting/ literature.

རྩོམ་ཐུང་ (dzōmduŋ) short essays/ poems/ stories.

རྩོམ་འཐབ་ (dzōmdəb) sm. རྩོམ་རྩོད་.

རྩོམ་དེབ་ (dzōmdeb) a book (that has been authored rather than translated).

རྩོམ་བསྡུ་ (dzōmdüù) collecting/ bringing together; va.—བྱེད་.

རྩོམ་བསྡུས་ (dzōmdüù) anthology, collection of essays/ literary works.

རྩོམ་པ་ (dzōmba) author, writer.

རྩོམ་པ་པོ་ (dzōmbabo) sm. རྩོམ་པ་.

རྩོམ་པ་པོའི་གཏམ་ (dzōmbabö dām) editor's note, author's note.

རྩོམ་པ་པོའི་དབང་ཆ་ (dzōmbabö wāŋja) copyright.

རྩོམ་འཕྲོ་ (dzōmdro) unfinished written works.

རྩོམ་འབྲི་ (dzōmdri) creative/ artistic/ literary writing; va.—བྱེད་.

རྩོམ་རྩོད་ (dzōmdzöö) an argument made via essays/ articles/ rejoinders.

རྩོམ་མཛོད་ (dzōmdzöö) library.

རྩོམ་ཞིབ་ (dzōmshib) editing; va.—བྱེད་ to edit.

རྩོམ་ཞུས་ (dzōmshüù) correcting, proofreading (a piece of writing).

རྩོམ་གཞི་ (dzōmshi) subject of an essay/ composition/ writing.

རྩོམ་གཞུང་ (dzōmshuŋ) composition, main text.

རྩོམ་ཟིན་ (dzōmsin) draft of an article.

རྩོམ་ཡིག (dzūmyiì) literary composition/ work, article, essay.

རྩོམ་ཡིག་གི་བཞག་པ་ (dzūmyiìgi sha̲gba) literature heritage.

རྩོམ་ཡིག་སྒྲིག་གཞི་ (dzūmyiì dri̲gshi) structure of an essay, book, etc.

རྩོམ་ཡིག་གཅེས་བསྡུས་ (dzūmyiì jēēdüù) sm. རྩོམ་བསྡུས་.

རྩོམ་ཡིག་ཕུལ་བྱུང་ (dzūmyiì pǖǖjuŋ) the best literary composition/ work, article/ essay.

རྩོམ་ཡིག་འབྲི་སྟངས་ (dzūmyiì dri̲daŋ) the style of a literary composition/ article/ essay.

རྩོམ་ཡིག་རྩག་རྩིག (dzūmyiì dzəgdzig) miscellaneous writing/ essays/ articles.

རྩོམ་ཡོན་ (dzōmyön) author's/ writer's fee, literary royalties.

རྩོམ་རིག (dzūmriì) literature.

རྩོམ་རིག་གི་སྐད་ཆ་ (dzūmriìgi gɛ̄ɛ̀ja) literary language.

རྩོམ་རིག་གི་རིགས་པའི་གཞུང་ལུགས (dzūmriìgi ri̲gbɛ shu̲ŋluù) literary theory.

རྩོམ་རིག་སྒྱུ་རྩལ་གྱི་ལས་རིགས་ (dzūmriì gyu̲dzɛɛgi lɛ̲ɛ̀riì) art and literary professions.

རྩོམ་རིག་རྙིང་པ་ (dzūmriì ñiŋbə) classical/ ancient literature.

རྩོམ་རིག་དང་སྒྱུ་རྩལ་ (dzūmriì da̲ŋ gyu̲dzɛɛ) literature and art.

རྩོམ་རིག་པ་ (dzūmrigbə) man of letters, scholar.

རྩོམ་རིག་ཞིབ་འཇུག་ཁང་ (dzūmriì shi̲mjuùgaŋ) institute of literature.

རྩོམ་རིག་ལོ་རྒྱུས་ (dzūmriì lu̲gyüù) literary history, history of literature.

རྩོམ་རིག་གསར་པ་ (dzūmriì sāāba) modern literature.

རྩོམ་རིགས་ (dzūmriì) literary works.

རྩོམ་རིང་ (dzōmriŋ) full-length literary work (usu. novel).

རྩོམ་ལན་རྩོམ་འབུལ་ (dzōmlɛn dzōmbüü) correspondence between authors, literary correspondence.

རྩོམ་ལུགས་ (dzōmluù) literary style.

རྩོམ་ལུས་ (dzōmlüù) the body or main part of an article.

རྩོམ་གཤིས་ (dzōmshiì) sm. རྩོམ་ལུགས་.

རྩོམ་བཤེར་ (dzōmsher) proofreading, editing.

རྩོམ་སློལ་ (dzōmsöö) sm. རྩོམ་ལུགས་.

རྩོམས་ (dzōm) 1. imp. of རྩོམ་.

རྩོལ་: p. བརྩལ་; f. བརྩལ་; imp. རྩོལ་ (dzöö) va. to strive, to endeavor, to do zealously, to work hard (for).

རྩོལ་སྒྲུབ་ (dzöödrub) achieving/ obtaining through hard work or striving; va.—བྱེད ¶ ཆ་རྐྱེན་དེ་དག་རྩོལ་སྒྲུབ་ཀྱི་ཆེད་དུ་ For the purpose of striving to achieve these conditions. ¶ ང་ཚོས་རང་དབང་རྩོལ་སྒྲུབ་བྱེད་པའི་ལས་འགན་གལ་ཆེ་འདི་ཉིད་བརྗེད་མེད་སྙིང་ལ་འཇོག་དགོས་ We must never forget our important task of endeavoring to achieve our freedom.

རྩོལ་བསྒྱུར་ (dzöögyur) tib. ch. reforming through hard work or striving.

རྩོལ་ཅག (dzööjaà) quick.

རྩོལ་བཅགས་ (dzööjaà) sm. རྩོལ་ཅག.

རྩོལ་འཆག (dzööjaà) sm. རྩོལ་ཅག.

རྩོལ་སྟུན་ཐོབ་སྒྲོད་ (dzöödün tōbdröö) sm. རྩོལ་བསྟུན་ཐོབ་སྒྲོད་.

རྩོལ་དྲག (dzöödraà) abbr. of ལས་རྩོལ་དྲག་པོ་.
རྩོལ་འདོན་ (dzöödön) working hard; va.—བྱེད་.
རྩོལ་པོ་ (dzööbo) h. of མགྱོགས་པོ་.
རྩོལ་བ་ (dzööwa) zeal, endeavor, diligence ¶ རྩོལ་བ་ཆེན་པོས་བྱས་པ་རེད་ (They) did it with great zeal.
རྩོལ་བ་མི་ལྷོད་པ་ (dzööwɛ milhööba) shung. working ceaselessly ¶ འགྲོ་བ་ཡོངས་ཀྱི་དོན་ལ་རྩོལ་བ་མི་ལྷོད་པར་ཚེས་འབད་པར་གྱིས་ཤིག (You should) work ceaselessly to bring comfort to all sentient beings.
རྩོལ་བྱུང་ (dzööjuŋ) man-made.
རྩོལ་མེད་ (dzöömeè) effortless, easily, without endeavor/ zeal, without effort ¶ ལས་དོན་འདི་རྩོལ་མེད་དུ་བསྒྲུབ་ཐུབ་ཀྱི་མ་རེད་ This work cannot be achieved without effort.
རྩོལ་མེད་སྐྱིད་རོལ་ (dzöömeè gyiiröö) living in comfort without working.
རྩོལ་མྱུར་ (dzööñur) h. of མགྱོགས་མྱུར་.
རྩོལ་ལམ་ (dzöölam) h. of མགྱོགས་ལམ་.
རྩོལ་ལོས་ (dzöölöö) h. of མགྱོགས་ལོས་.
རྩོལ་ཤུགས་ (dzööshüù) energy, drive, zeal; va.—རྒྱག; —སྐྱེད་ to do something with energy and zeal ¶ གསར་བརྗེའི་རྩོལ་ཤུགས་ Revolutionary zeal.
རྩོལ་ཤུགས་ཆེར་སྐྱེད་ (dzööshüù cēēgyeè) becoming more energetic/ driven/ zealous, increasing in energy/ zeal/ drive.
རྩྭ་ (dzā) grass, hay; va.—རྔ་; va.—འབྲེག to cut grass/ hay.
རྩྭ་ཀུན་དུ་བཟང་པོ་ (dzā gündu saŋbo) sm. རྩྭ་ཀུན་བཟང་.
རྩྭ་ཀུན་བཟང་ (dzā günsaŋ) wrinkled giant hyssop (used in traditional Tibetan medicine).
རྩྭ་བཀག (dzāgaà) protected grazing land (i.e., pastures on which animals are not permitted to forage, usu., until a certain time).
རྩྭ་སྐུད་ (dzāgüù) thread made from straw/ grass.
རྩྭ་སྐྱ་ (dzāgya) senescent grass.
རྩྭ་ཁ་ (dzāga) pasture area, grazing ground, grassland.
རྩྭ་ཁ་རེས་སྐོར་ (dzā kāreè gɔ̄ɔ̄) va. to engage in rotational grazing.
རྩྭ་ཁང་ (dzāgaŋ) 1. shed or hut made from grass/ straw. 2. storage house for grass or hay.
རྩྭ་ཁའི་ཟིལ་པ་ (dzāgɛ siibə) dew drops on grass.
རྩྭ་ཁུར་ (dzāgur) a load of grass.
རྩྭ་ཁྲ་ལག་འཛིན་ (dzādra ləŋdzin) shung. a document that demarcates and gives possession to a pasture area ¶ ན་སྲིད་ཁག་གསུམ་གུས་ཚོར་བསྩལ་བའི་རྫོང་བདང་རྩྭ་ཁྲ་ལག་འཛིན་ཡོད་པ་ We have a document issued by the District Commissioner in which three areas of pastureland were given to us.
རྩྭ་ཁྲིས་ (dzādreè) a large stack/ bundle of grass.
རྩྭ་མཁན་པ་ (dzā kɛ̄mbo) wormwood.
རྩྭ་འཁོར་མ་ (dzā kɔ̄ɔ̄ma) a ball of brown sugar wrapped in grass.
རྩྭ་གྲི་ (dzādri) grass cutting knife, scythe.
རྩྭ་འགེམས་སྨན་རྫས་ (dzāgem mēndzɛɛ̀) weed killer, herbicide.
རྩྭ་འགོའི་ཟིལ་པ་ (dzāngö silbə) shung. a small amount [Lit. a drop of dew on the tip of a blade of grass] ¶ ཆང་ནི་ཉེས་པ་ཀུན་གྱི་རྩ་བ་ཡིན་རྩྭ་འགོའི་ཟིལ་པ་ཙམ་སྤོང་བར་བྱ་ Barley beer is the root of all crimes, therefore, one should give up (drinking) even as much as a drop of dew on the tip of a blade of grass.
རྩྭ་སྒོར་ (dzāsgɔr) sm. རྩྭ་འཁོར་མ་.
རྩྭ་སྒྱེ་ (dzāgye) 1. sack made from grass/ straw, gunny bag. 2. bag for putting grass in.
རྩྭ་སྒྲོན་ (dzādrön) 1. torch made from grass. 2. ghost/ spirit fire seen flickering in the night.
རྩྭ་ངན་ (dzāŋɛn) sm. རྩྭ་ཡན་.
རྩྭ་ང་ (dzā ŋā) see རྩྭ་.
རྩྭ་ངའི་འཕྲུལ་འཁོར་ (dzāŋɛ trüügɔɔ) mowing machine, grass-cutting machine.
རྩྭ་སྔོ་ལྡུམ་བུ་ (dzāŋo dumbu) general term for grass and plants.
རྩྭ་བརྔ་ (dzā ŋā) va. to cut grass.
རྩྭ་བརྔ་སྦྲུལ་འདྲོགས་ (dzāŋa drüü drɔ̄ɔ̀) getting frightened by sth. [Lit. the snake got frightened when the grass was cut].
རྩྭ་བརྔའི་འུལ་མི་ (dzāŋɛɛ wüümi) shung. corvee laborers who cut grass/ mow hay.
རྩྭ་བཅུད་ (dzājüù) the nutritious value of grass.
རྩྭ་ལྕོག (dzājɔɔ̀) haystack.
རྩྭ་ཆག (dzājasà) hay and fodder.
རྩྭ་ཆུ་ (dzəju) grass/ vegetation and water ¶ རྩྭ་ཆུ་བཟང་བ་ Good grass and water.
རྩྭ་ཆུ་དབང་རིགས་ (dzəju wāŋrig) shung. ownership of grasslands and water.
རྩྭ་ཆུ་འཛོམས་པོ་ (dzəju dzombo) sm. རྩྭ་ཆུ་གཉིས་འཛོམས་.
རྩྭ་ཆུ་གཉིས་འཛོམས་ (dzəju ñiidzom) a lush area where there is both grass and water.
རྩྭ་ཆུ་གཉིས་བཟང་ (dzəju ñiisaŋ) sm. རྩྭ་ཆུ་གཉིས་འཛོམས་.
རྩྭ་མཆོག (dzājɔɔ̀) cogon grass.
རྩྭ་མཆོག་གྲོང་ (dzājɔɔ̀droŋ) Kushunagar— the place in India where the Buddha passed away.
རྩྭ་གཉེར་ལས་ཁུངས་ (dzāñee lɛɛ̀guŋ) shung. an office in the traditional Tibetan goverment that was in charge of feeding goverment horses and mules.
རྩྭ་སྙིགས་ (dzāñig) the leftover hay and grass stubble after the animals have grazed.
རྩྭ་གཏུབ་ (dzā dūb) va. to cut grass.
རྩྭ་གཏུབ་འཕྲུལ་འཁོར་ (dzādub trüügɔɔ) sm. རྩྭ་ངའི་འཕྲུལ་འཁོར་.
རྩྭ་ཐག (dzādaà) grass/ straw/ hemp rope.
རྩྭ་ཐང་ (dzādaŋ) grassy plain, grassland, pastureland.
རྩྭ་ཐུན་པ་ (dzā tümbə) a grass cutter, a person who cuts grass.
རྩྭ་ཐོ་ (dzāto) shung. a stone pile set up around a pasture to denote no grazing is permitted.
རྩྭ་ཐོས་གཅོད་ (dzādöö jöö) shung. to demarcate the boundary of a pasture by a pile of stones.
རྩྭ་འཐོག (dzā tɔ̄ɔ̀) va. to weed.
རྩྭ་དུག (dzəduù) poisonous grass; vi.—ཕོར་ to get poisoned from accidentally eating poisonous grass.
རྩྭ་དྭ་བྱིད་ (dzādajii) sm. དབྱར་རྩྭ་དགུན་འབུ་.
རྩྭ་གདན་ (dzādɛn) grass/ reed mat.
རྩྭ་གདན་ཐོག་ཁེབས་ (dzādɛn tɔ̄ɔ̀geb) grass or reed covered shed/ hut.
རྩྭ་བདག (dzādag) shung. owner of a pasture/ grassland area.
རྩྭ་འདམ་ (dzādam) marsh, grassy swamp.
རྩྭ་འདོན་ (dzādön) weeding; va.—རྒྱག; —བྱེད་.
རྩྭ་ལྡུམ་ (dzādum) abbr. of རྩྭ་སྔོ་ལྡུམ་བུ་.
རྩྭ་ལྡུམ་མཁན་པ་ (dzādum kɛ̄mbo) wormwood, artimisa.
རྩྭ་སྡུད་འཕྲུལ་འཁོར་ (dzādüù trüügɔɔ) grass/ hay harvesting machine.
རྩྭ་སྣ་འཛོམས་པོ་ (dzāna dzombo) a place having an abundance of different grasses.
རྩྭ་པད་མ་ (dzā pɛ̄ɛ̀ma) peony.
རྩྭ་སྤྱིལ་ (dzəjii) grass hut.
རྩྭ་ཕད་ (dzābɛɛ̀) abbr. of རྩྭ་རས་ཕད་གོག.
རྩྭ་ཕུང་ (dzāpuŋ) hay stack.
རྩྭ་འཕྱུགས་ (dzājaà) shung. taxes to be paid in hay; va.—རྒྱག.
རྩྭ་བྲིས་ (dzādreè) feeding trough for hay/ grass.
རྩྭ་དབྱི་ (dzə ī) lynx that lives in grassy fields/ grassland.
རྩྭ་འབུ་ (dzəmbu) bugs or insects that infest hay/ grass.
རྩྭ་འབུ་ཀ་ལ་ (dzəmbugāla) grasshopper, praying mantis.
རྩྭ་འབོལ་ (dzāmböö) mattress/ cushion stuffed with straw/ grass.
རྩྭ་འབྲུ་ (dzədru) 1. abbr. of རྩྭ་ and འབྲུ་. 2. the tuber

of dwarf lilyturf.

རྩྭ་འབྲིག་འཕྲུལ་འཁོར་ (dzādreè trũũgɔɔ) hay cutting machine.

རྩྭ་སྦུབས་ (dzābub) inner part of a stalk.

རྩྭ་མ་བཟས་ (dzā mas̲ɛɛ̀) being not sincere ¶ནང་དུ་གན་རྒོན་གྱིས་རྩྭ་མ་བཟས་ན་འཆམ་མཐུན་ཡོང་གི་མ་རེད་ If the elderly are not sincere there will be no harmony in the family. [Lit. did not eat grass].

རྩྭ་མི་ཤིང་མི་ (dzāmi shĩŋmi) sb. who does work with wood and grass.

རྩྭ་མུ་སུ་ (dzā mus̲u) alfalfa, lucerne.

རྩྭ་མུ་ཤུར་ (dzā mus̲hur) sm. རྩྭ་མུ་སུ་.

རྩྭ་མེ་ (dzāme) grass fire, prairie fire.

རྩྭ་སྨན་ (dzāmɛn) herbal medicine.

རྩྭ་རྩེ་ (dzādze) tip of grass/ hay.

རྩྭ་མཛོད་ར་བ་ (dzādzöö r̲awa) a fenced in pasture area.

རྩྭ་ཞིབ་ (dzəshib) grass cut into small/ fine pieces.

རྩྭ་ཞྭ་ (dzāsha) straw hat.

རྩྭ་གཞོན་ (dzāshön) new grass.

རྩྭ་ཟ་ (dzā s̲a) va. to respond positively to a male's flirting (for a female). 2. va. to eat grass.

རྩྭ་ཟ་མཁན་གྱི་གྲུས་ (dzā sañengi trɛɛ̀) sm. རྩྭ་ཟན་གྱི་རིགས་.

རྩྭ་ཟ་རེས་སྐོར་ (dzāsa r̲eègɔɔ) sm. རྩྭ་ཁ་རེས་སྐོར་.

རྩྭ་ཟན་ (dzāsɛn) animals that eat grass, herbivores.

རྩྭ་ཟན་གྱི་རིགས་ (dzāsɛngi rig) herbivores.

རྩྭ་ཟོར་ (dzāsɔr) sickle for cutting grass.

རྩྭ་གཟན་ (dzāsɛn) hay.

རྩྭ་ཡན་ (dzāyɛn) weeds; va.—འཐོག to weed.

རྩྭ་ཡུག་པོ་ (dzā y̲ugbu) weeds.

རྩྭ་ཡོག་པོ་ (dzā y̲ogbo) sm. རྩྭ་ཡུག་པོ་.

རྩྭ་གཡབ་ (dzāyəb) 1. grass roof. 2. fan made from grass.

རྩྭ་གཡོག (dzāyɔɔ̀) a servant who works feeding animals.

རྩྭ་གཡར་བྱེད་ (dzāyɔɔ c̲eè) va. to borrow pastureland.

རྩྭ་ར་ (dzāra) a demarcated/ set aside pasture area ¶དབྱར་དུས་འབྲོག་པ་ཚོ་ང་ཚོའི་དགོན་པའི་རྩྭ་རར་ཡོང་གི་ཡོད་པ་རེད་ In the summer, the nomads come to our monastery's pastureland.

རྩྭ་རམ་པ་ (dzā r̲amba) cogon grass.

རྩྭ་རམ་བུ་ (dzā r̲ambu) sm. རྩྭ་རམ་པ་.

རྩྭ་རས་ (dzārɛɛ̀) jute, gunny.

རྩྭ་རས་སྐུད་པ་ (dzārɛɛ̀ gũũbə) string/ thread made from jute/ hay.

རྩྭ་རས་ཕད་སྒོགས་ (dzārɛɛ̀ pɛ̀ɛgɔɔ̀) sm. རྩྭ་རས་ཕད་གོག.

རྩྭ་རས་ཕད་གོག (dzārɛɛ̀ pɛ̀ɛgɔɔ̀) gunnysack.

རྩྭ་རི་ (dzāri) grassy hill.

རྩྭ་རིགས་ (dzərii) types of grasses/ vegetation.

རྩྭ་རིགས་སྐྱེ་དངོས་ (dzərii gyēŋöö) plants, vegetation.

རྩྭ་རིགས་རིག་པ་ (dzərii r̲igbə) botany.

རྩྭ་རིན་ (dzərin) 1. price of hay. 2. fees paid for grazing animals on a pasture.

རྩྭ་ལིང་ལན་ (dzā l̲iŋlɛn) lily of the valley.

རྩྭ་ཤིང་ (dzəshiŋ) grass and trees, vegetation.

རྩྭ་ཤིང་སྣུམ་ (dzəshiŋ nūm) sm. རྩི་ཤིང་སྣུམ་.

རྩྭ་ཤིང་རིག་པར་མཁས་པ་ (dzəshiŋ r̲igbar kɛɛ̀ba) botanist.

རྩྭ་ཤོག (dzəshoò) a local nomad administrative unit in the TAR consisting of a few families who share pastureland.

རྩྭ་ས་ (dzāsa) grazing field, pasture.

རྩྭ་ས་འཛུགས་སྐྲུན་ཅུས་ (dzāsa dzugdrün jū) tib. ch. grassland development bureau.

རྩྭ་སའི་རྩོད་གཞི་ (dzāsɛ dzööshi) dispute over pasture.

རྩྭ་སོན་ (dzāsön) grass seed.

རྩྭ་གསེབ་ (dzāseb) in between grass.

རྩྭ་གསེར་སྒུད་ (dzā sērgüü) Chinese alpine rush (Eulapiopsis binata).

རྩྭ་གསོ་ (dzāso) a place with good grass where horses and mules are left to graze for long periods; va.—འཇོག to leave animals in such a place.

རྩྭ་བསེད་སྦྲུལ་འདྲོགས་ (dzāseè drũũ drɔɔ̀) getting frightened by sth. happening [Lit. the snake got frightened when the grass was chosen].

རྩྭ་བསྲེས་འདམ་པ་ (dāsɛɛ̀ d̲amba) mud that has been mixed with straw (for building).

རྩྭ་བསླས་ (dālɛɛ̀) sm. རྩྭ་སླས་.

རྩྭ་སླས་སྒྲོད་ཆས་ (dzālɛɛ̀ jööjɛɛ̀) goods woven from grass, jute, etc.

རྩྭ་ལྷམ་ (dzālham) grass/ straw sandals.

རྩྭ་ཨ་ལྭ་ (dzā āwa) Chinese Alpine rush.

རྩྭའི་ད་བྱིད་ (dzē t̲ajii) a green lizard that lives in grass.

སྩལ་ (dzɛɛ̄) sm. སྩོལ་.

སྩོགས་པ་ (dzɔ̄gba) arc. sm. སོགས་པ་.

སྩོལ་: p. བསྩལ་; f. བསྩལ་; imp. སྩོལ་ (dzöö) 1. va. to give ¶ཁོང་ལ་གསོལ་རས་ཆེན་པོ་ཞིག་བསྩལ་འདུག (They) gave him a large gift. 2. va. to let/ allow/ permit ¶གོང་རིམ་ནས་ལས་ཀ་དེ་ཁོང་ལ་བྱེད་དུ་བསྩལ་འདུག The higher authorities allowed him to do the work.

སྩོལ་འགྲེམས་མཛད་ (dzöndrem dz̲ɛɛ̀) va. to distribute.

སྩོལ་གནང་ (dzöönaŋ) h. of སྩོལ་.

བརྩགས་དོ་ (dzāgdo) sm.* བརྩེགས་དོ་.

བརྩགས་པ་ (dzāgba) sm.* བརྩེགས་པ་.

བརྩམ་ (dzām) f. of རྩོམ་.

བརྩམ་ཆོས་ (dzāmja) sm. བརྩམ་བྱ་.

བརྩམ་བྱ་ (dzāmja) literary work/ article, book.

བརྩམ་གཞི་ (dzāmshi) sm. རྩོམ་གཞི་.

བརྩམས་ (dzām) p. of རྩོམ་.

བརྩམས་སྒྲུང་ (dzāmdruŋ) novel, fictional story.

བརྩམས་སྒྲུང་རིང་པོ་ (dzāmdruŋ r̲iŋgu) a novel.

བརྩམས་ཆོས་ (dzāmjöö) commentaries on religious subjects.

བརྩམས་དེབ་ (dzāmdeb) sm. རྩོམ་དེབ་.

བརྩམས་འབྲས་ (dzāmdrɛɛ̀) the result of one's literary work.

བརྩམས་འབྲས་དང་པོ་ (dzāmdrɛɛ̀ t̲aŋbo) first/ maiden book or article.

བརྩམས་ཡོན་ (dzāmyön) royalty, fee for writing sth.

བརྩལ་ (dzɛɛ̄) p. and f. of རྩོལ་.

བརྩལ་ཚགས་ (dzɛɛ̄dzaà) a filter; va.—རྒྱག to filter.

བརྩི་ (dzī) f. of རྩི་.

བརྩི་བཀུར་ (dzīgur) respect; va.—བྱེད་; —ཞུ་.

བརྩི་འཁུར་ (dzīgur) sm. བརྩི་བཀུར་.

བརྩི་སྒོ་ (dzīgu) sth. that should be respected.

བརྩི་འཇོག (dzīnjoò) sm. བརྩི་བཀུར་.

བརྩི་ཐང་ (dzīdaŋ) sm. བརྩི་མཐོང་.

བརྩི་མཐོང་ (dzīdoŋ) respect, regard, esteem, value; va.—བྱེད་ to have high regard/ esteem for, to respect, to value ¶རྒྱ་གར་དུ་བུད་མེད་ནམས་ལ་བརྩི་མཐོང་ཁྱད་འཕགས་བྱེད་ཀྱི་ཡོད་པ་མ་རེད་ In India they do not have very high esteem for women.

བརྩི་མཐོང་ཆེན་པོ་ (dzīdoŋ cēmbo) highly thought of, highly regarded.

བརྩི་སྣང་ (dzīnaŋ) sm. བརྩི་འཇོག.

བརྩི་བྱ་ (dzīja) sm. བརྩི་སྒོ་.

བརྩི་མེད་ (dzīmeè) 1. disrespecting; va.—བྱེད་ to be disrespectful ¶ཁོ་ཚོས་བླ་མ་ལ་བརྩི་མེད་བྱས་པ་རེད་ They were disrespectful to the lama. 2. disregarding; va.—བྱེད་; —དུ་གཏོང་; —དུ་བསྐྱུར་ ¶ང་ཚོས་ཆིངས་ཡིག་ལ་བརྩི་མེད་བྱེད་དགོས་ We have to disregard the treaty.

བརྩི་མེད་སྣང་ཆུང་ (dzīmeè nəŋjuŋ) being disrespectful in the sense of not obeying or paying attention to someone older or above you; va.—བྱེད་; vi.—ཤོར་; —དུ་ལུས་.

བརྩི་འཛིན་ (dzīndzin) sm. བརྩི་བཀུར་.

བརྩི་བཞག (dzīshaà) roll call, review (military), inventory; va.—གཏོང་ to take roll, to review troops, to do inventory ¶དམག་དཔོན་ཚོས་དམག་མི་བརྩི་བཞག་བཏང་བ་རེད་ The officers reviewed the troops. ¶ང་ཚོས་ཚོང་ཟོག་བརྩི་བཞག་གཏོང་དགོས་ We have to do an inventory of the merchandise.

བརྩི་སེམས་ (dzīsem) respecting, honoring.

བརྩི་སྲུང་ (dzīsuŋ) adhering to, supporting; va.—བྱེད ¶ མང་ཚོགས་ལམ་ཕྱོགས་ལ་བརྩི་སྲུང་བྱེད་ཀྱི་ཡོད་པ་རེད་ (They) adhere to the mass line.

བརྩི་སྲུང་དང་ལེན་ (dzīsuŋ taŋlen) voluntarily respecting/ honoring.

བརྩིག (dzīì) f. of རྩིག.

བརྩིགས་ (dzīì) p. of རྩིག.

བརྩིས་ (dzīì) p. of རྩི་.

བརྩེ་ (dzē) 1. f. of. རྩེ་. 2. vi. (with སོ་) to have the cringing sensation at the noise caused by scratching a fingernail on glass or a blackboard ¶ ཤེལ་སྒོར་སེན་མོས་འབྲད་འབྲད་བཏང་ན་སོ་བརྩེ་གི་རེད་ If you scratch a window with your fingernail you will cringe at the sound. 3. va. to love, to have concern/ compassion for ¶ ཉམས་དགའ་ལ་ཞེན་དུ་བརྩེ་ནས་ Having compassion for the poor.

བརྩེ་སྐྱོང་ (dzēgyoŋ) loving care; va.—བྱེད་ to give loving care, to love and cherish ¶ མོས་ཕ་མ་མེད་པའི་ཕྲུ་གུ་ཚོར་བརྩེ་སྐྱོང་བྱས་པ་རེད་ She gave loving care to the orphans.

བརྩེ་གུས་ (dzēgüù) affection and respect; va.—བྱེད་; —ཞུ་ ¶ ཁྱེད་རྣམས་ལ་བརྩེ་གུས་ཆེན་པོ་གནང་གི་ཡོད་པ་རེད་ (They) are showing great affection and respect for you.

བརྩེ་གྲོགས་ (dzēdrɔɔ̀) lover, girl or boy friend.

བརྩེ་འཇུག་པ་ (dzē jugbə) lovers.

བརྩེ་གཏམ་ (dzēdam) lover's talk.

བརྩེ་དུང་ (dzēduŋ) love, affection ¶ གྲལ་རིམ་གྱི་བརྩེ་དུང་ Class love.

བརྩེ་གདུང་ (dzēduŋ) sm. བརྩེ་དུང་.

བརྩེ་མདངས་ (dzēdaŋ) sm. བརྩེ་དུང་.

བརྩེ་ལྡན་ (dzēdɛn) having love, lovingly; a standard phrase used in letters ¶ བརྩེ་ལྡན་རྡོ་རྗེ་ལགས་ཀྱི་དྲུང་དུ་ My dearest Dorje.

བརྩེ་ལྡན་གྲོགས་པོ་ (dzēdɛn trogbo) a dear or cherished friend.

བརྩེ་པོ་ (dzēbo) devoted, loving ¶ བཟའ་ཚང་དེ་གཉིས་བརྩེ་པོ་ཡོད་པ་རེད་ This couple loves each other.

བརྩེ་བ་ (dzēwa) love; va.—བྱེད་ to love; va.—འདོར་ to stop loving sb., to fall out of love ¶ ཕྲུ་གུ་དེས་ཕ་མར་བརྩེ་བ་ཆེན་པོ་བྱེད་ཀྱི་ཡོད་པ་རེད་ That child loves his parents a lot.

བརྩེ་བའི་དུང་སེམས་ (dzēwɛ tuŋsem) sm. བརྩེ་དུང་.

བརྩེ་བློན་ (dzēlön) beloved minister.

བརྩེ་མོ་ (dzēmo) sm. བརྩེ་བ་.

བརྩེ་ཞེན་ (dzēshɛn) cherished, loved, loving; va.—བྱེད་ to cherish ¶ བརྩེ་ཞེན་བྱེད་པའི་རང་དབང་རང་བཙན་ Cherished freedom.

བརྩེ་གཟིགས་བདག་རྐྱེན་ (dzēsiì daggyen) awarded with great affection.

བརྩེ་སེམས་ (dzēsem) love, affection.

བརྩེག (dzēè) f. of རྩེག.

བརྩེགས་ (dzēè) 1. p. of རྩེག. 2. story ¶ ཁང་ཐོག་སུམ་བརྩེགས་ A three story house.

བརྩེགས་ (dzēg) stacking, piling up; va.—རྒྱག.

བརྩེགས་པ་ (dzēgba) sm. བརྩེགས་ཏོ་.

བརྩེགས་པའི་ཚིག་གྲུབ་ (dzēgbɛ tsīgdrub) compound sentence.

བརྩེགས་པའི་ཡི་གེ་ (dzēgbɛ yigi) words with suffixed and superfixed letters.

བརྩེགས་འཕུལ་ (dzēgbüü) suffixed and superfixed letters.

བརྩེགས་མ་ (dzēgma) sm. བརྩེགས་པའི་ཡི་གེ་.

བརྩེང་ (dzēŋ) f. of རྩེང་.

བརྩེངས་ (dzēŋ) p. of རྩེང་.

བརྩེད་ (dzēè) vi. to get lame due to a horseshoe wearing out.

བརྩེས་ (dzɛ̄ɛ̀) p. of བརྩེ་.

བརྩོན་ (dzȫn) va. to strive for, to endeavor, to be diligent toward a goal ¶ ཁོས་དུས་རྟག་ཏུ་སློབ་སྦྱོང་ལ་བརྩོན་པ་རེད་ He was always diligent in his studies.

བརྩོན་འགྲུས་ (dzǖndrüù) industry, diligence; va.—བྱེད་ to be diligent/ industrious/ energetic ¶ ཏང་མི་ཚོས་གསར་བརྗེ་ལ་བརྩོན་འགྲུས་བྱས་པ་རེད་ The party members worked diligently at revolution.

བརྩོན་འགྲུས་ཀོ་ལོག (dzǖndrüù kolɔɔ̀) person who works hard at doing illegal/ wrong/ evil things.

བརྩོན་པ་ (dzȫmba) industriousness, diligence ¶ བརྩོན་པ་དྲག་པོས་ With great diligence.

བརྩོན་པ་བརྒྱ་འགྱུར་ (dzȫmba gyagyur) with a great deal of effort.

བརྩོན་པ་ལྷོད་ (dzȫmba lhȫò) vi. to relax/ lessen (one's) resoluteness to work hard.

བརྩོན་པོ་ (dzȫmbo) diligent.

བརྩོན་ཤིང་དཔའ་སྙིང་ཆེ་བ་ (dzȫnshiŋ pāñiŋ cēwa) industrious and courageous.

བརྩོན་ཞིབ་ (dzȫnshib) thorough study/ investigation/ research; va.—བྱེད་.

བརྩོན་ལེན་ (dzȫnlen) striving, working hard, exerting oneself (for some goal); va.—བྱེད་ to strive for, to exert oneself, to do one's best ¶ ལོ་ལེགས་ཡོང་བའི་བརྩོན་ལེན་བྱེད་ཀྱི་ཡོད་པ་རེད་ (They) are striving to get a good crop. 2. va. to bring or win sb. over to one's side/ point of view ¶ འབྱོར་ལྡན་གྲལ་རིམ་པ་རྣམས་ང་ཚོའི་ཕྱོགས་སུ་བརྩོན་ལེན་བྱེད་དགོས་ We have to bring over the bourgeoisie to our views.

བརྩོན་སེམས་ (dzȫnsem) diligent, industrious, enthusiastic.

བརྩོན་སེམས་ལྷོད་མེད་ (dzȫnsem lhȫòmeè) sm. བརྩོན་སེམས་.

བརྩོན་བསྲི་ (dzȫnsi) industriousness and thrift/ economy/ frugality; va.—བྱེད་; —གཉེར་ ¶ བརྩོན་བསྲིས་ཁེ་ལས་གཉེར་དགོས་ (One) must run a business diligently and economically.

བརྩོན་བསྲིས་ཁྱིམ་སྐྱོང་ (dzȫnsiì kyīmgyoŋ) running a household industriously and economically/ thriftily.

བརྩོན་བསྲིས་རྒྱལ་འཛུགས་ (dzȫnsiì gyɛɛ dzuù) developing the nation industriously and economically/ thriftily; va.—བྱེད་.

བརྩོན་བསྲིས་ཧྲེ་གཉེར་ (dzȫnsiì hrēñer) tib. ch. managing a commune industriously and economically/ thriftily.

བསྐྱལ་ (dzɛ̄ɛ̄) p. and f. of སྐྱོལ་.

བསྐྱལ་དམ་ (dzɛ̄ɛ̄dam) shung. a seal that was given by sb. ¶ ད་ཆ་མི་དབང་པོ་ལྷས་མི་ལུག་བསྐྱལ་དམ་དུ་སྤོ་རོང་གི་གཡོག་འཕྲིག་རྡུང་མི་ཆོག་ཅེས་གསལ་བ་ It was mentioned in the document accompanying the seal of Miwang Pola, that no one is allowed to beat Porong's servant.

བསྐྱལ་གནས་ (dzɛ̄ɛ̄nɛɛ̀) a letter (correspondence).

བསྐྱལ་ཕྱག (dzɛ̄ɛ̄jaà) sm. བསྐྱལ་གནས་.

ཚ་ (tsā) 1. the letter ཚ་ (used in alphabetical ordering). 2. abbr. of ཚ་པོ་ 3. vi. to get a sharp/ burning/ painful sensation ༑ རྐང་པའི་རྨ་ཚ་ནས་འགྲོ་མ་ཐུབ་པ་རེད་ (He) wasn't able to go because the sore in his leg pained him.

ཚ་རྐུབ་སྒྲོག (tsāgub drɔ̱ɔ̀) vi. to be afraid ༑ དགེ་རྒན་ཚ་པོ་དེ་ཡོང་དུས་སློབ་ཕྲུག་ཚང་མ་ཚ་རྐུབ་སྒྲོག་གི་ཡོད་པ་རེད་ When the strict teacher comes all the students are afraid.

ཚ་སྐམ་ (tsāgam) drying (by heat); vi.—ཐེབས་ to get dried (by heat); va.—གཏོང་ to dry (by heat) ༑ ཁོ་ཚོས་ཤ་ཚ་སྐམ་བཏང་བ་རེད་ They dried the meat (by heat).

ཚ་སྐྲང་ (tsādraŋ) inflammation, swelling; vi.—ཐེབས་ to get inflamed, to swell up.

ཚ་ཁ་ (tsāga) marksmanship, target shooting; va.—ལྟ་ to do target shooting.

ཚ་ཁ་འགྲན་སྡུར་ (tsāga drḛndur) target shooting contest.

ཚ་ཁ་བརྟན་པོ་ (tsāga dēmbo) accurate in shooting, a good marksman.

ཚ་ཁ་ལོན་པོ་ (tsāga lö̱mbo) sm. ཚ་ཁ་བརྟན་པོ་.

ཚ་ཁང་ (tsāgaŋ) a temple/ chapel where clay images of the Buddha and deities are kept.

ཚ་ཁམ་ཁམ་ (tsā kāmgam) sm. ཚ་སོབ་སོབ་.

ཚ་ཁུལ་ (tsəgüü) tropical area, tropics.

ཚ་ཁུལ་སྐྱེ་དངོས་ (tsəgüü gyēŋöö) tropical plants/ organisms, tropical biology.

ཚ་ཁུལ་གྱི་གནམ་གཤིས་ (tsəgüügi nəmshii) tropical climate.

ཚ་ཁུལ་གྱི་རྩི་ཤིང་ (tsəgüügi dzīshiŋ) tropical plant.

ཚ་ཁུལ་གྱི་ལོ་ཏོག (tsəgüü) tropical crop.

ཚ་ཁོག་ཁོག (tsā kɔ̄ɔgɔɔ) warm, cozy.

ཚ་ཁྲུག (tsəgyuù) having a sharp painful sensation; vi.—རྒྱག.

ཚ་ཁྲ་ (tsādra) shung. རྫས་པ་ given to the monks at Monlam and Tsongjö by the རྫས་བཞེལ་པ་.

ཚ་འཁྲུག (tsəkyuù) sm. ཚ་ཁྲུག.

ཚ་འཁྲུ་ (tsā trū) diarrhea cause by fever.

ཚ་གས་འཐེབས་ (tsəgɛɛ̀ tēb) vi. to break (for glass bottles) because of having too hot a liquid poured into it.

ཚ་གི་ཚི་གི་ (tsəgi tsīgi) nervous, jittery, restless; va.—བྱེད་ to do hurriedly, hastily; to act nervous/ jittery ༑ མི་འདི་ཚ་གི་ཚི་གི་ཞི་དྲག་འདུག He's a very nervous person. ༑ ཁོས་ཁ་ལག་ཚ་གི་ཚི་གི་བྱས་ནས་བཟས་པ་རེད་ He ate hurriedly.

ཚ་གི་ཚི་གི་མེད་པ་ (tsəgi tsīgi mḛèba) 1. calm, cool, unhurriedly ༑ འདི་ཚ་གི་ཚི་གི་མེད་པར་གོ་བསྡུར་བྱེད་དོ་ཞེས་བཤད་ (He) said, "let's discuss this unhurriedly."

ཚ་གེགས་ (tsāgeg) heat barrier (in physics).

ཚ་གོང་ (tsāgoŋ) the time before breakfast.

ཚ་གྲ་ (tsādra) shung. donation of རྫས་པ་ given by the traditional Tibetan government to the monks during Monlam.

ཚ་གྲང་ (tsādraŋ) 1. temperature. 2. hot and cold.

ཚ་གྲང་གཡལ་མདོ་ (tsādraŋ kḛḛndo) the point between fever and no fever.

ཚ་གྲང་ལྟ་ཆས་ (tsādraŋ dājɛɛ̀) thermometer.

ཚ་གྲང་བརྟག་དཔྱད་ཡོ་ཆས་ (tsādraŋ dāgjɛɛ̀ yo̱jɛɛ̀) sm. ཚ་གྲང་ལྟ་ཆས་.

ཚ་གྲང་ཐུབ་པ་ (tsādraŋ tūbə) a person or material that can face/ withstand any condition or situation [Lit. able to manage heat or cold].

ཚ་གྲང་འཐབ་ (tsādraŋ tə̄b) vi. to experience a radical change of temperature that causes pain (e.g., a toothache after drinking ice cold water).

ཚ་གྲང་ལྡོག་ཕྱོགས་ (tsādraŋ dɔ̱gjɔɔ̀) sm. ཚ་གྲང་ཡ་འགལ་.

ཚ་གྲང་ཡ་འགལ་ (tsādraŋ ya̱gɛɛ) incompatible, irreconcilable, conflicting, opposing ༑ ལྟ་གྲུབ་ཚ་གྲང་ཡ་འགལ་ Irreconcilable ideologies. [Lit. contradiction between hot and cold].

ཚ་གྲུམ་ (tsədrum) a kind of arthritis.

ཚ་གློག (tsālɔɔ) thermoelectricity.

ཚ་གློག་གདོང་འཕྲིན་གྱི་ནུས་པ་ (tsālɔɔ dōŋdengi nṳ̄übə) pyroelectric effect (in physics).

ཚ་གློག་ས་ཚིགས་ (tsālɔɔ sədzii) thermoelectric plant/ station.

ཚ་དགོངས་ (tsāgoŋ) summer vacation.

ཚ་རྒྱས་ (tsāgyɛɛ̀) thermal expansion.

ཚ་རྒྱས་གྲང་འཁུམས་ (tsāgyɛɛ̀ tra̱ŋgum) thermal expansion and contraction.

ཚ་རྒྱས་ནད་གཞི་ (tsāgyɛɛ̀ nḛ̀ɛshi) sm. ཚ་ནད་.

ཚ་རྒྱུ་ (tsəgyu) material/ source of heat.

ཚ་རྒྱུད་ (tsəgyüü) generations of grandchildren.

ཚ་རྒྱུན་ (tsəgyün) thermal current, heat current.

ཚ་ངད་ (tsāŋɛɛɛ̀) heat/ hotness (of a fire).

ཚ་ངམ་ངམ་ (tsā ŋamŋam) warm, warmly.

ཚ་ངར་ (tsāŋar) sm. ཚ་ངད་.

ཚ་ཅོལ་འོ་ཅོལ་ (tsājöö wo̱jöö) all at once, hurriedly, haphazardly, erratically ༑ ལས་ཀ་ཚ་ཅོལ་འོ་ཅོལ་ལ་བྱས་ན་ནོར་འཁྲུལ་ཤོར་ཉེན་ཡོད་ If you work hurriedly there is a danger that you will make errors.

ཚ་གཅིག་མ་ (tsā jīgmə) 1. disease that a person gets only once (e.g., measles). 2. a rug with thick pile.

ཚ་གཙུན་གྲང་འདོམས་ (tsājün tra̱ŋdom) sm. ཚ་འཛུན་གྲང་འདོམས་.

ཚ་ཕྱིབས་ (tsājib) piece of cloth used when handling a hot object/ pot.

ཚ་ལྕུག (tsājuù) welding/ soldering rod.

ཚ་ཆས་ (tsājɛɛ̀) provisions for use on the road or on a trip.

ཚ་ཆིལ་ཆིལ་ (tsā cīījii) warm.

ཚ་ཆུ་ (tsəju) 1. urine of a person who has fever. 2. hot springs. 3. illness which causes blockage of urine.

ཚ་ཆུ་ཁ་ (tsəjuka) hot springs.

ཚ་ཆུའི་འཁྲུད་ཁང་ (tsəjü trṻügaŋ) bath house.

ཚ་ཇ་ (tsāja) 1. noon tea. 2. tea on a trip, tea made on the road/ trail.

ཚ་འཇམ་ (tsānjam) rough/ harsh and gentle.

ཚ་འཇམ་རྒྱས་བསྡུས་ (tsānjam gyḛ̀ɛdüü) abbr. harsh, gentle, elaborate and abbreviated.

ཚ་འཇམ་རན་པོ་ (tsānjam rḛmbo) neither harsh nor gentle/ soft but appropriate in both.

ཚ་འཛུན་གྲང་འདོམས་ (tsānjün dra̱ŋdom) shung. strict discipline and forceful advice.

ཚ་ཉོར་ཉོར་ (tsā ñɔ̱rñɔr) warm and wet feeling (usu. used to convey state of the vagina during intercourse).

ཚ་བཏུང་ (tsə̄duŋ) hot drinks/ beverages.

ཚ་རྟགས་ (tsādaà) the mark made on the top of the letter ཙ that converts it to ཚ་.

ཚ་ཏིང་ (tsə̄diŋ) midmorning.

ཚ་ཏིང་ཁ་ལག (tsə̄diŋ kālaà) meal before noon.

ཚ་ཐག་ཆོད་ (tsādaà cȫö̀) effective, to the point, appropriate, excellent ༑ ཁོས་ལན་ཚ་ཐག་ཆོད་ཅིག་སྤྲད་པ་རེད་ He gave an answer that was right to the point. ༑ ཁོ་མེ་མདའ་ཚ་ཐག་ཆོད་འདུག He is an excellent shot.

ཚ་ཐབ་ (tsātəb) a heatable brick bed.

ཚ་ཐལ་ཤོར་ (tsādɛɛ shɔ̄ɔ) vi. to overheat.

ཚ་ཐིང་ཐིང་ (tsā tīŋdiŋ) sm. ཚ་སོབ་སོབ་.

ཚ་ཐུབ་ (tsədub) heat resistant.

ཚ་ཐུར་ (tsādur) a spoon-like Tibetan medical instrument that is heated and applied to an area where there is pain.

ཚ་ཐོག (tsādɔɔ) while sth. is hot ༑ ཁ་ལག་ཚ་ཐོག་ལ་ཟ་

དགོས་ One should eat food while it is hot.

ཚ་ཐོག་ལས་སྣོན་ (tsādɔɔ lɛɛ̀nön) hot processing (in metallurgy).

ཚ་ཐོར་ (tsādɔɔ) heat rash/ pimple; vi.—སྐྱེ་ to get a heat rash/ pimple, to get prickly heat.

ཚ་འཐབ་ (tsādəb) a hot war (in contrast to the cold war).

ཚ་འཐུང་ (tsāduŋ) drinking sth. (such as tea) while it is hot; va.—རྒྱག.

ཚ་འཐོར་ (tsā tɔ̄ɔ) vi. to break down/ disintegrate/ disperse ། རྒྱུ་ཆ་དུས་ཐོག་ལ་མ་འབྱོར་ཙང་ཁང་པ་རྒྱག་རྒྱུའི་ལས་ཀ་ཚ་འཐོར་བཞག Because the materials didn't come on time, the house construction work broke down.

ཚ་དམ་ (tsādam) a container/ flask to carry food that keeps it hot, thermos bottle.

ཚ་དམ་གྱི་ནང་བུམ་ (tsādamgi naŋbum) glass liner of a thermos flask.

ཚ་དར་ (tssādar) the ceremonial scarf given to the winner of a race or a marksmanship competition.

ཚ་དུབ་ (tsədub) sm. ཚ་གདུག.

ཚ་དུས་ (tsədüü) the period of warm/ hot weather, hot season, summer.

ཚ་དུས་ཐ་མ་ (tsədüü tāma) the end of the hot season/ summer.

ཚ་དུས་ཐོག་མ་ (tsədüü tɔ̄ɔma) the beginning of the hot season/ summer.

ཚ་དུས་བར་མ་ (tsədüü parma) the middle of hot season/ summer.

ཚ་དུས་འབྲུབ་ཆུ་ (tsədüü drubju) summer floods.

ཚ་དུས་གསུམ་ (tsədüü sūm) the three periods/ months of summer (beginning, middle, and end).

ཚ་དེམ་ (tsādem) thermos bottle.

ཚ་དྲག (tsādraà) 1. urgent, critical. 2. harsh, strict, drastic.

ཚ་དྲག་ཆེ་དྲགས་པ་ (tsādraà cē tragba) 1. very critical/ urgent. 2. very harsh/ strict/ drastic.

ཚ་དྲག་པ་ (tsādragba) sm. ཚ་དྲག.

ཚ་དྲག་ཡིག་ཆ་ (tsādraà yigja) an urgent document/ letter/ dispatch.

ཚ་དྲོ་ (tsādro) sm. ཚ་དྲོད.

ཚ་དྲོད་ (tsādröö) heat; vi.—རྒྱས་; —འཕེལ་ to get warm/ hot.

ཚ་དྲོད་འགྱེད་འཕྲོ་ (tsādröö gyeèdro) heat waves, heat/ thermal radiation.

ཚ་གདུག (tsəduù) heat; vi.—འཚིག to feel/ be hot; vi.—ཕོག to get sunstroke/ heat prostration ། ཉི་མའི་ནང་ཡུན་རིང་གོམ་པ་བརྒྱབ་པས་ཚ་གདུག་འཚིགས་པ་རེད་ He felt hot because he walked in the sun for a long time.

ཚ་གདུག་ཕོག (tsəduù pɔ̄ɔ) see ཚ་གདུག.

ཚ་གདུག་ཚིག (tsəduù tsīi) see ཚ་གདུག.

ཚ་གདུང་ (tsəduŋ) sm. ཚ་གདུག.

ཚ་འདེད་ (tsāndeè) using force/ coercion to pursue repayment of sth. (usu. a loan/ tax); va.—བྱེད་; —གཏོང་.

ཚ་འདེད་དྲག་དུང་ (tsāndeè tragduŋ) vigorously pursue and fiercely beating/ attacking; va.—གཏོང་; —བྱེད་.

ཚ་འདེད་ཕྱིར་ལེན་ (tsāndeè cīrlen) shung. paying back a loan after repeated attempts at forcible collection.

ཚ་འདེད་ཝུར་འདེད་ (tsāndeè wurdeè) sm. ཚ་འདེད་.

ཚ་འདོན་རྒྱག (tsāndön gyaà) va. to pour boiled water on barley before roasting it for grinding into རྩམ་པ་.

ཚ་འདྲི་ (tsəndri) interrogation with torture; va.—བྱེད་; —གཏོང་.

ཚ་འདྲི་མགོ་སྤྲོད་ (tsəndri godröö) shung. a type of interrogating in tt. wherein two people are placed face-to-face on their belly and whipped while they tell their version (to compare their different accounts of an incident); va.—བྱེད་.

ཚ་དིབ་ཤོར་ (tsədib shɔ̄ɔ) vi. to have stunted/ abnormal growth.

ཚ་དུང་ལས་སྣོན་ (tsəduŋ lɛɛ̀nön) sm. ཚ་ཐོག་ལས་སྣོན་.

ཚ་སྡུག (tsəduù) sm. ཚ་གདུག.

ཚ་ནད་ (tsānɛɛ̀) 1. illness due to heat/ fever/ sunstroke; vi.—ན་; —ཕོག. 2. pain ། ཉེས་དུང་ཚད་མེད་བཏང་ཙང་ཚ་ནད་མ་ཐེག་པས་པར་ཤོད་དགོས་བྱུང་ Because he was beaten endlessly, he couldn't bear the pain and had to tell (what they were asking).

ཚ་ནན་ (tsānɛn) strict, stern, harsh ། ཉེས་དུང་ཚ་ནན་གཏོང་ཡས་ Giving a harsh beating.

ཚ་ནུས་ (tsānüü) heat/ thermal power.

ཚ་ནུས་ཚོད་ཚད་ (tsānüü cöödzeɛ̀) thermal/ heat efficiency.

ཚ་ནུས་འཁྲུལ་འཁོར་ (tsānüü trüügɔɔ) heat engine.

ཚ་ནུས་ལས་ཚོད་ (tsānüü lɛɛ̀jöö) sm. ཚ་ནུས་ཚོད་ཚད་.

ཚ་ནོན་ (tsānön) an iron (for ironing clothing); va.—རྒྱག.

ཚ་གནོན་ (tsānön) sm. ཚ་ནོན་.

ཚ་སྣ་ (tsāna) a hole in the nose of an cow or yak (for placing a rope); va.—བརྒྱུ་ to make such a hole.

ཚ་པོ་ (tsābo) 1. hot ། ཇ་འདི་ཚ་པོ་འདུག This tea is hot. 2. attributive noun adding the meaning of "very," "extremely," or "excellently" ། ཁོ་སྐྱག་རྫུན་ཚ་པོ་འདུག He is a extremely mendacious. 3. sharp or biting (for a reply/ response); va.—རྒྱག ། ཁོང་གིས་དྲི་བ་དེ་ར་ལན་ཚ་པོ་ཞིག་བརྒྱབ་སོང་ He responded to the question in a sharp manner.

ཚ་པོ་རྒྱག (tsābo gyaà) 1. va. to shoot accurately. 2. va. to reply in a sharp/ biting manner.

ཚ་པོ་ཚ་རྒྱང་ (tsābo tsāgyaŋ) extremely hot.

ཚ་སྤུན་ (tsābün) nephews and brothers.

ཚ་སྤུན་ཕྱི་མ་ (tsābün cīmə) youngest brother.

ཚ་ཕོགས་ (tsābɔɔ) a stop for meal when traveling; va.—རྒྱག to stop for meal while traveling. 2. a quick sexual rendezvous; va.—རྒྱག.

ཚ་ཕྱིས་ (tsəjii) sm. ཚ་ཕྱིབས་.

ཚ་ཕུ་ (tsəju) sm. ཚ་ཕུ་མ་.

ཚ་ཕུ་མ་ (tsəjumə) Mongolian dress/ robe.

ཚ་ཕུར་ཕུར་ (tsā cūūjuu) warm.

ཚ་བ་ (tsāwa) 1. heat; vi.—རྒྱས་ to have warm weather come. ། ང་ཚ་བ་ལ་དགའ་པོ་མེད་ I don't like the heat. 2. fever; vi.— རྒྱས་; —འཁྱིད་; —འབར་ to have fever; va.—གཅོག; —སེལ་ to bring down fever; vi.—འཇགས་ to have fever decline/ subside; va.—ལྟ་; —གཟིགས་ to take sb.'s temperature ། ཁོང་ལ་ཚ་བ་ཆེན་པོ་འདུག He has a high fever. ། ཁོ་ཚ་བ་རྒྱས་བཞག He has fever. ། སྨན་པས་ནད་པར་ཚ་བ་བལྟས་པ་རེད་ The doctor took the temperature of the patient. 3. hot food, hot drinks.

ཚ་བ་གྲམ་ (tsāwa dram) vi. to have fever spread.

ཚ་བ་ཆུང་ (tsāwa cūŋ) 1. slightly hot. 2. the start of the 6th month of the Tibetan calendar when the climate is only slightly warm.

ཚ་བ་ཆེ་ (tsāwa cē) 1. very hot. 2. the part of the 6th month of the Tibetan calendar when the climate is hot.

ཚ་བ་ཆེ་བའི་ས་ཁུལ་ (tsāwa cēwɛ sōgüü) the tropics, tropical areas.

ཚ་བ་ཐེག་ཐུབ་པ་ (tsāwa tēgdubbə) heat resistant.

ཚ་བ་སྡེ་དྲུག (tsāwa dedruù) the six types of the fever according to Tibetan medicine.

ཚ་བ་བྱེར་འགྲེམས་ (tsāwa cendrem) thermal or heat diffusion.

ཚ་བ་འབར་ (tsāwa bar) 1. see ཚ་བ་. 2. vi. to be/ get sexually exited.

ཚ་བ་འབྱེར་ (tsāwa cee) sm. ཚ་བ་གྲམ་.

ཚ་བ་སྨིན་ (tsāwa mīn) vi. to be at the point when a fever is ready to break.

ཚ་བ་རྩུགས་ (tsāwa tsuù) the start of the warm weather (after the summer solstice).

ཚ་བ་ཡོད་ས་ (tsāwa yöösa) the tropics, places where the climate is hot.

ཚ་བ་རི་ཐང་མཚམས་ཀྱི་ཞིང་ (tsāwa ridaŋ tsāmgi

le̲wu) the name of a text in Tibetan medicine that deals with methods of treating of fever.

ཚ་བ་ལ་འདས་ (tsāwala dɛ̲ɛ̀) vi. a type of fever that is incurable/ fatal.

ཚ་བ་གསུམ་ (tsāwa sūm) three medicines: ginger, pepper and པི་པི་ལིང་.

ཚ་བའི་འགུལ་སྐྱོད་ (tsāwɛ gü̲ügyöö) thermal motion.

ཚ་བའི་ན་ཚ་ (tsāwɛ na̲dza) sm. ཚ་ནད་.

ཚ་བའི་ནད་ (tsāwɛ nɛ̲ɛ̀) sm. ཚ་ནད་.

ཚ་བའི་ནུས་པ་ (tsāwɛɛ̀ nü̲ùbə) thermal energy.

ཚ་བའི་སྨུམ་ཅན་ (tsāwɛ nūmjɛn) mustard.

ཚ་བའི་ཐ་རླབས་ (tsāwɛ bə̲ləb) heat wave.

ཚ་བའི་རིག་པ་ (tsāwɛ ri̲gbə) thermology (a branch of physics that studies heat).

ཚ་བའི་ཤོང་ཚད་ (tsāwɛ shōŋdzɛɛ̀) heat/ thermal capacity.

ཚ་བའི་ས་ཁུལ་ (tsāwɛ səgüü) tropical region, the tropics.

ཚ་བའི་ས་རྒྱུད་ (tsāwɛ sōgyüù) sm. ཚ་བའི་ས་ཁུལ་.

ཚ་བའི་སེམས་ཅན་དམྱལ་བ་བརྒྱད་ (tsāwɛ sēmjɛn mɛ̄ɛ̲wa gyɛ̲ɛ̀) sm. ཚ་དམྱལ་བརྒྱད་.

ཚ་བིར་བིར་ (tsā bi̲bir) a feeling of warmth (as when sitting by a fire).

ཚ་བུན་ (tsābün) painful burning sensation.

ཚ་བོ་ (tsāwo) 1. nephew. 2. grandson, grandchild.

ཚ་བྲ་ (tsādra) gifts for the dead (a Chinese custom).

ཚ་འབུམ་ (tsāmbum) 1. a hundred thousand religious clay images (stamped from a mold). 2. sm. ཚ་ཁང་.

ཚ་འབོག (tsāmbɔɔ̀) 1. a stop for a meal/ tea on a journey; va.—རྒྱག. 2. having quick sexual intercourse; va.—རྒྱག.

ཚ་འབྲུམ་ (tsəndru) heat rash.

ཚ་སྦིད་སྦིད་ (tsā bi̲ibiì) sm.* ཚ་སྦྲིད་སྦྲིད་.

ཚ་སྦྱོར་ (tsā jɔ̲ɔ) va. to weld/ join together by heat.

ཚ་སྦྲིད་སྦྲིད་ (tsā drii̲drii) a hot sensation.

ཚ་མོ་ (tsāmo) 1. niece. 2. granddaughter, grandchild.

ཚ་རྨུགས་ (tsāñaà) rotting because of heat; vi.—ཐེབས་.

ཚ་དམྱལ་བརྒྱད་ (tsāñɛɛ gyɛ̲ɛ̀) the 8 hot hells.

ཚ་སྨན་ (tsāmɛn) sm. དོད་སྨན་.

ཚ་ཚ་ (tsādza) 1. small religious images stamped from clay by means of a mold. 2. hot foods/ beverages ¶ དེའི་རིང་ཚ་ཚ་ཐིག་པ་གཅིག་ཀྱང་ཐོབ་མ་བྱུང་ During that time I did not get one drop of hot drink. 3. the stone under the grinding wheel.

ཚ་ཚག (tsādzaà) dress made from lambskin (with the fleece on the inside).

ཚ་ཚ་ཝུར་ཝུར་ (tsādza wu̲rwur) 1. quickly, fast ¶ དེ་རིང་ང་ཚོ་ཉ་པི་ཉོ་པི་མིན་ད་ཚ་ཚ་ཝུར་ཝུར་ཡིན་ Today we are not going to be lazy but will be fast. 2. in discussions: one after another (e.g., criticisms or suggestions). 3. urgently.

ཚ་ཚད་ (tsādzɛɛ̀) temperature, degrees of heat ¶ དེ་རིང་གི་ཚ་ཚད་བརྒྱད་ཅུ་ཐམ་པ་རེད་ Today's temperature is 80 degrees.

ཚ་ཚད་ལྟ་བྱེད་ (tsādzɛɛ̀ dājeè) thermometer.

ཚ་ཚད་མཐོ་ཐིག (tsādzɛɛ̀ tōdeg) high temperature ¶ ཚ་ཚད་མཐོ་ཐིག་བཞུ་ཐབ་ High temperature furnace.

ཚ་ཚད་མཐོན་པོ་ (tsādzɛɛ̀ tõmbo) high temperature.

ཚ་ཚད་མཐོན་པོའི་ལྕགས་བཞུ་ (tsādzɛɛ̀ tõmbö jāgshu) high temperature metallurgy.

ཚ་ཚད་མཐོན་པོའི་ལུད་ཕུང་ (tsādzɛɛ̀ tõmbö lü̲übuŋ) high temperature compost.

ཚ་ཚིགས་ (tsədzii) pain in the joints; vi.—ན་ to have pain in the joints.

ཚ་ཚུགས་ (tsādzuù) a place on the road where you stop for a meal.

ཚ་ཚོར་གློག་འགོག (tsātsɔr lōŋgɔɔ̀) thermal resister, thermister.

ཚ་ཞག (tsāshaà) abbr. of ཚ་འབོག and ཞག་སྡོད་.

ཚ་ཞང་ (tsāshaŋ) nephew and maternal uncle. 2. a nurturing relationship between someone senior and junior.

ཚ་བཞེས་ (tsāsheè) sm. ཞོགས་ཇ་.

ཚ་ཟིང་ངེ་བ་ (tsā si̲ŋsiŋ) sm. ཚ་ཟིང་ཟིང་.

ཚ་ཟིང་ཟིང་ (tsā si̲ŋsiŋ) feeling frightened, having a feeling of fright.

ཚ་ཟུག (tsāsug) pain, ache.

ཚ་ཟེར་ (tsāser) 1. sun rays. 2. heat rays.

ཚ་ཟེར་ཉི་མ་ (tsāser ñi̲mə) sm. ཚ་ཟེར་.

ཚ་ཟླ་ (tsānda) springtime.

ཚ་གཟིགས་ (tsāsii) shung. the custom of taking a share of tea and food (from the monastic prayer chanting sessions) to the higher authority monks in a monastery who are not attending.

ཚ་གཟེར་ (tsāser) sm. ཚ་ཟུག.

ཚ་བཙོས་རི་མོ་ (tsāsöö ri̲mu) a design burnt by a brand.

ཚ་ཝུར་ཝུར་ (tsā wu̲rwur) sm. ཚ་སོབ་སོབ་.

ཚ་ཝུར་རྒྱག (tsāwur gya̲à) vi. to get/ feel afraid, to get/ feel ashamed ¶ སྐད་ཅ་དེ་གོ་མ་ཐག་ངའི་སྙིང་ལ་ཚ་ཝུར་བརྒྱབ་བྱུང་ As soon as I heard the talk I got afraid.

ཚ་འོག་ཉིང་རྡུལ་འགྱུར་འགྱུར་ (tsāwɔɔ̀ ñi̲ŋdüü gyu̲rjuŋ) thermonuclear reaction.

ཚ་འོབ་འོབ་ (tsā wɔ̲bwɔb) engulfed by heat.

ཚ་འོར་ (tsāwɔɔ) dropsy caused by fever.

ཚ་ཡལ་གྲང་འཆར་ (tsāyɛɛ tra̲ŋjar) summer ends and winter comes.

ཚ་ཡུལ་ (tsəyüü) tropics, tropical country.

ཚ་གཡོལ་ (tsā yöö) 1. avoiding the heat; va. ཚ་གཡོལ་; va.—བྱེད་.

ཚ་གཡོལ་རི་གྲོང་ (tsāyöö ri̲droŋ) a summer resort in the mountains (to get away from the heat).

ཚ་གཡོལ་བྱེད་ས་ (tsāyöö ce̲èsa) a place to go to avoid the heat, a summer resort.

ཚ་རུ་ (tsəru) lambskin.

ཚ་རུ་མགོ་ (tsərugo) curly hair (like lamb's fleece).

ཚ་རུ་པགས་རྩག (tsəru bāgdzaà) lambskin dress (with fleece on the inside).

ཚ་རུམ་ (tsārum) center/ middle of a tropical place.

ཚ་རེག (tsāreg) 1. feeling of warmth/ heat. 2. a stinging sensation like that of being pricked by a thorn or nail.

ཚ་རེག་སི་སོང་བ་ (tsāreg sēsoŋwa) a sudden feeling of burning/ pain.

ཚ་རོ་ (tsāro) a dormant fever/ infection.

ཚ་རོང་ (tsāroŋ) name of an aristocratic family.

ཚ་རླངས་ (tsālaŋ) hot steam.

ཚ་རླབས་ (tsələb) 1. heat wave. 2. upsurging, swelling, rising; vi.—ལངས་; —འཁོལ་ to upsurge, to swell, to rise ¶ ཟློས་གར་གསར་བརྗེ་ཅན་ཤུགས་ཆེན་འཁྲབ་པའི་ཚ་རླབས་ལངས་པའི་སྐབས་སུ་ At the time of the upsurge of performing powerful revolutionary dramas.

ཚ་རླབས་མང་ཚོགས་ (tsəlab ma̲ŋdzɔɔ̀) the aroused masses, the surging masses.

ཚ་རླུང་ (tsəluŋ) hot air.

ཚ་རླུང་གི་ཐབ་ཀ་ (tsāluŋgi təbga) blast furnace.

ཚ་ལ་ (tsāla) 1. solder; va.—གཏོང་; —རྒྱག to solder, to weld. 2. borax.

ཚ་ལ་དཀར་པོ་ (tsāla gāābo) borax.

ཚ་ལ་རྒྱག་མཁན་བཟོ་པ་ (tsāla gya̲añɛn so̲ba) a welder, a solderer.

ཚ་ལ་རྒྱག་བྱེད་ (tsāla gya̲gjeè) sm. ཚ་ལ་གཏོང་བྱེད་.

ཚ་ལ་རྒྱག་བྱེད་ཀྱི་མདའ་ (tsāla gya̲gjeègi da̲) welding torch.

ཚ་ལ་གཏོང་བྱེད་ (tsāla dōŋjeè) soldering/ welding equipment.

ཚ་ལ་སྦུབས་སྦྱོར་བ་ (tsāla sūbjɔɔwa) welding seam/ line.

ཚ་ལག (tsālaà) sm. ཚ་རྟགས་.

ཚ་ལམ་ (tsālam) a half-day journey.

ཚ་ལམ་ལམ་ (tsā la̲mlam) sm. ཚ་སོབ་སོབ་.

ཚ་ལའི་སྐྱུར་ (tsālɛ gyūr) boracic acid, boric acid.

ཚ་ལའི་ལྕུག་མ་ (tsālɛ jūgmə) welding rod.

ཚ་ལའི་ལས་ཀ་ (tsālɛ lɛ̲ɛ̀ga) welding/ soldering work.

ཚ་ལུ་མ་ (tsəlumə) orange (the fruit).

ཚ་ལུད་ (tsālüü) composted human or pig excrement/ manure.

ཚ་ལུམ་ལུམ་ (tsā lumlum) describes a liquid that is boiling with bubbles.

ཚ་ལུམས་ (tsəlum) medicine mixed with hot water (usu. for soaking); va.—རྒྱག.

ཚ་ལེན་ (tsālen) requisitioning, commandeering; va.—གཏོང་ to requisition, to commandeer.

ཚ་ལོག (tsāləɔ̈) reheating; va.—གཏོང་.

ཚ་ལོང་ལོང་ (tsā loŋloŋ) 1. sm. ཚ་ལུམ་ལུམ་. 2. afraid, scared; vi.—བྱེད་ ¶ སྙིང་ཚ་ལོང་ལོང་བྱས་བྱུང་ I got scared.

ཚ་ལོས་ (tsālöö) the degree of hotness (as in temperature).

ཚ་ཤར་རྒྱག (tsāsaa gyaà) va. to be in pain (with a burning sensation).

ཚ་ཤུགས་ (tsəshuù) heat/ thermal power.

ཚ་ཤུགས་འབྱུང་ས་ (tsəshuù juŋsə) heat source.

ཚ་ཤུར་རྒྱག (tsāshur gyaà) 1. va. to be afraid/ scared.

ཚ་ཤུར་ཤུར་ (tsā shūrshur) frightened.

ཚ་གཤེར་ (tsāsher) hot and humid (weather).

ཚ་བཤལ་ (tsāshεε) 1. rinsing with hot water; va.—གཏོང་. 2. diarrhea caused by heat.

ཚ་ས་ (tsāsa) 1. sm. ཚ་ལམ་. 2. place to break for lunch on a journey. 3. place where sth. hurts/ burns/ pains.

ཚ་སུབ་རྒྱག (tsāsub gyaà) vi. to get sudden sharp pain.

ཚ་སུབ་སྦྱོང་རྫས་ (tsāsub gyoŋdzεὲ) soldering materials.

ཚ་སུབས་ཐེབས་ (tsāsub têè) 1. vi. to get overheated/ overcooked. 2. vi. to be stuffy (in a room).

ཚ་སིལ་གཏོང་ (tsāsii dōŋ) va. to warm tea.

ཚ་སེལ་ (tsā sēē) 1. va. to cool sth. down. 2. medicine to bring down fever.

ཚ་སོབ་སོབ་ (tsā sōnsob) 1. warm ¶ ཉལ་ཆས་ཚ་སོབ་སོབ་ཅིག་ནང་ཉལ་རྒྱུ་བྱུང་ I slept in a warm and cozy bed.

ཚ་སྲན་ཆེན་པོ་ (tsāsεn cēmbo) the ability to tolerate heat well.

ཚ་སྲེག (tsāseg) burning sth.; va.—གཏོང་.

ཚ་གསུར་ (tsāsur) a mixture of རྩམ་པ་, butter, yogurt, milk, honey and rock sugar that is burnt as an offering.

ཚ་གསེར་ (tsāsee) gilding; va.—གཏོང་ to gild.

ཚ་བསིལ་ (tsāsii) reheating sth. a little, warming a food (without bringing it to a boil); va.—གཏོང་.

ཚ་ཧུར་ཧུར་ (tsā hūrhuu) warm.

ཚ་ལྷག (tsālhaà) 1. sm. ཚ་དྲགས་. 2. a warm wind.

ཚ་ལྷང་ལྷང་ (tsā lhālhaŋ) hot.

ཚ་ཧྲིལ་ (tsəhrii) sm. ཚིད་ཧྲིལ་.

ཚ་ཧྲེན་ཆེན་པོ་ (tsāhren cēmbo) sm.* ཚ་སྲན་ཆེན་པོ་.

ཚག (tsāà) 1. the bas-relief style of metal working or carving; va.—རྒྱག; —འདེབས་ to do bas-relief style of metal work carving ¶ སེར་ཚག Gold bas-relief engraving. 2. abbr. of ཚག་པོ་.

ཚག་གུར་གླིང་ག (tsəgur liŋgə) a park about twenty miles west of Lhasa.

ཚག་སྒྲ་ (tsāgdra) a cracking sound.

ཚག་སྒྲ་དིག་སྒྲ་ (tsāgdra digdra) sound of people walking upstairs on a floor, roof, etc.

ཚག་ཐིག (tsəgdig) dotted lines.

ཚག་ཐོ་ (tsāgdo) small hammer used for engraving.

ཚག་དེབ་ (tsāgdeb) a journal.

ཚག་འདེབས་ (tsāà deb) va. to engrave.

ཚག་པ་ (tsāgba) person who does relief engraving on silver and gold implements.

ཚག་པར་ (tsāgbaa) sm. ཚགས་པར་.

ཚག་པོ་ (tsāgbo) sm. ཚགས་པོ་.

ཚག་དཔར་ (tsāgbaa) sm. ཚགས་པར་.

ཚག་མ་ (tsāgma) bas-relief type of metal work and wood carving ¶ དངུལ་བསྐྲམས་ཚག་མའི་བུམ་པ་ A vase with silver bas-relief work.

ཚག་ཚག་བྱེད་ (tsāgdzaà cee) sm. ཐིག་མོ་བྱེད་.

ཚག་ཚིག (tsəgdzii) abbr. of ཚག་གི་ཚིག་གི་.

ཚག་ཚིལ་ (tsəgdzii) sm. ཚགས་ཚིལ་.

ཚག་གཟོང་ (tsāgsoŋ) a chisel used for engraving.

ཚག་རིམ་ (tsəgrim) carving or engraving.

ཚག་རིས་ (tsəgrii) engraving; va.—རྒྱག.

ཚག་ལས་ (tsāglεὲ) engraving work.

ཚག་ལུག (tsəgluù) sm. ཚགས་ལུག.

ཚག་ཤ་ (tsāgsha) sm. ཚགས་ཤ་.

ཚག་ཤོག (tsāgshoò) sm. ཚགས་པར་.

ཚགས་ (tsāà) 1. strainer, sieve, filter; va.—རྒྱག to filter/ strain/ sift ¶ ཇ་ཚགས་ Tea strainer ¶ མོས་གྲོ་ཞིབ་ཚགས་བརྒྱབ་པ་རེད་ She sifted the flour. 2. sm. ཚག. 3. gap, space ¶ ཚགས་སྙོམས་པོ་ Even space/ gap (usu. for woven textiles). 4. abbr. of ཚགས་པོ་.

ཚགས་དཀྲོལ་ (tsāgdröö) engraving.

ཚགས་རྒྱན་ (tsāggyεn) engraved teapot.

ཚགས་ཁོག (tsāàgɔɔ̀) a yak carcass.

ཚགས་གླིང་ (tsəgliŋ) 1/4 of a yak carcass.

ཚགས་མགོ་ (tsāàgo) 1. yak head (of a slaughtered animal). 2. word used to scold a stupid person.

ཚགས་འགོད་ (tsāggöö) reported/ written in the news; va.—བྱེད་.

ཚགས་སྒྲིག (tsəgdrig) va. to put in order, to prepare, to streamline; va.—བྱེད་ ¶ དམག་མི་ཚོས་གོ་མཚོན་ཚང་མ་ཚགས་སྒྲིག་བྱས་སོང་ The soldiers prepared all the weapons.

ཚགས་བཅོས་ (tsāg jöö) va. to make the length of sth. even.

ཚགས་མཐུག་པོ་ (tsāà tūgbu) sm. ཚགས་དམ་པོ་.

ཚགས་དམ་པོ་ (tsāà dambo) compact, tight, tightly/ closely packed (or woven).

ཚགས་དེབ་ (tsāgdeb) abbr. newspapers and magazines.

ཚགས་དེབ་ལྟ་ཀློག་ཁང་ (tsāgdeb dāləɔ̈gaŋ) periodical/ newspaper-magazine reading room.

ཚགས་སྣོད་ (tsāgnöö) a vessel for straining.

ཚགས་པར་ (tsāgbar) 1. newspaper ¶ ཉིན་རེའི་ཚགས་པར་ A daily newspaper. 2. a type of thanka painting wherein needle holes are poked on the lines of a drawing which is placed on top of a blank canvas and then white powder is put into the holes to make an impression on the canvas so that the artist can replicate/ copy the outline of the drawing.

ཚགས་པར་ཀློག་མཁན་ཚོགས་ཆུང་ (tsāgbaa ləgñεn tsɔ̄gjuŋ) newspaper reading group.

ཚགས་པར་ཀློག་ཚན་ (tsāgbaa lɔ̄gdzεn) sm. ཚགས་པར་ཀློག་མཁན་ཚོགས་ཆུང་.

ཚགས་པར་ཁང་ (tsāgbargaŋ) newspaper office.

ཚགས་པར་འགོད་མི་ (tsāgbaa göömi) newspaper reporter.

ཚགས་པར་བལྟ་ཁང་ (tsāgbaa dāgaŋ) newspaper reading room (in a library).

ཚགས་པོ་ (tsāgbo) 1. yak that is killed for food ¶ འདི་ལོ་ཚག་པོ་དྲུག་བསད་པ་ཡིན་ This year I killed six yak. 2. cattle to be killed for meat.

ཚགས་དཔར་ (tsāgbaa) sm. ཚགས་པར་.

ཚགས་སྦྱད་ (tsāgjεὲ) sm. ཚགས་མ་.

ཚགས་ཕོར་ (tsāgbɔɔ) a kind of wooden snuff box with a sifter.

ཚགས་བུབས་ (tsāgbub) sm. ཚགས་ཁོག.

ཚགས་བྱེད་ (tsāà cee) va. to keep/ hold.

ཚགས་བྲིས་ (tsəgdrii) tattoo.

ཚགས་མ་ (tsāgma) 1. sieve. 2. anything sifted. 3. dense, compact.

ཚགས་ཚིགས་ (tsəgdzii) joint (in the body).

ཚགས་ཚིལ་ (tsəgdzii) yak fat.

ཚགས་ཚུད་ (tsəgdzuù) well-organized. efficient; va. ཚགས་ཚུད་; —བྱེད་ to be well organized ¶ མཉམ་ལས་ཁང་འདི་ཚགས་ཚུད་ཅིག་འདུག This cooperative is one that is well-organized.

ཚགས་ཚུད་པོ་ (tsāà tsūübu) well-organized.

ཚགས་འཛུགས་ (tsāà dzuù) va. to appoint/ assign/ delegate.

ཚགས་ཞིབ་མོ་ (tsaāà shi̱bmu) sm. ཚགས་དམ་པོ་.

ཚགས་ཞུ་ (tsāàshu) sm. ཚགས་ཞྭ་.

ཚགས་ཞྭ (tsāàsha) bamboo hat.

ཚགས་བཟང་ (tsāàsaŋ) physically fit and nimble ། ལུས་རྩལ་བྱས་ན་གཟུགས་པོ་ཚགས་བཟང་བར་འགྱུར་གྱི་རེད་ If (one) exercises (one) will become fit and nimble.

ཚགས་ཡིག (tsəgyiì) shung. records, documents ། ཉོ་ཚོང་ཚགས་ཡིག Trade records.

ཚགས་རས་ (tsāgrɛ̀ɛ̀) cloth used for sifting/ straining.

ཚགས་རིས་ (tsāgriì) tattoo.

ཚགས་ལིང་ (tsəgliŋ) sm. ཚགས་གླིང་.

ཚགས་ལུག (tsāàluù) 1. sheep to be slaughtered for meat. 2. abbr. of yak and sheep.

ཚགས་ཤ་ (tsāgsha) yak meat.

ཚགས་སུ་ཚུད་ (tsāgsu tsüü) vi. to be efficient, to be well-organized ། ཁོང་གི་དབུ་ཁྲིད་ལ་བརྟེན་ནས་ལས་ཀ་ཚགས་སུ་ཚུད་པ་རེད་ Because of his leadership the work became efficient.

ཚགས་ལྷོད་པོ་ (tsāà lhö̀öbo) loose, not compact/ dense.

ཚང་ (tsāŋ) 1. nest, den, lair ། སྟག་མོ་དེ་ཚང་ནས་ཐོན་པ་རེད་ The tigress came out of the den. 2. household, family ། གྲུང་ཏོག་ཚང་ Dungtok family. 3. vi. to be complete/ whole/ full/ entire ། ངའི་ཅ་ལག་ཚང་མ་ཚང་འདུག All my things were there complete (nothing was missing). 4. dwelling, abode ། གནས་ཚང་ Inn. ། ཐབ་ཚང་ Kitchen.

ཚང་འཁོར་ཅན་ (tsāŋgɔɔjɛn) round in shape/ design.

ཚང་འགོ་ (tsāŋgo) the first born in a litter.

ཚང་གཅིག་མ་ (tsāŋ ji̱gmə) an animal giving birth to one offspring in a litter.

ཚང་མཇུག (tsəŋjuù) the last born in a litter.

ཚང་ཉལ་ (tsāŋñɛɛ) hibernating; va.—བྱེད་.

ཚང་པོ་ (tsāŋbo) complete, entire ། ཚོགས་འདུར་ཡོང་མཁན་མི་ཚང་པོ་བྱུང་མི་འདུག All those who should have come to the meeting did not come.

ཚང་སྒྲུགས་སུ་ (tsāŋ dru̱gsu) completely, entirely.

ཚང་བང་ (tsāŋbaŋ) kitchen.

ཚང་འབྱོར་ (tsāŋjɔɔ) arriving completely, all the people having arrived.

ཚང་མ་ (tsāŋma) all, every, entire ། མི་ཚང་མ་འདིར་ཡོང་པ་རེད་ All the people came here.

ཚང་མ་འདྲ་མཉམ་ (tsāŋma dra̱ñam) equality, without discrimination, everyone equal.

ཚང་མ་ལོག (tsāŋmalɔɔ̀) everybody, all.

ཚང་མལ་ (tsāŋmɛɛ) bird's nest.

ཚང་རྫིས་ (tsāŋdziì) sm. ཚང་བཤེར་.

ཚང་ཚང་རུག་རུག (tsāŋdzaŋ ru̱gruù) sm. ཚང་འཛོམས་.

ཚང་ཚིང་ (tsəŋdziŋ) a dense grove/ thicket/ forest.

ཚང་འཛོམས་ (tsāŋdzom) 1. all gathering together ། དགེ་སློབ་ཚང་འཛོམས་བྱུང་སོང་ All the teachers and students gathered together. 2. plenary session.

ཚང་འཛོམས་གྲོས་ཚོགས་ (tsāŋdzom trö̱ödzɔɔ̀) plenary session/ meeting.

ཚང་ཞེན་ (tsāŋshen) attachment to one's home/ family.

ཚང་ཟླ་ (tsāŋda) relative.

ཚང་ར་ (tsāŋra) sm. མཚང་ར་.

ཚང་རག (tsāŋraà) horsemanship; va.—གཏོང་.

ཚང་རའི་རུས་སྒྲོམ་ (tsāŋrɛ rü̱üdrom) hip bones.

ཚང་ལ་མ་ཚང་ (tsāŋla ma̱dzaŋ) not complete.

ཚང་ལ་མ་ནོར་བ་ (tsāŋla ma̱nɔɔwa) complete and without mistakes.

ཚང་ལེན་ (tsāŋ le̱n) va. to spade a dog.

ཚང་ལོག (tsāŋ lɔ̱ɔ̀) 1. va. to return to one's nest/ den. 2. vi. to get completely destroyed/ finished/ dissolved (people and things). 3. see རི་བོང་ཚང་ལོག.

ཚང་བཤེར་ (tsāŋsher) examining to see if sth. is complete or not; va.—རྒྱག ། མཛོད་ཁང་གི་ཅ་ལག་རྣམས་ཚང་བཤེར་གཏོང་དགོས་ (We) have to examine whether all the things in the warehouse are there (complete).

ཚངས་ (tsāŋ) 1. abbr. of ཚངས་པ་. 2. the middle lining of clothes. 3. wadding.

ཚངས་སྐུད་ (tsəŋgüü) an ornament worn by tantric female deities.

ཚངས་སྐྱེས་ (tsāŋgyeè) poet. Saturday.

ཚངས་ཐིག (tsāŋdig) diameter.

ཚངས་ཐུག (tsāŋduù) white tassel that is put on temple roofs.

ཚངས་པ་ (tsāŋba) 1. Brahma. 2. clean.

ཚངས་པ་ལྷའི་མེ་ཏོག (tsāŋba lɛ̄ me̱doò) 1. the root of Chinese pulsatilla. 2. name for King Trisrong Detsan.

ཚངས་པའི་བུ་ག (tsāŋbɛ pu̱ga) a hole in the center of the skull that is used in acupuncture.

ཚངས་སྤྱོད་ (tsāŋjöö) 1. a gelong monk. 2. monks who have maintained their vows.

ཚངས་སྤྱོད་དགེ་བསྙེན་ (tsāŋjöö ge̱ñen) sm. དགེ་བསྙེན་.

ཚངས་ཕྱེད་ (tsāŋjeè) radius.

ཚངས་བུག (tsāŋbuù) sm. ཚངས་པའི་བུ་ག.

ཚངས་དབྱངས་རྒྱ་མཚོ་ (tsāyaŋ gya̱dzo) name of the 6th Dalai Lama.

ཚངས་མ་ (tsāŋma) 1. clean; va.—བཟོ་ to make clean. 2. a virgin. 3. house flies. 4. the mother of Brahma.

ཚད་ (tsɛ̄ɛ̀) 1. measurement, size, scale, degree; va.—འཇལ་; va.—རྒྱག་; —ལེན་ to take measurements, to measure ། སྟོད་ཐུང་གི་ཚད་ The size of the shirt. 2. limit, norm, level ། ཚད་ལས་བརྒལ་ཆོག་གི་མ་རེད་ (One) may not surpass the limit. 3. va. to compete with/ against ། ཁོང་གཉིས་ལག་ཤུགས་ཚད་པ་རེད་ Those two competed in arm wrestling. 4. every, whatever ། སློབ་ཕྲུག་ཡོད་ཚད་གླིང་ཀར་ཕྱིན་པ་རེད་ Every student went to the picnic. 5. whenever, every time ། སློབ་གྲྭར་ཕྱིན་ཚད་ལ་ཁོ་མཐོང་བྱུང་ Every time (I) went to school I saw him. 6. vi. (with neg.) to be more than stated ། འཛིན་གྲྭ་འདིའི་ནང་སློབ་ཕྲུག་བཅུ་ཚད་ཀྱི་མ་རེད་ There are more than ten students in this class.

ཚད་བཀག (tsɛ̄ɛ̀gaà) norm, standard, limitation (for time, amount, quality) ། དགེ་རྒན་གྱིས་སློབ་ཕྲུག་ཚོར་ལས་ཀ་ཚད་བཀག་མེད་པ་སྐྱལ་གྱི་ཡོད་པ་རེད་ The teacher makes the students work without any limits.

ཚད་བཀག་གྲངས་བཅད་ (tsɛ̄ɛ̀gaà tra̱ŋjɛɛ̀) a targeted amount, limited number.

ཚད་སྒམ་ (tsɛ̄ɛ̀gam) sculptor's tool.

ཚད་བགོས་ཐིག་ཤིང་ (tsɛ̄ɛ̀göö ti̱gshiŋ) ruler.

ཚད་ཁྲ་ (tsɛ̄ɛ̀dra) numeral, figure, quantity, amount.

ཚད་མཁྲིས་ (tsɛ̄ɛ̀ triì) fever and jaundice.

ཚད་འཁྱོལ་ (tsɛ̄ɛ̀gyöö) sm. ཚད་ལོངས་.

ཚད་འཁྲུ་ (tsɛ̄ɛ̀ trū) vi. to have diarrhea (in hot climates/ areas).

ཚད་གྲངས་ (tsɛ̄ɛ̀draŋ) quota ། བཟོ་གྲྭ་འདིའི་ཐོན་སྐྱེད་ཀྱི་ཚད་གྲངས་ནི་ཉིན་གཅིག་ནང་དངོས་པོ་ངོ་གྲངས་ ༡༠༠༠༠ ཙམ་བཟོ་གི་ཡོད་པ་རེད་ The production quota of that factory is to make10,000 items in one day.

ཚད་དགུང་ (tsɛ̄ɛ̀guŋ) 1. noon. 2. middle of summer.

ཚད་འགལ་ (tsɛ̄ɛ̀ gɛ̱ɛ) sm. ཚད་བརྒལ་.

ཚད་འགོད་ (tsɛ̄ɛ̀ gö̱ö) va. to set a quota, standard/ scale/ measurement ། བཟོ་པ་རེ་རེས་ཉིན་རེ་མེ་མདའ་གསུམ་བཟོ་དགོས་པའི་ཚད་བཀོད་པ་རེད་ They set a quota that each worker has to make three guns per day.

ཚད་འགྲིགས་པོ་ (tsɛ̄ɛ̀ dri̱gbu) fitting/ suitable in size.

ཚད་རྒྱག་སྐམ་པ་ (tsɛ̄ɛ̀gyaà gāmba) caliper.

ཚད་བརྒལ་ (tsɛ̄ɛ̀ gɛ̱ɛ) vi. to exceed a standard/ limit/ quota.

ཚད་བརྒལ་སྐར་ཆེན་ (tsɛ̄ɛ̀gɛɛ gārjen) supergiant star.

ཚད་བརྒལ་གྱི་ཁེ་སྤོགས་ (tsɛ̄ɛ̀gɛɛgi kēbɔɔ̀) super profit, excessive profit.

ཚད་བརྒལ་འགུལ་ཚད་ (tsɛ̄ɛ̀gɛɛ gü̱ü̱dzɛɛ̀) ultrahigh frequency (UHF).

ཚད་བརྒལ་གྱི་རིན་ཐང་ལྷག་མ་ (tsɛ̄ɛ̀gɛɛgi ri̱ndaŋ lhāgma) excessive surplus value.

ཚད་བརྒལ་གློག་གནོན་ (tsɛ̃ɛ̀gɛɛ lɔ̃ɔ̀nün) extra high voltage.

ཚད་བརྒལ་སྒྲ་རླབས་ (tsɛ̃ɛ̀gɛɛ dr̲aləb) ultrasonic (wave), supersonic (wave).

ཚད་བརྒལ་སྒྲ་རླབས་གློག་ཆས་ནད་བརྟག་ཁང་ (tsɛ̃ɛ̀gɛɛ dr̲aləb lɔ̃gjɛɛ̀ n̲ɛ̃ɛ̀daàgaŋ) ultrasonic diagnostic room.

ཚད་བརྒལ་དུལ་ཕྲན་ (tsɛ̃ɛ̀gɛɛ d̲ü̲ü̲drɛn) hyperon.

ཚད་བརྒལ་ནུས་པ་ (tsɛ̃ɛ̀gɛɛ n̲ü̲ü̲bə) extrahigh energy.

ཚད་བརྒལ་མྱུར་ཤུགས་ (tsɛ̃ɛ̀gɛɛ ñ̲u̲rshuù) ultrarapid, ultrafast.

ཚད་བརྒལ་དམའ་དྲོད་ (tsɛ̃ɛ̀gɛɛ m̲adröö) ultralow temperature.

ཚད་བརྒལ་ཚ་ཤུགས་ (tsɛ̃ɛ̀gɛɛ tsãshuù) superhigh temperature.

ཚད་བརྒལ་རང་བཞིན་ (tsɛ̃ɛ̀gɛɛ r̲aŋshin) the nature or the character of excessiveness.

ཚད་བརྒལ་རིན་ཐང་ལྷག་མ་ (tsɛ̃ɛ̀gɛɛ r̲indaŋ lhãàma) excess surplus value.

ཚད་བརྒལ་རླབས་ཐུང་ (tsɛ̃ɛ̀gɛɛ lə̃bduŋ) ultra short wave.

ཚད་བརྒལ་རླུང་གནོན་ (tsɛ̃ɛ̀gɛɛ lũŋnün) super high pressure.

ཚད་བརྒལ་ལེགས་འགྲུབ་ (tsɛ̃ɛ̀gɛɛ l̲egdrub) overfulfillment of a quota.

ཚད་བརྒལ་སྲ་གཟུགས་ (tsɛ̃ɛ̀gɛɛ trə̃suù) super hard material.

ཚད་ངེས་ (tsɛ̃ɛ̀ŋeè) a definite limit/ ration/ allowance/ quota.

ཚད་ངེས་ཅན་ (tsɛ̃ɛ̀ŋeèjɛn) having a definite limit/ ration, allowance/ quota.

ཚད་གཅིག་ཚད་གཉིས་ (tsɛ̃ɛ̀jig tsɛ̃ɛ̀ñii) on/ at the verge of competing ༎ ང་གཉིས་ཨབ་དང་ཚད་གཅིག་ཚད་གཉིས་ལ་ཁོ་ཕྱིན་སོང་ While we were on the verge of wrestling, he went.

ཚད་འཇལ་ (tsɛ̃ɛ̀ j̲ɛ̲ɛ̲) va. to measure.

ཚད་འཇལ་སྐམ་པ་ (tsɛ̃ɛ̀jɛɛ gãmba) sm. ཚད་རྒྱུག་སྐམ་པ་.

ཚད་འཇལ་རྟགས་རིས་ (tsɛ̃ɛ̀jɛɛ də̃grii) scale on a ruler/ gauge.

ཚད་འཇལ་པི་ཙི་ (tsɛ̃ɛ̀jɛɛ bĩdzi) tib. ch. measuring glass/ cup/ flask.

ཚད་འཇལ་རུ་ཁག (tsɛ̃ɛ̀jɛɛ r̲ugaà) survey team.

ཚད་རྙོག (tsɛ̃ɛ̀ñoò) lethargic/ lazy because of heat.

ཚད་རྟགས་ (tsɛ̃ɛ̀daà) abbr. of ཚད་འཇལ་རྟགས་རིས་.

ཚད་ལྟ་ (tsɛ̃ɛ̀da) sm. ཚོད་ལྟ་.

ཚད་བལྟ་ (tsɛ̃ɛ̀da) sm. ཚོད་ལྟ་.

ཚད་ཐིག (tsɛ̃ɛ̀dig) marking line, plumb line.

ཚད་ཐུབ་ (tsɛ̃ɛ̀dub) sm. ཚད་ལྡན་.

ཚད་མཐུན་ (tsɛ̃ɛ̀dün) in accordance with a standard/ quota/ size/ quality/ limit.

ཚད་མཐོ་ (tsɛ̃ɛ̀to) 1. high standard/ limit. 2. high tension, high voltage.

ཚད་མཐོ་གློག་སྒོ་བཟོ་གྲྭ (tsɛ̃ɛ̀to lɔ̃ɔ̀go s̲odra) high voltage switch factory.

ཚད་མཐོ་གློག་སྤྲོད་ཁང་ (tsɛ̃ɛ̀to) high voltage power supply office.

ཚད་འཐིབས་ (tsɛ̃ɛ̀dib) sm. ཚད་རྙོག.

ཚད་འདུམས་ (tsɛ̃ɛ̀dum) sm. ཚད་རྙོག.

ཚད་དང་འགལ་བ་ (tsɛ̃ɛ̀daŋ g̲ɛ̲ɛ̲wa) sm. ཚད་འགལ་.

ཚད་དང་མཐུན་ (tsɛ̃ɛ̀daŋ tũmbə) sm. ཚད་མཐུན་.

ཚད་དུག (tsɛ̃ɛ̀duù) a type fever that makes people crazy or muddleheaded.

ཚད་དྲོད་ (tsɛ̃ɛ̀dröö) 1. fever. 2. confidence.

ཚད་གདུགས་ (tsɛ̃ɛ̀duù) umbrella.

ཚད་གདུང་ (tsɛ̃ɛ̀duŋ) extremely hot; vi.—འཚིག to feel extremely hot.

ཚད་འདས་ (tsɛ̃ɛ̀dɛɛ̀) sm. ཚད་བརྒལ་.

ཚད་འདེབས་ (tsɛ̃ndeb) sm. ཚད་ལེན་.

ཚད་འདྲེན་ (tsɛ̃ɛ̀ dr̲en) va. to compete (in a competition).

ཚད་རྡུལ་ (tsɛ̃ɛ̀düü) quantum (physics) ༎ ཚད་རྡུལ་ཤུགས་རིགས་ Quantum mechanics.

ཚད་རྡོ་ (tsɛ̃ɛ̀do) shung. a stone pillar used to demarcate a boundary.

ཚད་ལྡང་ (tsɛ̃ɛ̀daŋ) sm. ཚད་ལོངས་.

ཚད་ལྡན་ (tsɛ̃ndɛn) 1. a standard, a term, limit; va.—བྱེད་ to make a standard/ term/ limit; vi.—དུ་འགྱུར་ to become standardized. 2. competent, qualified ༎ སྐྱེ་བོ་ཚད་ལྡན་ A competent person. 3. limited (iso. a company) ༎ ཚད་ལྡན་ཀུང་སི་ Limited Company.

ཚད་ལྡན་གྱི་སྐད་ (tsɛ̃ndɛngi gɛ̃ɛ̀) standard language.

ཚད་ལྡན་གྱི་སྒྲ་ (tsɛ̃ndɛngi dr̲a) standard pronunciation.

ཚད་ལྡན་གི་ལམ་ལྕགས་ (tsɛ̃ndɛngi l̲amjaà) standard size railroad track.

ཚད་ལྡན་འཇལ་ཆས་ (tsɛ̃ɛ̀dɛn j̲ɛɛjɛɛ̀) standard measure.

ཚད་ལྡན་དུ་འགྱུར་ (tsɛ̃ndɛndu gyu̲r) vi. to become standardized.

ཚད་ལྡན་དུས་ཚོད་ (tsɛ̃ndɛn t̲ü̲ü̲dzöö) standard time.

ཚད་ལྡན་སྦྱོང་བརྡར་ (tsɛ̃ndɛn jo̲ndar) regular/ standard training.

ཚད་ལྡན་དམག་དཔུང་ (tsɛ̃ndɛn mə̃gbuŋ) conventional regular/ troops.

ཚད་ལྡན་ཙིས་རྒྱུག་ཅུ (tsɛ̃ndɛn dzĩigyaà jũ) tib. ch. bureau of standard measurements.

ཚད་ལྡན་ཚད་ (tsɛ̃ndɛn tsɛ̃ɛ̀) standard quantity.

ཚད་ལྡན་ཡིག་ཆ་ (tsɛ̃ndɛn y̲igi) authentic/ genuine document.

ཚད་ལྡན་སློབ་གསོ་ (tsɛ̃ndɛn lõbso) standard education.

ཚད་སྡུར་ (tsɛ̃ɛ̀dur) comparing; va.—བྱེད་ to compare ༎ ལོ་གསར་རྙིང་གི་ཞིང་ལས་ཐོན་སྐྱེད་ཀྱི་ཚད་སྡུར་བྱེད་ཀྱི་ཡོད་པ་རེད་ (They) are comparing this year and last year's agricultural production.

ཚད་བསྡུར་ (tsɛ̃ɛ̀dur) p. of ཚད་སྡུར་.

ཚད་ནད་ (tsɛ̃ɛ̀nɛɛ̀) 1. fever. 2. malaria. 3. illness cause by heat.

ཚད་པ་ (tsɛ̃ɛ̀ba) 1. heat, hot (temperature) ༎ ལྡི་ལིར་དབྱར་ཀ་ཚད་པ་ཆེན་པོ་ཡོད་པ་རེད་ (It) is very hot in Delhi in the summer. 2. fever; vi.—ན་ to be ill with fever/ heat.

ཚད་པ་ཕོག (tsɛ̃ɛ̀ba pɔ̃ɔ̀) vi. to get/ be oppressed by heat, to get heat prostration.

ཚད་པ་ཞག་གཉིས་མ་ (tsɛ̃ɛ̀ba sh̲a̲à ñĩimə) fever which last for two days.

ཚད་དཔག (tsɛ̃ɛ̀baà) approximation, estimation, appraisal; va.—བྱེད་ to approximate, to estimate, to appraise ༎ ལུང་པ་འདིའི་མི་འབོར་ཚད་དཔག་བྱས་ན་ཁྲི་གསུམ་ཙམ་ཡོད་པ་རེད་ If we estimate the population of that country, it is approximately thirty thousand.

ཚད་དཔོག (tsɛ̃ɛ̀bɔɔ̀) sm. ཚད་དཔག.

ཚད་འཕེར་ (tsɛ̃mber) 1. meeting a standard ༎ བཟོ་གྲྭ་འདིའི་ཅ་ལག་ཚང་མ་སྤུས་ཚད་ཚད་འཕེར་ཡོད་པ་རེད་ All the things from that factory meet the quality standards. ༎ ཅ་ལག་འདི་ཚོ་ཚད་འཕེར་རེད་མི་འདུག These things do not meet the required standard.

ཚད་བྲལ་ (tsɛ̃ɛ̀drɛɛ) sm. ཚད་མེད་.

ཚད་འབོར་ (tsɛ̃ɛ̀mbɔɔ) the amount required to meet a standard or quota.

ཚད་མ་ (tsɛ̃ɛ̀ma) 1. logic (one of the five major parts of Buddhist teachings). 2. evident, true, proven ༎ སངས་རྒྱས་ཀྱི་བཀའ་ཚད་མ་ The true teachings of the Buddha. 3. standard ༎ སློབ་ཁྲིད་བྱེད་ཐབས་ཚད་མ་ Standard way of teaching. 4. just right ༎ ཁོང་གཟུགས་པོ་རིང་ཐུང་ཚད་མ་རེད་ He is just the right height.

ཚད་མ་གཉིས་ (tsɛ̃ɛ̀ma ñĩi) two types of logic.

ཚད་མ་རྣམ་འགྲེལ་ (tsɛ̃ɛ̀ma nãmdree) a religious text on logic.

ཚད་མ་པ་ (tsɛ̃ɛ̀maba) a monk who studies logic.

ཚད་མ་རིག་པ་ (tsɛ̃ɛ̀ma r̲igbə) logic (one of the five major parts of Buddhist teachings).

ཚད་མེད་ (tsɛ̃ɛ̀meè) 1. immense, boundless, limitless, infinite, complete/ total ༎ དགའ་སྤྲོ་ཚད་མེད་ Immense happiness. ༎ ཕམ་ཉེས་ཚད་མེད་ Total defeat.

ཚད་མེད་གྲངས་མེད་ (tsɛ̃ɛ̀meè tr̲a̲ŋmeè) countless,

innumerable.

ཚད་མེད་པ་ (tsɛ̄ɛ̀meèba) sm. ཚད་མེད་.

ཚད་མེད་བཞི་ (tsɛ̄ɛ̀meè shi) the four immeasurables: love, compassion, joy and equanimity.

ཚད་སྨྱོས་ (tsɛ̄ɛ̀ñöö) delirious with fever.

ཚད་སྨིན་ནགས་ཚལ་ (tsɛ̄ɛ̀min nagdzɛɛ) mature forest.

ཚད་སྨྱོ་ (tsɛ̄ɛ̀ño) sm. ཚད་སྨྱོས་.

ཚད་ཚད་ (tsɛ̄ɛ̀dzɛɛ̀) 1. (vb. + —) about to do, almost doing the verbal action. 2. (— + གཏོང་) trying to have sexual intercourse.

ཚད་ཚད་སྡུར་སྡུར་ (tsɛ̄ɛ̀dzɛɛ̀ durdur) measuring/ comparing carefully; va.—བྱེད་.

ཚད་ཚིག་ (tsɛ̄ɛ̀dziì) words that classify, measure word that go together (e.g., school of fish, flock of birds, etc.).

ཚད་མཚམས་ (tsɛ̄ɛ̀dzam) limit; va.—གཏོད་ to put/ make/ set a limit.

ཚད་འཛིན་ (tsɛ̄ɛ̀ dzin) vi. to meet/ adhere to a standard/ limit.

ཚད་འཛིན་འཕེར་ (tsɛ̄ndzin pēr) 1. vi. to be able to meet a standard/ limit. 2. a limit.

ཚད་འཛིན་བྱེད་ (tsɛ̄ɛ̀ndzin ceè) va. to make a rule/ standard.

ཚད་འཛིན་ས་ (tsɛ̄ɛ̀ dzīnsə) the standard for sth., the standard against which sth. is measured.

ཚད་གཞལ་ (tsɛ̄ɛ̀ shɛɛ) va. to measure, to survey.

ཚད་གཞི་ (tsɛ̄ɛ̀shi) 1. standard, criteria, specification ། ཚད་གཞི་མཐོ་ཤོས་ཀྱིས་པར་རྒྱག་གི་ཡོད་པ་རེད་ (They) are printing it according to the highest standards. 2. rate, level ། ཚོང་ཟོག་ཁག་ལ་ཁྲལ་འཇལ་བའི་ཚད་གཞི་ཉུང་དུ་གཏོང་དགོས་ (We) must reduce the tax rate on commodities.

ཚད་ཡངས་ (tsɛ̄ɛ̀yaŋ) spacious.

ཚད་ཡོད་ (tsɛ̄ɛ̀yöö) limited, bounded ། ཚད་ཡོད་ཀུང་སི་ A limited company.

ཚད་ཡོད་དམག་འཁྲུག་ (tsɛ̄ɛ̀yöö məgdruù) limited war.

ཚད་ཡོད་རང་བཞིན་ (tsɛ̄ɛ̀yöö rəŋshin) the nature of limits/ limitation.

ཚད་ཡོལ་ (tsɛ̄ɛ̀yöö) vi. to exceed a limit/ standard ། དམག་མིར་ཞུགས་པའི་ལོ་ཚད་ཡོལ་བ་རེད་ (He) exceeded the age standard for joining the army.

ཚད་རན་པོ་ (tsɛ̄ɛ̀ rɛmbo) appropriate in limit/ size/ amount.

ཚད་རེས་བྱེད་ (tsɛ̄ɛ̀reè ceè) va. to compete.

ཚད་རོ་ (tsɛ̄ɛ̀ro) an old illness; vi.—ལང་ to have an old sickness flare up again.

ཚད་ལ་ (tsɛ̄ɛ̀la) every time, whenever ། མི་དེས་ཁ་གདངས་ཚད་ལ་རྫུན་གཏོང་གི་རེད་ This man lies whenever he opens his mouth.

ཚད་ལས་རྒལ་ (tsɛ̄ɛ̀lɛɛ̀ gɛɛ) sm. ཚད་ལས་བརྒལ་.

ཚད་ལས་བརྒལ་ (tsɛ̄ɛ̀lɛɛ̀ gɛɛ) vi. to surpass/ exceed (a quota, norm, limit, etc.) ། ཐོན་སྐྱེད་ད་ལོའི་འཆར་གཞི་ཚད་ལས་བརྒལ་བ་རེད་ Production surpassed this year's plan. ། ཚད་ལས་བརྒལ་བའི་དགའ་སྤྲོ་ Immense joy.

ཚད་ལས་བརྒལ་བར་འགྲུབ་ (tsɛ̄ɛ̀lɛɛ̀ gɛɛwar drub) vi. to achieve more than the limit, to overfulfill a limit/ norm.

ཚད་ལས་འདའ་ (tsɛ̄ɛ̀lɛɛ̀ daa) sm. ཚད་ལས་བརྒལ་.

ཚད་ལས་འདས་པ་ (tsɛ̄ɛ̀lɛɛ̀ dɛ̄ɛ̀ba) sm. ཚད་ལས་བརྒལ་.

ཚད་ལེན་ (tsɛ̄ɛ̀len) measuring, surveying; va. ཚད་ལེན་; —བྱེད་ to survey, to measure.

ཚད་ལེན་རྩིས་རྒྱག (tsɛ̄ɛ̀len dziìgyaà) checking whether some job met a standard; va.—བྱེད་.

ཚད་ལོངས་ (tsɛ̄ɛ̀ loŋ) vi. to reach/ meet a standard (measurement, qualification, etc.) ། ཡིག་ཚད་ཀྱི་བརྒྱ་ཆའི་ཚད་ལོངས་པ་རེད་ (He) met the required percentage in his examination.

ཚད་ལོན་ (tsɛ̄ɛ̀ lön) sm. ཚད་ལོངས་.

ཚད་ཤིང་ (tsɛ̄ɛ̀shiŋ) a ruler (for measuring).

ཚན་ (tsɛ̄n) part, section, unit, segment.

ཚན་དཀར་དམན་པ་ (tsɛ̄ngar memba) stalagmite.

ཚན་སྒོར་ (tsɛ̄ngɔɔ) group, team.

ཚན་ཁ་ (tsɛ̄nga) power, energy.

ཚན་ཁག (tsɛ̄ngaà) department, division, section ། ལས་ཁུངས་འདིའི་དྲུང་ཡིག་ཚན་ཁག་རྣམས་ The secretarial division of this office. ། ལོ་རྒྱུས་ཚན་ཁག History department.

ཚན་གྲངས་ (tsɛ̄ndraŋ) the number of various items.

ཚན་བསྒོས་སློབ་ཁྲིད་ (tsɛ̄ngöö lōbdriì) team/ unit teaching.

ཚན་གཅིག (tsɛ̄njig) a unit/ cell/ section/ division/ group.

ཚན་ཆུང་ (tsɛ̄njuŋ) a small unit/ cell/ section/ division/ group.

ཚན་ཆེ་བ་ (tsɛ̄n cēwa) the most, the majority.

ཚན་ཆེན་ (tsɛ̄n cēn) sm. ཚན་པོ་ཆེ་.

ཚན་དེ་ (tsɛ̄nde) sm. ཚ་པོ་.

ཚན་དོད་ (tsɛ̄ndöö) money given as a substitute for a gift.

ཚན་པ་ (tsɛ̄mba) 1. department ། བོད་ཡིག་གི་ཚན་པ་ Tibetan language department. 2. paragraph, section, an act (in a play etc.).

ཚན་པོ་ཆེ་ (tsɛ̄mbo cē) 1. large quantity/ volume. 2. strong person.

ཚན་དབྱི་ཡོན་ (tsɛ̄nyiyön) ch. senator.

ཚན་དབྱི་ཡོའན་ (tsɛ̄nyiyön) ch. Senate, House of Councilors (Japan).

ཚན་དབྱི་ཡོའན་གྲོས་ཁང་ (tsɛ̄nyiyön tröögaŋ) ch.tib. sm. ཚན་དབྱི་ཡོའན་.

ཚན་འབྱིད་རྒྱུགས་ལེན་ (tsɛ̄njeè gyuùlen) imperial examination (in China).

ཚན་མོ་ (tsɛ̄nmo) hot.

ཚན་མོའུ་ (tsɛ̄nmowu) ch. staff officer (in the military).

ཚན་མོའུ་ཀྲང་ (tsɛ̄nmodraŋ) ch. chief of staff.

ཚན་དམར་ (tsɛ̄nmar) a type of herb.

ཚན་ཙན་ (tsɛ̄ndzen) ch. advisor, attache, secretary (of a legation).

ཚན་གཙོ་ (tsɛ̄ndzo) ch. sm. ཙུའུ་ཀྲང་.

ཚན་རྩལ་ (tsɛ̄ndzɛɛ) abbr. of ཚན་རིག་ལག་རྩལ་.

ཚན་རྩལ་དཔེ་སྐྲུན་ཁང་ (tsɛ̄ndzɛɛ bēdrüngaŋ) science and technology publishing house.

ཚན་རྩལ་དཔེ་མཛོད་ཁང་ (tsɛ̄ndzɛɛ bēndzögaŋ) science and technology library.

ཚན་རྩལ་སྒྱུལ་འཕྲིན་ཞིབ་འཇུག་ཁང་ (tsɛ̄ndzɛɛ ñüündrin shimjuùgaŋ) institute of scientific and technical information.

ཚན་རྩལ་པ་ (tsɛ̄ndzɛɛba) scientific/ technical worker.

ཚན་ཚན་ (tsɛ̄ndzɛn) in groups/ batches/ sections.

ཚན་ཚན་རིག་པ་ (tsɛ̄ndzɛɛ rigbə) sm. ཚན་རིག.

ཚན་ཞིབ་པ་ (tsɛ̄nshibə) scientist, researcher.

ཚན་ཟླ་ (tsɛ̄nda) brothers.

ཚན་རིག (tsɛ̄nriì) science; va.—སྤྱོད་ to use/ apply science.

ཚན་རིག་ཁང་ (tsɛ̄nriìgaŋ) Academy of Sciences ། ཀྲུང་གོའི་ཚན་རིག་ཁང་ The Chinese Academy of Sciences.

ཚན་རིག་ཁྱབ་གདལ་ཕྲུའུ་ (tsɛ̄nriì kyəbdee trū) tib. ch. popular science division/ unit.

ཚན་རིག་ཁྱབ་སྤེལ་ (tsɛ̄nriì kyəbbee) popularizing science; va.—གཏོང་.

ཚན་རིག་ཁྱབ་སྤེལ་ཀློག་དེབ་ (tsɛ̄nriì kyəbbee lōgdeb) popular science book.

ཚན་རིག་མཁས་པ་ (tsɛ̄nriì kēēbə) scientist.

ཚན་རིག་གི་གདེང་ཕབ་པ་ (tsɛ̄nriìgi deŋpəbbə) scientific fact/ finding.

ཚན་རིག་གི་དཔྱད་ཆས་ (tsɛ̄nriìgi jɛ̄ɛ̀jɛɛ̀) scientific equipment.

ཚན་རིག་གི་ཚོད་ལྟ་ (tsɛ̄nriìgi tsōöda) scientific experimentation; va.—བྱེད་.

ཚན་རིག་གི་རང་བཞིན་ (tsɛ̄nriìgi rəŋshin) imbued with a scientific character/ scientific nature.

ཚན་རིག་གི་ལག་ལེན་ (tsɛ̄nriìgi laglen) using science, putting science into practice; va.—བྱེད་.

ཚན་རིག་གི་ཤེས་བྱ་ (tsɛ̄nriìgi shēēja) scientific knowledge.

ཚན་རིག་ཀུང་ཕྲན་རིང་ལུགས་ (tsɛ̄nriì kuŋdrɛn riŋluù)

scientific communism.

ཚན་རིག་ཉམས་ཞིབ་ (tsɛ̄nrii̇ ñamshib) scientific research; va.—བྱེད་ ¶ ཚན་རིག་ཉམས་ཞིབ་པ་ A scientific researcher.

ཚན་རིག་ཉམས་ཞིབ་པ་ (tsɛ̄nrii̇ ñamshibbə) scientist, scientific researcher.

ཚན་རིག་རྟོག་ཞིབ་ (tsɛ̄nrii̇ dōgshib) scientific investigation.

ཚན་རིག་བརྟག་དཔྱད་ (tsɛ̄nrii̇ dāgjɛɛ̀) sm. ཚན་རིག་ཉམས་ཞིབ་.

ཚན་རིག་བརྟག་དཔྱད་ལྟེ་གནས་ (tsɛ̄nrii̇ dāgjɛɛ̀ dēnɛɛ̀) scientific research center.

ཚན་རིག་དང་མཐུན་པ་ (tsɛ̄nrii̇ dan̲ tūmbə) scientific, in accordance with science.

ཚན་རིག་དང་མཐུན་པའི་སྒྲུབ་བྱེད་ (tsɛ̄nrii̇ dan̲ tūmbɛ drubjeè) scientific proof/ demonstration.

ཚན་རིག་དང་མཐུན་པའི་ཚོད་གདམ་ (tsɛ̄nrii̇ dan̲ tūmbɛ cōōdam) scientific reference/ thesis.

ཚན་རིག་དང་མཐུན་པའི་འཆར་སྣང་ (tsɛ̄nrii̇ dan̲ tūmbɛ cārnaŋ) scientific illusion/ fantasy.

ཚན་རིག་དང་མཐུན་པའི་རྟོག་ཞིབ་ (tsɛ̄nrii̇ dan̲ tūmbɛ dōgshib) sm. ཚན་རིག་རྟོག་ཞིབ་.

ཚན་རིག་དང་མཐུན་པའི་སྤྱི་ཚོགས་རིང་ལུགས་ (tsɛ̄nrii̇ dan̲ tūmbɛ jīdzoò riŋluù) scientific socialism.

ཚན་རིག་དང་མཐུན་པའི་སྤྱོད་ཚུལ་ (tsɛ̄nrii̇ dan̲ tūmbɛ jōōdzüü) scientific attitude/ approach.

ཚན་རིག་དང་མཐུན་པའི་དབྱེ་ཞིབ་ (tsɛ̄nrii̇ dan̲ tūmbɛ yēshib) scientific analysis.

ཚན་རིག་པ་ (tsɛ̄nriibə) scientist.

ཚན་རིག་དཔྱད་ཆས་ (tsɛ̄nrii̇ jɛ̀ɛjɛɛ̀) scientific apparatus/ equipment.

ཚན་རིག་སྤྱི་ཚོགས་རིང་ལུགས་ (tsɛ̄nrii̇ jīdzoò ri̲ŋluù) scientific socialism.

ཚན་རིག་ཚོད་ལྟ་ (tsɛ̄nrii̇ tsōōda) scientific experiment/ test/ trial; va.—བྱེད་.

ཚན་རིག་ཞིབ་འཇུག (tsɛ̄nrii̇ shi̲mjuù) scientific research; va.—བྱེད་.

ཚན་རིག་ཞིབ་འཇུག་གི་གྲུབ་འབྲས་ (tsɛ̄nrii̇ shi̲mjuùgi dru̲mdrɛɛ̀) scientific achievement.

ཚན་རིག་ཞིབ་འཇུག་གི་འགག་གནད་སྒྲོལ་ (tsɛ̄nrii̇ shi̲mjuùgi ga̲gnɛɛ̀ drö̲ö) va. to solve a scientific impasse.

ཚན་རིག་ཞིབ་འཇུག་གི་རྣམ་གྲངས་ (tsɛ̄nrii̇ shi̲mjuùgi nāmdraŋ) subject of science research.

ཚན་རིག་ཞིབ་འཇུག་གི་ལས་ཁུངས་ (tsɛ̄nrii̇ shi̲mjuùgi lɛ̲ɛ̀guŋ) institution/ office of scientific research.

ཚན་རིག་ཞིབ་འཇུག་པ་ (tsɛ̄nrii̇ shi̲mjuùbə) scientist, scientific researcher.

ཚན་རིག་ཞིབ་འཇུག་བྱ་གཞི་ (tsɛ̄nrii̇ shi̲mjuù cə̲shi) scientific research project.

ཚན་རིག་ཡར་རྒྱས་ཀྱི་མཐུན་ཚོགས་ (tsɛ̄nrii̇ ya̲rgyɛɛ̀gi tündzɔɔ̀) association for the advancement of science.

ཚན་རིག་ཡར་རྒྱས་ལ་གཉེར་བའི་ཨ་མེ་རི་ཀའི་མཐུན་ཚོགས་ (tsɛ̄nrii̇ ya̲rgyɛɛ̀la ñērwɛ əmērikɛ tündzɔɔ̀) American Association for the Advancement of Science.

ཚན་རིག་ཡོན་ (tsɛ̄nrii̇ yo̲an) tib. ch. sm. ཚན་རིག་ཁང་.

ཚན་རིག་ལ་ཆེས་དགའ་བ་ (tsɛ̄nrii̇ cēè ga̲wa) scientific enthusiast.

ཚན་རིག་ལ་དབྱིངས་ཞུགས་ (tsɛ̄nriila yīŋ shu̲ù) sm. ཚན་རིག་ལ་ཆེས་དགའ་བ་.

ཚན་རིག་ལ་དབྱིངས་ཡོད་པ་ (tsɛ̄nriila yīŋ yö̲öba) sm. ཚན་རིག་ལ་དབྱིངས་ཞུགས་པ་.

ཚན་རིག་ལ་མོངས་པ་ (tsɛ̄nriila mōŋba) ignorant of science.

ཚན་རིག་ལག་རྩལ་ (tsɛ̄nrii̇ la̲gdzɛɛ) 1. scientific technique, scientific skills. 2. science and technology ¶ ཚན་རིག་ལག་རྩལ་སློབ་གྲྭ་ཆེན་མོ་ University of Science and Technology.

ཚན་རིག་ལག་རྩལ་གྱི་མི་སྣ་ (tsɛ̄nrii̇ la̲gdzɛɛgi mi̲nə) scientific and technical personnel.

ཚན་རིག་ལག་རྩལ་པ་ (tsɛ̄nrii̇ la̲gdzɛɛba) science and technology researcher, scientist.

ཚན་རིག་ལག་རྩལ་ལྷན་ཚོགས་ (tsɛ̄nrii̇ la̲gdzɛɛ lhēndzoò) society for science and technology.

ཚན་རིག་ལས་བྱེད་པ་ (tsɛ̄nrii̇ lɛ̲ɛ̀jeèba) scientist.

ཚན་རིག་སློབ་གསོ་ཁྲུའུ་ (tsɛ̄nrii̇ lōbso trū) tib. ch. science and education division.

ཚན་རིག་སློབ་གསོའི་གློག་བརྙན་ (tsɛ̄nrii̇ lōbsö lɔ̄ɔ̀ñɛn) popular science film.

ཚན་ཧྲི་ (tsɛ̄nhri) ch. councilor, senator.

ཚབ་ (tsə̄b) 1. substitute, replacement, in place of, on behalf of; va.—བྱེད་ to act as a substitute/ replacement, to act on behalf of sb; va.—གཏོང་ to send as a replacement/ substitute ¶ མོ་ཊ་རྙིང་པ་དེ་བཙོངས་པའི་ཚབ་ལ་གསར་པ་ཞིག་ཉོས་པ་རེད་ (They) bought a new car in place of the old one (they) sold. ¶ མི་དམངས་ཀྱི་ཚབ་བྱས་ནས་ Acting on behalf of the people. ¶ ཁོས་ཚགས་ཤོག་དེ་དག་མེ་ཤིང་གི་ཚབ་བྱས་པ་རེད་ He used newspaper as a substitute for firewood. ¶ ལས་བྱེད་པ་རྙིང་པ་འཕོས་ཚབ་གསར་པ་ཞིག་བཏང་བ་རེད་ A new officer was sent as the replacement of the old one.

ཚབ་སྐྱིན་ (tsə̄bgyin) replacement, repayment, substitute; va.—སྤྲོད་; —སྤྲིག; —སྤྲུབ་ to replace or pay for sth. (lost/ damaged/ loaned) ¶ དཔེ་མཛོད་ཀྱི་དེབ་བརླགས་པའི་ཚབ་སྐྱིན་སྤྲོད་དགོས་ (You) have to replace the library book (you) lost.

ཚབ་ཁྲིད་དགེ་རྒན་ (tsə̄bdrii̇ ge̲gɛn) temporary/ substitute teacher; va.—བྱེད་.

ཚབ་དངོས་ (tsə̄bŋöö) a replacement item, a substitute.

ཚབ་གཉེར་ (tsə̄bñer) trusteeship.

ཚབ་གཉེར་ས་ཁུལ་ (tsə̄bñer səgüü) trust territory, mandate territory.

ཚབ་གཏོང་ (tsə̄b dōŋ) see ཚབ་.

ཚབ་དུ་ (tsə̄bdu) sm. ཚབ་ལ་.

ཚབ་པོ་ (tsə̄bbo) sm. ཚབ་དངོས་.

ཚབ་སྤྱོད་ (tsə̄bjöö) replacing, substituting (for sth. in use).

ཚབ་སྤྱོད་དངོས་རྫས་ (tsə̄bjöö ŋöödzɛɛ̀) a substitute/ replacement item.

ཚབ་བི་ཚུབ་བི་ (tsə̄bbi tsūbbi) nervous, jittery, jumpy.

ཚབ་བྱེད་མཁན་ (tsə̄bjeèñɛn) agent, representative.

ཚབ་བྱེད་དངོས་རིགས་ (tsə̄bjɛɛ̄ ŋöörig) sm. ཚབ་དངོས་.

ཚབ་བྱེད་མི་སྣ་ (tsə̄bjɛɛ̀ mi̲nə) a representative ¶ འབྱོར་ལྡན་གྲལ་རིམ་གྱི་ཚབ་བྱེད་མི་སྣ་ Representatives of the bourgeois class.

ཚབ་བྱེད་རང་བཞིན་ (tsə̄bjɛɛ̀ rə̲ŋshiŋ) representation.

ཚབ་མ་ (tsə̄bmə) sm. ཚབ་དངོས་.

ཚབ་རྩིས་རིག་པ་ (tsə̄bdzii ri̲gbə) algebra.

ཚབ་ཚིག (tsə̄bdzii) pronoun.

ཚབ་ཚུབ་ (tsə̄bdzub) sm. ཚབ་བི་ཚུབ་བི་.

ཚབ་ཚུབ་དངངས་སྐྲག (tsə̄bdzub ŋāŋdraà) nervous/ jittery and scared; va.—བྱེད་.

ཚབ་མཚོན་མི་སྣ་ (tsə̄bdzün mi̲nə) people who are representatives/ substitutes.

ཚབ་ཞུ་ (tsə̄b shu̲) h. of ཚབ་བྱེད་.

ཚབ་རུང་དངོས་རྫས་ (tsə̄bruŋ ŋöödzɛɛ̀) sm. ཚབ་དངོས་.

ཚབ་ལ་ (tsə̄bla) instead of, in place of ¶ ཁོས་སློབ་གྲྭར་འགྲོ་རྒྱུའི་ཚབ་ལ་ Instead of going to school, he ...

ཚབ་གསར་ (tsə̄bsar) new replacement/ substitute.

ཚབས་ (tsə̄b) vi. to be/ get excited/ nervous/ agitated ¶ དམག་མ་བརྒྱབ་གོང་ལ་ཁོ་ཞེ་དྲགས་ཚབས་སོང་ He was very nervous before the battle.

ཚབས་ཆེ་ (tsə̄bje) serious, severe, grave ¶ ནད་པ་ཚབས་ཆེ་རྣམས་ The serious patients. ¶ རང་བྱུང་གི་གནོད་སྐྱོན་ཚབས་ཆེ་ A severe natural calamity.

ཚབས་ཆེན་གྱི་རང་བཞིན་ (tsə̄bcengi rə̲ŋshin) seriousness, importance.

ཚབས་ཆེན་པོ་ (tsə̄b cēmbo) brazen, impertinent, insolent.

ཚབས་ལྗིད་པོ་ (tsə̄b ji̲ibu) sm. ཚབས་ཆེན་པོ་.

ཚབས་པོ་ཆེ་ (tsə̄bboje) sm. ཚབས་ཆེ་.

ཚབས་ཤ་ (tsə̄bsha) nervous, agitated; va.—ལངས་.

ཚབས་ཤར་ (tsə̄bshaa) stinging, burning (pain); vi.—རྒྱག.

ཚམ་ངམ་ (tsāmŋam) panic, fright; vi.—བྱེད་ to get panicky/ frightened/ scared.

ཚམ་རྔམས་འཇིགས་འཇིགས་ (tsāmŋam jigjig) sm. རྔམ་རྔམ་རྔིག་རྔིག.

ཚམ་རྔམས་ (tsāmŋam) sm. ཚམ་ངམ་.

ཚམ་མི་ཚོམ་མི་ (tsəmmi tsōmmi) doubt, hesitation, wavering, shrinking back; va.—བྱེད་.

ཚམ་མེ་ཚོམ་མེ་ (tsāmme tsōmme) sm. ཚམ་མི་ཚོམ་མི་.

ཚམ་ཚོམ་ (tsāmtsom) sm. ཚམ་མི་ཚོམ་མི་.

ཚམ་ཚོམ་མེད་པ་ (tsāmdzom me̱èba) decisive, intrepid, daring.

ཚམས་ངམ་ (tsāmŋam) sm. ཚམ་ངམ་.

ཚམས་རྔམས་ (tsāmŋam) sm. ཚམ་ངམ་.

ཚའུ་ (tsəwu) 1. sifter, sieve; va.—རྒྱག to sift, to strain in a sieve. 2. sm. ཚ་བོ་.

ཚར་ (tsāā) 1. vi. to be finished, to be completed ¶ དེབ་དེ་བཀླགས་ཚར་སོང་ (I) finished reading the book. 2. times. ¶ ང་བོད་ལ་ཚར་གསུམ་ཕྱིན་པ་ཡིན་ (I) went to Tibet three times. 3. a line, series ¶ མཆོད་མེ་སྟོང་ཚར་ A line of 1000 butter lamps.

ཚར་རྒྱུག (tārgyuù) switch/ whip made from a branch of a tree.

ཚར་གཅིག (tsārjig) for once, one time.

ཚར་གཅོད་ (tsārjöö) annihilation, eradication, extermination; va.—བྱེད་; —གཏོང་ to annihilate, to kill, to eradicate, to exterminate ¶ དགྲ་བོ་ཚར་གཅོད་བྱེད་པའི་དམག་འཐབ་ནང་ In the fight to annihilate the enemy.

ཚར་གཅོད་དམག་འཐབ་ (tsārjöö məgdəb) war of annihilation.

ཚར་གཅོད་གཙང་དག (tsārjöö dzāŋdaà) complete annihilation/ eradication/ extermination.

ཚར་ལྷུག (tssārjɔɔ̀) pile/ stack of grains stalks (in the field).

ཚར་དུ་དངར་བ་ (rsārdu ŋārwa) a series, a line; va.—སྒྲིག to order/ arrange in a series/ row/ line ¶ གྲོས་མཐུན་ཚར་དུ་དངར་བ་ཞིག A series of agreements. ¶ འོད་སྣང་འབར་བའི་དགོངས་པ་ཚར་དུ་དངར་བ་ཞིག་མཚོན་གྱི་འདུག It shows a series of brilliant thoughts.

ཚར་པ་ (tsārba) chestnut tree.

ཚར་སྦེ་ (tsārbe) sm. ཚར་ལྷུག.

ཚར་སྦེའུ་ (tsārbewu) sm. ཚར་སྦེ་.

ཚར་ཕུང་ (tsārbuŋ) sm. ཚར་ལྷུག.

ཚར་ཕུད་ (tsārbüü) tassel.

ཚར་ཕོད་ (tsārböö) sm. ཚར་ཕུད་.

ཚར་ཕོན་ (tsārbön) bunch of grain.

ཚར་ཕྱིན་པ་ (tsārjinbə) sm. མཐར་ཕྱིན་པ་.

ཚར་བའི་ལས་ལ་ལྡོག་ཐབས་མེད་ (tsārwɛ le̱èla dəgdəb me̱è) sm. ཚར་ལས་བཅོས་ཐུབ་.

ཚར་བུ་ (tsārbu) 1. sm. ཚར་པ་. 2. tassel.

ཚར་བོང་ (tssārboŋ) Chinese cynomorium (cynomorium songaricum).

ཚར་མ་ (tsārma) unthreshed grains.

ཚར་རྩག (tsārdzaà) dress made from lambskin (with its fleece worn on the inside).

ཚར་ཚག (tsārdzaà) sm. ཚར་རྩག.

ཚར་ཚར་ (tsāādzar) a dangling tassel.

ཚར་ཚར་གྱི་པར་ལ་ (tsāādzāāgi pa̱rla) sm. ཚར་ཚར་པར་ལ་.

ཚར་ཚར་པར་ལ་ (tsāādzāā pa̱rla) until finished/ completed ¶ ང་ལས་ཀ་ཚར་ཚར་པར་ལ་ནང་ལ་ལོག་གི་མིན་ Until I finish working, I won't go home.

ཚར་ཞྭ་ (tsāāsha) a hat made from lamb skin (with its fleece on the inside).

ཚར་རུ་བྱེད་ (tsāra cɛ̱è) va. to work to finish sth. ¶ ལས་ཀ་འདི་ཉིན་མ་གཉིས་ལ་ཚར་རུ་བྱེད་ཀྱི་ཡིན་ I will work to finish this job in two days.

ཚར་རུའི་ཞྭ་མོ་ (tsərrü sha̱mo) sm. ཚར་ཞྭ་.

ཚར་ལས་བཅོས་ཐུབ་ (tsārlɛ jöödrɛɛ) there is no way to correct things that have been finished/ completed ¶ ཁ་སང་ཅ་ལག་བཙོངས་པ་དེ་ཕམ་ཚོང་ཤོར་འདུག་ཀྱང་ཚར་ལས་བཅོས་ཐུབ་རེད་ I sold the things yesterday, and even though I sold them at a loss there is no way to correct that since it is completed.

ཚར་ལེབ་ (tsārleb) a type of herb.

ཚར་ཤས་ (tsārsheɛ̀) (vb. + —) seems likely to be finished; vi.—ཆེ་ ¶ ཁང་པ་དེ་ཟླ་བ་གསུམ་ནང་བརྒྱབ་ཚར་ཤས་ཆེ་ That house will likely be finished in three months.

ཚར་སློག (tsārlɔɔ̀) sm. ཚར་རྩག.

ཚལ་ (tsɛ̄ɛ) 1. garden, park, grove ¶ མེ་ཏོག་གི་ཚལ་ Flower garden. 2. vegetables ¶ ཚལ་བཏབ་པ་ཡིན (I) planted vegetables. 3. a cooked vegetable dish ¶ པེ་ཅིང་གི་སྲོལ་རྒྱུན་ལྟར་པའི་ཚལ་ཞིག་བཟོས་པ་རེད་ (They) made a Beijing style vegetable dish.

ཚལ་དཀར་ (tsɛ̄ɛgar) a middle size porcelain bowl.

ཚལ་སྐྱོགས་ (tsɛ̄ɛgyɔɔ̀) ladle.

ཚལ་ཁྲོམ་ (tsɛ̄ɛdrom) vegetable market.

ཚལ་གད་རྒྱག (tsɛ̄ɛ kɛ̱è gya̱à) va. to pick out the fresh vegetables and throw away the bad ones (before cooking).

ཚལ་གླང་ (tsɛ̄ɛlaŋ) frying pan.

ཚལ་རྒོད་ (tsɛ̄ɛgöö) vegetables growing wild.

ཚལ་སྒྲོམ (tsɛ̄ɛdrɔɔ̀) rope to tie the legs of animals.

ཚལ་རྔོད་པ་ (tsɛ̄ɛ ŋöòba) fried vegetables.

ཚལ་རྗེན་ (tsɛ̄ɛjen) raw vegetables.

ཚལ་སྙོལ་ (tsɛ̄ɛ ñöö) va. to pickle vegetables.

ཚལ་བསྙལ་མ་ (tsɛ̄ɛ ñɛ̄ɛma) pickled vegetables, kim chee.

ཚལ་ཏོའོ་ (tsɛ̄ɛdo) ch. chopping cleaver.

ཚལ་ལྡུམ་ (tsɛ̄ɛdum) 1. vegetables. 2. vegetable garden.

ཚལ་སྣོད་ (tsɛ̄ɛnöö) container for putting vegetables.

ཚལ་པ་ (tsɛ̄ɛba) 1. pieces ¶ དཀར་ཡོལ་ཆག་པའི་ཚལ་པ་ A piece of broken China. 2. half.

ཚལ་པར་བཀས་ (tsɛ̄ɛbaa gɛ̱è) broken into pieces.

ཚལ་པར་སོང་ (tsɛ̄ɛbaa sōŋ) vi. to get broken into pieces.

ཚལ་པ་བཀའ་བརྒྱུད་ (tsɛ̄ɛba gāgyüù) one of the four Kagyu sects.

ཚལ་ཕྱུ་མ་ (tsɛ̄ɛjumə) a kind of men's dress.

ཚལ་བུ་ (tsɛ̄ɛbu) small pieces.

ཚལ་འབྲས་ (tsɛ̄ndrɛɛ̀) 1. rice and vegetables, a dish with rice and vegetables.

ཚལ་མ་ (tsɛ̄ɛma) breakfast.

ཚལ་མོག་མོག (tsɛ̄ɛ mo̱moò) dumplings with vegetable filling.

ཚལ་སྨྱུག་ར་བ་ (tsɛ̄ɛñug ra̱wa) a vegetable nursery/ garden.

ཚལ་ཞིང་ (tsɛ̄ɛshiŋ) 1. vegetable field, vegetable garden. 2. arc. an agricultural field.

ཚལ་གཡང་ཅན་ (tsɛ̄ɛ yāŋjɛn) ch. sm. ཚལ་ཞིང་.

ཚལ་གཡང་ཙེ་ (tsɛ̄ɛ yāŋdze) ch. sm. ཚལ་གཡང་ཅན་.

ཚལ་རུལ་ (tsɛ̄ɛrüü) rotten vegetables.

ཚལ་རུལ་མ་ (tsɛ̄ɛ rü̱ümə) sm. ཚལ་རུལ་.

ཚལ་ལ་དཔག་ནས་ཟས་ཟ་ ལུས་ལ་དཔག་ནས་གོས་འཚེམ་ (tsɛ̄ɛreè) adapting oneself to the circumstance [Lit. eat in accordance with the dish of food, sew clothes in accordance with the body].

ཚལ་རེས་ (tsɛ̄ɛreè) the turn for serving vegetables (e.g., the day vegetables are served in a prison).

ཚལ་གླང་ (tsɛ̄ɛlaŋ) frying pan.

ཚལ་སོན་ (tsɛ̄ɛsön) vegetable seed.

ཚལ་སོས་པ་ (tsɛ̄ɛ sööba) fresh vegetables.

ཚལ་གསེད་ (tsɛ̄ɛseè) sm. ཚལ་གད་རྒྱག.

ཚི་ (tsī) sticky, gluey, adhesive ¶ སྤྱིན་དེ་ལ་ཚི་ཡག་པོ་མི་འདུག This glue is not very adhesive.

ཚི་ཀ་ (tsīgə) furrow.

ཚི་གུ་ (tsīgu) the pit (in fruits).

ཚི་གུའི་ནང་སྙིང་ (tsīgü na̱ŋñiŋ) kernel, pit.

ཚི་ཅན་ (tsījɛn) sticky, gluey, adhesive.

ཚི་ཆད་ (tsījɛɛ̀) vi. to lost adhesiveness/ stickiness. 2. vi. to lose hope.

ཚི་ཐུང་ཐུང་ (tsī tūŋduŋ) 1. not very sticky. 2. short-tempered, not tolerant.

ཚི་དམ་པོ་ (tsī ta̱mbo) sticky, gluey, adhesive.

ཚི་དྲེག (tsīdreg) an oily spot/ stain.

ཚི་འདམ་ (tsīndam) 1. clay. 2. daub (in chemistry).

ཚི་སྣ་ (tsīnə) a fiber ¶ མིས་བཟོས་ཚི་སྣ་ Synthetic fiber.

ཚི་སྣ་རྟོག་བཤེར་ཅུས་ (tsīnə dōgsher jū) tib. ch. fibre inspection bureau.

ཚི་སྣའི་སྐྱེ་དངོས་ (tsīnɛ gyēŋöö) fibrous plants.

ཚི་སྣའི་རྒྱུ་ (tsīnɛ gyu) fibrous materials.

ཚི་སྣའི་པང་ལེབ་ (tsīnɛ bāŋleb) fiberboard.

ཚི་སྣའི་རྩི་ཤིང་ (tsīnɛ dzīshiŋ) a fibrous plant.

ཚི་བ་ (tsīwə) resin.

ཚི་རིང་པོ་ (tsī riŋbu) 1. sticky (usu.for wool). 2. tolerant, not losing one's temper easily.

ཚི་རེ་གནོན་ (tsīre nōn) va. to press down hard/ tight.

ཚི་ལུ་ (tsīlu) fat.

ཚི་ལེན་ (tsīlen) shirt.

ཚིག (tsīì) 1. word. 2. p. of འཚིག.

ཚིག་ཀྱལ་པ་ (tsīì gyɛɛbə) idle/ meaningless words or talk.

ཚིག་རྐང་ (tsīìgaŋ) a line in a verse.

ཚིག་རྐང་བཞི་ (tsīìgaŋ shi) a verse with four lines.

ཚིག་སྐམ་པོ་ (tsīì gāmbo) empty talk/ words.

ཚིག་སྐམ་སྟོང་བཤད་ (tsīìgām dōŋshɛɛ) sm. ཚིག་སྐམ་པོ་.

ཚིག་སྐམ་བྲོ་མེད་ (tsīìgam tromeè) empty and tasteless words/ talk.

ཚིག་སྐྱོན་ (tsīìgyön) mistakes in wording or in the use of words.

ཚིག་སྐུམ་ (tsīì gūm) va. to not divulge things in speech.

ཚིག་ཁ་ (tsīìga) edge, border, boundary.

ཚིག་ཁ་སྐོང་ (tsīì kāgoŋ) va. to add extra words to verses that do not have the required number of words.

ཚིག་ཁྱིམ་ (tsīìgyim) syllable (in Tibetan).

ཚིག་མཁྲེགས་པོ་ (tsīì trēgbo) words that are difficult/ unclear/ obscure ¶ ཡི་གེ་འདི་ཚིག་མཁྲེགས་པོ་འདུག This writing has words that are difficult to (understand).

ཚིག་འཁྱེར་ (tsīì kyōr) vi. to be able to recite memorized verses fluently.

ཚིག་འཁྲི་ (tsīìndri) paying too much attention on the words instead of the meaning; va.—བྱེད་.

ཚིག་འཁྲུན་ཆོད་ (tsīìdrün cōō) sm. ཚིག་ཐག་ཆོད་.

ཚིག་གི་གོང་འོག (tsīìgi goŋwɔɔ) the context of words.

ཚིག་གི་གདང་རག (tsīìgi dāŋraà) expressing one's thanks (in speech); va.—འབུལ་.

ཚིག་གི་དེབ་ (tsīìgi dēn) a letter in the alphabet.

ཚིག་གི་ཐབ་རྡོ་སྒྲིལ་ (tsīìgo tābdo drii) to slander, malign/ defame.

ཚིག་གི་བདུད་རྩི་ (tsīìgi düüdzi) pleasant sounding words.

ཚིག་གི་ནང་དུ་ཚིག (tsīìgi naŋdu tsīì) words that have a deep meaning.

ཚིག་གི་ཚོགས་ (tsīìgi tsɔɔ) sm. ཚིག་ཚོགས་.

ཚིག་གི་ལོ་མ་ (tsīìgi loma) wordy.

ཚིག་གྱོང་པོ་ (tsīì gyoŋbo) harsh/ rough/ coarse words or language ¶ ཁོས་སྐད་ཆ་ཚིག་གྱོང་པོ་ཤོད་ཀྱི་འདུག He is speaking harshly. 2. difficult to understand, obscure, unclear ¶ ཡི་གེ་འདི་ཚིག་གྱོང་པོ་འདུག This writing is difficult (to understand). 3. obstinate, stubborn (verbally).

ཚིག་གྲུབ་ (tsīgdrub) sentence; va.—བཟོ་ to make a sentence.

ཚིག་གྲུབ་སྒྲོར་སྟངས་ (tsīgdrub jɔɔdaŋ) structure of a sentence.

ཚིག་གྲུབ་རྩེག་མ་ (tsīgdrub dzēgma) compound sentence.

ཚིག་གྲོགས་ (tsīgdrɔɔ) auxiliary words.

ཚིག་འགལ་བ་ (tsīì gɛɛwa) contradiction of words.

ཚིག་འགོ་ (tsīŋgo) 1. prefix. 2. words that start a topic/ conversation/ talk.

ཚིག་འགྲེལ་ (tsīŋdrel) commentary, explanatory note.

ཚིག་རྒོལ་ (tsīì göö) va. to refute/ repudiate/ renounce.

ཚིག་རྒྱག (tsīggyaà) a type of Tibetan song competition where men and women alternate singing verses that answer each other; va.—རྒྱག.

ཚིག་རྒྱག་གདམ་རྒྱག (tsīggyaà dāmgyaà) sarcastic talk.

ཚིག་རྒྱན་ (tsīggyɛn) 1. words used for their beauty/ elegance/ aesthethic value; va.—རྒྱག. 2. the particles ཀྱང་ཡང་འང་ in Tibetan grammar.

ཚིག་སྒྲ་ (tsīgdra) pronunciation, sound of words.

ཚིག་སྒྲིག (tsīgdrig) va. to arrange or order words in writing, to compose a sentence.

ཚིག་སྒྲུག (tsīg druù) va. take/ pick out what is important from sb.'s words.

ཚིག་སྒྲུབ་ (tsīgdrub) sm. ཚིག་གྲུབ་.

ཚིག་བརྒྱ་མདོ་གཅིག (tsīggya dojig) saying a lot but in essence conveying little in meaning/ content.

ཚིག་བརྒྱད་བརྒྱ་བཤད་པའི་མདོ་ (tsīg gyɛɛgya shɛɛbɛ do) sm. ཚིག་བརྒྱ་མདོ་གཅིག.

ཚིག་བསྒྱུར་ (tsīggyur) word-for-word translation, literal translation; va.—བྱེད་.

ཚིག་ངན་ (tsīgŋɛn) insulting/ abusive/ nasty/ mean words or speech; va.—ཤོད་; —རྗོད་ to use insulting/ abusive/ nasty/ mean speech. 2. scolding; va.—ཤོད་; —རྗོད་ to scold.

ཚིག་ང་ (tsīgŋa) sm. ཚིག་མཇུག, 2.

ཚིག་ང་མཇལ་ཡིས་བསྐུལ་ཀས་ (tsīgŋa nāyi gaà) va. to swear at the end of a statement/ talk.

ཚིག་བཅོས་ (tsīgjöö) correction of words in a written draft, editing; va.—རྒྱག to correct words/ phrases, to edit.

ཚིག་ཆ་ཟུང་ (tsīgja suŋ) two syllables joined to form a compound term.

ཚིག་འཆལ་ (tsīgjɛɛ) meaningless words.

ཚིག་མཇུག (tsīŋjuù) 1. suffix. 2. the ending/ final word in a conversation/ statement/ talk.

ཚིག་འཇམ་ (tsīgjam) gentle/ kind/ pleasant talk.

ཚིག་འཇམ་པོ་ (tsīg jambo) sm. ཚིག་འཇམ་.

ཚིག་འཇུག་སྒྲིལ་ (tsīŋjuù drii) va. to conclude one's talk.

ཚིག་འཇུག་པོ་ (tsīg jugbu) appropriate in wording, the right word/ phrase.

ཚིག་རྗེས་དོན་གསལ་ (tsījeè tönsəb) sm. ཚིག་ཐོག་དུ་གནས་.

ཚིག་ཉམས་ (tsīgñam) beauty/ elegance of words; vi.—ཤོར་ to lose the beauty/ elegance of one language (usu. when translating into another).

ཚིག་ཉམས་དོད་པོ་ (tsīgñam tööbo) elegant speech/ writing.

ཚིག་ཉུང་དོན་དྲིལ་ (tsīgñuŋ töndrii) sm. ཚིག་ཉུང་དོན་སྡུད་.

ཚིག་ཉུང་དོན་སྡུད་ (tsīgñuŋ töndüü) concise, few words but concentrated meaning.

ཚིག་ཉུང་དོན་ཚང་ (tsīgñuŋ töndzaŋ) sm. ཚིག་ཉུང་དོན་སྡུད་.

ཚིག་ཉུང་དོན་ཟབ་ (tsīgñuŋ tönsəb) concise, few words but deep meaning.

ཚིག་ཉུང་དོན་གསལ་ (tsīgñuŋ tönsɛl) concise, few words brief but clear meaning.

ཚིག་གཉེན་པོ་ (tsīg ñɛmbo) sm. ཚིག་བཙན་པོ་.

ཚིག་རྙོག་ཅེ་བ་ (tsīgñoò cēwa) highly / overly complex sentence.

ཚིག་སྙན་དོན་དབེན་ (tsīgñɛn tönwen) beautiful words/ language that lacks meaning.

ཚིག་སྙན་དོན་བཟང་ (tsīgñɛn tönsaŋ) beautiful words/ language with good content.

ཚིག་རྟགས་ (tsīgdaà) comma.

ཚིག་ལྟར་ (tsīgdar) a line of words.

ཚིག་སྟོང་པ་ (tsīg dōŋbə) sm. ཚིག་སྐམ་པོ་.

ཚིག་ཐག་གཅོད་ (tsīgdaà jöö) va. to assert/ say emphatically, to state definitely ¶ ང་ཚོ་རང་བཙན་རྒྱལ་ཁབ་ཡིན་ཞེས་ཚིག་ཐག་བཅད་ནས་བཤད་པ་རེད་ (He) said emphatically, "We are an independent nation."

ཚིག་ཐག་ཆོད་ (tsīgdaà cöö) vi. to have said sth. emphatically/ definitely ¶ བཟོ་པ་ཚོས་ལས་མཚམས་འཇོག་རྒྱུའི་སྐད་ཆ་ཚིག་ཐག་ཆོད་མི་འདུག The workers have not said anything definitely about the strike.

ཚིག་ཐག་གཅང་བཅད་ (tsīgdaà dzāŋjɛ̀ɛ̀) saying emphatically, stating definitely.

ཚིག་ཐལ་ (tsīgdɛɛ) saying the wrong thing, a slip of the tongue; vi.—ཤོད་.

ཚིག་ཐུང་ (tīgduŋ) a short phrase.

ཚིག་ཐོ་ (tsīgdo) statement (written or spoken); va.—རྒྱག to make a statement, va.—ལེན་ to take a statement ¶ ཁོང་གིས་བོད་ཀྱི་གནས་ཚུལ་གྱི་ཚིག་ཐོ་ཞིག་བརྒྱབ་པ་རེད་ He made a statement on the situation in Tibet. ¶ བསྐོར་སྲུང་བས་ཁོའི་ཙ་ནས་ཚིག་ཐོ་ཞིག་བླངས་པ་རེད་ The police took a statement from him.

ཚིག་ཐོག་འཁེལ་ (tsīgdɔɔ̀ kēē) sm. ཚོས་ཚིག་ཐོག་ཏུ་གནས་.

ཚིག་ཐོག་ཏུ་གནས་ (tsīgdɔɔ̀du nɛ̄ɛ̀) va. to keep a promise, to stick to one's word, to maintain a trust ¶ ཁོ་ཚོས་ཚིག་ཐོག་ཏུ་མ་གནས་པར་དམག་མི་ཕྱིར་འཐེན་བྱས་པ་རེད་ Breaking (their) promise, they withdrew their soldiers.

ཚིག་ཐོག་དོན་འཁེལ་ (tsīgdɔɔ̀ tö̱ngee) sm. ཚིག་ཐོག་ཏུ་གནས་.

ཚིག་ཐོག་དོན་གནས་ (tsīgdɔɔ̀ tö̱nnɛ̀ɛ̀) sm. ཚིག་ཐོག་ཏུ་གནས་.

ཚིག་ཐོན་པོ་ (tsīg tȫmbo) sm. ཚིག་མཐོན་པོ་.

ཚིག་མཐའ་ (tsīgtaa) 1. suffix. 2. the last word.

ཚིག་མཐའི་སྒྲ་རྒྱན་ (tsīgtɛ dra̱gyɛn) rhyming words (as in poems), rhymes.

ཚིག་མཐོན་པོ་ (tsīg tȫmbo) words/ language that is difficult to understand.

ཚིག་འཐེང་པོ་ (tsīg tēŋbo) having too many or to few words (in a sentence etc.), sentences that do not flow well.

ཚིག་དན་ (tsīgdɛn) sm. ཁ་དན་.

ཚིག་དམ་པོ་ (tsīg ta̱mbo) words or language that is difficult to understand.

ཚིག་དུམ་འཁྱེར་ནས་ཀོ་ལོག་ལེན་ (tsīgdum kyērnɛ ko̱loò le̱n) va. to make a deliberate misinterpretation of sth. sb. said to distort the meaning.

ཚིག་དེབ་ (tsīgdeb) dictionary, word list, glossary.

ཚིག་དོན་ (tsīgdön) meaning of a word/ phrase.

ཚིག་དོན་གཉིས་ལྡན་ (tsīgdön ñīindɛn) a word with double meaning.

ཚིག་དོན་གཏིང་ཟབ་ (tsīgdön dīŋsəb) words or language that are profound/ deep.

ཚིག་དོན་དཔྱད་ཞིབ་ (tsīgdön yɛ̄ɛ̀shib) paying attention to the shades of meaning of words; va.—བྱེད་.

ཚིག་དོན་དམར་རྗེན་ (tsīgdön mārjen) saying clearly/ succinctly/ baldly.

ཚིག་དོན་མཚན་ཉིད་རིག་པ་ (tsīgdön tsɛ̄nñii ri̱gbə) semantic philosophy.

ཚིག་དོན་རིག་པ་ (tsīgdön ri̱gbə) semantics.

ཚིག་གདངས་ (tsīgdaŋ) tone/ pronunciation of a word ¶ ཚིག་གདངས་མཐོ་པོ་ High tone.

ཚིག་བདེན་ (tsīgden) truthful word/ language/ speech.

ཚིག་མདའ་ (tsīŋda) words that hurt others; va.—འཕེན་ to say things that hurt others [Lit. arrow word].

ཚིག་འདུམ་པོ་ (tsīg du̱mbu) sm. ཚིག་ཉུང་དོན་ཚང་.

ཚིག་ལྡབ་ (tsīgdəb) repeating/ saying again and again; va.—ཤོད་.

ཚིག་ལྡབ་ལྡིབ་ (tsīg də̱bdib) unclear/ stuttering words.

ཚིག་སྡུད་ (tsīgdüü) compound words.

ཚིག་བརྡ་ (tsīgda) verbal signal, verbal expression; va.—བྱེད་.

ཚིག་བསྡུས་དོན་ཟབ་ (tsīgdüü tö̱nsəb) sm. ཚིག་ཉུང་དོན་ཟབ་.

ཚིག་ནན་ (tsīgnɛn) abbr. ཚིག་ནན་པོ་.

ཚིག་ནན་དོན་དྲང་ (tsīgnɛn tö̱ndraŋ) firm/ forceful and true (in speech).

ཚིག་ནན་པོ་ (tsīg nɛ̱mbo) forceful/ emphatic/ firm speech.

ཚིག་གནག་པོ་ (tsīg nāgbo) harsh words/ language.

ཚིག་གནད་ (tsīgnɛ̀ɛ̀) the main meaning/ point (of words/ speech, etc).

ཚིག་གནད་སྒྲུག (tsīgnɛ̀ɛ̀ dru̱ù) va. take what is important from sb.'s words.

ཚིག་རྣོ་དོན་དྲིལ་ (tsīgno tö̱ndrii) words that are harsh but to the point.

ཚིག་རྣོ་དོན་ཟབ་ (tsīgno tö̱nsəb) words that are harsh or cutting but deep and profound.

ཚིག་རྣོན་པོ་ (tsīg nȫmbo) harsh/ sharp/ cutting words.

ཚིག་སྣ་ (tsīgna) the point/ meaning of words.

ཚིག་སྣ་བསྡུས་པོ་ (tsīgna dü̱übo) abbreviated words.

ཚིག་སྣག (tsīgnaà) a traditional Tibetan brown ink made from grain (used mainly for writing on wooden slates).

ཚིག་པ་ (tsīgbə) anger; vi.—ཟ་ to be/ get angry; vi.—འཇགས་ to have one's anger subside/ cool off; va.—སློང་ to cause sb. to be angry (deliberately).

ཚིག་པ་འབྲོང་ལ་ཟ་ནས་མགོ་ཡུག་རྟ་ལ་གཞུས་ (tsīgbə dro̱ŋla sa̱nɛ go̱jaà dāla shü̱ü) being angry at one person but showing one's anger to another [Lit. being angry with the wild yak but whipping the horse].

ཚིག་པ་གཡག་ལ་ཟ་ནས་རྡོག་རྒྱག་བོང་བུར་གཞུ་བ་ (tsīgbə yāàla sa̱nɛ do̱ŋgyaà pu̱ŋgu shu̱wa) being angry at one person but showing one's anger to another [Lit. being angry with the yak but beating the donkey].

ཚིག་དཔེ་ (tsīgbə) the original sample or model of words/ letters that students use when practicing their writing skill.

ཚིག་ཕྲད་ (tsīgdrɛɛ̀) connective particle, conjunction.

ཚིག་འཕྲད་ (tsīgdrɛɛ̀) sm. ཚིག་ཕྲད་.

ཚིག་འཕྲོ་ (tsīgdro) 1. half-burnt wood. 2. the unfinished words of a conversation/ talk.

ཚིག་བྲུས་ (tsīgdrüü) sm. སྐད་ཆ་སློག.

ཚིག་བླ་དྭགས་ (tsīg lādaŋ) neologisms.

ཚིག་འབྱམས་ (tsīŋjam) letters or writings that are too wordy.

ཚིག་འབྲུ་ (tsīŋdru) word, syllable.

ཚིག་འབྲེལ་ (tsīŋdree) syntax.

ཚིག་སྦོམ་པོ་ (tsīg bo̱mbo) sm. ཁ་རྒྱགས་པ་.

ཚིག་སྦྱངས་གསེད་བཀྲོལ་ (tsīgjaŋ sēèdröö) giving a clear/ thorough explanation.

ཚིག་སྦྱོར་ (tsīgjɔɔ) phrasing, composition, style of wording, rhetoric; va.—བྱེད་.

ཚིག་སྦྱོར་མཁྲེགས་པོ་ (tsīgjɔɔ trēgbo) heavy/ dull style of writing.

ཚིག་སྦྱོར་སྙན་མོ་ (tsīgjɔɔ ñɛ̄mbo) eloquent/ good style of writing.

ཚིག་སྦྱོར་བདེ་པོ་ (tsīgjɔɔ de̱bo) easy and smooth style of phrasing/ composition/ wording.

ཚིག་སྦྱོར་འདྲ་ཆགས་ (tsīgjɔɔ dra̱jaà) sm. ཚིག་སྦྱོར་སྙན་མོ་.

ཚིག་སྦྱོར་རིག་པ་ (tsīgjɔɔ ri̱gbə) the study of rhetoric.

ཚིག་མ་ (tsīgmə) burnt (food) ¶ ཏ་ཡང་ནང་ལ་འབྲས་ཚིག་མ་འདུག There is burnt rice in the pot.

ཚིག་མར་ (tsīgmaa) butter put in sth. to keep the food from getting burnt.

ཚིག་དམའ་པོ་ (tsīg ma̱abo) words/ language that are easy to understand [Lit. low words].

ཚིག་བཙན་ (tsīgdzɛn) forceful, emphatic, firm (with respect to speech) ¶ སྲིད་བློན་མཆོག་གིས་ཚིག་བཙན་གྱི་ཐོག་ནས་དམག་རྒྱག་གི་མ་རེད་ཅེས་གསུངས་པ་རེད་ The Prime Minister said emphatically, "We will not make war."

ཚིག་བཙན་པོ་ (tsīg dzɛ̄mbo) forceful/ emphatic words or orders, an order that cannot be violated.

ཚིག་བཙུན་པོ་ (tsīg dzū̄mbo) truthful/ reliable/ dependable words or language.

ཚིག་རྩ་འཛུ་ (tsīgdza ju̱) sm. ཚིག་སྣག.

ཚིག་རྩུབ་ (tsǐgdzub) harsh/ mean/ nasty/ abusive words or speech.

ཚིག་རྩུབ་ངག་འཁྱལ་ (tsǐgdzub ŋa̱àgyɛɛ) harsh and meaningless words/ language.

ཚིག་རྩོད་ (tsǐgdzöö) verbal debate; va.—རྒྱག.

ཚིག་བརྩི་ (tsǐg dzǐ) va. to be/ act obedient, to adhere to what one says.

ཚིག་ཚོགས་ (tsǐgdzɔɔ̀) 1. dictionary, glossary. 2. a chapter, a section of a book ¶ཚིག་ཚོགས་ཆེ་བ་ A large chapter. 3. a collection of writing ¶ཚིག་ཚོགས་ཆེ་བ་ Wordy.

ཚིག་མཚམས་ (tsǐŋdzam) space between syllables.

ཚིག་མཚོན་ (tsǐgdzön) slandering, denigrating, defaming; va.—འདེབས་ to slander/ malign/ defame.

ཚིག་འཚོ་པོ་ (tsǐg tsōbo) fine wording and meaning, pleasant language with good content.

ཚིག་མཛོད་ (tsǐŋdzöö) dictionary, glossary.

ཚིག་མཛོད་དེབ་ཆུང་ (tsǐŋdzöö te̱bjuŋ) pocket dictionary.

ཚིག་རྫུན་ (tsǐgdzün) a lie.

ཚིག་རྫོགས་ (tsǐgdzɔɔ̀) sm. གཏམ་ཟད་.

ཚིག་ཞུས་ (tsǐgshüü) correcting and editing.

ཚིག་གཞི་ (tsǐgshi) 1. main point/ item. 2. slogan.

ཚིག་གཞུང་ (tsǐgshuŋ) a large/ unabridged dictionary.

ཚིག་ཟ་ (tsǐgsə) anger, angry; va.—སློང་ to make sb. angry.

ཚིག་ཟ་ཀོ་ལོང་ (tsǐgsə gōloŋ) anger.

ཚིག་ཟུར་ (tsǐgsur)1. secondary mention of a subject; casual reference/ mention ¶བོད་དོན་སྐོར་གྲོས་ཆོད་སོགས་ཀྱི་ནང་ཚིག་ཟུར་ཙམ་ཡང་འཁོད་པའི་ཐབས་ཤེས་ངེས་པར་བྱེད་དགོས་ (You) have to definitely make sure that there is some (secondary) mention in the resolution about the Tibet question. 2. va.—རྒྱག to say sth. negative in an indirect way.

ཚིག་བཟོ་ (tsǐg so̱) va. to make words/ sentences.

ཚིག་ཡུལ་ (tsǐgyüü) topic (of a book, chapter, etc.).

ཚིག་རན་པོ་ (tsǐg re̱mbo) sm. ཚིག་འཇུག་པོ་.

ཚིག་རིས་ (tsǐgrii) 1. manner/ style of talking. 2. words written in books, etc.

ཚིགས་རོ་ (tsǐgro) 1. sm. ཚིག་མ་. 2. filler words in spoken Tibetan.

ཚིག་རོ་རྙོག་བཤད་ (tsǐgro ñōgshɛɛ̀) hackneyed phrase, stock/ stereotyped argument.

ཚིག་རོ་ཤོད་ (tsǐgro shöö) va. to speak meaninglessly.

ཚིག་རོ་སུབ་ (tsǐgro sūb) va. to delete/ erase useless words.

ཚིག་རོ་སྙོལ་སྙིང་ (tsǐgro sööñiŋ) sm. ཚིག་རོ་རྙོག་བཤད་.

ཚིག་རོགས་ (tsǐgrɔɔ̀) auxiliary words/ particles used to link clauses (e.g., དུས་, སྐབས་).

ཚིག་བརླང་པོ་ (tsǐg lāŋbo) harsh/ degrading words.

ཚིག་ལ་གནས་ (tsǐgla nɛɛ̀) vi. to keep one's promise.

ཚིག་ལ་མཚམས་གཅོད་བྱེད་ (tsǐgla tsāmjöö ce̱è) va. to stop someone talking/ conversing.

ཚིག་ལན་ཚིག་རྒྱག (tsǐglɛn tsǐggyaà) va. to exchange words. 2. a duel/ competition in words.

ཚིག་ལེན་ (tsǐg le̱n) 1. va. to memorize (words of a book, scripture, etc.). 2. sm. ཚིག་སྒྲུག.

ཚིག་ལེའུ་ (tsǐg li̱wu) chapter of a book.

ཚིག་ལོ་ (tsǐglo) abbr. of ཚིག་གི་ལོ་མ་.

ཚིག་ལོ་མང་པོ་ (tsǐglo ma̱ŋlo) writing/ talking off the main point, wordy, rambling.

ཚིག་ལོག (tsǐglɔɔ̀) 1. talking back (usu. to one's parents); va.—བྱེད་. 2. saying the opposite; va.—བྱེད་; —ཤོད་.

ཚིག་ཤུགས་ (tsǐgshuù) way/ manner of talking.

ཚིག་ཤོར་ (tsǐg shɔ̄ɔ̄) vi. to have a slip of the tongue.

ཚིག་བཤེར་ (tsǐgsher) checking to see the truth of a word/ statement/ speech; va.—བྱེད་.

ཚིག་གསར་ (tsǐgsaa) new words.

ཚིག་གསལ་དོན་གསལ་ (tsǐgsɛɛ tö̱nsɛɛ) clear writing.

ཚིག་གསུམ་ཤོད་དབང་དང་ གོམ་གསུམ་སྤོ་དབང་མེད་པ་ (tsǐgsum shȫöwaŋ da̱ŋ go̱msum bōwaŋ me̱èba) utterly powerless [Lit. powerless to say three words, powerless to take three steps].

ཚིག་གསོལ་ (tsǐg sȫö) va. to say sth., to express sth. verbally.

ཚིག་ལྷག (tsǐglhaà) 1. sm. ཚིག་འཕྱོ་. 2. unnecessary words.

ཚིག་ལྷུག (tsǐglhuù) prose.

ཚིགས་ (tsǐì) 1. any joint; vi.—བུད་ to dislocate a joint; vi.—འཆུས་; —འཁྲོག to sprain a joint; va.—སྒྱུད་ to reset a dislocated joint; vi.—ཟུག to have pain in a joint ¶ལག་ཚིགས་ Knuckles. ¶ཁོས་མཆོང་བརྒྱབ་ནས་རྐང་ཚིགས་བུད་པ་རེད་ He jumped and dislocated his ankle. 2. knot of a tree. 3. vi. to get burned ¶ང་མེས་ཚིགས་བྱུང་ I got burned by the fire.

ཚིགས་ཁེབས་ (tsǐìgeb) sm. ཚིགས་གོག.

ཚིགས་གོག (tsǐìgɔɔ̀) ring (for the finger).

ཚིགས་གྲུམ་ (tsǐìdrum) arthritis ¶ཚིགས་གྲུམ་དལ་ནད་ Chronic arthritis.

ཚིགས་གྲུམ་དལ་ནད་ (tsǐìdrum tɛ̱ɛnɛɛ̀) chronic arthritis.

ཚིགས་གྲུམ་ནད་སྙིང་ (tsǐìdrum nɛ̱èñiŋ) sm. ཚིག་གྲུམ་དལ་ནད་.

ཚིགས་རྒྱུད་ (tsǐìgyüü) see ཚིགས་.

ཚིགས་རྒྱུས་ (tsǐìgyüü) 1. ligament. 2. p. of ཚིགས་རྒྱུད་.

ཚིགས་བརྒྱུ་ (tsǐì gyu̱) f. of ཚིགས་རྒྱུད་.

ཚིགས་བཅད་ (tsǐgjɛɛ̀) verse, stanza.

ཚིགས་བཅད་མ་ (tsǐgjɛma) sm. ཚིགས་བཅད་.

ཚིགས་ཆེན་བཅུ་གཉིས་ (tsǐgjen jūñiì) twelve joints of the body according to Tibetan medicine.

ཚིགས་འཆུས་ (tsǐì jüù) see ཚིགས་.

ཚིགས་བརྗོད་ (tsǐgjöö) sm. ཚིགས་བཅད་.

ཚིགས་ཏགས་ (tsǐgdaà) sm.* ཚིག་ཏགས་.

ཚིགས་དོག (tsǐgdɔɔ̀) protruding joints (such as elbow, knuckles).

ཚིགས་ནད་ (tsǐìnɛɛ̀) any illness affecting the joints.

ཚིགས་ཕྲན་ (tsǐìtrɛn) the small joints in the body.

ཚིགས་བུག (tsǐgbüü) stumbling; vi.—རྒྱག་; —ལོག་; —ཐེབས་; —ཤོར་; to stumble (usu. animals falling onto their front knees).

ཚིགས་བུད་ (tsǐìbüü) see ཚིགས་.

ཚིགས་བུབ་ (tsǐìbub) sm. ཚིགས་བུག.

ཚིགས་མ་ (tsǐìmə) sediment, residue, dirt, filth.

ཚིགས་མལ་ (tsǐìmɛɛ) sm. བབས་ཚུགས་.

ཚིགས་མཚམས་ (tsǐìdzam) the space between the joints.

ཚིགས་གཞི་ (tsǐìshi) sm. ཚིགས་.

ཚིགས་ཟུག (tsǐìsuù) see ཚིགས་.

ཚིམ་: p. ཚིམས་; f. ཚིམ་ (tsǐm) vi. to be satisfied/ content/ satiated ¶ཁོར་སྐལ་བ་ཕྱེད་ཙམ་སྤྲད་ཙང་བློ་ཚིམས་སོང་ He was satisfied because they gave him half a share.

ཚིམ་པར་ (tsǐmbar) being satisfied/ content/ satiated ¶གསོལ་བ་ཚིམ་པར་མཆོད་ Eat until (you) are satiated.

ཚིམ་པར་སྐོང་ (tsǐmbar gōŋ) sm. ཚིམ་པར་བྱེད་.

ཚིམ་པར་བྱེད་ (tsǐmbar ce̱è) va. to satisfy sb.

ཚིམ་པར་སྦྱིན་ (tsǐmbar ji̱n) va. to give sth. to satisfy sb.

ཚིམ་པོ་ (tsǐmbu) satisfied; va.—བྱེད་ to satisfy, to do sth. to satisfy sb.

ཚིམ་བྱེད་བད་ཀན་ (tsǐmjeè pɛ̱ɛ̀gɛb) one type of བད་ཀན་.

ཚིམ་བྱེད་ཤིང་ (tsǐmjeè shǐŋ) 1. fuel (wood). 2. wood used in exorcisms.

ཚིམས་ (tsǐm) p. of ཚིམ་.

ཚིར་ (tsǐǐ) 1. imp. of འཚིར་. 2. the sizzling sound made when water is poured on a fire.

ཚིར་གྱིས་འཛིན་ (tsǐǐgi dzi̱n) va. to hold/ grasp tightly with the fist.

ཚིར་ཚིར་ (tsǐǐdzii) sm. ཚིར་, 2.

ཚིལ་ (tsǐǐ) fat, suet ¶ཕག་ཚིལ་ Pork fat.

ཚིལ་སྐྱུར་ (tsǐǐgyur) fatty acid.

ཚིལ་སྐྱུར་སྲ་མོ་ (tsǐǐgyur drāmu) stearic acid.

ཚིལ་ཁུ་ (tsīīgu) melted/ liquid fat, oil.

ཚིལ་རྒྱུ་ (tsīīgyu) sausage.

ཚིལ་ཆེན་ (tsīījen) human fat.

ཚིལ་ཉུང་ (tsīīñuŋ) low fat.

ཚིལ་བུ་ (tsīūbu) sm. ཚིལ་.

ཚིལ་མར་ (tsīīmar) ཚིལ་ཁུ་.

ཚིལ་མེད་ (tsīīmeè) lean, without fat.

ཚིལ་སྨིན་ (tsīīmen) tumor in the fatty tissue.

ཚིལ་ཤག (tsīīshaà) sm. ཤག་ཚིལ་.

ཚིལ་རོ་ (tsīīro) leftover fat.

ཚིལ་ལེན་ (tsīīlen) shirt ¶ ཚིལ་ལེན་བཟོ་གྲྭ་ Shirt factory.

ཚིལ་ལུ་ (tsīīlu) sm. ཚིལ་.

ཚིལ་ཤ་ལུག (tsīīsha lu̲ù) sm. རྫི་ཤ་ལུག.

ཚིས་ (tsīì) 1. ways, means, method ¶ མི་མང་ཆེ་བའི་འཚོ་ཚིས་ཞིང་པ་རེད་ The way of making a living for the majority of people is agriculture. 2. of help, beneficial.

ཚུ་ཁ་ (tsūga) this side (of a stream).

ཚུ་རི་ (tsūri) mountain/ hill on one's own side.

ཚུ་རོལ་ (tsūröö) one's own side, this side.

ཚུ་རོལ་བ་ (tsūröòwa) a person on our side of sth. (e.g., of a river).

ཚུག (tsūù) a Tibetan treatment used to cure sores/ boils by sticking a hot golden needle in it.

ཚུགས་ (tsūù) 1. imp. of འཛུགས་. 2. vi. to be established/ set up/ founded, to be able to stand on one's own feet ¶ གཞིས་ཆགས་འདི་སྤྱི་ལོ་ ༡༩༦༣ ནང་ཚུགས་པ་རེད་ This settlement was established in 1963. 3. shung. station, stopover place ¶ རྒྱལ་རྩེ་ནས་ལྷ་ས་བར་དྲིལ་ཚུགས་བདུན་ཡོད་པ་རེད་ There are seven mule stations between Gyantse and Lhasa. (this also conveys that it is a seven day trip). 4. (with negatives) unable to harm ¶ མེས་མི་ཚུགས་པ་ Fireproof. ¶ ཆུས་མི་ཚུགས་པ་ Waterproof.

ཚུགས་ཀ་ (tsūùgə) shape, form.

ཚུགས་ཁང་ (tsūùgaŋ) shung. caravan station, way station, overnight stopping place.

ཚུགས་འཁྱུག (tsūggyuù) sm. ཚུགས་མ་འཁྱུག.

ཚུགས་རྒྱ་ (tsūùgya) platform scale.

ཚུགས་ཆུང་ (tsūgjuŋ) small type of ཚུགས་ཐུང་ letters.

ཚུགས་ཆེན་པོ་ (tsūù cēmbo) reliable, dependable.

ཚུགས་འཆར་ (tsūgjar) a plan to establish sth.

ཚུགས་ཇ་ (tsūgja) tea served when an office opens/ starts/ is created; va.—གཏོང་.

ཚུགས་རྟེན་ (tsūgden) base, foundation.

ཚུགས་ཐུང་ (tsūgduŋ) a form of alphabet that is not quite as small as cursive.

ཚུགས་ཐུབ་པོ་ (tsūg tūbbo) sm. ཚུགས་ཆེན་པོ་.

ཚུགས་ཐེངས་ (tsūgdeŋ) number of meetings/ periods (as in a class period) ¶ ཟླ་བ་རེ་རེར་ཚུགས་ཐེངས་བཞི་རེ་ཡོད་པ་རེད་ There are four meetings a month.

ཚུགས་དལ་ (tsūgdɛɛ) a laid-back/ easygoing person.

ཚུགས་པོ་ (tsūgbo) reliable, dependable.

ཚུགས་ཕད་ (tsūgpɛɛ̀) a huge sack.

ཚུགས་བབས་ (tsūù bə̲b) va. to make an overnight stop/ camp ¶ དེའི་དགོངས་མོ་རི་མཚམས་དེར་ཚུགས་བབས་པ་རེད་ That night they camped at the foot of the hill.

ཚུགས་བར་གྲོལ་གསུམ་ (tsūgbar drö̲ö̲sum) the beginning, the middle and the end, the starting point, halfway through and the finish.

ཚུགས་བྱད་ (tsūgjeè) sm. ཚུགས་ཀ་.

ཚུགས་འབབ་ས་ (tsūù bə̲bsa) place where one spends a night on the road.

ཚུགས་མ་འཁྱུག (tsūg ma̲ kyūù) cursive writing that is mixed with ཚུགས་ཐུང་ style.

ཚུགས་གཙང་ (tsūgdzaŋ) 1. good looking, pretty, beautiful. 2. good in character/ behavior.

ཚུགས་ཚད་ (tsūgdzɛɛ̀) the length between one way station and the next, the length of one day's journey.

ཚུགས་ཞག (tsūgshaà) a trip that is the distance of one day ¶ ཚུགས་ཞག་གསུམ་ A three day journey.

ཚུགས་བཞི་ (tsūgshi) the beginning months of the four seasons.

ཚུགས་ཟིན་པོ་ (tsūù si̲mbu) reliable, dependable, stable.

ཚུགས་ཡིག (tsūgyiì) sm. ཚུགས་ཐུང་.

ཚུགས་རིང་ (tsūgriŋ) a type of ཚུགས་ཐུང་.

ཚུགས་ས་ཞག་ས་ (tsūgshaà bə̲bsa) overnight stopping place/ camp.

ཚུགས་ཤིང་ (tsūgshiŋ) poles for putting up a tent.

ཚུགས་ས་ (tsūgsa) sm. ཚུགས་ས་འབབ་ས་.

ཚུད་ (tsūù) 1. imp. of འཛུད་. 2. vi. to be included in, including ¶ ཨང་རྩིས་ཚུད་པའི་ཡིག་ཚད་རྣམ་གྲངས་ཚང་མ་ལོན་བཞག (He) passed all the exams including mathematics.

ཚུད་ཤུགས་ (tsūùshuù) admitting (into) an organization/ unit; va.—བྱེད་.

ཚུན་ (tsūn) 1. hither, on this side ¶ ཤིང་སྡོང་སྐམ་པོ་ཆེན་པོ་དེ་ཚུན་ཆད་ང་ཚོའི་ས་ཆ་རེད་ The land from that dead tree hither is ours. 2. from...until, within ¶ བོད་ལ་རྒྱ་མི་སླེབས་ཚུན་ From when the Chinese arrived in Tibet until now ¶ ལོ་བཅུ་ཚུན་ Within the last ten years 3. including ¶ སྐྱེ་དམན་དང་ཕྲུ་གུ་ཚུན་བཙོན་ལ་བཅུག་པ་རེད་ (They) imprisoned woman including their children. 4. ch. village. 5. ch. a traditional small unit of length.

ཚུན་ཀྲང་ (tsūn) ch. head of a ཚུན་ (village).

ཚུན་ཆད་ (tsūnjɛɛ̀) sm. ཚུན་.

ཚུན་ཆོད་ (tsūnjöö̀) sm. ཚུན་.

ཚུབ་མ་ (tsūbmə) sm. འཚུབ་མ་.

ཚུམ་ཙམ་ཚུམ་ཙམ་ (tsūmdzam tsūmdzam) sm. ཀྲུབ་ཙམ་ཀྲུབ་ཙམ་.

ཚུམས་ (tsūm) imp. of འཛུམ་.

ཚུའུ་ (tsūū) ch. vinegar.

ཚུའུ་སྐྱུར་ (tsūūgyur) ch.tib. acetic acid.

ཚུའུ་སོན་ (tsūūsön) sm. ཚུའུ་སྐྱུར་.

ཚུར་ (tsūū) 1. hither, towards this side ¶ ཕར་མ་འགྲོ་ཚུར་ཤོག Don't go away; come hither. ¶ ཚུར་ཕྱོགས་ One's own side. 2. a group of substances used in Tibetan medicine.

ཚུར་དཀར་ (tsūūgar) aluminum.

ཚུར་སྐོང་ (tsūūgoŋ) recalling, bringing back; va.—བྱེད་.

ཚུར་ཁ་ (tsūūga) this side, one's own side.

ཚུར་འགུག (tsūūguù) converting, winning over to one's side; va.—བྱེད་.

ཚུར་གོལ་ (tsūūgöö) an attack/ offensive against one's side; va.—བྱེད་ to have sb. launch an offensive/ attack against one's side ¶ ཁོ་ཚོས་ཚུར་གོལ་བྱས་ན་མ་གཏོགས་ང་ཚོས་ཕར་གོལ་བྱ་རྒྱུ་མིན་ Unless they attack (us) we will not attack them.

ཚུར་ཉོ་ (tsūūño) buying; va.—བྱེད་ to buy ¶ ཁོང་གིས་ཚུར་ཉོ་ཕར་འཚོང་བྱེད་ཀྱི་ཡོད་པ་རེད་ He buys and sells.

ཚུར་འཐེན་ (tsūūden) withdrawing (to one's side); va.—བྱེད་.

ཚུར་བསྡུ་ཚུར་ལེན་ (tsūūdüù tsūulen) collecting, taking in, drawing in; va.—བྱེད་.

ཚུར་སྣང་ (tsūūnaŋ) a reflection.

ཚུར་སྣང་སྨྲ་བ་ (tsūūnaŋ māwa) theory of reflection.

ཚུར་སྤྱོན་ (tsūūjön) va. to ask sb. to come.

ཚུར་ཕུལ་ (tsūūbüü) sth. that was given/ sent to this side ¶ ཚུར་ཕུལ་གནས་འཕྲིན་ཚང་མར་ཡིག་ལན་བཏང་བ་ཡིན་ I sent replies to all the letters I received (that were sent to me).

ཚུར་ཕྱོགས་ (tsūūjɔɔ̀) this side, this direction, one's own side.

ཚུར་གཅིག་ཚུར་ལ་ (tsūūjig tsūūlə) here, over here ¶ ཚུར་གཅིག་ཚུར་ལ་གསན་དང་ Listen here.

ཚུར་འཕྲོ་ (tsūū trō) vi. to shine hither (toward one's side) ¶ འོད་ཟེར་ཚུར་འཕྲོས་པ་རེད་ Light rays shining hither.

ཚུར་ཕྱུང་ཕར་སོང་ (tsūūjuŋ pāasoŋ) income and expenditures.

ཚུར་བླུ་ (tsūū lū) va. to redeem/ ransom (from hostage) ¶ དངུལ་སྤྲད་ནས་བུ་མོ་ཚུར་བླུས་པ་རེད་

(They) gave the money and ransomed back the girl.

ཚུར་ཙམ་ (tsūūdzam) a little bit toward here/ hither/ this side.

ཚུར་ཤོར་ (tsūūshɔɔ) sm. ཚུར་ལམ་.

ཚུར་རི་ (tsūūri) the hill/ mountain on this side ¶ཆུ་ཚུར་རི་ The hill on this (our) side of the river. 2. this side.

ཚུར་རོལ་ (tsūūröö) this side/ hither.

ཚུར་ལམ་ (tsūūlam) on the way hither/ back home.

ཚུར་ལེན་ (tsūū len) va. 1. to take (toward oneself/ hither) ¶ཁོས་འཇོར་ཞིག་ཚུར་བླངས་ནས་ཞིང་པ་ཚོར་རོགས་བྱས་པ་རེད་ He took a pickaxe and helped the farmers. 2. va. to take back (to oneself) ¶ངས་ཁོ་ལ་དེབ་གཡར་བ་དེ་ཚུར་ལེན་གྱི་ཡིན་ I will take back (to myself) the book I lent him.

ཚུར་ལོག (tsūūlɔɔ) returning back (to this side/ place); va.—བྱེད་ to return ¶ཁོ་རྒྱ་གར་ནས་ཚུར་ལོག་བྱས་པ་རེད་ He returned from India.

ཚུར་ལོག་པའི་ནུས་པ་ (tsūūlɔɔbɛ nüübə) chemical reaction.

ཚུར་ལོགས་ (tsūūlɔɔ) sm. ཚུར་ཕྱོགས་.

ཚུལ་ (tsūū) 1. manner, way, method ¶ཞིང་པ་ཚོའི་འཚོ་བའི་འཕོ་འགྱུར་བྱུང་ཚུལ་ལ་བལྟས་ན་ If (one) looks at how (the manner in which) changes occurred in the farmer's livelihood. ¶ངར་ལྕགས་དུམ་པོ་བླུགས་ཚུལ་འགྲེལ་བཤད་བརྒྱབ་པ་རེད་ He explained the method by which they cast steel ingots. 2. symbolizing ¶ཞིང་ལས་བྱས་པའི་ཚུལ་གྱི་ཞབས་བྲོ་ A dance symbolizing agricultural work. 3. pretext, pretension, pretending (ཡིན་ or ཡོད་ + —) ¶དམག་མི་ཡིན་ཚུལ་བྱས་པ་རེད་ He pretended to be a soldier. ¶ཁོས་སྨྱོན་པ་ཡིན་ཚུལ་བྱས་གང་བྱུང་བྱས་པ་རེད་ Under the pretext of madness, he did all sorts of things. 4. morality, ethical principles ¶ཁོས་ཚུལ་དང་མ་མཐུན་པའི་ལས་ཀ་བྱས་འདུག He has done sth. against morality. 5. particle conveying that sth. is said to have happened ¶ལྷ་སར་ཕེབས་ཚུལ་གོ་ཐོས་བྱུང་. It is said that (you) were coming to Lhasa.

ཚུལ་ཁྲིམས་ (tsūūdrim) vows; va.—འཆལ་ to break one's vows; va.—སྲུང་ to uphold one's vows. 3. person's name.

ཚུལ་ཁྲིམས་ཀྱི་དྲི་བསུང་ (tsūūdrimgi trisuŋ) a pleasant smell associated with monks who have not lost their celibacy.

ཚུལ་ཁྲིམས་རྒྱ་མཚོ་ (tsūūdrim gyadzo) the name of the 10th Dalai Lama.

ཚུལ་ཁྲིམས་ལྔའི་ཆིངས་ཡིག (tsūūdrim ŋɛ cīŋyiì) Panch Shila (the 5 point treaty between India and China).

ཚུལ་འགལ་ (tsūū gɛɛ) doing sth. against morality, overstepping norms/ customs, going too far.

ཚུལ་ངན་ (tsūūŋɛn) bad appearance, bad behavior/ morals/ ethics.

ཚུལ་ཅན་ (tsūūjɛn) sm. ཚུལ་བྱད་.

ཚུལ་བཅོས་ (tsūūjöö) sm. ཚུལ་འཆོས་.

ཚུལ་འཆོས་ (tsūūjöö) pretending to be sth. one is not; va.—བྱེད་.

ཚུལ་འཆོས་ངོ་སྲུང་ (tsūūjöö ŋosuŋ) flattering in an insincere/ affected manner.

ཚུལ་འཆོས་ལྟར་སྣང་ (tsūūjöö dārnaŋ) pretending to be sth. one is not.

ཚུལ་མཐུན་ (tsūūdün) lawful, lawabiding, moral, ethical; va.—བྱེད་ to be lawful/ law—abiding ¶ཚུལ་མཐུན་གྱི་ཁྱད་ཆོས་གསུམ་ལ་གཞི་བཞག་ཡོད་ (It) is based on three ethical characteristics. 2. logical, rational ¶ཚུལ་མཐུན་གྱི་བསམ་འཆར་ A rational plan (proposal).

ཚུལ་མཐུན་ལུགས་མཐུན་ (tsūūdün lugdün) lawful, ethical, moral, proper ¶ཚུལ་མཐུན་ལུགས་མཐུན་གྱི་ཚོང་ལས་བྱེད་པ་རེད་ They do lawful business.

ཚུལ་དང་ཚུལ་མིན་ (tsūūdaŋ tsūūmin) virtuous and not virtuous ¶གོང་རིམ་ནས་ཚུལ་དང་ཚུལ་མིན་གྱི་བྱ་བའི་བཀའ་སློབ་གནང་སོང་ The superiors advised us regarding what work is virtuous and what is nonvirtuous.

ཚུལ་དུ་ (tsūūdu) as, as if, in the manner/ way of ¶ཁོང་ཚོའི་དྲིལ་བསྒྲགས་ནང་མི་དམངས་ལ་རང་དབང་ཡོད་ཚུལ་དུ་བཤད་ཡོད་ In their propaganda, (they) speak as if the people have freedom. ¶ཤིང་དེ་མེ་མདའི་ཚུལ་དུ་འཁྱེར་དེ་ Carrying the stick as if it were a gun.

ཚུལ་འདས་ལུགས་འགལ་ (tsūū dɛ̀ɛ lug gɛɛ) contrary to tradition/ morality/ customs/ virtue.

ཚུལ་ལྡན་ (tsūndɛn) moral, upright, honorable, decent, proper, good, civilized.

ཚུལ་སྤྱོད་ (tsūūjöö) conduct, behavior.

ཚུལ་བྱད (tsūūjɛɛ) abbr. of སྤྱོད་ཚུལ་ and ཆ་བྱད་.

ཚུལ་བྱེད་ (tsūū cee) va. to pretend ¶མོས་ཤེས་ཚུལ་བྱས་པ་རེད་ She pretended she understood it.

ཚུལ་མིན་ (tsūūmin) improper, immoral, not in accordance with customs or rules, nonvirtuous.

ཚུལ་མིན་སྤྱོད་ལམ་ (tsūūmin jöölam) unethical/ immoral/ nonvirtuous behavior.

ཚུལ་མིན་སྤྱོད་ངན་ (tsūūmin jöölam) sm. ཚུལ་མིན་སྤྱོད་ལམ་.

ཚུལ་མིན་གཞོན་ནུ་ (tsūūmin shönnu) juvenile delinquent, youth without morals.

ཚུལ་གཙང་བ་ (tsūū dzāŋwa) 1. good conduct/ behavior. 2. able to maintain one's vows.

ཚུལ་ཞིག (tsūūshi) 1. vi. to have one's pretension be found out. 2. vi. to have one's vows. get broken.

ཚུལ་བཞིན་ (tsūūshin) in the right manner/ way, morally, ethically, properly ¶ཆབ་འབངས་ཚུལ་བཞིན་སྐྱོང་བའི་རྒྱལ་པོ་ A king who rules his subject morally.

ཚུལ་གཟབ་ (tsūūsob) sm. ཚུལ་འཆོས་.

ཚུལ་ལུགས་ (tsūūluù) customs, manners, traditions.

ཚུལ་ཤིང་ (tsūūshiŋ) the stick used for counting the monks during prayer assembly meetings.

ཚུལ་སྲུང་ (tsūūsuŋ) complying or adhering to discipline/ regulations/ vows.

ཚེ་ (tsē) 1. life ¶ཚེ་རིང་པོ་ Long life. 2. if (vb.+ —) ¶འདི་མ་བྱས་ཚེ་ If (they) didn't do it. 3. when, at the time ¶དེའི་ཚེ་ཁོང་བོད་ལ་ཡོད་པ་རེད་ At that time, he was in Tibet.

ཚེ་སྐྲ་ (tsēdra) hair that has never been cut.

ཚེ་འཁྱོལ་ (tsē kyöö) vi. to pass one's life ¶ཁོང་སྐྱིད་པོ་བྱས་ནས་ཚེ་འཁྱོལ་སོང་ He passed his life happily.

ཚེ་གང་ (tsēgaŋ) a lifetime, a whole life ¶ཚེ་གང་སྤྲང་པོ་བྱས་པ་རེད་ (They) were beggars all their lives. ¶ཚེ་གང་གཉེན་གྲོགས་ Lifelong spouse.

ཚེ་གང་གི་གྲོགས་པོ་ (tsēgaŋgi trogbo) lifelong partner (spouse).

ཚེ་གང་གི་གཉེན་གྲོགས་ (tsēgaŋgi dɛ̄ndrɔɔ) sm. ཚེ་གང་གི་གྲོགས་.

ཚེ་གང་སྒྲུབ་པ་བརྒྱབ་པ་ཞོགས་གཅིག་གཡང་ལ་དབྱུག (tsēgaŋ drubba gyəbba shɔ̄ɔjiì yāŋla yūù) a lifetime of great accomplishments in the end is thrown away in a moment [Lit. meditating one's whole life but throwing it away in one morning].

ཚེ་གྲོགས་ (tsēdrɔɔ) sm. ཚེ་གང་གི་གྲོགས་.

ཚེ་འགུགས་ (tsēguù) a ritual of longevity.

ཚེ་སྒོ་ (tsēgo) a lifetime (punishment) of wearing a cangue; va.—གཡོགས་ to fasten/ affix such a cangue.

ཚེ་སྒོ་བཙོན་འཇུག (tsēgo dzōnjuù) life imprisonment wearing a cangue.

ཚེ་སྒོ་ཆེ་ལྕགས་ (tsēgo tsejaà) life sentence of wearing a cangue and shackles; va.—རྒྱག.

ཚེ་སྒྲུབ་ (tsēdrub) ritual/ prayer for longevity.

ཚེ་སྔ་མ་ (tsē ŋāma) past/ previous life.

ཚེ་སྔ་མ་རིག (tsē ŋāma rig) vi. to know/ see one's previous life.

ཚེ་སྔོན་ (tsēŋön) sm. ཚེ་སྔ་མ་.

ཚེ་སྔོན་ལས་ (tsēŋön lɛ̄ɛ) karma from one's previous life.

ཚེ་གཅིག (tsējig) a lifetime, a whole life.

ཚེ་གཅིག་གི་དོན་ཆེན་ (tsējiggi tö̱njen) an important event in one's life.

ཚེ་གཅིག་ལུས་གཉིས་ (tsējig lṳ̄ṳ̄ñii) 1. tadpole. 2. animals that come from eggs.

ཚེ་བཅུད་ (tsējüü) sm. ཚེའི་ཟུངས་.

ཚེ་ཆང་ (tsējaŋ) beer blessed to bring longevity.

ཚེ་ཆུ་ (tsēju) a spring that has been blessed to bring longevity.

ཚེ་མཆོག་གླིང་ (tsējoliŋ) 1. a famous incarnate lama who has served as regent. 2. name of the monastery of that lama.

ཚེ་མཇུག (tsēnjuù) the later part of a life ¶ཁོང་གི་ཚེ་མཇུག་ལ་རྒྱ་གར་ལ་བཞུགས་པ་རེད་ He lived in India during the later part of his life.

ཚེ་མཇུག་ངལ་གསོ་ (tsējuù ŋɛ̱ɛ̱so) taking it easy in old age.

ཚེ་རྗེས་མ་ (tsē je̱èma) the next/ future life.

ཚེ་བརྗེ་ (tsē je̱) vi. to die [Lit. to change one's life (form)].

ཚེ་སྙིགས་མ་ (tsē ñīgmə) an era when the life span is shorter.

ཚེ་སྟོད་ (tsēdöö) the earlier/ younger part of one's life.

ཚེ་བརྟན་ (tsēdɛn) 1. name of a person. 2. longevity, long life.

ཚེ་བརྟན་པོ་ (tsē dɛ̄mbo) long life.

ཚེ་ཐར་ (tsēdaa) saving/ sparing a life; va.—གཏོང་ to spare/ save a life (that otherwise would be killed) ¶ལུག་འདི་མ་བསད་གོང་ལ་ཁོས་ཉོས་ནས་ཚེ་ཐར་བཏང་བ་རེད་ Before they killed the sheep he bought it and spared its life.

ཚེ་ཐུང་ (tsēduŋ) short life span.

ཚེ་ཐུང་ལ་རྒྱག (tsēduŋlə gya̱à) vi. to die an untimely death.

ཚེ་ཐོག་གཅིག་པ་ (tsēdɔɔ̀ jīgbə) (people of) the same generation.

ཚེ་མཐའ་ (tsēta) sm. ཚེ་མཇུག.

ཚེ་དང་ལྡན་པ་ (tsēdaŋ dɛ̱mba) a living person.

ཚེ་ལྡན་ (tsēdɛn) living, alive.

ཚེ་འདས་ (tsē dɛ̱ɛ̀) 1. vi. to die. 2. dead person, deceased.

ཚེ་འདས་ཕ་མ་ (tsēdɛɛ̀ pāma) parents who are deceased.

ཚེ་འདི་ཕྱི་ (tsē di̱ cī) this and the next life.

ཚེ་གནས་པའི་རྩ་ (tsēnɛɛ̀bɛ dzā) a vein (according to traditional Tibetan medicine) on which life depends.

ཚེ་ཕྱི་མ་ (tsē cīmə) the next life.

ཚེ་ཕྱིད་ (tsējīi) sm. ཚེ་འཕྱིལ་.

ཚེ་ཕྱེད་ (tsē cēè) half a life span.

ཚེ་འཕོ་ (tsē pō) vi. to die.

ཚེ་བུམ་ (tsēbum) the vase of longevity (used in the ritual of longevity).

ཚེ་འབར་ (tsēmbar) burning continuously night and day.

ཚེ་འབར་ཀོང་ (tsēmbar gōŋ) a lamp container that burns continuously (night and day).

ཚེ་སྨད་ (tsēmɛɛ̀) sm. ཚེ་མཇུག.

ཚེ་སྨོན་གླིང་ (tsēmönliŋ) 1. a famous incarnate lama who has served as regent. 2. name of the monastery of that lama.

ཚེ་བཙོན་ (tsēdzön) life imprisonment; va.—དུ་འཇུག to imprison for life.

ཚེ་ཚད་ (tsēdzɛɛ̀) life span, life expectancy.

ཚེ་ཚེ་ (tsēdze) goat.

ཚེ་ཚེ་ར་ (tsēdzera) sm. ཚེ་ཚེ་.

ཚེ་རྫས་ (tsēdzɛɛ̀) materials used in the longevity ritual/ empowerment.

ཚེ་རྫོགས་ (tsē dzɔɔ̀) to have one's life span end ¶རྩིས་ཀྱི་ནང་དུ་ནད་པ་དེ་ཚེ་རྫོགས་བཞག་ཟེར་འཁོར་འདུག According to astrological calculation the patient's life span has ended (i.e., he will die soon).

ཚེ་གཞུག (tsēshuù) the latter part of one's life.

ཚེ་ཟད་ (tsē sɛ̱ɛ̀) sm. ཚེ་རྫོགས་.

ཚེ་གཟུངས་ (tsēsuŋ) name of a prayer for long life.

ཚེ་བཟང་དུས་བཟང་ (tsēsaŋ tṳ̄ṳ̄saŋ) 1. an auspicious era/ time. 2. the auspicious Buddhist days of the month (the 1st, 8th, and 30th).

ཚེ་ཡི་དུས་བྱེད་ (tsēyi tṳ̄ṳ̄jeè) death.

ཚེ་ཡི་རིག་བྱེད་ (tsēyi ri̱gjeè) medical science.

ཚེ་ཡི་རིག་བྱེད་པ་ (tsēyi ri̱gjeèba) medical doctor.

ཚེ་གཡོག (tsēyɔɔ̀) a lifetime (hereditary) slave/ serf; va.—སྐྱེལ་ to enslave; va.—རྒྱག to be a serf/ slave for life.

ཚེ་རབས་ (tsērəb) generations.

ཚེ་རབས་ལས་རྩིས་ (tsērəb lɛ̱ɛ̀ dzīi) a horoscope done at birth telling what will happen in one's life.

ཚེ་རིང་ (tsēriŋ) 1. long life. 2. person's name.

ཚེ་རིང་སྐྱིན་ཁེབས་ (tsēriŋ gyīŋgeb) a type of brocade Tibetan hat with a long front brim.

ཚེ་རིང་སྐྲ་ཕུད་ (tsēriŋ drābüü) offering a high lama pieces of hair of children for their longevity.

ཚེ་རིང་མཆེད་ལྔ་ (tsēriŋ cēèŋa) the five female deities of longevity.

ཚེ་རིང་དྲུག་སྐོར་ (tsēriŋ tru̱ùgɔɔ) the six symbols of longevity.

ཚེ་རིང་ནད་མེད་ (tsēriŋ nɛ̄ɛ̀meè) long life without illness.

ཚེ་རིང་རྣམ་དྲུག (tsēriŋ nāmdruù) sm. ཚེ་རིང་དྲུག་སྐོར་.

ཚེ་རིང་པོ་ (tsē ri̱ŋbu) long-lived, long life.

ཚེ་རིང་ལོ་བརྒྱ་ (tsēriŋ m̀ōgya) a greeting that literally means, "long life, 100 years".

ཚེ་རིལ་ (tsērii) long-life pills.

ཚེ་རོགས་ (tsēroò) see ཚེ་གྲོགས་.

ཚེ་ལ་གཟན་པོ་ (tsēla sɛ̱mbo) harming one's longevity ¶སྲོག་གཅོད་མང་པོ་བྱས་ན་རང་ཉིད་ཀྱི་ཚེ་ལ་གཟན་པོ་ཡོང་གི་རེད་ If you do a lot of killing you will harm your longevity.

ཚེ་ལས་འདས་ (tsēlɛ dɛ̱ɛ̀) vi. to die.

ཚེ་ལུག (tsēluù) a sheep bought in order to spare its life.

ཚེ་ལོ་ (tsēlo) life span.

ཚེ་སྲིང་ (tsē sīŋ) va. to lengthen/ increase a person's life.

ཚེ་སྲིང་གཡང་རྟགས་ (tsēsīŋ yāŋdaà) a symbol of longevity.

ཚེ་སྲོག (tsēsɔɔ̀) life; vi.—ཆད་ to die; va.—འཕྲོག to kill.

ཚེ་སྲོག་ཉེན་སྲུང་ (tsēsɔɔ̀ ñensuŋ) life insurance.

ཚེ་སྲོག་ཆད་ (tsēsɔɔ̀ cɛɛ̀) see ཚེ་སྲོག.

ཚེ་བསོད་ (tsē sȫȫ) abbr. of ཚེ་ and བསོད་ནམས་.

ཚེ་ལྷ་རྣམ་གསུམ་ (tsēlha nāmsum) the three deities of longevity.

ཚེ་ལྷག (tsēlhaà) the life span left over from a previous existence.

ཚེག (tsēg) the dot used between syllables in Tibetan orthography; va.—རྒྱག to insert dots between words.

ཚེག་ཅོམ་ (tsēgjom) a sound made by rats, mice, etc.

ཚེག་རྟགས་ (tsēgdaà) 1. sm. ཚེག. 2. punctuation marks.

ཚེག་ཐིག (tsēgdig) a dotted line.

ཚེག་ཐུང་ (tsēgduŋ) sm. ཚེག.

ཚེག་དྲག (tsēgdraà) sm. རྣམ་བཅད་.

ཚེག་བར་ (tsēgbar) syllable.

ཚེག་བར་ཅན་གྱི་ཡི་གེ་ (tsēgbarjɛngi yi̱gi) a syllabic language.

ཚེག་འབྲེང་ (tsēgdreŋ) comma.

ཚེག་རིང་ (tsēgriŋ) a vertical line in the printed Tibetan script which is equivalent to a period or a full stop.

ཚེག་ཤད་ (tsēgshɛɛ̀) abbr. of ཚེག and ཤད་.

ཚེག་ཤིང་ (tsēgshiŋ) a type of tree from Kongpo.

ཚེགས་ (tsēg) 1. difficulty, trouble. 2. p. of འཚེག.

ཚེགས་ཆུང་ (tsēgjuŋ) easy.

ཚེགས་ཆེ་ (tsēgje) difficult.

ཚེགས་བར་ (tsēgbar) sm. གིགས་བར་.

ཚེགས་མེད་ (tsēgmeè) easy.

ཚེགས་མེད་ལྷུན་གྲུབ་ (tsēgmeè lhũndrub) able to achieve a lot without much hard work/ effort.

ཚེགས་ཚེགས་སུ་སྒྲུབ་ (tsēgdzegsu drub) va. to achieve sth. through much hard work/ effort.

ཚེགས་ཡང་ (tsēgyaŋ) a hard worker.

ཚེགས་ལེན་ (tsēglen) bearing hardship; va.—བྱེད་.

ཚེབ་ (tsēm) pitchfork.

ཚེམ་ (tsēm) abbr. of ཚེམ་བུ་.

ཚེམ་སྐུད་ (tsēmgüü) stitching thread.

ཚེམ་འཁོར་ (tsēmgɔɔ) sewing machine.

ཚེམ་གླ་ (tsēmla) sewing fee.

ཚེམ་སྦྱོང་རྒྱག (tsēmdoŋ gyaà) va. to practice sewing without thread.

ཚེམ་དྲུབ་ (tsēmdrub) needlework, embroidery, applique, decorative stitching; va.—བྱེད་.

ཚེམ་དྲུབ་མ་ (tsēmdrubmə) needlework, embroidery, decorative stitching ། ཞྭ་མོ་ཚེམ་དྲུབ་མ་ A hat with decorative stitching.

ཚེམ་བུ་ (tsĩmbu) sewing, stitching; va.—རྒྱག to sew, to stitch.

ཚེམ་བུ་ཁང་ (tsimbugaŋ) tailor's shop.

ཚེམ་བུ་ལྕགས་སྒྲོག (tsēmbu jāgdrɔɔ) a type of stitching.

ཚེམ་བུ་བ་ (tsēmbɔɔ) tailor.

ཚེམ་བུ་བྲལ་ (tsēmbu trɛɛ) vi. to come unstitched.

ཚེམ་བུ་ཧྲལ་པོ་ (tsēmbu hrēēbo) wide stitching.

ཚེམ་བུའི་འཁོར་ལོ་ (tsēmbü kɔ̄ɔlo) sewing machine.

ཚེམ་ཚེམ་ (tsēmdzem) arc. armor.

ཚེམ་ཞུ་ (tsēmshu) arc. helmet.

ཚེམ་ཞྭ་ (tsēmsha) ཚེམ་ཞུ་.

ཚེམ་བཟོ་ (tsēmso) tailoring, sewing; va.—བྱེད་ to do tailoring ། ཚེམ་བཟོ་བཟོ་གྲྭ་ A tailoring factory.

ཚེམ་བཟོ་ཁང་ (tsēmsogaŋ) tailoring/ mending workshop.

ཚེམ་སུབ་ (tsēmsub) sm. ཚེམ་སུབས་.

ཚེམས་ (tsēm) 1. h. of སོ་. 2. imp. of འཚེམ་.

ཚེམས་གྲལ་འཁྲིག་པོ་ (tsēmdrɛɛ drigbu) h. of སོ་གྲལ་འཁྲིག་པོ་.

ཚེམས་བརྗེ་ (tsēmje) h. of སོ་བརྗེ་.

ཚེམས་རྙིལ་ (tsēmñii) h. of སོ་རྙིལ་.

ཚེམས་ཐགས་བཟང་པོ་ (tsēmdaà saŋbo) h. of སོ་ཐགས་བཟང་པོ་.

ཚེམས་དྲེག (tsēmdreg) h. of སོ་དྲེག.

ཚེམས་འབམ་ (tsēmbam) h. of སོ་འབམ་.

ཚེམས་སྨན་ (tsēmmɛn) h. of སོ་སྨན་.

ཚེམས་ཚབ་ (tsēmdzəb) h. of སོ་ཚབ་.

ཚེམས་ཚེགས་དམ་པོ་ (tsēmdzem tambo) h. of སོ་ཚེགས་དམ་པོ་.

ཚེམས་རོང་རོང་ (tsēm roŋroŋ) h. of སོ་རོང་རོང་.

ཚེམས་ཤིང་ (tsēmshiŋ) h. of སོ་ཤིང་.

ཚེམས་ལྷུ་ (tsēmlhu) h. of སོ་ལྷུ་.

ཚེམས་ཧྲལ་ཧྲལ་ (tsēm hrɛ̄ɛhrɛɛ) h. of སོ་ཧྲལ་ཧྲལ་.

ཚེའི་འདུ་བྱེད་ (tsēē dujeè) death, dying; vi.—གཏོང་ to die.

ཚེའི་འདུ་བྱེད་སྟོངས་ (tsēē dujeè dōŋ) sm. ཚེའི་འདུ་བྱེད་གཏོང་.

ཚེའི་མེ་ཏོག (tsēē medoò) peach flower design.

ཚེའི་ཟུངས་ (tsēēsuŋ) lifespan; vi.—རྫོགས་ to have one's life expire (die).

ཚེར་ (tsēr) 1. abbr. of ཚེར་མ་. 2. zipper. 3. canceling/ balancing out a debt; va.—གཏོང་ ། དེ་རིང་ང་ལ་སྦག་ཐོབ་པ་དེས་ཁ་སའི་བུ་ལོན་ཚེར་བཏང་བ་ཡིན་ My winning today in mahjong, canceled my debt (from previous games).

ཚེར་དཀར་ (tsēēgar) type of herb.

ཚེར་ཁབ་ (tsērgəb) needle made from a thorn.

ཚེར་སྔོན་ (tsēr ŋōn) abbr. of ཨ་དུག་ཚེར་སྔོན་.

ཚེར་ཅན་ལྕགས་སྐུད་ (tsērjɛn jāggüü) barbed wire.

ཚེར་སྣར་ (tsērdar) fence made from thorn bushes.

ཚེར་ཐགས་ (tsērdaà) sm. ཚེར་སྣར་.

ཚེར་སྡོང་ (tsērdoŋ) thorn bush.

ཚེར་ཕུང་ (tsērbuŋ) 1. sm. ཚེར་སྡོང་. 2. a pile of thorn bushes that has been cut.

ཚེར་ཕུང་ལ་བསྐོར་ནས་རི་བོང་ལ་འཇབ་རྡོ་ (tsērpuŋla gɔ̄ɔnɛ riboŋla jəbdo) sm. ཕ་བོང་ལ་བསྐོར་ནས་རི་བོང་ལ་འཁྲུམ་ལྕུག.

ཚེར་མ་ (tsēēma) thorn; va.—ཟུག to get pricked by a thorn.

ཚེར་མ་དར་བདུམས་ (tsēēma tardum) iron fist in a velvet glove [Lit. thorn wrapped in silk].

ཚེར་མ་འདོམ་གཞལ་ (tsēēma domshɛɛ) exaggerating, making a mountain out of a molehill [Lit. measuring a thorn by འདོམ་ (length of one's outstretched arms)].

ཚེར་མ་ཚང་ཚིང་ (tsēēma tsəŋdziŋ) an area with a lot of thorn bushes.

ཚེར་མའི་ཁ་ (tsēēmɛ kā) the tip/ point of a thorn.

ཚེར་མའི་ཐོག་ཏུ་བསྡད་པ་བཞིན་ (tsēēmɛ tɔ̄ɔdu dɛ̄ɛba shin) a precarious/ dangerous situation [like sitting on top of a thorn].

ཚེར་མོ་ (tsērmo) two year old female sheep and goats.

ཚེར་རྟང་ (tsērdaŋ) a thorn that is stuck in a torma.

ཚེར་འཛིན་ (tsērdzin) sm. རྨུངས་འཛབ་.

ཚེར་ཤིང་ (tsērshiŋ) sm. ཚེར་སྡོང་.

ཚེར་ཤུག (tsērshug) Chinese thorny juniper.

ཚེར་ལྷོག (tsērlhoò) infection caused by a thorn.

ཚེས་ (tsēè) 1. date, day of the month ། ཚེས་ལྔ་ལ་འབྱོར་པ་རེད་ (They) arrived on the fifth. ། ཟླ་དང་པོའི་ཚེས་གཅིག The first day of the first month. 2. vi. to begin, to commence ། དུས་རབས་ཉི་ཤུ་པ་འདི་མ་ཚེས་གོང་ Before the twentieth century begins. ། ཟླ་བཞི་པ་ཚེས་པ་དང་ལྷ་སར་འགྲོ་གི་རེད་ (We) will go to Lhasa as soon as April starts.

ཚེས་ཁ་ (tsēèga) the beginning days of a month.

ཚེས་གྲངས་ (tsēèdraŋ) 1. date, day of the month ། ཚེས་གྲངས་ཡོད་པའི་ཆུ་ཚོད་ A calendar clock/ watch. ། ངས་ཚེས་གྲངས་བརྗེད་བཞག I've forgotten the date.

ཚེས་གྲངས་གཏན་འཁེལ་ (tsēèdraŋ dɛ̄nkee) fixed date/ time, definite schedule.

ཚེས་གྲངས་འགོག (tsēèdraŋ gɔɔ) va. to fix/ set a date or day for doing sth.

ཚེས་གྲངས་ཡག་པོ་ (tsēèdraŋ yagbo) sm. ཚེས་ཆ་བཟང་པོ་.

ཚེས་དགེ་བ་ (tsēè gewa) an auspicious day.

ཚེས་མགོ་ (tsēngo) sm. ཚེས་འགོ་.

ཚེས་འགོ་ (tsēŋgo) beginning of a month ། ཟླ་བ་བདུན་པའི་ཚེས་འགོར་ At the beginning of July (the seventh month).

ཚེས་བཅུ་ (tsēèju) see མར་ངོའི་ཚེས་བཅུ་ and ཡར་ངོའི་ཚེས་བཅུ་.

ཚེས་ཆ་ (tsēèja) date for going somewhere or doing sth., date on which sth. is to take place or be done ། ཚེས་ཆ་གཏན་འཁེལ་བྱུང་ The date has been decided.

ཚེས་ཆ་བཟང་པོ་ (tsēèja saŋbo) auspicious day/ date.

ཚེས་ཆད་ལྷག (tsēè cɛ̄ɛlhaà) months that have extra days or are short days.

ཚེས་ཆབ་ (tsēècəb) sm. ཚེས་ཆུ་.

ཚེས་ཆུ་ (tsēèju) water drawn from the well on New Year's day.

ཚེས་ཆེན་ (tsēèjen) the 15th day of the lunar month.

ཚེས་མཉམ་ (tsēèñam) days when the Tibetan and Western calendars are the same day.

ཚེས་གཏོར་ (tsēèdɔɔ) offering torma on the New Year's day.

ཚེས་སྟོད་ (tsēèdöö) sm. ཟླ་སྟོད་.

ཚེས་ཐམ་ (tsēèdam) date stamp, datemark.

ཚེས་ཐོ་ (tsēèto) calendar.

ཚེས་གནམ་གང་ (tsēè nāmgaŋ) the 30th day of the month.

ཚེས་པ་ (tsēèba) sm. ཚེས་.

ཚེས་འབྲས་ལྟ་ (tsēndrɛɛ dā) va. to check for an auspicious day to perform a ceremony.

ཚེས་རྩིས་ (tsēèdzii) astrological calculations of dates.

ཚེས་གཞུག (tsēèshuù) latter part of the month.

ཚེས་བཟང་ (tsēèsaŋ) abbr. of ཚེས་ཆ་བཟང་པོ་.

ཚེས་བཟང་དུས་བཟང་ (tsēèsaŋ t̲ṻsaŋ) 1. auspicious days (such as the 8th, 15th, 30th of the Tibetan calendar) and auspicious times.

ཚེས་བཟང་པོ་ (tsēè s̲aŋbo) sm. ཚེས་ཆ་བཟང་པོ་.

ཚེས་རི་ (tsēèri) start of a lunar month.

ཚེས་ལོ་ (tsēèlo) lunar year.

ཚེས་ཤར་ (tsēshaa) beginning of a month.

ཚེས་བཤོལ་ (tsēèshöö) an extra day (added to a month to even out the lunar calendar).

ཚེས་ལྷག (tsēèlhaà) sm. ཚེས་བཤོལ་.

ཚོ་ (tsō) 1. plural particle ¶ དམག་མི་ཚོ་ Soldiers. 2. herd, flock, group ¶ བྱ་ཚོ་གཅིག A flock of birds.

ཚོ་ཁ་ (tsōga) sm. ཚོ་ཁག.

ཚོ་ཁག (tsōgaà) tribes, groups.

ཚོ་ཁག་གི་གཉེན་སྒྲིག (tsōgaàgi ñēndrig) group or communal marriage.

ཚོ་ཁང་ (tsōgaŋ) a police station in Lhasa in tt.

ཚོ་ཆུང་ (tsōjuŋ) small group/ unit/ tribe.

ཚོ་ཆེན་ (tsōjen) big group/ unit/ tribe.

ཚོ་ཆེས་པ་ (tsōjeèba) foods that are very greasy.

ཚོ་དང་ཚོ་ (tsōdaŋ tsō) groups and groups; va.—བྱེད་ to form into groups, to be formed in groups; va.—བགོ་ to divide into groups ¶ སྐྱིད་ཚལ་གྱི་ནང་དུ་གཞོན་ནུ་ཚོ་དང་ཚོ་བྱས་ནས་རྩེད་མོ་རྩེ་གི་འདུག There are groups and groups of youths playing in the garden.

ཚོ་པ་ (tsōba) tribe, group, unit.

ཚོ་པའི་འགོ་དཔོན་ (tsōbɛ g̲obön) sm. ཚོ་དཔོན་.

ཚོ་པའི་བརྒྱ་དཔོན་ (tsōbɛ gy̲abön) leader of a hundred households.

ཚོ་པའི་སྟོང་དཔོན་ (tsōbɛ dōŋbön) leader/ chief/ head of a thousand households.

ཚོ་པོ་ (tsōbo) foods that are very greasy.

ཚོ་དཔོན་ (tsōbön) chief of a tribe, leader of a group.

ཚོ་དཔོན་རྒྱལ་ཁབ་ (tsōbön gy̲ɛɛgəb) emirate, sheikdom.

ཚོ་བ་ (tsōwa) sm. ཚོ་པོ་.

ཚོ་སྨོན་གླིང་ (tsōmönliŋ) sm. ཚེ་སྨོན་གླིང་.

ཚོ་གཙོ་ (tsōdzo) sm. ཚོ་དཔོན་.

ཚོ་ཚོ་ (tsōdzo) groups.

ཚོ་ཟིན་ (tsō s̲in) vi. to be independent/ self-sufficient ¶ ཕོགས་ཆེན་པོ་མེད་ཀྱང་ཚོ་ཟིན་ཐུབ་ཀྱི་ཡོད་པ་རེད་ Even though (I) don't get a large salary, (I'm) able to be self-sufficient.

ཚོ་ཟིན་པོ་ (tsō s̲imbu) well-behaved, stable, mature, having good judgment ¶ ཕྲུ་གུ་འདི་ཚོ་ཟིན་པོ་འདུག This child is well-behaved.

ཚོག (tsɔ̄ɔ) imp. of འཚོག.

ཚོགས་ (tsɔ̄ɔ) 1. p. of འཚོག. 2. assembly, meeting, gathering (esp. monk's prayer assembly); va.—འཚོག to convene an assembly/ gathering/ prayer assembly. 3. a religious offering; va.—གཏོང་. 4. imp. of འཚོག. 5. vi. to be able to collect/ hold ¶ སྣོད་ཆས་ལ་ཨེ་ཁུང་ཡོད་ཙང་ཆུ་ཚོགས་ཀྱི་མི་འདུག Because the container has holes, it can't hold water.

ཚོགས་བསྐོང་ (tsɔ̄ɔgoŋ) convening/ calling a meeting; va.—བྱེད་.

ཚོགས་བསྐོང་འགན་འཛིན་ (tsɔ̄ɔgoŋ g̲ɛndzin) convener/ caller/ organizer of a meeting.

ཚོགས་ཁག (tsɔ̄ɔgaà) bloc, clique, group.

ཚོགས་ཁག་ཆུང་ཆུང་རིང་ལུགས་ (tsɔ̄ɔgaà cūŋjuŋ r̲iŋluù) cliquishnessism, small group mentalityism.

ཚོགས་ཁག་ནག་པོ་ (tsɔ̄ɔgaà n̲agbo) the black cliques (an epithet for antiparty, antisocialist groups).

ཚོགས་ཁང་ (tsɔ̄ɔgaŋ) assembly hall, meeting hall, auditorium.

ཚོགས་ཁང་ཆེན་པོ་ (tsɔ̄ɔgaŋ cēmbo) large auditorium/ meeting hall.

ཚོགས་ཁང་ཆེན་མོ་ (tsɔ̄ɔgaŋ cēmmo) sm. ཚོགས་ཁང་ཆེན་པོ་.

ཚོགས་ཁུག (tsɔ̄ɔguù) small bag used to carry རྩམ་པ་ to a prayer assembly meeting (ཚོགས་).

ཚོགས་ཁྲོ་ (tsɔ̄ɔdro) sm. ཚོགས་ཟངས་.

ཚོགས་གྲལ་ (tsɔ̄ɔdrɛɛ) a row (in a meeting/ assembly); va.—སྒྲིག to order/ arrange the rows at a meeting.

ཚོགས་གྲོལ་ (tsɔ̄ɔ tr̲öö) 1. vi. to have a meeting/ assembly disperse/ adjourn/ dismiss. 2. vi. to die.

ཚོགས་མགོན་ (tsɔ̄ɔgön) presiding over a religious gathering ¶ སྨོན་ལམ་ཆེན་མོའི་ཚོགས་མགོན་དུ་གོང་ས་མཆོག་ཆིབས་བསྒྱུར་གནང་ The Dalai Lama came to preside over the Monlam ceremony.

ཚོགས་མགྲོན་ (tsɔ̄ɔdrön) guest at a meeting.

ཚོགས་བརྒྱ་ (tsɔ̄ɔgya) a religious offering of one hundred ཚོགས་.

ཚོགས་དངུལ་ (tsɔ̄ɔŋüü) dues of a society/ association/ party.

ཚོགས་ཆུ་ (tsɔ̄gju) water for use in monks' prayer assemblies.

ཚོགས་ཆུང་ (tsɔ̄gjuŋ) committee, subcommittee; small group ¶ གསར་བརྗེའི་ཚོགས་ཆུང་ A revolutionary committee.

ཚོགས་ཆེན་ (tsɔ̄gjen) 1. congress, conference, meeting, plenary session 2. General Assembly (in United Nations). 3. central prayer assembly hall in large monasteries. 4. term used to refer to the overall monastery in contrast to its constituent colleges.

ཚོགས་ཆེན་སྤྲུལ་སྐུ་ (tsɔ̄gjen drṻṻgu) high level/ rank of incarnate lamas within a monastery.

ཚོགས་ཆེན་དབུ་མཛད་ (tsɔ̄gjen ūmdzɛɛ̀) shung. the title of the monk chant master who starts the prayers during the prayer assembly meetings.

ཚོགས་ཆེན་ཞལ་ངོ་ (tsɔ̄gjen sh̲ɛɛŋo) shung. the two monk officials in charge of monitoring discipline in large monasteries.

ཚོགས་ཆོས་ (tsɔ̄gcöö) 1. religious teaching given to a large gathering of people. 2. abbr. of ཚོགས་ and ཆོས་ར་.

ཚོགས་མཆོད་ (tsɔ̄ŋjöö) shung. name of the religious prayer festival held in Lhasa in the 2nd lunar month.

ཚོགས་མཆོད་སེར་སྦྲེང་ (tsɔ̄ŋjöö sēēdreŋ) shung. the religious procession that takes place on the 30th day of the 2nd lunar month.

ཚོགས་མཇལ་ཞུ་ (tsɔ̄ŋjɛɛ sh̲u) va. to make a religious visit to observe a prayer assembly of monks.

ཚོགས་གཉིས་ (tsɔ̄ɔñii) two types of accumulation—merit and wisdom.

ཚོགས་གཏམ་ (tsɔ̄gdam) 1. sm. ཚོགས་བཤད་. 2. scolding; va.—གཏོང་ to scold; vi.—གཟེད་ to be/ get scolded ¶ རྒན་ལགས་ཀྱིས་ང་ལ་ཚོགས་གཏམ་བཏང་བྱུང་ The teacher scolded me.

ཚོགས་གཏོར་ (tsɔ̄ɔ dɔ̄ɔ) abbr. of ཚོགས་ and གཏོར་མ་.

ཚོགས་ཐང་ (tsɔ̄ɔdaŋ) sm. ཚོགས་ར་.

ཚོགས་འདུས་ (tsɔ̄ɔdüü) delegate to a meeting/ assembly.

ཚོགས་དར་ (tsɔ̄ɔdar) the flag of an association/ organization.

ཚོགས་དུང་ (tsɔ̄ɔduŋ) the conch shell used to call monks to assemble for prayers; va.—གཏོང་.

ཚོགས་དུས་ (tsɔ̄ɔdüü) a session of a meeting.

ཚོགས་དོན་ (tsɔ̄ɔdön) the purpose of a meeting.

ཚོགས་དྲུག (tsɔ̄ɔ tr̲uù) the six sense organs in Tibetan medicine: eyes, ears, nose, tongue, body and mind.

ཚོགས་གདན་ (tsɔ̄gdɛn) the long runner-type rugs used on seating rows in monastery prayer halls.

ཚོགས་འདུ་ (tsɔ̄ndu) 1. meeting, assembly, conference, congress; va.—འཚོག to hold meeting; va.—སྡུད་; —སྐོང་ to call/ convoke/ convene a meeting; vi.—གྲོལ་ to be adjourned/ dismissed (meetings, etc.). 2. shung. the National Assembly in precommunist Tibet. 3. the National Assembly in Bhutan.

ཚོགས་འདུ་རྒྱས་འཛོམས་ (tsɔ̄ndu gy̲ɛndzom) 1. a large/ plenary meeting. 2. shung. the large national assembly in tt.

ཚོགས་འདུ་ཚང་འཛོམས་ (tsōndu tsāŋdzom) assembly/ meeting at which everyone comes/ participates.

ཚོགས་འདུ་པ་ (tsōŋduwa) representative to a meeting.

ཚོགས་འདུ་འཚོགས་ས་ (tsōndu tsɔ̄ɔsa) meeting/ assembly place.

ཚོགས་འདུ་ཧྲག་བསྡུས་ (tsōndu hrāgdüü) shung. the abbreviated national assembly in tt.

ཚོགས་འདུ་ཧྲག་བསྡུས་རྒྱས་པ་ (tsōndu hrāgdüü gyɛ̱ɛ̀ba) shung. the enlarged abbreviated national assembly in tt.

ཚོགས་འདུར་ཞུགས་ (tsōndur shu̱ù) va. to participate in a meeting, to attend a meeting ¶ མི་དམངས་ཁྲི་ཕྲག་གིས་ཚོགས་འདུར་ཞུགས་པ་རེད་ Tens of thousands of people participated in the meeting.

ཚོགས་སྡེ་ (tsɔ̄ɔde) group, company, unit ¶ ཚོགས་མི་རྣམས་ཚོགས་སྡེ་བཞི་ལ་བགོས་པ་རེད་ (They) divided the members (of the meeting) into four groups.

ཚོགས་བརྡ་ (tsɔ̄ɔda) notice for a meeting; va.—རྒྱག.

ཚོགས་གནས་ (tsɔ̄ɔnɛɛ̀) the site of a meeting/ conference.

ཚོགས་པ་ (tsɔ̄gba) organization, association, group, party; va.—འཛུགས་ to found an organization/ party/ group.

ཚོགས་པ་ཆུང་ཆུང་རིང་ལུགས་ (tsɔ̄gba cūnjuŋ ri̱ŋluù) cliquish; small-group mentality.

ཚོགས་པའི་གྲི་ཕུའུ་ (tsɔ̄gbɛ drībuu) tib. ch. branch of an organization/ party.

ཚོགས་པའི་གྲི་ཧྲུའུ་ (tsɔ̄gbɛ drīhruu) tib. ch. secretary of a branch of an organization/ party.

ཚོགས་པའི་སྐྱིད་སྡུག (tsɔ̄gba gyīiduù) the membership of a club/ association.

ཚོགས་པའི་བྱེད་སྒོའི་ཉིན་མོ་ (tsɔ̄gba ce̱ègö ñi̱nmo) anniversary of the establishment of an organization/ party.

ཚོགས་པའི་སློབ་གྲྭ་ (tsɔ̄gbɛ lābdra) a school sponsored by an organization/ party.

ཚོགས་དཔོན་ (tsɔ̄gbön) 1. head of an association/ organization.

ཚོགས་སྤྱི་ (tsɔ̄gji) 1. the collective. 2. the whole meeting/ assembly ¶ ཚོགས་སྤྱིའི་བསམ་འཆར་ག་རེ་ཡོད་དམ་ What is the opinion of the meeting as a whole?

ཚོགས་ཕོར་ (tsɔ̄gbɔɔ) large wooden eating bowl brought by monks to monastic prayer assemblies.

ཚོགས་བྱིངས་ (tsɔ̄ɔjiŋ) the ordinary members in an association/ organization.

ཚོགས་དབུ་ (tsɔ̄ɔ ū) the main seat (throne) in a monks' prayer assembly hall.

ཚོགས་མ་བསགས་ (tsɔ̄ɔ ma̱ sāà) vi. to not to accumulate merit.

ཚོགས་མི་ (tsɔ̄ɔmi) member of a society/ organization/ association/ group.

ཚོགས་གཙོ་ (tsɔ̄gdzo) leader or chief of an organization/ association/ assembly/ delegation, chairman or president of a council/ committee ¶ ཚོགས་གཙོ་བགྲེས་གཞོན་ The Chairman and the Vice Chairman.

ཚོགས་ཚོགས་ (tsɔ̄ɔ tsɔ̄ɔ) 1. p. of ཚོགས་འཚོག. 2. gathering; va.—བྱེད་ ¶ མི་དམངས་ཚོས་དེང་སང་ཚོགས་ཚོགས་མང་པོ་བྱེད་ཀྱི་འདུག Nowadays, the people are assembling in many gatherings.

ཚོགས་འཚོག (tsɔ̄ɔ tsɔ̄ɔ) va. to gather/ convene a meeting.

ཚོགས་འཛོམས་ (tsɔ̄ɔ dzo̱m) 1. gathering, meeting, assembly; va.—བྱེད་ to assemble, to gather.

ཚོགས་རྫས་ (tsɔ̄gdzɛɛ̀) small things like candies, cookies, fruits that are offered with ཚོགས་ offerings.

ཚོགས་ཞུགས་ (tsɔ̄gshuù) a participant in a conference.

ཚོགས་ཞུགས་རྒྱལ་ཁབ་ (tsɔ̄gshuù gyɛ̱ɛgɔb) member state ¶ མཉམ་འབྲེལ་རྒྱལ་ཚོགས་ཀྱི་ཚོགས་ཞུགས་རྒྱལ་ཁབ་ A member state of the United Nations.

ཚོགས་ཞུགས་ཐོབ་ཐང་ (tsɔ̄gshuù tōbdaŋ) the right to attend meetings.

ཚོགས་ཞུགས་ཆད་ (tsɔ̄gshuù cɛ̀ɛ) vi. to be absent from a meeting.

ཚོགས་ཞུགས་ལག་ཁྱེར་ (tsɔ̄gshuù la̱ggyer) a permit to attend a meeting/ assembly.

ཚོགས་ཟངས་ (tsɔ̄gsaŋ) a large cauldron for making the monk's tea/ soup that is served at prayer assembly meetings.

ཚོགས་རྡུམ་ (tsɔ̄ɔ du̱m) 1. va. to accumulate merit. 2. va. to gather many people in one place.

ཚོགས་གཟིགས་ (tsɔ̄gsii) shung. government officials looking at/ inspecting a gathering of monks.

ཚོགས་ར་ (tsɔ̄ɔra) meeting place/ site, assembly place, conference hall ¶ ཚོགས་རའི་གྱང་ངོས་སུ་ On the wall of the meeting place.

ཚོགས་རམ་དགེ་བཤེས་ (tsɔ̄gram ge̱sheè) sm. ཚོགས་རམས་པ་.

ཚོགས་རམས་པ་ (tsɔ̄ɔramba) a geshe degree obtained during ཚོགས་མཆོད་ (lower than ལྷ་རམ་པ་).

ཚོགས་ལང་ (tsɔ̄ɔlaŋ) 1. two monks debating in the midst of large gathering of monks. 2. standing up at a meeting to be criticized; va.—བྱེད་ ¶ སློབ་ཕྲུག་དེས་སྒྲིག་ལམ་འགལ་ཙང་དགེ་རྒན་གྱིས་ཚོགས་ལང་བྱེད་དུ་བཅུག་འདུག Because the student violated the rules, the teacher made him stand up at a meeting and be criticized.

ཚོགས་ཤ་ (tsɔ̄gsha) meat that is offered with a ཚོགས་ offering.

ཚོགས་བཤད་ (tsɔ̄gshɛɛ̀) speech or comment at a meeting; va.—བྱེད་ ¶ བསམ་འཆར་ཚོགས་བཤད་བྱེད་དགོས་ We have to speak our opinions at the meeting.

ཚོགས་ས་ (tsɔ̄gsa) sm. ཚོགས་ར་.

ཚོགས་གསོག (tsɔ̄ɔ sɔ̄ɔ) va. to accumulate good merit (good karma).

ཚོང་ (tsōŋ) business, trading, buying and selling; va.—རྒྱག to do business, to do trading ¶ ཁོས་བོད་ལ་ཚོང་བརྒྱབ་པ་རེད་ He did business in Tibet.

ཚོང་ཀུབ་དིབ་ (tsōŋ gūb di̱b) vi. to go bankrupt, to lose all one's capital in business.

ཚོང་སྐད་ (tōŋgɛɛ̀) commercial language, business terminology.

ཚོང་སྐོར་ (tsōŋgɔɔ) 1. going around the market; va.—ལ་འགྲོ་. 2. business/ trading completed in one period or season.

ཚོང་སྐུར་ (tsōŋguu) sending sb. to do trading for oneself.

ཚོང་ཁ་ (tsōŋga) selling; vi.—རྒྱུག to be selling well.

ཚོང་ཁ་རྒྱུག་པོ་ (tsōŋga gyu̱gbu) doing good business, selling well ¶ དེང་སྐབས་ཁ་གདན་གྱི་ཚོང་ཁ་རྒྱུག་པོ་འདུག The carpets are selling well nowadays.

ཚོང་ཁང་ (tsōŋgaŋ) shop, store.

ཚོང་ཁེ་ (tsōŋge) business profit.

ཚོང་ཁེ་སྤོགས་ (tsōŋ kēbɔɔ) sm. ཚོང་ཁེ་.

ཚོང་ཁྲལ་ (tsōŋtrɛɛ) commercial tax, tax on trade or business, sales tax, duty, tariff.

ཚོང་ཁྲལ་མེད་པའི་གྲུ་ཁ་ (tsōŋdrɛɛme̱èbɛ tru̱ga) free port.

ཚོང་ཁྲོམ་ (tsōŋdrom) sm. ཚོང་འདུ་.

ཚོང་མཁན་ (tsōŋñɛn) seller, trader.

ཚོང་འགྲོས་ (tsōŋgöö) trading; va.—བྱེད་.

ཚོང་འགྲོས་འཐབ་ལེན་ (tsōŋgöö tāblen) sm. ཚོང་འགྲོས་.

ཚོང་གུན་ (tsōŋgün) a loss in business/ trading.

ཚོང་གྲུ་ (tsōŋdru) commercial boat, merchant marine vessel/ ship, freighter.

ཚོང་གྲོགས་ (tsōŋdrɔɔ) business partner, business colleague.

ཚོང་འགོ་འཁྱོངས་ (tsōŋgo kyōŋ) va. to be able to manage one's business.

ཚོང་འགྲིག (tsōŋ dri̱g) vi. to have a transaction/ deal/ sale get settled ¶ ངས་སྒོར་མོ་བཅུ་སྤྲད་ནས་ཚོང་འགྲིགས་སོང་ After I gave him ten dollars, the deal was settled.

ཚོང་འགྲིམ་ (tsōŋ drim) va. to take one's goods from place to place to sell.

ཚོང་འགྲུལ་ (tsōŋdrüü) trading activities/ dealings, commercial intercourse, commerce, trade.

ཚོང་འགྲུལ་བཀག་འགོག (tsōŋdrüü gāŋgɔɔ̀) trade/ commercial embargo.

ཚོང་འགྲུལ་གྲུ་ཁ་ (tsōŋdrüüu trugə) sm. ཚོང་དོན་གྲུ་ཁ་.

ཚོང་འགྲུལ་གྲོང་ཁྱེར་ (tsōŋdrüü troŋgyee) commercial town/ city.

ཚོང་འགྲུལ་པ་ (tsōŋdrüübə) traveling salesman, trader.

ཚོང་འགྲེམས་ (tsōŋdrem) 1. sales, selling things; va.—བྱེད་ to sell. 2. va. to show/ display one's merchandise.

ཚོང་རྒྱག (tsōŋ gyaà) va. to do trading, to buy and sell.

ཚོང་རྒྱུ་དངོས་པོ་ (tsōŋgyu ŋö̀öbo) goods or merchandise for sale.

ཚོང་རྒྱུ་འཇོག (tsōŋgyu jɔ̀ɔ) va. to leave sth. to be sold.

ཚོང་རྒྱུག་པོ་ (tsōŋ gyugbo) good business, good turnover in sales.

ཚོང་རྒྱུག་པོའི་ཚོང་ཟོག (tsōŋ gyugbü tsōŋsɔɔ̀) fast-selling items.

ཚོང་སྒར་ (tsōŋgar) shopping stall (in a market).

ཚོང་སྒོ་འབྱེད་ (tsōŋgo jeè) va. to open a business, to begin trading.

ཚོང་སྒྲིག (tsōŋdrig) arranging the terms of trade/ sale, bargaining; va.—བྱེད་.

ཚོང་སྒྱུར་ (tsōŋgyur) selling; va.—བྱེད་ to sell ¶ཁོང་ཚོའི་ཁང་པ་ཚོང་སྒྱུར་བྱེད་ཀྱི་ཡོད་པ་རེད་ (They) are selling their house.

ཚོང་བཅོལ་ (tsōŋjöö) consigning sth. to sell; va.—འཇོག; —བྱེད་ to leave sth. on consignment; va.—ཉར་ to keep goods on consignment.

ཚོང་བཅོལ་ཁང་ (tsōŋjöögaŋ) a store that sells things on consignment, commission shop.

ཚོང་བཅོལ་ཉོ་སྡུས་ཚོང་ཁང་ (tsōŋjöö ñodüü tsōŋgaŋ) sm. ཚོང་བཅོལ་ཁང་.

ཚོང་བཅོལ་ཚོང་ཁང་ (tsōŋjöö tsōŋgaŋ) sm. ཚོང་བཅོལ་ཁང་.

ཚོང་ཆང་ (tsōŋjaŋ) toasting with liquor/ beer after a business deal; va.—གཏོང་.

ཚོང་ཆིངས་ (tsōŋciŋ) trade agreement/ pact/ treaty.

ཚོང་ཆུང་ཉི་ཚེ་བ་ (tsōŋjuŋ ñidzewa) small trader, shopkeeper, peddler, vendor.

ཚོང་ཉེས་ (tsōŋ ñeè) sm. ཚོང་ཕམ་.

ཚོང་ཉེས་སྒོ་རྒྱག (tsōŋñeè gogyaà) bankruptcy, insolvency.

ཚོང་ཉོ་ (tsōŋño) buying and selling, (doing) commerce; va.—བྱེད་.

ཚོང་གཉེར་ (tsōŋñer) business enterprise.

ཚོང་གཉེར་ཁང་ (tsōŋñergaŋ) business enterprise, store, shop.

ཚོང་གཉེར་ཁྲུའུ་ (tsōŋñer trū) tib. ch. business division.

ཚོང་གཉེར་པ་ (tsōŋñerba) salesman in a store.

ཚོང་གཉེར་གྱི་དུས་ཚོད་ (tsōŋñergi tüüdzöö) the time a shop is open for business.

ཚོང་གཉེར་རུ་ཁག (tsōŋñer rugaà) a company of traveling merchants.

ཚོང་གཏམ་ (tsōŋdam) trader's talk, business talk/ conversation; va.—ཤོད་.

ཚོང་རྟགས་ (tsōŋdaà) trademark.

ཚོང་རྟགས་ཀྱི་བཅའ་ཁྲིམས་ (tsōŋdaàgi jādrim) trademark law.

ཚོང་རྟགས་རྒྱག་དབང་ (tsōŋdaà gyaàwaŋ) right to use a trademark.

ཚོང་རྟགས་ཆེད་སྤྱོད་ཀྱི་དབང་ཆ་ (tsōŋdaà cēèjöögi wāŋja) exclusive right to use a trademark.

ཚོང་རྟགས་ཐོ་འགོད་ (tsōŋdaà tōgöö) trademark registration.

ཚོང་སྟེགས་ (tsōŋdeg) counter or table on which things are sold.

ཚོང་ཐག་གཅོད་ (tsōŋdaà jöö) va. to settle a business deal or sale.

ཚོང་ཐག་ཆོད་ (tsōŋdaà cöö) vi. to come to an agreement on a business deal/ sale.

ཚོང་ཐོ་ (tsōŋto) list of things sold, account book/ ledger of sales; va.—རྒྱག to record sales in an account book/ ledger.

ཚོང་དུས་ (tsōŋdüü) the time a store or market is open.

ཚོང་དོན་ (tsōŋdön) commerce, trade ¶ཚོང་དོན་དྲིལ་བསྒྲགས་ Commercial advertisement.

ཚོང་དོན་ཀུང་སི་ (tsōŋdön gūŋsi) tib. ch. trading company.

ཚོང་དོན་ཁང་ (tsōŋdöngaŋ) department of commerce, commerce/ business bureau.

ཚོང་དོན་གྱི་ཆན་ཙན་ (tsōŋdöngi tsɛndzɛn) tib. ch. sm. ཚོང་དོན་ལས་ཚབ་.

ཚོང་དོན་གྲུ་ཁ་ (tsōŋdön trugə) commercial port.

ཚོང་དོན་འགག་སྒོ་ (tsōŋdön gaàgo) customs, duties (for importing and exporting).

ཚོང་དོན་ཆིངས་ཡིག (tsōŋdön ciŋyii) commercial treaty.

ཚོང་དོན་ཆོད་ཡིག (tsōŋdön cööyii) commercial agreement.

ཚོང་དོན་དྲིལ་བསྒྲགས་ (tsōŋdön triidraà) commercial advertisement.

ཚོང་དོན་སྤྱི་གཉེར་ཁང་ (tsōŋdön jiñergaŋ) commercial company/ corporation, general trading company/ corporation.

ཚོང་དོན་སྤྱི་ཁྱབ་པ་ (tsōŋdön jigyəbba) trade agent.

ཚོང་དོན་པུའུ་ (tsōŋdön būū) tib. ch. Commerce Department (U.S.A.).

ཚོང་དོན་བློན་ཆེན་ (tsōŋdön lönjen) Minister/ Secretary of Commerce.

ཚོང་དོན་མ་རྐང་ཀུང་སི་ (tsōŋdön magaŋ gūŋsi) tib. ch. shareholding company.

ཚོང་དོན་ལས་ཁངས་ (tsōŋdön lɛ̀ɛgun) Department of Commerce (U.S.A.).

ཚོང་དོན་ལས་ཚབ་ (tsōŋdön lɛ̀ɛdzəb) commercial charge d'affaires, commercial agent, trade agent/ representative.

ཚོང་དོན་ལས་ཚབ་ཁང་ (tsōŋdön lɛ̀ɛdzəbgaŋ) trade agent/ representative's office.

ཚོང་དོན་ལས་ཚབ་ཁྲུའུ་ (tsōŋdön lɛ̀ɛdzəb trūū) tib. ch. trade agency, trade representative's office.

ཚོང་བདག (tsōŋdaà) shopkeeper, merchant.

ཚོང་འདུས་ (tsōŋdüü) market place, bazaar, trade fair.

ཚོང་འདུས་མགྲོན་པོ་ (tsōŋdüü drömbo) 1. people at a market/ bazaar. 2. a temporary gathering [Lit. visitors/ guests at a bazaar].

ཚོང་འདུས་ཉིན་མོ་ (tsōŋdüù ñinmo) market day, the day a market is held.

ཚོང་རྡལ་ (tsōŋdɛɛ) 1. sm. ཚོང་འདུས་. 2. village, hamlet.

ཚོང་ན་ཕ་ཡང་འཚོང་ཞིང་ ཚོང་ན་མ་ཡང་བཤའ་བ་ (tsōŋna pāyŋ tsōŋshiŋ tōŋna mayaŋ shāwa) an extremely evil person who is capable of doing the worst evil [Lit. a person who will sell his father if he can be sold and slaughter his mother is she can be sold].

ཚོང་པ་ (tsōŋba) trader, merchant.

ཚོང་པ་ཁྲམ་པ་ (tsōŋba trāmba) dishonest trader.

ཚོང་པ་ཚོང་ཤག (tsōŋba tsōŋshaà) sm. ཚོང་ཤག.

ཚོང་པར་ (tsōŋbar) sm. ཚོང་རྟགས་.

ཚོང་དཔོན་ (tsōŋbön) merchant, large trader.

ཚོང་སྤོགས་ (tsōŋbɔɔ̀) business profit.

ཚོང་སྤྱི་ (tsōŋji) shung. trade agent (of traditional Tibetan government) ¶རྒྱལ་རྩེ་ཚོང་སྤྱི་ The Gyantse Trade Agent.

ཚོང་ཕམ་ (tsōŋpam) business loss ¶ཁོ་ཚོར་ཚོང་ཕམ་ཆེན་པོ་བྱུང་པ་རེད་ They incurred a large loss (in their business); vi.—ཤོར་ to incur a loss (in business).

ཚོང་ཕྱུགས་ (tsōŋjuù) animals/ livestock for sale.

ཚོང་ཕྲུག (tsōŋdruù) trader's assistant; va.—བྱེད་.

ཚོང་བྱང་ (tsōŋjaŋ) brand name, trademark.

ཚོང་ཁྲིན་ (tsōŋdrin) the manner in which sth. is selling ། དེང་སང་ཚོང་ཁྲིན་ཆེ་ཤོས་བཟའ་བཅའ་རེད་ Nowadays the thing that is selling best is foodstuffs.

ཚོང་ཁྲིན་པོ་ (tsōŋ dri̱mbu) good sales, selling well ། དེ་རིང་ཚོང་ཁྲིན་པོ་འདུག་གས་ Did you have good sales today?

ཚོང་དབང་གཅིག་བདག (tsōŋwaŋ jīgdaà) trade/ commercial monopoly; va.—བྱེད་.

ཚོང་འབོར་གཏན་འབེབས་ (tsōŋbɔɔ dɛ̄mbeb) sales limit/ ceiling.

ཚོང་འབྲུ (tsōŋdru) 1. grain sold as a commodity, commodity grain. 2. the grain that the government sells to urban residents and workers.

ཚོང་འབྲུ་ཐོན་སའི་རྟེན་གཞི་ (tsōŋdru tönsɛ dēnshi) a commodity grain base (selected villages and xiang with large grain output from which large amounts of grain are bought as quotas by the government).

ཚོང་འབྲེལ་ (tsōŋdree) trade relations, trade; va.—བྱེད་ to have trade relations ། ཡུལ་གཉིས་བར་ཚོང་འབྲེལ་གསར་དུ་འཛུགས་ཀྱི་ཡོད་པ་རེད་ The two countries are establishing trade relations.

ཚོང་འབྲེལ་གྲོས་མཐུན་ (tsōŋdree tro̱ödün) trade agreement.

ཚོང་འབྲེལ་མཉམ་ལས་ (tsōŋdree ñāmlɛɛ̀) marketing cooperative.

ཚོང་འབྲེལ་དོན་གཅོད་ (tsōŋdree to̱njöö̀) trade office/ bureau.

ཚོང་འབྲེལ་གསར་ཤོག (tsōŋdree sārshoò) Journal of Commerce.

ཚོང་འབྲེལ་ལྷན་ཚོགས་ (tsōŋdree lhēndzoò) 1. trade conference. 2. trade association.

ཚོང་སྦྲེལ་ (tsōŋdree) business partner ། ང་གཉིས་ཚོང་འབྲེལ་ཡིན་ We two are business partners.

ཚོང་རྩ་ (tsōŋdza) business capital.

ཚོང་རྩིས་ (tsōŋdzii̇) calculating business profit or loss; va.—རྒྱག.

ཚོང་ཚབ་ (tsōŋdzəb) sales agent, trade agent.

ཚོང་ཚོགས་ (tsōŋdzɔɔ̀) trade group/ association.

ཚོང་མཚམས་འཇོག (tsōŋdzam jɔ̱ɔ̀) 1. va. to stop selling/ doing business ། དཔྱིད་ཀ་དགུན་ཆས་ཚོང་མཚམས་འཇོག་གི་རེད་ In the spring they stop selling winter clothes. 2. va. to close down stores in a boycott.

ཚོང་རྫས་ (tsōŋdzɛɛ̀) sm. ཚོང་ཟོག.

ཚོང་ཟོག (tsōŋsɔɔ̀) commodities, merchandise, goods.

ཚོང་ཟོག་ལྐོག་འཁྱེར་ (tsōŋsɔɔ̀ gɔ̄gkyer) smuggling; va.—བྱེད་.

ཚོང་ཟོག་སྐོར་འགྲིམ་ (tsōŋsɔɔ̀ gōndrem) commodity circulation, trade circulation.

ཚོང་ཟོག་སྐྱེལ་ཐོ་ (tsōŋsɔɔ̀ gyēēdo) invoice, manifest.

ཚོང་ཟོག་ཁ་རྒྱུག་པོ་ (tsōŋsɔɔ̀ kā gyu̱gbu) things that sell well.

ཚོང་ཟོག་འཁོར་རྒྱུག (tsōŋsɔɔ̀ kɔ̄ɔgyuù) circulation of commodities.

ཚོང་ཟོག་གི་རྣམ་པ་ (tsōŋsɔɔ̀gi nāmba) forms of commodities, commodity types.

ཚོང་ཟོག་གི་ཚོང་ར་ (tsōŋsɔɔ̀gi tsōŋra) commodity market.

ཚོང་ཟོག་འགྲོ་རྒྱུག (tsōŋsɔɔ̀ dro̱gyuù) circulation of commodities.

ཚོང་ཟོག་འགྲོ་རྒྱུག་གི་འབྲེལ་རིམ་ (tsōŋsɔɔ̀ dro̱gyuùgi dre̱erim) the process of commodity circulation.

ཚོང་ཟོག་རྒྱུག་པོ་ (tsōŋsɔɔ̀ gyu̱gbu) sm. ཚོང་ཟོག་ཁ་རྒྱུག་པོ་.

ཚོང་ཟོག་རྒྱུན་འཁོར་ (tsōŋsɔɔ̀ gyü̱ngɔɔ) circulation of commodities.

ཚོང་ཟོག་མངགས་ (tsōŋsɔɔ̀ ŋāà) va. to order goods/ commodities.

ཚོང་ཟོག་མངགས་ཐོ་ (tsōŋsɔɔ̀ ŋāàdo) a list of goods that were ordered.

ཚོང་ཟོག་ཆུང་བ་ (tsōŋsɔɔ̀ cūŋwa) petty commodities.

ཚོང་ཟོག་ཆུང་བའི་དཔལ་འབྱོར་ (tsōŋsɔɔ̀ cūŋwɛ bēnjɔɔ) petty commodity economy.

ཚོང་ཟོག་བརྗེ་རེས་ (tsōŋsɔɔ̀ je̱ereè) exchange of commodities.

ཚོང་ཟོག་རྟོག་བཤེར་ཅུའུ་ (tsōŋsɔɔ̀ tōgsher jū) tib. ch. bureau for the inspection of commodities.

ཚོང་ཟོག་ཐོན་སྐྱེད་ (tsōŋsɔɔ̀ tōngyeè) commodity merchandise production.

ཚོང་ཟོག་བདག་གཉེར་ (tsōŋsɔɔ̀ da̱gñer) management of commodities.

ཚོང་ཟོག་སྣ་བརྒྱའི་ཀུང་སི་ (tsōŋsɔɔ̀ nāgyɛ gūŋsi) tib. ch. department store, general store.

ཚོང་ཟོག་སྣ་མང་ (tsōŋsɔɔ̀ nāmaŋ) general merchandise, many different kinds of goods/ merchandise ། ཚོང་ཟོག་སྣ་མང་ཚོང་ཁང་ department store.

ཚོང་ཟོག་སྣ་མང་ཀུང་སི་ (tsōŋsɔɔ̀ nāmaŋ gūŋsi) sm. ཚོང་ཟོག་སྣ་བརྒྱའི་ཀུང་སི་.

ཚོང་ཟོག་དཔལ་འབྱོར་ (tsōŋsɔɔ̀ bēnjɔɔ) commodity economy.

ཚོང་ཟོག་ཕྱིར་ལོག (tsōŋsɔɔ̀ cīīlɔɔ̀) sales returns, return of merchandise sold.

ཚོང་ཟོག་དབོར་འདྲེན་ (tsōŋsɔɔ̀ wɔ̱ndren) transporting goods/ merchandise; va.—བྱེད་.

ཚོང་ཟོག་ཙག་ཙིག (tsōŋsɔɔ̀ dzəgdzig) miscellaneous goods/ merchandise.

ཚོང་ཟོག་འཚོང་མཁན་ (tsōŋsɔɔ̀ tsōŋgɛn) salesman, trader.

ཚོང་ཟོག་ལྷར་བསྐུར་ཆོས་ལུགས་ (tsōŋsɔɔ̀ lhāāguu cōōluù) commodity fetishism.

ཚོང་ཟོང་ (tsōŋsoŋ) sm. ཚོང་ཟོག.

ཚོང་ཟླ་ (tsōŋda) sm. ཚོང་གྲོགས་.

ཚོང་ཡ་ (tsōŋya) sm. ཚོང་གྲོགས་.

ཚོང་ཡིག (tsōŋyiì) business letter, business documents.

ཚོང་ཡུལ་ (tsōŋyüü) market, bazaar.

ཚོང་གཡོག (tsōŋyɔɔ̀) 1. clerk, salesperson. 2. servant of a trader.

ཚོང་ར་ (tsōŋra) marketplace, bazaar.

ཚོང་ར་གློད་ (tsōŋra lȫȫ) va. to liberalize the market (system).

ཚོང་རའི་སྒོ་འབྱེད་ (tsōŋrɛ go̱ je̱è) va. to open a market/ bazaar.

ཚོང་རའི་སྔོན་ཚོད་ (tsōŋrɛ ŋōndzöö̀) market forecast.

ཚོང་རའི་གནས་ཚུལ་ (tsōŋrɛ nɛ̄ɛdzüü) market conditions/ situation.

ཚོང་རོགས་ (tsōŋrɔɔ̀) 1. sales assistance. 2. sb. helping one sell; va.—བྱེད་ ། ཁྱེད་རང་གིས་ངའི་ཅ་ལག་འདི་ཚོང་རོགས་བྱེད་དང་ Please help me to sell my things.

ཚོང་ལམ་ (tsōŋlam) 1. trade route. 2. a market; va.—བཤངས་ to open new markets, to clear a new path for business.

ཚོང་ལས་ (tsōŋlɛɛ̀) business, commerce, trade; va.—བྱེད་ to do business ། མང་ཆེ་བས་འཚོ་ཐབས་ལ་ཚོང་ལས་བྱས་པ་རེད་ Most (of the people) did business for their livelihood.

ཚོང་ལས་ཀྱི་ལྟེ་གནས་ (tsōŋlɛɛ̀gi dēnɛɛ̀) commercial center.

ཚོང་ལས་ཀྱི་མ་རྩ་ (tsōŋlɛɛ̀gi ma̱dza) commercial capital.

ཚོང་ལས་ཁང་ (tsōŋlɛɛ̀gaŋ) trade office.

ཚོང་ལས་ཁོངས་ཀྱི་བཟོ་ཚོགས་ (tsōŋlɛɛ̀goŋgi so̱dzɔɔ) trade union.

ཚོང་ལས་གོང་ཁྱད་ (tsōŋlɛɛ̀ go̱ŋgyɛɛ̀) trade price difference.

ཚོང་ལས་གྲོས་མཐུན་ (tsōŋlɛɛ̀ tro̱ödün) trade agreement.

ཚོང་ལས་འཇོག (tsōŋlɛɛ̀ jɔ̱ɔ̀) va. to go out of business.

ཚོང་ལས་ཐིང་ (tsōŋlɛɛ̀ tīŋ) tib. ch. trade office.

ཚོང་ལས་དྲ་བ་ (tsōŋlɛɛ̀ tra̱wa) commercial network, trade network.

ཚོང་ལས་སྡེ་ཚན་ཁག་གི་སྒྲིག་འཛུགས་ (tsōŋlɛɛ̀

dedzɛngaàgi drigdzuù) Chamber of Commerce.

ཚོང་ལས་པ་ (tsōŋlɛɛ̀ba) employee in a shop, salesman, businessman.

ཚོང་ལས་འབྱོར་ལྡན་གྲལ་རིམ་ (tsōŋlɛɛ̀ jɔbdɛn trɛɛrim) commercial bourgeoisie.

ཚོང་ལས་གཙོགས་འཛིན་རིང་ལུགས་ (tsōŋlɛɛ̀ dzīŋdzin riŋluù) mercantilism.

ཚོང་ལས་ཚོགས་པ་ (tsōŋlɛɛ̀ tsɔ̄gba) Chanber of Commerce.

ཚོང་ལས་བཞག (tsōŋlɛɛ̀ shaà) p. of ཚོང་ལས་འཇོག.

ཚོང་ལས་ལམ་འགྲོ་ (tsōŋlɛɛ̀ lāmdro) fortune/ luck in business.

ཚོང་ལས་སིལ་ཚོང་ཚན་པ་ (tsōŋlɛɛ̀ sīīdzoŋ tsēmba) retail sale unit/ office.

ཚོང་ལོག (tsōŋlɔɔ̀) black marketing.

ཚོང་ཤག (tsōŋshaà) regular customer.

ཚོང་ཤོག (tsōŋshɔɔ̀) a group/ association of traders.

ཚོང་བཤམས་ས་ (tsōŋshamsa) vender's stand/ booth.

ཚོང་སྲང་ (tsōŋsaŋ) a scale for measuring commodities for sale.

ཚོང་སློག (tsōŋlɔɔ̀) reneging/ going back on a deal; va.—རྒྱག.

ཚོང་ལྷ་ (tsōŋlha) deity of wealth/ fortune.

ཚོངས་ (tsōŋ) imp. of འཚོང་.

ཚོད་ (tsȍȍ) 1. judgement, guess, estimation; va.—བྱེད་ to guess, to estimate, to approximate ¶ ངས་ཚོད་བྱས་ན་ཁོ་ལ་དངུལ་སྒོར་ལྔ་སྟོང་ཡོད་པ་རེད་ I would estimate that he has five thousand dollars. 2. the correct/ right amount; va.—བྱེད་; —འཛིན་ to do in the correct/ right amount ¶ ཁ་ལག་ཟ་ཚོད་མ་བྱས་ན་ན་གི་རེད་ If (you) don't eat correctly (you) will get sick. 3. seems, looks like ¶ རྒྱ་ནག་ཏུ་དེང་སང་ནང་འཁྲུག་ཡོད་ཚོད་འདུག It looks like there is civil war in China. ¶ ད་ཕྲུག་གུ་ཚོ་ལྟོགས་ཚོད་ཡིན་ It seems that the children are hungry now. 4. abbr. of ཚོད་མ་. 5. abbr. of ཆུ་ཚོད་.

ཚོད་བགམ་ (tsȍȍgam) estimating, assessing, judging; va.—བྱེད་ to estimate/ judge/ assess; va.—ཐེབས་ to have an estimate work out ¶ ངས་ཚོད་བགམ་བྱས་ན་ If I were to estimate.

ཚོད་རྒྱུགས་ (tsȍȍ gyu̱ù) va. to give an exam at the start of school to assess the level/ standard students are at.

ཚོད་བརྒལ་ (tsȍȍ gɛɛ̱) vi. to pass/ exceed a limit ¶ སློབ་གྲྭའི་ལོ་ཚོད་ལས་བརྒལ་ན་སློབ་གྲྭར་འཛུགས་གི་མ་རེད་ Once you exceed the age limit for school you won't be admitted.

ཚོད་ཅན་ (tsȍȍjɛn) sm. ཚོད་འཛིན་པོ་.

ཚོད་འཇལ་ (tsȍȍ jɛɛ̱) va. to measure.

ཚོད་ཉུལ་ (tsȍȍ ñu̱u̱) va. to check/ test.

ཚོད་བཏུམ་ (tsȍȍdum) steamed stuffed bun.

ཚོད་ལྟ་ (tsȍȍda) 1. test, trial, experiment; —བྱེད་ ¶ ས་གནས་དེ་ཚོར་གྲོ་སྐྱེ་ཐུབ་ཀྱི་ཡོད་མེད་ཚོད་ལྟ་བྱས་པ་རེད་ (They) tested whether wheat can be grown in those regions.

ཚོད་ལྟ་ཁང་ (tsȍȍdagaŋ) experimental laboratory, testing room.

ཚོད་ལྟ་བྱེད་ས་ (tsȍȍda ce̱èsa) test ground, experimental site.

ཚོད་ལྟ་ཚོད་བགམ་ (tsȍȍda tsȍȍgam) sm. ཚོད་ལྟ་.

ཚོད་ལྟ་ཞིང་ར་ (tsȍȍda shiŋrə) experimental farm/ plot.

ཚོད་ལྟའི་རྟེན་གཞི་ (tsȍȍdɛ dēnshi) testing base, experimental site.

ཚོད་ལྟའི་ཕྱུགས་ར་ (tsȍȍdɛ cūùrə) experimental/ test pasture.

ཚོད་ལྟའི་ཞིང་ཁ་ (tsȍȍdɛ shiŋgə) sm. ཚོད་ལྟ་ཞིང་ར་.

ཚོད་ལྟའི་ཡོ་བྱད་ (tsȍȍdɛ yo̱jɛɛ̀) experimental tools.

ཚོད་ལྟའི་ར་བ་ (tsȍȍdɛ ra̱wa) proving ground, testing ground/ site.

ཚོད་ལྟའི་ཤེལ་སྦུག (tsȍȍdɛ shēēbuù) test tube.

ཚོད་ལྟའི་ཤོག་བུ་ (tsȍȍdɛ shɔ̄gbu) litmus paper, test paper.

ཚོད་ལྟའི་ས་གནས་ (tsȍȍdɛ sānɛɛ̀) sm. ཚོད་ལྟ་བྱེད་ས་.

ཚོད་ལྟར་འཚོང་བའི་ཐོན་རྫས་ (tsȍȍdar tsōŋwɛ tȍndzɛɛ̀) sm. འཚོང་ཚོད་ཐོན་ཚད་.

ཚོད་ལྟར་འཛུགས་ (tsȍȍdar dūù) va. to put into operation as a trial, to establish on a trial basis.

ཚོད་བལྟས་ར་སྤྲོད་ (tsȍȍdɛɛ̀ ra̱dröö) verify/ prove by testing or by having a trial; va.—བྱེད་.

ཚོད་སྟོན་ཁང་ (tsȍȍdöngaŋ) kitchen (for vegetable dishes).

ཚོད་བལྟ་ (tsȍȍda) sm. ཚོད་ལྟ་.

ཚོད་ཐིག (tsȍȍ tīg) vi. to appraise, to estimate, to judge, to guess. ¶ ཟ་ཚོད་མ་ཐིག་ན་ If you don't judge correctly (how much) to eat. ¶ ད་རེས་ཚོང་འདི་ཡག་པོ་ཡོང་མིན་ཚོད་ཐིག་གི་མི་འདུག I can't estimate whether sales these days will be good or bad.

ཚོད་ཐིག་པ་བྱེད་ (tsȍȍ tīgbə ce̱è) va. to estimate, to appraise/ judge.

ཚོད་ཐིག་པོ་ (tsȍȍ tīgbu) good appraiser/ estimater.

ཚོད་འདེབས་ (tsȍndeb) trial/ test/ experimental planting; va.—བྱེད་.

ཚོད་དོ་དཔྱད་ (tsȍȍdo yūù) va. to test/ check sth. ¶ ངས་གནས་ཚུལ་དེ་གོ་ཡོད་མེད་ཁོས་ང་ལ་ཚོད་དོ་དཔྱད་གི་འདུག He is testing to see if I had heard that information. [Lit. to throw a stone to test (the depth of) a water].

ཚོད་ལྡན་ (tsȍndɛn) sm. ཚོད་འཛིན་པོ་.

ཚོད་སྡེར་ (tsȍȍder) a plate for serving/ eating vegetable dishes.

ཚོད་སྡོར་ (tsȍȍdɔr) meat used in vegetable dishes.

ཚོད་དཔག (tsȍȍbaà) estimating, guessing; va.—བྱེད་ to guess, to estimate ¶ ད་ལོའི་སྟོན་ཐོག་ག་ཚོད་ཡོང་མིན་ཚོད་དཔག་བྱེད་ཁག་པོ་རེད་ It's hard to estimate how much this year's harvest will be.

ཚོད་དཔག་གྲངས་ཚད་ (tsȍȍbaà tra̱ndzɛɛ̀) probability (in math).

ཚོད་དཔག་ཆུང་དྲགས་ (tsȍȍbaà cūŋdraà) underestimation, underrating; va.—བྱེད་.

ཚོད་དཔག་ཆེ་དྲགས་ (tsȍȍbaà cēdraà) overestimation, overrating; va.—བྱེད་.

ཚོད་དཔག་ཐིག་པོ་ (tsȍȍbaà tīgbu) an accurate estimate/ guess/ prediction.

ཚོད་དཔག་དམའ་བ་ (tsȍȍbaà ma̱awa) underestimating, underrating.

ཚོད་དཔག་རན་པོ་ (tsȍȍbaà rɛ̱mbo) sm. ཚོད་དཔག་ཐིག་པོ་.

ཚོད་སྤྱོད་ (tsȍȍ jȍȍ) testing and utilizing.

ཚོད་སྤྱོད་དངོས་རྫས་ (tsȍȍjȍȍ ŋȍȍzɛɛ̀) trial/ test products.

ཚོད་སྤྱོད་དུས་ཡུན་ (tsȍȍjȍȍ tu̱u̱yün) probation period, trial period.

ཚོད་སྤྱོད་དཔེ་དེབ་ (tsȍȍjȍȍ) trial book.

ཚོད་བྱེད་ (tsȍȍjeè) 1. sm. ཚོད་འཛིན་. 2. va. to estimate, to guess ¶ ཚོད་བྱས་ན་ཨ་རི་རུ་བོད་མི་ཉིས་སྟོང་ཙམ་ཡོད་པ་རེད་ If (I) take a guess, there are about two thousand Tibetans in America. 3. (vb. + —) to limit/ restrict/ restrain sth. ¶ བྲོད་ཟ་ཚོད་མ་བྱས་ན་ན་གི་རེད་ If you don't restrain your eating you will get ill.

ཚོད་བྱེད་དབང་རྩ་ (tsȍȍjeè wāŋdza) sensory nerves.

ཚོད་བྲིས་ (tsȍȍdrii) freehand drawing/ painting.

ཚོད་མ་ (tsȍȍma) vegetable dishes/ meals.

ཚོད་མ་མཁན་ (tsȍȍmagɛn) a cook.

ཚོད་མ་འཁྱག་པོ་ (tsȍȍma kyāgbo) cold vegetable dish.

ཚོད་མ་རྒྱང་བསྙལ་ (tsȍȍma gya̱ŋñɛɛ) pickled vegetables.

ཚོད་མ་སྙོལ་ (tsȍȍma ñȍȍ) va. to pickle vegetables.

ཚོད་མ་གསེར་སྐྱུད་ (tsȍȍma sēēgüü) asparagus.

ཚོད་མེད་ (tsȍȍmeè) sm. ཚད་མེད་.

ཚོད་མེད་པ་ (tsȍȍmeèba) sm. ཚད་མེད་.

ཚོད་རྩིས་ (tsȍȍdzii) 1. anticipating/ calculating sb.'s reaction (and acting accordingly); va.—བྱེད་ ¶ འཛམ་གླིང་ཡུལ་ཁག་གི་གནས་བབ་ལ་ཚོད་རྩིས་བྱས་ནས་དམག་བརྒྱབ་པ་རེད་ Calculating the situation of the nations of the world, (they) made war. 2. estimating, guessing; va.—བྱེད་ ¶ ཚོད་རྩིས་བྱས་ན་

བོད་ལ་མི་འབོར་ས་ཡ་དྲུག་ཙམ་ཡོད་པ་རེད་ If I make a guess, the population in Tibet is about 6 million.

ཚོད་རྩིས་རྣམ་བཤད་ (tsȫȫdzii nāmshɛɛ̀) theory of probability.

ཚོད་རྩིས་རིན་གོང་ (tsȫȫdzii ringoŋ) estimated cost/ price.

ཚོད་ཚོད་ (tsȫȫodzȫȫ) 1. unreliable ¶ མི་འདི་ཚོད་ཚོད་ཅིག་འདུག This person is unreliable. 2. guessing, speculating, doing sth. when one is not certain about it; va.—བྱེད་ to make a guess, to speculate ¶ ཚོད་ཚོད་བྱས་ན་བོད་ལ་མི་འབོར་ས་ཡ་དྲུག་ཙམ་ཡོད་པ་རེད་ If I make a guess, the population in Tibet is about 6 million.

ཚོད་ཚོད་ཚ་པོ་ (tsȫȫdzȫȫ tsābo) 1. person who does things when he is not certain, a person who talks about a subject even when he doesn't know about it. 2. an unreliable/ undependable person ¶ མི་འདི་ཚོད་ཚོད་ཚ་པོ་ཞིག་འདུག This man is unreliable.

ཚོད་ཚོད་ཚོད་ལ་ (tsȫȫdzȫȫ tsȫȫla) going or doing sth. without knowing clearly where to go or what to do; va.—འགྲོ་; —བྱེད་.

ཚོད་དཔག (tsȫȫbaà) estimate, guess, estimating, guessing; va.—བྱེད་.

ཚོད་དཔག་བྱས་པར་གཞིགས་ན་ (tsȫȫbaà jɛɛ̀bar shignə) basing on an estimate/ guess.

ཚོད་འཛིན་ (tsȫndzin) 1. see ཚོད་. 2. controlling, regulating, restricting; va.—བྱེད་ to control/ to restrict/ regulate ¶ ནས་འདེབས་རྒྱ་ཨེ་ཀར་ ༡༠༠༠ ཙམ་ལ་ཚོད་འཛིན་བྱས་པ་རེད་ They restricted the planting of barley to 1000 acres. ¶ གཞུང་ནས་ནང་འདྲེན་ཚོང་ཟོག་ཚོད་འཛིན་བྱེད་ཀྱི་ཡོད་པ་རེད་ The government regulates the imports of goods. ¶ ཁོ་མོ་ཊ་རར་གཏོང་དགོས་ཡོད་ཙང་ཨ་རག་འཐུང་ཚོད་འཛིན་དགོས་བྱུང་བ་རེད་ Since he had to drive, he had to restrict his drinking of alcohol. 3. slang. 'you'd better watch out' ¶ ཁྱོད་རང་གཉིས་ཚོད་ཟུངས་ཨང་རྒན་པའི་ཁ་མ་ཉན་ན་ངས་གཏོར་གྱི་ཡིན་ You two had better watch out. If you don't listen to your elders I will beat you.

ཚོད་འཛིན་གྲངས་ཀ་ (tsȫndzin traŋga) regulated/ controlled/ scheduled figure or number.

ཚོད་འཛིན་འགག་སྒོ་ (tsȫndzin gaggo) water flow regulator, check gate, regulating sluice dam.

ཚོད་འཛིན་དམ་པོ་ (tsȫndzin tambo) tight or strict regulation/ control.

ཚོད་འཛིན་པོ་ (tsȫȫ dzimbu) self-controlled ¶ མི་འདི་ཚོད་འཛིན་པོ་འདུག The man has great self-control.

ཚོད་འཛིན་ཡོ་བྱད་ (tsȫndzin yojɛɛ̀) regulation/ control implements.

ཚོད་འཛུགས་ (tsȫȫdzuù) sm. ཚོད་ལྟར་འཛུགས་.

ཚོད་ཟིན་ (tsȫȫsin) sm. ཚོད་འཛིན་.

ཚོད་ཟིམ་པོ་ (tsȫȫ simbu) ཚོད་འཛིན་པོ་.

ཚོད་ཟུངས་ (tsȫȫ suŋ) see ཚོད་འཛིན་, 3.

ཚོད་གཟིགས་ (tsȫȫ sii) va. to experiment/ try/ test.

ཚོད་བཟུང་ (tsȫȫ suŋ) p. of ཚོད་འཛིན་.

ཚོད་བཟོ་ (tsȫȫso) trial manufacture, trying out, making sth. as a test; va.—བྱེད་ to try out, to trial manufacture ¶ ཞིང་ལས་ལག་ཆ་དཔེ་གསར་ཚོད་བཟོ་བྱས་པ་རེད་ They manufactured the new agricultural implements on a trial basis.

ཚོད་ར་ (tsȫȫra) sm. ཚལ་ཞིང་.

ཚོད་རན་པོ་ (tsȫȫ rɛmbo) good estimate/ guess, not too much or too little, the right amount ¶ ཁ་ལག་ཚོད་རན་པོ་བཟས་པ་རེད་ (They) ate the right amount of food.

ཚོད་ལ་སླེབས་ (tsȫȫla lēb) vi. the time for sth. has arrived/ occurred ¶ ཁོས་ང་ལ་ད་ལོག་ཚོད་དུ་སླེབས་འདུག་ཟེར་བྱུང་ He said to me, "now it has reached the time to go home."

ཚོད་ལེན་ (tsȫȫlen) sm. ཚོད་ལྟ་.

ཚོད་ལོངས་ (tsȫȫloŋ) sm. ཚོད་ལོན་.

ཚོད་ལོན་ (tsȫȫ lön) vi. to take the measure of sb. and act accordingly ¶ སློབ་ཕྲུག་རྣམས་ནས་དགེ་རྒན་གྱི་ཚོད་ལོན་ནས་གང་བྱུང་བྱེད་ཀྱི་ཡོད་པ་རེད་ The students took measure of the teacher and were misbehaving.

ཚོད་ཤེས་ (tsȫȫsheè) knowing or understanding what is suitable/ appropiate/ correct.

ཚོད་བཤད་ (tsȫȫshɛɛ̀) supposition, hypothesis.

ཚོད་གསོ་ (tsȫȫso) raising/ breeding/ cultivating/ rearing as a trial or test or experiment; va.—བྱེད་.

ཚོན་ (tsȫn) 1. color ¶ ཚོན་དམར་པོ་ Red color. 2. paint; va.—གཏོང་; —འདྲུག་ to paint ¶ ཚོན་དམར་པོ་བཏང་བ་ཡིན་ I painted (it) red. 3. ch. inch ¶ སྐུད་པ་ཚོན་གང་ An inch of thread. 4. ch. a village (an administrative unit immediately below a xiang in TAR).

ཚོན་བཀྲ་ (tsȫndra) 1. colorful, multicolored, bright, gay. 2. color ¶ དཔར་ཚོན་བཀྲ་ Color photograph. ¶ གློག་ཤོག་ཚོན་ཁྲ་ Color film.

ཚོན་བཀྲག (tsȫndraà) sm. ཚོན་བཀྲ་.

ཚོན་སྐུད་ (tsȫngüü) dyed thread.

ཚོན་ཁྲ་ (tsȫntra) sm. ཚོན་བཀྲ་.

ཚོན་ཁྲའི་གློག་བརྙན་ (tsȫndrɛ lōŋñɛn) technicolor motion picture.

ཚོན་ཅན་གློག་སྒྲོན་ (tsȫnjen lōgdrön) colored lights.

ཚོན་ཆེན་ (tsȫnjen) color that does not fade.

ཚོན་ལྗང་ (tsȫnjaŋ) 1. green color. 2. a mineral used in Tibetan medicine (malechite green).

ཚོན་དར་ (tsȫndar) colored flag.

ཚོན་གདན་ (tsȫndɛn) the base color for painting.

ཚོན་མདངས་ (tsȫndaŋ) color, sheen, hue (of color).

ཚོན་མདངས་རྣམ་པར་བཀྲ་བ་ (tsȫndaŋ nāmbar drāwa) very colorful, brilliantly colored.

ཚོན་མདོག (tsȫndɔɔ̀) color ¶ ཚོན་མདོག་དམར་པོ་ Red color.

ཚོན་ལྡན་ (tsȫndɛn) colored, having color, colorful ¶ གློག་ཤོག་ཚོན་ལྡན་ Color film.

ཚོན་ལྡན་བརྙན་འཕྲིན་ (tsȫndɛn ñɛ̄ndrin) color television.

ཚོན་སྣ་རྡེབ་ (tsȫnna deb) va. to draw in color.

ཚོན་སྣུམ་ (tsȫnnum) oil based paint (as opposed to water color paint).

ཚོན་པིར་ (tsȫnbir) tib. ch. paint brush.

ཚོན་པོ་ (tsȫmbo) fat, fatty ¶ ཤ་ཚོན་པོ་ Fatty meat.

ཚོན་བྲིས་ (tsȫndrii) color painting ¶ འདི་ནི་བོད་པའི་ཚོན་བྲིས་ཤིག་རེད་ This is a Tibetan painting done in color.

ཚོན་མེད་སྐྱ་བྲིས་ (tsȫnmeè) the sketching in black and white that is done before the actual painting.

ཚོན་མེད་གློག་བརྙན་ (tsȫnmeè lōɔñɛn) black and white motion picture.

ཚོན་དམར་ (tsȫnmar) red color.

ཚོན་རྩི་ (tsȫndzi) lacquer, enamel, varnish; va.—གཏོང་.

ཚོན་རྩི་བ་ (tsȫndziwə) painter.

ཚོན་རྩིའི་ཡོ་ཆས་ (tsȫndzii yojɛɛ̀) lacquered porcelain, lacquerware.

ཚོན་རྩིའི་ཡོ་བྱད་ (tsȫndzii yojɛɛ̀) lacquered porcelain, lacquerware.

ཚོན་རིས་ (tsȫnrii) decorative painting.

ཚོན་ལས་ (tsȫnlɛɛ̀) painting work.

ཚོན་ལེན་པོ་ (tsȫn lembo) a material/ substance that takes paint well.

ཚོན་ལོང་ (tsȫnloŋ) color blind.

ཚོན་གསོལ་ (tsȫnsöö) painting sth. such as a walls; va.—གཏོང་.

ཚོམ་ (tsōm) 1. see ཐེ་ཚོམ་. 2. abbr. of ཚོམ་པ་. 3. sm. ཚོམ་བུ་.

ཚོམ་ཆུང་མཐུག་འདེབས་ (tsōmjuŋ tūŋdeb) sm. ཚོམ་ཆུང་འཐུག་འདེབས་.

ཚོམ་ཆུང་འཐུག་འདེབས་ (tsōmjuŋ tūŋdeb) close serried planting, cluster planting.

ཚོམ་པ་ (tsōmba) 1. sm. ཚོམ་བུ་. 2. hesitation, doubt.

ཚོམ་བུ་ (tsōmbu) 1. bunch, bundle ¶ མེ་ཏོག་ཚོམ་བུ་ A bunch of flowers.

ཚོམ་མེ་བ་ (tsōmmewa) with hesitation/ doubt.

ཚོམས་ (tsōm) 1. a hall. 2. imp. of འཚམ་.

ཚོམས་ཁང་ (tsōmgaŋ) assembly hall.
ཚོམས་ཆེན་ (tsōmjen) 1. a reception/ audience room. 2. an assembly hall.
ཚོམས་ཆེན་ཤར་ (tsōmjen shāā) shung. the East Audience Hall in the Potala Palace.
ཚོམས་ཇ་ (tsomja) a prayer assembly meeting of the monastic ཁང་ཚན་ unit at which tea is served.
ཚོར་ (tsɔ̄ɔ̄) vi. to feel, to sense ༡འཚོ་བ་ཡར་རྒྱས་བྱུང་ཙང་དགའ་སྣང་ཚོར་གྱི་འདུག Because (my) livelihood improved, I feel happy. ༡སྒྲ་གོ་ནས་མི་ཡོད་པ་ཚོར་བྱུང་ I sensed there was someone there after hearing the sound.
ཚོར་རྒྱུ་ (tsɔ̄ɔ̄gyu) see གོ་རྒྱུ་ཚོར་རྒྱུ་.
ཚོར་ངད་ (tsɔ̄ɔ̄ŋeè) the power of sense/ feeling.
ཚོར་ཉམས་ (tsɔ̄rñam) feeling, sensation, perception.
ཚོར་འདུ་ (tsɔ̄ɔ̄ndu) sm. ཚོར་ཉམས་.
ཚོར་སྣང་ (tsɔ̄rnaŋ) sm. ཚོར་བ་.
ཚོར་སྣང་སྐྱེན་པོ་ (tsɔ̄rnaŋ gyēnbo) sm. ཚོར་བ་རྣོན་པོ་.
ཚོར་བ་ (tsɔ̄rwa) sense, feeling ༡ཚོར་བ་བདེ་བ་ Pleasant (happy) feeling/ sensation.
ཚོར་བ་ཉམས་ (tsɔ̄rwa ña̱m) vi. to be paralyzed, to lose the sense of feeling.
ཚོར་བ་བཏང་སྙོམས་ (tsɔ̄rwa dāŋñom) feeling of equanimity.
ཚོར་བ་དྲུག (tsɔ̄rwa tru̱ù) the six senses according to Tibetan medicine: sight, smell, hearing, taste, touch and consciousness.
ཚོར་བ་རྣོན་པོ་ (tsɔ̄rwa nōnbo) sensitive/ keen in perception, quick to sense.
ཚོར་བ་གསུམ་ (tsɔ̄rwa sūm) the three feelings: happiness, sadness and equanimity.
ཚོར་བའི་ཟུག་ཟུ་ (tsɔ̄rwɛ su̱gŋu) feeling of pain.
ཚོར་བའི་རང་བཞིན་ (tsɔ̄rwɛ ra̱ŋshin) sensitivity.
ཚོར་དབང་ (tsɔ̄rwaŋ) organs of the senses.
ཚོར་བྱེད་དབང་པོ་ (tsɔ̄rjeè wāŋbo) sm. ཚོར་དབང་.
ཚོར་མེད་ (tsɔ̄rmeè) without feeling/ sensation.
ཚོར་ཤེད་ (tsɔ̄rshuù) the power of feeeling/ sensation.
ཚོལ་ (tsȫȫ) imp. of འཚོལ་.
ཚོས་ (tsȫȫ) 1. dye, paint; va.—རྒྱག་; —བྱེད་ to dye; vi.—འགོ་ to accidentally get paint (on oneself or things); vi.—ཐེབས་ to take or absorb dye/ paint well. 2. vi. to be/ get cooked ༡ཤ་ཚོས་སོང་ The meat is cooked. 3. imp. of འཚོད་. 4. vi. to be steeped/ imbued/ permeated with sth. ༡སྣུམ་གྱིས་ཚོས་ Permeated with oil. 5. color ༡རུ་དར་ཚོས་ཚོགས་འདུ་མིན་ The unit's flags with various different colors.
ཚོས་སྐྱུག (tsȫȫ gyūù) vi. to run (for a color/ dye).
ཚོས་སྒྱུར་ (tsȫȫgyur) sm. ཚོས་དག.
ཚོས་ཁང་ (tsȫȫgaŋ) dyeing shop/ plant.
ཚོས་ཁུ་ (tsȫȫgu) liquid paint.
ཚོས་ཁོག (tsȫȫgɔɔ̀) dyeing pot.
ཚོས་ཁྲ་ (tsȫȫdra) sm. ཚོས་གྲ་.
ཚོས་ཁྲལ་ (tsȫȫdrɛɛ) 1. tax on dye. 2. tax requiring provision of dyes.
ཚོས་མཁན་ (tsȫȫñɛn) sb. who does dyeing work.
ཚོས་གྲ་མ་སྙོམས་པ་ (tsȫȫ tra̱ma ñōmba) uneven color (of sth, that has been dyed.
ཚོས་གྲ་ཤོར་ (tsȫȫdra shɔ̄ɔ̄) vi. to get uneven coloring (when dyeing).
ཚོས་འགོ་ (tsȫȫ go̱) vi. to have a color run onto another ༡སྟོད་ཐུང་དཀར་པོ་དེར་སྟོད་ཐུང་དམར་པོ་དེའི་ཚོས་འགོས་བཞག The red shirt's dye ran onto the white shirt.
ཚོས་འགྲིབ་ (tsȫȫ dri̱b) vi. to not take/ absorb a dye.
ཚོས་རྒྱག་འཁོར་ཁང་ (tsȫȫgyaà kɔ̄ɔ̄gaŋ) dyeing shop.
ཚོས་རྒྱུ་ (tsȫȫgyu) pigment, coloring material.
ཚོས་རྒྱུག (tsȫȫgyuù) a pole to mix dyes/ paints.
ཚོས་སྒྱུར་བཟོ་གྲྭ་ (tsȫȫgyur so̱dra) printing and dyeing mill ༡སྲིང་བལ་གྱི་འཁིལ་ཐག་ཚོས་སྒྱུར་བཟོ་གྲྭ་ Cotton textile printing and dyeing mill.
ཚོས་སྒྲིག (tsȫȫdrig) layers of colored materials arranged on sth. ༡གུར་འགོ་སྣམ་ཚོས་སྒྲིག A tent with layers of colored woolen cloth arranged on it.
ཚོས་གཅིག་མ་ (tsȫȫ ji̱gmə) monochromatic.
ཚོས་བཅད་ (tsȫȫ jɛ̱ɛ̀) a thin line between two different colors.
ཚོས་ཆེན་ (tsȫȫjen) vegetable dye.
ཚོས་ཉིས་མ་ (tsȫȫ ñi̱imə) things with only two colors.
ཚོས་ཉེས་ཤོར་ (tsȫȫ ñeè shɔ̄ɔ̄) vi. to not take a dye.
ཚོས་ཏ་ (tsȫȫda) coloring agent added when dyeing.
ཚོས་རྟགས་ (tsȫȫdaà) identification mark on things to be dyed indicating the color to be dyed.
ཚོས་འཐག་བཟོ་གྲྭ་ (tsȫȫdaà so̱dra) dyeing and textile mill.
ཚོས་ཐེབས་ (tsȫȫ tēb) vi. to take or absorb a dye.
ཚོས་དག་ (tsȫȫ ta̱à) vi. to have color wash/ fade away.
ཚོས་གདན་ (tsȫȫdɛn) the base dye.
ཚོས་མདངས་ (tsȫȫdaŋ) color.
ཚོས་མདོག་ (tsȫndɔɔ̀) color; va.—སྒྲིལ་ to match colors to see which ones go together or complement each other. va.—སྒྱུར་ to change colors ༡སྟོད་ཐུང་ཚོས་མདོག་དམར་པོ་གཅིག A red colored shirt.
ཚོས་མདོག་ཡལ་ (tsȫȫdɔɔ̀ yɛ̱ɛ) sm. ཚོས་དག.
ཚོས་མདོག་ལོག (tsȫȫdɔɔ̀ lɔ̱ɔ̀) vi. to have a color change into another color (e.g., due to exposure to sunlight).
ཚོས་ལྡན་འཁེལ་འཐག་བཟོ་གྲྭ་ (tsȫȫdɛn kēldaà so̱dra) yarn-dyeing textile mill.
ཚོས་ལྡན་ཤེལ་སྒོ་ (tsȫȫdɛn shēēgo) colored glass.
ཚོས་ནག (tsȫȫnaà) black dye/ paint.
ཚོས་སྣག (tsȫȫnaà) an ink made from dye.
ཚོས་པ་ (tsȫȫba) a person who does dyeing.
ཚོས་པོད་ (tsȫȫbii) sm. ཚོས་བུད་.
ཚོས་པོ་ (tsȫȫbo) well-cooked ༡ཤ་ཚོས་པོ་བྱུང་མི་འདུག The meat hasn't been well cooked.
ཚོས་བུད་ (tsȫȫbüü) ཚོས་དག.
ཚོས་བྱི་ (tsȫȫ ji̱) sm. ཚོས་དག.
ཚོས་བྱེད་ (tsȫȫjeè) 1. ཚོས་རྒྱག. 2. red sandalwood.
ཚོས་འབུད་ (tsȫȫ bü̱ü) va. to wash/ bleach out a color.
ཚོས་སྦྱོར་རྫས་ (tsȫȫjɔɔ dzɛ̱ɛ̀) a mordant (for dyeing).
ཚོས་མ་ (tsȫȫma) 1. a person who does dyeing (female). 2. anything that has been dyed.
ཚོས་འཛིན་ (tsȫȫ dzi̱n) sm. ཚོས་ཐེབས་.
ཚོས་གཞི་ (tsȫȫshi) sm. ཚོས་མདོག.
ཚོས་ཚོགས་ (tsȫȫdɔɔ̀) see ཚོས་, 4.
ཚོས་ཛ་ (tsȫȫdza) dyeing bowl/ pot.
ཚོས་ཞུད་ (tsȫȫ shü̱ü) sm. ཚོས་དག.
ཚོས་གཞི་ (tsȫȫshi) color; vi.—འགྱུར་ to have a color change (e.g., due to sunlight).
ཚོས་གཞི་ནོན་པོ་ (tsȫȫshi no̱mbo) a deep color.
ཚོས་གཞི་མ་སྙོམས་པ་ (tsȫȫ shi̱mə ñōmba) sm. ཚོས་གྲ་མ་སྙོམས་པ་.
ཚོས་གཞི་ཟབ་པོ་ (tsȫȫshi sa̱bbo) sm. ཚོས་གཞི་ནོན་པོ་.
ཚོས་གཞི་ཡལ་ (tsȫȫshi yɛ̱ɛ) sm. ཚོས་མདོག་ཡལ་.
ཚོས་ཟ་ (tsȫȫ sa̱) sm. ཚོས་ལེན་.
ཚོས་ཟ་བྱེད་རྫས་ཕྲ་ (tsȫȫ sa̱jeè dzɛ̱ɛ̀dra) chromosome.
ཚོས་ཟུག (tsȫȫsug) ཚོས་ཐེབས་.
ཚོས་ལངས་ (tsȫȫ la̱ŋ) vi. to have dye "rise" (come out) after fermenting.
ཚོས་ལས་ (tsȫȫlɛɛ̀) dyeing work.
ཚོས་ལེན་ (tsȫȫlen) sm. ཚོས་ཐེབས་.
ཚོས་ལེན་རྫས་ཕྲ་ (tsȫȫlen dzɛ̱ɛ̀dra) sm. ཚོས་ཟ་བྱེད་རྫས་ཕྲ་.
ཚོས་ལོག (tsȫȫ lɔ̱ɔ̀) vi. to have a color change or fade.
ཚོས་བཤུ་ (tsȫȫ shū) sm. ཚོས་འབུད་.
ཚོས་སར་ (tsȫȫsaa) sm. ཚོས་གསར་.
ཚོས་སེར་སྡོང་པོ་ (tsȫȫsee do̱ŋbo) Chinese pagoda tree.
ཚོས་སེར་ཤིང་ཐུར་དཔྱང་མ་ (tsȫȫsee shi̱ŋdur jāŋma) Chinese pagoda tree.
ཚོས་གསར་ (tsȫȫsaa) 1. chemical dye/ paint. 2. new

paint/ dye.

ཚོས་བཙང་རྒྱག (tsōōsaŋ gyaà) va. to rinse a material after being dyed.

ཚོས་གསར་ (tsōōsaa) new paint; va.—གཏོང་ ། ཁང་པར་ཚོས་གསར་བཏང་བ་རེད་ The house was given a new coat of paint.

ཚྭ་ (tsā) salt.

ཚྭ་ཁ་ (tsāga) salt field.

ཚྭ་ཁ་མཐོན་པོ་ (tsāga tōmbo) salty.

ཚྭ་ཁང་ (tsāgaŋ) storage house for salt.

ཚྭ་ཁས་ (tsāgɛɛ̀) sm. ཚྭ་ཁུག, 2.

ཚྭ་ཁུ་ (tsə̄gu) 1. salty; vi.—ཆགས་; vi.—བྱེད་ to become salty; va.—བཟོ་ to make salty. 2. salty liquid.

ཚྭ་ཁུ་ཚ་ཀྱང་ (tsə̄gu tsāgyaŋ) completely salty.

ཚྭ་ཁུ་བཟོ་གྲྭ (tsə̄gu sodra) salt factory.

ཚྭ་ཁུག (tsə̄guù) 1. pouch/ bag for holding salt. 2. vi. to be too salty (for foods).

ཚྭ་ཁྲོག་ཁྲོག (tsā trɔ̄ɔ̀drɔɔ̀) slightly salty.

ཚྭ་ཁྲོན་ (tsādrön) salt well.

ཚྭ་ཁྲོམ་ (tsādrom) salt market.

ཚྭ་གོང་ (tsāgoŋ) price of salt.

ཚྭ་རྒྱག (tsā gyaà) va. to salt, to put salt on sth.

ཚྭ་རྒྱུ་ (tsə̄gyu) halogen.

ཚྭ་རྒྱུ་འགྱུར་རྫས་ (tsə̄gyu gyurdzɛɛ̀) halogenide, halide.

ཚྭ་སྒོ་ (tsāgo) sm. བ་ཚྭ་.

ཚྭ་སྒོ་བ་ཚྭ་ཅན་ (tsāgo tsājɛn) sm. བ་ཚྭ་ཅན་.

ཚྭ་ཅང་ (tsā jāŋ) vi. to be under salted (for tea, food, etc.) ། ཁ་ལག་ཚྭ་ཅང་བཞག The food doesn't have enough salt.

ཚྭ་གཅག (tsājaà) sm. ཚྭ་ཅང་.

ཚྭ་ཆུ་ (tsə̄ju) salt water.

ཚྭ་ཉུང་ (tsāñuŋ) sm. ཚྭ་ཅང་.

ཚྭ་གཏེར་ (tsāder) salt mine.

ཚྭ་ལྟ་ (tsāda) va. to taste (tea or food) to see if there is enough salt.

ཚྭ་ལྟས་ལང་ (tsādɛɛ̀ laŋ) vi. to desire sth. salty to eat.

ཚྭ་ཐུབ་ (tsədub) salt resistant.

ཚྭ་ཐུབ་ལོ་ཏོག (tsədub lodoò) salt-resistant crops.

ཚྭ་མཐོས་ (tsədöö) sm. ཚྭ་ཁུག, 2.

ཚྭ་དུགས་ (tsəduù) a warm salt-soaked compression used to treat aches and pains.

ཚྭ་འདམ་ཐང་གཞུང་ (tsādam tāŋshuŋ) Tsaidam Basin.

ཚྭ་འདམ་གཞུང་ (tsādam shuŋ) sm. ཚྭ་འདམ་ཐང་.

ཚྭ་འདམ་གཞོངས་ས་ (tsādam shoŋsa) sm. ཚྭ་འདམ་ཐང་གཞུང་.

ཚྭ་རྡོག (tsādɔɔ̀) salt in the shape of a ball.

ཚྭ་ལྡན་ཆུ་མིག (tsādɛn cūmiì) saline spring.

ཚྭ་པ་ (tsāba) a person who goes to collect salt.

ཚྭ་བུལ་དོག (tsā büüdoò) salt and baking soda.

ཚྭ་བུལ་སྣོད་ (tsā büünöö) container for salt and soda.

ཚྭ་སྦྲངས་ (tsājaŋ) marinating food in salty water.

ཚྭ་མང་ (tsāmaŋ) too much salt.

ཚྭ་མེད་ (tsāmeè) without salt.

ཚྭ་མེད་ཆུ་ (tsāmeè cū) unsalted water, fresh water.

ཚྭ་མེད་མཚེའུ་ (tsāmeè tsēwu) fresh water lake.

ཚྭ་ཚལ་ (tsātsɛɛ) salted vegetables.

ཚྭ་ཚོང་ (tsādzoŋ) 1. salt selling business. 2. salt seller.

ཚྭ་ཚོད་ (tsādzöö) salted dishes, pickled vegetables.

ཚྭ་ཚྭ་ (tsādza) 1. sm. ཚ་ཚ་. 2. spark (of fire).

ཚྭ་མཚེའུ་ (tsā tsēwu) salt/ saline lake.

ཚྭ་མཚོ་ (tsātso) sm. ཚྭ་མཚེའུ་.

ཚྭ་རྫིང་ (tsādziŋ) salt pond.

ཚྭ་ཞན་ (tsāshɛn) too little salt.

ཚྭ་ཞིང་ (tsāshiŋ) salt field, salt flat.

ཚྭ་རུ་ (tsāra) salt field, salt flat.

ཚྭ་རུ་ (tsāra) a horn/ utensil used to feed salt to animals.

ཚྭ་ལ་དཀར་པོ་ (tsāla gāābo) borax.

ཚྭ་ལས་ (tsālɛɛ̀) salt work.

ཚྭ་ཤོ་ (tsāsho) 1. shung. tax paid on the sale of salt in tt. 2. shung. salt tax collector in tt.

ཚྭ་གསུར་ (tsāsur) burning salt to expel demons; va.—གཏོང་.

མཚག (tsāg) sm. འཚག.

མཚང་ (tsāŋ) wrongdoing, crime, fault; va.—རྟོལ་; —འབྱིན་ to reveal or expose a crime/ wrongdoing/ fault; va.—འཚྭ་ to try to find faults/ crimes/ wrongdoing; vi.—རྟོལ་ to be/ get exposed.

མཚང་ཁོག (tsāŋgɔɔ̀) 1. pelvis bone. 2. pelvic cavity.

མཚང་ཁོང་ (tsāŋgoŋ) sm. མཚང་ཁོག.

མཚང་འགོས་ (tsāŋgöö) the firstborn puppy or kitten in a litter.

མཚང་ར་ (tsāŋra) buttocks.

མཚང་རའི་ནང་ལོག (tsāŋrɛ naŋlɔɔ̀) pelvic cavity.

མཚན་ (tsɛ̄n) 1. name (h.) ། ཁོང་གི་མཚན་ལ་རྡོ་རྗེ་ཞུ་བ་རེད་ His name is Dorje. 2. night, evening ། མཚན་ལ་ལས་ཀ་འགྲོ་དགོས་ཡོད་ I have to go to work at night.

མཚན་དཀྱིལ་ (tsɛ̄ngyii) 1. middle of the night, midnight. 2. health.

མཚན་རྐུན་ (tsɛ̄ngün) burglar/ thief who comes during the night.

མཚན་རྐུབ་པར་ (tsɛ̄ngubbar) a point around the buttock used for acupuncture.

མཚན་སྐོར་ (tsɛ̄ngɔɔ) night patrol.

མཚན་ཁྲོམ་ (tsɛ̄ndrom) night market/ bazaar.

མཚན་མཁན་ (tsɛ̄nñɛn) abbr. of མཚན་ལྟས་མཁན་པོ་.

མཚན་འཁུར་ (tsɛ̄ngur) shung. responsibilities, duties; va.—བསྐྱངས་; —བཞེས་ to take the responsibility ། ཁོང་གིས་སྲིད་སྐྱོང་གི་མཚན་འཁུར་ལོ་བཞིའི་རིང་བསྐྱངས་སོང་ He took the responsibility of being regent for four years.

མཚན་འཁུར་དམ་བཅའ་ (tsɛ̄ngur tamja) swearing an oath to do sth.

མཚན་འཁྱོངས་ (tsɛ̄ngyoŋ) the whole night continuously.

མཚན་འགྱོལ་ (tsɛ̄n kyöö) vi. to pass/ go through the whole night.

མཚན་གང་ (tsɛ̄ngaŋ) all night, the whole night ། ཁོས་མཚན་གང་ལང་བསྡད་པ་རེད་ He stayed up all night.

མཚན་གུང་ (tsɛ̄nguŋ) sm. མཚན་དགུང་.

མཚན་གྲགས་ (tsɛ̄ndraà) renown, fame.

མཚན་དགུང་ (tsɛ̄nguŋ) midnight.

མཚན་འགེབས་གཏོང་ (tsɛ̄ngeb dōŋ) sm. མཚན་རྒོལ་ (བྱེད་).

མཚན་འགྱུར་ (tsɛ̄ngyur) 1. vi. to have one's name be/ get changed. 2. vi. to have one's sex changed.

མཚན་འགྲུལ་ (tsɛ̄ndrüü) 1. traveling at night; va.—རྒྱག ། ལྷ་སར་མཚན་འགྲུལ་བརྒྱབ་སོང་ (They) traveled at night to Lhasa. 2. going/ roaming around at night looking for fun.

མཚན་རྒོལ་ (tsɛ̄ngöö) night assault/ attack; va.—བྱེད་.

མཚན་རྒྱ་སྡོམ་པ་ (tsɛ̄ngya domba) night curfew.

མཚན་རྒྱག (tsɛ̄n gyaà) va. to go somewhere at night.

མཚན་བརྒལ་ (tsɛ̄ngɛɛ) crossing a river at night; va.—བྱེད་.

མཚན་སྒང་ (tsɛ̄ngaŋ) sm. མཚན་གང་.

མཚན་ངན་ (tsɛ̄nŋɛn) bad reputation/ name ། འདི་འདྲ་གནང་ན་མི་ཚང་ལ་མཚན་ངན་ཡོང་གི་རེད་ If you do this (your) family will get a bad name.

མཚན་ངུ་ (tsɛ̄nŋu) babies crying at night; va.—རྒྱག.

མཚན་གཅིན་ (tsɛ̄njin) night urination/ bed-wetting; vi.—ཤོར་ to accidentally urinate at night.

མཚན་གཅིག་པ་ (tsɛ̄njigbə) 1. h. of མིང་གཅིག་པ་. 2. a bed wetter (at night).

མཚན་མཇུག (tsɛ̄njuù) the period of night that comes after midnight.

མཚན་ཉིད་ (tsɛ̄nñii) 1. essential or natural characteristics. 2. logic, philosophy, dialectics, Buddhist philosophy; va.—རྩོད་ to formally debate Buddhist dialectics/ philosophy, to engage in religious debate.

མཚན་ཉིད་མཁན་པོ་ (tsɛ̄nñii kɛ̄mbo) teacher of Buddhist logic/ dialectics.

མཚན་ཉིད་མཁས་པ་ (tsɛ̄nñii kɛ̀ɛba) an expert in Buddhist logic/ dialectics.

མཚན་ཉིད་གྲྭ་ཚང་ (tsɛ̄nñii tra̱dzaŋ) a monastic college in which Buddhist dialectics is taught.

མཚན་ཉིད་དང་ལྡན་པ་ (tsɛ̄nñiidaŋ dɛ̱mba) having all the qualities/ characteristics associated with a standard ¶ བླ་མ་མཚན་ཉིད་དང་ལྡན་པ་ A lama with all the qualities associated with being a lama.

མཚན་ཉིད་པ་ (tsɛ̄nñiibə) 1. sm. མཚན་ཉིད་མཁས་པ་. 2. having all the characteristics of sth. or sb.

མཚན་ཉིད་ཚང་བ་ (tsɛ̄nñii tsāŋwa) sm. མཚན་ཉིད་པ་, 2.

མཚན་ཉིད་ཡིག་ཆ་ (tsɛ̄nñii yi̱gja) Buddhist texts on dialectics.

ཚན་ཉིད་རིག་པ་ (tsɛ̄nñii ri̱gbə) philosophy, metaphysics.

མཚན་གཉིས་པ་ (tsɛ̄nñiibə) person having dual organs/ genitals, hermaphrodite.

མཚན་གཉིས་མ་ནིང་ (tsɛ̄nñii mə̱niŋ) མཚན་གཉིས་པ་.

མཚན་གཉིས་མེ་ཏོག (tsɛ̄nñii mḛdoò) hermaphrodite flower.

མཚན་སྙན་ (tsɛ̄nñɛn) 1. title, designation. 2. reputation, renown, fame; va.—འཇང་ to lose one's reputation.

མཚན་སྙན་གྲགས་ (tsɛ̄n ñɛ̱ndraà) reputation, renown, fame ¶ མཚན་སྙན་གྲགས་ཡག་པོ་མི་འདུག (His) reputation is not good.

མཚན་སྙན་ཆེན་པོ་ (tsɛ̄nñɛn cēmbo) famous, well-known.

མཚན་སྙན་དམག་མི་ (tsɛ̄nñɛn mɔ̄ɔmi) disabled soldier who was honorably discharged.

མཚན་སྙན་གཟི་བརྗིད་ཅན་ (tsɛ̄nñɛn si̱jijɛn) sm. མཚན་སྙན་ཆེན་པོ་.

མཚན་གཏིབ་གདོང་ (tsɛ̄ndib dōŋ) sm. མཚན་དུང་གཏོང་.

མཚན་གཏོང་མེ་འཁོར་ (tsɛ̄ndoŋ mḛgɔɔ) evening/ night train.

མཚན་བཏགས་ (tsɛ̄ndaà) p. of. མཚན་འདོགས་.

མཚན་རྟགས་ (tsɛ̄ndaà) 1. h. of མིང་རྟགས་. 2. medal (h.) ¶ གསེར་གྱི་མཚན་རྟགས་ Gold medal. 3. the ceremony giving the geshe's degree.

མཚན་ལྟས་ (tsɛ̄ndɛɛ̀) 1. omen, prophecy ¶ མཚན་ལྟས་ངན་པོ་ Bad omen. 2. h. of རྨི་ལྟས་.

མཚན་ལྟས་མཁན་པོ་ (tsɛ̄ndɛɛ̀ kɛ̄mbo) a person who forecasts the future by studying signs.

མཚན་སྟོད་ (tsɛ̄ndöö̀) evening time prior to midnight, first part of the evening.

མཚན་སྟོན་ (tsɛ̄ndön) evening dinner, evening banquet.

མཚན་ཐུན་ (tsɛ̄ndün) the three segments making up a night in tt.

མཚན་ཐུབ་ (tsɛ̄ndub) a butter lamp that burns all night.

མཚན་ཐུབ་གོང་བུ་ (tsɛ̄ndub gōŋbu) sm. མཚན་ཐུབ་.

མཚན་ཐོ་ (tsɛ̄ndo) 1. list of names, a roll (h.). 2. the roll of monks registered in a monastery (by seniority).

མཚན་ཐོབ་ (tsɛ̄ndob) h. of མིང་ཐོབ་.

མཚན་ཐོག་ཐག (tsɛ̄n tɔ̄ɔdaà) the whole/ entire/ all night.

མཚན་མཐུན་དགའ་རོགས་ (tsɛ̄ndün ga̱rɔɔ̀) homosexuality, homosexual partner.

མཚན་མཐོང་ཆུ་ཚོད་ (tsɛ̄ndoŋ cūdzöö̀) illuminated watch.

མཚན་འཐབ་ (tsɛ̄ndəb) night combat; va.—བྱེད་.

མཚན་དུས་ (tsɛ̄ndüǜ) nighttime.

མཚན་དོད་པའི་དུས་ (tsɛ̄ndüübɛ tü̱ǜ) a period during conception when the genitals are beginning to form.

མཚན་དོན་ (tsɛ̄ndön) 1. name, reputation (h.). 2. abbr. of name and meaning.

མཚན་འདོགས་ (tsɛ̄n dɔ̱ɔ̀) h. of མིང་འདོགས་.

མཚན་འདོན་ (tsɛ̄n dö̱n) saying prayers at night.

མཚན་ལྡན་ (tsɛ̄ndɛn) qualified, authentic.

མཚན་དུང་ (tsɛ̄nduŋ) night raid, night assault; va.—གཏོང་.

མཚན་ནག་གུང་ (tsɛ̄nnaàgoŋ) at night, during the night.

མཚན་གནས་ (tsɛ̄nnɛɛ̀) h. of གོ་གནས་.

མཚན་གནས་ཚོ་ལོ་ (tsɛ̄nnɛɛ̀ cōlo) title (h.).

མཚན་སྣང་ (tsɛ̄nnaŋ) lamp.

མཚན་བསྣམས་ (tsɛ̄n nām) h. of མིང་ཁྱེར་.

མཚན་པ་ (tsɛ̄mba) sm. བརྒྱན་པ་.

མཚན་དཔེ་ (tsɛ̄mbe) marks, signs.

མཚན་ཕྱེད་ (tsɛ̄njeè) midnight.

མཚན་ཕྱེད་ཀ་ (tsɛ̄n cēga) half of the night, midnight.

མཚན་བྱ་ (tsɛ̄nja) owl.

མཚན་བྱང་ (tsɛ̄njaŋ) h. of མིང་བྱང་.

མཚན་བྱི་ (tsɛ̄nji) bat.

མཚན་འབྲེལ་ (tsɛ̄ndree) successive nights.

མཚན་སྦག (tsɛ̄nbaà) playing mahjong all night; va.—རྒྱག.

མཚན་སྦྱོང་ (tsɛ̄njoŋ) study or training in the evening/ night.

མཚན་མ་ (tsɛ̄nma) 1. mark, sign, label, symbol. 2. sex; vi.—འགྱུར་ to have one's sex get changed.

མཚན་མ་གཅིག་པའི་འཁྲིག་སྤྱོད་ (tsɛ̄nma ji̱gbɛ tri̱gjöö̀) homosexual.

མཚན་མ་རྟོག་བརྟགས་ (tsɛ̄nma dōgdaà) diagnosing/ assessing a person by his looks.

མཚན་མུན་ (tsɛ̄nmün) the darkness of night.

མཚན་མེད་ (tsɛ̄nmeè) 1. without signs. 2. asexual.

མཚན་མེད་སྐྱེ་འཕེལ་ (tsɛ̄nmeè gyēbel) asexual reproduction.

མཚན་མེད་རྒྱུད་འདྲེས་སྦྱོར་སྡེབ་ (tsɛ̄nmeè gyü̱ndreè jɔ̱deb) asexual reproduction/ crossing/ propagation.

མཚན་མེད་རྒྱུད་འཕེལ་ (tsɛ̄nmeè gyü̱mbel) asexual reproduction/ crossing/ propagation.

མཚན་མེད་རྒྱུད་སྦྱོར་ (tsɛ̄nmeè gyü̱ü̱jɔɔ) sm. མཚན་མེད་རྒྱུད་འཕེལ་.

མཚན་མེད་མ་ནིང་ (tsɛ̄nmeè mə̱niŋ) a person that does not have any sex organs.

མཚན་མེད་མ་ནིང་གི་འཇུག་རྫུལ་ (tsɛ̄nmeè mə̱niŋgi ju̱gdzüü) the 3 neuter finals (ན་ར་ལ་) that take a post final suffix ད་, e.g., ཕྱིནད་.

མཚན་མོ་ (tsɛ̄nmo) night, evening ¶ མཚན་མོའི་སློབ་གྲྭ་ Night school.

མཚན་མོ་གནངས་ཅག (tsɛ̄nmo nāŋjaà) every other night, alternating nights.

མཚན་མོ་ཕྱི་པོ་ (tsɛ̄nmo cību) late at night.

མཚན་མོའི་ཆབ་སྲིད་སློབ་གྲྭ་ (tsɛ̄nmö cəbsii lōbdra) political night school.

མཚན་མོའི་ཐུན་ཚོད་ (tsɛ̄nmö tǖndzöö̀) one fourth of a night.

མཚན་མོའི་ཞུ་འབུལ་ (tsɛ̄nmö shu̱mbüü) evening report (saying Long Live Chairman Mao, etc., in the evening during the Cultural Revolution era).

མཚན་མོའི་རོལ་རྩེད་ཁང་ (tsɛ̄nmö rö̱ö̱dzegaŋ) nightclub.

མཚན་མོའི་ལས་རེས་ཁང་ (tsɛ̄nmö lḛɛreègaŋ) night shift room.

མཚན་མོའི་སློབ་གྲྭ་ (tsɛ̄nmö lōbdra) night school.

མཚན་མོར་ཉིན་ཟློན་སྐོར་གཡེང་ (tsɛ̄nmɔ ñḛnsön gɔ̄ryeŋ) night patrolling.

མཚན་དམས་ (tsɛ̄nmɛɛ̀) denouncing; va.—ཞུ་ ¶ ཁོང་ལ་མཚན་དམས་ཞུས་པ་རེད་ They denounced him.

མཚན་སྨད་ (tsɛ̄nmɛɛ̀) sm. ནམ་སྨད་.

མཚན་ཚད་ (tsɛ̄ndzɛɛ̀) length of a night.

མཚན་ཚོགས་ (tsɛ̄ndzɔɔ̀) evening party/ banquet, evening gathering/ meeting.

མཚན་འཚོ་ (tsɛ̄ndzo) letting animals graze at night.

མཚན་འཛིང་ (tsɛ̄ndziŋ) night fighting/ combat.

མཚན་འཛིན་ (tsɛ̄ndzin) honorary (sb. with a title who does not have to attend or work) ¶ ཚོགས་པའི་མཚན་འཛིན་ཀྲུའུ་ཞི་ The honorary chairman of the party.

མཚན་ཞབས་ (tsɛ̄nshəb) shung. title of monks who assist the Dalai Lama in debating practice, tutor.

མཚན་ཟས་ (tsɛ̄nsɛɛ̀) midnight snack, evening snack.

མཚན་ཟོན་སྐོར་གཡེང་ (tsɛ̄nsön gɔ̄ɔ̄yeŋ) abbr. of མཚན་མོར་ཉིན་ཟོན་སྐོར་གཡེང་.

མཚན་བཟང་པོ་ (tsɛ̄n sa̲ŋbo) auspicious marks/ signs ¶ མཚན་བཟང་པོ་སུམ་ཅུ་རྩ་གཉིས་ The thirty-two auspicious marks of a Buddha.

མཚན་གཟིམ་ཁང་ (tsɛ̄nsimgaŋ) h. of ཉལ་ཁང་.

མཚན་ཡིག (tsɛ̄nyii) signature (h.); va.—འབྲི་; —འགོད་ to sign sth.

མཚན་ཡོད་ (tsɛ̄nyöö) sexual.

མཚན་ཡོད་རྒྱུད་འདྲེས་སྦྱོར་སྡེབ་ (tsɛ̄nyöö gyündreè jɔ̲ɔ̲deb) sexual reproduction/ propagation.

མཚན་ཡོད་རྒྱུད་འཕེལ་ (tsɛ̄nyöö gyü̲mbee) sexual reproduction/ propagation.

མཚན་རངས་པོ་ (tsɛ̄n ra̲ŋbo) the entire/ whole night.

མཚན་ལ་ (tsɛ̄nla) name, reputation (h.) ¶ རང་རིགས་ཀྱི་མཚན་ལ་ The reputation of our nationality.

མཚན་ལ་དཀྱུང་འདེགས་ (tsɛ̄nla gu̲ŋdeg) shung. advancing/ improving the reputation of sth. ¶ གཞུང་སའི་མཚན་ལ་དཀྱུང་འདེགས་ཀྱི་ཞབས་ཞུ་ཧུར་སྐྱེད་བྱུང་བར་བྱ་དགའ་བཙལ་ A award was given (to him) for advancing the reputation of the government.

མཚན་ལམ་ (tsɛ̄nlam) h. of རྨི་ལམ་.

མཚན་ལས་ (tsɛ̄nlɛɛ̀) night shift, night work; va.—བྱེད་ to work at night.

མཚན་ལོང་ (tsɛ̄nloŋ) night blindness.

མཚན་ཤས་ (tsɛ̄nshɛɛ̀) bad reputation/ name; va.—བཟོ་ to give sb. a bad reputation/ name.

མཚན་ཤས་དམའ་འབེབས་ (tsɛ̄nshɛɛ̀ mānjin) slandering/ degrading/ discrediting a reputation; va.—བྱེད་.

མཚན་ཤིང་ (tsɛ̄nshiŋ) a torch.

མཚན་ཤོག (tsɛ̄nshoò) business card, name card (h.).

མཚན་ཤོད་ (tsɛ̄nshöö) va. to interpret/ explain the meaning of a word.

མཚན་བཤར་ (tsɛ̄nshar) marching/ traveling at night.

མཚན་སོ་ (tsɛ̄nso) making the rounds at night, patrolling at night; va.—བྱེད་.

མཚན་སྲུང་ཞོད་བྱ་ (tsɛ̄nsuŋ dü̲ǜja) night duty.

མཚན་གསོལ་ (tsɛ̄nsöö) va. to give a title to sb. (h.).

མཚམས་ (tsām) 1. in between, an interval ¶ གཟིགས་མོ་ལེའུ་དང་པོ་དང་གཉིས་པའི་མཚམས་ Between the first and second part of the show. 2. place where two or more things meet, demarcation line, junction, border, boundary ¶ རི་མཚམས་དེར་གྲོང་ཆུང་ཞིག་ཡོད་པ་རེད་ At the foot of the hill is small town. 3. at/ by the time (usu. vb. + —) ¶ ན་ནིང་ཁོང་ཡོང་བའི་མཚམས་སུ་ At the time he came last year ¶ དེ་མཚམས་ At that time ¶ སྟོན་མཚམས་ At the time of autumn 4. abbr. of མཚམས་འདྲི་. 5. a religious retreat; va.—ལ་སྡོད་; —སྡོམ་ to go/ be on retreat.

མཚམས་ཀྱི་བྱེད་པོ་ (tsāmgi ce̲èbo) 1. arbitrator, mediator. 2. poet. bandits, thieves, robbers.

མཚམས་སྐྱེས་ (tsāmgyeè) abbr. of མཚམས་འདྲི་ and ལེགས་སྐྱེས་.

མཚམས་ཁང་ (tsāmgaŋ) place to do a retreat, hermit's cottage.

མཚམས་འགལ་ (tsām gɛ̲ɛ̲) vi. to exceed or go beyond a limit/ boundary.

མཚམས་བགལ་ (tsām gɛ̲ɛ̲) sm. མཚམས་འགལ་.

མཚམས་བརྒྱད་ (tsāmgyɛɛ̀) the eight intermediate directions, e.g., SE, NW.

མཚམས་སྒོ་ (tsāmgo) the door of a room or cave where a person is in retreat.

མཚམས་གཅིག་ལ་ (tsāmjiglə) at one time, once.

མཚམས་གཅོད་ (tsāmjöö̀) 1. va. to stop/ terminate, to cut off ¶ དགྲ་བོའི་དམག་རྒྱགས་ཀྱི་འོར་འདྲེན་མཚམས་བཅད་པ་རེད་ (They) cut off the enemy's supply lines. 2. person's name (given when parents hope this will be the last child).

མཚམས་ཆད་ (tsām cɛ̄ɛ̀) vi. to come to a halt/ stop ¶ འཕྲུལ་འཁོར་ལ་སྐྱོན་ཤོར་ཙང་ལས་མཚམས་ཆད་པ་རེད་ Work stopped because the machinery broke down. ¶ སྐྱོབ་གསོའི་རོགས་རམ་མཚམས་ཆད་ནས་ལོ་གཅིག་ཙམ་སྲིན་པ་རེད་ It's been about a year since relief aid stopped. ¶ ད་ལྟ་ཙ་ལག་ཉོ་མཁན་མཚམས་ཆད་མ་སོང་ The shoppers haven't stopped coming.

མཚམས་ཆད་མེད་པ་ (tsāmjɛɛ̀ me̲èba) without stopping/ halting/ suspending/ ceasing.

མཚམས་ཆེན་གཅོད་ (tsāmjen jöö̀) 1. va. to cut off/ terminate/ stop all relations. 2. va. to go into total religious retreat.

མཚམས་ཆོད་ (tsām cöö̀) sm. མཚམས་ཆད་.

མཚམས་འཇོག (tsāmjɔɔ̀) stopping, terminating, ending, suspending, leaving off doing; va.—བྱེད་ to stop, to end, to terminate, to cease, to suspend ¶ བཙན་འཛུལ་མཚམས་འཇོག་བྱེད་དགོས་ (You) must stop the aggression. ¶ ཁོ་ཚོའི་ཐོན་སྐྱེད་མཚམས་བཞག་པ་རེད་ They terminated production.

མཚམས་མཉམ་རོལ་འདེབས་ (tsāmñam rö̲ndeb) seeding in rows.

མཚམས་རྟགས་ (tsāmdaà) comma, period (a mark which causes a stop/ pause).

མཚམས་ཐིག (tsāmdig) demarcation line, boundary line.

མཚམས་ཕོ་ (tsāmdo) 1. demarcation line (usu. of a border). 2. a pile of stones placed near a religious retreat to indicate the point beyond which no one may cross; va.—འཛུགས་; —རྒྱག.

མཚམས་གདམ་ (tsām da̲m) va. to stay in a religious retreat.

མཚམས་འདྲི་ (tsāmdri) sm.* འཚམས་འདྲི་.

མཚམས་རྡོ་ (tsāmdo) stone boundary marker.

མཚམས་སྡོམ་ (tsāmdom) see མཚམས་.

མཚམས་པ་བ་ (tsāmbawa) a hermit, a person in religious retreat.

མཚམས་སྤྲིན་ (tsāmdrin) red sky, clouds at sunset; vi.—འཁོར་.

མཚམས་སྦྱོར་ (tsāmjɔɔ) 1. connection, linkage, joining; va.—བྱེད་ to connect/ link up/ join (people) ¶ ངས་ཁོང་ལས་ཁུངས་གསར་པ་ཞིག་ལ་མཚམས་སྦྱོར་བྱས་པ་ཡིན་ I made a connection for him with the new office. 2. introduction ¶ མཚམས་སྦྱོར་ཡི་གེ་ Letter of introduction.

མཚན་སྦྱོར་ངོས་པོ་ (tsāmjɔɔ ŋöö̀bo) connector.

མཚམས་སྦྱོར་ལྷག་བཅས་ཀྱི་སྒྲ་ (tsāmjɔɔ lhāgjɛɛ̀gi dra̲) words in Tibetan grammar that act as a conjunction.

མཚམས་མེད་ (tsāmmeè) without a break, without stop ¶ ལོ་བརྒྱད་རིང་མཚམས་མེད་སློབ་སྦྱོང་བྱས་པ་རེད་ (They) studied eight years without a break.

མཚམས་ཚད་ (tsāmdzɛɛ̀) limit, limitation, restriction (time, amount, quality).

མཚམས་ཚད་མེད་པ་ (tsāmdzɛɛ̀ me̲èba) endless, without limit.

མཚམས་ཚིགས་ (tsāmdzii̖) 1. rhythm ¶ རོལ་མོའི་མཚམས་ཚིགས་ Musical rhythm. 2. limit, restriction ¶ མཚམས་ཚིགས་མེད་པར་འགྲོ་སོང་བཏང་བ་རེད་ (They) spent (money) without any limits.

མཚམས་མཚམས་ (tsāmdzam) sometimes ¶ མོ་མཚམས་མཚམས་ལ་ཡོང་གི་ཡོད་པ་རེད་ She sometimes comes.

མཚམས་ཞུ་ (tsāmshu) 1. sm.* འཚམས་ཞུ་. 2. the section that introduces the main body of a letter.

མཚམས་བཞག (tsām sha̲à) p. of མཚམས་འཇོག.

མཚམས་བཞི་ (tsāmshi) the four intermediate directions: NE, NW, SE, SW.

མཚམས་འགོག་ལ་འཛུག (tsāmwɔɔ̀la ju̲ù) va. to allow/ let people to visit a person who is in retreat (as prearranged by the person in retreat).

མཚམས་ཡས་ (tsāmyɛɛ) sm. མཚམས་མེད་.

མཚམས་རི་ (tsāmri) a mountain that demarcates a boundary.

མཚམས་རེ་ (tsāmre) sm. མཚམས་མཚམས་.

མཚམས་ལ་སྡོད་ (tsāmla dö̲ö) see མཚམས་.

མཚམས་ལན་ (tsāmlɛn) sm.* འཚམས་ལན་.

མཚམས་སྲུང་ (tsāmsuŋ) 1. border guard, guarding the border; va.—བྱེད་ to guard a border.

མཚའ་ལུ་ (tsālu) 1. red rooster. 2. horses or mules with a white patch on their heels.

མཚར་ (tsāā) 1. strange, weird. 2. beautiful.

མཚར་དགའ་ (tsāāga) finding/ considering sth. interesting; va.—བྱེད་.

མཚར་ཆོས་ (tsāājöö) beautiful.

མཚར་གཏམ་ (tsāādam) interesting conversation/ talk.

མཚར་མཐོང་བློ་འགྱུར་ (tsārdoŋ lōgyur) easily swayed, impressionable [Lit. changing one's mind at the sight of sth. beautiful].

མཚར་མདངས་ (tsārdaŋ) beautiful and gleaming/ shining.

མཚར་སྡུག (tsāāduù) beauty, beautiful, gorgeous.

མཚར་སྡུག་ལྡན་པ་ (tsərduù dɛmba) beautiful.

མཚར་སྣང་ (tsārnaŋ cèè) sense or feeling of amazement/ wonder; va.—བྱེད་.

མཚར་པོ་ (tsārbo) beautiful, gorgeous.

མཚར་བ་ (tsārwa) 1. beautiful ། མེ་ཏོག་ལྟར་མཚར་བའི་བུ་མོ་ཞིག་འདུག There is a girl that is beautiful like a flower. 2. remarkable, noteworthy, exceptional, unusual, strange.

མཚར་མེད་ (tsārmeè) usual, common.

མཚར་མེད་བྱིར་བཏང་ (tsārmeè jīidaŋ) sm. མཚར་མེད་.

མཚར་བཟང་ (tsārsaŋ) beautiful, good looking.

མཚལ་ (tsɛ̄ɛ) 1. red (ink). 2. cinnabar (used in Tibetan medicine). 3. h. of ཁྲག.

མཚལ་ཀ་ (tsɛ̄ɛga) sm. མཚལ་མདོག.

མཚལ་དཀར་ (tsɛ̄ɛgar) a type of cinnabar.

མཚལ་སྐྱེས་ (tsɛ̄ɛgyeè) mercury.

མཚལ་ཁ་ (tsɛ̄ɛga) sm. མཚལ་ཀ་.

མཚལ་རྒོད་ (tsɛ̄ɛgöö) cinnabar.

མཚལ་ཐལ་ (tsɛ̄ɛtɛɛ) the ash that remains after extracting mercury from cinnabar.

མཚལ་མདོག (tsɛ̄ndɔɔ) bright red, vermilion red.

མཚལ་པར་ (tsɛ̄ɛbar) scriptures printed with vermilion red ink.

མཚལ་པར་མ་ (tsɛ̄ɛ bārma) sm. མཚལ་པར་.

མཚལ་ཕྱུ་མ་ (tsɛ̄ɛjūmə) sm. ཚ་ཕྱུ་མ་.

མཚལ་བྲིས་ (tsɛ̄ɛdrii) scriptures written with vermilion red ink.

མཚལ་སྦྲམ་ (tsɛ̄ɛdram) small slabs of cinnabar.

མཚལ་མོ་ (tsɛ̄ɛmo) a slightly reddish colored mule.

མཚལ་དམར་ (tsɛ̄ɛmar) 1. cinnabar. 2. a reddish colored mule.

མཚལ་སྨུག (tsɛ̄ɛmug) a dark reddish/ brown colored mule.

མཚལ་ཚྭ་ (tsɛ̄ɛdza) a type of salt used as medicine.

མཚལ་ཡིག (tsɛ̄ɛyii) 1. anything written with red ink. 2. red ink (in sense of a deficit) ། ནོར་སྲིད་ཀྱི་མཚལ་ཡིག Financial deficit.

མཚལ་རིས་ (tsɛ̄ɛrii) a painting done with vermilion paint.

མཚལ་ལུ་ (tsɛ̄ɛlu) sm. མཚའ་ལུ་.

མཚལ་གཤར་ (tsɛ̄ɛshaa) red woolen cloth used on the arch of a Tibetan boot.

མཚུངས་ (tsūŋ) 1. vi. to be alike/ similar ། འདི་གཉིས་མཚུངས་ཀྱི་མི་འདུག These two are not alike. 2. like, just like, similar, along with ། དྲིལ་བསྒྲགས་དེ་མཚུངས་ ༡༩༦༣ དང་ ༦༤ བྱས་པ་རེད་ (They) made a similar announcement in 1963 and 1964. ། ས་ཞིང་བཅོས་སྒྱུར་བྱས་པ་དང་མཚུངས་སྒེར་གྱི་བཟོ་གྲྭ་ཚང་མ་གཞུང་འཛིན་བྱས་པ་རེད་ Just as they reformed the land, (they) nationalized the private factories.

མཚུངས་རྟགས་ (tsūŋdaà) the equal sign (=).

མཚུངས་ལྡན་ (tsūŋdɛn) alike, similar.

མཚུངས་པ་ (tsūŋbə) sm. མཚུངས་, 2.

མཚུངས་པ་གསལ་བྱེད་ཀྱི་སྒྲ་ (tsūŋbə sɛ̄ɛjeègi dra) general term for words that convey two or more things being the same.

མཚུངས་པའི་ཟུར་ (tsūŋbɛ sur) equal angle.

མཚུངས་པོ་ (tsūŋbo) compatible ། འདི་གཉིས་ཚོས་གཞི་མཚུངས་པོ་འདུག These two are compatible colors.

མཚུངས་བྲལ་ (tsūŋdrɛɛ) sm. མཚུངས་མེད་.

མཚུངས་མེད་ (tsūŋmeè) incomparable, matchless ། བཀའ་དྲིན་མཚུངས་མེད་ Incomparable gratitude.

མཚུངས་ཟླ་མེད་པ་ (tsūŋda meèba) sm. མཚུངས་མེད་.

མཚུངས་ཟུར་ (tsūŋsur) abbr. of མཚུངས་པའི་ཟུར་.

མཚུན་ (tsũn) 1. paternal ancestors. 2. protective deities worshipped by paternal ancestors/ lineage. 3. a deceased person.

མཚུན་ཁང་ (tsũngaŋ) the chapel in which one's fathers/ grandfather's deities are kept. 2. tomb.

མཚུན་མཆོད་ (tsũnjöö) paying homage to one's deceased paternal ancestors (fathers/ grandfathers).

མཚུན་གཏོར་ (tsũndɔɔ) torma offered to the deities of one's paternal ancestors.

མཚུན་འཐོར་ (tsũndɔɔ) offerings of blood and meat made to the deities of one's paternal ancestors.

མཚུན་ཞལ་ (tsũnshɛɛ) 1. fire. 2. fire deity.

མཚུན་གསོལ་ (tsũnsöö) sm. མཚུན་འཐོར་.

མཚུན་ལྷ་ (tsũnlha) paternal ancestor's deities.

མཚུར་དཀར་ (tsūrgar) aluminum.

མཚུར་སྔོ་ (tsūrŋo) chalcanthitum (used in Tibetan medicine).

མཚུར་སྔོན་ (tsūrŋön) sm. མཚུར་སྔོ་.

མཚུར་ནག (tsūrnaà) black fibroferitum (used in Tibetan medicine).

མཚུར་དམར་ (tsūrmar) red fibroferitum (used in Tibetan medicine).

མཚུར་སེར་ (tsūrser) yellow fibroferitum (used in Tibetan medicine).

མཚུལ་པ་ (tsǖübə) lips and nose.

མཚུལ་ཤུ་ (tsǖüshu) hissing sound made from the nose.

མཚེ་ (tsē) 1. sm. མཚེ་ལྡུམ་. 2. abbr. of མཚེ་མ་.

མཚེ་དཀར་ (tsēgar) twins (boys).

མཚེ་ཁྲ་ (tsēdrra) boy and a girl twin.

མཚེ་ལྡུམ་ (tsēdum) a type of Chinese ephedra.

མཚེ་ནག (tsēnaà) twins (both girls).

མཚེ་མ་ (tsēma) twins.

མཚེ་མ་སྤུན་ཟླ་ (tsēma būndə) twins.

མཚེ་ཟོར་ (tsēsor) torma containing ephedra that is used to expel evil spirits.

མཚེད་ (tsēè) arc. to bury in a graveyard/ cemetery.

མཚེད་པ་ (tsēèba) graveyard, cemetery.

མཚེའུ་ (tsēwu) small lake, pond.

མཚེའུ་གཉིས་ (tsēwuñii) name of a district in Nagchuka.

མཚེའུ་ཚྭ་ (tsēwu tsā) salt that comes from a lake.

མཚེར་ (tsēr) 1. vi. to be shy ། ཁོང་མཚེར་སོང་ He was shy. 2. shung. temporary residence/ dwelling place, nomad's encampment; va.—སྦྱོར་ to send a person to put names on the doors of private homes that have to provide temporary residence for visiting dignitaries.

མཚེར་རྒྱག (tsērgyaà) a traditional method of treating sick animals.

མཚེར་རྙིང་ (tsērñiŋ) an old/ former/ previous nomad camp.

མཚེར་རྡོ་ (tsērdo) pile of stones used to mark the place where nomads are going to move next.

མཚེར་སྣང་ (tsērnaŋ) 1. shy ། མིའི་ནང་ལ་ཁ་ལག་ཟ་དུས་མཚེར་སྣང་བྱེད་དགོས་མ་རེད་. When eating at sb.'s house you should not be shy. 2. embarrassed ། ཁོང་ར་ཞི་དྲགས་བཟི་ནས་སྐད་ཆ་གང་བྱུང་བཤད་ཙང་གྲོགས་པ་ཚོ་མཚེར་སྣང་བྱུང་སོང་ Because he got very drunk his friends got embarrassed.

མཚེར་པ་ (tsērba) spleen.

མཚེར་པོ་ (tsērbo) sm. མཚེར་སྣང་.

མཚེར་བག (tsērbaà) frightened, scared; va.—བྱེད་.

མཚེར་ཤུལ་ (tsērshüü) remains of a nomad encampment.

མཚེར་ས་ (tsērsa) nomad encampment.

མཚེས་ (tsēè) neighbor.

མཚེས་དཀར་ (tsēègar) horses and other animals

with white heels.

མཚོ་ (tsō) lake.

མཚོ་སྐམ་རྡོ་རུལ་ (tsōgam dorüü) the great and powerful falling, a great family becoming bankrupt [Lit. ocean drying up, stone rotting].

མཚོ་སྐར་ (tsōgar) starfish, sea star.

མཚོ་སྐོར་དམག་གྲུ་ (tsōgɔr māgdru) cruiser (warship).

མཚོ་སྐོར་དམག་གྲུ་ཆེ་གྲས་ (tsōgɔr māgdru cēdrεὲ) heavy cruiser.

མཚོ་སྐྱེས་སྔོ་རིགས་ (tsōgyeè ŋōrig) marine algae/ seaweed.

མཚོ་སྐྱེས་རྡོ་རྗེ་ (tsōgyeè dɔɔje) Padmasambava.

མཚོ་སྐྱོད་ (tsōgyöö) sailing, going on the water; va.—བྱེད་.

མཚོ་ཁ་ (tsōga) bank, shore, harbor, coast.

མཚོ་ཁའི་གྲམ་སྡོང་ (tsōgε tramdoŋ) sm. མཚོ་གྲམ་.

མཚོ་ཁུག (tsōguù) bay, inlet.

མཚོ་ཁུག་ག་ཁྲལ་ (tsōguù katrεε) anchorage tax.

མཚོ་ཁུལ་ (tsōgüü) sea/ ocean area.

མཚོ་ཁོངས་ (tsōgoŋ) territorial waters.

མཚོ་ཁོངས་བཟོ་སྐྲུན་ (tsōgoŋ sodrün) ocean industries.

མཚོ་ཁྱི་ (tsōgyi) sm. མཚོ་དོམ་.

མཚོ་ཁྲི་ཤོར་རྒྱལ་མོ་ (tsōtrishɔɔ gyεεmo) sm. མཚོ་སྔོན་པོ་.

མཚོ་འཁོར་ (tsōgɔɔ) whirlpool.

མཚོ་འཁྱོམ་ཉ་མོ་བཟོད་མ་བདེ་ (tsōgyom ñamo söö made) when there are disturbances in an area people will not be safe anywhere [Lit. when the sea is in turmoil fishes will not be safe].

མཚོ་འཁྲུག (tsōdruù) rough seas, sea in turmoil.

མཚོ་གྲམ་ (tsōdram) tidal land.

མཚོ་གླང་ (tsōlaŋ) a mythological ocean buffalo.

མཚོ་གྲུ་ (tsōdru) ship, seagoing vessel.

མཚོ་གྲུའི་ལས་བྱེད་པ་ (tsōdrüü lεὲjeèba) sm. མཚོ་གྲུའི་ལས་བཟོ་པ་.

མཚོ་གྲུའི་ལས་བཟོ་པ་ (tsōdrü lεὲsowa) seaman, sailor.

མཚོ་གླིང་ (tsōliŋ) island.

མཚོ་འགག (tsōgaà) straits ¶ ཐའི་ཝན་མཚོ་འགག Taiwan straits.

མཚོ་འགྲམ་ (tsōdram) coast, shore.

མཚོ་འགྲིབ་ (tsō drib) vi. to be ebb tide.

མཚོ་འགྲུལ་ (tsōndrüü) sea/ ocean travel; va.— བྱེད་.

མཚོ་འགྲུལ་བཀག་སྡོམ་བཀའ་རྒྱ་ (tsōndrüü gāgdom gāgya) ban on maritime trade/ intercourse.

མཚོ་འགྲུལ་མཁས་པ་ (tsōndrüü kεὲba) navigator.

མཚོ་འགྲུལ་ས་བཀྲ་ (tsōndrüü sābdra) sea/ ocean/ nautical chart.

མཚོ་འགྲུལ་སྲུང་སྐྱེལ་ (tsōndrüü sūŋgyee) 1. defending sea lanes/ sea travel. 2. a convoy for defense.

མཚོ་འགྲུལ་སྲུང་སྐྱེལ་གྱི་སྐྱོགས་གྲུ་ (tsōndrüü sūŋgyeegi gyɔɔdru) frigate.

མཚོ་རྒྱས་ (tsō gyεὲ) vi. to be high tide.

མཚོ་རྒྱུད་ (tsōgyüü) along the coast, offshore, coastal.

མཚོ་རྒྱུད་གླིང་ཕྲན་ (tsōgyüü liŋdrεn) an offshore island.

མཚོ་རྒྱུན་དྲོ་པོ་ (tsōgyün trobo) warm winds blowing from the sea.

མཚོ་མཆིང་ (tsōjiŋ) sm. མཚོ་འཛིངས་.

མཚོ་འཛིངས་ (tsōjiŋ) the middle of the sea.

མཚོ་ངོགས་ (tsōŋɔɔ) harbor, port.

མཚོ་ངོས་ (tsōŋöö) sea level ¶ མཚོ་ངོས་ལས་ཕི་ཀྲི་ ༦༠༠༠ གི་ས་གནས་ A region that is six thousand feet above sea level.

མཚོ་སྔོན་ (tsōŋön) 1. Lake Kokonor. 2. Qinghai (province) ¶ མཚོ་སྔོན་ཞིང་ཆེན་ Qinghai Province.

མཚོ་སྔོན་པོ་ (tsō ŋōmbo) Lake Kokonor.

མཚོ་ཆུ་འགྲིབ་ (tsōju drib) sm. མཚོ་འགྲིབ་.

མཚོ་ཆུས་རྡེབ་ཟད་ (tsōjü debsεὲ) vi. to be eroded by water.

མཚོ་ཇག (tsōjaà) pirate, buccaneer.

མཚོ་མཇལ་ (tsō jεε) seeking guidance from visions in a holy lake; va.—ཞུ་ to request/ seek visions from a holy lake; va.—ལྟ་/ གཟིགས་ to look for a vision in a holy lake.

མཚོ་ཉ་ (tsōña) ocean/ sea fish.

མཚོ་སྙིང་ (tsōñiŋ) 1. a channel/ vent in the ocean floor. 2. name of a mountain at the middle of Lake Kokonor.

མཚོ་གཏིང་ (tsōdiŋ) sm. མཚོ་མཐིལ་.

མཚོ་རྟ་ (tsōda) legendary sea horse.

མཚོ་ལྟར་ཟབ་ལ་མེ་ལྟར་ཚ་བ་ (tsōdar sabla medar tsāwa) conveys great/ extreme suffering ¶ མི་དམངས་ཚོས་མཚོ་ལྟར་ཟབ་ལ་མེ་ལྟར་ཚ་བའི་གཉའ་གནོན་མྱངས་པ་རེད་ The people experienced extreme oppression as deep as ocean and as hot as fire. [Lit. deep as the ocean and hot as a fire].

མཚོ་ལྟས་ (tsōdεὲ) sm. མཚོ་མཇལ་.

མཚོ་ཐོག (ནས་) (tsōdɔɔ (nε)) by/ via sea, maritime.

མཚོ་ཐོག་སྐྱེལ་འདྲེན་ (tsōdɔɔ gyēndren) maritime transport; va.—བྱེད་.

མཚོ་ཐོག་བསྐོར་གཡེང་གྲུ་གཟིངས་ (tsōdɔɔ gɔ̄ɔyeŋ trusiŋ) cruiser (ship).

མཚོ་ཐོག་ཁ་ལོ་སྒྱུར་དབང་ (tsōdɔɔ kālo gyurwaŋ) sea control, sea power, sea supremacy.

མཚོ་ཐོག་གོད་ཁ་ (tsōdɔɔ gööga) perils of the sea.

མཚོ་ཐོག་འགྲིམ་འགྲུལ་ (tsōdɔɔ drimdrüü) sea travel; va.—བྱེད་.

མཚོ་ཐོག་བདེ་སྲུང་ཐིང་ (tsōdɔɔ desuŋ tiŋ) Maritime Safety Bureau.

མཚོ་ཐོག་དམག་འཁྲུག (tsōdɔɔ māgdru) naval battle, sea war; va.—རྒྱག.

མཚོ་ཐོན་ (tsōdön) ocean/ marine resources, ocean/ marine products.

མཚོ་ཐོན་དངོས་རྫས་ (tsōdön ŋöödzεὲ) ocean/ marine products.

མཚོ་ཐོན་བཟའ་བཅའ་ (tsōdön saja) foods from the sea.

མཚོ་མཐའ་ (tsōda) sm. མཚོ་ཁ་.

མཚོ་མཐིལ་ (tsōdil) the bottom of the sea.

མཚོ་དོན་ཁྲིམས་ཁང་ (tsōdön trimgaŋ) admiralty court, maritime court.

མཚོ་དོན་བཅའ་ཁྲིམས་ (tsōdön jādrim) law of the sea.

མཚོ་དོམ་ (tsōdom) seal (the animal).

མཚོ་དྲུག (tsōdruù) the seven items: honey, butter, yogurt, milk, water and chang (beer).

མཚོ་དྲུང་ (tsōdruŋ) ocean bank/ shore.

མཚོ་མདོག (tsōdɔɔ) color of the sea/ ocean.

མཚོ་སྣ་ (tsōna) area in southern Tibet.

མཚོ་པྲ་ (tsōdra) sm. མཚོ་མཇལ་.

མཚོ་དཔྱད་ (tsōjεὲ) sm. མཚོ་མཇལ་.

མཚོ་ཕག (tsōbaà) hippopotamus.

མཚོ་ཕྲན་ (tsōdrεn) small lake, pond.

མཚོ་བོད་ (tsōböö) abbr. Qinghai-Tibet ¶ མཚོ་བོད་རླངས་འཁོར་འགྲོ་ལམ་ Qinghai-Tibet highway.

མཚོ་བོད་ཐོག་སྒང་ (tsōböö tɔ̄ɔgaŋ) sm. མཚོ་བོད་ས་མཐོ་.

མཚོ་བོད་གཞུང་ལམ་ (tsōböö shuŋlam) Qinghai-Tibet highway.

མཚོ་བོད་ས་མཐོ་ (tsōböö sāto) Qinghai-Tibet Plateau.

མཚོ་བྱ་ (tsōja) water bird.

མཚོ་འབུ་ཞ་སྨི་ (tsōmbu shəmi) ocean shrimp.

མཚོ་འབུ་ཤ་སྐམ་ (tsōmbu shāgam) dried shrimp.

མཚོ་འབྲུག (tsōdruù) 1. sm. མཚོ་སྲུམ་. 2. pipefish.

མཚོ་མ་ཕམ་ (tsō mabam) Lake Manasarowa.

མཚོ་མ་དྲོས་པ་ (tsōma dröoba) sm. མཚོ་མ་ཕམ་.

མཚོ་མིག (tsūmii) small pools of water in a swamp.

མཚོ་མོ་ (tsōmo) 1. lake. 2. a female name.

མཚོ་དམག (tsōmaà) navy, marines, sailors ¶ མེ་གོའི་མཚོ་དམག The U.S. Navy.

མཚོ་དམག་སྐམ་འཐབ་རུ་ཁག (tsōmaà gāmdəb rugaà) sm. མཚོ་དམག་སྐམ་འཛིང་རུ་ཁག.

མཚོ་དམག་སྐམ་འཛིང་རུ་ཁག (tsōmaà gāmdziŋ rugaà) marine corps, marines.

མཚོ་དམག་མཁའ་སྐྱོད་དཔུང་སྡེ་ (tsōmaà kāgyöö būŋde) naval air force.

མཚོ་དམག་རྟེན་གཞི་ (tsōmaà dēnshi) naval base.

མཚོ་དམག་གནས་གཞི་ (tsōmaà nɛ̄ɛ̀shi) sm. མཚོ་དམག་རྟེན་གཞི་.

མཚོ་དམག་སྦྱོང་བདར་སློབ་གྲྭ་ (tsōmaà jo̲ŋdar lōbdra) naval training school.

མཚོ་དམར་པོ་ (tsō mārbo) the Red Sea.

མཚོ་ཚྭ་ (tsōdza) sea salt.

མཚོ་རྫིང་ (tsōdziŋ) reservoir.

མཚོ་འཛུལ་དམག་གྲུ་ (tsōndzüü māgdru) military submarine.

མཚོ་གཟིག (tsōsii) seal (the animal).

མཚོ་གཟིགས་ (tsō si̲i) va. to look for signs and visions in a holy lake.

མཚོ་འོག (tsōwɔɔ̀) sm. མཚོ་མཐིལ་.

མཚོ་འོག་གྲོག་རོང་ (tsōwɔɔ̀ drɔ̲groŋ) ocean trench.

མཚོ་འོག་གཤོང་ས་ (tsōwɔɔ̀ shōŋsa) ocean basin.

མཚོ་ཡུར་ (tsōyur) canal ¶ སུད་སི་མཚོ་ཡུར་ Suez Canal.

མཚོ་རགས་ (tsōraà) protective embankments in lakeside areas, revetment, seawall.

མཚོ་རླབས་ (tsōləb) waves; vi.—འཕྱུར་ to ebb and flow (waves).

མཚོ་རླབས་གློག་འདོན་ (tsōləb lōndön) making electricity from waves/ tides.

མཚོ་ལག (tsōlaà) a small/ branch lake.

མཚོ་ལམ་ (tsōlam) marine route, shipping route, navigation lane.

མཚོ་ལམ་སྟོར་ (tsōlam dōr) va. to cause a ship to go off course.

མཚོ་ལས་པ་ (tsōlɛɛ̀ba) seaman, sailor.

མཚོ་ལི་ (tsōle) nautical mile.

མཚོ་སེང་ (tsōseŋ) sea lion.

མཚོ་སྲིན་ (tsōsin) sea monster.

མཚོ་སྲུང་ (tsōsuŋ) sea/ coastal defense.

མཚོ་སྲུང་དཔུང་སྡེ་ (tsōsuŋ būŋde) coast guards (a branch of the military service), forces deployed to defend a coast.

མཚོ་བསུབས་ (tsō sūb) va. to fill in a lake.

མཚོག་གང་ (tsōggaŋ) sm. མཚོག་མ་.

མཚོག་མདུད་ཀྱི་སྒོ་ (tsōgdüügi go̲) center of the head.

མཚོག་མ་ (tsōgma) fontanel; vi.—སྲིམ་ to harden (the fontanel).

མཚོག་མ་མ་བསྐམས་པ་ (tsōgma ma̲gamba) young and inexperienced, not knowledgeable [Lit. the fontanel has not hardened].

མཚོག་གསང་ (tsōgsaŋ) a point in the fontanel for acupuncture.

མཚོན་ (tsōn) 1. vi. to express, to show, to symbolize, to illustrate, to represent ¶ དུས་མཚམས་གསར་པ་ཞིག་ཏུ་སླེབས་པ་མཚོན་ཡོད་ It shows that (they) have reached a new period. ¶ འཛམ་གླིང་ཞི་བདེའི་ལས་འགུལ་མཚོན་པའི་རི་མོ་ Paintings symbolizing the world peace movement. ¶ ཕྱོགས་ལྷུང་དང་པོ་ནི་ཁྲིན་གྱིས་མཚོན་གྱི་ཡོད་པ་རེད་ The first deviation is illustrated by Chen. 2. led by, the principal one ¶ རྒྱ་ནག་གིས་མཚོན་གུང་ཁྲན་རྒྱལ་ཁབ་ཁ་ཤས་ A few Communist countries led by Red China. 3. weapon ¶ རྡུལ་ཕྲན་གྱི་མཚོན་ Atomic weapons. 4. see མཚོན་པར་བྱེད་.

མཚོན་སྐྱོབ་ (tsōngyob) protective armor.

མཚོན་བསྐལ་ (tsōngɛɛ) abbr. of མཚོན་གྱི་བསྐལ་པ་.

མཚོན་ཁ་འགྲན་ (tsōn kā dre̲n) va. to compete with weapons.

མཚོན་ཁྱེར་ལག་འཛིང་ (tsōngyer lə̲ndzin) hand-to-hand combat with weapons; va.—བྱེད་.

མཚོན་ཁུང་ (tsōnguŋ) the opening/ hole in a wall from which a gun is shot.

མཚོན་ཁྲག (tsōndraà) bleeding caused by a weapon.

མཚོན་གྱི་བསྐལ་པ་ (tsōngi gɛ̄ɛwa) a Buddhist aeon when weapons become obsolete in the world.

མཚོན་འགོག (tsōngɔɔ̀) sth. that protects against weapons, e.g., armor.

མཚོན་སྒྲོམ་ (tsōndrom) a stand or frame on which weapons are placed.

མཚོན་ངར་མ་ (tsōn ŋ̲arma) sharp weapons.

མཚོན་ཆ་ (tsōnja) weapons; va.—བྱེད་ to use as a weapon, to be armed with ¶ མའོ་ཡི་དགོངས་པས་མཚོན་ཆ་བྱས་ནས་ Using Mao's thought as a weapon.

མཚོན་ཆ་འཁོར་ལོ་ (tsōnja kɔ̄ɔlo) star anise.

མཚོན་ཆ་ཅན་ (tsōnjajɛn) armed.

མཚོན་ཆ་ལྗི་རིགས་ (tsōnja ji̲rii) sm. མཚོན་ཆ་ཆེ་རིགས་.

མཚོན་ཆ་ཆེ་རིགས་ (tsōnja cērii) heavy weapons, heavy artillery.

མཚོན་ཆ་འཇོག (tsōnja jɔ̲ɔ̀) va. to lay down arms/ weapons.

མཚོན་ཆ་རྣོ་ངར་ཅན་ (tsōnja nōŋarjɛn) sharp-edged weapons.

མཚོན་ཆ་རྣོན་པོ་ (tsōnja nōmbo) sm. མཚོན་ཆ་རྣོ་ངར་ཅན་.

མཚོན་ཆ་འབུ་ཕྲ་ཅན་ (tsōnja bu̲drajɛn) bacteriological/ germ weapon.

མཚོན་ཆ་གཙོ་བོར་སྨྲ་བ་ (tsōnja dzōwor māwa) the theory that weapons decide everything.

མཚོན་ཆ་ཡང་རིགས་ (tsōnja ya̲ŋrii) light weapons, light artillery.

མཚོན་ཆའི་བཟོ་གྲྭ་ (tsōnjɛ so̲dra) military ordnance/ munitions factory.

མཚོན་རྟགས་ (tsōndaà) manifestation, symbol, sign ¶ དེ་ནི་མཐུན་སྒྲིལ་གྱི་མཚོན་རྟགས་འོད་སྣང་འབར་བ་ཞིག་རེད་ That is a brilliant manifestation of unity. 2. insignia ¶ བོད་དམག་གི་མཚོན་རྟགས་ The Tibetan army's insignia.

མཚོན་སྟངས་ (tsōndaŋ) appearance, attitude.

མཚོན་སྟོན་ (tsōndön) symbol, representation.

མཚོན་ཐུབ་ (tsōn tūb) 1. vi. to be able to express/ convey/ show ¶ གཏམ་བཤད་དེས་ཁོང་གི་སེམས་ཤུགས་མཚོན་ཐུབ་པ་རེད་ That speech was able to convey his enthusiasm. 2. bulletproof.

མཚོན་ཐུབ་འཁྲུལ་འཁོར་ (tsōndub drü̲ü̲gɔɔ) armored vehicle, bulletproof car.

མཚོན་འཐབ་ (tsōndəb) hot war, shooting war.

མཚོན་དོན་ (tsōndön) meaning, significance ¶ རྒྱལ་དར་གྱི་མཚོན་དོན་ག་རེ་རེད་ What is the significance of the national flag.

མཚོན་དོན་རི་མོ་ (tsōndön ri̲mu) caricature, cartoon.

མཚོན་ལྡན་ (tsōndɛn) armed ¶ མཚོན་ལྡན་མི་གཅིག An armed man.

མཚོན་ལྡན་ཁྲབ་འཁོར་ (tsōndɛn trābgɔɔ) tank, armored vehicle.

མཚོན་ལྡན་ལྕགས་འཁྲབ་རླངས་འཁོར་ (tsōndɛn jāgdrəb lāŋgɔɔ) sm. མཚོན་ལྡན་ཁྲབ་འཁོར་.

མཚོན་ན་ (tsōnna) for example, as an example ¶ པེ་ཅིང་དུ་མཚོན་ན་ For example, in Beijing.

མཚོན་ནགས་མདེལ་ཆར་ (tsōnnaà de̲ejar) heavy shooting/ firing [Lit. forest of weapons, rain of bullets].

མཚོན་ནད་ (tsōnnɛɛ̀) injury caused by weapons, wounded by weapons.

མཚོན་པ་ (tsōmba) sm. མཚོན་.

མཚོན་པར་བྱེད་ (tsōmbar ce̲è) va. to show/ manifest/ express ¶ ཐུན་མོང་གི་བསམ་འདུན་མཚོན་པར་བྱས་པ་རེད་ (They) manifested common wishes. ¶ ལག་གཉིས་ཐལ་མོ་སྦྱར་ནས་ཐུགས་རྗེ་ཆེ་ཞུ་རྒྱུ་མཚོན་པར་བྱས་ (He) clasped his hands together (as in namaste) to show thanks.

མཚོན་དཔེ་ (tsōnbe) diagram, chart.

མཚོན་བྱ་ (tsōnja) subject matter ¶ ཁོང་གི་རི་མོའི་མཚོན་བྱ་མང་ཆེ་བ་ཡུལ་ལྗོངས་རེད་ The subject matter of most of his painting is scenery.

མཚོན་བྱེད་ (tsōnjeè) 1. an object used to illustrate or show the nature/ character/ quality of a thing or person, indicator, symbol ¶ མི་རིགས་ཀྱི་ཁྱད་ཆོས་མཚོན་བྱེད་ཀྱི་རི་མོ་ Paintings illustrating national characteristics. 2. see མཚོན་, 4.

མཚོན་བྱེད་ཀྱི་རྟགས་ (tsōnjeègi dāà) the key (of a map, chart); marker, signal ¶ མཚོ་ལམ་མཚོན་བྱེད་ཀྱི་རྟགས་ A buoy.

མཚོན་བྱེད་ཀྱི་པར་རིས་ (tsōnjeègi bārrii) chart, diagram, sketch ¶ གནམ་གཤིས་མཚོན་བྱེད་ཀྱི་པར་རིས་

A weather chart.

མཚོན་བྱེད་དཔེ་རིས་ (tsŏnjeè bērii) sm. མཚོ་བྱེད་ཀྱི་པར་རིས་.

མཚོན་བྱེད་མི་སྣ་ (tsŏnjeè minə) representative personages, representatives ¶ འབྱོར་ལྡན་གྲལ་རིམ་གྱི་མཚོན་བྱེད་མི་སྣ་ Representatives of the bourgeoisie.

མཚོན་བྱེད་རང་བཞིན་ (tsŏnjeè rəŋshin) representativeness, representative ¶ མཚོན་བྱེད་རང་བཞིན་གྱི་གྲོང་ཁྱེར་ Representative cities.

མཚོན་བྱེད་རི་མོ་ (tsŏnjeè rimu) sm. མཚོ་བྱེད་ཀྱི་པར་རིས་.

མཚོན་བྱེད་རིང་ལུགས་ (tsŏnjeè riŋluù) symbolism.

མཚོན་རྨ་གསོ་སླ་ ཚིག་རྨ་གསོ་དཀའ་ (tsŏnma sōla tsīgma sōga) it is easy to heal a wound caused by a weapon but a hurt caused by harsh word is difficult to heal.

མཚོན་རྨས་ (tsŏnmεὲ) bullet/ weapon wound.

མཚོན་ཙམ་ (tsŏndzam) just a token of one's feeling/ thought, sth. in brief ¶ ལག་རྟགས་འདི་ང་རང་གི་བསམ་པ་མཚོན་ཙམ་ཡིན་ This gift is just a token of my feelings.

མཚོན་རྩེ་ (tsŏndze) spearhead.

མཚོན་རྫུལ་ (tsŏndzüü) manifestation ¶ འབྱོར་མེད་གྲལ་རིམ་གྱི་བསམ་བློ་མིན་པ་སྣ་ཚོགས་ཀྱི་མཚོན་རྫུལ་དང་འབྱུང་ཁུངས་ The sources and manifestations of various nonproletarian ideas.

མཚོན་འོག་ཤོར་ (tsŏnwɔɔ shɔɔ) vi. to die in battle ¶ དམག་མི་འགའ་ཤས་མཚོན་འོག་ཤོར་བའི་ས་གནས་ The place where several soldiers died in battle.

མཚོན་གཡོལ་ (tsŏnyöö) an amulet that protects the wearer against weapons.

མཚོན་ལམ་ (tsŏnlam) wound inflicted by a weapon.

མཚོན་སྲུང་ (tsŏnsuŋ) protective amulet/ charm/ talisman.

མཚོན་གསར་ (tsŏnsar) modern/ new weapons ¶ མཚོན་གསར་འཕྲུལ་མདའ་ Modern automatic guns.

མཚོན་ལྷ་ (tsŏnlha) god/ deity of war.

མཚོའི་མཐའ་ (tsŏdaa) on the edge of the sea.

འཚག་: p. **བཙགས་**; f. **བཙག**; imp. **ཚོགས་** (tsāà) 1. vi. to strain, to filter, to sift ¶ ཁོས་ཇ་དེ་ཕོར་པའི་ནང་བཙགས་སོང་ He strained the tea in the cup. 2. va. to press, to squeeze out ¶ པད་ཁ་ནས་སྣུམ་བཙགས་པ་རེད་ (They) pressed oil out of the mustard (seeds).

འཚག་རྒྱས་ (tsāggyεὲ) fat (for people).

འཚག་ཆས་ (tsāgjεὲ) filter, sieve, sifter, strainer.

འཚག་དམ་པོ་ (tsāà tambo) tightly woven.

འཚག་པ་ (tsāgba) sm. འཚག་རྒྱས་.

འཚག་ཕོར་ (tsāgbɔɔ) a sieve, sifter, strainer.

འཚག་བྱེད་ (tsāgjeè) sm. འཚག་ཆས་.

འཚག་བཟང་ (tsāgsaŋ) sm. འཚག་རྒྱས་.

འཚག་ཡིག (tsāgyii) archives, files, records.

འཚག་ཤོག (tsāgshɔɔ) filter paper.

འཚགས་ (tsāà) p. of འཚག.

འཚང་: p. **བཙངས་**; f. **བཙང་**; imp. **ཚོངས་** (tsāŋ) va. to stuff in, to squeeze in ¶ སྒམ་ནང་གི་ཅ་ལག་གི་གསེབ་ཏུ་ཤོག་བུ་བཙངས་འདུག When packing (they) stuffed paper between the things.

འཚང་: p. **འཚངས་**; f. **འཚང་**; imp. **འཚོངས་** (tsāŋ) va. to push/ squeeze oneself in ¶ ཀུན་མས་སྐྱེའུ་ཁུང་ནས་འཚངས་འདུག The thief squeezed in through the window. 2. vi. to pant ¶ གྱེན་འཛེགས་དུས་དབུགས་འཚངས་བྱུང་ When climbing uphill, I panted.

འཚང་ཀ་ (tsāŋga) crowd, crowded, packed, congested; va.—རྒྱག to crowd in, to push/ squeeze ahead ¶ ལྟད་མོ་ལྟ་མཁན་འཚང་ཀ་འདུག There's a big crowd to see the show. ¶ འཚང་ཀ་བརྒྱབ་ན་མ་གཏོགས་ལག་འཁྱེར་རག་གི་མ་རེད་ Unless you push (your way in) you won't get a permit.

འཚང་ཁ་ (tsāŋga) sm. འཚང་ཀ་.

འཚང་ཁ་ཤིག་ཤིག (tsāŋga shīgshiì) shoulder to shoulder, packed together, crowded together, congested, many people squashed together.

འཚང་ག (tsāŋga) sm. འཚང་ཀ་.

འཚང་ག་ཤིག་ཤིག (tsāŋga shīgshiì) sm. འཚང་ཁ་ཤིག་ཤིག.

འཚང་རྒྱ་ (tsāŋgya) vi. to become enlightened, to reach nirvana.

འཚང་ཚིགས་ (tsāŋdziì) tail bone.

འཚང་ར་ (tsāŋra) sm. མཚང་ར་.

འཚང་གཤིབ་ (tsāŋshib) sm. འཚང་ཁ་ཤིག་ཤིག.

འཚང་བཤད་རྟ་ལྕག (tsāŋshaŋ dējaà) shung. whip used to clear a path in a crowd.

འཚངས་ (tsāŋ) p. of འཚང་.

འཚངས་འཛུལ་ (tsāŋdzüü) coming between people or countries in a bad sense; va.—བྱེད་ ¶ བུད་མེད་དེས་བཟའ་ཚང་དབར་འཚང་འཛུལ་བྱས་ནས་བཟའ་ཚང་ཁ་བྲལ་བ་རེད་ That girl came between the couple and they got divorced.

འཚབ་: p. **འཚབས་**; f. **འཚབ་**; imp. **འཚོབས་** (tsāb) 1. va. to repay, to replace or pay for sth. lost or damaged (usu. used with སྐྱིན་པ་) ¶ ཁོང་གི་དེབ་བརླག་པའི་སྐྱིན་པ་འཚབ་དགོས་ཡོད་ (I) have to replace the book of his that was lost. 2. vi. to be anxious/ frantic ¶ ཁོ་ཕྱི་དྲགས་ཙང་སེམས་འཚབས་སོང་ He was anxious because he was late.

འཚབ་སྤྱོད་ཀྱི་རང་བཞིན་ (tsābgyöògi rəŋshin) fanatical enthusiasm/ zealousness.

འཚབ་པེ་འཚུབ་པེ་ (tsābbe tsūbbe) 1. nervous; va.—བྱེད་ ¶ ཡིག་ཚད་གཏོང་ཁར་སློབ་ཕྲུག་དེ་འཚབ་པེ་འཚུབ་པེ་བྱེད་ཀྱི་འདུག Just before the exam the student is acting nervous. 2. hurried, hurriedly, hastily ¶ ཨ་མ་ན་བའི་གནས་ཚུལ་ཐོས་འཕྲལ་ཁོང་འཚབ་པེ་འཚུབ་པེ་བྱས་ནས་ཐོན་སོང་ As soon as he heard the news that his mother was ill, he hurriedly departed (to see her).

འཚབ་མ་འཚབ་ (tsāb madzub) 1. hurriedly, hastily. 2. nervously, anxiously.

འཚབ་འཚབ་ (tsābdzub) sm. འཚབ་པེ་འཚུབ་པེ་.

འཚབ་འཚབ་འཚུབ་འཚུབ་ (tsābdzəb tsūbdzub) sm. འཚབ་པེ་འཚུབ་པེ་.

འཚབ་འཚུབ་ (tsābdzub) sm. འཚབ་པེ་འཚུབ་པེ་.

འཚབ་འཚུབ་བབ་ཅོལ་ (tsābdzub pəbjöö) talking hastily, talking without thinking; va.—སྨྲ་.

འཚབ་འཚུབ་ཧོད་རྒྱུག (tsābdzub hōōgyuù) hurried and not careful; va.—བྱེད་.

འཚབ་ཤ་སྐྱེ་ (tsābsha gyē) sm. འཚབ་ཤ་ལང་.

འཚབ་ཤ་ལང་ (tsābsha laŋ) vi. to get nervous/ jittery/ worried.

འཚབས་ (tsāb) p. of འཚབ་.

འཚབས་པོ་ (tsābbo) hurried, hasty.

འཚམ་: p. **བཙམས་**; f. **བཙམ་**; imp. **ཚོམས་** (tsām) 1. va. to compete. 2. va. to insult ¶ སློབ་ཕྲུག་དེས་དགེ་རྒན་ལ་འཚམ་པའི་སྐད་ཆ་བཤད་འདུག The student said sth. that insulted the teacher.

འཚམ་: p. **འཚམས་**; f. **འཚམ་** (tsām) vi. to be suitable/ appropiate ¶ རང་ཉིད་ཀྱི་ཤེས་ཡོན་དང་འཚམས་པའི་ལས་ཀ་འཚོལ་དགོས་ One should search for work that is appropriate to one's knowledge.

འཚམ་པོ་ (tsāmbo) sm. འཚམས་པོ་.

འཚམ་ཚོད་ (tsāmdzöö) controlling/ regulating sth.; va.—འཛིན་ to control/ regulate sth. ¶ མི་ཚང་གི་འགྲོ་སོང་ཚང་མ་ཨ་མས་འཚམ་ཚོད་འཛིན་གྱི་ཡོད་པ་རེད་ The mother regulates all the household expenses.

འཚམས་མཇལ་ (tsām jεε) a meeting to greet sb.

འཚམས་དར་ (tsāmdar) a telegram of greeting.

འཚམས་རྟགས་ (tsāmdaà) a greeting gift.

འཚམས་རྟེན་ (tsāmden) sm. འཚམས་རྟགས་.

འཚམས་ལྟེབ་ (tsāmdeb) a way of folding a ceremonial scarf into a square shape.

འཚམས་འདྲི་ (tsəmdri) 1. visiting/ calling on sb., making a courtesy/ goodwill visit; va.—ལ་འགྲོ་ ¶ མི་རིགས་རང་སྐྱོང་ས་གནས་ཁག་ལ་མཚམས་འདྲིར་འགྲོ་སྐབས་ When we were going to visit the nationality autonomous areas. ¶ ད་ལོ་ང་ཚོའི་སྲིད་འཛིན་གྱིས་རྒྱ་གར་དུ་མཚམས་འདྲི་གནང་བ་རེད་ This year our president paid a courtesy visit to India. 2. regards, well-wishes; va.—བྱེད་; —ཞུ་ (h.) to give/ send regards or well wishes ¶ ལྷ་སར་ཕེབས་ནས་བསོད་ནམས་ལ་འཚམས་འདྲི་ཞུ་རོགས་གནང་ After you arrive in Lhasa please give my regards to Sonam. 3. congratulations; va.—བྱེད་; —ཞུ་ to congratulate ¶ མཚོ་དམག་དམག་དཔུང་ལ་རྒྱལ་ཁ་ཆེན་པོ་ཐོབ་ཙང་དམག་སྤྱིས་མཚམས་འདྲིའི་ཡི་གེ་ཞིག་བཏང་བ་རེད་ Because the navy troops won a big battle, the commander in chief sent a letter of congratulations. 4. va.—བྱེད་ to interview ¶ བ་གླང་གསོ་མཁན་དུད་ཚང་ལ་རྡོ་རྗེ་འཚམས་འདྲི་བྱེད་པར་སླེབས་སོང་ Dorje came to interview a family who raises cattle.

འཚམས་འདྲི་ཚོགས་པ་ (tsəmdri tsɔ̄gba) a visiting or goodwill team/ committee/ delegation / mission.

འཚམས་འདྲི་གཟིགས་སྐོར་ (tsāmdri si̱ìgɔɔ) a visit and inspection tour.

མཚམས་འདྲིའི་ཚོགས་པ་ (tsāmdrii tsɔ̄gba) sm. འཚམས་འདྲི་ཚོགས་པ་.

མཚམས་འདྲིར་བཅར་ (tsəmdrii jāā) va. to call on (a person), to visit (h.).

འཚམས་པོ་ (tsāmbo) proper, suitable, appropriate ¶ ཤེས་ཚད་དང་འཚམས་པའི་ལས་འགན་སྤྲད་པ་རེད་ (They) gave responsibilities appropriate to one's learning. ¶ ཆེ་ཆུང་འཚམས་པོ་ Appropriate size.

འཚམས་འབུལ་མཇལ་ཁ་ (tsāmbüü je̱ɛga) an audience to give greetings.

འཚམས་ཞུ་ (tsāmshu) a greeting; va.— བྱེད་.

འཚམས་ཞུའི་འབུལ་མཆོད་ (tsāmshü bü̱ü̱dzön) gifts given when visiting someone.

འཚམས་གཟིགས་ (tsəmsi̱ì) abbr. of འཚམས་འདྲི་གཟིགས་སྐོར་.

འཚམས་ལན་ (tsāmlɛn) reciprocating sb.'s greeting/ good wishes; va.—ཞུ་; —འབུལ་.

འཚམས་ཤོག (tsāmshɔɔ̀) letters or cards for sending greetings or well wishes.

འཚར་ (tsār) 1. vi. to grow ¶ ཕྲུ་གུ་འདི་ཞེ་དྲག་འཚར་འདུག The child has grown up a lot. 2. sm. ཚར་.

འཚར་སྐྱེས་ (tsārgyeè) sm. འཚར་ལོང་.

འཚར་སྟོབས་རྒྱས་པ་ (tsārdob gye̱ɛ̀ba) growing luxuriantly.

འཚར་ལོང་ (tsārloŋ) growing up ¶ གསར་བརྗེའི་འགོ་འཁྲིད་འོག་འཚར་ལོང་བྱུང་བའི་གཞོན་ནུ་ The youth who grew up under the leadership of the revolution.

འཚར་ལོངས་སྐུལ་རྒྱུ་ (tsārloŋ gü̃ü̃gyu) growth hormone.

འཚལ་: p. **བཙལ་**; f. **བཙལ་**; imp. **འཚོལ་** (tsɛ̄ɛ) 1. a verb conveying the idea of prostration ¶ ཕྱག་འཚལ་ To prostrate. 2. I beg, I ask, I request, please ¶ སྐུ་གཟུགས་ལ་ཐུགས་ཅག་གནང་བར་འཚལ་ Please take care of yourself. 3. to be okay/ permissible ¶ ང་ཕྱིན་ན་འཚལ་ལམ་ Is it okay if I go. 4. I hope, I wish ¶ ནད་ལས་མྱུར་དུ་གྲོལ་བར་འཚལ་ I hope to recover soon from my illness. 5. va. to know/ comprehend/ understand ¶ མ་འོངས་པར་གནས་ཚུལ་ཇི་ཡོང་ཆ་མི་འཚལ་ It is unknown what will happen in the future.

འཚལ་མ་ (tsɛ̄ɛ̄ma) food.

འཚལ་མ་ནར་མ་ (tsɛ̄ɛ̄ma na̱rma) regular/ every day food.

འཚལ་འཚོལ་ (tsɛ̄ɛ̄dzöö) searching, looking for; va.—བྱེད་ to search, to look for ¶ འདི་ཁུལ་ལས་ཀ་ཞིག་འཚལ་འཚོལ་བྱེད་ཀྱི་ཡོད་ I'm looking for a job here.

འཚིག: p. **ཚིག**; f. **འཚིག** (tsīì) vi. to get burned, to burn ¶ སྣོད་ཚས་ཚ་པོས་ཁོའི་ལག་པ་ཚིག་པ་རེད་ The hot pot burnt his hand.

འཚིག་དོ་ (tsīìdo) 1. the burnt/ charred remains of sth., ashes 2. heat (season of animals). 3. sb. who is "hot" sexually.

འཚིག་དྲི་ (tsīìdri) smell of sth. burning; vi.—ཁ་ to smell burnt, to smell sth. burning.

འཚིག་པ་ (tsīgbə) 1. anger; vi.—ཟ་ to be angry. 2. vi. to be in heat.

འཚིག་རྨས་ (tsīgmɛɛ̀) a burn injury.

འཚིག་རིལ་ཐེབས་ (tsīgrii tēè) vi. to get burnt.

འཚིག་རོ་ (tsīgro) sm. འཚིག་དོ་, 1.

འཚིག་རོ་ལུག་སྣོན་ (tsīgro lu̱gnön) a pan for putting ashes/ charred remains.

འཚིག་ཤི་ (tsīgshi) death by fire; vi.—ཐེབས་ to get killed by fire, to burn to death.

འཚིགས་ (tsīì) p. of འཚིག.

འཚིམས་པོ་ (tsīmbu) sm. ཚིམ་པོ་.

འཚིར་: p. and f. **བཙིར་**; imp. **ཚིར་** (tsīr) va. to squeeze, to wring, to crush ¶ ཁོས་ངའི་ལག་པ་བཙིར་བྱུང་ He squeezed my hand. 2. va. to squeeze in the sense of squeezing sth. out of a person (e.g., information, confession, money) ¶ ཁྲིམས་དཔོན་གྱིས་ག་ཚོད་བཙིར་ཀྱང་ཉེས་ཅན་དེས་ངོས་ལེན་བྱས་མི་འདུག No matter how the judge squeezed the criminal, he didn't confess.

འཚུག: p. **ཚུགས་**; f. **འཚུག** (tsūg) vi. to get started, to begin ¶ ཚོགས་འདུ་ཆུ་ཚོད་གསུམ་པར་ཚུགས་པ་རེད་ The meeting began at 3 o'clock. 2. vi. to be firm ¶ ལྕོག་ཙེའི་རྐང་པ་གཅིག་འཚུག་གི་མི་འདུག One of the table legs doesn't rest firmly on the ground.

འཚུད་: p. **ཚུད་** (tsǖù) vi. to get admitted into, to get included in ¶ ཁོ་སློབ་གྲྭར་ཚུད་པ་རེད་ He got admitted to the school. 2. vi. to fit into ¶ སྒམ་ཆེན་པོ་འདི་སྒོ་དེའི་ནང་ལ་ཚུད་ཀྱི་མི་འདུག The big box doesn't fit in the door. 3. vi. to be/ get put into or under ¶ ཡུལ་དེ་ཕྱི་རྒྱལ་གྱི་དྲག་ཤུགས་འོག་ཏུ་ཚུད་པརེད་ That country was put under the military power of the foreigners. ¶ གྲྭ་པ་ཚོ་མགོ་སྐོར་འོག་ཚུད་པ་རེད་ The monks were tricked [Lit. were put into the state of being tricked].

འཚུབ་: p. **འཚུབས་**; f. **འཚུབ་** (tsūb) 1. vi. to whirl/ swirl around (wind, smoke), to be turbulent, to storm ¶ བུ་ཡུག་འཚུབས་ནས་ལམ་ཀ་ལྷགས་པ་རེད་ (It) stormed and (they) lost their way. 2. vi. to be in trouble/ harm/ injury (for health) ¶ སྐུ་ཁྲྭ་ཤིན་ཏུ་འཚུབ་པར་བརྟེན་ Because his health was fraught with danger. 3. vi. to drown ¶ ཁོང་ཆུ་ནང་དུ་འཚུབ་འདུག He drowned in the water.

འཚུབ་སྐོར་ (tsūbgɔɔ) tornado, cyclone, hurricane.

འཚུབ་ཆ་ (tsūbja) 1. unrest, trouble, turmoil, disorder ¶ ཤོག་ཁག་གཉིས་པོའི་དབར་འབྲེལ་ཐག་ཆད་ནས་ཡུལ་ནང་འཚུབ་ཆ་ཆེན་པོ་འདུག Since the relations between the two groups were severed, there is great unrest in the region. 2. bad portent/ apparition/ appearance.

འཚུབ་སྟོན་ (tsūbdön) sm. འཚུབ་ཆ་, 3.

འཚུབ་པོ་ (tsūbu) 1. (with regards to children) mischievous, naughty; va.—བྱེད་ to act/ be mischievous/ naughty. 2. (with regards to adults) one who has lots of affairs with the opposite sex. 3. trouble, turmoil, disorder ¶ དུས་སྐབས་འཚུབ་པོ་ A time of turmoil. 2. bad (e.g., for weather, dreams, etc.). 4. sm. འཚུབ་ཆ་.

འཚུབ་མ་ (tsūbmə) whirlwind, vortex (sandstorm, snowstorm).

འཚུབ་འཚུབ་ (tsubdzub) whirling, swirling.

འཚུབ་ལང་ (tsūb la̱ŋ) vi. to get nervous/ jittery/ worried.

འཚུབ་ལྟོངས་ (tsūblhoŋ) sign/ portent of sth. bad.

འཚུབས་ (tsūb) p. of འཚུབ་.

འཚུམ་ (tsūm) sm.* འཛུམ.

འཚུམ་འཚུམ་ (tsūmdzum) blinking, twinkling; va.—བྱེད་.

འཚེ་ (tsē) harm, harmful.

འཚེ་བྱ་ (tsēja) harmful birds.

འཚེ་བྱེད་ (tsējeè) harm.

འཚེ་མེད་ (tsēmeè) nonviolent, nonharmful ¶ འཚེ་མེད་ཞི་བའི་ལམ་ The path of peaceful nonviolence.

འཚེང་: p. **འཚེངས་**; f. **འཚེང་** (tsēŋ) 1. vi. to be satisfied, content. 2. vi. to gain profit, to win.

འཚེངས་ (tsēŋ) p. of འཚེང་.

འཚེད་ (tsēè) va. to cook.

འཚེད་མཁན་ (tsēèñɛn) a cook.

འཚེད་གནས་ (tsēènεὲ) kitchen.

འཚེད་སྣུམ་ (tsēènum) cooking oil.

འཚེད་ཤིང་ (tsēèshiŋ) firewood, fuel.

འཚེམ་: p. **བཙེམས་**; f. **བཙེམ་**; imp. **ཚེམས་** (tsēm) va. to sew, to stitch.

འཚེམ་: p. **འཚེམས་**; f. **འཚེམ་** (tsēm) vi. to be overlooked, to be left out, to be omitted/ missing ། སློབ་ཕྲུག་ལ་སྒྲིག་ཆས་སྤྲོད་དུས་སློབ་ཕྲུག་ཅིག་འཚེམས་འདུག One student was overlooked when distributing the uniforms.

འཚེམ་སྐུད་ (tsēmgüù) thread/ string for sewing.

འཚེམ་ཁབ་ (tsēmgəb) sewing needle.

འཚེམ་འཁོར་ (tsēmgɔɔ) sm. ཚེམ་འཁོར་.

འཚེམ་དྲུབ་ (tsēmdrub) sm. ཚེམ་དྲུབ་.

འཚེམ་དྲུབ་མ་ (tsēmdrubmə) sm. ཚེམ་དྲུབ་མ་.

འཚེམ་བུ་བྲལ་ (tsēmbu trεε) vi. to come unsewn.

འཚེམ་བཟོ་ཁང་ (tsēmsogaŋ) sewing factory.

འཚེམ་བཟོ་བ་ (tsēmsowa) tailor.

འཚེམ་ལས་ (tsēmlεὲ) sewing, tailoring.

འཚེམ་ལུས་ (tsēmlüù) sth. missing, left out, omitted; vi.—ཤོར་ to get omitted/ left out.

འཚེམ་ཤུལ་ (tsēmshüù) the mark left by the stitches.

འཚེམ་སྲུབ་ (tsēmsub) seam; vi.—བྲལ་ to have a seam come undone.

འཚེམ་ཧབ་ (tsēmhəb) the size/ space between stitches.

འཚེམས་ (tsēm) p. of འཚེམ་.

འཚེར་ (tsēr) 1. vi. to be shy. 2. vi. to involuntarily yell/ cry out, to neigh. 3. vi. to sparkle/ glitter ། ཉི་འོད་རབ་ཏུ་འཚེར་ The sunlight glittered greatly. 4. va. to be unwilling or afraid of doing hard work.

འཚེར་སྐད་ (tsērgεὲ) neighing of a horse; va.—རྒྱག.

འཚེར་རྒྱངས་ (tsērgεὲ) sm. འཚེར་སྐད་.

འཚེར་དིར་ (tsēēdir) sm. འཚེར་སྐད་.

འཚེར་ཕྱིར་ (tsēēdir) sm. འཚེར་སྐད་.

འཚེར་སྣང་ (tsēēnaŋ) 1. shy, bashful; vi.—བྱེད་; —སྐྱེ་ to feel bashful/ shy. 2. embarrassed; vi.—བྱེད་; —སྐྱེ་ to feel embarrassed.

འཚེར་སྣང་ཚ་པོ་ (tsēēnaŋ tsābo) sb. who is very shy/ bashful.

འཚེར་པོ་ (tsēēbo) sm. འཚེར་སྣང་.

འཚེར་ཤུར་ཤུར་ (tsēr shūūshuu) a feeling of embarrassment, a feeling of shyness.

འཚེར་ཤས་ཆེ་བ་ (tsēr shεὲ cēwa) sm. འཚེར་ཤུར་ཤུར་.

འཚེལ་ (tsēē) sm. འཚོལ་.

འཚོ་ (tsō) 1. vi. to live, exist ། དཀའ་ངལ་དེ་འདྲའི་འོག་ཡུན་རིང་འཚོ་ཐུབ་ཁག་པོ་རེད་ It is hard to be able to live long under such hardships. 2. va. to look after, to take care of ། ལུག་འཚོ་རྒྱུ་ Looking after sheep.

འཚོ་རྐང་ (tsōgaŋ) livelihood; vi.—ཆགས་ to establish a livelihood ། རིམ་པས་སྐྱབས་བཅོལ་བ་ཚོ་འཚོ་རྐང་ཆགས་ཐུབ་པ་རེད་ Gradually the refugees were able to establish their livelihood.

འཚོ་སྐབས་སླར་རྙེད་ (tsōgəb lārñeè) getting a new lease on life/ livelihood.

འཚོ་སྐྱིད་ལས་སྒྲོ་ (tsōgyiì lεὲdro) happy at work and having a good livelihood.

འཚོ་སྐྱོང་ (tsōgyoŋ) looking after, bringing up, supporting, sustaining, rearing; va.—བྱེད་ to look after, to bring up, to rear, to support, to sustain ། ཕྲུ་གུ་འདི་ཕ་མ་ཤི་ནས་ངས་འཚོ་སྐྱོང་བྱས་པ་ཡིན་ I brought up the child after it's parents died.

འཚོ་སྐྱོང་རོགས་ཕན་ (tsōgyoŋ rɔ̀ɔbεn) supporting/ looking after and helping.

འཚོ་ཁམས་ (tsōgam) well-being.

འཚོ་འཁོས་ (tsōgöò) livelihood.

འཚོ་གོས་ (tsōgöò) livelihood, subsistence ། འཚོ་གོས་སློབ་སྦྱོང་ཡར་རྒྱས་ Improvement of livelihood and education.

འཚོ་གོས་གནས་མལ་ (tsōgöò nεὲmεε) livelihood/ subsistence and shelter.

འཚོ་གླ་ (tsōla) fee for grazing animals somewhere.

འཚོ་རྒྱགས་ (tsōgyaà) supplies.

འཚོ་བཅུད་ (tsōjüù) nutrition, nutriment, nourishment 2. vitamins.

འཚོ་བཅུད་རིག་པ་ (tsōjöò rigbə) the study of nutrition.

འཚོ་ཆས་ (tsōjεὲ) foodstuffs.

འཚོ་འཆིའི་ཁེ་ཉེན་ (tsōjii kēñen) a matter of life and death.

འཚོ་ཇུས་ (tsōjüù) strategy of livelihood.

འཚོ་རྟེན་ (tsōden) sm. འཚོ་ཐབས་.

འཚོ་རྟེན་གྱི་ལག་དངུལ་ (tsōdengi lagŋüü) pocket money for living expenses.

འཚོ་རྟེན་དུ་བྱེད་ (tsōdendu ceè) va. to use sth. as one's source of livelihood/ subsistence.

འཚོ་རྟེན་མེད་པ་ (tsōden meèba) poor, bankrupt.

འཚོ་རྟེན་ཡོང་ཁུངས་ (tsōden yoŋguŋ) source of income/ livelihood/ subsistence.

འཚོ་རྟེན་ཤོར་ (tsōden shɔ̄ɔ) vi. to lose one's livelihood/ source of subsistence.

འཚོ་ཐབས་ (tsōdəb) means of livelihood; occupation, trade; vi.—ཤོར་ to lose one's livelihood; va.—བྱེད་ to earn a livelihood ། ངའི་འཚོ་ཐབས་འབྲོག་པ་ཡིན་ My occupation is nomad.

འཚོ་ཐབས་ཀྱི་དབང་ཆ་ (tsōdəbgi wāŋja) the right to earn a living.

འཚོ་ཐབས་མེད་པ་ (tsōdəb meè) destitute, without any means of livelihood.

འཚོ་ཐབས་བྲལ་ (tsōdəb trεε) sm. འཚོ་ཐབས་མེད་པ་.

འཚོ་ཐེབས་ (tsōdeb) 1. resources for subsistence/ livelihood. 2. trust fund/ endowment for livelihood.

འཚོ་དོད་ (tsōdöò) 1. money that provides livelihood. 2. alimony.

འཚོ་སྡོད་ (tsōdöò) sm. འཚོ་བཞུགས་.

འཚོ་གནས་ (tsō nεὲ) vi. to be able to survive, to be able to get a livelihood.

འཚོ་སྣོན་ (tsōnön) food supplement, extra foodstuffs ། འཚོ་སྣོན་སྐྱེལ་དགོས་ (They) had to deliver extra food.

འཚོ་གནས་ (tsōnεὲ) living condition.

འཚོ་ཕྱེད་སློབ་ཕྱེད་ (tsōjeè lōbjeè) half doing herding and half studying, part-time herding and part-time studying.

འཚོ་འཕེལ་ (tsōbee) surviving and increasing (usu. for livestock).

འཚོ་བ་ (tsōwa) 1. life ། དེང་རབས་ཀྱི་ཆབ་སྲིད་འཚོ་བ་ Contemporary political life. ། བོད་ལ་འཚོ་བའི་རྟེན་གཞི་ངོ་མ་ཆོས་རེད་ In Tibet the main foundation of life is religion. 2. livelihood; va.—སྐྱེལ་; —བརྟེན་ to earn one's livelihood ། དབྱིན་སྐད་མ་ཤེས་ན་ཨ་རི་ར་འཚོ་བ་སྐྱེལ་ཁག་པོ་རེད་ It's hard to earn a living in America if you don't know English.

འཚོ་བ་བརྟེན་ལུགས་ (tsōwa dēnluù) sm. འཚོ་ལུགས་.

འཚོ་བ་བདེ་འཇགས་ (tsōwa denjaà) peaceful life.

འཚོ་བ་སྐྱོད་ (tsōwa jöò) vi. to enjoy life, to live ། ཆོས་སྲིད་རང་དབང་གི་འཚོ་བ་སྐྱོད་པ་རེད་ They enjoyed political and religious freedom. ། འཚོ་བ་སྐྱོད་སྟངས་ A way of life (lifestyle).

འཚོ་བ་བྱ་འཚོལ་བྱིའུ་འཚོལ་ (tsōwa cadzöö ciwudzöö) living from hand to mouth; va.—བྱེད་.

འཚོ་བ་མྱོང་ (tsōwa ñoŋ) vi. to experience life ། ཤིན་ཏུ་སྐྱོ་བའི་འཚོ་བ་མྱོང་གི་ཡོད་པ་རེད་ They are experiencing a life of extreme poverty.

འཚོ་བ་གཞན་རྟེན་ (tsōwa shenden) depending/ living on other people; va.—བྱེད་ to be dependent on others.

འཚོ་བ་བཟང་ངན་ (tsōwa saŋŋεn) standard of living.

འཚོ་བ་རིག་པའི་གཞུང་ (tsōwa rigbε shuŋ) name of a Tibetan medical text.

འཚོ་བ་ལེགས་བཅོས་ (tsōwa legjöò) betterment/ improvement of livelihood.

འཚོ་བ་གསར་བརྗེ་ (tsōwa sārje) revolutionary life.

འཚོ་བ་གསུམ་ (tsōwa sūm) the three conditions that allows a person to live according to Buddhism: human life, good merit and karma.

འཚོ་བའི་ཁ་གསབ་ (tsōwε kāsəb) extra allowance for

living expenses.

འཚོ་བའི་མཁོ་ཆས་ (tsōwɛ kōjɛɛ̀) sm. འཚོ་བའི་ཉེར་སྤྱོད་.

འཚོ་བའི་རྒྱུ་ཆས་ (tsōwɛ gyojɛɛ̀) means of securing a livelihood.

འཚོ་བའི་ཆུ་ཚད་ (tsōwɛ cūdzɛɛ̀) standard of living.

འཚོ་བའི་ཉེར་སྤྱོད་ (tsōwɛ ñerjöö) daily necessities (of subsistence/ livelihood).

འཚོ་བའི་ལྡད་མོ་ (tsōwɛ dɛ̄ɛ̀mo) soap opera (on TV).

འཚོ་བའི་ཐོབ་ཐང་ (tsōwɛ tōbdaŋ) the right to earn one's livelihood.

འཚོ་བའི་མདུན་ལམ་ (tsōwɛ dünlam) future livelihood ¶ འཚོ་བའི་མདུན་ལམ་ས་བརྟན་ཞིག A stable future livelihood.

འཚོ་བའི་གནས་སྟངས་ (tsōwɛ nɛ̄ɛ̀daŋ) standard of living/ livelihood.

འཚོ་བའི་རྣམ་པ་ (tsōwɛ nāmba) living condition, pattern of life ¶ མི་དམངས་ཀྱི་འཚོ་བའི་རྣམ་པ་ཡག་ཏུ་ཕྱིན་པ་རེད་ The living conditions of the people became better.

འཚོ་བའི་སྣང་རྒྱལ་ (tsōwɛ nāmdzüü) sm. འཚོ་བའི་རྣམ་པ་.

འཚོ་བའི་སྤྲོ་བ་ (tsōwɛ drōwa) joy of life.

འཚོ་བའི་དབང་པོ་ (tsōwɛ wāŋbo) life.

འཚོ་བའི་མ་མ་ (tsōwɛ mama) nanny.

འཚོ་བའི་ཚད་ (tsōwɛ tsɛ̄ɛ̀) 1. life span. 2. living standard.

འཚོ་བའི་ཟླ་བ་ (tsōwɛ dawa) the 9th month of the Tibetan calendar.

འཚོ་བའི་ཡོ་བྱད་ (tsōwɛ yobjɛɛ̀) 1. food. 2. utensils for livelihood.

འཚོ་བའི་རིག་པ་ (tsōwɛ rigbə) medical science.

འཚོ་བའི་རོགས་དངུལ་ (tsōwɛ rɔ̄ɔ̀ŋüü) money to help one's livelihood/ subsistence.

འཚོ་བར་ཉམས་ཞིབ་ (tsōwar ñəmshib) observing and learning from life; va.—བྱེད་.

འཚོ་བར་རོལ་ (tsōwar rö̤ö) sm. འཚོ་བ་སྤྱོད་.

འཚོ་བྱེད་ (tsōjeè) 1. necessities, essentials of life ¶ ལྟོ་ཆས་ནི་སེམས་ཅན་འཚོ་བྱེད་ཅིག་རེད་ Food is an essential of life. 2. water. 3. fire. 4. medicine. 5. doctor. 6. moon. 7. Thursday. 8. Wednesday.

འཚོ་ཆེས་ (tsōdzii) sm. འཚོ་ཐབས་.

འཚོ་ཆེས་བྱམས་གཟིགས་ (tsōdzii camsii) providing subsistence and treating kindly.

འཚོ་རྒྱུལ་ (tsōdzüü) sm. འཚོ་ལུགས་.

འཚོ་འཛིན་ (tsōndzin) shung. a guardian appointed to assist a household, monastery or Labrang in livelihood/ subsistence/ economic affairs.

འཚོ་ཞིང་གནས་ (tsōshiŋ nɛ̄ɛ̀) vi. to live, to exist ¶ མཁས་པ་དེ་ནི་བརྒྱ་ཕྲག་བདུན་པའི་ནང་འཚོ་ཞིང་གནས་པ་ཞིག་རེད་ The scholar was one who lived in the seventh century.

འཚོ་ཞིབ་ (tsōshib) shung. officials sent to a place where there has been a natural calamity to investigate the need for relief and assistance.

འཚོ་གཞིས་ (tsōsheè) shung. alive ¶ གནས་ཚུལ་དེ་ལྔ་རྒྱལ་དབང་སྐུ་གོང་མ་འཚོ་གཞིས་སྐབས་བྱུང་བ་ཞིག་རེད་ That event is one that occurred when the previous Dalai Lama was alive.

འཚོ་བཞུགས་ (tsōshuù) shung. alive ¶ ཏཱ་ལའི་བླ་མ་འཚོ་བཞུགས་སྐབས་ When the Dalai Lama was alive.

འཚོ་བཞུགས་དུས་རབས་ (tsōshuù tüürəb) the period of someone's lifetime.

འཚོ་ཟིན་ (tsō sin) va. to be able to stand on one's own feet.

འཚོ་རླུང་ཉུང་བ་ (tsōluŋ ñuŋwə) thin air/ oxygen.

འཚོ་རླུང་སྡབ་པོ་ (tsōluŋ drābbu) sm. འཚོ་རླུང་ཉུང་བ་.

འཚོ་རླུང་གསར་པ་ (tsōluŋ sāāba) fresh air.

འཚོ་ལམ་ (tsōlam) the way one secures livelihood/ subsistence.

འཚོ་ལུགས་ (tsōluù) way/ mode of life, manner of living/ livelihood.

འཚོ་ས་རྟེན་ས་ (tōsa dēnsa) basis of one's livelihood.

འཚོ་སྲུང་ (tsōsuŋ) caring and protecting; va.—བྱེད་ to care for and protect, to defend ¶ འཛམ་གླིང་ཞི་བདེ་འཚོ་སྲུང་བྱེད་ཆེད་ For the purpose of defending world peace.

འཚོ་སློབ་ཕྱིད་བགོས་ (tsōlob cēègöö) sm. འཚོ་ཕྱིད་སློབ་ཕྱིད་.

འཚོག: p. **བཙོགས་**; f. **བཙོག**; imp. **འཚོགས་** (tsɔ̄ɔ̀) va. to beat, to break, to smash, to pulverize.

འཚོག: p. **འཚོགས་** or **ཚོགས་**; f. **འཚོག**; imp. **འཚོགས་** (tsɔ̄ɔ̀) 1. va. to assemble, to gather together, to hold a meeting ¶ ཁ་ས་ཚོགས་འདུ་ཞིག་ཚོགས་ཡོད་པ་རེད་ (They) held a meeting yesterday. 2. vi. to hold/ contain.

འཚོག་རྐྱེན་ (tsɔ̄ɔ̀gyen) arc. provisions taken by people attending a gathering/ meeting.

འཚོག་ཆས་ (tsɔ̄ɔ̀jɛɛ̀) arc. sm. འཚོག་རྐྱེན་

འཚོག་རྟེན་ (tsɔ̄ɔ̀den) arc. sm. འཚོག་རྐྱེན་

འཚོགས་ (tsɔ̄ɔ̀) p. and imp. of འཚོག.

འཚོང་: p. **བཙོངས་**; f. **བཙོང་**; imp. **ཚོངས་** (tsōŋ) va. to sell ¶ ཚལ་དེ་ཚོ་གྲོང་ཁྱེར་ནང་འཚོང་གི་ཡོད་པ་རེད་ (They) sell vegetables in the city.

འཚོང་མཁན་ (tsōŋñɛn) trader, businessmen, merchant.

འཚོང་གོས་ (tsōŋgöö) clothes for sale.

འཚོང་འདུས་ (tsōŋdüü) sm. ཚོང་འདུ་.

འཚོང་ཕྱོགས་ཀྱི་ཚོང་ར་ (tsōŋjɔ̄ɔ̀gi tsōŋra) seller's market.

འཚོང་ཚོད་ཐོན་ཚད་ (tsōŋdzöö tōndzɛɛ̀) trial sale goods, test products for sale.

འཚོང་ཡུལ་ (tsōŋyüü) market ¶ ལག་ཤེས་ཐོན་སྐྱེད་འཚོང་ཡུལ་ཆེན་པོ་ཡོད་པ་རེད་ There is a big market for handicraft products.

འཚོང་རེས་ (tsōŋreè) reciprocal sales/ trading, exchange sales; va.—བྱེད་ to sell each other, to sell reciprocally.

འཚོང་ལམ་ (tsōŋlam) avenue or channel for selling.

འཚོངས་ (tsōŋ) imp. of འཚོང་.

འཚོད་: p. **བཙོས་**; f. **བཙོ་**; imp. **ཚོས་** (tsöö) 1. va. to cook, to boil ¶ ཤ་འདི་ཁོག་མའི་ནང་བཙོས་པ་རེད་ (They) cooked the meat in the pot. 2. va. to smelt gold/ iron. 3. va. to dye.

འཚོད་སྣུམ་ (tsöönum) cooking oil.

འཚོད་མར་ (tsöömaa) melted butter (used for cooking/ frying).

འཚོད་རེས་ཤོར་ (tsööreè shɔ̄ɔ̀) vi. to be semicooked, to be half cooked.

འཚོད་ལ་མ་འཚོད་ (tsööla mandzöö) 1. semicooked, half cooked. 2. person who has only a vague understanding.

འཚོབ: p. **འཚོབས་**; f. **འཚོབ** (tsōb) 1. vi. (fontanel) to harden ¶ ཕྲུ་གུ་དེའི་མཚོག་མ་འཚོབས་འདུག The child's fontanel has hardened. 2. vi. to be/ get healed. 3. vi. to become frozen ¶ གཙང་པོའི་དར་ཁ་འཚོབས་འདུག The river has become frozen.

འཚོབས་ (tsōb) p. and imp. of འཚོབ.

འཚོར་ (tsōr) see ཚོར་.

འཚོལ་: p. and f. **བཙལ་**; imp. **ཚོལ་** (tsöö) va. to search for, to look for, to seek ¶ སོ་པ་འཚོལ་བར་བསྐྱོད་པ་རེད་ (They) went to search for spies.

འཚོལ་ཆས་ (tsööjɛɛ̀) searching equipment.

འཚོལ་ཉུལ་ (tsööñüü) searching/ looking for, investigating; va.—བྱེད་.

འཚོལ་སྙེག (tsööñeg) investigating, searching to find sth. out.

འཚོལ་འདེམས་ (tsööndem) searching/ looking for/ seeking and then selecting; va.—བྱེད་.

འཚོལ་འདོན་ (tsööndön) searching and extracting, exploration and mining; va.—བྱེད་ ¶ རྡོ་སྣུམ་གཏེར་ཁ་འཚོལ་འདོན་བྱེད་ཀྱི་ཡོད་པ་རེད་ (They) are exploring for and mining oil.

འཚོལ་འདྲི (tsööndri) sm. ཚད་གཅོད་.

འཚོལ་སྡུད་ (tsöödüü) searching out and assembling/ gathering together/ collecting; va.—བྱེད་ ¶ དངོས་རྫས་རྙིང་རིགས་མང་པོ་འཚོལ་སྡུད་བྱས་པ་རེད་ (They) collected many old artifacts.

འཚོལ་བསྡུ་ (tsȫȫdu) sm. འཚོལ་སྡུད་.

འཚོལ་ཙམ་བྱེད་ (tsȫȫdzam c̲è) va. to search for cursorily.

འཚོལ་ཞིབ་ (tsȫȫshib) investigating, searching, exploring; va.—བྱེད་.

འཚོལ་ཞིབ་ཐིག་ལེན་ (tsȫȫshib tīglen) surveying; va.—བྱེད་ to survey (in connection with exploration/ prospecting).

འཚོས་ (tsȫö̀) 1. p. of འཚོ་. 2. vi. to comprehend, understand.

འཚོས་སྡོད་ (tsȫö̀döö̀) va. to keep under close watch/ scrutiny ། ཁོ་གང་དུ་ཕྱིན་ཀྱང་མི་དམངས་ཀྱིས་འཚོས་སྡོད་ཀྱི་ཡོད་པ་རེད་ Whereever he goes, the people are keeping close watch on him.

ཛ་ (dza) 1. the letter ཛ་ (used in alphabetical ordering). 2. abbr. of ཛ་དྲག.

ཛ་སྐུ་ (dzagu) shung. abbr. of ཛ་སག་སྐུ་ཞབས་.

ཛ་གད་ (dzāgɛɛ) an offering of meat and ཆང་ to deities.

ཛ་གལ་ (dzāgɛɛ) urgent and important, urgency and importance.

ཛ་གལ་ཅན་ (dzāgɛɛjɛn) urgent and important.

ཛ་རྟགས་ (dzadaà) the mark on the letter ཙ་ which makes it a ཛ་.

ཛ་ཐའི་ (dzadɛɛ) shung. abbr. of ཛ་སག and ཐའི་ཇི་.

ཛ་དྲག (dzadraà) 1. emergency, urgent, critical །ཛ་དྲག་རོགས་རམ་ Emergency aid/ help. 2. intensive.

ཛ་དྲག་གི་གནས་ཚུལ་ (dzadraàgi nɛ̄ɛdzüü) state of emergency, emergency situation.

ཛ་དྲག་གི་ཚོགས་འདུ་ (dzadraàgi tsōndu) emergency session/ meeting/ conference.

ཛ་དྲག་ཅན་ (dzadraàjɛn) 1. urgent, critical, emergency །ལས་ཀ་འདི་ཛ་དྲག་ཅན་ཞིག་རེད་ This work is urgent. 2. intense, drastic ། དྲག་པོའི་འཐབ་རྩོད་ཛ་དྲག་ཅན་བྱེད་ཀྱི་ཡོད་པ་རེད་ (They) are carrying out an intense militant armed struggle.

ཛ་དྲག་ཆེ་བ་ (dzadraà cēwa) sm. ཛ་དྲག་ཅན་.

ཛ་དྲག་ཆེན་པོ་ (dzadraà cēmbo) sm. ཛ་དྲག་ཅན་.

ཛ་དྲག་འདུ་འཛོམས་ (dzadraà dundzom) urgent/ emergency mobilization, urgent call for action.

ཛ་དྲག་གནས་བབ་ (dzadraà nɛ̄ɛbəb) urgent or emergency situation/ position/ condition.

ཛ་དྲག་པོ་ (dza tragbo) sm. ཛ་དྲག་ཅན་.

ཛ་དྲུང་ (dza truŋ) shung. abbr. of ཛ་སག and དྲུང་ཡིག་ཆེན་མོ་.

ཛ་འཕྲུག (dzandruù) sm. ཛ་རྟགས་.

ཛ་བླ་ (dzala) shung. abbr. of ཛ་སག་བླ་མ་.

ཛ་ཛོང་ལྷན་རྒྱས་ (dzadoŋ lhēŋgyɛɛ) shung. the council consisting of the ཛ་སག of Tashilhumpo and the ཛོང་དཔོན་.

ཛ་ཛོར་ (dzadzɔɔ) sm. ཛ་རེ་ཛོ་རེ་.

ཛ་རག (dzaraà) 1. a long necked vase used for religious offerings. 2. a type of silver kettle/ pot. 3. small clay vase.

ཛ་རེ་པ་རེ་ (dzare pare) sm. ཛ་རེ་ཛོ་རེ་.

ཛ་རེ་མོ་རེ་ (dzare more) sm. ཛ་རེ་ཛོ་རེ་.

ཛ་རེ་ཛོ་རེ་ (dzare dzore) messy, untidy, dishevelled, scattered, disorderly.

ཛ་ལག (dzalaà) sm. ཛ་རྟགས་.

ཛ་ལང་ (dzalaŋ) 1. rash, impudent, rude, reckless. 2. having bad manners, being spoiled; vi.—ཤོར་ to get spoiled (behaviorally).

ཛ་ལས་སྡེ་གསོལ་ (dzalɛɛ desöö) shung. abbr. of ཛ་སག, ལས་སྡེ་, སྡེ་འཆང་, and གསོལ་དཔོན་.

ཛ་ལེབ་ལ་ (dzalebla) the pass between Tibet and Sikkim.

ཛ་སག (dzasaà) mong. shung. an official of the third rank in the tt. government.

ཛ་སག་སྐུ་ཞབས་ (dzāsaà gūshəb) shung. a term of address for ཛ་སག.

ཛ་སག་བླ་མ་ (dzāsaà lāma) shung. the monk ཛ་སག sent to rule Tashilhunpo while the Panchen Lama was in exile in China.

ཛ་སག་སེར་སྐྱ་ངོ་ལས་ (dzasaà sērgya ŋolɛɛ) shung. a team consisiting of one lay and one monk dzasa and other subordinate officials.

ཛ་ལྷག (dzalhaà) sm. ཛ་རྟགས་.

ཛཱ་ཏི་ (dzadi) round cardamom.

ཛམ་བྷ་ལ་ (dzambhala) deity of wealth.

ཛར་ཛར་ (dzardzar) sm. འཛར་འཛར་.

ཛར་ཛོར་ (dzardzɔr) abbr. of ཛ་རེ་ཛོ་རེ་.

ཛར་རེ་བ་ (dzarrewa) sth. left unfinished/ undone.

ཛུ་རི་ཅི་ (dzuriji) Zurich.

ཛུའི་ཆི་ཝུ་ (dzü cīwu) ch. soccer.

ཛེན་ནང་པའི་ཆོས་ལུགས་ (dzen naŋbɛ cōōluù) Zen Buddhism.

ཛོར་རྟགས་ (dzɔrdaà) sth. shameful, embarassing, disgraceful; va.—བྱེད་; —སྨྲ་; —དབྱུག་; —སློང་ to do or say sth. shameful/ embarassing/ disgraceful །ཉུན་མཆེད་ཡོད་སར་བཙོག་གཏམ་བཤད་ནས་ཛོར་རྟགས་དབྱུགས་སོང་ Talking dirty in the presence of relatives, he embarassed them.

ཛོར་པོ་ (dzɔrbo) dirty.

ཛོར་པོ་ (dzɔrwo) sm. ཛོར་པོ་.

མཛངས་ (dzaŋ) 1. shyness; va.—བྱེད་ to be shy །ཁོ་མཛངས་ཆེན་པོ་འདུག He is very shy. །མཛངས་མ་གནང་ Don't be shy. 2. sm. མཛངས་པ་.

མཛངས་པ་ (dzaŋba) 1. brave. 2. wise, intelligent, smart.

མཛངས་སྤྱོད་ (dzaŋjöö) conduct/ behavior that is brave and wise.

མཛངས་བླུན་ (dzaŋlün) learned and stupid, wise and foolish.

མཛངས་བླུན་ཞེས་བྱ་བའི་མདོ་ (dzaŋlün sheèjawɛ do) a sutra that contains stories of the ways of learned and stupid people.

མཛངས་མ་ (dzaŋma) an intelligent woman.

མཛངས་ཤིང་མཁས་པ་ (dzaŋshiŋ kɛ̄ɛba) brave and learned.

མཛངས་ཤེས་ (dzaŋsheè) sm. མཁས་མཛངས་.

མཛད་ (dzɛɛ̀) h. of བྱེད་.

མཛད་འཁུར་ (dzɛɛ̀gur) sm. འགན་འཁུར་.

མཛད་དགེ་ (dzɛɛ̀gɛ) it is better to do sth. །ངས་ཁོང་ལ་ཕྱིར་ཕེབས་མཛད་དགེ་པའི་བསམ་འཆར་ཞུས་པ་ཡིན་ I suggested to him that it would be better if he goes back.

མཛད་འགན་ (dzɛɛ̀gɛn) sm. ལས་འགན་.

མཛད་རྒྱ་ (dzɛɛ̀gya) scope of one's work/ business.

མཛད་རྒྱུ་ (dzɛɛ̀gyu) sm. མཛད་རྒྱ་.

མཛད་བརྒྱ་ (dzɛɛ̀gya) the 108 stories of the previous lives of the Buddha.

མཛད་སྒོ་ (dzɛɛ̀go) ceremony, function, official celebration; va.—བྱེད་ to conduct a ceremony/ function.

མཛད་སྒོ་ཆེན་མོ་ (dzɛɛ̀go cēmmo) an important or grand ceremony/ function/ official celebration.

མཛད་སྒོ་རྟེན་འབྲེལ་ (dzɛɛ̀go dēmdree) sm. མཛད་སྒོ་.

མཛད་སྒོ་གཟབ་རྒྱས་ (dzɛɛ̀go səbgyɛɛ) an elaborate/ grand ceremony or function.

མཛད་སྒོའི་སྒྲིག་རྒྱབ་པ་ (dzɛɛ̀gö jīgyəbbə) shung. person in charge of ceremonies/ functions/ celebrations.

མཛད་སྒོའི་རིམ་པ་ (dzɛɛ̀gö rimba) procedural steps in ceremonies/ functions/ celebrations.

མཛད་ཆེན་ (dzɛɛ̀jen) an important ceremony/ official function/ celebration/ ritual །གཞུང་འབྲེལ་མཛད་ཆེན་ Important government ceremonies.

མཛད་འཆར་ (dzɛɛ̀jar) plan of procedures for a ceremony or function.

མཛད་རྗེས་ (dzɛɛ̀jeè) h. of བྱས་རྗེས་.

མཛད་རྗེས་མདོར་བསྡུས་ (dzɛɛ̀jeè dɔrdüü) a brief account of one's achievements, a biographical sketch, resume.

མཛད་གཉེར་ཆེ་མོ་ (dzɛɛ̀ñer cēmo) the main person in charge of arrangements for a ceremony or function.

མཛད་སྟངས་ (dzɛɛ̀daŋ) sm. བྱེད་སྟངས་.

མཛད་སྟོན་ (dzɛɛ̀dön) sm. མཛད་སྒོ་.

མཛད་ཐབས་ (dzɛɛ̀dəb) sm. བྱ་ཐབས་.

མཛད་རྣམ་ (dzɛɛ̀nam) biography (h.).

མཛད་པ་ (dzɛɛ̀ba) h. of ལས་དོན་.

མཛད་པ་ཅན་ (dzɛɛ̀bajɛn) h. of བྱས་རྗེས་ཅན་.

མཛད་པ་བཅུ་གཉིས་ (dzɛɛ̀ba jūñii) the twelve deeds of the Buddha Sakyamuni.

མཛད་པ་པོ་ (dzɛɛ̀babo) 1. h. of བྱེད་མཁན་. 2. author,

writer.

མཛད་པ་ཕུལ་བྱུང་ (dzɛ̱ɛ̀ba pǖūjuŋ) masterpiece, outstanding deed/ act/ work.

མཛད་སྤྱོད་ (dzɛ̱ɛ̀jöö) h. of བྱ་སྤྱོད་.

མཛད་ཕྱོགས་ (dzɛ̱ɛ̀jɔɔ̀) h. of བྱེད་ཕྱོགས་.

མཛད་འཕྲིན་ (dzɛ̱ndrin) h. of འཕྲིན་ལས་.

མཛད་འཕྲིན་རྒྱས་པོ་ (dzɛ̱ndrin gyɛ̱ɛ̀bo) good achievements/ accomplishments, successful.

མཛད་བྱང་ (dzɛ̱ɛ̀jaŋ) colophon of a book.

མཛད་བྱུས་ (dzɛ̱ɛ̀jüü) h. of ལས་དུས་.

མཛད་བྲེལ་ (dzɛ̱ɛ̀dree) h. of ལས་བྲེལ་.

མཛད་གཙོ་ (dzɛ̱ɛ̀dzo) h. of བྱེད་གཙོ་.

མཛད་ཚུལ་ (dzɛ̱ɛ̀dzüü) h. of བྱེད་སྟངས་.

མཛད་ཞབས་པ་ (dzɛ̱ɛ̀shəbbə) shung. government officials attending ceremonies in tt. government.

མཛད་གཞུང་ (dzɛ̱ɛ̀shuŋ) shung. schedule of events, program for a ceremony/ celebration/ function.

མཛད་གཟིགས་ (dzɛ̱ɛ̀sii) reviewing sth. (e.g., a ceremony/ procession); va.—གནང་ to review sth.

མཛད་གཟིགས་སྡིངས་ཆ་ (dzɛ̱ɛ̀sii di̱ŋja) rostrum, reviewing stand.

མཛད་ལུགས་ (dzɛ̱ɛ̀luù) h. of བྱེད་སྟངས་.

མཛད་རིམ་ (dzɛ̱ɛ̀rim) abbr. of མཛད་སྒོ་རིམ་པ་.

མཛད་སེང་ (dzɛ̱ɛ̀seŋ) spare time (h.).

མཛད་སྲོལ་ (dzɛ̱ɛ̀söö) custom/ tradition of doing sth. ¶ དེ་སྔའི་མཛད་སྲོལ་ལ་ According to the previous custom.

མཛའ་ (dza̱) abbr. of མཛའ་པོ་.

མཛའ་གྲོགས་ (dza̱drɔɔ̀) friendship, goodwill, a friend; va.—བྱེད་ to make friends with, to act friendly towards ¶ མཛའ་གྲོགས་ཀྱི་འཚམས་འདྲི་ Friendship visit.

མཛད་འཁུར་དམ་བཅའ་ (dza̱drɔɔ̀ ta̱mja) sm. མཚན་འཁུར་དམ་བཅའ་.

མཛད་གྲོགས་རྒྱལ་ཁབ་ (dza̱drɔɔ̀ gyɛ̱ɛ̱gəb) friendly nation/ country.

མཛའ་གྲོགས་མཐུན་སྒྲིལ་ (dza̱drɔɔ̀ tǖndrii) friendship and unity; va.—བྱེད་ to act with friendship and unity.

མཛའ་གྲོགས་མཐུན་ཚོགས་ (dza̱drɔɔ̀ tǖndzɔɔ̀) friendship association.

མཛའ་གླུ་ (dza̱lu) love song.

མཛའ་འགྲོགས་ (dza̱drɔɔ̀) sm. མཛའ་གྲོགས་.

མཛའ་གཅུགས་ (dza̱juù) friendly, friendship ¶ རྒྱལ་ཁབ་གཉིས་བར་མཛའ་གཅུགས་ཀྱི་འབྲེལ་བ་བྱུང་སོང་ A friendly relationship was established between the two countries.

མཛའ་གཅུགས་མི་ཕྱེད་ (dza̱juù mi̱jeè) close friendship.

མཛའ་ཉེ་ (dza̱ñe) abbr. of མཛའ་མཛའ་ཉེ་ཉེ་.

མཛའ་མཐའ་བཟང་འཁྱོལ་ (dza̱da sa̱ŋgyöö) loving each other until the end of one's life.

མཛའ་མཐུན་ (dzədün) friendship, goodwill, cordialty; va.—བྱེད་ to act with friendship/ goodwill, to be friends ¶ ཀྲུང་ཨར་རྒྱལ་ཁབ་གཉིས་ཀྱི་མི་དམངས་ཀྱི་མཛའ་མཐུན་ The friendship of the people of China and Albania.

མཛའ་མཐུན་གྱི་འབྲེལ་བ་ (dza̱düngi dre̱ewa) friendly relations, ties/ bonds of friendship.

མཛའ་མཐུན་གྱི་འཚམས་འདྲི་ (dza̱düngi tsəmdri) friendship visit.

མཛའ་མཐུན་གྲོས་མོལ་ (dza̱dün trö̱ömöö) friendly discussion.

མཛའ་མཐུན་རྒྱལ་ཁབ་ (dza̱düng gyɛ̱ɛ̱gəb) friendly country.

མཛའ་མཐུན་ཆིངས་ཡིག (dza̱dün ci̱ŋyiì) treaty of friendship.

མཛའ་མཐུན་མཉམ་འབྲེལ་ (dza̱dün ñāmdree) friendly relations.

མཛའ་མཐུན་མཉམ་ལས་ (dza̱dün ñāmlɛɛ̀) friendship and cooperation.

མཛའ་མཐུན་མཉམ་ལས་ཀྱི་འབྲེལ་བ་ (dza̱dün ñāmlɛɛ̀gi dre̱ewa) relations of friendship and cooperation.

མཛའ་མཐུན་མཉམ་ལས་ཀྱི་ཆིངས་ཡིག (dza̱dün ñāmlɛɛ̀gi ci̱ŋyiì) treaty of friendship and cooperation.

མཛའ་མཐུན་འཐུས་ཚོགས་ (dza̱dün tǖūdzɔɔ̀) friendship mission/ delegation.

མཛའ་མཐུན་གདན་ཞུའི་འགྲན་བསྡུར་ (dza̱dün de̱nshü tre̱ndur) friendship invitational tournament or competition.

མཛའ་མཐུན་མནའ་འབྲེལ་རོགས་རེས་ཆིངས་ཡིག (dza̱dün nāndree ro̱greè ci̱ŋyiì) treaty of friendship, alliance and mutual assistance.

མཛའ་མཐུན་སེལ་མེད་ (dza̱dün sēlmeè) perfect friendship, friendship without problems.

མཛའ་དུང་ (dza̱duŋ) sm. བརྩེ་དུང་.

མཛའ་ན་མོ་ (dza̱ na̱mo) darling, dearest.

མཛའ་པོ་ (dzabo) friendly ¶ ཁོ་གཉིས་མཛའ་པོ་ཞེ་དྲགས་འདུག They are very friendly.

མཛའ་སྤུན་ (dza̱bön) relatives with whom one is friendly.

མཛའ་ཕྱོགས་ (dza̱jɔɔ̀) relatives.

མཛའ་འཕྲིན་ (dza̱drin) love letter.

མཛའ་བ་ (dza̱wa) friendship, friendly.

མཛའ་བོ་ (dza̱wo) 1. friend. 2. spouse.

མཛའ་འབྲེལ་ (dza̱ndree) friendship, friendly relations; va.—བྱེད་ to be friends, to have friendly relations.

མཛའ་མོ་ (dza̱mo) girlfriend.

མཛའ་བརྩེ་ (dza̱dze) love; va.—བྱེད་ to love.

མཛའ་བརྩེ་མཉམ་ལས་ (dza̱dze ñamlɛɛ̀) loving/ friendly cooperation.

མཛའ་རྩེ་ལྡན་པ་ (dza̱dze de̱mba) dear, beloved ¶ མཛའ་བརྩེ་ལྡན་པའི་བློ་མཐུན་རྣམས་ལ་ To the dear comrades.

མཛའ་བརྩེ་རོགས་རེས་ (dza̱dze ro̱greè) fraternal help.

མཛའ་མཛའ་ཉེ་ཉེ་ (dza̱dza ñe̱ñe) beloved and intimate/ dear.

མཛའ་གཞས་ (dza̱drɔɔ̀) sm. མཛའ་གླུ་.

མཛའ་ལོག (dza̱ lɔɔ̀) vi. to become unfriendly.

མཛའ་གཤིབ་ (dza̱shib) friendly, close.

མཛའ་གཤིས་ (dza̱shiì) friendly in character/ personality.

མཛའ་བཤེས་ (dza̱sheè) sm. མཛའ་གྲོགས་.

མཛའ་བཤེས་མཉམ་ལས་ (dza̱sheè) sm. མཛའ་བརྩེ་མཉམ་ལས་.

མཛའ་བཤེས་སྨོན་འདྲིན་ (dza̱sheè mōndrin) sm. མཛའ་གཅུགས་མི་ཕྱེད་.

མཛའ་བཤེས་ཚོང་ཁང་ (dza̱sheè tsōŋgaŋ) Friendship Store (in People's Republic of China).

མཛའ་སེམས་ (dza̱sem) feeling of friendship, friendly thoughts/ thinking.

མཛར་པ་ (dzārwa) food/ provisions taken to work or on a trip.

མཛར་མར་ (dzārmar) butter taken with food being carried to work or on a trip.

མཛུ་གུ་ (dzu̱gu) sm. མཛུག་གུ་.

མཛུག་གུ་ (dzu̱gu) finger, toe; va.—འཛུགས་ to point a finger; to accuse/ blame.

མཛུག་གུ་གང་ (dzu̱gu ka̱ŋ) sm. མཛུབ་གང་.

མཛུག་གུ་བཙིར་གནོན་ (dzu̱gu dzīrnün) squeezing a person's fingers between sticks (a form of torture).

མཛུག་གུ་འཛུགས་ས་ (dzu̱gu dzūgsa) 1. sb. to blame or accuse of sth. ¶ ལས་ཁུངས་ནང་གི་ཡིག་ཆ་བརླགས་པ་དེའི་སྐོར་མཛུག་གུ་འཛུགས་ས་མི་འདུག Conecerning the official documents that were lost, there is no one to blame (a place to point one's finger at). 2. sth. concrete to point to ¶ ཁོང་གིས་ལས་ཀ་འདི་ནང་མཛུག་གུ་འཛུགས་ཡོད་པའི་གྲུབ་རྗེས་གང་ཡང་བཀག་མི་འདུག There is no accomplishment in his work that we can point to.

མཛུག་ཆུང་ (dzu̱gjuŋ) littlle finger/ toe.

མཛུག་ཐེལ་ (dzu̱gtee) fingerprint; va.—རྒྱག to put a fingerprint (in Tibet, thumbprint) on sth.

མཛུག་རྩིས་ (dzu̱gdziì) counting on/ by one's fingers; va.—རྒྱག.

མཛུབ་ (dzu̱b) finger, toe.

མཛུབ་ཀྲབ་ལྕགས་པར་ (dzu̱bdrəb jāgbar) typewriter;

va.—རྒྱག to type on a typewriter.

མཛུབ་དཀྲིས་ (dzubdrii) ring made in the form of coils (usu. of gold).

མཛུབ་ཁྲིད་ (dzubdrii) guiding, instructing, directing (usu. by showing firsthand); va.—བྱེད་ to instruct, to teach, to direct.

མཛུབ་འཁྲིད་ (dzubdrii) sm. མཛུབ་ཁྲིད་.

མཛུབ་གང་ (dzubgaŋ) a measure consisting of the distance on the second finger from the tip to the first joint.

མཛུབ་གུ་ (dzubgu) sm. མཛུག་གུ.

མཛུབ་བརྒྱུས་ (dzubgyüü) ring.

མཛུབ་ངོ་ (dzubŋo) tool for making copperware.

མཛུབ་ལྕིབས་ (dzubjib) 1. thimble. 2. gloves.

མཛུབ་ཆུང་ (dzubjuŋ) sm. མཛུག་ཆུང་.

མཛུབ་རྗེས་ (dzubjeè) fingerprint.

མཛུབ་ཉུལ་ (dzubñüü) eating རྩམ་པ་ by kneading with the fingers; va.—རྒྱག.

མཛུབ་ཉོག (dzubñog) eating with one's fingers; va.—རྒྱག.

མཛུབ་སྟོན་ (dzubdön) guiding, instructing, pointing out, directing; guidance, instruction; va.—བྱེད་ ། ཚོགས་འདུའི་མཛུབ་སྟོན་གཞིར་བཟུང་ Based on the instructions of the meeting. ། གསར་བརྗེའི་ལས་འགུལ་གྱི་དམིགས་ཡུལ་མཛུབ་སྟོན་བྱེད་པ་རེད་ (They) pointed out the aims of the revolutionary movement. ། ཁོང་གིས་ཚད་སྐྱོབ་ཀྱི་ལས་ཀའི་ཐད་ལ་མཛུབ་སྟོན་བྱས་པ་རེད་ He directed the relief (aid) work.

མཛུབ་སྟོན་གྱི་ནུས་པ་ (dzubdöngi nüübə) guiding function/ power.

མཛུབ་སྟོན་གྱི་བསམ་བློ་ (dzubdöngi sāmlo) guiding thought/ theory/ idea.

མཛུབ་སྟོན་དམིགས་བསལ་ (dzubdön migsεε) special directive.

མཛུབ་ཐུང་ (dzubduŋ) sm. མཛུབ་ཆུང་.

མཛུབ་ཐེལ་ (dzubdee) fingerprint; va.—རྒྱག to make a fingerprint.

མཛུབ་མཐོ་ (dzubto) a measure consisting of the length from the outstretched thumb to the tip of the outstretched second finger.

མཛུབ་དྲུག (dzubdruù) sb. with six fingers.

མཛུབ་བཏད་ (dzubda) 1. indicating a direction with a finger; va.—བྱེད་. 2. pointing with the index finger to emphasize a point; va.—བྱེད་.

མཛུབ་གནོན་ (dzūbnün) a button to be pressed down (as on a recorder).

མཛུབ་གནོན་ཀྱིབ་དཔར་རྒྱག (dzūbnün drēbbar gyaà) sm. མཛུབ་ཀྱིབ་ལྕགས་པར་རྒྱག.

མཛུབ་གནོན་ལྕགས་པར་ (dzūbnün jāgbar) sm. མཛུབ་ཀྱིབ་ལྕགས་པར་.

མཛུབ་སྣེ་ (dzubne) finger tip.

མཛུབ་མོ་ (dzummo) sm. མཛུག་གུ་.

མཛུབ་མོ་གང་སྟོན་ཤར་ (dzummo kaŋdön shār) doing whatever is ordered [Lit. rising wherever the finger points].

མཛུབ་མོ་འགུགས་ཐབས་བྱེད་ (dzummo gugdəb ceè) sm. བློ་འགུགས་ཐབས་བྱེད་.

མཛུབ་མོས་གནམ་འདེགས་ (dzubmöö nāmdeg) having unrealistic expectations, trying to do the impossible, sth. that is impossible to do [Lit. finger holding up the sky].

མཛུབ་མོས་གནམ་འབིགས་ (dzubmöö nāmbig) sm. མཛུབ་མོས་གནམ་འདེགས་.

མཛུབ་མོས་གནམ་མི་འཕིགས་ (dzubmöö nām mibig) having unrealistic expectations, trying to do the impossible, sth. that is impossible to do [Lit. finger poking a hole in the sky].

མཛུབ་མོས་གནམ་མི་འབིགས་ (dzubmöö nām mibig) sm. མཛུབ་མོས་གནམ་མི་འཕིགས་.

མཛུབ་མོས་རི་སྟོན་ (dzubmö ridön) talking generally/ vaguely, not being specific, explaining roughly [Lit. finger shows a mountain].

མཛུབ་བཙུགས་ (dzubdzuù) sm. མཛུབ་མ་འཛུགས་.

མཛུབ་རྩེ་ (dzubdze) fingertip.

མཛུབ་རྩིས་ (dzubdzii) counting/ calculating with the fingers; va.—རྒྱག.

མཛུབ་རྩིས་མི་ཐེབས་པ་ (dzubdzii mitebba) too numerous to be counted on the fingers.

མཛུབ་ཚད་ (dzubdzεε) a specified quantity, a norm/ target/ quota.

མཛུབ་ཚིགས་ (dzubdzii) finger joint.

མཛུབ་ཚུགས་ (dzubdzuù) sm. མཛུབ་མ་འཛུགས་.

མཛུབ་ཞྭ་ (dzubsha) thimble.

མཛུབ་གཟུགས་ (dzubsuù) a type of chisel.

མཛུབ་བཟོ་མགོ་སྒོན་ (dzubso gogön) a coppersmith's tool.

མཛུབ་རིས་ (dzubrii) fingerprint.

མཛུབ་རུས་ (dzubrüü) finger bone.

མཛུབ་ཤུབས་ (dzubshub) gloves, coverings for the fingers.

མཛུབ་ཤུབས་ལྕིབས་མོ་ (dzubshub jībmu) thimble.

མཛུབ་གསང་ (dzubsaŋ) space between fingers.

མཛུབ་ཧྲག (dzubhraà) between the fingers.

མཛེ་ (dze) leprosy; vi.—རྒྱག to have/ get leprosy.

མཛེ་སྐྱ་ (dzegye) a type of leprosy.

མཛེ་ཁྲག (dzedraà) the blood of a person with leprosy.

མཛེ་གོད་འབྲུམ་ (dze göndrum) a kind of leprosy.

མཛེ་ཐོག་ཕོལ་བརྩེགས་ (dzedɔɔ pöödzeè) one disaster after another occuring [Lit. on top of leprosy, abcess].

མཛེ་ནད་ (dzenεε) sm. མཛེ་.

མཛེ་པོ་ (dzebo) male leper.

མཛེ་ཕོ་ (dzebo) sm. མཛེ་པོ་.

མཛེ་མོ་ (dzemo) female leper.

མཛེ་རྫ་ (dzedza) mirabilite, Glauber's salt.

མཛེར་དུམ་ (dzerdum) gall.

མཛེར་པ་ (dzerba) 1. wart; vi.—སྐྱེ་ to have wart appear/ grow; va.—འགོག to cut off a wart. 2. goitre. 3. a knot (in wood).

མཛེར་ཕྲན་ (dzerdrεn) 1. small wart. 2. small goitre.

མཛེར་བུ་ (dzerbu) sm. མཛེར་ཕྲན་.

མཛེས་ (dzeè) abbr. of མཛེས་པོ་.

མཛེས་ཁོང་ (dzeègoŋ) dimple.

མཛེས་ཀྱོང་ (dzeègyoŋ) sm. མཛེས་ཁོང་.

མཛེས་སྐུ་ (dzeègu) beautiful body/ figure.

མཛེས་བཀྲག (dzeèdraà) beautiful and bright/ lustrous/ gleaming.

མཛེས་ཁྱད་ (dzeègyεε) the quality of beauty.

མཛེས་གྲགས་ (dzeèdraà) famous and beautiful.

མཛེས་རྒྱན་ (dzeègyεn) ornament, decoration; va.—སྤྲས་ to ornament/ decorate/ beautify/ glorify.

མཛེས་སྒོ་ (dzeègo) decorated door.

མཛེས་སྒྲོན་ (dzeèdrön) lantern.

མཛེས་བཅོས་ཁང་ (dzeèjöögaŋ) beauty parlor/ shop.

མཛེས་ཆོས་ (dzeèjöö) decorations to make sth. beautiful; va.—བྱེད་; —སྤྲས་ to make oneself beautiful, to dress up, to beautify sth.

མཛེས་ཆོས་ཀྱི་སྤྲ་བ་ (dzeèjöögi bāwa) beautiful.

མཛེས་ཆོས་མཚར་སྒེག་ཅན་ (dzeèjöö cɔrgegjεn) beautiful but coquettish.

མཛེས་འཆོས་ (dzeèjöö) sm. མཛེས་ཆོས་.

མཛེས་འཆོས་སྤྲས་སྟེགས་ (dzeèjöö drεεdeg) dressing table.

མཛེས་ལྗོངས་ (dzeèjoŋ) beautiful scenery, scenic.

མཛེས་བརྗིད་གཉིས་ལྡན་ (dzeèjii ñiidεn) both beautiful and grand.

མཛེས་ཉམས་ (dzeèñam) charm, beauty, attractiveness.

མཛེས་ཉམས་ཅན་ (dzeèñamjεn) beautiful, attractive.

མཛེས་ཉམས་དོད་པོ་ (dzeè töòbo) beautiful, stylish.

མཛེས་སྙན་ (dzeèñam) beautiful and famous.

མཛེས་ཐོག་མཛེས་བརྩེགས་ (dzeèdɔɔ dzeèdzeg) adding good on top good [Lit. adding beauty on top of beauty].

མཛེས་མདངས་ (dzeèdaŋ) radiant beauty.

མཛེས་མདངས་ཅན་ (dzeèdaŋjεn) beautiful, gorgeous.

མཛེས་སྡུག (dzeèduù) beauty ། མཛེས་སྡུག་ལྡན་པ་

Beautiful.
མཛེས་སྡུག་ཉམས་འགྱུར་ (dzeèduù ñamgyur) beautiful, stylish.
མཛེས་སྡུག་ཡོད་འོང་ (dzeèduù yioŋ) sm. མཛེས་སྡུག.
མཛེས་སྣང་ (dzeènaŋ) sm. མཛེས་སྡུག.
མཛེས་པ་ (dzeèba) sm. མཛེས་པོ་.
མཛེས་པར་བརྒྱན་ (dzeèbar gyɛn) va. to beautify.
མཛེས་པོ་ (dzeèba) beautiful, lovely, pretty.
མཛེས་དཔྱད་རིག་པའི་སློབ་གསོ་ (dzeèjɛɛ̀ rigbɛ lōbso) sm. མཛེས་དཔྱད་སློབ་གསོ་.
མཛེས་དཔྱད་སློབ་གསོ་ (dzeèjeè lōbso) aesthetic education, fine arts education.
མཛེས་བྱད་ (dzeèjɛɛ̀) a beautiful face.
མཛེས་བྱེད་ (dzeèjeè) jewelry, ornaments.
མཛེས་མ་ (dzeèma) a beautiful girl.
མཛེས་མ་བུ་མོ་ (dzeèma pomo) sm. མཛེས་མ་.
མཛེས་མོ་ (dzeèmo) beauty.
མཛེས་རྩལ་ (dzeèdzɛɛ) art ། ཚགས་པར་འདིའི་མཛེས་རྩལ་རྩོམ་སྒྲིག་པ་ The art editor of this newspaper.
མཛེས་རྩལ་ཁང་ (dzeèdzɛɛgaŋ) art gallery, art museum.
མཛེས་རྩལ་མཁས་པའི་ཚོགས་ (dzeèdzɛɛ kɛ̄ɛ̀bɛ tsɔ̄ɔ̀) artists' association.
མཛེས་རྩལ་གྱི་ཡི་གེ་ (dzeèdzɛɛgi yigi) artistic calligraphy, artistic lettering.
མཛེས་རྩལ་གློག་བརྙན་ (dzeèdzɛɛ lɔ̄ɔ̀ñɛn) 1. art film. 2. animated film, cartoon flim.
མཛེས་རྩལ་པ་ (dzeèdzɛɛba) artist.
མཛེས་རྩལ་པའི་མཐུན་ཚོགས་ (dzeèdzɛɛbɛ tǖndzɔɔ̀) artists' association.
མཛེས་རྩལ་རིག་པ་ (dzeèdzɛɛ riigbɔ) aesthetics.
མཛེས་རྩལ་སློབ་གྲྭ་ (dzeèdzɛɛ lōbdra) school of fine arts.
མཛེས་རྩལ་སློབ་གྲྭ་ཆེན་མོ་ (dzeèdzɛɛ lōbdra cēmmo) college of fine arts.
མཛེས་རྩལ་སློབ་གསོ་ (dzeèdzɛɛ lōbso) fine arts education.
མཛེས་རྩོམ་ (dzeèdzom) artistic article/ essay.
མཛེས་ཚོར་ (dzeè tsɔ̄r) vi. to perceive beauty.
མཛེས་མཚོན་ (dzeèdzön) putting on an act (to please), not acting honestly/ genuinely in accordance with one's true feeling; va.—བྱེད་.
མཛེས་མཚོན་གྱི་སྐད་ཆ་ (dzeèdzöngi gɛ̀ɛja) nice sounding/ pleasant speech (that is not genuine or frank).
མཛེས་མཚོན་མཐུན་སྒྲིལ་ (dzeèdzön tǖndrii) getting along well with everyone (but not being honest/ frank).
མཛེས་མཛེས་བྱེད་ (dzeèdzeè ceè) 1. sm. མཛེས་བྱེད་. 2. va. to act shy.
མཛེས་ཞལ་ (dzeèshɛɛ) h. of མཛེས་བྱད་.
མཛེས་བཞིན་ (dzeèshin) sm. མཛེས་བྱད་.
མཛེས་ཟོལ་ (dzeèsöö) deceptive facade (that all is fine).
མཛེས་ཟོལ་མེད་པ་ (dzeèsöö meèba) truthful, straightforward.
མཛེས་བཟང་ (dzeèsaŋ) beautiful and of good character.
མཛེས་བཟོ་ (dzeèsö) cosmetics, makeup.
མཛེས་བཟོའི་ཕྱུག་རྫས་ (dzeèsö cugdzɛɛ) sm. མཛེས་བཟོ་.
མཛེས་ཡིག (dzeèyiì) beautifully written letters, calligraphy.
མཛེས་རིག (dzeèrig) sm. མཛེས་རྩལ་.
མཛེས་རིག་པར་ཁང་ (dzeèrig bārgaŋ) fine arts publishing house.
མཛེས་རིག་རྩོམ་རིགས་ (dzeèrig dzōmriì) fine arts literary works.
མཛེས་རིག་ལག་རྩལ་ (dzeèrig lagdzɛɛ) sm. མཛེས་རྩལ་.
མཛེས་རིག་སློབ་ཚན་ (dzeèrig lōbdzɛn) art lesson/ class.
མཛེས་རིས་ (dzeèriì) a beautiful picture/ painting.
མཛེས་ལམ་ (dzeèlam) sm. མཛེས་ཚོས་.
མཛེས་ལམ་གང་ཆགས་ (dzeèlam kaŋjaà) acting outwardly agreeably, doing sth. for outward appearance; va.—བྱེད་ ། གཅིག་ཕན་གཅིག་ཐོགས་མཐུན་གཞིབ་མཛེས་ལམ་གང་ཆགས་དགོས་རྒྱུར་སྣང་ཡང་ It is deemed necessary to help each other for outward appearance but.
མཛེས་ལས་ (dzeèlɛɛ̀) art work, art designing.
མཛེས་ལས་བྱེད་མཁན་ (dzeèlɛɛ̀ ceèñɛn) art designer.
མཛེས་ལེགས་ (dzeèleg) beautiful and good.
མཛོ་ (dzo) hybrid between a yak and cattle.
མཛོ་ཀོ་ (dzogɔɔ) hide of a མཛོ་.
མཛོ་ཁལ་ར་འགེལ་ (dzokɛɛ ragee) a task for which a person is not qualified or is way above his head, being unequal to one's responsibility/ work [Lit. a goat carrrying a load intended for a dzo].
མཛོ་ཁལ་ར་ཡིས་མི་ཐེག (dzokɛɛ rayiì midig) sm. མཛོ་ཁལ་ར་འགེལ་.
མཛོ་ཁལ་ལུག་ཁལ་ (dzokɛɛ luùkɛɛ) giving people appropriate/ suitable (tasks) [Lit. dzo load, sheep load].
མཛོ་གྭ་པ་ (dzo gaba) a dzo with a white face.
མཛོ་རྒོད་ (dzo göö) dzo that has not been trained to plow.
མཛོ་གཉའ་སྦྲེལ་ (dzo ñādree) va. to put two dzo together (for plowing).
མཛོ་རྟ་གསན་པ་ (dzoda sɛmba) shung. va. grazing horses and dzo ། འདི་པ་རྣམས་ནས་མཛོ་རྟ་གསན་པ་དང་རྔོན་རྒྱག་དུ་མ་བཅུག Grazing and hunting are not allowed in the area.
མཛོ་རྟ་གསན་མི་ (dzoda sɛnmi) shung. person who feeds dzo and horses.
མཛོ་རྡང་ (dzodaŋ) sm. མཛོ་གདང་.
མཛོ་མདུན་སྦལ་པས་བཅད་པ་ (dzodün bɛ̀ɛbɛ jɛ̀ɛba) doing sth. that's impractible/ impossible [Lit. a frog crossing in front of a dzo].
མཛོ་གདང་ (dzodaŋ) horizontal stretched rope/ tether line used to tie dzo.
མཛོ་བདག་ལ་མཛོ་རྒྱུས་ (dzodaàla dzogyüù) showing one's ignorance by talking about a subject that one knows very little about with a person who is an expert in that particular field [Lit. telling the owner of a dzo all about dzo].
མཛོ་སྣ་ (dzona) part of a Tibetan lock.
མཛོ་པ་ (dzoba) person who looks after dzo.
མཛོ་དཔོན་ (dzobön) person in charge of dzo.
མཛོ་ཕྲུག (dzodruù) མཛོ་ calf.
མཛོ་སྦྲེལ་ (dzodree) two dzo tied together.
མཛོ་མོ་ (dzomo) female མཛོ་.
མཛོ་མོ་ཁྱུ་འཛིན་རྒྱག (dzomo kyūndzin gyaà) shung. va. to catch the best female dzo amongst a herd ། མཛོ་མོ་ཁྱུ་འཛིན་བརྒྱབ་རྐྱེན་སོགས་ས་གནས་རྫོང་དུ་གཏུགས་བཞིར་བགྱིས་པ་ Because (he) caught the best female dzo amongst the herd, they brought a lawsuit to the district head.
མཛོ་མོ་ཤིང་ (dzomo shīŋ) a type of tree.
མཛོ་མོའི་རྟོལ་ (dzomö dȫö) calf of a dzo.
མཛོ་གཡུང་པོ་ (dzo yūŋbu) a riding dzo.
མཛོ་ར་ (dzora) a dzo shed/ corral.
མཛོ་ཤད་ (dzoshɛɛ̀) a three year old dzo.
མཛོག (dzɔɔ̀) sm. ཛོག་འགོ་.
མཛོག་འགོ་ (dzɔŋgo) fist; va.—བཀུག to raise one's fist.
མཛོག་རུམ་ (dzɔgrum) fist; va.—སྒྲིམ་ to make a fist; va.—གཞུ་ to hit with a fist.
མཛོད་ (dzöö) 1. treasury, storehouse. 2. polite imperative (imp. of མཛད་) ། མི་དམངས་བདེ་སྐྱིད་ཡོང་བ་མཛོད་ Make it so that the people will become happy.
མཛོད་ཀྱི་འགོ་པ་ (dzöögi goba) head of the treasury/ warehouse/ storehouse.
མཛོད་སྐོང་ (dzöö gōŋ) filling a storehouse/ warehouse; va.—བྱེད་.
མཛོད་ཁང་ (dzöögaŋ) storehouse, warehouse, treasury.
མཛོད་ཁང་ཞིབ་བཤེར་ (dzöögaŋ shibsher) checking the inventory of a warehouse/ storehouse/ treasury.

མཛོད་གོས་ (dzö̱ögöö) shung. brocade robe with a dragon pattern that was worn by officials of the 4th rank and higher (in tt.).

མཛོད་འགྲེལ་ (dzö̱ö dre̱e) an explanation/ commentary on the major Buddhist text on metaphysics.

མཛོད་དངུལ་ (dzö̱öŋüü) money deposited in a savings account.

མཛོད་ཅིག (dzö̱öjig) h. of བྲིས་ཤིག.

མཛོད་ཆུང་ (dzö̱öjuŋ) shung. a smaller treasury of the Dalai Lama.

མཛོད་ཆེན་ (dzö̱öjen) large warehouse/ storehouse/ treasury.

མཛོད་རྫས་ (dzö̱öjüü) a type of brocade.

མཛོད་འཛོག (dzö̱njɔɔ) stockpile; va.—བྱེད་ to stockpile/ store up.

མཛོད་ཉར་ (dzö̱öñar) keeping in storage, storing; va.—བྱེད་.

མཛོད་ཉར་ཚོང་ཟོག (dzö̱öñar tsōŋsoò) commodity/ stock inventory.

མཛོད་གཉེར་ (dzö̱öñer) storehouse/ warehouse/ treasury manager.

མཛོད་བཏགས་ (dzö̱ödaà) shung. a high quality ceremonial scarf.

མཛོད་བཏགས་འདོམས་འཁོར་མ་ (dzö̱ödaà do̱mkɔɔma) shung. a type of high quality long ceremonial scarf.

མཛོད་དམ་ཁ་ (dzö̱ö da̱mga) shung. tax collection for land and trade ¶ དམག་འཛམས་མཛོད་དམ་ཁས་མགོ་བྱས་ཁྲིམས་ཀྱི་བྱ་བ་ཅི་དགག་རྣམས་དུས་ལ་སྐྱིབས་པར་སྒྲུབས་ You shall handle matters concerning military affairs, postal stations and land and trade tax collection without delay.

མཛོད་ལྡེ་ (dzö̱öde) shung. abbr. of ཕྱག་མཛོད་ and ལྡེ་འཆང་.

མཛོད་པ་ (dzö̱öba) person (steward, manager) in charge of a storehouse/ warehouse/ treasury.

མཛོད་དཔོན་ (dzö̱öbön) sm. མཛོད་ཀྱི་འགོ་པ་.

མཛོད་སྤུ་ (dzö̱öbu) a black spot on the forehead of the Buddha.

མཛོད་སྤུངས་དངོས་རྫས་ (dzö̱öbuŋ ŋö̱ödzεὲ) sm. མཛོད་བསགས་དངོས་རྫས་.

མཛོད་སྤྲག (dzö̱öbuù) shung. the private treasury of the Dalai Lama (in tt.).

མཛོད་སྤྲག་ཁོངས་ (dzö̱öbuù kōŋ) shung. belonging to the Dalai Lama's treasury.

མཛོད་འཛིན་ (dzö̱ndzin) shung. sm. ཕྱག་མཛོད་.

མཛོད་བཞག (dzö̱öshaà) sm. མཛོད་ཉར་.

མཛོད་ཟུར་ (dzö̱ösur) shung. abbr. ཕྱག་མཛོད་ཟུར་པ་.

མཛོད་ལས་ (dzö̱ölεὲ) shung. abbr. of ཕྱག་མཛོད་ and ལས་བྱེད་པ་.

མཛོད་བསགས་དངོས་རྫས་ (dzö̱ösaà ŋö̱ödzεὲ) goods kept in stock; reserve materials/ goods.

མཛོའི་སྐེ་རྒྱན་ (dzö̱ö gēgyεn) ornaments put around the neck of a dzo.

མཛོའི་སྣ་ (dzö̱ö nā) sm. མཛོ་སྣ་.

མཛོལ་བུ་ (dzö̱öbu) 1. snare, trap. 2. a son of a prostitute, a bastard.

འཛག : p. ཟག; f. **འཛག** (dza̱à) 1. vi. to fall. 2. vi. to leak/ drip (water) ¶ སྣོད་འདིའི་སེར་ཀ་ནས་ཆུ་འཛགས་ཀྱི་འདུག Water drips through the crack in this container.

འཛག་གེ་འཛོག་གེ་ (dza̱àge dzo̱ge) dirty, muddy.

འཛག་ཆུ་ (dza̱gju) dripping/ leaking water.

འཛག་དམ་ (dza̱gdam) hourglass.

འཛག་སྣོད་ (dza̱gnöö) a pail/ container for putting under a leak.

འཛག་འཛོག (dza̱gdzog) abbr. of འཛག་གེ་འཛོག་གེ་.

འཛགས་གེར་ (dza̱gger) all covered, full of, all over ¶ རི་ལུང་ཤིང་ནགས་ཀྱིས་འཛག་གེར་ཁེབས་ཡོད་པ་རེད་ The mountains and plains are covered with forests.

འཛང་འཛང་ (dza̱ŋdzaŋ) 1. being short (for clothes/ dress). 2. scarce, short.

འཛང་པོ་ (dza̱ŋbo) sm. འཛང་འཛང་.

འཛང་སེ་བ་ (dza̱ŋsewa) a little short/ scarce.

འཛངས་ (dza̱ŋ) arc. sm. ཟད་.

འཛངས་པོ་ (dza̱ŋbo) scarce, short ¶ ལུང་པ་འདིར་ཤ་འཛངས་པོ་འདུག Meat is scarce in this country.

འཛད་ : p. ཟད་; f. **འཛད་** (dzε̱ὲ) vi. to be exhausted/ spent, to be consumed, to run out ¶ དུས་ཚོད་མང་བ་ལམ་དུ་ཟད་སོང་ Most of the time was spent on the road. ¶ མུ་གེ་ལོ་གཉིས་བྱུང་ཙང་མཛོད་ཁང་གི་འབྲུ་མང་ཆེ་བ་ཟད་པ་རེད་ Because there was famine for two years most of the stored grain was exhausted.

འཛད་སྒྲོན་ (dzε̱ὲdrön) expenditure, consumption ¶ མོ་ཊ་འདི་སྣུམ་འཛད་སྒྲོན་ཆེན་པོ་འདུག The gas consumption of this car is high.

འཛད་སྒྲོན་གྱི་ཚད་ (dzε̱ὲdröngi dzεὲ) the amount/ level of consumption.

འཛད་མཐའ་མེད་པ་ (dzε̱ὲta me̱èba) inexhaustible, limitless, endless.

འཛད་པ་མེད་པ་ (dzε̱ὲba me̱èba) sm. འཛད་མཐའ་མེད་པ་.

འཛད་སྤྱོད་ (dzε̱ὲjöö) utilization, consumption; va.—བྱེད་.

འཛད་སྤྱོད་ཁང་ (dzε̱ὲjöögaŋ) consumer's cooperative.

འཛད་སྤྱོད་རྒྱུ་ཆས་ (dzε̱ὲjöö gyu̱jεὲ) sm. འཛད་རྫས་.

འཛད་སྤྱོད་ཐེབས་རྩ་ (dzε̱ὲjöö tēbdza) consumer's fund/ endowment.

འཛད་སྤྱོད་པ་ (dzε̱ὲjööba) consumer.

འཛད་སྤྱོད་བྱེད་ཚད་ (dzε̱ὲjöö ce̱èdzεὲ) level of consumption.

འཛད་སྒྲོ་ཁང་ (dzε̱ὲdrogaŋ) abbr. of འཛད་སྤྱོད་ཁང་.

འཛད་མེད་ (dzε̱ὲmeè) abbr. of མཛད་པ་མེད་པ་.

འཛད་མེད་ཆད་མེད་ (dzε̱ὲmeè cεὲmeè) inexhaustable.

འཛད་མེད་རིམ་འབྱུང་ (dzε̱ὲmeè ri̱mjuŋ) occurring continously, occurring without break.

འཛད་རྫས་ (dzε̱ὲdzεὲ) consumer goods.

འཛད་རྫས་མཉམ་ལས་ཁང་ (dzε̱ὲdzεὲ ña̱mlεὲgaŋ) consumer's cooperative.

འཛད་ཟོག (dzε̱ὲsɔɔ) consumer goods.

འཛད་ཟོང་ (dzε̱ὲsoŋ) sm. འཛད་ཟོག.

འཛབ་བཟླས་ (dza̱b dε̱ὲ) va. to recite a mantra.

འཛབས་ (dza̱b) length (of anything hanging down) ¶ ཁྲ་ཡོལ་གྱི་འཛབས་རིང་པོ་འདུག The (length of the) window curtains are long.

འཛབས་ཐུང་ཐུང་ (dza̱b tūŋduŋ) short pants, short dress, short sleeves.

འཛབས་རིང་པོ་ (dza̱b ri̱ŋgu) long pants, long dress, long slevees.

འཛམ་ (dza̱m) abbr. of འཛམ་གླིང་.

འཛམ་ཁྲགས་ (dza̱mdraà) a special rifle made in Tibet and used at the New Year's celebration in Lhasa.

འཛམ་གླིང་ (dza̱mliŋ) the world, the earth.

འཛམ་གླིང་ཁ་ལོ་སྒྱུར་དབང་ (dza̱mliŋ kālo gyu̱rwaŋ) world domination, world supremacy.

འཛམ་གླིང་གི་ཁྲིམས་ (dza̱mliŋgi tri̱m) international law.

འཛམ་གླིང་གི་འགོད་པོ་ (dza̱mliŋgi gö̱ödo) sm. འཛམ་གླིང་གི་ཟིན་པོ་.

འཛམ་གླིང་གི་རྒྱལ་འདུས་ (dza̱mliŋgi gye̱ndüü) sm. འཛམ་གླིང་རྒྱལ་ཚོགས་.

འཛམ་གླིང་གི་རྒྱུ་ལམ་ (dza̱mliŋgi gyu̱lam) earth's orbit.

འཛམ་གླིང་གི་འཇིའུ་མཐུན་ཚོགས་ (dza̱mliŋgi ji̱wu tūndzɔɔ) World Jewish Congress.

འཛམ་གླིང་གི་གནམ་གཤིས་རྩ་འཛུགས་ (dza̱mliŋgi nāmshiì dza̱ndzuù) World Meteorological Organization.

འཛམ་གླིང་གི་གནས་སྟངས་ (dza̱mliŋgi nε̱ὲdaŋ) world situation.

འཛམ་གླིང་གི་སྤྱི་སྐད་ (dza̱mliŋgi ji̱gεὲ) universal language, Esperanto.

འཛམ་གླིང་གི་བོད་དོན་གནས་ཚུལ་ཁྱབ་སྤེལ་ལས་ཁང་ (dza̱mliŋgi pö̱ödön nεὲdzüü kyəbbel le̱ὲgaŋ) WTN (World Tibet Network).

འཛམ་གླིང་གི་ཁྲིན་ཡུལ་ (dza̱mliŋgi dri̱nyüü) world market.

འཛམ་གླིང་གི་ཚད་ལྡན་དུས་ཚོད་ (dzamliŋgi tsɛndɛn tüüdzöö) universal time.

འཛམ་གླིང་གི་ཚོང་ར་ (dzamliŋgi tsōŋra) sm. འཛམ་གླིང་གི་ཁྲོན་ཡུལ་.

འཛམ་གླིང་གི་ཟིན་ཐོ་ (dzamliŋgi sindo) world record.

འཛམ་གླིང་གི་བཟོ་ཚོགས་མཉམ་འབྲེལ་ཚོགས་པ་ (dzamliŋgi sodzoò ñamdree tsōgba) world united trade union/ association.

འཛམ་གླིང་གི་ཡང་སྟེང་ (dzamliŋgi yaŋdeŋ) the "roof of the world."

འཛམ་གླིང་གི་ཡང་རྩེ་ (dzamliŋgi yaŋdze) sm. འཛམ་གླིང་གི་ཡང་སྟེང་.

འཛམ་གླིང་གི་རང་བཞིན་ (dzamliŋgi raŋshin) internationalism.

འཛམ་གླིང་གི་ཨང་དང་པོ་ (dzamliŋgi āŋ taŋbo) world champion [Lit. number one in the world].

འཛམ་གླིང་རྒྱ་ཕིབས་ (dzamliŋ gyabib) the "roof of the world."

འཛམ་གླིང་རྒྱན་དྲུག་མཆོག་གཉིས་ (dzamliŋ gyɛndruù cɔ̄ɔ̄ñii) sm. རྒྱན་དྲུག་མཆོག་གཉིས་.

འཛམ་གླིང་རྒྱལ་སྤྱི་ (dzamliŋ gyɛɛji) sm. འཛམ་གླིང་རྒྱལ་ཚོགས་.

འཛམ་གླིང་རྒྱལ་སྤྱིའི་འབྲེལ་བ་ (dzamliŋ gyɛɛjii dreewa) international relations.

འཛམ་གླིང་རྒྱལ་ཚོགས་ (dzamliŋ gyɛɛdzɔ̀ɔ) the United Nations.

འཛམ་གླིང་རྒྱས་བཤད་ (dzamliŋ gyɛ̀ɛsheɛ̀) 1. world geography. 2. name of a Tibetan geography book on the world.

འཛམ་གླིང་དངུལ་ཁང་ (dzamliŋ ŋǖügaŋ) the World Bank.

འཛམ་གླིང་ཆོས་ལུགས་རིས་མེད་ཀྱི་གྲོས་ཚོགས་ (dzamliŋ cǖüluù riimeègi trööödzɔ̀ɔ) World Parliament of Religion.

འཛམ་གླིང་ཆོས་ལུགས་རིས་མེད་ཀྱི་ལྷན་ཚོགས་ (dzamliŋ cǖüluù riimeègi lhɛ̄ndzɔ̀ɔ) World Parliament of Religion.

འཛམ་གླིང་ཆོས་ལུགས་རིས་མེད་ཀྱི་ལྷན་ཚོགས་ (dzamliŋ cǖüluù riimeègi lhɛ̄ndzɔ̀ɔ) World Council of Churches.

འཛམ་གླིང་ཉོ་ཚོང་རྩ་འཛུགས་ (dzamliŋ ñodzoŋ dzɔ̄ndzuù) World Trade Organization (WTO).

འཛམ་གླིང་གཉིས་པ་ (dzamliŋ ñiibə) the second world.

འཛམ་གླིང་མཉམ་སྡེབ་རྒྱལ་ཚོགས་ (dzamliŋ ñamdree gyɛɛdzɔ̀ɔ) United Nations (UN).

འཛམ་གླིང་སྙིང་ཐིག (dzamliŋ ñiŋdig) earth's axis.

འཛམ་གླིང་ལྟ་རྟོག་ཞིབ་པའི་ཉམས་ཞིབ་ཁང་ (dzamliŋ dādoò sheèbɛ ñamshibgaŋ) World Watch Institute.

འཛམ་གླིང་ནང་པའི་ཆོས་གྲོགས་ཚོགས་པ་ (dzamliŋ naŋbɛ cöödrɔɔ̀ tsɔ̄gba) sm. འཛམ་གླིང་ནང་པའི་ཆོས་ཚོགས་.

འཛམ་གླིང་ནང་པའི་ཆོས་ཚོགས་ (dzamliŋ naŋbɛ cöötsɔ̄ɔ̀) World Buddhist Association.

འཛམ་གླིང་གནས་རྒྱལ་ (dzamliŋ nɛ̄ɛ̀dzüü) world news, world situation.

འཛམ་གླིང་སྤྱི་སྐད་ (dzamliŋ jīgɛɛ̀) sm. འཛམ་གླིང་གི་སྤྱི་སྐད་.

འཛམ་གླིང་སྤྱི་ཁྲིམས་ (dzamliŋ jīdrim) international law.

འཛམ་གླིང་སྤྱི་སྙོམས་ཆེན་པོ་ (dzamliŋ jīñom cēmbo) world equality.

འཛམ་གླིང་སྤྱི་བསང་ (dzamliŋ jīsaŋ) the universal incence offering holiday in Lhasa commemorating the preparation of the founding of Samye monastery (15th day of the 5th lunar month).

འཛམ་གླིང་འཕྲོད་བསྟེན་ལྷན་ཁང་ (dzamliŋ trööden lhɛ̄ngaŋ) World Health Organization (WHO).

འཛམ་གླིང་བྱིས་པ་གསོ་སྐྱོང་གི་མཐུན་ཚོགས་ (dzamliŋ ciibə sōgyoŋgi tǖndzɔ̀ɔ) Save the Children Federation.

འཛམ་གླིང་དམག་ཆེན་ (dzamliŋ māgjen) world war ¶ འཛམ་གླིང་དམག་ཆེན་གཉིས་པ་ The Second World War.

འཛམ་གླིང་དམངས་གཙོའི་གཞོན་ནུ་མཐའ་འབྲེལ་ (dzamliŋ māŋdzö shōnnu namdree) the World Federation of Democratic Youth.

འཛམ་གླིང་དམར་ཤོག་ཚོགས་ཆེན་ (dzamliŋ mārshoò tsɔgjen) the world communist assembly/ meeting.

འཛམ་གླིང་ཚོང་དོན་སྒྲིག་འཛུགས་ (dzamliŋ tsōŋdön drigdzuù) World Trade Organization.

འཛམ་གླིང་ཞི་བདེ་ (dzamliŋ shide) world peace.

འཛམ་གླིང་ཞི་བདེ་དོན་གཅོད་ལྷན་ཚོགས་ (dzamliŋ shide tönjöö lhɛ̄ndzoò) sm. འཛམ་གླིང་ཞི་བདེ་ལས་སྐྱོང་ལྷན་ཚོགས་.

འཛམ་གླིང་ཞི་བདེའི་ལས་སྐྱོང་ལྷན་ཁང་ (dzamliŋ shidee lɛɛ̀gyoŋ lhɛ̄ngaŋ) World Peace Council.

འཛམ་གླིང་ཞི་བདེའི་ལས་འཛིན་ལྷན་ཚོགས་ (dzamliŋ shidee lɛndzin lhɛ̄ndzɔ̀ɔ) sm. འཛམ་གླིང་ཞི་བདེའི་ལས་སྐྱོང་ལྷན་ཚོགས་.

འཛམ་གླིང་ཟ་འབྲུའི་ལས་འཆར་ (dzamliŋ səndü lɛɛ̀car) World Food Program.

འཛམ་གླིང་བཟོ་ཚོགས་མཉམ་འབྲེལ་ཚོགས་པ་ (dzamliŋ sodzoò ñamdree tsɔ̄gba) World Federation of Trade Unions.

འཛམ་གླིང་ཡུལ་ཁག (dzamliŋ yüügaà) the nations of the world.

འཛམ་གླིང་ཡོངས་ (dzamliŋ yoŋ) world, worldwide ¶ འཛམ་གླིང་ཡོངས་ཀྱི་ཞི་བདེར་དགའ་བའི་མི་དམངས་ The peace loving people of the world.

འཛམ་གླིང་རི་དྭགས་གཅེས་སྐྱོང་གི་ཐེབས་རྩ་ (dzamliŋ ridaà jēèsuŋgi tēbdza) World Wildlife Fund (WWF).

འཛམ་གླིང་རིང་ལུགས་ (dzamliŋ riŋluù) cosmopolitanism, internationalism.

འཛམ་གླིང་རིལ་པོའི་ས་ཁྲ་ (dzamliŋ riibü sādra) globe, map.

འཛམ་གླིང་སེང་ཆེན་རྒྱལ་པོ་ (dzamliŋ sēŋjen gyɛɛbo) King Gesar of Ling.

འཛམ་གླིང་གསར་བརྗེ་ (dzamliŋ sārje) world revolution.

འཛམ་གླིང་གསུམ་པ་ (dzamliŋ sūmbə) the third world.

འཛམ་གླིང་ཧམ་འཛིན་ (dzamliŋ hāmdzin) domination of the world.

འཛམ་ཐག (dzamdaà) a leather band/ rope.

འཛམ་བུ་གླིང་ (dzəmbuliŋ) sm. འཛམ་གླིང་.

འཛམ་བུ་ནད་ (dzəmbu nade) highest quality gold.

འཛམ་བུར་ (dzāābur) a cannon; va.—རྒྱག to fire a cannon.

འཛམ་རིལ་ (dzamrii) sm.* ཛམ་རིལ་.

འཛམ་ཤིང་ (dzamshiŋ) sm.* ཛམ་ཤིང་.

འཛའ་ (dza) abbr. of འཛའ་ཐང་.

འཛའ་ཆག (dza cāà) vi. to have a drop in the currency value/ rate.

འཛའ་ཆུང་ཆུང་ (dza cūŋjuŋ) low exchange rate.

འཛའ་ཆེན་པོ་ (dza cēmbo) high exchange rate.

འཛའ་ཐང་ (dzadaŋ) currency value/ rate, exchange rate; va.— བརྩི་ to convert/ compute/ calculate the exchange rate ¶ འཛའ་ཐང་འཕར་ཆག Fluctuation in the exchange rate. ¶ ཨ་རི་སྒོར་རེར་འཛའ་ཐང་དུ་པི་བཅུ་བརྩིས་ If (we) compute the exchange rate at one U.S. dollar for ten rupees.

འཛའ་སྤྲོད་ (dza drȫȫ) va. to pay the currency exchange rate.

འཛའ་འཕར་ (dza pār) vi. to have the exchange rate go up.

འཛའ་ལེན་ (dza len) va. to take/ accept the currency exchange rate.

འཛའ་སློག (dza lɔɔ̀) va. to return the currency rate difference.

འཛར་ (dzaa) 1. vi. to hang out ¶ སྣམ་ནང་ནས་རས་འཛར་ཙང་ཁོ་ཚོ་ཚང་མས་ལྟས་པ་རེད་ They all looked at the box because a piece of cloth was hanging out. 2. unfinished ངའི་ལས་ཀ་འགྲོས་འཛར་སྣང་ཡོད་ I still have unfinished work. 3. tassels, fringe.

འཛར་ཁ་བཞག (dzarga shaà) va. to leave sth.

unfinished or unanswered.

འཛར་ཆབ་ (dzarjəb) sm. འཛར་, 3.

འཛར་ལྡན་ (dzardɛn) things with tassels.

འཛར་པོད་འཕྱང་འཕྲུལ་ (dzārböö jāŋdrüü) shung. a kind of hanging fringe or tassle strung around the outside of a palanquin.

འཛར་བུ་ (dzarbu) sm. འཛར་, 3.

འཛར་མ་ (dzarma) sm. ཛེས་སུ་.

འཛར་མ་ཆད་པ་ (dzar ma cɛ̀ɛba) continuous, uninterrupted, without stopping ༑ མི་འཛར་མ་ཆད་པ་སླེབས་སོང་ People arrived continuously.

འཛར་མེད་ (dzarmeè) sm. འཛར་མ་ཆད་པ་.

འཛར་འཛར་ (dzardzaa) 1. things that are hanging or dangling. 2. unfinished, incomplete ༑ ལས་ཀ་འཛར་འཛར་ལུས་བཞག There is work that is unfinished. 3. (sth. coming) continuously.

འཛར་ལོ་ (dzarlo) end of a tassle.

འཛི་ (dzi) a white spot on the forehead of cattle.

འཛི་བོ་ (dziwo) cattle with a white spot on their forehead.

འཛིང་: p. འཛིངས་; f. འཛིང་; imp. འཛིངས་ (dziŋ) 1. va. to fight, to clash ༑ ཁོ་ཚོས་རྒྱ་དམག་ལ་ཐེངས་མང་པོ་འཛིངས་ཡོད་པ་རེད་ They fought with the Chinese army many times. 2. tangled ༑ མོའི་སྐྲ་ཞི་དྲག་འཛིངས་ཤག Her hair is all tangled.

འཛིང་སྐོར་ (dziŋgɔɔ) a round of fights.

འཛིང་ག་ (dziŋgə) 1. hand-to-hand fighting (people), head-to-head fighting (for animals, kites); va.—འགྱིད་; —རྒྱག. 2. tangled; va.—ཐེབས to get tangled ༑ སྐུད་པ་དེ་འཛིང་ཁ་ཐེབས་འདུག The thread got tangled.

འཛིང་ཐེབས་ (dziŋ tēè) vi. to get tangled ༑ མོའི་སྐྲ་འཛིང་ཐེབས་འདུག Her hair got all tangled.

འཛིང་ཕྱོགས་ (dziŋjɔ̀ɔ) the front (line), the battle area ༑ བཙན་རྒོལ་རྒྱལ་གཅེས་འཛིང་ཕྱོགས་དེ་ The front line of opposing imperialism and being patriotic to the nation.

འཛིང་མོ་ (dziŋmo) sm. འཛིང་རེས་.

འཛིང་རྩལ་ (dziŋdzɛɛ) martial arts.

འཛིང་ར་ (dzìiŋrə) fortification, bunker; va.—རྒྱག; —རྟིག to construct a fortification/ bunker.

འཛིང་རག (dziŋraà) sm. འཛིང་ར་.

འཛིང་རེས་ (dziŋreè) 1. fighting/ combating, hand-to-hand combat; va.—གཏོང་; —བྱེད་. 2. fighting as a sport.

འཛིང་ལུགས་ (dziŋluù) 1. military customs. 2. military tactics.

འཛིང་བཤར་ (dziŋshaa) sm. འཛིང་ར་.

འཛིངས་ (dziŋ) p. and imp. of འཛིང་.

འཛིངས་ཆེན་པོ་ (dziŋ cēmbo) muddled, confused, disorderly, chaotic ༑ ལས་ཀ་འདི་འཛིངས་ཆེན་པོ་གཅིག་འདུག This work is one that is badly confused.

འཛིངས་རྙོགས་ཆེན་པོ་ (dziŋñog cēmbo) chaotic, disorderly, tangled (letters, thread and documents, etc.).

འཛིངས་ཕྱོགས་ (dziŋjɔ̀ɔ) sm. འཛིང་ཕྱོགས་.

འཛིངས་ར་ (dziŋrə) sm. འཛིང་ར་.

འཛིངས་ལུགས་ (dziŋluù) sm. འཛིང་ལུགས་.

འཛིན་: p. བཟུང་; f. གཟུང་; imp. ཟུངས་ (dzin) 1. va. to hold, to grasp ༑ ལག་ཏུ་མེ་ཏོག་འཛིན་ནས་དགའ་བསུ་ཞུས་པ་རེད་ Holding flowers in their hand (they) welcomed them. ༑ འགལ་བ་གཙོ་བོ་འཛིན་ཐུབ་པ་བྱུང་བ་རེད་ (They) were able to grasp the principal contradiction. 2. va. to adhere to ༑ དམར་པོའི་ལྟ་བ་འཛིན་གྱི་ཡོད་པ་རེད་ (They) adhere to communist ideology. ༑ གུང་ཁྲན་གྱི་ལྟ་བ་འཛིན་མི་ A communist (a person who adheres to communism). 3. va. to catch, to seize ༑ ཉ་མང་པོ་བཟུང་འདུག (He) caught many fish. 4. va. to consider, to hold as ༑ ཚང་མས་ཁོ་དྲང་པོར་འཛིན་པ་རེད་ (They) all considered him honest. 5. receipt, invoice, voucher, check ༑ འཛིན་མེད་ན་དངུལ་སྤྲོད་ཀྱི་མེད་ If (you) don't have a receipt, (I) won't pay. 6. va. to be costumed/ attired ༑ དམག་ཆས་འཛིན་པའི་དམག་མི་ Soldiers in military uniform.

འཛིན་བཀའ་ཁྱབ་བསྒྲགས་ (dzinga kyəbdraà) a wanted poster/ notice (for criminals).

འཛིན་སྐྱོང་ (dzingyoŋ) 1. administration, administering, governing, ruling; va.—བྱེད་ to administer, to govern, to rule ༑ ༡༩༦༠ བར་སྲིད་གཞུང་རྙིང་པས་འཛིན་སྐྱོང་བྱས་པ་རེད་ Until 1960 (it) was ruled by the old government. ༑ འཛིན་སྐྱོང་རྒྱལ་སྲས་ A ruling prince. 2. va. to maintain, to protect/ defend ༑ རང་གི་རིག་གནས་འཛིན་སྐྱོང་བྱས་པ་རེད་ (They) maintained their own culture.

འཛིན་སྐྱོང་པ་ (dzingyoŋbə) ruler, administrator ༑ དམག་པོའི་འཛིན་སྐྱོང་པ་ཚོ་ The military administrators.

འཛིན་སྐྱོང་དོ་དམ་ (dzingyoŋ todam) an administrator.

འཛིན་སྐྱོང་སྤེལ་གསུམ་ (dzin gyōŋ bēl sūm) the three: keeping, defending and spreading ༑ རང་གི་ཐུན་མོང་མ་ཡིན་པའི་ཆོས་དང་རིག་གཞུང་འཛིན་སྐྱོང་སྤེལ་གསུམ་ཐུབ་ཆེད་སློབ་གྲྭ་མང་པོ་བཙུགས་ཡོད་པ་ They established many schools to enable themselves to keep, defend and spread their unique religion and culture.

འཛིན་སྐྱོང་ཚན་པ་ (dzingyoŋ tsēmba) administrative department.

འཛིན་སྐྱོང་ཚོགས་ཆུང་ (dzingyoŋ tsɔ̄gjuŋ) administrative/ executive committee.

འཛིན་སྐྱོང་ཨུ་ཡོན་ལྷན་ཁང་ (dzingyoŋ ūyön lhēngaŋ) tib. ch. administrative council/ committee.

འཛིན་ཁང་ (dzingaŋ) classroom.

འཛིན་ཁོངས་ (dzingoŋ) shung. estates under the adminstration/ control of a lord ༑ གཞིས་ཀ་དེ་ལུང་ཤར་གྱི་འཛིན་ཁོངས་རེད་ That estate is under the administrative control of Lungshar.

འཛིན་ཁྲིད་ (dzindrii) arresting and taking away; va.—བྱེད་ ༑ མི་གཉིས་དོན་མེད་དུ་འཛིན་ཁྲིད་བྱས་སོང་ (They) arrested and took away two men for no reason.

འཛིན་གྲས་ (dzindrɛɛ̀) shung. sm. བདག་གཅེས་.

འཛིན་གྲས་ཡ་མ་བྲལ་བ་ (dzindrɛɛ̀ yama trɛɛwa) shung. taking good care of ༑ འབྲིད་གཏན་བཙན་དམིགས་རིམ་འབྲེལ་ལ་དོ་ཕོག་མི་འབྱུང་བའི་བདག་དོན་བདག་གཅེས་ཀྱིས་ཀྱི་ཐེམ་དུ་མ་ལུས་པ་འཛིན་གྲས་ཡ་མ་བྲལ་བ་དགོས་རྒྱུ་ One shall not violate the series of land tenure documents and should take good care of the (property).

འཛིན་གྲྭ་ (dzindra) 1. class (in a school); vi.—གྲོལ་ to be finished, to let out (class); —འཕར་ to be/ get promoted to the next class; vi.—འཚོག; —ཚུགས་ to start/ begin (class); va.—བཙོ་ to organize a class ༑ ཉིན་གུང་ལ་འཛིན་གྲྭ་གྲོལ་པ་དང་། At noon, as soon as the class is over. 2. a grade (in school) ༑ སློབ་གྲྭ་ཆུང་བའི་འཛིན་གྲྭ་བཞི་པ་ The 4th grade in primary school.

འཛིན་གྲྭ་རང་འཇགས་སུ་འཇོག (dzindra ranjaàsu jɔ̀ɔ) va. to be left in the same class, to not be advanced to the next class.

འཛིན་འགོག (dzingɔ̀ɔ) stopping and capturing.

འཛིན་རྒྱུའི་ལུང་བྱིན་པ་ (dzingyu luŋ cinbə) shung. an edict issued to an individual.

འཛིན་སྒྲུབ་དབྱེ་འབྱེད་ (dzindrub yējeè) shung. to clarify/ distinguish what is to be paid in taxes and what is to be taken possession of ༑ ཁྲ་མ་ནང་གསལ་ས་ཞིང་ཁྲལ་རིགས་འཛིན་སྒྲུབ་དབྱེ་འབྱེད་བྱ་དགོས་ (You) must clarify according to the verdict which fields are to be taken as possessions and what taxes should be paid.

འཛིན་དངོས་ནང་རྫས་ (dzinŋöö nandzɛɛ̀) household things/ possessions.

འཛིན་ཆ་ (dzinja) a partial eclipse.

འཛིན་ཆགས་ (dzinjaà) attachments.

འཛིན་ཆས་ (dzinjɛɛ̀) furniture; va.— སྒྲིག to arrange furniture.

འཛིན་ཆོས་ (dzinjöö) scriptures to be memorized.

འཛིན་འཛབ་ (dzinjəb) a clamping apparatus.

འཛིན་རྩབ་ (dzinñəb) catching, holding by the hand; va.—བྱེད་ ། ངང་ལ་གྲུམ་བུའི་ནད་ཡོད་ཙང་ལག་པས་ཅ་ལག་འཛིན་རྩབ་བྱེད་ཁག་པོ་འདུག Because I have arthritis, it is hard to hold anything in my hand.

འཛིན་གཏོར་ (dzindɔɔ) a type of torma.

འཛིན་བདང་འགོ་མཆན་འབྱར་མ་ (dzindaŋ gojɛn jarma) shung. a receipt with a note that indicates the decision ། འཛིན་བདང་འགོ་མཆན་འབྱར་མ་བཅས་ གཟིགས་ཞིབ་ཡོད་པ་ Please take a look at the receipt with the note that indicates the decision.

འཛིན་བཅེན་ནང་ཞུགས་ (dzinden naŋshuù) admission by ticket only.

འཛིན་བསྟན་དངུལ་ལེན་ (dzindɛn ŋǖülen) showing a receipt/ check/ voucher and receiving or taking money.

འཛིན་སྟངས་ (dzindaŋ) 1. outlook, point of view. 2. manner/ way of holding.

འཛིན་སྟངས་ཀྱི་ཡུལ་ (dzindaŋgi yüü) the object of one's outlook/ view.

འཛིན་ཐབས་ (dzindəb) 1. means of holding/ grasping/ adhering/ memorizing. 2. manner of perceiving.

འཛིན་ཐམ་ (dzindam) receipt (for money and goods).

འཛིན་ཐེབས་ (dzinteb) shung. a trust for managing sth. ། དགོན་མ་ལག་གང་ཅི་བླ་བྲང་འཛིན་ཐེབས་སུ་ཇེ་སྲིད་ བར་བསྐུལ་པ་ The entire possessions of the monastery were granted forever to the labrang to be managed as a trust.

འཛིན་མཐུ་ (dzindu) ability to memorize.

འཛིན་དམ་ (dzindam) seal on a receipt.

འཛིན་བདག (dzindaà) owner.

འཛིན་བསྡུས་ (dzindüü) shung. a short/ abbreviated receipt.

འཛིན་སྣོན་ (dzinnöö) shung. an additional receipt.

འཛིན་སྤྲད་ (dzindrɛɛ̀) shung. sm. བདག་གཅེས་.

འཛིན་སྲུས་ (dzindrɛɛ̀) looking after, caring for.

འཛིན་འབྲི་ (dzin dri) va. to write a receipt.

འཛིན་ཕྱོགས་ (dzinjɔɔ) 1. the manner of holding (an attitude/ opinion) ། ཁོ་ཚོས་ང་ཚོར་སྲིད་དོན་འཛིན་ ཕྱོགས་ As for the manner of their political policy towards us. 2. the directions in which the eclipse of the sun or the moon occur.

འཛིན་ཕྱོགས་ཁ་རྒྱག་མིན་ (dzinjɔɔ kāgyaà min) shung. holding a different opinion.

འཛིན་ཕྱོགས་ལོག་སྒྲུབ་ (dzinjɔɔ lɔgdrub) shung. sm. ལོ་ བ་ལོག་སྒྲུབ་.

འཛིན་བུ་ (dzimbu) wild garlic/ leek.

འཛིན་བྱང་ (dzinjaŋ) ticket.

འཛིན་བྱང་བཙོང་ས་ (dzinjaŋ dzōŋsa) ticket office, booking office, box office.

འཛིན་བྱེད་ (dzinjeè) sth. to hold things (e.g., a hook, pliars).

འཛིན་དབང་ (dzinwaŋ) ownership right, right to hold or use sth. ། ཁང་པ་འདིའི་འཛིན་དབང་ཡོད་པ་རེད་ He has the right to this house.

འཛིན་མ་ (dzinma) sm. ས་གཞི་.

འཛིན་བཙོངས་ (dzindzoŋ) ticket sales, box office.

འཛིན་ཟིན་ (dzinsuŋ) annexing.

འཛིན་གཟུང་ (dzinsuŋ) arresting, capturing, seizing; va.—བྱེད་ ། དམག་འཁྲུག་སྐབས་འཛིན་གཟུང་བྱས་པའི་ས་ ཆ་ The areas seized during the war.

འཛིན་གཟུང་དམག་མི་ (dzinsuŋ māəmi) prisoner of war.

འཛིན་གཞིབ་ (dzinseb) birdcage.

འཛིན་བཟུང་ (dzinsuŋ) sm. འཛིན་གཟུང་.

འཛིན་བཟུང་ཆད་གཅོད་ (dzinsuŋ cɛ̄ɛ̀jöö) arrest and punishment.

འཛིན་བཟུང་ད་དམ་ (dzinsuŋ todam) arrest and surveillance.

འཛིན་འོས་ (dzinwöö) worthwhile, appropriate.

འཛིན་ཡིག (dzinyii) sm. འཛིན་ཤོག.

འཛིན་རིམ་ (dzinrim) grade, class (in a school).

འཛིན་རེས་བྱེད་ (dzinreè ceè) va. to take turns to manage/ administrate/ run.

འཛིན་ཤོག (dzinshoò) bill, invoice, receipt, postal registration.

འཛིན་ཤོག་འདྲ་གསུམ་མ་ (dzinshoò drasummə) triplicate form, a receipt with three copies.

འཛིན་ཤོག་གསུམ་སྦྲེལ་ (dzinshoò sūmbel) sm. འཛིན་ ཤོག་འདྲ་གསུམ་མ་.

འཛིན་བཤར་ (dzinshaa) reciting what has been memorized; va.—བྱེད་.

འཛིན་གསར་ (dzinsar) shung. newly appointed, newly taking power ། ང་རང་ཚོ་ཆུང་ཁོངས་ཡིན་མིན་ གུ་ར་འཛིན་གསར་ལ་བརྟེན་ངེས་གསལ་ཞུ་རྒྱུ་མེད་ Because I am newly appointed, I am not clear about whether Gura belongs to Tsochung.

འཛིམ་འཛིམ་ཝུར་ཝུར་ (dzimdzim wurwur) clamor of sounds.

འཛིམ་བུ་ (dzimbu) sm. འཛིན་བུ་.

འཛིར་ (dzir) vi. to seep through, to ooze out.

འཛུགས་: p. **བཙུགས་**; f. **གཟུགས་**; imp. **ཚུགས་** (dzuù) 1. va. to establish, to start, to found, to construct ། སྤྱི་པའི་ཟ་ཁང་དང་བུ་བཙོལ་ཁང་བཙུགས་ཡོད་པ་རེད་ (They) established a communal dining room and a nursery. 2. va. to set up, to put up, to hoist (flags, poles, etc.) ། ཐོག་ཁར་དར་ཆ་གཅིག་བཙུགས་པ་ རེད་ They set up a flag on the roof. 3. va. to plant (seedlings) ། ལམ་གྱི་གཡས་གཡོན་ལ་ལྕང་མ་མང་ པོ་བཙུགས་ཡོད་པ་རེད་ (They) have planted many willow trees on both sides of the road. 4. va. to poke/ prick/ stick/ stab ། ཁོས་ང་ར་གྲི་བཙུགས་བྱུང་ He stabbed me with a knife. 5. va. to bet ། དངུལ་ འཛུགས་ཚོག་གི་མ་རེད་ You are not allowed to bet money.

འཛུགས་དཀར་ (dzuùgar) a serving bowl.

འཛུགས་སྐྲུན་ (dzugdrün) construction, constructing; va.—བྱེད་ ། སྤྱི་ཚོགས་རིང་ལུགས་ཀྱི་འཛུགས་སྐྲུན་ Socialist construction.

འཛུགས་སྐྲུན་ཁོར་ཡུག་སྲུང་སྐྱོབ་ཐིང་ (dzugdrün kōōyuù sūŋgyob tiŋ) tib. ch. office of environmental protection.

འཛུགས་སྐྲུན་གྱི་རང་བཞིན་ (dzugdrüngi rəŋshin) constructiveness ། གྲོས་མོལ་དེ་འཛུགས་སྐྲུན་གྱི་རང་ བཞིན་ལྡན་པ་བྱུང་བཞག The talks were constructive.

འཛུགས་སྐྲུན་རྒྱུ་ཆས་ (dzugdrün gyujɛɛ̀) construction materials.

འཛུགས་སྐྲུན་དངུལ་ཁང་ (dzugdrün ŋǖügaŋ) construction bank.

འཛུགས་སྐྲུན་དངོས་པོ་ (dzugdrün ŋöòbo) sm. འཛུགས་ སྐྲུན་རྒྱུ་ཆས་.

འཛུགས་སྐྲུན་བྱ་བ་ (dzugdrün cawa) construction work/ activities.

འཛུགས་སྐྲུན་རིག་རྩལ་ (dzugdrün rigdzɛɛ) architecture.

འཛུགས་སྐྲུན་ལག་རྩལ་པ་ (dzugdrün lagdzɛɛba) construction/ building/ development expert.

འཛུགས་སྐྲུན་ལས་ས་ (dzugdrün lɛ̀ɛsa) construction site.

འཛུགས་ཁྲིམས་ (dzugdrim) laws or constitution of an organization.

འཛུགས་འཁོད་ (dzuggöö) shung. va. to erect ། རླུང་རྟ་ ཅོད་པན་སྲ་བརྟན་འཛུགས་འཁོད་ཐོག One must erect the prayer flags well and firm.

འཛུགས་སྒྱེ་ (dzuggye) a bag/ sack for grain.

འཛུགས་སྒྲིག (dzugdrig) establishing and arranging, setting up; va.—བྱེད་.

འཛུགས་གཉེར་ (dzugñer) organizing and managing/ running; va.—བྱེད་ ། མཚན་མོའི་སློབ་གྲྭ་འདི་ཞིང་པ་ ཚོས་འཛུགས་གཉེར་བྱས་པ་རེད་ The night school was organized and run by farmers.

འཛུགས་གཉེར་མཉམ་བྱེད་ (dzugñer ñamjeè) jointly organizing and managing.

འཛུགས་གཉེར་ད་དམ་ (dzugñer todam) person in charge of organizing and managing.

འཛུགས་གཏེ་ (dzugde) shung. sth. left on pawn.

འཛུགས་གཏོར་ (dzugdɔɔ) a kind of torma that is offered regularly/ all the time.

འཛུགས་སྟོན་ (dzugdön) a party given at the start of

a project; va.—གཏོང་; — གཤོམ་.

འཛུགས་དར་ (dzugdar) shung. a ceremonial scarf given to monks attending the Monlam.

འཛུགས་སྐྱེལ་ (dzugbeè) establishing and flourishing/ expanding/ spreading.

འཛུགས་བྱེད་འཕྲུལ་འཁོར་ (dzugjeè trüügɔɔ) a planting machine.

འཛུགས་འབྲུ་ (dzugdru) a large sack of grain put in the wedding hall/ room as a symbol of a good harvest.

འཛུགས་ཞིང་ (dzugshiŋ) a field left as a collateral/ pawn for a loan.

འཛུགས་གཞི་ (dzugshi) structure ¶ དཔལ་འབྱོར་འཛུགས་གཞི་ Economic structure.

འཛུགས་ལུང་ (dzugluŋ) a handle in which spears are set.

འཛུགས་ཤ་ (dzugsha) a full carcass put in the wedding hall/ room as a symbol of good livestock management.

འཛུགས་ཤིང་ (dzugshiŋ) 1. a planted tree. 2. the tree set up in the center of the Tibetan Opera stage.

འཛུགས་གསོ་ (dzugso) planting and taking care of/ nurturing; va.—བྱེད་ ¶ ཤིང་ནགས་འཛུགས་གསོ་རྒྱ་ཆེན་པོ་བྱེད་ཀྱི་ཡོད་པ་རེད་ (They) are planting and taking care of forests on a large scale.

འཛུགས་སྲོལ་ (dzugsöö) adminstrative framework, organizational regulations.

འཛུད་: p. **བཙུད་**; f. **གཟུད་**; imp. **ཚུད་** (dzüü) 1. va. to put in, to insert. 2. va. to lead, to guide.

འཛུམ་: p. **བཙུམས་**; f. **བཙུམ་**; imp. **ཚུམས་** (dzum) va. to shut, to close ¶ མེ་མདའ་རྒྱག་དུས་མིག་མ་ཚུམས་ When shooting a gun don't close your eyes.

འཛུམ་: p. **འཛུམས་**; f. **འཛུམ་**; imp. **འཛུམས་** (dzum) va. to smile ¶ ཁོང་གིས་འཛུམས་ཏེ་གསུང་བ་རེད་ He said it smiling.

འཛུམ་: p. **ཟུམ་**; f. **ཟུམ་** or **འཛུམ་** imp. **ཟུམ་** (dzum) vi. to get shut/ closed.

འཛུམ་གྱི་ཉམས་ (dzumgi ñam) sm. འཛུམ་མདངས་.

འཛུམ་དཀར་ (dzumgar) a smiling/ pleasant appearance; va.—སྟོན་ to manifest a smiling/ pleasant appearance.

འཛུམ་ཁ་པོ་ (dzumgabo) a person who always is smiling.

འཛུམ་གོད་བྱེད་ (dzumgöö ceè) sm. འཛུམ་པག་སྟོན་.

འཛུམ་བརྒྱར་བཞད་ (dzumgyaa shɛɛ) vi. to bloom totally/ completely.

འཛུམ་ཆུང་ (dzumjuŋ) a slight smile; va.—སྟོན་; — སྒྲོལ་.

འཛུམ་སྟོན་ (dzum dõn) va. to smile.

འཛུམ་ལྷག་དགྱེ་ (dzumdaàgye) tetanus.

འཛུམ་དྲུག (dzumdruù) stripes of a tiger.

འཛུམ་མདངས་ (dzumdaŋ) a pleasant/ smiling appearance; va.—སྟོན་; —འཕྱུང་; —རྒྱས་ to smile, to show a pleasant appearance.

འཛུམ་པའི་མདངས་ (dzumbɛ daŋ) sm. འཛུམ་མདངས་.

འཛུམ་དཔལ་སྒྲོལ་ (dzumbɛɛ dröö) va. to smile pleasantly.

འཛུམ་ཕྲེང་ (dzumdreŋ) smiling appearance.

འཛུམ་པག་སྟོན་ (dzumbaà dõn) sm. འཛུམ་མདངས་.

འཛུམ་འབག (dzumbaà) false front, pretense of liking; va.—གྱོན་ to put on a false front, to pretend to like [Lit. a smiling mask].

འཛུམ་མུལ་མུལ་ (dzum müümüü) a smiling/ pleasant appearance, all smiles.

འཛུམ་མེར་མེར་ (dzum meemee) a smiling face, all smiles.

འཛུམ་མོལ་ (dzummüü) talking with a smile on one's face; va.—བྱེད་.

འཛུམ་དམུལ་ (dzummüü) a smile; va.—བྱེད་ to smile.

འཛུམ་དམུལ་དམུལ་ (dzum müümüü) sm. འཛུམ་མུལ་མུལ་.

འཛུམ་དམུལ་ལེ་ (dzum müüle) sm. འཛུམ་མུལ་མུལ་.

འཛུམ་འཚེར་འཚེར་ (dzum tsẽrdzer) sm. འཛུམ་དམུལ་དམུལ་.

འཛུམ་འཛུམ་ (dzumdzum) sm. འཛུམ་དམུལ་.

འཛུམ་ཝང་ཝང་ (dzum wãŋwaŋ) sm. འཛུམ་མུལ་མུལ་.

འཛུམ་ཞལ་ (dzumshɛɛ) a smiling face/ countenance.

འཛུམ་ཞལ་ལྷུག་པར་སྒྲོལ་བ་ (dzumshɛɛ̀ lhūgbar drööwa) with a pleasant, smiling countenance.

འཛུམ་བཞད་ (dzumshɛɛ̀) laughter.

འཛུམ་ཡལ་ཡལ་ (dzum yɛɛyɛɛ) sm. འཛུམ་མུལ་མུལ་.

འཛུམ་ལང་ (dzumlaŋ) sm. འཛུམ་དམུལ་.

འཛུམ་ཤིག་གེར་ (dzum shĩger) sm. འཛུམ་ཤིག་ཤིག.

འཛུམ་ཤིག་ཤིག (dzum shĩgshiì) sm. འཛུམ་དམུལ་དམུལ་.

འཛུམ་ཤོར་ (dzum shɔ̃ɔ) vi. to break into a smile.

འཛུམས་ (dzum) p. and imp. of འཛུམ་.

འཛུར་: p. **བཟུར་**; f. **གཟུར་**; imp. **ཟུར་** (dzur) va. to step, move aside, to give way, to avoid sth. in one's path, to avoid/ shy away from work ¶ ང་ཡོང་དུས་ཁོས་བཟུར་མ་བྱུང་ When I came he didn't move aside. ¶ ལས་ཀ་ལ་བཟུར་མ་གནང་ Don't shy away from work.

འཛུལ་ (dzüü) va. to enter, to join ¶ ཁོ་ད་ལོ་སློབ་གྲྭར་འཛུལ་པ་རེད་ He entered school this year. ¶ ང་ཚོའི་ཉ་རར་འཛུལ་ནས་ Having entered our fishing area. ¶ གུར་ནང་འཛུལ་ཡོང་ནས་ Having entered (our) tent.

འཛུལ་བསྐྱོད་ (dzüügyöö) entering; va.—བྱེད་ to enter, to go into ¶ མི་གཞན་གྱི་ཞིང་ཁའི་ནང་འཛུལ་བསྐྱོད་བྱེད་ཆོག་གི་མ་རེད་ (One) isn't allowed to go into other people's fields.

འཛུལ་ཁུང་ (dzüüguŋ) a hole sb. goes into to hide.

འཛུལ་སྒོ་ (dzüügo) entrance.

འཛུལ་ཇ་ (dzüüja) the custom of serving tea to all members when sb. first joins a monastery or a school.

འཛུལ་གནོད་ (dzüünöö) entering and causing harm; va.—བྱེད་.

འཛུལ་འཛུལ་པར་ (dzüübar) being indoors; va.—སྡོད་ ¶ ང་ནང་ལ་འཛུལ་འཛུལ་པར་སྡོད་ཀྱི་ཡོད་ I stay home all the time.

འཛུལ་ཞུགས་ (dzüüshuù) sm. འཛུལ་.

འཛུལ་ས་ཐོན་ས་ (dzüüsə tõnsə) exit and entrance.

འཛུལ་སའི་སྒོ་ (dzüüsɛ go) entrance.

འཛེག: p. **འཛེགས་**; f. **འཛེག**; imp. **འཛེགས་** (dzeg) to climb up, to ascend ¶ རི་འཛེགས་དུས་ When climbing the mountain.

འཛེག་སྐས་ (dzeggɛɛ̀) ladder, stairs, steps.

འཛེག་རྟེན་ (dzegden) sm. འཛེག་སྐས་.

འཛེག་འཕེབས་འཕྲུལ་སྐས་ (dzegbeb trüügɛɛ̀) elevator.

འཛེགས་ (dzeg) p. and imp. of འཛེག.

འཛེགས་བསྐྱོད་ (dzeggyöö) climbing, ascending, mountaineering; va.—བྱེད་ to climb (mountains, etc.).

འཛེང་ (dzeŋ) a stone tool.

འཛེད་: p. and f. **བཟེད་**; imp. **ཟེད་** (dzeè) 1. va. to hold out (as a recepticle for sth. being poured) ¶ དཀར་ཡོལ་གཟེད་རོགས་གནང་ (Please) hold out your cup. 2. vi. to bear/ suffer ¶ བཙན་དབང་འདི་བཟེད་ཐུབ་ཀྱི་མ་རེད་ (We) cannot bear this oppression. ¶ ཁོས་ཉེས་གདུག་བཟེད་སོང་ He suffered a beating.

འཛེད་ཞལ་ (dzeèshɛɛ) a container for collecting liquids (usu. butter from the top of a cup of Tibetan tea).

འཛེམ་: p. **འཛེམས་**; f. **འཛེམ་**; imp. **འཛེམས་** (dzem) to avoid, to refrain from, to shy away from ¶ ང་གཅིག་པོར་མཚན་ལ་འགྲོ་རྒྱུ་འཛེམ་གྱི་ཡོད་ (I) avoid going out alone at night. ¶ ཆར་པར་མ་འཛེམས་པར་ཁོ་ཚོ་དགའ་བསུ་ཞུ་བར་ཡོང་པ་རེད་ Braving the rain, (they) came to welcome them.

འཛེམ་ཆ་ (dzemja) doubts, fears, qualms; va.—བྱེད་ to refrain from doing sth. because of doubts/ fears ¶ དེང་སང་ཁོང་གིས་ཤ་འཛེམས་ཆ་བྱེད་ཀྱི་ཡོད་པ་རེད་ These days he is refraining from eating meat.

འཛེམ་དོགས་ (dzemdɔɔ̀) sm. འཛེམ་ཟོན་.

འཛེམ་དོགས་ (dzemdɔɔ̀) sm. འཛེམ་དོགས་.

འཛེམ་དོགས་མེད་པ་ (dzemdɔɔ̀ meèba) without restraint/ doubts/ qualms.

འཛེམ་མདོག (dzemdɔɔ̀) pretending to abstain/ refrain; va.—བྱེད་.

འཛེམ་པ་ཅན་ (dzembajɛn) sm. འཛེམ་བག་ཅན་.

འཛེམ་པ་མེད་པ་ (dzemba meèba) sm. འཛེམ་མེད་.

འཛེམ་བག་ཅན་ (dzembaàjɛn) modest, unassuming.

འཛེམ་བག་མེད་པ་ (dzembaà meèba) 1. unbridled, rampant, audacious, shameless. 2. directly, without hesitation.

འཛེམ་བྱ་ (dzemja) sm. འཛེམ་ཡག.

འཛེམ་བྱེད་ (dzem cèè) va. to be shy/ bashful/ reserved ¶ཁོང་མིའི་དཀྱིལ་ལ་ཁ་ལག་ཟ་དུས་འཛེམ་བྱེད་ཀྱི་རེད་ He is shy when eating among people.

འཛེམ་མེད་ (dzemmeè) without shyness/ restraint/ reservation ¶ཁོས་གནས་ཚུལ་དངོས་གནས་འཛེམ་མེད་བཤད་པ་རེད་ He told the truth without any reservations.

འཛེམ་འཛེམ་ (dzemdzem) sm. འཛེམ་བག་ཅན་.

འཛེམ་འཛེམ་ཐུག་ཐུག (dzemdzem tūgduù) sm. འཛེམ་བྱེད་, 2.

འཛེམ་འཛེམ་ཐོགས་ཐོགས་མེད་མེད་ (dzemdzem tōgtɔɔ̀ meèmeè) sm. འཛེམ་བག་མེད་པ་.

འཛེམ་ཟོན་ (dzemsön) 1. heedfulness, carefulness, cautiousness; va.—བྱེད་ to heed, to be careful/ cautious ¶ས་ཆ་འདིར་རྐུན་མའི་འཛེམས་ཟོན་བྱེད་དགོས་ Around here (you) should be cautious of thieves. 2. reluctance, qualms, compunctions; va.—བྱེད་ to be reluctant, to have qualms/compunctions ¶ཁོས་ཚོགས་འདུའི་སར་སྐད་ཆ་ཤོད་པར་འཛེམས་ཟོན་བྱེད་ཀྱི་འདུག He is reluctant to talk at meetings.

འཛེམ་ཡག (dzemyaà) abstaining/ refraining from. doing sth; va.—བྱེད་.

འཛེམ་སྲོལ་ (dzemsöö) a custom to be abstained/ refrained from.

འཛེམས་ (dzem) p. and imp. of འཛེམ་.

འཛེམས་བྱེད་ (dzemjeè) sm. འཛེམ་བྱེད་.

འཛེམས་མེད་ཉེན་མཆོངས་ (dzemmeè ñenjoŋ) doing sth. without fear of consequences ¶འཛེམས་མེད་ཉེན་མཆོངས་ཀྱི་སྒོ་ནས་ཟིང་ཆ་བསླངས་པ་རེད་ (They) stirred up trouble without fear of the consequences. [Lit. without fear jumping into danger].

འཛེམས་ཟོན་ (dzemsön) sm. འཛེམ་ཟོན་.

འཛེར་ (dzer) 1. vi. to become hoarse ¶སྐད་མ་འཛེར་བར་བཤད་སོང་ (They) spoke until (they) became hoarse. 2. arc. va. to hang up sth. 3. arc. va. to bore a hole.

འཛེར་དུམ་ (dzerdum) sm. མཛེར་དུམ་.

འཛེར་རྡོ་ (dzerdo) a stone weight. attached to a fishing net.

འཛེར་པ་ (dzerba) sm. མཛེར་པ་.

འཛེར་བུ་ (dzerbu) a small wood nail.

འཛེར་མ་ (dzerma) sm. མཛེར་བུ་.

འཛེར་འཛེར་པོ་ (dzer dzerbo) hoarse (voice).

འཛོག་པ་ (dzɔgba) arc. fist.

འཛོག་རྡུང་ (dzɔgduŋ) banging/ hitting with a fist, crushing sth.

འཛོག་སྦྱོར་ (dzɔgjɔɔ) mixing everything together; va.—བྱེད་.

འཛོང་འཛོང་ (dzoŋdzoŋ) elongated, long and upright (e.g., a pillar-like shape).

འཛོབ་འཛོབ་ (dzobdzob) 1. pile, heap, stack ¶ཁ་ལག་ལ་ཤ་འཛོབ་འཛོབ་བརྒྱབ་བཞག (They) put heaps of meat on the food.

འཛོམ་: p. འཛོམས་; f. འཛོམ་; imp. འཛོམས་ (dzom) 1. vi. to be present, to be complete ¶ཁ་ལག་འདིར་ཤ་སྨན་སྣ་ཁ་ཚང་མ་འཛོམས་བཞག All the necessary spices are present in this dish. 2. vi. to gather, to congregate, to meet, to come together ¶ལོ་མང་རྗེས་ལ་ཁོ་གཉིས་སླར་ཡང་འཛོམས་པ་རེད་ After many years they got together again.

འཛོམ་དུས་ (dzomdüü) a time to meet/ get together; va.—བཟོ་ to make a time to meet ¶ང་ཚོ་འཛོམ་དུས་ཤིག་བཟོ་དགོས་ (Let) us make a time to meet.

འཛོམ་པོ་ (dzombo) complete, all present ¶ལུང་པ་འདི་མཐུན་རྐྱེན་འཛོམ་པོ་འདུག In this area all the necessary resources/ facilities/ living conditions are present.

འཛོམ་ཚོང་འགྲན་བསྡུར་ (dzomdzoŋ trenduu) auctioning; va.—བྱེད་.

འཛོམ་འཛོམ་རུབ་རུབ་ (dzomdzom rubrub) gathering, assembling, coming together.

འཛོམས་ (dzom) 1. p. of འཛོམ་. 2. gathering point or place.

འཛོམས་བཀག (dzomgaà) sm. མདུད་འཛིན་.

འཛོམས་འཁྲབ་ (dzomdrəb) a joint performance given by many theatrical groups.

འཛོམས་སྟོན་ (dzomdön) party, banquet, feast, social gathering.

འཛོམས་དུས་ (dzomdüü) sm. འཛོམ་དུས་.

འཛོམས་བརྡ་ (dzomda) shung. a notice sumnmoning officials to a meeting or gathering.

འཛོམས་འཛོམས་ (dzomdzom) 1. sometimes, occasionally ¶འཛོམས་འཛོམས་ལ་ཐ་མ་འཐེན་གྱི་ཡོད་ (I) smoke sometimes. 2. gathering, assembling, getting together; va.—བྱེད་ ¶ང་ཚོ་སྤུན་མཆེད་ཚོ་སྐབས་རེ་འཛོམས་འཛོམས་བྱེད་ཀྱི་ཡོད་ My relatives and I get together sometimes.

འཛོམས་ཟླ་ (dzomda) sm. འཛོམ་དུས་.

འཛོམས་ཡུལ་ (dzomyüü) meeting place.

འཛོམས་རེ་ (dzomre) sm. འཛོམས་འཛོམས་.

འཛོལ་ (dzöö) vi. to be mistaken, to be reversed/ inverted ¶ཁོས་ཕྱི་ནང་འཛོལ་ནས་བཙེམས་པ་རེད་ He sewed it inside out.

འཛོལ་འགན་ (dzöngɛn) responsibility for a mistake; vi.—འཁྲི་ to have responsibility for a mistake fall on oneself.

ཛ་ (dza) 1. clay (used for making pottery, tiles). 2. clay/ earthenware pottery.

ཛ་ཀོར་ (dzagɔɔ) a small earthenware bowl/ dish.

ཛ་ཀྱོག (dzagyɔɔ̀) a clay item (bowl, cup, etc.).

ཛ་དཀར་ (dzagaa) 1. clay used for making bowls/ cups.

ཛ་དཀར་བཟོ་གྲྭ་ (dzagaa sodra) ceramic/ earthenware bowl factory.

ཛ་སྐུ་ (dzōgu) clay icons/ statues.

ཛ་ཁང་ (dzagaŋ) a place/ building where they make earthernware items.

ཛ་ཁུང་ (dzəguŋ) clay pit.

ཛ་ཁོ་ (dzago) clay.

ཛ་ཁོག (dzagɔɔ̀) clay/ earthenware pot.

ཛ་ཁོག་ཆེན་པོ་ (dzagɔɔ̀ cēmbo) 1. insensitive, thick-skinned. 2. bold, arrogant.

ཛ་ཁོག་ཆག་པས་ཡག་བྱུང་ ཁྲོ་ཟངས་ལག་ཏུ་ཐེབས་བྱུང་ (dzagɔɔ̀ cāgbɛ yaàjuŋ trōsaŋ lagdu tēbjuŋ) lucky, fortunate [Lit. broke an earthenware pot, acquired a brass pot].

ཛ་ཁྱི་འཇིམ་བྱ་ (dzakyi jimja) useless things [Lit. clay dog, clay bird].

ཛ་ཁྲ་ (dzadra) colored/ painted pottery.

ཛ་ཁྲལ་ (dzatrɛɛ) shung. tax levied on clay goods.

ཛ་མཁན་ (dzañɛn) potter.

ཛ་གོ་ (dzagɔ) sm. ཛ་ཁོ་.

ཛ་གྲི་ (dzədri) tool for making clay pottery, etc.

ཛ་ང་ (dzaŋa) drum that has skin (striking face) on both sides.

ཛ་ང་ཁ་གཅིག་པ་ (dzaŋa kājigbə) drum that has skin (striking face) only on one side.

ཛ་ཆག (dzajaà) piece of broken clay pot, pot shard.

ཛ་ཆས་ (dzajɛɛ̀) 1. pottery, earthenware; va.—བཟོ་ to make pottery/ earthernware. 2. fuel for a stove; va.—སྒྲིག; —སྒྲོད་ to prepare a stove for burning by putting in fuel.

ཛ་ཆས་བཟོ་གྲྭ་ (dzajɛɛ̀ sodra) pottery/ earthenware factory.

ཛ་ཆུ་ (dzəju) 1. Mekong River. 2. a stream flowing down a rocky mountain.

ཛ་ཆུང་ (dzajuŋ) small pot.

ཛ་ཆེན་ (dzajen) large pot.

རྫ་ཏི་ (dzədi) nutmeg.

རྫ་གདུགས་ (dzaduù) repairing/ mending a broken clay pot; va.—རྒྱག.

རྫ་དམ་ (dzadam) a type of clay flask.

རྫ་དར་དྭ་ཐའི་ (dzadar dāā tɛ̄ɛ) shung. abbr. of a type of རྫ་སག, དར་དན་, དྭ་ལྦ་མ་, ཐའི་ཧེ་.

རྫ་དུག (dzəduù) high altitude sickness; vi.—རྒྱག to get high altitude sickness.

རྫ་དུབ་ (dzədub) mending/ repairing clay pots; va.—རྒྱག.

རྫ་མདོག (dzandɔɔ̀) brown.

རྫ་མདོང་ (dzandoŋ) sm. རྫ་སྨུག.

རྫ་སྡེར་ (dzader) clay plate.

རྫ་ནག་རི་ (dza nagri) black rocky mountain.

རྫ་ནང་ (dzanaŋ) rows of tiles on a roof.

རྫ་སྣོད་ (dzanöö) clay/ earthenware utensils.

རྫ་པག (dzabaà) clay tile/ brick.

རྫ་པར་ (dzabar) clay mould.

རྫ་སྤང་ (dzabaŋ) abbr. of རྫ་རི་དང་སྤང་རི་.

རྫ་ཕག (dzabaà) sm. རྫ་པག.

རྫ་ཕོར་ (dzabɔɔ) clay/ earthenware cup.

རྫ་ཕྲུ་ (dzadru) clay pot.

རྫ་བེན་ (dzaben) large clay pot/ vessel.

རྫ་བུམ་ (dzabum) earthenware vase/ bottle/ jar.

རྫ་བྲ་ (dzabra) a kind of rodent/ pica.

རྫ་བྲག (dzadraà) boulders in rocky mountains.

རྫ་སྦུག (dzəbuù) earthenware pipe.

རྫ་མ་ (dzama) clay/ earthenware pot.

རྫ་མི་ (dzəmi) a kind of mythical human-like creature that lives in rocky mountains.

རྫ་མུ་ (dzamu) Jammu (part of Kashmir).

རྫ་མོ་རོང་ (dzamoroŋ) rocky gorge.

རྫ་སྨུག (dzəmuù) grey.

རྫ་རྫི་རྒྱག (dzədzi gyaà) va. to glaze pottery.

རྫ་རྫི་གཏོང་ (dzədzi dōŋ) va. to glaze pottery.

རྫ་གཞོང་ (dzashoŋ) earthenware basin.

རྫ་གཟོང་ (dzasoŋ) a tool for making clay pots.

རྫ་བཟི་རྫུ་བཟི་ (dzasi dzusi) a person who acts without really understanding things.

རྫ་བཟོ་བ་ (dza sowa) sm. རྫ་མཁན་.

རྫ་ཡུང་ (dzāyuŋ) the bulb of fritillary (used in Tibetan medicine).

རྫ་ཡུལ་ (dzayüü) a place in S. E. Tibet.

རྫ་གཡམ་ (dzayam) tile, brick.

རྫ་གཡམ་རྫི་མ་ (dzayam dzīmə) glazed tile.

རྫ་གཡམ་གཡུ་རྫི་ཅན་ (dzayam yūdzijɛn) glazed turquoise-color roof tiles.

རྫ་རི་ (dzəri) a rocky mountain.

རྫ་རི་ཁ་སྦྱོར་ (dzəri kājɔɔ) getting two persons to go against each other or fight each other [Lit. to get two mountains to clash].

རྫ་རོང་ (dzaroŋ) abbr. of རྫ་མོ་རོང་.

རྫ་ལ་ (dzala) a small iron stove.

རྫ་ལས་ (dzalɛɛ̀) pottery work.

རྫ་ལེབ་ (dzaleb) a clay tile.

རྫ་ལེབ་ལ་ (dzalebla) a mountain pass between Yadong and India.

རྫ་ས་ (dzasaà) earth used for making pottery.

རྫ་ས་ཐོན་ཁུངས་ (dzasa tōnguŋ) shung. resources used for making clay items.

རྫ་སི་རྫུ་སི་ (dzasi dzusi) sm. རྫ་བཟི་རྫུ་བཟི་.

རྫ་སུལ་ (dzasüü) sm. རྫ་གསེང་.

རྫ་སོ་ (dzaso) the firing of potery; va.—གཏོང་.

རྫ་སོའི་ར་སྒོར་ (dzasö ragɔɔ) hearth/ kiln for firing clay.

རྫ་སླང་ (dzalaŋ) clay/ earthenware pan (used to roast barley).

རྫ་གསར་ (dzasaa) new earthernware utensil.

རྫ་གསེང་ (dzaseŋ) among the rocks on a rocky mountain.

རྫ་གསེབ་ (dzaseb) sm. རྫ་གསེང་.

རྫ་ལྷེབ་གཡུ་རྫི་ཅན་ (dzalheb yūdzijɛn) glazed roof tiles.

རྫག་གོག་ཆེན་པོ་ (dzaàgɔɔ̀ cēmbo) sm. རྫ་ཁོག་ཆེན་པོ་.

རྫག་ཏོ་ (dzagdo) sm. རྫག་དོ་.

རྫག་དོ་ (dzagdo) many, lots, much ༈ཁོ་ཚོར་མེ་མདའ་རྫག་དོ་ཡོད་པ་རེད་ They have lots of guns.

རྫག་ཚ་པོ་ (dzaà tsābo) sm. རྫག་གོག་ཆེན་པོ་.

རྫག་རྫག (dzagdzaà) full, saturated; vi.—ཁེངས་ to be full/ saturated.

རྫག་རྫོག (dzagdzɔɔ̀) sm. འཛོག་འཛོག.

རྫབ་ (dzəb) 1. mud, mire. 2. va. to dump/ merge/ put together ༈ཁ་ལག་ལྷག་མ་སྣོད་ཆས་གཅིག་གི་ནང་དུ་རྫབ་པ་རེད་ (They) dumped the leftover food into one pot.

རྫབ་ཀྱེ་ (dzəbgye) sm. རྫབ་ཅན་.

རྫབ་ཅན་ (dzəbjɛn) callous, hardened, unscruplous, unprincipled.

རྫབ་ཆུ་ (dzəbju) ditch water, dirty/ muddy water.

རྫབ་ཅེ་བ་ (dzab cēwa) 1. muddy. 2. insolently, contemptuously, impertinently.

རྫབ་ཆེན་ (dzabjen) sm. རྫབ་ཅན་.

རྫབ་ཆེན་སྨྱོན་པ་ (dzabjen ñomba) sb. who is རྫབ་ཅན་ to the point of madness.

རྫབ་ཆེན་ཨ་ར་དཀར་པོ་ (dzabjen āraà gāābo) sb. who is extremely རྫབ་ཅན་.

རྫབ་རྟོལ་མཆིན་མ་ (dzabdöö cīnmə) a kind of burl used for making wooden bowls.

རྫབ་དུང་ (dzabduŋ) dumping/ putting/ merging together; va.—གཏོང་; —སྤྱོད་.

རྫབ་དོང་ (dzabdoŋ) cesspool, sewer, muck, mire.

རྫབ་ཕག་སྦུ་མ་ (dzabpaà būmə) a kind of burl used for making wooden bowls.

རྫབ་ཕོར་ (dzəbpɔɔ) highest quality wooden bowl made from a burl.

རྫབ་བི་རྫུབ་བི་ (dzəbbi dzubbi) sb. who is deceitful/ duplicitous.

རྫབ་བེ་རྫོབ་བེ་ (dzabe dzobe) 1. sm. རྫབ་བི་རྫུབ་བི་. 2. rubbish, waste, trash.

རྫབ་ཚལ་ (dzabdzɛɛ) mixed vegetable dishes.

རྫབ་འཛོང་ (dzab dzōŋ) 1. va. to not listen/ obey, to not follow customs/ rules. 2. va. to loaf on a job.

རྫབ་རྫུབ་ (dzəbdzub) abbr. of རྫབ་བི་རྫུབ་བི་.

རྫབ་རྫོབ་ (dzabdzob) abbr. of རྫབ་བེ་རྫོབ་བེ་.

རྫབ་ཞལ་ (dzabshɛɛ) wooden bowl made from the burl/ knot of a tree.

རྫབ་འབུག་སྒྲོ་མ་ (dzəbwuù droma) a kind of burl used for making bowls.

རྫབ་ཡ་ (dzəbya) a very high quality wooden bowl made from a tree burl.

རྫབ་ཡ་མེ་འབར་མ་ (dzəbya me barwa) a type of high quality wooden bowl made from a burl "that shines like it is on fire."

རྫབ་ཡའི་ (dzəbyɛ) sm. རྫབ་ཡ་.

རྫབ་ཡའི་ཕོར་པ་ (dzəbyɛ pɔɔba) sm. རྫབ་ཕོར་.

རྫབ་ཡུར་ (dzəbyur) sewage canal.

རྫབ་ར་ (dzəbra) sm. རྫ་ར་.

རྫབ་རལ་འཛར་འཛར་ (dzəbrɛɛ dzandzar) full of mud.

རྫབ་རླུང་ (dzəbluŋ) marsh gas (methane gas).

རྫབ་ལུད་ (dzəblüü) manure, dung.

རྫབ་ཤོག (dzəbshɔɔ̀) straw board.

རྫབ་བཤང་ (dzəbshaŋ) dregging ༈རྫབ་བཤང་གྲུ་གཟིངས་ Dregging boat.

རྫབ་སུལ་ (dzəbsüü) boiled entrails of animals.

རྫམ་ལྡིག (dzamdig) an unorthodox/ unusual shape.

རྫམ་རིལ་ (dzamrii) a decorative ball attached to the རྫམ་ཤིང་.

རྫམ་ཤིང་ (dzəmshiŋ) short wooden pole that is tied horizontally behind the legs of mule and attached to the saddle; va.—རྒྱག.

རྫས་ (dzɛɛ̀) materials, things ༈ཐོན་རྫས་ Products. 2. chemical. 3. gunpowder.

རྫས་བཀྲམ་ཁང་ (dzɛɛ̀dramgaŋ) exhibit/ display hall.

རྫས་ཁང་ (dzɛɛ̀gaŋ) 1. ammunition dump. 2. storeroom.

རྫས་ཁུག (dzɛɛ̀guù) 1. pouch. 2. gunpowder pouch.

རྫས་ཁུང་ (dzɛɛ̀guŋ) 1. a hole drilled in the rock for putting explosives; va.—འབིགས་ to bore such a hole. 2. a small hole in Tibetan rifles for gunpowder. to ignite the barrel.

རྫས་གྲི་ (dzɛɛ̀dri) a small wooden knife used for grinding gunpowder.

རྫས་འགྱུར་ (dzɛɛ̀gyur) chemistry, chemical.

རྫས་འགྱུར་གྱི་རྒྱུ་ (dzɛɛ̀gyurgi gyu) chemical element.

རྫ་འགྱུར་གྱི་རྒྱུ་ཆ་ (dzɛɛ̀gyurgi gyuja) chemical raw materials, chemicals.

རྫས་འགྱུར་གྱི་འགྱུར་ལྡོག (dzɛɛ̀gyurgi gyundoò) chemical reaction/ change.

རྫས་འགྱུར་གྱི་འགྱུར་བ་ (dzɛɛ̀gyurgi gyuwə) chemical reaction/ change.

རྫས་འགྱུར་གྱི་ངོ་བོ་ (dzɛɛ̀gyurgo ŋowo) chemical property.

རྫས་འགྱུར་གྱི་ནུས་པ་ (dzɛɛ̀gyurgi nüübə) chemical action/ force/ power.

རྫས་འགྱུར་གྱི་ལུད་ (dzɛɛ̀gyurgi lüü) chemical fertilizer.

རྫས་འགྱུར་འགྱུར་འབྱུང་ (dzɛɛ̀gyur gyurjuŋ) chemical reaction.

རྫས་འགྱུར་གྲུབ་ཆ་ (dzɛɛ̀gyur trubja) chemical composition.

རྫས་འགྱུར་དངོས་པོ་ (dzɛɛ̀gyur ŋööbo) chemical materials.

རྫས་འགྱུར་ཉམས་ཞིབ་ (dzɛɛ̀gyur ñəmshib) chemical experiment/ study/ investigation.

རྫས་འགྱུར་བརྟག་དཔྱད་ (dzɛɛ̀gyur dāgjɛɛ̀) chemical test, chemical examination/ investigation.

རྫས་འགྱུར་འདྲེས་སྦྱོར་འདྲ་ཚད་ (dzɛɛ̀gyur dreèjɔɔ dradzɛɛ̀) chemical equivalent.

རྫས་འགྱུར་སྡེ་ཁག (dzɛɛ̀gyur degaà) department of chemistry.

རྫས་འགྱུར་ནུས་པ་ (dzɛɛ̀gyur nüübə) sm. རྫས་འགྱུར་གྱི་ནུས་པ་.

རྫས་འགྱུར་དབྱེ་ཞིབ་ (dzɛɛ̀gyur yēshib) chemical analysis.

རྫས་འགྱུར་དམག་འཁྲུག (dzɛɛ̀gyur məgdruù) chemical warfare.

རྫས་འགྱུར་སྨན་རིགས་བཟོ་གྲྭ་ (dzɛɛ̀gyur mɛ̄nriì sodra) chemical pharmaceutical factory.

རྫས་འགྱུར་སྨན་རྫས་བཟོ་གྲྭ་ (dzɛɛ̀gyur mɛ̄ndzɛɛ̀ sodra) chemical pharmaceutical factory.

རྫས་འགྱུར་ཚི་སྣ་ (dzɛɛ̀gyur tsīnə) chemical fibres.

རྫས་འགྱུར་ཚོད་ལྟའི་སྨན་རྫས་ (dzɛɛ̀gyur tsöödɛ mɛ̄ndzɛɛ̀) chemical reagent.

རྫས་འགྱུར་མཚོན་ཆ་ (dzɛɛ̀gyur tsõnja) chemical weapon.

རྫས་འགྱུར་འཚོ་ལུད་ (dzɛɛ̀gyur tsōlüü) sm. རྫས་འགྱུར་གྱི་ལུད་.

རྫས་འགྱུར་ཞིང་ལུད་ (dzɛɛ̀gyur shiŋlüü) sm. རྫས་འགྱུར་གྱི་ལུད་.

རྫས་འགྱུར་ཞིབ་འཇུག་ཁང་ (dzɛɛ̀gyur shimjuùgaŋ) institute of chemistry.

རྫས་འགྱུར་གཞི་རྒྱུ་ (dzɛɛ̀gyur shigyu) chemical elements.

རྫས་འགྱུར་བཟོ་གྲྭ་ (dzɛɛ̀gyur sodra) chemical factory/ plant.

རྫས་འགྱུར་བཟོ་ལས་ (dzɛɛ̀gyur solɛɛ̀) chemical industry ¶ རྫས་འགྱུར་བཟོ་ལས་བུའུ་ Ministry of chemical industry.

རྫས་འགྱུར་རིག་པ་ (dzɛɛ̀gyur rigbə) chemistry, the science of chemistry.

རྫས་འགྱུར་ས་ལུད་ (dzɛɛ̀gyur sālüü) chemical fertilizer.

རྫས་རྒྱུ་ (dzɛɛ̀gyu) matter, substance.

རྫས་ངན་ (dzɛɛ̀ŋɛn) a poison.

རྫས་གཅིག་པ་ (dzɛɛ̀ jīgbə) the container and the content.

རྫས་ཆའི་དོད་ (dzɛɛ̀jɛ töö) shung. a money payment that is a substitute for things needed to perform a religious ritual.

རྫས་ཆས་ (dzɛɛ̀jɛɛ̀) gunpowder case.

རྫས་ཐག (dzɛɛ̀daà) fuse for firing gunpowder.

རྫས་ཐུན་ (dzɛɛ̀dün) amount of gunpowder needed to fire a single shot.

རྫས་ཐུམ་ (dzɛɛ̀dum) sm. རྫས་འཐུམ་.

རྫས་འཐུམ་ (dzɛɛ̀dum) satchel charge; va.—རྒྱག to set off/ explode a satchel charge.

རྫས་དམ་ (dzɛɛ̀dam) sm. རྫས་ཁུག.

རྫས་དོད་ (dzɛɛ̀döö) shung. abbr. of རྫས་ཆའི་དོད་.

རྫས་མདའ་ (dzɛnda) matchlock rifle.

རྫས་མདེལ་ (dzɛndee) bullet and gunpowder, ammunition.

རྫས་མདིའུ་ (dzɛɛ̀ diwu) sm. རྫས་མདེལ་.

རྫས་དཔྱད་ཁང་ (dzɛɛ̀jɛɛ̀gaŋ) chemistry laboratory.

རྫས་ཕྲ་ (dzɛɛ̀dra) bacteria, microbe.

རྫས་སྦྱོར་ (dzɛɛ̀jɔɔ) chemistry, chemicals; va.—བྱེད་ to mix/ compound chemicals ¶ རྫས་སྦྱོར་ཞིང་ལུད་ Chemical fertilizer.

རྫས་སྦྱོར་རྒྱུ་ཆ་ (dzɛɛ̀jɔɔ gyuja) chemical raw materials.

རྫས་སྦྱོར་བཟོ་ལས་ (dzɛɛ̀jɔɔ solɛɛ̀) sm. རྫས་འགྱུར་བཟོ་ལས་.

རྫས་མ་ཡིན་པ་ (dzɛɛ̀mə yimbə) intangible, formless.

རྫས་མེ་ (dzɛɛ̀me) explosives, dynamite; va.—རྒྱག to dynamite, to blow up, to blast (with explosives).

རྫས་མེ་མདའ་ (dzɛɛ̀ menda) matchlock rifle.

རྫས་མེ་མེ་ཏོག (dzɛɛ̀me medoò) fireworks display.

རྫས་མེད་སྒྲོགས་མདེལ་ (dzɛɛ̀meè gyɔŋdee) blank artillery shell.

རྫས་མཚུངས་པ་ (dzɛɛ̀dzuŋba) things made from the same ingredients.

རྫས་རྫོང་རྒྱག (dzɛɛ̀dzoŋ gyaà) va. to ramrod powder (into the barrel of a matchlock gun).

རྫས་གཞོང་ (dzɛɛ̀shoŋ) a stone slab on which gunpowder is ground.

རྫས་བཟོ་འཕྲུལ་ཆས་བཟོ་གྲྭ་ (dzɛɛ̀so trüüjɛɛ̀ sodra) chemical equipment factory.

རྫས་བཟོ་ཚི་སྣ་བཟོ་གྲྭ་ (dzɛɛ̀so tsīnə sodra) chemical fiber factory.

རྫས་ཟོམ་ (dzɛɛ̀som) powder and keg.

རྫས་ཡོད་ (dzɛɛ̀yöö) tangible things, things that have form.

རྫས་རགས་པ་ (dzɛɛ̀ ragba) those things that have form (and can be seen with the naked eye).

རྫས་ར་ (dzɛɛ̀ra) sm. རྫས་རུ་.

རྫས་རིགས་ (dzɛɛ̀rig) goods, things.

རྫས་རིལ་ (dzɛɛ̀rii) 1. a stone for grinding gunpowder. 2. small balls of gunpowder.

རྫས་རུ་ (dzɛɛ̀ru) gunpowder container made from a hollowed horn.

རྫས་རླུང་ (dzɛɛ̀luŋ) gas (natural).

རྫས་ལུད་ (dzɛɛ̀lüü) sm. རྫས་འགྱུར་གྱི་ལུད་.

རྫས་ལི་ལ་ (dzɛɛ̀lela) sm. རྫས་ལེབ་ལ་.

རྫས་ལེབ་ལ་ (dzɛɛ̀lebla) a pass between India and Tibet.

རྫས་སུ་གྲུབ་པ་ (dzɛɛ̀su trubbə) sm. རྫས་ཡོད་.

རྫས་སུ་མེད་པ་ (dzɛɛ̀su meèba) formless.

རྫས་སུ་ཡོད་པ་ (dzɛɛ̀su yööba) sm. རྫས་ཡོད་.

རྫས་ལྷད་ (dzɛɛ̀lhɛɛ̀) a material that has been adulterated/ diluted/ mixed with sth. else.

རྫི་ (dzi) 1. the sense of smell ¶ རྫི་ནོ་པོ་ A sharp sense of smell. 2. sm. རླུང་. 3. a herder ¶ ར་རྫི་ Goat herder. 4. white spot on the forehead of animals.

རྫི་: p. བརྫིས་; f. བརྫི་; imp.; རྫིས་ (dzi) va. to knead ¶ ཁོས་བག་ལེབ་བཟོ་བྱེད་གྲོ་ཞིབ་རྫི་གི་འདུག He is kneading the flour to make bread. 2. va. to trample, to run over ¶ ཁོ་མོ་ཀྲས་བརྫིས་ནས་སྨན་ཁང་ལ་ཁྲིད་སོང་ A car ran over him and he was taken to the hospital.

རྫི་སྐོར་ (dzigɔɔ) 1. herder's stone enclosure, a shelter for herdsman. 2. sniffing around; va.—རྒྱག.

རྫི་སྐྱོར་ (dzigyɔɔ) sm. རྫི་སྐོར་.

རྫི་སྒྱེ་ (dzigye) a small bag carried by herders for holding their provisions.

རྫི་ཆར་ (dzijar) wind and rain.

རྫི་དུག (dziduù) poison gas.

རྫི་རྡིབ་ (dzi dib) 1. vi. to have one's memory deteriorate/ degenerate (usu. with age); to become senile. 2. vi. to loose one's sense of smell/ scent (usu. for dogs).

རྫི་ནོ་པོ་ (dzi̱ nōbo) sm. རྫི་གསང་པོ་.

རྫི་རྣོན་པོ་ (dzi̱ nõmbo) sm. རྫི་ནོ་པོ་.

རྫི་པ་ (dzi̱bə) sm. རྫི་བོ་.

རྫི་ཕྱོགས་ (dzi̱jɔɔ̀ direction of the wind (usu. upwind or downwind).

རྫི་བོ་ (dzo̱wo) herdsman, herder.

རྫི་བོ་མེ་ཏོག (dzi̱wo me̱doò) winter jasmine.

རྫི་མ་ (dzi̱mə) eyelash.

རྫི་མེད་ (dzi̱meè) 1. without the sense of smell. 2. not clever/ alert/ astute. 3. unguarded. 4. without eyelashes.

རྫི་མེད་སྣང་ཆུང་ (dzi̱meè nāŋjuŋ) not taking notice of, not paying attention to.

རྫི་གཞས་ (dzi̱shɛɛ̀) shepherd/ herdsmen's songs.

རྫི་ཡག་པོ་ (dzi̱ yagbo) sm. རྫི་རྣོན་པོ་.

རྫི་ར་ (dzi̱rə) sm. རྫི་སྣར་.

རྫི་རིག (dzi̱ rig) 1. vi. to smell. 2. vi. come to understand/ know/ learn ། ཁོས་གནོད་པ་སྐྱེལ་རྩིས་བྱས་པ་དེ་ངས་རྫི་རིག་བྱུང་ I came to know of his plan to harm me.

རྫི་རླུང་ (dzi̱luŋ) wind.

རྫིཞེན་ (dzi̱sha le̱n) vi. to pick up a smell/ scent from a distance (for animals).

རྫི་ཤ་ལུག (dzi̱sha lu̱ù) vi. to get a prolapse of the anus.

རྫི་ཤིང་ (dzi̱shiŋ) fuel collected by herders while herding.

རྫི་གསང་ (dzi̱saŋ) sensitivity, alertness, quickness in knowing to know; va.—བྱེད་ to be alert/ sensitive/ quick to know or sense or learn ། འདིའི་ཁུལ་སོ་པ་མང་པོ་ཡོད་ཙང་རྫི་གསང་བྱེད་དགོས་ Because there are many spies around here (you) have to be alert.

རྫི་གསང་པོ་ (dzi̱ sāŋbo) sm. རྫི་གསང་དོད་པོ་.

རྫི་གསང་དོད་པོ་ (dzi̱saŋ tö̱öbo) 1. acute sense of smell. 2. sensitive, alert, quick to know or sense ། ཁོ་འདི་འདྲ་ལ་རྫི་གསང་དོད་པོ་ཡོད་པ་རེད་ He is very sensitive to things like this.

རྫིག་ངམ་ཆེན་པོ་ (dzi̱ŋŋam cēmbo) imposing, grand, regal.

རྫིག་ཉམས་ (dzi̱ŋñam) elegance, grandness, magnificence, dignity, prestige ། གནས་ཚུལ་དེ་བྱུང་ནས་ཁོ་ཚོའི་རྫིག་ཉམས་ཐད་དེ་ཤོར་པ་རེད་ After that incident, they completely lost their dignity/ grandness.

རྫིག་ཉམས་ཆེ་མདོག (dzi̱ŋñam cēndɔɔ̀) the appearance of being magnificent.

རྫིག་ཉམས་སྟོན་ (dzi̱ŋñam dõn) va. to show or manifest one's grandeur/ elegance/ dignity.

རྫིག་ཉམས་དོད་པོ་ (dzi̱ŋñam tö̱öbo) sm. རྫིག་ཉམས་ལྡན་པ་.

རྫིག་ཉམས་ལྡན་པ་ (dzi̱ŋñam de̱mba) grand, elegant, dignified ། འགོ་ཁྲིད་དེ་རྫིག་ཉམས་ལྡན་པ་ཞིག་འདུག The leader is someone who looks grand.

རྫིག་གདམ་ (dzi̱gdam) sth. said to scare/ intimidate; va.—ཤོད་.

རྫིག་འཐེན་ (dzi̱den) pulling with all its might (usu. refers to a dog); va.—བྱེད་.

རྫིག་མདོག་ཁ་པོ་ (dzi̱ŋdoò kābo) grand, dignified, elegant, imposing.

རྫིག་མདོག་གོང་མདོག (dzi̱ŋdoò gö̱ndoò) showoffish, arrogantly ostentatious.

རྫིག་པོ་ (dzi̱gbu) 1. rich, wealthy. 2. grand, imposing ། མི་དེའི་གདོང་རྫིག་པོ་འདུག This man has an imposing face.

རྫིག་རྫིག་སྐྲུལ་ (dzi̱gdzii gü̃ü) va. to scare/ frighten.

རྫིག་རྫིག་ངམ་ངམ་ (dzi̱gdzii ŋāmŋam) scary and fierce.

རྫིག་རྫིག་གདོང་ (dzi̱gdzii dõŋ) sm. རྫིག་རྫིག་སྐྲུལ་.

རྫིག་རྫིག་བྱེད་ (dzi̱gdzii ce̱è) sm. རྫིག་རྫིག་སྐྲུལ་.

རྫིག་རལ་ (dzi̱rɛɛ) sm. རྫིག་རྫིག་ངམ་ངམ་.

རྫིག་རལ་སྐྲུལ་ (dzi̱rɛɛ gü̃ü) sm. རྫིག་རྫིག་སྐྲུལ་.

རྫིག་རལ་དོད་པོ་ (dzi̱grɛɛ tö̱öbo) scary and fierce; va.—བྱེད་.

རྫིང་ (dzi̱ŋ) pond, reservoir, pool; va.—གཏོང་ to irrigate from a reservoir.

རྫིང་སྐོར་ (dzi̱ŋgyɔɔ) wall around a pond/ reservoir.

རྫིང་ཆུ་ (dzi̱nju) water in a pond/ reservoir.

རྫིང་བུ་ (dzi̱ŋbu) sm. རྫིང་.

རྫིང་ལུད་ (dzi̱ŋlüü) fertilizer formed at the bottom of the pool.

རྫིངས་ (dzi̱ŋ) raft; va.—གཏོང་ to float/ paddle a raft.

རྫིའུ་ (dzi̱wu) sm. རྫི་བོ་.

རྫིའི་ཤིང་ (dzi̱shiŋ) firewood/ dung collected by herders when they are out with their animals.

རྫིས་ (dzi̱i) p. and imp. of རྫི་.

རྫུ་: p. བརྫུས་; f. བརྫུ་; imp. རྫུས་ (dzu̱) va. to pose as, to impersonate, to deceive, to disguise ། ཁོས་ཞིང་པ་ཞིག་ལ་བརྫུས་ནས་སོ་པ་བྱེད་པར་ཕྱིན་པ་རེད་ He disguised himself as a farmer and went to spy.

རྫུ་འདེབས་ (dzu̱ de̱b) va. to pretend, to pose as ། ཁོས་ན་རྫུ་བཏབ་ནས་ལས་ཀར་མ་ཡོང་པ་རེད་ He pretended to be sick and didn't come to work.

རྫུ་འཕྲུལ་ (dzu̱ndrüü) magic, illusion, deception, miracle; va.—སྟོན་ to do magic, to create an illusion.

རྫུ་འཕྲུལ་ལ་དབང་བ་ (dzu̱ndrüüla wāŋwa) person who can perform miracles/ magic.

རྫུ་བག (dzu̱baà) impersonation, deception, sham, pretense, hypocrisy; va.—སྟོན་;—བྱེད་ ། ཁོས་མཁས་པའི་རྫུ་བག་སྟོན་གྱི་འདུག He is pretending to be an expert.

རྫུ་བྱེད་ (dzu̱ ce̱è) va. to act false/ deceptive, to pretend ། ཁོང་གིས་ཤེས་ཡོད་ཀྱང་མི་ཤེས་པའི་རྫུ་བྱེད་ཀྱི་འདུག Even though he knows, he falsely pretends that he doesn't.

རྫུ་བཟང་ (dzu̱saŋ) a hypocrite, sb. who pretends to be kind/ good.

རྫུ་ཤོད་ (dzu̱ shöö) va. to lie.

རྫུན་ (dzü̱n) lying; va.—ཤོད་ ། དཀའ་ངལ་མི་འདུག་ཟེར་ན་རྫུན་རེད་ Its a lie if they say there are no problems.

རྫུན་ཀྲུབ་ (dzü̱ngub) exposing/ uncovering lies; va.—རྡོལ་ to expose/ uncover a lie or deception.; vi.—རྡོལ་; —ལུག to have a lie/ deceit get exposed ། ང་ཚོས་ཁོའི་རྫུན་ཀྲུབ་བརྡོལ་ཙང་ཁོ་བྲོས་ཕྱིན་པ་རེད་ He ran away because we exposed him.

རྫུན་རྒྱལ་ (dzü̱ngyɛɛ) a liar, sb. who lies a lot.

རྫུན་ཁག་བཀལ་ (dzü̱ngaà gɛ̄ɛ) shung. va. to bring a false charge against sb.

རྫུན་འགེབས་ (dzü̱ngeb) hiding/ covering up a lie; va.—བྱེད་ to hide/ conceal/ cover up a lie.

རྫུན་རྒྱབ་རྫུན་གནོན་ (dzü̱ngyəb dzü̱nnön) backing/ supporting a liar; va.—བྱེད་.

རྫུན་སྒྲིག (dzü̱ndrig) making lies, fabricating; va.—བྱེད་ to fabricate/ concoct lies.

རྫུན་བསྒྲིགས་ (dzü̱ndrig) sm. རྫུན་སྒྲིག.

རྫུན་བསྔགས་ (dzü̱nŋaà) false praise/ flattery.

རྫུན་ཆས་ (dzü̱njɛɛ̀) disguises, things for disguising; va.—གྱོན་ to wear a disguise.

རྫུན་གཏམ་ (dzü̱ndam) lie, falsehood; va. རྫུན་གཏམ་; —ཤོད་ to lie.

རྫུན་གཏམ་ཐེར་འདོན་ (dzü̱ndam tērdön) sm. རྫུན་ཀྲུབ་རྡོལ་.

རྫུན་མཐིལ་བརྡོལ་ (dzü̱ndii dö̱ö) sm. རྫུན་ཀྲུབ་རྡོལ་.

རྫུན་པ་ (dzü̱mba) lie, falsehood.

རྫུན་སྤངས་བདེན་འཛིན་ (dzü̱nbaŋ de̱ndzin) renouncing/ discarding the false and keeping or holding on to the truth (political slogan).

རྫུན་ཕུག་བརྡོལ་ (dzü̱nbuù dö̱ö) sm. རྫུན་ཀྲུབ་བརྡོལ་.

རྫུན་འབག (dzü̱nbaà) false face/ front, a false look; va.—གྱོན་ to put on a false face/ front ། ཞི་བདེའི་རྫུན་འབག་གྱོན་ནས་ཟིང་ཆ་སློང་དུ་བཅུག་པ་རེད་ Putting on the false face of peace he incited an uprising.

རྫུན་མ་ (dzü̱nmə) false, not genuine; va.—བཟོ་ to make false, to falsify, to counterfeit ། སྙན་ཞུ་རྫུན་མ་ False report.

རྫུན་མ་དོན་ (dzü̱nmə tö̱n) 1. va. to pretend to be sth.,

to act falsely ། ཁོས་ཁང་བདག་ཛུན་མ་དོན་ནས་ཁང་གླ་བསྡུས་བཞག He pretended to be a landlord and collected rent.

ཛུན་མ་གཏོང་ (dzü̲nmə dōŋ) va. to use counterfeit things (usu. money).

ཛུན་སྨྲ་ (dzü̲n mā) va. to lie.

ཛུན་ཚིག (dzü̲ndzii̖) sm. ཛུན་གཏམ་.

ཛུན་ཚུལ་ (dzü̲ndzüü) false/ deceitful appearance.

ཛུན་མཚང་ (dzü̲ndzaŋ) sm. ཛུན་ཀུབ་.

ཛུན་ཤུ་ (dzü̲nshu) false report; va.—བྱེད་ to make a false report.

ཛུན་བཟོ་ (dzü̲nso) sm. ཛུན་སྒྲིག.

ཛུན་བཟོས་མགོ་སྐོར་ (dzü̲nsöö go̲gɔɔ) cheating/ duping through deceit.

ཛུན་བཟོས་དངོས་པོ་ (dzü̲nsöö ŋööbo) counterfeit goods.

ཛུན་བཟོས་བདེན་འགྱུར་ (dzü̲nsöö de̲ngyur) having what was made up/ fabricatied come true.

ཛུན་ལབ་ (dzü̲n lə̲b) va. to lie.

ཛུན་བཤད་མགོ་སྐོར་ (dzü̲nshεὲ go̲gɔɔ) swindling/ duping by telling lies.

ཛུན་ཤོད་ (dzü̲n shöö) sm. ཛུན་ལབ་.

ཛུབ་ (dzu̲b) sm. ཛུན་.

ཛུའོ་ཅིའུ་ (dzu̲woci) ch. football, soccer.

ཛུལ་ (dzü̲ü̲) ch. jade.

ཛུས་ (dzü̲ü) imp. of ཛུ་.

ཛུས་གོལ་ (dzü̲ügöö) 1. feinting/ faking an attack; va.—བྱེད་.

ཛུས་རྟགས་ (dzü̲üdaà) disguise, disguising; va.—བྱེད་ ། བུ་མོ་དེས་སྤྲང་པོ་ཡིན་པར་ཛུས་རྟགས་བྱས་པ་རེད་ The girl disguised herself as a beggar.

ཛུས་མ་ (dzü̲ümə) 1. counterfeit, imitation, fake ། དངུལ་ཛུས་མ་ Fake money. 2. puppet ། སྲིད་དབང་ཛུས་མ་ A puppet government.

ཛུས་དམག (dzü̲ümaà) puppet troops (derogatory term used for enemy troops).

ཛུས་བཟོ་ (dzü̲üso) forging, faking, counterfeiting; va.—བྱེད་.

ཛེ་: p. བཛེས་; f. བཛེ་; imp. ཛེས་ (dze̲) 1. va. to raise up (e.g., curtains), to roll up ། གུ་ཐུང་ཡར་བཛེས་ནས་ Having rolled up the pants. 2. va. to push back hair from one's forehead.

ཛེ་མ་ (dze̲ma) wooden cover on a water mill.

ཛེ་ལོ་ (dze̲lo) rolling up ones sleeves/ pants; va.—བྱེད་.

ཛེའུ་ (dze̲wu) small clay pot.

ཛེའུ་བུམ་ (dzēbum) small clay pot/ vase.

ཛེའུ་ཚོས་ཁ་ཟས་ (dze̲wudzöö kāsεὲ) food individually cooked in a small clay pot.

ཛེས་ (dze̲è) imp. of ཛེ་.

ཛོ་ག་ར་ (dzo̲gara) eng. joker (in cards).

ཛོག (dzɔ̲ɔ̀) 1. va. to pound, to pulverize ། སྨོག་དེང་ནང་ལ་སྨན་སྣ་ཛོག་གི་འདུག (They) are pounding spices in the mortar. 2. vi. to unintentionally fall down.

ཛོག་ཁུང་ (dzɔ̲ɔ̀guŋ) holes/ space in the walls of a fort where attackers can be stoned from above.

ཛོག་མགོ་ (dzɔ̲ɔ̀go) fist.

ཛོག་དུང་གཏོང་ (dzɔ̲gduŋ dōŋ) 1. va. to thrash, beat. 2. va. to pulverize/ pound into powder.

ཛོག་རྡོ་དབྱུགས་ (dzɔ̲gdo yūù) va. to stone people from above.

ཛོག་སྣོད་ (dzɔ̲gnöò) mortar (for pulverizing).

ཛོགས་ (dzɔ̲ɔ̀) 1. vi. to come to the end, to run out of, to be exhausted, to be finished ། སྡུག་བསྔལ་གྱི་དུས་ཚོད་ཛོག་སོང་ The time of suffering came to an end. 2. vi. to be complete/ fulfilled/ met ། མཐུན་རྐྱེན་ཚང་མ་ཛོགས་བཞག All the conditions are met.

ཛོགས་རྒྱུ་མེད་པ་ (dzɔ̲ɔ̀gyu me̲èba) endless, inexhaustable.

ཛོགས་ཆེན་ (dzɔ̲gjen) a Nyingma subsect.

ཛོགས་ཉེ་ (dzɔ̲gñe) just before the end, almost finished ། མོ་ཊའི་སྣུམ་ཛོགས་ཉེའི་སྐབས་ When the gas in the car was about to run out.

ཛོགས་རྟགས་ (dzɔ̲gdaà) a period, the sign for a full stop.

ཛོགས་མཐའ་ (dzɔ̲gta) the end, the limit to sth.

ཛོགས་མཐའ་མེད་པ་ (dzɔ̲gta me̲èba) endless, limitless.

ཛོགས་ལྡན་ (dzɔ̲gdεn) complete, perfect.

ཛོགས་ལྡན་གྱི་དུས་ (dzɔ̲gdεngi tü̲ü̲) golden/ perfect age.

ཛོགས་ལྡན་གྱི་དུས་རབས་ (dzɔ̲gdεngi tü̲ürəb) golden/ perfect age.

ཛོགས་པ་ཆེན་པོ་ (dzɔ̲gba cēmbo) sm. ཛོགས་ཆེན་.

ཛོགས་པའི་སངས་རྒྱས་ (dzɔ̲gbε sāŋgyεὲ) 1. Buddha. 2. sm. བླ་མ་དཀོན་མཆོག, 2.

ཛོགས་པར་ (dzɔ̲gbar) fully, completely ། ཁོས་གནས་ཚུལ་འདི་ཛོགས་པར་བྱས་བཤད་སོང་ He told the story completely.

ཛོགས་ཚིག (dzɔ̲gdzii̖) particles indicating the end of a sentence.

ཛོགས་མཚམས་ (dzɔ̲gdzam) at the time/ point of (sth.) being depleted.

ཛོགས་འཚང་རྒྱ་ (dzɔ̲gdzaŋ gya̲) vi. to be enlightened.

ཛོགས་ལ་ཁད་ (dzɔ̲gla kε̄è) sm. ཛོགས་ཉེ་.

ཛོང་ (dzo̲ŋ) 1. district. 2. fort. 3. a county/ xian.

ཛོང་: p. བཛོངས་; f. བཛོང་; imp. ཛོངས་ (dzo̲ŋ) 1. va. to stuff in ། ཁོས་རས་ཁུག་ནང་ཅ་ལག་མང་པོ་བཛོངས་སོང་ He stuffed many things into the bag. 2. sm. གཏོང་.

ཛོང་ཀང་ (dzo̲ŋgaŋ) shung. tax land held by peasants that belongs to a district (where the district is equivalent to the lord).

ཛོང་སྐལ་ (dzo̲ŋgεε) dowry.

ཛོང་སྐྱེལ་ (dzo̲ŋgyee) shung. tax requiring corvee labor to transport goods from one district to another.

ཛོང་སྐྱེལ་རྟ་འུལ་ (dzo̲ŋgyee dāwu) shung. tax requiring corvee people and animals to transport goods from one district to another.

ཛོང་སྐྱོང་གཞིས་ཀ་ (dzo̲ŋgyoŋ shi̲igə) shung. estate governed by a district.

ཛོང་ཁག (dzo̲ŋgaà) districts.

ཛོང་ཁང་ (dzo̲ŋgaŋ) shung. the building/ residence of a district.

ཛོང་མཁར་ (dzo̲ŋgar) fortress, castle.

ཛོང་གི་རིམ་པ་ (dzo̲ŋgi ri̲mbə) a level/ category of officials and offices below the autonomous region level (roughly equavalent to the level of county/ xian).

ཛོང་འགོ་ (dzo̲ŋgo) 1. head of a ཛོང་. 2. distict ། ཛོང་འགོ་སོ་སོ་ Each district.

ཛོང་རྒྱག (dzo̲ŋgyaà) sm. ཛོང་.

ཛོང་རྒྱབ་ (dzo̲ŋgyəb) sm. ཛོང་རྒྱབ་ཀླུ་ཁང་.

ཛོང་རྒྱབ་ཀླུ་ཁང་ (dzo̲ŋgyəb lūgaŋ) the nāga temple behind the Potala palace.

ཛོང་རྒྱབ་ཞར་ཕེན་ (dzo̲ŋgyəb sha̲rben) shung. the ceremony after the Great Prayer Festival on the 26th of the first month in which ancient customs of marksmanship (riding, archery, spear throwing) are performed.

ཛོང་ཆོས་ (dzo̲ŋjöö) shung. the district and the monastery.

ཛོང་བཏང་ཁྲ་མ་ (dzo̲ŋdoŋ trāma) shung. a verdict issued by a district head.

ཛོང་ཐམ་ (dzo̲ŋdam) shung. the seal of the district head.

ཛོང་ཐུར་ (dzo̲ŋdur) ramrod (for bullets).

ཛོང་བདག (dzo̲ŋdaà) sm. ཛོང་དཔོན་.

ཛོང་བདའ་ (dzo̲ŋda) sm. ཛོང་བཏད་.

ཛོང་བཏད་ (dzo̲ŋda) 1. shung. an order from the government sending sb. somewhere ། ཛོང་སྡོད་ཀྱིས་ཁ་མཆུའི་ཁ་གཏད་གཉིས་ལྷ་སར་ཛོང་བཏད་བཀྱབ་པ་རེད་ The district head ordered the two disputing parties to go to Lhasa. 2. shung. sending a messenger ། ཡི་གེ་དེ་སྐྱེལ་བར་བང་ཆེན་ཞིག་ཛོང་བཏད་བཀྱབ་པ་རེད་ (They) sent a messeger to deliver the message. 3. shung. va. to expel/ ban/ banish/

deport ། ཁོ་གཉིས་རྒྱ་གར་ནས་རྫོང་བཏང་བརྒྱབ་པ་རེད་ The two were expelled from Lhasa.

རྫོང་འདུ་ (dzoŋdu) shung. district meeting; va.—འཚོག to convene a meeting between the district and representatives of the subjects.

རྫོང་སྡོད་ (dzoŋdöö) shung. sm. རྫོང་དཔོན་.

རྫོང་དཔོན་ (dzoŋbön) shung. head/ governor of a རྫོང་.

རྫོང་བྲེ་ (dzoŋdre) shung. a volume measure used by a district.

རྫོང་འབངས་ (dzoŋbaŋ) shung. abbr. the district and its subjects.

རྫོང་སྤྱིལ་ (dzoŋdree) shung. the (two) joint heads of a district ། བཀའ་ཤག་ནས་རྫོང་སྤྱིལ་ལ་བཀའ་རྒྱ་ཞིག་བཏང་པ་རེད་ The Kashag sent an order to the two heads of the district.

རྫོང་གཙོ་ (dzoŋdze) shung. in districts with joint monk and lay official heads, this term refers to the monk official district head.

རྫོང་གཙོ་ཤོད་ (dzoŋ dzē shöö) shung. the two heads of a district (one monk and the other lay).

རྫོང་གཙོ་ (dzoŋdzo) shung. abbr. of རྫོང་དཔོན་ and གཙོ་དག.

རྫོང་བཙན་ (dzoŋdzɛn) a safe or secure castle/ fort.

རྫོང་ཚགས་ (dzoŋdzaà) packing things tightly; va.—རྒྱག.

རྫོང་ཞོལ་ (dzoŋshöö) shung. the area immediately below (at the foot of) a district.

རྫོང་གཞིས་ (dzoŋshii) shung. 1. districts and estates. 2. estates held by a district.

རྫོང་གཞིས་སྣེ་སྡོད་ (dzoŋshii nēdöö) shung. abbr. of རྫོང་དཔོན་ and གཞིས་སྡོད་.

རྫོང་གཞིས་སྣེ་མོ་བ་ (dzoŋshii nēmowa) shung. sm. རྫོང་གཞིས་སྣེ་སྡོད་.

རྫོང་བཞུགས་ (dzoŋshuù) shung. sm. རྫོང་དཔོན་.

རྫོང་རིམ་པ་ (dzoŋ rimbə) sm. རྫོང་གི་རིམ་པ་.

རྫོང་ཤོད་ (dzoŋshöö) shung. in districts where there are two heads (one monk and one lay), this refers to the lay official.

རྫོང་སྲུང་ (dzoŋsuŋ) people who guard a district fort.

རྫོང་ཨུ་ (dzoŋ ū) tib. ch. abbr. a county party committee.

རྫོངས་ (dzoŋ) 1. imp. of རྫོང་. 2. gift; va.—སྐུར་ to send a gift/ present.

རྫོངས་སྐྱེས་ (dzoŋgyeè) sm. རྫོངས་སྣ་.

རྫོངས་ཆས་ (dzoŋjɛè) 1. gift to a person leaving. 2. provisions for a trip.

རྫོངས་ད་ (dzoŋda) sm. རྫོངས་སྣ་.

རྫོངས་སྣ་ (dzoŋda) gift to a person leaving.

རྫོངས་པ་ (dzoŋba) 1. a share (of sth.). 2. a gift/ present; va.—སྤྲོད་.

རྫོད་: p. and f. བརྫོད་; imp. རྫོད་ (dzöö) 1. va. to spoil (a child). 2. va. to dirty/ soil (one's) clothes.

རྫོབ་རྡགས་ (dzobdaà) stupid, foolhardy; va.—སྟོན་ to display stupidity.

རྫོབ་ཐེབས་ (dzob tēb) vi. to have ink unintentionally drip from a pen.

རྫོབ་དྲེག (dzobdreg) dirt (on hands, etc.).

རྫོབ་པོ་ (dzobbo) a lying/ cheating man.

རྫོབ་མ་ (dzobmo) a lying/ cheating woman.

རྫོབས་ (dzob) imp. of རྫོབ་.

བརྫང་ (dzaŋ) f. of རྫོང་.

བརྫང་ཐོ་ (dzaŋdo) shung. list of things sent somewhere.

བརྫང་ཐོ་འབའ་མཚན་ (dzaŋdo bajɛn) shung. a list of items that was sent somewhere.

བརྫངས་རྒྱ་ (dzaŋgya) sm. བརྫང་ཐོ་.

བརྫངས་ (dzaŋ) p. of རྫོངས་.

བརྫངས་ཐོ་ (dzaŋdo) sm. བརྫང་ཐོ་.

བརྫད་ (dzɛɛ̀) p. and f. of རྫོད་.

བརྫབ་ (dzəb) f. of རྫོབ་.

བརྫབས་ (dzəb) p. of རྫོབ་.

བརྫི་ (dzi) f. of རྫི་.

བརྫི་གནོན་ (dzinün) pressing down, trampling down, stepping on, not respecting; va.—བྱེད་ ། དམངས་གཙོའི་རྩ་དོན་ལ་བརྫི་གནོན་བྱས་པ་རེད་ (They) trampled on the principles of democracy.

བརྫིས་ (dzii) p. of རྫི་.

བརྫིས་ཤི་ (dziishi) being killed by getting trampling on/ run over; vi.—ཐེབས་ to get killed by being trampled on/ run over.

བརྫུ་ (dzu) f. of རྫུ་.

བརྫུན་ (dzün) sm. རྫུན་.

བརྫུས་ (dzüü) p. of རྫུ་.

བརྫུས་སྐྱེས་ (dzüügyeè) sm. རྫུས་སྐྱེས་.

བརྫུས་མ་ (dzüümə) sm. རྫུན་མ་.

བརྫེ་ (dze) f. of རྫེ་.

བརྫེས་ (dzeè) p. of རྫེ་.

ཝ

ཝ་ (wa) 1. drain pipe (on a roof), gutter. 2. abbr. for ཝ་མོ་. 3. the letter ཝ་ (used in alphabetical ordering. 4. sm. ཏའི་ཤུར.

ཝ་དཀར་ (wagar) white fox.

ཝ་སྐད་ (wagɛɛ̀) the cry of a fox; va.—རྒྱག.

ཝ་སྐོར་ (wagɔɔ) complete skin of a fox worn as a hat.

ཝ་སྐྱེས་ (wagyeè) 1. fox. 2. a sly/ foxy/ cunning person.

ཝ་སྐྱེས་རྒྱལ་པོར་བསྐོས་གྱུར་ན། ཁྱད་པར་ཝ་ཡིས་ཕྱོགས་སུ་སྣང་ (wagyeè gyɛɛwɔɔ gōò gyurna kyɛ̄ɛ̀bar wayiì cōgsu daŋ) people who look down on their own kind when they reach a position of power [Lit. if the fox becomes king, he hates foxes].

ཝ་སྐྱེས་རྒྱལ་པོར་བསྐོས་ (wagyeè gyɛɛwɔɔ) abbr. of ཝ་སྐྱེས་རྒྱལ་པོར་བསྐོས་གྱུར་ན། ཁྱད་པར་ཝ་ཡིས་ཕྱོགས་སུ་སྣང་.

ཝ་སྐྱེས་རྒྱལ་པོ་ (wagyeè gyɛɛbo) abbr. of ཝ་སྐྱེས་རྒྱལ་པོར་བསྐོས་གྱུར་ན། ཁྱད་པར་ཝ་ཡིས་ཕྱོགས་སུ་སྣང་.

ཝ་སྐྱེས་སྡར་མ་ (wagyeè darma) cowardly.

ཝ་ཁ་ (waga) drain pipe (on a roof).

ཝ་ཁུང་ (waguŋ) fox den/ lair.

ཝ་ཁྱུ་ (wa kyū) pack of a foxes.

ཝ་འཁྱིལ་ (wagyii) shung. black fox fur hat worn by high ranking officials of tt.

ཝ་འཁྱུག (wagyuù) running like a fox in a zigzag manner.

ཝ་འཁྱུགས་ (wagyuù) sm. ཝ་འཁྱུག.

ཝ་གར་ (wagar) fox hat.

ཝ་གྲོ་གྲོ་ (wa drodro) a fox fur that is pale yellow with a tinge of other colors.

ཝ་གླིང་ (waliŋ) abbr. of ཝ་པག་གླིང་.

ཝ་གློ་ (walo) lung of a fox (used in Tibetan medicine).

ཝ་རྒན་ (wagɛn) 1. an old fox. 2. a crafty/ sly/ cunning person.

ཝ་རྒྱ་ (wagya) fox trap; va.—འགྲིམས་ to lay a fox trap.

ཝ་བརྒྱལ་ (wagyɛɛ) the noise made by foxes when drinking water (negative connotation).

ཝ་སྔོན་ (waŋön) blue fox.

ཝ་ཆུ་ (waju) sm. ཝ་ཁ་.

ཝ་མཆུ་ (wanju) the end/ tip of a ཝ་ཁ་.

ཝ་ཆུ་རྒྱུག་མདོང་ (wanju gyugdoŋ) downspout.

ཝ་ཆུ་འདྲེན་སྦུག (wanju drembuù) sm. ཝ་ཆུ་རྒྱུག་མདོང་.

ཝ་སྙིང་ (wañiŋ) heart of a fox (used in Tibetan medicine).

ཝ་སྙིང་སྟག་གདོང་ (wañiŋ dāgdoŋ) sb. who looks or acts tough but is cowardly [Lit. heart of a fox and the face of a lion].

ཝ་ད་ (wada) white cloth.

ཝ་བདགས་ (wadaà) sm. ཝ་ཟུར་.

ཝ་ལྡར་འཁྱུག་པ་ (wadar kyūgbə) sm. ཝ་འཁྱུག.

ཝ་ལྡེམ་ (wadem) fox trap.

ཝ་སྡར་མ་སེང་གེ་ལ་འགྲན་པ་ (wa darma sēŋgela drɛmba) not knowing one's limitations [Lit. the cowardly fox challeging the lion].

ཝ་ནག (wanaà) black fox.

ཝ་པག་གླིང་ (wabaliŋ) ch.tib. an area in Lhasa that used to be inhabited mainly by Muslims.

ཝ་ལྤགས་ (wabaà) fox skin.

ཝ་སྤྱང་དུ་བསྡེབས་ (wajaŋ tradeb) evil people in cahoots [Lit. fox and wolf linked together].

ཝ་ཕྱིད་ (wajeè) sm. ཝ་ཟུར་.

ཝ་ཕྲུག (wadruù) fox cub.

ཝ་འབྲོས་ (wadröò) running scared like a fox; va.—རྒྱག.

ཝ་མི་བརྒྱལ་ཀ་མེད་འདྲེའི་འགྲམ་ལྕག (wa migyɛɛ gāmeè dree dramjaà) forcing sb. to do sth. [Lit. the fox was made to cry by the slap of the ghost].

ཝ་མོ་ (wamo) fox.

ཝ་མོ་ཁྲབ་གྱོན་ (wamo trābgyön) a coward trying to act brave [Lit. fox putting on armor].

ཝ་མོ་ཕོ་ (wāmo pō) male fox.

ཝ་མོ་མོ་ (wamo mo) female fox.

ཝ་ཙི་ (wadzi) ch. stockings.

ཝ་ཚང་ (wadzaŋ) sm. ཝ་ཁུང་.

ཝ་འཛུམ་སྟག་བརྫུས་ (wadzum dāgdzüù) a coward pretending to be brave. [Lit. a fox diguised as a tiger].

ཝ་ཞྭ་ (washa) fox fur hat.

ཝང་ཞུ་ (wāŋshu) shung. communication, commnique ¶ ཨམ་བན་ལྷན་རྒྱས་ནས་ཝང་ཞུ་བསྒྲུབ་ཕེབས་དགོངས་དོན་དུ་ The communique from the Ambans states.

ཝ་ཟུར་ (wasur) the letter ཝ་ subfixed to certain letters.

ཝ་ཡེ་ (wāye) 1. a phrase used to call attention ¶ སྐབས་དེ་ར་ཕྱི་སྒོ་དག་དག་ཅེས་ལན་འགག་བརྡུངས་པས་མོས་ཝ་ཡེ་སུ་ཡིན་ཞེས་བརྗོད་པ་རེད་ At that time there was a knocking on the outer door and she said, "Yes. Who is it?" 2. standard phone greeting in China/ Tibet that is equivalent to "hello."

ཝ་ར་ཎ་སི་ (wara nasi) Benaras.

ཝ་རོག་པོ་ (wa rogbo) a black fox.

ཝ་རོགས་ཁྱི་གྲོགས་ (warog kyīdrɔɔ̀) sm. ཁྱི་སྤྱང་ངན་འགྲིལ་.

ཝ་ལ་ (wala) completely black (for horse).

ཝ་ལུང་ (waluŋ) the Walung valley (E. Nepal).

ཝ་ལེ་ཝ་ལེ་ (wale wale) sm. ཝ་ལེར་.

ཝ་ལེར་ (waler) clear, distinct; vi.—འཆར་ to appear clearly in mind; vi.—དྲན་ to remember clearly ¶ རང་གི་ལུང་པར་སེམས་ལ་ཝ་ལེར་དྲན་བྱུང་ (I) remember clearly my own country.

ཝ་ཤི་ཡང་ཁྲ་མི་ཉམས་ (wa shīyaŋ tra miñam) one's deeds continue after one dies [Lit. even though the fox dies, the sheen (of the fur) doesn't deteriorate].

ཝ་ཤིག (washig) sm. སྣུ་མཁྲིན་.

ཝ་ཤུ་ (washu) sm. ཝ་ཞུ་.

ཝ་ཤུར་ (washur) roof drain pipe.

ཝ་ཤུལ་ (washüü) name of an ancient lineage in Tibet.

ཝ་སི་ (wasi) ch. gas.

ཝ་སི་ལིན་ (wasilin) vaseline.

ཝ་སློག (walɔɔ̀) fox fur dress.

ཝ་ཧའ་ (waha) ch. gas.

ཝ་ཧྲེང་ཏོན་ (wahreŋdön) Washington, D.C.

ཝང་ (waŋ) shung. ch. an ancient Chinese title (used in Tibet).

ཝང་གུང་ (waŋguŋ) shung. ch. prince and duke (two ancient Chinese titles used in Tibet).

ཝང་ཆིའུ་ (waŋ cīwu) ch. tennis; va.—རྒྱག to play tennis.

ཝང་བུ་ (waŋbu) shung. ch. an order issued by the Amban ¶ གོང་མའི་བཀའ་འགྲིལ་ཨམ་བན་ནས་ཝང་བུ་གནང་དོན་ལྟར་ According to the order issued by the Amban based on the instructions of the Emperor.

ཝང་མོ་ (waŋmo) licorice root.

ཝང་ཡེ་ (waŋye) ch. king.

ཝང་ལུང་ (wāŋluŋ) Bandung ¶ ཝང་ལུང་གྲོས་ཚོགས་ The Bandung Conference.

ཝང་ལེ་མོ་ (waŋlemo) shung. a type of hat Tibetan aristocrats wear when traveling.

ཝང་ཤུ་ (waŋshu) shung. ch. a report sent from the Tibetan Government to the Amban.

ཝང་ཧོའུ་ (waŋhowu) ch. empress.

ཝར་ཎ་དབུས་བོད་ཀྱི་ཆེས་མཐོའི་སློབ་གཉེར་ཁང་ (warna üügi cēèdö lōbñergaŋ) Central Institute of higher

Tibetan Studies (Varanasi).

ཝལ་གྱིས་ (wangyii) sm. ཝ་ལེར་.

ཝལ་གྱིས་ཤར་བ་ (wangyii shārwa) sm. ཝལ་གྱིས་.

ཝལ་ཝལ་ (wεεwεε) abbr. of ཝ་ལེ་ཝ་ལེར་.

ཝལ་ལེ་ (wεεle) sm. ཝ་ལེར་.

ཝིའ་ན་ (winə) Vienna.

ཝུ་ཆང་བཟོ་གྲྭ (wujaŋ) ch.tib. beer brewery.

ཝུ་རྡོ་ (wudo) pumice stone.

ཝུ་ཙེ་པེ་ཁེ་ (wudze bēge) Uzbeb (nationality).

ཝུ་ལན་པ་ཐུར་ (wulεn bātar) Ulanbator.

ཝུང་ཙི་ (wuŋdzi) ch. container for making liquor.

ཝུན་གྲུའུ་ (wün druwu) ch. asparagus fern (used in Tibetan medicine).

ཝུན་ཤིང་ཀོང་ཇོ་ (wünshiŋ gōŋjo) Princess Wenchen (Chinese wife of King Songtsen Gampo).

ཝུའུ་ལྕགས་ (wuujaà) ch.tib. tungsten.

ཝུའུ་ལུའུ་མུའུ་ཆ་ (wuuluu muuja) Urumuchi.

ཝུའུ་སུའུ་རིའི་ (wuusuuri) Ussuri River.

ཝུའུ་ནེ་རུའི་ལ་ (wuune rula) Venezuela.

ཝུའི་ཡེ་ན་ (wuyena) Vienna.

ཝེ་ཆི་མིག་མངས་ (weci miŋmaà) ch.tib. the game "go."

ཝེ་ཧྲེང་སུའུ་ (wehreŋsuu) ch. vitamin.

ཝེར་མ་ (werma) a god of war.

ཝོར་ག (woga) Volga River.

ཞ་ (sha̱) 1. the letter ཞ་ (used in alphabetical numbering). 2. vi. to get or be paralyzed/ crippled ¶ཁོའི་རྐང་པ་ཞ་བ་རེད་ His leg got paralyzed. ¶ལག་ཞ་ A crippled hand. 2. moisture, wetness.

ཞ་ཀྱོག (sha̱gyɔɔ̀) crippled, disabled, lame.

ཞ་དཀར་ (sha̱gar) 1. tin. 2. zinc.

ཞ་དཀར་ཤོག (sha̱gar shɔ̄ɔ̀) tinfoil.

ཞ་སྐུད་ (sha̱güù) galvanized wire.

ཞ་ཁུང་ (sha̱guŋ) hole made by animals like foxes, marmots.

ཞ་ཁུམ་ (sha̱ kūm) vi. to be/ get paralyzed.

ཞ་གི་ཞི་གི་ (shə̱gi shi̱gi) sth. that is about to or ready to crumble.

ཞ་གོང་ (sha̱goŋ) shotput, lead ball.

ཞ་གོང་སྦོ་ལོ་ (sha̱goŋ bōlo) shotput; va.—དབྱུག to throw the shotput.

ཞ་ང་ (shāŋa) arc. sm. ཞལ་ང་.

ཞ་ཅང་ (shājaŋ) ch. shrimp paste.

ཞ་ལྕུག (shə̱juù) lead (for a mechanical pencil).

ཞ་ཆག (sha̱jaà) incomplete, deficient, imperfect, defective.

ཞ་ཆག་མེད་པ་ (sha̱jaà me̱èba) complete, in full, in sound/ perfect condition.

ཞ་ཉེ་ (sha̱ñe) lead.

ཞ་ཉེ་དངུལ་མདོག་སྟོན་ (sha̱ñe ŋū̃ūndɔɔ̀ dō̃n) faking/ pretending sth. is good when it is bad [Lit. making lead appear as silver].

ཞ་ཉེ་མདོག (sha̱ñedɔɔ̀) lead color.

ཞ་ཉེ་རྡོ་ (sha̱ñe do̱) lead ore.

ཞ་ཉེའི་གཏེར་ཁ་ (sha̱ñee dērga) lead mine.

ཞ་ཉེའི་མདུང་རྩེ་ (sha̱ñee du̱ŋdze) an impressive looking but useless person [Lit. a lead spear head].

ཞ་ཉེའི་ཡིག་པར་ (sha̱ñee yi̱gbar) lead type (used in printing).

ཞ་ཉེའི་ཡིག་འབྲུ་ (sha̱ñee yi̱ŋdru) lead type (used in printing).

ཞ་ཉེའི་ལྷམ་གྱོན་པ་ཞིག (sha̱ñee lhāmgyönba shi̱g) going very slowly [Lit. like wearing a lead shoe].

ཞ་སྙུག (shə̱ñuù) lead pencil.

ཞ་གཏེར་ (sha̱der) lead mine.

ཞ་སྡོང་ (sha̱doŋ) shung. money paid as compensation for causing sb. to become crippled.

ཞ་ཐུལ་ (shə̱düü) a sleeveless Tibetan gown worn inside the house to keep warm.

ཞ་འཐེང་ (sha̱deŋ) lame, crippled (foot), sb. who walks with a limp ¶མི་ཞ་འཐེང་དེ་ That lame man.

ཞ་འཐེང་འཐེང་ (sha̱ tēŋdeŋ) sm. ཞ་འཐེང་.

ཞ་འཐེང་པོ་ (sha̱ tēŋbo) lame, crippled.

ཞ་རྡོ་ (sha̱do) lead ore.

ཞ་རྡོག་དཔྱང་ཐིག (shādog jāŋdig) plumb line.

ཞ་སྡེ་ (shāde) the group of four letters: ཞ་ཟ་འ་ཡ་ (in the Tibetan alphabet).

ཞ་ནེ་ (sha̱ne) sm. ཞ་ཉེ་.

ཞ་པར་ (sha̱bar) lead type, lead plate (for printing).

ཞ་ཕྱེ་ (sha̱je) lead powder.

ཞ་བོ་ (sha̱wo) sm. ཞ་འཐེང་.

ཞ་དམར་ (sha̱mar) a kind of lead.

ཞ་སྨི་ (shə̱mi) ch. shrimp.

ཞ་སྨྱུག (shə̱ñuù) sm. ཞ་སྙུག.

ཞ་སྨྱུག་རི་མོ་ (shə̱ñuù ri̱mu) a pencil drawing.

ཞ་ཞ་ (sha̱sha) bending one's body at the knees; va.—བྱེད་.

ཞ་ཞི་ (sha̱shi) children.

ཞ་ར་ (sha̱ra) blind.

ཞ་རིལ་ (shə̱rii) person with a crippled/ contracted leg.

ཞ་རེ་ཞོ་རེ་ (sha̱re sho̱re) during spare time ¶ངས་ཞ་རེ་ཞོ་རེར་ལུས་རྩལ་བྱེད་ཀྱི་ཡོད་ I exercise during my spare time.

ཞ་ལ་ (sha̱la) 1. plaster, plastering; va.—རྒྱག to plaster (usu. walls); vi.—གོག to have plaster peal. 2. floor; va.—འདིང་ to lay/ put down a floor. 3. wall.

ཞ་ལུ་ (shə̱lu) a district in Western Tibet.

ཞ་ལུ་སྐྱེས་ (shə̱lu gyēè) vi. to sprout a shoot.

ཞ་ཤེལ་ (sha̱shee) lead glass, lead crystal.

ཞ་ཤོག (sha̱shɔɔ̀) abbr. of ཞ་དཀར་ཤོག.

ཞ་སེར་ (sha̱ser) a type of lead ore.

ཞ་བསྲེས་ (sha̱seè) sth. alloyed with lead.

ཞ་བསྲེས་ལྕགས་པར་ (sha̱seè jāgbar) type for printing (iron mixed with lead for type setting).

ཞ་བསྲེས་ཤེལ་སྒོ་ (sha̱seè shēēgo) sm. ཞ་ཤེལ་.

ཞ་ཧྲི་ (shə̱hri) ch. corporal.

ཞ་ལྷེབ་ (sha̱lheb) lead (for a mechanical pencil).

ཞག (sha̱à) 1. the grease from meat or butter that is either floating or coagulated on the top of a liquid. 2. a period including a night and day ¶ཕྱིར་ལམ་རྒྱལ་རྩེར་ཞག་གསུམ་བསྡད་པ་ཡིན་ (I) stayed three days and nights in Gyantse on the way back.

ཞག་ཀག (sha̱àgaà) an ominous day on which disaster/ misfortune is likely to occur (according to one's astrology).

ཞག་གེག (sha̱àgeg) sm. ཞག་ཀག.

ཞག་སྐེག (sha̱àgeg) sm. ཞག་ཀག.

ཞག་སྐྱེས་ (sha̱àgeè) the amount of growth that occurs in one day (usu. for an infant).

ཞག་གྲངས་ (sha̱gdraŋ) number of nights sb. stayed at a place.

ཞག་གྲལ་ (sha̱gdrɛɛ) shung. the line of monks at Monlam where the better butter tea is served.

ཞག་འགའ་ (sha̱àga) few days.

ཞག་འགོར་ལུས་ (sha̱àgɔɔ lü̱ù) vi. to be or get delayed/ postponed for a few days.

ཞག་འགྱང་ (sha̱àgyaŋ) postponing, delaying for a few days; va.—བྱེད་.

ཞག་རྒྱགས་ (sha̱àgyaà) provisions for an overnight journey.

ཞག་ཅན་ (sha̱gjɛn) 1. greasy, oily. 2. a liquid that has a layer of oil on top.

ཞག་གཅིག (sha̱gjig) one night, one day and night.

ཞག་རྗེང་མ་ (sha̱à dĩŋmə) the day after, the next day.

ཞག་དྲི་ (shə̱gdri) smell of grease/ oil; vi.—ཁ་ to smell the aroma of oil/ grease.

ཞག་འདོན་ (sha̱à dö̱n) va. to remove the coagulated butter/ fat/ oil from the surface of a liquid.

ཞག་ལྡན་ (sha̱gdɛn) oily, greasy.

ཞག་སྡོད་ (sha̱gdöö̀) staying overnight on a trip; va.—བྱེད་ ¶ལུང་པ་དེར་ཞག་སྡོད་བྱེད་ས་ཡོད་པ་རེད་དམ Is there a place to stay overnight in that place?

ཞག་སྡོད་སློབ་མ་ (sha̱gdöö̀ lōbma) boarders in a school.

ཞག་པོ་ (sha̱gbo) sm. ཞག་གཅིག.

ཞག་པོར་སྡོད་ས་ (sha̱gbo dö̱ösa) sm. ཞག་ས་.

ཞག་པར་ (shāgbar) sm. ཞག་སླུག.

ཞག་པོར་ (sha̱gbɔr) sm. ཞག་སླུག.

ཞག་འཕུལ་ (sha̱gbüü) sm. ཞག་འགྱང་.

ཞག་འཕུལ་ཉིན་འགྱངས་ (sha̱gbüü ñi̱ngyaŋ) sm. ཞག་འགྱང་.

ཞག་སླུག (shə̱gluù) a container for collecting the melted butter that coagulates on top of tea (usu. refers to monks).

ཞག་མ་ (shāgma) sm. ཞག.

ཞག་མལ་ (shāgmɛɛ) sm. ཞག་ས་.

ཞག་རྫི་ (shə̱gdzi) grease, fat; va.—འདོན་ to extract/ take out the fat ¶ཞག་རྫི་བཏོན་པའི་འོ་མ་ Fat-free milk.

ཞག་ཚི་ཁོག་ཁོག (shəgdzi kōggɔɔ̀) greasy, oily.

ཞག་ཚི་ཙུང་ཙུང་ (shəgdzi cūŋjuŋ) very little fat/ grease.

ཞག་ཚི་ཆེན་པོ་ (shəgdzi cēmbo) a lot of fat, grease.

ཞག་ཚི་བདོན་པའི་སྲིང་བལ་ (shəgdzi dōnbɛ sīŋbɛɛ) absorbent cotton.

ཞག་ཚི་མཐུག་པོ་ (shəgdzi tūgbu) oily, greasy.

ཞག་ཚེ་ (shəgdzi) sm. ཞག་ཚི་.

ཞག་ཚིལ་ (shəgdzii) 1. sm. ཞག་ཚི་. 2. abbr. of ཞག and ཚིལ་.

ཞག་ཚུགས་ (shəgdzuù) a day's distance on a journey ། ཞག་ཚུགས་གཅིག A day's journey.

ཞག་ཚོན་དམར་པོ་ (shəgdzön māābo) red lipstick.

ཞག་ཤིག (shaàshiì) abbr. of ཞ་གི་ཤི་གི་.

ཞག་རེངས་ (shəgreŋ) coagulated fat.

ཞག་ལ་མི་སྒྱུར་ (shaàla miŋgyur) va. to not delay doing sth.

ཞག་ལེན་ (shaà len) va. to skim off the floating layer of fat/ grease from a liquid.

ཞག་ལེབ་ (shagleb) a flat slab of fat.

ཞག་ལོན་ (shaà lön) 1. a day old. 2. food from which the grease has been taken out.

ཞག་ཤས་ (shəgshɛɛ̀) a few days and nights.

ཞག་ཤུལ་ (shəgshüü)1. a grease or oil spot/ stain. 2. oily residue.

ཞག་ས་ (shagsa) halting place/ station for travelers, a place to stop overnight on a trip; va.—བྱེད་ to make an overnight stop at a halting place; va.—སྡོད་ to stay overnight at a halting place ། ཉི་མ་ནུབ་ཁར་ཞག་ས་དེར་སླེབས་བྱུང་ At sunset (we) arrived at the overnight halting place.

ཞག་གསུམ་གྱི་གྲོད་པ་རྒྱགས་ཀྱང་ ལོ་གསུམ་གྱི་སྡུག་བསྔལ་འཁུར་པ་ (shagsumgi trööba gyaàgyaŋ losumgi dugŋɛɛ kūrwə) a temporary gain that causes long term hardship/ trouble/ suffering [Lit. a full stomach for three days causing three years of suffering].

ཞག་ཧབ་ (shaà həb) va. to collect the layer of coagulated butter from the top of a tea cup.

ཞགས་ (shaà) lasso, lassoing; va.—རྒྱག; —འདེབས་ to lasso.

ཞགས་ཐག (shaàdaà) a lasso; va.—རྒྱག; —འདེབས་ to lasso.

ཞགས་པ་ (shagba) lasso; va.—རྒྱག; —འདེབས་ to lasso.

ཞང་ (shaŋ) 1. abbr. ཞང་པོ་. 2. wide, width. 3. sm.* ཤང་ (an ancient Tibetan lineage).

ཞང་ཀུ་ (shaŋgwa) ch. muskmelon.

ཞང་གོ་ (shaŋgo) a term used for elderly monks.

ཞང་གོ་ཤིང་གཉེར་ (shaŋgo sīŋñer) shung. monk in charge of fuel during Monlam.

ཞང་ལྕམ་ (shaŋjam) maternal uncle and his wife.

ཞང་ཆི་ (shaŋji) ch. Chinese checkers.

ཞང་ཉེ་ (shaŋñe) kinsman/ relatives on the mother's side.

ཞང་པོ་ (shaŋbo) maternal uncle.

ཞང་བློན་ (shaŋlön) ministers from the maternal/ matrilateral side of the Tibetan king.

ཞང་བློན་ལྷན་ཚོགས་ (shaŋlön lhɛ̄ndzɔɔ̀) a council consisting of ministers from the maternal/ matrilateral side of the Tibetan king and other ministers.

ཞང་དཔོན་ (shaŋbön) abbr. maternal uncle and nephew.

ཞང་འབོག (shaŋbɔɔ̀) see ཞབས་འབོག.

ཞང་ཚན་ (shaŋdzɛn) sm. ཞང་ཉེ་.

ཞང་ཞང་ (shaŋshaŋ) sm. ཞང་པོ་.

ཞང་ཞང་ལགས་ (shaŋshaŋlaà) sm. ཞང་ལགས་.

ཞང་ཞུང་བཟའ་ (shaŋshuŋ sa) one of the wives of king Srongtsen Gampo.

ཞང་ལགས་ (shaŋlaà) h. of ཞང་པོ་.

ཞང་ཧྲེང་ (shaŋhreŋ) ch. comic dialogue (between two people); va.—ཤོད་ to perform a comic dialogue.

ཞད་ (shɛɛ̀) bad influence.

ཞན་ (shɛn) sm.* ཤན་. 2. abbr. of. ཞན་པ་. 3. ch. ray.

ཞན་ཀང་ (shɛngaŋ) Danang (S. Vietnam).

ཞན་འགྱུར་ (shɛngyur) declining, waning, deteriorating.

ཞན་ཆ་ (shɛnja) damage, harm; va.—སེལ་ to clear or eliminate damage/ harm.

ཞན་བརྙས་དྲག་གཡོལ་ (shɛnñɛɛ̀ tragyöö) fearing/ avoiding the strong and bullying the weak.

ཞན་པ་ (shɛmba) inferior, bad, weak, poor ། རྒྱུ་ཞན་པ་ Inferior materials. ། གནམ་གཤིས་ཞན་པ་ Bad weather. ། གཟུགས་པོ་ཞན་པ་ Weak body.

ཞན་པའི་གྲས་ (shɛmbɛ trɛɛ̀) inferior type/ kind/ sort.

ཞན་པར་ (shɛmbar) printing plate; va.—རྒྱག.

ཞན་པིང་ (shɛmbiŋ) ch. sm. ཞན་པིང་དམག་དཔུང་.

ཞན་པིང་དམག་དཔུང་ (shɛnbiŋ māgbuŋ) ch.tib. military police; va.— བྱེད་ to police, to act as gendarme ། རྒྱལ་སྤྱིའི་ཞན་པིང་དམག་དཔུང་བྱེད་རྒྱུ་ Acting as international gendarmes.

ཞན་པོ་ (shɛmbo) weak, poor, inferior.

ཞན་ཙམ་ (shɛndzam) slightly inferior.

ཞན་ཚལ་ (shɛndzɛɛ) ch. pickled vegetables.

ཞན་ས་ (shɛnsa) weak spot/ place.

ཞན་ཨུ་ (shɛn ū) sm. ཤན་ཨུ་.

ཞབས་ (shəb) 1. foot, feet (h.) ། ཁོང་གི་ཞབས་ His feet. 2. the bottom part ། སྣོད་ཞབས་དོང་ཅིག A pot with a hole in the bottom.

ཞབས་ཀྱག (shəbgya) chair, stool (h.); va.—གནང་ to sit down ། ཁོང་གི་སྒམ་གཅིག་གི་ཐོག་ལ་ཞབས་ཀྱག་གནང་སོང་ He sat down on a box.

ཞབས་བཀྱག (shəbgya) sm. of ཞབས་ཀྱག.

ཞབས་ཀྱིས་བཅག (shəbgi jāà) va. to visit (h.) ། ས་འདི་རུ་བླ་མ་དུ་མས་ཞབས་ཀྱིས་བཅག་པ་རེད་ This place has been visited by many lamas.

ཞབས་ཀྱུ་ (shəbgyu) name of the vowel 'u' (ུ).

ཞབས་ཀྱོག (shəbgyɔɔ̀) h. of རྐང་ཀྱོག.

ཞབས་ཀྱོག་ཀྱོག (shəb gyɔggyɔɔ̀) sm. ཞབས་ཀྱོག.

ཞབས་དཀྲིས་ (shəbdrii) h. of རྐང་དཀྲིས་.

ཞབས་རྒྱན་ (shəbgyen) h. of གུ་དུང་.

ཞབས་སྐས་ (shəbgɛɛ̀) h. of སྐས་འཛེགས་.

ཞབས་སྐུལ་ཞུ་ (shəbgüü shu) va. to repeatedly request/ remind sb. higher to do sth. one has asked ། སྐབས་འདུག་ཞུས་པ་དེར་ཞབས་སྐུལ་ཞུས་པ་ཡིན་ I reminded him repeatedly of the request I made.

ཞབས་སྐོར་སྐྱོན་ (shəbgɔɔ gyōn) va. to circumambulate sth. (h.).

ཞབས་སྐོར་ཡག (shəbgɔɔ yaà) term of greeting used by people circumambulating.

ཞབས་སྐྱིལ་ཀྲུང་ (shəbgyee drūŋ) h. of སྐྱིལ་ཀྲུང་.

ཞབས་སྐྱེས་ (shəbgyeè) h. of འཁོར་ཡག.

ཞབས་བསྐུལ་ (shəbgüü) sm. ཞབས་སྐུལ་.

ཞབས་འཁོར་ (shəbgɔɔ) abbr. of ཞབས་ཕྱི་འཁོར་བཅས་.

ཞབས་འཁོད་ (shəbgöö) abbr. of ཞབས་སོར་འཁོར་.

ཞབས་འཁྱོགས་ (shəbgyɔɔ̀) h. of རྐང་འཁྱོགས་.

ཞབས་གོམ་ (shəbgom) h. of གོམ་པ་.

ཞབས་གྱོན་ (shəbgyön) h. of གུ་དུང་.

ཞབས་གྲ་འདྲིགས་པོ་ (shəbdra drigbu) h. of རྐང་གྲ་འདྲིགས་པོ་.

ཞབས་གྲུམ་གྱི་ནད་ (shəbdrumgi nɛɛ̀) h. of རྐང་གྲུམ་གྱི་ནད་.

ཞབས་གྲས་ (shəbdrɛɛ̀) servant (h.).

ཞབས་གླ་ (shəbla) h. of གླ་ཆ་.

ཞབས་འགྲིད་ཤོར་ (shamdreè shɔ̄ɔ̄) sm. ཞབས་འདྲེད་ཤོར་.

ཞབས་འགྲོས་ (shamdröö) h. of རྐང་འགྲོས་; གོམ་འགྲོས་.

ཞབས་འགྱུར་ (shəbgyur) aid, help (h.); va.—ཞུ་ to aid, to help.

ཞབས་རྒྱན་ (shəbgyɛn) a tool for carving wooden bowls.

ཞབས་སྒྲོག (shəbdrɔɔ̀) h. of ལྕགས་སྒྲོག; འདུག་སྒྲོག.

ཞབས་ངར་ (shəbŋar) h. of རྐང་པའི་ངར་གདང་.

ཞབས་ངོས་ (shəbŋöö) along the bottom.

ཞབས་ཅག (shəbjaà) shoes (h.).

ཞབས་བཅགས་ (shabjaà) stepping in, putting one's foot in.

ཞབས་བཅིངས་ (shəbjiŋ) sm. ཞབས་སྒྲོག.
ཞབས་འཇམ (shamjaà) sm. ཞབས་བཅག.
ཞབས་འཇམ་ (shamjam) h. of འཇམ་འཇམ་.
ཞབས་མཇུག (shamjuù) a ritual offered after a person dies.
ཞབས་འཇུར་ (shamjur) shoe (h.).
ཞབས་རྗེན་མ་ (shabjemma) h. of རྐང་རྗེན་མ་.
ཞབས་རྗེས་ (shabjeè) footprint.
ཞབས་རྗེས་ཕྱག་བསྒྲུབ་ (shabjeè cāgsub) h. of རྐང་རྗེས་ལག་བསྒྲུབ་.
ཞབས་རྣོངས་ (shab ñōŋ) vi. to have one's feet be paralyzed/ contracted.
ཞབས་ཏོག (shabdoò) serving (a superior) (h.); va.—ཞུ་; —སྒྲུབ་; —བྱེད་ to serve.
ཞབས་ཏོག་སྡེ་ཚན་ (shəbdoò dedzɛn) public works department.
ཞབས་ཏོག་པ་ (shabdogba) servant (male).
ཞབས་ཏོག་བློན་པོ་ (shabdo lōnbo) Minister of Public Works.
ཞབས་ཏོག་མ་ (shabdoòma) servant (female).
ཞབས་ཏིང་ (shəbdiŋ) h. of རྟིང་ག.
ཞབས་རྟེན་ (shabden) 1. shung. an estate given by the government in compensation for service [Lit. the base for one's foot]. 2. h. of རྐང་ཁྲི་; རྐུབ་བཀྱག.
ཞབས་རྟེན་པ་གཞིས་ (shabden pāshiì) shung. an estate held (owned) by an aristocratic family from which they derive their subsistence and from which the obligation to provide an official to the government derives.
ཞབས་བརྟན་ (shabdɛn) religious prayer service done by monks; va.—ཞུ་ to request monks to perform a religious prayer service; va.—གནང་/ བྱེད་ to perform a religious prayer service.
ཞབས་བརྟན་ཁང་ (shabdɛngaŋ) shung. office in tt. that does prayer services for the Dalai Lama's long life and to prevent harm coming to him.
ཞབས་སྟེགས་ (shəbdeg) h. of རྐང་སྟེགས་.
ཞབས་ཐང་ (shəbdaŋ) h. of རྐང་ཐང་.
ཞབས་ཐང་མ་ (shəbdaŋma) sm. ཞབས་ཐང་.
ཞབས་ཐང་ལ་ཕེབས་ (shəbdaŋla pēè) h. of རྐང་ཐང་ལ་འགྲོ་.
ཞབས་ཐིག (shəbdig) bottom/ lower line.
ཞབས་ཐུང་ (shəbduŋ) h. of གུ་ཐུང་.
ཞབས་མཐའ་ (shəbda) bottom.
ཞབས་མཐིལ་ (shəbdii) h. of རྐང་མཐིལ་.
ཞབས་ཐོ་ (shabdo) h. of དོག་ཐོ་.
ཞབས་ཐོག (shəbdɔ̀) sm. ཞབས་ཏོག.
ཞབས་དག (shabdaà) bottom's up; va.—རྒྱག; va.—སྐྱོན་ to drink bottom's up.
ཞབས་དོར་ (shabdɔɔ) sm. ཞབས་ཐུང་.

ཞབས་དྲུང་ (shəbdruŋ) 1. presence (of) (h.) ¶ སློབ་མ་དེ་ཁོང་གི་ཞབས་དྲུང་དུ་ཡུན་རིང་བསྡད་པ་རེད་ The disciple stayed with him (in his presence) for a long time. 2. used in headings and in letters to indicate the person to whom a letter is sent (h.) ¶ རྡོ་རྗེ་ལགས་ཀྱི་ཞབས་དྲུང་དུ་ To Dorje. 3. an attendant. 4. a polite form of addressing one's superior.
ཞབས་དྲུང་ངག་དབང་རྣམ་རྒྱལ་ (shəbdruŋ ŋaàwaŋ nāmgyɛɛ) Shabdrung Ngawang Namgyal (the 17th century founder of Bhutan).
ཞབས་དྲུང་རིན་པོ་ཆེ་ (shəbdruŋ rimboce) title of the highest lama in Bhutan (the lineage starting with Shabdrung Ngawang Namgyal).
ཞབས་གདུབ་ (shəbdub) h. of རྐང་གདུབ་.
ཞབས་གདན་ (shabdɛn) h. of རྐང་གདན་.
ཞབས་འདེགས་ (shamdeè) serving, service (h.); va.—ཞུ་ to serve, to work for ¶ ཁོས་གཞུང་གི་ཞབས་འདེགས་ལོ་མང་པོ་ཞུས་པ་རེད་ He served the government for many years.
ཞབས་འདེགས་ཀྱི་དྲྭ་ཚིགས་ (shəmdeègi tradzii) service network.
ཞབས་འདེགས་ཀྱི་རྣམ་འགྱུར་ (shəmdeègi nāmgyur) one's attitude in attending to or waiting on guests, customers, etc.
ཞབས་འདེགས་སྐོར་གྱི་ལས་རིགས་ (shəmdeè gɔ̄ɔgi lɛ̄ɛrii) the service industry/ trades.
ཞབས་འདེགས་པ་ (shəmdeèba) 1. government servant/ official. 2. waiter, bearer, attendant, one who serves others.
ཞབས་འདེགས་དམག་མི་ (shəmdeè māāmi) service personnel in the military.
ཞབས་འདེགས་ཞུ་སྟངས་ (shəmdeè shudaŋ) manner/ attitude in which one serves.
ཞབས་འདེགས་ཞུ་བའི་ལས་རིགས་ (shəmdeè shuwɛ lɛ̄ɛrii) sm. ཞབས་འདེགས་སྐོར་གྱི་ལས་རིགས་.
ཞབས་འདེགས་ལས་རིགས་ (shəmdeè lɛ̄ɛrii) service trade/ industry.
ཞབས་འདེགས་ས་ཚིགས་ (shəmdeè sādzii) service station, neighborhood service center ¶ ཕྱུགས་ལས་འཕྲུལ་ཆས་ཞབས་འདེགས་ས་ཚིགས་ Animal husbandry machinery service station.
ཞབས་འདྲེད་ཤོར་ (shamdreè shɔ̄ɔ) h. of རྐང་པ་འདྲེད་རྡར་ཤོར་.
ཞབས་འདྲེད་རྡར་ཤོར་ (shəb drēèdaa shɔ̄ɔ) h. of རྐང་པ་འདྲེད་རྡར་ཤོར་.
ཞབས་འདྲེན་ (shamdren) disgrace, shame; va.—ཞུ་ to disgrace ¶ ཁོས་ང་ཚོའི་ཞབས་འདྲེན་ཞུ་གི་འདུག He is disgracing us.
ཞབས་འདྲེན་གྱི་གནས་ཚུལ་ (shamdrengi nɛ̄ɛdzüü) a disgraceful/ scandalous situation or event.

ཞབས་འདྲེན་པ་ (shamdrenba) disgraceful person.
ཞབས་རྡུལ་ (shabdüü) the dust of feet (h.).
ཞབས་རྡོལ་ (shəb döö) 1. vi. to have cuts on feet through too much walking. 2. vi. to get a hole in the bottom of a container.
ཞབས་སྡོད་ (shabdöö) shung. entering of government service by lay aristocrats/ and monk officials; va.—ཞུ་ to request to enter government service ¶ མི་རྒྱུད་རིམ་པ་ནས་ས་གནས་སྲིད་གཞུང་གི་ཞབས་སྡོད་ཞུས་པ་རེད་ ¶ Each generation, one after another, enters government service. ¶ སྒེར་པ་ཞབས་སྡོད་མ་ཞུས་པའི་ཕ་གཞིས་ An estate that has no aristoctratic serving as a government official.
ཞབས་སྡོད་པ་ (shabdööba) shung. aristocratic officials of the tt.
ཞབས་ནས་འཐེན་ (shabnɛ tēn) sm. ཞབས་ལ་ཐག་པ་འདོགས་.
ཞབས་སྣེར་འགོད་ (shabner kȫö) shung. va. to be written/ recorded in (the government) official's register (i.e., to be appointed/ admitted as a government official).
ཞབས་པད་ (shab bɛɛ̀) shung. 1. Council Minister (member of the བཀའ་ཤག, the highest lay office in the tt.) 2. high honorific used when writing to sb. higher up (similar to ཞབས་དྲུང་) ¶ འདི་ཕྱིའི་སྐྱབས་གནས་རིན་པོ་ཆེ་མཆོག་གི་ཞབས་པད་མདུན་མཐའི་དྲུང་དུ་ To Rimpoche, who is the protector in this and the future life.
ཞབས་པད་དྲུང་ (shabbɛɛ̀ truŋ) sm. ཞབས་པད་, 2.
ཞབས་པུང་ངར་དུང་ (shəbbuŋ ŋarduŋ) shinbone.
ཞབས་པུས་ (shəbbüü) h. of པུས་མོ་.
ཞབས་དཔངས་ (shəbbaŋ) foot length.
ཞབས་སྤྱི་བོར་བླངས་ (shəb jīwor lāŋ) doing whatever is asked by one's superior [Lit. taking the foot (of one's root guru, etc.) on one's head].
ཞབས་འཕོངས་ (shamboŋ) h. of རྐུབ་.
ཞབས་ཕྱག (shabjaà) h. of རྐང་ལག.
ཞབས་ཕྱགས་ (shabjaà) h. of ལྷམ་.
ཞབས་ཕྱི་ (shəbji) h. of གཡོག་པོ་.
ཞབས་ཕྱི་ཁང་ (shəbjigaŋ) servant quarters.
ཞབས་ཕྱི་འཁོར་བཅས་ (shəbji kɔ̄ɔjɛɛ̀) retinue of servants (h.).
ཞབས་ཕྱི་སྟེགས་བུ་ (shəbji dēgbu) check-in desk, front desk, service desk.
ཞབས་ཕྱི་ནང་མ་ (shəbji naŋma) household servants.
ཞབས་ཕྱིད་ (shəbjiì) shung. accompanying (h.) ¶ རྒྱལ་པོ་དང་ཞབས་ཕྱིད་རྩིས་བློན་ The king with the finance minister accompanying him.
ཞབས་ཕྱིས་ (shəbjiì) shung. sm. ཞབས་ཕྱི་.

ཞབས་འཕེན་ (shamben) running (h.); va.—གཏོང་; —རྒྱག to run.
ཞབས་བོལ་ (shamböö) h. of རྐང་འབམ་.
ཞབས་བྲོ་ (shəbdro) dance, dancing; va.—རྒྱག to dance.
ཞབས་བྲོ་མཉམ་རྒྱག་དང་སྐེད་གཞིར་ལོགས་བཀར་ (shəbdro) doing sth. different from the rest of a group [Lit. dancing together but puttings one's hands on one's hip in a different manner].
ཞབས་བྲོ་ཐན་གོ་ (shəbdro tɛngo) tib.eng. tango (dance).
ཞབས་བྲོ་དབྱང་གོ་ (shəbdro yāŋgo) tib. ch. a popular Chinese rural folk dance.
ཞབས་བྲོའི་དགོང་ཚོགས་ (shəbdrö goŋdzɔɔ̀) dancing party.
ཞབས་བྲོའི་འདུ་ཚོགས་ (shəbdrö dudzɔɔ̀) dancing party, a dance.
ཞབས་བྲོའི་རོལ་དབྱངས་ (shəbdrö rööyaŋ) dance music.
ཞབས་བྲོའི་སློབ་གྲྭ་ (shəbdrö lōbdra) dance school.
ཞབས་འབམ་ (shambam) rheumatism of leg (h.).
ཞབས་འབོག (shambɔɔ̀) sm.* ཞབས་འཕོངས་.
ཞབས་འབོག་ལྦིད་པོ་ (shambɔɔ̀ jiibu) h. of རྐུབ་ལྦིད་པོ་.
ཞབས་འབོལ་ (shamböö) sm.* ཞབས་འཕེན་.
ཞབས་འགྱུར་སྒྲིག (shamjɔɔ) sm. མིང་བྱང་བཟོ་.
ཞབས་འདྲང་ (shamdraŋ) going with sb. who knows the way and can explain things; va.—བྱེད་ ། ངས་ཁོང་གི་ཞབས་འདྲང་བྱས་ནས་ལྷ་སྐོར་ལ་ཕྱིན་པ་ཡིན་ I went with him on a pilgrimage.
ཞབས་འདྲིང་པ་ (shəmdriŋbə) shung. government officials.
ཞབས་མ་ (shəbma) under, below, lower ། བང་ཁྲི་ཞབས་མ་ The lower shelf.
ཞབས་དམིགས་ (shəbmii) shung. sb. who will be able to serve as a government official ། སྐྱིར་པ་དེ་ར་ཞབས་དམིགས་མེད་ཙང་ངོ་དོད་འབུལ་གྱི་ཡོད་པ་རེད་ Because that aristocratic family had no one to serve as a government official, they are giving a money substitute.
ཞབས་ཚོགས་འཁྲུག (shəbdzii trɔɔ̀) h. of རྐང་ཚོགས་འཁྲུག.
ཞབས་འཛུགས་དགའ་སྟོན་ (shəbdzuù gadön) a party given when a child first walks (in ancient times).
ཞབས་མཛུབ་ (shəbdzub) h. of རྐང་པའི་མཛུབ་མ་.
ཞབས་བརྗེས་ (shəbdzii) h. of རྡོག་བརྗེས་.
ཞབས་ཞུ་ (shəbshu) sm. ཞབས་འདེགས་.
ཞབས་ཞུ་པ་ (shəbshuwə) servant, service person.
ཞབས་ཞུའི་ཏྲ་ཚོགས་ (shəbshü tradzii) sm. ཞབས་འདེགས་ཀྱི་ཏྲ་ཚོགས་.
ཞབས་ཞུའི་ལས་རིགས་ (shəbshü lɛɛ̀rii) service jobs, service trades.
ཞབས་ཞུའི་ས་ཚིགས་ (shəbshü sādzii) service center.
ཞབས་གཞས་ (shəbshɛɛ̀) h. of རྐང་བྲོ་གླུ་གཞས་.
ཞབས་ཟུར་ (shəbsur) shung. a ex/ former government official.
ཞབས་ཡང་པོ་ (shəb yaŋbo) h. of རྐང་ས་པ་ཡང་པོ་.
ཞབས་ཡུན་ (shəbyün) sm. ཞབས་ལོ་.
ཞབས་གཡར་ (shəbyar) shung. borrowing an official from one department to another (used in Tibetan government in exile).
ཞབས་གཡོག (shəbyɔɔ̀) sm. ཞབས་ཕྱི.
ཞབས་ར་ (shəbra) base/ stem of a cup or bowl.
ཞབས་རིམ་ (shəbrim) sm. ཞབས་བརྟན་.
ཞབས་རོགས་སྲིད་ཚབ་ (shəbrɔɔ̀ siidzəb) term for the three Bhutanese officials (regents) who helped the present king rule when he was a minor.
ཞབས་ལ་གཏུགས་ (shəbla dūg) va. to request a lama to be one's root teacher [Lit. to touch one's head at the feet].
ཞབས་ལ་ཐག་པ་འདོགས་ (shəbla tāgba dɔɔ̀) sm. ཞབས་འདྲེན་ཞུ་.
ཞབས་ལ་འདུད་ (shəbla düü) sm. ཞབས་ལ་གཏུགས་པ་.
ཞབས་ལོ་ (shəblo) working years.
ཞབས་ལོང་ (shəbloŋ) h. of རྐང་ལོང་.
ཞབས་ཤོག (shəbshɔɔ̀) 1. open space/ margin at the bottom of a page.
ཞབས་སུ་ (shəbsu) h. of རྐང་སུ་.
ཞབས་སུག (shəbsuù) sm. ཞབས་སུ་.
ཞབས་སེན་ (shəbsen) h. of སེན་མོ་.
ཞབས་སོར་འཁོད་ (shəbsɔɔ gȫö) vi. to arrive, to come (h.) ། གོང་ས་ཆེན་པོ་འཕགས་ཡུལ་དུ་ཞབས་སོར་འཁོད་ནས་ His Holiness the Dalai Lama, having come to India.
ཞབས་སོར་ཕྱིར་འཁོད་ (shəbsɔɔ cīgöö) sm. ཞབས་སོར་འཁོད་.
ཞབས་གསར་པ་ (shəb sāāba) shung. new official.
ཞབས་བསིལ་ (shəb sīī) h. of རྐང་པ་འཁྲུད་.
ཞབས་ཧད་ (shəbhɛɛ̀) slipper.
ཞབས་ལྷམ་ (shəblham) h. of ལྷམ་.
ཞམ་མེ་ཞོམ་མེ་ (shame shome) uneven, dented.
ཞམ་ཞམ་ (shamsham) dripping with sweat.
ཞམ་ཞོམ་ (shamshom) abbr. of ཞམ་མེ་ཞོམ་མེ་.
ཞམ་རིང་ (shəmriŋ) sm. ཞབས་ཕྱི་.
ཞའུ་ལི་ (shəwuli) shung. lower ranking clerk (jola) in the Tseja and Laja offices.
ཞའོ་ཀྲང་ (shawodraŋ) ch. school principal.
ཞའོ་ཐི་ཆིན་ (shawo tījin) ch. violin ། ཞའོ་ཐི་ཆེན་གཏོང་མཁན་དང་པོ་མཛད་ The lead violinist.
ཞའོ་དཔོན་ (shawobön) ch.tib. officer (in army).
ཞའོ་དཔོན་ཆུང་བ་ (shawobön cūŋwə) ch.tib. major (in army).
ཞའོ་དཔོན་ཆེ་བ་ (shawobön cēwa) ch.tib. senior colonel.
ཞའོ་དཔོན་འབྲིང་པ་ (shawobön driŋwə) ch.tib. lieutenant colonel.
ཞའོ་ཟེན་ (shawosön) sm. ཞའོ་སོན་.
ཞའོ་སོན་ (shawosön) ch. nitric acid.
ཞར་ (shar) vi. to be/ get blind.
ཞར་གོག (shārgɔɔ̀) blind.
ཞར་ལྟ་ (shār dā) looking when blind; va.—བྱེད་. 2. looking with crooked/ crossed eyes; va.—བྱེད་.
ཞར་དང་ཞོར་ (shardaŋ shɔɔ) whenever time permits, in one's spare time ། ངས་ཞར་དང་ཞོར་ལ་སློབ་སྦྱོང་བྱེད་གྱི་ཡོད་ I am studying during all my spare time.
ཞར་དུ་ (shardu) sm. ཞར་ལ་.
ཞར་བ་ (sharwa) blind.
ཞར་བྱུང་ (sharjuŋ) 1. additional, supplementary, appended, extra. 2. appendix, supplement.
ཞར་བྱུང་ཐོན་ཆས་ (sharjuŋ tönjɛɛ̀) a by-product.
ཞར་བྱུང་ཚགས་པར་ (sharjuŋ tsāgbar) supplement of a newspaper or magazine.
ཞར་ཞོར་ (sharshɔɔ) sm. ཞར་རེ་ཞོར་རེ་.
ཞར་ར་ (sharra) blind.
ཞར་ལ་ (shaala) sm. ཞོར་ལ་.
ཞར་ལ་བྱུང་བ་ (shaala cuŋwə) sm. ཞར་བྱུང་.
ཞལ་ (shɛɛ) 1. mouth (h.). 2. face (h.). 3. term added to others to make honorifics ། ཞལ་དཀར་ Honorific. of དཀར་ཡོལ་.
ཞལ་ཀང་ (shɛɛgaŋ) h. of མཛེས་ཀོང་.
ཞལ་ཀྱག (shɛɛgyaà) 1. h. of ཁྲི་བཀྱག. 2. h. of ཁས་ཀྱག.
ཞལ་ཀྱག་གནང་མཁན་ (shɛɛgyaà nāŋñɛn) h. of ཁས་ཀྱག་བྱེད་མཁན་.
ཞལ་ཀྱལ་ (shɛɛgyɛɛ) a joke.
ཞལ་དཀར་ (shɛɛgaa) h. of དཀར་ཡོལ་.
ཞལ་དཀར་ཕྱོགས་གཅིག (shɛɛgaa cɔɔ̀jig) people in the same organization/ government/ committee/ party.
ཞལ་དཀྱིལ་ (shɛɛgyii) h. of གདོང་.
ཞལ་དཀྲིས་ (shɛɛdrii) h. of ཁ་དཀྲིས་.
ཞལ་བཀག (shɛɛgaà) h. of ཁ་བཀག.
ཞལ་བཀོད་ (shɛɛgöö) h. of ཁ་བཀོད་.
ཞལ་བཀྱག (shɛɛgyaà) h. of ཁྲི་བཀྱག.
ཞལ་བཀྱག་བཀྱག (shɛɛ gyāàgyaà) h. of ཁ་བཀྱག་བཀྱག.
ཞལ་རྐན་ (shɛɛgɛn) h. of རྐན་.
ཞལ་སྐྱལ་ (shɛɛgüü) h. of ཞབས་སྐྱལ་.
ཞལ་སྐོམ་ (shɛɛgom) h. of ཁ་སྐོམ་.
ཞལ་སྐོར་ (shɛɛgɔɔ) h. of ཁ་སྐོར་.
ཞལ་སྐྱིན་ (shɛɛgyin) sm. ཞལ་དཀྱིལ་.
ཞལ་སྐྱུག (shɛɛgyuù) h. of སྐྱུག་པ་.
ཞལ་སྐྱིངས་ (shɛɛgyeŋ) sm. ཁ་སྐྱིངས་.

ཞལ་སྐྱིམས་ (shεεgyem) sm. ཞལ་སློམ་.

ཞལ་སྐྱིལ་ (shεεgyee) h. of ཁ་སྐྱིལ་.

ཞལ་སྐྱོགས་ (shεεgyɔɔ) sm. ཞལ་དཀར་.

ཞལ་བསྒོས་ (shεεgöö) h. of བསྒོ་གཞག.

ཞལ་ཁ་ཕྱེ་ (shεεka cē) vi. to bloom.

ཞལ་ཁ་འབྱེད་ (shεεka jeè) sm. ཞལ་ཁ་ཕྱེ་.

ཞལ་ཁ་བཞུགས་ (shεεka shuù) va. to keep quiet (h.).

ཞལ་ཁུ་སིམ་པོ་ (shεεgu sīmbu) h. of ཁ་ཁུ་སིམ་པོ་.

ཞལ་ཁུངས་ (shεεguŋ) h. of ཁ་ཁུངས་.

ཞལ་ཁེབས་ (shεεgeb) sm. ཞལ་གཙོད་.

ཞལ་ཁྱག (shεεgyaà) h. of ཁས་ཁྱག.

ཞལ་ཁྲིམས་ (shεεgyim) h. of གདོང་.

ཞལ་ཁྲུས་སྐྱོན་ (shεεdrüü gyön) h. of གདོང་འཁྲུད་.

ཞལ་ཁྲུས་གནང་ (shεεdrüü nāŋ) sm. ཞལ་ཁྲུས་སྐྱོན་.

ཞལ་མཁན་ (shεεñεn) a plasterer.

ཞལ་འཁྲིད་ (shεεdrīì) h. of ངག་ཁྲིད་.

ཞལ་གང་ (shεεgaŋ) 1. h. of ཁམ་གང་. 2. a measurement in tangka painting that is equal to 12 finger widths.

ཞལ་གྱི་དཀྱིལ་འཁོར་ (shεεgi gyīngɔɔ) sm. ཞལ་དཀྱིལ་.

ཞལ་གྱིས་བཞེས་ (shεεgi sheè) h. of ཁས་ལེན་.

ཞལ་གྲིས་ (shεεgyeè) h. of ཁ་གྲིས་.

ཞལ་གྲིས་ཞུ་ཡིག (shεεgyeè shuyiì) farewell/ goodbye letter.

ཞལ་གྲིས་གསོལ་སྟོན་ (shεεgyeè sōōdön) a farewell dinner/ banquet.

ཞལ་གྱོང་པོ་ (shεε gyoŋbo) h. of ཁ་གྱོང་པོ་.

ཞལ་གྲངས་ (shεεdraŋ) h. of ཁ་གྲངས་.

ཞལ་གྲངས་མང་པོ་ (shεεdraŋ maŋbo) a huge number, a big sum.

ཞལ་གླིང་ (shεεliŋ) h. of གླིང་བུ་.

ཞལ་བགྲད་ (shεεdrεὲ) h. of ཁ་འཕྲད་འཕྲད་.

ཞལ་འགྲམ་ (shεεdram) h. of འགྲམ་པ་.

ཞལ་འགྲིས་ (shεε gyeè) h. of ཁ་འགྲིས་.

ཞལ་རྒྱན་ (shεεgyεn) h. of ཁ་སྒྱུ་.

ཞལ་རྒྱས་ (shεεgyεὲ) sm. ལྷན་རྒྱས་.

ཞལ་རྒྱུག (shεεgyuù) h. of འཁར་རྒྱུག.

ཞལ་རྒྱུན་ (shεεgyün) h. of ངག་རྒྱུན་.

ཞལ་བརྒྱ་ (shεεgya) sm. ཞལ་ཕོབ་.

ཞལ་སྒོ་ (shεεgo) h. of ཁ་.

ཞལ་སྒྲོན་ (shεεdrön) h. of ཁ་སྒྲོན་.

ཞལ་སྒྲུང་ (shεεdruŋ) h. of ཁ་སྒྲུང་.

ཞལ་སྒྲོག (shεεdrɔɔ) h. of ཁ་སྒྲོག.

ཞལ་ངོ་ (shεεŋo) 1. h. of གདོང་. 2. shung. monk in charge of monastic discipline. 3. shung. a traditional Tibetan army rank (officer in charge of twenty five soldiers).

ཞལ་ངོ་མི་འདོག་པ་ (shεεŋo midɔgba) h. of ངོ་མི་འདོག་པ་.

ཞལ་ངོ་ཚོར་ (shεεŋo tsɔ̄ɔ) h. of ངོ་ཤེས་.

ཞལ་དངོས་ (shεεŋöö) in person (h.).

ཞལ་དངག (shεεŋaà) h. of ཁ་དངག.

ཞལ་སྔ་ (shεεŋa) presence ། བླ་མ་འི་ཞལ་སྔ་ནས་ཡོང་བ་ཡིན་ (I) came from the presence of the Lama.

ཞལ་གཅིག་ལྕགས་གཉིས་ (shεεjig jagñii) h. of ཁ་གཅིག་ལྕེ་གཉིས་.

ཞལ་གཅོད་ (shεεjöö) h. of ཁ་གཅོད་.

ཞལ་ཅོར་ (shεεjɔɔ) h. of ཨ་ཅོར་.

ཞལ་བཅོས་ (shεεjöö) h. of བཀོད་ཇུས་.

ཞལ་ལྕག (shεεjaà) h. of འགྲམ་ལྕག.

ཞལ་ལྕེ་ (shεεje) 1. decision, judgement (h.); va.— གཅོད་ to decide, to pass judgement. 2. law.

ཞལ་ལྕེ་བ་ (shεεjewa) 1. judge. 2. arbitrator.

ཞལ་ལྕེ་བཅུ་གཉིས་ (shεεje jūñii) the twelve codes/ edicts/ laws established by the 5th Dalai Lama.

ཞལ་ལྕེ་བཅུ་དྲུག (shεεje jūdruù) the sixteen codes/ laws/ edicts established in the 17th century by the King of Tsang.

ཞལ་ལྕེ་བཅུ་གསུམ་ (shεεje jōgsom) the thirteen codes/ laws/ edicts established by the King of Tsang.

ཞལ་ལྕེ་བཅོ་ལྔ་ (shεεje jōŋa) the fifteen codes/ laws/ edicts established by the Phamodru King in the 14th century.

ཞལ་ཆད་ (shεεjεὲ) h. of. ཁ་ཆད་.

ཞལ་ཆབ་ (shεεjəb) h. of. མཆི་མ་.

ཞལ་ཆོད་ (shεεjöö) h. of ཁ་དན་.

ཞལ་ཆུ་འཁོར་ (shεεju kɔ̄ɔ) h. of ཁ་ཆུ་འཁོར་.

ཞལ་ཆེ་ (shεεje) sm. ཞལ་ལྕེ་.

ཞལ་ཆེམས་ (shεεjem) h. of ཁ་ཆེམས་.

ཞལ་ཆོར་ (shεεjɔɔ) sm. ཞལ་ཅོར་.

ཞལ་འཆམ་ (shεnjam) h. of ཁ་འཆམ་.

ཞལ་འཆེས་ (shεεjeè) h. of ཁས་ལེན་.

ཞལ་མཆུ་ (shεεju) h. of མཆུ་ཏོ་.

ཞལ་ཇ་ (shεεja) tea offering served to an oracle when he/ she is trance.

ཞལ་རྗེས་ (shεεjüü) h. of ངག་བཀོད་.

ཞལ་མཇལ་ (shεε jεε) h. of ངོ་ཐུག.

ཞལ་མཇལ་གནང་ (shεεjεε nāŋ) va. to give an audience.

ཞལ་མཇལ་ཞུ་ (shεεjεε shu) va. to ask for an audience/ meeting.

ཞལ་འཇམ་ (shεε jam) h. of ཁ་འཇམ་པོ་.

ཞལ་འཇུག་མཛད་ (shεεjuù dzεὲ) va. to interrupt sb. talking.

ཞལ་ལྗིད་པོ་ (shεε jiību) h. of ཁ་ལྗིད་པོ་.

ཞལ་ཉུང་ཉུང་ (shεε ñuŋñuŋ) h. of ཁ་ཉུང་ཉུང་.

ཞལ་ཏ་ (shεεda) h. of ཁ་ཏ་.

ཞལ་ཏ་ཇོན་ (shεεda jön) sm. of བཀའ་གནང་.

ཞལ་ཏ་བ་ (shεεdawa) 1. a monk who works in a monastery (usu. as cook). 2. servant.

ཞལ་ཏ་མ་ (shεεdama) female servant (h.).

ཞལ་ཏོག (shεεdoò) h. of ཁ་ཏོག.

ཞལ་ཏོན་ (shεεdön) h. of ཁ་ཏོན་.

ཞལ་གཏུགས་ (shεε dūù) h. of ཁ་སྐྱིལ་; གདོང་གཏུགས་.

ཞལ་གཏོང་ (shεε dōŋ) h. of ཁ་གཏོང་.

ཞལ་བཏགས་ (shεεdaà) h. of ཁ་གཡར་.

ཞལ་སྟོང་ (shεεdoŋ) h. of ཨ་སྟོང་.

ཞལ་བརྟན་པོ་ (shεε dεmbo) h. of ཁ་བརྟན་པོ་.

ཞལ་ཐག་ཤང་པོ་ (shεεdaà shāŋbo) h. of ཁ་ཐག་ཤང་པོ་.

ཞལ་ཐང་ (shεεdaŋ) h. of ཐང་ཁ་.

ཞལ་ཐང་གི་གོང་གཤམ་ (shεεdaŋgi koŋsham) brocade on which a thanka is attached.

ཞལ་ཐང་གི་བྲིས་ཇུ་ (shεεdaŋgi driija) style of painting a thanka.

ཞལ་ཐལ་ (shεεtεε) sm. ཁ་ཐལ་.

ཞལ་ཐེག (shεεdeg) h. of ཁག་ཐེག.

ཞལ་ཐོན་པོ་ (shεε tōmbo) h. of ཁ་ཐོན་པོ་.

ཞལ་མཐུན་ (shεεdün) h. of ཁ་མཐུན་.

ཞལ་དན་ (shεεdεn) h. of ཁ་དན་.

ཞལ་དྲོ་བ་ (shεε trobo) h. of ཁ་དྲོ་བ་.

ཞལ་གདན་ (shεεdεn) h. of ཁ་གདན་.

ཞལ་གདངས་ (shεεdaŋ) h. of ཁ་གདངས་.

ཞལ་གདམས་ (shεεdam) sm. ཞལ་བཀོད་.

ཞལ་གདམས་བསླབ་བྱ་ (shεεdam lōbja) an important teaching/ directive, a famous dictum.

ཞལ་བདག (shεεdaà) monk in charge of monastery treasury, monastery treasurer.

ཞལ་མདངས་ (shεεdaŋ) h. of བཞིན་མདངས་.

ཞལ་མདངས་རྒྱས་པོ་ (shεεdaŋ gyεὲbo) h. of བཞིན་མདངས་རྒྱས་པོ་.

ཞལ་མདངས་ཡག་པོ་ (shεεdaŋ yagbo) sm. ཞལ་མདངས་རྒྱས་པོ་.

ཞལ་མདོག (shεεdɔɔ) h. of བཞིན་མདོག.

ཞལ་འདེབས་ (shεndeb) contribution, donation; va.—འབུལ་; —རྒྱག to give a contribution/ donation; va.—བསྡུ་ to collect donations/ contributions; va.—སློང་ to beg or solicit donations/ contributions.

ཞལ་འདེབས་རོགས་སྐྱོར་ (shεndeb rɔɔ̀gyɔɔ) donation/ contribution and help; va.—བྱེད་ to donate/ contribute and help.

ཞལ་འདོན་ (shεε dön) h. of ཁ་འདོན་.

ཞལ་དབས་བསགས་ (shεεdəb sāà) h. of ཁ་དབས་.

ཞལ་བདར་ (shεεda) h. of ཁ་བདར་.

ཞལ་ནག་སྡུད་ (shεεnaà düü) h. of ངོ་ནག་སྡུད་.

ཞལ་ནས་ (shεεnε) verbally, orally, from the mouth (h.).

ཞལ་པ་མཁན་ (shεεbagεn) plasterer.

ཞལ་པར་ (shεεbaa) h. of ཁ་པར་.

ཞལ་པར་བཞེས་ (shεεbaa sheè) h. of ཁ་པར་ལེན་.

ཞལ་པར་གསན་ (shεεbaa sε̄n) h. of ཁ་པར་ཉན་.

ཞལ་དཔར་ (shεεbaa) sm. ཞལ་པར་.

ཞལ་དཔོན་ (shεεbön) head plasterer.

ཞལ་སྒྲོ་ (shεεdro) inauguration of a temple, etc.

ཞལ་སྒྲོད་ (shεεdröö) h. of ཁ་སྒྲོད་.

ཞལ་ཕུད་ (shεεbüü) the first offering (h.); va.—འབུལ་ to offer the first (of anything).

ཞལ་ཕོར་ (shεεbɔɔ) h. of ཕོར་པ་.

ཞལ་ཕྱེ་ (shεεje) h. of ཁ་ཕྱེ་.

ཞལ་ཕྱོགས་ (shεεjɔ̄ɔ) h. of ཁ་ཕྱོགས་.

ཞལ་འཕངས་ (shεε pāŋ) sm. ཁ་འཕངས་.

ཞལ་འཕེར་པོ་ (shεε pērbo) h. of ཁ་འཕེར་པོ་.

ཞལ་བ་ (shεεwa) sm. ཞ་ལ་.

ཞལ་བབ་ (shεεbəb) h. of ཁ་བབ་.

ཞལ་བབ་ཕྱིད་པོ་ (shεεbəb jiibu) h. of ཁ་བབ་ཕྱིད་པོ་.

ཞལ་བྱང་ (shεεjaŋ) h. of ཁ་བྱང་.

ཞལ་བྲལ་ (shεεdrεε) sm. ཁ་བྲལ་,1.

ཞལ་དབུགས་ (shεε ūg) h. of དབུགས་.

ཞལ་དབུགས་དལ་ (shεε ūùhεὲ) h. of དབུགས་དལ་.

ཞལ་དབྱེ་ (shεε yē) va. to light a butter lamp offering.

ཞལ་འབག (shεmbaà) h. of འབག.

ཞལ་འབུག (shεmbuù) sm. ཁ་ཕུགས་.

ཞལ་འབེལ་པོ་ (shεε beebo) sm. ཁ་འབེལ་པོ་.

ཞལ་དབྱིབས་ (shεεyib) h. of གདོང་དབྱིབས་.

ཞལ་དབྱེ་ (shεε yē) sm. ཞལ་འབྱེད་.

ཞལ་འབྱེད་ (shεε jeè) h. of ཁ་འབྱེད་.

ཞལ་བད་ (shεεbεὲ) 1. joking around. 2. boasting.

ཞལ་སྦུག་དོག་པོ་ (shεεbuù tɔgbo) h. of ཁ་སྦུག་དོག་པོ་.

ཞལ་སྦྱོར་ (shεεjɔɔ) sm. ཞལ་སྐྱེལ་.

ཞལ་མལ་ (shεεmεε) h. of མལ་ལེ་.

ཞལ་མི་གསལ་བ་ (shεε mi sε̄εwa) h. of ཁ་མི་གསལ་བ་.

ཞལ་མོ་ (shεεmo) laughter, laughing, smile (h.); va.—བཞེས་ to laugh, to smile; vi.—ཤོར་ to (burst into) laughter.

ཞལ་མོ་ཁྲོ་པོ་ (shεεmo trobo) h. of གད་མོ་ཁྲོ་པོ་.

ཞལ་མོ་ཤོར་པོ་ (shεεmo shɔ̄ɔbo) sm. གད་མོ་ཤོར་པོ་.

ཞལ་བཙན་པོ་ (shεε dzε̄mbo) h. of ཁ་བཙན་པོ་.

ཞལ་བཙོག་པ་ (shεε dzɔ̄gba) h. of ཁ་བཙོག་པ་.

ཞལ་རྩེད་ (shεεdze) h. of ཁ་རྩེད་.

ཞལ་རྩོད་ (shεεdzöö) h. of ཁ་རྩོད་.

ཞལ་ཚ་པོ་ (shεε tsābo) h. of ཁ་ཚ་པོ་.

ཞལ་ཚས་ཚས་ (shεε tsεὲdzεὲ) h. of ཁ་ཚས་ཚས་.

ཞལ་ཚོགས་པོ་ (shεε tsɔ̄gbo) h. of ཁ་ཚོགས་པོ་.

ཞལ་ཚོན་གཅོད་ (shεε tsönjöö) h. of ཁ་ཚོན་གཅོད་.

ཞལ་ཚོམ་ (shεεdzom) h. of ཨོག་ཚོམ་.

ཞལ་ཚོར་ (shεε dzɔ̄ɔ) h. of ངོ་ཤེས་.

ཞལ་ཚོས་ (shεε dzöö) h. of མཁུར་ཚོས་.

ཞལ་འཚོགས་པོ་ (shεε tsɔ̄gba) h. of ཁ་ཚོགས་པོ་.

ཞལ་འཚོར་ (shεε tsɔ̄ɔ) sm. ཞལ་ཚོར་.

ཞལ་རྫོར་པོ་ (shεε dzɔrbo) sm. ཞལ་བཙོག་པ་.

ཞལ་འཛུམ་ (shεε dzum) h. of ཁ་འཛུམ་.

ཞལ་འཛུམ་ཐུགས་དགྱེས་ (shεεdzum tūùgyeè) smiling and happy (h.).

ཞལ་འཛེམ་ (shεε dzem) h. of ཁ་འཛེམ་.

ཞལ་འཛོམས་ (shεε dzom) h. of ཁ་འཛོམས་.

ཞལ་རྫུན་ (shεεdzün) h. of ཁ་རྫུན་.

ཞལ་ཞལ་ (shεεshεε) plastering; va.—བྱེད་ to plaster.

ཞལ་ཞལ་མཁན་ (shεεshεεñεn) sm. ཞལ་བ་མཁན་.

ཞལ་ཞོལ་ (shεεshöö) sm. ཞལ་ལི་ཞོལ་ལི་.

ཞལ་བཞིན་ (shεεshin) h. of གདོང་.

ཞལ་བཞུགས་ (shεεshuù) h. of འཚོ་སྡོད་.

ཞལ་བཞེས་ (shεε sheè) h. of ཁས་ལེན་.

ཞལ་བཞེས་ཕྱག་ལེན་ (shεεsheè cāàlen) h. of ཁ་བཤད་ལག་ལེན་.

ཞལ་བཞེས་བཟང་ཐོབ་ (shεεsheè saŋdob) shung. vi. to obtain sb.'s word, to get a favorable promise or assurance ¶ ཁོང་གི་ང་ཚོར་རྒྱབ་སྐྱོར་གནང་བའི་ཞལ་ཞེས་བཟང་ཐོབ་བྱུང་ (We) got an assurance (from him) that he would support us.

ཞལ་ཟག (shεεsaà) h. of ཁ་ཟག.

ཞལ་ཟས་ (shεεsεὲ) 1. h. of ཁ་ཟས་. 2. food for gods, torma ¶ ཞལ་ཟས་ཁྱིས་ཁྱེར་ཀྱང་འཛུམ་ཤིག་ཤིག ལྷ་ཁང་མེས་འཚིགས་ཀྱང་འཛུམ་ཤིག་ཤིག (shεεsεὲ kyīì kyērgyaŋ dzum shīìshii lhāgaŋ meè tsīìgyaŋ dzum shīìshiì) not paying attention to what is going on around one whatever happens [Lit. smiling when the dog takes the torma, smiling when the temple burns down].

ཞལ་གཟིགས་ (shεε siì) 1. va. to face a direction ¶ ཞལ་ཤར་ལ་གཟིགས་ནས་ Having faced east. 2. vi. to have a deity manifest itself ¶ བླ་མ་དེ་ལ་འཇམ་དཔལ་དབྱངས་ཞལ་གཟིགས་པ་རེད་ Manjusri manifested himself to the lama.

ཞལ་གཟེར་པོ་ (shεε serbo) h. of ཁ་གཟེར་པོ་.

ཞལ་བཟེད་ (shεεseè) h. of ཁ་གཟེད་.

ཞལ་བཟོ་སྐྱི་འདྲས་ (shεεso gyēndrεὲ) h. of ཁ་བཟོ་སྐྱི་འདྲས་.

ཞལ་བཟོ་དོད་པོ་ (shεεso töōbo) sm. ཁ་བཟོ་འཕེར་པོ་.

ཞལ་བཟོ་འཕེར་པོ་ (shεεso pērbo) h. of ཁ་བཟོ་འཕེར་པོ་.

ཞལ་ཡ་ (shεεya) h. of ཁ་ཡ་.

ཞལ་ཡང་པོ་ (shεε yaŋbo) h. of ཁ་ཡང་པོ་.

ཞལ་ཡམ་ (shεεyam) sm. ཞལ་བད་.

ཞལ་གཡོགས་ (shεεyɔɔ) h. of ཁ་གཡོགས་.

ཞལ་ར་ (shεεra) h. of སྣ་ར་.

ཞལ་རས་ (shεεrεὲ) h. of གདོང་.

ཞལ་རས་གཉེར་མ་ (shεεrεὲ ñērma) h. of གདོང་གི་གཉེར་མ་.

ཞལ་རས་ནག་པོ་ (shεεrεὲ nagbo) h. of གདོང་ནག་པོ་.

ཞལ་རུབ་ (shεεrub) h. of ཁ་རུབ་.

ཞལ་རོག (shεεrɔ̄ɔ) h. of ཁ་རོག.

ཞལ་ལ་ (shεεla) sm. ཞ་ལ་.

ཞལ་ལ་ཉན་ (shεεla ñε̄n) h. of ཁ་ལ་ཉན་.

ཞལ་ལ་ཉན་པོ་ (shεεla ñεmbo) obedient (h.).

ཞལ་ལག (shεεlaà) h. of ཁ་ལག.

ཞལ་ལག་ཀྱག (shεεlaà gyāà) h. of ཁ་ལག་འདྲེན་.

ཞལ་ལག་མཆོད་ (shεεlaà cöö) h. of ཁ་ལག་ཟ་.

ཞལ་ལག་འབུལ་ (shεεlaà büü) sm. ཞལ་ལག་ཀྱག.

ཞལ་ལག་བཞེས་ (shεεlaà sheè) sm. ཞལ་ལག་མཆོད་.

ཞལ་ལན་སློག (shεεlεn lɔ̄ɔ) h. of ཁ་ལན་སློག.

ཞལ་ལས་ (shεεlεὲ) h. of ཁ་ལས་.

ཞལ་ལུ་ (shεεlu) bowl, pot (h.).

ཞལ་ལུང་ (shεεluŋ) oral instructions/ teachings (h.).

ཞལ་ལུད་ (shεεlüü) h. of ལུད་པ་.

ཞལ་ལེ་ (shεεle) h. of ཁ་ལེ་.

ཞལ་ལེ་ཞོལ་ལེ་ (shεεle shööle) 1. untidy. 2. wearing dresses very low.

ཞལ་ཤུ་སྒྱོན་ (shεεshu gyön) h. of ཤུ་རྒྱག.

ཞལ་ཤེལ་ (shεεshee) h. of ཤེལ་སྒོ་.

ཞལ་ཤེས་ (shεεsheè) oral teachings.

ཞལ་ཤོབ་ (shεεshob) h. of ཀ་རེ་.

ཞལ་ཤོར་ (shεεshɔɔ) h. of ཁ་ཤོར་.

ཞལ་གཤིས་འགྱུར་ (shεεshiì gyur) h. of གདོང་གཤིས་འགྱུར་.

ཞལ་བཤུས་ (shεεshüü) h. of ངོ་བཤུས་.

ཞལ་སློབ་ (shεεlob) h. of སློབ་མ་.

ཞལ་གསང་ཐུགས་དྲང་ (shεεsaŋ tūgdraŋ) straightforward and honest (h.).

ཞལ་གསང་ (shεεsaŋ) h. of ཁ་གསང་.

ཞལ་གསང་པོ་ (shεε sāŋbo) h. of ཁ་གསང་པོ་.

ཞལ་གསལ་འཁོད་ (shεεsεε kööö) shung. written/ stated clearly ¶ ཞུ་ཐོ་འགོ་མཆན་དུ་གཞིས་ཀའི་ཁ་འཛིན་མུ་མཐུད་འཛིན་ཐུབ་ཆོག་པའི་ཞལ་གསལ་འཁོད་ It was written clearly in the notation made on the report that we can take the possession of the estate (and keep it) continuously.

ཞལ་གསུང་ (shεεsuŋ) talk, conversation (h.).

ཞལ་གསེར་ (shεεser) liquid gold used for gilding the faces of icons and statues (h.).

ཞལ་གསོ་ (shεε sō) va. to replenish sth. (h.).

ཞལ་བསིལ་ (shεε siì) h. of གདོང་འཁྲུད་.

ཞལ་བསྒྲོ་ (shεε sō) va. to consecrate a icon/ statue, etc.

ཞི་ (shi) 1. abbr. of ཞི་བ་. 2. vi. to calm down, to be pacified, to decrease/ diminish (e.g., anger.) ¶ ཁོའི་ཁོང་ཁྲོ་ཞི་བ་དང་ As soon as his anger was pacified.

ཞི་ཀྭ་ (shigwa) ch. watermelon.

ཞི་ཀུང་ (shiguŋ) Saigon.

ཞི་བསྒྱུར་དྲག་ཞུགས་ (shigyur tragshuù) renouncing peace and advocating violence/ war.

ཞི་གྲོས་ (shidröö) peace talks ། རྒྱ་བོད་དབར་ཞི་གྲོས་བྱུང་བ་རེད་ China and Tibet had peace talks.

ཞི་འགུག་བདེ་འགོད་ (shiguù degöö) peacefully summoning people and settling sth.

ཞི་འགྲིག་ལྷན་ཚོགས་ (shidrig lhɛndzɔɔ) peace conference.

ཞི་རྒོལ་ (shigöö) 1. peace protest. 2. abbr. of ཞི་བའི་རྒོལ་སྟངས་.

ཞི་ཙུན་ (shijün) ch. bacteria.

ཞི་ཆས་ (shijɛɛ̀) civilian clothes ། དམག་དཔོན་ཚོ་ཞི་ཆས་གྱོན་ནས་ཕེབས་འདུག The military leaders came in civilian clothes.

ཞི་ཆིངས་ (shijiŋ) peace treaty.

ཞི་ཆོས་ (shijöö) gentle/ peaceful manner.

ཞི་འཇགས་ (shijaà) quelling, calming, pacifying; va.—གཏོང་ to calm, to pacify, to quell, to suppress, to put down ། ངོ་ལོག་ཟིང་འཁྲུགས་ཞི་འཇགས་སུ་བཏང་ནས་ Having calmed the rebellion.

ཞི་འཇམ་ (shinjam) peaceful, gentle ། ཞི་འཇམ་གྱི་སྒོ་ནས་བཅིངས་བཀྲོལ་བཏང་བ་རེད་ (They) liberated (it) peacefully.

ཞི་ཐབས་ (shidəb) peaceful means/ methods.

ཞི་མཐུན་ (shidün) peace.

ཞི་མཐུན་མཉམ་གནས་ (shidün ñāmnɛɛ̀) peaceful coexistence.

ཞི་མཐུན་གྱི་ཆིངས་ (shidün jījiŋ) peace treaty.

ཞི་མཐུན་ཕུག་རོན་ (shidün pūgrön) peace dove.

ཞི་འཐབ་ (shindəb) a nonviolent/ peaceful struggle.

ཞི་དུལ་ (shidüü) gentle, peaceful, well-behaved.

ཞི་དུལ་གུས་ལུགས་ལྡན་པ་ (shidüü güüluù dɛmba) gentle/ peaceful and respectful.

ཞི་དུལ་ཅན་ (shidüüjɛn) gentle, peaceful.

ཞི་དུལ་པོ་ (shi düübu) mild tempered, tolerant, patient.

ཞི་དུལ་བག་ཡོད་ (shidüü pagyöö) gentle and humble.

ཞི་དོར་དྲག་ཞུགས་ (shidɔɔ trəgshuù) sm. ཞི་བསྒྱུར་དྲག་ཞུགས་.

ཞི་དྲག་ (shidraà) civil and military, peaceful and violent/ militant ། ཞི་དྲག་དཔོན་རིགས་ Civil and military officials.

ཞི་དྲག་གཉིས་འཛིན་ (shidraà ñīijön) capable in war and peace or in civil and military affairs.

ཞི་དྲག་དཔོན་རིགས་ (shidraà būnriì) civil and military officials.

ཞི་བདེ་ (shide) peace.

ཞི་བདེ་རྒྱ་མཚོ་ཆེན་པོ་ (shide gyadzo cēmbo) Pacific Ocean.

ཞི་བདེ་མཉམ་གནས་ (shide ñāmnɛɛ̀) peaceful coexistence ། ཞི་བདེ་མཉམ་གནས་ཀྱི་རྩ་དོན་ལྔ་པོ་ The five principles of peaceful coexistence.

ཞི་བདེ་ནམ་མཁའི་རྒྱལ་ཁབ་ཀྱི་ལས་འགུལ་ (shide nāmkɛ gyɛɛgəbgi lɛngüü) the Taiping Heavenly Kingdom Movement (1851-1864).

ཞི་བདེ་ཡུན་བརྟན་ (shide yündɛn) lasting/ enduring peace.

ཞི་བདེ་ཡུན་གནས་ (shide yünnɛɛ̀) sm. ཞི་བདེ་ཡུན་བརྟན་.

ཞི་བདེ་རང་དབང་ (shide raŋwaŋ) peace and freedom.

ཞི་བདེ་རུ་ཁག (shide rugaà) Peace Corps (U.S.A.).

ཞི་བདེ་ལས་སྐྱོང་ལྷན་ཁང་ (shide lɛɛ̀gyoŋ lhēngaŋ) committee for the defense of peace.

ཞི་བདེ་སྲུང་སྐྱོབ་ (shide sūŋgyob) defending/ safeguarding peace.

ཞི་བདེ་ལྷ་རྒྱལ་ (shide lhāgyɛɛ) sm. ཞི་བདེ་ནམ་མཁའི་རྒྱལ་ཁབ་ཀྱིས་ལས་འགུལ་.

ཞི་བདེ་ལྷ་རྒྱལ་ལས་འགུལ་ (shide lhāgyɛɛ lɛngüü) sm. ཞི་བདེ་ནམ་མཁའི་རྒྱལ་ཁབ་ཀྱིས་ལས་འགུལ་.

ཞི་བདེའི་ཕྱི་འབྲེལ་ (shidee cīndree) peaceful diplomacy/ foreign relations.

ཞི་བདེའི་མི་སྣ་ (shidee minə) pacifist, peace partisan.

ཞི་བདེའི་རིང་ལུགས་ (shidee riŋluù) pacifism.

ཞི་བདེའི་ལས་འགན་ (shidee lɛngɛn) peaceful mission/ task.

ཞི་བདེར་དགའ་བ་ (shider gawa) peace loving ། ཞི་བདེར་དགའ་བའི་མི་དམངས་ Peace loving people.

ཞི་འདུལ་པོ་ (shi düübu) person who is learned as well as amiable.

ཞི་གནས་ (shinɛɛ̀) peaceful place, peaceful.

ཞི་གནས་ལྷིང་འཇགས་ (shinɛɛ̀ lhīŋjaà) calm, peaceful, tranquil, serene.

ཞི་པན་ཡ་ (shibɛnya) Spain.

ཞི་དཔོན་ (shibün) shung. civil officials.

ཞི་བ་ (shiwə) 1. peaceful. 2. civil, nonmilitary.

ཞི་བ་འཚོ་ (shibədzo) name of a famous pandit from India (Shantarakshita).

ཞི་བ་ལྷ་ (shibəlha) 1. name of a famous pandit from India (Shantideva). 2. name of a lama in Chamdo.

ཞི་བའི་འགྲན་བསྡུར་ (shiwɛ trɛnduu) peaceful competition.

ཞི་བའི་རྒོལ་སྟངས་ (shiwɛ göödaŋ) peaceful offensive.

ཞི་བའི་རྒྱ་མཚོ་ (shiwɛ gyadzo) Pacific Ocean.

ཞི་བའི་དྲང་སླང་དཔུང་སྡེ་ (shiwɛ taŋlaŋ būŋde) Peace Corps.

ཞི་བའི་བཅིངས་འགྲོལ་ (shiwɛ jīŋdröö) peace liberation.

ཞི་བའི་མཐུན་སྣེ་གདུགས་ (shiwɛ tũnne dūù) va. to make a peaceful settlement, to settle peacefully through someone's good offices.

ཞི་བའི་སྦྱིན་སྲེག (shiwɛ jinseg) a peaceful rite of exorcism.

ཞི་བའི་ཚིག (shiwɛ tsīi) calm, peaceful words.

ཞི་བའི་རིམ་འགྱུར་ (shiwɛ rimgyur) peaceful evolution.

ཞི་བར་བྱེད་ (shiwar cee) va. to quell, to pacify, to subdue, to put down.

ཞི་དབྱི་སྨན་པ་ (shiye memba) tib. ch. western doctor.

ཞི་དབྱིངས་སུ་མནལ་ (shijiŋsu nɛɛ) sm. དགོངས་པ་ཞི་བར་གཤེགས་.

ཞི་མ་ཁྲོ་ (shima trō) half-peaceful, half-wrathful (usu. with respect to deities).

ཞི་མི་ (shimi) cat.

ཞི་མི་གཉིད་ལ་འཁོར་ཡང་བསམ་རྒྱུ་ཙི་གུ (shimi ñīilə kɔ̄ɔyaŋ sōmgyu dzīgu) absorbed/ obsessed with sth. [Lit. even when the cats sleeps, all it thinks about is mice].

ཞི་མི་གཉིད་ལ་ཤོར་ན་བསམ་རྒྱུ་ཙི་ཙི་ལས་མི་འདུག (shimi ñīilə shɔ̄ɔna sōmgyu dzīdzilɛ minduù) sm. ཞི་མི་གཉིད་ལ་འཁོར་ཡང་བསམ་རྒྱུ་ཙི་གུ.

ཞི་མིས་འཕུར་བཞིན་པའི་བྱིའུར་ལྟོགས་སྐྱ་བྱེད་པ་ (shimi pūrshimbɛ ciwur dōgla cɛɛ̀ba) sm. ཞི་མི་གཉིད་ལ་འཁོར་ཡང་བསམ་རྒྱུ་ཙི་གུ.

ཞི་མི་ལིང་མའོ་ (shimi liŋmao) tib. ch. civet (cat).

ཞི་མིའི་གཞུག་གུ (shimii shuggu) cattail.

ཞི་མོ་ (shimu) sm. བུ་མོ་.

ཞི་མོལ་ (shimüü) peace talks; va.—བྱེད་ to hold peace talks.

ཞི་མོལ་གྲོས་མཐུན་ (shimüü tröödün) sm. ཞི་མོལ་.

ཞི་སྨན་ (shimɛn) tranquilizer, sleeping pill.

ཞི་ཚོགས་ (shidzɔɔ) peace conference.

ཞི་ཞིང་དལ་བ་ (shishiŋ tɛɛ̀wa) sm. ཞི་དུལ་.

ཞི་ཡའོ་སྨན་རིགས་ (shiyao mɛnriì ch.tib. Western/ allopathic medicine.

ཞི་ལ་ (shila) Greece.

ཞི་ལུ་ (shilu) boy.

ཞི་ལམ་ (shilam) nonviolence/ peaceful path.

ཞི་སྲུང་ (shisuŋ) protecting/ defending/ maintaining/ keeping the peace ། ཞི་སྲུང་དམག་སྡེ་ Peace keeping force.

ཞི་ཧུང་ཧྲི་ (shi hūŋhri) ch. tomato.

ཞི་ལྷིང་ (shilhiŋ) peace and tranquillity.

ཞི་ལྷོད་ (shilhöö) 1. softening, easing, toning down, relaxing, lessening; va.—དུ་གཏོང་; vi.—དུ་འགྲོ་ to get softened/ eased/ toned down/ relaxed/ lessened ། རྒྱལ་སྤྱིའི་ཟིང་འཚུབ་གནས་ཚུལ་ཞི་ལྷོད་དུ་གཏོང་རྒྱུ་ The easing of international tensions. 2. calm, peaceful, gentle, mild, moderate.

ཞི་ཨན་ (shian) Xi'an.

ཞི་ཨན་དུས་འགྱུར་ (shian tüügyur) the Xi'an Incident (1936).

ཞིག (shii) 1. in one, at one, a ¶ མི་ཞིག་དང་རྟ་ཞིག A man and a horse. 2. p. of འཇིག. 3. vi. to become unfastened ¶ མདུད་པ་ཞིག་བཞག The knot has become unfastened.

ཞིག་ཏུ་ (shigdu) 1. at/ in/ to one, to a ¶ ཁོང་དགོན་པ་ཞིག་ཏུ་ཡོད་པ་རེད་ He is in a monastery. 2. as one/ a ¶ གྲོང་ཁྱེར་འདི་ཆེ་པོ་ཞིག་ཏུ་རྩི་གི་ཡོད་པ་རེད་ They consider this a large city.

ཞིག་པོ་ (shigbu) sm. ཞིག་རོ་.

ཞིག་རལ་ (shigrεε) ruined, demolished ¶ དེ་རིང་ང་ཚོ་ཁང་པ་ཞིག་རལ་གཏོང་བབབར་འགྲོ་དགོས་ Today we have to go to demolish the old house.

ཞིག་རོ་ (shigro) a ruin/ demolished (building).

ཞིག་ལ་ (shiglə) Greece.

ཞིག་ཤུལ་ (shigshüü) ruins, remains.

ཞིག་གསོ་ (shigso) maintaining, restoring, repairing; va.—བྱེད་ to do maintenance work, to repair, to restore ¶ གནམ་གྲུ་གཅིག་ཞིག་གསོ་བྱས་ཚར་ནས་ After completing the repair work on the airplane.

ཞིག་གསོ་ཁང་ (shigsogaŋ) repair workshop/ factory/ plant.

ཞིག་གསོ་འཛིན་སྐྲས་ (shigso dzindrεὲ) maintenance work.

ཞིག་གསོ་བཟོ་གྲྭ (shigso sodra) repair factory/ plant.

ཞིང་ (shiŋ) 1. conjunctive particle for adjectives and verbs ¶ འདི་གོང་ཁེ་ཞིང་སྤུས་ཀ་ཡག་པོ་ཡོད་པ་རེད་ This is cheap and good quality. ¶ ཁོས་ཚ་ལག་འཚོང་ཞིང་མོས་ནང་དུ་བསྡད་པ་རེད་ He did business and she stayed at home. 2. field ¶ འབྲས་ཞིང་ Rice field. 3. farmer ¶ བཟོ་ཞིང་ Workers and farmers.

ཞིང་སྐལ་ (shiŋgεε) one's share of fields.

ཞིང་བསྒྱུར་ནགས་གཉེར་ (shiŋgyur nagñer) giving up farming and adopting forestry.

ཞིང་བསྒྱུར་ཕྱུགས་སྐྱེལ་ (shiŋgyur cūgbel) giving up farming for animal husbandry.

ཞིང་བསྒྱུར་ཚོང་གཉེར་ (shiŋgyur tsōŋñer) giving up farming for trading/ business.

ཞིང་ཁ་ (shiŋgə) agricultural field; va.—བཟོ་ to make a field (newly); va.—རྨོ་ to plow a field.

ཞིང་ཁ་ཆུ་མ་ (shiŋgə cūmə) fields that can be irrigated.

ཞིང་ཁ་ཐ་གོག (shiŋgə tāgɔ̀ɔ̀) an uncultivated/ waste field.

ཞིང་ཁ་བདག་གཉེར་ (shiŋgə dagñer) managing an agricultural field.

ཞིང་ཁ་སེར་འཇགས་ (shiŋgə sērlaŋ) after watering a field the earth cracks (indicating that the field is ready to be plowed).

ཞིང་ཁ་གསར་པར་སློལ་ (shiŋgə sārba bōō) sm. ཞིང་ཁ་བཟོ་.

ཞིང་ཁང་ (shiŋgaŋ) a house in the midst of agricultural fields.

ཞིང་ཁམས་ (shiŋgam) 1. planet. 2. realm, place.

ཞིང་ཁའི་ཆུ་བེད་ (shiŋgε cūbeè) irrigation for farming.

ཞིང་ཁའི་རྣང་མ་ (shiŋgε nāŋma) sm. ཞིང་གི་རྣང་མ་.

ཞིང་ཁའི་མུ་ (shiŋgε mu) sm. ཞིང་མུ་.

ཞིང་ཁའི་མུ་ཁ་ (shiŋgε mugə) the edges of a field.

ཞིང་ཁའི་ལས་ཀ་ (shiŋgε lεὲga) farming, agriculture.

ཞིང་ཁྲལ་ (shiŋdrεε) agricultural tax.

ཞིང་ག (shiŋga) sm. ཞིང་ཁ་.

ཞིང་གི་ཐ་གྲུ་ (shiŋgi tōdru) area/ size of a field.

ཞིང་གི་ཐོག་ཕྲས་ (shiŋgi tōgshεὲ) a portion of the first yield of grain that is given as a tax (in tt.).

ཞིང་གི་རྣང་མ་ (shiŋgi nāŋma) the bunds surrounding fields.

ཞིང་ཁུལ་ (shiŋgüü) agricultural area.

ཞིང་གྲོང་ (shiŋdroŋ) field and village; farmers and townsfolk.

ཞིང་གླ་ (shiŋla) 1. rent/ lease fee for agricultural land.

ཞིང་གླ་པ་ (shiŋ lāba) sm. ཞིང་པ་གླ་པ་.

ཞིང་བགེགས་ (shiŋgeg) disasters (usu. natural) that occur in agricultural fields.

ཞིང་འགན་གཙང་ལམ་ལུགས་ (shiŋ gεndzaŋ ləmluù) the agricultural responsibility system (implemented in post 1978 China).

ཞིང་རྒོད་ (shiŋgöò) wild/ uncultivated land.

ཞིང་ངན་ (shiŋŋεn) poor land, low-yield land.

ཞིང་ཅང་ (shinjaŋ) Xinjiang (Province).

ཞིང་ཆས་ (shinjεὲ) agricultural implements, farmer's tools.

ཞིང་ཆས་བཅོས་བསྒྱུར་ (shinjεὲ jǖügyur) improvement/ reform of agricultural implements.

ཞིང་ཆས་ཆུང་རིགས་ (shinjεὲ cūŋrii) small size/ scale farming tools.

ཞིང་ཆས་གསོ་སྐྱོན་བཟོ་ཁང་ (shinjεὲ sōdrün sogaŋ) farm implements repair plant.

ཞིང་ཆས་བཟོ་གྲྭ (shinjεὲ sōdra) farm implements factory.

ཞིང་ཆུ་ (shinju) irrigation (for agricultural fields); va.—འདྲེན་; —གཏོང་ to irrigate.

ཞིང་ཆུ་གཏོར་འགྲེམ་ (shinju dōndrem) irrigation by a sprinkling system.

ཞིང་ཆུ་འདྲེན་འབྱུད་ (shinju drenbüü) irrigation operations.

ཞིང་ཆུ་མ་ (shinjumə) sm. ཞིང་ཁ་ཆུ་མ་.

ཞིང་ཆེན་ (shinjen) 1. province. 2. large field/ farm.

ཞིང་ཆེན་གྱི་ལྟེ་གནས་ (shinjengi dēnεὲ) provincial capital.

ཞིང་ཆེན་ཨུ་ཡོན་ལྷན་ཁང་ (shinjen ūyün lhēngaŋ) tib. ch. Provincial Party Committee.

ཞིང་མཆོག (shinjɔɔ̀) 1. the best/ most excellent area or place. 2. the highest realm.

ཞིང་བརྗེ་ (shiŋ je) vi. to die.

ཞིང་བཏབ་ (shiŋ dəb) p. of ཞིང་འདེབས་.

ཞིང་གཉའ་ (shiŋña) edge of a field.

ཞིང་གཉེར་ (shiŋñer) field manager/ steward.

ཞིང་ཐ་ཆད་ (shiŋ tājεὲ) the most inferior type of agricultural field.

ཞིང་ཐང་ (shindaŋ) sm. ཞིང་ར་.

ཞིང་ཐོན་ (shindön) abbr. of ཞིང་ལས་ཐོན་སྐྱེད་.

ཞིང་ཐོན་དངོས་རྫས་ (shindön ŋȫödzεὲ) agricultural products.

ཞིང་དུ་གཤེགས་ (shindu shēg) vi. to die (h.).

ཞིང་དུད་ (shindüü) agricultural/ peasant household.

ཞིང་དོར་ (shindɔɔ) the amount of land that can be plowed in one day.

ཞིང་དྲོད་མོ་ (shiŋ trȫōma) fertile land/ fields.

ཞིང་བདག (shindaà) agricultural landlord, landowner.

ཞིང་བདག་གྲལ་རིམ་ (shindaà treerim) agricultural landlord class.

ཞིང་བདག་གཉིས་པ་ (shindaà ñīibə) sublandlord, landlord of a landlord.

ཞིང་བདག་གཤེད་མ་ (shindaà shēgma) despotic landlord.

ཞི་འདེབས་ (shiŋ deb) va. to plant, to cultivate, to sow ¶ དཔྱིད་ཀ་སོ་ནམ་པ་ཚོས་ཞིང་འདེབས་དུས་ In the spring, when the farmers plant the fields.

ཞིང་སྡེ་ (shinde) village, rural town.

ཞིང་ནགས་ (shiŋnaà) agriculture and forestry ¶ ཞིང་ནགས་ཚན་རིག Agriculture and forestry science.

ཞིང་ནགས་སྤུའུ་ (shiŋnaà bū) tib. ch. ministry of agriculture and forestry.

ཞིང་ནགས་ཕྱུགས་གསུམ་ (shiŋnaà cūgsum) the three: farming, forestry and animal husbandry.

ཞིང་ནགས་ཕྱུགས་ཞོར་ཉ་ (shiŋnaà cūgshɔɔ ña) farming, forestry, animal husbandry, sideline work and fishery.

ཞིང་ནགས་ཚན་རིག་ལག་རྩལ་ས་ཚིགས་ (shiŋnaà tsēnrii lagdzεε sōdzii) agricultural and forestry technology station.

ཞིང་ནགས་ལག་རྩལ་ས་བོན་ཁྱབ་སྤེལ་ས་ཚིགས་ (shiŋnaà lagdzεε nābön kyəbbel sōdzii) agricultural seed extension station.

ཞིང་ནགས་ལས་རིགས་ (shiŋnaà lεerii) agriculture and

forestry professions.

ཞིང་པ་ (shiŋbə) farmer, peasant.

ཞིང་པ་ཕྱུག་པོ་ (shiŋbə cūgbu) rich peasant.

ཞིང་པ་བོགས་ལེན་པ་ (shiŋbə bɔ̄ɔlemba) farmer holding leased land, tenant farmer.

ཞིང་པ་བྲན་གཡོག (shiŋbə trɛnyɔɔ̀) sm. ཞིང་བྲན་.

ཞིང་པ་བྲན་གཡོག་བདག་པོ་ (shiŋbə trɛnyɔɔ̀ dagbo) sm. ཞིང་བྲན་བདག་པོ་.

ཞིང་པ་དབུལ་པོ་ (shiŋbə ǖǖbu) poor peasant/ farmers.

ཞིང་པ་འབྲིང་པ་ (shiŋbə driŋbə) sm. ཞིང་འབྲིང་.

ཞིང་པ་ཚེ་གཡོག (shiŋbə tsēyɔɔ̀) sm. ཞིང་བྲན་.

ཞིང་པའི་ཁྱིམ་ལུད་ (shiŋbɛ kyīmlüü) house manure (used on fields).

ཞིང་པའི་མཐུན་ཚོགས་ (shiŋbɛ tǖndzɔɔ̀) peasant association.

ཞིང་པའི་དུད་ཚང་ (shiŋbɛ tǖüdzaŋ) peasant household.

ཞིང་པའི་ཚོགས་ (shiŋbɛ tsɔɔ̀) sm. ཞིང་ཚོགས་.

ཞིང་པའི་འོས་ལངས་ (shiŋbɛ wȫölaŋ) peasant's revolt/ insurrection.

ཞིང་པའི་གསར་བརྗེ་ (shiŋbɛ sārje) peasant's revolution.

ཞིང་པའི་གྱེན་ལོག (shiŋbɛ gyenlɔɔ̀) farmer or peasant revolt/ insurrection.

ཞིང་པའི་ལྷན་ཚོགས་ (shiŋbɛ lhɛ̄ndzɔɔ̀) farmer/ peasant association.

ཞིང་དཔོན་ (shiŋbün) an official in charge of fields.

ཞིང་སྦྱོད་འཁྱིག་ཤོག་སྲབ་པོ་ (shiŋjöö gyigshoò drābbu) thin polyurethance plastic sheets used on fields.

ཞིང་ཕེབས་དམ་པ་ (shiŋpeb tamba) the deceased, the late.

ཞིང་ཕྱུག (shiŋcuù) rich farmers/ peasants.

ཞིང་ཕྱུགས་ (shiŋcuù) agriculture and animal husbandry.

ཞིང་ཕྱུགས་ཆུ་བེད་ཅུའུ་ (shiŋcuù cūbeè jū) tib. ch. bureau of agriculture, animal husbandry and water conservancy.

ཞིང་ཕྱུགས་ཉ་ལས་པུའུ་ (shiŋcuù ñalɛɛ̀ bū) tib. ch. ministry of agriculture, animal husbandry and fisheries.

ཞིང་ཕྱུགས་མཉམ་སྦྲེལ་ (shiŋcuù ñāmbee) agropastoralist.

ཞིང་ཕྱུགས་ནགས་ཆུ་གཞུང་ལས་ཁང་ (shiŋcuù nagju shuŋlɛɛ̀gaŋ) office of agriculture, animal husbandry, forestry and water resources.

ཞིང་ཕྱུགས་པུའུ་ (shiŋcuù bū) tib. ch. ministry of agriculture and animal husbandry.

ཞིང་ཕྱུགས་ཚན་རིག (shiŋcuù tsɛ̄nrii) agricultural and animal husbandry sciences.

ཞིང་ཕྱུགས་ཟུང་སྦྲེལ་ (shiŋcuù suŋdree) sm. ཞིང་ཕྱུགས་ཟུང་འབྲེལ་.

ཞིང་ཕྱུགས་ཟུང་འབྲེལ་ (shiŋcuù suŋdree) agropastoralism, the subsistence type that combines agriculture and animal husbandry.

ཞིང་ཕྱུགས་དོ་དམ་ཅུའུ་ (shiŋcuù todam jū) tib. ch. bureau of agriculture and animal husbandry.

ཞིང་ཕྱུགས་ལས་འཕྲུལ་ཆས་ (shiŋ cūglɛɛ̀ trǖüjɛɛ̀) farming and animal husbandry machinery/ mechanical equipment.

ཞིང་ཕྱེད་སློབ་གྲྭ་ (shiŋjeè lōbdra) school of agriculture and animal husbandry.

ཞིང་ཕྱེད་སློབ་གྲྭ་ཆེན་མོ་ (shiŋjeè lōbdra) college of agriculture and animal husbandry.

ཞིང་ཕྱེད་སློབ་ཕྱེད་ (shiŋjeè lōbjeè) part farming and part studying.

ཞིང་འཕྲུལ་ (shiŋdrüü) sm. ཞིང་ལས་འཕྲུལ་ཆས་.

ཞིང་འཕྲུལ་མཁོ་སྤྲོད་ཀུང་སི་ (shiŋdrüü kōdrüü gūŋsi) tib. ch. agricultural machinery supply company.

ཞིང་འཕྲུལ་ཆུ་ལོག་ཅུའུ་ (shiŋdrüü cūloò jū) tib. ch. bureau of agricultural machinery and water conservancy.

ཞིང་འཕྲུལ་ཉོ་སྒྲུབ་ས་ཚིགས་ (shiŋdrüü ñodrub sādzii) tib. ch. agricultural machinery purchasing station.

ཞིང་འཕྲུལ་དོ་དམ་ཁྲུའུ་ (shiŋdrüü todam trū) tib. ch. agricultural machinery management office.

ཞིང་བུན་ (shiŋbün) agricultural loan.

ཞིང་བོགས་ (shiŋbɔɔ̀) lease/ rental fee for agricultural land; va.—ལེན་ to lease/ rent agricultural land.

ཞིང་བྲན་ (shiŋdrɛn) agricultural serf.

ཞིང་བྲན་བདག་པོ་ (shiŋdrɛn dagbo) serf owner, serf lord.

ཞིང་བྲན་ཕྱུག་པོ་ (shiŋdrɛn cūgbo) rich serf.

ཞིང་བྲན་དབུལ་པོ་ (shiŋdrɛn ǖübu) poor serf.

ཞིང་བྲན་འབྲིང་རིམ་ (shiŋdrɛn driŋrim) middle serf.

ཞིང་བྲན་འོས་ལངས་ (shiŋdrɛn wȫölaŋ) serf revolt.

ཞིང་བྲན་རིང་ལུགས་ (shiŋdrɛn riŋluù) sm. ཞིང་བྲན་ལམ་ལུགས་.

ཞིང་བྲན་ལམ་ལུགས་ (shiŋdrɛn ləmluù) serf system, agricultural serfdom, feudal system.

ཞིང་དབུལ་ (shiŋüü) abbr. of ཞིང་པ་དབུལ་པོ་.

ཞིང་དབུལ་ཞིང་འབྲིང་འོག་མ་ (shiŋüü shiŋdriŋ wɔɔ̀ma) poor peasants and lower middle peasants.

ཞིང་འབངས་ (shiŋbaŋ) farmers, peasants.

ཞིང་འབུ་ (shiŋbu) agricultural insects.

ཞིང་འབྲིང་ (shiŋdriŋ) middle peasant/ farmer.

ཞིང་འབྲིང་གོང་མ་ (shiŋdriŋ koŋma) upper-middle peasant/ farmer.

ཞིང་འབྲིང་ཕྱུག་པོ་ (shiŋdriŋ cūgbu) rich middle peasant.

ཞིང་འབྲིང་འོག་མ་ (shiŋdriŋ wɔɔ̀ma) lower-middle peasant.

ཞིང་མིག (shiŋmii) quantity/ amount of fields.

ཞིང་འབྲོག (shiŋdrɔɔ̀) farmers and nomads.

ཞིང་རྨོ་ (shiŋ mō) va. to plow a field.

ཞིང་རྨོ་རུ་ཁག (shiŋmo rugaà) planting brigade.

ཞིང་རྨོ་ཡུར་རྒྱག (shiŋmo yurgyaà) plowing and weeding.

ཞིང་སྨན་ (shiŋmɛn) agricultural insecticides/ pesticides ¶ ཡུལ་གྱི་ཞིང་སྨན་ Indigenous insecticides/ pesticides.

ཞིང་རྩལ་པ་ (shiŋdzɛɛba) sm. ཞིང་ལས་ལག་རྩལ་པ་.

ཞིང་ཚན་ (shiŋdzɛn) sm. ཞིང་མིག.

ཞིང་ཚིགས་ (shiŋdzii) sm. ཞིང་མཚམས་.

ཞིང་ཚོགས་ (shiŋdzɔɔ̀) peasant association.

ཞིང་མཚམས་ (shiŋdzam) the border/ boundary of a field.

ཞིང་རྫས་ (shiŋdzɛɛ̀) agricultural products.

ཞིང་ཞོར་ (shiŋshɔɔ) 1. agricultural sideline (work/ products) ¶ ཞིང་ཞོར་ཐོན་རྫས་ Agricultural sideline products. 2. agricultural and sideline work.

ཞིང་བཟང་ (shiŋsaŋ) rich agricultural fields.

ཞིང་བཟོ་ཚོང་གསུམ་ (shiŋso tsōŋsum) the three: farmers, workers and traders.

ཞིང་ཡན་ (shiŋyɛn) uncultivated/ ruined/ waste fields.

ཞིང་ཡུར་ (shiŋyur) canal/ irrigation ditch in agricultural fields.

ཞིང་ཡོད་དབང་ཆ་ (shiŋyöö wāŋja) the right to own fields.

ཞིང་གཡོག (shiŋyɔɔ̀) sm. ཞིང་བྲན་.

ཞིང་གཡོག་བདག་པོ་ (shiŋyɔɔ̀ dagbo) sm. ཞིང་བྲན་བདག་པོ་.

ཞིང་གཡོག་ལམ་ལུགས་ (shiŋyɔɔ̀ ləmluù) sm. ཞིང་བྲན་ལམ་ལུགས་.

ཞིང་ར་ (shiŋrə) state farm.

ཞིང་རིན་ (shiŋrin) price/ value of a field.

ཞིང་རེངས་ (shiŋreŋ) disused/ abandoned land; vi.—ལུས་ to fall into disuse (farmland).

ཞིང་རོལ་ (shiŋrüü) furrow.

ཞིང་ལ་སྔ་ཆུ་གཏོང་ (shiŋla ŋaju dōŋ) va. to do the first watering of agricultural fields.

ཞིང་ལས་ (shiŋlɛɛ̀) agriculture, farming; va.—བྱེད་ to farm, to do agricultural work.

ཞིང་ལས་ཀྱི་འཐབ་ཕྱོགས་ (shiŋlɛɛ̀gi tōbjɔɔ̀) agricultural front.

ཞིང་ལས་ཀྱི་དཔྱ་ཁྲལ་ (shiŋlɛɛ̀gi jɛ̄drɛɛ) agricultural tax.

ཞིང་ལས་ཀྱི་སྤྱི་ཚོགས་རིང་ལུགས་བསྒྱུར་བཀོད་ (shiŋlɛɛ̀gi jīdzoò riŋluù gyurgöö) socialist transformation of agriculture.

ཞིང་ལས་ཀྱི་ཡིག་བརྒྱད་ཚ་ཁྲིམས་ (shiŋlɛɛ̀gi yiggyɛɛ̀ dzə̄drim) the eight point charter of agriculture (the eight areas of technological development proposed by Mao Zedong in 1958).

ཞིང་ལས་སྐྱེ་དངོས་ (shiŋlɛɛ̀ gyēŋuoȍ) crops.

ཞིང་ལས་སྐྱེ་དངོས་རིག་པ་ (shiŋlɛɛ̀ gyeŋuoȍ rigbə) agrobiology.

ཞིང་ལས་ཁང་ (shiŋlɛɛ̀gaŋ) agricultural cooperative.

ཞིང་ལས་ཁའོ་ (shiŋlɛɛ̀ kāwu) agricultural section.

ཞིང་ལས་གོང་འཕེལ་སྐོར་གྱི་ཚ་གནད་ (shiŋlɛɛ̀ koŋbelgɔɔgi dzānɛɛ̀) national program of agricultural development.

ཞིང་ལས་འགྲེམས་སྟོན་ (shiŋlɛɛ̀ dremdön) agricultural exhibit.

ཞིང་ལས་རྒྱལ་ཁབ་ (shiŋlɛɛ̀ gyɛɛgəb) agricultural nation/ country.

ཞིང་ལས་སྒྱུ་རྩལ་ (shiŋlɛɛ̀ gyudzɛɛ) agronomy.

ཞིང་ལས་ངལ་རྩོལ་ (shiŋlɛɛ̀ ŋɛɛdzöö) agricultural labor.

ཞིང་ལས་དངུལ་ཁང་ (shiŋlɛɛ̀ ŋüügaŋ) agricultural bank.

ཞིང་ལས་དངུལ་བུན་ (shiŋlɛɛ̀ ŋüübün) agricultural loan.

ཞིང་ལས་ཅུའུ་ (shiŋlɛɛ̀ cū) tib. ch.bureau of agriculture.

ཞིང་ལས་ཆུང་བ་ (shiŋlɛɛ̀ cūŋwa) small-scale farming/ agriculture.

ཞིང་ལས་ཆུང་བའི་དཔལ་འབྱོར་ (shiŋlɛɛ̀ cūŋwɛ bɛ̄njɔɔ) small peasant economy.

ཞིང་ལས་ཆེད་སྦྱོང་སློབ་གྲྭ་ (shiŋlɛɛ̀ cēèjoŋ lōbdra) agricultural specialized school.

ཞིང་ལས་མཉམ་སྒྲུབ་ཁང་ (shiŋlɛɛ̀ ñāmdrubgaŋ) agricultural cooperative.

ཞིང་ལས་མཉམ་ལས་ཅན་ (shiŋlɛɛ̀ ñamlɛɛ̀jɛn) collectivized/ cooperativized farming or agriculture; vi.—དུ་འགྱུར་ to be cooperativized/ collectivized (farming); va.—དུ་སྒྱུར་ to collectivize/ cooperativize farming ¶ དམངས་གཙོའི་བཅོས་བསྒྱུར་བཏང་ནས་ཞིང་ལས་མཉམ་ལས་ཅན་དུ་གྱུར་པ་རེད་ After the socialist reforms agriculture was collectivized.

ཞིང་ལས་ཐུན་མོང་ཅན་ (shiŋlɛɛ̀ tünmoŋjɛn) sm. ཞིང་ལས་མཉམ་ལས་ཅན་.

ཞིང་ལས་ཐོན་སྐྱེད་ (shiŋlɛɛ̀ tōŋgyeè) agricultural production/ output.

ཞིང་ལས་ཐོན་སྐྱེད་མཉམ་ལས་ཁང་ (shiŋlɛɛ̀ tōŋgyeè ñamlɛɛ̀gaŋ) agricultural producer's cooperative.

ཞིང་ལས་ཐོན་སྐྱེད་རུ་ཆེན་ (shiŋlɛɛ̀ tōŋgyeè rujen) agricultural production brigade.

ཞིང་ལས་ཐོན་སྐྱེད་རོགས་རེས་ཚོགས་ཆུང་ (shiŋlɛɛ̀ tōŋgyeè rɔgreè tsōgjuŋ) agricultural producer's mutual aid group/ team.

ཞིང་ལས་ཐོན་དངོས་ (shiŋlɛɛ̀ tōnŋoȍ) sm. ཞིང་ལས་ཐོན་རྫས་.

ཞིང་ལས་ཐོན་རྫས་ (shiŋlɛɛ̀ tōndzɛɛ̀) farm goods/ produce, agricultural products.

ཞིང་ལས་ཐོན་རྫས་ཁྲོམ་ར་ (shiŋlɛɛ̀ tōndzɛɛ̀ trōmra) agricultural products market.

ཞིང་ལས་ཐོན་རྫས་རིན་ཐང་བསྡོམས་འབོར་ (shiŋlɛɛ̀ tōndzɛɛ̀ rindaŋ dombɔɔ) value of total agricultural production/ output.

ཞིང་ལས་འཐབ་ཕྱོགས་ (shiŋlɛɛ̀ tə̄bjɔɔ̀) agricultural front.

ཞིང་ལས་དལ་དུས་ (shiŋlɛɛ̀ tɛɛdüü) slack farming season, agricultural off-season.

ཞིང་ལས་དལ་སྐབས་ (shiŋlɛɛ̀ tɛɛgəb) sm. ཞིང་ལས་དལ་དུས་.

ཞིང་ལས་དུས་སྐབས་ (shiŋlɛɛ̀ tüügəb) agricultural/ farming season.

ཞིང་ལས་དུས་ཚོད་ (shiŋlɛɛ̀ tüüdzöö) agricultural/ farming season.

ཞིང་ལས་གནམ་གཤིས་བརྟག་དཔྱད་ས་ཚིགས་ (shiŋlɛɛ̀ nāmshiì dāgjɛɛ̀ sədziì) agricultural weather station.

ཞིང་ལས་གནམ་གཤིས་རིག་པ་ (shiŋlɛɛ̀ nāmshiì rigbə) agrometeorology, agroclimatology.

ཞིང་ལས་གནམ་གཤིས་ས་ཚིགས་ (shiŋlɛɛ̀ nāmshiì sədziì) agricultural weather station.

ཞིང་ལས་པུའུ་ (shiŋlɛɛ̀ bū) tib. ch. Ministry of Agriculture.

ཞིང་ལས་དཔལ་འབྱོར་ (shiŋlɛɛ̀ bɛ̄njɔɔ) agricultural economy.

ཞིང་ལས་དཔེ་ལེགས་ཅན་ (shiŋlɛɛ̀ bēlegjɛn) model agricultural worker.

ཞིང་ལས་ཕྲན་ཆུང་བ་ (shiŋlɛɛ̀ trɛ̄njuŋwa) small farmer.

ཞིང་ལས་འཕྲུལ་འཁོར་ (shiŋlɛɛ̀ trǖügɔɔ) sm. ཞིང་ལས་འཕྲུལ་ཆས་.

ཞིང་ལས་འཕྲུལ་ཆས་ (shiŋlɛɛ̀ trǖüjɛɛ̀) agricultural machinery/ equipment.

ཞིང་ལས་འཕྲུལ་ཆས་ཅན་ (shiŋlɛɛ̀ trǖüjɛɛ̀jɛn) mechanized agriculture; vi.—དུ་འགྱུར་ to become mechanized (farming); va.—དུ་སྒྱུར་ to mechanize farming.

ཞིང་ལས་འཕྲུལ་ཆས་པུའུ་ (shiŋlɛɛ̀ trǖüjɛɛ̀ bū) tib. ch. bureau of agricultural machinery/ equipment.

ཞིང་ལས་འཕྲུལ་ཆས་བཟོ་གྲྭ་ (shiŋlɛɛ̀ trǖüjɛɛ̀ sodra) agricultural machinery/ equipment. factory.

ཞིང་ལས་བྱེད་ (shiŋlɛɛ̀ ceè) sm. ཞིང་ལས་.

ཞིང་ལས་བྱེད་མཁན་ (shiŋlɛɛ̀ ceèñɛn) farmers.

ཞིང་ལས་བྲེལ་དུས་ (shiŋlɛɛ̀ dreedüü) busy period in farming, agricultural peak season.

ཞིང་ལས་བྲེལ་ཟིང་ (shiŋlɛɛ̀ dreesiŋ) sm. ཞིང་ལས་བྲེལ་ཆེ་.

ཞིང་ལས་མི་གྲངས་ (shiŋlɛɛ̀ midraŋ) farm population.

ཞིང་ལས་སྨོན་འདེབས་བྱེད་ལུགས་ (shiŋlɛɛ̀ mōndeb ceèluù) agrotechnology, agrotechnics.

ཞིང་ལས་སྨན་རིགས་ (shiŋlɛɛ̀ mɛ̄nriì) agricultural insecticides/ pesticides.

ཞིང་ལས་ཚན་ཁག (shiŋlɛɛ̀ tsɛ̄ngaà) department of agriculture.

ཞིང་ལས་ཚན་རིག་ཁང་ (shiŋlɛɛ̀ tsɛ̄nriìgaŋ) academy of agricultural sciences.

ཞིང་ལས་ཚན་རིག་བརྟག་དཔྱད་ཁང་ (shiŋlɛɛ̀ tsɛ̄nriì dāgjɛɛ̀gaŋ) agricultural science research institute.

ཞིང་ལས་ཚན་རིག་ཞིབ་འཇུག་ཁང་ (shiŋlɛɛ̀ tsɛ̄nriì shimjuùgaŋ) institute of agricultural sciences.

ཞིང་ལས་ཚན་རིག་སུའོ་ (shiŋlɛɛ̀ tsɛ̄nriì sūo) tib. ch. institute of agricultural sciences.

ཞིང་ལས་ཚོད་ལྟ་ (shiŋlɛɛ̀ tsȫöda) agricultural experiment/ trial/ test.

ཞིང་ལས་ཚོད་ལྟའི་ས་ཚིགས་ (shiŋlɛɛ̀ tsȫödɛ sədziì) agricultural experiment station.

ཞིང་ལས་བཟོ་པ་ (shiŋlɛɛ̀ soba) agricultural worker.

ཞིང་ལས་ཡོ་བྱད་ (shiŋlɛɛ̀ yobjɛɛ̀) agricultural implements.

ཞིང་ལས་རིག་པ་ (shiŋlɛɛ̀ rigbə) agronomy.

ཞིང་ལས་ལག་རྩལ་ (shiŋlɛɛ̀ lagdzɛɛ) agricultural techniques/ skills/ technology, agrotechnology, agrotechnical.

ཞིང་ལས་ལག་རྩལ་ཁྱབ་སྤེལ་ས་ཚིགས་ (shiŋlɛɛ̀ lagdzɛɛ kyə̄bbel sədziì) agrotechnical extention station.

ཞིང་ལས་ལག་རྩལ་དགེ་རྒན་ (shiŋlɛɛ̀ lagdzɛɛ gegɛn) agronomist.

ཞིང་ལས་ལག་རྩལ་པ་ (shiŋlɛɛ̀ lagdzɛba) agronomist, agrotechnician, agricultural expert.

ཞིང་ལས་ལག་རྩལ་རིག་པ་ (shiŋlɛɛ̀ lagdzɛɛ rigbə) agronomy.

ཞིང་ལས་ལོ་ཏོག (shiŋlɛɛ̀ lodoò) crops.

ཞིང་ལས་ས་ཁུལ་ (shiŋlɛɛ̀ sə̄güü) agricultural region/ area.

ཞིང་ལས་ས་བོན་ས་ཚིགས་ (shiŋlɛɛ̀ sābön sədzig) agricultural seed station.

ཞིང་ལས་སློབ་གྲྭ་ (shiŋlɛɛ̀ lōbdra) agricultural school/ institute.

ཞིང་ལས་སློབ་གྲྭ་ཆེ་བ་ (shiŋlɛɛ̀ lōbdra cēwa) agricultural college/ university.

ཞིང་ལས་སློབ་གྲྭ་ཆེན་མོ་ (shiŋlɛɛ̀ lōbdra cēmmo)

agricultural college/ university.

ཞིང་ལས་སློབ་གྲྭ་འབྲིང་བ་ (shi̲ŋlɛɛ̀ lōbdra dri̲ŋgə) agricultural secondary school.

ཞིང་ལས་སློབ་འབྲིང་ (shi̲ŋlɛɛ̀ lōbdriŋ) agricultural secondary school.

ཞིང་ལུད་ (shi̲ŋlüǜ) fertilizer, manure.

ཞིང་ལུད་ཕྱེ་མ་ (shi̲ŋlüǜ cēma) chemical fertilizer.

ཞིང་ཤག་པ་ (shi̲ŋshagba) the Rimpung ruler who seized power in Tibet during the 16th century (Tseden Dorje).

ཞིང་གཤིན་པོ་ (shi̲ŋ sīmbu) good/ fertile land.

ཞིང་གཤེགས་ (shi̲ŋsheg) 1. the late, the deceased ¶ སྲིད་བློན་ཞིང་གཤེགས་ The late Prime Minister. 2. vi. to die, to pass away.

ཞིང་ས་ (shi̲ŋsə) soil, arable land.

ཞིང་སྲུང་ཤིང་ནགས་ (shi̲ŋsuŋ shīŋnaà) a forest planted to protect fields.

ཞིང་སྲུང་ནགས་ཚལ་ (shi̲ŋsuŋ n̲agdzɛɛ) sm. ཞིང་སྲུང་ཤིང་ནགས་.

ཞིང་ཧུང་རེ་ (shi̲ŋ hūŋre) ch. scarlet fever.

ཞིན་ (shi̲n) ch. zinc.

ཞིན་ཅང་ (shi̲njaŋ) Xinjiang (Province).

ཞིན་ཧྭ་ (shi̲nhwa) ch. Xinhua (news Agency) ¶ ཞིན་ཧྭ་དཔར་ཁང་ Xinhua printing house ¶ ཞིན་ཧྭ་དཔེ་ཚོང་ཁང་ Xinhua book store.

ཞིབ་ (shi̲b) 1. abbr. of ཞིབ་ཕྲ་. 2. abbr. of ཞིབ་ཞིབ་. 3. abbr. of ཞིབ་འཇུག. 4. sm. རྩམ་པ་.

ཞིབ་ཁང་ལས་ཁུངས་ (shi̲bgaŋ l̲ɛɛ̀guŋ) shung. an auditor's office in the traditional Tibetan government.

ཞིབ་ཁུག (shi̲bguù) h. of རྩམ་ཁུག.

ཞིབ་གྲོས་ (shi̲bdröö̀) discussing in detail; va.—བྱེད་.

ཞིབ་གླེང་ (shi̲bleŋ) saying/ talking in detail; va.—བྱེད་.

ཞིབ་འགོ་ (shi̲mgo) students who check the handwriting of other students in some Tibetan schools (in Lhasa in tt.).

ཞིབ་འགོད་ (shi̲mgüǜ) detailed statement/ account; va.—བྱེད་; —ཞུ་ to give a detailed account/ statement.

ཞིབ་འགྲེལ་ (shi̲mdree) detailed explanation; va.—བྱེད་ to explain in detail.

ཞིབ་རྒྱས་ (shi̲bgyɛɛ̀) detailed.

ཞིབ་རྒྱས་མེད་པ་ (shi̲bgyɛɛ̀ m̲eèba) vague, not detailed, cursory.

ཞིབ་མངགས་ (shi̲bŋaà) detailed order, va.—བྱེད་ to give detailed orders.

ཞིབ་ཅིང་ཕྲ་བ་ (shi̲bjiŋ trāwa) thorough, careful, painstaking.

ཞིབ་ཅིང་མཚར་བ་ (shi̲bjiŋ tsārwa) detailed and beautiful.

ཞིབ་གཅོད་ (shi̲bjöö̀) thorough investigation/ examination/ research; va.—བྱེད་ to investigate/ examine/ research thoroughly.

ཞིབ་གཅོད་པ་ (shi̲bjöö̀ba) investigator, member of an investigatory committee.

ཞིབ་ཆ་ (shi̲bja) detailed, thorough, minute; va.—ལྟ་ to look into a matter in detail.

ཞིབ་ཆ་ནང་གསལ་ (shi̲bja n̲aŋsɛɛ) phrase conveying that the details of sth. are enclosed.

ཞིབ་ཆ་མེད་པ་ (shi̲bja m̲eèba) vague, not detailed.

ཞིབ་མཆན་ (shi̲bjɛn) sm. ཞིབ་བཤེར་ཚོག་མཆན་.

ཞིབ་ཆེན་ (shi̲bjen) the best quality རྩམ་པ་ flour.

ཞིབ་འཇུག (shi̲mjuù) investigation, research, researching; va.—བྱེད་ to research.

ཞིབ་འཇུག་སྡེ་གནས་ (shi̲mjuù dēnɛɛ̀) research center.

ཞིབ་འཇུག་ཁང་ (shi̲mjuùgaŋ) research institute, investigation office ¶ ཉི་འོད་ནུས་ཤུགས་ཞིབ་འཇུག་ཁང་ Research institute for solar energy.

ཞིབ་འཇུག་བྱ་གཞི་ (shi̲mjuù c̲əshi) a question for study/ research.

ཞིབ་འཇུག་བྱ་ཡུལ་ (shi̲mjuù c̲əyüü) research subject/ object.

ཞིབ་འཇུག་མི་སྣ་ (shi̲mjuù mi̲nə) researcher.

ཞིབ་འཇུག་རྩད་དཔྱོད་ (shi̲mjuù dzɛ̄ɛ̀jöö̀) researching, investigating.

ཞིབ་འཇུག་ཚད་ལེན་ (shi̲mjuù tsɛ̄ɛ̀len) surveying (land, etc.).

ཞིབ་འཇུག་ཚོགས་པ་ (shi̲mjuù tsɔ̄gba) inspection/ research/ investigation group, team., or committee.

ཞིབ་འཇུག་བཟོ་བཅོས་ (shi̲mjuù s̲objöö̀) investigating and making corrections; va.—བྱེད་.

ཞིབ་འཇུག་ལྷན་ཚོགས་ (shi̲mjuù lhɛ̄ndzɔɔ̀) research association/ organization.

ཞིབ་བརྗོད་ (shi̲bjöö̀) detailed explanation/ narration; va.—བྱེད་.

ཞིབ་ཏིག (shi̲bdig) sm. ཞིབ་ཕྲ་.

ཞིབ་ཏུ་ (shi̲bdu) in detail, minutely, thoroughly, carefully ¶ རྒྱ་ནག་ནས་ལོག་རྗེས་ཁོ་པའི་བསམ་ཚུལ་ཞིབ་ཏུ་བཀོད་པའི་དེབ་ཅིག་བྲིས་པ་རེད་ After returning from China (he) wrote a detailed book of his opinions. ¶ གནས་དོན་དེ་ཚོ་ཞིབ་ཏུ་བརྟག་ནས་ཐག་གཅོད་བྱས་པ་རེད་ (We) examined that matter thoroughly and made a decision.

ཞིབ་ཏུ་དབྱེ་ (shi̲bdu yē) va. to dissect, to analyze in detail.

ཞིབ་བཏགས་བྱེད་ (shi̲bdaà c̲eè) va. to grind grain into flour.

ཞིབ་རྟོག (shi̲bdɔɔ̀) sm. ཞིབ་ཏུ་རྟོག.

ཞིབ་བརྟག (shi̲bdaà) checking sth. written for mistakes, proofreading; va.—བྱེད་.

ཞིབ་ལྟ་ (shi̲bda) looking carefully into sth.; examining/ investigating thoroughly or in detail; va.—བྱེད་.

ཞིབ་བལྟས་ (shi̲bdɛɛ̀) sm. ཞིབ་ལྟ་.

ཞིབ་ཐལ་ (shi̲bdɛɛ) རྩམ་པ་ that is added to broths/ soups.

ཞིབ་ཐུད་ (shi̲bdüǜ) a Tibetan food made of dried cheese, butter, རྩམ་པ་ and brown sugar.

ཞིབ་ཐོ་ (shi̲bdo) a detailed list; va.—རྒྱག to make a detailed list.

ཞིབ་ཐོན་ (shi̲bdön) precision, precise.

ཞིབ་ཐོན་འཁོར་སྡེགས་ (shi̲dön kɔ̄ɔ̄deg) precision lathe.

ཞིབ་ཐོན་དཔྱད་ཆས་ (shi̲dön jɛ̄ɛ̀jɛɛ̀) precision tools/ instruments.

ཞིབ་འཐག (shi̲bdaà)1. fine and closely woven. 2. finely ground (grains); va.—བྱེད་.

ཞིབ་འཐག་འཕྲུལ་འཁོར་ (shi̲bdaà trüǖgɔɔ) a fine milling/ grinding machine.

ཞིབ་འཐེམས་ (shi̲mdem) detailed and thorough.

ཞིབ་འདང་རྒྱག (shi̲mdaŋ gya̲à) va. to think about sth. thoroughly.

ཞིབ་འདྲི་ (shi̲mdri) asking in detail; va.—བྱེད་.

ཞིབ་འདྲོང་ (shi̲mdoŋ) sm. ཞིབ་འཐེམས་.

ཞིབ་རྡུང་ (shi̲bduŋ) pounding (into powder); va.—བྱེད་.

ཞིབ་བལྡད་དལ་མིད་ (shi̲bdɛɛ̀ t̲ɛɛmiì) taking one's time eating; va.—བྱེད་ [Lit. chew carefully and swallow slowly].

ཞིབ་སྡུར་ (shi̲bdur) sm. ཞིབ་བསྡུར་.

ཞིབ་བསྡུར་ (shi̲bdur) detailed discussion/ review/ comparison; va.—བྱེད་.

ཞིབ་པ་ (shi̲bbə) precise, exact, thorough, detailed.

ཞིབ་པོ་ (shi̲bbu) sm. ཞིབ་ཞིབ་.

ཞིབ་པོར་ (shi̲bbor) sm. ཞིབ་ཏུ་.

ཞིབ་དཔང་ (shi̲bbaŋ) shung. investigators sb. sent to check on sth. or sb.

ཞིབ་དཔྱད་ (shi̲bjɛɛ̀) inspection, investigation, examination; va.—བྱེད་ to inspect, investigate, examine, research ¶ སྐད་རིགས་ ༣༣ ལ་ཞིབ་དཔྱད་བྱས་པ་རེད་ They researched 33 languages.

ཞིབ་དཔྱད་བསྡུར་བཤེར་ (shi̲bjɛɛ̀ d̲ursher) examining/ investigating/ inspecting/ researching and comparing.

ཞིབ་དཔྱོད་ (shi̲bjöö̀) procuratorial work, prosecutorial work, investigatory work; va.—བྱེད་ to do procuratorial work.

ཞིབ་དཔྱོད་ཁང་ (shi̲bjöö̀gaŋ) chief procurator (public

procurator-general).
ཞིབ་དཔྱོད་པ་ (shibjööba) procurator, prosecutor, investigator.
ཞིབ་དཔྱོད་དབང་ཆ་ (shibjöö wāŋja) right of prosecution.
ཞིབ་དཔྱོད་ཡོན་ (shibjöö yoan) tib. ch. sm. ཞིབ་དཔྱོད་ཁང་.
ཞིབ་དཔྱོད་ལས་ཁུངས་ (shibjöö lɛ̱ɛ̀guŋ) sm. ཞིབ་དཔྱོད་ཁང་.
ཞིབ་དཔྱོད་ཨུ་ཡོན་ (shibjöö ūyün) tib. ch. investigative committee, procuratorial committee.
ཞིབ་ཕོར་ (shibbɔɔ) h. of རྩམ་ཕོར་.
ཞིབ་ཕྲ་ (shibdrə) 1. detailed, thorough ¶ རྩིས་ཁྲ་ཞིབ་ཕྲ་ A detailed account. 2. precise ¶ མཐོ་རིམ་ཞིབ་ཕྲའི་ཐོན་རྫས་ High precision products.
ཞིབ་ཕྲ་རྩད་གཅོད་ (shibdrə dzɛ̀ɛjöö) detailed/ thorough investigation.
ཞིབ་འཕར་ (shimbar) shung. a new tax levied on monastic and aristocratic estates in the 1920's (organized by Lungshar).
ཞིབ་འཕར་འབབ་འབྲུ་ (shimbar bəbdru) shung. the grain obtained by the ཞིབ་འཕར་ tax.
ཞིབ་འཕར་ལས་ཁུངས་ (shimbar lɛ̱ɛ̀guŋ) the office started by Lungshar to collect the ཞིབ་འཕར་ tax.
ཞིབ་བྲ་ (shibdrə) flour made from buckwheat.
ཞིབ་བྲིས་རི་མོ་ (shibdrii) intricate/ delicate drawings or designs.
ཞིབ་འབྱེད་ (shibjeè) analyzing/ examining and distinguishing between, checking and classifying, sorting out; va.—བྱེད་ ¶ དངོས་ཆས་གསར་རྙིང་ཞིབ་འབྱེད་བྱས་པ་རེད་ They sorted the new goods from the old.
ཞིབ་དཔྱོད་ཁང་ (shibjöögaŋ) investigation office, procurator's office.
ཞིབ་འབྲི་ (shibdrii) writing in detail.
ཞིབ་མ་ (shibmə) 1. basket made of bamboo for sifting; va.—རྒྱག་ to sift with a bamboo basket.
ཞིབ་མོ་ (shibmo) sm. ཞིབ་ཞིབ་.
ཞིབ་མོལ་ (shibmüü) negotiations, discussions, talks; va.—བྱེད་.
ཞིབ་སྨྱུལ་ (shibñüü) reconnoitering/ observing in secret; va.—བྱེད་.
ཞིབ་རྩ་ (shibdzə) sm. ཞིབ་ཕྲ་.
ཞིབ་རྩད་ (shibdzɛɛ̀) detailed inquiry/ investigation; va.—གཅོད་; —བྱེད་.
ཞིབ་རྩིང་ (shibdziŋ) fine and coarse.
ཞིབ་རྩིས་ (shibdzii) shung. a thorough/ detailed calculation/ accounting; va.—ལེན་ to make a detailed accounting when sb. new takes office; va.—རྒྱག་ to calculate/ do accounts in detail.
ཞིབ་རྩོད་ (shibdzöö) detailed interrogation/ question; va.—བྱེད་.
ཞིབ་བརྩད་ (shibdzɛɛ̀) sm. ཞིབ་ཕྲ་རྩད་གཅོད་.
ཞིབ་ཚགས་ (shibdzaà) precise, detailed, thorough; va.—བྱེད་ to do in precise/ detailed/ thorough manner ¶ མི་འདི་ལས་ཀའི་ཐོག་ཞིབ་ཚགས་འདུག་ས་ This man is thorough in his work. ¶ སྨན་པས་ཞིབ་འཇུག་ཞིབ་ཚགས་བྱས་པ་རེད་ The doctor gave a thorough examination.
ཞིབ་ཚགས་ཅན་ (shib tsāgjɛn) precise, thorough, detailed ¶ ཞིབ་ཚགས་ཅན་གྱི་འཕྲུལ་འཁོར་ A precision machine.
ཞིབ་ཚགས་པོ་ (shib tsāgbo) detailed, thorough, careful, precise ¶ ལས་ཀ་གང་ལ་ཡང་ཞིབ་ཚགས་པོ་འདུག (They) are thorough in whatever work (they do).
ཞིབ་ཚགས་འཕྲུལ་ཆས་ (shibdzaa trũũjɛɛ̀) pecision instruments/ equipment.
ཞིབ་ཚགས་མེད་པ་ (shibdzaà meèba) careless, slipshod, sloppy.
ཞིབ་ཚགས་ལས་བརྒལ་བ་ (shibdzaàlɛ gɛɛwa) ultra precise, ultra precision ¶ ཞིབ་ཚགས་ལས་བརྒལ་བའི་འཕྲུལ་འཁོར་ An ultra precision machine.
ཞིབ་ཚད་ (shibdzɛɛ̀) 1. accuracy, precision. 2. measuring or checking accurately/ precisely; va.—རྒྱག.
ཞིབ་འཚོལ་ (shibdzöö) searching thoroughly/ detailed; va.—བྱེད་.
ཞིབ་ཞིབ་ (shibshib) fine (in weave or texture); va.—བཟོ་; va.—རྡོག་ to make into fine texture (such as powder/ flour) ¶ སྨན་རིགས་ཁ་ཤས་ཞིབ་ཞིབ་རྡོག་དགོས་ (We) have to pound some medicines ingredients very finely. 2. close ¶ ཐིག་ཞིབ་ཞིབ་གཉིས་ཀྱི་བར་ལ་ Between two lines that are close together.
ཞིབ་གཞིགས་ (shibshii) analyzing, investigating; va.—བྱེད་.
ཞིབ་ཞུ་ (shibshu) telling in detail (usu. to a higher person); va.—བྱེད་ ¶ ལྷ་སར་ཐེབས་རྒྱུའི་སྐོར་སོགས་ཞིབ་ཞུ་བྱས་པ་ཡིན་ I told (him) in detail about (their) coming to Lhasa, etc.
ཞིབ་གཞུང་ (shibshuŋ) shung. government edict result from an investigation/ survey of an issue (usu. land and taxes).
ཞིབ་ཟོ་ (shibso) a wooden tsamba container.
ཞིབ་གཟིགས་ (shibsii) h. of ཞིབ་ལྟ་.
ཞིབ་གཟིགས་གནང་ (shibsii nāŋ) h. of ཞིབ་ལྟ་.
ཞིབ་གཟིགས་ཆོག་མཆན་ (shibsii cɔ̄gjɛn) shung. investigating/ scrutinizing thoroughly and giving approval.
ཞིབ་བཟོ་འཕྲུལ་འཁོར་ (shibso trũũgɔɔ) milling machine for flour.
ཞིབ་རོ་ (shibro) dregs, leftover.
ཞིབ་རོགས་ (shibrɔɔ̀) an assistant/ aide.
ཞིབ་ལས་ (shiblɛɛ̀) detailed work; va.—བྱེད་ to do detailed work.
ཞིབ་ལས་ཚགས་དཀྲོལ་ (shiblɛɛ̀ tsāgdröö) detailed, fine ¶ ཞིབ་ལས་ཚགས་དཀྲོལ་གྱིས་དངུལ་ཆས་བཟོ་བ་ Making fine silverware.
ཞིབ་བཤད་ (shibshɛɛ̀) sm. ཞིབ་བརྗོད་.
ཞིབ་བཤེར་ (shibsher) checking up, inspecting, investigating, searching, examining, auditing; va.—གཏོང་; —བྱེད་ to check/ inspect/ examine/ investigate/ search ¶ ཐོན་རྫས་རེ་རེ་བཞིན་ཞིབ་བཤེར་བྱེད་ཀྱི་ཡོད་པ་རེད་ (They) inspect the products individually.
ཞིབ་བཤེར་འཁྲུན་གཅོད་ (shibsher trũnjöö) shung. coming to a verdict after an investigation; va.—བྱེད་.
ཞིབ་བཤེར་ཆོག་མཆན་ (shibsher cɔ̄gjɛn) shung. giving approval after an investigation; va.—བྱེད་.
ཞིབ་བཤེར་གཏན་འབེབས་ (shibsher dɛ̄mbeb) deciding/ finalizing after an investigation; va.—བྱེད་.
ཞིབ་བཤེར་པ་ (shibsherba) sm. ཞིབ་བཤེར་བ་.
ཞིབ་བཤེར་བ་ (shibsherwa) inspector, investigator.
ཞིབ་བཤེར་རྩིས་ལེན་ (shibsher dzīilen) investigating/ examining and then taking charge (e.g., when an office changes hands); va.—བྱེད་.
ཞིབ་བཤེར་ལས་ཁུངས་ (shibsher lɛ̱ɛ̀guŋ) shung. investigatory office, prosecutor's office.
ཞིབ་བཤེར་ས་ཚིགས་ (shibsher sədzii) checkpoint, inspection station.
ཞིབ་བཤེར་གསུམ་ (shibsher sūm) the three checkups (political slogan).
ཞིབ་ས་ (shibsə) shung. a special office established for settling a particular case.
ཞིབ་གསལ་ (shibsɛl) thorough, clear and in detail, vivid, explicit ¶ ཁོའི་འགྲོ་སོང་གི་རྩིས་ཁྲ་ཞིབ་གསལ་ A clear and detailed account of his expenditures.
ཞིབ་གསལ་སྲིད་ཇུས་ (shibsɛl sīijüü) specific/ detailed/ explicit policy.
ཞིབ་གསེད་ཕྱེ་འབྱེད་ (shibseè shɛ̄njeè) investigating and differentiating or classifying; va.—བྱེད་.
ཞིབ་གསོལ་ (shibsüü) telling in detail; va.—བྱེད་ to tell in detail.
ཞིབ་ལྷིང་ (shiblhiŋ) person who is reliable/ dependable and meticulous.
ཞིབ་ལྷུག (shiblhug) discussing openly/ frankly and in detail; va.—བྱེད་.

ཞིབ་ལྷོངས་ (shiblhoŋ) shung. reporting in detail; va.—ཞུ་ to report/ tell in detail.

ཞིབ་ལྷོད་ (shiblhöö) (discussing/ talking in a manner that is) leisurely and in detail.

ཞིམ་ (shim) 1. abbr. of ཞིམ་པོ་. 2. abbr. of ཞིམ་མོ་.

ཞིམ་དགུ་ (shimgu) all the delicious food.

ཞིམ་མངར་ (shimŋar) sweet tasting ། ཞིམ་མངར་རྒུན་འབྲུམ་ Sweet tasting grapes.

ཞིམ་ལྷོ་ (shimlho) tasty, delicious.

ཞིམ་པ་ (shimbə) sm. ཞིམ་པོ་.

ཞིམ་པོ་ (shimbu) tasty, delicious.

ཞིམ་ཕྲུག (shimdruù) kitten.

ཞིམ་བུ་ (shimbu) tasty, delicious.

ཞིམ་རྩེད་ (shimdzeè) cats playing when they are in heat.

ཞིམ་རྫས་འབྲུག་མཆིལ་ (shimzεὲ drugjii) ambergris.

ཞིམ་ཞིམ་མངར་མངར་ (shimshim, ŋārŋar) delicious, tasty.

ཞིམ་ཟས་ (shimsεὲ) delicious foods.

ཞིམ་ཤིང་ (shimshiŋ) sm. ཤུམ་རྩ་.

ཞིའན་ཐྲན་གྱེན་ལངས་ (shiandün gyenlaŋ) ch.tib. Taiping rebellion/ uprising.

ཞིས་ཨན་ (shian) Xi'an.

ཞུ་: p. ཞུས་; f. ཞུ་; imp. ཞུས་ (shu) 1. va. to tell, to say, to ask ། ངས་ཁོང་ལ་བཀའ་འདྲི་ཞུ་གི་ཡིན་ I will ask him. ། ངས་ཁོང་ལ་ཞུ་གི་ཡིན་ I will tell him. 2. va. to ask a superior for sth. ། མ་འགྲོ་གོང་ལ་ཡཀའ་གྲོལ་ཞུ་དགོས་ One should ask for permission before one goes. ། ངས་ཁོང་གདན་འདྲེན་ཞུས་པ་ཡིན་ I invited him (asked him to come). 3. va. to receive/ get sth. from a superior ། ངས་ཁོང་གི་ཕྱག་ནས་ཞུས་པ་ཡིན་ I got it from him (his hands). 4. va. to be called ། ཁོང་ལ་རྡོ་རྗེ་ལགས་ཞུ་བ་རེད་ He is called Dorje. 5. va. to eat/ drink ། ད་ང་གསོལ་ཇ་ཞུ་གི་མིན་ I will not have tea now.

ཞུ་: p. ཞུས་; f. ཞུ་ (shu) vi. to melt (unintentionally/ spontaneously).

ཞུ་བསྐུལ་ (shugüü) appealing, requesting; va.—བྱེད་; —ཞུ་ to make an appeal/ request.

ཞུ་སྐྱོག (shugyɔɔ̀) ladle.

ཞུ་ཁ་མ་ལོན་ (shu kā malön) shung. not being able to report/ explain sth. to superiors.

ཞུ་ཁུ་ (shugu) liquid resulting from melting sth.

ཞུ་མཁན་ (shuñεn) sm. ཞུ་བ་པོ་.

ཞུ་མཁན་འབྲས་བུ་ (shuñεn drεὲbu) loquat (the tree and its fruits).

ཞུ་ཁྲ་ (shudra) shung. a petition/ request and the verdict or decision.

ཞུ་གོ་འཕེར་ (shu kober) sm. གོ་འཕེར་.

ཞུ་གླེང་ (shuleŋ) reporting orally/ verbally; va.—བྱེད་.

ཞུ་འགབ་མཆིས་མིན་ (shugəb cii min) shung. whether (this) is appropriate to do or not (a standard ending to a request to a superior) ། དེ་འདྲ་ཞུ་འགབ་མཆིས་མིན་བཀའ་ལན་ཡོད་པ་ཞུ་ Please give me an answer whether it is appropriate to do like that or not.

ཞུ་རྒྱ་ (shugya) shung. sealed letter (to a superior).

ཞུ་བརྒྱུད་ (shugyüü) helping on behalf of sb. in dealing with higher authorities, mediator; va.—བྱེད་ ། ཆོག་མཆན་ཞུ་རྒྱུ་དེ་ཁོང་གིས་གོང་རིམ་ལ་ཞུ་བརྒྱུད་བྱས་བྱུང་ He acted on my behalf with the higher authorities to obtain permission.

ཞུ་སྒོ་ (shugo) 1. shung. duty, responsibility ། ཡུལ་གྱི་བདེ་འཇགས་སྲུང་ཡས་ནི་སྐོར་བའི་ཞུ་སྒོ་རེད་ Safeguarding the peace of the region is the duty of the police. 2. all the work, activities ། འགོ་ཁྲིད་དེ་འཁོར་ཞག་ལ་མ་འགྲོ་གོང་ལས་ཁུངས་ཀི་སྒོ་རྣམས་གཤམ་རིམ་ལ་མངགས་པ་རེད་ Before the band went on vacation, he assigned all the work of his office to his subordinates.

ཞུ་སྒོ་འཐུས་ཚང་ (shugo tũüdzaŋ) shung. completing/ accomplishing (one's) work and tasks; va.—ཞུ་ ། ཞབས་འདེགས་ཞུ་སྒོ་འཐུས་ཚང་ཞུས་པ་རེད་ (He) completed his work serving (his lord).

ཞུ་ངོ་ (shuŋo) sm. ཞུས་ངོ་.

ཞུ་ངོ་མགྲོན་བརྒྱུད་ (shuŋo dröngyüü) shung. reporting to a higher official through his chamberlain/ aide.

ཞུ་ངོ་འཐེན་ (shuŋo tēn) va. to ask for a favor/ concession for sb. else. ། སློབ་ཕྲུག་གིས་སྒྲིག་ལམ་འགལ་བར་ཆད་པ་མེད་པ་ཞིག་ཕ་མས་དགེ་རྒན་ལ་ཞུ་ངོ་འཐེན་པ་རེད་ The parents asked the teacher not to punish the student for violating the regulation.

ཞུ་ཆག (shujaà) shung. requesting and giving a reduction/ concession ། བུ་ལོན་རྣམས་ཞུ་ཆག་ཆོག་གི་མ་རེད་ One is not permitted to request or give reductions for these loans.

ཞུ་ཆས་ (shujεὲ) shung. gift when requesting sth.

ཞུ་ཆུང་ (shujuŋ) shung. the junior proofreader.

ཞུ་ཆེན་ (shujen) the main proofreader.

ཞུ་མཆིད་ (shujii) 1. a letter. 2. discussion, conversation, talking.

ཞུ་སྙན་པ་ (shuñεmba) person who submits a report.

ཞུ་རྙོག་ཀ་ཀོར་ (shuñog gāgɔɔ) causing complications and creating disorder; va.—བྱེད་.

ཞུ་གཏུག (shuduù) 1. appealing (to authorities) about an issue, taking a case to court; va.—བྱེད་; —རྒྱག.

ཞུ་གཏུག་པ་ (shudugba) sm. ཞུ་གཏུག་བྱེད་མཁན་.

ཞུ་གཏུག་བྱེད་མཁན་ (shuduù ceēñεn) plaintiff, accuser, complainant.

ཞུ་གདུགས་ (shuduù) sm. ཞུ་གཏུག.

ཞུ་རྟགས་སུ་ཕུལ་ (shudagsu pǖǖ) shung. reporting with one's signature (usu. written at the end of a report or petition).

ཞུ་རྟེན་ (shuden) 1. a present/ gift given when asking a favor from sb. 2. a flower or ceremonial scarf sent with a letter.

ཞུ་ཐབ་ (shudəb) smelting furnace.

ཞུ་ཐོ་ (shuto) written petition, written request.

ཞུ་ཐོ་འགོ་མཆན་ (shuto gojεn) shung. a notation made on a report ། ཞུ་ཐོ་འགོ་མཆན་དུ་གཞིས་ཀའི་ཁ་འཛིན་མུ་མཐུད་འཛགས་གནས་སོང་བ་ཞལ་གསལ་འཁོད་ It was written clearly in the notation made on the report that we can take possession of the estate continuously.

ཞུ་ཐོ་ཕུལ་བའི་ཕྱིར་ཞིབས་ (shuto pǖüwε ciibeè) shung. a response to a report ། གྱོད་གཞི་དེའི་སྐོར་དོ་བདག་ནས་ཞུ་ཐོ་ཕུལ་བའི་ཕྱིར་ཞིབས་སུ་ As for the response to the report regarding the lawsuit made by the protagonist.

ཞུ་དག (shudaà) proofreading, correcting mistakes; va.—བྱེད་; —གཏོང་ ། ཞུ་དག་ཞིབ་ཚགས་ Careful proofreading.

ཞུ་དག་ཁང་ (shudaàgaŋ) proofreading/ proofreader's office.

ཞུ་དག་དང་པོ་ (shudaà taŋbo) the first proofreading.

ཞུ་དོན་ (shudön) shung. the points being petitioned/ appealed/ requested ། ཁྲིམས་ཁང་ནས་གྱོད་ཡ་གཉིས་ཀྱི་ཞུ་དོན་ལ་ཞིབ་འཇུག་མཐར་ཕྱིན་བྱས་རེད་ The court investigated thoroughly all the points raised by the two disputants.

ཞུ་འདུལ་ (shudüü) smelting; va.—བྱེད་.

ཞུ་འདེགས་ (shudeg) sm. ཞུ་རྟེན་.

ཞུ་ལྡེབ་ (shudeb) notes/ letters attached to the main letter.

ཞུ་སྣ་ (shuna) sm. ཞུ་ངོས་.

ཞུ་སྣོད་ (shunöö) smelting pot.

ཞུ་ནོར་ (shunɔɔ) making a mistake in saying sth., saying the wrong thing; vi.—ཐེབས་.

ཞུ་གནང་མཛད་ (shunaŋ dzεὲ) h. of ཞུ་.

ཞུ་ཕོད་ཆེན་པོ་ (shuböö cēmbo) sb. who is unafraid to speak or make a request to one's superiors or to the authorities.

ཞུ་ཕྱོགས་ནོར་ (shujɔɔ nɔɔ) h. of ནོར་ཕྱོགས་ནོར་.

ཞུ་འཕྲིན་ (shundrin) h. of འཕྲིན་ཡིག.

ཞུ་བ་ (shuwə) petitioning, appealing, requesting; va.—འབུལ་ to petition, to appeal, to make a request; va.—ཞིན་; —བཞེས་ to hear a petition/ appeal/ request; to cross-examine/ inquire into a petition/ appeal/ request, to interrogate; va.—

འཐེན་ to make a plea for sth.

ཞུ་བ་པོ་ (shuwəbo) petitioner, appealer, requester.

ཞུ་བ་གློང་འབེབས་ (shuwə lōŋbeb) shung. a mediator having a case returned from court so that he can try to settle it through mediation.

ཞུ་བའི་ཁམས་ (shuwɛ kām) 1. melted liquids. 2. sperm.

ཞུ་བྱ་ (shuja) sm. ཞུ་སྒོ་.

ཞུ་བྱས་ (shujɛɛ̀) 1. shung. a payment/ gift traditionally paid when asking for a loan. 2. asking for sth.; va.—བྱེད་.

ཞུ་བྱུས་ (shujüü) planning to report sth. to authorities; va.—བྱེད་ ། གནས་ཚུལ་དེའི་སྐོར་ཁོང་གིས་ལས་ཁུངས་ལ་ཞུ་བྱུས་བྱེད་ཀྱི་འདུག He is planning to report about this matter to the authorities.

ཞུ་བྱེད་ (shujeè) solvent, a substance that helps to melt sth.

ཞུ་བྱེད་ཀྱི་སྨན་ (shujeègi mɛ̄n) medicine that helps digestion.

ཞུ་བྱེད་དངོས་པོ་ (shujeè ŋȫöbo) sm. ཞུ་བྱེད་.

ཞུ་བྱེད་དྲོད་ཚད་ (shujeè tröödzɛɛ̀) melting temperature.

ཞུ་དབང་མེད་པ་ (shuwaŋ meèba) shung. not letting sb. say sth. or respond ། གནས་ལུགས་ཞུ་དབང་མེད་པར་ལམ་སེང་ཉེས་གཏགས་པ་རེད་ Without letting (them) say anything (he) whipped them.

ཞུ་དབང་མེད་པར་མགོ་འདོགས་ (shuwaŋ meèbar go dɔ̀ɔ) unconditional surrender.

ཞུ་འབུལ་ (shumbüü) 1. petitioning/ requesting to superiors; va.—བྱེད་. 2. sm. ཞུ་བ་འཐེན་.

ཞུ་འབོད་ (shumböö) shung. making a report/ appeal of hardship to a superior; va.—བྱེད་ ། མི་དམངས་ཚོས་སྲིད་གཞུང་ལ་སྡུག་བསྔལ་ཞུ་འབོད་བྱས་པ་རེད་ The people appealed to the government about their suffering.

ཞུ་འབོད་ཡི་གེ་ (shumböö yigi) a letter of ཞུ་འབོད་.

ཞུ་སྦྱོར་ (shujɔɔ) shung. reporting/ filing a case to legal authorities.

ཞུ་སྦྱོར་སྔ་མ་ (shujɔɔ ŋāma) plaintiff.

ཞུ་སྦྱོར་ཕྱི་མ་ (shujɔɔ cīmə) defendant.

ཞུ་མར་ (shumaa) lamp; va.—སྦྱོར་ to light a lamp; va.—གསོད་ to turn off a lamp.

ཞུ་མེད་ས་འཁྱག (shumeè sāgyaà) permafrost (soil).

ཞུ་མོས་ལྟར་ (shumöödar) as (stated) in a request/ appeal ། བཀྲ་ཤིས་ཀྱི་ཞུ་མོས་ལྟར་གཞུང་གིས་ལག་ལེན་བསྟར་ The government acted in accordance with Tashi's request.

ཞུ་སྨན་ (shumɛn) sm. ཞུ་བྱེད་.

ཞུ་ཙམ་ཞིག་བྱེད་ (shudzamshig ceè) va. to just tell sth. to superiors/ authorities (i.e., to not insist/ press).

ཞུ་ཚིག (shudzii) 1. shung. deposition, testimony, affidavit. 2. the content of a petition, notes taken while sb. is being questioned; va.—བྲི་; —འབེབས་. 3. a request.

ཞུ་ཚིག་ཟིན་ཐོ་ (shudzii sindo) interrogation/ questioning notes.

ཞུ་མཚུན་རྩལ་འགྲན་ (shudzün tsɛ̄ndrɛn) boxing.

ཞུ་འཚང་བྱེད་ (shudzaŋ ceè) va. to shove/ push/ squeeze in to ask a superior for sth.

ཞུ་འཛོལ་ (shudzöö) sm. ཞུ་ནོར་.

ཞུ་རྫས་ (shudzɛɛ̀) sm. ཞུ་བྱེད་.

ཞུ་ཞུ་དག་དག (shushu tagdaà) sm. མགོ་འདྲིན་འཚོལ་.

ཞུ་ཞི་ཆེན་པོ་ (shushe cēmbo) shung. a person/ official who easily agrees to the requests of others.

ཞུ་བཞེས་ (shu sheè) sm. ཞུ་བ་བཞེས་.

ཞུ་བཞེས་བདེན་རྫུན་གྱི་ཞལ་ལྕེ་ (shusheè dendzüngi shɛɛje) shung. one of the sixteen laws that deals with interrogating two parties in a dispute to learn the truth.

ཞུ་ཡིག (shuyii) 1. shung. written petition/ appeal/ request/ application/ message; va.—འབུལ་ to submit a written petition/ appeal/ request/ application. 2. a summary of one's life from age eight that was written in a law case or in prison (in PRC).

ཞུ་ཡིག་གི་ཆིངས་ (shuyiìgi cīŋ) a piece of paper in which petitions are rolled.

ཞུ་ཡིག་མགོ་མཆན་ (shuyiì gonjɛn) shung. a petition/ request on the top of which the superior official has written a decision and placed a seal it.

ཞུ་ཡིག་ཆེ་ཐང་མ་ (shuyiì cēdaŋma) shung. an important petition/ request.

ཞུ་འོད་ (shuwöö) light from a lamp.

ཞུ་འོས་ (shuwöö) sth. that is worthy/ deserving/ appropriate/ suitable to be said.

ཞུ་རལ་ (shurɛɛ) the torn hem of a dress.

ཞུ་རེ་ཀ་ཀོར་ (shure gāgɔɔ) delaying by dillydallying and requesting things (when receiving a superior's order).

ཞུ་ལན་ (shulɛn) questioning, interrogating; va.—ལེན་; —འབུལ་ ། ཞིབ་དཔྱོད་པས་ཞུ་ལན་རེ་གཉིས་བླངས་ The prosecutor questioned (them) once or twice.

ཞུ་ལི་ཡ་ (shuliya) Syria.

ཞུ་ལེན་པ་ (shulemba) interrogator.

ཞུ་ལོག (shulɔɔ̀) shung. causing trouble for someone by lying/ or instigating a higher authority; va.—རྒྱག; —འབུལ་.

ཞུ་བཤགས (shushaà) expressing regret, repenting; va.—འབུལ་; —བྱེད་.

ཞུ་ཤོག (shushɔɔ̀) 1. shung. a petition/ document submitted to a court. 2. sm. ཞུ་ཡིག.

ཞུ་བཤེར་ (shusher) asking questions and investigating (usu. in a dispute or court case); va.—རྒྱག ། ང་ཚོས་གྲོད་གཞི་དེའི་སྐོར་ཞུ་བཤེར་ཐེངས་མང་བྱས་པ་རེད་ We questioned and investigated the case many times.

ཞུ་སླའི་དངོས་རྫས་ (shulɛ ŋȫödzɛɛ̀) foodstuffs that are easy to digest.

ཞུ་སློག (shulɔɔ̀) turning down or deciding against a lawsuit/ legal case/ dispute; va.—བྱེད་.

ཞུ་གསོལ་ (shusüü) 1. sm. ཞུ་དོན་. 2. asking/ requesting; va.—བྱེད་ 3. in letters this is a phrase that indicates that the body of the letter follows.

ཞུ་ཧམ་ (shuham) 1. asking boldly/ arrogantly. 2. informing falsely.

ཞུ་ལྷད་ (shulhɛɛ̀) a false report/ statement.

ཞུགས་ (shuù) 1. va. to participate in, to attend ། གྲོས་ཚོགས་སུ་ཞུགས་མཁན་ Those participating in the meeting. 2. va. to join ། བཅིང་འགྲོལ་དམག་གི་ནང་དུ་ཞུགས་པ་རེད་ (He) joined the People's Liberation Army. 3. a term that makes honorifics ། ཞུགས་ཆར་ Rain. 4. arc. sm. སྲོན་མེ་.

ཞུགས་མཁན་ (shuùñɛn) participant, attendant.

ཞུགས་ཆར་ (shuùjar) h. of ཆར་པ་.

ཞུགས་ཉི་ (shuùñi) h. of ཉི་མ་.

ཞུགས་ཉི་དཔང་འཛུགས་ (shuùñi bāŋdzuù) swearing by the sun as witness; va.—བྱེད་.

ཞུགས་གཏོང་ (shugdoŋ) sending to join an organization; va.—བྱེད་ ། མི་ཚང་དེའི་ཕྲུ་གུ་གཅིག་དམག་མིར་ཞུགས་གཏོང་བྱས་པ་རེད་ That family sent one of its children to join the army.

ཞུགས་འཐུས་ (shugdüü) 1. permission to participate/ join ། ཁོས་སྲིད་དོན་ཚོགས་པར་ཞུགས་འཐུས་ཀྱི་བཀའ་འཁྲོལ་བ་རེད་ He got permission to participate in the political party. ། ཁྱེད་རང་སློབ་གྲྭར་ཞུགས་འཐུས་ཆོག་པའི་ཡི་གེ་འབུལ་རྩིས་ཡོད་པས་ Do you plan to submit a request to enter the school?

ཞུགས་འཐུས་ལག་འཛིན་ (shugdüü ləŋdzin) entrance/ admission ticket.

ཞུགས་གནམ་ (shugnam) h. of གནམ་གཤིས་.

ཞུགས་སྣུམ་ (shugnum) h. of སྣུམ་.

ཞུགས་འབུལ་ (shuŋbüü) cremation (h.); va.—བྱེད་ to cremate.

ཞུགས་སྦྱང་ (shugjaŋ) sm. ཞུགས་འབུལ་.

ཞུགས་མར་ (shugmaa) sm. ཞུ་མར་.

ཞུགས་མེ་ (shoome) h. of མེ་.

ཞུགས་ལམ་ (shuùlam) h. of. འགྲོ་ལམ་.

ཞུགས་ཤིང་ (shuùshiŋ) h. of མེ་ཤིང་.

ཞུགས་ལྷུགས་ (shuùlhaà) h. of ལྷུགས་པ་.

ཞུགས་སྔོང་སློབ་གྲྭ་ (shuùñoŋ lōbdra) one's former school, alma mater.

ཞུང་ནུའུ་ (shuŋnu) Huns.

ཞུང་ཡ་ལི་ (shuŋyali) Hungary.

ཞུད་ (shüù) 1. vi. to be peeling off, to fade ། དབ་ལོག་འདིའི་ཚོན་ཞུད་བཞག The color on this clothing has faded. 2. vi. to be too little/ low (to reach a certain weight on a scale) ། རྒྱ་མ་དོག་ཙམ་ཞུད་བཞག མར་ཁ་སྣོན་རྒྱག་དགོས་ The it is a little low on the wieghing scale. Add some more butter. 3. vi. to deteriorate/ decline ། བར་ལམ་ཁོང་སྙུང་ནས་ལུས་སྟོབས་ཞུད་བཞག Recently he has been sick and his physical strength has deteriorated. 4. rolling two or more strands of thread/ yarn together to make one; va.—རྒྱག ། སྐུད་པ་འདི་ཞུད་རྒྱག་དགོས་ You have to spin the thread (to make two-ply).

ཞུད་འཁལ་ (shüù kɛɛ) va. to spin a thread/ yarn.

ཞུད་ལྡ་ (shüùdaà) a tool for rolling two or more strands of thread/ yarn together to make one.

ཞུད་ཐག (shüùdaà) a dangling rope/ string.

ཞུད་མ་ (shüùmə) a high quality woven woolen material.

ཞུད་འོག (shüùwɔ̀ɔ) medium quality woven woolen material.

ཞུན་ (shün) 1. sm. ཞུ་མ་. 2. melted, molten ། སེར་ཞུན་ Melted gold.

ཞུན་ཆུ་ (shünju) molten ། ངར་ལྕགས་ཞུན་ཆུ་ Molten steel.

ཞུན་ཐབ་ (shündəb) smelting furnace.

ཞུན་ཐར་ (shündar) 1. smelting and refining, va.—གཅོད་, —སྐོལ་ to smelt. 2. scrutinizing, investigating, examining, va.—གཅོད་, —སྐོལ་ to clear up sth. by scrutinizing/ examining.

ཞུན་ཐར་ཆོད་ (shündar cȫò) vi. to have one's doubts/ suspicions/ hesitation cleared up due to investigation/ examination.

ཞུན་ཐིགས་ (shündiì) 1. molten drops. 2. crystallization; vi.—ཆགས་ to crystallize.

ཞུན་ཐིགས་བསྐྱར་དུ་ཆགས་ (shündiì gyārdu cāà) vi. to recrystallize.

ཞུན་ཐིགས་སླར་ཆགས་ (shündiì lārjaà) sm. ཞུན་ཐིགས་བསྐྱར་དུ་ཆགས་.

ཞུན་དག (shündaà) thorough, intensive.

ཞུན་དག་པོ་ (shün tagbo) doing thoroughly/ carefully ། མི་དེ་རྒྱུན་དུ་ལས་ཀ་ཞུན་དག་པོ་བྱེད་མཁན་ཞིག་རེད་ That person is sb. who always does his work thoroughly.

ཞུན་རྡར་ (shündar) sm. ཞུན་བརྡར་.

ཞུན་རྡོ་ (shündo) lava rock.

ཞུན་བརྡར་ (shündar) training, disciplining, practicing; va.—གཅོད་; —བྱེད་.

ཞུན་པ་ (shümba) sm. ཞུན་མ་.

ཞུན་པོར་ (shümbɔɔ) beaker/ flask (used in a laboratory).

ཞུན་བུམ་ (shümbum) sm. ཞུན་པོར་.

ཞུན་བྲག (shündraà) sm. ཞུན་རྡོ་.

ཞུན་མ་ (shünmə) melted, molten, liquefied ། མར་ཞུན་མ་ Melted butter.

ཞུན་མར་ (shünmar) melted butter.

ཞུབ་ (shub) 1. abbr. of ཞུབ་པ་. 2. va. to put on armor.

ཞུབ་པ་ (shubbə) armor.

ཞུབ་ཅན་ (shünjɛn) having armor, armored.

ཞུམ་ (shum) 1. vi. to be disheartened/ discouraged, to be low in spirits, to lose confidence ། ལན་གཅིག་དཀའ་ངལ་དང་འཕྲད་པར་སེམས་ཞུམ་རྒྱུ་མེད་ (One) shouldn't be disheartened at encountering a problem. 2. vi. to fear, to be afraid ། ཁོ་ཚོའི་དམག་ཤུགས་ལ་ང་ཚོ་ཞུམ་དགོས་མ་རེད་ (We) need not fear their military power. 3. abbr. of ཞུམ་བུ་.

ཞུམ་སྐད་ (shumgɛɛ̀) crying/ yelling with fright; vi.—ཤོར་ to cry out in fright.

ཞུམ་ཉམས་ (shumñam) weakness, fear, timidity; va.—སྟོན་ to show one's weakness.

ཞུམ་རྟགས་ (shumdaà) sign of weakness/ fear/ timidity/ cowardice; vi.—སྟོན་ to show weakness/ fear/ timidity/ cowardice.

ཞུམ་པ་མེད་པ་ (shumbə meèba) dauntless, fearless, courageous.

ཞུམ་ཕྲུག (shumdruù) kitten.

ཞུམ་བུ་ (shumbu) cat.

ཞུམ་བུའི་མཇུག་མར་རས་ཐུལ་བཏགས་པ་ལྟར་ (shumbüü jugmaa rɛɛ̀düü dāgbadar) following sb. wherever he goes [Lit. like attaching a ribbon on a cat's tail].

ཞུམ་བུའི་ཨ་སྟོང་ཙམ་ (shumbüü ādoŋdzam) a very short time, a moment [Lit. as much as the yawning of a cat].

ཞུམ་མེད་ (shummeè) sm. ཞུམ་པ་མེད་པ་.

ཞུམ་མེད་སྟོབས་ལྡན་ (shummeè dōbdɛn) courageous/ fearless and strong.

ཞུམ་མེད་སྲི་ཞུ་ (shummeè sīshu) performing a task without being disheartened/ discouraged; va.—བྱེད་.

ཞུམ་འཛེར་ (shumdzer) shy and bashful; vi.—བྱེད་ to be shy.

ཞུམ་ཞུམ་ (shumshum) crouching position (as that of a cat before pouncing).

ཞུམ་བཤོལ་ (shumshöö) shrinking away from, shying away from; va.—བྱེད་.

ཞུར་ (shur) going straight ། རྟ་ཞུར་གྱིས་རྒྱུགས་པ་རེད་ The horse ran straight.

ཞུར་ཐག (shurdaà) a rope used to slide down from a height.

ཞུལ་ (shüü) 1. va. to stroke (one's) beard/ head/ hair. 2. vi. to lessen/ fall/ decrease in amount.

ཞུལ་ཞུལ་ (shüüshüü) stroking (head, hair, beard); va.—བྱེད་.

ཞུས་ (shüù) p. of ཞུ་.

ཞུས་འགྲོལ་ (shüùtröö) getting permission after asking for sth. (usu. for leave of absence) ། ཁོང་དགོངས་པ་ཞུས་འགྲོལ་གྱིས་ནང་དུ་ལོག་པ་རེད་ He asked and received permission for leaving and returned home.

ཞུས་ངོ་ (shüùŋo) 1. doing sth. because of one's connection/ friendship with sb. ། ངས་གྲོགས་པོའི་ཞུས་ངོར་བལྟས་ནས་ཁྱེད་རང་ལ་ཁང་པ་གཡར་པ་ཡིན་ Because of (your) relationship with my friend, I rented you the house. ། ཁོང་གིས་ངའི་ཞུ་ངོ་བྱས་ནས་ཁྱེད་རང་ལ་ཁང་པ་གཡར་པ་ཡིན་ He is using his relationships to search for a job for me.

ཞུས་ཆེན་ (shüùjen) professor.

ཞུས་དག (shüùdaà) proofreading; va.—བྱེད་; —གཏོང་ to proofread, to check through.

ཞུས་དག་པ་ (shüùdaàba) proofreader.

ཞུས་དག་གཏན་འབེབས་ (shüùdaà dɛ̄mbem) final proofreading, finalizing a ms.; va.—བྱེད་.

ཞུས་ཆུང་ (shüùjuŋ) title of assistant professor in translation work.

ཞུས་ཆེན་ (shüùjen) title of professor in translation work.

ཞུས་ཆེན་ལོ་ཙཱ་བ་ (shüùjen lodzawa) sm. ཞུས་ཆེན་.

ཞུས་སྙིགས་ (shüùñig) slag.

ཞུས་འབྲས་ (shündrɛɛ̀) result/ decision of an appeal ། བོད་གཞུང་ནས་ང་ཚོའི་སྙན་ཞུར་ཞུས་འབྲས་གང་ཡང་ཐོན་མ་སོང་ No result came from the Tibetan Government regarding our appeal.

ཞུས་ཙང་ (shüùdzaŋ) that's right (Lhasa slang).

ཞུས་རྫས་ (shüùdzɛɛ̀) material/ substance to be melted.

ཞུས་ཡིག (shüùyiì) sm. ཞུ་ཡིག.

ཞུས་ལི་ཡ་ (shüùliyə) Syria.

ཞུས་ལེན་ (shüùlem) asking for and receiving/ getting; va.—བྱེད་.

ཞུས་བསྲེས་དངོས་པོ་ (shüùseè ŋȫòbo) the materials mixed through smelting/ melting.

ཞེ་ (she) 1. numerical particle for the forties ། ཞེ་བཅུ་ཞེ་གཉིས་ Forty two. 2. deep down, innermost (in feelings) ། ཁ་ཞེ་གཉིས་མེད་ Sincere [Lit.

without a difference between surface and inner]. 3. type, kind.

ཞེ་གླུད་པར་རྒྱག (she lɛɛ̀bargyaà) hurting deeply ¶ མོས་ང་ཞེ་གླུད་པར་རྒྱག་པ་བཏོས་བྱུང་ She hurt me deeply.

ཞེ་བཀོན་ (shegön) bitter hatred, hostility from deep down; va.—བྱེད་.

ཞེ་བཀམ་ (she gām) va. to envy ¶ གཞན་གྱི་རྒྱུ་ནོར་ལ་ཞེ་ཀམ་ནས་ Envying the wealth of others.

ཞེ་བཀམ་ཅན་ (shegamjɛn) greedy, covetous, envious.

ཞེ་སྐྱུག་སྤྲོ་ (shegyuù tro) vi. to vomit.

ཞེ་སྐྱིད་ (shegyeè) sm. ཉར་ཐག.

ཞེ་ཁ་ (shega) 1. what one says and really feels. 2. disliking, hating.

ཞེ་ཁྲེལ་ (shedree) va. to dislike, to hate.

ཞེ་ཁོན་ (shegön) sm. ཞེ་འཁོན་.

ཞེ་འཁམ་ (shengam) vi. to be angry/ agitated/ annoyed.

ཞེ་འཁོན་ (shegön) hatred ¶ གྲལ་རིམ་གྱི་ཞེ་འཁོན་ Class hatred.

ཞེ་འཁོན་སྡང་འཛིན་ (shegön dəŋdzin) sm. ཞེ་འཁོན་.

ཞེ་འཁྲེལ་ (shedree) sm. ཞེ་ཁྲལ་.

ཞེ་གྱོང་ (shegyoŋ) sm. གྱོང་པོ་.

ཞེ་དགུ་ (shigu) 1. forty nine. 2. the 49th day after sb. died; vi.—རྫོགས་ to be the end of the 49 days of mourning after a person dies.

ཞེ་མགུ་ (shegu) liking/ loving very much.

ཞེ་འགྲང་ (she draŋ) vi. to have been satisfied/ fulfilled.

ཞེ་འགྲས་ (shedrɛɛ̀) animosity, hostility, hate.

ཞེ་འགྲས་འཁོན་འགྲས་ (shedrɛɛ̀ kōndrɛɛ̀) hatred, animosity, hating; va.—བཟོ་ to cause hatred/ animosity.

ཞེ་རྒོད་ (shīegöö̀) volatile, quick-tempered, aggressive; vi.—འཁྲུགས་ to get angry.

ཞེ་སྒུག (sheguù) 1. waiting for a result; va. ཞེ་སྒུག;—བྱེད་. 2. keeping in mind one's hatred and waiting to take revenge; va. ཞེ་སྒུག; va.— བྱེད་.

ཞེ་བརྒྱད་ (shebgyɛɛ̀) forty eight.

ཞེ་ངན་པ་ (sheŋɛmba) a mean/ cruel person.

ཞེ་ལྔ་ (sheŋa) forty five.

ཞེ་གཅིག (shijiì) 1. forty one. 2. only, solely ¶ ངས་ཤ་ཞེ་གཅིག་ཉོས་པ་ཡིན་ I bought only meat.

ཞེ་གཅོད་ (she jöö̀) va. to hurt/ upset ¶ མི་རྣམས་ཀྱི་ཞེ་གཅོད་པའི་སྐད་ཆ་ཤོད་མི་རུང་ It is wrong to say (things) that upset a person.

ཞེ་བཅད་དྲག་པོ་ (shejɛɛ̀ tragbo) making up one's mind, deciding to do sth.; va.—བཟོག.

ཞེ་ཆགས་ (shejaà) sm. སེམས་ཆགས་.

ཞེ་འཇམ་ (shenjam) kind, gentle.

ཞེ་གཉིས་ (shiñiì) forty two.

ཞེ་གཏིང་ (shediŋ) deep in one's heart, deep down ¶ ཞེ་གཏིང་ལ་གཞུང་འདིའི་འོག་སློབ་སྦྱོང་དང་ལས་ཀ་བྱེད་འདོད་མེད་ཀྱང་ Although deep down (I) had no desire to study and work under this government.

ཞེ་ཐག་པ་ (shedagba) sincerely, truly, deeply felt ¶ ཞེ་ཐག་པ་ནས་ངོ་རྒོལ་བྱས་པ་རེད་ (They) sincerely opposed it.

ཞེ་ཐོགས་པ་ (she tōgba) sm. ཞེ་ཐོགས་ས་.

ཞེ་ཐོགས་ས་ (she tɔ̄ɔ̀gsa) sb. or sth. to be worried about ¶ ཕ་མ་གཉིས་ཀྱི་ཞེ་ཐོགས་ས་དེ་བུ་གཅིག་བུ་དེ་ཡིན་ For the parents, the thing they worried about was their only son.

ཞེ་མཐུན་ (shedün) compatible, in agreement, harmonious, with one heart.

ཞེ་དྲག (shedraà) much, many, a lot, very ¶ ཁོས་དཔེ་ཆ་ཞེ་དྲག་ཀློག་ཡོད་པ་རེད་ He has read many books. ¶ དེའི་ནང་ལ་ཡོང་མཁན་ཞེ་དྲག་ཉུང་ཉུང་རེད་ There are very few people who come there.

ཞེ་དྲགས་ (shedraà) sm. ཞེ་དྲག.

ཞེ་དྲུག (shedruù) forty six.

ཞེ་བདུན་ (shibdün) forty seven.

ཞེ་འདོད་ (shendöö̀) desire, wish, aspiration, hope ¶ རང་ཉིད་ཁོ་རའི་ཞེ་འདོད་འགྲུབ་ཆེད་དུ་ In order to fulfill one's own desires.

ཞེ་ལྡོག (shedɔɔ̀) sm. ཞེ་ལོག.

ཞེ་སྡང་ (shedaŋ) hatred, anger, animosity; va.—འཛིན་;—བྱེད་ to hate, to be angry (with).

ཞེ་སྡང་སྤྲ་གཟེངས་ (shedaŋ drāseŋ) exceptionally angry [Lit. hairs standing on end].

ཞེ་སྡང་གིས་འཆིང་ (shedaŋgi cīŋ) vi. to be filled with hatred/ anger/ animosity.

ཞེ་སྡང་མཉམ་སྐྱེས་ (shedaŋ ñamgyeè) sharing/ shared hatred.

ཞེ་སྡང་བྱེད་རེས་ (shedaŋ cɛɛ̀reè) hating one another reciprocally; va.—བྱེད་.

ཞེ་ན་ (shena) sm. ཟེར་ན་.

ཞེ་ནག་གཏིང་ནས་འཁྲུག (she nagdiŋnɛ trūù) vi. to have/ get deep hatred.

ཞེ་ནད་ (shenɛɛ̀) deeply held hatred.

ཞེ་ནད་འཁོན་འཛིན་ (shenɛɛ̀ kōndzin) sm. ཞེ་ནད་.

ཞེ་ནས་ (shenɛɛ̀) from deep down, deeply, sincerely ¶ དེ་ནི་ཞེ་ནས་དགའ་པོ་བྱེད་དགོས་པ་ཞིག་རེད་ This is sth. one should sincerely like.

ཞེ་ནས་སྡང་ (shenɛɛ̀ daŋ) va. to hate from the bottom of (one's) heart.

ཞེ་གནག་ཁོག་བཅངས་ (shenaà kɔ̄gjaŋ) harboring thoughts to harm others, holding hatred within oneself.

ཞེ་གནག་པོ་ (she nagbo) cruel, mean, evil, merciless.

ཞེ་གནོང་ (she nōŋ) vi. to be sorry, to regret, to feel guilty.

ཞེ་གནོན་ (she nōn) va. to hurt other people's feelings.

ཞེ་མནའ་ (shena) a deeply held oath/ vow.

ཞེ་སྣང་ (shenaŋ) sm. སྣང་བ་.

ཞེ་པ་ (sheba) sm. ཞེ་སྡང་.

ཞེ་པོ་ (shebo) sm.* ཞེད་པོ་.

ཞེ་པོ་ཅིག (shebojiì) sm.* ཞེད་པོ་ཅིག.

ཞེ་སྤོ་ (shebo) sm. ཞེ་ལ་རྒྱག.

ཞེ་བློ་བདེ་ (shelo de) vi. to be happy/ glad ¶ ཁྱེད་རང་དེར་བདེ་འགྱོར་བྱུང་བ་ཞེ་བློ་བདེ་བྱུང་ (I) am glad that you arrived there safely.

ཞེ་བློ་ལོག (shelo lɔɔ̀) va. to turn against sb.

ཞེ་མ་བདེ་ (she made) unhappy, not glad.

ཞེ་མེར་ (shemee) nausea, vomiting; vi.—ལོག; —ལངས་; —རྒྱག to feel nauseous. 2. fed up with sth.; vi.—ལོག; —ལངས་; —རྒྱག.

ཞེ་སྨོན་ (shemön) sm. ཡིད་སྨོན་.

ཞེ་གཙང་ (shedzaŋ) sincere, well-meaning, well intended ¶ ཞེ་གཙང་ཞབས་འདེགས་ Serving sincerely.

ཞེ་རྩ་འཁྲུགས་ (shedza trūù) vi. to be angry/ disturbed.

ཞེ་རྩ་བ་ (shedzawa) sm. ཞེ་ནས་.

ཞེ་རྩིས་ (shedziì) 1. having respect for sth.; va.—བྱེད་. 2. an inward/ inner plan.

ཞེ་རྩུབ་ (shedzub) sm. སེམས་ནག.

ཞེ་ཚིག (shedziì) honorific words.

ཞེ་ཚིམ་ (she tsīm) vi. to be satisfied/ content ¶ ལས་འགན་ལེགས་སྒྲུབ་བྱུང་བས་ཞེ་ཚིམ་པ་རེད་ Having completed the task successfully, he felt satisfied.

ཞེ་མཚེར་ (shendzer) shy, bashful.

ཞེ་འཛིན་ (shendzin) keeping in mind sth. bad that sb. has done; va.—བྱེད་.

ཞེ་བཞག (sheshaà) sm. ཞེ་འཛིན་.

ཞེ་བཞི་ (shishi) forty four.

ཞེ་ཟིན་ (shesön) sm. དོགས་ཟོན་.

ཞེ་རེ་ཁྲེལ་ (sheredrɛɛ) sm. ཞེ་ཁྲེལ་.

ཞེ་རུས་ (sherüù) sm. བརྩོན་འགྲུས་.

ཞེ་ལ་ (shela) in the mind/ heart ¶ ཁོའི་ཞེ་ལ་ཕོག་པའི་སྐད་ཞིག་ཆ་བཤད་སོང་ (They) said (sth.) that touched his heart.

ཞེ་ལ་རྒྱག (shela gyəb) 1. va. to be fed up with sth., to feel nauseated/ disgusted by sth. 2. vi. to be bothered/ annoyed.

ཞེ་ལ་འཛོག (shela gyəb) sm. སེམས་ལ་འཛོག.

ཞེ་ལ་མེད་པ་ (shela meèba) insincere, not deeply felt/ held.

ཞེ་ལ་འཛིན་ (shela dzin) sm. སེམས་ལ་འཛིན.
ཞེ་ལང་ (shelaŋ) sm. ཞེ་སྡང་.
ཞེ་ལོག (shelɔɔ̀) sm. ཞེ་ལ་རྒྱུག.
ཞེ་ས་ (shesa) honorific speech; va.—ཞུ་; —བྱེད་ to use honorific speech/ language ¶ བྱེད་ལ་ཞེ་ས་བྱས་ན་གནང་རེད་ The honorific of བྱེད་ is གནང་.
ཞེ་ས་ཆག་འཁྱོག (shesa cāŋgyɔɔ̀) using honorifics inconsistently, mixing honorific and nonhonorific terms.
ཞེ་སུན་ (shesün) irritating, annoying.
ཞེ་གསུམ་ (shesum) forty-three.
ཞེ་སེམས་ (shesem) 1. deep feelings/ thoughts. 2. sm. སེམས་པ་.
ཞེ་ལྷོད་ (shelhöö) calm, relaxed.
ཞེ་ལྷོད་ངང་རིང་ (shelhöö ŋaŋriŋ) calm/ relaxed and patient.
ཞེང་ (sheŋ) width ¶ ཆུ་ཞེང་ The width of a river.
ཞེང་དཀྱུས་ (sheŋgyüü) length and width.
ཞེང་ཁ་ (sheŋga) width.
ཞེང་ཁ་ཆེན་པོ་ (sheŋga cēmbo) spacious, wide.
ཞེང་ཁ་ཆེ་ཆུང་ (sheŋga cījuŋ) the size of the width.
ཞེང་ག (sheŋga) sm. ཞེང་ཁ་.
ཞེང་ཅན་ (sheŋjɛn) wide.
ཞེང་ཆུང་ (sheŋjuŋ) narrow.
ཞེང་ཆུང་ལྕགས་ལམ་ (sheŋjuŋ jāglam) narrow gauge railway.
ཞེང་ཕྲ་མོ་ (sheŋ trāmo) sm. ཞེང་ཆུང་.
ཞེང་ཚད་ (sheŋdzɛɛ̀) 1. width. 2. bore, caliber (of a gun).
ཞེད་ (sheè) vi. to be afraid/ scared ¶ རི་བོང་ཤིན་ཏུ་ཞེད་ནས་ The rabbit, getting very scared.
ཞེད་སྐྲག (sheèdraà) sm. ཞེད་སྣང་.
ཞེད་སྐྲག་ཚ་པོ་ (sheèdraà tsābo) sm. ཞེད་སྣང་ཚ་པོ་.
ཞེད་ཛམ་ཚ་པོ་ (sheèŋam tsābo) very scary/ frightening.
ཞེད་ཐག་ཆོད་ (sheèdaà cöö) vi. to be completely scared/ frightened.
ཞེད་དོན་ (sheèdön) the reason for being afraid/ scared.
ཞེད་སྣང་ (shenaŋ) fear, fright, dread; vi.—བྱེད་; —ལང་; —སྐྱེ་ to be afraid, to fear; va.—སྐུལ་; —སློང་ to scare, to frighten.
ཞེད་སྣང་ཚ་པོ་ (sheènaŋ tsābo) 1. frightening, scary. 2. tough, aggressive ¶ མི་འདིའི་གདོང་ཞེད་སྣང་ཚ་པོ་ཞིག་འདུག This man's face is very frightening.
ཞེད་པ་ (sheèba) sm. ཞེད་སྣང་.
ཞེད་པོ་ (shebo) 1. very much, great deal ¶ ཕྲུ་གུ་དེས་དངུལ་ཞེ་པོ་གཏོར་བཞག The child has wasted a lot of money. 2. sm. ཞེད་སྣང་ཚ་པོ་. 3. doing sth. well ¶ རྐང་རྩེད་པོ་ལོའི་འགྲན་སྡུར་ཐོབ་པ་ཞེད་པོ་བྱུང་ (They) did well in winning the soccer match.
ཞེད་མ་དངངས་ (sheèma ŋāŋ) somewhat afraid.
ཞེད་ཟོན་ (sheèsön) cautious and afraid.
ཞེད་རོགས་ (sheèrɔɔ̀) knife, gun, etc. [Lit. sth. to help one's fright].
ཞེན་ (shen) loyalty, attachment, sincerity, fidelity, love, affection ¶ རང་ཡུལ་ལ་ཞེན་ཆེན་པོ་ཡོད་པའི་མི་ཚོ་ Those people who have great loyalty to their own country.
ཞེན་སྐུལ་ (shengüü) encouraging loyalty; va.—བྱེད་; —ཞུ་.
ཞེན་ཁ་ (shenga) 1. sm. ཞེན་ཆགས་. 2. appetite; vi.—ལོག to lose one's appetite, to be fed up with eating a particular food.
ཞེན་ཁ་ལོག (shenga lɔɔ̀) sm. ཞེན་པ་ལོག.
ཞེན་ཁོག (shengɔɔ̀) loyalty; va.—བྱེད་ ¶ རང་སྲིད་ཀྱི་རྒྱལ་ལ་ཞེན་ཁོག་བྱ་དགོས་ One should be loyal to one's nation.
ཞེན་ཆགས་ (shenjaà) attachment, fondness; vi.—བྱེད་ to be attached to, to be fond of ¶ ཆོས་ཡག་པོ་བྱེད་འདོད་ཡོད་ན་འཇིག་རྟེན་ལ་ཞེན་ཆགས་བྱ་མ་རེད་ If you want to practice religion well, you can't be attached to worldliness.
ཞེན་དོན་ (shendön) the object of attachment/ fondness/ love.
ཞེན་པ་ (shemba) sm. ཞེན་.
ཞེན་པ་ལོག (shemba lɔɔ̀) 1. vi. to be sick of, to be fed up with ¶ དམག་འཁྲུག་ལ་ཞེན་པ་ལོག་ནས་ Having become fed up with war. 2. appetite; vi.—ལོག to lose one's appetite, to be fed up with eating a particular food.
ཞེན་པ་སློག (shemba lɔ̄ɔ̀) va. to make sb. fed up/ sick of.
ཞེན་ཕྱོགས་ (shenjɔ̄ɔ̀) one's position of loyalty.
ཞེན་འཛིན་ (shendzin) sm. ཞེན་ཁོག.
ཞེན་ལོག (shēnlɔɔ̀) abbr. of ཞེན་པ་ལོག.
ཞེན་ལོག་སློག (shenlɔɔ̀ lɔ̄ɔ̀) sm. ཞེན་པ་སློག.
ཞེན་ཤ་གཏིང་ལོག (shensha dīŋlɔɔ̀) completely fed up, totally sick of.
ཞེའོ་ (shewo) sm. ཟེར་རོ་.
ཞེར་འདེབས་ (sherdeb) sm. ཞེ་གཅོད་.
ཞེར་པོ་ (sherbo) bad/ coarse/ poor/ inferior in quality.
ཞེར་བ་ (sherwa) sm. ཞེར་པོ་.
ཞེལ་ཕོར་ (sheebɔɔ) sm.* ཞེབ་ཕོར་.
ཞེས་ (sheè) sm. ཅེས་ (used after final vowels and after final ང་ ན་ མ་ འ་ ར་ ལ་).
ཞེས་བགྱི་བ་ (sheègyiwa) called.
ཞེས་པ་ (sheèba) the one called, that called, so called ¶ ནག་ཆུ་ཞེས་པ་བོད་བྱང་ཕྱོགས་ཁུལ་གྲོང་ཁྱེར་གཅིག་ཡོད་ There is a town called Nagchuka in the northern region of Tibet.
ཞེས་བྱ་བ་ (sheècawa) sm. ཞེས་པ་.
ཞེས་སུ་གྲགས་ (sheèsu traà) vi. to be known as, to be called.
ཞོ་ (sho) 1. curds, yogurt; va.—སྙོལ་ to make yogurt (by fermenting milk); — ལྡོག to eat yogurt. 2. shung. a traditional Tibetan monetary unit (10 སྐར་ = 1 ཞོ; 10 ཞོ་ = 1 སྲང་).
ཞོ་དཀྲོག (sho drɔ̄ɔ̀) va. to churn yogurt to make butter.
ཞོ་དཀྲོག་འཕྲུལ་ཆས་ (shodrɔɔ̀ trüüjɛɛ̀) yogurt churning machine for making butter.
ཞོ་སྐ་བ་ (sho kāwa) thick yogurt.
ཞོ་སྐྱ་ (shogya) buttermilk.
ཞོ་སྐྱེད་ (shogyeè) a monthly interest of 1 ཞོ་ for each 1 སྲང་ borrowed (10% interest).
ཞོ་སྐྱེས་ (shogyeè) 1. a type of livestock parasite. 2. sm. སྲིག་པ་.
ཞོ་ཁ་ཆུ་ (sho kāju) sm. ཞོ་སྐྱ་.
ཞོ་ཁོག (shogɔɔ̀) pot for holding yogurt.
ཞོ་གང་ (shogaŋ) one ཞོ་ in the Tibetan monetary system.
ཞོ་གྲོད་ (shodröö) the stomach of animal made into a yogurt container.
ཞོ་འགྱེད་ (shogyeè) a celebration/ party at which yogurt is served; va.—གཏོང་.
ཞོ་མངར་ (shoŋar) yogurt from which the butter has not been extracted.
ཞོ་ཆ་ (shoja) 1/10 of a ཞོ་ (i.e., 1 karma).
ཞོ་འཇོ་ (shojo) milking; va.—བྱེད་ to milk.
ཞོ་སྙོལ་ (sho ñöö) va. to ferment milk to make yogurt.
ཞོ་ཏྟ་ (shoda) fermenting agent/ starter (for making yogurt).
ཞོ་སྟོན་ (shodön) Lhasa Summer Opera Festival [Lit. the yogurt festival].
ཞོ་དོ་ (shodo) two ཞོ་.
ཞོ་བདུན་སྒོར་མོ་ (shodün gormo) Chinese silver dollar.
ཞོ་མདོང་ (shodoŋ) a yogurt churner (to make butter).
ཞོ་པད་ (shobɛɛ̀) sm. ཞོ་.
ཞོ་དཔྱང་ (shojaŋ) buttermilk.
ཞོ་སྤྲིས་ (shodrii) the layer of cream that forms on top of milk.
ཞོ་ཕབ་ (shobəb) sm. ཞོ་ཏྟ་.
ཞོ་ལྷུག (sholuù) yogurt container.
ཞོ་འབྲས་ (shomdrɛɛ̀) yogurt and rice meal.
ཞོ་མར་ཁུ་ (sho mərgu) a food that consists of yogurt

and melted butter.

ཞོ་རྫབས་ (shodzəb) sm. ཞོ་དྲ་.

ཞོ་རྫི་ (shodzi) sm. ཞོ་དྲ་.

ཞོ་རལ་ (sho rɛɛ) vi. to go bad/ sour, to become spoiled (regarding yogurt).

ཞོ་ཟོ་ (shoso) yogurt churn.

ཞོ་ལོ་མོ་ལོ་ཀྱག (sholo molo gyāà) sm. གཞོགས་ལོག་མོ་ལོག་ཀྱག.

ཞོ་ཤ་ (shosha) 1. arc. strength, energy. 2. arc. wage, salary. 3. arc. tax.

ཞོ་ཤས་འཚོ་ (shoshɛɛ̀ tsō) va. to earn one's livelihood/ subsistence.

ཞོག (shɔɔ̀) imp. of འཛོག.

ཞོག་ཁོག (shɔɔ̀gɔɔ̀) potato.

ཞོག་ཁོག་མངར་མོ་ (shɔɔ̀gɔɔ̀ ŋāāmo) sweet potato.

ཞོག་ཁོག་ཡུས་ཐོའུ་ (shɔɔ̀gɔɔ̀ yüüto) tib. ch. sweet potato.

ཞོག་ཁོག་ས་དོང་ (shɔɔ̀gɔɔ̀ sādoŋ) ditch/ hole dug to store potatoes for the winter; va.—འབྲུ་ to dig such a pit.

ཞོག་ཁོག་བསྲེགས་མ་ (shɔɔ̀gɔɔ̀ drēgma) baked potato.

ཞོག་ཁོག་ཧྲུའུ་ཡུས་ (shɔɔ̀gɔɔ̀ hrūyüü) tib. ch. Chinese yam (dioscorea batatas).

ཞོག་གོག (shɔɔ̀gɔɔ̀) sm. ཞོག་ཁོག.

ཞོག་གོག་གོབ་ཚོས་ (shɔɔ̀gɔɔ̀ kobdzöö) potato and meat stew.

ཞོག་གོག་སྦུ་རུ་ (shɔɔ̀gɔɔ̀ buru) type of edible wild plant.

ཞོག་གཅིག་མ་གཉིས་གསུམ་པའི་ཐོག (shɔɔ̀jig mañii sūmbɛ tɔ̄ɔ̀) phrase used when synchronizing work: one, two, three (pull, heave).

ཞོག་མ་ (shɔɔ̀ma) sm. ཞོགས་མ་.

ཞོགས་ཀ་ (shɔɔ̀ga) in the morning.

ཞོགས་སྐད་ (shɔɔ̀gɛɛ̀) sm. ཞོགས་ཀ་.

ཞོགས་ཁྲོམ་ (shogdrom) market that opens in the morning, morning market; vi.—གྲོལ་ to have the morning market end/ close; va.— སྤེན་ to open a stall/ booth for the morning market; vi.—ཚུགས་ to have the morning market start.

ཞོགས་གང་ (shɔɔ̀gaŋ) a full/ whole morning ¶ ཞོགས་གང་གཅིག་རིང་ During one whole morning.

ཞོགས་གུང་མཚན་གསུམ་ (shɔɔ̀guŋ tsēnsum) the three: morning, noon and night.

ཞོགས་རྒྱུགས་ (shɔɔ̀gyuù) running after being startled.

ཞོགས་སྔ་ (shɔɔ̀) early morning. ¶ ཞོགས་སྔ་ལངས་དགོང་ཕྱི་ཉལ་ Getting up early and going to bed late.

ཞོགས་ཆོས་ (shɔɔ̀) morning offering/ prayer.

ཞོགས་ཇ་ (shɔɔ̀ja) morning tea, breakfast.

ཞོགས་མཇལ་ (shogjɛɛ) morning audience (e.g., of a king).

ཞོགས་ཉག (shɔɔ̀ñuù) morning hunt.

ཞོགས་ཉལ་ (shɔɔ̀ñɛɛ) sleeping in late; vi.—རྒྱག to sleep late.

ཞོགས་ལྟར་ (shɔɔ̀dar) every morning.

ཞོགས་ལྟར་རེ་བཞིན་ (shɔɔ̀daa reshin) each and every morning.

ཞོགས་གཏོང་འཁོར་ལོ་ (shɔɔ̀doŋ kɔ̄ɔlo) a vehicle that goes early in the morning.

ཞོགས་ཐུག (shogduù) morning soup/ stew.

ཞོགས་དྲོ་ (shogdro) driving animals back to the corral in the morning after a stint of early morning grazing.

ཞོགས་པ་ (shogba) morning.

ཞོགས་པ་བདེ་ལེགས་ (shogba deleè) "good morning" (neologism used in exile).

ཞོགས་པའི་མཚམས་སྦྲིན་ (shogbɛ tsəmdrin) a greeting used in the morning.

ཞོགས་པའི་ལུས་རྩལ་ (shogbɛ lüüdzɛɛ) morning exercises/ calisthenics.

ཞོགས་སྤགས་ (shɔɔ̀baà) breakfast of རྩམ་པ་.

ཞོགས་སྦྱོང་ (shɔɔ̀jɔŋ) morning exercise/ practice.

ཞོགས་མ་ (shɔɔ̀ma) wood shavings, sawdust.

ཞོགས་རྩལ་ (shɔɔ̀dzɛɛ) sm. ཞོགས་པའི་ལུས་རྩལ་.

ཞོགས་ཚོགས་ (shɔɔ̀dzɔɔ̀) morning meeting.

ཞོགས་ཟས་ (shɔɔ̀sɛɛ̀) breakfast, morning food/ meal.

ཞོགས་འུར་ (shɔɔ̀wur) a sudden fright/ panic; vi.—ལང་ to be suddenly panic stricken/ frightened ¶ དམག་འཁྲུག་ཡོང་རྒྱུའི་གྱི་དགུག་གཏམ་དེས་ཞོགས་འུར་ལངས་བཞག They were panic stricken by the false news that war is coming.

ཞོགས་ལས་ (shɔɔ̀lɛɛ̀) 1. morning's work (usu. refers to the work in the house in the early morning). 2. morning shift.

ཞོང་ (shoŋ) abbr. of ཞོང་ཞོང་.

ཞོང་ཞོང་ (shoŋshoŋ) a depression, a concave area ¶ ས་ཆ་ཞོང་ཞོང་དེ་ཚོར་ཆུ་འཁྱིལ་འདུག Water formed puddles in those depressions.

ཞོད་ (shöö) rainfall.

ཞོད་ཀྱི་གེགས་ (shöögi geg) disaster caused by (heavy) rain.

ཞོད་སྐྱོན་ (shöögyön) damage/ destruction caused by (heavy) rainfall.

ཞོད་སྐྱོན་འགོག་པ་ (shöögyön gogba) waterproof.

ཞོད་གེགས་ (shöögeg) sm. ཞོད་ཀྱི་གེགས་.

ཞོད་འགོག (shöögɔɔ̀) sm. ཞོད་སྐྱོན་འགོག་པ་.

ཞོད་ཆར་ (shööjar) rain, rainfall.

ཞོད་ཆུ་ (shööju) rainfall.

ཞོད་ཆེ་ (shööje) heavy rainfall.

ཞོད་འཇགས་ (shönjaà) quelling, quieting, calming, putting down; va.—གཏོང་ ¶ ལྷ་སའི་ཐེང་འཁྲུག་ཞོད་འཇགས་བཏང་པ་རེད་ (They) quelled the revolt in Lhasa.

ཞོད་ཐན་ (shöötɛn) flood and drought.

ཞོད་སླ་ (shööla) rainy weather.

ཞོན་ (shön) va. to ride, to mount ¶ རྐང་འཁོར་ཞོན་ནས་ཁྲོམ་ལ་ཕྱིན་སོང་ He rode the bicycle and went to the market. ¶ ཁོས་རྟ་ཞོན་ནས་ལྷ་སར་ཕྱིན་པ་རེད་ He went on horseback to Lhasa.

ཞོན་ཁལ་ (shön kɛɛ̄) shung. riding and carrying animals.

ཞོན་ཇག (shönjaà) bandits on horseback.

ཞོན་རྟ་ (shönda) a riding horse.

ཞོན་སྟེགས་ (shöndeg) stone or mound on which to stand to mount a horse.

ཞོན་དྲེལ་ (shöndree) a riding mule.

ཞོན་པ་ (shömba) a riding animal.

ཞོན་དམག (shönmaà) cavalry/ mounted troops.

ཞོན་ཤོག (shönshɔɔ̀) tib. ch. xuan paper (a high quality paper made in Anhui Province).

ཞོམ་ (som) sm. གཞོམ་.

ཞོར་ (shɔɔ) coincidental/ secondary to another main activity ¶ ཁོས་ལས་ཀའི་ཞོར་དུ་སློབ་སྦྱོང་བྱེད་ཀྱི་ཡོད་པ་རེད་ He studied during his spare time at work.

ཞོར་སྐྱོང་ (shɔɔgyoŋ) sideline work, doing sth. on the side ¶ ཚགས་པར་ལས་ཁངས་ཀྱིས་ཟ་ཁང་ཞོར་སྐྱོང་བྱེད་ཀྱི་ཡོད་པ་རེད་ The newspaper office manages a restaurant on the side.

ཞོར་སྐྱོན་ (shɔɔgyön) an undesirable/ damaging side effect.

ཞོར་ཁྲིད་ (shɔɔ trii) teaching on the side, side/ extra class or instruction.

ཞོར་འགུམ་སོང་ (shɔɔdrum sōŋ) vi. to have been killed accidentally.

ཞོར་སྒྲུབ་ (shɔɔdrub) doing sth. secondarily; va.—བྱེད་.

ཞོར་ཕྱོགས་ (shɔɔjɔɔ̀) secondary ¶ གཞུང་གཙོ་བོ་དང་ཁྱིམ་ཚང་ཞོར་ཕྱོགས་སུ་འཛིན་གྱི་ཡོད་པ་རེད་ (They) consider the government as the main one and the family as secondary.

ཞོར་ཕྱོགས་སུ་གཉེར་ (shɔɔjɔɔ̀su ñēr) va. to take charge of sth. secondary to one's main duty/ office.

ཞོར་གཉེར་ (shɔɔñer) abbr. of ཞོར་ཕྱོགས་སུ་གཉེར་.

ཞོར་གདོགས་ (shɔɔdɔɔ̀) an appendage, a subordinate entity. ¶ བོད་ནི་བཙན་རྒྱལ་རིང་ལུགས་ཀྱིས་ཞོར་གདོགས་རྒྱལ་ཁབ་དུ་བསྒྱུར་རྩིས་བྱས་པ་རེད་ The imperialists tried to change Tibet into one of their subordinate (appendages/ countries).

ཞོར་ཐོན་དངོས་རྫས་ (shɔɔdön ŋöödzɛɛ̀) by-product.

ཞོར་དུ་ (shɔɔdu) sm. ཞོར་.

ཞོར་དེབ་ (shɔɔdeb) supplementary book.

ཞོར་འདྲུད་ (shɔndrüü) getting involved in sth. on account of sb. else, getting drawn into sth., being implicated; vi.—ཐེབས་; —འཁྱིལ་ ¶ མི་དེས་ཟིང་ཆའི་ནང་མི་ཡང་ཞོར་དྲུད་ཐེབས་ནས་བཙོན་དུ་ཚུད་བཞག Because that person participated in the disturbances, his family got implicated and were jailed.

ཞོར་སྣོན་གྱི་ཆ་རྐྱེན་ (shɔɔnöngi cāgyen) additional conditions.

ཞོར་ཕུང་ (shɔɔbuŋ) getting implicated/ involved; vi.—བྱེད་.

ཞོར་འཕྲོས་སུ་ (shɔɔ drȫosu) at the same time, along with/ incidental to sth. else ¶ ཁོའི་ནང་མིའི་སྐོར་ཡང་ཞོར་འཕྲོས་སུ་དྲི་བ་བྱས་པ་རེད་ (I) asked about his family at the same time (incidental to sth. else).

ཞོར་འཛིན་ལས་འགན་ (shɔndzin lɛngɛn) side job, supplementary duty.

ཞོར་འཛུགས་ (shɔndzuù) secondarily started/ established ¶ ཟ་ཁང་འདི་དགོན་པའི་ཞོར་འཛུགས་བྱས་པ་ཞིག་རེད་ This restaurant is one that the monastery established secondarily.

ཞོར་ཟས་ (shɔɔsɛɛ̀) nonstaple foods, snacks.

ཞོར་ཟས་ཚོང་ཁང་ (shɔɔsɛɛ̀ tsōŋgaŋ) grocery store (nonstaple food store).

ཞོར་ལ་ (shɔɔla) sm. ཞོར་.

ཞོར་ལ་ཐེབས་ (shɔɔla tēb) sm. ཞོར་ལ་ཚུད་.

ཞོར་ལ་ཚུད་ (shɔɔla tsüü) vi. to be involved in sth. coincidentally/ incidentally.

ཞོར་ལས་ (shɔɔlɛɛ̀) sideline job/ work, secondary job/ occupation, work done after hours, spare time work; va.—བྱེད་ to work at a sideline job ¶ ཞིང་པ་ཚོས་འཐག་ལས་སོགས་ཀྱི་ཞོར་ལས་བྱས་པ་རེད་ The farmers did sideline work such as weaving.

ཞོར་ལས་ཐོན་སྐྱེད་ (shɔɔlɛɛ̀ tōngyeè) sideline production.

ཞོར་ལས་ཐོན་རྫས་ (shɔɔlɛɛ̀ tōndzɛɛ̀) sideline products.

ཞོལ་ (shöö) shung. 1. lower part, bottom, the area below a structure such as a fort ¶ རིའི་ཞོལ་ The area around the base of the mountain. 2. the name of the walled town below the Potala (now a part of Lhasa).

ཞོལ་ཁུལ་ (shöögüü) the area beneath or at the base of a fort or castle or mountain.

ཞོལ་རྒན་པོ་ (shöö gɛmbo) shung. the Panchen Lama's office that was in charge of Shigatse's Shol area.

ཞོལ་ལྕགས་རི་ (shöö jāəri) shung. the wall around a ཞོལ་.

ཞོལ་ཆེན་ (shööjen) sm. ཞོལ་པོ་.

ཞོལ་གཉེར་ (shööñer) shung. the head of the ཞོལ་པ་ལས་ཁུངས་.

ཞོལ་མགར་དོད་དཔལ་ (shöö dööbɛɛ) shung. an association of smiths and craftsmen.

ཞོལ་འདབས་ (shöndəb) sm. ཞོལ་, 1.

ཞོལ་དྲུང་ (shöödruŋ) shung. a clerk in ཞོལ་པ་ལས་ཁུངས་.

ཞོལ་རྡོ་རིང་ཕྱི་མ་ (shöö doriŋ cīmə) outer stone pillar in ཞོལ་.

ཞོལ་སྡེ་པ་ (shöö gɛmbo) shung. ཞོལ་རྒན་པོ་.

ཞོལ་པ་ (shööba) shung. 1. a resident of ཞོལ་. 2. sm. ཞོལ་གཉེར་.

ཞོལ་པ་ལས་ཁུངས་ (shööba lɛɛ̀guŋ) shung. the office that is responsible for law and order in ཞོལ་ and the area around Lhasa.

ཞོལ་པོ་ (shööbo) sm. ཞོལ་ཕོ་.

ཞོལ་ཕོ་ (shööbo) stud yak.

ཞོལ་མོ་ (shöömo) milch འབྲི་.

ཞོལ་ཞོལ་ (shööshöö) a style of wearing one's Tibetan dress long.

ཞོལ་གཡག (shööyaà) sm. ཞོལ་ཕོ་.

ཞོལ་ལས་ཁུངས་ (shöö lɛɛ̀guŋ) shung. sm. ཞོལ་པ་ལས་ཁུངས་.

ཞོས་ (shöö) imp. of འཞོ་.

ཞྭ་ (sha) abbr. of ཞྭ་མོ་.

ཞྭ་དཀར་ (shagaa) 1. white hat. 2. shung. a ceremonial hat worn by monk officials.

ཞྭ་གོས་ (shagöö) hat and clothes.

ཞྭ་གོས་ལྷམ་གསུམ་ (shagöö lhāmsum) the three: hat, clothes and boots.

ཞྭ་སྒབ་པ་ (shagəbba) an aristocratic family.

ཞྭ་སྒམ་ (shāgam) hat box.

ཞྭ་མཆུ་ (shəmju) peak (of a cap), visor.

ཞྭ་ཏོག (shādoò) an button/ ornament on top of a hat.

ཞྭ་རྟགས་ (shadaà) abbr. of ཞྭ་མོའི་རྟགས་.

ཞྭ་རྟོགས་ (shadɔ̀ɔ) badge that is worn on a hat.

ཞྭ་སྟེགས་ (shādeg) hat stand.

ཞྭ་ཐེབ་ (shādeb) shung. a kind of hat worn by monks and monk officials.

ཞྭ་གདན་ (shadɛn) a cap worn under a helmet.

ཞྭ་འདབས་ (shandəb) the brim of a hat.

ཞྭ་ནག (shanaà) 1. the black hat worn by Ngagpa. 2. black hat that is worn by the Head of the Black Hat Karmapa sect. 3. blaming innocent people; va.—གཡོག to unjustly blame/ accuse.

ཞྭ་སྣ་རིང་ (sha nāriŋ) a cone shaped cap with long ear flaps worn by very high lamas.

ཞྭ་སྣེ་ (shane) edge/ border of a hat.

ཞྭ་པར་ (shabar) wooden head (mold) used for making hats.

ཞྭ་དཔེ་ལྷམ་འགེབ་ (shabe lhāmgeb) being obstinate and doing things that are not suitable or appropriate, a farfetched argument; va.—བྱེད་ [Lit. to use the design of the hat on the shoe].

ཞྭ་འབུད་ (sha büü) va. to take off one's hat.

ཞྭ་སྦྲགས་སྟོད་གོས་ (shdraà dȫögöö) parka, anorak (coat with an attached hat).

ཞྭ་འབོག (shambɔ̀ɔ) shung. a type of hat worn by tt. officials and རགས་རྒྱབ་པ་.

ཞྭ་མོ་ (shamo) hat, cap; va.—གྱོན་; —གོན་ to put on/ wear a hat; va.—གཡོག (see ཞྭ་མོ་གཡོག).

ཞྭ་མོ་ཁ་ལེབ་ (shamo kāleb) cap with a brim extending over forehead (sth. like baseball cap).

ཞྭ་མོ་མགོ་ལ་སྙམ་པ་ མེ་ཏོག་སྤང་ལ་མཛེས་པ་ (shamo gola bāmba medoò bāŋla dzeèba) arranging people in suitable positions [Lit. the hat looks good on the head and flowers look beautiful on the meadow].

ཞྭ་མོ་ལྕུགས་མདའ་ (shamo jānda) shung. hat worn by the officials above the 4th rank in tt. in the summer.

ཞྭ་མོ་སྤྱགས་ཞྭ་ (shamo bāgsha) fur hat.

ཞྭ་མོ་ཡོད་པ་ (shamo yööba) 1. a communist ex-prisoner who is out on probation but has no status or position. 2. sb. who has been branded/ labeled a counterrevolutionary.

ཞྭ་མོ་གཡོག (shamo yɔ̀ɔ) 1. va. to put a hat on sb. 2. va. to label (a person) ¶ མི་དེ་ཚོར་སྐབས་འཚོལ་རིང་ལུགས་པའི་ཞྭ་མོ་གཡོགས་པ་རེད་ They labeled those people opportunists. 3. va. to be branded as a counterrevolutionary, to be officially declared a counterrevolutionary.

ཞྭ་མོའི་ལྕེ་ལེབ་ (shamö jēleb) flaps on a hat, peak of a cap, visor.

ཞྭ་མོའི་ལྕེ་འཛར་ (shamö jēdzar) sm. ཞྭ་མོའི་ལྕེ་ལེབ་.

ཞྭ་མོའི་རྟགས་ (shamö dāà) badge/ insignia worn on the front of a hat.

ཞྭ་མོའི་སྟོང་ཆབ་ (shamö dōŋjəb) tassel of a hat.

ཞྭ་མོའི་ཚོང་ཁང་ (shamö tsōŋgaŋ) hat shop.

ཞྭ་མོའི་ཨ་མཆོག (shamö āmjɔ̀ɔ) ear flap of a hat.

ཞྭ་དམར་ (shamar) 1. red hat. 2. subsect of the Kagyu sect.

ཞྭ་དམར་ནག (sha mārnaà) the Black and Red Hat subsects of the Karma Kagyu sect.

ཞྭ་དམར་བ་ (shamārwa) follower of the Red Hat Karma subsect.

ཞྭ་རྨོག (shamɔ̀ɔ) military helmet.

ཞྭ་ཙོག (shadzoò) a hat worn by the attendants of a

monastic abbot.

ཞྭ་ཟེ་ (sha̱se) feather(s) worn on caps/ hats.

ཞྭ་ལྡུམ་ (sha̱ndum) a type of hat worn by monks from Amdo.

ཞྭ་རིང་ (shə̱riŋ) tall hat.

ཞྭ་སེར་ (sha̱ser) 1. a yellow hat. 2. Yellow Hat sect (the Gelugpa sect).

ཞྭ་སེར་གྱི་བསྟན་པ་ (sha̱sergi dɛ̄mba) the Gelugpa doctrine.

ཞྭ་སེར་བ་ (sha̱serwa) the followers of the Yellow Hat (Gelugpa) sect.

གཞག (sha̱à) f. of འཇོག.

གཞགས་ (sha̱à) sm. བཞགས་.

གཞང་ (sha̱ŋ) the lower part of the female body, vagina, anus.

གཞང་ཁ་ (sha̱ŋga) h. of ཀུབ་.

གཞང་ཁང་ (sha̱ŋgaŋ) brothel.

གཞང་གྲིབ་ (sha̱ŋdrib) sexually transmitted disease.

གཞང་གྲུམ་ (shə̱ŋdrum) sm. གཞང་འབྲུམ་.

གཞང་འབོག (sha̱ŋbɔ̀ɔ) h. of ཀུབ་.

གཞང་འབོག་ཕྱིད་པོ་ (sha̱ŋbɔ̀ɔ ji̱ibu) h. of ཀུབ་ཕྱིད་པོ་.

གཞང་འབྲུམ་ (shə̱ŋdrum) hemorrhoids.

གཞང་ཚོང་མ་ (sha̱ŋdzoŋma) prostitute.

གཞང་ལུག (sha̱ŋ lu̱ù) vi. to have a prolapse of the anus.

གཞང་ལོག (sha̱ŋ lɔ̱ɔ̀) sm. གཞང་ལུག.

གཞང་སྲིན་ (shə̱ŋsin) a disease that causes itchiness around the anus.

གཞན་ (shɛ̱n) other, another ¶ ཡུལ་གཞན་གྱི་མི་རིགས་ Nationalities of other countries.

གཞན་རྐྱེན་ (shɛ̱ngyen) the external cause of sth.

གཞན་སྐྱོན་ཐེར་འདོན་ (shɛ̱ngyön tērdön) exposing other's mistakes; va.—བྱེད་.

གཞན་སྐྱོར་ངོ་སྲུང་ (shɛ̱ngyoŋ ŋo̱suŋ) supporting a person and hiding his/ her faults/ wrong doings.

གཞན་བཀོལ་ (shɛ̱ngöö) controlled by sb. else.

གཞན་བཀོལ་སྲིད་གཞུང་ (shɛ̱ngöö sīishuŋ) puppet regime/ government.

གཞན་ཁ་ (shɛ̱nga) sm. གཞན་དག.

གཞན་འཁྱུད་སྡོང་པོ་ (shɛ̱ngyüù do̱ŋbo) a vine.

གཞན་གྱི་ལྗེ་རྟེན་ (shɛ̱ngi jēden) the advice of others.

གཞན་གྱི་གདོང་ལ་ཤིག་འགྲོ་བ་མཐོང་པ་ལས་ རང་གི་གདོང་ལ་གཡག་འགྲོ་བ་མ་མཐོང་བ་ (shɛ̱ngi do̱ŋla shīì dro̱walɛ ra̱ŋgi do̱ŋla yāà dro̱a matoŋwa) someone who sees other people's faults but does not see his own faults [Lit. someone who can see a louse going on another's face but can not see a yak going on his own face].

གཞན་གྱིས་མི་ཐུབ་པ་ (shɛ̱ngi mi̱tubbə) 1. (one) that cannot be subdued/ defeated by others. 2. a wrathful deity.

གཞན་འགན་འཕྲོག་སྒྲུབ་ (shɛ̱ngɛn trɔ̄ɔ̀drub) 1. stealing/ appropriating sb.'s duties/ power/ position. 2. monopolizing activities/ business/ responsibilities; va.—བྱེད་.

གཞན་འགན་ཚབ་ཁུར་ (shɛ̱ngɛn tsə̄bgur) substituting for sb. else, acting in sb.'s place, taking on sb.'s responsibilities.

གཞན་འགའ་ཞིག (shɛ̱n ga̱shig) a few others, some others.

གཞན་འགྱུར་ (shɛ̱ngyur) transforming, changing over; va.—བྱེད་.

གཞན་འགྲན་མེད་པ་ (shɛ̱ndrɛn me̱èba) unequaled, unrivaled.

གཞན་རྒྱུད་ (shɛ̱ngyüù) the feeling/ mind/ thoughts of others.

གཞན་ངོ་ (shɛ̱nŋo) for the sake of others.

གཞན་ངོམ་འཕོར་ཤོབ་ (shɛ̱nŋom bɔ̱rshob) showing off to other people.

གཞན་ངོམ་ཡོད་ལྟོམ་ (shɛ̱nŋor yö̱ölom) sm. གཞན་ངོམ་འཕོར་ཤོབ་.

གཞན་ངོས་ (shɛ̱nŋöö̀) 1. the others, the other side ¶ གཞན་ངོས་ནས་བསམ་འཆར་ག་རེ་ཡོད་ལམ་སེང་ཤེས་ཀྱི་མ་རེད་ (We) won't know at once what opinions the other side has. 2. the view of others (opposite of རང་ངོས་).

གཞན་དངོས་ཀྱི་ཆ་རྐྱེན་ (shɛ̱nŋöògi cāgyen) objective condition.

གཞན་ཉེན་སྐབས་བསྣུན་ (shɛ̱nñen gəbdün) taking advantage of sb.'s precarious position/ disaster.

གཞན་ཉེས་གོང་ཞུ་ (shɛ̱nñeè ko̱ŋshu) reporting crimes/ misdeeds of others to superiors.

གཞན་ཉེས་ཐེར་འདོན་ (shɛ̱nñeè tērdön) uncovering/ exposing an offense of another.

གཞན་རྗེས་རང་སྐྱོད་ (shɛ̱njeè ra̱ŋgyöö̀) following others (rather than making one's own decisions), imitating another person.

གཞན་རྟེན་ (shɛ̱nden) 1. dependent on others. 2. parasitic.

གཞན་རྟེན་སྐྱེ་དངོས་ (shɛ̱nden gyēŋöö̀) parasitic plants.

གཞན་རྟེན་རྒྱལ་ཁབ་ (shɛ̱nden gyɛ̱ɛ̱gəb) dependent/ satellite country.

གཞན་རྟེན་འཚོ་སྐྱེལ་ (shɛ̱nden tsōgyee) making a living by exploiting others.

གཞན་རྟེན་འཚོ་འབུ་ (shɛ̱nden tsōmbu) sm. གཞན་རྟེན་སྲིན་འབུ་.

གཞན་རྟེན་སྲིན་འབུ་ (shɛ̱nden sīmbu) parasites.

གཞན་བརྟེན་ (shɛ̱nden) sm. གཞན་རྟེན་ས.

གཞན་དག (shɛ̱ndaà) other, another ¶ ཁོ་དང་སློབ་གཉེར་བ་གཞན་དག་ཚོ་ He and other students. ¶ དེབ་གཞན་དག་དགོས་ (I) need another (different) book. ¶ ས་ཆ་གཞན་དག་ནས་ From other places.

གཞན་དང་མི་འདྲ་བ་ (shɛ̱ndaŋ mi̱ndrawa) unlike anything else, extraordinary ¶ ཁོའི་ལས་ཀའི་གྲུབ་འབྲས་གཞན་དང་མི་འདྲ་བ་དེར་བསྟོད་བསྔགས་བྱས་པ་རེད་ (They) praised the extraordinary success of his work.

གཞན་དུ་ (shɛ̱ndu) another, other.

གཞན་དུ་ན་ (shɛ̱nduna) if not ... otherwise ¶ ཕྲུ་གུ་ཆུང་དུས་གཙུན་དགོས་ གཞན་དུ་ན་འཕྲོ་བརླག་འགྲོ་གི་རེད་ Children should be disciplined when young, otherwise they will be spoiled.

གཞན་དོན་ (shɛ̱ndön) the interest/ benefit/ good of others; va.— སྒྲུབ་ to work for the good/ benefit/ interests of others.

གཞན་དོན་ཚབ་སྒྲུབ་ (shɛ̱ndön tsə̄bdrub) sm. གཞན་འགན་ཚབ་ཁུར་.

གཞན་དྲིང་མི་འཇོག (shɛ̱ndriŋ mi̱njɔɔ̀) free/ independent of others.

གཞན་བདེ་རང་སྐྱིད་ (shɛ̱nde ra̱ŋgyiì) others good and oneself happy.

གཞན་འདུལ་རང་རྒྱལ་ (shɛ̱ndüü ra̱ŋgyɛɛ) others being defeating and oneself being victorious.

གཞན་འདྲེན་ཞོར་དྲུད་ (shɛ̱ndren shɔ̱ɔ̱drüù) sm. ཞོར་འདྲེད་ཐེབས་.

གཞན་རྡུགས་ (shɛ̱nduù) having exhausted all means/ alternatives.

གཞན་སྡུག་སྙིང་ཚིམ་ (shɛ̱nduù ñīŋdzim) taking pleasure in the difficulties/ misfortunes of others; va.—བྱེད་.

གཞན་སྡེ་ (shɛ̱nde) sm. གཞན་སྡེ་པ་.

གཞན་སྡེ་པ་ (shɛ̱ndeba) infidel, heathen.

གཞན་གནོད་རང་ཕན་ (shɛ̱nnöö̀ ra̱ŋbɛn) causing misfortune to others to benefit oneself.

གཞན་པ་ (shɛ̱mba) sm. གཞན་དག.

གཞན་པའི་ཁོག་རྟེན་ (shɛ̱mbɛ kɔ̄gden) endoparasite.

གཞན་དཔེ་འདྲ་བཤུས་ (shɛ̱mbe drə̱shüù) copying sb. else's work; va.—བྱེད་.

གཞན་དཔེ་རང་སྤྱོད་ (shɛ̱mbe ra̱ŋjöö̀) acting in accordance with sb. else's example.

གཞན་ཕན་ (shɛ̱mbɛb) sb. else's benefit.

གཞན་ཕན་བརྩོན་འགྲུས་ (shɛ̱mbɛn dzȫndröö̀) working diligently for the well being/ benefit of others.

གཞན་ཕན་རིང་ལུགས་ (shɛ̱mbɛn ri̱ŋluù) altruism.

གཞན་ཕྱོགས་ (shɛ̱njɔɔ̀) 1. sm. གཞན་སྡེ་པ་. 2. the other side.

གཞན་བོར་རང་འདུ་ (shɛ̱nbɔɔ ra̱ŋdu) collecting other's lost things.

གཞན་དབང་དུ་ (shɛ̱nwaŋdu) under another's power/

authority/ control; vi.—འགྲོ་; —འགྱུར་; —ཚུད་ to fall under another's power ། ང་ཚོ་ནང་ཁུལ་གཅིག་སྒྲིལ་མ་བྱས་ན་གཞན་དབང་དུ་འགྲོ་གི་རེད་ If we aren't unified internally we'll fall under the power of another country.

གཞན་མ་ (shenma) sm. གཞན་པ་.

གཞན་སྨོད་ (shenmöö) slander/ calumny/ defamation/ derision of others.

གཞན་ཛོད་འཐེན་འཁྱེར་ (shendzöö tēngyer) taking sides and arguing with others.

གཞན་ཞོར་རང་དྲུད་ (shenshɔɔ randrüü) sm. ཞོར་འདྲུད་ ཐེབས་.

གཞན་ཟེར་རྗེས་འབྲང་ (shensee jeèdran) following what other's say.

གཞན་ཡང་ (shenyan) also, furthermore, moreover ། སྲིད་བློན་མཆོག་དང་གཞན་ཡང་བློན་ཆེན་ཁག་བཅས་ཡོད་པ་རེད་ The prime minister and, furthermore, the ministers were there.

གཞན་ཡུལ་ (shenyüü) the place/ country of another.

གཞན་གཡམ་ (shenyam) sm. གཞན་ཟེར་རྗེས་འབྲང་.

གཞན་ལ་ངོམ་ངོམ་ (shenla ŋomŋom) showing off to other people, va.—བྱེད་.

གཞན་ལ་ལྟ་བའི་མིག་ཡོད་ཀྱང་རང་ལ་ལྟ་བར་མེ་ལོང་དགོས་ (shenla dāwɛ miggyan ranla dāwaa melon göö) one should look at one's own faults/ actions/ behavior [Lit. you have eyes to watch other people but need a mirror to watch oneself].

གཞན་ལ་བརྟེན་ (shenla dēn) va. to depend on others ། འཚོ་བ་གཞན་ལ་བརྟེན་དགོས་བྱུང་ན་ If one has to depend on others for one's livelihood.

གཞན་ལས་མགོ་འཕང་མཐོ་བ་ (shenlɛɛ goban tōwa) rising above others, standing out among one's fellows.

གཞན་ལས་ལྷག་པ་ (shenlɛɛ lhāgba) more than others.

གཞན་ལུགས་ (shenluù) other's view/ outlook/ idea.

གཞན་བཤད་རྗེས་བཟློས་ (shenshɛɛ jendöö) repeating/ echoing/ parroting what others say, repeating/ echoing/ parroting the views of others.

གཞན་ས་ (shensa) other's place/ area ། ཉིན་གསུམ་ནས་གཞན་ས་ཐུག་ཀྱུ་ (One) will reaching another's area in three days.

གཞན་སེམས་ (shensem) other's wish/ thought.

གཞབ་ (shəb) f. of འཇབས་.

གཞའ་ (sha) 1. arc. sm. ཡིབས་. 2. arc. sm. ཤགུ. 3. arc. sm. གབ་.

གཞའ་མཚོན་ (shadzön) rainbow, rainbow color.

གཞའ་རིས་ (sharii) sm. འཇའ་རིས་.

གཞའ་རིས་ཡིབས་རིས་ (shareè yibreè) sm. གབ་རིས་ ཡིབས་རིས་.

གཞའ་རློན་ (shalön) dampness.

གཞའ་གསང་ (shasan) 1. arc. sm. ཕྱིན་ལས་. 2. arc. sm. གཡུང་དྲུང་. 3. arc. sm. མཐུ་ནང་.

གཞར་: p. བཞར་; f. གཞར་; imp. གཞོར་ (shaa) va. to shave (hair, beard, etc.) ། གྲྭ་པ་ཚོ་སྐྲ་གཞར་གྱི་ཡོད་པ་རེད་ The monks are shaving their hair.

གཞར་སྤྱད་ (shaajeèè) shaving utensils/ implements.

གཞར་ཡང་ (sharyan) sm. སླར་ཡང་.

གཞལ་ (shee) f. of འཇལ་.

གཞལ་གྱིས་མི་ལང་བ་ (sheegi milanwa) countless, infinite, limitless, immeasurable.

གཞལ་ལུགས་ (sheèluù) sm. འབོ་.

གཞལ་མེད་ (sheemeè) sm. གཞལ་གྱི་མི་ལང་བ་.

གཞལ་མེད་ཁང་ (sheemeègan) sm. གཞལ་ཡས་ཁང་.

གཞལ་ཚད་ (sheedzeè) sm. གཞལ་ཚད་.

གཞལ་ཡས་ (sheeyeè) sm. གཞལ་གྱིས་མི་ལང་བ་.

གཞལ་ཡས་ཁང་ (sheeyeègan) 1. abode of the gods. 2. a great/ wonderful dwelling.

གཞས་ (sheè) song, music; va.—གཏོང་ to sing.

གཞས་ཀྱི་ཕུའུ་ཙི་ (sheègi pūüdzi) tib. ch. musical notation.

གཞས་སྐྱལ་ (sheègüü) leading a group in singing.

གཞས་ཁང་ (sheègan) a hall for a show (singing, dancing).

གཞས་འགོ་ (shengo) start of a song.

གཞས་ཆུང་ (sheèjun) ballad, ditty.

གཞས་ཆེན་ (sheèjen) special type of song sung at ceremonies such as weddings.

གཞས་རྙིང་ (sheèñin) old songs.

གཞས་རྙིང་བསྐྱར་གཏོང་ (sheèñin gyärdon) reviving/ restoring old customs [Lit. sing old songs again].

གཞས་གདམ་ཚོགས་པ་ (sheèdam tsōgba) recitation and song troupe.

གཞས་དེབ་ (sheèdeb) song book.

གཞས་གདངས་ (sheèdan) tune, melody; va.—སྒྲིགས་ to compose music.

གཞས་གདངས་སྒྲིག་རྩོམ་ (sheèdan drigdzom) music composition; va.—བྱེད་ to compose music.

གཞས་གདངས་སྒྲིག་རྩོམ་པ་ (sheèdan drigdzomba) musical composer.

གཞས་གདངས་བཟོ་འགོད་ (sheèdan sogöö) sm. གཞས་ གདངས་སྒྲིག་རྩོམ་.

གཞས་སྣེ་འཁྲིད་མཁན་ (sheène triiñɛn) lead singer (of a chorus).

གཞས་སྣེ་འདྲེན་པ་ (sheène dremba) sm. གཞས་སྣེ་འཁྲིད་ མཁན་.

གཞས་པ་ (sheèba) singer (male).

གཞས་དཔོན་ (sheèbön) lead singer, head of a group, conductor of singers.

གཞས་ཕུད་ (sheèbüü) sm. གཟིགས་ཕུད་.

གཞས་མ་ (sheèma) singer (female).

གཞས་མ་གདམ་ (sheèma dām) type of folk art that includes ballad singing, story telling, comic dialogues.

གཞས་མ་རྣམ་ཐར་ (sheèma nāmdar) a type of singing that has both song and opera arias.

གཞས་ཚིག་ (sheèdzii) words of songs.

གཞས་ཞབས་བྲོ་ (sheè shabdro) song and dance.

གཞས་གཞུག་ (sheèshuù) the end of a song.

གཞས་བཟོ་ (sheè so) va. to compose a song.

གཞས་ར་ (sheèra) stage.

གཞས་ཤགས་ (sheèshaà) contest between two people/ groups wherein each side uses words of songs to respond to each other; va.—རྒྱག.

གཞས་སུ་གཏོང་ (sheèsu dōn) va. to set to music ། ཚིག་དེ་ཚོ་ཁོ་ཚོས་གཞས་སུ་གཏོང་བ་རེད་ (They) set those words to song.

གཞི་ (shi) 1. basis, foundation; vi.—འཛུག; —བཟུང་; —བཙུགས་ to base upon, on the basis of ། རྒྱལ་ཁབ་ཀྱི་སྟོབས་ཤུགས་ཀྱི་གཞི་ The basis of the strength and power of the country. ། བཟོ་ལས་ལ་གཞི་བཞག་པའི་དཔལ་འབྱོར་ An economy based on industry. ། རྩ་ཁྲིམས་ལ་གཞི་བཟུང་ནས་ Basing it on the constitution. 2. (vb. + —) cause, source, basis ། ནང་འཁྲུག་ཡོང་གཞི་དེ་ནི་ As for the cause of the civil war. 3. the predominant background color or pattern ། གཞི་སྔོན་པོའི་ཐོག་མེ་ཏོག་དམར་ཡོད་པའི་རས་ Cloth with red flowers on a blue background.

གཞི་ཀ་ང་ (shigan) 1. actually, really ། གཞི་ཀ་ང་ཁོང་མི་ཡག་པོ་ཡོད་ཀྱང་ཁྲུང་ལང་ཙམ་ཡོད་པ་རེད་ Actually, even though he is a good person, he has a slight temper. 2. core, base, basic, foundation.

གཞི་ཀ་ངང་ཐོག (shigandɔɔ) in the main, essentially, basically ། གཞི་ཀ་ང་ཐོག་སློབ་ཆུང་སློབ་གསོ་ཁྱབ་གདལ་དུ་བཏང་བ་རེད་ In the main, primary education has become universal.

གཞི་ཁུངས་ (shigun) origin, roots, class origins ། ཁོ་ཚོ་གཞི་ཁུངས་སྐྱོ་པོ་རེད་ They are of poor (class) origin.

གཞི་ཁུངས་འཕོངས་དམན་ (shigun kööman) poor class background.

གཞི་ཁྱོན་ (shigyön) scale, size, extent ། རྒྱལ་ཡོངས་ཀྱི་གཞི་ཁྱོན་ལྡན་པའི་ནང་འཁྲུག A country-wide civil war.

གཞི་ཁྱོན་ཆུང་བ་ (shigyön cūŋwə) small scale.

གཞི་ཁྱོན་ཆེ་བ་ (shigyön cēwa) large scale, large in size.

གཞི་ཁྱོན་ཆེན་པོ་ (shigyön cēmbo) sm. གཞི་ཁྱོན་ཆེ་བ་.

གཞི་ཁྱོན་ཆེན་པོའི་བསད་རྒྱས་རང་བཞིན་གྱི་མཚོན་ཆ་ (shigyön cēmbö sɛ̄ɛmɛɛ rəŋshingi tsōnja) weapons of mass destruction.

གཞི་གྲངས་ (shidraŋ) data.

གཞི་གྲངས་ཀྱི་མཛོད་ (shidraŋgi dzöö) database, databank.

གཞི་གྲངས་བཀོད་སྒྲིག (shidraŋ gōödrig) data processing.

གཞི་གྲངས་ཆགས་ཚུལ་ (shidraŋ cāgdzüü) data structure.

གཞི་གྲངས་སྤོལ་སྐྱེལ་ (shidraŋ bōögyee) data transmission.

གཞི་གྲངས་མཛོད་བདག་གཉེར་ (shidraŋdzöö dagñer) database management system.

གཞི་དགོན་ (shigün) sm. གཞིས་དགོན་.

གཞི་རྒྱ་ (shigya) sm. གཞི་ཁྲོན་.

གཞི་རྒྱུ་ (shigyu) elements (in chemistry).

གཞི་རྒྱུ་དུས་འཁོར་རེའུ་མིག (shigyu tüügɔɔ riwumii) periodic table of elements.

གཞི་རྒྱུད་ (shigyüü) bow string; va.—འཐེན་ to draw a bow string.

གཞི་རྒྱུར་ཙ་རྒྱུར་ (shigyur dzəgyur) radical reform/ change, thorough/ complete reform; va.—བྱེད་.

གཞི་སྒྱུར་ཙ་སྒྱུར་ (shigyur dzəgyur) sm. གཞི་རྒྱུར་ཙ་རྒྱུར་.

གཞི་སྒྲོམ་ (shidrom) a frame.

གཞི་དངུལ་ (shiŋüü) stock (in a company).

གཞི་གཅིག་ཏུ་འདྲིལ་ (shi jīgdu dree) vi. to come together into a single unit (e.g., political parties, streams).

གཞི་བཅོས་ (shijöö) curing/ healing/ correcting sth. from the root; va.—བྱེད་.

གཞི་ལྕི་ (shiji) sm. གཞི་ལྕིད་པོ་.

གཞི་ཆགས་ (shi cāà) vi. to become the basis/ foundation for sth. ¶ ལས་དགེ་བ་བསྒྲུབས་ན་བདེ་བའི་གཞི་ཆགས་ཀྱི་རེད་ If (you) do virtuous deeds, they will be the foundation for happiness.

གཞི་ཆེས་ (shijeè) very important/ significant.

གཞི་ལྕིད་པོ་ (shi jibu) serious, grave.

གཞི་རྟགས་ (shidaà) radical sign (in math).

གཞི་རྟེན་ (shiden) base, foundation; va.—བཙུ་ to make a base, foundation ¶ ཞིང་ལས་ནི་ཁོང་ཚོའི་འཚོ་བའི་གཞི་རྟེན་རེད་ Farming is the basis of their livelihood.

གཞི་ཐིག (shidig) plumb line.

གཞི་མཐུན་ (shidün) objects having similar qualities.

གཞི་མཐུན་པོ་ (shi tũmbu) matching, suitable, getting along.

གཞི་དེབ་ (shideb) the main book.

གཞི་དོན་ (shidön) sm. ཙ་དོན་.

གཞི་གདན་ (shidɛn) rug used under another rug, rug pad.

གཞི་གདན་གོག་རྡུལ་ (shidɛn gəghrüü) a shambles, an awful mess.

གཞི་བདག (shidaà) deity of a particular area or place, local deity.

གཞི་བདག་གཉུག་མར་གནས་པ་ (shidaà ñūgmaa nɛ̄ɛba) the local deity of a particular place or area.

གཞི་དུལ་ཁ་པ་ (shidüü kāba) beta particle.

གཞི་མདའ་ (shida) radical axis.

གཞི་ནས་ (shinɛɛ̀) only then, only after ¶ གསར་བརྗེ་བྱས་ནས་གཞི་ནས་གྲལ་རིམ་གྱི་སྡུག་བསྔལ་བསལ་ཐུབ་པ་རེད་ They were able to remove the sufferings of class only after the revolution. 2. from scratch, from the beginning ¶ ལས་ཀ་འདི་གཞི་ནས་བྱེད་དགོས་རེད་ (They) have to do this work from scratch.

གཞི་ཕྲན་ཚེགས་ (shi trɛ̄ndzeg) a small/ minute matter.

གཞི་པོ་ (shiwo) permanent resident.

གཞི་བྱེས་ (shijeè) sm. གཞིས་བྱེས་.

གཞི་མ་ (shimə) 1. sm. གཞི་ཙ་. 2. homebase encampment of nomads.

གཞི་མ་གྲུབ་པ་ (shimə trubbə) 1. not existing. 2. (person of) bad character.

གཞི་མེད་ (shimeè) 1. (usu. vb. + —) without foundation/ basis, no basis. 2. emptiness, the void.

གཞི་མེད་རང་བྱུང་ (shimeè rəŋjuŋ) sth. that is borne without any foundation, sth. that is groundless.

གཞི་ཙ་ (shidzə) basis, foundation; va.—འཇོག to leave/ have as the basis of doing sth. ¶ ཁོང་ཚོའི་དམིག་ཡུལ་གྱི་གཞི་ཙ་ The foundation of their aims.

གཞི་ཙའི་ཁེ་ཕན་ (shidzɛ kēbɛn) vital interest, fundamental benefit.

གཞི་ཙའི་ཆ་ནས་ (shidzɛ cānɛ) 1. mostly, pretty much ¶ གཞི་ཙ་འི་ཆ་ནས་ལོ་འདིའི་ལས་འགན་བསྒྲུབས་ཟིན་པ་རེད་ We have mostly fulfilled this year's work assignment. 2. in principle ¶ གཞི་ཙའི་ཆ་ནས་ཡུལ་དེ་ར་ཆོས་དད་རང་དབང་ཡོད་ In principle, there is religious freedom in that place.

གཞི་ཙའི་ཐོག (shidzɛtɔɔ̀) sm. གཞི་ཙའི་ཆ་ནས་.

གཞི་ཙའི་ཐོབ་ཐང་ (shidzɛ tōbdaŋ) fundamental rights ¶ འགྲོ་བ་མིའི་གཞི་ཙའི་ཐོབ་ཐང་ Fundamental human rights.

གཞི་ཙའི་ཆོས་གཞི་ (shidzɛ tsũũshi) sm. གཞི་ཚོན་.

གཞི་ཙའི་སློབ་སྦྱོང་ (shidzɛ lōbjoŋ) basic training.

གཞི་ཙར་བཟུང་ (shidzaa suŋ) va. to base sth. upon, to do on the basis of ¶ རང་གི་མི་རིགས་དང་གོམས་གཤིས་སོགས་གཞིས་ཙར་བཟུང་སྟེ Based on one's own nationality and customs.

གཞི་ཙེ་ (shidze) abbr. of གཞིས་ཀ་ཙེ་.

གཞི་ཙུགས་ (shi tsūù) vi. to establish a base/ foundation.

གཞི་ཚུལ་ (shidzüü) a radical (in math); va.—ཙོ་.

གཞི་ཚུལ་མཉམ་བྱ་ (shidzüü ñāmja) radical equation (in math).

གཞི་ཚོན་ (shidzön) primary colors.

གཞི་འཛིན་ (shindzin) using/ holding as the basis or foundation or starting point; va.—བྱེད་.

གཞི་འཛིན་ས་མེད་པ་ (shidzinsə meèba) unfounded, baseless.

གཞི་འཛིན་སའི་གྲངས་ཀ་ (shidzinsɛ traŋga) sm. གཞི་གྲངས་.

གཞི་བཞག (shi shaà) va. to base on ¶ ཁོང་གི་བསམ་བློ་ནི་ཚུལ་མཐུན་གྱི་ཁྱད་ཆོས་གསུམ་ལ་གཞི་བཞག་ཡོད་པ་རེད་ His thoughts are based on these three moral characteristics. ¶ ཙ་ཁྲིམས་ལ་གཞི་བཞག་སྟེ་ཐག་གཅོད་བྱས་པ་རེད་ They made a decision based on the constitution. ¶ སྙན་སྒྲོན་ནང་འཁོད་དོན་གཞི་བཞག་གིས་ Based on what was written in the report.

གཞི་བཞག་ན་ (shi shaàna) on the basis of, in view of ¶ ཁོས་བཤད་པར་གཞི་བཞག་ན་ On the basis of what he said.

གཞི་བཞག་བྱེད་ (shishaà ceè) va. to be based on ¶ ཚོགས་མི་མང་བའི་དགོངས་འཆར་ལ་གཞི་བཞག་བྱས་ནས་ཐག་གཅོད་བྱས་པ་རེད་ Based on the suggestions of the majority of the members, they decided (it).

གཞི་བཟུང་ (shisuŋ) sm. གཞི་བཞག.

གཞི་བཟུང་ན་ (shisuŋna) sm. གཞི་བཞག་ན་.

གཞི་བཟུང་བྱེད་ (shisuŋ ceè) sm. གཞི་བཞག་བྱེད་.

གཞི་ཡངས་ཆེ་བ་ (shiyaŋ cēwa) large scale, large in size.

གཞི་ཡུལ་ (shiyüü) basic, foundation.

གཞི་རིམ་ (shirim) basic/ local level (cadre and officials), grassroots level ¶ གཞི་རིམ་དུ་བརྟག་དཔྱད་བྱས་པ་རེད་ (He) did grassroots level research and examination.

གཞི་རིམ་འདེམས་བསྐོ་ (shirim demgo) local election.

གཞི་རིམ་ཙ་འཛུགས་ (shirim dzəndzuù) local/ primary organization.

གཞི་རིམ་ལས་བྱེད་ (shirim lɛɛ̀jeè) local officials.

གཞི་རིམ་ལས་བྱེད་པ་ (shirim lɛɛ̀jeba) sm. གཞི་རིམ་ལས་བྱེད་.

གཞི་རིམ་སློབ་གྲྭ་ (shirim lōbdra) local/ primary school.

གཞི་རིམ་སློབ་དེབ་ (shirim lōbdeb) local/ primary text book.

གཞི་རིམ་སློབ་སྦྱོང་ (shirim lōbjoŋ) sm. གཞི་རིམ་སློབ་གསོ་.

གཞི་རིམ་སློབ་གསོ་ (shirim lōbso) local/ primary education.

གཞི་རིམ་ཨུ་ཡོན་ལྷན་ཁང་ (shirim ūyün lhɛ̄ngaŋ) local party committee.

གཞི་ལ་ (shilə) sm. གཞིར་.

གཞི་ཕླིང་པོ་ (shi̲ lhīŋbu) cool headed, composed, calm.

གཞིག: p. གཞིགས་; f. གཞིག; imp. གཞིགས་ (shi̲i) 1. va. to examine, to look into ¶ གནས་ཚུལ་དེ་ཚོར་ནན་གཏན་གཞིགས་ནས་ཐག་གཅོད་བྱས་པ་རེད་ (They) made the decision after carefully examining the circumstances. 2. vi. to be based on, to be in accordance with ¶ གནས་ཚུལ་དེར་གཞིགས་གནས་ནས་ Based on that situation.

གཞིབ་ (shi̲b) f. of འཇིབ་.

གཞིབ་འཐུང་ (shi̲bduŋ) sucking, suckling; va.—བྱེད་.

གཞིབ་སྣབས་ (shi̲bbub) sm. འཇིབ་རུ་.

གཞིའི་སྒྲ་ལུས་ (shi̲i gyu̲lüü) body of a person while he is in the bardo state.

གཞིའི་སྒྱུར་ཆད་ (shi̲i gyu̲rjεὲ) radical deviation.

གཞིའི་སྟོན་གྲངས་ (shi̲i dõndraŋ) radical exponent (in math).

གཞིར་ (shi̲r) (vb. + —) the cause/ source of the verbal action ¶ ས་བདག་གི་བཙུ་གནོན་ནི་ཞིང་པས་ཕྱིན་ལང་བྱེད་གཞིར་གྱུར་པ་རེད་ The exploitation of the landlords became the cause of the uprising of the peasants.

གཞིར་བཅས་ (shi̲rjεὲ) presuming (used at the end of a clause) ¶ ཁྱེད་རང་ཚོ་ཚང་མ་སྐུ་ཁམས་བདེ་ཐང་དུ་ཡོད་པ་གཞིར་བཅས་ (I) presume that you all are in good health.

གཞིར་འཛིན་ (shi̲rdzin) sm. གཞིར་བཟུང་.

གཞིར་བཞག (shi̲rshaà) sm. གཞིར་བཟུང་.

གཞིར་བཟུང་ (shi̲rsuŋ) va. to hold or take as the basis/ foundation, to base on, to do in accordance with ¶ མང་ཚོགས་ཀྱི་བསམ་འཆར་ལ་གཞིར་བཟུང་ནས་ Taking the opinion of the people as the foundation. ¶ཁོང་གི་མཛུབ་སྟོན་གཞིར་བཟུང་ལས་དོན་ལག་ལེན་བསྒྲུར་དགོས་ (They) should carry out the task in accordance with his instructions.

གཞིལ་ (shi̲i) f. of འཇིལ་.

གཞིས་ shi̲i) 1. abbr. of གཞིས་ཀ་. 2. shung. home (in contrast to away) ¶ གཞིས་གཞུང་ The government in the main place (in contrast to a government in exile).

གཞིས་ཀ་ (shi̲igə) estate (agricultural).

གཞིས་ཀ་རྩེ་ (shi̲igədze) Shigatse.

གཞིས་ཀ་རྩེ་སྤྱི་ཁྱབ་ (shi̲igadze jīdzoŋ) shung. the head official of Shigatse district (in tt.).

གཞིས་སྐྱེལ་ (shi̲igyee) shung. corvee tax consisting of transporting goods from one estate to the next.

གཞིས་བསྐོར་ (shi̲igɔɔ) shung. officials getting leave from Lhasa and going to their estate; va.—དུ་འགྲོ་ to go on leave to one's estate; — ཞུ་ to ask for such a leave.

གཞིས་ཁག (shi̲igaà) different estates.

གཞིས་ཁང་ (shi̲igaŋ) manor house on an estate.

གཞིས་འཁོད་ (shi̲igöö) sm. གཞིམ་ལུས་.

གཞིས་འཁོར་ (shi̲igɔɔ) sm. གཞིམ་བསྐོར་.

གཞིས་མགྲོན་ (shi̲ndrün) 1. a traveler from (one's) home/ country. 2. abbr. a resident of a place and a traveler.

གཞིས་དགོན་ (shi̲igün) small branch monastery, village monastery.

གཞིས་འགོ་ (shi̲ngo) settlement leader, camp leader.

གཞིས་རྒྱལ་ (shi̲i gyε̲ε̲) shung. abbr. Shigatse and Gyantse.

གཞིས་རྒྱལ་དིང་གསུམ་ (shi̲igyεε ti̲ŋsum) shung. abbr. Shigatse, Gyantse and Dingri (the three).

གཞིས་སྒར་ (shi̲igar) a settlement; vi.—ཆགས་ to become settled.

གཞིས་སྒྲིལ་ (shi̲idrii) 1. two families joining together/ merging/ combining into one. 2. going somewhere to settle with all one's possessions; va.—རྒྱག.

གཞིས་བཅའ་ (shi̲ijaa) sm. གཞིས་ཆགས་.

གཞིས་བཅས་ (shi̲ijεὲ) sm. གཞིས་ཆགས་.

གཞིས་ཆགས་ (shi̲ijaà) a settlement, settling down somewhere new; va.—བྱེད་ to settle ¶ སྐྱབས་བཅོལ་བ་མང་པོ་ས་ཞིང་ཐོག་གཞིས་ཆགས་བྱས་ཡོད་པ་རེད་ Many refugees have been settled on farms.

གཞིས་ཆགས་ལས་ཁུངས་ (shi̲i lε̲ὲguŋ) office in charge of settlements.

གཞིས་ཆགས་ལས་རྟགས་ (shi̲ijaà lε̲ὲdzuù) settling down and establishing a livelihood/ business/ occupation, permanently settling down.

གཞིས་གཉེར་ (shi̲iñer) shung. manager/ foreman/ steward of an estate (who generally lives on the estate); va.—བྱེད་.

གཞིས་དུད་ (shi̲idüü) shung. དུད་ཆུང་ households that are attached to an estate but do not hold tax land and are not required to provide corvee labor.

གཞིས་དེབ་ (shi̲ideb) shung. the record (book) of the income and expenditures of an estate.

གཞིས་བདག (shi̲idaà) shung. landowner, lord of an estate.

གཞིས་སྡོད་ (shi̲idüü) shung. sm. གཞིས་གཉེར་.

གཞིས་པ་ (shi̲ibə) inhabitant, resident ¶ ཆུ་རྒྱུད་དེའི་གཞིས་པ་རྣམས་ The inhabitants along that river.

གཞིས་དཔོན་ (shi̲ibün) shung. sm. གཞིས་གཉེར་.

གཞིས་སྤོ་ (shi̲i bō) va. to move (one's place of residence).

གཞིས་བྱེས་ (shi̲ijeè) shung. those at home and those away from home ¶ གཞིས་བྱེད་བོད་མི་ The Tibetans in Tibet and those away/ outside (in exile).

གཞིས་བྱེས་མཉམ་འཛོམས་ (shi̲ijeè ñamdzom) relatives/ family getting together after being apart.

གཞིས་བྱེས་ཞལ་འཛོམས་ (shi̲ijeè she̲ndzom) sm. གཞིས་བྱེས་མཉམ་འཛོམས་.

གཞིས་བྲན་ (shi̲idrεn) shung. estate serf.

གཞིས་འབབ་ (shi̲ibəb) shung. the income of an estate.

གཞིས་འབྲུ་ (shi̲ndu) shung. grain harvested from an estate.

གཞིས་འབྲོག (shi̲i drɔ̲ɔ̀) shung. abbr. farmers and nomads.

གཞིས་མ་ལག (shi̲imalaà) shung. the main estate and its branches.

གཞིས་མི་ (shi̲imə) settler, a person who has been settled.

གཞིས་མིན་པོ་བྲང་ (shi̲imin pōdraŋ) temporary palace.

གཞིས་དམག (shi̲imaà) soldiers on/ from an estate.

གཞིས་རྩ་ལེན་ (shi̲idzə le̲n) shung. va. to confiscate an estate completely (by the government).

གཞིས་རྩེ་ (shi̲idze) abbr. of གཞིས་ཀ་རྩེ་.

གཞིས་འོག (shi̲iwɔɔ̀) shung. people owned by an estate, people belonging to an estate.

གཞིས་གཡོག (shi̲iyɔɔ̀) shung. servants on an estate.

གཞིས་ལག (shi̲ilaà) shung. the branches of an estate.

གཞིས་ལས་ (shi̲lεὲ) abbr. for གཞིས་ཆགས་ལས་ཁུངས་.

གཞིས་ལུས་ (shi̲lüü) those left at home (used by Tibetans in India for those left in Tibet) ¶ ང་ཚོའི་གཞིས་ལུས་སྤུན་ཟླའི་དཀའ་ངལ་ལ་བསམས་ན་ If we think about the hardships of (our) brethren who are left behind in Tibet.

གཞིས་ཤུལ་ (shi̲ishüü) shung. hereditary estate; va.—འཛིན་ to hold an estate hereditarily.

གཞིས་སྲུང་ (shi̲isuŋ) guarding/ looking after an estate; va.—བྱེད་.

གཞུ་: p. བཞུས་; f. གཞུ་; imp. གཞུས་ (shu̲) va. to hit, to strike, to throw at ¶ ཁོས་ཁྱི་ལ་རྡོ་གཞུས་པ་རེད་ He hit the dog with a stone. ¶ ཁོས་དེ་ལ་ཐོ་བ་གཞུ་གྲབས་བྱེད་སྐབས་ When he was about to strike it with a hammer. 2. a bow (the weapon) va.; —འགེང་; —འཐེན་; —འགུག; —བདུང་ to pull the string of a bow. 3. the plank of wood between the pillar and beam.

གཞུ་ཀྲད་ (shu̲drεὲ) string of a bow.

གཞུ་གང་ (shu̲gaŋ) sm. འདོམ་གང་.

གཞུ་གང་ཚད་ (shu̲gaŋdzεὲ) sm. འདོམ་གང་.

གཞུ་གར་མ་ (shu̲garma) a strong/ tough bow.

གཞུ་གུ་ (shu̲gu) 1. tail ¶ ཁྱིའི་གཞུ་གུ་ The tail of a dog.

2. the end of sth. ། གྲལ་གྱི་གཞུ་གུར་ At the end of the line (row). 3. va.—བཀྱག to rise up again, to resurrect oneself [Lit. to lift one's tail].

གཞུ་གུ་སྐྱིལ་ (shugu gyēē) va. to complete/ conclude ། ངས་ཁ་སང་ལས་ཀའི་གཞུ་གུ་བསྐྱིལ་བ་ཡིན་ I completed the work yesterday.

གཞུ་གུ་སྒྲིལ་ (shugu drii) va. to see things to their conclusion, to wrap up things, to finish doing the last bit.

གཞུ་གུ་སྡོག (shugu dɔɔ̀) sm. གཞུ་གུ་སྒྲིལ་.

གཞུ་གུ་སྡོམ་ (shugu dom) va. to sum/ add up at the end.

གཞུ་གུ་འཛིན་ (shugu dzin) va. to inherit, to carry on sth. ། མི་ཚང་དེ་རང་པ་མ་གཉིས་ཀྱི་གཞུ་གུ་འཛིན་མཁན་མེད་པ་རེད་ That family has no one to carry on after them. [Lit. hold on to the tail].

གཞུ་གུ་གཞུག་རྒྱང་ (shugu shuùgyaŋ) sm. གཞུ་གུ་གཞུག་གུ་.

གཞུ་གུ་གཞུག་གུ་ (shugu shuùgu) the very last.

གཞུ་གུ་གཞུག་དེད་ (shugu shuǹdeè) pursing, chasing; va.—གཏོང་ ། རྐུན་མ་དེ་གཞུ་གུ་གཞུག་དེད་བཏང་ནས་འཛིན་བཟུང་བྱས་པ་རེད་ They pursued the thief and arrested him.

གཞུ་གུ་རིལ་རིལ་ (shugu riirii) 1. dog's tail wagging out of joy; va.—བྱེད་. 2. curled up tail.

གཞུ་གུར་ (shugur) later, after ། ཁྱེད་རང་ལས་ཀ་ངན་པ་བྱས་ན་གཞུ་གུར་ཡག་པོ་ཡོང་གི་མ་རེད་ If you do bad work, later it will not be good.

གཞུ་གུར་འགྲོ་ (shugur dro) va. to follow after.

གཞུ་རྒྱུད་ (shugyüü) bow string; va.—སྣར་ to string a bow.

གཞུ་སྒྲ་ (shudra) sound of a bow string.

གཞུ་སྒྲིལ་ (shudrii) sm. གཞུ་གུ་སྒྲིལ་.

གཞུ་མཆོག (shujɔɔ̀) a high quality bow.

གཞུ་མཆོག་དཀར་ (shujɔɔ̀gar) sm. གཞུ་མཆོག.

གཞུ་དོ་ (shudo) 1. tail bone. 2. end of the tail.

གཞུ་ཐིག (shudig) a curved line.

གཞུ་ཐིག་གུག་ཚད་ (shudig kuùdzɛɛ̀) the degree of an arc/ curved line.

གཞུ་ཐུང་ (shuduŋ) 1. a short bow. 2. the piece of wood between a beam and pillar. 3. the tail bone.

གཞུ་འཐེན་ (shu tēn) va. to draw a bow string.

གཞུ་འཐེན་རོལ་ཆ་ (shuden rööja) percussion and string instruments.

གཞུ་འདོམ་ (shundom) an ancient unit of measurement equal to 4 cubits (roughly 6 feet).

གཞུ་དབྱིབས་ (shuyib) bow shaped.

གཞུ་དབྱིབས་ཅན་ (shuyibjɛn) bow shaped.

གཞུ་དབྱིབས་ཅན་གྱི་ཆུ་སྦུག (shuyibjɛngi cūbuù) a siphon.

གཞུ་དབྱིབས་ཅན་གྱི་མཆོངས་སྟེགས་ (shuyibjɛngi cōŋdeg) diving board.

གཞུ་མོ་ (shumo) a bow (the weapon).

གཞུ་རིང་ (shuriŋ) 1. longbow. 2. a long piece of wood that is placed between a beam and pillar.

གཞུ་རེས་གཏོང་ (shureè dōŋ) va. to fight/ hit back and forth.

གཞུ་ལན་སློག (shulɛn lɔ̄ɔ̀) va. to hit back after being hit, to respond to a blow with a blow.

གཞུ་ཤུབས་ (shushub) bow case/ sheath.

གཞུག (shuù) f. of འཇུག.

གཞུག་གུ་ (shugu) sm. གཞུ་གུ་.

གཞུག་རྒྱན་ (shuùgyɛn) a type of ornament/ decoration put on a horse's tail (or mane).

གཞུག་འཆིང་ (shugjiŋ) an ornament/ decoration for a horse's tail; va.—རྒྱག to put on such an ornament.

གཞུག་ཐུང་ (shugduŋ) short tail.

གཞུག་དེད་ (shugdeè) sm. གཞུ་གུ་གཞུག་དེད་.

གཞུག་འདེད་ (shugdeè) གཞུ་གུ་གཞུག་དེད་.

གཞུག་རྡུམ་གཏོང་ (shugdum dōŋ) va. to cut off the tail of an animal, to make the tail shorter.

གཞུག་རྡུམ་པ་ (shugdumbə) 1. tailless animal. 2. an animal that has a short tail.

གཞུག་འཕྱ་རྒྱག (shundra gyaà) va. to buck with hind legs (horses/ mules).

གཞུག་མ་ (shuùmə) latter.

གཞུག་མ་གཤག་མ་ (shuùmə shagma) at last, in/ at the very end ། ཁོའི་མི་ཚེའི་གཞུག་མ་གཤག་མ་དེ་ར་འབུལ་ཕོངས་སུ་གྱུར་པ་རེད་ At the very end of his life that person had become poor.

གཞུག་འཛར་ (shugdzar) 1. unfinished, leftover. 2. an heir.

གཞུག་འཛར་ཟིན་ (shugdzar sin) va. to inherit.

གཞུག་འཛར་ཟིན་མཁན་ (shugdzar singɛn) inheritor, heir.

གཞུག་གཞུག་ལ་ (shuùshuùlə) sm. གཞུག་མ་གཤག་མ་.

གཞུག་ཟིན་ (shug sin) va. to catch up, to reach ། ང་འགྲོ་རྒྱུ་ཕྱི་དྲགས་ནས་གནམ་གྲུ་གཞུག་ཟིན་མ་སོང་ I was late in going and didn't catch the plane (missed the plane).

གཞུག་རིལ་ (shugrii) curled-up tail.

གཞུག་ལ་ (shuùlə) 1. afterwards, after, in the future ། དེའི་གཞུག་ལ་ང་སློབ་གྲྭ་འགྲོ་གི་ཡིན་ After this I am going to school. 2. as long as ། སོ་སོའི་ལས་ཀ་དྲག་བྱས་པའི་གཞུག་ལ་གཞན་གྱིས་གང་བཤད་ཀྱང་གནད་འགག་མེད་ As long as one works diligently, it doesn't matter what others say.

གཞུག་ལ་འགྲོ་ (shuùla dro) 1. va. to go afterwards. 2. va. to follow.

གཞུག་ལ་ལས་ (shuùla lɛɛ̀) sm. གཞུག་ལ་ལུས་.

གཞུག་ལ་ལུས་ (shuùla lüü) vi. to have dropped behind, to be/ get left behind.

གཞུག་ཤོས་ (shugshöö) the very last.

གཞུང་ (shuŋ) 1. central, middle ། ལམ་གྱི་གཞུང་དུ་ In the middle of the road. ། དབྱར་གཞུང་ In the middle of summer. 2. government ། རྒྱ་གར་གཞུང་ The government of India. 3. treatise, text book ། སྨན་གཞུང་ Medical text. 4. va.—བསྒྲིག to compose (a treatise). 5. theory ། ཆོས་ཀྱི་གཞུང་ Religious theory. 6. length. 7. character ། མི་དེ་གཞུང་དྲང་པོ་ཞིག་རེད་ That person is honest. 8. the main valley. 9. lengthwise (as opposed to crosswise).

གཞུང་ཀོ་ (shuŋgɔ) traveling by coracle down a river (as opposed to across) ། ང་གཞུང་ཀོའི་ནང་ལྷ་ས་ནས་ཆུ་ཤུལ་བར་ཕྱིན་པ་ཡིན་ I went by coracle down the river from Lhasa to Chushul.

གཞུང་བཀའ་འཁྲིད་གནང་ (shuŋ gātrīī nāŋ) h. of གཞུང་འཁྲིད་.

གཞུང་བཀའ་ཡོད་ལྔ་ (shuŋ gāböö ŋā) sm. གཞུང་ཆེན་བཀའ་ཡོད་ལྔ་.

གཞུང་བཀལ་ (shuŋgɛɛ) sth. that is hanging from top to bottom.

གཞུང་བཀུར་དམངས་གཅེས་ (shuŋguu māŋjeè) support the government and cherish the people (political slogan).

གཞུང་རྒྱང་ (shuŋgyaŋ) shung. family household.

གཞུང་སྐུལ་ (shuŋgüü) shung. an order by the government conscripting/ requisitioning sth. ། གཞུང་ལམ་བཟོ་སར་གཞུང་སྐུལ་ཞུས་མི་མང་པོ་ཞིག་སླེབས་འདུག Many people who were conscripted by the government arrived at the road building site.

གཞུང་བསྐོས་ (shuŋgöö) shung. government appointed ། གཞུང་བསྐོས་དགེ་རྒན་ Government appointed teacher.

གཞུང་ཁ་ (shuŋga) the Bhutanese government dialect.

གཞུང་ཁང་ (shuŋgaŋ) 1. the main/ principal rooms (in a courtyard these are usually the ones facing south). 2. government houses/ buildings. 3. sm. གཞུང་ལས་ཁང་.

གཞུང་ཁོངས་ (shuŋgoŋ) shung. belonging to the government, the government sector ། གཞུང་ཁོངས་བཟོ་གྲྭ་ Government owned factories.

གཞུང་ཁྲ་ (shundra) a detailed list.

གཞུང་ཁྲལ་ (shundrɛɛ) shung. government taxes.

གཞུང་ཁྲལ་དངོས་གཞི་ (shundrɛɛ ŋöòshi) shung. main government tax.

གཞུང་ཁྲིམས་ (shundrim) government law/

regulations.

གཞུང་འཁྲིད་ (shuŋ trii) va. to teach, to give a lecture ༑ མི་རིགས་རིག་པའི་གཞུང་འཁྲིད་ཀྱི་ཡོད་པ་རེད་ (They) are teaching a course on anthropology.

གཞུང་གི་ཀང་དངུལ་ (shuŋgi gāŋŋüü) sm. གཞུང་ཕྱོགས་ཀྱི་མ་དངུལ་.

གཞུང་གི་དཔར་བསྐྲུན་ཁང་ (shuŋgi bərdrüngaŋ) Government Printing Office (GPO, in U.S.A.).

གཞུང་སྒྲོན་ (shuŋdrön) government/ public expenditure; va.—གཏོང་. to pay expenses from a government fund.

གཞུང་སྒྲོན་ཐོབ་ཐང་ (shuŋdrön tōbdaŋ) the right to do sth. at public/ government/ state expense.

གཞུང་སྒྲོན་སྨན་བཅོས་ (shuŋdrön mēnjöö) government paid/ funded medical treatment.

གཞུང་སྒྲོན་འཚོ་སྐྱོང་ (shuŋdrön tsōgyoŋ) government support, government economic welfare.

གཞུང་སྒྲོན་སློབ་མ་ (shuŋdrön lōbma) a student on government expense, a student funded by the government.

གཞུང་གླིང་ (shuŋliŋ) 1. a vertically held flute, a flute held straight in front of the mouth. 2. parks belonging to the government.

གཞུང་གླིང་ལྦི་གཅིག་མ་ (shuŋliŋ jējigmə) clarinet.

གཞུང་མགྲོན་ (shuŋdrön) shung. government guest.

གཞུང་འགལ་ལུགས་འགལ་ (shuŋgɛɛ luggɛɛ) in breach of customs and rules.

གཞུང་འགྲེལ་ (shuŋdree) footnote.

གཞུང་རྒྱུ་ (shuŋgyu) shung. government wealth/ property.

གཞུང་རྒྱུག (shuŋgyuù) shung. abbr. of གཞུང་རྒྱུག་པ་.

གཞུང་རྒྱུག་འཁྱེར་ཞེན་ (shuŋgyuù kyērshɛn) shung. the poorer people amongst the government taxpayer serfs.

གཞུང་རྒྱུག་པ་ (shuŋgyuùbə) shung. government taxpayer serfs.

གཞུང་རྒྱུག་མི་སེར་ (shuŋgyuù misee) shung. sm. གཞུང་རྒྱུག་པ་.

གཞུང་རྒྱུག་ས་འཛིན་ (shuŋgyuù səndzin) shung. sm. གཞུང་རྒྱུག་པ་.

གཞུང་རྒྱུགས་ཁྲལ་པ་ (shuŋgyuù trɛ̄ɛba) shung. sm. གཞུང་རྒྱུག་པ་.

གཞུང་རྒྱུད་ (shuŋgyüü) sm. གཞུང་, 7.

གཞུང་རྒྱུད་དྲང་པོ་ (shuŋgyüü traŋbo) sm. གཞུང་དྲང་.

གཞུང་སྒེར་ (shuŋger) 1. shung. government and private ༑ གཞུང་སྒེར་བཟོ་གྲྭ་ Government and privately (owned) factories. 2. shung. the government and the aristocracy.

གཞུང་སྒེར་ཆོས་གསུམ་ (shuŋger cöösum) shung. the three: the government, the aristocracy and the monasteries.

གཞུང་སྒེར་གཉིས་མཐོང་ (shuŋger ñiidoŋ) looking after both public and private interests.

གཞུང་སྒེར་གཉིས་ཕན་ (shuŋger ñiibɛn) beneficial to both public and private interests.

གཞུང་སྒེར་མཉམ་གཉེར་ (shuŋger ñamñer) joint government/ private management or enterprise.

གཞུང་སྒོ་ (shuŋgo) main door, the main gate.

གཞུང་སྒོར་ (shuŋgɔɔ) government money/ funds.

གཞུང་སྒྲུབ་ (shuŋdrub) sm. གཞུང་བཙུགས་.

གཞུང་སྒྲུབ་ཁང་ (shuŋdrubgaŋ) sm. གཞུང་ལས་ཁང་.

གཞུང་བསྒྱུར་ (shuŋgyur) nationalization; va.—བྱེད་; —གནང་ to nationalize.

གཞུང་བསྒྲིགས་ (shuŋ drig) va. to edit/ organize/ arrange a text.

གཞུང་ངན་པོ་ (shuŋ ŋɛmbo) sm. རྒྱུ་དངུལ་མེད་པ་.

གཞུང་ངོ་མ་ (shuŋ ŋoma) the legal/ recognized government.

གཞུང་དངུལ་ (shuŋŋüü) government money/ funds.

གཞུང་དངུལ་སྒེར་སྤྱོད་ (shuŋŋüü gerjöö) private use/ embezzlement/ misappropriation of public funds; va.—བྱེད་.

གཞུང་དངོས་ (shuŋŋöö) 1. original text, the main text. 2. government property.

གཞུང་སྔོན་སྒེར་རྗེས་ (shuŋŋön gerjeè) putting public interest ahead of one's own; va.—བྱེད་.

གཞུང་གཅོད་ (shuŋjüü) 1. va. to fix/ settle/ set by the government. 2. va. to traverse or cross sth. lengthwise (in contrast to crosswise).

གཞུང་བཅད་ཀྱི་ངོས་ (shuŋjɛ̀ɛgi ŋöö) 1. government set/ fixed ༑ གཞུང་བཅད་རིན་གོང་ A government fixed price. 2. a longitudinal/ lengthwise section.

གཞུང་ཆག (shuŋ cāà) 1. vi. to crack (longitudinally or from top to bottom). 2. a government exemption/ concession.

གཞུང་ཆུ་ (shuŋju) main current/ flow of a river.

གཞུང་ཆེན་བཀའ་པོད་ལྔ་ (shuŋjen gāböö ŋā) a key set of texts used by monks in their studies of Buddhist dialectics.

གཞུང་ཆོད་ (shuŋjüü) 1. vi. to be fixed/ settled/ set by the government. 2. va. to be able to traverse or cross sth. lengthwise (in contrast to crosswise).

གཞུང་གཉེར་ (shuŋñer) government run, government managed (e.g., an office, business).

གཞུང་བསྙད་སྒེར་ཕན་ (shuŋñɛ̀ɛ gerbɛn) promoting private interests under the guise of serving the public; va.—བྱེད་.

གཞུང་ཏོག (shuŋdoò) a government official/ employee.

གཞུང་གཏུག (shuŋduù) bringing a lawsuit to the government; va.—རྒྱག to bring a lawsuit to the government.

གཞུང་བཏང་མི་འགྲོ་ (shuŋdaŋ migro) shung. an official sent on a long task/ trip by the government.

གཞུང་རྟགས་ (shuŋdaà) ordinate (in math).

གཞུང་སྟོན་ (shuŋdön) party/ banquet given to calligraphers when they come to the middle part of a copying project.

གཞུང་བསྟེན་དགྲ་ལྷ་ (shuŋden dralha) State Oracles of the Government of Tibet (e.g., Nechung, Gatong, Samye).

གཞུང་བསྟེན་སྲུང་མ་ (shuŋden sūŋmə) shung. sm. གཞུང་བསྟེན་དགྲ་ལྷ་.

གཞུང་ཐག (shuŋdaà) a rope that goes lengthwise across a tent.

གཞུང་ཐམ་ (shuŋdam) shung. government seal.

གཞུང་ཐིག (shuŋdig) (lines of) longitude, vertical line.

གཞུང་ཐིག་གི་ཚད་ (shuŋdiggi tsɛ̄ɛ) degree of longitude.

གཞུང་ཐེལ་ (shuŋdee) shung. government seal, official seal.

གཞུང་དར་ (shuŋdar) a country's flag, national flag.

གཞུང་དོན་ (shuŋdön) 1. government/ public affairs, official business ༑ ས་ཆ་གཞན་དག་ལ་གཞུང་དོན་དུ་འགྲོ་སྐབས་ While going to other places on official business. 2. the main subject of a text/ treatise.

གཞུང་དོན་ཁང་ (shuŋdöngaŋ) the office/ bureau in an organization that handles administrative activities like daily schedules and relations with other offices and people.

གཞུང་དོན་སྒང་ (shuŋdöngaŋ) a bureau, chancellery.

གཞུང་དོན་བཙོན་པ་ (shuŋdön dzōmba) political prisoner.

གཞུང་དོས་ (shuŋdöö) shung. Tibetan goverment cargo (loads) that are moved by corvee labor.

གཞུང་དྲང་ (shuŋdraŋ) fair-minded, upright, honest.

གཞུང་དྲང་ཁ་སངས་ (shuŋdraŋ kāsaŋ) honest and open/ straightforward.

གཞུང་དྲང་འཁྱོག་མེད་ (shuŋdraŋ kyɔ̄gmeè) just, fair, honest.

གཞུང་དྲང་ཅན་ (shuŋdraŋjɛn) truthful, honest.

གཞུང་དྲང་འཇོན་ཆེ་ (shuŋdraŋ jönce) just/. honest and capable.

གཞུང་དྲང་པོ་ (shuŋ traŋbo) sm. གཞུང་དྲང་.

གཞུང་དྲང་བློ་བརྟན་ (shuŋdraŋ lōdɛn) honest and dependable.

གཞུང་དྲང་ཟོལ་མེད་ (shuŋdraŋ söömeè) honest and straightforward/ sincere.

གཞུང་བདག (shuŋdaà) owned by the government.

གཞུང་ལྡན་ (shuŋdɛn) person with good character/ honesty.

གཞུང་སྡུད་ (shuŋdüü) shung. collecting (taxes) by the government; va.—བྱེད་.

གཞུང་བསྡུ་ (shuŋdu) sm. གཞུང་སྡུད་.

གཞུང་ནག (shuŋnaà) person with bad/ cruel character.

གཞུང་ནས་ (shuŋnɛ) 1. from top to bottom, lengthwise. 2. from or by the government.

གཞུང་གནས་ (shuŋnɛɛ̀) shung. the government ¶ གཞུང་གནས་ཀྱི་ཆེད་བསྒྲགས་ A special government announcement.

གཞུང་སྣེ་ (shuŋne) shung. government officials.

གཞུང་པ་ (shuŋbə) sm. གཞུང་རྒྱགས་པ་.

གཞུང་པོ་ཏི་ལྔ་ (shuŋ bōdi ŋā) the five subjects of monks studying dialectics (ཕར་ཕྱིན་; དབུ་མ་; ཚད་མ་; འདུལ་བ་; མཛོད་).

གཞུང་དཔོན་ (shuŋbön) shung. government officials.

གཞུང་སྤེལ་ (shuŋ bēē) va. to spread traditions/ customs.

གཞུང་སྤྱོད་ (shuŋjöö) things used by the government (as opposed to private persons) ¶ ཅ་ལག་འདི་ཚོ་གཞུང་སྤྱོད་རེད་ These things are for use by the government.

གཞུང་སྤྲོད་ (shuŋdröö) 1. given/ supplied by the government; va.—བྱེད་. 2. requisitioned/ taken over for use by the government.

གཞུང་ཕྱི་ཐག (shuŋ cīdaà) sm. ཕྱི་ཐག.

གཞུང་ཕྱོགས་ (shuŋjɔ̀ɔ) the government side/ sector (as opposed to the private).

གཞུང་ཕྱོགས་ཀྱི་ཁྲིམས་སྐྱོར་བྱེད་མཁན་ (shuŋjɔ̀ɔgi trīmjɔɔ ceèñɛn) public/ government prosecutor.

གཞུང་ཕྱོགས་ཀྱི་མ་དངུལ་ (shuŋjɔ̀ɔgi məŋüü) government share/ capital (in a joint state-private enterprise).

གཞུང་ཕྱོགས་མཉམ་འབྲེལ་ (shuŋjɔ̀ɔ ñāmdree) 1. top to bottom connection. 2. a connection/ joint relationship with the government sector.

གཞུང་བུན་ (shuŋbün) 1. loan taken from the government. 2. government bonds/ loans/ debt.

གཞུང་ཁྱིན་པོ་ (shuŋ cimbu) the whole text/ treatise/ book.

གཞུང་བྲིས་ (shuŋdriì) 1. vertical writing, writing from top to bottom. 2. sm. གཞུང་རིས་.

གཞུང་འབབ་ (shuŋbəb) shung. government revenue/ income.

གཞུང་འབུལ་ (shuŋbüü) shung. giving (as a donation) to the government; va.—ཞུ་ to give (as a donation) to the government ¶ ཕོགས་ནས་ཟླ་རེ་སྒོར་གསུམ་རེ་གཞུང་འབུལ་ཞུས་པ་རེད་ (He) gave three rupees from his salary to the government each month.

གཞུང་འབྲུ་ (shuŋdru) 1. shung. government grain. 2. grain given to the government in post 1959 Tibet technically as a donation (but really a kind of tax).

གཞུང་འབྲུ་སྤྱི་མཛོད་ཁང་ (shuŋdru jīdzöögaŋ) shung. government grain storage office in tt.

གཞུང་འབྲེལ་ (shuŋdree) 1. shung. government related/ connected, governmental, official ¶ གཞུང་འབྲེལ་གསར་འགྱུར་ཁང་ Government news agency. ¶ གཞུང་འབྲེལ་གཟིགས་སྐོར་ Official state visit.

གཞུང་འབྲེལ་མ་ཡིན་པ་ (shündree mə yimbə) nongovernmental ¶ གཞུང་འབྲེལ་མ་ཡིན་པའི་ལྷ་ཞིབ་ཚོགས་པ་ Nongovernmental organizations (NGO).

གཞུང་བླ་ (shuŋla) shung. the Tibet government and the Panchen Lama's (Labrang) government ¶ གཞུང་བླའི་མི་སེར་ The subjects of the Dalai Lama's government and the Panchen Lama's Labrang.

གཞུང་བླ་ཁམས་གསུམ་ (shuŋla kāmsum) term used in the 1950s to refer to the (Tibetan) Lhasa government, Panchen Lama's area, and the Chamdo area.

གཞུང་བླ་ས་གསུམ་ (shuŋla sāsum) shung. traditional term referring to the Tibetan government, the Panchen lama's area and Sakya.

གཞུང་མ་ (shuŋmə) middle, center.

གཞུང་མང་ (shuŋmaŋ) shung. the government and the people.

གཞུང་དམག (shuŋmaà) government troops.

གཞུང་དམངས་ (shuŋmaŋ) sm. གཞུང་མང་.

གཞུང་བཙུགས་ (shuŋdzuù) established by the government ¶ གཞུང་བཙུགས་སློབ་གྲྭ་ A government established school.

གཞུང་རྩ་ (shuŋdza) main root, basic root, taproot.

གཞུང་ཚད་ལོན་ངེས་ (shuŋdzɛɛ̀ lönŋeè) sb. who has learned the main Tibetan medical texts (sth. like a medical graduate).

གཞུང་ཚབ་ (shuŋdzəb) government representative, envoy, consul.

གཞུང་ཚབ་ཀྱིས་ཁྲིམས་གཅོད་བྱེད་ཆོག་པའི་དབང་ཆ་ (shuŋdzəbgi trīmjöö ceèjɔgbɛ wāŋja) right of consular jurisdiction.

གཞུང་ཚབ་ཁང་ (shuŋdzəbgaŋ) sm.གཞུང་ཚབ་ལས་ཁུངས་.

གཞུང་ཚབ་ཆེན་པོ་ (shuŋdzəb cēmbo) ambassador.

གཞུང་ཚབ་ཆེན་པོའི་ལས་ཁུངས་ (shuŋdzəb cēmbö lɛɛ̀guŋ) embassy.

གཞུང་ཚབ་དོན་གཅོད་ཁང་ (shuŋdzəb tönjöögaŋ) consulate, legation.

གཞུང་ཚབ་དོན་བྱེད་ཁང་ (shuŋdzəb tönjeègaŋ) sm. གཞུང་ཚབ་དོན་གཅོད་ཁང་.

གཞུང་ཚབ་དཔང་ཡིག (shuŋdzəb bāŋyiì) diplomatic credentials.

གཞུང་ཚབ་ལས་ཁུངས་ (shuŋdzəb lɛɛ̀guŋ) embassy, consulate, legation.

གཞུང་ཚིག (sjuŋyiì) the words in a text/ treatise/ book.

གཞུང་ཚོང་ (shuŋdzoŋ) shung. trading by the government, a government trader.

གཞུང་མཛོད་ (shuŋdzöö) shung. government treasury/ exchequer.

གཞུང་འཛིན་ (shuŋdzin) 1. ruling, in power; va.—བྱེད་ ¶ ད་ལྟའི་གཞུང་འཛིན་ཚོགས་པ་དེ་ནི་ As for the present ruling party. 2. nationalizing, taking over by the government; va.—བྱེད་ to nationalize ¶ གྲུ་གཟིངས་འཁབས་ཚུགས་ཁག་གཞུང་འཛིན་བྱས་པ་རེད་ (They) nationalized the docks. 3. va. to learn a religious text by heart.

གཞུང་འཛུགས་ (shuŋ dzuù) sm. གཞུང་བཙུགས་.

གཞུང་ཞབས་ (shuŋshəb) shung. government official; va.—བྱེད་ to become a government official, to work as a government official; va.—ཞུ་ to request appointment as a government official ¶ གཞུང་ཞབས་སེར་སྐྱ་ Monk and lay officials.

གཞུང་ཞབས་འདེམས་བསྒྲོ་ལྷན་ཚོགས་ (shuŋshəb demgo lhēndzɔɔ̀) Depertment of Personnel in the Tibetan exile government.

གཞུང་ཞབས་ཞལ་དཀར་ཕྱོགས་གཅིག (shuŋshəb shɛɛgar cɔ̄ɔ̀jig) shung. government officials united/ harmonious [Lit. government officials (fed) in one bowl].

གཞུང་ཞིང་ (shuŋshiŋ) 1. fields on the plains, fields in a main valley. 2. government owned fields.

གཞུང་ཞེ་རྩིས་ཅན་ (shuŋshe dziijɛn) sm. གཞུང་དྲང་.

གཞུང་ཞེན་ཅན་ (shuŋ shenjɛn) shung. loyal to the government ¶ གཞུང་གཞེན་ཅན་གྱི་འབྲོག་པ་ Nomads loyal to government.

གཞུང་གཞིས་ (shuŋshiì) shung. government estate.

གཞུང་བཞི་འཕྲེད་དྲུག (shuŋshi trēèdruù) short and fat person [Lit. four in height, six in width].

གཞུང་བཞེས་ (shuŋsheè) shung. confiscating, expropriating (by the governemnt); va.—གཏོང་; va.—གནང་ to confiscate, to expropriate ¶ མི་ཚང་དེས་ངོ་ལོག་བརྒྱབ་ཙང་ཕ་གཞིས་གཞུང་བཞེས་བཏང་བ་རེད་

Because that family rebelled (the government) confiscated its estate.
གཞུང་བཟང་ (shuŋsaŋ) sm. གཞུང་དྲང་.
གཞུང་བཟོ་བ་ (shuŋsowa) 1. an organization of government related craftsmen (sth. like a craft association). 2. government craftsmen.
གཞུང་ཡིག (shuŋyii) shung. 1. official paper/ document. 2. sm. གཞུང་རིས་.
གཞུང་གཡོག (shuŋyɔɔ) shung. government servant.
གཞུང་རིས་ (shuŋrii) shung. the style of writing that was taught to student's in the traditional Tibetan government's Tselabdra school.
གཞུང་རུ་ (shuŋru) shung. a government owned herd.
གཞུང་རླབས་ (shuŋləb) longitudinal wave.
གཞུང་ལམ་ (shuŋlam) main path or road, highway ¶ ངས་གཞུང་ལམ་བརྒྱུད་ནས་ཕྱིན་པ་ཡིན་ I went via the main road.
གཞུང་ལམ་གཅེས་སྐྱོང་ (shuŋlam jēègyoŋ) road checkpost.
གཞུང་ལམ་སྤྱི་ཁྱབ་བཟོ་ཁག (shuŋlam jīgyəb sōgaà) highway district.
གཞུང་ལམ་བཟོ་སྐྲུན་ཁྲུའུ་ (shuŋlam sodrün trū) tib. ch. highway engineering division.
གཞུང་ལས་ (shuŋlɛɛ̀) shung. government work, official business; va.—སྒྲུབ་; —བྱེད་ to do government work/ official business.
གཞུང་ལས་ཁང་ (shuŋlɛɛ̀gaŋ) 1. government office. 2. sm. གཞུང་དོན་ཁང་.
གཞུང་ལས་འགྲོ་སྒྲོན་ (shuŋlɛɛ̀ drodrön) government expenditure/ expenses.
གཞུང་ལས་ཆེན་མོ་ (shuŋlɛɛ̀ cēmbo) shung. a tax wherein skilled craftsmen were requisitioned by the government for a project.
གཞུང་ལས་ཆེན་མོ་བ་ (shuŋlɛɛ̀ cēmowa) shung. skilled government technical/ craftsmen.
གཞུང་ལས་ཐིང་ (shuŋlɛɛ̀ tiŋ) sm. གཞུང་ལས་ཁང་.
གཞུང་ལས་པ་ (shuŋlɛɛ̀ba) shung. 1. monk who is in charge of debating examinations in the monastery. 2. government official.
གཞུང་ལུགས་ (shuŋluù) theory, doctrine, system ¶ མར་ཁེ་སི་ལེ་ནིན་རིང་ལུགས་ཀྱི་འགྱུར་མེད་གྲལ་རིམ་གྱི་སྲིད་དབང་སྒེར་འཛིན་གྱི་གཞུང་ལུགས་ The Marxist-Leninist theory of the dictatorship of the proletariat. ¶ བརྡ་དག་གི་གཞུང་ལུགས་ The system of spelling.
གཞུང་ལུགས་ཀྱི་རྨང་གཞི་ (shuŋluùgi mɔ̄ŋshi) theoretical basis.
གཞུང་ལུགས་སྐོར་གྱི་རྫས་འགྱུར་རིག་པ་ (shuŋluùgɔɔgi dzɛɛ̀gyur rigbə) theoretical chemistry.
གཞུང་ལུགས་སྐོར་གྱི་ཤུགས་རིག (shuŋluùgɔɔgi shūgriì) theoretical mechanics.
གཞུང་ལུགས་དང་བྱ་བ་དངོས་ (shuŋluùdaŋ cawaŋöö) theory and practice.
གཞུང་ལུགས་པ་ (shuŋluùbə) theoretician.
གཞུང་ལུགས་ཕུའུ་ (shuŋluù bū) tib. ch. theory department.
གཞུང་ལུགས་སྨྲ་བ་ (shuŋluù māwa) theory.
གཞུང་ལུས་ (shuŋlüü) the main body/ context of a text.
གཞུང་ལེན་ (shuŋlen) sm. གཞུང་བཞེས་.
གཞུང་ཤག (shuŋshaà) shung. government houses/ buildings.
གཞུང་ཤིང་ (shuŋshiŋ) the main beams and pillars (of a house).
གཞུང་གཤག (shuŋshaà) splitting down the middle; va.—གཏོང་.
གཞུང་ས་ (shuŋsa) shung. sm. གཞུང་གནས་.
གཞུང་ས་ཆེན་མོ་ (shuŋsa chēmmo) shung. the great Tibetan government.
གཞུང་ས་མཆོག (shuŋsa cɔ̄ɔ) the great Tibetan government.
གཞུང་སེམས་ (shuŋsem) patriotic/ loyal thought ¶ ཁོ་གཞུང་སེམས་དག་པོ་ཡོད་པ་རེད་ He has loyalty to the government.
གཞུང་སེམས་དྲང་པོ་ (shuŋsem traŋbo) honest, moral, sincere and loyal ¶ གཞུང་སེམས་དྲང་པོའི་མི་ལ་ཀུན་གྱིས་དགའ་ An honest and loyal person is loved by all.
གཞུང་སེམས་རྣམ་དག (shuŋsem nàmdaà) faithful, loyal.
གཞུང་སྲིད་ (shuŋsiì) shung. administration, government; va.—སྐྱོང་ to rule/ administer a government.
གཞུང་སྲིད་འཛིན་སྐྱོང་ (shuŋsiì dzingyoŋ) sm. གཞུང་སྲིད་.
གཞུང་སྒྲོང་ (shuŋ sōŋ) 1. va. to narrate the story in a Tibetan opera ¶ མི་དཔོན་གྱིས་ཁྲིམས་ཀྱི་གཞུང་སྒྲོང་གི་ཡོད་པ་རེད་ (He) is narrating the Tibetan opera. 2. va. to settle honestly/ fairly.
གཞུང་སྒྲོང་བ་ (shuŋsoŋwa) narrator in a Tibetan opera performance.
གཞུང་སྲོལ་ (shuŋsöö) shung. governmental rules and regulations.
གཞུང་སྲོལ་ཡིག་ཆ་ (shuŋsöö yigjə) red tape, routine bureaucratic papers/ documents.
གཞུང་བསྒྲུངས་ (shuŋ sāŋ) p. of གཞུང་སྒྲོང་.
གཞུང་བསྲིངས་ (shuŋ siŋ) sm. རྒྱུན་བསྲིངས་.
གཞུངས་བརྒྱུངས་ (shuŋ gyuŋ) spinal cord.
གཞུངས་པ་ (shuŋbə) sm. གཞུངས་བརྒྱུངས་.
གཞུངས་རིངས་ (shuŋriŋ) spinal column.
གཞུན་ (shün) f. of འཇུན་.
གཞུན་པོ་ (shünbu) 1. good, attractive. 2. diligent, hard working.
གཞུམ་ (shüm) f. of འཇུམ་.
གཞུའུ་ (shuu) small bow.
གཞུར་ (shur) center, middle.
གཞུས་ (shüü) imp. of གཞུ་.
གཞེ་ (she) arc. time, period, era.
གཞེན་བསྐུལ་ (shengüü) encouraging, stimulating, appealing; va.—བྱེད་; —ཞུ་ to encourage/ stimulate/ appeal ¶ རང་རིགས་གཞོན་ནུ་རྣམས་ལ་གཞེན་བསྐུལ་ཞུ་རྒྱུར་ (I) have an appeal for our youths. ¶ ཨ་རི་གཞེན་བསྐུལ་གནང་དོན་ལྟར་ན་ According to the appeal to the U.S.
གཞེན་འདེབས་ (shendeb) sm. གཞེན་བསྐུལ་.
གཞེན་པ་ (shemba) arc. sm. དྲན་སྐུལ་.
གཞེར་ (sher) sm. བསྙེན་.
གཞེས་ཀྱི་ལྷ་ཉིན་དཀར་པོ་ (sheègi lhāñin gārbo) sm. གཞེས་ཉིན་.
གཞེས་འཆར་ (shenjar) every three days ¶ ང་སློབ་གྲྭར་གཞེས་འཆར་འགྲོ་གི་ཡོད་ I go to school every three days.
གཞེས་འཛགས་ (shenjaà) 1. sm. གཞེས་འཆར་. 2. (please) sit down.
གཞེས་ཉིན་ (sheèñin) three days from today ¶ གཞེས་ཉིན་ཁྱེད་རང་ངའི་ནང་ལ་ཕེབས་རོགས་གནང་ Please come to my home three days from now.
གཞེས་ཉིན་ཀ་ (sheè ñingə) sm. གཞེས་ཉིན་.
གཞེས་ཉིན་མོ་ (sheè ñinmu) sm. གཞེས་ཉིན་.
གཞེས་བརྡ་ (sheèda) a message to do sth. three days from today.
གཞེས་ནིང་ (sheèniŋ) the year before last, two years ago.
གཞེས་ནིང་ལོ་ (sheèniŋ lo) sm. གཞེས་ནིང་.
གཞེས་ཕོད་ (sheèböö) two years from now.
གཞོག (shɔɔ) f. of འཇོག.
གཞོག: p. གཞོགས་; f. གཞོག (shɔɔ) va. to whittle wood, to plane down.
གཞོག་དཀྲུག (shɔgdruù) lathe.
གཞོག་དཀྲུག་བཟོ་པ་ (shɔgdruù soba) lathe operator.
གཞོག་གྲི་ (shɔgdri) whittling/ paring knife, lathe blade.
གཞོག་རྒྱག (shɔɔ gyaà) va. to pare/ shave/ whittle (wood).
གཞོག་སྡེགས་ (shɔgdeg) lathe.
གཞོགས་ (shɔɔ) side ¶ གཞོགས་གཡས་གཡོན་ The right and left side. ¶ ཁོའི་གཞོགས་སུ་བསྡད་པ་རེད་ (They) sat beside him.
གཞོགས་ཀྱི་གནོན་ཤུགས་ (shɔɔgi nōnshuù) lateral pressure.
གཞོགས་འཁྱིལ་ (shɔngyee) a type of stitching.

གཞོགས་འགྲུད་ཤོར་ (shɔndrüü shɔ̄ɔ̄) vi. to have one's heel wear more on one side.

གཞོགས་ངོས་ (shɔ̄ɔ̄ŋöö) sm. གཞོགས་.

གཞོགས་གཅིག (shɔ̄ɔ̄jig) 1. one side ¶ གཞོགས་གཅིག་གཙོ་བོར་འཛིན་ Holding one side as the main one. 2. counting when sth. is being lifted or pulled in unison, e.g. one, two, three, pull).

གཞོགས་གཅིག་མར་གཉིས་སྐྱལ་ (shɔ̄ɔ̄jii maãñii gũü) va. to count one, two, three when doing sth. in unison (usu. lifting or pulling).

གཞོགས་གཅིག་མར་གཉིས་གསུམ་པའི་ཐོག (shɔ̄ɔ̄jii maãñii sũmbɛ tɔ̄ɔ̄) counting in unison when lifting or pulling (i.e., one, two, three, pull).

གཞོགས་གཅིག་ལ་ཕྱོགས་པ་ (shɔ̄ɔ̄jiilə cɔ̄gba) leaning to one side, unbalanced, partial.

གཞོགས་ཆ་ (shɔ̄ɔ̄ja) a radical (i.e., a Chinese character).

གཞོགས་ཉལ་ (shɔ̄ɔ̄ñɛɛ) laying down on one's side; va.—རྒྱག to lie down on one's side.

གཞོགས་སྙེས་ (shɔ̄ɔ̄ñeè) leaning against sth. like a wall; va.—རྒྱག to lean/ rest the side of the body (against a wall, etc.) ¶ ཁོས་རྩིགས་པར་གཞོགས་སྙེས་བརྒྱབ་ནས་བསྡད་འདུག He was leaning against the wall.

གཞོགས་གཉིས་ (shɔ̄ɔ̄ñii) bilateral, two sides ¶ གཟུགས་པོའི་གཞོགས་གཉིས་ལ་རྨ་བཟོས་བཞག He got injured on both sides of his body.

གཞོགས་གཉིས་ཀ་ (shɔ̄ɔ̄ ñiigə) both sides.

གཞོགས་སྡེགས་ (shɔgdeg) sm. གཞོག་སྡེགས་.

གཞོགས་དྲུང་ (shɔgdruŋ) beside, near.

གཞོགས་འདེགས་ (shɔŋdeg) assisting, supporting; va.—བྱེད་ ¶ ཁོ་ཚོས་དཀའ་ངལ་ཆེན་པོ་ཡོད་པའི་ཞིང་པ་ཚོར་གཞོགས་འདེགས་བྱེད་ཀྱི་ཡོད་པ་རེད་ They are giving assistance to the farmers who are having great difficulties. ¶ ཁོ་ཚོས་བཟོ་པར་གཞོགས་འདེགས་བྱེད་ཆེད་ལས་མཚམས་བཞག་པ་རེད་ They went on strike to support the workers.

གཞོགས་འདེགས་གནམ་གྲུ་ (shɔŋdeg) support planes.

གཞོགས་འདེགས་འབར་དངོས་ (shɔŋdeg barŋöö) booster rocket stage.

གཞོགས་འདེགས་དམག་དཔུང་ (shɔŋdeg māgbuŋ) auxiliary/ support troops.

གཞོགས་འདེགས་རོལ་མོ་ (shɔŋdeg röömo) background music.

གཞོགས་འདྲིད་ (shɔndrii) tricking, deceiving.

གཞོགས་འདྲུད་ (shɔndrüü) crawling on one's side (e.g., a dog with crippled leg on one side); va.—རྒྱག.

གཞོགས་རྡུང་ (shɔ̄ɔ̄duŋ) flanking attack; va.—གཏོང་.

གཞོགས་གནས་པོ་བྲང་ (shɔ̄ɔ̄nɛɛ̄ pōdraŋ) a side hall or compartment.

གཞོགས་ཕྱེད་ (shɔ̄ɔ̄jeè) one side/ half of sth. ¶ ཁོང་གི་གཟུགས་པོའི་གཞོགས་ཕྱེད་ལ་གཟའ་ཕོག་བཞག Half his body was paralyzed.

གཞོགས་འཕྱས་ (shɔ̄ɔ̄jɛɛ̀) making fun/ ridiculing indirectly.

གཞོགས་སྦྲར་པོ་བྲང་ (shɔ̄ɔ̄jar pōdraŋ) side hall in a palace.

གཞོགས་སྦྲར་ལྷ་ཁང་ (shɔ̄ɔ̄jar lhāgaŋ) side hall in a temple.

གཞོགས་སྨས་ (shɔ̄ɔ̄mɛɛ̀) butting in/ interfering while two people are talking; va.—བྱེད་.

གཞོགས་ཟུར་ (shɔ̄ɔ̄sur) a side of sth.

གཞོགས་ཡ་གཅིག (shɔ̄ɔ̄ yajii) one side.

གཞོགས་གཡས་ (shɔ̄ɔ̄yɛɛ̀) the right side.

གཞོགས་གཡོན་ (shɔ̄ɔ̄yön) the left side.

གཞོགས་ལེབ་ (shɔ̄ɔ̄leb) slices.

གཞོགས་ལོག་མོ་ལོག་ཀྱག (shɔ̄ɔ̄lɔɔ̄ molɔɔ̄ gyāà) va. to lift sth. up (by a group of people working together).

གཞོགས་བཤལ་ (shɔ̄ɔ̄shɛɛ) walking with one side of the body/ leg/ arm drooping (usu. after a stroke).

གཞོགས་གཞིབ་ (shɔ̄ɔ̄shib) seated side-by-side.

གཞོགས་སུ་ (shɔ̄ɔ̄su) just next to, beside ¶ ཁོང་ངའི་གཞོགས་སུ་བསྡད་སོང་ He sat beside me.

གཞོགས་སློང་ (shɔ̄ɔ̄loŋ) asking indirectly, hinting; va.—བྱེད་ to ask for indirectly, to hint.

གཞོང་ཀོར་ (shoŋgɔɔ) sm. གཞོང་པ་.

གཞོང་ཁུང་ (shoŋguŋ) sm. གཞོང་པ་.

གཞོང་སྐོར་ (shoŋgɔɔ) a round wooden trough/ basin (usu. wood).

གཞོང་སྒྲོམ་ (shoŋdrom) sm. སྒྲོམ་སྐོར་.

གཞོང་པ་ (shoŋba) a rectangular basin/ tub/ trough.

གཞོང་བུ་ (shoŋbu) a small trough/ basin.

གཞོང་དབྱིབས་ས་ཁུལ་ (shoŋyib sāgüü) a place situated in an area that is like a basin.

གཞོངས་ (shoŋ) arc. scenery.

གཞོངས་སྤྱོད་ (shoŋjöö) sm. ལྗོངས་རྒྱུ་.

གཞོན་ (shön) young ¶ ཁོ་ལོ་གཞོན་དུས་ When he was young. ¶ ཕོ་གཞོན་དང་མོ་གཞོན་ Young men and woman.

གཞོན་སྐྱེས་ (shöngyeè) young people.

གཞོན་ཁྲལ་ (shöndrɛɛ) tasks/ obligations ("taxes") of the young (usu. refers to obligations of young monks).

གཞོན་ཉམས་དོད་པོ་ (shönñam tööbo) youthful looking.

གཞོན་དུས་ (shöndüü) when young, early years, youth.

གཞོན་དྲུང་ (shöndruŋ) a junior clerk (in Dharamsala).

གཞོན་ནུ་ (shönnu) youth ¶ གཞོན་ནུའི་ཚོགས་པ་ Youth League.

གཞོན་ནུ་མཐུན་སྒྲིགས་ཚོགས་པ་ (shönnu tũndrɔɔ tsɔ̄gba) Youth Union/ Alliance.

གཞོན་ནུ་གདོང་ལེན་རུ་ཁག (shönnu doŋlen rugaà) Young Pioneers.

གཞོན་ནུ་སྡེ་ཚོགས་ (shönnu dedzɔɔ) Youth League.

གཞོན་ནུ་འཕྲུལ་སྒྲུབ་པ་ (shönnu trɛɛ̄drubbə) Youth Congress Members, in youth shock worker.

གཞོན་ནུ་འཕྲུལ་སྒྲུབ་རུ་ཁག (shönnu trɛɛ̄drub rugaà) youth shock brigade.

གཞོན་ནུ་མ་ (shönnumə) young girl, maiden.

གཞོན་ནུ་ཚོགས་པ་ (shönnu tsɔ̄gba) Youth League/ Association, Youth Congress.

གཞོན་ནུ་ཚོགས་མི་ (shönnu tsɔ̄gmi) Member of a Youth League/ Association.

གཞོན་ནུ་ཤེས་ཡོན་ཅན་ (shönnu shēèyünjɛn) young intellectuals.

གཞོན་ནུ་ལྷན་ཚོགས་ (shönnu lhɛ̄ndzɔɔ) Youth Association, Youth Congress.

གཞོན་ནུའི་དང་བླངས་རུ་ཁག (shönnü doŋlen rugaà) Pioneer Youth Organization (Young Pioneers).

གཞོན་ནུའི་དུས་ཆེན་ (shönnü tüüjen) Youth Day (May 4).

གཞོན་ནུའི་གདོང་ལེན་རུ་ཁག (shönnü doŋlen rugaà) Pioneer Youth Organization (Young Pioneers).

གཞོན་ནུའི་པོ་བྲང་ (shönnü pōdraŋ) Youth Palace.

གཞོན་ནུའི་མི་རབས་ (shönnü mirəb) the young/ younger generation.

གཞོན་ནུའི་ཚོགས་པ་ (shönnü tsɔ̄gba) Youth League/ Association, Youth Congress.

གཞོན་ནུའི་ལང་འཚོ་ (shönnü laŋdzo) health and good looks of youth.

གཞོན་པ་ (shömba 1. a young man ¶ གཞོན་པ་རྣམས་ The young men. 2. junior, younger ¶ ཁོའི་བུ་གཞོན་པ་ His younger son. 3. vice (in position) ¶ ཚོགས་གཙོ་གཞོན་པ་ The vice-chairman.

གཞོན་བབ་ (shön bəb) vi. to become younger looking, to look young again (for older people).

གཞོན་མ་ (shömma) sm. གཞོན་ནུ་མ་.

གཞོན་གཞོན་ (shönshön) young ¶ ཁོ་ཚོ་གཞོན་གཞོན་རེད་ They are young.

གཞོན་བཟོ་དོད་པོ་ (shönso tööbo) sm. གཞོན་ཤ་དོད་པོ་.

གཞོན་རབས་ (shönrəb) younger generation.

གཞོན་ཤ་ (shönsha) youthfulness.

གཞོན་ཤ་ཆགས་པ་ (shönsha cāba) sm. གཞོན་ཤ་དོད་པོ་.

གཞོན་ཤ་ཅན་ (shönshajɛn) sm. གཞོན་ཤ་དོད་པོ་.

གཞོན་ཤ་དོད་པོ་ (shönsha tööbo) youthful, young looking ¶ མི་ཐོན་གཞོན་ཤ་དོད་པོ་ The youthful

looking old man.
གཞོན་ཤེས་ (shönsheē̃) educated youth.
གཞོན་སོ་དཀར་ (shönsogar) youth.
གཞོན་ལྷན་ (shönlhɛn) abbr. of གཞོན་ནུ་ལྷན་ཚོགས་.
གཞོབ་ (shob) vi. to be singed/ scorched/ burnt.
གཞོབ་དྲི་ (shobdri) smell of sth. singed/ scorched/ burnt; vi.—ཁ་ to smell sth. singed/ scorched/ burnt.
གཞོབ་རལ་ (shobraà) singed, seared, scorched; vi.—ཐེབས་ to get singed/ seared/ scorched; va.—གཏོང་ to singe/ sear/ scorch.
གཞོམ་ (shom) 1. f. of འཇོམས་. 2. vi. to be subdued/ demolished/ destroyed/ quelled ༈ དགྲ་བོའི་སྟོབས་ཤུགས་གཞོམ་པར་བྱེད་དགོས་ (We) must do sth. to subdue the power of the enemy.
གཞོམ་མེད་ (shommeè) sm. གཞོམ་ཤིག་མེད་པ་.
གཞོམ་ཤིག་མེད་པ་ (shomshig meèba) indestructible, unbreakable, incontrovertible ༈ གཞོམ་ཤིག་མེད་པའི་བདེན་དོན་ The incontrovertible truth.
གཞོར་ (shɔɔ) 1. sm. འཇོར་. 2. imp. of གཞར་.
གཞོར་བུ་ (shɔɔbu) sm. འཇོར་, 1.
གཞོལ་ (shöö) 1. vi. to descend/ fall ༈ ཆར་པ་གཞོལ་དུས་ When it is raining. 2. va. to participate in, to take part in ༈ ལས་འགུལ་ལ་གཞོལ་བཞིན་དུ་ While taking part in the campaign. 3. vi.—གྲོ་ to flow down (rivers, etc.). 3. va. to devote oneself, to do sth. diligently and energetically. 4. va. to descent/ dismount ༈ ང་ཚོ་ཉི་མ་མ་གཞོལ་གོང་ལ་འགྲོ་དགོས་ We have to go before sunset.
གཞོལ་འགྲོ་ (shöö dro) to flow down.
གཞོལ་འབབ་ (shömbəb) river, stream (that flows down).
བཞག་ (shaà) 1. p. of འཇོག་. 2. (linking or existential vb. + —) expresses the idea of not knowing firsthand or having specific knowledge ༈ དེ་ཚོ་ཚང་མ་ཆབ་སྲིད་ཐད་ཀྱི་དབྱེ་བ་ཤ་སྟག་རེད་བཞག These are all differentiated only on political grounds. 3. a spiral-like design. 4. back part of the thigh.
བཞག་སྒོར་ (shaàgɔr) small intestine.
བཞག་དངུལ་ (shaàŋüü) bank deposit, bank savings.
བཞག་སྟེགས་ (shaàdeg) a stand ༈ བུམ་པ་བཞག་སྟེགས་གཅིག་གི་སྟེང་ལ་བཞག་ན་ If you put the vase on a stand.
བཞག་པག་བྲོ་ (shaà paàdro) sb. who seems capable but is really all front, sb. who is all talk but no action.
བཞག་འོག་ (shaàwɔɔ) armpit.
བཞག་ཤ་ (shaàsha) back part of the thigh.
བཞངས་ (shaŋ) sm. བཞེངས་.
བཞད་ (shɛɛ̀) 1. vi. to bloom ༈ མེ་ཏོག་མི་འདྲ་བ་མང་པོ་རིམ་པ་བཞིན་དུ་བཞད་ཀྱི་ཡོད་ Many different kinds of flowers are blooming one after the other. 2. vi. to laugh (h.) ༈ ཁོང་གིས་བཞད་མོ་བཞད་སོང་ He laughed.
བཞད་ཁ་འབྱེད་ (sheèga jeè) vi. to bloom/ blossom.
བཞད་ཁ་མ་ (sheègama) flowers just about to bloom.
བཞད་གད་ (sheègɛɛ̀) sm. བཞད་མོ་.
བཞད་གད་བྱེད་ (sheègɛɛ̀ ceè) sm. ཞལ་རྫེད་གནང་.
བཞད་གད་ཅི་ལི་ (sheègɛɛ̀cile) (sound of) laughter by many people.
བཞད་གད་པ་ (sheègɛɛ̀ba) joker, comedian.
བཞད་གད་ཟློས་གར་ (sheègɛɛ̀ döögar) comedy show/ play.
བཞད་གད་སློང་ (sheègɛɛ̀ lōŋ) va. to make laugh.
བཞད་སྒྲ་ (sheèdra) sound of laughter; va.—སྒྲོག to laugh.
བཞད་ཐོག་སྨོན་ (sheè tōŋmön) one of the largest estate of the Panchen Lama.
བཞད་འཛུ་ (sheènja) making people laugh by making fun of sth.; va.—སློང་ to make people laugh by making fun of sth.
བཞད་འཛུ་དིང་དིང་ (sheènja tiŋdiŋ) laughing.
བཞད་དྲོ་བ་ (shɛɛ̀ trobo) funny, farcical, hilarious.
བཞད་མོ་ (shɛɛ̀mo) laughter, laughing (h.); va.—བཞད་; —ཤོར་ to laugh; va.—སློང་ to make sb. laugh; vi.—ཤོར་ to burst out into laughter; vi.—ཡོ་ to feel like laughing.
བཞམས་ (sham) va. to collect together.
བཞམས་བསྒོ་ (shamgo) 1. mentioning, reminding; va.—བྱེད་ to mention, to remind. 2. advising tactfully.
བཞམས་པ་ (shamba) sm. བཞམས་པོ་.
བཞམས་པོ་ (shambo) sm. འཇམ་པོ་.
བཞའ་ (sha) wetness, dampness; va.—རྒྱག to moisturize, to wet; vi.—ཐེབས་ to become damp/ wet/ moist (usu. from humidity).
བཞའ་སྐམ་ (shagam) dehydration; va.—བྱེད་ to dry, to dehydrate.
བཞའ་སྐྱོན་ཐེབས་ (shagyön tēb) vi. to be damaged by humidity/ moisture/ dampness.
བཞའ་ཁུག (shəguù) vi. to become moist/ wet/ damp (e.g., from humidity).
བཞའ་རྒྱག (sha gyaà) va. to make sth. wet.
བཞའ་ཐེབས་ (shaà tēb) vi. to get damp, wet/ moist (usu. from humidity).
བཞའ་སྡོད་ (sha döö) vi. to be/ remain wet ༈ ཁ་གདན་ལ་ད་དུང་བཞའ་བསྡད་བཞག The rug is still wet.
བཞའ་སྦབས་ (shabəb) slightly wet/ damp.
བཞའ་པེམ་པེམ་ (sha pembem) damp, moist, clammy.
བཞའ་འབེན་འབེན་ (sha pembem) sm. བཞའ་པེམ་པེམ་.
བཞའ་ཚད་ (shadzɛɛ̀) degree of humidity/ moisture.
བཞའ་ཚན་ (shadzɛn) moisture, wetness, humidity; vi.—ཡོག to get damp/ moist/ wet (usu. from humidity); va.—འགོག to stop/ block moisture, dampness, humidity ༈ དབྱར་ཀ་ཡུལ་པ་འདི་བཞའ་ཚན་ཆེན་པོ་འདུག In the summer this place is very humid.
བཞའ་ཚན་ཆེ་བ་ (shadzɛn cēwa) sm. བཞའ་ཚན་ཆེན་པོ་.
བཞའ་ཚན་ཆེན་པོ་ (shadzɛn cēmbo) very damp/ moist/ humid.
བཞའ་རླན་ (shalɛn) sm. བཞའ་ཚན་.
བཞར་ (shaa) p. of གཞར་.
བཞར་གྲི་ (shaadri) razor, razor blade.
བཞར་རྒྱག (shar gyaà) va. to plane a piece of wood.
བཞི་ (shi) four.
བཞི་སྐོར་ (shigɔɔ) shung. 1. an agricultural yield that is four times the seed sown. 2. in barter exchanges, one item getting four units of the other in exchange.
བཞི་ཁྲི་ (shidri) forty thousand.
བཞི་ག་ (shigə) the four of them, all four ༈ སློབ་གྲྭ་བ་བཞི་ག་ཕྱིན་པ་རེད་ All four students went.
བཞི་གླིང་ (shiliŋ) a quarter, a fourth ༈ དེའི་བཞི་གླིང་གཅིག One fourth of that.
བཞི་བརྒྱ་ (shibgya) four hundred.
བཞི་ལྔ་འགྲོ་ (shiŋa dro) shung. twenty five percent interest.
བཞི་བཅུ་ (shibju) forty ༈ བཞི་བཅུ་ཞེ་གཉིས་ Forty two.
བཞི་བཅུ་ཐམ་པ་ (shibju tāmba) sm. བཞི་བཅུ་.
བཞི་ཆ་ (shija) a quarter, a fourth ༈ དེའི་བཞི་ཆ་གཉིས་ Two fourths of that.
བཞི་མཆོད་ (shijöö) festival commemorating the death of Jamchen Chöje, the founder of the Sera Monastery (24th of the 10th month).
བཞི་སྟོང་ (shidoŋ) four thousand.
བཞི་མཐའ་ (shida) the four times table.
བཞི་སྡེ་ (shede) the monastery in Lhasa belonging to Reting Rinpoche.
བཞི་སྡེ་གྲྭ་ཚང་ (shede) sm. བཞི་སྡེ་.
བཞི་མདོ་ (shido) the point where the two roads cross.
བཞི་མདོ་ཁ་ (shidoga) crossroads.
བཞི་སྣ་ (shinə) shung. an additional conscription/ levy of soldiers from existing military tax units (in the 19th century).
བཞི་པ་ (shibə) the fourth ༈ མི་བཞི་པ་ The fourth person.
བཞི་པའི་གནས་སྐབས་ (shibɛ nɛɛ̀gəb) old age [Lit. the fourth stage of life].

བཞི་པོ་ (shibu) the four together ། ཁོང་ཚོ་བཞི་པོ་འདིར་ཡོང་པ་རེད་ The four of them came here together.

བཞི་མེས་ (shimeè) great great great grandfather.

བཞི་ཚོ་ (shidzo) a unit of four villages/ households.

བཞི་ཟུར་ (shisur) sm. བཞི་ཆ་.

བཞི་ལིང་ (shiliŋ) sm. བཞི་གླིང་.

བཞི་ལིང་ལྔ་ལིང་འཕྲལ་ (shiliŋ ŋāliŋ trɛ̄ɛ) va. to break/ divide/ separate into pieces ། ལྕོག་ཙེ་དེ་བཞི་ལིང་ལྔ་ལིང་འཕྲལ་ནས་འཁྱེར་ཕྱིན་པ་རེད་ (They) broke the table down into pieces and took it with them.

བཞི་ཤད་ (shishɛɛ̀) the mark used after the end of a chapter in Tibetan books.

བཞིན་ (shin) 1. just like, just as, according to ། ངས་བྱེད་པ་བཞིན་བྱིས་རོགས་ Please do as I do. ། ཁོང་ཚོའི་གསལ་འདེབས་བཞིན་ In accordance with (their) advice. 2. present particle conveying in the process of doing sth. (vb.+ —) ། ཁོ་དཔེ་ཆ་ཀློག་བཞིན་པ་རེད་ He is reading a book (now). ། ང་ལྷ་སར་ཉིན་རེ་བཞིན་འགྲོ་གི་ཡོད་ I go to Lhasa each day. 3. face ། བཞིན་གྱི་འཛུམ་བག The smile on the face. 4. (vb. + — dat.loc.) while, during ། ལས་ཀ་འདི་བྱེད་བཞིན་དུ་སློབ་སྦྱོང་བྱེད་ལོང་མི་འདུག While I'm doing this work I don't have time to study. 5. as well as ། མཛེས་སྡུག་ང་རྒྱལ་བཞིན་སྤོབས་པ་བྱེད་ཀྱི་འདུག (She) is acting showoffish as well as proud about (her) beauty. 6. even though ། ཁོང་གིས་ཤེས་བཞིན་དུ་ང་ལ་སྐད་ཆ་འདྲི་གི་འདུག Even though he knows (it), he is asking me. 7. (vb. — vb. —) the more one does sth. ། དེ་སྔའི་ལོ་རྒྱུས་ལ་བསམས་བཞིན་བསམས་བཞིན་འགྱོད་པ་སྐྱེ་གི་འདུག The more one thinks about past history one regrets.

བཞིན་ཁྱིམ་ (shingyim) face, countenance (h.).

བཞིན་གྱི་དཀྱིལ་འཁོར་ (shingyi gyīngɔɔ) face.

བཞིན་གྱི་འཁོར་ལོ་ (shingi kɔ̄ɔlo) sm. བཞིན་གྱི་དཀྱིལ་འཁོར་.

བཞིན་འགྱུར་ (shingyur) vi. to change one's facial expression ། ངའི་སྐད་ཆ་དེ་གོ་མ་ཐག་ཁོང་གི་བཞིན་འགྱུར་སོང་ As soon as (he) heard what I said his facial expression changed.

བཞིན་ངན་ (shinŋɛn) ugly.

བཞིན་སྣབས་ (shindəb) facial expression/ appearance.

བཞིན་དུ་ (shindu) see བཞིན་.

བཞིན་མདངས་ (shindaŋ) sm. བཞིན་སྣབས་.

བཞིན་མདངས་རྒྱས་པོ་ (shindaŋ gyɛ̀ɛbo) a healthy look/ appearance (face).

བཞིན་མདངས་ཡག་པོ་ (shindaŋ yagbo) sm. བཞིན་མདངས་རྒྱས་པོ་.

བཞིན་མདོག (shindɔɔ̀) facial complexion/ color.

བཞིན་མདོག་ལོག (shindɔɔ̀ lɔ̀ɔ) sm. གདོང་གཉིས་ལོག.

བཞིན་སྡུད་ (shindüü) vi. to get a sad/ long look (facial expression) ། ཁོང་གི་ཕུན་མཆེད་གྲོངས་པའི་གནས་ཚུལ་ཐོབ་འཕྲལ་བཞིན་བསྡུས་སོང་ As soon as he heard the news that his parents died, he got a sad look. 2. vi. to get/ have an angry looking face.

བཞིན་ཁྲོག (shindɔɔ) sm. བཞིན་འགྱུར་.

བཞིན་སྡུག་པོ་ (shin dugbu) pretty face.

བཞིན་ནག་པོ་ (shin nagbo) sm. གདོང་ནག་པོ་.

བཞིན་གནག་པོ་ (shin nagbo) sm. བཞིན་ནག་པོ་.

བཞིན་གནག་པ་ (shin nagba) sm. གདོང་ནག་པོ་.

བཞིན་སྣུམ་པ་ (shin nūmbə) healthy looking face.

བཞིན་པར་ (shinbar) sm. བཞིན་དུ་.

བཞིན་པ་ (shimbə) see བཞིན་, 4.

བཞིན་དཔལ་ (shimbɛɛ) beautiful face.

བཞིན་དམན་ (shin mɛ̄n) vi. to be embarrassed, to feel shy.

བཞིན་སྨད་ (shin mɛ̄ɛ̀) va. to bow (one's) head because of shyness/ embarrassment.

བཞིན་འཛུམ་ (shindzum) smile, smiling face; va.— མཛད་; —གནང་.

བཞིན་བཟང་ (shinsaŋ) beautiful/ pretty face.

བཞིན་བཟང་མཆོག་མ་ (shinsaŋ cōgba) exceedingly beautiful.

བཞིན་བཟང་མ་ (shin saŋma) a beautiful/ pretty girl.

བཞིན་རང་སྡོད་ (shin raŋ dö̀ö) doing sth. continuously ། མཚན་གང་ངལ་གསོ་མེད་པར་འགྲོ་བཞིན་རང་བསྡད་པ་རེད་ (They) kept on going all night without rest ། ཕྲུ་གུ་འདི་དཔེ་དེབ་ཀློག་བཞིན་རང་སྡོད་ཀྱི་འདུག The child reads books continuously.

བཞིན་རས་ (shinrɛɛ̀) face.

བཞིན་རས་ཚར་པོ་ (shinrɛɛ̀ tsārbo) beautiful face.

བཞིན་ལག (shinlaà) body shape.

བཞིན་ལེགས་ (shinleg) 1. sm. བཞིན་བཟང་. 2. king of the Nagas.

བཞུ་: p. བཞུས་; f. བཞུ་; imp. བཞུས་ (shu) va. to melt, to smelt, to dissolve.

བཞུ་ (shu) abbr. of བཞུ་མར་.

བཞུ་བཀྱག (shugyaà) stand for an oil lamp.

བཞུ་སྐྱོགས་ (shugyɔɔ̀) a ladle used for melting sth.

བཞུ་ཁུ་ (shugu) molten liquid made by melting ། མར་གྱི་བཞུ་ཁུ་ Melted (liquid) butter.

བཞུ་གྲིབ་ (shudrib) a lamp shade.

བཞུ་འཇུག (shunjuù) melting, smelting, dissolving; va.—བྱེད་.

བཞུ་དྲི་ (shudri) sm.* གཞོབ་དྲི་.

བཞུ་འདུལ་ (shundüü) smelting metals; va.—བྱེད་.

བཞུ་ལྡུག་བཟོ་གྲྭ་ (shuduù sodra) casting factory, foundry.

བཞུ་སྣུམ་ (shunum) oil for lamp.

བཞུ་སྣོད་ (shunüü) a vessel/ receptacle in which sth. is melted.

བཞུ་བྱེད་ (shujeè) 1. sth. for melting/ smelting. 2. chemical solvent.

བཞུ་བྱེད་སྒྲིག་ཆས་ (shujeè drigjɛɛ) smelting equipment.

བཞུ་བྱེད་བཟོ་གྲྭ་ (shujeè sodra) smelting factory.

བཞུ་སྦྱང་ (shujaŋ) melting, smelting; va.—བྱེད་.

བཞུ་སྦྱང་བཟོ་གྲྭ (shujaŋ sodra) smelting factory.

བཞུ་མར་ (shumaa) a lamp; va.—སྦར་ to light a lamp; va.—གསོད་ to extinguish/ turn off a lamp.

བཞུ་སྙུལ་ (shuñuu) searching with a lamp/ lantern/ torch; va.—རྒྱག.

བཞུ་ཚད་ (shudzɛɛ̀) melting point.

བཞུ་རྫས་ (shudzɛɛ) sm. བཞུ་བྱེད་.

བཞུ་འོད་ (shuwö̀ö) light of a lamp.

བཞུགས་ (shuù) va. to sit, to stay, to dwell, to reside (h.) ། ཁོང་དགུན་ཁ་རྒྱ་གར་ལ་བཞུགས་ཀྱི་ཡོད་པ་རེད་ He resides in India in the winter. ། བོད་བཞུགས་སྐུ་ཚབ the representative residing in Tibet.

བཞུགས་སྐུ་ (shuùgu) a statue that is seated on sth.

བཞུགས་ཁྲི་ (shugdri) h. of ཁྲི་.

བཞུགས་གྲ་ཁྲིག (shug trədrii) sm. བཞུགས་ཁྲིག.

བཞུགས་གྲལ་ (shugdrɛɛ) a row of seats.

བཞུགས་གྲལ་བཤག (shugdrɛɛ shāà) va. to make people laugh ། དེ་རིང་མི་དེས་བསྟན་བཤིག་བཤད་ནས་བཞུགས་གྲལ་བཤགས་སོང་ Today that person told a joke and made people laugh.

བཞུགས་གྲུ་ (shugdru) h. of གྲུ.

བཞུགས་གྲོགས་ (shugdrɔɔ) h. of སྡོད་རོགས་.

བཞུགས་གླིང་ (shugliŋ) h. of གླིང་ག.

བཞུགས་སྒར་ (shuùgar) 1. camp, nonpermanent/ temporary residence. 2. the "temporary" residence of the Dalai Lama in India, i.e., Dharamsala ། གནས་ཚུལ་འདི་བཞུགས་སྒར་ནས་འབྱོར་དོན་ལྟར་ According to the news arriving from Dharamsala.

བཞུགས་སྒྲིག (shugdrii) shung. making living arrangements for visitors/ travelers (h.); va.— བྱེད་ ། ཚོགས་འདུའི་འཐུས་མི་རྣམས་ཀྱི་བཞུགས་སྒྲིག་བྱ་དགོས་ (You) have to make living arrangements for the delegates to the conference.

བཞུགས་སྒྲོམ་ (shugdrom) h. of སྡོད་སྒྲོམ་.

བཞུགས་སྟངས་ (shuùdaŋ) h. སྡོད་སྟངས་.

བཞུགས་སྟན་ (shugdɛn) h. of གདན་.

བཞུགས་སྟེན་ (shugden) h. of ཀྱག་བཀྱག.

བཞུགས་གདན་ (shugdɛn) h. of གདན་.

བཞུགས་གདན་འཇགས་ (shuùdɛnjaà) 1. please be seated. 2. good-bye (said by the person leaving to the person staying). 3. part of the response to the greeting ཕྱག་ཕེབས་གནང་བྱུང་.

བཞུགས་གདན་འཛུགས་ས་ (shu̱ùdɛn ja̱àsa) place of residence (h.).
བཞུགས་གནས་ (shu̱gnɛὲ) residence, place where sb. stays (h.).
བཞུགས་འབོལ་ (shumböö) sm. འབོལ་གདན་.
བཞུགས་བྱ་ (shu̱gja) shung. term for the "on duty" བཀའ་བློན་ (i.e., the one Kalon was always on "duty" at the residence of the Dalai Lama).
བཞུགས་བྲང་ (shu̱ùdraŋ) sm. བཞུགས་གནས་.
བཞུགས་མོལ་ (shu̱ùmöö) discussion, talk (h.); va.—བྱེད་, —གནང་.
བཞུགས་མོལ་ཚོགས་འདུ་ (shu̱ùmöö tsöndu) round table discussion, symposium, seminar, forum.
བཞུགས་མཚེར་ (shu̱ŋdzer) shung. 1. temporary residence/ home. 2. name (of guest) that are fastened on doors of houses that are being used as guest houses for visiting dignitaries at the order of the government.
བཞུགས་ཞག (shu̱ùshaà) sm. ཞག་སྡོད་.
བཞུགས་གཞིས་ (shu̱ùshiì) sm. སྡོད་གཞིས་.
བཞུགས་ཡུལ་ (shu̱ùyüü) sm. བཞུགས་ས་, 2.
བཞུགས་ཤག (shu̱ùshaà) sm. བཞུགས་ས་, 2.
བཞུགས་ས་ (shu̱ùsə) 1. seat (h.). 2. place of residence (h.). 3. h. of ཞག་ས་.
བཞུགས་ས་སྒྲིག (shu̱ùsə drig) h. of སྡོད་སྒྲིག་བྱེད་.
བཞུད་ (shü̱ü) 1. vi. to set (for sun and moon) ¶ཉི་མ་བཞུད་ནས་ After the sun set. 2. va. to go.
བཞུད་ཆུ་ (shü̱üju) fast flowing stream.
བཞུན་ (shü̱n) abbr. of བཞུན་པོ་.
བཞུན་ཐིགས (shü̱ndig) drops of melted/ molten material.
བཞུན་ཐུད་དཀར་པོ་ (shü̱ndüü gāābo) a Tibetan food made of melted butter and cheese.
བཞུན་བདར་ (shü̱ndar) sm. བཞུ་འདུལ་.
བཞུན་པོ་ (shü̱nbu) diligent, conscientious.
བཞུར་ (shu̱r) 1. va. to strain, to filter. 2. sm. བཞར་.
བཞུར་འགྲོ་ (shu̱rdro) running/ flowing (water).
བཞུར་རྒྱུག (shu̱u gyaà) va. to buzz (by airplanes).
བཞུར་ཆུ་ (shu̱uju) 1. the liquid produced by melting. 2. a stream, a small river.
བཞུར་པོ་ (shu̱rbu) rushing/ fast flowing (water).
བཞུར་ཚད་ (shu̱rdzɛὲ) volume of flow (for water, electricity).
བཞུར་གཟུགས་ཤུགས་རིག (shu̱rsuù shūgriì) fluid mechanics.
བཞུས་ (shü̱ü): p. and imp. of བཞུ་; p. of གཞུ་.
བཞུས་མ་ (shü̱ümə) 1. solution (chemical). 2. molten ¶ལྕགས་བཞུས་མ་ Molten iron.
བཞུས་ཤེལ་ (shü̱üshee) man-made crystal.
བཞེང་: p. བཞེངས་ (she̱ŋ) 1. va. to get up, to rise (h.) ¶ཁོང་བཞེངས་ནས་ཕེབས་པ་རེད་ He got up and went. 2. va. to erect, to build ¶ལྷ་ཁང་བཞེང་རྒྱུ་ The building of temples.
བཞེངས་ (she̱ŋ) p. of བཞེང་.
བཞེངས་སྒྲུན་ (she̱ŋdrün) sm. བཞེངས་, 2.
བཞེངས་སྟབས་ (she̱ŋdəb) standing up ¶ཚོགས་འདུ་འགོ་ཚུགས་སྐབས་ཚོགས་མི་ཚང་མ་བཞེངས་སྟབས་སུ་གྲལ་བསྒྲིགས་འདུག When the meeting started, all the attendees were arranged to be standing in a rows.
བཞེངས་བཞུགས་ (she̱ŋshuù) va. to stand (h.).
བཞེད་ (she̱è) aim, thought, idea, intention (vb.+ —) ¶གསང་ཕེབས་གནང་བཞེད་ཀྱང་ (They) also/ even had the idea of secretly fleeing. 2. va. to accept a (view) ¶འཛམ་གླིང་རིལ་མོ་ཡིན་པར་བཞེད་པ་རེད་ (He) accepted the (view) that the world is round. 3. va. to be willing to do sth. ¶ཁོང་ལྷ་སར་འབྱོན་པར་བཞེད་ནས་ཕྱག་བྲིས་གནང་འདུག In his letter (he) said he was willing to go to Lhasa.
བཞེད་དགོངས་ (she̱ègoŋ) h. of རེ་འདོད་.
བཞེད་དོན་ (she̱èdön) sm. བཞེད་དགོངས་.
བཞེད་དོན་འབོད་ཚིག (she̱èdön bö̱ödziì) slogan of the type that ends in—may sth. come to pass.
བཞེད་ཚུལ་ (she̱èdzüü) thoughts, doctrine, opinion ¶གྲུབ་མཐའ་སོ་སོའི་བཞེད་ཚུལ་སྐོར་ Concerning the doctrines of each sect. ¶གན་དྷི་མཆོག་གི་བཞེད་ཚུལ་ Gandhi's thoughts.
བཞེད་གཞི་ (she̱èshi) sm. དགོངས་གཞི་.
བཞེད་ལུགས་ (she̱èluù) sm. བཞེད་ཚུལ་.
བཞེད་སྲོལ་ (she̱èsöö) a convention, custom, tradition.
བཞེར་ (she̱e) respecting, honoring.
བཞེས་ (she̱è) 1. h. of ལེན་. 2. h. of ཟ་. 3. an honorifizer. 4. h. of གོན་.
བཞེས་ཁམ་ (she̱ègam) h. of ཁམ་བུ་.
བཞེས་ཁུག (she̱èguù) h. of ཐ་ཁུག.
བཞེས་ཁྲུང་ (she̱èdruŋ) h. of ཆང་.
བཞེས་གྲོ་བཞེས་འབྲས་ (she̱dro she̱ndrɛὲ) h. of གྲོ་མ་འབྲས་སིལ་.
བཞེས་འགམ་སྒྱོན་ (she̱ngam gyōn) h. of རྩམ་འགམ་རྒྱག.
བཞེས་སྒོ་ (she̱ègo) h. of ཡོང་སྒོ་.
བཞེས་རྒྱུ་ (she̱ègyu) h. of རྒྱུ་མ་.
བཞེས་སྒོང་ (she̱ègoŋ) h. of སྒོང་ང་.
བཞེས་ཆ་ཡོད་པ་ (she̱èja yō̱ōbə) please accept responsibility for sth.
བཞེས་ཇས་ (she̱èjɛὲ) cup (h.).
བཞེས་འཛམ་ (she̱njam) h. of རྩམ་ཐུག.
བཞེས་ཉ་ (she̱èña) h. of ཉ་.
བཞེས་ཉན་པ་ (she̱è ñe̱mba) h. of ཟ་ཉན་པ་.
བཞེས་ཉིན་ (she̱èñin) day after tomorrow.
བཞེས་ཉུང་ (she̱èñuŋ) h. of ཉུང་མ་.
བཞེས་ཉེས་ཤོར་ (she̱èñeè shɔ̄ɔ) h. of ཟ་ཉེས་ཤོར་.
བཞེས་ཐ་ (she̱èda) sm. བཞེས་ཐག.
བཞེས་ཐག (she̱èdaà) tobacco, cigarette (h.); va.—བཞེས་; —མཆོད་ to smoke.
བཞེས་ཐལ་ཤོར་ (she̱èdɛɛ shɔ̄ɔ) h. of ཟ་ཐལ་ཤོར་.
བཞེས་ཐུག (she̱èduù) h. of ཐུག་པ་.
བཞེས་ཐུག་རྒྱ་ཐུག (she̱èduù gyə̱duù) h. of. རྒྱ་ཐུག.
བཞེས་ཐུག་བག་ཐུག (she̱èduù pə̱duù) h. of བག་ཐུག.
བཞེས་ཐུག་མིང་བཏགས་ (she̱èduù mi̱ŋdaà) h. of ཐུག་པ་མིང་བཏགས་.
བཞེས་ཐུད་ (she̱èdüü) h. of ཐུད་.
བཞེས་ཐུར་ (she̱èdur) h. of ཐུར་མ་.
བཞེས་ལྷན་ (she̱èdɛn) h. of ཀློལ་ལྷན་.
བཞེས་ལྷུར་ (she̱èdur) h. of ཛ་ལྷུར་.
བཞེས་སྡོར་ (she̱èdɔr) h. of སྡོར་.
བཞེས་པོ་ (she̱èbo) h. of ལེན་པོ་.
བཞེས་སྒྲོ་ (she̱èdro) h. of ཁ་ཟས་.
བཞེས་སྒྲོ་པ་ (she̱è drōba) person who makes deep fried pastries.
བཞེས་ཕོར་ (she̱èbɔɔ) sm. རྩམ་ཕོར་.
བཞེས་ཕྱུར་ (she̱èjur) h. of ཕྱུར་བ་.
བཞེས་འཕྲོ་ (she̱èdro) used, leftover.
བཞེས་བག (she̱èbaà) h. of བག་ལེབ་.
བཞེས་འབྲས་ (she̱ndrɛὲ) h. of འབྲས་.
བཞེས་མི་ལོ་བ་ (she̱è mi̱lowa) h. of ཟ་མི་ཉན་པ་.
བཞེས་མོག (she̱èmɔɔ̀) h. of མོག་མོག.
བཞེས་ཙེ་ (she̱èdze) h. of ཁོའི་ཙེ་.
བཞེས་ཚལ་ (she̱èdzɛɛ) h. of ཚལ་.
བཞེས་ཚིལ་ (she̱èdzii) h. of ཚིལ་ལུ་.
བཞེས་ཚོགས་ (she̱èdzɔɔ̀) banquet (h.).
བཞེས་གཟར་ (she̱èsar) h. of དཀར་གཟར་ and གཟར་བུ་.
བཞེས་ཡོས་ (she̱èyöö) h. of ཡོས་.
བཞེས་རག (she̱èraà) h. of ཨ་རག.
བཞེས་རག་མཉེས་དགའ་གནང་ (she̱èraà ñe̱daà nāŋ) h. of ཨ་རག་ཞབས་དགའ་རྒྱག.
བཞེས་རག་སྨོན་ཚིག (she̱èraà mō̱ndziì) a toast (made when drinking).
བཞེས་ལབ་ (she̱èləb) radish (h.).
བཞེས་ལུམ་མ་ (she̱èlummə) h. of ཚ་ལུམ་མ་.
བཞེས་ལོ་ (she̱èlo) h. of ཟ་ལོ་.
བཞེས་ཤ་ (she̱èsha) h. of ཤ་.
བཞེས་ཤ་སྐམ་པོ་ (she̱èsha gāmbo) h. of ཤ་སྐམ་པོ་.
བཞེས་ཤུ་ (she̱èshu) h. of ཀ་ཤུ་.
བཞེས་ཤེད་ (she̱èsheè) h. of ཟ་ཤེད་.
བཞེས་སོན་ལ་ཕྱུག (she̱èsōnlabuù) h. of སོན་ལ་ཕྱུག.
བཞེས་སྲོལ་ (she̱èsöö) sm. བཞེས་ཚུལ་.
བཞེས་སློམ་ (she̱èlom) h. of སློ་མ་.
བཞེས་ཏྲའུ་ (she̱èhuu) h. of ཏྲའུ་.

བཞོ་: p. **བཞོས་**; f. **བཞོ་** (sho) 1. va. to milk. 2. f. of འཇོ་.

བཞོ་སྡེགས་ (shodeg) a stool used when milking.

བཞོ་ཐག (shodaà) a rope used for tying the legs of animals when milking.

བཞོ་དབྱངས་ (shoyaŋ) song sung when milking.

བཞོ་མ་ (shoma) sm. བཞོན་མ་.

བཞོ་ཞྭ་ (shosha) a hat worn by people who milk.

བཞོ་གཞས་ (shoshɛɛ̀) sm. བཞོ་དབྱངས་.

བཞོ་ཟོ་ (shojo) sm. བཞོ་ཟོམ་.

བཞོ་ཟོམ་ (shosom) milking bucket.

བཞོ་གཟུང་ (shosuŋ) a type of ornament worn by women in eastern Tibet.

བཞོག་སྐྱུད་ (shogjɛɛ̀) a carpenter's tool for cutting and carving.

བཞོག་ས་ (shogsa) sm.* འཇོག་ས་.

བཞོགས་ (shɔɔ̀) p. of འཇོག.

བཞོད་ (shöö̀) imp. of བཞད་.

བཞོན་ (shön) 1. va. to ride ¶ རྟ་བཞོན་ནས་ཕྱིན་པ་ཡིན་ (I) went riding a horse. 2. va. to milk.

བཞོན་ཁལ་ (shöngɛɛ) shung. riding animals and transport animals.

བཞོན་རྟ་ (shönda) riding horse.

བཞོན་དྲེལ་ (shöndree) riding mule.

བཞོན་ཕྱུགས་ (shönjuù) milking animals.

བཞོན་བྱ་ (shönja) a riding animal.

བཞོན་མ་ (shönma) 1. milch animal. 2. person who milks animals.

བཞོན་མ་ར་བ་ (shönma rawa) dairy farm.

བཞོན་མཛོ་ (shöndzo) a milch dzo.

བཞོན་ར་ (shönra) dairy farm.

བཞོར་ (shɔ̄r) imp. of བཞར་.

བཞོས་ (shöö̀) p. of འཇོ་.

བཞོས་སྐམ་ (shöö̀gam) dry animal (one that no longer gives milk).

ཟ་: p. ཟོས་ or བཟས་; f. བཟའ་; imp. ཟོ་ (sa) 1. va. to eat ། ཁོས་ཟ་ཁང་ལ་ཁ་ལག་བཟས་པ་རེད་ He ate at the restaurant. 2. vi. to get/ be angry ། ཁོ་ཁོང་ཁྲོ་བཟའ་གི་རེད་ He will be angry. 3. vi. to itch ། ང་སྣོད་སྒལ་ཟ་གི་འདུག My back is itching. 4. va. to take a bribe, to take money/ embezzle from a fund ། དངུལ་འདི་ང་གཉིས་ཀྱིས་བཟས་ཡོད་པ་མ་རེད་ We two didn't embezzle any of the money. ། ཁྲིམས་དཔོན་དེས་སྐྱབས་རྟེན་མང་པོ་བཟས་འདུག The judge took many bribes.

ཟ་ཀྱེ་ (sagye) a useless person.

ཟ་རྐང་བཀོད་ (sagaŋ gööba) shung. va. to create a source of income ། བུན་འདེད་པས་འདེད་གླ་སོགས་མིང་སློས་སྒྲིག་བཅད་ལས་ཀྱང་གཙོ་ཆེ་བའི་ཟ་རྐང་བཀོད་པ་རེད་ The debt collector has created additional sources of income on top of what he is being paid.

ཟ་སྐོང་ (sagoŋ) a disease of the skin characterized by itching.

ཟ་རྒྱང་འཐུང་རྒྱང་ (sagyaŋ tüŋgyaŋ) eating and drinking freely/ without hestitation.

ཟ་སྐད་འཐུང་སྐད་ (sagεε tüŋgεε) daily used language.

ཟ་སྐལ་ (sagεε) good fortune/ benefit due to past karma.

ཟ་ཁ་བུད་ (saga büü) just enough to live on ། ཁོང་གི་གླ་ཕོགས་དེས་ཟ་ཁ་བུད་ཙམ་ཡོད་པ་རེད་ His salary is just enough to live on.

ཟ་ཁ་ལོབ་ (saga lob) 1. vi. to get/ become accustomed ། ད་ང་རྒྱ་གར་གྱི་ལྟོ་ཆས་ཟ་ཁ་ལོབ་བཞག Now I have become accustomed to eating indian food.

ཟ་ཁང་ (sagaŋ) restaurant.

ཟ་ཁང་གི་སྣེ་ལེན་པ་ (sagaŋgi nēlemba) host/ hostess/ receptionist in a restaurant.

ཟ་ཁང་གི་ཞབས་ཕྱི་པ་ (sagaŋgi shəbcīmə) waiter, waitress.

ཟ་ཁུ་ (sagu) a digestive illness in Tibetan medicine.

ཟ་མཁས་འཐུང་མཁས་ (sageè tüŋkεè) sm. ཟ་མཁས་སྦྱོང་མཁས་.

ཟ་མཁས་སྦྱོང་མཁས་ (sageè jöökεè) economical/ frugal living; va.—བྱེད་ to act/ be economical.

ཟ་ག (saga) showing off; va.—བྱེད་ to show off.

ཟ་གོས་སྡོད་གསུམ་ (sagöö döösum) the three: eating, clothing and housing ། དེང་སང་ཟ་གོས་སྡོད་གསུམ་ཕྱི་ལུགས་ཅན་དུ་གྱུར་འདུག These days, eating, clothing and housing have become Westernized.

ཟ་དགའ་འཐུང་སྐྱིད་ (saga tüŋgyii) sb. who seeks pleasure, a hedonist.

ཟ་དགའ་ངལ་འཛེམ་ (saga ŋendzem) lazy, indolent [Lit. likes to eat but shies away from work].

ཟ་སྒོང་མཉམ་འཁུར་ (sagyoŋ ñamgur) shung. sharing the profit and loss together/ equally ། ཁྲ་མ་འདིས་དཔྱད་རྗེས་ཕྱོགས་གཉིས་ཀས་ཟ་སྒོང་མཉམ་འཁུར་བྱ་དགོས་ After the arrival of this verdict, both parties should share the profit and loss together/ equally.

ཟ་གྱོན་ (sagyön) food and clothing.

ཟ་གྱོན་ཆེན་པོ་ (sagyön cēmbo) large scale bribe taking/ corruption; va.—བྱེད་.

ཟ་གྱོན་བདུང་གསུམ་ (sagyön dūŋsum) shung. abbr. of ཟ་རྒྱུ་གྱོན་རྒྱུ་.

ཟ་གྲི་ (sadri) table knife.

ཟ་གྲོགས་ (sadrɔɔ) eating partner, sb. with whom one goes out to eat, people who reciprocally visit each other for meals.

ཟ་འགྲམ་ (sandram) cheeks.

ཟ་འགྲོ་སྡོད་གསུམ་ (sandro döösum) the three: eating, going and staying.

ཟ་རྒྱག་སྦྱོད་གསུམ་ (sagyaà jöösum) acting as a spendthrift (in excess of customs/ norms).

ཟ་རྒྱུ་ (sagyu) food ། ཁོ་ཚོ་སྐྱོ་པོ་བྱུས་ནས་ཟ་རྒྱུ་དཀོན་པོ་འདུག They have become poor and food is scare.

ཟ་རྒྱུ་གྱོན་རྒྱུ་ (sagyu gyöngyu) necessities of life [Lit. things for eating and wearing].

ཟ་རྒྱུ་འཐུང་རྒྱུ་ (sagyu tüngyu) foodstuffs, things for eating and drinking.

ཟ་རྒྱུ་འཐུང་རྒྱུ་མང་ན་དགའ་ ལབ་རྒྱུ་གླེང་རྒྱུ་ཉུང་ན་དགའ་ (sagyu tüngyu maŋna ga ləbgyu lēŋgyu ñuŋnə ga) one should avoid disputes/ quarrels [Lit. it is good to have more food and drink to eat; it is good to have few disputes/ quarrels].

ཟ་སྒོ་ (sago) shung. a bribe or other illegal income derived from a position or office; va.—བྱེད་; vi.—བྱུང་ to receive a bribe or other illegal income from a position or office ། གཞིས་སྡོད་ཀྱིས་ཟ་སྒོ་མང་པོ་བྱས་པ་རེད་ The estate steward took much income in bribes.

ཟ་ངེ་ཟིང་ངེ་ (saŋe siŋŋe) bedlam, turmoil, commotion; vi.—ཆགས་ to become bedlam/ commotion; va.—བྱེད་ to cause things to be in commotion/ bedlam.

ཟ་རྔམ་ (saŋam) sm. ཟ་སྒོ་.

ཟ་རྔམ་ཆེན་པོ་ (saŋam cēmbo) greedy, avaricious, covetous.

ཟ་རྔམ་འཐུང་རྔམ་ (saŋam tüŋŋam) greedy, avaricious, covetous.

ཟ་རྔམ་ཚ་པོ་ (saŋam tsābo) sm. ཟ་རྔམ་འཐུང་རྔམ་.

ཟ་བཅུད་ (sajüü) nutrient, nutrition, nutritious.

ཟ་བཅུད་ཆུང་ཆུང་ (sajüü cūŋjuŋ) 1. low in nutrients, not nutritious. 2. low value/ worth.

ཟ་བཅུད་ཆེན་པོ་ (sajüü cēmbo) 1. high in nutrients, very nutritious ། ཁ་ལག་འདི་ཟ་བཅུད་ཆེན་པོ་འདུག This food is highly nutritious. 2. high value/ worth ། རང་ཉིད་ཀྱིས་དཀའ་ལས་བརྒྱབ་པའི་དངོས་པོ་དེ་ཟ་བཅུད་ཆེན་པོ་ཡོད་པ་རེད་ Things one obtained from hard work have great value.

ཟ་ལྕག (saja) a whip made of nettles.

ཟ་ཆ་ (saja) sm. ཟ་ཆས་.

ཟ་ཆེ་བ (sajewa) overeating.

ཟ་ཚོག་འཐུང་ཚོག (sajɔɔ tüŋjɔɔ) 1. ready for eating and drinking. 2. ready to do, well prepared ། ཨར་པོའི་རྒྱུ་ཆ་རྣམས་ཟ་ཚོག་འཐུང་ཚོག་ནང་བཞིན་གྲ་སྒྲིག་བྱས་བཞག They prepared the building materials well (like having food and drink ready to eat).

ཟ་ཆས་ (sajεὲ) foodstuffs.

ཟ་རྗེས་ (sajeè) shung. abbr. of ཟ་ལས་རྗེས་འབྲེལ་.

ཟ་ཉན་ (sañεn) sm. ཟ་ཉན་པ་.

ཟ་ཉན་པ་ (sañεmba) edible.

ཟ་ཉན་ཡོད་པ་ (sañεn yööba) sm. ཟ་ཉན་པ་.

ཟ་ཉལ་ (sa ñεε) eating and sleeping.

ཟ་ཉེས་པ་ (sañeèba) sm. ཟ་ཉེས་ཤོར་.

ཟ་ཉེས་ཤོར་ (sañeè shɔ̄ɔ) vi. to eat eat sth. that make one sick/ ill.

ཟ་མཉམ་ (sañam) eating at the same time, eating together; va.—བྱེད་ ། ད་རང་ང་གཉིས་ལྟོ་ཆས་ཟ་མཉམ་ཡིན་ This morning we two were eating at the same time.

ཟ་སྙད་ (sañεὲ) sm. ཟ་སྙད་.

ཟ་བསྙད་ (sañεὲ) causing difficulties in order to get a bribe; va.—བྱེད་ ། འགག་སྒོའི་ལས་བྱེད་པས་འགྲུལ་པ་རྣམས་ལ་ཟ་བསྙད་བྱེད་ཀྱི་ཡོད་པ་རེད་ The custom officers are causing difficulties for the passengers in order to get them to pay bribes.

ཟ་བསྙེགས་སྲོལ་ལམ་ (sañeg söölam) shung. system/ custom of grazing animals ། བཀའ་མཆན་དུ་ཟ་བསྙེགས་སྲོལ་ལམ་གང་ཅི་སྔར་རྒྱུན་ད་ལྟ་ཕན་བཞིན་བྱེད་དགོས་གསལ་བ་ It was mentioned in the note written above the petition that the custom of grazing animals must be done.

ཟ་བདུང་ (sədun) eating and drinking.

ཟ་བདུང་རྒྱས་སྤྲོས་ (sədun gyɛɛ̀dröö) living lavishly.
ཟ་སྡེར་ཨྣ་ (sadera) sm. ལྡོ་ཟ་སྡེར་ཨྣ་.
ཟ་སྡོབས་ཆུང་ཆུང་ (sadob cūnjun) sm. གྲོད་ཁོག་ཆུང་ཆུང་.
ཟ་སྡོབས་ཆེན་པོ་ (sadob cēmbo) sm. གྲོད་ཁོག་ཆེན་པོ་.
ཟ་ཐང་ (sadaŋ) 1. good fortune ། ཁོ་ལ་ལས་ཀ་ཡག་པོ་དེ་རག་པ་ནི་ཁོ་པའི་ཟ་ཐང་རང་རེད་ It is his good fortune to get that job. 2. arc. salary.
ཟ་ཐལ་ (satɛɛ) eating excessively; vi.—ཤོར་ to eat excessively. 2. eating badly; vi.—ཤོར་.
ཟ་ཐུར་ (sədur) 1. spoon. 2. chopsticks.
ཟ་ཐེངས་གཅིག (sa tēnjig) eating sth. at one time.
ཟ་འཐུང་ (sədun) sm. ཟ་བདུང་.
ཟ་འཐུང་འཛོམས་པོ་ (sədun dzombo) 1. a variety of foods and drinks. 2. a prosperous area/ region.
ཟ་དུས་མིད་པ་འགག་རྒྱུར་ཉེན་ འགྲོ་དུས་རྐང་འདྲེད་ཤོར་རྒྱུར་ཉེན་ (sədüü miibə gəggyu sön drodüü gāndreè shōrgyu sön) one should be very careful in all things [Lit. when eating beware of choking, when walking beware of slipping].
ཟ་འདོད་ (sandöö) 1. the desire to eat, hunger; vi.—ལངས་ to have the desire to eat arise. 2. sm. ཟ་བསྐྱད་. 3. desire for corruption/ bribes.
ཟ་འདོད་འཁྱལ་འཆེར་ (sandöö gündzer) greedy/ desirous but lazy.
ཟ་འདོད་བསྙད་འཚོལ་ (sandöö ñɛɛ̀ndzöö) sm. ཟ་བསྐྱད་.
ཟ་འདོད་གཙོ་འདོན་ (sandöö dzōndön) shung. avaricious in embezzling/ being corrupt ། ས་གནས་སྐྱི་སྤྱོད་ནས་ཟ་འདོད་གཙོ་འདོན་གྱི་དབང་དུ་མ་སོང་བ་དྲང་པོས་གཞུང་བསྲུངས་དགོས་རྒྱུ་ The local officials are not to be avaricious in corruption, and should settle matters justly.
ཟ་འདྲེ་ (sandre) sm. ཟ་ཀྱི་.
ཟ་ནམ་ཟིན་ལྡེ་ (sanam sinde) the 16th ancient Tibetan king.
ཟ་མནར་འཐུང་མནར་ (sanar tūnnar) suffering hunger and thirst.
ཟ་སྣུམ་ (sanum) cooking oil.
ཟ་སྤྱད་ (sajɛɛ̀) 1. eating. 2. eating implements.
ཟ་སྤྱད་སྟག་གི་ཁ་ཡོད་ན་ ཞུ་སྤྱད་ཀོ་བོའི་པོ་བ་དགོས་ (sajɛɛ̀ dāāgi kā yōōna shūjɛɛ̀ kowö pōwa gɔɔ̀) if one has the courage to do risky things one should have the ability to deal with the consequences, if one has the guts to start something risky one should have the ability to see it through to the end [Lit. if one has the mouth of a tiger one should have the stomach of a gobo bird (a bird that is said to be able to digest stones)].
ཟ་པ་ (saba) head of a household.
ཟ་པ་སྤྱི་ (sabaji) shung. the head of a family and the other members of the family.
ཟ་ཕོད་ (sa pöö) vi. to not be afraid of eating sth., to dare to eat sth. ། མི་དེ་ཚོས་ཉ་གསོན་པ་ཟ་ཕོད་ཀྱི་འདུག Those people are not afraid of eating raw fish.
ཟ་འཕྲུག (səndruù) itching; vi.—ལང་ to itch.
ཟ་འཕྲོ་ (sandro) leftover (food); vi.—ལུས་ to have food be leftover; va.—འཇོག་ to leave food ། ང་ཁ་ལག་ཟ་འཕྲོ་བཞག་ནས་འགྲོ་དགོས་བྱུང་ I had to leave my food and go.
ཟ་འཕྲོས་ (sāndröö) sm. ཟ་འཕྲོ་.
ཟ་བ་ (sawa) food.
ཟ་བ་པོ་ (sawabo) eater of food.
ཟ་བབས་ (sabəb) a type of brocade.
ཟ་བེ་ཟོ་བེ་ (sabe sobe) indolent, slothful, careless ། མི་དེས་རྟག་པར་ལས་ཀ་ཟ་བེ་ཟོ་བེ་བྱེད་ཀྱི་འདུག He always does work carelessly.
ཟ་བེད་ (sabeè) sm. ཟ་བསྐྱད་.
ཟ་བེར་ (sa per) vi. to itch.
ཟ་དབང་ཕྱོགས་ཤེད་ (sawaŋ cɔ̄ɔ̀sheè) shung. ganging up to gain bribes/ corruption.
ཟ་འབོར་ཁ་འཐབ་ (sabɔr kādəb) one's income and expenditures in balance.
ཟ་འབྲུ་ (səndru) 1. edible grains. 2. grains for consumption (as opposed to those kept for seed).
ཟ་འབྲུ་དང་སྨན་རྫས་འཛིན་སྐྱོང་ལས་ཁང་ (səndru daŋ mɛndzɛɛ dzingyoŋ lɛɛ̀gaŋ) Food and Drug Administration (FDA, in U.S.A.).
ཟ་འབྲུ་དང་སོ་ནམ་ལས་དོན་ཁང་ (səndru daŋ sōnam lɛɛ̀döngaŋ) Food and Agriculture Organization (FOA, of UN).
ཟ་འབྲུ་ལོ་ཏོག (səndru lodoò) food crops.
ཟ་མ་ (sama) food; va.—ཟ་ to eat food.
ཟ་མ་ཏོག (sama dōò) 1. utensil/ container for food. 2. name of a religious text.
ཟ་མ་གདན་ཐོག (sama dɛndɔɔ̀) a job that pays well but doesn't require doing much work.
ཟ་མ་མ་ནིང་ (sama məniŋ) men and women who are incapable of sexual relations.
ཟ་མ་མོ་ (samamo) woman.
ཟ་མ་ཟིན་ (sama sin) (with numbers) very close ། མི་ཁྲི་གཅིག་ཟ་མ་ཟིན་ About 10,000 people (very close to being 10,000).
ཟ་མི་ཉན་པ་ (sa miñɛmba) inedible, not fit to eat.
ཟ་མི་ལོ་བ་ (sa milowa) sm. ཟ་མི་ཉན་པ་.
ཟ་རྩྭ་ (sadza) grasslands used for grazing, pastureland.
ཟ་རྩོད་ (sadzöö) shung. conflict/ quarrel over using grasslands.
ཟ་ཚད་ (sadzɛɛ̀) the amount of food one eats, appetite.
ཟ་ཚན་ (sādzɛn) appetite ། མི་དེ་ཟ་ཚན་ཆེན་པོ་ཞིག་འདུག That man has a big appetite.
ཟ་ཚོད་ (sadzöö) restraining/ restricting/ controlling one's eating; va.—བྱེད་; —རྒྱག.
ཟ་ཚྭ་ (sādza) salt.
ཟ་ཟ་འཐུང་འཐུང་ (sasa tūndun) drinking and eating.
ཟ་ཟི་ (səsi) 1. sm. ཟང་ཟིང་. 2. sm. ཟ་ཆས་.
ཟ་འོག (sawɔɔ̀) a type of high quality brocade.
ཟ་འོས་ (sāwöö) edible, fit to eat.
ཟ་འོས་པ་ (sawööbə) sm. ཟ་འོས་.
ཟ་ཡོན་ (sayön) 1. sm. ཟ་པ་. 2. fee for helping others. 3. fee for reading scriptures.
ཟ་ར་ཚགས་ (sara tsāà) sm. ཕྱ་ཁ་.
ཟ་རི་ཟི་རི་ (səri siri) 1. unclear, vague, indistinct ། གསར་འགྱུར་ཟ་རི་ཟ་རི་ Unclear news. 2. helter-skelter, disorganized ། ལས་ཀ་ཟ་རི་ཟ་རི་བྱས་ན་མི་འགྲིགས་ (One) should not work in a disorganized way. 2. stunned, dazed ། མི་དེའི་མགོ་ལ་མུར་མཛོག་ཅིག་གཞུས་ནས་ཟ་རི་ཟི་རི་བཟོས་པ་རེད་ (He) punched the man in the head and dazed him.
ཟ་རི་ཟེ་རི་ (səri seri) sm. ཟ་རི་ཟི་རི་.
ཟ་རུ་ (səru) 1. left-handed ། ཁོ་ལག་པ་ཟ་རུ་རེད་ He is left-handed. 2. a wooden ladle.
ཟ་རུ་བདུབ་ (sərudub) arc. eatable.
ཟ་རེག (sareg) itching; vi.—ལང་ to itch; va.—འཕྲུག; —འཕྲད་ to scratch an itch.
ཟ་རོ་ (saro) sm. ཟ་ཀྱི་.
ཟ་རོགས་ (sarɔɔ̀) an eating partner.
ཟ་ལས་རྗེས་འབྲེལ་ (salɛɛ jendree) shung. income and work being related/ linked ། གླ་ཕོགས་ཆེན་པོ་ཡིན་ཙང་ཟ་ལས་རྗེས་འབྲེལ་གྱི་ལས་ཀ་མང་པོ་བྱེད་དགོས་ཀྱི་འདུག Because (his) salary is high and income and work are linked, (he) has to do lot of work.
ཟ་ལོ་ (salo) sm. ཟ་འོས་.
ཟ་ཤུགས་ཆུང་ཆུང་ (sashug cūnjun) sm. གྲོད་ཁོག་ཆུང་ཆུང་.
ཟ་ཤུགས་ཆེན་པོ་ (sashug cēmbo) sm. གྲོད་ཁོག་ཆེན་པོ་.
ཟ་ཤེད་ (sasheè) appetite ། ཟ་ཤེད་ཆེན་པོ་ A big appetite.
ཟ་སེམས་ (sasem) sm. ཟ་འདོད་.
ཟ་སྲུང་ (sasuŋ) arc. a guarantee given to caligraphers who are copying scriptures to provide them food regularly.
ཟ་བསོད་ (sasöö) sm. ཟ་ཐང་.
ཟ་ཧམ་ (saham) greedy, avaricious.
ཟ་ཧོར་ (sahɔr) Bengal.
ཟ་ཧོར་ཀུ་ཤུ་ (sahɔɔ gūshu) a type of apple.
ཟ་ལྷག་འཐུང་ལྷག (salhaà tūnlhaà) leftover/ excess food.
ཟག: p. ཟགས་; f. ཟག (saà) 1. vi. to fall/ drop ། ཐོག་

ཁ་ནས་ཟགས་པ་རེད་ (He) fell from the roof ¶ གནས་ཚུལ་དེ་གོ་ནས་མཆི་མ་ཟགས་པ་རེད་ Tears fell when he heard the news. 2. p. of འཛག.

ཟག་ཁ་ (sa̱gu) sm. ཉིང་ཁ་.

ཟག་ཁུང་ (sa̱guŋ) a gaping hole, a hole through which things fall.

ཟག་ཁུང་བརྒྱ་གྲོན་ (sa̱guŋ gya̱dön) sm. རྨ་བརྒྱ་བུག་སྟོང་.

ཟག་མགོ་ (sa̱ŋgo) pipe (for smoking).

ཟག་སྒོ་ (saggo) sm. ཟག་ཁུང་.

ཟག་བཅས་ (sa̱gjɛɛ̀) having delusions.

ཟག་ཐིག་དབྱིབས་ (sa̱gdig yi̅b) 1. streamlined (for cars, boats, etc.). 2. cone shaped.

ཟག་ཐིག་གཟུགས་ (sə̱gdig su̱ù) sm. ཟགས་ཐིག་དབྱིབས་.

ཟག་གྲོན་ (sagdön) a secretion.

ཟག་བདེ་ (sa̱gde) happiness caused by delusion.

ཟག་པ་ (sa̱gba) 1. delusions. 2. bodily excrements/ secretions.

ཟག་པ་གསོག (sa̱gba sɔ̄ɔ̀) va. to bother/ annoy/ agitate.

ཟག་ཕུང་ (sa̱gbuŋ) body.

ཟག་རྫས་ (sa̱gdzɛɛ̀) the bodily wastes: urine, stool, snot, sweat.

ཟག་ཟོག (sāgsōg) fraud, cheating, deceiving ¶ བླ་མ་འདི་ཟག་ཟོག་རེད་ This lama is a fraud.

ཟག་ཟད་ (sa̱gsɛɛ̀) abbr. of ཟག་པ་ཟད་.

ཟགས་ (sa̱g) p. of ཟག.

ཟང་ངེ་ཟིང་ངེ་ (sa̱ŋŋe si̱ŋŋe) turmoil, unrest, disorder; vi.—ཆགས་ to come into a state of disorder/ unrest/ turmoil; va.—བཟོ་; —བྱེད་ to create turmoil/ unrest/ disorder.

ཟང་ཐལ་ (sa̱ŋdɛɛ) going straight through sth. (in a magical way) ¶ རྫུ་འཕྲུལ་གྱིས་བྲག་ལ་ཟང་ཐལ་དུ་འགྲོ་གི་འདུག By magic, (he) goes straight through rocks.

ཟང་མ་ (sa̱ŋma) apparent, conspicuous.

ཟང་ཟིང་ (sə̱ŋsiŋ) 1. abbr. of ཟང་ངེ་ཟིང་ངེ་. 2. material things (as opposed to spiritual things).

ཟང་ཟིང་གི་དངོས་པོ་ (sə̱ŋsiŋgi ŋ̄ö̀bo) material objects/ things.

ཟང་ཟིང་གི་སྦྱིན་པ་ (sə̱ŋsiŋgi ji̱mbə) donations/ charity in kind.

ཟང་ཟིང་མེད་པ་ (sa̱ŋsiŋ me̱èba) 1. no things. 2. without disturbance or turmoil, peaceful and quiet.

ཟང་ཟིང་ཡོ་སྲང་ (sə̱ŋsiŋ yo̱saŋ) calming/ correcting/ eliminating disorder or unrest or turmoil; va.—བྱེད་.

ཟངས་ (sa̱ŋ) 1. copper. 2. a vessel made from ཟངས་.

ཟངས་ཀྱི་རྟགས་མ་ (sa̱ŋgi dāŋma) the bronze medal (in sports).

ཟངས་ཀྱི་འཛིར་བུ་ (sa̱ŋgi dzi̱rbu) eugenia aromatica baill (used in Tibetan medicine).

ཟངས་དཀར་ (sa̱ŋgar) Zangkar (a region in Ladakh).

ཟངས་རྒྱན་ (sa̱ŋgyɛn) a kind of tea pot made of copper.

ཟངས་སྐུ་ (sa̱ŋgu) copper statue.

ཟངས་སྐུད་ (sa̱ŋgüü) copper wire.

ཟངས་སྐྱེས་ (sa̱ŋgyeè) molded copper.

ཟངས་སྐྱོགས་ (sa̱ŋgyɔɔ̀) copper ladle.

ཟངས་སྐོལ་ (sa̱ŋ gȫȍ) va. to smelt copper.

ཟངས་ཁོག (sa̱ŋgɔɔ̀) 1. copper pot. 2. bald ¶ ཟངས་ཁོག་མགོ་ Bald head.

ཟངས་ཁོལ་ (sa̱ŋgöö) liquid/ melted copper.

ཟངས་ཁྲབ་ (sa̱ndrəb) copper armor.

ཟངས་ཁྲུ་ (sa̱ŋdru) shung. copper pot.

ཟངས་ཁྲོ་ (sa̱ŋdro) copper caldron.

ཟངས་མཁན་ (sa̱ŋñɛn) coppersmith.

ཟངས་གྱང་ལྕགས་རིག (sa̱ŋgyaŋ jə̄ə̄dziì) an impregnable fortress [Lit. fence of copper, wall of iron].

ཟངས་གྲི་ (sə̱ŋdri) 1. knife for cutting copper. 2. copper knife.

ཟངས་མགར་ (sa̱ŋgar) coppersmith.

ཟངས་ངོ་མ་ཆོད་ (sa̱ŋ ŋ̱oma cȫö) vi. to be unable to recognize a good person.

ཟངས་རྔ་ (sa̱ŋŋa) copper drum.

ཟངས་གཅོག་གྲུ་སྣུབ་ (sa̱ŋjɔɔ̀ tru̱nub) fighting to the death [Lit. break copper, sink boats].

ཟངས་ཆས་ (sa̱ŋjɛɛ̀) copperware.

ཟངས་ཆུང་ (sa̱ŋjuŋ) small copper pot.

ཟངས་ཆེན་ཁ་སྦྱོར་ (sa̱ŋjen kājɔɔ) copper box used to throw corpses into the river in ancient Tibet.

ཟངས་ཏིག (sə̱ŋdig) swertia mussofi franch (used in Tibetan medicine).

ཟངས་ཏིལ་ (sa̱ŋdee) copper moxibustion instrument.

ཟངས་གཏེར་ (sa̱ŋder) copper mine.

ཟངས་གཏེར་དམར་པོ་ (sa̱ŋder mārbo) copper ore, cuprite.

ཟངས་ཐུར་ (sa̱ŋdur) copper spoon.

ཟངས་ཐལ་ (sa̱ŋdɛɛ) copper powder/ dust. 2. sm. ཟང་ཐལ་.

ཟངས་དུང་ (sa̱ŋduŋ) copper pipe.

ཟངས་དུང་རོལ་ཆ་ (sa̱ŋduŋ rö̱öja) musical instruments made of brass ¶ ཟངས་དུང་རོལ་ཆ་རུ་ཁག Brass band/ orchestra.

ཟངས་དེམ་ (sa̱ŋdem) sm. ཟངས་ཏིག.

ཟངས་དྲེག (sa̱ŋdreg) the dregs/ scraps/ remains from copper work.

ཟངས་མདོག (sa̱ŋdɔɔ) copper color.

ཟངས་འདོན་ (sa̱ŋdön) copper mining; va.—བྱེད་ to mine copper.

ཟངས་ཏིག (sa̱ŋdig) copper pot.

ཟངས་རྡུང་ (sa̱ŋ du̱ŋ) va. to forge copper.

ཟངས་རྡུང་བ་ (sa̱ŋduŋwa) coppersmith.

ཟངས་རྡོ་ (sa̱ŋdo) copper ore.

ཟངས་རྡོ་དམར་པོ་ (sa̱ŋdo mārbo) copper ore, cuprite.

ཟངས་སྣོད་ (sa̱ŋnöö) copperware, copper utensils.

ཟངས་པར་ (sa̱ŋbar) copper plates for printing.

ཟངས་ཕག (sa̱ŋbaà) copper brick.

ཟངས་ཕོར་ (sa̱ŋbɔr) copper cup/ bowl.

ཟངས་བན་ (sa̱ŋbɛn) 1. copper basin. 2. copper ཆང་ container.

ཟངས་བུམ་ (sa̱ŋbum) copper vase.

ཟངས་བྱང་ (sa̱ŋjaŋ) strip of copper used in making curses.

ཟངས་སྦུག (sa̱ŋbuù) copper pot.

ཟངས་མ་ (sa̱ŋma) natural copper, ordinary quality copper.

ཟངས་དམར་ (sa̱ŋmar) copper.

ཟངས་ཚགས་ (sa̱ŋdzaà) copper strainer.

ཟངས་ཞུན་ (sa̱ŋshün) liquid smelted copper.

ཟངས་ཟོག (sa̱ŋsɔɔ̀) copperware.

ཟངས་བཟོ་བ་ (sa̱ŋsowa) sm. ཟངས་མགར་.

ཟངས་ཡིག (sa̱ŋyii) letters engraved on copperware.

ཟངས་གཡའ་ (sa̱ŋya) copper tarnish.

ཟངས་རུ་བཞི་མ་ (sa̱ŋru shi̱mə) a traditional copper pot with four handles.

ཟངས་ལུང་བཞི་མ་ (sa̱ŋluŋ shi̱mə) sm. ཟངས་རུ་བཞི་མ་.

ཟངས་ལོང་ (sa̱ŋloŋ) copper rings.

ཟངས་ཤན་ (sa̱ŋshɛn) copper band put around churns/ barrels.

ཟངས་ཤོག (sa̱ŋshɔɔ̀) thin copper sheet.

ཟངས་ས་ལེ་སྦྲམ་ (sa̱ŋ sāledram) a high quality copper.

ཟངས་སེར་ (sa̱ŋser) yellowish copper.

ཟངས་ཧྲུག (sa̱ŋhruù) small bits and pieces of copper.

ཟད་ (sɛ̱ɛ̀) vi. to run out of, to wear out, to be finished/ exhausted ¶ ལྷམ་ཁོག་དེ་ཟད་འདུག The shoes have worn out.

ཟད་སྐྱོན་ (sɛ̱ɛ̀gyön) wear and tear, wearing out; vi.—ཐེབས་ to wear out.

ཟད་གྲོན་ (sɛ̱ɛ̀drön) depreciation, wearing out, using up, exhausting. 2. attrition; va.—བཟོ་ to cause things to wear out/ use up/ break ¶ ཟད་གྲོན་གྱི་ཚད་ The rate of attrition. ¶ མི་སོ་སོའི་དུབ་ལོག་ཟད་གྲོན་འདྲ་མིན་ཡོང་གི་ཡོད་པ་རེད་ Each person has a different rate of clothing wearing out. ¶ ཟླ་བ་འདིའི་ནང་ལས་ཁུངས་ཀི་ཡིག་ཆས་ཟད་གྲོན་ག་འདྲ་བྱུང་འདུག How much stationery has been used up in the office this month?

ཟད་སྒྲོན་ཆེན་པོ་ (sɛ̱ɛ̀drön cēmbo) wearing out quickly, exhausting/ using up rapidly ། མི་ཁ་ཤས་ཕྱུ་པ་ཟད་སྒྲོན་ཆེན་པོ་ཡོད་པ་རེད་ Some people wear out their clothes quickly. ། ལས་ཁུངས་ཀྱི་ཡིག་ཆས་ཟད་སྒྲོན་ཆེན་པོ་བྱུང་ཙང་ཡིག་ཆས་གསར་པ་ཉོ་དགོས་རེད་ Because the office used up a lot of stationery (it) had to buy new stationery.

ཟད་སྒྲོན་མཉམ་ལས་ཁང་ (sɛ̱ɛ̀drön na̱mlɛɛ̀gaŋ) consumer's cooperative.

ཟད་སྒྲོན་དམག་འཐབ་ (sɛ̱ɛ̀drön mə̄gdəb) war of attrition.

ཟད་སྒྲོན་གྱི་ཚད་ (sɛ̱ɛ̀dröngi dzɛ̄ɛ̀) consumption rate.

ཟད་སྒྲོན་གསོག་འཇོག (sɛ̱ɛ̀drön sōnjɔɔ̀) replacement fund.

ཟད་འགྱུར་ (sɛ̱ngyur) declining, wearing out.

ཟད་འགྲོ་ (sɛ̱ɛ̀dro) sm. ཟད་.

ཟད་སྒོ་ (sɛ̱ɛ̀go) source of expenditures.

ཟད་ཀྱུང་ཀྱུང་ (sɛ̱ɛ̀ cūŋjuŋ) 1. durable ། རས་དེ་ཟད་ཀྱུང་ཀྱུང་ཡོད་པ་རེད་ That material is durable. 2. a person who is careful with things so they last long ། མི་དེ་དུ་ལོག་ཟད་ཀྱུང་ཀྱུང་རེད་བཞག That person takes care of his clothing well so they last long.

ཟད་གདུགས་ (sɛ̱ɛ̀duù) almost depleted/ exhausted/ finished; vi.—ལ་སྒྱུར་; —ལ་ཐུག to reach a state of being almost exhausted/ depleted/ finished.

ཟད་སྟོངས་ (sɛ̱ɛ̀doŋ) the dying out of a family/ group; va.—སུ་འགྱུར་.

ཟད་མཐའ་ (sɛ̱ɛ̀da) wearing out, being exhausted.

ཟད་མཐའ་མེད་པ་ (sɛ̱ɛ̀da me̱èba) sm. ཟད་མེད་.

ཟད་འཐུད་ (sɛ̱ɛ̀düù) replenishing sth., replacing sth. that is used up or worn out. 2. spare/ replacement parts.

ཟད་པར་ (sɛ̱ɛ̀bar) all, entire.

ཟད་མེད་ (sɛ̱ɛ̀meè) inexhaustible, endless, not able to wear out.

ཟད་ཚད་ (sɛ̱ɛ̀dzɛɛ̀) abbr. of ཟད་སྒྲོན་གྱི་ཚད་.

ཟད་ཟད་ (sɛ̱ɛ̀sɛɛ̀) until worn out, until nothing is left ། དུག་ལོག་དེ་ཟད་ཟད་གོན་པ་ཡིན་ (I) wore the clothing until it wore out.

ཟད་ལེན་ (sɛ̱ɛ̀len) having a spare ready for when sth. wears out ། དུ་ལོག་ཟད་ལེན་འགའ་ཤས་དགོས་ཀྱི་འདུག One needs several spare changes of clothing.

ཟད་སོང་ (sɛ̱ɛ̀soŋ) sm. འགྲོ་སོང་.

ཟད་ཧྲུལ་ (sɛ̱ɛ̀hrüü) worn out, tattered ། དོར་མ་ཟད་ཧྲུལ་ Worn out trousers.

ཟན་ (sɛ̱n) 1. food; va.—ཟ་ to eat food.

ཟན་སྐལ་ (sɛ̱ngɛɛ) share of food.

ཟན་ཁམ་ (sɛ̱ngam) sm. ཟན་གོང་.

ཟན་གོང་ (sɛ̱ngoŋ) a "dough ball" of kneaded རྩམ་པ་ the size of a mouthful.

ཟན་སྒྲིལ་ (sɛ̱ndrii) sm. ཟན་རིལ་.

ཟན་བསྒོངས་ (sɛ̱ngoŋ) sm. ཟན་གོང་.

ཟན་བསྒོངས་ (sɛ̱n go̱ŋ) va. to knead རྩམ་པ་ into a mouth-size ball.

ཟན་ཆག (sɛ̱njaà) fodder.

ཟན་ཆང་ (sɛ̱njaŋ) 1. a type of snack made from རྩམ་པ་ and ཅང་ that is mixed together and squeezed into strips that are dried. 2. sm. ཟན་གོང་.

ཟན་བདག (sɛ̱ndaà) sm. ཟན་རིལ་, 1.

ཟན་དོག (sɛ̱ndɔɔ̀) sm. ཟན་གོང་.

ཟན་དྲོན་ (sɛ̱ndrön) warm རྩམ་པ་ dough (usu. used medically as a compress).

ཟན་སློག་པ་ (sɛ̱n nɔ̄ɔ̀ba) food that is plentiful.

ཟན་པོ་ (sɛ̱mbo) sm.* གཟན་པོ་.

ཟན་ཕྱེ་ (sɛ̱nje) kneaded རྩམ་པ་ balls that is then crumbed and eaten.

ཟན་སྦྲུས་ (sɛ̱n drȫö) va. to knead རྩམ་པ་.

ཟན་མ་ (sɛ̱nma) sm. རྩམ་པ་.

ཟན་བཙོས་ (sɛ̱n dzȫö) va. to boil རྩམ་པ་.

ཟན་རྫུ་ (sɛ̱ndza) fodder.

ཟན་གཡོ་ (sɛ̱n yō) va. to knead རྩམ་པ་ into a dough-like consistency.

ཟན་རིལ་ (sɛ̱nrii) 1. a religious lottery wherein names/ options are put in small balls made of རྩམ་པ་ and shaken in a bowl until one pops out; va.—སྒྲིལ་; va.—དཀྲུག to roll a lottery (bowl), to consult this kind of lottery; va.—ཞུ་ to ask a question via this lottery; vi.—བབ་; —ཐེབས་ to receive an answer to a question from the lottery ། གྲོས་མོལ་བྱ་རྒྱུ་དེ་ཟན་རིལ་ལ་ཐེབས་པ་རེད་ The lottery answered that we should have discussions.

ཟན་རིལ་གང་ཐོན་ (sɛ̱nrii ka̱ŋdön) shung. whatever comes out from the lottery.

ཟན་ཤིང་ (sɛ̱nshiŋ) fodder and wood.

ཟབ་ (sə̱b) abbr. of ཟབ་པོ་.

ཟབ་དཀྱིལ་ཆེ་བ་ (sə̱bgyee cēwa) sm. དཀྱིལ་ཆེ་བ་.

ཟབ་སྐུད་ (sə̱bgüù) silk thread (usu. used in brocade).

ཟབ་ཁྱད་ཐོན་པ་ (sə̱bgyɛɛ̀ tõmba) effective ། ནད་གཞི་འདིར་ཟབ་ཁྱད་ཐོན་པའི་སྨན་ཞིག་དགོས་ཀྱི་འདུག One needs an effective medicine for this illness.

ཟབ་གོས་ (sə̱bgöö) good quality brocade/ clothing.

ཟབ་རྒྱས་ (sə̱bgyɛɛ̀) sm.* གཟབ་རྒྱས་.

ཟབ་ཅིང་འཐུག་པ་ (sə̱bjiŋ tūgbə) deep/ profound and lasting.

ཟབ་ཅིང་མཚར་བ་ (sə̱bjiŋ tsārwa) deep/ profound and interesting.

ཟབ་ཆེན་ (sə̱bjen) brocade.

ཟབ་འཇུག (sə̱mjuù) deeply/ totally involved; va.—བྱེད་ to go into deeply, to get totally involved ། འཐབ་རྩོད་ཀྱི་ནང་དུ་ཟབ་འཇུག་བྱེད་ཀྱི་འདུག (They) are totally involved in the struggle.

ཟབ་འཇུག་མེད་པ་ (sə̱mjuù me̱èbə) superficial, not deep/ profound.

ཟབ་ཉོག (sə̱bñog) family members who do not have jobs or income.

ཟབ་ཏུ་འགྲོ་ (sə̱mjuù dro̱) vi. to go/ become deeper.

ཟབ་ཏུ་གཏོང་ (sə̱bdu dōŋ) va. to make deeper, to deepen/ intensify ། ཁྲོན་པ་གཏིང་ཟབ་ཏུ་བཏང་སོང་ They made the well deeper.

ཟབ་ནན་ (sə̱bnɛn) sm. གཟབ་ནན་.

ཟབ་པ་ (sə̱bbə) deep, profound; deeper, more profound.

ཟབ་པོ་ (sə̱bbo) deep, profound, thorough ། དགོངས་པ་ཟབ་པོ་ Profound thoughts.

ཟབ་པོ་བཟོ་ (sə̱bbo so̱) sm. ཟབ་ཏུ་གཏོང་.

ཟབ་ཕྱུག (sə̱bjuù) deep (and rich) ། བརྩེ་དུང་ཟབ་ཕྱུག Deep affection.

ཟབ་བེ་ཟོབ་བེ་ (sə̱bbe so̱bbe) 1. sm. ཟ་བེ་ཟོ་བེ་. 2. loosely tied.

ཟབ་དབྱངས་ (sə̱bjaŋ) tunes/ melodies that convey deep feelings.

ཟབ་འབོལ་ (sə̱bböö) a cushion/ mat that is edged with brocade.

ཟབ་སྦྱོང་ (sə̱bjoŋ) in-depth study, advanced study.

ཟབ་མོ་ (sə̱bmo) sm. ཟབ་པོ་.

ཟབ་མོའི་དོན་ (sə̱bmö tö̱n) emptiness.

ཟབ་མོར་འགྱུར་ (sə̱bmɔɔ gyu̱r) sm. ཟབ་ཏུ་འགྲོ་.

ཟབ་རྨོ་ (sə̱bmo) deep plowing; va.—རྒྱག.

ཟབ་རྨོ་ཞིབ་ལས་ (sə̱bmo shi̱blɛɛ̀) deep plowing and intensive cultivation; va.—བྱེད་.

ཟབ་རྨོའི་ཐོང་གཤོལ་ (sə̱bmö tōŋshöö) sm. ཟབ་སློག་ཐོང་གཤོལ་.

ཟབ་རྩར་ (sə̱bdzar) slapping/ hitting on the cheeks; va.—ལ་གཞུ་ to slap on the cheek.

ཟབ་ཚད་ (sə̱bdzɛɛ̀) (degree of) depth ། ཆུ་འདིའི་ཟབ་ཚད་ཡག་པོ་ཤེས་ཀྱི་མི་འདུག We don't know the depth of the water.

ཟབ་ཞུགས་ (sə̱bshuù) doing/ entering/ participating in depth; va.—བྱེད་ ། ཁོང་དམངས་གཙོའི་ལས་འགུལ་ནང་ཟབ་ཞུགས་བྱས་འདུག He participated deeply in the democratic campaign.

ཟབ་ཟབ་སིག་སིག (sə̱bsəb sīisii) carefully; va.—བྱེད་ to do carefully.

ཟབ་ཟོབ་ (sə̱bsob) abbr. of ཟབ་བེ་ཟབ་བེ་.

ཟབ་ཡངས་ (sə̱byaŋ) deep and wide/ extensive.

ཟབ་རག་ (sabraà) itching; vi.—ལང་ to itch.

ཟབ་བླིང་ (səbliŋ) profound, deep, lofty.

ཟབ་ལག་ཅན་ (səblajɛn) rheum spiciforme royle (used in Tibetan medicine).

ཟབ་ལམ་ (səblams) profound doctrine.

ཟབ་སིམ་ (səbsim) water seeping/ sinking into sth. ¶ ཞིང་གའི་ནང་ཆུ་ཟབ་སིམ་བྱུང་བཞག The water seeped into the field.

ཟབ་སློག་ཐོང་གཤོལ་ (səblɔɔ tõŋshöö) a deep plowing plow.

ཟབ་ཕྲུག (səbhruù) small children.

ཟབས་ (səb) deep.

ཟམ་ (sam) 1. abbr. of ཟམ་པ་. 2. continuation.

ཟམ་བཀག (samgyaà) pier/ foundation of a bridge.

ཟམ་ཁ་ (samga) end or start of a bridge.

ཟམ་ཁའི་འཐབ་འཛིན་ (samgɛ tə̃mdzin) bridgehead (in warfare).

ཟམ་རྒྱུག (səmgyuù) wooden planks or long pieces of wood used in making a bridge.

ཟམ་ངོས་ (samŋöö) sm. ཟམ་སྟེང་.

ཟམ་ཆུ་ (səmju) water under a bridge.

ཟམ་ཆུང་ (samjuŋ) small bridge.

ཟམ་ཆེན་ (samjen) large bridge.

ཟམ་རྟེན་ (samden) foundation/ pilings of a bridge.

ཟམ་སྟེགས་ (samdeg) sm. ཟམ་རྟེན་.

ཟམ་སྟེང་ (samdeŋ) surface of a bridge ¶ ཟམ་སྟེང་ལ་མི་མང་པོ་འགྲོ་གི་འདུག Many people are going on the bridge.

ཟམ་གདན་ (samdɛn) sm. ཟམ་རྟེན་.

ཟམ་གདུང་ (samduŋ) bridge girder.

ཟམ་ལྡེམ་ (samdem) a suspension bridge.

ཟམ་སྣ་ (sãmne) the two ends of a bridge.

ཟམ་སྣེ་ (samne) sm. ཟམ་ཁ་.

ཟམ་པ་ (samba) bridge; va.—རྒྱག; —འཛུགས་ to build a bridge.

ཟམ་པ་བསླངས་གཟུགས་ (samba lãŋsuù) an overpass (on a highway).

ཟམ་པའི་ནུས་པ་ (sambɛ nüübə) a bridge connecting places ¶ ཁྱེད་རང་གིས་ཚོགས་པ་གཉིས་དབར་ཟམ་པའི་ནུས་པ་འདོན་དགོས་ You have to act as a bridge between the two organizations.

ཟམ་པོ་ཆེ་ (samboje) shung. postal/ courier stations.

ཟམ་འཕྲེང་ངོ་དམ་ (samdreŋ todam) shung. tax collectors located on bridges and narrow passes.

ཟམ་མ་ཆད་པ་ (sam ma cɛ̃ɛba) uninterrupted, continuous, without a break ¶ ང་ཚོས་ལྷ་སར་གནས་ཚུལ་ཛ་དྲག་ཆེ་ལུགས་སྐོར་ཟམ་མ་ཆད་པར་ཉན་པ་ཡིན་ We listened continuously to the urgent news about Lhasa.

ཟམ་མི་ཆད་པ་ (sammi cɛ̃ɛba) sm. ཟམ་མ་ཆད་པ་.

ཟམ་མི་ཟིམ་མི་ (sammi simmi) 1. not deep, superficial, (for rain) light. 2. squinting one's eyes; va.—ལྟ་. 3. dozing, slumbering; vi.—ཁུག ¶ གནམ་གྲུའི་ནང་གཉིད་ཟམ་མི་ཟིམ་མི་ཞིག་ཁུག་བྱུང་ I was dozing on the plane.

ཟམ་མིག (səmmiì) the arch of a bridge.

ཟམ་མེ་ཟོམ་མེ་ (samme somme) sm. ཟ་པེ་ཟོ་པེ་.

ཟམ་ཞང་ (samshaŋ) sm. ཟམ་ཞེང་.

ཟམ་ཞེང་ (samseŋ) width of a bridge.

ཟམ་ཟིམ་ (samsim) abbr. of ཟམ་མི་ཟིམ་མི་.

ཟམ་ཟུམ་ (samsum) flickering/ turning on and off continuously (lights); va.—བྱེད་.

ཟམ་ཟོམ་ (samsom) abbr. of ཟམ་མེ་ཟོམ་མེ་.

ཟར་འགྲོ་ (sandro) shung. reductions.

ཟར་འགྲོ་མཆན་དཀྲུས་ (sandro cɛ̃ngyüü) shung. approval/ permission to reduce.

ཟར་བུ་ (sarbu) sm. གཟར་བུ་.

ཟར་མ་ (sarma) linen usitatssimum (used in Tibetan medicine).

ཟར་ཟིར་ (sarsir) abbr. of ཟ་རི་ཟི་རི་.

ཟར་རི་ཟིར་རི་ (sarri sirri) sm. ཟར་ཟིར་.

ཟལ་ཐོན་ (sɛɛdön) sm. ངོ་སོ་ཐོན་པོ་.

ཟལ་པོ་ (sɛɛbo) multicolored (for animals).

ཟལ་མོ་ (sɛɛmo) female cattle with white fur along the back.

ཟས་ (sɛɛ) 1. food ¶ དཀར་ཟས་ Vegetarian/ dairy foods.

ཟས་དཀར་ (sɛɛgar) vegetarian/ dairy foods.

ཟས་དཀར་གསུམ་ (sɛɛgar sũm) the three dairy foods: yogurt, milk and butter.

ཟས་དཀོན་ (sɛɛgön) food scarcity.

ཟས་སྐོམ་ (sɛɛgom) food and drink, solid and liquid foods.

ཟས་སྐོལ་ (sɛɛ gõõ) va. to cook food.

ཟས་ཁ་ (sɛɛga) appetite; vi.—ཤི་ to lose one's appetite.

ཟས་ཁ་ནང་དུ་ཡོད་དུས་ཕྱིས་འབུད་ (sɛɛga) sm. གྲོག་ཁ་ལ་ཡོད་པ་ཕྱིས་སྦུད་.

ཟས་ཁུ་བ་ཅན་ (sɛɛ kũwəjɛn) food that is liquid (not solid).

ཟས་གོང་ (sɛɛgoŋ) food prices.

ཟས་གོས་ (sɛɛgöö) food and clothing.

ཟས་གོས་སྒྲོན་ཆུང་ (sɛɛgöö drönjuŋ) living cheaply/ frugally.

ཟས་གོས་གཉིས་མེད་ (sɛɛgöö ñiimeè) poor livelihood, poor in both food and clothing.

ཟས་གོས་གཉིས་འཛོམས་ (sɛɛgöö ñiidzom) having an abundance of both food and clothing, good livelihood.

ཟས་གོས་འཛོམས་པོ་ (sɛɛgöö dzombo) sm. ཟས་གོས་གཉིས་འཛོམས་.

ཟས་གོས་གནས་མལ་ (sɛɛgöö nɛ̃ɛmɛɛ) food, clothing and housing/ residence ¶ ཟས་གོས་གནས་མལ་ལ་དཀའ་བ་མེད་ Not having difficulty with food, clothes and residence.

ཟས་གོས་སྤྱོད་གསུམ་ (sɛɛgöö jõõsum) the three: food, clothing and behavior ¶ མི་འདིའི་ཟས་གོས་སྤྱོད་གསུམ་ཁ་ཆེ་རང་རེད་ This man's food, clothing and behavior are that of a Muslim.

ཟས་གོས་བཟང་འབོལ་ (sɛɛgöö saŋböö) sm. ཟས་གོས་གཉིས་འཛོམས་.

ཟས་གྱོན་ (sɛɛgyön) food and clothing.

ཟས་གྲོགས་ (sɛɛdrɔɔ) spices.

ཟས་གྲིབ་ (sɛɛdrib) unclean/ polluted food.

ཟས་གྲོན་ (sɛɛdrön) food expenses.

ཟས་འགག (sɛɛ gaà) vi. to lose one's appetite.

ཟས་ངན་ (sɛɛŋɛn) 1. poisoned/ tainted food. 2. low-grade food.

ཟས་ངོ་ (sɛɛŋo) the quality of foodstuffs.

ཟས་མངར་ (sɛɛŋar) sweets, sweet foods.

ཟས་གཅོད་ (sɛɛ jöö) 1. va. to abstain from eating certain foods. 2. va. to go on a hunger strike ¶ བཙོན་པས་ཟས་བཅད་ནས་ངོ་རྒོལ་བྱས་པ་རེད་ The prisoners rose in opposition by having a hunger strike.

ཟས་བཅད་ངོ་རྒོལ་ (sɛɛjɛɛ ŋogöö) hunger strike; va.—བྱེད་.

ཟས་བཅུད་ (sɛɛjüü) nourishment, nutrients, nutritious.

ཟས་བཅུད་གཉིད་བྲལ་ (sɛɛjüü ñiidrɛɛ) unable to eat or sleep ¶ ཕྱི་རྒྱལ་ལ་བྲོས་རྒྱུའི་གྲ་སྒྲིག་དང་དངས་སྐྲག་ཟས་བཅུད་གཉིད་བྲལ་སྐབས་ At the time of preparing to flee, they were frightened and were unable to eat or sleep.

ཟས་མཉེན་པོ་ (sɛɛ ñembo) a soft diet, soft foods.

ཟས་སྙི་མོ་ (sɛɛ ñimu) sm. ཟས་མཉེན་པོ་.

ཟས་མཆོག (sɛɛjɔɔ) the best quality food.

ཟས་འཇུ་ (sɛɛ ju) vi. to digest food ¶ ཕོ་བ་ནད་ན་ཚ་ཡོད་ཙང་ཟས་འཇུ་ཐུབ་ཀྱི་མི་འདུག Because he had a stomach illness he couldn't digest food.

ཟས་བརྗེད་གཉིད་བྲལ་ (sɛɛjeè ñiidrɛɛ) working extremely hard [Lit. forgetting food and not sleeping].

ཟས་སྙོག (sɛɛ ñõò) va. to look/ search for food.

ཟས་སྙོད་ (sɛɛ ñõõ) va. to feed a baby directly from one's mouth.

ཟས་ཐལ་གྲོད་སྦོས་ (sɛɛdɛɛ trööböö) a bloated stomach from excessive eating.

ཟས་ཐོ་ (sɛɛdo) list of foods, recipe.

ཟས་འཐུ་ (sɛɛ tũ) 1. va. to pick up food. 2. va. to

pool food (e.g., when several people go on a picnic each bringing some food).

ཟས་དུག (sɛɛ̀duù) food poisoning, illness caused by bad/ tainted food; va.—ཕོག; —ཕོར་.

ཟས་དུལ་མ་ (sɛɛ̀ tüümə) sm. ཟས་འབོལ་པོ་.

ཟས་དུས་ཉོ་ཐང་ (sɛɛ̀düü ñodaŋ) price of foodstuffs.

ཟས་དྲངས་ (sɛɛ̀ traŋ) p. of ཟས་འདྲེན་.

ཟས་བདའ་པོ་ (sɛɛ̀ dabo) tasty/ delicious food.

ཟས་འདྲེན་ (sɛɛ̀ dren) va. to serve food ¶ གྲོགས་པོ་ཚོར་ཟས་དྲངས་པ་རེད་ (He) served food to his friends.

ཟས་བསྡམས་ (sɛɛ̀ dam) sm. ཟས་གཅོད་.

ཟས་ནོར་ (sɛɛ̀nɔɔ) food and possessions/ wealth.

ཟས་ནོག་པོ་ (sɛɛ̀ nōgbo) delicious and plentiful food.

ཟས་སྣ་འཛོམས་པོ་ (sɛɛ̀na dzombo) having a variety of foods and drinks.

ཟས་སྣ་གཡོས་སྦྱོར་དཔེ་དེབ་ (sɛɛ̀na yōōjɔɔ bēdeb) cook book.

ཟས་སྣོད་ (sɛɛ̀nöö) food container.

ཟས་སྤྱོད་ (sɛɛ̀jöö) 1. va. to eat food ¶ ནད་པས་ཟས་སྤྱོད་དུས་གཟབ་གཟབ་བྱ་དགོས་ An ill person must be careful when eating. 2. eating and behavior, the manner of eating and behaving ¶ བོད་སྨན་གཏོང་དུས་ཟས་སྤྱོད་འཛེམས་དགོས་པ་རེད་ When taking Tibetan medicine, one must be careful about what one eats and does.

ཟས་ཕུད་ (sɛɛ̀büü) an offering one makes to deities before one eats.

ཟས་ཕྱི་མི་ལེན་པ་ (sɛɛ̀ cī milenba) abstaining from eating after lunch (a practice followed by gelong monks).

ཟས་བྲིམས་ (sɛɛ̀ drim) va. to give/ serve food to one after another.

ཟས་འབོལ་པོ་ (sɛɛ̀ bööbo) mashed, pulpy (food).

ཟས་འབྲེལ་ (sɛndree) relationship in which sbs. gives or receives food, a relationship in which people eat together ¶ ཁྱེད་རང་མི་དེ་དང་ཟས་འབྲེལ་ཡོད་པས་ Do you have an eating relation with that person?

ཟས་སྦྱིན་ (sɛɛ̀ jin) va. to give food.

ཟས་མ་ (sɛɛ̀ma) food.

ཟས་མང་གོས་མང་ (sɛɛ̀maŋ köömaŋ) having plenty to eat and wear.

ཟས་གཙང་ (sɛɛ̀dzaŋ) 1. clean food. 2. name of the Buddha's father. 3. sm. ཡུང་དཀར་.

ཟས་གཙང་སྲས་ (sɛɛ̀ dzāŋsɛɛ̀) sm. ཟས་གཙང་.

ཟས་བཙོས་མ་ (sɛɛ̀ dzōōma) cooked food.

ཟས་རྩོད་ (sɛɛ̀dzöö) an argument over food; va.—རྒྱག.

ཟས་ཚོད་ (sɛɛ̀dzöö) a portion, a serving, a ration.

ཟས་ཞིམ་ (sɛɛ̀shim) tasty/ delicious food.

ཟས་ཞིམ་སློབ་གྲྭ་ (sɛɛ̀shin lōbdra) the 1st modern primary school started in Lhasa in 1952.

ཟས་ཟ་ཉེས་པ་ (sɛɛ̀ sañeèba) sm. ཟ་ཉེས་པ་.

ཟས་ཡོན་ (sɛɛ̀yün) payment for food.

ཟས་རིགས་ (sɛɛ̀rii) foodstuffs, edibles.

ཟས་རིགས་ཕྱི་གཏོང་ཀུང་སི་ (sɛɛ̀rii cīdoŋ gūŋsi) tib. ch. foodstuffs export company.

ཟས་རིགས་བཙོས་མ་ (sɛɛ̀rii dzōōma) sm. ཟས་བཙོས་མ་.

ཟས་རིགས་ཚོང་ཁང་ (sɛɛ̀rii tsōŋgaŋ) food store.

ཟས་རིགས་ལས་སྣོན་ (sɛɛ̀rii lɛɛ̀nön) food processing; va.—བྱེད་.

ཟས་རོ་ (sɛɛ̀ro) food remnants/ leftovers.

ཟས་ལ་ཟ་ཚོད་བྱས་ན་ཟ་ཡུན་རིང་ (sɛɛ̀ro) one should be careful with how one uses things so one doesn't run out [Lit. if one is thrifty in eating the food will last a long time].

ཟས་སུ་འཁོད་ (sɛɛ̀su kōō) va. to sit down to eat.

ཟས་སློང་ (sɛɛ̀ lōŋ) va. to beg for food.

ཟས་བསོད་པ་ (sɛɛ̀ sōōba) food delicacy, tasty food.

ཟས་ལྷག་བཏུངས་ལྷག (sɛɛ̀lhaà tūŋlhaà) leftover food and drink.

ཟི་ཁྲན་ (sidrɛn) a kind of cloth.

ཟི་ཁྲོན་ (sidrön) Sichuan Province.

ཟི་འཁོར་ (sikɔɔ) dizzy, giddy; vi.—ལང་ to get/ be dizzy/ giddy.

ཟི་འཁྱོམས་ (singyom) sm. ཟི་འཁོར་.

ཟི་སྔོན་འབོག (siŋön bɔ̀ɔ̀) a square blue cloth used for wrapping clothes into bundles.

ཟི་དིར་ (sidir) sound of flying insects/ bees.

ཟི་ལྡི་ར་ (sidirə) a kind of small flying insect.

ཟི་བེར་ (sibe) 1. a sound. 2. sm. ཟི་རི་བི་རི་.

ཟི་མ་ (simə) eyelash; va.—ཚུམ་ཚུམ་བྱེད་ to blink one's eyes/ eyelashes.

ཟི་ར་ (sirə) caraway.

ཟི་ར་དཀར་པོ་ (sirə gāābo) fennel.

ཟི་ར་སེར་པོ་ (sirə sērbo) the root of Chinese thorowax (Bupleurum chinense).

ཟི་རི་བི་རི་ (siri biri) dizzy, tipsy, drowsy; vi.—བྱེད་.

ཟི་རི་རི་ (si riri) humming/ buzzing/ droning noise (of insects).

ཟི་རུ་ (sirə) a wooden frame/ brace for bamboo baskets (usu. on the four corners or the bottom).

ཟི་ལ་ (silə) a kind of metal.

ཟི་ལིང་ (siliŋ) Xining (capital of Qinghai Province).

ཟི་ལིང་སྒ་དམར་ (siliŋ gamar) ginger from Qinghai Province.

ཟི་ལིང་དགུ་ལིང་ (siliŋ guliŋ) 1. tumultuous, turbulent, noisy, disorderly, chaotic. 2. (with "mind") being upset due to troubles or conflicts.

ཟི་ལིང་ལྕགས་ཁྲ་ (siliŋ jāgdra) a type of Tibetan matchlock gun.

ཟི་ལིང་པགས་སློག (siliŋ baglɔɔ̀) a type of Tibetan fur cap.

ཟི་ལིང་བི་ལིང་ (siliŋ biliŋ) sm. ཟི་ལིང་དགུ་ལིང་.

ཟིང་ (siŋ) 1. disturbance, unrest, turmoil, uprising; vi.—ལང་ to be disturbed, to be in a state of unrest/ turmoil, to have an uprising. 2. vi. to be tangled/ disheveled (hair) ¶ ཁོའི་སྐྲ་ཟིང་འདུག His hair is tangled and disheveled. 3. vi. to stand on end (out of fear) ¶ ཤིན་ཏུ་སྐྲག་ཆོད་ནས་ལུས་ཀྱི་སྤུ་ཟིང་བྱུང་ Being very frightened, my body hair stood on end.

ཟིང་དཀར་ (siŋgar) pink.

ཟིང་སྐྱ་ (siŋgya) sm. ཟིང་དཀར་.

ཟིང་འཁོལ་ (siŋ kōō) sm. ཟིང་ཆང་འཁོལ་/ལང་.

ཟིང་འཁྲུག (siŋdruù) disturbance, turmoil, unrest, riot, uprising; va.—སློང་ to cause a turmoil/ unrest/ disturbance, to incite a riot/ uprising; vi.—ལངས་ to be/ get into a state of turmoil/ unrest/ disturbance, to have a riot/ uprising occur.

ཟིང་འཁྲུག་སྐོག་སློང་ (siŋdruù gōglɔŋ) secretly stirring up trouble.

ཟིང་རྒྱག (siŋ gyaà) sm. ཟིང་ཆང་རྒྱག.

ཟིང་ངེ་བ་ (siŋŋewa) 1. unkempt, tangled, disheveled (hair). 2. disturbance, unrest, trouble.

ཟིང་བཅོས་ (siŋjöö) controlling or putting down an uprising/ disturbance/ unrest; va.—བྱེད་.

ཟིང་བཅོས་ཡོ་བསྲང་ (siŋjuoǒ yosaŋ) putting down a disturbance and restoring order.

ཟིང་ཆ་ (siŋjə) 1. turmoil, disturbance, unrest ¶ གྲོང་ཁྱེར་གྱི་ཟིང་ཆ་ནས་ཐག་རིང་དབེན་གནས་སུ་སྤོས་པ་རེད་ He moved far from the turmoil of the city into a deserted place. 2. sm. ཟིང་འཁྲུག.

ཟིང་ཆང་ (siŋjaŋ) a small disturbance/ turmoil; va.—བཀོལ་; —རྒྱག; —བཟོ་; —སློང་ to create/ make a disturbance, to cause turmoil; vi.—འཁོལ་; —ལང་.

ཟིང་ཆང་ཚ་པོ་ (siŋjaŋ tsābo) very disturbing/ disorderly/ noisy.

ཟིང་རྙོག (siŋñog) sm. ཟིང་འཁྲུག.

ཟིང་རྟ་ (siŋda) a kind of horse from Xining.

ཟིང་དྲེལ་ (siŋdree) a type of mule from Xining.

ཟིང་ལྡི་ར་ (siŋdirə) sm. ཟི་ལྡི་ར་.

ཟིང་ནག (siŋnaà) dark pink.

ཟིང་པོ་ (siŋbu) 1. sm. ཟིང་ངེ་བ་. 2. sm. ཟང་ཟིང་.

ཟིང་བ་ (siŋwə) sm. ཟིང་ངེ་བ་.

ཟིང་དམར་ (siŋmar) reddish pink.

ཟིང་སྨུག (siŋmuù) sm. ཟིང་ནག.

ཟིང་འཚུབ་ (siŋdzub) tense, strained ¶ རྒྱལ་སྤྱིའི་ཟིང་

འཚུབ་གནས་ཚུལ་ A tense international situation.

ཟིང་ཟིང་ (siŋsiŋ) sm. ཟིང་.

ཟིང་ཟིང་ལོང་ལོང་ (siŋsiŋ loŋloŋ) disturbed disorderly, in turmoil ། ཟིང་ཟིང་ལོང་ལོང་གི་རྣམ་པ་ཞིག་ཆགས་བཞག (They) are in a disorderly state.

ཟིང་ཡོད་ (siŋyöö) (sb.) involved in the 1959 uprising.

ཟིང་ལོང་ལོང་ (siŋ loŋloŋ) sm. ཟིང་ཟིང་ལོང་ལོང་.

ཟིང་བཤིག (siŋshii) shung. sm. ཟིང་འཁྲུག.

ཟིང་བཤིག་ལོག་པར་འགྲོ་རིགས་ (suŋshii ləgbar drorii) shung. chaos, disturbances ། ཟིང་བཤིག་ལོག་པར་འགྲོ་རིགས་སུ་ཙམ་བྱས་ན་འཁྲུས་རྒྱུ་མེད་པ་ No one is allowed to create chaos or disturbances.

ཟིང་སེལ་ཡོ་བསྲང་ (siŋsee yosaŋ) sm. ཟིང་བཙོས་ཡོ་བསྲང་.

ཟིང་སློང་དོན་རྐྱེན་ (siŋloŋ töngyen) the cause of a disturbance/ uprising/ riot.

ཟིང་སློང་བྱེད་ (siŋloŋ ceè) sm. ཟིང་འཁྲུག་(སློང་).

ཟིད་ཐུང་བ་ (sii tūŋwə) time passing quickly.

ཟིན་ (sin) 1. vi. to be over with, to be finished, to be done ། ཡི་གེ་བྲིས་ཟིན་པ་རེད་ (I) am finished writing the letter. 2. va. to catch, to capture, to get a hold of ། ཐག་པ་ཟིན་ནས་མ་བཏང་བ་རེད་ (He) caught hold of the rope and didn't let go. 3. vi. to reach (an amount) ། མི་འབོར་ ༡༠༠༠༠ ཙམ་ཟིན་གྱི་ཡོད་པ་རེད་ The population reached about ten thousand. 4. abbr. of ཟིན་བྲིས་ ། སྙན་ཟིན་ A draft/ petition. 5. sm. གཉེར་. 6. va. to learn by heart ། གྲྭ་པས་དཔེ་ཆ་ཟིན་དགོས་ Monks have to learn books by heart.

ཟིན་འཁྲིད་ (sindrii) capturing, taking prisoner; va.—བྱེད་ to capture, to take prisoner.

ཟིན་ཏིག (sindii) 1. name of a Tibetan medical text. 2. gentian violet. 3. motherwort (leonurus heterophyllus).

ཟིན་ཐུན་ (sintün) sm. ཟིན་བྲིས་.

ཟིན་ཐོ་ (sindo) 1. making notes, recording; va.—འགོད་ to make a note of, to record. 2. a record (as set in a sporting event); va.—གཏོར་ to break a record.

ཟིན་ཐོ་གསར་གཏོད་ (sindo sārdöö) breaking a record, making a new record.

ཟིན་ཐོ་ལས་བརྒལ་ (sindo lɛ̀ɛgɛɛ) breaking/ exceeding a record.

ཟིན་བྲིས་ (sindrii) 1. a draft; va.—རྒྱག; — བཟོ་; — འགོད་ to make a draft ། ཚོགས་མིས་གྲོས་ཆོད་ཀྱི་ཟིན་བྲིས་ཤིག་བཀོད་པ་རེད་ The delegates at the meeting wrote a draft resolution. 2. sm. ཟིན་ཐོ་.

ཟིན་བྲིས་གནད་བསྡུས་ (sindrii nɛ̀ɛdüü) rough outline/ draft.

ཟིན་མེད་སོ་ནམ་ (sinmeè sōnam) endless.

ཟིན་གཟན་ (sinsɛn) monk's shawl.

ཟིན་རིས་པ་ (sinrìibə) a person who takes notes.

ཟིན་ཤོག (sinshoò) 1. paper for writing a draft. 2. sm. ཟིན་བྲིས་.

ཟིམ་ (sim) sm.* འཛིན་.

ཟིམ་ཆར་ (simjar) light rain, drizzle.

ཟིམ་པོར་ལྟ་ (simbu dā) sm. ཟིམ་མེར་ལྟ་.

ཟིམ་བུ་ (simbu) 1. light drizzle ། ཆར་པ་ཟིམ་བུ་ Light drizzle/ rain. 2. sm. ཟིམ་མེར་.

ཟིམ་མེར་ (simmee) squinting one's eyes; va.—ལྟ་ to look with squinting eyes.

ཟིམ་ཟིམ་ (simsim) sm. ཟིམ་མེར་.

ཟིར་སྒྲ་ (sirdra) buzzing sound.

ཟིར་པོ་ (sirbu) accurate ། ཁོ་མེ་མདའ་ཟིར་པོ་འདུག He is an accurate marksman.

ཟིར་ཟིར་ (sirsir) sm. ཟིར་སྒྲ་.

ཟིལ་ (sii) sm. གཟི་བརྗིད་.

ཟིལ་གྱིས་གནོན་ (siigi nōn) va. to intimidate by one's power/ status.

ཟིལ་དངར་ (siiŋar) sm. ཟིལ་མངར་.

ཟིལ་མངར་ (siiŋar) nectar.

ཟིལ་རྔམ་ (siiŋam) sm. ཟིལ་ཤུགས་.

ཟིལ་ཆགས་དྲོད་ཚད་ (siijaà tröödzɛɛ̀) dewpoint.

ཟིལ་ཆགས་པོ་ (sii cāgbo) majestic, magnificent, exalted.

ཟིལ་ཆུ་ (siiju) dew.

ཟིལ་ཉམས་ (siiñam) sm. ཟིལ་བརྗིད་.

ཟིལ་ཐིགས་ (siidig) abbr. of ཟིལ་པའི་ཐིགས་པ་.

ཟིལ་དྲོད་ (siidröö) abbr. of ཟིལ་ཆགས་དྲོད་ཚད་.

ཟིལ་གནོན་ (siinün) abbr. of ཟིལ་གྱིས་གནོན་.

ཟིལ་པ་ (siibə) 1. dew; vi.—འཚེར་ to shine with dew ། ལོ་མའི་སྟེང་གི་ཟིལ་པ་ Dew on a leaf. 2. condensation (that forms on eyeglasses); vi.—ཆགས་ to get fogged over (glasses) ། མིག་ཤེལ་ལ་ཟིལ་པ་ཆགས་འདུག The glasses fogged over.

ཟིལ་པ་དཀར་པོ་ (siibə gāābo) whitish dew.

ཟིལ་པ་ཁྲུམ་ཁྲུམ་ (siibə trūmdrum) shimmering/ glittering (from dew).

ཟིལ་པའི་ཐིགས་པ་ (siibɛ tigbə) a drop of dew.

ཟིལ་པས་བངས་ (siibɛ baŋ) vi. to be/ get wet with dew.

ཟིལ་ཤུགས་ (siishuù) strength, power ། ང་ཚོའི་དམག་དཔུང་གི་ཟིལ་ཤུགས་འོག་ཇག་པ་ཚོ་བྲོས་ཕྱིན་པ་རེད་ Due to the strength of our army, the bandits fled.

ཟིལ་ཤུགས་ལྡན་པ་ (siishuù dembə) grand, majestic.

ཟིས་པོ་ (siibu) woven basket.

ཟུག (suù) 1. sharp/ acute pain; vi.—རྒྱག to hurt/ pain. 2. vi. to be stuck into, to be buried ། ཤིང་སྡོང་འདིའི་རྩ་བ་གཏིང་རིང་ཟུག་བཞག The root of this tree is buried deep. 3. vi. to be pricked, to be pierced ། རྐང་པར་ཚེར་མ་ཟུག་པ་རེད་ A thorn pricked his foot. 4. vi. to be attracted to ། མོའི་མཛེས་སྡུག་ལ་སེམས་ཟུག་པ་རེད་ (He) was attracted to her beauty. 5. va. to bark.

ཟུག་སྐད་ (suggɛɛ̀) dog's barking.

ཟུག་ག (suggə) sharp/ acute pain.

ཟུག་གེ་བ་ (sugewa) sm. ཟུག་ག.

ཟུག་རྔུ་ (sugŋu) pain; vi.—འབྱིན་; —འདོན་; —རྒྱག to get or have sharp/ acute pain.

ཟུག་ནུས་ (sugnüü) the power/ energy to pierce.

ཟུག་པོ་ (sugbu) effective, influenced, touched ། བླ་མའི་བཀའ་སློབ་སེམས་ལ་ཟུག་པོ་བྱུང་ The lama's advice touched me.

ཟུག་སྨན་ (sugmɛn) pain-killing medicine.

ཟུག་གཟེར་ (sugser) pain; vi.—རྒྱག; —ལངས་ to have pain; va.—སློང་ to cause pain.

ཟུག་ཤུགས་ (sugshuù) sm. ཟུག་ནུས་.

ཟུང་ (suŋ) 1. two, a pair/ couple ། ཁོང་ཟུང་ The two of them. 2. the Sung dynasty. 3. imp. of འཛིན་.

ཟུང་གྲངས་ (suŋdraŋ) even numbers.

ཟུང་ང་ (suŋŋa) 1. a pair. 2. door latch. 3. wooden peg. 4. rope (for drying clothes).

ཟུང་འཇུག (suŋ juù) 1. va. to combine two different things into one. 2. unification (in a religious sense).

ཟུང་འཇུག་གི་གོ་འཕང་ (suŋjuùgi kobaŋ) the stage of being enlightened.

ཟུང་དུ་འབྲེལ་ (suŋdu dree) va. to join together, to combine.

ཟུང་དུས་རབས་ (suŋ tüürəb) Sung dynasty.

ཟུང་འདུ་ (suŋ du) va. to join together.

ཟུང་ལྡན་ (suŋdɛn) things or people that have two of something ། ཕ་མ་ཟུང་ལྡན་གྱི་ཕྲུ་གུ A child with both parents.

ཟུང་ལྡན་གྱི་ཚིག་རྒྱན་ (suŋdɛngi tsiggyɛn) Tibetan style of poetry where the first or last two words of a verse are same.

ཟུང་སྡེབ་ (suŋdeb) sm. ཟུང་འབྲེལ་.

ཟུང་སྣ་ (suŋna) sm. ཟོག་སྣ་.

ཟུང་འབྲེལ་ (suŋdree) 1. jointly, combined together, in conjunction with; va.—བྱེད་ to join together, to do combined ། ཁོང་གཉིས་ཟུང་འབྲེལ་གྱིས་ཚོང་བརྒྱབ་པ་རེད་ They did trading jointly. ། ཡུལ་དམག་ནི་གཞུང་གི་དམག་དང་ཟུང་འབྲེལ་བྱས་ནས་བརྩུགས་པ་ཞིག་རེད་ As for the militia, they joined with the government troops. 2. connected with, in conjunction with.

ཟུང་འབྲེལ་བཀའ་ཤོག (suŋdree gāshoò) joint statement; va.—འདོན་ to release/ issue a joint statement.

ཟུང་སྦྱོར་ (su̲ŋjɔɔ) sm. འཁྲིག་སྦྱོར་.

ཟུང་སྦྲེལ་ (su̲ŋdree) sm. ཟུང་འབྲེལ་.

ཟུང་ཟུང་ (su̲ŋsuŋ) in pairs.

ཟུངས་ (su̲ŋ) 1. energy, strength; vi.—ཟད་ to lose energy/ strength. 2. imp. of འཛིན་.

ཟུངས་ཁྲག་ཉམས་པ་ (su̲ŋdraà ña̲mba) anemia, weak blood.

ཟུངས་ཁྲག་ཕྲ་ཕུང་ (su̲ŋdraà trəbuŋ) blood cell.

ཟུངས་རྒྱག་ (su̲ŋgyaà) sm. ཡིན་རྒྱག.

ཟུངས་ངན་ (su̲ŋŋɛn) sm. ཟུངས་ཞན་.

ཟུངས་ཐག་ཆད་ (sa̲ŋdaà cɛ̀ɛ̀) sm. ཟུངས་ཟད་.

ཟུངས་གདབ་ (su̲ŋdəb) sm. ཟུངས་རྒྱག.

ཟུངས་ཞན་ (su̲ŋshɛn) weak/ poor health.

ཟུངས་ཞན་ནད་མང་ (su̲ŋshɛn nɛ̲ɛ̀maŋ) weak from many illnesses.

ཟུངས་ཞན་ཤུགས་མེད་ (su̲ŋshɛn shūgmeè) weak, debilitated.

ཟུངས་ཟད་ (su̲ŋ sɛ̲ɛ̀) vi. to lose physical strength, to get weak.

ཟུངས་ཤོར་ (su̲ŋ shɔ̄ɔ) sm. ཟུངས་ཟད་.

ཟུངས་ཤོར་ངལ་དུབ་ (su̲ŋshɔɔ ŋɛ̲ɛdub) tired and weak.

ཟུབ་ (su̲b) vi. to disappear, to vanish, to be erased ། རྨ་རྗེས་དེ་རིམ་པས་ཟུབ་སོང་ The scar disappeared gradually.

ཟུབ་ཕྱི་ (su̲bji) an type of scarf.

ཟུབ་ཕྱི་དཀྱུས་མ་ (su̲bji gyǖüma) an ordinary ཟུབ་ཕྱི་.

ཟུབ་ཕྱི་ཆུ་རིས་ (su̲bji cūrii) shung. a type of scarf with a design of water ripples.

ཟུབ་ཤེ་ (su̲bshe) sm. ཟུབ་ཕྱི་.

ཟུམ་ (su̲m) vi. to have one's eyes semiclosed, to squint.

ཟུམ་པོར་ལྟ་ (su̲mbar dā) squinting one's eyes; va.—ལྟ་ to look with squinting eyes.

ཟུར་ (su̲r) 1. corner, angle, side ། ཅོག་ཙེའི་ཟུར་ལ་ On the corner of the table. 2. ex-, former ། སྲིད་འཛིན་ཟུར་པ་ Ex-president. 3. fraction, part, percent ། བཅུ་ཟུར་གསུམ་ Three tenths. 4. separately ། ངས་ཁོང་ལ་ཡི་གེ་ཞིག་ཟུར་དུ་བཏང་བ་ཡིན་ I sent him a letter separately.

ཟུར་ཀྱོག་ཀྱོག (su̲r gyɔ̄ɔgyɔɔ) hanging sth. (pictures, etc.) at an angle.

ཟུར་བཀར་ (su̲rgar) separating, isolating (from a group); va.—བྱེད་.

ཟུར་བཀར་ཞིབ་བཤེར་ (su̲rgar shi̲bsher) isolating/ separating and investigating; va.—བྱེད་.

ཟུར་བཀོད་ (su̲rgöö) written/ listed separately.

ཟུར་བཀོད་རེའུ་མིག (su̲rgöö re̲wumig) an index.

ཟུར་བཀོལ་ (su̲rgöö) appendix, supplement ། ཟུར་བཀོལ་དུ་བསྒྲིགས་ Arranged as a supplement/ appendix.

ཟུར་བཀོལ་དཀར་ཆག (su̲rgöö gārjaà) index.

ཟུར་བཀོལ་དཔྱད་གཞི་ (su̲rgöö jɛ̀ɛ̀shi) list or citation of references/ footnotes.

ཟུར་བཀོལ་མ་ (su̲rgööma) separate edition.

ཟུར་སྐྱུར་ (su̲rgyur) discarding, throwing aside.

ཟུར་ཁང་ (su̲rgaŋ) name of an aristocratic family.

ཟུར་ཁྲལ་ (su̲rdrɛɛ) surtax, surcharge, additional tax.

ཟུར་ཁྲིད་ (su̲rdrii) sm. ཟུར་འཁྲིད་.

ཟུར་ཁྲོམ་འདོན་ (su̲rdrom dö̲n) va. to peddle/ hawk goods.

ཟུར་འཁྲིད་ (su̲rdrii) tutoring or coaching that is given outside the classroom, private tutoring; va.—བྱེད་.

ཟུར་གང་རུང་ (su̲r ka̲ŋruŋ) arbitrary angle.

ཟུར་གོན་རྒྱག (su̲rgön gya̲à) va. to wear (a hat) off to one side of the head.

ཟུར་གྱུར་ (su̲rgya) shung. misplacing sth.

ཟུར་གྱི་ཐོག་ཕེབས་ (su̲rgi tɔ̄ɔ̀beb) overlapping roofs.

ཟུར་གྲས་ (su̲rdrɛɛ̀) attending, auditing; va.—སུ་སྡོད་ to sit off to a side, to audit, to attend unofficially ། གྲངས་བཅད་ཀྱིས་མ་ཚུད་པ་རྣམས་ཟུར་གྲས་སུ་སྡོད་ཆུགས་པ་ (Those students) that exceed or surpass the class limit were allowed to audit the class.

ཟུར་གྲོགས་ (su̲rdrɔɔ̀) girlfriend or boyfriend (of sb. who is married).

ཟུར་འགོད་ (su̲rgöö) sm. ཟུར་བཀོད་.

ཟུར་སྒོ་ (su̲rgo) sidedoor.

ཟུར་སྒྲོན་ (su̲rdrön) sth. that is attached or accompanies sth. else.

ཟུར་བརྒྱད་པ་ (su̲rgyɛɛ̀ba) octagon, octagonal.

ཟུར་ལྔའི་སྐར་མ་ (su̲rŋɛ gārma) five-pointed star.

ཟུར་ལྔའི་ཁང་ཆེན་ (su̲rŋə kāŋjen) U.S. Pentagon.

ཟུར་གཅིག (su̲rjig) one part of sth.

ཟུར་ལྕམ་ (su̲rjam) rafter placed at the corner of a house.

ཟུར་ཕྱུག (su̲rjoò) a small room built on the roof of a main house.

ཟུར་ཆག (su̲rjaà) vi. to change the way sth. is pronounced ། ཚིག་དེའི་སྒྲ་ཟུར་ཆགས་བཞག This word's pronunciation has changed.

ཟུར་ཆག་གི་སྐད་ (su̲rjaàgi gɛ̀ɛ) words whose the pronunciation has changed.

ཟུར་ཆས་ (su̲rjɛɛ̀) 1. special gifts. 2. personal belongings.

ཟུར་མཆན་ (su̲rjɛn) 1. reference, citation, note, footnote. 2. a supplementary note, e.g., in a treaty.

ཟུར་མཇལ་ (su̲rjɛɛ) meeting separately (usu. nonofficially); va.—ཞུ་ ། ངས་ལས་ཁུངས་ཀྱི་འགོ་ཁྲིད་ཟུར་མཇལ་ཞུས་པ་ཡིན་ I asked the head of the office to meet separately with me.

ཟུར་འཇུག་ཤོག་ལྷེ་ (su̲rjuù shɔ̄ɔ̀lhe) supplementary page/ section.

ཟུར་འཇོག (su̲rjɔɔ̀) setting aside, reserving; va.—བྱེད་ to reserve ། སྦ་སིའི་ཀྱི་ཀ་སི་སྔོན་ཚུད་ཟུར་འཇོག་བྱེད་ཆོག Reserving bus tickets in advance is permitted.

ཟུར་འཇོག་ཁང་ (su̲rjɔɔ̀gaŋ) isolation room, room where sth. is kept separately.

ཟུར་ཉན་ (su̲rñɛn) nonvoting observer at a meeting, auditor (in a course); va.—བྱེད་.

ཟུར་ཉན་གྱི་གྲལ་གནས་ (su̲rñɛngi trɛ̲ɛnɛɛ̀) auditor's row (e.g., in a classroom), visitor's row/ seats.

ཟུར་ཉན་གྲལ་ (su̲rñɛn trɛ̲ɛ) sm. ཟུར་ཉན་གྱི་གྲལ་གནས་.

ཟུར་ཉན་སློབ་མ་ (su̲rñɛn lōbma) auditor (in a class).

ཟུར་ཉམས་ (su̲rñam) an incomplete/ broken edge, an edge that is worn away.

ཟུར་གདད་ཐིག (su̲rdɛɛ̀dig) diagonal (line).

ཟུར་གཏོགས་ (su̲rdɔɔ̀) adjunct to, appended to, attached to, subsidiary to.

ཟུར་གཏོགས་རྒྱལ་ཁབ་ (su̲rdɔɔ̀ gyɛ̲ɛgəb) dependent/ subsidiary country.

ཟུར་གཏོགས་དངོས་པོ་ (su̲rdɔɔ̀ ŋɔ̀ɔ̀bo) accessories.

ཟུར་གཏོགས་བདག་དབང་ (su̲rdɔɔ̀ da̲àwaŋ) suzerainty.

ཟུར་བདོན་ (su̲rdön) sm. ཟུར་འདོན་.

ཟུར་ལྟ་ (su̲rda) observing/ looking on (without participating as full member); va.—བྱེད་. 2. reference (book) ། ཟུར་ལྟའི་དཔེ་ཆ་ Reference book. 3. sidelong glance, askance look.

ཟུར་ལྟེབ་ (su̲rdeb) the side fold of Tibetan dresses.

ཟུར་བལྟ་ (su̲rda) sm. ཟུར་ལྟ་.

ཟུར་བསྟན་ (su̲rdɛn) supplementary, extra.

ཟུར་བསྟན་ལེབ་མཐོང་ (su̲rdɛn le̲bdoŋ) understanding the whole from seeing a part, sth. that is clear at a glance.

ཟུར་བསྟར་ (su̲rdar) as shown in an attached document.

ཟུར་བསྟེན་ (su̲rden) on the side, incidental ། ང་དགེ་ཀན་ཟུར་བསྟེན་བྱས་ནས་དབྱིན་ཇི་སློབ་སྦྱོང་བྱེད་ཀྱི་ཡོད་ I am studying English on the side.

ཟུར་བསྟེན་ཚུང་མ་ (su̲rden cūŋmə) sm. ཟུར་མོ་.

ཟུར་ཐིག (su̲rdiì) diagonal (line).

ཟུར་ཐོ་ (su̲rdo) supplementary note; va.—རྒྱག to take or make a supplementary note.

ཟུར་ཐོག (su̲rdɔɔ̀) sm. ཟུར་ཕྱུག.

ཟུར་མཐོང་ལེབ་གསལ་ (su̲rdoŋ le̲bsɛɛ) sm. ཟུར་བསྟན་ལེབ་མཐོང་.

ཟུར་འཕྲེན་ (su̲rden) separating from others, taking or placing aside; va.—བྱེད་ ། ལས་བྱེད་པ་གསུམ་ཟུར་

འཐེན་བྱས་ནས་ཨ་རི་ར་བཏང་བ་རེད་ They took aside three cadre and sent them to America.

ཟུར་འཐེན་རྒྱུགས་ལེན་ (surden gyuùlen) picking one student from many and giving him/ her a test or quiz; va.—བྱེད་.

ཟུར་འཐེན་ཞིབ་དཔྱད་ (surden shibjɛɛ̀) testing a batch of sth. by picking one item at random and testing it.

ཟུར་དུ་ (surdu) separately, aside, apart from ¶ཁོང་ཟུར་དུ་བཞུགས་ཡོད་པ་རེད་ He lives separately.

ཟུར་དུ་བཀོལ་ (surdu gȫö) sm. ཟུར་བཀོལ་.

ཟུར་དུ་འཇུག (surdu juù) va. to put aside/ separate.

ཟུར་དུ་འཇོག (surdu jɔ̄ɔ̀) va. to set aside.

ཟུར་དུ་འདོན་ (surdu dön) va. to take out sth. ¶ངས་དངུལ་ཁང་ནས་དངུལ་ཁག་ཅིག་ཟུར་དུ་བཏོན་ནས་ཞལ་འདེབས་བརྒྱབ་པ་ཡིན་ I took out a part of the money from the bank to give a donation.

ཟུར་དུ་དབྱུག (surdu yūù) va. to throw away, to discard.

ཟུར་དུ་འབུད་ (surdu büü) va. to set aside, to exclude.

ཟུར་དུ་བཞག (surdu shaà) p. of ཟུར་དུ་འཇོག.

ཟུར་དེབ་ (surdeb) secondary book/ register.

ཟུར་དྲིལ་ (surdrii) bells hung on the corner of temples/ roofs.

ཟུར་འདེབས་ (surdeb) sm. ཟུར་སྣོན་.

ཟུར་གདོང་ (surdoŋ) outer corner of a house/ building.

ཟུར་འདུག་བྱེད་ (surduù cɛ̄ɛ̀) 1. va. to sit side saddle. 2. va. to sit on the edge/ side of sth.

ཟུར་འདོན་ (surdön) abbr. of ཟུར་དུ་འདོན་.

ཟུར་རྡོ་ (surdo) cornerstone.

ཟུར་ལྡན་ཀ་བ་ (surdɛn gāā) a pillar that has edges.

ཟུར་ལྡན་སྦྱང་བུ་ (surdɛn ñūŋbu) 1. awl with edges. 2. pyramid.

ཟུར་སྡོད་ (surdöö) 1. sm. ཟུར་ཉན་. 2. state of neutrality.

ཟུར་བརྡ་ (surda) hint, signal; va.—སྟོན་ to give a hint/ signal.

ཟུར་ནས་ (surnɛ) from a side.

ཟུར་ནས་འགྲོ་ (surnɛ dro) va. to go from the side (rather than directly from the front).

ཟུར་ནས་ལྟད་མོ་ལྟ་ (surnɛ dɛ̄ɛ̀mo dā) sm. ཟུར་ལྟ་བྱེད་.

ཟུར་གནས་ (surnɛɛ̀) neutral ¶ཟུར་ནས་ཡུལ་ཁག Neutral countries.

ཟུར་སྣོན་ (surnön) 1. supplement, subsidy, addition; va.—བྱེད་; —རྒྱག to supplement/ subsidize. 2. sm. ཟུར་ཡིག.

ཟུར་སྣོན་གྱི་བརྡ་ (surnüngi da) inflection (in grammar).

ཟུར་སྣོན་ཤོག་ལྷེ་ (surnün shɔ̄ɔ̀lhe) supplement (of a magazine/ newspaper).

ཟུར་པ་ (surbə) 1. former, previous, ex- ¶སྲིད་འཛིན་ཟུར་པ་ Ex-president. 2. secondary branch of a family (i.e., when a member separates from the main family and sets up his own household).

ཟུར་དཔང་ (surbaŋ) circumstantial evidence.

ཟུར་ཕུད་ (surbüü) excluding, treating exclusively/ separately; va.—བྱེད་ ¶ཁོ་གསང་བའི་ཚོགས་འདུ་ནས་ཟུར་ཕུད་བྱས་བཞག He was excluded from the secret meeting. 2. topknot (hair tied into a knot on the top of a head).

ཟུར་ཕོ་ (surbo) a secret (male) lover.

ཟུར་ཕོགས་ (surbɔɔ̀) a supplement to one's basic salary.

ཟུར་འཕྲད་ (surdreɛ̀) nh. of ཟུར་མཇལ་.

ཟུར་ཕྱུང་ (surjuŋ) sm. ཟུར་འདོན་.

ཟུར་ཕྱིན་ (surjin) sm. མཐར་ཕྱིན་.

ཟུར་ཕྱོགས་ (surjɔɔ̀) side.

ཟུར་འཕྱོང་རབ་གསལ་ (surjoŋ rəbsɛɛ) corner room of a house with windows on both sides.

ཟུར་ཕྱོལ་ (surjüü) avoiding; va.—བྱེད་.

ཟུར་བྲལ་ (surdrɛɛ) separated from one's group/ unit/ party.

ཟུར་བྲིས་ (surdrii) sm. ཟུར་ཡིག.

ཟུར་འབུད་ (sumbüü) expelling; va.—གཏོང་.

ཟུར་འབུལ་ (sumbüü) giving separately/ privately; va.—ཞུ་ to send or give separately/ privately.

ཟུར་འབེན་ (sumben) carpentry plane.

ཟུར་སྦྱིན་ (surjin) an additional gift.

ཟུར་མ་ (surmə) sb. who is not the main one but rather is secondary.

ཟུར་མང་གི་དབྱིབས་ (surmaŋgi yīb) polygon.

ཟུར་མང་ངོས་དབྱིབས་ (surmaŋ ŋööyib) having many angles.

ཟུར་མིག (surmii) sm. ཟུར་ལྟ་.

ཟུར་མེད་ (surmeè) round, circular.

ཟུར་མོ་ (surmo) girlfriend of a man who is married, mistress.

ཟུར་ཙམ་ (surdzam) a little, a bit; va.—བྱེད་ ¶ཟུར་ཙམ་ལས་མ་བཤད་ནའི་ལམ་སེང་ཤེས་སོང་ Even though he only said a little, (I) knew right away.

ཟུར་ཙམ་ཞིག (surdzamjig) sm. ཟུར་ཙམ་.

ཟུར་ཚད་ (surdzɛɛ̀) degree of an angle.

ཟུར་ཚིག (surdzii) sarcasm; va.—གཏོང་ to speak sarcastically.

ཟུར་ཚོགས་ (surdzɔɔ̀) a side meeting outside of or separate from the main one; va.—བྱེད་.

ཟུར་འཚོགས་ (surdzɔɔ̀) sm. ཟུར་ཚོགས་.

ཟུར་འཛར་ (surdzar) sm. ཟུར་ཡིག.

ཟུར་ཞིག (surshig) a corner.

ཟུར་ཞུ་ (sur shu) va. to report sth. separately/ aside.

ཟུར་ཞུགས་ (surshuù) observing or looking on (without participating).

ཟུར་བཞི་བླ་ཁག (surshi lāgaà) shung. term used in Tashilunpo Labrang for all its monks and lamas.

ཟུར་བཞི་ཞབས་འབྲིང་ (surshi shəbdriŋ) shung. term used in Tashilhunpo Labrang to refer to all its subjects and officials.

ཟུར་བཞུགས་ (surshuù) h. of ཟུར་སྡོད་.

ཟུར་ཟ་ (sursə) satire, sarcasm; va.—བྱེད་ to act/ be sarcastic.

ཟུར་ཟའི་སྐད་ཆ་ (sursɛ gɛ̄ɛ̀ja) smart/ witty/ sarcastic remarks.

ཟུར་ཟའི་སྐོར་གཏམ་ (sursɛ gɔ̄ɔ̄dam) sm. ཟུར་ཟའི་སྐད་ཆ་.

ཟུར་ཟའི་རི་མོ་ (sursɛ rimu) cartoon.

ཟུར་ཡིག (suryii) 1. index, appendix. 2. side note (to some other document/ agreement).

ཟུར་གཡོལ་ (suryöö) going to the side to avoid sth.; va.—བྱེད་.

ཟུར་ལ་ (surla) 1. to/ or at the side. 2. separately.

ཟུར་ལམ་ (surlam) sidewalk.

ཟུར་ལུགས་སྐྱི་བ་ (surluù ñīwə) an herbal medicine (codonopsis pilosula).

ཟུར་ལོག་ལོག (surlɔɔ̀lɔɔ̀) turning one's body to one side to indicate disappointment or anger; va.—བྱེད་.

ཟུར་བཤད་ (surshɛɛ̀) an aside, a side comment.

ཟུར་སོང་ (sursoŋ) shung. to send something attached to sth. else.

ཟུར་སོང་རྩིས་ལེན་ (sursoŋ tsīìlen) sending sth. along with sth. and asking the other to take possession of it; va.—བྱེད་.

ཟུར་སློག (sur lɔ̄ɔ̀) 1. sm. ཟུར་སློང་. 2. va. to lay on a slope/ incline.

ཟུར་སློང་ (sur lōŋ) va. to make (sb. or sb.) stand up.

ཟུར་གསན་ (sursɛn) h. of ཟུར་ཉན་.

ཟུར་གསལ་ (sursɛɛ) supplement, addition (usu. in a document/ agreement).

ཟུར་གསུམ་ (sursum) triangle.

ཟུར་གསུམ་ཁྲི་ཙེ་ (sursum trēdze) tib. ch. triangular ruler.

ཟུར་གསུམ་གླིང་ (sursumliŋ) delta, peninsula.

ཟུར་གསུམ་གླིང་ཕྲན་ (sursum līŋdrɛn) sm. ཟུར་གསུམ་གླིང་.

ཟུར་གསུམ་རྟེན་འབྱུང་གྲངས་ (sursum dēnjuŋ traŋ) trigonometric function.

ཟུར་གསུམ་རྣོ་ཟུར་ཅན་ (sursum nōsurjɛn) acute triangle.

ཟུར་གསུམ་པ་ (sursumba) sm. ཟུར་གསུམ་.

ཟུར་གསུམ་དབྱིབས་ (sursum yib) triangular, triangle shaped.

ཟུར་གསུམ་མ་ (sursummə) triangular.

ཟུར་གསུམ་རྩིས་རིག (sursum dziirii) trigonometry.

ཟུར་གསུམ་རིག་པ་ (sursum rigbə) sm. ཟུར་གསུམ་རྩིས་རིག.

ཟུར་གསོས་ (sursöö) sm. ཟུར་སྦྱིན་.

ཟུར་བསལ་ (sursεε) acting or treating specially; va.—བྱེད་.

ཟུར་བསྒྲིངས་ (sursiŋ) sending sth. along with something else; va.—བྱེད་.

ཟུལ་གྱིས་ (süügi) gradually.

ཟུལ་ཕུད་ལྔ་པ་ (süübüü ŋāba) Manjushri.

ཟེ་ (se) 1. mane, hump, crest ¶ རྟའི་ཟེ་ Horse's mane. 2. direct discourse/ speech particle ("said") ¶ ཁོ་ཚོས་ལས་ཀ་བྱེད་ཀྱི་ཡིན་ཟེ་བཤད་པ་རེད་ They said, "(they) will work."

ཟེ་ཀ་ (sega) sm. ཟེ་, 1.

ཟེ་ཁ་ (sega) edge of a hill /mountain.

ཟེ་ཁེབས་ (segeb) satin/ brocade covering for the mane of the horses of high ranking officials and lamas.

ཟེ་ཁྲག (sedraà) blood from a cock's comb.

ཟེ་སྒྲོ་ (sedro) 1. mane and feather. 2. feather worn on a hat.

ཟེ་ངོག (seŋɔɔ̀) mane of (a horse).

ཟེ་མཇུག (senjuù) mane and tail.

ཟེ་དའོ་ (sedawo) ch. sm. ཟེ་རྡའོ་.

ཟེ་རྡའོ་ (sedawo) ch. a bayonet.

ཟེ་དམ་ (sedam) to put a seal on the braided mane of a horse (to identify it); va.—རྒྱག.

ཟེ་རྡུམ་ (sedum) a short mane.

ཟེ་ཕྲོག (sedrɔɔ̀) cockscomb.

ཟེ་བ་ (sewa) 1. sm. ཟེ་. 2. sm. ཟེ་ཕྲོག. 3. sm. ཟེ་འབྲུ་.

ཟེ་འབྲུ་ (sendru) anther of a flower.

ཟེ་མ་ (sema) eyelash.

ཟེ་མ་ར་མགོ་ (sema raŋgo) sm. གཟེ་མ་ར་མགོ་.

ཟེ་མོ་ (semo) sm. ཟེ་མོང་.

ཟེ་མོང་ (semoŋ) porcupine.

ཟེ་ཚ་ (sedza) sm. ཟེ་ཚྭ་.

ཟེ་ཚྭ་ (sedza) nitrum (used in Tibetan medicine).

ཟེ་ཚྭ་སྣུམ་མངར་ (sedza nūmŋar) nitroglycerine.

ཟེ་ཚྭའི་སྐྱུར་ (sedzε gyūr) sm. ཟེ་ཚྭའི་སྐྱུར་རྩི་.

ཟེ་ཚྭའི་སྐྱུར་རྩི་ (sedzε gyūrdzi) nitric acid.

ཟེ་ལངས་ (selaŋ) 1. a horse mane that stands upright. 2. vi. to have sth. negative finally come out in the open. 3. vi. to have a negative result ¶ དཀྲོག་གཏམ་དེས་ཟེ་ལངས་ནས་མི་མང་པོ་མ་སྐྱིད་པ་བཟོས་སོང་ The gossip had a negative effect and caused lots of people to be unhappy.

ཟེ་གཞུག (seshuù) mane and tail.

ཟེ་སློང་ (seloŋ) va. to cause a negative result.

ཟེག་པ་ (segba) a brownish red colored horse.

ཟེགས་པ་ (segba) 1. sm. ཞྭང་. 2. old ¶ གོས་རྡུལ་ཟེགས་པ་ Old tattered clothes.

ཟེགས་མ་ (segma) a small drop/ particle ¶ ཆུའི་ཟེགས་མ་ A drop of water.

ཟེད་ (seè) imp. of འཛེད་.

ཟེད་ལངས་ (seè laŋ) vi. to have a hangnail grow.

ཟེབ་ (seb) small basket.

ཟེམ་ (sem) wooden container (for liquids).

ཟེའུ་ (sewu) small wooden bowl.

ཟེའུ་འབྲུ་ (sendru) anther of flowers, pollen; va.—ལེན་ to pollinate.

ཟེའུ་འབྲུ་ཕོ་མོ་སྡེབ་སྦྱོར་ (sendru pōmo debjɔɔ) pollination of plants.

ཟེའུ་འབྲུ་མོ་ (sendrumo) pistil.

ཟེའུ་འབྲུའི་སྦྱོར་བ་ (sēndrü jɔɔwa) sm. ཟེའུ་འབྲུ་ཕོ་མོ་སྡེབ་སྦྱོར་.

ཟེར་ (ser) 1. ray/ beam of light. 2. va. to say, to call, to address ¶ ཁོས་ཟེར་གྱི་འདུག He says it. ¶ ཁོའི་མིང་ལ་ཉི་མ་ཟེར་བ་རེད་ They call him Nyima (His name is Nyima). 3. the direct discourse/ speech particle ¶ དེ་བྱེད་མི་ཐུབ་ཟེར་བཤད་པ་རེད་ (They) said, "(One) cannot do that." 4. a zipper; va.—རྒྱག to zip up.

ཟེར་སྐད་ལ་ (sergεὲla) it is said, they say.

ཟེར་ཁ་སྦུ་ལོང་ (serga būloŋ) shung. to cause trouble verbally.

ཟེར་དགུ་ཅོག (ser gujoò) everything that is said.

ཟེར་རྒྱུ་ལབ་རྒྱུ་མེད་པ་ (sergyu ləbgyu meèba) giving or having no reason for others to speak ill of one ¶ མི་གཞན་གྱིས་ཟེར་རྒྱུ་ལབ་རྒྱུ་མེད་པའི་ལས་ཀ་ཞིག་བྱ་དགོས་ One should work so that no one can speak ill of you later on.

ཟེར་སྒྲོས་ (serdröö) sm. ཟེར་སྲོལ་.

ཟེར་སྒྲོས་སུ་འབྲངས་ (ser dröösu draŋ) va. to echo (sb's) words/ thoughts/ ideas, to follow tradition/ custom.

ཟེར་ཅི་དགོས་ (serjigöö) really good ¶ མི་དེ་ལ་ཟེར་ཅི་དགོས་ བློས་འཁེལ་ཐག་ཆོད་ཡོད་པ་རེད་ That man is really good. He is absolutely reliable.

ཟེར་ཆེན་ (serjen) a great/ big ray of light ¶ ཉི་མའི་ཟེར་ཆེན་ The great rays of the sun.

ཟེར་རྗེས་སུ་འབྲང་ (ser jeèsu draŋ) va. to follow what sb. says.

ཟེར་དུས་ (serdüü) as sth. that is called a ... ¶ ཁོ་མི་ཟེར་དུས་གསེར་འདྲ་པོ་ཅིག་ཡོད་པ་རེད་ As a man, he is as good as gold. ¶ མོ་བུ་མོ་ཟེར་དུས་མེ་ཏོག་པད་མ་ནང་བཞིན་ཞིག་འདུག As a girl, she is as pretty as a lotus.

ཟེར་སྣང་ (sernaŋ) appearance.

ཟེར་ཕྲེང་ (serdreŋ) rays (of light).

ཟེར་མ་ (serma) sm. ཟེགས་མ་.

ཟེར་མོ་ (sermo) porcupine.

ཟེར་ཚད་ (serdzεὲ) sm. ཟེར་དགུ་ཅོག.

ཟེར་ཚད་ལ་ཡོན་མི་རུང་ བྱིན་ཚད་ལ་ཟ་མི་རུང་ (serdzεὲla lõn miruŋ cindzεὲla sa miruŋ) one should be cautious/ careful [Lit. one should not believe whatever one hears, one should not eat whatever someone gives you].

ཟེར་རིགས་ (serrig) a saying.

ཟེར་རིས་ (serrii) painting of light rays.

ཟེར་ལོ་ (serlo) gossip, mere talk.

ཟེར་ལུགས་ (serluù) sm. ཟེར་སྲོལ་.

ཟེར་སྲོལ་ (sersöö) a traditional/ customary saying.

ཟེལ་ (sel) wood chip/ shaving ¶ ཤིང་ཟེལ་ Wood shavings.

ཟེལ་མ་ (selma) wood chip/ shaving.

ཟོ་ (so) 1. imp. of ཟ་. 2. arc. nature. 3. abbr. of ཟོ་ལག.

ཟོ་ཆགས་ (sojaà) sm. ཟོ་ཤེ་.

ཟོ་ཆུན་ (sojün) water mill.

ཟོ་ཆུན་འཁོར་ལོ་ (sojün kɔ̄ɔlo) sm. ཟོ་ཆུན་.

ཟོ་ཆུན་འཁྱུད་མོ་ (sojün kyüümu) the buckets attached to a large water wheel.

ཟོ་ཆུན་རྒྱུད་མོ་ (sojün kyüümu) sm. ཟོ་ཆུན་འཁྱུད་མོ་.

ཟོ་མདོག (sondɔɔ̀) physical strength, physical well-being.

ཟོ་མདོག་ཡང་པ་ (sondɔɔ̀ yaŋwa) 1. healthy, well. 2. good complexion.

ཟོ་བ་ (sowa) sm. ཟོ་ལག.

ཟོ་བའི་ལྕུག་དཀྲིས་ (sowε jūgdrii) a thin band of branches tied around a butter churn.

ཟོ་མར་ (somar) butter-like cream that forms in a butter churn.

ཟོ་མོ་ (somo) sm. ཟོ་མར་.

ཟོ་བཟང་ (sosaŋ) kind/ generous person.

ཟོ་རིས་ (sorii) facial makeup.

ཟོ་ལག (solaà) bucket, pail.

ཟོ་ཤེ་ (soshe) sm. ཟོ་མར་.

ཟོག (sɔɔ̀) 1. goods, merchandise, commodities. 2. cattle, livestock. 3. abbr. of ཟོག་པོ་.

ཟོག་རྒྱལ་ (soggyεε) sm. ཟོག་རྫུན་.

ཟོག་སྐྱེལ་ (soggyee) sm. ཟོག་པོ་.

ཟོག་སྐྱེལ་གླངས་འཁོར་ (soggyee lāŋgɔɔ) sm. ཟོང་སྐྱེལ་གླངས་འཁོར་.

ཟོག་ཁང་ (sɔɔ̀gaŋ) warehouse.

ཟོག་ཁྱུ་ (soggyu) a herd of cattle.

ཟོག་ཁྲལ་ (sɔgdrɛɛ) 1. excise tax, commodity tax. 2. animal tax.

ཟོག་གི་ཁྲ་ཁྲ་ཕྱི་ མིའི་ཁྲ་ཁྲ་ནང་ (sɔ̀gi trādra cī mii trādra naŋ) sm. མིའི་རི་མོ་ནང་ ལྟག་གི་རི་མོ་ཕྱི་.

ཟོག་གོག་རུལ་དངོས་ (sɔggɔ̀ hrũũŋöö) worthless leftover goods, rubbish, trash.

ཟོག་གོང་ (sɔ̀goŋ) price (of goods/ merchandise).

ཟོག་གོང་འགྱུར་བའི་སྟོན་གྲངས་ (sɔ̀goŋ gyurwɛ dõndraŋ) price index.

ཟོག་གོང་གཏན་འཇགས་ (sɔ̀goŋ dẽnjaà) a fixed/ stabilized price.

ཟོག་གྲུ་ (sɔgdru) cargoship, freighter.

ཟོག་འགྲུལ་ (sɔndrüü) commodity circulation.

ཟོག་སྒྲོམ་ (sɔgdrom) display for merchandise.

ཟོག་སྒྲོམ་སྒྲིགས་འཁོར་ (sɔgdrom dēggɔɔ) a movable cart for selling merchandise.

ཟོག་ཆས་ (sɔgjɛɛ̀) fodder for cattle.

ཟོག་སྙིགས་ (sɔgñig) unsold goods/ merchandise.

ཟོག་སྟོང་ (sɔgdoŋ) deceitful talk.

ཟོག་ཐང་ (sɔgdaŋ) sm. ཟོག་གོང་.

ཟོག་ཐོ་ (sɔgdo) list of goods, shipping list.

ཟོག་དོས་ (sɔgdöö) a load of goods/ merchandise.

ཟོག་བདག (sɔ̀daà) 1. term for Nepalese merchants in Tibet. 2. owner of goods/ merchandise.

ཟོག་འདྲེན་ (sɔndren) freight transportation; va.—བྱེད་.

ཟོག་འདྲེན་གྲུ་གཟིངས་ (sɔndren trusiŋ) cargo ship.

ཟོག་འདྲེན་མེ་འཁོར་ (sɔndren megɔɔ) freight train.

ཟོག་འདྲེན་ལྡང་འཁོར་ཁ་ལོ་བའི་མཐུན་ཚོགས་ (sɔndren lãŋgɔɔ kālowɛ tũndzɔɔ̀) Teamsters Union (U.S.A.).

ཟོག་འདྲེན་ཤིང་གྲུ་ (sɔndren shĩŋdru) freight/ transport barge.

ཟོག་ནག་པོ་ (sɔ̀ nagbo) black market goods.

ཟོག་སྣ་ (sɔgna) a variety of goods/ items.

ཟོག་པོ་ (sogbo) hypocritical, deceitful, false.

ཟོག་པོ་ཁྱི་དཀྲུག་མཁན་ (sogbo kyīdrɔɔ̀ñɛn) sb. who causes trouble by lying.

ཟོག་དཔེ་ (sɔgbe) sample of goods/ merchandise.

ཟོག་དཔོན་ (sɔgbön) sm. ཚོང་དཔོན་.

ཟོག་སྤུས་ (sɔgbüü) the quality of goods/ merchandise.

ཟོག་ཕུད་ (sɔgbüü) the small portion of goods taken by tax collectors in the guise of an initial offering/ sample.

ཟོག་མ་ (sɔgma) 1. a lying/ deceitful woman. 2. deceit.

ཟོག་མོ་ (sɔgmo) sm. ཟོག་མ་.

ཟོག་ཙག་ཙིག་ (sɔ̀ dzɔ̄gdzig) miscellaneous goods.

ཟོག་རྩ་ (sɔgdza) shung. the original number of animals leased ། དེ་སྔའི་ཟོག་རྩའི་ཐོག་གཞུང་ལུག་ཁག་ཅིག་རྗེས་འཁྱིར་བསྣལ་པ་ (The government) gave addition sheep to be added to the original number of animals leased.

ཟོག་ཚོང་པ་ (sɔ̀dzoŋba) sm. ཚོང་པ་.

ཟོག་འཚོ་ཡག (soŋ tsōyaà) a nomad greeting.

ཟོག་འཛིན་ (sɔŋdzin) a receipt for goods/ merchandise, an invoice.

ཟོག་རྫི་ (sɔgdzi) herder.

ཟོག་རྫུ་ (sɔgdzu) sm. ཟོག་རྫུན་.

ཟོག་རྫུན་ (sɔgdzün) deceiving, lying cheating; va.—བྱེད་.

ཟོག་བརྫུས་ (sɔgdzüü) fake/ false/ bogus/ counterfeit goods.

ཟོག་རིན་ (sɔgrin) sm. ཟོག་གོང་.

ཟོག་རིན་ཆད་འཇོག (sɔgrin cẽnjɔɔ̀) buying/ selling on credit; va.—བྱེད་.

ཟོག་རིན་རྗེས་འཇོག (sɔgrin jenjɔɔ̀) sm. ཟོག་རིན་ཆད་འཇོག.

ཟོག་རིན་གཏན་ཆགས་ (sɔgrin dẽnjaà) goods/ merchandise with fixed price.

ཟོག་རིན་འཐེན་ (sɔgrin tēn) va. to deduct the cost or purchase price of goods.

ཟོག་རོ་ (sɔgro) 1. rejects, rejected merchandise/ products. 2. unsold merchandise.

ཟོག་ལ་ཟོག་རྒྱག (sɔgla sɔ̀gyaà) exchanging of goods, bartering; va.—བྱེད་.

ཟོག་ལུད་ (sɔglüü) cattle manure.

ཟོག་ལེགས་གོང་ཁེ་ (sɔ̀leg koŋke) goods/ merchandise that are cheap and good quality.

ཟོང་ (soŋ) goods, merchandise.

ཟོང་སྐྱེལ་ལྡང་འཁོར་ (soŋgyee lãŋgɔɔ) freight truck.

ཟོང་ཁྲལ་ (soŋdrɛɛ) sm. ཟོག་ཁྲལ་.

ཟོང་གོང་ (soŋgoŋ) sm. ཟོག་གོང་.

ཟོང་གྲུ་ (soŋdru) sm. ཟོག་གྲུ་.

ཟོང་འགྲུལ་ (soŋdrüü) sm. ཟོག་འགྲུལ་.

ཟོང་འགྲེམ་གནས་ (soŋdrem nɛ̃ɛ̀) sm. ཁྲོམ་ར་.

ཟོང་དོས་ (soŋdöö) loads of merchandise/ goods.

ཟོང་འདྲེན་ (soŋdren) sm. ཟོག་འདྲེན་.

ཟོང་པ་ (soŋba) sm. ཚོང་པ་.

ཟོང་མང་ཉར་ཚགས་ཁང་ (soŋmaŋ ñardzaàgaŋ) storeroom for groceries/ sundry goods.

ཟོང་མང་ཀུང་སི་ (soŋmaŋ ñardzaàgaŋ) tib. ch. 1. a company selling groceries/ sundry goods. 2. department store.

ཟོང་མང་ཚོང་ཁང་ (soŋmaŋ tsõŋgaŋ) sm. ཟོང་མང་ཀུང་སི་.

ཟོང་དཔེ་ (soŋbe) sm. ཟོག་དཔེ་.

ཟོང་ཐང་ (soŋdaŋ) sm. ཟོག་ཐང་.

ཟོང་འཛིན་ (soŋdzin) sm. ཟོག་འཛིན་.

ཟོང་ཟོག (soŋsɔɔ̀) goods, merchandise.

ཟོང་རོ་ (soŋro) sm. ཟོག་རོ་.

ཟོན་ (sön) 1. precautions, caution, heed; va. ཟོན་; —བྱེད་ to take precautions, to be cautious, to heed; va.—སྐྱོང་ to not be cautious. 2. ch. one of the eight trigrams. 3. abbr. of ཟོན་པ་. 4. relief, rest.

ཟོན་ཀོ་བརྩེགས་ (söngodzeg) shung. a type of Tibetan boot.

ཟོན་སྐྱོར་ཆེན་པོ་ (söngyön cēmbo) comfortable (for shoes).

ཟོན་གྲབས་ (söndrəb) sm. ཟོན་, 1.

ཟོན་མགོ་ (söngo) the toe/ tip of a Tibetan boot.

ཟོན་ཆ་ (sönja) sm. ཟོན་, 1.

ཟོན་མཐིལ་ (söndii) heel of a Tibetan boot; va.—འདེབས་ to make/ sew the heel of a Tibetan boot.

ཟོན་པ་ (somba) Tibetan woolen boot.

ཟོན་པན་ (sõmbɛn) ch. abacus; va.—རྒྱག་; —གཏོང་ to use an abacus.

ཟོན་བྱ་ར་ (sönjara) shung. defending the border.

ཟོན་བྱེད་ (sön ceè) va. to be cautious/ watchful, to take precautions.

ཟོན་མེད་ (sönmeè) negligent, incautious, heedless. 2. frank, candid.

ཟོན་ཡུ་ (sönyu) the leg of a Tibetan woolen boot.

ཟོན་ལྷམ་ (sönlham) Tibetan style woolen boots.

ཟོབ་ (sob) arc. sm. ཟོག་པོ་.

ཟོབ་ཟོབ་ཀྱི་ར་བ་ (sobsobgi rawa) hedge, hedgerow.

ཟོམ་ (som) 1. wooden barrel/ bucket/ cask. 2. amidst ། རི་བོའི་ཟོམ་ནས་ From the midst of the mountains. 3. top, peak. 4. sm. ཟོན་པ་.

ཟོམ་སྐྱོན་ (somgyön) error, mistake (in accounting).

ཟོམ་བསྒྱུར་ (somgyur) sm. ཟོམ་འཇོག.

ཟོམ་ཁོག (somgɔɔ̀) the capacity of a ཟོམ་.

ཟོམ་མགོ་ (somgo) sm. ཟོན་མགོ་.

ཟོམ་རྔ་ (somŋa) a drum that is beaten on both sides.

ཟོམ་ཆེན་ (somjen) large wooden barrel/ bucket/ cask.

ཟོམ་འཇོག (somjɔɔ̀) not taking care of, neglecting; va.—བྱེད་ ། ལས་འགན་དེ་གལ་ཆེན་པོ་ཡིན་པས་རང་བཞིན་ཟོམ་འཇོག་བྱས་ན་མི་འགྲིགས་ This task is very important so it is not okay to neglect it.

ཟོམ་ཐག (somdaà) rope for carrying a bucket.

ཟོམ་མཐིལ་ (somdii) sm. ཟོན་མཐིལ་.

ཟོམ་དུ་ལུས་ (somdu lüü) sm. ཟོམ་ལུས་.

ཟོམ་པ་ (somba) sm. ཟོན་པ་.

ཟོམ་རྫི་ (somdzi) sm. ཟོ་མར་.

ཟོམ་ལུས་ (som lüü) vi. to unintentionally leave sth. out, to miss/ neglect.

ཟོམ་ལྷམ་ (somlham) sm. ཟོན་ལྷམ་.

ཟོམ་ལྷམ་མཐིལ་གཅིག་མ་ (somlham tīi jīgbə) a kind of Tibetan woolen boot where the sole is made of a single piece of leather.

ཟོའི་ (sowo) ch. branch office/ unit ¶ ཞིང་ལས་ཚན་རིག་ཞིབ་འཇུག་ཟོའི་ Agricultural Scientific Research Branch Office.

ཟོའི་ཙེ་ (sowodze) ch. gravy.

ཟོར་ (sɔr) 1. cursing sb.; va.—རྒྱག; —འཕེན་. 2. the amount or degree of sth. ¶ འཕྲུལ་འཁོར་གྱིས་མིའི་ངལ་རྩོལ་ཟོར་ཡང་དུ་བཏང་བ་རེད་ The machine made the amount of people's work lighter.

ཟོར་ཁ་ (sɔrga) target to whom a curse is directed.

ཟོར་བ་ (sɔrwa) sickle ¶ ཐོ་བ་དང་ཟོར་བ་ Hammer and sickle.

ཟོར་བ་ཡུ་རིང་ (sɔrwa yuriŋ) long handled sickle.

ཟོར་བུ་ (sɔrbu) a small sickle.

ཟོར་མ་ (sɔrma) auspicious words.

ཟོར་མའི་གླུ་དབྱངས་ (sɔrmɛ lūyaŋ) songs with auspicious words.

ཟོར་ཡང་ (sɔryaŋ) 1. convenient, easy (to do) ¶ ལས་ཀ་འདི་ཟོར་ཡང་ཆེད་དུ་རོགས་པ་གཅིག་གཏོང་གི་ཡིན་ I will send a helper to make the job easier. 2. briefer, shorter, more condensed/ simplified (for writing); va.—དུ་གཏོང་ ¶ ཡི་གེའི་ཟོར་ཡང་དུ་གཏོང་དགོས་ You must condense the writing.

ཟོར་ཡང་པོ་ (sɔr yaŋbo) easy, simple ¶ ལས་ཀ་འདི་ཟོར་ཡང་པོ་འདུག This work is easy.

ཟོལ་ (söö) 1. deceit. 2. with verbs: "pretend" ¶ ཁོས་གྲོགས་པོ་ཡིན་པའི་ཟོལ་བྱས་ནས་མགོ་སྐོར་བཏང་བྱུང་ He pretended he was a friend and tricked me.

ཟོལ་སྒྲིབ་ (söödrib) hiding (one's) faults/ errors through deceit; va.—བྱེད་.

ཟོལ་ཅན་ (sööjɛn) deceitful.

ཟོལ་བཅོས་ (söö) tampering, falsifying, altering; va.—རྒྱག; —བྱེད་; —འདེབས་ ¶ སློབ་གྲྭའི་འགོ་ཁྲིད་ཀྱིས་སྲིད་ཇུས་ལ་ཟོལ་བཅུག་ནས་འགྲོ་གྲོན་ཉུང་དུ་བཏང་བ་རེད་ The head of the school tampered with the policy and reduced expenses.

ཟོལ་འཆོས་ (sönjöö̀) sm. ཟོལ་བཅོས་.

ཟོལ་འཇོག (sönjɔɔ̀) letting sb. get away with sth.

ཟོལ་གཏོང་ (söö dōŋ) va. to make counterfeit, to make fake, to adulterate ¶ མི་དེས་མར་ལ་ཟོལ་བཏང་ནས་འཚོང་གི་འདུག That person has adulterating butter and selling it.

ཟོལ་བསྟོད་ (söödöö̀) praising falsely.

ཟོལ་པོ་ (sööbo) swindler, deceiver, liar, conniver.

ཟོལ་བུ་ (sööbu) sm. ཟོལ་པོ་.

ཟོལ་སྦྱོར་ (sööjɔɔ) deceit, falseness.

ཟོལ་སྦྱོར་བསླུ་བྲིད་ (sööjɔɔ lūdrii) tricking or swindling through falsehood/ pretense/ guile.

ཟོལ་མ་ (söömа) sm. ཟོལ་ཟོག.

ཟོལ་མེད་ (söömeè) 1. genuine, pure. 2. frank, candid, straightforward.

ཟོལ་བཛུ་ (söödzu) sm. ཟོལ་ཟོག.

ཟོལ་ཚིག (söödzii) deceiving words, false/ duplicitous talk.

ཟོལ་ཟོག (söösɔɔ̀) deceitful, false, duplicitous.

ཟོས་ (söö̀) p. of ཟ་. 2. p. of འཛད་.

ཟོས་བདེ་ (söö̀de) (vb. + —) at ease, free from worry/ anxiety ¶ ཞིང་འཁྲུག་སྐྱིང་འཛགས་བྱུང་བ་ནས་མི་ནམས་སྡོད་ཟོས་བདེ་བ་བྱུང་བ་རེད་ After the disturbance was over all the people lived at ease.

ཟོས་བདེ་ག་ཡངས་ (söö̀de guyaŋ) free from worry/ anxiety, peaceful.

ཟོས་པོ་ཁ་བརྙོགས་ (söö̀bo kāñog) getting into a bad habit ¶ ཚོང་པ་ཟོས་པོ་ཁ་བརྙོགས་དེས་རྟག་པར་མི་དམངས་ལ་མགོ་སྐོར་གཏོང་གི་ཡོད་པ་རེད་ The trader got into the bad habit of always tricking the people.

ཟོས་ཟོས་ (söö̀söö̀) a sparkler type of firecracker; va.—སྦྱོར་ to light a sparkler firecracker.

ཟྭ་ (sa) abbr. of ཟྭ་པོ་.

ཟྭ་ཁུ་ (sɔgu) sm. ཟྭ་ཚོད་.

ཟྭ་ཁྱམ་ (sagyam) sm. ཟྭ་པོ་.

ཟྭ་གོད་ (sagöö̀) sm. ཟྭ་པོ་.

ཟྭ་ལྕག (sajaà) a whip made from nettles.

ཟྭ་འདྲ་ (sandra) a nettle-like plant used in Tibetan medicine.

ཟྭ་པོ་ (sabo) nettles (urtica tibetica).

ཟྭ་པོས་ལྕུག (saböö̀ dɔɔ̀) vi. to be irritated by sb. [Lit. to be stung by nettles].

ཟྭ་སྤྱི་ཨ་ཡ་ (saji āya) sm. ཟྭ་པོ་.

ཟྭ་འཐོད་ (sadröö) vi. to be closed tightly ¶ སྒམ་དེའི་ཟྭ་འཐོད་མི་འདུག That box is not closed tightly.

ཟྭ་འབྲུམ་ (sandrum) 1. rash (caused by nettles). 2. nettle seeds.

ཟྭ་ཚོད་ (sadzöö) nettle soup.

ཟླ་ (da) abbr. of ཟླ་བ་.

ཟླ་དཀར་ (dagar) moon; vi.—ཤར་ to rise (the moon).

ཟླ་དཀྱིལ་ (dəgyii) middle of the month.

ཟླ་བཀྲག (dabdraà) moonlight ¶ ཟླ་བཀྲག་མཚན་མོ་ A moonlit night.

ཟླ་སྐར་ (dagar) moon and stars.

ཟླ་སྐྱེད་ (dagyeè) monthly interest.

ཟླ་སྐྱེས་ (dagyeè) 1. wednesday. 2. the amount a child grows in one month.

ཟླ་བསྐང་ (dagaŋ) monthly prayers made to portector deities; va.—འབུལ་.

ཟླ་བསྐྱོད་འཕུར་འཁོར་ (dagyöö̀ pūngɔɔ) moon rocket.

ཟླ་ཁ་མ་གང་བར་སྐྱེ་ (da kāmagaŋwar gyē) vi. to be born prematurely.

ཟླ་ཁ་མ་ཚང་བ་ (da kāmadzaŋwa) premature/ not full term birth.

ཟླ་ཁར་ཟླ་བཞག (dagar dashaà) month after month continuously.

ཟླ་འཁོར་ (dagɔɔ) monthly ¶ ཟླ་འཁོར་འཆར་གཞི་ Monthly plan.

ཟླ་འཁྲིམས་ (dəgyim) halo around the moon.

ཟླ་གང་ (dagaŋ) full moon.

ཟླ་གམ་ (dagam) 1. semicircular. 2. a cloak worn by Buddhist monks at prayer sessions.

ཟླ་གམ་མ་ (da gamma) sm. ཟླ་གམ་, 2.

ཟླ་གམ་གཟུགས་ (dagam sug) semicircular shape.

ཟླ་གྲངས་ (dadraŋ) number of months.

ཟླ་གྲས་ (dadrɛɛ̀) servant.

ཟླ་གྲས་གཡོག་རིགས་ (dadrɛɛ̀ yɔɔ̀rii) shung. servants.

ཟླ་གྲོགས་ (dadrɔɔ̀) friend, companion.

ཟླ་གླ་ (dala) monthly salary/ wage.

ཟླ་གླ་པ་ (da lāba) monthly salaried (worker).

ཟླ་དགུ་ངོ་བཅུ་ (dəgu ŋoju) nine months and ten days (period of pregnancy according to Tibetan medicine).

ཟླ་འགོ་ (dango) the beginning part of the month.

ཟླ་འགོ་ཚང་བ་ (dango tsāŋwa) one month old baby.

ཟླ་འགོར་འཐེབས་ (dangɔɔ tēb) vi. to have childbirth delayed past nine months.

ཟླ་འགྲིལ་ (da drii) vi. to get merged or combined.

ཟླ་རྒྱགས་ (dagyaà) monthly provision of food salary.

ཟླ་སྒོར་བག་ལེབ་ (dagɔɔ paàleè) moon cake (cookie/ cake eaten at Chinese Mid-Autumn Festival).

ཟླ་སྒྲིག (da drii) va. to find or arrange a companion/ helper.

ཟླ་སྒྲིལ་ (dəndrii) merging, combining together; va.—བྱེད་; —གཏོང་ to merge, to combine ¶ མི་ཚང་འདི་གཉིས་ཟླ་སྒྲིལ་བཏང་བ་རེད་ These two families merged (into one).

ཟླ་ངོ་ (daŋo) month ¶ ཟླ་ངོ་བཞི་རིང་ For the duration of four months.

ཟླ་ལྔའི་དུས་ཆེན་ (daŋɛ tüüjen) the Dragon Boat Chinese Festival (in the 5th month).

ཟླ་བཅུ་སྤྱི་ཚོགས་རིང་ལུགས་ཀྱི་གསར་བརྗེ་ (daju jīdzoò riŋluùgi sārje) the October Socialist Revolution (in Russia in 1917).

ཟླ་ཆུ་ (dəju) abbr. of. ཛ་ཆུ་ and ངོམ་ཆུ་.

ཟླ་མཆོད་དུས་ཆེན་ (dajöö̀ tüüjen) a Chinese festival occurring during the middle of autumn (15th of the 8th lunar month).

ཟླ་མཇུག (dənjuù) the latter part of a month.

ཟླ་ཉིན་ (dəñin) sm.* ན་ཉིང་.

ཟླ་སྙིང་ (dəñiŋ) last month.

ཟླ་གདུགས་པོ་ (da dūgbu) short of, scarce, in short

supply ¶ དེང་སང་ཁོང་ལག་དངུལ་ཟླ་གདུགས་པོ་འདུག These days he is short of pocket money.

ཟླ་ལྷར་ (dadar) monthly, every month.

ཟླ་སྟོད་ (dadöö) the beginning part of a month.

ཟླ་སྟོན་ (dadön) arc. a monthly party/ banquet given to calligraphers when they are copying scriptures/ books.

ཟླ་ཐུང་ཐུང་ (da tūŋduŋ) sm. ཟླ་གདུགས་པོ་.

ཟླ་ཐོ་ (dado) a calendar/ almanac.

ཟླ་ཐོག་ལོ་བརྩེགས་ (datɔɔ̀ lodzeg) for years on end, year after year.

ཟླ་ཐོག་ལོ་བཞག་ (datɔɔ̀ loshaà) a long time ago.

ཟླ་ཐོབ (dadob) 1. a share of an allotment (money or supplies) that one is due for the period of a month ¶ དཀོན་གཉེར་གྱིས་ལས་ཁུངས་ལ་ཟླ་ཐོབ་ཞུ་བར་ཕྱིན་པ་རེད་ The chapel caretaker went to the office to ask for that month's share (allotment). 2. amount paid for a month's work based on the profit of the enterprise.

ཟླ་དུམ་ (dadum) half moon/ crescent shape.

ཟླ་དུས་ (dədüü) a period equal to a month (30 days).

ཟླ་དུས་ཚེས་གྲངས་ (dədüü tsēèdraŋ) the date (day and month) ¶ ཁྱེད་རང་འདིར་ཕེབས་པའི་ཟླ་དུས་ཚེས་གྲངས་གསུང་རོགས་གནང་ Tell (me) the date when you came here.

ཟླ་དྲུག་སོང་ཁྲ་ (dadruù sōŋdra) shung. a six month report of purchases/ expenditures.

ཟླ་འདྲེས་ (dandreè) vi. to get mixed together ¶ ངའི་ཅ་ལག་གི་ནང་དུ་མི་གཞན་གྱི་ཅ་ལག་ཟླ་འདྲེས་བྱུང་བཞག Other people's things got mixed in with mine.

ཟླ་སྡུད་ (dədüü) sm. སྒྲར་བསྡུ་.

ཟླ་སྡེབ་ (da deb) va. to go together as traveling companions ¶ གྲོགས་པོ་གཉིས་ཟླ་བསྡེབས་ནས་རྒྱ་གར་དུ་ཕྱིན་འདུག The two friends went to India as travel companions.

ཟླ་སྡོང་ (dadoŋ) comrade-in-arms, helpers, associates.

ཟླ་ནག (danaà) an inauspicious month according to Tibetan astrological calculations.

ཟླ་ཕོགས་ (dabɔɔ̀) monthly salary.

ཟླ་ཕྱེད་ (dajeè) 1. half a month. 2. half moon.

ཟླ་ཕྱེད་དམར་པོ་ (dajeè māābo) Red Crescent (organization).

ཟླ་ཕྱེད་གཟུགས་ (dajeè sug) half moon shape.

ཟླ་འཕྱུལ་ (dəmbüü) delaying, postponing; va.—བྱེད་.

ཟླ་བ་ (dawa) 1. moon ¶ ཟླ་བའི་འོད་ Moonlight. 2. month ¶ ཟླ་བ་དང་པོ་ The first month (in the Tibetan calendar). 3. (གཟའ་—) Monday.

ཟླ་བ་གང་བ་ (dawa gaŋwa) full moon.

ཟླ་བ་གོང་མ་ (dawa koŋma) the previous month.

ཟླ་བ་རྒྱས་པ་ (dawa gyɛɛ̀ba) full moon.

ཟླ་བ་ངོ་རེ་བཞིན་ (dawa ŋoreshin) shung. every month.

ཟླ་བ་སྔ་མ་ (dawa ŋāma) sm. ཟླ་བ་གོང་མ་.

ཟླ་བ་སྔོན་མ་ (dawa ŋōnma) sm. ཟླ་བ་གོང་མ་.

ཟླ་བ་བཅུ་པའི་གསར་བརྗེ་ (dawa jūbɛ sārje) the October Revolution (in Russia in 1917).

ཟླ་བ་ཆ་ (dawa cā) even months (e.g., the 2nd, 4th, 6th month).

ཟླ་བ་ཆ་འཛིན་ (dawa cāndzin) partial lunar eclipse.

ཟླ་བ་མཇུག་མ་ (dawa juùmə) next month.

ཟླ་བ་ཉ་གང་ (dawa ñagaŋ) full moon.

ཟླ་བ་ཉ་རྒྱས་པ་ (dawa ñagyɛɛ̀ba) sm. ཟླ་བ་ཉ་གང་.

ཟླ་བ་ཉ་པ་ (dawa ñaba) sm. ཟླ་བ་ཉ་གང་.

ཟླ་བ་གཉིས་པ་ (dawa ñiìbə) the second month (in the Tibetan calendar).

ཟླ་བ་གཉིས་རེའི་དུས་དེབ་ (dawa ñiiree tüüdeb) bimonthly magazine.

ཟླ་བ་རྟིང་མ་ (dawa dīŋmə) next month.

ཟླ་བ་དང་པོ་ (dawa taŋbo) the first month (in the Tibetan calendar).

ཟླ་བ་གདུབ་འཛིན་ (dawa dubdzin) lunar eclipse.

ཟླ་བ་ཕྱི་མ་ (dawa cīmə) next month.

ཟླ་བ་ཕྱེད་ (dawa cēè) sm. ཟླ་ཕྱེད་.

ཟླ་བ་འཕེལ་འགྲིབ་ (dawa pēndrib) the waxing and waning of the moon.

ཟླ་བ་བྱུང་ངོ་ཅོག་ (dawa cuŋ ŋojoò) shung. sm. ཟླ་བ་ངོ་རེ་བཞིན་.

ཟླ་བ་མར་ངོ་ (dawa marŋo) the second half of the month.

ཟླ་བ་མོག་པ་ (dawa məgba) moon hidden by clouds.

ཟླ་བ་ཚང་ (dawa tsāŋ) 1. vi. to have reached full term in a pregnancy ¶ ཕྲུ་གུ་ཟླ་བ་ཚང་ནས་སྐྱེ་རན་འདུག The child has reached full term (in the pregnancy) so it is now time for it to be born. 2. vi. to reach the end of a term (for a loan/ contract) ¶ གན་རྒྱ་ནང་གསལ་ལས་ཀའི་དུས་ཚོད་ཀྱི་ཟླ་བ་ཚང་བཞག The time specified for the job (to be completed) in the agreement is over (has been reached).

ཟླ་བ་ཚེས་པ་ (dawa tsēèba) the 3rd and 4th day of the Tibetan month.

ཟླ་བ་འཛིན་ (dawa dzin) sm. ཟླ་འཛིན་.

ཟླ་བ་གཞོན་ནུ་ (dawa shönnu) sm. ཟླ་བ་ཚེས་པ་.

ཟླ་བ་གཟའ་འཛིན་ (dawa səndzin) lunar eclipse.

ཟླ་བ་ཡ་ (dawa ya) odd numbered months.

ཟླ་བ་ཡར་ངོ་ (dawa yarŋo) the time from the 1st to the 15th day of the month.

ཟླ་བ་རིལ་པོ་ (dawa riibu) a full month.

ཟླ་བ་རིལ་འཛིན་ (dawa rindzin) full lunar eclipse.

ཟླ་བའི་གོ་ལ་ (dawɛ kola) 1. the lunar orbit. 2. the moon.

ཟླ་བའི་འཇིག་རྟེན་ (dawɛ jigden) moon.

ཟླ་བའི་ཐོག་མ་ (dawɛ tɔɔ̀ma) 1. the first month. 2. the first day of the month.

ཟླ་བའི་འཐེན་ཤུགས་ (dawɛ tēnshuù) the moon's gravitational pull.

ཟླ་བའི་མ་མ་ (dawɛ mama) poet. ocean, sea.

ཟླ་བའི་འོད་ཟེར་ (dawɛ wöösee) moonlight.

ཟླ་བའི་ར་རི་ (dawɛ rari) the darker part of the moon's surface that appears as a design from earth (e.g., for Tibetans the rabbit on the moon).

ཟླ་བས་འཕེལ་ (dawɛ pēl) poet. ocean, sea.

ཟླ་བུ་ (dəbu) wednesday.

ཟླ་བོ་ (dəwu) 1. spouse. 2. friend.

ཟླ་བྲལ་ (dadrɛɛ) sm. ཟླ་མེད་.

ཟླ་དབྱིབས་ (dəyib) 1. the moon. 2. moon-shaped.

ཟླ་མི་ཐུང་བ་ (də mitūŋwə) abundant, plentiful ¶ དམག་སར་དམག་རྒྱགས་ཟླ་མི་ཐུང་བ་བསྐྱལ་བཞག They sent abundant military provisions to the battlefield.

ཟླ་མེད་མཚན་མོ་ (dameè tsēnmo) a moonless night.

ཟླ་མེད་ (dameè) matchless, unequaled, unrivaled.

ཟླ་མོ་ (damo) girlfriend.

ཟླ་སྨད་ (damɛɛ̀) sm. ཟླ་མཇུག.

ཟླ་སྨད་ནག་པོ་ (dameè nagbo) the latter part of the month that is considered inauspicious according to Tibetan astrology.

ཟླ་ཙམ་ (dədzam) a little bit ¶ ཁ་ལག་ལ་སི་པན་ཟླ་ཙམ་བརྒྱབ་འདུག The food has a little bit of chili in it.

ཟླ་རྩིས་ (dədzii) calculated on a monthly basis (usu. wages); va.—རྒྱག.

ཟླ་ཚེས་ (dadzeè) month and date/ day.

ཟླ་ཚེས་ཕྱོགས་ཀྱི་དང་པོ་ (dadzeè cɔɔ̀gi taŋbo) 1st day of the month.

ཟླ་མཚན་ (dadzɛn) menstruation; vi.—འབབ་; —ཐེབས་ to menstruate, to start menstruating; vi.—ཆད་ to have menstruation stop (e.g., at menapause); vi.—འཁྱིལ་ to have menstruation not arrive on time.

ཟླ་མཚན་གྱི་དུས་འཁོར་ (dadzɛngi tüügɔɔ) menstrual cycle.

ཟླ་མཚན་འབབ་དུས་ (dadzɛn bəbdüü) menstrual period.

ཟླ་མཚན་འོས་སུ་སྒྲིག (dadzɛn wöösu drig) va. to regulate menstruation (menstrual flow).

ཟླ་མཚན་གསང་རས་ (dadzɛn sāŋrɛɛ̀) sanitary napkin.

ཟླ་མཚམས་ (dadzam) end of a month.

ཟླ་མཚམས་སོ་སོར་ (dadzam sōso) shung. due date in a month ¶ སྐྱིད་འབབ་རྣམས་ཟླ་མཚམས་སོ་སོར་ལི

མེད་འཇལ་སྤྲོད་དགོས་རྒྱུ་ The interest on the loan should be paid on the due dates in the month.

ཟླ་འཛིན་ (dəndzin) sm. ཟླ་བ་གཟའ་འཛིན་.

ཟླ་ཞག (dashaà) abbr. of ཟླ་བ་ and ཞག་མ་.

ཟླ་ཞག་གི་དགོངས་པ་ (dashaàgi goŋba) shung. a leave for months and days.

ཟླ་ཞལ་ (dashɛɛ) beautiful (for women).

ཟླ་ཞལ་མ་ (da shɛɛma) a beautiful woman.

ཟླ་གཞུག (dəshuù) latter part of the month.

ཟླ་གཟུགས་ (dəsuù) moon shaped.

ཟླ་ཟེར་ (daser) lunar rays, moon beams.

ཟླ་ཟོ་ (daso) a wooden utensil used for measuring.

ཟླ་ཟླུམ་ (dadum) the full (round) moon.

ཟླ་འོད་ (dawöö) moonlight.

ཟླ་ཡ་ (daya) 1. rival, opponent, opposition; va.—བྱེད་ to act as a rival/ opponent/ opposition. 2. arc. divorce.

ཟླ་རེ་ (dare) each month, monthly.

ཟླ་རེ་ངོ་རེ་ (dare ŋore) every month, monthly.

ཟླ་རེའི་འཆར་གཞི་ (daree cārshi) monthly plan/ schedule.

ཟླ་རེའི་དུས་དེབ་ (daree tüüdeb) monthly journal/ magazine/ periodical.

ཟླ་རེའི་ཞུ་ཐོ་ (daree shudo) monthly report.

ཟླ་ལམ་ (dalam) a trip or journey that takes a month.

ཟླ་ཤས་ (dashɛɛ̀) several months.

ཟླ་ཤོག (dashɔɔ̀) a monthly personal report in which ones thoughts and feelings had to be conveyed for the communist party officials.

ཟླ་བཤོལ་ (dashöö) intercalary month.

ཟླ་བཤོལ་ཡོད་པའི་ལོ་ (dashöö yööbɛ lo) a year with an intercalary month.

ཟླ་སྲང་སྐར་སྐྱེད་ (dasaŋ gārgyeè) shung. 60% annual interest rate (5 སྐར་མ་ interest for each one སྲང་ borrowed).

ཟླ་སྲང་ཁ་སྐྱེད་ (dasaŋ kāgyeè) shung. 30% interest rate (2 1/2 སྐར་མ་ of interest each month for each one སྲང་ borrowed).

ཟླ་སྲང་ཞོ་སྐྱེད་ (dasaŋ shogyeè) shung. 120% interest rate (one ཞོ་ interest per month for each one སྲང་ borrowed).

ཟླ་གསར་ (dasar) new moon.

ཟླ་ལྷག (dalhaà) sm. ཟླ་བཤོལ་.

ཟླས་འབྱེད་ (dɛɛ̀ jeè) va. to differentiate.

ཟླུག་: p. བཟླུགས་; f. བཟླུག་; imp. ཟླུགས་ (duù) 1. va. to pour into a container, to fill up ། ཕོར་པའི་ནང་དུ་འོ་མ་བཟླུགས་བཞག (He) filled up the cup with milk. 2. va. to ask about, to inquire about. 3. arc. va. to give.

ཟླུགས་ (duù) imp. of ཟླུག.

ཟླུམ་: p. བཟླུམས་; f. བཟླུམ་; imp. ཟླུམས་ (dum) 1. va. to collect/ bring together, to gather ། ས་གནས་ཁག་གི་འཐུས་མི་རྒྱལ་སར་བཟླུམས་འདུག They brought the local representatives to the capital. 2. va. to settle, to mediate to bring to an end ། ཁ་མཆུ་དེ་གྲོགས་པོ་ཚོས་བཟླུམས་ཐུབ་པ་བྱུང་འདུག The friends were able to mediate (and solve) the dispute. 3. abbr. of ཟླུམ་པོ་.

ཟླུམ་སྐོར་ (dumgɔɔ) circular paintings/ drawings.

ཟླུམ་འཁོར་ (dumgɔɔ) 1. round, ball- shaped. 2. sm. སྒོར་འགྲིལ་དུ་འཁོར་བ་.

ཟླུམ་ངོས་ (dumŋöö) surface of a sphere/ globe/ ball.

ཟླུམ་འཆོས་ (dumjöö) 1. mediating, arbitrating; va.—བྱེད་. 2. making sth. round in shape.

ཟླུམ་སྣུང་ (dumñuŋ) a round awl.

ཟླུམ་ཐིག (dumdiì) a circular line.

ཟླུམ་པོ་ (dumbo) 1. globular, spherical, round. 2. bald, shaved head.

ཟླུམ་ཞྭ་ (dumsha) a round hat/ cap.

ཟླུམ་གཟུགས་ (dumsuù) sm. ཟླུམ་པོ་.

ཟླུམ་སྲིན་མཚེ་མ་ (dumsin tsēma) diplococcus.

ཟླུམས་ (dum) imp. of ཟླུམ་.

ཟློ་: p. བཟློས་; f. བཟློ་; imp. ཟློས་ (do) va. to intone/ recite ། རྗེས་སུ་བཟློས་ To repeat after (someone).

ཟློག་: p. བཟློགས་; f. བཟློག; imp. ཟློག (dɔɔ̀) va. to force/ drive back, to repel, to repulse ། ནད་ཡམས་ཟློག་པའི་ཆེད་དུ་སྔོན་འགོག་ཁབ་བརྒྱབ་པ་རེད་ To repulse an epidemic they gave inoculations.

ཟློག་སྒྱུར་ (dɔggyur) prayers to stop disasters from happening.

ཟློག་ཐབས་ (dɔgdəb) ways of forcing/ driving back/ repelling; va.—བྱེད་.

ཟློག་ཐབས་བྲལ་ (dɔɔ̀dəb trɛɛ) impossible to repel/ repulse, unavoidable.

ཟློག་པ་ (dɔgba) clapping; va.—རྒྱག to clap/ applaud.

ཟློག་རིམ་ (dɔgrim) prayers and rites done for stopping disasters.

ཟློས་ (döö) 1. imp. of ཟློ་. 2. vi. to repeat (in speech). 3. a legal case/ lawsuit. 4. vi. to appear, to become manifest ། འདྲེ་མོ་དེ་སླར་ཡང་མིའི་གཟུགས་སུ་ཟློས་ནས་ཡོང་བ་རེད་ The witch appeared in a human form and came.

ཟློས་གར་ (döögar) drama, play, show; va.—འཁྲབ་ to perform a show/ play.

ཟློས་གར་ཁང་ (döögargaŋ) theater.

ཟློས་གར་མཁན་ (döögarñɛn) actor, performer, dancer.

ཟློས་གར་འཁྲབ་ཚན་ (döögar trəbdzɛn) program for a play/ drama.

ཟློས་གར་འཁྲབ་ཚིག (döögar trəbdziì) stage lines, dialogue.

ཟློས་གར་འཁྲབ་རོགས་ (döögar trəbrɔɔ̀) supporting actor/ actress.

ཟློས་གར་གྱི་ནང་དོན་ (döögargi naŋdön) the main plot/ story of the drama or play.

ཟློས་གར་གདམ་མོལ་ (döögar dāmmöö) dialogue in a play.

ཟློས་གར་ཚོགས་པ་ (döögar tsɔ̄gba) theatrical group/ troupe.

ཟློས་གར་བཞད་གད་ཅན་ (döögar shɛɛ̀gɛɛ̀jɛn) comedy play.

ཟློས་གྱར་ (döö gyar) vi. to get involved in a dispute/ lawsuit.

ཟློས་སྒྲ་ཅན་ (döödrajɛn) words containing two different syllables with the same meaning.

ཟློས་གདམ་ (döödam) sth. that is repeated again and again.

ཟློས་བུ་ (dööbu) repetitive; va.—བཤད་ to say repeatedly/ repetitively.

ཟློས་རྩོད་ (döödzöö) a case (in court); va.—བྱེད་.

ཟློས་གཞི་ (dööshi) shung. the principal in a law case; va.—གྱར་ to be involved in a lawsuit/ legal case.

ཟློས་ཡ་ (dööya) one of the parties in a legal case/ lawsuit.

ཟློས་ཧྲལ་ (dööhrɛɛ) Tibetan letters with suffixed y or r.

གཟག (saà) sm. an alternative way to write the present and future of གཟགས་.

གཟགས་: p. གཟགས་; f. གཟགས་; imp. གཟོགས་ (saà) 1. va. to pour/ throw away (a liquid) ། མདོང་མོའི་ཆུ་གཟགས་པ་རེད་ They poured the water out of the churn. 2. va. to turn over a container to let the (water) drip out ། སྣོད་ཆས་ནང་གི་ཆུ་གཟགས་པ་རེད་ They let the water drip out from the container.

གཟང་ (saŋ) 1. point, tip, edge (of a knife). 2. a leather piece used under a saddle.

གཟང་རིང་ (saŋriŋ) a long object with a sharp tip/ edge/ point.

གཟད་ (sɛɛ̀) sm. འཛད་.

གཟན་ (sɛn) 1. shawl. 2. top part of a monk's dress. 3. hay, fodder. 3. p. and f. of གཟོན་. 4. vi. to wear out. 5. vi. to be bothersome/ harmful.

གཟན་སྒྱུར་ (sɛngyur) monks paying respect when greeting by removing their shawl from the shoulder and bowing; va.—འཕེབ་.

གཟན་ཁང་ (sɛnga) barn or room for hay/ fodder.

གཟན་གོད་ (sɛngöö) sth. that wears out or gets wasted quickly.

གཟན་སྒྲོག (sɛndrɔɔ̀) sm. གཟན་སྒྲོམ་.

གཟན་རྒྱག (sengyaà) wasting, wearing out; va.—བྱེད་.

གཟན་ཆག (senjaà) fodder; hay and fodder ། ཕག་གཟན་ Pig fodder.

གཟན་ཆག་ཚོང་ཁང་ (senjaà tsōŋgaŋ) fodder store.

གཟན་ཆག་ཞིང་ར་ (senjaà siŋrə) fodder farm.

གཟན་ཆག་རིལ་བུ་ (senjaà riibu) granulated fodder.

གཟན་ཆས་ (senjɛɛ̀) sm. གཟན་ཆག.

གཟན་ཆས་ལོ་ཏོག (senjɛɛ̀ lodoò) fodder crops.

གཟན་འཇའ་སྒྲིག་མ་ (senja drigmə) a type of rainbow colored shawl (worn with the རྒྱ་ལུ་ costume).

གཟན་སྙིགས་ (senñii) hay/ fodder leftover after animals eat.

གཟན་སྟན་ (sendɛn) monk's shawl and mat/ rug.

གཟན་ཐག (sendaà) rope attached to a monk's shawl.

གཟན་འཐུད་ (sendüù) shung. a money substitute for a fodder tax obligation.

གཟན་དྲོན་ (sendrön) sm. ཟན་དྲོན་.

གཟན་སྡོམ་ (sendom) sm. གཟན་ཐག.

གཟན་སྣ་ལྔ་ (sen nāŋa) a kind of shawl with five colors worn by officials of the traditional Tibetan government.

གཟན་པ་ (semba) 1. hay, straw; va.—རྒྱག to feed hay/ straw to animals.

གཟན་པོ་ (sembo) 1. bothersome, harmful, bad ། འདི་ན་ཅོག་ལ་གཟན་པོ་འདུག This is bothersome to the ear. ། འོད་ཆེན་པོ་དེ་མིག་ལ་གཟན་པོ་འདུག The bright light is bad for the eyes. 2. (སེམས་ལ་ —) hurting sb.'s feeling. 3. wearing away, wearing out, corroding. ། ཐག་རིང་པོ་གོམ་པ་བརྒྱབ་ན་ལྷམ་ལ་གཟན་པོ་ཡོང་གི་རེད་ (If) you walk a great distance you'll wear out your shoes. 4. see མིག་ལ་གཟན་པོ་.

གཟན་མེ་ཤིང་ (sen mesiŋ) fodder and firewood/ dung.

གཟན་རྩ་ (sendza) hay/ grass used as fodder.

གཟན་རིལ་ (senrii) shung. sm. ཟན་རིལ་.

གཟན་ཤམ་ (sensham) monk's shawl and skirt (upper and lower garments).

གཟན་ཤིང་ (senshiŋ) fodder/ hay and firewood/ dung.

གཟབ་ (səb) 1. va. to be earnest/ serious ། སྤྱི་དོན་ལ་ཚང་མས་གཟབ་དགོས་ Everyone must be earnest with respect to the common cause. 2. abbr. of གཟབ་གཟབ་.

གཟབ་གོས་ (sabgöò) sm. གཟབ་སྤྲོས་.

གཟབ་གྲུང་ (səbdruŋ) careful and alert.

གཟབ་རྒྱས་ (sabgyɛɛ̀) elaborate, grand ། མཇལ་ལེན་གཟབ་རྒྱས་ An elaborate reception.

གཟབ་བཅགས་ (səbjaà) shung. sm. གཟབ་ནན་.

གཟབ་ལྕག་རྒྱུན་འཁྱོངས་ (səbjaà gyüŋgyoŋ) shung. being consistently careful.

གཟབ་མཚར་ (sabjɔɔ) dressed up, decorated; va.—སྤྲོས་ to dress up ། དུས་ཆེན་གྱི་ཉིན་མོ་མི་ཚང་མ་གཟབ་མཚར་སྤྲས་འདུག All the people got dressed up on the day of the holiday.

གཟབ་འཚོས་ (sabjöò) trying perform a task with great care; va.—བྱེད་.

གཟབ་ཉན་ (sabñɛn) listening carefully; va.—བྱེད་.

གཟབ་བརྟན་ (sabdɛn) careful, thorough, deliberate; va.—བྱེད་.

གཟབ་ནན་ (sabnɛn) careful, serious; va.—བྱེད་ ། ལས་ཀ་གཟབ་ནན་མ་བྱས་ན་ནོར་འཁྲུལ་ཤོར་གྱི་རེད་ If you don't do your work carefully you will make a mistake.

གཟབ་ནན་ཞིབ་ཚགས་ (sabnɛn shibdzaà) careful and detailed.

གཟབ་སྤྲོས་ (sabdröò) dressy clothing, Sunday best clothing; va.—རྒྱག་; —སྤྲས་; —གཏོང་ to dress up, to wear one's Sunday best.

གཟབ་སྤྲོས་ཆེན་པོ་ (sabdröò cēmbo) sm. གཟབ་སྤྲོས་.

གཟབ་སྤྲོས་བཞེས་ (sabdröò sheè) h. of གཟབ་སྤྲོས་རྒྱག.

གཟབ་སྤྲིང་རུ་ཁག (sabdreŋ rugaà) sm. གཟབ་གཟེངས་རུ་ཁག.

གཟབ་བཞེས་ (sabsheè) 1. h. of གཟབ་ནན་. 2. dressed up in fine clothes.

གཟབ་གཟབ་ (səbsəb) careful, serious, attentive, cautious, watchful; va.—བྱེད་ ། རྒྱུན་དུ་མོ་ཊ་གཏོང་དུས་གཟབ་གཟབ་བྱེད་ཀྱི་ཡོད་པ་རེད་ (He) is usually careful when driving. ། གཟབ་གཟབ་བྱས་ནས་ཉན་པ་རེད་ (He) listened carefully. 2. doing one's best, treating well, acting hospitable ། ཁོང་གིས་ང་ཚོར་གཟབ་གཟབ་གནང་བྱུང་ (He) treated us very well.

གཟབ་གཟབ་ནན་ཏན་ (səbsəb nendɛn) careful, cautious, attentive, serious.

གཟབ་གཟབ་ནན་ནན་ (səbsəb nennɛn) sm. གཟབ་གཟབ་ནན་ཏན་.

གཟབ་གཟབ་སིལ་སིལ་ (səbsəb siisii) sm. གཟབ་གཟབ་, 1.

གཟབ་གཟབ་གཟེངས་གཟེངས་ (səbsəb seŋseŋ) happily/ gladly and respectfully.

གཟབ་གཟེངས་ (səbseŋ) abbr. of གཟབ་གཟབ་གཟེངས་གཟེངས་.

གཟབ་གཟེངས་རུ་ཁག (səbseŋ rugaà) guard of honor.

གཟབ་གཟོབ་ (səbsɔr) sm. གཟབ་གཟབ་.

གཟབ་ཡིག (səbyii) sm. དབུ་ཅན་.

གཟབ་བརླིང་ (səbliŋ) careful and stable.

གཟབ་བརླིང་བརྟན་འགྲོ་ (səbliŋ dēndro) va. to go carefully.

གཟབ་བརླིང་བརྟན་གསུམ་ (səbliŋ dēnsum) careful and stable.

གཟབ་བརླིང་ཚུགས་ཆེ་ (səbliŋ tsügje) sm. གཟབ་བརླིང་བརྟན་གསུམ་.

གཟབ་ཤར་ (səbshar) དབུ་ཅན་ and དབུ་མེད་.

གཟབ་གསོལ་ (səbsüü) ritual ceremony at which offerings are made to protective deities.

གཟབ་ལྷིང་ (səblhiŋ) careful and calm.

གཟབས་ (səb) p. of གཟོབ་.

གཟའ་ (sa) 1. planet ། གཟའ་མིག་དམར་ The planet mars (also Tuesday). 2. day of the week ། གཟའ་ཟླ་བ་ Monday.

གཟའ་སྐར་ (sagar) planets and stars ། གཟའ་སྐར་བཟང་བ་ Astrologically auspicious (planets and stars).

གཟའ་སྐར་མཁན་ (sagarñɛn) astrologer.

གཟའ་སྐར་དགེ་བ་ (sagar gewa) an auspicious constellation of the planets and stars, an auspicious day.

གཟའ་སྐར་ཚེས་རྩིས་ (sagar tseèdzii) Tibetan astrological calculation.

གཟའ་སྐར་བཟང་པོ་ (sagar saŋbo) an auspicious day.

གཟའ་འཁོར་ (sagɔɔ) week ། གཟའ་འཁོར་སྔོན་མ་ Last week.

གཟའ་འཁོར་གཉིས་རེའི་དུས་དེབ་ (sagɔɔ ñiiree tüüdeb) a fortnightly publication/ magazine/ journal.

གཟའ་འཁོར་སྔོན་མ་ (sagɔɔ ŋōnma) previous week.

གཟའ་འཁོར་དུས་དེབ་ (sagɔɔ tüüdeb) a weekly magazine/ periodical/ paper.

གཟའ་འཁོར་གཞུག་མ་ (sagɔɔ shugmə) next week.

གཟའ་འཁོར་རེའི་དུས་དེབ་ (sagɔɔree tüüdeb) weekly magazine/ journal.

གཟའ་འཁོར་རེའི་ཚགས་པར་ (sagɔɔree tsāgba) weekly newspaper.

གཟའ་གྲིབ་ (sədrib) a stroke; vi.—ཕོག to have a stroke.

གཟའ་རྒྱག (sa gyaà) sm. གཟའ་ཕོག.

གཟའ་ངན་པ་ (sa ŋemba) inauspicious day.

གཟའ་ལྔ་ (saŋa) the five days of the week excluding Sunday and Monday.

གཟའ་མཇུག (sanjuù) weekend (days).

གཟའ་མཇུག་མཚན་ཚོགས་ (sanjuù tsɛ̄ndzɔɔ̀) weekend party.

གཟའ་མཇུག་རིང་ (sa jugriŋ) Haley's comet.

གཟའ་ཉི་མ་ (sa ñimə) Sunday.

གཟའ་བདག (sadaà) the sun.

གཟའ་ནད་ (sanɛɛ̀) epilepsy.

གཟའ་བདུན་ (sādün) the seven days of the week.

གཟའ་པ་སངས་ (sa bāsaŋ) 1. Friday. 2. the planet Venus.

གཟའ་སྤེན་པ་ (sa bēmba) 1. Saturday. 2. the planet Saturn.

གཟའ་ཕུར་བུ་ (sa pūrbu) 1. Thursday. 2. the planet Jupiter.

གཟའ་ཕོག (sa pɔ̃ɔ̀) vi. to have/ get a stroke.

གཟའ་མིག་དམར་ (sa miŋmar) 1. Tuesday. 2. the planet Mars.

གཟའ་ཚེས་ (sadzeè) the day of the week and the date.

གཟའ་འཛིན་ (sandzin) an eclipse ¶ ཉི་མ་གཟའ་འཛིན་ Solar eclipse.

གཟའ་ཟིན་ (sasin) sm. གཟའ་འཛིན་.

གཟའ་ཟླ་བ་ (sa dāwa) Monday.

གཟའ་ཡན་སྐར་ཡན་ (sayɛn gāryɛn) inauspicious days (and stars) in astrology.

གཟའ་ཡི་དེན་ (səyi dēn) the north star.

གཟའ་རོ་ (saro) paralysis, apoplexy.

གཟའ་ལྷག་པ་ (sa lhāgba) 1. Wednesday. 2. the planet Mercury.

གཟའ་ཨོག་རལ་ (sa ɔ̄grɛɛ) name of the mythical dog who eats the moon (i.e., the eclipse of the moon).

གཟར་ (saa) 1. fringe, tassel. 2. va. to hang down. 3. abbr. of གཟར་པོ་.

གཟར་མགོ་ (sango) the bowl of a pipe (for smoking).

གཟར་ཆེན་ (saājen) a satin/ brocade piece used under a saddle.

གཟར་སྟན་ (saadɛn) a cushion/ rug used under a saddle.

གཟར་ཐག (saadaà) rope for hanging sth., a clothesline.

གཟར་དུར་ (saadur) a steep slope.

གཟར་པོ་ (sarbo) steep (slope or pitch) ¶ རི་གཟར་པོ་ A steep hill.

གཟར་པོད་ (sarbö̀ö) tassles.

གཟར་བུ་ (sarbu) wooden ladle.

གཟར་འབབ་ (sambəb) slope, gradient.

གཟར་འབུ་ (sambu) ladybug.

གཟར་མོ་ (sarmo) sm. གཟར་པོ་.

གཟར་ཚད་ (sardzɛɛ̀) degree of incline/ slope, degree of steepness.

གཟར་ཡུ་ (saryu) the stem of a smoking pipe.

གཟར་རུ་ (sərru) wooden ladle.

གཟས་ (sɛɛ̀) sm. འཕུར་.

གཟས་འཛིན་ (sɛndzin) sm. གཟས་འཛིན་.

གཟས་ས་ (sɛɛ̀sa) grazing areas for nomad animals.

གཟི་ (si) 1. a type of stone highly valued in Tibet as jewelry. 2. brightness, splendor.

གཟི་རྒྱག (si gyaà) va. to rub a གཟི་ stone on thankas painted in gold to bring out the sheen.

གཟི་རྡམ་ (siŋam) dignity, majestic, grand, awe imposing, commanding; va.—འདོན་ to show one's majesty, to act imposing ¶ གཟི་རྡམ་ཅན་གྱི་ སྟོབས་ཤུགས་ An imposing power.

གཟི་རྡམ་ཆེ་བ་ (siŋam cēwa) majestic looking, grand.

གཟི་བརྗིད་ (sijiì) 1. magnificent, majestic, dignified, grand. 2. honor, esteem, glory.

གཟི་བརྗིད་ཀྱི་མིང་བྱང་ (sijiìgi miŋjaŋ) a board containing names of honored people.

གཟི་བརྗིད་ཅན་ (sijiìjɛn) magnificent, majestic, dignified, grand, glorious. 2. honorable, esteemed, glorious.

གཟི་བརྗིད་ཅན་གྱི་སྙན་གྲགས་ (sijiìjɛngi ñɛ̄ndraà) a majestic/ grand reputation.

གཟི་བརྗིད་ཆེན་པོ་ (sijiì cēmbo) very majestic/ honorable/ glorious.

གཟི་བརྗིད་སྙན་གྲགས་ (sijiì ñɛ̄ndraà) sm. གཟི་བརྗིད་ཅན་གྱི་སྙན་གྲགས་.

གཟི་བརྗིད་དང་ལྡན་པ་ (sijiìdaŋ dɛmba) sm. གཟི་བརྗིད་ཅན་.

གཟི་བརྗིད་དཔལ་འབར་ (sijiì bɛ̄mbar) glorious, splendid.

གཟི་བརྗིད་བརྩོན་ལེན་ (sijiì dzɔ̃nlen) a fight/ struggle/ competition for honor or glory.

གཟི་བརྗིད་འོད་སྡོང་འབར་བ་ (sijiì wö̀ödoŋ barwa) remarkably magnificent/ glorious.

གཟི་ཉམས་ལྡན་པ་ (siñam dɛmba) grand, magnificent, glorious.

གཟི་མདུ་ (situ) sm. གཟི་བརྗིད་ཅན་.

གཟི་མདངས་ (sidaŋ) radiance, a healthy/ good complexion.

གཟི་ནར་ནར་ (si narnar) an oval shaped (elongated) གཟི་.

གཟི་ལྡན་ (sīndɛn) sm. གཟི་བརྗིད་ཅན་.

གཟི་པང་ (sibaŋ) a polishing/ rubbing board.

གཟི་དཔལ་ (sibɛɛ) sm. གཟི་བརྗིད་.

གཟི་སྤོབས་ (sibob) glory and pride.

གཟི་ཕྲུག (sidruù) a very small piece of གཟི་.

གཟི་བྱིན་ (sijin) sm. གཟི་བརྗིད་.

གཟི་མ་ (simə) eyelash.

གཟི་མིག (simiì) the eyes (circles) on གཟི་.

གཟི་འོད་ (siwö̀ö) brilliance, luster; vi.—འཕྲོ་ to shine majestically.

གཟི་རིལ་ (sirii) a type of གཟི་ that is round.

གཟི་ལོག (siloò) cross-eyed; va.—ལྟ་ to look cross-eyed.

གཟི་ལོར་ (siloo) sm. གཟི་ལོག.

གཟིག (sii) leopard.

གཟིག་ཁྱི་ (siìgyi) dogs that are extremely fierce.

གཟིག་ཁྲ་ (siìdra) a design or pattern that is spotted like that of a leopard skin.

གཟིག་རྒམ་ (siìgam) snare /trap for catching leopards.

གཟིག་རྒྱུག (siìgyuù) a staff/ pole that is covered by leopard skin which is hung beside the doors of the Potala and Norbulinka palaces.

གཟིག་སྙིང་སྟག་མཁྲིས་བཟས་པ་ (sigñiŋ dāgdriì sɛɛ̀ba) a saying used to convey extreme boldness [Lit. ate the heart of the leopard and the gall bladder of the tiger].

གཟིག་ཐིག་མ་ (sii tīgmə) materials that are designed to look like a leopard skin.

གཟིག་གདན་ (siìdɛn) leopard skin rug.

གཟིག་ཤྭགས་ (siìbaà) leopard skin.

གཟིག་ཕྲུག (sigdruù) leopard cub.

གཟིག་དམར་ (siìmar) red leopard.

གཟིག་ཚང་ (sigdzaŋ) leopard's den.

གཟིག་ཚང་སྒོ་འགྲམ་གྱི་གླ་བའི་འཕར་འཚག (sigdzaŋ godramgi lāwɛ pāgdzaà) tempting fate [Lit. the musk deer jumping around at the door of the leopard's den].

གཟིག་རིས་ (sigriì) leopard's spots.

གཟིག་ཤུབས་ (sigshub) an arrow case that is covered with leopard skin.

གཟིག་སློག (siglɔ̀ɔ) dress lined with leopard skin fur.

གཟིགས་ (sii) 1. vi. to see (h.) ¶ ཁོང་གིས་ང་གཟིགས་སོང་ He saw me. 2. va. to look at ¶ ཁོང་གིས་ང་ལ་གཟིགས་ཀྱི་འདུག He is looking at me. 3. va. to buy (h.) ¶ ཁོང་གིས་དེབ་འདི་གཟིགས་སོང་ He bought this book.

གཟིགས་སྐོར་ (siìgɔɔ) h. of ལྟ་སྐོར་.

གཟིགས་བསྐོར་ (siìgɔɔ) sm. གཟིགས་སྐོར་.

གཟིགས་སྐྱོང་ (siìgyoŋ) 1. looking after, caring for (h.); va.—གནང་ ¶ དཔོན་པོ་རེས་གཡོག་པོ་ཚོར་གཟིགས་སྐྱོང་ཡག་པོ་གནང་གི་ཡོད་པ་རེད་ The lord looks after his servants well. 2. looking after in a negative sense, i.e., favoritism, partiality.

གཟིགས་སྐྱོང་གི་སྲིད་ཇུས་ (siìgyoŋgi sīìjùù) the policy of looking after/ caring for sb. well.

གཟིགས་སྐྱོང་དངུལ་ (siìgyoŋ ŋǜü) relief funds.

གཟིགས་སྐྱོང་དངུལ་བུན་ (siìgyoŋ ŋǜübün) a loan on favorable terms.

གཟིགས་བསྐྱངས་ (siìgyaŋ) sm. གཟིགས་སྐྱོང་.

གཟིགས་བསྐྱངས་ཆེན་པོ་ (siìgyaŋ cēmbo) h. of ལྟ་སྐྱོང་ཆེན་པོ་.

གཟིགས་བསྐྱངས་ཆེ་ཤོས་བྱ་ཡུལ་རྒྱལ་ཁབ་ (siìgyaŋ cēshö̀ö cəyüü gyɛɛ̀gəb) most favorable nation status.

གཟིགས་མཁྱེན་སྤྲིངས་ཡིག (siìgyen drīŋyiì) a government-to-government communique.

གཟིགས་རྒྱ་ཆེན་པོ་ (siìgya cēmbo) 1. well read, learned (person). 2. sb. who is experienced/ has been around.

གཟིགས་རྒྱང་ (siigyaŋ) h. of མིག་རྒྱང་.

གཟིགས་ངོ་ (siiŋo) view/ opinion (based on seeing sth.) ¶ཕོ་ཚོའི་གཟིགས་ངོར་མི་དེ་སྡུག་ཅག་ཅིག་ཏུ་མཐོང་པ་རེད་ That man looked bad in their opinion.

གཟིགས་མཆན་ (siijɛn) notes written on a text.

གཟིགས་རྟགས་ (siidaà) a sign or mark on document submitted for approval showing that one has read it; va.—སྒྲོན་; —རྒྱག.

གཟིགས་རྟོག (siidoò) h. of ལྟ་རྟོག.

གཟིགས་རྟེན་ (siiden) sth. that is sent along with a letter (e.g., a dried flower, scarf).

གཟིགས་སྟངས་ (siidaŋ) h. of ལྟ་སྟངས་.

གཟིགས་སྟེགས་ (siideg) bleachers, grandstand, review stand (h.).

གཟིགས་ཐོག་གནང་ (siidɔɔ nāŋ) sm.* གཟིགས་རྟོག་གནང་.

གཟིགས་མཐོང་ས་ (siidoŋ) 1. sm. གཟིགས་ལམ་. 2. esteem.

གཟིགས་དང་ (siidaà) Look!

གཟིགས་སྡུར་ (sigdur) h. of ལྟ་སྡུར་.

གཟིགས་སྣང་ (siinaŋ) h. of མཐོང་སྣང་.

གཟིགས་སྣང་གཟིགས་ཕྱོགས་ (siinaŋ siijɔɔ) h. of ལྟ་སྣང་མཐོང་ཕྱོགས་.

གཟིགས་པ་པོ་ (siibəbo) readers (of a book, journal, etc.).

གཟིགས་པ་ཆེན་པོ་ (siibə cēmbo) regarded highly by superiors.

གཟིགས་པ་གཡོ་རྟེན་ (siibə yōden) sm. གཟིགས་རྟེན་.

གཟིགས་དཔྱད་ (siijɛɛ̀) h. of བརྟག་དཔྱད་.

གཟིགས་ཕུད་ (siibüü) a preview performance giving samples of the full show; va.—འབུལ་ to give a preview performance; va.—བཞེས་ to attend the preview performance.

གཟིགས་ཕུལ་ཞུ་དག (siibüü shudaà) inspection or test done before superiors (e.g., troops on parade).

གཟིགས་ཕྱོགས་ (siijɔɔ) h. of མཐོང་ཕྱོགས་.

གཟིགས་བབ་ (siibəb) the way someone looks at events or things.

གཟིགས་བྱང་ (siijaŋ) 1. address. 2. title of a book.

གཟིགས་འབུལ་ (simbüü) 1. showing/ presenting/ demonstrating/ displaying sth. for inspection and the approval of superior(s); va.—ཞུ་. 2. a stamp used to indicate that a book has been paid for in Tibet.

གཟིགས་མོ་ (siimo) h. of ལྟད་མོ་.

གཟིགས་མོ་ཆེན་པོ་ (siimo cēmbo) 1. a good/ interesting show (h.). 2. the Tibetan opera and religious dance festival in Tashilhunpo.

གཟིགས་མོ་བ་ (siimowa) spectator, audience (h.).

གཟིགས་མོ་འབུལ་ (siimo büü) h. of ལྟད་མོ་སྟོན་.

གཟིགས་མོ་གཟིགས་ (siimo sii) h. of ལྟད་མོ་ལྟ་.

གཟིགས་མོའི་ལེའུ་ (siimü lewu) a skit or scene in a show.

གཟིགས་ཚུལ་ (siidzüü) h. of ལྟ་ཚུལ་.

གཟིགས་ཚོད་ (sigdzöö) h. of ཆ་ཚོད་.

གཟིགས་ཚོལ་ (sigdzöö) h. of ལྟ་ཚོལ་.

གཟིགས་འཚལ་ (siidzɛɛ) Please look ¶ངའི་ཞུ་ཡིག་འདི་ལ་གཟིགས་འཚལ་ Please look at my request.

གཟིགས་མཛད་ (siidzɛɛ̀) sm. གཟིགས་, 2.

གཟིགས་ཞིབ་ (siishib) h. of ལྟ་ཞིབ་.

གཟིགས་བཟོས་ (sigsüü) award, prize.

གཟིགས་བཟོས་སྐྱལ་ལྕག (sigsüü gǖüjaà) sm. གཟིགས་བཟོས་.

གཟིགས་བཟོས་ཉེས་འགེལ་ (sigsüü ñengee) awards/ prizes and punishments.

གཟིགས་བཟོས་རྟགས་མ་ (sigsüü dāŋma) award, medal.

གཟིགས་བཟོས་ཡིག་རིགས་ (sigsüü yigrii) letter of commendation/ award.

གཟིགས་བཟོས་གསོལ་རས་ (sigsüü sȫȫrɛɛ̀) gift/ prize accompanying an awards.

གཟིགས་ཡུལ་ (sigyüü) h. of ལྟ་ཡུལ་.

གཟིགས་རོགས་ (siiroò) h. of ལྟ་རོགས་.

གཟིགས་ལམ་ (siilam) shung. the field of vision of the Dalai Lama or a high official when watching sth. ¶གོང་ས་མཆོག་གི་གཟིགས་ལམ་དུ་རྟ་པ་ཚོས་རྟ་ཐོག་ནས་མེ་མདའ་བརྒྱབ་པ་རེད་ The riders shot guns while the Dalai Lama watched.

གཟིགས་ལུགས་ (siiluù) h. of ལྟ་ལུགས་.

གཟིགས་སུ་འབུལ་ (sigsu büü) sm. གཟིགས་འབུལ་ཞུ་.

གཟིང་: p. གཟིངས་; f. གཟིང་ (siŋ) vi. to be/ get tangled (for hair/ beard), to be/ get unkempt.

གཟིངས་ (siŋ) p. of གཟིངས་. 2. boat, ship.

གཟིང་གཟིང་ (siŋsiŋ) boisterous, disorderly, riotous; va.—བྱེད་.

གཟིངས་ཁ་ (siŋgə) port, dock.

གཟིམ་ (sim) f. of གཟིམས་.

གཟིམ་དཀར་ (simgar) h. of ཉིན་ཁང་.

གཟིམ་དཀྱིལ་ (simgyii) abbr. of གཟིམ་ཆུང་དཀྱིལ་.

གཟིམ་རྐྱོང་ (simgyoŋ) h. of རྐྱང་བསྡད་.

གཟིམ་ཁང་ (simgaŋ) 1. home (h.). 2. bedroom (h.).

གཟིམ་ཁང་སྟེང་ (simgaŋ dēŋ) the name of an extinct Labrang in Loseling College in Drepung Monastery (in the Dalai Lama's incarnation line).

གཟིམ་ཁང་འོག (simgaŋ wɔɔ̀) the name of the Dalai Lama's Labrang in Loseling College in Drepung Monastery.

གཟིམ་ཁྲི་ (simgyi) h. of ཁྲི་.

གཟིམ་ཁྲི་ (simdri) h. of ཉལ་ཁྲི་.

གཟིམ་གུར་ (simgur) h. of གུར་.

གཟིམ་འགག (siŋgaà) shung. 1. guard, bodyguard. 2. the lay officials who serve as guards to high officials (actually they serve more like attendants).

གཟིམ་འགག་ཁྲི་པ་ (siŋgaà tribə) shung. the senior གཟིམ་འགག.

གཟིམ་སྒམ་ (simgam) shung. boxes in which the Dalai Lama's things for daily use are put.

གཟིམ་སྒོ་ (simgo) h. of སྒོ་.

གཟིམ་སྒྲོམ་ (simdrom) h. of ཉལ་སྒྲོམ་.

གཟིམ་ཆང་ (simjaŋ) h. of ཉལ་ཆང་.

གཟིམ་ཆས་ (simjɛɛ̀) h. of ཉལ་ཆས་.

གཟིམ་ཆུང་ (simjuŋ) 1. living room (h.). 2. living quarters (h.).

གཟིམ་ཆུང་དཀྱིལ་ (simjuŋ gyii) h. of དབུས་ཁང་.

གཟིམ་ཆུང་འཁྲུགས་ (simjuŋ trüù) vi. to fight/ quarrel (between spouses/ family members).

གཟིམ་ཆུང་འགག (simjuŋ gaà) shung. the secretariat office of the regent.

གཟིམ་ཆུང་ང་ (simjuŋŋə) sm. གཟིམ་ཆུང་བ་.

གཟིམ་ཆུང་ངའི་གོ་རྩེད་ (simjuŋŋɛ kodzeè) shung. military/ martial arts demonstration at Monlam (in costumes of ancient soldiers).

གཟིམ་ཆུང་མཇལ་ཁ་ (simjuŋ jɛɛga) private audience (h.).

གཟིམ་ཆུང་མདོ་ཕྲུག (simjuŋ dobuù) inner and outer connecting rooms.

གཟིམ་ཆུང་བ་ (simjuŋwə) bodyguard.

གཟིམ་འཇོ་ (simjo) cloth/ leather case or bag in which bedding is packed when traveling (h.).

གཟིམ་འཇམ་གནང་དགོས་ (simjam nāŋgɔɔ) good night, sleep tight.

གཟིམ་འཇམ་བདེ་འཐོད་ (simjam dendröö) sm. གཟིམས་འཇམ་གནང་དགོས་.

གཟིམ་ཏོག (simdoò) h. of ཅས་ཏོག.

གཟིམ་སྟན་ (simdɛn) h. of ཉལ་སྟན་.

གཟིམ་སྟེང་ (simdeŋ) abbr. of གཟིམ་ཁང་སྟེང་.

གཟིམ་ཐུལ་ (simdüü) h. of ཐུལ་པ་.

གཟིམ་དུང་གཏོང་ (simduŋ dōŋ) h. of ཉལ་དུང་གཏོང་.

གཟིམ་དོས་ (simdöö) shung. loads in which the Dalai Lama's things for daily use are packed.

གཟིམ་དྲེལ་ (simdree) shung. Dalai Lama's mules.

གཟིམ་དྲེལ་ཞལ་ངོ་ (simdree shɛɛŋo) shung. the person in charge of the Dalai Lama's mules.

གཟིམ་གདན་ (simdɛn) h. of ཉལ་གདན་.

གཟིམ་བདེ་གཏོང་ (simda dōŋ) h. of ཉལ་བདེ་གཏོང་.

གཟིམ་གནང་ (simnaŋ) h. of ཉལ་.

གཟིམ་མནལ་ (simnɛɛ) h. of གཉིད་.

གཟིམ་དཔོན་ (simbön) h. of གཡོག་པོ་.

གཟིམ་དཔོན་མཁན་པོ་ (simbön kɛ̄mbo) shung. one of the chief personal attendants of the Dalai Lama.

གཟིམ་སྤོས་ (simböö) h. of སྤོས་.

གཟིམ་སྤྱིལ་ (simjii) sm. སྤྱིལ་བུ་.

གཟིམ་སྤྱོད་ (simjöö) h. of གསང་སྤྱོད་.

གཟིམ་སྤྲོ་པོ་ (sim drōbo) h. of གཉིད་སྐྱིད་པོ་.

གཟིམ་འཕོག (simbɔɔ̀) shung. h. of འཕོག.

གཟིམ་སྦུག (simbuù) h. of ཉལ་ཁང་.

གཟིམ་མལ་ (simmɛɛ) h. of ཉལ་ས་.

གཟིམ་མལ་བ་ (simmɛɛwa) shung. servants who serve in the bedroom.

གཟིམ་མལ་བརྩིགས་ཁབ་ (simmɛɛ dzīggəb) arc. person in charge of the bedding of the early kings of Tibet.

གཟིམ་དམག (simmaà) sm. གཟིམ་ཆུང་བ་.

གཟིམ་བཞུ་ (simsu) h. of བཞུ་མར་

གཟིམ་གཟན་ (simsɛn) h. of ཉལ་ཟན་.

གཟིམ་གཡོག (simyɔɔ̀) house servant.

གཟིམ་ཡོལ་ (simyüü) h. of སྒོ་ཡོལ་.

གཟིམ་ཤག (simshaà) 1. h. of ཁང་པ་. 2. an aristocratic family ༖ གཟིམ་ཤག་རྡོ་རིང The aristocratic family Doring.

གཟིམ་ས་ (simsə) h. of ཉལ་ས་.

གཟིམ་སར་ལུས་ (siimsaa lüü) h. of ཉལ་སར་ལུས་.

གཟིམས་: p. **གཟིམས་**; f. **གཟིམ་** (sim) va. to sleep, to go to bed (h.).

གཟིམས་ (sim) 1. p. of གཟིམ་. 2. h. of ཉལ་.

གཟིམས་ཀྱོང་ (simgyoŋ) sm. གཟིམ་ཀྱོང་.

གཟིམས་ཁེབས་ (simgeb) h. of ཉལ་ཆས་ཁེབས་.

གཟིམས་སྒོ་མཚན་འབྱར་མ་ (simgo tsɛ̄njarma) h. of སྒོ་མིང་འབྱར་མ་.

གཟིམས་ཕྲུག (simdruù) h. of བཙུགས་ཕྲུག.

གཟིམས་འཕོག (simbɔɔ̀) 1. h. of འཕོག. 2. the bedding of the Dalai Lama.

གཟིམས་མལ་ (simmɛɛ) h. of ཉལ་ས་.

གཟིམས་ཐུལ་ (simdüü) h. of ཀླུ་གམ་.

གཟིམས་ལམ་ (simlam) h. of རྨི་ལམ་.

གཟིམས་ཤག (simshaà) sm. གཟིམ་ཤག.

གཟིམས་ས་ (simsə) sm. གཟིམ་ས་.

གཟིམས་མལ་བ་ (simmɛɛwa) bedroom servants of ancient Tibetan kings.

གཟིར་ (sir) 1. vi. to be tormented, to suffer, to be afflicted ༖ ཚ་བས་གཟིར་ནས་ Suffering from heat. 2. va. to take aim ༖ འབེན་ལ་གཟིར་ནས་མེ་མདའ་བརྒྱབ་པ་རེད་ (He) took aim at the target and shot.

གཟིར་བལྟས་ (sirdɛɛ̀) va. to stare (in anger).

གཟིར་པོ་ (sirbu) accurate (in shooting) ༖ཁོ་མེ་མདའ་གཟིར་པོ་འདུག He is an accurate shot.

གཟིལ་ (sii) vi. to break into pieces.

གཟུ་ (su) abbr. of གཟུ་བོ་.

གཟུ་སྒོ་ (sugo) mediator's home.

གཟུ་གཅོད་ (su jöö) va. to settle sth. fairly/ unbiased, to mediate/ arbitrate.

གཟུ་དོན་ (sudön) shung. outcome of a mediation, option for mediation ༖ སྒྲོད་ལ་གཉིས་པོས་གཟུ་དོན་གསུམ་པོ་གང་རུང་འདོད་འདེམས་བྱ་དགོས་ The two parties choose from the three options that the mediator offered.

གཟུ་གནས་དྲང་འབྲེལ་ (sunɛɛ̀ traŋdree) unbiased/ not taking sides; va.—བྱེད་.

གཟུ་པ་ (subə) 1. mediator, arbitrator ༖ ང་ཚོའི་གྲོད་གཞིར་གཟུ་པས་བར་འདུམ་བཏང་ The mediator has mediated our case. 2. an honest person. 3. a witness.

གཟུ་དཔང་ (subaŋ) witness.

གཟུ་འཕེན་ (su pēn) va. to mediate.

གཟུ་བོ་ (suwo) sm. གཟུ་པ་.

གཟུ་བློ་ (sulo) honest, trustworthy, straightforward.

གཟུ་བློན་ (sulön) an honest minister.

གཟུ་བློས་ཞིབ་བརྟག (sulöö shibdaà) shung. investigating thoroughly with an unbiased mind.

གཟུ་མས་བཀོད་ (sumɛɛ̀ gö̃ö) va. to make inappropriate decisions at a lower level rather than pass the issue on to a higher level ༖ ཆེས་མཐོའི་ཁྲིམས་ཁང་ནས་ཐག་གཅོད་བྱ་དགོས་པའི་གྲོད་གཞི་དེ་འབྲིང་རིམ་ཁྲིམས་ཁང་ནས་གཟུ་མས་བཀོད་ཀྱིས་ཐག་གཅོད་བྱས་འདུག That case which should have been decided by the supreme court, was decided inappropriately by the middle court.

གཟུ་ལུམ་ (sulum) 1. concocted, false ༖ འདི་ངས་གཟུ་ལུམ་དུ་བཤད་པ་ཞིག་མ་ཡིན་པར་ཚན་རིག་གི་གཞི་འཛིན་ས་ཡོད་པ་ཞིག་ཡིན་ It is not sth. that I concocted, there is scientific proof. 2. rash, impetuous. 3. pretentious.

གཟུ་ལུམ་ཅན་ (sulumjɛn) 1. a person who concocts things. 2. pretentious. 3. rash, impetuous.

གཟུ་བཤད་ (sushɛɛ̀) mediation, conciliation, arbitration.

གཟུག (suù) quarter of a carcass of meat.

གཟུགས་ (suù) form, figure, body. 2. f. of འཛུགས་.

གཟུགས་ཀྱི་གླུད་ (suùgi lüü) an effigy made of a sick person and left on the roadside in the belief that the sickness will be carried by the effigy.

གཟུགས་ཀྱི་ཆུང་མཐའ་ (suùgi cūŋda) atoms.

གཟུགས་ཀྱི་ཉི་མ་ (suùgi ñimə) name of a famous Tibetan opera.

གཟུགས་དཀྱུས་ (suggyüü) length of the body (of horses, etc.).

གཟུགས་བཀོད་ (suùgöö) abbr. of གཟུགས་སུ་བཀོད་.

གཟུགས་སྐམ་སྟོབས་ཉམས་ (suùgam dōbñam) physically thin and weak.

གཟུགས་སྐུ་ (suùgu) h. of གཟུགས་པོ་.

གཟུགས་སྐུ་ཆོས་དབྱིངས་སུ་འཐིམས་པ་ (suggu cõõyiŋsu tīmbə) shung. vi. to die (usu. used for lamas).

གཟུགས་སྐུའི་བཀོད་པ་ཆོས་དབྱིངས་སུ་བསྡུས་ (suggü gõõba cõõyiŋsu düü) shung. vi. to die (usu. used for lamas).

གཟུགས་སྐུའི་བཀོད་པ་བསྡུས་ (suggü gõõba düü) shung. sm. དགོངས་པ་ཆོས་དབྱིངས་སུ་བསྡུས་.

གཟུགས་ཁམས་ (suùgam) 1. the realm. of form. 2. the body ༖ གཟུགས་ཁམས་ཀྱི་འཕྱོད་བསྟེན་ Physical hygiene.

གཟུགས་ཁམས་ཆགས་ཚུལ་གྱི་རིག་པ་ (suùgam cāgdzüügi rigbə) physiology.

གཟུགས་ཁམས་གཤགས་ལས་ (suùgam shāglɛɛ̀) anatomy.

གཟུགས་ངན་ (sugŋɛn) ugly.

གཟུགས་ཅན་ (sugjɛn) having physical body, having solid form.

གཟུགས་ཅན་གྱི་དངོས་པོ་ (sugjɛngi ŋõõbo) all things that are tangible (have physical bodies).

གཟུགས་བཅོས་ (sug jöö) va. 1. to make icons/ statues. 2. false image.

གཟུགས་ཆེན་པོ་ (sug cēmbo) tall.

གཟུགས་མཆོག (sugjɔɔ̀) 1. good looking, handsome. 2. name of a Buddha.

གཟུགས་རྗེས་གྲིབ་འབྲང་ (sugjeè tribdraŋ) inseparable [Lit. shadow follows the body].

གཟུགས་ལྗིད་ (sugjiì) body weight ༖ གཟུགས་ལྗིད་ཡང་བའི་རིམ་པ་ Lightweight (in sports events like boxing).

གཟུགས་ལྗིད་ཡང་ཤོས་ཀྱི་རིམ་པ་ (sugjiì yaŋshöögi rimbə) flyweight (in sports events like boxing).

གཟུགས་མཉམ་ (sugñam) 1. similar looking, alike in body. 2. of the same body size/ height.

གཟུགས་བརྙན་ (sugñɛn) 1. an image; vi.—འཆར་ to appear (images); va.—སྟོན་ to show/ make/ manifest an image. 2. dummy, effigy; va.—བཟོ་ to make an effigy/ dummy. 3. movie, film ༖ རྒྱུ་རྩལ་གཟུགས་བརྙན་ Art film.

གཟུགས་བརྙན་བཀྲ་བ་ (sugñɛn drāwa) an attractive image.

གཟུགས་བརྙན་འཆར་འཕྲུལ་ (sugñɛn cāndrüü) movie projector.

གཟུགས་སྟོབས་ (sugdob) physical strength, body size.

གཟུགས་སྟོབས་ཆེན་པོ་ (sugdob cēmbo) tall and well built/ sturdy/ robust.

གཟུགས་ཐང་ (sugdaŋ) healthy.

གཟུགས་ཐང་ཤུགས་ཆེ་ (sugdaŋ shūgje) healthy and

strong.

གཟུགས་ཐུང་ (sugduŋ) short.

གཟུགས་མཐོང་གློག་བརྙན་ (sugdoŋ lɔ̄ɔñɛn) sm. གཟུགས་མཐོང་གློག་འཕྲིན་.

གཟུགས་མཐོང་གློག་འཕྲིན་ (sugdoŋ lɔ̄ndrin) sm. གཟུགས་མཐོང་རླུང་འཕྲིན་.

གཟུགས་མཐོང་གློག་འོད་ཡོ་བྱད་ (sugdoŋ lɔ̄ɔwöö yobjɛɛ̀) fluoroscope.

གཟུགས་མཐོང་རླུང་འཕྲིན་ (sugdoŋ lūŋdrin) television.

གཟུགས་དྭངས་པོ་ (sug daŋbo) well, healthy.

གཟུགས་འདས་རིག་པ་ (suŋdɛɛ̀ rigbə) metaphysics.

གཟུགས་སྡུག་པ་ (sug dugbo) beautiful attractive.

གཟུགས་ནུས་ཚད་བརྒལ་ (sugnüü tsɛɛ̀gɛɛ) hyperfunction.

གཟུགས་སྣང་ (sugnaŋ) form, shape, image.

གཟུགས་སྣང་དུ་འགྱུར་ (sugnaŋdu gyur) vi. to change form/ shape ¶ བུ་དེ་བུ་མོ་ཞིག་གི་གཟུགས་སྣང་དུ་འགྱུར་བ་མཐོང་ (I) saw that boy change into a girl's body.

གཟུགས་པོ་ (sugbu) body ¶ གཟུགས་པོ་སྙོ་པོ་ Weak body (poor health).

གཟུགས་པོ་འཁོར་ (sugbu kɔ̄ɔ) vi. to become pregnant.

གཟུགས་པོ་གཅོང་པོ་ (sugbu jōŋbo) weak in body, poor in health.

གཟུགས་པོ་ཆེན་པོ་ (sugbu cēmbo) tall.

གཟུགས་པོ་གཏེ་པོ་ (sugbu dēbo) short.

གཟུགས་པོ་ཐང་པོ་ (sugbu tāŋbo) healthy, well.

གཟུགས་པོ་མཐོ་པོ་ (sugbu tōbo) pregnancy in its latter stage.

གཟུགས་པོ་བདེ་པོ་ (sugbu debo) sm. གཟུགས་པོ་ཐང་པོ་.

གཟུགས་པོ་ཕྲ་ལྡེམ་ལྡེམ་ (sugbu trā demdem) flexible/ slender body (of women).

གཟུགས་པོ་ཞན་པོ་ (sugbu shɛmbo) poor health, weak body.

གཟུགས་པོ་ཡག་པོ་ (sugbu yāgbo) sm. གཟུགས་པོ་ཐང་པོ་.

གཟུགས་པོ་ཡོད་པ་ (sugbu yööba) pregnant.

གཟུགས་པོ་རིང་པོ་ (sugbu riŋbu) tall.

གཟུགས་པོ་ཤོར་ (sugbu shɔ̄ɔ) vi. to have a miscarriage.

གཟུགས་པོ་གསོ་ (sugbu sō) vi. to recuperate.

གཟུགས་པོ་གསེག་ལོག (sugbu sēglɔɔ̀) facing/ lying sideways.

གཟུགས་པོ་ཧྲིལ་པོ་ (sugbu hrīibu) whole body.

གཟུགས་པོའི་གདོས་ཚད་ (sugbü döödzɛɛ̀) height (body).

གཟུགས་པོའི་དྲོད་ཚད་ (sugbü trööd zɛɛ̀) body temperature.

གཟུགས་པོར་ཆུ་གསོག (sugbor cūsɔɔ̀) edema.

གཟུགས་དཔངས་ (sugbaŋ) height of the body.

གཟུགས་ཕུང་ (sugbuŋ) 1. human corpse. 2. human body.

གཟུགས་ཕྲ་བ་ (sug trāwə) atom.

གཟུགས་ཕྲ་མོ་ (sug trāmo) 1. skinny/ lean body. 2. things that are very small. 3. the life force during the བར་དོ་ state.

གཟུགས་བབ་ (sugbəb) health, physical status.

གཟུགས་བྱད་ (sugjɛɛ̀) physique, stature, bodily form/ shape/ figure/ build.

གཟུགས་དབྱིབས་ (sugyib) body form/ figure/ shape.

གཟུགས་དབྱིབས་ཐོན་པ་ (sugyib tōmba) the body form/ figure/ shape can be seen too clearly because the clothing is too tight.

གཟུགས་མི་སྡུག་པ་ (sug midugbə) ugly.

གཟུགས་མེད་ (sugmeè) immaterial, without substance/ body, formless.

གཟུགས་མེད་ཁམས་ (sugmeè kām) the realm of formlessness.

གཟུགས་མེད་གྲིབ་འཇལ་ (sugmeè tribjɛɛ) levying taxes when there is no basis [Lit. measuring the shadow when there is no body].

གཟུགས་མེད་གྲིབ་བཟོ་ (sugmeè tribso) fabricating a case or charge against somebody, trumping up. [Lit. making a shadow when there is no body].

གཟུགས་མེད་འཆིང་ཐག (sugmeè ciŋdaà) invisible bonds.

གཟུགས་མེད་སྟོང་སྒྲུབ་ (sugmeè dōŋdrub) shung. having to pay tax on sth. that does not exist.

གཟུགས་མོ་ (sugmu) sm. གཟི་མོ་.

གཟུགས་མོ་གྱི་ཐུར་ (sugmu cidur) sm. གཟི་མོ་.

གཟུགས་སྨད་ཞ་ཁུམ་ (sugmɛɛ̀ shəgum) paraplegia; vi.—ཆགས་ to become paraplegic.

གཟུགས་ཚད་ (sugdzɛɛ̀) height of a person.

གཟུགས་མཚུངས་ (sugdzuŋ) sm. གཟུགས་མཉམ་.

གཟུགས་འཛིན་ (suŋdzin) beholding with the eyes, seeing firsthand.

གཟུགས་འཛིན་དྲ་སྐྱི་ (suŋdzin trəgyi) retina.

གཟུགས་མཛེས་ (sugdzeè) beautiful/ attractive (usu. of females).

གཟུགས་མཛེས་བློ་གསལ (sugdzeè lōsɛɛ) beautiful/ attractive and intelligent.

གཟུགས་གཞི་ (sugshi) physical constitution, physique, physical well-being; vi.—འཁྱོངས་ to have one's physical condition enable one to do sth. ¶ གཟུགས་གཞི་བདེ་ཐང་ Good health. ¶ ལས་ཀ་འདི་ངའི་གཟུགས་གཞི་འཁྱོངས་པ་མི་འདུག I am physically unable to do this work.

གཟུགས་བཟང་ (sugsaŋ) 1. good physical shape. 2. tall person.

གཟུགས་རགས་པ་ (sugragba) solid or tangible things.

གཟུགས་རིང་ (sugriŋ) sm. གཟུགས་ཆེན་པོ་.

གཟུགས་རིང་ཐུང་ (sug riŋduŋ) body height.

གཟུགས་ལངས་གྲིབ་མཐོན་ (suglaŋ tribdön) get immediate/ instant results [Lit. stand up and see the shadow].

གཟུགས་གཤིས་ (sugshii) degree of health.

གཟུགས་སུ་བཀོད་ (sugsu gōō) va. to be liken to ¶ ཁོང་གི་ཤེས་ཡོན་དེ་རྒྱ་མཚོའི་གཟུགས་སུ་བཀོད་པ་རེད་ His knowledge is likened to be like an ocean (vast).

གཟུགས་སུ་དོད་ (sugsu töö) vi. to take form/ shape.

གཟུང་ (suŋ) 1. f. of འཛིན་. 2. sm. གཟུངས་.

གཟུང་སྔགས་ (suŋŋaà) mantra, mantric prayer; va.—འདོན་.

གཟུང་བ་ཡུལ་ (suŋwa yüü) objects that can be perceived/ visualized.

གཟུང་བྱའི་ཡུལ་ (suŋjɛ yüü) sm. གཟུང་བ་ཡུལ་.

གཟུང་མ་ (suŋma) sm. ཆུང་མ་.

གཟུང་འཛིན་ (suŋdzin) the object and the object perceiver.

གཟུང་ཡུལ་ (suŋyüü) sm. གཟུང་བ་ཡུལ་.

གཟུངས་ (suŋ) 1. mantras. 2. items placed inside statues.

གཟུངས་ཁེབས་ (suŋgeb) silk or satin that is used to wrap the sacred mantras that are put inside an icon or statue.

གཟུངས་སྔགས་ (suŋŋaà) mantra.

གཟུངས་གཞུག (suŋshuù) rolls of prayers and mantras that are put inside of statues; va.—འབུལ་ to insert a roll of prayers and mantras inside a statue. 2. va. to instill/ influence sb. in a negative way.

གཟུངས་གཟེར་ (suŋser) a hook used to close doors.

གཟུངས་རིང་ (suŋriŋ) long mantra.

གཟུངས་སུ་བཟུང་ (suŋsu suŋ) va. to remember, to bear in mind, to not forget.

གཟུངས་སུ་རུང་བ་ (suŋsu ruŋwə) objects that can be seen, touched, smelled, heard and tasted.

གཟུད་ (süü) f. of འཛུད་.

གཟུར་ (sur) f. of འཛུར་.

གཟུར་གནས་ (surnɛɛ̀) neutral, impartial ¶ གཟུར་གནས་ཡུལ་ཁག Neutral countries.

གཟུར་གནས་དྲང་འབྲེལ་ (surnɛɛ̀ traŋdree) shung. unbiased, fair.

གཟུར་རེས་ (surreè) 1. mutually stepping aside so the other can pass. 2. letting sb. have their own way.

གཟུར་ཤོལ་ (surshöö) stepping or moving aside, letting sb. have their own way; va.—བྱེད་.

གཟུར་བཤོལ་ (surshöö) sm. གཟུར་ཤོལ་.

གཟུལ་ (sɛɛ) f. of འཛུལ་.

གཟི་ཆུང་ (sejuŋ) blunt, not pointed.

གཟི་དབྱིབས་ (seyib) thorn shaped, barbed-wire

shaped.

གཟི་མ་འཕང་ཆེན་ (sema pāŋjen) water chestnut.

གཟི་མ་ར་མགོ་ (sema raŋgo) thorn, barbed wire.

གཟི་མ་ར་མགོའི་དབྱིབས་ (sēma raŋgö yīb) sm. གཟི་དབྱིབས་.

གཟི་མོ་ (semo) porcupine.

གཟེགས་མ་ (segma) a drop ༐ ཆུའི་གཟེགས་མ་ Drop of water.

གཟེངས་ (seŋ) height, elevation ༐ གཟེངས་མཐོ་བ་ Lofty. 2. va. to raise/ lift.

གཟེངས་རྟགས་ (seŋdaà) award, medal.

གཟེངས་བསྟོད་ (seŋdöö) 1. praise, compliment; va.—བྱེད་; —འབུལ་ to praise, to compliment. 2. medal, award.

གཟེངས་བསྟོད་ཀྱི་མཚན་རྟགས་ (seŋdöögi tsɛndaà) sm. གཟེངས་རྟགས་.

གཟེངས་བསྟོད་པང་ལེབ་ (seŋdöö pāŋleb) a billboard that lists pictures and stories of the praiseworthy.

གཟེངས་བསྟོད་ལག་ཁྱེར་ (seŋdöö laggyee) certificate of merit, testimonial.

གཟེངས་ཐོན་ (seŋdön) 1. praiseworthy, meritorious, outstanding ༐ ཁོང་ལ་གཞུང་གི་ལས་དོན་གཟེངས་ཐོན་བྱུང་བའི་བྱ་དགའ་ཐོབ་པ་རེད་ He was awarded a prize for his outstanding work for the government. 2. lofty, exhaulted.

གཟེངས་མཐོ་པོ་ (seŋ tōbo) lofty, exhaulted.

གཟེངས་མཐོན་པོ་ (seŋ tōnbo) sm. གཟེངས་མཐོ་.

གཟེངས་པོ་ (seŋbo) 1. high in elevation, tall. 2. meritorious, outstanding in achievement.

གཟེངས་ཞྭ་ (seŋsha) a tall/ long hat.

གཟེངས་གཟེངས་ (seŋseŋ) raising (one's) eyebrows.

གཟེངས་སུ་བསྟོད་ (seŋsu dōö) shung. sm. གཟེངས་བསྟོད་.

གཟེངས་སུ་ཐོན་ (seŋsu tōn) sm. གཟེངས་ཐོན་.

གཟེངས་སུ་མཐོ་བའི་རྟགས་ (seŋsu tōn) sm. གཟེངས་རྟགས་.

གཟེད་ (seè) 1. f. of འཛེད་. 2. va. to hold sth. 3. vi. to receive (a beating/ scolding).

གཟེན་ (sen) ch. fried dough.

གཟེབ་ (seb) 1. basket. 2. tent.

གཟེབ་ཀྱི་སྒྲོག་མ་ (sebgi drōòma) a woven bamboo container/ basket.

གཟེབ་སྣོད་ (sebnöö) sm. གཟེབ་ཀྱི་སྒྲོག་མ་.

གཟེབ་མ་ (sebma) 1. sm. གཟེབ་སྣོད་. 2. bamboo bird cage.

གཟེམ་ (sem) f. of འཛེམ་.

གཟེར་ (ser) 1. nail, rivet; va.—རྒྱག to nail or rivet sth. 2. va. to wear (a sword or knife). 3. acute/ sharp pain; vi.—རྒྱག to have/ get sharp pain; vi.—འཇགས་ to have sharp pain subside. 4. a tap/ cleat (on the sole of a shoe).

གཟེར་དཀར་ (seegar) nail.

གཟེར་དཀར་རྟ་མགོ་ (seegar dāŋgo) a type of nail that has a hooked head.

གཟེར་ཁ་ (seega) sharp/ acute pain; vi.—རྒྱག to get/ have sharp/ acute pain.

གཟེར་མགོ་ (seŋgo) abbr. of གཟེར་དཀར་རྟ་མགོ.

གཟེར་རྒྱག་བཟོ་པ་ (sergyaà soba) riveter.

གཟེར་རྒྱན་ (sergyɛn) nail decoration.

གཟེར་འཇགས་སྨན་ཁབ་ (senjaà mɛ̄ngəb) injection to relieve pain.

གཟེར་འཇགས་སྨན་ (senjaà mɛ̄n) pain relief medicine.

གཟེར་འཇགས་སྨན་ལེབ་ (senjaà mɛ̄nleb) pain relief tablet.

གཟེར་འཇོམས་སྨན་ (senjaà mɛ̄n) sm. གཟེར་འཇགས་སྨན་.

གཟེར་ཏེན་ (serden) washer, nut.

གཟེར་ཐུང་ (serduŋ) 1. short but acute pain. 2. a short nail.

གཟེར་མཐུད་ (serdüü) riveting, rivet joints; va.—རྒྱག.

གཟེར་གདན་ (serdɛn) washer.

གཟེར་འདེབས་ (sēr deb) 1. va. to nail. 2. vi. to have acute pain.

གཟེར་སྡོམ་ (serdom) putting/ fastening together by nailing; va.—རྒྱག.

གཟེར་ནད་ (sernɛɛ̀) illness characterized by acute pain.

གཟེར་མིག (sermiì) 1. place where the pain is located. 2. the hole where the nail has to go.

གཟེར་དམིགས་ (sermiì) sm. གཟེར་མིག.

གཟེར་མོ་ (sermo) sm. གཟེ་མོ་.

གཟེར་རྩེ་གཉིས་མ་ (sērdze ñīimə) cotter pin, split pin.

གཟེར་ཚེམ་ (sērdzem) a type of stitch.

གཟེར་ཟུག (sērsug) pain; vi.—རྒྱག; —ལངས་ to get/ have pain.

གཟོ་ (so) va. to remember kindness, to repay/ return kindness.

གཟོང་ (soŋ) chisel; va.—རྒྱག to chisel.

གཟོང་ཁ་ (soŋga) the point of a chisel.

གཟོང་ཁ་གཅིག་སྒྲིལ་ (soŋga jīgdrii) working in unity/ cooperation; va.—བྱེད་ ༐ ཚང་མ་གཟོང་ཁ་གཅིག་སྒྲིལ་གྱིས་དགྲ་བོ་ལས་རྒྱལ་བ་བྱ་དགོས་ All must work in unity and defeat our enemy.

གཟོང་ཆག (soŋjaà) a type of carpenter's chisel.

གཟོང་བུ་ (soŋbu) sm. གཟོང་.

གཟོང་རིལ་ (soŋrii) a round pointed chisel for making holes in metal.

གཟོད་མ་ (söòma) sm. གདོད་མ་.

གཟོན་ (sön) imp. of གཟན་.

གཟོབ་: p. གཟབས་; f. གཟབ་; imp. གཟོབས་ (sob) va. to do/ act with care ༐ ལས་ཀ་འདི་གལ་ཆེན་པོ་ཡིན་པས་གཟབ་དགོས་ This work is very important so you should be careful.

གཟོབ་པོ་ (sobbo) carefully; va.—བྱེད་.

བཟང་ (saŋ) abbr. of བཟང་པོ་.

བཟང་ཁྱི་ (saŋgyi) a good watch dog.

བཟང་ཁྲག (saŋdraà) the kind of blood according to Tibetan medicine that is considered good blood.

བཟང་ཁྲག་ བླུག (saŋdraà lūù) va. to have a blood transfusion.

བཟང་གོམས་ (saŋgom) good habits.

བཟང་གོས་ (saŋgöö) good quality clothes.

བཟང་གྲས་ (saŋdrɛɛ̀) good kind, good rank.

བཟང་དགུ་ (saŋgu) everything that is good, all good things.

བཟང་འགྲོ་ (saŋdro) sm. བདེ་འགྲོ་.

བཟང་མགུ་ (saŋgu) sm. བཟང་དགུ་.

བཟང་བསྒྱུར་ (saŋgyur) reforming; va.—བྱེད་.

བཟང་ངན་ (saŋŋɛn) good or bad, how good how bad, quality ༐ གནས་སྟངས་བཟང་ངན་མ་ཤེས་པར་ Not knowing how good or bad the situation is. ༐ བཟང་ངན་ག་རེ་བྱུང་ན་ཡང་ Whatever happens good or bad.

བཟང་ངན་མཉམ་འདུས་ (saŋŋɛn ñamdüü) the good and the bad intermingled.

བཟང་ངན་མཉམ་གནས་ (saŋŋɛn ñamnɛɛ̀) good and bad together, wise and foolish joined.

བཟང་བཅའ་ (saŋ jā) va. to help well/ kindly.

བཟང་བརྗོད་ (sanjöö) sm. ཐུགས་བརྗོད་.

བཟང་ཉམས་ (saŋñam) a good or auspicious sign/ omen.

བཟང་ཉམས་ཁ་པོ་ (sāŋñam kābo) giving just the appearance of being generous/ honest/ kind.

བཟང་ལྟས་ (saŋdɛɛ̀) sm. བཟང་ཉམས་.

བཟང་བསྟོད་ངན་སྨད་ (saŋdöö ŋɛnmɛɛ̀) praising the good and denigrating the bad.

བཟང་ཐག་ངན་ཐག་ཆོད་ (saŋdaà ŋɛndaà cōö) deciding a result whether it. is good or bad ༐ ང་གཉིས་ཀྱི་གནད་དོན་འདི་ད་རེས་བཟང་ཐག་ངན་ཐག་ཆོད་པ་དགོས་ We two must settle our problem whether the result is good or bad.

བཟང་ཐལ་ཤོར་ (saŋdɛɛ shɔ̄ɔ) vi. to be/ get carried away in one's generosity.

བཟང་དྲུག (saŋdruù) abbr. of བཟང་པོ་དྲུག.

བཟང་བདམས་ (saŋdam) choosing/ selecting the best ༐ བཟང་བདམས་བཀོལ་སྤྱོད་ Selecting the best and putting it to use.

བཟང་འདེམས་ (saŋdem) sm. བཟང་བདམས་.

བཟང་པོ་ (saŋbo) 1. good, fine ༐ དམིགས་ཡུལ་བཟང་པོ་

A good goal. 2. kind, sincere, well-meaning ¶ སེམས་པ་བཟང་པོའི་བསླབ་བྱ་ Kind advice. 3. a male name. 4. one of the sixteen arhats.

བཟང་པོ་བཙུ་འཛོམས་ (sanbo jūndzom) an auspicious day after the holiday of ངན་པ་དགུ་འཛོམས་ on which parties are given.

བཟང་པོ་བློས་འཁེལ་ (sanbo lōōgee) trusting sb. without any doubts/ reservations.

བཟང་པོ་མ་ (sanboma) person who is kind/ generous/ honest.

བཟང་པོ་ལང་ཤོར་ (sanbo lanshɔɔ) spoiled (behaviourally); vi.—ཆགས་ to get spoiled.

བཟང་པོ་གསུམ་ལྡན་གྱི་སློབ་ཕྲུག (sanbo sūmdengi lōbdruù) the three good students: an honorific title given to students who are good in the three areas of physical health, academic studies and work.

བཟང་པོའི་ཤོག་ལ་ཇ་ཚང་ ངན་པའི་ཤོག་ལ་རྒྱུག་དུང་ (sanbö shɔ̄ɔla cajan ŋembɛ shɔ̄ɔla gyugduŋ) one benefits by associating with good people and is harmed by associating with bad company [Lit. getting tea and ཚང་ with good (people), getting beaten with bad (people)].

བཟང་པོའི་ཟླ་བ་ (sanbö dawa) the 2nd month of the Tibetan calendar.

བཟང་པོར་བཟང་མ་བསྔས་ན་ བཟང་པོ་ཁོ་ཆད་ ངན་པར་ངན་མ་བསྔས་ན་ ངན་པ་ངོར་ལྡང་ (sanbor sān mameɛ̀na sanbo kōjɛɛ̀ ŋambar ŋɛn mameɛ̀na ŋemba ŋɔrdan) if you do not praise good people they will be discouraged; if you do not criticize evil people they will be proud/ arrogant.

བཟང་པོར་བཟང་ལན་ (sanbor sānlɛn) rewarding/ returning good with good.

བཟང་སྤྱོད་ (sanjöö) moral/ upright behavior.

བཟང་ཕེབས་བྱུང་ (sanpebjuŋ) shung. to have a divination come out well, to be selected in a divine lottery ¶ གཉེན་སྒྲིག་འདིའི་སྐོར་ཐུགས་དམ་བཟང་ཕེབས་བྱུང་སོང་ Concerning the marriage, the divination came out favorably.

བཟང་བ་ (sanwa) sm. བཟང་པོ་.

བཟང་འབྲས་ (sandrɛɛ̀) good result/ accomplishment.

བཟང་འབྲེལ་ (sandree) good relationship.

བཟང་མོ་ (sanmo) a girl's name.

བཟང་བཙོན་ (sandzön) house arrest/ confinement/ detention.

བཟང་བཙོན་དོ་དམ་ (sandzön todam) sm. བཟང་བཙོན་.

བཟང་བཙོན་ལ་འཇུག (sandzönla juù) va. to be put under house arrest, to be detained (but not treated like a prisoner).

བཟང་རྩལ་རྒྱན་རྩལ་ (sandzüü gyɛndzüü) the good points/ advantages of sth.

བཟང་འཛོམས་ (sandzom) having many good qualities combined.

བཟང་ཞན་ (sānshɛn) 1. good and bad. 2. the quality of sth.

བཟང་ཟླ་ (sānda) the 8th month of the Tibetan calendar.

བཟང་རབ་དང་རྒྱན་རབ་ (sanrəb dan gyɛnraŋ) (commenting on) a person's good qualities.

བཟང་ལན་ (sanlɛn) repaying/ paying back sth. good with good.

བཟང་ལན་བཟང་ལྡོག (sānlɛn sandɔɔ̀) paying back good with good; va.—བྱེད་.

བཟང་ལན་ངན་འདེབ་ (sanlɛn ŋenjɛɛ) repaying good with evil; va.— བྱེད་.

བཟང་ལེན་ངན་དོར་ (sanlen ŋendɔɔ) eliminate the evil and retain the good; va.—བྱེད་.

བཟང་ས་ཤན་ཐེབས་ (sanshɛn tēb) vi. to have a good influence on sb./ sth.

བཟང་ས་མཛའ་མཐུན་ (sansa dzadün) good friends.

བཟང་ལྡ་ང་གང་པོ་ ངན་ཐོམ་བུ་གང་གིས་སྐྱག (san lāŋa kanbo ŋɛn tōmbu kangi baà) one bad act can spoil many good acts [Lit. one full roasting pan filled with good deeds being spoiled by one ladle of bad deeds].

བཟང་སློབ་ (san lōb) va. to give good advice ¶ ཕྲུ་གུ་ཚོར་བཟང་སློབ་དགོས་པ་རེད་ One should give good advice to children.

བཟེད་ (sɛɛ̀) gentle, mild mannered.

བཟབ་ (səb) f. of གཟབ་.

བཟབས་ (səb) p. of གཟབ་.

བཟའ་ (sa) 1. abbr. of བཟའ་བཅའ་. 2. abbr. of བཟའ་ཚང་.

བཟའ་སྐྱོན་ (sagyön) paralyzed, paralysis.

བཟའ་གྱོད་ (sagyöö) marital dispute, law case between spouses.

བཟའ་གྲོགས་ (sadrɔɔ̀) spouse.

བཟའ་མགྲོན་ (sadrön) feast, banquet.

བཟའ་རྒྱུ་ (səgyu) things to be eaten.

བཟའ་རྒྱུ་མེད་པའི་ལས་རྒྱུ་ (səgyu meèbɛ lɛɛ̀gyu) working hard but to no avail/ profit.

བཟའ་བཅའ་ (sabja) food, foodstuffs ¶ བཟའ་བཅའི་ཚོང་ཁང་ Food/ grocery store.

བཟའ་བཅའ་དཀྱུས་མ་ (sabja gyüümə) ordinary/ common/ plain food.

བཟའ་བཅའ་འབོལ་པོ་ (sabja bööbo) sm. ཟས་དུལ་མ་.

བཟའ་བཅའི་སྦྱོར་རྡ་ (sabjɛ jɔrda) food ingredients.

བཟའ་བཅའི་བཟོ་ལས་ (sabjɛ solɛɛ̀) food industry.

བཟའ་བཅའི་ལས་སྣོན་ (sabjɛ lɛɛ̀nön) food manufacturing/ processing.

བཟའ་བཅུད་ (sabjüü) nutrition.

བཟའ་ཆས་ (sajɛɛ̀) sm. food, foodstuffs; va.—འཚོལ to seek one's livelihood, to earn a living.

བཟའ་ཆས་གཙོ་བོ་ (sajɛɛ̀ dzōwo) staple food.

བཟའ་ཆས་བཟོ་ལས་ (sājɛɛ̀ solɛɛ̀) food industry.

བཟའ་ཆས་སོས་སྲུང་ (sajɛɛ̀ sōōsuŋ) protection of food's freshness.

བཟའ་བཏུང་ (səduŋ) food and drink.

བཟའ་རྟགས་ (sadaà) 1. a marriage gift. 2. a gift given to one's wife/ lover.

བཟའ་དྲུག་འཛོམས་པ་ (sadruù dzomba) a situation where the couples (husbands and wives) from three generations in a household are all alive.

བཟའ་སྡོད་གྱོན་གསུམ་ (sadöö gyön sūm) the three things the government provides to school children (in Tibet): room, board and clothes.

བཟའ་སྣུམ་ (sənum) cooking oil.

བཟའ་སྣོད་ (sanöö) kitchen/ cooking utensils or vessels.

བཟའ་དཔོན་ (sabön) head of a household/ family.

བཟའ་དཔོན་རྒས་ན་ལུག་རྫི་ (sabön gɛɛ̀na lugdzi) when one gets old he or she is no longer held in esteem, looking down on the elderly [Lit. when the household head becomes old, he become a shepherd].

བཟའ་པ་ (sapa) sm. བཟའ་དཔོན་.

བཟའ་ཕྲན་ (sadrɛn) married couple.

བཟའ་བ་ (sawa) sm. བཟའ་ཕྲན་.

བཟའ་བ་པོ་ (sawapo) sm. བཟའ་དཔོན་.

བཟའ་བ་མོ་ (sawamo) 1. female head of a household. 2. wife.

བཟའ་བྱ་ (saja) edibles.

བཟའ་བྱའི་ཤ་མོ་ (sajɛ shāmo) edible mushrooms.

བཟའ་འབྲུ་ (səndru) 1. grain ration. 2. grain for household consumption.

བཟའ་འབྲུ་ཐེམ་ཐོ་ (səndru tēmdo) grain ration card (used in China).

བཟའ་འབྲུའི་དམིགས་ཞིང་ (səndrü mīgsiŋ) grain ration field, field from which people get grain for their own subsistence.

བཟའ་མ་ (sama) 1. food. 2. wife.

བཟའ་མང་ (samaŋ) many people in a family.

བཟའ་མི་ (səmi) husband and wife, couple ¶ དོན་གྲུབ་བཟའ་མི་གཉིས་ Thondup, husband and wife.

བཟའ་མི་གཉིས་ (səmi ñīì) sm. བཟའ་མི་.

བཟའ་མི་བུ་ཕྲུག (səmi pudruù) members of a family/ household (a married couple and their children).

བཟའ་མོ་ (səmo) 1. female head of household. 2. wife.

བཟའ་དམག (səmaà) arc. militia.

བཟའ་ཚང་ (sa̲dzaŋ) sm. བཟའ་མི་.

བཟའ་ཚང་ཁ་བྲལ་ (sa̲dzaŋ kādrɛɛ) vi. to get divorced/ separated.

བཟའ་ཚང་ཁྱིམ་ཐབས་ (sa̲dzaŋ kyīmdəb) sm. བཟའ་ཚང་.

བཟའ་ཚང་གྱེས་ (sa̲dzaŋ gye̲è) sm. བཟའ་ཚང་ཁ་བྲལ་.

བཟའ་ཚང་ལམ་འདྲིད་ (sa̲dzaŋ la̲mdrɛ̲ɛ̀) couple living together (without parents arranging it, i.e., based on their own wishes).

བཟའ་ཚལ་ (sa̲dzɛɛ) vegetables, greens.

བཟའ་ཚོ་ (sa̲dzo) sm. བཟའ་མི་.

བཟའ་ཟུང་ (sa̲suŋ) sm. བཟའ་མི་.

བཟའ་ཟླ་ (sa̲nda) wife.

བཟའ་ཟླ་མོ་ (sa̲ndamo) wife.

བཟའ་ཟླ་མོ་ཆེ་བ་ (sa̲ndamo cēwa) legal or principal wife (in contrast to concubine).

བཟའ་ཡ་ (sa̲ya) shung. life partner/ spouse ¶ གུས་པའི་བཟའ་ཡ་བུ་ཕྲུག་འདྲིལ་བ་ My spouse together with my children.

བཟའ་ཡོན་ (sa̲yön) sm. བཟའ་དཔོན་.

བཟའ་རོགས་འཐུང་རོགས་ (sa̲rɔɔ̀ tūŋrɔɔ̀) eating and drinking partner/ buddy.

བཟའ་ཤིང་ (sə̲shiŋ) fruit tree.

བཟའ་ཤིང་ར་བ་ (sə̲shiŋ ra̲wa) orchard.

བཟའ་སིལ་ (sə̲sii) snack.

བཟའ་སིལ་ཟ་ཁང་ (sə̲sii sa̲gaŋ) snack bar.

བཟའ་གསུམ་པ་ (sə̲sumbə) marriages with multiple spouses (polyandry or polygyny).

བཟར་ (sa̲r) p. of འཛེར་.

བཟས་ (sɛ̲ɛ̀) p. of ཟ་.

བཟས་ན་མི་འཕུང་ཉལ་ན་ཕུང་ (sɛ̲ɛ̀na mipuŋ ñɛ̲ɛna pūŋ) one should work hard and not loaf [Lit. one will not get ruined if one eats, but one will get ruined if one sleeps].

བཟི་ (si̲) vi. to be intoxicated, to get drunk.

བཟི་འཁྱོམ་ (si̲gyom) slightly drunk; vi.—ལང་ to get slightly drunk. 2. giddy, dizzy; vi.—ལང་.

བཟི་འཁྱོམ་འཁྱོམ་ (si̲ kyōgyom) 1. slightly drunk. 2. giddy, dizzy.

བཟི་འཐོམ་ (si̲ndom) sm. བཟི་འཁྱོམ་.

བཟི་འཐོམ་འཐོམ་ (si̲ tōmdom) sm. བཟི་འཁྱོམ་འཁྱོམ་.

བཟི་དྭངས་ (si̲ ta̲ŋ) vi. to sober up.

བཟི་བེར་ (si̲bee) slightly tipsy (from drinking alcohol); vi.—བྱེད་.

བཟི་བོའི་སྙིང་གཏམ་ཁ་འབབ་ (si̲wö ñīŋdam kābəb) a drunk will tell things that are secret.

བཟི་བྱེད་སྨན་ཐང་ (si̲jeè mēndaŋ) medicine that makes one drunk.

བཟི་མིག (si̲mii) eyes that show the effects of drinking alcohol.

བཟི་སྨྱོས་ (si̲ñöò) intoxication, intoxicated.

བཟི་རྫུ་ (si̲dzu) pretending to be drunk; va.—བྱེད་.

བཟི་ཡོམ་ (si̲yom) sm. བཟི་འཁྱོམ་.

བཟི་ཡོམ་ཡོམ་ (si̲ yo̲myom) sm. བཟི་འཁྱོམ་འཁྱོམ་.

བཟི་ཤུགས་ (si̲shuù) the alcoholic content of liqueur.

བཟུང་ (su̲ŋ) 1. p. of འཛིན་. 2. (with ནས་—) from then on ¶ ཁོང་སླེབས་པ་ནས་བཟུང་ From the time he arrived on.

བཟུང་བཀྱིག (su̲ŋgyii) sm. བཟུང་བཀྱིགས་.

བཟུང་བཀྱིགས་ (su̲ŋgyii) apprehending/ arresting and tying up; va.—བྱེད་.

བཟུང་བཀྱིགས་ཁྲིམས་རའི་ཞལ་ལྕེ་ (su̲ŋgyig trīmrɛ shɛ̲ɛje) laws regarding arresting people.

བཟུང་སྐྱེལ་ (su̲ŋgyee) arresting/ apprehending and delivering them somewhere.

བཟུང་ཁྲིད་ (su̲ndrii) 1. kidnapping; va.—བྱེད་. 2. seizing and taking away (a suspect, hostage), arresting.

བཟུང་འཇོམས་བརྐུས་བསད་ (su̲ndzom gūüsɛɛ̀) kidnapping, robbing and killing.

བཟུང་འདྲུད་ (su̲ndrüü) arresting/ apprehending/ seizing and dragging off.

བཟུང་ན་ལག་འཚིག (su̲ŋna la̲gdzii dāŋna dza̲ cāà) a very difficult situation/ dilemma [Lit. if you hold it it burns your hand].

བཟུང་དམག (su̲ŋmaà) prisoner of war.

བཟུང་དམག་ཕྱིར་སློག (su̲ŋmaà cīīlɔɔ̀) repatriation of prisoners of war.

བཟུང་དམག་རྨས་མ་ (su̲ŋmaà mɛ̄ɛma) wounded prisoners of war.

བཟུང་ཡིག (su̲nyii) arrest warrant.

བཟུར་ (su̲r) 1. p. of འཛུར་. 2. sm. འཛུར་.

བཟི་རེ་ (se̲re) sm. བཟོད་སྲན་ཆུང་བ་.

བཟེད་ (se̲è) 1. p. and f. of འཛེད་. 2. vi. to receive/ get sth. ¶ ཁོས་ཉེས་རྡུང་ཞི་དྲག་བཟེད་སོང་ He received a heavy beating. ¶ ལག་པའི་ནང་ལ་ཆུ་བཟེད་ To receive/ get water in one's cupped hand.

བཟེད་ཞལ་ (se̲èshɛɛ) h. of ཞག་སྣུག. 2. ལུད་ཕོར་.

བཟོ་: p. བཟོས་; f. བཟོ་; imp. བཟོས་ (so̲) 1. va. to make, to create, to manufacture ¶ ཁོས་སྒམ་ཆུང་ཆུང་ཞིག་བཟོས་པ་རེད་ He made a small box. 2. (vb. + —) to seem, to look like, to show a sign of, to appear ¶ ཁོ་ཚོ་མགྱོགས་པོ་ཡོང་བཟོ་འདུག It seems like they are coming. ¶ ཁོ་སོ་པ་ཡིན་བཟོ་འདུག It is seems he is a spy. ¶ ཁོ་སོ་པ་མིན་བཟོ་འདུག It is doesn't seem he is a spy.

བཟོ་བཀོད་ (so̲göò) 1. model, design; va.—བྱེད་ to model, design, to engineer ¶ བཟོ་བཀོད་དཔེ་གསར་ A new model. ¶ གནམ་གྲུའི་བཟོ་བཀོད་ལ་སློབ་སྦྱོང་བྱས་པ་རེད་ (They) studied designing and making airplanes. 2. projects, works.

བཟོ་བཀོད་སྐྲུན་དངོས་ (so̲göò drūnŋüü) the results of engineering (i.e., buildings, etc.).

བཟོ་བཀོད་དྲོད་དཔྱད་རིག་པ་ (so̲göò trö̲öjɛɛ̀ ri̲gbə) engineering thermodynamics.

བཟོ་བཀོད་པ་ (so̲göòbə) engineer, designer, draftsman.

བཟོ་བཀོད་མཛེས་རྩལ་ (so̲göò dze̲èdzɛɛ) arts and crafts.

བཟོ་བཀོད་ཤུགས་དཔྱད་རིག་པ་ (so̲göò shūgjɛɛ̀ ri̲gbə) engineering mechanics.

བཟོ་ཀུན་ (so̲gün) scab, strike breaker.

བཟོ་བརྐོས་ (so̲göò) the art of carving.

བཟོ་སྐྱོར་རྒྱག (so̲gyɔr gya̲à) remaking; va.—རྒྱག.

བཟོ་སྐྲུན་ (so̲drün) constructing, building, manufacturing; va.— བྱེད་.

བཟོ་སྐྲུན་ཀུང་སི་ (so̲drün gūŋsi) tib. ch. engineering/ construction company.

བཟོ་སྐྲུན་དགེ་རྒན་ (so̲drün ge̲gɛn) engineer.

བཟོ་སྐྲུན་ཅུའུ་ (so̲drün jū) tib. ch. bureau of engineering.

བཟོ་སྐྲུན་ཇུས་འགོད་ཁང་ (so̲drün jü̲ngöògaŋ) institute of engineering design.

བཟོ་སྐྲུན་ལྟེ་བ་ (so̲drün dēwa) the main project/ work.

བཟོ་སྐྲུན་སྤྱི་ཁྱབ་རུ་ཁག (so̲drün jīgyəb ru̲gaà) general construction brigade.

བཟོ་སྐྲུན་རིག་པ་ (so̲drün ri̲gbə) engineering (as a field).

བཟོ་སྐྲུན་རིས་འགོད་སློབ་ཚོགས་ (so̲drün ri̲igöò lōbdzoò) society of engineering graphics.

བཟོ་སྐྲུན་ལས་ཁུངས་ (so̲drün lɛ̲ɛguŋ) construction office.

བཟོ་སྐྲུན་ལས་ཡུལ་ (so̲drün lɛ̲ɛyüü) construction site.

བཟོ་སྐྲུན་ལས་རིགས་ (so̲drün lɛ̲ɛrii) manufacturing/ construction industry.

བཟོ་བསྐྲུན་ (so̲drün) sm. བཟོ་སྐྲུན་.

བཟོ་བསྐྲུན་དམག (so̲drün māà) engineering corps (in the army).

བཟོ་ཁང་ (so̲gaŋ) 1. plant, workshop, factory. 2. shung. association of tailors in traditional Tibet.

བཟོ་ཁང་དོ་དམ་པ་ (so̲gaŋ to̲damba) shung. person in charge of workers for the tt. government.

བཟོ་ཁང་བ་ (so̲gaŋwa) tailor's association in traditional Tibet.

བཟོ་ཁག (so̲gaà) section of a factory.

བཟོ་མཁན་ (so̲ñɛn) sm. བཟོ་པ་.

བཟོ་གྲྭ་ (so̲dra) factory, plant.

བཟོ་གླ་ (so̲la) 1. cost of manufacturing/ making. 2. wages for making sth., the making charge.

བཟོ་འགོ་ (so̲ngo) overseer, foreman.

བཟོ་འགྲིམ་ཅུའུ་ (sondrim jū) tib. ch. industrial and communications bureau.

བཟོ་རྒྱུན་ (sogyön) the tradition of handicrafts/ crafts.

བཟོ་དངོས་འགན་ལེན་ (soŋöö gɛnlen) warranty/ guarantee for a product.

བཟོ་བཅོས་ (sobjöö) repairs, alterations, revisions; va.—རྒྱག་ to repair, to alter, to revise.

བཟོ་བཅོས་རྒྱག་མཁན་ (sobjöö gyaàñɛn) repairman.

བཟོ་བཅོས་དཔར་གཞི་ (sobjöö bārshi) revised edition.

བཟོ་བཅོས་རིང་ལུགས་ (sobjöö riŋluù) revisionism.

བཟོ་བཅོས་ལྷ་སྒྲིག་ (sobjöö lhūdrig) repair and assembling (of machinery) ¶ བཟོ་བཅོས་ལྷ་སྒྲིག་གི་བཟོ་གྲྭ་ Repair shop/ plant.

བཟོ་ཆག (sojaà) shung. tax exemption received by families for providing workers for the tt. government.

བཟོ་ཆས་ (sojɛɛ̀) sm. བཟོ་སྤྱད་.

བཟོ་ཚུང་ (sojuŋ) a small association of painters in traditional Tibet.

བཟོ་ཆེན་འོག་ནས་བཟོ་ཚུང་དོན་ (sojen wɔ̀ɔnɛ sojuŋ tön) sm. གཟུ་མས་བཀོད་.

བཟོ་ཚོ་ (sojo) form, shape, appearance; vi.—ཐོན་ to take shape/ form/ appearance ¶ ད་ཆ་བཟོ་གྲྭ་འཛུགས་སྐྲུན་གྱི་བཟོ་ཚོ་ཡག་པོ་ཐོན་གྱི་འདུག Now the factory construction is taking a good shape (going along well). ¶ ནད་པ་འདིའི་བཟོ་ཚོ་ག་པར་བལྟས་ཀྱང་ཚེ་རིང་པོ་ཡོང་ས་མ་རེད་ However one looks at the appearance of the patient, it doesn't look like he will live long.

བཟོ་ཉེས་ (soñeè) 1. sm. བཟོ་ཉེས་དྲས་ཐལ་. 2. disgraceful/ shameful behavior; va.—སྟོན་ to do sth. disgraceful/ shameful/ embarrassing ¶ མི་ཡོད་སར་རང་གིས་བཟོ་ཉེས་བསྟན་ན་ང་ཚོ་ངོ་ཚ་གི་འདུག If you act disgraceful in a place where there are people around we will be embarrassed. 3. ugly; va.—སྟོན་ to make oneself ugly.

བཟོ་ཉེས་དྲས་ཐལ་ (soñeè trɛ̀ɛdee) ruined, wasted; vi.—ཤོར་ to get ruined and wasted ¶ འཆར་གཞི་ལག་ལེན་བསྟར་སྟངས་སྐོར་བཟོ་ཉེས་དྲས་ཐལ་ཤོར་ནས་ད་ཆ་བཅོས་ཐབས་མེད་པ་ཆགས་བཞག The plan to put this into practice has gotten ruined and there is no way to correct it.

བཟོ་ཏ་ (sobda) sm. བཟོ་ལྟ་.

བཟོ་ཏང་ (sodaŋ) the Labor Party.

བཟོ་ཏན་ (sodɛn) definitely/ certainly making sth. ¶ ངའི་ཕྲུ་གུ་འདིའི་དུ་ལོག་གཞན་ལས་ཡག་པ་ཞིག་བཟོ་ཏན་ཡིན I will definitely make my child's clothes better than the others.

བཟོ་གཏེར་ (soder) industry and mining, manufacturing and mining.

བཟོ་གཏེར་ཁུལ་ (soderküü) industry and mining area.

བཟོ་གཏེར་ཁེ་ལས་ (soder kēlɛɛ̀) industrial/ factory and mining enterprises or businesses.

བཟོ་ལྟ་ (sobda) shape, form, appearance, look; va.—སྟོན་ to show or manifest an appearance/ look; vi.—ཤོར་ to lose one's front/ facade, to lose one's good/ healthy appearance; vi.—ཤོར་ i. to be down/ dejected/ under the weather, ii. to be defeated, to collapse; va.—སྤྲོད་; —བཟོ་ to teach sb. a lesson (through some harsh means); va.—ལྟ་ to look at a situation or circumstance; va.—འདོན་ to apply makeup ¶ འགྲོ་འདོད་མེད་པའི་བཟོ་ལྟ་སྟོན་གྱི་འདུག (They) are showing signs of not wanting to go. ¶ བར་ལམ་ཁོང་ན་ནས་བཟོ་ལྟ་ཤོར་བཞག Recently, he got sick and looks bad. ¶ སློབ་ཕྲུག་དེ་ཡིག་ཚད་མ་ཐོན་ཙང་བཟོ་ལྟ་ཤོར་བཞག The student was dejected because he didn't pass the exam. ¶ བཟོ་ལྟར་བལྟས་ན་འདི་ལོ་ཚོང་ལས་ཡག་པོ་ཡོང་ས་མ་རེད་ If one looks at the situation, this year business will not be good.

བཟོ་ལྟ་ངན་པ་ (sobda ŋamba) sm. བཟོ་བལྟ་ཉེས་པོ་.

བཟོ་ལྟ་འཆོས་ (sobda cȍȍ) va. to make an image.

བཟོ་ལྟ་ཉེས་པོ་ (sobda ñeèbo) 1. ugly. 2. bad behavior/ actions; va.—བྱེད་.

བཟོ་ལྟ་ཐོན་ (sobda tön) sm. བཟོ་ཚོ་ (ཐོན་).

བཟོ་ལྟ་ཤོར་ (sobda shɔ̄ɔ) see བཟོ་ལྟ་.

བཟོ་ལྟའི་རིང་ལུགས་ (sobdɛ riŋluù) formalism.

བཟོ་བལྟ (sobda) sm. བཟོ་ལྟ་.

བཟོ་བལྟ་ཡ་མཚན་ (sobda yamdzɛn) odd looking, strange shaped.

བཟོ་བལྟ་ར་བོ་ (sobda rawo) pretending; va.—བྱེད་ ¶ ཁོས་གནས་ཚུལ་དེ་ཤེས་ཀྱི་མེད་པའི་བཟོ་བལྟ་ར་བོ་བྱེད་ཀྱི་འདུག He is pretending that he does not know about that matter.

བཟོ་བལྟར་ལྟ་ (sobda dā) sm. བཟོ་ལྟ་ (ལྟ་).

བཟོ་སྟེགས་ (sodeg) anvil.

བཟོ་སྟོན་ (sodön) abbr. of བཟོ་ལྟ་སྟོན་.

བཟོ་ཐོན་ (sodön) sm. བཟོ་ཚོ་ (ཐོན་).

བཟོ་བདག (sodaà) workers and owners, labor and management.

བཟོ་འདོན་ (sondön) production, manufacturing; va.—བྱེད་ to produce, to manufacture.

བཟོ་འདྲ་ (sondra) sm. བཟོ་བལྟ་ར་བོ་.

བཟོ་འདྲ་པོ་ (so drabo) sm. བཟོ་བལྟ་ར་བོ་.

བཟོ་འདྲ་པོ་ཞིག (so draboshig) 1. sm. བཟོ་བལྟ་ར་བོ་. 2. just like sth. ¶ ཁོས་ཁང་པ་དེའི་བཟོ་འདྲ་པོ་ཞིག་བརྒྱབ་བཞག He built a house just like that house.

བཟོ་གནང་མཛད་ (sonaŋdzɛɛ̀) h. of བཟོ་.

བཟོ་གནས་ (sonɛɛ̀) place where crafts/ handicrafts are done.

བཟོ་གནས་ཀྱི་རིག་པ་ (sonɛɛ̀gi rigbə) the field of crafts/ handicrafts.

བཟོ་སྣོན་ (sonön) processing of (products); va.—བྱེད་.

བཟོ་པ་ (soba) worker, laborer.

བཟོ་པ་གྲལ་རིམ་ (soba trɛɛrim) sm. བཟོ་པའི་གྲལ་རིམ་.

བཟོ་པ་སྔོན་ཐོན་པ་ (soba ŋöndönba) advanced worker.

བཟོ་པ་མཉམ་འབྲེལ་རིང་ལུགས་ (soba ñamdree riŋluù) trade unionism.

བཟོ་པ་ཕྲུ་གུ་ (soba trūgu) child laborer, child labor.

བཟོ་པ་བུད་མེད་ (soba püümɛɛ̀) female worker.

བཟོ་པ་བྱང་མ་ (soba caŋma) skilled worker.

བཟོ་པ་ལག་རྩལ་ཅན་ (soba lagdzɛɛjɛn) skilled worker, craftsman.

བཟོ་པ་ལྷག་འགྲོ་ (soba lhāgdrȍȍ) unemployed workers.

བཟོ་པའི་གྲལ་རིམ་ (sobɛ trɛ̀ɛrim) the working class.

བཟོ་པའི་འགོ་པ་ (sobɛ goba) foreman, overseer.

བཟོ་པའི་ནང་རུལ་ (sobɛ nəŋrüü) sm. བཟོ་ཀུན་.

བཟོ་པའི་རྫ་འཛུགས་ (sobɛ dzāndzuù) sm. བཟོ་ཚོགས་.

བཟོ་པའི་རླུང་རླབས་ (sobɛ lūŋləb) tide/ wave of labor.

བཟོ་པའི་ལས་འགུལ་ (sobɛ lɛngüü) labor (workers') movement.

བཟོ་པའི་ལས་མཚམས་ (sobɛ lɛndzam) workers' strike; va.—འཛུགས་ to go on strike.

བཟོ་པའི་ལས་མཚམས་ཆེད་འཛུགས (sobɛ lɛndzam cēnjɔɔ̀) workers' strike.

བཟོ་པོ་ (sobo) careful; va.—བྱེད་ to act/ be careful ¶ ཁོང་རྣམ་ཀུན་ནས་དུ་ལོག་བཟོ་པོ་ཞི་དྲག་རེད་ He is usually very careful with his clothes.

བཟོ་དཔོན་ (sobön) foreman, work boss, overseer.

བཟོ་སྤྱད་ (sojöö) equipment, tools, instruments.

བཟོ་ཕྲུག (sodruù) sm. བཟོ་པ་ཕྲུ་གུ་.

བཟོ་བ་ (sowa) sm. བཟོ་པ་.

བཟོ་བའི་ཁམས་གསོ་གླིང་ (sowɛ kāmsoliŋ) workers' sanitarium.

བཟོ་བའི་མཉམ་སྐྱོ་ཁང་ (sowɛ ñamdrogaŋ) workers' social club.

བཟོ་བའི་རིག་གནས་པོ་བྲང་ (sowɛ rignɛɛ̀ pōdraŋ) workers' cultural palace.

བཟོ་བའི་རིག་གནས་སློབ་གྲྭ (sowɛ rignɛɛ̀ lōbdra) workers' cultural/ literacy school.

བཟོ་བའི་ལག་རྩལ་སློབ་གྲྭ (sowɛ lagdzɛɛ lōbdra) workers' technical school.

བཟོ་བའི་སློབ་གྲྭ་ཆེན་པོ་ (sowɛ rignɛɛ̀ lōbdra) workers' university.

བཟོ་བོ་ (sowo) sm. བཟོ་པ་.

བཟོ་བྱེད་ (sojeè) 1. shung. expressing deep

gratitude. 2. the material from which sth. is made.

བཟོ་དབྱིབས་ (soyib) shape, form, appearance; vi.—འགྱུར་ to change shape/ form/ appearance, to be transformed.

བཟོ་འབྲེལ་རིང་ལུགས་ (sodree riŋluù) labor federalism.

བཟོ་མོ་ (somo) female worker.

བཟོ་མོ་ཕྱུའུ་ (somo bū) tib. ch. female workers' bureau.

བཟོ་རྨས་ (somɛɛ̀) work injury.

བཟོ་རྩལ་ (sodzɛɛ) work skill, craft skill ¶ བལ་ལུགས་ཀྱི་བཟོ་རྩལ་ Nepalese style craft skills. 2. technology.

བཟོ་རྩལ་བཀོལ་སྤྱོད་བྱ་རིམ་ (sodzɛɛ) technological operating rules/ instructions.

བཟོ་རྩལ་མཁས་པ་ (sodzɛɛ kɛ̀ɛ̀ba) skilled craftsman, skilled worker, skilled labor.

བཟོ་རྩལ་གོ་རིམ་ (sodzɛɛ korim) technological procedures.

བཟོ་རྩལ་གྱི་དགོས་མཁོ་ (sodzɛɛgi göòko) technological requirements/ necessities.

བཟོ་རྩལ་གྱི་བརྒྱུད་རིམ་ (sodzɛɛgi gyüùrim) technological process.

བཟོ་རྩལ་གྱི་ཆུ་ཚད་ (sodzɛɛgi cūdzɛɛ̀) technological level.

བཟོ་རྩལ་གྱི་ཇུས་འགོད་ (sodzɛɛgi jüùgöò) technological design.

བཟོ་རྩལ་གྱི་ཐོན་རྫས་ (sodzɛɛgi tōndzɛɛ̀) technological products, industrial products, manufactured goods.

བཟོ་རྩལ་གྱི་ཚད་ལྡན་བྱ་རིམ་ (sodzɛɛgi tsɛ̀ɛ̀dɛn carim) technological regulations.

བཟོ་རྩལ་རྒྱན་ཆ་ (sodzɛɛ gyɛnja) technological decoration.

བཟོ་རྩལ་རྒྱན་སྤྲས་ (sodzɛɛ gyɛndrɛɛ̀) sm. བཟོ་རྩལ་རྒྱན་ཆ་.

བཟོ་རྩལ་དངོས་པོ་ (sodzɛɛ ŋöòbo) technological products, high tech products.

བཟོ་རྩལ་ཐོན་རྫས་བཟོ་གྲྭ (sodzɛɛ tōndzɛɛ̀ sodra) handicraft factory.

བཟོ་རྩལ་མཛེས་དངོས་ (sodzɛɛ dzeèŋöò) handicrafts, arts and crafts.

བཟོ་རྩལ་མཛེས་རྩལ་ཚོང་ཁང་ (sodzɛɛ dzeèdzɛɛ tsōŋgaŋ) handicrafts/ arts and crafts shop.

བཟོ་རྩལ་མཛེས་རྩལ་སློབ་ཚོགས་ (sodzɛɛ dzeèdzɛɛ lōbdzoò) association of handicrafts/ arts and crafts.

བཟོ་ཚན་ (sodzɛn) division/ unit in factory.

བཟོ་ཚོགས་ (sodzɔ̀ɔ̀) trade/ labor union.

བཟོ་ཚོགས་མཉམ་འབྲེལ་ཚོགས་པ་ (sodzɔ̀ɔ̀ ñamdree tsɔ̄gba) federation of trade unions.

བཟོ་ཚོགས་ལས་བྱེད་སློབ་གྲྭ (sodzɔ̀ɔ̀ lɛ̀ɛ̀jeè lōbso) labor union cadre's school.

བཟོ་ཚོགས་རིང་ལུགས་ (sodzɔ̀ɔ̀ riŋluù) trade unionism.

བཟོ་ཚོང་ (sodzoŋ) industry and commerce, industrial and commerical.

བཟོ་ཚོང་དངུལ་ཁང་ (sodzoŋ ŋǖūgaŋ) bank of industry and commerce.

བཟོ་ཚོང་ཁྱིམ་དུད་ (sodzoŋ tēmdüù) industrial and commerical households.

བཟོ་ཚོང་དཔྱ་ཁྲལ་ (sodzoŋ jādrɛɛ) tax on industry and commerce.

བཟོ་ཚོང་ཞིང་ཕྱུགས་ (sodzoŋ shiŋjuù) industry, commerce, agriculture and animal husbandry.

བཟོ་ཚོང་ལས་རིགས་ (sodzoŋ lɛ̀ɛrig) industry and commerce, business circles, industrial and commercial circles.

བཟོ་ཚོང་ལས་རིགས་མཉམ་འབྲེལ་ལྷན་ཚོགས་ (sodzoŋ lɛ̀ɛrig ñamdree lhēndzɔ̀ɔ̀) Federation of Industry and Commerce, Association of Industrial and Commerical workers.

བཟོ་ཚོད་ (sodzöò) experimenting, trying out, doing a pilot test; va.—བྱེད་; —ལྟ་ ¶ འཕྲུལ་འཁོར་གསར་པ་དངོས་སུ་མ་བཟོས་གོང་བཟོ་ཚོད་བལྟས་པ་རེད་ They did a trial of the new equipment before actually putting it into production.

བཟོ་མཚམས་བཞག (sodzam shaà) va. to leave a job half-finished/ unfinished.

བཟོ་ཚོང་ལས་རིགས་ (sodzoŋ lɛ̀ɛriì) industrial and commercial enterprises.

བཟོ་རྫས་ (sodzɛɛ̀) industrial/ manufactured products.

བཟོ་རྫས་ཆེས་ལྷག (sodzɛɛ̀ cēèlhaà) excess products, over produced products.

བཟོ་ཞྭ་ (sosha) a kind of cap typically worn by workers.

བཟོ་ཞིང་ (soshiŋ) 1. workers and farmers. 2. industry and agriculture.

བཟོ་ཞིང་གི་བུ་ཕྲུག་དམག (soshiŋgi pudruù māà) the army that consists of the children of famers/ peasants and workers (i.e., the Chinese communist's army).

བཟོ་ཞིང་གཉིས་ཤེས་ (soshiŋ ñīisheè) knowing both farming and industrial work.

བཟོ་ཞིང་མཐའ་འབྲེལ་ (soshiŋ nandree) worker and peasant/ farmer alliance.

བཟོ་ཞིང་འབྲོག་ཞོར་ཉ་ལྔ་ (soshiŋ drogshɔɔ ñaŋa) abbr. the five: workers, farmers/ peasants, pastoralists/ nomads, sideline workers and fishermen.

བཟོ་ཞིང་མང་ཚོགས་ (soshiŋ maŋdzoò) the masses of workers and peasants/ farmers.

བཟོ་ཞིང་དམག (soshiŋ māà) sm. བཟོ་ཞིང་དམག་གསུམ་.

བཟོ་ཞིང་དམག་སློབ་ཚོང་ (soshiŋ māglob tsōŋ) abbr. workers, farmers/ peasants, soldiers, students and businessmen.

བཟོ་ཞིང་དམག་གསུམ་ (soshiŋ māgsum) abbr. the three: workers, peasants and soldiers.

བཟོ་ཞིང་དམར་དམག (soshiŋ mārmaà) workers' and peasants' Red Army.

བཟོ་ཞིང་ལས་བྱེད་པ་ (soshiŋ lɛ̀ɛ̀jeèba) workers' and peasants' cadre.

བཟོ་ཞིང་ལས་རིགས་ (soshiŋ lɛ̀ɛ̀riì) industrial and agricultural enterprises.

བཟོ་གཞིས་ (soshiì) industrial settlement.

བཟོ་ཤེས་ (soshee̋) knowledge of a craft.

བཟོ་ར་ (sora) workshop, work site.

བཟོ་རིག (soriì) technology.

བཟོ་རིག་མཁས་པ་ (soriì kɛ̀ɛ̀ba) technical expert, technician, engineer.

བཟོ་རིགས་ (soriì) types of work.

བཟོ་རིགས་སློབ་སྦྱོང་ (soriì lōbjoŋ) vocational training.

བཟོ་རིགས་སློབ་གྲྭ (soriì lōbdra) vocational/ technical school.

བཟོ་ལ་ལྟ་ (sola dā) va. to look at the shape/ manner form of sth. or sb. ¶ སྔོན་ལ་འགྲོ་མཁན་རྣམས་ཀྱི་བཟོ་ལ་བལྟས་ན་ If one looks at the manner of those who are going in front.

བཟོ་ལག་ཤེས་ (so lagsheè) handicrafts.

བཟོ་ལམ་གཞིས་གསུམ་ (solam shiisum) abbr. the three: industries, road construction, and settlements.

བཟོ་ལས་ (solɛɛ̀) industry, industrial ¶ རྡོ་སོལ་བཟོ་ལས་ Coal industry.

བཟོ་ལས་ཀྱི་ཁེ་ལས་ (solɛɛ̀gi kēlɛɛ̀) industrial enterprise.

བཟོ་ལས་ཀྱི་རྒྱལ་ཁབ་ (solɛɛ̀gi gyɛɛgəb) industrial country/ nation.

བཟོ་ལས་ཀྱི་ཆུ་འཐེན་འཁོར་ལོ་ (solɛɛ̀gi cūden kɔ̄ɔlo) industrial water pump.

བཟོ་ལས་ཀྱི་སྙིགས་རོ་ (solɛɛ̀gi ñīgro) industrial waste.

བཟོ་ལས་ཀྱི་སྙིགས་རོ་གསུམ་ (solɛɛ̀gi ñīgrosum) the three wastes products of industry: waste gas, waste water, and industrial residue.

བཟོ་ལས་ཀྱི་འཐབ་ཕྱོགས་ (solɛɛ̀gi tābjɔ̀ɔ̀) industrial front.

བཟོ་ལས་ཀྱི་སྤྱི་ཐོན་རྫས་ (solɛɛ̀gi jīdöndzɛɛ̀) gross value of industrial output.

བཟོ་ལས་ཀྱི་བེད་མེད་རྒྱུ་ཆ་ (solɛɛ̀gi beèmeè gyuja) sm.

བཟོ་ལས་ཀྱི་སྙིགས་རོ་.

བཟོ་ལས་ཀྱི་ལས་ནད་ (soleègi leènee) industrial disease/ illness.

བཟོ་ལས་ཀྱི་ཨ་རག་ཉིང་ཁུ་ (soleègi āraà ñiŋgu) cleaning alcohol.

བཟོ་ལས་ཁང་ (soleègaŋ) workshop.

བཟོ་ལས་ཁྱབ་བཤེར་ (soleè kyəbsher) industrial survey.

བཟོ་ལས་གོང་འཕེལ་ (soleè koŋbee) industrial development.

བཟོ་ལས་གྲོང་ཁྱེར་ (soleè troŋgyer) industrial city.

བཟོ་ལས་དགེ་རྒན་ (soleè gegen) 1. industrial teacher. 2. engineer.

བཟོ་ལས་འཁྲིམ་འགྲུལ་ (soleè drimdrüü) industry and transportation.

བཟོ་ལས་རྒྱལ་ཁབ་ (soleè gyeegəb) industrialized/ industrial country.

བཟོ་ལས་རྒྱལ་ཁབ་ལ་དབང་བ་ (soleè gyeegəbla wāŋwa) state ownership of industry, industry owned by the state.

བཟོ་ལས་རྒྱུ་ཆ་ (soleè) industrial raw materials.

བཟོ་ལས་རྒྱུ་ཆའི་ལོ་ཏོག (soleè gyujɛ lodoò) industrial crops.

བཟོ་ལས་ཅན་ (soleèjen) industrialized.

བཟོ་ལས་ཅན་དུ་འགྱུར་ (soleèjendu gyur) vi. to be/ get industrialized.

བཟོ་ལས་ཅན་དུ་སྒྱུར་ (soleèjendu gyur) va. to industrialize.

བཟོ་ལས་ལྗི་བ་ (soleè jīwə) heavy industry.

བཟོ་ལས་ཆུང་ཚགས་འཛིན་སྐྱོང་ཁང་ (soleè cūŋdzaà dziŋgyoŋgaŋ) Small Business Administration (U.S.A.).

བཟོ་ལས་འཆར་འགོད་ (soleè cārgöö) industrial planning.

བཟོ་ལས་ཐད་ཀྱི་གནམ་གཤིས་རིག་པ་ (soleè teègi nāmshiì rigbə) industrial meteorology.

བཟོ་ལས་ཐོན་ཆས་ (soleè tōnjeè) sm. བཟོ་ལས་ཐོན་རྫས་.

བཟོ་ལས་ཐོན་རྫས་ (soleè tōndzeè) industrial products, industrial production.

བཟོ་ལས་ཐོན་ཟོག (soleè tōnsɔɔ̀) sm. བཟོ་ལས་ཐོན་རྫས་.

བཟོ་ལས་པ་ (soleèba) engineer, technical expert.

བཟོ་ལས་དཔལ་འབྱོར་ (soleè bēnjɔɔ) industrial economy.

བཟོ་ལས་མ་ལག (soleè malaà) industrial system.

བཟོ་ལས་མི་མང་གི་སྲུང་སྐྱོབ་དང་འཕྲོད་བསྟེན་བདག་སྐྱོང་ཁང་ (soleè mimaŋgi sūŋgyobdaŋ trööden dāgyoŋgaŋ) Occupational Safety and Health Administration (OSHA).

བཟོ་ལས་ཚན་ཁག (soleè tsēngaà) technical department, engineering department.

བཟོ་ལས་འཛུགས་སྐྲུན་ (soleè dzugdrün) industrial construction/ development.

བཟོ་ལས་གཞིས་ཆགས་ (soleè shiijaà) industrial settlement.

བཟོ་ལས་ཡང་བ་ (soleè yaŋwa) light industry.

བཟོ་ལས་ལག་རྩལ་གྱི་བྱ་རིམ་ (soleè lagdzeegi carim) technological process.

བཟོ་ལས་བཤོལ་ (soleè shöö) va. to go on strike (workers).

བཟོ་ལས་ས་ཁུལ་ (soleè səgüü) industrial area/ district.

བཟོ་ལས་སློབ་གྲྭ་ (soleè lōbdra) engineering school, technical school.

བཟོ་ལས་སློབ་གྲྭ་ཆེན་མོ་ (soleè lōbdra cēmmo) engineering college, technical college.

བཟོ་ཤེས་ (sosheè) knowledge of crafts.

བཟོ་ཤེས་ཞིང་ཤེས་ (sosheè shiŋsheè) sm. བཟོ་ཞིང་གཉིས་ཤེས་.

བཟོ་ཤོར་ (soshɔɔ) sm. བཟོ་ལྟ་ཤོར་ (see བཟོ་ལྟ་).

བཟོ་སློབ་ཁང་ (solobgaŋ) technical/ vocational school.

བཟོང་ (soŋ) shung. abbr. of བཟང་པོ་.

བཟོད་ (söö) vi. to be able to bear/ tolerate/ withstand ¶ཁོ་ཚོའི་བཙན་གནོན་མ་བཟོད་ནས་ Not being able to bear their oppression.

བཟོད་དཀའ་ (sööga) sm. བཟོད་ཁག་པོ་.

བཟོད་ཁག་པོ་ (söö kāgbo) difficult to bear/ tolerate/ withstand.

བཟོད་སྒོམ་ (söögom) tolerating, enduring, forbearing; va.—བྱེད་ to tolerate/ bear/ endure.

བཟོད་སྒོམ་གཞན་བསྟུན་ (söögom shendün) being tolerant/ conciliatory with others.

བཟོད་བླགས་ (söölaà) tolerating/ bearing/ suffering adversity or hardship, va.—བྱེད་.

བཟོད་བླགས་བྲལ་བ་ (söölaà treewa) unbearable, intolerable.

བཟོད་བླགས་མེད་པ་ (söölaà meèba) sm. བཟོད་བླགས་བྲལ་བ་.

བཟོད་ཐབས་གདན་བྲལ་ (söödəb dendree) sm. བཟོད་ཐབས་བྲལ་བ་.

བཟོད་ཐབས་བྲལ་བ་ (söödəb treewa) intolerable, unbearable ¶བཟོད་ཐབས་བྲལ་བའི་བཤུ་གཞོག Unbearable exploitation.

བཟོད་ཐབས་མེད་པ་ (söödəb meèba) sm. བཟོད་ཐབས་བྲལ་བ་.

བཟོད་ཐེག (söödeg) sm. བཟོད་སྒོམ་.

བཟོད་དུ་མེད་པ་ (söödu meèba) sm. བཟོད་ཐབས་བྲལ་བ་.

བཟོད་བདེ་བག་ཕེབས་ (söödе pagbeb) safe and secure.

བཟོད་པ་ (sööba) sm. བཟོད་སྒོམ་.

བཟོད་པ་སྒོམ་ (sööba gom) vi. to tolerate/ endure/ bear.

བཟོད་པ་སྒོམ་ཐབས་མེད་པ་ (sööba gomdəb meèba) impossible to tolerate/ bear/ endure.

བཟོད་པ་བྱེད་ (sööba ceè) va. to tolerate, to endure, to bear.

བཟོད་པའི་སྟོབས་ (sööbɛ dōb) the power of tolerance.

བཟོད་པར་གསོལ་ (sööbar söö) sm. བཟོད་གསོལ་ཞུ་.

བཟོད་མ་ཐུབ་པ་ (sööma tūbbə) sm. བཟོད་ཐབས་བྲལ་བ་.

བཟོད་མ་བདེ་ (söömade) sm. བཟོད་ཐབས་བྲལ་བ་.

བཟོད་སེམས་ (söösem) a tolerating mind.

བཟོད་གསོལ་ (söösöö) apologizing, excusing, forgiving; va.—ཞུ་ to apologize, to ask pardon/ forgiveness ¶ངས་ཁྱེད་ལ་སྐྱ་གསུང་ཐུགས་ཡོག་ཞུས་པར་བཟོད་གསོལ་གནང་རོགས་གནང་ Please forgive my comments that caused you hurt.

བཟོད་བསྲན་ (söösen) sm. བཟོད་སྒོམ་.

བཟོད་བསྲན་སྒོམ་པ་ (sösen gomba) able to tolerate/ endure /bear.

བཟོད་བསྲན་མེད་པ་ (söösen meèba) unable to tolerate.

བཟོའི་བསྟན་བཅོས་ (sö denjöö) a text on the arts and crafts.

བཟོའི་ཕྱག་ཆས་ (sö cāàjeè) h. of ལག་ཆ་.

བཟོས་ (söö) p. of བཟོ་.

བཟོས་གྲུབ་འབྲུ་རིགས་ (söödrub drurig) processed grains.

བཟོས་སྒོ་ (söögo) award, prize.

བཟོས་དངུལ་ (sööŋüü) embezzled money.

བཟོས་སྨན་ (söömen) medicine that has already been prepared/ mixed.

བཟོས་རྫས་ (söödzeè) products.

བཟོས་ལམ་ (söölam) custom of giving an award.

བཟླ་ (da) f. of ཟླ་.

བཟླ་བཞིན་ལོགས་པ་བྱེད་ (dashin ləgba ceè) shung. violating a decree/ edict.

བཟླས་ (deè) p. of ཟླ་.

བཟླས་བརྗོད་ (deèjöö) reciting mantras; va.—བྱེད་.

བཟླུག (duù) f. of ཟླུག.

བཟླུགས་ (duù) p. of ཟླུག.

བཟླུམ་ (dum) f. of ཟླུམ་.

བཟླུམས་ (dum) p. of ཟླུམ་.

བཟློ་བ་ (dowa) shung. make the following known ¶སེར་སྐྱ་མཆོག་དམན་མཐའ་དག་ལ་བཟློ་བ་ Make the following known to all laymen and monks.

བཟློག (dɔɔ̀) f. of ཟློག.

བཟློག་རིམ་ (dɔgrim) shung. prayers/ pujas for driving back disasters/ misfortunes.

བཟློགས་ (dɔɔ̀) p. of ཟློག.

བཀློས་ (dö̱ö̀) p. of ཀློ་.

བཀློས་ཀྱར་ (dö̱ö̀gyar) sm. བཀློས་ཐུག.

བཀློས་ཐུག (dö̱ö̀duù) shung. va. to have a law case.

བཀློས་ཡ་ (dö̱ö̀ya) shung. party in a law case/ lawsuit.

འ་ (a) the letter 'a' (used in alphabetical ordering).

འ་ཅག་ (ajaà) sm. ང་ཅག.

འ་ཆ་ (aja) jeering, laughing; va.—རྒྱག་ to jeer.

འ་ཆ་ཐིང་ཐིང་ (aja tiŋdiŋ) roars of laughter.

འ་ཆད་འུ་ཐུག་ (ajɛɛ̀ wuduù) in total despair/ desperation.

འ་ཆུང་ (əjuŋ) the small འ་ that is placed under a letter.

འ་ཛི་འུ་ཛི་ (əji uji) sm. འ་འཁྱོར་འུ་འཁྱོར་.

འ་ན་ (ana) sm. ཨོ་ན་.

འ་ན་ཡང་ (anayaŋ) although, even though.

འ་ནི་འོན་ནི་ (ani önni) 1. ambiguous, vague. 2. pretending to be hard of hearing; va.—བྱེད་ ། ངས་བཤད་པའི་སྐད་ཆ་ར་ཁོས་འ་ནི་འོན་ནི་བྱས་ནས་ལན་ཡག་པོ་རྒྱག་གི་མི་འདུག Pretending he is hard of hearing, he is not answering my comments well.

འ་པ་ (aba) arc. paternal uncle.

འ་འཁྱོར་འུ་འཁྱོར་ (ajɔɔ ujɔɔ) blurry vision; vi.—བྱེད་ ། བརྙན་འཕྲིན་ལྟ་དུས་མིག་འ་འཁྱོར་འུ་འཁྱོར་བྱེད་ཀྱི་འདུག When I watch television I see it blurry.

འ་མ་ (ama) slang exclamation expressing surprise: oh!, oh my! ། འ་མ་ དེ་འདྲའི་ཁང་པ་དེ་ཆེ་བ་ལ་ཨང་ Oh! Such a big building.

འ་ཚིས་ (ədzi) sm. འ་མ་.

འ་ཚིས་རྫུ་མ་ (ədziì dzumə) sb. who pretends to be timid but is really bold.

འ་ཝུབ་ (əwub) extent, size, degree.

འ་ཝུབ་མ་འདུས་ (əwub mandüù) sm. འབ་སུ་མ་འདུས་.

འ་ཝུར་ (əwur) abbr. of འ་རི་འུ་རི་.

འ་འོན་ (əwön) abbr. of འ་ནི་འོན་ནི་.

འ་ཡའི་ཀྱིད་ (ayɛ gyē) a positive expression of surprise: wow, not bad! ། འ་ཡའི་ཀྱིད་ ཁོ་ཡིག་ཚད་ཡག་པོ་དེ་འདྲ་ཡོན་བཞག Wow. He did well on the exam.

འ་རི་འུ་རི་ (əri uri) disorganized, disorderly, erratic, scatterbrained, careless; va.—བྱེད་ ། མི་དེས་འ་རི་འུ་རི་བྱས་ནས་ཡི་གེ་ནོར་འཁྲུལ་མང་པོ་བཏང་བཞག That man was careless and made many mistakes in writing.

འ་ལས་ (ālɛɛ̀)1. oh ། འ་ལས་ངས་འདི་འདྲ་ཏ་གོ་མ་སོང་ Oh. I didn't know that. 2. an exclamatory term of disapproval: oh my ། འ་ལས་སྐད་ཆ་བཙོག་པ་དེ་འདྲ་མ་ཤོད་དྲ་ Oh my. Dont talk such dirty talk! 3. in some Eastern Tibetan dialects this means vagina.

འག་སྒྲ་ (aŋdra) the crying of a monkey when it is frightened.

འག་འདེབས་ (aŋdeb) the yelp or cry of foxes.

འང་ (aŋ) sm. ཀྱང་.

འང་ཀ་ (aŋga) sm. ངང་པ་.

འང་གུ་ (əŋgu) pigeon, dove.

འང་གུ་མདོག་ (əŋgu dɔɔ̀) bluish-grey color.

འང་གུའི་རྐུབ་ནས་ཨ་ལོང་ (əŋgü gūbnɛ āloŋ) sth. impossible [Lit. an earring from the ass of a pigeon].

འང་པན་ (aŋbɛn) ch. chopping board.

འན་ནེ་འོན་ནེ་ (ane öne) sm. འ་ནི་འོན་ནི་.

འན་བུ་ (ambu) I.

འན་འོན་ (anwön) abbr. of འ་ནི་འོན་ནི་.

འབ་ (əb) va. to bark ། ས་རུབ་ནས་ཁྱིས་འབ་ཀྱི་འདུག After it becomes dark dogs bark.

འབ་སྒྲ་ཚ་པོ་ (əbdra tsābo) brash, impudent, loud, boastful.

འབ་ལྕགས་ (əbjaà) a wall, a wall-like fence.

འབ་པེ་འོབ་པེ་ (abe obe) hasty, careless, haphazard ། ལས་ཀ་བྱེད་དུས་འབ་པེ་འོབ་པེ་བྱས་ན་ཡག་པོ་ཡོང་གི་མ་རེད་ When you work it will not be good if you are careless.

འབ་བྲེད་ (abdreè) sm. འབ་རས་རྒྱག.

འབ་ཝུབ་ (əbub) sm. འབ་སུ་.

འབ་རས་རྒྱག་ (abrɛɛ gyaà) sm. འདྲད་.

འབ་སུ་ (əbsu) able to manage/ cope with; va.—འདུ་ to manage, to cope with ། ཚོང་ཁང་རྒྱ་ཆེ་དྲགས་ནས་མི་ཉུང་ཉུང་གིས་འབ་སུ་འདུས་ཀྱི་མི་འདུག The store is too big so a small number of people are unable to manage it.

འབ་སུ་མ་འདུས་ (əbsu məndüù) unable to cope/ manage ། ལས་གཞི་རྒྱ་ཆེ་དྲགས་ནས་འབ་སུ་མ་འདུས་པ་བྱུང་བ་རེད་ Because the project was too big they were unable to handle with it.

འམ་ (am) 1. interrogative particle (used after vowel finals) ། ཁྱེད་ལྷ་སར་འགྲོ་འམ་ Will you go to Lhasa? 2. "or" particle (used after vowel finals) ། ཆེ་འམ་ཆུང་ Big or small.

འམ་འཇུར་ (amjur) sm. འར་གྲིས་འདུལ་.

འམ་བུ་ (ambu) red willow.

འམ་གཙིགས་སྡོམ་ (əmdzi dom) va. to place one's upper teeth over the lower lip in an expression of anger.

འར་ (ar) 1. vi. to come apart, to become unsewn ། ཚེམ་བུ་འར་བཞག The stitching came apart. 2. abbr. of འར་པོ་.

འར་སྐད་ (argɛɛ̀) boisterous/ raucous/ loud talk or noise; va.—རྒྱག; —ཤོད་.

འར་སྐད་ཚ་པོ་ (argɛɛ̀ tsābo) boisterous, raucous, loud (in talk).

འར་གྲིས་འདུལ་ (argi düü) va. to intimidate by harsh words/ criticism ། དགེ་རྒན་གསར་པ་དེས་སློབ་ཕྲུག་རྣམས་འར་གྲིས་བདུལ་ཙང་ཚང་མས་ཞེད་སྣང་བྱེད་ཀྱི་འདུག The students are frightened because the new teacher intimidated them (with harsh words and criticism).

འར་སྒྲ་ (ardra) sm. འར་སྐད་.

འར་སྒྲ་ཆེན་པོ་ (ardra cēmbo) sm. འར་སྐད་ཚ་པོ་.

འར་ཆད་ཐེབས་ (arjɛɛ̀ tēb) vi. to become exhausted by work ། བཟོ་པ་རྣམས་ལ་ལས་ཀ་ཚད་ལས་བརྒལ་བ་བསྐྱལ་ན་འར་ཆད་ཐེབས་ཀྱི་རེད་ If one makes the workers work in excess of norms they will become exhausted (and be unable to work).

འར་འདེད་ (andeè) 1. pushing a person or animal to work too much or too hard; va.—གཏོང་ ། ལས་རྒྱབ་པས་ལས་མི་རྣམས་འར་འདེད་བཏང་དྲགས་ཙང་མི་མང་པོ་ཆད་འདུག The supervisor pushed the workers too much so many people became exhausted (unable to work). 2. pursuing/ collecting a debt excessively; va.—གཏོང་.

འར་འདེད་བཙན་སྐྱོར་ (andeè dzɛnjɔɔ) shung. sm. འར་འདེད་.

འར་པ་ (arba) a crude/ unreasonable/ arbitrary person.

འར་པོ་ (arbo) 1. crude, rude, arbitrary, unreasonable, exaggerated ། མི་དེ་སྐད་ཆ་འར་པོ་ཤོད་མཁན་ཞིག་རེད་ That man speaks in a crude manner. 2. va.—སྐྱལ་; sm. འར་འདེད་གཏོང་.

འར་མི་སྤུངས་ (arme būŋ) va. to pile up.

འར་ཚ་པོ་ (ar tsābo) sm. འར་སྐད་ཚ་པོ་.

འར་ཟེར་འོར་ཟེར་ (arser worsee) speaking in a loud and arrogant manner.

འར་ཝུར་ (arwur) abbr. of འ་རི་འུ་རི་.

འལ་འོལ་ (alüül) abbr. of འལ་ལི་འོལ་ལི་.

འལ་འོལ་ཕར་འགྱངས་ (alwüü pāgyaŋ) wasting time and delaying; va.—གཏོང་.

འལ་ལི་འོལ་ལི་ (ale ööle) 1. unclear due to darkness. 2. sb. who doesn't focus on one topic/ task, sb. who is erratic; va.—བྱེད་ ། མི་དེས་རྟག་པར་འལ་ལི་འོལ་ལི་བྱས་ནས་ལས་ཀ་དུས་ཐོག་ལ་བྱེད་ཀྱི་མི་འདུག He always doesn't focus on the main task so he doesn't do his work on time.

འི་ (i) genitive particle suffixed to vowel final stems ། ཁོའི་ His.

འུ་ (wu) diminutive particle ། རྟའུ་ Baby horse.

ཝུ་གུ་ (wugu) I.

ཝུ་གུ་ཆུང་ (wugujuŋ) owl.

ཝུ་ཅག (wujaà) sm. ང་ཚོ་.

ཝུ་གཉིས་ (wuñii) we two.

ཝུ་ཐུག (wuùduù) vi. to be in desperate straits, to be left with no choices in a hopeless situation ¶ཁོ་ཚོ་ཝུ་ཐུག་ནས་དྲག་པོའི་ངོ་རྒོལ་བྱེད་དགོས་བྱུང་བ་རེད་ They were in a desperate situation and revolted.

ཝུ་ཐུག་ཁྱི་རྒན་གྱང་ལ་མཆོང་ (wuùduù kyīgɛn gyaŋla cōŋ) acting out of desperation, doing sth. dangerous out of desperation [Lit. a desperate old dog jumps at the wall].

ཝུ་ཐུག་ཆིངས་ཡིག (wuùduù cīŋyii) a treaty signed out of desperation (because there was no other option).

ཝུ་ཐུག་མཆོང་རྒྱག (wuùduù cōŋgyaà) sm. ཝུ་ཐུག་ཁྱི་རྒན་གྱང་ལ་མཆོང་.

ཝུ་ཐུག་ཉེན་མཆོང་ (wuùduù ñenjoŋ) sm. ཝུ་ཐུག་མཆོང་རྒྱག.

ཝུ་ཐུག་ཐབས་རྙེད་ (wuùduù tōbñii) finding a means or way out of a desperate situation.

ཝུ་ཐུག་ཐབས་ཟད་ (wuùduù tōbsɛɛ̀) vi. to be at one's wits end, to be in a desperate/ hopeless situation.

ཝུ་ཐུག་མཐར་ལྷུང་ (wuùduù tārlhuŋ) sm. ཝུ་ཐུག་ཐབས་ཟད་.

ཝུ་ཐུག་པའི་གནས་ (wuùduùbɛ nɛ̄ɛ̀) a desperate/ hopeless situation; vi.—སུ་གྱུར་ to fall into desperate straits, to come into a desperate situation.

ཝུ་ཐུག་བཟོད་བྲལ་ (wuùduù sööödrɛɛ) desperate and unbearable/ intolerable.

ཝུ་ཐོམ་མེར་སྡོད་ (wuùdüü merdöö) standing looking stupified/ stunned.

ཝུ་དུམ་ (wudum) pieces of broken things.

ཝུ་དུམ་བཙན་ (wudumdzɛn) King Langdarma.

ཝུ་བུ་ (wubu) I.

ཝུ་བུ་ཅག (wubujaà) we.

ཝུ་ཚང་ (wudzaŋ) our family.

ཝུ་ཟུབ་ (wusub) down in spirits, depressed ¶སློབ་ཕྲུག་དེ་ཡིག་ཚད་མ་ལོན་ཙང་ཝུ་ཟུབ་ནས་བསྡད་བཞག Because the student didn't pass the test, he was depressed.

ཝུ་ཟུབ་པོ་ (wu subbu) down in spirits, despirited, depressed.

ཝུ་རང་ (wuraŋ) we.

ཝུ་རུ་རུ་ (wu ruru) a whizzing/ whistling sound.

ཝུ་ལག (wulaà) shung. corvee labor; va.—རྒྱུགས་ to do corvee labor; va.—སྐྱལ་; —གཏོང་ to make/ send sb. to do corvee labor.

ཝུ་ལག་ཉིས་སྐྱལ་ (wulaà ñīigüü) shung. corvee labor that involves working on alternating days.

ཝུ་ལག་རྟག་རྒྱུགས་ (wulaà dāggyuù) shung. corvee labor that involves working every day.

ཝུ་ལུ་ (wulu) physalis alkekengi (used in Tibetan medicine).

ཝུ་ཤན་ཏན་ (wushɛndɛn) ch. wireless.

ཝུ་སུ་ (wusu) coriander.

ཝུག (wug) abbr. of ཝུག་པ་.

ཝུག་སྐད་ (wuggɛɛ̀) owl's hooting.

ཝུག་སྒྲོ་ (wugdro) owl's feather.

ཝུག་ཆུང་ (wugjuŋ) abbr. ཝུག་གུ་ཆུང་.

ཝུག་པ་ (wugbə) owl.

ཝུག་པ་ཁ་གཅིག (wugbə kājig) being single-minded in what one says and not deviating from it [Lit. owl's have one mouth (sound)].

ཝུག་པ་མཆོད་བྱེད་ (wugbə cöòjeè) sm. སྲམ་.

ཝུག་པའི་ཁ་ནས་ཝུག་གཅིག (wugbɛ kānɛ wugjig) sm. ཝུག་པ་ཁ་གཅིག.

ཝུག་ཕྲུག (wugdruù) baby owl.

ཝུང་དེ་ (wuŋde) sm. འོན་ཀྱང་.

ཝུང་དེང་ (wuŋdeŋ) sm. འོན་ཀྱང་.

ཝུང་སྡེ་ (wuŋde) sm. འོན་ཀྱང་.

ཝུང་ཝུང་ (wuŋwuŋ) sound of sth. exploding.

ཝུད་ (wüù) 1. exaggeration, overstatement; va.—སྒྲོག to exaggerate, to overstate. 2. sm. ཡུད་ཙམ་. 3. sm. ཤུགས་.

ཝུད་སྒྲོག (wüùdrɔɔ̀) sm. ཝུད་.

ཝུད་གདམ་ (wüùdam) sm. ཝུད་.

ཝུད་བསྟོད་ (wüùdöö) exaggerated praise; va.—བྱེད་.

ཝུད་བསྟོད་སྤྲེལ་ལད་ (wüùdöö bēēlɛɛ̀) sm. ཝུད་བསྟོད་.

ཝུད་བསྟོད་ཚད་མེད་ (wüùdöö tsɛɛ̀meè) sm. ཝུད་བསྟོད་.

ཝུད་པོ་ཆེ་ (wüùboje) sm. ཝུད་.

ཝུད་ཤོབ་ (wüùshob) boasting, bragging, exaggerating; va.—ཤོད་; —བྱེད་ to boast, to brag, to exaggerate.

ཝུད་ཤོབ་ཚ་པོ་ (wüùshob tsābo) sb. who boasts/ brags/ exaggerates a lot.

ཝུན་ཤིང་ཀོང་ཇོ་ (wünshiŋ kōŋjo) Chinese wife of King Songtsen Gampo.

ཝུབ་ (wub) collecting all at once, taking in one fell swoop.

ཝུབས་ (wub) sm. ཝུབ་.

ཝུབས་བསྡུས་ (wub düü) 1. va. to frighten ¶དགེ་རྒན་ཚ་པོ་དེས་སློབ་གྲྭ་བ་རྣམས་ཝུབས་བསྡུས་ཀྱི་ཡོད་པ་རེད་ The harsh teacher frightens the students. 2. vi. to be frightened ¶སློབ་ཕྲུག་ཚོ་དགེ་རྒན་ཚ་པོ་དེར་ཝུབས་བསྡུས་ཀྱི་ཡོད་པ་རེད་ The students are frightened by the harsh teacher. 3. to gather all together. 4. (va.—རྒྱག) to stitch poorly/ carelessly.

ཝུར་ (wur) 1. vi. to be startled (due to a noise) ¶མེ་མདའི་སྒྲ་གྲགས་པ་དང་བྱ་ཚང་མ་ཝུར་སོང་ The gun noise startled all the birds. 2. exaggerating; boasting; va.—ཤོད་. 3. pushing and shoving by a crowd, commotion, clamor; va.—རྒྱག ¶ཚོང་ཁང་དུ་མི་མང་པོས་ཝུར་རྒྱག་བཞིན་འདུག Many people were pushing and shoving to go into the shop.

ཝུར་དཀྲོག (wurdrɔɔ̀) turmoil/ agitation/ disturbance caused by sth. said or by rumors; vi.—ཐེབས་ to have great turmoil/ disturbance occur due to sth. said or by rumors; va.—བྱེད་; —སློང་ to cause turmoil, to agitate, to make/ incite a disturbance.

ཝུར་སྐད་ (wurgɛɛ̀) 1. roaring, yelling, hubbub, uproar, tumult (usu. made by a crowd or audience); va.—རྒྱག ¶བཟོ་པ་ཚོས་གླ་ཆ་སྤྲོར་དགོས་ཞེས་ཝུར་སྐད་བརྒྱབ་པ་རེད་ The workers were yelling they want wages. 2. sound of howling wind, the thundering sound of an earthquake, a droning sound (e.g., a cloud of locusts).

ཝུར་སྒྱ་ (wurgya) sm. ཝུར་རྡོ་.

ཝུར་བསྐྱོད་ (wurgyöö) making a disturbance/ commotion/ clamor/ while going somewhere.

ཝུར་འགྲོས་ (wurdröö) sm. ཝུར་བསྐྱོད་.

ཝུར་རྒྱག (wur gyaà) the hubbub of a large crowd of people talking together, the sound/ commotion/ clamor of many people in a crowd.

ཝུར་རྒྱག་ཟིང་སློང་ (wurgyaà siŋloŋ) making commotion and turmoil; va.—བྱེད་.

ཝུར་སྒྲ་ (wurdra) 1. clamor, loud noise, yelling, boisterous noise; va.—བྱེད; —རྒྱག; —སྒྲོག.

ཝུར་སྒྲ་ཆེན་པོ་ (wurdra cēmbo) very boisterous/ noisy.

ཝུར་སྒྲ་ཐིང་ཐིང་ (wurdra tīŋdiŋ) boisterous, loud, noisy.

ཝུར་སྒྲ་ཚ་པོ་ (wurdra tsābo) sm. ཝུར་སྒྲ་ཆེན་པོ་.

ཝུར་སྒྲ་ཤིག་ཤིག (wurdra shīgshii) sm. ཝུར་སྒྲ་ཐིང་ཐིང་.

ཝུར་སྒྲོག་རྒྱག (wurdrɔɔ̀ gyaà) sm. ཝུར་སྒྲ་(སྒྲོག).

ཝུར་ཅིལ་ལི་ (wur cīīli) 1. noisy, boisterous. 2. sm. ཝུར་པོ་.

ཝུར་ཅེམ་ (wurjen) abbr. of ཝུར་ཝུར་ཅེམ་ཅེམ་.

ཝུར་ཅོམ་ (wurjom) a loud thundering sound.

ཝུར་ལྡགས་ཕོག (wurjaà pɔ̄ɔ̀) vi. to get hit by a slingshot's rope.

ཝུར་དོན་ (wurdün) sm. ཝུར་འདོན་.

ཝུར་གདམ་ (wurdam) sm. ཝུད་.

ཝུར་གདམ་དཀྲོག་རྐྱེན་ (wurdam drɔ̄ggyen) sm. ཝུར་དཀྲོག.

ཝུར་བསྟོད་ (wurdöö) sm. ཝུད་བསྟོད་.

ཝུར་ཐིང་ངེ་ (wur tīŋŋe) sm. ཝུར་ཅིལ་ལི་.

ཝུར་མཐིལ་ (wurdii) the part of the sling where the

stone is placed.

ཝུར་དིར་དིར་ (wur tirdir) sm. ཝུར་ཅིལ་ལི་.

ཝུར་འདར་གཡོ་ (wurdar yō) vi. to tremble ¶ མེ་སྒྲོགས་ཀྱི་སྒྲ་ཡིས་ས་གཞི་ཝུར་འདར་གཡོས་སོང་ The sound of the artillery made the earth tremble.

ཝུར་འདོན་ (wurdün) loud chanting/ reciting in unison; va.—བྱེད་.

ཝུར་འདྲོག (wurdrɔɔ̀) scared/ started by a noise; vi.—ཐེབས་.

ཝུར་རྡོ་ (wurdo) slingshot; va.—རྒྱག; —གཞུ་; —འཕེན་ to shoot a slingshot.

ཝུར་རྡོ་ཆུ་མིག་དགུ་སྐྱིལ་ (wurdo cũmig gudrii) the nine-eyed sling (a type sligshot in which nine eye-like designs are braided into the design).

ཝུར་རྡོའི་ཚར་ལྕེ་ (wurdö tsārje) the tip of a slingshot that is used to make a cracking sound to drive animals.

ཝུར་པའི་ཕྱི་སློགས་ (wurbɛ cigɔɔ̀) cicada slough.

ཝུར་པ་ (wurba) 1. locust. 2. skylark.

ཝུར་པོ་ (wurbu) working fast; va.—བྱེད་ ¶ ལས་ཀ་ཝུར་པོ་མ་བྱས་ན་དུས་བཀག་གོང་ཚར་ས་མ་རེད་ If we don't work fast we won't finish before the time fixed (to finish).

ཝུར་ཕྲུག (wurdruù) sm. བྱི་ཕྲུག.

ཝུར་མ་ (wurmə) early morning mist/ fog.

ཝུར་ཞིང་ (wursiŋ) abbr. of ཝུར་རྒྱག་ཞིང་སྐྱོང་.

ཝུར་ཚ་པོ་ (wur tsābo) sm. ཝུད་ཤོབ་ཚ་པོ་.

ཝུར་ཤོགས་ (wurshɔɔ̀) sm. ཝུར་གཏམ་.

ཝུར་ཝུར་ (wurwur) sm. ཝུར་སྐད་.

ཝུར་ཝུར་ཅིལ་ཅིལ་ (wurwur ciijii) sm. ཝུར་ཅི་ལི་.

ཝུར་ཝུར་ཅེམ་ཅེམ་ (wurwur cēmjem) loud sound of drums and cymbals.

ཝུར་ཝུར་སིལ་སིལ་ (wurwur siisii) loud sound of music.

ཝུར་རུ་ (wurru) sm. ཝུར་ཤོབ་.

ཝུར་རུ་རུ་ (wur ruru) sm. ཝུ་རུ་རུ་.

ཝུར་ལངས་ (wur laŋ) 1. vi. to have a disturbance/ turmoil occur/ arise ¶ ཉེན་རྟོག་པས་མེ་མདའ་བརྒྱབ་ཙང་མི་དམངས་ཀྱི་ཁྲོད་དུ་ཝུར་ལངས་པ་རེད་ Because the police opened fire, a disturbance broke out among the people. 2. vi. to create a sensation ¶ སྲིད་འཛིན་གསར་པའི་གཏམ་བཤད་དེས་མང་ཚོགས་ཀྱི་ཁྲོད་དུ་ཝུར་ལངས་པ་རེད་ The newly elected president's speech caused a sensation amongst the people.

ཝུར་ཤོག་ཚ་པོ་ (wurshoò tsābo) sm. ཝུར་ཤོབ་ཚ་པོ་.

ཝུར་ཤོད་ (wurshöö) sm. ཝུར་ཤོབ་.

ཝུར་ཤོབ་ (wurshob) sm. ཝུད་ཤོབ་.

ཝུར་སིལ་ (wursii) abbr. ཝུར་ཝུར་སིལ་སིལ་.

ཝུར་སློང་ (wurloŋ) sm. ཝུར་རྒྱག་ཞིང་སྐྱོང་.

ཝུལ་ (wüü) abbr. of ཝུ་ལག.

ཝུལ་མི་ (wüümi) a corvee laborer.

འེ་ལེ་ (ele) shame on you! ¶ འེ་ལེ་ད་ལྟ་ཁྱེད་རང་བུ་མོར་བརྩས་བགྲོ་རྒྱུ་ལོ་ཆུང་དྲགས་པ་རེད་ Shame on you ! You are too young to be teasing girls.

འོ་ (o) 1. sentence ending particle used after vowel finals. 2. a kiss; va.—སྐྱེལ་; —བྱེད་ to kiss ¶ ངང་ལ་འོ་བྱོས་ཤིག Give me a kiss. 3. abbr. of འོ་མ་. 4. Oh my!

འོ་ཀྲིང་ (odriŋ) sm. འོ་ཀྲིན་.

འོ་ཀྲིན་ (odrin) canned milk.

འོ་ཀྲིན་མངར་མོ་ (odrin ŋārmo) condensed milk.

འོ་དཀྲོག་འཕྲུལ་ཆས་ (odrɔɔ̀ drũũjɛɛ̀) milk churning machine.

འོ་རྐྱལ་ (ogyɛɛ) milk bag.

འོ་སྐམ་ (ogam) powdered milk.

འོ་སྐོལ་ (ogöö) sm. ང་ཅག.

འོ་སྐྱུར་ (ogyur) 1. sour milk, curdled milk. 2. lactic acid.

འོ་ཁེབས་ (ogeb) bra.

འོ་ཁྲུས་ (odrüü) washing one's face with milk (to make the skin lighter and softer); va.—རྒྱག.

འོ་བརྒྱལ་ (opgyɛɛ) 1. fatigue, weariness, tiredness ¶ ཁྱེད་དེ་རིང་འོ་བརྒྱལ་བྱུང་ངམ་ Did you get tired today? 2. a common greeting asked of people arriving from a journey ¶ ཁྱེད་ཚོ་འོ་བརྒྱལ་བྱུང་ངམ་ Did you get tired on the trip (Are you tired from the trip).

འོ་བརྒྱལ་རང་ཉོ་ (opgyɛɛ raŋño) creating one's own difficulties.

འོ་མངར་ (oŋar) milk before the butter is removed.

འོ་ཅག (ojaà) we.

འོ་ཅོག (ojoò) all.

འོ་ཆང་ (ojaŋ) kumiss, fermented milk.

འོ་ཆུ་ (oju) 1. milk and water. 2. sm. འོ་བཙུད་.

འོ་ཆུ་གཅིག་འདྲེས་ (oju jĩŋdreè) sm. འོ་ཆུ་མཉམ་འདྲེས་.

འོ་ཆུ་མཉམ་འདྲེས་ (oju ñamdreè) having a good relationship or close friendship [Lit. milk and water mixed together].

འོ་ཆུ་འདྲེས་པ་ (oju dreèba) sm. འོ་ཆུ་མཉམ་འདྲེས་.

འོ་ཆོལ་སྟོར་ (ojöö dōr) va. to sprinkle milk as an offering.

འོ་ཇ་ (oja) tea made with milk.

འོ་རྗེན་ (ojen) fresh milk.

འོ་སྙིགས་ (oñig) milk residue.

འོ་ཐག་གཅོད་ (odaà jöö) va. to wean ¶ ཕྲུ་གུའི་འོ་ཐག་གཅོད་རན་འདུག It is time to wean that child.

འོ་ཐག་ཆོད་ (odaà cöö) vi. to be/ get weaned.

འོ་ཐུག (oduù) a soup/ broth made with milk.

འོ་ཐོན་ཁྱིམ་ཕྱུགས་ (odön kyĩmjuù) domestic milch livestock.

འོ་ཐོན་སྒོ་ཕྱུགས་ (odön gojuù) sm. འོ་ཐོན་ཁྱིམ་ཕྱུགས་.

འོ་འཐུང་ཕྲུ་གུ་ (oduŋ drūgu) a nursing baby.

འོ་འཐུང་སྲོག་ཆགས་ (oduŋ sōgjaà) mammals.

འོ་ད་ (oda) now.

འོ་དུས་ (odüü) the time of lactation.

འོ་དོད་ (odöö) wailing; va.—འབོད་.

འོ་དྲི་ (odri) smell of milk.

འོ་དྲི་ཁ་མཁན་ (odri kāñɛn) sm. འོ་དྲི་དྲོ་བ་.

འོ་དྲི་དྲོ་བ་ (odri trowo) young and inexperienced [Lit. smelling of (mother's) milk].

འོ་དྲི་མ་ཡལ་བ་ (odri ma yɛɛwa) a baby still nursing.

འོ་དྲི་མ་བསང་བ་ (odri ma sāŋwa) sm. འོ་དྲི་མ་ཡལ་བ་.

འོ་མདོག (ondɔɔ̀) color of milk.

འོ་མདོང་ (odoŋ) wooden milk churn.

འོ་ཏོག (odɔɔ̀) nipple.

འོ་ན་ (ona) well then, in that case.

འོ་སྤྲི་ (odri) cream.

འོ་ཕུད་ (obüü) the first milk from a milking that is offered to the deities.

འོ་ཕྱེ་ (oje) powdered milk.

འོ་བྱམས་ (o cam) va. to love/ cherish.

འོ་བྱེད་ (o ceè) va. to kiss.

འོ་འབོད་བྱེད་ (omböö ceè) va. to call/ yell.

འོ་མ་ (oma) milk; va.—འཛོ་ to milk.

འོ་མ་དཀྲོག (oma drɔɔ̀) va. to churn milk (to make butter).

འོ་མ་སྐམ་པོ་ (oma gāmbo) powdered milk.

འོ་མ་སྟེར་ (oma dēr) 1. va. to breast feed. 2. va. to give milk.

འོ་མ་བཞུར་ (oma shur) sm. འོ་མ་དཀྲོག.

འོ་མ་བཞོ་ (oma sho) sm. འོ་མ་འཛོ་.

འོ་མ་བཞོས་ (oma shöö) p. of འོ་མ་འཛོ་.

འོ་མ་རུལ་ (oma rüü) sm. འོ་མ་ཤི་.

འོ་མ་ལས་སྣོན་བཟོ་གྲྭ་ (oma lɛɛ̀nün sodra) 1. condensed milk factory. 2. dairy products plant.

འོ་མ་ཤེལ་ཏོག (oma shēēdɔɔ̀) frosted light bulb.

འོ་མ་ཤི་ (oma shī) vi. to have milk turn sour/ curdle.

འོ་མ་སྲུབ་ (oma sūb) sm. འོ་མ་དཀྲོག.

འོ་མ་སྲུབ་བྱེད་འཕྲུལ་འཁོར་ (oma sūnjeè trũũgɔɔ) milk churning machine.

འོ་མའི་ཁ་སྤྲིས་ (omɛ kədrii) cream.

འོ་མའི་རྒྱ་མཚོའི་ནང་ ཁྲག་གི་ཐིག་པ་འཕེན་ (omɛ gyadzö naŋ trāāgi tigbə pēn) causing hatred/ anger amongst people living in harmony and peace [Lit. dripping blood in an ocean of milk].

འོ་མའི་རྒྱ་མཚོའི་ནང་གི་སྦལ་པ་ཁྲག་ཅན་ (omɛ gyadzönaŋgi bɛɛba trāājɛn) an evil person amongst a group of good people [Lit. a wounded frog amongst a sea of milk].

འོ་མའི་ཐོན་རྫས་ (omɛ töndzɛɛ̀) milk products.

འོ་མའི་རྩེ་ (o̲mɛ dzē) nipple.
འོ་རྫམ་ (o̲dzam) powdered milk.
འོ་ཚགས་ (o̲dzaà) milk strainer; va.—རྒྱག to strain milk.
འོ་ཚབ་ (o̲dzəb) milk substitute.
འོ་ཚབ་ཕྱེ་མ་ (o̲dzəb cēma) powdered milk subsitute.
འོ་ཚབས་ (o̲dzəb) disease of the breast (women).
འོ་འཛིན་ (o̲ndzin) woman's breasts.
འོ་འཛིན་བུམ་བཟང་ (o̲ndzin pu̲msaŋ) woman's breasts.
འོ་ཞོ་ (o̲sho) yogurt.
འོ་བཞོའི་འཕྲུལ་འཁོར་ (o̲shö trüügɔɔ) sm. འོ་བཞོའི་འཕྲུལ་ཆས་.
འོ་བཞོའི་འཕྲུལ་ཆས་ (o̲shö trüüjɛɛ̀) milking machine.
འོ་བཟང་ (o̲saŋ) well done.
འོ་ཟས་ (o̲sɛɛ̀) dairy products/ foods.
འོ་ཟོ་ (o̲so) sm. འོ་ཟོམ་.
འོ་ཟོམ་ (o̲som) milking bucket.
འོ་བཟེ་ (o̲se) efficient in work.
འོ་བཟོས་ཀ་ར་ (o̲söö gāra) a kind of cheese candy made from milk.
འོ་བཟོས་ཐོན་རྫས་ (o̲söö tōndzɛɛ̀) milk dairy products.
འོ་བཟོས་བྱི་རིལ་ (o̲söö ci̲rii) sm. འོ་བཟོས་ཀ་ར་.
འོ་བཟོས་བཟའ་ཆས་ (o̲söö sajɛɛ̀) foods made from milk, diary products.
འོ་ཤི་ (o̲shi) abbr. of འོ་མ་ཤི་.
འོ་སེ་ (o̲se) sm. འོ་སེ་ཤིང་.
འོ་སེ་ཤིང་ (o̲se shīŋ) pyrus pashia tree (used in Tibetan medicine).
འོ་གསར་ (o̲sar) 1. fresh milk.
འོ་གསོ་ (o̲so) sm. འོ་མ་སྤྲིར་.
འོ་གསོ་ཁང་ (o̲sogaŋ) a room set aside for breast feeding.
འོ་གསོ་སྲོག་ཆགས་ (o̲so sōgjaà) mammals.
འོ་བསུ་ (o̲su) the custom of the mother-in-law welcoming the new bride with a bowl of milk.
འོག (wɔ̲ɔ̀) 1. under, beneath, below ¶ གནམ་གྲུའི་འོག Under the plane. ¶ དཀའ་ཚེགས་ཏ་ཅང་ཆེ་བའི་འོག Under very difficult conditions. 2. because of, due to, by, though, with ¶ སྐབས་དེར་བཙན་རྒྱལ་རིང་ལུགས་པའི་རྒྱུད་བསྐུལ་འོག Because of incitement by the imperialists. 3. testacles; va.—འདོན་ to castrate.
འོག་སྐས་ (wɔ̲ɔ̀gɛɛ̀) the lower stairs/ staircase.
འོག་སྐོར་ (wɔ̲ɔ̀gɔɔ) 1. underspin, backspin (in tennis). 2. sm. འོག་བསྐོར་.
འོག་བསྐོར་ (wɔ̲ɔ̀gɔɔ) crop rotation; va.—འདེབས་ to rotate crops.
འོག་བསྐོར་བསྐྱར་འདེབས་ (wɔ̲ɔ̀gɔɔ gyāndeb) crop rotation and multiple cropping.
འོག་ཁྲིམས་ (wɔ̲gdrim) laws made secretly/ illegally.
འོག་འཁྲུ་ (wɔ̲ɔ̀ trū) vi. to have diarrhea.
འོག་གོས་ (wɔ̲ɔ̀göö̀) 1. clothes worn under an outer garment. 2. underwear.
འོག་གྲབས་ (wɔ̲ɔ̀drəb) preparing, getting ready; va.—བྱེད་ ¶ ལས་ཀ་འགོ་མ་བཙུགས་གོང་འོག་གྲབས་ཡག་པོ་བྱེད་དགོས་ Before you start work you must make good preparations.
འོག་འགྱུ་དམར་པོ་ (wɔ̲ɔ̀gyu mārpo) extremely suspicious.
འོག་སྒོ་ (wɔ̲ɔ̀go) anus.
འོག་སྒོ་གཉིས་ (wɔ̲ɔ̀go ñīì) genitals and anus.
འོག་ཅན་ (wɔ̲ɔ̀jɛn) uncastrated (animals).
འོག་གཅིན་ (wɔ̲ɔ̀jin) urine.
འོག་འཆིང་ (wɔ̲ɔ̀jiŋ) belt tied under one's dress.
འོག་འཇུག (wɔ̲njuù) shirt (without a collar) worn under one's dress/ gown.
འོག་འཇུག་སྨན་དབྱུག (wɔ̲njuù mɛ̄nyuù) sm. འོག་འཇུག་སྨན་རིལ་.
འོག་འཇུག་སྨན་རིལ་ (wɔ̲njuù mɛ̄nrii) rectal suppository medicine.
འོག་ཏུ་ (wɔ̲gdu) below, under, beneath.
འོག་རྟ་ (wɔ̲gda) riding horse.
འོག་སྟན་ (wɔ̲gdɛn) a pad/ rug put under another rug.
འོག་ཐུ་ (wɔ̲gdu) sm. ཐུ་བ་ནང་མ་.
འོག་མཐའ་ (wɔ̲gda) lowest.
འོག་གདན་ (wɔ̲gdɛn) anvil.
འོག་གདུང་ (wɔ̲gduŋ) beam.
འོག་འདྲི་ (wɔ̲gdri) asking in an indirect manner; va.—རྒྱག.
འོག་རྡོ་ (wɔ̲gdo) 1. anvil. 2. the lower stone of a flour mill. 3. stones placed on the bottom part of a wall.
འོག་ལྡན་ (wɔ̲gdɛn) sm. འོག་ཅན་.
འོག་བསྡོམས་ (wɔ̲gdɔɔ) sm. འོག་གྲབས་.
འོག་ནས་གོང་ལ་ (wɔ̲nɛ go̲ŋla) from the lower/ bottom to the higher/ top ¶ གྲྭ་པ་ཚོས་འོག་ནས་གོང་ལ་ངོ་རྒོལ་བྱས་པ་རེད་ All the monks (the monks from lower to higher) opposed (it).
འོག་གནོན་ (wɔ̲gnön) holding/ pinning down, oppressing; va.—བྱེད་.
འོག་པག (wɔ̲gbaà) a decorated/ embroidered belt.
འོག་དཔོན་ (wɔ̲gbön) arc. junior official.
འོག་ཕྱུང་ (wɔ̲ɔ̀ cūŋ) va. to castrate.
འོག་ཕྱོགས་ (wɔ̲ɔ̀jɔɔ̀) the bottom or lower realm/ section/ part.
འོག་དབང་ (wɔ̲ɔ̀waŋ) genitals.
འོག་མ་ (wɔ̲ɔ̀ma) 1. lower, later ¶ གྲོས་ཚོགས་འོག་མ་ The lower house (in parliament). 2. for siblings/ relatives, the younger.
འོག་མིག་ལྟ་ (wɔ̲ɔ̀mii dā) va. to have one's head facing down and peek up.
འོག་རྩ་ (wɔ̲gdza) anvil.
འོག་བརྩེགས་ (wɔ̲gdzeg) sm. བཙོ་སྦྲིགས་.
འོག་ཚ་ (wɔ̲gdza) sm. བཙོ་སྦྲིགས་.
འོག་ཚེམ་ (wɔ̲gdzem) h. of འོག་གོས་.
འོག་ཚུད་ (wɔ̲ɔ̀dzüü) see འཚུད་, 3.
འོག་གཞི་ (wɔ̲ɔ̀shi) 1. earth, the world. 2. base, foundation.
འོག་གཞིའི་དཀྱིལ་འཁོར་བཞི་ (wɔ̲ɔ̀shii gyīŋgɔɔ shi̲) the four mandalas: of earth, wind, fire, water.
འོག་རིམ་ (wɔ̲ɔ̀rim) lower ranks/ levels ¶ འོག་རིམ་ལས་བྱེད་པ་ The lower level officials.
འོག་རོལ་ (wɔ̲ɔ̀röö) 1. bottom, below. 2. after, later.
འོག་རླུང་ (wɔ̲ɔ̀luŋ) flatus; vi.—གཏོང་.
འོག་ལ་ (wɔ̲ɔ̀la) under, below, beneath.
འོག་ལམ་ (wɔ̲ɔ̀lam) sm. འོག་སྒོ་.
འོག་ལུད་ (wɔ̲ɔ̀lüü) base fertilizer.
འོག་ལེན་ (wɔ̲ɔ̀len) 1. estimating, guessing; va.—རྒྱག. 2. castrated.
འོག་ཤག (wɔ̲gshaà) apartments/ rooms on the bottom floor.
འོག་ཤལ་ (wɔ̲gshɛɛ) the fleshy skin below the neck of chickens/ and oxen.
འོག་གཤམ་ (wɔ̲ɔ̀sham) lower part, bottom, under, beneath.
འོག་སོ་ (wɔ̲gso) lower teeth.
འོག་གསང་ (wɔ̲gsaŋ) sm. གསང་གནས་.
འོང་: p. འོངས་; f. འོང་ (o̲ŋ) 1. va. to come. 2. a field with crops on it.
འོང་སྐོར་ (o̲ŋgɔɔ) a summer festival involving walking around fields with religious objects to insure a good harvest; va.—ལ་འགྲོ་ to go on an འོང་སྐོར་; va.—གཏོང་ to do/ conduct a འོང་སྐོར་ festival.
འོང་སྐོར་དུས་ཆེན་ (o̲ŋgɔɔ tü̲üjen) sm. འོང་སྐོར་.
འོང་ཁ་ (o̲ŋga) a field with crops on it.
འོང་ཁྲིམས་ (o̲ŋdrim) regulations/ restrictions/ taboos practiced during summertime in the fields.
འོང་གོར་ (o̲ŋgɔɔ) sm. འོང་སྐོར་.
འོང་འཕྱུར་ (o̲ŋ cār) sm. འོང་སིང་.
འོང་དབྱུག (o̲ŋyuù) wooden flail for threshing; va.—རྒྱག.
འོང་མཚམས་ (o̲ŋdzam) the edges of fields.
འོང་ཞིང་ (o̲ŋshiŋ) a field with crops on it.
འོང་བཞེས་ (o̲ŋsheè) taking winnowed grain from the threshing ground to the storeroom.
འོང་སིང་ (o̲ŋ sīŋ) va. to winnow with a pitchfork like stick (to separate straw from grain).

འོང་སྲུང་ (o̱ŋsuŋ) protecting fields (with crops); va.—བྱེད་.

འོང་སྲུང་བ་ (o̱ŋsuŋwa) person who guards/ watches over fields (with crops).

འོང་བསེར་ (o̱ŋser) sm. འོང་སེང་.

འོང་ར་ (o̱ŋra) 1. fence around a field with crops. 2. winnowing area.

འོངས་ (o̱ŋ) p. of འོང་.

འོད་ (wö̱ö̀) light; vi.—རྒྱག to shine, to glow ¶ཉི་མའི་འོད་ Sunlight.

འོད་ཀོར་ (wö̱ö̀gɔɔ) halo.

འོད་ཀྱི་སྣང་བ་ (wö̱ö̀gi nāŋwa) sm. འོད་སྣང་.

འོད་ཀྱི་མཚན་མ་ (wö̱ö̀gi tsε̄mma) 1. sm. འོད་སྣང་. 2. an omen based on the quality of a light.

འོད་ཀྱི་གསོ་ཐབས་ (wö̱ö̀gi sōdəb) 1. phototherapy. 2. raising sth. by artificial light.

འོད་ཁྲིག་ཁྲིག (wö̱ö̀drigdiì) shiny.

འོད་བཀྲ་ (wö̱ö̀dra) brilliant, dazzling, shining.

འོད་བཀྲག (wö̱ö̀draà) shining/ glowing of light.

འོད་བཀྱེ་ (wö̱ö̀ gyē) va. to produce light, to shine, to radiate.

འོད་སྐོར་ (wö̱ö̀gɔɔ) 1. a round light. 2. halo.

འོད་ཁང་ (wö̱ö̀gaŋ) lantern.

འོད་ཁྱུག་ཁྱུག (wö̱ö̀ kyūùgyuù) sm. འོད་ཆེམ་ཆེམ་.

འོད་འཁྱིམ་པ་ (wö̱ö̀ kyīmbə) vi. to have a halo around the sun/ moon.

འོད་འཁྱུག་འཁྱུག (wö̱ö̀ kyūùgyuù) sm. འོད་ཆེམ་ཆེམ་.

འོད་འཁྱུག་སེ་ (wö̱ö̀ kyūgse) sm. འོད་ཐིང་ངེར་.

འོད་གྱེས་པ་ (wö̱ö̀ gye̱èba) chromatic dispersion.

འོད་གློག (wö̱ö̀lɔɔ̀) optics and electronics.

འོད་འགྱེད་སྡེ་ཚན་ (wö̱ö̀gyeè de̱dzεn) x-ray department.

འོད་རྒྱག (wö̱ö̀ gya̱à) vi. to shine.

འོད་སྒོར་ (wö̱ö̀gɔɔ) camera aperture.

འོད་སྔོན་ (wö̱ö̀ŋön) 1. blue light, blue rays. 2. the first light of dawn.

འོད་ཅན་ (wö̱ö̀jεn) 1. shinny ¶རས་འོད་ཅན་ A shinny cloth. 2. Friday. 3. stars. 4. firefly.

འོད་ཆག (wö̱ö̀ cāà) vi. to fall out of favor ¶དེང་སང་བློན་ཆེན་དེ་འོད་ཆག་བཞག These days the minister has fallen out of favor.

འོད་ཆགས་པ་ (wö̱ö̀ cāgba) illuminated with (bright) light.

འོད་ཆིབ་ཆིབ་ (wö̱ö̀ cībjib) sm. འོད་ཆིམ་ཆིམ་.

འོད་ཆིམ་ཆིམ་ (wö̱ö̀ cīmjim) glittering, twinkling, sparkling.

འོད་ཆེན་མ་ (wö̱ö̀ cēmma) a bright/ shinning light.

འོད་ཆེམ་ཆེམ་ (wö̱ö̀ cēmjem) sm. འོད་ཆིམ་ཆིམ་.

འོད་འཇམ་ (wö̱njam) soft/ subdued light.

འོད་སྟོང་ (wö̱ö̀doŋ) 1. brilliant, splendid ¶འོད་སྟོང་ལྡན་པའི་གསར་བརྗེ་ The brilliant revolution. 2. a thousand rays of light.

འོད་སྟོང་འཕྲོ་བ་ (wö̱ö̀doŋ drōwa) sm. འོད་སྟོང་འབར་བ་.

འོད་སྟོང་འབར་བ་ (wö̱ö̀doŋ ba̱rwa) brilliant, splendid, lustrous, glorious, magnificient.

འོད་ཐིང་ངེར་ (wö̱ö̀ tiŋŋer) shining, shiny.

འོད་ཐིང་ཐིང་ (wö̱ö̀ tiŋdiŋ) sm. འོད་ཐིང་ངེར་.

འོད་མདངས་ (wö̱ö̀daŋ) rays of light.

འོད་མདངས་བཀྲ་བ་ (wö̱ö̀daŋ drāwa) sm. འོད་སྟོང་འབར་བ་.

འོད་མདངས་འབྱེད་ཆས་ (wö̱ö̀daŋ je̱èjεὲ) sm. འོད་འབྱེད་འཕྲུལ་ཆས་.

འོད་མདངས་འབྱེད་ཤེལ་ (wö̱ö̀daŋ je̱èshee) sm. འོད་ཟེར་འབྱེད་ཤེལ་.

འོད་མདའ་ (wö̱nda) ray of light, light beam.

འོད་མདེལ་ (wö̱ndee) flare; va.—རྒྱག; —འཕེན་ to shoot a flare.

འོད་འདུས་སློག་ཤུ་ (wö̱ndüù lɔ̄gshu) spotlight.

འོད་འདོན་ (wö̱ö̀ dö̱n) va. to polish.

འོད་ལྡན་ (wö̱ndεn) 1. sm. འོད་ཅན་. 2. sexual desire. 3. Friday. 4. stars.

འོད་ལྡན་འཁྲི་ཤིང་ (wö̱ndεn trīshiŋ) hyacinth.

འོད་ལྡོག་མེ་ལོང་ (wö̱ö̀ndεn me̱loŋ) light reflector.

འོད་ལྡོང་ (wö̱ndoŋ) brilliant, splendid ¶འོད་ལྡོང་དང་ལྡན་པའི་གསར་བརྗེ་ The brilliant revolution.

འོད་སྣང་ (wö̱ö̀naŋ) shinning light.

འོད་པ་ (wö̱ö̀ba) flooding; vi.—རྒྱག to have a flood.

འོད་པོ་ཆེ་ (wö̱ö̀boje) a bright/ shinning light.

འོད་དཔག་མེད་ (wö̱ö̀baàmeè) Amitabha Buddha.

འོད་སྤྲོ་ (wö̱ö̀dro) sm. འོད་བཀྱེ་.

འོད་ཕོག་དཔྱད་ཆས་ (wö̱ö̀pɔɔ̀ jε̄ὲjεὲ) exposure meter.

འོད་ཕོག་སྒྲིན་ཤོག (wö̱ö̀pɔɔ̀ ji̱nshoò) photosensitive paper.

འོད་འཕྲོ་ (wö̱ö̀ trō) vi. to shine, to glow, to emit light, to sparkle.

འོད་འབར་ (wö̱mbar) abbr. of འོད་སྟོང་འབར་བ་.

འོད་འབར་ལམ་ (wö̱mbar la̱m) Shining Path guerrillas (in Peru).

འོད་འབྱེད་འཕྲུལ་ཆས་ (wö̱ö̀jeè trūùjεὲ) spectrometer, spectroscope.

འོད་སྦྱོར་ནུས་པ་ (wö̱ö̀jɔɔ nu̱ùbə) photosynthesis.

འོད་མའི་སྨྱུ་གུ་ (wö̱ö̀mε ñu̱gu) 1. bamboo shoot. 2. rattan.

འོད་མའི་ཚལ་ (wö̱ö̀mε tsε̄ε) a grove of bamboo/ rattan.

འོད་དམར་ (wö̱ö̀mar) 1. red light/ rays. 2. red sky just before sunrise.

འོད་ཚད་ (wö̱ö̀dzεὲ) illuminating power, light intensity.

འོད་ཚད་འཇལ་བྱེད་ (wö̱ö̀dzεὲ je̱εjeè) sm. འོད་ཕོག་དཔྱད་ཆས་.

འོད་ཚད་ལེན་པའི་ཡོ་ཆས་ (wö̱ö̀dzεὲ le̱mbε yo̱jεὲ) sm. འོད་ཕོག་དཔྱད་ཆས་.

འོད་འཚེར་ (wö̱ö̀ tsēr) vi. to shine, to glow, to emit light.

འོད་འཚེར་རྡོ་ (wö̱ö̀ tsērdo) amphibole.

འོད་འཚེར་འཚེར་ (wö̱ö̀ tsērdzer) sm. འོད་ཆེམ་ཆེམ་.

འོད་ཞགས་ (wö̱ö̀shaà) rays of light that look like a lasso.

འོད་ཞུ་ (wö̱ö̀ shu̱) vi. to become a light ray.

འོད་ཟེར་ (wö̱ö̀see) light rays; vi.—འཕྲོ་ to emit light, to glow, to radiate, to shine, to sparkle.

འོད་ཟེར་སྟོང་ལྡན་ (wö̱ö̀see dōŋdεn) sm. འོད་སྟོང་འབར་བ་.

འོད་ཟེར་འབྱེད་ཤེལ་ (wö̱ö̀see je̱èshee) spectroscope.

འོད་གཟེར་ (wö̱ö̀see) sm. འོད་ཟེར་.

འོད་ཡོང་ཁུངས་ (wö̱ö̀ yo̱ŋguŋ) source of light.

འོད་རིག (wö̱ö̀riì) optics.

འོད་རིག་འཁོར་ཁང་ (wö̱ö̀riì kɔ̄ɔ̄gaŋ) optical shop.

འོད་རིག་དཔྱད་ཆས་ (wö̱ö̀riì jε̄ὲjεὲ) optics/ optical instruments.

འོད་རིམ་ (wö̱ö̀rim) light spectrum.

འོད་ལམ་མེ་ (wö̱ö̀ la̱mme) shinning brightly.

འོད་རླབས་ (wö̱ö̀ləb) light waves.

འོད་ལོ་ (wö̱ö̀lo) a light year.

འོད་ཤི་ (wö̱ö̀ shī) 1. vi. to lose brightness/ glitter/ shine. 2. vi. to fade/ pass away/ die/ end.

འོད་གསལ་ (wö̱ö̀ sεε) vi. to shine.

འོད་ཧྲིལ་ཧྲིལ་ (wö̱ö̀ hrīīhrii) shiny, glittering.

འོད་ཧྲིབ་ཧྲིབ་ (wö̱ö̀ hrēbhreb) sm. འོད་ཧྲིལ་ཧྲིལ་.

འོད་ལྷག་གེ་ (wö̱ö̀ lhāgge) sm. འོད་ལམ་མེ་.

འོད་ལྷག་ལྷག (wö̱ö̀ lhāglhaà) sm. འོད་ལམ་མེ་.

འོད་ལྷབ་ལྷབ་ (wö̱ö̀ lhəblhəb) sm. འོད་ལྷག་ལྷག.

འོད་ལྷམ་ལྷམ་ (wö̱ö̀ lhāmlham) sm. འོད་ཆེམ་ཆེམ་.

འོན་ (wö̱n) vi. to be/ get deaf.

འོན་ཀྱང་ (wö̱ngyaŋ) but, however, yet, nevertheless ¶ཁོས་སློབ་སྦྱོང་ཡག་པོ་བྱས་མི་འདུག འོན་ཀྱང་ལས་ཀ་ཡག་པོ་བྱས་བཞག He didn't do well in his studies but he has worked well.

འོན་ལྐུགས་ (wö̱nguù) deaf and dumb.

འོན་ལྐུགས་སློབ་གྲྭ་ (wö̱nguù lōbdra) school for the deaf and dumb.

འོན་ལྐུགས་ལྷན་ཚོགས་ (wö̱nguù lōbdra) association for the deaf and dumb.

འོན་ཁོག (wö̱ngɔɔ̀) sm. འོན་པ་.

འོན་གོག (wö̱ngɔɔ̀) sm. འོན་པ་.

འོན་དང་ (wö̱ndaŋ) sm. འོན་ཀྱང་.

འོན་ཏེ་ (wö̱nde) sm. འོན་ཀྱང་.

འོན་པ་ (wö̱mba) deaf.

འོན་བྲ་ (wö̱ndra) a nomad district in Nagchuka

Prefecture.

འོན་ཟུ་འདེབས་ (wöndzu deb) va. to pretend to be deaf.

འོན་ལོང་ (wönloŋ) deaf and blind.

འོན་ལོང་སྐུགས་པའི་སློབ་གྲྭ (wönloŋ gūgbɛ lōbdra) school for the deaf, blind and mute.

འོན་སངས་ (wön sāŋ) vi. to recover one's lost hearing.

འོན་སེང་ (wönseŋ) sm. འོན་གསང་.

འོན་གསང་ (wönsaŋ) waiting for sth. in readiness, being on the alert ¶ སོ་སོས་ཐུག་དགོས་པའི་བཙོན་པ་དེ་ཡོང་མིན་བཙོན་ཁང་སྒོ་རྩར་འོན་གསང་ཞུས་ཏེ་བསྡད་པ་རེད་ They sat in readiness at the door of the prison waiting for the prisoner they wanted to meet to come.

འོབས་ (wob) pit, trench.

འོབས་དེ་ཉེད་ (wobdeñeè) sm. ཉེན་མེད་ཁོན་མེད་.

འོབས་དོང་ (wobdoŋ) sm. འོབས་.

འོབས་ལྤགས་ (wobjaà) sm. འབ་ལྤགས་.

འོབས་ཆུ་ (wobju) water in a trench/ moat around a wall.

འོབས་རྩིག (wobdzii) sm. འོབས་ལྤགས་.

འོབས་ཞུ་ (wobshu) a type of hat worn by Bon religious practitioners.

འོམ་བུ་ (wömbu) tamarisk.

འོམ་བུ་གླ་སྒང་ (wömbu lāgaŋ) the first palace/ fortress in Tibet.

འོའོ་ཙི་ (woodzi) an expression of surprise: oh my! wow ¶ འོའོ་ཙི་ ང་ཚོའི་གྲོགས་པོའི་བཟའ་ཟླ་ཁ་ས་གྲོངས་བཞག Oh my, our friend's wife died yesterday.

འོར་ (wɔr) 1. (— + vb. of motion) va. to bring, to take ¶ ཅ་ལག་རྣམས་འོར་ཡོང་པ་རེད་ (They) brought the things. ¶ ཅ་ལག་རྣམས་འོར་ཕྱིན་པ་རེད་ (They) took the things away. 2. a type of dropsy in Tibetan medicine that is characterized by many pimples.

འོར་འཁྱེར་ (wɔrgyer) sm. འོར་འདྲེན་.

འོར་འགའ་ (wɔnga) some, several.

འོར་འདྲེན་ (wɔndren) transporting, taking/ bringing, transferring; va.—བྱེད་ to transport, to take/ bring, to transfer.

འོར་འདྲེན་བཟོ་པ་ (wɔndren soba) transport worker, mover.

འོར་ནད་ (wɔrnɛɛ̀) sm. འོར་, 2.

འོར་མ་ (wɔrma) sm. ཐེངས་.

འོར་རྫ་ (wɔrdza) plugged up (as in a drain); vi.—ཤོར་ to get plugged up.

འོར་ལྷུང་ (wɔrlhuŋ) 1. sm. འོར་, 2. 2. vi. to become physically weak.

འོར་ཀ་ (wɔrga) a drain.

འོར་ཁ་ (wɔrga) 1. dark brown. 2. name of a place in southern Tibet.

འོར་མདུད་ (wɔndüǜ) Adam's apple.

འོལ་ཀ་ (wööga) an irrigation/ water canal.

འོལ་ནད་ (wöönɛɛ̀) a type of skin disease in Tibetan medicine.

འོལ་སྤྱི་ (wööji) sm. འོལ་ཚོད་.

འོལ་སྤྱོད་ (wööjöö̀) rash behavior; va.—བྱེད་.

འོལ་བ་ (wööwa) sparrow hawk.

འོལ་མོ་ (wöömo) 1. the root of bidenate achyranthes (used in Tibetan medicine). 2. name of a place.

འོལ་ཚོད་ (wöö̀dzöö̀) approximation, guess, assumption; va.—བྱེད་ to approximate, to guess, to assume ¶ འོལ་ཚོད་ཀྱིས་བཤད་པའི་གཏམ་དེ་ཁྲིམས་ར་ར་མི་འགྲོ་ Words based on guesses are not acceptable in a court of law.

འོས་ (wöö̀) 1. vi. to be worthwhile, to be worthy, to be right ¶ དཀའ་ལས་རྒྱག་འོས་པ་ཞིག་རེད་ It is worthy of hard work. ¶ འདི་ཞུ་འོས་ཆེ་ན་ཡང་ Even though this is worthy of saying. 2. abbr. of འོས་མི་. 3. vote.

འོས་ཁོངས་ (wöö̀goŋ) candidates, nominees.

འོས་མཁན་ (wöngɛn) a worthy person, qualified candidate.

འོས་འགན་ (wöngɛn) duty, obligation ¶ རྒྱལ་སྤྱིའི་འོས་འགན་ International obligation.

འོས་འགན་འཁྲི་སྒྲུབ་ (wöngɛn trīdrub) performance of duty.

འོས་འགན་གྱི་ངལ་རྩོལ་ (wöngɛngi ŋɛɛdzöö) compulsory labor, labor for which there is no wage.

འོས་འགན་གྱི་སློབ་གསོ་ (wöngɛngi lōbso) compulsory education.

འོས་འགན་དམག་སྐུལ་ལམ་ལུགས་ (wöngɛn mə̄ggüü ləmluù) system of compulsory military service/ conscription.

འོས་འགན་དམག་མི་ (wöngɛn mə̄ə̄mi) conscriptee, drafted soldier.

འོས་འགན་དམག་ཞབས་ལམ་ལུགས་ (wöngɛn mə̄gshəb ləmluù) sm. འོས་འགན་དམག་སྐུལ་ལམ་ལུགས་.

འོས་འགབ་ (wöngəb) sm. འོས་འཚམ་.

འོས་སྒྲིག (wöö̀drig) arranging candidates/ nominees for a vacancy.

འོས་སྣག (wöö̀guù) alternate candidate/ nominee.

འོས་ངོ་མ་ (wöö̀ ŋoma) actual candidate/ nominee.

འོས་ཚོས་ (wöö̀jöö̀) qualifications of candidates.

འོས་འཆར་ (wöö̀car) an appropriate/ worthy plan; va.—འདོན་ to put forward/ originate a worthy plan; va.—སྤྲོད་/འབུལ་ to submit a plan.

འོས་འཆར་ཁྲུའུ་ (wöö̀cardru) tib. ch. planning office.

འོས་ཐང་ (wöö̀daŋ) suitable/ appropriate value.

འོས་ཐོ་ (wöö̀do) list of candidates; va.—སྤྲོད་ to submit the list of candidates.

འོས་ཐོབ་ (wöö̀dob) 1. votes received. 2. deserving.

འོས་དང་པོ་ (wöö̀ taŋbo) the first candidate.

འོས་འདུ་ (wöndu) sm. འོས་བསྡུ་.

འོས་འདེམས་ (wöndeb) election, electing; va.—བྱེད་ to hold an election ¶ རྒྱལ་ཡོངས་འོས་འདེམས་ National election.

འོས་བསྡུ་ (wöö̀du) voting, electing, election; va.—བྱེད་.

འོས་བསྡུ་ལས་ཁང་ (wöö̀du lɛɛ̀gaŋ) election commission.

འོས་འདྲ་ (wöndra) an alternate (candidate/ delegate/ nominee).

འོས་པ་ (wöö̀ba) worthwhile, worthy, proper, appropriate, right ¶ འདི་སྐྱོ་པམ་འོས་པ་ཞིག་རེད་ This is something that is appropriate to be sad about.

འོས་པའི་ཁོང་ཁྲོ་ (wöö̀bɛ kōŋdro) righteous indignation.

འོས་པའི་འགན་ (wöö̀bɛ gɛn) a worthy responsibility.

འོས་པའི་ཤིང་ལ་སེར་ཁ་མེད་པ་འཕྲལ་ མི་དགོས་རྡོ་ལ་སྦྱིན་སྦྱར་གང་འདྲ་ཟེ་ (wöö̀bɛ shīŋlə sērga meèba trɛ̄ɛ migöö̀ dola jīnjar kaŋdre) separating well matched things and joining together inappropriate things [Lit. separating wood that does not have cracks, trying to stick stones together with glue].

འོས་པར་དཀའ་བ་ (wöö̀bar gāwa) inconceivable, impossible.

འོས་པོ་ (wöö̀bo) proper, fitting, worthy.

འོས་སྤྲུལ་ (wöö̀drüü) candidate for selection as a reincarnation ¶ ཁོང་ཏཱ་ལའི་བླ་མའི་འོས་སྤྲུལ་རེད་ He is a candidate for the reincarnation of the Dalai Lama.

འོས་བབས་ (wöö̀bəb) sm. འོས་པོ་.

འོས་བབས་ལོ་རྒྱུས་ (wöö̀bəb lugyüǜ) resume (usu. of a candidate).

འོས་བབས་སུ་རུང་ (wöö̀bəb sūruŋ) whoever is worthy/ deserving (should be appointed or get a job) ¶ དམག་མི་འོས་བབས་སུ་རུང་ལ་མདའ་དཔོན་བསྐོ་གཞག་གནང་རོགས་གནང་ Please appoint a worthy soldier as commander.

འོས་འབབ་ (wömbəb) the amount that is deserved.

འོས་འབུལ་ (wömbüü) 1. va. to recommend, to nominate. 2. recommending, nominating; va.—འབུལ་.

འོས་སྦྱོར་ (wo̲ö̀jɔɔ) recommending, nominating; va.—བྱེད་.

འོས་མ་མཆིས་པ་ (wo̲ö̀ mə̲ciìbə) extremely inappropriate, not good/ worthy ¶ འགོ་ཁྲིད་ལ་ཁ་ལན་བརྒྱབ་པ་དེ་འོས་མ་མཆིས་པ་རེད་ Talking back to one's boss is inappropiate.

འོས་མི་ (wo̲ö̀mi) candidate, nominee.

འོས་མིན་ (wo̲ö̀min) unacceptable, unworthy, inappropriate ¶ དྲི་བ་བྱས་པ་ལུགས་འགལ་འོས་མིན་རེད་ The questioning was unacceptable and in violation of custom.

འོས་མེད་ (wo̲ö̀meè) unworthy, undeserving, inappropriate, unfitting, improper.

འོས་མེད་འགྲིག་ཐབས་ (wo̲ö̀meè dri̲gdəb) coming to terms, compromising ¶ བཙན་རྒྱལ་རིང་ལུགས་དང་འོས་མེད་འགྲིགས་ཐབས་བྱེད་མི་རུང་ It is not okay to compromise with imperialism.

འོས་མེད་བསྡུན་ཐབས་ (wo̲ö̀meè dǖndəb) sm. འོས་མེད་འགྲིག་ཐབས་.

འོས་མེད་མཐུན་ཐབས་ (wo̲ö̀mɛɛ̀ tǖndəb) sm. འོས་མེད་འགྲིག་ཐབས་.

འོས་མེད་ཧམ་ཤེད་ (wo̲ö̀mɛɛ̀ hāmsheè) using excesive force that is improper.

འོས་མོ་ (wo̲ö̀mo) root of bidentate achyranthes (used in Tibetan medicine).

འོས་ཚད་ (wo̲ö̀dzɛɛ̀) conditions, standards, degree of suitability.

འོས་ཚོད་ (wo̲ö̀dzö̀ö̀) estimating/ approximating; va.—བྱེད་.

འོས་ཚོད་རང་བཟོ་ (wo̲ö̀dzö̀ö̀ ra̲ŋso) doing (sth.) on guesswork; va.—བྱེད་.

འོས་འཚམ་ (wo̲ndzam) abbr. of འོས་ཤིང་མཚམས་པ་.

འོས་འཛུགས་ (wo̲ndzug) nominating candidates; va.—བྱེད་.

འོས་གཞི་ (wo̲ö̀shi) candidate in an election.

འོས་རིགས་ (wo̲ö̀rig) abbr. of འོས་ཤིང་རིགས་པ་.

འོས་ལ་ཚུད་ (wo̲ö̀la tsǖù) vi. to be included as a candidate for a position.

འོས་ལངས་ (wo̲ö̀laŋ) a just revolt/ uprising; va.—བྱེད་.

འོས་ལངས་མགོ་འདོགས་མི་སྣ་ (wo̲ö̀laŋ go̲dɔɔ̀ mi̲nə) persons who rebelled and surrendered to the enemy (usu. Guomindang troops who rebelled and joined the communists).

འོས་ལངས་དམག་ (wo̲ö̀laŋ mā̀à) soldiers who justly rebel.

འོས་ཤིང་འཚམས་པ་ (wo̲ö̀shiŋ tsāmba) fitting and proper, appropriate ¶ ཐག་གཅོད་འོས་ཤིང་འཚམས་པ་ An appropriate decision.

འོས་ཤིང་རིགས་པ་ (wo̲ö̀shiŋ ri̲gbə) appropriate, fitting.

འོས་ཤོག་ (wo̲ö̀shoò) vote, ballot; va.—ལྷུག་ to cast ballots, to vote.

འོས་སུ་ཆེ་བ་ (wo̲ö̀su cēwa) suitable, appropiate, worthy.

འོས་སུ་མ་མཆིས་པ་ (wo̲ö̀su mə̲ciìbə) sm. འོས་མ་མཆིས་པ་.

འོས་སུ་འཐད་པ་ (wo̲ö̀su tɛ̄ɛ̀ba) suitable, appropriate, worthy.

ཡ་ (ya) 1. the letter ཡ་ (used in alphabetical ordering). 2. one of a pair ¶ལག་པ་ཡ་གཅིག་ལས་མེད་པའི་དམག་དཔོན་ནང་བཞིན་ Like a one armed general. 3. sm. ཡས་. 4. rival, match ¶མི་དེ་ལ་ཡ་ཡོད་པ་མ་རེད་ That person has no match.

ཡ་ཀྲའུ་གླིང་ (yadrawu līŋ) ch.tib. Asia, Asian continent.

ཡ་གླད་ (yalɛɛ̀) sm. ཡ་ཐོད་.

ཡ་དཀན་ (yagɛn) sm. ཡ་རྐན་.

ཡ་བཀྱག (wagyaà) sm. ཡ་རྒྱག.

ཡ་རྐན་ (yagɛn) 1. upper palate. 2. sm. ཡས་སོ་.

ཡ་རྐྱང་ (yagyaŋ) odd piece, one of a pair ¶ལྷམ་ཁོག་ཡ་རྐྱང་ཁ་ཤས་འདུག There are several odd shoes.

ཡ་སྐྲ་ (yadra) hair on the temple.

ཡ་ཁ་ (yaga) 1. sm. ཡ་རྐན་. 2. upper, above. 3. upper lip.

ཡ་ཁུང་ (yaguŋ) temple (of the head) ¶ཡ་ཁུང་གཡས་གཡོན་ལ་ On the right and left temple.

ཡ་ཁོག (yagɔɔ̀) abdomen.

ཡ་ཁོལ་ (yagöö) arc. sm. ཤུབས་.

ཡ་ཁྱོར་ (yagyɔɔ) a handful.

ཡ་མཁལ་ (yagɛɛ) sm. ཡ་མགལ་.

ཡ་ག (yaga) sm. ཡ་ཁ་.

ཡ་གི (yəgi) up there.

ཡ་གྱད་ (yagyɛɛ̀) rung (of a ladder).

ཡ་གྱར་ (ya gyar) vi. to be scattered/ separated ¶དཔེ་ཆ་ཤོག་ལེ་མང་པོ་ཡ་གྱར་བཞག Many pages of the book have been scattered.

ཡ་གྱལ་ (ya gyɛɛ) 1. one part of sth. ¶གསོ་བ་རིག་པ་ནི་རིག་གནས་ཆེ་བ་ལྔའི་ཡ་གྱལ་ཞིག་རེད་ Medicine is one of the five major Tibetan sciences. 2. sm. ཁ་བྲལ་.

ཡ་གྱེས་སུ་འགྲོ་བ་ (yagyeèsu dro) vi. to be/ get separated.

ཡ་གྲངས་ (yadraŋ) odd numbers (e.g., 1, 3, 5).

ཡ་གླིང་ (yəliŋ) Asia, Asian Continent.

ཡ་གླིང་ཤར་ལྷོ་ (yəliŋ shārlho) Southeast Asia.

ཡ་གླིང་ལྷོ་མ་ (yəliŋ lhōma) South Asia.

ཡ་མགལ་ (yagɛɛ) upper jaw.

ཡ་འགལ་ (yangɛɛ) disagreement, conflict; vi.—(དུ་) འགྱུར་ to come into conflict/ disagreement, to break down (in talks) ¶ཕྱོགས་གཉིས་བར་གྱི་གྲོས་མོལ་དེ་ཆ་གྲང་ཡ་འགལ་དུ་གྱུར་བཞག There was complete disagreement in the negotiations between the two parties.

ཡ་རྒྱག (yagyaà) pestle.

ཡ་ང་ (yaŋa) 1. sympathy, pity, compassion; va.—བྱེད་. 2. cruel, terrible, brutal. 3. fear ¶དགྲ་བོའི་མདུན་དུ་ཡ་ང་མེད་པར་མཆོངས་པ་རེད་ They leapt to (fight) the enemy without any fear.

ཡ་ང་སྙིང་རྗེ་ (yaŋa ñīŋje) pity and compassion ¶ཡ་ང་སྙིང་རྗེ་མེད་པ་ Without pity and compassion.

ཡ་ང་བ་ (yaŋawa) pitiful, sad, pathetic ¶ལོ་མང་དམག་ས་ཡིན་པས་གནས་སྟངས་ཡ་ང་བ་ཞིག་འདུག Because it has been a battlefield for many years, the condition of the farmers is pitiful.

ཡ་ང་མེད་པ་ (yaŋa meèba) 1. merciless, pitiless, ruthless. 2. fearless.

ཡ་ངེ་ཡེ་ངེ་ (yaŋe yeŋe) lacking concentration, inattentive ¶སློབ་ཕྲུག་འཛིན་གྲྭའི་ནང་ཡ་ངེ་ཡེང་ངེ་ཁོ་ན་བྱས་ཙང་ཡིག་ཚད་ལོན་མི་འདུག Because the student was been inattentive in class he failed his exam.

ཡ་ངེ་ཡེང་ངེ་ (yaŋe yaŋŋe) sm. ཡ་ངེ་ཡེ་ངེ་.

ཡ་གཅིག (yajig) sm. ཡ་, 2.

ཡ་གཅོག (ya jōò) va. to compete against.

ཡ་མཆུ་ (yaju) upper lip.

ཡ་མཆེ་ (yanje) upper canine teeth.

ཡ་ཆོག (ya cɔ̄ɔ̀) vi. to be able to compete against ¶རྒྱ་མཆན་རྩལ་འགྲན་ནང་རྒྱ་མིས་ཨུ་རུ་སུའི་ཡ་ཆོག་མི་འདུག The Chinese cannot compete against the Russians in boxing.

ཡ་མཆོག (yajɔɔ̀) upper tip of a bow (the weapon).

ཡ་འཆམ་ (yanjam) sinus cold, cold affecting the sinuses.

ཡ་འཆོར་ (yanjɔɔ) sm. ཡ་ཆོག.

ཡ་ཇུ་ཁ་ཡ་ (yəju kāya) a type of tea.

ཡ་ཇུ་ཁོར་གསུམ་ (yəju kɔ̄rsum) a type of tea.

ཡ་ཉག (ya ñaà) 1. vi. to sink down (for earth). 2. vi. to lose one's wealth.

ཡ་གཉག (yañaà) a flat area on the slope of a mountain.

ཡ་གཉིས་མ་གཉིས་ (yəñiì məñiì) four year old horses and mules.

ཡ་ཏོག (yadɔɔ̀) top, peak, apex, summit.

ཡ་བཏགས་ (yadaà) the subjoined "ཡ་" letter.

ཡ་ཐུབ་ (ya tūb) vi. to be able to compete ¶འབྲུག་ཡུལ་གྱིས་རྒྱ་གར་གྱི་ཡ་ཐུབ་ཀྱི་མ་རེད་ Bhutan can't compete with India.

ཡ་ཐེམ་ (yadem) lintel (over door).

ཡ་ཐོག (yadɔɔ̀) 1. primitive, primeval ¶ཡ་ཐོག་གུང་ཁྲན་སྤྱི་ཚོགས་ Primitive communist society. 2. old times, antiquity. 3. roof.

ཡ་ཐོད་ (yadöö̀) 1. skull. 2. upper part of a door.

ཡ་ཐོད་ཀྱི་མིག་དང་ཡ་ཁོག་གི་སྙིང་ (yadöö̀gi miìdaŋ yadöö̀gi ñīŋ) sm. དཔྲལ་བའི་མིག་དང་ཁོག་པའི་སྙིང་.

ཡ་མཐའ་ (yada) at the utmost, at the highest/ most.

ཡ་མཐར་ (yadar) sm. ཡ་མཐའ་.

ཡ་དོ་ (yado) 1. an odd one of a pair, one from a pair ¶ལྷམ་དེ་ཡ་དོ་རེད་ That boot is one of a pair. 2. sm. ཡ་ཆོག. 3. matched ¶བུ་འདི་དང་བུ་མོ་འདི་གཉིས་གཤིས་ཀ་ཡག་པོ་འདུག་པས་གཉེན་སྒྲིག་བྱས་ན་ཡ་དོ་བ་ The boy and girl have good character so if they get married they will be well matched.

ཡ་དོ་བ་ (yadowa) sm. ཡ་དོ་.

ཡ་པ་ (yaba) 1. title for aristocratic families in traditional Sikkimese society.

ཡ་པད་ (yabɛɛ̀) a kind of lotus design in art.

ཡ་པེ་ཡོ་པེ་ (yabe yobe) carelessly, hastily; va.—བྱེད་.

ཡ་པོ་ (yabo) 1. rival, adversary; va.—བྱེད་. 2. sb. who subsists from hunting. 3. wanderer, vagabond.

ཡ་ཕུབ་ (yabub) 1. thatch used on the roofs of farmer's houses. 2. the upper floor of a house.

ཡ་ཕུབས་ (yabub) sm. ཡ་ཕུབ་.

ཡ་བ་ (yawa) shung. partner.

ཡ་བེ་ཡོ་བེ་ (yabe yobe) sm. ཡ་པེ་ཡོ་པེ་.

ཡ་བོ་ (yabo) sm. ཡ་པོ་.

ཡ་བྱེད་ (ya ceè) 1. va. to be attentive ¶མགྲོན་པོ་གདན་འདྲེན་ཞུས་ཀྱང་ཁོང་གི་ཡ་མ་བྱས་པ་རེད་ Even though he invited guests he wasn't attentive to them. 2. va. to take notice of ¶ཁོས་ང་ལ་བརྙས་བཅོས་བྱས་ཀྱང་ངས་ཡ་མ་བྱས་ Even though he bullied me, I didn't take notice of it.

ཡ་བྲལ་ (yadrɛɛ) disrupted, dislocated, separated, split up; va.—བྱེད་.

ཡ་མ་ (yama) 1. temple. 2. sinuses; vi.—ན་ to have a sinus infection/ cold.

ཡ་མ་དཀར་པོ་ (yama gārbo) a type of sinus illness in Tibetan medicine.

ཡ་མ་སྐྱོང་ (yama gyoŋ) va. to aggravate/ irritate/ displease ¶ཁོས་ང་ལ་ཡ་མ་སྐྱོང་ཡས་ཀྱི་སྐད་ཆ་བཤད་བྱུང་ He said sth. to irritate me.

ཡ་མ་དུང་ (yama duŋ) va. to touch one's temple with one's index finger to indicate liking a girl.

ཡ་མ་ནག་པོ་ (yama nagbo) a type of sinus illness in Tibetan medicine.

ཡ་མ་ཟུང་ (yamasuŋ) sm. ཡ་མ་གཟུགས་.

ཡ་མ་གཟུགས་ (yama suù) 1. disfiguration, abnormality. 2. unpaired, asymmetrical.

ཡ་མ་སོ་མ་ (yama sōma) flax.

ཡ་མ་སློང་ (yama lōŋ) sm. ཡ་མ་སྐྱོང་.

ཡ་མ་བརླ་ (yama lā) arc. having no substance, having no intrinsic value.

ཡ་མ་གསོ་མ་ (yama sōma) flax, linen.

ཡ་མའི་ནད་ (yamɛ nɛ̱ɛ̀) sinus illness.

ཡ་མས་ཁ་ (yamɛga) Jamaica.

ཡ་མིན་ཆ་ཡོད་ (yamin cāyöö) in pairs, not single.

ཡ་མེ་ཡོམ་མེ་ (yame yomme) shaky, unsteady, swaying, wavering; va.— བྱེད་ ། ལྷགས་པ་རྒྱག་དུས་ལྗོན་ཤིང་གི་ཡལ་ག་ཡ་མེ་ཡོམ་མེ་བྱེད་ཀྱི་འདུག When the wind blows the branches sway.

ཡ་མེ་ཡོ་མེ་ (yame yome) sm. ཡམ་ཡོམ་.

ཡ་མེད་ (yameè) 1. matchless. 2. wild, reckless; va.—བྱེད་; —འཚོང་. 3. in pairs, not single.

ཡ་མེད་དོ་མེད་ (yameè tomɛɛ̀) matchless, unequaled.

ཡ་མེད་ཚ་པོ་ (yameè tsābo) wild, reckless.

ཡ་མོན་ (yamön) Yamen (a government office in traditional China).

ཡ་ཙི་ (yədzi) ch. duck.

ཡ་ཙི་གདང་ལ་འདེད་ (yədzi daŋla deè) trying to make sb. do sth. that is beyond his capacity [Lit. chasing a duck onto a chicken's perch].

ཡ་ཙེ་ (yādze) ch. sm. ཡ་ཙི་.

ཡ་ཚ་བ་ (yadzawa) fearing, being afraid.

ཡ་ཚད་ (yadzɛɛ̀) 1. a little way up ། ཁང་པ་འདི་ཡ་ཚད་ལ་ཡོད་པ་རེད་ The house is a little way up there. 2. combating, competing, challenging ། མི་འདིའི་ལག་ཤུགས་ལ་ཡ་ཚད་ཐུབ་མཁན་མེད་པ་རེད་ No one can match the strength of his arms.

ཡ་ཚེས་ (yadzeè) odd-numbered days.

ཡ་མཚན་ (yamdzɛn) 1. strange, weird, bizarre, surprising, astonishing, amazing; vi.—སྐྱེ་ to be or get surprised/ amazed; va.—བྱེད་ to act strange/ weird/ bizarre/ unusual ། ཁོའི་སྤྱོད་པ་ཡ་མཚན་ཞིག་འདུག He behaves strangely.

ཡ་མཚན་ཅན་ (yamdzɛn) strange, weird, bizarre.

ཡ་མཚན་པོ་ (yam dzɛ̄mbo) 1. surprising, amazing, astonishing, wondrous. 2. strange, weird, unusual.

ཡ་མཚན་འཚོལ་ཐབས་ (yamdzɛn tsöödəb) hunting/ seeking novelty.

ཡ་མཚར་ (yamdzar) sm. ཡ་མཚན་.

ཡ་ཞར་ (yashar) blind in one eye.

ཡ་ཞི་ཡ་གླིང་ (yashi yəliŋ) ch.tib. Asia, Asian Continent.

ཡ་ཟད་ (yasɛɛ̀) sm. ཡ་ཚད་, 1.

ཡ་ཟི་ཡོ་ལངས་ (yəsi yolaŋ) risky situation/ actions ། ཡ་ཟི་ཡོ་ལངས་ཆེན་པོའི་ཚོང་རྒྱག་རྒྱུ་མེད་ You shouldn't do risky business.

ཡ་ཟི་ཡོ་ལངས་ཚ་པོ་ (yəsi yolaŋ tsābo) sb. who takes big risks.

ཡ་ཟིན་ (yəsin) sm. ཡ་ཐུབ་.

ཡ་ཟླ་ (yanda) months with odd numbers.

ཡ་བཟུང་ (yasuŋ) opposing; va.—བྱེད་ ། བཙན་འཛུལ་པར་ཡ་བཟུང་བྱེད་པའི་དམག་འཁྲུག་བརྒྱབ་པ་རེད་ (They) waged war in opposition to the invaders.

ཡ་འུ་བྱེད་ (yawu cee) sm. ཡ་བྱེད་.

ཡ་ཡ་ (yaya) okay, I accept.

ཡ་ཡ་པོ་ (ya yawo) unsteady/ troubled mind.

ཡ་ཡུག་ (yəyuù) 1. risky, bold, gutsy, adventurous, rash; va.—བྱེད་ ། ཚོང་ཡ་ཡུག་ཆེན་པོ་འདི་འདྲ་རྒྱག་རྒྱུ་མེད་ You shouldn't do risky business like that. 2. exaggerated, unbelievable (speech); va.—ཤོད་ ། ཁོ་རང་གཅིག་པོས་གཞུང་ལ་ངོ་རྒོལ་བྱེད་ཀྱི་ཡིན་ཞེས་སྐད་ཆ་ཡ་ཡུག་དེ་འདྲ་ཤོད་ཀྱི་འདུག He is saying unbelievable things like he will oppose the government alone.

ཡ་ཡུག་ཆེན་པོ་ (yəyuù cēmbo) sm. ཡ་ཡུག་ཚ་པོ་.

ཡ་ཡུག་ཚ་པོ་ (yəyuù tsābo) gutsy, bold, adventurous.

ཡ་ཡུད་ (yəyüü) 1. sm. ཡ་ཡུག. 2. large scale, major, big ། འཕོ་འགྱུར་ཡ་ཡུད་ཆེན་པོ་བྱུང་པ་རེད་ A great change took place.

ཡ་ཡོ་ (yayo) bent, curved, crooked.

ཡ་ཡོ་མེད་པ་ (yayo meèba) straight, straightforward.

ཡ་ཡོར་ (yayɔɔ) loose with regards to weaving.

ཡ་ཡོལ་ (yayöö) procrastinating, making excuses or pretexts to avoid doing sth.; va.—བྱེད་ ། མི་དེས་ལས་ཀར་ཡ་ཡོལ་ཁོ་ན་བྱས་ཙང་མཐའ་མ་ལས་ཁངས་ནས་ཕུད་འདུག Because that person only procrastinated with his work he was eventually fired.

ཡ་གཡོག་ (yayɔɔ) shung. lower officials who act as servants of the ཡ་སོར་ཁྲི་པ་.

ཡ་རབས་ (yərəb) principled (person), genuinely good/ decent in character.

ཡ་རབས་དྲ་མའི་སྤྱོད་རྒྱལ་ (yərəb trame jöödzüü) shung. a noble character/ personality.

ཡ་རབས་མ་རབས་སྤྱོད་པས་ཤེས་ (yərəb marəb jüübɛ shēè) one can know whether sb. is principled or not by his behavior.

ཡ་རུ་ (yəru) yak baby.

ཡ་རེ་ཡོ་རེ་ (yare yore) unsteady; vi.—བྱེད་ to be unsteady.

ཡ་ལ་ (yala) blaming, accusing (wrongly); va.—འཛུག; —དཀྲི; —འཛུགས་; —བཞག to blame/ accuse wrongly; va.—འཁྱེར་ to accept blame; vi.—གཟེད་ to get blamed/ accused.

ཡ་ལ་སྐྱོན་འཛུགས་ (yala gyöndzuù) blaming, accusing (wrongly); va.—བྱེད་ ། ང་ལ་ཡ་ལ་སྐྱོན་འཛུགས་མ་བྱེད་ Don't blame me.

ཡ་ལད་ (yalɛɛ̀) armor, mail.

ཡ་ལན་ (yalɛn) response, answer; va.—བྱེད་; —སྤྲོད་; —འཛལ་; —ཤོག; —སློག to retaliate, to respond, to answer back, to pay back ། ང་ཚོས་སྲིད་ཕྱོགས་དེ་ལ་ཡ་ལན་བྱེད་རྒྱུའི་གྲ་སྒྲིག་བྱེད་དགོས་ཀྱི་རེད་ We have to prepare to retaliate to that policy. ། དགེ་རྒན་གྱི་འདྲི་བར་སློབ་ཕྲུག་ཚོས་ཡ་ལན་བསྒྲགས་པ་རེད་ The students responded to the teacher's question.

ཡ་ལི་ཧྲན་ད་ (yali hrɛ̄nda) Alexandria.

ཡ་ལི་ (yale) very ། དགའ་ཡ་ལི་ Very happy.

ཡ་ལི་མ་ལི་འབྲལ་ (yale male drɛɛ) vi. to fall apart.

ཡ་ལི་ཡོ་ལི་ (yale yole) sm. ཡ་ཡོལ་.

ཡ་ལུའི་གཙང་པོ་ (yalü dzāŋbo) Yalu Chiang River.

ཡ་ཤེལ་ (yashee) shung. a type of plain brocade.

ཡ་ཤེར་ (yasher) black brocade/ satin/ silk.

ཡ་སེ་ཡོ་ལངས་ (yase yolaŋ) sm. ཡ་ཡུག་ཚ་པོ་.

ཡ་སེ་ཡོ་སེ་ (yase yose) undependable, unreliable.

ཡ་སོ་ (yaso) upper teeth.

ཡ་སོར་ཁྲི་པ་ (yasor tribə) shung. leader of the ancient army that is displayed during Monlam.

ཡ་སྲིན་ (yasin) microorganisms that cause sinus infections (in Tibetan medicine).

ཡ་ཧ་ད་ (yahada) Djakarta.

ཡ་ཧུ་དི་ (yahudi) Jew.

ཡ་ཧྥེ་ (yāfe) ch. abbr. Asian and African ། ཡ་ཧྥེ་མཐུན་སྒྲིལ་ Afro-Asian solidarity.

ཡུ་གླིང་ (yəliŋ) sm. ཡ་གླིང་.

ཡུ་གླིང་ལྷོ་མ་ (yəliŋ lhoma) sm. ཡ་གླིང་ལྷོ་མ་.

ཡག་ (yaà) 1. abbr. of ཡག་པོ་. 2. sm. ཡས་.

ཡག་ག་ (yaga) better ། དེབ་འདི་ལས་དེ་ཡག་གི་རེད་ That book is better than this one.

ཡག་སྒྲུག་ (yag druù) selecting the better ones; va.—རྒྱག; —བྱེད་ ། ས་བོན་ཡག་སྒྲུ་བྱེད་རྒྱུ་ Selecting the better seeds.

ཡག་ཉེས་ (yaàñeè) 1. quality of sth., good or bad; vi.—ཤོར་ to be different in quality ། ཁང་པ་འདི་གཉིས་ཡག་ཉེས་ཡོད་པ་རེད་ Is there a difference in the quality of these two houses? 2. va.—གཏོང་ to treat unfairly/ discriminatingly/ with partiality/ with bias ། ཕ་མས་ཕྲུ་གུ་གཉིས་ལ་ཡག་ཉེས་གཏོང་གི་ཡོད་པ་རེད་ The parents treated the children with partiality.

ཡག་ཉེས་མེད་པ་ (yañeè meèba) 1. without any difference in quality. 2. without any partiality/ discrimination.

ཡག་དགས་ (yaàdaà) a good omen/ sign ། ཁོས་སྨན་ཁང་ལ་ཨ་མ་ཐུག་པར་རྒྱུག་ཕྱིན་པ་འདི་ཡག་དགས་མ་བྱུང་ His running to the hospital to see his mother was a bad sign (that his mother's condition had worsened).

ཡག་ཐག་ཆོད་ (yaà tāgjöö) 1. very/ extremely good ། ཁོང་ཚོགས་འདུར་ཡོང་པ་འདི་ཡག་ཐག་ཆོད་རེད་ That he came to the meeting is very good. 2. too good ། ཞྭ་མོ་འདི་ང་ལ་ཡག་ཐག་ཆོད་བཞག This hat is too good for me.

ཡག་ཐོག་བཟང་ཐོག (yaàdɔɔ̀ saŋdɔɔ̀) good relations between people or families.

ཡག་ཐོག་ཡག་རྩེག (yaàtɔɔ̀ yaàdzeg) though doing well (still) do better ། ད་ལྟ་ཁྱེད་རང་སློབ་སྦྱོང་ཡག་པོ་ཡོད་པ་ད་དུང་ཡག་ཐོག་ཡག་རྩེག་ཡོང་བ་གནང་དགོས་ You are good in your studies; in the future you must do even better.

ཡག་པ་ (yaga) better ། ང་ཁང་པ་འདི་ལས་ཡག་པ་ཞིག་ཉོ་དགོས་ཡོད་ I have to buy a house that is better than this.

ཡག་པོ་ (yagbo) good; va.—བརྩི་ to consider good, to regard highly, to value ། དེབ་འདི་ཡག་པོ་ཞི་དྲག་འདུག This book is very good.

ཡག་པོ་གསུམ་ལྡན་གྱི་སློབ་ཕྲུག (yagbo sūmdɛngi lōbdruù) sm. བཟང་པོ་གསུམ་ལྡན་གྱི་སློབ་ཕྲུག.

ཡག་བྱུང་ (yaàju) thanks ། དཔལ་ལྡན་ཡག་བྱུང་ Palden, thank you.

ཡག་བྱུང་ཨ་མའི་ཇ་ཆང་མེད་པ་ (yaàjuŋ) sm. དྲིན་ལན་ལོག་འཇལ་.

ཡག་མ་ (yagma) 1. a thick rug placed under saddles. 2. new. 3. good.

ཡག་མོ་ (yagmo) good.

ཡག་བཙོག (yagdzɔɔ̀) sm. ཡག་ཉེས་.

ཡག་ཡག (yaàyaà) 1. as good as; va.—བྱེད་ ། I did the work as good as possible. 2. doing or saying for sb.'s own good ། ངས་ཁོ་ལ་ཡག་ཡག་བྱས་ནས་བཤད་ཀྱང་ཁོ་ཐུང་ལངས་སོང་ I advised him for his own good, he got angry.

ཡག་ཡག་དག་དག (yaàyaà) sm. བཟང་ཚུལ་རྒྱན་ཚུལ་.

ཡག་རིགས་ཡག་ཚད་ (yərii yagdzɛè) the very best.

ཡག་རུ་གང་འགྲོ་ (yaàru kaŋdro) va. to get better and better ། ལུང་པ་འདིའི་གནས་སྟངས་ཡག་རུ་གང་འགྲོ་རེད་ The situation in this area is getting better and better.

ཡག་རུ་འགྲོ་ (yaàru dro) vi. to become better.

ཡག་རུ་གཏོང་ (yaàru dōŋ) va. to make better.

ཡག་རུ་ཡག་རུ་ (yaàru yaàru) better and better.

ཡག་ལོས་ (yaglöö) how good; va.—ལྟ་ to look at sth. to see how good it is ། ཁང་པ་འདི་ཡག་ལོས་འདུག How good is this house? ། ཁང་པ་འདི་ཡག་ལོས་ལྟ་བར་ཡོང་པ་ཡིན་ I came to look at the quality of the house.

ཡག་ཤོས་ (yagshöö) the best.

ཡགས་ (yaà) utensils for offering prayers for the deceased.

ཡང་ (yaŋ) 1. see ཀྱང་. 2. light ། སྐྱེད་ཡང་ Light interest. 3. also, again ། ཡང་དེ་རྗེས་ Also, after that. ། ཡང་ཁོང་སླེབ་བྱུང་ He came again.

ཡང་གྲོའུ་ (yaŋdro) Yangchow.

ཡང་ཀློག་སྐྱར་ཀློག (yaŋlɔɔ̀ gyāŋlɔɔ̀) reading again and again.

ཡང་དཀར་ (yaŋgar) whitewash.

ཡང་སྐོར་བསྐྱར་སྐོར་ (yaŋgɔɔ gyargɔɔ) again and again.

ཡང་སྐྱར་ (yaŋgyar) sm. ཡང་བསྐྱར་.

ཡང་བསྐྱར་ (yaŋgyar) again, once more ། ཁོང་གི་ཡང་སྐྱར་སྤུན་མཆེད་ཐུག་པར་སླེབས་སོང་ He came to see his relatives again.

ཡང་བསྐྱར་ཐོན་སྐྱེད་ (yaŋgyar tōŋgyeè) reproducing/ recycling; va.—བྱེད་ to reproduce, to produce again, to recycle.

ཡང་བསྐྱར་འདྲི་གཅོད་ (yaŋgyar drijöö) reexamination of a case/ investigation, va.—བྱེད་.

ཡང་བསྐྱར་ཚུར་རྒོལ་ (yaŋgyar tsūūgöö) attacking again; va.—བྱེད་.

ཡང་བསྐྱར་སློབ་གསོ་ (yaŋgyar lōbso) reeducation; va.—གཏོང་.

ཡང་ཁུ་ (yəŋgu) sm. ཉིང་ཁུ་.

ཡང་ཁེང་ (yaŋgeŋ) servant's servant.

ཡང་མགོ་ (yaŋgo) sm. ཡང་པོ་.

ཡང་དགོས་ (yaŋgöö) sm. ཡང་སྒོས་.

ཡང་སྒོས་ (yaŋgöö) 1. specially, in particular, particularly ། སྤྱིར་ཁོང་བོད་སྨན་མཁས་པ་ཡིན་ལ་ཡང་སྒོས་མེ་རྒྱག་རྒྱུར་ད་ཅང་མཁས་པ་ཡོད་པ་རེད་ In general he is expert in Tibetan medicine and in particular in moxibustion. 2. in addition ། ཁོང་སྐད་ཡིག་མཁས་པ་ཡིན་ལ། ཡང་སྒོས་ཚན་རིག་ལ་ཡང་མཁས་པོ་ཡོད་ He is expert in language and in addition is expert also in science.

ཡང་ངེ་ཡིང་ངེ་ (yəŋi yiŋi) inattentive, not concentrating, wandering mind; va.—བྱེད་.

ཡང་ཅིག (yaŋjig) once again ། ཡང་ཅིག་གསུང་དང་ Please say it once again.

ཡང་ལྗི་ (yəŋji) sm. ཡང་ལྗིད་.

ཡང་ལྗུན་མེ་ཏོག (yəŋjün) passion flower.

ཡང་ཆ་ (yaŋja) sm. ཆག་ཡང་.

ཡང་ཆད་ (yaŋjɛɛ̀) shung. the final balance ། སྔོན་ཞུས་ངོ་སྐྱེད་རྣམས་རྩིས་བྱས་ཡང་ཆད་འབྲུ་ཁྲེ་ ༦༠༠ ལུས་པ་ After paying the previous principle and interest, the final balance is 600 ཁྲེ་ of grain.

ཡང་ཆམ་ (yaŋjam) things light in weight ། ཡང་ཆས་བཟོ་ལས་ Light industry/ manufacturing.

ཡང་ཆིན་ (yaŋjin) ch. dulcimer.

ཡང་འཇུག (yəŋjuù) post-suffixed letter (e.g., the ས་ in ལངས་).

ཡང་ལྗིད་ (yəŋjiì) weight; va.—འགྲོགས་ to weigh (both material things and the skills/ qualities of a person) [Lit. light and heavy].

ཡང་ལྗིད་ཀོ་ལོག (yəŋjiì kodɔɔ̀) reversing/ inverting the important and unimportant.

ཡང་ལྗིད་མེད་པ་ (yəŋjiì meèba) balanced evenly/ equally in weight.

ཡང་ལྗིད་ཤོར་ (yəŋjiì shɔ̄ɔ) vi. to have come to be different in weight (e.g., two animal loads). 2. vi. to be different in assertiveness/ bossiness ། བཟའ་ཚང་དེ་གཉིས་དབང་ཆེ་ཆུང་ཡང་ལྗིད་ཤོར་བཞག The couple is unequal in authority (one is more assertive/ bossy than the other).

ཡང་སྙིང་ (yəŋñiŋ) in reality, in fact, in effect, in any case, in essence ། པ་ལེའི་སྒྲུ་རྩལ་དེ་ཡང་སྙིང་མང་ཚོགས་ལ་ཞབས་འདེགས་ཞུ་རྒྱུ་རེད་དམ་ Does the ballet, in fact, serve the masses?

ཡང་ཏིག (yəŋdii) last price ། ཡང་ཏིག་ཅིག་གསུང་དང་ Please (tell me) your last price.

ཡང་ཏིག་སྙིང་པོ་ (yəŋdiì ñīŋbu) essence, main topic.

ཡང་སྟེང་ (yaŋdeŋ) roof, penthouse ། ཁང་པ་སོགས་ཀྱི་ཡང་སྟེང་དུ་ On the roofs of houses, etc.

ཡང་ཐ་ (yaŋda) worst of the worst.

ཡང་ཐོག (yaŋdɔɔ̀) 1. highest story of a building. 2. dome.

ཡང་དག (yaŋdag) sm. ཡང་དག་པ་.

ཡང་དག་པ་ (yaŋdagba) correct, accurate, perfect, complete, faultless ། ཏང་གི་ལམ་ཕྱོགས་ཡང་དག་པ་ The correct party line.

ཡང་དག་པའི་དགེ་སློང་ (yaŋdagbɛ geloŋ) a gelong who has remained faithful to his vows.

ཡང་དག་པའི་ཞི་མོང་ཕྱུངས་ (yaŋdagbɛ shēmoŋ cūŋ) shung. having a good sense of responsibility ། ཁྱེད་སངས་རྒྱས་ཀྱི་བསྟན་པ་ལ་དད་ཅིང་གོང་ལ་སེམས་བཟང་པོ་བསམ་ནས་བཀུར་སྐྱེ་བྱས་ཡང་དག་པའི་ཞི་མོང་ཕྱུངས་པར་ད་ལྟ་ནན་གྱིས་སི་ཏུའི་མིང་དང་ལས་ཀ་བསྒོ་རྒྱུ་ You are a pious Buddhist who respects the will of heaven and has a good sense of responsibility and I therefore grant you the title of Situ.

ཡང་དག་པར་ (yaŋdagbar) perfectly, completely, correctly, without error.

ཡང་དང་ཡང་དུ་ (yaŋdaŋ yaŋdu) sm. ཡང་ཡང་.

ཡང་དུ་ཆུག (yaŋdu cūù) shung. to be absolved ། དོ་བདག་འཕྱིར་ཞན་ཉམས་ཐག་ལ་བསམས་ད་ལམ་རེང་ཉེས་པ་ཡང་དུ་ཆུག In consideration of the poverty of the accused, this time the penalty has been absolved.

ཡང་དུ་ཡང་དུ་ (yaŋdu yaŋdu) 1. sm. ཡང་ཡང་. 2. lighter and lighter; vi.—འགྲོ་ to become lighter and lighter; va.—གཏོང་ to make lighter and lighter.

ཡང་དུ་གཏོང་ (ya̲ŋdu dōŋ) va. to lighten/ reduce/ relieve/ ease.

ཡང་འདམ་ (ya̲ŋdam) an old loan.

ཡང་འདུལ་གཙུག་ལག་ཁང་ (yəŋdüü dzūglagaŋ) one of the four cathedrals built during the time of king Srongtsen Gampo.

ཡང་འདྲི་ (yəŋdri) interrogating, asking again and again; va.—བྱེད་.

ཡང་ན་ (ya̲ŋna) or, either or, otherwise ¶ཁོ་བོད་པ་ཡིན་དང་ཡང་ན་རྒྱ་མི་ཡིན་ན་གོ་གི་མི་འདུག I can't make out whether he is Tibetan or Chinese.

ཡང་ནས་ཡང་དུ་ (ya̲ŋnɛ ya̲ŋdu) over and over again, repeatedly ¶གཏམ་དེ་ཡང་ནས་ཡང་དུ་ཞུས་པ་རེད་ (He) said it over and over again.

ཡང་པོ་ (ya̲ŋbo) 1. light (in weight). 2. lenient (in punishments).

ཡང་སྤྲུལ་ (yəŋdrüü) reincarnation of an incarnation.

ཡང་ཕྱི་ (yəŋji) great grandmother.

ཡང་ཕྱི་ཡང་མེས་ (ya̲ŋji ya̲ŋmeè) great grandmother and great grandfather.

ཡང་བ་ (ya̲ŋwa) light, lighter ¶མེ་ཆ་ཡང་བ་ Light machine gun. ¶ཡང་བའི་བཟོ་ལས་ Light industry.

ཡང་བའི་ལྕགས་རིགས་ (ya̲ŋwɛ jārii) light metals.

ཡང་བའི་བཟོ་ལས་ (ya̲ŋwɛ so̲lɛ̀ɛ) light industry.

ཡང་བའི་བཟོ་ལས་པུའུ་ (ya̲ŋwɛ so̲lɛ̀ɛ bū) tib. ch. ministry of light industry.

ཡང་བྲན་ (ya̲ŋdrɛn) sm. ཡང་ཁེང་.

ཡང་འབད་བསྐྱར་འབད་ (ya̲ŋbɛ̀ɛ gyārbɛ̀ɛ) a determined/ persistent effort, persevering again and again, pressing on persistently; va.—བྱེད་.

ཡང་མ་དག་པ་ (yaŋ ma̲dagba) incorrect, imperfect.

ཡང་མིན་ན་ (yaŋ mi̲nnə) either ¶ཡང་མིན་ན་ཁྱེད་སྔོན་ལ་ཐེག ཡང་མིན་ན་ངས་སྔོན་ལ་ཕྱིན་ཆོག Either you will go first or I will go first.

ཡང་མེས་ (ya̲ŋmeè) 1. great grandfather. 2. founder of a family/ lineage, the first ancestor.

ཡང་མོའོ་ (ya̲ŋmo) ch. a type of felt hat.

ཡང་རྨོའོ་ (ya̲ŋmoo) grandmother.

ཡང་རྩལ་ (ya̲ŋdzɛɛ) light on one's feet, lithe, limber.

ཡང་རྩལ་དོད་པོ་ (ya̲ŋdzɛɛ tö̲öbo) light on one's feet, dexterous, agile, athletic.

ཡང་རྩེ་ (ya̲ŋdze) 1. top, peak, acme, summit ¶མའོ་ཙེ་ཏུང་གི་དགོངས་པ་ནི་དེང་རབས་ཀྱི་མར་ཁེ་སི་ལེ་ནིན་རིང་ལུགས་ཀྱི་ཡང་རྩེ་ཡིན་ Mao Zedong's thought is the acme of Marxism-Leninism in this era. 2. the highest peak (of a mountain range).

ཡང་རྩེ་ལྷུར་ལེན་ (ya̲ŋdze lhūrlen) aiming high (in goals), striving for first place, striving to be the best.

ཡང་རྩེའི་སྐང་ལ་ཡས་སྐྲན་ (ya̲ŋdze ga̲ŋla yɛ̲̀ɛ dr̲ɛn) one experience of good luck/ fortune after another ¶ད་རེས་གྱོང་ལ་ལས་ཀ་ཡག་པོ་ཞིག་རག་པ་དེའི་ཐོག་ད་དུང་གཟེངས་རྟགས་ཐོབ་པ་ནི་ཡང་རྩེའི་སྐང་ལ་ཡས་སྐྲན་རང་རེད་བཞག His getting a good job and on top of that winning an award is like having one good fortune on top of another.

ཡང་རྩེར་སོན་ (ya̲ŋdzer sōn) vi. to reach the summit, to attain perfection, to be a masterpiece ¶ཡང་རྩེར་སོན་པའི་རོལ་མོ་ A musical masterpiece.

ཡང་ཚ་མོ་ (yaŋ tsāmo) great granddaughter.

ཡང་ཚ་ (ya̲ŋtsa) great grandson.

ཡང་ཚ་བུ་མོ་ (ya̲ŋdza po̲mo) great granddaughter.

ཡང་ཚའི་རབས་ (ya̲ŋdzɛ ra̲b) great grand child's generation.

ཡང་ཞིང་མྱུར་བ་ (ya̲ŋshiŋ ñu̲rwə) light and quick ¶གནམ་གྲུ་འདི་ལ་ཡང་ཞིང་མྱུར་བའི་ཁྱད་ཆོས་ལྡན་ཡོད་པ་རེད་ One of the characteristics of this plane is that it is light and fast.

ཡང་ཟབ་ (ya̲ŋsəb) in great depth, very deeply.

ཡང་ཟོར་ཅན་ (ya̲ŋsɔrjɛn) lithe/ limber/ flexible/ graceful (of body).

ཡང་ཟོར་ཆེ་བ་ (ya̲ŋsɔr cēwa) very lithe/ limber/ flexible/ graceful (of body).

ཡང་བཟླས་བསྐྱར་བཟླས་ (ya̲ŋdöö gyārdöö) repeating again and again.

ཡང་བཟོ་ (ya̲ŋso) light industry.

ཡང་བཟོས་ (ya̲ŋsöö) maker light, easing, reducing, mitigating; va.—གཏོང་ ¶མི་དེའི་ཉེས་ཆད་ཡང་བཟོས་བཏང་འདུག (They) lightened the person's punishment.

ཡང་ཡང་ (ya̲ŋyaŋ) again and again, over and over again, repeatedly ¶ཐ་ཚིགས་ཡང་ཡང་བསྒྲགས་པ་ལ་ To the repeated warnings.

ཡང་ཡང་ཨ་ཕྱིའི་གཞས་ལ་སྙན་རྒྱུ་མེད་ (ya̲ŋyaŋ ājee shɛ̲̀ɛla ñɛ̃ngyu me̲è) repeating sth. over and over is not interesting [Lit. the woman's singing songs over and over is not interesting].

ཡང་ཡང་ཨ་ཕོའི་གཞས་ལ་སྙན་རྒྱུ་ག་རེ་ཡོད་དམ་ (ya̲ŋyaŋ ābö shɛ̲̀ɛla ñɛ̃mbo ka̲ra yö̲ödam) repeating sth. over and over is not interesting [Lit. how could the man's singing songs over and over again be interesting].

ཡང་ཡའི་ (ya̲ŋyɛ) again.

ཡང་ཡེང་ (ya̲ŋyeŋ) abbr. of ཡང་དེ་ཡེང་དེ་.

ཡང་གཡོག (ya̲ŋyɔɔ) sm. ཡང་ཁེང་.

ཡང་རུ་འགྲོ་ (ya̲ŋru dro̲) vi. to become lighter.

ཡང་རུ་གཏོང་ (ya̲ŋru dōŋ) va. to make lighter.

ཡང་རླུང་ (ya̲ŋluŋ) oxygen.

ཡང་རླུང་འབར་མདེའུ་ (yəŋluŋ ba̲ndee) hydrogen bomb.

ཡང་ལྭ་ (ya̲ŋla) ch. candle, wax.

ཡང་ལྭ་དཀར་པོ་ (ya̲ŋla gārbo) wax, tallow.

ཡང་ལའ་ (ya̲ŋla) sm. ཡང་ལྭ་.

ཡང་ལའི་འཛུགས་སྒྲིགས་ (ya̲ŋlɛ dzu̲gdeg) ch.tib. a stand for a candle.

ཡང་ལྡོག་འོར་ལྡོག (ya̲ŋlɔɔ̀ wo̲rlɔɔ̀) returning again and again.

ཡང་ལོས་ (ya̲ŋlöö̀) degree of lightness, how light? ¶ཁུར་པོ་འདི་ཡང་ལོས་འདུག How light is this load?

ཡང་ཤ་ (ya̲ŋsha) agility, nimbleness, light of foot, lithe.

ཡང་ཤ་དོད་པོ་ (ya̲ŋsha tö̲öbo) agile, nimble, light of foot.

ཡང་ཤིག་ཤིག (yaŋ shīishii) sm. ཡང་སིར་སིར་.

ཡང་སིར་སིར་ (yaŋ sīisii) feeling light/ nimble, having a big burden removed ¶ལོ་མཇུག་ཡིག་ཚད་བཏང་རྗེས་སྟོད་སྐྱལ་ཡང་སིར་སིར་བྱུས་བྱུང་ After the final examination, (I) felt a big burden removed from my shoulders.

ཡང་སིལ་སིལ་ (yaŋ sīisii) sm. ཡང་སིར་སིར་.

ཡང་སེ་ (ya̲ŋse) often ¶ཡང་སེ་ཕེབས་རོགས་ Come often.

ཡང་སོན་ (ya̲ŋsön) seeds that ripen quickly, quick growing crops.

ཡང་སོར་གཏོང་ (ya̲ŋsɔɔ dōŋ) sm. ཡངས་གསོལ་.

ཡང་སོས་ (ya̲ŋsöö) one of the eight hot hells in Tibetan Buddhism.

ཡང་སྲིད་ (yəŋsii) 1. reincarnation. 2. an incarnate lama; vi.—ཕེབས་ to be reincarnated as a lama.

ཡང་སྲིད་མཆོག་སྤྲུལ་རིན་པོ་ཆེ་ (yəŋsiì cɔ̄gdrüü ri̲mboce) shung. honorific term used for reincarnated lamas.

ཡང་སྲིད་ཕྱི་མ་ (yəŋsiì cīmə) the next life, the next reincarnation.

ཡང་སློབ་ (ya̲ŋlob) disciple of a disciple.

ཡང་གསང་ (ya̲ŋsaŋ) 1. top secret. 2. sm. རྫོགས་ཆེན་.

ཡང་གསེད་ (ya̲ŋseè) sifting, differentiating, sorting out; va.—རྒྱག ¶གྱོན་ཆས་གསར་རྙིང་ཚང་མ་ཡང་གསེད་ཅིག་རྒྱག་དགོས་ཀྱི་འདུག (We) have to sort out the old and new clothes.

ཡང་བསང་དོད་པོ་ (ya̲ŋsaŋ tö̲öbo) sb. who is too unilateral in making decisions or is too frank.

ཡང་ཧུ་སི་བན་ཌྲི་ (ya̲ŋhusi be̲ndri) Younghusband.

ཡང་ལྷམ་ (ya̲ŋlham) cloth shoes/ slippers/ sneakers.

ཡངས་ (ya̲ŋ) 1. wide, broad, spacious, roomy ¶ཡངས་ཤིང་རྒྱ་ཆེ་བའི་རྩྭ་ཐང་ A vast pasture. 2. abbr. of ཡངས་པོ་.

ཡངས་དོག (ya̲ŋdoò) abbr. of ག་ཡང་པོ་ and ག་དོག་པོ་.

ཡངས་ལྡན་ (ya̲ŋdɛn) sm. ཡངས་ཤིང་རྒྱ་ཆེ་.

ཡངས་པ་ (yaŋbə) sm. ཡངས་.

ཡངས་པ་ཅན་ (yaŋbəjɛn) see ཡངས་.

ཡངས་པོ་ (yaŋbo) wide, broad, spacious, roomy.

ཡངས་གསལ་ (yaŋsɛɛ) wide and bright.

ཡངས་ཤིང་རྒྱ་ཆེ་ (yaŋshiŋ gyace) open and wide, large and spacious, vast.

ཡངས་ཤིང་དབེན་པ་ (yaŋshiŋ wēmbə) large/ vast and deserted.

ཡངས་གསོས་ (yaŋsöö̀) lessening or reducing hardship/ suffering/ difficulty ¶ ལས་འགན་ཉུང་དུ་བཏང་ཙང་ཁོ་ཚོ་ཡངས་གསོས་བྱུང་སོང་ Because (they) lessened their responsibilities, their hardship was reduced.

ཡད་དེ་ཡུད་དེ་ (yɛɛ̀de yüǜde) 1. unclear, obscure. 2. talking without regard for the consequences; va.—བྱེད་.

ཡད་ཡུད་ (yɛɛ̀yüǜ) abbr. of ཡད་དེ་ཡུད་དེ་.

ཡན་ (yɛn) 1. sm. ཡན་ཆད་. 2. sm. འཁྱམས་. 3. vi. to lose ¶ ཅ་ལག་དེ་མ་ཡན་པ་བྱེད་དགོས་ You must not lose these things. 4. even ¶ རང་ཉིད་ཀྱི་གྱོན་ཆས་ཡན་ཕུད་ནས་སྤྲད་ཀྱང་ཁྲལ་འཇལ་ཐུབ་མེད་པ་རེད་ Even though they gave even their clothes, they weren't able to pay the tax.

ཡན་ཁྱར་ (yɛngyar) vi. to be/ get scattered/ dispersed.

ཡན་ག (yɛnga) see ཡལ་ག.

ཡན་གར་ (yɛngar) isolated, alone, single.

ཡན་ཆད་ (yɛnjɛɛ̀) 1. (usu. with numbers) above, upwards of, more than, over ¶ སུམ་བཅུ་ཡན་ཆད་ Thirty and above. 2. before ¶ ཟླ་བ་གསུམ་པ་ཡན་ཆད་ Before March. 3. including (even) ¶ ཁོ་ཚོས་སྤག་གཡོ་རྒྱུ་ཡན་ཆས་ཡག་པོ་ཞི་དྲག་བྱས་བྱུང་ They did many good things for us including even kneading སྤག.

ཡན་ཆད་མན་ཆད་ (yɛnjɛɛ̀ mɛnjɛɛ̀) more or less, approximately, around ¶ དམག་མི་འཛུགས་ཡས་དེ་ལོ་ཉིས་ཅུ་ཡན་ཆད་མན་ཆད་གདན་འབེབས་བཟོས་བཞག (They) have decided to recruit soldiers who are around twenty years of age.

ཡན་ཆོད་ (yɛnjöö̀) sm. ཡན་ཆད་.

ཡན་མཆུ་ (yɛnju) upper lip.

ཡན་ཐབས་ (yɛndəb) sm. ཡན་ཆད་.

ཡན་དུ་ (yɛndu) sm. ཡན་ཆད་.

ཡན་ནས་ (yɛnnɛ) 1. from before ¶ ཟླ་བ་བཞི་པ་ཡན་ནས་ From before the 4th month.

ཡན་པ་ (yɛmba) 1. another, other ¶ དེབ་ཡན་པ་གཅིག་དགོས་ I need another book. 2. sm. ཡན་པོ་.

ཡན་པ་བ་ (yɛnbawa) another, other.

ཡན་པོ་ (yɛmbo) lenient, permissive, letting people evade punishment; va.—གཏོང་ ¶ ཉེས་པ་ཅན་རྣམས་ཡན་པོར་གཏོང་མི་རུང་ One should not let the criminals evade punismments.

ཡན་པོར་གཏོང་ (yɛmbor dōŋ) va. to spoil (a child).

ཡན་ལྤགས་ (yɛmbaà) sm. མིག་ལྤགས་ཡས་མ་.

ཡན་མན་ (yɛnmɛn) abbr. of ཡན་ཆད་མན་ཆད་.

ཡན་ཚོང་ཁང་ (yɛndzoŋgaŋ) branch store/ shop.

ཡན་ལ་ (yɛnla) sm. ཡན་ཆད་.

ཡན་ལག (yɛnlaà) 1. limb ¶ ལུས་ཀྱི་ཡན་ལག The limbs of the body. 2. branch ¶ ཡན་ལག་བཟོ་གྲྭ་ A branch factory.

ཡན་ལག་གི་བྲན་གཅོད་ (yɛnlaàgi trɛnjöö̀) arc. to cut off the limbs.

ཡན་ལག་གི་ཚིག་གྲུབ་ (yɛnlaàgi tsīgdrub) a clause (in a longer sentence).

ཡན་ལག་བརྒྱད་ལྡན་གྱི་རྩོམ་རྩལ་ (yɛnlaà gyɛndɛngi dzōmdzüü) sm. ཡན་ལག་བརྒྱད་པའི་རྩོ་རྩལ་.

ཡན་ལག་བརྒྱད་པའི་རྩོམ་རྩལ་ (yɛnlaà gyɛɛ̀bɛ dzōmdzüü) 1. eight part essay (a literary composition prescribed for Chinese civil service examinations). 2. jargon, stereotypical writing.

ཡན་ལག་བརྒྱད་པའི་རྩོམ་རྩལ་གསར་པ་ (yɛnlaà gyɛɛ̀bɛ dzōmdzüü sārba) new/ modern jargon.

ཡན་ལག་སྒྲིག་འཛུགས་ (yɛnlaà drigdzuù) branch organization.

ཡན་ལག་ལྔ་ (yɛnlaà ŋā) the five: arms and legs and the head.

ཡན་ལག་ལྔ་ས་ལ་ཕབ་པའི་ཕྱག (yɛnlaà ŋā sāla pəbbɛ cāà) a type of prostration where the hands, feet and head touch the ground.

ཡན་ལག་ཅན་ (yɛnlaàjɛn) the main body, the headquarters.

ཡན་ལག་གཅོད་བྲེགས་ (yɛnlaà jȫö̀dreg) shung. sm. ཡན་ལག་གཅོད་འབྲེག.

ཡན་ལག་གཅོད་འབྲེག (yɛnlaà jȫö̀dreg) shung. cutting off the limbs as corporal punishment.

ཡན་ལག་བཅོས་མ་ (yɛnlaà jȫö̀ma) artificial limbs.

ཡན་ལག་ཉེ་འབྲེལ་ (yɛnlaà ñendree) family and friends.

ཡན་ལག་དང་ཡན་ལག་ཅན་གྱི་འབྲེལ་བ་ (yɛnlaà dāŋ yɛnlaàjɛngi dreewa) relations between the main entity and its branches.

ཡན་ལག་པུའུ་ཁང་ (yɛnlaà būgaŋ) branch unit/ office. tib. ch.

ཡན་ལག་ཕྱོགས་ཁག (yɛnlaà cɔ̄ɔ̀gaà) branch/ offshoot group.

ཡན་ལག་དམག་ཁུལ་ (yɛnlaà māggüü) military subcommand (area).

ཡན་ལག་དམག་ཁོངས་ (yɛnlaà māggoŋ) military subdivision, military branch district.

ཡན་ལག་དམག་ཁུལ་ (yɛnlaà məggüü) sm. ཡན་ལག་དམག་ཁོངས་.

ཡན་ལག་ཚིག་གྲུབ་ (yɛnlaà tsīgdrub) a clause (in grammar).

ཡན་ལག་ཚོགས་པ་ (yɛnlaà tsōgba) branch association.

ཡན་ལག་ཚོང་ཁང་ (yɛnlaà tsōŋgaŋ) branch store.

ཡན་ལག་ཞ་བོ་ (yɛnlaà shawo) crippled (in limbs).

ཡན་ལག་བཞི་ (yɛnlaà shi) the four limbs.

ཡན་ལག་བཞི་པའི་དཔུང་ (yɛnlaà sibɛ būŋ) four ancient branches of the military: cavalry, elephant, chariot, infantry.

ཡན་ལག་རུ་ཁག (yɛnlaà rugaà) subunit, branch of a unit/ brigade.

ཡན་ལག་ལས་ཁུངས (yɛnlaà lɛɛ̀guŋ) branch office.

ཡན་ལག་ལས་དོན་ཨུ་ཡོན་ལྷན་ཁང་ (yɛnlaà lɛɛ̀dön ūyün lhɛ̄ngaŋ) branch committee, subcommittee.

ཡན་ལག་ལྷན་ཁང་ (yɛnlaà lhɛ̄ngaŋ) subcommittee.

ཡན་ལག་ལྷན་ཚོགས་ (yɛnlaà lhɛ̄ndzɔɔ̀) branch committee/ association.

ཡན་སོན་ (yɛnsön) ch. hydrochloric acid.

ཡན་སོང་མེད་པ་ (yɛnsoŋ meèba) shung. not letting people evade punishment.

ཡན་ཨན་ (yɛnan) Yenan.

ཡན་ཨན་གྱི་སྙིང་སྟོབས་ (yɛnnangi ñīŋdob) the Yenan Spirit (the spirit of self-reliance and hard struggle).

ཡན་ཨོའོ་ (yɛno) ch. edible bird nest (used in making a type of soup).

ཡབ་ (yəb) 1. h. of ཕ་. 2. sm. སྐྱེབས་.

ཡབ་གུང་ (yəbguŋ) shung. the father of the Dalai (who has the title of གུང་).

ཡབ་གུང་གསར་རྙིང་ (yəbguŋ sərñiŋ) shung. the fathers of theold and new Dalai Lamas.

ཡབ་རྒྱལ་པོ་ (yəb gyɛɛbo) king (who also is a father).

ཡབ་གཅིག (yəbjig) sm. ཡབ་, 1.

ཡབ་ཆེན་ (yəbjen) honorific term for fathers in aristocratic families.

ཡབ་རྗེ་ (yəbjen) sm. ཡབ་, 1.

ཡབ་སྟག (yəbdaà) shung. abbr. of ཡབ་གཞིས་སྟག་འཚེར་.

ཡབ་དམ་པ་ (yəb tamba) h. of ཕ་དམ་པ་.

ཡབ་རྗེ་དམ་པ་ (yəbje tamba) h. of ཕ་དམ་པ་.

ཡབ་འབངས་ (yəbbaŋ) subjects/ miser/ serfs from the father's side.

ཡབ་མེས་ (yəbmeè) paternal forefathers.

ཡབ་མོ་ (yəbmo) sm. གཡབ་མོ་.

ཡབ་ཚང་ (yəbdzaŋ) family, household.

ཡབ་གཞིས་ (yəbshiì) title/ name of families who have produced Dalai Lamas ¶ ཡབ་གཞིས་སྟག་

འཚེར་ The Taktse family (the family of the 14th. Dalai Lama).

ཡབ་གཞིས་ཀུང་ (yəbshiì kuŋ) father of the Dalai Lama who has the title of ཀུང་.

ཡབ་ཡབ་པོ་ (yəb yəbbo) sb. who is unable to concentrate/ focus.

ཡབ་ཡུམ་ (yəbyum) h. of ཕ་མ་.

ཡབ་ཡོབ་ (yəbyob) abbr. of ཡབ་བེ་ཡོབ་བེ་.

ཡབ་སྲས་ (yəbsɛɛ̀) 1. h. of ཕ་བུ་. 2. a son from a ཡབ་གཞིས་ family. 3. the father and son (used to refer to the Dalai Lama and the Panchen Lama respectively) ། རྒྱལ་བ་ཡབ་སྲས་གཉིས་ The two: the Dalai Lama and Panchen Lama. 4. lama/ master and his main disciples.

ཡབ་སྲས་གསུང་འབུམ་ (yəbsɛɛ̀ sūŋbum) the collected works of Tsongkapa and his two main disciples.

ཡམ་ (yam) sm. ཡམས་ནད་.

ཡམ་བུ་ (yəmbu) Kathmandu.

ཡམ་མེ་བ་ (yammewa) approximately, roughly.

ཡམ་མེ་ཡོམ་མེ་ (yamme yomme) shaky, unsteady, swaying, wavering, influx. ། ཡམ་མེ་ཡོམ་མེ་ཆེ་བའི་ལྕགས་ཟམ་ An iron bridge that sways a lot.

ཡམ་ཡོམ་ (yamyom) abbr. of ཡམ་མེ་ཡོམ་མེ་.

ཡམ་ཤིང་ (yamshiŋ) firewood used in tantric exorcisms.

ཡམས་ (yam) sm. ཡམས་ནད་.

ཡམས་འགོག (yamgɔɔ̀) epidemic prevention.

ཡམས་ནད་ (yamnɛɛ̀) epidemic.

ཡའ་ཙེ་ (yadze) ch. duck.

ཡའུ་ (yəwu) sm. ཡ་བྱིད་.

ཡའི་ (yɛ) sm. ཡང་.

ཡའོ་ (yao) Yao (minority nationality in Southern China).

ཡར་ (yar) 1. up, upwards ། ཡར་འཐེན་མ་ཐུབ་པ་རེད་ (They) were unable to pull it up. 2. facing inside, facing away from the door ། ཁོ་སྒོ་ནས་ཡར་ཡོང་གི་འདུག He is coming inside from the door.

ཡར་ཀྱག (yaa gyā) va. to lift up, to raise.

ཡར་ཀླུང་ (yərluŋ) the Yarlung valley and river (in S. Tibet).

ཡར་ཀླུངས་ (yərluŋ) sm. ཡར་ཀླུང་.

ཡར་ཀླུང་ཁ་རིལ་ (yərluŋ kārii) a type of sole on Tibetan woolen boots made in Yarlung.

ཡར་ཀླུང་གཙང་པོ་ (yərluŋ dzāŋbo) the Yarlung Tsangpo River.

ཡར་དཀན་ (yargɛn) steep.

ཡར་དཀྲུག་མར་དཀྲུག (yaadrug maadrug) causing/ instigating trouble everywhere (above and below); va.—བྱེད་.

ཡར་བཀྱག (yaa kyāà) sm. ཡར་ཀྱག.

ཡར་སྐྱེལ་ (yəəgüü) stimulating/ promoting development or improvement; va.—གཏོང་ ། ཐོན་འཕེལ་ཡོང་རྒྱུར་ཡར་སྐྱེལ་བཏང་བ་རེད་ They stimulated an increase in production.

ཡར་སྐྱེལ་བ་ (yəəgüüwə) promoter, developer.

ཡར་སྐྱིད་ (yargyeè sm. ཡར་རྒྱས་.

ཡར་སྐྱེལ་མར་སྐྱེལ་ (yargyeè maagyee) taking/ delivering things everywhere (up and down, hither and thither).

ཡར་སྐྱེས་ (yaagyeè) sm. ཡར་རྒྱས་.

ཡར་སྐྱུག་མར་བཤལ་ (yərgyuù maashɛɛ) vomiting and having diarrhea; va.—བྱེད་.

ཡར་སྐྱོར་ (yaa gyɔ̄ɔ̄) va. to support/ hold sb. up (to stand) ། ནད་པ་འདི་ཡར་སྐྱོར་ནས་སྨན་ཁང་ལ་འཁྲིད་པ་རེད་ (They) supported the sick person and took him to the hospital.

ཡར་ཁྱུང་ (yərguŋ) temple.

ཡར་ཁྱིམ་ (yargyim) Yarkhand.

ཡར་འཁྱམ་མར་ཉུལ་ (yərgyam maañüü) wandering up and down.

ཡར་འཁྱིལ་སྨ་ར་ (yərgyii māra) handlebar moustache.

ཡར་འཁྱོག (yar kyɔ̄ɔ̀) vi. to be able to lift up.

ཡར་འགེལ་ (yar gee) va. to hang up.

ཡར་འགོ་མར་འབབ་ (yar go maa bəb) climbing up and going down a slope.

ཡར་འགུལ་མར་འགུལ་ (yangüü mangüü) moving/ going up and down or here and there.

ཡར་འགྲོ་ (yaa dro) 1. va. to go upwards. 2. vi. to improve. 3. improving, improved.

ཡར་འགྲོ་བརྒྱ་དང་མར་འགྲོ་སྟོང་ (yandro gya taŋ mandro dōŋ) many people going up and down, a place or road where many people pass [Lit. a hundred going up and a thousand going down].

ཡར་འགྲོ་མར་འགྲོ་ (yandro mandro) going up and down, going to and fro; va.—བྱེད་.

ཡར་འགྲོའི་བསམ་པ་ (yandrö sāmba) progressive.

ཡར་རྒྱག (yaa gyaà) sm. ཡས་རྒྱག.

ཡར་རྒྱས་ (yargyɛɛ̀) progress, development, improvement; va.—གཏོང་ to make progress, to develop, to get improved; va.—འགྲོ་ to get/ have progress/ development/ improvement.

ཡར་རྒྱས་དམན་པ་ (yargyɛɛ̀ mēmba) underdeveloped ། ཡར་རྒྱས་དམན་པའི་རྒྱལ་ཁབ་ Underdeveloped countries.

ཡར་རྒྱས་སུ་འགྲོ་བཞིན་པའི་ (yargyɛɛ̀su droshimbɛ) developing ། ཡར་རྒྱས་སུ་འགྲོ་བཞིན་པའི་ཡུལ་ཁབ Developing countries.

ཡར་རྒྱུག་མར་རྒྱུག (yaagyuù maagyuù) going back and forth, going hither and thither/ to and fro; va.—བྱེད་.

ཡར་རྒྱུགས་མར་རྒྱུགས་ (yaagyuù maagyuù) sm. ཡར་རྒྱུག་མར་རྒྱུག.

ཡར་རྒྱུགས་མར་འདུར་ (yaagyuù mandur) sm. ཡར་རྒྱུག་མར་རྒྱུག.

ཡར་སྒྲིད་ (yaagyeè) the front stone or the front iron leg of a stove.

ཡར་སྒྲུག (yaa druù) va. to pick up.

ཡར་བགྲལ་མར་བགྲལ་ (yaagɛɛ maagɛɛ) more or less the same (usu. for age) ། ལོ་ཚད་ཡར་བགྲལ་མར་བགྲལ་གྱི་ཕྲུ་གུ་གསུམ་སླེབས་སོང་ Three children came whose ages are more or less the same.

ཡར་ངོ་ (yaaŋo) the first half of the lunar month (from the 1st to the 15th).

ཡར་ངོ་ཚེས་བཅུ་ (yaaŋo tsēèju) the 10th day of the Tibetan lunar month.

ཡར་ངོའི་ཟླ་བ་ (yaaŋö dawa) sm. ཡར་ངོ་.

ཡར་བཅད་པ་ (yar jɛ̀ɛ̀ba) except for, excluding ། ལོ་རྒན་པ་རྣམས་ཡར་བཅད་པའི་དེ་མིན་ཚང་མ་ངལ་རྩོལ་ལ་འགྲོ་དགོས་ Excluding the elderly, everyone has to work.

ཡར་ཆོབ་ཆོབ་ (yaa cōbjob) 1. bouncing; va.—བྱེད་. 2. piling up; va.—བྱེད་.

ཡར་མཆོང་མར་མཆོང་ (yaajoŋ maajoŋ) jumping up and down; va.—བྱེད་.

ཡར་མཆོད་མར་སྦྱིན་ (yaacöö maajin) (giving) offerings above to the gods and alms below to beggars.

ཡར་བཏེག (yaa dēg) sm. ཡར་བཀྱག.

ཡར་ལྟ་ (yaa dā) 1. va. to look up. 2. va. to follow/ learn from/ look up to good examples ། ཕྲུ་གུ་ཚོར་ཁ་མིག་ཡར་ལྟ་བྱེད་དགོས་པའི་བསླབ་བྱ་རྒྱག་དགོས་ One should advise the children to follow good examples.

ཡར་ལྟོས་ (yaa dōō) sm. ཡར་ལྟ་.

ཡར་ཐོན་ (yardön) 1. advanced, developed ། ཡར་ཐོན་གྱི་ལག་རྩལ་ Advanced skills. ། འཛམ་གླིང་ཡར་ཐོན་གྱི་ཡུལ་རྣམས་ The developed countries. 2. progressive ། སྐུ་དྲག་འདི་ཡར་ཐོན་ཅན་ཞིག་རེད་ That aristocrat is a progressive.

ཡར་ཐོན་གྱི་སྤོབས་པ་ (yardöngi bōbba) vigor, animation, vitality, life.

ཡར་ཐོན་རྒྱལ་ཁབ་ (yardön gyɛ̀ɛ̀gəb) advanced/ developed country.

ཡར་ཐོན་ཅན་ (yardönjɛn) progressive, advanced.

ཡར་ཐོན་ཅན་གྱི་དུལ་ལྡན་མགོ་མཚོན་ཚོད་འཛིན་བྱེད་པའི་གྲོས་མཐུན་ (yardönjɛngi tüüdren kodzön tsöndzin cəèbɛ tröödzɔɔ̀) Strategic Arms Limitation Talks (SALT).

ཡར་ཐོན་ཞིང་ལས་མཉམ་ལས་ཁང་ (yardön shiŋlɛɛ̀

ñāmlɛ̀ɛ̀gaŋ) advanced farm cooperative.

ཡར་ཐོན་ཅན་གྱི་ལས་རྩོལ་ཚོགས་པ་ (yardönjɛngi lɛ̀ɛ̀dzöö tsɔ̄gba) Progressive Labor Party.

ཡར་ཐོན་ལྷུར་ལེན་ (yardön lhūū len) making an effort to progress/ advance/ develop; va.—བྱེད་.

ཡར་འཐེན་ (yaa tēn) 1. va. to pull up. 2. va. to promote, to advance.

ཡར་དར་ (yardar) sm. ཡར་རྒྱས་.

ཡར་འདུལ་མ་འདུར་ (yandur mandur) sm. ཡར་རྒྱུག་མར་རྒྱུག.

ཡར་འདེབས་མར་གཡུག (yandeb maryuù) throwing things here and there or up and down.

ཡར་འདོན་ (yardön) va. to take out, to pull out ¶ ཁྲོན་པའི་ནང་ནས་ཕྲུ་གུ་དེ་ཡར་བཏོན་པ་རེད་ (They) pulled the child out of the well.

ཡར་རྡོ་ཕོག (yardo pɔ̄ɔ̀) vi. to have a stone hit sb. accidentally.

ཡར་ལྡང་ (yardaŋ) sm. ཡར་ལང་.

ཡར་ལྡན་གོང་འཕེལ་ (yardɛn koŋbel) shung. sm. གོང་འཕེལ་.

ཡར་ལྡིང་ (yaa dīŋ) vi. to float/ soar.

ཡར་ལྡིང་མར་མཆོང་ (yaa dīŋ maa cōŋ) hopping and jumping (usu. when angry).

ཡར་ལྡོག (yaa dɔ̄ɔ̀) sm. གྱེན་ལོག.

ཡར་སྣེ་ (yarne) the upper end (of a stick, etc.).

ཡར་ལྤགས་ (yarbaà) skin of a one year old yak.

ཡར་དཔེར་འགྲན་པ་ (yarber drɛmba) shung. to set a good example ¶ བླ་འབངས་ཀྱི་མ་སྤྲིན་དྲལ་གྱིས་དམ་ཚིག་ལ་རྒྱ་ཡར་དཔེར་འགྲན་པ་ The friendship and the loyalty between the Lama and the subject is just like cloudless sunshine which sets a good example for all the people.

ཡར་འཕགས་པ་ (yaa pāgba) to be elevated, to reach a high position.

ཡར་འཕར་ (yaa pār) sm. ཡར་འཕེལ་.

ཡར་འཕར་མར་ཆག (yaa pāā maa cāà) going up and down, increasing and decreasing (usu. prices).

ཡར་ཕེབས་ (yaa pēè) come in (h.).

ཡར་འཕེལ་ (yaa pēl) vi. to be/ get increased ¶ ལུང་པ་འདིའི་འབྲུ་རིགས་ཐོན་སྐྱེད་ཡར་འཕེལ་བྱུང་བཞག The production of grain in this place has increased. ¶ འབྲུ་རིགས་ཐོན་སྐྱེད་ཡར་འཕེལ་གཏོང་དགོས་ (We) need to increase the production of grain.

ཡར་འཕྱུལ་མར་སྒྱུར་ (yaabüü maagyur) obsequious/ respectful to superiors and arrogant to inferiors.

ཡར་འཕྱུར་ (yaa cār) sm. ཡར་བཀྲག.

ཡར་འཕྱུར་རླུང་རྒྱུན་ (yaa cār lūŋgyün) up draft of air, up current (of air).

ཡར་བེའུ་ (yarbewu) one year old calf.

ཡར་འབྲོག (yamdrɔ̀ɔ̀) Yamdrok (lake and area).

ཡར་འབྲོག་སྐམ་སོས་ (yamdrɔ̀ɔ̀ gāmsöö) dried meat from the Yamdrok area.

ཡར་འབྲོག་གཡུ་མཚོ་ (yamdrɔ̀ɔ̀ yūmdzo) Lake Yamdrok.

ཡར་མ་ (yārma) cattle that have given birth to a calf last year.

ཡར་མར་ (yaa maa) up and down.

ཡར་ཙམ་ (yədzə) up a little bit.

ཡར་བརྩོན་ (yardzön) sm. ཡར་ཐོན་ལྷུར་ལེན་.

ཡར་ཚེས་ (yardzeè) first part of the month.

ཡར་འཛེག (yaa dzeg) va. to climb up.

ཡར་ཞུ་ (yar shu) va. to submit or present a report or make a request/ appeal to a superior.

ཡར་ཞུ་མར་གནང་ (yarshu manaŋ) shung. one who takes messages up to a superior and transmits his instructions/ orders to subordinates.

ཡར་ཞོ་ (yarsho) yogurt made from the milk of an animal that gave birth the previous year.

ཡར་བཞེང་ (yaa sheŋ) 1. h. of ཡར་ལང་. 2. va. to erect, to build.

ཡར་ཟ་མར་ལུག (yaasa maaluù) vi. to have diarrhea immediately after one has eaten.

ཡར་གཟེད་ (yaa seè) 1. va. to hold out (a hand/ cup) to receive sth. 2. sm. ཡར་སྙོན་.

ཡར་ཡར་ (yaryar) gradually going up and up ¶ ང་ཚོ་ཡར་ཡར་ཕྱིན་ནས་གངས་རིའི་རྩེ་ལ་སླེབས་བྱུང་ We gradually went up and up and came to the top of the mountain.

ཡར་རེ་ཡོར་རེ་ (yaare yorre) unsteady, shaky, wobbly.

ཡར་རླངས་མར་ཐིགས་མེད་པ་ (yar laŋ maa tīg meèba) without slip up/ loss/ damage/ hindrance [Lit. no steam above and no drops below].

ཡར་ལ་ (yaala) up, upwards.

ཡར་ལངས་ (yaa laŋ) 1. va. to get up, to stand up. 2. va. to rise up (in rebellion).

ཡར་ལངས་ན་མགོ་བརྡབ་ མར་བསྡད་ན་རྐུབ་བརྡབ་ (yaa laŋna godəb maa dɛ̀ɛna gūb dəb) in a dilemma, facing a problem whatever one does [Lit. if one get up one bangs one's head, if one sits down one bangs one's ass].

ཡར་ལངས་ཞིང་བྲན་ (yaalaŋ shiŋdrɛn) the poorest agricultural serfs who "rose up" (were emancipated after democratic reforms in 1959).

ཡར་ལིང་མར་ལིང་ (yarliŋ marliŋ) pulled, torn apart, torn asunder; va.—ཤུལ་ ¶ གཟིགས་གཉིས་ཀྱིས་ལུག་བསད་ནས་ཡར་ལིང་མར་ལིང་ཤུལ་བཞག Two leopards killed a sheep and tore it apart.

ཡར་ལོག (yaa lɔ̀ɔ̀) 1. sm. གྱེན་ལོག. 2. va. to climb from the bottom up.

ཡར་ལོག་བླ་མ་ (yarlɔ̀ɔ̀ lāma) a defrocked monk taking the vows of monk again.

ཡར་ཤན་མར་ཤན་ (yarshɛn marshɛn) shung. dragging up and down; va.—བྱེད་.

ཡར་ཤོག (yaa shōò) come in!

ཡར་བཤད་མར་བཤད་ (yaashɛɛ̀ maashɛɛ̀) 1. saying things to those above and below ¶ ཁོང་གིས་ཡར་བཤད་མར་བཤད་བྱས་ནས་དོན་དག་དེ་སྒྲུབ་ཐུབ་པ་བྱུང་བཞག He spoke to those above and below and has been able to accomplish his task. 2. saying this and that, talking in circles, avoiding sth. in speech. ¶ ཁོས་ཡར་བཤད་མར་བཤད་བྱས་ནས་དོན་ངོ་བཤད་མ་སོང་ He said this and that but didn't say the real meaning.

ཡར་ས་མར་སྐྱེལ་ (yaasa maagyee) causing trouble everywhere, turning upside down; va.—བྱེད་.

ཡར་གསོལ་ (yaasöö) reporting to superiors (saying "long live Mao," etc.) every morning during the Cultural Revolution.

ཡར་བསུ་མར་སྐྱེལ་ (yaasu maagyee) 1. welcoming and seeing people off. 2. sm. ཨས་བསུ་མས་འགེབས་.

ཡལ་ (yɛɛ) vi. to disappear, to vanish, to fade away ¶ ཚོན་འདི་ཡལ་འདུག The paint has faded.

ཡལ་ག (yɛɛga) branch, bough (of a tree).

ཡལ་ག་མཐུད་སྦྱོར་ (yɛɛga tǖǖjɔɔ) grafting (of trees).

ཡལ་ག་འདྲེག་གཅོད་ (yɛɛga dreèjöö) pruning/ trimming of trees.

ཡལ་ག་འདྲེག (yɛɛga dreè) va. to prune/ trim (trees).

ཡལ་ག་འདྲེག་གཅོད་ (yɛɛga dreèjöö) sm. ཡལ་ག་འདྲེག་གཅོད་.

ཡལ་གཅོད་བྱེད་ (yɛɛga dreèjöö) sm. ཡལ་ག་འདྲེག.

ཡལ་འདབ་ (yɛndəb) branches and leaves.

ཡལ་སྡོང་ (yɛɛdoŋ) branches and trunk.

ཡལ་བར་འདོར་ (yɛɛwar dɔɔ) va. to leave uncared for ¶ དབུལ་ཕོངས་རྣམས་ཡལ་བར་འདོར་མི་རུང་ It isn't proper to not look after the poor.

ཡལ་མ་ཡོལ་ (yɛɛma yöö) just before or after ¶ ནམ་ཕྱེད་ཡལ་མ་ཡོལ་ཞིག་ལ་ཁ་པར་ཞིག་འབྱོར་བྱུང་ I received a phone call around midnight.

ཡལ་མེད་རྟག་པ་ (yɛɛmɛ dāgba) all the time, everytime ¶ ཁོང་གི་གདོང་ལ་ཡལ་མེད་རྟག་པའི་འཛུམ་ཞིག་ཡོད་ He has a smile on his face all the time.

ཡལ་རྩེ་ (yɛɛdze) the tip of a branch.

ཡལ་བཤུར་རྒྱག (yɛɛshuu gyaà) 1. va. to prune. 2. va. to weed out (people).

ཡལ་ཡུལ་ (yɛɛyüü) a short time, a brief period.

ཡལ་ཡོལ་ (yɛɛyöö) sm. ཡལ་ལི་ཡོལ་ལི་.

ཡལ་ཡོལ་ཆ་མེད་དུ་ཐལ་ (yɛɛyöö cāmeèdu tɛɛ) vi. to completely disappear, to vanish without a trace.

ཡལ་ལི་ཡོལ་ལི་ (yɛɛle yööle) idly passing away time ། ཡལ་ལི་ཡོལ་ལི་བྱས་ནས་མ་སྡོད་ སློབ་སྦྱོང་ཡག་པོ་བྱེད་ Don't sit around idly; do (your) studies well.

ཡལ་སེ་རྒྱག (yɛɛse gyaà) sm. ཡར་བཞེད་རྒྱག.

ཡས་ (yɛɛ̀) 1. verbal nominalizing particle ། དམག་འཁྲུག་སློང་ཡས་ཀྱི་གྲ་སྒྲིག་བྱས་པ་རེད་ (They) made preparation for starting a war. ། བོད་སྐད་སློབ་སྦྱོང་བྱེད་ཡས་ཀྱི་དེབ་འདི་ཡག་པོ་འདུག This book is good for studying Tibetan. ། པེ་ཅིང་ལ་འགྲོ་ཡས་ཁག་པོ་རེད་ Going to Beijing is difficult. 2. future action particle ། ཁོ་སང་ཉིན་འགྲོ་ཡས་རེད་ He will be going tomorrow. 3. (vb. — + བྱུང་) having no chance to do the verbal action ། ཁོ་ལ་ཁང་པ་རྒྱག་ཡས་བྱུང་བ་རེད་ He had a chance to build a house.

ཡས་ཀན་ (yɛ̀ɛgɛn) the upper jaw.

ཡས་ཁོད་ (yɛ̀ɛgöö) 1. the top stone of a grinding stone. 2. pestle.

ཡས་འཁོན་མས་འཁོན་ (yɛ̀ɛgön mɛ̀ɛgön) troubles and difficulties everywhere (above and below).

ཡས་གུང་ (yɛ̀ɛguŋ) shirt, jacket.

ཡས་གླུད་ (yɛ̀ɛlüü) sm. གླུད་.

ཡས་འགེམ་ (yɛngem) animals whose lower teeth/ jaw are longer than the upper.

ཡས་འགྲམ་ (yɛ̀ɛdram) the upper jaw.

ཡས་རྒྱག (yɛ̀ɛgyaà) pestle.

ཡས་སྒྲོན་ (yɛ̀ɛdrön) va. to put butter on the rim of a ཆང་ cup (good luck custom).

ཡས་མཆིག (yɛ̀ɛjii) 1. sm. ཡས་རྒྱག. 2. the top/ upper grinding stone.

ཡས་མཆུ་ (yɛ̀ɛju) upper lip.

ཡས་གཉིས་མས་གཉིས་ (yɛ̀ɛñii mɛ̀ɛñii) sm. ཡ་གཉིས་མ་གཉིས་.

ཡས་གདུན་ (yɛ̀ɛdün) sm. ཡས་མཆིག.

ཡས་སྡ་མས་འཇོར་ (yɛ̀ɛda mɛnjɔɔ) pick axe.

ཡས་ཐིག (yɛ̀ɛdig) fishing string.

ཡས་ཐེམ་ (yɛ̀ɛdem) wooden frame above the door.

ཡས་དོ་ (yɛ̀ɛdo) top/ upper grinding stone.

ཡས་སྣོད་ (yɛ̀ɛnöö) a kind of butter lamp.

ཡས་པ་ (yɛ̀ɛba) without, less ། མཐའ་ཡས་པ་ Limitless.

ཡས་ཕྱིན་ (yɛ̀ɛjin) sm. གོང་འོག.

ཡས་བབ་ (yɛ̀ɛbəb) flowing/ falling down from above.

ཡས་མ་ (yɛ̀ɛma) previous, prior, above, upper.

ཡས་མས་ (yɛ̀ɛmɛɛ̀) 1. up and down, all over ། བོད་ས་ཡས་མས་གང་སར་ཐེབས་འདུག (They) went all over Tibet. 2. about, around, approximately, more or less ། ད་ལམ་མི་ཁྲི་བརྒྱ་ཡས་མས་ཤིག Approximately one million people.

ཡས་མས་ཕྱི་ནང་ (yɛ̀ɛmɛɛ̀ cĩnaŋ) everything, everywhere (up, down, inside, outside).

ཡས་ཚེམས་ (yɛ̀ɛdzem) h. of ཡས་སོ་.

ཡས་མཚམས་ (yɛndzam) the upper boundary (of a place).

ཡས་རྫོང་ (yɛ̀ɛdzoŋ) sm. སྟོད་གདོང་.

ཡས་བཟེད་ (yɛ̀ɛseè) sm. ཡས་སྒྲོན་.

ཡས་ཡས་མས་མས་ (yɛ̀ɛyɛɛ̀ mɛ̀ɛmɛɛ̀) this and that (used to describe what sb. said); va.—ཤོད་ to make excuses ། མི་དེས་ཡས་ཡས་མས་མས་ཁོ་ན་བཤད་ནས་བུ་ལོན་དུས་ཐོག་སྤྲོད་ཀྱི་མི་འདུག That person is only making excuses and not paying the debt on time.

ཡས་སོ་ (yɛ̀ɛso) upper teeth.

ཡས་སོ་ཅན་ (yɛ̀ɛsojɛn) animals that have upper teeth.

ཡས་བསུ་མས་སྐྱེལ་ (yɛ̀ɛsu mɛ̀ɛgyee) sm. ཡས་བསུ་མས་འགེབས་.

ཡས་བསུ་མས་འགེབས་ (yɛ̀ɛsu mɛ̀ɛgeb) the amount ། བཟོ་གྲྭ་འདིའི་ཟླ་རེའི་ཡོང་འབབ་ཡས་བསུ་མས་འགེབས་ཀྱིས་ཁྲི་གཉིས་བྱུང་སོང་ The amount of monthly income for the factory was twenty thousand.

ཡས་ལྷེ་མས་ལྷེ་ཆད་ (yɛ̀ɛlhe mɛ̀ɛlhe cɛ̀ɛ) vi. to be tattered/ mangy.

ཡི་ (yi) genitive particle (used after vowels).

ཡི་ག (yigə) taste, appetite; vi.—འགག to lose one's appetite ། དེང་སང་ཁ་ལག་གི་ཡི་ག་འགག་བཞག These days I have lost my appetite. 2. mind; vi.—འོང་ to like, to find appealing, to be attracted to, to come to mind ། རང་གི་ཡི་གར་འོང་བའི་གྲོགས་མོ་ཞིག་འཚོལ་དགོས་ I have to search for a girl I find appealing (will come into my mind).

ཡི་གར་འཕྲོད་ (yigar trõõ) vi. to be pleasing, to like, to be attracted to.

ཡི་གར་འོང་ (yigar oŋ) sm. ཡི་གར་འཕྲོད་.

ཡི་གེ་ (yigi) 1. letters, writing, handwriting; va.—གཏོང་; —བསྐུར་ to send/ mail a letter; va.—དཔོད་ to dictate a letter; va.—སྐྱེལ་ to deliver a letter ། ཁོའི་ཡི་གེ་ཡག་པོ་འདུག His handwriting is good. ། ངར་ཡི་གེ་ཞིག་འབྱོར་བྱུང་ I received a letter.

ཡི་གེ་རྐྱང་པ་ (yigi gyãŋba) 1. a single letter. 2. syllables that do not have any affixed letters.

ཡི་གེ་སྐྱེལ་གླ་ (yigi gyēēla) postal rates.

ཡི་གེ་མཁན་ (yigiñɛn) sm. ཡི་གེ་པ་.

ཡི་གེ་རྒྱ་མ་ (yigi gyama) shung. a letter with an envelope.

ཡི་གེ་སྒྱུར་ (yigi gyur) va. to translate.

ཡི་གེ་བཅོས་བསྒྱུར་ (yigi jöögyur) language reform.

ཡི་གེ་བཅོས་བསྒྱུར་ཨུ་ཡོན་ལྷན་ཁང་ (yigi jöögyur ūyön lhɛngaŋ) language reform commission.

ཡི་གེ་མཆན་བཀོད་ (yigi cēngöö) explanations/ comments/ notes written in a text or on a letter.

ཡི་གེ་འཇོག (yigi jɔɔ̀) va. to sign/ agree to a document.

ཡི་གེ་འཇོན་པོ་ (yigi jõmbo) good at reading/ writing.

ཡི་གེ་གཉིས་ (yigi ñīī) the vowels and consonants.

ཡི་གེ་གཏོང་རེས་ (yigi dōŋreè) writing to each other (back and forth).

ཡི་གེ་གཏོང་ཡུལ་ (yigi dōŋyüü) the person/ address to which sth. is sent.

ཡི་གེ་གཏོང་ས་ (yigi dōŋsa) sm. ཡི་གེ་གཏོང་ཡུལ་.

ཡི་གེ་རྟགས་འབྱར་མ་ (yigi dāà jarma) sealed letters and documents.

ཡི་གེ་དྲུག་མ་ (yigi truŋmə) the six word "mani" mantra (of Avalokitesvara—o mani padme hum).

ཡི་གེ་ན་གཅིག་མི་ཤེས་པ་ (yigi nəjig misheèbə) totally illiterate (one who doesn't know even a single word).

ཡི་གེ་ནག་ཆུང་ (yigi nəgjuŋ) letters.

ཡི་གེ་པ་ (yigibə) scribe, writer.

ཡི་གེ་དཔོད་ (yigi bǒǒ) va. to dictate a letter.

ཡི་གེ་དཔོད་རྩོམ་ (yigi bǒǒdzom) composing a letter by dictating.

ཡི་གེ་དབུ་ཅན་ (yigi ūjɛn) sm. དབུ་ཆེན་.

ཡི་གེ་དབུ་ཆེན་ (yigi ūcen) sm. དབུ་ཅན་.

ཡི་གེ་དབུ་མེད་ (yigi ūmeè) sm. དབུ་མེད་.

ཡི་གེ་འབྲི་ (yigi dri) va. to write a letter.

ཡི་གེ་སྦྱོར་ (yigi jɔɔ) va. to paste a poster/ letter on a wall.

ཡི་གེ་མི་ཤེས་མཁན་ (yigi misheèñɛn) an illiterate person.

ཡི་གེ་མི་ཤེས་པ་ (yigi misheèba) illiterate.

ཡི་གེ་བཟོ་མི་ (yigi somi) recorder, note taker.

ཡི་གེ་ཤ་ཆེན་ (yigi shājen) aesthetically pleasing writing/ calligraphy.

ཡི་གེ་ཤེས་པ་ (yigi sheèba) sm. ཡི་གེ་མི་ཤེས་མཁན་.

ཡི་གེའི་སྐྱེས་གནས་ (yigii gyēènɛɛ̀) point of articulation (in linguistics).

ཡི་གེའི་མཁན་པོ་ (yigii kēmbo) calligrapher.

ཡི་གེའི་རྟགས་གསུམ་ (yigii dāgsum) male, female and neuter genders in the Tibetan alphabet.

ཡི་གེའི་གནས་ཚད་ (yigii nɛ̄ɛdzɛɛ̀) the length of time it takes to pronounce a particular Tibetan letter in the alphabet.

ཡི་གེའི་ཕྱི་མོ་ (yigii cĩimu) the consonants.

ཡི་གེའི་བྱེད་རྩོལ་ (yigii ceèdzöö) articulation, pronunciation.

ཡི་གེའི་དབྱངས་ (yigii yāŋ) the vowels.

ཡི་གེའི་མ་དཔེ་ (yigii mabe) original manuscript, original copy of a letter or document.

ཡི་གེའི་གཞི་ (yigii shi) the sound and shape of the Tibetan letters.

ཡི་གེའི་རིག་པ་ (yigii rigbə) philology.

ཡི་གེར་ཕབས་ (yigii bəb) va. to copy, to take notes.

ཡི་གཅོད་ (yi jöö) to cause sadness, to make sad ¶ གནས་ཚུལ་ངན་པ་དེ་བཤད་ནས་ཁོང་གི་ཡི་བཅད་པ་རེད་ (He) told the bad news and made him sad.

ཡི་ཆད་ (yijɛɛ̀) sm. ཡིག་ཆད་.

ཡི་ཏ་ལི་ (yidali) Italy.

ཡི་ཐང་ཆད་ (yidaŋ cɛ̀ɛ̀) vi. to be fed up ¶ ཕྲུ་གུ་དེ་ར་ག་ཚོད་ལབ་ཀྱང་མ་ཉན་ཙང་ཡི་ཐང་ཆད་བཞག (He) is fed up with the child because he won't listen no matter how much one talks to him. 2. vi. to become bereft of hope ¶ ཁོང་ལ་ཚོང་ཉེས་ཐེངས་མང་པོ་བྱུང་ཙང་ཡི་ཐང་ཆད་བཞག Because he suffered loses in business many times he has become bereft of hope.

ཡི་དྭགས་ (yidaà) hungry ghosts: one of the three realms of bad rebirths.

ཡི་དམ་ (yidam) 1. tutelary deity, main meditative deity. 2. promise, vow, oath; va.—བྱེད་; —བཅའ་ to promise, to make a vow, to give an oath.

ཡི་མི་རང་ (yi miraŋ) vi. to dislike, to be disgruntled, to be dissatisfied ¶ བཟོ་པ་ཚོའི་གླ་ཆ་ཆུང་ཆུང་ཡིན་ཙང་ཡི་མི་རངས་པ་རེད་ Because the worker's wages are low, they were dissatisfied.

ཡི་མུག (yimuù) sm. ཡིད་མུག.

ཡི་ཙི་ (yidzi) ch. soap; va.—ཕྱག to wash with soap.

ཡི་ཚེ་ (yidze) sm. ཡི་ཙི་.

ཡི་སི་རེ་ལ་ (yisirela) Israel.

ཡི་སི་རོ་ (yisiro) sm. ཡི་སི་རེ་ལ་

ཡི་རག (yiraà) Iraq.

ཡི་རང་ (yiraŋ) 1. va. to rejoice, to be happy ¶ གཞན་གྱི་བདེ་བ་ལ་ཡི་རང་བྱེད་དགོས་ One should rejoice at other's happiness. 2. agreement, endorsement, approval; va.—བྱེད་ ¶ འགོ་ཁྲིད་ཀྱི་གསུང་བཤད་དེ་ལ་མང་ཚོགས་ཚོས་ཡི་རང་བའི་རྣམ་འགྱུར་བསྟན་པ་རེད་ The people made an expression of approval and happiness at the leader's speech.

ཡི་རང་གོང་བཀུར་ (yiraŋ koŋgur) admiring/ approving and respecting.

ཡི་རེ་མུག (yiremuù) sm. ཡི་མུག་པ་.

ཡི་ལའ་ཁེ་ (yilage) sm. ཡི་ལའ་ཁོ་.

ཡི་ལའ་ཁོ་ (yilago) Iraq.

ཡི་ལང་ (yilaŋ) Iran.

ཡི་ཤི་ (yi shi) sm. ཡི་ཆད་.

ཡི་ཤུ་ (yishu) eng. 1. Jesus. 2. Christianity.

ཡི་ཤུའི་ཆོས་དད་པའི་མཐའ་མཐུན་ (yishü cöödɛɛ̀bɛ nədün) Christian Coalition (U.S.A.).

ཡི་ཤུའི་ལྟ་བ་མཆོག་ཏུ་འཛིན་པའི་སྒྲིག་འཛུགས་ (yishü dāwa cōgdu dzinbɛ drigdzuù) the Moral Majority (in U.S.A.).

ཡི་ཤུའི་བླ་ཆེན་སློབ་ཀྱི་གདན་ས་ (yishü lājen lōbgi dɛnsa) Vatican.

ཡི་ཤུའི་བླ་ཆེན་སློབ་ཀྱི་འཛིན་སྐྱོང་ཁང་ (yishü lājen lōbgi dziŋgyoŋgaŋ) Roman Curia.

ཡི་ཧོ་ཐོན་ལས་འགུལ་ (yihotön lɛŋgüü) tib. ch. the Boxer Rebellion.

ཡིག (yii) sm. ཡི་གེ་.

ཡིག་དཀར་ (yiigar) the དབུ་ཆེན་ script.

ཡིག་དཀྱུས་ (yiggyüü) the length of letters in a single line of text.

ཡིག་ཀོག (yiigɔɔ̀) sm. ཡིག་སྐོགས་.

ཡིག་ཀོག་གི་འཛིན་རྟགས་ (yiigɔɔ̀gi dzindaà) postmark.

ཡིག་ཀོ་ཁང་ (yiggogaŋ) shop/ room where seals are carved.

ཡིག་རྐྱང་ (yiggyaŋ) abbr. of ཡི་གེ་རྐྱང་པ་.

ཡིག་ཀློག (yiigɔɔ̀) sm. ཡིག་ཀློགས་.

ཡིག་སྐད་ (yiigɛɛ̀) literary language.

ཡི་སྐོགས་ (yiigɔɔ̀) envelope; va.—སྦྱར་ to seal an envelope.

ཡིག་སྐོགས་ཁ་སྦྱོར་ (yiigɔɔ̀ kājɔɔ) va. to seal/ close an envelope.

ཡིག་སྐྱུར་ (yiggyur) a (protest) wall poster; va.—སྦྱར་ to stick up a (protest) wall poster; va.—བཀྱལ་; —དབྱུགས་; འགྲེམས་ to distribute (protest) wall posters.

ཡིག་སྐྱེལ་ (yiggee) postal service, delivering letters.

ཡིག་སྐྱེལ་ཅུས་ (yigyee jüü) tib. ch. post office.

ཡིག་སྐྱེལ་གྲུ་གཟིངས་ (yiggyee trusiŋ) postal freighter, ship that carries mail.

ཡིག་སྐྱེལ་གློག་ཕྲིན་ཁང་ (yiggyee lɔ̄gdriŋgaŋ) post and telegraph office/ building.

ཡིག་སྐྱེལ་དྲ་བ་ (yiggyee trawa) postal network.

ཡིག་སྐྱེལ་ཀླངས་འཁོར་ (yiggyee lāŋgɔɔ) mail delivery car.

ཡིག་སྐྱེལ་པ་ (yiggyeeba) mailman.

ཡིག་སྐྱེལ་ཕུག་རོན་ (yiggyee pūrön) carrier pigeon.

ཡིག་སྐྱེལ་བ་ (yiggyeewa) sm. ཡིག་སྐྱེལ་པ་.

ཡིག་སྐྱོན་ (yiggyön) misspelled words.

ཡིག་བརྐོས་ (yiggüü) carving/ engraving letters; va.—རྐྱག.

ཡིག་བསྐུར་ (yiggur) corresponding; va.—བྱེད་ to correspond by letter.

ཡིག་བསྐུར་ཁང་ (yiggurgaŋ) post office.

ཡིག་བསྐུར་རང་དབང་ (yiggur raŋwaŋ) freedom of communication.

ཡིག་བསྐུར་རྣམ་གཞག (yiggur nāmshaà) name of a Tibetan language book on letter writing.

ཡིག་སྐྱུར་ (yiggyur) sm. ཡིག་སྐྱུར་.

ཡིག་ཁང་ (yiggaŋ) sm. ཡིག་བསྐུར་ཁང་.

ཡིག་ཁྲ་ (yigdra) verdict.

ཡིག་མཁན་ (yiggɛn) secretary, clerk, scribe.

ཡིག་མཁན་དྲུང་ཡིག (yiggɛn truŋyii) shung. clerk, scribe.

ཡིག་འཁོད་ལོ་རྒྱུས་ (yiggöö lugyüü) recorded history.

ཡིག་འཁོད་ཁྲིམས་ལུགས་ (yiggöö trimluù) formal written law, statute.

ཡིག་འཁྱེར་དམག (yiggyer māà) signal corps, communication troops.

ཡིག་གྲངས་ (yigdraŋ) number of lines (in a letter/ poem).

ཡིག་གློག (yiglɔɔ̀) post and telegraph, post and telecommunications.

ཡིག་མགོ (yiŋgo) 1. the first letter of the alphabet. 2. letter heading.

ཡིག་འགྲུལ་ (yiŋdrüü) correspondence; va.—བྱེད་ to correspond (with).

ཡིག་སྒམ་ (yiigam) mailbox.

ཡིག་རྒྱ་ (yiggya) sm. ཡིག་སྐོར་.

ཡིག་རྒྱུགས་ (yiggyuù) exam, test; va.—གཏོང་ to take an exam; va.—ལེན་ —བསྡུ་ལེན་ to give an exam.

ཡིག་རྒྱུགས་གྲུབ་འབྲས་རེའུ་མིག (yiggyuù) grade sheet.

ཡིག་རྒྱུགས་དྲིས་ལན་ (yiggyuù) answer sheet (exam).

ཡིག་སྒྱུར་ (yigyur) translation, translating; va.—བྱེད་.

ཡིག་སྒྱུར་པ་ (yigyurbə) translator, interpreter.

ཡིག་སྒྲིག་ལས་ཚན་ (yigdrii lɛɛ̀dzɛn) composing room.

ཡིག་སྒྲིལ་ (yigdrii) 1. tied bundles of files/ archives. 2. mail bag.

ཡིག་སྒྲོམ་ (yigdrom) a frame/ cabinet for putting documents.

ཡིག་བསྒྱུར་ (yiggyur) sm. ཡིག་སྒྱུར་.

ཡིག་ངོ་ (yiŋŋo) letters, writing; vi.—ཚོད་ to be able to see/ read letters ¶ མིག་ཤེལ་མ་བརྒྱབ་ན་ཡིག་ངོ་ཚོད་ཀྱི་མི་འདུག If I don't wear glasses I can't read the letters.

ཡིག་གཅིག་སྒྲ་མང་ (yigjii dramaŋ) a character or word that can be pronounced in different ways.

ཡིག་ལྕོག (yiŋjoò) desk.

ཡིག་ཆ་ (yigja) documents, records, notes.

ཡིག་ཆ་ཚད་ལྡན་ (yigja tsɛ̄ndɛn) reliable/ authentic documents or records.

ཡིག་ཆའི་རིང་ལུགས་ (yigjɛ riŋluù) red-tapism, bureaucratism.

ཡིག་ཆས་ (yigjɛɛ̀) writing materials, stationery.

ཡིག་ཆས་རྒྱས་དཔྱད་ (yigjɛɛ̀ gyɛɛ̀jɛɛ̀) shung. fixed/ confirmed by a document.

ཡིག་ཆུང་ (yigjuŋ) 1. a small or minor note/ letter/ memo. 2. an essay.

ཡིག་ཆེན་ (yigjen) 1. the main document. 2. large letters.

ཡིག་ཆེན་སྦྱར་འགྲེམས་ཚགས་པར་ (yigjen jandrem tsāgbar) sm. ཡིག་ཆེན་ཚགས་པར་.

ཡིག་ཆེན་ཚགས་པར་ (yigjen tsāgbar) big character poster/ newspaper.

ཡིག་ཇ་ (yigja) shung. tea served during the break between classes.

ཡིག་མཇུག (yinjuù) the end of a letter/ article/ book; va.—སྡུད་; —སྒྲིལ་ to end a letter/ article/ book.

ཡིག་འཛོག (yinjoò) signing a contract or agreement; va.—བྱེད་.

ཡིག་ཧྲོག (yiñoò) trash paper, waste paper.

ཡིག་ཧྲོག་སི་ར་ (yigño sīrə) waste paper basket.

ཡིག་གཉེར་ (yigñer) abbr. of ཡིག་ཚང་གཉེར་པ་.

ཡིག་རྙིང་ (yigñiŋ) classical/ ancient literature, ancient writing/ terms.

ཡིག་རྙོག (yigñog) 1. sm. ཡིག་ཧྲོག. 2. useless/ pointless writing.

ཡིག་བརྙན་ (yigñɛn) subtitles (for movies).

ཡིག་གདགས་ཁང་ (yigdaàgaŋ) typing room.

ཡིག་གདགས་འཕྲུལ་ཆས་ (yigdaà trüüjɛɛ̀) typewriter.

ཡིག་རྟགས་འགོད་ས་ (yigdaà göösa) registration window (at the a post office).

ཡིག་རྟེན་ (yigden) sm. གཟིགས་རྟེན་.

ཡིག་སྟོང་ (yigdoŋ) a letter without a gift [Lit. an empty letter].

ཡིག་ཐུམ་ (yigdum) 1. envelope, letter wrapper. 2. a letter wrapped with other things; va.—གཏོང་; —སྐུར་ to send a letter wrapped with other things. 3. parcel.

ཡིག་ཐུམ་སྐྱེལ་འདྲེན་བྱེད་པའི་མཉམ་སྦྲེལ་ (yigdum gyēndren ceēbɛ ñambel) United Parcel Service (UPS).

ཡིག་ཐེའུ་ (yigdeu) postage stamp.

ཡིག་ཐོག (དུ་) (yigdɔɔ̀du) by letter, in written form. ¶ ཡིག་ཐོག་གི་སྙན་ཞུ་ A report in writing. ¶ ཡིག་ཐོག་གི་གཏམ་བཤད་ Written speech/ lecture/ statement.

ཡིག་ཐོག་ནས་རྒྱུགས་ལེན་ (yigdɔ̀nɛ gyulen) va. to give a written examination.

ཡིག་ཐོག་མ་འཁོད་པའི་ཁྲིམས་ལུགས་ (yigdɔ̀ magööbɛ trīmluù) unwritten law.

ཡིག་ཐོག་ལ་འགོད་ (yigdɔɔ̀la gööò) va. to put down in writing.

ཡིག་ཐོག་ལ་འབྲི་ (yigdɔɔ̀la dri) sm. ཡིག་ཐོག་ལ་འགོད་.

ཡིག་ཐོག་སློབ་ཁྲིད་ (yigdɔɔ̀ lōbdriì) teaching by correspondence.

ཡིག་ཐོག་སློབ་གྲྭ (yigdɔɔ̀ lōbdra) correspondence school.

ཡིག་འཐུམས་ (yigdum) sm. ཡིག་ཐུམ་.

ཡིག་དན་ (yigdɛn) 1. written agreement. 2. files, records, archives.

ཡིག་དུག (yigduù) eyestrain from reading; vi.—ཕོག to get eyestrain from reading a lot.

ཡིག་དྲུག (yigdruù) abbr. of ཡིག་གི་དྲུག་མ་.

ཡིག་གདང་ (yigdaŋ) ropes and poles for hanging bundles of files (as storage).

ཡིག་མདའ་རྒྱག (yiŋda gyaà) vi. to misplace letters/ papers.

ཡིག་ནག་ཆུ་བཤལ་ (yignaà cūshɛɛ) shung. disregarding contracts/ agreements etc.; va.—གཏོང་ ¶ བཀའ་གདན་རྣམས་ཡིག་ནག་ཆུ་བཤལ་དུ་གཏོང་མི་ཆོག It is not permitted to disregard the land tenure documents.

ཡིག་ནོར་ (yignɔɔ) incorrect character/ letter.

ཡིག་སྣོད་ཤོག་སྒམ་ (yinöö shōgam) shung. a drawer/ box for keeping documents.

ཡིག་པར་ (yigbar) wood printing block.

ཡིག་དཔར་ (yigbar) sm. ཡིག་པར་.

ཡིག་དཔེ་ (yigbe) copy book.

ཡིག་ཕོན་སྦྲག་གཏོང་ (yigbön dragdoŋ) bulk mailing.

ཡིག་ཕྲན་ (yigdrɛn) sm. ཡིག་ཆུང་.

ཡིག་ཕྲེང་ (yigdreŋ) a line of words.

ཡིག་འཕྲིན་ (yigdrin) correspondence, letters; va.—གཏོང་ to correspond.

ཡིག་འཕྲེང་ (yigdreŋ) sm. ཡིག་ཕྲེང་.

ཡིག་བར་ (yigbar) 1. the space/ gap between letters. 2. gap between lines (of letters).

ཡིག་བྲིས་ (yigdriì) 1. scribe, recording secretary. 2. recording secretary of the Tibetan National Assembly.

ཡིག་བློན་ (yiglön) chief secretary, grand secretary.

ཡིག་བློན་ཆེན་མོ་ (yiglön cēmbo) a form of address for a grand secretary in the Ming and Qing Dynasties.

ཡིག་འབྲི་ (yiŋdri) writing; va.—བྱེད་ ¶ ཁོང་ཡིག་འབྲིའི་ཀ་འགན་ལེན་མཁན་རེད་ He is the one taking the main responsibility for writing (it).

ཡིག་འབྲི་མཁས་པའི་ལྷན་ཚོགས་ (yigdri kɛɛ̀bɛ lhɛ̄ndzoò) calligrapher's association.

ཡིག་འབྲི་བ་ (yigdribə) secretary.

ཡིག་འབྲིའི་ཅོག་ཙེ་ (yigdrii jōgdze) desk.

ཡིག་འབྲིའི་ཉེར་སྤྱད་ (yigdrii ñerjɛɛ̀) writing materials, stationery.

ཡིག་འབྲུ་ (yiŋdru) 1. syllable, character (in Chinese); va.—སྒྲིག to set type. 2. point ¶ ཡིག་འབྲུ་བརྒྱད་ཀྱི་རྩ་ཁྲིམས་ The eight point charter/ constitution.

ཡིག་འབྲུ་གསར་པ་ (yiŋdru sārba) new/ simplified Chinese character system.

ཡིག་འབྲེལ་གྱི་གྲོགས་པོ་ (yindreegi trogbo) penpal.

ཡིག་སྦྱོང་འཛིན་གྲྭ་ (yigjoŋ dzindrə) literacy class, class to teach reading.

ཡིག་སྦྱོང་རྨོངས་སེལ་ (yigjoŋ mōŋsel) studying to end illiteracy.

ཡིག་སྦྱོང་སློབ་དེབ་ (yigjoŋ lōbdeb) textbook for learning to read.

ཡིག་རྨོངས་ (yigmoŋ) illiterate; va.—སེལ་ to eliminate/ wipe out illiteracy ¶ ཡིག་རྨོངས་སེལ་བའི་འཛིན་གྲྭ་ A class to teach literacy (eliminate illiteracy).

ཡིག་རྩ་ (yigdza) the root of letters.

ཡིག་རྩ་བཟང་པོ་ (yigdza saŋbo) person who understands the meaning of documents/ articles well.

ཡིག་རྩ་ལོན་པོ་ (yigdza lömbo) persons who understand the meaning of articles or documents thoroughly.

ཡིག་རྩིས་ (yigdziì) writing/ reading and calculating.

ཡིག་རྩིས་མཁས་པ་ (yigdziì kɛɛ̀ba) sm. ཡིག་རྩིས་གཉིས་མཁས་.

ཡིག་རྩིས་གཉིས་མཁས་ (yigdziì ñīigɛɛ̀) skilled in both in writing and calculating.

ཡིག་རྩོམ་ (yigdzom) article, essay.

ཡིག་རྩོམ་མཁས་ཅན་ (yigdzom kɛɛ̀jɛn) writer, author.

ཡིག་རྩོམ་རིག་གནས་ (yigdzom rignɛɛ̀) literature.

ཡིག་ཚགས་ (yigdzaà) 1. official in charge of documents/ records. 2. archives. 3. dossiers/ records of individuals.

ཡིག་ཚང་ (yigdzaŋ) 1. office ¶ འབྲས་སྤྱི་བློན་ཆེན་གྱི་ཡིག་ཚང་ནས་ From the office of the political officer in Sikkim. 2. shung. highest monk official office in tt. 3. sm. ཐོབ་ཐང་.

ཡིག་ཚང་ཁང་ (yigdzaŋgaŋ) archives.

ཡིག་ཚང་གཉེར་པ་ (yigdzaŋ ñēēba) shung. a monk official under the དྲུང་ཡིག་ཆེན་མོ་ in the ཡིག་ཚང་ office in tt.

ཡིག་ཚང་ལས་ཁུངས་ (yigdzaŋ lɛɛ̀guŋ) shung. the highest monk official office in the Tibetan government.

ཡིག་ཚད་ (yigdzɛɛ̀) test, examination (written); va.—གཏོང་ to take a test, va.—ལེན་ to give a test.

ཡིག་ཚད་འབྲི་ས་ (yigdzɛɛ̀ drisə) exam. paper.

ཡིག་ཚད་རྫུས་མ་ (yigdzɛɛ̀ dzüümə) cheating during an exam.

ཡིག་ཚད་ལོན་ (yīgdzɛɛ̀ lön) vi. to pass an exam.

ཡིག་རྫུགས་ (yigdzuù) sm. ཡིག་གཟུགས་.

ཡིག་ཚོགས་ (yigdzɔɔ̀) abbr. of ཡི་གེའི་ཚོགས་པ་.

ཡིག་མཛོད་ (yiŋdzöö) dictionary.

ཡིག་འཛིན་ (yiŋdzin) receipt.

ཡིག་རྫུས་ (yigdzüü) counterfeit letter/ writing.

ཡིག་རྫོབ་ (yigdzob) wordy.

ཡིག་རྫོབ་ཆུང་བ་ (yigdzob cūŋwə) not wordy, to the point.

ཡིག་རྫོབ་ཆེ་བ་ (yigdzob cēwa) wordy, long-winded, verbose.

ཡིག་གཞི་ (yigshi) shung. land tenure document ། རྩྭ་རིགས་སྐོར་ཡིག་གཞི་ཁུངས་ཐུབ་མེད་པ་ They do not have any land tenure documents regarding the grasslands.

ཡིག་ཟམ་ (yigsam) post office.

ཡིག་ཟམ་གྲུ་གཟིངས་ (yigsam trusiŋ) mail ship.

ཡིག་ཟམ་གློག་འཕྲིན་ (yigsam lōgdrin) post and telegraph.

ཡིག་ཟམ་གློག་འཕྲིན་ཅུས་ (yigsam lōgdrin jüü) tib. ch. post and telegram office.

ཡིག་ཟམ་ཐེལ་ཙེ་ (yigsam tēēdze) tib. ch. post mark, cancellation mark (for stamps).

ཡིག་ཟམ་རླངས་འཁོར་ (yigsam lāŋgɔɔ) postal delivery truck.

ཡིག་ཟམ་ལས་དོན་ཁང་ (yigsam lɛ̱ɛ̱döngaŋ) postal office building.

ཡིག་ཟིན་ (yigsin) letter, message, statement.

ཡིག་ཟོམ་ (yigsom) mail box.

ཡིག་ཟོར་ (yigsɔr) sm. ཡིག་རྫོབ་.

ཡིག་ཟོར་ཡང་པོ་ (yigsɔr yaŋbo) sm. ཡིག་རྫོབ་ཆུང་བ་.

ཡིག་གཟུགས་ (yigsuù) handwriting, penmanship, calligraphy; va.—སྦྱོང་ to practice calligraphy/ handwriting.

ཡིག་གཟུགས་མཁན་པོ་ (yigsuù kɛ̄mbo) skilled calligrapher.

ཡིག་གཟུགས་མཁས་པ་ (yigsuu kɛ̄ɛ̀ba) sm. ཡིག་གཟུགས་མཁན་པོ་.

ཡིག་གཟུགས་འབྲི་རྩལ་ (yigsuù dridzɛɛ) the art of calligraphy.

ཡིག་རིག (yigrii) literature.

ཡིག་རིག་པ་ (yigrigbə) literary critic/ expert.

ཡིག་རིགས་ (yigrii) 1. documents, dispatches. 2. scripts/ orthographies/ letters.

ཡིག་རིགས་བརྐོས་མ་ (yigrii gōōma) carved inscription.

ཡིག་རིགས་མཁས་པ་ (yigrii kɛ̄ɛ̀ba) man of letters.

ཡིག་རིགས་ཁོ་ནར་ལྟ་བའི་རིང་ལུགས་ (yigrii kōnar dāwɛ riŋluù) red-tapism, bureacratism.

ཡིག་རིས་ (yigrii) style of hand writing/ calligraphy.

ཡིག་རིས་འགྲེམ་སྟོན་ (yigrii dremdön) exhibition of calligraphy.

ཡིག་རུས་ (yigrüü) sm. ཡིག་རིས་.

ཡིག་ལན་ (yiglɛn) answer/ reply (by letter); va.—གཏོང་; —སླར་; —སྤྲོད་; —ស្លོག to reply, to answer.

ཡིག་ལམ་ (yiglam) 1. by mean of/ through writing. 2. writing prize.

ཡིག་ལོང་ (yigloŋ) 1. illiteracy. 2. unclear cursive handwriting.

ཡིག་ཤུབས་ (yigshub) envelope.

ཡིག་ཤེས་ (yigsheè) literacy.

ཡིག་ཤེས་སློབ་གྲྭ་ (yigsheè lōbdra) literacy school (school to teach illiterates to read).

ཡིག་ཤོག (yigshoòs) writing paper, note pad.

ཡིག་སློབ་འཛིན་གྲྭ་ (yiglob dzindrə) sm. ཡིག་ཤེས་སློབ་གྲྭ་.

ཡིག་གསལ་འགོད་ (yigsɛɛ göö) va. to record clearly, to keep a clear record.

ཡིག་བསང་ (yigsaŋ) weeding through papers, reorganizing papers that have become messed up; va.—རྒྱག.

ཡིག་ཧྲུལ་ (yighrüü) sm. ཡིག་རྙིག.

ཡིག་ལྷད་ (yiglhɛɛ̀) errors/ mistakes in writing.

ཡིང་ (yiŋ) ch. military battalion (around 1000 soldiers).

ཡིང་གོང་འོད་ཟེར་ (yiŋgoŋ wöösee) ch.tib. fluorescent light.

ཡིང་ཀྲང་ (yiŋdraŋ) ch. commander of a battalion.

ཡིང་ཤོག (yiŋshoò) sm. ཡིང་.

ཡིད་ (yii) 1. mind. 2. thought.

ཡིད་ཀྱི་ཁམས་ (yiigi kām) mental consciousness.

ཡིད་ཀྱི་འཆར་སྒོ་ (yiigi cārgo) opinion, view.

ཡིད་ཀྱི་ཉེས་པ་ (yiigi ñeèba) the three mental nonvirtuous deeds: greed, harming others and holding wrong views.

ཡིད་ཀྱི་དང་བ་སྟོན་ (yiigi taŋwa dön) va. to like sb., to be fond of, to find pleasing.

ཡིད་ཀྱི་འདུ་བྱེད་ (yiigi dujeè) mental acts.

ཡིད་ཀྱི་སྡོམ་པ་ (yiigi domba) mental vow/ oath.

ཡིད་ཀྱི་དབང་པོ་ (yiigi wāŋbo) mental consciousness.

ཡིད་ཀྱི་སྨན་ཡོན་དུ་འདྲོངས་ (yiigi mēnyöndu droŋ) shung. vi. to be extremely happy to receive a letter/ advice, etc. ། གང་ཉིད་ཐུགས་བརྩེའི་འཆིང་ཞག་མ་དོར་བའི་ནང་མའི་སློབ་སྟོན་རྣམས་གསུང་བའི་ཡིད་ཀྱི་སྨན་ཡོན་དུ་འདྲོངས་ I am extremely happy to receive your kind advice.

ཡིད་ཀྱི་ཟེའུ་འབྲུ་ (yiigi sendro) the jewel of one's heart.

ཡིད་ཀྱི་ཟླ་གསར་ (yiigi dasar) close friends/ buddies.

ཡིད་དཀྱིལ་ (yiigyee) sm. བློ་རྒྱ་.

ཡིད་གླིང་ (yiiloŋ) in the mind.

ཡིད་སྐྱུལ་ (yiigüü) encouraging; va.—བྱེད་ to encourage.

ཡིད་སྐྱོ་ (yii gyō) vi. to be sad/ depressed.

ཡིད་སྐྱོ་བློ་ཕམ་ (yiigyo lōpam) shung. feeling sad.

ཡིད་སྐྱོད་ (yii gyööba) shung. vi. to disturb/ upset the mind ། དེ་སྐབས་ངོ་ལོག་པ་རྣམས་ཀྱིས་འཁྲུག་པ་བསླངས་ཏེ་མི་དམངས་ཀྱི་ཡིད་བསྐྱོད་པ་ At that time rebellion caused trouble and disturbed the minds of the people.

ཡིད་ཀློང་ (yiiloŋ) sm. སེམས་ཀྱི་དཀྱིལ་.

ཡིད་ཁ་ (yiiga) sm. ཡིད་ཀྱི་ཁམས་.

ཡིད་ཁམས་ (yiigam) sm. ཡིད་ཀྱི་ཁམས་.

ཡིད་ཁུག (yiiguù) sm. སེམས་ཁུག.

ཡིད་ཁེངས་ (yii kēŋ) 1. vi. to be satisfied/ fulfilled. 2. vi. to proud/ arrogant ། བཟོ་པ་ཚོར་ཡིད་ཁེངས་པའི་གླ་ཆ་སྤྲད་པ་རེད་ (They) paid the workers a wage that satisfied them.

ཡིད་འཁུལ་ (yii küü) vi. to become gentle/ calm/ peace loving.

ཡིད་འཁུགས་པར་བྱེད་ (yii kūgbar cee) va. to move/ influence.

ཡིད་འཁོལ་ (yii köö) 1. vi. to be happy/ elated. 2. vi. to be nervous.

ཡིད་ཀྱི་རྒྱ་མཚོ་འཁོལ་ (yiigi cūtso köö) sm. སྤྲོ་སེམས་འཁོལ་བ་.

ཡིད་གྲོགས་ (yiidrɔɔ) sm. ཡིད་འགྲོགས་.

ཡིད་དགའ་ (yii ga) vi. to be happy/ elated.

ཡིད་མགུ་བ་ (yii gu) 1. to be satisfied, to like ། ཁོ་རང་གི་ཡིད་མགུ་བའི་གླ་ཆ་ཞིག་རག་བཞག He got a wage that satisfied him.

ཡིད་འགུག (yii guù) sm. སེམས་འགུག.

ཡིད་འགུལ་ (yii güü) moving, touching (emotionally); vi.—ཐེབས་ to be moved/ touched.

ཡིད་འགྲོགས་ (yiidrɔɔ) sweetheart, girl friend, boyfriend.

ཡིད་རྟོད་པོ་ (yii gööbo) a very imaginative person.

ཡིད་ངོ་ (yiiŋo) in the mind.

ཡིད་ངོམ་ (yii ŋom) vi. to be satisfied/ content.

ཡིད་ཅན་ (yiijɛn) sm. ཡིད་ལྡན་.

ཡིད་གཅུགས་པ་ (yiijugbə) close, intimate.

ཡིད་གཅོང་ (yii jōŋ) sm. སེམས་གཅོང་.

ཡིད་གཅོད་ (yii jöö) va. to make sb. discouraged/ lose hope ། འགོ་ཁྲིད་དེས་གཞམ་རིམ་གྱི་རེ་འདུན་ཐེངས་མང་མཁས་ལེན་མ་བྱས་པར་ཁོ་ཚོའི་ཡིད་བཅད་པ་རེད་ The leader made the lower officials lose hope by not agreeing to their request on many occasions.

ཡིད་ཆགས་ (yii cāà) vi. to get/ be attached ། མེ་ཤོར་དུས་ཁོ་ཅ་ལག་ལ་ཡིད་ཆགས་ནས་བྲོས་མ་ཕྱིན་པར་བཙན་མེས་འཚིག་པ་རེད་ When the fire broke out, he got burned because he was so attached to his things he didn't flee.

ཡིད་ཆད་ (yii cɛ̄ɛ) vi. to get discouraged, to lose hope.

ཡིད་ཆས་གྲོས་ (yi̱ijɛɛ trö̱ö) discussions held to make sb. come to believe in one's side/ policy, etc.

ཡིད་ཆེས་ (yi̱ijɛɛ̀) belief; va. ཡིད་ཆེས་; —སྐྱེ་; —བྱེད་ to believe; vi.—ཤོར་ to lose one's belief in sth. ། ཁོས་བཤད་པའི་སྐད་ཆ་ར་ཡིད་ཆེས་ཀྱི་མི་འདུག (I) don't believe what he said. ། འདི་ནི་བོད་མི་ཚང་མས་ཡིད་ཆེས་བྱེད་ཀྱི་ཡོད་པ་རེད་ All Tibetans believe in this.

ཡིད་ཆེས་ཀྱིས་ཁེངས་པ་ (yi̱ijɛɛ̀gi kē̱ŋba) sm. ཡིད་ཆེས་ཆེན་པོ་.

ཡིད་ཆེས་དགེ་རྒྱུའི་ལས་ཁུངས་ (yi̱ijɛɛ̀ ge̱dzɛ lɛ̱ɛ̀guŋ) Charity Trust Fund (of Tibetan exile government).

ཡིད་ཆེས་བརྒྱ་འགྱུར་ (yi̱ijɛɛ̀ gyaŋgyur) with unbounded belief/ trust.

ཡིད་ཆེས་ཆེན་པོ་ (yi̱ijɛɛ̀ cēmbo) deep belief/ trust/ faith.

ཡིད་ཆེས་མཉམ་ལས་ཁང་ (yi̱ijɛɛ̀ ña̱mlɛɛ̀gaŋ) credit association/ union.

ཡིད་ཆེས་གདེང་འཁེལ་ (yi̱ijɛɛ̀ de̱ŋgee) belief, confidence, trust.

ཡིད་ཆེས་བུན་གཏོང་ (yi̱ijɛɛ̀ pü̱ndoŋ) giving credit/ loans; va.—བྱེད་.

ཡིད་ཆེས་བློ་གཏད་ (yi̱ijɛɛ̀ lōdɛɛ̀) believing and trusting.

ཡིད་ཆེས་བློས་འཁེལ་ (yi̱ijɛɛ̀ lōōgee) believing and trusting.

ཡིད་ཆེས་ཚད་མེད་ (yi̱ijɛɛ̀ tsɛɛ̀meè) boundless faith/ belief.

ཡིད་ཆེས་སླ་བ་ (yi̱ijɛɛ̀ lāwa) gullible, credulous.

ཡིད་འཆུས་ (yi̱i cüü) vi. to have a change of heart.

ཡིད་འཇགས་ (yi̱njaà) remembering, keeping/ bearing in mind; va.—བྱེད་ ། དེ་དོན་ཡིད་འཇགས་བྱེད་ Please keep that in mind.

ཡིད་འཇོག (yi̱njɔ̀ɔ) paying attention, noticing; va.—བྱེད་ to pay/ give attention to, to keep/ bear in mind, to take care of ། ངས་བཤད་པ་དེ་ཁོས་ཡིད་འཇོག་བྱས་མ་བྱུང་ He didn't keep in mind what I said.

ཡིད་གཉིས་ (yi̱iñii) of two minds, having doubts/ hesitation.

ཡིད་གཏད་ (yi̱idɛɛ̀) 1. sm. བློ་འཁེལ་. 2. va. to concentrate/ focus on sth.

ཡིད་རྟོན་ (yi̱idön) 1. confidence, trust, reliance; va.—འཕེར་ to have confidence in, to rely on, to depend on, to have trust in. 2. credit.

ཡིད་རྟོན་ཁང་ (yi̱idöngaŋ) credit cooperative.

ཡིད་རྟོན་དངུལ་ཁང་ (yi̱idön ŋü̱ügaŋ) credit bank.

ཡིད་རྟོན་དངུལ་བུན་ (yi̱idön ŋü̱übün) credit loans.

ཡིད་རྟོན་དངུལ་བུན་ཁྲུའུ་ (yi̱idön ŋü̱übün) finance department, fiduciary loan office.

ཡིད་རྟོན་དངུལ་གསོག (yi̱idön ŋü̱üsɔɔ̀) a deposit in a credit bank.

ཡིད་རྟོན་མཉམ་ལས་ཁང་ (yi̱idön ña̱mlɛɛgaŋ) credit cooperative.

ཡིད་བརྟན་ (yi̱idɛn) sm. ཡིད་རྟོན་.

ཡིད་བརྟན་དངུལ་བུན་ (yi̱idɛn ŋü̱übün) sm. ཡིད་རྟོན་དངུལ་བུན་.

ཡིད་བསྟུན་ (yi̱idün) acting according to the will/ needs/ wish of others; va.—བྱེད་.

ཡིད་ཐང་ཆད་ (yi̱idaŋ cɛɛ̀) 1. vi. to be discouraged/ disappointed/ sad/ down/ dismayed. 2. vi. to be fed up.

ཡིད་མཐུན་ (yi̱idün) agreeing with; va.—བྱེད་ to agree with ། ཚང་མ་ཡིད་མཐུན་བྱུང་ All agreed.

ཡིད་མཐུན་མོས་མཐུན་ (yi̱idün mo̱ödün) in agreement, in accord.

ཡིད་མཐུན་རོགས་རམ་ (yi̱idün ro̱gram) support, backing, help.

ཡིད་འཐད་ (yi̱i tɛɛ̀) sm. ཡིད་དུ་འོང་བ་.

ཡིད་དལ་ (yi̱i tɛ̱ɛ) vi. to be relaxed/ at ease/ calm.

ཡིད་དལ་པོ་ (yi̱i tɛ̱ɛbo) relaxed, at ease ། དེང་སང་ང་ནས་ཡོལ་ཞུས་ནས་ཡིད་དལ་པོ་འདུག These days I have retired so I am relaxed.

ཡིད་དུ་འཆང་ (yi̱idu cāŋ) va. to keep/ bear in mind, to hold in one's heart.

ཡིད་དུ་འཐད་པོ་ (yi̱idu tɛɛ̀bo) sm. ཡིད་དུ་འོང་བ་.

ཡིད་དུ་འཛིན་ (yi̱idu dzi̱n) sm. ཡིད་དུ་འཆང་.

ཡིད་དུ་འོང་བ་ (yi̱idu o̱ŋwa) beautiful, pleasing, pleasant, pretty ། ཡིད་དུ་འོང་བའི་རི་མོ་ A beautiful painting.

ཡིད་དུང་ངེ་བ་ (yi̱i du̱ŋ ŋ̱ewa) a feeling of sadness ། ནང་མི་གནས་ཚུལ་ངན་པ་དེ་གོ་ནས་ཡིད་དུང་ངེ་བ་ཞིག་བྱུང་ I heard the bad news about that family and became sad.

ཡིད་དུང་དུང་ (yi̱i du̱ŋduŋ) sm. ཡིད་དུང་ངེ་བ་.

ཡིད་དུངས་ (yi̱i du̱ŋ) 1. vi. to like, to be very fond of ། ཁོང་གི་ཡིད་དུང་པའི་གྲོགས་མོ་དང་ཁ་བྲལ་དགོས་བྱུང་སོང་ He had to separate from the girlfriend he was very fond of. 2. vi. to have an attachment.

ཡིད་དོགས་ (yi̱idɔɔ̀) doubts; vi.—ཤར་ to have doubts arise.

ཡིད་དྲངས་ (yi̱i dra̱ŋ) vi. to get inspired/ encouraged by sth. or sb. ། དེད་པས་ཡིད་དྲངས་ཏེ་ངས་བླ་མ་དེ་མཇལ་བ་ཡིན་ I got inspired with faith toward that lama and went to meet him.

ཡིད་གདུང་ (yi̱iduŋ) sadness, misery, suffering; vi. ཡིད་གདུང་; —བྱེད་ to be sad/ miserable, to suffer ། དགེ་རྒན་གྲོང་པའི་གནས་ཚུལ་གོ་ནས་སློབ་ཕྲུག་ཚང་མ་ཡིད་གདུངས་པ་རེད་ Having heard the news that the teacher died, all the students were sad.

ཡིད་གདུང་ངུ་འབོད་ (yi̱iduŋ ŋ̱u bö̱ö) sad and crying.

ཡིད་བདེ་བ་ (yi̱i de̱wa) mentally well, psychologically fit.

ཡིད་འདུན་ (yi̱ndün) sm. རེ་འདུན་.

ཡིད་འདོམས་ཀྱིས་ (yi̱ndomgi) shung. bearing/ keeping in mind as ordered ། དེ་དོན་ཡིད་འདོམས་ཀྱིས་ Keeping in mind that information.

ཡིད་ལྡན་ (yi̱ndɛn) human beings, humans, humanity.

ཡིད་ལྡོག (yi̱i dɔ̱ɔ) sm. བློ་ལྡོག.

ཡིད་སྡུག་སེམས་སྐྱོ་ (yi̱idug sēmgyo) sadness, sad.

ཡིད་ནང་དུ་ཆུད་ (yi̱ina̱ŋdu cüü) vi. to become sad ། དགེ་རྒན་གྲོང་པའི་གནས་ཚུལ་གོ་ནས་ཡིད་ནང་དུ་ཆུད་པ་རེད་ They got sad when they heard the news that the teacher died.

ཡིད་གནོངས་ (yi̱i nōŋ) vi. to get embarrassed.

ཡིད་རྣལ་དུ་ཕབ་ (yi̱i nɛɛ̄du pāb) vi. to be dispassionate/ cool/ calm ། གནད་དོན་འདིའི་སྐོར་ཁྱེད་རང་ཡིད་རྣལ་དུ་ཕབ་བསམ་བློ་བཏང་དགོས་ Concerning this issue, you must think about it in a calm manner.

ཡིད་སྤྲོ་ (yi̱idro) happy, pleased.

ཡིད་སྤྲོ་བློ་ཚིམ་ (yi̱idro lōdzim) pleased, satisfied.

ཡིད་ཕངས་ (yi̱i pāŋ) vi. to feel regret/ sadness ། ངའི་སྨྱུ་གུ་ཡག་པོ་དེ་བརླགས་ནས་ཡིད་ཕངས་བྱུང་ I felt regret that I lost my good pen.

ཡིད་ཕངས་པོ་ (yi̱i pāŋbo) having regret/ sadness, lamenting ། ངའི་སྨྱུ་གུ་ཡག་པོ་དེ་བརླགས་ནས་ཡིད་ཕངས་པོ་བྱུང་ I felt regret that I lost my good pen.

ཡིད་ཕམ་ (yi̱i pām) vi. to be disappointed/ sad.

ཡིད་ཕེབས་ (yi̱i pēb) vi. to be trusted/ trustworthy ། མང་ཚོགས་ལ་གདམ་ཡིད་ཕེབས་པར་སྨྲས་ནས་བློ་བཀུག་ཐུབ་པ་བྱུང་བ་རེད་ (He) spoke in a trustworthy way so was able to win over the masses.

ཡིད་ཕྱུང་ (yi̱i cūŋ) sm. ཡིད་སྐྱོ་.

ཡིད་འཕྲེང་ (yi̱i trēŋ) 1. sm. ཡིད་ཆགས་. 2. vi. to miss sb.

ཡིད་འཕྲོག (yi̱i trɔ̄ɔ) vi. to attract, to impress, to fascinate, to captivate ། ཞིང་འཛུགས་འཕྲུལ་འཁོར་གསར་པས་ཞིང་པ་ཚོའི་ཡིད་འཕྲོག་གི་ཡོད་པ་རེད་ The new transplanting machines are impressing the farmers.

ཡིད་འཕྲོག་པོ་ (yi̱i trɔ̄ɔbo) attractive, fascinating, arresting, charming.

ཡིད་འཕྲོག་མ་ (yi̱i trɔ̄ɔma) an attractive/ fascinating/ arresting/ charming woman.

ཡིད་འཕྲོས་ (yi̱i trö̱ö) vi. to be unable to concentrate, to have one's mind wander ། ཆོས་ཞུ་སྐབས་གཞན་དུ་ཡིད་འཕྲོས་རྒྱུ་མེད་ When receiving religious teachings,one should not let one's mind wander.

ཡིད་བག་ཕེབས་ (yiibaà pēè) vi. to be at peace mentally.

ཡིད་བག་ཕེབས་པོ་ (yiibaà pēèbo) mentally at peace/ calm.

ཡིད་བྱང་ (yiijaŋ) sm. ཤེས་བྱང་.

ཡིད་བློ་ (yiilo) mind; vi.—ཚིམ་ to be satisfied/ content.

ཡིད་བློང་བློང་ (yii lōŋloŋ) 1. blurry/ dim/ unclear mind. 2. unhappy state of mind, being at a lost, having a dilemma.

ཡིད་དབང་འཕྲོག (yiiwaŋ trɔ̄ɔ̀) vi. to be spontaneously attracted by, to be involuntarily captivated by ¶ གཞོན་ནུ་མ་དེས་ཁོང་གི་ཡིད་དབང་འཕྲོག་པ་རེད་ He was captivated by the young woman.

ཡིད་དབང་འཕྲོག་ཤུགས་ (yiiwaŋ trɔ̄gshuù) the quality of being able to captivate/ attract/ fascinate.

ཡིད་དབང་མེད་དུ་ཤོར་ (yiiwaŋ meèdu shɔ̄ɔ̀) sm. ཡིད་དབང་འཕྲོག.

ཡིད་དབང་ཤོར་ (yiiwaŋ shɔ̄ɔ̀) sm. ཡིད་དབང་འཕྲོག.

ཡིད་འབྱུང་ (yii juŋ) 1. vi. to be melancholy/ depressed/ sad. 2. sm. ཡིག་འཁྱལ་.

ཡིད་མ་ཚིམ་ (yii ma tsīm) vi. to be dissatisfied/ discontent.

ཡིད་མི་བདེ་བ་ (yii midewa) 1. unhappy. 2. mentally ill.

ཡིད་རྨུག (yii muù) vi. to be gloomy/ pessimistic/ depressed/ down.

ཡིད་སྨུན་གཙང་སེལ་ (yiimün dzāŋsel) completely clearing doubts and confusions; va.—བྱེད་.

ཡིད་སྨུན་སེལ་ (yiimün sēl) vi. to have doubts and confusions cleared up/ clarified.

ཡིད་སྨུན་གསལ་ (yiimün sɛ̄ɛ̀) sm. ཡིད་སྨུན་སེལ་.

ཡིད་མོས་ (yii möö) vi. to like.

ཡིད་མོས་གོང་བཀུར་ (yiimöö koŋgur) liking/ admiring and respecting.

ཡིད་སྨྱོས་ (yii ñöö) vi. to be mad/ crazy with anger or desire or joy ¶ ཁོ་འདོད་ཆགས་ཀྱིས་ཡིད་སྨྱོས་ནས་བུ་མོ་ན་ཆུང་དེ་ར་ལོག་གཡེམ་བྱས་འདུག Because of his lust for the girl, he became crazy and raped her.

ཡིད་རྨུགས་ (yii mūg) sm. ཡིད་རྨུག.

ཡིད་སྨོན་ (yiimün) admiring, liking; va.—བྱེད་ ¶ གོས་གསར་པ་དེ་ཚོར་ཡིད་སྨོན་དེ་ Admiring those new clothes.

ཡིད་སྨོན་གུས་བཀུར་ (yiimün küügur) admiring and respecting; va.—བྱེད་.

ཡིད་སྨོན་དད་གུས་ (yiimün tɛɛ̀güü) admiring and respecting; va.—བྱེད་.

ཡིད་རྩལ་ (yiidzɛɛ) power of the mind, mental power.

ཡིད་རྩེ་གཅིག (yiidzɛɛ jīg) the utmost concentration, single-minded ¶ ཡིད་རྩེ་གཅིག་གིས་སློབ་སྦྱོང་བྱས་ན་གྲུབ་འབྲས་ཡག་པོ་ཡོང་ If one studies single-mindedly one will achieve good success.

ཡིད་རྩེར་རྒྱག (yiidzɛɛ gyaà) va. to be badly hurt, to be badly disturbed.

ཡིད་ཚིམ་ (yiidzim) satisfying, being content; vi.ཡིད་ཚིམ་; —བྱེད་ to be satisfied/ content ¶ ཁོ་རང་གླ་ཆ་དེར་ཡིད་ཚིམ་བཞག He is satisfied with that wage.

ཡིད་ཚིམ་པོ་ (yii tsīmbu) satisfied, content.

ཡིད་ཚིམས་པོ་ (yii tsīmbu) sm. ཡིད་ཚིམ་པོ་.

ཡིད་འཛིན་ཆེན་པོ་ (yiidzin cēmbo) having a good memory.

ཡིད་ཞུམ་ (yii shum) vi. to be disheartened/ dismayed/ down/ discouraged. 2. sm. སེམས་ཞུམ.

ཡིད་ཞུམ་རིང་ལུགས་ (yiishum riŋluù) pessimism.

ཡིད་གཞུངས་ (yiishuŋ) intelligent, knowledgeable.

ཡིད་བཞིན་ (yiishin) according to (one's) wishes/ desires ¶ རང་ཉིད་ཀྱི་ཡིད་བཞིན་གྱི་དོན་ཐམས་ཅད་གྲུབ་པ་རེད་ He achieved all in accordance with his wishes.

ཡིད་བཞིན་གྱི་ཁོག་རྩིས་ (yiishingi kɔ̄gdzii) inner calculations based on what one wishes (rather than facts).

ཡིད་བཞིན་ནོར་བུ་ (yiishin nɔɔbu) 1. name for the Dalai Lama. 2. a precious stone that fulfill one's wishes.

ཡིད་བཟོ་ (yii sho) va. to console.

ཡིད་ཟབ་ (yiisəb) sm. ཡིད་གཟབ་.

ཡིད་ཟུག (yii suù) vi. to fall in love, to lose one's heart to sth.

ཡིད་གཟབ་ (yiisəb) careful, attentive, alert, mindful, cautious; va.—བྱེད་.

ཡིད་བཟང་མ་ (yii saŋma) a kindhearted, generous woman.

ཡིད་འོང་ (yiioŋ) sm. ཡིད་དུ་འོང་.

ཡིད་འོང་འདྲ་ཆགས་ (yiioŋ drajaà) attractive, good-looking.

ཡིད་འོང་མ་ (yii oŋma) 1. a beautiful woman. 2. a kind of goddess.

ཡིད་ཡུལ་ (yiiyüü) realm of thinking/ conception ¶ ཡིད་ཡུལ་ལས་འདས་པ་ Beyond the realm of thought (i.e., inconceivable).

ཡིད་ཡུལ་དུ་འདོམས་ (yiiyüüdu dom) shung. keeping/ bear in mind.

ཡིད་ཡུལ་དུ་འདོམས་པ་བྱེད་ (yiiyüüdu domba cɛ̀ɛ̀) shung. you should bare this in mind.

ཡིད་གཡོ་ (yii yō) sm. སེམས་འཁྲུལ་ཐེབས་.

ཡིད་རང་ (yiiraŋ) sm. ཡི་རང་.

ཡིད་རེ་ (yiire) hope, wish.

ཡིད་ལ་ (yiilə) in the mind; va.—བྱེད་; —འཛོག to keep/ bear in mind, to remember, to take to heart.

ཡིད་ལ་འཁོར་འཁོར་ (yiilə kɔ̄ɔ̄gɔɔ) coming to mind again and again, remembering over and over again; va.—བྱེད་.

ཡིད་ལ་འཆང་ (yiilə cāŋ) va. to bear/ keep in mind.

ཡིད་ལ་འཇོག (yiilə jɔ̀ɔ̀) see ཡིད་ལ་.

ཡིད་ལ་འཐད་ (yiilə tɛ̄ɛ̀) sm. ཡིད་དུ་འོང་.

ཡིད་ལ་དྲན་དྲན་ (yiilə trɛndrɛn) thinking/ remembering again and again; va.—བྱེད་.

ཡིད་ལ་མནགས་ (yiilə nāg) sm. ཡིད་ལ་བརྣགས་.

ཡིད་ལ་བརྣགས་ (yiilə nāg) 1. va. to bear/ keep in mind ¶ རང་དབང་ནི་མི་དམངས་ཀྱི་ཡིད་ལ་བརྣགས་པའི་འདོད་དོན་ཞིག་རེད་ Freedom is a wish that the people keep in mind. 2. va. to endure/ tolerate.

ཡིད་ལ་བྱེད་ (yiilə cɛ̀ɛ̀) 1. va. to remember, to keep in mind. 2. va. to consider/ think.

ཡིད་ལ་འབབ་ (yiilə bəb) sm. ཡིད་དུ་འོང་.

ཡིད་ལ་བཟུང་ (yiilə suŋ) sm. ཡིད་ལ་འཛོག.

ཡིད་ལ་ཤར་ (yiilə shāā) vi. to have a thought/ idea come to mind.

ཡིད་ལས་ (yiilɛ) abbr. of ཡིད་ཆེས་དགེ་རྒྱའི་ལས་ཁུངས་.

ཡིད་ལས་འདས་པ་ (yiilɛ dɛɛ̀ba) sm. བསམ་ཡུལ་ལས་འདས་པ་.

ཡིད་ལོག (yii lɔɔ̀) sm. བློ་ལྡོག.

ཡིད་ཤི་ (yii shī) 1. sm. ཡིད་ཐང་ཆད་. 2. vi. to lose one's anger.

ཡིད་ཤེས་ (yiisheè) mental attitude, consciousness.

ཡིད་སུན་སྐྱེ་ (yiisün gyē) vi. to be annoyed/ bothered/ tired ¶ འཇིག་རྟེན་གྱི་བྱ་གཞག་ལ་ཡིད་སུན་སྐྱེད་ནས་ཆོས་བྱས་པ་རེད་ He was bothered by the worldly life and embraced religion.

ཡིད་སེམས་ (yiisem) mind; va.—འཕྲོག to captivate, to attract ¶ མའོ་ཀྲུའུ་ཞིའི་གསུང་རྩོམ་གྱི་འགྲེམས་སྟོན་དེས་རྒྱ་ཁྱབ་ལྟ་མཁན་རྣམས་ཀྱི་ཡིད་སེམས་ཕྲོགས་པ་རེད་ That exhibition of Chairman Mao's works captivated large numbers of visitors.

ཡིད་སྲུབ་ (yii sūb) va. to stir up/ agitate sb. mentally.

ཡིད་སྲུབས་ (yiisub) devil, demon.

ཡིད་གསོ་ (yii sō) sm. སེམས་གསོ་.

ཡིད་གསོད་ (yii sɔ̄ɔ̀) va. to make (sb.) sad/ disappointed ¶ བཟོ་གྲྭའི་བདག་པོས་བཟོ་པ་ཚོའི་གླ་ཆ་བཅག་ནས་ཁོ་ཚོའི་ཡིད་བསད་པ་རེད་ The factory owner reduced the worker's wages and made them sad.

ཡིད་བསྐྱང་ (yii sāŋ) sm. ངོ་སྐྱོང་.

ཡིད་ལྷག་པར་སྨོན་ (yii lhāgbar mōn) va. to admire very much.

ཡིན་ (yin) 1. linking verb (to be) ། དེབ་འདི་ངའི་ཡིན་ This book is mine. ། ང་དམག་མི་ཡིན་ I am a soldier. 2. auxiliary verb used in active verb construction to indicate first person ། ངས་ལས་ཀ་བྱས་པ་ཡིན་ I worked.

ཡིན་སྐད་ (yingɛɛ̀) it is said །ཁོང་ང་ཚོའི་ལས་ཁུངས་ཀྱི་འགོ་ཁྲིད་གསར་པ་ཡིན་སྐད་འདུག It is said that he is the new boss of the office.

ཡིན་ཁུལ་ (yingüü) pretending to be; va.—བྱེད་ ། ཁོས་མཁས་པ་ཡིན་ཁུལ་བྱེད་ཀྱི་འདུག He is pretending to be an expert.

ཡིན་ཁུལ་གནང་ (yingüü nāŋ) sm. ཡིན་ཁུལ་བྱེད་.

ཡིན་འཁྱུག་འཁྱུག་བྱེད་ (yingyuggyug cee̱) va. to continue to act as if nothing has happened.

ཡིན་གོ་ལེ་ཤོག (yinkoleshōò) may, hope.

ཡིན་གྲང་ (yindraŋ) sm. ཡིན་དུང་.

ཡིན་གྲང་ན་ (yindraŋna) if this is so.

ཡིན་དགོས་བྱུང་ (yingɔjuŋ) of course, sure, certainly ། ཁོང་མཁས་པ་ཡིན་དགོས་བྱུང་སློབ་སྦྱོང་ལོ་བཅུ་བྱུང་ས་བྱས་ཡོད་པ་རེད་ He is certainly an expert; he has studied for ten years.

ཡིན་འགྲོ་ (yindro) probably/ apparently is, seems to be ། ཁོ་དགེ་རྒན་ཡིན་འགྲོ་ It seems he is a teacher.

ཡིན་རྒྱུ་དག (yingyudaà) even though ། ཁོང་ཡིན་རྒྱུ་དག་དགེ་རྒན་ཞིག་ཡིན་ནའང་ཉམས་མྱོང་དེ་ཙམ་མེད་པ་རེད་ Even though he is a teacher, he doesn't have much experience.

ཡིན་བརྒྱ་མིན་སྟོང་ (yingya mindoŋ) talking at great length but much of it being false.

ཡིན་གཅིག་མིན་གཅིག (yinjii minjii) must, in any case, without fail ། བོད་ལ་འགྲོ་སྐབས་ལྷ་སར་ཡིན་གཅིག་མིན་གཅིག་འགྲོ་དགོས་རེད་ When you go to Tibet you must go to Lhasa.

ཡིན་གཅིག་ཡིན་གཉིས་ (yinjii yinñii) sm. ཡིན་གཅིག་མིན་གཅིག.

ཡིན་ལྟ་ཡིན་ (yindəyin) certainly, by all means.

ཡིན་ཐག་ཆོད་ (yin tāgcōò) certainly, surely, definitely ། ཁོང་ཞིང་པ་ཡིན་ཐག་ཆོད་རེད་ He is definitely a farmer.

ཡིན་ཐང་ (yindaŋ) most probably it is, seems to ། གནས་ཚུལ་དེ་བདེན་པ་ཡིན་ཐང་སྣམ་ This information seems to be true.

ཡིན་དང་མིན་ (yindaŋ min) sm. ཡིན་ལྟ་མིན་.

ཡིན་དུ་ཆུག (yindu cūù) if we assume ། ཁོས་བཤད་པ་དེ་ཡིན་དུ་ཆུག ཡིན་ནའང་ང་ཚོས་ད་དུང་བརྟག་དཔྱད་བྱེད་ཀྱི་ཡིན་ Even if we assume what he said is true, we will continue investigating.

ཡིན་དུ་གཤའ་བ་ (yindu shawa) most likely it is.

ཡིན་མདོག་ཁ་པོ་ (yindo kābo) 1. it seems to be ། ཁོ་སོ་པ་ཡིན་མདོག་ཁ་པོ་འདུག He seems to be a spy. 2. attractive, good/ nice looking ། ཁང་པ་འདི་ཡིན་མདོག་ཁ་པོ་འདུག This house looks good.

ཡིན་མདོག་ཁ་མོ་ (yindo kāmo) sm. ཡིན་མདོག་ཁ་པོ་.

ཡིན་མདོག་མིན་མདོག (yindo mindo) abbr. of ཡིན་མདོག་མདོག མིན་མདོག་མདོག.

ཡིན་མདོག་མདོག མིན་མདོག་མདོག (yindondoò min dondoò) giving the run around ། བུ་མོ་དེས་ཡིན་མདོག་མདོག མིན་མདོག་མདོག་བཤད་ནས་ང་ལ་མགོ་སྐོར་སྐྱེར་བྱུང་ The girl tricked me by giving me the run around.

ཡིན་ན་མིན་ན་ (yinna minna) sm. ཡིན་གཅིག་མིན་གཅིག.

ཡིན་ན་གཅིག་དང་མིན་ན་གཉིས་ (yinnajig daŋ minnəñìì) forcefully insisting on doing sth.; va.—བྱེད་ ། ང་སྐྱིད་ཁར་འགྲོ་འདོད་མེད་ཀྱང་ཡིན་ན་གཅིག་དང་མིན་ན་གཉིས་བྱས་ནས་ཁྲིད་བྱུང་ (They) forcefully took me to the picnic even though I didn't want to go.

ཡིན་ནམ་མིན་ནམ་ (yinnam minnam) uncertain whether sth. is or is not, uncertain whether or not to do sth. ། ང་ལྷ་སར་འགྲོ་དགོས་ཡིན་ནམ་མིན་ནམ་ I am uncertain whether I should go to Lhasa or not.

ཡིན་ན་ཡང་ (yinnayaŋ) sm. ཡིན་ནའང་.

ཡིན་ནམ་མིན་ (yinnam min) will you do it or not ། འདི་བྱེད་ཀྱི་ཡིན་ནམ་མིན་ Will (you) do this or not?

ཡིན་ནའང་ (yinnaaŋ) nevertheless, even though ། ཡིན་ནའང་ང་ཚོས་བྱེད་དགོས་ Nevertheless, we have to do (it).

ཡིན་ནའང་འདྲ་ (yinnaŋdra) whether ། ལས་ཁུངས་འདི་ཉིན་མོ་ཡིན་ནའང་འདྲ་མཚན་མོ་ཡིན་ནའང་འདྲ་ཁྲོལ་བ་ཚ་པོ་ཞིག་དུག་འདུག Whether it is daytime or nighttime, this office is very busy.

ཡིན་ནའི་ (yinnɛ) sm. ཡིན་ནའང་.

ཡིན་ནོ་ཅོག (yinnojoò) all/ everyone who is ... ། ལོ་གཞོན་པ་ཡིན་ནོ་ཅོག་ལས་ཀར་སྐད་བཏང་པ་རེད་ Everyone who is young was called to work.

ཡིན་པ་གང་ཞིག་ལ་ (yinbə kaŋshiglə) for a ... ། ཁོ་ནང་པ་ཡིན་པ་གང་ཞིག་ལ་ཤ་ཟ་གི་ཡོད་པ་རེད་ For a Buddhist, he eats meat.

ཡིན་པ་འདྲ་ (yimbədra) probably it is, it seems to be ། ཁོ་དམག་མི་ཡིན་པ་འདྲ་ It seems he is a soldier.

ཡིན་པ་ནམ་ (yimbənam) a polite question ending ། ཁོང་གཞུང་ཞབས་ཡིན་པ་ནམ་ Is he a government official?

ཡིན་པ་ཡོད་ (yimbəyöò) might have, might be ། ཁོང་དགེ་རྒན་ཡིན་པ་ཡོད་ He might be a teacher.

ཡིན་པ་རེད་ (yimbəreè) sm. རེད་ (implies speaker has a source for the question) ། ཁོ་སྨན་པ་ཡིན་པ་རེད་ He is a doctor.

ཡིན་པས་ (yimbɛ) 1. a question term (is it?) ། དེབ་འདི་ཁྱེད་རང་གི་ཡིན་པས་ Is this your book? 2. because it is ། ལས་ཀ་འདི་གལ་ཆེན་པོ་ཡིན་པས་གཟབ་གཟབ་བྱེད་དགོས་ Because this work is important, we should be careful.

ཡིན་པའི་ཁུལ་ (yimbɛgüü) 1. pretending to be; va.—བྱེད་ to pretend to be ། ཁོང་འགོ་ཁྲིད་ཡིན་པའི་ཁུལ་བྱས་ནས་ཚོགས་འདུར་ཡོང་བ་རེད་ He pretended to be a teacher and came to the meeting. 2. supposed to be ། ཁོང་དགེ་རྒན་ཡིན་པའི་ཁུལ་རེད་ཡིན་ནའང་འཛིན་ཐང་མེད་པ་རེད་ He is supposed to be a teacher but he is not capable. 3. a humble way of saying that one is sth. ། ང་དགེ་རྒན་ཡིན་པའི་ཁུལ་རེད་ I am a teacher. [Lit. I am supposed to be a teacher].

ཡིན་པའི་རྣམ་འགྱུར་སྟོན་ (yimbɛ nāmgyur dȫn) va. to pretend to be sth., to falsely pose as sth.

ཡིན་པའི་དབང་དུ་བཏང་ནའང་ (yimbɛ wāŋdu dāŋnaaŋ) even if we suppose/ say it is ... ། ཁང་པ་འདི་ཁྱེད་རང་གི་ཡིན་པའི་དབང་དུ་བཏང་ནའང་ཁང་གླ་བཏང་མི་ཆོག Even if we suppose this house is yours, you cannot rent it out.

ཡིན་པར་སྒྲུབ་ (yimbar drub) va. to prove/ justify/ authenticate/ substantiate ། ཁོང་གིས་གནས་ཚུལ་དེ་བདེན་པ་ཡིན་པར་བསྒྲུབ་པ་རེད་ He proved the truth of that information.

ཡིན་པར་ཆ་ཞོགས་ (yimbar cāshoò) taking for granted ། གནད་དོན་ཆུང་ཙག་འདིར་ངས་རྩོད་རྒྱག་གི་མིན་ཁྱེད་རང་གིས་བཤད་པ་དེ་ཡིན་པར་ཆ་ཞོགས་ I will not argue on this minor point. I will take for granted what you told me.

ཡིན་ཕྱིན་ (yinjin) as long as, whenever ། བརྩོན་འགྲུས་ལྡན་པ་ཞིག་ཡིན་ཕྱིན་བསྒྲུབ་མི་ཐུབ་པའི་བྱ་བ་གང་ཡང་མེད་ There is nothing one cannot achieve as long as one is hard working.

ཡིན་མིན་ (yinmin) whether or not ། ཁོ་སྨན་པ་ཡིན་མིན་ཤེས་ཀྱི་མིན་འདུག (I) don't know whether or not he is a doctor.

ཡིན་མིན་གོ་ལྡོག (yinmin kodɔɔ̀) reversing right and wrong, doing or saying the opposite.

ཡིན་མིན་ཕྱིན་ཅི་ལོག (yinmin cīnjilɔɔ̀) turning upside down, sowing discord.

ཡིན་མིན་ཆེན་པོ་ (yinmin cēmbo) a major question of right or wrong, a major question of principle ། འབྱོར་ལྡན་གྲལ་རིམ་གྱིས་སྲིད་དབང་འཛིན་དང་འབྱོར་མེད་གྲལ་རིམ་གྱིས་སྲིད་དབང་འཛིན་རྒྱུ་དེ་ཡིན་མིན་ཆེན་པོའི་གནད་དོན་རེད་ Whether the proletarian or the bourgeoisie will hold political power is a major question of principle.

ཡིན་མིན་མཉམ་བསྲེས་ (yinmin ñamseè) confusing right and wrong.

ཡིན་མིན་དབྱེ་འབྱེད་ (yinmin yējeè) sm. ཡིན་མིན་གསལ་

འཇོག་བྱེད་.

ཡིན་མིན་ཞིབ་དཔྱད་ (yinmin shibjɛɛ̀) judging/ investigating right and wrong.

ཡིན་མིན་གསལ་འབྱེད་ (yinmin sēējeè) distinguishing right and wrong; va.— བྱེད་.

ཡིན་མིན་གསལ་ཤེས་ (yinmin sɛ̄ɛ̄sheè) knowing/ understanding the difference between right and wrong.

ཡིན་མོད་ (yinmöö̀) although, despite, even though ། མི་དེ་ཡོན་ཏན་ཅན་པོ་ཡིན་མོད་ འོན་ཀྱང་ཉམས་མྱོང་མེད་པ་རེད་ Although that man is learned, nevertheless, he has no experience.

ཡིན་ཙམ་མིན་ཙམ་བྱེད་ (yindzam mindzam ceè) va. to not do/ say consistently ། མི་དེས་ལས་ཀ་ཡིན་ཙམ་མིན་ཙམ་ཁོ་ན་བྱས་ནས་མཐའ་སྐྱོལ་གྱི་མི་འདུག That person is not working consistently and is not completing the work.

ཡིན་ཚད་ (yindzɛɛ̀) all, entire ། བོད་པ་ཡིན་ཚད་ཚོགས་འདུར་སྐད་བཏང་འདུག All the Tibetans were invited to the meeting.

ཡིན་ཚུལ་ (yindzüü) shung. pretending to be ། ཁོས་སྐུ་མགྲོན་ཡིན་ཚུལ་གྱིས་ཐུགས་སྒྲོར་ཕྱིན་བཞག He pretended to be guest and went to the party.

ཡིན་ཚུལ་འདུག (yindzüüduù) seems likely to be ། མི་དེ་སོ་པ་ཡིན་ཚུལ་འདུག That man seems to be a spy.

ཡིན་ཚུལ་བྱེད་ (yindzüü ceè) va. to pretend to be.

ཡིན་ཚོད་འདུག (yindzöö̀ duù) maybe it is like that.

ཡིན་ཚོད་ཙམ་ལས་ (yindzöö̀ dzāmlɛ) shung. not proven, not certain, only hearsay ། ཁོང་དགེ་འདུན་ཡིན་ཚོད་ཙམ་ལས་ཡིག་ཆ་ཁུངས་སྐྱེལ་རྒྱུ་མི་འདུག It's a only hearsay that he is a monk; he has no documents to prove it.

ཡིན་ཟོལ་བྱེད་ (yinsöö jeè) va. to make believe, to pretend ། ཁོ་ཕྱུག་པོ་ཡིན་ཟོལ་བྱེད་ཀྱི་འདུག He is pretending to be rich.

ཡིན་བཟོ་ (yinso) sm. ཡིན་ཟོལ་འདུག.

ཡིན་ཡང་ (yinyaŋ) but, however, nevertheless.

ཡིན་ཡིན་པ་ (yin yimbə) already ། ཁོང་སློབ་གྲྭར་མ་སླེབས་གོང་མཁས་པ་ཡིན་ཡིན་པ་རེད་ He was already an expert before he came to school.

ཡིན་རེ་སྐན་ (yinregɛn) to swear that one is not sth. ། ང་རྐུན་མ་རྐུ་མཁན་ཡིན་རེ་སྐན་ I swear that I am not the thief.

ཡིན་རེ་ཤི་ (yinreshi) sm. ཡིན་རེ་སྐན་.

ཡིན་ལ་མིན་ལ་ (yinlə minlə) ambivalent, uncertain, equivocal ། ཁོས་ཡིན་ལ་མིན་ལ་བཤད་ནས་ངའི་དུས་ཚོད་འཕྲོ་བརླག་བཏང་སོང་ He was ambivalent in what he said and wasted my time.

ཡིན་ལས་ཆེ་ (yinlɛɛ̀je) perhaps, maybe ། གནས་ཚུལ་དེ་བདེན་པ་ཡིན་ལས་ཆེ་ Maybe this information is true. ། དེ་ཡིན་ལས་ཆེ་ འོན་ཀྱང་ང་ཡིད་མ་ཆེད་ Perhaps that is so, but I do not believe it.

ཡིན་ལུགས་ (yinluù) see ལུགས་.

ཡིན་ལུགས་ངོ་ཐོག (yinluù ŋodoò) the real factual situation ། ངས་ཁོང་ལ་ཡིན་ལུགས་ངོ་ཐོག་བཤད་ཀྱང་ཡིད་ཆེས་མ་སོང་ Even though I told him the real factual situation, he didn't believe me.

ཡིན་ལུགས་དྲང་པོར་སྨྲོང་བ་ (yinluù traŋbor sōŋwa) sm. ཡིན་ལུགས་ངོ་ཐོག.

ཡིན་ལུགས་དཔྱོད་པའི་ཆོས་ཚོགས་ (yinluù jȫȍbɛ cȫȍdzɔɔ̀) Church of Scientology.

ཡིན་ལུགས་མིན་ལུགས་ (yinluù minluù) what happened exactly; va.—ཤོད་; —ལབ་ to say what is and what is not, to state what happened exactly.

ཡིན་ལུགས་ཚུལ་ལྡན་ (yinluù tsǖǖdɛn) virtuous and just, law abiding, honest.

ཡིན་ལུགས་ཡིན་སྣངས་ (yinluù yindaŋ) how sth. is or happened ། ང་རྐུ་མ་ཡིན་ལུགས་ཡིན་སྣངས་ཁུངས་སྐྱེལ་རོགས་གནང་ Please prove to me in detail how I am a thief.

ཡིན་ལོ་ (yinlo) pretending, acting ། མི་དེ་ལ་ཚད་ལྡན་གྱི་ཤེས་ཡོན་གང་ཡང་མེད་ཀྱང་མཁས་པ་ཡིན་ལོ་བྱེད་ཀྱི་འདུག Although he doesn't even have a standard education, he pretends to be a scholar.

ཡིན་ལོག (yinlɔɔ̀) sm. མ་ཡིན་པ་.

ཡིན་ཤག (yinshaà) thinking sth. is, assuming/ taking for granted ། ལས་ཀ་དེ་ལས་སླ་པོ་ཡིན་ཤག་བྱས་པ་ཡིན་ཀྱང་ལག་ལེན་བསྟར་དུས་ལས་སླ་པོ་མི་འདུག Even though I thought the work was easy, when I tried to do it it wasn't easy.

ཡིན་ཤས་ཆེ་ (yinshɛɛ̀je) sm. ཡིན་ལས་ཆེ་.

ཡིན་ས་མིན་སྐྱེལ་ (yinsə mingyee) proving the truth and falseness of sth. ། ངས་ཁྲིམས་ཁང་ལ་ཡིན་ས་མིན་སྐྱེལ་གྱི་རྒྱུ་རྐྱེན་ཞུས་ནས་ཁ་མཆུ་དེ་ཐག་གཅོད་དྲང་པོ་ཞིག་བྱུང་སོང་ I proved the truth and falseness (of the case) in court and the case was decided justly.

ཡིན་སྲིད་ཆེ་ (yinsiìje) sm. ཡིན་ལས་ཆེ་.

ཡིབ་: p. **ཡིབས་**; f. **ཡིབ་**; imp. **ཡིབས་** (yib) va. to hide (oneself) ། ཉིན་མཚན་མང་པོ་རི་ལ་ཡིབས་པ་ཡིན་ I hid in the mountains for many days.

ཡིབ་ཁུང་ (yibguŋ) shelter, refuge, sanctuary ། གནམ་གྲུར་ཡིབ་ཁུང་ Air raid shelter.

ཡིབ་ཁུངས་ (yibguŋ) sm. ཡིབ་ཁུང་.

ཡིབ་ལྟའི་རྒྱང་ཤེལ་ (yibdɛ gyaŋshee) periscope.

ཡིབ་སྡོད་ (yibdöö̀) hiding, concealing; va. ཡིབ་སྡོད་; —བྱེད་ to be in hiding, to stay concealed.

ཡིབ་འབྲོལ་ (yibjöö) running away and hiding; va.—བྱེད་.

ཡིབ་མ་ (yibma) hidden, concealed.

ཡིབ་དམག (yibmaà) military attack from hiding/ ambush; va.—རྒྱག to ambush.

ཡིབ་ཞུ་ (yibshu) a dress from Kongpo that is like a poncho.

ཡིབ་བཞུགས་ (yibshuù) sm. ཡིབ་སྡོད་.

ཡིབ་ཤིང་ (yibshiŋ) a mythical tree that becomes invisible when held by a person.

ཡིབ་ས་ (yibsə) hideout, hiding place.

ཡིབས་ (yib) p. of ཡིབ་.

ཡིབས་བསྡད་ (yibdɛɛ̀) 1. p. of ཡིབ་སྡོད་. 2. hiding, concealing; va.—བྱེད་.

ཡིའི་མའི་ (yiimɛ) ch. castor oil plant.

ཡིའི་རིགས་ (yiiriì) Yi nationality.

ཡིའུ་ཁྲ་སྣུམ་ཤིང་ (yidru nūmshiŋ) tea-oil tree, oil-tree camellia.

ཡིའུ་ཏ་ (yiwuda) 1. Judas. 2. ch. uranium.

ཡིའུ་གཏེར་ (yiwuder) ch.tib. uranium mine.

ཡིའུ་ཐའི་རྒྱལ་ཁབ་སླར་གསོའི་རིང་ལུགས་ (yiwude gyɛɛgəb lārsö riŋluù) Zionism.

ཡིའུ་ཐའི་ཆོས་ལུགས་ (yiwude cȫȍluù) Judaism.

ཡིའུ་ཐའི་པ་ (yiwudebə) a Jew.

ཡིའུ་ཐའི་མི་ (yiwutemi) ch. ཡིའུ་ཐའི་པ་.

ཡིའུ་པིང་ (yiwubiŋ) ch. oil cake.

ཡིའུ་པེའུ་ (yiwubeu) ch. postage stamp.

ཡིའུ་པེའུ་བསྡུ་གསོག (yibe dusɔɔ̀) ch.tib. stamp collecting.

ཡིའུ་མུའུ་ཤིང་ (yiwumu shīŋ) ch.tib. teak tree.

ཡིའུ་ཚལ་ཚོད་མ་ (yiwudzɛɛ tsȫȍma) ch.tib. bok choy.

ཡིའུ་ཞང་ (yiwushaŋ) ch. deep fried dough bread.

ཡིའུ་ཧའེ་ཤིང་ (yiwuheshiŋ) ch. starfish.

ཡིས་ (yiì) by (instrumental particle used following vowel final syllables).

ཡིས་ཀྲང་ (yiìdraŋ) ch. speaker, president (of a congress, parliament).

ཡིས་ཙི་ (yiìdzi) ch. soap.

ཡུ་ཁུ་ (yugu) sm. ཡུ་གུ.

ཡུ་ག (yugə) a stick that is rubbed to make fire.

ཡུ་གན་ཊ་ (yugandra) Uganda.

ཡུ་གུ་ (yugu) oats.

ཡུ་གུ་ཤིང་ (yugushiŋ) ch. ginseng.

ཡུ་གུ་ས་ལ་ཝི་ཀི་ཡ་ (yugusala wigiyə) Yugoslavia.

ཡུ་གུར་ (yugur) Uighur.

ཡུ་མགོ་ (yungo) handle.

ཡུ་ནེ་ས་ཀོ་ (yunesago) eng. UNESCO.

ཡུ་པི་ཨའི་གསར་སྤེལ་ལས་ཁང་ (yu bīyi sārbel lɛɛ̀gaŋ) eng.tib. United Press International (UPI).

ཡུ་བ་ (yuwa) 1. handle ། གྲི་ཡུ་ Knife handle. 2. leg (of a boot).

ཡུ་བ་ཅན་ (yuwajɛn) things with a handle.

ཡུ་བོ་ (yuwo) hornless male animal.

ཡུ་མ་ (yuma) weeding, weeds; va.—རྒྱག to weed.

ཡུ་མའི་ཆི་འུ་ (yumo cīwu) ch. shuttlecock, badminton.

ཡུ་མེད་ (yumeè) handleless.

ཡུ་མོ་ (yumo) 1. hornless female animals. 2. female deer.

ཡུ་རིང་ (yuriŋ) long (for boots, bowls).

ཡུ་རོབ་ (yurob) Europe.

ཡུ་རོབ་ཀྱི་རིག་གཞུང་དང་དམངས་གཙོ་དར་སྤེལ་གྱི་སྒྲིག་འཛུགས་ (yurobgi rigshuŋ daŋ māŋdzo tarbelgi driŋdzuù) Council of Europe.

ཡུ་རོབ་གྲོས་ཚོགས་ (yurob tröödzoò) European parliament.

ཡུ་རོབ་གླིང་ཆེན་ (yorob līŋdrɛn) European continent.

ཡུ་རོབ་འགན་འཛིན་ལྷན་ཚོགས་ (yurob gɛndzin lhɛ̄ndzɔɔ̀) European Commission.

ཡུ་རོབ་འགྲོ་བ་མིའི་ཐོབ་ཐང་འགན་འཛིན་ལྷན་ཚོགས་ (yurob drowɛ tōndaŋ gɛndzin lhɛ̄ndzɔɔ̀) European Commission of Human Rights.

ཡུ་རོབ་དཔལ་འབྱོར་མཉམ་སྦྲེལ་སྡེ་ཚོགས་ (yorob benjɔɔ ñamdree dedzoò) European Economic Community (EEC).

ཡུ་རོབ་དཔལ་འབྱོར་ཐུན་མོང་ཚོགས་པ་ (yorob benjɔɔ tūnmoŋ tsɔ̄gba) European Economic Community (EEC).

ཡུ་རོབ་ཚོང་དོན་ལྷན་ཚོགས་ (yorob tsōŋdön lhɛ̄ndzɔɔ̀) European Trade Commission.

ཡུ་རོབ་རང་དབང་རླུང་འཕྲིན་ཁང་ (yorob raŋwaŋ lūŋdringaŋ) Radio Free Europe.

ཡུ་ལུ་མ་ (yuluma) sm. ཡུ་མོ་.

ཡུ་ཤ་ (yusha) a thin/ light soup.

ཡུག (yug) 1. a whole (uncut) roll of cloth. 2. joined together.

ཡུག་གཅིག་ཏུ་ (yugjigdu) in one piece, joined together; vi.—འགྱུར་ to become one with, to merge with, to form a whole; vi.—གནས་ to stay in one piece, to stay joined together.

ཡུག་གཅིག་ལ་འབྲེལ་ (yugjigla dree) va. to link/ join together.

ཡུག་གཅོག (yugjöö) the whole thing, everything.

ཡུག་བཅད་ (yugjɛɛ̀) cutting down completely; va.—གཏོང་.

ཡུག་ཆད་སྙེ་མཐུད་ (yugjɛɛ nēdüü) reconciling, coming back together.

ཡུག་རྐྱང་ (yugjuŋ) a small roll of cloth.

ཡུག་ཆོད་ (yugjöö) fantastic, great, extremely, very. ། ཁོས་ལས་ཀ་ཡུག་ཆོད་པ་བྱས་བཞག He has done a fantastic job. ། ཚོང་ཁང་ཕ་གིའི་ཅ་ལག་གི་རིན་གོང་ཡུག་ཆོད་འདུག The goods in that store are extremely expensive.

ཡུག་དོག (yugdɔɔ̀) sole of a shoe.

ཡུག་སྣམ་ (yugnam) 1. a complete roll of woolen cloth. 2. a stone from which a red dye is made.

ཡུག་པོ་ (yugbo) oats.

ཡུག་ཕོ་ (yugbo) widower.

ཡུག་ཕོ་ཡུག་མོ་དྭ་ཕྲུག་མི་ཧྲེང་ (yugbu yugmo tədruù mihraŋ) widower, widow, orphan and the homeless.

ཡུག་ཕྲན་ (yugdrɛn) sm. ཡུག་ཆུང་.

ཡུག་འཕྱུག (yugjaà) robbing/ destroying completely; va.—བྱེད་.

ཡུག་སྦྲེལ་ (yugdree) 1. parallel. 2. va. to link/ join together.

ཡུག་སྦྲེལ་གློག་ལམ་ (yugdree lōglam) parallel electric circuit.

ཡུག་སྦྲེལ་གློག་འགོག (yugdree lōŋgɔɔ̀) parallel resistance (in electricity).

ཡུག་མོ་ (yugmo) widow.

ཡུག་ཚང་ (yugdzaŋ) whole/ complete roll of material ། གོས་ཆེན་ཡུག་ཚང་ A whole roll of brocade.

ཡུག་ཚར་ (yugdzar) roll of silk/ brocade/ wool/ cloth with tassels at the end still uncut.

ཡུག་ཟ་མ་ (yugsama) 1. widow. 2. bitch (derogatory term for women).

ཡུག་ཟ་མོ་ (yugsamo) sm. ཡུག་ཟ་མ་.

ཡུག་ཟའི་བུ་ (yugsɛ pu) children born after their father died.

ཡུག་ཡུག (yugyuù) waving, swaying; va.—བྱེད་;—གཏོང་ to wave, to sway ། སྲིད་འཛིན་གནམ་ཐང་དུ་འབྱོར་རྗེས་མང་ཚོགས་ལ་ལག་པ་ཡུག་ཡུག་བཏང་བ་རེད་ After the president arrived at the airport, he waved his hand at the people.

ཡུག་ལེན་ (yuglen) the whole thing, everything.

ཡུག་ས་མ་ (yugsama) sm. ཡུག་མོ་.

ཡུག་ས་མའི་ཟླ་བ་ (yugsamɛ dawa) the 6th month of the Tibetan lunar calendar.

ཡུག་གསོད་ (yugsöö) sm. སྲིབ་གསོད་.

ཡུགས་ཕོ་ (yugbo) sm. ཡུག་ཕོ་.

ཡུགས་རྡོ་ (yugdo) ochre.

ཡུགས་མོ་ (yugmo) sm. ཡུག་མོ་.

ཡུགས་མོ་དམ་གཙང་ (yugmo tamdzaŋ) widow who decides not to remarry.

ཡུགས་ཟ་མ་ (yug sama) sm. ཡུག་མོ་.

ཡུགས་ཟ་ཕོག (yugsa pɔ̄ɔ̀) sm. ཡུགས་ཟར་ལུས་.

ཡུགས་ཟར་ལུས་ (yugsa lüü) vi. to become a widow.

ཡུགས་ས་མ་ (yugsama) sm. ཡུག་ས་མ་.

ཡུང་ང་ (yuŋŋa) sm. ཡུང་བ་.

ཡུང་མདོག (yuŋdɔɔ̀) turmeric color.

ཡུང་རྡོག (yuŋdog) sm. ཡུང་མ་.

ཡུང་བ་ (yuŋwa) turmeric.

ཡུང་མ་ (yuŋma) turnip.

ཡུངས་དཀར་ (yuŋgar) white mustard (seed).

ཡུངས་ནག (yuŋnaà) black mustard (seed).

ཡུངས་འབྲུ་ (yuŋdru) mustard seed.

ཡུངས་མར་ (yuŋmar) mustard seed oil.

ཡུད་ (yüü) a brief/ short time.

ཡུད་ཀྱིས་ (yüügi) in a moment, quickly.

ཡུད་ཅིག (yugjig) sm. ཡུད་ཙམ་.

ཡུད་པོ་ (yugbo) lonely ། ཨ་མ་གཅིག་པུ་ཁང་པའི་ནང་ལ་བསྡད་ན་ཡུད་པོ་ཡོང་གི་རེད་ Mother will get lonely if she stays at home alone.

ཡུད་ཙམ་ (yugdzam) for a short/ brief time, for awhile ། ཡུད་ཙམ་ངལ་གསོ་བརྒྱབ་པ་ཡིན་ (I) rested briefly.

ཡུད་ཙམ་གྱི་སྔོན་ (yugdzamgi ŋōn) a brief instant ago, a moment ago.

ཡུད་ཙམ་ཅིག (yugdzamjig) a brief moment, a short time.

ཡུད་ཡུད་ (yüüyüü) praising, glorifying; va.—བྱེད་.

ཡུན་ (yün) 1. duration, period, time ། ལས་ཀ་བྱེད་ཡུན་རིས་གཏན་མི་འདུག The duration of work (in the office) is not fixed.

ཡུན་ཀུའི་མཐོ་སྒང་ (yüngu tōgaŋ) ch.tib. the Yunnan-Guizhou Plateau.

ཡུན་འགོར་ (yüngɔɔ) 1. delaying ། ཟླ་ཕྱེད་ཙམ་ཡུན་འགོར་བྱུང་བ་རེད་ (They) delayed about half a month. 2. duration, time ། ཁང་པ་འདི་རྒྱག་པར་ཡུན་འགོར་ག་ཚོད་ཙམ་འགོར་གྱི་རེད་ How much time will it take to build that house?

ཡུན་འགྱངས་ (yüngyaŋ) prolonging, delaying; va.—བྱེད་ ། མའོ་རང་ཉིད་ཀྱི་དབང་ཆ་ཡུན་འགྱངས་ཀྱི་ཐབས་ཤེས་ཤིག (It) is strategy to prolong Mao's own power.

ཡུན་གཏན་ (yündɛn) permanent, lasting, long term, enduring, eternal ། ཡུན་གཏན་གྱི་ཕྱུགས་ར་ A permanent cattle corral ། མན་ཇུ་དམག་རྣམས་ཡུན་གཏན་མ་ཐུབ་པར་ཆབ་མདོ་བར་ཕྱིར་འཐེན་བྱེད་དགོས་བྱུང་འདུག The Manchu army could not remain permanently and had to withdraw up to Chamdo.

ཡུན་གཏན་འཁྱག་ས་ (yündɛn kyāgsa) permafrost.

ཡུན་བརྟན་ (yündɛn) sm. ཡུན་གཏན་.

ཡུན་ཐུང་ (yünduŋ) short time, little while, short term ། ཡུན་ཐུང་སྦྱོང་གྲྭ་ Short term training class. ། ཡུན་ཐུང་གླ་པ་ Short term worker.

ཡུན་མཐུད་ (yündüü) continuously ། ཕར་རྒོལ་ཡུན་མཐུད་བྱས་པ་རེད་ (They) continuously attacked.

ཡུན་དུ་ (yündu) for a long time.

ཡུན་དུ་གནས་ (yündu nɛ̀ɛ̀) va. to exist/ stay for a long time ¶ ཚེ་ཡུན་དུ་གནས་པའི་སྨོན་འདུན་ཞུ་ I wish you a long life.

ཡུན་དུ་འཚོ་ (yündu tsō) sm. ཡུན་འཚོ་.

ཡུན་ནན་ཞིང་ཆེན་ (yünnɛn shinjen) Yunnan Province.

ཡུན་ནས་ཡུན་དུ་ (yünnɛ yündu) sm. ཡུན་དུ་.

ཡུན་གནས་ (yünnɛ̀ɛ̀) sm. ཡུན་དུ་གནས་.

ཡུན་ཙམ་ (yündzam) short time, briefly, momentarily ¶ ཡུན་ཙམ་སོང་བ་དང་ A short time passed and.

ཡུན་ཚད་ (yündzɛ̀ɛ̀) duration, time limit, term, space of time ¶ ཚོགས་འདུའི་ཡུན་ཚད་ནི་ As for the time limit of the meeting.

ཡུན་འཚོ་ (yündzo) existing/ surviving for a long time.

ཡུན་རིང་ (yünriŋ) for a long time.

ཡུན་རིང་གི་ཁེ་ཕན་ (yünriŋgi kēbɛn) long term interest/ benefit.

ཡུན་རིང་རྒྱུན་སྲིང་ (yünriŋ gyünsiŋ) continuing for a long time.

ཡུན་རིང་མཉམ་གནས་ (yünriŋ ñamnɛ̀ɛ̀) coexisting for a long time.

ཡུན་རིང་བརྟན་གནས་ (yünriŋ dɛnnɛ̀ɛ̀) long-term stability.

ཡུན་རིང་ཐུབ་པ་ (yünriŋ tūbbə) durable.

ཡུན་རིང་འཐབ་པ་ (yünriŋ tābbə) protracted war/ warfare.

ཡུན་རིང་པོ་ (yün riŋbu) long time, long term, long range ¶ ཡུན་རིང་པོའི་འཆར་གཞི་ Long range plan.

ཡུན་རིང་མ་མཇལ་ (yünriŋ manjɛɛ) a term of address conveying: long time no see.

ཡུན་རིང་མི་ལག (yünriŋ milaà) long-term hired hand.

ཡུན་རིང་རང་བཞིན་ (yünriŋ rəŋshin) long-term.

ཡུན་སྲན་ (yünsɛn) kidney bean.

ཡུན་སྲིངས་ (yünsiŋ) postponing, delaying; va.—བྱེད་ to postpone, to delay.

ཡུན་ཧྲན་གསོམ་ཤིང་ (yünhrɛn sōmshiŋ) spruce tree.

ཡུམ་ (yum) h. of ཨ་མ་.

ཡུམ་སྐུ་ཞབས་ (yum gūshəb) h. of ཨ་མ་.

ཡུམ་རྒྱུད་ (yumgyüü) arc. sm. མ་རྒྱུད་.

ཡུམ་ཆེན་ (yumjen) sm. ཡུམ་སྐུ་ཞབས་.

ཡུམ་བུ་བླ་སྒང་ (yumbu lāgaŋ) the oldest castle in Tibet.

ཡུམ་བུ་ལྷ་མཁར་ (yumbu lāgɛn) sm. ཡུམ་བུ་བླ་སྒང་.

ཡུམ་བུ་ལྷ་སྒང་ (yumbu lhāgaŋ) sm. ཡུམ་བུ་བླ་སྒང་.

ཡུམ་སྲས་ (yümsɛ̀ɛ̀) h. of མ་བུ་.

ཡུའན་ཏུང་ (yunduŋ) ch. the Far East.

ཡུའན་ཙེ་ (yundze) ch. atomic, nuclear.

ཡུའན་ཧྲུའི་ (yünhru) ch. marshal (in the army).

ཡུ་གོ་སི་ལ་ཝ་ས་ (yugosilawasa) Yugoslavia.

ཡུ་ཕྲུ་ར་ཏེས་ (yufurati) Euphrates River.

ཡུའི་ཏན་ (yudɛn) Jordan.

ཡུའི་ཧན་ཞུན་སྲིད་གཞུང་ (yuhɛnshün sīishuŋ) ch.tib. the Johnson administration.

ཡུར་ (yur) sm. ཡུར་བུ་.

ཡུར་ཆུ་ (yurju) irrigation water, water from an irrigation canal/ ditch; va.— འདྲེན་; —གཏོང་ to irrigate.

ཡུར་འཇོར་ (yurjɔɔ) hoe.

ཡུར་སྟོན་ (yurdön) a party given after the wedding is over.

ཡུར་འདྲུ་འཕྲུལ་འཁོར་ (yundru trüügɔɔ) trench digging machine.

ཡུར་ཕྲན་ (yurdrɛn) small irrigation canal/ ditch.

ཡུར་བ་ (yurwa) sm. ཡུར་བུ་.

ཡུར་བུ་ (yurbu) irrigation canal/ ditch, drain, gutter.

ཡུར་བྱེད་འཕྲུལ་འཁོར་ (yurjeè trüügɔɔ) weeding machine.

ཡུར་མ་ (yurmə) weeding; va.—རྒྱག; —ཡུར་ to weed.

ཡུར་རྩྭ་ (yürdza) 1. grass that has been weeded. 2. grass growing along an irrigational canal.

ཡུར་གསངས་ (yürsaŋ) cleaning a ditch/ canal; va.— རྒྱག.

ཡུལ་ (yüü) 1. country, region, location ¶ ཕ་ཡུལ་ Fatherland. ¶ ཡུལ་གྱི་སློབ་གཞི་ Local teaching materials. 2. the object (in philosophy). 3. (vb. + —) place/ location/ source of verbal action ¶ སྐྱེས་ཡུལ་ག་པར་རེད་ Where were you born? ¶ ཁོ་ཚོས་ཁང་པ་རྒྱག་ཡུལ་ལྷ་ས་རེད་ The place where they built the house is Lhasa.

ཡུལ་བགོད་ (yüügöö) sm. ཡུལ་ལྡོངས་.

ཡུལ་སྐད་ (yüügɛ̀ɛ̀) dialect, language of an area.

ཡུལ་སྐབས་ (yüügəb) time and place.

ཡུལ་སྐོར་ (yüügɔɔ) tour, touring, travel; va.—དུ་འགྲོ་; —བྱེད་ to tour, to travel, to go on a tour.

ཡུལ་སྐོར་ཛུས་ (yüügɔɔ jüü) tib. ch. tourist agency.

ཡུལ་སྐོར་སྐྱོ་འཆམ་ (yüügɔɔ drōnjm) tour, tourism.

ཡུལ་བསྐོར་སྐྱོ་འཆམ་པ་ (yüügɔɔ drōnjamba) tourist.

ཡུལ་སྐོར་སྐྱོ་འཆམ་དྲན་རྟེན་ (yüügɔɔ drōnjam trɛnden) tourist souvenir.

ཡུལ་སྐོར་སྐྱོ་གསེང་ས་ཁུལ་ (yüügɔɔ drōseŋ sōgüü) tourist area.

ཡུལ་སྐོར་ཚོང་པ་ (yüügɔɔ tsōŋba) traveling salesman.

ཡུལ་སྐོར་ལག་དེབ་ (yüügɔɔ lagdeb) travel guide (book).

ཡུལ་སྐོར་རླངས་འཁོར་ (yüügɔɔ lāŋgɔɔ) tour car/ bus.

ཡུལ་སྐོར་ལས་དོན་ཁང་ (yüügɔɔ lɛ̀ɛ̀döngaŋ) travel/ tourist agency.

ཡུལ་སྐོར་ལས་དོན་མཁན་ (yüügɔɔ mɛ̀ɛ̀döngɛn) travel agent.

ཡུལ་སྐྱོང་ (yüügyoŋ) king, monarch.

ཡུལ་སྐྱོང་ཚོགས་པ་ (yüügyoŋ tsōgba) peace preservation association (a local organization during the Sino-Japanese war, 1937-1945.

ཡུལ་ཁག (yüügaà) nations, countries.

ཡུལ་ཁལ་ (yüügɛɛ) a local ཁལ་ grain measure that is different (usu. more) than the official government ཁལ་.

ཡུལ་ཁམས་ (yüügam) 1. country, area, nation ¶ ཡུལ་ཁམས་ཀྱི་ཚོགས་འདུ་ National Assembly. 2. condition, degree.

ཡུལ་ཁུག (yüüguù) the backwoods, remote areas.

ཡུལ་ཁྱིམ་ (yüügyim) country and home.

ཡུལ་ཁྲིམས་ (yüüdrim) laws of a country/ nation.

ཡུལ་འཁོར་ (yüügɔɔ) territory, province, country, district.

ཡུལ་འཁོར་དབང་པོ་ (yüügɔɔ wāŋbo) head of a province/ state/ country.

ཡུལ་འཁོར་སྲུང་ (yüügɔɔ sūŋ) King of the East (one of the four guardians - Dhritarasrtra).

ཡུལ་འཁྱམ་ (yüügyam) sm. ཡུལ་འཁྱར་.

ཡུལ་འཁྱར་ (yüügyar) moving from place to place, wandering around.

ཡུལ་འཁྱར་སྲིད་གཞུང་ (yüügyar sīishuŋ) exile government.

ཡུལ་འཁྱར་པ་ (yüügyarba) refugee, wanderer, vagabond.

ཡུལ་འཁྲུད་ (yüüdrüü) shung. a ritual exorcising of the land.

ཡུལ་གངས་ཅན་ (yüü kaŋjɛn) Tibet.

ཡུལ་གོང་ (yüügoŋ) market price.

ཡུལ་གོམས་ (yüügom) local custom.

ཡུལ་གོམས་གཤིས་ལུགས་ (yüügom shīiluù) native customs/ habits/ way of life.

ཡུལ་གྱར་ (yüügyar) sm. ཡུལ་འཁྱར་.

ཡུལ་གྱི་བསྐལ་པ་ (yüügi gɛlba) shung. extreme/ long distance.

ཡུལ་གྱི་ཁྱད་རྫས་ (yüügi kyɛ̀ɛ̀dzɛ̀ɛ̀) local specialty products.

ཡུལ་གྱི་ཐོན་ཁུངས་ (yüügi tõnguŋ) sm. ཡུལ་གྱི་ཁྱད་རྫས་.

ཡུལ་གྱི་ཐོན་ཟོག (yüügi tõnsɔɔ) sm. ཡུལ་གྱི་ཁྱད་རྫས་.

ཡུལ་གྱི་ཚུགས་པ་ (yüügi tsūgba) tax collector.

ཡུལ་གྱི་གཤེད་མ་ (yüügi shēèma) local tyrant.

ཡུལ་གྲུ་ (yüüdru) country, region ¶ འཛམ་གླིང་ཡུལ་གྲུ་གཞན་དག་ཁག་ལ་ In the other countries of the world.

ཡུལ་གྲུ་ཀུན་དུ་ (yüüdru gündu) everywhere.

ཡུལ་གླུ་ (yüülu) folk song, ballad.

ཡུལ་དགོན་ (yüügön) village and monastery.

ཡུལ་འགུགས་ཁྲངས་འཛུག (yüüguù kũŋjuù) shung. recapturing one's runaway serfs from other areas and making them farm one one's estate.

ཡུལ་ངན་ (yüüŋɛn) 1. a poor country/ area/ place. 2. famine, calamity.

ཡུལ་ལྔ་ (yüüŋa) the five dimensions: form, sound, taste, smell, touch.

ཡུལ་ཅང་ཅང་ (yüü jãŋjaŋ) lonely, desolate.

ཡུལ་ཆུ་བཏུངས་རྗེས་ ཡུལ་ཁྲིམས་འཁུར་དགོས་ (yüüju dũŋjeè yüüdrim kũrgöö) one must adhere to the laws of the place where one resides [Lit. after drinking the area's water, one must abide by the area's law].

ཡུལ་ཆུང་ (yüüjuŋ) small, local areas.

ཡུལ་ཆོས་ (yüüjöö) sm. ཡུལ་ཁྲིམས་.

ཡུལ་ལྗོངས་ (yünjoŋ) landscape, scenery.

ཡུལ་ལྗོངས་གྲགས་ཅན་ (yünjoŋ tragjɛn) famous spot, place of interest.

ཡུལ་ལྗོངས་བརྫུས་མ་ (yünjoŋ dzüümə) setting/ background for theatrical productions.

ཡུལ་ལྗོངས་རི་མོ་ (yünjoŋ rimu) landscape painting.

ཡུལ་གདད་ (yüüdɛɛ̀) a derogatory term used for bad/ evil people.

ཡུལ་བཏགས་ (yüüdaà) local weaving, sth. woven locally.

ཡུལ་རྟ་ (yüüda) local horse.

ཡུལ་ཐང་ (yüüdaŋ) local price/ value.

ཡུལ་ཐབས་ (yüüdəb) native/ indigenous/ local methods ¶ ཡུལ་ཐབས་ཀྱི་མཁས་པ་ Experts in local methods. ¶ ཡུལ་ཐབས་ཀྱི་འཕྲུལ་འཁོར་ An indigenous machine.

ཡུལ་ཐོན་ (yüüdön) 1. produced locally ¶ ཡུལ་ཐོན་དངོས་ཟོག Local products. 2. va. to flee/ leave an area.

ཡུལ་ཐོན་ཁྱད་ཐོན་ (yüüdön kyɛɛ̀dün) local specialty products.

ཡུལ་མཐའ་འཁོབ་ (yüü tãgob) places where Buddhism has not spread.

ཡུལ་དུ་འགྱུར་ (yüüdu gyur) vi. to become an object of sth. ¶ བསྔགས་བརྗོད་ཀྱི་ཡུལ་དུ་གྱུར་པའི་རྒྱལ་ཁ་ The victory which is the object of praise.

ཡུལ་དུས་ (yüüdüù) time and place; condition.

ཡུལ་དུས་སྐྱ་ཐམ་ (yüüdüù gyãbam) a bad year for crops.

ཡུལ་དུས་ཀུན་དུ་ (yüüdüù gũndu) always and everywhere.

ཡུལ་དུས་གནས་ཚུལ་ (yüüdüù nɛɛ̀dzüü) sm. ཡུལ་དུས་.

ཡུལ་དུས་བབས་འབྲེལ་ (yüüdüù bəmdree) in accordance with the place and time.

ཡུལ་གདངས་ (yüüdaŋ) local accent/ pronunciation.

ཡུལ་འདུག་བྱེད་ (yüüduù cɛè) va. to stay put in a place.

ཡུལ་སྡེ་ (yüüde) province, district, settlement.

ཡུལ་སྡེའི་སྲུང་སྐྱོབ་ (yüüdee sũŋgyob) homeguards.

ཡུལ་ནང་ (yüünaŋ) internal ¶ ཡུལ་ནང་གི་དཀའ་ངོག Internal difficulties.

ཡུལ་པ་ (yüüba) inhabitants of a country, natives.

ཡུལ་པོ་ (yüübu) loneliness ¶ གྲོགས་པོ་ཕྱིན་ནས་ང་ཡུལ་པོ་བྱུང་ I got lonely when my friend went away.

ཡུལ་དཔོན་ (yüübön) local official, local headman/ chief.

ཡུལ་དཔོན་སྲུང་པ་ (yüübön sũŋba) shung. sm. ཡུལ་སྲུང་.

ཡུལ་ཕག (yüü) local pig.

ཡུལ་ཕྱི་ཟུང་སྦྲེལ་ (yüü) combining native and foreign methods.

ཡུལ་ཕུད་ (yüü) va. to expel, to exile.

ཡུལ་ཕྱོགས་ (yüüjɔɔ̀) district, region.

ཡུལ་ཕྱོགས་ཚོགས་པ་ (yüüjɔɔ̀ tsõgba) an association of fellow provincials or townsmen.

ཡུལ་ཕྲ་བ་ (yüüdrawa) very small particles (e.g., atoms).

ཡུལ་བབ་ (yüübəb) local conditions, local character ¶ ཡུལ་བབ་དང་བསྟུན་ In accordance with local conditions.

ཡུལ་བབ་དང་བསྟུན་ (yüübəbdaŋ dũn) in accordance with local conditions.

ཡུལ་བབ་དང་མཐུན་ (yüübəbdaŋ tũn) vi. in harmony/ compatibility with local conditions.

ཡུལ་བལ་ (yüüpɛɛ) local wool.

ཡུལ་བྲོལ་ (yüüjöö) taking refugee, going into exile, fleeing, deserting (for soldiers); va.—(དུ་)འགྲོ་; —བྱེད་ to go into exile, to flee, to seek refugee ¶ དམག་ཕོར་ནས་མི་མང་པོ་ཡུལ་བྲོལ་དུ་ཕྱིན་པ་རེད་ Having lost the war, many people fled into exile.

ཡུལ་བྲོལ་ཞིང་བདག (yüüjöö shiŋdaà) runaway landlords, landlords who have fled/ gone into hiding.

ཡུལ་བྲེ་ (yüüdre) shung. a བྲེ་ volume measure that is used in a particular local area.

ཡུལ་དབུས་ (yüü üü) 1. shung. central Tibet. 2. the central area/ region.

ཡུལ་འབྲོག (yündroò) farmers and nomads.

ཡུལ་མ་རྒྱག (yüüma gyaà) sm. ཡུར་མ་རྒྱག.

ཡུལ་མ་འདྲོག (yüüma drɔɔ̀) sm. ས་མ་འདྲོག.

ཡུལ་མི་ (yüümi) local inhabitant/ resident/ native, fellow villager/ countryman.

ཡུལ་མི་གནས་སྤོས་ (yüümi nɛɛ̀böö) sm. ཡུལ་མི་གཞན་སྤོས་.

ཡུལ་མི་སྤུན་ཟླ་ (yüümi bũnda) fellow countrymen, sb. from one's homeland.

ཡུལ་མི་གཙོ་ཆེན་ (yüümi dzõjen) prominent citizens in a locality.

ཡུལ་མི་གཞན་སྤོས་ (yüümi shɛnböö) emigrating; va.—བྱེད་.

ཡུལ་མི་ལས་པ་ (yüümi lɛɛ̀ba) local people conscripted for work on public projects (this work can involve payment).

ཡུལ་མིའི་ལྡི་གནས་ (yüümii dēnɛɛ̀) housing estate, residential quarters, central place where people live.

ཡུལ་མིའི་ཨུ་ཡོན་ལྷན་ཁང་ (yüümii ũyön lhẽngaŋ) neighborhood committee.

ཡུལ་མེད་ (yüümeè) 1. having no chance or hope of being accepted or agreed to ¶ འགོ་ཁྲིད་དེ་ལ་ལྷ་སར་འགྲོ་རྒྱུའི་ཆོག་མཆན་སྤྲོར་སྐད་ཆ་ཤོད་པའི་ཡུལ་མེད་པ་རེད་ There is no chance of the boss agreeing to give permission to go to Lhasa. 2. homeless, a wanderer.

ཡུལ་མོ་ངན་ (yüümo ŋɛn) a poor/ infertile place.

ཡུལ་དམག (yüümaà) local militia.

ཡུལ་དམག་ལམ་ལུགས་ (yüümaà ləmluù) the system of militias.

ཡུལ་སྨུས་ (yüümüù) bad climate/ weather.

ཡུལ་གཙོ་ (yüüdzo) sm. ཡུལ་མི་གཙོ་པོ་.

ཡུལ་ཚན་ (yüüdzɛn) sm. ཡུལ་ཚོ་.

ཡུལ་ཚོ་ (yüütso) small rural district/ area.

ཡུལ་མཚམས་ (yündzam) border between areas.

ཡུལ་མཛེས་ཐོན་ཕྱུག (yüüdzeè tõnjuù) an area that is atrractive and rich.

ཡུལ་འཛིན་ (yüüdzin) va. to live on, to graze on ¶ ས་གནས་དེ་ར་རི་དྭགས་ཀྱི་ཡུལ་འཛིན་གྱི་ཡོད་ Wild animals live in that place.

ཡུལ་རྫས་ (yüüdzɛɛ̀) local products, native products.

ཡུལ་རྫས་ཀུང་སི་ (yüüdzɛɛ̀ gũŋsi) local products company.

ཡུལ་རྫས་ཁྱད་རྫས་ (yüüdzɛɛ̀ kyɛɛ̀dzɛɛ̀) local specialty products.

ཡུལ་རྫས་ཚོང་ཁང་ (yüüdzɛɛ̀ tsõŋgaŋ) local products store.

ཡུལ་གཞས་ (yüüshɛɛ̀) local song.

ཡུལ་གཞིས་ (yüüshii) manorial estates.

ཡུལ་ཟོག (yüüsɔɔ̀) sm. ཡུལ་རྫས་.

ཡུལ་ཟོག་ཐོན་རྫས་ (yüüsɔɔ̀ tõndzɛɛ̀) local products, products from a local area.

ཡུལ་བཟང་ (yüüsaŋ) a good area/ place.

ཡུལ་ཡུལ་པོ་ (yüü yüübu) 1. missing sb. ¶ ཕྲུ་གུ་དེ་ཕ་མ་དང་ཁ་བྲལ་ནས་ཡུལ་ཡུལ་པོ་ཞིག་བྱུང་བ་རེད་ That child was separated from his parents and missed

them a lot. 2. being embarrassed.
ཡུལ་གཡང་ (yüüyaŋ) the good fortune of a country.
ཡུལ་རགས་པ་ (yüüragba) large things that can be seen.
ཡུལ་རུབ་ (yüürub) a village ganging up and beating sb.; va.—རྒྱག.
ཡུལ་ལ་བདེ་སྐྱིད་བྱུང་ན་རྒྱལ་པོ་ཨ་ནེ་བྱས་ཀྱང་འགྲིགས་ (yüüla degyii cuŋnə gyɛɛbo āne cɛ̀ɛgyaŋ drig) if it benefits the area, any kind of person can be the ruler [Lit. as long as there is peace and happiness in the land it is okay even if a nun were to become the king].
ཡུལ་ལག (yüülaà) small place, hamlet.
ཡུལ་ལས་འགོངས་པ་ (yüülɛ̀ɛ goŋba) shung. sm. ཡུལ་ལས་འདས་པ་.
ཡུལ་ལས་འདས་པ་ (yüülɛ̀ɛ dɛ̀ɛba) passed beyond a stage/ status ¶ མི་སྤྱོད་ཡུལ་ལས་འདས་པ་ Inhuman (human behavior that has passed beyond human norms).
ཡུལ་ལས་མ་འདས་ (yüülɛ̀ɛ madɛ̀ɛ) no doubt about sth. happening ¶ ཁྱེད་རང་གིས་ལས་ཀ་དེ་འདྲ་བྱས་ན་དེ་ནི་འཕྱ་སྨོད་ཀྱི་ཡུལ་ལས་མ་འདས་ If you work like that there is no doubt that people will ridicule you.
ཡུལ་ལུགས་ (yüüluù) local customs.
ཡུལ་ལུང་ (yüüluŋ) sm. ཡུལ་.
ཡུལ་ལོག (yüülɔ̀ɔ) being sick from staying in a foreign area/ country, having a bad negative reaction to the conditions in a new area, being not acclimatized to a new place; vi.—རྒྱག; —ཐེབས་.
ཡུལ་ས་ (yüüsa) land; va.—འཛིན་ to settle down in a place and establish a household.
ཡུལ་སེལ་ (yüüsii) apricot, peach.
ཡུལ་སྲིད་ (yüüsii) local government.
ཡུལ་སྲིད་འཕབས་ (yüüsiibaŋ) shung. abbr. of ཡུལ་སྲིད་གཞུང་མི་སེར་.
ཡུལ་སྲིད་གཞུང་མི་སེར་ (yüüsiishuŋ misee) shung. local government and the people/ citizens/ subjects/ serfs.
ཡུལ་སྲུང་ (yüüsuŋ) 1. guarding/ defending an area. 2. garrison commander.
ཡུལ་སྲུང་དམག་སྡེ་ (yüüsuŋ māgde) homeguard.
ཡུལ་སྲོལ་ (yüüsöö) local customs.
ཡུལ་སྲོལ་གོམས་འདྲིས་ (yüüsöö komdrii) sm. ཡུལ་སྲོལ་གོམས་གཤིས་.
ཡུལ་སྲོལ་གོམས་གཤིས་ (yüüsöö komshii) local habits/ customs (of an area).
ཡུལ་སྲོལ་དམངས་ཁྲིམས་ (yüüsöö māŋdrim) local rules and customary law.
ཡུལ་སྲོལ་དམངས་འཆིངས་ (yüüsöö māŋjiŋ) sm. ཡུལ་སྲོལ་དམངས་ཁྲིམས་.
ཡུལ་ལྷ་ (yüülha) guardian deity of an area/ locality.
ཡུལ་ལྷ་གཞི་བདག (yüülha shidaà) local gods/ spirits.
ཡུས་ (yüü) reminding sb. what you did for them, making a big deal about sth. one has done, tooting one's own horn.; va.—ཕོད་ ¶ ཁོང་ང་ལ་དངུལ་གཡར་བའི་སྐོར་ཡུས་བཤད་བྱུང་ He made a great deal about lending me money.
ཡུས་ཀྱིས་བནྡངས་ (yüügi nāŋ) sm. ཡུས་ (ཕོད་).
ཡུས་མའོ་ཆེའུ་པོ་ལོ་ (yüümoce bōlo) ch.tib. badminton.
ཡུས་ཤགས་རྒྱག (yüüshaà gyaà) sm. ཡུས་ (ཕོད་).
ཡུས་ལེའི་དམག་གྲུ་ (yüülee māgdru) ch.tib. torpedo boat.
ཡེ་ (ye) the start, the beginning ¶ ཡེ་ནས་ From the beginning.
ཡེ་མཁྱེན་ (ye kyēn)1. vi. to have prior knowledge, to know beforehand. 2. name of a Bon deity. 3. astrologer.
ཡེ་སྟོང་ (yedoŋ) the initial emptiness/ void.
ཡེ་ནས་ (yenɛ) 1. from the beginning/ start; always. 2. (— + neg.) never, not at all ¶ ངས་ལྟ་བ་དེ་ལ་གོ་བ་ཡེ་ནས་ལེན་ཐུབ་ཀྱི་མི་འདུག I cannot understand that concept at all.
ཡེ་མི་བྲ་བ་ (yemi drawa) not daring to do sth.
ཡེ་མིན་ (yemin) sm. ཡེ་མེན་.
ཡེ་མེན་ (yemin) Yemen.
ཡེ་མེད་ (yemeè) sm. ཙ་མེད་.
ཡེ་སྨོན་ནག་པོ་ (yemön nagbo) one of the ancient clans/ tribes in Tibet.
ཡེ་རྫོགས་ (yedzɔ̀ɔ) being complete from the start/ beginning.
ཡེ་ཞུ་ (yeshu) sm. ཡེ་ཤུ་.
ཡེ་ར་ཝ་དི་ (yera wadi) Irrawaddy River.
ཡེ་རེ་ (yere) once, one time.
ཡེ་རེ་བུད་ (yere büü) vi. to be conspicuous/ salient ¶ དམག་མི་མང་པོའི་དཀྱིལ་ནས་དཔའ་བོ་དེ་ཡེ་རེ་བུད་འདུག The hero was conspicuous among the soldiers.
ཡེ་རེ་ལྷོད་དེ་ (yere lhööde) unhurried manner.
ཡེ་ཤུ་ (yeshu) Jesus.
ཡེ་ཤུའི་འཁྲུངས་སྐར་ (yeshü trüŋgar) Jesus' birthday, Christmas.
ཡེ་ཤུའི་འཁྲུངས་སྐར་གྱི་རྟེན་འབྲེལ་ལྗོན་ཤིང་ (yeshü trüŋgargi dēmdree jönshiŋ) Christmas tree.
ཡེ་ཤུའི་ཆོས་ (yeshü cöö) Christianity, the Christian religion.
ཡེ་ཤུའི་ཆོས་འཆད་མཁན་ (yeshü cöö cɛ̀ɛñɛn) Christian clergyman/ pastor/ priest/ minister.
ཡེ་ཤུའི་ལྟ་བ་མཆོག་ཏུ་འཛིན་པའི་སྒྲིག་འཛུགས་ (yeshü dāwa cōgdu dzimbɛ driŋdzuù) Moral Majority.
ཡེ་ཤུའི་ཆོས་དད་པའི་མནའ་མཐུན་ (yeshü cöödɛɛbɛ nādün) Christain Coalition.
ཡེ་ཤུའི་ཆོས་སྤེལ་མཁན་ (yeshü cööbeeñɛn) Christian missionary.
ཡེ་ཤུའི་ཆོས་ལུགས་ (yeshü cööluù) Christianity.
ཡེ་ཤུའི་ཆོས་ལུགས་མཉམ་འབྲེལ་གྱི་ཆོས་ལུགས་ (yeshü cööluù ñamdreegi cööluù) Unification Church.
ཡེ་ཤུའི་ཆོས་ལུགས་པ་ (yeshü cöölugbə) a Christian.
ཡེ་ཤུའི་ཆོས་ལུགས་གསར་པ་ (yeshü cöölug sääba) Protestanism.
ཡེ་ཤུའི་འདས་ལོ་ (yeshü dɛ̀ɛlo) AD. ¶ ཡེ་ཤུའི་འདས་ལོ་བརྒྱ་ཕྲག་བདུན་པ་ The 7th. century AD.
ཡེ་ཤུའི་ཕོ་གཞོན་གྱི་མཐུན་ཚོགས་ (yeshü pōshöngi tündzɔ̀ɔ) Young Men's Christian Association (YMCA).
ཡེ་ཤུའི་བླ་ཆེན་སྤོབ་ཀྱི་གདན་ས་ (yeshü lājen bōbgi dɛnsa) the Vatican.
ཡེ་ཤུའི་བླ་ཆེན་སྤོབ་ཀྱི་འཛིན་སྐྱོང་ཁང་ (yeshü lājen bōbgi dziŋgɔ̀ɔgaŋ) the Vatican's Curia.
ཡེ་ཤུའི་མ་ཡུམ་མཆོད་ཁང་ (yeshü mayum cöögaŋ) shrine of virgin Mary.
ཡེ་ཤུའི་མོ་གཞོན་གྱི་མཐུན་ཚོགས་ (yeshü pōshöngi tündzɔ̀ɔ) Young Women's Christian Association (YWCA).
ཡེ་ཤུའི་ཡུམ་ (yeshü yum) the mother of Jesus (Mary).
ཡེ་ཤེས་ (yesheè) 1. wisdom, knowledge. 2. a Tibetan name.
ཡེ་ཤེས་ཀྱི་མཁའ་འགྲོ་མ་ (yesheègi kāndroma) sm. ཡེ་ཤེས་མཁའ་འགྲོ་.
ཡེ་ཤེས་མཁའ་འགྲོ་ (yesheè kāndro) dakini.
ཡེ་ཤེས་པ་ (yesheèba) deity possessing a medium.
ཡེ་ཤེས་གཟིགས་དཔྱད་ (yesheè siijɛ̀ɛ) shung. contemplating and deciding on an issue (by a superior).
ཡེ་སག་དཀར་པོ་ (yesag gārbo) an ancient lineage in Tibet. 2. a deity in the Bon religion.
ཡེགས་པ་ (yegba) unkempt, disheveled ¶ སྐྲ་ཡེགས་པ་ Unkempt hair.
ཡེང་ (yeŋ) sm. གཡེང་.
ཡེང་ངེ་བ་ (yeŋŋewa) sm. ཡང་ངེ་ཡེང་ངེ་.
ཡེངས་ (yeŋ) sm. གཡེང་.
ཡེངས་མ་ལམ་ (yeŋmalam) sm. རྣམ་གཡེང་.
ཡེན་ (yen) sm. གཡེང་.
ཡེར་ (yer) 1. va. to raise/ lift up ¶ ལག་པས་དཀར་ཡོལ་བྱིན་དུ་ཡེར་ནས་མཆོད་ཆང་བཀྲུག་པ་རེད་ (He) offered ཆང་ with both hands raised up. 2. vi. to wake up, to get cleared up ¶ མདང་དགོང་རྨི་ལམ་འཚུབ་པོ་ཞིག་བཏང་ནས་གཉིད་ཡེར་སོང་ Last night I had a

nightmare and woke up. 3. quickly, suddenly.

ཡེར་གྱིས་ (yergi) quickly, suddenly.

ཡེར་བུ་ (yerbu) a type of wind disease in Tibetan medicine.

ཡེར་ཡེར་བ་ (yēryerwa) shaking, trembling.

ཡེར་རེ་ (yērre) pure, clear ¶ སྔོ་ཡེར་རེ་ Pure blue. ¶ རིག་པ་ཡེར་རེ་ Clear intelligence.

ཡེར་རེ་སེང་ངེ་ (yere sēŋŋe) sm. ཡེར་རེ་.

ཡོ་ (yo) 1. vi. to be leaning towards one side ¶ ཁོའི་གཟུགས་པོ་ཡོ་བྱས་འགྲོ་གི་འདུག He is going along with his body leaning to one side. 2. arc. all.

ཡོ་ཀྱོག (yogyɔɔ̀) crooked.

ཡོ་འཁྱོག (yogyɔɔ̀) 1. crooked. 2. biased.

ཡོ་འཁྱོམས་ (yogyom) unstable, vacillating, in turmoil.

ཡོ་ག (yoga) 1. spindle; va.—ཡོག to spin thread on a spindle. 2. yoga.

ཡོ་ག་པ་ (yogaba) yogi.

ཡོ་ག་མ་ (yogama) yogini.

ཡོ་གི་ནི་ (yogini) sm. ཡོ་ག་མ་.

ཡོ་གླིང་ (yoliŋ) Europe ¶ ཡོ་གླིང་ཤར་མ་ East Europe.

ཡོ་བཅོས་ (yojöö) sm. ཡོ་བསྲང་.

ཡོ་ཆས་ (yojɛɛ̀) sm. ཡོ་བྱད་.

ཡོ་རྡན (yodɛn) Jordan.

ཡོ་དོག (yodoò) having a big nose.

ཡོ་ནན་ (yonɛn) Vietnam ¶ ཡོ་ནན་དམངས་གཙོའི་སྤྱི་མཐུན་རྒྱལ་ཁབ་ Democratic Republic of Vietnam.

ཡོ་ནན་ལྷོ་རྒྱུད་ (yonɛn lhōgyüü) sm. ཡོ་ནན་ལྷོ་མ་.

ཡོ་ནན་ལྷོ་ཕྱོགས་ (yonɛn lhōjɔɔ̀) sm. ཡོ་ནན་ལྷོ་མ་.

ཡོ་ནན་ལྷོ་མ་ (yonɛn lhōma) South Vietnam.

ཡོ་སྦྱད་ (yojɛɛ̀) sm. ཡོ་བྱད་.

ཡོ་བྱད་ (yojɛɛ̀) 1. implement, tool, utensil, equipment, instrument. 2. necessities, needs ¶ ཨར་ལས་བྱེད་ཡས་ཀྱི་ཡོ་བྱད་དང་རྒྱུ་ཆ་ Equipment and materials for construction. ¶ འཚོ་བའི་ཡོ་བྱད་ Necessities of life.

ཡོ་བྱད་བཅོས་སྒྱུར་ (yojɛɛ̀ jöögyur) tool improvement.

ཡོ་འབོག (yombɔɔ̀) elm tree.

ཡོ་འབོག་ཤིང་ (yombɔɔ̀ shiŋ) sm. ཡོ་འབོག.

ཡོ་མེད་ (yomeè) just, honest, fair.

ཡོ་མེད་གཞུང་དྲང་ (yomeè shuŋdraŋ) honest, just, fair.

ཡོ་ཡོན་པོ་ (yo yömbo) crooked, curved.

ཡོ་རེ་བ་ (yorewa) unclear due to darkness/ shadows.

ཡོ་རོབ་ (yorob) sm. ཡོ་གླིང་.

ཡོ་རོབ་གླིང་ (yorobliŋ) sm. ཡོ་གླིང་.

ཡོ་རོབ་པ་ (yorobba) European.

ཡོ་རོབ་དཔལ་འབྱོར་ཐུན་མོང་ཚོགས་པ་ (yorob bēnjɔɔ tũnmoŋ tsōgba) the European Economic Community (E.E.C.).

ཡོ་ལ་ (yola) sm. ཡོལ་བ་.

ཡོ་ལ་ཤོར་ (yola shōō) vi. to be twisted/ crooked ¶ རྩིག་པ་དེ་ཡོ་ལ་ཤོར་བཞག The wall has become crooked.

ཡོ་ལང་ (yolaŋ) sm. ཡོ་ལངས་.

ཡོ་ལང་ཆེན་པོ་ (yolaŋ cēmbo) 1. enormous, extremely big. 2. grand and spectacular in scale. 3. risky.

ཡོ་ལངས་ (yolaŋ) 1. enormous, great, very much ¶ བཟོ་གྲྭ་དེའི་གཏོང་ཡོང་ཡོ་ལངས་ཆེན་པོ་ཡོད་པ་རེད་ The factory has enormous expenditures and income. 2. on a grand and spectacular scale. 3. risky (actions/ situations).

ཡོ་ལེ་ཕྱོད་དེ་ (yole jööde) biased.

ཡོ་ལོ་ (yolo) arc. sm. གོ་ཆོད་.

ཡོ་ལོག (yo lɔɔ̀) va. to dislike.

ཡོ་སྲོང་ (yosaŋ) sm. ཡོ་བསྲང་.

ཡོ་བསྲང་ (yosaŋ) 1. straightening sth. that is crooked or bent. 2. correcting, rectifying; va.—བྱེད་ to correct, to rectify ¶ ངས་ལས་ཀར་ཕྱི་འབྱོར་བྱེད་པ་དེ་ཡོ་བསྲང་བྱེད་ཀྱི་ཡིན་ I will correct my coming late to work.

ཡོ་བསྲང་ཚད་བརྒལ་ (yosaŋ tsɛ̃ɛ̀gɛɛ) exceeding the proper limits in righting a wrong and thereby creating a new mistake, overcorrecting; va.—བྱེད་.

ཡོ་བསྲང་ལེགས་བཅོས་ (yosaŋ leggjöö) sm. ཡོ་བསྲང་.

ཡོག (yɔɔ̀) 1. sm.* འོག. 2. sm. ཡོད་.

ཡོག :p. **ཡོགས་**; f. **ཡོག**; imp. **ཡོགས་** (yɔɔ̀) va. to spin (thread).

ཡོག་སྐྱུལ་རྒྱུག (yɔɔ̀güü gyaà) revolving credit association (a type of economic association where a group of people deposit money monthly and use the total amount in turn).

ཡོག་ཁང་ (yɔɔ̀gaŋ) sm. འོག་ཁང་.

ཡོག་ག (yɔɔ̀ga) spindle for spinning thread; va.— ཡོག to spin thread.

ཡོག་མགོ་ (yɔɔ̀go) spindle head.

ཡོག་ཆེན་ (yɔɔ̀jen) capillary artemisa.

ཡོག་ཐོད་ (yɔɔ̀töö) wooden stick used to stir grain when roasting.

ཡོག་པ་ (yɔgba) stick.

ཡོག་པ་གཅན་སྒྲིལ་ (yɔgba sɛndrii) consolidated in one figure/ amount ¶ གླ་པ་རྣམས་ལ་གླ་ཕྱོགས་པ་གཅན་སྒྲིལ་གྱིས་ཟླ་རེ་སྒོར་ ༡༠༠ སྤྲོད་ཀྱི་ཡོད་ (I) pay the hired hands the consolidated figure of 100 dollars a month for their salary and food.

ཡོག་པོ་ (yɔgbo) 1. poker/ stick for stirring a fire. 2. the part of a spindle where the thread is wrapped.

ཡོག་བུ་ (yɔgja) twisted wool that is wrapped around the wrist for use in spinning wool into thread.

ཡོག་ཡོག (yɔgyɔɔ̀) a lot, much.

ཡོག་རེད་ (yɔɔ̀reè) sm.* ཡོད་པ་རེད་.

ཡོག་ཤིང་ (yɔgshiŋ) sm. ཡོག་པོ་, 1.

ཡོགས་ (yɔɔ̀) p. and imp. of ཡོག.

ཡོང་ (yoŋ) 1. va. to come ¶ གཞོན་ནུ་ ༧༠ ཙམ་ང་ཚོའི་བཟོ་གྲྭར་ཡོང་བ་རེད་ About 70 youths came to our factory. 2. (vb. + —) conveys simultaneous verbal action together with coming ¶ ཁོས་འདིར་འཕུར་ཡོང་པ་རེད་ He flew here (came flying). 3. future auxiliary verb ¶ འདི་འདྲ་བྱས་ན་ན་ཡོང་གི་རེད་ If you do that you will get sick. 4. vi. to be okay ¶ འདི་འདྲ་བྱས་ན་ཡོང་གི་མ་རེད་ It is not okay to do that.

ཡོང་རྐྱེན་ (yoŋgyen) cause/ origin of sth. coming or occurring ¶ དགོང་པ་ཞུ་དགོས་བྱུང་པའི་སྐབས་དེའི་ཡོང་རྐྱེན་གནས་ཚུལ་སྐོར་ Concerning the cause of (his) having to resign.

ཡོང་སྐྱོད་ (yoŋgyöö) coming and going.

ཡོང་ཁང་ (yoŋgaŋ) shung. an officer in charge of collecting taxes from small shopkeepers.

ཡོང་ཁུངས་ (yoŋguŋ) resources ¶ དཔལ་འབྱོར་ཡོང་ཁུངས་ Economic resources.

ཡོང་མཁན་ (yoŋgɛn) visitors, people that are coming.

ཡོང་སྒོ་ (yoŋgo) income ¶ ཡོང་སྒོ་སྒོར་བཞི་ཁྲི་ཡན་མན་ཙམ་ཐོབ་པ་རེད་ (He) received an income of about forty thousand dollars.

ཡོང་སྒོ་སིལ་མ་ (yoŋgo sĩima) side income.

ཡོང་ང་ (yoŋŋa) okay, certainly.

ཡོང་ངེས་ (yoŋŋeè) (sth.) will definitely come/ happen.

ཡོང་ཉག་འཁེལ་ (yoŋñaà kēē) vi. to come at the right time ¶ ཨེམ་ཇི་དེ་ཡོང་ཉག་འཁེལ་སོང་ The doctor came at the right time.

ཡོང་ཉུང་གཏོང་མང་ (yoŋñuŋ dōŋmaŋ) loss, deficit [Lit. little coming, much going].

ཡོང་སྟངས་ (yoŋdaŋ) sm. ཡོང་བབས་.

ཡོང་སྟངས་ཡོང་ལུགས་ (yoŋdaŋ yoŋluù) 1. sm. ཡོང་བའི་ཡོང་རབས་. 2. all about how sth. came about/ happened.

ཡོང་ཐག་ཆོད་ (yoŋ tāàjöö) 1. certain to come. 2. decided to come. 3. stopped coming.

ཡོང་ཐང་ (yoŋdaŋ) income.

ཡོང་ཐབས་བྱེད་ (yoŋdəb ceè) va. to plan to come.

ཡོང་དང་ཡོང་ (yoŋdaŋ yoŋ) certainly, definitely.

ཡོང་དེབ་ (yoŋdeb) shung. a book in which income is listed.

ཡོང་མདོག་ཁ་པོ་ (yoŋdɔɔ̀ kābo) likely to come/ occur.

ཡོང་སྡུད་ (yoŋdüü) collecting income; va.—བྱེད་ ། དགོན་པས་བུ་ལོན་དང་བོགས་མ་ཡོང་སྡུད་བྱས་པ་རེད་ The monastery collected income from its loans and leases.

ཡོང་སྡུད་པ་ (yoŋdüübə) an income collector.

ཡོང་གནས་མ་མཆིས་པ་ (yoŋnɛɛ̀ maciibə) shung. can not be, will not be ། བདེན་དཔང་འབྲེལ་བའི་རྒྱ་རྐྱེན་ཞིབ་གསལ་མ་ཕུལ་བར་གྱོད་དོན་ཐག་གཅོད་ཡོང་གནས་མ་མཆིས་པ་ Until a detailed report with proof is submitted, the case will not be settled.

ཡོང་པའི་ཡོང་རབས་ (yoŋbɛ yoŋrəb) sm. ཡོང་བའི་ཡོང་རབས་.

ཡོང་སྤར་གཏོང་འཕྲི་ (yoŋbar dōŋdri) increase income (and) decrease expenditures.

ཡོང་བ་འདུག (yoŋwa duù) can do sth. ། ལས་ཀ་འདི་ཡོང་བ་འདུག I can do this work.

ཡོང་བ་མི་འདུག (yoŋwa miduù) cannot do ། ངས་ལས་ཀ་འདི་ཡོང་བ་མི་འདུག I cannot do this work.

ཡོང་བབས་ (yoŋbəb) the manner of coming ། མི་དེ་ཕྱི་པོ་དེ་འདྲ་ཡོང་བབས་ལ་གཞིགས་ན་གནས་ཚུལ་ཡག་པ་ཞིག་མ་རེད་ His coming late is not a good a situation.

ཡོང་འབབ་མི་གྲ (yoŋbəb midrə) shung. sm. མི་བོགས་.

ཡོང་བའི་ཡོང་རབས་ (yoŋwɛ yoŋrəb) all about how sb. came somewhere ། ཁོས་ལྷ་ས་ནས་ཨ་རི་ར་བར་ཡོང་བའི་ཡོང་རབས་བཤད་བྱུང་ He told me everything about his trip from Lhasa to America.

ཡོང་འབབ་ (yoŋbəb) income.

ཡོང་འབབ་ཁེ་གཙང་ (yoŋbəb kēdzaŋ) net income.

ཡོང་འབབ་བསྡོམས་གྲངས་ (yoŋbəb domdraŋ) gross total income.

ཡོང་འབབ་བསྡོམས་འབོར་ (yoŋbəb dombɔɔ) gross total income.

ཡོང་དམིགས་ (yoŋmig) the source of income.

ཡོང་རྩིས་ (yoŋdzii) 1. calculating one's income; va.—རྒྱག. 2. planning to come ། ཁོ་ལས་ཁུངས་ལ་ཡོང་རྩིས་འདུག He plans to come to the office.

ཡོང་ཚོད་ཀྱི་མཐུན་རྐྱེན་ (yoŋdzöögi tũngyen) as much as one can afford to give ། ཁྱེད་རང་གིས་ང་ལ་ཡོང་ཚོད་ཀྱི་མཐུན་རྐྱེན་ཞིག་སྦྱོར་རོགས་གནང་ Please give me as much as you can afford.

ཡོང་གཞི་ (yoŋshi) 1. source of income. 2. cause of sth. that has occurred.

ཡོང་ཡོང་འབབ་པོ་ (yoŋyoŋ bɛɛbo) lots of misfortunes occurring ། ད་ལོ་མི་ཚང་དེ་ར་ཡོང་ཡོང་འབབ་པོ་བྱུང་སོང་ This year that family has had a lot of misfortunes.

ཡོང་རབས་ (yoŋrəb) sm. ཡོང་པའི་ཡོང་རབས་.

ཡོང་ལམ་ (yoŋlam) a route used for coming.

ཡོང་ས་ (yoŋsa) 1. road, route. 2. source of a product.

ཡོང་སོང་ག་མི་འདུམ་པ་ (yoŋsoŋ ka mindumba) sm. གཏོང་མང་ཡོང་ཉུང་.

ཡོང་སོང་ག་མི་མཚུངས་པ་ (yoŋsoŋ ka mindzuŋba) sm. གཏོང་མང་ཡོང་ཉུང་.

ཡོངས་ (yoŋ) all, the whole ། ཏང་ཡོངས་དང་མི་ཡོངས་ All the party and all the people.

ཡོངས་ཁུངས་ (yoŋguŋ) sm. ཡོང་ཁུངས་.

ཡོངས་ཁྱབ་ (yoŋgyəb) 1. widespread, large scale, universal, broad, general ། ཞིབ་འཇུག་ཡོངས་ཁྱབ་བྱེད་རྒྱུ་ Making a widespread investigation. 2. completely. ། དམངས་གཙོ་ནི་ཡོངས་ཁྱབ་ཀྱི་ལམ་ལུགས་ཤིག་རེད་ Democracy is a system that is universally accepted.

ཡོངས་ཁྱབ་ཀྱི་ཆོས་ཉིད་ (yoŋgyəbgi cöönii) general rule, universal law.

ཡོངས་ཁྱབ་ཀྱི་བདེན་དོན་ (yoŋgyəbgi dendön) universal truth.

ཡོངས་ཁྱབ་ཀྱི་ཞིབ་འཇུག (yoŋgyəbgi shimjuù) general investigation/ research.

ཡོངས་ཁྱབ་ཀྱི་རང་བཞིན་ (yoŋgyəbgi rəŋshin) universality.

ཡོངས་ཁྱབ་ཀྱི་འདེམས་བསྐོ་ (yoŋgyəbgi demgo) general election.

ཡོངས་ཁྱབ་ཏུ་ (yoŋgyəbdu) 1. broad, widely, all over, general, all encompassing ། ལམ་ལུགས་དེ་ཡོང་ཁྱབ་ཏུ་དར་ཡོད་པ་རེད་ That system has spread all over. 2. completely, entirely ། ལྟོ་གོས་ནི་ཁ་ཆེ་དགོས་གཏུགས་ཤིག་ཡིན་པ་ཡོངས་ཁྱབ་ཏུ་ངོས་འཛིན་བྱེད་ཀྱི་ཡོད་པ་རེད་ It is completely recognized by everyone that food and clothing are the most important things (in life).

ཡོངས་ཁྱབ་བརྡ་ཡིག (yoŋgyəb dəyii) public notice/ communication (that is spread all over).

ཡོངས་ཁྱབ་ངེས་འགན་ (yoŋgyəb wöŋgɛn) universal/ widespread/ nationwide obligation ། ཡོངས་ཁྱབ་ངེས་འགན་སློབ་གསོ་ Nationwide compulsory education.

ཡོངས་ཁྱབ་གསལ་བསྒྲགས་ (yoŋgyəb sɛɛdraà) universal declaration.

ཡོངས་གྲགས་ (yoŋdraà) 1. well known, famous; va.—བྱེད་ to make well known, to make known all over; vi.—སུ་འགྱུར་ to become well known/ famous ། ཡོངས་གྲགས་བདུན་རེའི་ཚགས་པར་ A well known weekly newspaper. 2. public, open ། ཡོངས་གྲགས་རྩོད་ཞུ་ཞིབ་ཉན་ Public hearing/ trial.

ཡོངས་གྲུབ་ (yoŋdrub) completely achieved/ attained/ finished.

ཡོངས་འགྲེམ་ (yoŋdrem) disseminated all over.

ཡོངས་བསྒྲགས་ (yoŋdraà) proclamation, declaration; va.—གཏོང་; —བྱེད་ to proclaim, to declare, to promulgate ། སྲིད་ཇུས་གསར་པ་འདི་ཡོངས་བསྒྲགས་བྱས་པ་རེད་ They proclaimed the new policy all over.

ཡོངས་སྒྲགས་གློག་འཕྲིན་ (yoŋdraà lōŋdrin) an open telegram (to all).

ཡོངས་བསྔོ་ (yoŋŋo) completely dedicated/ devoted.

ཡོངས་རྟོགས་ (yoŋdoò) 1. thorough/ comprehensive/ detailed examination or consideration. 2. complete understanding/ comprehension.

ཡོངས་འདུ་ (yoŋdu) 1. everyone gathered together; va.—བྱེད་. 2. sm. དཔག་བསམ་ཤིང་.

ཡོངས་བསྡུས་ (yoŋdüü) completely collected, collecting all; va.—བྱེད་.

ཡོངས་བསྡོམས་ (yoŋdom) in all, all told ། ཚོགས་འཛོམས་ཀྱི་སྐུ་མི་ཡོངས་བསྡོམས་ ༡༥༠ ཡོད་པ་རེད་ There are one hundred and fifty assembly members in all.

ཡོངས་སྤྱོད་ (yoŋ jöö) va. to utilize everything.

ཡོངས་འཛིན་ (yoŋdzin) tutor, teacher (of a high lama) ། སྐྱབས་རྗེ་ཡོངས་འཛིན་རྣམ་གཉིས་ The two tutors of the Dalai Lama.

ཡོངས་འཛིན་སྐུ་བགྲེས་ (yoŋdzin gūdreè) sm. ཡོངས་འཛིན་བགྲེས་པ་.

ཡོངས་འཛིན་སྐུ་གཞོན་ (yoŋdzin gūshön) junior tutor.

ཡོངས་འཛིན་བགྲེས་པ་ (yoŋdzin dreèba) senior tutor.

ཡོངས་འཛིན་ཆུང་བ་ (yoŋdzin cūŋwə) junior tutor.

ཡོངས་རྫོགས་ (yoŋdzɔɔ̀) all, entire, whole, total.

ཡོངས་རྫོགས་གྲོས་ཚོགས་ (yoŋdzɔɔ̀ tröödzɔɔ̀) plenary session.

ཡོངས་རྫོགས་དགེ་བསྙེན་ (yoŋdzɔɔ̀ geñen) the complete layman's vow.

ཡོངས་རྫོགས་འདྲ་མཉམ་ (yoŋdzɔɔ̀ drañam) complete equality.

ཡོངས་རྫོགས་མི་དམངས་ (yoŋdzɔɔ̀ mimaŋ) the whole people, all the people.

ཡོངས་རྫོགས་ལས་མཚམས་འཇོག་པ་ (yoŋdzɔɔ̀ lendzam jɔgba) general strike.

ཡོངས་ཤེས་ (yoŋsheè) omnipotent, all knowing.

ཡོངས་སུ་ (yoŋsu) thoroughly, fully, completely, exhaustively.

ཡོངས་སུ་ཁྱབ་ (yoŋsu kyāb) sm. ཡོངས་ཁྱབ་.

ཡོངས་སུ་གྲགས་ (yoŋsu traà) sm. ཡོངས་གྲགས་.

ཡོངས་སུ་སྤྱོད་ (yoŋsu jöö) sm. ཡོངས་སྤྱོད་.

ཡོངས་སུ་རྫོགས་ (yoŋsu dzɔɔ̀) sm. ཡོངས་རྫོགས་.

ཡོད་ (yöö) 1. existential verb (there is, there are ...) ། ངར་ཁྱི་གཅིག་ཡོད་ I have a dog. ། ཁོར་ཁྱི་གཅིག་ཡོད་ཙང་ Because he has a dog. 2. (vb. past + —) present perfect complement ། ངས་དེབ་ཁྱེར་ཡོད་ I have brought a book.

ཡོད་ཀྱི་རེད་ (yöögireè) 1. probably ༈ཁོ་ལ་དངུལ་ཡོད་ཀྱི་རེད་ He probably has money.

ཡོད་དགུ་ (yöögu) sm. ཡོད་རྒུ་.

ཡོད་འགྲོ་ (yöödro) 1. probably doesn't have, probably not ༈ཁོ་ལ་དངུལ་ཡོད་འགྲོ། ཁོའི་ས་ནས་གཡར་ལོས་ཡོད་པ་མ་རེད་ He probably doesn't have money. There is no point in you trying to borrow from him. 2. probably ༈ཁོ་ལ་དངུལ་ཡོད་འགྲོ། ཁྱེད་རང་གིས་གཡར་ན་འགྲིགས་ He probably has money. Its okay to borrow from him.

ཡོད་རྒུ་ (yöögu) whatever there is, all, everything ༈ཐབས་ཤེས་ཡོད་རྒུས་ By every means.

ཡོད་རྒུ་རྩལ་སྒྲུག་ (yöögu dzɛ̄ɛ̄druù) with all one's strength/ might, doing the best ༈ངས་ཐབས་ཤེས་ཡོད་རྒུ་རྩལ་སྒྲུག་གིས་ལས་ཀ་ཞིག་རྩལ་བ་ཡིན་ I have done my best to find a job.

ཡོད་ཐང་ (yöödaŋ) probably.

ཡོད་དོ་ཅོག་ (yöödojoò) 1. everything, all, everybody ༈བོད་རིགས་སུ་གཏོགས་པ་ཡོད་དོ་ཅོག་གི་ཡིད་ལ་ In the hearts of all Tibetans. 2. the best.

ཡོད་མདོག་ཁ་པོ་ (yöndo kābo) seems likely, may have.

ཡོད་ན་མེད་ན་ (yööna meèna) 1. whether it is or not, whether has or doesn't have, whether does sth. or doesn't. ༈མི་དེ་ང་ཚོའི་ལས་ཁུངས་ནང་ལ་ལས་ཀ་བྱེད་ཀྱི་ཡོད་ན་མེད་ང་ས་མི་ཤེས་ I don't know whether that man is working in our office or not. 2. the best ༈མི་དེ་ང་ཚོའི་ལས་ཁུངས་ནང་གི་ཡོད་ན་མེད་ན་རེད་ That person is the best in the office.

ཡོད་འདུག་ (yööduù) sm. ཡོད་པ་རེད་.

ཡོད་པ་འདྲ་ (yööbadra) probably is/ has.

ཡོད་པ་ནམ་ (yööbanam) do you have, are there ༈ཁྱེད་རང་ལ་ཕྱུག་དངུལ་ཡོད་པ་ནམ་ Do you have money?

ཡོད་པས་ (yööbɛ) 1. do you have, are there ༈ཁྱེད་རང་ལ་དངུལ་ཡོད་པས་ Do you have money? 2. because there is/ are sth.

ཡོད་པ་རེད་ (yööbareè) existential verb: there is/ are ༈འདི་ཡག་པོ་ཞི་དྲག་ཡོད་པ་རེད་ This is very good.

ཡོད་འཕྱོར་བྱེད་ (yööjɔɔ ceè) va. to show off, to put on airs.

ཡོད་འབྲུ་ (yöndru) shung. grain collected (as tax) from households who have grain.

ཡོད་མེད་ (yöömeè) whether sth. exists or not ༈དེབ་ཡོད་མེད་ཤེས་ཀྱི་མེད་ (I) don't know whether or not there is a book.

ཡོད་ཚད་ (yöödzɛɛ) all that there is/ was ༈ནུས་ཤུགས་ཡོད་ཚད་བཏོན་ནས་ Exerting all (their) strength. ༈མི་ཡོད་ཚད་ All the people.

ཡོད་ཚད་ཁས་ལེན་ (yöödzɛɛ kɛ̄ɛlen) complete agreement.

ཡོད་ཚད་ཐམས་ཅད་ (yöödzɛɛ tāmjɛɛ̀) all, entire, everything.

ཡོད་ཚད་ཚང་མ་ (yöödzɛɛ tsāŋma) all, everything.

ཡོད་རྒྱུལ་ (yöödzüü) existence, presence ༈ནས་ཡོད་རྒྱུལ་གོ་མ་ཐག་ལམ་སང་ནས་དེ་ཉོས་ནས་བཏབ་པ་རེད་ As soon as (they) heard of the existence of barley, (they) at once bought the barley and planted it.

ཡོད་ཤན་འདྲ་ (yööshɛndra) probably there is/ are.

ཡོད་བཞིན་པ་ (yööshinbɔ) existing, having ༈ཁོ་ལ་དངུལ་མང་པོ་ཡོད་བཞིན་པར་དུ་ཡང་དངུལ་གསོག་གི་འདུག While having much money, he still is accumulating (more) money.

ཡོད་ཡོད་པ་ (yööyööba) sm. ཡོད་བཞིན་པ་.

ཡོད་ཡོད་སྐད་ (yööyöö gɛɛ̀) shung. acting as if ༈ཁོས་དངུལ་མང་པོ་ཡོད་ཡོད་སྐད་བྱེད་ཀྱི་འདུག He is acting as if he has lots of money.

ཡོད་རལ་ཤོད་ (yöörɛɛ shöö) va. to boast/ brag ༈ཁོ་ཕྱུག་པོ་ཡིན་རྒྱལ་ཡོད་རལ་བཤད་པ་མ་གཏོགས་དོན་དངོས་དེ་འདྲ་མ་རེད་ He boasted of being rich but in reality that is not the case.

ཡོད་རིགས་ (yöörii) all kinds ༈འབྲུ་ཡོད་རིགས་ནས་ From all those kinds of grain. ༈དཀའ་ངོགས་ཡོད་རིགས་ All kinds of difficulties.

ཡོད་རེ་སྐན་ (yööregɛn) a phrase swearing that there is not sth. ༈ང་ལ་དངུལ་ཡོད་རེ་སྐན་ I swear that I have no money.

ཡོད་རེ་ཤི་ (yööreshi) sm. ཡོད་རེ་སྐན་.

ཡོད་ལ་མེད་ལ་ (yööla meèla) having little of, having hardly any of ༈ཚོང་ཁང་དེ་ལ་ཅ་ལག་ཉོ་མཁན་ཡོད་ལ་མེད་ལ་རེད་བཞག That store has hardly any customers.

ཡོད་རེད་ (yööreè) sm. ཡོད་པ་རེད་.

ཡོད་ཧླམ་ (yöölom) pretending/ making believe one has sth. ༈མི་དེས་ཡོན་ཏན་ཡོད་ཧླམ་བྱས་ཀྱང་དོན་དུ་ཡོན་ཏན་ངོ་མ་གང་ཡང་མེད་པ་རེད་ That person pretends to be learned but in reality he is not at all knowledgeable.

ཡོད་ཤག་ (yööshaà) certain to be/ have.

ཡོད་ས་ (yöösa) the place where sth. exists.

ཡོད་སྲིད་ (yöösii) may possibly exist ༈དཔེ་མཛོད་ཁང་དེར་དེབ་དེ་ཡོད་སྲིད་ཀྱི་རེད་ That book may be in the library.

ཡོན་ (yön) 1. present, gift, offering (usu. to monks) va.—(དུ་)འབུལ་ to give a present/ gift/ offering. 2. ch. member ༈ཧྲེ་ཡོན་ Commune member ༈དང་ཡོན་ Party member. 3. fee, price ༈སྨན་ཡོན་ Doctor's/ medicine fee. 4. ch. office ༈སྲིད་འཛིན་ཡོན་ Administrative Yuan (office).

ཡོན་གྱི་བདག་པོ་ (yöngi dagbo) shung. sm. སྦྱིན་བདག.

ཡོན་ཀྱོག་ (yöngyɔɔ) crooked, not straight.

ཡོན་ཀྲང་ (yöndraŋ) ch. sm. ཡོའན་ཀྲང་.

ཡོན་གྱི་གནས་ (yöngi nɛ̄ɛ) priest, lama (one to whom a patron gives offerings to).

ཡོན་བསྔོ་ (yön ŋō) va. to say prayers of dedication for a patron.

ཡོན་ཆབ་ (yönjɔb) holy water (used in religious offerings); va.—འབུལ་ to make a water offering.

ཡོན་མཆོད་ (yönjöö) patron and priest.

ཡོན་ཏན་ (yöndɛn) knowledge.

ཡོན་ཏན་ཁྱད་པར་ཅན་ (yöndɛn kyɛ̄ɛbarjɛn) one who has specialized ability/ knowledge, a specialist.

ཡོན་ཏན་གྱི་ཚད་ (yöndɛngi tsēè) sm. ཡོན་ཚད་.

ཡོན་ཏན་རྒྱ་མཚོ་ (yöndɛn gyadzo) the 4th Dalai Lama (1589-1616).

ཡོན་ཏན་ངོ་མ་ (yöndɛn ŋoma) real/ true knowledge.

ཡོན་ཏན་ཅན་ (yöndɛnjɛn) knowledgeable person/ educated person.

ཡོན་ཏན་ཆེན་པོ་ (yöndɛn cēmbo) knowledgeable, educated.

ཡོན་ཏན་མེད་པ་ (yöndɛn meèba) ignorant.

ཡོན་ཏན་བརྩོན་ཤིབ་ (yöndɛn dzönshib) diligent with regard to knowledge.

ཡོན་དུང་ས་ཁུལ་ (yönduŋ sōgüü) ch. tib. the Far East.

ཡོན་བདག (yöndaà) patron, donor.

ཡོན་ནུས་ (yönnüü) skill, technical proficiency, craftsmanship.

ཡོན་གནས་ (yönnɛɛ̀) 1. abbr. of ཡོན་བདག. and མཆོད་གནས་ 2. sm. མཆོད་གནས་.

ཡོན་པོ་ (yönbo) crooked, curved.

ཡོན་འབུལ་ (yön büü) va. to give a gift, present (usu. to monks, lamas, doctors).

ཡོན་མེད་རྩལ་མེད་ (yönmeè dzɛ̄ɛmeè) no knowledge and no skills.

ཡོན་མི་དགོས་པ་ (yönmi gööba) free of charge.

ཡོན་ཙེ་ (yöndzi) ch. atom, atomic.

ཡོན་ཙེ་དན་ (yöndzdɛn) ch. atomic bomb, nuclear bomb.

ཡོན་ཙེ་རྡུལ་སྙིང་ (yöndzi düüñiŋ) sm. ཡོན་ཙེའི་སྙིང་པོ་.

ཡོན་ཙེ་རྡུལ་ཕྲན་ (yöndzi düüdrɛn) ch.tib. atomic, nuclear ༈ཡོན་ཙེ་རྡུལ་ཕྲན་མེ་ཤུགས་འཕུར་མདའི་རྟེན་གཞི་ Atomic missile base.

ཡོན་ཙེ་ནང་སྙིང་ (yöndzi naŋñiŋ) sm. ཡོན་ཙེའི་སྙིང་པོ་.

ཡོན་ཙེ་ནང་སྙིང་དངོས་གཤིས་ (yöndzi naŋñiŋ ŋööshii) ch.tib. nuclear physics, atomic physics.

ཡོན་ཙེའི་འཁྱགས་གཏོར་གྲུ་གཟིངས་ (yöndzii kyāgdɔɔ trusiŋ) ch.tib. atomic/ nuclear icebreaker boat.

ཡོན་ཙེའི་ཚན་པོ་ (yöndzii cünbu) ch.tib. atomic group.

ཡོན་ཅེའི་ལྗིད་ཚད་ (yö̱ndzii ji̱ìdzɛɛ̀) ch.tib. atomic weight.

ཡོན་ཅེའི་སྙིང་པོ་ (yö̱ndzii ñi̱ŋbu) ch.tib. atomic nucleus.

ཡོན་ཅེའི་འདྲེས་སྦྱོར་ཚད་གྲངས་ (yö̱ndzi dre̱èjɔɔ tsɛɛ̀draŋ) ch.tib. valance; atomicity.

ཡོན་ཅེའི་ནུས་འདོན་སྒྲིག་ཆས་ (yö̱ndzii nü̱ndön dri̱gjɛɛ̀) ch.tib. atomic/ nuclear reactor.

ཡོན་ཅེའི་ནུས་པ་ (yö̱ndzii nü̱ùbə) ch.tib. atomic/ nuclear energy.

ཡོན་ཅེའི་ནུས་པས་གློག་གཏོང་བའི་བབས་ཚུགས་ (yö̱ndzii nü̱ùbɛ lɔ̄gdoŋwɛ ba̱bdzuù) ch.tib. nuclear electric generating station.

ཡོན་ཅེའི་ནུས་པའི་གློག་འདོན་ས་ཚིགས་ (yö̱ndzii nü̱ùbɛ lɔ̄gdön sə̄dzii̇) ch.tib. atomic/ nuclear power station.

ཡོན་ཅེའི་དམག་འཁྲུག་ (yö̱ndzii mə̄gdruù) ch.tib. nuclear war.

ཡོན་ཅེའི་མཚོན་ཆ་ (yö̱ndzii tsȫnja) ch.tib. atomic/ nuclear weapon.

ཡོན་ཅེའི་རིམ་གྲངས་ (yö̱ndzii ri̱mdraŋ) ch.tib. atomic number.

ཡོན་ཚད་ (yö̱ndzɛɛ̀) ability, qualifications, standard, degree ༡ སོ་སོའི་ཡོན་ཚད་ལ་བལྟས་ནས་ In accordance with each one's ability.

ཡོན་ཚད་གཅིག་མཚུངས་ (yö̱ndzɛɛ̀ ji̱gdzuŋ) having the same educational level/ standard/ degree/ qualification.

ཡོན་ཞའོ་ (yö̱nshao) ch. sweet dumplings made of glutinous rice flour.

ཡོན་ཧྲུའུ་ཤོག་བུ་ (yö̱nhru shɔ̄gbu) ch.tib. type of traditional Chinese paper.

ཡོན་ཟོང་ (yö̱nsoŋ) offerings to monks.

ཡོན་ཧྲི་ (yö̱nhri) sm. ཡོའན་ཀྲང་.

ཡོན་ཧྲོའེ་ (yö̱nhrowe) ch. commander in chief, field marshal.

ཡོབ་ (yo̱b) 1. stirrup. 2. sm. གཡོབ་. 4. pedal of a bike.

ཡོབ་སྐྱུལ་ (yo̱bgüü) sm. ཡོབ་བརྡུངས་.

ཡོབ་གོང་ (yo̱bgoŋ) instep of foot.

ཡོབ་རྒྱན་ (yo̱bgyɛn) engravings on a stirrup.

ཡོབ་ཆེན་ (yo̱bjen) sm. ཡོབ་, 1.

ཡོབ་སྟན་ (yo̱bdɛn) piece of felt used to protect the horse's belly from the stirrups.

ཡོབ་ཐག་ (yo̱bdaà) stirrup strap.

ཡོབ་མཐིལ་ (yo̱bdii) the part of the stirrup where the foot is placed.

ཡོབ་འདྲུད་ (yo̱bdrüù) being dragged by a horse with one foot stuck in the stirrup; vi.—གཏོང་.

ཡོབ་རྡུང་ (yo̱bduŋ) sm. ཡོབ་བརྡུངས་.

ཡོབ་བརྡུངས་ (yo̱bduŋ) spurring on by hitting the horse with one's stirrups; va.—གཏོང་.

ཡོབ་སྦྲུགས་ (yo̱bdruù) sm. ཡོབ་བརྡུངས་.

ཡོབ་ལང་ (yo̱blaŋ) standing up in the stirrups; va.—རྒྱག.

ཡོབ་ལུང་ (yo̱bluŋ) 1. the strap/ rope to which the stirrup is attached. 2. the stirrup ring.

ཡོམ་ (yo̱m) vi. to totter, to rock, to swing, to shake, to sway.

ཡོམ་འགུལ་ (yo̱mgüü) shaking, trembling.

ཡོམ་པོ་ (yo̱mbo) sm. ཡོམ་ཡོམ་.

ཡོམ་ཡོམ་ (yo̱myom) rocking, swaying, tottering, shaking; va.—བྱེད་.

ཡོམ་འབོག (yo̱mbɔɔ̀) 1. elm tree. 2. the bark of an elm tree.

ཡོམ་འབོགས་ཤིང་ (yo̱mbɔɔ̀ shi̱ŋ) sm. ཡོམ་འབོག.

ཡོམ་རིམ་ (yo̱mrim) sm. གཡོ་རིམ་.

ཡོའན་ (yo̱an) ch. office, yuan.

ཡོའན་ཀྲང་ (yo̱andraŋ) ch. dean or president of a college/ institute, director/ superintendent (of a hospital), chief justice (of a law court).

ཡོར་ (yɔ̱r) rinderpest.

ཡོར་དན་ (yɔ̱rdɛn) Jordan.

ཡོར་པོ་ (yɔ̱rbo) abbr. of ཡོར་ཡོར་པོ་.

ཡོར་ཡོར་ (yɔ̱ryɔɔ) sm. ཡོམ་ཡོམ་.

ཡོར་ཤིང་ (yɔ̱rshi̱ŋ) 1. sm. རྒྱ་ལྕང་. 2. sm. འོམ་བུ་.

ཡོལ་ (yö̱ö̱) 1. vi. to pass/ elapse (for time) ༡ ལོ་རྒྱུས་ཀྱི་དུས་རིམ་ཞིག་ཡོལ་ཚར་བ་རེད་ A historical period has passed. 2. curtain, drape, veil ༡ སྒོ་ཡོལ་ Door curtain.

ཡོལ་དཀར་ (yö̱ö̱gar) 1. white curtain. 2. movie screen.

ཡོལ་གོ་ (yö̱ö̱go) container.

ཡོལ་སྒོ་ (yö̱ö̱go) a cloth fence set up on all four sides (usu. in a park for privacy by those picnicking).

ཡོལ་སྒྲོམ་ (yö̱ö̱drom) 1. the wooden frame for a cloth screen/ partition/ divider. 2. a a cloth screen/ partition/ divider with a wooden frame.

ཡོལ་བཅད་ (yö̱ö̱jɛɛ̀) cloth screen/ partition divider (without a wooden frame); va.—འཐེན་ to put up such a partition/ divider.

ཡོལ་ཆེན་གློག་བརྙན་ (yö̱ö̱jen lɔ̄ɔ̀ñɛn) wide screen (for films), cinemascope.

ཡོལ་སྒྲིད་ (yö̱ö̱jɛɛ̀) shung. sm. ཤེར་པ་.

ཡོལ་བ་ (yö̱ö̱wa) 1. curtain, drape, veil, screen; va.—ཕྱེ་ to open/ raise a curtain; to inaugurate, to unveil; va.—རྒྱག་ to draw/ close a curtain; va.—གཏོང་ to put up curtains; va.—འཐེན་ to open/ close a curtain. 2. sm. དར་དཀར་ཡོལ་བ་.

ཡོལ་བའི་རྒྱབ་ (yö̱ö̱wɛ gya̱b) 1. behind the curtain. 2. behind the scenes.

ཡོལ་བའི་མདུན་ (yö̱ö̱wɛ dü̱n) 1. in front of the curtain. 2. open, not behind the scenes.

ཡོལ་འབྱེད་མཛད་སྒོ་ (yö̱ö̱jeè dzɛ̱ɛ̀go) inauguration ceremony.

ཡོལ་ལེ་ཡོད་ (yö̱ö̱le cȫö̀) not firm, undependable.

ཡོས་ (yö̱ö̀) 1. popped/ roasted grain; va.—རྔོ་ to pop/ roast grains. 2. rabbit, hare.

ཡོས་དཀྲུག (yö̱ö̀druù) wooden stick for turning and stirring grain when it is being popped/ roasted.

ཡོས་བཀྲ་ (yö̱ö̀dra) grain that has popped.

ཡོས་ཁུར་ (yö̱ö̀gur) basket used to keep roasted grain.

ཡོས་ཁྲ་ (yö̱ö̀dra) sm. ཡོས་བཀྲ་.

ཡོས་འགྲོ་ (yö̱ö̀dro) the hole where the popped grains are put in a water mill for grinding to tsamba.

ཡོས་སྒྱེ་ (yö̱ö̀gye) sack for popped grain.

ཡོས་ཆང་ (yö̱ö̀jaŋ) ཆང་ made from popped grain.

ཡོས་ནན་ (yö̱ö̀nɛn) sm. ཡོ་ནན་.

ཡོས་ཐུག (yö̱ö̀duù) soup made with popped grains.

ཡོས་དུགས་ (yö̱ö̀duù) hot popped grain applied to the body as a compress to treat certain ailments.

ཡོས་བུ་ (yö̱ö̀bu) 1. sm. ཡོས་. 2. domesticated/ tame rabbit.

ཡོས་བུ་གསོ་ར་ (yö̱ö̀bu sōra) rabbit farm.

ཡོས་ཟླ་ (yö̱nda) the second month of the Tibetan calendar.

ཡོས་ལོ་ (yö̱ö̀lo) year of the rabbit.

ཡོས་ལོ་པ་ (yö̱ö̀loba) a male born in the year of the rabbit.

ཡོས་ལོ་མ་ (yö̱ö̀loma) a female born in the year of the rabbit.

ཡོས་རྡལ་ (yö̱ö̀hrɛɛ) 1. coarsely ground popped grain that is used in soups; va.—འཐག་ to grind coarsely. 2. boasting, bragging; va.—འཐག་ to boast, to brag.

ཡོས་རྡལ་ཐུག་པ་ (yö̱ö̀hrɛɛ tūgbə) soup/ gruel made from coarsely ground popped barley.

གཡག (yāà) yak.

གཡག་ཀོ་ (yāàgɔ) yak skin/ hide.

གཡག་ཁྱུ་པ་ (yāà kyūwa) breeding/ stud yak.

གཡག་གྲུ་པ་ (yāà ga̱ba) white-faced yak.

གཡག་གི་ཁུ་ལུ་ (yāàgi kūlu) yak wool (the undercoat on the upper body of yaks).

གཡག་གི་རྫིད་པ་ (yāàgi dzībə) yak hair (the hair on the lower body/ belly of yaks).

གཡག་གློད་ (yāà lȫö̀) vi. to fart.

གཡག་མགོ་ (yāàŋgo) yak head.

གཡག་རྒོད་ (yāàgöö) wild yak.
གཡག་སྒ་ (yāàgaà) saddle for a yak.
གཡག་རྒྱབ་ (yāàgyəb) a load for a yak.
གཡག་རྔ་ (yāàŋa) yak tail.
གཡག་བཅག་ (yāgjaà) using yaks to walk over the grains to thresh the grain; va.—སྐོར་; —སྐོར་ to thresh with yaks.
གཡག་འཆག་ (yāgjaà) sm. གཡག་བཅག་སྐོར་.
གཡག་ཆེ་བས་ལྗི་བ་ཆེ་བ་གཏོང་གི་མ་རེད་ (yāg cēwɛɛ̀ jīwa cēwa dōŋgi mareè) rich people will not give big presents or be more generous [Lit. big yaks will not pass big dung].
གཡག་ཆེན་ (yāgjen) bullheaded, obstinate, disorderly, rebellious.
གཡག་རྗེས་ (yāgjeè) shung. sm. གཡག་པ་.
གཡག་ཐེར་ (yāgder) a type of woolen cloth made in གཡག་སྡེ་.
གཡག་སྡེ་ (yāgde) a place in central Tibet.
གཡག་པ་ (yāgba) 1. yak herder. 2. a small hoe-like implement.
གཡག་ལྤགས་ (yāgbaà) yak skin.
གཡག་ཕྲུག (yəgdruù) yak calf.
གཡག་ཚུགས་ (yəgdzuù) a day's journey with a loaded yak ¶ གཡག་ཚུགས་ལྔ་ A five day trip (for men with yaks).
གཡག་འཚོང་ (yāgdzoŋ) sm. ཁྱིབ་འཚོང་.
གཡག་རྫི་ (yəgdzi) sm. གཡག་པ་, 1.
གཡག་ཞར་བས་རྩྭ་བཟས་པ་ལྟར་ (yāà sharwɛɛ̀ dzā sɛ̀ɛbadar) blindly doing things, not doing things completely [Lit. like a blind yak eating grass].
གཡག་ཡུ་བོ་ (yāà yuwo) hornless yak.
གཡག་ར་ (yāgra) yak corral.
གཡག་རུ་ (yəgru) yak horn.
གཡག་རུ་དྲག་ཆོས་ (yəgru drajöö) a curse/ spell that is put in the horn of a yak.
གཡག་རོག་ཤོལ་ཆེན་ (yəgroò shööjen) uncastrated/ stud yak.
གཡག་ལག་ (yāglag) a set/ unit of twenty (or sometimes ten) transport yaks.
གཡག་ཤ་ (yāgsha) yak meat.
གཡག་ཤི་འབྲོང་ཆད་ (yāàshi droŋcɛɛ̀) persisting to the very end [Lit. yaks die, wild yaks get exhausted].
གཡག་ཤུག་ (yāgshuù) a type of thorny juniper tree.
གཡག་ཤིང་ (yāgshiŋ) latch, bolt.
གཡག་བཤས་ (yāgshɛɛ̀) slaughtering/ buthcering yaks; va.—གཏོང་ to slaughter/ buthcher yaks (for food).
གཡག་ཨ་ཡུ་ (yāg āyu) hornless yak.
གཡང་ (yāŋ) 1. sm. གཡང་ས་. 2. auspicious, lucky, good fortune; va.—ཤོར་ to lose one's luck/ fortune/ prosperity; va.—འགུགས་ to do things to restore one's fortune/ luck. 3. ch. sheep.
གཡང་དཀར་ (yāŋgar) sheep.
གཡང་དཀར་ལུག (yāŋ gārlug) sm. གཡང་དཀར་.
གཡང་བཀྲག (yāŋ gyāà) sm. གཡེང་བཀྲག.
གཡང་ཁ་ (yāŋga) 1. sm. གཡང་ས་. 2. the lid/ door of a གཡང་སྒམ་.
གཡང་ཁང་ (yāŋgaŋ) the room in which the "fortune" box (གཡང་སྒམ་) is kept to bring wealth to the family.
གཡང་ཁུག (yəŋguù) 1. bag/ pouch for auspicious/ good-luck objects. 2. vi. to have good fortune come.
གཡང་གྲོད་རལ་ (yāŋdröö rɛɛ) vi. to have a person who has had good fortune die.
གཡང་སྒམ་ (yāŋgam) box with religious objects and precious things that is considered to bring luck and good fortune.
གཡང་འགུགས་ (yāŋguù) doing rites/ practices that brings luck and good fortune; va. གཡང་འགུགས་; —བྱེད་.
གཡང་སྒྲུབ་ (yāŋdrub) a ritual for bringing luck and good fortune; va.—བྱེད་.
གཡང་སྒྲོམ་ (yāŋdrom) sm. གཡང་སྒམ་.
གཡང་ཅན་ (yāŋjɛn) sm. གཡང་ཆེན་པོ་.
གཡང་ཆགས་ (yāŋ cāà) vi. to have/ get good fortune and luck.
གཡང་ཆས་ (yāŋjɛɛ̀) auspicious/ lucky things.
གཡང་ཆེན་པོ་ (yāŋ cēmbo) good luck/ fortune.
གཡང་ཏྲི་ (yəŋdri) sm. གཡང་ཏི་.
གཡང་ཏི་ (yəŋdi) a jade-like stone (nephrite).
གཡང་ཏི་སྔོན་མོ་ (yəŋdi ŋōmbo) green nephrite.
གཡང་ཏིའི་དཀར་ཡོལ་ (yəŋdi gāàyöö) bowl made from nephrite.
གཡང་རྟེན་ (yāŋden) an auspicious/ lucky object (that a family keeps to bring it good fortune).
གཡང་དར་ (yāŋdar) a ceremonial arrow having ribbons of different colors that is used in the གཡང་འགུགས་ rite.
གཡང་མདའ་ (yāŋda) good fortune/ good luck arrow.
གཡང་ནོར་ (yāŋnɔɔ) an object that is a symbol of good fortune and luck.
གཡང་བུམ་ (yāŋbum) a good fortune/ good luck vase.
གཡང་འབོད་ (yāŋböö) a ritual that calls for good fortune.
གཡང་མོ་ (yāŋmo) sm. གཡང་དཀར་.
གཡང་ཙེ་ (yāŋdze) ch. pattern.
གཡང་རྩེ་ (yāŋdze) sm. ཡང་རྩེ་.
གཡང་རྩེའི་སྟེང་གི་ཡས་སྒྲོན་ (yāŋdzee dēŋgi yɛɛ̀drön) sm. ཡག་ཐོག་ཡག་རྩེག.
གཡང་རྩེའི་སྟེང་དུ་མ་ར་ཀྱི་ཡས་བཞེད་རྒྱང་པ་ (yāŋdzee dēŋgdu maagi yɛɛ̀seè gyagba) sm. ཡག་ཐོག་ཡག་རྩེག.
གཡང་རྫས་ (yāŋdzɛɛ̀) the contents of the good luck/ good fortune vase or box (གཡང་སྒམ་).
གཡང་གཞི་ (yāŋshi) 1. a complete human skin. 2. complete animal skin including the head and feet.
གཡང་བཞག (yāŋshaà) sm. གཡང་ཤ་.
གཡང་ཟ་པོ་ (yāŋ sabo) overly cautious, frightened ¶ མི་དེ་གཡང་ཟ་པོ་སོང་ཙང་ལས་ཀ་དེ་བྱེད་ཡོད་ཀྱི་མ་རེད་ Because that person is overly cautious, he doesn't dare to do the work.
གཡང་ཟ་ (yāŋ sawa) vi. to get frightened/ scared.
གཡང་ཟེ་ (yāŋse) edge of a precipice.
གཡང་གཟའ་ (yāŋsa) Saturday.
གཡང་གཟར་པོ་ (yāŋ sarbo) steep.
གཡང་རོང་ (yāŋroŋ) steep/ precipitous ravine.
གཡང་ལུག (yāŋluù) good luck/ good fortune sheep.
གཡང་ལུགས་ (yəŋluù) a dress worn without being tied at the waist by a belt.
གཡང་ཤ་ (yāŋsha) meat used in the (གཡང་སྒམ་) "fortune box" for good luck.
གཡང་ཤོར་ (yāŋ shɔɔ) vi. to lose one's good fortune/ luck.
གཡང་ཤམ་ (yāŋsham) draping sth. (usu. coats) over one's shoulder; va.—བྱེད་.
གཡང་ས་ (yāŋsa) a deep ravine/ gorge/ precipice/ abyss.
གཡང་གསོལ་ (yāŋsöö) sm. གཡང་སྒྲུབ་.
གཡང་ལྷ་ (yāŋlha) deity of good fortune.
གཡངས་ (yāŋ) 1. sm. ཡིང་. 2. sm. གཡེང་.
གཡན་པ་ (yɛ̄mba) ringworm and similar skin diseases that cause itching.
གཡན་པ་རྒྱ་ཐོར་ (yɛ̄mba gyadɔr) a pimples that grow into sores after scratching.
གཡན་པ་འཕྲུག (yɛ̄mba trūù) va. to scratch an itch.
གཡབ་ (yəb) any roof-like projection, a verandah/ porch; va.—རྒྱག to put up a verandah/ overhanging roof.
གཡབ་ (yəb) 1. f. of གཡོབ་. 2. va. to beckon. 3. va. to have sexual intercourse.
གཡབ་འཁོར་ (yəbgɔɔ) verandah running around a house.
གཡབ་ཆུང་ (yəbjuŋ) 1. a narrow verandah. 2. taking sth. lightly; va.—བྱེད་; —གཏོང་ to take work lightly; to look down on sb. (take them lightly).

གཡབ་སྡེང་ (yābdeŋ) verandah (on an upper floor).

གཡབ་དར་ (yābdar) pieces of colored silk that hang down.

གཡབ་ལྡན་ར་བ་ (yābdɛn r̲awa) a corral with a verandah-like roof.

གཡབ་པ་ (yābba) wooden farm implement used to collect grains on the threshing flour.

གཡབ་མེད་འཁོར་ལོ་ (yābmeè kɔ̄ɔlo) convertible car/ truck, vehicle without a roof.

གཡབ་མོ་ (yābmu) a hand signal/ gesture indicating come; va.—འདེབས་; —རྒྱག to wave with hand to come.

གཡབ་གཡུག (yābyuù) sm. གཡབ་གཡོབ་.

གཡབ་གཡུབ་ (yābyub) sm. གཡབ་གཡོབ་.

གཡབ་གཡོབ་ (yābyob) waving, beckoning, signaling (with hands to come); va.—བྱེད་; —རྒྱག to wave, to beckon, to give a sign/ signal with one's hands.

གཡབ་རིང་ (yābriŋ) a long covered corridor/ verandah.

གཡབ་ཤིང་ (yābshiŋ) sm. གཡབ་པ་.

གཡབས་ (yāb) p. of གཡོབ་.

གཡམ་རྒྱུགས་ (yāmgyuù) going astray by following other's views; va.—བྱེད་ ། མི་གཞན་གྱི་རྗེས་སུ་གཡམ་རྒྱུགས་བྱེད་རྒྱུ་མེད་ One should not follow others.

གཡམ་པ་ (yāmba) a slate.

གཡམ་ལ་རྒྱུག (yāmla gyu̲ù) sm. གཡམ་རྒྱུགས་བྱེད་.

གཡམ་ལེབ་ (yāmleb) sm. གཡམ་པ་.

གཡའ་ (yā) 1. tarnish, oxidation; va.—རྒྱག; —ཆགས་; —འཁོར་; —འདུལ་ ། དངུལ་གཡའ་ Silver tarnish. 2. sm. གཡའ་ཤིང་. 3. manner, style, shape (negative connotation) ། མི་དེ་ལ་རྐུ་མའི་གཡའ་ཞིག་འདུག That man has the manner of a thief. 4. vi. to feel itchy, to itch. 5. a symptom/ sign ། ན་ཚའི་གཡའ་ A sign of illness. 6. a mountain that contains slate.

གཡའ་ཁྲོད་ (yādröö) hills containing slate.

གཡའ་མཁྲང་བ་ (yā trāŋwa) the dead skin caused by scratching.

གཡའ་རྒྱག་དཀའ་བ་ (yāgyaà gāāwa) anticorrosive, rustproof, tarnishproof.

གཡའ་སྒོག (yā g̲ɔɔ̀) 1. va. to tickle. 2. a kind of wild garlic.

གཡའ་ཆུ་ (yāju) a stream coming from a གཡའ་རི་.

གཡའ་དག (yā t̲aà) 1. vi. to clear up (for sky, weather). 2. vi. to be/ get cleared/ cleaned of tarnish.

གཡའ་དུག (yāduù) tarnish; vi.—ཐོག to get tarnished.

གཡའ་རྡོ་ (yādo) slate.

གཡའ་དྭངས་ (yā t̲aŋ) clear (cloudless) sky; vi.—(སུ་) འགྲོ་ to become clear ། ལྷ་སའི་གནམ་གཤིས་མང་ཆེ་བ་གཡའ་དྭངས་རེད་ The weather in Lhasa is mainly clear.

གཡའ་ནད་ (yānɛɛ̀) a disease characterized by itching.

གཡའ་སྤང་ (yābaŋ) 1. abbr. of གཡའ་རི་ and སྤང་རི་. 2. an area on a mountain with both grass/ meadows and slate.

གཡའ་ཕིན་ (yābin) ch. opium.

གཡའ་ཕྱིས་ (yājii) wiping off the tarnish; va.—རྒྱག.

གཡའ་བག (yābaà) 1. sign, symptom. 2. tarnish.

གཡའ་བྲག (yādraà) abbr. of གཡའ་རི་ and བྲག་རི་.

གཡའ་བྲལ (yādrɛɛ) cloudless, fogless, clear ། གཡའ་བྲལ་ནམ་མཁའ་ Cloudless sky.

གཡའ་མ་ (yāma) sm. གཡའ་རྡོ་.

གཡའ་སྨྱུག (yāñuù) slate pencil.

གཡའ་མཚམས་ (yāndzam) the dividing line between the upper and lower part of a slate hill.

གཡའ་ཡང་མེད་ (yā ya̲ŋmeè) no trace ། ང་ཨ་རི་ལ་འགྲོ་དུས་བོད་པ་ཡིན་པའི་གཡའ་ཡང་མེད་པའི་བོད་པའི་བུད་མོ་ཞིག་ཐུག་བྱུང་ When I went to America I met a Tibetan girl who did not show a trace of being Tibetan.

གཡའ་རི་ (yāri) slate mountain.

གཡའ་ཤིང་ (yāshiŋ) bolt (of a door); va.—རྒྱག to bolt a door.

གཡའ་སེལ་ (yā sēl) 1. va. to clean tarnish. 2. va. to correct/ edit writing.

གཡར་: p. and f. གཡར་; imp. གཡོར་ (yāā) 1. va. to borrow, to lend ། ངས་ཁོང་གི་ས་ནས་དངུལ་གཡར་བ་ཡིན་ I borrowed money from him. ། ངས་ཁོང་ལ་དངུལ་གཡར་བ་ཡིན་ I lent him money. 2. face (h.).

གཡར་སྐྱི་ (yārgyi) sm. གཡར་.

གཡར་ཁང་ (yārgaŋ) rental house, a house that is rented or for rent.

གཡར་ཁམས་ (yārkam) the body.

གཡར་ཁམས་བདེ་ཞིང་ (yārkam d̲eshiŋ) being in good health.

གཡར་ཁྲལ་ (yārdrɛɛ) work that one must do.

གཡར་གྲངས་ (yārdraŋ) borrowed number (in math).

གཡར་གླ་ (yārla) rental fee.

གཡར་ངོ་ (yārŋo) face.

གཡར་དངུལ་ (yārŋüü) money borrowed/ loaned.

གཡར་དངོས་ (ya̲rŋuoò) borrowed/ lent goods.

གཡར་སྔ་ (yārŋa) sm. སྤྱན་སྔ་.

གཡར་སྔར་ (yārŋar) gift, present.

གཡར་གཏོང་ (yār dōŋ) va. to lend ། ངས་ཁོ་ལ་དངུལ་གཡར་བཏང་བ་ཡིན་ I lent him money.

གཡར་དམ་ (yārdam) oath, pledge, vow.

གཡར་དེབ་ (yārdeb) book in which things that are lent are recorded.

གཡར་པོ་ (yārbo) lending; va.—གཏོང་ to loan, to give a loan; va.—ཞུ་ to ask for a loan, to borrow from sb.

གཡར་པོ་བདག་རེངས་ (ya̲rbo da̲àreŋ) not returning things that have been borrowed; va.—བྱེད་.

གཡར་པོ་གནང་ (yārbo nāŋ) h. of གཡར་པོ་ (གཏོང་).

གཡར་པོ་འབུལ་ (ya̲rbo bü̲ü) h. of གཡར་པོ་ (གཏོང་).

གཡར་དཔེ་ (yārbe) metaphor, figurative example.

གཡར་འབུལ་ (yārbüü) abbr. of གཡར་པོ་འབུལ་.

གཡར་འབུལ་ཞུ་ (yārbüü shu̲) sm. གཡར་པོ་འབུལ་.

གཡར་འབྲུ་ (yār dru̲) summer barley.

གཡར་ཚ་ (yārdza) arc. sm. ངོ་ཚ་.

གཡར་ཚིག (yārdzii) borrowed words (from another language).

གཡར་ཚུས་ (ya̲rdzüü) arc. food.

གཡར་འཛིན་ (yāŋdzin) certificate of indebtedness, receipt for a loan.

གཡར་ཞལ་ (yārshɛɛ) h. of གདོང་.

གཡར་ཞུ་ (yār shu̲) abbr. of གཡར་པོ་ཞུ་.

གཡར་གཞུང་ (yārshuŋ) shung. government lists of things that are borrowed (from monasteries and big aristocratic families).

གཡར་ལེན་ (yārlen) va. to borrow.

གཡལ་ (yɛ̄ɛ) sm. གཡལ་སྡོང་.

གཡལ་སྡོང་ (yɛ̄ɛdoŋ) yawning; vi.—རྒྱག to yawn.

གཡལ་འདར་ (yɛ̄ɛdar) the shiver that often accompanies yawning.

གཡལ་སྙལ་ (yɛ̄ɛñɛɛ) sm. གཡལ་སྙོང་.

གཡལ་སྙོང་ (yɛ̄ɛñoŋ) yawning and stretching; va.—བྱེད་.

གཡལ་ལི་གཡོལ་ལི་ (yɛ̄ɛle yööle) fooling around, not doing diligently, avoiding work ། མི་དེ་ནས་ལས་ཀར་གཡལ་ལི་གཡོལ་ལི་བྱས་ནས་དུས་ཚོད་འཕྲོ་བརླག་གཏོང་གི་འདུག That person is fooling around and wasting time instead of working.

གཡས་ (yɛ̄ɛ̀) right (side).

གཡས་དཀར་གཡོན་ནག (yɛ̄ɛ̀gar yönnaà) unfair, unjust; va.—བྱེད་.

གཡས་དཀར་གཡོན་ནག་མེད་པ་ (yɛ̄ɛ̀gar yönnaà me̲èba) impartial, unbiased, fair.

གཡས་སྐོར་ (yɛ̄ɛ̀gɔɔ) clockwise; va.—རྒྱག; —འགྲོ་ to go around sth. clockwise/ to the right.

གཡས་སྐྱོར་གཡོན་སྐྱོར་ (yɛ̄ɛ̀gɔɔ yöngyɔɔ) supporting sb. from both sides; va.—བྱེད་.

གཡས་བསྐོར་ (yɛ̄ɛ̀gɔɔ) sm. གཡས་སྐོར་.

གཡས་ཁག་གཡོན་དཀྲི་ (yɛ̄ɛ̀gaà yöndri) blaming each other; va.—བྱེད་.

གཡས་འཁྱིལ་ (yɛ̄ɛ̀gyii) circular patterns that go

clockwise.

གཡས་འཁྱིལ་གཡོན་འཁྱིལ (yɛ̄ɛ̀kyɔɔ̀ yǒnkyɔɔ̀) 1. meandering, winding (of rivers, roads). 2. biased; va.—བྱེད་ to be biased.

གཡས་འཁྱིལ་གཡོན་འཁྱིལ་མེད་པ་ (yɛ̄ɛ̀kyɔɔ̀ yǒnkyɔɔ̀ me̱ɛ̀ba) va. to be unbiased/ just/ fair.

གཡས་གུམ་རྒྱག (yɛ̄ɛ̀gum gya̱à) va. to make one's kite make circles to the right side in the sky.

གཡས་གོང་ (yɛ̄ɛ̀goŋ) upper right side.

གཡས་གྲལ་ (yɛ̄ɛ̀drɛɛ) the row(s) on the right side.

གཡས་སྐྱུར་ (yɛ̄ɛ̀ gyu̱r) turn right! (as in drill commands).

གཡས་ངོས་ (yɛ̄ɛ̀ŋöö̀) right side/ direction.

གཡས་ཆུང་ (yɛ̄ɛ̀juŋ) sm. གཡབ་ཆུང་.

གཡས་འཛགས་གཡོན་ལངས་ (yɛ̄njaà yǒnlaŋ) uprising that is difficult to control because one side rises up as another gets suppressed or dies down [Lit. the right side calms, the left side rises].

གཡས་སྙིང་ཤག (yɛ̄ɛ̀ñīŋ shāà) right ventricle.

གཡས་ལྟ་གཡོན་ལྟ་ (yɛ̄ɛ̀da yǒnda) looking left and right, looking around.

གཡས་ཐལ་ (yɛ̄ɛ̀ tēē) ultraright, too far right (politically).

གཡས་དུང་ (yɛ̄ɛ̀duŋ) sm. དུང་གཡས་.

གཡས་དར་གཡོན་དར་ (yɛ̄ɛ̀dar yǒndar) a file that is rough on both sides.

གཡས་སྡེ་ (yɛ̄ɛ̀de) village/ town situated on the right side.

གཡས་ནས་རྩི་ (yɛ̄ɛ̀nɛ dzī) va. to calculate/ count from right to left.

གཡས་པ་ (yɛ̄ɛ̀ba) right ༡ལག་པ་གཡས་པ་ Right-handed.

གཡས་སྤྱན་གཡོན་མིག (yɛ̄ɛ̀jɛn yǒnmiì) sm. གཡས་དཀར་གཡོན་ནག.

གཡས་ཕྱེད་ (yɛ̄ɛ̀jeè) the right half (of body, etc.).

གཡས་ཕྱོགས་ (yɛ̄ɛ̀jɔɔ̀) sm. གཡས་ངོས་.

གཡས་ཕྱོགས་པ་ (yɛ̄ɛ̀jɔɔ̀ba) rightist, right winger.

གཡས་ཕྱོགས་ཤོག་ཁ་ (yɛ̄ɛ̀jɔɔ̀ shɔ̄ɔ̀gaà) rightist clique/ group.

གཡས་བྱས་གཡོན་ཤོར་ (yɛ̄ɛ̀cɛ̄ɛ̀ yǒnshɔɔ) unable to take care of the whole situation [Lit. do the right, lose the left].

གཡས་སྨད་ (yɛ̄ɛ̀mɛɛ̀) lower right section of sth.

གཡས་ཞ་གཡོན་འཕྱིང་ (yɛ̄ɛ̀sha yǒndeŋ) treating people in a biased/ unfair way.

གཡས་ཞར་མ་ (yɛ̄ɛ̀ sha̱rma) a female who is blind in the right eye.

གཡས་གཞོགས་ (yɛ̄ɛ̀shɔɔ̀) sm. གཡས་ངོས་.

གཡས་གཞོགས་གུང་བློན་ (yɛ̄ɛ̀shɔɔ̀ ku̱nlön) a minister who is the right side assistant of the Emperor.

གཡས་གཞོགས་གཡོན་འདེགས་ (yɛ̄ɛ̀shɔɔ̀ yǒndeg) cooperating, helping each other in a united effort; va.—བྱེད་ to cooperate together.

གཡས་འོག (yɛ̄ɛ̀wɔɔ̀) sm. གཡས་སྨད་.

གཡས་ཟིན་གཡོན་ཤོར་ (yɛ̄ɛ̀sin yǒnshɔɔ) sm. གཡས་བྱས་གཡོན་ཤོར་.

གཡས་གཡུག (yɛ̄ɛ̀yuù) beckoning, waving; va.—རྒྱག to beckon, to wave.

གཡས་གཡོན་ (yɛ̄ɛ̀yön) right and left, both sides, either side ༡ལམ་ཁའི་གཡས་གཡོན་ལ་ཁང་པ་འདུག There are houses on both sides of the street.

གཡས་གཡོན་མེད་པ་ (yɛ̄ɛ̀yön me̱ɛ̀ba) neither right nor left.

གཡས་རུ་ (yɛ̄ɛ̀ru) 1. right wing, right flank. 2. one of the four ancient རུ་ of དབུས་གཙང་.

གཡས་རུ་དང་ཤོག (yɛ̄ɛ̀ru dāŋshɔɔ̀) rightist party/ clique.

གཡས་རུ་ཕྱོགས་ཁག (yɛ̄ɛ̀ru cɔ̄ɔ̀gaà) sm. གཡས་རུ་དང་ཤོག.

གཡས་རུ་པ་ (yɛ̄ɛ̀rubə) right-winger, conservative.

གཡས་རུ་དཔུང་སྒར་ (yɛ̄ɛ̀ru būŋgar) rightist camp.

གཡས་ལག (yɛ̄ɛ̀laà) right-handed.

གཡས་ལམ་ (yɛ̄ɛ̀lam) the road/ route on the right side.

གཡས་ལོགས་ (yɛ̄ɛ̀lɔɔ̀) sm. གཡས་ངོས་.

གཡས་ཤོག (yɛ̄ɛ̀shɔɔ̀) abbr. of གཡས་ཕྱོགས་ཤོག་ཁ་.

གཡས་ཤོར་གཡོན་འདེགས་ (yɛ̄ɛ̀shɔ̄ɔ̀ yo̱ndeg) helping/ supporting each other.

གཡས་བཤད་གཡོན་ཤུ་ (yɛ̄ɛ̀shɛɛ̀ yǒnshu) saying sth. everywhere [Lit. say from the left, say from the right].

གཡས་སུ་ལྷུང་བ་ (yɛ̄ɛ̀su lhūŋwa) right wing, deviation.

གཡས་གསེག (yɛ̄ɛ̀sii) leaning/ sloping to the right.

གཡས་ལྷུང་ (yɛ̄ɛ̀lhuŋ) sm. གཡས་སུ་ལྷུང་བ་.

གཡས་ལྷུང་སྐབས་འཚོལ་རིང་ལུགས་ (yɛ̄ɛ̀luŋ gābdzöö ri̱ŋluù) rightist opportunism.

གཡས་ལྷུང་སྐབས་འཚོལ་རིང་ལུགས་པ་ (yɛ̄ɛ̀lhuŋ gābdzöö ri̱ŋluù) rightist viewpoint opportunist.

གཡས་ལྷུང་གི་ལྟ་ཚུལ་ (yɛ̄ɛ̀lhuŋgi də̄dzüü) rightist, rightist-deviationist viewpoint.

གཡས་ལྷུང་གི་བསམ་ཚུལ་ (yɛ̄ɛ̀lhuŋgi sāmdzüü) right wing deviationist sentiment/ thought.

གཡས་ལྷུང་བག་འཁུམས་ (yɛ̄ɛ̀lhuŋ pa̱ggum) right-wing conservative.

གཡི་ (yī) lynx.

གཡི་བརྡར་ཤོར་ (yīdaa shɔ̄ɔ̄) vi. to slip.

གཡི་ལྤགས་ (yībaà) lynx skin.

གཡི་སྤྱང་ (yījaŋ) abbr. of གཡི་ and སྤྱང་ཀི་.

གཡིག : p. གཡིགས་; f. གཡིག (yiì) 1. vi. to hiccup. 2. vi. to have one's mouth tingle (as when one eats Sichuan peppercorns).

གཡིག་པ་ (yīgbə) hiccup; vi.—རྒྱག.

གཡིགས་ (yīì) tingling sensation.

གཡིགས་ (yīì) p. of གཡིག.

གཡིའུ་ (yīwu) young yak.

གཡིས་ (yīì) mustard seed oil.

གཡིས་ཁང་ (yīìgaŋ) building where mustard seed is pressed into oil.

གཡིས་རྡོ་ (yīìdo) stone used for crushing/ pressing mustard seeds.

གཡིས་འཚག་ཁང་ (yīìdzaàgaŋ) oil pressing factory.

གཡིས་ཟོ་ (yīìso) oil drum/ container.

གཡུ་ (yū) turquoise.

གཡུ་བརྐོས་ (yūgöö̀) etching/ engraving turquoise; va.—རྒྱག.

གཡུ་སྔོན་ (yūŋön) woman's name.

གཡུ་ཆུང་གྲུ་དཀར་ (yūjuŋ dru̱gar) a type of whitish turquoise.

གཡུ་རྙིང་ (yūñiŋ) old turquoise (used in Tibetan medicine).

གཡུ་ཐོག (yūtoò) 1. name of aristocratic family in Tibet. 2. turquoise color glazed roof.

གཡུ་ཐོག་ཟམ་པ་ (yūtoò sa̱mba) the name of a famous covered bridge in Lhasa.

གཡུ་དང་དུ་ལོ་མཉམ་བསྲེས་ (yūdaŋ to̱lo ñāmseè) mixing the good and the bad [Lit. mixing real turquoise with blue beads].

གཡུ་དྲུག་དམར་ (yū dru̱gmar) a type of reddish-color turquoise.

གཡུ་མདོག (yūdɔɔ̀) turquoise color.

གཡུ་ནར་ནར་ (yū na̱rnar) an elongated piece of turquoise.

གཡུ་སྦུར་ (yūbur) a turquoise stud earring worn both by Tibetan women and men.

གཡུ་ཕྲ་ (yūdra) turquoise pieces stuck on gold or other ornaments.

གཡུ་བུར་ (yūbur) 1. sm. གཡུ་སྦུར་. 2. turquoise and coral.

གཡུ་བྱུར་ (yūcur) turquoise and coral.

གཡུ་འབྲུག (yūndruù) type of dragon design.

གཡུ་སྦྲང་ (yūdraŋ) bee, wasp.

གཡུ་རྫི་ (yūdzi) turquoise (green) glaze.

གཡུ་རྫི་སྔོ་དཀར་ (yūdzi ŋōgar) light blue turquoise glaze.

གཡུ་རྫི་བརྐོས་མ་ (yūdzi gö̀ōma) turquoise glazed statue.

གཡུ་མཚོ་ (yūmdzo) blue lake/ sea.

གཡུ་ཞགས་སྒོར་མོ་ (yūshaà go̱rmo) turquoise with a circular hole.

གཡུ་ལོ་ (yūlo) turquoise colored leaves.

གཡུ་ལོ་རྒྱས་པ་ (yūlo gyɛ̀ɛba) 1. luxuriant flourishing. 2. with regard to work: abundant, lots of success, good achievement.

གཡུ་གཤོངས་ (yūshoŋ) lush green (for scenery).

གཡུ་བཤད་ (yūshɛ̀ɛ) custom of a mother-in-law welcoming a new bride by placing a turquoise on the bride's head and a person reciting auspicious sayings.

གཡུ་གསར་ (yūsar) new turquoise (used in Tibetan medicine).

གཡུག: p. གཡུགས་; f. གཡུག; imp. གཡུགས་ (yūù) 1. va. to throw ¶ཁོས་རྡོ་ཞིག་གཡུགས་པ་རེད་ He threw a stone. 2. va. to swing ¶ཁོས་གྲི་གཡུགས་ནས་མིའི་མགོ་བཅད་པ་རེད་ He swung his sword and cut off the man's head. ¶ཁོང་ལག་པ་གཡུགས་ནས་འགྲོ་གི་འདུག He is going along swinging his hands.

གཡུག་འཇོག (yūg jɔ̀ɔ) va. to leave off/ stop doing sth., to set sth. aside, to leave alone ¶ལས་ཀ་མ་ཚར་གོང་གཡུག་འཇོག་རྒྱུ་མེད་ You should not leave off the work before completing it.

གཡུག་སྨན་ (yūgmɛn) weed killer, weed killing herbicide.

གཡུག་བརྡ་ (yūgda) the sword and spear carried by Tibetan oracles when going into trance.

གཡུག་གཡུག (yūùyuù) waving; va.—བྱེད་; —གཏོང་ to wave, to shake, to wag ¶མེ་ཏོག་ཆུན་པོ་གཡུག་གཡུག་བྱས་ཏེ་ Waving a bouquet of flowers. ¶གཞུག་མ་གཡུག་གཡུག་བྱས་ཏེ་ Wagging (their tails).

གཡུགས་ (yūù) p. of གཡུག.

གཡུགས་ཤོག (yūgshoò) an idiom conveying: never mind, forget it, leave it alone.

གཡུགས་བཞག (yūgshaà) p. of གཡུགས་འཇོག.

གཡང་དགོན་ (yūŋgön) abbr. of གཡུང་ཧོ་གོང་.

གཡུང་ཛ་ (yūŋdza) abbr. of གཡང་དགོན་ཛ་སག.

གཡུང་དགོན་ཛ་སག (yūŋgön dza̱saà) shung. title of the Tibetan monk official sent as abbot to གཡུང་ཧོ་གོང་ Monastery in Beijing.

གཡུང་དྭགས་ (yūŋdag) domestic animals.

གཡུང་དྲུང་ (yūŋdruŋ) swastika.

གཡུང་དྲུང་གི་མདུད་རྒྱ་ (yūŋdruŋgi dü̱ügya) shung. a permanent contract ¶གཉེན་ཡིག་རྟགས་ཅན་གཡུང་དྲུང་གི་མདུད་རྒྱ་གཉིས་ Two copies of the permanent marriage contract.

གཡུང་དྲུང་པ་ (yūŋdruŋbə) sm. བོན་པོ་.

གཡུང་དྲུང་ལག་འབྱུད་ (yūŋdruŋ la̱ggyüù) a type of design containing swastikas.

གཡུང་པོ་ (yūŋbu) person of low caste in India.

གཡུང་བ་ (yūŋwə) 1. well-tamed (for animals). 2. feeble/ weak in body. 3. inferior goods/ items. 4. sm. གཡུང་པོ་.

གཡུང་བབ་ (yūŋ bə̱b) vi. to become well-tamed. 2. vi. to run slowly (of water).

གཡུང་མ་ (yūŋma) sm. གཡུང་བ་.

གཡུང་མོ་ (yūŋmo) female of low caste in India.

གཡུང་ལག (yūŋlaà) sm. གཡུང་དྲུང་ལག་འབྱུད་.

གཡུང་ཧོ་དགོན་ (yu̱ŋhogön) name of the major Gelugpa Monastery in Beijing.

གཡུར་དུ་ཟ་ (yūrdu sa̱) abbr. of གཡུར་ཟ་.

གཡུར་བ་ (yūrwə) sm. ཡུར་བ་.

གཡུར་ཟ་ (yūrsa) fully ripe ¶ཤིང་སྡོང་ལ་ཤིང་འབྲས་གཡུར་ཟ་བ་བཏགས་འདུག The fruit on the tree is fully ripe. ¶སློབ་སྦྱོང་གི་འབྲས་བུ་གཡུར་ཟ་བ་ཐོབ་པ་རེད་ (His) education was fruitful (got excellent results).

གཡུར་ཟ་བ་ (yūrsawa) sm. གཡུར་ཟ་.

གཡུལ་ (yǖǖ) 1. battle, war, fighting ¶དམག་དཔུང་གཡུལ་དུ་འགྲོ་ The army is going/ marching to battle. 2. abbr. of གཡུལ་ཁ་.

གཡུལ་ཀ་ (yǖǖgə) sm. གཡུལ་ཁ་.

གཡུལ་ཁ་ (yǖǖgə) 1. threshing ground; va.—གཏོང་; —གཙོག; —རྡུང་ to thresh; va.—སྐེམ་ to dry grain on a threshing ground. 2. battlefield.

གཡུལ་མཁའི་ཁྲ་སྒྲིག (yǖǖgö tra̱driì) sm. གཡུལ་གཤོམ་.

གཡུལ་མཁའི་ཡོ་ཆས་ (yǖǖgö yo̱jɛ̀ɛ) war implements/ materials.

གཡུལ་འཁྲུག (yǖǖdruù) war.

གཡུལ་གྱི་ཁ་ལོ་པ་ (yǖǖgi kāloba) military commander.

གཡུལ་གྱི་ངོ་ (yǖǖgi ŋo̱) 1. battlefield. 2. a sign of pending war.

གཡུལ་གྱི་ལས་གཤོམ་ (yǖǖgi lɛ̀ɛshom) sm. གཡུལ་གཤོམ་.

གཡུལ་གྲུ་ (yǖǖdru) warship, battleship.

གཡུལ་འགྱེད་ (yǖǖgyeè) battle, conflict, war.

གཡུལ་འགྱེད་ས་ཁུལ་ (yǖǖgyeè səgüü) war zone, battle area.

གཡུལ་རྒྱགས་ (yǖǖgyaà) military provisions.

གཡུལ་རྒྱལ་ (yǖǖgyɛɛ) military victory ¶གཡུལ་རྒྱལ་བཀྲ་ཤིས་བདེ་ལེགས་ Congratulations on a military victory.

གཡུལ་རྒྱལ་ཕྱིར་ལོག (yǖǖgyɛɛ cīīlɔ̀ɔ) returning from a war after victory.

གཡུལ་རྒྱལ་ལེགས་འབུལ་ (yǖǖgyɛɛ le̱nbüü) congratulations on a military victory.

གཡུལ་ངོ་ (yǖǖŋo) sm. གཡུལ་ས་.

གཡུལ་ངོ་བསུ་ (yǖǖŋo sū) va. to challenge/ confront somebody who is fighting.

གཡུལ་ཆས་ (yǖǖjɛ̀ɛ) abbr. of གཡུལ་མཁའི་ཡོ་ཆས་.

གཡུལ་ཐང་ (yǖǖdaŋ) threshing ground.

གཡུལ་ཐིག (yǖǖdig) battle line/ front.

གཡུལ་ཐོན་ (yǖǖdön) 1. party given after harvesting. 2. va. to leave to go to war.

གཡུལ་འཐབ་ (yǖǖdəb) warfare, battle, war, fight; va.—བྱེད་.

གཡུལ་དུས་ (yǖǖdüù) 1. the time of harvesting. 2. time of war.

གཡུལ་སྤྲོད་ (yǖǖ drȫò) sm. དམག་རྒྱག.

གཡུལ་ཕམ་ (yǖǖ pām) vi. to lose a battle, to be defeated.

གཡུལ་ཕྱོགས་ (yǖǖjɔɔ̀) sm. གཡུལ་ས་.

གཡུལ་འགྲིམས་ (yǖǖdreè) sm. དམག་རྒྱག.

གཡུལ་གཞི་ (yǖǖshi) place of harvesting.

གཡུལ་བཟློག (yǖǖ dɔ̱ɔ̀) va. to retaliate, to counterattack in war/ battle.

གཡུལ་ལས་ (yǖǖlɛɛ̀) 1. battle, fight, war; vi.—རྒྱལ་ to win a battle, to be victorious, to triumph; vi.—ཕམ་ to lose a battle, to be defeated ¶གཡུལ་ལས་རྒྱལ་ནས་ལོག་པ་རེད་ (They) returned in triumph. 2. threshing grain; va.—བྱེད་; —གཏོང་ to thresh grain.

གཡུལ་ལས་རྒྱལ་ (yǖǖlɛɛ̀ gyɛ̱ɛ̱) vi. to be victorious in war.

གཡུལ་ལས་གཏོང་ (yǖǖlɛɛ̀ dōŋ) va. to thresh.

གཡུལ་ལོག (yǖǖlɔɔ̀) enemy soldiers retreating.

གཡུལ་གཤོམ་ (yǖǖshom) war/ battle preparations; va. གཡུལ་གཤོམ་; —བྱེད་ to make war preparations.

གཡུལ་ས་ (yǖǖsə) battlefield, war zone.

གཡུལ་ས་མདུན་ས་ (yǖǖsə dü̱nsə) front lines (in war).

གཡུལ་བསྲུང་ (yǖǖsuŋ) sentry, guard, va.—བྱེད་ to do sentry duty, to act as a sentry.

གཡུལ་བསྲི་ (yǖǖ sē) va. to wage war, to fight.

གཡེང་: p. གཡེངས་; f. གཡེང་ (yēŋ) 1. vi. to wander (of mind), to be inattentive ¶སློབ་ཕྲུག་དེ་སེམས་གཡེང་ནས་ཡིག་ཚད་ལོན་མི་འདུག The student's mind wandered so he didn't pass the exam. 2. vi. to worry. 3. vi. to float (on water) ¶ཕོར་པ་ཆུའི་ནང་ལ་འཕངས་པས་ཆུ་ཁར་གཡེངས་ནས་བསྡད་སོང་ (I) threw the (wooden) bowl in the water and it floated.

གཡེང་བཀྲག (yēŋ gyāà) vi. to be worried or afraid.

གཡེང་གཏམ་ (yēŋdam) silly/ idle talk.

གཡེང་སྤྲིན་ (yēŋdrin) thin/ floating clouds.

གཡེང་འཕྱོ་ (yēŋjo) suspended ¶གཡེང་འཕྱོའི་ཟམ་པ་ Suspension bridge.

གཡེང་བ་ཆེན་པོ་ (yēŋwa cēmbo) absentedminded.

གཡེང་བག (yēŋbaà) abbr. of གཡེང་བ་ and བག་ཡང་.

གཡེང་མེད་ (yēŋmeè) being attentive, concentrating well.

གཡེང་རྫེད་ (yēŋdzeè) abbr. of གཡེང་བ་ and རྫེད་མོ་.

གཡེང་གཡེང་བ་ (yēŋyeŋwa) sm. གཡེང་.

གཡེངས་ (yēŋ) p. of གཡེང་.

གཡེན་ (yēn) 1. va. to chase, to frighten. 2. vi. to be shy/ embarrassed.

གཡེན་དཀྲུག (yēndruù) sm. གཡེན་སྦྱོ་, 1.

གཡེན་སྦྱོ་ (yēn jō) 1. va. to sow/ instigate discord, to cause trouble. 2. va. to hate. 3. va. to frighten/ scare. 4. va. to chase.

གཡེན་སྦྱོར་ (yēnjɔɔ) sm. གཡེན་སྦྱོ་, 1.

གཡེམ་ (yēm) fornication, sexual intercourse; va.—བྱེད་.

གཡེམ་སྦྱོར་ (yēmjɔɔ) adultery.

གཡེམ་མ་ (yēmma) 1. whore. 2. a loose woman.

གཡེམ་ཟ་པོ་ (yēm sabo) sm. གཡང་ཟ་པོ་.

གཡེར་ཁ་ (yērga) small bell.

གཡེར་ཆུང་ (yērjuŋ) very small bell.

གཡེར་དྲིལ་ (yēr trimə) sm. གཡེར་ཁ་.

གཡེར་པོ་ (yērbu) 1. wise, intelligent, knowledgeable. 2. stylish.

གཡེར་པོ་ཆེ་ (yērboje) famous, well-known.

གཡེར་བ་ (yērwa) 1. stylish. 2. a container with a large mouth.

གཡེར་མ་ (yēēma) 1. Sichuan peppercorn. 2. sm. གཡེར་མོ་.

གཡེར་མོ་ (yērmo) female who is a stylish dresser.

གཡེར་ཤིང་པ་ (yērsiŋbə) root of Zhejiang figwort.

གཡེལ་ (yēē) 1. vi. to be inattentive, to wander mentally, to be forgetful, to not concentrate. 2. vi. to be careless/ slipshod over work.

གཡེལ་ཅན་ (yēējɛn) abbr. of གཡེལ་བག་ཅན་.

གཡེལ་བག་ཅན་ (yēēbaàjɛn) sb. who likes to play games/ fool around.

གཡེལ་མ་ (yēēma) sm. གཡེམ་མ་.

གཡོ་ (yō) deceit, cunning, guile, trickery, hoodwinking; va.—བྱེད་ to use trickery/ deceit.

གཡོ་: p. **གཡོས་**; f. **གཡོ་**; imp. **གཡོས་** (yō) 1. va. to move, to shake, to agitate; to manipulate ¶ ས་ཡོམ་གྱིས་གྲོང་གསེབ་ཀྱི་ས་གཞི་རབ་ཏུ་གཡོས་པ་རེད་ The earthquake shook the village. 2. vi. to be touched/ moved emotionally ¶ ཁོ་ཚོས་གནས་ཚུལ་འདི་ཐོས་སྐབས་སེམས་པ་གཡོས་སོང་ They were moved (emotionally) when they heard the news. 3. va. to make/ knead dough ¶ མོས་གྲོ་ཞྱེ་གཡོས་པ་རེད་ She kneaded the dough.

གཡོ་ཀྱི་ (yōgye) deceitful, deceptive.

གཡོ་བཀོལ་ (yō gȍȍ) getting things done through trickery/ deceit/ sham; va.—བྱེད་.

གཡོ་སྐྱོད་ (yōgyöö) shaking; va.—གཏོང་; —བྱེད་ to shake ¶ ས་ཡོམ་གྱིས་ས་གཞི་གཡོ་སྐྱོད་བྱས་སོང་ The earthquake shook the earth.

གཡོ་བསྐོར་ (yūgɔɔ) trickery, deceit, deception; va.—བྱེད་.

གཡོ་ཁུངས་སུ་ཚུད་ (yōguŋsu tsȕȕ) vi. to fall into a trap, to get tricked, deceived/ duped.

གཡོ་ཁྲམ་ (yōdram) deception, deceit, trickery.

གཡོ་ཁྲམ་མཁན་ (yōdramñɛn) sm. གཡོ་ཁྲམ་ཅན་.

གཡོ་ཁྲམ་ཅན་ (yōdramjɛn) one who practices deception/ deceit, trickery.

གཡོ་མཁན་ (yōñɛn) sb. who is a deceiver/ faker/ trickster.

གཡོ་འཁྲུལ་ (yōdrüü) tricking and lying/ deceiving; va.—བྱེད་.

གཡོ་གྲུ་ (yōdru) swingboat.

གཡོ་འགུལ་ (yōgüü) shaking, vacillating, wavering; va.—གཏོང་; —བྱེད་; vi.—ཐེབས་; —འཐེབས་ to be moved/ touched (emotionally) ¶ གྲལ་རིམ་གཡོ་འགུལ་ཅན་ A vacillating class ¶ ཁོས་བུམ་པར་གཡོ་འགུལ་བཏང་ཡང་ Even though he shook the vase ¶ ཁོང་གི་བཀའ་སློབ་དེས་ངའི་སེམས་ལ་གཡོ་འགུལ་ཐེབས་སོང་ His advice moved me.

གཡོ་འགེབས་ (yōngeb) covering up, deceiving, befuddling; va.—བྱེད་ to cover up, to deceive, to befuddle ¶ ཁོག་ཚོང་གི་བྱ་བ་གཡོ་འགེབས་བྱེད་ཀྱི་འདུག (They) are covering (their) smuggling activities.

གཡོ་འགྱེལ་ (yōgye) moving and falling (e.g., a tree).

གཡོ་རྒན་ (yōgɛn) an old person who is deceitful.

གཡོ་རྒོད་ (yōgöö) sm. གཡོ་ངན་ཁོག་འཆང་.

གཡོ་སྒྱུ་ (yōgyu) deceit, cunning, guile, trickery; va.—བྱེད་; —འཁྲབ་; —རྩེ་ ¶ ཁོས་གཡོ་སྒྱུ་བྱས་ནས་མི་ལ་མགོ་སྐོར་གཏོང་གི་ཡོད་པ་རེད་ He uses deceit to trick people.

གཡོ་སྒྱུ་ཁྲམ་གསུམ་ (yōgyu trāmsum) trickery, outrageous audacity, lying.

གཡོ་སྒྱུ་མགོ་སྐོར་ (yōgyu gogɔɔ) sm. གཡོ་སྐོར་.

གཡོ་སྒྱུ་སྐྱལ་རལ་ (yōgyu gɛɛrɛɛ) deceitful and insubordinate.

གཡོ་སྒྱུ་ཅན་ (yūgyujɛn) sm. གཡོ་ཅན་.

གཡོ་སྒྱུ་ཆེན་པོ་ (yūgyu cēmbo) tricky, deceitful, cunning, sly.

གཡོ་སྒྱུ་དྲན་འཕྲུལ་ (yōgyu trendrüü) sm. གཡོ་སྒྱུ་.

གཡོ་སྒྱུ་མེད་པ་ (yōgyu meèba) a truthful/ deceitless person.

གཡོ་སྒྱུ་ཚ་པོ་ (yōgyu tsābo) sm. གཡོ་སྒྱུ་ཆེན་པོ་.

གཡོ་ངན་ (yōŋɛn) sm. གཡོ་.

གཡོ་ངན་ཁོག་བཅང་ (yōŋɛn kɔ̄gjaŋ) sm. གཡོ་ངན་ཁོག་འཆང་.

གཡོ་ངན་ཁོག་འཆང་ (yōŋɛn kɔ̄gjaŋ) plotting, intriguing (covertly); va.—བྱེད་ to plot, to intrigue.

གཡོ་ཅན་ (yōjɛn) cunning, crafty, shy, deceitful, tricky.

གཡོན་ཅན་དྲང་བརྫུ་ (yōjɛn traŋdzu) a deceitful person who pretends to be honest.

གཡོ་ཅན་ཝ་མོ་ (yōjɛn wamo) cunning as a fox.

གཡོ་བཅོས་ (yōjöö) deliberately distorting/ misconstruing/ misrepresenting/ tampering with/ falsifying; va.—བྱེད་ ¶ ཁོས་ཡིག་ཆ་ར་གཡོ་བཅོས་བྱས་ནས་རང་གི་དགྲ་བོར་ཡ་ལ་བཙུགས་པ་རེད་ He tampered with the records and accused his enemy (of some wrongdoing).

གཡོ་ཇུས་ (yōjüù) intriguing, plotting, a deceitful plan/ scheme; va.—བྱེད་; —གཞོམ་ to intrigue, to plot, to scheme ¶ དགྲ་བའི་གཡོ་ཇུས་ལ་མགོ་འཁོར་རྒྱུ་མེད་ You should not be tricked by the enemy's deceitful scheme.

གཡོ་གཏམ་ (yōdam) deceitful talk, lying; va.—ཤོད་.

གཡོ་ཐབས་ (yōdəb) deceitful methods/ means, crafty practices, underhanded methods/ means ¶ མི་གོ་བཙན་རྒྱལ་རིང་ལུགས་ཀྱིས་ངོ་ཚ་ཁྲེལ་མེད་ཀྱི་གཡོ་ཐབས་ག་འདྲ་ཞིག་སྤྱད་རུང་ Whatever shameless deceitful methods the U.S. imperialists use.

གཡོ་ཐོ་རྐྱང་པ་ (yōdo gyāŋba) simple pendulum. (in physics).

གཡོ་དྲག་ཟུང་འབྲེལ་ (yōdraà suŋdree) joining together both cunning/ guile/ deceit and force ¶ སྲིད་གཞུང་གིས་གཡོ་དྲག་ཟུང་འབྲེལ་གྱི་ཐོག་ནས་མི་དམངས་སྤྱི་ཁང་བཙུགས་པ་རེད་ The government established the people's communes through cunning and force.

གཡོ་བདའ་ (yōdar) sm. གཡོས་སྦྱོར་.

གཡོ་འདར་ (yō dar) vi. to tremble/ shiver.

གཡོ་འདས་ (yōndɛɛ̀) trembling; va.—བྱེད་ ¶ ཁོང་ཁྲོ་ལངས་ནས་གཟུགས་པོ་གཡོ་འདར་བྱས་སོང་ (He) got angry and his body trembled.

གཡོ་གནོན་ (yōnön) suppressing or oppressing by cunning/guile/ deceit; va.—བྱེད་.

གཡོ་སྣོད་ (yōnöö) a utensil for kneading flour, etc.

གཡོ་འཕར་ (yōmbar) pulsating; vi.—བྱེད་.

གཡོ་འཕྲུལ་ (yōndrüü) 1. cunning, guile, deceit; va.—འཁྲབ་; —བྱེད་. 2. flirting; va.—སྟོན་ to flirt.

གཡོ་འཕྲུལ་དྲག་སྦྱོད་འདྲེས་མ་ (yōndrüütragjöö dreèma) sm. གཡོ་དྲག་ཟུང་འབྲེལ་.

གཡོ་འཕྲོག (yōndɔɔ̀) stealing by guile/ trickery/ deceit/ usurping; va.—བྱེད་ to steal by guile/ trick, to usurp ¶ སུའུ་ལན་གྱི་ཏང་དང་རྒྱལ་ཁབ་དེ་དེང་རབས་ཀྱི་བཟོ་བཅོས་རིང་ལུགས་ཀྱི་ཚོགས་ཁག་གིས་གཡོ་འཕྲོག་བྱས་པ་རེད་ The modern revisionist clique usurped the Soviet party and state.

གཡོ་འཕྲོག་བཙན་ལེན་ (yōndrɔɔ̀ dzɛ̄nlen) stealing by deceit and taking by force.

གཡོ་བ་མེད་པ་ (yōwa me̱èba) 1. without wavering/ vacillation ༡ དུས་མཚུངས་སུ་གཡོ་བ་མེད་པའི་སྒོ་ནས་ཆོས་དད་རང་མོས་ཀྱི་སྲིད་ཇུས་ལག་བསྟར་བྱེད་ཀྱི་རེད་ At the same time, the policy of religious freedom will be carried out without wavering. 2. honest, upright, straightforward.

གཡོ་སྒྲིད་ (yōdriì) sm. ལྷ་སྒྲིད་.

གཡོ་མིག་ལྟ་ (yōmiì dā) va. to look at sb. in a deceitful way.

གཡོ་མེད་ (yōmiì) abbr. of གཡོ་བ་མེད་པ་.

གཡོ་མེད་ཀྱི་རང་བཞིན་ (yōme̱ègi rə̱ŋshin) 1. firmness, steadfastness, resoluteness. 2. honesty, uprightness, straightforwardness.

གཡོ་མེད་པ་ (yōmeèba) sb. without guile/ trickery, an honest/ straight forward person.

གཡོ་རྫིད་མགོ་སྐོར་ (yōdzeè go̱gɔɔ) tricking, deceiving.

གཡོ་ཚོ་པོ་ (yō tsābo) a person who is tricky/ deceitful.

གཡོ་རྫོང་ (yōdzoŋ) betraying, betrayal; va.—བྱེད་ ༡ ཁོས་རང་ཉིད་ཀྱི་གྲོགས་པོ་གཡོ་རྫོང་བྱས་ནས་ཁེ་བཟང་ཆེན་པོ་བཟས་འདུག He betrayed his own friend and made a great deal of profit.

གཡོ་འཛུལ་ (yō dzṳ̀ṳ) va. to enter/ get into a position or organization through deceit/ guile.

གཡོ་ཛུ་ (yōdzu) pretending, acting as if; va.—འདེབས་ ༡ ཁོས་ཚན་རིག་མཁས་པ་ཡིན་པའི་གཡོ་ཛུ་བཏབ་ནས་སློབ་གྲྭའི་གོ་ས་རག་པ་རེད་ He pretended he was a scientist and obtained a title/ position from the school.

གཡོ་ཛུན་ (yōdzün) sm. གཡོ་ཛུ་

གཡོ་ཟ་ (yōsa) embezzling; va.—བྱེད་ to embezzle ༡ ཁོས་དངུལ་གཡོ་ཟ་ཞེ་དྲག་བྱས་པ་རེད་ He embezzled lots of money.

གཡོ་ཟམ་ (yōsam) a suspension bridge.

གཡོ་ཟོལ་ (yōsöö) 1. avoiding doing sth. one ought to do, being lazy; va.—བྱེད་. 2. dishonesty, fraud, deception; va.—བྱེད་.

གཡོ་ཟོལ་མེད་པ་ (yōsöö me̱èba) honest, pure, sincere ༡ མཐུན་འབྲེལ་གཡོ་ཟོལ་མེད་པ་ Sincere friendship.

གཡོ་ཟོལ་ཅན་པོ་ (yōsöö tsābo) 1. sb. who is lazy, sb. who doesn't work diligently. 2. sb. who is dishonest/ deceptive.

གཡོ་འོག་ཏུ་ཚུད་ (yōwɔgdu tsṻṻ) vi. to be fooled/ hoodwinked/ deceived/ cheated/ tricked.

གཡོ་ཛུས་ (yōdzṻṻ) sm. གཡོ་ཛུ་.

གཡོ་རོལ་ (yōröö) sm. གཡོ་ལྷད་.

གཡོ་རིམ་ (yōrim) magnitude of an earthquake (e.g., richter scale).

གཡོ་རུ་ (yōru) one of the four ancient central Tibetan regions.

གཡོ་ལས་ (yōlɛɛ̀) tricking, deceiving, swindling, cheating, defrauding; va.—བྱེད་.

གཡོ་ལེན་ (yōlen) defrauding, taking sth. by guile/ deceit; va.—བྱེད་ to defraud, to take by guile / deceit.

གཡོ་ལེན་བཙན་འཕྲོག (yōlen dzɛ̄ndrɔɔ̀) stealing by force and trickery.

གཡོ་ལེན་ཧམ་འཕྲོག (yōlen hāmdrɔɔ̀) sm. གཡོ་ལེན་བཙན་འཕྲོག.

གཡོ་ཤོད་ (yō shȍȍ) va. to deceive/ trick/ defraud verbally.

གཡོ་བཤད་ (yōshɛɛ̀) verbal deceit/ guile/ fraud; va.—བྱེད་ to deceive/ trick/ defraud verbally.

གཡོ་ཧམ་ (yōham) sm. གཡོ་ཛུ་.

གཡོ་ལྷད་ (yōlhɛɛ̀) tricking/ deceiving through adulterating.

གཡོ་ལྷད་མེད་པ་ (yōlhɛɛ̀ me̱èba) sincere, genuine.

གཡོ་ལྷད་དྲན་འཁྱུལ་ (yōlhɛɛ̀ tre̱ndrüü) false front; va.—བྱེད་ to show a false front.

གཡོག (yɔ̄ɔ̀) servant, servanting; va.—རྒྱུག; —བྱེད་ to serve as a servant, to take care of sb. ༡ གཡོག་རྡོ་རྗེ་ Servant Dorje. ༡ དཔོན་གཡོག Lord and servant.

གཡོག: p. གཡོགས་; f. གཡོག; imp. གཡོགས་ (yɔ̄ɔ̀) 1. va. cover ༡ དེ་སྟེང་ས་གཡོགས་ཏེ་མཐོང་རྒྱུ་མེད་པ་བཟོས་པ་རེད་ (They) covered it with earth and so that it couldn't be seen. 2. va. to dress, to clothe ༡ ཨ་མས་ཕྲུ་གུ་ལ་ཕྱུ་པ་གཡོགས་པ་རེད་ The mother dressed the child (put on its dress). 3. va. to serve/ assist ༡ ང་ནད་པ་ལ་གཡོག་དགོས་བྱུང་སོང་ I had to serve the sick person.

གཡོག་སྐལ་ (yɔ̄ɔ̀gɛɛ̀) sm. ཇ་གཡོག.

གཡོག་སྐུལ་ (yɔ̄ɔ̀güü) compelling sb. to serve as a servant; va.—གཏོང་ to compel/ make sb. serve as a servant, to enslave.

གཡོག་འཁོར་ (yɔ̄ɔ̀gɔɔ) servant and retinue.

གཡོག་གོས་ (yɔ̄ɔ̀göö) servant's clothes.

གཡོག་གླ་ (yɔ̄ɔ̀la) servant's salary.

གཡོག་རྒྱུག (yɔ̄ɔ̀ gyṳṳ̀) va. to go serve as a servant.

གཡོག་ངན་དཔོན་དཀྲུག (yōgŋɛn bōndruù) shung. evil servants causing trouble among the masters.

གཡོག་ཏུ་བཀོལ་ (yōgdu gȍȍ) sm. གཡོག་སྐུལ་.

གཡོག་ནང་ཟན་ (yɔ̄ɔ̀ na̱ŋsɛn) household servants/ nangsen.

གཡོག་པོ་ (yōgbo) 1. male servant; va.—རྒྱུག; —བྱེད་ to serve as a servant. 2. waiter.

གཡོག་ཕྲུག (yōgdruù) 1. a child servant. 2. the child of a servant.

གཡོག་བྱས་ནག་འགེལ་ (yōgjɛɛ̀ na̱ggel) shung. servants being blamed as criminals.

གཡོག་བྱེད་ (yōgjeè) see གཡོག.

གཡོག་བྱས་མཐའ་མ་ནག (yōgjɛɛ̀ tāma na̱à) being accused as a criminal after serving sb. for a long time.

གཡོག་མོ་ (yōmo) female servant.

གཡོག་ཞིང་ (yōgshiŋ) land given to servants as compensation.

གཡོག་བཞུན་པོ་ (yōg shṳ̄mbu) an obedient servant.

གཡོག་ཟས་ (yōgsɛɛ̀) food given to servants.

གཡོགས་ (yɔ̄ɔ̀): p. and imp. of གཡོག.

གཡོགས་དར་ (yɔ̄ɔ̀dar) ceremonial scarfs given to people.

གཡོགས་མ་ (yɔ̄ɔ̀ma) outer covering of a garment.

གཡོང་མ་ (yɔ̄ŋma) another, other.

གཡོན་ (yȍn) left (side, direction).

གཡོན་སྐོར་ (yȍngɔɔ) going counterclockwise; va.—ལ་འགྲོ་; —རྒྱག to go counterclockwise.

གཡོན་བསྐོར་ (yȍngɔɔ) sm. གཡོན་སྐོར་.

གཡོན་གུམ་རྒྱག (yȍngum gya̱à) va. to make one's kite make circles on the left side in the sky.

གཡོན་གྱི་སྐྱོན་ཆ་ (yȍngi gyȍnja) mistakes of the left, leftism.

གཡོན་གྲལ་ (yȍndrɛɛ) a row on the left side.

གཡོན་སྒྱུར་ (yȍngyur) turn left! (a drill command).

གཡོན་ངོས་ (yȍnŋöö) left side, left direction.

གཡོན་ཅན་ (yȍnjɛn) sm. གཡོ་སྒྱུ་ཅན་.

གཡོན་གདམ་ (yȍndam) deceiving/ cunning/ tricking talk.

གཡོན་ཐལ་ (yȍntɛɛ) too left (in ideology), ultra leftism.

གཡོན་ཐལ་ཆེ་བའི་ལམ་ཕྱོགས་ (yȍn tɛ̄ɛcewɛ la̱mjɔɔ̀) excessive leftist policy (refers usu. to the Red Guards and the Cultural Revolution).

གཡོན་དུ་ (yȍndu) to/ on the left.

གཡོན་ན་ (yȍnna) sm. གཡོན་དུ་.

གཡོན་པ་ (yȍmba) left, left one ༡ མིག་གཡོན་པ་ The left eye.

གཡོན་པོ་ (yȍmbo) crooked, not straight.

གཡོན་ཕྱེད་ (yȍnjeè) the left half (of body, etc.).

གཡོན་ཕྱོགས་ (yȍnjɔɔ̀) 1. left side (direction). 2. leftist (in ideology) ༡ གཡོན་ཕྱོགས་དར་དམར་པོའི་ཚོགས་མི་ A member of the leftist Red Flag party.

གཡོན་ཕྱོགས་པ་ (yȍnjɔɔ̀ba) leftist, left-winger.

གཡོན་ཕྱོགས་པའི་བྱིས་བློའི་སྐྱོན་ (yȍnjɔɔ̀bɛ ci̱ilö gyȍn) left wing infantile disorder.

གཡོན་ཕྱོགས་ཤོག་ཁག (yȍnjɔɔ̀ shɔ̄ɔ̀gaà) left wing association, leftist group.

གཡོན་ཕྱོགས་སུ་ལྷུང་བ་ (yȍnjɔɔ̀su lhṻŋwə) left wing

deviation.

གཡོན་མ་ (yǒnma) 1. the left one ¶ ལག་པ་གཡོན་མ་ Left handed. 2. woman, female. 3. prostitute, whore.

གཡོན་གཞོགས་ (yǒnshɔ̀ɔ) leftist, left side.

གཡོན་གཞོགས་གུང་བློན་ (yǒnshɔ̀ɔ kuŋlön) a minister who is the left side assistant of the Emperor.

གཡོན་རུ་ (yǒnru) left wing/ flank.

གཡོན་རུའི་རྩོམ་མཁན་མནའ་འབྲེལ་ (yǒnrü dzōmgɛn nāndree) Union of Left-Wing Writers.

གཡོན་རོལ་ (yǒnröö) left side.

གཡོན་ལ་ཕྱོགས་པ་ (yǒnla cǒgba) sm. གཡོན་ལྷུང་.

གཡོན་ལག (yǒnlaà) left hand.

གཡོན་ལམ་ (yǒnlam) 1. deceitful ways/ path. 2. leftist path.

གཡོན་ལོགས་ (yǒnlɔ̀ɔ) sm. གཡོན་ངོས་.

གཡོན་གསེག (yǒnseg) sloping to the left.

གཡོན་ལྷུང་ (yǒnlhuŋ) left deviation, leftism.

གཡོན་ལྷུང་སྐབས་འཚོལ་རིང་ལུགས་ (yǒnlhuŋ gābdzöö riŋluù) left opportunism.

གཡོན་ལྷུང་ཉེན་མཆོང་རིང་ལུགས་ (yǒnluŋ ñenjoŋ riŋluù) left adventurism.

གཡོབ་: p. གཡོབས་; f. གཡོབ་; imp. གཡོབས་ (yōb) 1. va. to wave ¶ ཁོས་ལག་པ་གཡབས་ནས་ང་སྐད་གཏོང་གི་འདུག He is calling to me by waving his hands. 2. va. to pile on one side.

གཡོབ་བྱེད་ (yōbjeè) 1. oar (for a boat). 2. sm. གཡང་མདའ་. 3. fan.

གཡོབས་ (yōb) imp. of གཡོབ་.

གཡོམ་འདས་ཆེན་པོ་ (yōmdɛɛ̀ cēmbo) sb. who thinks big in business and planning.

གཡོར་ (yɔ̄r) 1. imp. of གཡར་. 2. vi. to be covered/ shaded.

གཡོར་མཁན་ (yɔ̄rñɛn) squint-eyed, cross-eyed.

གཡོར་གྲུ་ (yɔ̄rdru) sailboat, sailing vessel; va.—གཏོང་.

གཡོར་ཆེན་པོ་ (yɔ̄ɔ cēmbo) large amount, large quantity.

གཡོར་དག (yɔ̄ɔdaà) cooking/ kitchen work.

གཡོར་ལྡན་དམག་གྲུ་ (yɔ̄ɔdɛn māgdru) military sailing vessel.

གཡོར་པོ་ (yɔ̄ɔbo) lender, borrower.

གཡོར་མ་སོ་ (yɔ̄ɔmaso) numerous, very many ¶ མི་གཡོར་མ་སོ་སླེབས་འདུག Many people arrived.

གཡོར་མོ་ (yɔ̄ɔmo) a sail.

གཡོར་ཡོལ་ (yɔ̄ɔyüü) sm. གཡོར་མོ་.

གཡོར་ཤིང་ (yɔ̄ɔshiŋ) mast.

གཡོལ་ (yö̌ö) va. to avoid, to refrain from, to shirk, to shun ¶ མུ་གེ་གཡོལ་བར་ཡོང་བ་རེད་ (They) came to avoid the famine.

གཡོལ་ཐབས་བྱེད་ (yö̌ödəb jeè) va. to avoid/ evade/ dodge sth.

གཡོལ་ཐབས་མེད་པ་ (yö̌ödəb meèba) inevitable, unavoidable.

གཡོལ་སྡོད་བྱེད་ (yö̌ödöö ceè) va. to stay somewhere avoiding sth.

གཡོལ་བྱ་བྱེད་ (yö̌öja ceè) sm. གཡོལ་ཐབས་བྱེད་.

གཡོལ་བྲོལ་(དུ་)འགྲོ་ (yö̌öjöödu dro) va. to flee to escape sth. ¶ བལ་ཡུལ་ལ་གཡོལ་བྲོལ་དུ་འགྲོ་རྒྱུ་བྱས་པ་རེད་ They planned to flee to Nepal.

གཡོས་ (yö̌ö) 1. p. of གཡོ་. 2. large intestine. 3. cooked food.

གཡོས་སྐྱོག (yö̌ögyɔ̀ɔ) ladle.

གཡོས་ཁང་ (yö̌ögaŋ) kitchen.

གཡོས་ཆང་ (yö̌öjaŋ) cooking wine.

གཡོས་ཐབ་ (yö̌ödəb) kitchen stove.

གཡོས་སྣོད་ (yö̌önöö) sm. གཡོས་སྦྱོར་.

གཡོས་དཔོན་ (yö̌öbön) head cook, chef.

གཡོས་བྱེད་ (yö̌öjeè) va. to cook.

གཡོས་སྦྱོར་ (yö̌öjɔɔ) cooking food; va.—བྱེད་.

གཡོས་མ་ (yö̌öma) a cook.

གཡོས་མལ་ (yö̌ömɛɛ) sm. གཡོས་ཁང་.

གཡོས་རྫ་ (yö̌ödza) sm. གཡོས་སྣོད་.

གཡོས་ར་མ་ (yö̌örama) flesh in the intestines.

གཡོས་ས་ (yö̌ösa) sm. གཡོས་ཁང་.

ར་ (ra) 1. the letter (used in alphabetical ordering). 2. a fence/ wall surrounding an enclosure, an enclosed place ། ལུག་ར་ Sheep corral. ། ཉ་ར་ A fishery. 3. a dative-locative particle that is used with vowel finals ། ཁོར་དེབ་ཅིག་འདུག He (to him) has a book. 4. goat.

ར་ཀ་བརྡགས་གཏོང་ (raga dadoŋ) va. to check sth. carefully/ in detail/ seriously.

ར་ཀླད་ (ralɛɛ̀) goat's brain (used in Tibetan medicine).

ར་རྐྱལ་ (ragyee) bag made from goat skin.

ར་སྐད་ལུག་སྐད་ (ragɛɛ̀ luùgɛɛ̀) term used to describe many people singing out of tune; va.—རྒྱག [Lit. sound of goat, sound of sheep].

ར་སྐོར་ (ragɔɔ) 1. sm. ར་བ་. 2. a courtyard surrounded by apartments (usu. in monasteries).

ར་སྐོར་ཁང་པ་ (ragɔɔ kāŋba) a house surrounded by a fence. 2. houses surrounding a main house/ courtyard.

ར་སྐྱ་ཚོམ་ཚོམ་ (ragyeè) sm. སྐྱ་ཕྱིད་ཐོ་ཕྱིད་.

ར་སྐྱེས་ (ragyeè) goat.

ར་སྐྱོར་ (ragyɔɔ) low fence.

ར་བསྐོར་ཁང་པ་ (ragɔɔ kāŋba) sm. ར་སྐོར་ཁང་པ་.

ར་ཁུལ་ (rəgüü) cashmere.

ར་ཁུལ་མདོག (rəgüü dɔ̀ɔ) the color of cashmere.

ར་ཁྲག (radraà) goat blood (used in Tibetan medicine).

ར་འཁོར་ (ragɔɔ) sm. ར་སྐོར་.

ར་གན་ (ragɛn) brass.

ར་གན་གསེར་མདོག་སྟོན་ (ragɛn sērdɔ̀ɔ dön) sm. ར་གན་གསེར་བརྫུས་.

ར་གན་གསེར་བརྩི་ (ragɛn sērdzi) considering sth. that is bad as good, being unable to distinguish the good from the bad ། ལས་ཁུངས་ནས་མི་དེ་ར་གན་གསེར་བརྩི་བྱས་ནས་ལས་ཀ་སྤྲད་སྐབས་རྗེས་སུ་གྱོང་རག་པ་རེད་ Because the office considered that (bad) person as good and gave him a job, later it suffered. [Lit. considering brass as gold].

ར་གན་གསེར་བརྫུས་ (ragɛn sērdzüù) acting/ pretending sth. is good when it is bad; va.—བྱེད་ ། མི་ངན་པ་དེས་ར་གན་གསེར་བརྫུས་བྱས་ནས་ལས་ཀ་རག་ཐབས་བྱས་བཞག That bad person passed himself off as a good person in order to get a good job. [Lit. faking brass as gold].

ར་གུ (rəgu) kid (baby goat).

ར་གུར་ (rəgur) sm. ར་བ་.

ར་མགོ་ (raŋgo) superfixed ར་.

ར་མགོ་ཅན་ (rangojɛn) having a ར་མགོ་.

ར་མགོ་ལུག་སྦྱར་ (rango lugjaa) combining two things inappropriately [Lit. attaching a goat's head to a sheep].

ར་རྒན་ (ragɛn) old goat.

ར་རྒན་མར་མར་ རི་བུ་ཡར་ཡར་ (ragɛn marmar riwu yaryar) old people are on the decline and young people are on the ascent (are developing) [Lit. the old goat goes down and down, the baby goat goes up and up].

ར་རྒོད་ (ragöö) wild goat.

ར་རྒྱ་ (ragya) a kind of mountain goat.

ར་རྒྱབ་ (ragyəb) 1. a load that can be carried by a single goat. 2. the cashmere plucked from a single goat.

ར་རྒྱུ་ (ragyu) goat's intestines.

ར་སྒོ་ (rago) a door in a wall/ fence.

ར་སྒོག (ragɔ̀ɔ) wild garlic.

ར་སྒོར་ (ragɔ̀ɔ) a round fence, a fence that goes around sth.

ར་སྒྲེང་ (radreŋ) 1. Reting (Monastery). 2. Reting Rimpoche (name of a line of high incarnations some of whom have served as regent of Tibet).

ར་ངོ་ (raŋo) goat mange.

ར་ཆེན་ (rajen) 1. a large fenced/ walled in enclosure. 2. a big goat.

ར་ཉག (rañaà) a nomad tax where nomads pay a fixed amount (a ཉ་ག་) of butter per horn of their animals.

ར་མཉེ་ (ramñe) sealwort (used in Tibetan medicine).

ར་ཏི་རོ་ཏི་ (radi rodi) bumpy, uneven, rough.

ར་གཏུགས་ (raduù) sm. ར་སྤྲོད་.

ར་བཏགས་ (radaà) subjoined/ suffixed ར་.

ར་སྟག (rəadaà) 1. abbr. the two incarnations Reting and Taktra (these were the two regents during the period 1934-1950). 2. goat and tiger.

ར་ཐུག (rəduù) sm. ར་འཕྲོད་.

ར་ཐུལ་ (radüü) a sleeping container/ bag made from goat skin (with the fleece on the inside).

ར་ཐོང་ (radoŋ) three year old goat.

ར་དྭངས་ (ra taŋ) vi. to sober up.

ར་དྲི་ (rədri) 1. the smell of goat's meat. 2. the smell of goats.

ར་འདག་པ་འདྲ་པོ་ཞིག་བཟི་ (ra dagba drāboshig si) vi. to be/ get completely drunk.

ར་ཌར་ (radrar) eng. radar.

ར་དེ་རོ་དེ་ (rade rode) sm. ར་ཏི་རོ་ཏི་.

ར་གདང་ (radaŋ) sm. ར་ཐང་.

ར་མདའ་ (ramda) 1. a traditional defense system in which each household must send an armed man on horseback to chase bandits; va.—གཏོང་ ། འགོ་པས་ཁྱིམ་ཚང་རེ་རེ་ནས་ལམ་སེང་མི་རེ་ར་མདར་ཕྱོག་ཅེས་སྐད་བཏང་བ་རེད་ The headman called out, "Each household immediately send a person for ར་མདའ་." 2. reinforcements, auxiliary/ supplementary troops or militia ། དམག་ས་དེར་དམག་མི་ཉུང་དྲགས་འདུག་པས་ར་མདའ་གཏང་དགོས་ Because there are too few soldiers at the front, the government must send reinforcements.

ར་མདའ་པ་ (ramdaba) persons going on ར་མདའ་.

ར་མདའི་དཔུང་ཚོགས་ (ramdɛ būŋdzɔ̀ɔ) 1. auxiliary troops, reinforcements, supplementary troops. 2. a group going on ར་མདའ་.

ར་མདར་སྒྲོན་ (ramda drön) va. to call for a ར་མདའ་.

ར་འདེགས་ (ramdeè) sm. ར་མདའ་.

ར་ཐང་ (radaŋ) a rope strung along the ground for tying goats.

ར་སྡེ་ (rade) the four letter set in the Tibetan alphabet consisting of: ར་ལ་ཤ་ས་.

ར་ནད་ལུག་དཀྲིས་ (ranɛɛ̀ lugdriì) blaming others for one's own misdeeds [Lit. tying the sickness of the goat on the sheep].

ར་སྣ་བསམ་འཕེལ་ (rana sāmbel) a traditional Tibetan medicine that includes powdered pearls.

ར་པི་རི་པི་ (rəbi ribi) unclear, indistinct (visually).

ར་པི་རུ་པི་ (rəbi rubi) the quality of light at the start of dusk ། ས་ར་པི་རུ་པི་ཞིག་ལ་ཁོང་ངའི་སར་སླེབས་བྱུང་ He came to see me when dusk was just starting.

ར་པེ་རོ་པེ་ (rabe robe) sm. ར་ཏི་རོ་ཏི་. 2. shabby, uneven.

ར་ལྤགས་ (rabaà) goat skin, goat hide.

ར་སྤུ་ (rəbu) goat's hair.

ར་སྤུའི་འུར་རྡོ་ར་ཡི་མཇིང་པར་འཁོར་ (rəbü wurdo rayi jiŋbar kɔ̄ɔ) suffering the negative consequences of one's actions, having sth. backfire [Lit. the goat hair sling hitting the goat's neck].

ར་སྤུའི་འུར་རྡོ་ར་ལ་འཁོར་ (rəbü wurdo rala kɔ̄ɔ) sm. ར་སྤུའི་འུར་རྡོ་ར་ཡི་མཇིང་པར་འཁོར་.

ར་སྤྲགས་ (radraà) sm. ར་སྤྲོད་.

ར་སྤྲགས་ཐུག (radraà tūù) sm. ར་སྤྲོད་ཐུག.

ར་སྤྲོད་ (radröö) 1. disputants going face-to-face before a third person to argue their case; va.—གཏོང་ ། ཁ་མཆུའི་གྲོད་ཡ་གཉིས་ཀྱིས་ཁྲིམས་ཁང་དུ་ར་སྤྲོད་

བཏང་བ་རེད་ The two disputants in the dispute went to the court to make their case face-to-face. 2. proving, confirming; va.—བྱེད་; — འསྒྲོད་ to get/ receive proof ༎ གནས་ཚུལ་དེའི་སྐོར་ཁོ་ལ་ར་སྒྲོད་བྱ་རྒྱུ་གང་ཡང་མི་འདུག Concerning this issue, he has no proof at all.

ར་སྒྲོད་ཁུངས་འཚོལ་ (radröö kūŋdzüü) looking for proof/ evidence.

ར་སྒྲོད་ཐུག (radröö tūù) vi. to meet face-to-face to give one's side in a dispute.

ར་སྒྲོད་ཕེར་ (radröö pēr) sm. ར་སྒྲོད་འཕེར་.

ར་སྒྲོད་འཕེར་ (radröö pēr) vi. to be able to prove sth. ༎ གནས་ཚུལ་དེའི་སྐོར་ཁོ་ལ་ར་སྒྲོད་འཕེར་བ་གང་ཡང་ཡོད་རྒྱུ་མི་འདུག Concerning this issue, he has no proof (can say nothing that will be able to prove it).

ར་ཕོ་ (rabo) ram.

ར་ཕོ་ཁ་ལུག (rabo) vi. to be out of control, to be without discipline.

ར་ཕྲུག (rədruù) kid (baby goat).

ར་འསྒྲོད་ (ra tröö) vi. to get/ be proved ༎ གྱོད་དོན་དེའི་སྐོར་ཁྲིམས་ཁང་ནང་ར་སྒྲོད་བཏང་ཡང་ར་འསྒྲོད་མ་སོང་ Concerning this case, even though the court called the disputants face-to-face, they could not prove the allegation. ༎ ལུང་བསྟན་ནང་གི་གནས་ཚུལ་དེ་དེང་སང་ར་འསྒྲོད་བྱུང་སོང་ The events in his prophecy have come true these days.

ར་འསྒྲོད་ཁུངས་འཚོལ་ (radröö kūŋdzüü) sm. ར་སྒྲོད་ཁུངས་འཚོལ་.

ར་འསྒྲོད་བརྡ་ (radröö da) identification.

ར་བ་ (raba) 1. fence/ wall enclosing sth. ༎ ཁང་པ་དེར་ར་བ་བསྐོར་བཞག That house is surrounded by a wall. 2. coral, pen, yard ༎ རྟ་དྲེལ་གྱི་ར་བ་ A corral for horses and mules. 3. place, farm ༎ ཉ་འཛིན་ར་བ་ Fish farm. ༎ སྦྱོང་བརྡར་ར་བ་ Training ground.

ར་བི་རི་བི་ (rəbi ribi) sm. ར་བེ་རིབ་བེ་.

ར་བེ་རིབ་བེ་ (rabe ribe) blurry, unclear, (visually).

ར་བེ་རོ་བེ་ (rabe robe) in shoddy/ careless manner; va.—བྱེད་ ༎ ལས་ཀ་ར་བེ་རོ་བེ་བྱས་ན་ལས་ཁུངས་ནས་འབུད་ཀྱི་རེད་ If you do shoddy work, you will get fired from the office.

ར་བྱ་གཅོད་ (raja jöö) va. to castrate a goat.

ར་མ་ (ram) adult female goat.

ར་མ་སྒང་ (ramagaŋ) ferry site on the Lhasa river south of the city.

ར་མ་ཐུག (rama tūù) shung. sth. that does not correlate/ tally ༎ ཁོས་བཤད་པ་དང་བྱས་པ་གཉིས་ར་མ་ཐུག་རེད་བཞག What he said and what he did, did not correlate.

ར་མ་འཕགས་ན་ཀ་བ་འགྲེལ་མི་ཐུབ་ (rama pāgna gāwa gyee mi tūb) the subordinates/ subjects can not overthrow the government/ superiors [Lit. the goat can never pull down the pillar].

ར་མ་ལུག (ramaluù) 1. a hybrid, any mixture of two things [Lit. neither goat nor sheep].

ར་མར་ (ramar) butter made from goat's milk.

ར་མི་རུ་མི་ (rami rumi) aching all over; vi.—བྱེད་ ༎ ཉིན་གང་གོམ་པ་བརྒྱབ་ནས་རྐང་པ་ར་མི་རུ་མི་ཆགས་བཞག Having walked all day, my feet are aching all over.

ར་མ་རོ་འགྱུར་ (rama ro gyur) vi. to become almost like corpses, to almost die (usu. after fighting).

ར་མེ་རོ་མེ་ (rame rome) sm. ར་མི་རུ་མི་.

ར་མོ་ (ramo) female goat.

ར་མོ་ཆེ་ (ramoce) the Ramoche Temple in Lhasa.

ར་དམར་ (ramar) cattle that have gored sb. to death.

ར་རྫག (radzaà) dress/ robe made from goat skin (with fleece on the inside).

ར་ཚ་ (radza) a mineral used in Tibetan medicine.

ར་ཚང་ (radzaŋ) goat pen/ corral.

ར་ཚིལ་ (rədzii) goat fat.

ར་མཚེ་ (ramdze) Ephedra Sinica (used in Tibetan medicine).

ར་རྫི་ (radzi) goat herder.

ར་གཞུག་སྦང་ (rəshuù baŋ) losing one's celibacy (for monks) ༎ གྲྭ་པ་དེ་ནས་འཁོགས་ཆགས་ནས་ར་གཞུག་སྦངས་བཞག That monk lost his celibacy after he became elderly. [Lit. goat soaks its tail in the water].

ར་བཟི་ (ra si) vi. to be/ get drunk.

ར་བཟི་བ་ (rasiwə) drunkard.

ར་བཟི་ཤོད་ (rasi shöö) va. to talk when intoxicated (and cause trouble), to talk drunk talk.

ར་ཡི་ཝུར་རྡོ་ར་ལ་ཕོག (rəyi wurdo rala pɔ̄ɔ̀) ར་ཡི་ཝུར་རྡོ་ར་ལ་འཁོར་.

ར་ཡེ་བཧ་དུར་ (raye bədur) hind. Rai Bahadur, a title in the British Government of India.

ར་ར་ (rara) a container that has a wide/ flat opening.

ར་རི་ (rəri) dirt, blemish, spot.

ར་རི་མེད་པ་ (rəri meèba) clean, not dirty.

ར་རིའི་དྲི་མ་ (rərii trimə) shung. sm. ར་རི་.

ར་རོ་ (raro) sm. ར་བཟི་.

ར་ལང་ཅ་ལང་ (ralaŋ calaŋ) undisciplined, uncontrolled, chaotic, disorganized; va.—བྱེད་.

ར་ལུག (rəluù) goats and sheep.

ར་ལུང་ (rəluŋ) a village near Gyantse.

ར་ལུད་ (rəlüü) goat's dung.

ར་ལེབ་ (rəlüü) sm. ཨན་དར་.

ར་ཤ་ (rasha) 1. goat meat. 2. sb. who does not get fat ༎ བུ་མོ་དེ་ར་ཤ་རེད་བཞག That girl is sb. who doesn't get fat (however much she eats).

ར་ཤ་ཟ་དུས་ཁ་ཚིག་ཚིག ཤ་རིན་སྤྲོད་དུས་ངོ་ནག་སྡོང་རྒྱུ་མེད་ (rasha sədüü kā dzēgdzeè shārin düdüü ŋonaà dōngyu meè) one should not smile when enjoying sth. and show a long face when paying for it, one should accept the consequences of doing things [Lit. one should not smile when eating goat meat and show a long face when paying the fee for goat meat].

ར་ཤི་ཡའི་གྲོས་ཚོགས་འོག་མ་ (rashiyɛ tröödzɔɔ̀ wɔ̄ɔma) Duma (Russia).

ར་ཤེལ་འཁྲུད་ཁང་ (rashel trüügaŋ) darkroom (for photography).

ར་ས་ (rasa) an old name for Lhasa.

ར་ས་འཕྲུལ་སྣང་ (rasa trüünaŋ) the main temple/ cathedral in Lhasa (the Tsuglhakhang).

ར་སའི་ཤ་ཙལ་ (rasɛ shādzɛɛ) arc. sm. ར་ས་.

ར་བསད་ན་ལུག་འདར་ ཁྱི་བརྡུངས་ན་ཕག་པ་འབྲོས་ (ra sɛ̄ɛna lug dar kyī dunna pāgba tröö) teaching others a lesson by imposing a harsh penalty on sb., punishing sb. as a warning to others [Lit. killing a goat makes the sheep shiver, beating a dog makes the pig flee].

ར་སློག (ralɔɔ̀) sm. ར་རྫག.

ར་ཨ་ད་ (ra āda) type of goat with small ears.

རག (raà) 1. brass. 2. vi. to obtain, to get ༎ ལས་ཀ་མ་བྱས་ན་དངུལ་རག་གི་མ་རེད་ If (you) don't work you won't get money. 3. va. to touch ༎ འདི་ལ་ལག་པ་མ་རག Don't touch this.

རག་དཀར་ (raàgar) yellowish whitish color (for horses).

རག་དཀྲོལ་རྒྱག (raàdröö gyaà) va. to engrave/ etch brass.

རག་སྐུད་ (rəgüü) brass wire.

རག་སྐྱོགས་ (raàgyɔɔ̀) brass ladle.

རག་ག་ཤག (raàgashar) name of an important aristocratic family.

རག་གེ་རོག་གེ་ (raàge roòge) describes a dark and blurry vision of sth. at a distance.

རག་ཆས་ (ragjɛɛ̀) brassware.

རག་ཆེ་བ་ (ragjewa) tall and manly in appearance.

རག་གཏེར་ (ragder) a place/ mine where རག་དོ་is obtained.

རག་སྟེགས་ (raàdeg) a cup stand made of brass.

རག་ཐག (raàdaà) brass chain.

རག་ཐབས་བྱེད་ (ragdəb ceè) va. to try to get/ obtain sth.

རག་ཐུར་ (rəgdur) brass spoon.

རག་དུང་ (rəgduŋ) brass trumpet/ horn.

རག་མདོང་ (ragdoŋ) a churn that has brass bands.
རག་འདན་ (raŋdɛn) a soup containing liquor, melted butter and tsampa.
རག་དུལ་ (rəgdüü) sm. རག་བདུལ་.
རག་རྡོ་ (ragdo) chalcopyrite (the ore from which brass is made).
རག་སྡེར་ (ragder) brass plate (for food).
རག་པ་ (ragba) tan colored horse/ mule (usu. with a black mane and tail).
རག་མ་ (ragma) tan female horse/ mule.
རག་མོ་ (ragmo) sm. རག་མ་.
རག་རག (ragraà) tan colored horses and mules.
རག་རོག (ragrog) abbr. of རག་གི་རོག་གི་.
རག་ལས་ (raà lɛɛ̀) vi. to depend on ¶ བོད་ཡར་རྒྱས་འགྲོ་ཡས་འདི་བོད་པ་རང་ལ་རག་ལས་པ་རེད་ Tibet's progress depends on Tibetans themselves.
རག་ལས་པའི་རྒྱུ་རྐྱེན་ (ralɛɛ̀bɛ gyugyen) the cause on which sth. depends.
རག་ལས་ས་ (ralɛɛ̀sa) the main link, the chief factor, that upon which one depends ¶ བཟོ་པ་ཚོས་ལས་ཀ་ཡག་པོ་བྱ་རྒྱུའི་རག་ལས་ས་དེ་གླ་ཕོགས་རེད་ The main factor concerning the workers working well is salary.
རག་ལུས་ (raàlüü) sm. རག་ལས་.
རག་ལེབ་ (raàleb) a brass plate (usu. on which names/ numbers of houses are engraved).
རག་ཤན་ (ragshɛn) a brass binding band (usu. on found on wooden butter churns).
རག་ཤོག (raàshoò) brass foil.
རགས་ (raà) 1. dam, dike, embankment; va.—རྒྱག to build a dam/ dike/ embankment. 2. sm. རག. 3. rough, crude, not fine ¶ ཁོང་ཚོས་རགས་རྩིས་བརྒྱབ་སོང་ They did a rough accounting.
རགས་ཁ་ (raàga) 1. sm. རགས་. 2. vi. a crack/ breach in a dam or dike; vi.—ཤོར་ to get a crack/ breach in a dam or dike.
རགས་འཁེལ་ (ragkel) rough/ crude spinning; va.—བྱེད་.
རགས་སྒོ་ (raàgo) a gate or door in a dam/ dike.
རགས་རྒྱག (raàgyaà) see རགས་.
རགས་རྒྱབ་པ་ (rəgyəbbə) 1. an untouchable caste of people who take corpses to the sky-burial ground in Lhasa. 2. a person with no manners/ class, sb. who is obnoxious/ rude/ crude.
རགས་རྒྱབ་དཔོན་པོ་ (rəgyəb bõnbo) the head of the རགས་རྒྱབ་པ་.
རགས་རྒྱབ་ཨ་ཕ་ (rəgyəb āba) a male རགས་རྒྱབ་པ་.
རགས་རྒྱབ་ཨ་མ་ (rəgyəb āma) a female རགས་རྒྱབ་པ་.
རགས་བསྒྲིགས་ཟིན་དཔེ་ (ragdrig simbe) galley proof.
རགས་ཐིག (rəgdig) roughly, crudely, in draft form, cursorily; va.—ལེན་ to measure sth. roughly, to take a rough survey; va.—རྒྱག to make a rough outline/ sketch.
རགས་རྡོ་ (ragdo) stones for building dams.
རགས་བསྡུས་ (rəgdüü) cursory, in summary, in outline, general, brief ¶ ཁོང་གིས་ཚོགས་འདུའི་ཐོག་གཏམ་བཤད་རགས་བསྡུས་ཤིག་གནང་སོང་ He gave a brief speech at the meeting. ¶ རྒྱལ་རབས་ལོ་རྒྱུས་སྙིང་དོན་རགས་བསྡུས་ཙམ་ཞིག་འབྲི་གི་ཡིན་ I will write briefly on the essence of the history.
རགས་པ་ (ragba) 1. rough, coarse ¶ བྱེ་མ་རགས་པ་ Coarse sand. 2. cursory, not in detail ¶ གཏམ་བཤད་རགས་པ་ A cursory speech.
རགས་པ་ཆེ་ལོང་ (ragba cēloŋ) the more important/ essential aspect.
རགས་བྲིས་ (ragdriì) rough sketch, outline drawing.
རགས་དབྱིབས་ (rəgyib) outline, initial sketch/ form, model.
རགས་རྨོ་རགས་འདེབས་ (ragmo randeb) plowing roughly and sowing roughly.
རགས་ཙམ་ (rəgdzam) in general, not in detail, cursorily ¶ གནས་ཚུལ་དེའི་སྐོར་ཁོང་གིས་རགས་ཙམ་བཤད་སོང་ He spoke generally (not in detail) about this situation.
རགས་ཙམ་མཐོང་བ་ (ragdzam tõŋwa) superficial view.
རགས་བཙིར་བཟོ་གྲྭ་ (ragdzii sodra) cogging factory.
རགས་བཙེམས་དཔེ་དེབ་ (ragdzem bēdeb) a crudely bound book.
རགས་རྩིས་ (rəgdziì) rough estimate/ approximation; va.—རྒྱག.
རགས་རྩིས་ཁྲུའུ་ (rəgdziì drūwu) tib. ch. budget office.
རགས་ཞིབ་ (rəgshib) rough and coarse, fine and detailed.
རགས་བཟོ་ (ragso) sm. རགས་ལས་.
རགས་བཟོ་རྫོབ་ལས་ (ragso dzoblɛɛ̀) roughly/ crudely manufactured; va.—བྱེད་.
རགས་རིམ་ (rəgrim) sm. རགས་པ་.
རགས་རོབ་ (ragrob) sm. རགས་པ་.
རགས་ལས་ (raàlɛɛ̀) 1. roughly/ simply/ crudely done work, superficial job. 2. sm. རག་ལས་.
རགས་བཤད་ (ragshɛɛ̀) talking in generalities, speaking cursorily; va.—བྱེད་ to speak in generalities/ approximations, to talk cursorily.
རགས་བཞིར་ཀུའུ་ (ragshee gūwu) tib. ch. preliminary hearing/ trial.
རགས་སྲུང་ཤིང་ནགས་ (ragsuŋ shiŋnaà) protective belt of trees planted along an embankment.
རང་ (raŋ) 1. self, oneself, own ¶ རང་གི་ཕ་ཡུལ་ One's own homeland. 2. (pronoun + —) makes reflectives ¶ ཁོ་རང་ He himself. ¶ ང་རང་ I myself. 3. really, definitely, surely ¶ བསམ་བློ་འདི་རེ་སྟོང་ཞིག་རང་རེད་ This is really a hopeless idea. ¶ འདི་འདྲ་བྱས་ན་ཏང་གི་གཅིག་སྒྲིལ་གཏོར་བཤིག་བྱས་པ་རང་རེད་ If (you) do this it will definitely disrupt the unity of the party. ¶ ཁོ་རྒྱ་མི་རང་རེད་ He is really Chinese. 4. (adj. + — + neg.) not so, not entirely, not quite ¶ འདི་བཟོ་སྐབས་སྤུས་ཚད་ཡག་པོ་རང་བྱུང་མི་འདུག When they made this, the quality wasn't so good. ¶ ང་འདི་དགའ་པོ་རང་མི་འདུག I don't like this too much. 5. precisely, exactly, the very ¶ ང་དེབ་འདི་རང་དགོས་ I want this very book. 6. (neg. + vb. + — + vb.) no choice but to do verbal action ¶ ང་ཚོས་ལས་ཀ་མ་བྱས་རང་བྱས་རེད་ We have no choice but to work.
རང་: p.**རངས་** (raŋ) vi. to be happy/ joyful/ glad/ satisfied ¶ བཟོ་པ་དེ་རར་གླ་ཆ་སྤྲོད་སྐབས་ཤིན་ཏུ་རང་བའི་ཉམས་འགྱུར་སྟོན་གྱི་འདུག When (I) paid the worker he appeared to be very glad.
རང་བཀུར་ (raŋgur) self-esteem, self-respect.
རང་བཀུར་གྱི་བསམ་པ་ (raŋgurgi sāmba) sm. རང་བཀུར་.
རང་རྐང་རང་ཚུགས་ (raŋgaŋ randzuù) sm. རང་རྒྱ་.
རང་རྐང་རང་ལང་ (raŋgaŋ raŋlaŋ) sm. རང་རྒྱ་.
རང་རྒྱ་ (raŋgya) independent, standing on one's own two feet; vi.—འཐེར་ to be independent, to be able to stand on one's own two feet ¶ ཁྱོད་ཚོ་རང་རྒྱ་མ་འཐེར་བར་དུ་ང་འགྲོ་གི་མིན་ I won't go until you are able to stand on your own two feet. ¶ རང་རྒྱ་འཐེར་བའི་བསམ་གཞིགས་ Independent thinking.
རང་སྐལ་ (raŋgɛɛ) one's share (of sth.).
རང་སྐལ་ལྕགས་ཡིན་ཡང་མུར་ (raŋgɛɛ jāà yinyaŋ mur) sm. རང་སྐལ་ཆུ་རྡོ་ཡིན་རུང་མུར་ [Lit. if one's share is an iron, suck on it].
རང་སྐལ་ཆུ་རྡོ་ཡིན་རུང་མུར་ (raŋgɛɛ cūdo yinruŋ mur) fulfilling one's duty no matter what it takes to get it done [Lit. if one's share is a river stone, suck on it].
རང་སྐེ་རང་བསྡམས་ (raŋge random) 1. strangling/ hanging oneself; va.—བྱེད་. 2. doing sth. that causes one's own harm/ downfall/ demise; va.—བྱེད་.
རང་སྐྱ་ (raŋgya) sm. རང་རྒྱ་.
རང་སྐྱིད་གཞན་སྨོན་ (raŋgyiì shɛnmön) being the envy of others due to one's well-being/ happiness.
རང་སྐྱེངས་ (raŋgyeŋ) being ashamed/ embarrassed ¶ དེ་འདྲ་བྱས་ན་རང་སྐྱེངས་ཡོང་གི་རེད་ If you do that you will get embarrassed.
རང་སྐྱེས་ (raŋgyeè) 1. growing by itself. 2. born to

oneself.

རང་སྐྱོང་ (raŋgyoŋ) autonomy, self-government, self-rule; va.—བྱེད་ ། ས་གནས་དེ་གའི་འགོ་ཁྲིད་ཀྱིས་རང་སྐྱོང་བྱེད་ཀྱི་ཡོད་པ་རེད་ That area's officials are ruling autonomously.

རང་སྐྱོང་ཁུལ་ (raŋgyoŋ küü) autonomous area.

རང་སྐྱོང་གི་རྣམ་པ་ (raŋgyoŋgi nāmba) appearance/ form of autonomy.

རང་སྐྱོང་མངའ་ཁུལ་ (raŋgyoŋ ŋəəgüü) autonomous dominion, self-governing territory.

རང་སྐྱོང་ལྗོངས་ (raŋgyoŋjoŋ) autonomous region ། བོད་རང་སྐྱོང་ལྗོངས་གྲ་སྒྲིག་ཨུ་ཡོན་ལྷན་ཁང་ The Preparatory Committee for the Tibet Autonomous Region.

རང་སྐྱོང་མནའ་མཐུན་ (raŋgyoŋ nadün) autonomous/ self-governing league.

རང་སྐྱོང་དབང་ཆ་ (raŋgyoŋ wāŋja) the right of autonomy.

རང་སྐྱོང་གཙང་མ་ (raŋgyoŋ dzāŋma) complete autonomy.

རང་སྐྱོང་རྫོང་ (raŋgyoŋ dzoŋ) sm. རང་སྐྱོང་ཞིན་.

རང་སྐྱོང་ཞིན་ (raŋgyoŋ shen) tib. ch. autonomous county.

རང་སྐྱོང་ལམ་སྲོལ་ (raŋgyoŋ lamsöö) custom or tradition of self rule/ autonomy.

རང་སྐྱོང་ལས་ཁུངས་ (raŋgyoŋ lɛ̀ɛ̀guŋ) autonomous office.

རང་སྐྱོང་ས་ཁོངས་ (raŋgyoŋ sāgoŋ) autonomous region/ area.

རང་སྐྱོང་ས་གནས་ (raŋgyoŋ sānɛɛ̀) sm. རང་སྐྱོང་ས་ཁོངས་.

རང་སྐྱོན་ (raŋgyēn) one's own mistakes, self-criticism; va.—ཤོད་; —བརྗོད་ to say or tell one's own mistakes, to do self-examination/ self-criticism; va.—བརྟག to examine one's own mistakes/ errors ། ཁོང་གིས་ཚོགས་འདུའི་ཐོག་རང་སྐྱོན་བཤད་པ་རེད་ He did self-criticism at the meeting.

རང་སྐྱོན་ངོས་ལེན་ (raŋgyön ŋöölen) confessing/ admitting one's own mistakes; va.—བྱེད་.

རང་སྐྱོན་བརྗོད་ (raŋgyēn jöö) see རང་སྐྱོན་.

རང་སྐྱོན་བརྟག (rəŋgyön dāà) see རང་སྐྱོན་.

རང་སྐྱོན་ཐལ་མོས་བཀབ་ནས་མི་སྐྱོན་མཛུབ་མོས་འདྲུ་ (raŋgyön tɛ̄ɛ̄möö gābnɛ migyön dzubmü dru) not admitting one's mistakes while digging up faults of others [Lit. to hide one's mistakes with one's palm and dig the faults of the others with one's fingers].

རང་སྐྱོན་ཐུག་ཁྲུ་གང་དེ་ས་ལ་སྦས་ མི་སྐྱོན་གཟར་བུ་གང་དེ་འཕྱར་འཕྱར་བྱེད་ (raŋgyön tūgdru kaŋde sāla bɛɛ̀ migyön sarbu kaŋde cārcār cee) hiding one's own big errors and exposing other people's small errors [Lit. hiding one's own errors which are as much as a full pot, showing other peoples' errors which are (only) as much as a full ladle].

རང་སྐྱོན་གཞན་འགེལ་ (raŋgyön shengee) putting the blame of one's errors onto others; va.—བྱེད་.

རང་སྐྱོན་རང་བརྗོད་ (raŋgyön raŋjöö) self-criticism, criticizing one's own mistakes; va.—བྱེད་.

རང་སྐྱོན་རང་བརྟག (raŋgyön raŋdaà) searching/ investigating/ looking for one's own mistakes; va.—བྱེད་.

རང་སྐྱོན་རང་ཞིབ་ (raŋgyön raŋshib) investigating one's own faults/ errors; va.—བྱེད་.

རང་སྐྱོན་གཞན་གཡོག (raŋgyön shɛnyɔɔ̀) putting the blame on others for one's own mistakes; va.—བྱེད་.

རང་སྐྱོན་ལ་བརྟག (raŋgyönla dāà) see རང་སྐྱོན་བརྟག.

རང་སྐྱོན་ཤོད་ (raŋgyön shöö) sm. རང་སྐྱོན་རང་བརྗོད་.

རང་སྐྱོན་ཤེས་པ་ (raŋgyön shēèba) knowing one's faults; va.—བྱེད་.

རང་སྐྱོན་སུན་འབྱིན་ (raŋgyön sũnjin) rebuking oneself for one's errors; va.—བྱེད་.

རང་སྐྱོན་སྲོང་ (raŋgyön sāŋ) va. to correct/ mend one's faults.

རང་སྐྱོབ་ (raŋgyob) saving/ helping oneself; va.—བྱེད་.

རང་ཁ་ (raŋga) one's own mouth; va.—གསོ་ to live by one's own toil, to be self-sufficient.

རང་ཁ་འཁྱིད་ཙམ་ (raŋga ciidzam) just enough to manage.

རང་ཁ་གསོ་ (raŋga sō) see རང་ཁ་.

རང་ཁ་རང་གསོ་ (raŋga rāŋso) sm. རང་ཁ་གསོ་.

རང་ཁག་གཞན་འགེལ་ (raŋgaà shengee) sm. རང་སྐྱོན་གཞན་འགེལ་.

རང་ཁུ་རང་སིམ་ (raŋgu raŋsim) 1. boiling meat, etc. unitl the juice is absorbed in the meat. 2. using sth. of one's own on oneself.

རང་ཁུངས་ (raŋguŋ) 1. belonging to oneself, one's own ། རང་ཁུངས་མི་སེར་ One's own subjects/ serfs. 2. one's origin/ source.

རང་ཁུངས་བརྗེད་ (rəŋguŋ jee) vi. to forget one's origin.

རང་ཁུངས་མི་རྫ་ (rəŋguŋ midza) shung. one's own serf.

རང་ཁུངས་རང་སྐྱེལ་ (rəŋguŋ raŋgyee) proving sth. oneself; va.—བྱེད་.

རང་ཁུངས་ལས་བྱེད་ (raŋguŋ lɛ̀ɛ̀jee) sm. རང་ཁོངས་ལས་བྱེད་.

རང་ཁུལ་ (raŋgüü) one's own place/ area.

རང་ཁེ་ (rəŋge) self-interest, self-benefit; va.—གཉེར་ to look after one's self interest.

རང་ཁེ་གང་ལོན་ (rəŋge kaŋlön) looking after one's self-interest as much as possible, seeking as much profit for oneself as possible.

རང་ཁེ་ཅི་ལོན་ (rəŋge jīlön) sm. རང་ཁེ་གང་ལོན་.

རང་ཁེ་ཕུགས་སུ་ཞེན་ (raŋge pūgsu shen) va. to hold one's own future interest as the most important.

རང་ཁེ་བློ་མང་ (raŋge lōmaŋ) having many ideas or thoughts of making profit for oneself.

རང་ཁེ་རང་ཕན་ (raŋge raŋben) sm. རང་ཁེ་.

རང་ཁོངས་ (raŋgoŋ) part of one's own unit/ area.

རང་ཁོངས་ལས་བྱེད་ (raŋgoŋ lɛ̀ɛ̀jee) sb. employed directly by an office (rather than appointed by the government, this is a term used in exile).

རང་ཁྱིམ་ (raŋgyim) one's home.

རང་ཁྱིམ་རང་བདག (raŋgyim raŋdaà) being the master of one's own household/ affairs/ fate; va.—བྱེད་.

རང་ཁྲལ་གཞན་འགེལ་ (raŋtrɛɛ shengee) transferring one's taxes/ responsibilities to others.

རང་ཁྲིམས་ཐེག་པ་ཁུར་ལེན་ (raŋ trīm tēgba kūrlen) shung. adhering to the law, law abiding.

རང་ཁྲིམས་སྤྱི་ཁུར་ (rəŋdrim jīgur) shung. law abiding ། རང་ཁྲིམས་སྤྱི་ཁུར་གྱི་རྒྱལ་མཐུན་སྡོད་མཁས་དགོས་རྒྱུ་ One must be a good law abiding citizen.

རང་མགོ་ (rango) one's own needs ། རང་མགོའི་དངོས་པོ་ཚང་མ་ཉོས་པ་རེད་ I bought all the things I need.

རང་མགོ་རང་སྒྲུབ་ (rango raŋdrub) sm. རང་ཁ་རང་གསོ་.

རང་མགོ་རང་འདང་ (rango raŋdaŋ) sm. རང་ཁ་རང་གསོ་.

རང་མགོ་རང་ལྡང (rango raŋdaŋ) sm. རང་ཁ་རང་གསོ་.

རང་མགོ་རང་ལྡིང་ (rango raŋdeŋ) sm. རང་ཁ་རང་གསོ་.

རང་མགོ་རང་སྒྲོད་ (rango raŋdröö) sm. རང་ཁ་རང་གསོ་.

རང་འཁོར་ (raŋgɔɔ) 1. self-revolving, automatically revolving; vi.—རྒྱག to automatically revolve/ turn around ། ས་གཞི་རིལ་མོས་རང་འཁོར་རྒྱག་བཞིན་པར་ཉི་མར་སྐོར་བ་རྒྱག་གི་ཡོད་པ་རེད་ The world revolves by itself around the sun. 2. retribution, sth. bad coming back to harm oneself ། མི་ངན་པ་དེ་ལ་ལས་འབྲས་རང་འཁོར་བྱུང་སོང་ That bad person got karmic retribution (for his bad deeds).

རང་འཁྲི་ (rəŋdri) one's own responsibility ། འདི་ངའི་རང་འཁྲིའི་ལས་འགན་མ་རེད་ This is not my responsibility.

རང་འཁྲིའི་ཁྲལ་འབབ་ (rəŋdrii trɛ̀ɛ̀bəb) shung. payable taxes.

རང་འཁྲིའི་བྱེད་སྒོ་ (rəŋdrii ceego) sm. རང་འཁྲིའི་ལས་འགན་.

རང་འཁྲིའི་ལས་འགན་ (rəŋdrii lɛŋen) one's duty/ assignment, work that one is responsible for.

རང་འཁྲིའི་ལས་དོན་ (rəŋdrii lɛ̀ɛ̀dön) one's own

work, work that one is responsible for.

རང་ག་བ་ (ra̱ŋgawa) ordinary ། ཁོ་མི་རང་ག་བ་ཞིག་རེད་ He is an ordinary person.

རང་ག་མ་ (ra̱ŋgama) sm. རང་ག་བ་.

རང་གི་ (ra̱ŋgi) one's own ། རང་གི་དེབ་ One's own book.

རང་གི་ངང་ (ra̱ŋgi ŋa̱ŋ) sm. རང་ཤུགས་.

རང་གི་ངོ་བོ་ (ra̱ŋgi ŋowo) one's nature/ character.

རང་གི་ངོས་འཛིན་ (ra̱ŋgi ŋöndzin) sth. one has accepted, one's opinion ། རང་གི་ངོས་འཛིན་ཡིན་མ་གཏོགས་ཁྱེད་རང་ལ་ཨུ་ཚུགས་རྒྱག་གི་མེད་ This is just sth. I accept. I will not insist you (do also).

རང་གི་མཚན་ཉིད་ (ra̱ŋgi tsɛ̄nñii) one's own characteristics.

རང་གི་ལོ་རྒྱུས་ (ra̱ŋgi lu̱güü) autobiography.

རང་གི་ཤེས་པ་ (ra̱ŋgi shēèba) one's own views/ concepts/ knowledge.

རང་གིར་བྱེད་ (ra̱ŋgir cɛ̱̀ɛ) va. to take ownership/ possession ། ཁང་པ་དེ་ཁོས་རང་གིར་བྱས་བཞག He took possession of the house.

རང་གིར་བཟུང་ (ra̱ŋgir su̱ŋ) sm. རང་གིར་བྱེད་.

རང་གིས་ (ra̱ŋgi) by oneself ། ནང་སྦྱོང་དེ་རང་གིས་བྱ་དགོས་པ་རེད་ One should do homework oneself. ། རང་གིས་དེ་འདྲ་བྱས་ན་གྱོང་རག་གི་རེད་ If one does that, one will suffer a loss.

རང་གིས་ངང་གིས་ (ra̱ŋgi ŋa̱ŋgi) naturally/ unconsciously adopting another's character, one's character being influenced by another ། ཕྲུ་གུ་དེ་གྲོགས་པོ་ངན་པ་མཉམ་དུ་འཁྱིན་ཙང་རང་གིས་ངང་གིས་གོམས་གཤིས་ངན་པ་འགོས་བཞག Because that child went around with bad friends, he unconsciously adopted bad habits.

རང་གིས་དཔེ་སྟོན་ (ra̱ŋgi bēdön) setting an example oneself; va.—བྱེད་.

རང་གུས་དང་བའི་སྒོ་ནས་ (rə̱bgüü ta̱ŋwɛ go̱nɛ) shung. with great respect.

རང་གྲངས་ཉིས་སྒྱུར་ (ra̱ndraŋ ñīīgyur) square, squared (in math).

རང་གྲངས་ཉིས་སྒྱུར་གྱི་གཞི་ (ra̱ndraŋ ñīīgyurgi shi̱) square root (in math).

རང་གྲུབ་ (rə̱ndrub) naturally occurring ། རང་གྲུབ་ཀྱི་ཤིང་ནགས་ Natural forest.

རང་གྲུབ་འགག་བཙན་ (rə̱ndrub ga̱gdzɛn) natural barriers.

རང་གྲུབ་བཙན་ས་ (rə̱ndrub dzɛ̄nsa) sm. རང་གྲུབ་འགག་བཙན་.

རང་གྲུབ་སྲུང་ཡོལ་ (rə̱ndrub sūŋyüü) natural line of defense.

རང་སྒྲོན་ (ra̱ndrön) one's own expenses; va.—གཏོང་ to pay one's own expenses.

རང་སྒྲོན་གཞན་གཏོང་ (ra̱ndrön sẖɛndoŋ) sb. else paying one's expenses.

རང་སྒྲོན་རང་གཏོང་ (ra̱ndrön rāŋdoŋ) paying one's own expenses; va.—བྱེད་.

རང་དགའ་ (ra̱ŋga) 1. doing whatever one likes, acting without restraints, unfettered behavior; va.—འཛོག; —གཏོང་. to let sb. do what they want or act as they wish ། སྐད་ཆ་རང་དགར་ཤོད་རྒྱུ་མེད་པར་བསམ་བློ་བཏང་ནས་ཤོད་དགོས་ You shouldn't say whatever you like; you should think then speak. ། སྡིག་ལམ་མི་སྲུང་མཁན་དེ་ཚོ་རང་དགར་འཛོག་རྒྱུ་མེད་ You should let the bad people who don't adhere to the rules do what ever they like. 2. va. to leave sb./ sth. unattended or not cared for, to leave sth. as it is without doing sth. to correct/ change it. 3. vi. to be/ get left unattended or not looked after, to leave sth. as it is without doing sth. to correct/ change it ། པ་ཕས་ཨ་རག་མང་པོ་བཏུངས་ཙང་ཕྲུ་གུ་དེ་བདག་པོ་རྒྱག་མཁན་མེད་པར་རང་དགར་ལུས་བཞག Because the father drank a lot of liquor, the child was left alone without being looked after. 4. va. to pay sb. back ། ཁོས་ང་ལ་རྙོགས་དྲ་མང་པོ་བཟོས་ཙང་ཉི་མ་གཅིག་ཁོ་རང་དགར་འཛོག་གི་མིན་ Because he caused me a lot of trouble, one day I'll pay him back for this.

རང་དགར་འཛོག (ra̱ŋga jɔ̱ɔ̀) va. to leave sb./ sth. unattended or not cared for, to leave sth. as it is without doing sth. to correct/ change it.

རང་དགར་སྡོད་ (ra̱ŋga döö) va. to sit around idly, to hang around without doing anything.

རང་དགར་ལུས་ (ra̱ŋga lü̱ü) vi. to be/ get left unattended or not looked after, to leave sth. as it is without doing sth. to correct/ change it ། པ་ཕས་ཨ་རག་མང་པོ་བཏུངས་ཙང་ཕྲུ་གུ་དེ་བདག་པོ་རྒྱག་མཁན་མེད་པར་རང་དགར་ལུས་བཞག Because the father drank a lot of liquor, the child was left alone without being looked after.

རང་མགོ་ཆུ་འདྲེན་ (ra̱ŋgo cūndren) bringing misfortune/ harm on oneself (by one's own action) [Lit. bringing water on one's own head].

རང་མགོ་ཆུ་ལླུག (ra̱ŋgo cūluù) sm. རང་མགོ་ཆུ་འདྲེན་.

རང་མགོ་ཐོན་ (ra̱ŋgo tȫn) vi. to become self-sufficient/ self-reliant, to stand on one's own two feet.

རང་མགོ་འདོན་ (ra̱ŋgo dö̱n) va. to take actions to become self-sufficient.

རང་མགོ་རང་ཐོན་ (ra̱ŋgo ra̱ndön) sm. རང་མགོ་རང་འདོན་.

རང་མགོ་རང་འདོན་ (ra̱ŋgo ra̱ndön) being self-reliant, self-sufficient; va.—བྱེད་.

རང་མགོ་རང་ཡུགས་ཀྱིས་འཚམས་པ་ (ra̱ŋgo ra̱nbaàgi tũmbə) having just enough to take care of oneself.

རང་མགོན་བཀའ་དྲིན་ཟླ་མེད་ (ra̱ŋgön gādrin da̱meè) our greatful savior.

རང་འགན་ (ra̱ŋgɛn) one's own responsibility/ duty; va.—སྒྲུབ་ to accomplish/ fulfill one's responsibilities.

རང་འགན་གཞན་དྲི་ (ra̱ŋgɛn sẖɛndri) shifting one's responsibility to sb. else; va.—བྱེད་.

རང་འགར་གང་བྱུང་ (ra̱ŋgar ka̱ŋjuŋ) shung. doing whatever one likes/ desires.

རང་འགུལ་ (rə̱ŋgüü) 1. automatic, moving by itself ། རང་འགུལ་གྱི་འཁོར་སྐྱོགས་ An automatic lathe. 2. voluntarily ། རང་འགུལ་གྱིས་རོགས་རམ་བྱེད་ཀྱི་འདུག (They) are voluntarily helping. 3. taking the initiative; va.—བྱེད་ ། ངས་རང་འགུལ་གྱིས་བསམ་འཆར་སྔོན་ལ་སྨྲས་པ་ཡིན་ I took the initiative and told my opinion first.

རང་འགུལ་ཁ་པར་ (rə̱ŋgüü kābaa) direct dial telephone ། རང་འགུལ་ཁ་པར་བརྗེ་རེས་ཀྱི་འཕྲུལ་འཁོར་ A direct dial telephone exchange machine.

རང་འགུལ་གྱི་འཁོར་སྐྱོགས་ (rə̱ŋgüügi kɔ̄ɔdeg) automatic lathe.

རང་འགུལ་གྱི་མཚོན་ཆ་ (rə̱ŋgüügi tsō̃nja) automatic weapons.

རང་འགུལ་ཅན་ (rə̱ŋgüüjɛn) automatic; vi.—དུ་འགྱུར་ to get automated; va.—དུ་གཏོང་ to automate.

རང་འགུལ་ཅན་ཕྱེད་ཙམ་ (rə̱ŋgüüjɛn cēdzam) semiautomatic, semiautomated.

རང་འགུལ་ཆེད་སྤྱོད་ཀྱི་འཕྲུལ་སྐྱོགས་ (rə̱ŋgüü cēèjöögi trũũdeg) automatic lathe.

རང་འགུལ་འཕྲུལ་འཁོར་ (rə̱ŋgüü trũũgɔɔ) an automatic machine.

རང་འགུལ་འཕྲུལ་ཆས་ཅན་ (rə̱ŋgüü trũũjɛɛ̀jɛn) automated and mechanized.

རང་འགུལ་འཕྲུལ་མདའ་ (rə̱ŋgüü trũnda) machine gun, automatic weapon.

རང་འགུལ་ཚོད་འཛིན་ (rə̱ŋgüü tsöndzin) automatic control; va.—བྱེད་.

རང་འགུལ་མེ་མདའ་ (rə̱ŋgüü me̱nda) automatic rifle/ gun.

རང་འགུལ་མཚོན་ཆ་ (rə̱ŋgüü tsō̃nja) automatic arms/ weapons.

རང་འགོ་ཐོན་ (ra̱ŋgo tö̃n) sm. རང་མགོ་ཐོན་.

རང་འགོ་གང་ཐོན་ (ra̱ŋgo ka̱ndön) acting with one's own gains in mind, selfishly individualistic; va.—བྱེད་.

རང་འགྲིགས་ (ra̱ndrig) sth. completely provided for by oneself.

རང་འགྲུབ་བཙན་ས་ (rəŋdrub dzensa) sm. རང་གྲུབ་འགག་བཙན་.

རང་འགྲེལ་ (raŋdrel) giving one's own explanation.

རང་འགྲོགས་འོད་ (raŋdrɔɔ wöö) natural brightness.

རང་འགྲོས་ལ་འཇོག (raŋdröölа jɔɔ) va. to let a person do his thing without interfering, to leave sb. alone ¶ ཕྲུ་གུ་དེ་རང་འགྲོས་ལ་བཞག་ན་སློབ་སྦྱོང་ཡག་པོ་བྱེད་ཀྱི་མ་རེད་ If you leave that child alone, he won't do well in his studies.

རང་རྒོལ་ལངས་མཆོང་ (raŋgöö laŋjoŋ) rising up and revolting against sb.

རང་རྒྱལ་ (raŋgyɛɛ) 1. our nation/ country. 2. one's own victory.

རང་རྒྱལ་གྱི་དངོས་ཟོག (raŋgyɛɛgi ŋōösɔɔ) native goods, goods from our own country.

རང་རྒྱལ་གྱིས་བཟོས་པ་ (raŋgyɛɛgi sööba) products made in one's own country.

རང་རྒྱལ་གཞན་ཕམ་ (raŋgyɛɛ shembam) sm. རང་རྒྱལ་གཞན་ཕུང་.

རང་རྒྱལ་གཞན་ཕུང་ (raŋgyɛɛ shempuŋ) acting with one's own victory and another's loss in mind; va.—བྱེད་.

རང་རྒྱུ་ (raŋgyu) one's own wealth/ property.

རང་རྒྱུད་ (raŋgyüü) 1. state of mind ¶ ཆོས་བྱས་ན་རང་རྒྱུད་དུལ་པོ་ཆགས་ཀྱི་རེད་ If one practices religion, one's mind will become calm. 2. one's ancestors/ lineage.

རང་རྒྱུད་པ་ (raŋgyüüba) a follower of the Svatantrika school of Madhyamika Buddhism.

རང་རྒྱུད་ལུགས་ (raŋgyüüba) the Svatantrika school of Madhyamika Buddhism.

རང་རྒྱུད་རང་ལོན་ (raŋgyüü raŋlön) knowing oneself, knowing one's capabilities; va.—བྱེད་.

རང་རྒྱུད་ལ་སྦྱར་ (raŋgyüüla jar) va. to take to heart/ mind.

རང་རྒྱུད་ལ་ལོན་ (raŋgyüüla lön) va. to take to heart/ mind.

རང་རྒྱུས་རང་ལོན་ (raŋgyüü raŋlön) sm. རང་རྒྱུད་རང་ལོན་.

རང་སྒེར་ (raŋger) individual, personal.

རང་སྒེར་གཅིག་གཅོད་ (raŋger jīgjöö) va. to decide things by oneself.

རང་སྒྱུར་ (rəŋgyur) power (in math).

རང་སྒྱུར་གྲངས་ (rəŋgyur traŋ) power (in math).

རང་སྒྱུར་ཐེངས་གྲངས་ (rəŋgyur tēŋdraŋ) ascending power (in math).

རང་སྒྱུར་རིམ་གྲངས་ (rəŋgyur rimdraŋ) power series (in math).

རང་སྒྲིག (rəŋdrig) sm. རང་འགྲིག.

རང་ངེ་རོང་ངེ་ (raŋŋe roŋŋe) rough, coarse, rocky, uneven, bumpy.

རང་ངོ་ (raŋŋo) one's face.

རང་ངོ་མ་ (raŋ ŋoma) yourself, oneself.

རང་ངོམ་ (raŋŋom) praising oneself, flattering oneself, being proud/ arrogant/ conceited/ self-important; va.—བྱེད་.

རང་ངོམ་ཚ་པོ་ (raŋŋom tsābo) a braggart, sb. who praises himself, sb. who is proud/ conceited and shows off or likes to be in the limelight.

རང་ངོམ་རང་ཆེ་ (raŋŋom raŋce) sm. རང་ངོམ་.

རང་ངོམ་རང་བསྟོད་ (raŋŋom raŋdöö) sm. རང་ངོམ་.

རང་ངོམ་རིང་ལུགས་ (raŋŋom riŋluù) showing offism, limelightism (being fond of being in the limelight).

རང་ངོས་ (raŋŋöö) oneself, one's own, one's own view ¶ རང་ངོམ་ནས་ཁྱེད་རང་ལ་ལྷག་བསམ་རྣམ་དག་གི་བསམ་འཆར་ཞུས་པ་ཡིན་ From my point of view, I gave you sincere suggestions.

རང་ངོས་ཀྱི་ཆ་རྐྱེན་ (raŋŋöögi cāgyen) one's own conditions (effort, intelligence, wealth, etc.) ¶ སློབ་སྦྱོང་ཡག་པོ་ཡོང་མིན་རང་ངོས་ཀྱི་ཆ་རྐྱེན་ལ་རག་ལས་པ་རེད་ Whether one does well in school or not depends on one's conditions.

རང་དངོས་ (raŋŋöö) one's own property/ possessions/ things.

རང་ཅག (raŋjaà) we.

རང་གཅུན་ (raŋjün) self-discipline, self-restraint, self-control; va.—བྱེད་.

རང་གཅུན་ལྷོད་མེད་ (raŋjün lhōömeè) sm. རང་རང་ནན་གཅུན་.

རང་གཅུན་སྤྱི་གཅེས་ (raŋjün jījeè) whole hearted devotion to public duty; working selflessly for the public interest.

རང་གཅུན་ལུགས་གསོ་ (raŋjün lugso) to restrain oneself and restore/ revive customs (a slogan coined by Lin Biao during the Cultural Revolution).

རང་གཅེས་ཐེག་པ་ཁུར་ལེན་ (raŋjeè tēgba kūrlen) shung. abiding by the law.

རང་གཅོད་ (raŋjöö) decided by oneself.

རང་གཅོད་ཀྱི་དབང་ཆ་ (raŋjöögi wāŋja) right of self-determination.

རང་ཅྲེབ་ (raŋjeb) committing suicide; va.—བྱེད་.

རང་ཆ་ (raŋja) one's own share/ portion.

རང་ཆགས་ (raŋjaà) naturally formed/ created.

རང་ཆས་ (raŋjɛɛ) 1. sm. རང་བྱུང་. 2. one's own things/ possessions.

རང་ཆེ་ (raŋce) sm. རང་ངོམ་རང་བསྟོད་.

རང་ཆེ་རང་བསྟོད་ (raŋce raŋdöö) sm. རང་ངོམ་.

རང་ཆེ་རང་མཐོ་ (raŋce raŋto) sm. རང་ངོམ་.

རང་ཆེ་རང་སློམ་ (raŋce raŋlom) sm. རང་ངོམ་.

རང་ཇུས་ (raŋjüü) one's plan/ strategy.

རང་ཇུས་རང་འཁོར་ (raŋjüü raŋgɔɔ) one's own strategy to benefit oneself backfires and causes harm to oneself.

རང་ཇུས་རང་ཕོག (raŋjüü raŋpɔɔ) sm. རང་ཇུས་རང་འཁོར་.

རང་འཇགས་ (raŋjaà) as was, as before, unchanged; va.—འཇོག to leave as was, to leave without change, to leave as before ¶ སྲིད་བློན་རང་འཇགས་ཐོབ་རྒྱུའི་ཡིད་ཆེས་བྱས་ཡོད་པ་རེད་ (He) believed that he would win the Prime Minister position as before. ¶ འདི་རང་འཇགས་གནས་ཡོད་པ་རེད་ It has stayed as before without change.

རང་འཇགས་ཕྱིར་ལོག (raŋjaà cīīlɔɔ) returning back (to one's previous home); va.—གཏོང་ to send back to one's previous home; va.—བྱེད་ to go back to one's previous home.

རང་འཇགས་སུ་འཇོག (raŋjaàsu jɔɔ) sm. རང་འཇགས་འཇོག.

རང་འཇིག་རང་སྐྱོབ་ (raŋjig raŋgyob) overcoming one's hardships/ difficulties by oneself; va.—བྱེད་.

རང་ལྗོངས་ (raŋjoŋ) our region, one's own area ¶ རང་ལྗོངས་ཀྱི་ཞིང་ལས་ཐོན་སྐྱེད་ལེགས་པོ་བྱུང་ཡོད་ Agriculture production from our region was good.

རང་བརྗོད་ (raŋjöö) one's own comments/ speech; va.—བྱེད་ ¶ ཁོང་གིས་རང་སྐྱོན་རང་བརྗོད་བྱས་པ་རེད་ He criticized himself.

རང་ཉམས་ (raŋñam) 1. one's mind/ thought. 2. thinking poorly of oneself.

རང་ཉིད་ (rəŋñii) oneself, itself, one's own, its own, myself, ourself ¶ རང་རྒྱལ་གྱིས་གཞི་ནས་རང་ཉིད་ཀྱི་གློག་འདོན་སྒྲིག་ཆས་བཟོ་བའི་བཟོ་ལས་བཙུགས་པ་རེད་ It was only then that our country established an industry for making its own power generating equipment. ¶ ཁོང་རང་ཉིད་ཀྱི་ནང་ལ་ལོག་སོང་ He returned to his own house. ¶ ང་རང་ཉིད་ཀྱི་ནང་ལ་ལོག་པ་ཡིན་ I returned to my house. ¶ རང་ཉིད་ནས་ཁྱེད་རང་ལ་ལྷག་བསམ་རྣམ་དག་གིས་བསམ་འཆར་ཞུས་པ་ཡིན་ From myself, I gave you sincere suggestions. ¶ ལས་ཀ་དེ་རང་ཉིད་ཀྱིས་བྱས་པ་ཡིན་ I did the work myself.

རང་ཉིད་ཀྱི་ཁྲིང་ཕྱུང་ (rəŋñiigi trēŋfuŋ) tib. ch. one's class status.

རང་ཉིད་ཀྱི་མྱོང་ཚོར་ (rəŋñii ñoŋdzɔɔ) personal experience.

རང་ཉིད་ཀྱི་གཞི་ཁུངས་ (rəŋñiigi shiguŋ) sm. རང་ཉིད་ཀྱི་ཁྲིང་ཕྱུང་.

རང་ཉིད་ཀྱི་ལོ་རྒྱུས་ (rang̱ñiigi lugyüü) autobiography.

རང་ཉིད་ཀྱི་ཤེས་ཚོར་ (rang̱ñiigi shēēdzɔɔ) understanding oneself.

རང་ཉིད་སྒྲིད་སློམ་ (rang̱ñii gyiilom) sm. རང་ཉིད་ཆེ་སློམ་.

རང་ཉིད་ཁེར་རྐྱང་ (rang̱ñii kērgyang) oneself/ itself alone ¶ ཨ་རིའི་གཞུང་གིས་རང་ཉིད་ཁེར་རྐྱང་ལ་རྒྱལ་ཁ་ལོན་ཐབས་བྱེད་ཀྱི་ཡོད་པ་མ་རེད་ The U.S. government isn't trying to get victory for itself alone.

རང་ཉིད་མཁས་སློམ་ (rang̱ñii kɛ̄ɛlom) showing off one's knowledge/ skill/ ability.

རང་ཉིད་བསྒྱུར་བཀོད་ (rang̱ñii gyurgöö) self-remolding, self-reeducation, self-reformation; va.—བྱེད་; —གཏོང་.

རང་ཉིད་ངོ་སྤྲོད་ (rang̱ñii ng̱odröö) self- introduction; va.—བྱེད་.

རང་ཉིད་ངོམ་ (rang̱ñii ng̱om) va. to glorify/ flatter/ praise oneself, to show off ¶ ཁོས་རང་ཉིད་ངོམ་གྱི་འདུག He is praising himself.

རང་ཉིད་གཅུན་ (rang̱ñii jüün) va. to restrain/ control oneself.

རང་ཉིད་ཆེ་སློམ་ (rang̱ñii cēlom) conceited, self-glorifying, praising oneself; va.—བྱེད་.

རང་ཉིད་དཔལ་སློམ་རིང་ལུགས་ (rang̱ñii bɛ̄ɛlom ring̱luù) individual pridism/ conceitism.

རང་ཉིད་སློབ་སྦྱོང་ (rang̱ñii lōbjong) self-study; va.—བྱེད་.

རང་ཉིད་སློབ་གསོ་ (rang̱ñii lōbso) self-education; va.—བྱེད་.

རང་ཉིད་རང་བརླག (rang̱ñii rang̱laà) damaged/ destroyed/ harmed by oneself.

རང་ཉིས་སྒྱུར་འབྱེད་ (rang̱ñii gyurlaà) va. to extract the square root (in math).

རང་ཉེས་ (rang̱ñeè) one's own crime.

རང་ཉེས་ངོས་ལེན་ཞུ་ཡིག (rang̱ñeè ng̱öòle shuyii) self-confession letter/ report.

རང་ཉེས་ཁས་ལེན་ (rang̱ñeè kɛ̄ɛlen) confessing/ admitting one's guilt; va.—བྱེད་.

རང་ཉེས་འགྱོད་བཤགས་ (rang̱ñeè gyöòshaà) repenting/ regretting one's own crime; va.—བྱེད་.

རང་ཉེས་རྗེན་བརྗོད་ (rang̱ñeè jenjöö) sm. རང་ཉེས་ཁས་ལེན་.

རང་ཉེས་གཞན་འགེལ་ (rang̱ñeè sheng̱ee) blaming sb. else for one's own crime; va.—བྱེད་.

རང་ཉེས་གཞན་གཡོགས་ (rang̱ñeè sheng̱yɔɔ) sm. རང་ཉེས་གཞན་འགེལ་.

རང་ཉེས་རང་ཞུ་ (rang̱ñeè rang̱shu) confessing one's crimes/ wrongdoing; va.—བྱེད་.

རང་ཉེས་གསལ་ཞུ་ (rang̱ñeè sɛ̱ɛshu) confessing one's crime/ wrongdoing clearly; va.—བྱེད་.

རང་ཉོས་ཀྱི་བྱ་བ་ (rang̱ñöògi c̱awa) one's own actions.

རང་གཉེར་ (rang̱ñer) managed by oneself ¶ རང་གཉེར་ས་ཞིང་ A farm managed by oneself.

རང་རྟགས་ (rang̱daà) intrinsic/ true characteristics, one's real charter/ nature; va.—སྟོན་ to show one's true characteristic/ nature/ self; vi.—མཚོན་ to have one's true character appear, to symbolize ¶ ཁོས་སྒྱུང་པོ་ཡིན་ཁུལ་བྱས་ཀྱང་གླེན་པའི་རང་རྟགས་བསྟན་སོང་ Even though he pretended to be clever, he showed his true nature of being stupid. ¶ བཅིངས་བཀྲོལ་ཐོབ་པའི་རང་རྟགས་མཚོན་པའི་མིང་ཞིག་རེད་ It is a name which symbolizes the achievement of liberation. ¶ ཁོས་སྒྱུང་པོ་ཡིན་ཁུལ་བྱས་ཀྱང་གླེན་པའི་རང་རྟགས་མཚོན་པ་རེད་ Even though he pretended to be clever, his true nature of being stupid appeared.

རང་རྟོགས་ (rang̱dɔɔ) understanding on one's own ¶ ཚིག་སྒྲུབ་འདི་དགེ་རྒན་གྱིས་འགྲེལ་བཤད་གསལ་པོ་མ་བརྒྱབ་ན་སློབ་ཕྲུག་ཚོས་རང་རྟོགས་ཀྱིས་ཤེས་ཁག་པོ་རེད་ Unless the teacher explains the sentence clearly, it is difficult for the students to understand it on their own. 2. volunteering, one's own initiative ¶ ཁོ་ཚོས་རང་རྟོགས་ཀྱིས་རང་ཉིད་མང་ཚོགས་ཀྱི་ལྟ་ཞིབ་འོག་ཏུ་འཇོག་གི་ཡོད་པ་རེད་ They voluntarily are putting themselves under the supervision of the masses.

རང་རྟོགས་རང་མོས་ (rang̱dɔɔ rang̱möö) voluntarily, willingly, of one's own free will/ initiative; va.—བྱེད་.

རང་སྟོབས་ (rang̱dob) (via) one's own efforts/ initiative. 2. one's own strength/ power.

རང་སྟོབས་རང་སྐྱེལ་ (rang̱dob rang̱bel) development/ improvement through one's own efforts, self-reliance; va.—བྱེད་.

རང་སྟོབས་རང་སྐྱེལ་ (rang̱dob rang̱bel) sm. རང་ཁ་རང་གསོ་.

རང་བསྟོད་ (rang̱döö) self-praise, bragging, self-glorification; va.—བྱེད་.

རང་བསྟོད་གཞན་སྨད་ (rang̱döö shenmɛɛ̀) praising oneself and degrading/ denigrating others.

རང་བསྟོད་རང་བསྔགས་ (rang̱döö rang̱draà) sm. རང་བསྟོད་.

རང་ཐག་གཅོད་ (rang̱daà jöö) va. to decide by oneself.

རང་ཐག་རང་གཅོད་ (rang̱daà rang̱jöö) deciding by oneself, self-determination ¶ མི་རིགས་རང་ཐག་རང་གཅོད་ Nationality self-determination.

རང་ཐག་རང་གཅོད་ཀྱི་དབང་ཆ་ (rang̱daà rang̱jöögi wāngja) the right of self-determination.

རང་ཐག་རང་བསྡམས་ (rang̱daà rang̱dam) getting harmed by one's own actions [Lit. to tie oneself with one's own rope].

རང་ཐད་ (rang̱dɛɛ̀) sm. རང་ངོས་.

རང་ཐོན་རང་འཚོང་ (rang̱dön rang̱dzong) producing and selling by oneself; va.—བྱེད་.

རང་མཐོ་ (rang̱to) shung. a measure of distance equal to the length between one's outstretched middle finger and thumb.

རང་མཐོ་རང་ཆེ་ (rang̱to rang̱ce) vain, conceited, arrogant, self-important.

རང་མཐོང་ (rang̱tong) sm. རང་མཐོ་རང་ཆེ་.

རང་མཐོང་ཆེ་བ་ (rang̱tong cēwa) sm. རང་མཐོ་རང་ཆེ་.

རང་མཐོང་ཆེན་པོ་ (rang̱tong cēmbo) sm. རང་མཐོ་རང་ཆེ་.

རང་མཐོང་ཚ་པོ་ (rang̱tong tsābo) sm. རང་མཐོ་རང་ཆེ་.

རང་མཐོང་རང་སྐྱེས་ (rang̱tong rang̱gyeè) sm. རང་མཐོང་རང་གཙོ.

རང་མཐོང་རང་གཙོམ (rang̱tong rang̱jɔɔ) underestimating one's achievements, putting oneself down, demeaning oneself, having an inferiority complex, va.—བྱེད་.

རང་མཐོང་རང་ཆེའི་ཕྱོགས་རིས་རིང་ལུགས་ (rang̱tong rang̱cee cɔ̄ɔrii ring̱luù) arrogant sectarianism.

རང་འཐག (rang̱daà) grindstone, millstone, va.—སྐོར་ to mill grain on a grindstone/ mill, to turn a grindstone.

རང་འཐག་སྐོར་ (rang̱daà gɔɔ̄) va. to turn a grindstone/ millstone.

རང་དག་ཁ་འཐབ་ (rang̱dag kādəb) just enough to subsist ¶ ཟླ་རེའི་གླ་ཕོགས་དེ་འགྲོ་སོང་དང་རང་དག་ཁ་འཐབ་ཏུ་འགྲོ་གི་འདུག (My) monthly salary is just enough to subsist on.

རང་དད་འདོད་མོས་ (rang̱dɛɛ dö̱ömöö) shung. sm. དད་པ་རང་མོས་.

རང་དོན་ (rang̱dön) one's own private affairs; va.—བྱེད་; —སྒྲུབ་ to do one's own private purpose affairs/ work/ activities (in contrast to those of a group).

རང་དོན་ཁོ་ནའི་རིང་ལུགས་ (rang̱dön kōnɛ ring̱luù) solipsism (in philosophy).

རང་དོན་ཁོག་ཏུ་བཅུག་ནས་གཞན་དོན་སྙིན་མ་ཟེར་ཟེར་ (rang̱dön kɔ̄gdu jüünɛ sheṉdön mīnma siṉsin) doing sth. for one's own benefit but acting as if its for the benefit of others; va.—བྱེད་.

རང་དོན་རྒྱབ་བསྒྱུར་ (rang̱dön gyạbgyur) selflessly, without concern for one's own interests; va.—བྱེད་.

རང་དོན་སྒྲིམ་པོ་ (rang̱dön dṟimbu) skillful in achieving one's own interests/ goals/ ends.

རང་དོན་སྒྲུབ་ཕྱོགས་ (rang̱dön dṟubjɔɔ) putting the main effort on getting one's own interests/ ends met or achieved ¶ མི་དེ་རང་དོན་སྒྲུབ་ཕྱོགས་ལ་ཏ་ཅང་འཛིན་པོ་ཡོད་པ་རེད་ That person is skillful in getting his own interests achieved.

རང་འདོད་ངན་རྒྱབ་ (ra̲ŋdöö ŋɛngyəb) shung. supporting an evil person with the aim of achieving one's own wishes/ desires.

རང་དོན་གཉིད་བརྗེད་ (ra̲ŋdön di̲ŋjeè) sm. རང་དོན་རྒྱབ་སྐྱུར་.

རང་དོན་ཐེར་ལ་བོར་ གཞན་དོན་ཏང་དུ་བླངས་ (ra̲ŋdön tērla bɔ̲r shɛ̲ndön ta̲ŋdu lāŋ) sacrificing one's own interests for the good of others.

རང་དོན་འབའ་ཞིག (ra̲ŋdön ba̲shig) selfishness, thinking only of oneself; va.—བྱེད་; —སྒྲུབ་.

རང་དོན་སྦུག་འདྲེན་ (ra̲ŋdön bu̲gdren) keeping one's interests internal/ hidden; va.—བྱེད་.

རང་དོན་རང་གཅེས་ (ra̲ŋdön ra̲ŋjeè) considering one's own interest/ benefits/ advantages as the most important.

རང་དོན་རང་བརྗོད་ (ra̲ŋdön ra̲ŋjöö) telling about one's affairs/ interests/ ends in one's own words.

རང་དོན་རིང་ལུགས་ (ra̲ŋdön ri̲ŋluù) individualism.

རང་དོར་སྤྱི་སྐྱོང་ (ra̲ŋdɔɔ ji̲gyoŋ) putting aside one's own interests for the interest of the public; va.—བྱེད་.

རང་དོར་གཞན་སྐྱོབ་ (ra̲ŋdɔɔ shɛ̲ngyob) putting aside one's interest to help others, to sacrifice oneself to save others; va.—བྱེད་.

རང་དོར་གཞན་བསྟུན་ (ra̲ŋdɔɔ shɛ̲ndün) following others without thinking of one's own interests, making personal sacrifices to accomplish a broader goal; va.—བྱེད་.

རང་དྲིན་རང་ཆུང་དུ་གཏོང་ (rə̲ŋdrin ra̲ŋju̲ŋdu dōŋ) va. to waste/ ruin/ harm oneself.

རང་གདན་ (ra̲ŋdɛn) one's monastery.

རང་གདེང་ (ra̲ŋdeŋ) self-confidence; va.—འཁྱིལ་ to exhibit self-confidence ¶ ཡིག་ཚད་གཏོང་སྐབས་རང་གདེང་འཁྱིལ་བའི་བསམ་པ་ཞིག་ཡོད་དགོས་ཀྱི་རེད་ When you take your exam you must have self-confidence.

རང་བདག (ra̲ŋdaà) independent/ privately owned, belonging to oneself ¶ རང་བདག་རྒྱལ་ཁབ་ Independent country. ¶ ཟ་ཁང་རང་བདག A privately owned restaurant.

རང་མདངས་སྟོན་ (ra̲ŋdaŋ dön) va. to declare one's position/ views.

རང་མདའ་རང་འཕེན་ (ra̲ŋda ra̲ŋben) shooting oneself; va.—རྒྱག.

རང་མདོག (ra̲ŋdɔɔ̀) one's true nature/ character; va.—སྟོན་ to reveal one's true nature/ character; vi.—ཐོན་ to have one's true nature / character revealed.

རང་འདོད་ (ra̲ŋdöö) 1. one's own desire/ wishes; va.—བྱེད་ to act in accordance with one's own desire/ wishes ¶ ཁོས་ལས་ཁུངས་ཀྱི་ལས་ཀ་ཚང་མ་རང་འདོད་ཀྱི་ཐག་གཅོད་ཀྱི་ཡོད་པ་རེད་ He decides all issues in the office according to his own wishes. 2. volunteering (on one's own wishes/ desire) ¶ ལས་འགན་རང་འདོད་ཀྱིས་བླངས་པ་རེད་ (He) volunteered to take the responsibility.

རང་འདོད་ཁེར་སྒྲུབ་ (ra̲ŋdöö kēēdrub) getting one's own desires/ wishes fulfilled; va.—བྱེད་.

རང་འདོད་གང་དྲན་ (ra̲ŋdöö ka̲ŋdrɛn) doing whatever comes to mind without concern for others, acting willfully; va.—བྱེད་.

རང་འདོད་གང་ཡོད་ (ra̲ŋdöö ka̲ŋyöö) sm. རང་འདོད་ལྟར་.

རང་འདོད་ངན་རྒྱབ་ (ra̲ŋdöö ŋɛngyəb) siding with evil doers for selfish reasons (i.e., to get what one desires); va.—བྱེད་.

རང་འདོད་ཆེན་པོ་ (ra̲ŋdöö cēmbo) egoistic, selfish, self-centered.

རང་འདོད་ལྟར་ (ra̲ŋdöödar) as one likes, at will, according to one's wishes/ desires.

རང་འདོད་མཐའ་སྐྱེལ་ (ra̲ŋdöö tāgyee) seeing one's own desires fulfilled insistently or by all means [Lit. until the end].

རང་འདོད་པ་ (ra̲ŋdööba) egotist, self-centered person.

རང་འདོད་སྦུག་བཅུག (ra̲ŋdöö bu̲gjuù) sm. རང་འདོད་སྦུག་འདྲེན་.

རང་འདོད་སྦུག་འཚང་ (ra̲ŋdöö bu̲gdzaŋ) sm. རང་འདོད་སྦུག་འདྲེན་.

རང་འདོད་གཙོར་བཟུང་ (ra̲ŋdöö) holding/ placing one's own desires/ interest as the most important; va.—བྱེད་.

རང་འདོད་བཙན་བཀོལ་ (ra̲ŋdöö) imposing one's wishes/ desires on others; va.—བྱེད་.

རང་འདོད་རྩ་དོན་ (ra̲ŋdöö) the principle of volanteerism, the principle of acting on one's own accord; va.—བྱེད་.

རང་འདོད་ཆ་པོ་ (ra̲ŋdöö) sm. རང་འདོད་ཆེན་པོ་.

རང་འདོད་རང་འཐད་ (ra̲ŋdöö) thinking that whatever one thinks is the truth, thinking oneself always in the right.

རང་སྡུག་རང་ཉོ་ (ra̲nduù ra̲ŋño) causing or creating one's own troubles/ harm/ misfortune/ calamity.

རང་སྡུག་རང་བཟོ་ (ra̲nduù ra̲ŋso) sm. རང་སྡུག་རང་ཉོ་.

རང་སྡེ་ (ra̲ndwe) sm. རང་ཕྱོགས་.

རང་སྡོད་སར་མི་བཞག་མི་སྡོད་སར་རང་བཞག (ra̲ŋdöö sāā mi̲shaà mi̲döö sāā ra̲ŋshaà) putting oneself in another person's shoes, thinking of the other person's position/ situation [Lit. putting a person in one's house; putting oneself in a person's house].

རང་འདྲ་ (ra̲ŋdra) assimilation, acculturation, like oneself; va.—སྒྱུར་ to assimilate, to make/ change like oneself ¶ སྲིད་གཞུང་གསར་པ་དེས་མི་རིགས་རང་འདྲར་སྒྱུར་བའི་སྲིད་ཇུས་ལག་བསྟར་བྱས་པ་རེད་ The new government put into practice the policy of assimilating minority nationalities into their own culture.

རང་ནུས་ (ra̲ŋnüü) one's own strength/ force/ power ¶ རང་ནུས་ཀྱིས་བྱེད་ཐུབ་པའི་ལས་ཀ་ Work one is able to do oneself. ¶ གྲལ་རིམ་གྱི་རང་ནུས་ The strength of a class.

རང་ནུས་གང་ཡོད་ (ra̲ŋnüü ka̲ŋyöö) doing the best one can given one's own strength and ability.

རང་ནུས་ངོམ་པ་ (ra̲ŋnüü ŋ̲omba) boastful, egoistic.

རང་ནོངས་ (ra̲ŋnoŋ) one's guilt/ crime/ wrongdoing; va.—ཤེས་ to know one's own guilt/ crimes; va.—ངོས་ལེན་བྱེད་ to confess/ acknowledge one's guilt or crimes.

རང་ནོངས་སྐྱོན་བརྗོད་ (ra̲ŋnoŋ gyõnjöö) self-criticism; va.—བྱེད་.

རང་ནོངས་འགྱོད་མེད་ (ra̲ŋnoŋ gyö̲ömeè) not regretting one's crimes/ wrongdoing.

རང་ནོངས་ངོས་ལེན་ (ra̲ŋnoŋ ŋ̲öölen) confessing/ admitting one's mistakes, crimes.

རང་ནོར་ངོམས་ (ra̲ŋnɔɔ ŋ̲om) va. to show off one's wealth.

རང་གནས་ (ra̲ŋnɛɛ̀) 1. one's place of residence. 2. sm. རང་འཇགས་.

རང་གནས་རིང་ལུགས་ (ra̲ŋnɛɛ̀ ri̲ŋluù) localism, local parochialism. 2. selfish departmentalism.

རང་གནོང་ (ra̲ŋnoŋ) sm. རང་ནོངས་.

རང་མནར་གཞན་སླུའི་ཐབས་ཇུས་ (ra̲ŋnar shɛ̲nlü tə̄bjüü) the strategy of inflicting an injury on oneself to win the confidence of the enemy, a trick of having oneself tortured to win the confidence of the enemy.

རང་རྣ་བཀབ་ནས་དྲིལ་བུ་རྐུ་བ་ (ra̲ŋna gə̄bnɛ dri̲ibu gūwə) fooling/ deceiving oneself [Lit. covering one's ears when stealing the bell].

རང་སྣང་ (ra̲ŋnaŋ) one's own view/ perception/ outlook, subjective view/ perspective.

རང་སྣང་གང་དྲན་ (ra̲ŋnaŋ ka̲ŋdrɛn) unrestrained/ reckless behavior, unbridled actions, doing whatever one likes; va.—བྱེད ¶ ལས་ཁུངས་ཀྱི་སྒྲིག་ཁྲིམས་སྲུང་དགོས་པ་ལས་རང་སྣང་གང་དྲན་བྱེད་མི་ཆོག One is not allowed to do whatever one wants; one has to uphold the office's rules.

རང་སྣང་གང་ཤར་ (ra̲ŋnaŋ ka̲ŋshar) sm. རང་སྣང་གང་དྲན་.

རང་སྣང་གང་ཤར་མིང་འདོགས་ཅི་རིགས་ (ra̲ŋnaŋ

kaŋshar miŋdɔɔ jïrii) shung. inventing all sorts of excuses.

རང་སྣང་གི་སྒོ་ནས་ (raŋnaŋgi gonɛ) subjectively, from a subjective viewpoint.

རང་སྣང་གི་འཇིག་རྟེན་ (raŋnaŋgi jigden) the subjective world.

རང་སྣང་གི་རེ་འདུན་ (raŋnaŋgi rendün) subjective wishes/ desires/ hopes.

རང་སྣང་ཆ་རྐྱེན་ (raŋnaŋ cāgyen) sm. རང་ངོས་ཆ་རྐྱེན་.

རང་སྣང་དག་ (raŋnaŋ taà) vi. to feel that what one has done is fine/ okay, to have a clear conscience.

རང་སྣང་རིང་ལུགས་ (raŋnaŋ riŋluù) subjectivism.

རང་སྣང་སེམས་གཙོའི་རིང་ལུགས་ (raŋnaŋ sēmdzö riŋluù) subjective idealism.

རང་དཔུང་ (raŋbuŋ) one's own troops/ forces/ soldiers, our own troops/ forces/ soldiers.

རང་དཔེ་གཞན་འགེབས་ (raŋbe shɛngeb) sm. རང་ཚོད་གཞན་དཔག.

རང་དཔེ་གཞན་སྟོན་ (raŋbe shɛndön) setting an example with one's own conduct; va.—བྱེད་.

རང་དཔེ་གཞན་སྦྱར་ (raŋbe shɛnjar) sm. རང་ཚོད་གཞན་དཔག.

རང་སྤེལ་ (raŋbel) self-improvement/ development; va.—བྱེད་.

རང་སྤེལ་རང་གསོ་ (raŋbel raŋso) self- improvement and self-support; va.—བྱེད་.

རང་སྤྲོད་ (randröö) self-sufficient (providing for sth. oneself); va.—བྱེད་.

རང་ཕན་ (raŋbɛn) one's own benefit/ profit; va.—བྱེད་.

རང་ཕན་གཞན་གནོད་ (raŋben shɛnnöö) beneficial to oneself and harmful to others, injuring others to benefit oneself; va.—བྱེད་.

རང་ཕན་རིང་ལུགས་ (raŋbɛn riŋluù) egotism, self-beneficialism.

རང་འཕུང་ (rəŋbuŋ) self-defeating, self-ruining; va.—བྱེད་ to do sth. that brings ruin/ defeat to oneself.

རང་འཕུང་རང་གིས་སྒྲུབ་ (raŋbuŋ raŋgi drub) shung. ruining oneself, causing one's own ruin.

རང་ཕྱོགས་ (raŋjɔɔ) our side/ group/ party, one's own side/ group/ party.

རང་ཕྱོགས་མ་ཡིན་པ་ (raŋjɔɔ məyimbə) not part of one's own side, alien, opposing.

རང་འཕེལ་ (raŋ pēl) 1. spontaneously arising/ developing ¶ རང་འཕེལ་འཐབ་རྩོད་ Spontaneous struggle. ¶ རང་འཕེལ་སྟོབས་ཤུགས་ Spontaneously arising authority/ power. 2. naturally increasing ¶ ཁོང་གི་ཕྱུགས་ཟོག་རང་འཕེལ་ཆེན་པོ་བྱུང་བཞག His livestock had a large natural increase (conveys from birth not purchase).

རང་འཕེལ་རང་གསོ་ (raŋ pēl raŋ sō) sm. རང་སྤེལ་རང་གསོ་.

རང་བབ་ (raŋbəb) 1. one's situation/ affairs/ circumstances. 2. sm. རང་འཇགས་.

རང་བབས་ (raŋbəb) sm. རང་བབ་.

རང་བབས་ཚོག་ཤེས་ (raŋbəb cōgsheè) being content/ satisfied with one's situation; va.—བྱེད་.

རང་བུ་ (raŋbu) 1. alone, single. 2. one's own son.

རང་བྱན་ཆུད་པ་ (raŋjɛn cüübə) skilled, knowledgeable.

རང་བྱན་ཚུད་པ་ (raŋjɛn tsüübə) sm. རང་བྱན་ཆུད་པ་.

རང་བྱས་རང་ཁུར་ (raŋjɛɛ raŋgur) being responsible for one's actions; va.—བྱེད་.

རང་བྱས་རང་འཕུང་ (raŋjɛɛ raŋbuŋ) shung. bringing about one's own downfall.

རང་བྱས་རང་མྱོང་ (raŋjɛɛ raŋñom) suffering from one's own actions, experiencing sth. negative due to one's own acts, to suffer the consequences of one's actions.

རང་བྱས་བདེན་འཛིན་ (raŋjɛɛ dendzin) considering one's acts as true.

རང་བྱས་རང་ལ་སྨིན་པ་ (raŋjɛɛ raŋla mīmbə) sm. རང་བྱས་རང་མྱོང་.

རང་བྱུང་ (rəŋjuŋ) 1. nature, the natural world, natural. 2. self-grown, naturally occurring.

རང་བྱུང་སྐྱེ་དངོས་ཀྱི་ཁོར་ཡུག (rəŋjuŋ gyēŋöögi kɔɔyuù) natural environment.

རང་བྱུང་སྐྱེ་ཚུལ་གྱི་ཁོར་ཡུག (rəŋjuŋ gyēdzügi kɔɔyuù) natural environment.

རང་བྱུང་ཁམས་ (rəŋjuŋgam) nature ¶ རང་བྱུང་ཁམས་ཀྱི་ཐོན་ཁུངས་ Natural resources; va.—འདུལ་ to conquer nature.

རང་བྱུང་ཁམས་ཀྱི་སྐད་སྒྲ་ (rəŋjuŋgamgo gɛɛdra) sounds of nature.

རང་བྱུང་ཁམས་ཀྱི་ཆ་རྐྱེན་ (rəŋjuŋgamgi cāgyen) sm. རང་བྱུང་གི་ཆ་རྐྱེན་.

རང་བྱུང་ཁམས་ཀྱི་གནས་ཚུལ་ (rəŋjuŋgamgi nɛɛdzüü) sm. རང་བྱུང་གི་ཁོར་ཡུག.

རང་བྱུང་ཁམས་འདུལ་ (rəŋjuŋ kāmdüü) conquering/ controlling nature.

རང་བྱུང་ཁམས་དབང་དུ་འདུ་ (rəŋjuŋgam wāŋdu du) va. to conquer nature or the natural world.

རང་བྱུང་ཁམས་ལས་འདས་པ་ (rəŋjuŋgamlɛ dɛɛba) the supernatural, beyond the natural world.

རང་བྱུང་ཁོར་ཡུག (rəŋjuŋ kɔɔyuù) the natural environment/ surroundings ¶ རི་ཁུལ་གྱི་རང་བྱུང་ཁོར་ཡུག The mountain environment.

རང་བྱུང་ཁོར་ཡུག་སྲུང་སྐྱོབ་ (rəŋjuŋ kɔɔyuù sūŋgyob) protecting/ saving the environment, environmental protection; va.—བྱེད་.

རང་བྱུང་ཁོར་ཡུག་སྲུང་སྐྱོབ་བྱེད་པའི་སྒེར་གྱི་སྒྲིག་འཛུགས་ (rəŋjuŋ kɔɔyuù sūŋgyob cɛɛbɛ gergi drigdzuù) Nature Conservancy.

རང་བྱུང་གི་རྐྱེན་ངན་ (rəŋjuŋgi gyēnŋɛn) a natural disaster.

རང་བྱུང་གི་ཁྲིམས་ (rəŋjuŋgi trīm) natural law, law of nature.

རང་བྱུང་གི་གེགས་བར་ (rəŋjuŋgi gegbar) natural calamity/ obstacle/ obstruction.

རང་བྱུང་གི་ཆ་རྐྱེན་ (rəŋjuŋgi cāgyen) natural condition.

རང་བྱུང་གི་ཆོས་ཉིད་ (rəŋjuŋgi cōōñii) sm. རང་བྱུང་གི་གནས་ལུགས་.

རང་བྱུང་གི་ཐོན་ཁུངས་ (rəŋjuŋgi tönguŋ) natural resources.

རང་བྱུང་གི་མཐུན་རྐྱེན་ (rəŋjuŋgi tüŋgyen) natural resources.

རང་བྱུང་གི་གནས་ཚུལ་ (rəŋjuŋgi nɛɛdzüü) natural or environmental condition/ situation.

རང་བྱུང་གི་གནས་ལུགས་ (rəŋjuŋgi nɛɛluù) natural laws, law of nature.

རང་བྱུང་གི་གནོད་སྐྱོན་ (rəŋjuŋgi nöögyön) sm. རང་བྱུང་གི་རྐྱེན་ངན་.

རང་བྱུང་གི་རྣམ་པ་ (rəŋjuŋgi nāmba) natural phenomena.

རང་བྱུང་གི་འོབས་ཆེན་ (rəŋjuŋgi objen) "the natural moat" (i.e., the River Yangtse that bisects China into north and south).

རང་བྱུང་གི་ཡུལ་མཚམས་ (rəŋjuŋgi yündzam) natural division/ boundary.

རང་བྱུང་གི་ལྡོག་ཏུ་མེད་པའི་ཆོས་ཉིད་ (rəŋjuŋgi dɔgdu meèbɛ cōōñii) inevitable law of nature.

རང་བྱུང་གི་ལྡོག་མེད་རང་བཞིན་ (rəŋjuŋgi dɔgmeè rəŋshin) sm. རང་བྱུང་གི་ལྡོག་ཏུ་མེད་པའི་ཆོས་ཉིད་.

རང་བྱུང་གི་མཚན་ཉིད་རིག་པ་ (rəŋjuŋgi tsɛnñii rigbə) natural philosophy.

རང་བྱུང་གི་ས་གཤིས་ (rəŋjuŋgi sāshii) physical geography.

རང་བྱུང་གྲངས་ (rəŋjuŋ traŋ) a natural number (in math).

རང་བྱུང་གྲངས་ཕྲེང་ (rəŋjuŋ traŋpeŋ) natural sequence of numbers (in math).

རང་བྱུང་གྲོང་སྡེ་ (rəŋjuŋ troŋde) natural village/ township.

རང་བྱུང་གྲོང་ཚོ་ (rəŋjuŋ troŋdzo) sm. རང་བྱུང་གྲོང་སྡེ་.

རང་བྱུང་རྒྱུད་འདྲེས་ (rəŋjuŋ gyündreè) natural crossing of species (hybridizing).

རང་བྱུང་ངང་ཚུལ་ (rəŋjuŋ ŋandzüü) natural

phenomena.

རང་བྱུང་དངོས་མང་འགྲེམ་སྟོན་ཁང་ (rəŋjuŋ ŋöòmaŋ dremdöngaŋ) sm. རང་བྱུང་དངོས་མང་བཤམས་སྟོན་ཁང་.

རང་བྱུང་དངོས་མང་བཤམས་སྟོན་ཁང་ (rəŋjuŋ ŋöòmaŋ shāmdöngaŋ) natural history museum.

རང་བྱུང་དངོས་རྫས་བཤམས་སྟོན་ཁང་ (rəŋjuŋ ŋöòdzɛè shāmdöngaŋ) natural history museum.

རང་བྱུང་ཨ་ལྡན་ (rəŋjuŋ ŋādɛn) name of a statue of Avalokitesvara in Lhasa's Tsuglakhang.

རང་བྱུང་ཆ་རྐྱེན་ (rəŋjuŋ cāgyen) sm. རང་བྱུང་གི་ཆ་རྐྱེན་.

རང་བྱུང་ཆ་སྙོམས་ (rəŋjuŋ cāñom) natural balance.

རང་བྱུང་ཆོས་ཉིད་ (rəŋjuŋ cöòñii) natural characteristics (of nature), law of nature.

རང་བྱུང་གཏེར་ཆུ་ (rəŋjuŋ dērju) natural spring, mineral water.

རང་བྱུང་ཐོན་ཁུངས་ (rəŋjuŋ tōnguŋ) natural resources.

རང་བྱུང་ནུས་ཁུངས་ (rəŋjuŋ nüüguŋ) natural energy resources.

རང་བྱུང་ནུས་པའི་འབྱུང་ཁུངས་ (rəŋjuŋ nüübɛ juŋguŋ) sm. རང་བྱུང་ནུས་ཁུངས་.

རང་བྱུང་ནུས་ཤུགས་ (rəŋjuŋ nüüshuù) natural forces.

རང་བྱུང་གནོད་པ་ (rəŋjuŋ nöòba) sm. རང་བྱུང་གི་རྐྱེན་ངན་.

རང་བྱུང་སྣོད་ཀྱི་འཇིག་རྟེན་ (rəŋjuŋ nöògi jigden) the physical world.

རང་བྱུང་སྣུམ་ (rəŋjuŋ nūm) natural oil.

རང་བྱུང་སྣུམ་གྱི་རླངས་པ་ (rəŋjuŋ nūmgi lāŋba) sm. རང་བྱུང་རླངས་པ་.

རང་བྱུང་དཔལ་འབྱོར་ (rəŋjuŋ bēnjɔɔ) natural economy.

རང་བྱུང་བུལ་ཏོག་ཀུང་ཟི་ (rəŋjuŋ büüdoò gūŋsi) tib. ch. natural alkali company.

རང་བྱུང་རྩོད་སྒྲུབ་རིག་པ་ (rəŋjuŋ dzöògrub rigbə) dialectics of nature.

རང་བྱུང་ཚད་མ་རིག་པ་ (rəŋjuŋ tsɛ̀ɛma rigbə) natural philosophy.

རང་བྱུང་ཚན་ཉིད་ (rəŋjuŋ tsɛ̄nñii) sm. རང་བྱུང་ཚན་རིག.

རང་བྱུང་ཚན་རིག (rəŋjuŋ tsɛ̄nrii) natural sciences.

རང་བྱུང་ཚན་རིག་སློབ་གྲྭ་ཆེན་མོ་ (rəŋjuŋ tsɛ̄nrii lōbdra cēmmo) natural science university.

རང་བྱུང་ཚི་སྣ་ (rəŋjuŋ tsīnə) natural fiber.

རང་བྱུང་མཚེའུ་ (rəŋjuŋ tsēwu) natural lake.

རང་བྱུང་ཟངས་ (rəŋjuŋ saŋ) natural copper.

རང་བྱུང་ཡུལ་ལྗོངས་ (rəŋjuŋ yünjoŋ) natural scenery.

རང་བྱུང་རགས་ (rəŋjuŋ raà) a natural dam.

རང་བྱུང་རང་གྲུབ་ (rəŋjuŋ rəndrub) sm. རང་བྱུང་.

རང་བྱུང་རིང་ལུགས་ (rəŋjuŋ riŋluù) naturalism.

རང་བྱུང་རླངས་པ་ (rəŋjuŋ lāŋba) natural gas.

རང་བྱུང་རླངས་པའི་ཐོན་ཁུངས་ (rəŋjuŋ lāŋbɛ tōnguŋ) natural gas field.

རང་བྱུང་རླངས་རིགས་ (rəŋjuŋ lūŋrii) sm. རང་བྱུང་རླངས་པ་.

རང་བྱུང་ལ་བརྟེན་པའི་རིང་ལུགས་ (rəŋjuŋlə dēnbɛ riŋluù) sm. རང་བྱུང་རིང་ལུགས་.

རང་བྱུང་ལས་བགོས་ (rəŋjuŋlɛ̀ɛ göò) natural division of labor.

རང་བྱུང་ལེགས་ཆ་ (rəŋjuŋ legja) good natural conditions.

རང་བྱུང་ལུད་ (rəŋjuŋ lüü) organic/ natural manure.

རང་བྱུང་ས་ཁམས་ (rəŋjuŋ sāgam) physical geography.

རང་བྱུང་ས་ཁམས་ཀྱི་རིག་པ་ (rəŋjuŋ sāgamgi rigbə) physical geography.

རང་བྱུང་ས་རྒྱུས་ (rəŋjuŋ sāgyüü) sm. རང་བྱུང་ས་ཁམས་.

རང་བྱུང་སོལ་རླངས་ (rəŋjuŋ söòlaŋ) sm. རང་བྱུང་རླངས་པ་.

རང་བྱུང་སྲུང་སྐྱོབ་ས་ཁུལ་ (rəŋjuŋ) a nature reserve.

རང་བྱོན་ (rəŋjön) miraculously formed (usu. for rocks, bones).

རང་བྱོན་ཨ་ལྡན་ (rəŋjön ŋādɛn) sm. རང་བྱུང་ཨ་ལྡན་.

རང་བྲན་དུ་འགྱུར་ (rəndrɛndu gyur) shung. vi. to become one's subject/ serf.

རང་བྲིས་ (rəndrii) written by oneself ¶ རང་བྲིས་ཁ་ཆེམས་ A will written by oneself.

རང་བྲིས་གླེང་གཞི་ (rəndrii lēŋshi) sm. རང་བྲིས་འགོ་བརྗོད་.

རང་བྲིས་འགོ་བརྗོད་ (rəndrii gojöö) author's preface.

རང་བློ་རང་འཁེལ་ (raŋlo raŋkee) self-confident.

རང་བློ་རང་སྦྱོང་ (raŋlo raŋjoŋ) self- training of one's mind.

རང་བློས་གང་ལྷོག (raŋlöö kaŋjaà) doing/ thinking as much as one can according to one's mental ability.

རང་བློས་གཏོང་ (raŋlöö dōŋ) va. to sacrifice oneself (for sth. or sb.).

རང་དབང་ (raŋwaŋ) freedom, liberty, independence.

རང་དབང་གི་གྲུ་ཁ་ (raŋwaŋgi trugə) a free port.

རང་དབང་གི་རྒྱལ་ཁབ་ (raŋwaŋgi gyɛɛgəb) independent country/ nation.

རང་དབང་གི་དབང་ཆ་ (raŋwaŋgi wāŋja) right of freedom/ independence.

རང་དབང་གི་ཡུལ་ (raŋwaŋgi yüü) the realm of freedom, an area/ region/ country where there is freedom.

རང་དབང་གི་རླུང་འཕྲིན་ (raŋwaŋgi lūŋdrin) Radio Liberty.

རང་དབང་གླེང་སྟེགས་ (raŋwaŋ lēŋdeg) Freedom Forum.

རང་དབང་སྒེར་ལངས་ (raŋwaŋ gerlaŋ) an uprising for freedom.

རང་དབང་སྒེར་ལངས་པ་ (raŋwaŋ gerlaŋba) freedom fighter.

རང་དབང་ཅན་ (raŋwaŋjɛn) free, independent.

རང་དབང་ཅན་དུ་འགྱུར་ (raŋwaŋjɛndu gyur) vi. to become free/ independent.

རང་དབང་འཇིག་རྟེན་ (raŋwaŋ jigden) the free world.

རང་དབང་ཏང་ (raŋwaŋ dāŋ) 1. freedom party. 2. (Britain) Liberal Party.

རང་དབང་དོན་གཉེར་གྱི་ཚོགས་པ་ (raŋwaŋ tönñergi tsōgba) Libetarian Party.

རང་དབང་བག་ཕེབས་ (raŋwaŋ pagpeè) being free (of work/ duties) and relaxing.

རང་དབང་མེད་པ་ (raŋwaŋ meèba) without freedom/ independence, having no choice/ freedom.

རང་དབང་མེད་པར་ (raŋwaŋ meèbar) 1. having no choice/ freedom, being forced/ compelled to do sth. ¶ ང་ལམ་བཟོར་རང་དབང་མེད་པར་འགྲོ་དགོས་བྱུང་ I had no choice but to go to do road construction. 2. uncontrollably, spontaneously, without planning ¶ རང་དབང་མེད་པར་མིག་ཆུ་ཤོར་བ་རེད་ (She) cried uncontrollably (burst out into tears).

རང་དབང་དམངས་ (raŋwaŋ māŋ) people who are free, freemen.

རང་དབང་དམངས་གཙོའི་ཏང་ (raŋwaŋ māŋdzö dāŋ) Liberal-Democratic Party, People's Freedom Party.

རང་དབང་རྩོལ་སྒྲུབ་ཚོགས་པ་ (raŋwaŋ dzōdrub tsōgba) Liberty Lobby.

རང་དབང་བརྩོན་ལེན་ (raŋwaŋ dzōnlen) freedom fight/ struggle.

རང་དབང་ཞི་བདེར་གཅེས་པ་ (raŋwaŋ shidee jēèba) peace and freedom loving.

རང་དབང་རང་འཐད་ (raŋwaŋ raŋdɛɛ̀) the freedom/ power to choose one's own spouse.

རང་དབང་རང་བདག (raŋwaŋ randaà) sm. རང་དབང་རང་བཙན་.

རང་དབང་རང་བཙན་ (raŋwaŋ randzɛn) independent, free ¶ ལུང་པ་དེ་རང་དབང་རང་བཙན་རེད་ That country is independent.

རང་དབང་རིང་ལུགས་ (raŋwaŋ riŋluù) liberalism.

རང་དབང་ལས་རིགས་ (raŋwaŋ lɛɛ̀rig) professions.

རང་དབང་ལས་རིགས་པ་ (raŋwaŋ lɛɛ̀rigbə) a professional.

རང་འབབ་ (raŋbəb) 1. naturally falling/ flowing. 2. one's own share.

རང་འབབ་ཁྲོན་པ་ (raŋbəb trōmba) artesian well.

རང་འབབ་ཆུ་ (raŋbəb cū) 1. running water. 2. water from a tap.

རང་འབབ་ཆུ་མདོང་ (raŋbəb cūdoŋ) pipe carrying running water.

རང་འབབ་ཆུའི་གཙུས་སྒོ་ (raŋbəb cū jūùgo) water tap.

རང་འབབ་ཞིང་ཆུ་ (raŋbəb shiŋju) irrigation system using naturally flowing water.

རང་སྦྱོང་ (raŋjoŋ) homework, independent study, studying at home, self-education; va.—བྱེད་.

རང་མ་གདོགས་ (raŋ mandoò) sm. རང་ལས་.

རང་མལ་ (raŋmɛɛ) 1. sm. རང་འཇགས་. 2. རང་བཞིན་.

རང་མི་ (rəŋmi) one's own people, people of one's own nationality ¶ ཕྱི་སྡོད་རང་མི་ Overseas nationals (e.g., if a Chinese uses this it would mean oversees Chinese).

རང་མིང་ (rəŋmiŋ) one's own name.

རང་མིང་ཐོན་ཐབས་ (rəŋmiŋ tōndəb) seeking to be in the limelight, seeking fame for oneself.

རང་མེད་གཞན་མེད་ (raŋmeè shɛnmeè) sm. རང་མེད་མི་མེད་.

རང་མེད་མི་མེད་ (raŋmeè mimeè so) destroying oneself as well as others; va.—བཟོ་.

རང་མེད་གཞན་འཚོལ་ (raŋmeè shɛndzöö) using all possible means to do sth. ¶ ཁྱེད་རང་ལ་དགོས་པའི་དེབ་དེ་ངས་རང་མེད་གཞན་འཚོལ་བྱེད་ཀྱི་ཡིན་ I will do everything possible to find the book that you want.

རང་མོས་ (raŋmöö) agreeable to oneself, one's own choice/ initiative, voluntarily; va.—བྱེད་ to agree, to accept voluntarily, to do according to one's wish ¶ ཁྱེད་རང་ལས་ཀ་དེ་བྱེད་མིན་རང་མོས་བྱེད་ཆོག Whether or not to do this work, it's okay to decide according to your own wish. ¶ རང་མོས་ཀྱིས་མགོ་བཏགས་ཞུས་པ་རེད་ (They) voluntarily surrendered.

རང་མོས་ཀྱི་འགྲན་རྩོད་ (raŋmöögi trɛndzöö) voluntary/ free competition.

རང་མོས་ཀྱི་འཇིག་རྟེན་ (raŋmöögi jigden) free world.

རང་མོས་སྙན་རྩོམ་ (raŋmöö ñɛ̄ndzom) free verse.

རང་མོས་འདོད་འདེམས་ (raŋmöö döndem) freedom of choice; va.—བྱེད་ to choose freely, to select according to one's wish/ desire.

རང་མོས་འབྱོར་ལྡན་གྲལ་རིམ་ (raŋmöö jondɛn trɛɛrim) liberal bourgeoisie.

རང་མོས་རིང་ལུགས་པ་ (raŋmöö riŋluù) liberalism, laissez-faireism.

རང་མོས་ལས་རིགས་ (raŋmöö lɛɛ̀rii) the professions.

རང་དམག (raŋmaà) one's own troops/ army.

རང་དམན་ (raŋmɛn) looking on oneself negatively, a feeling of inferiority ¶ རང་དམན་གྱི་འདུ་ཤེས་ Inferiority complex.

རང་དམའ་རང་འབེབས་ (raŋma raŋbeb) shaming/ disgracing oneself; va.—བྱེད་.

རང་མོ་ཕྱེད་ཙམ་གྱི་ཞིང་པ་ (raŋmo cēèdzamgi shiŋbə) part owning farmer/ peasant.

རང་མོའི་ཞིང་པ་ (raŋmö shiŋbə) peasant landowner/ landholder.

རང་སྨད (raŋmɛɛ̀) holding oneself as lower/ subordinate/ inferior ¶ མི་སེར་སྐྱིལ་ཡུལ་གྱི་མི་དམངས་རྣམས་རང་སྨད་ཀྱི་འདུ་ཤེས་བཟུང་ནས་སྡོད་དགོས་བྱུང་བ་རེད་ The people in colonial countries had to consider themselves inferior.

རང་གཙོ་ (rāŋdzo) self-centered, conceited.

རང་བཙན་ (randzɛn) 1. independence, freedom; va.—བྱེད་ to be/ get independent. 2. name of a publication in India.

རང་བཙན་གྱི་དབང་ཆ་ (randzɛngi wāŋja) right of independence.

རང་བཙན་རྒྱལ་ཁབ་ (randzɛn gyɛɛ̀gəb) independent country.

རང་བཙན་རྒྱལ་པོའི་རྒྱལ་ཁབ་ (randzɛn gyɛɛbö gyɛɛgəb) independent kingdom.

རང་བཙན་ཐོབ་པའི་མཐུན་ཚོགས་རྒྱལ་ཁབ་ (randzɛn tōbbɛ tūnjɔɔ gyɛɛgəb) Commonwealth of Independent States (CIS).

རང་བཙན་རང་བདག (randzɛn randaà) independent.

རང་བཙས་ (randzɛɛ̀) one's own child.

རང་རྩིས་ (rəndzii) sm. རང་བརྩི་.

རང་རྩོམ་ (randzom) written by oneself.

རང་རྩོམ་རང་འཁྲབ་ (randzom randrəb) writing as well as acting in a play.

རང་རྩོམ་རང་གདོང་ (randzom randoŋ) composing and singing (a song).

རང་བརྩི་ (rəndzi) self-respect, self-pride, self-esteem.

རང་བརྩིའི་བསམ་པ་ (rəndzii sāmba) self-esteem, self-pride, self-respect.

རང་ཚགས་ (randzaà) keeping sth. oneself; va.—བྱེད་ ¶ མེ་མདའ་འདི་ཁྱེད་ཀྱིས་ཉར་ཚགས་བྱས་ན་ཡག་གི་རེད་ It is better if you keep the gun yourself.

རང་ཚང་དུ་སྤྱང་ཀི་འཁྲིད་པ་ (randzaŋdu jəŋgi triībə) bringing disaster upon oneself [Lit. leading a wolf to one's house/ den].

རང་ཚང་གཟིག་ལ་སྟོན་པ་ (randzaŋ siglə dōmba) sm. རང་ཚང་དུ་སྤྱང་ཀི་འཁྲིད་པ་.

རང་ཚིག (randzii) one's own words, what one has said.

རང་ཚིག་རང་འགལ་ (randzii raŋgɛɛ) contradicting oneself; va.—བྱེད་.

རང་རྐྱགས་ (rəndzuù) 1. sm. རང་རྐྱ་. 2. independent in action, under one's own command ¶ རང་རྐྱགས་རྟ་དམག Cavalry under their own command.

རང་རྐྱགས་ཟིན་པ་ (rəndzuù simbə) 1. self-controlled, not impulsive, having good judgement. 2. standing on one's own two feet, able to act on one's own.

རང་རྐྱགས་ཟིན་པོ་ (rəndzuù simbu) sb. who is self-controlled. 2. sb. who is able to stand on one's own feet.

རང་རྐྱགས་རང་བཞིན་ (rəndzuù rəŋshin) independent, under one's own control.

རང་རྐྱལ་བརྗེད་ (rəndzüü jeè) vi. to forget one's own situation/ circumstances ¶ མི་དབུལ་པོ་དེ་ཕྱུག་པོ་ཆགས་རྗེས་རང་རྐྱལ་བརྗེད་ནས་དབུལ་པོ་ལ་མཐོང་ཆུང་བྱེད་ཀྱི་འདུག After the poor person got rich, he forgot his circumstances and looks down on the poor.

རང་རྐྱལ་རྟོགས་ (rəndzüü dɔ̄ɔ̀) vi. to know one's capacity/ strength/ capability.

རང་ཚོད་ (randzöö) one's own circumstances/ capacity/ capabilities; va.—ཟིན་; —འཛིན་ to know one's condition/ situation/ conditions/ limits, to control oneself/ one's behavior.

རང་ཚོད་མ་ལོན་ (randzöö malön) not knowing one's own situation/ conditions/ limits.

རང་ཚོད་མི་ཐིག་པ་ (randzöö midegba) sm. རང་ཚོད་མ་ལོན་.

རང་ཚོད་གཞན་དཔག (randzöö shɛmbaà) judging/ evaluating others by oneself, thinking others are same as oneself; va.—བྱེད་ ¶ སློབ་ཕྲུག་སོ་སོའི་རིག་པ་ཡག་ཉེས་ལ་དཔག་པའི་སློབ་ཁྲིད་བྱ་དགོས་པ་ལས་དགེ་རྒན་གྱིས་རང་ཚོད་གཞན་དཔག་བྱ་རྒྱུ་མེད་ One should teach in accordance with each students intelligence not by the teacher thinking others are like him.

རང་ཚོད་རང་འཛིན་ (randzöö randzin) self-discipline, self-control, self-restraint; va.—བྱེད་.

རང་ཚོད་རང་ལོན་ (randzöö ranlön) knowing one's limitations/ situation, controling one's behavior/ actions.

རང་མཚང་རྟོལ་ (randzaŋ döö) vi. to give oneself away, to reveal one's own secret or fault (unintentionally).

རང་མཆམས་ (randzam) on one's own decision/ initiative ¶ བཀའ་ཤག་ལ་དགོངས་སྐོར་ཙམ་མ་ཞུས་པར་རང་མཆམས་ཀྱིས་ཁྲིམས་གཅོད་བྱས་པ་རེད་ (He) punished (them) without as much as asking the opinion of the Kashag.

རང་མཆམས་བསྒྱུར་འཇོག (randzam gyūrjɔɔ̀) shung. abandoning one's own decision.

རང་མཆམས་ཁྲིམས་ཀུན་ (randzam trīmgün) shung. to take the law into one's own hands.

རང་མཆམས་ཚ་པོ་ (randzam tsābo) sb. who decides/ does things on his own.

རང་འཆམས་ (randzam) sm. རང་མཆམས་.

རང་འཚོ་ (randzo) economic independence/ self-sufficiency; va.—ཐུབ་; —ཐེན་ to be able to stand on one's own two feet ¶ རང་འཚོའི་བཟོ་གྲྭ་ A factory that is self-sufficient.

རང་རྫས་རང་ཐོབ་ (randzεὲ randob) acquiring one's wealth oneself.

རང་ཞབས་ (ranshəb) one's subjects/ servants, one's government's officials.

རང་ཞལ་ (ranshεε) h. of རང་ངོ་.

རང་ཞིག (ran shii) coming undone /untied by itself.

རང་ཞུས་སྤྱི་གྲོས་ (ranshüü jidröö) self assessment and public discussion; va.—བྱེད་.

རང་གཞན་ (ranshεn) oneself and others.

རང་གཞན་གྱི་ཆ་རྐྱེན་ (ranshεngi cāgyen) subjective and objective conditions.

རང་གཞན་གཉིས་ཕན་ (ranshεn ñiipεn) vi. to do well for others as well as for oneself.

རང་གཞན་གཉིས་འཕུང་ (ranshεn ñiibun) destroying oneself as well as others.

རང་གཞན་གཉིས་བསླུ་ (ranshεn ñiilu) deceiving both oneself and others.

རང་གཞིས་ (ranshii) one's own estate.

རང་གཞུང་ (ranshun) our government, one's own government.

རང་བཞག་ཕྱུགས་རིགས་ (ranshaà cüùrii) animals given to households for their private use during the commune period.

རང་བཞག་ས་ཞིང་ (ranshaà səshin) private plot (of land), household plot.

རང་བཞིན་ (ranshin) 1. nature, character, essence ¶ ཞི་བདེའི་རང་བཞིན་ The nature of peace. 2. (— + vb. + ཐབས་བྲལ་/མེད་) being unable to do verbal action ¶ ང་ཚོས་ཆིངས་ཡིག་འདི་རང་བཞིན་འཇོག་ཐབས་མེད་པ་རེད་ We cannot leave the treaty as it is. 3. natural, ordinary.

རང་བཞིན་གྱི་ནད་འགོག་នུས་པ་ (rənshingi nεngɔɔ nüübə) natural immunity to disease.

རང་བཞིན་གྱི་ཐོག་ནས་ (rənshingi tɔ̄ɔnε) naturally ¶ གཏུགས་བར་དེ་རང་བཞིན་གྱི་ཐོག་ནས་བྱུང་བ་རེད་ The disaster occurred naturally.

རང་བཞིན་གྱི་ནུས་པ་ (rənshingi nüübə) instinct, natural ability.

རང་བཞིན་གྱི་དཔའ་ (rənshingi bā) natural bravery.

རང་བཞིན་གྱི་ལམ་ (rənshingi lam) sm. རང་བཞིན་གྱི་ཐོག་ནས་.

རང་བཞིན་གྱིས་ (rənshingi) naturally, spontaneously, automatically ¶ སྨན་གཏོང་མ་དགོས་པར་ནད་ཚ་རང་བཞིན་གྱིས་དྲག་སོང་ Without having to take medicine, the illness got better spontaneously.

རང་བཞིན་བརྗོད་ (rənshin jöö) va. to describe/ talk about a thing's nature or character.

རང་བཞིན་ཉིས་བརྩེགས་ (rənshin ñiidzeg) dual nature.

རང་བཞིན་དུ་ (rənshindu) sm. རང་བཞིན་གྱིས་.

རང་བཞིན་ལྡན་པ་ (rənshin dεmba) having the nature of, occurring naturally ¶ བཙན་འཛུལ་རང་བཞིན་ལྡན་པའི་དམག་དོན་ཚོགས་ཁག A naturally aggressive military bloc. ¶ ལོ་རྒྱུས་ཀྱི་རང་བཞིན་ལྡན་པའི་རྒྱལ་ཁ་ A historic victory.

རང་བཞིན་ནས་ (rənshinnε) sm. རང་བཞིན་གྱིས་.

རང་བཞིན་གཞི་གྲུབ་ཀྱི་གནས་བབ་ (rənshingi shidrubgi nεὲbəb) objective position.

རང་བཞིན་ཨོ་ཚོད་དུ་སྡོད་ (rənshin ōdzöödu döö) va. to hang around idly ¶ དགོངས་ཞག་གཙང་ནས་རང་བཞིན་ཨོ་ཚོད་དུ་བསྡད་ན་མི་འགྲིགས་ Having finished one's vacation, it isn't okay to hang around (conveys the idea of hanging around without notifying one's boss or office).

རང་ཟས་ (ransεὲ) one's own food.

རང་ཟིན་ (ransin) occupied/ reserved by oneself.

རང་ཟོན་ (ransön) cautious, timid.

རང་ཟོན་ངོ་བསྟོད་ (ransön nodöö) cautious and sycophantic.

རང་ཟོན་ཚ་པོ་ (ransön tsābo) excessively cautious/ timid/ afraid.

རང་ཟོན་འཛེམ་མེད་ (ransön dzemmeè) not cautious/ timid/ afraid.

རང་གཟུགས་ (rənsuù) 1. true or real shape/ appearance; va.—སྟོན་ to manifest one's true form (e.g., really being a witch). 2. own body.

རང་གཟུགས་ཧྲེན་མངོན་ (rənsuù jennön) showing one's true shape/ form, revealing the real person, showing/ revealing one's true colors.

རང་གཟུགས་རང་བདག (rənsuù randaà) freedom over one's own body.

རང་བཟོ་ (ranso) made up/ concocted by oneself; va.—བྱེད་.

རང་བཟོ་འཕེར་ (ranso pēr) sm. རང་འགོ་ཐོན་.

རང་བཟོ་ཡལ་ (ranso yεε) 1. vi. to lose one's front/ facade, to lose one's good/ healthy appearance. 2. vi. to be down/ dejected/ under the weather, to be defeated, to collapse.

རང་བཟོའི་ཐ་སྙད་ (ransö tāñεὲ) a coined word.

རང་ཡིད་རང་ཆེས་ (ranyii rancēè) self-confident, believing in oneself.

རང་ཡིད་དབང་མེད་དུ་ཐལ་ (rənyii ran cēè) vi. to spontaneously be very attracted by, to be captivated by ¶ གཞོན་ནུ་མ་དེས་ཁོང་གི་རང་ཡིད་དབང་མེད་དུ་ཐལ་པ་རེད་ He was captivated by the young woman.

རང་ཡུ་ (ranyu) handle on a hand-powered grinding mill.

རང་ཡུལ་ (rənyüü) one's own country/ area/ locality, homeland.

རང་ཡུལ་གྲོགས་རོང་ཁ་རུ་ཆགས་ཀྱང་སྐྱིད་ (rənyüü trogron kāru chāggyan gyii) sm. རང་ཡུལ་ཕག་ཚང་ཡིན་ཡང་གཞལ་ཡས་ཁང་ [Lit. one's homeland, even if it is located on a cliff is nice].

རང་ཡུལ་སྟོང་པ་བཞག་ནས་མི་ཡུལ་འོད་ཀྱིས་གྱོང་བ་ (rənyüü dōnba shaànε miyüü wöögi gyōnwa) not doing anything in one's own country but doing a lot in other countries/ places [Lit. leaving one's own country empty and filling other countries/ areas with brightness].

རང་ཡུལ་ཕག་ཚང་ཡིན་ཡང་གཞལ་ཡས་ཁང་ (rənyüü pāgdzan yinyan shεεyεὲ kān) there is no place like home [Lit. one's homeland, even if its a pig sty, is a god's house].

རང་ཡོད་ (ranyöö) sth. that comes natually or is natural ¶ ཁོང་གི་རང་ཡོད་ཀྱི་རྣམ་པའི་ཐོག་རྒྱན་ཆས་དེ་དུ་ཙང་མཛེས་པོ་འདུག Those ornaments look very beautiful together with her natural beauty.

རང་རང་ (ranran) one's own, each person ¶ ཁོ་ཚོ་རང་རང་གི་ཁྱིམ་ལ་ཕྱིན་སོང་ They (each) went to their own homes.

རང་རང་ནན་གཅུན་ (ranran nεnjün) strict self-control, strict self-discipline.

རང་རང་སོ་སོ་ (ranran sōso) sm. རང་རང་.

རང་རིགས་ (ranrig) one's own race/ ethnic group/ nationality, our race/ ethnic group/ nationality.

རང་རིགས་ཀྱི་མྱུ་གུ་ (ranriìgi ñugu) 1. one's descendants. 2. new generation. 3. children of one's own race/ ethnic group/ nationality.

རང་རེ་ (ranre) we, us, our ¶ རང་རེའི་ཁང་པ་ Our house.

རང་རེ་གཉིས་ (ranre ñii) we two, the two of us.

རང་རོང་ (ranron) rough, rocky.

རང་རོང་འབར་འབུར་ (ranron barbur) rocky, and bumpy/ uneven.

རང་ལ་སྐྱོན་ཞིབ་ (ranla gyönshib) investigating one's mistakes, doing self-criticism; va.—བྱེད་.

རང་ལ་བསྟོད་ (ranla döö) va. to praise oneself.

རང་ལ་འཁོར་ (ranla kɔ̄ɔ) vi. to do sth. bad and have it result in misfortune for oneself, to have one's actions backfire ¶ གཞན་ལ་གནོད་པ་བསྐྱལ་བའི་ངན་འབྲས་རང་ལ་འཁོར་བ་རེད་ The consequences of causing trouble to others backfired and resulted in (him) being harmed.

རང་ལ་ཡིད་ཆེས་ (ranla yiicēè) believing in oneself, self-confidence.

རང་ལམ་རང་འགྲོ་ (ranlam randro) going one's own way.

རང་ལམ་རང་འགོག (ran̲lam ran̲gɔɔ̀) blocking one's own progress/ way.

རང་ལམ་རང་བཀག (ran̲lam ran̲gaà) sm. རང་ལམ་རང་འགོག.

རང་ལུགས་ (ran̲luù) 1. one's tradition/ custom, one's own ideology/ doctrine. 2. one's own point of view.

རང་ལུགས་ལྟ་སྤྱོད་ (ran̲luù dājöö) one's customs/ views/ and traditions ¶ མི་མང་པོས་རང་ལུགས་ལྟ་སྤྱོད་འགྱུར་གཞི་འབྱུང་བའི་དོགས་པ་བྱེད་ཀྱི་ཡོད་པ་རེད་ Many people doubt that our customs will be changed.

རང་ལུས་ (ran̲lüü) one's own body; va.—བླུ་ to buy back or ransom oneself; va.—འབུལ་ to sacrifice one's life (for a cause).

རང་ལུས་ཁྲིམས་ལེན་ (ran̲lüü trimlen) bringing harm/ penalty to oneself.

རང་ལུས་གདིང་བཞེད་ (ran̲lüü din̲jeè) selflessness, without thought of one's life and body.

རང་ལུས་ཚུལ་བཞིན་སྲུང་བ་ (ran̲lüü tsüüshin sūnwa) 1. va. to not have sexual relations with women other than one's wife. 2. va. to not have sexual relations while someone is ill.

རང་ལུས་རང་དབང་ (ran̲lüü ran̲wan) 1. individual freedom. 2. freedom over one's body.

རང་ལུས་སྲུང་དཀའ་ (ran̲lüü dūnga) difficult/ unable to defend one's body.

རང་ལོ་ (ran̲lo) one's age.

རང་ཤག (ran̲shaà) one's own quarters/ apartment.

རང་ཤི་ (rən̲shi) committing suicide, killing oneself; va.—རྒྱག to commit suicide.

རང་ཤུགས་ (rən̲shuù) 1. naturally, spontaneously ¶ དབྱིན་སྐད་རྒྱག་སའི་ལུང་པ་ཞིག་ལ་བསྡད་ན་རང་ཤུགས་ཀྱིས་དབྱིན་སྐད་ཤེས་ཀྱི་རེད་ If one lives in a place where English is spoken, one will learn English spontaneously (without formally studying it). 2. one's own strength.

རང་ཤུགས་ཀྱི་གདམ་ག (rən̲shuùgi d̲amga) the theory of natural selection.

རང་ཤུགས་ཀྱིས་ (rən̲shuùgi) sm. རང་ཤུགས་.

རང་ཤུགས་སུ་བྱུང་ (rən̲shuùsu jūn) vi. to appear spontaneously ¶ རང་ཤུགས་སུ་བྱུང་བའི་འཐབ་རྩོད་ A spontaneous struggle. ¶ རང་ཤུགས་སུ་བྱུང་བའི་ཕྱོགས་ལྷུང་ A spontaneous trend/ tendency.

རང་ཤུགས་སུ་ཡོང་བའི་རང་བཞིན་ (rən̲shuùsu yo̲nwɛ rən̲shin) spontaneity.

རང་ཤེད་ (ran̲sheè) 1. obstinate in always thinksing one's thoughts/ ideas are right and others are wrong; va.—བྱེད་. 2. arbitrarily, unilaterally ¶ ཁོས་རང་ཤེད་ཀྱིས་ཐག་གཅོད་བྱས་པ་རེད་ He decided arbitrarily.

རང་ཤེད་ཆེན་པོ་ (ran̲sheè cēmbo) kind of person who is obstinate and is always thinking his thoughts/ ideas are right and others are wrong.

རང་ཤེད་ཚ་པོ་ (ran̲sheè tsābo) sm. རང་ཤེད་ཆེན་པོ་.

རང་ཤེད་རིང་ལུགས་ (ran̲sheè ri̲nluù) subjectivism.

རང་ཤེད་ཨུ་ཚུགས་ (ran̲sheè ūdzuù) sm. རང་ཤེད་ཚ་པོ་.

རང་ཤེས་ (ran̲sheè) shung. to take one's own initiative.

རང་གཤིས་ (ran̲shii) one's character/ personality/ nature ¶ མི་འདི་རང་གཤིས་བཟང་པོ་ཞིག་འདུག This man has a good character. ¶ རང་གཤིས་གྱོང་པོ་ A capable personality.

རང་གཤོམ་ (ran̲shom) making one's own preparations; va.—བྱེད་.

རང་བཤད་རང་འགལ་ (ran̲shɛ̀ɛ ran̲gɛɛ) contradicting things one said earlier.

རང་ས་ (ran̲sa) sm. རང་སོ་.

རང་ས་གཞན་ཤོར་ (ran̲sa shɛ̲nshɔɔ) vi. to lose one's country to another/ others.

རང་ས་རང་གནས་འཇོག (ran̲sa ran̲nɛ̀ɛ jɔ̲ɔ) va. to keep things as they are.

རང་སར་ (ran̲sar) one's own place/ area/ position; va.—འཇོག to leave in one's own place/ area/ position.

རང་སར་མི་བཞག (ran̲sar mi̲shaà) judging others as if one were in their place, putting oneself in the place of others [Lit. putting another in one's place].

རང་སར་མི་བཞག་ མི་སར་རང་བཞག (ran̲sar mi̲shaà mi̲sar ran̲shaà) sm. རང་སར་མི་བཞག.

རང་སར་ཞི་ (ran̲saa shi̲) shung. to disappear naturally ¶ འགལ་རྐྱེན་ཡོད་རིགས་རང་སར་ཞི་ནས་ After all of the disasters will naturally disappeared.

རང་སྲུན་རང་རྙོ་ (ran̲sün rāñño) sm. རང་སྲུན་རང་བཙེས་.

རང་སྲུན་རང་བཙེས་ (ran̲sün rtan̲söö) vi. to cause one's own bother/ annoyance/ trouble.

རང་སུམ་སྒྱུར་ (ran̲sum gyu̲r) cube, cubic equation (in math).

རང་སུམ་སྒྱུར་འབྱེད་ (ran̲sum gyu̲rjeè) va. to extract the cube root (in math).

རང་སུམ་སྒྱུར་གྱི་གཞི་ (ran̲sum gyu̲rgi shi̲) cube root (in math).

རང་སེམས་ (ran̲sem) one's thought/ mind; va.—གཅུན་ va. to control/ restrain oneself.

རང་སེམས་བདེན་རློམ་ (ran̲sem d̲enlom) thinking or perceiving that one knows the truth, considering oneself infallible.

རང་སེམས་རང་ཚུགས་ (ran̲sem ran̲dzuù) shung. controlling oneself, restraining oneself.

རང་སེམས་རང་གསོ་ (ran̲sem ran̲so) consoling oneself; va.—བྱེད་.

རང་སེམས་ལ་ཉེས་པ་མེད་ན་ གཤིན་རྗེ་ལ་ཡང་འཇིགས་རྒྱུ་ཅི་ཡོད་ (ran̲semla ñe̲èba me̲èna shi̲njelayan jiggyu jīyöö) if one is innocent there is nobody to be afraid of [Lit. if one is innocent, one does not have to be afraid of even the Lord of the Dead].

རང་སོ་ (ran̲so) as before; va.—འཇོག to leave as before; vi.—གནས་ to be left as before, to keep sth./ sb. as before. ¶ ཁོང་གི་དེ་སྔའི་ལས་འགན་རང་སོར་བཞག་པ་རེད་ (They) left him in the same position he had before.

རང་སྲིད་ (rən̲sii) shung. one's own politics/ policy.

རང་སྲུང་ (ran̲sun) self-defense, self protection; va.—བྱེད་ to defend/ protect oneself ¶ དྲག་པོའི་རང་སྲུང་ལས་འགུལ་ An armed self-defense movement. ¶ རང་སྲུང་རྡུལ་མཚོན་ Defensive nuclear weapons.

རང་སྲུང་རྒོལ་ལན་ (ran̲sun gö̲ö̲lɛn) defensive counterattack; va.—སློག; —སྤྲོད་.

རང་སྲུང་དཔུང་སྡེ་ (ran̲sun būnde) self-defense force (usu. refers to Japan).

རང་སྲུང་དམག (ran̲sun māà) sm. རང་སྲུང་དཔུང་སྡེ་.

རང་སྲུང་དམག་འཁྲུག (ran̲sun māgdruù) war of self-defense.

རང་སྲུང་དམག་འཐབ་ (ran̲sun māgdəb) sm. རང་སྲུང་དམག་འཁྲུག.

རང་སྲུང་རུ་ཁག (ran̲sun ru̲gaà) self-defense brigade/ unit.

རང་སྲོག (ran̲soò) one's own life; va.— གཅོད་; —ཕྲེལ་ to commit suicide; va.—གཏོང་; —འདོར་ to risk/ give up/ sacrifice one's life (for a cause).

རང་སྲོག་བློས་གཏོང་ (ran̲sɔɔ̀ lȫö̀ dōn) giving up/ sacrificing/ risking one's life (for a cause); va. རང་སྲོག་བློས་གཏོང་; —བྱེད་.

རང་སྲོག་འབེན་བཙུགས་ (ran̲sɔɔ̀ be̲njuù) sm. རང་སྲོག་ལ་མ་འཛེམས་པ་.

རང་སྲོག་རང་གིས་གཅོད་ (ran̲sɔɔ̀ ran̲gi jöö) sm. རང་སྲོག་རང་གཅོད་བྱེད་.

རང་སྲོག་རང་གཅོད་ (ran̲sɔɔ̀ ran̲jöö) suicide; va. རང་སྲོག་རང་གཅོད་; —བྱེད་ to commit suicide.

རང་སྲོག་ལ་མ་འཛེམས་པ་ (ran̲sɔɔ̀la m̲andzemba) sm. རང་སྲོག་བློས་གཏོང་.

རང་བསགས་གཞན་འཁྱེར་ (ran̲saà she̲ngyer) others taking what one has saved/ accumulated, others taking away the benefit of what one has done.

རང་བསགས་རང་སྨྱོང་ (ran̲saà ran̲ ño̲n) vi. to experience the consequences of one's deeds/ actions/ accumulations.

རང་བསམ་བདེན་ལྡོམ་ (raŋsam denlom) sm. རང་སེམས་བདེན་ལྡོམ་.

རང་བསམ་རང་འདོད་ (raŋsam raŋdöö) doing as one wants/ wishes; va.—བྱེད་.

རངས་པོ་ (raŋbo) all, complete (set).

རད་པ་ (rɛ̀ba) 1. dry. 2. shriveled up, wilted.

རད་རོད་ (rɛ̀röö) dry and bumpy ground.

རད་སྲབ་ (rɛ̀drəb) thin clothing.

རན་ (rɛn) (vb. + —) the time to do sth. ¶ཁ་ལག་ཟ་རན་བཞག It's time to eat.

རན་ཁར་ (rɛngaa) at the time just before sth. is starting ¶ང་གློག་བརྙན་སྟོན་རན་ཁར་སླེབས་བྱུང་ I arrived at the time the movies was just about to start.

རན་གུན་ (rɛngün) Rangoon.

རན་པ་ (rɛmba) 1. fitting well in size. 2. cocongrass (used in Tibetan medicine).

རན་པོ་ (rɛmbo) fitting well in size; va.—བཟོ་ to make fit well ¶ཁོང་གིས་དུག་ལོག་ཆེ་ཆུང་རན་པོ་ཞིག་གྱོན་འདུག He wore clothes that fit him well.

རན་མ་ (rɛmma) the warp (in weaving); va.—བྲན་ to set up the warp in weaving.

རན་ཙམ་ (rɛndzam) 1. close to or about to be the time to do sth. ¶ལས་ཀར་འགྲོ་རན་ཙམ་འདུག It's about time to go to work. 2. just fitting.

རབ་ (rəb) 1. the best ¶རབ་འབྲིང་མཐའ་ The best, the middle and the worst. 2. shallow water, a place to ford; va.—རྒྱག to cross a shallow part of a river on foot. ¶ཆུ་ལ་རབ་མེད་ A river without a place to ford. 3. abbr. of རབ་ཏུ་.

རབ་དཀར་ (rəbgar) very white.

རབ་བཀྲུས་ (rəbdrüü) purified, cleansed.

རབ་བསྐྱེད་ (rəbgyeè) growth, development.

རབ་ཁ་ (rəbga) 1. a place where a river can be forded. 2. ferry site (for crossing a river).

རབ་དཀར་ལྷ་རྫས་ (rəbgar lhâdzɛ̀ɛ̀) shung. a kind of ceremonial scarf.

རབ་གུས་ (rəbgüü) with great respect.

རབ་གྲས་ (rəbdrɛ̀ɛ̀) the best type/ category.

རབ་དགའ་ (rəbga) 1. the plant Mercury. 2. thoroughly happy.

རབ་དགའི་འདབ་སྲེང་རྒྱས་པ་ (rəbgɛ dəbdreŋ gyɛ̀ɛ̀ba) shung. to have the flower of happiness bloom.

རབ་རྒྱག (rə̄ gyaà) see རབ་.

རབ་རྒྱན་ (rəbgyɛb) name for 17th རབ་བྱུང་.

རབ་རྒྱལ་ (rəbgyɛɛ) name for 16th རབ་བྱུང་.

རབ་རྒྱས་ (rəbgyɛ̀) 1. developing the best, increasing greatly. 2. name of a person.

རབ་བསྔགས་ (rəbŋaà) praising, lauding.

རབ་མཆོག (rəbcɔ̀ɔ̀) the best, the most excellent.

རབ་འཇེབས་ (ramjeb) very pleasant (tune/ song).

རབ་ཉམས་ (rəb ñam) extremely deteriorated.

རབ་ཏུ་ (rəbdu) thoroughly, completely, very ¶སེམས་རབ་ཏུ་འགུལ་བ་ Being completely moved.

རབ་ཏུ་འཁྱུག (rəbdu kyüù) darting/ moving a lot.

རབ་ཏུ་འཁྲུག (rəbdu trüù) vi. to tremble/ shake/ move vigorously (as in an earthquake).

རབ་ཏུ་འགུལ་ (rəbdu güü) vi. to tremble/ shake/ move vigorously (as in an earthquake).

རབ་ཏུ་ཆེམ་ཆེམ་ (rəbdu cēmjen) shining bright (usu. for sunlight).

རབ་ཏུ་བརྟན་པ་ (rəbdu dɛmba) extremely stable/ firm.

རབ་ཏུ་ལྡེག (rəbdu deg) vi. to tremble/ shake/ move vigorously (as in an earthquake).

རབ་ཏུ་འཕྱང་བའི་རྨ་ (rəbdu cāŋwɛ mā) wounds with flesh dangling.

རབ་ཏུ་བྱུང་ (rəbdu cuŋ) va. to take monastic vows when entering a monastery.

རབ་ཏུ་དམར་ཞིང་མཆོག་ཏུ་མཁས་པ་ (rəbdu māāshiŋ cɔ̄gdu kɛ̄ɛba) thoroughly red and expert (political slogan).

རབ་ཏུ་ཧུར་ཧུར་ (rəbdu ṭurwur) a loud rumbling sound/ noise.

རབ་ཏུ་གཡོ་ (rəbdu yū) vi. to shake/ move vigorously (as in an earthquake).

རབ་བརྡབས་ (rəbdaà) exaggerating; va.—བྱེད་.

རབ་བརྡབས་རི་མོ་ (rəbdaà rimu) cartoon, caricature; va.—བྲིས་ to draw a cartoon/ caricature.

རབ་རྟོག་རོ་དབྱངས་ (rəbdoò royaŋ) rhapsody.

རབ་ཏུ་བརྟན་པ་ (rəbdu dɛ̄mba) extremely firm/ steady/ stable.

རབ་བརྟན་ (rəbdɛn) 1. abbr. of རབ་ཏུ་བརྟན་པ་. 2. person's name.

རབ་དང་རིམ་པ་ (rabdaŋ rimbə) a series of many things, many things, various kinds ¶སྲིད་འགྱུར་རབ་དང་རིམ་པ་ཞིག་རྟུས་འགོད་བྱས་པ་རེད་ (They) instigated a series of coups.

རབ་ན་ (rabna) the best ¶རབ་ན་ལས་ཀ་ཆུ་ཚོད་གཅིག་ལ་ཚར་བ་དགོས་ The best is that you finish the work in an hour.

རབ་གནས་ (rabnɛɛ̀) consecration, consecrating; va.—བྱེད་.

རབ་པི་རུ་པི་ (rəbbi rubi) sm. རབ་བེ་རིབ་བེ་.

རབ་འཕྲུལ་ (rəbdrüü) one of the six gods of desire.

རབ་བེ་རིབ་བེ་ (rəbbi ribbi) sm. རབ་བེ་རི་བེ་.

རབ་བེ་རི་བེ་ (rabbe ribi) 1. blurred, dim, hard to see, unclear, vague. 2. sb. who is unreliable.

རབ་བེ་རོབ་བེ་ (rabbe robbe) 1. slipshod, carelessly, not detailed ¶ལས་ཀ་རབ་བེ་རོབ་བེ་བྱས་ན་འགྲིགས་ཀྱི་མ་རེད་ It is not okay to do a slipshod job. 2. uneven ¶ལམ་ལ་རྡོ་རབ་བེ་རོབ་བེ་འདུག The road is filled with uneven rocks.

རབ་འབྱམས་པ་ (rəbjamba) shung. a type of geshe degree.

རབ་བྱུང་ (rəbjuŋ) 1. the sixty year cycle in the Tibetan calendar. 2. a monk. 3. abbr. of རབ་ཏུ་བྱུང་.

རབ་བྱུང་མཁན་པོ་ (rəbjuŋ kēmbo) the monk or lama who gives a monk his vows.

རབ་བྱུང་སྡོམ་པ་སླར་འབུལ་ (rəbjuŋ domba lārbüü) giving back/ relinquishing one's monastic vows.

རབ་བྱུང་སྡོམ་བཞེས་ (rəbjuŋ domsheè) taking monastic vows.

རབ་བྱུང་མ་ (rəbjuŋmə) a nun.

རབ་བྱུང་ལག་འཛིན་ (rəbjuŋ ləŋdzin) certificate of being a monk.

རབ་བྱེད་ (rabjeè) a chapter.

རབ་འབར་མེ་ལྕེ་ (rambar meje) a raging flame/ fire.

རབ་འབྱམས་ (rəbjam) profound knowledge.

རབ་འབྱམས་རྒྱ་མཚོ་ (rəbjam gyadzo) the big/ great ocean.

རབ་འབྲིང་མཐའ་གསུམ་ (rəbdriŋ tāsum) the three: (the) best, the middle and the worst.

རབ་མང་ (rəbmaŋ) very many.

རབ་ཚའི་ས་ཁུལ་ (rəbdzɛɛ sə̄əgüü) the tropics ¶རབ་ཚའི་ས་ཁུལ་གྱི་ལོ་ཏོག Tropical crops.

རབ་ཚེས་རབ་བྱུང་ (rabdzeè rəbjuŋ) a name for the 15th རབ་བྱུང་.

རབ་མཛེས་མ་ (rəbdzeèma) a beautiful woman.

རབ་བཞེས་ (rabsheè) va. to take one's monastic vows.

རབ་འོག (rab wɔ̀ɔ̀) the second in rank/ status/ level, that which is just below the best.

རབ་ཡིད་ (rəbyii) a name for the 14th རབ་བྱུང་.

རབ་ཡོལ་ (rəbyöö) a monk/ lama who has broken his vows, usu. implies via heterosexual intercourse.

རབ་རིབ་ (rəbrib) sm. རབ་བེ་རི་བེ་.

རབ་རིབ་སེལ་ (rəbrib sīī) daybreak.

རབ་རོབ་ (rabrob) abbr. of རབ་བེ་རོབ་བེ་.

རབ་ལ་ (rəbla) sm. རབ་ན་.

རབ་ལོ་ (rəblo) a year in Tibetan calendar.

རབ་སོན་ (rəbsön) the best quality seed.

རབ་གསལ་ (rəbsɛl) 1. a balcony in front of a window. 2. very/ extremely clear.

རབ་གསུམ་རབ་ལ་ (rəbsum rəbla) at best ¶རབ་གསུམ་རབ་ལ་བྱུང་ན་ལོ་གཅིག་བཞུགས་རོགས་གནང་ དེ་མ་བྱུང་ན་ཟླ་བ་གསུམ་བཞུགས་རོགས་གནང་ At best, please stay for one year, but if you can't do this, stay for three months.

རབས་ (rəb) a generation.

རབས་གཅོད་ (rəb jöö) va. to make extinct.

རབས་ཆད་ (rəbjɛɛ̀) 1. childless, barren (woman). 2. vi. to have become extinct. 3. vi. to be barren/ childless.

རབས་ཆད་མ་ (rəb cɛɛ̀ma) a barren/ childless woman.

རབས་མཚུངས་ (rəbdzuŋ) the same generation.

རབས་རིམ་པ་ (rəb rimbə) shung. sm. མི་རབས་རིམ་པ་.

རམ་ (ram) 1. interrogative particle for words ending in 'r.' 2. 'or' particle for word ending in 'r' ། མར་རམ་སྣུམ་ Butter or oil.

རམ་སྐྱོར་ (ramgyɔr) vocal/ choral accompaniment, the technique used in Tibetan opera singing where the accompaniers fill in while the soloist catches his breath; va.—བྱེད་.

རམ་འདེགས་ (ramdeg) 1. supplementary, subsidiary, auxiliary; va.—བྱེད་ ། རམ་འདེགས་ཀྱི་ཐབས་ལམ་ Supplementary means. ། ཕར་རྒོལ་ལ་རམ་འདེགས་བྱེད་ཡས་ For supplementing the attack. 2. sm. རམ་སྐྱོར་.

རམ་འདེགས་དགེ་རྒན་ (ramdeg gegɛn) teaching assistant.

རམ་འདེགས་པ་ (ramdegba) assistant, aide, helper.

རམ་པ་ (ramba) 1. name of an aristocratic family in traditional Tibet. 2. cocongrass.

རམ་བུ་ (rəmbu) helping, assisting; va.—འདེགས་ to help/ assist/ aid; to sing accompaniment in Tibetan opera.

རམ་འབྱམས་ (ramjaŋ) an official in the Bhutanese government.

རམས་ (ram) indigo.

རམས་ཀྱོང་ (ramgyoŋ) stoneware bowl/ pot for grinding indigo dye.

རམས་ཁོག་ (ramkɔɔ̀) pot for boiling indigo.

རམས་རྡིལ་ (ramdee) stone pestle slab for pulverizing indigo.

རམས་པ་ (ramba) abbr. རབ་འབྱམས་པ་.

རམས་ཚོས་ (ramdzöö) indigo dye.

རམས་ཤིང་ (ramshiŋ) indigo plant.

རའི་ཊར་ (rɛdrar) eng. Reuters.

རའི་རིལ་མ་ལ་ལུག་གིས་ངོ་སོ་འཁྱེར་ (rɛ riimala luùgi ŋoso kyēr) taking credit for another's work. [Lit. the sheep takes credit for the goat's dung].

རལ་ (rɛɛ) 1. vi. to get torn/ ripped ། ངའི་སྟོད་ཐུང་རལ་བཞག My blouse got torn. 2. abbr. of རལ་པ་; 1.

རལ་སྐོར་མཁན་ (rɛɛ gɔ̄ɔ̄ñɛn) a person expert with the sword.

རལ་སྐྱོག་ (rɛɛgyɔɔ̀) torn, ripped ། རང་དག་ལོག་རལ་སྐྱོག་དེ་འདྲ་མ་གོན་ You shouldn't wear torn clothes like that.

རལ་སྐྱོན་ (rɛɛgyön) torn, ripped; vi.—ཤོར་ to get torn/ ripped.

རལ་ཁ་ (rɛɛga) 1. blade of a sword. 2. a kind of blouse worn by female Gelong.

རལ་ཁ་དཔུང་ཆད་ (rɛɛga būŋjɛɛ̀) a kind of sleeveless shirt/vest worn by male Gelong.

རལ་གྲི་ (rɛɛdri) sword; va.—གཡུག་ to swing a sword, to hit with a sword.

རལ་གྲི་གནམ་གཡུག (rɛɛdri nāmyuù) deciding things unilaterally in a domineering/ autocratic way; va.—བྱེད་ [Lit. to strike a sword at the sky].

རལ་གྲི་ལ་ཁུ་ཚུར་རྡེག་པ་ (rɛɛdri kūrdzur degba) doing sth. stupid that harms oneself [Lit. to hit a sword with one's fist].

རལ་རྒྱལ་འཆལ་རྒྱལ་ (rɛɛgyɛɛ cɛ̄ɛ̄gyɛɛ) shung. leaving sth. in a state of disrepair.

རལ་ཅན་ (rɛɛjɛn) 1. torn dilapidated, worn out. 2. abbr. of རལ་པ་ཅན་.

རལ་ཅོག་ (rɛɛjoò) hair tied in a knot/ bundle on the head; va.—རྒྱག.

རལ་ལྕང་ (rɛɛjaŋ) 1. weeping willow tree. 2. braided hair.

རལ་ལྕོག (rɛɛjoò) sm. རལ་ཅོག.

རལ་རྡོག་ཁྲུལ་ཁྲུལ་ (rɛɛdog trüüdrüü) a person with a lot of matted hair.

རལ་རྡོལ་ (rɛɛdöö) torn with holes, tattered, dilapidated.

རལ་རྡོལ་མཐའ་རུལ་ (rɛɛdöö tāhrüü) shung. tattered, ragged, worn-out.

རལ་པ་ (rɛɛba) 1. a person with long hair. 2. person with matted, disheveled hair. 3. a type of dance in which the woman carry drums and the men carry small cymbals. 4. sm. སྐྲ་མ་.

རལ་པ་ཅན་ (rɛɛbajɛn) 1. the 41st ancient King of Tibet. 2. sb. with long hair (usu. shaggy, unkempt hair).

རལ་པ་སྤྲོག་སྤྲོག (rɛɛba trɔ̄gdrɔɔ̀) having long shaggy/ unkempt hair.

རལ་པ་ས་འདྲུད་ (rɛɛba sāndrüù) a riding skill wherein a rider touches his hair on the ground while his horse is galloping.

རལ་པའི་གདེངས་ཀ་ (rɛɛbɛ deŋga) hair tied in a knot/ bundle and fastened on top of the head.

རལ་པོ་ (rɛɛbo) sm. རལ་སྐྱོག.

རལ་པོ་ལྷན་པས་མི་ཁེབས་པ་ (rɛɛbo lhɛmbɛ mi kēbba) a situation out of control ། ཁྱེད་རང་གི་སྐྱོན་ཆ་དེ་ད་ལྟ་ཡོ་བསྲང་མ་བྱས་ན་རྗེས་སུ་རལ་པོ་ལྷན་པས་མི་ཁེབས་པ་ཡོང་གི་རེད་ If you don't correct the error now, later it will be out of control. [Lit. holes that can't be covered with patches].

རལ་པོ་ལྷན་པའི་སྐྱོ་རོགས་ (rɛɛbo lhɛnbɛ gyōrɔɔ̀) poor people helping each other [Lit. patches help the torn clothing].

རལ་མོ་ (rɛɛmo) a female རལ་པ་.

རལ་བཙེམས་ (rɛɛdzem) mending torn clothes; va.—བྱེད་.

རལ་བ་འཛིན་ (rɛɛwa dzin) va. to look for mistakes/ faults (in others), to seize on shortcomings.

རལ་རུལ་ (rɛɛrüü) abbr. of རལ་ལི་རུལ་ལི་.

རལ་ལི་ (rɛɛli) eng. train, railway.

རལ་ལི་རུལ་ལི་ (rɛɛle rüüli) torn, shredded.

རལ་སུབས་ (rɛɛsub) a crack, fissure.

རས་ (rɛɛ̀) cloth.

རས་ཀ་ཅི་ (rɛɛ̀ gāji) sm. རས་དཀར་ཅི་.

རས་དཀར་ཅི་ (rɛɛ̀ gārji) white cloth.

རས་རྐྱང་ (rɛɛ̀gyaŋ) clothes without any lining.

རས་སྐུད་ (rɛɛ̀güü) cotton thread.

རས་ཁུག (rɛɛ̀guù) a cloth bag/ satchel/ pouch.

རས་ཁྲ་ (rɛɛ̀dra) dyed fabric/ cloth, printed cotton cloth.

རས་གུག (rɛɛ̀guù) cloth bag.

རས་གུར་ (rɛɛ̀gur) cloth tent.

རས་གོས་ (rɛɛ̀göö) cloth clothing.

རས་འགའ་ (rɛɛ̀ga) thick cloth woven from jute.

རས་སྒྱེ་ (rɛɛ̀gye) large cloth bag.

རས་སྒྲིལ་ (rɛɛ̀drii) cloth for wrapping.

རས་གཅོད་ (rɛɛ̀jöö) treating as trivial/ unimportant; va.—བྱེད་ ། ནོར་འཁྲུལ་ཆུང་ཙག་ལའང་རས་གཅོད་བྱ་རྒྱུ་མེད་ One shouldn't treat even small mistakes as trivial.

རས་ཆ་ (rɛɛ̀ja) cotton cloth.

རས་ཆ་འཁུམས་གཉེར་ཅན་ (rɛɛ̀ja kūmñerjɛn) cloth that is wrinkled.

རས་ཆུང་ (rɛɛ̀juŋ) a disciple of Milarepa.

རས་ཆེན་ (rɛɛ̀jen) one of the 13 articles that a gelong may possess - a type of overcoat/ raincoat.

རས་སྙིགས་ (rɛɛ̀ñii) rags.

རས་སྟོད་ (rɛɛ̀döö) cotton shirt.

རས་ཐག (rɛɛ̀daà) rope made from cotton.

རས་ཐིག་མ་ (rɛɛ̀ tīgmə) striped cloth.

རས་ཐུམ་ (rɛɛ̀dum) sm. རས་སྒྲིལ་.

རས་མཐིལ་ (rɛɛ̀tii) shoes with cloth soles.

རས་འཐག (rɛɛ̀daà) weaving cloth; va.—བྱེད་.

རས་འཐག་འཕྲུལ་འཁོར་ (rɛɛ̀daà trüügɔɔ) cloth weaving machine.

རས་འཐག་བཟོ་གྲྭ་ (rɛɛ̀daà sodra) textile factory/

mill, weaving mill.

རས་འཐུམ་ (r̲ɛ̀ɛdum) cloth bundle/ package.

རས་གདན་ (r̲ɛ̀ɛdɛn) bed sheet.

རས་པ་ (r̲ɛ̀ɛba) sadhus and yogis who are clad only with a small piece of cloth.

རས་སྤྲ་སངས་ཁམ་པ་ (r̲ɛ̀ɛ) gauze cloth used for bandages.

རས་སྤུ་མ་ (r̲ɛ̀ɛ pūmə) cotton flannel.

རས་ཕད་ (r̲ɛ̀ɛbüü) sm. རས་ཁུག.

རས་ཕྱགས་ (r̲ɛ̀ɛjaà) cloth broom/ duster; va.—རྒྱག.

རས་ཕྱར་ (r̲ɛ̀ɛjaa) large cloth sheet.

རས་ཕྲན་ (r̲ɛ̀ɛdrɛn) undergarment, underwear.

རས་བལ་ (r̲ɛ̀ɛbɛɛ) 1. cotton. 2. abbr. of རས་ and བལ.

རས་བུབས་ (r̲ɛ̀ɛbub) a roll of cotton.

རས་བོར་ (r̲ɛ̀ɛbɔɔ) shung. sm. རས་སུ་བོར་

རས་བོར་དུ་གཏོང་ (r̲ɛ̀ɛbɔɔdu dōŋ) shung. sm. རས་སུ་བོར་

རས་བྱང་ (r̲ɛ̀ɛjaŋ) label written on pieces of cotton cloth that are attached to boxes, etc.

རས་བྲིས་ (r̲ɛ̀ɛdrii) paintings done on cloth.

རས་འབྲས་ (r̲ɛndrɛɛ̀) seed/ fruit of cotton plant.

རས་སྦྱར་མ་ (r̲ɛ̀ɛjarma) layers of cloth stuck together (e.g., to make a sole).

རས་མ་ (r̲ɛ̀ɛma) 1. cotton. 2. cotton shreds.

རས་མ་སེང་ (r̲ɛ̀ɛma sēŋ) cross between cotton cloth and cotton net.

རས་རྩི་མ་ (r̲ɛ̀ɛ dzi̲mə) varnished cloth.

རས་བརྩེགས་ (r̲ɛ̀ɛdzeg) sole made of layers of cotton cloth.

རས་ཚགས་ (r̲ɛ̀ɛdzaà) a cloth used to filter tea, etc.

རས་འཚེམ་ (r̲ɛndzem) sewing pieces of cloth; va.—རྒྱག.

རས་འཛར་ (r̲ɛndzar) 1. leftover pieces of cloth (after making sth.). 2. dangling end of a piece of cloth. 3. sm. རས་བྱང་.

རས་གཞི་ (r̲ɛ̀ɛshi) 1. type of cloth on which thankas are painted. 2. motion picture screen.

རས་ཟོན་ (r̲ɛ̀ɛsön) sm. རས་ཟོམ་.

རས་ཟོམ་ (r̲ɛ̀ɛsom) a type of boot worn by lamas and monk officials.

རས་ཟོམ་རྒྱང་འགོ་ (r̲ɛ̀ɛsom gyo̲ŋgo) a traditional shoe tree for རས་ཟོམ་.

རས་གཟན་ (r̲ɛ̀ɛsɛn) cloth shawls worn by monks.

རས་ཡུག (r̲ɛ̀ɛyuù) sm. རས་བུབས་.

རས་ཡོལ་ (r̲ɛ̀ɛyöö) cloth curtain.

རས་གཡབ་ (r̲ɛ̀ɛyəb) cloth canopy.

རས་ལྭ་ (r̲ɛ̀ɛla) sm. རས་གོས་.

རས་ཤག (r̲ɛ̀ɛshaà) rags.

རས་སག (r̲ɛ̀ɛsaà) a type of cloth that is loosely woven.

རས་སག་སག (r̲ɛ̀ɛ sāgsaà) sm. རས་སག.

རས་སང་ (r̲ɛ̀ɛsaŋ) loosely woven cotton (usu. used for curtains).

རས་སུ་བོར་ (r̲ɛ̀ɛsu bɔ̲ɔ) va. to shun/ avoid/ not do well ¶ ཁོས་གཞུང་དོན་རས་སུ་བོར་ནས་སྒེར་དོན་གཉེར་གྱི་འདུག He avoided working to achieve the interests of the government and instead looked after his own private affairs.

རས་སུལ་མ་ (r̲ɛ̀ɛ sǖümə) cotton crepe.

རས་བསེ་ (r̲ɛ̀ɛse) varnished cloth (so the surface is shinny).

རས་བསེ་ནག་པོ་ (r̲ɛ̀ɛse n̲agbo) electrical tape.

རས་བསེ་དཀར་པོ་ (r̲ɛ̀ɛse gārbo) medical (white) adhesive tape.

རས་ཧམ་ (r̲ɛ̀ɛham) sm. རས་ལྷམ་.

རས་ལྷམ་ (r̲ɛ̀ɛlham) canvas shoes, sneakers, cloth shoes.

རས་ཧྲུག (r̲ɛ̀ɛhruù) pieces of leftover material (after making sth.).

རས་ཧྲུལ་ (r̲ɛ̀ɛhrüü) sm. རས་ཧྲུག.

རས་ལྷེ་ (r̲ɛ̀ɛlhe) sm. རས་ཧྲུག.

རི་ (r̲i) 1. hill, mountain. 2. abbr. of རི་ཡིན་. 3. vi. to have value, to be worth sth. ¶ འདི་སྒོར་ལྔ་ལས་རི་གི་མ་རེད་ This is worth only five dollars. 4. the part of a fingerprint that looks like a hill. 5. the part of a shoe from the sole to the first strip on the sides.

རི་ཀྲུང་ (r̲idruŋ) abbr. of Japan and China.

རི་ཀླུང་ (r̲iluŋ) 1. rivers and hills; scenery. 2. country, state, territory ¶ རི་ཀླུང་ཕྱེད་ཀ་ཙམ་ About half of the country.

རི་ཀླུང་ཀུན་ལ་ཁྱབ་ (r̲iluŋ gǖnla kyəb) vi. to be widespread, to be spread everywhere.

རི་ཀླུང་རྒྱ་སྡོམ་ (r̲iluŋ gya̲dom) shung. a ban on killing wild animals (wolves, mice/ rats were usually excluded from this).

རི་ཀླུང་རྩ་ཚིག (r̲iluŋ dzədzii) shung. edict prohibiting the killing of wild animals (wolves, mice/ rats were usually excluded from this).

རི་བཀག་རྫ་སྲུང་ (r̲igaà dzāsuŋ) building walls on the mountainsides to protect the vegetation from erosion.

རི་བཀྲ་ (r̲idrə) 1. multicolored painting/ patterns. 2. a beautiful pattern or painting.

རི་རྐེད་ (r̲igeè) half way up a mountain, the middle section of a mountain.

རི་སྐེ་ (r̲ige) sm. རི་འགུལ་.

རི་སྐེགས་ (r̲igeg) myna (bird).

རི་སྐེད་ (r̲igeè) sm. རི་རྐེད་.

རི་སྐེད་པ་ཉག་ཉག (r̲igeèba ñagñaà) a mountain shaped like a saddle.

རི་སྐོར་ (r̲igɔɔ) circumambulating a holy mountain.

རི་སྐྱ་རྫ་མེད་ (r̲igya dzāmeè) an area with poor vegetation.

རི་སྐྱེགས་ (r̲igyeg) sm. རི་སྐེགས་.

རི་སྐྱེས་ (r̲igyeè) things that grow on hills and mountains ¶ རི་སྐྱེས་རྩྭ་ཤིང་ Mountain vegetation/ plants.

རི་སྐྱེས་སྐྱེ་དངོས་ (r̲igyeè gyēŋöö) wild/ plants/ vegetation.

རི་སྐྱེས་ཚི་སྣ་ (r̲igyeè tsīnə) wild fibres.

རི་སྐྱེས་སྔོ་ཚལ་ (r̲igyeè ŋōdzɛɛ) wild vegetables.

རི་སྐྱེས་རྩི་ཤིང་ (r̲igyeè dzīshiŋ) wild plants.

རི་སྐྱེས་ཚོད་མ་ (r̲igyeè tsöōma) sm. རི་སྐྱེས་སྔོ་ཚལ་.

རི་སྐྱེས་སྲོག་ཆགས་ (r̲igyeè sōgjaà) wild animals.

རི་སྐྱེས་སྲོག་ཆགས་འདུས་གསོ་ར་བ་ (r̲igyeè sōgjaà d̲üüso r̲awa) wildlife (rearing) farm.

རི་སྐྱོད་འགྲོགས་བྱམས་ (r̲igyöö gyɔ̲gjam) a type of sedan chair that was used in mountain areas.

རི་ཁ་བ་ཅན་ (r̲i kāwajɛn) 1. snow mountain. 2. Tibet.

རི་ཁམ་ (r̲ikam) mountain grown peach.

རི་ཁུག (r̲iguù) mountain gorge/ valley/ ravine.

རི་ཁུག་ལུང་ཁུག (r̲iguù l̲uŋguù) a remote/ barren/ wilderness area.

རི་ཁུད་ (r̲igüü) sm. རི་སུལ་.

རི་ཁུལ་ (r̲igüü) hills, mountains, mountainous areaa ¶ རི་ཁུལ་རྩྭ་ར་ Mountain pasture area.

རི་ཁོག་སྦུག་ལམ་ (r̲igɔɔ̀ b̲uglam) tunnel through a mountain.

རི་ཁྱི་ (r̲igyi) wolf.

རི་ཁྱི་སྔོན་པོ་ (r̲igyi ŋōmbo) a bluish colored wolf.

རི་ཁྱིམ་ (r̲igyim) house built on a hill/ mountain slope.

རི་ཁྲ་ (r̲idra) sm. རི་བཀྲ་.

རི་ཁྲོད་ (r̲idröö) hermitage located in the mountains.

རི་ཁྲོད་པ་ (r̲idröōba) sb. who lives in a hermitage, hermit.

རི་མཁར་ (r̲igar) a house built on a hill/ mountain.

རི་གུ་ (r̲igu) baby goat.

རི་གོང་ (r̲igoŋ) sm.* རི་བོང་.

རི་གྲོང་ (r̲idroŋ) mountain village.

རི་གླག (r̲ilaà) eagle.

རི་གླུ་ (r̲ilu) songs of/ from the mountains.

རི་མགུལ་ (r̲ingüü) near the top of a mountain [Lit. neck of the mountain].

རི་མགོ་ (r̲ingo) mountain top/ peak.

རི་མགོ་ལོགས་འཛུགས་ (r̲ingo lɔ̲gdzuù) creating a faction/ clique in a party or organization; va.—

བྱེད་ [Lit. mountain top put separately].

རི་མགོའི་རིང་ལུགས་ (ringü rinluù) mountaintopism (seeing one's own party or group as more important than the government).

རི་འགོ་ (ringo) sm. རི་མགོ་.

རི་འགག (ringaà) place situated between two hills or mountains.

རི་འགོག (riŋgɔɔ̀) resist the Japanese; va.—བྱེད་ (political slogan referring to the Sino-Japanese War).

རི་འགོག་མི་རིགས་འཐབ་ཕྱོགས་གཅིག་སྒྲིལ་ (riŋgɔɔ̀ miriì təbjɔɔ̀ jìgdrii) united front of the antiJapanese nations/ peoples.

རི་འགོག་དམག་འཁྲུག (riŋgɔɔ̀ məgdruù) war of resistance against Japan, the Sino-Japanese War of 1937-45.

རི་འགོག་གཡུལ་འགྱེད་ (riŋgɔɔ̀ yüügyeè) sm. རི་འགོག་དམག་འཁྲུག.

རི་རྒལ་ལ་རྒྱབ་ (rigyɛɛ la gyəb) crossing over many mountains, traveling over hills and dales [Lit. cross mountain, go over pass].

རི་རྗོད་ (rigüü) bare mountain.

རི་རྒྱ་ (rigya) 1. Japan and China, Sino-Japanese ¶ རི་རྒྱ་དམག་འཁྲུག The Sino-Japanese War. 2. shung. a ban on the killing of wild animals.

རི་རྒྱ་ལུང་རྒྱ་སྡོམ་ (rigya lüŋgya dom) shung. ban on killing wild animals.

རི་རྒྱ་ནགས་གསོ་ (rigya nagso) reforestation of a mountain.

རི་རྒྱུད་ (rigyüù) mountain range.

རི་རྒྱུད་གུན་གསབ་ (rigyüù günsəb) an allowance for being posted in the mountains.

རི་རྒྱུད་འབྲེལ་མ་ (rigyüù dreema) sm. རི་རྒྱུད་.

རི་རྒྱབ་ (rigyəb) back of a mountain.

རི་རྒྱལ་ (rigyɛɛ) sm. རི་རྒྱལ་ལྷུན་པོ་.

རི་རྒྱལ་ལྷུན་པོ་ (rigyɛɛ lhünbu) Mt. Mehru.

རི་སྒང་ (rigaŋ) ridge of a mountain.

རི་སྒུལ་མཚོ་སྐྱོམ་ (rigüü tsögyom) sm. རི་སྙིལ་མཚོ་སྐྱོམ་.

རི་སྒོག (rigɔɔ̀) wild garlic.

རི་བརྒྱུད་ (rigüü) sm. རི་རྒྱུད་.

རི་བརྒྱུད་མི་དམངས་ཀྱི་གཞིས་སྦྱོད་ཉམས་ཞིབ་ཁང་ (rigyüù mimaŋgi shiìjöö ñamshibgaŋ) Woodlands Mountain Institute.

རི་ངུ་ (riŋu) a wailing sound that comes from mountains that is considered a bad omen [Lit. mountain crying].

རི་ངོས་ (riŋöö) side of a mountain.

རི་སྔོ་ཆུ་དྭངས་ (riŋo cüdaŋ) green mountains and clear water.

རི་ཅན་ (rijɛn) hilly, mountainous.

རི་བཅོས་ཆུ་བཅོས་ (rijöö cüjüü) sm. རི་འདུལ་ཆུ་འདུལ་.

རི་ཆུ་ (riju) hills/ mountains and rivers.

རི་ཆུ་ཁྲི་སྟོང་ (riju tridoŋ) very many mountains and rivers [Lit. hills rivers 10,000,000].

རི་ཆུ་བཅོས་བསྒྱུར་ (rijüü jüügyur) sm. རི་འདུལ་ཆུ་འདུལ་.

རི་ཆུ་ཡུལ་ལྗོངས་ (riju yüüjoŋ) landscape, scenery.

རི་ཆུང་ (rijuŋ) a small hill.

རི་ཆེ་ (rice) 1. abbr. of རི་བོ་ཆེ་. 2. a large hill.

རི་ཇག (rijaà) Japanese gangsters/ bandits (derogatory name used for the Japanese army).

རི་འཇུ་ (rinju) a thick thread made from goat hair.

རི་ཉག (riñaà) the saddle of a mountain.

རི་ཉལ་ (riñɛɛ) a name for people who don't come home often [Lit. sleeping in the mountains].

རི་ཉིལ་ (riñii) vi. to have/ get a landslide.

རི་ཉིལ་མཚོ་འཁྱོམ་ (riñii tsögyom) a momentous event [Lit. mountains have landslides and oceans shake].

རི་གཉན་ (riñɛn) hills and mountains that possess ghosts and demons.

རི་གཉའ་ (riñaa) sm. རི་སྙེ་.

རི་སྙིལ་ (ri ñii) vi. to have/ get a landslide.

རི་སྙིལ་ས་གས་ (riñii sāgɛɛ̀) sm. རི་ཉིལ་མཚོ་འཁྱོམ་ [Lit. mountains have landslides and the earth splits].

རི་བསྙིལ་ (riñii) sm. རི་སྙིལ་.

རི་ཏོག་ཏོག (ri dogdoò) 1. a small hill. 2. a cone shaped hill/ mountain.

རི་གདོས་ (ridöö) the size of a mountain.

རི་ལྟར་གཡོ་མེད་གནས་པ་ (ridar yōmeè nɛɛ̀ba) steadfast, dependable (like a mountain).

རི་ལྟས་ (ridɛɛ̀) signs and omens that come from hills and mountains.

རི་སྟེང་ (rideŋ) sm. རི་རྩེ་.

རི་སྟོང་ (ridoŋ) barren hills.

རི་ཐང་ (ridaŋ) mountains and plains.

རི་ཐང་མཚམས་ (ridaŋ tsām) the area between the hills/ mountains and the plains.

རི་ཐོད་ (ridöö) sm. རི་རྩེ་.

རི་ཐོན་ (ridön) sth. that comes from or grows in the mountains ¶ རི་ཐོན་ཤིང་ཏོག Fruits that come from mountains.

རི་མཐའ་ (ridaa) the edge of a mountain.

རི་མཐོ་བྲག་གཟར་ (rito tragsar) a high and steep mountain.

རི་མཐོ་ལ་གཟར་ (ri tō la sar) sm. རི་མཐོ་བྲག་གཟར་.

རི་མཐོ་ས་གཙང་ (ri tō sā dzāŋ) high mountains that are clean/ pure.

རི་མཐོའི་གྲོས་ཚོགས་ (ritö tröödzɔɔ̀) summit conference.

རི་མཐོའི་ན་ཚ་ (ridö nadza) high altitude sickness (hypoxia).

རི་མཐོན་པོ་མགོ་སྒུར་དུ་འཇུག ཆུ་ཆེན་པོ་ལམ་བཟུར་དུ་འཇུག (ri tōmbo gogurdu jug cū cēmbo lamsurdu juù) conquering nature [Lit. to make the mountains bow their heads and the rivers give way].

རི་འཐབ་སྨན་ཁང་ (rindəb mɛ̄ngaŋ) field hospital.

རི་དེའུ་ (ri dewu) small hill.

རི་དྭགས་ (ridaà) wild animals (usu. refers to herbivores); va.—རྒྱག; —རྔོན་ to hunt wild animals (usu. refers to herbivores).

རི་དྭགས་ཀྱི་ནགས་ (ridaàgi nag) Deer Park in Sarnath.

རི་དྭགས་རྔོན་པ་ (ridaà ŋōmba) hunter.

རི་དྭགས་རྔོན་ར་ (ridaà ŋōnra) hunting zone/ area.

རི་དྭགས་རྔོན་ཆས་ (ridaà ŋōnjɛɛ̀) hunting tools/ equipment.

རི་དྭགས་རྔོན་ས་ (ridaà ŋōnsa) sm. རི་དྭགས་རྔོན་ར་.

རི་དྭགས་ཆོས་འཁོར་ (ridaà cöögɔɔ̀) the statue/ ornament that consists of two deer and a wheel that is found on the roofs of temples and monasteries.

རི་དྭགས་རྙི་ཐག (ridaà ñīdaà) snare for trapping animals.

རི་དྭགས་རྟགས་ཅན་ (ridaà dāgjɛn) 1. poet. moon. 2. a physical characteristics of a person that sets him off from others (in a good or bad way).

རི་དྭགས་ཐེད་རོ་ (ridaà tēero) leftover carcass of an animal killed by another animal.

རི་དྭགས་དྲ་བ་ (ridaà trawa) a net for trapping animals.

རི་དྭགས་པ་ (ridagba) hunter.

རི་དྭགས་རྨས་མ་བཞིན་དུ་ (ridaà mɛ̄ɛ̀ma shindu) extremly dangerous/ alert/ on guard [Lit. like a wounded wild animal].

རི་དྭགས་ཚེ་རིང་ (ridaà tsēriŋ) the long-lived deer (one of the six symbols of longevity).

རི་དྭགས་ར་བ་ (ridaà rawa) zoo.

རི་དྭགས་རུ་རུ་ (ridaà ruru) deer.

རི་གདོང་ (ridoŋ) sm. རི་ཟུར་.

རི་འདབས་ (rindəb) base/ foot of a mountain.

རི་འདུལ་ཆུ་འདུལ་ (rindüü cündüü) conquering nature; va.—བྱེད་ [Lit. tame the mountains and tame the rivers].

རི་རྡོ་ལུང་འབེབས་ (rido lüŋbeb) moving people and things in an inappropriate/ unsuitable way; va.—བྱེད་ [Lit. move mountain stone to the valley].

རི་རྡོག་རྡོག (ri dogdoò) small hills.

རི་སྡེ་ (ride) a mountain community.

རི་ལྡེབས་ (rideb) hillside, mountain slope, face of a mountain side.

རི་ནེ་ཝ་ (rinewa) Geneva.

རི་སྣ་ (rinə) the end of a རི་ཟུར་.

རི་པ་ (ribə) 1. mountain dweller. 2. mountaineer.

རི་པིན་ (ribin) Japan.

རི་དཔྱད་ (rijɛɛ̀) the shape of mountains.

རི་སྤུ་མེད་ (ri būmeè) a bare mountain, a mountain without trees.

རི་སྤོས་མཚོ་སྐྱོང་ (ribüü tsōgyoŋ) doing an impossible or very difficult task [Lit. move mountains, stretch the ocean].

རི་སྤོས་མཚོ་སྐྱོམ་ (ribüü tsōgyom) doing impossible/ very difficult tasks [Lit. move the mountain and shake the ocean].

རི་སྤོས་མཚོ་ཕྱུང་ (ribüü tsōcuŋ) sm. རི་སྤོས་མཚོ་སྐྱོམ་.

རི་སྤོས་མཚོ་སློག (ribüü tsōlɔ̄ɔ̀) sm. རི་སྤོས་མཚོ་སྐྱོམ་.

རི་སྤྱི་ (riji) shung. a major administrative committee consisting of the abbots of colleges that teach religious philosophy (e.g., in large Geluk monasteries such as Drepung).

རི་སྤྲེལ་ (ridree) mountain monkey.

རི་ཕག (ribaà) 1. wild boar. 2. pigs living in mountains. 3. in/ amongst the mountains.

རི་ཕུག (ribuù) mountain cave.

རི་ཕྱུགས་ (rijuù) cattle.

རི་བོ་ (riwo) mountain.

རི་བོ་གྲུ་འཛིན་ (riwo trundzin) Potala Palace.

རི་བོ་དགའ་ལྡན་པ་ (riwo gandɛmba) the Gelugpa Sect.

རི་བོ་ཆི་ལེན་ (riwo cīlen) Qilian Mountains.

རི་བོ་ཆེ་ (riwoje) an area in Kham northwest of Chamdo.

རི་བོ་ཆེན་པོ་གསུམ་ (riwo cēmbo sūm) the three powerful (kinds) of lords: aristocrats, monasteries and the government [Lit. the three great mountains] (a political slogan).

རི་བོ་མཆོག་རབ་ (riwo cɔ̄grəb) sm. རི་རབ་.

རི་བོ་ཐང་ལྷ་ (riwo tāŋlha) Tangla Mountains.

རི་བོ་ཐའི་ཧྲན་ (riwo tɛ̄hɛn) Taishan Mountains.

རི་བོ་དྭངས་བསིལ་ (riwo taŋsii) Mt. Wutai.

རི་བོ་སྤོ་མཐོ་ (riwo bōto) high hills/ mountains.

རི་བོ་རྩེ་ལྔ་ (riwo dzēŋa) sm. རི་བོ་དྭངས་བསིལ་.

རི་བོ་བཟས་ཀྱང་མ་འགྲངས་ རྒྱ་མཚོ་བཏུངས་ཀྱང་མ་ངོམས་ (riwo sɛ̄ɛ̀gyaŋ mandraŋ gyadzo dūŋgyaŋ maŋom) extremely greedy/ avaricious [Lit. having eaten the mountain still not full, having drunken the ocean still not quenched].

རི་བོ་ཧི་མ་ལ་ཡ་ (riwo hīmalaya) the Himalayan Mountains.

རི་བོ་ལྷུན་སྟུག (riwo lhūnduù) a big/ grand mountain.

རི་བོགས་ (ribɔ̄ɔ̀) shung. payment for leasing hills and mountains and utilizing things that grow there; va.—རྒྱག.

རི་བོང་ (reboŋ) rabbit.

རི་བོང་ཀླད་པ་ (reboŋ lɛ̄ɛ̀ba) rabbit's brain (used in Tibetan medicine).

རི་བོང་སྐར་ཚོམ་ (riboŋ gārdzom) the constellation Lepus.

རི་བོང་གི་རྭ་ (riboŋgi ra) sth. that is impossible or extremely rare [Lit. a rabbit with horns].

རི་བོང་ཅལ་འདྲོགས་ (reboŋ jɛ̄ɛ̀drɔɔ̀) being frightened for no reason, alarming oneself needlessly [Lit. rabbit frightened by the sound of sth. falling in the water causing a splash].

རི་བོང་རྡོར་རྫུས་ (reboŋ dordzüù) pretending to be someone else, impersonating sb. [Lit. rabbit pretending to be a stone].

རི་བོང་གནམ་དིབ་ཀྱི་སྡུག་བསྔལ་ (reboŋ nāmdibgi duŋŋɛɛ) worrying unnecessarily, worrying about imaginary troubles [Lit. the rabbit worrying that the sky will fall].

རི་བོང་སྙིང་ (reboŋ ñīŋ) heart of a rabbit (used in Tibetan medicine).

རི་བོང་མིག (reboŋ miì) rabbit eyes (used in Tibetan medicine).

རི་བོང་ཚང་ལོག (riboŋ tsāŋlɔɔ̀) a bride or groom returning home after a failed marriage [Lit. a rabbit going back to its den].

རི་བོང་འཛིན་ (reboŋ dzin) poet. moon.

རི་བོང་རྭ་ (reboŋ ra) sth. impossible [Lit. rabbit's horn].

རི་བྱ་ (rija) mountain bird.

རི་བྱིའུ་ (ri ciwu) mountain sparrow.

རི་བྱོལ་ (rijöö) fleeing/ escaping to the mountains; va.—བྱེད་.

རི་བྲག (ridraà) sm. བྲག་རི་.

རི་བྲག་པ་ (ridragba) people living on hills.

རི་དབང་ (riwaŋ) sm. རི་རབ་.

རི་དབྲག (ridraà) mountain gorge.

རི་འབུར་ (rimbur) a small hill.

རི་འབོག (ribɔɔ) mountain spur.

རི་སྦུག (ribug) mountain cave/ cavern.

རི་སྦོག་སྦོག (ri bɔgbɔɔ̀) hilly.

རི་མ་ (rimə) nonirrigated farmland.

རི་མ་ལུང་ (riməluŋ) sm. རི་མ་ཐང་.

རི་མ་ཐང་ (rimədaŋ) an area not quite mountainous and not quite a valley.

རི་མ་འདབས་ (rimadəb) an area where a mountain meets a plain.

རི་མང་ཡུལ་གྲུ་ (rimaŋ yüüdru) a country with many mountains.

རི་མིན་པིས་ (riminbi) ch. currency unit in the PRC equivalent to the dollar unit in America (renminbi).

རི་མེ་ (rime)1. ch. abbr. of Japan-U.S. 2. volcano. 3. mountain fire; vi.—ཤོར་ to have a mountain fire breakout.

རི་མོ་ (remo) 1. picture, painting; vi.—འབྲི་ ¶ རི་མོ་འགྲེམས་སྟོན་ཚོགས་འདུ་ Art exhibition. 2. sketches, drawings.

རི་མོ་མཁན་ (remogɛn) sm. རི་མོ་བ་.

རི་མོ་མཁས་པ་ (remo kɛ̄ɛ̀ba) sm. རི་མོ་བ་.

རི་མོ་དེབ་ཆུང་ (remo tebjuŋ) illustrated book, picture book, comic book.

རི་མོ་ནག་བྲིས་ (remo nəgdriì) ink drawing; va.—འབྲི་.

རི་མོ་བ་ (remowa) artist, painter.

རི་མོ་བྱེད་ (remo ceè) 1. va. to paint, to draw. 2. va. to serve food respectfully (to lamas or one's parents).

རི་མོ་ཚོན་ཁྲ་ཅན་ (remo tsōndrajɛn) color painting.

རི་མོ་རགས་པ་ (remo ragba) sketch for a painting/ drawing.

རི་མོ་ཤ་ཤུར་ (remo shəshur) sketch/ drawing with wavy lines.

རི་མོའི་འགྲེམས་སྟོན་ (remö dremdön) exhibit of paintings.

རི་མོའི་དེབ་ (remö teb) picture book, illustrated book.

རི་མོའི་དེབ་ཆུང་ (remö tebjuŋ) sm. རི་མོ་དེབ་ཆུང་.

རི་མོའི་དཔེ་དེབ་ (remö bēdeb) pictorial magazine/ book.

རི་མོའི་བཤད་པ་ (remö shɛ̄ɛ̀ba) a narrating a painting; va.—རྒྱག to narrate/ explain a painting.

རི་མོར་བཀོད་པའི་མི་བཞིན་ (remɔɔ gɔ̄ɔ̀bɛ mishin) astonished, extremely surprised [Lit. like a person in a painting.

རི་མོར་བྱེད་ (rimɔɔ ceè) 1. va. to draw. 2. sm. བཀུར་སྐྱེ་བྱེད་.

རི་མོས་དོན་འགྲེལ་ (remö töndrel) illustrating/ explaning using charts and pictures.

རི་དམག (rimaà) 1. mountain troops. 2. Japanese army/ soldiers.

རི་སྨན་ (rimɛn) herbal medicines growing on hills/ mountains.

རི་བཙོང་ (ridzoŋ) onions that grow on mountains.

རི་རྩ་ (ridza) the foot/ base of a mountain.

རི་རྫིབས་ (ridzib) the craggy part of hills/ mountains.

རི་རྩེ་ (ridze) mountain top/ peak.

རི་རྩྭ (ri̱dza) grass that grows on hills and mountains.

རི་ཚད་ (ri̱dzɛɛ̀) the size of a hill or mountain.

རི་ཚིག་ལྷ་དཔང་ (ri̱dzii̇ lhābaŋ) swearing or taking an oath by the mountains and gods.

རི་ཚོགས་ (ri̱dzɔɔ̀) mountain range.

རི་མཛེས་ཆུ་གཙང་ (ri̱dzeè cūdzaŋ) a good environment [Lit. beautiful mountains and clear water].

རི་འཛེག (ri̱dzeg) mountain climbing; va.—བྱེད་ to climb mountains.

རི་འཛེགས་འགྲུལ་བཞུད་ལྷ་སྐོར་ (ri̱dzeg drü̱ü̱shüǜ dāgɔɔ) trekking; va.—འགྲོ་.

རི་འཛེགས་མཐུན་ཚོགས་ (ri̱dzeg tũndzɔɔ̀) mountaineering association.

རི་འཛེགས་པ་ (ri̱dzegba) a mountaineer.

རི་འཛེགས་རུ་ཁག (ri̱dzeg ru̱gaà) mountain climbing group, mountaineering party/ team/ expedition.

རི་འཛེགས་རུ་མི་ (ri̱dzeg ru̱mi) mountain climber, mountaineer.

རི་འཛེགས་ལུས་རྩལ་ (ri̱dzeg lü̱ü̱dzɛɛ) mountain climbing, mountaineering.

རི་འཛེགས་ལུས་རྩལ་པ་ (ri̱dzeg lü̱ü̱dzɛɛba) mountaineer.

རི་རྫས་ (ri̱dzɛɛ̀) mountain products ¶ རི་རྫས་ལས་སྒྱུར་བཟོ་གྲྭ Mountain products processing factory.

རི་རྫོང་ (ri̱dzoŋ) a fort/ district headquarters situated on hill/ mountain.

རི་ཞབས་ (ri̱shəb) base/ foot of a mountain.

རི་ཞིང་ (ri̱shiŋ) a terraced mountain field/ farm.

རི་ཞུམ་ (ri̱shum) a wild mountain cat.

རི་ཞིམ་ (ri̱shim) sm. རི་ཞུམ་.

རི་ཞོད་ (ri̱shöö) mountain slope.

རི་ཞོལ་ (ri̱shöö) sm. རི་འདབས་.

རི་ཟུར་ (ri̱sur) the end of a mountain range (the part that extends into a valley like a finger).

རི་ཟེ་ (ri̱se) mountain top.

རི་ཟོམ་ (ri̱som) 1. sm. རི་རྩེ་. 2. cave.

རི་ཟོར་ (ri̱sɔr) abbr. of hill/ mountain (grass) and sickle.

རི་ཟོར་ག་འཛོལ་ (ri̱sɔr ka̱dzöö) a large task with few resources [Lit. mountain and sickle imbalance (a small sickle for cutting grass on a mountain)].

རི་གཟར་ (ri̱sar) a towering/ steep mountain.

རི་གཟར་པོ་ (ri̱ sarbo) mountain with steep slopes/ precipices.

རི་གཟར་རྡབ་རྡོ་ (ri̱sar bəbdo) things that are unstoppable [Lit. steep mountain, falling stones].

རི་བཟོས་མ་ (ri̱ sö̱öma) man-made mountain.

རི་འོ་དི་རན་ནེ་རོ་ (ri̱wo te̱rɛnnero) Rio de Janeiro.

རི་རབ་ (ri̱rəb) sm. རི་རབ་ལྷུན་པོ་.

རི་རབ་ལྷུན་པོ་ (ri̱rəb lhũmbo) Mount Mehru.

རི་ལ་མཛེས་པ་ ཐང་ལ་སྙམ་པ་ (ri̱la dze̱èba tāŋla bāmba) settling sth. appropriately [Lit. good looking to the mountain, appropriate to the plain].

རི་ལ་འོས་པའི་ཐང་ཤིང་ (ri̱la wö̱öbɛ tāŋshiŋ) suitable or appropriate arrangements/ conditions [Lit. it is suitable for pine trees to be in the moutains].

རི་ལག (ri̱laà) mountain range.

རི་ལང་ (ri̱ la̱ŋ) va. to flee, to escape into exile.

རི་ལམ་ (ri̱lam) mountain path/ road/ trail.

རི་ལི་ (ri̱li) eng. train, railroad.

རི་ལིའི་གྲི་སིང་ (ri̱lii drisiŋ) eng. railway station.

རི་ལིའི་ཁང་པ་ (ri̱lii kāŋba) eng.tib. train carriage/ compartment.

རི་ལིའི་མགོ་ (ri̱lii go̱) eng.tib. sm. རི་ལིའི་ཨ་མ་.

རི་ལིའི་ལྕགས་ལམ་ (ri̱lii jāglam) eng.tib. railway track.

རི་ལིའི་ཏེ་སིན་ (ri̱lii dri̱sin) eng. train station.

རི་ལིའི་བབས་ས་ (ri̱lii bə̱bsa) eng.tib. sm. རི་ལིའི་ཏེ་སིན་.

རི་ལིའི་ཨ་མ་ (ri̱lii āma) eng.tib. locomotive.

རི་ལུ་ (ri̱lu) sm. རིལ་བུ་.

རི་ལུག་པ་ཐག་པས་མི་འདུམ་ (ri̱ lu̱gbə tāgbɛ mi̱ndum) a situation out of control [Lit. when the mountain has a landslide ropes cannot keep it together].

རི་ལུང་ (ri̱luŋ) abbr. of རི་ and ལུང་པ་.

རི་ལོགས་ (ri̱lɔɔ̀) the face/ side of a mountain.

རི་ཤུར་ (ri̱shur) a ravine.

རི་ཤོད་ (ri̱shöö) the foot of a hill/ mountain.

རི་གཤགས་ (ri̱ shāà) va. to break up a mountain (in order to make stones and build roads, etc.).

རི་གཤགས་ཆུ་བཀག (ri̱ shāà cū gāà) a magnificent/ powerful undertaking [Lit. split the mountain and dam the river].

རི་གཤགས་ལ་གཏོར་ (ri̱ shāà la̱ dɔ̄r) sm. རི་གཤགས་ཆུ་བཀག [Lit. split the mountain and destroy the pass].

རི་གཤགས་ལམ་བཅོས་ (ri̱ shāà la̱mjöö) sm. རི་གཤགས་ཆུ་བཀག [Lit. split the mountain and fix the road].

རི་གཤམ་ (ri̱sham) bottom of a hill/ mountain.

རི་བཤུས་རྒྱག (ri̱shüü gya̱à) va. to search the mountains and hills for bandits.

རི་སུག (ri̱suù) the root of the Chinese pulsatilla (used in Tibetan medicine).

རི་སུལ་ (ri̱süü) mountain valley/ ravine/ gully.

རི་སྲུང་བ་ (ri̱suŋwə) hill/ mountain ranger or guard.

རི་གསེབ་ (ri̱seb) on/ in a mountain.

རི་བསང་ (ri̱saŋ) offering incense on hills and mountain tops; va.—གཏོང་.

རི་བསང་རླུང་སྐྱེད་ (ri̱saŋ lhūŋgyeè) offering incense and putting up prayer flags on hills and mountain tops; va.—འཛུགས་.

རི་ཧན་ཆིངས་ཡིག (ri̱hɛn ci̱ŋyii̇) the Japan-South Korea Treaty.

རིག (ri̱i̇) vi. to see ¶ ངས་མིག་བལྟས་ཀྱང་ཁོང་རིག་མ་སོང་ Even though I looked, I didn't see him.

རིག་འགྲེ་ (ri̱ŋdre) sm. རིགས་འགྲེ་.

རིག་གྱོད་ (ri̱gbə gyōbo) abbr. of རིག་པ་གྱོད་པོ་.

རིག་རྒྱུད་ (ri̱ggyüü) character/ nature of the mind.

རིག་བགྲེ་ (ri̱gdre) sm. རིག་འགྲེ་.

རིག་དངོས་ (ri̱ŋŋoò) 1. cultural relics ¶ པེ་ཅིང་དུ་གནས་པའི་བོད་ཀྱི་རིག་དངོས་སྐོར་ Concerning Tibetan cultural relics located in Peking. 2. archaeological data/ collections.

རིག་དངོས་རྙིང་པ་ (ri̱ŋŋoò ñi̱ŋbə) ancient relics.

རིག་དངོས་གཤམས་སྟོན་ཁང་ (ri̱ŋŋoò shāmdöngaŋ) cultural relic exhibition hall/ center.

རིག་སྔགས་འཛིན་ (ri̱gŋaà dzi̱n) 1. va. to practice tantra. 2. va. to memorize mantras.

རིག་ཅན་ (ri̱gjɛn) intelligent.

རིག་བཅོས་ (ri̱gjöö) sm. རང་བཟོ་.

རིག་སྟོབས་ (ri̱gdob) intellectual power, intelligence; va.—འགྲན་ to compete in intellectual power.

རིག་རྟུལ་ (ri̱gdüü) low intelligence, dull mentally ¶ རིག་རྟུལ་བྱིས་པ་ Retarded child.

རིག་སྟོབས་འཕེལ་རྒྱས་ (ri̱gdob pēlgyɛɛ̀) intellectual development/ progress.

རིག་དོན་ཚོགས་པ་ (ri̱gdön tsɔ̄gba) art/ cultural troupe.

རིག་འདེད་ (ri̱ndeè) analogical/ comparative reasoning, reasoning by inference; va.—བྱེད་.

རིག་དིབ་ (ri̱ŋdib) sm. རིག་པ་རྟུལ་པོ་.

རིག་ལྡན་ (ri̱ŋdɛn) sm. རིག་ཅན་.

རིག་སྡུར་ (ri̱ŋdur) battle of wits; va.—བྱེད་ to engage in a battle of wits.

རིག་ནུས་ (ri̱gnüü) brain power, intellectual faculties.

རིག་གནས་ (ri̱gnɛɛ̀) culture.

རིག་གནས་ཀུན་བསྡུས་ཀྱི་དཔེ་དེབ་ (ri̱gnɛɛ̀ gũndüügi bēdeb) sm. རིག་གནས་ཀུན་འཛོམས་ཀྱི་དཔེ་དེབ་.

རིག་གནས་ཀུན་འཛོམས་ཀྱི་དཔེ་དེབ་ (ri̱gnɛɛ̀ gũndzomgi bēdeb) encyclopedia.

རིག་གནས་ཀྱི་ཆུ་ཚད་ (ri̱gnɛɛ̀gi cūdzɛɛ̀) cultural level.

རིག་གནས་ཀྱི་བརྟན་རྒྱུན་ (ri̱gnɛɛ̀gi dɛ̃ngyün) shung. cultural prevailing custom.

རིག་གནས་ཀྱི་འཐབ་ཕྱོགས་ (ri̱gnɛɛ̀gi tə̄bjɔɔ̀) cultural

front.

རིག་གནས་ཀྱི་བཙན་འཛུལ་ (rignɛɛ̀gi tsɛ̄ndzüü) cultural aggression.

རིག་གནས་ཀྱི་ཡོན་ཚད་ (rignɛɛ̀gi yöndzɛɛ̀) cultural level.

རིག་གནས་ཀྱི་བཞག་པ་ (rignɛɛ̀gi shagba) cultural heritage.

རིག་གནས་ཀྱི་ཡོ་ཆས་ (rignɛɛ̀gi yojɛɛ̀) cultural materials/ things.

རིག་གནས་ཀྱི་གསར་བརྗེ་ (rignɛɛ̀gi sārje) the Cultural Revolution.

རིག་གནས་ཀྱི་གསར་བརྗེའི་ཨུ་ཡོན་ལྷན་ཁང་ (rignɛɛ̀gi sārjee ūyön lɛ̄ngaŋ) Cultural Revolutionary Committee.

རིག་གནས་སྐུ་ཚབ་ཚོགས་པ་ (rignɛɛ̀ gūdzəb tsɔ̄gbə) cultural delegation.

རིག་གནས་ཁང་ (rignɛɛ̀gaŋ) cultural center.

རིག་གནས་ཁྲུའུ་ (rignɛɛ̀ trū) tib. ch. cultural divison.

རིག་གནས་མཁས་པ་ (rignɛɛ̀ kɛ̄ɛ̀ba) scholar of culture.

རིག་གནས་མཁོ་ཆས་ཚོང་ཁང་ (rignɛɛ̀ kōjɛɛ̀ tsōŋgaŋ) stationery store.

རིག་གནས་དངོས་རྫས་ (rignɛɛ̀ ŋȫȍdzɛɛ̀) sm. རིག་གནས་ཤུལ་དངོས་.

རིགས་གནས་ལྔ་ (rignɛɛ̀ ŋā) the five major and minor sciences.

རིག་གནས་ཅུའུ་ (rignɛɛ̀ jū) tib. ch. cultural bureau.

རིག་གནས་བཅུ་ (rignɛɛ̀ jū) ten fields of knowledge, the ten sciences.

རིག་གནས་ཆུང་བ་ལྔ་ (rignɛɛ̀ cūŋwa ŋā) the five minor sciences: poetry, semantics, lexicography, astrology, and dance/ drama.

རིག་གནས་ཆེ་བ་ལྔ་ (rignɛɛ̀ cēwa ŋā) the five major sciences: grammar, sanskrit, medicine, logic/ philosophy, painting/ handicrafts.

རིག་གནས་བརྗེ་རེས་ (rignɛɛ̀ jereè) sm. རིག་གནས་སྤེལ་རེས་.

རིག་གནས་རྙིང་པ་ (rignɛɛ̀ ñīŋbə) old culture.

རིག་གནས་ཆུ་ཚད་ (rignɛɛ̀ cūdzɛɛ̀) educational standard, cultural level/ standard.

རིག་གནས་འཐུས་མིའི་ཚོགས་པ་ (rignɛɛ̀ tűǜmii tsōgba) sm. རིག་གནས་སྐུ་ཚབ་ཚོགས་པ་.

རིག་གནས་པ་ (rignɛɛ̀ba) scholar.

རིག་གནས་པུའུ་ (rignɛɛ̀ bū) Ministry of Culture.

རིག་གནས་སྤེལ་རེས་ (rignɛɛ̀ bēēreè) cultural exchange ¶ རྒྱལ་ཁབ་གཉིས་ཀྱི་རིག་གནས་སྤེལ་རེས་ Cultural exchange between the two countries.

རིག་གནས་ཕོ་བྲང་ (rignɛɛ̀ pōdraŋ) Cultural Palace (opposite the Potala in current Lhasa).

རིག་གནས་སྦྱོང་ (rignɛɛ̀ joŋ) va. to study culture, language, poetics.

རིག་གནས་ཚན་ཁག (rignɛɛ̀ tsɛ̄ngaà) department of cultural studies.

རིག་གནས་འཚོ་བ་ (rignɛɛ̀ tsōwa) cultural life.

རིག་གནས་ཡོ་བྱད་བཟོ་གྲྭ (rignɛɛ̀ yobjɛɛ̀ sodra) cultural equipment factory.

རིག་གནས་རོལ་རྩེད་ (rignɛɛ̀ rȫȍdzeè) cultural recreation/ entertainment.

རིག་གནས་རོལ་རྩེད་ཁང་ (rignɛɛ̀ rȫȍdzeègaŋ) cultural recreation/ entertainment room.

རིག་གནས་ལས་དོན་དོ་དམ་ཅུའུ་ (rignɛɛ̀ lɛɛ̀dön todam jū) tib. ch. administrative bureau of culture.

རིག་གནས་ལོ་རྒྱུས་ (rignɛɛ̀ logyüǜ) cultural history.

རིག་གནས་ལོ་རྒྱུས་ཁང་ (rignɛɛ̀ logyüǜgaŋ) institute of cultural history.

རིག་གནས་ལོ་རྒྱུས་ཞིབ་འཇུག་ཁང་ (rignɛɛ̀ logyüǜ shimjuùgaŋ) research institute of cultural history.

རིག་གནས་ཤུལ་དངོས་ (rignɛɛ̀ shűűŋöȍ) relics, artifacts.

རིག་གནས་ཤུལ་རྫས་ (rignɛɛ̀ shűűdzɛɛ̀) cultural heritage.

རིག་གནས་ཤུལ་བཞག (rignɛɛ̀ shűűshaà) sm. རིགས་གནས་ཤུལ་རྫས་.

རིག་གནས་སློབ་གསོ་ (rignɛɛ̀ lōbso) cultural education.

རིག་གནས་གསབ་སྦྱོང་སློབ་གྲྭ (rignɛɛ̀ səbjoŋ lōbdra) literacy continuation school.

རིག་གནས་གསར་གཏོད་ (rignɛɛ̀ sārdȍȍ) cultural creation.

རིག་གནས་གསར་བརྗེ་ (rignɛɛ̀ sārje) sm. རིག་གནས་ཀྱི་གསར་བརྗེ་.

རིག་གནས་གསར་བརྗེའི་ལས་འགུལ་ (rignɛɛ̀ sārjee lɛngüü) the movement of the Cultural Revolution.

རིག་སྣ་ (rigna) subject of knowledge/ study ¶ རིག་སྣ་འཛོམས་པའི་སློབ་གྲྭ་ཆེ་བ་ A university that includes many subjects of knowledge.

རིག་པ་ (rigbə) 1. intelligent, intelligence ¶ ཁོ་རིག་པ་ཡག་པོ་འདུག He has good intelligence. 2. ology: any science or body of knowledge ¶ མི་རིགས་ཀྱི་རིག་པ་ Anthropology (the science of ethnic groups/ ethnicity).

རིག་པ་སྐྱེན་པོ་ (rigbə gyēmbo) sm. རིག་པ་གསལ་པོ་.

རིག་པ་སྐྱོ་པོ་ (rigbə gyōbo) 1. dull, unintelligent. 2. having bad memory.

རིག་པ་གྲོད་པོ་ (rigbə gȫȍbo) clever, skillful.

རིག་པ་སྒྲིམ་ (rigbə drim) sm. རིག་པ་བསྒྲིམས་.

རིག་པ་སྒྲིམ་ཚད་ (rigbə drimdzɛɛ̀) attention/ concentration span.

རིག་པ་བསྒྲིམས་ (rigbə drim) va. to concentrate on sth.

རིག་པ་ཅན་ (rigbəjɛn) intelligent.

རིག་པ་རྙེད་ (rigbə ñēè) vi. to get/ find an idea.

རིག་པ་གཏོང་ (rigbə dōŋ) va. to think, to use one's intelligence/ mind.

རིག་པ་རྟུལ་པོ་ (rigbə dűűbu) stupid, unintelligent, foolish.

རིག་པ་དྭངས་གསལ་ (rigbə taŋsɛl) clear/ bright mind, intelligent.

རིག་པ་སྡུར་ (rigbə dur) sm. རིག་སྡུར་.

རིག་པ་ནང་པར་འཆི་ཡང་སློབ་སྦྱོང་ སྐྱེ་བ་ཕྱི་མར་བཙོལ་བ་ (rigbə naŋbar cīyaŋ lōbjoŋ gyēwa cīmar jȫȫwə) it is never too late [Lit. even if one will die tomorrow, one's study will be carried onto the next rebirth].

རིག་པ་རྣོ་པོ་ (rigbə nōbo) mentally sharp, intelligent, clever.

རིག་པ་བ་ (rigbəwə) intellectual.

རིག་པ་མི་གསལ་ (rigbə misɛl) ignorant.

རིག་པ་རྩེ་གཅིག་ཏུ་སྒྲིམ་ (rigbə dzējigdu drim) va. to concentrate/ completely/ whole-heartedly ¶ ཁོང་གིས་སློབ་སྦྱོང་ཐོག་རིག་པ་རྩེ་གཅིག་ཏུ་སྒྲིམ་གྱི་འདུག He is concentrating completely on his studies.

རིག་པ་ཟབ་པོ་ (rigbə səbbo) 1. able to think deeply. 2. a body of knowledge that is deep/ profound.

རིག་པ་ཡག་པོ་ (rigbə yagbo) 1.sm. རིག་པ་རྣོ་པོ་. 2. having a good memory.

རིག་པ་གསར་པ་ (rigbə sārba) new ideas/ thoughts.

རིག་པ་གསལ་པོ་ (rigbə sɛɛ̄bo) clear in thought, intelligent.

རིག་པ་གསལ་མ་གསལ་ (rigbə sɛɛ̄ masɛɛ) unclear mind.

རིག་པ་བསིལ་པོ་ (rigbə sīību) fresh/ clear thoughts.

རིག་པའི་གློང་རྡོལ་བ་ (rigbɛ lōŋdööwa) sb. who is extremely intelligent.

རིག་པའི་འཕྲུལ་རྩལ་ (rigbɛ trűűdzɛɛ) shung. with intelligence and skill.

རིག་པའི་སློབ་གསོ་ (rigbɛ lōbso) intellectual education.

རིག་པས་འདུམ་བྲལ་ (rigbɛ dumdrɛɛ) shung. sm. རིག་པས་མི་འདུམ་པ་.

རིག་པས་འདུམ་མེད་ (rigbɛ dummeè) shung. sm. རིག་པས་མི་འདུམ་པ་.

རིག་པས་མི་འདུམ་པ་ (rigbɛ midumbə) beyond all expectation, beyond the realm of thought ¶ ས་གཡོས་ཀྱིས་རྐྱེན་པས་ལུང་པ་འདིར་སྐྱོན་ཆག་རིག་པས་མི་འདུམ་པ་ཞིག་བྱུང་བཞག The damage caused by the earthquake in this place is beyond all expectations (inconceivable).

རིག་དཔྱད་ (rigjɛɛ̀) theory (as opposed to practice).

རིག་པའི་འཕྲུལ་ (rigbɛ drũũ) mental skill.

རིག་བྱེད་ (rigjeè) intelligence, wisdom.

རིག་མ་ (rigmə) 1. consort. 2. wife of a lama.

རིག་མྱོང་ (rigñoŋ) seeing and experiencing.

རིག་མོངས་ (rigmoŋ) ignorant, illiterate.

རིག་རྩལ་ (rigdzɛɛ) literature and art, art and culture ¶ རིག་རྩལ་གྱི་ལྟད་མོ་ An artistic show/ play.

རིག་རྩལ་སྐྱར་དར་ (rigdzɛɛ gyãrdar) the Renaissance Era.

རིག་རྩལ་ཁྲུའུ་ (rigdzɛɛtru) tib. ch. literature and art division.

རིག་རྩལ་མཁན་ (rigdzɛɛñɛn) sm. རིག་རྩལ་པ་.

རིག་རྩལ་འཁྲབ་ཚན་ (rigdzɛɛ trəbdzɛn) artistic performance/ program.

རིག་རྩལ་གྱི་སྐྱོན་ཡོན་བརྗོད་པ་ (rigdzɛɛgi gyõnyön jö̱öba) literary/ artistic criticism.

རིག་རྩལ་གྱི་གར་སྟེགས་ (rigdzɛɛgi kardeg) performing stage.

རིག་རྩལ་གྱི་རྩོམ་རིག (rigdzɛɛgi dzõmrig) works of literature and art.

རིག་རྩལ་གྱི་ལེ་ཚན་ (rigdzɛɛgi ledzɛn) a programme of entertainment, a theatrical performance.

རིག་རྩལ་གློག་བརྙན་ (rigdzɛɛ lõgñɛn) art movie/ film.

རིག་རྩལ་བརྟག་དཔྱད་ (rigdzɛɛ dãgjɛɛ̀) cultural/ artistic investigation.

རིག་རྩལ་པ་ (rigdzɛɛba) artist, writer.

རིག་རྩལ་པའི་གྲྭས་ (rigdzɛɛbɛ trɛɛ̀) literary and artistic circle.

རིག་རྩལ་རྩོམ་སྒྲིག་པུའུ་ (rigdzɛɛ dzõmdrig bũ) tib. ch. ministry of art and literature.

རིག་རྩལ་རྩོམ་རིག (rigdzɛɛ dzõmrig) artistic and literary works.

རིག་རྩལ་ཚོ་ཆུང་ (rigdzɛɛ tsõjuŋ) small artistic group/ troupe.

རིག་རྩལ་ཚོགས་པ་ (rigdzɛɛ tsõgba) 1. ensemble, troupe. 2. literature and art organization.

རིག་རྩལ་རིག་པ་ (rigdzɛɛ rigbə) study of literature and art.

རིག་རྩལ་ལས་བྱེད་པ་ (rigdzɛɛ lɛɛ̀jeèba) artistry and literary cadre, official people who work in cultural affairs.

རིག་རྩལ་ལས་རིགས་ (rigdzɛɛ lɛɛ̀rig) artistic (literary and art) professional/ workers.

རིག་རྩལ་སླར་གསོ་ (rigdzɛɛ lãrso) artistic/ cultural renaissance or revival.

རིག་རྩལ་གསར་རྩོམ་ (rigdzɛɛ sãrdzom) literary/ artistic new creation.

རིག་རྩལ་ལྷན་ཚོགས་ (rigdzɛɛ lhẽndzoò) Literary and Art Association.

རིག་རྩལ་ལྷན་འཛོམས་འཁྲབ་སྟོན་ (rigdzɛɛ lhẽndzom trəbdön) theatrical festival.

རིག་རྩེད་ (rigdzeè) cultural entertainment.

རིག་འཚོ་མ་ཟིན་པ་ (rigdzo masimbə) unable to control one's senses/ intellect, crazy, insane.

རིག་འཚོ་ཟིན་པོ་མེད་ (rigdzo simbu meè) sm. རིག་འཚོ་མ་ཟིན་པ་.

རིག་མཛོད་འཕྲུལ་སྒམ་ (riŋdzöö trũũgam) computer.

རིག་འཛིན་ (riŋdzin) 1. sm. རིག་ཅན་. 2. person's name.

རིག་འཛིན་མ་ (riŋdzinmə) honorific term of address for nuns.

རིག་རྫས་ (rigdzɛɛ̀) relic, momento, artifact ¶ གསར་བརྗེའི་རིག་རྫས་ Revolutionary momento.

རིག་རྫས་རྗེས་ཤུལ་ (rigdɛɛ̀ jeèshüü) cultural relic/ artifact/ remnant.

རིག་གཞུང་ (rigshuŋ) 1. culture ¶ བོད་པའི་རིག་གཞུང་ Tibetan culture. 2. academic, scholarly.

རིག་གཞུང་མཁས་དབང་ (rigshuŋ kɛɛ̀waŋ) cultural authority.

རིག་གཞུང་གི་ཆེད་རྩོམ་ (rigshuŋgi cẽdzom) academic thesis/ essay/ article.

རིག་གཞུང་གི་ཐ་སྙད་ (rigshuŋgi tãñɛɛ̀) technical/ scientific terms or jargon.

རིག་གཞུང་གྲོས་མོལ་གྱི་ཚོགས་འདུ་ (rigshuŋ trö̱ömöögi tsõndu) academic conference.

རིག་གཞུང་བརྒྱུད་ཤུལ་ (rigshuŋ gyü̱üshüü) cultural heritage.

རིག་གཞུང་བརྗེ་རེས་ (rigshuŋ je̱ereè) cultural exchange.

རིག་གཞུང་བརྟག་དཔྱད་ (rigshuŋ dãgjɛɛ̀) academic research.

རིག་གཞུང་དུས་དེབ་ (rigshuŋ tü̱üdeb) scientific/ academic journal.

རིག་གཞུང་པུའུ་ (rigshuŋ bũ) tib. ch. Ministry of Culture.

རིག་གཞུང་ཕོ་བྲང་ (rigshuŋ põdraŋ) palace of culture.

རིག་གཞུང་འཕེལ་རྒྱལ་ (rigshuŋ pẽẽdzüü) academic movement.

རིག་གཞུང་ཚན་ཁག (rigshuŋ tsẽngaà) academic department/ section.

རིག་གཞུང་ཚོགས་པ་ (rigshuŋ tsõgba) academic society/ association.

རིག་གཞུང་ལས་རིགས་ (rigshuŋ lɛɛ̀rig) academic/ cultural work.

རིག་གཞུང་སློབ་ཚོགས་ (rigshuŋ lõbdzɔ̀ɔ) academic society/ association.

རིག་གཞུང་སློབ་གསོ་ (rigshuŋ lõbso) cultural education.

རིག་གཞུང་ཨུ་ཡོན་ལྷན་ཁང་ (rigshuŋ ũyön lhẽngaŋ) academic committee, cultural committee.

རིག་བཟང་ (rigsaŋ) 1. name of a person. 2. bright, intelligent.

རིག་རིག (rigrìi) looking with wide glaring eyes; va.—ལྟ་.

རིག་རིག་གི་མིག་རྩ་དང་གོ་གོའི་རྣ་རྩར་འཛོག་པ་ (rigrìigi migdzə daŋ kokẽo nãdzar jo̱gba) keeping in mind whatever one sees or hears.

རིག་ལམ་ (riglam) logic; va.—སློབ་ to study/ teach logic.

རིག་ལམ་དཔྱད་ཚོགས་ (riglam jɛɛ̀dzɔ̀ɔ) academic conference.

རིག་ཤེད་ཅན་ (rigsheèjɛn) scholar-tyrant.

རིག་ཤེས་པ་ (rigsheèba) intelligentsia, intellectual.

རིག་སློབ་ (riglob) culture and education, cultural education ¶ རིག་སློབ་ཁྲུའུ་ Office of culture and education.

རིག་གསར་ (rigsar) 1. new sciences, new fields of study. 2. innovations, new ways of doing things, new ideas.

རིག་གསལ་ (risɛɛ) educated, intelligent, smart.

རིག་གསལ་ལག་བདེ་ (rigsɛɛ lagde) smart and dexterous.

རིགས་ (rig) 1. race, ethnic group, nationality, lineage ¶ བོད་རིགས་ Tibetan nationality/ ethnic group. 2. kind, category ¶ གྲོའི་རིགས་ག་རེ་ཡོད་པ་རེད་ What kinds of wheat are there? ¶ ལས་བྱེད་འོས་རིགས་ Those worthy of being cadre. ¶ སྟོབས་ཤུགས་ཆེ་རིགས་ Those who are powerful. 3. vi. to be okay ¶ འདི་འདྲ་བྱས་ན་མི་རིགས་ Its not okay to do this.

རིགས་ཀྱི་རྒན་རབས་ (riggi gɛnrəb) older generations.

རིགས་ཀྱི་ཅོད་པན་ (riggi jö̀öbɛn) one held in great respect/ esteem.

རིགས་ཀྱི་ཐ་མ་ (riggi tãma) the lower castes, untouchables.

རིགས་ཀྱི་ཐུ་བོ་ (riggi tũwo) the Brahman caste.

རིགས་ཀྱི་བུ་ (riggi pu̱) term used by a root lama for his close followers/ disciples.

རིགས་ཀྱི་བུ་མོ་ (riggi po̱mo) term used by a root lama for his female close followers/ disciples.

རིགས་ཀྱི་དབང་ཕྱུག (riggi wãŋjuù) shung. the Emperor.

རིགས་ཀྱི་མ་ (riggi ma̱) 1. bride. 2. female head of a household.

རིགས་ཀྱི་ཉུ་གུ་ (riggi ñugu) shung. descendant.

རིགས་ཀྱི་གཙོ་བོ་ (riggi dzõwo) clan elder, head of a clan.

རིགས་འཁྲིད་ (rig trìi) vi. to acquire certain traits (from one's parents) ¶ ཕྲུ་གུ་དེ་ཕ་ཡི་རིགས་ཁྲིད་ནས་

རིག་པ་ཡག་པོ་འདུག This child has acquired traits from his father and is intelligent and smart.
རིགས་གྲྭ་ (rigdrə) the committee consisting of abbots that governs the monastery as a whole.
རིགས་འགྲེ་ (rigdre) logical reasoning/ inference; va.—གཏོང་; —བྱེད་.
རིགས་རྒྱུགས་ (riggyuù) sm. རིགས་འཁྲིད་.
རིགས་རྒྱུད་ (riggyüü) lineage, race, species ¶ རིགས་རྒྱུད་ནག་པོ་ Negroid race.
རིགས་རྒྱུད་ཀྱི་ཕྱོགས་འཛིན་ (riggyüügi cōgden) racial prejudice.
རིགས་རྒྱུད་ཀྱི་མྱུ་གུ་ (riggyüügi ñugu) ancestry, lineage.
རིགས་རྒྱུད་འགོ་བའི་ལྷ་ (riggyüü gowɛ lhā) family/ lineage deity.
རིགས་རྒྱུད་མཐོང་ཆུང་ (riggyüü tōŋjuŋ) racial discrimination.
རིགས་རྒྱུད་ཆད་ (riggyüü cɛ̀ɛ̀) vi. to have a lineage die out.
རིགས་རྒྱུད་འདྲེས་མ་ (riggyüü dreèma) mixed ancestry, mixed race.
རིགས་རྒྱུད་སྣང་ཆུང་ (riggyüü naŋjuŋ) sm. རིགས་རྒྱུད་མཐོང་ཆུང་.
རིགས་རྒྱུད་སྤེལ་ (riggyüü bēl) va. to increase one's race/ lineage/ caste.
རིགས་རྒྱུད་འཕེལ་ (riggyüü pēl) vi. to have one's race/ lineage/ caste increase.
རིགས་རྒྱུད་བར་གྱི་དམག་འཁྲུག (riggyüübargi mōgdruù) racial war; va.—རྒྱག.
རིགས་རྒྱུད་སྨན་པ་ (riggyüü mɛ̄mba) a Tibetan doctor from a lineage of doctors.
རིགས་རྒྱུད་གཞན་ལ་གཉའ་གནོན་ (riggyüü shenla ñanön) racial/ caste/ lineage oppression.
རིགས་རྒྱུད་གཞན་ལ་མཐོང་ཆུང་ (riggyüü shenla tōŋjuŋ) racial/ ethnic discrimination.
རིགས་རྒྱུད་རིང་ལུགས་ (riggyüü riŋluù) racism.
རིགས་བརྒྱའི་བདག་པོ་ (riggyɛ dagbo) Vajradhara.
རིགས་སྒྲེ་ (rigdre) sm. རིགས་འགྲེ་.
རིགས་བསྒྲེ་ (rigdre) sm. རིགས་འགྲེ་.
རིགས་ངན་ (rigŋɛn) impure or unclean caste/ birth/ lineage (e.g., untouchables in India, or blacksmiths in Tibet).
རིགས་ངན་ཐ་ཆད་ (rigŋɛn tājɛɛ̀) sm. རིགས་ངན་.
རིགས་གཅིག་པ་ (rig jīgbə) of the same race/ lineage/ nationality/ ethnic group.
རིགས་ཆས་ (rigjɛɛ̀) sm. རིགས་, 2.
རིགས་ཆེན་ (rigjen) high birth/ caste.
རིགས་མཉམ་ (rigñam) equal rank/ status/ birth/ caste.
རིགས་མཐུན་ (rigdün) of the same race/ caste/ status/ ethnic group ¶ མནའ་མ་ལེན་དུས་རིགས་མཐུན་པ་ཞིག་དགོས་ When one takes a bride one should take one from one's own race/ caste/ status/ ethnic group.
རིགས་མཐོ་བ་ (rig tōwa) high caste/ birth/ race.
རིགས་འདྲ་ (riŋdra) similar or equivalent or equal race/ caste/ status/ birth.
རིགས་ལྡན་ (riŋdɛn) 1. sm. རིགས་མཐོ་བ་. 2. the king of the mythical shambala.
རིགས་པ་ (rigbə) 1. one of the components of the Four Noble Truths (the antidote for delusion). 2. reason, reasoning ¶ ཚན་རིག་གི་ཆོད་གཏན་འདི་ནི་རིགས་པས་ཁུངས་སྐྱེལ་ཐུབ་ཡོད་པ་ཞིག་རེད་ This scientific law has been proven by reasoning (inference).
རིགས་པ་སྨྲ་བ་ (rigbə māwa) theory.
རིགས་པའི་གཞུང་ལུགས་ (rigbɛ shuŋluù) theory, thesis.
རིགས་པའི་གཞུང་ལུགས་ཀྱི་སྤྱི་མཚན་ (rigbɛ shuŋluùgi jīdzɛn) abstract theory.
རིགས་པས་ཁུངས་སྐྱེལ་ (rigbɛ kūŋgyee) proving by means of reasoning, using reason to make inferences; va.—བྱེད་.
རིགས་པས་སྒྲུབ་པ་ (rigbɛ drubbə) sm. རིགས་པས་ཁུངས་སྐྱེལ་.
རིགས་པས་ཐག་གཅོད་ (rigbɛ tāàjöö) deciding/ concluding by reasoning or inference.
རིགས་པས་དཔྱད་ (rigbɛ jɛ̄ɛ̀) va. to analyse through reason.
རིགས་དཔྱད་ (rigjɛɛ̀) theory ¶ རིགས་དཔྱད་དང་ལག་ལེན་ Theory and practice.
རིགས་དབྱེ་ (rigje) 1. sm. རིགས་འབྱེད་. 2. f. of རིགས་འབྱེད་.
རིགས་འབྱེད་ (rig jeè) va. to classify/ sort/ differentiate into types, to catalogue.
རིགས་འབྱེད་ཕྱོགས་བསྒྲིགས་ (rigjeè cōgdrig) sorting out and arranging/ ordering; va.—བྱེད་.
རིགས་མང་ (rigmaŋ) many kinds/ things.
རིགས་མེད་ (rigmeè) 1. sm. རིགས་ངན་. 2. mongoose.
རིགས་མྱུག (rigñug) abbr. of རིགས་ཀྱི་མྱུ་གུ་.
རིགས་དམའ་ (rigmaa) sm. རིགས་ངན་.
རིགས་དམན་ (rigmɛn) sm. རིགས་ངན་.
རིགས་བཙུན་པ་ (rig dzūmba) a high caste/ lineage/ race.
རིགས་མཚུངས་ (rigdzuŋ) sm. རིགས་འདྲ་.
རིགས་ཞེན་ (rigshɛn) racial/ nationalistic/ ethnic/ lineage/ caste loyalty.
རིགས་ཞེན་ཅན་ (rigshɛnjɛn) sb. who has racial/ nationalistic/ ethnic/ caste loyalty.
རིགས་བཟང་ (rigsaŋ) high or good or clean race/ nationality/ ethnic group/ caste/ species.
རིགས་རུས་ (rigrüü) lineage, race, caste.
རིགས་རུས་སྐྱེ་རྒྱུད་ (rigrüü gyēgyüü) lineage, caste.
རིགས་རུས་འཆོལ་བར་སྤྱོད་ (rigrüü cōōwar jōō) va. to have sexual intercourse with sb. of a lower caste/ lineage/ clan.
རིགས་རུས་གཙང་མ་ (rigrüü dzāŋma) pure or clean caste/ race/ lineage.
རིགས་ལམ་བཤད་ལུགས་ (riglam shɛ̄ɛ̀lug) traditional theory/ teachings ¶ ཆོས་ལུགས་ཀྱི་རིགས་ལམ་བཤད་ལུགས Traditional religious theory.
རིགས་སྲས་ (rigsɛɛ̀) 1. male offsprings of a tantric practitioner. 2. sons of kings and high lineage/ caste families.
རིགས་གསུམ་མགོན་པོ་ (rigsum gömbo) 1. the three meditation deities: Avalokestisvara, Manjusri and Vajrapani. 2. pansy (flower).
རིགས་གསུམ་ལྷ་ཁང་ (rigsum lhāgaŋ) the temples of the three meditation deities Avalokestisvara, Manjusri and Vajrapani.
རིང་ (riŋ) 1. abbr. of. རིང་པོ་. 2. when, during the time of ¶ ལོ་ཤས་རིང་ During the period of several years. ¶ ཁོས་ལས་ཀ་བྱེད་རིང་ When he worked.
རིང་སྐི་རག་ཐུང་ལྷམ་སྒྲོག (riŋ gēraà tūŋ lhādrɔɔ̀) helping at all levels [Lit. at the longest the belt, at the shortest the bootstrap].
རིང་སྐྱེལ་ (riŋgyee) shung. sending corvee labor from one district (dzong) to another. 2. going a great distance to see/ send off a person; va.—བྱེད་.
རིང་སྐྱོད་ (riŋgyöö) traveling a long distance, going on a long journey; va.—འགྲོ.
རིང་ཁྱད་ (riŋgyɛɛ̀) sm. རིང་ཚད་.
རིང་གི་བཟོད་དཀའ་བའི་གྲལ་རིམ་ (riŋgi söögawɛ trɛɛrim) long suffering classes.
རིང་འགག (riŋgaà) a long sleeveless coat worn by monks.
རིགས་རྒྱུག (riggyuù) a long distance run/ race; va.—བྱེད་.
རིང་ཅང་ (riŋjaŋ) a tall and thin person (derogative term).
རིང་བཅད་ཐུང་མཐུད་ (riŋjɛɛ̀ tūŋtüü) making up a deficiency from a surplus [Lit. cutting off from the long to join the short].
རིང་ཆ་ (riŋja) 1. the longer part ¶ ཀ་ཐུང་དེའི་རིང་ཆ་དེ་ཐུང་དུ་གཏོང་དགོས་ You have to shorten the longer part of the pants. 2. the length of sth.
རིང་ཐུང་ (riŋduŋ) length, distance, height [Lit. long and short].
རིང་ཐུང་རན་པོ་ (riŋduŋ rɛmbo) appropriate size/ length/ height.
རིང་མཐོང་ (riŋdoŋ) 1. learned person. 2. sm. རིང་དུ་

མཐོང་.

རིང་དུ་ (riŋdu) sm. རིང་, 2.

རིང་དུ་ཁྱབ་ (riŋdu kyəb) 1. vi. to have become widespread. 2. sweet smell/ fragrance/ odor.

རིང་དུ་འགྲོ་ (riŋdu dro) vi. to become longer.

རིང་དུ་གཏོང་ (riŋdu dōŋ) va. to lengthen, to make longer.

རིང་དུ་མཐོང་ (riŋdu tōŋ) vi. to see far.

རིང་དུ་སྤང་ (riŋdu bāŋ) 1. va. to throw sth. far away. 2. va. to give up doing sth. like smoking completely.

རིང་དུས་ (riŋdöö) sm. རིང་, 2.

རིང་མདའ་ (riŋda) rifle.

རིང་པོ་ (riŋgu) 1. long, tall. 2. far.

རིང་པོར་མི་ཐོགས་པར་ (riŋbor mitɔgba) soon, shortly ¶ རིང་པོར་མི་ཐོགས་པར་ཡོང་གི་རེད་ (He) will come soon.

རིང་འཕུར་ (riŋbur) flying a long distance. 2. name of a star. 3. vulture.

རིང་བ་ (riŋwə) 1. long/ longer, tall/ taller. 2. far/ farther.

རིང་བའི་རྒྱུ་རྐྱེན་ (riŋwɛ gyugyen) remote cause.

རིང་མིན་ (riŋmin) soon, quickly, in a short time ¶ རིང་མིན་ཉིན་ཤས་ Soon, in a few days.

རིང་མིན་ཐུང་མིན་ (riŋmin tūŋmin) not long and not short ¶ ཁོང་གིས་ག་ཐུང་རིང་མིན་ཐུང་མིན་ཞིག་གོན་བཞག He is wearing pants that are neither long nor short.

རིང་མིན་དུས་ཀྱི་ཆར་ (riŋmin tüügi cār) shung. soon, in a short time.

རིང་མོ་ (riŋmo) sm. རིང་པོ་.

རིང་མོ་ཅན་ (riŋmojɛn) long ¶ ལོ་མ་རིང་མོ་ཅན་གྱི་ཤིང་ A tree with long leaves.

རིང་ཚད་ (riŋdzɛɛ̀) length, distance, height for people.

རིང་ཚད་འབྲིང་གྲས་ (riŋdzɛɛ̀ driŋdrɛɛ̀) medium range ¶ རིང་ཚད་འབྲིང་གྲས་བསྐྱོད་ཐུབ་པའི་མེ་ཤུགས་འཕུར་མདེལ་ Medium range ballistic missile.

རིང་ཞིག་ཏུ་ (riŋshigdu) for a long time.

རིང་ཞིག་ལོན་པ་ (riŋshig lömba) taking a long time.

རིང་ལ་ (riŋla) sm. རིང་དུ་.

རིང་ལུགས་ (riŋluù) doctrine, principle, -ism ¶ བཙན་རྒྱལ་རིང་ལུགས་ Imperialism.

རིང་ལོས་ (riŋlöö) 1. how big/ far/ long? ¶ སློབ་ཚན་གྱི་དུས་ཚོད་རིང་ལོས་ཡོད་དམ་ How long is the class? ¶ མི་དེ་གཟུགས་པོ་རིང་ལོས་ཡོད་རེད་ How tall is that person. ¶ འདི་ནས་ལྷ་ས་བར་ཐག་རིང་ལོས་ཡོད་དམ་ How far is Lhasa from here. 2. sm. རིང་ཐུང་.

རིང་ཤར་ (riŋshaa) the Far East.

རིང་སེ་བ་ (riŋsewa) slightly long.

རིང་བསྲེལ་ (riŋsee) relics.

རིངས་ཁྱད་ (riŋgyɛɛ̀) shung. hastily, in a hurry, urgently.

རིངས་གལ་གསང་ཡིག (riŋgɛɛ sāŋyiì) important/ urgent confidential letters.

རིངས་ནས་རིངས་པར་ (riŋnɛ riŋbar) sm. རིངས་པ་.

རིངས་པ་ (riŋbə) quick, fast, speedy, in a hurry ¶ རིངས་པར་འདིར་ཕེབས་ Come here quickly.

རིངས་པར་ (riŋbar) sm. རིངས་པ་

རིད་ (rii) 1. a flat piece of wood used in tanning leather. 2. vi. to become thin, emaciated ¶ ཁོང་དེང་སང་ལུས་པོ་རིད་འདུག These days he (his body) has become thin.

རིན་ (rin) 1. price, value, va.—གཅོག to reduce price ¶ དེབ་འདིའི་རིན་ག་ཚོད་རེད་ What is the price of this book? 2. (vb. + —) worthwhile doing sth. ¶ གླ་ཕོགས་ཉུང་དྲགས་ནས་ལས་ཀ་འདི་བྱེད་རིན་མི་འདུག The work is not worthwhile doing because the salary is so little.

རིན་སྐྱིན་ (ringyin) payment (and replacement).

རིན་སྐྱིན་མི་དགོས་པ་ (ringyin migööbə) without the need for payment/ reward, without remunerative considerations.

རིན་སྐྱིན་ཚབ་གསུམ་ (ringyin tsəbsum) the three: the price of sth. bought, the return of sth. borrowed, the replacement of sth.

རིན་ཁྱད་ (ringyɛɛ̀) cost/ price differential.

རིན་གོང་ (ringoŋ) price; va.—འགོད་; —རྒྱག; to fix a price; vi.—ཆག; —ལྷུང་ to have a fall/ drop (in prices); vi.—འཕར་ to have prices rise/ increase ¶ རིན་གོང་མཐོ་པོ་ A high price.

རིན་གོང་གི་ཁྱད་པར་ (ringoŋgi kyɛɛ̀bar) sm. རིན་ཁྱད་.

རིན་གོང་གི་སྲིད་ཇུས་ (ringoŋgi sììjüù) price policy.

རིན་གོང་གང་མཐོ་བ་འཚོང་ (ringoŋ kaŋ tōwa tsōŋ) selling at as high a price as possible.

རིན་གོང་འགོད་ (ringoŋ göö) see རིན་གོང་.

རིན་གོང་རྒྱས་དཔྱད་ (ringoŋ gyɛɛ̀jɛɛ̀) installment payment; va.—སྤྲོད་ to make installment payments.

རིན་གོང་ངོ་མ་ (ringoŋ ŋoma) the true price/ value.

རིན་གོང་གཅོད་ (ringoŋ jöö) see རིན་གོང་.

རིན་གོང་ཆག (ringoŋ cāà) see རིན་གོང་.

རིན་གོང་ཆེན་པོ་ (ringoŋ cēmbo) expensive.

རིན་གོང་མཉམ་པ་ (ringoŋ ñamba) sm. རིན་མཉམ་.

རིན་གོང་བསྡོམས་འབོར་ (ringoŋ dombɔr) gross value.

རིན་གོང་འཕར་ (ringoŋ pār) see རིན་གོང་.

རིན་གོང་འཕར་ཆག་མེད་པ་ (ringoŋ pārjaa meèba) prices that don't fluctuate.

རིན་རྒྱན་ (ringyɛn) shung. sm. རིན་ཆེན་རྒྱན་ཆ་བ་.

རིན་རྒྱན་ཁྲི་པ་ (ringyɛn tribə) shung. the head of the རིན་ཆེན་རྒྱན་ཆ་བ་.

རིན་དངུལ་ (rinŋüü) money used to pay sth.

རིན་དངུལ་སྡུད་ས་ (rinŋüü drööso) place for collecting money/ fees.

རིན་ཅན་ (rinjɛn) valuable, precious.

རིན་བཅག་དངོས་ཟོག (rinjaà ŋǖüsɔɔ̀) goods/ merchandise on sale (with reduced price).

རིན་བཅག་ཚོང་སྒྱུར་ (rinjaà tsōŋgyur) selling goods at a reduced price, selling things on sale; va.—བྱེད་.

རིན་ཆུང་ (rinjuŋ) 1. cheap, inexpensive. 2. inferior ¶ རིན་ཆུང་ལོ་ཏོག་གི་རིགས་ An inferior strain of crops.

རིན་ཆུང་ཕན་ཆེ་ (rinjuŋ pēnce) sth. that is inexpensive but useful.

རིན་ཆེན་ (rinjen) 1. precious, valuable. 2. person's name.

རིན་ཆེན་རྒྱན་ཆ་བ་ (rinjen gyɛnjawa) shung. a group of lay officials in the tt. government who wore precious jewel ornaments on special ceremonies such as New Year in the Potala.

རིན་ཆེན་མགྲོན་ཆེ་ (rinjen gyɛnjawa) shung. one of the junior heads of the རིན་ཆེན་རྒྱན་ཆ་བ་.

རིན་ཆེན་གཏེར་མཛོད་ (rinjen dērdzöö) 1. a treasure house (where precious gems/ jewelry are kept). 2. a major Nyingmapa text.

རིན་ཆེན་དང་པོ་ (rinjen taŋbo) gold.

རིན་ཆེན་གཉིས་པ་ (rinjen ñiìbə) silver.

རིན་ཆེན་ནོར་བུ་ (rinjen nɔɔbu) a precious stone/ gem.

རིན་ཆེན་སྣ་ལྔ་ (rinjen nāŋa) 1. the five precious gems and metals: gold, silver, turquoise, coral, and pearl. 2. the precious metals: gold, silver, brass, iron and tin. 3. an apron worn by women on their back.

རིན་ཆེན་སྣ་བདུན་ (rinjen nādün) the seven auspicious royal symbols.

རིན་ཆེན་སྤུངས་ཤད་ (rinjen būŋshɛɛ̀) name of a type of ཤད་ used in writing དབུ་ཅན་.

རིན་ཆེན་བང་མཛོད་ (rincen paŋdzöö) sm. རིན་ཆེན་གཏེར་མཛོད་, 1.

རིན་ཆེན་དབང་སྔོན་ (rincen wāŋŋön) sapphire.

རིན་ཆེན་དམར་པོ་ (rincen mārbo) ruby.

རིན་ཆེན་རིལ་བུ་ (rincen riìbu) a type of Tibetan medicine that includes pulverized precious gems.

རིན་ཆེན་གསུམ་ (rinjen sūm) shung. sm. དཀོན་མཆོག་གསུམ་.

རིན་གཉིས་ཏམ་ཀ་ (rinñiì drāŋga) shung. a silver Tibetan coin.

རིན་གཉིས་ཏམ་དཀར་ (rinñiì drāŋga) shung. sm. རིན་

གཉིས་ཏམ་ཀ་.

རིན་མཉམ་ (rinñam) equal value.

རིན་མཉམ་དངོས་རྫས་ (rinñam ŋöödzɛɛ̀) sm. རིན་མཉམ་དངོས་ཟོག.

རིན་མཉམ་དངོས་ཟོག (rinñam ŋöösɔɔ̀) products of equal value.

རིན་མཉམ་དངོས་རྫས་ (rinñam ŋöödzɛɛ̀) sm. རིན་མཉམ་དངོས་ཟོག.

རིན་མཉམ་བརྗེ་ཚོང་ (rinñam jedzoŋ) equitable exchange, fair trade in buying and selling.

རིན་མཉམ་བརྗེ་ཚོང་ (rinñam) bartering with products of equal value.

རིན་མཉམ་བརྗེ་ལེན་ (rinñam jelen) exchanging at equal value.

རིན་མཉམ་ཚབ་སྒྲོད་ (rinñam tsəbdrɛɛ̀) substituting a product of equal value; va.—བྱེད་.

རིན་རྟོགས་ (rin dɔɔ̀) va. to find out or learn the price/ value.

རིན་ཐང་ (rindaŋ) value, price, worth; vi.—ཆག to have the price or value get decreased/ devaluated/ depreciated; vi.—ཕབ་ to reduce the price; vi.—འཕར་ to have the price get increased ¶ དེང་སང་བཟའ་བཅའི་རིན་གོང་འཕར་བཞག These days the price of foodstuffs has increased.

རིན་ཐང་གློག་བཅད་ (rindaŋ gōgdzaŋ) secret price fixing.

རིན་ཐང་ཁེར་གཙང་ (rindaŋ kērdzaŋ) net value ¶ ཞིང་ལས་ཀྱི་རིན་ཐང་ཁེར་གཙང་ The net value of agricultural production.

རིན་ཐང་གི་ཆོས་ཉིད་ (rindaŋgi cööñii) law of value (in economics).

རིན་ཐང་ཅན་ (rindaŋjɛn) very expensive/ valuable.

རིན་ཐང་གཅོག (rindaŋ jɔɔ̀) va. to reduce the price.

རིན་ཐང་ཆག (rindaŋ cāà) see རིན་ཐང་.

རིན་ཐང་འཆག (rindaŋ cāà) vi. to have the price to come down/ fall.

རིན་ཐང་གཏན་འབེབས་ (rindaŋ dēnbeb) fixed value/ price; va.—བྱེད་.

རིན་ཐང་ཕབ་ (rindaŋ pāb) see རིན་ཐང་.

རིན་ཐང་བྲལ་པ་ (rindaŋ trɛɛwa) sm. རིན་ཐང་མེད་པ་.

རིན་ཐང་མེད་པ་ (rindaŋ meèba) invaluable, priceless.

རིན་ཐང་ལྷག་མ་ (rindaŋ lhāgba) surplus value.

རིན་དོད་ (rindüü) payments that include nonmonetary things like housing, food, etc.; va.—གཏོང་.

རིན་པ་ (rimbə) price.

རིན་པ་ཁུག (rimbə kūù) vi. to command/ get a price, to be able to sell for a price ¶ ཅ་ལག་འདི་ཚོར་རིན་པ་ཁུག་ས་མ་རེད་ བྱས་ཙང་གད་སྙིགས་ནང་དབྱུག་པ་ཡིན་ These things won't command any price so I threw them away.

རིན་པོ་ཆེ་ (rimboche) 1. precious ¶ རྩ་ཁྲིམས་རིན་པོ་ཆེ་ The precious constitution. 2. a term of address/ title for incarnate lamas.

རིན་པོ་ཆེ་སྣ་བདུན་ (rimboce nadün) seven kinds of precious gems.

རིན་པོ་ཆེའི་གཏེར་ (rimbocee dēr) treasury, storehouse.

རིན་པོ་ཆེའི་གདུགས་ (rimbocee dug) one of the eight auspicious symbols: the umbrella.

རིན་སྤུངས་ (rimbuŋ) sm. རིན་སྤུངས་.

རིན་སྤུངས་པ་ (rimbuŋba) historical figure whose family held power over parts of Tibet from the 14th to the 16th centuries.

རིན་སྤུངས་རྫོང་ (rimbuŋ dzoŋ) Rimpung District.

རིན་ཕིའུ་ (rinbe) ch. sm. རིན་མིན་པི་.

རིན་བྱིན་ (rin jin) va. to give payment ¶ཁོས་ང་ལ་ཅ་ལག་གི་རིན་བྱིན་མ་བྱུང་ He didn't pay me for the things.

རིན་བྲལ་ (rintrɛɛ) sm. རིན་ཐང་མེད་པ་.

རིན་འབབ་ (rinbəb) price, cost ¶ཁ་ལག་གི་རིན་འབབ་རྩིས་རོགས་ Please calculate the cost of the food.

རིན་སྦྲག་གཉིས་མེད་ (rindraà ñiimeè) free of cost and shipping fees ¶ཁོང་གིས་ང་ལ་རིན་སྦྲག་གཉིས་མེད་ཀྱི་དེབ་ཅིག་བསྐུར་བཞག He sent me a book free.

རིན་མེད་ (rinmeè) without cost, free.

རིན་ཚད་ (rindzɛɛ̀) price, cost.

རིན་ཚབ་ (rindzəb) price and substitution for goods borrowed; va.—སྤྲོད་ ¶ཅ་ལག་མང་པོ་ཉོས་གཡར་བྱས་པ་དེ་ཚོའི་རིན་འབབ་དུས་ཐོག་སྤྲད་པ་རེད་ The things that were bought and borrowed they paid for and returned on time.

རིན་རྫོང་ (rindzoŋ) shung. abbr. of རིན་སྤུངས་རྫོང་.

རིན་ཧྲིན་ (rinhrin) ch. ginseng.

རིབ་ (rib) 1. cheating (usu. in gambling); va.—རྩེ་ to cheat in gambling ¶ཁོས་སྦག་རྒྱག་དུས་རིབ་རྩེ་གི་འདུག He cheats when playing mahjong. 2. a brief/ short time.

རིབ་མ་ (ribmə) fence, wall.

རིབ་ཙམ་ (ribdzam) 1. brief/ short time ¶ རིབ་ཙམ་མཐོང་བྱུང་ I got a brief look at it. 2. deceitful, duplicitous ¶ མི་དེ་རིབ་ཙམ་ཡོད་པས་གཟབ་གཟབ་བྱེད་དགོས་ Because that person is deceitful, (you) should be careful.

རིབ་ཚ་པོ་ (rib tsābo) sb. who cheats a lot.

རིབ་གཞི་ (ribshi) sm. རུ་གཞི་.

རིབ་རིབ་ (ribrib) 1. unclear visually ¶ མིག་ཡག་པོ་མེད་ཙང་རིབ་རིབ་ཅིག་ལས་མཐོང་གི་མི་འདུག Because I have a bad eyesight, I can't see clearly. 2. short/ brief time.

རིམ་ (rim) (— + vb.) to do gradually ¶ དཀའ་ངལ་རིམ་སེལ་བྱེད་དགོས་ (We) must solve difficulties gradually. ¶ ཚོགས་འདུའི་གོ་སྒྲིག་རིམ་ཞུས་ཆོག་པ་ཞུ་རྒྱུ (We) will gradually make arrangements for the meeting.

རིམ་གྱི་ (rimgi) shung. abbr. of རིམ་གྱི་.

རིམ་སྐྱོད་ (rimgyöö) going gradually/ in stages; va.—བྱེད་ ¶ དམག་མི་རྣམས་ཡུལ་དེར་རིམ་སྐྱོད་བྱས་འདུག The soldiers went to that place gradually.

རིམ་བསྐྲུན་ (rimdrün) building gradually/ in stages; va.—བྱེད་ ¶ གྲོང་ཁྱེར་ནང་ཁང་པ་གསར་པ་མང་པོ་རིམ་བསྐྲུན་བྱས་འདུག They have built new buildings in the city in stages.

རིམ་གས་འགྱུར་འབྱུང་ (rimgɛɛ̀ gyurjuŋ) chain reaction (in chemistry/ physics).

རིམ་གོང་ (rimgoŋ) sm. གོང་རིམ་.

རིམ་གྱིས་ (rimgyi) gradually, by degrees; va.—བྱེད་ ¶ འཛུགས་སྐྲུན་བྱེད་སྒོ་རྣམས་རིམ་གྱིས་བྱེད་བཞིན་པ་རེད་ (They) are doing the construction projects gradually.

རིམ་གྱིས་འགྱུར་ (rimgyi gyur) vi. to evolve, to change gradually.

རིམ་གྲངས་ (rimdraŋ) ordinal numerals/ numbers, mathematical progression/ series (in math).

རིམ་གྲས་ (rimdrɛɛ) stratum, class ¶ དབང་སྒྱུར་མཁན་གྱི་རིམ་གྲས་ Ruling class.

རིམ་གྲོ་ (rimdro) a religious ceremony/ rite to eliminate difficulties.

རིམ་གྲོ་བ་ (rimdrowa) 1. person who does the རིམ་གྲོ་ rite. 2. a servant.

རིམ་བགྲོད་ (rimdröö) gradually, stage by stage ¶ རིམ་བགྲོད་གོང་འཕེལ་ Progressing stage-by-stage/ gradually.

རིམ་འགྲོས་ (rimdröö) sm. རིམ་བགྲོད་.

རིམ་འགྱུར་ (rimgyur) evolution, gradual change ¶ ཞི་བའི་རིམ་འགྱུར་ Peaceful evolution.

རིམ་བཀལ་ (rimgɛɛ) irregular, not gradual or by degrees ¶ ལས་བྱེད་པ་གཞོན་ནུ་ཁག་ཅིག་རིམ་བཀལ་གནས་སྤར་བྱས་འདུག Some young officials were promoted irregularly (not by regular stages).

རིམ་བཀལ་ཞུ་གདུག (rimgɛɛ shuduù) bypassing the bureaucracy and appealing (out of sequence) to a higher level of court/ officials; va.—བྱེད་; —རྒྱག ¶ གྱོད་གཞི་དེའི་སྐོར་ཁྲིམས་ས་གོང་མར་རིམ་བཀལ་ཞུ་གདུགས་བྱས་པ་རེད་ (He) appealed (out of sequence) to a higher court concerning that case.

རིམ་རྒྱུད་ (rimgyüü) sm. རིམ་བརྒྱུད་.

རིམ་བརྒྱུད་ (rimgyüü) gradually from one to another.

རིམ་ཅན་ (rimjɛn) sm. རིམ་བཞིན་.

རིམ་ཅན་དུ་ (rimjɛndu) successively, occurring one after another ¶ རྒྱལ་རབས་རིམ་ཅན་དུ་ In successive generations/ dynasties.

རིམ་བཅར་ (rimjaa) 1. gradually coming close to/ meeting ¶ རྔོན་པས་རི་དྭགས་དེའི་སར་རུམ་བཅར་བྱེད་སྐབས་རི་དྭགས་དེ་བྲོས་པ་རེད་ As the hunter gradually moved close to the animal, the animal ran away. 2. going to meet a superior several times in succession ¶ ངས་འགོ་ཁྲིད་ལ་རིམ་བཅར་ཞུས་པ་ཡིན་ I went to meet the leader several times (one after another).

རིམ་བཙོལ་སྡེབ་ལེན་ (rimjöö deblen) putting money in the bank gradually but withdrawing it at once.

རིམ་ཆག (rim cāà) vi. to decrease by degrees/ gradually/ in stages.

རིམ་མཆེད་ (rim cēè) gradual dissemination/ spreading/ diffusion.

རིམ་ཉམས་ (rimñam) gradually declining/ deteriorating.

རིམ་ཉམས་རིམ་སྡོང་ (rimñam rimdoŋ) gradually becoming weak and poor (declining) and becoming extinct ¶ ཁྲལ་རིགས་བཙན་མནར་ཆེ་བས་གཞུང་རྒྱུགས་ཁྲལ་པ་རྣམས་རིམ་ཉམས་རིམ་སྡོང་དུ་གྱུར་པ་ Because of the hardship causes by high taxes, the government taxpayer serfs gradually declined and became extinct.

རིམ་གཉིས་ (rimñīì) abbr. of རིམ་པ་གཉིས་པ་.

རིམ་བསྡར་ (rimdar) in series/ stages ¶ རྟ་དམག་རྣམས་རིམ་བསྡར་གྱིས་འབྱོར་སོང་ The cavalry arrived in stages.

རིམ་མཐུད་ (rimdüù) one after another, in succession (without a break).

རིམ་ཐོག་རིམ་རྩེག (rimdɔɔ̀ rimdzeg) va. to add one on top of another.

རིམ་དག (rimdaà) shung. being gradually exhausted.

རིམ་འདས་ (rimdɛɛ̀) 1. super ¶ རིམ་འདས་རྒྱལ་ཁབ་ Superpower country. 2. special.

རིམ་ལྡན་ (rimdɛn) sm. རིམ་པ་ཡོད་པ་.

རིམ་པ་ (rimbə) rank, level, grade, degree ¶ རིམ་པ་ལྔ་པའི་གཞུང་ཞབས་ Officials of the fifth rank.

རིམ་པ་ཁག (rimbəgaà) different levels ¶ རིམ་པ་ཁག་གི་ལས་ཁུངས་ལ་ཕོགས་མི་འདྲ་བ་ཡོད་ Offices of different levels have different salaries.

རིམ་པ་འཁྲུགས་ (rimbə trūù) vi. to have ranks/ levels/ grades/ degrees get mixed up/ disordered.

རིམ་པ་གོང་མ་ (rimbə koŋma) 1. higher level/ grade, superior ¶ རིམ་པ་གོང་མའི་ལས་བྱེད་པ་ Higher level cadre. 2. higher authorities ¶ གནད་དོན་དེ་རིམ་པ་གོང་མས་ཐག་བཅད་པ་རེད་ This issue was decided by the higher authorities.

རིམ་པ་གོང་འོག (rimbə koŋ wɔɔ̀) higher and lower level/ grades.

རིམ་པ་སྒྲིག (rimbə drig) va. to put sth. in order/ series.

རིམ་པ་གཉིས་པ་ (rimbə ñīìbə) the second rank.

རིམ་པ་ལྟར་བྱེད་ (rimbə dārjeè) doing things orderly/ gradually/ step-by-step.

རིམ་པ་བསྟར་ཆགས་ (rimbə dārjaà) one after another (without break).

རིམ་པ་མཐོ་བ་ (rimbə towa) higher rank.

རིམ་པ་དང་གཉིས་ (rimbə taŋñīì) the first and the second ranks.

རིམ་པ་སྤབས་ (rimbə bōb) va. to demote ¶ ཁོང་ནོར་འཁྲུལ་ཤོར་ཙང་རིམ་པ་ལྔ་པ་ནས་དྲུག་པར་སྤབས་པ་རེད་ Because he made a mistake he was demoted from the fifth to the sixth rank.

རིམ་པ་སྤར་ (rimbə bār) va. to promote.

རིམ་པ་ཕབ་ (rimbə pāb) vi. to be/ get demoted.

རིམ་པ་བཞིན་ (rimbə shin) sm. རིམ་བཞིན་.

རིམ་པ་བཟོ་ (rimbə so) sm. རིམ་པ་སྒྲིག.

རིམ་པ་འོག་མ་ (rimbə wɔɔ̀ma) lower level/ rank, subordinate.

རིམ་པ་སོ་སོ་ (rimbə soso) each level/ rank.

རིམ་པ་གསུམ་པ་ (rimbə sūmbə) third rank.

རིམ་པ་གསུམ་པའི་དོག་གནས་ (rimba sūmbɛ dōgnɛɛ̀) shung. the third rank (in tt.).

རིམ་པ་གསུམ་ལ་དབང་བའི་ལམ་ལུགས་ (rimbə sūmla wāŋwɛ ləmluù) the three level ownership system: the commune, the production brigade and the production team.

རིམ་པའི་ལམ་ལུགས་ (rimbɛ ləmluù) a system of organizational hierarchy where ranks/ levels are used.

རིམ་པར་རིམ་སྐོར་ (rimbar rimgɔɔ) layer upon layer, one after another (usu. a series of walls/ fences) ¶ ཕོ་བྲང་ལ་ལྕགས་རི་ཕྱི་ནང་རིམ་པ་རིམ་སྐོར་བྱས་ཡོད་པ་རེད་ The palace has layer upon layer of walls.

རིམ་པས་ (rimbɛ) sm. རིམ་གྱིས་.

རིམ་པས་སྐྱོང་ (rimbɛ gyōŋ) va. to rule/ govern by degrees/ gradually.

རིམ་ཕྱེ་འགན་འཁུར་ (rimce gɛnkur) classifying and taking responsibility; va.—བྱེད་; —ལེན་.

རིམ་ཕྱེ་དོ་དམ་ (rimce todam) classifying and managing; va.—བྱེད་.

རིམ་འཕར་ (rim pār) 1. vi. to progressively increase. 2. promoted.

རིམ་འཕེལ་གྱིས་ (rimpelgi) gradually occurring.

རིམ་བྱུས་ (rimjɛɛ̀) shung. sth. done several times.

རིམ་བྱུང་ (rimjuŋ) gradual/ successive occurrences, occurring in stages ¶ རྒྱ་ནག་གོང་མ་རིམ་བྱུང་གིས་དབང་སྒྱུར་བྱས་ཡོད་པ་རེད་ The Emperors of China ruled successively.

རིམ་བྱུང་ཚད་ཐོ་ (rimjuŋ tsɛɛ̀do) a record ¶ འཛམ་གླིང་རིམ་བྱུང་ཚད་ཐོ་ A world record.

རིམ་བྱོན་ (rimjön) arriving or coming in succession/ stages/ gradually.

རིམ་བྲལ་ (rimdrɛɛ) disorderly, irregular, sporadic.

རིམ་འབྱོར་ (rimjɔɔ) vi. to arrive gradually/ one after another.

རིམ་འབྲིང་ (rimdriŋ) middle rank.

རིམ་འབྲེལ་འགྱུར་འབྱུང་ (rimdree gyurjuŋ) chain reaction.

རིམ་མིན་ (rimmin) out of order/ sequence; va.—བྱེད་.

རིམ་མེད་ (rimmeè) sm. རིམ་བྲལ་.

རིམ་བརྩེགས་ (rimdzeg) 1. stacked/ piled up. 2. progressive.

རིམ་བརྩེགས་ཐོབ་འབབ་དཔྱ་ཁྲལ་ (rimdzeg tōbbəb jādrɛɛ) graduated/ progressive income tax.

རིམ་མཚུངས་མཉམ་འགྲན་ (rimdzuŋ ñāmdrɛn) league or division matches (in sports).

རིམ་འཛར་དུ་ (rimdzardu) in order, in sequence.

རིམ་བཞི་ (rimshi) shung. 1. fourth rank. 2. a fourth rank official in tt.

རིམ་བཞིན་ (rimshin) 1. gradually ¶ དམག་འཁྲུག་དེ་རིམ་བཞིན་རྒྱ་ཆེར་གཏོང་དགོས་ (We) must gradually widen the war. ¶ གོ་རྟོགས་ནི་རིམ་བཞིན་ཇེ་མཐོར་ཕྱིན་པ་རེད་ (Their) comprehension increased gradually. 2. (va. + —) whenever ¶ བསོད་ནམས་ཐུག་རིམ་བཞིན་ཁོང་གིས་ང་ལ་དངུལ་གཡར་གྱི་འདུག Whenever I meet Sonam, he lends me money.

རིམ་བཞིན་འགྱུར་ (rimshin gyur) vi. to be altered gradually, to evolve.

རིམ་ཡོད་ (rimyöö) sm. རིམ་པ་.

རིམ་ལད་ (rimlɛɛ̀) imitating/ adopting/ following gradually.

རིམ་ལེན་དངུལ་བུན་ (rimlen ŋüübün) a loan acquired over a period of time.

རིམ་སྲབ་གཏེར་ཁ་ (rimdrəb dērga) a shallow mine, a mine that is near the surface.

རིམ་གསབ་ (rim sāb) replacing sb. one after another/ successively ¶ རྫོང་སོ་སོའི་རྫོང་སྡོད་རིམ་གསབ་ཀྱིས་བཏང་ཡོད་པ་རེད་ They sent district officials to each district one after another (as the old term expired).

རིམ་གསོག (rimsɔɔ̀) accumulating gradually; va.—བྱེད་.

རིམ་བསགས་ (rimsaà) sm. རིམ་གསོག.

རིམ་བསགས་ཀྱི་བརྩི་ (rimsaàgi dzī) an accounting of what has been accumulated to date.

རིམས་ (rim) sm. རིམ་ནད་.

རིམས་འགོག (rimgɔ̀ɔ) epidemic prevention; va.—བྱེད་ to prevent the spread of epidemics.

རིམས་འགོག་ཁྲུའུ་ (rimgɔ̀ɔ trū) tib. ch. quarantine office.

རིམས་འགོག་ཏོ་དམ་ཁའོ་ (rimgɔ̀ɔ todam kāwo) tib. ch. quarantine control/ management section.

རིམས་འགོག་སྨན་ཁབ་ (rimgɔ̀ɔ mɛ̄ngəb) vaccination, inoculation.

རིམས་འགོག་ས་ཚིགས་ (rimgɔ̀ɔ sādzii) quarantine station.

རིམས་ཆམ་ (rimjam) influenza, flu.

རིམས་རྙིང་ (rimñīŋ) an epidemic disease which lasts for a long time.

རིམས་དྲག་པོ་ (rim tragbo) serious epidemic.

རིམས་ནད་ (rimnɛ̀ɛ) epidemic.

རིམས་ཚད་ (rimdzɛ̀ɛ) epidemic which causes fever.

རིམས་གསར་ (rimsar) start of an epidemic.

རིའི་སྐེད་པ་ (rii gēèba) the middle of a mountain.

རིའི་གྱེན་ (rii gye) mountain slope.

རིའི་མགུལ་པ་ (rii gǖüwa) sm. རིའི་ངོས་.

རིའི་སྒང་ (rii gaŋ) 1. on top of a mountain. 2. a ridge.

རིའི་ངོས་ (rii ŋȫö) face of a mountain.

རིའི་ཆུ་ལོག (rii cūlɔ̀ɔ) a flood starting in the mountains.

རིའི་ཉིན་སྲིབ་ (rii ñindrib) the south and the north side of a mountain.

རིའི་ལྟག (rii dāà) sm. རི་སྒལ་.

རིའི་མཐའ་ (rii tā) edge of a mountain.

རིའི་ལྡེབས་ (rii deb) face of a mountain.

རིའི་དཔུང་པ་ (rii būŋbə) the "shoulder" of a mountain.

རིའི་ཕར་རྒྱབ་ (rii pār gyəb) back of a mountain, on the other side of a mountain.

རིའི་རྩེ་ (rii dzē) the top of a mountain.

རིའི་འོག (rii wɔ̀ɔ) the bottom of a mountain.

རིར་འཛེག (rii dzeg) mountain climbing; va.—བྱེད་.

རིལ་ (rii) 1. vi. to fall ¶ ང་ལམ་ཁར་འདྲེད་དེ་ར་ཕྱིར་ནས་རིལ་བྱུང་ I slipped on the road and fell. 2. abbr. of རིལ་པོ་.

རིལ་གྲངས་ (riidraŋ) a whole number, integer (in math).

རིལ་ངོས་ (rii ŋȫö) surface of a globe/ ball/ sphere.

རིལ་པོ་ (riibu) 1. whole, complete, entire. 2. round.

རིལ་པོར་ (riibor) wholly, entirely.

རིལ་བ་ཞབས་ཚགས་ཅན་ (riiwa shəbdzaàjɛn) a canister (with small holes at the bottom for sprinkling water).

རིལ་བུ་ (riibu) pill; va.—གཏོང་ to take a pill.

རིལ་དབྱིབས་ (riiyib) sm. རིལ་གཟུགས་.

རིལ་མ་ (riimə) the dung of sheep and goats.

རིལ་མོ་ (riimu) sm. རིལ་པོ་.

རིལ་རྩི་ (riidzi) the shiny coating of pills.

རིལ་ཚང་ (riidzaŋ) place where goat and sheep dung is stored (for fuel).

རིལ་འཛིན་ (rindzin) total eclipse of sun/ moon.

རིལ་གཟུགས་ (riisuù) spheroid, globular, round-shaped.

རིལ་རིལ་ (riirii) 1. sm. རིལ་པོ་. 2. wagging (tails); va.—བྱེད་ to wag one's tail.

རིལ་རིལ་འཇོང་འཇོང་གང་བཟོ་ན་ཡང་ (riirii joŋjoŋ kaŋ sonayaŋ) whatever decision one wants to make ¶ རིལ་རུལ་འཇོང་འཇོང་གང་བཟོ་ན་ཡང་འགོ་ཁྲིད་ཀྱི་ལག་པ་རེད་ It is up to the leaders to make whatever decision they want.

རིལ་རིལ་རྡོག་རྡོག (riirii dɔgdɔ̀ɔ) 1. complete, a complete entity. 2. sm. རིལ་པོ་.

རིལ་ལུད་ (riilǜü) sheep and goat dung fertilizer.

རིལ་ལེ་ (riile) arc. directly, straight.

རིལ་གསོག (riisɔ̀ɔ) sm. རིལ་ཚང་.

རིས་ (rii) 1. figure, form, design. 2. party, team, side.

རིས་འགུལ་གློག་བརྙན་ (riigǖü lɔ̀ɔñɛn) animated picture/ cartoon.

རིས་སྣ་འཆར་མདོང་ (riina cārdoŋ) kaleidoscope.

རིས་ཅན་ (riijɛn) prejudiced, partial, biases.

རིས་བྲལ་ (riidrɛɛ) sm. རིས་མེད་.

རིས་འབུར་གོས་ཆེན་ (riibur kȫöjen) a type of brocade with relief design.

རིས་མེད་ (riimeè) impartial, unprejudiced, without discrimination/ distinction; va.—བྱེད་.

རིས་ཚན་ (riidzɛn) sm. སྡེ་ཚན་.

རིས་བཤད་ (riishɛ̀ɛ) explanation of a painting.

རིས་སུ་བོར་ (riisu bɔ̄ɔ) 1. va. to biased/ partial/ prejudiced. 2. va. to look down on.

རིས་སུ་མ་ཆོད་ (riisu majȫö) sm. རིས་མེད་.

རིས་སུ་མ་ཆད་པ་ (riisu majɛ̀ɛ) sm. རིས་མེད་.

རུ་ (ru) 1. dative-locative particle (see དུ་) ¶ ང་ལྟ་རུ་མ་བཅུག་ན་ང་ཕྱིར་ལོག་རྒྱུ་གི་ཡིན་ If you don't let me see (it) I'll return (home). 2. abbr. of ཨུ་རུ་སུ་. 3. horn. 4. abbr. of བསྟན་འཛིན་མཁར་རུ་. 5. abbr. of རུ་དཔོན་. 6. sm. རུ་སྟར་. 7. a battalion/ brigade/ group.

རུ་ཀྲི་ (rudri) hind. bread.

རུ་བཀལ་ (rugɛɛ) sm. རུ་བསྐུས་སྒོ་.

རུ་སྐོར་ (rugɔɔ) 1. a group of nomads. 2. neighbors/ community of nomads.

རུ་སྐྱ་ (rugya) an oar.

རུ་ཁ་ (ruga) the horn brace of a Tibetan rifle.

རུ་ཁག (rugaà) unit, team, brigade ¶ ཐོན་སྐྱེད་རུ་ཁག Production brigade.

རུ་ཁག་ཆུང་བ་ (rugaà cūŋwa) squad, small team.

རུ་ཁལ་ (rugɛɛ) shung. the basic vaolue measurement unit in the tt. equaling about 28 རྒྱ་མ་ (30.8 lbs.) (same as བསྟན་འཛིན་མཁར་རུ་).

རུ་གྱོང་པོ་ (ru gyoŋbo) stubborn.

རུ་གྲལ་ (rudrɛɛ) row, file.

རུ་གླུ་ (rula) the song of a unit/ team/ brigade.

རུ་མགོ (rungo) the head of a line/ row/ formation (usu. when marching).

རུ་འགོ (rungo) sm. རུ་མགོ་.

རུ་རྒྱ་ (rugya) abbr. Russia and China; Russia and India.

རུ་སྒྲིག (rudrig) sm. རུ་བསྒྲིགས་.

རུ་སྒྲིག་སྒྲིག (rudrig drig) va. to line up in formation.

རུ་སྒྲིག་གཏོང་ (rudrig dōŋ) sm. རུ་སྒྲིག་སྒྲིག.

རུ་བརྒྱ་ (rugya) shung. abbr. of Rupon and Gyapon (in Tibetan army).

རུ་བརྒྱ་ལྡིང་གསུམ་ (rugya diŋsum) shung. abbr. of Rupon, Gyapon and Shengo (military officers in the traditional Tibetan army).

རུ་བསྒྲིགས་ (rudrig) marching in formation, lining up in rows/ formation; va. རུ་བསྒྲིགས་; —གཏོང་.

རུ་ང་ (ruŋa) sm. རུ་ངར་པོ་.

རུ་ང་དན་དིག (ruŋa dēndig) shung. careful, meticulous.

རུ་ངར་པོ་ (ru ŋarbo) 1. fastidious, meticulous (in appearance and/ or work); va.—བྱེད་ ¶ ཁོང་རང་ལས་ཀར་རུ་ངར་པོ་སོང་ཙང་གཞན་གྱིས་བྱས་པ་ལས་སྣ་པོར་ལོ་གི་མེད་པ་རེད་ Because he does meticulous work, he isn't easily satisfied with the work of others. 2. sb. who gets angry easily, sb. who is short tempered ¶ ཁྱེད་རང་དེ་འདྲའི་རུ་ངར་པོ་མ་གནང་དང་ བཀའ་མོལ་ག་ལེར་གསུང་དང་ Don't be short-tempered like that, speak calmly. 3. a stingy, miserly person.

རུ་ངར་ཞིབ་ཚགས་ (ruŋar shidzaà) sm. རུ་ངར་པོ་.

རུ་ཅན་ (rujɛn) 1. having horns. 2. Tibetan guns that have a rifle brace made of antelope horns.

རུ་གཅིག (rujig) one battalion/ brigade/ unit/ team.

རུ་ཆུང་ (rujuŋ) abbr. of རུ་ཁག་ཆུང་བ་.

རུ་ཆེན་ (rujen) battalion, large team/ unit/ brigade ¶ ལམ་བཅོས་རུ་ཆེན་ A large road construction team.

རུ་མཇུག (runjuù) the end of row.

རུ་རྟ་ (ruda) 1. saussurea lappa. 2. yeast. 3. cavalry horses.

རུ་སྟར་ (rudar) lined up in formation; va.—སྒྲིག to

line up in formation.

རུ་སྟར་གྲབས་སྦྱོང་ (rudar trəbjoŋ) rehearsal drill/ practice for a parade or march.

རུ་ཐུང་ (rudaŋ) a point on the arm for draining blood.

རུ་ཐུར་ (rudur) horn (of an animal).

རུ་ཐོག (rudoò) name of a place in W. Tibet.

རུ་དར་ (rudar) flag of an battalion/ brigade/ unit/ team/ army.

རུ་འདུད་ (rudüü) military salute/ greeting; va.—ཞུ་ to give a military salute, to present arms in greeting.

རུ་འདྲེན་ (rudren) sm. རུ་སྣེ་.

རུ་འདྲེན་སྡེ་བཞི་ (rudren deshi) units of soldiers marching at the front, back, right, and left side of a king.

རུ་འདྲེན་པ་ (rudrenba) sm. རུ་སྣེ་.

རུ་སྣེ་ (rune) 1. leader or head of a column/ line/ row/ brigade. 2. the front of a line or row; va.—འཁྲིད་ to lead a group/ unit/ column.

རུ་སྣེ་འཁྲིད་མཁན་ (rune triìñɛn) the leader of a group.

རུ་པ་ (rubə) army, troops, members of a unit/ column/ group.

རུ་པི་ (rubi) hind. rupee.

རུ་དཔུང་ (rubuŋ) sm. རུ་ཁག.

རུ་དཔོན་ (rubön) 1. leader or head of a རུ་ཁག. 2. shung. military officer in the Tibetan army immediately under a མདའ་དཔོན་ (in charge of 500 troops).

རུ་ཕྱག (rujaà) sm. རུ་འདུད་.

རུ་བ་ (roo) herd of livestock.

རུ་བ་སྐྱུས་སྤོ་ (roo gyɛ̄ɛ̀bo) moving into a new pasture area (nomads with their tents and herds); va.—བྱེད་.

རུ་འབྲིང་ (rudriŋ) 1. a middle size military unit corresponding to a company or battalion. 2. a middle size work unit/ group/ unit/ column.

རུ་མ་ (rumə) fermenting agent/ yeast for making beer and yogurt.

རུ་མི་ (rumi) member of a རུ་ཁག.

རུ་མིང་ (rumiŋ) name of a རུ་ཁག.

རུ་མིན་ (rumin) a red fez worn by Moslems.

རུ་མེ་ནི་ཡ་ (rumeniya) sm. རུ་མེན་ཉི་ཡ་.

རུ་མེན་ཉི་ཡ་ (rumeniya) Rumania.

རུ་དམག (rumaà) 1. soldiers in formation. 2. soldiers in a unit.

རུ་དམར་ (rumar) an animal that has killed people by goring.

རུ་གཙོ་ (rudzo) head/ leader of a རུ་ཁག.

རུ་རྩི་ (rudzi) fermenting agent/ yeast for making beer and yogurt.

རུ་ཚན་ (rudzɛn) sm. སྡེ་ཚན་.

རུ་ཚོགས་ (rudzɔɔ̀) sm. རུ་ཁག.

རུ་མཚན་ (rudzɛn) military color/ standard.

རུ་མཚམས་དབྱེ་ (rudzam yē) va. to make a demarcation between units.

རུ་མཚོན་ (rudzön) 1. sm. རུ་དར་. 2. military equipment. 3. abbr. of རུ་དར་ and མཚོན་ཆ་.

རུ་འཛིངས་ (rudziŋ) 1. many disasters and misfortunes occurring at the same time. 2. animals fighting with horns.

རུ་གཞི་ (rushi) frame.

རུ་བཞི་ (rushi) four ancient division of Central Tibet (དབུས་གཙང་).

རུ་ཡོང་བཟའ་ (ruyoŋsa) one of the wives of King Srongtsen Gampo.

རུ་རུ་ (ruru) 1. deer. 2. the barking or crying sound of deer.

རུ་ལག (rulaà) shung. one of the four རུ་ of དབུས་གཙང་.

རུ་ལེབ་ (ruleb) flat horn.

རུ་ཤོག (rushɔɔ̀) a large subdivision of a regiment ¶ བོད་དམག་རུ་ཤོག A Tibetan army unit.

རུ་ས་ (rusə) place where nomads make camp.

རུ་སུ་ (rusu) Russia.

རུ་སུ་དཀར་པོ་ (rusu gārbo) White Russian, White Russia, Tsarist Russia.

རུ་སོག (rusoò) Russia.

རུག (ruù) 1. va. to collect/ gather ¶ སློབ་ཕྲུག་རྣམས་སློབ་ཁང་དུ་རུག་དགོས་ The students have to gather in the classroom.

རུག་གི་ (ruggi) sm. རུག་དེ་ཁ་ལ་.

རུག་སྒོག (rugɔg) garlic that grows in the shade on hills and mountains.

རུག་དེ་ཁ་ལ་ (rugdekala) all together ¶ ནང་མི་ཚང་མ་རུག་དེ་ཁ་ལ་འཛོམས་སོང་ All the family members gathered together.

རུག་བསྡུས་ (rugdüü) sm. རུག་རུག.

རུག་པ་ (rūgbə) a kind of garlic that grows in the shade on mountains.

རུག་འཚོགས་ (rugdzɔɔ̀) gathering/ assembling together; va.—བྱེད་.

རུག་འཛོམ་ (rugdzom) sm. རུག་འཚོགས་.

རུག་རུག (ruùruù) collecting/ gathering together; va.—བཟོ་; —བྱེད་ to collect/ gather (together) ¶ ཞིང་ལོང་པ་སྟོང་ཕྲག་འགའ་ཞིག་རུག་རུག་བྱས་པ་རེད་ Several thousand demonstrators gathered together.

རུང་ (ruŋ) 1. even though, although ¶ ཁོ་རྒྱ་མི་ཡིན་རུང་རྒྱ་གར་ལ་སྡོད་ཀྱི་ཡོད་པ་རེད་ Even though he is Chinese he lives in India. 2. proper, suitable, appropriate, allowed ¶ སྦྲང་བུ་ཙམ་ལའང་གནོད་ཚེ་བྱེད་མི་རུང་ It is not allowed to harm even a fly. 3. (interrogative + —) —ever ¶ ཅི་རུང་ Whichever/ whatever. ¶ སུ་རུང་ Whomever. ¶ རས་ཆོས་གཞི་དཀར་པོ་དང་སྔོན་པོ་ཅི་རུང་ཞིག་ཉོས་ཤོག Buy either blue or white or cloth (whichever). ¶ ཚོགས་འདུ་དེ་ར་ཁྱེད་རང་གཉིས་སུ་རུང་ཞིག་ཕྱིན་ན་འགྲིགས་ Whichever (of you two) go to that meeting it is okay.

རུང་ཁང་ (rumgaŋ) kitchen in a monastery.

རུང་རུང་བྱེད་ (ruŋruŋ ceè) shung. va. to make a display of, to show off.

རུང་ཧོ་ཕུང་ (ruŋhobuŋ) Younghusband.

རུད་ (rüü) vi. to cave in, to crumble, to avalanche, to landslide ¶ གངས་རི་རུད་བཞག The snow mountain had an avalanche.

རུད་རྒྱག (rüü gyaà) vi. to avalanche, to landslide.

རུད་རུད་པོ་ (rüü rüübo) avalanche, landslide, cave in.

རུབ་ (rub) 1. va. to join up, to join together ¶ མི་ཚང་མས་ལས་ཀ་རུབ་ནས་བྱས་སོང་ All the people got together and worked. 2. hind. rupee.

རུབ་རྒོལ་ (rubgöö) joining together to attack; va.—བྱེད་.

རུབ་རྒྱག (rubgyaà) 1. va. to attack (in a gang), to gang up on ¶ ཁོ་ཚོས་མི་དེ་རུབ་བརྒྱབ་ནས་ཉེས་བཞག They ganged up on that person and beat him up. 2. sm. རུག.

རུབ་རྒྱག་གློད་ (rubgyaà lö̀ö) va. to gang up on.

རུབ་བཅོམ་ (rubjom) robbing done by a gang (rather than a single thief); va.—རྒྱག.

རུབ་ཆས་ (rubjɛɛ̀) sm. འགྲོ་ཆས་.

རུབ་གཏོར་ (rubdɔɔ) ganging up and destroying; va.—བྱེད་.

རུབ་སྡོད་ (rubdöö) staying together; va.—བྱེད་.

རུབ་འཛོམ་ (rubdzom) sm. རུག་འཛོམ་.

རུབ་རུབ་ (rubrub) sm. རུག་རུག.

རུབས་ (rub) sm. རུབ་.

རུམ་ (rum) 1. womb. 2. rug, carpet; va.—འཐག to weave a rug/ carpet. 3. bed ¶ ཁོ་རུམ་ལ་ཉལ་བཞག He slept in a bed. 4. va. to put to bed ¶ ཁོས་ཉལ་སའི་ནང་བུ་མོ་ཞིག་རུམ་བཞག He put the girl to sleep in the bed. 5. va. to hatch ¶ བྱ་མོས་སྒོ་ང་རུམ་འདུག The hen has hatched eggs. 6. a pocket, the pouch in a Tibetan dress.

རུམ་གྲི་ (rumdri) a knife kept in one's pocket, a knife kept in the pouch of a Tibetan dress.

རུམ་འཐག་མཁན་ (rum tāāñɛn) carpet/ rug weaver.

རུམ་འཐག་བཟོ་གྲྭ་ (rumdaà sodra) a rug weaving factory.

རུམ་དུ་འཛུག (rumdu juù) 1. va. to put in (one's) pocket. 2. vi. to become pregnant/ to conceive. 3. va. to put in bed.

རུམ་གདན་ (rumdɛn) woven carpet/ rug.

རུམ་མ་ (rummə) a pregnant woman.

རུའི་ཁལ་ (rü kɛ̀ɛ) the standardized ཁལ་ volume measure for grains (same as བསྟན་འཛིན་མཁར་རུ་).

རུའི་ཕུལ་ (rü pǖü) a volume unit equal to one sixth of a བྲེ་.

རུའི་བྲེ་ (rü tre) a volume unit equal to one twentieth of a ཁལ་.

རུའུ་ལུགས་རིགས་པ་ (rüluù rigbə) ch.tib. Confucianism.

རུའུ་སོན་ (rüsön) 1. sour curdled milk. 2. lactic acid.

རུའི་ཌེན་ (rüden) Sweden.

རུའི་ཧྲི་ (ruhri) Switzerland.

རུལ་ (rüü) 1. vi. to rot/ spoil/ decay/ decompose ¶ ཤ་འདི་མགྱོགས་པོ་རུལ་བཞག The meat spoiled quickly. ¶ ང་ཚོའི་གཞུང་རུལ་བཞག Our government has become rotten. 2. rotten, spoiled, decomposed ¶ ཤ་རུལ་ Rotten meat.

རུལ་སྐྱུར་ (rüügyur) rotten and sour.

རུལ་སྐྱོན་ (rüügyön) sm. རུལ་, 2.

རུལ་འགྱུར་འགོག (rüügyur gɔ̀ɔ) va. to stop sth. from decaying/ getting rotten.

རུལ་དྲི་ (rüüdri) the smell of sth. rotting/ decaying; vi.—ཁ་; —བྲོ་ to smell rotten/ decayed/ putrid.

རུལ་པ་ (rüübə) rotten ¶ ཤ་འདི་རུལ་པ་རེད་ This meat is rotten.

རུལ་པོ་ (rüübu) sm. རུལ་པ་.

རུལ་བར་འགྱུར་ (rüübar gyur) sm. རུལ་, 1.

རུལ་སྨན་ (rüümɛn) corrosive agent, corrodent.

རུལ་བཟོ་ (rüü so) va. to decay, to spoil. (e.g., when making some cheeses).

རུལ་ལད་ (rüülɛɛ̀) 1. rotten, spoiled. 2. sm. སྐྱོན་ཆ་.

རུལ་ལུད་ (rüülüü) manure, compost.

རུལ་སུངས་ (rüüsuŋ) putrid/ rotten smelling; vi.—ཁ་ to smell rotten/ putrid ¶ ཤ་འདི་ལ་རུལ་སུངས་ཁ་གི་འདུག The meat smelled putrid. 2. rotten, corrupt ¶ རུལ་སུངས་ཅན་གྱི་སྲིད་གཞུང་དེ་མགོ་རྟིང་བསློགས་པ་རེད་ The corrupt rotten government was overthrown.

རུལ་སུངས་འགོག་རྫས་ (rüüsuŋ gɔgdzɛɛ̀) antispoiling/ decaying agent, preservative.

རུལ་སུངས་ཚད་མེད་ (rüüsuŋ rsɛɛ̀meè) unlimited/ limitless corruption/ rotting/ getting spoiled.

རུལ་སུངས་སུ་འགྱུར་ (rüüsuŋsu gyur) vi. to become rotten/ spoiled, to become corrupt.

རུལ་བསླད་ (rüülɛɛ̀) making corrupt, spoiling; va.—གཏོང་ to corrupt ¶ བུད་མེད་ལ་བརྟེན་ནས་དམག་དཔུང་ལ་རུལ་བསླད་བཏང་བ་རེད་ (They) corrupted the army by means of women.

རུལ་ལྷུང་ (rüülhuŋ) corrupt, rotten, decadent.

རུས་ (rüü) 1. bone ¶ མི་རུས་ Human bone. 2. lineage, descent group, clan.

རུས་ཀོ་ (rüügo) sm. རུས་, 1.

རུས་ཀྲང་ (rüüdraŋ) skeleton.

རུས་དཀར་བདུད་མོ་ (rüügar düümu) the White Bone Demon (in the Chinese novel "Pilgrimage to the West").

རུས་རྐང་ (rüügaŋ) 1. bone marrow. 2. human thigh bone. 3. human thigh bone trumpet.

རུས་རྐྱང་ (rüügyaŋ) only the bones themselves.

རུས་སྐྱ་ (rüügya) oars (of a boat).

རུས་བཀྲ་ (rüüdra) drawing of the human skeleton structure.

རུས་སྐོགས་ཅན་གྱི་སྲོག་ཆགས་ (rüügɔ̀jɛngi sōgjaà) crustaceans.

རུས་བཀོས་རྩིས་འབྲས་ (rüügɔ̀ dzīndrɛɛ̀) bone divination.

རུས་བཀོས་ཡི་གེ་ (rüügöò yigi) the inscriptions/ marks on bones and tortoise shells that are read in divination.

རུས་ཁུ་ (rüügu) broth made from bones.

རུས་ཁུངས་ (rüüguŋ) lineage, descent group/ line.

རུས་ཁུངས་གཙང་མ་ (rüüguŋ dzāŋma) a clean lineage/ descent group/ line (i.e., not impure like blacksmiths, butchers, etc.).

རུས་ཁོག (rüügɔ̀ɔ) 1. sm. རུས་.

རུས་ཁོག་པགས་བདུམས་ (rüügɔ̀ bāgdum) sm. རུས་པ་པགས་བདུམས་.

རུས་མཁྲེགས་ (rüüdreg) sm. རུས་པ་མཁྲེགས་པོ་.

རུས་གོང་ (rüügoŋ) sm. རུས་, 1.

རུས་གྱོང་པོ་ (rüü gyoŋbo) stubborn, headstrong.

རུས་གླིང་ (rüüliŋ) bone flute.

རུས་མགོ་ལྤགས་གཡོགས་ (rüügo bāgyɔ̀ɔ) very skinny/ thin [Lit. bones covered with skin].

རུས་རྒན་ (rüügɛn) lineage elder, clan elder.

རུས་རྒྱན་ (rüügyɛn) full length necklace made from bones (used in Tantric Buddhism).

རུས་རྒྱུད་ (rüügyüü) lineage, clan, descent group.

རུས་རྒྱུད་འཁྲིད་ (rüügyüü trīī) vi. to inherit the genetic characteristics of one's forefathers.

རུས་རྒྱུད་སྤྱི་ཚོགས་ (rüügyüü jīdzoò) clan organized society, tribal society.

རུས་རྒྱུད་ཚོ་པ་ (rüügyüü tsōba) tribe based on a lineage or clan.

རུས་རྒྱུད་ལམ་ལུགས་ (rüügyüü ləmluù) clan/ lineage system.

རུས་སྒྲོམ་ (rüüdrom) bone frame, skeleton.

རུས་གཅིག་པ་ (rüü jīgbə) kinsman.

རུས་བཅག་རྐང་འཇིབ་ (rüüjaà gāŋjib) excessively oppressive, cruelly exploiting. [Lit. break bones and suck marrow].

རུས་ཆག (rüüjaà) broken bone; vi.—ཤོར་ to break a bone; va.— མཐུད་ to join/ set a (broken) bone.

རུས་ཆས་ (rüüjɛɛ̀) things made from bone.

རུས་ཆེན་ (rüüjen) 1. big bone. 2. high caste/ lineage.

རུས་ཆོད་ (rüü cöö) vi. to be completely cured.

རུས་འཆིང་ (rüüjiŋ) binding broken bones; va.—རྒྱག.

རུས་སྙིའི་ནད་ (rüüñii nɛɛ̀) osteomalacia.

རུས་བརྡོག་རྒྱག (rüüdoò gyaà) va. to gnaw on bones.

རུས་ཐང་ (rüüdaŋ) soup/ broth made from boiled bones.

རུས་ཐལ་ (rüütɛɛ) bones and ashes (usu. after a cremation), the ashes from bones.

རུས་ཐོན་ (rüü tön) vi. to shown a clear sign ¶ ཁོང་ནི་དགྲ་གཉེན་གང་ལ་ཡང་ཆགས་སྡང་གི་རུས་ཐོན་པའི་མི་ཞིག་རེད་ He is a person who shows a clear signs of love towards one's relatives and hatred towards one's enemies.

རུས་མཐོ་ (rüüto) high birth/ lineage/ caste.

རུས་མཐུད་ཐེབས་ (rüütüü tēb) vi. to have a bone that was broken heal (join back together) naturally.

རུས་འཐོག (rüüdɔ̀ɔ) gnawing; va.—རྒྱག to gnaw on bones.

རུས་གདོང་ (rüüdoŋ) shin bone.

རུས་བདག (rüüdaà) lineage head, clan elder.

རུས་སྡོར་ (rüüdɔr) bones put in broth/ soup.

རུས་པ་ (rüübə) sm. རུས་.

རུས་པ་དཀར་པོ་ (rüübə gārbo) 1. white bone. 2. sm. རིགས་རུས་གཙང་མ་.

རུས་པ་མཁྲེགས་པ་ (rüübə trēgba) a person of strong character and convictions (a positive connotation) ¶ ཁོང་ནི་རུས་པ་མཁྲེགས་པའི་མི་ཞིག་ཡིན་ཙང་དགྲ་བོའི་འཇིགས་སྐུལ་གྱི་འོག་ཏུ་མགོ་སྒུར་མེད་ Because he is person of strong character, he did not surrender under the enemy's threat.

རུས་པ་གྱོང་པོ་ (rüübə gyoŋbo) sm. གཤིས་ཀ་གྱོང་པོ་.

རུས་པ་ཅན་ (rüübəjɛn) 1. diligent. 2. loyal.

རུས་པ་ཆག (rüübə cāà) vi. to break a bone.

རུས་པ་ཆག་མཐུད་ (rüübə cāgdüü) joining/ setting a broken bone; va.—བྱེད་.

རུས་པ་མཉེན་པོ་ (rüübə ñēnbo) brittle bones.

རུས་པ་མཐུད་ (rüübə tüü) sm. རུས་ཆག་མཐུད་.

རུས་པ་པགས་བདུམས་ (rüübə bāgdum) extremely thin [Lit. bone wrapped in skin].

རུས་པ་འབྲུད་ (rüübə drɛɛ̀) sm. རུས་བཅག་རྒྱག.

རུས་པ་གཞུང་ཆག (rüübə shuŋjaà) horizontal fracture of the bone.

རུས་པའི་དྲ་ཕྱེད་ (rüübɛ trajeè) beads made of bones that are worn by tantric practitioners.

རུས་པའི་དྲ་བ་ (rüübɛ trawa) རུས་པའི་དྲ་ཕྱེད་.

རུས་པའི་པ་ཏ་ (rüübɛ bādra) bone lattice.

རུས་སྤྱད་ (rüüjɛɛ̀) bone implements.

རུས་སྤྱིན་ (rüüjin) glue made from bones.

རུས་སྤྱིན་བཟོ་གྲྭ་ (rujin sodra) bone glue factory.

རུས་ཕྱེ་ (rüüce) powdered/ pulverized bones.

རུས་བུ་ (rüübu) small bones.

རུས་དབང་ (rüüwaŋ) clan authority.

རུས་འབྲུད་རྒྱག (rüüdrɛɛ̀ gyaà) sm. རུས་བཅག་རྒྱག.

རུས་སྦལ་ (rüübɛɛ) turtle, tortoise.

རུས་སྦལ་གྱེན་དུ་འགྲོད་པ་བཞིན་ (rüübɛɛ gyendu dröòbashin) doing sth. slowly/ gradually [Lit. a turtle going uphill].

རུས་སྦལ་ཅན་ (rüübɛɛjɛn) the 4th month of the Tibetan calendar.

རུས་མིག (rüümiì) bone joint.

རུས་མིང་ (rüümiŋ) 1. clan name. 2. family name, surname.

རུས་སྨྱོ་ (rüüño) a kind of bone disease.

རུས་ཚན་ (rüüdzɛn) paternal/ patrilateral relatives.

རུས་ཚི་གཉེན་ཚན་ (rüüdzi ñēndzɛn) relatives and clansmates.

རུས་ཚིགས་ (rüüdzii) bone joint; vi.—ན་ to be ill with arthritis.

རུས་ཚིགས་ཀྱི་ནད་ (rüüdziigi nɛɛ̀) arthritis.

རུས་ཚིགས་སྐྲང་ནད་ (rüüdzii drāŋnɛɛ̀) disease characterized by swollen joints.

རུས་རྩུགས་ (rüüdzuù) bone structure.

རུས་ཚོ་ (rüüdzo)1. paternal relatives. 2. a tribe/ group based on a patrilineal descent.

རུས་འཛེར་ (rüü dzer) thickening of the bones at the joint where it was broken.

རུས་ཞག (rüüshaà) 1. bone marrow. 2. the fat that is extracted after boiling bones.

རུས་ཞེན་ (rüüshen) loyalty to one's lineage/ clan/ tribe.

རུས་གཞོང་ (rüüshoŋ) pelvis.

རུས་ཟུག (rüüsuù) aches/ pain in the bone/ joints; vi.—རྒྱག to have pain in the bones/ joints ¶ རུས་ཟུག་རྒྱག་པའི་གྲང་ལྷང་ Freezing cold air that causes the bones to ache.

རུས་ཟུག་གྲང་ངད་ (rüüsuù traŋŋɛɛ̀) extreme cold (cold that makes the bones pain).

རུས་ཟོང་ (rüüsoŋ) small shells, cowry shells.

རུས་གཟེབ་ (rüüseb) the space between the bone/ joints.

རུས་རིགས་ (rüürig) sm. རུས་རྒྱུད་.

རུས་རིགས་འཁྲིལ་ (rüürii kēl) sm. རུས་རྒྱུད་འཁྲིད་.

རུས་ལུད་ (rüülüü) bone fertilizer.

རུས་ལེབ་སོག་ལེ་ཁ་ཅན་ (rüüleb sòòle kājɛn) an ancient weapon made from bone with saw-shaped edges (teeth).

རུས་ཤིང་ (rüüshiŋ) sm. སྟོག་ཤིང་.

རུས་བཤུས་རྒྱག (rüüshüü gyaà) sm. རུས་འབྲུད་རྒྱག.

རུས་གསེབ་ (rüüseb) inside of bones.

རེ་ (re) 1. each, every ¶ ཉིན་རེ་ Each day. ¶ གནས་ཚུལ་དེ་འདྲ་རེ་བྱུང་ཚེ་དམག་མི་ཁྲིན་ཆེ་བཏང་ནས་ཁུལ་དེར་དག་གནོན་རེ་བྱེད་པ་རེད་ Each time an event like that occurred, many Chinese soldiers would be sent to these regions to forcibly put it down. 2. (vb. + —) worth doing verbal action ¶ ལས་ཀ་འདི་བྱེད་རེ་ཡོད་པ་རེད་ This work is worth doing. 3. particles for the sixties ¶ དྲུག་ཅུ་རེ་གཅིག Sixty one. 4. abbr. for རེ་བ་. 5. va. to depend on ¶ ཁྱེད་རང་མི་ལ་རེ་དགོས་མ་རེད་ You don't have to depend on others.

རེ་སྐན་ (regɛn) (vb. + —) a term conveying absolutely not ¶ ལས་ཀ་དེ་ངས་བྱེད་རེ་སྐན་ I absolutely will not do that work. ¶ གནས་ཚུལ་དེ་བྱུང་ཡོད་རེ་སྐན་ I swear that event never occurred.

རེ་སྐྱེལ་ (regɛɛ) sm. རེ་བསྐྱལ་.

རེ་ཀྲི་ཡོའོ་ (dedreyo) eng. radio.

རེ་སྐོང་ (regoŋ) granting/ satisfying/ fulfilling a wish ¶ གོང་རིམ་ནས་ངའི་རེ་སྐོང་གནང་བྱུང་ The higher authorities fulfilled my wish.

རེ་བསྐུལ་ (regüü) request, favor; va.—ཞུ་; —བྱེད་ to make a request, to ask a favor ¶ ངས་ཁོང་ལ་ལས་ཀ་ཞིག་གནང་རོགས་ཟེར་རེ་སྐུལ་ཞུས་པ་ཡིན་ I asked a favor of him, "Please give me a job."

རེ་སྐྱབས་ཞུ་ (regyəb shu) 1. va. to request help/ support, to seek refuge ¶ བོད་པ་ཚོས་བོད་ནས་བྲོས་ཏེ་རྒྱ་གར་ལ་རེ་སྐྱབས་ཞུས་པ་རེད་ The Tibetans fled Tibet and sought refuge in India.

རེ་ཁ་ (rega) sm. རེ་མོ་.

རེ་ཁྲལ་མཉམ་འདྲུག (redrɛɛ ñamjug) hoping and worrying at the same time.

རེ་འཁང་ (regaŋ) frustrated/ angry because one's request was not granted.

རེ་འཁོན་ (regön) hope and hatred.

རེ་གྲོན་ (redrön) 1. hopeless, an empty hope. 2. sm. དོན་མེད་འགྲོ་སོང་.

རེ་དགོངས་ (regoŋ) sm. རེ་སེམས་.

རེ་འགའ་ (renga) a few, some.

རེ་སྒུག (reguù) waiting for a wish/ hope; va.—བྱེད་ to wait in hope of sth. happening ¶ རས་ཕྱིང་པ་གཅིག་བཏིང་ནས་སྦྱིན་པའི་རེ་སྒུག་བྱས་པ་རེད་ (They) laid out a piece of cloth and waited in hope of getting alms.

རེ་ངན་ (reŋɛn) evil or malicious intent/ scheme/ hope/ plan, conspiracy; va.—འཆང་ to hold an evil or malicious intent/ schemes/ plan, to conspire ¶ ཀུན་མ་ཀུ་རྒྱུའི་རེ་ངན་བཅངས་པ་རེད་ (They) held the evil hope of stealing.

རེ་ངན་ཁོག་བཅངས་ (reŋɛn kōgjaŋ) holding evil or malicious intent/ schemes/ plans (inside/ secret).

རེ་ལྕུག (rejaà) Euphorbia fisheriana.

རེ་གཅིག (rejig) 1. emphatically/ insistingly asking sb. to do a favor; va.—བྱེད་ ¶ ཁྱེད་རང་གིས་ཁོང་ལ་རེ་གཅིག་བྱས་ན་རོགས་པ་བྱེད་ངེས་རེད་ If you ask him emphatically, he will definitely help. 2. sixty one.

རེ་བཅོལ་རེ་སྐུལ་ (rejöö regüü) sm. རེ་སྐུལ་.

རེ་འཆར་ (renjar) hoping/ aspiring for; va.—འཛིན་ to hope for, to hold a hope, to aspire to ¶ ཁོང་གི་ཕྲུ་གུ་མགྱོགས་མྱུར་སློབ་གྲྭ་ཐོན་རྒྱུའི་རེ་འཆར་འཛིན་བཞིན་པ་རེད་ He hopes his child will graduate soon.

རེ་གཉིས་ (reñii) one or two, a few ¶ ཉི་མ་རེ་གཉིས་ཀྱི་རྗེས་སུ་ After a few days.

རེ་གཉིས་ཙམ་ (reñiidzam) sm. རེ་གཉིས་.

རེ་ད་ (reda) sm. རེ་ལྡི་.

རེ་ལྟོས་ (redöö) hope, expectation; va.—བྱེད་ to hope for, to expect (from), to look forward for help, to depend on ¶ ཨུ་རུ་སུ་ལ་རེ་ལྟོས་བྱེད་མི་དགོས་ We do not have to look to Russia for help.

རེ་ལྟོས་འཆའ་ཡུལ་ (redöö cāyüü) a person on whom one depends/ counts/ relies.

རེ་སྟོང་ (redoŋ) 1. empty/ illusory hope; va.—འཆང་; —བྱེད་ to hold an empty hope; vi.—དུ་འགྱུར་; —དུ་འགྲོ་ to become hopeless ¶ ཁོ་ཚོ་རྩ་མེད་གཏོང་རྒྱུའི་རེ་སྟོང་འཆང་གི་ཡོད་པ་རེད་ Holding the illusion of (being able to) annihilate them. ¶ ཁོས་བུ་མོ་དེ་ཆང་ས་རྒྱག་བསམ་པ་དེ་རེ་སྟོང་དུ་གྱུར་པ་རེད་ His hope of marrying the girl has become hopeless.

རེ་སྟོང་འཆང་ (redoŋ) see རེ་སྟོང་.

རེ་སྟོང་བཅངས་ (redoŋ jāŋ) p. of རེ་སྟོང་འཆང་.

རེ་ལྟོས་ (redöö) counting on, depending/ relying on.

རེ་ཐག་ཆད་ (redaà cɛɛ̀) vi. to have given up all hopes.

རེ་ཐག་ཆོད་ (redaà cöö) sm. རེ་ཐག་ཆད་.

རེ་དུག་རེ་ལྕུག (reduù rejaà) Euphorbia fisheriana.

རེ་དོགས་ (redɔɔ) hopes and fears/ doubts.

རེ་དོན་ (redön) hope, wish; vi.—འགྲུབ་ to achieve/ get one's hope, to have a hope fulfilled.

རེ་དྭོགས་ (redɔɔ) sm. རེ་དོགས་.

རེ་འདུན་ (rendön) hope, wish; va.—འདོན་ —ཞུ་ to

request/ ask sb. to fulfill a hope/ wish; va.—འཆང་ to hope for sth. ¶ངའི་ཕ་ཡུལ་ལ་ལོག་རྒྱུ་ཡོང་བའི་རེ་འདུན་འཆང་བཞིན་ཡོད་ I hope to return to my native homeland. ¶ངས་ཁོང་ལ་དངུལ་གཡར་རོགས་ཞེར་རེ་འདུན་བཏོན་པ་ཡིན་ I asked him to lend me money.

རེ་འདུན་ནན་པོ་ (rendün nɛnbo) fervently hope, ardently wish.

རེ་འདུན་ཞུ་ཡིག (rendün shuyii) written petition, application seeking sth.

རེ་ལྡེ་ (rede) 1. coarse material woven from yak hair. 2. bamboo basket.

རེ་འདོད་ (rendöö) hope, wish ¶རེ་འདོད་བྲལ་བའི་གནས་ A hopeless state.

རེ་ནག (renaà) sm. རེ་ལྡེ་.

རེ་ནན་ཞུ་ (renɛn shu) va. to make an earnest request.

རེ་ནས་ (renɛ) from each/ every ¶ལོ་རེ་ནས་སྒོར་ 100 སྣར་རྒྱུ་ཡིན་ Each year (we) will increase (it) by 100 dollars.

རེ་ནས་ཙམ་ (renɛɛ̀dzam) just one or two, just a couple.

རེ་གནས་ (renɛɛ̀) sm. རེ་ལྟོས་འཆའ་ཡུལ་.

རེ་སྣམ་ (renam) woven yak hair fabric.

རེ་ཕད་ (rebɛɛ̀) sack, bag.

རེ་ཕྱར་ (rejar) large sheet of yak hair cloth (used for drying grains, cheese, etc.).

རེ་བ་ (rewa) 1. hope, wish; va.—བྱེད་ to hope/ wish for; va.—འཛིན་; —འཆང་ to hold hopes/ wishes; va.—སྐོང་ to fulfill/ satisfy a hope; va.—འདོན་ to express a wish/ hope ¶ཕྲུ་གུ་དེ་སློབ་གྲྭ་མཐོ་པོ་ཐོན་པའི་རེ་བ་བྱེད་ཀྱི་ཡོད་པ་རེད་ The child hopes to graduate from college (in the future). ¶གོང་རིམ་ནས་ངའི་གླ་ཕོགས་སྤོར་དགོས་པའི་རེ་བ་བསྐངས་བྱུང་ The authorities fulfilled my request (hope) that my salary be increased. 2. sm. རེ་ལྡེ་.

རེ་བ་སྐོང་ (rewa gōŋ) see རེ་བ་.

རེ་བ་འགྲུབ་ (rewa drub) vi. to have one's hope/ wish be fulfilled.

རེ་བ་བཅོལ་ས་ (rew jöösa) sm. རེ་ལྟོས་འཆའ་ཡུལ་.

རེ་བ་འཆོལ་ (rewa cöö) sm. རེ་ལྟོས་བྱེད་.

རེ་བ་སྟོང་པ་ (rewa dōŋba) sm. རེ་སྟོང་.

རེ་བ་སྟོང་ཟད་ (rewa dōŋsɛɛ̀) being disappointed (in one's hopes); va.—དུ་གཏོང་ to cause disappointment, to cause sb. to lose hope; vi.—དུ་འགྱུར་ to come to lose hope ¶ཁོང་ལ་བུ་མོ་དེ་རག་ནི་བསམ་པ་རེ་བ་སྟོང་ཟད་དུ་གྱུར་པ་རེད་ He lost all hope of getting that girl.

རེ་བ་ནན་པོ་ (rewa nɛmbo) urgent hope/wish; va.—ཞུ་.

རེ་བ་བྱེད་ (rewa cee) see རེ་བ་.

རེ་བ་མེད་པ་ (rewa meèba) see རེ་མེད་.

རེ་བ་རྫོགས་ (rewa dzɔɔ̀) 1. vi. to lose all hope. 2. vi. to have all one's wishes/ hopes fulfilled.

རེ་བ་ཞུ་ (rewa shu) see རེ་བ་.

རེ་བ་ཟད་ (rewa sɛɛ̀) vi. to lose all hopes.

རེ་བྲལ་ (remdrɛɛ) having no hope, hopeless.

རེ་བློ་ (relo) sm. རེ་བ་.

རེ་འབོད་ (remböö) appealing, calling; va.—བྱེད་ to appeal to/ for, to issue a call for ¶མི་མང་གིས་ཞི་བདེ་ཡོང་བའི་རེ་འབོད་བྱེད་ཀྱི་ཡོད་པ་རེད་ The people are appealing for peace.

རེ་འབྱམས་ (renjam) crocodile, alligator.

རེ་འབྲས་ (rendrɛɛ̀) sm. རེ་བ་.

རེ་འབྲས་དོན་སྨིན་ (rendrɛɛ̀ tönmin) realizing one's hope/ wish.

རེ་མང་ (remaŋ) sb. having many hopes and wants; va.—བྱེད་.

རེ་མིག (rimii) sm. རེའུ་མིག.

རེ་མེད་ (remeè) hopeless, without hope.

རེ་མེད་ཐབས་མེད་ (remeè tābmeè) a hopeless situation (without hope or the means to do sth.).

རེ་མེད་སྤོབས་མེད་ (remeè bōbmeè) without hope or inclination/ motivation, in a state of depressed inertia; va.—བྱེད་; —འཆང་ ¶ཁྱེད་རང་རེ་མེད་སྤོབས་མེད་མ་བྱེད་ཡིག་ཚད་གཏན་གཏན་ལོན་གྱི་རེད་ Don't stay in a state of depression, you will definitely pass the exam.

རེ་མོས་ (remöö) alternating, by turns; va.—བྱེད་ to do by turns, to alternate ¶བཟོ་པ་ཚོས་ཉིན་མཚན་རེ་མོས་ཀྱིས་ལས་ཀ་བྱེད་ཀྱི་ཡོད་པ་རེད་ The workers alternate working days and nights.

རེ་དམིགས་ (remii) hopes and goals/ objectives/ aims.

རེ་རྨ་ (rema) arc. sm. བུད་མེད་.

རེ་སྨོན་ (remön) hoping and praying; va.—བྱེད་; —ཞུ་ ¶ཁྱེད་རང་སྐུ་གཟུགས་བདེ་པོ་ཡོང་བའི་སྨོན་འདུན་ཞུ་གི་ཡོད་ I hope and pray you will be well.

རེ་ཙམ་ (redzam) a few, one or two.

རེ་ཙམ་གཉིས་ཙམ་ (redzam ñiidzan) one or two, a few.

རེ་ཚིག (redzii) words expressing a wish/ hope.

རེ་ཞིག (reshii) for awhile, temporarily ¶ང་རེ་ཞིག་ཨ་རིར་སྡོད་རྩིས་ཡོད་ I plan to stay in America for awhile. ¶རེ་ཞིག་ཐོན་སྐྱེད་ཐོག་དཀའ་ངལ་བྱུང་བ་རེད་ They encountered difficulties in production for a short time.

རེ་ཞིག་དར་ཁྱབ་ (reshii targyəb) the rage, in fashion/ vogue.

རེ་ཞིག་དར་བ་ (reshii tarwa) sm. རེ་ཞིག་དར་ཁྱབ་.

རེ་ཞིག་བར་ (reshiiwar) sm. རེ་ཞིག.

རེ་ཞིག་རིང་ (reshiiriŋ) sm. རེ་ཞིག.

རེ་བཞིན་ (reshin) each one ¶ཟླ་རེ་བཞིན་ Each month.

རེ་ཞུ་བྱེད་ (reshu ceè) sm. རེ་བ་ཞུ་.

རེ་ཟུང་ (resuŋ) 1. one or two, a few, a little.

རེ་ཡུལ་ (reyüü) sm. རེ་ལྟོས་འཆའ་ཡུལ་.

རེ་རེ་ (rere) each ¶མི་རེ་རེ་ལ་དངུལ་སྤྲད་པ་རེད་ (They) gave money to each person. ¶མི་རེ་རེས་དེབ་རེ་རེ་ཉོས་པ་རེད་ Each person bought a book.

རེ་རེ་གཉིས་གཉིས་ (rere ñiiñii) 1. sm. རེ་གཉིས་. 2. one by one, one after another ¶ངས་ལས་ཁུངས་ཀྱི་ཅ་ལག་རྣམས་རེ་རེ་གཉིས་གཉིས་བྱས་ནས་རྩིས་སྤྲད་པ་ཡིན་ I turned over all the office's things one by one to him.

རེ་རེ་བྱས་ནས་ (rere cɛɛ̀nɛ) one by one ¶མི་རེ་རེ་བྱས་ནས་དངུལ་ལེན་དགོས་རེད་ (You) have to get the money from each person one by one.

རེ་རེ་བྱེད་ (rere ceè) sm. རེ་རེ་བྱས་.

རེ་རེ་བཞིན་ (rēreshin) one by one, bit by bit ¶ནོར་འཁྲུལ་ཡོད་པ་ཤེས་རྗེས་རེ་རེ་བཞིན་ལེགས་བཅོས་བཏང་བ་རེད་ After finding the mistakes (they) corrected them one by one.

རེ་རེ་རེ་རེ་བྱེད་ (rere rēre ceè) sm. རེ་རེ་བྱས་.

རེ་རེའི་གོང་ (reree koŋ) unit price, price of each.

རེ་རེར་ (reree) to each ¶མི་རེ་རེར་སྤྲད་པ་རེད་ (They) gave (it) to each person.

རེ་རེས་ (rereè) by each ¶མི་རེ་རེས་བྱས་པ་རེད་ Each person did it.

རེ་ཤིག (reshig) sm. རེ་ཞིག.

རེ་ས་ (resa) sm. རེ་ཡུལ་.

རེ་ས་རྟེན་ས་མེད་པ་ (resa dēnsa meèba) having no one or place to turn to.

རེ་ས་ལྟོས་ས་ (resa dōōsa) sm. རེ་ཡུལ་.

རེ་ས་སྡོད་ས་ (resa döōsa) sm. རེ་ཡུལ་.

རེ་སེམས་ (resem) sm. རེ་བ་.

རེ་ཧོ་ (reho) Jehol Province.

རེ་ཧོ་ཙེའི་མཚོན་ཆ་ (reho dzīī tsōnja) ch.tib. thermonuclear weapon.

རེག (reg) va. to touch ¶ཁོས་ང་ར་ལག་པ་རེག་བྱུང་ He touched me.

རེག་འཁྱུད་ (reggyüü) hugging.

རེག་དགའ་ (regga) prostitute.

རེག་འཇམ་ (regjam) soft (to the touch).

རེག་དུག (regduù) 1. any disease transmitted by contact. 2. venereal disease (syphilis, gonorrhea).

རེག་ནད་ (regnɛɛ̀) sm. རེག་དུག.

རེག་བྱ་ (regja) sense of touch/ feeling.

རེག་བྱ་བཅུ་གཅིག (regja jūgjii) the eleven sensations: earth, water, fire, wind, soft, coarse, light (weight), cold, heavy, hunger and thirst.

རེག་བྱ་དྲུག (reja truù) the six sensations: soft, coarse, light, heavy, cold, hunger/ thirst.

རེག་བྱེད་དབང་པོ་ (regja wāŋbo) sense of touch.

རེག་ཚོར་ (regdzɔr) sm. རེག་བྱ་.

རེག་ཚོར་གསུམ་ (regdzɔɔ sūm) the three feelings: happiness, suffering, and equanimity.

རེག་འཛིན་ (reŋdzin) sm. རེག་དགའ་.

རེག་ཟིན་ (regsin) arc. sm. ཟིན་བྲིས་.

རེགས་ (reg) va. to cut.

རེང་ (reŋ) sm. རེངས་.

རེང་བ་ (reŋwa) sm. རེངས་པོ་.

རེང་བུ་ (reŋbu) alone, individually.

རེངས་ (reŋ) vi. to become rigid/ stiff/ hard ¶ཀོ་བ་དེ་རེངས་བཞག The leather has become stiff. 2. vi. to become frozen ¶ཤ་ཁོག་དེ་ཁང་པའི་ཕྱི་ལ་བཞག་ཙང་རེངས་འདུག Because (they) put the carcass outside, it has frozen. 3. vi. to coagulate ¶དྭ་ལྔ་མར་ཁུ་རེངས་མི་འདུག The melted butter is not now coagulated. 4. vi. to be stubborn/ inflexible.

རེངས་འཁུམས་ (reŋ kūm) vi. to become rigid/ stiff and unable to straighten out (usu. legs).

རེངས་པའི་རང་བཞིན་ (reŋbɛ rəŋshin) nature of solidification/ coagulation.

རེངས་པོ་ (reŋbo) 1. rigid, stiff, hard. 2. sm. སྲོང་པོ་. 3. inflexible; vi.—འགྱུར་ to become inflexible/ deadlocked (politically).

རེངས་པོའི་གནས་རྩུལ་ (reŋbö nɛ̀ɛdzüü) deadlock, stalemate.

རེངས་པོར་གནས་ (reŋbɔɔ nɛ̀ɛ) 1. vi. to be deadlocked/ stalemated. 2. vi. to become rigid/ stiff/ hard.

རེངས་བསླད་ (reŋlɛ̀ɛ) spoiled (behaviorally).

རེད་ (reè) 1. linking verb "is" ¶འདི་དེབ་རེད་ This is a book. 2. auxillary verb in present, past and future verb complements ¶ཁོས་ལས་ཀ་བྱས་པ་རེད་ He worked. ¶ཁོས་ལས་ཀ་བྱེད་ཀྱི་རེད་ He will work.

རེད་དམ་ (reèdam) interrogative form of རེད་ ¶འདི་དེབ་རེད་དམ་ Is this a book?

རེད་འདུག (reè duù) is (conveys more certainty than རེད་ alone) ¶ཁོང་རྒྱ་རིགས་རེད་འདུག He is Chinese.

རེད་པས་ (rebɛ) sm. རེད་དམ་.

རེད་མ་རེད་ (reè mareè) whether it is or not ¶ཁོ་བོད་པ་རེད་མ་རེད་ངས་མི་ཤེས་ I don't know whether or not he is Tibetan.

རེད་མི་འདུག (reè minduù) sth. definitely is not ¶ལས་ཁུངས་ལ་མེ་ཤོར་བ་དེ་ཁོང་གི་ཉེས་སྐྱོན་རེད་མི་འདུག The fire in the office definitely was not his fault.

རེན་མིན་ (renmin) ch. people ¶རེན་མིན་ཀུང་ཧྲེ་ people's commune.

རེམ་: p. རེམས་; f. རེམ་; imp. རེམས་ (rem) 1. va. to concentrate one's mind ¶ཁོང་དེ་རིང་སློབ་སྦྱོང་ཐོག་རེམ་གྱི་ཡོད་པ་རེད་ ¶Nowadays he is concentrating his mind on his studies. 2. va. to work hard ¶ཁྱེད་རང་ལས་ཀར་རེམས་དགོས་ You should work hard.

རེམ་མ་ (remma) quickly, fast, hurrying up ¶དུ་རེམ་མ་མེ་གཏོང་ Hurry up and light the fire.

རེམ་རེམ་ (remrem) diligent, industrious.

རེམས་ (rem) p. and imp. of རེམ་.

རེའི་དར་ (reedar) eng. radar.

རེའུ་ (riwu) a baby goat, kid.

རེའུ་དཀར་ (riwugar) a type of ancient white woven material.

རེའུ་མིག (riwumii) 1. chart, table, diagram, graph, form.

རེའུ་མིག་བཀོད་འབུལ་ (riwumii gōmbüü) filling in a form and submitting it to the authorities.

རེའུ་མིག་དེབ་ཐོ་ (riwumii tebdo) books containing figures, charts, tables (usu. statistics).

རེའུ་ལུག (riwuluù) lambs and kids.

རེར་ (ree) to/ in/ for each ¶ལོ་རེར་ In each year. ¶དམག་རྒྱག་ཐེངས་རེར་རྒྱལ་ཁ་ཆེན་པོ་ཐོབ་པ་རེད་ In each battle they won a great victory.

རེས་ (reè) 1. by each ¶མི་རེས་བྱས་པ་རེད་ Each person did it. 2. (vb. + — + བྱེད་) to do reciprocally/ in turns/ back and forth ¶ཁོང་ཚོས་ཕན་ཚུན་ཆང་འབུལ་རེས་བྱས་པ་རེད་ They gave (each other) ཆང་ back and forth. ¶ལག་གཏོང་རེས་གནང་པ་རེད་ (They) exchanged handshakes.

རེས་སྐོར་ (reègɔɔ) turning, shifting, rotating, va.—བྱེད་ to do in shifts, to do by rotation, to do in turns ¶གཡོག་པོ་ཚོས་རེས་སྐོར་བྱས་ནས་མགྲོན་པོར་ཆང་ཞུགས་སོང་ The servants served the ཆང་ to the guests in turns. ¶རེས་སྐོར་དང་པོ་ First shift.

རེས་སྐོར་ཀྲུའུ་རིན་ (reègɔɔ drūrin) tib. ch. production/ shift manager.

རེས་སྐོར་འགྲན་སྡུར་ (reègɔɔ drendur) round robin contest.

རེས་སྐོར་སྦྱོང་བརྡར་ (reègɔɔ joŋdar) rotation training (either training a person on different things on a rotation basis or training a group of people by rotating a portion at any one time for training).

རེས་འཁོར་ (reègɔɔ) sm. རེས་སྐོར་.

རེས་འཁྱག་རེས་ཚ་ (reègyaà reèdza) abruptly changing temperature (sometimes hot, sometime cold).

རེས་འགའ་ (rengaa) sometimes, occasionally ¶མི་དེས་རེས་འགའ་གཞས་གཏོང་བ་དང་རེས་འགའ་གད་མོ་དགོད་ཀྱི་འདུག Sometimes he sings songs and sometimes he laughs.

རེས་སྒྲུབ་ (reèdrub) rotating, taking turns, in shifts; va.—བྱེད་ ¶བཟོ་པ་ཚོས་བཟོ་གྲྭའི་ལས་ཀ་རེས་སྒྲུབ་བྱེད་ཀྱི་ཡོད་པ་རེད་ The workers work in the factory in shifts.

རེས་གཅིག (reèjig) once.

རེས་འཇོག (renjɔɔ̀) doing things in alternation/ rotation ¶ང་ཚོང་ཁང་ལ་གཟའ་འཁོར་རེས་འཇོག་བྱས་ནས་འགྲོ་གི་ཡོད་ I go for shopping at the store in alternate weeks. ¶ཞིང་ཁ་འདི་ཚོ་ལོ་དུས་འདེབས་རེས་འཇོག་བྱེད་ཀྱི་ཡོད་པ་རེད་ They plant the fields in rotation (by years).

རེས་སྡབས་ (reèdəb) sm. རེས་མོས་.

རེས་འདེབས་ (rendeb) crop rotation; va.—བྱེད་ to rotate crops.

རེས་བྱེད་ (reèjeè) see རེས་.

རེས་སྦྱོང་ (reèjoŋ) sm. རེས་སྐོར་སྦྱོང་བརྡར་.

རེས་མ་ (reèma) 1. sm. བུད་མེད་. 2. whore, prostitute.

རེས་མོས་ (reèmöö) rotation, rotating, by turns, in shifts; va.—བྱེད་ to rotate, to take turns, to do in shifts, to alternate.

རེས་མོས་ངལ་གསོ་ (reèmöö ŋɛɛso) resting in turn, taking a day off or a holiday in turn; va.—རྒྱག.

རེས་མོས་སྡོད་བྱ་ (reèmöö dööja) on duty by turns; va.—བྱེད་.

རེས་གཟའ་ (reèsa) day (of the week) ¶རེས་གཟའ་ཟླ་བ་ Monday.

རེས་གཟའ་ལྷའི་བླ་མ་ (rɛ̀ɛsa lhē lāma) shung. Thursday.

རེས་གསོ་ (reèso) raising/ feeding in rotation or in alternation; va.—བྱེད་ ¶བཟའ་ཚང་ཁ་བྲལ་རྗེས་ཕ་མ་གཉིས་ཀྱིས་ཕྲུ་གུ་རེས་གསོ་བྱེད་ཀྱི་ཡོད་པ་རེད་ After the couple got divorced, they alternated raising the child.

རོ་ (ro) 1. corpse. 2. taste, flavor ¶ཁ་ལག་འདི་རོ་ཞིམ་པོ་འདུག This food tastes good. 3. dregs, waste, residue, remains ¶ཤོག་རོ་ Waste paper. 4. sentence final particle used after words ending in ར་.

རོ་སྐམ་ (rogam) dried/ dessicated corpse.

རོ་བསྐམས་ (rogam) deserted place.

རོ་སྐོར་ (rogɔɔ) examining the place sb. was killed; va.—རྒྱག.

རོ་སྐྱུར་ (rogyur) sour taste.

རོ་བསྒྲ་ (roga) sm. རོ་ཁ་བ་.

རོ་ཁ་བ་ (rokawa) bitter taste.

རོ་ཁང་ (rogaŋ) crypt, mausoleum.

རོ་ཁུང་ (roguŋ) hole in which corpses are buried.

རོ་ཁེབས་ (rogeb) shroud to cover the dead.

རོ་ཁོག (rogɔɔ̀) corpse, dead body.

རོ་ཁྲལ་འཁྱོལ་ (rotrɛɛ kyö̃ö) shung. vi. to get a tax exemption for sending a soldier as a result of the corvee tax soldier of one's household dying in battle.

རོ་གོས་ (rogöö) clothes worn by a corpse.

རོ་གྱོང་པོ་ (ro gyoŋba) sb. who doesn't listen to what people tell him to do.

རོ་གྲིབ་ (rudrib) contamination/ pollution/ defilement from a corpse.

རོ་གླ་ (rola) fee for killing someone; va.—ལེན་ to take a fee to kill sb.

རོ་རྒྱབ་པ་ (rogyəbbə) a person who accompanies the corpse to the sky burial site.

རོ་སྒམ་ (rogam) coffin.

རོ་སྒྲུང་ (rodruŋ) a book of stories about ghosts/ zombies.

རོ་བརྒྱ་ (rogya) sm. རོ་མཆོག.

རོ་བརྒྱའི་བཅུད་ལྡན་ (rogyɛ jündɛn) a meal that includes many flavors.

རོ་མངར་བ་ (ro ŋarwa) sweet taste.

རོ་མངར་ཤིང་ (roŋar shĩŋ) sugar cane.

རོ་ལྔ་ (roŋa) the five tastes.

རོ་བཅུད་ (rojüü) tasty and nutritious.

རོ་བཅུད་ལྡན་ (ro jündɛn) tasty and nutritious.

རོ་མཆོག (rojɔɔ̀) best flavor/ taste.

རོ་འཇམ་པོ་ (ro jambo) a smooth taste.

རོ་འཇོག (ro jɔɔ̀) va. to kill ༎ཁྱོད་མགོ་སྒྲུར་རམ་རོ་འཇོག Surrender or (we) will kill you.

རོ་ཉལ་ (roñɛɛ) sleeping like a corpse; va.—རྒྱག ༎ ཁྱོད་རང་རོ་ཉལ་བརྒྱབ་ནས་མ་སྡོད་ ལས་ཀ་བྱེད་པར་རྒྱུགས་ Don't sleep here like a corpse. Go to work.

རོ་ཉེ་ (roñe) 1. lead. 2. zinc.

རོ་སྙོམ་ (roñam) equal.

རོ་དོ་ (rodo) leftover dregs ༎ཇ་རོ་དོ་ Leftover tea leaves.

རོ་སྟོད་ (rodöö) the upper part of the body.

རོ་ཐག (rodaà) 1. rope to tie a corpse. 2. negative term for cigarettes.

རོ་ཐབ་ (rodəb) crematory.

རོ་ཐལ་ (rotɛɛ) cremation ashes.

རོ་ཐོ་ (rodo) shung. a pile of stones placed on a field that was obtained in compensation for a murder of a family member.

རོ་དར་ (rodar) cloth for wrapping up a corpse.

རོ་དོང་ (rodoŋ) a burial hole for a corpse.

རོ་དྲུག (rodruù) six tastes: sweet, sour, salty, hot (from chilli), bitter, astringent.

རོ་བདག (rodaà) family of a person who was killed.

རོ་མདོག (rodɔɔ̀) ghostly pallor (implies poor health); vi.—སྟོན་ to exhibit/ manifest a ghostly pallor.

རོ་ལྡན་ (rondɛn) tasty.

རོ་ལྡན་གནས་ (rondɛn nɛɛ̀) graveyard, cemetery.

རོ་ལྡན་ཤིང་ (rondɛn shĩŋ) 1. grapevine. 2. sugar cane.

རོ་གནས་ (ronɛɛ̀) sm. རོ་ལྡན་གནས་.

རོ་ཕུང་ཞིབ་བཤེར་ (ropuŋ shibsher) autopsy; va.—བྱེད་.

རོ་བམ་ (ro bam) vi. to have a corpse decompose/ rot/ decay.

རོ་བུམ་ (robum) grave, tomb.

རོ་བྲན་ (rodrɛn) servants of the main corpse (in the རོ་སྒྲུང་ stories).

རོ་སྦས་ས་ (ro bɛ̀ɛsa) graveyard, cemetery.

རོ་སྦེད་ (ro beè) va. to bury a corpse.

རོ་སྦེད་ས་ (ro beèsa) sm. རོ་ལྡན་གནས་.

རོ་སྦྱོར་ (rojɔɔ) derogatory term for Khampas.

རོ་མ་ (roma) 1. Rome. 2. dirt, dregs, sediments, residue.

རོ་མ་མཐོང་གོང་ནས་ངུ་བ་ (ro matoŋgoŋnɛ ŋuwa) complaining before a problem starts [Lit. crying before seeing the corpse].

རོ་མ་ཉི་ཡ་ (romañiya) Rumania.

རོ་མའི་ཨང་གི་ (romɛ āŋgi) eng.tib. Roman numerals.

རོ་མེད་ (romeè) tasteless.

རོ་རྨུགས་ (ro ñaà) 1. vi. to decompose (for a corpse). 2. slush, muddy.

རོ་རྨུགས་འདམ་ (roñaàdam) one of the eight hot hells.

རོ་མྱང་ (roñaŋ) f. of རོ་མྱོང་.

རོ་མྱང་དུ་གསོལ་ (ro ñaŋdu sö̃ö) va. to taste (h.) ༎ ཁྱེད་ཀྱིས་ཞལ་ལག་འདིའི་རོ་མྱང་དུ་གསོལ་ Please taste the food.

རོ་མྱངས་ (roñaŋ) p. of རོ་མྱོང་.

རོ་མྱོང་ (roñoŋ) va. to taste ༎ངས་ཁ་ལག་གི་རོ་མྱངས་པ་ཡིན་ I tasted the food.

རོ་སྨད་ (romɛɛ̀) lower part of the body.

རོ་ཙ་ (rodza) 1. carnal/ sexual desire, sex; vi.—ལངས་ to have or get carnal/ sexual desire. 2. fertility; vi.—ཉམས་ to become infertile, to become impotent.

རོ་ཚ་པོ་ (ro tsābo) hot, spicy.

རོ་ཚ་བ་ (ro tsāwa) hot tasting, spicy ༎རོ་ཚ་བའི་བཟའ་ཆ་ Hot tasting food.

རོ་འཛིན་ (rondzin) 1. tongue. 2. person who takes care of a corpse.

རོ་འཛིན་འབུར་མ་ (rondzin burmə) taste buds.

རོ་ཞིབ་ (rushib) autopsy; va.—བྱེད་.

རོ་ཞིམ་པ་ (ro shimbə) tasty.

རོ་བཞུ་ཐབ་ (ro shudəb) crematory.

རོ་ཟན་ (rosɛn) sm. རོ་ཟས་.

རོ་ཟས་ (rosɛɛ̀) 1. food taken to the cemetery for the deceased. 2. man eating demon. 3. vultures.

རོ་གཟན་ (rosɛn) shroud used for wrapping corpses.

རོ་འོག་རྨ་ཞི་ (rowɔɔ̀ māshi) shung. an ancient custom in Tibet where the injury of a person who has killed someone is not considered—only the murder.

རོ་རས་ (rorɛɛ̀) shroud for wrapping corpses.

རོ་རེངས་པོ་ (ro reŋbo) corpses that have become stiff.

རོ་ལངས་ (rolaŋ) 1. zombie-like creature. 2. comeback, restoration (usu. in politics); va.—རྒྱག to come back from the dead, to make a comeback, to get restored/ revived ༎མ་རྩའི་རིང་ལུགས་རོ་ལངས་རྒྱག་རྒྱུ་སྔོན་འགོག་བྱ་རྒྱུའི་སྲིད་ཇུས་ The policy of preventing the comeback of capitalism.

རོ་ལན་ཚྭ་ (ro lɛndza) spicy taste.

རོ་ལས་ (rolɛɛ̀) 1. the work of cutting up corpses at sky burial; va.—བྱེད་. 2. funeral arrangements.

རོ་ལས་པ་ (rolɛɛ̀ba) person who cuts up corpses at sky burial.

རོ་ཤད་རྒྱག (roshɛɛ̀ gyaà) sm. ཤི་ཁའི་འཕག་འཆག་རྒྱག.

རོ་བཤུས་རྒྱག (roshüü gyaà) va. to disrobe/ undress the corpse.

རོ་ས་འོག་གཏམ་ས་སྟེང་ (rosa wɔgdam sādeŋ) the evil deeds of a person will outlive him [Lit. corpse under the ground, talk on top of the ground].

རོ་སོ་དྲུག (roso truù) six kinds of sweet tastes: sweet, sweet and sour, sweet and bitter, sweet and astringent, sweet and hot, sweet and salty.

རོ་སྲེག (ro sēg) va. to cremate a corpse.

རོག་གེ་བ་ (roggewa) long faced (in appearance).

རོག་རྒྱས་ (roggyɛɛ̀) sm. རོག་པོ་.

རོག་པོ་ (rogbo) black-colored (for animals such as a yaks, cows).

རོག་པོ་འཛོམས་སྐྱེས་ (rogbo dzomgyeè) an plant used in Tibetan medicine.

རོག་མ་ (rogma) placenta.

རོག་རོག (rogrɔɔ̀) dark/ black figures (usu. seen at the distances).

རོགས་ (rɔɔ̀) 1. help, aid, assistance; va.—བྱེད་ ༎ཁོས་ང་ཚོར་རོགས་བྱས་པ་རེད་ He helped us. 2. helper, companion ༎ལམ་རོགས་ Traveling companion. 3. (vb. + — + བྱེད་) to help ༎ང་ཚོས་དཀའ་ངལ་འདི་སེལ་རོགས་བྱེད་དགོས་ We must help eliminate this hardship. 4. (vb. + —) please do sth. ༎སང་ཉིན་འདི་རུ་ཕེབས་རོགས་ Please come here tomorrow.

རོགས་སྐྱབས་ (rɔ̀gyəb) rescuing, relieving; va.—བྱེད་ to rescue, to relieve.
རོགས་སྐྱོར་ (rɔ̀gyɔɔ) aid, help, assistance, support, relief; va.—བྱེད་ ། ང་ཚོ་ཕན་ཚུན་རོགས་རམ་བྱེད་ཐུབ་ཀྱི་རེད་བསམས་ཀྱི་འདུག We think we can mutually help one another.
རོགས་ཁྲིད་ (rɔ̀trii) sm. རོགས་འཁྲིད་.
རོགས་འཁྲིད་ (rɔ̀trii) 1. guiding, assisting; va.—བྱེད་ ། ཁོང་ལ་གྲོང་ཁྱེར་འདིའི་རྒྱུས་མེད་སྐབས་རོགས་འཁྲིད་བྱེད་མཁན་ཞིག་དགོས་ཀྱི་འདུག Because he didn't know the city, he needs a guide. 2. tutoring; va.—བྱེད་ ། སློབ་ཕྲུག་དེ་ལ་དགེ་རྒན་གྱིས་རོགས་ཁྲིད་བྱེད་དགོས་ཀྱི་ཡོད་པ་རེད་ The teacher needs to tutor the student.
རོགས་དགའ་ (rɔ̀ga) a friend.
རོགས་འགྲིག (rɔgdrig) a couple/ spouse.
རོགས་དངུལ་ (rɔ̀ŋüü) relief/ aid money, subsidy, grant.
རོགས་གཅེས་ (rɔ̀jeè) close/ dear friend.
རོགས་དན་ (rɔ̀dɛn) sm. རོགས་རམ་.
རོགས་འདེགས་ (rɔŋdeg) 1. sm. རོགས་རམ་. 2. blending colors to make a new shade.
རོགས་གནང་ (rɔ̀naŋ) 1. h. of རོགས་བྱེད་. 2. (vb. + —) please ། སང་ཉིན་འདིར་ཕེབས་རོགས་གནང་ Please come here tomorrow.
རོགས་སྣོན་ (rɔ̀nön) reinforcing, subsidizing, making up a deficiency; va.—བྱེད་ ། དམག་སར་དམག་མི་ཉུང་དྲགས་ཀྱི་འདུག་པས་རོགས་སྣོན་གཏོང་དགོས་ཀྱི་འདུག Because there are too few soldiers at the battlefield, (they) need to send reinforcements.
རོགས་པ་ (rɔgba) helper, assistant; va.—བྱེད་ to help/ assist; va.—སྒྲིག to arrange helper/ assistant (usu. to accompany one on a journey); va.—འཚོལ་ to look for a helper.
རོགས་ཕན་ (rɔgbɛn) helping, assisting; va.—བྱེད་.
རོགས་བྱས་ན་ (rɔ̀ cɛ̀ɛna) (vb.+ —) if only one would do the verbal action ། ཁོ་ཚོས་ཁང་པ་གཅིག་ཉོ་རོགས་བྱས་ན་ If only they would buy a house.
རོགས་བྱས་ཡོད་ན་ (rɔ̀ cɛ̀ɛ yö̀ona) (vb.+ —) if only one had done the verbal action ། ཁོས་སྨན་ཁང་ལ་དུས་ཐོག་འགྲོ་རོགས་བྱས་ཡོད་ན་ If only he had gone to the hospital in time.
རོགས་བྱེད་ (rɔ̀ cèè) 1. see རོགས་. 2. (vb. + —) please do the verbal action ། འདི་ང་ར་སྤྲོད་རོགས་བྱེད་ Please give this to me.
རོགས་འབྲེལ་ (rɔndree) alliance, union; va.—བྱེད་ to ally, to join in union, to combine.
རོགས་སྦྲེལ་ (rɔ̀dree) sm. རོགས་འབྲེལ་.
རོགས་མེད་ (rɔ̀meè) without help/ assistance.
རོགས་མོ་ (rɔ̀mo) female partner/ helper.
རོགས་ཚོགས་ (rɔgdzɔ̀) aid or relief agency/ organization.
རོགས་ཟླ་ (rɔnda) 1. companion. 2. helper (as in an office).
རོགས་རམ་ (rɔ̀ram) help, assistance, aid; va.—བྱེད་ to help, to assist, to aid.
རོགས་རམ་བྱེད་རེས་བྱེད་ (rɔ̀ram cèèreè cèè) va. to help each other, to assist/ aid mutually.
རོགས་རམ་ཚོགས་པ་ (rɔ̀ram tsɔ̄gba) sm. རོགས་ཚོགས་.
རོགས་རེས་ (rɔgreè) 1. mutual assistance/ help/ aid; va.—བྱེད་. 2. work exchange between families in a village.
རོགས་རེས་མཉམ་ལས་ (rɔgreè ñamlɛ̀ɛ) mutual assistance and cooperation.
རོགས་རེས་ཚན་ཆུང་ (rɔgreè tsɛ̄njuŋ) sm. རོགས་རེས་ཚོ་ཆུང་.
རོགས་རེས་ཚོ་ཆུང་ (rɔgreè tsōjuŋ) mutual aid team (several families cooperating in work but keeping their own fields' yields).
རོགས་རེས་ཚོགས་ཆུང་ (rɔgreè tsɔ̄gjuŋ) sm. རོགས་རེས་ཚོ་ཆུང་.
རོགས་རེས་ཆིངས་ཡིག (rɔgreè cīŋyii) mutual assistance treaty/ pact.
རོགས་ལམ་ (rɔglam) supply line.
རོགས་ལས་ (eɔ̄glɛ̀ɛ) cooperation, help, assistance; va.—བྱེད་.
རོང་ (roŋ) 1. deep valley, gorge, ravine. 2. abbr. of རོང་པ་. 3. a farming area. 4. name of an area in Rimpung county.
རོང་སྐོར་ (roŋgɔɔ) a place of pilgrimage in southeast Tibet.
རོང་ཁུང་ (roŋguŋ) narrow valley.
རོང་ཁུལ་ (roŋgüü) 1. an area around a narrow valley. 2. a farming/ agricultural area (in contrast to a pastoral area).
རོང་འགྲོ་ (roŋ dro) going to a farming area. ། རོང་འགྲོ་བཤས་ལུག Sheep going to farming areas for slaughter.
རོང་ངེ་ (roŋŋe) protruding, sticking out.
རོང་ལྗང་ (roŋjaŋ) trees in farming areas.
རོང་ཅ་ག་པ་ (roŋ cāgaba) cicada.
རོང་ཆེན་ (roŋjen) a big/ deep gorge or canyon.
རོང་རྟ་ (roŋda) horses from རོང་ཡུལ་.
རོང་པ་ (roŋba) 1. agriculturalist, farmer. 2. person from རོང་.
རོང་ཕྱོགས་ (roŋjɔ̀ɔ) farming/ valley areas.
རོང་མ་འབྲོག (roŋmadrɔ̀ɔ) agropastoral, seminomad (people practicing agriculture and animal husbandry).
རོང་བོད་ (roŋpöö) Tibet and the valley/ farming areas (e.g., Nepal or China).
རོང་འབེབ་ (raŋbeb) shung. bringing goods down to the lower valley (to trade) ། ད་ནས་བཟུང་རོང་འབེབ་མི་ཆོག་པའི་བཀའ་འདོམས་ཡོད་པ་ཞུ We request you order that from now on goods be prohibited from being brought to the valley areas.
རོང་མ་འབྲོག (roŋmadrɔ̀ɔ) seminomad, agropastoralist.
རོང་ཚད་ (roŋdzɛ̀ɛ) hot weather in the farm areas/ valleys.
རོང་ཡུལ་ (roŋyüü) farming area.
རོང་རོང་ (roŋroŋ) craggy, precipitous.
རོང་ལ་གཏོང་ (roŋla dōŋ) va. to have anal intercourse, to do sodomy.
རོང་ཤུར་ (roŋshur) valley.
རོང་ས་ (roŋsa) farming area.
རོང་སེལ་ (roŋsɛɛ) the fruit of Cherokee rose (used in Tibetan medicine).
རོང་གསལ་མེ་ཏོག (roŋsɛɛ medoò) wild rose.
རོད་ (röö) 1. physical appearance, health ། དེང་སང་ཁོང་གི་གཟུགས་པོའི་རོད་ཉམས་འདུག Nowadays his physical health has deteriorated. 2. vi. to be chronic (for an illness) ། ན་ཚ་རོད་ནས་སྨན་བཅོས་བྱེད་དཀའ་པོ་འདུག The disease is chronic so it is difficult to cure.
རོད་ཕྱི་བ་ (röö jīwə) severe illness.
རོད་ཉམས་པ་ (röö ñamba) weak, feeble.
རོབ་ (rob) abbr. of རོབ་ཙམ་.
རོབ་རྒྱག (rob gyaà) va. to cause bedlam/ commotion ། ལས་བྱེད་པ་ཚོས་སྒྲིག་ལམ་མ་སྲུང་པར་རོབ་རྒྱག་གི་འདུག The cadres are not following the rules and are causing bedlam.
རོབ་ཅོར་ (robjɔr) sm. རོ་སྐྱོར་.
རོབ་ཆགས་ཙམ་ (rob cāgdzam) sm. ར་ལང་ཆ་ལང་.
རོབ་བསྡུས་ (robdüü) rough, brief, sketchy.
རོབ་ཙམ་ (robdzam) brief, rough, not detailed, cursory ། གནས་ཚུལ་རོབ་ཙམ་ཕྱོགས་སྒྲིགས་བྱས་པ་རེད་ They compiled a rough account of the events. ། རོབ་ཙམ་མཐོང་བ་ Seeing at a glance (catching a glimpse). ། བོད་ཡིག་རོབ་ཙམ་ཤེས་ (He) knew a little literary Tibetan.
རོབ་ཙམ་ལྟ་ (robdzam dā) va. to glance/ glimpse at sth.
རོམ་པོ་ (rombo) thick, massive, deep (sounds).
རོའི་སྐྱེ་མཆེད་ (rö gyējeè) taste.
རོའུ་དའོ་ (rodo) ch. judo, karate.
རོལ་ (röö) 1. side ། ཕྱི་རོལ་ Outside. 2. a furrow, row ། རོལ་ ༢༤ ཅན་གྱི་སོན་འདེབས་འཕྲུལ་འཁོར་ A twenty four row planting machine. 3. vi. to enjoy ། རང་དབང་ལ་རོལ་སྐབས་ When enjoying freedom. ། སྤྱིའུས་བློན་ཤིང་གི་འབྲས་བུ་ལ་རོལ་བ་རེད་

The monkey enjoyed (ate) the fruit of the tree. 4. abbr. of རོལ་ཆ་.

རོལ་དཀྲོལ་གཞས་གཏོང་ (röödröö shɛɛ̀ dōŋ) va. to enjoying oneself (playing and singing).

རོལ་ཁ་ (röōga) sm. རོལ་, 2.

རོལ་གར་ (röö gar) music and dance.

རོལ་འགྲོས་ (röö dröö) dancing according to a musical beat.

རོལ་གྲལ་ (röögɛɛ) sm. རོལ་, 2.

རོལ་སྒལ་ (röögɛɛ) sm. རོལ་, 2.

རོལ་སྒེག (röögeg) graceful/ elegant when dancing.

རོལ་སྒེག་མ་ (röö gegma) 1. female dancer. 2. graceful/ elegant woman.

རོལ་ཆ་ (rööja) 1. musical instrument ¶ འབུད་གཏོང་ རོལ་ཆ་ A wind instrument. 2. music; va.—གཏོང་; —དཀྲོལ་ to play/ perform music ¶ དམག་མིའི་རོལ་ཆ་ Martial/ military music.

རོལ་ཆ་རྐྱང་དཀྲོལ་ (rööja gyāŋdröö) solo performance (in music).

རོལ་ཆ་མཉམ་གཏོང་ (rööja ñamdoŋ) playing together as an orchestra/ band/ ensemble.

རོལ་ཆ་པ་ (rööjawa) sm. རོལ་ཆ་གཏོང་མི་.

རོལ་ཆ་གཏོང་མི་ (rööja dōŋmi) musicians.

རོལ་ཆ་དབྱངས་ཆིན་ (rööja yāŋjin) dulcimer.

རོལ་ཆའི་རུ་ཁག (rööjɛ rugaà) orchestra, band, ensemble.

རོལ་ཆའི་དབྱངས་གདངས་ (rööjɛ yāŋdaŋ) composition/ tune/ melody for a musical instrument.

རོལ་ཆས་ (rööjɛɛ̀) musical instruments.

རོལ་ཆས་རྐྱང་དཀྲོལ་ (rööjɛɛ̀ gyāŋdröö) solo musical performance.

རོལ་སྙེད་ (rööñeè) sm. རོལ་རྩེད་.

རོལ་གདངས་ (röödaŋ) musical tune; va.—བཟོ་ to compose a musical tune.

རོལ་གདངས་ལེ་ཚན་ (röödaŋ ledzɛn) movement in a musical composition.

རོལ་འདེབས་ (röndeb) row seeding/ drilling, sowing in furrows; va.—བྱེད་.

རོལ་འདེབས་འཐུག་འཛུགས་ (röndeb tūgdzuù) row seeding/ drilling with close planting.

རོལ་གནས་ (röönɛɛ̀) 1. dance, musical hall, theatre, auditorium. 2. public park.

རོལ་པ་ (rööba) 1. structure, arrangement. 2. manifestation.

རོལ་དཔོན་ (rööbön) bandmaster, band leader, conductor.

རོལ་དབྱངས་ (rööyaŋ) music; va.—འཁྲོལ་; —དཀྲོལ་ to play music.

རོལ་དབྱངས་མཐོ་དམའ་མཉམ་གཏོང་ (rööyaŋ tōmaa ñamdoŋ) playing together as an orchestra/ symphony/ ensemble.

རོལ་དབྱངས་སྡེ་ཚན་ (rööyaŋ dedzɛn) orchestra, band, ensemble.

རོལ་དབྱངས་རྩོམ་རིག (rööyaŋ dzōmriì) musical composition.

རོལ་དབྱངས་བརྩམ་བྱ་ (rööyaŋ dzāmja) instrumental music.

རོལ་དབྱངས་ཚོགས་པ་ (rööyaŋ tsɔ̄gba) 1. philharmonic/ symphony orchestra. 2. music association.

རོལ་དབྱངས་ལེ་ཚན་ (rööyaŋ ledzɛn) movement in a musical score.

རོལ་དབྱངས་ལེའུ་ (rööyaŋ lewu) sm. རོལ་དབྱངས་ལེ་ཚན་.

རོལ་དབྱངས་སློབ་གྲྭ་ཆེན་མོ་ (rööyaŋ lōbdra cēmmo) conservatory of music.

རོལ་མོ་ (röömo) 1. music; va.—དཀྲོལ་; —འཁྲོལ་ to play music ¶ རོལ་མོའི་སློབ་ཚན་ Music class/ lesson. 2. cymbals; va.—དཀྲོལ་ to play the cymbals. 3. musical instruments.

རོལ་མོ་རྐྱང་གཏོང་ (röömo gyāŋdoŋ) solo performance (in music).

རོལ་མོ་ཁང་ (röömogaŋ) music hall, concert hall.

རོལ་མོ་མཁས་པ་ (röömo kēèba) musical expert, composer, musician.

རོལ་མོ་གླུ་གཞས་འདུ་འཛོམས་ (röömo lūshɛɛ̀ tudzom) concert, musical performance.

རོལ་མོ་ཉིས་སྒྲགས་ (röömo ñīidraà) duet.

རོལ་མོ་མཉམ་གཏོང་ (röömo ñamdoŋ) playing together as an orchestra/ symphony/ ensemble.

རོལ་མོ་མཉམ་གཏོང་རུ་ཁག (röömo ñamdoŋ rugaà) philharmonic/ symphony orchestra.

རོལ་མོ་བ་ (röömowa) musician.

རོལ་མོ་རྩེད་ཁང་ (röömo dzēègaŋ) club, cabaret.

རོལ་མོ་ཚོགས་པ་ (röömo tsɔ̄gba) sm. རོལ་མོ་མཉམ་གཏོང་རུ་ཁག.

རོལ་མོའི་སྒྲ་གདངས་ (röömö dradaŋ) melody, musical composition.

རོལ་མོའི་འདུ་ཚོགས་ (röömö dudzɔɔ̀) music festival.

རོལ་མོའི་སྡེ་ཚན་ (röömö dedzɛn) band, orchestra.

རོལ་མོའི་གནས་ (röömö nɛɛ̀) place where music is played.

རོལ་མོའི་ཕུའུ་ཙི་ (röömö pūdzi) tib. ch. music book, musical score.

རོལ་མོའི་རྩོམ་རིགས་ (röömö dzōmriì) musical composition.

རོལ་མོའི་མཚམས་ཚིགས་ (röömö tsāmdziì) musical rhythm.

རོལ་མོའི་གཞུང་ལུགས་ (röömö shuŋluù) musical theory.

རོལ་མོའི་རིགས་པའི་གཞུང་ལུགས་ (röömö rigbɛ shuŋluù) sm. རོལ་མོའི་གཞུང་ལུགས་.

རོལ་མོའི་རུ་ཁག (röömö rugaà) sm. རོལ་མོ་ཚོགས་པ་.

རོལ་མོའི་སློབ་གྲྭ་ (röömö lōbdra) conservatory of music.

རོལ་མོས་རམ་འདེགས་ (röömö ramdeg) musical accompaniment.

རོལ་སྨོད་ (röömöò) sm. རོལ་འདེབས་.

རོལ་རྩེད་ (röödzeè) amusement, entertainment, pleasure; va.—བྱེད་.

རོལ་རྩེད་ཁང་ (röödzeègaŋ) recreation place/ building, clubhouse.

རོལ་རྩེད་ཐང་ (röödzeèdaŋ) playground ¶ བྱིས་པའི་རོལ་རྩེད་ཐང་ Children's playground.

རོལ་རྩེད་དོ་ར་ (röödzeè tora) place of entertainment/ amusement/ pleasure.

རོལ་རྩེད་ཡོ་བྱད་ (röödzeè yojɛɛ̀) things or implements for entertainment/ amusement.

རོལ་ཚན་ (röötsɛn) musical program/ performance.

རོལ་གཞས་མཉམ་གཏོང་ (rööshɛɛ̀ ñamdoŋ) va. to sing and play instruments at the same time.

རོལ་རིས་ (röörii) furrow made after plowing a field.

རོལ་སོན་འདེབས་ (röösön deb) va. to sow seeds in furrows/ rows after plowing.

རོལ་སོན་གསོ་ (röösön shō) sm. རོལ་སོན་འདེབས་.

རོས་དེན་ (rööden) Sweden.

རོས་སི་ (röösi) Switzerland.

རྭ་ (ra) horn.

རྭ་ཀེར་ཤིང་ཀེར་ (rager shiŋger) shung. seeking or being in the limelight.

རྭ་དཀྲི་ (ra drī) va. to tell the age of animals by the rings on theirs horn.

རྭ་ཁ་ (raga) 1. the hole/ opening in the top of a water mill in which the grain is poured during grinding. 2. horn; va.—ལེན་ to pick up/ lift up sth. with its horn (for animals).

རྭ་རྒྱག (ra gyaà) a method of treatment in which blood is sucked out through a horn.

རྭ་རྒྱན་ (ragyɛn) ornaments put on the horns of plowing animals.

རྭ་སྒ་ (raga) a part of a རྭ་རྡེ་.

རྭ་སྒྲེང་ (radreŋ) Reting (monastery or incarnate lama).

རྭ་ཅན་ (rajɛn) having horns, horned.

རྭ་ཅིའི (rajii) a kind of knife with a handle made from bone.

རྭ་ཅོ་ (rajo) 1. horn. 2. handlebar (bike).

རྭ་ཅོ་རྒྱེ་ལུག (rajo gyēluù) chaotic, disorderly,

disorganized ¶ ཚོགས་པ་འདིའི་ནང་གི་མང་ཆེ་བ་ར་ཅོ་སྒྱེ་ཁུག་ནང་བཞིན་རེད་ Most people in this organization are disorderly. [Lit. putting horns in a sack].
ར་ཅོ་གཟུགས་ (rajosug) horn shaped.
ར་ཉག (rañaà) scorpion.
ར་རྙི་ (rəñi) trap made from horns.
ར་སྣུང་ (rəñuŋ) an awl made from bone.
ར་སྟག (radaà) abbr. of ར་སྒྲེང་ and སྟག་བྲག (the two Regents who ruled between 1934-50).
ར་ཐག (radaà) rope tied to the horns of plowing animal so it can be led when plowing.
ར་ཐམ་ (ratam) sm. ར་དམ་.
ར་མཐོང་སོ་འགོས་ (ratoŋ sōgöö) shung. stupid and simpleminded.
ར་དམ་ (radam) a brand on an animal's horn; va.—རྒྱག.
ར་དུང་ (raduŋ) animals horn used as a trumpet/ bugle.
ར་ཕོར་ (rabɔɔ) type of medical instrument used to drain blood; va.—རྒྱག.
ར་བླ་ (rala) abbr. Reting's labrang.
ར་ཡོད་བརྒྱ་ཐར་སར་ར་མེད་གཅིག་མ་ཐར་བ་མེད་ (rayöö gya tārsaa rameè jīg matarwa meè) if many have done sth, there is no reason why you should not [Lit. there is no reason why one hornless animal should not pass where hundreds of horned animals have passed].
ར་ཙེ་ (radze) cigarette holder made from a horn.
ར་ཙ་ (radza) bottom/ lower part of the horn.
ར་རྩེ་ (radze) tip of a horn.
ར་རྩེད་རྩེ་ (radzeè dzē) va. to play with one's horns (for animals).
ར་ཚིགས་ (rədzii) sm. ར་དཀྲི་.
ར་ཚུགས་ (ra dzuù) va. to apply a horn made hot by rubbing it against wood to the area of the body that is to be treated (a Tibetan medical treatment).
ར་གཞུ་ (rashu) bow made from horn.
ར་ལུགས་ (raluù) name of a tantric sect founded by the translator ར་ལོ་ཙཱ་བ་.
ར་ལོ་ (ralo) abbr. of ར་ལོ་ཙཱ་བ་.
ར་ལོ་ཙཱ་བ་ (ra lodzawa) the famous translator Dorje Tragba.
རླག (lāà) sm.* བརླག.
རླག་འཐོར་ (lāàdɔɔ) sm.* བརླག་འཐོར་.
རླག་བོང་ (lāàboŋ) a derogatory term used for donkeys.
རླག་མོ་ (lāàmo) 1. sm. རྙང་མ་. 2. delusion. 3. derogatory term for women.

རླངས་ (lāŋ) sm. རླངས་པ་.
རླངས་བཀག་རྒྱག (lāŋgaà gyaà) va. to steam sth.
རླངས་བཀག་ཧ་ཡང་ (lāŋgaà hāyaŋ) pressure cooker.
རླངས་བསྐོར་འཁྲུལ་ཆས་ (lāŋgɔɔ trüüjɛɛ̀) steam turbine.
རླངས་འཁུར་ (lāŋgur) steamed dumplings.
རླངས་འཁོར་ (lāŋgɔɔ) vehicle, automobile; va.—གཏོང་ to drive a vehicle/ automobile.
རླངས་འཁོར་གྱི་གློག་ཞུ་ (lāŋgɔɔgi lōgshu) automobile headlights.
རླངས་འཁོར་གྱི་འཁྱིག་འཁོར་ (lāŋgɔɔgi gyiggɔɔ) automobile/vehicle tires.
རླངས་འཁོར་མགྱོགས་ལོད་སྒྱུར་ཆས་ (lāŋgɔɔ gyoglöö gyurjɛɛ̀) gears (for automobiles).
རླངས་འཁོར་འགྲོ་ལམ་ (lāŋgɔɔ drolam) highway, motorway.
རླངས་འཁོར་སྐུལ་བྱེད་འཁྲུལ་འཁོར་བཟོ་གྲྭ་ (lāŋgɔɔ güüjeè trüügɔɔ sodra) car engine factory.
རླངས་འཁོར་ཆུང་གྲས་ (lāŋgɔɔ cūŋdrɛɛ̀) small cars.
རླངས་འཁོར་ཆུང་བའི་གླ་གཏོང་ཀུང་སི་ (lāŋgɔɔ cūŋwɛ lādoŋ gūŋsi) taxi company.
རླངས་འཁོར་ཆེན་པོ་ (lāŋgɔɔ cēmbo) truck.
རླངས་འཁོར་འཛིབ་ཆུང་ (lāŋgɔɔ jibjuŋ) 1. car. 2. jeep.
རླངས་འཁོར་འཛོག་ཁང་ (lāŋgɔɔ jɔ̀ɔgaŋ) garage for keeping cars/ vehicles.
རླངས་འཁོར་ལྗིད་འདེགས་འཁྲུལ་འཁོར་ (lāŋgɔɔ jiìdeg trüügɔɔ) derrick/ crane (vehicle) for lifting.
རླངས་འཁོར་ཉམས་གསོ་བཅོས་སྒྲིག་ཁང་ (lāŋgɔɔ ñamso jöödriggaŋ) automobile/ vehicle repair shop.
རླངས་འཁོར་འཁྲུལ་ལས་པའི་མཉམ་སྒྲིལ་ (lāŋgɔɔ trüüulɛɛ̀bɛ ñāmdree) United Automobile Workers (UAW).
རླངས་འཁོར་འབབ་ཚུགས་ (lāŋgɔɔ bəbdzuù) bus station.
རླངས་འཁོར་ཞིབ་བཤེར་ས་ཚིགས་ (lāŋgɔɔ shibsher sədzii) car inspection station, car checkpost.
རླངས་འཁོར་བཟོ་གྲྭ་ (lāŋgɔɔ sodra) automobile factory.
རླངས་འཁོར་བཟོ་བཅོས་བཟོ་གྲྭ་ (lāŋgɔɔ sobjöö sodra) sm. རླངས་འཁོར་ཉམས་གསོ་བཅོས་སྒྲིག་ཁང་.
རླངས་འཁོར་རུ་ཁག (lāŋgɔɔ rugaà) sm. རླངས་འཁོར་རུ་ཚོགས་.
རླངས་འཁོར་རུ་ཚོགས་ (lāŋgɔɔ rudzɔɔ̀) 1. motor transport corps, a fleet of cars. 2. motorcade, convoy.
རླངས་འཁོར་ས་ཚིགས་ (lāŋgɔɔ sədzii) vehicle station/ depot/ stop.
རླངས་འཁོར་གསོ་སྒྲིག་བཟོ་གྲྭ་ (lāŋgɔɔ sōdrig sodra) motor car repair and assembly plant.

རླངས་འཁོར་ལྷུ་སྒྲིག་ཀུང་སི་ (lāŋgɔɔ lhūdrig gūŋsi) tib. ch. motor parts company.
རླངས་གྲུ་ (lāŋdru) motorboat.
རླངས་འགུལ་གློག་སྐྱེད་མ་འཁོར་ (lɔ̄ŋgüü lōggyeè magɔɔ) sm. རླངས་འགུལ་གློག་འདོན་འཁྲུལ་འཁོར་.
རླངས་འགུལ་མ་འཁོར་གྱི་འཁོར་ལོ་ (lɔ̄ŋgüü magɔɔgi kɔ̄ɔlo) steam turbogenerator.
རླངས་འགུལ་མ་འཁོར་བཟོ་གྲྭ་ (lɔ̄ŋgüü magɔɔ sodra) steam turbine factory.
རླངས་འགུལ་མེ་འཁོར་ཨ་མ་ (lɔ̄ŋgüü megɔɔ āma) sm. རླངས་འགུལ་མེ་འཁོར་མགོ་.
རླངས་འགྱུར་ (lāŋ gyur) vaporization.
རླངས་འགྱུར་ཚ་ཚད་ (lāŋgyur tsādzɛɛ̀) heat from vaporization.
རླངས་སྐུལ་གློག་འདོན་འཁྲུལ་འཁོར་ (lɔ̄ŋgüü lōgdön trüüjɛɛ̀) turbogenerator, steam generator.
རླངས་སྐུལ་ཐོ་བ་ (lɔ̄ŋgüü tōwa) steam hammer.
རླངས་སྐུལ་འདེགས་འཁོར་ (lɔ̄ŋgüü deggɔɔ) steam powered crane.
རླངས་སྐུལ་འཁྲུལ་འཁོར་ (lɔ̄ŋgüü trüügɔɔ) steam powered machine.
རླངས་སྐུལ་འཁྲུལ་འཁོར་བཟོ་གྲྭ་ (lɔ̄ŋgüü tüügɔɔ sodra) steam turbine plant.
རླངས་སྐུལ་མེ་འཁོར་མགོ་ (lɔ̄ŋgüü megɔɔ go) steam powered locomotive.
རླངས་སྐུལ་ལམ་བཅག་འཁྲུལ་འཁོར་ (lɔ̄ŋgüü lamjaà trüügɔɔ) steamroller.
རླངས་སྒྱུར་དྭངས་འབྱེད་ (lɔ̄ŋgyur tanjeè) distillation.
རླངས་སྒྱུར་འཁྲུལ་ཆས་ (lɔ̄ŋgyur trüüjɛɛ̀) 1. vaporizing machine. 2. carburetor.
རླངས་སྒྱུར་ཚ་བ་ (lɔ̄ŋgyur tsāwa) sm. རླངས་འགྱུར་ཚ་ཚད་.
རླངས་ཆང་ (lāŋjaŋ) sparkling wine.
རླངས་ཆུ་ (lāŋju) 1. distilled water; va.— འདོན་; —ཕབ་; —སྦྱངས་ to distill. 2. the top of a pressure cooker from which the steam blows out.
རླངས་ཆུ་བཟོ་བྱེད་འཁྲུལ་ཆས་ (lɔ̄ŋju sojeè trüüjɛɛ̀) distillation apparatus.
རླངས་གཏེར་ (lāŋder) natural gas field.
རླངས་ཐབ་ (lāŋdəb) radiator.
རླངས་ཐོན་ཁྲོ་ཐབ་ (lāŋdön trōdəb) steam boiler.
རླངས་དུག (lɔ̄ŋduù) poison gas.
རླངས་དུང་ (lɔ̄ŋduŋ) steam whistle/ siren.
རླངས་སྣུམ་ (lāŋnum) petrol, gasoline.
རླངས་སྣུམ་འབར་མདེལ་ (lāŋnum bandee) gasoline bomb, molotov cocktail.
རླངས་སྣུམ་གསོག་སྣོད་ (lāŋnum sōgnöö) gasoline can.
རླངས་སྣོད་ (lāŋnöö) gas tank, gasoline can.
རླངས་པ་ (lāŋ) steam, vapor.
རླངས་པ་འཁྱགས་འགྱུར་ (lāŋba kyāggyur) a vapor

condensing into a solid.

རླངས་པ་འགྱུར་ (lāŋba gyur) vi. to evaporate.

རླངས་པ་འགྱུར་ཚད་ (lāŋba gyurdzɛɛ̀) volume of evaporation.

རླངས་པ་ཐུལ་ལེ་བ་ (lāŋba tůlewa) sm. རླངས་པ་འཚུབ་འཚུབ་.

རླངས་པ་འཕུར་འཕུར་ (lāŋba cūrjur) steamy.

རླངས་པ་འཚུབ་འཚུབ་ (lāŋba tsūbdzub) steaming hot.

རླངས་པས་དྲོད་གཏོང་ (lāŋbɛ trö̀ödoŋ) steam heating.

རླངས་འབར་སྐུལ་ཤུགས་འཁྱུལ་འཁོར་ (lāŋbar güüshuù trǘǘgɔɔ) gas engine.

རླངས་འབུད་ (lāŋ bǜǜ) va. to force out steam (as in a jet).

རླངས་སྤུད་གནམ་གྲུ་ (lāŋbüü nəmdru) jet airplane.

རླངས་བཙོས་ (lāŋjöö) steaming food; va.—རྒྱག; —གཏོང་ to steam food.

རླངས་བཙོས་ཁུར་གོར་ (lāŋdzöö kūrrgɔɔ) steamed dumpling.

རླངས་བཙོས་བག་ལེབ་ (lāŋdzöö paàleè) steamed bread.

རླངས་བཙོས་བཟའ་བཅའ་ (lāŋdzöö saja) steamed foods.

རླངས་ཚགས་ (lāŋdzaà) food steamer.

རླངས་ཚོས་མ་ (lāŋdzöma) steamed food.

རླངས་འཚོད་ (lāŋdzöö) va. to steam food.

རླངས་གཟུགས་ (lāŋsuù) gas.

རླངས་གཟུགས་སུ་འགྱུར་ (lāŋsuù drāngyur) sm. རླངས་པ་འཁྱུགས་འགྱུར་.

རླངས་གཟུགས་གནོན་བཙིར་ (lāŋsuù nöndzir) compressed air.

རླངས་གཟུགས་འབར་རྫས་ (lāŋsuù bandzɛɛ̀) gaseous fuel (e.g., propane gas).

རླངས་ཞིང་ (lāŋshiŋ) natural gas field.

རླངས་ལུམས་ (lāŋlum) a type of medical therapy that uses steam.

རླངས་ཤུགས་ (lāŋshuù) steam energy/ power/ force.

རླངས་ཤུགས་ཁྲོ་ཐབ་ (lāŋshuù trödəb) steam boiler.

རླངས་ཤུགས་འཁྱུལ་འཁོར་ (lāŋshuù trǘǘgɔɔ) steam engine/ turbine.

རླངས་སུབ་གཏོང་ (lāŋsub dōŋ) sm. རླངས་བཙོས་རྒྱག.

རླན་ (lɛ̄n) 1. moisture, humidity, dampness. 2. abbr. of རླན་པ་.

རླན་གྲང་ (lɛ̄ndraŋ) damp and cold.

རླན་ཅན་ (lɛ̄njɛn) moist, humid, damp.

རླན་ནེ་རླན་ནེ་ (lɛ̄nne lēnne) damp, wet.

རླན་པ་ (lɛ̄mba) wet.

རླན་མེད་ (lɛnmeè) not moist/ humid/ damp.

རླན་ཚད་ (lɛ̄ndzɛɛ̀) degree of humidity, level of moisture.

རླན་སློན་ (lɛ̄nlön) sm. རླན་ཅན་.

རླན་གཤེར་ (lɛ̄nsher) humidity, moisture, dampness.

རླབས་ (ləb) waves (sea, sound and radio).

རླབས་ཀྱི་རི་མོ་ (ləbgi rimo) ripples of water.

རླབས་ཀྱི་རིང་ཚད་ (ləbgi riŋdzɛɛ̀) wave length.

རླབས་དཀྲུག (ləbdruù) agitating/ stirring up; va.—བྱེད་.

རླབས་གྱེན་འཕུར་ (ləbgyen cūr) vi. the movement of the tides.

རླབས་རྒྱུན་ (ləbgyün) current, tide ¶ རླབས་རྒྱུན་འཕེལ་ཕྱོགས་ The direction of the tide. ¶ གཡོན་ལྡང་གི་བསམ་པའི་རླབས་རྒྱུན་གྱི་དེབ་གཞུ་ཐོག་པ་རེད་ They were impacted by the tide of leftist thinking.

རླབས་རྒྱུན་སླར་ལོག (ləbgyün gyārlɔɔ̀) resurgence.

རླབས་རྒྱུན་བཟློག (ləbgyün dɔɔ̀) va. to go against the tide.

རླབས་ཆེ་ (ləbje) 1. great, powerful ¶ རླབས་ཆེ་བའི་མཐའ་གྲོགས་ A great ally. 2. large waves. 3. efficient, competent, deft.

རླབས་ཆེན་ (ləbjen) great, powerful.

རླབས་ཆེན་གྱི་གྲུ་པ་ (ləbjengi truba) great helmsman.

རླབས་ཆེན་སྤྱི་ཁྱབ་བཀོད་འདོམས་པ་ (ləbjen jīgyəb göödomba) great supreme commander.

རླབས་ཆེན་གཙོ་འཛིན་ (ləbjen dzōndzin) great leader.

རླབས་ཆེན་ཟླ་བ་བཅུ་པའི་གསར་བརྗེ་ (ləbjen dawa jūbɛ sārje) the Great October Revolution.

རླབས་འཇགས་ (ləbjaà) sm. རླབས་ཞི་.

རླབས་གཉེར་ (ləbñee) waves like wrinkles.

རླབས་ཐག (ləbdaà) sm. རླབས་ཀྱི་རིང་ཚད་.

རླབས་ཐུང་ (ləbduŋ) short wave.

རླབས་དྲག་པོ་ (ləb tragbo) tidal wave, turbulent waves.

རླབས་པོ་ (ləbbo) sm. ནུས་པ་.

རླབས་པོ་ཆེ་ (ləbboje) great ¶ རླབས་པོ་ཆེའི་མཐའ་འབྲེལ་ The great alliance.

རླབས་ཕྲན་ (ləbdrɛn) ripples.

རླབས་ཕྲེང་ (ləbdreŋ) waves.

རླབས་དབྱིབས་ཚད་ནད་ (ləbyib tsɛ̄ɛnɛɛ̀) undulant fever.

རླབས་འབྲིང་ (ləmdriŋ) medium wave.

རླབས་རྩེ་ (ləbdze) crest of a wave.

རླབས་ཞི་ (ləbshi) mild/ gentle waves.

རླབས་ཟུར་གྱེན་ལྡོག (ləbsur gyendɔɔ̀) going against the current, adverse/ counter current.

རླབས་རིང་ (ləbriŋ) long waves.

རླབས་ལོག་དེབ་སྒྲ་ (ləblɔɔ debdra) the sound made by the crashing of waves.

རླབས་ཤུགས་ (ləbshuù) force of waves.

རླབས་ཤུར་ (ləbshur) sm. རླབས་གཤོང་.

རླབས་གཤགས་མདུན་སྐྱོད་ (ləbsham düngyöö) moving forward with great force (e.g., a political campaign) [Lit. split the waves and go forward].

རླབས་གཤོང་ (ləbshoŋ) the trough of a wave.

རླམ་འགོག་སྨན་རྫས་ (lāmgɔɔ̀ mɛ̄ndzɛɛ̀) fungicide.

རླམ་པ་ (lāmba) sm. ཏམ་སྐྱུ་.

རླམ་ཕྲ་ (lāmdra) mold, mildew.

རླམ་ཚེར་ (lāmdzer) a type of thorn.

རླའ་ཏིང་མེ་གླིང་ (lādin meliŋ) ch. Latin America.

རླིག་སྒོང་ (līggoŋ) 1. testicles. 2. penis and testicles.

རླིག་ཐང་ (līgdaŋ) testicles.

རླིག་པ་ (līgbə) penis; va.—འབྱིན་; —ཕུང་ to castrate; vi.—སྒྲིང་ to get an erection.

རླིག་པ་འབྱིན་ (līgbə jin) see རླིག་པ་.

རླིག་ཕུང་བ་ (līgjuŋwa) eunuch.

རླིག་འབྲས་ (līŋdrɛɛ̀) sm. རླིག་རིལ་.

རླིག་མེད་ (līgmeè) castrated, without testicles.

རླིག་རིལ་ (līgrii) testicles; va.—འདོན་ to castrate.

རླིག་རླུགས་ (līglum) orchitis.

རླིག་རླུགས་པ་ (līglugbə) sm. རླིག་རླུགས་.

རླིད་པུ་ (lī̀ibu) skin of an animal to be used for taxidermy purposes.

རླིད་སྦུབས་ (lī̀ibub) sm. རླིད་པུ་.

རླིབས་པ་ (lībbə) arc. wide.

རླུག: p. བརླུགས་; f. བརླུག; imp. རླུགས་ (lūù) 1. va. to believe/ trust. 2. va. to dismantle/ take down. 3. va. to expose an error. 4. vi. to have diarrhea. 5. vi. to leak. 6. va. to demolish.

རླུགས་ (lūù) 1. imp. of རླུག. 2. diarrhea.

རླུང་ (lūŋ) 1. anger; vi.—ལངས་ to get angry; —སྟོན་ to show anger. 2. wind, air; vi.—རྒྱག to blow (of wind) ¶ ཐལ་རླུང་ Dust storm. 3. a class of depression-like disorders in Tibetan medicine.

རླུང་རྒྱལ་ (lūŋgyɛɛ) short-tempered.

རླུང་སྐམ་ (lūŋgam) drying by air; va.—གཏོང་.

རླུང་སྒོར་འཚུབ་ (lūŋ gɔ̄ɔdzub) wind swirling around.

རླུང་སྐྲན་ (lūŋdrɛn) tumor caused by རླུང་ disease.

རླུང་སྐྱོད་དར་ལྕོག (lūŋgyöö tarjɔɔ̀) a flag erected to bring good luck.

རླུང་སྐྱོན་ (lūŋgyön) wind/ storm damage.

རླུང་སྐྱོར་ (lūŋgyɔɔ) a windbreak.

རླུང་ཁམས་ཆེན་པོ་ (lūŋgam cēmbo) the atmosphere.

རླུང་ཁམས་ཆེན་པོའི་ཆགས་རིམ་ (lūŋgam cēmbö cəgrim) atmospheric layer.

རླུང་ཁམས་ཆེན་པོའི་ནུས་ཤུགས་ (lūŋgam cēmbö nüüshuù) atmospheric pressure.

རླུང་ཁམས་པ་ (lūŋ kāmba) sb. with a depression like disorder.

རླུང་ཁའི་མར་མེ་ (lūŋgɛ marme) things that are about to come to an end, end of an era/ period [Lit. flame flickering in the wind].

རླུང་ཁུང་ (lūŋguŋ) air vent, air hole, air passage.

རླུང་འཁོར་ (lūŋgɔɔ) 1. electric fan. 2. a mani prayer wheel turned by wind. 3. windmill. 5. a magical wheel that is used for going fast.

རླུང་འཁོར་དྲག་པོ་ (lūŋgɔɔ tragbo) tornado.

རླུང་འཁོར་རྩུབ་ (lūŋ kɔ̄ɔdzub) 1. sm. རླུང་འཁོར་འཚུབ་.

རླུང་འཁོར་འཚུབ་ (lūŋ kɔ̄ɔdzub) whirlwind.

རླུང་འཁྱིལ་ (lūŋgyii) sm. རླུང་འཁོར་འཚུབ་.

རླུང་འབྲུགས་ (lūŋ trūù) 1. vi. to have a wind storm. 2. vi. to have a wind (illness) disorder. 3. vi. to get/ be angry.

རླུང་གི་དཀྱིལ་འཁོར་ (lūŋgi gyīngɔɔ) atmosphere.

རླུང་གི་ཁམས་ (lūŋgi kām) the element wind.

རླུང་གི་གྲུ་ (lūŋgi tru) sailboat.

རླུང་གི་མགྱོགས་ཚད་ (lūŋgi gyɔgdzɛɛ̀) wind velocity.

རླུང་གི་ནད་ (lūŋgi nɛɛ̀) sm. རླུང་, 2.

རླུང་གི་རྣལ་འབྱོར་ (lūŋgi nɔ̄njɔɔ) tantric practitioner who meditates on "wind energy".

རླུང་གི་འཕྲུལ་འཁོར་ (lūŋgi trṻṻgɔɔ) machine driven by wind/ air.

རླུང་གི་རྒྱུ་བ་ (lūŋgi gyuwə) ventilation/ air current.

རླུང་གི་སོ་ནད་ (lūŋgi sōnɛɛ̀) a type of toothache caused by wind disease.

རླུང་གིས་དེད་པ་ལྟར་ (lūŋgi teèbadar) quickly [Lit. like being pursued by the wind].

རླུང་གིས་མི་གཡོ་ (lūŋgi mi yō) unshakable, unwavering, determined.

རླུང་གིས་ཟད་ (lūŋgi sɛɛ̀) vi. to weather, to get eroded by weather.

རླུང་གོས་ (lūŋgöö) windbreaker, wind jacket.

རླུང་གྲིབ་ (lūŋdrib) stroke caused by wind disease.

རླུང་གྲུ་ (lūŋdru) 1. dirigible, blimp. 2. glider plane; va.—གཏོང་. 3. sailboat.

རླུང་འགུལ་ (lūŋgüü) air powered, pneumatic ¶ རླུང་འགུལ་ཐོ་བ་ Pneumatic hammer.

རླུང་འགོག་ (lūŋgɔɔ̀) protecting from the wind; va.—བྱེད་ to protect against the wind.

རླུང་འགོག་བཙུགས་ཤིང་ (lūŋgɔɔ̀ dzūgshiŋ) sm. རླུང་འགོག་ཤིང་ནགས་.

རླུང་འགོག་ཚལ་ཞིང་ (lūŋgɔɔ̀ tsɛ̄ɛshiŋ) indoor vegetable garden, vegetable garden protected from the wind.

རླུང་འགོག་ཤིང་ནགས་ (lūŋgɔɔ̀ shīŋnaà) forest which acts as a windbreaker.

རླུང་འགྲོ་ (lūŋdro) sm. རླུང་འགྲོས་.

རླུང་འགྲོ་ས་ (lūŋ dosa) ventilation chute/ opening.

རླུང་འགྲོའི་སྒྲིག་ཆས་ (lūŋdrö drigjɛɛ̀) ventilation equipment/ facilities.

རླུང་འགྲོའི་ལྦུགས་མདོང་ (lūŋdrö jāgdoŋ) exhaust pipe, ventilation duct.

རླུང་འགྲོས་ (lūŋdröö) shaking/ swaying caused by the wind.

རླུང་རྒྱུན་ (lūŋgyün) air current.

རླུང་སྒུལ་ (lūŋgüü) sm. རླུང་འགུལ་.

རླུང་སྒུལ་ཐོ་བ་ (lūŋgüü tōwa) pneumatic hammer.

རླུང་སྒུལ་འབིགས་ཆས་ (lūŋgüü bigjɛɛ̀) pneumatic drill.

རླུང་སྒུལ་ཡོ་བྱད་ (lūŋgüü yobjɛɛ̀) pneumatic tools/ equipment.

རླུང་སྒོ་ (lūŋgo) a hole or opening through which air comes in or goes out (e.g., a ventilation vent).

རླུང་སྒོམ་ (lūŋgom) breathing meditation.

རླུང་སྒོམ་པའི་བཅོས་ཐབས་ (lūŋgombɛ jöödəb) sm. རླུང་སྒོམ་པའི་གསོ་ཐབས་.

རླུང་སྒོམ་པའི་གསོ་ཐབས་ (lūŋgombɛ sōdəb) a method of curing illness by using breathing meditation.

རླུང་ངན་ (lūŋŋɛn) 1. bad atmosphere/ environment. 2. adverse wind. 3. unhealthy trend.

རླུང་བཅོས་ (lūŋjöö) treatment for alleviating wind disease.

རླུང་ཆེན་ (lūŋjen) atmosphere.

རླུང་མཆིག (lūŋjii) windmill.

རླུང་འཇམ་ (lūŋjam) gentle breeze.

རླུང་འཇམ་ཆར་ཟིམ་ (lūŋjam cārsim) gentle breeze and light rain/ drizzle.

རླུང་འཇགས་སྤྲིན་ཡལ་ (lūŋjaà drīnyɛɛ) peaceful/ calm situation [Lit. wind subsides and the clouds disappear].

རླུང་འཇགས་ཆར་སིལ་ (lūŋjaà cārsii) sm. རླུང་འཇམ་ཆར་ཟིམ་.

རླུང་འཇགས་རླབས་གཞིམ་ (lūŋjaà lābshöö) sm. རླུང་འཇགས་སྤྲིན་ཡལ་.

རླུང་འཇིལ་ (lūŋ jii) vi. to stop breathing, to suffocate.

རླུང་འཇོར་ (lūŋjɔɔ) pneumatic pick.

རླུང་གཏོར་རླབས་གཤག (lūŋdɔɔ lābshaà) forcefully eliminate obstacles [Lit. destroy the wind and clean the waves].

རླུང་རྟ་ (lūŋda) luck, fortune; vi.—རྒྱགས་; —དར་; —སྐྱེད་; —འགྲོ་ to have good luck; —ཆགས་; —གུད་; —ཉམས་ to have one's luck go down ¶ དེང་སྐབས་ངའི་རླུང་རྟ་དམའ་པོ་རེད་ These days my luck is low.

རླུང་རྟ་དར་བའི་དུས་སུ་ལྷ་ལས་བླ་མ་བཟང་བ་ རླུང་རྟ་ཆག་པའི་དུས་སུ་ཁྱི་ལས་ཞུམ་བུ་སྡང་བ་ (lūŋda tarwɛ tüüsu lhālɛ lāma saŋ lūŋda cāgbɛ tüüsu kyīlɛ shumbu daŋ) when one's luck is good everybody likes you but when one's luck is bad even low people will insult you [Lit. when fortune is good the lama is better than god, when fortune is bad even cats hate you more than dogs].

རླུང་རྟ་མེད་པ་ (lūŋda meèba) unfortunate unlucky.

རླུང་ལྟར་གྲགས་ (lūŋdar traà) vi. to spread like the wind.

རླུང་སྟོན་ (lūŋ dōn) va. to show one's anger.

རླུང་ཐབ་ (lūŋdəb) a stove that burns through air convection rather than through use of a bellows.

རླུང་འཐེན་འཕྲུལ་འཁོར་ (lūŋden trṻṻgɔɔ) air pumping machine.

རླུང་འཐེན་འཕྲུལ་ཆས་ (lūŋden trṻṻjɛɛ̀) sm. རླུང་འཐེན་འཕྲུལ་འཁོར་.

རླུང་དར་ (lūŋdar) prayer flags to bring good luck.

རླུང་དྲོན་ (lūŋdrön) heating system in a house.

རླུང་འདེགས་གྲུ་གཟིངས་ (lūŋdeg trusiŋ) hovercraft.

རླུང་ནང་གི་མར་མེ་ (lūŋnaŋgi marme) insecure, unsteady, precarious [Lit. a butter lamp in the wind].

རླུང་ནག (lūŋnaà) wind storm.

རླུང་ནད་ (lūŋnɛɛ̀) sm. རླུང་, 3.

རླུང་གནོན་ (lūŋnön) 1. air pressure. 2. the two long red strips of silk on the front of tankas.

རླུང་གནོན་མཐོན་པོ་ (lūŋnön tōmbo) high air pressure.

རླུང་གནོན་དཔྱད་ཆས་ (lūŋnön jɛɛ̀jɛɛ̀) air pressure gauge.

རླུང་གནོན་འཕྲུལ་ཆས་ (lūŋnön trṻṻjɛɛ̀) air pump.

རླུང་གནོན་དམའ་བ་ (lūŋnön maabo) low air pressure.

རླུང་ཕྱོགས་ (lūŋjɔɔ̀) 1. wind direction.

རླུང་ཕྱོགས་ལྟ་ (lūŋjɔɔ̀ dā) va. to look at how a situation is developing or has developed [Lit. look at the direction of the wind].

རླུང་འཕར་ (lūŋ pār) 1. to have a རླུང་ disease arise. 2. vi. to get angry.

རླུང་འཕྲིན་ (lūŋdrin) wireless, radio.

རླུང་འཕྲིན་ཁང་ (lūŋdrin) radio/ broadcasting station.

རླུང་འཕྲིན་གློག་ཁང་ (lūŋdrin) sm. རླུང་འཕྲིན་ཁང་.

རླུང་འཕྲིན་སྙམ་ (lūŋdrin) radio receiver.

རླུང་འཕྲིན་གཏོང་བྱེད་འཕྲུལ་འཁོར་ (lūŋdrin) radio transmitter.

རླུང་འཕྲིན་སྡུད་ལེན་འཕྲུལ་འཁོར་ (lūŋdrin) radio receiver.

རླུང་འཕྲིན་ཟློས་གར་ (lūŋdrin döögar) radio play/ show.

རླུང་འཕྲིན་ལུས་སྦྱོང་ (lūŋdrin lüüjoŋ) radio exercises.

རླུང་བུ་ (lūŋbu) wind; va.—རྒྱག to blow (the wind).

རླུང་འབུད་ (lūŋ büü) va. to force out air, to blast out air.

རླུང་འབུད་སྒུལ་བྱེད་འཕྲུལ་འཁོར་ (lūŋbüü güüjeè trṻṻgɔɔ) sm. རླུང་སྤུད་འཕྲུལ་འཁོར་.

རླུང་འབུད་ཅན་ (lūŋbüüjɛn) jet-propelled.

རླུང་འབུད་གནམ་གྲུ་ (lūŋbüù nəmdru) jet plane.

རླུང་འབུད་རྣམ་པ་ (lūŋbüù nāmba) sm. རླུང་འབུད་ཅན་.

རླུང་སྦུད་འཕྲུལ་འཁོར་ (lūŋbüù trü̃ü̃gɔɔ) jet engine.

རླུང་སྙུར་དཔྱོད་སྤྱད་ (lūŋñur jȫȍjɛɛ̀) wind velocity measuring machine.

རླུང་དམར་ (lūŋmar) 1. wind. 2. dust storm.

རླུང་དམར་ཐོག་དྲག (lūŋmar tɔ̄gdraà) wind and thunder storm.

རླུང་ཅེ་ (lūŋdzi) cage.

རླུང་ཅེ་ (lūŋdzi) sm. རླུང་ཅེ་.

རླུང་ཅེའི་ནང་གི་བྱིའུ་ (lūŋdzii na̲ŋgi ci̲wu) losing one's freedom. [Lit. a bird in a cage].

རླུང་ཚ་བ་ (lūŋ tsābo) 1. windy. 2. hot-tempered.

རླུང་ཚབས་ (lūŋdzəb) windy.

རླུང་རྩུབ་ (lūŋdzub) sm. རླུང་འཚུབ་.

རླུང་ཚོམ་ (lūŋdzom) air mass.

རླུང་འཚང་ (lūŋdzaŋ) 1. a sickness characterized by gasping and difficulty breathing. 2. vi. to have air blow in through cracks in a wall, etc.

རླུང་འཚུབ་ (lūŋdzub) a fierce wind, a cyclone, a whirlwind; vi.—རྒྱག.

རླུང་འཚུབ་ཐོག་དྲག (lūŋdzub tɔ̄gdraà) sm. རླུང་དམར་ཐོག་དྲག.

རླུང་འཚུབ་དྲག་ཆར་ (lūŋdzub tra̲gjar) a hurricane/ cyclone/ tornado/ whirlwind with heavy rain.

རླུང་འཚུབ་སྤྲིན་འཁྲིགས་ (lūŋdzub drīndrig) hurricane/ cyclone/ tornado/ whirlwind with huge black clouds.

རླུང་འཚུབ་དྲག་པོ་ (lūŋdzub tra̲gbo) hurricane, typhoon, cyclone.

རླུང་འཚུབ་འཚུབ་ (lūŋ dzūbdzub) 1. a fierce wind. 2. angry, furious; va.—བྱེད་.

རླུང་འཚུབ་རླབས་དྲག (lūŋdzub lābdraà) hurricane/ typhoon/ cyclone with high waves.

རླུང་འཚུབ་རླབས་རྡབ་ (lūŋdzub lābdəb) hurricane, typhoon, cyclone with smashing/ pounding waves.

རླུང་འཚུབ་སླར་ལོག (lūŋdzub lārlɔɔ̀) staging a comeback (perjorative) [Lit. the whirlwind returning again].

རླུང་རྗེ་ (lūŋdzi) 1. smell/ odor carried by the wind. 2. an acute sense of smell certain animals have.

རླུང་ཞི་ (lūŋshi) 1. vi. to subside (for wind, anger, རླུང་ disease).

རླུང་ཞི་རླབས་འཇགས་ (lūŋshi lābjaà) calm, tranquil [Lit. wind calm, waves gentle].

རླུང་ཤུགས་གློག་འདོན་འཕྲུལ་འཁོར་ (lūŋshuù lɔ̄gdön trü̃ü̃gɔɔ) wind driven electric generator.

རླུང་ཟུག (lūŋsuù) pain caused by རླུང་ disease.

རླུང་ཟློག་མུན་གསལ་ (lūŋdɔɔ̀ mü̲nsɛl) turning back the wind and clearing away the darkness (a magical feat).

རླུང་གཞེར་ (lūŋser) sm. ཪ་.

རླུང་གཟུགས་ (lūŋsug) gas.

རླུང་གཟུགས་འབར་རྫས་ (lūŋsug ba̲rdzɛɛ̀) gaseous fuel.

རླུང་ཝུར་ (lūŋwur) sound of howling wind.

རླུང་ཡན་ (lūŋyɛn) unhealthy trend, bad influence; va.—རྒྱག [Lit. false wind].

རླུང་ཡབ་ (lūŋyəb) sm. རླུང་གཡབ་.

རླུང་ཡབ་དབྱིབས་ (lūŋyəb yīb) fan-shaped.

རླུང་ཡོལ་ (lūŋyöö) curtain to stop the wind.

རླུང་གཡབ་ཀྱི་རྩིབས་ (lūŋyəbgi dzīb) fan blade.

རླུང་གཡབ་འཕྲུལ་འཁོར་ (lūŋyəb trü̃ü̃gɔɔ) a fan (machine).

རླུང་གཡབ་མེ་སྦར་ (lūŋyəb me̲bar) inciting/ instigating/ stirring up trouble [Lit. fanning wind to light a fire].

རླུང་ཡོར་ (lūŋyɔɔ) sail (of a ship).

རླུང་གཡབ་ (lūŋyəb) fan; va.—རྒྱག to fan, to fan with a fan.

རླུང་གཡབ་ལྡེབ་མ་ (lūŋyəb dēbma) folding fan.

རླུང་གཡུག (lūŋ yūù) vi. to be blowing (the wind).

རླུང་གཡོ་སྤྲིན་འཁྱུར་ (lūŋyo drīnjur) sm. རླུང་འཚུབ་སྤྲིན་འཁྲིགས་.

རླུང་གཡོ་རླབས་འཁྲུག (lūŋyo lābdruù) sm. རླུང་གཡོབ་རླབས་དཀྲུག.

རླུང་གཡོབ་ (lūŋyob) fan.

རླུང་གཡོབ་གྲུ་ (lūŋyob tru̲) sailboat.

རླུང་གཡོབ་རླབས་དཀྲུག (lūŋyob lābdruù) stirring up trouble/ disorder [Lit. fanning the wind, stirring up the waves].

རླུང་གཡོར་ (lūŋyɔɔ) sm. རླུང་ཡོར་.

རླུང་རས་ (lūŋrɛɛ̀) 1. prayer flags. 2. a short loin cloth worn by tantric practitioners.

རླུང་རླབས་ (lūŋləb) 1. unrest, agitation, ferment [Lit. wind and tide]. 2. wind current.

རླུང་རིམས་ཡེར་བུ་ (lūŋrim ye̲rbu) insomnia caused by རླུང་ disease.

རླུང་རློན་ཚིགས་གྲུམ་ (lūŋlön tsīgdrum) rheumatoid arthritis.

རླུང་ལ་སྐུར་ (lūŋla gūū) 1. va. to spread rumors/ information [Lit. send to the wind]. 2. va. to abandon/ quit/ relinquish.

རླུང་ལ་ཞགས་པ་འཕེན་ (lūŋla sha̲gba pēn) attempting to do something impossible [Lit. lassoing the wind].

རླུང་ལྭ་ (lūŋla) sm. རླུང་གོས་.

རླུང་ལང་ (lūŋlaŋ) sm. རླུང་ལངས་.

རླུང་ལང་པོ་ (lūŋ la̲ŋbo) sm. རླུང་ལངས་པོ་.

རླུང་ལངས་ (lūŋlaŋ) see རླུང་.

རླུང་ལངས་པོ་ (lūŋ la̲ŋbo) short-tempered, quick-tempered.

རླུང་ལམ་ (lūŋlam) air passage.

རླུང་ལུམས་ (lūŋlum) a method of treating an illness by steam.

རླུང་ལོག (lūŋlɔɔ̀) returned by the wind (a saying conveying that a new born boy changes to a girl).

རླུང་ཤུགས་ (lūŋshuù) wind power/ force.

རླུང་ཤུགས་སྐུད་འཁེལ་ (lūŋshuù gü̃ù kēl) wind powered thread spinning machine.

རླུང་ཤུགས་གློག་འདོན་ས་ཚིགས་ (lūŋshuù lɔ̄gdön sə̄dziì) wind-power station.

རླུང་ཤུགས་ཆུ་འཐེན་འཁོར་ལོ་ (lūŋshuù cēden kɔ̄ɔlo) wind-powered water wheel.

རླུང་ཤུགས་རང་འཐག (lūŋshuù ra̲ŋdaà) wind powered grinding mill.

རླུང་ཤོར་ (lūŋ shɔ̄ɔ) 1. vi. to have wind draft, to have wind seep through. 2. vi. to lose air (e.g., from a sealed container).

རླུང་གཤག་རླབས་གཏོར་ (lūŋshaà lābdɔɔ) making a great effort, overcoming all difficulties [Lit. split the wind, destroy the waves].

རླུང་གསང་ (lūŋsaŋ) a རླུང་ disorder characterized by intermittently getting angry; va.—ལྟ to see whether sb. is angry or not; va.—འགོག; —སྡེམ་ to put hot melted butter on the temple of patients suffering from nervous disorders.

རླུང་སློང་ (lūŋ lōŋ) va. to make sb. angry.

རླུང་བསིལ་ཟླ་གསལ་ (lūŋsil da̲sɛɛ) at leisure, relaxed [Lit. cool breeze and bright moon].

རླུང་གསེབ་ཀྱི་མར་མེ་ (lūŋsebgi ma̲rme) in danger of destruction/ annihilation [Lit. a butter lamp in the wind].

རླུང་གསོར་ (lūŋsor) pneumatic/ air drill.

རླུང་བསེར་བུ་ (lūŋ sērbu) calm/ gentle breeze.

རླུང་ལྷག (lūŋlaà) air and wind.

རླུང་གྲུ་ (lūŋdru) steamboat.

རླུབས་ (lūb) pit, hole.

རློག: p. བརླགས་; f. བརླག; imp. རློགས་ (lɔ̄ɔ̀) 1. va. to destroy, obliterate ༈ ལུགས་སྲོལ་རྙིང་པ་དེ་ཤུལ་མེད་དུ་བརླགས་འདུག They totally destroyed that old custom. ༈ སྐྱོན་ཆ་དེས་ཁོང་གི་མཚན་སྙན་བརླགས་འདུག His errors destroyed his fame.

རློགས་ (lɔ̄ɔ̀) imp. of རློག.

རློན་ཅག་ཅག (lȭn jāgjaà) dripping wet, drenched.

རློན་: p. བརླན་; f. བརླན་; imp. རློན་ (lȭn) va. to make wet.

རློན་ (lȭn) 1. abbr. of རློན་པ་. 2. beverages like tea

and beer ། ལས་ཀ་བྱེད་དུས་ཙམ་པ་སྤྲད་ཀྱང་རློན་སྤྲད་མ་བྱུང་ When they worked they were given ཙམ་པ་ but they were not given beverages.

རློན་ཆབ་ཆབ་ (lõn cōbjob) wet, damp.

རློན་ཐོར་ (lõndɔɔ) eczema.

རློན་དོད་ (lõndöö) giving money instead of beverages/ drinks (as part of wages).

རློན་འདྲེད་ (lõndreè) wet and slippery.

རློན་པ་ (lõmba) 1. wet, damp, moist; vi.—ཆགས་ to become wet; va.—བཟོ་ to make wet ། སྟོད་ཐུང་འདི་རློན་པ་རེད་ The shirt is wet. 2. uncooked, raw, unripe.

རློན་པ་ཙོབ་རྒྱལ་ (lõmba dzōbgyɛɛ) sm. རློན་པ་རློན་རྒྱང་.

རློན་པ་རློན་རྒྱང་ (lõmba lõngyaŋ) completely wet.

རློན་པོ་ (lõmbo) sm. རློན་པ་.

རློན་ཕོགས་ (lõmbɔɔ̀) salary involving beverages (usu. tea and ཆང་).

རློན་འབྲུམ་ (lõndrum) sm. རློན་ཐོར་.

རློན་ཚད་ (lõndzɛɛ̀) degree of humidity.

རློན་ཤིག་ཤིག (lõn shĩgshiì) wet, damp.

རློན་གཤེར་ (lõnsher) wet; va.—གཏོང་ to make wet, to moisten.

རློན་གསོལ་ (lõnsöö) shung. a type of offering made to protective deities.

རློམ་ (lōm) 1. va. to possess sb. (demons, ghost, etc.). 2. vi. to pretend/ act ། དབང་ཆ་ཡོད་རློམ་བྱེད་དགོས་ (We) have to pretend we have authority.

རློམ་པ་ (lōmba) 1. arrogance, conceit, pride; vi.—སྐྱེ་ to become arrogant/ proud/ conceited.

རློམ་སེམས་སྐྱེ་ (lōmsem gyē) sm. རློམ་སེམས་སྐྱེད་.

རློམ་སེམས་སྐྱེད་ (lōmsem gyɛ̃ɛ̀) vi. to be conceited/ arrogant/ overbearing, to think one is better than others.

རློམ་སེམས་ང་རྒྱལ་ (lōmsem ŋagyɛɛ) egotism, conceit; va.—བྱེད་.

བརླ་ཀང་ (lāgaŋ) thigh bone.

བརླ་ལྕག་རྒྱག (lājaà gyaà) va. to hit/ slap one's thigh (in anger).

བརླ་བསྣོལ་ (lā nõõ) va. to cross one's leg while sitting.

བརླ་བར་ (lābar) between the thighs.

བརླ་ཛར་ (lādzar) wool from the thigh of a sheep.

བརླ་མཛེས་ (lādzeè) good looking/ beautiful thigh.

བརླ་རུས་ (lārüù) thigh bone.

བརླ་ལེགས་ཟླུམ་པོ་ (lāleg dumbo) sm. བརླ་མཛེས་.

བརླ་ཤ་ (lāsha) thigh.

བརླ་ཤ་སྒྲིམ་ (lāsha drim) va. to hold one's thighs together (usu. when monks have sexual relations between the thighs).

བརླག: p. བརླགས་; f. བརླག (lāà) 1. vi. to lose ། གཟབ་མ་བྱས་ན་དངུལ་བརླག་གི་རེད་ If you are not careful, you will lose the money. 2. f. of རློག.

བརླག་འགྱུར་ (lāàgyar) sm.བརླག་སྟོར་.

བརླག་དངོས་ (lāàŋöö) lost item.

བརླག་གཏོར་ (lāàdɔɔ) sm. བརླག་སྟོར་.

བརླག་སྟོར་ (lāàdɔɔ) 1. destroying, annihilating; vi.—འགྱུར་; —འགྲོ་; —ཤོར་; va.—གཏོང་.

བརླག་འཐོར་ (lādɔɔ) sm.བརླག་སྟོར་.

བརླག་དོར་ (lādɔɔ) things lost or stolen.

བརླག་བརྡ་ (lāàda) a notice that sth. is lost.

བརླག་བཙུན་མ་ (lāgdzümma) a derogatory term used to berate nuns.

བརླག་རྫུ་ (lāgdzu) pretending that sth. is lost; va.—བྱེད་.

བརླགས་ (lāà) p. of རློག and བརླག.

བརླང་པོ་ (lāŋbo) coarse, rough.

བརླང་སྤྱོད་ (lāŋjöö) cruel/ coarse/ rough behavior.

བརླང་ཚིག (lāŋdzii) harsh/ crude/ rough words.

བརླན་ (lɛ̄n) p. of རླན་.

བརླན་གཤེར་ (lɛ̄nsher) moisture, humidity.

བརླབ་ (lāb) f. of རློབ་.

བརླམ་ (lām) f. of རླམ་.

བརླའི་ཤ་ (lɛ̄sha) sm. བརླ་ཤ་.

བརླིང་པོ་ (lĩŋbu) unmoved, firm, steady, impassive.

བརླིང་བ་ (lĩŋwə) sm. བརླིང་པོ་.

བརླུག (lūù) f. of va.རླུག.

བརླུགས་ (lūù) p. of རླུག.

ལ་ (la) 1. sm. དུ་ (used after all final letters) 2. adjective and verbal connective particle: "as well as" ། ལས་སླ་ལ་ཐོན་ཆེ་བ་ཡོད་ It is easy to do well as well as highly in productivity. ། ཁོ་རྒྱ་སྐད་ཤེས་ལ་བོད་ཀྱང་ཤེས་ As well as knowing Chinese, he also knows Tibetan. ། ཆུང་ལ་དཀྱུས་མ་ཡིན་པའི་ཚོང་ཁང་ A small and common store. 3. mountain pass; va.—རྒྱག་ to cross a mountain pass. 4. wax, candle wax. 5. the letter "ལ་" (used in alphabetical ordering). 6. after having done ། སྔོན་ལ་རྒྱ་ནག་ཏུ་ཕྱིན་ལ་གཞི་ནས་བོད་ལ་ཕྱིན་པ་རེད་ First he went to India, and after having done that only then did he go to Tibet.

ལ་ལུང་ (ləluŋ) mountains and valleys; va.—རྒྱག་ to cross mountains and valleys.

ལ་བཀྱག་ (lagyaà) candle holder.

ལ་སྐེད་ (lageè) middle of a mountain pass.

ལ་ཁ་ (laga) 1. top of a mountain pass. 2. mountain pass.

ལ་ཁད་ (lagɛɛ̀) (vb. + —) at the time/ point of ། ཤི་ལ་ཁད་ At the point of death.

ལ་ཁའི་ཉི་མ་ (lagɛ ñimə) 1. at twilight, at the time of the setting sun. 2. the end of a person's life.

ལ་ཁའི་ས་སྲུང་ (lagɛ sə̄suŋ) sentries/ guards posted along a mountain pass.

ལ་ཁའི་སོ་བ་ (lagɛ sōba) sm. ལ་ཁའི་ས་སྲུང་.

ལ་ཁྱི་ (ləkyi) 1. a large apso. 2. sm. ཤོ་ཁྱི་.

ལ་ཁྲལ་ (ladrɛɛ) tax paid for collecting herbs and firewood from mountain areas.

ལ་ག (laga) two year old sheep.

ལ་གོར་ (lagɔɔ) fast, quick.

ལ་གྲགས་ལུང་གྲགས་ (lətraà luŋdraà) sth. that is spread/ heard/ known everywhere [Lit. known on the mountain pass, known in the valley].

ལ་གླུ་ (ləlu) songs sung on mountains by herders.

ལ་དགུ་ལུང་དགུ་ (ləgu luŋgu) 1. many mountain passes and valleys [Lit. nine mountain passes and nine valleys]. 2. corduroy.

ལ་མགོ་ (lango) 1. sm. ལ་རྩེ. 2. the ལ་ superfixed letter.

ལ་མགོ་ཅན་ (laŋgojɛn) the letters which have the letter ལ་ superfixed.

ལ་རྒན་བཤགས་པའི་བོང་རྒན་ (lagɛn shāgbɛ poŋgɛn) well experienced [Lit. an old donkey who has crossed many mountain passes].

ལ་རྒྱ་ (lagya) 1. loyalty; va.—རྩེ་; —འཛིན་ —དགོངས་ to have a sense of loyalty ། ཁོང་ཚོ་གཞུང་ལ་ལ་རྒྱ་ཆེན་པོ་འདུག They have great loyalty towards the government ། ཁོང་གིས་རྒྱལ་ཁབ་ཀྱི་ལ་རྒྱ་བརྩིས་ནས་གཞུང་ལ་ཞབས་ཕྱི་དྲུར་ཐག་ཞུ་གི་ཡོད་པ་རེད་ He is working very hard because of his loyalty towards the country. 2. generally, on the whole ། ལ་རྒྱ་ལ་བཤད་ན་ Generally speaking.

ལ་རྒྱུག་ལུང་རྒྱུག (lagyaà luŋgyuù) going all over, going hither and thither; va.—བྱེད་ ། ཉེན་རྟོག་པས་ལ་རྒྱུག་ལུང་རྒྱུག་བྱས་ནས་ཀུན་མ་དེ་འཚོལ་བར་ཕྱིན་པ་རེད་ The police went all over searching for the thief.

ལ་རྒྱུགས་ལུང་རྒྱུགས་ (lagyuù luŋgyuù) sm. ལ་རྒྱུག་ལུང་རྒྱུག.

ལ་རྒྱུགས་ལྐུང་རྒྱུགས་ (lagyuù lūŋgyuù) sm. ལ་རྒྱུག་ལུང་རྒྱུག.

ལ་སྒོ་ (lago) 1. sm. ལ་ཁ་. 2. arc. places of trade/ business.

ལ་སྒོ་ཏ་ཟམ་ (lago dāsam) shung. a post station in Purang county in Ngari at the Nepalese border.

ལ་སྒོ་འབྱེད་ (lago ceè) sm. ཚོང་སྒོ་འབྱེད་.

ལ་བརྒྱབ་ཆུ་བརྒལ་ (lagyəb cūgɛɛ) crossing mountains and rivers, traveling far; va.—བྱེད་.

ལ་བརྒྱབ་རི་བརྒལ་ (ləgyəb rigɛɛ) sm. ལ་བརྒྱབ་ཆུ་བརྒལ་.

ལ་བརྒྱབ་ལུང་བརྒྱབ་ (ləgyəb luŋgyəb) sm. ལ་བརྒྱབ་རི་བརྒལ་.

ལ་ངེ་ལིང་ངེ་ (laŋŋe liŋŋe) sm. ལང་ངེ་ལིང་ངེ་.

ལ་གཅན་པ་ (lajɛnba) arc. 1. a tax collector for mountain passes. 2. a person protecting a mountain pass.

ལ་ཅོ་ (lajo) ch. hot pepper.

ལ་ཆ་ (laja) sealing wax; va.— རྒྱག་ to seal sth. with wax.

ལ་ཆེན་ (lajen) sm. མ་གཞི་.

ལ་ཆེན་གཅིག་དང་མ་འཕྲད་ན་རྟ་པོའི་ཤེད་ཤུགས་ག་ནས་ཤེས་ དགྲ་ཆེན་གཅིག་དང་མ་འཕྲད་ན་གྲོགས་པོའི་སློ་རྩ་ག་ནས་ཤེས་ (lajen jīdaŋ madrɛɛ̀na dābö shēèshuù kənɛɛ̀ shēè drajen jīgdaŋ madrɛɛ̀na trɔgbö lōdza kənɛɛ̀ shēè) one can not know the real character/ strength of others until encountering adversity [Lit. if you do not come to a high mountain pass you will not know the strength of a horse, if you do not meet a serious enemy, you will not know the courage of your friend].

ལ་འཇམ་པོ་ (la jambo) 1. a peaceful mountain pass that is devoid of danger from bandits and wild animals. 2. an mountain pass that is easy to cross.

ལ་འཇོར་ (lajɔɔ) a hoe/ pickaxe for digging sod.

ལ་ཉག (lañа) saddle/ concave shaped mountain pass.

ལ་ཉག་མཛོ་གཟེངས་ (lañag dzoseŋ) needing to compromise, finding a middle course [Lit. the mountain pass is concave, the dzo stands erect].

ལ་ཉུང་ (ləñuŋ) radish and turnip.

ལ་ཉེ་ (lañe) 1. mark, sign. 2. ability, energy.

ལ་ཏ་ (lada) 1. a type of string. 2. a thin/ fine cloth.

ལ་ཏྲ་ (lada) a container made of shell for keeping urine to be tested by doctors.

ལ་ཏིང་གླིང་ (ladin līŋ) Latin America.

ལ་ཏིང་མེ་གླིང་ (ladiŋ meliŋ) sm. ལ་ཏིང་གླིང་.

ལ་ཏིང་དབྱངས་གསལ་ཡི་གེ (ladiŋ yāŋsɛɛ yigi) the Latin alphabet, romanization.

ལ་སྟོང་ (ladoŋ) a hill mountain that is uninhabited.

ལ་གཏམ་ལུང་གཏམ་ (ladam luŋdam) empty/ idle/ useless talk.

ལ་བཏགས་ (ladaà) the name of the subjoined "ལ་."

ལ་རྟིང་གི་གྲིབ་མ་ (ladiŋgi tribmə) an old person who is going to die soon [Lit. the shadow of a mountain (pass) at sunset].

ལ་བརྟེན་ནས་ (ladennɛ) by means of, through, because of ། ལུང་པ་འདིའི་འཚོ་བའི་གནས་སྟངས་ཡག་པོ་ཡོད་པ་ལ་བརྟེན་ནས་མི་མང་པོ་སྤོས་ཡོང་གི་ཡོད་པ་རེད་ Many people are moving to this place because of its good living conditions.

ལ་སྟེགས་ (ladeg) candlestick, candle holder.

ལ་ཐག (ladaà) the distance to cross a hill/ mountain pass ། ལ་འདིའི་ལ་ཐག་རིང་པོ་ཡོད་པ་རེད་ This pass is very long.

ལ་ཐིགས་ (ladig) 1. a drop of sealing wax; va.—རྒྱག to seal sth. with sealing wax. 2. va.—རྒྱག an ancient form of torture involving dripping hot wax on a person.

ལ་ཐུ་ (lədu) sm. ལ་དུ་.

ལ་ཐུར་ (laduu) 1. downhill side of a mountain pass ། ལ་ཐུར་ལ་འགྲོ་དུས་རྟ་བབ་དགོས་ When going downhill one should dismount from one's horse. 2. abbr. of ལ་ and ཐུར་.

ལ་ཐིན་ཨ་མེ་རི་ཀ་ (laden āmerikgə) sm. ལ་ཏིང་གླིང་

ལ་ཐེལ་ (ladee) seal stamped on sealing wax; va.—རྒྱག.

ལ་ཐོག (ladɔɔ̀) sm. ལ་རྩེ་.

ལ་ཐོད་ (ladöö) a bandanna tied around the head.

ལ་ད་ (lada) sm. ལ་ཏ་.

ལ་དྭ་ཡུགས་ (ladayug) a roll of thick cloth.

ལ་དྭགས་ (ladaà) Ladakh.

ལ་དུ་ (lədu) food to be eaten when crossing a pass.

ལ་དུག (ləduù) high altitude sickness; vi.—ཤོར; —ཕོག [Lit. mountain pass poison].

ལ་དོན་ (ladön) the dative-locative particles.

ལ་སྣམ་ (lanam) soft woolen cloth.

ལ་ཕིན་ (ləbin) ch. bean starch (noodles).

ལ་སྤང་སྐོར་ལོག (labaŋ gɔ̄ɔ̄lɔɔ̀) shung. a fence built with sod/ turf.

ལ་ཕུག (ləbuù) radish.

ལ་ཕུག་དཀར་རིལ་ (ləbuù gāārii) small white round radish.

ལ་ཕུག་གོབ་ཚོས་ (ləbuù gobdzöö̀) stew made with meat and radish.

ལ་ཕུག་སྐོར་འཚོད་ (ləbuù gɔɔdzöö̀) sm. ལ་ཕུག་གོབ་ཚོས་.

ལ་ཕྲེང་ཟམ་པ་ (ladreŋ samba) precipitous mountain trails and bridges ༎ལ་ཕྲེང་ཟམ་པ་སོགས་ལ་ཉམས་བཟོ་བྱེད་ Repair the precipitous mountain trails and bridges.

ལ་འཕྲང་ (ladraŋ) precipitous mountain trails (overlooking ravines/ rivers).

ལ་བ་ (lawa) 1. sm. ལ་སྣམ་. 2. ch. horn, va.—རྒྱག to blow a horn.

ལ་བོ་ཆེ་ (lawoje) a high mountain pass.

ལ་དབྱངས་ (layaŋ) sm. ལ་གཞིས་.

ལ་འབོལ་ (laböö) wax for mounting stones/ gems in settings.

ལ་འབྲུག (ladrug) abbr. of Ladakh and Bhutan.

ལ་སྦར་ (labar) ch. rubber. 2. rubber tire.

ལ་མ་ (lama) sod, turf; va.—རྒྱག to lay sod; va.—འདྲུ་ to dig up sod.

ལ་མ་ལུང་ས་ (lamaluŋ) neither mountain (pass) nor plain.

ལ་མག (lamaà) sm. ལ་མ་.

ལ་མོ་ (lamo) 1. mountain pass. 2. fast, quick ༎དགེ་རྒན་གྱིས་ཁྱེད་ལ་མོ་ཤོག་ཟེར་གྱི་འདུག The teacher is asking for you to come quickly.

ལ་སྨན་ (lamɛɛ̀) 1. a Tibetan medicine used for jaundice. 2. any compounded Tibetan medicine.

ལ་སྨུག (ləmuù) crayon.

ལ་བཙས་ (ladzɛɛ̀) 1. sm. ལ་རྫས་. 2. sm. ལ་ཁྲལ་.

ལ་རྩ་ (ladza) foot of a hill/ mountain.

ལ་རྩི་ (lədzi) mending cracks with melted wax; va.—རྒྱག.

ལ་རྩེ་ (ladze) mountain summit/ peak.

ལ་ཚད་ (ladzɛɛ̀) size/ height of a mountain.

ལ་ཚིགས་ (lədzii) sm. ལ་ཉག.

ལ་ཚུགས་པ་ (ladzugbə) tax collector for trade goods located on mountain passes.

ལ་རྫབ་ (ladzəb) gall/ burl on trees (that are used to make wooden bowls).

ལ་རྫས་ (ladzɛɛ̀) prayer flags and stone cairns at the summit of mountain passes.

ལ་གཞིས་ (lashɛɛ̀) sm. ལ་སྒྲུ་.

ལ་ཟུར་ (lasur) the sides of a mountain pass.

ལ་གཟར་ (lasar) a steep slope.

ལ་ཝར་པན་ཌི་ (lawar pɛ̄ndi) Rawalpindi.

ལ་ཝུར་ (lawur) sm. འཕྲུལ་དུ་.

ལ་འོ་གོ་ (lawogo) Laos.

ལ་འོག (lawɔɔ̀) 1. foot of a mountain. 2. area just below a mountain pass.

ལ་འོང་ (laoŋ) yes! okay!

ལ་འོད་ (lawöö̀) light from a candle.

ལ་ཡོགས་ (layɔɔ̀) sth. bad happening as retribution for one's own bad act; vi.—རྒྱག; —ཐེབ ༎ཁོས་ཕ་མར་ཞབས་ཕྱི་མ་ཞུས་པའི་ལ་ཡོགས་བརྒྱབ་ནས་ནད་ངན་ཕོག་འདུག He suffered a serious illness as retribution for not looking after his parents.

ལ་གཡོགས་ (layɔɔ̀) sm. ལ་ཡོགས་.

ལ་རགས་ (laraà) a fence/ wall/ barrier built of sod slabs.

ལ་རེ་ (lare) sm. ལ་ལ་.

ལ་རོང་ (laroŋ) mountains and valley.

ལ་ལ་ (lala) some ༎མི་ལ་ལ་དྲང་པོ་ཡོད་ཀྱང་ལ་ལ་དྲང་པོ་མེད་ Some people are truthful and some are not.

ལ་ལ་ཁ་བ་མེད་པར་ལུང་ལ་བ་མོ་ཡོང་དོན་མེད་ (lalə kāwa meèbaa lūŋlə pamo yoŋdön meè) sth. will not happen without a cause [Lit. if there is no snow on the mountains there is no reason for frost to come to the valley].

ལ་ལ་གཏོང་ (lala dōŋ) va. to have anal intercourse.

ལ་ལ་ཕུད་ (la labüǜ) cnidium monnieri (used in Tibetan medicine).

ལ་ལུང་ (ləluŋ) 1. abbr. of ལ་ and ལུང་པ་. 2. hills/ mountains and plains/ valleys. 3. everywhere.

ལ་ཤགས་ (lashaà) a type of long Tibetan men's dress.

ལ་ཤན་དབྱེ་ (lashen yē) va. to pick out/ select.

ལ་ཤས་ (lashɛɛ̀) sm. ལ་ལ་.

ལ་ཤོག (lashoò) sm. ལྒ་ཤོག.

ལ་སང་ (lasaŋ) very much, extremely ༎འདི་འདྲ་བྱུང་ན་དངོས་གནས་ཡག་པ་ལ་སང་ If this happens, it will really be so good.

ལ་སོ་ (laso) abbr. of ལ་ཁའི་སོ་པ་.

ལ་སོགས་པ་ (lasogba) etc., so forth (see སོགས).

ལ་ཧོར་ (lahɔr) Lahore.

ལྒ་ (la) wax, candle.

ལྒ་ཀྱག (lagyaà) candle stand.

ལྒ་ཤོག (lashɔɔ̀) 1. wax paper. 2. stencil paper.

ལྦ་ (la) sm. ལ་བ་.

ལག (lag) 1. hand, arm. 2. a unit of ten horses or mules used for transporting. 3. the hinge/ joint of a cover.

ལག་གོར་ (laggɔɔ) bangles, bracelets.

ལག་གྱོག (laggyɔɔ̀) crooked/ crippled hand or arm.

ལག་དཀར་མོ་ (lag gārmo) white hands from kneading dough (this is said to make a person more suseptible to harm from ghosts/ demons).

ལག་དགྲིས་ (lə̄gdrii̇̀) sm. ལག་གདུབ་.

ལག་སྐམ་ (lagam) sm. ལག་པ་སྐམ་པོ་.

ལག་སྐར་ (lagar) sm. སྐར་མ་.

ལག་སྐེའི་ཆུ་ཚོད་ (laggee cūdzöö̀) wrist watch.

ལག་སྐོར་ (laggɔɔ) hand turned, hand operated, manually operated ༎ལག་སྐོར་བལ་བྲེག་འཕྲུལ་འཁོར་ A hand operated wool shearing machine. 2. the act of doing sth. from hand to hand; va.—བྱེད་ ༎སྐུ་མགྲོན་ཚོར་བྱེ་རིལ་ལག་སྐོར་བྱས་ནས་བཏང་བ་རེད་ They served the candies to the guests one by one (from hand to hand).

ལག་སྐོར་འཁེལ་འཁོར་ (laggɔɔ kēēkɔɔ) hand operated spinning machine.

ལག་སྐོར་འཁོར་སྡེགས་ (laggɔɔ kɔ̄ɔ̄deg) hand operated lathe.

ལག་སྐྱེས་ (laggyeè) an animal born from one's own animal rather than bought from outside.

ལག་སྐྱོགས་ (laggyɔɔ̀) small ladle.

ལག་སྐྱོར་ (laggyɔɔ) supporting by the hand; va.—བྱེད་.

ལག་སྐྱོར་འདྲུད་འཁོར་ (laggyɔɔ drüǜgɔɔ) abbr. of ལག་སྐྱོར་འདྲུད་འཐེན་འཁོར་ལོ་.

ལག་སྐྱོར་འདྲུད་འཐེན་འཁོར་ལོ་ (laggyɔɔ drüǜden kɔ̄ɔ̄lo) a small handlebar steered tractor in use in Tibet.

ལག་བསྐོར་གཏོང་ (laggɔɔ dōŋ) va. to be arm-in-arm ༎ཁོང་གཉིས་ལག་སྐོར་བཏང་ནས་འགྲོ་གི་འདུག Those two are going arm-in-arm.

ལག་བསྐོར་འཕྲུལ་ཆས་ (laggɔɔ trūūjɛɛ̀) hand operated machines.

ལག་བསྐོར་བའི་རྟགས་ (laggɔɔwɛ dāà) shung. seal put on a document collectively for others.

ལག་བསྐོར་བའི་ཞུ་ཐེལ་ (laggɔɔwɛ shudee) shung. sm. ལག་བསྐོར་བའི་རྟགས་.

ལག་བསྐོར་དབུ་ཁྲིད་ (laggɔɔwɛ ūdrii̇̀) shung. the person who represents people and puts a seal on a document on their behalf.

ལག་ཁུག (lagguù) handbag, pouch held in the hand.

ལག་ཁུར་གློག་བཞུ་ (laggur lɔ̄gshu) hand held lantern/ flashlight/ torch.

ལག་ཁོག (lagkɔɔ̀) the upper half of an animal carcass.

ལག་ཁྱི་ (lәggyi) sm. ཤོ་ཁྱི་.

ལག་ཁྱེར་ (laggyer) sm. ལག་འཁྱེར་.

ལག་ཁྱོར་ (laggyɔɔ) holding one's hand(s) cupped to receive sth.; va.—བྱེད་.

ལག་ཁྲིད་ (lәgdrii) 1. instructions or directions given firsthand via an example; va.—བྱེད་ ¶ བཟོ་པའི་དགེ་རྒན་གྱིས་དགེ་ཕྲུག་ལ་ལག་ཁྲིད་བྱས་པ་རེད་ The worker's teacher taught the students by showing them firsthand.

ལག་འཁར་ (laggar) walking stick, cane.

ལག་འཁོར་ (laggɔɔ) things turned/ spun with the hand.

ལག་འཁྱེར་ (laggyee) 1. pass, permit, certificate, diploma 2. passport. 3. hand carried/ held ¶ ལག་འཁྱེར་མེ་མདའ་ཐག་ཐག Hand held machine gun. 4. style of hand movement used when dancing.

ལག་འཁྱེར་བཀའ་ཤོག (laggyer gāshoò) sm. ལག་ཁྱེར་.

ལག་འཁྱེར་གློག་བཞུ་ (laggyer lɔ̄gshu) flashlight.

ལག་ཁྱེར་རྩ་ཚིག (laggyer dzәdzii) shung. a proclamation/ order that is carried on person.

ལག་ཁྱེར་ཞིབ་འབྱར་མ་ (laggyer shibjarma) shung. a permit/ pass with the seal of the investigator on it.

ལག་མགོ་ (laŋgo) hand, arm.

ལག་མགྱོགས་པིག་རྣོ་ (laggyɔɔ̀ bigno) skilled worker [Lit. sharp eyes and quick hands].

ལག་འགྱོག (laggyɔɔ̀) hitting/ striking with the hand; va.—བྱེད་.

ལག་འགྲིམ་ (lagdrim) having a hand in doing sth. ¶ ཐོན་དངོས་འདི་ཚོ་མི་མང་པོའི་ལག་འགྲིམ་ནས་བཟོས་པ་ཞིག་རེད་ A lot of people had a hand in making these products.

ལག་རྒྱན་ (laggyɛn) bracelet, bangle.

ལག་རྒྱུགས་ (lәggyuù) walking stick, cane.

ལག་རྒྱུན་ (lәggyün) customary technique/ practice; vi.—ཆད་ to have a skill come into disuse, to lose a customary skill/ tradition/ practice ¶ བོད་ལུགས་སྨན་པའི་གཤག་བཅོས་ཀྱི་ལག་རྒྱུན་ཆད་པ་རེད་ The Tibetan medical technique of doing (surgical) operations has been lost.

ལག་སྒམ་ (laggam) 1. a small box/ chest. 2. briefcase.

ལག་སྒུལ་ (laggüü) hand operated, manual.

ལག་སྒྲོག (lagdrɔɔ̀) rope used to tie a horse's front leg to one of its back legs.

ལག་བརྒྱུད་ (lәggyüü) shung. to pass sth. from hand to hand.

ལག་ངར་ (lagŋar) the arm from the shoulder to the wrist.

ལག་ངར་རུས་པ་ (lagŋar rüüba) the bones extending from the shoulder to the wrist.

ལག་དངུལ་ (lәgŋüü) 1. cash, money on hand. 2. petty cash (for daily expenses). 3. pocket money, expense money.

ལག་དངུལ་དེབ་ཆུང་ (lәgŋüü tebjuŋ) petty cash book.

ལག་ང་ (lagŋa) hand held drum.

ལག་ངོ་ (lagŋo) skin diseases of the hand such as mange/ scabies.

ལག་སྔ་བ་ (lag ŋāwa) the first one to hit/ strike ¶ ཕྲུ་གུ་གཉིས་རྒྱག་རེས་བརྡུང་དུས་ཕྲུ་གུ་ཆུང་བ་དེ་ལག་སྔ་བ་བྱུང་སོང་ When the two boys fought, the younger one struck first.

ལག་གཅིག་ལག་མ་ (lagjig lagma) person with only one arm.

ལག་བཅག (lagjaà) an implement for tapping down the edge of a Tibetan roof.

ལག་ལྕག (lagjaà) sm. ལག་བཅག.

ལག་ལྕགས་ (lagjaà) handcuffs hand shackles; va.—རྒྱག to handcuff.

ལག་ལྕིབ་ (lagjib) pot holder.

ལག་ཆ་ (lagja) 1. implement, tool. 2. weapon. 3. penis (slang).

ལག་ཆའི་དཔེ་དེབ་ (lagjɛ bēdeb) instruction manual.

ལག་འཆང་ (lagjaŋ) va. to get involved with, to pay attention to; va.—བྱེད་ ¶ དུས་གཅིག་ལ་ལས་ཀ་མང་པོར་ལག་འཆང་བྱ་རྒྱུ་མེད་ One shouldn't get involved with many tasks at the same time.

ལག་འཇམ་ (lagjam) abbr. of ལག་པ་འཇམ་པོ་.

ལག་འཇུ་ (lagju) 1. door handle. 2. banister.

ལག་འཇུས་ (lagjüü) holding hands; va.—བྱེད་.

ལག་རྗེས་ (lagjɛɛ̀) 1. handprint. 2. an accomplishment, achievement ¶ འདས་པའི་དཔའ་བོའི་ལག་རྗེས་ The accomplishments of past heroes.

ལག་རྗེས་ཐོན་འབྲས་ (lagjɛɛ̀ töndrɛɛ̀) sm. ལག་རྗེས་, 2.

ལག་ཉ་ (lagña) fleshy part of the arm.

ལག་ཉར་ (lagñar) holding, keeping; va.—བྱེད་ ¶ དངོས་པོ་མཁོ་གལ་ཆེ་བ་ཁག་ཅིག་ལག་ཉར་བྱས་ནས་དེ་བྱིངས་ཚང་མ་བཙོངས་པ་ཡིན་ I kept the more useful things and sold all the remainder.

ལག་ཉུལ་ (lagñüü) searching/ groping with one's hand; va.—བྱེད་.

ལག་ཉེས་ཁུར་ (lagñeè kūr) vi. to cause sth. bad happen to happen accidentally, to make a mistake with one's hands ¶ བཟོ་པ་དེས་ལག་ཉེས་ཁུར་ནས་འཕྲུལ་འཁོར་དེ་སྐྱོན་ཤོར་བ་རེད་ The worker accidentally made a mistake and broke the machine.

ལག་ཉེས་ཤོར་ (lagñeè shɔ̄ɔ) sm. ལག་ཉེས་ཁུར་.

ལག་མཉེད་ (lagñeè) kneading sth. in one's hand to tan it; va.—གཏོང་.

ལག་ཏུ་འཆང་ (lagdu cāŋ) 1. va. to hold in one's hand. 2. sm. ལག་འཆང་.

ལག་ཏུ་ཐེབས་ (lagdu tēb) vi. to fall/ come into one's hand. ¶ སོ་པ་བདུན་ལག་ཏུ་ཐེབས་པ་རེད་ Seven spies fell into our hands.

ལག་ཏུ་འབྱོར་ (lagdu jɔɔ) sm. ལག་ཏུ་ཐེབས་.

ལག་ཏུ་ཚུད་ (lagdu tsüü) sm. ལག་ཏུ་ཐེབས་.

ལག་ཏུ་ལེན་ (lagdu len) 1. va. to put into practice ¶ ཁ་ནས་བཤད་པ་ལག་ཏུ་བླངས་པ་རེད་ (They) put what they said into practice. 2. va. to take into one's hand, to seize.

ལག་ཏུ་ཤོར་ (lagdu shɔ̄ɔ) vi. to lose, to fall into the hands of another (e.g., an enemy).

ལག་ཏུ་སོན་ (lagdu sȫn) sm. ལག་ཏུ་ཐེབས་.

ལག་གཏམ་ (lagdam) a way of doing business by putting one's hand in the sleeve of another person and making an offer or giving a price by extending fingers to indicate the price.

ལག་གདུགས་ (lagdug) sm. ལག་ཐུག.

ལག་བཏགས་ (lagdaà) 1. handwoven. 2. sm.* ལག་རྟགས་, 2.

ལག་བཏང་ཁ་བྲལ་ (lagdaŋ kādrɛɛ) shaking hands and departing.

ལག་བཏང་འཆང་ (lagdaŋ cāŋ) sm. ལག་བཏང་གཏོང་.

ལག་བཏེགས་འབོག་རས་ (lagdeg bɔgreè) handbag.

ལག་བཏང་གཏོང་ (lagdaŋ dōŋ) va. to hold hands.

ལག་རྟགས་ (lagdaà) present, gift, presentation; va.—སྐུར་ to send presents/ gifts; va.—སྤྲོད་ to give a gift/ present.

ལག་རྟགས་ཆུང་ཡང་བསམ་པའི་ཁྱད་ (lagdaà cūŋyaŋ sāmbɛ kyɛ̄ɛ̀) it's the thought that counts, not the size of the gift.

ལག་རྟེན་ (lagden) 1. walking stick, cane. 2. stair railing. 3. a potter's tool.

ལག་སྟབས་ (lagdәb) sm. ལག་འཁྱེར་, 4.

ལག་སྟོང་ (lagdoŋ) empty-handed.

ལག་སྟོང་ཁྱིམ་འཛུགས་ (lagdoŋ kyīmdzuù) starting from scratch; va.—བྱེད་ [Lit. starting a household with no possessions].

ལག་སྟོང་མཚོན་མེད་ (lagdoŋ tsȫnmeè) unarmed.

ལག་སྟོང་ལུས་སྦྱོང་ (lagdoŋ lüüjoŋ) freestyle exercises, calisthenics.

ལག་བརྟེན་ (lagden) sm. ལག་རྟེན་.

ལག་བསྟར་ (lagdar) 1. sm. ལག་ལེན་བསྟར་. 2. sm. ལག་བསྟར་མ་. 3. acting ¶ ལག་བསྟར་ཀྲུ་ཞི་ Acting chairman.

ལག་བསྟར་དོན་འགྲུབ་ (lagdar töndrub) implementing and succeeding.

ལག་བསྟར་བྱེད་ (lagdar ceè) va. to put into practice, to implement.

ལག་བསྟར་མ་ (lagdarma) in one's own handwriting ¶ འཛིན་འདི་ཁོའི་ལག་བསྟར་མ་རེད་ This receipt is in his own handwriting.

ལག་ཐགས་ (lagdaà) 1. handwoven. 2. handloom.

ལག་ཐལ་ (lagdεε) inadvertently doing sth. incorrectly, doing sth. mistakenly with the hands; vi.—ཤོར་.

ལག་ཐིའུ་ (lagtiwu) sm. ལག་ཐིལ་.

ལག་ཐུག (lag tüù) vi. to fist fight, to hit one another with the hand ¶ ཁོ་གཉིས་སྔོན་ལ་ཁ་ཚོད་ཤོར་རྗེས་ཕན་ཚུན་ལག་ཐུག་བཞག First they argued and then they hit each other.

ལག་ཐུག་རྒྱག (lagtuù gyaà) vi. to be out of sth. and in great need of it ¶ ངའི་ནམ་རྒྱུན་གྱི་ན་ཚའི་སྨན་མ་ཁྱེར་ཙང་ལག་ཐུག་རྒྱག་བྱུང་ I was in great need of the medicine that I forgot to take with me.

ལག་ཐུག་རྒྱག་པོ་ (lagtuù gyagbo) sm. ལག་ཐུག་རྒྱག.

ལག་འཐེན་རླུང་འབུད་འབབ་ཆ་ (lagten lūŋbüü baja) accordion; va.—གཏོང་.

ལག་ཐེལ་ (lagdee) a seal stamped on bracelets worn by soldiers of the tt.

ལག་ཐོ་ (lagdo) 1. handwritten notes. 2. a type of small hammer.

ལག་ཐོ་གཞུ་ (lagdo shu) va. to kick with the front legs (of horses).

ལག་ཐོག (lagdɔɔ̀) 1. on hand ¶ ལག་ཐོག་དངུལ་ཞེ་དྲགས་མེད་ I don't have much money on hand. 2. by hand; va.— སྤྲོད་ to give by hand.

ལག་ཐོགས་ (lagdɔɔ̀) 1. for the time being, temporarily ¶ ལག་ཐོགས་སྡོད་ས་འདི་འགྲིགས་ཀྱི་རེད་ For the time being, this will do for a place to stay. 2. essential items, sth. badly needed ¶ ང་དངུལ་ལག་ཐོགས་ཀྱི་འདུག་པས་ངས་གཡར་བའི་དངུལ་སླར་སྤྲོད་རོགས་ I am badly in need of money so please give back the money that I lent you.

ལག་ཐོགས་པ་ (lagdɔgba) sm. ལག་ཐོགས་པོ་

ལག་ཐོགས་པོ་ (lagdɔgbo) sm. ལག་ཐོགས་, 2.

ལག་ཐོབ་ (lagdɔb) net amount, amount in one's hand.

ལག་མཐིལ་ (lәgdii) palm of the hand.

ལག་མཐུ་ (lәgdu) arm strength.

ལག་མཐིལ་དུ་བླངས་པ་ལྟར་ (lәgdiidu lāŋbadar) sm. སྐར་མཐིལ་ནང་དུ་བླུགས་འདྲ་.

ལག་འཐག (lagdaà) handwoven, handloomed; va.—རྒྱག ¶ ལག་འཐག་རས་ Handwoven cloth.

ལག་འཐེན་ཐུག་པ་ (lagden tūgbә) hand pulled noodles.

ལག་དག (lagdaà) vi. to be okay ¶ ཁྱེད་རང་གིས་ལས་ཀ་དེ་འདྲ་བྱས་པས་ལག་དག་གི་མ་རེད་ If you do work like this it wont be okay.

ལག་དམ་ (lagdam) 1. seal, stamp. 2. stingy, tightfisted.

ལག་དམ་པོ་ (lag tambo) stingy, tightfisted.

ལག་དར་ (lagdar) hand held flag.

ལག་དལ་ (lagdεε) leisure time; va.—བྱེད་; —བྲིས་བྲིས་ to write sth. during leisure time, to doodle ¶ འགོ་ཁྲིད་ཀྱིས་གཏམ་བཤད་བྱེད་སྐབས་ཁོས་ལག་དལ་གྱིས་རི་མོ་བྲིས་བཞག When the leader was giving a speech he doodled.

ལག་དེབ་ (lagdeb) small notebook.

ལག་དོ་ (lagdo) person who loads transport mules, muleteer.

ལག་དོ་བ་ (lagdowa) sm. ལག་དོ་.

ལག་དོག (lagdɔg) bundle of yarn; va.—རྒྱག to make yarn into a roll/ bundle by holding one end in one's hand and wrapping the other around one's elbow in a figure eight.

ལག་གདང་ (lagdaŋ) holding hands, hand-in-hand; va.—སྒྲིལ་; —གཏོང་; —འཆང་ to hold hands ¶ ཁོ་གཉིས་ལག་གདང་བདང་ནས་འགྲོ་གི་འདུག Those two are walking holding hands.

ལག་གདང་དཔུང་སྒྲིག (lagdaŋ būŋdrig) sm. ལག་གདང་དཔུང་སྒྲིལ་.

ལག་གདང་དཔུང་སྒྲིལ་ (lagdaŋ būŋdree) hand-in-hand, shoulder-to-shoulder, side-by-side; va.—བྱེད་ ¶ ཁོང་ཚོ་ལག་གདང་དཔུང་སྒྲིལ་བྱས་ནས་དམག་ས་ར་བསྐྱོད་པ་རེད་ They marched to the battlefield shoulder-to-shoulder.

ལག་གདང་དཔུང་གཤིབ་ (lagdaŋ būŋshib) sm. ལག་གདང་དཔུང་སྒྲིལ་.

ལག་གདན་ (lagdεn) a wooden board used under a lathe when hollowing out wooden bowls.

ལག་གདུང་ (lәgduŋ) sm.* ལག་གདབ་.

ལག་གདུབ་ (lәgdub) bracelet.

ལག་གདུབ་ཆུ་ཚོད་ (lәgdub cūdzüü) wrist watch.

ལག་བདར་ (lag dar) va. to do work with one's own hands.

ལག་བདེ་ (lagde) 1. talented, clever, dexterous (with hand tasks). 2. monks who serve tea in monastic prayer assemblies.

ལག་བདེ་བ་ (lagdewa) sm. ལག་བདེ་.

ལག་བདེ་ལས་མགྱོགས་ (lagde lεègyɔɔ̀) dexterous and quick at work.

ལག་མདའ་ (laŋda) 1. any hand held gun including rifles ¶ ལག་མདའ་དབྱིན་ཇི་ཁ་རེང་ The English carbine rifle. 2. pistol, revolver.

ལག་མདུང་ (lagduŋ) a short spear.

ལག་འདབ་ (lagdab) hand.

ལག་འདེབས་ (lag deb) shung. va. plowing a field for one's own use.

ལག་འདེབས་ས་ཞིང་ (lagdeb shiŋ) 1. shung. a field whose yield is for one's own use. 2. tenement land/ field (on an estate).

ལག་འདོགས་ཆུ་ཚོད་ (lagdɔɔ̀ cūdzüü) wrist watch.

ལག་འདོགས་ཆུ་ཚོད་འཁོར་ལོ་ (lagdɔɔ̀ cūdzüü kɔ̄ɔ̄lo) sm. ལག་འདོགས་ཆུ་ཚོད་.

ལག་འདོགས་དུས་ཚོད་ (lagdɔɔ̀ tüüdzüü) sm. ལག་འདོགས་ཆུ་ཚོད་.

ལག་འདོན་ (laŋdün) shung. 1. a type of traditional tax payment in kind/ cash (in contrast to work); va.—བྱེད་ to pay a tab in cash or kind. 2. expenses that one has paid; va.—རྒྱག; —སྤྲོད་ to give money by one's own hand ¶ སྔོན་ལ་འགྲོ་སོང་ཚང་མ་ལག་འདོན་བཏང་ནས་རྗེས་སུ་རྩིས་རྒྱག་བྱེད་དགོས་ First pay all the expenses yourself and then later you can do an accounting.

ལག་དྲུགས་ (lәgduù) sm. ལག་ཐུག་རྒྱག.

ལག་རྡུམ་ (lәgdum) handless (sb. whose hand has been cut off); va.—བཅད་ to cut off sb.'s hands (as corporal punishment).

ལག་རྡུམ་པ་ (lәgdumbә) handless person.

ལག་རྡུམ་བྲག་ལ་འཛེགས་པ་ (lәgdum tragla dzegba) trying to do sth. that is impossible, a foolish/ stupid endeavor [Lit. a person without hands trying to climb a rock].

ལག་རྡེལ་ (lagdee) hand grenade.

ལག་རྡོ་ (lagdo) 1. a rock for throwing by hand; va.—གཡུག to throw a rock by hand.

ལག་བརྡ་ (lagda) hand gesture/ sign, va.—བྱེད་ to gesture/ signal by hand.

ལག་བརྡབ་ (lagdәb) sm. ལག་པ་བརྡབ་.

ལག་བརྡུལ་ (lagdüü) 1. waving one's hands. 2. grinding/ pulverizing by hand; va.— བྱེད་.

ལག་ལྡན་ (lagεn) 1. sm. ལག་ཐོག. 2. occupation, skill.

ལག་སྡུག་རྒྱག (lәgdug gyaà) sm. ལག་ཐོགས་པོ་.

ལག་སྡོག (lagdɔɔ̀) sm. ལག་བསྡོགས་.

ལག་སྡོད་པ་ (lagdöö) a person who stops hail storms by means of tantric practices.

ལག་བསྡོགས་ (lagdɔɔ̀) 1. fried twisted dough. 2. preparing to do sth.; va.—བྱེད་.

ལག་བསྡོགས་ཁ་ཟས་ (lagdɔɔ̀ kāpsεὲ) sm. ལག་བསྡོགས་, 1.

ལག་ན་ཐོད་པ་ (laàna tȫȍbә) sm. དབང་ཕྱུག.

ལག་ན་རྡོ་རྗེ་ (laàna dɔɔje) sm. ཕྱག་ན་རྡོ་རྗེ་.

ལག་ནས་ (lagnε) 1. grain in one's possession/ on hand. 2. grains that is used in bartering. 3. from one's hand.

ལག་ནོམ་ (lagnom) sm. ལག་རྩལ་.

ལག་ནོར་ (lagnɔɔ) possessions/ property/ wealth that is in hand or on hand.

ལག་སྣེ་ (lagne) expense money for daily necessities; va.—གཏོང་ to spend money for daily necessities; vi.—ཇོགས་ to exhaust (one's daily expenses) ¶ ཕོགས་དུས་ཐོག་ལ་མ་འབྱོར་ཙང་ཁོང་གི་ལག་སྣེ་ཇོགས་བཞག Because his salary didn't come on time his money for daily expenses was exhausted.

ལག་སྣེ་གཏོང་བྱེད་ (lagne dōŋjeè) sm. ལག་སྣེ་.

ལག་སྣོད་ (lagnöö) measuring utensil used when selling milk and ཆང་.

ལག་གནད་ (lagnɛɛ̀) sm. ལག་ཐོགས་པོ་.

ལག་པ་ (lagba) 1. hand, arm; va.—གཏོང་ to shake hands; —རྒྱག to touch sth. with one's hand; va.—འགྱོགས་ to raise one's hand to hit; va.—གཡར་ to lend a hand, to help; va.—རྐྱོང་ to stretch/ raise one's hand ¶ མི་གཞན་དག་གི་ཅ་ལག་ལ་ལག་པ་རྒྱག་རྒྱུ་མེད་ You shouldn't touch other people's things. ¶ གྲོགས་པོ་གཉིས་ལག་པ་བཏང་སོང་ The two friends shook hands. ¶ ཁོས་ང་ལ་ལག་པ་བརྒྱབ་བྱུང་ He hit me with his hand. ¶ ང་ཕྱོགས་ཅོག་ཙེ་འདི་དབོར་དགོས་ཡོད་པས་ལག་པ་གཡར་དང་ Please lend me a hand I have to move the table. ¶ འཐུས་མི་ཚོ་མོས་མཐུན་ཡོད་ན་ལག་པ་རྐྱོང་ཞིག Delegates. If you agree, please raise your hands. 2. the forelegs of a quadruped.

ལག་པ་བཀྲིན་པོ་ (lagba drēnbo) sm. ལག་པ་སྐམ་པོ་.

ལག་པ་སྐམ་པོ་ (lagba gāmbo) stingy, tightfisted.

ལག་པ་སྐྱིད་པར་གཟེར་ (lagba gēèbar seè) sm. སྐྱིད་གཟེར་བྱེད་.

ལག་པ་རྐྱོང་ (lagba gyōŋ) see ལག་པ་.

ལག་པ་ཁ་སྦྱར་ (lagba kājar) cupping one's hands (as in greeting or namaste); va.— བྱེད་.

ལག་པ་མཁས་པོ་ (lagba kɛ̄ɛbo) adept, skillful.

ལག་པ་ཁོབ་དོ་ (lagba kōbdo) clumsy, not dexterous.

ལག་པ་འཁོལ་ (lagba kȫö) vi. to be itching to hit or beat sb. ¶ ཁོས་ང་ལ་ཁོང་ཁྲོ་བསླངས་ཐག་ཆོད་ནས་ང་ལག་པ་འཁོལ་བྱུང་ He made me so angry that I was itching to beat him up.

ལག་པ་གློད་ (lagba lȫö) vi. to get let go, to get released.

ལག་པ་གློད་གཏོང་ (lagba lȫö dōŋ) va. to let go, to take one's hands off, to release.

ལག་པ་མགྱོགས་པོ་ (lagba gyɔgbo) dexterous, nimble with the hands.

ལག་པ་འཁྲིམ་ (lagbə drim) vi. to do work that many people had a hand in ¶ ཐོན་རྫས་འདི་བཟོ་པ་མང་པོའི་ལག་པ་འཁྲིམ་པ་རེད་ Many workers had a hand in making this product.

ལག་པ་འགྲོ་ (lagba dro) vi. to be lucky in gambling.

ལག་པ་སྒྲུལ་ (lagba güü) va. to do sth. oneself ¶ རང་གི་ལག་པ་སྒྲུལ་ན་ཡག་གི་རེད་ If you do it yourself it will be better.

ལག་པ་སྒྲིང་ (lagba dreŋ) sm. ལག་པ་རྐྱོང་.

ལག་པ་སྔ་དིང་ (lagba ŋədiŋ) taking the initiative to gain the upper hand, striking first to gain the advantage; va.—གཏོང་ ¶ ད་ཆ་ལག་པ་སྔ་དིང་གཏོང་རྒྱུ་ལས་གཞན་བྱེ་བྲ་ཐབས་མེད་ Now there is no choice but to take the initiative to strike first to gain the upper hand.

ལག་པ་ཆད་མཐུད་ (lagba cɛ̄ɛdüü) resetting a broken hand/ arm; va.—རྒྱག.

ལག་པ་གཅུས་རིལ་ (lagba jüürii) twisting an arm into a hammer lock (behind the back); va.—རྒྱག.

ལག་པ་འཆང་ (lagba cāŋ) va. to touch with the hand.

ལག་པ་འཇམ་པོ་ (lagba jambo) a person who is gentle with his hands [Lit. soft hands].

ལག་པ་འཛུ་ (lagba ju) va. to hold sb.'s hands, to hold with or in the hand.

ལག་པ་གཏོང་ (lagba dōŋ) 1. va. to shake hands. 2. sm. ལག་གཏམ་. 3. va. to extend/ reach out one's hand.

ལག་པ་གཏོང་རེས་ (lagba dōŋreè) shaking hands; va.—བྱེད་ to shake hands back and forth, to shake each other's hand.

ལག་པ་སྟོང་པ་ (lagba dōŋba) sm. ལག་སྟོང་.

ལག་པ་འཐེན་ (lagba tēn) va. to pull sb.'s hands.

ལག་པ་དམ་པོ་ (lagba tambo) sm. ལག་པ་སྐམ་པོ་.

ལག་པ་བདེ་པོ་ (lagba debo) sm. ལག་བདེ་, 1.

ལག་པ་རྡབ་ (lagba dəb) 1. va. to clap, to applaud. 2. vi. to bang one's hand against sth. (accidentally). 3. va. to bang one's hand on a table, etc. (in anger).

ལག་པ་གནམ་ཀེར་ (lagba nāmger) holding up hands (e.g., to surrender); va.—བྱེད་ ¶ ལག་པ་གནམ་ཀེར་བྱས་ནས་མགོ་བཏགས་ཞུས་པ་རེད་ Holding up their hands, they surrendered.

ལག་པ་སྤྲོད་ (lagba drȫö) sm. ལག་པ་རྩིས་སྤྲོད་.

ལག་པ་ཕྱིས་ས་ (lagba cīisə) an excuse/ pretext ¶ ཚོགས་མི་འགའ་ཤས་མ་སླེབས་ཙང་ཚོགས་འདུ་འཚོག་ཐུབ་མ་སོང་ཟེར་བ་དེ་ལག་པ་ཕྱིས་ས་བཟོས་པ་རང་རེད་ The fact that some members did not show up was used as an excuse for not holding the meeting. 2. passing off responsibility to others ¶ གནད་དོན་དེ་གོང་རིམ་ནས་ཐག་གཅོད་སྔོན་ཀྱང་འཐུས་མི་ཚོ་གྲོས་སྡུར་བྱེད་བཅུག་པ་དེ་ལག་པ་ཕྱིས་བཟོས་པ་ཞིག་རང་རེད་ Even though the superior already decided the issue, they passed off the responsibility to others by convening delegates to discuss it.

ལག་པ་འཕྱིད་ (lagba cīi) 1. va. to wipe one's hands. 2. va. to pass off responsibility to another ¶ འགོ་ཁྲིད་དེས་ནམ་རྒྱུན་མི་ལ་ལག་པ་ཕྱིས་ནས་གནད་དོན་ཐག་གཅོད་བྱེད་ཀྱི་མེད་པ་རེད་ That official always passes off responsibility to others and doesn't make decisions.

ལག་པ་འབྱིད་ (lagba jii) sm. ལག་པ་འཕྱིད་.

ལག་པ་རྩིས་སྤྲོད་ (lagba dzīidröö) giving in/ yielding/ surrendering ¶ བཙོན་བྲོས་བྱོལ་ཕྱིན་པའི་བཙོན་པ་དེས་ལག་པ་རྩིས་མ་སྤྲོད་ན་གསོད་ཅིག If the runaway prisoner doesn't give in, kill him.

ལག་པ་གཙང་མ་ (lagba dzāŋma) 1. clean hands. 2. not guilty of sth. such as stealing ¶ ངའི་གཡོག་པོ་འདི་ལག་པ་གཙང་མ་ཡོད་ My servant does not steal. [Lit. has clean hands].

ལག་པ་བཙིར་ (lagba dzīr) va. to squeeze the hand. 2. vi. to get crushed/ squashed ¶ ཁོའི་ལག་པ་སྒོའི་བར་ལ་བཙིར་སོང་ His hand got crushed in the door.

ལག་པ་རྗེ་ (lagba je) va. to roll up one's sleeves.

ལག་པ་ཞ་རིལ་ (lagba sharii) maimed/ crippled hands.

ལག་པ་གཟེད་ (lagba seè) 1. va. to hold out one's cupped hands (to receive alms, etc.) ¶ ཚེས་བཅོ་ལྔའི་ཉིན་བར་སྐོར་ནང་སྤྲང་པོ་ཚོ་ལག་པ་གཟེད་ནས་བསྡད་འདུག Beggars sit with their hands held out (for alms) on the Bagor road on the 15th of the month. 2. va. to ask for help/ aid ¶ སྡུག་པོ་ག་ཚོད་བྱུང་ན་ཡང་ཁོ་ཚོར་ལག་པ་གཟེད་ཀྱི་མ་རེད་ However much difficulty they experience they will not ask for help.

ལག་པ་གཟེར་པོ་ (lagba sirbu) accurate in throwing things.

ལག་པ་གཟེར་པོ་ (lagba serbo) sb. who easily angers and hits others.

ལག་པ་ཡང་པོ་ (lagba yaŋbo) sm. ལག་པ་གཟེར་པོ་.

ལག་པ་གཡབ་གཡུག (lagba yābyuù) waving hands; va.— རྒྱག.

ལག་པ་གཡར་ (lagba yār) see ལག་པ་.

ལག་པ་གཡས་པ་ (lagba yɛ̄ɛba) 1. right hand. 2. right-handed. 3. right hand man ¶ ལས་བྱེད་པ་འདི་འགོ་ཁྲིད་ཀྱི་ལག་པ་གཡས་པ་རེད་ That person is the leader's right hand man.

ལག་པ་གཡུག (lagba yūù) 1. va. to wave one's hand. 2. va. to swing the hand (e.g., while walking).

ལག་པ་གཡུག་གཡུག (lagba yūùyuù) sm. ལག་པ་གཡུག, 1.

ལག་པ་གཡོན་མ་ (lagba yōnma) 1. left hand. 2. left-handed.

ལག་པ་རིང་པོ་ (lagba riŋbu) 1. long arms. 2. sb. who

takes other's belongings (usu. small things).

ལག་པ་ཤངས་པོ་ (lagba shōŋbo) sm. ལག་པ་ཤོགས་པོ་

ལག་པ་ཤོགས་པོ་ (lagba shōgbo) generous.

ལག་པ་ཤོར་ (lagba shɔ̄ɔ) vi. to have sth. slip/ fall out of one's hands accidentally ༑ དཀར་ཡོལ་དེ་ངའི་ལག་པ་ཤོར་ནས་ཆག་སོང་ That cup slipped out of my hand and broke.

ལག་པ་སྡིང་ (lagba siŋ) sm. ལག་པ་རྟིང་.

ལག་པ་ལྷུག་པོ་ (lagba lhūgbu) sm. ལག་པ་ཤོགས་པོ་.

ལག་པའི་གྲུ་མོ་ (lagbɛ trumo) elbow.

ལག་པའི་རྒྱབ་མདུན་ (lagbɛ gyəmdün) differentiating good from bad ༑ ལག་པ་རྒྱབ་མདུན་མ་ཤེས་ཙང་ Because he doesn't know who is good and who is bad. [Lit. front and back of the hand].

ལག་པའི་ཕྱག་རྒྱ་ (lagbɛ cāggya) mudra made with the hands.

ལག་པའི་མཛུབ་མོ་ལྔ་ (lagbɛ dzubmo ŋā) 1. the five fingers of the hand. 2. phrase used to convey its easy to find out sth. ༑ གནས་ཚུལ་འདི་ལས་ཁུངས་འདིའི་ནང་བྱུང་ཙང་ལག་པའི་མཛུབ་མོ་ལྔ་ལ་གྲངས་ཀ་མ་ཐེབས་པ་མེད་པ་ནང་བཞིན་བརྟག་གཅོད་བྱེད་བདེ་པོ་ཡོད་པ་རེད་ Because this incident occurred in the office, it is easy to investigate it just like it is easy to count one's fingers.

ལག་པའི་རི་མོ་ (lagbɛ rimu) fingerprints.

ལག་པར་ཐེབས་ (lagbaa tēè) sm. ལག་ཏུ་ཐེབས་.

ལག་པར་ལེན་ (lagbaa len) va. to take in one's hands.

ལག་པས་བཀོལ་སྤྱོད་ (lagbɛ̀ɛ gōōjöö) 1. handmade. 2. manually operated.

ལག་པོད་ (lagböö) 1. reciprocating (gift, labor, etc.). 2. doing sth. in return; va.—སློག ༑ ཁོང་གིས་ང་ལ་ལག་རྟགས་སྤྲད་པ་དེའི་ལག་པོད་སློག་དགོས་ཡོད་ I have to reciprocate (with a gift) for the gift he gave me. 3. taking revenge, striking back; va.—སློག.

ལག་སྤྲོད་ (lagdröö) giving by hand; va.—བྱེད་.

ལག་སྤྱད་ (lagjɛ̀ɛ) sm. ལག་ཆ་.

ལག་དཔོན་ (lagbön) 1. head craftsman. 2. leader.

ལག་ཕུབ་ (lagbub) hand held shield.

ལག་ཕྱིས་ (ləgjii) 1. handkerchief. 2. towel.

ལག་འཕུར་ (lagbur) rubbing with the hand; va.—གཏོང་.

ལག་འཕེན་པོ་ལོ་ (lagben bōlo) volleyball.

ལག་འཕེན་འབར་འདེལ་ (lagben bandee) hand grenade.

ལག་འཕོས་ (lagböö) sm. ལག་པོད་.

ལག་འཕྱིད་ (ləgjii) 1. handkerchief. 2. abbr. of ལག་པ་འཕྱིད་.

ལག་བྱང་མ་ (lag jaŋma) a person skilled with his hands.

ལག་བྱུང་ (lagjuŋ) shung. what was actually received (in one's hand) ༑ ལག་བྱུང་འབྲུ་རུའི་ཁལ་ ༡༠ (He) actually received 10 ཁལ་ of grain.

ལག་བྲིས་ (ləgdrii) 1. hand written, hand painted. 2. teaching new students how to write by holding their hand and forming the motions; va.—རྒྱག.

ལག་འབབ་ (lagbəb) net (profit/ yield).

ལག་འབབ་ཁེ་སྐྱེད་ (lagbəb kēgyeè) net interest/ profit.

ལག་འབམ་ (lagbam) sm. ལག་འབོམ་.

ལག་འབུད་འཁོར་ལོ་ (lagbüü kɔ̄ɔlo) hand powered/ hand pushed vehicles or carts, etc.

ལག་འབུད་གད་རྒྱག་འཕྱུལ་འཁོར་ (lagbüü kɛ̀ɛgya trǖūgɔɔ) vacuum cleaner.

ལག་འབུད་ཐེར་རྒྱང་ (lagbüü tērjuŋ) sm. ལག་འབུད་འཁོར་ལོ་.

ལག་འབོམ་ (lagbom) hand grenade.

ལག་འབྱོར་ (lag jɔɔ) va. to receive (in hand) ༑ ཁྱེད་ཀྱི་ཕྱག་ཐིས་ལག་འབྱོར་བྱུང་ I received your letter.

ལག་འབྲས་གཙང་མ་ (laŋdrɛ̀ɛ dzāŋma) excellent in quality, exquisite.

ལག་འབྲེག (laŋdreè) shung. amputating the hand as punishment; va.—བྱེད་.

ལག་འབྲེལ་ (laŋdree) scheming/ plotting together; va.—བྱེད་ to scheme/ plot together ༑ ཁོ་གཉིས་ལག་འབྲེལ་བྱས་ནས་ཀུན་མ་བརྐུས་སོང་ Those two schemed together and stole things. 2. holding hands; va.—གཏོང་ to join/ hold hands. 3. accomplice (in sth. bad).

ལག་འབྲེལ་དཔུང་སྒྲིག (laŋdree būŋdrii) sm. ལག་གདང་དཔུང་གཤིབ་.

ལག་སྦུབ་ (ləgbub) sm. ཆོགས་སྦུབ་.

ལག་སྦོམ་ (lagbom) hand grenade.

ལག་སྦྲིང་ (lagdreŋ) poet. beggar.

ལག་སྦྲིང་རོལ་ཆ་ (lagdreŋ rööja) accordion.

ལག་སྦྲེལ་ (lagdree) 1. sm. ལག་འབྲེལ་ 2. sm. ལས་སྦྲེལ་.

ལག་མར་ (lagmar) 1. bartering butter for grains. 2. butter that is in (one's) possession or is on hand.

ལག་མང་ཀྱག་བདེ་ (lagmaŋ gyāàde) 1. many people working make the work seem easy [Lit. many hands, easy work].

ལག་སྨྱུལ་ (lagñüü) groping/ feeling/ searching blindly; va.—རྒྱག. 2. doing sth. without knowing exactly what should be done, doing sth. without a plan; va.—རྒྱག.

ལག་དམར་ (lagmar) 1. murderer. 2. butcher.

ལག་རྩལ་ (lagdzɛɛ) 1. skill in crafts ༑ བཟོ་པ་ལག་རྩལ་ཅན་ A skilled craftsman. 2. technology.

ལག་རྩལ་སྐོར་གྱི་དཔྱད་གཞིའི་ཡིག་རིགས་ (lagdzɛɛ gɔ̄ɔgi jɛ̀ɛshii yigrii) technical/ technological data.

ལག་རྩལ་མཁན་ (lagdzɛɛñɛn) technician.

ལག་རྩལ་ཁྱབ་སྤེལ་ས་ཚིགས་ (lagdzɛɛ kyābbel sādzii) technical dissemination station.

ལག་རྩལ་གྱི་བདེ་འཇགས་ (lagdzɛɛgi denjaà) technical safety.

ལག་རྩལ་གོ་མིང་ (lagdzɛɛ komiŋ) titles for technical personnel.

ལག་རྩལ་སྒྲིག་ཆས་ (lagdzɛɛ drigjɛ̀ɛ) technical equipment.

ལག་རྩལ་གྱི་དཔེ་ཚད་ (lagdzɛɛgi bēdzɛ̀ɛ) technical/ technological specifications.

ལག་རྩལ་གྱི་རང་བཞིན་ (lagdzɛɛgi rəŋshin) technical.

ལག་རྩལ་དགེ་གན་ (lagdzɛɛ gegɛn) technical expert/ instructor.

ལག་རྩལ་བསྒྱུར་བཅོད་ (lagdzɛɛ gyurgöö) sm. ལག་རྩལ་བཙོས་བསྒྱུར་.

ལག་རྩལ་བཙོས་བསྒྱུར་ (lagdzɛɛ jöögyur) technical transformation/ innovation.

ལག་རྩལ་ཆུ་ཚད་ (lagdzɛɛ cūdzɛ̀ɛ) technical level, technical standard.

ལག་རྩལ་ཆེན་པོ་ (lagdzɛɛ cēmbo) high technical level/ standard.

ལག་རྩལ་འཆར་འགོད་ (lagdzɛɛ cārgöö) technical designing/ planning.

ལག་རྩལ་བརྟག་དཔྱད་ (lagdzɛɛ dāgjɛ̀ɛ) technological research/ investigation.

ལག་རྩལ་ཐོན་རྫས་ (lagdzɛɛ tōndzɛ̀ɛ) handicraft products/ goods.

ལག་རྩལ་ནང་བཤུག (lagdzɛɛ naŋshuù) technology transfer.

ལག་རྩལ་སྣ་མང་ཅན་ (lagdzɛɛ nāmaŋjɛn) versatile/ skilled in many crafts.

ལག་རྩལ་པ་ (lagdzɛɛba) technician, craftsman.

ལག་རྩལ་བྱང་འཆུབ་པའི་མི་སྣ་ (lagdzɛɛ caŋjubbɛ minə) sm. ལག་རྩལ་འབྱོངས་གོམས་མི་སྣ་.

ལག་རྩལ་འབྱོངས་གོམས་མི་སྣ་ (lagdzɛɛ coŋgom minə) technical personnel.

ལག་རྩལ་མི་སྣ་ (lagdzɛɛ minə) technician, craftsman, technical experts, technical personnel.

ལག་རྩལ་དམག་རིགས་ (lagdzɛɛ məgrii) 1. technical weapons. 2. technical troops.

ལག་རྩལ་རྩ་བ་ (lagdzɛɛ dzāwa) basic skills.

ལག་རྩལ་མཛེས་རིག (lagdzɛɛ dzeèrii) industrial arts.

ལག་རྩལ་ཞིང་ལས་ (lagdzɛɛ shiŋlɛ̀ɛ) agrotechnics.

ལག་རྩལ་བཟོ་པ་ (lagdzɛɛ soba) sm. ལག་རྩལ་པ་.

ལག་རྩལ་བཟོ་པའི་སློབ་གྲྭ་ (lagdzɛɛ sobɛ lōbdra) sm. ལག་རྩལ་སློབ་གྲྭ

ལག་རྩལ་ལས་བྱེད་པ་ (lagdzɛɛ lɛ̀ɛjeèba) technical cadre (e.g., engineers).

ལག་རྩལ་ལས་མི་ (lagdzεε lὲεmi) sm. ལག་རྩལ་མི་སྣ་.

ལག་རྩལ་བཤུག་སྒྲོད་ (lagdzεε shūgdröö) sm. ལག་རྩལ་ནང་བཤུག.

ལག་རྩལ་སློབ་གྲྭ (lagdzεε lōbdra) technical school.

ལག་རྩལ་སློབ་པའི་དང་བླང་ཚོགས་པ་ (lagdzεε lōbbε taŋlaŋ tsōgba) Volunteers in Technical Assistance.

ལག་རྩལ་གསར་བཅོས་ (lagdzεε sārjöö) technical innovation.

ལག་རྩལ་གསར་སྤེལ་ (lagdzεε sārbel) technological development.

ལག་རྩལ་གསར་བརྗེ་ (lagdzεε sārje) technical/ technological revolution.

ལག་རྩལ་གསལ་འབྱེད་ (lagdzεε sε̄ε̄jeè) technical appraisement.

ལག་རྩིས་ (ləgdzii) 1. palmistry. 2. using (one's) fingers to count.

ལག་རྩེད་སྤོ་ལོ་ (lagdzeè bōlo) basketball, handball; va.—རྒྱག.

ལག་རྩེད་རྩེ་ (lagdzeè dzē) 1. to play with one's hands. 2. to use a woman sexually. 3. to doodle (on paper).

ལག་བསྩལ་ (lagdzεε) shung. sth. that was given by hand or into one's hand ¶ ས་གླང་ལོ་ལག་བསྩལ་དངུལ་འབབ་ Money that was handed to me in the Earth-Ox year.

ལག་ཚབ་ (ləgdzub) 1. a substitute for sb. working; va.—བྱེད་. 2. reciprocating for sb.'s work on one's behalf.

ལག་ཚིགས་ (ləgdzii) joints of the hand.

ལག་ཚེམ་ (lagdzem) hand stitching; va.—རྒྱག.

ལག་ཚོར་ (lagdzɔɔ) sensing/ feeling by hand; va.—བྱེད་ ¶ ལོང་བས་ལག་ཚོར་ལ་བརྟེན་ནས་ཡི་གེ་ཀློག་གི་འདུག The blind read by feeling with their hands.

ལག་མཛོད་ (laŋdzöö) storeroom.

ལག་འཛངས་ (laŋdzaŋ) being short of money/ food/ etc. ¶ དེང་སང་དངུལ་ལག་འཛངས་འདུག་པས་དངུལ་སྐྱིན་བུ་གཡར་རོགས་ These days I am short of money so please lend me some money.

ལག་འཛངས་དགོས་གདུགས་ (lagdzaŋ gööduù) shung. to being short of money/ food/ etc., being in great need of things ¶ བླ་བྲང་ནས་གང་ཅིའི་ལག་འཛངས་དགོས་གདུགས་སྐབས་རོགས་རམ་བླ་མེད་བསྩལ་པ་ When I was in great need of everything, Labrang extended great help.

ལག་འཛངས་ཅི་ཆེ་ (lagdzaŋ jïje) sm. ལག་འཛངས་དགོས་གདུགས་.

ལག་འཛངས་པོ་ (lag dzaŋbo) sm. ལག་འཛངས་.

ལག་འཛིང་ (ləŋdziŋ) hand-to-hand combat; va.—གཏོང་; —རྒྱག.

ལག་འཛིངས་ (ləŋdziŋ) sm. ལག་འཛིང་.

ལག་འཛིན་ (ləŋdzin) 1. receipt. 2. shung. document authorizing sth.

ལག་འཛིན་དྲུད་འཁྱིན་འཁོར་ལོ་ (ləŋdzin dründen kɔɔlo) hand steered (with handlebars) tractor.

ལག་འཛུགས་ (ləgdzuù) planting by hand; va.—བྱེད་; —འདེབས་ to plant by hand.

ལག་བརྫེས་ (ləgdzeè) rolling up one's sleeve.

ལག་ཞ་བ་ (lag shawa) sm. ལག་པ་ཞ་རིལ་.

ལག་ཞུ་ (ləgshu) flashlight.

ལག་ཤོར་ (lagshɔɔ) accidentally/ unintentionally taking or doing sth.; va.—གཏོང་ ¶ ཁོས་ལས་ཁུངས་ནས་སྨྱུ་གུ་ལག་ཤོར་བཏང་ནས་ཁྱེར་བཞག He accidentally took the pen from the office.

ལག་བཞག (lagshaà) va. to carry out, to put into practice, to execute; va.—གཏོང་ ¶ ཁོས་ལས་ཀ་དེ་ཁ་ཐོག་ལག་བཞག་བཏང་སོང་ He carried out the work just like he said.

ལག་བཞུ་ (ləgshu) lantern, flashlight.

ལག་ཟད་དུ་གཏོང་ (lagsεεdu dōŋ) va. to ruin by wearing out.

ལག་ཟད་དཔུང་ཐུག (lagsεὲ būŋduù) at the end of one's rope, desperate, hopeless [Lit. hand wears out (until) one reaches the shoulder].

ལག་ཟིན་ (ləgsin) 1. held by the hand. 2. firsthand knowledge, eyewitness information ¶ ཁོ་ཚོས་མངོན་སུམ་ལག་ཟིན་བྱུང་ཡོད་པ་རེད་ (They) had firsthand knowledge (of it).

ལག་ཟུང་ཉིས་སྐྱོར་ (lagsuŋ ñïïgyɔɔ) holding or talking sth. with the two palms held together.

ལག་གཟུང་ (lagsuŋ) (door) handle, railing (on stairs), banister.

ལག་གཟེབ་ (lagseb) a small basket.

ལག་གཟེར་རྒྱག (lagser gyaà) shung. a form of punishment whereby prisoners are tortured by inserting sharp bamboo under their fingernails.

ལག་གཟོང་ (lagsoŋ) stone mason's tool, chisel.

ལག་བཟོ་ (lagso) sm. ལག་བཟོས་.

ལག་བཟོ་བ་ (lagsowa) sm. ལག་ཤེས་པ་.

ལག་བཟོས་ (lagsöö) handmade.

ལག་བཟོས་དངོས་ཆས་ (lagsöö ŋööjεὲ) handicraft products, handmade products.

ལག་བཟོས་མཛེས་ཆས་ (lagsöö dzeejεὲ) handicraft (handmade) art products.

ལག་བཟོས་མཛེས་རིག་ཐོན་རྫས་ (lagsöö dzeèrig tōndzεὲ) sm. ལག་བཟོས་མཛེས་ཆས་.

ལག་ཡངས་ (lagyaŋ) sm. ལག་པ་ཡང་པོ་.

ལག་ཡར་ (lagyar) female yak that gave birth the previous year.

ལག་ཡུ་ (ləgyu) arm.

ལག་ཡོད་ (lagyöö) 1. on hand, in hand, at hand ¶ ལག་ཡོད་ཚོང་ཟོག Merchandise on hand. 2. net ¶ ལག་ཡོད་ཡོང་འབབ་ Net income (take-home pay). 3. brave.

ལག་གཡབ་ (ləgyəb) putting one's hand to one's forehead when looking into the distance; va.—བྱེད་.

ལག་གཡུག (ləgyuù) sm. ལག་པ་གཡུག.

ལག་གཡུག་འབར་མདེལ་ (ləgyuù bandee) hand grenade.

ལག་གཡོག (lagyɔɔ) 1. assistant, helper. 2. servant's servant.

ལག་གཡོག་རྒྱག (lagyɔɔ̀ gyaà) vi. to get bad karma because of mistreating sb. ¶ མི་དེ་ཕ་མར་ཞབས་ཕྱི་ཡག་པོ་མ་ཞུས་ཙང་ཁོ་ལ་ལ་གཡོག་བརྒྱབ་སྟེ་ནད་ངན་ཕོག་པ་རེད་ That person incurred bad karma because he did not serve his parents well and got ill.

ལག་གཡོབ་ (lagyob) gesturing a (person) to come by waving (one's) hand; va.—བྱེད་.

ལག་གཡོར་ (lagyɔɔ) assisting/ helping/ aiding back and forth; va.—བྱེད་.

ལག་རས་ (lagrεὲ) sm. ལག་ཕྱིས.

ལག་རིལ་ (ləgrii) 1. crippled hand. 2. illiterate person.

ལག་རིས་ (ləgrii) 1. fingerprint. 2. accomplishment.

ལག་རུ་འགོག (ləgru gɔɔ̀) va. to obstruct/ to block (physically) ¶ ང་ལས་ཀ་བྱེད་སར་ཁོས་ལག་རུ་བཀག་བྱུང་ He obstructed me from my workplace.

ལག་རུབ་རྒྱག (ləgrub gyaà) va. to collect/ bring together many people to do some task.

ལག་རེག་རྒྱག (lagreg gyaà) sm. ལག་ཐོ་གཞུ་.

ལག་རོགས་ (lagrɔɔ̀) 1. assistant. 2. helper with regard to loading transport mules.

ལག་ལན་ (laglεn) sm. ལག་ཡོད་, 2.

ལག་ལས་ (laglεὲ) work done by hand, manual labor; va.—བྱེད་.

ལག་ལས་ཡོ་ཆས་ (laglεὲ yobjεὲ) hand implements.

ལག་ལེན་ (laglen) 1. putting into practice, implementing; va.—བྱེད་; —བསྟར་ ¶ ཁོ་ཚོས་སྲིད་ཇུས་དེ་ལག་ལེན་བསྟར་ཐུབ་མ་སོང་ They were unable to put the policy into practice. ¶ རིག་དཔྱད་དང་ལག་ལེན་ Theory and practice. 2. custom of doing ¶ ཁོ་ཚོར་སྒོ་ཕྱུགས་གསོ་སྐྱོང་གི་ལག་ལེན་ཡོད་པ་མ་རེད་ (They) do not have the custom of breeding livestock.

ལག་ལེན་གྱི་རྣམ་བཤད་ (laglengi nāmshεὲ) "On Practice" (an essay by Mao Zedong).

ལག་ལེན་དངོས་ (laglen ŋöö) practical ¶ ལག་ལེན་དངོས་ཀྱི་དོན་སྙིང་ Practical significance.

ལག་ལེན་བསྟར་ (laglen dār) see ལག་ལེན་.

ལག་ལེན་དོན་འཁེལ་ (laglen töngee) sm. ལག་ལེན་བསྟར་.

ལག་ལེན་བྱེད་ཐབས་ (laglen cḛèdəb) the ways/ means to put into practice or implement.

ལག་ཤ་ (lagsha) pad of an animal's paw, human palm.

ལག་ཤུབས་ (lagshub) gloves.

ལག་ཤེས་ (lagsheè) handicrafts.

ལག་ཤེས་ངལ་རྩོལ་ (lagsheè ŋɛɛdzöö) handicraft work.

ལག་ཤེས་པ་ (lagsheèba) craftsman, artisan.

ལག་ཤེས་བཟོ་གྲྭ་ (lagsheè sodra) handicraft center/ factory.

ལག་ཤེས་བཟོ་ལས་ (lagsheè solɛɛ̀) handicraft work.

ལག་ཤེས་བཟོ་ལས་པ་ (lagsheè solɛɛ̀ba) handicraft worker.

ལག་ཤེས་བཟོ་ལས་ཐོན་སྐྱེད་མཉམ་ལས་ཁང་ (lagsheè solɛɛ̀ töngyeè ñamlɛgaŋ) handicraft cooperative.

ལག་ཤོགས་ (lagshɔɔ̀) abbr. of ལག་པ་ཤོགས་པོ་.

ལག་ཤོར་ (lag shɔ̄ɔ) 1. abbr. of ལག་པ་ཤོར་. 2. escaping from one's hand/ control/ possession ¶ ཀུན་མ་དེ་ལག་ཤོར་མི་ཡོང་བ་བྱ་དགོས་ You must be sure not to let the thief escape from your control.

ལག་གཤོར་རྫིས་སྤྲོད་ (lagshɔɔ dzı̄idröö) shung. measuring when handing over; va.—བྱེད་ ¶ འབྲུ་འབབ་གྲངས་ཚང་རྫོང་དཔོན་ནས་ལག་གཤོར་རྫིས་སྤྲོད་དགོས་ཀྱི་ The amount of grain due must be measured by the District Commissioner when being handed over (paid).

ལག་བཤད་ (lagshɛɛ̀) arms flailing while talking, gesturing with one's hands while talking (in a disrespectful manner); va.—གཏོང་.

ལག་སག (lagsaà) sm. ལག་གསག.

ལག་སུག (lagsuù) nudging (with the elbow to give a signal); va.—རྒྱག.

ལག་སོན་ (lagsön) in hand ¶ ཁྱེད་རང་གི་ཡི་གེ་ལག་སོན་དུ་བྱུང་ I received your letter (in my hand).

ལག་སོར་ (lagsɔɔ) fingers.

ལག་སླེལ་ (lagleè) a small basket.

ལག་སློག (laglɔɔ̀) abbr. of ལག་པོད་སློག.

ལག་གསག (lagsaà) sm. ལག་པ་ཡང་པོ་.

ལག་གསར་ (lagsar) novice, rookie.

ལག་གསར་པ་ (lag sārba) sm. ལག་གསར་.

ལག་གསོས་ (lagsöö) animals raised at home; va.—རྒྱག.

ལགས་ (laà) 1. honorific term ¶ བློ་བཟང་ལགས་ Lobzang-la. ¶ ལགས་རེད་ It is. (Yes). 2. linking verb (to be) ¶ ཁོང་རྣམས་སང་ཉིན་ཕེབས་རྒྱུ་ལགས་ They are coming tomorrow. ¶ ཁྲལ་རྒྱུག་ཁྲིམས་འབྱུར་ཞུ་ཞུས་ལགས་ཀྱང་ Even though we are law abiding and tax paying. 3. yes. ¶ ལགས་བཀའ་གནང་རང་ Yes, it is as you say.

ལགས་འདུག (laà duù) h. of འདུག.

ལགས་ཡོད་ (laà yöö) 1. yes. 2. yes I have, a response to the greeting ཕྱག་ཕེབས་གནང་བྱུང་.

ལགས་འོང་ (laà oŋ) yes.

ལགས་ལགས་ལུགས་ལུགས་ (laàlaà lugluù) being very respectful and using honorific language.

ལགས་སོ་ (laàso) yes.

ལགས་ལགས་སོ་ (laàlaàso) yes! yes!

ལང་: p. ལངས་ (laŋ) 1. va. to get up, to stand up, to rise ¶ མོ་ཞོགས་པ་ལྟར་ཆུ་ཚོད་དྲུག་པར་ལང་གི་ཡོད་ She gets up at six every morning. 2. vi. to occur, to come to be, to get started ¶ དམག་འཁྲུག་ཆེན་པོ་ལངས་པ་རེད་ A big war occurred (broke out). 3. vi. to rise/ ferment (for dough, beer, etc.).

ལང་ཀ་ (laŋga) Sri Lanka, Ceylon.

ལང་ཀ་མགྲིན་བཅུ་ (laŋga drinju) the king of the སྲིན་པོ་ (with ten heads).

ལང་ཀག (laŋgaà) road.

ལང་རྒྱལ་ (laŋgyɛɛ) treading water; va.—རྒྱག.

ལང་རྐྱེན་ (laŋgyen) the cause (of sth. occuring).

ལང་ངེ་ལིང་ངེ་ (laŋŋe liŋŋe) 1. swaying, rocking. 2. rolling ¶ ནམ་མཁར་སྤྲིན་པ་ལང་ངེ་ལིང་ངེར་འཁྱིམས་པ་འདུག Clouds rolling in the sky.

ལང་ངེ་ལོང་ངེ་ (laŋŋe loŋŋe) sm. ལང་ལོང་.

ལང་མཉམ་ (laŋñam) standing up at the same time, standing up simultaneously; va.—བྱེད་.

ལང་ཐང་ཙེ་ (laŋdaŋdzi) (black) henbane seed (used in Tibetan medicine).

ལང་དུ་ཤོར་ (laŋdu shɔ̄ɔ) vi. to be spoiled/ pampered.

ལང་ཕྱོགས་ (laŋjɔɔ̀) sm. ལངས་ཕྱོགས་.

ལང་ཚོ་ (laŋdzo) youth, young adult; vi.—དར་; —རྒྱས་ to be in the young adult period, to be in the prime of life ¶ ལང་ཚོ་དར་བའི་སྐབས་སུ་ཆང་ས་རྒྱག་དགོས་པ་རེད་ One should marry during the young adult period.

ལང་ཚོ་ཅན་ (laŋdzojɛn) a young adult.

ལང་ཚོ་དར་ (laŋdzo tar) see ལང་ཚོ་.

ལང་ཚོ་དར་ལ་བབ་པ་ (laŋdzo tarla bəbba) in the prime of life (usu. in the late twenties/ mid thirties).

ལང་ཚོ་ཡོལ་ (laŋdzo yöö) vi. to age, to pass the prime of life.

ལང་ཚོའི་དཔལ་འབར་ (laŋdzo bēmbar) sm. ལང་ཚོ་དར་.

ལང་འཛར་ཅན་ (laŋdzarjɛn) sth. with tassels on the handle.

ལང་ལ་ཤོར་ (laŋdu shɔ̄ɔ) sm. ལང་དུ་ཤོར་.

ལང་ལིང་ (laŋliŋ) abbr. of ལང་ངེ་ལི་ངེ་.

ལང་ལོང་ (laŋloŋ) bubbling (for water), rolling (for clouds), moved, touched (emotionally) ¶ ནམ་མཁར་སྤྲིན་ནག་ལང་ལོང་དུ་འཕྱུར་བཞིན་འདུག Black clouds rolling in the sky. ¶ གློག་བརྙན་ཡག་པོ་དེ་ལྟ་སྐབས་སེམས་པ་ལང་ལོང་བྱས་བྱུང་ When watching the good movie I was moved.

ལང་ཤོར་ (laŋshɔɔ) spoiling, pampering; va.—གཏོང་ to spoil, to pamper.

ལངས་ (laŋ) p. of ལང་.

ལངས་རྐྱེན་ (laŋgyen) sm. ལང་རྐྱེན་.

ལངས་ཁར་ (laŋkar) on the eve, at the moment, just before an event happens ¶ ཟིང་ཆ་ལངས་ཁར་ཁོས་བྲོས་ཐུབ་འདུག At the time the unrest was about to start he was able to escape.

ལངས་དུང་གཏོང་ (laŋduŋ dōŋ) va. to sound the bugle call to wake people up.

ལངས་སྡོད་ (laŋ döö) va. to stand up, to be standing up.

ལངས་བརྡ་གཏོང་ (laŋda dōŋ) va. to send a wake up call or signal.

ལངས་ཕྱོགས་ (laŋjɔɔ̀) position, stand; va.—འཛིན་ to take a position/ stand; va.—ལང་ to accept/ go over to a position/ stand ¶ དྲང་བདེན་གྱི་ལངས་ཕྱོགས་ A just position. ¶ འདི་གུང་ཁྲན་ཏང་གི་ལངས་ཕྱོགས་རེད་ This is the position of the Chinese Communist Party. ¶ མ་རྩའི་རིང་ལུགས་ནས་ཁོས་གུང་ཁྲན་ཏང་གི་ལང་ཕྱོགས་སུ་ལངས་པ་རེད་ From capitalism, he went over to the position of the Chinese Communist Party.

ལངས་ཕྱོགས་དོར་ (laŋjɔɔ̀ tɔɔ) va. to give up/ renounce one's position or stand.

ལངས་གཟུགས་ (laŋsuù) a three-dimensional (object).

ལངས་གཟུགས་དབྱིབས་རྩིས་ (laŋsuù yı̄bdzii) solid geometry.

ལངས་ཤོར་ (laŋshɔɔ) sm. ལང་ཤོར་.

ལངས་ས་ (laŋsa) place where sth. originated/ arose.

ལད་ (lɛɛ̀) vi. to deteriorate, to worsen.

ལད་འགྲོས་ (lɛndröö) copying/ imitating the way sb. walks/ moves.

ལད་པོ་ (lɛɛ̀bo) vagabonds, wanderers.

ལད་པོད་ (lɛɛ̀böö) sm. ལག་པོད་.

ལད་སྤོད་ (lɛɛ̀böö) sm. ལག་པོད་.

ལད་མོ་ (lɛɛ̀mo) imitating, copying; va.—བྱེད་ to imitate, to copy ¶ ཕྲུ་གུ་དེས་དགེ་རྒན་གྱི་ལད་མོ་བྱེད་ཀྱི་འདུག The child is imitating his teacher.

ལད་སྣོས་ (lɛndöö) sm. ལད་མོ་.

ལད་བཟོ་ (lɛɛ̀so) reproducing, copying; va.—བྱེད་ to reproduce/ copy ¶ འཕྲུལ་ཆས་གསར་པ་དེ་བཟོ་གྲྭ་གཞན་

དག་གིས་ལད་བཟོས་བྱས་འདུག The new machine was copied by other factories.

ལད་སོད་ (lɛ̱ɛ̀söö̀) sm. ལད་ཟློས་.

ལན་ (lɛ̱n) 1. response, answer, reply; va.—འདེབས་; —རྒྱག; —སྤྲོད་; —རྗོད་; —གླན་; —སློན་; —ལྡོན་ to respond/ answer/ reply ¶ཁོང་གི་དྲི་བ་ར་ངས་ལན་བརྒྱབ་པ་ཡིན་ I answered his question. 2. message (usu. verbal); va.—སྐུར་; —གཏོང་ to send a message; va.—སྤྲོད་; —སྐྱེལ་ to deliver a message ¶སང་ཉིན་ཚོགས་འདུ་ཚོགས་རྒྱུའི་ལན་གཏོང་དགོས་ We must send a message that the meeting will convene tomorrow. 3. times ¶ལན་མང་པོ་ Many times. 4. ch. company (an army unit of about 1000, three of which comprise a battalion). 5. vi. to be responsible for sth. ¶འཕྲུལ་འཁོར་ལ་སྐྱོན་ཤོར་བ་དེ་ངས་ལན་ཡོད་པ་མ་རེད་ I am not responsible for the machine breaking.

ལན་ཀན་ (lɛ̱ngɛn) ch. railing, banister.

ལན་ཀའོ་པད་ཚལ་ (lɛ̱ngao bɛ̀ɛ̀dzɛɛ) ch.tib. cabbage.

ལན་ཀྲང་ (lɛ̱ndraŋ) ch. head of a army company.

ལན་ཀྲུའུ་ (lɛ̱ndro) Lanzhou.

ལན་རྐྱེན་ (lɛ̱ngyen) the cause/ basis for a mishap or disaster ¶མེ་ཤོར་བའི་ལན་རྐྱེན་བརྟག་ཚོད་མི་འདུག (They) could not find the cause of the fire.

ལན་སྐུར་ (lɛ̱n gūr) see ལན་, 2.

ལན་སྐྱེལ་ (lɛ̱n gyɛ̄ɛ) see ལན་, 2.

ལན་ཁག (lɛ̱ngaà) blaming; vi.—འཁྲི་ to get blamed; va.—འགེལ་ to blame sb.

ལན་ཁག་མེད་པ་ (lɛ̱ngaà me̱èba) blameless.

ལན་ཁན་ (lɛ̱ngɛn) sm. ལན་ཀན་.

ལན་འཁྱོལ་ (lɛ̱n kyöö̀) vi. to be able to deliver a message ¶ཕྲུ་གུ་ཆུང་ཆུང་འདིས་ལན་འཁྱོལ་གྱི་མ་རེད་ The small child will not be able to deliver the message.

ལན་འཁྱོལ་པོ་ (lɛ̱n kyöö̀bo) sb. able to deliver a message.

ལན་གྱུག (lɛ̱ngyɔɔ̀) sm. ལན་ཆགས་.

ལན་གྲངས་ (lɛ̱ndraŋ) 1. a number of times ¶ཁོ་ལ་ལན་གྲངས་བཤད་པ་ཡིན་ཡང་ Even though I told him many times. 2. schedule number (of a flight/ bus/ train).

ལན་གློན་ (lɛ̱njön) see ལན་.

ལན་དགུ་ཆད་མཐུད་ (lɛ̱ngu cɛ̀ɛ̀düü) repeatedly trying sth. ¶ངས་ཁོ་ལ་ལན་དགུ་ཆད་མཐུད་གྱིས་སློབ་གསོ་བརྒྱབ་ཀྱང་ཉན་མ་བྱུང་ I repeatedly gave him advice but he didn't listen. [Lit. nine times joining what is broken].

ལན་འགའ་ (lɛ̱nga) several times.

ལན་རྒྱག (lɛ̱ngyaà) see ལན་.

ལན་སྒྲ་ (lɛ̱ndra) an echo; vi.—འཁོར་ to echo.

ལན་གཅིག་མ་ (lɛ̱njigmə) the first (best) ཆང་.

ལན་ལྕོག (lɛ̱njɔɔ̀) sm. ཐོར་ཅོག.

ལན་ཆགས་ (lɛ̱njaà) a karmic debt from a former life that results in sth. happening in this life; vi.—འཁོར་ ¶ཚེ་འདིར་ཕྲུ་གུ་མང་པོ་འདི་འདྲ་སྐྱེས་པ་ནི་ཚེ་སྔོན་མའི་ལན་ཆགས་རེད་ As for having borne so many children in this life, it is due to a debt to people in a former life (who are reborn as one's children in this life).

ལན་ཆགས་རྒྱབ་ཁུར་ (lɛ̱njaà gyə̱bgur) a symbolic shaped dough that is put in the soup eaten on the 29th of the 12th lunar month indicating a child will be born.

ལན་ཆགས་བུ་ལོན་ (lɛ̱njaà pu̱lön) sm. ལན་ཆགས་.

ལན་ཆིའུ་ (lɛ̱nciwu) ch. basketball; va.—རྒྱག.

ལན་ཆིའུ་པོ་ལོ་ (lɛ̱nciwu pōlo) ch.tib. sm. ལན་ཆིའུ་.

ལན་འཆོལ་ (lɛ̱n cöö̀) vi. to mistakenly give a wrong message.

ལན་འཇོག (lɛ̱n jɔ̱ɔ̀) va. to leave a message.

ལན་འཇོག་འཕྲུལ་འཁོར་ (lɛ̱njɔɔ̀ trüüjɛ̀ɛ) phone answering machine.

ལན་གཏོར་ (lɛ̱ndɔɔ) a གཏོར་མ་ for cleansing ལན་ཆགས་.

ལན་ཐེན་གྱི་སྤྲ་མི་ (lɛ̱ndengi drāmi) Lantian Man (fossil of a primitive man 600,000 years old found in Lantian, Shaanxi).

ལན་དུ་ (lɛ̱ndu) in answer to, in response to.

ལན་འདེབས་ (lɛ̱ndeb) 1. answering, replying; va.—བྱེད་ to answer/ reply/ respond. 2. see ལན་.

ལན་འདོམས་ (lɛ̱ndom) shung. a communication or answer to a report/ petition.

ལན་ལྡོག (lɛ̱ndɔɔ̀) reaping the fruit (good or bad) of one's past acts (karmic retribution).

ལན་ལྡོན་ (lɛ̱ndön) see ལན་.

ལན་བརྡ་ (lɛ̱nda) a message; va.—སྐྱེལ་ to deliver a message.

ལན་པ་ (lɛ̱mba) cause/ responsibility for sth. bad ¶ཁང་པ་མེ་ཤོར་བའི་ལན་པ་ང་ལ་མེད་ I am not responsible for the house catching fire.

ལན་པ་མེད་པ་ (lɛ̱mba me̱èba) shung. not to be blamed or held responsible for sth. bad. ¶དེ་སྐོར་ཁོང་ལ་ལན་པ་མེད་པ་ Regarding that matter, he is blameless.

ལན་པར་ (lɛ̱mbar) eng. label, brand name.

ལན་པོ་ (lɛ̱mbo) suitable, appropriate ¶ཚོས་གཞི་དེ་ཁྱེད་རང་ལ་ལན་པོ་འདུག This color is suitable for you.

ལན་སྤྲོད་ (lɛ̱ndröö̀) see ལན་.

ལན་ཕྲིན་ (lɛ̱ndrin) message, reply ¶ཐུག་འཕྲད་དུ་ཡོང་དགོས་ཞེས་ལན་ཕྲིན་འབྱོར་བྱུང་ (I) received a message asking (me) to come to meet (him). ¶ཁོང་སང་ཉིན་ཡོང་ཐུབ་ཀྱི་མི་འདུག་ཅེས་ལན་ཕྲིན་འབྱོར་བྱུང་ He replied that he couldn't come tomorrow.

ལན་བུ་ (lɛ̱mbu) a braid (of hair).

ལན་བློན་ (lɛ̱nlön) sm. ལན་གློག.

ལན་འབུལ་ (lɛ̱mbüü) h. of ལན་སྤྲོད་.

ལན་མ་ (lɛ̱mma) several times ¶དགོངས་སེལ་ལན་མར་ཞུས་ He apologized several times.

ལན་མང་ (lɛ̱nmaŋ) sm. ལན་གྲངས་.

ལན་མེད་ཆ་མེད་ (lɛ̱nmeè cāmeè) no words, no answer/ reply/ message ¶དེང་སང་ངའི་ནང་ནས་ལན་མེད་ཆ་མེད་རེད་བཞག Nowadays there is no word from my home.

ལན་མོ་ (lɛ̱nmo) a clay container for ཆང་.

ལན་རྩ་ (lɛ̱ndza) the cause of sth. bad ¶ལྷ་སའི་ཞིང་ཆའི་ལན་རྩ་འདི་འབྲས་སྤུངས་དགོན་པ་རེད་ The cause of the disturbance in Lhasa was Drepung Monastery.

ལན་རྩ་གཏལ་མེན་ (lɛ̱ndza kɛ̱ɛmin) shung. sm. ལན་པ་མེད་པ་.

ལན་རྩེ་ (lɛ̱ndze) ch. false hair (worn by woman in the old Tibetan society).

ལན་ཚ་བ་ (lɛ̱n tsāwa) salty (taste).

ལན་ཚར་ (lɛ̱ndzɔɔ) 1. sm. སྐྲ་གཞུག. 2. sm. ལན་བུ་.

ལན་ཚྭ་ (lɛ̱ndza) salt.

ལན་ཚིག (lɛ̱ndzii) reply, answer.

ལན་ཚེ་ (lɛ̱ndze) inferior porcelain.

ལན་འཚལ་ (lɛ̱n dzɛ̄ɛ) sm. ལན་འཚོལ་.

ལན་འཚོལ་ (lɛ̱n dzöȫ) va. to search for an answer (iso. a rebuttal).

ལན་འཛོལ་ (lɛ̱ndzöö) 1. responsibility for an error/ problem. 2. a mistaken/ erroneous message.

ལན་ཤོག (lɛ̱nshoò) sm. ལན་, 4.

ལན་སློག (lɛ̱n lɔ̄ɔ̀) va. to act in response to sth., to respond/ reciprocate ¶ཁ་སྔོན་ཁོང་གིས་ང་ལ་ལག་རྟགས་སྤྲད་པ་དེའི་ལན་སློག་དགོས་ཡོད་ I have to reciprocate for the gift he gave me recently.

ལབ་ (lə̱b) va. to say, to tell ¶ངས་ཁོང་ལ་གནས་ཚུལ་དེའི་སྐོར་ལབ་པ་ཡིན་ I told him about this situation. 2. abbr. of ལ་ཕུག.

ལབ་སྐྱོར་ (lə̱bgyɔɔ) saying again, repeating oneself; va.—རྒྱག.

ལབ་གད་རྒྱག (lə̱bgɛ̀ɛ gya̱à) va. to peel a radish.

ལབ་གླེང་ (lə̱bleŋ) 1. controversy, altercation, complaint ¶ཁོང་གི་དགོངས་ཞུའི་སྐོར་ལབ་གླེང་ཆེན་པོ་བྱུང་ There was a great controversy over his resignation. 2. discussion, talk.

ལབ་གླེང་མེད་པ་ (lə̱bleŋ) 1. without controversy/ altercation. 2. without discussions/ talk, without delay ¶ཡུལ་གྱི་ནུ་བང་དངོས་བཞག་བོད་གཏོང་ལབ་གླེང་

མེད་པ་དགོས་རྒྱུ་ (You) should send the salt to Tibet without delay according to the local price.

ལབ་རྒྱུ་ (lәbgyu) controversy, altercation; vi.—ལྷགས་ to become a controversy/ disagreement/ complaint/ altercation ¶ ཁྱེད་རང་ཚུགས་ལས་འདི་འདྲ་གནང་ན་ལབ་རྒྱུ་ལྷགས་ཀྱི་རེད་ If you work like that there will be controversy.

ལབ་རྒྱུ་གླིང་རྒྱུ་ (lәbgyu lēŋgyu) sm. ལབ་རྒྱུ་.

ལབ་རྒྱུ་གླིང་རྒྱུ་མེད་པ་ (lәbgyu lēŋgyu mēēba) blameless.

ལབ་རྒྱུ་འཚོལ་ (lәbgyu tsȫȫ) va. to look for things that provoke trouble/ controversy.

ལབ་རྒྱུ་བཟོ་ (lәbgyu so̲) 1. va. to say things that cause others trouble. 2. va. to do things that provoke others to harm/ criticize you.

ལབ་རྒྱུ་ཕ་བསད་བུ་ལ་ཡང་ཡོད་ (lәbgyu pā sɛ̄ɛ̀ pu̲layaŋ yȫȫ) there are reasons for everything [Lit. an explanation can even be made if a son kills his father].

ལབ་ངོ་མ་ཤེས་ (lәbŋo mashee̲) not knowing what or how to say.

ལབ་བཅོས་ (lәbjöö) a method of treating a swollen leg by soaking it in hot water that has radishes in it.

ལབ་ཆང་ (lәbjaŋ) shung. ཆང་ served for saying sth. (according to the ancient Tibetan law).

ལབ་འཆོལ་ (lәb cȫȫ) vi. to talk in one's sleep.

ལབ་བརྗོད་ (lәbjöö) talk ¶ གཞུང་རྒྱུ་ཟོག་ཟ་ སྣག་འཛིན་བྱས་སྐོར་ལབ་བརྗོད་རྣམ་གྲངས་མ་ཉུང་ཙམ་འདུག་ན་ There was a lot of talk about embezzlement.

ལབ་ཉེས་ཤོར་ (lәbñeè shɔ̄ɔ̄) vi. to say things that should not have been said, to have a slip of the tongue.

ལབ་རྙོག (lәbñoò) an argument, dispute; va.—བཟོ་.

ལབ་རྙོག་ལོ་མས་འགྲིབ་གྲིབ་སྒྲིབ་ (lәbñoò lomɛ dr̲ɛ̄èdrib) shung. the secondary comments supersede the primary. [Lit. the leaves shading the fruit].

ལབ་སྟངས་ (lәbdaŋ) the manner/ way of saying.

ལབ་དོང་ (lәbdoŋ) pit used to preserve radishes during the winter.

ལབ་དྲི་ (lәbdri) the smell of radishes cooking.

ལབ་དར་ (lәbdar) a radish grater.

ལབ་དོལ་ (lәbdöö) superfluous talk, nonsensical talk, gibberish, rubbish.

ལབ་ཕིང་ (lәbbiŋ) ch. sm. ལ་ཕིན་.

ལབ་བེ་ལོབ་བེ་ (labbe lo̲be) term used to describing objects that are undulating in shape (not round or square).

ལབ་མེད་གླིང་བསང་ (lәbmeè lēŋsaŋ) shung. settled in a way that no criticism can be levied ¶ རྙོག་དྲ་འདིའི་སྐོར་ལབ་མེད་གླིང་བསང་རེད་བཞག Concerning this problem, it has been settled in a way that no one can give criticism.

ལབ་ཙམ་ཅིག་བྱེད་ (lәbdzamjig ce̲è) va. to mention sth. cursorily/ casually to sb. ¶ ལས་ཀའི་དུས་ཚོད་ལ་ཁྲོམ་ལ་འགྲོ་དགོས་ཡོད་ན་འགོ་ཁྲིད་ལ་ལབ་ཙམ་ཅིག་བྱེད་དགོས་ If you have to go to the market during work hours you should mention it cursorily to the boss.

ལབ་རྩོད་ (lәbdzöö) arguing, quarreling; va.—རྒྱག to get into a quarrel/ conflict.

ལབ་རྩོད་དོན་འབྱུང་ (lәbdzöö to̲nbüü) shung. arguing/ quarreling and having conflicts.

ལབ་གཞི་ (lәbshi) 1. sm. ལབ་གླིང་

ལབ་ཟླ་ (lәmda) 1. a talking partner, sb. to talk to/ with. 2. a singing partner, a chorus.

ལབ་ལབ་ (lәblәb) 1. talking back and forth; va.—བྱེད་ ¶ གསར་འགྱུར་དེའི་སྐོར་ལས་ཁུངས་ནང་ལབ་ལབ་མང་པོ་བྱེད་ཀྱི་འདུག They are talking back and forth about the news in the office. 2. talking behind sb's back; va.—གཏོང་.

ལབ་ལེབ་ (lәbleb) flat.

ལབ་ལོང་ (lәbloŋ) sm. ལབ་རྡོལ་.

ལབ་ཤད་ (lәbshɛɛ̀) sm. ལབ་དར་.

ལབ་ཤེད་པོ་ (lәb shēèbo) sm. ཁ་ཤེད་ཆེན་པོ་.

ལབ་སོན་ (lәbsön) radish seed.

ལབ་སློག (lәblɔɔ̀) sm. ཁ་ལན་སློག.

ལབས་ (lәb) sm. ལོབ་.

ལམ་ (lam) 1. road, path, way; vi.— ཤུག to have a road washed out by rain, etc. ¶ འཁོར་ལམ་ Motor road. 2. tradition, custom ¶ སྔར་གྱི་ལམ་ལྟར་ In accordance with the old customs. 3. interrogative and "or" particle for word ending in "l." 4. (vb. + —) custom/ precedent for sth. ¶ ཕྱོགས་ཕྱིན་སྐབས་ཕོགས་ཐོབ་གཞུང་ཕྱོགས་ནས་བརྒྱལ་ལམ་འདུག There is a custom of receiving salary from the government when traveling. 5. (— + vb.) a little ¶ བོད་ཡིག་ཀྱང་ལམ་ཤེས་ (He) also knows a little written Tibetan. 6. ways, means, method ¶ ཚན་རིག་གི་ལམ་ནས་ཞིང་ག་འདེབས་ཀྱི་ཡོད་པ་རེད་ They are farming with scientific methods.

ལམ་ཀ་ (laŋga) sm. ལམ་, 1.

ལམ་ཀག (laŋga) sm. ལམ་, 1.

ལམ་ཀག་ཁ་ (laŋga kā) by the side of the road.

ལམ་ཀག་འཁྱིལ་ (laŋga kēē) vi. to be on/ along a road ¶ གྲོང་གསེབ་འདི་ལ་མོ་ཊའི་ལམ་ཀག་འཁྱིལ་གྱི་ཡོད་པ་རེད་ This village is on the motor road.

ལམ་ཀག་འགག (laŋga gaà) vi. to be blocked (for a road).

ལམ་ཀག་འགོག (laŋga gɔ̲ɔ̀ va. to block off a road.

ལམ་ཀག་སྟོན་ (laŋga dön) va. to guide/ show a road.

ལམ་ཀག་མཐའ་ (laŋga tā) 1. end of the road. 2. sides of a road.

ལམ་ཀག་འཐོམ་ (laŋga tōm) vi. to get/ be lost on the road, to lose one's way.

ལམ་ཀག་ནོར་ (laŋga nɔ̲ɔ) vi. to be on the wrong road.

ལམ་ཀག་པ་རུའུ་ (laŋga bәruu) in between the roads ¶ ལམ་ཀག་པ་རུའུ་ལ་མེ་ཏོག་བཏབ་འདུག They planted flowers between the roads.

ལམ་ཀག་པར་ (laŋgabar) sm. ལམ་ཀག་པ་རུའ་.

ལམ་ཀག་འཚོལ་ (laŋga tsȫȫ) va. to search for a road.

ལམ་ཀག་གཞོགས་ལ་ (laŋga shɔ̲ɔ̀la) by/ on the road side.

ལམ་ཀག་བཞི་མདོ་ཁ་ (laŋga shi̲doga) crossroads (four-way).

ལམ་ཀྱོག (lamgyɔɔ̀) zigzag/ crooked/ curving road.

ལམ་བཀག (la̲m gāà) p. of ལམ་འགོག.

ལམ་བཀྲ་ཤིས་པ་ (la̲m drāshiìbә) auspicious signs encountered on the way to somewhere.

ལམ་བཀྲིས་ (lәmdriì) guiding on a path/ road (spiritual and physical); va.—བྱེད་.

ལམ་རྒྱང་ (la̲mgyaŋ) sm. ལམ་སེང་.

ལམ་རྐྱེན་ (lamgyen) mishaps/ accidents on the road.

ལམ་སྐོག (lamgɔɔ̀) secret road/ path.

ལམ་སྐོར་ (la̲mgɔɔ) going round about/ detouring; va. ལམ་སྐོར་; —གཏོང་; —རྒྱག.

ལམ་སྐྱོང་ (la̲mgyoŋ) road upkeep/ repair.

ལམ་སྐྱོང་པ་ (la̲mgyoŋba) person who does road upkeep/ repairs.

ལམ་ཁ་ (laŋga) sm. ལམ་ཀ་.

ལམ་ཁ་དབྲག (la̲m kādraà) a fork in a road.

ལམ་ཁག (laŋga) sm. ལམ་ཀག.

ལམ་ཁུག (lәmguù) street corner, curve on a road.

ལམ་ཁུངས་སྟོན་ (lәmguŋ dȫn) va. to guide.

ལམ་ཁྱིལ་ (la̲mgee) sm. ལམ་འཁྱིལ.

ལམ་མཁན་ (lamgɛn) guide.

ལམ་མཁྱེན་པ་ (la̲m kyēmba) one who knows the road/ trail.

ལམ་འཁྱིལ་ (la̲mkee) shung. a place on a road/ trail where one's journey will pass, a place one will encounter along on a journey ¶ ལམ་འཁྱིལ་གྲོང་ཚོ་ The villages along the road (we will go).

ལམ་ཁྲིད་ (lәmdriì) 1. guiding others on a trip/ journey; va.—བྱེད་. 2. sm. ལམ་ཁྲིད་པ་.

ལམ་ཁྲིད་མཁན་ (lәmdriñɛn) sm. ལམ་ཁྲིད་པ་.

ལམ་ཁྲིད་པ་ (lәmdribә) a guide on a trip.

ལམ་འགོད་ (lamgöö) shung. sm. ལམ་འཁྱིལ་.

ལམ་ག (laŋga) sm. ལམ་ཀ་.

ལམ་གོལ་ (lamgöö) 1. wrong road/ path (in

religion). 2. a small road in a remote area.

ལམ་གྱི་བདེན་པ་ (lamgi demba) one of the noble truths: the truth of the path.

ལམ་སྒྲོ་ (lamdro) provisions for a journey.

ལམ་གྲོགས་ (lamdrɔɔ̀) fellow traveler, traveling companion.

ལམ་གྲོན་ (lamdrön) traveling expenses, travel allowance.

ལམ་བགྲོད་ (lamdröö) traveling on a road/ trip; va.—བྱེད་ ¶ ང་ཚོ་མོ་ཊ་ལམ་བགྲོད་མགྱོགས་པོ་བྱས་ནས་ཡོང་བ་ཡིན་ We came by car traveling quickly. ¶ འགལ་རྐྱེན་གང་ཡང་མེད་པར་ལམ་བགྲོད་ཐུབ་པ་བྱུང་སོང་ I was able to travel (here) without misfortune.

ལམ་མགྱོགས་ (lamgyɔɔ̀) traveling quickly.

ལམ་མགྲོན་ (lamdrön) traveler.

ལམ་འགག (lam gaà) 1. vi. to be blocked (road). 2. checkpost on a road.

ལམ་འགོག (lam gɔɔ̀) 1. va. to block a road. 2. blockading a road; va.—བྱེད་.

ལམ་འགོར་ (lam gɔɔ) vi. to be delayed on the road.

ལམ་འགོལ་ས་ (lam göösa) a remote/ wilderness road or trail.

ལམ་འགྲམ་ (lamdram) alongside a road.

ལམ་འགྲིམ་ (lamdrim) va. to go on the road.

ལམ་འགྲུལ་ (lamdrüü) 1. travelers. 2. pedestrian traffic.

ལམ་འགྲོ་ (lamdro) 1. luck, good fortune; vi.—འགྲོ་; —རྒྱག to be lucky, to have things go one's way ¶ ཁྱེད་ལ་བྱ་བ་ལམ་འགྲོ་ཡོང་བར་ཤོག May you have good luck in whatever you do. 2. people going on the road.

ལམ་འགྲོ་རྒྱག་པོ་ (lamdro gyugbo) lucky, fortunate, successful ¶ ད་རེས་ཀྱི་ཚོང་འདི་ལམ་འགྲོ་རྒྱག་པོ་བྱུང་ Business these days has been successful.

ལམ་འགྲོ་མེད་པ་ (lamdro meèba) unlucky, unfortunate.

ལམ་འགྲོ་ཡོད་པ་ (lamdro yööba) lucky, fortunate.

ལམ་གླ་ (lamla) road fee/ toll.

ལམ་རྒྱ་ (lamgya) 1. blocking off a road; va.—སྡེམ་ to block off a road. 2. scope of a project/ task/ work. 3. consort.

ལམ་རྒྱགས་ (lamgyaà) provisions/ food for a journey/ trip.

ལམ་རྒྱུད་ (ləmgyüü) 1. on/ during a journey ¶ ལམ་རྒྱུད་ལ་རྐྱེན་ངན་གང་ཡང་བྱུང་མ་སོང་ I had no mishaps on the journey. 2. sm. ལམ་འཁོལ་.

ལམ་རྒྱུན་འཛགས་མུས་ (ləmgyün jagmüü) shung. customs that are still being practiced.

ལམ་རྒྱུས་ (ləmgyüü) 1. knowledge of a route/ road/ trip. 2. a guide; va.—བྱེད་ to guide ¶ གྲོང་ཁྱེར་གསར་པར་འགྲོ་དུས་ལམ་རྒྱུས་བྱེད་མཁན་ཞིག་དགོས་ཀྱི་འདུག When (one) goes to a new city one needs a guide.

ལམ་རྒྱུས་པ་ (ləmgyüübə) a (tour/ trip) guide.

ལམ་རྒྱུས་བྱེད་མཁན་ (ləmgyüü ceèñɛn) sm. ལམ་རྒྱུས་པ་.

ལམ་སྒྱུར་ལམ་ལྕགས་ (ləmgyur lamjaà) railroad switch track.

ལམ་སྒོ་ (lamgo) archway (on a road).

ལམ་སྒྲོན་ (lamdrön) street lamp, road lamp.

ལམ་བརྒྱུད་ (ləmgyüü) sm. ལམ་རྒྱུད་.

ལམ་སྐྱོལ་ (lamdröö) escorting; va.—བྱེད་ ¶ མི་དེ་ལམ་སྐྱོལ་དམག་མི་དང་སྦྲགས་ནས་ལྷ་སར་བཏང་བ་རེད་ They sent him with an escort of soldiers to Lhasa.

ལམ་ངན་ (lamŋɛn) 1. a dangerous/ treacherous road. 2. a bad system/ custom.

ལམ་ངན་དོད་རིགས་ (lamŋɛn tööriì) shung. bad customs.

ལམ་ངན་མུ་འབྱམས་ (lamŋɛn munjam) bad practices that have become customs/ routine matters.

ལམ་ངོས་ (lamŋöö) surface of a road.

ལམ་ངོ་ཚོད་ (lam ŋojöö) knowing the way/ road/ trail.

ལམ་དངུལ་ (ləmŋüü) traveling expenses.

ལམ་བཅག་འཕྲུལ་འཁོར་ (lamjaà trüügɔɔ) a steamroller that flattens the surface of roads.

ལམ་བཅོས་ (lamjöö) repairing roads; va.—བྱེད་ to repair roads.

ལམ་བཅོས་བཟོ་པ་ (lamjöö soba) road repair worker.

ལམ་བཅོས་ས་ཚིགས་ (lamjöö sədziì) a road repair/ road upkeep station.

ལམ་ལྕགས་ (lamjaà) railroad track/ rails; va.—འདིང་ to lay rail tracks.

ལམ་ལྕགས་ཉིས་གཤིབ་ (lamjaà ñiìshib) double-track railroad. 2. a dual policy.

ལམ་ལྕགས་ནས་ཟགས་ (lamjaànɛ saà) vi. to get derailed (train).

ལམ་ལྕགས་མེད་པའི་གློག་འཁོར་ (lamjaà meèbɛ lɔɔ̀gɔɔ) electric trolley.

ལམ་ལྕགས་ཞེང་ཆུང་ (lamjaà shenjuŋ) narrow gauge railroad track.

ལམ་ཆང་ (lamjaŋ) ཆང་ served to travelers.

ལམ་ཆས་ (lamjɛɛ̀) luggage, baggage ¶ ལམ་ཆས་ལེན་ས་ Baggage retrieving area.

ལམ་ཆས་ཁང་ (lamjɛɛ̀gaŋ) luggage compartment.

ལམ་ཆེན་ (lamjen) major route/ road, highway.

ལམ་མཆོག་ (lamjɔɔ̀) 1. the correct path. 2. a good road.

ལམ་འཆག་འཕྲུལ་འཁོར་ (lamjaà trüügɔɔ) steamroller.

ལམ་འཆོལ་ (lam cöö) vi. to take the wrong road.

ལམ་ཉག་ (lamñaà) sm. ལམ་ཟུར་.

ལམ་ཉལ་ (lamñɛɛ) a "scout" responsible for watching a road.

ལམ་ཉེན་གཟར་ས་ (lamñen sarsa) road sign (warning of danger).

ལམ་ཉེས་ (lamñeè) sm. ལམ་ངན་, 2.

ལམ་རྙིང་ (lamñiŋ) an old road.

ལམ་རྙེད་ (lam ñeè) vi. to find a road/ trail ¶ ཤིང་ནགས་ཀྱི་ལ་འགྲོ་བའི་ལམ་རྙེད་མ་བྱུང་ I didn't find the road going through the forest.

ལམ་གཏམ་ (lamdam) 1. talking about roads/ routes/ travel. 2. hearsay, rumor/ gossip.

ལམ་གཏོད་ (lamdöö) 1. va. to make a new road. 2. va. to make or create or invent a new means/ custom/ way/ path ¶ སྲིད་འཛིན་གསར་པས་མི་སེར་དབུལ་ཕོངས་རྣམས་ལ་སྐྱབ་གསོ་བྱ་རྒྱུའི་ལམ་གཏོད་པ་རེད་ The new president created a new way to give aid to the poor.

ལམ་རྟགས་ (lamdaà) road sign.

ལམ་རྟགས་རྡོ་རིང་ (lamdaà doriŋ) stone pillar (indicating distance on road).

ལམ་རྟོག (lamdoò) 1. investigating the state of a road/ path/ route; va.—བྱེད་ ¶ འགོ་ཁྲིད་མ་ཐོན་གོང་སྔོན་ལ་ལམ་རྟོག་བྱེད་མཁན་ཞིག་བཏང་བ་རེད་ (They) sent sb. to investigate the route before the leader departed. 2. va. to distinguish the wrong and right path (in religion).

ལམ་སྟོན་ (lamdön) 1. guiding, leading; va.—བྱེད་ to guide, to lead ¶ ཡུལ་སྐོར་སྐྱོ་འཆམ་པ་ཚོར་ལམ་སྟོན་བྱེད་མཁན་ཞིག་དགོས་ཀྱི་རེད་ Tourists need guides. 2. showing the way to do sth; va.—བྱེད་ ¶ ང་ལ་ལས་ཀ་གསར་པ་ཞིག་འཚོལ་རྒྱུའི་ལམ་སྟོན་བྱེད་རོགས་ Please show me how to find a new job.

ལམ་སྟོན་མཁན་ (lamdönñɛn) sm. ལམ་སྟོན་པ་.

ལམ་སྟོན་སྒྲོན་མེ་ (lamdön drönme) 1. lighthouse, beacon. 2. street light.

ལམ་སྟོན་པ་ (lamdömba) guide.

ལམ་སྟོན་བྱང་བུ་ (lamdön cəŋbu) signpost, guidepost.

ལམ་བསྟན་ (lamdɛn) sm. ལམ་སྟོན་.

ལམ་ཐག (lamdaà) distance ¶ ལམ་ཐག་ཀུང་ལི་ཉིས་སྟོང་ལྷག་ཙམ་ཡོད་པ་རེད་ The distance is more than two thousand (li) kilometers.

ལམ་ཐག་རིང་ཐུང་ (lamdaà rinduŋ) the distance/ length of a road ¶ ལྷ་ས་དང་རྒྱལ་རྩེའི་བར་ལམ་ཐག་རིང་ཐུང་ག་འདྲ་ཡོད་པ་རེད་ What is the distance between Lhasa and Gyantse?

ལམ་ཐག་རིང་ན་ཏ་ཤུགས་ཤེས་ ཡུན་རིང་གཤིབ་ན་མི་རྒྱུས་ལོན་ (lamdaà riŋnə dāshug shēè yünriŋ shībnə migyüü lön) knowing about sb. from a long period of contact/ interaction [Lit. a long distance shows a horse's strength, being together a long time shows a person's character].

ལམ་ཐིག (lamdig) 1. lines marking roads/ paths on map. 2. lines dividing lanes on a road.

ལམ་ཐོ་ (lamdo) traveling notes/ diary.

ལམ་ཐོག་གི་བཀག་དོ་ (lamdɔ̀ɔgi gāgdo) stumbling block, obstruction.

ལམ་ཐོག་གི་ཁྲལ་རིགས་ (lamdɔ̀ɔgi trɛ̄ɛrii) corvee transportation taxes.

ལམ་ཐོག་མི་ཁལ་ (lamdɔ̀ɔ migɛɛ) travelers and transport animals (on the road).

ལམ་མཐུན་པ་ (lam tʰunbə) 1. (taking) the same road/ path. 2. the same work/ role/ task.

ལམ་དུ་རྒྱུག (lamdu gyuù) 1. va. to run on the road. 2. sm. ལམ་དུ་འགྲོ་.

ལམ་དུ་འགྲོ་ (lamdu dro) va. to go on the road, to travel. 2. vi. to have good luck in business or in some venture.

ལམ་དུ་འཛུག (lamdu juù) sm. ལམ་དུ་ཞུགས་.

ལམ་དུ་ཞུགས་ (lamdu shuù) 1. va. to start/ enter/ participate in (a doctrine, faith, course of action). 2. va. to start on a journey.

ལམ་དུ་སློང་ (lamdu lhōŋ) sm. ལམ་དུ་འགྲོ་.

ལམ་དོད་ (lamdöö) shung. sm. ལམ་བྱངས་.

ལམ་བདེ་པ་ (lam debo) good road, easy route.

ལམ་བདེན་ (lamden) abbr. of ལམ་གྱི་བདེན་པ་.

ལམ་མདོ་ (lamdo) an intersection of roads, crossroads.

ལམ་མདོ་ཁ་ (lamdoga) sm. ལམ་མདོ་.

ལམ་འདེགས་ (lamdeg) sm. ལམ་དུ་ཞུགས་.

ལམ་མདོའི་རྩྭ་བཞིན་འདོར་བ་ (lamdö dzāshin dɔ̄ɔwa) kicking sb. out [Lit. throwing away like grasss on the road].

ལམ་འདྲི་ (lamdri) asking directions; va. ལམ་འདྲི་; —བྱེད་.

ལམ་འདྲེན་ (lamdren) sm. ལམ་སྟོན་.

ལམ་རྡུང་ (lamduŋ) ambushing on the road and robbing; va.—གཏོང་.

ལམ་རྡུལ་ (lamdüü) road dust.

ལམ་རྡེའུ་ (lamdewu) pebbles used as roadbed.

ལམ་སྡུག་ (lamduù) hardships of the road; vi.—མྱོང་ to experience the hardships of the road.

ལམ་བརྡ་ (lamda) message sent overland.

ལམ་ནོར་ (lam nɔɔ) vi. to lose one's way, to take the wrong road/ trail.

ལམ་ནོར་ཐེབས་ (lamnɔɔ tēè) vi. to lose one's way, to take the wrong road (in both the political and geographic sense).

ལམ་ནོར་ལོག་ཤེས་ (lamnɔɔ dɔgsheè) 1. returning from a wrong road to the correct one. 2. reforming/ correcting one's mistakes; va.—བྱེད་.

ལམ་ནོར་ལོག་ཤེས་མེད་པ་ (lamnɔɔ dɔgsheè meeba) persisting in one's errors.

ལམ་གནད་འདུ་འགག (lamnɛɛ̀ tungaà) the main or important juncture(s) of roads.

ལམ་སྣ་ (lamna) 1. the start of a trip, the beginning of a journey. 2. leading, guiding (a journey); va.—ཁྲིད་ to guide/ lead on a trip or journey.

ལམ་སྣེ་ (lamne) sm. ལམ་སྣ་.

ལམ་སྣེ་པ་ (lamnewa) a guide.

ལམ་པ་ (lamba) 1. traveler. 2. beggar. 3. the lead animal. 4. a guide.

ལམ་པོ་ (lambo) sm. འགྲོ་ལམ་.

ལམ་ཕྱེད་ (lamjeè) halfway/ midway on a trip or journey.

ལམ་ཕྱོགས་ (lamjɔɔ̀) road, path, course ¶ སྤྱི་ཚོགས་རིང་ལུགས་ཀྱི་ལམ་ཕྱོགས་ The path of socialism. ¶ ལམ་ཕྱོགས་འདི་བརྒྱུད་པ་རེད་ He went via this road.

ལམ་ཕྱོགས་ཁ་སྒྱུར་ (lamjɔɔ̀ kagyur) shung. changing a route/ direction.

ལམ་ཕྱོད་ (lamjöö) the pace at which one travels.

ལམ་ཕྲན་ (lamdrɛn) a small path/ trail.

ལམ་འཕྱག་མཁན་ (lamjaàñɛn) a sweeper.

ལམ་འཕྲང་ (lamdraŋ) a narrow mountain road overlooking a gorge/ river.

ལམ་འཕྲལ་ (lamdrɛɛ) at once, immediately.

ལམ་བར་ (lambar) 1. on the way/ journey. 2. between two roads.

ལམ་བུ་ (lambu) sm. ལམ་.

ལམ་བྱངས་ (lam jaŋ) vi. to become a tradition or way of doing things ¶ ཐོག་མར་དང་བླངས་ཀྱིས་ཞལ་འདེབས་ཕུལ་བ་དེ་ལམ་བྱངས་ནས་རྗེས་སུ་ལུགས་སྲོལ་དུ་གྱུར་པ་རེད་ What was initially a voluntary donation has become a tradition.

ལམ་བྲོ་ (lamdro) provisions for a trip/ journey.

ལམ་དབུ་མ་ (lam ūmə) the middle path.

ལམ་འབྱེད་ (lamjeè) sm. ལམ་གཏོད་.

ལམ་འབྱེད་གཏོང་ལེན་ (lamjeè doŋlen) pathbreaking, pioneering.

ལམ་མི་འདྲ་ཡང་འགྱུར་ས་གཅིག་པ་ (lam mindrayaŋ jɔɔsa jīgbə) different strategies/ methods leading to the same goal [Lit. different roads but one arrival place].

ལམ་མི་ཟ་ (lam misa) sm. མོ་མཚན་.

ལམ་མི་ལུམ་མི་ (lammi lummi) shredding/ falling apart due to overcooking ¶ ཤ་ཚོད་ཐག་ཆོད་ནས་ལམ་མི་ལུམ་མི་ཆགས་བཞག The meat was overcooked and has become shredded.

ལམ་མིན་ (lammin) wrong way/ path.

ལམ་མེ་བ་ (lammewa) bright, shinning.

ལམ་མེར་ (lammee) bright, shinning.

ལམ་ཙམ་ (lamdzam) roughly, briefly, tentatively ¶ དང་པོ་དབྱེ་ཞིབ་ལམ་ཙམ་བྱེད་དགོས་ First you must analyze it roughly.

ལམ་ཙམ་ཞིག (lamdzamshig) sm. ལམ་ཙམ་.

ལམ་རྩིས་ (lamdzii) shung. a rough calculation.

ལམ་ཚད་ (lamdzɛɛ̀) mileage distance.

ལམ་ཚད་རྡོ་བཙུགས་ (lamdzɛɛ̀ dodzuù) milepost.

ལམ་ཚད་རྡོ་རིང་ (lamdzɛɛ̀ doriŋ) sm. ལམ་ཚད་རྡོ་བཙུགས་.

ལམ་འཛིན་ (lamdzin) travel permit.

ལམ་འཛོལ་ (lamdzöö) getting lost on the way/ road.

ལམ་འཛོས་ (lamdzöö) sm. ལམ་མདོ་.

ལམ་ཞང་ (lamshaŋ) sm. ལམ་ཞེང་.

ལམ་ཞལ་ (lamshɛɛ) macadam tar used to cover roads.

ལམ་ཞིབ་ (lamshib) 1. road surveying; va.—བྱེད་. 2. shung. investigating corvee transportation taxes.

ལམ་ཞིབ་ལས་ཁངས་ (lamshib lɛ̀ɛguŋ) shung. the office in charge of investigating corvee transport taxes.

ལམ་ཞུ་ (lamshu) street lamp.

ལམ་ཞུགས་འགྲུལ་པ་ (lamshuù drüüba) passenger on a journey/ trip.

ལམ་ཞེང་ (lamsheŋ) the width of a road.

ལམ་ཞོར་ (lamshɔɔ) doing sth. incidental to going somewhere, stopping somewhere on the way to somewhere else ¶ ལྷ་སར་འགྲོ་དུས་ལམ་ཞོར་རྒྱལ་རྩེར་ཕྱིན་པ་ཡིན་ On the way to Lhasa (I) went Gyantse.

ལམ་ཞོར་ལ་ (lam shɔɔla) sm. ལམ་ཞོར་.

ལམ་གཞི་ (lamshi) road base/ foundation.

ལམ་གཞུང་ (lamshuŋ) main road/ street, highway.

ལམ་བཞི་མདོ་ཁ་ (lamshi doga) crossroads (of four roads).

ལམ་ཟད་ (lamsɛɛ̀) sm. ལམ་བཟའ་.

ལམ་ཟས་ (lamsɛɛ̀) sm. ལམ་རྒྱགས་.

ལམ་ཟན་པ་ (lamaemba) sm. སྣང་པོ་.

ལམ་ཟུར་ (lamsur) side of a road.

ལམ་གཟུར་ (lam sur) va. to divert/ move/ detour to make room for another one encouters on a trail/ road.

ལམ་བཟང་ (lamsaŋ) the right path/ way/ doctrine.

ལམ་བཟོ་ (lamso) road construction, road repair; va.—བྱེད་ to do road construction/ road repair.

ལམ་བཟོ་འཕྲུལ་ཆས་ (lamso trüüjɛɛ̀) road building machinery.

ལམ་བཟོ་པ་ (lamsowa) a road construction/ repair worker.

ལམ་འོད་སྲིན་བུ་ (lamwöö sïmbu) firefly.

ལམ་ཡིག (lamyiì) shung. 1. travel documents permitting the requisition of corvee labor and transport animals. 2. passport.

ལམ་ཡིག་ནང་གསལ་ (lamyiì naŋsεε) shung. contents of the corvee requisition document.

ལམ་གཡར་གླ་ (lamyöö lā) fee for using a road.

ལམ་གཡོལ་ (lamyöö) sm. ལམ་གཟུར་.

ལམ་རིང་གིས་རྟ་ཤེད་ལོན་ འདྲི་རིང་གིས་མི་ཁོག་ལོན་ (lamriŋgi dāsheè lön driringi migɔɔ̀ lön) sm. ལམ་ཐག་རིང་ན་རྟ་ཤུགས་ཤེས་ ཡུན་རིང་གཤིབ་ན་མ་རྒྱུས་ལོན་.

ལམ་རིམ་ (lamrim) 1. the "graded path" text of Tsongkapa. 2. stages of one's journey/ trip/ voyage.

ལམ་རོགས་ (lamrɔɔ̀) traveling companion.

ལམ་ལ་འགྲོ་ (lamla dro) vi. to be successful ¶ གནས་ཚུལ་ལ་བལྟས་ན་ཚོང་འདི་ལམ་ལ་འགྲོ་གི་མ་རེད་བསམས་ཀྱི་འདུག Looking at the situation, I think this trading will not be successful.

ལམ་ལ་ཆས་ (lamla cεὲ) sm. ལམ་ལ་འགྲོ་.

ལམ་ལམ་ (lamlam) 1. clearly remembering/ recalling. 2. flickering (of light).

ལམ་ལས་ (lamlεὲ) road building/ construction work.

ལམ་ལས་བཟོ་སྐྲུན་ཀུང་སི་ (lamlεὲ sodrün gūŋsi) tib. ch. road building/ construction company.

ལམ་ལུམ་ (lamlum) abbr. of ལམ་མི་ལུམ་མི་.

ལམ་ལ་ཞུགས་ (lamla shuù) sm. ལམ་དུ་ཞུགས་.

ལམ་ལུགས་ (lamluù) way, system ¶ སྤྱི་ཚོགས་རིང་ལུགས་ཀྱི་ལམ་ལུགས་ The socialist system.

ལམ་ལོག (lamlɔɔ̀) the wrong path/ faith/ doctrine.

ལམ་ཤུལ་ (lamshüü) track/ trace on a road; va.—འདེད་ to follow a track/ trace (on a road).

ལམ་ཤོག (lamshoò) sm. ལམ་ཡིག.

ལམ་བཤང་ (lamshaŋ) clearing the road for sb. or sth.; va.—རྒྱག to clear the way for, to make way for ¶ འགོ་ཁྲིད་ཡོང་དུས་ཉེན་རྟོག་པས་ལམ་བཤང་བརྒྱབ་པ་རེད་ When the leader came, police cleared the road (before him).

ལམ་སང་ (lamsaŋ) sm. ལམ་སེང་.

ལམ་སངས་ (lamsaŋ) sm. ལམ་སང་.

ལམས་སེ་ལམ་ (lamselam) flickering (of light).

ལམ་སེང་ (lamseŋ) immediately, right away, at once ¶ འདིར་ལམ་སེང་ཤོག Come here at once.

ལམ་སེལ་ (lamsel) sm. ལམ་བཤང་.

ལམ་སྲོན་ (lamsön) shung. sm. ལམ་ཡིག.

ལམ་སྲུང་ (lamsuŋ) protecting/ defending a road. 2. taking care of/ maintaining a road.

ལམ་སྲུང་དམག་མི་ (lamsuŋ māəmi) police/ militia guarding a road or highway.

ལམ་སྲོལ་ (lamsöö) custom, rule, regulation, precedent.

ལམ་གསལ་ (lamsεε) shung. abbr. of ལམ་ཡིག་ནང་གསལ་.

ལམ་གསོ་ (lamso) looking after/ maintaining a road, railway/ highway maintenance.

ལམ་གསོ་ཁག (lamsogaà) road maintenance stations.

ལམ་གསོ་ལས་གྲྭ་ (lamso lεὲdra) railway/ highway maintenance unit.

ལམ་བསང་ (lamsaŋ) sm. ལམ་བཤང་.

ལམ་ལྷོངས་ (lamlhoŋ) sm. ལམ་དུ་ལྷོངས་.

ལའ་ཏིང་ཨ་མེ་རི་ཀ་ (ladiŋ āmerika) Latin America.

ལའན་ཀྲིའོ་ (landre) Lanzhou.

ལའན་ཅིའུ་སྦོ་ལོ་ (lanci bōlo) ch.tib. basketball; va.—རྒྱག to play basketball.

ལའོ་ཀོ་ (lago) ch. sm. ལའོ་ལྦོ་.

ལའོ་ལྦོ་ (lawo) Laos.

ལའོ་སེ་ (lase) sm. ལའོ་ལྦོ་.

ལར་དགོངས་ (largoŋ) shung. abbr. of ལ་རྒྱར་དགོངས་ (see ལ་རྒྱར་).

ལར་རྒྱ་ (largya) sm. ལ་རྒྱ་.

ལར་ནས་ (larnε) 1. actually, in reality ¶ ལར་ནས་ཁྱེད་རང་གིས་བརྟག་དཔྱད་གཟབ་ནན་མ་བྱས་པ་དེ་གང་ཡིན་ནམ་ Actually why didn't you investigate this carefully? 2. in general ¶ ལར་ནས་ལས་ཀ་གལ་ཆེ་བ་རྣམས་གོང་རིམ་ལ་དགོངས་སྐོར་ཞུ་དགོས་ In general, one must ask one's superiors when the task is important.

ལར་ཡང་ (laryaŋ) again.

ལར་ཞེན་ (larshen) loyalty; va.— འཛིན་ to have loyalty.

ལས་ (lεὲ) 1. action, deeds, work. 2. result, fruit, merit, karma ¶ འདི་ཁོའི་ལས་རེད་ This is his karma. 3. from ¶ སྐུ་འདྲ་འདི་དངུལ་ལས་བཞེངས་པ་རེད་ The statue was made from silver. 4. except for, other than ¶ འདི་ལས་མེད་ (I) don't have anything other than this. 5. comparative particle: 'than' ¶ དེ་ལས་འདི་མངར་བ་འདུག This is sweeter than that. 6. va. to do ¶ ལས་ཀ་ལས་ To do work. ¶ ཟ་མ་ལས་ To cook.

ལས་ཀ་ (lεὲga) work, job, task; va.—བྱེད་ to work.

ལས་ཀ་འགན་ལེན་ (lεὲga gεnlen) a labor contract/ agreement.

ལས་ཀ་བགོད་ (lεὲga göö) va. to dispense/ distribute/ divide work.

ལས་ཀ་རྒོད་པོ་ (lεὲga gööbo) good/ capable at working.

ལས་ཀ་ཅག་པོ་ (lεὲga jāgbo) sb. who works fast/ promptly.

ལས་ཀ་ཆད་ (lεὲga cεὲ) vi. to be unable to work ¶ རྒྱུ་ཆ་དུས་ཐོག་ལ་མ་འབྱོར་ཙང་བཟོ་པ་ཚོའི་ལས་ཀ་ཆད་པ་རེད་ Because the (raw) materials didn't arrive in time, the laborers were unable to work.

ལས་ཀ་འཇོན་པོ་ (lεὲga jömbo) capable/ competent/ able in work.

ལས་ཀ་བརྗེ་ (lεὲga je) va. to change work.

ལས་ཀ་མཉམ་སྒྲུབ་ (lεὲga ñamdrub) working together, working cooperatively; va.—བྱེད་.

ལས་ཀ་འཐེན་ (lεὲga tēn) va. to quit/ resign from work.

ལས་ཀ་ཐོབ་ (lεὲga tōb) vi. to get a job, to obtain work.

ལས་ཀ་འདྲ་བ་ལ་ཐོབ་ཆ་འདྲ་བ་ (lεὲga drawala tōbja drawa) equal pay for equal work.

ལས་ཀ་འཕེར་པོ་ (lεὲga pērbo) sm. ལས་ཀ་འཇོན་པོ་.

ལས་ཀ་བྱ་ཡུལ་ (lεὲga cayüü) place of work.

ལས་ཀ་བྱེད་ (lεὲga ceè) see ལས་ཀ་.

ལས་ཀ་བྱེད་སྟངས་ (lεὲga ceèdaŋ) way/ style of doing things.

ལས་ཀ་བྱེད་ཐབས་ (lεὲga ceèdəb) method of work.

ལས་ཀ་བྱེད་ལུགས་ (lεὲga ceèluù) sm. ལས་ཀ་བྱེད་སྟངས་.

ལས་ཀ་ཙ་གི་ཙ་གི་ (lεὲga dzə̄gi dzīgi) odd jobs, miscellaneous work.

ལས་ཀ་ཤོར་ (lεὲga shɔ̄ɔ̄) vi. to lose a job.

ལས་ཀ་འཇོག (lεὲga jɔɔ̀) va. to go on strike.

ལས་ཀ་ཧུར་པོ་ (lεὲga hūrbu) diligent/ ardent/ enthusiastic worker.

ལས་ཀའི་སྐར་གྲངས་ (lεὲgε gārdraŋ) the value in money of a work point (in a socialist commune).

ལས་ཀའི་རྣམ་འགྱུར་ (lεὲgε nāmgyur) work attitude.

ལས་ཀའི་རྣམ་འགྱུར་འཛིན་སྟངས་ (lεὲgε nāmgyur dzindaŋ) sm. ལས་ཀའི་རྣམ་འགྱུར་.

ལས་ཀའི་དབྱེ་བ་ (lεὲgε yēwa) differences in the rank/ title of workers.

ལས་ཀའི་མིང་ (lεὲgε miŋ) occupation title.

ལས་ཀའི་ལག་ཁྱེར་ (lεὲgε laggyer) sm. ལས་རྟགས་.

ལས་ཀར་གཡོལ་ (lεὲgaa yöö) va. to avoid work.

ལས་ཀར་སྒྱིད་ལུགས་ (lεὲgaa gyiìluù) 1. laziness with respect to work; va.—བྱེད་. 2. slowdown tactics (at work); va.—བྱེད་.

ལས་ཀྱང་ (lεὲgyaŋ) comparative construction: 'even...than' ¶ འདི་ལས་ཀྱང་འདི་ཆེ་བ་འདུག This is even bigger than this.

ལས་ཀྱི་བསྐོས་བཞག (lεὲgi gööshaà) sm. ལས་ཀྱིས་བསྐོས་.

ལས་ཀྱི་མཐའ་ (lεὲgi tā) the end of one's task/ work/ job.

ལས་ཀྱི་སྣེ་ (lεὲgi nē) 1. workers/ officials in

monasteries. 2. start and finish of work. 3. stages of work.

ལས་ཀྱི་བླ་ (lɛ̱ɛ̀gi lā) supervisor.

ལས་ཀྱིས་བསྒོས་ (lɛ̱ɛ̀gi göö) vi. to be determined by past karma ¶ ཚེ་འདིའི་སྐྱིད་སྡུག་ལེགས་ཉེན་ནི་ཚེ་སྔོན་མའི་ལས་ཀྱིས་བསྒོས་པ་རེད་ This life's joy and suffering is the karmic consequence of one's past life.

ལས་ཀྱིས་འཁོར་ (lɛ̱ɛ̀gi kɔ̄ɔ) vi. to come naturally because of sth. else ¶ ཟ་ཁང་གི་ཁ་ལག་ཞིམ་པོ་ཡོད་ན་ཁ་ལག་ཟ་མཁན་ལས་ཀྱིས་འཁོར་ཡོང་གི་རེད་ If the restaurant's food is good people will come naturally (without having to try to find customers).

ལས་དཀྱུས་ (lɛ̱ɛ̀gyüü) 1. common workers. 2. shung. abbr. of ལས་ཚན་པ་ and དུད་འཁོར་དཀྱུས་མ་.

ལས་ཀཱང་ (lɛ̱ɛ̀gaŋ) post, position ¶ ལས་ཀཱང་སྟོང་པ་ A vacant position.

ལས་སྐར་ (lɛ̱ɛ̀gar) sm. སྐར་མ་, 5.

ལས་སྐལ་ (lɛ̱ɛ̀gɛɛ) 1. karmic effect/ consequences ¶ ཚེ་འདིའི་སྐྱིད་སྡུག་ལེགས་ཉེན་ནི་ཚེ་སྔོན་མའི་ལས་སྐལ་རེད་ One's joy and suffering in this life is the karmic consequence of one's past life. 2. one's portion/ share of work.

ལས་སྐལ་ཅི་བབ་ (lɛ̱ɛ̀gɛɛ jībəb) sm. ལས་ཀྱིས་བསྒོས་པ་.

ལས་སྐོར་ (lɛ̱ɛ̀gɔɔ) overseeing, supervising; va.—བྱེད་.

ལས་སྐྲུན་ (lɛ̱ɛ̀drün) building, constructing; va.—བྱེད་ ¶ གྲོང་ཁྱེར་ནང་ཁང་པ་གསར་པ་མང་པོ་ལས་སྐྲུན་བྱས་འདུག (They) constructed many new buildings in the city.

ལས་སྐྱོང་ལྷན་ཚོགས་ (lɛ̱ɛ̀gyoŋ lhēndzɔɔ) council ¶ ཞི་བདེའི་ལས་སྐྱོང་ལྷན་ཚོགས་ Peace council.

ལས་བསྐོས་ (lɛ̱ɛ̀göö) sm. ལས་སྐོས་.

ལས་ཁང་ (lɛ̱ɛ̀gaŋ) 1. office. 2. workshop.

ལས་ཁུངས་ (lɛ̱ɛ̀guŋ) office, department, bureau.

ལས་ཁུངས་ཀྱི་ཚགས་པར་ (lɛ̱ɛ̀guŋgi tsāgbar) governmental/ office newspaper, party organ.

ལས་ཁུངས་ཁ་འདུ་ (lɛ̱ɛ̀guŋ kūdu) streamlining/ simplifying offices or administrative structures to make them more efficient.

ལས་ཁུངས་གྲོལ་ (lɛ̱ɛ̀guŋ dr**öö**) vi. to adjourn/ let out/ finish/ close (for an) office.

ལས་ཁུངས་ཚུགས་ (lɛ̱ɛ̀guŋ tsüù) 1. to begin/ start (for an) office ¶ ཞོགས་པ་ཆུ་ཚོད་བརྒྱད་པར་ལས་ཁུངས་ཚུགས་ཀྱི་རེད་ The office starts in the morning at 8 am. 2. vi. to be in session/ progress ¶ ད་ལྟ་ལས་ཁུངས་ཚུགས་བསྡད་བཞག The office is in session now.

ལས་ཁུངས་འཚོག (lɛ̱ɛ̀guŋ tsɔ̄ɔ) sm. ལས་ཁུངས་ཚུགས་.

ལས་ཁུངས་འཛིན་སྐྱོང་ (lɛ̱ɛ̀guŋ dzi̱ngyoŋ) office administration.

ལས་ཁུངས་དང་ཨུ་ (lɛ̱ɛ̀guŋ dāŋ ū) tib. ch. party committee of an office.

ལས་ཁུངས་ཟ་ཁང་ (lɛ̱ɛ̀guŋ sa̱gaŋ) dinning hall/ canteen of an office.

ལས་ཁུར་ (lɛ̱ɛ̀gur) job, position; va.—འཛིན་ to hold an office/ position/ job; va.—སྤྲོད་ to give sb. an office job/ position ¶ ལས་ཁུར་དུས་ཡུན་ Term of office.

ལས་ཁུར་དགོངས་ཞུ་ (lɛ̱ɛ̀gur go̱ŋshu) resignation (from office); va.—བྱེད་.

ལས་ཁུར་ཕྱིར་འཐེན་ (lɛ̱ɛ̀gur ci̱rden) resignation from an office/ position/ job; va.—བྱེད་ to ask sb. to resign ¶ གྲོས་ཚོགས་ཀྱི་འཐུས་མི་དེ་ལས་ཁུར་ཕྱིར་འཐེན་བྱས་འདུག The senator was asked to resign.

ལས་ཁུར་ལོ་དུས་ (lɛ̀ɛgur lo̱düü) term of office; vi.—རྫོགས་ to end/ complete a term of office.

ལས་ཁྲལ་ (lɛ̱ɛ̀drɛɛ) corvee labor tax.

ལས་ཁྲལ་གྱི་ས་བོགས་ (lɛ̱ɛ̀drɛɛgi bɔ̱ɔ) leasing land on the basis of paying in labor.

ལས་ཁྲི་ (lɛ̱ɛ̀dri) 1. scaffold. 2. ལས་ཐོག.

ལས་འཁུར་ (lɛ̱ɛ̀gur) sm. ལས་ཁུར་.

ལས་མཁན་ (lɛ̱ɛ̀gɛn) worker.

ལས་མཁོའི་དཔེ་དེབ་ (lɛ̱ɛ̀gö bēdeb) reference book or manual for work/ job.

ལས་འགྱུར་ (lɛ̱ɛ̀gyur) leaving an office/ job/ position ¶ ཁོང་གི་ང་ཚོའི་ལས་ཁུངས་ལས་འགྱུར་བྱུང་བ་རེད་ He left our office.

ལས་འགྱུར་ངལ་གསོ་ (lɛ̀ɛgyur ŋɛ̱ɛso) retirement; va.—བྱེད་ to retire.

ལས་འགྱུར་པ་ (lɛ̀ɛgyurwə) retired person.

ལས་ཀོ་ (lɛ̱ɛ̀go) capability to do a job/ task; vi.—འཕེར་ to be able/ capable of doing a job or task.

ལས་ཀོ་འཕེར་པོ་ (lɛ̱ɛ̀go pērbo) capable, able, competent.

ལས་གོས་ (lɛ̱ɛ̀göö) work clothes, work uniform.

ལས་གྲྭ་ (lɛ̱ɛ̀dra) 1. workshop, worksite ¶ ཨར་རྒྱག་ལས་གྲྭ་ Construction worksite. 2. a work group/ crew ¶ གློག་རིན་ལས་གྲྭ་ Electric bill collecting crew.

ལས་གྲི་ (lɛ̱ɛ̀dri) knife for cutting corpses at sky burial site.

ལས་སྒྲིབ་ (lɛ̱ɛ̀drib) karmic pollution/ negativities ¶ རང་སེམས་པ་བཟང་པོ་བྱས་ན་ཚེ་སྔོན་གྱི་ལས་སྒྲིབ་དག་གི་རེད་ If (one) acts kind the karmic negativities of (one's) past life will be cleansed.

ལས་གྲྭའི་མ་གནས་ (lɛ̱ɛ̀drɛ ma̱nɛɛ) cost of production.

ལས་གྲངས་ (lɛ̱ɛ̀draŋ) work point (in the PRC's commune system); va.—འགོད་ to record one's work points.

ལས་གྲོགས་ (lɛ̱ɛ̀drɔɔ) assistant, helper.

ལས་གླ་ (lɛ̱ɛ̀la) wages, labor charges.

ལས་བགོ་ (lɛ̱ɛ̀go) sm. ལས་བགོས་.

ལས་བགོས་ (lɛ̱ɛ̀göö) division of labor; va.—རྒྱག; —བྱེད་ to divide up labor.

ལས་འགན་ (le̱ngɛn) task, responsibility, duty, mission; va.—ཁུར་; —འཁྱེར་; —ལེན་ to take on a responsibility/ task ¶ ཆབ་སྲིད་ལས་འགན་ Political responsibility. ¶ སྐབས་དེར་ང་བླ་གཉེར་གྱི་ལས་འགན་འཁུར་མུས་ At that time I was working as a བླ་གཉེར་.

ལས་འགན་ཁུར་ཡུན་ (le̱ngɛn kūryün) term of office, duration of office.

ལས་འགན་སྒྲུབ་ (le̱ngɛn dru̱b) va. to accomplish a task/ job/ duty/ responsibility.

ལས་འགན་གཅིག་ལྡོགས་ (le̱ngɛn ji̱gjoò) having responsibility for more than one office at the same time.

ལས་འགན་སྙིག་སྒྲུབ་ (le̱ngɛn ñēgdrug) vi. to finish/ complete/ accomplish a responsibility quickly.

ལས་འགན་སྤོ་ (le̱ngɛn bō) va. to transfer an official from one post/ position to another.

ལས་འགན་བར་མཚམས་འཇོག (le̱ngɛn pa̱rdzam jɔ̱ɔ) va. to suspend sb. from an office/ duty/ responsibility.

ལས་འགན་གཙང་ལེན་ (le̱ngɛn dzāŋlen) taking complete responsibility; va.—བྱེད་.

ལས་འགན་ཚབ་སྒྲུབ་ (le̱ngɛn tsābdrub) carrying out a responsibility in place of someone else.

ལས་འགན་བཞེས་ (le̱ngɛn she̱e) h. of ལས་འགན་ཁུར་.

ལས་འགན་ལེགས་སྒྲུབ་ (le̱ngɛn le̱gdrub) successfully accomplishing a task/ duty/ responsibility; va.—བྱེད་.

ལས་འགུགས་གཞོན་ནུ་ (lɛ̱ɛ̀guù sho̱nnu) unemployed youth [Lit. youth waiting for jobs].

ལས་འགུལ་ (le̱ngüü) a movement, campaign; va.—བྱེད་; —སྤེལ་ to do a campaign/ movement ¶ ལོ་ལྟར་ཏང་གིས་ལས་འགུལ་གསར་པ་རེ་སྤེལ་གྱི་ཡོད་པ་རེད་ Every year the party makes a new campaign.

ལས་འགུལ་པ་ (le̱ngüüwə) an activist.

ལས་འགོ་ (le̱ngo) start/ beginning of work; va.—འཛུགས་; —རྩོམ་ to start work/ job.

ལས་འགོ་ཚུགས་ (le̱ngo tsüù) vi. to begun a project/ job.

ལས་འགྱུར་ (le̱ngyur) sm. ལས་སྒྱུར་.

ལས་འགྱུར་དམག་མི་ (le̱ngyur mā̱əmi) soldiers transferred to civilian work/ duty.

ལས་འགྲུབ་མཛད་སྒོ་ (lɛ̱ɛ̀drub dzɛ̱ɛgo) celebration on

the completion of a project.

ལས་འགྲོ་ (lɛndro) sm. ལས་ཕྱོ་, 2.

ལས་རྒྱབ་པ་ (lɛ̀ gyəbbə) supervisor, foreman, overseer.

ལས་རྒྱུ་འབྲས་ (lɛ̀ gyundrɛɛ̀) karmic consequences/ retribution/ result (for one's past actions), the result of one's karma; vi.—འཁོར་ to have the consequences of one's past actions impact one ¶ གཞན་ལ་གནོད་པ་བསྐྱལ་བའི་ལས་རྒྱུ་འབྲས་འཁོར་ནས་ཁོ་རང་རྐྱེན་ངན་མང་པོ་འཕྲད་པ་རེད་ As a karmic retribution for his harming others he met many disasters.

ལས་རྒྱུན་ (lɛ̀ɛgyün) 1. term of office; va.—འཛིན་ to succeed (to an office/position) ¶ རྒྱལ་སྲས་ཀྱིས་ཡབ་རྒྱལ་པོའི་ལས་རྒྱུན་འཛིན་གྱི་ཡོད་པ་རེད་ The prince is succeeding his father the king. ¶ཁོང་གི་ལས་རྒྱུན་རིང་ During his term of office.

ལས་སྒུག (lɛ̀ɛguù) waiting for a job (i.e., unemployed) ¶ ལས་སྒུག་གཞོན་ནུ་ Unemployed youth (waiting to get a job).

ལས་སྒུག་གི་སྐྱབས་གསོ་ (lɛ̀ɛguùgi gyəbso) unemployment benefits for the unemployed.

ལས་སྒུག་ངལ་རྩོལ་པ་ (lɛ̀ɛguù ŋɛɛdzübə) unemployed workers/ laborers.

ལས་སྒོ་ (lɛ̀ɛgo) 1. a vocation, profession; va.—ཞུགས་ to work in a vocation ¶ ཕྲུ་གུ་སློབ་གྲྭ་ཐོན་ནས་ལས་སྒོར་ཞུགས་ཐུབ་པ་བྱུང་བ་རེད་ The child graduated from school and entered into a vocation. 2. factory, company ¶ ལས་སྒོའི་རྟགས་ Brand of a company. ¶ ལས་སྒོ་རང་གི་ཅ་ལག Real factory goods. 3. a department. 4. sm. ལས་སྐལ་.

ལས་སྒྲ་ (lɛ̀ɛdra) sm. ལས་སུ་བྱ་བའི་སྒྲ་.

ལས་སྒྲུབ་ (lɛ̀ɛdrub) doing work.

ལས་སྒྲུབ་ཀྱི་ལས་རིམ་ (lɛ̀ɛdrubgi lɛ̀ɛrim) production line [Lit. doing work in sequence/ stages].

ལས་སྒྲུབ་འཆར་གཞི་ (lɛ̀ɛdrub cərshi) work schedule/ plan.

ལས་སྒྲུབ་པ་ (lɛ̀ɛdrubbə) working personnel, staff members.

ལས་སྒྲུབ་ཚོགས་ཆུང་ (lɛ̀ɛdrub tsɔ̄gjuŋ) work group/ team.

ལས་སྒྲུབ་རུ་ཁག (lɛ̀ɛdrub rugaà) work unit.

ལས་བསྒྱུར་ (lɛ̀ɛgyur) 1. changing one's work/ job, transferring from one job to another ¶ དམག་མི་ཁག་ཅིག་ལས་བསྒྱུར་བྱས་ནས་ལས་ཁུངས་ནང་དུ་བཅུག་འདུག A group of soldiers were transferred and put in offices.

ལས་བསྒྱུར་དམག་མི་ (lɛ̀ɛgyur mə̄əmi) a demobilized soldier, an soldier transferred to a civilian job.

ལས་ངན་ (lɛ̀ɛŋɛn) 1. bad karma; va.—གསོག to accumulate bad karma.

ལས་ང་ (lɛ̀ɛŋa) beating a drum to summon people to start work.

ལས་ཅན་ (lɛ̀ɛjɛn) fortunate/ lucky person.

ལས་བཅས་ (lɛ̀ɛjɛɛ̀) shung. together with officials ¶ བློན་ཆེན་ལས་བཅས་ཚོགས་འདུར་ཕེབས་འདུག The minister attended the meting together with his officials.

ལས་ཆག (lɛ̀ɛjaà) shung. tax exemption received by families for providing certain types of workers.

ལས་ཆད་ (lɛ̀ɛjɛɛ̀) being absent from work ¶ ཁོ་ལས་ཁུངས་ནང་ལས་ཆད་མང་པོ་བྱུང་འདུག He was absent from work many times. ¶ ལས་ཁུང་ནང་ལ་ལས་ཆད་མང་པོ་འདུག There are many people absent from work in the office.

ལས་ཆས་ (lɛ̀ɛjɛɛ̀) work clothes.

ལས་ཆུང་ཕན་ཆེ་ (lɛ̀ɛjuŋ pēnje) a little work but a great benefit.

ལས་ཆུང་བ་ (lɛ̀ɛjuŋwa) 1. unfortunate/ unlucky person. 2. a person who is not able to work quickly. 3. easy task/ work.

ལས་ཆེ་བ་ (lɛ̀ɛjewa) 1. a fortunate/ lucky person. 2. person able to work quickly/ do lots of work. 3. difficult work/ task. 4. bigger than ¶ ཁོང་ང་ལས་ཆེ་བ་འདུག He is bigger than me.

ལས་ཆོད་ (lɛ̀ɛjöö) work output/ productivity ¶ ལས་ཀ་བྱེད་ཐབས་གསར་པ་དེ་ལས་ཆོད་ཆེ་བ་འདུག The new method has greater output. ¶ ལས་ཆོད་ཆེན་པོ་ High productivity/ efficiency.

ལས་འཆར་ (lɛ̀ɛjar) sm. ལས་གཞི་.

ལས་ཇུས་ (lɛ̀ɛjüü) plans/ methods for work; va.—འགོད་; —འདིང་ to make a work plan.

ལས་མཇུག (lɛnjuù) end of work/ project/ job; va.—སྒྲིལ་; —སྒྲིལ་; —སྒྲོག; —སྒྲུབ་ to finish/ complete work/ project.

ལས་མཇུག་འགྲིལ་ (lɛnjuù drii) vi. to have a project/ job be finished or completed.

ལས་མཇུག་ལེགས་སྒྲིལ་ (lɛnjuù lɛgdrii) sm. ལས་མཇུག་ལེགས་བསྡུས་.

ལས་མཇུག་ལེགས་བསྡུས་ (lɛnjuù lɛgdüü) successfully completing a job/ projectx; va.—བྱེད་ ¶ ང་ཚོ་ཟླ་བ་སྔོན་མའི་ལས་མཇུག་བྱས་པ་རེད་ We successfully completed the job last month.

ལས་རྗེས་ (lɛ̀ɛjee) work output/ result ¶ མི་དེ་ས་ལས་ཀ་བྱས་པའི་ལས་རྗེས་སྟོན་རྒྱུ་མི་འདུག That person shows little result for his work.

ལས་བརྗེས་ (lɛ̀ɛjee) work exchange; va.—རྒྱག.

ལས་ཉིས་ལས་ (lɛ̀ɛ ñīilɛɛ̀) redoing a job; va.—བྱེད་.

ལས་ཉེས་ (lɛ̀ɛñee) doing work incorrectly; vi.—ཤོར་ to do work incorrectly/ wrong.

ལས་གཉེར་ (lɛ̀ɛñer) work management; va.—བྱེད་ to manage work ¶ ལས་གཉེར་མཁས་པ་ Somebody skilled in managing work.

ལས་གཉེར་ཁང་ (lɛ̀ɛñergaŋ) sm. ལས་གཉེར་ཁྲུའུ་.

ལས་གཉེར་ཁྲུའུ་ (lɛ̀ɛñer trū) tib. ch. management office, managing office.

ལས་གཉེར་དུས་ཚོད་ (lɛ̀ɛñer tüüdzöö) working hours ¶ ལས་གཉེར་དུས་ཚོད་ ༦ - ༩ བར་ Working hour are between 6 and 9 o'clock.

ལས་གཉེར་པ་ (lɛ̀ɛñērba) a manager.

ལས་རྟོས་ (lɛ̀ɛdoò) sm.* ལ་ཐོད་.

ལས་རྟགས་ (lɛ̀ɛdaà) 1. product brand/ trademark. 2. official position and title.

ལས་སྟེགས་ (lɛ̀ɛdeg) sm. ལས་ཁྲི་.

ལས་ཐག་གཅོད་ (lɛ̀ɛ tāàjöö) va. to stop/ end work for the day.

ལས་ཐང་ (lɛ̀ɛdaŋ) ability, capability.

ལས་ཐབས་ (lɛ̀ɛdəb) 1. a way or means to do some work/ job; va.—བྱེད་. ¶ དེ་སྐོར་ལས་ཐབས་མེད་ I had no way to do that. 2. arc. sm. ལས་སླ་, 2.

ལས་ཐམ་ (lɛ̀ɛdam) seal used by an office, official seal.

ལས་ཐེབས་གཅོག (lɛ̀ɛdeb jōò) va. to hinder/ impede/ delay one's work ¶ གྲོགས་པོ་ཞིག་ང་ཐུག་པར་ཡོང་ཙང་ངའི་ལས་ཐེབས་བཅག་སོང་ Because a friend came to meet me, it hindered my work.

ལས་ཐེབས་ཆག (lɛ̀ɛdeb cāà) vi. to be hindered/ delayed/ impeded in work ¶ གྲོགས་པོ་ཞིག་ང་ཐུག་པར་ཡོང་ཙང་ངའི་ལས་ཐེབས་ཆག་སོང་ Because a friend came to meet me, my work was hindered.

ལས་ཐོ་ (lɛ̀ɛdo) record of work done, record of workers who came to work; va.—རྒྱག; —འགོད་.

ལས་ཐོག (lɛ̀ɛdɔ̀ɔ) 1. present, current, the one in office, the incumbent ¶ སློབ་སྤྱི་ལས་ཐོག The present principal (of a school).

ལས་ཐོག་སྔ་མ་ (lɛ̀ɛdɔ̀ɔ ŋāma) predecessor in an office/ position.

ལས་ཐོག་དང་པོ་ (lɛ̀ɛdɔ̀ɔ taŋbo) the first to be appointed to an office.

ལས་ཐོག་པ་ (lɛ̀ɛdɔ̀ɔba) the present incumbent, one in active service.

ལས་ཐོག་འབྱོར་ཚད་ (lɛ̀ɛdɔ̀ɔ jɔ̄ɔdzɛɛ̀) rate of attendance.

ལས་ཐོག་མ་པ་ (lɛ̀ɛ tɔ̄ɔmaba) sm. ལས་དང་པོ་བ་.

ལས་ཐོག་ལས་བྱེད་པ་ (lɛ̀ɛdɔ̀ɔ lɛ̀ɛjeèba) the current cadres/ officials in office.

ལས་ཐོག་ལས་འཚོལ་ (lɛ̀ɛdɔ̀ɔ lɛ̀ɛdzöö) searching for a job when one has a job; va.—བྱེད་.

ལས་ཐོགས་པ་ (lɛ̀ɛdɔ̀ɔba) work not done with precision/ exactness/ accuracy, work that is not well done.

ལས་མཐུད་ (lɛeɛ̀düǜ) succeeding in work/ job; va.—རྒྱག.

ལས་མཐུད་པ་ (lɛɛ̀ tü̃ǜba) successor to a position/ office.

ལས་མཐུན་ (lɛeɛ̀dün) having a karmic relationship.

ལས་འགྲུབ་ཤོར་ (lɛɛ̀düǜ shɔ̄ɔ̄) vi. to be unable to accomplish a job/ task successfully.

ལས་འཐེན་ངལ་གསོ་ (lɛɛ̀den ŋɛɛso) retiring; va.—བྱེད་ to retire from work.

ལས་དང་པོ་བ་ (lɛɛ̀ taŋbowa) beginners, rookies, trainees.

ལས་དམ་ (lɛɛ̀dam) sm. ལས་ཐམ་.

ལས་དུས་ (lɛɛ̀düǜ) working hours.

ལས་དུས་བཅད་གྲངས་ (lɛ̄ɛ̀düǜ jɛ̄ɛ̀draŋ) fixed hours of labor/ work.

ལས་དུས་འཕར་སྣོན་ (lɛ̄ɛ̀düǜ pārnön) overtime work.

ལས་དོན་ (lɛɛ̀dön) work, job, business, affairs; va.—སྒྲུབ་ to accomplish one's work; va.—བྱེད་ to do work.

ལས་དོན་ཁང་ (lɛɛ̀döngaŋ) agency ¶ རྒྱལ་སྤྱིའི་ཡར་རྒྱས་ལས་དོན་ཁང་ Agency for International Development (AID).

ལས་དོན་སྒྲུབ་སེམས་ (lɛɛ̀dön grubsem) devotion/ dedication to work (to accomplish one's work).

ལས་དོན་ཆེ་ཁག (lɛɛ̀dön cēgaà) important work; important affairs.

ལས་དོན་ཆེ་ཕྲ་གང་ཅི་ (lɛɛ̀dön cēdra kaŋji) shung. all phases of work big and small.

ལས་དོན་བྱ་རིམ་ (lɛɛ̀dön cərim) work procedures/ steps.

ལས་དོན་ཚོ་ཆུང་ (lɛɛ̀dön tsōjuŋ) sm. ལས་དོན་ཚོགས་ཆུང་

ལས་དོན་ཚོགས་ཆུང་ (lɛɛ̀dön tsɔ̄gjuŋ) work team (usu. comprised of officials taken from different offices to go somewhere to oversee a campaign or solve a problem).

ལས་དོན་ཚོགས་འདུ་ (lɛɛ̀dön tsōndu) meeting regarding work.

ལས་དོན་ཨུ་ཡོན་ལྷན་ཁང་ (lɛɛ̀dön ūyön lhɛ̄ngaŋ) administrative council/ bureau.

ལས་དོན་རུ་ཁག (lɛɛ̀dön rugaà) sm. ལས་དོན་ཚོགས་ཆུང་.

ལས་དྲུང་ (lɛɛ̀druŋ) shung. clerk (in tt.).

ལས་འདོད་གྲིམ་འདོད་ (lɛɛ̀döö̀ drimdöö̀) willing to work hard.

ལས་བསྡུར་སྐར་འགོད་ (lɛɛ̀dur gārgöö̀) evaluating work and giving/ awarding work points for the work; va.—བྱེད་.

ལས་སྡེབ་ (lɛɛ̀deb) mutual assistance, joint/ combined work.

ལས་བསྡོམས་ (lɛɛ̀dom) work report, progress report; va.—རྒྱག; —བྱེད་ to give a progress or work report ¶ ལོ་མཇུག་ཏུ་ལས་ཁུངས་སོ་སོའི་ལས་བསྡོམས་རྒྱག་དགོས་པ་རེད་ At the end of the year each office has to give a work report.

ལས་ནག (lɛɛ̀naà) nonvirtuous deeds.

ལས་ནད་ (lɛɛ̀nɛɛ̀) occupational disease/ illness.

ལས་ནད་སྨན་ཁང་ (lɛɛ̀nɛɛ̀ mɛ̄ngaŋ) hospital for occupational diseases/ illnesses.

ལས་གནས་ (lɛnnɛɛ̀) post, rank, position.

ལས་གནས་རྒན་གཡོལ་ (lɛɛ̀nɛɛ̀ gɛnyöö) retirement from work due to age; va.—བྱེད་.

ལས་གནས་རྒན་གཡོལ་དོད་ (lɛɛ̀nɛɛ̀ gɛnyöö töö̀) retirement pension.

ལས་གནས་སྟོང་པ་ (lɛɛ̀nɛɛ̀ dōŋba) vacant position.

ལས་གནས་ནད་གཡོལ་ (lɛɛ̀nɛɛ̀ nɛɛ̀yöö) retirement from work due to illness.

ལས་སྣ་ (lɛɛ̀na) 1. post, appointment, position. 2. the main person in charge of a job/ project.

ལས་སྣ་པ་ (lɛɛ̀naba) official, functionary.

ལས་སྣ་ཚོགས་ (lɛɛ̀ nādzoò) 1. different kinds of work. 2. virtuous and nonvirtuous deeds.

ལས་སྣ་ཚོགས་པ་ (lɛɛ̀nā tsōgba) person who does odd jobs.

ལས་སྣེ་ (lɛɛ̀ne) monastic officials.

ལས་སྣེ་ཐོན་ཟིན་ (lɛɛ̀ne tȭnsin) shung. ex-monastic officials.

ལས་སྣོན་ (lɛɛ̀nön) 1. processing, manufacturing; va.—བྱེད་ to process/ manufacture. 2. overtime work, extra work.

ལས་སྣོན་བཙོ་སྦྱང་བཟོ་གྲྭ་ (lɛɛ̀nön dzōjaŋ sodra) processing and refining plant.

ལས་སྣོན་བཟོ་གྲྭ་ (lɛɛ̀nön sodra) processing or manufacturing factory/ plant.

ལས་སྣོན་བཟོ་ལས་ (lɛɛ̀nön solɛɛ̀) processing/ manufacturing industry.

ལས་པ་ (lɛɛ̀ba) a worker.

ལས་སྤོ་ (lɛɛ̀bo) transferring/ changing work or job; va.—བྱེད་ to transfer one's work; va.—ཞུ་ to request a work transfer.

ལས་སྤོས་ (lɛɛ̀böö̀) transferring/ changing work or job.

ལས་སྤོས་གནས་སྤོས་ (lɛɛ̀bȫö̀ nɛɛ̀bȫö̀) transferring/ changing work and area.

ལས་སྤོས་དམག་མི་ (lɛɛ̀böö̀ mə̄əmi) sm. ལས་སྒྱུར་དམག་མི་.

ལས་དཔོན་ (lɛɛ̀bön) work supervisor, foreman, overseer.

ལས་ཕོགས་ (lɛɛ̀bɔɔ̀) wages.

ལས་སྦྱིད་སློབ་སྦྱིད་ (lɛɛ̀jeè lōbjeè) part-time working and part-time studying.

ལས་སྦྱོད་ (lɛɛ̀jöö̀) labor productivity, work output.

ལས་ཕྲན་ (lɛɛ̀drɛn) a minor task/ work/ job.

ལས་འཕར་ (lɛmbar) shung. an additional/ extra official ¶ བཀའ་བློན་ལས་འཕར་ An additional Council Minister.

ལས་འཕར་འདོན་ (lɛmbar don) shung. a འདོན་ land unit on which additional taxes/ corvee work has been imposed.

ལས་འབྲོ་ (lɛndro) 1. incomplete/ unfinished work. 2. karma.

ལས་འབྲོ་ཅན་ (lɛndrojɛn) having good karma effects because of past good deeds.

ལས་འབྲོའི་མདུད་པ་ (lɛndröö düǜbə) a connection/ link caused by karma.

ལས་བུམ་ (lɛɛ̀bum) a vase used for Buddhist religious rites.

ལས་བྱ་ (lɛɛ̀ca) shung. an official ¶ ལས་བྱ་རིམ་བཞི་ A 4th rank official under the Governor General of Eastern Tibet (in tt.). ¶ ཁོང་ཡིག་ཚང་གི་ལས་བྱ་བསྐོས་པ་རེད་ He was appointed as an official (lower) in the Ecclesiastic Office (in tt.).

ལས་བྱུས་ (lɛɛ̀jüǜ) sm. ལས་ཇུས་.

ལས་བྱེད་ (lɛɛ̀jeè) sm. ལས་བྱེད་པ་.

ལས་བྱེད་ཁམས་གསོ་ཁང་ (lɛɛ̀jeè kāmsogaŋ) sm. ལས་བྱེད་ཁམས་གསོ་གླིང་.

ལས་བྱེད་ཁམས་གསོ་གླིང་ (lɛɛ̀jeè kāmsoliŋ) cadre's sanatorium.

ལས་བྱེད་དོ་དམ་ཁའོ་ (lɛɛ̀jeè todam kə̄wo) tib. ch. cadre management section.

ལས་བྱེད་བདག་གཉེར་ (lɛɛ̀jeè dagñee) managing personnel/ staff ¶ ལས་བྱེད་བདག་གཉེར་ཁང་ Personnel office. 2. the head of a personnel office.

ལས་བྱེད་བདེ་སྐྱོང་ཨུ་ཡོན་ལྷན་ཁང་ (lɛɛ̀jeè degyoŋ ūyön lhɛ̄ngaŋ) cadre health care committee.

ལས་བྱེད་ནང་མ་ (lɛɛ̀jeè naŋma) shung. the inner attendants of the Dalai Lama.

ལས་བྱེད་སྣེ་ལེན་ཁང་ (lɛɛ̀jeè nēlengaŋ) cadre's guset house.

ལས་བྱེད་པ་ (lɛɛ̀jeèba) official, civil servant, cadre.

ལས་བྱེད་ཕན་གཉེར་དོ་དམ་ཨུ་ཡོན་ལྷན་ཁང་ (lɛɛ̀jeè pɛ̄nñer todam ūyön lhɛ̄ngaŋ) cadre welfare management committee.

ལས་བྱེད་སྦྱོང་བརྡར་འཛིན་གྲྭ (lɛɛ̀jeè joŋdar dzindra) cadre's training class.

ལས་བྱེད་མི་སྣ་ (lɛɛ̀jeè minə) sm. ལས་བྱེད་པ་.

ལས་བྱེད་ཚན་ཆུང་ (lɛɛ̀jeè minə) sm. ལས་དོན་ཚོགས་ཆུང་.

ལས་བྱེད་ལས་ཞོར་སློབ་གྲྭ་ (lɛɛ̀jeè lɛɛ̀shɔɔ lōbdra)

cadre's sparetime school.

ལས་བྱེད་རིག་གནས་སློབ་གྲྭ་ (lɛ̱ɛ̀jeè ri̱gnɛɛ̀ lōbdra) cadre's literacy school.

ལས་བྱེད་སློབ་གྲྭ་ (lɛ̱ɛ̀jeè lōbdra) cadre school, school to train officials.

ལས་བྱེད་སློབ་སྦྱོང་ (lɛ̱ɛ̀jeè lōbjoŋ) administrative/ cadre training.

ལས་བྲོལ་ (lɛ̱ɛ̀jöö) 1. absent from work; va.—བྱེད་ ། ལས་ཀའི་དུས་ཚོད་ལ་ལས་བྲོལ་བྱེད་མི་ཆོག One is not permitted to be absent during work time. 2. avoiding work; va.—བྱེད་.

ལས་བྲོལ་ཆ་པོ་ (lɛ̱ɛ̀jöö tsābo) sb. who avoids/ shies away from work.

ལས་བྲེལ་ (lɛ̱ɛ̀dree) busy with/ at work ། དེང་སང་ལས་ཁངས་ནང་ལས་བྲེལ་ཆེན་པོ་འདུག These days the office is very busy with work.

ལས་བློན་ (lɛ̱ɛ̀lön) ministers (under the Chinese Emperor).

ལས་དབང་ (lɛ̱ɛ̀waŋ) sm. ལས་སྐལ་.

ལས་དབང་ཅི་བབས་ (lɛ̱ɛ̀waŋ ji̋bəb) sm. ལས་ཀྱིས་བསྐོས་.

ལས་དབང་སྨྲ་བ་ (lɛ̱ɛ̀waŋ māwa) 1. the belief in karmic causation. 2. fatalism.

ལས་འབོ་ (lɛ̱mbo) an unstandardized/ local འབོ་ measure.

ལས་འབོར་ (lɛ̱mbɔɔ) sm. ལས་ཚད་.

ལས་འབྲས་ (lɛ̱ɛ̀drɛɛ̀) sm. ལས་རྒྱུ་འབྲས་.

ལས་འབྲས་ཁྱད་གསོད་ (lɛ̱ndrɛɛ̀ kyɛɛ̀söö) sm. ལས་འབྲས་རྨོག.

ལས་འབྲས་རྨོག (lɛ̱ndrɛɛ̀ ñöò) vi. to not honor/ adhere to moral norms (the karmic law of cause and effect) ། ཕྲུ་གུ་དེས་ལས་འབྲས་བརྩིགས་ནས་ཕ་མར་ཞབས་ཕྱི་ཞུས་མ་སོང་ The child did not act in accordance with moral norms and didn't serve his parents.

ལས་འབྲས་དཔང་བཞག (lɛ̱ndrɛɛ̀ bāŋshaà) accepting/ adhering to the morality associated with karmic cause and effect.

ལས་འབྲེལ་ (lɛ̱ndree) relations/ associations due to the karma in a previous life ། ཆེ་འདེ་རང་གཉིས་བཟའ་ཚང་འབྲེལ་བ་ནི་ཚེ་སྔོན་མའི་ལས་འབྲེལ་རེད་ As for we two being married in this life, it is a result of our karmic relationship in our past life.

ལས་སྦྲང་ (lɛ̱ɛ̀draŋ) worker bee.

ལས་སྦྲེལ་ (lɛ̱ɛ̀dree) shung. a jointly held position/ job ། ཁོང་གཉིས་སྟག་རྩེ་རྫོང་སྡོད་ལས་སྦྲེལ་རེད་ Those two are jointly holding the position of Taktse's district commission.

ལས་མ་ (lɛ̱ɛ̀ma) man-made materials.

ལས་མང་ཐོབ་མང་ (lɛ̱ɛ̀maŋ tōbmaŋ) more work, more gain/ profit/ income.

ལས་མི་ (lɛ̱ɛ̀mi) worker, workman, laborer ། བུད་མེད་ལས་མི་ Women workers.

ལས་མི་འགུལ་སྐྱོད་ (lɛ̱ɛ̀mi g̱üügyöö) labor movement.

ལས་མེད་ (lɛ̱ɛ̀meè) jobless, unemployed.

ལས་མེད་སྐྱིད་སྡོད་ (lɛ̱ɛ̀meè gyi̋idöö) sb. who is happy to have no work/ job.

ལས་མེད་ལྟོ་མེད་ (lɛ̱ɛ̀meè dōmeè) no work no food.

ལས་མེད་ལྟོ་བཟས་ (lɛ̱ɛ̀meè dōsɛɛ̀) eating without having to work, reaping the fruits of other people's toil.

ལས་མེད་ཐོབ་མེད་ (lɛ̱ɛ̀meè tōbmeè) sm. ལས་མེད་ལྟོ་མེད་.

ལས་མེད་དལ་སྡོད་ (lɛ̱ɛ̀meè tɛ̱ɛ̱döö) relaxing without working.

ལས་མེད་སྤྲང་འཁྱམ་ (lɛ̱ɛ̀meè drāŋgyam) wandering without work like a beggar; va.—རྒྱག.

ལས་དམག (lɛ̱ɛ̀maà) engineer corps (in the army).

ལས་དམངས་ (lɛ̱ɛ̀maŋ) abbr. of ལས་བྱེད་པ་ and མི་དམངས་.

ལས་རྨས་ (lɛ̱ɛ̀mɛɛ̀) work accident/ injury.

ལས་སྨོན་ (lɛ̱ɛ̀mön) karma and prayers ། ཚེ་འདིར་སྐྱིད་པོ་བྱུང་བ་ནི་ཚེ་སྔོན་མའི་ལས་སྨོན་ལ་བརྟེན་ནས་བྱུང་བ་རེད་ Being happy in this life is the result of karma and prayers in one's past life.

ལས་གཙོ་ (lɛ̱ɛ̀dzo) foreman, supervisor, overseer.

ལས་བཙུན་མ་ (lɛ̱ɛ̀dzünmə) nuns who stay at home and do regular work there.

ལས་བཙུན་ (lɛ̱ɛ̀dzün) monks who work.

ལས་རྩལ་དགེ་རྒན་ (lɛ̱ɛ̀dzɛɛ g̱egɛn) 1. teacher of craft skills. 2. teacher of technicians/ technical skills.

ལས་རྩལ་པ་ (lɛ̱ɛ̀dzɛɛba) technician, skilled worker.

ལས་རྩལ་ལྡན་པའི་ལས་མི་ (lɛ̱ɛ̀dzɛɛ d̲ɛmbɛ lɛ̱ɛ̀mi) sm. ལས་རྩལ་པ་.

ལས་རྩལ་ཞིབ་འཇུག་ཁང་ (lɛ̱ɛ̀dzɛɛ shi̱mjuùgaŋ) technology research institute.

ལས་རྩལ་བཟོ་པ་ (lɛ̱ɛ̀dzɛɛ s̱oba) sm. ལས་རྩལ་པ་.

ལས་རྩལ་བཟོ་པའི་སློབ་གྲྭ (lɛ̱ɛ̀dzɛɛ s̱obɛ lōbdra) technician's school.

ལས་རྩལ་སློབ་གྲྭ (lɛ̱ɛ̀dzɛɛ lōbdra) technical school.

ལས་རྩལ་གསར་བཅོས་ (lɛ̱ɛ̀dzɛɛ sārjöö) technology innovation.

ལས་རྩི་པ་ (lɛ̱ɛ̀dziba) a person who forecasts the karma of an individual through astrological calculation.

ལས་རྩིས་ (lɛ̱ɛ̀dzii) abbr. of ཚེ་རབས་ལས་རྩིས་.

ལས་རྩོམ་ (lɛ̱ɛ̀dzom) labor, work; va.—ཟ་; —བྱེད་ to lay the foundation of work.

ལས་རྩོལ་ (lɛ̱ɛ̱dzöö) labor.

ལས་རྩོལ་སྡོམ་རྩིས་ལས་ཁངས་ (lɛ̱ɛ̱dzöö d̲omdzi̋i lɛ̱ɛ̀guŋ) Bureau of Labor Statistics.

ལས་རྩོལ་ནུས་ཤུགས་ (lɛ̱ɛ̱dzöö n̲üüjöö) labor productivity.

ལས་རྩོལ་པ་ (lɛ̱ɛ̱dzööba) laborer.

ལས་རྩོལ་མི་མང་ (lɛ̱ɛ̱dzöö m̲imaŋ) laboring masses.

ལས་རྩོལ་མི་མང་དང་བཟོ་ལས་མཉམ་སྤྱིལ་སྒྲིག་འཛུགས་ (lɛ̱ɛ̱dzöö m̲imaŋdaŋ s̲olɛɛ̀ ñamdreemdr̲igdzuù) American Federation of Labor and the Congress of Industrial Organizations (AFL-CIO).

ལས་རྩོལ་མི་དམངས་ཀྱི་ཉིན་རེའི་ཚགས་པར་ (lɛ̱ɛ̱dzöö m̲imaŋgi ñinre tsāgba) Worker's Daily.

ལས་རྩོལ་ཚོགས་པ་ (lɛ̱ɛ̱dzöö tsōgbə) Labor Party.

ལས་རྩོལ་ལས་ཁངས་ (lɛ̱ɛ̱dzöö lɛ̱ɛ̀guŋ) Department of Labor (U.S.A.).

ལས་བརྩོན་ཅན་ (lɛ̱ɛ̀dzönjɛn) hardworking, diligent.

ལས་བརྩོན་དཔའ་ལྡན་ (lɛ̱ɛ̀dzön bēndɛn) brave and hardworking.

ལས་བརྩོན་ཕྱུག་བསྒྱུར་ (lɛ̱ɛ̱dzön cūggyur) becoming prosperous through hard work.

ལས་ཚད་ (lɛ̱ɛ̀dzɛɛ̀) 1. evaluating work to determine what work points it should receive. 2. work quota.

ལས་ཚན་ (lɛ̱ɛ̀dzɛn) 1. department/ section of an office or entity. 2. a position ། ཁོང་གིས་བཀའ་བློན་རྣམས་ལ་ལས་ཚན་ཡག་ཞིག་གནང་རོགས་ཞིབ་ཞུས་པ་རེད་ He asked the ministers to give him a good position. 3. workshop.

ལས་ཚན་ཆེ་ཁག (lɛ̱ɛ̀dzɛn cēgaà) shung. the higher ranking positions.

ལས་ཚན་འཇོག་དུ་འཇུག (lɛ̱ɛ̀dzɛn j̲ogdu j̲uù) shung. va. to let some one resign from their position.

ལས་ཚན་དྲག་པ་ (lɛ̱ɛ̀dzɛn tr̲agba) shung. important/ good positions.

ལས་ཚན་དྲག་རིམ་ (lɛ̱ɛ̀dzɛn tragrim) shung. sm. ལས་ཚན་དྲག་པ་.

ལས་ཚན་པ་ (lɛ̱ɛ̀dzɛmba) a 5th rank official in the tt.

ལས་ཚན་ཤིག་ལ་ཟ་རྒྱུ་སྒོ་མ་ (lɛ̱ɛ̀dzɛn shi̋glə s̲əgyu drōma) even a low position can gets small bribes [Lit. a position like lice can get bribes like nits].

ལས་ཚན་གསར་འཕར་ (lɛ̱ɛ̀dzɛn sārmbar) shung. newly added positions.

ལས་ཚབ་ (lɛ̱ɛ̀dzəb) 1. an acting official ། ཁྲི་པ་ལས་ཚབ་ The acting chairman. 2. chargé d'affaires, deputy. 3. a substitute worker. 4. agent, representative.

ལས་ཚབ་བསྒོ་གཞག (lɛ̱ɛ̀dzəb gōshaà) shung. an appointment to fill a vacancy.

ལས་ཚབ་པ་ (lɛ̱ɛ̀dzəbbə) sm. ལས་ཚབ་.

ལས་ཚིག (lɛ̱ɛ̀dzii) verb.

ལས་ཚུལ་ (lɛ̱ɛ̀dzüü) the manner of doing sth.

ལས་ཚོགས་ (lɛ̲ɛ̀dzɔɔ̀) worker's association/ guild.

ལས་མཚམས་ (lɛ̲ndzam) stopping work for a break or at the end of day; va.—འཇོག ། ཉིན་དགུང་ལ་ལས་མཚམས་བཞག་ནས་ཁ་ལག་ཟ་བར་འགྲོ་གི་ཡོད་ At noon we take a break and go to eat. 2. a work/ labor strike ། བཟོ་པ་ཚོས་གླ་ཆ་སྣོན་ཆེད་ལས་མཚམས་བཞག་པ་རེད་ The workers went on strike to increase their wages.

ལས་འཚེར་ (lɛ̲ɛ̀dzer) shying away from/ avoiding work; va.—བྱེད་.

ལས་འཛིན་ (lɛ̲ɛ̀dzin) 1. job, position ། དམག་སྤྱིའི་ལས་འཛིན་དུ་གསར་བསྐོ་གནང་བ་རེད་ (They) appointed (him) to a new position as commander in chief. 2. director, manager, head of an office.

ལས་འཛིན་ཀྲུའུ་ཞི་ (lɛ̲ndzin trūshi) tib. ch. executive chairman.

ལས་འཛིན་ཁའོ་ (lɛ̲ndzin kāwo) tib. ch. executive section.

ལས་འཛིན་འགོ་གཙོ་ (lɛ̲ndzin go̲dzo) chairman of the board, chief executive officer.

ལས་འཛིན་གཉེར་པ་ (lɛ̲ndzin ñērba) shung. the current manager/ steward.

ལས་འཛིན་པ་ (lɛ̲ndzimbə) manager.

ལས་འཛིན་ལྷན་ཚོགས་ (lɛ̲ndzin lhɛ̄ndzɔɔ̀) administrative executive committee, board of directors.

ལས་འཛོལ་ (lɛ̲ɛ̀dzöö) 1. a mistake/ error in work. 2. mishap, accident, injury (regarding work).

ལས་རྫོབ་ (lɛ̲ɛ̀dzob) shung. problems with work/ job.

ལས་ཞག (lɛ̲ɛ̀shaà) a working day.

ལས་ཞབས་ (lɛ̲ɛ̀shəb) shung. sm. ལས་ཞབས་ཆབས་ཅིག.

ལས་ཞབས་ཆབས་ཅིག (lɛ̲ɛ̀shəb cābjiì) shung. one's specific position in the government and one's overall position as a government official ། ཁོངས་ལས་ཞབས་ཆབས་ཅིག་གནས་དབྱུང་བཏང་འདུག He was demoted from his position and expelled from government service.

ལས་ཞིང་ (lɛ̲ɛ̀shiŋ) a field that has been leased in return for a number of days of work.

ལས་ཞུགས་ (lɛ̲ɛ̀shuù) employed ། ལས་བྱེད་པ་སོ་སོའི་ལས་ཞུགས་ཀྱི་དུས་ཡུན་ལ་གཞིགས་པའི་རྒས་གསོའི་དངུལ་སྤྲད་ཀྱི་ཡོད་པ་རེད་ They are giving pensions based on the amount of time officials have been employed.

ལས་ཞུགས་མི་གྲངས་ (lɛ̲ɛ̀shuù mi̲draŋ) the employed population, the number of people employed.

ལས་ཞུགས་ཞིབ་བཤེར་ (lɛ̲ɛ̀shuù shi̲bsher) checking. employment history; va.— བྱེད་.

ལས་ཞུགས་སོང་ལོ་ (lɛ̲ɛ̀shuù sōŋlo) length of time employed.

ལས་ཞོར་ (lɛ̲ɛ̀shɔɔ) 1. spare time, time outside of work ། ལས་ཞོར་སློབ་གྲྭ་ A school to attend in one's spare time. 2. amateur, nonprofession ། ལས་ཞོར་གྱི་རོལ་མོ་བ་ Nonprofessional musicians.

ལས་ཞྭ་ (lɛ̀ɛ̀sha) shung. a hat worn as part of the official uniform of dress of governmental officials.

ལས་ཞྭ་ལས་གོས་ (lɛ̲ɛ̀sha lɛ̲ɛ̀göö) shung. the official dress (including hats) worn by officials of the tt.

ལས་གཞས་ (lɛ̲ɛ̀shɛɛ̀) work songs; va.—གཏོང་.

ལས་གཞི་ (lɛ̲ɛ̀shi) a project, an undertaking ། ཚིག་མཛོད་ཀྱི་ལས་གཞི་ Dictionary project.

ལས་གཞུག་སྡོག (lɛ̲ɛ̀shuù dɔɔ̀) va. to finish/ complete work.

ལས་གཞུག་ཞིབ་བཤེར་ (lɛ̲ɛ̀ shi̲bsher) the final evaluation of the work on a job project; va.— བྱེད་.

ལས་གཞུངས་པ་ (lɛ̲ɛ̀shugba) 1. good/ skillful worker. 2. sincere/ diligent work.

ལས་བཞག (lɛ̲ɛ̀shaà) leaving/ quitting one's job; va.—བྱེད་ ། ཁོང་གིས་ལས་བཞག་བྱས་ནས་ཕ་ཡུལ་དུ་ལོག་པ་རེད་ He quit his job and returned to his homeland.

ལས་བཞག་ངལ་གསོ་ (lɛ̲ɛ̀shaà ŋɛ̲ɛ̲so) leaving one's work to rest/ recuperate; va.—བྱེད་.

ལས་བཞག་སློབ་སྦྱོང་ (lɛ̲ɛ̀shaà lōbjoŋ) (sabbatical) leave for study.

ལས་བཞིའི་ཁ་ལོ་པ་ (lɛ̲ɛ̀shii kālaba) shung. the officials in charge of the four work areas: politics, economics, tax collecting and military.

ལས་བཞིའི་སྣེ་འཛིན་ (lɛ̲ɛ̀shii nēndzin) shung. sm. ལས་བཞིའི་ཁ་ལོ་པ་.

ལས་ཟད་ཕོགས་གཅོད་ (lɛ̲ɛ̀sɛɛ̀ pɔ̄ɔ̀jöö) leaving/ quitting one's job and having one's salary terminated.

ལས་ཟམ་ (lɛ̲ɛ̀sam) sm. ལས་ཁྲི་.

ལས་ཟུར་ (lɛ̲ɛ̀sur) shung. the present office holder and the ex-office holder ། ཛ་སག་ལས་ཟུར་གཉིས་ The Dzasa and the Ex-Dzasa.

ལས་བཟང་ (lɛ̲ɛ̀saŋ) good deeds, meritorious work.

ལས་བཟོ་ (lɛ̲ɛ̀so) 1. cadre/ officials and workers ། ལས་བཟོ་མི་བརྒྱད་ Eight workers and cadre. 2. workers.

ལས་བཟོ་བའི་སྨན་ཁང་ (lɛ̲ɛ̀sowɛ mɛ̄ngaŋ) worker's hospital.

ལས་བཟོ་ཚོགས་པ་ (lɛ̲ɛ̀so tsɔ̄gba) trade/ labor union.

ལས་བཟོའི་སློབ་གྲྭ་ (lɛ̲ɛ̀sö lōbdra) cadre and worker's school.

ལས་འོང་འོང་འདྲ་མོ་ (lɛ̲ɛ̀ wo̲ŋoŋ dra̲mo) sb. who appears capable but isn't ། མི་དེའི་ཕྱི་ཚུལ་ལ་བལྟས་ན་ལས་འོང་འོང་འདྲ་མོ་ཡོད་ནའང་དོན་དུ་བྱབས་ཆུང་ཞིག་འདུག Outwardly the person seems capable but in reality he isn't.

ལས་ཡུན་ (lɛ̲ɛ̀yün) 1. the time a job takes. 2. the time one works ། ལས་ཡུན་ཆུ་ཚོད་བརྒྱད་ཀྱི་ལམ་ལུགས་ The eight hour system of work.

ལས་ཡུལ་ (lɛ̲ɛ̀yüü) work area, construction site, building area.

ལས་ཡུལ་དངོས་ (lɛ̲ɛ̀yüü nȫö) at the sight of a work project ། ལས་ཡུལ་དངོས་ཀྱི་གྲོས་ཚོགས་ A meeting at the work site.

ལས་གཡོག་རྒྱག (la̲yɔr gya̲à) sm. ལ་གཡོག་རྒྱག.

ལས་གཡོར་ (lɛ̲ɛ̀yɔr) shung. a borrowed labor force.

ལས་གཡོལ་ (lɛ̲ɛ̀ yȫö) sm. ལས་ཐོལ་.

ལས་ར་ (lɛ̲ɛ̀ra) work site.

ལས་རིགས་ (lɛ̲ɛ̀rig) occupation, vocation, profession ། བཟོ་ཞིང་གི་ལས་རིགས་ Industrial and agricultural occupations. ། ལས་རིགས་སློབ་སྦྱོང་ Vocational training. ། དཔལ་འབྱོར་ལས་རིགས་ Economic professionals/ occupations.

ལས་རིགས་ཁག (lɛ̲ɛ̀rii kāà) various occupations/ trades/ professions ། ལས་རིགས་ཁག་གི་མི་དམངས་ People from all occupations.

ལས་རིགས་གཅོང་ནད་ (lɛ̲ɛ̀rii jōŋnɛɛ̀) occupational illness/ sickness.

ལས་རིགས་གཅིག་པ་ (lɛ̲ɛ̀rii ji̲gbə) from the same occupational background.

ལས་རིགས་སོ་དྲུག (lɛ̲ɛ̀rii sōdruù) all types of work [Lit. 36 types of work].

ལས་རིགས་སློབ་གསོ་ (lɛ̲ɛ̀rii lōbso) vocational education.

ལས་རིམ་ (lɛ̲ɛ̀rim) work stage, work level/ phase/ step ། ཁང་པ་རྒྱག་རྒྱུའི་ལས་རིམ་དང་པོ་དེ་ནི་རྨང་གཞི་འདིང་རྒྱུ་དེ་ཡིན་ The first stage in building a house is laying the foundation.

ལས་རུང་ (lɛ̲ɛ̀ruŋ) abbr. of ལས་སུ་རུང་བ་.

ལས་རེས་ (lɛ̲ɛ̀reè) taking turns working, on duty, a work shift; va.—སྐོར་ to take a turn on duty, to work a shift; va.—བརྗེ་ to change shifts; va.—བཟོ་ to make a work system by shifts ། དེ་རིང་ང་ལས་རེས་ཡིན་ Today I am on duty. ། སྨན་ཁང་གི་ནད་སྐྱོང་བ་ཚོ་ཆུ་ཚོད་བརྒྱད་རེའི་ལས་རེས་བྱེད་ཀྱི་ཡོད་པ་རེད་ The nurses of the hospital are working in eight hour shifts.

ལས་རེས་ཁང་ (lɛ̲ɛ̀reègaŋ) on duty room/ office.

ལས་རེས་མི་སྣ་ (lɛ̲ɛ̀reè mi̲nə) on duty personnel.

ལས་རོ་ (lɛ̲ɛ̀ro) unfinished work/ task.

ལས་རོགས་ (lɛ̲ɛ̀rɔɔ̀) assistant, helper.

ལས་རོགས་ངལ་རྩོལ་པ་ (lɛ̲ɛ̀rɔɔ̀ ŋɛ̲ɛ̲dzööba) auxiliary

laborer/ worker.

ལས་རོགས་པ་ (lɛ̀ɛrɔ̀ɔba) assistant, helper.

ལས་ལུང་རྒྱུགས་ (lɛ̀ɛluŋ gyuù) vi. to have a plan/ project/ job go smoothly.

ལས་ལ་བཀོད་པ་ (lɛ̀ɛgö̀öba) sm. ལས་ཀྱིས་བསྐོས་.

ལས་ལ་བསྐོས་ (lɛ̀ɛla gö̀ö) sm. ལས་ཀྱིས་བསྐོས་.

ལས་ལ་གང་བསྐོས་ (lɛ̀ɛla kaŋ gö̀ö) sm. ལས་ཀྱིས་བསྐོས་.

ལས་ལ་གང་བསྐོས་མ་གཏོགས་སྣང་བ་གང་དྲན་མི་འདུག (lɛ̀ɛla kaŋ gö̀ö məndoò nāŋwa kandrɛn minduù) things are determined by one's past karma not one's own wishes (a saying).

ལས་ལ་བརྩོན་པ་ (lɛ̀ɛla dzö̃mba) hardworking, diligent.

ལས་ལམ་ལ་བུད་ (lɛ̀ɛlamla büù) having good effects due to karma.

ལས་ལས་ (lɛ̀ɛlɛɛ̀) sm. ལས་ལག.

ལས་ལུགས་ (lɛ̀ɛluù) work style, work system, work custom.

ལས་ལོ་ (lɛ̀ɛlo) length of time employed, number of years working.

ལས་ལོ་བསྡོམས་འབོར་ (lɛ̀ɛlo dombɔr) total number of years worked.

ལས་ལོག (lɛ̀ɛlɔ̀ɔ) redoing work/ job, doing sth. again; va.—རྒྱག; —བྱེད་.

ལས་ལོག་མ་ (lɛ̀ɛlɔ̀ɔma) a woman who does things in an opposite or wrong way.

ལས་སློབ་གཉིས་མེད་ (lɛ̀ɛlob ñı̃imeè) neither working nor going to school.

ལས་ཤག (lɛ̀ɛshaà) work hostel, room or apartment for workers at their place of work.

ལས་ཤུ་ (lɛ̀ɛshu) a whistle blown when workers are to start; va.—རྒྱག.

ལས་ཤུགས་ (lɛ̀ɛshuù) the effectiveness/ efficiency of work.

ལས་ཤུགས་ཅན་ (lɛ̀ɛshuùjɛn) capable/ effective (with regard to work).

ལས་ཤོག (lɛ̀ɛshoò) office/ business stationery.

ལས་ཤོགས་ (lɛ̀ɛshoò) sm. ལས་ཡོད་.

ལས་ཤོབ་ (lɛ̀ɛshob) sm. ལས་ཡོད་.

ལས་ཤོར་ (lɛ̀ɛshɔɔ) laid off, unemployed (workers).

ལས་ཤོར་རྒྱུད་སྐྱོབ་ (lɛ̀ɛshɔɔ gyüùgyob) unemployment relief/ benefits.

ལས་ཤོར་དཔུང་ཆེན་ (lɛ̀ɛshɔɔ bū̃ŋjen) the mass of unemployed people.

ལས་ཤོར་བཟོ་པ་ (lɛ̀ɛshɔɔ soba) a laid off worker.

ལས་ཤོར་བཟོ་ཚོགས་ (lɛ̀ɛshɔɔ sodzɔ̀ɔ) laid off worker's union.

ལས་བཤེར་ (lɛ̀ɛsher) checking/ inspecting work; va.—གཏོང་.

ལས་བཤེར་བསྡོམས་རྩིས་ (lɛ̀ɛsher domdziì) checking on work and calculating work points.

ལས་སུ་སྒྲུབ་ (lɛ̀ɛsu drub) sm. ལས་ཀྱིས་བསྐོས་.

ལས་སུ་བྱ་བ་ (lɛ̀ɛsu cawa) the dative case.

ལས་སུ་བྱ་བའི་ཚིག (lɛ̀ɛsu cawɛ tsı̃i) dative/ locative particles.

ལས་སུ་རུང་བ་ (lɛ̀ɛsu ruŋwa) sth. that works ¶འཕྲུལ་འཁོར་དེ་བཟོ་བཅོས་བརྒྱབ་ན་ལས་སུ་རུང་བ་ཆགས་ཀྱི་རེད་ The machine will work well if it is repaired.

ལས་སེ་ (lɛ̀ɛse) yes.

ལས་སེང་ (lɛ̀ɛseŋ) sm. ལས་གསེང་.

ལས་སླ་འབབ་ཆེ་ (lɛ̀ɛla bəbje) easy and good income.

ལས་སློབ་ (lɛ̀ɛlob) work-study.

ལས་སློབ་གཉིས་བརྩོན་ (lɛ̀ɛlob ñı̃idzön) work-study program.

ལས་སློབ་སློབ་གྲྭ་ (lɛ̀ɛlob lōbdra) work-study school.

ལས་སྲོལ་ (lɛ̀ɛsöö) sm. ལས་ལུགས་.

ལས་སྲོལ་གཞི་རྒྱ་ (lɛ̀ɛsöö shigya) large-scale with regards to work ¶ལས་སྲོལ་གཞི་རྒྱ་ཆེ་བའི་ཁེ་ལས་ Large-scale enterprise.

ལས་སླ་ (lɛ̀ɛla) sm. ལས་སླ་པོ་.

ལས་སླ་སྒྲུབ་བདེ་ (lɛ̀ɛla drubde) easy to accomplish or complete.

ལས་སླ་བཅོས་བདེ་ (lɛ̀ɛla jö̀öde) easy to do and fix.

ལས་སླ་སྟབས་བདེ་ (lɛ̀ɛla dābde) easy and convenient.

ལས་སླ་པོ་ (lɛ̀ɛ lābo) easy, convenient ¶ལས་ཀ་འདི་ལས་སླ་པོ་ཞེ་དྲག་འདུག This work is very easy.

ལས་སློབ་ (lɛ̀ɛlob) 1. working and studying. 2. students and workers.

ལས་གསར་ (lɛ̀ɛsar) 1. a new worker, trainee, rookie. 2. new work.

ལས་གསེང་ (lɛ̀ɛseŋ) vacation, holiday, day off from work.

ལས་གསེང་ལུས་སྦྱོང་ (lɛ̀ɛseŋ lǖüjoŋ) exercise break during working hours.

ལས་བསམ་དུ་མི་འགྲོ་གསེག་ཏུ་འགྲོ་ རྡོ་གཡའ་མའི་བཀས་ཁ་འཁྱིད་དུ་འགྲོ་ (lɛ̀ɛ sāmdu mindro sēgdu dro do yāmɛ gɛ̀ɛ kādreèdu dro) things not going one's way [Lit. to not have things go as one wishes, the stone breaks toward the wrong side].

ལི་ (li) 1. bronze, bell metal. 2. pear.

ལི་ཀ་ར་ (ligara) sm. ལི་ཁ་ར་.

ལི་ཀིན་ (ligin) Reagan.

ལི་ཀུ་ (ligu) sm. ལི་གུ་.

ལི་སྐུ་ (ligu) bronze statue.

ལི་ཁ་ར་ (ligara) 1. sugar cane. 2. a place in India.

ལི་ཁུད་ཚོགས་པ་ (ligud tsɔ̄gba) Likud Party.

ལི་གུ་ (ligu) a store or businessman who sells sth. to a person everyday; va.—བཟོ་ to make an arrangement with sth. to sell sth. daily ¶ངས་འོ་མའི་ལི་གུ་བཟོས་པ་ཡིན་ I made an arrangement for sb. to sell me milk everyday.

ལི་ཆས་སྤྱོད་པའི་དུས་རབས་ (lijɛɛ drȫöbɛ tǖürəb) the Bronze Age.

ལི་ཐང་ (lidaŋ) Litang (area in Eastern Tibet).

ལི་ཐོ་ (lido) sm. ལོ་ཐོ་.

ལི་དྲིལ་ (lidrii) bronze bell.

ལི་སྡེར་ (lider) plate made of bronze.

ལི་ནག (linaà) black bell metal.

ལི་པ་ནོན་ (libanün) Lebanon.

ལི་པི་ལིའི་ཡ་ (libi lɛya) Liberia.

ལི་བ་ (liwə) 1. curly hair. 2. cockeyed.

ལི་མ་ (limə) 1. sm. ལི་. 2. Lima (Peru).

ལི་མའི་མེ་ལོང་ (limɛ meloŋ) bronze plate/ mirror.

ལི་དམར་ (limar) 1. orange reddish color. 2. the red dot Hindu women put on their foreheads.

ལི་སྨི་ (limi) sm. ལི་སྨི་.

ལི་སྨུག (limuù) 1. dark purple. 2. dark colored bell metal.

ལི་ཙི་ (lidzi) ch. pear.

ལི་ཙི་ཕོ་ (lidzipo) ch.tib. positive ions.

ལི་ཙི་མོ་ (limimo) ch.tib. negative ions.

ལི་ཝང་ (liwaŋ) orange (color).

ལི་ལི་ (lili) cat.

ལི་ཤི་ (lishi) 1. clove. 2. lilac.

ལི་ཤིང་ར་བ་ (lishi rawa) a type of wooden fence used around a garden.

ལི་སི་པོང་ (lisiboŋ) Lisbon.

ལི་སེར་ (liser) 1. yellowish bell metal. 2. yellowish orange color.

ལི་ཧང་ (lihaŋ) sm. ཝང་.

ལི་ཧྭ་མེ་ཏོག (liha medoò) ch.tib. plum flower.

ལིང་ (liŋ) 1. a type of silk. 2. sm. ལིངས་.

ལིང་སེ་ (liŋse) sm. ལིངས་སེ་.

ལིང་བསྒྱུར་ (liŋgyur) tossing down one's load, heaving/ throwing down a load; va.—བྱེད་ ¶ཁོ་དཀའ་ལས་ཁག་ཐག་ཆོད་ནས་དོག་ཁྲིས་ལིང་བསྒྱུར་བྱས་སོང་ He was completely exhausted and threw down his load.

ལིང་བསྒྲལ་ (liŋ drɛɛ) va. to destroy demons through exorcism.

ལིང་ངེ་ (liŋŋe) swaying/ waving back and forth.

ལིང་ཏོག (liŋdoò) cataract.

ལིང་སྡེ་ (liŋde) sm. ལིངས་སེ་.

ལིང་ཐོག (liŋdɔ̀ɔ) sm. ལིང་ཏོག.

ལིང་ཚེ་ (liŋdze) a table, a form.

ལིང་རོ་ (liŋru) a type of eye disease according to Tibetan medicine that is similar to cataracts.

ལིང་ལིང་ (linlin) sm. ལང་ལིང་.

ལིང་ལིང་འགོག (linlin gɔɔ̀) vi. to break/ peel off in chunks.

ལིང་ལོང་ (linlon) sm. ལང་ལིང་.

ལིང་ཤང་ (linshan) ch. small bells (that are tied on animals).

ལིང་སིའི་ (linsii) ch. ལིང་ཧྲི་.

ལིང་ཧྲི་ (linhri) ch. consul ། ལིང་ཧྲི་ལས་ཁུངས་ Consulate.

ལིངས་ (lin) 1. entire, entirely, completely ། བློ་གཏད་ལིངས་བཙོལ་ Complete confidence. 2. one quarter of a carcass. 3. a trap/ snare.

ལིངས་ཁྱི་ (lingyi) sm. ཤ་ཁྱི་.

ལིངས་གྲིབ་མིག་ནད་ (lindrib mignɛɛ̀) cataracts; vi.—ཕོག to get cataracts.

ལིངས་དེ་ (linde) sm. ལིངས་.

ལིངས་དུང་ (lindun) a horn blown when hunting to call/ entice animals.

ལིངས་པ་ (linbə) hunter.

ལིངས་པོ་ (linbu) complete, all, whole.

ལིངས་སེ་ (linse) entire, completely, whole, all ། ལས་ཀ་ལིངས་སེ་མོས་བྱས་པ་རེད་ She did the work entirely (by herself). ། ལུང་པ་ལིངས་སེ་ཤོར་བ་རེད་ They lost the whole country.

ལིངས་སེ་ཁ་ལ་ (linsegala) sm. ལིངས་སེ་.

ལིན་ (lin) ch. phosphorus.

ལིན་དགག་སྤྱོད་བཅོས་ (lingaà jö̀öder) oppose Lin Biao and reform one's own behavior.

ལིན་རྒྱུའི་ཚིལ་ལུ་ (lingyü tsīīlu) ch.tib. lecithin.

ལིན་ཐའི་རྡོ་ (lindɛ do) ch.tib. apatite.

ལིན་རྡོའི་གཏེར་ཁ་ (lindö dērga) ch.tib. phosphorous mine.

ལིན་རྡོ་དམར་པོ་ (lindo mārbo) ch.tib. red phosphorous.

ལིན་པ་ (limbə) lymph.

ལིན་པ་རྩ་མདུད་ (limba dzādüù) lymph nodes.

ལིན་པིའོ་ (linbio) Lin Biao.

ལིན་མེ་ (linme) ch.tib. phosphorescent light.

ལིན་ཞག (linshaà) ch.tib. phosphatide.

ལིན་ལུད་ (linlüù) ch.tib. phosphate fertilizer.

ལིམ་ལོག (limlɔɔ̀) sm. ཉིན་ལན་ལོག་འཇལ་.

ལིའང་ཙེ་ (lindze) ch. quantum.

ལིའན་ (lian) ch. a company (in the army) ། ལའན་ཀྲང་ Company commander.

ལིའི་པི་ཡ་ (liibiyə) Libya.

ལིའི་ཡོ་ཆས་སྤྱོད་པའི་དུས་རབས་ (lii yojɛɛ̀bɛ tüù̀rəb) the Bronze Age.

ལིའུ་ཐོ་ (liwudo) sm. ལིའུ་ཐོ་.

ལིའུ་སོན་ (liwusön) ch. sulphuric acid.

ལིའུ་ཧྲའོ་ཆི་ (liwu hrāoci) Liu Shaoqi.

ལིའོ་ཉིང་ (lioñin) Liaoning (Province).

ལིའོ་ཉིན་ (liwoñin) sm. ལིའོ་ཉིང་.

ལིའོ་ཧྲོ་ཆིས་ (lihoji) Liu Shaoqi.

ལུ་ (lu) vi. to cough.

ལུ་གུ་ (lugu) lamb.

ལུ་གུ་རྒྱགས་ཀྱང་རྐང་མར་ཁྲག (lugu gyaggyan gāŋmar trāà) however strong they are they can't cope with me [Lit. although the lamb is fat, the marrow in its legs is blood].

ལུ་གུ་རྒྱུད་ (lugu gyüù) continuously, one after another ། ང་ཚོའི་ལས་ཀ་འདི་ལུ་གུ་རྒྱུད་པ་ནང་བཞིན་ཡིན་ Our work is like an assembly line. [Lit. lambs in a line/ row].

ལུ་གུ་རྒྱུད་འབྲེལ་དུ་ (lugu gyündreedu) sm. ལུ་གུ་རྒྱུད་.

ལུ་གུ་བཙའ་ལེན་ (lugu dzālen) helping to deliver lambs; va.—བྱེད་

ལུ་གུ་ལག་སྐྱེས་ (lugu laggyeè) product from one's own country/ area/ school/ monastery ། དགོན་པ་འདི་རང་ནས་ལུ་གུ་ལག་སྐྱེས་ཀྱི་དགེ་བཤེས་མང་པོ་ཞིག་ཐོན་ཡོད་ From this very monastery, they produced many geshe.

ལུ་གུ་ལྷོག་རྩྭ་ (lugu lɔ̄gdza) pasture that has been set aside for lambs.

ལུ་ཐེ་རན་རྒྱལ་སྤྱིའི་རོགས་རམ་ཚོགས་པ་ (luderɛn gyɛɛjii rɔɔ̀ram tsɔ̄gba) Lutheran World Relief.

ལུ་མ་ (lumə) water hole, spring.

ལུ་ཡིན་ཅི་ (luyinji) ch. tape recorder.

ལུ་ལུ་ (lulu) coughing constantly.

ལུ་ཧང་ (luhan) ch. sulphur.

ལུག (luù) sheep.

ལུག : p. ལུགས་; f. ལུག; imp. ལུགས་ (luù) 1. vi. to fall down, to slip away, to collapse ། ཆར་པ་མང་པོ་བབས་ནས་ཁང་པ་ལུགས་བཞག It rained a lot and the house has collapsed. 2. vi. to burst out ། ཆུ་རགས་ལུགས་བཞག The dam burst.

ལུག་ཀླད་ (luùlɛɛ̀) sheep brain.

ལུག་སྐོར་ (luùgɔɔ) a herd of sheep.

ལུག་ཁལ་བ་ (luù kɛ̄ɛwa) an adult male sheep.

ལུག་ཁོག (luùgɔɔ̀) carcass of a sheep.

ལུག་ཁྱུ་ (luùgyu) flock of sheep.

ལུག་ཁྱུའི་སྣ་ཁྲིད་མཁན་ (luùgyü nā drīìñɛn) a leader, an influential person [Lit. one who leads a flock].

ལུག་གུ་ (lūùgu) sm. ལུ་གུ་.

ལུག་མགོ་ (lungo) sheep's head.

ལུག་མགོ་འཀལ་ནས་ཁྱི་ཤ་འཚོང་བ་ (lungo gɛ̄ɛnɛ kyīsha tsōŋwa) prov. faking, tricking, deceiving [Lit. to display a sheep's head and then to sell dog meat (as mutton)].

ལུག་རྒྱུད་གསོ་སྐྱོང་ (luùgyüù sōgyon) improving sheep via breeding; va.—བྱེད་.

ལུག་ཇ་ལེབ་ (luù ŋāləb) the fat-tailed breed of sheep.

ལུག་གཉེ་ (lugñe) lily.

ལུག་ཐུག (lugduù) ram.

ལུག་ཐུལ་ (lugdüü) cloak made of sheepskin.

ལུག་ཐོང་པ་ (luù tōnba) three year old male sheep.

ལུག་གདང་ (luùdan) sm. ལུག་རྡང་.

ལུག་རྡང་ (luùdan) rope for tying sheep.

ལུག་པ་ (lugbə) sm. ལུག་རྫི་.

ལུག་ལྤགས་ (lugbaà) sheepskin.

ལུག་ལྤགས་གྱོན་པའི་སྤྱང་ཀྱི་ (lugbaà gyönbɛ jəngi) a dangerous evil person among good people [Lit. wolf in sheep's skin].

ལུག་ཕྲུག (lugdruù) lamb.

ལུག་བལ་ (lugpɛɛ) sheep wool/ fleece.

ལུག་མ་ (lugmə) female sheep.

ལུག་མ་མོ་ (lug mamo) adult female sheep.

ལུག་མིག (lugmiì) sheep's eye.

ལུག་མིག་མེ་ཏོག (lugmiì medoò) chrysanthemum, aster.

ལུག་ཚང་ (lundzan) sheep pen/ enclosure/ corral.

ལུག་ཚང་དང་གི་སྤྱང་ཀི་ (lundzannangi jəngi) a dangerous evil person among good people [Lit. a wolf in a sheep pen].

ལུག་ཚིལ་ (lugdzii) sheep fat.

ལུག་ཚུགས་ (lugdzuù) a day's journey of a person with sheep ། ལུག་ཚུགས་ལྔ་ A five days (trip).

ལུག་རྫི་ (lugdzi) shepherd.

ལུག་རྫི་བ་ (lugdziwə) sm. ལུག་རྫི་.

ལུག་གཞུག (lugshuù) 1. sheep's tail. 2. armpit.

ལུག་ཟླ་ (lunda) the 6th month of the Tibetan calendar.

ལུག་ར་ (lugrə) sheep pen.

ལུག་རིལ་ (lugrii) sheep dung.

ལུག་རུ་ (lugru) ram's horn.

ལུག་བརླག་གླང་རྙེད་ (luglaà lāñeè) losing a little and gaining a lot [Lit. to lose a sheep and gain an ox].

ལུག་ལུག (lugluù) hanging, protruding (usu. clothing, stomach).

ལུག་ལུག་ལ་དོན་ (lugluùla tön) vi. to come out continuously (usu. refers to tears).

ལུག་ལོ་ (luglu) year of the sheep.

ལུག་ཤ་ (lugsha) mutton.

ལུག་ཤིག (lugshi) sheep lice.

ལུག་ཤུབས་ (lugshəb) a utensil used by goldsmiths.

ལུག་ཤེད་ངན་དཔྱིད་ཀ་ལས་ཐར་བ་ལྟར་ (lugsheèŋɛn jīìgəlɛ tārwa dār) poor people having passsed the worst season/ period [Lit. weak sheep having been able to survive spring].

ལུག་ཤོར་རྟ་ཐོབ་ (lugshɔɔ dābəb) sm. ལུག་བརླག་གླང་

རྗེད་.

ལུག་ས་ (lugsə) a place where sheep are kept/ grazed.

ལུག་ལྷས་ (luglhɛɛ̀) sm. ལུག་ར་.

ལུག་ཨ་ད་ (luù āda) a sheep with curved horns.

ལུག་ཨ་ཡུ་ (lug āyu) hornless sheep.

ལུགས་ (luù) custom, manner, way, mode, fashion ¶ སྔར་གྱི་ལུགས་ Old customs. ¶ ཁོང་རང་རང་ཉིད་ཀྱི་སློབ་ལུགས་ཐུན་མོང་མ་ཡིན་པ་ His own unique way of teaching. 2. about, concerning, how, the reasons for, the manner of ¶ ཉི་མས་སློབ་སྦྱོང་བྱས་ལུགས་ཁྱེད་ཀྱི་ཤེས་སམ་ Do you know the details of how Nyima studied? ¶ སང་ཉིན་འབྲུག་ཡུལ་བརྒྱུད་རྒྱ་གར་དུ་གསང་བྲོས་བྱ་རྒྱུ་ཡིན་ལུགས་བརྗོད་ (He) told all about how he was going to secretly flee to India via Bhutan tomorrow. ¶ ཁོ་ཚོས་བོད་ནས་ཡོང་ལུགས་སྐོར་བཤད་པ་རེད་ They spoke about their reasons for coming from Tibet (or, depending on context, the details of how they came from Tibet). ¶ ཁོ་ས་ཉིན་འགྲོ་གི་ཡིན་ལུགས་ང་ལ་ཡབ་བྱུང་ He told me all the details about his going tomorrow. 3. casting molds, foundry work; va.—རྒྱག; —བླུག to cast, to mold, to do foundry work. 4. p. of ལུག.

ལུགས་ཀ་ (luggə) sm. སྲོལ་རྒྱུན་.

ལུགས་ཀོང་ (luggoŋ) crucible, mold.

ལུགས་ཀྱི་སྤྱན་པ་ (luùgi jɛ̃mba) sm. ཁྲིམས་དཔོན་.

ལུགས་ཀྱི་ལུང་ (luùgi luŋ) shung. sm. ཁྲིམས་སྐོང་.

ལུགས་དཀྲུག (lugdruù) sm. ཁྲིམས་འགལ་ལུགས་དཀྲུག.

ལུགས་སྐུ་ (luùgu) icons and statues made from brass molds.

ལུགས་ཁང་ (luùgaŋ) a building/ room used for making casts from molds.

ལུགས་མགར་ (luggar) abbr. people who do casting and blacksmiths.

ལུགས་འགལ་ (luùgɛɛ) against a rule or custom, in violation of a custom.

ལུགས་འགལ་སྲོལ་འགལ་ (luùgɛɛ sōōgɛɛ) immoral, unethical, in violation of customs.

ལུགས་རྒྱག (luù gyaà) va. to cast/ make from a mold.

ལུགས་རྒྱག་བཟོ་ཁང་ (luùgyaà sogaŋ) molding/ casting workshop, foundry.

ལུགས་སྒྱུར་ (luùgyur) changing customs; va.—བྱེད་.

ལུགས་སྒྱུར་སྲོལ་སྒྱུར་ (luùgyur sōōgyur) sm. ལུགས་སྒྱུར་.

ལུགས་ངན་ (luùŋen) bad custom/ manner/ way.

ལུགས་ཆས་ (luùjɛɛ̀) sm. ལུགས་པར་.

ལུགས་གཉིས་ (luùñii) the "dual system/ way" (spiritual and temporal) ¶ ལུགས་གཉིས་ཀྱི་དབུ་ཁྲིད་ Spiritual and temporal leader (usu. refers to the Dalai Lama).

ལུགས་གཉིས་ཟུང་འབྲེལ་ (luùñii suŋdree) shung. the spiritual and temporal combined (usu. refers to the Tibetan government).

ལུགས་རྙིང་ (lugñiŋ) old customs/ traditions/ styles ¶ ལུགས་རྙིང་གི་ཐོན་སྐྱེད་ Old style production.

ལུགས་རྙིང་ལེ་ཐོ་ (lugñiŋ ledo) sm. ལུགས་རྙིང་ལོ་ཐོ་.

ལུགས་རྙིང་ལོ་ཐོ་ (lugñiŋ lodo) lunar calendar, traditional calendar.

ལུགས་རྙིང་སྲོལ་ངན་ (lugñiŋ sōōŋɛn) old and bad conventions/ ways/ customs.

ལུགས་རྙིང་རྩ་སྒྱུར་ (lugñiŋ dzāgyur) transforming old ways/ customs.

ལུགས་བསྟུན་དོན་སྒྲུབ་ (lugdün tõndrub) achieving or succeeding by doing sth. in accordance with the rules/ the system/ customs.

ལུགས་མཐུན་ (lugdün) proper, lawful, correct, valid; in accordance with custom/ law, va.—བྱེད་.

ལུགས་མཐུན་དྲང་འབྲེལ་ (lugdün traŋdree) sm. ལུགས་མཐུན་དྲང་བཞག.

ལུགས་མཐུན་དྲང་བཞག (lugdün traŋshaà) fair, honest, impartial, lawfully; va.—བྱེད་.

ལུགས་མཐུན་སྨོས་མེད་ (lugdün mōōmeè) in accordance with the law/ custom so that no one can criticize it; va.—བྱེད་.

ལུགས་དང་མཐུན་པ་ (luùdaŋ tũmbə) sm. ལུགས་མཐུན་.

ལུགས་ལྡོག (luùdɔɔ̀) counting from the bottom up; va.—རྒྱག.

ལུགས་ལྡོན་གྲངས་ (lugdön traŋ) rational numbers (in math).

ལུགས་ལྡོག་སྐྱེས་ (lugdɔɔ̀ gyēè) va. to give breech birth.

ལུགས་སྣོད་ (lugnüü) sm. ལུག་སྣོད་.

ལུགས་པ་ (lugbə) a person who makes casts/ molds. 2. foundry worker.

ལུགས་པར་ (lugbar) a mold, cast; va.—རྒྱག.

ལུགས་བླུག (lugluù) see ལུགས་.

ལུགས་བླུག་འཕྲུལ་འཁོར་ (lugluù cūrgɔɔ) molding/ casting machine.

ལུགས་འབྱུང་ (lugjuŋ) in sequence from the top of a list down.

ལུགས་འབྱུང་ལུགས་ལྡོག (lunjuŋ lugdɔɔ̀) style of writing verse where each line starts with a letter of the alphabet from a - z, and then from z - a.

ལུགས་མ་ lugmə) sth. that has been casted/ molded.

ལུགས་མ་གྲངས་ (lugma traŋ) irrational number (in math).

ལུགས་བཞིན་ (lugshin) according to the system/ culture.

ལུགས་ཟུང་ (lugsuŋ) abbr. of ལུགས་གཉིས་ཟུང་འབྲེལ་.

ལུགས་བཟང་ (lugsaŋ) good custom/ manner/ way.

ལུགས་ཤུབས་ (lugshub) sm. ལུག་ཤུབས་.

ལུགས་ཤོག (lugsɔɔ̀) 1. ch. noodle strainer. 2. paper-mache mold/ model.

ལུགས་སུ་བླུག (lugsu lūù) sm. ལུགས་བླུག.

ལུགས་སྲོལ་ (lugsüü) custom, tradition, practice ¶ བོད་པའི་ལུགས་སྲོལ་རྙིང་པ་ Old Tibetan customs.

ལུགས་སྲོལ་གོམས་གཤིས་ (lusüü komshii) sm. ལུགས་སྲོལ་.

ལུགས་གསར་ (lugsaa) new custom, manner/ way ¶ ལུགས་གསར་ཨེམ་ཆི་ New custom (allopathic medicine) doctor.

ལུགས་གསར་ལེ་ཐོ་ (lugsar ledo) solar (Gregorian) calendar.

ལུགས་གསར་ལོ་ཐོ་ (lugsar lodo) solar calendar.

ལུང་ (luŋ) 1. handle. 2. religious initiation reading transmission (a text that is read by one who has received the transmission himself and is read to others giving them the authority to study/ read and meditate on those teachings). 3. prediction, prophesy; va.—རྒྱག to predict/ prophesy. 4. scripture, religious text.

ལུང་གྱོག.(luŋgyoò) remote place/ area.

ལུང་བཀོད་གནང་.(luŋgöö nāŋ) shung. va. to give instructions/ orders (by an oracle/ shaman).

ལུང་སྐུགས་ (luŋguù) a remote place.

ལུང་བསྐུལ་ (luŋgüü) prophecy that urges sth. ¶ ལྷ་སར་ཕེབས་རྒྱུའི་སྐོར་ལྷ་བླ་རྣམས་ཀྱིས་གོང་ས་མཆོག་ལ་ལུང་བསྐུལ་གནང་བ་རེད་ The deities and lamas and oracles made prophecies that urged the Dalai Lama to go to Lhasa.

ལུང་ཁུག (luŋguù) a remote/ isolated region, the boondocks.

ལུང་ཁུངས་ (luŋguŋ) the source of a quotation.

ལུང་གི་རྗེས་འབྲང་ (luŋgi jeèdraŋ) dogmatism.

ལུང་གྲ་ (luŋdra) shung. a type of monastic gathering.

ལུང་ཆུང་ནང་གི་དཔོན་ཆུང་ (luŋjuŋ naŋgi bõnjuŋ) sb. who has power in only a small/ limited sphere, a big fish in a small pond [Lit. a small place with a small leader].

ལུག་ལྡས་ (luŋdɛɛ̀) sm. ལུང་བརྟག.

ལུང་སྟོང་ (luŋdoŋ) desolate/ deserted area.

ལུང་སྟོངས་ (luŋdoŋ) sm. ལུང་སྟོང་.

ལུང་རྟགས་ (luŋdaà) sm. ལུང་བརྟག.

ལུང་རྟོགས་རྒྱ་མཚོ་ (luŋdɔɔ̀ gyādzo) the name of the 9th Dalai Lama.

ལུང་བརྟག (luŋdaà) prophecy/ divination given by lamas and deities.

ལུང་སྟོན་ (luŋ dõn) va. to predict, to prophesy.

ལུང་སྟོན་མཁན་ (luŋdönñɛn) a person who predicts/ makes prophesies.

ལུང་བསྟན་ (lu̲ŋdɛn) prediction, prophecy; va.—རྒྱག; — གནང་ to prophesy, to predict the future.

ལུང་ཐག (lu̲ŋdaà) strap/ rope functioning as a handle.

ལུང་ཐག་སྐེ་ལ་བརྒྱུས་པ་ (lu̲ŋdaà gēla gyüùbə) explaining the important parts of sth. thoroughly/ precisely [Lit. attaching a strap on the neck].

ལུང་ཐང་ (lu̲ŋdaŋ) plain, plateau.

ལུང་ཐོབ་ (lu̲ŋtob) vi. to receive a ལུང་ initiation.

ལུང་དོན་གཅིག་གྱུར་ (lu̲ŋdön ji̲ggyur) agreement/ consensus between the predictions of two oracles or deities ། ལྷ་གཉིས་ཀྱི་ལུང་དོན་གཅིག་གྱུར་གནང་བྱུང་ (We) got predictions from two gods that coincided.

ལུང་དོན་བཞིན་ (lu̲ŋdönshin) shung. according to the prophecy.

ལུང་མདའ་ (lu̲ŋda) sm. ལུང་པའི་མདའ་.

ལུང་མདོ་ (lu̲ŋdo) sm. ལུང་པའི་མདའ་.

ལུང་འདྲེན་ (lu̲ŋdren) citing, quoting; va. ལུང་འདྲེན་; —བྱེད་ to quote/ cite ། ཁོང་གིས་གདམ་བཤད་བྱེད་སྐབས་དགེ་འདུན་ཆོས་འཕེལ་གྱི་གསུང་ལུང་འདྲེན་བྱས་སོང་ When he gave the speech, he quoted Gendun Chompel.

ལུང་པ་ (lu̲ŋbə) place, locality, area, country, region.

ལུང་པ་ཁུག་ཀྱོག (lu̲ŋbə kūggyoò) sm. ལུང་ཀྱོག.

ལུང་པ་གང་ (lu̲ŋbagaŋ) a great deal, a lot, much, plenty ། མི་དེས་རྙོག་དྲ་ལུང་པ་གང་བཟོས་བཞག That person caused much trouble.

ལུང་པ་ཆུས་འཇིག་ན་རྡོ་ལེབ་སྐམ་པོ་ལུས་མི་སྲིད་ (lu̲ŋba cũù ji̲gnə no̲lib gāmbo lü̲ù mi̲sii) when the country is at war, single families can not stay indifferent [Lit. when the country is covered by water, stones cannot remain dry].

ལུང་པ་ཐང་ཁུག་བཟོ་འདྲ་ (lu̲ŋba tãŋguù so̲ndra) a very narrow valley where one can only see the sky.

ལུང་པ་ལུང་ཀྱོག (lu̲ŋba lu̲ŋgyɔɔ̀) sm. ལུང་ཀྱོག.

ལུང་པའི་སྐད་ (lu̲ŋbɛ gɛ̃ɛ̀) local dialect.

ལུང་པའི་ཆགས་གཞི་ (lu̲ŋbɛ cə̃gshi) the geography of the place.

ལུང་པའི་མདའ་ (lu̲ŋbɛ da̲) the lower reaches of a valley.

ལུང་པའི་ཕུ་ (lu̲ŋbɛ pū) the upper part of a valley/ region.

ལུང་ཕོག (lu̲ŋpɔɔ̀) vi. to receive a ལུང་ initiation.

ལུང་ཕྲན་ (lu̲ŋdrɛn) small areas/ places/ countries.

ལུང་འབེབས་ (lu̲ŋbeb) sm. ལུང་བསྟན་རྒྱག.

ལུང་འབོགས་ (lu̲ŋbɔɔ̀) giving a ལུང་ initiation.

ལུང་འབོགས་པ་པོ་ (lu̲ŋbɔɔ̀babo) the lama who gives a ལུང་ initiation.

ལུང་མིག (lu̲ŋmii̇) a handle in shape of a ring (for doors, etc.).

ལུང་ཙམ་འཛིན་པའི་རིང་ལུགས་ (lu̲ŋdzam dzi̲mbɛ ri̲ŋluù) dogmatism, doctrinairism.

ལུང་ཚན་ (lu̲ŋdzɛn) region, province, locality.

ལུང་ཚན་ཕྱོགས་རིས་ (lu̲ŋdzɛn cɔ̃ɔ̀rii̇) prejudice in favor of one's region/ area/ locality.

ལུང་ཚིག (lu̲ŋdzii̇) 1. dogma, doctrine. 2. citation, quotation.

ལུང་མཚན་ (lu̲ŋdzɛn) abbr. of ལུང་ and དགས་མཚན་.

ལུང་འཛིན་རིང་ལུགས་ (lu̲ŋdzin ri̲ŋluù) dogmatism, doctrinairism.

ལུང་ཞུ་ (lu̲ŋshu) questions asked to a deity while it is possessing a medium's body; va.—འབུལ་ to ask questions to a deity possessing a medium.

ལུང་གཞུང་ (lu̲ŋshuŋ) valley.

ལུང་ཡིག (lu̲ŋyii̇) a written prophecy.

ལུང་རིགས་ (lu̲ŋrii̇) scriptures and reasoning.

ལུང་ལས་ (lu̲ŋlɛɛ̀) seal and title that grants authority to govern an area.

ལུང་ཤར་ (lu̲ŋshar) a Tibetan aristocratic family important in 20th century history.

ལུང་ཤུར་ (lu̲ŋshur) sm. ལུང་གཞུང་.

ལུང་ཧྲུལ་ (lu̲ŋhrüü) sm. ལུང་ཁུག.

ལུང་ཧྲེ་ལན་ (lu̲ŋhrelɛn) ch. century plant.

ལུད་ (lü̲ü) fertilizer; va.—རྒྱག to fertilize ། ཟླ་བ་གསུམ་པའི་ནང་ཞིང་གར་ལུད་རྒྱག་དགོས་ (They) must fertilize the fields in the third month. 2. vi. to overflow, to boil over ། མེ་ཚ་དྲགས་ནས་ཐུག་པ་ལུད་སོང་ Because the fire was too hot the soup boiled over.

ལུད་སྐྱེལ་ (lü̲ü gyēē) va. to transport manure/ fertilizer.

ལུད་སྐྱོགས་ (lü̲ügyɔɔ̀) ladle (used for removing manure).

ལུད་ཁུ་ (lü̲ügu) liquid fertilizer.

ལུད་རྒྱུའི་སྐྱེ་དངོས་ (lü̲ügyü gyēŋöö̀) plants used for fertilizer.

ལུད་སྒྲ་ (lü̲üdra) sound of clearing (one's) throat; va.—སྒྲིག.

ལུད་སྒྲག་སློ་པོ་ (lü̲üdruù lēbo) sm. ལུད་སློ་.

ལུད་ཆུ་ (lü̲üju) 1. ལུད་ཁུ་. 2. fertilizer and water.

ལུད་ཆུ་འཛོམས་པོ་ (lü̲üju dzombo) a rich land (i.e., a place where water and manure are plentiful).

ལུད་ཆེན་སྐྱེལ་ (lü̲üjen gyēè) va. to apply fertilizer/ manure (in the spring).

ལུད་གཏོར་མཁན་ (lü̲üdɔɔñɛn) the person who spreads manure/ fertilizer.

ལུད་དུང་ (lü̲üduŋ) sm. ལུད་ཟོ་.

ལུད་དོང་ (lü̲üdoŋ) pit/ ditch for keeping fertilizer.

ལུད་འདྲེན་འུ་ལག (lü̲üdren wu̲laà) shung. corvee labor to carry fertilizer to the fields.

ལུད་ནུས་ (lü̲ünüü) strength/ power/ effectiveness of fertilizer.

ལུད་པ་ (lü̲übə) phlegm, sputum; vi.—ཐོན་ to cough up phlegm/ sputum; va.—དབྱུག to spit phlegm.

ལུད་སྤུངས་ (lü̲ü būŋ) va. to heap up manure/ compost, to store up manure.

ལུད་ཕུང་ (lü̲übuŋ) manure pile, compost pile.

ལུད་ཕོར་ (lü̲üpɔɔ) spittoon.

ལུད་ཕྱེ་ (lü̲üce) powdered fertilizer.

ལུད་དབོར་ (lü̲ü wɔ̃ɔ̀) va. to transport fertilizer (to the fields).

ལུད་འབུ་ (lü̲mbu) bugs that grow in fertilizer.

ལུད་སྦྱོར་ (lü̲üjɔɔ) making fertilizer, composting manure; va.—བྱེད་.

ལུད་རྫས་ (lü̲üdzɛɛ̀) chemical fertilizer.

ལུད་གཞོང་ (lü̲üshoŋ) wooden manure bucket/ trough.

ལུད་ཟོ་ (lü̲üso) bucket used for carrying manure.

ལུད་ར་ (lü̲üra) a corral/ enclosure for keeping manure.

ལུད་ཤུགས་ (lü̲üshuù) the strength/ effectiveness of manure.

ལུད་ས་ (lü̲üsə) soil used in composting manure.

ལུད་སློ་ (lü̲üle) basket for collecting dung.

ལུད་གསོག (lü̲üsɔɔ̀) va. to store manure.

ལུན་དུན་ (lü̲ndün) London.

ལུམས་ (lu̲m) a treatment in Tibetan medicine where the patient soaks in a warm liquid made from a fermented mixture of barley and medicine.

ལུམས་བཅོས་ (lu̲mjöö̀) sm. ལུམས་.

ལུམ་བིའི་ཚལ་ (lu̲mbini) Lumbini: the birthplace of the Buddha (in Nepal).

ལུའེ་ (lu̲wɛ) ch. 1. brigade. 2. troops, forces.

ལུའེ་ལྕགས་ (lu̲wɛ jãà) ch.tib. aluminum.

ལུའེ་རླུང་ (lu̲wɛ lūŋ) ch.tib. chlorine gas.

ལུའུ་ཅུན་དམག (lu̲jun mãà) ch.tib. the name of the Chinese Army that entered Tibet at the end of 1909.

ལུའུ་མེན་ (lu̲mɛn) lumen.

ལུའི་ད་ (lu̲da) ch. radar.

ལུས་ (lü̲ü) 1. body, form ། ལུས་ཀྱི་ཡན་ལག Limbs of the body. 2. vi. to be left behind, to be left in a state of sth. ། ངའི་དེབ་དེ་ལུས་འདུག My book was left behind. ། ཟས་མེད་པར་ལུས་པ་རེད་ (We) were left without food. ། འདི་ར་ཞག་འགྱངས་ལུས་ཚེ་མི་ངན་གྱིས་འཕྲོག་བཅོམ་བྱ་རྒྱུའི་ཉེན་ཁ་འདུག If you get left behind for one day, there is a danger that evil people will rob you.

ལུས་ཀྱི་གྲོམ་ (lüügi drom) skeleton.

ལུས་ཀྱི་ངལ་རྩོལ་ (lüügi ŋəədzöö) physical/ manual labor.

ལུས་ཀྱི་ཉམས་སྟོབས་ (lüügi ñamdob) stature/ condition of the human body; vi.—རྒྱས་ to get physically healthy/ strong; vi.—གུད་ to get physically weak.

ལུས་ཀྱི་གཉན་ས་ (lüügi ñɛ̃nsa) important points on the human body.

ལུས་ཀྱི་དབང་པོ་ལྔ་ (lüügi wāŋbo ŋā) the five sense organs in Tibetan medicine (eyes, ear, nose, tongue, body).

ལུས་ཀྱི་གནས་ལྔ་ (lüügi nɛ̄ɛ̀ŋa) five parts of a body (for prostrating) forehead, palms of hands and knees.

ལུས་ཀྱི་རྣམ་ཤེས་ (lüügi nāmsheè) physical consciousness.

ལུས་ཀྱི་མཐལ་ལྔ་ (lüügi mɛɛŋa) sm. ལུས་ཀྱི་གནས་ལྔ་.

ལུས་ཀྱིས་ལས་ (lüügi lɛ̀ɛ̀) physical karma.

ལུས་རྐྱང་ (lüügyaŋ) naked.

ལུས་སྐེམ་པ་ (lüü gēmba) physically thin/ weakly.

ལུས་སྐྱིས་གཡོ་ (lüü gyēè yō) vi. to have one's hair stand on end.

ལུས་ཁམས་ (lüügam) the body.

ལུས་ཁམས་བདེ་ཐང་ (lüügam dedaŋ) good health ¶ ལུས་ཁམས་བདེ་ཐང་སླར་གསོ་ཐུབ་པ་རེད་ (They) were able to restore (his) good health.

ལུས་ཁམས་བདེ་སྲུང་ (lüügam desuŋ) health care, protecting health ¶ ལུས་ཁམས་བདེ་སྲུང་ཁང་ Health care center.

ལུས་ཁམས་བདེ་སྲུང་ཁང་ (lüügam desuŋgaŋ) health care center.

ལུས་ཁམས་བདེ་སྲུང་ས་ཚིགས་ (lüügam desuŋ sādzii) health care center.

ལུས་ཁོག་ (lüügɔɔ̀) the body.

ལུས་ཁྲག་ (lüüdraà) blood.

ལུས་ཁྲག་འཁོར་རྒྱུག་ (lüüdraà kɔ̄ɔ̄gyuù) blood circulation.

ལུས་ཁྲིམས་གཅོད་ (lüütrim jöö) va. to impose corporal punishment.

ལུས་འཁྲིལ་ (lüüdrii) twisting/ coiling the body during sexual intercourse.

ལུས་འཁྲུད་ཁང་ (lüü trüügaŋ) bath house.

ལུས་འཁྲུད་ས་ (lüü trüüsa) bath house.

ལུས་འཁྲིལ་པོ་ (lüü triibu) one who twists/ coils the body during sexual intercourse.

ལུས་འགྱིངས་ (lüügyiŋ) grandiose appearance.

ལུས་རྒྱགས་ (lüügyaà) fat (person).

ལུས་སྒྱུར་ (lüü gyur) 1. va. to emanate into sth., to transform into sth. 2. wearing clothes with patches of sun or moon to avoid bad luck.

ལུས་ངག་ཡིད་གསུམ་ (lüü ŋaà yii sūm) the thre: body, mind and speech.

ལུས་ངན་པོ་ (lüü ŋɛmbo) frail, skinny, thin (body).

ལུས་ངལ་འཛེམ་མེད་ (lüüŋɛɛ dzemmeè) working hard, striving all out; va.—བྱེད་.

ལུས་ངོས་ (lüüŋöö) surface of the body.

ལུས་དངོས་ (lüüŋöö) the main part or section of a text/ book/ scripture.

ལུས་རྔུལ་ (lüüŋüü) sweat, perspiration; vi. ལུས་རྔུལ་; —རྒྱག; —ཐོན་ to sweat.

ལུས་སྔ་མ་ (lüü ŋāma) past/ previous life.

ལུས་ཅན་ (lüüjɛn) living beings, sentient beings.

ལུས་གཅོང་ (lüüjoŋ) infirm, weak (in body).

ལུས་བཅུད་ (lüüjüü) sperm.

ལུས་ལྕི་མ་ (lüüjimə) pregnant woman.

ལུས་ཆགས་རྩལ་གྱི་རིག་པ་ (lüü cāgdzüügi rigbə) science of physiology.

ལུས་ཆགས་ས་དང་སེམས་རྟེན་ས་ (lüü cāgsa taŋ sēm dēnsa) sm. ལུས་སེམས་ཆགས་རྟེན་.

ལུས་ཆད་ (lüüjɛɛ̀) corporal punishment; va.—གཅོད་; —འགེལ་ to give corporal punishment; vi.—འཁེལ; —ཐོག to receive corporal punishment ¶ ཀུན་མ་དེ་ལ་ལུས་ཆད་བཅད་པ་རེད་ They inflicted physical punishment on the thief.

ལུས་ཆས་ (lüüjɛɛ̀) clothing.

ལུས་ཆས་སྦོང་ཐག (lüüjɛɛ̀ bōŋdaà) giving away one's clothes as alms.

ལུས་ཆེན་ (lüüjen) tall (person).

ལུས་འཆལ་ (lüüjɛɛ) illegal/ immoral acts.

ལུས་འཆོས་ (lüüjöö) changing one's appearance; va.—བྱེད་.

ལུས་ཉམས་རྒྱས་པོ་ (lüüñam gyɛɛ̀bo) strong and healthy.

ལུས་གདོས་ (lüüdöö) size of a body.

ལུས་རྟེན་ (lüüden) body, form ¶ མི་ཡི་ལུས་རྟེན་ Human form/ body.

ལུས་སྟེང་ལ་ཆ་འཇུན་ (lüüdeŋla tsānjün) shung. corporal punishment ¶ ཉེས་འཆལ་ཆེ་བའི་བྱེད་གཏེ་རྣམས་ལ་ལུས་སྟེང་ཆ་འཇུན་དུ་རྒྱུ་ The main culprits will receive corporal punishment.

ལུས་སྟོད་ (lüüdöö) upper part of the body.

ལུས་སྟོབས་ (lüüdob) physical strength; va.—སྦྱོང་ to build/ increase strength, to do body building; vi.—ཤོར་; —ཟད་ to lose physical strength/ vitality.

ལུས་སྟོབས་སྐྱེད་སྨན་ (lüüdob gyēèmɛn) vitamins, tonic.

ལུས་ཐང་པོ་ (lüü tāŋbo) physically healthy.

ལུས་ཐིག་དྲུག་ (lüüdig truù) sm. འཛམ་དྲུག.

ལུས་ཐོག་ཉེས་ཆད་ (lüüdɔɔ̀ ñeèjɛɛ̀) corporal punishment.

ལུས་ཐོག་གི་ཁྲིམས་གཅོད་ (lüüdɔɔ̀gi trimjöö) sm. ལུས་ཐོག་ཉེས་ཆད་.

ལུས་དང་གྲིབ་མ་བཞིན་དུ་འགྲོགས་པ་ (lüüdaŋ trubmə shindu drɔgba) inseparable, closely associated [Lit. accompanying like a body and its shadow].

ལུས་དང་གྲིབ་མ་མཉམ་འགྲོགས་ (lüüdaŋ tribmə ñāmdrɔɔ̀) sm. ལུས་དང་གྲིབ་མ་བཞིན་དུ་འགྲོགས་པ་.

ལུས་དལ་པོ་ (lüü tɛɛbo) without work, not busy, at leisure ¶ དེང་སང་ང་ལུས་དལ་པོ་ཡོད་ These days I am not busy.

ལུས་དུབ་སེམས་འཁྲུག (lüüdub sēmdruù) being physically tired and mentally depressed/ upset.

ལུས་དོགས་སྔོན་འཚང་ (lüüdɔɔ̀ ŋöndzaŋ) crowding/ pushing oneself to the front out of fear of being left behind.

ལུས་བདེ་སེམས་སྐྱིད་ (lüüde sēmgyii) healthy and happy.

ལུས་དྲོད་དཔྱད་ཆས་ (lüüdröö jɛ̀ɛ̀jɛɛ̀) thermometer.

ལུས་འདོར་ (lüüdɔɔ) 1. vi. to sacrifice one's life. 2. vi. to die.

ལུས་འདུད་ (lüüdüü) gestures of respect with the body (e.g., bowing).

ལུས་འདྲིས་ (lündreè) copulation; va.—བྱེད་ to have sexual intercourse ¶ ང་མདང་དགོང་བུ་མོ་དེ་དང་ལུས་འདྲིས་བྱུང་སོང་ I had sexual intercourse with that girl last night.

ལུས་དོས་ (lüüdöö) sm. ལུས་གདོས་.

ལུས་ལྡན་ (lüündɛn) sm. ལུས་ཅན་.

ལུས་སྡོད་ (lüü döö) vi. to be left behind ¶ ཁོང་ནི་ནང་མི་རྣམས་ཕ་ཡུལ་ལ་ལུས་བསྡད་ཡོད་པ་རེད་ His family members have been left behind in his homeland.

ལུས་གནད་ (lüünɛɛ̀) sm. ལུས་ཀྱི་གཉན་ས་.

ལུས་སྣེད་ (lüü nēè) vi. to be handicapped physically.

ལུས་པོ་ (lüübo) body; vi.—རྒྱས་ to grow (body) ¶ ཕྲུ་གུ་ལུས་པོ་རྒྱས་པའི་སྐབས་སུ་ལྟོ་ཆས་ཡག་པོ་སྟེར་དགོས་པ་རེད་ The child is at the time when his body is growing so you should give him good food.

ལུས་པོ་ཞིབ་བཤེར་ (lüübo shibsher) 1. health or physical checkup. 2. body search; va.—བྱེད་.

ལུས་པོའི་ལྗིད་ཚད་ (lüübo jiidzɛɛ̀) body weight.

ལུས་སྤུ་ (lüübu) body hair.

ལུས་ཕུང་ (lüübuŋ) sm. ལུས་པོ་.

ལུས་ཕུང་འཚོ་སྐྱོང་ (lüübuŋ tsōgyoŋ) keeping fit, taking care of oneself; va.—བྱེད་.

ལུས་ཕུང་རྒྱས་པའི་དུས་སྐབས་ (lüübuŋ gyɛɛ̀bɛ tüügəb) the growing period (of the body).

ལུས་ཕྱི་མ་ (lüü cīmə) future life.

ལུས་ཕྱེད་ (lüüjeè) half of the body, one side of the body.

ལུས་ཕྱེད་འགུལ་མི་ཐུབ་པ་ (lüüjeè güü mitubbə) vi. to be paralyzed on one side of the body.

ལུས་འཕགས་པོ་ (lüü pāgbo) one of the continents surrounding Mount Mehru.

ལུས་བོངས་ (lüüboŋ) sm. ལུས་གདོས་.

ལུས་བྱད་ (lüüjɛɛ̀) 1. sm. གཟུགས་བྱད་. 2. body and face.

ལུས་བྲེལ་པོ་ (lüü dreebo) busy ། ཉིང་སང་ང་ལུས་བྲེལ་པོ་འདུག These days I am busy.

ལུས་དབང་ (lüüwaŋ) the five sense organs of the body.

ལུས་དབྱིབས་ (lüüyiɔ̀) shape of the body.

ལུས་འབྱར་ (lünjar) 1. underclothes, underwear. 2. personal effects ། བཙོན་པའི་ལུས་འབྱར་གྱི་དངོས་པོ་གཞུང་བཞེས་གཏོང་གི་མེད་པ་རེད་ They don't confiscate the personal effects that a prisoner brings along with him.

ལུས་འབྲེལ་ (lündree) sexual intercourse; va.—བྱེད་ to have sexual intercourse.

ལུས་སྦྱིན་ (lüüjin) meditating and visualizing that one is sacrificing one's body; va.—གཏོང་.

ལུས་སྦྱོང་ (lüüjoŋ) physical exercise; va.—བྱེད་ to exercise.

ལུས་སྦྱོར་ (lüüjɔɔ) having sexual intercourse; va.—བྱེད་.

ལུས་མ་ (lüümə) remainder, balance.

ལུས་མ་བསྲུངས་ (lüü masuŋ) a loose, promiscuous woman.

ལུས་མི་གཅིག་ཁག་ཁག སེམས་མི་གཅིག་སོ་སོ་ (lüü mijig kāgaà sēm mijig sōso) being separated physically and mentally.

ལུས་མི་བདེ་ (lüü mide) 1. not feeling well. 2. pregnant woman.

ལུས་མི་སྡུག (lüü miduù) ugly.

ལུས་བཙོངས་ཁེ་གཉེར་ (lüüdzoŋ kēñer) 1. selling one's soul and body for personal gains. 2. selling family members for one's own gain.

ལུས་བཙོངས་གན་རྒྱ་ (lüüdzoŋ kengya) contract selling oneself as a slave.

ལུས་བཙོངས་མགོ་བདགས་ (lüüdzoŋ godaà) bartering one's honor for sb.'s help/ patronage.

ལུས་རྩལ་ (lüüdzɛɛ) sports, athletics, physical exercise; va.—རྩེད་ to do physical exercise, to perform gymnastics, to play sports; va.—སྦྱོང་ to practice sports.

ལུས་རྩལ་ཁང་ (lüüdzɛɛgaŋ) gymnasium.

ལུས་རྩལ་མཁས་པ་ (lüüdzɛɛ kɛ̄ɛba) master of sports, expert sportsman.

ལུས་རྩལ་གྱི་བྱེད་སྒོ་ (lüüdzɛɛgi cēègo) sports/ athletic activities.

ལུས་རྩལ་འགུལ་སྐྱོད་ཨུ་ཡོན་ལྷན་ཁང་ (lüüdzɛɛ güügyöö ūyün lhēngaŋ) physical culture and sports committee.

ལུས་རྩལ་འགྲན་ཚོགས་ (lüüdzɛɛ trēndzɔɔ̀) sports competition, athletic meet.

ལུས་རྩལ་ཐང་ (lüüdzɛɛdaŋ) sports field, athletic ground, stadium.

ལུས་རྩལ་སྡུར་ (lüüdzɛɛ dur) va. to compete in sports/ athletics.

ལུས་རྩལ་པ་ (lüüdzɛɛba) athlete.

ལུས་རྩལ་སྒྲོ་ཁང་ (lüüdzɛɛ drōgaŋ) sports club.

ལུས་རྩལ་པོ་བྲང་ (lüüdzɛɛ podraŋ) gymnasium, indoor stadium.

ལུས་རྩལ་བྱེད་ས་ (lüüdzɛɛ cɛ̄ɛsa) athletic field/ ground.

ལུས་རྩལ་སྦྱོང་ (lüüdzɛɛjoŋ) see ལུས་རྩལ་.

ལུས་རྩལ་རྩེ་ (lüüdzɛɛ dzē) see ལུས་རྩལ་.

ལུས་རྩལ་རྩེ་ཐང་ (lüüdzɛɛ dzēdaŋ) sports stadium, athletic field.

ལུས་རྩལ་ཚགས་པར་ (lüüdzɛɛ tsāgbaa) sports newspaper.

ལུས་རྩལ་ཚོགས་ཆེན་ (lüüdzɛɛ tsōgjen) sports meeting/ competition.

ལུས་རྩལ་ཚོགས་འདུ་ (lüüdzɛɛ tsōndu) sm. ལུས་རྩལ་ཚོགས་ཆེན་.

ལུས་རྩལ་ཚོགས་པ་ (lüüdzɛɛ tsōgba) sports or athletic association.

ལུས་རྩལ་ར་བ་ (lüüdzɛɛ rawa) sm. ལུས་རྩལ་ཐང་.

ལུས་རྩལ་ལ་བརྟེན་པའི་གསོ་ཐབས་ (lüüdzɛɛla dēmbɛ sōdəb) physical therapy.

ལུས་རྩལ་སློབ་གྲྭ་ (lüüdzɛɛ lōbdra) sports school.

ལུས་རྩལ་སློབ་གྲྭ་ཆེན་མོ་ (lüüdzɛɛ lōbdra cēmbo) sports college.

ལུས་རྩལ་སློབ་གསོ་ (lüüdzɛɛ lōbso) physical education.

ལུས་རྩལ་ཨུ་ཡོན་ལྷན་ཁང་ (lüüdzɛɛ ūyün lhēngaŋ) sm. ལུས་རྩལ་འགུལ་སྐྱོད་ཨུ་ཡོན་ལྷན་ཁང་.

ལུས་ཚགས་ (lüüdzaà) sm. ལུས་ཀྱི་མཉམ་སྡོམས་.

ལུས་ཚད་ (lüüdzɛɛ̀) size of the body.

ལུས་འཚམ (lüüdzaà) sm. ལུས་ཀྱི་མཉམ་སྡོམས་.

ལུས་འཚོ་ (lüü tsō) vi. to sustain life, to subsist ། མུ་གེའི་སྐབས་གྲོང་གསེབ་པ་རྣམས་ལུས་འཚོ་ཁག་པོ་བྱུང་བ་རེད་ During the famine the villagers had a difficult time surviving.

ལུས་ཛོགས་ (lüüdzɔɔ̀) fully grown.

ལུས་གཞི་ (lüüshi) body.

ལུས་གཞུང་ (lüüshuŋ) body.

ལུས་བཟུངས་ (lüüsuŋ) physical strength, vitality; vi.—ཟད་; —ཤོར་ to lose physical strength/ vitality.

ལུས་བཟུངས་དྭངས་མ་ (lüüsuŋ taŋma) sperm.

ལུས་ཟོས་ཡང་པོ་ (lüüsöö yaŋbo) agile, nimble, quick of foot.

ལུས་གཟུགས་ (lüüsuù) sm. ལུས་གཞི་.

ལུས་བཟོ་ (lüüso) the art of drawing bodies in thanka painting.

ལུས་ལ་འཕྲིལ་པོ་ (lüüla trīibu) (clothing) that fits the body well.

ལུས་ལ་སྦྱར་ (lüüla jar) va. to hold sth/ put sth. against one's body ། ཨ་མས་ཕྲུ་གུ་ལུས་ལ་སྦྱར་ནས་དྲོད་བཀུག་པ་རེད་ The mother kept the child warm by putting (him) against her body.

ལུས་ལེན་ (lüü len) vi. to take a form/ body, to be born as ། མིའི་ལུས་ལེན་ཁག་པོ་རེད་ It is difficult to be born as a human.

ལུས་ཤུགས་ (lüüshuù) body strength.

ལུས་ཤེད་ (lüüsheè) sm. ལུས་ཤུགས་.

ལུས་ཤེས་ (lüüsheè) body consciousness.

ལུས་བཤེར་ (lüüsher) searching/ frisking the body; va.—གཏོང་; —བྱེད་ to search/ frisk ། བཙོན་འཇུག་མ་བྱས་གོང་བཙོན་པ་ལུས་བཤེར་གཏོང་གི་ཡོད་པ་རེད་ Before putting (them) in prison they searched the prisoners.

ལུས་སེམས་ (lüüsem) body and mind, physical and mental.

ལུས་སེམས་ཆགས་རྟེན་ (lüüsem cāgden) person (or place) to whom one is attached ། རང་གི་ལུས་སེམས་ཆགས་པའི་གྲོགས་མོ་དེ་དང་ཁ་བྲལ་དགོས་བྱུང་སོང་ I had to separate from my girl friend with whom I was very attached.

ལུས་སེམས་གཉིས་བདེ་ (lüüsem ñīide) physical and mental well being, healthy body and mind.

ལུས་སེམས་རྟེན་ས་ (lüüsem dēnsa) sm. ལུས་སེམས་གཉིས་བདེ་.

ལུས་སེམས་བདེ་ཐང་ (lüüsem dedaŋ) sm. ལུས་སེམས་གཉིས་བདེ་.

ལུས་སོ་ (lüüso) the physical body.

ལུས་སྲུང་ (lüüsuŋ) 1. body armor. 2. va. to protect/ guard one's body. 3. va. to be sexually faithful (for women) ། བུད་མེད་དེས་རང་ཉིད་ཀྱི་ཁྱོ་ག་ཕྱོགས་ལ་འགྲོ་དུས་ལུས་སྲུང་ཐུབ་མི་འདུག That woman can't remain faithful when her husband is away on trips.

ལུས་སྲོག (lüüsɔɔ̀) life ། ཁོང་གིས་རྒྱལ་ཁབ་ཀྱི་དོན་དུ་ལུས་སྲོག་བློས་གཏོང་བྱས་པ་རེད་ He sacrificed his life for the nation.

ལུས་སྲོག་གི་ཐོབ་ཐང་ (lüüsɔɔ̀gi tōbdaŋ) right to life.

ལུས་སྲོག་རྒྱུ་གསུམ་ (lüüsɔɔ gyusum) the three: body,

life and property.

ལུས་སྲོག་འཕངས་མེད་ (lüüsɔɔ pāŋmeè) risking one's life for another, disregarding one's safety ¶ཁོང་གིས་ལུས་སྲོག་འཕངས་མེད་བྱས་ནས་དམག་སར་ཕྱིན་པ་རེད་ Disregarding his own safety, he went to the battle.

ལུས་སྲོག་བློས་གཏོང་ (lüüsɔɔ lōōdoŋ) sacrificing one's life for another; va.—བྱེད་ ¶ཁོང་གིས་རྒྱལ་ཁབ་ཀྱི་ཆེད་དུ་ལུས་སྲོག་བློས་གཏོང་བྱས་པ་རེད་ He sacrificed his life on behalf of the nation.

ལུས་སྲོག་འཛེམས་མེད་ (lüüsɔɔ dzemmeè) sm. ལུས་སྲོག་འཕངས་མེད་.

ལུས་སྲོག་ལོངས་སྤྱོད་ (lüüsɔɔ lonjöö) shung. life and property.

ལུས་གསོ་ (lüüso) restoring health, physical therapy; convalescence, recuperation, va.—རྒྱག; —བྱེད་ to convalesce, to recuperate.

ལུས་གསོ་ཁང་ (lüüsɔɔgaŋ) sanitorium, rest home.

ལུས་ཧྲི་ (lüühri) ch. lawyer.

ལུས་ཧྲེ་ (lüühre) Port Arthur.

ལེ་ (le)1. sm. ལེ་བར་. 2. sm. ལེ་ལག.

ལེ་ཁག (legaà) 1. sm. ལེ་ཚན་. 2. blaming, reproaching; va.—དཀྲི་; —འཁྲིད་ to blame ¶ང་ལ་ཀུན་མའི་ལེ་ཁག་དཀྲིས་བྱུང་ I got blamed for stealing.

ལེ་ཁག་མེད་པ་ (legaà meèba) blameless ¶ལས་ཀ་འདིའི་སྐོར་ལ་ཁོང་ལ་ལེ་ཁག་མེད་པ་རེད་ He is blameless concerning this work.

ལེ་འགོན་ (legön) 1. sm. ལེ་ཁག. 2. error, mistakes ¶ཁོང་གིས་ལས་ཀ་བྱེད་པའི་རིང་ལེ་འགོན་གང་ཡང་བྱུང་མེད་པ་རེད་ When he was working, he didn't make any mistakes.

ལེ་འཁྲི་ (le trī) 1. vi. to be blamed ¶ཁོང་ལ་ཀུན་མའི་ལེ་འཁྲི་བྱུང་བཞག He got blamed for stealing. 2. vi. to be involved in a court case ¶ཁྲིམས་ཁང་ནས་གྱོད་དོན་འདིའི་སྐོར་ལེ་འཁྲི་ཡོད་པ་ཚང་མ་བསྐོངས་འདུག The court summoned all those involved in this case.

ལེ་འགྲིག (ledrig) settling via mediation/ arbitration; va. ལེ་འགྲིག; —བྱེད་ ¶གྱོད་གཞི་དེ་ཁྲིམས་སར་ཁུར་མ་དགོས་པར་བར་འདུམ་བཏང་ནས་ལེ་འགྲིགས་བཞག That case didn't have to go to court as it was settled via mediation.

ལེ་འགྲིག་པོ་ (le drigbu) sm. གྲ་འགྲིག་པོ་.

ལེ་བཙན་ (legɛn) 1. red color. 2. red silk. 3. liver. 4. a type of jaundice.

ལེ་བཙན་རྒྱས་པ་ (legɛn gyɛ̀ɛba) a liver disease in Tibetan medicine.

ལེ་ཅན་ (lejɛn) shung. sm. ལེ་ཐོགས་.

ལེ་ཆིའུ་ (leciwu) ch. softball.

ལེ་ཉིན་ (leñin) Lenin.

ལེ་ཉིན་གི་རད་ (leñin gerad) Leningrad.

ལེ་ཉིན་རིང་ལུགས་ (leñin rinluù) Leninism.

ལེ་ད་ (leda) ch. radar.

ལེ་ད་འཕྲུལ་ཆས་ (leda trũũjɛɛ̀) radar equipment.

ལེ་ཏར་ (ledar) eng. cigarette lighter.

ལེ་ཐོ་ (ledo) calendar.

ལེ་ཐོག (ledɔɔ̀) sm. ལེ་ཐོགས་.

ལེ་ཐོགས་ (ledɔɔ) 1. vi. to be involved with ¶དེ་རིང་གི་ལས་དོན་དེའི་ནང་ང་ལེ་ཐོགས་མེད་ I was not involved in that affair today. 2. person involved in sth. ¶ཆོས་སྲིད་ཁོངས་ནས་ལེ་ཐོགས་དོ་དམ་གཟུང་འཆར་ཡོད་པ་རེད་ There was a plan to arrest the monk and lay officials who were involved (in the affair). 3. vi. to make a mistake/ error ¶དུས་འགྱངས་ལེ་ཐོགས་ Not making the error of delaying.

ལེ་ཐོགས་གྲས་ (ledɔɔ trɛ̀ɛ̀) those involved (those people/ offices).

ལེ་བདའ་ (leda) blaming/ criticizing one's mistakes; va.—བྱེད་.

ལེ་འདོགས་ (le dɔɔ) 1. va. to use an excuse ¶ཁོས་སྙན་མཆེད་ན་བར་ལེ་བཏགས་ནས་ལས་ཁུངས་ལ་མ་ཡོང་བ་རེད་ He used as an excuse for not coming to the office that his relative was sick. 2. va. to blame ¶ཁོང་གིས་ལས་ཀ་ཡག་པོ་བྱས་ཀྱང་མི་གཞན་གྱིས་ཁོང་ལ་ལེ་འདོགས་ཀྱི་ཡོད་པ་རེད་ Even though he did the work well, others are blaming him.

ལེ་སྣ་ (lena) shung. a type of woolen material.

ལེ་པ་ནོན་ (lebanön) Lebanon.

ལེ་བར་ (lewar) a "li" — a tradition Chinese unit of distance equal to about 0.5 kilometers ¶ལེ་བར་ཉིས་ཁྲི་ལྔ་སྟོང་གི་རྒྱང་བསྐྱོད་ The "Long March" of 25,000 li.

ལེ་དབར་ (lewar) sm. ལེ་བར་.

ལེ་དབར་ཁྲི་ལྡན་ (lewar tridɛn) very long/ far.

ལེ་བྷ་ནོན་ (lebhanön) Lebanon.

ལེ་ཚན་ (ledzɛn) section, chapter, part; va.—སྒྲིག to arrange the sections/ parts/ chapters ¶དེབ་འདི་ལ་ལེ་ཚན་གསུམ་ཡོད་པ་རེད་ This book has three chapters.

ལེ་ལག (lelaà) part, branch; va.—ཕྲལ་ to take apart.

ལེ་ལན་ (lelɛn) 1. revenging; va.—སློག to revenge. 2. wrongdoings, mistakes, errors; vi.—ཐོག to suffer the bad results of one's past wrongdoings/ mistakes.

ལེ་ལོ་ (lelo) laziness; va.—བྱེད་ to be lazy in work, to act in lazy manner.

ལེ་ལོ་ཅན་ (lelojɛn) lazy.

ལེ་ལོ་ནར་འགྱངས་ (lelo nargyaŋ) lazy and procrastinating, lazy and delaying.

ལེ་ལོ་བག་གཡེང་ (lelo pagyeŋ) lazy and not diligent.

ལེ་ཤོར་ (leshɔr) sm. འབྲས་ཤོར་.

ལེ་སུ་ཐོག་ལ་ (lesu tōgba) shung. whoever is involved.

ལེ་སེ་ (lese) okay, yes.

ལེའུ་ཚན་ (leudzɛn) sm. ལེ་ཚན་.

ལེགས་ (leg) 1. abbr. of ལེགས་པོ་. 2. better ¶ད་ཕྱིན་ན་ལེགས་ If (we) go now it is better.

ལེགས་སྐྱེས་ (leggyeè) 1. award, tribute, medal ¶ཁོང་གིས་ལས་ཀ་ཡག་པོ་བྱས་ཙང་གཞུང་ནས་ལེགས་སྐྱེས་གནང་བ་རེད་ Because he did good work the government gave him an award. 2. contributing effort/ work; va.—འབུལ་ ¶ཟ་ཁང་གོང་འཕེལ་གཏོང་ཆེད་རང་ཉིད་ནས་ནུས་ཤུགས་ལེགས་སྐྱེས་འབུལ་གྱི་ཡིན་ I will do good work to improve the hotel. 3. gift, present ¶ངའི་གྲོགས་པོ་སླེབས་འདུག་པས་ལེགས་སྐྱེས་སྤྲོད་པར་ཕྱིན་པ་ཡིན་ Because my friend arrived, I went to give him a gift.

ལེགས་སྐྱེས་གཟེངས་རྟགས་ (leggyeè sendaà) the championship or medal contest/ competition.

ལེགས་འགྱུར་ (leggyur) sm. ལེགས་བཅོས་.

ལེགས་གྲས་ (legdrɛɛ̀) first class (e.g. in an airplane or train).

ལེགས་འགྲུབ་ (legdrub) sm. ལེགས་བསྒྲུབས་.

ལེགས་སྒྲིག (legdrig) 1. coordinating/ ordering/ arranging well; va.—བྱེད་ ¶ལས་ཀའི་གོ་རིམ་ལེགས་སྒྲིག་བྱས་ཙང་ལས་ཕྱོད་ཆེན་པོ་བྱུང་བ་རེད་ Because he arranged the work stages well, the work was very productive. 2. rectifying, reforming; va.—བྱེད་ ¶བཟོ་གྲྭའི་སྒྲིག་ལམ་ལེགས་སྒྲིག་བྱས་ཙང་ཐོན་ཚད་མཐོ་རུ་ཕྱིན་པ་རེད་ Because they rectified the factory's discipline, production increased.

ལེགས་སྒྲིག་དག་ཐེར་ (legdrig tagder) rectifying; va.—བྱེད་.

ལེགས་བསྒྲུབས་ (legdrub) successfully accomplishing/ achieving/ completing; vi.—ཟིན་; —བྱུང་ to complete successfully ¶འདི་ལོ་ཁང་པའི་འཛུགས་སྐྲུན་ལེགས་སྒྲུབ་བྱུང་བ་རེད་ This year building construction was successfully completed.

ལེགས་བརྒྱ་སྐོར་གཅིག (leggya gɔ̄ɔ̄jig) able to accomplish many good things with one deed.

ལེགས་བཅོས་ (legjöö) correcting, improving, rectifying, reforming; va.—བྱེད་; —གཏོང་; —འགྲོ་ ¶ཁྱབ་འགྲེམས་སྟངས་ལེགས་བཅོས་བྱས་སོང་ (They) improved the manner of distribution.

ལེགས་བཅོས་པ་ (legjööba) reformist, reformer.

ལེགས་བཅོས་ཕྱོགས་ཁག (legjöö cɔ̄ɔ̄gaà) reformist clique/ bloc.

ལེགས་བཅོས་རིང་ལུགས་ (legjöö rinluù) reformism.

ལེགས་ཆ་ (legja) good qualities, good points, goodness; va.—སྡུར་ to compare the good qualities of several people ། བོད་རིགས་ཀྱི་ལེགས་ཆ་ The good qualities of the Tibetan race.

ལེགས་ཚང་ (legjaŋ) ཚང་ offered as congratulations; va.—བཀུག; —འབུལ་.

ལེགས་བརྗོད་ (legjöö) 1. saying sth. well. 2. maxim, proverb, saying.

ལེགས་ཉེས་ (legñeè) good or bad, right or wrong; va.—བྱེད་ to distinguish/ discern good from bad or right from wrong; va.—ལྟ་; —འབྱེད་ to differentiate/ distinguish right from wrong.

ལེགས་ཉེས་རྒྱལ་ཕམ་ (legñeè gyɛɛpam) whether sth. will be successful or not or good or bad, whether one will win or lose ། ལེགས་ཉེས་རྒྱལ་ཁ་ཕམ་ག་འདྲ་ཡོང་གི་ཡོད་ཀྱང་འགྲན་སྡུར་འདིའི་ནང་ཞུགས་ཀྱི་ཡིན་ Whether I will win or lose I will participate in the competition.

ལེགས་ཉེས་སྣངས་འཛིན་ (legñeè də̄ŋdzin) observing the merits and demerits and coming to a decision ། ལས་ཀ་འདི་གལ་ཆེན་པོ་ཡིན་ཙང་ལེགས་ཉེས་སྣངས་འཛིན་ཡག་པོ་བྱ་དགོས་པ་རེད་ Because this matter is very important, (you) should observe the merits and demerits and make a good decision.

ལེགས་ཉེས་ཐོབ་ཤོར་ (legñeè tōbshɔɔ) sm. ལེགས་ཉེས་རྒྱལ་ཕམ་.

ལེགས་རྟོག (legdɔɔ) 1. understanding well; va.—བྱེད་. 2. investigating thoroughly/ well; va.—བྱེད་.

ལེགས་ཐོག་ལེགས་འཚོལ་ (legdɔɔ legdzöö) always seeking to improve; va.—བྱེད་.

ལེགས་དར་ (legdar) ceremonial scarf given as congratulations/ recognition/ tribute.

ལེགས་འདུམ་ཞུ་ (legdum shu) shung. to mediate.

ལེགས་འདེམས་ (legdem) selecting/ choosing the best; va.—བྱེད་.

ལེགས་ལྡན་ (legdɛn) 1. good, excellent. 2. man's name.

ལེགས་གནས་སྙམ་ (legnɛɛ̀ ñām) I think it will be good ། དེ་ལྟར་གནང་ན་ལེགས་གནས་སྙམ་ If you do like that, I think it will be good.

ལེགས་པར་འགྲོ་ (legbar dro) va. to go well/ safely.

ལེགས་པར་འོང་ (legbar oŋ) va. to arrive safely.

ལེགས་པོ་ (legbo) good, well ། ཁང་པ་འདི་ལེགས་པོ་འདུག This house is good.

ལེགས་སྤེལ་ (legbel) 1. spreading/ advancing/ increasing sth. good; va.—གཏོང་ ། ལམ་ལུགས་བཟང་པ་དེ་ལེགས་སྤེལ་བྱེད་དགོས་ We have to spread (advance) that good system.

ལེགས་སྤེལ་སྐྱོན་འདོན་ (legbel gyöndön) increasing/ advancing the good and revealing the faults/ errors.

ལེགས་སྤེལ་ཉེས་འགོག (legbel ñengɔɔ) increasing/ advancing the good and blocking the bad.

ལེགས་སྤེལ་ཞེན་བཅོས་ (legbel shɛnjöö) sm. ལེགས་སྤེལ་ཉེས་འགོག.

ལེགས་སྤྱད་ (legjɛɛ̀) virtuous/ good deeds.

ལེགས་ཕྱོགས་ཅི་འགྲིག (legjɔɔ̀ jindrig) shung. doing everything possible so that things will turn out for the better.

ལེགས་བྱས་ (legjɛɛ̀) virtuous deeds.

ལེགས་འབུལ་ (legbüü) gift/ award thanking or congratulating sb. for sth.

ལེགས་སྦྱར་ (legjaa) h. of གདམ་བཤད་.

ལེགས་སྦྱར་སྐད་ (legjar gɛ̄ɛ̀) Sanskrit language.

ལེགས་སྨོས་ཞིབ་ལས་ (legmöö̀ shiblɛɛ̀) intensive cultivation.

ལེགས་སྨོན་ (legmön) praying for good things to happen; va.—ཞུ་; —རྒྱག.

ལེགས་བཙའ་ལེགས་གསོ་ (legdza legso) giving birth to good children and raising them well.

ལེགས་ཚང་ (legdzaŋ) complete with regard to good qualities.

ལེགས་ཚུལ་ (legdzüü) the good way/ manner ། སྤྱོད་ལམ་ལེགས་ཚུལ་ Good behavior.

ལེགས་ཚོགས་ (legdzɔɔ̀) 1. combination of all good things. 2. good merit.

ལེགས་ཞན་ (legshɛn) good and bad; quality ། འཕྲུལ་ཆས་འདི་ལེགས་ཞན་ག་འདྲ་འདུག What is the quality of that machine?

ལེགས་ཤེར་ (legsher) sm. ལེགས་ཞན་.

ལེགས་བཞག་ཉེས་དོར་ (legshaà ñeèdɔɔ) leave the good and throw out the bad (political slogan).

ལེགས་འོང་ (legoŋ) a disciple of the Buddha.

ལེགས་བཤད་ (legshɛɛ̀) 1. maxim, aphorism. 2. correct speech.

ལེགས་སུ་གཏོང་ (legsu dōŋ) va. to improve ། གཞུང་གིས་སློབ་གྲྭ་ཚང་མ་ལེགས་སུ་བཏང་བ་རེད་ The government improved all the schools.

ལེགས་སོ་ (legso) 1. vi. to go well. 2. a cry expressing cheers/ applause; va.—བརྗོད་ to cheer, to applaud. 3. thanks ། ལེགས་སོའི་ལག་རྟགས་སྤྲད་སོང་ (They) gave him a gift of thanks.

ལེགས་སྲུང་འཛིན་ (legsuŋ dzin) va. to conserve.

ལེགས་སློབ་ཉེས་བཅོས་ (leglob ñeèjöö) shung. giving good advise and correcting mistakes/ errors.

ལེགས་གསོ་ (legso) repairing, restoring; va.—བྱེད་ to repair/ restore ། ཁང་པ་རྙིང་པ་དེ་ལེགས་གསོ་བྱས་པ་རེད་ They repaired the old house.

ལེགས་གསོལ་ (leg söö) 1. va. to report well/ correctly to higher authorities. 2. va. to repay sb.'s kindness fully.

ལེགས་བསླབས་ཉེས་བཅོས་ (legləb ñeèjöö) learning what is good and correcting one's evil ways, turning over a new leaf.

ལེང་བགྱིད་ (leŋ gyii) sm. མངོན་དུ་འགྱུར་.

ལེན་: p. བླངས་; f. བླང་; imp. ལོངས་ (len) va. to take, to receive, to collect ། ངའི་ལག་ནས་བླངས་སོང་ (He) took it from my hand.

ལེན་ (len) ch. a company-size military unit (containing about 100 troops) ། སྔོན་སྐྱོད་ལེན་ Advance strike company.

ལེན་དེབ་བསྡུ་གཞུང་ (lendeb dushuŋ) shung. account book for collecting lease fees.

ལེན་པོ་ (lembo) suitable, appropriate, becoming ། ཚོས་གཞི་དེ་ཁྱེད་རང་ལ་ལེན་པོ་འདུག This color is suitable for you.

ལེན་མི་སུའུ་ (lenmesu) ch. streptomycin.

ལེན་འཛིན་ (lendzin) a receipt for receiving sth.

ལེན་འོས་ (lenwöö) acceptable ། གཞན་གྱི་བཤད་པའི་ནང་ནས་བསླབ་བྱ་ལེན་འོས་འདུག་ན་ལེན་དགོས་ If there is acceptable advice in sb. else's comments, you should accept it.

ལེན་ཤེས་སྤྲོད་ཤེས་ (lensheè drööshee) taking a loan and repaying it on time.

ལེན་ཧོ་གོ་ (lenhogo) ch. the United Nations.

ལེན་ཧོ་པད་ཚལ་ (lenho bɛɛ̀dzɛɛ) ch. cabbage.

ལེབ་ (leb) 1. abbr. of ལེབ་ལེབ་. 2. all, entire, whole. 3. a basis for imposing taxes.

ལེབ་ཅ་ (lenja) Lepcha (an indigenous ethnic group in Sikkim).

ལེབ་གཅིག (lebjii) all over ། ཁང་པ་དེ་ལ་ཚོན་དཀར་པོ་ལེབ་གཅིག་ལ་བཏང་འདུག That house is painted white all over.

ལེབ་སྒྱེ་ (lebgye) large saddle bag.

ལེབ་ངོས་ (lenŋöö̀) flat surface.

ལེབ་ངོས་མཚོན་པའི་རི་མོ་ (lebŋöö̀ tsönbɛ remo) a one dimensional figure/ diagram.

ལེབ་ལྕུག (lebjuù) ingot ། གསེར་ལེབ་ལྕུག Gold ingot.

ལེབ་དེ་ (lebde) all, entire, whole.

ལེབ་སྟོངས་ (len dōŋ) vi. to become completely extinct ། ཡུལ་འདི་ར་ས་ཡོམ་བརྒྱབ་ནས་ཁྱིམ་ཚང་ལེབ་སྟོངས་བྱུང་བཞག The region had an earthquake and all the households became extinct.

ལེབ་འདུར་བྱེད་ (lebdur cee) shung. va. to show no favoritism, to make no exceptions.

ལེབ་རྡུང་ལེབ་གསོད་ (lebduŋ lebsöö) killing and attacking indiscriminately.

ལེབ་པ་ (lebba) sm. ལེབ་ལེབ་.

ལེབ་པོ་ (lebbo) sm. ལེབ་ལེབ་.

ལེབ་འཕྱག (lebjaà) sweeping away, annihilating; va.—བྱེད་; —གཏོང་ ། ལུང་པའི་ནང་གི་ཉལ་ཐ་འཐེན་མཁན་ཚང་མ་ལེབ་ཕྱག་བྱས་འདུག They swept away all the opium addicts in the country. ¶ སྒོ་ར་ནང་གི་གད་སྙིགས་ལེབ་འཕྱག་བྱ་དགོས་ You have to sweep away all the garbage in the courtyard.

ལེབ་འབྱར་ (lebjaa) shoetree.

ལེབ་སྦྱོར་ (lebjɔɔ) sm. ལེབ་འབྱར་.

ལེབ་མོ་ (lebmo) sm. ལེབ་ལེབ་.

ལེབ་མོ་བཙོས་ (lebmo jöö) sm. ལེབ་ལེབ་བཟོ་.

ལེབ་རྩིས་ (lendzii) counting everything, accounting for everything; va.—རྒྱག.

ལེབ་གཞོག (lebshɔɔ̀) slicing; va.—རྒྱག ¶ ཞོག་ཁོག་མ་རྔོས་གོང་ལེབ་གཞོག་རྒྱག་དགོས་ One should cut the potatoes into slices before frying.

ལེབ་ལེབ་ (lebleè) flat; va.—བཟོ་ to flatten, to make flat, to level.

ལེབ་ཤིང་ (lebshiŋ) a flat board, a plank.

ལེབ་བཤུས་ (lebshüü) shung. va. to copy exactly.

ལེམ་ཐང་ (lemdaŋ) a type of silk shawl.

ལེའུ་ (liwu) chapter (of a book), act (in a play).

ལེའུ་ཐོ་ (lēwudo) sm. ལེ་ཐོ་.

ལེའུ་ལྷན་ (lewulön) an extra chapter added to a text.

ལེའུ་ཚེ་ (lewudze) a form/ table.

ལེའོ་ཉིང་ཞིང་ཆེན་ (leoñiŋ shiŋjen) Liaoning Province.

ལེའན་ (lean) sm. ལེན་.

ལེའི་པེས་ཞི་ (lɛbishi) Leipzig.

ལོ་ (lo) 1. year, age ¶ ལོ་བཞི་ Four years. 2. vi. to meet a requirement/ standard, to be fit/ suitable for, to be satisfied with sth.'s quality ¶ འདི་ཟ་ལོ་གི་མ་རེད་ This is not fit for consumption. ¶ ཁོང་རང་ལས་ཀ་ར་དྭངས་རང་པོ་སོང་ཙང་གཞན་གྱིས་བྱས་པ་ལས་བློ་པོར་ལོ་གི་མེད་པ་རེད་ Because he does meticulous work, he isn't easily satisfied with the work of others.3. vi. to like ¶ ཁ་སང་ངས་ཁྱེད་རང་ལ་མིག་བསྟན་པའི་བུ་མོ་དེ་ལོ་སོང་ངམ་ Did you like the girl I pointed out to you the other day. 4. crop ¶ ད་ལོ་ལོ་ཡག་པོ་འདུག This year the crops are good.

ལོ་ཀེག (logeg) sm. སྐེག.

ལོ་ཀུན་ (logün) saying one is younger than one actually is; va.—རྒྱག ¶ ཁོང་སློབ་གྲྭ་ལ་འཛུལ་སྐབས་ལོ་ཀུན་ལོ་གསུམ་བརྒྱབ་བཤད་ When he entered he school, he said that he was three years younger than he was.

ལོ་སྐེག (logeg) sm. སྐེག.

ལོ་སྐོར་བཅུ་གཉིས་ (logɔɔ jūñii) the cycle of twelve animal years.

ལོ་སྒྲ་རྒྱས་ (lo gyāgyɛɛ̀) sm. ལོ་ལེགས་བྱུང་.

ལོ་སྒྲིན་ (logyin) giving sth. in place of crops.

ལོ་སྒྱུར་ཐང་ཤིང་ (logyur tōŋshiŋ) larch tree.

ལོ་སྐྱེག (logyeg) sm. སྐེག.

ལོ་སྐྱེད་ (logyeè) yearly interest.

ལོ་སྐྱེས་ (logyeè) yearly growth (usu. for children).

ལོ་སྐྲ་ (lodra) custom of not cutting a child's hair until the age of one.

ལོ་ཁམས་ (logam) year and element (the sixty cycle in the Tibetan calendar).

ལོ་ཁམས་བརྩི་སྟངས་ (logam dzīdaŋ) astrological calculations to prepare the calendar.

ལོ་ཁྱུད་འཁོར་ (lokyūūgɔɔ) complete/ full year ¶ ལོ་ཁྱུད་འཁོར་གཅིག་རིང་ང་ཡུལ་དེར་བསྡད་པ་ཡིན་ I lived here for one complete year.

ལོ་ཁྲལ་ (lodrɛɛ) yearly/ annual tax.

ལོ་ཁྲི་ཕྲག་དུ་བརྟན་པར་ཤོག (lo drīdraàdu dēmbar shō) "long live" ¶ མི་དམངས་དམག་འཁྲུག་གི་རྒྱལ་ཁ་ལོ་ཁྲི་ཕྲག་དུ་བརྟན་པར་ཤོག Long live the victory of the people's war! [Lit. May (he/ it) last for ten thousands of years].

ལོ་ཁྲིམས་ (lodrim) laws pertaining to the protection of crops.

ལོ་འཁོར་ (logɔɔ) 1. annual, yearly, anniversary ¶ ལོ་འཁོར་དུས་ཆེན་ An annual festival. 2. vi. to pass (for years), to be a certain number of years since sth. took place ¶ ང་ཚོ་འདིར་འབྱོར་ནས་ལོ་གསུམ་འཁོར་གྱི་ཡོད་པ་རེད་ Three years have passed since we arrived here. ¶ ལོ་གསུམ་འཁོར་བའི་དྲན་གསོ་ The third anniversary.

ལོ་འཁོར་སྔོན་རྩིས་ (logɔɔ ŋōndzii) annual budget or forecast (for the following year); va.—རྒྱག.

ལོ་འཁོར་བཅུ་སྐྱེད་ (logɔɔ jūgyeè) shung. twenty percent interest a year.

ལོ་འཁོར་འཆར་གཞི་ (logɔɔ cārshi) annual plan, plan for the year.

ལོ་འཁོར་མ་ (lo kɔ̄ɔma) an entire year, the whole year.

ལོ་འཁོར་མོ་ (lo kɔ̄ɔmo) an entire year, the whole year.

ལོ་འཁོར་མོ་ཡུག་དུ་ (logɔɔmo yugdu) throughout the whole year ¶ ལུང་པ་འདིར་ལོ་འཁོར་མོ་ཡུག་དུ་ཡུལ་སྐོར་སྐྱོ་འཆམ་པ་ཡོང་གི་ཡོད་པ་རེད་ Tourists come to this area throughout year.

ལོ་གོང་མ་ (lo koŋma) the previous year.

ལོ་གོའི་མོག་མོག (logö momoò) steamed dough dumplings that do not have stuffings.

ལོ་གྲངས་ (lodraŋ) number of years, age ¶ ཕྲུ་གུ་འདི་སློབ་གྲྭར་ལོ་གྲངས་ལ་ག་ཚོད་བསྡད་པ་རེད་ How many years did the child stay in school?

ལོ་གླ་ (lola) annual salary; va.—རྒྱག.

ལོ་བགྲེས་ (lodreè) sm. ལོ་རྒས་.

ལོ་འགོ་ (longo) the beginning or early part of a year.

ལོ་རྒན་གཞོན་ (lo gɛnshön) young and old, youth and old age.

ལོ་རྒས་ (lo gɛɛ̀) va. to age, to get old ¶ ཁོང་ལོ་རྒས་ནས་མིག་ཡག་པོ་མི་འདུག He has gotten old and his eyesight is poor.

ལོ་རྒྱགས་ (logyaà) 1. ཚམ་པ་ that is enough for one year. 2. the yearly provision of food.

ལོ་རྒྱུན་ (logyün) years ¶ ཁོང་བོད་ལ་ལོ་རྒྱུན་རིང་མིན་བསྡད་འདུག He lived in Tibet for a number of years.

ལོ་རྒྱུན་ཆགས་ (logyünjaà) sm. ལོ་ལྟར་.

ལོ་རྒྱུན་མང་བརྒྱུད་ (logyün maŋgyüù) after a continuous/ long period ¶ ཕྱི་རྒྱལ་དུ་གནས་སྡོད་ལོ་རྒྱུན་མང་བརྒྱུད་ཡུལ་དེའི་སྐད་ཡིག་ཀུང་ཤེས་བྱུང་ Having lived abroad for a long time he learned the local written and spoken language.

ལོ་རྒྱུད་རིག་པ་ (logyüü rigbə) history, the study of history.

ལོ་རྒྱུས་ (lugyüü) history.

ལོ་རྒྱུས་ཀྱི་འཁོར་ལོ་ (lugyüügi kɔ̄ɔlo) the wheel of history ¶ ལོ་རྒྱུས་ཀྱི་འཁོར་ལོ་མདུན་དུ་སྐྱོད་པར་སུས་ཀྱང་བཀག་ཐབས་མེད་ Nobody can stop the wheel of history.

ལོ་རྒྱུས་ཀྱི་འཁོར་ལོ་ལྡོག་དུ་གཏོང་ (lugyüügi kɔ̄ɔlo dɔgdu dōŋ) sm. ལོ་རྒྱུས་ཀྱི་འཁོར་ལོ་ཕྱིར་སློར་.

ལོ་རྒྱུས་ཀྱི་འཁོར་ལོ་ཕྱིར་སློར་ (lugyüügi kɔ̄ɔlo cīgɔɔ) turning back the wheel of history.

ལོ་རྒྱུས་ཀྱི་གད་སྙིགས་ཕུང་པོ་ (lugyüügi kɛ̄ñii pūŋbo) the garbage heap of history.

ལོ་རྒྱུས་ཀྱི་དགེ་མཚན་ (lugyüügi gedze) historical value/ merit.

ལོ་རྒྱུས་ཀྱི་འགྲོ་ཕྱོགས་ (lugyüügi drojɔɔ̀) historical trend/ direction.

ལོ་རྒྱུས་ཀྱི་རྒྱུ་ཆ་ (lugyüügi gyuja) historical materials.

ལོ་རྒྱུས་ཀྱི་དངོས་མང་བཤམས་སྟོན་ཁང་ (lugyüügi ŋöömaŋ shāmdön) historical museum.

ལོ་རྒྱུས་ཀྱི་དངོས་གཙོ་སྨྲ་བ་ (lugyüügi ŋöödzo māwa) historical materialism.

ལོ་རྒྱུས་ཀྱི་དངོས་གཙོའི་རིང་ལུགས་ (lugyüügi ŋöödzö riŋluù) historical materialism.

ལོ་རྒྱུས་ཀྱི་ཆ་གདོགས་ (lugyüügi cādɔɔ̀) the domain/ sphere of history.

ལོ་རྒྱུས་ཀྱི་རྒྱུན་རིང་པོ་ (lugyüügi gyün riŋbu) the long flow of history.

ལོ་རྒྱུས་ཀྱི་རྗེས་ཤུལ་ (lugyüügi jeèshüü) historical trace/ site/ relic.

ལོ་རྒྱུས་ཀྱི་སྙན་རྩོམ་ (lugyüügi ñēndzom) epic (in literature).

ལོ་རྒྱུས་ཀྱི་ལྟ་བ་ (lugyüügi dāwa) sm. ལོ་རྒྱུས་ཀྱི་ལྟ་ཚུལ་.

ལོ་རྒྱུས་ཀྱི་ལྟ་ཚུལ་ (lugyüügi dədzüü) historical point of view.

ལོ་རྒྱུས་ཀྱི་དུས་རིམ་ (lugyüügi tüürim) historical stage/ period.

ལོ་རྒྱུས་ཀྱི་དོན་དངོས་ (lugyüügi tönŋöö) historical fact.

ལོ་རྒྱུས་ཀྱི་དོན་སྙིང་ (lugyüügi tönñiŋ) historical significance/ importance.

ལོ་རྒྱུས་ཀྱི་གནས་ཚུལ་ (lugyüügi nɛ̄ɛ̀dzüü) historical situation, historical context/ background, historical information.

ལོ་རྒྱུས་ཀྱི་དཔྱད་ཡིག (lugyüügi jēèyiì) sm. ལོ་རྒྱུས་ཀྱི་ཡིག་རིགས་.

ལོ་རྒྱུས་ཀྱི་འཕེལ་ཕྱོགས་ (lugyüügi pēljɔɔ̀) historical trend.

ལོ་རྒྱུས་ཀྱི་འཕེལ་རིམ་ (lugyüügi pēlrim) the course of history.

ལོ་རྒྱུས་ཀྱི་བརྩམས་སྒྲུང་རིང་པོ་ (lugyüügi dzāmdruŋ riŋbu) historical novel.

ལོ་རྒྱུས་ཀྱི་ཡིག་རིགས་ (lugyüügi yigriì) historical documents/ data/ reference materials.

ལོ་རྒྱུས་ཀྱི་ཟློས་གར་ (lugyüügi döögar) historical play.

ལོ་རྒྱུས་ཀྱི་རང་བཞིན་ (lugyüügi rəŋshin) historical, history.

ལོ་རྒྱུས་ཀྱི་རིན་ཐང་ (lugyüügi rindaŋ) sm. ལོ་རྒྱུས་ཀྱི་དགེ་མཚན་.

ལོ་རྒྱུས་ཀྱི་རླབས་རྒྱུན་ (lugyüügi lābgyün) tide of history, historical trend.

ལོ་རྒྱུས་ཀྱི་ལམ་བུ་ (lugyüügi ləmbu) historical path.

ལོ་རྒྱུས་ཀྱི་ལམ་ཚད་ (lugyüügi ləmdzɛɛ̀) historical course.

ལོ་རྒྱུས་ཀྱི་ལས་འགན་ (lugyüügi lɛngɛn) historical responsibility.

ལོ་རྒྱུས་ཀྱི་ཤུལ་བཞག (lugyüügi shüüshaà) historical heritage.

ལོ་རྒྱུས་ཀྱི་སེམས་གཙོའི་སྨྲ་བ་ (lugyüügi sēmdzö māwa) sm. ལོ་རྒྱུས་ཀྱི་སེམས་གཙོའི་རིང་ལུགས་.

ལོ་རྒྱུས་ཀྱི་སེམས་གཙོའི་རིང་ལུགས་ (lugyüügi sēmdzö riŋluù) historical idealism.

ལོ་རྒྱུས་སྒྲུན་ (lugyüü drün) va. to make history.

ལོ་རྒྱུས་བསྒྲུན་པ་པོ་ (lugyüü drünbabo) history makers.

ལོ་རྒྱུས་དངོས་མང་བཤམས་སྟོན་ཁང་ (lugyüü ŋöömaŋ shāmdöngaŋ) museum of history.

ལོ་རྒྱུས་ཅན་ (lugyüüjɛn) sm. ལོ་རྒྱུས་ཀྱི་རང་བཞིན་ཅན་.

ལོ་རྒྱུས་ཐོག་གི་དོན་རྐྱེན་ (lugyüütɔɔ̀gi töŋgyen) historical events.

ལོ་རྒྱུས་ཐོག་གི་སྲོལ་རྒྱུན་ (lugyüütɔɔ̀gi sōōgyün) historical tradition.

ལོ་རྒྱུས་ཐོག་ཐེངས་དང་པོ་ (lugyüütɔɔ̀ tēŋ taŋbo) unprecedented in history, first time in history.

ལོ་རྒྱུས་ཐོག་བྱུང་མ་མྱོང་བ་ (lugyüütɔɔ̀ cuŋ maŋoŋbə) unprecedented in history.

ལོ་རྒྱལ་དུས་རབས་ (lugyüü tüürəb) historical era ¶ ལོ་རྒྱུས་དུས་རབས་གསར་པ་ཞིག་འགོ་བཙུགས་པ་རེད་ A new historical era started.

ལོ་རྒྱུས་དེབ་ (lugyüü teb) one's personal file (ch. dangan).

ལོ་རྒྱུས་དེབ་ཐེར་ (lugyüü tebter) history book.

ལོ་རྒྱུས་དོན་སྟོང་རིང་ལུགས་ (lugyüü töndoŋ riŋluù) historical nihilism.

ལོ་རྒྱུས་མདོར་བསྡུས་ (lugyüü dordüü) brief historical summary.

ལོ་རྒྱུས་ལྡན་པ་ (lugyüü dɛmba) sm. ལོ་རྒྱུས་ཀྱི་རང་བཞིན་.

ལོ་རྒྱུས་སྡེ་ཚན་ (lugyüü dɛdzɛn) department of history.

ལོ་རྒྱུས་པ་ (lugyüübə) historian.

ལོ་རྒྱུས་དཔྱད་གཞིའི་ཡིག་རིགས་ (lugyüü jɛ̄ɛ̀shii yigriì) historical data/ records/ reference materials.

ལོ་རྒྱུས་ཕྱིར་འཐེན་ (lugyüü ciīden) going back in history.

ལོ་རྒྱུས་འཕེལ་རྒྱས་ (lugyüü pēlgyɛɛ̀) historical development ¶ དེ་ནི་ལོ་རྒྱུས་འཕེལ་རྒྱས་ཀྱི་འབྲས་བུ་ཞིག་རེད་ As for that, it is the result of historical development.

ལོ་རྒྱུས་སྨྲ་བ་ (lugyüü māwa) historian, those who tell history.

ལོ་རྒྱུས་སྨྲ་བའི་བྱེད་པོ་ (lugyüü māwɛ cēèbo) historian.

ལོ་རྒྱུས་མཚོན་བྱེད་སྙན་ངག (lugyüü tsönjeè ñɛnŋaà) historical epic.

ལོ་རྒྱུས་ཞིབ་འཇུག་ཁང་ (lugyüü shimjuùgaŋ) institute of history.

ལོ་རྒྱུས་ཟློས་གར་ (lugyüü döögar) sm. ལོ་རྒྱུས་ཀྱི་ཟློས་གར་.

ལོ་རྒྱུས་རིག་དངོས་ (lugyüü rigŋöö) historical relics.

ལོ་རྒྱུས་རིག་པ་ (lugyüü rigbə) historical science, study of history.

ལོ་རྒྱུས་རིག་པ་བ་ (lugyüü rigbəbə) historian, historiographer.

ལོ་རྒྱུས་རིང་པོ་ (lugyüü riŋbu) sm. ལོ་རྒྱུས་ཀྱི་ཆུ་རྒྱུན་རིང་པོ་.

ལོ་རྒྱུས་ལས་འདས་པ་ (lugyüülɛ dɛ̀ɛ̀ba) beyond history.

ལོ་རྒྱུས་གསལ་ཐོ་ (lugyüù sɛ̄ɛ̄do) personal file/ dossier (ch. dangan).

ལོ་སྒང་ཚང་གཅིག (lo gaŋdzaŋ jīg) one whole year.

ལོ་སྒོར་པད་ཚལ་ (logɔɔ bɛ̄ɛ̀dzɛɛ) ch. cabbage.

ལོ་བརྒྱད་དྲི་ཆུ་ (logyɛɛ̀ triju) urine of an eight year child (used in Tibetan medicine).

ལོ་བརྒྱའི་ཇུས་ཆེན་ (logyɛ cüüjen) a long range plan, a long term strategy [Lit. plan for one hundred years].

ལོ་ངན་ (loŋɛn) a year of disaster/ famine, etc.

ལོ་ངོ་ (loŋo) years of age.

ལོ་ལྔའི་འཆར་གཞི་ (loŋɛ cāāshi) five year plan.

ལོ་སྔོན་ (loŋön) before a certain year ¶ ༡༩༥༦ ལོ་སྔོན་ Before 1956.

ལོ་བཅུ་ཐོག་ལྔ་ (lo jūtɔɔ̄ ŋā) fields that are planted only every second year.

ལོ་ཅང་ (lojaŋ) one year old ཅང་.

ལོ་ཅང་ཁམ་པ་ (lojaŋ kāmba) sm. ལོ་ཅང་.

ལོ་ཆུ་ (loju) crops and rainfall ¶ ལོ་ཆུ་ལེགས་པ་ Good rainfall and crops.

ལོ་ཆུ་ལམ་ལྷོང་ (loju lamlhoŋ) having good crops (harvest) due to good rainfall.

ལོ་ཆུང་ (lojuŋ) 1. youth, youngster, young person, teenager. 2. a junior translator.

ལོ་ཆུང་སྒྲ་དཀར་ (lojuŋ drāgar) sm. ལོ་ཆུང་མགོ་དཀར་.

ལོ་ཆུང་གི་ཁྱིམ་ཚང་ (lojuŋgi kyīmdzaŋ) children's home.

ལོ་ཆུང་མགོ་དཀར་ (lojuŋ gogaa) young person with premature grey hair.

ལོ་ཆུང་རྒྱུ་ཉུང་ (lojuŋ gyuñuŋ) young and inexperienced.

ལོ་ཆུང་གདོང་ལེན་རུ་ཁག (lojuŋ doŋlen rugaà) young pioneers (youth group in China).

ལོ་ཆུང་གདོང་ལེན་རུ་མི་ (lojuŋ doŋlen rumi) a young pioneer member.

ལོ་ཆུང་ཕོ་བྲང་ (lojuŋ pōdraŋ) children's palace (for amusement).

ལོ་ཆུང་བྱིས་པ་ (lojuŋ ciìbə) child.

ལོ་ཆུང་སྨོན་འདྲིན་ (lojuŋ mōndrin) childhood friendship.

ལོ་ཆུན་ (lojün) arc. patches (for clothes).

ལོ་ཆེན་ (lojen) 1. senior translator. 2. old.

ལོ་མཆོད་ (locöö) ritual done one year after the death of a person.

ལོ་མཇུག (lonjuù) latter part of a year, the end of a year.

ལོ་མཇུག་བསྡོམས་རྩིས་ (lonjuù domdziì) end of year accounting; va.—རྒྱག.

ལོ་མཇུག་རྩིས་རྒྱག (lonjuù dziigyaà) end of year accounting; va.—རྒྱག.

ལོ་རྗེས་མ་ (lo jeèma) next year.

ལོ་མཉམ་ (loñam) of the same age ¶ ང་གཉིས་ལོ་མཉམ་རེད་ We two are the same age.

ལོ་སྙིང་ (loñiŋ) sm. ལོ་རྙགས་.

ལོ་སྙིང་སྐྱེལ་ (loñiŋ gyēē) vi. to pass the old year, to see off the old year.

ལོ་ཉེས་ (loñeè) bad harvest, year of poor harvest/ crop failure.

ལོ་ཏོག (lodoò) crop; va.—འདེབས་ to plant crops.

ལོ་ཏོག་འགྱེལ་ (lodoò gyee) vi. to fall over (of crop stalks).

ལོ་ཏོག་ཉལ་ (lodoò ñɛɛ) sm. ལོ་ཏོག་འགྱེལ་.

ལོ་ཏོག་འདེབས་སྐྱོང་ཞིབ་འཇུག་ཁང་ (lodoò debgyoŋ shimjuùgaŋ) farming research institute.

ལོ་གཏོར་ (lodɔɔ) a གཏོར་མ་ that is left for a whole year.

ལོ་རྟགས་ (lordaà) an animal year in the twelve year animal calendar system ¶ཁོའི་ལོ་རྟགས་རྟ་རེད་ His animal year (of birth) is horse.

ལོ་རྟགས་ཀྱི་ལོ་ (lordaàgi lo) sm. ལོ་རྟགས་.

ལོ་རྟགས་གསོལ་རས་ཞུ་ (lordaà sööreɛ shu) asking for the animal birth year of a prospective bride/ groom so that an astrologer can check whether it is compatible.

ལོ་ལྟར་ (lodar) yearly, every year.

ལོ་ལྟར་རེ་བཞིན་ (lodar reshin) sm. ལོ་ལྟར་.

ལོ་སྟུད་མར་ (lo dǖüma) sm. ལོ་བསྟུད་.

ལོ་སྟོང་ཚོ་གསར་པ་ (lo dōŋdzo sāāba) the new millennium.

ལོ་སྟོད་ (lodöö) the first half of the year.

ལོ་བསྟུད་ (lodüü) continuously one year after another.

ལོ་ཐང་ (lodaŋ) 1. the tribute given during an annual audience. 2. yearly grain tax. 3. yearly income.

ལོ་ཐུག (loduù) a kind of vegetable soup.

ལོ་ཐོ་ (lodo) sm. ལེ་ཐོ་.

ལོ་ཐོག (lodoò) sm. ལོ་ཏོག.

ལོ་ཐོག་ལོ་རྩིགས་ (lodɔɔ̀ lodziì) one year on top of another, in repeated years ¶ཡུལ་འདི་ར་ལོ་ཐོག་ལོ་བརྩེགས་ཀྱི་མུ་གེ་བྱུང་བ་རེད་ In that place they experienced famine one year on top of another.

ལོ་མཐོ་ཁ་ཁྱེར་ (lodo kā kyēr) abbr. of ལོ་ན་མཐོ་བ་ཁ་ཁྱེར་.

ལོ་འཐག་འཇོག (lodaà jɔɔ̀) va. to leave woven material unfinished on the loom at the end of the year.).

ལོ་དར་མ་ (lo tarma) adult in the prime of life.

ལོ་དུས་ (lodüü) 1. term, period, time set as a limit; vi.—ཐིམ་; —རྫོགས་ to expire, to finish, to terminate (e.g., a term of office) ¶མདོ་སྨད་སྤྱི་ཁྱབ་པའི་ལོ་དུས་རྫོགས་ (His) term as Governor General of Kham ended. 2. yearly ¶ལུང་པ་དེ་ར་ལོ་དུས་ཀྱི་ཚོང་འདུས་རེ་འཚོགས་གི་ཡོད་པ་རེད་ There is a yearly trade fair in that place.

ལོ་དུས་འཁོར་རྩིས་ (lodüü kɔ̄ɔdzii) shung. calculating the term of payments on loans.

ལོ་དུས་གྲངས་བཅད་ (lodüü traŋjɛɛ̀) shung. loans with a set period of years for repayment.

ལོ་དུས་རིམ་སྤྲོད་ (lodüü rimdröö) installment payments over a period of years.

ལོ་དེབ་ (loteb) yearbook, annual book/ volume ¶བསྡོམས་རྩིས་ལོ་དེབ་ Statistical yearbook.

ལོ་འདབ་ (lodəb) leaves and petals; vi.—རྒྱས་ to be fully grown, to be in full bloom (for flowering plants).

ལོ་སྡོང་མེ་འབྲས་བཞི་ (lodoŋ mendrɛɛ̀ shi) the four: leaf, trunk/ stem, flower and fruit.

ལོ་ན་ (lona) age; vi.—རྒས་ to age, to grow old.

ལོ་ན་ཆུང་བ་ (lona jūŋwa) young, younger.

ལོ་ན་སྡོང་སྐྱེལ་ (lona dōŋgyee) sm. ལོ་ཟླ་སྡོང་སྐྱེལ་.

ལོ་ན་མཐོ་བ་ཁ་འཁྱེར་ (lona tōwa kāgyee) using old age as an excuse (usu. to avoid work or to get a better share of sth.).

ལོ་ན་ཕྲ་བ་ (lona trāwa) sm. ལོ་ན་ཆུང་བ་.

ལོ་ན་འཚམས་པ་ (lona tsāmba) of the right/ suitable age ¶ང་ཚོའི་བུ་ལ་ལོ་ན་མཚམས་པའི་མནའ་མ་ཞིག་ལེན་གྱི་ཡིན་ We will get a bride of a suitable age for our son.

ལོ་ན་གཞོན་པ་ (lona shōmba) sm. ལོ་ན་ཆུང་བ་.

ལོ་ན་རན་པ་ (lona rɛmba) sm. ལོ་ན་འཚམས་པ་.

ལོ་ན་སོན་ (lona sōn) vi. to grow up.

ལོ་ནག (lonaà) 1. an astrologically determined bad/ unpropitious year ¶ལོ་ནག་ལ་ཆང་ས་རྒྱག་མི་རུང་ One should not get married in a bad year. 2. a year of crop failure/ famine, etc.

ལོ་ནད་སྣན་འབྱར་ (lonɛɛ̀ dēnjar) people who have been bedridden for years.

ལོ་ནས་ལོ་བསྟུད་ (lonɛ lodǖü) sm. ལོ་བསྟུད་.

ལོ་ནས་ལོ་བར་ (lonɛ lobar) from year to year.

ལོ་གནངས་ག་ཁྲལ་ (lonaŋ kadrɛɛ) shung. animal taxes paid every other year.

ལོ་གནངས་འཆར་ (lo nāŋjar) alternate years, every other year.

ལོ་པ་ (loba) 1. acceptable/ suitable in age ¶མི་འདི་ལོ་པ་མི་འདུག This man's age is not acceptable. 2. the year in which one is born ¶སྟག་ལོ་པ་ཡིན་ (I) was born in the year of the tiger.

ལོ་པཎ་ (lobɛn) abbr. translator and scholar.

ལོ་ཕུད་ (lobüü) barley planted in a small container before the Tibetan New Year to enable making an auspicious offering to the gods during the New Year of the first stalks that appear.

ལོ་ཕོགས་ (lobɔɔ̀) yearly/ annual salary.

ལོ་ཕྱག (lojaà) shung. annual/ yearly tribute or gift.

ལོ་ཕྱུགས་ (lojuù) abbr. agriculture and animal husbandry.

ལོ་ཕྱེད་ (lojee) half a year.

ལོ་ཕྲ་ (lodra) young people.

ལོ་འཕོ་ (lo pō) vi. to transition to a new year.

ལོ་བ་ (lowa) sm. ལོ་པ་, 1.

ལོ་བོགས་ (lobɔɔ̀) lease for one year.

ལོ་འབབས་ (lobəb) yearly/ annual yield.

ལོ་འབུལ་ (lobüü) an annual gift/ present/ tribute; va.—འབུལ་.

ལོ་འབྲས་ (londrɛɛ̀) general term for grains.

ལོ་མ་ (loma) leaf ¶ལོ་མ་ཆེ་རིགས་ཤིང་ Broad-leafed tree.

ལོ་མ་ཁབ་དབྱིབས་ཅན་ (loma kəbyibjɛn) needle leaf (conifer trees).

ལོ་མ་ཆེ་བའི་ལྗོན་ཤིང་ (loma cēwe jönshiŋ) broadleaf tree.

ལོ་མ་ཆེ་བའི་རྩྭ་ཡན་ (loma cēwɛ dzəyɛn) broadleaf grasses.

ལོ་མ་ཆེ་བའི་ཤིང་ནགས་ (loma cewɛ shīŋnaà) forest of broad-leaved trees.

ལོ་མ་ཉི་ཡ་ (lomañiyə) Romania.

ལོ་མ་ཕྲ་རིགས་ (loma trārii) needle-leaf trees, conifers ¶ལོ་མ་ཕྲ་རིགས་ཀྱི་ཤིང་ནགས་ A conifer forest.

ལོ་མ་མང་པོ་ (loma maŋbo) talking a lot but saying very little [Lit. having many leaves].

ལོ་མ་ཟགས་ས་རྩ་བ་ (loma saàsa dzāwa) a person who had been residing elsewhere finally returning to his ancestral home [Lit. the leaves fall on the roots].

ལོ་མ་ལེབ་མོ་ (loma lebmo) blade of a leaf.

ལོ་མ་གསར་པ་ (loma sārba) new leaves.

ལོ་མང་ (lomaŋ) many years.

ལོ་མང་བུན་རྙིང་ (lomaŋ bünñiŋ) an old debt/ loan.

ལོ་མང་ཐུབ་པའི་རྩི་ཤིང་ (lomaŋ tūbbɛ dzəshiŋ) perennial plant.

ལོ་མའ་ (loma) Rome.

ལོ་མའི་སྐྱུར་རྒྱུ་ (lomɛ gyurgyu) folic acid, folacin.

ལོ་མའི་ལྗང་རྒྱུ་ (lomɛ jaŋgyu) chlorophyll.

ལོ་མའི་ལྗང་རྒྱུ་ཕུང་པོ་ (lomɛ jəŋgyu pūŋbo) chloroplast.

ལོ་མའི་འདབ་རིས་ (lomɛ dəbrii) vein of leaf.

ལོ་མའི་ཕུར་མ་ (lomɛ pūrmə) powdered incense made into a tiny bundle that is placed as decoration on altars.

ལོ་མའི་བང་རིམ་ (lomɛ pəŋrim) phylotaxy.

ལོ་མའི་དམར་རྒྱུ་ (lomɛ mərgyu) carotene.

ལོ་མའི་ཙ་ནད་ (lomɛ dzānɛɛ̀) leaf rust.

ལོ་མའི་ཙ་རིས་ (lomɛ dzərii) sm. ལོ་མའི་འདབ་རིས་.

ལོ་མའི་ཡུ་བ་ (lomɛlomɛ yuwə) leaf stalk.

ལོ་མའི་ཤ་ (lomɛ shā) mesophyll.

ལོ་མའི་སེར་རྒྱུ་ (lomɛ sērgyu) lutein, anthophyl.

ལོ་མའི་ར་རི་ནད་ (lomɛ rari nɛɛ̀) leaf spot.

ལོ་མའི་སྲིན་ (lomɛ sīn) looper, inchworm.

ལོ་མར་ (lomar) 1. Rome. 2. butter that had been stored for year.

ལོ་མས་འབྲས་སྒྲིབ་ (lomɛ drɛ̱ɛ̀drib) the secondary supersedes the primary [Lit. the leaves cover the fruit].

ལོ་མུར་ (lomur) continuously one year after another.

ལོ་སྨད་ (lomɛɛ̀) the latter half of the year.

ལོ་ཙཱ་ཁྲུའུ་ (lodza trū) tib. ch. translation department.

ལོ་ཙཱ་བ་ (lodzawa) translator.

ལོ་ཚད་ (lodzɛɛ̀) 1. age limit; vi.—ཡོལ་; —ལས་བརྒལ་ to exceed/ surpass an age limit; vi.—ལོངས་; —ལོན་ to reach an age limit ¶ དམག་མིར་ཞུགས་རྒྱུར་ལོ་ཚད་ཡོད་པ་རེད་ There is an age limit for joining the army. 2. seniority in work ¶ ཕོགས་ལོ་ཚད་ནས་སྤྲོད་ཀྱི་ཡོད་པ་རེད་ Salary is paid according to seniority.

ལོ་ཚད་ངོ་མ་ (lodzɛɛ̀ ŋoma) exact age, age in whole years.

ལོ་ཚོད་ (lodzöö̀) according to one's age; va.—སྡུར་ to compare differences of age.

ལོ་ཚན་ (lodzɛn) 1. quality of crops/ harvest. 2. the rhizome of Chinese monkshood (used in Tibetan medicine).

ལོ་ཚིགས་ (lodzii̇) chronological table/ record of events that have occurred.

ལོ་གཞུག (loshuù) end of the year.

ལོ་གཞིས་འཆར་ (lo shẹèjaa) every third year.

ལོ་གཞོན་ (loshön) youth, young people/ person ¶ ལོ་གཞོན་རྣམས་སྐྱིད་གར་ཕྱིན་འདུག The youths had gone for a picnic.

ལོ་གཞོན་པ་ (lo shömba) sm. ལོ་གཞོན་.

ལོ་གཞོན་གཞོན་ (lo shönshön) sm. ལོ་གཞོན་.

ལོ་ཟླ་ (londa) 1. year and month. 2. the same age ¶ ངའི་འཛིན་གྲྭའི་ནང་ལ་ལྷ་གུ་ལོ་ཟླ་ཡིན་པ་གཉིས་ཡོད་ In my class there are two students who are the same age as me. 3. time, period ¶ དམག་འཐབ་ཀྱི་ལོ་ཟླར་དྲན་གསོ་བྱེད་སྐབས་ At the time of commemorating the year of the battle.

ལོ་ཟླ་སྟོང་སྐྱེལ་ (londa dōŋgyee) wasting/ frittering away time.

ལོ་བཟང་ (losaŋ) a person whose year of birth is astrologically determined to be auspicious.

ལོ་ཡག་ལྗང་པ་ (loyaà jaŋba) good stalks (of crops).

ལོ་ཡི་ཐེག་པ་ (loyi tēgba) sm. ལོའི་ཐེག་པ་.

ལོ་ཡི་ཐོག་མ་ (loyi tɔ̄ɔma) the 11th month of the Tibetan calendar.

ལོ་ཡི་དང་པོ་ (loyi taŋbo) the 1st month of the Tibetan calendar. 2. the year of the rat.

ལོ་ཡུན་ (loyün) sm. ལོ་རྒྱུན་.

ལོ་ཡོན་ (loyön) annual salary.

ལོ་རན་མོ་ཕྱུགས་ (lorɛn mojuù) female livestock that have arrived at the breeding age.

ལོ་རན་གཞོན་ནུ་ (lorɛn shönnu) young people who are of the right age to do sth. (e.g., join the army or get married).

ལོ་རབས་ (lorəb) 1. decade ¶ ལོ་རབས་བཞི་བཅུ་པའི་ཁ་གདན་ A carpet from the decade of the (19)40's. 2. historical/ period/ era.

ལོ་རིམ་ (lurim) by year, one year after another ¶ ལོ་རིམ་ལྟར་སྒྲིག་རྒྱུ་ Arranging chronologically by (year). 2. class, grade (in school) ¶ སློབ་གྲྭ་འབྲིང་བར་ལོ་རིམ་གཉིས་ཡོད་ There are two grades in middle school. ¶ ལོ་རིམ་དང་པོ་ The first grade.

ལོ་རིམ་བརྒལ་སྤར་ (lurim gɛɛ bār) skipping a grade in school.

ལོ་རིམ་ལོ་རྒྱུས་ (lurim lugyüü) a chronicle, a history arranged year-by-year.

ལོ་རིམ་གསུང་སྒྲོག (lorim sūŋdrɔɔ̀) shung. scriptures read yearly.

ལོ་རིལ་པོ་ (lo riibu) whole year, all year round.

ལོ་རེ་ (lo re) sm. ལོ་རེ་རེ་.

ལོ་རེ་སྔོན་རྩིས་ (lore ŋōndzii) annual budget forecast.

ལོ་རེ་རེ་ (lo rere) every year ¶ ལོ་རེ་རེ་སློབ་ཕྲུག་གསར་པ་ཐེངས་རེ་རེ་སྡུད་ཀྱི་ཡོད་པ་རེད་ New students are recruited one time each year.

ལོ་རེ་བཞིན་ (loreshin) sm. ལོ་ལྟར་.

ལོ་རེའི་འཆར་གཞི་ (loree cāāshi) annual plan.

ལོ་རེས་ (loreè) sm. ལོ་རྟགས་.

ལོ་རོ་བ་ (lorowa) shung. horse trader.

ལོ་ལེགས་ (loleè) bumper harvest ¶ སྔར་བྱུང་མ་མྱོང་བའི་ལོ་ལེགས་བྱུང་ They got an unprecedented bumper harvest.

ལོ་ལོ་ (lolo) each year.

ལོ་ལོ་ཟླ་ (lo londa) sm. ལོ་ཟླ་.

ལོ་ལོན་ (lolön) vi. to reach/ arrive at a year ¶ ལོ་གཅིག་ལོན་པའི་ཤ་ Meat that is a year old (that has reached one year).

ལོ་ཤ་ (losha) meat that has been cured for a year.

ལོ་ཤས་ (loshɛɛ̀) a few years, several years.

ལོ་ཤས་ཅིག་ (loshɛɛ̀jii) sm. ལོ་ཤས་

ལོ་ཤོལ་ (loshöö) leap year.

ལོ་བཤད་ (loshɛɛ̀) astrological prediction/ prophecy for a year.

ལོ་ས་ (losa) okay, suitable ¶ མོ་ཊ་འདི་ལོ་ས་རེད་པས་ Is this car okay for you?

ལོ་སར་ (losar) sm. ལོ་གསར་.

ལོ་སོང་སྐྱེད་རྩིས་ (losoŋ gyēēdzii) shung. apportioning of payments of interest (on a loan).

ལོ་གསར་ (losar) new year ¶ ཕ་མ་གཉིས་ལ་ལོ་གསར་གྱི་བཀྲ་ཤིས་བདེ་ལེགས་ཞུས་པ་རེད་ (They) gave New Year's congratulations to their parents.

ལོ་གསར་དགའ་སྟོན་དུས་ཆེན་ (losar gadön tüüjen) New Year's Day celebration/ party.

ལོ་གསར་སྔ་ནུབ་ (losar ŋānub) New Year's Eve.

ལོ་གསར་ཉ་གང་ (losar ñagaŋ) 15th day of the 1st lunar month.

ལོ་གསར་དུས་ཆེན་ (losar tüüjen) New Year's celebration.

ལོ་གསར་གནམ་གང་ (losar nāmgaŋ) New Year's Eve.

ལོ་གསར་མེ་ཏོག (losar medoò) 1. a red flower put on the New Year's offering box. 2. cockscomb (used in Tibetan medicine).

ལོ་གསར་ཚེས་གཅིག (losar tsēējig) first day of the New Year.

ལོ་གསར་བཟང་ (losar saŋ) a new year greeting (in Amdo dialect).

ལོ་གསུམ་ཁམ་བུ་ (losum kāmbu) a peach tree that fruits every three years.

ལོ་གསུམ་ཕྱོགས་གསུམ་ (losum cɔ̄ɔsum) a religious retreat that goes on for three years and three months.

ལོ་ཧྲིལ་པོ་ (lo hriibu) sm. ལོ་རིལ་པོ་.

ལོག (lɔɔ̀) 1. va. to return, to come or go back ¶ དམག་བརྒྱབ་ནས་དམག་མི་ནང་ལ་ལོག་པ་རེད་ The soldiers returned home after the battle. 2. vi. to get in the wrong order, to be upside down/ inside out/ reversed/ inverted ¶ ཡིག་འབྲུ་འདི་མགོ་འཛུག་ལོག་ནས་པར་བརྒྱབ་བཞག They printed the letters upside down. 3. vi. to collapse, to fall down, to tumble down ¶ ཁང་པ་དེ་ལོག་སོང་ That house collapsed. 4. wrong, incorrect, backwards ¶ སྨན་ལོག་ཕུལ་ He gave (them) the wrong medicine. 5. vi. to lose shine/ sheen, to fade ¶ དུབ་ལོག་གི་ཆོས་གཞི་ལོག་བཞག The color of the clothes faded. 6. va.—གཏོང་ to send back/ home ¶ ཁོས་སློབ་ཕྲུག་ཚང་མ་ལོག་བཏང་སོང་ He sent all the students back (home). 7. vi. to die.

ལོག་སྐད་ (lɔggɛɛ̀) a language that others cannot understand, a secret language; va.—རྒྱག to talk in ལོག་སྐད་.

ལོག་གེ་བ་ (lɔggewa) describing a particular stance that is crooked/ sideways.

ལོག་རྒྱག (lɔɔ̀ gyaà) 1. to plow, to turn the soil over ¶ བཙས་མ་བསྡུས་པ་དང་ཞིང་གར་ལོག་རྒྱག་དགོས་ As soon as the harvest is done one must plow the field. 2. vi. to recur (for sickness/ illness) ¶ ངའི་ནད་ཚ་རྙིང་པ་ལོག་བརྒྱབ་བཞག My old sickness recurred.

ལོག་སྒྲུབ་ (lɔgdrub) misapprehension, misinterpretation (usu. used with གོ་བ་); va.—བྱེད་

¶ ཁོང་གིས་སྲིད་ཇུས་ལ་གོ་བ་ལོག་སྒྲུབ་བྱས་ནས་ལག་ལེན་བསྟར་སྟངས་ནོར་པ་རེད་ He misinterpreted the policy and implemented it wrongly.

ལོག་འགྲོ་ (lɔ̀ dro) va. to return, to go back.

ལོག་རྒོལ་ལོག་རྫིས་ (lɔ̀göö lɔ̀dzii) planning retaliation (to settle old scores).

ལོག་བསྔོ་ (lɔ̀ŋo) dedicating one's prays/ deeds in an opposite/ perverse way.

ལོག་ཆོས་ (lɔgjöö) 1. heresy, heretical religious beliefs. 2. nonBuddhist religions.

ལོག་འཆམ་རྒྱུག (lɔŋjam gyaà) va. to be time to leave ¶ ད་ཆུ་ཚོད་ལྔ་པར་སླེབས་འདུག་པས་ལོག་འཆམ་རྒྱུག་རན་འདུག Now it is 5 o'clock so it is time to leave.

ལོག་འཛལ་བྱེད་ (lɔnjɛɛ ceè) va. to act in an ungrateful, thankless manner ¶ ཁོས་རང་ཉིད་ཀྱི་ཕ་མར་དྲིན་ལན་ལོག་འཛལ་བྱས་པ་རེད་ He behaved in an ungrateful way toward his parents.

ལོག་གདམ་ (lɔgdam) saying sth. opposite of what it should be, wrong views/ talk/ advice ¶ མི་དེས་ལོག་གདམ་བཤད་པར་ཡིད་ཆེས་བྱས་ནས་ནོར་འཁྲུལ་ཤོར་བ་རེད་ They trusted his talk which was opposite of what it should have been and they made a mistake (in what they were doing).

ལོག་གདམ་སུན་འབྱིན་ (lɔgdam sũnjin) refuting wrong views; va.—བྱེད་.

ལོག་གདོང་ (lɔ̀ dōŋ) see ལོག.

ལོག་རྟོགས་ (lɔgdɔ̀) wrong/ distorted understanding, misconceiving, misunderstanding.

ལོག་ལྟ་ (lɔgda) heresy, heretical/ perverse view; vi.—སྐྱེ་ to have heretical views arise; va.—བྱེད་ to hold heretical views.

ལོག་ལྟ་ཅན་ (lɔgdajɛn) heretical, perverse in viewpoint.

ལོག་མཐོང་ (lɔgdoŋ) shung. despising, showing contempt for, looking down upon.

ལོག་གནོན་ (lɔgnön) suppressing wrong or heretical ideas/ thoughts/ views; va.—བྱེད་.

ལོག་པ་ (lɔgba) 1. opposite, reverse; vi.—སྐྱེད་ to get/ have arise opposite or reverse thoughts ¶ ཁོས་གཞུང་གི་ཅ་ལག་མ་ཉོས་པར་གཞུང་དངུལ་ཟ་རྒྱུའི་བསམ་རྩལ་ལོག་པ་སྐྱེད་པ་རེད་ He got the wrong (opposite) idea that he wouldn't buy the items from the government but would embezzle them. 2. incorrect, false, heretical, perverse.

ལོག་པའི་ཡི་གེ་བཞི་ (lɔgbɛ yige shi) the four reversed letters in the Tibetan alphabet (ཊ,ཋ,ཌ,ཎ).

ལོག་པར་འཁུ་ (lɔgba kū) vi. to become angry.

ལོག་པར་ལྟ་བ་ (lɔgbar dāwa) sm. ལོག་ལྟ་.

ལོག་པར་སྤྱོད་ (lɔgbar jöö) 1. va. to do things in an opposite (wrong) way. 2. va. to commit adultery.

ལོག་པར་གཡེམ་པ་ (lɔgba yēmba) sm. ལོག་གཡེམ་.

ལོག་པར་ལྷུང་ (lɔgbar lhũŋ) 1. vi. to fall on the wrong side of the government/ authorities, to get into trouble ¶ ཕྲུ་གུ་དེ་གྲོགས་པོ་ངན་པ་དང་འགྲོགས་ནས་ལོག་པར་ལྷུང་བཞག The child ran around with bad friends and got into trouble. 2. ངན་འགྲོ་.

ལོག་པོ་ (lɔgbo) sm. ལྡེབ་.

ལོག་སྤྱོད་ (lɔgjöö) reactionary action/ conduct, heretical/ perverted action or conduct.

ལོག་སྤྱོད་གྲལ་རིམ་ (lɔgjöö trɛɛrim) reactionary class.

ལོག་སྤྱོད་ཅན་ (lɔgjööjɛn) reactionary ¶ བསམ་བློ་ལོག་སྤྱོད་ཅན་ Reactionary ideas/ thoughts.

ལོག་སྤྱོད་པ་ (lɔgjööba) a reactionary.

ལོག་སྤྱོད་ཕྱོགས་ཁག (lɔgjöö cɔ̄ɔ̀gaà) reactionary clique/ bloc/ group, reactionaries.

ལོག་སྤྱོད་དབང་སྒྱུར་ (lɔgjöö wāŋgyur) reactionary rule.

ལོག་སྤྱོད་དབང་སྒྱུར་གྲལ་རིམ་ (lɔgjöö wāŋgyur trɛɛrim) reactionary ruling class.

ལོག་སྤྱོད་ཚོགས་ཁག (lɔgjöö tsɔ̄ɔ̀gaà) sm. ལོག་སྤྱོད་ཕྱོགས་ཁག.

ལོག་སྤྱོད་རུ་ཁག (lɔgjöö rugaà) sm. ལོག་སྤྱོད་ཕྱོགས་ཁག.

ལོག་ཕྱོགས་པ་ (lɔgjɔɔ̀ba) sm. ལོག་སྤྱོད་པ་.

ལོག་ཕྲུག (lɔgdruù) the children of a reactionaries.

ལོག་སྦྱོར་ (lɔgjɔɔ) 1. wrong use of grammar (e.g., using གི་ instead ཀྱི་). 2. prescribing or treating with the wrong medicine.

ལོག་སྨོན་ (lɔgmön) prayer for sth. evil, prayer to curse sb.; va.—རྒྱག.

ལོག་སྨྲ་ (lɔ̄gma) heterodox/ heretical theories.

ལོག་ཚོང་ (lɔgdzoŋ) trading that is illegal/ improper; va.—རྒྱག.

ལོག་འཚོ་ (lɔgdzo) living by perverse means, earning one's livelihood in illegal/ improper ways.

ལོག་ཞག (lɔgshaà) twenty four days after the winter solstice.

ལོག་ཡོང་ (lɔ̀ yoŋ) va. to come back, to return ¶ ཁོང་ན་ནིང་བོད་ནས་ལོག་ཡོང་བ་རེད་ Last year he returned from Tibet.

ལོག་གཡེམ་ (lɔgyem) 1. sexually immoral acts, sexual perversion. 2. (with བཙན་ཤེད་) rape; va.—བྱེད་ to rape.

ལོག་རླུང་ (lɔgluŋ) adverse wind, unhealthy trend.

ལོག་ལམ་ (lɔglam) false doctrine, wrong/ perverted path.

ལོག་ལོག (lɔglɔɔ̀) sth. round that is wrapped up.

ལོག་ཤུ་ (lɔgshu) a whistle blown when it is time for workers to end work; va.—རྒྱག.

ལོག་བཤད་ (lɔgshɛɛ̀) saying sth. in an opposite way; va.—བྱེད་.

ལོག་ཤེས་ (lɔgsheè) wrong/ perverted consciousness or conceptions.

ལོག་སེམས་ (lɔgsem) reactionary thinking/ thoughts.

ལོག་སྲིད་བསྐྱར་ལངས་ (lɔgsiì gyūrlaŋ) the restoring/ coming back of a reactionary government.

ལོག་གསོག་བྱེད་ (lɔgsɔɔ̀) amassing illegally; va.—བྱེད་.

ལོག་བསམ་ (lɔgsam) 1. sm. ལོག་སེམས་. 2. sm. ལོག་ཤེས་.

ལོགས་ (lɔ̀) 1. face/ surface of sth. ¶ དེ་གྱང་གི་ལོགས་ལ་སྦྱར་པ་རེད་ (They) stuck it on the (surface of the) wall. 2. (ནང་ + —) inside.

ལོགས་སྐད་ (lɔggɛɛ̀) sm. ལོག་སྐད་.

ལོགས་ཁང་ (lɔ̀gaŋ) room at the corner of a house.

ལོགས་དགར་ (lɔ̀gar) 1. separate, apart; va.—བྱེད་ to separate, to place apart; va.—འཛིན་ to hold a different view; va.—འཇོག to put separately/ apart ¶ བོད་ཡིག་གི་དེབ་ཚང་མ་ལོགས་དགར་འཇོག་དགོས་ You should leave all the Tibetan books separate. ¶ མི་ཚང་དེའི་བུ་སྤུན་གཉིས་ལོགས་དགར་བྱས་བསྡད་བཞག That household's two sons live separately. 2. divorcing, separating, splitting up; va.—བྱེད་ to divorce/ separate/ split up ¶ ཁོང་གཉིས་བཟའ་ཚང་ལོགས་དགར་བྱས་བཞག They got divorced.

ལོགས་འགེལ་ (lɔ̄ɔ̀gee) things hanging on a wall.

ལོགས་ངོས་ (lɔ̀ŋöö) face, surface, exterior.

ལོགས་བཅད་ (lɔgjɛɛ̀) shung. apart, separately ¶ ལོགས་བཅད་དུ་སྡོད་ཡུལ་ཁྱིམ་གསར་པ་ The new home in which he lived separately.

ལོགས་ཞལ་ (lɔgshɛɛ) plaster on a wall; va.—རྒྱག to plaster a wall.

ལོགས་རིས་ (lɔgrii) mural, fresco.

ལོགས་སུ་ (lɔgsu) 1. on the face/ surface ¶ རྩིག་པའི་ལོགས་སུ་པར་མང་པོ་བཀལ་འདུག (They) hung many pictures on the surface of the wall. 2. separately, apart ¶ ཁོ་སྡོད་ས་ལོགས་སུ་ཡོད་པ་རེད་ His residence is separate (from others).

ལོགས་སུ་དགར་ (lɔgsu gar) va. to separate, to put aside.

ལོགས་སུ་བཅར་ (lɔgsu jāā) sm. ཟུར་མཇལ་.

ལོགས་སུ་སྡོད་ (lɔgsu) va. to live separately.

ལོགས་སུ་ཕྱེ་ (lɔgsu cē) va. to separate/ differentiate.

ལོགས་སུ་ལུས་ (lɔgsu lüù) vi. to be left alone, to be isolated/ apart/ separated ¶ མི་ཚང་མ་ཕྱིན་ཚར་ནས་ཁོ་ལོགས་སུ་ལུས་འདུག Everyone went and he was left alone.

ལོང་ (loŋ) 1. vi. to become blind, to lose one's eyesight. 2. abdomen, stomach ¶ ལོང་ཁར་ན་ཚ་

བདང་གི་འདུག I have a pain in my abdomen. 3. (vb. + —) time to do the verbal act ¶ང་ལྟད་མོར་འགྲོ་ལོང་མེད་ I don't have time to go to the show. 4. sometimes used sm. ལོན་. 5. (vb. + — + མེད་པར་) soon after the verbal act ¶བོད་ལ་སླེབས་ལོང་མེད་པར་ཁང་པ་ཉོས་སོང་ He bought a house soon after arriving in Tibet.

ལོང་ཀ་ (loŋga) sm. ལོང་ཁ་.

ལོང་ལྐུགས་སློབ་གྲྭ་ (loŋguù lōbdra) school for the blind and dumb.

ལོང་ཁ་ (loŋga) sm. ལོང་, 2.

ལོང་ཁེབས་ (loŋgeb) a kind of blanket/ covering for horses that is placed over the hind area.

ལོང་ཁྲིད་ (loŋdrii) 1. sb. who leads the blind; va.—བྱེད་; —རྒྱག. 2. the walking stick carried by the blind.

ལོང་ག (loŋga) sm. ལོང་ཁ་.

ལོང་གོའི་པད་ཚལ་ (loŋgö bɛ̀ɛdzɛɛ) ch. cabbage.

ལོང་རྒྱུག (loŋgyuù) sm. ལོང་མཆོང་.

ལོང་མཆོང་ (loŋjoŋ) acting rashly/ blindly; va.—བྱེད་; —རྒྱག ¶ས་གནས་ཀྱི་གནས་ཚུལ་ལ་ཞིབ་དཔྱད་མ་བྱས་པར་ལོང་མཆོང་རྒྱག་རྒྱུ་མེད་ One shouldn't act rashly without investigating the local situation.

ལོང་མཆོང་རིང་ལུགས་ (loŋjoŋ riŋluù) putschism.

ལོང་གཏམ་ (loŋdam) talking without understanding the topic; va.—ཤོད་.

ལོང་ཐེར་ (loŋter) moxabustion points to the left and the right of the navel.

ལོང་ནད་ (loŋnɛɛ̀) diseases of the intestines.

ལོང་ཕྲེང་ (loŋdreŋ) woman's silver ornament worn around the waist.

ལོང་བ་ (loŋwa) a blind person.

ལོང་བའི་འཁར་རྒྱུག (loŋwɛ kārgyuù) a blind person's cane.

ལོང་བའི་རྗེས་འབྲང་ (loŋwɛ jeèdraŋ) following blindly.

ལོང་བའི་ལག་རྟེན་ (loŋwɛ lagden) sm. ལོང་བའི་འཁར་རྒྱུག.

ལོང་བར་ལམ་འདྲི་ (loŋwar lamdri) seeking advice from an ignorant person [Lit. to ask a blind man the way].

ལོང་བས་ཀང་ཀྱོག་བཟུང་བ་ (loŋwɛ gāŋgyɔɔ̀ suŋwə) a Tibetan game in which one is blindfolded and the other has his leg tied so that he is one-legged—the blind person then tries to catch the one-legged person.

ལོང་བས་ཉ་འཛིན་ (loŋwɛ ña dzin) acting blindly, acting without knowing the situation or the local conditions/ background [Lit. a blind person fishing].

ལོང་བས་རྟ་ཞར་གཞོན་པ་ (loŋwɛ dāshar shōmba) imminent danger [Lit. a blind man riding a blind horse).

ལོང་བས་བལྟས་ཀྱང་ཁམས་གསུམ་ (loŋwɛ dɛ̄ɛgyaŋ kāmsum) sth. obvious/ known to all [Lit. even the blind can see the three Buddhist realms].

ལོང་བས་རི་དྭགས་མདའ་འཕེར་ (loŋwɛ ridaà daber) sm. ལོང་བས་ཉ་འཛིན་ [Lit. the blind hunting wild animals].

ལོང་བས་ལག་རྟེན་གར་འཛུགས་ (loŋwɛ lagden kardzuù) blaming blindly (without really knowing) [Lit. blind person pointing his cane].

ལོང་བས་ལོང་བ་ཁྲིད་ (loŋwɛ loŋwa trii) blind leading the blind.

ལོང་བས་ཤིག་བཟུང་ (loŋwɛ shīgsuŋ) sm. ལོང་བས་ཉ་འཛིན་ [Lit. the blind trying to catch lice].

ལོང་བུ་ (loŋbu) anklebone.

ལོང་མོ་ (loŋmo) a blind female.

ལོང་ཙམ་ (loŋdzam) 1. just enough ¶ཞལ་འདེབས་བསྡུས་ནས་དངུལ་དེ་ལོང་ཙམ་བྱུང་སོང་ (They) collected donations and got just enough money. 2. roughly, cursorily, approximately ¶ཁོང་གིས་རྩོམ་ཡིག་དེའི་དཔལ་འབྱོར་སྐོར་ལ་ཆེ་ལོང་ཙམ་བཀོད་འདུག He wrote cursorily about economics in his articles.

ལོང་ཚད་ (loŋdzɛɛ̀) 1. the rate of growth (of a child). 2. an illness in the intestines in Tibetan medicine.

ལོང་ཚིགས་ (loŋdzii) sm. ལོང་བུ་.

ལོང་འོན་ལྐུགས་གསུམ་ (loŋ) blind, deaf and dumb.

ལོང་ཡིག (loŋyii) Braille.

ལོང་ལོང་ (loŋloŋ) 1. bubbling. 2. feeling sad; va.—བྱེད་.

ལོང་བཤད་ (loŋshɛɛ̀) sm. ལོང་གཏམ་.

ལོངས་ (loŋ) 1. imp. of ལེན་ and ལང་. 2. vi. to be able to make up, to reach an amount/ set number/ quantity ¶ཅ་ལག་ཉོས་པའི་རིན་པ་མ་ལོངས་ཙང་དངུལ་གཡར་པ་རེད་ Since (their money) didn't suffice for the price of the things they bought, (they) borrowed money. 3. vi. to grow ¶ཕྲུ་གུ་འདི་གཟུགས་པོ་ཞེ་དྲག་ལོངས་འདུག The child has grown a lot.

ལོངས་སྤྱད་ (loŋjɛɛ̀) p. of ལོངས་སྤྱོད་.

ལོངས་སྤྱོད་ (loŋjöö) enjoying, benefiting from, utilizing/ using; va.—ལོངས་སྤྱོད་; —བྱེད་; —གཏོང་ to enjoy, to benefit from,, to use ¶ཁོ་ལ་རྒྱ་ནོར་ག་ཚོད་ཡོད་ཀྱང་ལོངས་སྤྱོད་བྱེད་ཐུབ་ཡོད་པ་མ་རེད་ No matter how much wealth he had, he was unable to enjoy/ use it.

ལོངས་སུ་སྤྱད་ (loŋsu jɛɛ̀) p. of ལོངས་སུ་སྤྱོད་.

ལོངས་སུ་སྤྱོད་ (loŋsu jöö) va. to enjoy, to benefit from, to make use of ¶དེང་སང་མི་དམངས་རྣམས་རང་དབང་ལ་ལོངས་སུ་སྤྱོད་བཞིན་པ་རེད་ These days the people are enjoying freedom.

ལོད་ (löö) 1. (usu. vb. + — +) of use, making a difference ¶ཁོ་ལ་ཤོད་ལོད་ཡོད་པ་མ་རེད་ There is no use telling him. ¶ཁྱེད་རང་ཕེབས་ལོད་ཡོད་པ་མ་རེད་ It will not make any difference if you go. 2. (adjective + —) how (much, big, long, etc.) ¶ཚོགས་འདུར་མི་མང་ལོད་སླེབས་འདུག་གམ How many people came to the meeting? 3. vi. to be severe/ bad (illness) ¶ཁོང་གི་ན་ཚ་གཞི་ལོད་དུ་ཕྱིན་བཞག His illness got worse.

ལོད་པ་ (lööba) sm. ལོད་པོ་.

ལོད་པོ་ (lööbo) bad, poor ¶ནད་གཞི་ལོད་པོ་ Bad illness.

ལོན་ (lön) 1. vi. to get, to acquire, to obtain, to reach, to arrive at ¶ཁོ་སློབ་ལོ་ལོན་དུས་ When he reaches school age. 2. sm. ལན་.

ལོན་དན་ (löndɛn) London.

ལོན་པ་བྱེད་ (lömba cee) va. to do one's best to obtain a certain level/ goal ¶དངུལ་ཁྲི་གཅིག་ལོན་པ་བྱེད་དགོས་ཟེར་བ་རེད་ (He) said we must do our best to reach a level of ten thousand dollars.

ལོན་ཕྲིང་ (löndriŋ) reply/ answer to a letter.

ལོབ་ (lob) imp. of ལབ་.

ལོབ་མཚོ་ (lobnɔr) Lake Lobnor.

ལོབས་ (lob) vi. to become a habit ¶ཁོང་གསོལ་སྟོན་མང་པོར་ཕྱིན་ཙང་ཨ་རག་འཐུང་རྒྱུ་ལོབས་བཞག Because he went to many parties, drinking alcohol became a habit.

ལོའི་ཐེག་པ་ (lö tēgba) elderly/ aged man.

ལོའི་ཐོན་ཚད་ (lö tōndzɛɛ̀) annual production/ output.

ལོ་རའོ་གཏེར་ (loro dēr) ch. chromium.

ལོར་ (lɔr) paper money.

ལོར་ཁང་ (lɔrgaŋ) mint/ printing house for paper money.

ལོར་རོ་ (loroò) paper money.

ལོར་རོ་མ་བིན་ (loroò məbin) counterfeit money.

ལོར་རོ་མ་བྲིན་ (loro mədrin) sm. ལོར་རོ་མ་བིན་.

ལོར་རོ་རྫུན་མ་ (loro dzümə) sm. ལོར་རོ་མ་བྲིན་.

ལོས་ (löö) 1. certainly, definitely ¶འདི་ཁོས་ལོས་ཤེས་ He will certainly know it. 2. (adjective + —) how much with respect to the adjective ¶ལྷ་ས་ཆེ་ལོས་འདུག How big is Lhasa?

ལོས་ཀྱང་ཡིན་ (löögyaŋyin) of course!

ལོས་ཡིན་ (lööyin) of course!

ལྭ་བ་ (laa) 1. type of woven woolen material. 2. blanket. 3. clothing.

ལྭ་རིང་ (lariŋ) a type of long dress.

ལྭ་ཤ་ (lasha) a long Tibetan dress.

ཤ་ (shā) 1. the letter ཤ་ (used in alphabetical ordering). 2. meat, flesh ། ལུག་ཤ་ Mutton.

ཤ་ཀ་མ་ (shāgama) sm. ཁ་ཆེ་ཤ་ཀ་མ་.

ཤ་ཀ་ར་ (shāgara) sugarcane, brown sugar, rock sugar.

ཤ་ཀྲག (shādraà) sm.* ཤ་བསྲིགས་.

ཤ་ཀྲད་ (shādrɛɛ̀) ring worn on the thumb (made from deer horn).

ཤ་ཀྲིང་ (shādriŋ) tib.eng. canned meat.

ཤ་ཀླད་ (shālɛɛ̀) brain.

ཤ་དཀར་ (shāgar) 1. tin. 2. sheep meat.

ཤ་དཀར་ཤ་ནག (shāgar shānag) meat from cattle and sheep.

ཤ་བཀྲ་ (shābdra) vitiligo (a skin disease).

ཤ་བཀྲག་ཆེ་བ་ (shābdraà cēwa) healthy looking, splendid.

ཤ་རྐྱལ་ (shāgyɛɛ) a leather/ skin bag.

ཤ་སྐམ་ (shāgam) abbr. of ཤ་སྐམ་པོ་.

ཤ་སྐམ་པགས་སྐམ་ (shāgam bāggam) skinny, very thin.

ཤ་སྐམ་པོ་ (shā gāmbo) 1. dried meat. 2. thin.

ཤ་སྐམ་གཟུགས་ཆུང་ (shāgam sugjuŋ) thin and small.

ཤ་སྐམ་རུས་སྐམ་ (shāgam rṵṵgam) sm. ཤ་སྐམ་པགས་སྐམ་.

ཤ་སྐམ་རུས་པ་རོང་རོང་ (shāgam rṵṵba roŋroŋ) sm. ཤ་སྐམ་པགས་སྐམ་.

ཤ་སྐམ་སེང་ (shā gāmseŋ) meat dried by freezing.

ཤ་སྐམ་སོབ་ (shā gāmsob) dried meat that is soft.

ཤ་སྐལ་ (shāgɛɛ) 1. share of meat. 2. a person's soul taken by a witch when it is her turn to supply the other witches with flesh.

ཤ་སྐྱ་ (shā gyā) a type of whitish deer.

ཤ་སྐྱི་ (shāgyi) flesh and skin.

ཤ་སྐྱོ་བ་ (shā gyōba) sm. ཤ་སྐམ་པོ་, 2.

ཤ་སྐྲང་ (shā drāŋ) vi. to swell (flesh) ། ཉེས་དུང་བཏང་ནས་ཤ་སྐྲང་བཞག (He) was beaten and swelled up.

ཤ་སྐྲན་ (shādrɛn) cancer.

ཤ་ཁ་ (shāga) container made of horn that is used to hold gunpowder.

ཤ་ཁ་མ་ (shāgāma) saffron.

ཤ་ཁ་ར་ (shāgāra) sm. ཤ་ཀ་ར་.

ཤ་ཁ་ཤ་བཞག་ནས་ཉ་ཤ་འཛིན་ ཁ་ཤ་ནམ་མཁའི་མཐོངས་སུ་འཕུར་ ཉ་ཤ་ཆུ་མའི་གཏིང་དུ་འཛུལ་ (shā kāsha shaànɛ ñasha dzin kāsha nāmgɛ tōŋsu pūr ñasha cūmɛ dīŋdu dzṵṵ) if one is too greedy one will lose all [Lit. holding a bird in the mouth the animal tried to catch a fish but then the bird flew away to the sky and the fish dove to the bottom of the water].

ཤ་ཁག་ཁག་དྲི་སོ་སོ་ (shā kāàgaà tri sōso) completely separate/ apart/ different ། ང་ཚོ་སྤུ་ན་གཞོན་གཉིས་ཁྱིམ་ཚང་ཐ་དད་ཕྱེས་ནས་ཤ་ཁག་ཁག་དྲི་སོ་སོ་ཡིན་ We two brothers set up different households and are completely separate.

ཤ་ཁང་ (shāgaŋ) meat shop.

ཤ་ཁུ་ (shəgu) meat broth/ juice.

ཤ་ཁུ་ཚའི་ (shā kūdza) prunella vulgaris (used in Tibetan medicine).

ཤ་ཁུ་ཤ་ཐིམ་ (shəgu shā tīm) what is obtained for a purpose is used for that purpose ། དགོན་པར་ཞལ་འདེབས་ཕུལ་བ་རྣམས་དགོན་པ་རང་གི་འགྲོ་སོང་ཐོག་ཤ་ཁུ་ཤ་ཐིམ་བཏང་ཡོད་ The donations received for the monastery has been used for the expenses of the monastery. [Lit. the gravy of meat has soaking back into the meat].

ཤ་ཁུག (shəguù) 1. meat bag. 2. vi. dry meat to get rehydrated.

ཤ་ཁེབས་ (shāgeb) a patch of dark skin on the face (vitiligo).

ཤ་ཁོག (shāgɔɔ) dressed carcass of an animal.

ཤ་ཁོག་དང་སྡིག་གའི་དཔེ་ (shāgɔɔ daŋ dīgɛ bē) shung. sm. ཤ་ཁོག་ཕར་སྤྲད་སྡིག་ཆུར་ལེན་.

ཤ་ཁོག་ཕར་སྤྲད་སྡིག་ཆུར་ལེན་ (shāgɔɔ pāādrɛɛ̀ dīgə tsüülen) giving sth. precious/ valuable and getting back sth. mediocre/ small ། མི་དེའི་མཁར་རྗེ་དབང་ཐང་ཡོངས་རྫོགས་དགོན་པ་རེར་སྤྲད་ནས་ཕྱི་རང་ཟླ་རེ་དགོན་པ་ནས་ཕོགས་ཐོབ་ཕྲན་བུ་རེ་ལེན་པ་དེ་ནི་ཤ་ཁོག་ཕར་སྤྲད་ སྡིག་ཆུར་ལེན་པ་རང་རེད་ That person gave all of his property to the monastery and got in return from the monastery only a small monthly salary, this is like giving a carcass and receiving only a piece of meat. [Lit. giving a carcass and receiving only pieces of meat].

ཤ་ཁོན་ (shāgön) sm. ཤ་འཁོན་.

ཤ་ཁྱི་ (shəgyi) hunting dog.

ཤ་ཁྱེར་ལྤགས་ཁྱེར་ (shāgyer bāggyer) shung. taking whatever one can get one's hands on [Lit. carrying the meat, carrying the skin].

ཤ་ཁྲ་ (shādra) sm. ཤ་བཀྲ་.

ཤ་ཁྲག (shādraà) flesh and blood.

ཤ་ཁྲག་རྒྱུད་པ་ (shādraà gyṵṵbə) kinship.

ཤ་ཁྲག་གཅིག་འབྲེལ་ (shādraà jīgdree) closely related, flesh and blood relationship.

ཤ་ཁྲག་ལྷན་འབྲེལ་ (shādraà lhɛndree) sm. ཤ་ཁྲག་གཅིག་འབྲེལ་.

ཤ་ཁྲལ་ (shādrɛɛ) shung. tax on meat.

ཤ་ཁྲིམས་ (shədrim) law/ rule prohibiting the slaughtering of animals in the Tibetan 4th month; vi.—སྒྲོམ་ to apply/ impose such a ban; —གྲོལ་ to end such a ban.

ཤ་ཁྲོམ་ (shādrom) meat market.

ཤ་མཁྲེགས་ (shādreg) a callus.

ཤ་འཁོན་ (shāgön) 1. anger/ hatred where one seeks vengeance/ revenge; va.—ལེན་; —སྒྲོག.

ཤ་འཁྱེར་པགས་འཁྱེར་ (shāgyer bāggyer) taking everything [Lit. take the flesh, take the skin].

ཤ་གོས་ (shāgöö) undergarments.

ཤ་གྲི་ (shədri) knife for cutting meat.

ཤ་གླང་ (shālaŋ) stud bull kept for breeding.

ཤ་འགག (shāngɔɔ) vest.

ཤ་འགེལ་གདང་བུ་ (shāgee daŋbu) a long piece of wood on which meat is hung.

ཤ་རྒོད་ (shāgöö) muscles of the body; va.—ལོག to lose one's strength and get tired.

ཤ་རྒྱགས་པ་ (shā gyagba) 1. fat meat. 2. fat, plump (of people). 3. healthy.

ཤ་རྒྱགས་ལོས་ (shā gyaglöö) how fat a person or animals is.

ཤ་རྒྱངས་རྒྱུ་མ་ (shāgyaŋ gyumə) sausage.

ཤ་རྒྱས་ (shā gyɛɛ̀) 1. vi. to become fat, to put on weight. 2. sm. ཤ་རྒོད་.

ཤ་རྒྱས་ཁྲག་རྒྱས་ (shāgyɛɛ̀ trāggyɛɛ̀) hearty, healthy, strong.

ཤ་རྒྱུ་ (shəgyu) sausage.

ཤ་རྒྱུད་ (shəgyüü) matrilineal descent line, relatives on mother's size.

ཤ་རྒྱུས་ (shəgyüü) meat and sinew.

ཤ་རྒྱུས་མཉམ་གཅོད་ (shəgyüü ñamjöö) settling two matters simultaneously, killing two birds with one stone [Lit. cutting meat and sinew together].

ཤ་སྒ་ (shāga) hump of a camel.

ཤ་སྒོག (shāgɔɔ) wild garlic.

ཤ་སྒོང་བཟོ་གྲྭ་ (shāgoŋ sodra) meat and egg processing factory.

ཤ་སྒྲོ་ (shādro) 1. leather pouch used for keeping meat. 2. sm. སྒྲོ་.

ཤ་སྒྲོམ་ (shādrom) a frame or stand for hanging meat.

ཤ་ཇམས་ (shāŋam) amount of fat in an animal.

ཤ་ཇོག (shāŋɔɔ) meat on the tail of a fat-tail type of sheep.

ཤ་རྔོད་ (shā ŋȫȫ) va. to fry/ roast meat.

ཤ་གཅིག་པ་ (shā jĭgbə) 1. maternal kinsman. 2. of the same opinion/ ideas.

ཤ་གཅུས་ (shājöö) pinching; va.—རྒྱག to pinch.

ཤ་གཅོད་ (shā jȫȫ) va. to castrate.

ཤ་བཅག་པོ་ (shā jāgbo) 1. a sinewy, muscular person. 2. hard bamboo (usu. used for pens).

ཤ་ལྕུག (shājuù) strips of dried meat; va.—གདོང་ to dry strips of meat.

ཤ་ལྕོག (shājɔɔ̀) hump of a camel.

ཤ་ཆང་ (shā cāŋ) meat and ཆང་.

ཤ་ཆང་གི་གྲོགས་པོ་ (shājaŋgi tro̱gbo) drinking buddy/ pal.

ཤ་ཆུ་ (shəju) grouse.

ཤ་ཆུང་བ་ (shaā cūŋwə) skinny, thin.

ཤ་ཆེན་ (shājen) human flesh.

ཤ་ཆོད་རུས་ཆོད་ (shājöö rṳṳjöö) settling or deciding sth. clearly [Lit. meat cut, bone cut].

ཤ་ཆོབ་ (shājob) a type of wild mushroom.

ཤ་རྗེན་ (shājen) abbr. of ཤ་རྗེན་པ་. 2. naked.

ཤ་རྗེན་པ་ (shā je̱mba) raw meat.

ཤ་ཉམས་ (shā ñam) 1. vi. to lose weight. 2. body condition; vi.—རྒྱས་ to be/ get healthy or strong.

ཤ་ཉེ་ (shāñe) kinsman, descendent, blood relative.

ཤ་ཉོག་རུས་ཉོག (shāñog rṳṳñog) slaughtering man and animals (in battle) completely annihilating; va.—གཏོང་ ། དམག་སར་དགྲ་བོའི་དམག་མི་ཤ་ཉོག་རུས་ཉོག་ཏུ་བཏང་བ་རེད་ In the battle (they) destroyed the enemy soldiers completely.

ཤ་བསྙལ་མ་ (shā ñεεma) meat that has been marinated.

ཤ་ཏིག (shədig) small slices of meat.

ཤ་ཏོ་ར་ (shādora) a metal plate with cover.

ཤ་ཏྲེམ་ (shādrem) a type of arthritis.

ཤ་ཊོ་ར་ (shādora) sm. ཤ་ཏོ་ར་.

ཤ་གཏོར་རུས་གཏོར་ (shādɔɔ rṳṳdɔɔ) sm. ཤ་ཉོག་རུས་ཉོག.

ཤ་རྟགས་ (shādaà) 1. birthmark. 2. the mark/ scratch made by a witch on sb.'s face as a signal to take the soul of that person.

ཤ་རྟགས་སྔོན་པོ་ (shādaà ŋõmbo) blue birthmark.

ཤ་སྟག (shādaà) only, all ། སྒྲིག་ཆས་ཐབས་ཆག་ཤ་སྟག་ཡིན་རུང་ Even though the equipment was all only mediocre (in quality).

ཤ་སྟོབས་ (shādob) body condition ། ཤ་སྟོབས་རྒྱས་པ་ Strong/ healthy body.

ཤ་ཐག (shādaà) the front and back rope that keeps a saddle in place on the horse.

ཤ་ཐང་ (shādaŋ) meat soup/ broth.

ཤ་ཐང་ཆད་ (shādaŋ cεὲ) vi. to become tired/ exhausted.

ཤ་ཐུག (shətug) soup/ noodles with meat.

ཤ་ཐུད་ (shā tṻṻ) abbr. of ཤ་ and ཐུད་.

ཤ་ཐུམ་བག་ལེབ་ (shādum pa̱a̱leè) meat-filled pancakes.

ཤ་ཐོག་མར་རྫེག (shādɔɔ̀ ma̱a̱dzeg) 1. having plenty to eat. 2. helping those who don't need help [Lit. on top of meat piling butter].

ཤ་མཐང་ (shādaŋ) flesh of the lower part of the body.

ཤ་མཐུག་པོ་ (shā tūgbu) 1. fat ། མི་དེ་ཤ་མཐུག་པོ་འདུག That person is fat. 2. a kind of thick bamboo.

ཤ་འཐག་རུས་འཐག (shādaà rṳṳdaà) crushing flesh and bone.

ཤ་འཐོར་ཁྲག་འཐོར་ (shādɔɔ trāgdɔɔ) sm. ཤ་འཐོར་རུས་འཐོར་.

ཤ་འཐོར་རུས་འཐོར་ (shādɔɔ rṳṳdɔɔ) 1. ཤ་ཉོག་རུས་ཉོག་ཏུ. 2. body shattered into pieces by an explosion.

ཤ་དར་ཁྲག་རྒྱས་ (shādar traàgyεὲ) hearty, healthy, strong.

ཤ་དུག (shəduù) food poisoning (caused by bad meat); vi.—ཕོག to get food poisoning (from bad meat).

ཤ་དུམ་ (shədum) a piece of meat.

ཤ་དུམ་ཁྲག་དུམ་ (shədum trāgdum) sm. ཤ་ཉོག་རུས་ཉོག.

ཤ་དྲེག (shādreg) callus; vi.—ཆགས་ to have a callus grow.

ཤ་གདན་ (shādεn) muscles ། ཤ་གདན་ལྷུག་པོ་ Flabby muscles.

ཤ་མདངས་ (shādaŋ) sm. ཤ་ཉམས་, 2.

ཤ་མདོག (shāndɔɔ̀) color of skin.

ཤ་མདོག་དཀར་པོ་མིན་པའི་མི་རྒྱུད་ (shāndɔɔ̀ gārbo mi̱mbε mi̱gyṻṻ) people of color.

ཤ་མདོག་ཚོས་གཞི་ (shāndɔɔ̀ tsööshi) sm. ཤ་མདོག.

ཤ་འདྲེས་འདྲེས་ (shā dre̱e̱dreè) a dish consisting of vegetables mixed with meat.

ཤ་རྡོ་ཁྲག་རྡོ་ (shādo traàdo) tough, strong, in the prime of one's life [Lit. flesh like stone, blood like stone].

ཤ་རྡོག (shādɔg) 1. hump of a camel. 2. a chunk of meat.

ཤ་རྡོག་གཉིས་ལྡན་རྔ་མོང་ (shādɔg ñīidεn ŋāmoŋ) two-hump camel, Bactrian camel.

ཤ་ལྡབ་ (shā də̱b) vi. to rot/ spoil (meat).

ཤ་ལྡིག་ལྡིག (shā di̱gdig) 1. fat body (usu. sheep). 2. meat that has a lot of meat as opposed to bone.

ཤ་ལྡུར་ (shādur) pulpy/ tender meat (due to overcooking).

ཤ་སྡུག་ཁྱི་སྡུག (shādug kyīdug) both sides having a difficult time [Lit. dog and the deer both getting tired].

ཤ་སྡུག་འབུ་སྡུག (shādug bu̱dug) sm. ཤ་སྡུག་ཁྱི་སྡུག.

ཤ་ན་ (shāna) hemp, flax.

ཤ་ནག (shānaà) 1. black deer. 2. cattle meat.

ཤ་ནང་གི་ཚེར་མ་ (shānaŋgi tsērma) a thorn in one's side [Lit. a thorn in the flesh].

ཤ་ནའི་རས་ (shānε rε̱ὲ) cloth made of jute/ flax.

ཤ་གནད་ (shānεὲ) sm. ཤ་གནོད་.

ཤ་སྣག (shānag) meat with no bones, tendons.

ཤ་པ་ (shāba) 1. sm. ཨ་ཀ་རུ་. 2. sb. who is seeking revenge. 3. butcher.

ཤ་པ་གདོང་ཐུག (shāba do̱ŋduù) sm. དགྲ་ལ་འཁག་ཐུག.

ཤ་པ་འཕྲང་འཕྲད་ (shāba trāŋdrεὲ) sm. དགྲ་ལ་འཁག་ཐུག.

ཤ་པགས་ (shābaà) sm.* ཤ་ལྤགས་.

ཤ་ལྤགས་ (shābaà) meat and skin.

ཤ་པགས་ཀྱི་འཐབ་རྩོད་ (shābaàgi təbdzöö) political struggle session with physical beatings.

ཤ་སྤགས་ (shābaà) meat and skin.

ཤ་སྤུ་ (shəbu) flesh and hair/ fur.

ཤ་ཕུང་ཕྲ་མོ་ (shābuŋ trāmo) tiny cells.

ཤ་ཕོ་ (shābo) stag.

ཤ་ཕྱེ་རུས་ཕྱེ་ (shāje rṳṳje) sm. ཤ་འཐོར་རུས་འཐོར་.

ཤ་ཕྱིས་ (shəjii) potter's skin cloth used for polishing.

ཤ་ཕྲག (shādraà) in between the flesh.

ཤ་ཕྲུག (shədruù) baby deer.

ཤ་འཕྲུ་ (shəndru) comb (of chickens).

ཤ་བ་ (shāā) deer.

ཤ་བ་ཁ་དཀར་ (shāā kāgar) white-lipped deer.

ཤ་བ་རི་ (shāāri) hunter.

ཤ་བག་ལེབ་ (shā pa̱a̱leè) fried meat-filled pancakes.

ཤ་བམ་ (shābam) meat that is almost spoiled.

ཤ་བའི་ཁྲག (shāwe trāà) deer blood (used in Tibetan medicine).

ཤ་བའི་ཁྲག་རྭ་ (shāwε trāàra) pilose antler.

ཤ་བའི་གླིང་བུ་ (shāwε līŋbu) flute used to entice deer.

ཤ་བའི་འབག (shāwε ba̱à) mask of a stag used in religious (འཆམ་) dance.

ཤ་བའི་འབོག་རྭ་ (shāwε bɔ̱gra) sm. ཤ་བའི་ཁྲག་རྭ་.

ཤ་བའི་ཚིལ་བུ་ (shāwε tsīibu) deer fat (used in Tibetan medicine).

ཤ་བའི་རྭ་རྒན་ (shāwε ra̱gεn) stag antler (used in Tibetan medicine).

ཤ་བལ་ (shābεε) 1. moss, lichen. 2. white residue on alkaline soil.

ཤ་སྦུབས་ (shəbub) sm. ཤ་ཁོག.

ཤ་བེ་ཤོ་བེ་ (shābe shōbe) sm. ཤབ་བེ་ཤོབ་བེ་.

ཤ་བོ་ (shāwo) main ¶ དགྲ་ཤ་བོ་ Main enemy.

ཤ་བོ་ངལ་སོས་ (shāwo ŋɛ̱ɛ̱söö̀) tossing a pack/ load upward on one's shoulders when it is sliding downward.

ཤ་བེམ་ (shābem) body.

ཤ་དབྱེ་རུས་དབྱེ་ (shāmye rṳ̈ǜye) meat geeting separated from the bone due to overcooking; vi.—བྱེད་; —ཆགས་.

ཤ་འབུ་ (shāmbu) maggot.

ཤ་འབུར་ (shāmbur) any fleshy growth on the body.

ཤ་འབོལ་པོ་ (shā bö̱ö̱bo) tender meat.

ཤ་འབྱར་པགས་འབྱར་ (shānjar bāŋjar) keeping sth. close by oneself, keeping sth. in one's sight.

ཤ་འབྲས་ (shāmdrɛɛ̀) 1. dish consisting of meat, rice and curry. 2. sm. ཤ་འབྲས་.

ཤ་འབྲེག (shā drɛ̱ɛ̀) 1. va. to cut meat. 2. va. to castrate.

ཤ་སྦོས་ (shā bö̱ö̀) vi. to have one's skin swell up.

ཤ་སྦྱར་ (shājar) underwear.

ཤ་སྦྲང་ (shādraŋ) a kind of black fly commonly found around meat.

ཤ་མ་ (shāma) 1. placenta, afterbirth; vi.—ཐོན་ to have the afterbirth come out. 2. a kind of bird.

ཤ་མ་ཚིལ་ (shāma tsīì) mixed fat and meat.

ཤ་མ་རུས་ (shāmarüǜ) bone with meat on it.

ཤ་མར་ (shāmar) meat and butter.

ཤ་མར་ཁུ་ (shā mə̱ə̱gu) meat fried in butter.

ཤ་མིག་ཡོད་པ་ (shəmiì yö̱ö̀ba) a term used to describe a person who comes to visit precisely at the time for lunch or dinner [Lit. having (vulture's) eyes for meat].

ཤ་མིའི་ (shəmi) ch. shrimp.

ཤ་མེད་ (shāmeè) meatless.

ཤ་མོ་ (shāmo) 1. mushroom, fungus. 2. female deer.

ཤ་མོ་སྤྲེལ་མགོ (shāmo dre̱ngo) a type of mushroom.

ཤ་མོག་མོག (shā mo̱mo) dumpling stuffed with meat.

ཤ་མོང་ (shāmoŋ) sm. ཤ་མོ་.

ཤ་མོའི་རིགས་ (sha̱mö ri̱g) fungus/ mushroom plants.

ཤ་དམར་པོ་ (shā mārbo) sm. ཤ་རྗེན་.

ཤ་སྨིས་ (shəmiì) sm. ཤ་མིའི་.

ཤ་སྨིན་ (shāmen) 1. sm. ཤ་ནག. 2. scar.

ཤ་སྨན་ (shāmɛn) spices (for foods); va.—རྒྱག to spice foods.

ཤ་སྨན་ཝེ་ཅིང་ (shāmɛn we̱jin) tib. ch. monosodium glutinate.

ཤ་སྨིད་འབྲུག་དབྱིབས་མ་ (shəmiì dru̱gyibmə) lobster.

ཤ་སྨིད་ཉོ་སྐྱ་ (shəmiì ŋōgya) freshwater shrimp.

ཤ་ཙོག (shādzog) camel hump.

ཤ་གཙང་རུས་གཙང་ (shādzaŋ rṳ̈ǜdzaŋ) having a good/ clean caste or lineage.

ཤ་གཙབ་འཕྲུལ་འཁོར་ (shādzəb trüügɔɔ) meat-grinding machine.

ཤ་གཙབ་རུས་གཙབ་ (shādzəb rṳ̈ǜdzəb) sm. ཤ་འཐོར་རུས་འཐོར་.

ཤ་བཙོ་ (shā dzō) va. to cook meat.

ཤ་བཙོན་ (shādzön) captive/ prisoner of one's enemy.

ཤ་བཙོས་ (shādzöö̀) p. of ཤ་བཙོ་.

ཤ་རྩི་ (shā dzī) sm. ཤ་མདོག.

ཤ་རྩིད་གོ་རྩིད་ (shādziì go̱dziì) an inferior type of wool.

ཤ་ཆ་ (shādza) love, fondness, affection, concern, affinity, solidarity; va.—བྱེད་ to have love/ fondness/ affection/ concern/ affinity ¶ ངས་ཁོང་ལ་ཤ་ཆ་བྱས་ནས་སྐྱོན་བརྗོད་བྱས་པ་ཡིན་ I criticized him out of love.

ཤ་ཆ་ཆེན་པོ་ (shādza cēmbo) having great love, fondness, affection, concern, affinity; solidarity.

ཤ་ཆ་རྣམ་དག (shādza nāmdaà) loyal, faithful, loving.

ཤ་ཆ་པོ་ (shā tsābo) sm. ཤ་ཆ་ཆེན་པོ་.

ཤ་ཆ་མེད་པ་ (shādza mɛ̱ɛ̀ba) insincere, disloyal, not loving.

ཤ་ཆ་ཟོལ་མེད་ (shādza sö̱ö̱meè) sm. ཤ་ཆ་རྣམ་དག.

ཤ་ཆང་ཁྱི་འཁྲིད་ (shādzaŋ kyīdriì) shung. aiding evil people [Lit. leading a dog to a deer's den].

ཤ་ཚན་ (shādzen) 1. maternal relatives. 2. body heat.

ཤ་ཆའི་གདམ་ངན་ (shāwɛ dāmŋɛn) loving criticism.

ཤ་ཚལ་སྒོང་གསུམ་ (shā tsɛ̄ɛ go̱ŋ sūm) the three: meat, vegetables, eggs.

ཤ་ཚིལ་ (shədzii) 1. fat of meat. 2. meat and fat.

ཤ་ཚུགས་ (shādzuù) shape of a body.

ཤ་ཚེ་ (shā tsē) sm. གཤའ་དཀར་.

ཤ་ཚོང་ (shādzoŋ) selling meat; va.—རྒྱག.

ཤ་ཚོད་ལས་ (shā tsȫö̀ lɛ̱ɛ̀) va. to cook meat.

ཤ་ཚོན་པོ་ (shā tsȫmbo) fatty meat.

ཤ་ཚྭ་སྲོ་ (shā tsādro) salted meat.

ཤ་མཚན་ (shādzɛn) sm. ཤ་རྟགས་.

ཤ་འཚོང་ (shā tsōŋ) va. to sell meat.

ཤ་འཚོང་ཁང་ (shādoŋgaŋ) meat store.

ཤ་འཚོང་མཁན་ (shā tsōŋñɛn) meat seller.

ཤ་མཛེར་ (shādzer) wart.

ཤ་འཛར་ (shādzar) provisions of meat for a journey.

ཤ་འཛིན་ (shəndzin) prong/ hook for lifting meat when it is being cooked.

ཤ་འཛིན་ཐོག་གི་ཁྲོན་སྐྱོག (shəndzin tɔ̄ɔ̀gi trōmgyɔɔ̀) sth. that is ready/ poised to fall [Lit. a well ladle hanging on a hook].

ཤ་ཞག (shāshaà) the grease from meat that is either floating in liquids or coagulated.

ཤ་ཞན་པོ་ (shā she̱mbo) lean, thin.

ཤ་ཞིམ་པོ་ཨ་ཁུ་སྤྱང་ཀིས་བཟས་ ཁག་ངན་པ་ཨ་ལྕེ་ཝ་མོར་དཀྲིས་ (shā shi̱mbu əgu jəŋgi sɛ̱ɛ̀ kāà ŋɛ̱mba ājwe wa̱moo drīì) blaming the wrong person [Lit. the delicious meat was eaten by the wolf but the fox was blamed for it].

ཤ་ཞུ་ (shə shu̱) vi. to thaw.

ཤ་ཞུ་བ་ (shā shu̱wə) sm. ཤ་ཉམས་.

ཤ་ཞེན་ (shāshen) loyalty, love; va.—བྱེད་ ¶ རྒྱལ་ཁབ་ལ་ཤ་ཞེན་ Patriotism to the nation.

ཤ་ཞེན་དོར་མེད་ (shāshen tɔ̱rmeè) unchanging loyalty.

ཤ་ཞེན་མེད་པ་ (shāshen me̱èba) disloyal, unpatriotic.

ཤ་ཞོལ་ཆང་གསུམ་ (shāshö cāŋsum) shung. abbr. the three (Prime Ministers): Shatra, Zholkang and Changkyim.

ཤ་གཞའ་ (shā sa̱) a scar that heals leaving a concave hole.

ཤ་ཟ་ (shā sa̱) 1. sm. ཤ་ཟན་. 2. a kind of demon that feeds on human flesh.

ཤ་ཟ་ལྕེ་སྤྱང་གདོང་ (shāsa jējaŋ do̱ŋ) 1. a flesh eating ghost with a head of a jackal. 2. name of a protective deity.

ཤ་ཟད་རུས་ཐུག (shāsɛɛ̀ rṳ̈ǜduù) in a difficult or desperate situation [Lit. the meat is exhausted and one meets the bone (to eat)].

ཤ་ཟན་ (shāsɛn) 1. carnivorous. 2. wild beast ¶ ཤ་ཟན་སྲོག་ཆགས་ Carnivorous animals.

ཤ་ཟས་ (shāsɛɛ̀) foods/ dishes that include meat.

ཤ་ཟས་བསྙལ་མ་ (shāsɛɛ̀ ñɛ̄ɛ̄ma) meat that has been marinated/ cured.

ཤ་ཟིང་སྤུ་ཟིང་ (shəsiŋ būsiŋ) hair-raising fright.

ཤ་ཟུངས་ (shəsuŋ) sm. ཤ་འཛིན་.

ཤ་གཟུག (shā su̱g) one fourth of a carcass.

ཤ་གཟུགས་མ་ (shā su̱gmə) a type of leather boot worn by monks.

ཤ་གཟུར་རུས་འཛིན་ (shā su̱r rṳ̈ǜ dzi̱n) lack of judgement [Lit. throw meat, hold bone].

ཤ་བཟན་ (shāsɛn) a castrated sheep.

ཤ་ཡང་ཁུམས་ (shāyaŋ kūm) arc. va. to take revenge.

ཤ་ཡི་ཤ་ལན་ལེན་ (shāyi shālɛn le̱n) va. to take revenge.

ཤ་ཡོད་པགས་ཡོད་ (shāyöö̀ bāgyöö̀) a good result, successful ¶ ད་ལོའི་ལས་ཀ་དེ་ཤ་ཡོད་པགས་ཡོད་བྱུང་

སོང་ This year the work was successful. [Lit. having meat and having skin].

ཤ་ར་མ་ར་ (shāra mara) straight, direct ། ཁྱེད་རང་ཚོང་ཁང་ལ་ཤ་ར་མ་ར་རང་ཕྱིན་ནས་མགྱོགས་པོ་ལོག་ཤོག You should go straight to the store and return quickly.

ཤ་ར་ར་ (shā rara) 1. sm. ཤ་ར་མ་ར་. 2. sound of rain.

ཤ་ར་ཤོ་རེ་ (shāra shōre) muddy.

ཤ་རལ་སྙིང་གས་ (shārɛɛ ñiŋgɛɛ̀) great sadness [Lit. rip the flesh and split the heart].

ཤ་རི་ (shəri) oriole.

ཤ་རིགས་ (shərii̖) various kinds of meat.

ཤ་རིགས་ལྕགས་ཀྲིན་ (shərii̖ jēgdrin) canned meat.

ཤ་རིགས་མཉམ་འབྲེལ་བཟོ་གྲྭ་ (shərii̖ ñamdree sodra) coop meat factory.

ཤ་རིགས་ལས་སྣོན་བཟོ་གྲྭ་ (shərii̖ lɛ̀ɛnön sodra) meat processing factory.

ཤ་རི་ཤུ་རི་ (shəri shūri) 1. hurriedly, hastily; va.—བྱེད་ ། ཁོ་ཟ་ཆས་ཀྱང་ཟ་ལོང་མེད་པར་ཤ་རི་ཤུ་རི་བྱས་ནས་ཕྱིན་སོང་ He didn't have time to eat and left hurriedly. 2. mediocre, inferior quality ། ཁོང་གིས་ང་ལ་ཇ་ཤ་རི་ཤུ་རི་ཞིག་བླུགས་བྱུང་ He served me an inferior tea.

ཤ་རིད་ (shā rii̖) vi. to become thin.

ཤ་རིད་པོ་ (shā riibu) skinny, thin.

ཤ་རིད་དབུགས་ཉམས་ (shī rii̖ ū ñam) weak and skinny; vi.—ཆགས་ to become weak and skinny.

ཤ་རིན་ (shərin) the price of meat.

ཤ་རིལ་ (shərii) 1. meatballs. 2. a relic.

ཤ་རུ་ (shəru) deer antler.

ཤ་རུལ་ (shā rüü) vi. to rot (meat).

ཤ་རུལ་སྦྲང་འཚུབ་ (shārüü draŋdzub) people of the same ilk associating together/ getting along together [Lit. flies hovering over rotten meat].

ཤ་རུས་ (shā rüü̖) meat and bone, flesh and bone.

ཤ་རུས་གཅིག་པ་ (shərüü̖ jīgbə) 1. relatives. 2. of the same ethnic group.

ཤ་རུས་འདྲེས་པ་ (shārüü̖ dreèba) a very close relationship, very close ties [Lit. flesh and bone mixed].

ཤ་རུས་འབྲལ་མེད་ (shārüü̖ drɛɛmeè) sm. ཤ་རུས་འདྲེས་པ་.

ཤ་རེ་བ་ (shārewa) sm. ཤ་ར་མ་ར་.

ཤ་རེ་མ་རེ་ (shāre mare) sm. ཤ་ར་མ་ར་.

ཤ་རེ་ཚ་ (shāredza) 1. oh. too bad (in genuine sense). 2. too bad (in a pejorative sense).

ཤ་རེ་ཤ་རེ་ (shāre shāre) sm. ཤ་ར་མ་ར་.

ཤ་རེ་ཤོ་རེ་ (shāre shōre) 1. carelessly. 2. sm. ཤ་ར་མ་ར་.

ཤ་རོད་པ་ (shā reèba) sm. ཤ་སྐམ་པོ་.

ཤ་རོ་ (shāro) 1. corpse. 2. callus, scab; vi.—ཆགས་ to become callused/ scab.

ཤ་རྭ་ (shāra) antler.

ཤ་རློན་ (shālön) fresh meat.

ཤ་ལ་ (shāla) a tool for smoothing/ evening a plowed field.

ཤ་ལ་ཁྱི་འཁོར་འཁོར་ (shāla kyī kɔ̄ɔ̄gɔɔ) men attracted by sth. (e.g., a woman) [Lit. dog attracted by meat].

ཤ་ལན་ (shālɛn) revenge, vengeance; va.—སློན་; —ལེན་; —སློག to seek revenge.

ཤ་ལན་ཤ་དང་ཁྲག་ལན་ཁྲག (shālɛn shā daŋ trāàlɛn trāà) seeking revenge/ vengeance.

ཤ་ལམ་གྲི་བཅད་ (shālam trijɛ̀ɛ) shung. to lay a foundation before starting work [Lit. to draw a line before cutting the meat].

ཤ་ལས་ (shālɛɛ̀) working with meat (e.g., cutting, drying); va.—བྱེད་; —གཏོང་.

ཤ་ལེབ་ (shāleb) slab of meat (like a steak).

ཤ་ཤུན་ (shāshün) outermost layer of skin.

ཤ་ཤེད་ (shāsheè) coat, sheen, appearance (of an animal); vi.—རྒྱས་ to have good coat/ sheen, to grow fat, to put on flesh (for animals); vi.—ཉམས་; —གུད་; —འཛགས་ to grow thinner, to loose sheen ། ཤ་ཤེད་རྒྱས་པའི་ཕྱུགས་རིགས་ Healthy looking animals.

ཤ་ཤེད་འཁུམ་ (shāsheè kūm) vi. to have muscles atrophy.

ཤ་ཤེད་རྒྱས་པ་ (shāsheè gyɛ̀ɛba) sm. ཤ་ཤེད་ཡག་པོ་.

ཤ་ཤེད་བཟང་པོ་ (shasheè saŋbo) sm. ཤ་ཤེད་ཡག་པོ་.

ཤ་ཤེད་ཡག་པོ་ (shāsheè yagbo) having a healthy coat/ sheen.

ཤ་ཤུན་ (shāshün) flesh and skin.

ཤ་གཤིན་པོ་ (shā shīmbu) sm. ཤ་འབོལ་པོ་.

ཤ་བཤད་རུས་བཤད་ (shāshɛɛ̀ rüü̖ shɛ̄ɛ̀) narrating in full detail.

ཤ་བཤའ་ (shā shā) va. to slaughter animals for meat.

ཤ་སོབ་སོབ་ (shā sōbsoò) dried meat that is soft.

ཤ་སོས་པ་ (shā sɔ̄ɔ̀bo) fresh meat.

ཤ་སྲབ་པོ་ (shā drəbbu) sm. ཤ་རིད་པོ་.

ཤ་སྲེག (shā sēg) sm. ཤ་བསྲེགས་.

ཤ་སྲིད་ (shā sēa flesh eating demon.

ཤ་སློམ་ (shālom) a small woven basket used to hold meat.

ཤ་གསར་ (shāsar) sm. ཤ་རློན་.

ཤ་གསར་སྒང་ (shāsargaŋ) a place at the north side of the Tsuglagang temple in Lhasa where fresh meat is sold.

ཤ་གསོས་ (shāsöö̀) skin cream.

ཤ་བསྲེགས་ (shāseg) roast meat; va. ཤ་བསྲེགས་; —གཏོང་ to roast meat.

ཤ་བསྲེགས་མ་ (shā sēgma) roast meat.

ཤ་ཧྲུག (shəhruù) sm. ཤ་ཧྲུག་ཧྲུག.

ཤ་ཧྲུག་ཧྲུག (shā hrūghruù) minced meat, ground meat; va.—བཟོ་ to mince/ grind meat.

ཤ་ལྷག (shālhaà) 1. leftover meat. 2. goiter. 3. camel hump.

ཤ་ལྷུ་ (shəlhu) 1. meat cut into pieces. 2. one quarter of a carcass.

ཤ་ལྷེབ་ (shālheb) slice of flesh (usu. cut by a sword strike).

ཤ་ལྷེབ་ལྷེབ་ (shā lhēblheb) sm. ཤ་ལྷེབ་.

ཤཱཀྱ་ (shākya) Shakya lineage in ancient India.

ཤཱཀྱ་ཐུབ་པ་ (shākya tūbbə) the Shakyamuni Buddha.

ཤཱཀྱ་ཐུབ་པ་ཕེབས་ཀྱང་ཞྭ་མི་ཕུད་ གླང་ཆེན་སྨྱོན་པ་ཡོང་ཡང་ལམ་མི་བྲུར་ (shākya tūbbə pēègyaŋ sha mibüü lāŋjen ñōmba yoŋyaŋ lam mi sur) sb. who is so extremely proud/ arrogant that it makes his judgment poor [Lit. even when the Buddha comes one does not take off one's hat, even when a mad elephant comes one does not make room on the road].

ཤཱཀྱ་ཐུབ་པ་རིག་ན་ཞྭ་མི་ཕུད་ གླང་ཆེན་སྨྱོན་པ་ཐུབ་ན་ལམ་མི་གཟར་ (shākya tūbbə rignə sha mibüü lāŋjen ñomba tūbnə lammi saa) sm. ཤཱཀྱ་ཐུབ་པ་ཕེབས་ཀྱང་ཞྭ་མི་ཕུད་ གླང་ཆེན་སྨྱོན་པ་ཡོང་ཡང་ལམ་མི་བྲུར་.

ཤཱཀྱ་མུ་ནི་ (shākya muni) the Shakyamuni Buddha.

ཤཱཀྱ་སེང་གེ་ (shāgya sēŋge) shung. sm. ཤཱཀྱ་ཐུབ་པ་.

ཤཱཀྱའི་རིང་ལུགས་ (shāgyɛ riŋluù) Buddhism [Lit. the doctrine of Shakyamuni].

ཤཱ་རིའི་བུ་ (shāriibu) one of the ten disciples of the Buddha.

ཤག (shāà) 1. sm.* བཞག. 2. house, apartment, dwelling (usu. used for monks). 3. most probably, likely ། གནས་ཚུལ་དེ་བདེན་པ་ཡིན་ཤག་རེད་ Most probably that information is true. 4. abbr. of ཤག་ཚང་.

ཤག་གི་ཤིག་གེ་ (shāggi shīgge) loosely packed/ woven/ arranged.

ཤག་སྒྲ་ (shāàdra) the sound made by drawing out a sword.

ཤག་སྐོར་ (shāàgɔɔ) apartments surrounding a courtyard.

ཤག་དངོས་ (shāàŋuoò) the possessions of a ཤག་ཚང་.

ཤག་ཆས་ (shsāgjɛɛ̀) 1. furniture. 2. the belongings in a monk's apartment.

ཤག་ཆུང་ (shāgjuŋ) sm. ཤག་མིག.

ཤག་དི་ (shāgdi) a type of sword.

ཤག་པོ་ (shāgbo) close friends; va.—འགྲིགས་ to make good/ close friends.

ཤག་མ་ (shāgma) small stones/ pebbles, gravel.

ཤག་མིག (shəgmiì) a small room or dwelling.

ཤག་ཚང་ (shāgdzaŋ) a household/ family of monks in a monastery.

ཤག་མཚེས་ (shāgdzeè) sm. ཤག་མཚེས་པ་.

ཤག་མཚེས་པ་ (shāg dzēèma) neighboring ཤག in a monastery, neighbors in a monastery.

ཤག་རུག (shāgruù) sm. ཤག་མ་.

ཤག་རོགས་ (shāgrɔ̀ɔ) monk roommate.

ཤག་ལ་ (shāgla) (vb. + —) most probably ༑ཁོང་གིས་ཡི་གེ་བཏང་ཡོད་ཤག་ལ་ Most probably he sent the letter.

ཤག་ཤག (shāgshaà) 1. most probably. 2. the sound made by rain.

ཤག་ཤིག (shāgshig) abbr. of ཤག་གི་ཤིག་གི་.

ཤག་ས་ (shāgsa) rocky soil, soil having lots of pebbles.

ཤག་ཧྲུག (shāghruù) sm. ཤག་མ་.

ཤགས་རྒྱག (shāà gyaà) 1. va. to compete in singing where songs/ verses are sung back and forth in response to the previous song. 2. va. to debate in court.

ཤགས་འདེབས་ (shāà deb) sm. ཤགས་རྒྱག.

ཤགས་ལེན་ (shāglen) an answer/ response in a debate or song competition.

ཤང་ (shāŋ) ch. xiang/ township (a rural administrative unit consisting of several villages).

ཤང་ཀང་ (shāŋgaŋ) Hong Kong.

ཤང་ཀྲང་ (shāŋdraŋ) ch. head of a xiang.

ཤང་པོ་ (shāŋbo) 1. easy to get along with, outgoing. 2. generous ༑ཁོང་ལག་པ་ཤང་པོ་ཡོད་པ་རེད་ He is a generous person.

ཤང་པོར་ཉལ་ (shāŋbo ñɛɛ) to lie down face up.

ཤང་ལང་ (shāŋlaŋ) knife/ sword with a blade on one side only.

ཤང་ཤང་ (shāŋshaŋ) slim, slender.

ཤང་ཤང་དེའུ་ (shāŋshaŋ dēwu) 1. partridge. 2. a mythological bird with a human-like upper body.

ཤང་ཤྲི་ (shāŋshri) shung. a lama.

ཤང་ཧྲེང་ (shāŋhreŋ) see ཞང་ཧྲེང་.

ཤངས་ (shāŋ) 1. h. of སྣ་ཁུང་. 2. a district in Central Tibet.

ཤངས་སྐད་ (shāŋgeè) h. of སྣ་སྐད་.

ཤངས་ཁུང་ (shāŋguŋ) h. of སྣ་ཁུང་.

ཤངས་ཁྲག (shāŋdraà) h. of སྣ་ཁྲག.

ཤངས་གོང་ (shāŋgoŋ) h. of སྣ་གོང་.

ཤངས་ཆུ་ (shāŋju) h. of སྣ་ཆུ་.

ཤངས་ཐ་ (shāŋda) h. of སྣ་ཐ་.

ཤངས་ཐག (shāŋdaà) h. of སྣ་ཐག.

ཤངས་གདོང་ (shāŋdoŋ) h. of སྣ་གདོང་.

ཤངས་སྣབས་ (shāŋnəb) h. of སྣབས་ཐུག.

ཤངས་སྤུ་ (shāŋbu) nose hair.

ཤངས་ཕྱི་ (shāŋji) sm. ཤངས་འཕྱིད་.

ཤངས་ཕྱིས་ (shāŋjiì) h. of ཤངས་འཕྱིད་.

ཤངས་འཕྱིད་ (shāŋjiì) h. of སྣབས་ཕྱིས་.

ཤངས་རྩེ་ (shāŋdze) h. of སྣ་རྩེ་.

ཤངས་མཚལ་ (shāŋdzɛɛ) h. of སྣ་ཁྲག.

ཤངས་གཟེངས་མཐོ་བ་ (shāŋseŋ tōwa) h. of སྣ་གདོང་མཐོ་བ་.

ཤངས་རུ་ (shāŋru) h. of སྣ་རུ་.

ཤངས་གསང་པོ་ (shāŋ sāŋbo) h. of སྣ་གསང་པོ་.

ཤད་ (shɛ̄ɛ̀) 1. the vertical line used in Tibetan for punctuation. 2. a comb ༑སྐྲ་ཤད་འདི་གསར་པ་རེད་ This comb is new.

ཤད་: p. and f. བཤད་ (shɛ̄ɛ̀) 1. va. to comb (hair) ༑ང་སྐྲ་ཤད་དགོས་ཡོད་ I have to comb my hair. 2. va. to card wool ༑བལ་འདི་བཤད་རྗེས་སྐུད་པ་འཁལ་དགོས་ After carding the wool, one has to spin it into thread.

ཤད་རྒྱག (shɛ̄ɛ̀ gyaà) va. to churn (tea).

ཤད་མ་ (shɛ̄ɛ̀ma) 1. a type of high quality woolen cloth.

ཤད་མོ་ (shɛ̄ɛ̀mo) three year old female yak/ cow.

ཤད་མཚམས་ (shɛ̄ndzam) the place where a ཤད་ is written.

ཤད་ཟུག་པོ་ (shɛ̄ɛ̀ sugbo) sth. that is able to churn well.

ཤད་བཟང་པོ་ (shɛ̄ɛ̀ saŋbo) a quality animal skin.

ཤད་འོག (shɛ̄ɛ̀wɔ̀ɔ) a second quality ཤད་མ་.

ཤད་ཡར་ (shɛ̄ɛ̀yar) two or three year old cattle.

ཤད་ཤད་ (shɛ̄ɛ̀shɛ̄ɛ̀) 1. promptly, quickly. 2. combing; va.—རྒྱག.

ཤན་ (shɛ̄n) 1. a metal band holding a barrel/ churn together; va.—རྒྱག to affix a metal band. ༑རག་ཤན་ A brass band. 2. ch. xian/ county/ district (an administration unit consisting several ཤང་). 3. sm. བཤན་. 4. va. to beat ༑ཁོས་རྟག་པར་ཕྲུ་གུ་ཤན་གྱི་འདུག He beats the child every day.

ཤན་ཀྲང་ (shɛ̄ndraŋ) ch. head of a xian.

ཤན་ཁ་ (shɛ̄nga) ferry dock.

ཤན་ཁའི་གྲུ་ཁ་ (shɛ̄ngɛ trugə) name of ferry crossing just east of Lhasa.

ཤན་ཁང་ (shɛ̄ngaŋ) sm. བཤན་ཁང་.

ཤན་མཆུ་ (shɛ̄nju) the mouth of a bellows.

ཤན་འཇུག (shɛ̄njuù) sm. གུམ་ཤིང་.

ཤན་སྣངས་འབྱེད་ (shɛ̄ndaŋ jeè) shung. va. to differentiate what is true and what is false.

ཤན་དུ་འགྱུར་ (shɛ̄ndu gyur) sm. ཤན་ཞུགས་.

ཤན་བརྡེག (shɛ̄ndeg) 1. clean items being polluted or defiled by an unclean item. 2. suffering the consequences of someone else's wrongdoing.

ཤན་ཕྱེ་ (shɛ̄nje) p. of ཤན་འབྱེད་.

ཤན་འབྱེད་ (shɛ̄n ceè) distinguishing/ determining/ differentiating between things; va.—བྱེད་ ༑ཁྲིམས་ཁང་ནས་གྱོད་གཞི་དེའི་སྐོར་བདེན་རྫུན་ཤན་འབྱེད་བྱས་པ་རེད་ The court determined what is true and false in this case.

ཤན་སྦྱར་ (shɛ̄njar) bilingual or multilingual (texts/ book/ dictionary).

ཤན་ཙ་ (shɛ̄ndza) name of a nomad district in Nagchu Prefecture.

ཤན་ཞུགས་ (shɛ̄n shuù) vi. to be influenced/ spoiled by ༑ཕྲུ་གུ་འདི་ལ་གྲོགས་པོ་ངན་པའི་ཤན་ཞུགས་ནས་ཨ་རག་འཐུང་གི་འདུག The child was influenced by bad friends and (now) drinks liquor.

ཤན་ཤོར་ (shɛ̄n shɔ̄ɔ) sm. ཤན་ཞུགས་.

ཤབ་: p. ཤབས་; f. ཤབ་; imp. ཤོབས་ (shəb) va. to draw a sword.

ཤབ་ཀྲད་ (shəbdreè) sm. ཤ་ཀྲད་.

ཤབ་རྒྱུག (shəb gyuù) running after sth.; va.—བྱེད་.

ཤབ་བི་ཤུབ་བི་ (shəbbi shūbbi) whispering; va.—ཤོད་; —ལབ་ to whisper.

ཤབ་བེ་ཤོབ་བེ་ (shəbbe shōbbe) sm. ཤབ་བི་ཤུབ་བི་.

ཤབ་ཤུབ་ (shəbshub) sm. ཤབ་ཤོབ་.

ཤབ་ཤུབ་ཅབ་སྒྲ (shəbshub jəbdra) shung. sound of whispering and talking in a low voice.

ཤབ་ཤོབ་ (shəbshob) whispering; va.—ཤོད་; —གཏོང་; —ལབ་ to whisper.

ཤབས་ (shəb) p. of ཤབ་.

ཤམ་ (shām) sm. གཤམ་.

ཤམ་གོས་ (shāmgöö) lower garments.

ཤམ་ཐབས་ (shāmdəb) lower garment worn by monks.

ཤམ་ཐབས་ཀྱི་ཁྲལ་ (shāmdəbgi trɛ̄ɛ) 1. tax collected from monks. 2. shung. the duties (tax) for monastic work that falls on all monks.

ཤམ་ཐབས་ཀྱི་གཟན་ (shāmdəbgi sɛn) sm. ཤམ་ཐབས་.

ཤམ་ཐབས་ཁྲལ་འགེལ་ (shāmdəb trɛ̄ɛgee) sm. ཤམ་ཐབས་ཀྱི་ཁྲལ་.

ཤམ་ཐབས་སྣ་ལྡོག་ཕྱི་ལྡོག (shāmdəb ŋālɔ̀ɔ cīlɔ̀ɔ) folding up the lower garment of monks dress when running, etc.; va.—བྱེད་.

ཤམ་དུ་ (shāmdu) sm. གཤམ་དུ་.

ཤམ་བྷ་ལ་ (shāmbala) mythical place in Tibetan religious folklore (Shambala).

ཤམ་བུ་ (shāmbu) fringe, trimming (usu. on windows); va.—འདོགས་; —རྒྱག to put up a fringe on a window. ། སྒེའུ་ཁུང་ལ་ཤམ་བུ་གསར་པ་བརྒྱབ་འདུག They have put up new fringes on the windows.

ཤམ་བུ་སྒེད་རིས་ (shāmbu gēèrii) 1. paintings of cloth fringes on the upper part of the Tibetan houses. 2. three horizontal lines painted on the sides of some Tibetan houses.

ཤམ་སུལ་ (shāmsüü) the pleats used in ཤམ་བུ་.

ཤའང་ཀའང་ (shāŋgaŋ) Hong Kong.

ཤའི་ཁོག (shɛ̄gɔɔ̀) carcass.

ཤའི་སྤྱན་ (shɛ̄jɛn) human eye, naked eye.

ཤའི་འཛེར་པ་ (shɛ̄ dzerba) sm. ཤ་འཛེར་.

ཤར་ (shār) 1. east ། ཤར་དཀྲུག་ནུབ་རྒྱག Stirring up trouble in the east and attacking in the west. 2. vi. to rise, to arise, to come to be ། དུས་རབས་གསར་དུ་ཤར་བ་རེད་ A new era arose. 3. (— + vb.) verbal action done directly/ straight/ without obstacles ། ཁྱེད་རང་ཚོ་ཤར་གྱིས་ཕྱིན་ན་ལྷ་སར་མགྱོགས་པོ་སླེབས་ཀྱི་རེད་ If you go straight, you will reach Lhasa quickly.

ཤར་ཀྱག (shāāgyaà) sm. ཤར་རྒྱག.

ཤར་དཀྲུག་ནུབ་རྡེག (shāādrɔɔ̀ nubdeg) feint an attack on one side while really attacking on the other side [Lit. stir up the east and strike the west].

ཤར་སྐྱོད་ (shārgyöö) sm. ཤར་བསྐྱོད་.

ཤར་བསྐྱོད་ (shārgyöö) going straight ahead, proceeding directly; va.—བྱེད་ to go straight/ directly ། ཁྱེད་རང་ཚོ་ཤར་སྐྱོད་བྱས་ན་ལྷ་སར་མགྱོགས་པོ་སླེབས་ཀྱི་རེད་ If you go directly you will reach Lhasa quickly.

ཤར་གབ་ནུབ་ཡིབ (shārgəb nubyib) hiding all over; va.—བྱེད་ ། རྐུན་མ་དེ་ཤར་གབ་ནུབ་ཡིབ་བྱས་ཙང་འཛིན་མ་ཐུབ་པ་རེད་ Because the thief is hiding all over, they were not able to catch him.

ཤར་གྱི་གཞུང་ཐིག (shārgi shuŋdig) east longitude.

ཤར་གྱིས་ (shārgyi) straight, directly ། ཁྱེད་རང་ཚོ་ཤར་གྱིས་ཕྱིན་ན་ལྷ་སར་མགྱོགས་པོ་སླེབས་ཀྱི་རེད་ If you go straight you will reach Lhasa quickly.

ཤར་བགྲོད་ (shārdröö) sm. ཤར་བསྐྱོད་.

ཤར་རྒྱ་མཚོ་ཆེན་པོ་ (shār gyadzo cēmbo) Pacific Ocean.

ཤར་རྒྱག (shārgyaà) direct, straight ། ཤར་རྒྱག་ཀ་ལ་ཀ་ཏར་ཕྱིན་པ་ཡིན་ (It) went straight to Calcutta.

ཤར་རྒྱུག་ནུབ་རྒྱུག (shārgyuù nubgyuù) running all over the place, searching everywhere; va.—བྱེད་ ། ཁོང་གིས་ཤར་རྒྱུག་ནུབ་རྒྱུག་བྱས་ཀྱང་ལས་ཀ་ཡག་པོ་ཞིག་རག་མ་སོང་ He searched everywhere but was unable to find work.

ཤར་རྒྱུད་ (shārgyüü) eastern side/ area ། གཙང་པོའི་ཤར་རྒྱུད་ The eastern side of the river.

ཤར་སྒོ་ (shārgo) east door.

ཤར་སྒྲོལ་ (shārdröö) crossing a river, etc. without hindrance/ difficulty.

ཤར་ངོས་ (shārŋöö) easterly side/ direction.

ཤར་ལྕོག (sharjoò) abbr. of ཤར་ཆེན་ལྕོགས་.

ཤར་ཆེན་ལྕོགས་ (shārjenjɔɔ̀) a prison used for political prisoners in the east side of the Potala (in tt.).

ཤར་གཏོང་ (shārdoŋ) sending directly/ straight; va.—བྱེད་ ། ཁོང་གིས་ལྷ་སར་བང་ཆེན་ཤར་གཏོང་བྱས་འདུག He sent a messenger straight to Lhasa.

ཤར་རྟགས་ (shārdaà) a mark put on a juniper (tree's) east side so when it is later cut to make statues, the east will be on the side of god's face; va.—རྒྱག.

ཤར་བལྟ་ (shār dā) facing towards east ། ཁང་པའི་སྒོ་ཤར་བལྟ་རེད་ The door of the house faces east.

ཤར་མཐའ་ (shārta) Far East.

ཤར་བདལ་གཏོང་ (shārdo dōŋ) sm. སྐྱ་མདལ་གཏོང་.

ཤར་ནུབ་ (shārnub) east and west.

ཤར་པ་ (shārba) 1. easterner. 2. Sherpa.

ཤར་པོ་ (shārbo) person in the prime of his life.

ཤར་སྤྲིན་ (shārdrin) easterly clouds.

ཤར་ཕེབས་ (shārpeb) h. of ཤར་སྐྱོད་.

ཤར་ཕོ་ (shārpo) sm. ཤར་པོ་.

ཤར་ཕྱོགས་ (shārjɔɔ̀) the eastern side/ direction, the east.

ཤར་ཕྱོགས་དམར་ (shārjɔɔ̀ mār) "The East is Red" (title of song in China).

ཤར་ཕྱོགས་ལོ་གསར་ (shārjɔɔ̀ losar) farmer's New Year celebrated in Tibet in the 12th month of the Tibetan calendar.

ཤར་བུ་ (shərbu) decorative hanging used on the roof of monasteries/ temples.

ཤར་བྱང་ (shārjaŋ) northeast.

ཤར་བྲོས་ནུབ་བྱོལ་ (shārdröö nubjöö) fleeing all over; va.—བྱེད་ ། ཇག་པ་ལྷག་འཕྲོ་རྣམས་ཤར་བྲོས་ནུབ་བྱོལ་བྱས་སོང་ The remaining bandits fled all over. [Lit. flee to the east, flee to the west].

ཤར་མ་ (shārma) 1. eastern. 2. females in their twenties. 3. one, a single.

ཤར་མར་ (shārmar) directly, straight; va.—ཤོད་ to speak directly without hesitation.

ཤར་མོ་ (shārmo) sm. ཤར་མ་, 1.

ཤར་འཚོལ་ནུབ་བསྡུ་ (shārdzöö nubdu) patching/ scraping together from here and there, putting together odds and ends ། ཁང་པའི་ཅ་ཆ་རྣམས་ཤར་འཚོལ་ནུབ་འཚོལ་བྱས་ནས་ཁང་པ་དེ་རྒྱག་ཐུབ་ཙམ་བྱུང་བ་རེད་ They scraped together the construction materials from here and there and were just able to build the house.

ཤར་ཡོ་གླིང་ (shār yoliŋ) Eastern Europe.

ཤར་ཡོ་རོབ་ (shār yorob) Eastern Europe.

ཤར་རེར་ (shārre) directly, straight ། ཁོས་ངའི་ནང་ལ་ཤ་རེར་སླེབས་བྱུང་ He came straight to my house.

ཤར་རླུང་ (shārluŋ) easterly wind.

ཤར་ལུ་ (shārlu) sm. ཤར་པོ་.

ཤར་ལུས་འཕགས་པོ་ (shārlüü pāgbo) the eastern continent surrounding Mt. Mehru.

ཤར་ཤར་ (shārshar) sm. ཤར་ཤར་རྒྱང་.

ཤར་ཤར་རྒྱང་ (shār shārgyaŋ) directly to the east.

ཤར་ཤུར་ (shārshur) abbr. of ཤར་རེ་ཤུ་རེ་.

ཤར་ཤོར་ (shārshɔr) abbr. of ཤར་རེ་ཤོར་རེ་.

ཤར་སླེབས་མེ་འཁོར་ (shārleb megɔɔ) express train.

ཤར་ལྷོ་ (shārlho) southeast.

ཤར་ལྷོའི་ཨེ་གླིང་ (shārlhö ēliŋ) Southeast Asia.

ཤར་ཨེ་གླིང་ (shār ēliŋ) East Asia.

ཤལ་ (shɛ̄ɛ) sm. བཤལ་.

ཤལ་སྒོར་ (shɛ̄ɛgɔɔ) disc harrow.

ཤལ་བ་ (shɛ̄ɛwa) harrow.

ཤལ་འཛིན་ (shɛ̄ndzin) person who uses the harrow.

ཤལ་ལ་ (shɛ̄ɛla) sm. བཤལ་ལ་.

ཤལ་བཤལ་ (shɛ̄ɛ shɛ̄ɛ) va. to harrow the land.

ཤས་ (shɛ̀ɛ) 1. several, a few (abbr. of ཁ་ཤས་). 2. lease arrangement for land (half of yield to owner and half to leasee). 3. a part, fraction, share.

ཤས་ཁ་ (shɛ̀ɛga) part, share.

ཤས་ཆུང་ (shɛ̀ɛjuŋ) small part.

ཤས་ཆེ་ (shɛ̀ɛje) (vb. + —) maybe, perhaps ། ཁོ་སང་ཉིན་ཡོང་ཤས་ཆེ་ Maybe he will come tomorrow.

ཤས་ཆེ་བ་ (shɛ̀ɛjewa) most of, the major part.

ཤས་གཏོང་ (shɛ̀ɛ dōŋ) va. to lease land/ animals (on 50-50 basis) ། གཞིས་ཀ་དེས་ཞིང་ག་མང་པོ་ཞིག་ཤས་གཏོང་བྱས་འདུག That estate leased many fields on a 50-50 basis.

ཤས་ཞིང་ (shɛ̀ɛshiŋ) leased land/ fields.

ཤས་ལེན་ (shɛ̀ɛ len) va. to lease land or animals from the owner.

ཤས་སླེབས་ (shɛ̀ɛleb) profit/ income from leasing land or animals ། ལོ་འདིའི་ནང་གཞིས་ཀ་དེར་ཤས་སླེབས་ཆེན་པོ་བྱུང་ཡོད་པ་རེད་ This year the estate received large profit from its leases of land.

ཤི་ (shi) vi. to die ། ཁོ་ད་ལོ་ཤི་བ་རེད་ He died this year.

ཤི་སྐྱོན་ (shīgyün) death ། ནད་ཡམས་ཀྱིས་རྐྱེན་པས་སེམས་ཅན་མང་པོ་ཤི་སྐྱོན་བྱུང་འདུག Because of the epidemic many animals died.

ཤི་ཁ་ (shīgə) the moment of death.

ཤི་ཁ་ལྷ་མོ་ (shīgə lhāmo) just before dying ། ཁོ་ཤི་ཁ་ལྷ་མོར་ཁ་ཆེམས་བཞག་པ་རེད་ Just before dying he made a will.

ཤི་ཁའི་འཕག་འཛག (shīgɛ pāgdzaà) last-ditch struggle; va.—རྒྱག to make a last-ditch. struggle ། ཇག་པ་ལྷག་འཁྱོ་རྣམས་ཆ་མེད་གཏོང་ཁར་ཤི་ཁའི་འཕག་འཛག་བརྒྱབ་ནས་ཉེན་རྟོག་པར་ཚུར་རྒོལ་བྱས་འདུག The remaining bandits made a last-ditch struggle when they were about to be attacked and annihilated by the police.

ཤི་གོ་ལོག (shī ko lɔɔ̀) vi. to have children die before their parents ། འདི་ལོ་རྒན་རྒོན་གཉིས་ཀྱི་བུ་དེ་གྲོངས་ནས་ཤི་གོ་ལོག་བྱུང་སོང་ This year the son of the old couple died before them.

ཤི་གོད་ (shīgöö) sm. ཤི་སྐྱོན་.

ཤི་གོས་ (shīgöö) clothing/ shroud for the deceased.

ཤི་དགེ་ (shīge) prayers to create merit for the deceased.

ཤི་དགེ་གསོན་རིམ་དཀོར་ཁོངས་ (shīgesōnrim gōrgoŋ) shung. donations/ offerings and religious rites made by families of a deceased person.

ཤི་རྒྱགས་ (shīgyaà) good deeds to help one in one's next life.

ཤི་རྒྱུ་མེད་པ་ (shīgyu meèba) 1. immortal. 2. a term used when scolding the elderly.

ཤི་སྒུག (shīguù) waiting until sb. dies; va.—རྒྱག.

ཤི་སྒུག་སྨན་ཁང་ (shīguù mēngaŋ) hospice.

ཤི་ཚད་ (shīdzɛɛ̀) mortality rate.

ཤི་ཇུས་ (shījüü) plan for dying (by performing religious rites); va.—བྱེད་.

ཤི་ཉལ་རོ་ཉལ་ (shīñɛɛ roñɛɛ) sleeping well [Lit. sleeping like a corpse].

ཤི་མཉམ་ (shīñam) dying together; va.—བྱེད་.

ཤི་རྟགས་ (shīdaà) signs of dying; va.—སྟོན་ to show a sign of dying.

ཤི་ཐེ་ལེ་ (shīdele) ch. Hitler.

ཤི་འཐབ་ (shīndəb) a battle until death, a death struggle, fighting to the end; va.—བྱེད་.

ཤི་འཐབ་རོ་འཐབ་ (shīndəb rondəb) sm. ཤི་འཐབ་.

ཤི་འཐམ་རོ་འཐམ་ (shīndəb rondam) holding on to sth. until death; va.—བྱེད་ ། འགོ་ཁྲིད་རྒན་འཁོགས་དེས་མ་ཤི་བར་ལས་གནས་ལ་ཤི་འཐམ་རོ་འཐམ་བྱས་པ་རེད་ The old leader held on to his position until he died.

ཤི་དུར་ཁྲོད་སྐང་ལ་འཁྱེར་ (shī turdröö gaŋla kyēr) va. to be taken to the grave (usu. used with regard to secrets) ། རྒྱལ་ཁབ་ཀྱི་གསང་བ་འདི་ཤི་དུར་ཁྲོད་སྐང་ལ་འཁྱེར་རྒྱུ་ཞིག་རེད་ This state secret is one that will be taken to the grave.

ཤི་མདོག་ཁ་པོ་ (shīndo kābo) likely to die.

ཤི་འདྲེ་ (shīndre) ghost.

ཤི་ནའི་ཤི་ (shīnɛ shī) even if die (I will do sth. without regret) ། ང་མི་དམངས་ཀྱི་དོན་དུ་ཤི་ནའི་ཤི་ For the benefit of the masses, even if I die I have no regret.

ཤི་པན་ཡ་ (shībɛbya) Spain.

ཤི་པོ་ (shību) the deceased.

ཤི་པོའི་རྡིང་པར་རྡུང་ (shībü dīŋbar duŋ) saying bad things about a person who is dead [Lit. to hit the heel of a corpse].

ཤི་ལྤག (shībaà) the skin of animlas that died.

ཤི་ཕོད་ (shī pöö) vi. to dare to die (for sth.).

ཤི་འཕོས་ (shī pöö) vi. to die ། ཤི་འཕོས་རྗེས་སྐྱེ་བ་གསར་པ་ཞིག་ལེན་གྱི་རེད་ After dying, one will get reborn.

ཤི་བའི་ཉིན་མོ་ (shīwɛ ñinmu) the day of dying/ death.

ཤི་བྲལ་བྱེད་ (shīdrɛɛ ceè) vi. to be separated due to death (usu. one member of a married couple).

ཤི་བོ་ (shīwo) sm. གཤིན་པོ་.

ཤི་འབྱུར་རོ་འབྱུར་ (shījar rojar) 1. sm. ཤི་འཐམ་རོ་འཐམ་. 2. staying in one place for a long time; va.—བྱེད་.

ཤི་སྦར་འཐམས་ (shībɛɛ̀ tām) vi. to clutch to things at the time of death (conveys being stingy in one's life).

ཤི་མ་གསོན་ (shī masön) sm. ཤི་མིན་རོ་མིན་.

ཤི་མིག་གསོན་བལྟས་ (shīmig sōndɛɛ) trying to revive a dying person; va.—བྱེད་.

ཤི་མིན་རོ་མིན་ (shīmin romin) at the point of death [Lit. not alive, not dead] ། ཁོང་ཉེས་རྡུང་བཏང་ནས་ཤི་མིན་རོ་མིན་བཟོས་བཞག He was beaten to the point of death.

ཤི་མིན་གསོན་མིན་ (shīmin sōnmin) sm. ཤི་མིན་རོ་མིན་.

ཤི་མུ་ལ་ཆིངས་ཡིག (shīmula cīŋyiì) Simla Convention.

ཤི་སྨན་ (shīmɛn) anesthetic, pain killer; va.—རྒྱག; —སྲེར་ to give an anesthetic.

ཤི་རྨས་ (shīmɛɛ̀) dead and wounded, casualties.

ཤི་ཚད་ (shīdzɛɛ̀) death rate, mortality rate.

ཤི་ཚིགས་ (shīdziì) the one year anniversary of sb.'s death.

ཤི་འཛིང་ (shīdziŋ) sm. ཤི་འཐབ་.

ཤི་འཛིན་ (shīndzin) shung. a receipt given by the owner of animals to the leasee acknowledging having received the head and skin of an animal that died under the care of the leasee.

ཤི་རྫུ་འདེབས་ (shīdzu deb) va. to pretend to be dead.

ཤི་ཟན་ (shīsɛn) food offering made to the dead at the grave (Chinese custom).

ཤི་ཡང་དབུགས་མི་འགྲོ་བ་ (shīyaŋ ūùmi drowa) promising or swearing sth. before one dies [Lit. to not stop breathing even though one dies].

ཤི་ཡང་མི་སློད་པ་ (shīyaŋ milööba) sm. ཤི་འཐམ་རོ་འཐམ་.

ཤི་རག་བར་ (shīragbar) sm. ཤི་ཤི་བར་དུ་.

ཤི་རི་གུ་རི་ (shīri guri) Siliguri (a town in West Bengal, India).

ཤི་རིན་ཡོད་པ་ (shīrin yööbə) sth. worth dying for.

ཤི་རོ་ (shīro) corpse.

ཤི་ལ་ཁད་ (shīləkɛɛ̀) about to die.

ཤི་ལ་མ་ཤི་ (shilə məshi) almost dead; va.—བཟོ་ to almost kill.

ཤི་ལམ་ (shīlam) road to death ། ཁྱོད་རང་ནག་ཉེས་དེ་འདྲ་བསགས་ན་ཤི་ལམ་མ་གཏོགས་མེད་ If you amass crimes like this, there is no other option but the road of death (i.e., execution).

ཤི་ལམ་རང་འཚོལ་ (shīlam raŋdzöö) bringing about one's own destruction.

ཤི་ལོག (shīlɔɔ̀) returning from dead; va.—རྒྱག.

ཤི་ཤ་ (shīsha) meat from an animal that died.

ཤི་ཤ་སྤང་མ་ (shīsha bāŋma) Mt. Shisha pangma.

ཤི་ཤི་ན་ན་ (shīshi nana) working or doing sth. very hard or energetically; va.—བྱེད་.

ཤི་ཤི་བར་དུ་ (shīshi pərdu) until death ། ང་ཤི་ཤི་བར་དུ་འཛིང་གི་ཡིན་ I will fight until death.

ཤི་ཤི་ལ་ལ་ (shishi lala) ch. bad.

ཤི་ས་ (shīsə) the place of death.

ཤི་སོས་ (shī söö) sm. ཤི་ལོག.

ཤི་གསོན་ (shīsön) dead or alive, life and death ། ཤི་གསོན་ག་རེ་ཡོང་གི་ཡོད་ན་ཡང་དམག་སར་འགྲོ་གི་ཡིན་ Whatever will come whether it be life or death, I am going to the battlefield.

ཤི་གསོན་ཆགས་འཇིག (shīsön cəgjig) at the critical point/ juncture of death and life.

ཤི་གསོན་ཐག་གཅོད་ (shīsön tāgjöö) life and death struggle ། ད་རེས་ཀྱི་དམག་འཐབ་ནི་ཤི་གསོན་ཐག་གཅོད་ཀྱི་དམག་འཐབ་ཅིག་ཡིན་ This battle is a life and death struggle.

ཤི་གསོན་འབེན་འཛུགས་ (shīsön bendzuù) sm. ཤི་གསོན་འཛེམས་མེད་.

ཤི་གསོན་འཛེམས་མེད་ (shīsön dzemmeè) not afraid to die, no fear of death.

ཤི་གསོས་ (shīsöö) sm. ཤི་ལོག.

ཤི་ཨན་ (shīan) X'ian.

ཤིག (shīg) 1. the form of གཅིག used after final s ། ལུས་ཤིག A body. 2. imperative particle ། ལྟོས་ཤིག Look! 3. louse (lice); vi.—རྒྱག to have lice; va.—སྣུག to pick lice. 4. va. to shift, to move །

ཀུབ་བཀྱག་ཕྱི་ལ་ཤིག་སོང་ (He) moved the chair backwards. ། ཕར་ཤིག་ཚུར་ཤིག Make way for sb. [Lit. move this way and that way]. 5. imp. of འཇིག.

ཤིག་གི་ལོགས་ནས་རྒྱུས་པའི་རེ་བ་ (shīggi lɔ̀ɔnɛ gyṳ̈ṳbɛ rēwa) empty hope [Lit. hoping to get sinew from a louse].

ཤིག་གིས་ལ་བརྒྱབ་ཀྱང་འགྲོ་ས་དཔྱལ་མགོ་ (shīggi la gyəbgyaŋ drosa drɛ̄ngo) sm. ཤིག་ལ་བརྒྱབ་ཀྱང་གོང་ངའི་ཕྱི་ལོགས་.

ཤིག་སྒོང་ (shīggoŋ) louse egg, nit.

ཤིག་ཅན་ (shīgjɛn) infested with lice.

ཤིག་དོང་ (shīŋdoŋ) a punishment pit in which lice were kept.

ཤིག་འབུད་ (shīgdɛɛ̀) scratching lice bites; va.—བྱེད་.

ཤིག་ཚང་ (shīgdzaŋ) lice nest, a heavy infestation of lice.

ཤིག་ཟན་ (shīgsɛn) one's who eat lice (derogatory name for people from འཕན་པོ་).

ཤིག་སེ་ (shīgsɛ) a little bit, a small amount.

ཤིག་རལ་ (shīgrɛɛ) eng. cigarette ། ཤིག་རལ་སྒམ་ཆུང་ A packet of cigarettes.

ཤིག་རས་ (shīgrɛɛ̀) sm. ཤིག་རལ་.

ཤིག་ལ་བརྒྱབ་ཀྱང་གོང་ངའི་ཕྱི་ལོགས་ (shīg la gyəbgyaŋ koŋŋɛ cīloò) the bad can't escape/ flee away; evil people can't succeed [Lit. even though the lice climb to the mountain pass, it can only go as far as the collar.

ཤིག་ལ་བརྒྱབ་ཀྱང་གོང་བའི་ཕྱི་ནང་ (shīg la gyəbgyaŋ koŋwɛ cīnaŋ) sm. ཤིག་ལ་བརྒྱབ་ཀྱང་གོང་ངའི་ཕྱི་ལོགས་.

ཤིག་ཤིག (shīgshiì) moving over; va.—བྱེད་ to move ། འདི་ཕྱོགས་ལ་མི་མང་དྲགས་འདུག་པས་ཀུབ་བཀྱག་ཕར་ཤིག་ཤིག་བྱེད་དགོས་ There are too many people on this side so move your chair to that side.

ཤིག་སེན་ར་སྤྲོད་ (shīgsen rədröö) proving sth. clearly ། ཁྱོད་རང་ངོས་གནང་དོན་དེ་ཁས་ལེན་གྱི་མེད་ན་ཁྲིམས་ཁང་དུ་ཤིག་སེན་ར་སྤྲོད་གཏོང་གི་ཡིན་ If you don't agree on this matter, I will take you to the court and prove my position clearly. [Lit. proof like a louse between the fingernails].

ཤིག་སྒོ་ (shīgso) lice and nits.

ཤིག་གསོད་སྟ་རའི་འཕྱར་ (shī sȍȍ dārjar) should use appropriate methods; making a mountain out of a mole hill [Lit. wave an ax to kill a louse].

ཤིག་གསོད་པར་སྟ་རེ་འཕྱར་མི་དགོས་ (shīg sȍȍbar dāre cār migȍȍ) sm. ཤིག་གསོད་སྟ་ར་འཕྱར་ [Lit. you don't need an axe to kill a lice].

ཤིང་ (shīŋ) 1. connective particle used after final s words (see ཅིང་). 2. tree. 3. wood.

ཤིང་ཀང་ (shīŋgaŋ) 1. tree seedling; va.—འཛུགས་ to plant seedlings. 2. wooden leg.

ཤིང་སྐམ་ལས་གཉའ་རེངས་པ་དང་ཀོ་སྐྱོང་ལས་ཞེ་སྒྱོང་བ་ (shīŋgamlɛ ñareŋdaŋ gōgyoŋlɛ shegyoŋwa) extremely stubborn/ hardheaded [Lit. tougher than dry wood, harder than dry leather].

ཤིང་སྐུ་ (shīŋgu) wooden statue.

ཤིང་སྐོགས་ (shīŋgɔɔ̀) bark of a tree.

ཤིང་སྐྱོ་ (shīŋgyo) wood pulp.

ཤིང་སྐྱོའི་ཤོག་བུ་ (shīŋgyö shōgbu) paper made from wood pulp.

ཤིང་སྐྱོགས་ (shīŋgyɔɔ̀) wooden ladle.

ཤིང་བརྐོས་ (shīŋgöö) wood carving/ engraving; va.—རྒྱག་ to carve/ engrave wood.

ཤིང་བརྐོས་པར་རྒྱག (shīŋgöö bārgyaà) printing from carved woodblocks; va.—བྱེད་.

ཤིང་བརྐོས་པར་མ་ (shīŋgöö bārma) a book printed from a woodblock.

ཤིང་བརྐོས་པར་རིས་ (shīŋgöö bārrii) sm. ཤིང་བརྐོས་རི་མོ་.

ཤིང་བརྐོས་མ་ (shīŋ gȍȍma) carved wood.

ཤིང་བརྐོས་རི་མོ་ (shīŋgöö rimu) a picture printed from a woodblock.

ཤིང་ཁ་ (shīŋ kā) 1. on a tree. 2. the edge of boards put together.

ཤིང་ཁང་ (shīŋgaŋ) wooden house.

ཤིང་ཁམས་ (shīŋgam) one of the 5 elements (wood).

ཤིང་ཁུ་ (shīŋgu) sap/ juice of trees.

ཤིང་ཁུར་ (shīŋgur) load/ bundle of wood.

ཤིང་ཁེ་ལས་ (shīŋ kēlɛɛ̀) lumber industry, lumber enterprise/ company.

ཤིང་ཁོ་ (shīŋgo) 1. wooden mortar. 2. a kind of wooden bowl.

ཤིང་ཁྱེམ་ (shīŋgyem) wooden winnowing spade/ shovel.

ཤིང་ཁྱི་ (shīŋgyi) wood-dog year.

ཤིང་ཁྲལ་ (shīŋdrɛɛ) shung. tax on wood.

ཤིང་ཁྲི་ (shīŋdri) wooden scaffold.

ཤིང་ཁྲིས་པོ་ (shīŋ trrēēbo) sm. ཤིང་ཁུར་.

ཤིང་ཁྲོམ་ (shīŋdrɔɔ̀) wooden furniture.

ཤིང་ཁྲོལ་ (shīŋdröö) Tibetan wooden serving tray/ dish.

ཤིང་མཁན་ (shīŋgɛn) sm. ཤིང་བཟོ་བ་.

ཤིང་ག་པུར་ (shīŋ gəbur) sm. ཤིང་ག་བུར་.

ཤིང་ག་བུར་ (shīŋ gəbur) camphor tree.

ཤིང་ག (shīŋgə) 1. a cobbler's tool. 2. a wooden tool used by potters.

ཤིང་གི་གོང་སྙིང་ (shīŋgi kōŋñiŋ) the core of a tree.

ཤིང་གི་འདྲ་གཟུགས་ (shīŋgi drəsuù) wooden puppet.

ཤིང་གི་པ་དག (shīŋgi padaà) 1. spider web. 2. thin roots (of a tree).

ཤིང་གི་ལོ་ཚད་ (shīŋgi lodzɛɛ̀) age of a tree.

ཤིང་གི་སྲིན་བུ་ (shīŋgi sīmbu) insects that live on/ in trees.

ཤིང་གེལ་པ་ (shīŋ keeba) 1. tree branches. 2. a tree with many branches.

ཤིང་གྲུ་ (shīŋdru) wooden ship/ boat, junk (ship).

ཤིང་གླང་ (shīŋlaŋ) wood-ox year.

ཤིང་གླིང་ (shīŋliŋ) wooden flute.

ཤིང་གན་ (shīŋgɛn) old tree.

ཤིང་གནས་ནགས་ཚལ་ (shīŋgɛɛ̀ nagdzɛɛ) forest with old trees.

ཤིང་མགོན་ (shīŋgön) woodpecker.

ཤིང་རྒྱུད་ (shīŋgyṳ̈ṳ̀) sm. ཤིང་རིགས་.

ཤིང་སྒ་ (shīŋga) wooden saddle.

ཤིང་སྒམ་ (shīŋgam) wooden box/ chest.

ཤིང་སྒོ་ཅན་ (shīŋgojɛn) a house with a wooden door.

ཤིང་སྒྲོག (shīŋdroò) wooden furniture.

ཤིང་སྒྲོམ་ (shīŋdrom) wooden frame.

ཤིང་ང་དཔུང་བཅད་ (shīŋŋa būŋjɛɛ̀) a vest worn by female gelongs.

ཤིང་དངུལ་ (shīŋŋüü) shung. tax collected in cash for the fuel for the Monlam Prayer Festival.

ཤིང་མངར་ (shīŋŋar) licorice root.

ཤིང་ཅང་ (shīŋjaŋ) Xinjiang Province.

ཤིང་ཅི་ (shīŋji) ch. week.

ཤིང་བཅུད་ (shīŋjüü) sap, syrup (of trees).

ཤིང་གཅིག་ཀང་ཟམ་ (shīŋjig gāŋsam) a wooden trunk used as a bridge.

ཤིང་གཅོད་ (shīŋ jȍȍ) va. to cut wood/ lumber.

ཤིང་གཅོད་རྒྱག (shīŋjöö gyaà) sm. ཤིང་གཅོད་.

ཤིང་གཅོད་པ་ (shīŋjȍȍba) lumberjack.

ཤིང་ཆ་ (shīŋja) timber, lumber; va.—གཅོད་ to cut timber/ lumber ། ཤིང་ཆའི་ར་བ་ Lumber yard.

ཤིང་ཆ་འབྲེག་བྱེད་འཕྲུལ་འཁོར་ (shīŋja dregjeè trṳ̈ṳ̄gɔɔ) timber cutting machine, chain saw.

ཤིང་ཆ་ལས་སྒྲོན་བཟོ་གྲྭ (shīŋja lɛ̄ɛnön sodra) timber processing mill.

ཤིང་ཆ་བཟོ་གྲྭ་ (shīŋja sodra) lumber yard/ mill.

ཤིང་ཆགས་བྱ་རིགས་ (shīŋjaà cərii) birds that stay in trees.

ཤིང་ཆའི་ཀུང་སི་ (shīŋjɛ gūŋsi) tib. ch. timber company.

ཤིང་ཆའི་བཟོ་གྲྭ་ (shīŋjɛ sodra) timber yard/ mill.

ཤིང་ཆས་ (shīŋjɛɛ̀) wooden articles/ items/ utensils.

ཤིང་གྱོན་པ་འཁྱོག་ན་སྒྲོང་རྒྱུ་ཡོད། ཤིང་རྒས་པ་འཁྱོག་ན་སྒྲོང་རྒྱུ་མེད་ (shīŋjɛɛ̀) mistakes/ erros can be corrected in the early stage but cannot be correct if it is too late/ old [Lit. if a young tree is crooked it can be straightened, if an old tree is crooked it can not be straightened].

ཤིང་གཉེར་ (shīŋñer) stewards/ officials in charge of firewood.

ཤིང་མཉེན་པོ་ (shīŋ ñēmbo) cork.

ཤིང་སྙིང་ (shīŋñiŋ) sm. ཤིང་གི་ཁོང་སྙིང་.

ཤིང་བརྙན་ཟློས་གར་ (shīŋñɛn d̲öögar) puppet play/ theater.

ཤིང་ཏ་ལ་ (shīŋdala) palm tree ¶ ཤིང་ཏ་ལ་ལོ་མའི་དཔེ་ཆ་ Book written on palm tree leaves.

ཤིང་ཏོག་ (shīŋdoò) fruit ¶ ཤིང་ཏོག་སྐམ་པོ་ Dried fruits.

ཤིང་ཏོག་ཁུ་བའི་ཨ་རག་ (shīŋdoò kūwɛ āraà) liquor made from fruit.

ཤིང་ཏོག་གི་ཁུ་བ་ (shīŋdoògi kūwə) fruit juice.

ཤིང་ཏོག་ངང་ལག་ (shīŋdoò ŋaŋlaà) banana.

ཤིང་ཏོག་ལྕགས་ཀྲིན་ (shīŋdoò jāgdrin) canned fruits.

ཤིང་ཏོག་ཉིང་ཁུ་ (shīŋdoò n̲iŋgu) fruit juice.

ཤིང་ཏོག་ལྡུམ་ར་ (shīŋdoò d̲umrə) sm. ཤིང་ཏོག་ར་བ་.

ཤིང་ཏོག་པོ་ལུའོ་ (shīŋdoò bōlu) tib. ch. pineapple, jackfruit.

ཤིང་ཏོག་ཧྥིང་ལི་ (shīŋdoò fēŋli) tib. ch. sm. ཤིང་ཏོག་པོ་ལུའོ་.

ཤིང་ཏོག་བིལ་པ་ (shīŋdoò p̲iibə) calabash.

ཤིང་ཏོག་ཡ་ལི་ (shīŋdoò y̲əli) tib. ch. a kind of pear grown in Hebei Province.

ཤིང་ཏོག་ཡིའུ་ཙི་ (shīŋdoò y̲iwudzi) tib. ch. pomelo.

ཤིང་ཏོག་ར་བ་ (shīŋdoò r̲awa) orchard.

ཤིང་ཏོག་ལི་ཀྲི་ (shīŋdoò l̲idri) tib. ch. litchi (nut).

ཤིང་ཏོག་ལི་ཙི་ (shīŋdoò l̲idzi) tib. ch. plum.

ཤིང་ཏོག་སོས་པ་ (shīŋdoò sööba) fresh fruits.

ཤིང་ཏོག་ཨ་མྲ་ (shīŋdoò āmra) persimmon.

ཤིང་གཏུན་ (shīŋdün) wooden mortar.

ཤིང་རྟ་ (shīŋda) 1. horse drawn cart/ carriage/ chariot. 2. wood-horse year. 3. wooden rocking horse.

ཤིང་རྟ་མཁན་ (shīŋ dāñɛn) 1. the person who drives a horse cart. 2. person who makes horse carts.

ཤིང་རྟ་འཁོར་ལོ་ (shīŋda kōōlo) sm. ཤིང་རྟ་, 1.

ཤིང་རྟ་ཆེ་གཉིས་ (shīŋda cēñii) shung. sm. ཤིང་རྟ་ཆེན་ ཆེན་པོ་.

ཤིང་རྟ་ཆེན་པོ་ (shīŋda cēmbo) shung. 1. chariot. 2. two ancient Buddhist teachers: Nagarjuna and Asanga.

ཤིང་རྟ་པ་ (shīŋdaba) 1. sm. ཤིང་རྟ་མཁན་. 2. horse cart owner.

ཤིང་རྟ་པའི་སྐར་ཚོམ་ (shīŋdabɛ gārdzom) Auriga (constellation).

ཤིང་རྟ་མོ་ (shīŋ dāmo) woodpecker.

ཤིང་རྟ་ལེབ་གཞུང་ (shīŋda l̲ebshuŋ) shung. the wood horse year census (of land and taxes).

ཤིང་རྟའི་ཁ་ལོ་པ་ (shīŋdɛ kāloba) horse cart driver, charioteer.

ཤིང་རྟའི་ཐབས་ཇུས་ (shīŋdɛ təbjüü) the strategy of the Trojan horse.

ཤིང་སྟག་ (shīŋdaà) wood-tiger year.

ཤིང་སྟག་པ་ (shīŋ dāgba) birch tree.

ཤིང་སྟེགས་ (shīŋdɛg) wooden stool.

ཤིང་སྟན་ (shīŋdɛn) wooden chopping block.

ཤིང་སྟེང་ཉ་འཚོལ་ (shīŋdeŋ ñ̲adzöö) a fruitless/ hopeless/ impossible approach or strategy [Lit. searching for fish on top of a tree].

ཤིང་ཐགས་ (shīŋdaà) 1. a wooden fence. 2. wooden tower on the corner of a house. 3. wooden table.

ཤིང་ཐུན་པ་ (shīŋ tūmbə) 1. wood cutter, lumberjack. 2. person who gets firewood.

ཤིང་ཐུར་ (shīŋdur) 1. wooden spoon. 2. wooden chopstick.

ཤིང་ཐོག་ (shīŋdoò) sm. ཤིང་ཏོག.

ཤིང་མཐིལ་འདྲུད་ལྷམ་ (shīŋdii drü̲ülham) wooden slipper.

ཤིང་འཐུ་ (shīŋ tū) va. to collect firewood.

ཤིང་དུམ་ (shīŋdum) a log, a piece of wood.

ཤིང་མདུང་ (shīŋduŋ) wooden spear/ lance.

ཤིང་འདྲ་ཁང་ (shīŋdragaŋ) lumber mill, saw mill.

ཤིང་སྡེར་ (shīŋder) wooden plate/ dish.

ཤིང་སྡོང་ (shīŋdoŋ) tree.

ཤིང་སྡོང་སྐམ་པོ་ (shīŋdoŋ gāmbo) dead tree.

ཤིང་སྡོང་འགྱུར་རྡོ་ (shīŋdoŋ gyu̲ndo) petrified/ fossilized tree.

ཤིང་སྡོང་ལའི་མུའུ་ (shīŋdoŋ l̲emu) tib. ch. large-leaf dogwood (cornus macrophylla).

ཤིང་སྡོད་བྱ་རིགས་ (shīŋdöö c̲ərig) sm. ཤིང་ཆགས་བྱ་རིགས་.

ཤིང་ནག་པོ་ (shīŋ n̲agbo) 1. black wood. 2. ebony wood.

ཤིང་ནགས་ (shīŋnaà) forest; va.—སྲུང་ to protect the forest.

ཤིང་སྣ་ (shīŋna) kinds of trees ¶ ལུང་པ་འདི་ར་ཤིང་སྣ་འཛོམས་པོ་འདུག་ This place has many kinds of trees.

ཤིང་སྣུམ་ (sīŋnum) oil from trees, wood oil.

ཤིང་པད་མ་ (shīŋ bɛ̀ɛma) peony, peony tree.

ཤིང་པར་ (shīŋbar) a book printed by the woodblock method.

ཤིང་དཔོན་ (shīŋbün) shung. person in charge of fuel/ firewood.

ཤིང་སྤེ་ (shīŋbe) a pile/ heap of wood.

ཤིང་སྤྱིལ་ (shīŋjii) wooden cabin.

ཤིང་སྤྲེལ་ (shīŋdree) wood-monkey year.

ཤིང་ཕག་ (shīŋbaà) wood-pig year.

ཤིང་ཕུར་ (shīŋpur) wooden peg/ stake.

ཤིང་ཕོ་ (shīŋbo) male wood element (used in the Tibetan calendar).

ཤིང་ཕོར་ (shiŋbɔɔ) wooden bowl.

ཤིང་ཕྱེ་ (shīnje) sawdust.

ཤིང་ཕྲུག་ (shīŋdruù) sapling.

ཤིང་ཕྲུག་ར་བ་ (shīŋdruù r̲awa) a fence to protect saplings.

ཤིང་བལ་ (shīŋbɛɛ) the cotton-like down of the silk-cotton (kapok) tree.

ཤིང་བལ་རིགས་ལྔ་ (shīŋbɛɛ ri̲gŋa) five types of kapok trees.

ཤིང་བུ་ (shīŋbu) 1. chopstick. 2. an implement used in exorcism rites. 3. small pieces of wood.

ཤིང་བུད་ (shīŋbüü) va. to put wood into a stove/ fireplace.

ཤིང་བྱ་ (shīŋja) wood-bird year.

ཤིང་བྱང་ (shīnjaŋ) a long wooden placard which serves as a sign board.

ཤིང་བྱི་ (shīŋji) wood-mouse year.

ཤིང་འབག་ (shīŋbaà) wood mask.

ཤིང་འབག་ཁྲང་ཞི་ (shīŋbaà trāŋshi) tib. ch. puppet theater.

ཤིང་འབུ་ (shīŋbu) insects that live in trees.

ཤིང་འབྲས་ (shīndrɛɛ̀) fruit.

ཤིང་འབྲས་ཁོག་དམར་ (shīndrɛɛ̀ kōgmar) watermelon.

ཤིང་འབྲས་ལྡུམ་ར་ (shīndrɛɛ̀ d̲umrə) orchard.

ཤིང་འབྲས་མུའུ་ཧྲུའུ་ (shīndrɛɛ̀ mu̲hru) tib. ch. cassava.

ཤིང་འབྲུག་ (sīŋdruù) wood-dragon year.

ཤིང་འབྲུག་དམག་ (shīŋdruù māà) wood-dragon year war (fought against the British in 1904).

ཤིང་སྦར་ (shīŋbaa) wooden rake.

ཤིང་སྦུབས་ (shīŋbub) inside the trunk of a tree.

ཤིང་སྐྱག་ (shīŋjaà) wooden spade.

ཤིང་སྦྱར་མ་ (shīŋ ja̲rma) wooden planks stuck together, plywood, veneer.

ཤིང་སྦྲང་ (shīŋdraŋ) wood wasp/ bee.

ཤིང་སྦྲུལ་ (shīŋdrüü) wood-snake year.

ཤིང་མར་ (shīŋmar) margarine.

ཤིང་སྨུག་ (shīŋmug) sm. ཤིང་འབུ་.

ཤིང་སྙུག་ (shīŋñuù) sapling.

ཤིང་སྙུག་ར་བ་ (shīŋñuù r̲awa) tree nursery.

ཤིང་སྨན་ (shīŋmɛn) traditional herbal medicine.

ཤིང་ཙེ་ཧྲན་ (shīŋ dzīhrɛn) tib. ch. yew (tree).

ཤིང་བརྩུགས་ (shīn dzūù) p. of ཤིང་འཛུགས་.

ཤིང་རྩ་ (shīŋdzə) root of a tree.

ཤིང་རྩ་མ་རུལ་ན་ལོ་མ་མི་སྨམ་ (shīŋdzə ma̲rüüna l̲oma m̲igam) if the central part/ person is viable, then there is hope all will flourish [Lit. if the roots don't rot then the leaves will not become dry] ¶ ཤིང་རྩ་མ་རུལ་ན་ལོ་མ་མི་སྐམ་ཟེར་བའི་དཔེ་ལྟར་ཡུལ་དེའི་དམངས་གཙོའི་ལས་འགུལ་དེ་རྩ་མེད་དུ་མ་སོང་ཕྱིན་ནམ་ཞིག་རྒྱལ་ཁ་འཐོབ་ཀྱི་རེད་ Like the saying "if the roots don't rot then the leaves will not become dry," if the democratic organization is not totally destroyed, one day it will be victorious.

ཤིང་རྩབ་ (shīŋdzəb) 1. wooden wedge used to keep a table or chair from wobbling; va.—རྒྱག.

ཤིང་རྩི་ (shīŋdzi) gum, resin, sap.

ཤིང་རྩེད་རྩེ་ (shīŋdzeè dzē) va. to play by climbing a wooden pole.

ཤིང་ཚ་ (shīŋdza) cinnamon.

ཤིང་ཚལ་ (shīŋdzεε) 1. grove, park, forest. 2. wood shavings.

ཤིང་ཚི་ (shīŋdzi) sm. ཤིང་རྩི་.

ཤིང་ཚིལ་ (shīŋdzii) sm. ཤིང་རྩི་.

ཤིང་ཚུག (shīŋdzuù) a Tibetan medical treatment consisting of a hot stick that is applied to the body.

ཤིང་ཚེ་རིང་ (shīŋ tsēriŋ) the tree of longevity (one of the six symbols of longevity).

ཤིང་ཚོན་ (shīŋdzön) 1. paint for painting wooden things. 2. painting wooden things/ furniture; va.—གཏོང་.

ཤིང་ཚོས་ (shīŋdzöö) vegetable dye.

ཤིང་མཚེ་ (shīŋdze) tib. ch. Chinese ephedra.

ཤིང་འཛུགས་ (shīŋ dzu̲ù) va. to plant trees ¶ ན་ཉིང་ཤིང་སྡོང་ཁྲིག་མང་པོ་བཙུགས་པ་རེད་ Last year they planted many thousands of trees.

ཤིང་འཛུགས་ནགས་བཟོ་ (shīŋdzuù n̲agso) afforestation; va.—བྱེད་.

ཤིང་འཛེར་ (shīŋdzer) tree knot.

ཤིང་རྫིངས་ (shīŋdiŋ) raft.

ཤིང་ཝུའུ་ཐུང་ (shīŋ wu̲duŋ) tib. ch. parasol tree.

ཤིང་ཞོགས་ (shīŋshɔɔ) wood shavings.

ཤིང་གཞུ་ (shīŋshu) bow made from wood.

ཤིང་གཞོན་ (shīŋshön) a young tree.

ཤིང་ཟ་ (shīŋsə) drill (for boring holes in wood).

ཤིང་ཟན་ (shīŋsεn) 1. woodworm. 2. termite.

ཤིང་ཟན་མོ་ (shīŋ s̲enmo) sm. ཤིང་ཟན་.

ཤིང་ཟམ (shīŋsam) wooden bridge.

ཤིང་ཟོམ་ (shīŋsom) wooden bucket.

ཤིང་གཟུགས་ (shīŋsuù) shadow puppet.

ཤིང་གཟུགས་ཅེ་ཅས་ (shīŋsuù dzējεὲ) sm. ཤིང་གཟུགས་.

ཤིང་གཟེར་ (shīŋser) wooden peg/ stake.

ཤིང་གཟོང་ (shīŋsoŋ) sm. ཤིང་ཟ་.

ཤིང་བཟང་ (shīŋsaŋ) healthy tree.

ཤིང་བཟོ་ (shīŋso) carpentry; va.—བྱེད་ to do carpentry.

ཤིང་བཟོ་པ་ (shīŋsowə) carpenter.

ཤིང་བཟོས་ (shīŋsöö) made from wood ¶ ཤིང་བཟོས་ཚགས་མ་ ¶ A sieve made from wood.

ཤིང་བཟོས་ཆུ་འཁོར་ (shīŋsöö cūgɔɔ) wooden water mill.

ཤིང་བཟོས་ཐོ་བ་ (shīŋsöö tōwa) wooden hammer.

ཤིང་བཟོས་འདྲུད་ལྷམ་ (shīŋsöö drü̲ülham) wooden shoe/ clogs.

ཤིང་ར་ (shīŋrə) 1. wooden fence. 2. an enclosure for keeping firewood.

ཤིང་ར་ལས་ཁུངས་ (shīŋrə lεὲguŋ) shung. an office in charge of firewood.

ཤིང་ཡོས་ (shīŋyöö) wood-hare year.

ཤིང་རགས་ (shīŋraà) trees and bushes erected as an obstacle to prevent travel or block an enemy.

ཤིང་རིགས་ (shīŋrig) 1. trees, types of trees. 2. woody plants.

ཤིང་རིགས་སྐྱེ་དངོས་ (shīŋrig gyēŋöö) woody plants.

ཤིང་རིགས་སྣུམ་རྫས་ (shīŋrig nūmdzεὲ) oil bearing plants.

ཤིང་རུལ་ (shīŋrüü) a rotten tree.

ཤིང་རུལ་སྡོང་རུལ་ (shīŋrüü do̲ŋrüü) a rotten tree with a rotten inside.

ཤིང་རོ་ (shīŋro) wood shavings, left over pieces of wood.

ཤིང་ལམ་ (shīŋlam) wooden tracks (on railways).

ཤིང་ལས་ (shīŋlεὲ) lumber work.

ཤིང་ལས་བཟོ་གྲྭ (shīŋlεὲ) lumber/ wood factory.

ཤིང་ལུག (shīŋluù) wood-sheep year.

ཤིང་ལེབ་ (shīŋleb) board, plank.

ཤིང་ལེབ་ནག་པོའི་གསར་འགྱུར་ (shīŋleb n̲agbö sɔ̄ŋgyuu) wall newspaper.

ཤིང་ལུས་རྡོ་སྙིང་ (shi̲ŋlüü do̲ñiŋ) unfeeling, not swayed by emotion/ feeling [Lit. wood body, stone heart].

ཤིང་ལེབ་རོལ་ཆས་ (shīŋleb rö̲öjεὲ) wood clappers.

ཤིང་ལོ་ (shīŋlo) tree leaves.

ཤིང་ལོའི་རླུང་གཡབ་ (shīŋlö lūŋyəb) palm-leaf fan.

ཤིང་ཤ་རྒྱས་ (shīŋsha gyε̲ὲ) vi. to swell (wood) when wet.

ཤིང་ཤ་མོ་ (shīŋ shāmo) an edible fungus.

ཤིང་ཤུན་ (shīŋshün) sm. ཤིང་ལྤགས་.

ཤིང་ཤོག (shīŋsoò) paper made from wood.

ཤིང་གཤགས་མ་ (shīŋ shāgma) split logs, firewood.

ཤིང་གཤོལ་ (shīŋshöö) wooden plow.

ཤིང་སོག (shīŋsɔɔ) saw for cutting wood; va.—རྒྱག.

ཤིང་སོན་ (shīŋsön) tree seeds.

ཤིང་སོན་གྱི་ར་བ་ (shīŋsöngi r̲awa) sm. ཤིང་སོན་ལྡུམ་ར་.

ཤིང་སོན་ལྡུམ་ར་ (shīŋsön du̲mrə) tree seedling nursery.

ཤིང་སོབ་སོབ་ (shīŋ sōbsob) soft/ spongy wood, wood pitted with holes.

ཤིང་སྲང་ (shīŋsaŋ) a སྲང་ scale made of wood.

ཤིང་སྲིན་ (shīŋsin) insects that live on trees.

ཤིང་གསར་ (shīŋsar) a young/ new tree.

ཤིང་གསེག (shīŋseg) tool used to polish wood.

ཤིང་གསོམ་ (shīŋsom) fir tree.

ཤིང་ཧྲུག (shīŋhruù) pieces of leftover wood, wood scraps.

ཤིང་ཧྲུལ་ (shīŋhrüü) sm. ཤིང་ཧྲུག.

ཤིང་ཨ་རུ་ར་ (shīŋ ārura) olive tree.

ཤིང་ཨ་རུ་རའི་ཡལ་ག (shīŋ ārurε yε̲ε̲ga) olive branch.

ཤིད་ (shīi) sm. ཤིད་ཆོས་. 2. a type of fruit.

ཤིད་ཆོས་ (shīijöö) va. to do rites/ prayers for the deceased; va.—བྱེད་.

ཤིད་སྡོན་ (shīidön) sm. ཤིད་ཆོས་.

ཤིད་ཟན་ (shīisεn) sm. ཤི་ཟན་.

ཤིད་ལས་ (shīilεὲ) activities to be done when a person dies.

ཤིན་ཅང་ (shīnjaŋ) sm. ཤིང་ཅང་.

ཤིན་ཏུ་ (shīndu) very ¶ སྒམ་ཤིན་ཏུ་ལྕི་བ་ཞིག A very heavy box.

ཤིན་ཏུ་ནས་ (shīndunε) sm. ཤིན་ཏུ་.

ཤིན་ཏུ་མོ་ཡིག (shīndu m̲oyig) the letters ང་ཉ་ན་མ་ in the Tibetan alphabet.

ཤིན་ཏུ་སེམས་པ་ (shīndu sēmba) meticulous/ precise in thinking.

ཤིན་དེ་མ་ (shīndema) 1. feeble, weak. 2. leftover, residue.

ཤིན་བོད་ (shīn pö̲ö) Xinjiang-Tibet ¶ ཤིན་བོད་གཞུང་ལམ་ Xinjiang-Tibet Highway.

ཤིན་ཧྭ་གསར་འགྱུར་ཁང་ (shīnhwa sɔ̄ŋyugaŋ) ch.tib. Xinhua News Agency.

ཤིནྟུ (shīndu) shung. abbr. of ཤིན་ཏུ་.

ཤིའི་ཀྭ (shīgwa) ch. watermelon.

ཤིའི་ཛང་ (shīidzaŋ) ch. Tibet.

ཤིའི་ཨན (shīian) X'ian.

ཤིར་ཤིར་ (shīrshir) sound of water falling.

ཤིས་ཁང་ (shīigaŋ) ch. sm. ཤིས་ཁམས་.

ཤིས་ཁམས་ (shīigam) ch. Xigang province (a province created by the Kuomintang government of China that included much of Kham).

ཤིས་བརྗོད་ (shīijöö) auspicious words.

ཤིས་རྟགས་ (shīidaà) auspicious signs.

ཤིས་པ་ (shīibə) auspicious; va.—བརྗོད་ to say auspicious phrases.

ཤིས་པན་ཡ་ (shībεnya) Spain.

ཤིས་འཕྲིན་ (shīidrin) favorable/ good/ auspicious news ¶ དམག་འཁྲུག་ལ་རྒྱལ་ཁ་ཐོབ་པའི་ཤིས་འཕྲིན་འབྱོར་

བ་རེད་ We received the good news that we won the war.

ཤིས་ཚིག (shiidzii) 1. words of praise/ congratulations; va.—བརྗོད་; —ཞུ་; —སྨོད་ to utter words of greeting/ felicitation. 2. Chinese good luck character.

ཤིས་ཧུང་ཧྲི་ (shiihuŋhre) ch. tomato.

ཤིས་ཨན་ (shiian) X'ian.

ཤུ་ (shū) whistling; va.—རྒྱག to whistle.

ཤུ་གུ (shūgu) sm.* ཤོག་བུ་.

ཤུ་གླུ་ (shūlu) whistling a tune; va.—གཏོང་.

ཤུ་སྒྲ་ (shūdra) sound of whistling.

ཤུ་ཐོར་ (shūdɔɔ) sores and pimples.

ཤུ་བརྡ་ (shūda) signaling by whistling; va.—གཏོང་.

ཤུ་བ་ (shūwə) 1. a type of skin sore; vi.—རྒྱག; —སྐྱེ་ to get a skin sore.

ཤུ་བ་ཁ་བརྒྱ་ (shūwə kāgya) leprosy.

ཤུ་འབྲས་ (shūndrɛɛ̀) a cancerous sore.

ཤུག (shūg) wife ། ཁྱོ་ཤུག Husband and wife.

ཤུག : p. བཤུགས་; f. བཤུག; imp. ཤུགས་ (shūg) 1. va. to sell things internally without taking a profit. 2. va. to exile/ expel.

ཤུག་གུ་ (shūgu) sm.* ཤོག་བུ་.

ཤུག་དངུལ་ (shūgŋüü) shung. money to be paid according to the lease/ loan contract.

ཤུག་གཅིག་ཁྱོ་མང་ (shūùjiì kyōmaŋ) polyandry.

ཤུག་ལྕུག (shūùjɔɔ̀) a drawer; va.—འཐེན་ to open a drawer.

ཤུག་དུད་ (shūgdüü) smoke from burned Juniper (incense).

ཤུག་དྲི་ (shūgdri) smell of smoke from junipers.

ཤུག་སྡོང་ (shūgdoŋ) a Juniper tree.

ཤུག་པ་ (shūgbə) Juniper.

ཤུག་སྤྲོད་ (shūgdröö) lending things to another, letting sb. use sth. of yours; va.—བྱེད་ ། ང་གུང་སེང་དུ་འགྲོ་ཤུལ་ངའི་ཁང་པ་དེ་གྲོགས་པོར་ཤུག་སྤྲོད་བྱས་པ་ཡིན་ When I went for vacation, I let my friend use my house. 2. selling sth. to a friend at the original price with no profit.

ཤུག་ཕྱེ་ (shūgce) shung. powdered juniper (incense).

ཤུག་བོགས་ (shūbɔɔ̀) shung. lease, leasing.

ཤུག་འབྲས་ (shūndrɛɛ̀) fruit of the juniper tree.

ཤུག་འབྲུམ་ (shūndrum) sm. ཤུག་འབྲས་.

ཤུག་གཟང་ (shūgdzaŋ) a type of silk.

ཤུག་ཙང་ (shūgdzaŋ) a peg made from Juniper.

ཤུག་ལེབ་ (shūgleb) juniper-type needles.

ཤུག་ཤུག (shūgshuù) leaving quietly, slipping away ། ཚོགས་འདུ་འཚོགས་ས་ནས་མི་ཁ་ཤས་ཤུག་ཤུག་ལ་ལོག་ཕྱིན་བཞག Some people slipped away from the meeting and returned (to where they came from).

ཤུགས་ (shūg) strength, power, force ། ས་ཡོམ་གྱི་ཤུགས་ནི་ As for the force of the earthquake.

ཤུགས་ཀྱི་རིག་པ་ (shūggi rigbə) the science of mechanics.

ཤུགས་ཀྱིས་ (shūggi) 1. by the power/ strength/ force of ། ཆུ་ལོག་དྲག་པོའི་ཤུགས་ཀྱིས་ཁང་པ་ཡང་ཁྱེར་ཐེན་པ་རེད་ The force of the powerful flood carried away even houses. 2. with force, strongly, hard ། བཙོན་པར་རྟ་ལྕག་ཤུགས་ཀྱིས་བཞུས་པ་རེད་ They whipped the prisoner hard. 3. to indicate indirectly ། ཁོའི་སྐད་ཆའི་ཐོག་ནས་ལས་ཀ་བྱེད་འདོད་མེད་པ་ཤུགས་ཀྱིས་སྟོན་གྱི་འདུག Through his conversation he is indicating indirectly he doesn't want to work.

ཤུགས་རྐྱེན་ (shūggyen) effect; vi.—ཐེབས་ to have/ get an effect ། སྲིད་ཇུས་གསར་པ་དེས་དམངས་གཙོའི་འཚོ་བ་ལ་ཤུགས་རྐྱེན་ཆེན་པོ་ཐེབས་སོང་ The new policy had a great effect on the livelihood of the people.

ཤུགས་རྐྱེན་ངན་པ་ (shūggyen ŋɛmba) bad effect/ influence.

ཤུགས་རྐྱེན་བཟང་བ་ (shūggyen saŋwa) good effect/ influence.

ཤུགས་སྐད་ (shūggɛɛ̀) a loud voice.

ཤུགས་སྐྱིལ་ (shūggyiì) clamping down on, reining in, blocking the power of; va.—བྱེད་ ། དེ་ནི་དགྲ་བོའི་ཤུགས་སྐྱིལ་བྱེད་ཀྱི་སྲིད་ཇུས་ཤིག་རེད་ That is a policy that will rein in the power of our enemy.

ཤུགས་སྐྱེད་སྟོབས་སྐྱིལ་ (shūggyeè dōbbel) sm. ཤུགས་བསྐྱེད་སྟོབས་སྐྱིལ་.

ཤུགས་སྐྱོ་པོ་ (shūg gyōbo) weak.

ཤུགས་བསྐྱེད་སྟོབས་སྐྱིལ་ (shūggyeè dōbbel) striving vigorously, working hard, going all out to accomplish sth.; va.—བྱེད་ ། ཤུགས་བསྐྱེད་སྟོབས་སྐྱིལ་བྱས་ནས་དཔལ་འབྱོར་ཡར་རྒྱས་གཏོང་དགོས་ You must go all out to improve the economy.

ཤུགས་བསྐྱེད་དམག་འཐབ་ (shūggyeè məgdəb) a military strategy involving concentrating one's power.

ཤུགས་གང་ཡོད་ཀྱིས་ (shūggaŋ yöögi) with all one's strength/ force ། ཤུགས་གང་ཡོད་ཀྱིས་དཔལ་འབྱོར་ཡར་རྒྱས་བཏང་བ་རེད་ Using all their strength, (they) improved the economy.

ཤུགས་གླུ་ (shūglu) a type of folk song.

ཤུགས་འགྲན་ཐག་འཐེན་ (shūgdrɛn tāgden) tug-of-war competition; va.—བྱེད་.

ཤུགས་འགྲོ་ (shūgdro) mule.

ཤུགས་འགྲོའི་ཕ་ (shūdrö pā) donkey.

ཤུགས་འགྲོས་ (shūgdröö) walking energetically; va.—ཀྱིས་འགྲོ་.

ཤུགས་རྒྱག (shūg gyaà) va. to use strength, to make an effort, to work hard/ vigorously ། ཐོན་སྐྱེད་ཡར་རྒྱས་ཐོག་ཤུགས་རྒྱག་རྒྱུ་དེ་གལ་ཆེ་ It is important to work hard to increase production. 2. va. to use one's influence/ power ། ངའི་གྲོགས་པོས་ཤུགས་བརྒྱབ་ནས་ང་ལ་ལས་ཀ་དེ་རག་བྱུང་ My friend used his power to get me that job.

ཤུགས་ངོམ་ (shūgŋom) showing off one's strength; va.—བྱེད་.

ཤུགས་ངོམ་སྲིད་ཇུས་ (shūgŋom siijüü) policy of showing one's strength, big stick policy.

ཤུགས་དངོས་ (shūgŋöö) actual strength, real strength.

ཤུགས་ཅན་ (shūgjɛn) strong, powerful, forceful.

ཤུགས་ཅི་ཡོད་འདོན་ (shūg jiyöö dön) sm. ཤུགས་གང་ཡོད་ཀྱིས་.

ཤུགས་ཆད་ (shūg cɛɛ̀) vi. to fade/ weaken (in strength).

ཤུགས་ཆེ་བུལ་ཏོག (shūgje püüdoò) caustic soda.

ཤུགས་ཆེན་ (shūgjen) sm. ཤུགས་ཆེན་པོ་.

ཤུགས་ཆེན་པོ་ (shūg cēmbo) strong.

ཤུགས་ཆེ་རུ་འགྲོ་ (shūg cēru dro) vi. to become stronger, to become more powerful.

ཤུགས་ཆེ་རུ་གཏོང་ (shūg cēru dōŋ) va. to increase power, to make stronger, to reinforce in strength.

ཤུགས་མཉམ་པ་ (shūg ñāmba) balance of power.

ཤུགས་སྟོན་སྲིད་ཇུས་ (shūgdön siijüü) sm. ཤུགས་ངོམ་སྲིད་ཇུས་.

ཤུགས་བསྟན་ (shūgdɛn) see ཤུགས་ཀྱིས་.

ཤུགས་བསྟན་གོ་དོན་ (shūgdɛn kodön) implication, hidden meaning.

ཤུགས་བསྟན་གཏམ་དཔེ་ (shūgdɛn dāmbe) a proverb or saying with hidden meaning/ implications.

ཤུགས་བསྟན་ཚིག་དོན་ (shūgdɛn tsīgdön) words/ speech with hidden implications, indirect speech.

ཤུགས་བསྟུན་ལས་སྒྲུབ་ (shūgdün lɛɛ̀ drub) accomplishing tasks in accordance with one's strength.

ཤུགས་དྲག (shūgdraà) strong, intensive, powerful, violent ། ན་ནིང་བོད་ལ་ས་ཡོམ་ཤུགས་དྲག་ཆེན་པོ་བརྒྱབ་སོང་ Last year there was a violent earthquake in Tibet.

ཤུགས་འདོན་ (shūgdön) sm. ཤུགས་རྒྱག.

ཤུགས་ལྡན་ (shūŋdɛn) 1. powerful, strong. 2. name of a protective deity of the Gelugpa sect.

ཤུགས་ནར་ (shūgnar) sm. ཤུགས་རིང་.

ཤུགས་སྣོན་ (shūgnön) strengthening, reinforcing, augmenting; va.—བྱེད་; —རྒྱག ། དག་རྩལ་སྦྱོང་བརྡར་

བྱེད་རྒྱུར་ཤུགས་སྣོན་རྒྱག་དགོས་ (We) must strengthen military maneuvers.

ཤུགས་པ་འབྱིན་ (shūgbə ji̱n) va. to send a signal by whistling.

ཤུགས་དཔྱད་རིག་པ་ (shūgjɛɛ̀ ri̱gbə) dynamics.

ཤུགས་བྱས་ (shūgjɛɛ̀) sm. ཤུགས་ཀྱིས་.

ཤུགས་སྦྱོང་ (shūgjoŋ) exercising to build one's strength; va.—བྱེད་.

ཤུགས་མ་ཐུབ་ (shūg ma̱ tūb) having no choice (but to do sth.) ¶ གནད་དོན་དེའི་སྐོར་ཁོང་གིས་ཁྲིམས་ཁང་ནང་ཤུགས་མ་ཐུབ་ཀྱིས་ངོས་ལེན་བྱེད་དགོས་བྱུང་འདུག Concerning this matter, in court he had no choice but to confess. 2. naturally, without trying specially ¶ རང་ཉིད་ལ་ཡོན་ཏན་དང་འཇོན་ཐངས་ཡོད་ན་ཤུགས་མ་ཐུབ་ཀྱིས་ལས་ཀ་ཡག་པོ་ཞིག་རག་གི་རེད་ If you are well educated and capable, naturally you can get a good job.

ཤུགས་མེད་པ་ (shūg mɛ̱ɛ̀ba) having no strength, being not strong.

ཤུགས་མེད་ཤུགས་ངོམ་ (shūgmeè shūgŋom) making an empty show of strength.

ཤུགས་རྩལ་ (shūgdzɛɛ) skill in wrestling and games of strength.

ཤུགས་རྩེད་ (shūgdzeè) wrestling and other games of strength; va.—འགྲན་ to wrestle.

ཤུགས་ཚད་ (shūgdzɛɛ̀) strength, power; va.—བྱེད་ ¶ དེང་དུས་དང་འཚམས་པའི་དམག་དོན་ཤུགས་ཚད་ཇེ་མཐོར་ཕྱིན་ Their modern military strength increased. ¶ ང་གཉིས་ཤུགས་ཚད་བྱས་ང་ལ་ཐོབ་བྱུང་ We two had a contest to see who is strong and I won.

ཤུགས་ཚད་ (shūg dzɛ̄ɛ̀) va. to have a contest of strength, to see who is stronger.

ཤུགས་རྫོགས་ (shūg dzɔ̱ɔ̀) vi. to lose one's strength.

ཤུགས་ཞན་ (shūgshɛn) weak; va.—གཏོང་ to weaken/ soften, to bring to submission.

ཤུགས་ཞན་པ་ (shūg shɛ̱mba) sm. ཤུགས་ཞན་.

ཤུགས་ཞན་ས་ (shūg shɛ̄nsa) weak point/ spot, weakness, deficiency.

ཤུགས་ཟད་སྐད་འཛེར་ (shūgsɛɛ̀ gɛ̄ndzer) going all out to do sth. [Lit. strength exhausted, voice hoarse].

ཤུགས་རིག (shūgriì) abbr. of ཤུགས་ཀྱི་རིག་པ་.

ཤུགས་རིག་པའི་ཚོད་ལྟ་ཁང་ (shūgrigbɛ tsȫòdagaŋ) mechanics laboratory.

ཤུགས་རིང་ (shūùriŋ) a sigh; vi.—འབྱིན་; —འདོན་ to sigh.

ཤུགས་ལ་བསྟན་ (shūgla dɛ̄n) sm. ཤུགས་བསྟན་.

ཤུགས་ལས་ (shūglɛɛ̀) physical work/ labor; va.—བྱེད་.

ཤུགས་ལེན་ཆུ་རགས་ (shūglen cūraà) a dam across a river.

ཤུགས་གསོག (shūg sɔ̄ɔ̀) va. to gather or amass power/ strength.

ཤུང་ཡ་ལི་ (shūŋyali) sm. ཤུང་ཡ་ལོ་.

ཤུང་ཡ་ལོ་ (shūŋyalo) ch. Hungary.

ཤུང་ཤུང་ (shūŋshuŋ) hmph, a sound of disgust made through the nose.

ཤུངས་དམོད་ (shūŋmöò) talking behind sb.'s back; va.—བྱེད་.

ཤུད་ (shūùù) sm. བཤུད་.

ཤུད་དེ་ཁ་ལ་ (shūùde kāla) sm. ཤུག་ཤུག.

ཤུད་ཤུད་གཏོང་ (shūùshüù dōŋ) sm. བཤུད་.

ཤུན་སྐོགས་ (shūngɔɔ̀) outer skin, bark, peel.

ཤུན་བརྗེས་ (shūnjeè) sm. ཤུན་པ་བརྗེ་.

ཤུན་སྣུམ་ (shūnnum) husk oil.

ཤུན་པ་ (shūmba) skin, bark, peel; vi.—བརྗེ་ to shed skin/ bark ¶ སྦྲུལ་གྱི་ཤུན་པ་བརྗེས་འདུག The snake has shed its skin.

ཤུན་ལྤགས་ (shūmbaà) sm. ཤུན་པ་.

ཤུབ་ (shūb) va. to whisper.

ཤུབ་སྐད་ (shūbgɛɛ̀) whispering; va.—ཤོད་.

ཤུབ་བུ་ (shūbbu) sm. ཤུབ་ཤུབ་.

ཤུབ་བུའིབརླབས་པ་འདོན་ (shūbü dɛ̱ɛ̀ba dö̱n) va. to whisper to each other.

ཤུབ་སྦྲག (shūbdraà) sth. that has a sheath/ case.

ཤུབ་ཤུབ་ (shūbshub) whispering; va.—ཤོད་; —གཏོང་ ¶ ཁོ་ཚོས་སྐད་ཆ་ཤུབ་ཤུབ་མང་པོ་བཤད་སོང་ They talked a lot in whispers.

ཤུབ་ཤུབ་ཝུར་ཝུར་ (shūbshub wu̱rwur) the sound of many people talking softly/ praying/ etc.

ཤུབས་ (shūb) an outer covering/ case/ sheath ¶ གྲི་ཤུབས་ Knife sheath.

ཤུབས་བླངས་བཙོས་སྒོང་ (shūblaŋ dzȫògoŋ) poached egg.

ཤུམ་ (shūm) sm.* བཤུམ་.

ཤུམ་སྐད་ (shūmgɛɛ̀) h. of ངུ་སྐད་.

ཤུམ་ཆོག་ཆོག (shūm cɔ̄ɔ̀jɔɔ̀) h. of ངུ་ཆོག་ཆོག.

ཤུར་ (shūr) ravine, water channel, chute.

ཤུར་ཁ་ (shūrgə) breach, gap.

ཤུར་ཁུང་ (shūrguŋ) a chute.

ཤུར་སྒྲ་ (shūrdra) sound of wind, thunder etc.

ཤུར་ཅོག (shūūjoò) drawer; va.—རྒྱག to close a drawer.

ཤུར་ཐིག་ཅན་ (shūrdigjɛn) corduroy.

ཤུར་མདའ་ (shūnda) a type of arrow.

ཤུར་འདོན་འཁོར་སྟེགས་ (shūrdön kɔ̄ɔ̄deg) broaching machine.

ཤུར་བུ་ (shūrbu) a type of belt.

ཤུར་བུ་ཁྲེའུ་ (shūrbu trēwu) a belt woven with multicolored strings.

ཤུར་བྲོས་ (shūrdröò) sneaking away; slinking off.

ཤུར་འབེན་ (shūrben) a plane used to make depressions (on planks).

ཤུར་མ་ (shūrmə) corduroy.

ཤུར་མ་ངང་སྒྲོ་མ་ (shūrma ŋa̱ŋdroma) goose down.

ཤུར་མ་འབུར་འདོན་ (shūrmə bu̱rdön) sm. ཤུར་མ་.

ཤུར་རྩི་ (shūrdzi) ch. leather boots.

ཤུར་ཤུར་ (shūrshur) 1. narrow. 2. a feeling of sth. ¶ གྲངས་ཤུར་ཤུར་ A feeling of coldness. ¶ མཚེར་ཤུར་ཤུར་ A feeling of embarrassment.

ཤུལ་ (shūū) 1. anything left behind, remains, trace; vi.—ལྷག; —ལུས་; —ལུས་ ¶ ཕ་གྲོངས་རྗེས་ཁྱིམ་ཚང་གི་ཤུལ་ཚང་མ་བུ་ལ་རག་འདུག After the father died, the son got all the household's remaining things. 2. while, meanwhile ¶ ང་རང་གུང་སེང་དུ་འགྲོ་ཤུལ་ནང་ལ་རྐུན་མ་ཤོར་འདུག While I was gone on vacation, (my) house was robbed 3. distance ¶ མི་ཚེ་འདི་ལས་ཕྱི་མ་ཤུལ་ཐག་རིང་ The path of (our) future life is longer than the journey of our present life.

ཤུལ་རྒྱུན་ (shūūgyün) tradition, heritage, inheritance, legacy; va.—འཛིན་ to maintain a tradition/ heritage.

ཤུལ་བགྲོད་ (shūūdröò) va. to pass through/ complete a journey.

ཤུལ་བརྒྱུད་ (shūūgyüù) sm. ཤུལ་རྗེས་.

ཤུལ་དངོས་ (shūūŋöò) inherited property.

ཤུལ་བཅས་གཙང་སྒྲུབ་ (shūūjɛɛ̀ dzāŋdrub) shung. to pay sth. completely.

ཤུལ་རྗེས་ (shūūjeè) 1. legacy, inheritance; va.—འཇོག to leave a legacy/ inheritance, to leave sth. behind ¶ མཁས་པ་དེས་རིག་གནས་ཀྱི་ཤུལ་རྗེས་མང་པོ་བཞག་འདུག That scholar left a legacy of many cultural works.

ཤུལ་རྙིང་ (shūūñiŋ) old remains/ ruins.

ཤུལ་སྟོང་ (shūūoŋ) vi. to become extinct.

ཤུལ་དུ་ (shūūdu) a trace, a wake, remains ¶ སྦོམ་དབྱུགས་པའི་ཤུལ་དུ་ཁང་པ་ཞིག་བརྒྱབ་པ་རེད་ (They) built a house on the place where the bomb was thrown.

ཤུལ་དུ་འགོད་ (shūūdu gö̱ò) va. to leave sth. as an inheritance.

ཤུལ་སྡོད་ (shūūdöò) survivor ¶ མི་ཚང་དེའི་ཤུལ་སྡོད་ག་ཚོད་འདུག་གམ་ How many survivors are there in that family?

ཤུལ་པ་ (shūūbə) sm. ཤུལ་འཛིན་མཁན་.

ཤུལ་མ་ (shūūmə) things left behind.

ཤུལ་མི་ (shūūmi) sm. ཤུལ་འཛིན་, 2.

ཤུལ་མེད་ (shūūmeè) without a trace, without any remains; va.—དུ་གཏོང་ to annihilate/ obliterate, to make so there is no trace left.

ཞུལ་མེད་དུ་འགྲོ་ (shǘǘmeèdu dro̱) vi. to become extinct/ annihilated.

ཞུལ་མེད་བཟོ་ (shǘǘmeè so̱) va. to completely annihilate/ destroy.

ཞུལ་ཙམ་མེད་པ་ (shǘǘdzam me̱èba) destroyed without a trace, obliterated, annihilated.

ཞུལ་འཛར་ (shǘndzar) shung. sm. ཞུལ་འཛིན་.

ཞུལ་འཛིན་ (shǘndzin) 1. va. to inherit, to succeed, to carry on. 2. successor, heir ¶ མི་ཚང་འདི་ལ་ཞུལ་འཛིན་བུ་མོ་ཞིག་ལས་ལྷག་མེད་པ་རེད་ This family has as its successor only one daughter.

ཞུལ་འཛིན་མཁན་ (shǘǘ dzi̱ññɛn) successor, heir.

ཞུལ་འཛིན་པ་ (shǘǘ dzi̱mba) sm. ཞུལ་འཛིན་མཁན་.

ཞུལ་འཛིན་དབང་ཆ་ (shǘndzin wāṉja) right of succession/ inheritance.

ཞུལ་རྫས་ (shǘǘdzɛɛ̀) one's inheritance, that which one inherits.

ཞུལ་བཞག (shǘǘ sha̱à) legacy, inheritance ¶ ཞུལ་བཞག་རྒྱུ་དངོས་ Inherited property. ¶ མི་རབས་གོང་མའི་ཞུལ་བཞག་གི་གོམས་གཤིས་ངན་པ་ Bad habits inherited from the past generation.

ཞུལ་བཞག་རྒྱུ་རྫས་ (shǘǘshaà gyu̱dzɛɛ̀) sm. ཞུལ་བཞག.

ཞུལ་བཞག་བརྒྱུད་སྤྲོད་ (shǘǘshaà gyǘǘdruoò) passing on an inheritance to children ¶ ཕ་སྨན་པའི་ལག་རྩལ་དེ་བུ་ལ་ཞུལ་བཞག་བརྒྱུད་སྤྲོད་བྱས་འདུག The father passed on his medical skills to his son.

ཞུལ་བཞག་དངོས་རྫས་ (shǘǘshaà ŋṏòdzɛɛ̀) sm. ཞུལ་རྫས་.

ཞུལ་བཞག་གནད་དོན་ (shǘǘshaà nɛ̄èdön) issues/ questions left over from the past.

ཞུལ་བཞག་ཞེན་ཐྲིས་ (shǘǘshaà si̱ndri) will, last testament.

ཞུལ་བཞག་གསུང་རྩོམ་ (shǘǘshaà sūŋdzom) posthumous works (of an author).

ཞུལ་རིང་ལ་ (shǘǘ ri̱ŋlə) during, while ¶ ཕྲུ་གུ་དེ་སློབ་གྲྭར་འགྲོ་ཞུལ་རིང་ལ་ནང་དུ་ཀུན་མ་ཞུགས་འདུག While he was going to school his house was robbed.

ཞུལ་ལ་ (shǘǘlə) sm. ཞུལ་རིང་ལ་.

ཞུལ་ལམ་ (shǘǘlam) sm. འགྲོ་ལམ་.

ཞུལ་ལས་ (shǘǘlɛɛ̀) sm. ཞུལ་ལུས་.

ཞུལ་ལུས་ (shǘǘlüù) 1. sth. left behind, leftover ¶ ཁོས་ཞུལ་ལུས་ཟ་ཁང་རྩིས་ལེན་བྱས་པ་རེད་ (He) took over the restaurant that was left behind. 2. vi. to be unfinished ¶ ངའི་ལས་ཀའི་ཞུལ་ལུས་ཙང་སང་ཉིན་འགྲོ་དགོས་ཡོད་ Because my work was left unfinished, I have to go tomorrow.

ཞུལ་ལུས་གོམས་གཤིས་ (shǘǘlüù ko̱mshii) customs inherited from the past.

ཞུལ་ལུས་ནད་གཞི་ (shǘǘlüù nè̱èshi) an illness not completely cured.

ཞུལ་ཞུལ་ (shǘǘshüü) sm. ཞུལ་.

ཞུས་ (shǘǘ) sm. བཞུས་.

ཞུས་འདེབས་ (shǘǘ de̱b) va. to signal through whistling.

ཤེ་ (shē) leasing animals; va.—གཏོང་ to lease animals in return for a fixed amount of butter (and/ or wool) ¶ འབྲོག་བདག་གིས་འབྲོག་པ་དབུལ་པོ་ཚོར་ལ་འབྲི་མང་པོ་ཤེ་ལ་བཏང་བ་རེད་ The rich nomad leased many female yaks to the poor nomads.

ཤེ་ཁག (shēgaà) a herd of leased animals.

ཤེ་ཁྲལ་ (shēdrɛɛ) sm. ཤེ་ཐོབ་.

ཤེ་འགྲེམས་ (shēdrem) shung. animals distributed on lease ¶ བླ་བྲང་ནས་ཤེ་འགྲེམས་སེམས་སེམས་ཅན་ Animals distributed for leasing by the Labrang.

ཤེ་སྡག (shēdaà) sm. ཤེ་.

ཤེ་ཐོབ་ (shēdob) shung. the amount of an animal lease.

ཤེ་མཐུན་ (shēdün) sm. ཤེད་མཐུན་.

ཤེ་ན་ (shēna) if one says what was said/ written ¶ རྒྱལ་སྤྱིའི་ཚོགས་འདུའི་སར་ཁོང་གིས་གང་གསུངས་ཤེ་ན་ If one says what he said at the meeting of the UN.

ཤེ་དཔོན་ (shēbön) the person looking after leased animals.

ཤེ་བ་ (shēwa) white eyeballs.

ཤེ་བམ་ (shēbam) shung. land tenure document (usu. issued by Dalai Lama or regent).

ཤེ་བམ་ཆེན་མོ་ (shēbam cēmmo) shung. sm. ཤེ་བམ་.

ཤེ་བམ་གཏན་ཚིག (shēbam dɛ̄ndzii) land tenure document ¶ མི་ཚང་དེའི་གཞིས་ཀ་རེ་རེར་ཤེ་བམ་གཏན་ཚིག་རེ་ཡོད་པ་རེད་ This family has a land tenure document for each of its estates.

ཤེ་འབབ་ (shēbəb) sm. ཤེ་མར་.

ཤེ་འབྲི་ (shē dri̱) a leased female yak.

ཤེ་སྦྱོར་ (shējɔɔ) copulation; va.—བྱེད་ to copulate.

ཤེ་སྦྱོར་མ་ (shējɔɔma) a promiscuous woman.

ཤེ་མ་ (shēma) shung. a person who leases other people's livestock.

ཤེ་མར་ (shēmar) shung. the fee in butter received per head of leased animals.

ཤེ་མི་ཆོད་ (shē mi̱jöö) not useful.

ཤེ་མོ་ (shēmo) prosperity.

ཤེ་མོང་ (shēmoŋ) sm. ཤེད་མོ་.

ཤེ་ཟོག (shēsɔɔ̀) leased animals.

ཤེ་གཡོག (shēyɔɔ̀) servant of sb. who leases someone else's animals.

ཤེ་རུ་ (shēru) sm. ཤེ་ཁག.

ཤེད་ (shēè) 1. force, power, strength ¶ མི་དེ་ཤེད་ཆེན་པོ་ཞི་དྲག་འདུག That person is very strong. 2. sm. ཤེད་མོ་.

ཤེད་སྐྱེད་ shēègyeè) 1. va. to use one's strength. 2. va. increase one's strength.

ཤེད་ཁྱེར་ (shēègyer) sm. ཤེད་ངོམ་.

ཤེད་རྒྱུག (shēè gyu̱ù) wrestling and racing (as sports).

ཤེད་ངོམ་ (shɛ̄ɛ̀ŋom) bullying by showing off one's strength (through violence); va.—བྱེད་.

ཤེད་ངོམས་ (shēèŋom) sm. ཤེད་ངོམ་.

ཤེད་ཅན་ (shēèjɛn) powerful, strong.

ཤེད་ཆུང་ (shēèjuŋ) weak, feeble.

ཤེད་ཆེན་པོ་ (shēè cēmbo) strong, vigorous.

ཤེད་འཇགས་ (shēnjaà) vi. to lose vigor/ strength (for animals).

ཤེད་ཉམས་ཤུགས་མེད་ (shēèñam shūgmeè) weak, decrepit, worn out.

ཤེད་སྙོམས་ (shēèñom) fractions of a common denominator (in math).

ཤེད་སྟོབས་ (shēèdob) strength, vigor (animals).

ཤེད་མཐུན་ (shēèdün) 1. friend. 2. equal in strength.

ཤེད་དང་ཤེད་མོ་ (shēèdaŋ shēèmo) strength.

ཤེད་བྱས་ (shēèjɛɛ̀) with force/ strength ¶ ཁོས་ཤིང་དེ་ཤེད་བྱས་བཏོག་སོང་ He used a lot of strength and pulled out the tree.

ཤེད་དབང་ (shēèwaŋ) abuse, force, domination.

ཤེད་སྦྲུག (shēèjaà) sm. ཤེད་འཇགས་.

ཤེད་སྦྱངས་ (shēè ja̱ŋ) 1. va. to regret one's wrongdoing. 2. p. of ཤེད་སྦྱོང་.

ཤེད་སྦྱོང་ (shēèjoŋ) physical exercise; va.—བྱེད་ to exercise (physically).

ཤེད་སྦྱོང་རྒྱུ་མ་ (shēèjoŋ gyu̱mə) chest expander (a type of exercise machine).

ཤེད་སྦྱོང་ལྕགས་རིལ་ (shēèjoŋ jāgrii) weights for lifting, dumbbells; va.—འགྱོགས་ to lift weights.

ཤེད་མ་ (shēèma) sm. ཤེད་མོ་.

ཤེད་མེད་ (shēèmeè) weak, powerless, feeble.

ཤེད་མོ་ (shēèmo) 1. coat (animal's sheen); va.—ལེན་ to get good sheen coat, to gain weight; vi.—ཤོར་; —འཇགས་ to lose one's sheen/ good coat, to lose weight; ¶ ཤེད་མོ་ཡག་པོ་ A good sheen. 2. strength, force, power.

ཤེད་མོ་རྒྱས་པ་ (shēèmo gyè̱èba) having a good sheen.

ཤེད་མོ་ལེན་ (shɛ̄ɛmo lɛ̄n) see ཤེད་མོ་.

ཤེད་མོ་ཤུར་རྒྱུག (shēèmo shǖrgyuù) sm. ཤུར་རྒྱུག.

ཤེད་མོ་ཤོར་ (shēèmo shɔ̄ɔ̄) see ཤེད་མོ་.

ཤེད་མོང་ (shēèmoŋ) 1. physical strength. 2. sm. དབང་ཤུགས་.

ཤེད་མོང་འཛོང་ (shēēmoŋ dzōŋ) shung. va. to bully others by showing one's strength or using violence.

ཤེད་རྩལ་ (shēèdzεε) wrestling.

ཤེད་ཚན་ (shēèdzεn) sm. ཤེད་མོང་.

ཤེད་ཚོང་ (shēè tsōŋ) shung. to use violence/ force to bully others.

ཤེད་བཟང་ (shēèsaŋ) 1. strong, healthy. 2. good coat/ sheen, fat (of animals) ¶ཁོས་ལུག་ཤེད་བཟང་ཞིག་བསད་པ་རེད་ He killed a fat sheep.

ཤེད་ལང་ (shεὲ laŋ) see ཤེད་མོ་ལེན་.

ཤེད་ཤུགས་ (shēèshuù) power, strength, force; va.—སྒྲིམ་; —སྒྲིལ་ to concentrate strength.

ཤེད་ཤུགས་གཅིག་སྒྲིམ་ (shēèshuù jīgdrim) focusing all one's energy together, concentrating all one's strength; va.—བྱེད་.

ཤེད་ཤུགས་གཅིག་སྒྲིལ་ (shēèshuù jīgdrii) sm. ཤེད་ཤུགས་གཅིག་སྒྲིམ་.

ཤེད་ཤུགས་རིགས་པ་ (shēèshuù rigbə) dynamics.

ཤེད་ཤོར་ (shēèshɔɔ) sm. ཤེད་མོ་ཤོར་.

ཤེན་ (shēn) sm.* ཤེས་.

ཤེན་པ་ (shēmba) 1. sm. ཤན་པ་. 2. sm. ཤུར་བ་.

ཤེའུ་ (shēwu) fawn.

ཤེར་ (shēr) 1. eng. seer (= 2.06 pounds) 2. p. and imp. of བཤེར་.

ཤེལ་ (shēē) crystal, glass.

ཤེལ་ཀ་ར་ (shēēgara) sugar, rock candy.

ཤེལ་ཀ་ར་དིང་པར་ (shēēgara dīŋbar) rock sugar molded into the shape of a water offering bowl.

ཤེལ་དཀར་ (shēēgar) 1. name of a dzong. 2. glass cup.

ཤེལ་ཁང་ (shēēgaŋ) greenhouse.

ཤེལ་ཁེབས་ (shēēgeb) 1. window curtain. 2. covering for a greenhouse.

ཤེལ་ཁྲ་ (shēēdra) glass window.

ཤེལ་ག་བུར་ (shēē gəbur) borneol.

ཤེལ་གྱི་བཞུ་ཞུ་ (shēēgi shusha) glass lamp shade.

ཤེལ་གྱི་སྒྲོན་ཁེབས་ (shēēgi dröngeb) sm. ཤེལ་གྱི་བཞུ་ཞུ་.

ཤེལ་གྱི་ཚི་སྣ་ (shēēgi tsīnə) fiberglass.

ཤེལ་སྒམ་ (shēēgam) glass case/ showcase.

ཤེལ་སྒོ་ (shēēgo) 1. glass. 2. mirror; va.—ལྟ་ to look in a mirror.

ཤེལ་སྒོ་ངོས་འཇམ་ (shēēgo ŋönjam) plate glass.

ཤེལ་སྒོ་དཔྱད་ཆས་བཟོ་གྲྭ་ (shēēgo jέὲjεὲ sodra) glass instruments factory.

ཤེལ་སྒོ་ཚལ་ཞིང་ (shēēgo tsεεshiŋ) vegetable greenhouse.

ཤེལ་སྒོ་ཟུར་གསུམ་མ་ (shēēgo sursummə) prism.

ཤེལ་སྒོ་བཟོ་གྲྭ་ (shēēgo sodra) glassworks.

ཤེལ་སྒོ་གསུམ་མ་ (shēēgo) sm. ཤེལ་སྒོ་ཟུར་གསུམ་མ་.

ཤེལ་སྒོང་ (shēēgoŋ) marbles, glass ball.

ཤེལ་སྒོའི་ནང་གི་མོག་མོག (shēēgö naŋgi momoò) sth. that is not possible to get ¶བུ་མོ་མཛེས་མ་དེ་ཁྱེད་རང་ལ་རག་གི་མ་རེད་ དེ་ཤེལ་སྒོའི་ནང་གི་མོག་མོག་རེད་ You can't get that beautiful girl. It is like a dumpling in a display case. [Lit. dumpling in glass].

ཤེལ་སྒོར་གཟབ་ནན་ (shēēgɔɔ səbnεn) "beware/ be careful of the glass" (a sign on glass doors).

ཤེལ་སྒྲོམ་ (shēēdrom) frame for a mirror.

ཤེལ་ཆས་ (shēējεὲ) glassware.

ཤེལ་ད་ (shēēda) myrrh.

ཤེལ་དང་དཀར་ནག (shēēdaŋ gārnaà) large and small leaf gentian.

ཤེལ་དོག (shēēdoò) sm. ཤེལ་རྡོག.

ཤེལ་དམ་ (shēēdam) bottle.

ཤེལ་རྡོ་ (shēēdo) rock/ quartz crystal.

ཤེལ་རྡོ་ཟུར་གསུམ་ (shēēdo sursum) prism.

ཤེལ་རྡོག (shēēdɔɔ̀) light bulb, vacuum tube.

ཤེལ་བརྡ་ (shēēda) signaling with a mirror; va.—གཏོང་.

ཤེལ་སྣོད་ (shēēnöö̀) glass vessel/ container.

ཤེལ་པང་ (shēēbaŋ) sheet of glass.

ཤེལ་སྤྱད་ (shēējεὲ) sm. ཤེལ་ཆས་.

ཤེལ་ཕག (shēēbaà) glass brick/ block.

ཤེལ་ཕོར་ (shēēbɔɔ) drinking glass/ cup.

ཤེལ་ཕྲེང་ (shēēdreŋ) glass rosary.

ཤེལ་བུམ་ (shēēbum) sm. ཤེལ་དམ་.

ཤེལ་སྦུག (shēēbuù) glass tube, test tube.

ཤེལ་སྦུབས་ (shēēbub) sm. ཤེལ་སྦུག.

ཤེལ་མིག (shēēmiì) eyeglasses.

ཤེལ་ཚྭ་ (shēēdza) crystal salt.

ཤེལ་ཚོན་ནོར་བུར་རེ་བ་ (shēēdzön norbur rewa) having false/ unrealistic hopes [Lit. hoping colored glass would be a precious stone].

ཤེལ་འཛིན་ཁྲ་རུ་ (shēndzin trōru) shung. window frame.

ཤེལ་ཟུར་གསུམ་མ་ (shēēsur sūmmə) triangular prism.

ཤེལ་གཟུགས་ (shēēsuù) crystal.

ཤེལ་གཟུགས་ཆགས་ཚུལ་ (shēēsuù cəgdzüü) crystal lattice.

ཤེལ་གཟུགས་རྡུལ་ཕྲན་གྱི་ཕྲེང་བསྟར་ (shēēsuù düüdrεngi trēŋdar) sm. ཤེལ་གཟུགས་ཆགས་ཚུལ་.

ཤེལ་གཟུགས་སྦུ་གུ་ (shēēshuù bugu) transistor.

ཤེལ་གཟུགས་རིག་པ་ (shēēsuù rigbə) crystallography.

ཤེལ་བཟོས་ཡོ་བྱད་ (shēēsöö yojεὲ) glassware.

ཤེལ་བཟོ་བ་ (shēēsowa) glassware maker.

ཤེལ་ཡོལ་ (shēēyöö) sm. ཤེལ་ཁེབས་.

ཤེལ་རིགས་ཚི་སྣ་བཟོ་གྲྭ་ (shēērii tsīnə sodra) fiberglass factory.

ཤེལ་རིལ་ (shēērii) 1. electric bulb. 2. glass ball/ bead.

ཤེལ་ལེབ་ (shēēleb) 1. lens. 2. glass plate.

ཤེལ་ཤུར་ (shēēshur) sm. ཤུར་འབེབ་.

ཤེལ་ཤོག (shēēshoò) glassine.

ཤེས་ (shēè) 1. vi. to know, to understand ¶ཁོང་གིས་ལྕགས་བཟོའི་ལག་རྩལ་ཤེས་པ་རེད་ He knew the steel making techniques. ¶འདི་ངས་ཤེས་ཀྱི་འདུག I know this. 2. (vb. + —) to be possible/ able ¶ཡུལ་འདིའི་ནང་དམངས་གཙོའི་ལམ་ལུགས་ཡོང་ཤེས་ཀྱི་མ་རེད་ Its not possible for democracy to come to that country. 3. (vb.+ ཤེས་པ་བྱེད་དགོས་) to have to know how to do sth. ¶ཁེ་བཟང་ཆེན་པོ་དགོས་ན་ཚོང་གི་ཐབས་ཤེས་ཤེས་པ་བྱེད་དགོས་ If you want big profit, you have to know business methods. 4. (vb. + —) knowing how to do ¶དམག་མི་གཏོང་ཤེས་ན་དགོས་མཁོ་སྤྲོད་ཐུབ་པ་དགོས་ཀྱི་རེད་ If one knows to send troops, one needs to know how to supply them.

ཤེས་བཀྲ་གཟུགས་བཟང་ (shēèdra sugsaŋ) intelligent and physically strong/ healthy.

ཤེས་འགོས་གཉིས་ལྡན་ (shēègöò ñīndεn) having both knowledge and wealth.

ཤེས་རྒྱ་ (shēègya) scope (of one's) knowledge/ learning/ wisdom ¶ཁོ་ཤེས་རྒྱ་ཆུང་ཆུང་རེད་ He is sb. who is poorly informed.

ཤེས་རྒྱ་ཆུང་ཆུང་ (shēègya cūŋjuŋ) see ཤེས་རྒྱ་.

ཤེས་རྒྱ་ཆེན་པོ་ (shēègya cēmbo) having wide knowledge, learned, wise.

ཤེས་སྒོ་ (shēègo) sm. ཤེས་རྒྱ་.

ཤེས་སྒོ་ཞན་པ་ (shēègo shεmba) sm. ཤེས་རྒྱ་ཆུང་ཆུང་.

ཤེས་སྒོ་ཡངས་པ་ (shēègo yaŋba) sm. ཤེས་རྒྱ་ཆེན་པོ་.

ཤེས་འཆལ་ (shēèrcεε) 1. foolish, stupid. 2. perverse/ wrong knowldge.

ཤེས་འཇོན་ (shēè jön) knowledgeable and capable.

ཤེས་ཉེན་ (shēèñen) sm. ཡོན་དན་.

ཤེས་གཉེན་ (shēèñen) sm. ཤེས་ཉེན་.

ཤེས་གཉེན་ཅན་ (shēèñenjεn) learned, knowledgeable, wise.

ཤེས་རྟོགས་ (shēèdoò) understanding, knowledge, comprehension; va.—བྱེད་ to know, to comprehend, to understand ¶ཁག་འདོགས་དེ་ཕན་མེད་ཅིག་ཡིན་པ་ཤེས་རྟོགས་བྱུང་ (They) understood that that pretext was not useful. ¶ཡིག་བསྐྱར་དེ་སུས་བྲིས་མིན་ཤེས་རྟོགས་མ་བྱུང་ (I) didn't know who wrote the protest poster.

ཤེས་རྟོགས་ཀྱི་ནུས་པ་ (shēèdoògi nüübə) cognitive ability.

ཤེས་ཐབས་ (shēèdəb) method of learning ¶མགྱོགས་པོ་ཤེས་ཐབས་ A method of learning quickly.

ཤེས་ཐུབ་པའི་རང་བཞིན་ (shēèdubbε rənshin) knowable.

ཤེས་ཐོས་བྱུང་ (shēètööjuŋ) coming to know sth. ¶ སོ་པ་ཡོད་པ་གཞུང་ནས་ཤེས་ཐོས་བྱུང་ The government came to know there were spies. [Lit. knowing and hearing].

ཤེས་དོགས་ (shēèdɔɔ̀) having doubts/ suspicions that sb. will know; va.—བྱེད་ ¶ ཁོས་ཀུན་མ་བརྐུས་པ་དེ་མི་གཞན་གྱིས་ཤེས་དོགས་བྱེད་ཀྱི་འདུག He has suspicions that others know he stole (it).

ཤེས་ལྡན་མ་ (shēèdemma) learned woman.

ཤེས་འདོད་ (shēndöö) desiring/ wanting to know; va.—བྱེད་ ¶ གསར་འགྱུར་དེ་མི་ཚང་མས་ཤེས་འདོད་བྱེད་ཀྱི་ཡོད་པ་རེད་ Everyone wants to know that news.

ཤེས་ལྡན་ (shēndɛn) wise, learned, intelligent. 2. distinguished ¶ ཤེས་ལྡན་མགྲོན་པོ་ Distinguished guests.

ཤེས་ལྡན་མི་སྣ་ (shēèdɛn minə) experts.

ཤེས་ནུས་ (shēènüü) knowledge and ability.

ཤེས་པ་ (shēèba) knowledge, learning, understanding; va.—བྱེད་ to learn, to find out, to know ¶ ལུང་པ་གསར་པ་ཞིག་ལ་སླེབས་དུས་ཡུལ་དེའི་སྐད་ཤེས་པ་བྱེད་དགོས་ When one arrives in a new place one must learn that area's language.

ཤེས་པ་ཅན་ (shēèbəjɛn) 1. intellectual, learned, knowledgeable. 2. general term for all sentient beings.

ཤེས་པ་འཐིབས་ (shēèba tib) vi. to feel mentally dull ¶ མདང་དགོང་གཉིད་ཡག་པོ་མ་ཁུག་ཙང་དེ་རིང་ཤེས་པ་འཐིབས་འདུག Because I didn't sleep well last night, today I am mentally dull.

ཤེས་པ་སྨྲ་བ་ (shēè māwa) sm. ཤེས་པའི་རྣམ་བཤད་.

ཤེས་པ་ཡེར་རེ་སེང་ངེ་ (shēèb yere sēŋŋe) clear mind/ thoughts/ understanding.

ཤེས་པའི་སྟོབས་ (shēèbɛ dōb) intellectual power/ capacity.

ཤེས་པའི་རྣམ་བཤད་ (shēèbɛ nāmshɛɛ̀) theory of knowledge.

ཤེས་པའི་སློབ་གསོ་ (shēèbɛ lōbso) intellectual education.

ཤེས་སྤྱོད་ (shēèjöö) knowledge and behavior.

ཤེས་བྱ་ (shēè) knowledge, learning, understanding. 2. name of a Tibetan refugee magazine.

ཤེས་བྱ་ཆེན་པོ་ (shēèja cēmbo) a learned person, an intellectual.

ཤེས་བྱ་ཡོན་ཏན་ (shēèja yöndɛn) knowledge.

ཤེས་བྱ་སློབ་གཉེར་ (shēèja lōbñer) seeking knowledge, learning or acquiring education.

ཤེས་བྱེད་ (shēèjeè) the reason for sth.

ཤེས་འབྱོན་ (shēèjön) knowledge and capability.

ཤེས་མེད་ཚོར་མེད་ (shēèmeè tsɔ̄rmeè) sm. ཤེས་དམན་.

ཤེས་དམན་ (shēèmɛn) ignorant.

ཤེས་རྨོངས་ (shēèmoŋ) sm. ཤེས་དམན་.

ཤེས་རྨོངས་ཀྱི་དུས་རབས་ (shēèmoŋgi tüürəb) age of barbarism, uncivilized era.

ཤེས་རྩལ་ཅན་ (shēèdzɛɛ̀jɛn) intelligent, wise, learned.

ཤེས་ཚད་ (shēèdzɛɛ̀) level of knowledge, education level, degree.

ཤེས་ཚད་ལག་འཁྱེར་ (shēèdzɛɛ̀ laggyee) diploma.

ཤེས་ཚོད་ (shēèdzöö) knowledge, level of knowledge ¶ ངས་ཤེས་ཚོད་བྱས་ན་ To the best of my knowledge.

ཤེས་ཚོར་ (shēèdzɔɔ) 1. knowing, understanding ¶ ཁོང་ཚོགས་འདུར་ཡོང་གི་ཡོད་པ་ངས་ཤེས་ཚོར་མ་བྱུང་ I didn't know he is coming to the meeting.

ཤེས་ཚོར་མགྱོགས་པོ་ (shēèdzɔɔ gyogbo) keen, penetrating.

ཤེས་ཚོར་རྣོ་པོ་ (shēèdzɔɔ nōbo) sm. ཤེས་ཚོར་མགྱོགས་པོ་.

ཤེས་ཚོར་རྣོན་པོ་ (shēèdzɔɔ nōmbo) sm. ཤེས་ཚོར་མགྱོགས་པོ་.

ཤེས་ཞན་ (shēèsgɛn) ignorant, illinformed, uneducated.

ཤེས་བཞིན་ (shēèshin) knowingly, deliberately ¶ ཁོས་ཤེས་བཞིན་སྒྲིག་ལམ་དང་འགལ་བ་བྱེད་ཀྱི་འདུག He is deliberately going against the regulation.

ཤེས་བཞིན་ཁྱད་གསོད་ (shēèshin kyɛɛ̀söö) doing something knowingly; va.—བྱེད་.

ཤེས་བཞིན་སྒྲིབ་ཆགས་ (shēèshin dribjaà) shung. sm. ཤེས་བཞིན་སྒྲིབ་སྤྱང་.

ཤེས་བཞིན་སྒྲིབ་སྤྱང་ (shēèshin dribjaŋ) deliberate action ¶ ངས་ལས་ཀ་ནོར་འཁྲུལ་འདི་ཤེས་བཞིན་སྒྲིབ་སྤྱང་བྱས་པ་མིན་ I didn't knowingly do the work wrong.

ཤེས་བཞིན་དུ་ (shēèshindu) sm. ཤེས་བཞིན་.

ཤེས་བཞིན་དུ་འདྲི་ (shēèshindu dri) va. to ask while knowing the answer.

ཤེས་བཞིན་དུ་བྱེད་ (shēèshindu cee) va. to knowingly do sth. bad ¶ ཁོས་ལས་ཀ་ནོར་འཁྲུལ་འདི་ཤེས་བཞིན་དུ་བྱས་འདུག He knowingly did the work wrong.

ཤེས་ཡོན་ (shēèyön) knowledge, education.

ཤེས་ཡོན་ཁང་ (shēèyöngaŋ) institute ¶ ལུས་རྩལ་གྱི་ཤེས་ཡོན་ཁང་ Physical education institute.

ཤེས་ཡོན་ངེས་ཅན་ (shēèyön ŋeèjɛn) sb. with definite/ in depth knowledge in certain areas.

ཤེས་ཡོན་ཅན་ (shēèyönjɛn) an intellectual, a scholar, a learned person.

ཤེས་ཡོན་ཅན་གྱི་ཐོབ་ཐང་ (shēèyönjɛngi tōbdaŋ) academic degree.

ཤེས་ཡོན་ཆེན་པོ་ (shēèyön cēmbo) sm. ཤེས་བྱ་ཆེན་པོ་.

ཤེས་ཡོན་ཐོབ་ཐང་གི་ཆེད་རྩོམ་ (shēèyön tōbdaŋgi cēèdzom) thesis, dissertation (for an academic degree).

ཤེས་ཡོན་སྣ་འཛོམས་ (shēèyön nāndzom) learned/ knowledgeable in many ways.

ཤེས་ཡོན་ཚོགས་ཆུང་ (shēèyön tsɔ̄gjuŋ) study group.

ཤེས་ཡོན་འཛོམས་པོ་ (shēèyön dzōmbo) sm. ཤེས་ཡོན་སྣ་འཛོམས་.

ཤེས་ཡོན་རིག་གཅིག་ཀྱང་འཛིན་པ་ (shēèyön rigjig gāŋdzimbə) specialist.

ཤེས་ཡོན་སློབ་སྤེལ་ (shēèyön lōbel) spreading education; va.—བྱེད་ ¶ གཞོན་ནུ་རྣམས་ལ་ཤེས་ཡོན་སློབ་སྤེལ་བྱ་དགོས་ You must educate the youth.

ཤེས་རབ་ (shēèrəb) intelligence, wisdom ¶ ཁོང་ལ་བརྩོན་འགྲུས་ཡོད་ཀྱང་ཤེས་རབ་མེད་པ་རེད་ Even though he has diligence, he has no intelligence.

ཤེས་རབ་ཅན་ (shēèrəbjɛn) intelligent, wise, learned.

ཤེས་རབ་འཆལ་ (shēèrəb cɛɛ̀) 1. foolish, stupid. 2. perverse/ wrong knowledge.

ཤེས་རབ་སྤང་ལ་མེ་ཤོར་ བརྩོན་འགྲུས་བྲག་ལ་མདའ་ཟུག (shēèrəb bāŋla meshɔɔ dzöndrüü tragla dasuù) diligence is critical [Lit. wisdom is like a wild prairie fire, diligence is as permanent as an arrow stuck in a rock].

ཤེས་རབ་སྨྱུར་པོ་ (shēèrəb ñurwo) sm. ཤེས་ཚོར་རྣོན་པོ་.

ཤེས་རབ་རལ་གྲི་ (shēèrəb rɛɛdri) sword of wisdom.

ཤེས་རབ་གསལ་བ་ (shēèrəb sēèwa) intelligent.

ཤེས་རམས་པ་ (shēèrəma) 1. scholar. 2. bachelor.

ཤེས་རིག (shēèrii) 1. intelligence ¶ ངའི་བུ་འདི་ལ་ཤེས་རིག་ཡོད་པ་རེད་ My son is intelligent. 2. culture ¶ ཤེས་རིག་པར་ཁང་ Cultural Printing Press. ¶ ཤེས་རིག་བློན་ཆེན་ Minister of Culture; va.—དར་; —འཕེལ་ to be/ get civilized; va.—སྤེལ་ to civilize.

ཤེས་རིག་ཅན་ (shēèrigjɛn) 1. intelligent, clever. 2. sentient beings.

ཤེས་རིག་བཀྲ་བ་ (shēèrig drāwa) intelligent.

ཤེས་རིག་དར་ (shēèrig tar) see ཤེས་རིག.

ཤེས་རིག་དར་བའི་ལོ་རྒྱུས་ (shēèrii tarwɛ lugyüü) the history of civilization.

ཤེས་རིག་འཕེལ་ (shēèrig pēl) see ཤེས་རིག.

ཤེས་རིགས་མ་དར་བའི་མི་རིགས་ (shēèrig madarwɛ mirii) uncivilized/ primitive nationalities or ethnic groups.

ཤེས་རིག་གཙུག་ལག་ཁང་ (shēèrig dzūglaàgaŋ) institute of culture.

ཤེས་རིག་ལས་ཁུངས་ (shēèrig lɛɛ̀guŋ) cultural office, department of culture.

ཤེས་རིག་གསར་བརྗེ་ (shēèrig sārje) cultural revolution.

ཤེས་ཀློམ་ (shēèlom) pride in knowing sth. or having some knowledge.

ཤེས་རེ་སྐན་ (shēère gɛ̄n) va. to swear one does not know sth.

ཤེས་ལུགས་ (shēèluù) culture, customs.

ཤེས་གསལ་ (shēèsee) 1. well known, common knowledge ། འདི་ངས་ཤེས་གསལ་ཡིན་ I know this well. 2. abbr. of ཤེས་རབ་གསལ་བ་.

ཤེས་གསལ་ལྟར་ (shēèseldar) as is commonly/ well known ། ཚང་མས་ཤེས་གསལ་ལྟར་ As everyone knows.

ཤོ་ (shō) 1. dice; va.—རྒྱག; —འགྱེད་ to play dice. 2. a line/ column of animals; —སྒྲིག to be/ go in a line (animals). 3. a tax, custom's duty.

ཤོ་ཀ་ལི་ (shōgali) sm. ཤོག་ཀ་ལི་.

ཤོ་ཁ (shōga) shung. tribe, group.

ཤོ་ཁུག (shōguù) pouch in which dice and its associated paraphernalia are kept.

ཤོ་ཁྱི་ (shōgyi) the markers a player uses in Tibetan dice to move.

ཤོ་ཁྲལ་ (shōdrɛɛ) shung. tax, toll, customs duty.

ཤོ་ཁྲིད་ (shōdriì) leading/ heading a group of animals.

ཤོ་གམ་ (shōgam) sm. ཤོ་ཁྲལ་.

ཤོ་གམ་སྡུས་ (shōgam dö̱ö̀) va. to collect taxes.

ཤོ་གློད་ (shō lö̀ö̀) va. to let the line of mules go and start a journey.

ཤོ་འགྱེད་ (shōgyeè) see ཤོ་.

ཤོ་གལ་ (shōgɛɛ) flood, flooding.

ཤོ་རྒྱན་ (shōgyɛn) betting in a dice game; va.—འཛུགས་; —འཕེན་ to place bets in a dice game.

ཤོ་སྒོ་ (shōgo) shung. the door through which donkeys/ mules go to determine the customs' duty in tt.

ཤོ་སྒྲ་ (shōdra) rustling sound made by leaves when the wind blows; vi.—སྒྲོག.

ཤོ་སྒྲིག (shō drig) 1. see ཤོ་. 2. va. to arrange/ fit skins together when making men's and women's dresses. 3. sm. ཤོ་མིག.

ཤོ་ཆང་ (shōjaŋ) ཆང་ served when playing dice.

ཤོ་ཆས་ (shōjɛ̀ɛ̀) dice playing paraphernalia.

ཤོ་ཆེན་ (shōjen) a type of dice game played with big dice.

ཤོ་ཇུས་ (shōjüü) strategy in playing dice.

ཤོ་ཏོ་ (shōdo) harelip.

ཤོ་སྟར་ལྷོ་གསུམ་ (shōdaa lhōsum) area in Kham comprised of ཤོ་པ་མདོ་, དཔལ་འབར་, and ལྷོ་རྫོང་.

ཤོ་སྟན་ (shōdɛn) sm. ཤོ་གདན་.

ཤོ་ཐང་ (shōdaŋ) price.

ཤོ་ཐུག་རྒྱག (shōduù gya̱à) vi. to have two columns/ lines of animals meet on a road large enough for only one to pass.

ཤོ་ཐོ་ (shōto) shung. list of taxes.

ཤོ་དྲིལ་ (shōdrɛɛ) the lead mule.

ཤོ་གདན་ (shōdɛn) round leather mat/ pad used for playing dice.

ཤོ་དིའུ་ (sho di̱wu) cowry shells used when playing ཤོ་.

ཤོ་པ་ (shōba) 1. dice player. 2. shung. duty/ customs office or officer.

ཤོ་ཕོར་ (shōbɔɔ) wooden bowl in which dice are shaken before being flung down on a leather pad (ཤོ་སྟན་).

ཤོ་བ་ (shōwa) the saddle-like dips in mountain ranges.

ཤོ་བེ་ (shōbe) perpetual liar.

ཤོ་སྦག (shōbaà) dice and mahjong; gambling; va.—རྒྱག.

ཤོ་སྦག་གི་འཛིན་ (shōbaàgi dzi̱n) shung. permit for playing dice and mahjong.

ཤོ་སྦག་རྩེད་ས་ (shōbaà dzēèsa) gambling parlor (for dice and mahjong).

ཤོ་མིག (shūmiì) 1. eyes on dice cubes. 2. checker board pattern (e.g., on rugs).

ཤོ་མོ་ (shō mo̱) doing divination with dice; va.—རྒྱག; —ཚད་.

ཤོ་རྩེད་ (shōdzeè) the game of dice; va.—རྩེ་ to play dice.

ཤོ་ཚུགས་ (shōdzuù) a place where customs/ excise duties or taxes are collected.

ཤོ་གཟུགས་མ་ (shōsugmə) cube.

ཤོ་ར་ (shōra) a place where ཤོ་ is played.

ཤོ་རལ་ (shōrɛɛ) harelip, cleft lip.

ཤོ་རེ་ (shōre) sm. ཤོ་རལ་.

ཤོ་ལམ་ (shōlam) sm. ལམ་སྲོལ་.

ཤོ་ལི་ (shōli) abbr. of ཤོ་ཀ་ལི་.

ཤོ་ལོ་ཀ་གཅིག (shōlo gājig) a verse (in poetry).

ཤོ་ཤོར་ཉེས་པ་ (shōshɔɔ ñe̱èba) shung. losing a throw of dice to decide sth.

ཤོ་བཤད་ (shōbshɛ̀ɛ̀) sayings said while throwing dice; va.—གཏོང་.

ཤོ་ས་ (shōsa) alfalfa.

ཤོག (shōò) 1. va. to come ། འདིར་ཤོག Come here! 2. (vb. + པར་/བར་ + —) may the verbal action come to pass ། རྒྱལ་ཁ་ཐོབ་པར་ཤོག May (we) be victorious. 3. paper. 4. (vb. + —) imperative particle ། ཤོག་བུ་ཞིག་ལམ་སེང་ལོངས་ཤོག Get a piece of paper at once! 5. group, gang ། ཇག་ཤོག A gang of bandits.

ཤོག་ཀ་ལི་ (shōògali) book stand.

ཤོག་བཀག (shōògaà) decorative paper stuck into the mouth of a kettle which contains butter tea or chang.

ཤོག་བཀྲ་ (shōgdra) multicolored paper.

ཤོག་ཁ་ (shōòga) group, clique, faction, party, sector ། གཡས་ཕྱོགས་ཤོག་ཁ་ The right wing clique. ། སྒེར་གྱི་དཔལ་འབྱོར་ཤོག་ཁ་ The private economic sector.

ཤོག་ཁག (shōògaà) groups, cliques, factions, groups, parties.

ཤོག་ཁང་ (shōgaŋ) 1. a room for keeping papers. 2. factory/ work shop for making paper.

ཤོག་ཁུག (shōòguù) paper bag.

ཤོག་ཁྲ་ (shōgdra) 1. colored paper. 2. paper window.

ཤོག་ཁྲལ་ (shōgdrɛɛ) shung. 1. tax on paper. 2. tax requiring provision of paper.

ཤོག་གུ་ (shūgu) sm. ཤོག་བུ་.

ཤོག་གུ་བག་ཇུ་ལས་ཚན་ (shūgu pa̱gju lɛ̱èdzɛn) pulp workshop.

ཤོག་གྲངས་ (shōgdraŋ) 1. number of pages in a book. 2. page number in a book.

ཤོག་གྲི་ (shōgdri) knife for cutting paper.

ཤོག་གྲིལ་ (shōgdrii) a bundle/ roll of paper.

ཤོག་གླུད་ (shōglüü) a paper གླུད་.

ཤོག་གླེགས་ (shōgleg) wooden holder for traditional Tibetan texts.

ཤོག་གླེགས་ (shɔ̄gleg) paper board, cardboard.

ཤོག་སྒམ་ (shɔ̄ɔ̀gam) cardboard box.

ཤོག་སྒོར་ (shɔ̄ɔ̀gɔɔ) 1. paper money. 2. paper dollar (yuan in PRC).

ཤོག་སྒོར་གྱི་འཛའ་ཐང་ (shɔ̄gɔɔgi dza̱daŋ) currency value/ rate.

ཤོག་སྒོར་ཟུར་ (shɔ̄gɔɔ su̱r) a unit equal to one tenth of a Chinese paper dollar (yuan).

ཤོག་སྒྲིལ་ (shōgdrii) 1. rolled up paper. 2. joining together, combining forces; va.—བྱེད་; —སྒྲིལ་; —གཏོང་; —སློད་ ། རྒྱ་ནག་དང་པ་ཀི་སི་ཐན་ཤོག་བསྒྲིལ་གྱི་དམག་རྒོལ་ལ་གདོང་ལེན་བྱེད་ཐུབ་ཀྱི་རེད་ (We) can face the joint attack of China and Pakistan. 3. lottery, lots; va.—སྒྲུག to draw lots. 4. a scroll.

ཤོག་སྒྲོམ་ (shōgdrom) wooden frame with a cotton bottom where wood pulp is poured to make paper.

ཤོག་ངོ་ (shōŋo) page.

ཤོག་ངོས་ (shōgŋöö) sm. ཤོག་ངོ་.

ཤོག་དངུལ་ (shōŋüü) sm. ཤོག་སྒོར་.

ཤོག་དངུལ་གྱི་སྒོར་གྲངས་ (shōŋüügi gɔ̱ɔdraŋ) the currency value of paper money.

ཤོག་དངུལ་རྫུན་མ་ (shōŋüü dzü̱nma) counterfeit money.

ཤོག་ཆུ་ (shōgju) liquid from which paper is made.

ཤོག་ཆག (shōgjaà) 1. money wrapped and folded in

paper (the traditional Tibetan way of giving a money gift); va.—སྤྲོད་; —སྤྲོད་ to give a ཤོག་ཆག gift; va.—རྒྱག to make a ཤོག་ཆག gift. 2. a bribe; va.—སྤྲོད་ to give a bribe.

ཤོག་ཉོབ་ (shōgñob) sm. ཤོག་རོ་.

ཤོག་སྙིགས་ (shōgñii) sm. ཤོག་རོ་.

ཤོག་སྟོང་ (shōgdoŋ) blank paper.

ཤོག་སྟག (shōdaà) paper tiger.

ཤོག་ཐུག (shōgduù) paper pulp.

ཤོག་ཐུམ་ (shōgdum) sth. wrapped in paper.

ཤོག་ཐོག་སྟོང་བཤད་ (shōgdɔɔ̀ dōŋshɛɛ̀) including things on paper or in agreements that are not put into practice [Lit. on paper, empty talk].

ཤོག་ཐོག་ཕབ་པ་ (shōgdɔɔ̀ pābbə) getting promoted from the stage of writing on a writing board to the stage of writing on paper (in traditional Tibetan schools).

ཤོག་དུ་ (shōgdu) cigarette; va.—འཐེན་ to smoke.

ཤོག་དུ་བཟོ་གྲྭ་ (shōgdu sodra) cigarette factory.

ཤོག་དུད་ (shōgdüù) cigarette; va.—འཐེན་ to smoke.

ཤོག་དྲས་ (shōgdrɛɛ̀) cutting the rough edges of a paper; va.—རྒྱག.

ཤོག་དྲས་རི་མོ་ (shōgdrɛɛ̀ rimu) pictures made by cutting paper with scissors.

ཤོག་དྲིལ་ (shōgdrii) sm. ཤོག་སྒྲིལ་.

ཤོག་མདོང་ (shōgdoŋ) cylindrical tube/ container.

ཤོག་འདམ་ (shōŋdam) paper pulp mixed with mud to make icons/ statues.

ཤོག་འདེམས་ (shōg dem) electing/ voting by ballot.

ཤོག་ལྡེབ་ (shōgdeb) a piece of paper, a page.

ཤོག་སྣག་སྨྱུག་གསུམ་ (shōg nāg ñugsum) the three: paper, ink and pen.

ཤོག་པ་ (shōgba) sm. ཤོག་ཁ་.

ཤོག་པང་ (shōgbaŋ) cardboard.

ཤོག་སྤང་ (shōgbaŋ) sm.* ཤོག་པང་.

ཤོག་པོ་ (shɔ̄gbo)1. generous. 2. a friend.

ཤོག་འཕྲིན་ (shōgdrin) letter.

ཤོག་བམ་ (shōgbam) a bunch of paper tied together.

ཤོག་བུ་ (shōgbu) paper; va.—རྒྱག; —བཟོ་ to make paper.

ཤོག་བུ་ཀུར་ཀུར་ (shōgbu gyūrgyur) long thin paper.

ཤོག་བུ་རྒྱག་མཁན་ (shōgbu gyañɛn) paper maker.

ཤོག་བུ་བསྒྲིལ་མ་ (shōgbu driimə) sm. ཤོག་དྲིལ་.

ཤོག་བུ་གཏུབ་བྱེད་འཕྲུལ་འཁོར་ (shōgbu dūbjeè trǖgɔɔ) paper cutting machine.

ཤོག་བུ་དྲ་ (shōgbu tra) va. to cut paper.

ཤོག་བུ་དྲས་རོ་ (shōgbu trɛɛ̀ro) remnant pieces of torn/ cut paper.

ཤོག་བུ་སྣུམ་ཟན་ (shōgbu nūmsɛn) sm. ཤོག་བུ་སྣུམ་ཟེས་.

ཤོག་བུ་སྣུམ་ཟེས་ (shōgbu nūmsöö) gradually spreading out/ diffusing [Lit. oil spreading on paper].

ཤོག་བུ་སྦང་རྒྱག (shōgbu baŋgyaà) va. to dampen paper before using it with a printing block.

ཤོག་བུ་སྦྱར་མ་ (shōgbu jarma) papers that are stuck together to make them thicker (several ply).

ཤོག་བུ་བཟོ་གྲྭ་ (shōgbu sodra) paper mill.

ཤོག་བུ་བཟོ་ལས་ (shōgbu solɛɛ̀) paper industry.

ཤོག་བུ་རླུང་ཁྱེར་ (shōgbu lūŋgyer) easily swayed [Lit. paper carried by wind].

ཤོག་བུའི་སྐྱོ་མ་ (shōgbu gyōma) paper pulp.

ཤོག་བུའི་སྟག (shōgbü dāà) paper tiger.

ཤོག་བུའི་ལྡེ་གུ་ (shōgbü degu) pulp, va.—བཟོ་ to make pulp.

ཤོག་བུའི་པང་ལེབ་ (shōgbü bāŋleb) cardboard.

ཤོག་བུས་རས་ལྟོམ་ (shōgbü rɛɛ̀lom) pretending to be what one is not [Lit. paper pretending to be cloth].

ཤོག་བྱ་ (shōgja) kite; va.—གཏོང་ to fly a kite.

ཤོག་བྱང་ (shōgjaŋ) label, note on piece of paper.

ཤོག་དྲེགས་ (shōgdreg) paper that has been cut.

ཤོག་འབྲེག་རི་མོ་ (shōŋdreg rimu) design/ picture made from artistically cutting paper.

ཤོག་སྦག (shōbaà) firecracker; va.—རྒྱག to shoot a firecracker.

ཤོག་སྦུག་རླུང་འཚང་ (shōbug lūŋdzuŋ) sm. ངན་སྐྱལ་དཀྲུག་ཤོང་.

ཤོག་སྦུབས་རླུང་འཚང་ (shōbub lūŋdzaŋ) sm. ངན་སྐྱལ་དཀྲུག་ཤོང་.

ཤོག་ཚལ་ (shōgdzɛɛ) waste/ remnant paper.

ཤོག་ཚལ་གཏོང་ (shōgdzɛɛ dōŋ) 1. va. to pay no attention to, to not heed ¶ ཁོས་འགོ་ཁྲིད་ཀྱི་སྐད་ཆ་ཤོག་ཚལ་དུ་གཏོང་གི་ཡོད་པ་རེད་ He doesn't pay attention to what the leader says. 2. va. to do with ease ¶ བོད་སྐད་སློབ་ཀྱི་ཁོང་གིས་ཤོག་ཚལ་དུ་གཏོང་གི་ཡོད་པ་རེད་ As for teaching the Tibetan language, he could do it with ease.

ཤོག་འཛར་ (shōgdzar) paper used as a label; va.—བསྦྱར་ to affix a label on sth.

ཤོག་བཟོ་ (shɔ̄gso) 1. paper mill. 2. paper making.

ཤོག་རིལ་ (shōgrii) a roll of paper.

ཤོག་རས་ (shōgrɛɛ̀) cloth placed on the frame in preparation of making paper.

ཤོག་རོ་ (shōgro) sm. ཤོག་ཚལ་.

ཤོག་རོ་ལྕུག་ས་ (shōgro lūùsə) waste basket (for putting paper trash).

ཤོག་ལངས་བསྒྲོས་རྫོད་ (shōglaŋ dö̱ödzöö) shung. different groups banding together and filing law suits against one another.

ཤོག་ལེབ་ (shōgleè) sm. ཤོག་ལྡེ་.

ཤོག་ལོག་རྒྱག (shōglɔr gyaà) to recycle/ reuse paper.

ཤོག་ལོར་ (shōglɔr) paper money.

ཤོག་ལོར་ཤོག་དངུལ་ (shōglɔr shōgŋüü) sm. ཤོག་ལོར་.

ཤོག་ཤུབས་ (shɔ̄gshub) envelope.

ཤོག་ཤོག (shɔ̄gshɔɔ̀) 1. va. come, come. 2. sound of paper carried by the wind.

ཤོག་སག (shɔ̄gsaà) sandpaper; va.—རྒྱག to sand with sandpaper.

ཤོག་སྲང་ (shɔ̄gsaŋ) a paper currency note worth a སྲང་.

ཤོག་སྲབ་ (shɔ̄gdrəb) thin paper.

ཤོག་ལྡེ་ (shɔ̄ɔ̀leè) a page, a piece/ sheet of paper.

ཤོག་ལྡེ་སྙན་ཞུ་ (shɔ̄ɔ̀leè ñɛ̄nshu) shung. brief report.

ཤོག་ལྡེ་གསུམ་སྦྲེལ་མ་ (shɔ̄ɔ̀leè sūmdreema) bill/ invoice with three parts (sheets of paper).

ཤོགས་ (shɔ̄ɔ̀) sm. གཤོགས་.

ཤོགས་པོ་ (shɔ̄gbo) generous.

ཤོགས་ཆེན་ (shɔ̄ɔ̀jen) sm. ཤོགས་ཆེན་པོ་. 2. big (business, etc.).

ཤོགས་ཆེན་པོ་ (shɔ̄ɔ̀ cēmbo) 1. sm. ལས་ཕྱོད་ཆེན་པོ་. 2. big, large-scale (business, etc.).

ཤོང་ (shōŋ) 1. vi. to fit, to hold, to have room ¶ ང་ཚོ་ཁང་པའི་ནང་མ་ཤོང་ཙང་ཕྱུགས་རའི་ནང་སྡོད་དགོས་བྱུང་ Because (we) didn't fit in the house, we had to stay in the cattle shed. 2. sm.* གཤོང་.

ཤོང་དཀར་རྫེ་མོ་ (shōŋgar dzēmo) the tips of tea plants.

ཤོང་རྒྱ་ (shōŋgya) capacity ¶ ཤོང་རྒྱ་ཆེན་པོ་ Large capacity.

ཤོང་ཚད་ (shōŋdzɛ̀ɛ) the capacity or limit sth. can hold or be filled ¶ ཚོགས་ཁང་འདི་ཤོང་ཚད་ཆེན་པོ་འདུག This hall has a large capacity.

ཤོང་ཚད་ལས་བརྒལ་བ་ (shōŋdzɛɛ̀lɛ gɛɛwa) vi. to exceed the capacity of sth.

ཤོང་བུ་ (shōŋbu) see གཤོང་བུ་.

ཤོང་རྒྱ་ (shōŋgya) capacity, volume.

ཤོངས་ (shōŋ) imp. of གཤོང་.

ཤོད་ (shöö̀) 1. lower ¶ སྟེང་ཤོད་ Upper and lower. 2. shung. term used to refer to the regent ¶ ཤོད་མགྲོན་ Aide to the regent.

ཤོད་: p. and f. བཤད་; imp. ཤོད་ (shöö̀) va. to say, to talk, to speak.

ཤོད་སྐོར་ (shöö̀gɔɔ) shung. lay (aristocratic) officials in tt.

ཤོད་སྐྱོར་རྒྱག (shöö̀gyɔr gyaà) va. to repeat saying sth.

ཤོད་ཁང་ (shöö̀gaŋ) lower room / apartment in a house.

ཤོད་མཁན་ (shöö̀ñɛn) speaker, talker.

ཤོད་མཁས་པོ་ (shöö̀ kɛɛ̀bo) eloquent in speech,

verbal.

ཤོད་མགྲོན་ (shõ̀ndrön) shung. the regent's aide de camp.

ཤོད་འགག་ (shõ̀ gaà) shung. the secretariat office of the regent.

ཤོད་རྒྱུ་གདམ་རྒྱུ་ (shõ̀gyu dāmgyu) sth. to talk about.

ཤོད་ཛེ་ལགས་ (shõ̀ colaà) shung. sm. ཤོད་ཕྱག་ནང་.

ཤོད་སྟངས་ (shõ̀daŋ) the tone of a statement, the manner of saying sth.

ཤོད་སྟེགས་ (shõ̀deg) sm. འཆད་སྟེགས་.

ཤོད་ཐབས་ (shõ̀dəb) 1. abacus. 2. means of saying sth.

ཤོད་ཐོག་ (shõ̀dɔɔ̀) 1. abbr. of upstairs and downstairs. 2. first floor.

ཤོད་དུ་ (shõ̀du) downward ¶ ཤོད་དུ་འགྲོ་དགོས་ (You) have to go down.

ཤོད་དྲུང་ (shõ̀druŋ) shung. lay (aristocratic) official in tt.

ཤོད་ཕྱག་ནང་ (shõ̀ cāānaŋ) shung. clerks in the བླ་ཕྱག་ལས་ཁངས་ (one of the supply offices of the Dalai Lama).

ཤོད་བླ་བྲང་ཕྱག་མཛོད་ལས་ཁངས་ (shõ̀ lābraŋ cāndzöö lɛ̱ɛ̀guŋ) shung. sm. བླ་ཕྱག་ལས་ཁངས་.

ཤོད་མ་ཤེས་པ་ (shõ̀ ma̱sheèba) hard/ difficult to say ¶ ཚོགས་འདུའི་ཐོག་ཤོད་མ་ཤེས་པ་ཞིག་འདུག་པས་འགོ་ཁྲིད་ལ་ཟུར་དུ་ཤོད་ཀྱི་ཡིན་ Because it was hard to say (openly) at the meeting, I will tell the leaders separately. 2. va. not knowing how to say sth. properly ¶ ཁོས་སྐད་ཆ་ཤོད་མ་ཤེས་ཙང་འགོ་ཁྲིད་ཁྲོང་ལངས་པ་རེད་ Because he didn't know how to say it properly, the leader got angry.

ཤོད་རྩལ་ (shõ̀dzüü) sm. ཤོད་སྟངས་.

ཤོད་མཛོད་ (shõ̀dzöö) storage room on the lower floor.

ཤོད་གཟིམ་འགག་ (shõ̀ si̱mgaà) shung. the bodyguard officials of the regent.

ཤོད་གཟིམ་ཆུང་འགག་ (shõ̀ si̱mjuŋ gaà) shung. sm. ཤོད་འགག་.

ཤོད་བཟོ་དོད་པོ་ (shõ̀so tö̱öbo) articulate, eloquent, verbal.

ཤོད་རིན་མེད་པ་ (shõ̀rin me̱èba) insignificant, unimportant, not worth saying.

ཤོད་ལུགས་ (shõ̀luù) sm. ཤོད་སྟངས་.

ཤོད་སྲོལ་ (shõ̀söö) sm. ཤོད་སྟངས་.

ཤོན་ (shõn) ch. a type of long thin playing card; va.—རྒྱག.

ཤོན་པད་ (shõnbɛɛ̀) sm. ཤོན་.

ཤོན་བྱེད་ (shõn ce̱è) va. to dance without singing, to mime.

ཤོབ་ (shōb) 1. whispering. 2. bragging ¶ ཁྱོད་རང་ཤོབ་མ་ཤོད་ Don't brag.

ཤོབ་སྒྲ་ (shōbdra) whispering; va.—སྒྲོག to whisper.

ཤོབ་གདམ་ (shōbdam) bragging.

ཤོབ་པེ་ (shōbbe) sm. ཤོབ་, 2.

ཤོབ་པེ་ཤུ་པེ་ (shōbbe shūbe) sm. ཤོབ་ཤོབ་.

ཤོབ་ཚིག (shōbdzii) sm. ཤོབ་གདམ་.

ཤོབ་རལ་ཚ་པོ་ (shōbrɛɛ tsābo) a braggart, sb. who boasts a lot.

ཤོབ་ཤོབ་ (shōbshob) whispering; va.—སྒྲ་; —ཤོད་; —སྒྲོག; —གཏོང་ to whisper.

ཤོབ་ཤོབ་པོ་ (shōb shōbbo) sm. ཤོབ་, 2.

ཤོབས་ (shōb) imp. of ཤབ་.

ཤོམ་འགྱིང་ (shōmgyiŋ) proud.

ཤོམ་པག (shōmbaà) a type of large leaf plant that is used to wrap butter, etc.

ཤོམ་ར་ (shōmra) elaborate, grand.

ཤོམས་ (shōm) imp. of གཤོམ་.

ཤོར་ (shɔ̃ɔ) vi. to lose ¶ ཁོ་ལས་ཀ་ཤོར་བ་རེད་ He lost his job. 2. vi. to get away, to escape ¶ ཁོ་ཚོས་བཟུང་བའི་བྱིའུ་དེ་ཤོར་བ་རེད་ The bird they caught got away. 3. indicates sth. happens unintentionally or accidentally ¶ མེ་མདའ་ཁ་ཤོར་བ་རེད་ The gun fired accidentally. 4. to become unequal/ uneven ¶ དོ་པོ་དེ་གཉིས་ཆེ་ཆུང་ཤོར་བཞག The two loads became unintentionally unequal in size. 5. p. of འཆོར་. 6. sm. འཕོ་ཁ་རྒྱག.

ཤོར་ཁ་རྒྱག (shɔ̃ɔga gya̱à) sm. འཕོ་ཁ་རྒྱག.

ཤོར་ཕམ་ (shɔ̃ɔbam) vi. to lose ¶ ཁོ་ཚོ་དམག་ཤོར་ཕམ་བྱུང་བ་རེད་ They lost the war.

ཤོར་ཚད་ (shɔ̃ɔdzɛɛ̀) the amount of sth. lost (as in a game).

ཤོར་ར་རེ་ (shɔ̃ɔ ra̱re) likely to get lost/ flee/ run away ¶ ཁྱི་འདི་ཡག་པོ་མ་བཏགས་ན་ཤོར་ར་རེ་ Unless you tie the dog well, it will run away.

ཤོར་ཤོར་བྱེད་ (shɔ̃ɔshɔɔ ce̱è) va. to be enthusiastic about doing sth., to be chaffing at the bit ¶ ཁོ་དམག་རྒྱག་པར་འགྲོ་གི་ཡིན་ཟེར་ཤོར་ཤོར་བྱེད་ཀྱི་འདུག He is chaffing at the bit saying he wants to go to war.

ཤོལ་ (shõ̀) 1. imp. of བཤོལ་. 2. extra ¶ ཟླ་ཤོལ་ An extra (intercalary) month (in the Tibetan calendar).

ཤོལ་ཙེ་ (shõ̀dze) ch. leather boot.

ཤོལ་ཟླ་ (shõnda) an extra (intercalary) month (in the Tibetan calendar).

ཤོས་ (shõ̀) 1. superlative particle ¶ མཐོ་ཤོས་ The highest. 2. the other of two ¶ དགེ་རྒན་ཅིག་ཤོས་ The other teacher. 3. imp. of གཤོ་.

ཤྭ་ (shāā) deer.

ཤྭ་ཁྱུ་ (shāāgyu) a herd of deer.

ཤྭ་རྒལ་ (shāāgɛɛ) sm. ཤྭ་འོད་.

ཤྭ་རྒྱ་ (shāāgya) a type of mountain goat.

ཤྭ་སྒྲོས་ (shāādröö) sm. ཁ་ཤྭ་.

ཤྭ་ང་བསྣན་ནས་བོང་ཤ་བཙོངས་ (shāŋa dēnnɛ po̱ŋsha dzōŋ) sm. ལུག་མགོ་བཀལ་ནས་ཁྱི་ཤ་འཚོང་.

ཤྭ་ལྤགས་ (shāābaà) deer skin.

ཤྭ་ཕོ་ (shāābo) male deer.

ཤྭ་ཕོ་ཆེན་རྒྱུག་ལམ་ལ་ རྔོན་པ་རྒས་པོ་སྒུག་ལམ་ཁེལ་ (shāābo) experiences produces results [Lit. the old hunter waits where the deer run].

ཤྭ་ཕྲུག (shādruù) fawn.

ཤྭ་བ་ (shāā) deer.

ཤྭ་བ་གླེ་རིང་ (shāwa gēriŋ) giraffe.

ཤྭ་བ་སྒོ་ཁར་སླེབས་དུས་མདའ་གཞུ་བཟོ་བ་ (shāāwa go̱gar lēbdüü də̱shu so̱wa) doing sth. too late, lack of foresight [Lit. making a bow and arrow when the deer arrives at the door].

ཤྭ་བ་སྤང་ལ་བརྩེ་བ་ལྟར་ (shāwa bāŋla dzēwadar) very glad/ pleased, liking a lot [Lit. like a deer likes grass].

ཤྭ་བ་ཕོ་ཆེན་ (shāā pōjen) sm. ཤྭ་ཕོ་.

ཤྭ་བ་འཛིན་རྒྱུ་མེད་པར་ ལུང་ཆུང་ཁྱི་སྐད་བརྒྱངས་པ་ (shāwa dzi̱ngyu me̱èbaa lu̱ŋjuŋ kyīdrɛɛ̀ gya̱ŋba) making a big deal abou sth. all over but acomplishing nothing. [Lit. the dog's barking fills the area but does not result in catching the deer].

ཤྭ་བའི་ཁྲག་རྭ་ (shāāwɛ trāgra) pilose antler.

ཤྭ་བའི་རྭ་ཅོ་ (shāāwɛ ra̱jo) antler, deer horn.

ཤྭ་མོ་ (shāāmo) female deer.

ཤྭ་འོད་ (shāwöö) flooding; vi.—རྒྱག to flood; va.—འགོག to prevent/ protect against flooding.

ཤྭ་རྭ་ (shāāra) sm. ཤྭ་བའི་ཁྲག་རྭ་.

ཤྭ་ལོག (shāālɔɔ̀) sm. ཤྭ་འོད་.

ཤྭ་སློག (shāālɔɔ̀) a deerskin Tibetan dress.

ཤྭ་གསོ་ར་བ་ (shāāso ra̱wa) deer breeding farm.

གཤག (shāà) f. of གཤོག.

གཤག་གྲི་ (shāgdri) scalpel.

གཤག་བཅོས་ (shāgjöö) operation (medical); va.—བྱེད་ to operate, to have an operation.

གཤག་བཅོས་ཁང་ (shāgjöögaŋ) operating room.

གཤག་བཅོས་སྟེགས་བུ་ (shāgjöö dēgbu) operating table.

གཤག་པ་ (shāgba) sm. གཤོག་པ་.

གཤག་གཟེར་ (shāgsoŋ) large iron stake for splitting rock.

གཤག་ལས་ (shāglɛɛ̀) cutting open, dissecting, operating; va.—བྱེད་.

གཤག་ལས་སྨན་བཅོས་ (shāglɛɛ̀ mõnjöö) surgical

treatment.

གཤགས་ (shāà) 1. p. of གཤོག.

གཤགས་བགྱི་ (shāggye) wrangling/ quarreling/ fighting verbally.

གཤགས་ཁྲི་ (shāgdri) sm. གཤག་ཁྲི་.

གཤགས་འགྱེད་ (shāggyeè) sm. གཤགས་བགྱི་.

གཤགས་ངན་ (shāgŋɛn) hurtful/ mean talk.

གཤགས་བཅོས་ (shāgjöö) sm. གཤག་བཅོས་.

གཤགས་པའི་རྨ་ (shagbɛ mā) wounds caused by swords/ knifes.

གཤགས་མ་ (shāgma) wood cut for firewood.

གཤགས་ལས་ (shāglɛè) sm. གཤག་ལས་.

གཤང་ (shāŋ) sm. བཤང་.

གཤང་གཅི་ (shāŋji) sm. བཤང་གཅི་.

གཤང་ལྩི་ (shāŋji) sm. བཤང་གཅི་.

གཤང་ངེ་གཤོང་ངེ་ (shāŋŋe shōŋŋe) uneven (ground).

གཤང་བ་ (shāŋwa) sm. གཤང་ལྩི་.

གཤང་ལམ་ (shāŋlam) rectum.

གཤང་གཤོང་ (shāŋshoŋ) abbr. of གཤང་ངེ་གཤོང་ངེ་.

གཤན་པ་ (shɛ̄mba) sm. ཤན་པ་.

གཤན་འབྱེད་པ་ (shɛ̄mjeba) referee.

གཤམ་ (shām) 1. below, bottom, lower (of people and places), after ། གཤམ་གྱི་པར་གཡོན་མ་ The lower left picture. ། ཡིག་ཆ་དེའི་གཤམ་དུ་མིང་རྟགས་བཀོད་འདུག There were many names signed on the bottom of the document. ། གློག་བརྙན་འདིའི་གཤམ་དུ་ག་རེ་སྟོན་རྒྱུ་ཡིན་ནམ After this movie, what will they show? ། ལས་ཁུངས་ཨ་མ་འདིའི་གཤམ་དུ་ཡན་ལག་མང་པོ་ཡོད་པ་རེད་ There are many branch offices below this office. ། གཤམ་འོག་གི་གཞུང་ཞབས་ Lower officials.

གཤམ་སྐྱོད་ (shāmgyöö) going to the village for work (for cadres).

གཤམ་མཆན་ (shāmjɛn) shung. a note written under or at the bottom of a document.

གཤམ་འཇུག (shāmjuù) sleeveless shirt/ petticoat worn by the monks under their robes.

གཤམ་བདང་ལས་བྱེད་པ་ (shāmdaŋ lɛ̀ɛ̀jeba) cadres who have been transferred to lower levels.

གཤམ་ཐབས་ (shāmdəb) sm. ཤམ་ཐབས་.

གཤམ་ཐབས་ཀྱི་ཁྲལ་ (shāmdəbgi trɛ̄ɛ̄) monk's work obligations (tax) in monastery.

གཤམ་དུ་ (shāmdu) 1. after that ། གཤམ་དུ་ཁོང་གིས་གསུང་བཤད་གནང་གི་རེད་ After that he will give a talk. 2. the bottom of ། ཡི་གེ་དེའི་གཤམ་དུ་ས་ཡིག་བརྒྱབ་འདུག (He) has signed at the bottom of the letter. 3. below, under ། ལས་ཁུངས་འདིའི་གཤམ་དུ་ཡན་ལག་མང་པོ་འདུག There are many branches under that office.

གཤམ་འདོགས་ (shāmdɔ̀ɔ̀) sm.* ཤམ་ཐབས་.

གཤམ་འདོམས་ (shāmdom) shung. the summary at the end of a document.

གཤམ་ནས་རྩི་ (shāmnɛ dzī) va. to count/ calculate from the bottom.

གཤམ་སྤེལ་ (shāmbel) disseminating below (to people below); va.—བྱེད་ ། སྲིད་འཛིན་གྱིས་གནང་བའི་མཛད་སྟོན་གཤམ་སྤེལ་བྱས་སོང་ The instructions which the president issued were disseminated below.

གཤམ་བུ་ (shəmbu) traditional frills on Tibetan windows; va.—རྒྱག to put such frills on windows.

གཤམ་སྦྱར་ (shāmjar) lower part of the སྟོད་འགག monk's vest.

གཤམ་མ་ (shāmma) 1. the following one, the one lower/ below/ beneath ། ང་སྡོད་ས་ཁང་པ་གཤམ་མ་དེ་ར་བསྡད་ཡོད་ I live in the lower house (e.g., of two houses on a slope). 2. cursive letters/ script.

གཤམ་མི་ (shāmmi) underlings, subordinates.

གཤམ་མཚུངས་ (shāmdzuŋ) as written below.

གཤམ་འཛར་ (shāmdzar) tassels.

གཤམ་འོག (shāmwɔ̀ɔ̀) sm. གཤམ་, 1.

གཤམ་ཡོལ་ (shāmyöö) 1. frill and curtain on Tibetan windows. 2. a kind of curtain put under a windows (indicating rank).

གཤམ་རིམ་ (shəmrii) lower level/ rank/ status, subordinate rank ། གཤམ་རིམ་ལས་བྱེད་པ་ཚོར་སྲིད་ཇུས་དྲིལ་བསྒྲགས་བྱས་པ་རེད་ They publicized the policy to the lower officials.

གཤམ་ལ་ (shāmla) sm. གཤམ་དུ་.

གཤམ་ཤིང་ (shāmshiŋ) sm. གུམ་ཤིང་.

གཤམ་གསལ་ (shāmsɛl) listed/ presented/ cited below.

གཤམ་གསལ་ལྟར་ (shāmsɛldar) as listed/ presented/ cited below.

གཤའ་ (shā) sm. ཤག, 3.

གཤའ་དཀར་ (shāgar) tin.

གཤའ་མ་ (shāma) perfect, faultless, worthy.

གཤའ་ཚེ་ (shādze) sm. གཤའ་དཀར་.

གཤའ་ཚེ་དཀར་པོ་ (shādze gārbo) sm. གཤའ་དཀར་.

གཤའ་རིང་ (shāriŋ) a point on the arm for draining blood.

གཤར་: p. བཤར་; f. གཤར་; imp. གཤོར་ (shāā) va. to march/ move one after another.

གཤར་རྒྱག (shār gyaà) va. to sew with long stitches.

གཤར་སྦྱང་ (shārjaŋ) learning through repetition; va.—བྱེད་.

གཤར་མ་ (shārma) དབུ་མེད་ writing (style).

གཤར་ཡིག (shəryiì) དབུ་མེད་ writing (style).

གཤལ་གོས་ (shɛ̄ɛ̄ göö) vi. to have bad faults/ errors occur.

གཤིན་ (shīn) abbr. of གཤིན་པོ་.

གཤིན་དཀོར་ (shīngɔɔ) offerings that are made to monks after a person dies.

གཤིན་གྱི་ནགས་ (shīngi nag) cemetery, graveyard.

གཤིན་དགེ་ (shīnge) offerings made on behalf of a deceased person.

གཤིན་རྒྱལ་སྐར་མ་ (shīngyɛɛ gārma) the planet Pluto.

གཤིན་ཆོག (shīnjɔ̀ɔ̀) a ritual done for the deceased.

གཤིན་རྗེ་ (shīnje) abbr. of གཤིན་རྗེ་ཆོས་རྒྱལ་.

གཤིན་རྗེ་ཆོས་རྒྱལ་ (shīnje cȫögyɛɛ) Yama, the Lord of the Dead.

གཤིན་རྗེའི་འཆིང་ཞགས་ཀྱིས་འཆིང་ (shīnjee cīŋshaàgi cīŋ) vi. to be at the point of death.

གཤིན་རྗེའི་ཡུལ་ (shīnjee yüü) the realm of the Lord of the Dead.

གཤིན་རྗེའི་ལས་མཁན་ (shinjee lɛ̀ɛ̀ñɛn) the Lord of the Dead's workers, workers in hell.

གཤིན་སྟོང་ (shīndoŋ) an indemnity payment for murder.

གཤིན་འདྲེ་ (shīndre) a ghost/ spirit of a dead person.

གཤིན་ནགས་ (shīnnaà) abbr. of གཤིན་གྱི་ནགས་.

གཤིན་གནས་ (shīnnɛɛ̀) cemetery, graveyard, sky burial site.

གཤིན་པ་ (shīmbə) 1. nutritious. 2. sm. གཤིན་པོ་.

གཤིན་པོ་ (shīmbu) 1. fertile ། ས་རྒྱ་གཤིན་པོ་ Fertile fields. 2. dead, deceased, corpse ། གཤིན་པོ་ས་སྦས་བཏང་སོང་ (They) buried the dead. 3. close ། གཟིམ་ཤག་དེ་གཉིས་ཐུགས་སྣང་གཤིན་པོ་ཡོད་པ་རེད་ Those two aristocratic families are close. 4. gentle/ calm in personality ། བུ་མོ་དེ་སེམས་རྒྱུད་གཤིན་པོ་ཞིག་འདུག This girl has a gentle personality.

གཤིན་སྦྱང་ (shīnjaŋ) shung. religious rites performed for the deceased to liberate their consciousness from the world of samsara.

གཤིན་རྩིས་ (shīndzii) astrological calculation done after a person dies; va.—བཀོལ་ to make astrological calculations to determine what kind of funeral arrangements and activities should be done.

གཤིན་རྫས་ (shīndzɛɛ̀) belongings of a dead person.

གཤིན་ཟན་ (shīnsɛn) sm. གཤིན་ཟས་.

གཤིན་ཟས་ (shīnsɛɛ̀) 1. food paid from the money of a deceased person. 2. food given to increase the good karma of a deceased person.

གཤིན་བཟོ་ (shīnso) making land fertile.

གཤིན་ས་ (shīnsə) fertile land.

གཤིབ་: p. གཤིབས་; f. གཤིབ་; imp. གཤིབས་ (shīb) 1.

va. to be acquainted with, to have had contact with, to have work/ associate with sb. ༑ང་ཁོ་དང་གཤིབ་མ་མྱོང་ I've never had contact with him. 2. va. to arrange/ place close together.

གཤིབ་ཁག་པོ་ (shi̅b kāgbo) difficult to get along with, difficult to live with, difficult to get close to.

གཤིབ་རྒྱུན་ (shi̅bgyün) time spent together.

གཤིབ་སྙིང་འདོད་པོ་ (shi̅bñi tö̱öbo) sm. གཤིབ་འདོད་པོ་.

གཤིབ་ཐུག་རྒྱག (shi̅bduù gya̱à) va. to associate with, to be in contact with.

གཤིབ་བདེ་པོ་ (shi̅b de̱bo) easy to get along with.

གཤིབ་འདོད་པོ་ (shi̅b dö̱ö̀bo) being amiable, easy to get along with, friendly.

གཤིབ་པའི་སྨོས་འདྲིན་དུ་བརྩི་ (shi̅bbɛ mõndrindu dzi̅) va. to consider/ regard as a cherished friend.

གཤིབ་གཤིབ་ (shi̅bshiì) close together, side-by-side, crowded together; va.—བྱེད་ to move close together, to be side-by-side; va.—བཟོ་ to make sth. close together/ side-by-side.

གཤིབས་ (shi̅b) p. of གཤིབ་.

གཤིབས་ཆེན་པོ་ (shi̅b cēmbo) spending a lot of time together with sb.

གཤིས་ (shi̅i) nature, character, disposition. 2. (vb. + —) because ༑དེང་སྐབས་འཛམ་གླིང་ནང་འགྲོ་ཁྱབ་ཆེ་ཤོས་དབྱིན་ཇིའི་སྐད་ཡིག་ཡིན་གཤིས་ Because English is the most widely used language in the world today.

གཤིས་ཀ་ (shi̅igə) character, personality.

གཤིས་ཀ་སྒྱོང་པོ་ (shi̅igə gyo̱ŋbo) sm. གཤིས་ཀ་རྩུབ་པོ་.

གཤིས་ཀ་འཇམ་པོ་ (shi̅igə ja̱mbo) soft/ gentle/ calm character or personality.

གཤིས་ཀ་མཐུན་པ་ (shi̅igə tũmbu) similar or compatible personality/ character.

གཤིས་ཀ་རྩུབ་པོ་ (shi̅igə dzūbbu) harsh or rough personality/ character.

གཤིས་རྒྱུད་ (shi̅igyüü) sm. གཤིས་ཀ་.

གཤིས་རྒྱུད་ངར་པོ་ (shi̅igyüü ŋarbo) spirited/ aggressive/ militant in character or personality.

གཤིས་རྒྱུད་འཇམ་པོ་ (shi̅igyüü ja̱mbo) sm. གཤིས་ཀ་འཇམ་པོ་.

གཤིས་རྒྱུད་རྩིང་པོ་ (shi̅igyüü dziŋbu) sm. གཤིས་ཀ་རྩུབ་པོ་.

གཤིས་ངན་ (shi̅iŋɛn) evil/ bad nature or character.

གཤིས་འཇམ་མཇལ་བདེ་ (shi̅injam je̱ede) gentle and easy to meet.

གཤིས་དྲང་ (shi̅idraŋ) just/ upright/ honest in character or personality.

གཤིས་ནུས་ (shi̅inüü) performance/ function (of a machine).

གཤིས་སྤྱོད་ (shi̅ijöö) character/ personality and behavior.

གཤིས་སྤྱོད་གཉིས་ལྡན་ (shi̅ijöö ñi̅idɛn) having good behavior and character.

གཤིས་བཟང་ (shi̅isaŋ) kind/ good character or personality.

གཤིས་ཡོན་གཉིས་ལེགས་ (shi̅iyön ñi̅ileg) morally upright and highly educated.

གཤིས་རིག (shi̅irii) abbr. of གཤིས་ལུགས་ and རིག་གནས་.

གཤིས་ལུགས་ (shi̅iluù) tradition, custom.

གཤིས་ལོབས་ (shi̅ilob) getting into the habit of doing sth.

གཤིས་སྲོལ་ (shi̅isüü) sm. གཤིས་ལུགས་.

གཤུང་: p. གཤུངས་; f. བཤུང་; imp. ཤུངས་ (shūŋ) va. to reproach/ blame/ criticize.

གཤུངས་ (shūŋ) p. of གཤུང་.

གཤེ་ (shē) 1. sm. གཤེ་གཤེ་. 2. va. to scold.

གཤེ་གཤེ་ (shēshe) scolding; va.—གཏོང་ to scold, to yell at ༑དགེ་རྒན་གྱིས་སློབ་ཕྲུག་ལ་གཤེ་གཤེ་གཏོང་གི་འདུག The teacher is scolding the students.

གཤེག (shēg) sm. གཤོག.

གཤེག་བཅོས་ (shēgjöö) sm. གཤོག་བཅོས་.

གཤེགས་ (shēg) va. to come/ go ༑ཁོང་ཞལ་ལག་མཆོད་པར་གཤེགས་སོང་ He went to eat. 2. vi. to die ༑ཁོང་ན་ནིང་གཤེགས་སོང་ He died last year.

གཤེགས་སྐྱེམ་ (shēggyem) offering of tea and ཆང་ to a person going on a trip.

གཤེགས་ཁ་ (shēgga) h. of གྲོངས་ཁ་.

གཤེགས་མཁན་ (shēggɛn) the late, the deceased.

གཤེགས་མགྲོན་ (shēgdrön) a guest that has to be received or has to be bid goodbye to.

གཤེགས་གཏོར་ (shēgdɔɔ) གཏོར་མ་ offered when a medium goes into trance.

གཤེགས་ཟུ་འདེབས་ (shēgdzu de̱b) va. to pretend to die.

གཤེགས་རྫོང་ (shēgdzoŋ) sm. གཤིན་དགེ་.

གཤེགས་བཞུགས་ (shēgshuù) those dead and those still alive.

གཤེགས་བཞུད་ (shēgshüü) visiting, coming to see ༑དེང་སང་ཁོང་ང་འི་སར་གཤེགས་བཞུད་གནང་མ་བྱུང་ Thesedays he didn't come to visit me.

གཤེགས་ཤུལ་ (shēgshüü) sm. ཕྱིན་ཤུལ་.

གཤེད་ (shēè) 1. enemy, foe.

གཤེད་འདྲེ་ (shēndre) a derogatory name (murderous demon).

གཤེད་མ་ (shēèma) 1. executioner, murderer. 2. messenger of king of the dead.

གཤེད་དམག (shēèmaà) warlord, militarist.

གཤེན་ (shēn) the lineage of གཤེན་རབ་ (the founder of Bon religion).

གཤེན་རབ་ (shēnrəb) name of the founder of the Bon religion.

གཤེར་ (shēr) 1. vi. to get/ be wet ༑ཆར་པའི་དཀྱིལ་ལ་ཕྱིན་ནས་གོས་གཤེར་སོང་ He went in the rain and (his) clothes got wet. 2. dampness, wetness, moisture.

གཤེར་ཁུ་ (shērgu) juice of sth.

གཤེར་འགྱུར་ (shērgyur) vi. to become liquid, to be liquified.

གཤེར་ཆུ་ (shērju) liquids.

གཤེར་གནོན་ (shērnön) hydraulic pressure.

གཤེར་གནོན་འཕྲུལ་འཁོར་ (shērnün trũ̃gɔɔ) hydraulic press.

གཤེར་བའི་ཤེལ་གཟུགས་ (shērwɛ shēēsuù) sm. གཤེར་ཤེལ་.

གཤེར་དབྱིབས་ (shēryib) liquid state.

གཤེར་མ་ (shērma) pancreas.

གཤེར་མའི་གཉན་ཚད་ (shērmɛ ñēndzɛɛ̀) pancreatitis.

གཤེར་མའི་འབྲས་སྐྲན་ (shērmɛ drɛ̱ɛ̀drɛn) pancreatic cancer.

གཤེར་མའི་ཟགས་ཁུ་ (shērmɛ sa̱ggu) pancreatic juice.

གཤེར་སྨེན་ (shērmen) gland ༑ན་འོག་གཤེར་སྨེན་ Parotid gland.

གཤེར་ཚག (shērdzaà) conjunctivitis.

གཤེར་ཟས་ (shērsɛɛ̀) liquid foods.

གཤེར་གཟུགས་ (shērsuù) liquid, fluid.

གཤེར་གཟུགས་མཁའ་རླུང་ (shērsuù kāluŋ) liquid air.

གཤེར་གཟུགས་འབར་རྫས་ (shērsuù ba̱rdzɛɛ̀) liquid fuel.

གཤེར་ལུད་ (shērlüü) liquid fertilizer.

གཤེར་ཤེལ་ (shērshel) liquid crystal.

གཤེར་ས་ (shērsa) damp place.

གཤོ་: p. བཤོས་; f. བཤོ་; imp. ཤོས་ (shō) 1. va. to throw at or out (dirt or liquids) ༑ཁོས་མེའི་སྟེང་ལ་ཆུ་བཤོས་སོང་ He threw water on the fire.

གཤོག: p. བཤགས་; f. གཤག; imp. གཤོགས་ (shɔ̃ɔ̀) 1. va. to cut through, to split, to cleave ༑རི་བཤགས་ནས་མོ་ཊའི་འགྲོ་ལམ་བཟོས་པ་རེད་ (They) split the mountain and built the road.

གཤོག (shɔ̃g) abbr. of གཤོག་པ་.

གཤོག་ཀྱུར་ (shɔ̃ggyur) gliding; va.—བྱེད་.

གཤོག་བཀྲ་ (shɔ̃gdra) partridge.

གཤོག་སྒྲ་ (shɔ̃gdra) sound of wings flapping.

གཤོག་སྒྲོ་ (shɔ̃gdro) sm. གཤོག་པ་.

གཤོག་ཆགས་ (shɔ̃gjaà) birds.

གཤོག་རྡབ་ (shɔ̃gdəb) flapping of wings; va.—བྱེད་.

གཤོག་པ་ (shɔ̃gbə) wings; va.—གཡུག; —རྡབ་ to flap wings ༑བྱ་རྣམས་གཤོག་པ་བརྡབས་ནས་འཕུར་འགྲོ་གི་འདུག The birds are flapping their wings and flying.

གཤོག་པ་རྒྱང་ (shɔ̄gba gyōŋ) va. to soar with spread wings.

གཤོག་མེད་བྱ་ (shɔ̄gmeè ca) kiwi bird [Lit. bird without wings].

གཤོག་རྩལ་ (shɔ̄gdzɛɛ) ability to fly. flying skill.

གཤོག་ཟུང་ (shɔ̄gsuŋ) a pair of wings.

གཤོག་འོག་ལྷུང་རྒྱབ་ (shɔ̄gwɔɔ̀ lūŋgyəb) sm. ངན་སྐྱལ་དཀྲུག་ཤིང་.

གཤོག་རླབས་ (shɔ̄gləb) wings; va.—རྡེབ་ to flap one's wings.

གཤོགས་ (shɔ̄ɔ̀) imp. of གཤོག.

གཤོང་ (shōŋ) sm. གཤོང་ས་.

གཤོང་: p. བཤངས་; f. བཤང་; imp. ཤོངས་ (shōŋ) va. to clear (a blockage) ¶ ཡུར་བ་འགགས་པ་དེ་བཤང་དགོས་ (We) have to clear the blocked irrigation canal.

གཤོང་ཅན་ (shōŋjɛn) low-lying, concave.

གཤོང་བུ་ (shōŋbu) sm. གཤོང་ས་.

གཤོང་ཞིང་ (shōŋsiŋ) fields in the plains/ lowlands/ basin.

གཤོང་གཤོང་ (shōŋshoŋ) sm. གཤོང་ས་.

གཤོང་ས་ (shōŋsa) 1. basin (geological), depression, low-lying area ¶ ཐ་རིམ་གཤོང་ས་ The Tarim Basin. 2. sometimes used for a deep valley, ravine.

གཤོངས་ (shōŋ) 1. sm. ལྗོངས་. 2. sm. གཤོང་.

གཤོངས་ས་ (shōŋsa) sm. གཤོང་ས་.

གཤོམ་: p. བཤམས་; f. བཤམ་; imp. ཤོམས་ (shōm) 1. va. to prepare ¶ ཚོགས་འདུའི་གྲ་སྒྲིག་བཤམས་པ་རེད་ They prepared for the meeting. 2. va. to serve or offer food/ meal ¶ གསོལ་ཚིགས་བཤམས་པ་རེད་ (They) served food. 3. va. to draw a sword ¶ རྒྱག་རེས་རྒྱག་དུས་གྲི་བཤམས་སོང་ (He) drew his sword when he fought. 4. va. to throw/ cast out, to empty out ¶ དཀར་ཡོལ་ནང་གི་ཇ་གྲང་མོ་དེ་ཤོམས་ཤིག Empty out that cold cup of tea. 5. va. to spread, to lay out ¶ ཚོང་ཟོག་ཚང་མ་ལྕོག་ཙེའི་སྟེང་དུ་བཤམས་འདུག They spread the merchandise on the table.

གཤོམ་ར་ (shōmra) making preparations, arranging, setting up; va.—བྱེད་.

གཤོམ་ར་འཛིན་ (shōmra tēn) va. to act as if one is rich/ powerful.

གཤོམས་ (shōm) sm. གཤོམ་.

གཤོམས་ལས་ (shōmlɛɛ̀) planning work; va.—བྱེད་.

གཤོམས་ལས་ལག་ལེན་ཚོགས་པ་ (shōmlɛɛ̀ laglen tsōgba) committee for preparing and implementing programs.

གཤོར་: p. and f. བཤར་; imp. གཤོར་ (shɔ̄r) va. to level off the grain at the top of a measuring box so that it is exactly full ¶ གཞིས་སྡོད་ཀྱིས་གཡོག་པོའི་ཕོགས་འབྲུ་བཤར་ནས་སྤྲད་པ་རེད་ The estate steward leveled the grain in the measuring box and paid the servants their salary.

གཤོར་: p. and f. བཤོར་; imp. གཤོར་ (shɔ̄r) va. to hunt.

གཤོར་ཁ་རྒྱག (shɔ̄rga gyaà) va. to level off the grain at the top of a measuring box so that it is exactly full.

གཤོར་ཁུང་ (shɔ̄ɔ̄guŋ) shung. a hole in the wall of storage house from which grain is extracted.

གཤོར་སྤྲོད་ (shɔ̄ɔ̄dröö) shung. to measure out and hand over.

གཤོར་བྲེ་ (shɔ̄rdre) a grain measuring box whose size is the volume of one བྲེ་.

གཤོར་འབོ་ (shɔ̄mbo) a grain measuring box whosae size is the volume of one འབོ་.

གཤོར་ལྷག (shɔ̄ɔ̄lhaà) shung. remainder/ residue of grain left after measuring out.

གཤོལ་ (shɔ̄ɔ̄) a plow.

གཤོལ་སྒོར་ (shɔ̄ɔ̄gɔɔ) disc plow.

གཤོལ་མགོ་ (shɔ̄ŋgo) the head of a plow.

གཤོལ་ལྕགས་ (shɔ̄ɔ̄jaà) iron plowshare.

གཤོལ་རྟེན་ (shɔ̄ɔ̄den) wooden frame of a plow.

གཤོལ་འདེབས་ (shɔ̄ɔ̄ deb) shung. va. 1. to postpone/ delay (a departure) ¶ ཁོང་ཚོགས་འདུར་ཕེབས་རྒྱུ་གཤོལ་འདེབས་གནང་བཞག He postponed going to meeting. 2. va. to plow.

གཤོལ་མདའ་ (shɔ̄nda) plow shaft.

གཤོལ་པོ་ (shɔ̄ɔ̄bo) sm. གཤོལ་.

གཤོལ་སྤྱད་ (shɔ̄ɔ̄jɛɛ̀) parts of a plow.

བཤག (shāà) 1. sm.* གཤག. 2. f. of འཆགས་.

བཤག་བཅོས་ (shāgjöö) sm. གཤག་བཅོས་.

བཤག་འདོན་ (shāgdön) sm. གཤག་བཅོས་.

བཤགས་ (shāà) p. of གཤོག.

བཤགས་རྟེན་ (shāgden) giving sth. as a sign of repentance; va.—འབུལ་.

བཤགས་པ་ (shāgba) repenting; va.—འབུལ་; —བྱེད་.

བཤང་ (shāŋ) 1. va. to clean out, to unclog ¶ ང་ཚོས་ཡུར་བུ་བྱེ་བཤང་བརྒྱབ་པ་ཡིན་ We cleaned out the sand from the irrigation canal. ¶ ཆུ་ལོག་དོན་རྗེས་ལམ་བཤང་དགོས་བྱུང་ After the flood we had to clean off the road. 2. va. to clear a path. ¶ བླ་མ་ཕེབས་ཀྱི་ཡོད་ཙང་ལམ་བཤང་དགོས་རེད་ Because the lama is coming we have to clear a path (in a crowd). 3. f. of གཤོང་.

བཤང་བཀག (shāŋgaà) constipation.

བཤང་སྒོ་ (shāŋgo) anus.

བཤང་གཅི་ (shāŋji) stool and urine; va.—འདོར་ to defecate and urinate; vi.—འགག to be unable to defecate and urinate.

བཤང་གཅིའི་སྣོད་ཆས་ (shāŋjii nöòjɛɛ̀) bed pan.

བཤང་ཕྱི་ (shāŋji) sm. བཤང་གཅི་.

བཤང་གཅིན་ (shāŋjin) sm. བཤང་གཅི་.

བཤང་དྲི་ (shāŋdri) fart, flatus.

བཤང་པོ་ (shāŋbo) 1. generous ¶ ཁོང་ལག་པ་བཤང་པོ་ཡོད་པ་རེད་ He is very generous. 2. outgoing, extroverted.

བཤང་བ་ (shāŋwa) excrement; va.—འདོར་ to defecate.

བཤང་འབུ་ (shāŋbu) sm. སྦྲུག་འབུ་.

བཤང་འབྲུམ་ (shāŋdrum) sm. གཞང་འབྲུམ་.

བཤང་ལམ་ (shāŋlam) rectum.

བཤངས་ (shāŋ) p. of གཤོང་.

བཤད་ (shɛɛ̀) p. of ཤོད་.

བཤད་སྐྱོར་རྒྱག (shɛɛ̀) va. to repeat, to say again.

བཤད་ཁ་མ་ (shɛɛ̀kama) a woman who insults people.

བཤད་ཁྲིད་ (shɛɛ̀drii) lecture; va.—རྒྱག to give a lecture, to explain.

བཤད་ཀ་ལ་དགོས་ (shɛɛ̀ kalagöö) sm. སྨོས་ཅི་དགོས་.

བཤད་གླེང་ (shɛɛ̀leŋ) discussion, conversation; va.—བྱེད་.

བཤད་གྲྭ་ (shɛɛ̀dra) advanced institute/ school where Buddhist philosophy is taught (typical of Nyingma sect).

བཤད་དགོས་པ་གསུམ་ (shɛɛ̀göòba sūm) the three stresses (political campaign of 1999-2000).

བཤད་རྒྱུད་ (shɛɛ̀gyüü) 1. one of the four main texts on Tibetan medicine.

བཤད་རྒྱུན་ (shɛɛ̀gyün) legend, tale.

བཤད་སྒྲ་ (shādra) name of an important Tibetan aristocratic family.

བཤད་སྒྲུབ་ (shɛɛ̀drub) teaching and practice.

བཤད་སྒྲུབ་ཆོས་སྤྱོད་ (shɛɛ̀drub cööjöö) shung. teaching, practice and religious activities.

བཤད་སྒྲོས་ (shɛɛ̀dröö) sm. བཤད་རྒྱུན་.

བཤད་བཅོལ་བྱེད་ (shɛɛ̀jöö cee) va. to ask sb. to keep sth. for you.

བཤད་ཉན་ (shɛɛ̀ñɛn) speaking and listening.

བཤད་ཉེས་ (shɛɛ̀ñee) saying the wrong thing; vi.—ཤོར་ to inadvertently say the wrong thing.

བཤད་རྟགས་ (shɛɛ̀daà) exclamation mark.

བཤད་སྟངས་ (shɛɛ̀daŋ) manner/ style of talking; va.—བསྒྱུར་ to change the topic (during a conversation).

བཤད་སྟེགས་ (shɛɛ̀deg) rostrum, platform, pulpit.

བཤད་པ་བརྒྱ་ལས་ལྟ་བ་གཅིག་གསལ་ (shɛɛ̀ba gyalɛ dāwa ji sēē) looking one time is clearer than talking one hundred times.

བཤད་ཕྱོགས་ (shɛɛ̀jɔɔ̀) sm. བཤད་སྟངས་.

བཤད་ཕྱོགས་བྱེད་ (shɛ̀ɛjɔɔ jeè) va. to talk keeping in mind the person and situation.

བཤད་འཕྲོས་ (shɛ̀ɛdröö) sth. leftover to discuss.

བཤད་སྦྱངས་ (shɛ̀ɛjaŋ) explaining in speech.

བཤད་སྦྱར་ (shɛ̀ɛjar) the main topic and its commentary.

བཤད་མི་དགོས་ (shɛ̀ɛ migöö) sm. སྨོས་ཅི་དགོས་.

བཤད་ཅམ་སྐྱུང་ཅམ་ (shɛ̀ɛdzam gūmdzam) talking in a hesitating manner; va.—བྱེད་.

བཤད་ཚོལ་གྱི་ཐོན་ (shɛ̀ɛdzöögi tō̃n) shung. leaving immediately.

བཤད་ཚད་ཐམས་ཅད་ (shɛ̀ɛdzɛɛ tāmjɛɛ̀) sm. ཟེར་དགུ་ཅོག.

བཤད་ཚབ་ (shɛ̀ɛdzəb) spokesman, advocate.

བཤད་ཚིག་ (shɛ̀ɛdziì) wording.

བཤད་ཚུལ་ (shɛ̀ɛdzüü) sm. བཤད་སྟངས་.

བཤད་ཟུར་ (shəsur) name of an aristocratic family.

བཤད་བཟོ་དོད་པོ་ (shɛ̀ɛso tö̱öbo) eloquent, articulate.

བཤད་ཡམ་ (shɛ̀ɛyam) 1. wordy (in speech and writing). 2. irrelevant talk.

བཤད་ཡམ་ཚིག་ལོ་ (shɛ̀ɛyam tsi̱glo) wordy, verbose.

བཤད་རོགས་ (shɛ̀ɛrɔɔ̀) joining in when sb. is telling a story; va.—བྱེད་.

བཤད་རབས་ (shɛ̀ɛrəb) history of talk/ discussions; va.—འགོད་ to record the history of talk/ discussions ། ཁོང་གིས་སྐད་གཏམ་མང་པོ་བཤད་རབས་བཀོད་འདུག They recorded the many stories he told.

བཤད་ལུགས་ (shɛ̀ɛluù) sm. བཤད་ཚུལ་.

བཤད་བཤད་ (shɛ̀ɛshɛɛ̀) scolding; va.—གཏོང་ to scold; vi.—གཟེད་ to get scolded.

བཤད་བཤད་ཐག་ཐག་ (shɛ̀ɛshɛɛ̀ tāgdaà) many accounts or talk about sth. ། ཁོས་རྒྱལ་རབས་སྐོར་བཤད་བཤད་ཐག་ཐག་མང་པོ་ཞིག་ཟེར་གྱི་འདུག He is giving many accounts of history.

བཤད་ས་བུ་མོ་དང་ཕོག་ས་མནའ་མ་ (shɛ̀ɛsa po̱modaŋ pɔ̀ɔsa nāma) sb. getting hurt by comments meant for sb. else [Lit. sb. talked to the daughter but the in-marrying bride got hurt].

བཤད་སྲོལ་ (shɛ̀ɛsöö) a saying, legend.

བཤད་གསོལ་ (shɛ̀ɛsöö) sm. བཤད་རྒྱུན་.

བཤན་ཁང་ (shɛ̄ŋgaŋ) slaughterhouse, butcher store.

བཤན་གྲི་ (shɛ̄ndri) slaughtering knife.

བཤན་སྒྲིབ་ (shɛ̄ndrib) defilement caused by doing butchering.

བཤན་བླ་ (shɛ̄nla) butcher's fee.

བཤན་ཆས་ (shɛ̄njɛɛ̀) the costume worn by the butcher in Tibetan opera.

བཤན་གཏོང་ (shɛ̄n dōŋ) va. to slaughter/ butcher an animal.

བཤན་པ་ (shɛ̄mba) butcher.

བཤན་པོ་ (shɛ̄mbo) 1. true. 2. accurate/ straight; va.—འཕེན་ to throw straight/ accurate.

བཤན་པ་ལག་དམར་ (shɛ̄mba la̱gmar) a killer/ murderer.

བཤན་བུ་ (shɛ̄mbu) butcher's children.

བཤན་མོ་ (shɛ̄nmo) sm. བཤན་པོ་.

བཤན་ར་ (shɛ̄nra) slaughter house.

བཤམ་ (shām) f. of གཤོམ་.

བཤམས་ (shām) p. of གཤོམ་.

བཤམས་དངོས་ (shāmŋöö) goods or articles that are displayed or exhibited.

བཤམས་སྟོན་ (shāmdön) exhibit, display.

བཤམས་སྟོན་ཁང་ (shāmdöŋgaŋ) museum.

བཤམས་སྟོན་ཚོགས་འདུ་ (shāmdön tsōndu) exhibition, fair.

བཤམས་མ་ (shāmma) sm. བཤམས་དངོས་.

བཤམས་འཚོང་ (shāmdzoŋ) exhibition at which articles are for sale; va.—བྱེད་.

བཤམས་བཞེས་ (shāmsheè) eating what has been set out; va.—མཛད་; —གནང་ to eat what has been set out.;

བཤའ་: p. བཤས་; f. of བཤའ་; imp. བཤོས་ (shā) va. to slaughter, to kill (animals) ། དེ་རིང་ཁོ་ཚོས་གཡག་མང་པོ་བཤས་འདུག Today they slaughtered many yak.

བཤའ་དཀར་ (shā) sm. གཤའ་དཀར་.

བཤའ་གྲི་ (shədri) butcher's knife used in slaughtering.

བཤའ་རྒྱུ་ (shəgyu) an animal that is to be slaughtered.

བཤའ་རྡོ་ (shādo) stannite ore.

བཤའ་ནག (shānaà) abbr. of བཤའ་ཚེ་ནག་པོ་.

བཤའ་ཚེ་ (shādze) 1. stannite. 2. zinc.

བཤའ་ཚེ་དཀར་པོ་ (shādze gārbo) greyish stannite.

བཤའ་ཚེ་ནག་པོ་ (shādze na̱gbo) blackish stannite.

བཤའ་ར་ (shāra) butcher's place, site where slaughtering takes place.

བཤའ་ལས་ (shālɛɛ̀) slaughtering (work); va.—བྱེད་.

བཤའ་ལུག (shāluù) a sheep that is to be killed.

བཤར་ (shār) 1. p. of གཤོར་. 2. see ཐད་བཤར་.

བཤར་བཀག་གཏོང་ (shārgaà dōŋ) va. to line up to collect alms (monks).

བཤར་བཀག་འཛུགས་ (shārgaà dzu̱ù) va. to gang rape.

བཤར་སྦྱང་ (shārjaŋ) sm. གཤར་སྦྱང་.

བཤར་མ་ (shārma) grain that has already been measured container.

བཤར་མར་ཀློག་ (shārmar lɔ̄ɔ) va. to read easily/ fluently.

བཤལ་: p. བཤལ་; f. བཤལ་; imp. བཤོལ་ (shɛ̄ɛ) va. to rinse (when washing). 2. a harrow. 3. vi. to have diarrhea.

བཤལ་སྐོར་ (shɛ̄ɛgɔɔ) harrowing a field after sowing the seeds.

བཤལ་གཅོད་ (shɛ̄ɛ jöö) vi. to cause diarrhea to stop.

བཤལ་ཐག (shɛ̄ɛdaà) rope used for pulling a harrow.

བཤལ་འདྲུད་ (shɛ̄ɛdrüü) harrowing; va.—རྒྱག.

བཤལ་ནད་ (shɛ̄ɛnɛɛ̀) diarrhea; vi.—ན་; —ཕོག to have diarrhea.

བཤལ་འབྱེ་ (shɛ̄ɛje) sm. བཤལ་འདྲུད་.

བཤལ་སྨན་ (shɛ̄ɛmɛn) a laxative.

བཤལ་སྨན་སྦྲུམ་རིགས་ (shɛ̄ɛmɛn du̱mrig) a traditional Tibetan laxative.

བཤལ་རྫ་ (shɛ̄ɛdza) magnesium sulphate.

བཤལ་རིམས་ (shɛ̄ɛrim) an epidemic of diarrhea.

བཤལ་ལ་ (shɛ̄ɛla) harrowing (fields); va.—རྒྱག.

བཤལ་བཤལ་གཏོང་ (shɛ̄ɛ dōŋ) va. to rinse.

བཤས་ (shɛ̄ɛ) 1. p. of བཤའ་. 2. slaughtering, butchering; va.—གཏོང་.

བཤས་ཁང་ (shɛ̀ɛgaŋ) slaughterhouse.

བཤས་ཁྲངས་ (shɛ̀ɛguŋ) animals that are set aside/ identified to be slaughtered; va.—སྤུ་གཏོང་ to set aside/ identify animals for slaughtering.

བཤས་ཁྲལ་ (shɛ̀ɛdrɛɛ) tax on slaughtering animals.

བཤས་གྲི་ (shɛ̀ɛdri) knife for slaughtering animals.

བཤས་རྒྱུ་ (shɛ̀ɛgyu) set aside/ identified for slaughter.

བཤས་པ་ (shɛ̀ɛba) butcher.

བཤས་ཕག (shɛ̀ɛbaà) a pig identified for slaughter.

བཤས་ཕྱུགས་ (shɛ̀ɛjuù) livestock identified for slaughter.

བཤས་གཡག (shɛ̀ɛyaà) a yak identified for slaughter.

བཤས་ར་ (shɛ̀ɛra) 1. slaughterhouse. 2. goat identified for salughter.

བཤས་ལུག (shɛ̀ɛluù) sheep identified for slaughter.

བཤིག (shīì) p. and f. of འཇིག.

བཤིག་སྒྲིག (shīidrig) dismantling and reassembling; va.—བྱེད་.

བཤིག་གཏོར་ (shīgdɔɔ) destroying, demolishing; va.—བྱེད་.

བཤིག་ཐབས་མེད་པ་ (shīgdəb me̱eba) indestructible.

བཤིག་གསོ་ (shīgso) repairing, restoring; va.—བྱེད་.

བཤིགས་ཅམ་བྱེད་ (shīgdzam ce̱e) va. to move a little bit.

བཤིགས་བཤིགས་ (shīgshii) crowding/ moving close together; va.—བྱེད་.

བཤུ་ (shū) f. of ཤུ་.

བཤུ་: p. བཤུས་; f. བཤུ་; imp. ཤུས་ (shū) 1. va. to

peel, to skin, to pare ། ཞོག་ཁོག་འདི་པགས་པ་བཤུ་དང་ Please peel the potato. 2. va. to copy ། དེབ་རྙིང་པ་དེ་ཚོ་བཤུས་པ་རེད་ (He) copied the old books. 3. va. to defrock (official clothes when sb. is dismissed from government service) ། ཁོང་གི་ལས་ཞྭ་ལས་གོས་སོགས་བཤུས་ནས་རྒྱང་འབུད་བཏང་བ་རེད་ (They) took off his official clothes and exiled him.

བཤུ་གཞོག (shūshoò) exploitation, exploiting; va.—གཏོང་; —བྱེད་ to exploit; vi.—མྱོང་ to experience exploitation.

བཤུ་གཞོག་མཁན་ (shūshoòñɛn) exploiters.

བཤུ་གཞོག་གི་རྣམ་པ་ (shūshoògi nāmba) forms of exploitation.

བཤུ་གཞོག་གྲལ་རིམ་ (shūshoò tr̲ɛ̲ɛrim) the exploiting class.

བཤུ་གཞོག་བྱེད་མཁན་གྲལ་རིམ་ (shūshoò ce̲èñɛn tr̲ɛ̲ɛ̀rim) sm. བཤུ་གཞོག་གྲལ་རིམ་.

བཤུ་གཞོག་བྱེད་ཐབས་ (shūshoò ce̲èdəb) exploiting/ explo itive means.

བཤུ་གཞོག་བྱེད་པོ་ (shūshoò ce̲èbo) exploiters.

བཤུ་གཞོག་མྱོང་ (shūshoò ño̲ŋ) va. to experience exploitation.

བཤུ་གཞོག་མྱོང་མཁན་གྲལ་རིམ་ (shūshoò ño̲ŋñɛn tr̲ɛ̲ɛrim) the exploited class.

བཤུ་གཞོག་ལམ་ལུགས་ (shūshoò l̲ə̲mluù) the system of exploitation.

བཤུག (shūù) f. of ཤུག.

བཤུགས་ (shūg) p. of ཤུག.

བཤུང་ (sūŋ) f. of གཤུང་.

བཤུངས་ (shūŋ) p. of གཤུང་.

བཤུད་: p. **བཤུད་**; f. **བཤུད་**; imp. **ཤུད་** (shūù) 1. va. to rub, to scrape. 2. vi. to get frostbite.

བཤུམ་: p. **བཤུམས་**; f. **བཤུམ་**; imp. **ཤུམས་** (shūm) va. to cry (h.).

བཤུམས་ (shūm) p. of བཤུམ་.

བཤུར་མ་ (shūrmə) sm. ཤུར་མ་.

བཤུར་: p. **བཤུར་**; f. **བཤུར་**; imp. **ཤུར་** (shūr) va. to singe/ burn (usu. the long hair of woven wool cloth).

བཤུལ་ (shǖǖ) 1. sm. བཤུལ་ལམ་. 2. back (of a person or animal).

བཤུལ་ཀ་ (shǖǖga) sm. བཤུལ་ལམ་.

བཤུལ་ཁ་ (shǖǖga) sm. བཤུལ་ལམ་.

བཤུལ་རྒྱགས་ (shǖǖgyaà) provisions for a trip/ journey.

བཤུལ་ཐག (shǖǖdaà) distance traveled, distance of a trip.

བཤུལ་ཚིལ་ (shǖǖdzii) fat on the back of an animal.

བཤུལ་རིང་ (shǖǖriŋ) long distance.

བཤུལ་ལམ་ (shǖǖlam) trail, road ། བཤུལ་ལམ་རིང་བའི་འགྲུལ་པ་ A traveler on a long road.

བཤུལ་ཤ་ (shǖǖsha) 1. the flesh on the back of an animal. 2. thigh flesh.

བཤུལ་སེལ་ (shǖǖsel) clearing a path through a crowd, dispersing a crowd.

བཤུས་ (shǖǖ) 1. p. of ཤུ་. 2. (ཞལ་— or སྙན་—) sth. that follows is an exact transcription or verbatim account ། གསུང་བཤད་བཀའ་སློབ་གནང་བ་ཞལ་བཤུས་ཤིག A verbatim account of (his) advice (follows). 3. va. to take/ peel off (e.g., skin, clothes, saddle, etc.) ། དང་པོ་ཧ་སྒ་བཤུ་དགོས་ First one has to take off the saddle.

བཤུས་སྒྲིག (shǖǖdrig) copying and compiling.

བཤུས་བཅད་རྨ་ (shǖǖjɛ̀ɛ mā) a cut or wound caused by a stone or knife.

བཤུས་དེབ་ (shǖǖdeb) a book that has been copied from another.

བཤུས་འབྲིས་ (shǖǖdrii) copying, transcribing; va.—བྱེད་ to copy to transcribe.

བཤུས་མ་ (shǖǖmə) a copy, a duplicate.

བཤེར་ (shēr) 1. p. and f. of ཤེར་. 2. va. to compare, to examine, to investigate ། མིང་ཐོ་བཤེར་ནས་རྡོ་རྗེ་འདིར་མེད་པ་ཤེས་བྱུང་ Having checked the names on the list (I) learned that Dorje wasn't here.

བཤེར་ཁང་ (shērgaŋ) shung. a law court during the tt.

བཤེར་ཁང་ལས་ཁུངས་ (shērgaŋ l̲ɛ̲ɛ̀guŋ) sm. བཤེར་ཁང་.

བཤེར་ཁྲ་ (shērdra) judgment, verdict; va. གཏོང་ to render a verdict.

བཤེར་རྒྱག (shēr gya̲à) va. to dispute/ argue in a lawsuit/ law case.

བཤེར་བསྡུར་བྱེད་ (shērdur ce̲è) sm. བཤེར་རྒྱག.

བཤེར་དཔང་ (shērbaŋ) shung. 1. public prosecutor. 2. the judge/ head of the བཤེར་དཔང་ལས་ཁུངས་.

བཤེར་དཔོན་ (shērbön) sm. བཤེར་དཔང་.

བཤེར་བློན་ (shērlün) shung. sb. sitting in judgement over a dispute.

བཤེར་ཚགས་ (shērdzaà) saying/ talking in detail; va.—བྱེད་.

བཤེར་འཚོལ་ (shērdzüü) hunting for, searching for; va.—བྱེད་.

བཤེར་གཞུང་ (shērshuŋ) list of students in a class from which attendance is taken.

བཤེར་གཟུང་ (shērsuŋ) sm. བཤེར་བཟུང་.

བཤེར་བཟུང་ (sērsuŋ) abbr. of ཐོག་བཤེར་འཛིན་བཟུང་.

བཤེར་ལེན་ (shērlen) hearing a case; va.—བྱེད་.

བཤེས་ (shēè) friends, relatives.

བཤེས་ངོ་ (shēèŋo) showing partiality to one's friends.

བཤེས་གཉེན་ (shēèñen) 1. close friend. 2. teacher.

བཤེས་གཉེན་ངན་པ་ (shēèñen ŋ̲ə̲mba) bad friend and bad teacher.

བཤེས་པའི་སྤྲིང་ཡིག (shēèbɛ drīŋyiì) sm. བཤེས་སྤྲིངས་.

བཤེས་སྤྲིངས་ (shɛ̄ɛ̀driŋ) a letter said to be written by Nagarjuna that is widely studied in Tibet.

བཤེས་མེད་ (shēèmeè) friendless, alone.

བཤེས་མེད་སྐྱབས་བྲལ་ (shēèmeè gyəbdrɛɛ) sb. who has nobody to turn to.

བཤོ་ (shō) f. of གཤོ་.

བཤོག (shɔ̄ɔ̀) sm. གཤོག.

བཤོགས་ (shɔ̄ɔ̀) imp. of འཆགས་.

བཤོངས་ (shōŋ) 1. sm. གཤོང་.

བཤོར་ (shōr) p. and f. of གཤོར་.

བཤོལ་ (shȫȫ) 1. va. to withdraw/ resign ། རྒྱལ་ཚབ་སྲིད་ཁྲི་ལས་བཤོལ་བ་རེད་ The regent resigned. 2. va. to get off, to dismount/ disembark ། མེ་འཁོར་ནས་བཤོལ་དེ་ Disembarking from the train. 3. va. to throw/ cast.

བཤོལ་ཐབས་མེད་པ་ (shȫȫdəb me̲èba) unavoidable, irresistible.

བཤོལ་འདེབས་ (shȫndeb) asking sb. to delay/ postpone sth.; va.—བྱེད་ ། ཁོང་བོད་ལ་ཕེབས་རྒྱུ་བཤོལ་འདེབས་ཞུས་པ་རེད་ (They) asked him to postpone his visit to Tibet.

བཤོལ་བྱེད་མི་རུང་བ་ (shȫȫjeè mi̲ruŋbə) sm. བཤོལ་ཐབས་མེད་པ་.

བཤོལ་མ་ (shȫȫma) 1. Tibetan beer (ཆང་). 2. sm. བཤོལ་འདེབས་.

བཤོལ་ཟླ་ (shȫnda) sm. ཟླ་ལྷག.

བཤོལ་ལོ་ (shȫȫlo) leap year.

བཤོལ་ས་ (shȫȫsa) a place to get off/ dismount/ disembark.

བཤོས་ (shȫȫ) 1. imp. of བཤའ་. 2. p. of གཤོ་. 3. h. of ཟས་. 4. va. to have sexual intercourse.

བཤོས་བུ་ (shȫȫbu) a small torma.

བཤོས་ཞིང་ (shȫȫshiŋ) grain field.

ས

ས་ (sā) soil, land, earth, ground ¶ ས་གཤིན་པ་ Fertile soil. ¶ ས་རྒྱ་ཆེན་པོ་ A wide area of land. ¶ ས་སྟེང་གི་མི་ཐམས་ཅད་ All the people on the earth. ¶ བྱིའུ་དེ་ས་ལ་བབས་སོང་ The bird landed on the ground. 2. (vb. + —) the place where the verbal action takes place ¶ ཁོའི་ལས་ཀ་བྱེད་ས་ག་པར་འདུག་གམ་ Where is the place he works? ¶ ཁོང་ལ་སྐྱ་ཅེད་ཞུ་ས་མི་འདུག There is no room for teasing him (one cannot tease him). 3. the letter "sa" (used in alphabetical ordering). 4. instrumental particle suffixed to vowel finals ¶ ཁྱིས་ By the dog. 5. sm. གྲངས་ཀྱི་གནས་.

ས་ཀོང་ (sāgoŋ) a depression in the ground.

ས་གླུ་ (sā lū) abbr. of ས་བདག and གླུ་.

ས་དཀར་ (sāgar) whitewash, lime; va.—འཐུག; —གཞི་; —གཏོང་; —གསོལ་ to whitewash (a house).

ས་དཀར་ཁྲི་འཛིན་ (sāgar trindzin) shung. sm. ས་སྐྱ་ཁྲི་པ་.

ས་དཀར་ཝུ་ལག (sāgar wuulaà) shung. a corvee labor tax that involves whitewashing the Potatla Palace; va.—བྱེད་.

ས་དཀོར་རྡུག་པ་ (sāgɔɔ sugbə) land that produces bad yields due to overuse.

ས་བཀྲ་ (sābdra) 1. map; va.—འགོད་; —རྒྱག to draw/ make a map. 2. a sign whether a place is lucky or not ¶ ས་བཀྲ་ལེགས་པ་ཞིག་ལ་ཁང་པ་རྒྱག་གི་ཡིན་ I am building a house on a site that is considered to be lucky.

ས་བཀྲ་དཔེ་སྐྲུན་ཁང་ (sābdra bēdröngaŋ) cartographic publishing house.

ས་བཀྲ་ལེན་འགོད་ (sābdra lengöö) mapping; va.—བྱེད་.

ས་བཀྲབ་གནམ་བཀྲབ་ (sābdrəb nāmdrəb) working hard day and night; va.—བྱེད་.

ས་བཀྲའི་ཐིག་རིས་ (sābdrɛ tigrii) map coordinates.

ས་བཀྲའི་དཔེ་དེབ་ (sābdrɛ bēdeb) book of maps.

ས་བཀྲའི་འཕྲེད་ཐིག (sābdrɛ trēŋdig) degrees of latitude.

ས་བཀྲའི་གཞུང་ཐིག (sābdrɛ shuŋdig) degrees of longitude.

ས་བཀྲས་ (sā drɛ̄ɛ̀) abbr. of Sakya and Tashilunpo (monasteries).

ས་བཀྲེན་པོ་ (sā drēmbo) poor quality land.

ས་ཀོ་ (sā gō) va. to dig (the ground).

ས་ཀོ་རྡོ་སློག (sāgo dolɔɔ̀) digging up the soil and throwing aside the rocks; va.—བྱེད་.

ས་བཀོའི་འཕྲུལ་འཁོར་ (sāgö trüügɔɔ) a digging machine.

ས་སྐམ་ (sāgam) arid/ dry land.

ས་སྐམ་པོ་ (sā gambo) sm. ས་སྐམ་.

ས་སྐལ་ (sāgɛɛ) land share/ allotment.

ས་སྐུད་ (sōgüü) a wire going underground.

ས་སྐོར་ (sāgɔɔ) shung. an inspection tour of an area/ place; va.—འགྲོ་; —རྒྱག ¶ ཉེན་རྟོག་པས་མི་གསོད་བྱུང་སར་ས་སྐོར་བརྒྱབ་པ་རེད་ The police went to inspect the place where the murder took place.

ས་བསྐོར་ (sāgɔɔ) sm. ས་སྐོར་.

ས་སྐྱ་ (sāgya) Sakya (monastery).

ས་སྐྱ་ཁྲི་པ་ (sāgya tribə) sm. ས་སྐྱ་བདག་ཆེན་.

ས་སྐྱ་ཐེར་ (sā gyäder) barren land.

ས་སྐྱ་བདག་ཆེན་ (sāgya dagjen) the head of the Sakya sect.

ས་སྐྱ་འབག་མོ་ (sāgya baàmo) female protective deities (witches) of the Saya sect.

ས་སྐྱེ་རྡོ་སྐྱེས་ (sāgye dogyeè) 1. indigenous, native ¶ ང་ལུང་པ་འདིའི་ས་སྐྱེ་རྡོ་སྐྱེས་ཡིན་ I am a native of this place. 2. growing all over ¶ ལུང་པ་འདིར་དབྱར་དུས་མེ་ཏོག་ས་སྐྱེ་རྡོ་སྐྱེས་རེད་འདུག During the summer flowers grow all over in this area.

ས་སྐྱེས་རྡོ་སྐྱེས་ (sāgye dosgyeè) sm. ས་སྐྱེ་རྡོ་སྐྱེས་.

ས་སྐྱོ་ (sāgyo) a white paste spread on cloth in preparation of painting a thanka.

ས་སྐྱོང་ (sāgyoŋ) 1. sm. བཀའ་བློན་. 2. lord, king, ruler [Lit. ruler of the earth].

ས་སྐྱོང་མི་དབང་ (sāgyoŋ miwaŋ) shung. sm. ས་སྐྱོང་.

ས་སྐྱོན་ (sāgyön) anthrax.

ས་སྐྱོར་ (sāgyɔɔ) 1. wall made from earth; va.—རྒྱག; —འཛིན་.

ས་ཁ་ (sāga) the field/ ground/ earth ¶ ས་ཁར་སེམས་ཅན་མང་པོ་འདུག There are many animals on the fields.

ས་ཁ་འབྱེད་པ་ (sāga jeè) va. to do the first plowing [Lit. to open the soil].

ས་ཁང་ (sāgaŋ) 1. abbr. land and house. 2. mud brick house.

ས་ཁད་ (sāgɛɛ̀) sm. ས་ཐག.

ས་ཁད་རྒྱང་ (sāgɛɛ̀ gyaŋ) vi. to be far away (in distance).

ས་ཁད་རྒྱང་པོ་ (sāgɛɛ̀ gyaŋbo) far away (in distance).

ས་ཁད་ཡངས་པོ་ (sāgɛɛ̀ yaŋbo) large/ spacious/ open land.

ས་ཁད་རིང་པོ་ (sāgɛɛ̀ riŋbu) far (in distance).

ས་ཁམས་ (sāgam) 1. the five elements in Tibetan astrology: fire, wind, water, earth, iron. 2. geography.

ས་ཁམས་འཁོར་ཡུག (sāgam kɔ̄ɔ̄yuù) geographical environment.

ས་ཁམས་ཀྱི་རྒྱུན་ཤེས་ (sāgamgi gyünsheè) geography, geographical features.

ས་ཁམས་གནས་ཚུལ་ (sāgam nɛ̄ɛ̀dzüü) geographical conditions.

ས་ཁམས་རིག་པ་ (sāgam rigbə) the science of geography.

ས་ཁལ་ལེ་བ་ (sāgɛɛ lewa) dusty ¶ མི་རྣམས་ངལ་རྩོལ་བྱས་ནས་གྱོན་པ་ས་ཁལ་ལེ་བར་ལོག་སླེབས་བྱུང་ After doing manual labor, the workers returned home with dusty clothes.

ས་ཁུ་ (sōgu) loose mixture of water and earth.

ས་ཁུང་ (sōguŋ) pit, hole (in the ground); va.—བྲུ་ to dig a hole/ pit.

ས་ཁུངས་ (sāguŋ) an area in which one has duties/ responsibilities ¶ ཆུ་རགས་ཀྱི་ལས་གྲྭ་དེ་ས་ཁུལ་མང་པོར་བགོས་ནས་ལས་མི་རྣམས་ལ་སྤྲད་པ་རེད་ They divided the dam construction work site into many areas and gave them to the workers.

ས་ཁུལ་ (sāgüü) 1. region, zone, district ¶ བོད་བྱང་ཕྱོགས་ཀྱི་ས་ཁུལ་ The region of northern Tibet. 2. prefecture ¶ ས་ཁུལ་ཏང་ཨུ་ Prefectural party committee.

ས་ཁུལ་སྤྱི་ཁྱབ་ (sāgüü jigyəb) shung. district governor.

ས་ཁུལ་གསུམ་གྱི་གསར་བརྗེ་ (sāgüüsumgi sārje) the revolution in three region's (in Ili, Tarbagatai and Alta in Xinjiang).

ས་ཁོངས་ (sāgoŋ) belonging to sth. territorially; vi.—འགྱུར་; —ཚུགས་ to become a part of a country/ territory ¶ ཀ་ཤི་མིར་རྒྱ་གར་གྱི་ས་ཁོངས་སུ་གྱུར་པ་རེད་ Kashmir became part of India.

ས་ཁོངས་འཆར་འགོད་ (sāgoŋ cārgöö) regional planning.

ས་ཁོངས་རང་སྐྱོང་ (sāgoŋ raŋgyoŋ) regional autonomy.

ས་ཁོངས་རང་བཞིན་ (sāgoŋ rəŋshin) regionalism.

ས་ཁོད་སྙོམས་པོ་ (sāgöö ñōmbo) level/ flat land.

ས་ཁྱད་ (sāgyɛɛ̀) differences in the soil/ ground.

ས་ཁྱི་ (səgyi) earth-dog year.

ས་ཁྱི་ལོའི་ལུགས་སྒྱུར་ (səgyii luggyur) the Reform Movement of 1898 in China.

ས་ཁྱོན་ (sāgyön) land area.

ས་ཁྱོན་ཞིབ་འཇལ་ (sāgyön shimjɛɛ) shung. detailed measurement of fields/ land; va.—བྱེད་.

ས་བྲ་ (sābdra) sm. ས་བཀྲ་.

ས་བྲ་བོ་ (sā trāwo) multicolored earth/ soil.

ས་ཁྲལ་ (sādrɛɛ) land tax, tax on land holdings.

ས་ཁྲལ་སྤྱི་འདོམས་ (sādrɛɛ jindom) shung. chief person in charge of land taxes.

ས་ཁྲི་ (sədri) 1. earthen brick platform bed. 2. Chinese heated "kang" bed.

ས་བྲུ་སློག (sədru lɔ̃ɔ) va. to turn over fields before sowing.

ས་ཁྲོལ་ (sādröö) sieve, sifter (for earth).

ས་མཁན་ (sāñɛn) 1. guide. 2. a person who searches land for auspicious signs.

ས་མཁར་ (sāgar) sm. ས་ཁང་, 2.

ས་མཁྲགས་ (sādrag) sm. ས་མཁྲེགས་.

ས་མཁྲེགས་ (sādreg) 1. hard ground/ earth/ soil. 2. macadam road.

ས་མཁྲེགས་ལ་ཕུར་པ་བཏབ་པ་ལྟ་བུ་ (sādregla pūrba dəbbə dəbu) sth. that is very stable [Lit. a stake driven into solid earth].

ས་མཁྲེགས་ལམ་ཁ་ (sādreg laŋga) macadam covered road.

ས་འཁོར་ཁང་ཤིང་ (sāgɔɔ kāŋshiŋ) shung. land, house and trees.

ས་འཁོད་སྙོམ་ལ་རྡོ་འབུར་འདོན་ (sāgɔɔ ñomla dobur dön) sb. who stands out by being different [Lit. a rock on level ground].

ས་འཁོར་གནས་འཁོར་ (sāgɔɔ nɛ̀ɛgɔɔ) feeling of dizziness/ giddiness.

ས་འཁོལ་རྡོ་འཁོལ་ (sāgöö dogöö) intense activity [Lit. earth boiling, stones boiling].

ས་འཁྱག (sāgyaà) frozen ground/ earth.

ས་འཁྱག་གདན་དང་རྡོ་འཁྱག་སྔས་ (sāgyaà dendaŋ dogyaà ŋɛ̀ɛ) extreme hardship/ suffering [Lit. frozen earth as mattress, frozen rock as pillow].

ས་འཁྲུག (səndruù) one of six types of earthquakes in Tibetan belief.

ས་ག་ཟླ་བ་ (sāga dawa) the fourth (and holiest) month of the Tibetan calendar.

ས་གད་ (sāgɛɛ̀) sweeping the ground; va.—རྒྱག ། སྒོ་རའི་ནང་ས་གད་རྒྱག་དགོས་ (You) must sweep the ground in the courtyard.

ས་གས་ཉ་བ་ (sāgɛɛ̀ ñawa) the 15th day of the 4th month of the Tibetan calendar.

ས་གས་གནམ་རྡིབ་ (sāgɛɛ̀ nāmdib) violent political and social upheaval, earth shattering events [Lit. the earth splits open and the sky collapses].

ས་གས་རི་ཉིལ་ (sāgɛɛ̀ riñii) sm. ས་གས་གནམ་རྡིབ་ [Lit. earth splits open and the mountain slides down].

ས་གོང་ (sāgoŋ) lump of earth.

ས་གོལ་ (sāgöö) a remote/ out of the way place ། ཁོས་ང་ལུང་ཁུག་ས་གོལ་ལ་གཏོང་རྩིས་འདུག He plans to send me to a remote place.

ས་གྱོང་ (sāgyoŋ) hard/ poor quality soil.

ས་གྲགས་གནམ་གྲགས་ (sādrag nāmdrag) very famous [Lit. well known to the earth, well known to the sky].

ས་གླ་ (sāla) 1. rent/ lease paid for use of land. 2. the rent paid to government for the land a house is situated on. 3. parking fee.

ས་གླང་ (sālaŋ) earth-ox year.

ས་དགའ་ (sāga) a nomad district in southwestern Tibet.

ས་དགེ་བཀའ་རྙིང་ (sāge gāñiŋ) abbr. of the four major sects of Buddhism in Tibet (ས་སྐྱ་, དགེ་ལུགས་, བཀའ་བརྒྱུད་ and རྙིང་མ་).

ས་དགྲ་ (sādra) inauspicious land/ place ། ས་དགྲ་ངན་པ་ཡོད་སར་སྡོད་ཁང་རྒྱག་རྒྱུ་མེད་ One should not build house in an inauspicious place.

ས་མགོ་ (sāgo) the superfixed letter "s".

ས་མགོ་ཅན་ (sāgojɛn) words with the superfixed letter "s".

ས་འགག (sāŋgaà) a strategic pass.

ས་འགག་སོ་ཁང་ (sāŋgaà sōgaŋ) strategic checkpost.

ས་འགུལ་ (səngüü) earthquake; vi.—རྒྱག to have an earthquake.

ས་འགུལ་བརྟག་ཆས་ (səngüü dāgjɛɛ̀) seismograph.

ས་འགུལ་བརྟག་ཆས་ཅུའུ་ (səngüü dāgjɛɛ̀ jū) tib. ch. bureau of seismology.

ས་འགུལ་བརྟག་ཆས་ལས་ཁུངས་ (səngüü dāgjɛɛ̀ lɛ̀ɛguŋ) seismic station, seismologic station, bureau of seismology.

ས་འགུལ་གནམ་འདྲོག (səngüü nāmdrɔɔ̀) sm. ས་གས་གནམ་རྡིབ་ [Lit. the earth shakes and the sky collapses].

ས་འགུལ་སྣོད་སྐྱོབ་ (səngüü nööögyob) earthquake relief.

ས་འགོ་ (sāngo) sm. རྫོང་དཔོན་.

ས་འགོད་ (səngöö) abbr. of ས་ཡིག་འགོད་.

ས་རྒོད་ (sāgöö) uncultivated/ undeveloped land, virgin land, wasteland; va.—སློག་; —རྨོ་ to reclaim wild/ waste/ virgin land for cultivation.

ས་རྒོད་འདུལ་སྒྲིག (sāgöö düüseg) reclaiming virgin land/ wasteland; va.—བྱེད་.

ས་རྒོད་ཕུ་སློག (sāgöö trūlɔɔ) sm. ས་རྒོད་འདུལ་སྒྲིག.

ས་རྒོད་ཕུ་སློག་ཅུའུ་ (sāgöö trūlɔɔ jū) tib. ch. bureau of agricultural reclamation.

ས་རྒོད་ཕུ་སློག་རུ་ཁག (sāgöö trūlɔɔ rugaà) land reclamation team/ unit.

ས་རྒོད་སློག (sāgöö lɔɔ) see ས་རྒོད་.

ས་རྒོད་གསར་སྤེལ་ (sāgöö sārböö) sm. ས་རྒོད་ཕུ་སློག.

ས་རྒྱ་ (sāgya) area ། ས་རྒྱ་ཆུང་ཆུང་ A small area.

ས་རྒྱ་དཔངས་གྲུ་བཞི་ (sā gyabaŋ trushi) cubic meter of land.

ས་རྒྱུ་ (səgyu) 1. quality of the soil ། ས་རྒྱུ་ཞན་པ་ Poor soil. 2. land and property.

ས་རྒྱུ་ཆུ་གཤིས་ (səgyu cūshii) hydrogeology.

ས་རྒྱུ་གཞུང་ལེན་ (səgyu shuŋlen) shung. land and property confiscated by the government.

ས་རྒྱུ་ལེགས་བཅོས་ (səgyu legjöö) improvement of the soil/ land.

ས་རྒྱུ་གཤིན་པོ་ (səgyu shimbu) rich soil.

ས་རྒྱུའི་རིག་པ་ (səgyü rigbə) agronomy.

ས་རྒྱུད་ (səgyüü) area, region ། མདོ་སྨད་ས་རྒྱུད་ལ་དམག་མི་མང་པོ་འབྱོར་འདུག Many soldiers arrived in the Kham area.

ས་རྒྱུན་ (sāgyün) abbr. of ས་གནས་རྒྱུན་ལས་.

ས་རྒྱུས་ (səgyüü) knowledge of the geography of an area; vi.—འཕྲིངས་ to know the geography of an area.

ས་རྒྱུས་རྡོ་རྒྱུས་ (səgyüü dogyüü) sm. ས་རྒྱུས་.

ས་རྒྱུས་སྡེ་ཁག (səgyüü degaà) department of geography.

ས་རྒྱུས་མི་རྒྱུས་ (səgyüü migyüü) knowledge of people and geography in an area.

ས་རྒྱུས་ལམ་རྒྱུས་ (səgyüü lamgyüü) knowledgeable about an area and its road/ trails; va.—བྱེད་ to act as a guide ། ལུང་པ་རྒྱུས་མེད་ལ་སླེབས་དུས་ས་རྒྱུས་ལམ་རྒྱུས་བྱེད་མཁན་ཞིག་དགོས་ When one comes to a new land one needs a guide (sb. knowledgeable about an area).

ས་སྒོ་ (sāgo) ground breaking ceremony; va.—འབྱེད་ to break ground (for a construction project).

ས་སྒང་ (sāgaŋ) an elevated place, a higher place.

ས་སྒྲེ་བོ་ (sā drewo) barren land.

ས་སྒྲིབ་ (sədrib) sm.* ས་རུབ་.

ས་ངན་ (sāŋɛn) 1. harsh/ barren land. 2. poor quality soil.

ས་ངོས་ (sāŋöö) the surface of the ground.

ས་ངོས་ཆགས་ཚུལ་ (sāŋöö cəgdzüü) the general configuration of the earth's surface.

ས་ངོས་ཆགས་ཚུལ་གྱི་ས་བཀྲ་ (sāŋöö cəgdzüügi sābdra) relief map, geomorphological map.

ས་ངོས་ཆགས་ཚུལ་རིག་པ་ (sāŋöö cəgdzüü rigbə) geomorphology.

ས་ངོས་ཆགས་ཚུལ་རིག་པ་མཁས་ཅན་ (sāŋöö cəgdzüü rigbə kɛ̀ɛjɛn) geomorphology expert.

ས་ངོས་སྙོམས་ཐིག (sāŋöö ñomdig) the horizon (line).

ས་ངོས་འབར་འབུར་ (sāŋöö barbur) land that is uneven/ undulating.

ས་ངོས་དམག་དཔུང་ (sāŋöö məgbuŋ) ground troops/

soldiers.

ས་ངོས་རིག་པ་ (sāŋöö rigbə) topography.

ས་ངོས་སུ་བྱུང་པའི་གཏེར་རྡོ་ (sāŋöösu pṳübɛ dērdo) a vein of ore at the surface of the earth.

ས་སྔགས་ (sāŋaà) mud balls that have been blessed with tantric rituals.

ས་བརྡབ་བརྡབ (sā jāgjaà) beating/ stomping/ pounding on the ground to compress the surface; va.—བྱེད་.

ས་བཅད་ (sābjɛɛ̀) 1. general outline (of subjects or topics). 2. chapter or section (in a book) ༡ས་བཅད་གཉིས་པ་ The second chapter.

ས་བཅའ་ (sā jā) va. to establish a residence or home.

ས་བཅུ་ (sāju) the ten stages of a Bodhisattva.

ས་བཅུད་ (sājüü) fertility of the soil; vi.—ཉམས་ to have the fertility of the soil decline ༡ས་བཅུད་ཆེན་པོ་ Very fertile land.

ས་བཅུད་བུམ་པ་ (sājüü pṳmbə) shung. a vase that brings good luck and fertility of the land.

ས་བཅུད་འཛོམས་པོ་ (sājüü dzo̱mbo) fertile land.

ས་བཅུད་ཡོད་པ་ (sājüü yo̱öbə) sm. ས་བཅུད་འཛོམས་པོ་.

ས་ཆ་ (sāja) place, land, territory ༡ང་ཚོ་བོད་ནང་ས་ཆ་འདྲ་མིན་མང་པོར་འགྲོ་མྱོང་ We have been to many different places in Tibet.

ས་ཆ་ཀུ་ཡངས་པོ་ (sāja ku̱ ya̱ŋbo) an open/ spacious place or area.

ས་ཆ་ཅིག་ཅིག་ཅིག (sāja jījjigjig) so and so places ༡ང་ཚོ་ས་ཆ་ཅིག་ཅིག་ཅིག་ལ་ཕྱིན་པ་ཡིན་ We went to so and so places.

ས་ཆ་གཅོད་ (sāja jöö) va. to sever/ separate/ cede a territory ༡མི་ཚང་གི་བུ་གཅིག་ལོགས་དགར་དོན་སྐབས་ས་ཆ་ཁག་གཅིག་བཅད་ནས་སྐལ་བར་སྤྲད་པ་རེད་ When that household's son separated, (they) ceded a section of the land and gave it (to him) as his share.

ས་ཆ་གཉན་པོ་ (sāja ñēmbo) a place with many spirits/ minor supernaturals (གཉན་པོ་).

ས་ཆ་བརྩན་པོ་ (sāja dzēmbo) a secure or safe place/ land/ territory.

ས་ཆ་ཤོར་ (sāja shɔ̄ɔ) vi. to lose territory/ area.

ས་ཆགས་ (sājaà) 1. sm. ས་ཆགས་ཡུལ་འདྲིས་. 2. va. to live/ settle in peace ༡ལུང་པ་དེར་རྐག་པས་ས་ཆགས་འཇུག་གི་མེད་པ་རེད་ The bandits in that place did not let the people live in peace.

ས་ཆགས་ཡུལ་འདྲིས་ (sājaà yṳndriì) becoming settled/ accustomed/ familiar with a place.

ས་ཆགས་གཞིས་ཆགས་ (sājaà shi̱ijaà) settling down in a place; va.—བྱེད་.

ས་ཆའི་ཀུ་ཡུལ་ (sājɛ ku̱yüü) an open space.

ས་ཆའི་གཅོད་སྦྱོར་ (sājɛ cōōjɔɔ) taking away and adding land.

ས་ཆའི་ཆགས་རྩལ་ (sājɛ cə̄gdzüü) geography, geology.

ས་ཆའི་བདག་འཛིན་ (sājɛ də̱ŋdzin) ownership of a territory; va.—བྱེད་.

ས་ཆའི་བབས་དང་བསྟུན་ (sājɛ bə̱bdaŋ dǖn) in accordance with the situation of a place/ area.

ས་ཆའི་འཛིན་བདག (sājɛ dzi̱ndaà) landowner.

ས་ཆུ་ (səju) 1. earth and water. 2. the natural environment.

ས་ཆུ་གཉིས་འཚོ་ (səju ñīidzo) amphibian, living on land and water.

ས་ཆུ་མ་འཕྲོད་ (səju ma̱ndröö) climatically/ physically unsuitable.

ས་ཆུ་ཤོར་ (səju shɔ̄ɔ) vi. to have/ get soil erosion.

ས་ཆུ་སྲུང་འཛིན་ (səju sūŋdzin) water and soil conservation.

ས་ཆུང་དུ་རུབ་ (səjuŋŋu ru̱b) vi. to be dusk.

ས་ཆུའི་ཆགས་རྩལ་ (səjü cəgdzüü) structure/ composition of water and land.

ས་ཆེན་པོ་ (sā cēmbo) the world, the earth.

ས་ཆེམ་ཆེམ་ (sā cēmjem) one of the six types of earthquakes.

ས་ཆེའར་ (sājer) Thatcher.

ས་ཆོག (sājɔɔ̀) sanctification ritual conducted before breaking ground to build a monastery.

ས་ཆོད་ (sā cöö) vi. to be able to cover a distance traveling ༡དེ་རིང་སྔ་དྲོ་རངས་ལང་ནས་གྲུ་བཏང་ཙང་ས་ཞི་དྲག་ཆོད་སོང་ This morning, because we went by boat from dawn, we covered a great distance.

ས་ཆོད་ཆེན་པོ་ (sājöö cēmbo) covering a great distance traveling.

ས་མཆོག (sājɔɔ̀) 1. prime quality land. 2. white sandalwood.

ས་མཆོང་རྡོ་མཆོང་ (sājoŋ nāmjoŋ) sm. ས་མཆོང་གནམ་མཆོང་.

ས་མཆོང་གནམ་མཆོང་ (sājoŋ nāmjoŋ) great joy, jumping for joy/ excitement [Lit. jump on earth, jump on sky].

ས་རྗེན་པ་ (sā je̱mba) damp earth/ ground ༡ས་རྗེན་པའི་སྟེང་ལ་མ་སྡོད་ ན་གི་རེད་ Don't sit on the damp earth. You will become ill.

ས་ལྗན་ལྗིན་ (sā je̱njin) dirty soil/ ground.

ས་ཉམས་ (sāñam) vi. to become infertil (land).

ས་ཉལ་ (sāñɛɛ) sm. ཉམས་ཆོད་.

ས་ཉིལ་ཆུ་ཤོར་ (sā ñi̱i cū shɔ̄ɔ) 1. landslides and flooding. 2. soil erosion.

ས་ཉོར་ (sāñor) soft earth/ ground.

ས་གཉན་ (sāñɛn) 1. a kind of spirit/ minor diety of an area. 2. ས་ཆ་གཉན་པོ་.

ས་སྙིང་ (səñiŋ) the earth's core.

ས་སྙིང་འཐེན་ཤུགས་ (səñiŋ tēnshuù) gravity.

ས་སྣུག (səñuù) chalk.

ས་དི་ཨ་ལ་པི་ (sədi ālabe) Saudi Arabia.

ས་གཏེར་ (sāder) 1. minerals; va.—འདོན་; —སྔོག to mine/ extract minerals. 2. གཏེར་མ་ buried under the ground.

ས་གཏིང་ (sādiŋ) under the earth.

ས་རྟ་ (sāda) earth-horse year.

ས་རྟགས་ (sādaà) 1. property boundary marker. 2. trail/ road marker.

ས་རྟེན་ (sāden) 1. the world. 2. shung. the land basis for which one pays taxes ༡ས་རྟེན་པ་གཞིས་ The estate that is the basis for one's taxe obligations.

ས་རྟེན་ཆགས་འཇིག (sāden cāŋjig) shung. the creating and destroying of the land basis for paying taxes.

ས་སྟག (sādaà) earth-tiger year.

ས་སྟན་ (sādɛn) sm. ས་གདན་.

ས་སྟེང་ (sādeŋ) on the earth, on land.

ས་སྟེང་གི་ཆུ་ (sādeŋgi cū) surface water.

ས་སྟེང་གི་བདེ་བ་ཅན་ (sādeŋgi de̱wajɛn) heaven on earth.

ས་སྟེང་གི་དམྱལ་བ་ (sādeŋgi ñɛ̱ɛwa) hell on earth.

ས་སྟེང་འགྲོ་བ་ཐམས་ཅད་ (sādeŋ dro̱wa tāmjɛɛ̀) all sentient beings.

ས་སྟེང་བརྒྱུ་ལེན་ (sādeŋ du̱len) satellite receiving dish.

ས་སྟོང་ (sādoŋ) 1. waste land, vacant/ empty place; va.—སྤེལ་; —འདུལ་; —སྔོག to open up or utilize vacant land ༡ཁང་པ་རྒྱག་ས་ས་སྟོང་ A vacant area for building a house. 2. blank space; va.—འཇོག to leave a space ༡སྙན་ཞུ་འབུལ་མཁན་གྱི་མིང་རྟགས་འགོད་སའི་ས་སྟོང་ Space for the applicant to put his signature.

ས་སྟོང་ཁྲུ་སྔོག (sādoŋ trūlɔɔ̀) bringing waste/ empty land under cultivation; va.—བྱེད་.

ས་སྟོད་ (sādöö) high altitude land/ area.

ས་ཐ་ (sāda) the worst land/ field.

ས་ཐག (sādaà) distance ༡ཁྱེད་རང་སྡོད་ས་དང་ཁྲོམ་བར་ས་ཐག་ག་ཚོད་ཡོད་པ་རེད་དམ་ What is the distance between your house and the market?

ས་ཐག་ཐུང་ཐུང་ (sādaà tūŋduŋ) short distance.

ས་ཐག་རིང་ཐུང་ (sādaà ri̱ŋduŋ) the amount of distance ༡ཁྱེད་རང་སྡོད་ས་དང་ཁྲོམ་བར་ས་ཐག་རིང་ཐུང་ག་ཚོད་ཡོད་པ་རེད་དམ་ What is the distance between your house and the market?

ས་ཐག་རིང་པོ་ (sādaà ri̱ŋbo) long distance.

ས་ཐང་ (sādaŋ) sm. ཐང་.

ས་ཐབ་ (sādəb) abbr. of ས་སྨྱུ་ཐབ་ཀ་.

ས་ཐམ་ (sādam) 1. an area in Yunnan Province. 2. a type of earthen seal put on a pile of grain on the threshing ground; va.—རྒྱག.

ས་ཐམས་ (sādam) sm. ས་དོང་.

ས་ཐར་མ་ (sā tārma) an animal that is immune from anthrax.

ས་ཐལ་ (sādεε) dust.

ས་ཐིག (sədig) 1. a line of demarcation, a boundary line ¶ ས་ཐིག་སོ་བརྒྱད་ The 38th parallel (in Korea). 2. drawing/ setting out the shape or outline of a house on the ground; va.—རྒྱག.

ས་ཐེ་འཛུགས་ (sāde dzuù) sm. སར་ཏེ་འཛུགས་.

ས་ཐེར་ཐེར་ (sā tērder) flat land/ area, a plain.

ས་ཐོ་ལག་འཛིན་ (sāto ləŋdzin) shung. certificate of landholding.

ས་ཐོག (sādɔɔ) on the land/ earth, via. land, on the ground, by land ¶ ང་ཚོ་རྒྱ་གར་ལ་ས་ཐོག་ནས་ཡོང་བ་ཡིན་ We came to India by land.

ས་ཐོག་སྐྱེལ་འདྲེན་ (sādɔɔ gyēndren) transporting by land; va.—བྱེད་.

ས་ཐོག་གློག་སྐུད་ (sādɔɔ lɔɔgüü) electric wires strung on poles.

ས་ཐོག་ནས་བར་སྣང་རྒྱག་པའི་མེ་ཤུགས་འཕུར་མདའ་ (sādɔɔnε parnaŋ gyagbε meshuù pūnda) ground-to-air missile, surface-to-air missile.

ས་ཐོག་ནས་ས་ཐོག་ལ་རྒྱག་པའི་མེ་ཤུགས་འཕུར་མདའ་ (sādɔɔne sādɔɔla gyagbε meshuù pūnda) ground-to-ground missile, surface-to-surface missile.

ས་ཐོག་ཞབས་ཞུ་ (sādɔɔ shəbshu) ground service (e.g., at an airport).

ས་མཐའ་ (sāda) 1. a remote area, a distant place ¶ ས་མཐའི་ལུང་ཁག A remote village in the boondocks. ¶ མི་ཡུལ་ས་མཐའ་ Distant foreign lands. 2. the worst quality arable land. 3. the suffixed letter ས་.

ས་མཐའ་སྡེ་མཐའ (sāda deda) sm. ས་མཐའ་.

ས་མཐིལ་ (sədii) on the ground, on the floor ¶ སྤྲང་པོ་དེ་ཚོ་ས་མཐིལ་སྟེང་ལ་བསྡད་འདུག The beggars are sitting on the ground.

ས་མཐོ་ (sādo) plateau, highland.

ས་མཐོ་ས་ (sā tōsa) sm. ས་མཐོ་.

ས་མཐོངས་ (sātoŋ) a crack in the earth.

ས་མཐོའི་ཁ་སྣོན་དངུལ་ (sātö kānön ŋüü) extra salary for working at high altitude.

ས་མཐོའི་ན་ཚ་ (sātö nadza) high altitude sickness.

ས་འཐབ་གནམ་འཛིང་ (sādəb nāmdziŋ) combating nature, braving the elements [Lit. fighting against heaven and earth].

ས་འཐེན་ (sā tēn) va. to retreat/ pull back (from an area) ¶ དགྲ་བོའི་ཁ་གདང་གཅོག་མ་ཐུབ་པར་ས་འཐེན་དགོས་བྱུང་བ་རེད་ Because (they) were unable to combat their enemy, they had to retreat.

ས་དམ་ (sādam) sm. ས་ཐམ་, 2.

ས་དར་དོ་དར་ (sādar dodar) widely/ broadly spread or disseminated, very popular.

ས་དུག (sədùù) 1. humidity. 2. illness caused by dampness/ wetness.

ས་དུལ་མ་ (sā düümə) fertile land.

ས་དོ་ (sādo) load of earth/ dirt.

ས་དོང་ (sādoŋ) 1. pit/ hole in the ground; va.—རྡོག to dig a hole/ pit. 2. tunnel; va.—རྡོག to dig a tunnel.

ས་དྲག (sādraà) the suffixed letter ས་ which follows the letters ག་,ང་,བ་,མ་.

ས་དྲི་ (sədri) the smell of the earth; vi.—ཁ་ to smell the earth smell.

ས་དྲེག (sādreg) moss.

ས་དྲོད་ (sādröö) ground temperature/ warmth.

ས་གདན་ (sādεn) floor carpet.

ས་གདན་བཟོ་གྲྭ་ (sādεn sodra) carpet weaving mill.

ས་བདག (sādaà) 1. landlord, landowner. 2. king. 3. a spirit/ minor supernatural of a place/ land/ area.

ས་བདག་གྲལ་རིམ་ (sādaà treerim) landlord class.

ས་མདའ་ (sānda) animal trap set with an arrow.

ས་མདོག (sādɔɔ) khaki color, the color of earth.

ས་འདུལ་ (səndüü) 1. conducting a sanctifying/ purifying ritual before erecting a temple or house. 2. sm. ས་ཆོད་སྒྲོག.

ས་འདུས་ (səndüü) shung. the main juncture of many roads.

ས་འདྲེད་འཕྲུལ་འཁོར་ (sāndeè trüügɔɔ) bulldozer.

ས་འདོལ་ (sāndöö) soft soil.

ས་འདྲིས་ (sāndreè) sharing a boundary/ border, being contiguous ¶ རྒྱ་གར་དང་བོད་གཉིས་ས་འདྲིས་རེད་ India and Tibet share a boundary.

ས་དིབ་ (sədib) the ground sinking/ caving in; vi. ས་དིབ་; —གཏོར་ to have the ground sink/ cave in.

ས་དུལ་ (sədüü) dust.

ས་དུལ་བསགས་ན་རི་རབ་ (sədüü sāgna rirəb) many small things can make a great thing, doing little by little can produce a great result [Lit. if one accumulates dust you can make Mt. Meru].

ས་རྡོ་ (sādo) earth and rocks.

ས་རྡོག (sādog) sm. ས་རྡོག་རྡོག.

ས་རྡོག་རྡོག (sā dɔgdɔɔ) lump of earth.

ས་སྡེ་ (sāde) shung. fields/ land and communities (subjects) ¶ མངའ་བདག་དེར་ས་སྡེ་ད་ཅང་མང་པོ་ཡོད་པ་རེད་ The lord has very many fields and subject communities.

ས་སྡེ་མི་གསུམ་ (sāde misum) shung. the land, community and the people/ serfs.

ས་སྡེར་སྡེར་ (sā derder) a plain, a flat area.

ས་ནག (sānaà) "black beach" (a part of the grassland where the upper sod layer has been eroded).

ས་ནད་ (sānεè) sm. ས་སྐྱོན་.

ས་ནས་ (sānε) from, from the place of ¶ ཁོང་གི་ས་ནས་བཀའ་སློབ་ཞུས་པ་ཡིན་ (I) asked advice from him.

ས་ནི་མ་ནི་ (səni məni) small things, miscellaneous things.

ས་ནུས་ (sānüü) productivity of the land; va.—སྤེལ་ to increase land productivity.

ས་གནས་ (sānεè) region, district, locality ¶ ས་གནས་གཞུང་ Local government. ¶ ཀྲུང་དབྱང་དང་ས་གནས་ཀྱི་འབྲེལ་བ་ The relationship between the central government and the local (government).

ས་གནས་ཀྱི་བགོ་སྐལ་དབང་ཆ་ (sānεègi gogεε wāŋja) decentralized power/ authority.

ས་གནས་ཀྱི་མང་ཚོགས་ (sānεègi məŋdzoò) local masses.

ས་གནས་ཀྱི་དུས་ཚོད་ (sānεègi tüüdzöö) local time.

ས་གནས་ཁག (sānεègaà) different regions/ localities.

ས་གནས་རྒྱལ་གཉེར་ཁེ་ལས་ (sānεè gyeeñer kēlεè) locally administered state enterprises.

ས་གནས་རྒྱུན་ལས་ (sānεè gyünlεè) the local standing committee.

ས་གནས་དང་ཨུ་ (sānεè dāŋu) tib. ch. local party committee.

ས་གནས་དྲག་དཔུང་ (sānεè tragbuŋ) local army.

ས་གནས་དྲུང་ཆེ་ (sānεè truŋje) local secretary, secretary of a branch/ chapter (as opposed to the overall organization).

ས་གནས་འདེད་པ་ (sānεè deèba) shung. a person who goes to collect loans in the localities.

ས་གནས་སྡེ་སྡོད་ (sānεè nēdöö) shung. district head.

ས་གནས་དཔུང་སྡེ་ (sānεè būŋde) sm. ས་གནས་དམག་དཔུང་.

ས་གནས་མི་རིགས་རིང་ལུགས་ (sānεè mirii riŋluù) local nationalism/ chauvinism (a pejorative position that puts the local nationality's interests above that of the nation).

ས་གནས་དམག (sānεè māà) sm. ས་གནས་དམག་དཔུང་.

ས་གནས་དམག་དཔུང་ (sānεè məgbuŋ) local forces, regional troops.

ས་གནས་གཞོན་ནུ་ལྷན་ཚོགས་ (sānεè shənnu lhēndzɔɔ) regional youth congress.

ས་གནས་རང་སྐྱོང་ (sānɛɛ̀ raŋgyoŋ) regional autonomy.

ས་གནས་ལོ་རྒྱུས་ (sānɛɛ̀ lugyüü) history of a locality, regional history.

ས་གནས་ས་ཐོག (sānɛɛ̀ sādɔɔ̀) shung. on the spot, locally ༑ཁོང་ངོ་མ་ས་གནས་ས་ཐོག་ལ་རྟོག་ཞིབ་ལ་ཕེབས་སྐབས་ When he himself went for investigation on the spot.

ས་གནས་སྲིད་གཞུང་ (sānɛɛ̀ siìshuŋ) 1. local/ regional government. 2. used in China to refer to the tt. government.

ས་གནས་ཨུ་ཡོན་ལྷན་ཁང་ (sānɛɛ̀ ūyön lhjɛ̄ngaŋ) regional party committee.

ས་གནོན་ (sānön) occupying a place; va.—བྱེད་.

ས་སྣུམ་པོ་ (sā nūmbu) rich/ fertile land.

ས་སྣུམ་ (sənum) 1. kerosene. 2. oil.

ས་སྣུམ་ཐབ་ (sənum təb) kerosene stove.

ས་སྣུམ་འདོན་ས་ (sənum dönsa) oil field.

ས་སྣུམ་ཡང་རིགས་ (sənum yəŋrig) light oil.

ས་སྣེ་ (sāne) the edge/ border of a place; vi.—སླེབས་; —ཟིན་ to reach the border/ edge of a land ༑རྒྱ་གར་གྱི་ས་སྣེ་མ་སླེབས་བར་ Until you reach the edge of the territory belonging to India.

ས་སྣེ་ལམ་རྒྱུས་ (sāne ləmgyüü) sm. ལམ་རྒྱུས་.

ས་སྣོད་ (sānöö) 1. clay pot. 2. container for keeping soil/ earth.

ས་སྣོན་ (sānön) adding more soil (to a field); va.—རྒྱག.

ས་པག (sābaà) sm.* ས་ཕག, 2.

ས་པྲ་ (sā drā) to divine/ forecast by studying the earth.

ས་དཔྱད་ (sājɛɛ̀) an auspicious sign (that a place is good); va.—བརྟག to examine for auspicious signs; to survey/ investigate an area.

ས་སྤུངས་ (sābuŋ) piling up earth/ mud/ soil; va. ས་སྤུངས་; —རྒྱག.

ས་སྤྱིན་ (sājin) earth used for making pottery/ statues.

ས་སྤྱིལ་ (səjil) small mud hut.

ས་སྤྱོད་ (sājöö) shung. king, monarch ༑སྡེ་དགེ་ས་སྤྱོད་ The king of Derge.

ས་སྤྱོད་པ་ (sājööba) sm. ས་སྤྱོད་.

ས་སྤྱོད་མ་ (sājööma) shung. queen.

ས་སྤྱོད་པའི་གནས་ (sājööbɛ nɛ̄ɛ̀) palace of the queen.

ས་སྦྲུལ་ (sədrüü) earth-snake year.

ས་སྤྲེལ་ (sādree) earth-monkey year.

ས་ཕག (sābaà) 1. earth-hog year. 2. (mud) bricks; va.—རྒྱག to make bricks; —རྩིག to build sth. with bricks; —སྲེག; —བཀྲག to fire bricks.

ས་ཕུག (səbuù) cave, cavern. 2. tunnel.

ས་ཕུང་ (səbuŋ) mound/ pile earth of earth.

ས་ཕུད་ (səbüü) 1. the first sample/ offering of earth that is done before building temples, etc. 2. estates given to monasteries for the monks' subsistence.

ས་ཕོ་ (sāpo) male-earth element (in the Tibetan calendar).

ས་ཕྱིས་ (sā cii) vi. to be late ༑ང་ཚོ་དེ་ཉིན་ས་ཕྱིས་ནས་ས་གནས་དེར་ཞག་སྡོད་བྱེད་དགོས་བྱུང We were late that day and had to stay at that place overnight.

ས་ཕྱེ་རྡོ་ཕྱེ་ (sāje doje) dust from pulverized stones and earth.

ས་ཕྱོགས་ (sājɔɔ̀) 1. direction ༑ངས་འཛུགས་སྐྲུན་ལས་གྲྭའི་ས་ཕྱོགས་གང་ཡིན་ངས་ཤེས་མ་བྱུང་ I didn't know the direction of the construction site. 2. place, locality ༑ས་ཕྱོགས་མང་པོ་ནས་ཡོང་བའི་མི་ People who have come from many places.

ས་ཕྱོགས་གང་སར་ (sājɔɔ̀ kaŋsar) everywhere ༑ཁོ་ས་ཕྱོགས་གང་སར་འགྲོ་མྱོང་པ་རེད་ He has traveled everywhere.

ས་ཕྱོགས་མི་རིགས་རིང་ལུགས་ (sājɔɔ̀ mirii riŋluù) sm. ས་གནས་མི་རིགས་རིང་ལུགས་.

ས་ཕྱོགས་རིང་ལུགས་ (sājɔɔ̀ riŋluù) localism, local chauvinism.

ས་ཕྱོད་ (sājöö) sm. ས་ཚོད་.

ས་འཕུལ་འཕྲུལ་འཁོར་ (sābüü trüügɔɔ) bulldozer.

ས་འཕང་ (sābaŋ) thickness of the soil layer.

ས་འཕོས་ (sā pöö) 1. va. to move to another place. 2. va. to reach the higher level of the Bodhisattava stage.

ས་འཕྱུར་ན་རྡོ་ལྷང་ལ་ཕུད་ (sā cārna do lhāŋla büü) sm. ས་འཕྱུར་ན་རྡོ་བ་ལྷང་ལ་འབུད་.

ས་འཕྱུར་ན་རྡོ་བ་ལྷང་ལ་འབུད་ (sā cārna dowa lhāŋla büü) if one investigates thoroughly a group of suspects the culprit will surface [Lit. if you winnow the earth the stones will come out seperately].

ས་བ་ཚྭ་ཅན་ (sāwa tsājɛn) alkaline soil.

ས་བབ་ (sābəb) sm. ས་བབས་.

ས་བབས་ (sābəb) geographical features, terrain, topography ༑ང་ཚོས་མ་ཐོན་གོང་ལ་ས་བབས་ཞིབ་འཇུག་བྱེད་དགོས་རེད་ Before we leave we have to do research on the topography (of the place).

ས་བབས་ས་ཁྲ་ (sābəb sābdra) relief/ topographical map.

ས་བུག (səbuù) sm. ས་ཕུག.

ས་བོགས་ (sābɔɔ̀) 1. leasing fields/ lands; va.—གཏོང་ to lease out land; va.—ལེན་ to take land on lease. 2. the fee for leasing fields/ land; va.—རྒྱག to pay a lease fee.

ས་བོགས་ལས་ཁྲལ་ (sābɔɔ̀ lɛ̀ɛdrɛɛ) fee for leased land and the corvee labor tax.

ས་བོན་ (sābön) seeds; va.—སྣོར་; —གཤེ་; —གཏོར་ to broadcast seed; va.—གསོ་ to raise seeds/ seedlings; va.—འདེབས་ to sow seeds; va.—སྦོང་ to soak seeds. 2. sperm.

ས་བོན་སྐྲན་ (sābön drɛ̄n) tumor in the womb caused by sperm (in Tibetan medicine).

ས་བོན་ཅུའུ་ (sābön jū) tib. ch. seed bureau.

ས་བོན་དོ་དམ་ས་ཚིགས་ (sābön todam sədzii) seed management station.

ས་བོན་འདེབས་འཁོར་ (sābön debgɔɔ) seed sowing machine.

ས་བོན་སྦང་ (sābön bāŋ) sm. ས་བོན་སྦོང་.

ས་བོན་སྦོང་ (sābön bōŋ) va. to soak seeds.

ས་བོན་སྨན་བསྲེས་ (sābön mɛ̄nseè) seeds treated with insecticides.

ས་བོན་མཛོད་ཁང་ (sābön dzööganŋ) seed storehouse.

ས་བོན་འཛག (sābön dzaà) 1. vi. to have a wet dream. 2. vi. to have a discharge/ drip from the penis.

ས་བྱ་ (sāja) 1. earth-bird year. 2. field mouse.

ས་བྱི་ (sāji) earth-mouse year.

ས་བླ་ (sāla) sm. སྤྲར་སྣང་.

ས་དབང་ (sāwaŋ) shung. 1. ruler, governor, lord. 2. title for Council Ministers (བཀའ་བློན་) in tt.

ས་དབང་ཆེན་མོ་ (sāwaŋ cēmmo) 1. Council Ministers (བཀའ་བློན་) in tt. 2. term of address for Council Ministers in tt.

ས་འབར་རྡོ་འབར་ (sābar dobar) on a grand scale, magnificent, dynamic [Lit. earth burning, rocks burning].

ས་འབུ་མགོ་སེར་ (səmbu goser) cutworm.

ས་འབུམ་ (səmbum) earthen stupa where the body of a lama is placed.

ས་འབུམ་མཆོད་རྟེན་ (səmbum cööden) sm. ས་འབུམ་.

ས་འབུར་ (sāmbur) a mound.

ས་འབུས་ (sā büü) vi. to have the earth crack/ split open.

ས་འབོག (sābɔɔ̀) mounds of earth.

ས་དབྱིབས་ (səyib) topography, terrain.

ས་དབྱིབས་རིག་པ་ (səyib rigbə) the science of topography.

ས་དབྱིབས་ལས་བྱེད་པ་ (səyib lɛ̀ɛjeèba) topographer.

ས་དབྱིབས་ས་བཀྲ་ (səyib sābdra) topographical map.

ས་དབྱིབས་ས་ཁྲ་ (səyib sābdra) sm. ས་དབྱིབས་ས་བཀྲ་.

ས་འབུ་ (sāmbu) earthworm.

ས་འབུར་འབུར་ (sā bumbur) a mound, mounded earth.

ས་འབོག་འབོག (sā bɔ̱gbɔɔ̀) sm. ས་འབུར་འབུར་.

ས་འབོལ་ (sāmböö) soft earth/ soil.

ས་འབྱེད་ (sānjeè) sm. ས་འབུས་.

ས་འབྲི་ (sə̄ndri) 1. abbr. of ས་སྐྱ་ and འབྲི་གུང་. 2. vi. to sink (for earth/ ground).

ས་འབྲིང་ (sə̄driŋ) middle quality arable land.

ས་འབྲུ་ (sə̄ dru̱) vi. to dig up earth.

ས་འབྲུག (sə̄ndruù) earth-dragon year.

ས་འབྲེལ་ (sāndree) adjacent, adjoining, contiguous (having the same boundary).

ས་སྦས་ (sābɛɛ̀) burying under the ground; va.—གཏོང་ ། རོ་ཚང་མ་ས་སྦས་བཏང་སོང་ (They) buried all the corpses.

ས་སྦིར་ (sā bi̱r) vi. to shake/ tremor (earth/ ground) ། མེ་སྒྲོགས་ཀྱི་མདེའུ་ཕོག་དུས་ས་སྦིར་སོང་ When the cannon shell hit, the earth shook.

ས་སྦུག (sə̄bug) underground tunnel.

ས་སྦོལ་ (sāböö) 1. opening new fields; va.—བྱེད་. 2. wet mud that is used between stones as mortar when building walls.

ས་སྦྱང་བ་ (sā ja̱ŋma) one of the rituals included in ས་ཆོག.

ས་སྦྲུལ་ (sə̄drüü) earth-snake year.

ས་མ་འགག (sāmagaà) an animal disease.

ས་མ་རྡོ་ (sāmado) 1. mixture of earth and stone. 2. soft stone (used for carving).

ས་མ་འབྲོག (sāmadrɔɔ̀) seminomad, agropastoral (engaging in both agriculture and pastoral nomadism) ། ས་མ་འབྲོག་གི་ས་ཁུལ་ An agropastoral area.

ས་མ་རིབ་ (sāmarib) sm. ས་མ་ཧྲིབ་.

ས་མ་རུབ་གོང་ནས་བཞུ་མར་ (sā ma̱rub go̱ŋnɛ shu̱maa) doing sth. too early/ too soon [Lit. lighting a lamp before dusk].

ས་མ་ཧྲིབ་ (sāmahrib) before dusk/ darkness ། ས་མ་ཧྲིབ་གོང་ང་ཚོ་ཁ་ལག་བཟས་པ་ཡིན་ We ate just before darkness.

ས་མལ་ (sāmɛɛ) 1. a hole where the earth has been dug. 2. Chinese earthen “kang” bed.

ས་མི་ (sāmi) land and people.

ས་མི་འཁོར་ (sā mi̱ kɔ̄ɔ) shung. land, people/ serfs, and servants.

ས་མི་སེམས་མི་ (sāmi sī̱mi) sm. སེམས་སེམས་སེམས་ལ་.

ས་མིག (sə̄mii̖) 1. sm. ས་དམིགས་. 2. looking at the ground (when embarrassed); va.—བྱེད་.

ས་མིང་ (sə̄miŋ) name of places ། ས་མིང་ཐོ་བྱང་ List of place names.

ས་མིང་གཞུང་ལས་ཁང་ (sə̄miŋ shu̱ŋlɛɛ̀gaŋ) toponymy office.

ས་མིང་རིག་པ་ (sə̄miŋ ri̱gbə) toponymy.

ས་མུག (sə̄mug) ruined/ crumbling walls.

ས་མུན་ལ་ཐུག (sā mü̱nla tūù) sm. ས་རིབ་.

ས་མེ་ (sāme) a mine (the weapon), underground bomb; va.—རྒྱག ། ཁོང་ཚོས་ས་མེ་བརྒྱབ་ནས་དགྲ་བོའི་དམག་སྒར་གཏོར་འདུག They exploded an underground bomb and destroyed the enemy’s camp.

ས་མེད་མི་སེར་ (sāmeè mi̱ser) landless people/ subjects/ serfs.

ས་མོ་ (sāmo) female-earth year.

ས་མོ་ཕག (sāmo pāà) earth-female pig year.

ས་དམའ་ས་ (sā ma̱a̱sa) low lying land, low area.

ས་དམར་ (sāmar) red earth/ soil.

ས་དམིགས་ (sə̄mii̖) 1. position, job (e.g., in an office) ། དབྱིན་དགེའི་ས་དམིགས་གཉིས་འདུག There are two English teacher positions. 2. sm. ས་འགག.

ས་སྨད་ (sāmɛɛ̀) 1. low altitude area. 2. eastern part of Tibet.

ས་སྨུག (sə̄mug) maroon colored earth.

ས་སྙགས་ (sə̄ñaà) sm. འདམ་བག.

ས་སྙུག (sə̄ñuù) sm. ས་སྨུག.

ས་གཙང་རྡོ་གཙང་ (sādzaŋ do̱dzaŋ) unadulterated, pure, unmixed, clean [Lit. earth clean, stone clean].

ས་བཙན་པོ་ (sā dzɛ̄mbo) a strategically secure place/ area ། ས་བཙན་པོ་ཡིན་ཙང་དགྲ་བོས་ལས་སླ་པོར་གཏོར་ཐུབ་མེད་པ་རེད་ Because the place was located in a strategically secure place, the enemy was unable to easily destroy it.

ས་བཙོག (sādzɔg) sm. ས་སྙིན་.

ས་རྩ་ཆུ་རིས་ (sə̄dza cūrii̖) ownership/ authority over land, pasture and irrigation.

ས་རྫི་ (sə̄dzi) liquid made from mixing water and earth.

ས་རྩོད་ (sādzöö̖) disputes over land.

ས་ཚི་ཅན་ (stsī̱jɛn) soil with high clay/ adhesive content.

ས་ཚན་ (sādzɛn) thickness of the soil layer.

ས་ཚིགས་ (sə̄dzii̖) shung. a station/ stage in the corvee transportation system in tt.

ས་ཚིགས་ཀྱི་ཁྲལ་ (sə̄dzii̖) shung. corvee tax requiring taxpayer peasants to provide animals to transport goods from one stage on a transport network to the next.

ས་ཚིགས་ཀྱི་སྒྲུབ་ཆ་ (sə̄dzii̖gi dru̱bja) shung. sm. ས་ཚིགས་ཀྱི་ཁྲལ་.

ས་ཚིགས་ཀྱི་མི་ཧྲེང་ (sə̄dzii̖gi mi̱hreŋ) shung. a corvee person accompanying corvee transport animals from one stage to the next.

ས་ཚིགས་སྒྲུབ་རྟེན་ (sə̄dzii̖ dru̱bden) shung. land basis for having to perform the corvee transportation tax.

ས་ཚིགས་རྟ་ཁལ་མི་གསུམ་ (sə̄dzii̖ dākhɛɛ mi̱sum) shung. corvee transport tax consisting of horses, carrying animals and people.

ས་ཚིགས་དོད་ (sə̄dzii̖ tö̱ö̖) shung. money paid as a substitute for performing the corvee transportation tax.

ས་ཚུགས་ (sə̄dzuù) sm. ས་ཚིགས་.

ས་ཚུབ་འཁྱུར་རེ་བ་ (sə̄dzunb kyūrrewa) dusty (all over) ། དཔྱིད་ཀ་དྲོ་རླུང་རྒྱག་དུས་གང་སར་ས་ཚུབ་འཕྱུར་རེ་བར་འདུག The warm wind that blows in the spring makes everything dusty.

ས་ཚུར་ (sə̄dzur) sm. ས་མཚུར་.

ས་ཚོས་ (sādzöö̖) paint made from earth.

ས་མཚམས་ (sāndzam) border, boundary line ། ཁོ་ཚོས་ས་མཚམས་ཀྱི་རྡོ་གཙུགས་པ་རེད་ They placed stones to mark the boundary.

ས་མཚམས་ཀྱི་རྡོ་རིང་ (sāndzamgi do̱riŋ) shung. stone pillar marking a border/ boundary.

ས་མཚམས་བརྒལ་ (sāndzam gɛ̱ɛ̱) va. to cross a border.

ས་མཚམས་གཅོད་ (sāndzam jȫö̖) va. to demarcate the border.

ས་མཚམས་ཐོ་རྡོ་ (sāndzam tōdo) piles of stones demarcating a border or boundary.

ས་མཚམས་རྡོ་རིང་ (sāndzam do̱riŋ) stone pillar marking a border/ boundary.

ས་མཚམས་གནད་ཆེ་བ་ (sāndzam nɛ̄ɛ̀ cēwa) important/ strategic border area.

ས་མཚམས་འབྱེད་ (sāndzam je̱è) va. to determine/ delimit a boundary.

ས་མཚམས་འབྲེལ་ (sāndzam dre̱e̱) vi. to share a border.

ས་མཚམས་མེད་པའི་སྨན་པ་ (sāndzam me̱èbɛ mɛ̄mba) Doctors Without Borders.

ས་མཚམས་ཡིག་ཆས་རྒྱས་དཔྱད་ (sāndzam yi̱gjɛɛ̀ gyɛ̱ɛ̀jɛɛ̀) shung. a border/ boundary that is demarcated by documents.

ས་མཚུར་ (sə̄dzur) kind of yellow dye.

ས་འཚག (sādzaà) sifter for screening soil; va.—རྒྱག.

ས་མཚུར་ (sə̄dzur) soil used in making dyes.

ས་མཚོ་ (sādzo) land and sea.

ས་མཚོ་གནམ་ (sā tsō nām) land, sea and sky.

ས་མཚོ་གནམ་གསུམ་གྱི་དམག་དཔུང་ (sādzo nāmsumgi mə̄gbuŋ) the three: army, navy and air force.

ས་འཛད་མ་ (sā dzɛ̱ɛ̀ma) a derogatory term for a woman.

ས་འཛིན་ (sā dzi̱n) shung. 1. va. to seize/ capture

and occupy a territory ། ལུང་པ་དེའི་ས་འཛིན་པར་དམག་དཔུང་བཏང་བ་རེད་ They sent soldiers to capture the area. 2. banishment to a distant area (in this banishment the person is given land to farm); va.—གཏོང་ ། ཇག་པ་དེ་ས་འཛིན་དུ་བཏང་བ་རེད་ The court banished the bandit.

ས་འཛིན་གྱི་ཕྲེང་བ་ (sə̄ndzingi trēŋwa) poet. mountain.

ས་འཛིན་བདག་པོ་ (sə̄ndzin dagbo) 1. emperor. 2. landlord.

ས་འཛུལ་གནམ་འཛུལ་ (sə̄ndzüü nāmdzüü) trying to hide everywhere; va.—བྱེད་ [Lit. entering the earth, entering the sky].

ས་རྫོང་ (sādzoŋ) 1. shung. abbr. of ས་ཆགས་ and རྫོང་སྐྱིལ་. 2. shung. a district.

ས་ཞག (sāshaà) smooth/ slippery ground, muddy surface.

ས་ཞན་ (sāshɛn) poor quality earth/ fields.

ས་ཞན་འཁོས་དམན་ (sāshɛn kōōmɛn) poor quality land and a low standard of living.

ས་ཞན་མི་དབུལ་ (sāshɛn mi ǖü) land of poor quality and poor people.

ས་ཞན་ལུང་སྟོང་ (sāshɛn luŋdoŋ) a deserted area with land of poor quality.

ས་ཞིང་ (sə̄shiŋ) arable field, cultivated farmland ། མི་ཚང་འདི་ལ་ས་ཞིང་མི་འདུག That household has no arable land.

ས་ཞིང་ཁྱོད་སྙོམས་ (sə̄shiŋ kōōñom) evening/ equalizing arable land; va.—བྱེད་.

ས་ཞིང་བགོ་བཤའ་ (sə̄shiŋ goshaà) division of land/ fields; va.—རྒྱག.

ས་ཞིང་སྒེར་ཡོད་ལམ་ལུགས་ (sə̄shiŋ geryöö lə̄mluù) system of private ownership of land.

ས་ཞིང་བཅོས་བསྒྱུར་ (sə̄shiŋ jöögyur) land reform; va.—བྱེད་; —གཏོང་.

ས་ཞིང་ཆུ་བེད་ (sə̄shiŋ cūde) sm. ཞིང་ཁའི་ཆུ་བེད་.

ས་ཞིང་ཆུ་བེད་ས་ཚིགས་ (sə̄shiŋ cūbe sə̄dzii) irrigation and water conservancy station.

ས་ཞིང་སྙོམ་བགོ་ (sə̄shiŋ ñōmgo) equal distribution/ division of land.

ས་ཞིང་སྤྱི་ཡོད་ལམ་ལུགས་ (sə̄shiŋ jīyöö lə̄mluù) system of public ownership of land.

ས་ཞིང་གཏིང་སློག (sə̄shiŋ dīŋlɔɔ̀) va. to plow (turnover) the earth deeply.

ས་ཞིང་ཐ་རྐོད་ (sə̄shiŋ tāgöö) poor quality soil.

ས་ཞིང་དོ་དམ་ས་ཚིགས་ (sə̄shiŋ todam sə̄dzii) farmland management station.

ས་ཞིང་འདུ་ཆེ་ (sə̄shiŋ duce) shung. a place where many fields join together.

ས་ཞིང་དབང་ལུགས་ (sə̄shiŋ wāŋluù) system of land ownership.

ས་ཞིང་བཙོང་འཛིན་ (sə̄shiŋ dzōŋdzin) title/ deed for land that has been sold.

ས་ཞིང་ཞན་པ་ (sə̄shiŋ shemba) poor quality land.

ས་ཞིང་གཤིན་པོ་ (sə̄shiŋ shīmbu) fertile land.

ས་ཞིང་གསར་བརྗེ་ (sə̄shiŋ sārje) agrarian revolution; va.—བྱེད་.

ས་ཞིབ་ (sə̄shib)1. shung. land survey; va.—བྱེད་ to make a land survey. 2. earth that has been broken into small pieces; va.—བཟོ་.

ས་ཞིབ་ཞིབ་ (sā shibshii) sm. ས་ཞིབ་.

ས་ཞོམ་ (sāshom) sm. ས་རྡིབ་.

ས་གཞི་ (sə̄shi) 1. earth, the world ། སྲིད་འཛིན་གསར་པ་དེས་ས་གཞི་འདིའི་ཐོག་ཞི་བདེ་ཡོང་བ་བྱ་རྒྱུ་ཡིན་ཞེས་བཤད་པ་རེད་ The new president said that he will bring peace to the world. 2. land, soil ། ས་གཞི་བཟང་པོ་ Good fertile land.

ས་གཞི་ཆེན་པོ་ (sə̄shi cēmbo) the earth, the world.

ས་གཞི་དྲུལ་དག (sə̄shi düüdaà) sm. ནམ་མཁའི་གཡའ་དག.

ས་གཞི་རིལ་མོ་ (sə̄shi riibu) sm. ས་གཞི་ཆེན་པོ་.

ས་གཞི་རིལ་མོའི་འཐེན་ཤུགས་ (sə̄shi riimü tēnshuù) earth's gravity.

ས་གཞིའི་ཁབ་ལེན་སྣེ་མོ་ (sə̄shii kēblen nēmo) sm. སའི་ཁབ་ལེན་སྣེ་མོ་.

ས་གཞིའི་ཁབ་ལེན་ར་བ་ (sə̄shi kēblen rawa) sm. སའི་ཁབ་ལེན་ར་བ་.

ས་གཞིའི་ངོས་ (sə̄shii ŋöö) horizon.

ས་གཞིའི་མདངས་ (sə̄shii daŋ) painting of a grassy scene at the bottom of thankas.

ས་གཞིའི་ལྡོག་ཤུགས་ (sə̄shii dogshuù) crustal stress.

ས་གཞིའི་སྨུ་མཐའ་ (sə̄shii muda) sm. ས་ངོས་སྙོམས་ཐིག.

ས་གཞིས་ (sə̄shii) 1. sm. གཞིས་ཀ་. 2. land and house.

ས་གཞུང་ (sāshuŋ) 1. shung. the Sakya government. 2. local government.

ས་གཞོང་ (sāshoŋ) 1. basin (in geography). 2. rectangular wooden container with sand in which astrological calculations are done.

ས་གཞོན་ (sāshön) abbr. of ས་གནས་གཞོན་ནུ་ལྷན་ཚོགས་.

ས་གཞོམ་ (sāshom) sm. ས་ཞོམ་.

ས་བཞུ་ (sə̄shu) kerosene pressure lamp, Coleman lamp.

ས་བཞུའི་སྤྲོང་རས་ (sə̄shü doŋrɛɛ̀) kerosene pressure lamp's mantle.

ས་ཟད་རྡོ་ཐུག (sāsɛɛ̀ doduù) at the end of one's rope, without the means/ methods of overcoming sth., a desperate situation ། ས་ཟད་རྡོ་ཐུག་གིས་མཚམས་སུ་མ་སླེབས་བར་ཁོང་ཚོས་མགོ་བཏགས་ཞུས་མི་འདུག They did not surrender until they were completely desperate. [Lit. soil worn out, reach rock].

ས་ཟད་རྡོ་གདུགས་ (sāsɛɛ̀ doduù) sm. ས་ཟད་རྡོ་ཐུག.

ས་ཟླ་ (sānda) abbr. of ས་ག་ཟླ་བ་.

ས་ཟླའི་བཅོ་ལྔ་ (sāndɛ jōŋa) the 15th day of the 4th month.

ས་བཟང་ (sāsaŋ) fertile ground/ land.

ས་འོག (sāwɔɔ̀) underground ། ས་འོག་གི་ཆུའི་གནས་ཚད་ Underground water level.

ས་འོག་ཁང་པ་ (sāwɔɔ̀ kāŋba) sm. ས་འོག་གི་ཁང་པ་.

ས་འོག་གི་ཁང་པ་ (sāwɔɔ̀gi kāŋba) basement, cellar.

ས་འོག་གི་ལྕགས་ལམ་ (sāwɔɔ̀gi jāglam) underground railway/ subway.

ས་འོག་གི་ཆུ་ (sāwɔɔ̀gi cū) subsoil/ subsurface water.

ས་འོག་གི་ཆུ་ལམ་ (sāwɔɔ̀gi cūlam) underground sewer/ drain/ water passage.

ས་འོག་གློག་ཐག (sāwɔɔ̀ lōgdaà) underground electric wires.

ས་འོག་གློག་སྐུད་ (sāwɔɔ̀ gōggüü) sm. ས་འོག་གློག་ཐག.

ས་འོག་རྒྱུག་ཆུ་ (sāwɔɔ̀ gyugju) underground river/ stream.

ས་འོག་བགྲོད་ལམ་ (sāwɔɔ̀ dröölam) underground tunnel.

ས་འོག་སྐུགས་ལམ་ (sāwɔɔ̀ jāglam) subway.

ས་འོག་ཆུ་ (sāwɔɔ̀ cū) sm. ས་འོག་གི་ཆུ་.

ས་འོག་ཆུ་འགྲོ་ (sāwɔɔ̀ cūndro) sm. ས་འོག་གི་ཆུ་ལམ་.

ས་འོག་ཉིང་རྡུལ་འབར་གས་ (sāwɔɔ̀ ñiŋdüü bargɛɛ) underground nuclear explosion; va.—བྱེད་.

ས་འོག་ཉིང་རྡུལ་མཚོན་ཆ་ཚོད་ལྟ་ (sāwɔɔ̀ ñiŋdüü tsõnja tsööda) underground nuclear weapons test; va.—བྱེད་.

ས་འོག་དར་འཐག (sāwɔɔ̀ tardaà) using secret/ deceptive/ hidden means for evil; va.—བྱེད་ [Lit. to weave silk underground].

ས་འོག་འདམ་ལང་ (sāwɔɔ̀ damlaŋ) bringing sth. bad/ evil to light; va.—བྱེད་ [Lit. a marsh rising from underground].

ས་འོག་རྡོ་ཞུན་ (sāwɔɔ̀ doshün) underground magma.

ས་འོག་སྡེ་ (sāwɔɔ̀ de) 1. city of the nagas. 2. underground community.

ས་འོག་སྡོང་པོ་ (sāwɔɔ̀ doŋbo) trunk/ stem that is underground.

ས་འོག་ནས་ཐོན་པའི་རིག་རྫས་ (sāwɔɔ̀nɛ tõmbɛ rigdzɛɛ̀) excavated/ unearthed relics.

ས་འོག་ནས་འདོན་ (sāwɔɔ̀nɛ dön) va. to unearth/ excavate from underground.

ས་འོག་འབར་མདེལ་ (sāwɔɔ̀ bandee) land mine, underground explosive ། ས་འོག་འབར་མདེལ་དམག་འཐབ་ Mine warfare.

ས་འོག་སྦུ་གུ་ (sāwɔɔ̀ bugu) underground piping.

ས་འོག་དམག་འཁྲུག (sāwɔɔ̀ mə̄gdruù) tunnel warfare.

ས་འོག་བཙོན་ཁང་ (sāwɔɔ̀ dzõŋgaŋ) dungeon.

ས་འོག་ཚ་ནུས་ (sāwɔɔ̀ tsānüü) geothermal energy.

ས་འོག་ཚ་ནུས་གྲོན་པ་ (sāwɔɔ̀ tsānüü trōnba) geothermal well.

ས་འོག་ཚ་ནུས་གློག་འདོན་ (sāwɔɔ̀ tsānüü lōgdün) geothermal power.

ས་འོག་ཚ་ནུས་ཡོད་ས་ (sāwɔɔ̀ tsānüü yö̱ösa) geothermal field.

ས་འོག་ཚ་ནུས་རིག་པ་ (sāwɔɔ̀ tsānüü ri̱gbə) geothermics.

ས་འོག་ཚ་ནུས་འབྱུང་ཁུངས་ (sāwɔɔ̀ tsānüü ju̱ŋguŋ) geothermal energy resources.

ས་འོག་ཚོགས་པ་ (sāwɔɔ̀ tsōgba) an underground organization/ cell/ party.

ས་འོབས་ (sāob) trench, ditch, tunnel.

ས་འོབས་ཁ་སྒྲོད་ (sāob kābdröö) an approach tunnel (military tactic).

ས་འོབས་འདུ་བྱེད་འཕྲུལ་འཁོར་ (sāob dru̱jeè trǖügɔɔ) trench digging machine.

ས་ཡ་ (sāya) million ¶ སྒོར་ས་ཡ་བརྒྱ་ཐམ་པ་ One hundred million dollars.

ས་ཡངས་ (sāyaŋ) broad/ open country.

ས་ཡི་ལྷ་ (sāyi lhā) an earth god/ deity.

ས་ཡིག (səyiì) signature; va.—རྒྱག; —འགོད་ to sign one's signature.

ས་ཡུལ་ (səyüü) 1. place, area, country. 2. room, space ¶ མི་མང་པོ་གཤོང་སའི་ས་ཡུལ་མེད་ There is no room for many people.

ས་ཡུལ་གྱི་གཞིས་ཁ་པ་ (səyüügi shi̱igəbə) shung. owner of an estate.

ས་ཡོམ་ (sāyom) earthquake; vi.—རྒྱག to have an earthquake.

ས་ཡོམ་གྱི་སྔོན་བརྡ་ (sāyomgi dö̱öda) earthquake prediction/ forecasting.

ས་ཡོམ་གྱི་ལན་ (sāyomgi le̱n) aftershock of an earthquake.

ས་ཡོམ་ཡོམ་ (sā yo̱myom) trembling/ shaking/ vibrating of the ground or earth.

ས་ཡོམ་བརྟག་དཔྱད་ཁང་ (sāyom dāgjeèɡaŋ) seismograph (or seismic) station.

ས་ཡོམ་རླབས་ཕྲེང་ (sāyom lābdreŋ) seismic wave.

ས་ཡོམ་ས་རྒྱུད་ (sāyom sāgyüü) seismic belt, area of seismic activity.

ས་ཡོས་ (sāyöö) earth-hare year.

ས་གཡང་ (sāyaŋ) sm. ས་བཅུད་.

ས་གཡང་བུམ་པ་ (sāyaŋ pu̱mbə) shung. sm. ས་བཅུད་བུམ་པ་.

ས་གཡོ་ (sā yō) 1. vi. to have an earthquake. 2. va. to secretly plot/ connive/ stir up discord ¶ ད་ལྟ་མི་དེས་ཁ་མཁས་པོ་ཤོད་ཀྱི་འདུག་ཀྱང་རྗེས་སུ་ས་གཡོ་སྒྱིད་ཀྱི་རེད་ Although that person talks nicely now, it is possible that he will plot against you later.

ས་གཡོ་རི་འགུལ་ (sāyo ri̱güü) earthshaking, colossal.

ས་གཡོའི་གདོར་ཚད་ (sāyö dōrdzɛɛ̀) earthquake intensity.

ས་གཡོའི་རིམ་པ་ (sāyö ri̱mbə) magnitude of an earthquake (on the Richter scale).

ས་གཡོས་ (sāyöö) p. of ས་གཡོ་.

ས་གཡོས་པ་ (sā yö̱öba) plotter, conniver, one who stirs up discord.

ས་རགས་ (sāraà) earthen dam/ dike.

ས་རང་རོང་ (sā ra̱ŋroŋ) uneven ground.

ས་རབ་ (sā rə̱b) the best quality arable land.

ས་རི་ཆད་དུམ་ (səri cɛ̀ɛ̀dum) geologic fault.

ས་རིག (sərig) geography.

ས་རིགས་ (sərig) 1. shung. estates given to lay aristocratic officials in tt. government. 2. agricultural land.

ས་རིགས་རྒྱུ་དངོས་ (sərig gyu̱ŋöö) shung. land and property.

ས་རིགས་བདག་ཐོབ་ (sərig da̱gdob) shung. shung. ownership of a landed estate.

ས་རིགས་དེའུ་ངོས་འཛིན་ (sərig di̱wu ŋ̱öndzin) shung. making a clear demarcation of land with stone markers.

ས་རིན་ (sərin) land price.

ས་རིབ་ (sərib) sm.* ས་རུབ་.

ས་རིབ་མ་རིབ་ (sərib ma̱rib) just about dusk.

ས་རིམ་ (sərim) 1. grade of land/ soil. 2. thickness of soil ¶ ས་རིམ་སྲབ་མོ་ Thin layer of soil. 3. the stages/ posts/ stations of the corvee transportation system in tt.; va.—སྐྱེལ་ to transport loads from one corvee station to another.

ས་རིམ་བར་མ་ (sərim pa̱rma) (the earth's) mantle.

ས་རིས་ (səriì) doing astrological calculations made on a ས་གཞོང་; va.—རྒྱག. 2. drawings on ground. 3. sm. ས་ཁྲ་. 4. sm. ས་རིགས་, 1.

ས་རིས་ཐང་གསལ་ (səriì tāŋsɛl) clear for all to see ¶ ཁོང་གིས་བྱས་པའི་ལས་ཀ་རྣམས་ས་རིས་ཐང་གསལ་རེད་ The work that he did is clear for all to see [Lit. drawings clear on the ground].

ས་རུད་ (sā rü̱ü) landslide, mud slide; vi.—རྒྱག to have a landslide/ mud slide.

ས་རུབ་ (sā ru̱b) vi. to become night, to become dark ¶ ས་རུབ་ནས་ཕྱི་ལ་འགྲོ་གི་མེད་ (We) don't go out after dark.

ས་རུས་ (sərüü) sm. ས་གཞིས་.

ས་རེ་སོ་རེ་ (sāre sōre) sound of labored breathing made by a sick person.

ས་རེག (sāreg) 1. wealthy, rich. 2. va. to touch the earth.

ས་རེངས་ (sāreŋ) 1. hard ground/ soil. 2. name of a Hindu god.

ས་རོ་ (sāro) leftover earth.

ས་རོ་རྡོ་རོ་ (sāro do̱ro) 1. ruins [Lit. stone rubble, earth rubble]. 2. small peices of stone and earth.

ས་རོང་ (sāroŋ) rough road.

ས་རླངས་ (sālaŋ) moisture, humidity, dampness.

ས་ལ་ (sāla) 1. on the ground ¶ དེ་ས་ལ་ཟགས་པ་རེད་ That fell on the ground. 2. place/ presence (of sb.) ¶ ཁོང་གི་ས་ལ་ཕྱིན་སོང་ (They) went to his presence. ¶ ངའི་ས་ལ་ཤོག Come to me.

ས་ལ་སྦད་ (sāla bɛ̱ɛ̀) sm. ས་ལ་སྦེད་.

ས་ལ་སྦེད་ (sāla be̱è) va. to bury under the earth/ ground.

ས་ལམ་ (sālam) 1.a road, a way. 2. hind. (a salute) salaam; va.— ཞུ་.

ས་ལས་ (sālɛɛ̀) 1. working with earth, soil; va.— བྱེད་. 2. from the earth.

ས་ལས་རྡོ་ལས་ (sālɛɛ̀ do̱lɛɛ̀) building/ construction work.

ས་ལུག (səluù) earth-sheep year.

ས་ལུགས་ (səluù) the Sakya tradition.

ས་ལུད་ (səlüü) silt/ earth used as fertilizer.

ས་ལེ་བ་ (sālewa) sm. གསལ་ལེ་བ་.

ས་ལེ་སྦྲམ་ (sāledram) highest quality.

ས་ལོག་ཐེབས་ (sālɔɔ̀ tēb) sm. ཡུལ་ལོག་རྒྱག.

ས་ཤིང་ལས་གྲྭ་ (səshiŋ le̱èdra) an engineering/ construction site.

ས་ཤིང་བཟོ་སྐྲུན་ (səshiŋ so̱drün) civil engineering.

ས་ཤིང་བཟོ་སྐྲུན་སློབ་ཚོགས་ (səshiŋ so̱drün lōbdzɔɔ̀) society of civil engineering.

ས་ཤུན་ (səshün) earth's crust.

ས་ཤུར་ (səshur) trench, ditch, canal.

ས་ཤོར་ (sā shɔ̄ɔ) vi. to lose (control over) a territory ¶ ཆབ་མདོ་ས་ཤོར་སོང་བས་ Because they lost Chamdo.

ས་གཤིན་ (səshin) sm. ས་གཤིན་པོ་.

ས་གཤིན་པོ་ (sā shi̱mbu) fertile/ rich soil.

ས་གཤིས་ (səshiì) geology ¶ ས་གཤིས་རིག་པ་མཁས་པ་ Geological specialist.

ས་གཤིས་ཀྱི་གནས་རྩལ་ (səshiìgi nɛ̱ɛ̀dzüü) geological features/ structure.

ས་གཤིས་ཀྱི་འཕོ་ཤུགས་རིག་པ་ (səshiìgi pōshuù ri̱gbə) geomechanics.

ས་གཤིས་ཁྱབ་བཤེར་རུ་ཁག (səshiì kyābsher ru̱gaà) geology survey team.

ས་གཤིས་ཅུའུ་ (səshiìgi cū) tib. ch. bureau of geology.

ས་གཞིའི་ཆགས་ཚུལ་ (sāshiì cəgdzüü) geological structure.

ས་གཞིའི་ཆགས་ལོ་ (sāshiì cāglo) geological time.

ས་གཞིའི་ཆགས་ལོའི་རིག་པ་ (sāshiìgi cāglö rigbə) geochronology.

ས་གཞིའི་ཆུ་དཔྱད་རུ་ཁག (sāshiìgi cūjɛ̀ɛ rugaà) geological and hydrological survey team.

ས་གཞིའི་གཏེར་ཐོན་ཁྲུའུ་ (sāshiì dērdön trū) tib. ch. geology and mineral resources office.

ས་གཞིའི་བརྟག་ཞིབ་ལས་ཁུངས་ (sāshiì dəgsib lɛ̀ɛguŋ) geological survey office.

ས་གཞིའི་ཐིག་ལེན་ (sāshiì tīglen) geological survey.

ས་གཞིའི་དཔེ་རིས་ (sāshiì bērii) geologic map.

ས་གཞིའི་དཔྱད་ཆས་ (sāshiì jɛ̀ɛjɛɛ̀) geological instruments.

ས་གཞིའི་དཔྱད་གཞི་ཡིག་རིགས་ཁང་ (sāshiì jɛ̀ɛshi yigriìgaŋ) geological data office.

ས་གཞིའི་རྩད་གཅོད་རུ་ཁག (sāshiì dzɛ̀ɛjöö rugaà) geological survey team.

ས་གཞིའི་རྩད་ཞིབ་ (sāshiì dzɛ̀ɛshib) geological survey.

ས་གཞིའི་ཞན་པ་ (sāshiì shembə) sm. ས་རྒྱུ་ཞན་པ་.

ས་གཞིའི་ཡུལ་བབ་ (sāshiì yüübəb) sm. ས་བབ་.

ས་གཞིའི་རིག་པ་ (sāshiì rugbə) geology.

ས་གཞིའི་ལེགས་བཅོས་ས་ཚིགས་ (sāshiì legjöö sādzii) soil/ land improvement station.

ས་གཞིའི་སློབ་གྲྭ་ (sāshiì lōbdra) geological institute/ school.

ས་གཞིའི་སློབ་ཚོགས་ (sāshiì lōbdzoò) geological society.

ས་གཤོང་ (sāshoŋ) basin (geological).

ས་བཤངས་ (sāshaŋ) digging/ cleaning out old dirt or rubbish from a drain or canal; va.—རྒྱག ¶ ཡུར་བུ་འགགས་འདུག་པས་ས་བཤངས་རྒྱག་དགོས་ Because the drain is blocked, we must clean it out.

ས་བཤད་རྡོ་བཤད་ (sāshɛɛ̀ doshɛɛ̀) useless/ idle/ senseless/ gibberish talk; va.—ཤོད་.

ས་བཤིག་གི་ཨ་བྲ་ སྡེ་བཤིག་གི་ཇག་པ་ (shiìgi ābra deshiìgi cagba) things or people who cause destruction/ trouble [Lit. the pika who destroys the earth, the bandits who destroy a community].

ས་བཤེར་གློག་སྒྲོན་ (sāsher lōgdrön) searchlight.

ས་ས་མལ་མལ་ (sāsa mɛɛmɛɛ) shung. in one's own place.

ས་སེལ་རྡོ་སེལ་ (sāsee dosee) cleaning up rubble and earth after constuction is over.

ས་སོབ་སོབ་ (sā sōbsoò) soft/ loose earth.

ས་སྲིན་ད་ལ་ (sāsin dāla) centipede.

ས་སྲིབ་ (sāsib) sm. ས་རུབ་.

ས་སྲུང་ (sāsruŋ) 1. border defense, border police/ garrison; va.— བྱེད་ to defend the border. 2. those who guard/ defend the border.

ས་སྲུང་བ་ (sāsuŋwə) border policeman/ guards.

ས་སྲུང་དམག་མི་ (sāsuŋ māəmi) border defense troops.

ས་སྲུང་རི་འགོག (sāsuŋ rigɔɔ̀) defend the country and oppose the Japanese (political slogan).

ས་སྲུང་སོ་ལྟ་ (sāsuŋ sōda) guard/ sentry on duty.

ས་སྲུབ་ (sāsub) crack/ crevasse in the earth or ground.

ས་སྲུབ་སྦྲུལ་ཞུགས་ (sāsub drüüshuù) an evil person searching for opportunities to cause harm [Lit. snakes crawling into cracks in the ground].

ས་སྲོད་ (sāsöö) time from nightfall to midnight ¶ ས་སྲོད་ཀྱི་མཚམས་སུ་ཁྱིམ་ནས་ཐོན་ (He) left his house at night.

ས་སྲོད་རབ་རིབ་ (sāsöö rəbrib) getting dusky/ dark.

ས་སྲོས་ (sāsöö) sm. ས་སྲོད་.

ས་སློག (sālɔɔ̀) reclaiming/ opening (land for cultivation); va.—རྒྱག to reclaim land for cultivation, to bring unused land for cultivation.

ས་སློག་རྡོ་སློག (sālɔɔ̀ dolɔɔ̀) sm. ས་ཀོ་རྡོ་སློག.

ས་གསང་རྡོ་གསང་ (sāsaŋ dosaŋ) extremely secret [Lit. earth secret, rocks secret].

ས་གསུམ་ (sāsum) the three divisions of the universe: space, the ground and the underground.

ས་གསོག་ཀོ་མོག (sāsɔɔ̀ gōmɔɔ̀) shung. a hollow in which earth has accumulated.

ས་ཧ་ལིང་ (sāhalin) Sakhalin (Island).

ས་ཧེབ་ (sāheb) hind. sahib (term of respectful address).

ས་ཧྲུག་རྡོ་ཧྲུག (sāhruù dohruù) sm. ས་རོ་རྡོ་རོ་.

ས་ཧྲུལ་རྡོ་ཧྲུལ་ (sāhrüü dohrüü) sm. ས་རོ་རྡོ་རོ་.

ས་ལྷ་ (sālha) 1. shung. abbr. of ས་སྐྱ་ and ལྷ་རྒྱ་རི་. 2. local earth god in an area.

ས་ལྷག་མི་ཆད་ (sālhaà mijɛɛ̀) small populace living in a large area, an underdeveloped area.

སཱ་ལུ་ (sālu) ch. tangerine.

སག (sāà) 1. sm.* གསིག. 2. doing sth. suddenly (without other's knowing) ¶ ཁོས་ཚོགས་འདུའི་ས་ནས་སག་སྒྲི་ཕྱིན་བཞག He left the meeting suddenly.

སག་ངོས་ (sāgŋöö) a slanted/ inclined plane.

སག་གཅོད་ (sāgjöö) sm.* གསིག་གཅོད་.

སག་ཉལ་རྒྱག (sāgñɛɛ gyaà) sm. གསག་ཉལ་རྒྱག.

སག་སྙིས་ (sāgñeè) sm.* གསིག་སྙིས་.

སག་སྡེ་ཁ་ལ་ (sāgde kāla) see སག, 2.

སག་ཐག (sāgdaà) quiver for arrows.

སག་མཐིལ་མ་ (sāgdiimə) shung. a type of woolen Tibetan boot.

སག་ཐེབས་ (sāgdeb) sm. བསེ་ཐེབས་.

སག་དར་ (sāgdar) sm. གསིག་དར་.

སག་བདར་ (sāgdar) sm. སག་དར་.

སག་རྫུན་ (sāgdzün) fake སག་རི་.

སག་རམ་རྩི་ (sāà ramdzi) gold-colored paper.

སག་རི་ (sāgri) a blue leather from India. 2. caked up dirt on the hands; va.—འཁོར་; —ཆགས་ to get caked up dirt accumulating on one's hands/ feet.

སག་ལམ་ (sāglam) sm. གསིག་ལམ་.

སག་ས་ (sāgsa) dried intestines cut into pieces.

སག་སག (sāgsaà) 1. loosely woven cloth. 2. sm. སག་ས་.

སག་སིག (sāgsii) sound of a bell tinkling.

སག་ལྷམ་ (sāglham) shoes/ boots made partly with སག་རི་ leather.

སང་ (sāŋ) 1. tomorrow ¶ སང་འགྲོ་དགོས་ཡོད་ (I) have to go tomorrow. 2. drapes or curtains made from very fine linen. 3. sm.* སངས་.

སང་གྷ་ (sāŋgha) sangha (the order of monks).

སང་དགོང་ (sāŋgoŋ) tomorrow night.

སང་འགྱངས་གནངས་འགྱངས་ (sāgyaŋ nāŋgyaŋ) procrastinating [Lit. delay tomorrow, delay the day after tomorrow].

སང་འགྲོ་གནངས་འགྲོ་ (sāŋdro nāŋdro) leaving soon, about to leave ¶ འགྲུལ་པ་དེ་ཚོ་སང་འགྲོ་གནང་འགྲོ་རེད་བཞག The travelers are about to leave. [Lit. go tomorrow, go the day after tomorrow].

སང་ངེ་ (sāŋŋe) 1. bright, light (for a room). 2. clearing/ curing an illness ¶ གློ་སྨན་དེ་བཏང་ནས་ངའི་གློ་དེ་སང་ངེར་ཕྱིན་སོང་ I took cough medicine and my cough cleared up.

སང་ངེ་སེང་ངེ་ (sāŋŋe sēŋŋe) cracks in a wall that one can see through.

སང་ཉིན་ (sāñin) tomorrow, the next day.

སང་ཉིན་གནངས་ཉིན་ (səŋñin nəŋñin) tomorrow and/ or the day after tomorrow ¶ ཁོང་སང་ཉིན་གནངས་ཉིན་ཞིག་ཕེབས་ཀྱི་རེད་ He will come tomorrow or the day after.

སང་ནངས་པ་ (sāŋ naŋba) tomorrow morning.

སང་ནུབ་ (sāŋnub) sm. སང་དགོང་.

སང་གནངས་ (sāŋnaŋ) abbr. of སང་ཉིན་གནངས་ཉིན་.

སང་ཕོད་ (sāŋböö) next year, the following year.

སང་ཚགས་ (sāŋdzaà) a seive, a sifter; va.—རྒྱག to sift.

སང་ཞོགས་ (sāŋshɔɔ̀) tomorrow morning, the next morning.

སང་རས་ (sāŋrɛɛ̀) sm.* སང་, 2.

སང་ཤི་གནངས་ཤི་ (səŋshi nəŋshi) the uncertainty of death, impending death ¶ ནད་པ་དེ་ན་ཚ་ཕྱིད་པོ་འདུག་པས་སང་ཤི་གནང་ཤི་རེད་བཞག The patient's illness is very serious and (he) is about to die any day [Lit. die tomorrow, die the day after tomorrow].

སང་ལོ་ (sāŋlo) sm. སང་ཕོད་.

སང་སང་ (sāŋsaŋ) 1. upright; va.—བྱེད་ to sit or put upright ། གཟུགས་པོ་སང་སང་བྱས་སོང་ (He) sat upright. 2. having many holes.

སང་སང་གནངས་གནངས་ (sāŋsāŋ nāŋnaŋ) postponing/ delaying/ putting off; va.—བྱེད་ ། ཁོས་སང་སང་གནངས་གནངས་བྱས་ནས་བུ་ལོན་སྤྲོད་ཀྱི་མི་འདུག He is delaying and is not paying the loan.

སང་སང་པོ་ (sāŋ sāŋbo) clear, bright.

སང་སེང་ (sāŋseŋ) abbr. of སང་ངེ་སེང་ངེ་.

སངས་ (sāŋ) 1. vi. to be free from, to recover from, to get cleared up/ cured ། མ་རིག་པ་ལས་སངས་ To be free from ignorance. ། སྨན་དེ་བཏང་ནས་ན་ཚ་སངས་འདུག He took that medicine and his illness got cured.

སངས་རྒྱ་ (sāŋgya) va. to attain the state of nirvana, to become enlightened.

སངས་རྒྱས་ (sāŋgyɛɛ̀) 1. Buddha ། སངས་རྒྱས་ཀྱི་གོ་འཕང་ The state of being a Buddha. 2. p. of སངས་རྒྱ་.

སངས་རྒྱས་ཀྱི་བསྟན་པ་ (sāŋgyɛɛ̀gi dēmba) Buddhism [Lit. the teachings of the Buddha].

སངས་རྒྱས་རྒྱ་མཚོ་ (sāŋgyɛɛ̀ gyadzo) regent of the 5th Dalai Lama.

སངས་རྒྱས་ཆུང་ (sāŋgyɛɛ̀juŋ) disciples of the Buddha.

སངས་རྒྱས་ཆོས་པ་ (sāŋgyɛɛ̀ cȫȍba) Buddhist.

སངས་རྒྱས་ཆོས་ལུགས་ (sāŋgyɛɛ̀ cȫȍluù) Buddhism.

སངས་རྒྱས་པ་ (sāŋgyɛɛ̀ba) Buddhist.

སངས་རྒྱས་ལ་ཀ་ཁ་ (sāŋgyɛɛ̀la gāka) giving advice to sb. who knows more that oneself [Lit. teaching the alphabet to the Buddha].

སངས་དྲག་ (sāŋ traà) completely/ fully (cured) ། ཁོང་གི་ན་ཚ་སངས་དྲག་ཕྱིན་བཞག His illness got fully cured.

སངས་པོ་ (sāŋbo) sharp, keen ། རྣ་བ་སངས་པོ་ Sharp ears (i.e., hearing).

སངས་དམག་ (sāŋmaà) shung. troops.

སད་ (sɛ̀ɛ̀) 1. frost; vi.—རྒྱག་ to have/ get frost. 2. va. to awaken, to wake up ། དེ་རིང་ཞོགས་པ་ང་གཉིད་སྔ་པོ་སད་བྱུང་ I woke up early this morning. 3. va. to test, to examine, to try out ། མི་དེ་སོ་པ་ཡིན་མིན་ངས་ཉམས་སད་པ་ཡིན་ I tested that person to see if he was a spy or not.

སད་ཀྱིས་ཁྱེར་ (sɛ̀ɛ̀gi kyēr) sm. སད་, 1.

སད་སྐྱོན་ (sɛ̀ɛ̀gyön) frost damage.

སད་འཁོར་སྦྱོར་འགོད་ (sɛ̀ɛ̀gɔɔ jɔ̄ɔgöö) shung. putting a religious object somewhere (e.g., mountains) to prevent frost.

སད་རྒྱག་པའི་དུས་ (sɛ̀ɛ̀gyaàbɛ tüü) the time/ period when frost occurs.

སད་གདན་ (sɛ̀ɛ̀dɛn) permafrost.

སད་དུས་ (sɛ̀ɛ̀düü) sm. སད་རྒྱག་པའི་དུས་.

སད་འབོ་ (sɛ̄mbo) shung. an object for preventing frost.

སད་མི་མི་བདུན་ (sɛ̀ɛ̀mi midün) the first seven monks in Tibet (ordained as an experiment in the 8th. century A.D.).

སད་སེར་ (sɛ̀ɛ̀ sēr) frost and hail ། སད་སེར་གྱི་གནོད་འཚེ་ Damage from hail and frost.

སད་དེ་སུད་དེ་ (sɛ̀ɛ̀de sü̃üde) a few, a little.

སད་སུད་ (sɛ̀ɛ̀süü) abbr. of སད་དེ་སུད་དེ་.

སད་གཡོལ་སེར་གཡོལ་ (sɛ̀ɛ̀yöö seryöö) avoiding hail and frost.

སད་སེར་བཙའ་ཐན་ (sɛ̀ɛ̀ser dzādɛn) abbr. frost, hail, mildew, drought.

སད་ལྷུང་ (sɛ̀ɛ̀lhuŋ) the time when frost begins to occur.

སན་དེ་ཡ་གོ་ (sɛ̄nde yago) Santiago.

སན་ཧྥ་རན་སིས་ཀོ་ (sɛ̄nfurɛn sīigo) San Francisco.

སབ་བེ་སོབ་བེ་ (sābbe sōbe) soft.

སབ་སྦག་སྦག (sɔ̄b bagbaà) eng.tib. submachine gun.

སབ་མ་ (sɔ̄bma) fences made with entwined branches from trees. 2. straw/ bamboo mat.

སབ་སིབ་ (sɔbsib) drizzling (rain), light falling snow; vi.—དུ་འབབ་ to be drizzling lightly, to be snowing lightly.

སབ་མོ་ (sɔ̄bmu) sm. སབ་མ་.

སབ་སུབ་ (sɔ̄bsub) hiding/ concealing one's errors; va.—བྱེད་.

སབ་སོབ་ (sɔ̄bsob) abbr. of སབ་བེ་སོབ་བེ་.

སམ་ (sām) 1. interrogative particle used after final s ། ལས་ཀ་བྱས་སམ་ Did (you) work? 3. "or" particle (used after final s) ། རས་སམ་ཤོག་བུ་ Cloth or paper.

སམ་ཁྲ་ (sāmdra) traditional Tibetan message/ writing board; va.—གཏོང་ to send a message on a སམ་ཁྲ་.

སམ་ཏ་ (sāmdra) sm. སམ་ཁྲ་.

སམ་བྷོ་ཊ་ (sambhoda) skt. sm. ཐུ་མི་སམ་བྷོ་ཊ་.

སའི་དཀྱིལ་འཁོར་ (sɛ̄gyiŋgɔɔ) the earth, the world.

སའི་ཁབ་ལེན་སྣེ་མོ་ (sɛ kāblen nēmo) magnetic pole.

སའི་ཁབ་ལེན་ར་བ་ (sɛ kāblen rawa) terrestrial magnetism.

སའི་གོ་ལ་ (sɛ kolo) the earth ། མི་བཟོས་སྲུང་སྐར་གྱིས་སའི་གོ་ལ་སྐོར་གྱི་ཡོད་པ་རེད་ The satellite revolves around the earth.

སའི་གོ་ལའི་འཁོར་སྐར་ (sɛ̄golö kɔ̄ɔgar) satellite (revolving in the sky).

སའི་གོ་ལའི་དངོས་ཁམས་གཏེར་འཚོལ་རུ་ཁག (sɛ̄golö ŋȫȍgam dērdzöö rugaà) geophysical prospecting team.

སའི་གོ་ལའི་དངོས་ཁམས་ཞིབ་འཇུག་ཁང་ (sɛ̄golö ŋȫȍgam shimjuùgaŋ) institute of geophysics.

སའི་གོ་ལའི་དངོས་ཁམས་རིག་པ་ (sɛ̄golö ŋȫȍgam rigbə) geophysics.

སའི་གོ་ལའི་དངོས་ཁམས་སློབ་ཚོགས་ (sɛ̄golö ŋȫȍgam lōbdzoò) society of geophysics.

སའི་གོ་ལའི་མཉམ་འགྲོད་འཁོར་སྐར་ (sɛ̄golö ñāmdröö kɔ̄ɔgar) geostationary satellite, synchronous satellite.

སའི་གོ་ལའི་ཟླ་བ་ (sɛ̄golö dāba) sm. ས་སྙིང་.

སའི་གོ་ལའི་འཐེན་ཤུགས་ (sɛ̄golö tēnshuù) earth's gravity.

སའི་གོ་ལའི་འདྲེན་ཤུགས་ (sɛ̄golö drenshuù) sm. སའི་གོ་ལའི་འཐེན་ཤུགས་.

སའི་གོ་ལའི་སྣེ་གཉིས་ (sɛ̄golönēñii) the two terrestrial poles (the South and North Poles).

སའི་གོ་ལའི་དཔེ་དབྱིབས་ (sɛ̄golö bēyib) globe.

སའི་གོ་ལའི་ཕྱེད་ (sɛ̄golö cēè) hemisphere.

སའི་གོ་ལའི་ཕྱེད་ནུབ་མ་ (sɛ̄golö cēè nubmə) western hemisphere.

སའི་གོ་ལའི་ཕྱེད་བྱང་མ་ (sɛ̄golö cēè caŋma) northern hemisphere.

སའི་གོ་ལའི་ཕྱེད་ཤར་མ་ (sɛ̄golö cēè shārma) eastern hemisphere.

སའི་གོ་ལའི་ཕྱེད་ལྷོ་མ་ (sɛ̄golö cēè lhōma) southern hemisphere.

སའི་གོ་ལའི་ཚན་རིག (sɛ̄golö tsɛ̄nrii) earth sciences, geology.

སའི་གོ་ལའི་རྫས་འགྱུར་རིག་པ་ (sɛ̄golö dzɛ̀ɛ̀gyur rigbə) geochemistry.

སའི་གོ་ལའི་རྫས་འགྱུར་རྩད་བཤེར་རུ་ཁག (sɛ̄golö dzɛ̀ɛ̀gyur dzɛ̀ɛ̀sher rugaà) geochemistry exploring team.

སའི་གོ་ལའི་སྲོག་ཤིང་ (sɛ̄golö sɔ̄gshiŋ) the earth's axis.

སའི་ཆགས་རིམ་ (sɛ̄ cɔ̄grim) geological strata.

སའི་ཉིང་ཁུ་ (sɛ̄ ñiŋgu) sm. ས་བཅུད་.

སའི་རྟེན་ (sɛ̄den) spleen.

སའི་བཞའ་ཚན་ (sɛ̄ shadzɛn) ground (water) vapor.

སའི་ཞིན་ཚད་ (sɛ̄ shīndzɛɛ̀) soil fertility.

སའི་སྲོག་ཤིང་ (sɛ̄ sɔ̄gshiŋ) earth's axis.

སར་ (sāā) sm. ས་ལ་.

སར་འགྲིལ་སྤོ་ལོ་ (sāādrii bōlo) 1. baseball. 2. a ground ball (in baseball).

སར་ཝ་ཌོར་ (sāāwador) Salvador.

སར་ཉལ་རྩ་ལྡུམ་ (sāāñɛɛ dzādum) creeping plants.

སར་དི་འཛུགས་ (sāādi dzu̲ù) va. to give one's word you will settle in a place.
སར་པ་ (sārba) sm.* གསར་པ་.
སར་མི་ (sārmi)1. newcomer, new arrival. 2. arc. messenger.
སར་ཚུགས་གློག་ཤུ་ (sāādzug lōgshu) floor lamp, lamp fixed in the ground.
སར་ཚུགས་སྒྲ་སྡུད་འཕྲུལ་འཁོར་ (sāādzug dra̲dzüù trüügɔɔ) console (radio).
སར་འཛིན་སྡོང་པོ་ (sārdzin do̲ŋbo) sm. སར་ཉལ་རྟ་ལྷུལ་.
སར་བཞག་འདེགས་རྒྱ་ (sārshaà de̲ggya) drawbridge.
སལ་མོན་དབྱུག་སྲིན་ (sɛ̄ɛ̄mön yūgsin) eng.tib. salmonella.
སལ་སིལ་ (sɛ̄ɛ̄sii) sound of bells ringing.
སལ་སུལ་ (sɛ̄ɛ̄süü) narrow/ deep gorge.
སི་ (sī) 1. whistle, whistling; va.—རྒྱག to whistle. 2. ch. silk. 3. a type of high quality bamboo.
སི་དཀྲིས་གློག་སྐུད་ (sīdriì lɔ̄ɔ̄güù) fabric covered electrical wire.
སི་སྐད་ (sīgɛɛ̀) whistling; va.—རྒྱག.
སི་ཁྱིམ་ (sīgyim) eng. the second hand of a watch.
སི་ཁྲུའན་ (sīdruan) sm. སི་ཁྲོན་.
སི་ཁྲོན་ (sōdrön) Sichuan (Province).
སི་ཁྲོན་གཞོང་ས་ (sīdrön shōŋsa) Sichuan Basin.
སི་གླུ་ (sīlu) whistling a song; va.—གཏོང་ to whistle a song/ tune.
སི་རྒྱག (sīgyaà) see སི་.
སི་སྒྲ་ (sīdra) sm. སི་སྐད་.
སི་མེན་ (sīmɛn) silk wadding.
སི་སྨྱུག (sīñuù) bamboo pen.
སི་ཅིའི་ (sījii) ch. driver.
སི་ད་ལིན་ཀི་ལི་ (sīdalingile) Stalingrad.
སི་དུའི་སུམ་རྟགས་འགྲེལ་ཆེན་ (sīdü sūmdaà dre̲ejen) a commentary on Tibetan grammar.
སི་དོག་ཧོ་ལེམ་ (sīdog hōlerm) ch. Stockholm.
སི་བཏགས་ (sīdaà) woven silk.
སི་བརྡ་ (sīda) signaling by whistling; va.—གཏོང་.
སི་པན་ (sībɛn) cayenne pepper, hot chili.
སི་པན་སྦང་ཚབ་ (sībɛn ba̲ŋjəb) mixture of cayenne pepper soaked in salt and water that is eaten with རྩམ་པ་.
སི་ཝ་ཧི་ལི་ (sīwahili) Swahili.
སི་ཝེ་དེན་ (sīwɛdɛn) Sweden.
སི་སྨྱུག (sīñuù) a traditional Tibetan pen made of bamboo.
སི་འོད་ (sīwöö) the sheen of silk.
སི་ཝུའུ་ཀྲང་ (sīwudraŋ) ch. mess officer. (in the army).
སི་ར་ (sīrə) woven basket.
སི་རི་རི་ (sī ri̲ri) rustling sound of the wind.

སི་རི་ཡ་ (sīriyə) Syria.
སི་རུང་ (sīruŋ) ch. velvet.
སི་ལི་མ་ (sīlimə) a thin coat of ice.
སི་ལི་ལི་ (sī li̲li) tinkling sound of bells.
སི་ལིག (sīlig) eng. silk (and silk-like materials such as nylon).
སི་ལིང་ (sīliŋ) ch. military commander, head of སི་ལིང་པུའུ་.
སི་ལིང་ཀུ་ལིང་ (sīliŋ gu̲liŋ) sound of breaking glass.
སི་ལིང་ལྗང་མ་ (sīliŋ ja̲ŋma) fringed iris.
སི་ལིང་པུའུ་ (sīliŋbu) ch. command center, headquarters (in army).
སི་ལིང་ཡོན་ (sīliŋyön) ch. sm. སི་ལིང་.
སི་ལིན་པུའུ་ (sīlinbu) ch. command center, headquarters.
སི་ཤན་ (sīshɛn) silk thread.
སི་སི་པན་ (sīsipɛn) C-Span.
སི་ཧོན་སུའུ་ (sīhönsu) ch. tetracycline.
སི་ཨན་ཨན་ (sī ēnen) eng. CNN.
སིག (sīg) 1. Sikh (nationality in India). 2. va. to hike/ hitch up (a load on one's back); va.—རྒྱག. 3. abbr. of སིག་ར་.
སིག་བུ་ (sīgbu) sm. སིག་ར་.
སིག་ར་ (sīirə) bamboo basket.
སིག་སིག (sīgsiì) 1. sm. སིག. 2. shaking from fear/ cold; va.—གཏོང་.
སིག་སིག་དུ་འཕར་ (sīgsiìdu pār) vi. to shake/ tremble.
སིགས་ (sīì) imp. of གསིག.
སིགས་མ་ (sīgmə) residue, dregs.
སིང་: p. སིངས་ (sīŋ) va. to choose, to pick, to select.
སིང་སྒྱུར་ (sīŋgyur) an inferior (weak) Tibetan ཆང་.
སིང་ག་པུར་ (sīŋgabur) Singapore.
སིང་ག་ལ་ (sīŋgala) Ceylon, Sri Lanka.
སིང་གྷ་ལ་ (sīŋghala) sm. སིང་ག་ལ་.
སིང་སྒྲ་ (sīŋdra) ringing/ tinkling sounds of bells and metals striking.
སིང་ངེ་ (sīŋŋe) completely or absolutely well/ clean ། སྡོད་ས་ཚང་མ་གཙང་སིང་ངེ་འདུག All the residences were completely clean.
སིང་ངེ་ཡེ་རེ་བ་ (sīŋŋe ye̲rewa) extremely clear.
སིང་དྭངས་ (sīŋdaŋ) sm. སིང་སྒྱུར་.
སིང་པོ་ (sīŋbu) sm. སིང་སྒྱུར་.
སིང་ཕྱེ་ (sīŋjeè) starch.
སིང་རག (sīŋraà) ཆང་ and alcohol/ liqueur.
སིངྒ་པུར་ (sīŋgabur) Singapore.
སིངྒ་ལ་ (sīŋgala) Ceylon, Sri Lanka.
སིང་སིང་ (sīŋsiŋ) 1. ringing/ tinkling sounds of bells and metals striking. 2. completely ། སྔོ་སིང་སིང་ Completely green.

སིང་སིང་ཁྲོག་ཁྲོག (sīŋsiŋ trɔ̄gdrɔɔ̀) sm. སིང་སིང་.
སིང་སིང་པོ་ (sīŋ sīŋbu) sm. སིང་སིང་.
སིངས་ (sīŋ) p. of སིང་.
སིངས་པ་ (sīŋbə) sm. སིངས་པོ་.
སིངས་པོ་ (sīŋbu) weak (of ཆང་/ alcohol).
སིད་ (sīì) sm. སི་, 1.
སིད་སྒྲ་ (sīidra) sm. སི་སྒྲ་.
སིད་ཉི་ (sīiñii) Sidney.
སིན་དི་ (sīmdi) the ramrod used with gunpowder in Tibetan matchlock guns.
སིན་བུ་ (sīmbu) weaving shuttle; va.—རྒྱག to use the shuttle when weaving.
སིན་འབི་ (sīmbi) sm. སིན་དི་.
སིན་འབེན་ (sīmben) sm.* སིན་འབི་.
སིབ་ནད་ (sībnɛɛ̀) sm. སིབ་པི་.
སིབ་པི་ (sīnbbi) measles.
སིབ་པིའི་ནད་དུག (sībbii nɛ̲ɛ̀duù) vaccination for measles.
སིབ་བུ་ (sībbu) sm. སིབ་པི་.
སིབ་སིབ་ (sībsib) lightly/ softly falling rain/ snow.
སིམ་ (sīm) 1. vi. to seep through ། ཆུ་ས་ལ་སིམ་སོང་ The water seeped through the ground. 2. vi. to find joy, to feel happy.
སིམ་ཁུང་ (sīmguŋ) the groove on Tibetan rifles into which the ramrod is kept.
སིམ་འགྲོད་ (sīmdröö) sm. སིམ་སིམ་སིམ་ལ་.
སིམ་དོང་ (sīmdoŋ) seepage pit.
སིམ་པོ་ (sīmbu) 1. quiet, silent ། ཁང་པ་འདི་སིམ་པུ་འདུག This house is very quiet. 2. well, happy.
སིམ་མེ་བ་ (sīmmewa) sm. སིམ་པོ་, 2.
སིམ་འཛུལ་ (sīmdzuù) infiltrating; va.—བྱེད་ ། ང་ཚོས་ས་མཚམས་སུ་དགྲ་བོའི་དམག་མི་སིམ་འཛུལ་བྱས་པ་རེད་ The enemy troops infiltrated our border.
སིམ་ལའི་ཆིངས་ཡིག (sīmlɛ ciŋyii) eng.tib. Simla Convention.
སིམ་ཤུགས་ (sīmshuù) the force of sth. seeping or leaking.
སིམ་སིམ་ (sīmsim) sm. སིབ་སིབ་.
སིམ་སིམ་སིམ་ལ་ (simsim sīmlə) quietly, silently ། ཀུན་མ་དེས་སིམ་སིམ་སིམ་ལ་ཁང་པའི་ནང་ལ་འཛུལ་བ་རེད་ The thief walked silently into the house.
སིམས་ (sīm) vi. to be absorbed, to be soaked up.
སིའུ་ (sīwu) 1. sm.* སེའུ་. 2. steps.
སིར་སྒྲ་ (sīrdra) sm. སིར་སིར་.
སིར་སིར་ (sīrsir) a buzzing sound.
སིལ་ (sīì) sm. སིལ་སྙན་.
སིལ་ཁྲོལ་ (sīidröö) the small bells that are attached to the costumes of opera or religious dancers.
སིལ་གྲངས་ (sīīldraŋ) decimal (in math).
སིལ་གྲངས་བགོ་རྩིས་ (sīīldraŋ go̲dzii) divisions of

decimals.

སིལ་གྲངས་སྒྱུར་རྩིས། (sīildraŋ gyu̱rdzii) multiplication of decimals.

སིལ་གྲངས་སྣོན་རྩིས། (sīildraŋ nōndzii) addition of decimals.

སིལ་གྲངས་འཕྲི་རྩིས། (sīildraŋ trīdzii) subtraction of decimals.

སིལ་གྲངས་ཚག (sīitra̱ŋdzaà) decimal point.

སིལ་བཙོལ། (sīijöö) a savings account where one can withdraw money anytime.

སིལ་ཉོ། (sīiño) buying retail; va.—བྱེད།.

སིལ་སྙན། (sīiñɛn) type of cymbal; va.—དཀྲོལ། to play the cymbals.

སིལ་སྙན་མ། (sīiñɛnma) women who play the cymbals.

སིལ་ཏོག (sīidoò) arc. fruits.

སིལ་ཏོག་སྐྱ་དོ། (sīidoò gyādo) arc. unripe fruits.

སིལ་ཐོར། (sīidɔɔ) untied, loose, (e.g., flowers).

སིལ་སྡོང་། (sīidoŋ) fruit trees.

སིལ་སྡོང་ར་བ། (sīidoŋ ra̱wa) orchard.

སིལ་བལ། (sīibɛɛ) carded wool.

སིལ་བུ། (sīibu) in fragments, in pieces, disintegrated, individually (rather than in bulk); vi.—འགྱུར།; —འཐོར། to become fragmented/ scattered/ disintegrated.

སིལ་བུའི་དཔལ་འབྱོར། (sīibü bɛ̄njɔɔ) individual economy (as opposed to communal).

སིལ་བུར་འཐོར། (sīibur tɔ̄r) see སིལ་བུར།.

སིལ་བུར་གནས། (sīibur nɛ̱ɛ̀) va. to remain or exist fragmented/ disintegrated/ in small parts/ units ། ལོ་བརྒྱ་ཕྲག་ཁ་ཤས་རིང་ཡུལ་དེ་སིལ་བུར་གནས་པ་རེད། For several hundred years the country stayed fragmented.

སིལ་བུར་འཕྱང་། (sīibur cāŋ) vi. to hang down loosely (hair).

སིལ་མ། (sīimə) 1. sm. སིལ་བུ།. 2. loose/ small change (with respect to coins) ། དངུལ་སིལ་མ་ཡོད་པས། Do (you) have any small change?

སིལ་མ་ཉོ། (sīimə ño̱) va. to buy retail.

སིལ་མ་འཚོང་། (sīimə tsōŋ) va. to sell retail.

སིལ་ཙེ་ཙིག (sīidzijig) just a moment, a small amount ། ཁྱེད་རང་སིལ་ཙེ་ཙིག་བཞུགས་ཨ། Please wait for a moment.

སིལ་ཙེ། (sīidze) ch. shredded.

སིལ་ཚོང་། (sīidzoŋ) sm. སིལ་འཚོང་།.

སིལ་ཚོང་ཁང་། (sīidzoŋgaŋ) retail store.

སིལ་ཚོང་གོང་། (sīidzoŋ ko̱ŋ) retail price.

སིལ་འཚོང་། (sīidzoŋ) retail sales, selling retail; va.—བྱེད།; —རྒྱག to sell/ retail.

སིལ་འཚོང་ཁང་། (sīidzoŋgaŋ) retail outlet/ store.

སིལ་འཚོང་གི་གཏན་འབེབས་རིན་གོང་། (sīidzoŋgi dɛ̄nbeb ri̱ngoŋ) fixed retail price.

སིལ་འཚོང་གི་ཟོག་གོང་། (sīidzoŋgi sɔ̱ɔ̀goŋ) retail price.

སིལ་འཚོང་དངོས་ཟོག (sīidzoŋ ŋɔ̄ɔ̄sɔɔ̀) retail merchandise/ goods.

སིལ་འཚོང་རིན་གོང་། (sīidzoŋ ri̱ngoŋ) retail price.

སིལ་འཚོང་ལས་རིགས། (sīidzoŋ lɛ̱ɛ̀rii) retail trade/ business.

སིལ་འཚོང་བ། (sīidzoŋwa) retailer.

སིལ་ཟས། (sīisɛɛ̀) snack.

སིལ་ར། (sīirə) basket.

སིལ་ལི་མ། (sīilimə) sm. སི་ལི་མ།.

སིལ་ཤིང་། (sīishiŋ) firewood cut into pieces.

སིལ་སངས་ཙམ་བྱེད། (sīisaŋdzam ce̱è) va. to take a break (from work).

སིལ་སངས་སངས། (sīi sāŋsaŋ) feeling relief/ relaxed; va.—བྱེད། ། ལོ་འཇུག་ཡིག་ཚད་བཏང་ཚར་ནས་སིལ་སངས་སངས་བྱས་སོང་། I felt relief after taking the final exam.

སིལ་སིལ། (sīisii) sound of bells ringing/ tinkling.

སུ། (sū) 1. dative-locative particle (used after the final s) ། ཁོའི་སྡོད་གནས་སུ་ཕྱིན་པ་རེད། (They) went to his residence. 2. who? ། མོ་སུ་རེད། Who is she? ། འདི་སུ་ལ་སྤྲོད་དགོས་རེད། To whom should (I) give this? 3. "as" ། ཕྱག་རོགས་སུ་སྲིད་བློན་གླང་མདུན་ཡོད་པ་རེད། He had Prime Minister Langdun as his colleague.

སུ་དཀར་སུ་ནག (sūgaa sūnaà) who is innocent and who is guilty ། ཁ་རྒྱ་འདིའི་སྐོར་ང་གཉིས་སུ་དཀར་སུ་ནག་གི་ཐག་དེ་ཁྲིམས་ཁང་ནས་གཅོད་ཀྱི་རེད། Concerning this dispute, the court will decide which of us is innocent or guilty [Lit. who is white, who is black].

སུ་ཀུན། (sūgün) all, entire, everyone.

སུ་གང་། (sūgaŋ) whoever, anyone ། སྐད་ཆ་འདི་མི་སུ་གང་གིས་མ་ཤེས་པ་བྱ་དགོས། You must not let anyone know of this conversation.

སུ་མགྱོགས་སྡུར། (sūgyɔg du̱r) va. to compete who goes or does sth. quicker.

སུ་རྒྱལ་སུ་ཕམ། (sūgyɛɛ sūpam) who is the victor and who is the vanquished, who won and who lost ། དམག་འཁྲུག་དེ་དུས་ཡུན་རིང་པོར་སུ་རྒྱལ་སུ་ཕམ་གྱི་ཐག་མ་ཆོད་པ་རེད། That war went on for many years without it being decided who won and who lost.

སུ་བཏབ་དེས་སྡུད། (sūdəb te̱èdüü) the policy in Tibet in 1959 that whoever planted the land that year could collect the yield.

སུ་བཏབ་སུས་ལེན། (sūdəb süü le̱n) sm. སུ་བཏབ་དེ་སྡུད།.

སུ་ཐོད་ཐོད། (sū tōōdöö) whoever.

སུ་ཐོབ་གང་ལོན། (sūtob ka̱ŋlön) sm. དབ་ཐོབ།.

སུ་དང་སུ། (sūdaŋsu) whoever, everyone ། མི་སུ་དང་སུ་ཡིན་ནའང་རང་གི་ཁེ་ཕན་མ་བསམ་མཁན་མེད། There is no one who does not think of his own benefit. ། སང་ཉིན་ཚོགས་འདུར་མི་སུ་དང་སུ་འགྲོ་གི་རེད། Who all is going to the meeting tomorrow?

སུ་དྲག་འགྲན། (sū tra̱gdrɛn) va. to compete with sb.

སུ་འདྲ་ཞིག (sūndrajig) 1. who (what sort of a person) ། ལས་ཀ་འདི་སུ་འདྲ་ཞིག་གིས་བྱས་པ་རེད། Who did this work? 2. whoever, anyone ། མི་སུ་འདྲ་ཞིག་ལ་ཡང་རོགས་བྱེད་ཀྱི་རེད། Someone will help anyone.

སུ་ནས། (sūnɛ) from whom ། སྐད་ཆ་འདི་སུ་ནས་གོ་བྱུང་། From whom did you hear this talk?

སུ་ནི་ཁ་ཆེའི་ཆོས་བརྒྱུད། (sūni kājee cōōgyüü) Sunni Islam.

སུ་པན། (sūbɛn) sm. སི་པན།.

སུ་ཕྲི་ཁ་ཆེའི་ཆོས་བརྒྱུད། (sūbi kājee cōōgyüü) Sufism.

སུ་མ་ད་ར། (sūmadara) Sumatra.

སུ་ཕྲེ་ཨེད། (sūween) Soviet.

སུ་ཞིག (sūjig) whoever, anyone ། ཚོགས་པ་དེའི་ནང་མི་སུ་ཞིག་ཡིན་ནའང་འཛུལ་ཆོག་གི་རེད། Anyone can join that organization.

སུ་བཟང་སུ་སྐྱིད། (sūsaŋ sūgyii) whoever is better off/ happier.

སུ་ཡང་། (sūyaŋ) whoever, anybody, nobody (with neg.) ། ལག་ཁྱེར་ཡོད་པར་མི་སུ་ཡང་བོད་ལ་འགྲོ་ཆོག་གི་རེད། With a permit anybody can go to Tibet. ། ལག་ཁྱེར་མེད་པར་མི་སུ་ཡང་བོད་ལ་འགྲོ་ཆོག་གི་མ་རེད། Without a permit nobody can go to Tibet.

སུ་ཡིན་ན་ཡང་། (sūyinnayaŋ) whoever, whosoever.

སུ་ཡིས། (sūyii) sm. སུས།.

སུ་རུ། (sūru) sm. སུ་ལུ།.

སུ་རུ་པན་ཙ། (sūru bēndza) sm. སི་པན།.

སུ་རུག (sūruù) leather for making boots.

སུ་རུང་། (sūruŋ) whoever, whichever, either one (of you) ། ཁྱེད་རང་གཉིས་སུ་རུང་ཞིག་ངའི་རོགས་པར་ཡོང་དགོས། Either one of you two must come and help me.

སུ་ལ། (sūlə) to whom.

སུ་ལུ། (sūlu) 1. curly (hair). 2. a plant from which tinder for starting fires is made. 3. a type of azalea.

སུ་ལུ་གོང་གོང་། (sūlu ko̱ŋgoŋ) sm. སུ་ལུ།.

སུ་ལུ་མགོ། (sūlugo) curly (haired).

སུ་སུ། (sūsu) who, who all ། སང་ཉིན་ཚོགས་འདུར་མི་སུ་སུ་འགྲོ་གི་རེད། Who all are going to the meeting tomorrow.

སུག (sūg) abbr. of སུག་པ།, 1.

སུག་གྱོག (sūggyɔɔ) lame, limp.

སུག་དཀར། (sūgar) animals that have white legs.

སུག་བཀྱིགས་ (sūggyig) tying all four limbs together; va.—བྱེད་.

སུག་ཁྲལ་ (sūgdrɛɛ) animal head tax [Lit. hoof tax].

སུག་རྒྱག (sūg gya̠à) va. to nudge/ push.

སུག་རྟིང་ཀྱོག་ཀྱོག (sūgdiŋ gyɔ̄ggyɔɔ̀) sm. སུག་ཀྱོག.

སུག་རྟེན་ (sūgden) base, pedestal.

སུག་ཐུང་ (sūgduŋ) small feet/ hooves.

སུག་མཐིལ་ (sūgdii) 1. hoof. 2. palm of the hand.

སུག་རྡོག (sūgdɔɔ̀) sm. སུག་མཐིལ་.

སུག་པ་ (sūgbə) 1. hands and legs, limbs. 2. shung. hands; va.—སློན་ to receive sth. in one's hands. 3. a herb used for washing.

སུག་པོ་ (sūgbu) sm. སུག་པ་, 1.

སུག་བྲིས་ (sūgdriì) handwritten.

སུག་མེལ་ (sūgmee) sm.* སུག་སྨེལ་.

སུག་ཟྨེལ་ (sūgmee) sm. སུག་མེལ་.

སུག་སྨེལ་ (sūgmee) cardamom.

སུག་བཞི་ (sūgshi) four-legged animals; vi.—གྲམ་ to be lying on the ground with one's hand and legs spread out.

སུག་བཞིར་རྟེན་ཁྲལ་ (sūgshi dēndrɛɛ) shung. tax on animals.

སུག་བཞིར་བརྟེན་པའི་ཁྲལ་ (sūgshi dēmbɛ trɛ̄ɛ) sm. སུག་བཞིར་རྟེན་ཁྲལ་.

སུག་ཡོབ་ (sūgyob) sm. སུག་པ་, 1.

སུག་ལག (sūglaà) sm. སུག་པ་, 1.

སུག་ལས་ (sūglɛɛ̀) sm. ལག་ལས་.

སུག་སུག་གདོང་ (sūgsug dōŋ) sm. སུག.

སུང་རྒྱལ་རབས་ (sūŋ gyɛ̠ɛ̠rəb) the Sung Dynasty.

སུང་ཆིན་ལིང་ (sūŋ cīnliŋ) Madame Sun Yatsen.

སུང་ཧྭ་ཅའང་གཙང་པོ་ (sūŋhajaŋ dzāŋbo) Sungari River.

སུངས་ (sūŋ) sm. རུལ་.

སུད་དེ་ཤི་ (sūùde shī) vi. to die of suffocation.

སུད་པ་ (sūùbə) a bit, a little.

སུད་ཀྲར་ཚོང་མཁན་ (sūùdra tsōŋñɛn) eng.tib. sweater sellers (an occupation of some Tibetans in India).

སུད་ཚོང་ (sūùdzoŋ) abbr. of སུད་ཀྲར་ཚོང་མཁན་.

སུད་སི་ (sūùsi) Swiss, Switzerland.

སུད་སིའི་མཚོ་ཡུར་ (sūùsi tsōyur) Suez Canal.

སུད་སུད་སུད་ལ་ (sūùsuù sūùlə) gradually, little by little ¶ ངའི་དངུལ་ཚང་མ་སུད་སུད་སུད་ལ་འགྲོར་སོང་ Little by little all my money got spent.

སུན་: p. བསུན་; f. སུན་ (sūn) vi. to be irritated, to be fed up/ annoyed, to be sick/ tired of ¶ ཕྲུ་གུས་སྐད་ཅོར་བརྒྱབ་པར་བསུན་པ་རེད་ (He) was irritated by the children shouting.

སུན་ཀྲུང་ཧྲན་ (sūn drūŋhrɛn) Sun Yatsen.

སུན་ཆིན་ལིང་ (sūn cīnliŋ) sm. སུང་ཆིན་ལིང་.

སུན་སྣང་ (sūnnaŋ) irritated, bothered, fed up/ tired of; vi.—སྐྱེ་; —བྱེད་ ¶ ཉིན་ལྟར་སྐད་ཆ་དེ་རང་སྐྱར་ནས་སྐྱར་དུ་ཉན་པར་སུན་སྣང་སྐྱེས་པ་རེད་ (They) got fed up with having to listen to the same thing over and over again.

སུན་སྣང་མེད་པ་ (sūnnaŋ me̠èba) patient, tolerant, even-tempered.

སུན་སྣང་ཚ་པོ་ (sūnnaŋ tsābo) very irritable, easily bothered.

སུན་པོ་ (sūmbu) bothering, annoying; va.—བྱེད་; —བཟོ་ ¶ ཕྲུ་གུ་དེ་ཚོས་ཧྲན་པ་དགོས་ཡོད་ཟེར་ནས་རྟག་པར་སུན་པོ་བཟོ་གི་འདུག The children are always bothering them about wanting a present.

སུན་པོ་བཟོ་ (sūmbu so̠) see སུན་པོ་.

སུན་ཕྱུང་ (sūnjuŋ) p. of སུན་འབྱིན་.

སུན་འབྱིན་ (sūnjin) 1. refuting, repudiating; criticizing; va. སུན་ཕྱིན་; —བྱེད་ ¶ མི་དམངས་ལ་གནོད་པ་སྐྱེལ་བའི་བྱ་ངན་དེ་ཚོར་སུན་ཕྱུང་བ་རེད་ (They) criticized the bad people who were harming the masses. 2. va. to humiliate/ demean/ denigrate ¶ མི་དེ་ཁྲོ་པ་མཐོ་པོ་བྱས་ནས་མི་གཞན་ལ་སུན་འབྱིན་བྱེད་ཀྱི་ཡོད་པ་རེད་ That person is very proud and demeans other people.

སུན་འབྱིན་ལྟར་སྣང་ (sūnjindar nāŋ) being critical of those that are faultless and uncritical of those with faults.

སུན་མ་ (sūnmə) sm. བསུ་མ་.

སུན་མེད་སྐྱོ་མེད་ (sūnmeè gyōmeè) at ease, relaxed [Lit. not bothered, not sad].

སུན་མེད་ངང་རིང་ (sūnmeè ŋə̠ŋriŋ) tolerant, forbearing, patient.

སུན་གཙེར་ (sūndzer) annoying, bothering; va.—བཟོ་ to annoy, to bother.

སུན་འཛེམས་ (sūndzem) sm. སུན་སྣང་.

སུབ་: p. བསུབས་; f. བསུབ; imp. སུབས་ (sūb) 1. va. to erase, to rub out ¶ ནག་པང་ལོག་གི་རི་མོ་བསུབས་སོང་ (He) erased the drawing on the blackboard. 2. va. to suffocate, to choke ¶ དབུག་བསུབས་ནས་བསད་པ་རེད་ (They) killed (him) by suffocating.

སུབ་བཀྱིགས་ (sūbgyig) packing/ tying up a load for a trip; va.—བྱེད་.

སུབ་བཅོས་ (sūbjöö̀) erasing and correcting (editing); va.—རྒྱག.

སུབ་ཏུ་མེད་པ་ (sūbdu me̠èba) impossible to erase/ rub out/ obliterate; va.—འཛུགས to do sth. that cannot be erased/ obliterated/ eradicated ¶ ཁོང་གི་རྒྱལ་ཁབ་ཀྱི་ཆེད་དུ་བྱས་རྗེས་སུབ་ཏུ་མེད་པ་བཞག་ཡོད་པ་རེད་ His achievements on behalf of the country cannot be obliterable.

སུབ་ཐབས་མེད་པ་ (sūbdob me̠èba) sm. སུབ་ཏུ་མེད་པ་.

སུབ་ཐིངས་གཅིག་སུབ་ (sūndeŋ jīsub) va. to cancel/ reject with one stroke.

སུབ་སུབ་ (sūbsub) obliterating, erasing, rubbing out; va.—བྱེད་.

སུམ་ (sūm) three ¶ སུམ་ཅུ་ Thirty.

སུམ་: p. བསུམས་; f. བསུམ་; imp. སུམས་ (sūm) va. to close, to shut (a pouch or bag), to draw a pouch shut ¶ རས་ཁུག་གི་ཁ་བསུམས་སོང་ He tied shut the cloth bag.

སུམ་ཁྲི་ (sūmdri) thirty thousand.

སུམ་འགྱུར་ (sūmgyur) increasing three times, tripling ¶ ལོ་འདིའི་གནག་ཕྱུགས་ཀྱི་གྲངས་འབོར་སུམ་འགྱུར་བྱུང་འདུག The number of yaks tripled this year.

སུམ་བརྒྱ་ (sūmgya) three hundred.

སུམ་སྒྱུར་ (sūmgyur) sm.* སུམ་འགྱུར་.

སུམ་བསྒྲིགས་ (sūmdrig) three of a thing arranged together.

སུམ་ཅུ་ (sūmju) thirty.

སུམ་ཅུ་ཐམ་པ་ (sūmju tāmba) sm. སུམ་ཅུ་.

སུམ་ཅུ་པ་ (sūmjubə) the basic Tibetan text on Tibetan grammar.

སུམ་ཅུ་རྩ་གསུམ་ (sūmju dzāsum) 1. thirty three. 2. a realm of the gods.

སུམ་ཆ་ (sūmja) a third ¶ སུམ་ཆ་གཉིས་ Two thirds.

སུམ་གཉིས་ (sūmñiì) two thirds.

སུམ་རྟགས་ (sūmdaà) Tibetan grammar.

སུམ་ལྟེབ་ (sūmdəb) three folds (of sth.), sth. folded into thirds.

སུམ་སྟོང་ (sūmdoŋ) three thousand.

སུམ་ཐོག (sūmdɔɔ̀) three story (house, etc.).

སུམ་མདོ་ (sūmdo) a place where three roads intersect.

སུམ་པའི་རུ་ (sūmbɛ ru̠) one of the four areas in Central Tibet during the era of the kings.

སུམ་འབུམ་ (sūmbum) three hundred thousand.

སུམ་སྦྱར་པང་ལེབ་ (sūmjar bāŋleè) plywood, three-ply wood.

སུམ་སྒྲགས་ (sūmdraà) three things put together/ joined together; three things that occurred (one after another) together/ at one time—གཏོང་ ¶ ཚིག་མཛོད་ཀྱི་སྟོད་ཆ་དང་བར་ཆ་སྨད་ཆ་བཅས་སུམ་སྒྲགས་ཀྱི་དེབ་ཆེན་པོ་ཞིག་འདུག The fiirst, second and third volumes of the dictionary are put together in one large volume.

སུམ་སྒྲིལ་ (sūmdree) three of sth. joined together; va.—བྱེད་.

སུམ་རྩེག (sūmdzeg) anything stacked up in threes; e.g., three stories/ layers.

སུམ་རྩེན་ (sūmdzen) heaven, the realm of the gods.

སུམ་རྩེན་བདག་པོ་ (sūmdzen dagbo) shung. sm. ལྷའི་དབང་པོ་.

སུམ་རྩེན་མདུན་མ་ (sūmdzen dünmə) shung. sm. ལྷ་ཡུལ་.

སུམ་བརྩེགས་དུས་རབས་ (sūmdzeg tüürəb) the Triassic Period.

སུམ་ཚུགས་ (sūmdzuù) sth. that is triangular shaped.

སུམ་ཟུར་ (sūmsur) 1. one third. 2. three cornered.

སུམ་ཡར་ (sūmyar) three and above.

སུམ་རིམ་པ་ (sūm rimbə) three stages/ levels.

སུམ་ལོག (sūmlɔɔ̀) sm. སུམ་འགྱུར་.

སུམས་ (sūm) imp. of སུམ་པ་.

སུའི་ (sũũ) whose ། དེབ་འདི་སུའི་རེད་ Whose book is this?

སུའི་སྨན་ (sūmɛn) sm. སུག་སྨིལ་.

སུའི་ཛར་ལེན་ (sũũdzarlɛn) Switzerland.

སུའུ་ (sūū) abbr. of སུའུ་ཝེ་ཨེད་.

སུའུ་ཀེ་ལན་ (sūgelɛn) Scotland.

སུའུ་གུང་ཀྲུང་དབྱང་ (sūguŋ drūŋyaŋ) ch. the Central Committee of the Communist Party of the Soviet Union.

སུའུ་ཏན་ (sūūdɛn) Sudan.

སུའུ་ཌན་ (sūudɛn) Sweden.

སུའུ་དབྱི་ཧྲི་གཙང་པོ་ (sūūyihri) Suez Canal.

སུའུ་ཝེ་ཨེད་ (sūūwaed) ch. soviet.

སུའུ་མོང་ (sūūmoŋ) ch. Soviet-Mongol (abbr. of སུའུ་ལེན་དང་མོང་གོལ་).

སུའུ་ཝེའི་ཨེད་སྤྱི་ཚོགས་རིང་ལུགས་སྤྱི་མཐུན་རྒྱལ་ཁབ་མཉམ་འབྲེལ་གྱི་རྒྱལ་ཁབ་ (sūūwed jidzoò riŋluù jidün gyɛɛgəb nāndreegi gyɛɛgəb) ch.tib. the Union of Soviet Socialist Republics (USSR).

སུའུ་ལིའན་ (sūlin) sm. སུའུ་ལེན་.

སུའུ་ལེན་ (sūlen) ch. the Soviet Union ། སུའུ་ལེན་སྲིད་གཞུང་ The government of the Soviet Union.

སུའུ་ཏར་ཚང་བ་ (sūdar cūŋwə) tib. ch. sodium bicarbonate.

སུའོ་ལིའོ་ (sūliu) ch. plastic.

སུར་ (sūū) to whom.

སུར་དཀར་ (sūrgar) azalea.

སུར་རྒྱག (sūr gyaà) vi. to become rotten/ moldy ། མར་རྙིང་པ་དེ་ལ་སུར་བརྒྱབ་བཞག The old butter got moldy.

སུར་སྒྲ་ (sūrdra) sizzling sound when water is tossed on fire.

སུར་དུག (sūrduù) a disease that afflicts lambs.

སུར་པན་ (sūūbɛn) hot pepper, chili.

སུར་ཤོར་ (sūr shɔ̄ɔ̄) sm. སུར་རྒྱག.

སུར་ན་ (sūrna) sm. རྒྱ་སྣིང་.

སུལ་ (sũũ) 1. a pleat, fold. 2. a furrow/ groove. 3. folds in a mountain.

སུལ་སྡུད་ (sūū düü) va. to pleat/ fold sth., to gather into pleats/ folds.

སུལ་འཛིན་ (sũũjin) sm. སུན་འཛིན་.

སུལ་མ་ (sũũmə) creases, folds.

སུལ་རུབ་ (sũũ rub) vi. to become creased.

སུལ་རུབ་རུབ་བྱེད་ (sūū rubrub ceè) 1. sm. སུལ་སྡུད་. 2. sm. སུལ་རུབ་.

སུལ་ལམ་ (sũũlam) a twisting path on a mountain overlooking a gorge.

སུལ་སུལ་ (sũũsüü) having many creases/ folds/ pleats.

སུས་ (sũũ) 1. by whom ། སུས་བཤད་པ་རེད་ Who said it? [Lit. it was said by whom]. 2. (སུས་ + vb. + འདི་ + vb. མེད་པ་) not knowing who did sth. ། སུས་གཏོར་འདི་གཏོར་མེད་པ་ Not knowing who destroyed it.

སུས་བཏབ་དེས་བསྡུ་ (sũũdəb teè du) the policy in 1959 just following "democratic reforms" stipulating that whoever cultivated a field could keep the yield.

སུས་བཏབ་ན་དེས་བསྡུ་ (sũũdəbna teè du) sm. སུས་བཏབ་དེས་བསྡུ་.

སེ་ (sē) 1. one of the four ancient lineage of Tibet. 2. name of a bird. 3. a kind of white clay for making pottery. 4. abbr. Sera monastery.

སེ་གོ་དིང་ (sēgodiŋ) sm. གོ་བོ་སླག་པག.

སེ་གོ་བོ་ (sēgowo) sm. སེ་གོ་དིང་.

སེ་གོལ་ (sēgöö) snapping (of fingers); va.—རྡེབ་; —གཏོགས་ to snap (one's fingers).

སེ་གོལ་གཅིག་ལ་ (sēgöö jīglə) sm. སེ་གོལ་ཙམ་ལ་.

སེ་གོལ་གཏོགས་ཙམ་ (sēgöö dōgdzam) in the time it takes to snap one's fingers, in a moment.

སེ་གོལ་ཙམ་ལ་ (sēgöö dzāmla) sm. སེ་གོལ་གཏོགས་ཙམ་.

སེ་རྒོད་ (sēgöö̀) wild pomegranate.

སེ་ཆེན་རྒྱལ་པོ་ (sējen gyɛɛbo) Kublai Khan.

སེ་དུག (sēduù) sm. སེ་མོག.

སེ་བདར་ (sēdar) a file used on iron.

སེ་འདྲི་ (sēndri) body odor.

སེ་པན་སྐམ་སིལ་ (sēbɛn gāmsii) powdered hot pepper.

སེ་བ་ (sēwa) 1. rosa sericea (used in Tibetan medicine). 2. a unit for measuring gold (100 སེ་བ་ equals 1 ཞོ་).

སེ་བོ་ (sēwo) gray (color).

སེ་བོན་ (sēbön) a Bon sect.

སེ་བྱ་ (sēca) sm. སེ་གོ་དིང་.

སེ་འབྲས་དགའ་གསུམ་ (sēndrɛɛ̀ gasum,) abbr. of the three monastic seats of the Gelug sect: Sera, Drepung and Ganden.

སེ་འབྲུ་ (sĩndru) pomegranate.

སེ་འབྲུ་རྡོ་ (sĩndru do) garnet.

སེ་མན་ (sēmɛn) silk wadding.

སེ་མོག (sēmɔɔ̀) syphilis; vi.—རྒྱག.

སེ་ཞོ་ (sēsho) abbr. two units for measuring the weight of gold (སེ་ and ཞོ་).

སེ་ཡབ་ (sēyəb) papaya.

སེ་ཡོ་རེ་བ་ (sēyo rewa) whitish.

སེ་ར་ (sēra) 1. Sera monastery. 2. hail; vi.—རྒྱག; —གཏོང་ to hail.

སེ་ར་ཕུར་མཇལ་ (sēra pūnjɛɛ) religious festival when Lhasa people go to Sera Monastery to see the dagger of Sera's protective deity Tamdin.

སེ་རུས་ (sērüü) old and tattered.

སེ་ཤར་རེ་བ་ (sēshar rewa) whitish.

སེ་ཤིང་ (sēshiŋ) sm. བསེ་ཤིང་.

སེག (sēg) 1. sm. གསེག. 2. སོ་སེག.

སེག་སྐོར་ (sēggɔɔ) the part of a Tibetan woolen boot where green and red legging materials are used.

སེག་དར་ (sēgdar) metal file.

སེག་མ་ (sēgma) a type of bamboo container.

སེང་ (sēŋ) abbr. of སེང་གེ་.

སེང་དཀར་ (sēŋgar) white snow lion.

སེང་ཁྲ་ (sēŋdra) window screen, mesh screen, iron bars that are put over windows.

སེང་ཁྲི་ (sēŋdri) the snow lion throne.

སེང་ག་གླིང་ (sēŋgaliŋ) sm. སེང་ག་ལ་.

སེང་ག་པོར་ (sēŋgabor) Singapore.

སེང་ག་ལ་ (sēŋgala) Sri Lanka, Ceylon.

སེང་གེ་ (sēŋge) mythical snow lion.

སེང་གེ་ཁ་འབབ་ (sēŋge kābəb) Indus River.

སེང་གེ་རྒྱན་གཞི་ (sēŋge gyɛnshi) a type of brocade with a snow lion design.

སེང་གེ་ཅང་ཤེས་ (sēŋge jāŋsheè) a mythical snow lion.

སེང་གེ་མི་གདོང་ (sēŋge midoŋ) the sphinx (of Egypt).

སེང་གེ་གཙང་པོ་ (sēŋge dzāŋbo) Indus River.

སེང་གེའི་སྐར་ཚོམ་ (sēŋgee gārdzom) the constellation Leo.

སེང་གེའི་མགོ་ལ་སྤྲེའུས་ལག་རྩེད་ (sēŋgee gola drēwü lagdzeè) playing with fire, doing things that are dangerous [Lit. monkey playing with the snow lion's head].

སེང་གེའི་ང་རོ་ (sēŋgee ŋaro) roar of a snow lion.

སེང་གེའི་ཉལ་སྟབས་ (sēŋgee ñɛɛdəb) Buddha's sleeping position, i.e., sleeping on one's right side with the palm of the right hand under one's right cheek and the left hand resting on one's left thigh.

སེང་གེའི་ཡ་མགལ་ལ་ཁྱིའི་མ་མགལ་སྣད་པ་ (sēŋgee

yagεεla kyīī magεε drε̄èba) doing or saying things that are inappropriate [Lit. putting the lower jaw of a dog on the upper jaw of a snow lion].

སེང་གེའི་གཡུ་རལ་ལ་སྤྲེའུའི་ལག་རྫེད་ (sēŋgee yūrεεla drēwü lagdzεε) sm. སེང་གེའི་མགོ་ལ་སྤྲེའུས་ལག་རྫེད་.

སེངྒེ་ (sēŋge) sm. སེང་གེ་.

སེང་སྒམ་ (sēŋgam) a wire or net cover that is put over food to keep flies away.

སེང་སྒྲོན་ (sēŋgrön) sm. ས་བཞུ་.

སེང་ལྕམ་འབྲུག་མོ་ (sēŋjam drugmo) wife of the legendary King Gesar.

སེང་དྲག (sēŋdraà) recovering completely ¶ཁོང་སྣན་གཞི་སེང་དྲག་བྱུང་བ་རེད་ He recovered completely from his illness.

སེང་དྲག་བྱུང་ཚད་ (sēŋdraà cuŋdzεὲ) cure rate.

སེང་ལྡེང་ (sēŋdeŋ) a type of sandalwood.

སེང་པོ་ (sēŋbo) 1. a loose weave/ lattice. 2. a crack/ gap between planks, etc.

སེང་ཕྲུག (sēŋdruù) lion cub.

སེང་ཕྲུག་ལུས་སྟོབས་ཆུང་ཡང་སེང་གེའི་རྒྱུད་.(sēŋdrug lüüdob cūnyaŋ sēŋgee gyüü) one can't change one's birth status/ caste [Lit. even though a snow lion cub is small in body, it is still a snow lion].

སེང་འབྲུག (sēŋ drüù) abbr. snow lion and dragon.

སེང་མ་ (sēŋma) sm. སེང་པོ་.

སེང་རྩེད་ (sēŋdzeè) the snow lion dance.

སེང་ཚགས་ (sēŋdzaà) a very sheer gauze-like cloth used for straining things; va.—རྒྱག.

སེང་ཞྭ་ (sēŋsha) black gauze cap worn by officials in old society.

སེང་ཡོལ་ (sēŋyöö) a very sheer/ gauze-like curtain.

སེང་གཡབ་ (sēāyəb) the open area in the middle of some traditional Tibetan houses.

སེང་རས་ (sēŋrεε) gauze, very sheer cloth/ gauze, muslin cloth.

སེང་ཤོར་ (sēŋshɔɔ) shung. carelessness, negligence, oversight.

སེང་སེང་པོ་ (sēŋ sēŋbo) sm. སེང་པོ་.

སེངས་ (sēŋ) sm.* སེང་.

སེད་ (sēè) imp. of གསེད་.

སེན་ (sēn) abbr. of སེན་མོ་.

སེན་སྐྱི་ལོག (sēngyi lɔɔ̀) vi. to have a hangnail.

སེན་རྒྱ་ (sēngya) sth. the size of a fingernail ¶རང་ས་སེན་རྒྱ་ཙམ་ཡང་དགྲ་བོར་མི་སྤྲོད་ཐག་ཆོད་ཡིན་ We will never give any of our land to the enemy, even as much as a fingernail's worth.

སེན་གཙུས་ (sēnjüü) pinching; va.—རྒྱག to pinch.

སེན་གཏུབ་ (sēndub) nail cutter/ clipper.

སེན་བཏོག (sēndɔɔ̀) pinching; va.—རྒྱག; —འདེབས་ to pinch.

སེན་སྟོང་སེངས་པོ་ (sēndoŋ sēŋbo) weak ཆང་ (that has had water added for the fourth time).

སེན་འཐོག (sēndɔɔ̀) sm. སེན་བཏོག.

སེན་འདྲ་བཟོ་གྲྭ (sēndra sodra) nail clipper factory.

སེན་སྤྲོམ་ (sēndrom) areca, betel palm.

སེན་བར་ (sēnbar) the space between the nails.

སེན་མོ་ (sēnmo) fingernails, toenails ¶རྐང་པའི་སེན་མོ་ Toenails.

སེན་མོ་གང་ (sēnmo kaŋ) a little (bit), a moment ¶ཁྱེད་རང་སེན་མོ་གང་བཞུགས་ Stay just a little bit.

སེན་མོས་གཅོད་ (sēnmöö jöö) va. to cut/ break with one's nails.

སེན་མོའི་བཀྲག་རྩི་ (sēnmö drāgdzi) nail polish; va.—གཏོང་.

སེན་མོར་བྱུགས་ཡས་ (sēnmɔɔ cuùyεὲ) nail polish.

སེན་རྩ་ (sēndza) the part of the finger where the nail starts to grow.

སེན་ཚོས་ (sēndzöö) nail polish.

སེན་ཤ་ (sēnsha) the cuticle around the nail; vi.—བྲལ་ the cuticle becoming separated from the nail.

སེབ་རྒྱག (sēbgyaà) sm. སེབ་གཏོང་.

སེབ་གཏོང་ (sēb dōŋ) va. to fill a container only loosely with རྩམ་པ་ (i.e., to not compress it).

སེབ་སེབ་ (sēbseb) sm. སེབ་གཏོང་.

སེམས་ (sēm) 1. the mind ¶སེམས་ཀྱི་ངལ་རྩོལ་ Mental labor. ¶སེམས་བཟང་པོ་ Sb. with a kind mind. 2. (vb. + —) thinking of doing a verbal action ¶ང་བོད་ལ་འགྲོ་སེམས་མེད་ I have no thoughts of going to Tibet.

སེམས་: p. **བསམས་**; f. **བསམ་**; imp. **སོམས་** (sēm) vi. to think, to conceive ¶ཁྱེད་རང་ཕེབས་ཡོང་བསམས་མ་བྱུང་ (I) did not think you would come. ¶དེ་ཡོང་མི་སྲིད་པ་ཞིག་རེད་སེམས་ཀྱི་ཡོད་པ་རེད་ (They) think that it is impossible for that to happen.

སེམས་ཀྱི་དམ་པ་ (sēmgi tamba) bodhicitta.

སེམས་ཀྱི་ཁྱད་པར་ (sēmgi kyε̄èbar) 1. an expression or sign of one's thoughts/ feelings ¶ལག་རྟགས་འདི་ཆུང་ཆུང་ཡིན་ནའང་ངའི་སེམས་ཀྱི་ཁྱད་པར་ཡིན་པས་བཞེས་རོགས་གནང་ Even though the gift is small, it is an expression of my thoughts. 2. making a difference in someone's thoughts, fulfilling/ pleasing sb.'s wishes or thoughts ¶ནད་པ་འདི་ལ་ཕན་མིན་ལ་མ་ལྟོས་པར་སྔགས་རྒྱག་མཁན་དེ་སྐད་བཏང་ན་དགའ་གི་རེད་ ཁོ་རང་གི་སེམས་ཀྱི་ཁྱད་པར་རེད་ Regardless whether this benefits the patient, it is better to call the Ngagpa to please his wish.

སེམས་ཀྱི་ཁྱེར་སོ་ (sēmgi kyērso) attitude, viewpoint ¶ཁོའི་སེམས་ཀྱི་ཁྱེར་སོ་ཡག་པོ་མེད་ཙང་ལས་ཀ་ཡག་པོ་ཡོང་གི་མེད་པ་རེད་ Because his attitude is bad, he will not work well.

སེམས་ཀྱི་དོག་གྲོལ་ (sēmgi dogdröö) a mental burden; vi.—ཕབ་ to have a mental burden removed.

སེམས་ཀྱི་གཏིང་ (sēmgi diŋ) from the bottom of one's heart.

སེམས་ཀྱི་སྦུག་དུ་ (sēmgi bugdu) in one's inner thoughts ¶ཁོའི་སེམས་ཀྱི་སྦུག་དུ་གང་དྲན་ཡིན་མི་ཤེས་ཁ་མཁས་པོ་ཞིག་ཤོད་ཀི་འདུག I don't know what is in his inner thoughts. He is talking cautiously (on this issue).

སེམས་ཀྱི་ཅེ་བྲག (sēmgi cedraà) sm. སེམས་ཀྱི་ཁྱད་པར་, 2.

སེམས་ཀྱི་ཚོར་བ་ (sēmgi tsɔ̄rwa) sensations of the mind.

སེམས་ཀྱི་རི་མོ་ (sēmgi rimu) one's inner thoughts.

སེམས་དཀར་བ་ (sēm gārwa) kind, generous.

སེམས་དཀྲུག (sēm drūù) va. to make sb. deliberately angry.

སེམས་སྐྱིད་པོ་ (sēm gyīibu) happy, joyful.

སེམས་སློང་ཡངས་པ་ (sēmloŋ yaŋba) tolerant and openminded.

སེམས་སྐུལ་ (sēmgüü) encouraging, giving encouragement; va.—གཏོང་ ¶བཟོ་པ་རྣམས་ལ་སེམས་སྐུལ་བཏང་ནས་ལས་ཀ་མགྱོགས་པོ་ཚར་བ་བྱེད་དགོས་ (You) must encourage the workers to finish the work faster.

སེམས་སྐྱོ་ (sēm gyō) vi. to get/ feel sad.

སེམས་སྐྱོ་སྣང་བྱེད་ (sēmgyo nāŋceè) sm. སེམས་སྐྱོ་.

སོམས་སྐྱོ་པོ་ (sēm gyōbo) sad.

སེམས་ཁ་བདེ་ (sēmgade) sm. བློ་བདེ་.

སེམས་ཁ་མ་བདེ་བ་ (sēmga madewa) sm. བློ་མ་བདེ་བ་.

སེམས་ཁམས་ཀྱི་རིག་པ་ (sēmgamgi rigbə) psychology, psychiatry.

སེམས་ཁམས་ཀྱི་ཨམ་ཇི་ (sēmgamgi ə̄mji) psychiatrist, psychologist, mental health therapist.

སེམས་ཁམས་སློབ་ཚོགས་ (sēmgam lōbdzoò) society of psychology.

སེམས་ཁུག (sēm kūù) vi. to be brought around/ changed/ reformed in thinking (for the better) ¶མི་ངན་པ་དེ་སེམས་ཁུག་ནས་ཡག་པོ་ཆགས་བཞག The bad person became reformed in his thinking and became good.

སེམས་ཁུར་ (sēmgur) concern, interest; va.— བྱེད་ to show concern/ interest ¶མང་ཚོགས་ཀྱི་འཚོ་བ་ལ་སེམས་འཁུར་བྱེད་དགོས་ (We) should have concern for the livelihood of the masses.

སེམས་ཁུར་ཆེན་པོ་ (sēmgur cēmbo) having great concern/ interest.

སེམས་ཁེངས་ (sēm kēŋ) vi. to be satisfied/ content ¶ ཤིང་བཟོ་བ་དེ་གླ་ཆར་སེམས་ཁེངས་མ་སོང་ The carpenter was not satisfied with his wages.

སེམས་ཁོང་ (sēmnaŋ) sm. སེམས་ནང་.

སེམས་ཁྱད་ (sēmgyεὲ) sm. སེམས་ཀྱི་ཁྱད་པར་.

སེམས་ཁྲལ་ (sēmdrεε) worry, anxiety; va.—བྱེད་; —སེལ་ to remove/ anxiety, to make a person stop worrying ¶ ངའི་ནང་མི་བདེ་པོ་ཡིན་པའི་ཡིག་གི་འབྱོར་ནས་ངའི་སེམས་ཁྲལ་བསལ་སོང་ I received a letter saying my family is well so I stopped worrying.

སེམས་ཁྲིག་ཁྲིག (sēm drīgdriì) bad character/ morals.

སེམས་ཁྲིད་རྒྱག (sēmdriì gyaà) va. to teach the nature of the mind.

སེམས་ཁྲེལ་ (sēmdree) worry, anxiety; va.—བྱེད་ to worry, to be anxious ¶ སེམས་ཁྲལ་མ་བྱེད་ Don't worry.

སེམས་ཁྲིས་ (sēmdreè) abbr. of སེམས་ཀྱི་རྟོག་ཁྲིས་.

སེམས་མཁན་ (sēmgεn) sentient beings.

སེམས་མཁྲེགས་པོ་ (sēm drēgbo) 1. stubborn, hardheaded. 2. having no compassion, merciless.

སེམས་འཁུར་ (sēmgur) sm. སེམས་ཁུར་.

སེམས་འཁུལ་ (sēm kǖū) vi. to be able to overcome/ control/ subdue one's mental faculties ¶ ཆོས་ཉམས་ལེན་བྱས་པའི་འབྲས་བུ་དེ་རང་གི་སེམས་འཁུལ་ཐུབ་པ་ཞིག་དགོས་ The fruit of practicing dharma should be that one should be able to control one's mental faculties.

སེམས་འཁོལ་ (sēm kō̄ō) vi. to feel happy/ elated/ joyful.

སེམས་འཁྱོག་པོ་ (sēm kyōgbo) cunning, deceitful.

སེམས་འཁྲི་ (sēmdri) sm. དགའ་ཞེན་.

སེམས་འཁྲུལ་ (sēm trǖū) vi. to think about sth. in a wrong/ inappropriate way, to be misled/ wrong/ deluded in thinking about sth. 2. vi. to be/ have delusions.

སེམས་འཁྲུགས་ (sēm trūù) vi. to be upset/ disturbed/ agitated.

སེམས་ག་དོག་པོ་ (sēm ku̲ to̲gbo) narrow-minded, petty.

སེམས་ག་ཡངས་པོ་ (sēm ku̲ ya̲ŋbo) lighthearted, easygoing.

སེམས་དགའ་ (sēm ga̲) vi. to be happy.

སེམས་དགའ་པོ་ (sēm ga̲bo) a happy feeling ¶ དེ་འདྲ་བྱས་ན་ཁོང་དགའ་པོ་ཡོང་གི་རེད་ If you do that, he will be happy.

སེམས་སྒྱུ་མ་སྒྱུ (sēmgya mə̲gyu) cunning, deceiving.

སེམས་སྒོང་པོ་ (sēm gyo̲ŋbo) tough, hardhearted.

སེམས་འགག (sēm ga̲à) vi. to faint.

སེམས་འགྱུ (sēm gu̲ù) va. to change/ reform sb.'s thinking ¶ གཡོ་ཐབས་ཀྱིས་གཞན་སེམས་འགྱུག་གི་ཡོད་པ་རེད་ (They) are changing people's thinking by deceitful means.

སེམས་འགུལ་ (sēm gǖū) affected emotionally, deeply moved/ touched; vi.—ཐེབས་ to be emotionally moved/ touched ¶ ཁོང་གི་གསུང་བཤད་དེས་མི་ཚང་མར་སེམས་འགུལ་ཐེབས་པ་རེད་ His talk moved all the people.

སེམས་འགྱུར་ (sēm gyu̲r) vi. to have one's mind get changed ¶ འགོ་ཁྲིད་ཀྱིས་སློབ་གསོ་བརྒྱབ་རྗེས་ཁོའི་སེམས་འགྱུར་བཞག The leader gave him advice and his mind got changed.

སེམས་འགྱོད་ (sēm gyō̲ö) sm. སེམས་འགྱོད་གདུང་.

སེམས་འགྱོད་གདུང་ (sēm gyō̲ödu̲ŋ) regretting; vi.—སྐྱེ་ ¶ མི་དེས་སྔོན་བྱས་ཀྱི་ནག་ཉེས་ལ་སེམས་འགྱོད་གདུང་སྐྱེས་པ་རེད་ That person regretted his past evil deeds.

སེམས་རྒྱ་སྐྱིད་ (sēmgya gyēè) sm. བློ་རྒྱ་ཆེ་སྐྱིད.

སེམས་རྒྱ་མ་ཆུང་བ་ (sēmgya ma̲juŋwa) shung. sm. གདོང་ཡོད་ཆེན་པོ་.

སེམས་རྒྱུད་ (sēmgyüü) quality of the mind, character ¶ སེམས་རྒྱུད་བཟང་པོ་ A good/ generous character.

སེམས་རྒྱུད་ངང་རིང་ (sēmgyüü ŋə̲ŋriŋ) patient, tolerant.

སེམས་རྒྱུད་དག་པ་ (sēmgyüü ta̲gba) pure in heart.

སེམས་རྒྱུན་ (sēmgyün) sm. སེམས་པ་.

སེམས་སྒྱུར་ (ēm gyu̲r) va. to change sb.'s mind/ views.

སེམས་སྒྱུར་ལུས་སྒྱུར་ (sēmgyur lü̲ügyur) a complete change [Lit. change mind, change body].

སེམས་ངན་ (sēmŋεn) evil/ malicious thoughts.

སེམས་ང་རོ་པོ་ (sēm ŋa̲rbo) sb. who is very aggressive.

སེམས་ངལ་ (sēm ŋε̲ε̲) sm. སེམས་ཁྲལ་.

སེམས་ངེས་པོ་ (sēm ŋe̲èbo) sb. who has a good memory.

སེམས་ཅན་ (sēmjεn) 1. sentient beings. 2. animals ¶ མི་ཚང་དེར་སེམས་ཅན་མང་པོ་ཡོད་པ་རེད་ That household has many animals.

སེམས་ཅན་དཀར་ནག (sēmjεn gārnaà) shung. cattle/ yaks and sheep/ goats.

སེམས་ཅན་ལ་འཚེ་བ་འགོག་ཐབས་ཀྱི་སྒྲིག་འཛུགས་ (sēmjεnla tsēwa gə̲gdəbgi drigdzuù) Society for the Prevention of Cruelty to Animals.

སེམས་ཅན་སྤུ་ནག (sēmjεn būnaà) shung. yaks.

སེམས་ཅན་གསོ་མཁན་ (sēmjεn sōgεn) animal caretaker.

སེམས་གཅོང་ (sēmjoŋ) great sadness; vi.— ཞུགས་ to become sad; va.—འཇུག to cause sadness in sb.; vi.—སངས་ to have one's sadness disappear/ be relieved ¶ ཁོང་གི་གྲོགས་མོ་དེས་ཕྱི་ག་གཞན་དག་བཙལ་ཏེ་ཁོང་ལ་སེམས་གཅོང་བཙུག་བཞག His girlfriend going after another man caused him great sadness.

སེམས་ཆགས་ (sēm cāà) vi. to be attached to, to be fond of ¶ ཁོ་རྒྱ་ནོར་ལ་སེམས་ཆགས་ནས་དུས་ཐོག་ལ་བྲོས་མ་ཐུབ་པ་རེད་ Because (he) was attached to (his) wealth (he) was unable to escape in time.

སེམས་ཆགས་ཡུལ་ཆགས་ (sēm cāà yü̲ü̲jaà) sm. སེམས་ཆགས་.

སེམས་ཆུང་ (sēmjuŋ) humble, meek, timid; va.—བྱེད་ to be humble/ meek/ timid.

སེམས་ཆུང་ཆུང་ (sēm cūŋjuŋ) sm. སེམས་ཆུང་.

སེམས་ཆུང་བག་ཟོན་ (sēmjuŋ pa̲gsön) humble and unassuming.

སེམས་ཆེན་ (sēmjen) 1. brave, courageous. 2. Bodhisattva.

སེམས་ཆེན་པོ་ (sēm cēmbo) knowing everything.

སེམས་འཆལ་ (sēm cε̄ε) vi. to have a wanton, unbridled mind, to have a mind that is uncontrollable ¶ ར་བཟི་བ་ཡིན་ན་སེམས་འཆལ་ནས་གང་བྱུང་བྱེད་སྲིད་ If (one) becomes drunk, (one) is unable to control (one's) mind and is liable to do anything.

སེམས་འཆོལ་ (sēm cō̄ō) vi. to have delusions.

སེམས་འཛགས་ (sēmjaà) bearing, keeping in mind; va.—བྱེད་; —ཞུ་ to bear/ keep in mind, to remember ¶ ང་ཚོར་ཡི་གི་ཡང་ཡང་གཏོང་རྒྱུ་སེམས་འཛགས་བྱེད་རོགས་ Please remember to write us often.

སེམས་འཛོག (sēm jɔ̲ɔ̀) va. to concentrate (the mind on) ¶ ལས་ཀའི་ཐོག་ལ་སེམས་བཞག་ན་ལས་ཀ་ཡག་པོ་ཡོང་གི་རེད་ If you concentrate on work, the work will go well.

སེམས་ཉིད་ (sēmñii) the mind itself.

སེམས་མཉམ་སྟོབས་སྒྲིལ་ (sēmñam dōbdrii) making a united effort, pulling together; va.—བྱེད་ ¶ ང་ཚོ་ཚང་མས་སེམས་མཉམ་སྟོབས་སྒྲིལ་གྱིས་དཀའ་ལས་བརྒྱབ་ན་ང་ཚོའི་དམིགས་ཡུལ་བསྒྲུབ་ཐུབ་ངེས་རེད་ If we all pull together and work hard we can achieve our goals.

སེམས་གདད་ (sēm dε̄è) p. of སེམས་གཏོད་.

སེམས་གདམ་ (sēm dam) sm. སྙིང་གདམ་.

སེམས་གཏིང་ལ་འཛོག (sēmdiŋlə jɔ̲ɔ̀) va. to keep in the bottom of one's mind/ heart.

སེམས་གདོང་ (sēm dōŋ) va. to have a feeling that sb. is thinking of (oneself), to have an intuitive feeling ¶ དེ་རིང་ང་སེམས་བདན་ནི་བུ་ནི་བྱེད་ཀྱི་འདུག་མི་ཞིག་གིས་ང་ལ་སེམས་གདོང་གི་ཡོད་པ་འདྲ་ I feel troubled today. I have a feeling that sb. is thinking of me.

སེམས་གཏོད་ (sēm dȫȍ) va. to trust/ rely on ¶ མི་དེ་ལ་སེམས་གཏད་ཆོག་གི་རེད་ You can trust in that person. 2. sm. སེམས་འཇོག.

སེམས་རྟེན་ (sēmden) a remembrance, keepsake.

སེམས་སྡོང་ལྷང་ལྷང་ (sēmdoŋ lhāŋlhaŋ) lonely, desolate.

སེམས་སྡོབས་ (sēmdob) sm. སེམས་ཤུགས་.

སེམས་སྡོར་ (sēm dɔ̄ɔ) va. to make perplexed/ confused/ troubled.

སེམས་བརྟན་པོ་ (sēm dɛ̄mbo) 1. a good/ reliable memory. 2. sb. who doesn't get nervous, a careful/ steady person.

སེམས་ཐག (sēmdaà) 1. absolutely, certainly (usu. in a negative sense) ¶ ང་མ་འགྲོ་སེམས་ཐག་ཡིན་ I am absolutely not going. 2. hopeless/ no chance of getting sth. ¶ ཁྱེད་རང་ལ་ལས་ཀ་འདི་རག་རྒྱུ་སེམས་ཐག་རེད་ You have no chance of getting that job.

སེམས་ཐག་སྒོར་མོའི་རྡོ་ (sēmdaà g̲ɔ̲ɔmö d̲o̲) sm. སེམས་ཐག, 2.

སེམས་ཐག་གཅོད་ (sēmdaà jȫȍ) va. to decide, to make up one's mind ¶ གཤག་བཅོས་བྱེད་རྒྱུར་སེམས་ཐག་བཅད་ (He) made up his mind to undergo the operation.

སེམས་ཐག་ཆོད་ (sēmdaà cȫȍ) vi. to be decided/ convinced, to come to a decision, to make up one's mind ¶ ཁོ་ཕྱིར་ལོག་མི་ཡོང་རྒྱུར་སེམས་ཐག་ཆོད་སོང་ (I) am convinced that he will not return.

སེམས་ཐག་ཆོད་པོ་ (sēmdaà cȫȍbo) able to come a decision easily, sb. able to make up one's mind.

སེམས་ཐག་ཆོད་ཡིག (sēmdaà cȫȍyii) resolution.

སེམས་ཐག་ཐད་བཅད་ (sēmdaà b̲ɛ̲ɛ̀jɛɛ̀) resolutely, with complete determination ¶ འཐབ་འཛིངས་བྱེད་རྒྱུར་སེམས་ཐག་ཐད་བཅད་ཡིན་ (We) are determined to fight. ¶ ཁོ་ཚོས་སེམས་ཐག་ཐད་བཅད་ཀྱིས་འཐབ་འཛིང་བྱས་སོང་ They fought resolutely.

སེམས་ཐག་གཅང་བཅད་ (sēmdaà dzāŋjɛɛ̀) sm. སེམས་ཐག་ཐད་བཅད་.

སེམས་ཐག་རིང་པོ་ (sēmdaà r̲i̲ŋbu) having a feeling of helplessness because sth. will take a long time ¶ ཁང་པ་དེ་རྒྱག་པར་ལོ་བཅུ་འགོར་གྱི་རེད་ཟེར་དུས་ང་སེམས་ཐག་རིང་པོ་བྱུང་ When I heard that it will take ten years to build that house, I had a feeling of helplessness because of how long it was going to take.

སེམས་ཐང་ཆད་ (sēm tāŋjɛɛ̀) sm. ཡིད་ཐང་ཆད་.

སེམས་མཐུན་ (sēm tȫn) vi. to be of one mind, to agree.

སེམས་མཐུན་པོ་ (sēm tȫmbu) able to get along, seeing eye-to-eye, in harmony.

སེམས་མཐུན་སྡོབས་སྒྲིལ་ (sēmtün dōbdrii) sm. སེམས་མཉམ་སྡོབས་སྒྲིལ་.

སེམས་མདོ་ (sēmdo) conceit, pride, arrogance.

སེམས་དང་བ་ (sēm t̲a̲ŋwa) in total agreement ¶ ལས་ཀ་གསར་པ་དེ་ངས་སེམས་དང་བའི་སྒོ་ནས་ཁས་ལེན་ཞུས་པ་ཡིན་ I accepted the new job with total agreement.

སེམས་དྲང་པོ་ (sēm tr̲a̲ŋbo) honest, upright.

སེམས་དོགས་ (sēmdoò) worrying; va.—བྱེད་ ¶ ལས་ཀའི་ནང་ནོར་འཁྲུལ་ཡོང་གི་རེད་བསམས་པའི་སེམས་དོགས་བྱུང་ (I) worried that (I) would make mistakes in my work.

སེམས་དྲུག (sēmdruù) the six sense organs: eyes, nose, ears, tongue, body and mind.

སེམས་དུལ་མ་ཐུབ་པ་ (sēmdruù m̲a̲tubbə) unable to control oneself ¶ དོན་དངོས་ཐོག་རྐུན་མ་རྒྱུ་དགོས་ཡས་མེད་ཀྱང་སེམས་དུལ་མ་ཐུབ་པར་ཁོས་སྐབས་རེ་རྐུན་མ་རྒྱུ་གི་ཡོད་པ་རེད་ He steals sometimes even though there is no need because he is unable to control himself.

སེམས་གདིང་ཅན་ (sēmdiŋjɛn) shung. filled with grief ¶ དུ་ལའི་བླ་མ་ཞིང་དུ་གཤེགས་པ་ཐོས་པས་ ངའི་ནང་ལ་བྱམས་བརྩེ་ཆེན་པོ་སེམས་གདིང་ཅན་ When the Dalai Lama of the last incarnation passed away, my home was filled with grief and compassion.

སེམས་བདེ་པོ་ (sēm d̲e̲bo) happy; va.—བྱེད་.

སེམས་བདེ་བློ་བདེ་ (sēmde lōde) happy, content, glad; va.—བྱེད་.

སེམས་འདུལ་ (sēm d̲ü̲ü̲) va. to conquer/ pacify the mind.

སེམས་འདྲིས་ (sēmdriì) familiarity with sb.'s thinking.

སེམས་འདྲེན་མ་ (sēmdrenma) the mind being not consentrated/ focused/ clear, mentally mixed up ¶ སེམས་འདྲེན་མ་མ་ཡིན་པའི་རྩེ་གཅིག་གིས་སྒོམ་པ་ Meditating with a concentrated mind.

སེམས་འདྲེས་མ་ (sēmdreèma) sm. སེམས་འདྲེན་མ་.

སེམས་ལྡན་ (sēmdɛn) sm. སེམས་ཅན་.

སེམས་སྡུག (sēmduù) sadness, sorrow, depression; va.—བྱེད་ to be sad, to be depressed ¶ ངའི་སྤུན་མཆེད་གྲོངས་དུས་སེམས་སྡུག་བྱུང་ When my relative died I felt sad.

སེམས་སྡུག་པོ་ (sēm d̲u̲gbu) sad, unhappy.

སེམས་སྡུག་ཡིད་སྐྱོ་ (sēmduù y̲i̲igyo) sad, unhappy.

སེམས་སྡུག་ཉམ་ང་ (sēmduù ñ̲a̲ŋɛn) sad, unhappy, mournful.

སེམས་ན་ (sēm n̲a̲) 1. vi. to suffer mentally, to have mental illness. 2. vi. to be/ get hurt (mentally).

སེམས་ནག (sēmnaà) 1. cruel, vindictive, spiteful, mean, malicious, ill-willed; va.—བྱེད་ to act mean/ cruel/ spiteful/ malicious ¶ ཁོས་ང་ལ་སེམས་ནག་བྱས་ནས་ངའི་དེབ་སྦས་བཞག He acted mean to me by hiding my book. 2. rape; va.—བྱེད་ to rape.

སེམས་ནག་པོ་ (sēm n̲a̲gbo) sb. who is spiteful/ vindictive/ mean/ malicious.

སེམས་ནག་ཚ་པོ་ (sēmnaà tsābo) sm. བསམ་ནག་ཚ་པོ་.

སེམས་ནང་ (sēmnaŋ) in the mind.

སེམས་ནད་ (sēmnɛɛ̀) 1. sm. སེམས་གཅོང་. 2. mental illness; vi.—ན་; —ཐོག; —ལང་ to be/ get mentally ill; vi.—སངས་ to recover from mental illness.

སེམས་ནས་ཁས་བླངས་ (sēmnɛ kɛ̄ɛ̀laŋ) va. to give tacit consent.

སེམས་ནས་བསམ་ (sēmnɛ sām) va. to think sth. ¶ སེམས་ནས་བསམ་ཚད་ཁ་ནས་ཤོད་རྒྱུ་མེད་ (One) shouldn't say everything one thinks.

སེམས་གནག (sēmnaà) sm. སེམས་ནག.

སེམས་གནག་ལག་རྫུབ་ (sēmnaà l̲a̲gdzub) sm. སེམས་ནག་པོ་.

སེམས་གནོང་ (sēm nōŋ) vi. to feel regret.

སེམས་རྣལ་ (sēmnɛɛ) calm/ peaceful state of mind, cool-headed, unflustered; vi.—དུ་ཕབ་ to do or be calm/ unflustered ¶ སེམས་རྣལ་དུ་ཕབ་ནས་ལས་ཀ་བྱས་ན་ལས་ཀ་ཡག་པོ་ཡོང་གི་རེད་ If you work calmly, the work will go well.

སེམས་སྣང་ (sēmnaŋ) sm. འཚར་སྣང་.

སེམས་པ་ (sēmba) thoughts, thinking.

སེམས་པ་དཀར་པོ་ (sēmba gārbo) 1. kindhearted. 2. faithful.

སེམས་པ་འཁྱེང་ (sēmba trēŋ) vi. to be sad at parting/ separating.

སེམས་པ་འཁྲུག (sēmba trūù) vi. to be mentally disturbed/ upset.

སེམས་པ་སྙི་པོ་ (sēmba ñību) softhearted, tenderhearted.

སེམས་པ་ནག་པོ་ (sēmba nāgbo) spiteful, unkind.

སེམས་པ་དམར་པོ་ (sēmba māābo) sb. loyal to communism.

སེམས་པ་ཡངས་པོ་ (sēmba y̲a̲ŋbo) sm. སེམས་གཡེང་.

སེམས་པ་གསོད་ (sēmba sȫȍ) vi. to break a person's heart ¶ ཁྱེད་རང་གིས་བྱེད་སྟངས་དེ་ངའི་སེམས་པ་བསད་སོང་ Your behavior broke my heart.

སེམས་པ་ལྷོང་ལྷོང་ (sēmba lhōŋlhoŋ) an unpleasant/ uncomfortable feeling in one's mind.

སེམས་པའི་ཀུན་རྟོག (sēmbɛ gündoò) 1. sm. རྟོག་སྤྱོད་ 2. sm. རྣམ་རྟོག.

སེམས་པའི་ཡི་གེ་ (sēmbɛ y̲i̲ge) love letter.

སེམས་པས་ཕོད་ (sēmba pɔ̄ɔ) 1. vi. to do sth. without regret ¶ ལོ་མང་གཞིས་པའི་བཟའ་ཟླ་ནད་པ་དེ་དབྱུག་རྒྱ

སེམས་པས་ཡོད་པ་འདུག་གམ་ Can you leave your wife of many years who is sick without having regret? ¶ དབུལ་པོངས་རྣམས་ལ་སྦྱིན་པ་རྒྱ་ཆེན་པོ་འདི་ལྟ་བུ་གཏོང་རྒྱུ་སེམས་པས་ཡོད་པ་ངོ་མཚར་ཆེན་པོ་རེད་ It is miraculous that (he) could give so much alms to the poor people without having regrets.

སེམས་དཔངས་མཐོ་པོ་ (sēmbaŋ tōbo) sm. སེམས་མཐོ་.

སེམས་དཔའ་ (sēmba) brave.

སེམས་ཕུགས་སྲབ་པོ་ (sēmbaà drəbbu) softhearted.

སེམས་ཕངས་ (sēm pāŋ) vi. to feel sad, to feel it is a pity sth. happened ¶ ངའི་སྨྱུ་གུ་ཡག་པོ་དེ་བརླགས་ནས་སེམས་ཕངས་བྱུང་ I felt sad that I lost my good pen.

སེམས་ཕངས་པོ་ (sēm pāŋbo) felling sad.

སེམས་ཕམ་ (sēm pām) vi. to be disheartened/ despondent/ depressed ¶ ཚོགས་འདུའི་སར་ཁོང་གིས་ང་ལ་སྐྱོན་བརྗོད་བྱས་ནས་ང་སེམས་ཕམ་བྱུང་ I felt sad that he criticized me at the meeting.

སེམས་ཕམ་པོ་ (sēm pāŋbo) sad, despondent, disheartened, depressed.

སེམས་ཕམ་ཡིད་ཆད་ (sēmbam yi̱ìjɛɛ̀) despondent, sad, discouraged, depressed.

སེམས་འཕང་མཐོན་པོ་ (sēmpaŋ tȍnbo) sm. སེམས་མཐོ་.

སེམས་འཕྱོ་ (sēm cō) 1. va. to be proud/ arrogant/ conceited. 2. vi. to feel sad.

སེམས་འཕྲེང་ (sēmdreŋ) sm. སེམས་པ་འཕྲེང་.

སེམས་འཕྲོག་པ་ (sēm drɔ̄ɔ̀) vi. to be completely enraptured/ infatuated (usu. by a person's good looks).

སེམས་བག་ཆ་ (sēm pa̱gdzā) vi. to be nervous, shy, meek, timid.

སེམས་བག་ཡངས་པོ་ (sēm pa̱à ya̱ŋbo) easygoing, happy-go-lucky, carefree; va.—བྱེད་.

སེམས་བབ་ལྗི་བ་ (sēmbəb jēwa) heavyhearted, sad.

སེམས་བུན་ (sēmbün) vi. to regret.

སེམས་བུན་འཇལ་ (sēmbün ja̱ɛɛ) va. to do sth. to compensate sb. whose feelings were perviously hurt.

སེམས་བེམ་པོ་ (sēm pe̱mbo) sb. who is mute/ retarded.

སེམས་བློང་བློང་པོ་ (sēmloŋ lōŋbo) mentally troubled/ disturbed/ sad.

སེམས་སྦུག་དོག་པོ་ (sēmbug to̱gbo) downcast, gloomy, withdrawn; va.—བྱེད་.

སེམས་སྐྱོང་པོ་ (sēm jo̱ŋbo) sad ¶ གློག་བརྙན་དེ་སེམས་སྐྱོང་པོ་ཞིག་འདུག That film is sad.

སེམས་འབྲེལ་ (sēmdree) a very close relationship ¶ ང་གཉིས་སེམས་འབྲེལ་བའི་གྲོགས་པོ་ཡིན་ We are very close friends.

སེམས་མ་ (sēmma) female Bodhisattva.

སེམས་མ་སྐྱིད་པ་ (sēm ma̱gyiìbə) unhappy ¶ གནས་ཚུལ་དེ་གོ་ནས་ཁོང་སེམས་མ་སྐྱིད་པ་བྱུང་སོང་ After he heard the news he became very unhappy.

སེམས་མ་ཆགས་ (sēm ma̱jaà) sm. སེམས་མ་གནས་པ་.

སེམས་མ་གནས་པ་ (sēm ma̱nɛɛ̀ba) mentally unsettled/ unsteady ¶ རང་ཡུལ་དང་བྲལ་རྗེས་ལུང་པ་གང་དུ་སླེབས་ཀྱང་སེམས་མ་གནས་པ་ཞིག་ཡོང་གི་རེད་ Once you are separated from your country, you never feel at home anywhere else.

སེམས་མ་སྡོ་ (sēm ma̱do) sm. སེམས་མ་སྐྱིད་.

སེམས་མི་གཡོ་བ་ (sēm mi̱yowa) mentally not wandering/ wavering, concentrating mentally on sth.

སེམས་མེད་པ་ (sēm me̱èba) 1. a person whose anger dies quickly. 2. a fool. 3. things that do not have a mind (inanimate things).

སེམས་དམར་བ་ (sēm māāwa) having strong belief/ attachment to communist ideology.

སེམས་སྨད་ (sēm mɛ̄ɛ̀) vi. to be humble/ meek.

སེམས་ཙམ་པ་ (sēm dzāmba) Mahayana school of thought which asserts the true existence of dependent phenomena but does not accept their external existence.

སེམས་རྩ་ (sēmdza) nerve system related to the mind.

སེམས་རྩ་འཁོལ་པོ་ (sēmdza kȫȍbo) enthusiastic, zealous, ardent; va.—བྱེད་.

སེམས་རྩ་ཆུ་ལྟར་འཁོལ་བ་ (sēmdza cūdar kȫȍwa) sm. བློ་སེམས་འཁོལ་བ་.

སེམས་རྩ་གསལ་པོ་ (sēmdza sɛ̄ɛ̄bo) a clear mind, clear thinking.

སེམས་རྩེ་གཅིག (sēm dzējig) concentrating on one thing; va.—སྒྲིམ་ to concentrate/ focus attention on one thing; vi.—ཆགས་ to become attracted/ absorbed/ fascinated with sth. ¶ སེམས་རྩེ་གཅིག་ཏུ་སྒྲིམ་ནས་སློབ་སྦྱོང་བྱས་ན་གྲུབ་འབྲས་ཡག་པོ་ཡོང་གི་རེད་ If you concentrate on your studies you will be successful. ¶ ལུང་པ་སྐྱིད་པོ་དེ་ར་ཁོང་སེམས་རྩེ་གཅིག་ཆགས་ཏེ་ཡུན་རིང་བསྡད་པ་རེད་ He became fascinated with that place and lived there a long time.

སེམས་རྩེ་ཨུ་གིས་ (sēndze wu̱gi) shung. working devoutly.

སེམས་གཙོ་ (sēmdzo) idealistic.

སེམས་གཙོ་སྨྲ་བ་ (sēmdzo māwa) idealism.

སེམས་གཙོའི་རིང་ལུགས་ (sēmdzö ri̱ŋluù) sm. སེམས་གཙོ་སྨྲ་བ་.

སེམས་གཙོའི་ལོ་རྒྱུས་ལྟ་ཚུལ་ (sēmdzö lu̱gyüù dədzüü) historical idealism.

སེམས་ཆད་མཐོན་པོ་ (sēmdzɛɛ̀ tȍmbo) great enthusiasm.

སེམས་ཚབ་ཚུབ་ (sēm tsəbdzub) worried, nervous, anxious; va.—བྱེད་ to be worried/ nervous/ anxious.

སེམས་ཚབས་ (sēmdzəb) worried, anxious, nervous; vi. སེམས་ཚབས་; —བྱེད་ to be worried/ anxious/ nervous ¶ ཚོགས་འདུའི་ཐོག་གཏམ་བཤད་བྱེད་དུས་སེམས་ཚབས་རྒྱུ་མེད་ You shouldn't be nervous when giving a speech at a meeting. ¶ དེ་རིང་ང་ཡིག་ཚད་གཏོང་དགོས་ཡོད་པས་སེམས་ཚབ་གྱི་འདུག I am anxious because I have an exam today.

སེམས་ཚབས་ལག་འདར་ (sēmdzəb la̱gdar) trembling with worry/ anxiety.

སེམས་ཚེགས་ (sēmdzeg) sm. སེམས་ངལ་.

སེམས་ཚོར་ (sēmdzɔr) feelings ¶ མི་མང་གི་སེམས་ཚོར་ The feelings of the people.

སེམས་མཚེར་ (sēm tsēr) vi. to be shy/ embarrassed ¶ མི་མང་པོའི་དཀྱིལ་དུ་གཞས་གཏོང་བཅུག་ཙང་ང་སེམས་མཚེར་བྱུང་ Because I was made to sing in the midst of many people, I got embarrassed.

སེམས་འཚབ་ (sēm tsəb) sm. སེམས་ཚབས་.

སེམས་འཚབ་ (sēmdzəb) sm. སེམས་ཚབས་.

སེམས་འཚིག (sēmdzii) sm. སེམས་ཚབས་.

སེམས་འཚོལ་རྒྱག (sēmdzöö gya̱à) va. to search for the nature of the mind (in a religious sense).

སེམས་འཚེར་ (sēm tsēr) sm. སེམས་མཚེར་.

སེམས་འཛིན་ (sēmdzim) bearing hatred/ malice/ grudge; va.—བྱེད་ to bear hatred/ grudge/ malice/ grudge; vi.—སངས་ to have hatred/ malice/ grudges disappear ¶ གཞན་གྱིས་སེམས་བཟང་གིས་སྐྱོན་བརྗོད་བྱས་པར་སེམས་འཛིན་བྱེད་རྒྱུ་མེད་ One should not bear hatred because of sb.'s well-meaning criticism.

སེམས་ཞུགས་ (sēm shu̱g) sm. སེམས་ཤོར་.

སེམས་ཞུམ་ (sēm shu̱m) vi. to be discouraged/ dispirited/ sad ¶ ཡིག་ཚད་ཐེངས་གཅིག་མ་ལོན་པར་སེམས་ཞུམ་རྒྱུ་མེད་ You shouldn't be discouraged by not passing the exam once.

སེམས་གཞས་ (sēm shɛɛ̀) songs that express or convey feelings/ emotions.

སེམས་བཞག (sēmshaà) bearing/ keeping in mind; va.—བྱེད་ ¶ ཁྱེད་ཀྱིས་མངགས་པའི་ལས་ཀ་དེ་ངས་སེམས་བཞག་བྱས་ཡོད་ I have kept in mind the work you asked me to do.

སེམས་ཟང་ཟིང་ (sēm si̱ŋsiŋ) abbr. of སེམས་ཟང་ངེ་ཟིང་ངེ་.

སེམས་བཟང་ (sēmsaŋ) sm. སེམས་བཟང་པོ་.

སེམས་བཟང་ཅན་ (sēm sa̱ŋjɛn) sm. སེམས་བཟང་པོ་.

སེམས་བཟང་བསླབ་བྱ་ (sēmsaŋ ləbja) well-meaning advice.

སེམས་བཟང་པོ་ (sēm sa̱ŋbo) good-natured,

kindhearted.

སེམས་གཟན་པོ་ (sēm sɛmbo) sm. སེམས་ལ་གཟན་པོ་.

སེམས་བཟོ་དགེ་རྒན་ (sēmso gegɛn) psychologist, psychotherapist.

སེམས་ཡན་རོལ་དབྱངས་ (sēmyɛn röòyaŋ) rhapsody (in music).

སེམས་གཡང་ (sēmyaŋ) sm. སེམས་གཡེང་.

སེམས་གཡེང་ (sēmyeŋ) 1. vi. to be absentminded, to have one's mind wander, to be lost in thought, to lose one's concentration, to be inattentive ¶ མོ་ཊ་གཏོང་དུས་སེམས་གཡེང་རྒྱུ་མེད་ When driving a car you shouldn't let your mind wander. 2. worried, anxious; va.—བྱེད་ to be worried/ anxious ¶ ཁྱེད་རང་གི་ཕྲུ་གུ་འདིར་སེམས་གཡེང་བྱེད་དགོས་ཡས་མི་འདུག སློབ་སྦྱོང་ཡག་པོ་འདུག You don't have to worry about your child, he is doing well in his studies.

སེམས་གཡེང་པོ་ (sēm yēŋbo) absentminded, forgetful, sb. whose mind wanders.

སེམས་གཡོ་ (sēm yō) sm. སེམས་འཁྱལ་.

སེམས་ལ་འཁོར་ (sēmla kɔ̄ɔ) vi. to have some thought come to mind ¶ གནས་ཚུལ་དེ་དག་སེམས་ལ་རྟག་པར་འཁོར་གྱི་འདུག These events always come to mind (into my thoughts).

སེམས་ལ་རྒྱུག (sēmla gyuù) vi. to have one's feelings get hurt ¶ སེམས་ལ་རྒྱུག་ཡག་གི་སྐད་ཆ་མ་ཤོད་ Don't say things that will hurt sb.'s feelings.

སེམས་ལ་རྒྱུག་པོ་ (sēmla gyagbo) having one's feelings hurt ¶ ཁོས་མི་མང་པོ་ཡོད་སར་ང་ལ་མཐོང་ཆུང་བྱས་པ་དེ་སེམས་ལ་རྒྱུག་པོ་བྱུང་ His looking down on me in the presence of many people hurt my feelings.

སེམས་ལ་ངག (sēmla ŋaà) sm. སེམས་ལ་ངེས་.

སེམས་ལ་ངེས་ (sēmla ŋeè) vi. to remember ¶ ཁྱེད་རང་གི་གསུངས་པ་ཚང་མ་སེམས་ལ་ངེས་སོང་ I remember everything you said. (I have everything you said in my mind). ¶ ཁྱེད་རང་གིས་གསུངས་པ་ཚང་མ་ངས་སེམས་ལ་ངེས་པ་བྱེད་ཀྱི་ཡིན་ I will remember everything you said.

སེམས་ལ་ཆུ་འཁྱགས་བླུག (sēmla cūgyag lūù) va. to dampen sb.'s spirits/ enthusiasm [Lit. to pour cold water on the mind].

སེམས་ལ་འཇོག (sēmla jɔ̀ɔ) va. to keep in mind, to remember ¶ དེ་རིང་ཁོས་གང་བཤད་སེམས་ལ་འཇོག་གི་ཡིན་ (I) will keep in mind everything he says today.

སེམས་ལ་ན་ཚ་ཟིན་ (sēmla nadza sin) va. to bear hatred/ grudge/ malice.

སེམས་ལ་ཕན་ (sēmla pēn) vi. to help/ ease the mind.

སེམས་ལ་ཕན་པོ་ (sēmla pēmbo) sth. that helps/ eases the mind.

སེམས་ལ་ཕོག (sēmla pɔ̀ɔ) sm. སེམས་ལ་རྒྱུག.

སེམས་ལ་བབ་ (sēmla bəb) vi. to like, to find attractive/ good.

སེམས་ལ་བབས་པོ་ (sēmla bəbbo) liking sth. ¶ བུ་མོ་དེ་ཁོའི་སེམས་ལ་བབས་པོ་བྱུང་སོང་ He liked that girl.

སེམས་ལ་འབབ་ (sēmla bəb) sm. སེམས་ལ་བབ་.

སེམས་ལ་གཙེས་ཤུར་སྟེར་ (sēmla dzēèshuu dēr) va. to hurt sb.'s feelings badly.

སེམས་ལ་བཞག (sēmla shaà) p. of སེམས་ལ་འཇོག.

སེམས་ལ་ཟུག (sēmla sug) sm. སེམས་ལ་བབ་.

སེམས་ལ་གཟན་ (sēmla sɛn) sm. སེམས་ལ་གཟན་པོ་.

སེམས་ལ་གཟན་པོ་ (sēmla sɛmbo) sm. སེམས་ལ་རྒྱུག་པོ་.

སེམས་ལ་རིང་ཐུང་ཤོར་ (sēmla riŋduŋ shɔ̄ɔ) vi. to have a difference of opinions/ ideas.

སེམས་ལས་ (sēmlɛɛ̀) sm. སེམས་ཁྲལ་.

སེམས་ལས་སུ་རུང་བ་ (sēmlɛɛsu ruŋbə) peaceful/ calm in mind.

སེམས་ལོག (sēm lɔ̀ɔ) vi. to have a change of heart (usu. from positive to negative) ¶ གཡོག་པོ་དེ་སྦྱིན་བདག་ལ་སེམས་ལོག་ནས་བྲོས་ཕྱིན་བཞག The servant had a change of heart about his patron and ran away.

སེམས་ཞི་ (sēm shī) vi. to have one's anger subside/ recede ¶ དགེ་རྒན་དེ་ཁ་ས་ལྷུང་ཞེ་དྲག་ལངས་འདུག་ཀྱང་དེ་རིང་སེམས་ཞི་བཞག The teacher got very angry yesterday but today his anger subsided.

སེམས་ཤུགས་ (sīmshuù) 1. enthusiasm; vi.—སྐྱེ་; —སྐྱེད་ to get enthusiastic/ eager/ ardent; va.—སྒྲིམ་ to concentrate one's effort/ enthusiasm; va.—སྤར་ to boost sb.'s spirits/ enthusiasm ¶ བཟོ་པ་ཚོས་སེམས་ཤུགས་བསྒྲིམས་ནས་ལས་ཀ་བྱས་ཙང་ལས་ཀ་མགྱོགས་པོ་ཚར་པ་རེད་ The workers concentrated their enthusiasm (efforts) in their work and finished the work quickly. 2. effort; va.—སྒྲིམ་ to exert an effort, to strive for.

སེམས་ཤུགས་ངེས་མེད་ཀྱི་སྐྱོན་ (sīmsuù ŋeèmeègi gyȭn) fault of having fickle enthusiasms.

སེམས་ཤུགས་གཅིག་སྒྲིལ་ (sīmsuù jīgdrii) a united/ concerted effort or enthusiasm.

སེམས་ཤུགས་ཆག (sīmsuù cāà) vi. to lose enthusiasm, to get discouraged ¶ དམག་ཤོར་ཙང་དམག་མིའི་སེམས་ཤུགས་ཆགས་ནས་བྲོས་ཕྱིན་པ་རེད་ Because they lost the war, the soldiers lost their enthusiasm and fled.

སེམས་ཤུགས་ཆེན་པོ་ (sīmsuù cēmbo) being very enthusiastic/ eager/ ardent.

སེམས་ཤུགས་ཉམས་ (sīmsuù ñam) vi. to be discouraged, to lose one's enthusiasm.

སེམས་ཤེས་ (sēmsheè) 1. capable in thinking. 2. poet. scholar, pundit, expert.

སེམས་ཤོར་ (sēm shɔ̄ɔ) vi. to fall in love, to have a crush on ¶ རྡོ་རྗེ་བུ་མོ་དེར་སེམས་ཤོར་བ་རེད་ Dorje fell in love with that girl.

སེམས་སོང་ (sēm sōŋ) sm. སེམས་ཤོར་.

སེམས་སྲུང་ (sēm sūŋ) va. to control the mind.

སེམས་གསོ་ (sēmso) consoling, comforting; va.—གཏོང་; —བྱེད་ to console, to comfort ¶ ཁོང་གི་ཨ་མ་གྲོངས་དུས་ངས་ཁོང་ལ་སེམས་གསོ་བཏང་བ་ཡིན་ I consoled him when his mother died.

སེམས་གསོད་ (sēm sȫȫ) va. to (deliberately) hurt sb.'s feelings.

སེམས་གསོའི་ཁ་བཏགས་ (sēmsö kādaà) a ceremonial scarf given as consolation/ condolence.

སེམས་གསོའི་མཇལ་དར་ (sēmsö jɛɛdar) sm. སེམས་གསོའི་ཁ་བཏགས་.

སེམས་གསོའི་འཚམས་འདྲི་ (sēmsö tsəmdri) visit or message of consolation/ condolence; va.—ཞུ་ to offer consolation/ condolence ¶ ཁོང་གི་སྐུ་ཟླ་གྲོངས་སྐབས་ངས་གློག་འཕྲིན་ཐོག་ནས་སེམས་གསོའི་འཚམས་འདྲི་ཞུས་པ་ཡིན་ When his spouse died, I sent him a letter of condolence.

སེམས་ལྷོད་པོ་ (sēm lhȫȫbo) sm. སེམས་ལྷོད་ལྷོད་.

སེམས་ལྷོད་བག་ཡངས་ (sēm lhȫȫ pagyaŋ) relaxed, easygoing.

སེམས་ལྷད་ལ་འབབ་ (sēm lhɛ̄ɛla bəb) sm. སེམས་ལྷོད་ལྷོད་.

སེམས་ལྷོད་ལྷོད་ (sēm lhȫȫlhöö) relaxed, calm (mentally); va.—བྱེད་ to be relaxed/ calm (mentally).

སེའུ་ (sēwu) 1. pomegranate. 2. berry. 3. child.

སེའུ་མཐོང་སྐོམ་སེལ་ (sēwudoŋ gōmsel) consoling oneself with false hopes [Lit. quenching thirst by looking at berries].

སེའུ་སྡོང་ (sēwudoŋ) pomegranate tree.

སེའུ་འབྲས་ (sēwudrɛɛ̀) hawthorn.

སེའུ་འབྲུ་ (sēwu dru) pomegranate.

སེའུ་ཤིང་ (sēwushiŋ) sm. སེའུ་སྡོང་.

སེར་ (sēē) 1. abbr. of སེར་པོ་. 2. abbr. of སེར་བ་. 3. soil ready to plant (all irrigated and fertilized); vi.—ཡང་ to be ready to plant; vi.—སྐམ་ to have soil get dried so that it is ready for sowing.

སེར་ཀ་ (sērga) sm. སེར་ཁ་.

སེར་ཀ་མ་ (sēr gāma) sm. སེར་སྐམ་མ་.

སེར་རྐང་ (sērgaŋ) a heavy hail storm.

སེར་སྐམ་ (sēēgam) fields that have dried out and are ready for planting.

སེར་སྐམ་མ་ (sēē gāmma) a kind of dung.

སེར་སྐེ་ (sērge) a yellow fly that feeds on cow dung.

སེར་སྐེ་སྐེ་ (sēr gēge) sth. that looks yellow and

upright.

སེར་སྐྱ་ (sērgya) 1. light yellow in color. 2. shung. monks and layman ། གཞུང་ཞབས་སེར་སྐྱ་ Lay and monk officials.

སེར་སྐྱ་རྒན་གཞོན་ (sērgya genshön) everyone, all people [Lit. monks, layman, old and young].

སེར་སྐྱ་མཆོག་དམན་ (sērgya cɔ̃ɔ̀mɛn) everyone, all people [Lit. monks, layman, rich, poor].

སེར་སྐྱ་སྦྲེལ་པོ་ (sērgya dreebo) shung. joint appointment of one lay and one monk official to a post ། བཀའ་ཤག་གིས་རྫོང་སེར་སྐྱ་སྦྲེལ་པོ་ལ་བཀའ་རྒྱ་གནང་བ་རེད་ The Council of Ministers sent an order to the two (monk and lay) joint district heads.

སེར་སྐྱོན་ (sērgyön) damage caused by hail.

སེར་ཁ་ (sērga) crack. fissure, gap; vi.—གས་; —ཤོར་ to crack, to split, to have a fissure/ gap appear ། གྲོགས་པོ་གཉིས་ཀྱི་བར་ལ་སེར་ཁ་ཤོར་བཞག A split occurred between the two friends.

སེར་ཁ་མ་ (sērgama) sm. སེར་ཀ་མ་.

སེར་ཁྱིམ་ (sērgyim) a type of Buddhism wherein married householders are also monks.

སེར་ཁྱིམ་པ་ (sēr kyīmbə) a married householder who is also a monk.

སེར་ཁྱུག་གེ་ (sēr kyūgge) sth. that is yellowish and darting/ streaking.

སེར་ཁྲ་ (sērdra) sth. where the foundation/ base color is yellow.

སེར་ཁྲལ་ (sērdrɛɛ) shung. 1. taxes collected to pay a practitioner who stops hail. 2. a tax requiring families with more than one son to make one of the sons a monk.

སེར་འཁྱིལ་འཁྱིལ་ (sēr kyīigyii) yellowish and round.

སེར་ག (sērga) 1. sm. སེར་ཀ་. 2. a hole in a Tibetan stove where the tip of the bellows is inserted.

སེར་གས་ (sērgɛɛ̀) sm. སེར་ག.

སེར་གླ་ (sērla) fee paid to the practitioner who does rituals to prevent hail.

སེར་གོས་ (sērgöö) monk's robe [Lit. yellow clothes].

སེར་འགོག (sērgɔɔ̀) hail protection/ prevention.

སེར་རྒོད་ (sērgöö) hailstorm.

སེར་སྒོང་ (sērgoŋ) yolk (of egg).

སེར་ཅན་ (sērjɛn) sm. སེར་, 3.

སེར་ཆེན་ (sērjen) marigold.

སེར་མཆོད་ (sērjöö) offering of material goods to monks.

སེར་ཉི་ཀློད་ཀོ་ (sērñi lɛ̀ɛgo) a rise in temperature that signals a coming hail storm.

སེར་ལྡེམ་ལྡེམ་ (sēr dēmdem) yellowish in color.

སེར་བསྙལ་ (sēr ñɛ̄ɛ) va. to water the fields and let it to seep into the ground in preparation for planting.

སེར་ཐག་ཆོད་ (sērdaà cȫö) sm. སེར་སྐེམ་.

སེར་ཐིག (sērdiì) 1. egg yolk. 2. a design with yellow/ gold spots.

སེར་ཐིང་ཀུ་ཐིང་ (sērdiŋ gudiŋ) sm. སེར་ལྡེམ་ལྡེམ་.

སེར་ཐིང་ཐིང་ (sēr tīŋdiŋ) sm. སེར་ལྡེམ་ལྡེམ་.

སེར་དེབ་ (sērdeb) books/ documents pertaining to monks or religion, a book or register listing the names of monks.

སེར་དྲག (sērdraà) large hail; vi.—གཏོང་ to be hailing large hail.

སེར་མདངས་ (sērdaŋ) yellow radiance/ glow.

སེར་མདོག (sērdɔɔ̀) yellow color.

སེར་རྡུང་ (sērduŋ) damage done by hail; vi.—གཏོང་ to be damaged by falling hailstones.

སེར་རྡོག (sērdɔɔ̀) hailstone.

སེར་ནག (sērnaà) darkish yellow.

སེར་ནས་ (sērnɛɛ̀) grain given to the practitioners who do rites to prevent hail.

སེར་ནད་ (sērnɛɛ̀) jaundice.

སེར་སྣ་ (sērna) miserly, stingy, avaricious; va.—བྱེད་ ། ཁོ་སེར་སྣ་ཆེ་བས་ཁ་ལག་ཡག་པོ་ཟ་གི་ཡོད་པ་མ་རེད་ Because he is very miserly he doesn't eat well.

སེར་སྣ་ཅན་ (sērnajɛn) miserly, stingy.

སེར་སྣ་ཚ་པོ་ (sērna tsābo) miserly, stingy.

སེར་པོ་ (sērbo) yellow.

སེར་པོ་གསེར་ (sērbo sēē) yellow gold.

སེར་ཕྱུར་ཕྱུར་ (sēr cūūjuu) yellowish.

སེར་སྤྲིན་ (sērdrin) 1. egg yolk. 2. a hail-laden cloud.

སེར་ཕྲེང་ (sērdreŋ) 1. procession of monks carrying sacred items. 2. a yellow rosary.

སེར་འཕྲེང་ (sērdreŋ) sm. སེར་ཕྲེང་.

སེར་བ་ (sērwa) hail; vi.—གཏོང་; —རྒྱག to hail; va.—འགོག to stop/ block hail.

སེར་བྱེས་ (sērjeè) the བྱེས་ college of Sera Monastery.

སེར་སྦངས་ (sērbaŋ) sm. སེར་ཕྲེང་, 1.

སེར་སྦྲེང་ (sērdreŋ) sm. སེར་ཕྲེང་, 1.

སེར་སྦྲེངས་ཆེན་མོ་ (sērdreŋ cēmbo) the religious procession of monks held at the end of the ཚོགས་མཆོད་ festival in Lhasa on the 30th of the second lunar month.

སེར་འབྲས་ (sēndrɛɛ̀) abbr. of Sera and Drepung Monasteries.

སེར་མ་ (sērma) 1. sm. སེར་, 3. 2. nun.

སེར་མེད་ (sērmeè) very tight, close, intimate ། མཛའ་མཐུན་སེར་མེད་ Very close friendship [Lit. no cracks].

སེར་མོ་བ་ (sērmowa) Buddhist monks and nuns.

སེར་མོ་བའི་རྫོང་སྡོད་ (sērmowö dzo̲ŋdöö) shung. a district head who is a monk official.

སེར་དམག (sērmaà) monk troops/ soldiers.

སེར་སྨད་ (sērmɛɛ̀) the སྨད་ college of Sera Monastery.

སེར་སྨད་གྲྭ་ཚང་ (sērmɛɛ̀ tra̲dzaŋ) sm. སེར་སྨད་.

སེར་སྨུག (sērmuù) yellowish red/ brown.

སེར་ཚོགས་ (sērdzɔɔ̀) assembly of monks.

སེར་ཞགས་འཕེན་ (sērshaà pēn) vi. to be hit by hail/ hailstorm.

སེར་ཞིང་སྐམ་པ་ (sērshiŋ gāmba) pale and thin (face).

སེར་བཟའ་སེར་འཐུང་ (sērsa sērduŋ) stingy/ miserly in giving food and drink; va.—བྱེད་.

སེར་ཡོན་ (sēryön) sm. སེར་གླ་.

སེར་རིལ་ (sērrii) yolk (of eggs).

སེར་རོག་གེ་ (sērroge) assemblage of many yellow colored things.

སེར་ལང་ (sērlaŋ) see སེར་, 3.

སེར་ཤ་ (sērsha) 1. mushrooms (in general). 2. a kind of yellowish mushroom.

སེར་ཤང་ངེ་ (sērshaŋŋe) yellowish.

སེར་སྲུན་ (sēr sũn) shung. protecting from hail.

སེར་སྲུང་ (sēr sūŋ) va. to protect the fields from hail.

སེར་སྲུབས་ (sēr sūb) crack.

སེར་སློང་ (sēr lōŋ) shung. collecting donations for doing rites to protect from hail ། གཞན་ཡང་སེར་སློང་གིས་མཆོན་སྔར་ཕན་གསོལ་རས་སྦྱོད་ལམ་ཇེ་ཡོད་སྦྱོད་དགོས་ One should give donations for protecting from hail according to tradition.

སེར་བསང་ (sērsaŋ) a type yellow (color).

སེར་བསུབ་ (sērsub) patching/ filling cracks (of walls, etc.); va.—བྱེད་.

སེར་ཧང་ཧང་ (sēr hāŋhaŋ) sm. སེར་ཧུར་ཧུར་.

སེར་ཧུར་ཧུར་ (sēr hūrhur) bright yellow.

སེལ་: p. and f. བསལ་; imp. སོལ་ (sēē) 1. va. to remove, to get rid off, to clear, to eliminate ། ཐེ་ཚོམ་སེལ་ To remove doubts. ། རྩ་ཤིང་ནམས་བཅད་ནས་ལམ་ཁ་བསལ་བ་རེད་ (They) cut the trees and bushes and cleared the path. 2. va. to pay off (debts) ། བུ་ལོན་སེལ་ཐུབ་པ་བྱུང་ (He) was able to pay off (his) debts. 3. va. to cure ། ཁོའི་ན་ཚ་དེ་གཙང་མ་བསལ་འདུག His illness has been completely cured (through treatment). 4. dissension, discord ། ཁོ་གཉིས་གྲོགས་པོ་གཉིས་དབར་སེལ་ཞུགས་བཞག There was dissension between the two friends. 5. va. to distinguish/ differentiate ༡ ཅ་ལག་ལེགས་ཉེས་བསལ་ནས་བཞག་འདུག They have differentiated and separated between the good and bad items.

སེལ་བཀོད་ (sēē gȫȫ) shung. va. to eliminate/ write off/ get rid of.

སེལ་བཀྲོལ་བྱེད་ (sēēdröö cḛè) va. to explain/ clarify ༡ ཕྱོགས་གཉིས་དབར་གོ་བ་ལོག་སྣང་བྱུང་བ་རྣམས་ཕན་ཚུན་གཉིས་ཀས་སེལ་བཀྲོལ་ཡག་པོ་བྱུང་བཞག Both parties thoroughly explained the misunderstanding that occurred between them.

སེལ་མཚན་འགོད་ (sēēdzɛn gȫȫ) shung. va. to make a note on a loan contract indicating that payment has been made.

སེལ་འཇུག་བྱེད་ (sēnjuù cḛè) sm. སེལ་ཞུགས་.

སེལ་པོ་ (sēēbo) sm. སྙིལ་པོ་.

སེལ་ཞུགས་ (sēē shṵù) vi. to get a breach/ rift (in a relationship) ༡ བཟའ་ཚང་དེ་གཉིས་བར་སེལ་ཞུགས་བཞག A rift has occurred between the couple.

སོ་ (sō) 1. teeth; va.—རྒྱག་; —འདེབས་ to bite. 2. the clause ending particle used after final s ༡ དེར་གནས་སོ་ (They) lived there. 3. numerical particle for thirties ༡ སུམ་ཅུ་སོ་གཉིས་ Thirty two. 4. abbr. of སོ་པ་. 5. va.—གཏད་ to take aim. ༡ འབེན་ལ་སོ་གཏད་ནས་མེ་མདའ་བརྒྱབ་པ་རེད་ (He) took aim at the target and fired. 6. blade of a sword/ knife. 7. va.—གཏོང་ to fire (bricks, pots) ༡ ས་ཕག་ལ་སོ་བཏང་ན་ཆུས་འཇིག་མི་ཐུབ If you fire the bricks, they cannot be destroyed by water.

སོ་ཀ་ (sōga) sm. སོས་ཀ་.

སོ་ཌཱ་ (sōdra) eng. soda.

སོ་ཌཱར་ (sōdra) sm. སོ་ཌཱ་.

སོ་དཀར་ (sōgar) 1. white teeth. 2. four year old cattle.

སོ་སྐམ་ (sōgam) pliers for pulling out teeth; va.—རྒྱག.

སོ་སྐུད་ (sōgüü) 1. jute string. 2. dental floss.

སོ་སྐྱག (sōgyaà) sm. སོ་དྲེག.

སོ་སྐྱེ་ (sōgye) 1. vi. to get one's first tooth (for infants). 2. abbr. of teething. 2. abbr. of སོ་སོ་སྐྱེ་བོ་.

སོ་སྐྱེས་དྲི་ (sōgyeè dri̱) sm. སོ་དྲེག.

སོ་ཁ་ (sōga) 1. the aiming notch at the end of a gun, gunsight; va.—ལྟ་. 2. sm. སོ་ཁང་.

སོ་ཁང་ (sōgaŋ) sentry post, watch post, watch tower.

སོ་ཁའི་ཞིབ་བཤེར་པ་ (sōgɛ shi̱bsherba) custom's officer.

སོ་ཁུང་ (sōguŋ) turret, parapet.

སོ་མཁར་ (sōgar) fort.

སོ་འཁོར་ (sōgɔɔ) gear wheel.

སོ་འཁོར་སྒྲོམ་བུ་ (sōgɔɔ dro̱mbu) gear box.

སོ་འཁྲུ་ (sōdru) toothbrush.

སོ་འཁྲུད་ (sō drüü) va. to brush one's teeth.

སོ་ག (sōga) sm. སོས་ཀ.

སོ་གྲང་རྒྱག (sōdraŋ gya̱à) vi. to have teeth suddenly hurt due to drinking or eating sth. cold.

སོ་གྲལ་འགྲིགས་པོ་ (sōdrɛɛ dri̱gbu) straight teeth.

སོ་འགག (sōngaà) watch post, sentry post.

སོ་འགོག (so̱ gɔ̱ɔ̀) va. to extract a tooth.

སོ་འགྲིག (sō dri̱g) va. to clench (one's) teeth.

སོ་རྒྱག (sō gya̱b) 1. va. to bite ༡ ང་ལ་ཁྱིས་སོ་བརྒྱབ་བྱུང་ A dog bit me. 2. va. to bite/ chew (food) ༡ ཁ་ལག་ཟ་དུས་སོ་ཡག་པོ་རྒྱག་དགོས When you eat food you must chew well. 3. sm. སོ་ལྟ་.

སོ་སྒོ་ (sōgo) teeth.

སོ་སྒྱེ་ (sōgye) gunnybag, bag made from jute.

སོ་སྒྲ་ (sōdra) 1. sound made by grinding teeth (e.g., gnashing one's teeth in anger, chattering from cold, grinding one's teeth while sleeping); va.—རྒྱག; —སྒྲིག; —འདེབས་; —སྒྲོག.

སོ་སྒྲ་སྒྲིག (sōdra dri̱g) vi. to have the teeth clenched together (for corpses).

སོ་སྒྲ་འདེབས་ (sōdra de̱b) 1. sm. སོ་སྒྲ་. 2. va. to whistle through (one's) teeth.

སོ་འགྲམ་ (sōdram) jaw bone.

སོ་སྔོག (sōŋɔɔ̀) va. to pick one's teeth.

སོ་སྔོག་ཡས་ (sō ŋɔ̱ɔ̀yaà) toothpick.

སོ་སྔོག་ཡས་ཀྱི་རྒྱུག་པ་ (sō ŋɔ̱ɔ̀yaàgi gyu̱gbɔ) sm. སོ་སྔོག་ཡས་.

སོ་སྔོག་ཤིང་ (sō ŋɔ̱ɔ̀shiŋ) sm. སོ་སྔོག་ཡས་.

སོ་ཅོག་ལ་ (sōjoòla) (vb. + —) all/ everything/ whatever was done ༡ ཁོས་ལས་ཀ་བྱས་སོ་ཅོག་ལ་སྐྱོན་མཐོང་གི་ཡོད་པ་རེད་ (They) see fault in everything he did.

སོ་ཕྱིབས་ (sōjib) lips.

སོ་བརྗེ་ (sō je̱) vi. to have baby teeth replaced with permanent teeth.

སོ་ཉུལ་ (sōñüü) secret agent.

སོ་ཉུལ་གྱི་གནམ་གྲུ་ (sōñüügi nōmdru) reconnaissance spy plane.

སོ་ཉུལ་ས་སྐོར་ (sōñüü sāgɔɔ) shung. patrolling, make round to check up on sth.

སོ་རྙིལ་ (sōñii) gum (of mouth) ༡ སོ་རྙིལ་རྣུས་ནད་ Gum disease.

སོ་གཉིས་ (sōñii) 1. thirty two. 2. four year old cattle.

སོ་གསུམ་ (sōsum) thirty three.

སོ་གཏོང་ (sōdoŋ) see སོ་.

སོ་གཏོང་ཁུང་ (sō dōŋguŋ) kiln.

སོ་གཏོང་ཐབ་ཀ་ (sōdoŋ tābga) kiln.

སོ་བཏབ་ (sōdəb) p. of སོ་འདེབས་.

སོ་ལྟ་ (sō dā) 1. va. to be on watch, to stand guard/ sentry; va.—བྱེད་ ༡ སོ་ལྟ་དམག་མི་ Soldiers on guard duty.

སོ་ལྟ་ཁང་ (sōdagaŋ) watch post/ sentry post.

སོ་ལྟ་ཐོག་ཁང་ (sōda tɔ̄ɔ̀gaŋ) watchtower.

སོ་ལྟ་བྱེད་མཁན་ (sōda ceèñɛn) sentry, guard.

སོ་ལྟ་ཞིབ་བཤེར་ (sōda shi̱bsher) making rounds, inspecting; va.—བྱེད་.

སོ་སྟོ་ (sōdo) buck tooth.

སོ་ཐག (sōdaà) rope made from jute/ hemp/ flax.

སོ་ཐགས་ (sōdaà) row of teeth.

སོ་ཐགས་བཟང་པོ་ (sōdaà sa̱nbo) evenly aligned row of teeth.

སོ་ཐར་ (sōdar) abbr. of སོ་སོ་ཐར་པ་.

སོ་ཐར་གྱི་སྡོམ་པ་ (sōdargi do̱mba) vows of individual liberation.

སོ་ཐུབ་པ་ (sō tūbbə) 1. clay that can be fired/ baked. 2. va. to be able to stand on one's own two feet.

སོ་མཐའ་རུལ་ནད་ (sōdaa rü̱ü̱nɛɛ̀) periodontitis.

སོ་མཐིལ་ (sōdii) shoe sole made from jute.

སོ་དམ་པོ་ (sō ta̱mba) straight teeth.

སོ་དོགས་ (sōdɔɔ̀) sm. སོ་ལྟ་བྱེད་མཁན་.

སོ་དྲུག (sōdruù) 1. thirty six. 2. six year old cattle.

སོ་དྲེག (sōdreg) tartar on the teeth; vi.—འཁྱིར་ to have tartar accumulate on teeth.

སོ་འདེབས་ (sō de̱b) see སོ་.

སོ་འདྲུ་ (sōdru) toothpick.

སོ་འདྲུ་ (sō dru̱) va. to pick one's teeth.

སོ་ལྡན་བྱ་རིགས་ (sōdɛn cə̱rig) birds that have teeth.

སོ་བདར་ (sō da̱r) va. to gnash/ grind one's teeth.

སོ་ན་ (sō na̱) vi. to have a toothache.

སོ་ན་འཛོག (sōna jɔ̱ɔ̀) sm. རང་སོར་འཛོག.

སོ་ན་གནས་ (sōnanɛɛ̀) sm. སོར་གནས་.

སོ་ནད་ (sōnɛɛ̀) dental/ tooth disease.

སོ་ནད་སྡེ་ཚན་ (sōnɛɛ̀ de̱dzɛn) dental department.

སོ་ནད་སྨན་པ་ (sōnɛɛ̀ mɛ̄mba) dentist.

སོ་ནད་ཚན་ཁག (sōnɛɛ̀ tsɛ̄ngaà) dentistry department/ section.

སོ་ནམ་ (sōnam) farming, agriculture; va.—བྱེད་ to farm, to do agricultural work.

སོ་ནམ་ཁོ་ཆས་ (sōnam kōjɛɛ̀) agricultural implements.

སོ་ནམ་གྱི་ཡོ་ཆས་ (sōnamgi yo̱jɛɛ̀) agricultural implements.

སོ་ནམ་གྱི་ཡོ་བྱད་ (sōnamgi yo̱bjɛɛ̀) sm. སོ་ནམ་གྱི་ཡོ་ཆས་.

སོ་ནམ་གྱི་རིག་པ་ (sōnamgi ri̱gbə) agronomy.

སོ་ནམ་གྲོང་ (sōnam tro̱ŋ) agricultural village.

སོ་ནམ་གྲོང་ཚོ་ (sōnam troŋdzo) sm. སོ་ནམ་གྲོང་.
སོ་ནམ་གླ་པ་ (sōnam lāba) agricultural hired hand/ laborer.
སོ་ནམ་དུས་བཞི་ (sōnam tüüshi) the four agricultural seasons.
སོ་ནམ་པ་ (sōnamba) farmer, peasant ། སོ་ནམ་པ་བར་མ་ Middle peasant. ། སོ་ནམ་པ་ཕྱུག་པོ་ Rich peasant.
སོ་ནམ་བྱེད་མཁན་ (sōnam ceèñɛn) farmers.
སོ་ནམ་པུའུ་ཁང་ (sōnam būgaŋ) Ministry of Agriculture.
སོ་ནམ་ཞིང་ལས་ལས་ཁུངས་ (sōnam shiŋlɛɛ̀ lɛ̀ɛguŋ) Department of Agriculture.
སོ་ནམ་ཡོ་བྱད་ (sōnam yobjɛɛ̀) sm. སོ་ནམ་གྱི་ཡོ་བྱད་.
སོ་ནམ་རིག་པ་ (sōnam rigbə) agronomy.
སོ་ནམ་ལག་ཆ་ (sōnam lagja) agricultural tools/ implements.
སོ་ནམ་ལས་ཀ་ (sōnam lɛ̀ɛga) farm work; va.— བྱེད་.
སོ་ནམ་ལས་ཁུངས་ (sōnam lɛ̀ɛguŋ) shung. Agricultural Office/ Department (in tt.).
སོ་ནམ་ལོ་གསར་ (sōnam losar) farmer's New Year (1st day of the 12th month).
སོ་པ་ (sōba) 1. spy, secret agent; va.—བྱེད་ to spy; va.—གཏོང་ to send a spy.
སོ་པིད་ (sōbii) sm. སོ་འབུད་.
སོ་དཔོན་ (sōbön) head of an intelligence department.
སོ་ཕག (sōbaà) 1. toothbrush. 2. bricks (that have been fired); va.—རྒྱག; —བཟོ་ to make fired bricks; va.—རྩིག to stack bricks.
སོ་ཕག་ཁོག་སྟོང་ (sōbaà kɔ̄gdoŋ) hollow bricks.
སོ་ཕག་བཟོ་ (sōbaà so) va. to make bricks.
སོ་ཕག་བཟོ་གྲྭ་ (sōbaà sodra) brick factory, brickyard.
སོ་ཕག་སྲེག་ཁུང་ (sōbaà sēgguŋ) brick kiln.
སོ་ཕད་ (sōbɛɛ̀) gunny sack.
སོ་ཕི་ཡ་ (sōbeya) Sophia.
སོ་ཕྲ་ (sōdra) top, apex, pinnacle, summit.
སོ་ཕྲེང་ (sōdreŋ) row of teeth.
སོ་འཕུད་ (sōbüü) sm.* ཕུད་.
སོ་བ་ (sōwa) unhusked grain.
སོ་བུད་ (sō büü) vi. to fall out (teeth).
སོ་བློན་ (sōlön) sm. སོ་དཔོན་.
སོ་དབྲག (sōdraà) between the teeth.
སོ་འབམ་ (sōmbam) a gum disease.
སོ་འབུད་ (sō büü) va. to extract teeth.
སོ་འབུས་ (sō büü) vi. to have the first teeth grow (in infants).
སོ་དབྱིབས་ (sūyib) tooth shape.
སོ་འབྲས་ (sōndrɛɛ̀) jute kernel.
སོ་འབྲད་ (sōndrɛɛ̀) gnawing; va.—རྒྱག to gnaw.
སོ་འབྲུ་ (sōndru) sm. སོ་འདྲུ་.
སོ་མ་ (sōma) fresh, new ། ཤ་སོ་མ་ Fresh meat.
སོ་མ་ཁར་འཆང་ (sōma kānjaŋ) sm. ཨམ་གཙིགས་སྦོམ་.
སོ་མ་ཐུལ་མ་ (sōma tũũmə) newly fired pottery.
སོ་མ་ར་ཙ་ (sōma radza) flax, jute, hemp.
སོ་མ་ར་ཛ་ (sōma radza) sm. སོ་མ་ར་ཙ་.
སོ་མ་ར་ཛ་སེར་པོ་ (sōma radza sērbo) sm. སོ་མ་ར་ཙ་.
སོ་མ་རཱ་ཛཱ་ (sōma radza) sm. སོ་མ་ར་ཙ་.
སོ་མང་ (sōmaŋ) a fine-toothed comb.
སོ་མའི་རིགས་ཀྱི་སྐྱེ་དངོས་ (sōmɛ riggi gyēŋöö) fibrous crops.
སོ་སྨྱུལ་ (sōñüü) scouting, spying; va.—བྱེད་.
སོ་མེད་ (sōmeè) toothless.
སོ་དམག (sōmaà) 1. soldiers (in military intelligence). 2. watchman, sentry.
སོ་སྨན་ (sōmɛn) 1. toothpaste. 2. medicine for curing toothaches.
སོ་སྨན་ཕྱེ་མ་ (sōmɛn cēma) powdered toothpaste.
སོ་ཙག་ཆུང་ཆུང་ (sōdzag cūŋjuŋ) (chewing/ eating) with small bites.
སོ་གཙིགས་ (sō dzig) va. to show one's teeth in anger (a kind of grimace).
སོ་གཙེར་ (sō dzēr) 1. vi. to be pained/ annoyed/ irritated by a screeching noise like running fingernail on a blackboard. 2. vi. to bite on a stone while eating rice/ tsamba.
སོ་ཙ་ (sōdza) 1. nerves attached to the teeth. 2. root of tooth.
སོ་རྩི་ (sūdzi) toothpaste.
སོ་བཙེ་ (sō dze) va. to grind teeth.
སོ་བརྩེགས་མ་ (sō dzēgma) one tooth overlapping another.
སོ་བཙེབ་ (sōdzeb) sm. སོ་བཙེ་.
སོ་ཚོགས་དམ་པོ་ (sōdzɔɔ̀ tambo) well- fitted/ arranged teeth.
སོ་ཚང་ (sōdaŋ) alveolus.
སོ་ཚང་རུས་པ་ (sōdzaŋ rüübə) alveolus bone.
སོ་ཚབ་ (sōdzəb) false teeth; va.—སྒྲིར་ to put in false teeth/ dentures.
སོ་ཚི་ (sōdzi) sm. སོ་རྩི་.
སོ་ཚིས་ (sōdzii) livelihood.
སོ་ཚེག་གེ (sō dzege) showing one's teeth when smiling.
སོ་ཚེག་ཚེག (sō dzegdzeg) sm. སོ་ཚེག་གེ.
སོ་མཚམས་ (sōndzam) 1. border (of a country). 2. space between the teeth. 3. root of a tooth.
སོ་མཚམས་མེད་པའི་སྨན་པ་ (sōndzam meèbɛ mēmba) Doctors Without Borders.
སོ་འཚོག (sōndzii) gathering, assembling; va.—བྱེད་.
སོ་འཛིན་ (sōndzin) guarding/ protecting a border or frontier; va.—བྱེད་. 2. va. to scout. 3. gunsight.
སོ་ཞིབ་ (sūshib) abbr. of སོ་ལྟ་ཞིབ་བཤེར་.
སོ་ཞིབ་ཞིབ་རྒྱག (sō shibshib gyaà) va. to chew thoroughly.
སོ་ཞོ་སྡོན་ (sōsho dõn) va. to clench one's teeth over the lower lip (in order to look fierce/ show anger/ threaten).
སོ་ཟིང་ (sūsiŋ) sm. སོ་སྐྱེ་.
སོ་ཟིན་ (sō sin) va. to aim.
སོ་ཟེ་ (sōse) sm. སོ་ཕག, 1.
སོ་གཟེར་ (sō ser) vi. to have a toothache.
སོ་འོན་ (sōwön) 1. spying; va.—བྱེད་ to spy, to go secretly to see what sb. is doing (and report back); va.—གཏོང་ ། ངོ་དགོང་དམག་མི་སླེབས་ཡོད་མེད་སོ་འོན་དུ་མི་གཉིས་བཏང་བ་ཡིན་ I sent two men to secretly go and spy to see if the soldiers had arrived or not.
སོ་འོན་དམག་མི་ (sōwön mɔ̄ɔmi) shung. sm. སོ་དམག.
སོ་འོན་སེང་ (sōwönseŋ) shung. sm. སོ་འོན་.
སོ་གཡོགས་ (sōyɔɔ̀) the upper and lower lips.
སོ་ར་ (sōra) kiln.
སོ་རས་ (sōrɛɛ̀) cloth made from jute.
སོ་རུ་ (sōru) sm. སོ་ར་, 2.
སོ་རུལ་ (sōrüü) 1. decayed tooth. 2. dental cavity.
སོ་རིས་ (sōreè) one's turn to go on sentry duty.
སོ་རོང་བ་ (sō roŋwa) bucktooth.
སོ་རོང་རོང་ (sō roŋroŋ) sm. སོ་རོང་བ་.
སོ་ལ་ (sōla) sm. སོལ་བ་.
སོ་ལ་འགྲོ་ (sōla dro) va. to go on sentry duty, to go to spy.
སོ་ལ་མཆི་ (sōla cī) sm. སོ་ལ་འགྲོ་.
སོ་ལས་ (sōlɛɛ̀) shung. abbr. of སོ་ནམས་ལས་ཁུངས་.
སོ་ལོ་སྔོན་པོ་ (sōlo ŋõmbo) green pepper.
སོ་ཤད་ (sōshɛɛ̀) toothbrush.
སོ་ཤས་རྒྱག (sōshɛɛ̀ gyaà) va. to bite (by horses, mules, etc.).
སོ་ཤིང་ (sūshiŋ) toothpick.
སོ་ཤུན་ (shōshün) lips.
སོ་ཤོ་ (shōsh) the gap between the front teeth.
སོ་ཤོག (sōshoò) paper made from jute.
སོ་ཤྭ་ (sōsha) sm. སོ་ཤོ་.
སོ་སངས་ (sōsaŋ) gaps between the teeth.
སོ་སེག (sō sēg) vi. to bite on a stone when eating རྩམ་པ་ or rice.
སོ་སོ་ (sōso) individual, separate, distinct, each one ། སོ་སོའི་འདོད་པ་ Individual desires/ wishes (each one's desire/ wishes). ། གཞན་གྱི་རོགས་པ་མེད་པར་སོ་སོས་བྱེད་དགོས་ (One) should do it individually (on their own) without help from others. ། ཡི་གེ་རྣམས་མི་སོ་སོར་ལག་སྤྲོད་བྱས་པ་ཡིན་ (I) handed the

letters to each person.
སོ་སོ་སྐྱེ་བོ་ (sōso gyēwo) ordinary person.
སོ་སོ་ཅི་རིགས་པ་ (sōso jīrii) whatever, any ༑ དཀར་པོ་མེད་ན་དེ་མིན་ཁ་དོག་སོ་སོ་ཅི་རིགས་པ་བྱུང་ན་འགྲིག If you don't have white, whatever color you have will do.
སོ་སོ་གཅིག་པུ་ (sōso jīgbu) alone, by oneself.
སོ་སོ་ནས་ (sōsonɛ) separately, individually ༑ མི་རིགས་འདྲ་མིན་སོ་སོ་ནས་འཐུས་མི་བཅུ་རེ་ཚོགས་འདུར་བསྐོང་འདུག Ten delegates were summoned from each different nationality.
སོ་སོ་བ་ (sōsowa) sm. སོ་སོ་.
སོ་སོ་རང་ཉིད་ (sōso raŋñii) one's own, one's self ༑ སོ་སོ་རང་ཉིད་ཀྱི་བསམ་ཚུལ་ One's own opinion.
སོ་སོ་སོ་ (sōso sō) each one individually, separately, distinctly ༑ ང་ཚོ་བུ་སྤུན་གསུམ་སོ་སོ་སོ་བྱས་ནས་བསྡད་ཡོད་ We three brothers live separately.
སོ་སོ་སོ་སོ་ (sōso sōso) sm. སོ་སོ་སོ་.
སོ་སོ་སོ་སོས་བྱེད་ (sōso sōsö cèè) va. to do by oneself.
སོ་སོ་སོ་སོར་ (sōso sōsr) sm. སོ་སོར་.
སོ་སོའི་རང་ནུས་གང་ཐོན་ (sōsö raŋnüü kaŋdün) from each according to his ability.
སོ་སོའི་བློ་ངག་བཞིན་ (sōsö lōŋaàshin) shung. remembering, keeping/ bearing in one's mind.
སོ་སོར་ (sōsɔr) separately, individually, to each one.
སོ་སོར་ངེས་ (sōsɔr ŋèè) va. to learn each of sth. separately/ one by one, to keep in mind separately/ distinctly ༑ ལས་ཀའི་གོ་རིམ་སོ་སོ་ངེས་པ་བྱེད་དགོས་ One should keep in mind each of the work procedures.
སོ་སོར་ཐར་ (sōsɔr tār) vi. to be liberated from the cycle of existence.
སོ་སོར་ཐར་པའི་སྡོམ་པ་ (sōsɔr tāwɛ domba) vows of individual liberation.
སོ་སོར་ཕྱེ་ (sōsɔr cē) p. of སོ་སོར་འབྱེད་.
སོ་སོར་འབྱེད་ (sōsɔr jèè) va. to separate, to set apart individually.
སོ་སོར་གསལ་ (sōsɔr sēl) to be clearly separated/ differentiated ༑ ལས་ཁངས་ཀྱི་གྲོན་དངུལ་གཏོང་ཕྱོགས་སྐོར་ཡིག་ཆའི་ནང་སོ་སོར་གསལ་མི་འདུག Concerning the office's expenditures, they are not clearly differentiated in the documents.
སོ་སྲིན་ (sūsin) sm. སོ་རུལ་.
སོ་སྲུང་ (sō sūŋ) 1. va. to scout, to patrol. 2. patrolman, scout.
སོ་སུབས་ (sōsub) space/ gap between the teeth.
སོ་གསུམ་ (sōsum) thirty three.
སོ་གསེང་ (sōseŋ) sm. སོ་སུབས་.
སོ་གསོད་པ་.(sō sööbə) happy, joyful, peaceful.
སོ་གསོད་པོ་ (sō sööbo) sm. སོ་གསོད་པ་.
སོ་ལྷམ་ (sōlham) jute/ straw shoes.
སོ་ཕི་ཡ་ (sōpiya) Sophia.
སོ་ཧྲལ་ཧྲལ་ (sō hrɛ̄ɛ̄hrɛɛ) teeth with gaps.
སོ་ཧྲུབ་ (sōhrub) minced meat.
སོ་ཧྲུབས་ (sōhrub) a space between teeth.
སོ་ལྷུ་ (sōlhu).sm. སོ་གྲུལ་.
སོག (sɔ̄ɔ) 1. straw, hay. 2. Mongolia, Mongolian. 3. abbr. of སོག་ལེ་. 5. abbr. of སོག་མ་. 6. imp. of འཇོག.
སོག་ཀ་པ་ (sɔ̄ɔgaba) shepherd's pouch.
སོག་རྐང་ (sɔ̄ɔgaŋ) one straw of grain.
སོག་སྐད་ (sɔ̄ɔgɛɛ̀) Mongolian language.
སོག་ཁ་ (sɔ̄ɔga) triangular shaped.
སོག་ག་པ་ (sɔ̄ɔgaba) sm. སོག་ཁ་.
སོག་རྒྱན་.(sɔ̄ggyɛn) an onament put on the shoulders of plowing animals.
སོག་སྒྲོམ་.(sōgdrom) frame of a large saw.
སོག་གུར་ (sɔ̄ggur) yurt.
སོག་ཆས་ (sɔ̄gjɛɛ̀) Mongolian attire/ dress.
སོག་རྟ་ (sɔ̄gda) Mongolian horse.
སོག་ཐལ་ (sɔ̄gtɛɛ) ashes from human shoulder blade.
སོག་ཐག་བྱེད་ (sōgdaà cèè) va. to hang sth. (like a camera) on one's shoulder.
སོག་ཐུག (sɔ̄gtuù) sm. གུ་ཅི་རི་ཐུག.
སོག་དག (sɔ̄gdaà) Sogdians.
སོག་དར་ (sɔ̄gdar) a Mongolian style blue ceremonial scarf.
སོག་ལྡུམ་ (sɔ̄ŋdum) sm. སོག་ཤུལ་.
སོག་ལྡིར་ (sɔ̄ɔ) sm. སོག་ལྡུམ་.
སོག་པ་ (sɔ̄gba) shoulder blade.
སོག་པའི་མེ་ལོང་ (sōgbɛ meloŋ) sm. སོག་པ་.
སོག་པོ་ (sɔ̄gbo) Mongols, Mongolians.
སོག་པོ་སྟག་ཁྲིད་ (sōgbo dāgdrii) the auspicious symbol consisting of a painting of a Mongolian leading a tiger (found on the main gate of some Tibetan homes).
སོག་དཔྱད་ (sɔ̄gjɛɛ̀) a form of divining by burning the shoulder blade of animals and forecasting based on the manner in which the shoulders blades crack.
སོག་སྤུངས་ (sōgbuŋ) stack of straw/ hay.
སོག་ཕུང་ (sōgbuŋ) sm. སོག་སྤུངས་.
སོག་ཕྱེ་ (sōgje) sawdust.
སོག་ཕྲོག (sōgdrɔ̄ɔ) between the shoulder blades.
སོག་བྱིལ་ (sōòjii) the long turquoise earring worn by Tibetan lay officials on the left ear.
སོག་དབྲག (sōgdraà) between the shoulder blade.
སོག་འབུར་ (sɔ̄ŋbur) protruding shoulder blade bones.
སོག་འབོལ་ (sɔ̄mbüü) hay-straw stuffed mattress.
སོག་སྦུབས་ (sōgbub) sm. སོག་མ་.
སོག་མ་ (sōgma) straw, hay.
སོག་མོ་ (sōgmo) Mongolian woman.
སོག་བཙུན་ (sōgdzün) Mongolian monk.
སོག་ཚིགས་ (sōgdzii) joints on the stem of grain stalks. 2. joints on the shoulder blade.
སོག་ཚེམ་ (sōgdzem) rainbow colored pattern on the toe of Tibetan boots.
སོག་ཞྭ་ (sōgsha) type of hat (usu. worn by male servants).
སོག་གཞུང་ (sōgshuŋ) 1. center/ middle of Mongolia. 2. name of a place in northern Tibet. 3. government of Mongolia.
སོག་ཡིག (sōgyii) Mongolian alphabet/ script.
སོག་ཡུ་ (sōgyu) 1. སོག་རྐང་. 2. part of the shoulder blade.
སོག་ཡུལ་ (sōgyüü) Mongolia.
སོག་ར་ (sōgra) a corral for storing hay.
སོག་རིགས་ (sōgrii) the Mongolian race/ nationality/ ethnic group.
སོག་རུ་ (sōgru) a unit/ group of Mongolian nomads.
སོག་རུམ་ (sōgrum) Mongolian rugs/ carpets.
སོག་རུས་ (sōgrüü) shoulder blade.
སོག་ལུག (sōgluù) Mongolian sheep.
སོག་ལུགས་ (sōgluù) Mongolian customs.
སོག་ལེ་ (sɔ̄ɔle) a saw; va.—རྒྱག to saw ༑ གློག་གི་སོག་ལེ་ Electric saw.
སོག་ལེ་འཐེན་པ་ལྟ་བུའི་དམག་འཐབ་ (sɔ̄ɔle tēmba dəbü məgdəb) seesaw battle.
སོག་ལེ་བཟོ་གྲྭ་ (sɔ̄ɔle sodra) saw factory.
སོག་ལེའི་ཁ་ (sɔ̄ɔlee kā) the blade of a saw.
སོག་ལེའི་འཁོར་སྟེགས་ (sɔ̄ɔlee kɔ̄ɔdeg) sawhorse.
སོག་ལེའི་སེམས་ལྡན་མ་ (sɔ̄ɔlee sēmdemba) a harsh/ cruelhearted woman.
སོག་ཤུལ་ (sɔ̄gshüü) 1. grain stalks left on field after harvesting. 2. shung. after the harvest is completed.
སོག་སོག (sɔ̄gsɔ̄ɔ) hairy, bushy (in hair); vi.—ཆགས་ to become hairy/ bushy.
སོག་ལྷམ་ (sɔ̄glham) Mongolian boots.
སོགས་ (sɔ̄ɔ) 1. et cetera, such as (usu. preceded by ལ་) ༑ ལྷ་ས་སོགས་བོད་ཀྱི་གྲོང་ཁྱེར་ཆེ་ཁག Lhasa and other big cities of Tibet. ༑ བོད་པ་ལ་སོགས་པའི་མི་རིགས་མང་པོ་འཛོམས་ཡོད་ Many nationalities such as Tibetans have assembled. 2. vi. to have gotten accumulated/ amassed/ saved up ༑ ངས་དངུལ་མང་པོ་བསགས་ཡོད་བསམ་བྱུང་ཡང་སྐོར་སྐོང་ཕྱག་རེ་

གཉིས་ལས་སོག་མི་འདུག I thought I had saved up a lot of money but I only accumulated one or two thousand.

སོགས་ཁོངས་ (sōɔ̃goŋ) sth. included in a "such as" category ¶ སློབ་ཚན་འདུ་མིན་ཡོད་པའི་སོགས་ཁོངས་སུ་ཡང་རྩིས་དང་ས་གཞིས་ཚུད་ཡོད་ Included among the many classes are math and geography. ¶ ད་རེས་ཀྱི་ཚོགས་འདུར་སོག་པོ་ལ་སོགས་པའི་མི་རིགས་ཞུགས་ཡོད་ཅེས་བོད་པ་སོགས་ཁོངས་སུ་བཙུག་འདུག At the meeting nationalities such as Mongolians are participating. Tibetans have been included among those.

སོགས་སྒྲ་ (sōɡdra) sm. སོགས་ཁོངས་.

སོང་ (sōŋ) 1. past tense verb particle ¶ ཁོང་འདིར་ཕེབས་སོང་ He came here. 2. vi. to be past, to have been finished (in time) ¶ སྐར་མ་ལྔ་སོང་ནས་ After five minute passed/ elapsed. 3. expenditures ¶ ལོ་འདི་ལ་སོང་ག་ཚོད་འདུག This year how much were the expenditures. 4. see.སོང་ཙང་. 5. p. of འགྲོ. 6. sm. རྒྱུགས་.

སོང་ཁྲ་ (sōŋdra) written account/ list of expenses.

སོང་ཐོ་ (sōŋdo) record/ list/ account of expenditures; va.—འགོད་; —རྒྱག to record expenditures.

སོང་འབྲེལ་ (sōŋdrel) shung. as was told ¶ ཞིབ་གཅོད་དགོས་ཀྱི་སོང་འབྲེལ་ཅ་ཞིབ་བྱེད་མཚམས་སུ When they were doing the detailed investigation of the case they were told to investigate.

སོང་ཙང་ (sōŋdzaŋ) sm. སོང་གཙང་.

སོང་གཙང་ (sōŋdzaŋ) because, since ¶ ལས་སླ་པོར་བྱེད་ཐབས་མེད་པར་སོང་གཙང་ Since (we) do not have an easy way of doing it. ¶ དེ་འདྲ་སོང་གཙང་ང་ནང་ལ་ལོག་པ་ཡིན་ Because of that, I returned home.

སོང་རབས་ (sōŋrəb) accounting/ records/ accounts of things that occurred in the past.

སོང་ཙ་ན་ (sōŋdzana) sm. སོང་གཙང་.

སོང་གསལ་ (sōŋsɛɛ) shung. according to the list of expenditures.

སོངས་ (sōŋ) imp. of བསང་.

སོད་ (sōȯ) imp. of གསོད་.

སོཌ་ (sōɔ̃) sm. སོགས་.

སོན་ (sōn) 1. seeds; va.—རྒྱག; —འདེབས་ to plant/ sow seed ¶ དཔྱིད་ཀའི་སོན་ Spring seed. 2. vi. to arrive/ reach/ come to, to receive ¶ ང་ཚོར་འདིར་བདེ་བར་སོན་བྱུང་ (We) arrived here well. ¶ ཁྱེད་རང་གི་ཕྱག་བྲིས་སོན་བྱུང་ (I) received your letter. ¶ མོ་ལོ་བཞི་ལ་སོན་སྐབས་ When she reached the age of four.

སོན་ཁལ་ (sōngɛɛ) a ཁལ་ volume measure of seed (that is equal to about 31 lbs.) ¶ འདི་སོན་ཁལ་བཅུའི་ཞིང་ཁ་རེད་ This is a ten ཁལ་ field (i.e., ten ཁལ་ of seed can be sown on it).

སོན་ཁུག (sōnguù) leather bag for seed.

སོན་རྒྱག (sōngyaà) see སོན་.

སོན་འགྲོ་ (sōndro) the amount of seed a unit of land takes.

སོན་འགྲོ་བོགས་འགྲོ་ (sōndro bɔgdro) shung. lease arrangement where the lease fee is equal to the amount of seed sown.

སོན་བཏབ་ (sōn dəb) p. of སོན་འདེབས་.

སོན་ཐོབ་ (sōndob) shung. sm. སོན་འགྲོ་.

སོན་འདེབས་ (sōndeb) planting; va. སོན་འདེབས་; —བྱེད་ to plant/ sow seeds.

སོན་འདེབས་རྒྱ་ཁྱོན་ (sōndeb gyagyön) sm. སོན་འགྲོ་.

སོན་འདེབས་ཆས་ (sōn debjɛɛ) equipment used in sowing.

སོན་འདེབས་འཕྲུལ་འཁོར་ (sōndeb trüügɔɔ) seed planting machine.

སོན་འདེམས་ (sōndem) sm. སོན་དོག་འདེམས་.

སོན་འདྲེན་ (sōndren) shung. transportation of seeds.

སོན་དོགས་འདེམས་ (sōndɔɔ̃ dem) va. to select seeds for planting.

སོན་པན་ (sōmbɛn) abacus; va.—རྒྱག; —གཏོང་.

སོན་ཕྱུགས་ (sōnjuù) stud livestock.

སོན་ཕྱུགས་ར་བ་ (sōnjuù rawa) cattle breeding station.

སོན་བྱ་སྤེལ་ར་ (sūnja bēlra) a farm for raising chickens.

སོན་འབྲུ་ (sōndru) grain used for seed.

སོན་སྦྱོར་ (sōnjɔɔ) hybrid seed.

སོན་མེད་སྲིང་བལ་ (sōnmeè siŋbɛɛ) ginned cotton.

སོན་སྨྱུག (sōnñuù) seedlings (for transplanting).

སོན་དམིགས་ (sōnmiì) seed specially set aside for planting.

སོན་ཙ་ (sōndza) seeds for planting.

སོན་ཞིང་ (sōnshiŋ) seedbed, seeding field.

སོན་གཞུང་ (sōnshuŋ) shung. list of the amount of seed that each field takes at planting.

སོན་བཟང་ (sōnsaŋ) a good seed strain, a strain of high-yielding seed.

སོན་བཟང་ར་བ་ (sōnsaŋ rawa) seed breeding farm.

སོན་རིགས་ (sōnriì) types of seeds.

སོན་ལུག (sōnluù) ram.

སོན་ལུག་སྤེལ་ར་ (sōnluù bēlra) sheep breeding farm.

སོན་གཤོ་ (sōn shō) va. to broadcast/ scatter seeds.

སོན་གསོ་ (sōnso) raising seeds for sowing; va.—བྱེད་.

སོབ་ཀྱེ་ (sōbgye) brittle, fragile.

སོབ་དོ་ (sōbdo) sm. སོབ་ཀྱེ་.

སོབ་པ་ (sōbba) sm. གསོབ་པ་.

སོབ་པོ་ (sōbbo) sm. སོབ་སོབ་.

སོབ་སོབ་ (sōbsob) 1. soft, spongy. 2. see ཚ་སོབ་སོབ་.

སོབས་ (sōb) imp. of གསོབ་.

སོམ་ (sōm) equal, even.

སོམ་དཀར་ (sōmgar) white pine.

སོམ་ཉི་ (sūmñi) doubt, suspicion, uncertainty, hesitation; va.—བྱེད་ ¶ སོམ་ཉི་གི་དྲ་བར་ཚུད་པའི་མི་དེ་ That man who was hesitating (immersed in a net of doubts). ¶ ལས་ཀ་བརྗེ་སྒྱུར་བྱ་མིན་སྐོར་ཁོང་སོམ་ཉི་བྱས་ནས་བསྡད་བཞག He is hesitating about whether to change his job or not.

སོམ་ཉི་ཐེ་ཚོམ་ (sūmñi tēdzom) sm. སོམ་ཉི་.

སོམ་ཉི་མ་ཟློག་པ་ (sūmñi mandɔɔ̀ba) unable to stop from hesitating, unable to decide ¶ ཁོང་གནས་སྐོར་ལ་འགྲོ་མིན་སོམ་ཉི་མ་ཟློག་པར་བསྡད་འདུག He is staying herre unable to decide whether to go for a pilgrimage or not.

སོམ་ཉི་མེད་པ་ (sūmñi meèba) without hesitation/ doubts.

སོམ་ཉིའི་དྲ་བར་ཚུད་ (sūmñii trawar tsüü) vi. to hesitate, to be hesitant [Lit. to be involved in a net of doubts].

སོམས་ (sōm) imp. of སེམས་.

སོའི་རྩ་ (sōdza) tooth nerve/ root.

སོའི་གསེང་ (sō sēŋ) space between the teeth.

སོར་ (sɔ̄ɔ) 1. abbr. of སོར་མོ་. 2. a measurement equal to the width of one finger (excluding the thumb) ¶ པང་ལེབ་འདིའི་ཞེང་ཁ་སོར་བཞི་བཟོ་རོགས་གནང་ Please make the width of the plank equal to the width of four fingers. 3. sm.* གསོར་.

སོར་ཀྲུབ་ཡིག་པར་ (sɔ̄rdrəb yigbar) typewriter.

སོར་སྐོར་ (sɔ̄rgɔɔ) va. to spin thread.

སོར་སྐྱོབ་ (sɔ̄rgyob) sm. སོར་ཕྱིབས་.

སོར་འཁོར་ (sɔ̄r gɔ̄ɔ) sm.* གསོར་འཁོར་.

སོར་གང་ (sɔ̄rgaŋ) 1. the width of one finger. 2. not at all ¶ ངས་བཤད་པར་ཁོས་སོར་གང་ཉན་གྱི་མི་འདུག He is not listening at all to what I said.

སོར་ཕྱིབས་ (sɔ̄rjib) thimble.

སོར་ཆུད་ (sɔ̄rjüü) bringing back to a former condition or state, being or getting restored/ revived; va. སོར་ཆུད་; —ཡོང་བ་བྱེད་ ¶ དགོན་པ་རྣམས་སོར་ཆུད་ཐུབ་པ་བྱུང་བ་རེད་ The monasteries were able to be restored.

སོར་དོ་ (sɔ̄rdo) width of two fingers.

སོར་གདུབ་ (sɔ̄rdub) ring (for a finger).

སོར་དེའུ་ (sɔ̄rdewu) small stone (used in games); va.—འཕེན་ to flick a small stone with one's finger (in play).

སོར་རྡོ་ (sɔ̄rdo) sm. སོར་དེའུ་.

སོར་གནས་ (sɔ̄rnɛɛ) state of remaining unchanged,

old fashioned; va.—བྱེད་; —འཛིན་ to keep/ leave unchanged ༑ གཞུང་གསར་གྱིས་ཁོང་ཚོའི་སྔར་གྱི་གོ་གནས་སོར་གནས་སུ་བཞག་པ་རེད་ The new government left the previous titles/ ranks unchanged.

སོར་གནས་རྒྱུན་འཁྱོངས་ (sɔ̄rnɛɛ̀ gyü̲ngyoŋ) shung. sticking to one's (promise) ༑ གན་དོན་འདི་རང་ལ་སོར་གནས་རྒྱུན་འཁྱོངས་ཞུ་བ་ We will continuously stick to the promise made in the contract.

སོར་གནས་འཕེལ་མེད་ (sɔ̄rnɛɛ̀ pēlmeè) static, without change.

སོར་བྲིས་རི་མོ་ (sɔ̄rdriì ri̲mu) finger painting.

སོར་མོ་ (sɔ̄rmo) finger.

སོར་མོ་དང་པོ་ (sɔ̄rmo ta̲ŋmo) thumb.

སོར་མོ་ལྔ་ (sɔ̄rmo ŋā) the five fingers.

སོར་མོ་ཆུང་བ་ (sɔ̄rmo cūŋwa) little finger.

སོར་མོའི་འདབ་མ་ (sɔ̄rmö da̲bma) shung. hands/ palms clasped together ༑ ཕྱག་འབངས་ནས་སོར་མོའི་འདབ་མ་སྤྱི་བོར་བཀོད་དེ་ཕྱག་བཙལ་ཞུ་གསོལ་འདེབས་སྐྱིང་ I put my clasped hands on my head and pleaded.

སོར་རྩིས་ (sɔ̄rdziì) counting on one's fingers; va.—རྒྱག.

སོར་ཚད་ (sɔ̄rdzɛɛ̀) sm. སོར་, 2.

སོར་ཚིགས་ (sɔ̄rdziì) finger joint.

སོར་བཞག (sɔ̄rshaà) leaving/ keeping unchanged ༑ ཁྱེད་ཀྱི་གོ་གནས་སྔར་བཞིན་སོར་བཞག་བྱ་རྒྱུ་རེད་ (We) will leave your position unchanged as before.

སོར་ལྡུམ་ (sɔ̄ndum) a finger without its tip.

སོར་རིས་ (sɔ̄rriì) fingerprint, toe print.

སོར་སོར་ (sɔ̄rsɔr) 1. sound of labored breathing. 2. sound of snoring.

སོལ་ (sōō) 1. imp. of སེལ་. 2. abbr. of སོལ་བ་.

སོལ་ཁུང་ (sōōguŋ) sm. སོལ་དོང་.

སོལ་ཁྲལ་ (sōōdrɛɛ) tax on charcoal.

སོལ་འབྲུད་བཟོ་གྲྭ (sōōdrüü so̲dra) coal cleaning plant, coal washery.

སོལ་སྙིགས་ (sōōñii) coal tar/ residue.

སོལ་གཏེར་ (sōōder) coal mine.

སོལ་གཏེར་བཟོ་ལས་ (sōōder so̲lɛɛ̀) the coal industry.

སོལ་ཐལ་ (sōōdɛɛ) charcoal/ coal ash.

སོལ་དུག (sōōduù) carbon monoxide; vi.—ཕོག to get carbon monoxide poisoning.

སོལ་དོང་ (sōōdoŋ) 1. coal pit. 2. kiln (for making charcoal).

སོལ་མདོག (sōndɔɔ̀) black, charcoal (in color).

སོལ་འདོན་ (sōō dö̲n) va. to mine/ extract coal.

སོལ་ནག (sōōnaà) sm. སོལ་བ་.

སོལ་སྣུམ་ (sōōnum) coal oil.

སོལ་པིར་ (sōōbir) charcoal pen.

སོལ་ཕྱེ་ (sōōje) charcoal ash.

སོལ་བ་ (sōōla) charcoal; va.—རྒྱག; —བཟོ་; —སྲེག to make charcoal; va.—སྲེག; —མེ་གཏོང་ to burn charcoal.

སོལ་བ་བཀྲུས་ཀྱང་དཀར་དུ་མི་འགྲོ་བ་ (sōōwa drüügyaŋ gārdu mi̲ndrowə) things that cannot be changed [Lit. charcoal can not be washed to make it white].

སོལ་བ་མདོག (sōōwa dɔ̲ɔ̀) charcoal color.

སོལ་བ་གྲུག (sōōwa drāà) sm.* སོལ་བ་སྲེག.

སོལ་བ་སྲེག (sōōwa sēg) 1. va. to burn charcoal. 2. va. to make charcoal.

སོལ་བའི་ཕྱེ་མ་ (sōōwɛ cēma) sm. སོལ་ཕྱེ་.

སོལ་བྲིས་རི་མོ་ (sōōdriì ri̲mu) charcoal drawing.

སོལ་རྡུལ་ནག་པོ་ (sōōdzɛɛ̀ na̲gbo) soot.

སོལ་ར་ (sōōra) coal yard.

སོལ་རིལ་ (sōōrii) ball-shaped mixture of coaldust and mud (used in stoves as fuel), coal briquette.

སོལ་རིས་ (sōōriì) charcoal drawing.

སོལ་རླངས་ (sōōlaŋ) 1. coal (gas). 2. gas ༑ སོལ་རླངས་ཀྱི་འཕྲུལ་འཁོར་ Gas engine.

སོལ་རླངས་ཀྱི་སྒྲོན་མེ་ (sōōlaŋgi drö̲nmeè) gas lamp/ lantern, Coleman type lantern.

སོལ་རླངས་ལྕགས་མདོང་ (sōōlaŋ jāgdoŋ) gas exhaust pipe.

སོལ་རླངས་ཐབ་ཀ་ (sōōlaŋ tābga) gas stove.

སོལ་རླངས་ཐབ་སྣོད་ (sōōlaŋ tābnöö) gas can/ tank.

སོལ་རླངས་སྤྱོད་ཆས་བཟོ་གྲྭ (sōōlaŋ jööjɛɛ̀ so̲dra) gas utensils factory.

སོལ་རླངས་འབྱུང་གནས་ (sōōlaŋ ju̲ŋnɛɛ̀) gas field.

སོལ་ལ་བཀྲུས་ནས་མི་དཀར་ (sōōla drüünɛ mi̲ gār) things that cannot be changed [Lit. even if one washes charcoal it is not white].

སོས་ (sōō) 1. by/ with the teeth. 2. imp. of གསོ་ and འཚོ་. 3. vi. to be cured, to get well ༑ དེང་སང་ཁོང་གི་ནད་སོས་བཞག These days his sickness has been cured. 4. abbr. of སོས་ཀ་.

སོས་ཀ་ (sōōga) spring.

སོས་ཆར་ (sōōjar) spring rain.

སོས་དལ་ (sōōdɛɛ) leisurely, relaxed ༑ དེང་སང་ཁོང་ནས་ཡོལ་བྱས་ནས་སོས་དལ་དུ་བསྡད་འདུག These days he has retired and is living leisurely (not working).

སོས་དལ་བག་ཕེབས་ (sōōdɛɛ pa̲gbeb) leisurely and happy, carefree.

སོལ་གདལ་ (sōōdɛɛ) sm. སོས་དལ་.

སོས་བདེ་ཀུ་ཡངས་ (sōōde ku̲yaŋ) sm. སོས་དལ་བག་ཕེབས་.

སོས་ལྡད་ (sōō dɛ̲ɛ̀) va. to chew cud.

སོས་པ་ (sōōba) fresh ༑ ཚལ་སོས་པ་ Fresh vegetables.

སོས་ཕེད་ (sōō pēè) vi. to be unable to chew ༑ ཤ་མཁྲེགས་པོ་དེ་རྒན་འཁོགས་ཀྱི་སོས་ཕེད་ཀྱི་མི་འདུག Old people are unable to chew that hard meat.

སོས་འཕར་ (sōō pār) vi. to become spring.

སོས་ཚད་ (sōōdzɛɛ̀) rate of curing (illness).

སོས་ཟིན་ (sōō si̲n) 1. va. to hold sth. with one's teeth. 2. a type of disease which causes the penis to stay erect.

སོས་ལྡད་ (sōō lɛɛ̀) sm. སོས་ལྡད་.

སྲ་ (sā) abbr. of སྲ་བ་.

སྲ་སྐམ་ (sāgam) abbr. hard and dry.

སྲ་མཁྲེགས་ (sādreg) sm. སྲ་བརྟན་.

སྲ་མཁྲེགས་ཤེལ་སྒོ་ (sādreg shēēgo) unbreakable glass.

སྲ་འཁྱག (sā kyāà) hard and frozen (earth, etc.).

སྲ་འགྱུར་ (sāngyur) hardened, rigid.

སྲ་ངར་ (sāŋar) overbearing, willful, aggressive.

སྲ་ཆགས་ (sājaà) sm. སྲ་འགྱུར་.

སྲ་ཆུ་ (sāju) hard water.

སྲ་ཆུ་མཉེན་སྒྱུར་ (sāju ñēngyur) softening hard water.

སྲ་སྙི་ (sāñi) hard and soft; flexibility.

སྲ་བརྟན་ (sādɛn) firm, stable, durable, strong; va.—གཏོང་ to stabilize/ strengthen/ solidify/ consolidate ༑ ཞི་བདེ་སྲ་བརྟན་དུ་གཏོང་དགོས་ We must make the peace stable.

སྲ་བརྟན་འགྱུར་མེད་ (sādɛn gyu̲rmeè) unbreakable, indestructible, immutable ༑ མཛའ་འབྲེལ་སྲ་བརྟན་འགྱུར་མེད་ Unbreakable friendship.

སྲ་བརྟན་ཕུགས་ཐུབ་ (sādɛn pūgdub) sm. སྲ་བརྟན་འགྱུར་མེད་.

སྲ་བརྟན་ཕུགས་འཕེར་ (sādɛn pūgber) sm. སྲ་བརྟན་འགྱུར་མེད་.

སྲ་ཐང་ (sādaŋ) healthy ༑ ལུས་འཚོ་སྲ་ཐང་གི་དོན་དུ་ In order to be healthy.

སྲ་འཐས་ (sāndɛɛ̀) hard.

སྲ་པོ་ (sābo) sm. སྲ་བ་.

སྲ་བ་ (sāwa) hard, strong, firm, durable.

སྲ་བའི་གཟུགས་ (sāwɛ su̲ù) sm. སྲ་འཛིན་.

སྲ་མོ་ (sāmo) sm. སྲ་བ་.

སྲ་རྩི་ (sādzi) varnish, lacquer.

སྲ་རྩི་པོག (sādzi bɔ̲ɔ̀) sm. སྤོས་དཀར་.

སྲ་རྩི་སྤོག (sādzi bɔ̲ɔ̀) sm. སྤོས་དཀར་.

སྲ་རྩི་སྤོས་ (sādzi bōō) sm. སྤོས་དཀར་.

སྲ་རྩི་ཤིང་ (sēdzi shi̲ŋ) a tree that produces lacquer.

སྲ་རྩིའི་ཕོར་པ་ (sādzö pɔ̄rba) lacquered bowl.

སྲ་ཚད་ (sādzɛɛ̀) the degree of hardness.

སྲ་ཚིལ་ (sādzii) stearin.

སྲ་ཚུགས་ཟིན་ (sādzug si̲n) vi. to be able to stand on one's own two feet.

སྲ་འཚོ་ཟིན་ (sāndzo si̲n) vi. to be able to stand firm.

སྲ་འཛིན་ (sə̄ndzin) solid in body (not hollow or liquid).

སྲ་གཟུགས་ (sə̄suù) sm. སྲ་འཛིན་.

སྲ་གཟུགས་འབར་རྫས་ (drə̄suù bardzɛɛ̀) solid fuel.

སྲ་ཤིང་ (sə̄shiŋ) hardwoods.

སྲ་ཤོག (sāshoò) cardboard.

སྲ་སར་འགྲིད་ སྙེ་སར་ཟུག (sāsar dreè ñēsar sug) harassing the weak and leaving the strong alone [Lit. slipping where the earth is hard, sticking where the earth is soft].

སྲ་སྲེ་ (sā drē) va. to mix together.

སྲག (sāà) sm.* སྲིག.

སྲང་ (sāŋ) 1. balance scale; va.—འདེགས་ to weigh (on a traditional balance-scale). 2. a Tibetan currency unit equal to 10 ཞོ་. 3. alley ¶ ཁྲོམ་སྲང་ An alley in the bazaar. 4. in between (object or time) ¶ ལས་ཀའི་སྲང་ In between work. 5. ch. liang (1/10 of a jin or རྒྱ་མ་).

སྲང་སྐུད་ (sə̄ŋgüù) the string/ thread that holds the weighing scale.

སྲང་གང་ (sāŋgaŋ) one སྲང་.

སྲང་གང་བག་ལེབ་ (sāŋgaŋ paàleè) a kind of bread (the name comes from its cost in tt. of one སྲང་).

སྲང་འགག (sāŋgaà) sm. སྲང་ལམ་.

སྲང་སྒོ་ (sāŋgo) place where a main street joins a side street or alley.

སྲང་ཆ་ (sāŋja) a སྲང་ unit ¶ རྒྱ་མ་གང་སྲང་ཆར་འགོས་པ་ཡིན་ན་སྲང་བཅུ་ཡོད་པ་རེད་ If one divides one jin into “sang” units, there are ten sang.

སྲང་ཆག (drānjaà) sm. སྲན་ཆག.

སྲང་འཇལ་ (sāŋ jɛɛ) measuring gold and silver by སྲང་.

སྲང་ཐག (sāŋdaà) sm. སྲང་སྐུད་.

སྲང་མཐིལ་ (sāŋdii) sm. སྲང་ཐོར་.

སྲང་དོ་ (sāŋdo) two སྲང་.

སྲང་མདའ་ (sāŋda) the scale bar (on a Tibetan balance scale).

སྲང་མདའ་མི་གཡོ་བ་ (sāŋda miyowa) impartial and just [Lit. the scale bar on a balance scale not wavering/ moving].

སྲང་མདོ་ (sāŋdo) sm. སྲང་སྒོ་.

སྲང་འདེགས་ (sāŋdeg) sm. སྲང་ལ་འདེགས་.

སྲང་རྡོ་ (sāŋdo) the weight used on a balance-scale.

སྲང་པོ་ (sāŋbo) straight, direct, straight forward.

སྲང་ཕོར་ (sāŋbɔɔ) the bowl/ plate used to put the item to be weighed (on a balance scale).

སྲང་བར་ (sāŋbar) sm. སྲང་ལམ་.

སྲང་མིག (sə̄ŋmii) the measure units on a balance scale.

སྲང་གཞི་ (sə̄ŋshi) sm. སྲང་ཕོར་.

སྲང་ཚད་ (sāŋdzɛɛ) the amount of སྲང་.

སྲང་ལ་རྒྱག (sāŋla gyāà) sm. སྲང་ལ་འདེགས་.

སྲང་ལ་འདེགས་ (sāŋla deg) va. to weigh on a balance scale.

སྲང་ལམ་ (sāŋlam) side street, alley.

སྲང་ལམ་དོན་གྲུབ་ཁང་ (sāŋlam töndrubgaŋ) subdistrict office (in a city).

སྲང་གསུམ་སྒོར་མོ་ (sāŋsum gɔrmo) shung. a coin equal to three སྲང་.

སྲང་གསེང་ (sāŋseŋ) sm. སྲང་ལམ་.

སྲང་སྲང་ (sāŋsaŋ) sm. སྲང་ལམ་.

སྲད་ (drɛɛ̀) 1. grass, weeds. 2. stubble after harvest. 3. name of a place in Tsang.

སྲད་དཀར་ (drɛɛ̀gar) 1. white thread. 2. a type of herbal medicine.

སྲད་བུ་ (drɛɛ̀bu) thread, string.

སྲད་མ་ (drɛɛ̀ma) wild beans/ peas.

སྲན་ (drɛn) 1. abbr. for སྲན་མ་. 2. sm. བརྫེད་. 3. the smallest weighing unit (used for gold and silver).

སྲན་དཀར་ (drɛngar) white bean/ lentil/ pea.

སྲན་སྐྱོ་ (drɛngyo) bean/ lentil/ pea paste.

སྲན་ཁྲོལ་ (drɛndröö) bean/ lentil/ pea sifter.

སྲན་གོད་ (drɛngöö) sm. སྲད་མ་.

སྲན་སྔེའུ་ (drɛnŋewu) bean/ lentil/ pea grown in Mon-yul.

སྲན་ཆག (drɛnjaà) ground bean/ lentil/ peas used as fodder for livestock.

སྲན་ཆུང་ (drɛnjuŋ) lentils.

སྲན་ཆུང་དམར་པོ་ (drɛnjuŋ mārbo) red lentils.

སྲན་ཆེན་ (drɛnjen) sm. སྲན་མ་ཆེན་པོ་.

སྲན་ལྗང་ (drɛnjaŋ) mung bean.

སྲན་སྙིགས་ (drɛnñig) bean dregs.

སྲན་དེས་མ་ (drɛndema) generous/ tolerant woman.

སྲན་དོག (drɛndɔɔ̀) a grain of bean/ lentil/ pea.

སྲན་དོག་མགོ་ (drɛndɔɔ̀ go) derogatory term used for bald people [Lit. head like a bean].

སྲན་ཕུང་ (drɛnbuŋ) a pile of beans/ lentils/ peas.

སྲན་ཕུང་སྡོར་བ་ (drɛnbuŋ dōrwa) striking the enemy so that they scatter/ disperse/ disintegrate [Lit. to scatter a pile of peas].

སྲན་ཕུབ་ (drɛnbub) the skin/ peal from beans/ lentils/ peas.

སྲན་ཕྱེ་ (drɛnje) flour made from beans/ lentils/ peas.

སྲན་མ་ (drɛmma) the general name for beans, lentils, peas.

སྲན་མ་ཆེན་པོ་ (drɛmma cēmbo) large beans.

སྲན་མ་ཡུ་དུའུ་ (drɛmma yündu) tib. ch. kidney bean.

སྲན་མ་སེར་པོ་ (drɛmma sērbo) yellow beans.

སྲན་མའི་གང་བུ་ (drɛmmɛ kəŋbu) peapod.

སྲན་མའི་གམ་བུ་ (drɛmmɛ kəmbu) sm. སྲན་མའི་གང་བུ་.

སྲན་མའི་མེ་ཏོག (drɛmmɛ medog) bean/ lentil/ pea flower.

སྲན་མེ་ (drɛnme) abbr. of སྲན་མའི་མེ་ཏོག.

སྲན་སྨྱུག (drɛnñuù) bean/ lentil/ pea shoot.

སྲན་དམར་ (drɛnmar) red lentil.

སྲན་རྩམ་ (drɛndzam) རྩམ་པ་ from beans/ lentils/ peas.

སྲན་ཚོད་ (drɛndzöö) a meal/ dish made from cooked beans/ lentils/ peas.

སྲན་ཞིབ་ (drɛnshib) a high quality bean/ lentil/ pea རྩམ་པ་ (the skin being removed before grinding).

སྲན་ཞིབ་ཁ་ཟས་ (drɛnshib kāsɛɛ̀) an elongated fried pastry made from bean flour.

སྲན་ཞོ་ (drɛnsho) fermented bean curd.

སྲན་ཡོས་ (drɛnyöö) roasted beans/ lentils/ peas.

སྲན་རིལ་ (drɛnrill) peas.

སྲན་ལེབ་ (drɛnleb) flat peas.

སྲན་བཤོས་ (drɛnshöö) 1. things (foods) that are made from beans/ lentils/ peas. 2. གཏོར་མ་ that are made from bean flour.

སྲན་སེར་ (drɛnsee) abbr. of སྲན་མ་སེར་པོ་.

སྲན་སེར་གང་བུ་ (drɛnsee kəŋbu) soya bean sprouts.

སྲབ་ (drəb) 1. horse tack consisting of the bit and head stall; va.—གཡོགས་ to put on a bit and head stall. 2. abbr. of སྲབ་པོ་.

སྲབ་ཀྱི་ལྕེ་མདུད་ (drəbgi jēndüü) the rings attaching the bit to the head stall of a bridle.

སྲབ་བཀུག (drəb güù) pulling the rein of a horse so that its neck arches making it look attractive; va.—རྒྱག.

སྲབ་སྐྱོག (drəbgyɔɔ̀) sm. སྲབ་སྐྱོགས་.

སྲབ་སྐྱོགས་ (drəbgyɔɔ̀) sm. སྲབ་ཐག.

སྲབ་ཁུག (drəbguù) sm. སྲབ་བཀུག.

སྲབ་གོར་ (drəbgɔɔ) sm. སྲབ་སྒོར་.

སྲབ་འགུགས་ (drəbguù) sm. སྲབ་ཁུག.

སྲབ་སྒ་སྟན་ཆ་ཚང་ (drəb gadɛn cādzaŋ) a complete horse set: bit, saddle and saddle rug.

སྲབ་སྒོར་ (drəbgɔɔ) sm. སྲབ་ཀྱི་ལྕེ་མདུད་.

སྲབ་ལྕགས་ (drəbjaà) bit.

སྲབ་ཐག (drəbdaà) reins.

སྲབ་མཐུག (drəbduù) thin and thick; thickness ¶ སྲབ་མཐུག་སྙོམ་པ་ Even in thickness.

སྲབ་མཐུག་འཇལ་ཆས་ (drəbduù jɛɛjɛɛ̀) an instrument for measuring thickness.

སྲབ་མཐུར་ (drəbdur) abbr. of སྲབ་ and མཐུར་འགོ་.

སྲབ་འཐུག (drəbduù) sm. སྲབ་མཐུག.

སྲབ་མདའ་ (drəmda) rein; va.—གློད་ to let go of the rein (and let the horse go by itself); va.—འཐེན་

to pull on the rein.

སྲབ་འདེབས། (drəbdeb) a thin planting of seeds; va.—བྱེད་.

སྲབ་པོ། (drəbbu) thin, flat (as in paper) ། ཁོང་གིས་སྟོད་ཐུང་སྲབ་པོ་ཞིག་གྱོན་འདུག He wore a thin shirt.

སྲབ་བེ་སྲིབ་བེ། (drəbbi dribbi) 1. the time just before nightfall, dusk. 2. blurry, unclear.

སྲབ་མོ། (drəbmo) sm. སྲབ་པོ་.

སྲབ་ཞན། (drəbshɛn) thin/ poor in quality.

སྲབ་གཟེར། (drəbsee) the nail that is used to attach the reins to the bridle.

སྲབ་ལོས། (drəblöö) the flatness of sth.

སྲབ་ཤུ། (drəbshu) sores/ cuts caused by the bit on mouth of a horse; vi.—སྐྱེད་; —ཐོན་.

སྲབ་སྲིབ། (drəbsiŋ) abbr. of སྲབ་བེ་སྲིབ་བེ་.

སྲམ། (drām) otter.

སྲམ་རྒྱན་པ། (drām gyɛmba) a Tibetan dress with otter-skin trim.

སྲམ་མཐའ་ཅན། (drāmdajɛn) a dress that has a strip (hem) of otter skin along the edge for decoration.

སྲམ་མདོག (drāmdɔɔ) tan/ brown (color of otter skin).

སྲམ་ཕྲུགས། (drāmbaà) otter skin/ pelt.

སྲམ་ཤ། (drāmsha) otter meat (used in Tibetan medicine).

སྲལ། (drɛɛ) va. to do things with care and diligence.

སྲས། (sɛ̄ɛ) 1. son (h.). 2. disciple.

སྲས་ཀྱི་ཐུ་བོ། (sɛ̄ɛgi tūwo) the main disciple.

སྲས་སྐུ། (sɛ̄ɛgu) abbr. of སྲས་སྐུ་ཞབས་.

སྲས་སྐུ་ཞབས། (sɛ̄ɛ gūshəb) honorific term of address used for the sons of aristocrats (in Tibet).

སྲས་མཁར་དགུ་ཐོག (sɛ̄ɛgar gudoò) the nine story building built by Milarepa according to the order of his guru Marpa.

སྲས་ཐུ་བོ། (sɛ̄ɛ tūwo) the main disciple.

སྲས་རྣམ་པ། (sɛ̄ɛnamba) shung. an inherited rank for lay officials just under the 4th rank in the tt. government.

སྲས་པོ། (sɛ̄ɛbo) sm. སྲས་.

སྲས་འཕྱོར་པོ། (sɛ̄ɛ cɔ̄rbo) a richly attired young male aristocrat.

སྲས་མོ། (sɛ̄ɛmo) 1. h. of བུ་མོ་. 2. young unmarried female aristocrat.

སྲས་མོའི་སྐུ་ཞབས། (sɛ̄ɛmö gūshəb) honorific term of address for young unmarried female aristocrats.

སྲས་སྲོས། (sɛ̄ɛsöö) h. of བུ་ and བུ་མོ་.

སྲི: p. བསྲིས་; f. བསྲི་ (sī) va. to not waste time, to do or be thrifty ། དུས་ཚོད་ལེགས་པར་བསྲིས་ནས་ལས་ཀ་བྱེད་ཀྱི་ཡོད་པ་རེད་ (They) are working without wasting time. ། རྒྱུན་གཏན་ནས་དངུལ་གྱི་འགྲོ་སོང་བསྲི་ཆག་བྱེད་དགོས་ One should always spend money wisely.

སྲི། (sī) 1. demon, evil spirit. 2. vi.—ཡངས་ to have misfortune/ tragedy/ disaster come again at the same time or place ། ན་ལོ་མོ་ཊ་བརྡབས་ནས་མི་ཤི་སྐྱོན་བྱུང་པ་དེ་རང་དུ་འདི་ལོ་ཡང་དེ་ནང་བཞིན་ཞིག་བྱུང་འདུག་པ་དེ་ནི་སྲི་ལང་བ་ཞིག་ཡིན་ A similar accident took place at the same spot where last year a person was killed in a car accident.

སྲི་སྐྱེལ། (sī gyēē) va. to secretly inform, to tell on sb. ། སློབ་ཕྲུག་གིས་དགེ་རྒན་ལ་སྲི་བསྐྱལ་བ་རེད་ The student secretly informed the teacher.

སྲི་གནོན། (sīnün) subduing; va.—བྱེད་.

སྲི་མོ། (sīmu) a female demon/ evil spirit.

སྲི་ཞུ། (sīshu) service, serving; va.—བྱེད་; —སྒྲུབ་ to serve ། ཁོང་གི་ཕ་མ་སྲི་ཞུ་ཡག་པོ་བསྒྲུབས་པ་རེད་ He served his parents well.

སྲི་ཞུའི་འཛིན་སྒྲས། (sīshu dzindrɛɛ) shung. the service on taking care of sth.

སྲི་ཞུ་ཞབས་འདེགས། (sīshu shamdeè) sm. སྲི་ཞུ་.

སྲི་ཞུའི་མི་སྣ། (sīshü minə) government officials.

སྲི་བཟོ། (sī so) sm. བདག་དཀྱུག་རྒྱག.

སྲི་ལང་། (sī laŋ) vi. to cause trouble/ mischief.

སྲི་ཤིང་། (sīshiŋ) nutmeg.

སྲིང་། (sīŋ) cotton thread, cotton fiber.

སྲིང་: p. བསྲིངས་; f. བསྲིང་; imp. སྲིངས་ (sīŋ) 1. va. to prolong, lengthen ། ཐག་པ་དེ་རིང་དུ་བསྲིང་བ་རེད་ They lengthened the rope. 2. va. to rear/ raise/ bring up ། ཕ་མས་ཕྲུ་གུ་སྐྱིད་བསྲིངས་པ་རེད་ The parents raised the child. 3. va. to send (letters, etc.) ། ཁོང་གིས་ནང་ལ་ཡི་གེ་བསྲིངས་པ་རེད་ He sent a letter to his home.

སྲིང་སྐུད། (sīŋgüü) cotton yarn/ thread; —འཁལ་ to spin cotton yarn/ thread.

སྲིང་སྐུད་ཀྱི་བཏགས་རྫས། (sīŋgüügi dāgdzɛɛ) cotton goods.

སྲིང་སྐུད་འཁལ་འཁོར། (sīŋgüü) cotton spinning machine.

སྲིང་སྐུད་འཁལ། (sīŋgüü kēē) sm. སྲིང་སྐུད་འཁལ་.

སྲིང་སྐུད་འཁྱུལ་འཁོར། (sīŋgüü trüügɔɔ) cotton spinning machine.

སྲིང་འཁྱིལ་ཁབ་བརླས། (sīŋgee kəblɛɛ) cotton knitting.

སྲིང་འཁོར། (sīŋgɔɔ) reel for spinning/ rolling cotton thread.

སྲིང་བཏགས་ཐོན་རྫོག (sīŋdaà tōnsɔɔ) products made of cotton fabric.

སྲིང་འདེབས་ཞིང་པ། (sīŋdeb shiŋgə) cotton farmer.

སྲིང་ཕྱར། (sīŋjar) cotton blanket.

སྲིང་བལ། (sīŋbɛɛ) cotton; va.—འདེབས་ to plant cotton; va.—གསེད་ to card cotton.

སྲིང་བལ་ཁབ་འཐག་བཟོ་གྲྭ། (sīŋbɛɛ kəbdaà sodra) cotton knitwear mill.

སྲིང་བལ་འཁིལ་ཐག་ཚོས་སྒྱུར་བཟོ་གྲྭ། (sīŋbɛɛ kēēdaà sodra) cotton textile printing and dyeing mill.

སྲིང་བལ་འཁིལ་ཐག་བཟོ་གྲྭ། (sīŋbɛɛ kēēdaà sodra) cotton textile mill/ factory.

སྲིང་བལ་གྱི་འཁིལ་ཐག་བཟོ་གྲྭ། (sīŋbɛɛgi kēēdaà sodra) cotton textile mill/ factory.

སྲིང་བལ་གྱི་སྡོང་པོ། (sīŋbɛɛgi doŋbo) cotton plant.

སྲིང་བལ་གྱི་འབྲུ་གུ། (sīŋbɛɛgi drugu) cotton seed.

སྲིང་བལ་གྱི་ཚི་སྣ། (sīŋbɛɛgi tsīnə) cotton fiber.

སྲིང་བལ་གནོད་འབུ། (sīŋbɛɛ nönbu) insects that attack cotton plants.

སྲིང་བལ་འབྲུ་ལེན་འཁྲུལ་འཁོར། (sīŋbɛɛ drulen trüügɔɔ) cotton ginning mill.

སྲིང་བལ་མལ་སྟན། (sīŋbɛɛ mɛɛdɛn) cotton-stuffed mattress.

སྲིང་བལ་ཞིང་པ། (sīŋbɛɛ shiŋba) cotton farmer.

སྲིང་བལ་ཞྭ་མོ། (sīŋbɛɛ shamo) cotton-padded hat.

སྲིང་བལ་ཤད། (sīŋbɛɛ shɛ̄ɛ) va. to card cotton.

སྲིང་བལ་ཤད་བྱེད་འཁྲུལ་འཁོར། (sīŋbɛɛ shɛ̄ɛjeè trüügɔɔ) rotary carding machine, cotton carding machine/ gin.

སྲིང་བལ་གསེད། (sīŋbɛɛ sēè) see སྲིང་བལ་.

སྲིང་བལ་གསེད་བྱེད་འཁྲུལ་འཁོར། (sīŋbɛɛ sēèjeè trüügɔɔ) sm. སྲིང་བལ་ཤད་བྱེད་འཁྲུལ་འཁོར་.

སྲིང་བལ་གསེད་མ། (sīŋbɛɛ sēèma) ginned cotton.

སྲིང་འབྲུའི་སྣུམ། (sīŋdrü nūm) cottonseed oil.

སྲིང་མོ། (sīŋmo) younger sister.

སྲིང་ཞྭ། (sīŋsha) abbr. of སྲིང་བལ་ཞྭ་མོ་.

སྲིང་ཤུབས། (sīŋshub) cotton-padded sheath/ covering/ cozy for keeping things warm.

སྲིང་སོན། (sīŋsön) cotton seed.

སྲིང་ལྷམ། (sīŋlham) cotton-padded shoes.

སྲིངས། (sīŋ) imp. of སྲིང་.

སྲིད། (sīī) 1. length ། སྲིད་ལ་མི་བརྒྱད་ Eight meters in length. 2. vi. to be possible ། ནོར་འཁྲུལ་ཡོང་སྲིད་ཀྱི་རེད་ It is possible that there will be mistakes. 3. (neg. + vb. + ག་ལ་སྲིད་) vi. to not be possible ། དགའ་ཚོར་མི་སྐྱེ་ག་ལ་སྲིད་ How is it possible not to be happy. 3. reign, government, administration, dominion; va.—སྐྱོང་; —བྱེད་ to rule, to govern, to reign ། ཁོང་གིས་ལོ་ཤས་སྲིད་བསྐྱངས་པ་རེད་ He ruled for a couple of years. 4. political, politics ། སྲིད་དབང་ Political power. 5. abbr. for སྲིད་པ་ or སྲིད་བློན་ or སྲིད་ཆབ་.

སྲིད་ཀྱི་ཉེས་ཅན། (sīīgi ñeèjɛn) political offender/

criminal.

སྲིད་བཀའ་ (sīiga) shung. 1. abbr. of སྲིད་བློན་ and བཀའ་བློན་ 2. government/ administrative order.

སྲིད་བཀུར་དམངས་གཅེས་ (sīigur māŋjeè) support the government and cherish the people (political slogan).

སྲིད་སྐྱོང་ (sīigyoŋ) 1. a title for the regent of Tibet; va.—བྱེད་/ གཏང་ to rule as a regent ༑ སྲིད་སྐྱོང་རྭ་སྒྲེང་ Regent Reting. 2. va. to rule, to govern, to reign ༑ སྲིད་འཛིན་དེས་ལོ་བཞི་སྲིད་བསྐྱངས་པ་རེད་ The president ruled for four years.

སྲིད་སྐྱོང་དང་ (sīigyoŋ dāŋ) tib. ch. the ruling/ governing party.

སྲིད་སྐྱོང་ན་རིམ་ (sīigyoŋ nərim) shung. the succession of regents, the line of successive regents.

སྲིད་སྐྱོང་དཔོན་པོ་ (sīigyoŋ bōmbo) ruling officials.

སྲིད་སྐྱོང་བྱས་རྗེས་ (sīigyoŋ cɛ̀ɛjeè) achievements during one's rule.

སྲིད་སྐྱོབ་སྲུང་མ་ (sīigyob sūŋma) a protective deity who defends/ protects the political system or the government.

སྲིད་བསྐྱངས་ (sīi gyāŋ) p. of སྲིད་སྐྱོང་.

སྲིད་ཁྲི་ (sīidri) political power/ authority/ office (used for the top one or two positions/ officers in a government); vi.—འཁོད་; —སླེབས་ to come to power in a government/ country; —འཛེགས་ to achieve power in a country/ government ༑ སྲིད་འཛིན་དེ་སྲིད་ཁྲིར་ཁོད་ནས་ལོ་བརྒྱད་སོང་བ་རེད་ It has been eight years since the president came to power.

སྲིད་ཁྲི་ལས་བབ་ (sīidrilɛ bəb) va. to step down from office/ power, to give up office.

སྲིད་ཁྲིམས་ (sīidrim) politics/ political science and law.

སྲིད་ཁྲིམས་ཁྲུའུ་ (sīidrim) tib. ch. the office of politics and lawå.

སྲིད་ཁྲིམས་ལས་བྱེད་སློབ་གྲྭ་ (sīidrim lɛ̀ɛjeè lōbdra) school for cadres on political science and law.

སྲིད་ཁྲིར་སླེབས་ (sīidrii lēè) see སྲིད་ཁྲི་.

སྲིད་གྲོས་ (sīidröö) 1. political discussion/ conference. 2. abbr. of ཆབ་སྲིད་གྲོས་ཚོགས་.

སྲིད་གྲོས་ཁང་ (sīidröögaŋ) sm. ཆབ་སྲིད་གྲོས་ཚོགས་.

སྲིད་གྲོས་པ་ (sīidrööba) 1. political spokesman. 2. senator.

སྲིད་གྲོས་ཚོགས་འདུ་ (sīidröö tsōŋdu) 1. ཆབ་སྲིད་གྲོས་ཚོགས་. 2. political conference/ meeting.

སྲིད་དགྲ་ (sīidra) political enemy, political opposition.

སྲིད་འགན་ (sīngɛn) political responsibility/ authority.

སྲིད་འགྱུར་ (sīi gyu̱r) coup, coup d'ètat; va.—ཁུར་; —ལེན་ to seize power in a coup; va.—བྱེད་; —གཏོང་ to make a coup d'ètat ༑ དམག་དོན་སྲིད་འགྱུར་ A military coup.

སྲིད་རྒྱ་ (sīigya) abbr. of སྲིད་འཛིན་བཀའ་རྒྱ་.

སྲིད་སྒྱུར་ (sīigyur) sm. སྲིད་འགྱུར་.

སྲིད་རྙིང་ (sīiñiŋ) 1. the traditional Tibetan government. 2. the old government.

སྲིད་ཇུས་ (sīijüü) policy, plan, strategy; va.—གཏོང་; —འདོན་ to develop/ make a strategy ༑ ཐོན་སྐྱེད་ཡར་རྒྱས་གཏོང་རྒྱུའི་སྲིད་ཇུས་ A plan for increasing production.

སྲིད་ཇུས་སྐྱོང་སྟངས་ (sīijüü gyōŋdaŋ) sm. སྲིད་ཇུས་སྐྱོང་ཕྱོགས་.

སྲིད་ཇུས་སྐྱོང་ཕྱོགས་ (sīijüü gyōɔ̄jɔɔ̀) the manner/ way in which one holds a policy ༑ རྒྱ་ནག་གི་ཐད་ཨ་རིས་སྲིད་ཇུས་སྐྱོང་ཕྱོགས་ America's policy towards China.

སྲིད་ཇུས་དངོས་འཕེབས་ (sīijüü ŋōmbeb) carrying out a policy (to its fruition).

སྲིད་ཇུས་ཆེན་མོ་བཅུ་ (sīijüü cēmmo jū) the ten main policies: (the ten main points that were the basis of the 1951 Seventeen Point Agreement).

སྲིད་ཇུས་དོན་འཁྱོལ་ (sīijüü to̱ngyöö) 1. carrying out/ implementing a policy; va.—བྱེད་. 2. the policy that redresses the unjust wrongs done to persons during the Cultural Revolution.

སྲིད་ཇུས་ཞིབ་འཇུག་ཁང་ (sīijüü shi̱mjuùgaŋ) institute of policy.

སྲིད་ཇུས་ལག་ལེན་ (sīijüü la̱glen) carrying out a policy/ strategy, putting a policy/ strategy into practice; va.— བྱེད་; —བསྟར་.

སྲིད་འཇགས་པ་ (sīi ja̱gba) shung. a calm, stable political situation.

སྲིད་དང་ (sīidaŋ) political party.

སྲིད་སྟེགས་ (sīideg) political platform/ stage/ arena/ scene.

སྲིད་བསྟུན་ཐོབ་སྤྲོད་ (sīidün tōbdröö) distributing sth. according to political views or behavior.

སྲིད་ཐབས་ཀྱི་ཇུས་གཞི་ (sīitəbgi jü̱ushi) sm. སྲིད་ཇུས་.

སྲིད་མཐའ་ (sīida) 1. unlikely, improbably ༑ འཛམ་གླིང་ཡོངས་སུ་དུས་གཅིག་ལ་དམག་འཁྲུག་འབད་རྒྱུ་ནི་སྲིད་མཐའ་ཙམ་ཞིག་ཡིན་ It is unlikely that war will break out everywhere in the world at once. 2. the end of cyclic existence, end of rebirth.

སྲིད་དམ་ (sīidam) shung. the regent or prime minister's seal.

སྲིད་དུ་མི་རུང་བ་ (sīidu mi̱ruŋbə) impossible.

སྲིད་དོ་ཅོག (sīidojoò) all, entire, everything.

སྲིད་དོན་ (sīidün) politics, political ༑ སྲིད་དོན་གྱི་ཉམས་མྱོང་ Political experience. ༑ སྲིད་དོན་གྱི་བཙོན་པ་ Political prisoner.

སྲིད་དོན་མཁས་པ་ (sīidün kɛ̄ɛba) politician, political expert.

སྲིད་དོན་གྱི་སྐྱབས་བཅོལ་ (sīidüngi gyəbjüü) political asylum; va.—བྱེད་; —ཞུ་.

སྲིད་དོན་གྱི་སྐྱབས་བཅོལ་བ་ (sīidüngi gyəbjüüwa) sb. who has received political asylum.

སྲིད་དོན་གྱི་འགྱུར་སྐྱོད་ (sīidüngi gü̱ügyöò) political changes/ shifts; va.—བྱེད་.

སྲིད་དོན་གླེང་རྩོམ་ (sīidün lēŋdzom) political essay.

སྲིད་དོན་གྲོས་ཚོགས་ (sīidün trö̱ödzɔɔ̀) 1. political conference/ meeting. 2. sm. ཆབ་སྲིད་གྲོས་ཚོགས་.

སྲིད་དོན་ཆེད་རྩོམ་ (sīidün cēndzom) sm. སྲིད་དོན་གླེང་རྩོམ་.

སྲིད་དོན་བརྗོད་གཏམ་ (sīidün jö̱ödam) political commentary.

སྲིད་དོན་བརྗོད་པ་ (sīidün jö̱öba) political commentator.

སྲིད་དོན་ཉེས་ཅན་ (sīidün ñe̱èjɛn) political criminal.

སྲིད་དོན་གཉེར་མཁན་ (sīidün ñērñɛn) politician.

སྲིད་དོན་དཔྱད་གཏམ་ (sīidün jɛ̄ɛdam) sm. སྲིད་དོན་བརྗོད་གཏམ་.

སྲིད་དོན་དཔྱོད་པ་པོ་ (sīidün jöòbabo) political commentator.

སྲིད་དོན་སྤྱི་ཁྱབ་ཁང་ (sīidün jīgyəbgaŋ) the Government Administration Council (of the Central People's Government of the People's Republic of China that was replaced by the State Council in 1954).

སྲིད་དོན་གཙང་སྐྱོང་ (sīidün dzāŋgyoŋ) just or honest political administration/ rule.

སྲིད་དོན་ཚོགས་པ་ (sīidün tsōgba) political party.

སྲིད་དོན་འཛིན་སྐྱོང་ (sīidün dzi̱ngyoŋ) political rule/ administration; va.— བྱེད་.

སྲིད་དོན་ལས་འགུལ་ (sīidün lɛ̱ngüü) a political movement/ campaign; va.—སྤེལ་ to make a political campaign ༑ མང་ཚོགས་ཀྱི་བསམ་བློ་འགྱུར་ཆེད་དུ་སྲིད་དོན་གྱི་ལས་འགུལ་གསར་པ་ཞིག་སྤེལ་བ་རེད་ In order to change the thinking of the people, they made a new political campaign.

སྲིད་ན་དཀོན་པ་ (sīinə gōmbo) very rare.

སྲིད་ན་སྤྱོད་པ་ (sīinə jööba) politician, sb. working in politics.

སྲིད་ན་རིང་བ་ (sīinə ri̱ŋwə) shung. extremely long ༑ སྣན་ཤལ་སྲིད་ན་རིང་བ་འབུལ་གནང་མཛད་ (He) offered an extremely long ceremonial scarf.

སྲིད་པ་ (sīibə) existence, samsara; va.—གནས་ to live in the realm of samsara.

སྲིད་པ་བདུན་ (sīibə dün) seven different kinds of existence.

སྲིད་པ་བར་མ་ (sīibə parma) sm. བར་དོ་.

སྲིད་པ་བཟུང་ (sīibə suŋ) va. to be born in samsara ¶ བསམ་བཞིན་དུ་མིའི་སྲིད་པ་བཟུང་བའི་སྐྱེས་ཆེན་དམ་པ་རྣམས་ The great Lamas who took the human form purposely.

སྲིད་པ་གསུམ་ (sīibə sūm) the three realms of existence: the realm of the gods, the realm of humans, the realm of the demons and hell.

སྲིད་པ་ལྷོ་ (sīibə lhō) thanka which has the wheel of life in the center.

སྲིད་པའི་འཁོར་ལོ་ (sīibɛ kɔ̄ɔ̄lo) the wheel of life/ existence.

སྲིད་པའི་གངས་རི་ (sīibɛ kaŋri) an eternal snow mountain (used as a symbol of eternity).

སྲིད་པའི་མེས་པོ་ (sīibɛ meèbo) Brahma.

སྲིད་ཀྱི་ལས་ཁུངས་ (sīiji lɛɛ̀guŋ) administrative office.

སྲིད་ཕྱོགས་ (sīijɔɔ̀) politics, political activity.

སྲིད་ཕྱོགས་ཀྱི་མི་སྣ་ (sīijɔɔ̀gi minə) people in politics.

སྲིད་བྱུས་ (sīijüù) sm. སྲིད་ཇུས་.

སྲིད་བློན་ (sīilün) 1. chief minister (a post in tt. that was above the Council Ministers and was filled occassionally, usu. when the Dalai Lama fled from Lhasa). 2. prime minister.

སྲིད་བློན་ཕྱོགས་རོགས་ (sīilün cɔ̄grɔɔ̀) the three Council Ministers who were appointed by the Dalai Lama as assistants to the regent in 1908.

སྲིད་བློན་ཟུར་པ་ (sīilün surbə) ex-prime minister/ སྲིད་བློན་.

སྲིད་དབང་ (sīiwaŋ) 1. political power, political authority, secular power; va.—འཛིན་; — བྱེད་ to hold political power/ authority, to rule; va.—སྤྱོད་ to use political power ¶ སྲིད་དབང་འཛིན་མཁན་གྱི་ཚོགས་པ་ The political party in power. 2. political citizenship; va.—འཕྲོག to take away one's right of citizenship ¶ བཙོན་པ་དེ་ལོ་བཅུའི་བཙོན་འཇུག་དང་ལོ་གསུམ་རིང་སྲིད་དབང་འཕྲོག་པ་རེད་ That prisoner was imprisoned for ten years and had his political rights taken away for three years.

སྲིད་དབང་གི་ཁྲིམས་སྲོལ་ (sīiwaŋgi drigsöö) sm. སྲིད་དབང་གི་འཛུགས་ལུགས་.

སྲིད་དབང་གི་འཛུགས་ལུགས་ (sīiwaŋgi dzugluù) system of government.

སྲིད་དབང་འགན་འཛིན་ (sīiwaŋ gɛndzin) the power holders, the authorities.

སྲིད་དབང་སྐྱེར་གཅོད་ (sīiwaŋ gerjöö) dictatorship, autocracy, despotism; va.—བྱེད་ to act in a dictatorial/ autocratic/ despotic way.

སྲིད་དབང་སྐྱེར་གཅོད་ལམ་ལུགས་ (sīiwaŋ gerjöö ləmluù) despotic/ autocratic system, dictatorship.

སྲིད་དབང་སྐྱེར་འཛིན་ (sīiwaŋ gendzin) sm. སྲིད་དབང་སྐྱེར་གཅོད་.

སྲིད་དབང་གཅིག་འཛིན་ (sīiwaŋ jīgdzin) sm. སྲིད་དབང་སྐྱེར་གཅོད་.

སྲིད་དབང་རྙིང་པ་ (sīiwaŋ ñīŋbə) old regime/ government/ political system.

སྲིད་དབང་ཚབ་སྐྱོང་ (sīiwaŋ tsəbgyoŋ) ruling as a regent; va.—བྱེད་.

སྲིད་དབང་འཛིན་མཁན་ལས་ཁུངས་ (sīiwaŋ dzinñɛn lɛɛ̀guŋ) organs/ offices of political power.

སྲིད་དབང་འཛུགས་ལུགས་ (sīiwaŋ dzugluù) system of government, political system.

སྲིད་དབང་རྫུན་མ་ (sīiwaŋ dzünmə) sm. སྲིད་དབང་རྫུས་མ་.

སྲིད་དབང་རྫུས་མ་ (sīiwaŋ dzüümə) puppet government.

སྲིད་དབང་ཟིན་ (sīiwaŋ sin) va. to hold political power.

སྲིད་དབང་ལས་ཁུངས་ (sīiwaŋ lɛɛ̀guŋ) offices/ organs of political power.

སྲིད་འབྱོར་ (sīijɔɔ) the prosperity of this world.

སྲིད་ཚབ་ (sīidzəb) shung. the acting prime minister/ སྲིད་བློན་.

སྲིད་ཚོགས་ (sīidzɔɔ̀) 1. political party/ clique/ faction. 2. political meeting.

སྲིད་ཚོང་པ་ (sīi tsōŋba) politician (derogatory term).

སྲིད་འཚོ་བ་ (sīidzowa) kings and ministers, political leaders.

སྲིད་འཚོང་པ་ (sīidzoŋba) sm. སྲིད་ཚོང་པ་.

སྲིད་འཛིན་ (sīndzin) 1. president. 2. executive branch (as opposed to legislative).

སྲིད་འཛིན་ཀུང་ཧྲུའུ་ (sīndzin gūŋhru) tib. ch. administrative office.

སྲིད་འཛིན་བཀའ་རྒྱ་ (sīndzin gāgya) administrative decree/ order.

སྲིད་འཛིན་བཀའ་འབེབས་ (sīndzin gāmbeb) sm. སྲིད་འཛིན་བཀའ་རྒྱ་.

སྲིད་འཛིན་ཁྲུའུ་ (sīndzin trū) tib. ch. administrative office.

སྲིད་འཛིན་གྱི་ལྟ་སྐུལ་ (sīndzingi dəgüü) administrative supervision.

སྲིད་འཛིན་གྲོང་ཚོ་ (sīndzin troŋdzo) administrative village (a unit in Tibet beneath the xiang).

སྲིད་འཛིན་འགྲོ་སོང་ (sīndzin drosoŋ) the part of commune production used for the commune's administrative expenses.

སྲིད་འཛིན་དང་ (sīndzin dāŋ) tib. ch. the party holding political power.

སྲིད་འཛིན་ཐོག་གི་བཀའ་འབེབས་ (sīndzin tōgi gāmbeb) administrative order/ decree.

སྲིད་འཛིན་ཐོག་གི་ཆད་གཅོད་ (sīndzin tōgi cɛɛ̀jöö) administrative measure.

སྲིད་འཛིན་ཐོག་གི་བྱེད་ཐབས་ (sīndzin tōgi ceèdeb) administrative action/ methods/ means.

སྲིད་འཛིན་བདག་གཉེར་ (sīndzin dagñer) administration management; va.—བྱེད་.

སྲིད་འཛིན་སྡེ་ཚན་ (sīndzin dedzɛn) administrative unit ¶ རྫོང་གི་སྲིད་འཛིན་སྡེ་ཚན་གསར་དུ་བཙུགས་སོང་ They set up a new administrative unit in the district.

སྲིད་འཛིན་ནོར་དོན་ཁྲུའུ་ (sīndzin nɔɔdön trū) tib. ch. administrative financial office.

སྲིད་འཛིན་དཔོན་ (sīndzin bōn) head of a political administrative unit, chief executive.

སྲིད་འཛིན་མི་སྣ་ (sīndzin mina) executive/ administrative personnel.

སྲིད་འཛིན་གཞོན་པ་ (sīndzin shömba) vice president.

སྲིད་འཛིན་འཛིན་གྲྭ་ (sīndzin dzindrə) administrative course/ class.

སྲིད་འཛིན་འོག་མ་ (sīndzin wɔɔma) sm. སྲིད་འཛིན་གཞོན་པ་.

སྲིད་འཛིན་ལས་ཁུངས་ (sīndzin lɛɛ̀guŋ) administrative office.

སྲིད་འཛིན་ལས་བྱེད་པ་ (sīndzin lɛɛ̀jeèba) administrative officer/ cadre/ staff.

སྲིད་འཛིན་ས་ཁུལ་ (sīndzin sāgüü) administrative district/ region.

སྲིད་འཛིན་ས་ཁོང་ (sīndzin sāgoŋ) sm. སྲིད་འཛིན་ས་ཁུལ་.

སྲིད་ཞི་ (sīishi) the cyclic of existence and the state of peace/ nirvana.

སྲིད་ཞེང་ (sīisheŋ) length and breadth.

སྲིད་གཞུང་ (sīishuŋ) government ¶ ས་གནས་སྲིད་གཞུང་ Local government.

སྲིད་གཞུང་གི་གཙོ་འཛིན་ (sīishuŋgi dzōndzin) head of a government.

སྲིད་གཞུང་དྲང་གཙང་ (sīishuŋ taŋdzaŋ) a just/ honest government.

སྲིད་གཞུང་མེད་པའི་གནས་ཚུལ་ (sīishuŋ meèbɛ nɛɛ̀dzüü) anarchy [Lit. a situation without a government].

སྲིད་གཞུང་མེད་པའི་རིང་ལུགས་ (sīishuŋ meèbɛ riŋluù) anarchism.

སྲིད་གཞུང་དྲུང་ཆེ་ (sīishuŋ trünje) shung. sm. རྒྱལ་དོན་བློན་ཆེན་.

སྲིད་ལུགས་ sīiluù) system of government.

སྲིད་ཟུར་ (sīisur) 1. ex-prime minister/ སྲིད་བློན་ (in

tt.). 2. ex-regent (in tt.).

སྲིད་རིང་ (sīiriŋ) length of rule/ administration.

སྲིད་ལོ་ (sīilo) year of a Chinese Emperor (the number of years since he became emperor) ། གོང་མ་ཆན་ལུང་སྲིད་ལོ་གསུམ་པ་ The third year in the reign of the Emperor Qianlong.

སྲིད་ཧྲེ་ (sīihre) tib. ch. abbr. government and commune.

སྲིད་ཧྲེ་གཅིག་སྒྲིལ་ (sīihre jīgdrii) the merger of government administration with communal management.

སྲིད་སྲུང་ (sīisuŋ) protecting/ defending the government or country; va.—བྱེད་.

སྲིན་ (sīn) abbr. of སྲིན་བུ་ and སྲིན་པོ་.

སྲིན་སྐུད་ (sīngüü) silk yarn/ thread ། སྲིན་སྐུད་ཉིས་སྒྲིམ་ 2-ply silk thread.

སྲིན་སྐྲན་ (sīndrɛn) stomach cancer.

སྲིན་ཁུང་ (sīnguŋ) 1. temple (of the head). 2. nest of insects.

སྲིན་གོང་ (sīnguŋ) silkworm cocoon.

སྲིན་གླང་ (sīnlaŋ) ascariasis.

སྲིན་རྒྱལ་ (sīngyɛɛ) king of the flesh easting demons.

སྲིན་ཐག་ (sīndaà) silk thread, silk rope.

སྲིན་ཐོར་ (sīndɔɔ) a skin disease.

སྲིན་ནད་ (sīnnɛɛ̀) diseases of the digestive system caused by worms and parasites.

སྲིན་པོ་ (sīmbu) a flesh-eating demon.

སྲིན་པོ་ཁྲོས་པ་ (sīmbu drööba) a wrathful deity's appearance.

སྲིན་པོ་མི་བརྫུས་ (sīmbu midzüü) pretending to be what one isn't, the evil pretending to be good [Lit. a demon disguised as a man].

སྲིན་ཕོལ་ (sīmböö) a type of sore caused by an insect.

སྲིན་ཕྲུག་ (sīmdruù) children of flesh eating demons.

སྲིན་བལ་ (sīmbɛɛ) unprocessed/ raw silk.

སྲིན་བུ་ (sīmbu) 1. general term for insect. 2. silkworm.

སྲིན་བུ་གླང་འཐབ་ (sīmbu lāŋdəb) sm. སྲིན་གླང་.

སྲིན་བུ་འགུལ་ (sīmbu güü) the start of the 2nd month in the Tibetan calendar.

སྲིན་བུ་པད་པ་ (sīmbu bɛ̀ɛ̀ba) leech.

སྲིན་བུ་མི་བརྫུས་ (sīmbu midzüü) sm. སྲིན་པོ་མི་བརྫུས་.

སྲིན་བུ་མིར་ཁི་ (sīmbu migi) a type of worm in the brain that causes epilepsy according to Tibetan medicine.

སྲིན་བུ་མེ་ཁྱེར་ (sīmbu mekyer) firefly.

སྲིན་བུ་རང་དཀྲིས་ (sīmbu randrii) getting caught/ trapped by one's own actions [Lit. a silkworm coiling around itself].

སྲིན་འབུ་ (sīmbu) sm. སྲིན་བུ་.

སྲིན་བྱ་ (sīnja) owl.

སྲིན་མོ་ (sīnmu) female demon.

སྲིན་ཚང་ (sīndzaŋ) sm. སྲིན་ཁུང་.

སྲིན་མཛུབ་ (sīndzub) the fourth finger counting from the thumb.

སྲིན་ཞལ་ (sīnshɛɛ) sm. སྲིན་པོ་ཁྲོས་པ་.

སྲིན་ཟམ་ (sīnsam) a bridge between two houses.

སྲིན་ལག་ (sīnlaà) sm. སྲིན་མཛུབ་.

སྲིན་ལོང་ (sīnloŋ) part of the small intestines.

སྲིན་ཤིང་ (sīnshiŋ) mulberry tree.

སྲིན་ཤིང་དར་འབུ་ (sīnshiŋ tarbu) silkworm.

སྲིན་ཤིང་ར་བ་ (sīnshiŋ rawa) mulberry grove/ farm.

སྲིབ་ (drīb) 1. vi. to get dark/ night ། ས་སྲིབ་པ་དང་ནང་དུ་ལོག་པ་ཡིན་ As soon as it got dark I returned home.

སྲིབ་སྐྱེས་རྩི་ཤིང་ (drībgyeè dzīshiŋ) plants that grow in the shade.

སྲིབ་ནག་ (drībnaà) shadow, shade.

སྲིབ་ནད་ (drībnɛɛ̀) measles.

སྲིབ་ཚལ་ (drībdzɛɛ) forest located in the shade.

སྲིབ་རི་ (drībri) mountain located in the shade.

སྲིབ་ལུང་ (drībluŋ) a place in the shade.

སྲིབས་ (drīb) sm. སྲིབ་.

སྲིའུ་ (drīwu) new born baby, infant.

སྲིལ་ (drīi) moth.

སྲིས་ (drīi) imp. of སྲི་.

སྲིས་རྒྱ་ (drīigya) name of a kind of red paint.

སྲུ་ (srū) 1. abbr. of སྲུ་མོ་. 2. va. to pour ། ངས་ཇ་སྲུ་པ་ཡིན་ I poured tea.

སྲུ་མོ་ (sōmo) maternal aunt.

སྲུ་མོ་ལགས་ (sōmolaà) h. sm. སྲུ་མོ་.

སྲུང་: p. བསྲུངས་; f. བསྲུང་; imp. སྲུངས་ (sūŋ) va. to guard/ defend/ protect ། ཁོ་ཚོས་ཕོ་བྲང་སྲུང་གི་ཡོད་པ་རེད་ They are guarding the palace. ། རྒྱལ་ཁབ་ཀྱི་ས་མཚམས་སྲུང་ཡས་ Defending the borders of the country. ། མཁའ་སྲུང་ Air defense.

སྲུང་སྐར་ (sūŋgar) satellite (in the sky); va.—གཏོང་ to send/ launch a satellite.

སྲུང་སྐུད་ (sūŋgüü) sm. སྲུང་མདུད་.

སྲུང་སྐྱེལ་ (sūŋgyee) escorting sb. (for protection); va.—བྱེད་ to escort; va.—ཞུ་ to request an escort ། ཕྱི་རྒྱལ་གྱི་འཐུས་མི་རྣམས་ས་མཚམས་བར་སྲུང་སྐྱེལ་ཞུས་པ་རེད་ They escorted the foreign delegates to the border.

སྲུང་སྐྱེལ་སྐྱོགས་གྲུ་ (sūŋgyee gyɔgdru) escort gunboat.

སྲུང་སྐྱོང་ (sūŋgyoŋ) defending, safeguarding, taking care of, looking after the welfare of ། སྲིད་གཞུང་ནས་ཕྲུ་གུ་སྲུང་སྐྱོང་གི་སྡེ་ཚན་འགའ་ཤས་བཙུགས་པ་རེད་ The government established several units to look after the welfare of children.

སྲུང་སྐྱོབ་ (sūŋgyob) defending, safeguarding, protecting; va.—བྱེད་ ། འཛམ་གླིང་ཞི་བདེའི་སྲུང་སྐྱོབ་བྱེད་ཀྱི་ཡོད་པ་རེད་ (They) are defending world peace.

སྲུང་སྐྱོབ་ཀྱི་སྤྱི་ཁྱབ་ (sūŋgyobgi jīgyəb) defense minister.

སྲུང་སྐྱོབ་ཁྲུའུ་ (sūŋgyob trū) tib. ch. security section/ unit.

སྲུང་སྐྱོབ་རྒྱལ་ཁབ་ (sūŋgyob gyɛɛgəb) a protectorate (nation).

སྲུང་སྐྱོབ་སྡོངས་གྲོགས་མཛོད་ (sūŋgyob doŋdrɔɔ̀ dzö̀ö̀) shung. issuing a plea for protection and help ། ལྷ་སྲུང་དམ་ཅན་གང་གིས་ཉིན་མཚན་དུས་དྲུག་ཏུ་སྲུང་སྐྱོབ་སྡོངས་གྲོགས་མཛོད་ We plea to the protective deity to give protection and help during the days and nights.

སྲུང་སྐྱོབ་དྲུང་ཆེ་ (sūŋgyob trunje) Secretary of Defense (U.S.).

སྲུང་སྐྱོབ་བྱེད་མཁན་ (sūŋgyob cèèñɛn) guardian, protector, defender.

སྲུང་སྐྱོབ་བློན་ཆེན་ (sūŋgyob lönjen) Defense Minister.

སྲུང་སྐྱོབ་དམག་འཐབ་ (sūŋgyob məgdəb) defensive war.

སྲུང་སྐྱོབ་ལས་ཁུངས་ (sūŋgyob lɛ̀ɛ̀guŋ) defense ministry/ bureau.

སྲུང་སྐྱོབ་ལྷན་ཁང་ (sūŋgyob lhēngaŋ) Security Council (of the UN).

སྲུང་བཀག་ (sūŋgaà) sm. སྲུང་འགོག.

སྲུང་མཁན་དགྲ་དམག་ (sūŋgɛn dramaà) defending enemy army.

སྲུང་འཁོར་ (sūŋgɔɔ) a protective amulet.

སྲུང་འགེབས་ (sūŋgeb) protecting, shielding, harboring, hiding, covering up; va.—བྱེད་ ། ཉེས་ཅན་སྲུང་འགེབས་བྱས་པ་སྐོར་སྲུང་དམག་གིས་ཤེས་པ་རེད་ The police knew that they shielded the criminals.

སྲུང་འགོ་པ་ (sūŋgoba) shung. head of the guards.

སྲུང་འགོག་ (sūŋgɔɔ̀) defending, guarding, protecting; va.—བྱེད་ ། ས་མཚམས་སྲུང་འགོག་བྱེད་མཁན་དམག་མི་ཁག་ཅིག་བཏང་བ་རེད་ They sent a group of soldiers to guard the border.

སྲུང་འགོག་གི་ནུས་པ་ (sūŋgɔɔ̀gi nüüba) defense capability.

སྲུང་ཇ་ (sūŋja) guards; va.—སྡོད་ to stand/ stay on guard; va.—བྱེད་ to act as a guard; va.—འཛུག་ to leave a guard.

སྲུང་ཇ་བ་ (sūŋjawa) shung. sm. སྲུང་ཇ་.

སྲུང་མདུད་ (sūŋdüüs) protective string amulet (i.e.,

string that is knotted in a special way and blessed by a lama as protection).

སྲུང་འདོགས་ (sūŋdoò) protective talisman/ amulet.

སྲུང་འདོམས་ (sūŋdom) be on alert/ on guard; va.—བྱེད་ to keep a lookout/ to defend/ uphold sth. ¶ འགོ་ཁྲིད་ཀྱིས་ལས་ཁུངས་ཀྱི་སྒྲིག་ལམ་སྲུང་འདོམས་ཡག་པོ་བྱེད་དགོས་ The leader has to keep a sharp lookout regarding upholding the officer's discipline.

སྲུང་འདོམས་རྩ་ཚིག (sūŋdom dzādzii) shung. regulation/ proclamation issued for upholding discipline.

སྲུང་སྡོམ་ (sūŋdom) keeping one's vows/ oaths; va.—བྱེད་.

སྲུང་གནས་ (sūŋnɛɛ̀) place where sb. stands guard/ sentry.

སྲུང་སྤྱི་ (sūŋji) shung. all the protective deities in general.

སྲུང་བ་ (sūŋwə) protective charms/ amulets.

སྲུང་བ་པོ་ (sūŋwabo) sm. སྲུང་བྱ་.

སྲུང་བྱ་ (sūŋja) 1. guarding; va.—བྱེད་ to guard ¶ རྒྱལ་ཟུར་རྭ་སྒྲེང་དོ་དམ་སྐབས་སྲུང་བྱ་བྱེད་རིང་ While guarding the ex-Regent Reting during the time he was under arrest. 2. guard ¶ སྲུང་བྱ་ལུང་ཤར་བརྒྱུད་ Via the guard Lungshar.

སྲུང་བྱ་དོན་ཚན་ (sūŋja tö̱ntsɛn) regulations/ rules to be upheld.

སྲུང་བྱེད་ཁ་དོག (sūŋjeè kādoò) protective coloring (for animals).

སྲུང་མ་ (sūŋma) guardian/ protective deity.

སྲུང་མ་དམར་ནག (sūŋma mārnaà) the two state protective deities in tt.: གནས་ཆུང་ཆོས་སྐྱོང་ and དཔལ་ལྡན་ལྷ་མོ་.

སྲུང་མ་ཁང་ (sūŋmagaŋ) sm. མགོན་ཁང་.

སྲུང་དམག (sūŋmaà) 1. guards, bodyguards, security forces/ police; va.—བྱེད་. 2. defending troops.

སྲུང་དམག་དམར་པོ་ (sūŋmaà māābo) the Red Guards.

སྲུང་དམག་རུ་ཁག (sūŋmaà ru̱gaà) the corps of guardsmen/ bodyguards/ security police.

སྲུང་བརྩི་ (sūŋdzi) adhering to, respecting, honoring (rules, regulations, etc.); va.—བྱེད་; —ཞུ་ ¶ ཆིངས་ཡིག་ལ་སྲུང་བརྩི་མ་བྱས་པ་རེད་ (They) did not honor the treaty.

སྲུང་མཚམས་ (sūŋdzam) line of defense.

སྲུང་མཛད་ (sūŋdzɛɛ̀) 1. སྲུང་ཆ་. 2. another name for the Buddha.

སྲུང་རྫས་ (sūŋdzɛɛ̀) protective amulet.

སྲུང་འཛིན་ (sūŋdzin) conserving, preserving; va.—བྱེད་; —སྲིལ་ to conserve, to preserve ¶ ས་ཆུ་སྲུང་འཛིན་ Conserving soil and water.

སྲུང་ཡོལ་ (sūŋyüü) defense barrier, line of defense.

སྲུང་སེམས་ (sūŋsem) watchful/ vigilant mind.

སྲུངས་ (sūŋ) imp. of སྲུང་.

སྲུན་པོ་ (sūmbu) mild, tame, gentle.

སྲུབ་ (sūb) crack, fissure, gap.

སྲུབ་: p. **བསྲུབས་**; f. **བསྲུབ་**; imp. **སྲུབས་** (sūb) va. to churn ¶ མོ་ཇ་སྲུབ་ཀྱི་འདུག She is churning tea.

སྲུབ་དཀྲུག (sūbdruù) churning, mixing, stirring; va.—བྱེད་.

སྲུབ་དཀྲུག་འཕྲུལ་འཁོར་ (sūbdruù trǚǚgɔɔ) mixer, blending machine.

སྲུབ་ཇ་ (sūbja) churned (butter) tea.

སྲུབ་ཐག (sūbdaà) rope attached to a churner.

སྲུབ་སྣོད་ (sūbnöö) a churn; va.—བྱེད་ to churn.

སྲུབ་མདའ་ (sūmda) 1. the piston like stick that moves up and down in a churn. 2. a piston.

སྲུབ་མདའ་བཟོ་གྲྭ་ (sūmda so̱dra) piston factory.

སྲུབ་བྱེད་ (sūbjeè) a churn.

སྲུབ་མ་ (sūbmə) 1. churned ¶ ཇ་སྲུབ་མ་ Churned tea. 2. sm. སྲུབ་མདའ་. 3. fissure, gap, crack.

སྲུབ་འཚང་རྒྱག (sūbdzaŋ gyaà) va. to come between a couple or between a boyfriend and girlfriend.

སྲུབ་གཟན་ (sūbsɛn) piping (used for trimming clothes/ upholstery).

སྲུབས་ (sūb) 1. fissure, crack, gap. 2. imp. of སྲུབ་. 3. seam.

སྲུབས་ཀ་ (sūbga) a crack; vi.—ཤོར་ to crack.

སྲུབས་གནོན་ (sūbnün) an iron (for pressing clothes, etc.); va.—རྒྱག.

སྲུབས་དབར་ (sūbwar) sm. སྲུབལ་ཀ་.

སྲུབས་དྲག (sūbdraà) sm. སྲུབས་ཀ་.

སྲུབས་མེད་ (sūbmeè) seamless ¶ སྲུབས་མེད་ལྕགས་མདོང་ Seamless iron tube/ pipe. ¶ སྲུབས་མེད་ཇོ་སྦུག Seamless tubing.

སྲུབས་ཟན་ (sūbsɛn) piping, cording.

སྲུབས་ཤིང་ (sūbshiŋ) 1. sm. སྲུབས་མདའ་. 2. wood for patching cracks/ gaps.

སྲུབས་ལྷན་ (sūblhɛn) materials for patching cracks/ gaps.

སྲུལ་: p. and f. **བསྲུལ་** (sǖǖ) vi. to rot, to decompose, to putrefy.

སྲུལ་པོ་ (sǖǖbu) putrid, decomposed, rotten.

སྲུལ་མོ་ (sǖǖmu) sm. སྲུལ་པོ་.

སྲུས་ (sǖǖ) 1. new/ green/ unripe ears of grain. 2. unripened barley that is roasted and eaten as a snack.

སྲུས་ཇ་ (sǖǖja) sm. སྲུབ་ཇ་.

སྲུས་ཐུག (sǖǖdug) soup/ broth made with unripe grain.

སྲུས་མ་ (sǖǖmə) sm. སྲུབ་ཇ་.

སྲེ་: p. **བསྲེས་**; f. **བསྲེ་**; imp. **སྲེས་** (drē) va. to mix/ blend together ¶ ཆུ་དང་འོ་མ་བསྲེས་པ་རེད་ (He) mixed milk and water together.

སྲེ་སྐྱག (drēgyaà) 1. skunk's odor; va.—སྟེར་ to have a skunk emit its odor. 2. slang. swindling, conniving; va.—སྟེར་ ¶ ཁོང་གིས་མི་ངན་པ་དེར་བློས་བཀལ་ནས་མ་རྩ་བསྐུར་བ་དེ་མི་ངན་དེས་སྲེ་སྐྱག་སྟེར་བ་རེད་ He trusted that bad person and gave him capital and then that bad person swindled him.

སྲེ་ད་ (drēda) 1. an ear of grain that does not have kernels. 2. a flower that grows poorly.

སྲེ་ནག (drēnaà) soot.

སྲེ་ནག་མདོག (drēnaàdɔɔ̀) color of soot.

སྲེ་པོ་ (drēwo) sm. བསྲེ་པོ་.

སྲེ་མོ་ (drēmo) sm. སྲེ་མོང་.

སྲེ་མོག (drēmoò) sm. སྲེ་ནག.

སྲེ་མོང་ (drēmoŋ) 1. skunk. 2. weasel.

སྲེ་མོང་ཤ་ (drēmoŋ shā) སྲེ་མོང་ meat (used in Tibetan medicine).

སྲེ་ཟན་ (drēsɛn) millet flour.

སྲེ་ལོང་ (drēloŋ) 1. anklebone. 2. heel bone.

སྲེ་སྲེ་ (drēse) mixing; va.—གཏོང་ ¶ འབྲུ་དང་སྲན་མ་སྲེ་སྲེ་བཏང་ནས་རྩམ་པ་བཏག་འདུག (They) mixed barley and beans together and ground them into རྩམ་པ་.

སྲེག: p. **བསྲེགས་**; f. **བསྲེག**; imp. **སྲེགས་** (sēg) 1. va. to burn ¶ ཡིག་ཆ་རྣམས་མེ་ལ་བསྲེགས་པ་རེད་ (They) burned the documents in the fire. 2. va. to roast/ grill/ broil ¶ ཤ་བསྲེགས་ནས་ཟ་གི་ཡོད་པ་རེད་ (They) roasted the meat and are eating it. 3. va. to fry ¶ ཁ་ཟས་བསྲེགས་ Frying cookies (Tibetan pastries).

སྲེག་ཁང་ (sēggaŋ) crematory.

སྲེག་བཅད་བརྡར་གསུམ་ (sēgjɛɛ̀ da̱rsum) looking into, examining carefully/ thoroughly; va.—བྱེད་ ¶ གྱོད་དོན་འདི་སྐོར་ཁྲིམས་ཁང་ནས་སྲེག་བཅད་བརྡར་གསུམ་བྱས་ནས་ཐག་གཅོད་བྱས་འདུག Concerning this case, the court investigated thoroughly and made a decision. [Lit. the three: burn, cut and sharpen].

སྲེག་གཏོར་རུ་ཁག (sēgdɔɔ ru̱gaà) demolition squad.

སྲེག་ཐབ་ (sēgdəb) furnace, oven.

སྲེག་ཐལ་ (sēgdɛɛ) ashes.

སྲེག་འཐུད་བཟོ་གྲྭ་ (sēgdüǜ so̱dra) sintering plant/ factory.

སྲེག་མདེལ་ (sēgdee) incendiary shell/ bomb.

སྲེག་དོང་ལངས་མ་ (sēgdoŋ la̱ŋma) kiln/ oven for firing bricks.

སྲེག་གནས་ (sēgnɛɛ̀) place where corpses are cremated.

སྲེག་པ་ (sēgba) 1. sm. སྲེག་མ་. 2. quail, grouse.

སྲེག་བླུགས་ (sēgluù) exorcism rite.

སྲེག་མ་ (sēgma) anything burned/ roasted/ grilled ¶

ཤ་སྲེག་མ་ Grilled meat.

སྲེག་རྫས་ (sēgdzɛɛ̀) things used in the rite of exorcism.

སྲེག་ཟན་ (drāàsɛn) a thin pancake.

སྲེག་བསྣུག (sēglaà) destroying by burning; va.—གཏོང་.

སྲེག་ཤ་ (drāàsha) grilled/ broiled meat.

སྲེག་ཤིང་ (sēgshiŋ) 1. firewood. 2. wood used in exorcism rites.

སྲེག་ཤེལ་ (sēgshee) magnifying glass (used to start a fire).

སྲེག་གསོད་འཕྲོག་བཅོམ་ (sēgsöò trɔ̄ɔ̀jom) burning, killing and plundering.

སྲེད་ (drēè) vi. to be attached to, to have a desire for, to love, to lust for ¶ ནོར་ལ་སྲེད་ཆེ་བའི་རྐྱེན་གྱིས་མི་ལ་མགོ་སྐོར་བཏང་བ་རེད་ Because he is strongly attached to wealth, he swindled people.

སྲེད་ཉམས་ (drēèñam) lust, passion, desire, craving; va.—སྟོན་ to show lust/ passion/ desire.

སྲེད་ལྡན་ཟློས་གར་ (drēndɛn dö̱ögar) pornographic play/ show.

སྲེད་པོ་ (drēèbo) lustful.

སྲེལ་: p. and f. of བསྲེལ་; imp. སྲེལ་ (drēē) 1. va. to hold, to keep. 2. va. to rear, to raise, to bring up.

སྲེས་ (drēè) imp. of སྲེ་.

སྲོ་: p. བསྲོས་; f. བསྲོ་; imp. སྲོས་ (drō) va. to warm by heat ¶ དགུན་ཁ་ཉི་མ་སྲོ་བ་རེད་ In the winter they warm themselves in the sun. 2. va. to dry by heat ¶ གོས་རློན་པ་མེ་ལ་བསྲོས་པ་རེད་ (They) dried the wet clothes by fire.

སྲོ་ཁང་ (drōgaŋ) 1. hot house. 2. bath house/ sauna.

སྲོ་སྒམ་ (dōgam) oven, roaster.

སྲོ་སྒོང་ (drōgoŋ) sm. སྲོ་ཁང་.

སྲོ་སྟེགས་ (drōdeg) open veranda/ terrace/ porch.

སྲོ་མ་ (drōma) nit; vi.—རྒྱག to be infested with nits/ lice.

སྲོ་མར་ (drōmaa) sm.* སྲོ་མ་.

སྲོ་མོ་ (drōmo) sm. སྲོ་མོ་.

སྲོ་ཤད་ (drōshɛɛ̀) a fine comb for getting rid of nits/ lice.

སྲོ་ཞི་ (drō shi̱) vi. to lose courage.

སྲོ་ཤིག (drōshii) abbr. of སྲོ་མ་ and ཤིག.

སྲོག (sɔ̄ɔ̀) 1. life; vi.—ཤོར་ to lose (one's) life, to die ¶ རང་སྲོག One's own life. 2. durability ¶ སྲོག་མཁྲེགས་པོ་ Durable. ¶ སྲོག་མེད་པ་ Fragile.

སྲོག་རྐྱེན་དུ་གཏོང་ (sɔ̄ɔ̀gyendu dōŋ) shung. va. to kill.

སྲོག་སྐྱིན་ (sɔ̄ɔ̀gyin jɛ̱ɛ̱) taking a life for a life; va.—འཇལ་.

སྲོག་སྐྱེལ་ (sɔ̄ɔ̀ gyēē) va. to lose one's life unnecessarily ¶ ཁོས་དོན་མེད་དུ་རྒྱག་རེས་བརྒྱབ་ནས་སྲོག་བསྐྱལ་བཞག He fought for no reason and lost his life unnecessarily.

སྲོག་སྐྱོན་ (sɔ̄ɔ̀gyön) loss of life, casualties, deaths ¶ མི་མང་པོར་སྲོག་སྐྱོན་བྱུང་འདུག Many people lost their lives.

སྲོག་སྐྱོབ་ (sɔ̄ɔ̀gyob) saving a life; va. སྲོག་སྐྱོབ་; —བྱེད་ to save a life; va.—ཞུ་ to seek protection for one's life ¶ ཁོས་ཕྲུ་གུ་དེའི་སྲོག་བསྐྱབས་པ་རེད་ He saved the life of that child.

སྲོག་སྐྱོབ་འཁྱིག་འཁོར་ (sɔ̄ɔ̀gyob gyi̱ggɔɔ) sm. སྲོག་སྐྱོབ་འཁྱིག་སྐོར་.

སྲོག་སྐྱོབ་འཕྲུལ་སྒམ་ (sɔ̄ɔ̀gyob trü̱ü̱gam) mechanical life supporting unit (in a hospital).

སྲོག་སྐྱོབ་འཁྱིག་སྐོར་ (sɔ̄ɔ̀gyob gyi̱ggɔɔ) life buoy, life jacket.

སྲོག་བསྐྱབས་ (sɔ̄ɔ̀gyəb) p. of སྲོག་སྐྱོབ་.

སྲོག་མཁྲེགས་པོ་ (sɔ̄ɔ̀ trāgbo) sm.* སྲོག་མཁྲེགས་པོ་.

སྲོག་ཁྲིམས་ (sɔ̄gdrim) capital punishment, death sentence; va.—གཏོང་; —གཅོད་ to execute (legally) ¶ ཇག་པ་འགའ་ཤས་ལ་སྲོག་ཁྲིམས་བཅད་པ་རེད་ They executed some bandits.

སྲོག་མཁྲེགས་པོ་ (sɔ̄ɔ̀ trēgbo) durable, very hard.

སྲོག་གི་ཆད་པ་ (sɔ̄ɔ̀gi cɛ̄ɛ̀ba) sm. སྲོག་ཁྲིམས་.

སྲོག་གི་ཀ་བ་ (sɔ̄ɔ̀gi gāwa) sm. སྲོག་ཙ་.

སྲོག་གི་བར་ཆད་ (sɔ̄ɔ̀gi pa̱rjɛɛ̀) fatal accident, dying by accident.

སྲོག་མགོ་ (sɔ̄ŋgo) at the point of death, facing death; vi.—ཐོན་ to be in danger of dying or being killed but overcoming it ¶ ལམ་བར་དུ་ཇག་པ་མང་པོ་ཐུག་ཀྱང་ངའི་སྲོག་མགོ་ཐོན་ཙམ་བྱུང་ Even though I met many bandits on the road and was in danger of being killed, I didn't get killed.

སྲོག་འགན་འཁྱེར་ (sɔ̄ŋgɛn kyēr) va. to take responsibility for sb.'s life, to guarantee a person's life/ safety.

སྲོག་འགྲོ་ (sɔ̄ɔ̀ dro̱) vi. to die ¶ ངའི་སྲོག་འགྲོ་གི་ཡོད་ནའང་རྒྱལ་ཁབ་ཀྱི་དོན་དུ་དམག་ལ་འགྲོ་ཐག་ཆོད་ཡིན་ Even if I die, I have decided to fight for (my) country.

སྲོག་ཅན་ (sɔ̄gjɛn) having life, being animate, sentient beings.

སྲོག་ཅན་ཚོང་ཟོག (sɔ̄gjɛn tsōŋsɔɔ̀) live merchandise.

སྲོག་གཅོད་ (sɔ̄gjöö̀) killing; va.—བྱེད་ to kill, to take life; va.—སྤོང་ to give up/ renounce the taking of life.

སྲོག་གཅོད་གཤེད་མ་ (sɔ̄gjöö shēèma) killer, murderer.

སྲོག་བཅོལ་ (sɔ̄gjöö) placing one's life in the hands (protection) of another; va.—ཞུ་.

སྲོག་ཆགས་ (sɔ̄gjaà) living/ animate beings.

སྲོག་ཆགས་ཀྱི་རིག་པ་ (sɔ̄gjaàgi ri̱gbə) zoology.

སྲོག་ཆགས་གླིང་ག (sɔ̄gjaà li̱ŋgə) zoo.

སྲོག་ཆགས་ར་བ་ (sɔ̄gjaà ra̱wa) zoo.

སྲོག་ཆགས་སློབ་སྡེ་ (sɔ̄gjaà lōbde) zoology/ biology department.

སྲོག་ཆད་ (sɔ̄ɔ̀jɛɛ̀) sm. སྲོག་ཁྲིམས་.

སྲོག་འཆད་ (sɔ̄g cɛ̄ɛ̀) vi. to die.

སྲོག་ཉེན་ (sɔ̄gñen) danger to life, danger of dying; vi.—ཐར་ to escape from a danger to one's life.

སྲོག་ཉེན་འཛེམ་མེད་ (sɔ̄gñen dze̱mmeè) not afraid of losing one's life.

སྲོག་ཉེས་ (sɔ̄gñeè) sm. སྲོག་ཁྲིམས་.

སྲོག་གཏོང་ (sɔ̄ɔ̀ dōŋ) va. to sacrifice/ give one's life (for a cause) ¶ རྒྱལ་ཁབ་ཀྱི་དོན་དུ་སྲོག་བཏང་བའི་དཔའ་བོ་ Heroes who gave their lives for their country.

སྲོག་གཏོང་མེས་པོ་ (sɔ̄gdoŋ me̱èwo) martyred ancestors.

སྲོག་བཏང་དཔའ་བོ་ (sɔ̄gdaŋ bāwo) martyr.

སྲོག་རྟེན་ (sɔ̄gden) life, spirit, life essence (བླ་).

སྲོག་སྟེར་གཅེས་ (sɔ̄gder jēè) va. to consider/ cherish sth. as one's does one's own life ¶ ཁོང་གིས་རྒྱལ་ཁབ་ཀྱི་རྒྱུ་ནོར་ལ་སྲོག་སྟེར་གཅེས་ནས་སྲུང་སྐྱོབ་བྱེད་ཀྱི་ཡོད་པ་རེད་ He protects government property like it was his own.

སྲོག་ཐག (sɔ̄gdaà) lifeline ¶ ལམ་དེ་ནི་ས་མཐའི་མི་རྣམས་ཀྱི་སྲོག་ཐག་ལྟ་བུ་ཞིག་རེད་ That road is the lifeline for the people in remote areas.

སྲོག་ཐར་ (sɔ̄gdar) vi. to escape a danger of dying ¶ ས་ཡོམ་ཆེན་པོ་འདིའི་འོག་ནས་ང་སྲོག་ཐར་བྱུང་ I escaped the great earthquake with my life.

སྲོག་ཐུག་རྨས་སྐྱོན་ (sɔ̄gduù mɛ̄ɛ̀gyön) fatal wound/ injury.

སྲོག་ཐོག་ཁྲིམས་གཅོད་ (sɔ̄gdɔɔ̀ tri̱mjöö̀) capital punishment, execution; va.—གཏོང་.

སྲོག་ཐོག་ཉེས་ཆད་ (sɔ̄gdɔɔ̀ ñe̱èjɛɛ̀) sm. སྲོག་ཐོག་ཁྲིམས་གཅོད་.

སྲོག་ཐོག་ཉེས་སྤྱོད་ (sɔ̄gdɔɔ̀ ñe̱èjöö̀) capital crime; va.—བྱེད་ to commit a capital crime.

སྲོག་ཐོག་གཏོང་ (sɔ̄gdɔɔ̀ dōŋ) va. to execute ¶ ལྗོན་ཤིང་ལ་བཏགས་ནས་སྲོག་ཐོག་བཏང་བ་རེད་ They tied them to a tree and executed them.

སྲོག་དང་སྡོ་ (sɔ̄ɔ̀daŋ do̱) va. to risk one's life, to go all out even it means one's life ¶ ཁོ་ཚོས་སྲོག་དང་བསྡོས་ནས་རང་དབང་བསྲུངས་པ་རེད་ They risked their lives to protect (their) freedom.

སྲོག་དང་བྲལ་ (sɔ̄ɔ̀daŋ tre̱e̱) 1. vi. to die. 2. a way of swearing ("I promise") in Tsang.

སྲོག་དོར་ (sɔ̄ɔ̀dɔɔ) p. of སྲོག་འདོར་.

སྲོག་མདའ་ (sɔ̄ŋda) central axis, axle.

སྲོག་འདོར་ (sɔ̄ɔ̀ dɔ̱ɔ̱) sm. སྲོག་གཏོང་.

སྲོག་བསྡོས་ (sōɔ döö) sm. སྲོག་དང་སྡོ་.

སྲོག་ལྡན་ (sōŋdɛn) sm. སྲོག་ཅན་.

སྲོག་འཕྲོག་ (sōndrɔɔ) killing, taking sb.'s life; va.—བྱེད་.

སྲོག་བྲལ་ (sōɔ trɛɛ) vi. to die.

སྲོག་བླུ་ (sōɔ lū) 1. va. to save sb.'s life, to rescue ¶ གྲུ་པས་ཁོའི་སྲོག་བླུ་པ་རེད་ The boatman saved his life. 2. sm. སྲོག་བླུ་གཏོང་.

སྲོག་བླུ་གཏོང་ (sōɔ lū dōŋ) va. to save a life (animals) by buying an animal scheduled to be slaughtered.

སྲོག་བླུས་ (sōglüü) p. of སྲོག་བླུ་.

སྲོག་བློས་གཏོང་ (sōɔ lȫȫ dōŋ) va. to risk/ sacrifice one's life for sth. ¶ ཁང་པར་མེ་ཤོར་དུས་ཁོང་གིས་སྲོག་བློས་བཏང་ནས་མི་མང་པོ་བསྐྱབས་པ་རེད་ When the house caught fire, he risked his life and saved many people. ¶ ཁང་པར་མེ་ཤོར་སྐབས་མི་གཞན་དག་སྐྱབ་ཆེད་དུ་ཁོང་རང་གི་སྲོག་བློས་བཏང་བ་རེད་ When the house caught fire, he gave up his life to save others.

སྲོག་དབང་ (sōɔwaŋ) sm. སྲོག.

སྲོག་དབུགས་ (sōɔ ūù) the breath of life; —ཆད་ to have the breath of life be cut off, to die.

སྲོག་འབེན་འཛུགས་ (sōŋben dzuù) sm. སྲོག་བློས་གཏོང་.

སྲོག་སྦྱིན་ (sōɔ jīn) 1. va. to save a life. 2. va.—གཏོང་ to sacrifice/ give up one's life for others.

སྲོག་མེད་ (sōɔmeè) 1. inanimate, not living/ alive. 2. fragile.

སྲོག་མེད་པེམ་པོ་ (sōɔmeè pembo) sm. སྲོག་མེད་, 1.

སྲོག་མེད་བླ་འཁྱམ་ (sōɔmeè lāgyam) wandering consciousness (after sb. died).

སྲོག་མེད་པ་ (sōɔmeèba) sm. སྲོག་མེད་.

སྲོག་རྩ་ (sōgdza) lifeline, life essence, life blood.

སྲོག་རྩར་ཐུག (sōgdza tūg) vi. to reach the point of life and death, to reach a critical/ crucial point ¶ སྲོག་རྩར་ཐུག་པའི་གནས་སྐབས་ A crucial moment.

སྲོག་འཚོ་ (sōg tsō) vi. to sustain life, to survive ¶ ཞིང་ཁ་ཕར་སྣོན་མ་བྱུང་ན་ཞིང་པ་ཚོའི་སྲོག་འཚོ་ཐུབ་ས་མ་རེད་ Unless (they) get more fields, the farmers cannot survive.

སྲོག་ཟུངས་ (sōɔsuŋ) physical strength.

སྲོག་ཟོན་ (sōgsön) careful/ watchful/ mindful of losing one's life; va.—བྱེད་.

སྲོག་རླུང་ (sōɔluŋ) a type of mental depression/ illness.

སྲོག་ལ་ཐུག (sōɔla tūù) vi. to face death, to come into a situation where one's live is at risk ¶ ང་རང་གི་སྲོག་ལ་ཐུག་ཀྱང་ཆོས་དང་འགལ་བའི་ལས་ཀ་བྱེད་ཀྱི་མིན་ Even at the risk of my life, I will not do anything in violation of religion.

སྲོག་ལ་བབས་ (sōɔla bab) vi. to die ¶ སྲོག་ལ་བབས་པའི་ཁྲིམས་ཆད་མི་ཕོག་པ་མཛོད་ Please don't let me be given the death sentence.

སྲོག་ལ་མ་འཛེམས་པ་ (sōɔla mandzemba) not fearing death ¶ སྲོག་ལ་མ་འཛེམས་པར་དམག་སའི་གནས་ཚུལ་ལྟ་བར་ཕྱིན་པ་རེད་ Not fearing death, (he) went to look at the battlefield situation.

སྲོག་ལེན་འཇལ་ (sōɔlɛn jɛɛ) va. to take blood vengeance/ revenge (by killing sb.).

སྲོག་བརླག (sōɔ lāà) sm. སྲོག་ཤོར་.

སྲོག་ཤིང་ (sōgshiŋ) 1. backbone, nucleus, kernel, core ¶ ཁོ་ཚོའི་སྒྲིག་འཛུགས་ཀྱི་སྲོག་ཤིང་ The nucleus of their organization. 2. axle.

སྲོག་ཤིང་གི་ནུས་པ་ (sōgshinggi nüübə) central/ key role ¶ གུང་ཁྲན་ཏང་གིས་ཀྲུང་གོའི་སྲོག་ཤིང་གི་ནུས་པ་འདོན་གྱི་ཡོད་པ་རེད་ The communist party plays the central role in China.

སྲོག་ཤེད་ (sōɔ shēè) life and strength.

སྲོག་ཤོར་ (sōɔ shɔɔ) vi. to die, to lose one's life.

སྲོག་སྲུང་ (sōɔ sūŋ) protecting life; va. སྲོག་སྲུང་; —བྱེད་.

སྲོང་: p. བསྲངས་; f. བསྲང་; imp. སྲོངས་ (sōŋ) 1. va. to straighten (out) ¶ སྨྱུག་མ་དེ་འཁྱོག་བསྲངས་སོང་ (He) straightened out the bend in the bamboo. 2. va. to correct.

སྲོང་པོ་ (sāŋbo) 1. truthfully, honestly, straightforwardly ¶ གནས་ཚུལ་སྲོང་པོར་བཀོད་པ་ཡིན་ (I've) written these events truthfully. 2. straight ¶ མདའ་འདི་སྲོང་པོ་མི་འདུག This arrow isn't straight.

སྲོང་བཙན་སྒམ་པོ་ (sōŋdzɛn gambo) the first great king of the Tibetan empire (7th. century A.D.).

སྲོངས་ (sōŋ) imp. of སྲོང་.

སྲོད་ (drȫö̀) the time from when it becomes dark to about midnight.

སྲོད་འཁོར་ (drȫö̀gɔɔ) sm. སྲོད་.

སྲོད་འཇིང་ (drȫö̀jiŋ) a time in the middle of སྲོད་ (about 10 pm.).

སྲོད་ཐོ་ (drȫö̀do) abbr. of སྲོད་ and ཐོ་རངས་.

སྲོད་གདོང་ནག (drȫö̀doŋnaà) sm. སྲོད་.

སྲོད་ཐྲིངས་ (drȫö̀jiŋ) sm. of སྲོད་.

སྲོད་མུན་ (drȫö̀mün) sm. སྲོད་ཐྲིངས་.

སྲོད་ཡོལ་ (drȫö̀yö̀ö) the later part of སྲོད་ (just before midnight).

སྲོད་ལོང་ (drȫö̀loŋ) night blindness.

སྲོབས་ (drōb) imp. of སྲབས་.

སྲོལ་ (sȫö̀) customs, usage, tradition ¶ ལག་པ་གཏོང་སྲོལ་ The custom of shaking hands.

སྲོལ་ཀ་ (sȫȫga) sm. སྲོལ་ཁ་.

སྲོལ་ཁ་ (sȫȫga) sm. ལུགས་སྲོལ་.

སྲོལ་གོང་སེར་པོ་ (sȫȫgoŋ sērbo) soroseris hookeriana (used for in Tibetan medicine).

སྲོལ་འགལ་ (sȫngɛɛ) breach of customs/ rules/ tradition; va.—བྱེད་.

སྲོལ་འགལ་བྱ་སྤྱོད་ (sȫngɛɛ) unbecoming behavior, behavior in breach of a custom.

སྲོལ་རྒྱུན་ (sȫȫgyün) a tradition, custom, established practice; vi.—ཆགས་ to become a tradition/ custom ¶ མི་རིགས་གཞན་གྱི་རིག་གནས་སློབ་སྦྱོང་བྱེད་རྒྱུ་སྲོལ་རྒྱུན་ཆགས་པ་རེད་ It has become a tradition to study other people's cultures.

སྲོལ་ཆགས་ (sȫȫ cāà) vi. to become a custom/ tradition/ established practice.

སྲོལ་རྙིང་ (sȫȫñiŋ) old customs; va.—ཞེན་ to be conservative, to adhere to old customs, to be attached to old ways.

སྲོལ་གཏོད་ (sȫȫdȫȫ) introducing/ originating/ founding a custom; va. སྲོལ་གཏོད་; —བྱེད་ ¶ སློབ་གསོ་བྱེད་སྟངས་གསར་པ་ཁ་ཤས་སྲོལ་གཏོད་བྱས་པ་རེད་ (They) introduced several customs in educational training.

སྲོལ་གཏོད་མཁན་ (sȫȫdȫȫñɛn) originator, creator, founder, inventor.

སྲོལ་གཏོད་མེས་པོ་ (sȫȫdȫȫ meèbo) founding father, originator.

སྲོལ་དུ་འགྱུར་ (sȫȫdu gyur) sm. སྲོལ་ཆགས་.

སྲོལ་དབང་ (sȫȫwaŋ) a right, a privilege.

སྲོལ་འབྱེད་ (sȫȫjeè) sm. སྲོལ་གཏོད་.

སྲོལ་ཚུགས་ (sȫȫdzuù) sm. སྲོལ་ཆགས་.

སྲོལ་འཛིན་ (sȫȫ dzin) 1. va. to keep/ hold/ adhere to/ maintain traditions or customs. 2. person who adheres to or maintains customs or traditions ¶ ཁོང་གིས་དགེ་ལུགས་པའི་སྲོལ་འཛིན་གྱི་ཡོད་པ་རེད་ He adheres to the Gelug sect.

སྲོལ་འཛུགས་ (sȫȫ dzuù) sm. སྲོལ་གཏོད་.

སྲོལ་བཟང་ (sȫȫsaŋ) good customs/ traditions ¶ དམངས་གཙོའི་སྲོལ་བཟང་ Democratic (good) traditions.

སྲོལ་ཡིག (sȫȫyii) regulation, ordinance, rule.

སྲོལ་ལམ་ (sȫȫlam) sm. སྲོལ་རྒྱུན་.

སྲོལ་ལུགས་ (sȫȫluù) sm. སྲོལ་རྒྱུན་.

སྲོལ་བརླག་ཞབས་འདྲེན་ (sȫȫlaà shamdren) disgraceful behavior that goes against customs/ norms.

སྲོལ་གསར་གཏོད་ (sȫȫsar dȫö̀) va. to invent/ establish a new custom.

སྲོས་ (sȫö̀) 1. imp. of སྲོ་. 2. sm. རུབ་.

སྲོས་མ་ (sȫö̀ma) sth. that has been warmed ¶ ཆང་སྲོས་མ་ Warmed ཆང་.

སླ་ (lā) 1. abbr. of སླ་པོ་. 2. va. to weave (baskets),

to knit, to braid ¶ སླེ་པོ་སླ་གི་ཡོད་པ་རེད་ (They) are weaving baskets.

སླ་སྒྲུབ་ (lā drub) sth. easily accomplished/ done.

སླ་ང་ (lāŋa) a frying/ roasting pan.

སླ་བཅོས་ (lājöö) doing sth. in a perfunctory/ slipshod/ careless/ halfhearted way; va.—བྱེད་.

སླ་བཅོས་ངལ་འཛེམས་ (lājöö ŋɛndzem) shung. doing sth. in a perfunctory way and shying away from hard work ¶ རང་འཁྲིའི་ལས་སྒོ་གང་ཅི་སླ་བཅོས་ངལ་འཛེམས་སུ་མ་སོང་དགོས་རྒྱུ One should not perform one's duties in a perfunctory manner and be afraid of hard work.

སླ་ཆོབ་ཆོབ་ (lā cōbjob) slightly wet ¶ ཞལ་བ་འདི་སླ་ཆོབ་ཆོབ་ཞིག་ཆགས་འདུག The floor has become slightly wet.

སླ་ཆོས་ (lājöö) sm. སླ་བཅོས་.

སླ་ཆོས་ཁྲལ་ཆོས་ (lājöö trɛɛjöö) sm. ཁྲལ་མཛོད་སླ་བཅོས་.

སླ་དངས་ (lādaŋ) tea/ soup/ broth that is weak.

སླ་པོ་ (lābo) 1. thin (of soup) ¶ ཐུག་པ་སླ་པོ་ A thin broth. 2. weak, light (tea or alcohol, etc.) ¶ ཇ་སླ་པོ་ Weak tea. 3. easy, without difficulty (usu. ལས་ + —) ¶ འདི་བྱེད་རྒྱུ་ལས་སླ་པོ་རེད་ This is easy to do. ¶ དེབ་དེ་ཀློག་ལས་སླ་པོ་ཡོད་པ་རེད་ That book is easy to read. 4. wet ¶ གནམ་གཤིས་སླ་པོ་ Wet climate. 5. see ཀུབ་སླ་པོ་. 6. acting without the dignity/ respect associated with one's position ¶ ང་ཚོའི་འགོ་ཁྲིད་དེ་སླ་པོ་ཡིན་ཙང་གཞམ་རིམ་ལས་བྱེད་པས་བརྩི་བཀུར་བྱེད་ཀྱི་མེད་པ་རེད་ Because our leader does not behave with the dignity associated with his position, the lower officials do not respect him. 7. pliable, supple ¶ གཞུ་སླ་པོ་ A supple bow.

སླ་སྡུད་ (lājöö) a shortened/ abbreviated version of a name.

སླ་མོ་ (lāmo) sm. སླ་པོ་.

སླ་ཙ་ (lādza) sm. སླ་ཚ་.

སླ་གཡོས་ཚ་པོ་ (lāyöö tsābo) crybaby, whining brat.

སླ་གཡོས་པོ་ (lā yööbo) sm. སླ་གཡོས་ཚ་པོ་.

སླ་གཡོས་ཤོད་ (lāyöö shöö) va. to whine in a spoiled way ¶ ཕྲུ་གུ་དེ་ཕ་མར་རྩེད་ཆས་དགོས་ཡོད་ཟེར་ནས་རྟག་པར་སླ་གཡོས་ཤོད་ཀྱི་འདུག That child always whines to his parents that he wants a toy.

སླག་པ་ (lāàba) a sheep/ goat skin dress worn with the fleece on the inside.

སླགས་པ་ (lāgba) sm. སླག་པ་.

སླང་ (lāŋ) frying/ roasting pan ¶ ལྕགས་སླང་ An iron frying pan.

སླང་ང་ (lāŋŋa) sm. སླང་.

སླང་དྲེག་ (lāŋdreg) soot on a frying pan.

སླང་སྡེར་ (lāŋder) flat bottomed frying pan.

སླང་རྨོས་ (lāŋmöö) disc plowing; va.— རྒྱག.

སླད་ (lɛɛ) 1. for the purpose of, in order to ¶ གཏེར་འདོན་གྱི་ལས་དོན་ཡར་རྒྱས་གཏོང་སླད་ In order to improve the mining work. 2. later, in the future ¶ སླད་མ་མཇལ་བའི་བར་ Until (I) see (you) later ¶ སླད་དེ་འདྲ་བྱེད་རྩིས་མེད་ (We) do not plan to do like that again in the future. 3. sm. བསླད་. 4. sometimes used for ལྷད་.

སླད་དུ་ (lɛɛdu) sm. སླད་.

སླད་འདོམས་ཁྲིམས་གཅོད་ (lɛɛdom trimjöö) shung. to use harsh punishment to set an example as a deterrent; va.—བྱེད་ ¶ ཇག་པ་དེ་ཚོར་སླད་འདོམས་ཁྲིམས་གཅོད་བྱས་ན་ཇག་པ་ཉུང་རུ་འགྲོ་གི་རེད་ If we use harsh punishment on those bandits it will serve as a deterrent and the number of bandits will decrease.

སླད་ནས་ (lɛɛnɛ) sm. སླད་ཕྱིན་.

སླད་ཆ་ (lɛɛja) see སླད་, 2.

སླད་ཕྱིན་ (lɛɛjin) later, henceforth, in the future ¶ དེ་འདྲ་བྱས་ན་སླད་ཕྱིན་ང་ཚོ་སྡུག་རག་གི་རེད་ If (we) do like that, in the future we will suffer.

སླད་ཕྱིན་འབྱུང་ (lɛɛ cinjuŋ) sm. སླད་ཕྱིན་.

སླད་མ་ (lɛɛma) see སླད་ཕྱིན་.

སླད་མར་ (lɛɛmar) sm. སླད་ཕྱིན་.

སླད་ཙ་ (lɛɛdza) sm. སླད་ཚ་.

སླད་ཚ་ (lɛɛdza) excrement.

སླད་བཞིན་ (lɛɛshin) sm. སླར་ཡང་.

སླད་རོལ་དུ་ (lɛɛröödu) 1. sm. སླད་ཕྱིན་. 2. ཕྱི་རོལ་.

སླད་ལ་ (lɛɛla) patriotism, loyalty, devotion ¶ རང་གི་རྒྱལ་ཁབ་ཀྱི་སླད་ལ་མ་ལོག་པ་བྱ་དགོས་ One should not abandon loyalty to one's country.

སླད་ལམ་འདོམས་པ་ (lɛɛlam domba) shung. setting an example by imposing a harsh punishment.

སླད་ལར་མི་བདུབ་པ་ (lɛɛlar midubbə) shung. being disloyal.

སླད་ལར་བསམས་ (lɛɛlar sām) shung. va. to think loyally.

སླད་ས་ (lɛɛsa) sm. སླར་ཚ་.

སླན་ (lɛn) sometimes used for ལྷན་.

སླན་ཆད་ (lɛnjɛɛ) sm. སླད་ཕྱིན་.

སླར་ (lār) again, once again ¶ སླར་རྒྱ་གར་དུ་འགྲོ་སྐབས་ When he was going to India again.

སླར་སྐྲུན་ (lārdrün) reconstructing, rebuilding; va.—བྱེད་ ¶ དམག་འཁྲུག་ནང་གཏོར་སྐྱིན་བྱུང་བའི་ལྷ་ཁང་རྣམས་སླར་སྐྲུན་བྱས་འདུག The temples that were destroyed in the war were rebuilt.

སླར་བརྗོད་ (lār jöö) 1. va. to reply/ answer. 2. poet. Brahmin.

སླར་དར་ (lārdar) revival, renaissance; vi. སླར་དར་; —བྱེད་ to be revived, to have a renaissance ¶ རིག་གནས་གསར་བརྗེའི་རྗེས་སུ་ནང་ཆོས་སླར་དར་བྱུང་བ་རེད་ After the Cultural Revolution, Buddhism had a revival.

སླར་དུ་ (lārdu) sm. སླར་.

སླར་དུག་ (lārduù) sm. དུག་ལོང་.

སླར་ལྡོག་ (lār dɔɔ) vi. to make a comeback/ return, to revert back to ¶ མ་རྩ་རིང་ལུགས་སླར་མི་ལྡོག་པའི་ཐབས་ཤེས་བྱེད་དགོས་ (We) must prevent capitalism from making a comeback.

སླར་ལྡོག་མི་སྲིད་པ་ (lār dɔɔ misiibə) sth. that can't make a comeback/ revival ¶ སྤྱི་ཚོགས་རྙིང་པའི་དུས་ཚོད་ནི་སླར་ལྡོག་མི་སྲིད་པ་ཞིག་རེད་ The period of the old society cannot be revived.

སླར་ཕུལ་ཞུ་སྙན་ (lārbüü shuñɛn) submitting a report again, reporting for the second time.

སླར་ཞིང་ (lārshiŋ) again and again.

སླར་གཟུགས་ (lārsuù) image, statue, portrait, picture.

སླར་བཟོ་བྱེད་ (lārso jeè) va. to make again, to remake ¶ ཆུ་ལོག་གིས་བཤིག་པའི་གཞུང་ལམ་སླར་བཟོ་བྱས་པ་རེད་ They remade the highway that was destroyed by the flood.

སླར་ཡང་ (lāryaŋ) once again, once more ¶ ལུང་པ་དེ་ར་སླར་ཡང་ས་ཡོམ་ཆེན་པོ་ཞིག་བྱུང་འདུག That area once again was hit by a powerful earthquake.

སླར་ཡང་ཐོན་སྐྱེད་ (lāryaŋ tŏŋgyeè) producing sth. again; va.—བྱེད་ ¶ འཕྲུལ་འཁོར་གསར་པ་དེ་འགྲོ་རྒྱུགས་ཆེན་པོ་བྱུང་ཙང་སླར་ཡང་ཐོན་སྐྱེད་བྱས་པ་རེད་ The machine sold very well so they produced them again.

སླར་ལོག་ (lār lɔɔ) returning/ going back again; va.—བྱེད་ ¶ མི་དེ་ཚོ་ཕྱི་རྒྱལ་ནས་རང་ཉིད་ཀྱི་ཕ་ཡུལ་ལ་སླར་ལོག་བྱས་པ་རེད་ Those people returned again to their homeland from abroad.

སླར་ལོག་འགྲོ་ (lārlɔɔ dro) va. to return/ go back again.

སླར་གསོ་ (lārso) restoring, reviving, reestablishing, reconstructing; va.—བྱེད་ ¶ ཞི་བདེ་སླར་གསོ་བྱེད་ཆེད་ For the restoration of peace.

སླས་ (lɛɛ) 1. relatives. 2. servant, attendant.

སླས་ཀྱི་ལྷ་ཁང་ (lɛɛgi lhāgaŋ) a small branch temple or chapel.

སླས་འཐག་ (lɛɛdaà) knitting and weaving; va.—བྱེད་.

སླས་པ་ (lɛɛba) sm. སླས་མ་.

སླས་མ་ (lɛɛma) braided; va.—རྒྱག to make into braids ¶ སྐྲ་ལ་སླས་མ་རྒྱག་དགོས་ You must braid your hair.

སླས་ར་ (lɛɛra) corral, pen, stable.

སླུ་: p. **བསླུས་**; f. **བསླུ་**; imp. **སླུས་** (lū) va. to lure/ entice/ beguile.

སླུ་ཁྲིད་ (lūdrii) luring, enticing, beguiling; va.—བྱེད་.

སླུ་འབྲིད་ (lūdrii) sm. སླུ་ཁྲིད་.

སླུ་གུ་ (lūgu) a small cooking pot.

སླུ་འཐེན་ (lūden) sm. སླུ་ཁྲིད་.

སླུ་འདྲིད་ (lūdrii) sm. སླུ་ཁྲིད་.

སླུ་ཡོ་ (lūdo) bait (in fishing/ hunting).

སླུ་བྱེད་ (lūjeè) 1. sm. སླུ་ཁྲིད་. 2. person who does སླུ་ཁྲིད་.

སླུ་བྱེད་ཉ་ཟན་ (lūjeè ñasɛn) bait for catching fish.

སླུ་ཐྲིད་ (lūdrii) sm. སླུ་ཁྲིད་.

སླུ་འཐྲིད་ (lūdrii) sm. སླུ་ཁྲིད་.

སླུ་མེད་ (lūmeè) without deceit, sincere, genuine, upright.

སླུ་ཟན་ (lūsɛn) bait.

སླུ་ཟས་ (lūsɛɛ̀) sm. སླུ་ཟན་.

སླུག་རྒྱག་ (lūù gyaà) va. to marinate.

སླུས་ (lūù) imp. of སླུ་.

སླེ་ (lē) Leh (capital of Ladakh).

སླེ་ཀོག་ (lēgɔɔ) sm. སླེ་པོ་.

སླེ་འདམས་པ་ (lēdamba) a man without a complete penis.

སླེ་པོ་ (lēbo) sm.* སླེས་པོ་.

སླེ་བ་ (lēwa) 1. cock-eyed person. 2. handicapped person.

སླེ་པོ་ (lēbo) sm. སླེ་བ་.

སླེ་མིག་ (lēmii) sm. སླེ་བ་, 1.

སླེ་མོ་ (lēmo) 1. raincoat made of animal hide. 2. sm. ཕྱུ་ར་.

སླེ་ཡོན་ (lēyön) a crafty/ cunning/ deceitful person.

སླེབ་ (lēb) sm. སླེབས་.

སླེབས་: p. སླེབས་; f. སླེབ་ (lēb) vi. to reach, to arrive, to come to ། མོ་ལོ་བརྒྱད་ལ་བསླེབས་པ་རེད་ She reached the age of eight. ། ཁོ་ཚོ་གྲོང་ཚོར་དགོང་མོ་སླེབས་པ་རེད་ They arrived in the village at night. ། འགྲོ་ཡས་ཀྱི་དུས་ལ་སླེབས་དུས་ When the time comes to go.

སླེབས་པ་རྒན་གཞོན་ (lēbba gɛnshön) in accordance with age/ seniority.

སླེབས་ཧྲགས་ (lēbdaà) punching in the arrival time (e.g., on a time clock in a factory, etc.); va.—རྒྱག.

སླེབས་ཐོ་ (lēbdo) registration book/ list of people who arrive somewhere (e.g., at a conference).

སླེའུ་ (lēwu) a tightly woven wool blanket often use as a rain poncho.

སླེའོ་ (lēwo) talk, speech; va.—ཤོད་.

སླེལ་ཀོག་ (lēēgɔɔ) sm. སླེ་པོ་.

སླེལ་ཐག་ (lēēdaà) rope for carrying a basket.

སླེལ་པོ་ (lēēbo) basket (for carrying things on one's back).

སླེལ་ཕྱར་ (lēējar) sm. ཕྱར་བ་.

སླེས་པོ་ (lèèbo) sm. སླེལ་པོ་.

སློ་ (lō) sm. བཅོ་.

སློ་དྲོན་ (lōdrön) sm. བཅོ་ཚ་པོ་.

སློ་འབོ་ (lōmbo) sm. སློ་མ་.

སློ་མ་ (lōma) small woven basket.

སློག: p. བསློགས་; f. བསློག; imp. སློགས་ (lɔ̄ɔ) 1. va. to return, to send back ། ཁོ་ཕྱིར་བསློག་གི་རེད་ (They) are going to send him back. 2. va. to turn (upside down/ inside out) ། མོས་སྟོད་ཐུང་དེ་ཕྱི་ནང་བསློགས་སོང་ She turned the shirt inside out. 3. va. to turn over, to plow over the land ། ས་གསོད་སློག་པའི་སྐབས་ When (they) plowed the virgin land. 4. vi. to make change (in money) ། ང་སློག་ཡས་མེད་འདུག I have no change.

སློག་གོས་ (lɔ̄ɔgöö sheep or goatskin dress that is worn with fleece on the inside.

སློག་ཆ་ (lōgja) 1. compensation, restitution, fine, penalty ། ཁྲིམས་ཁང་ནས་ཁ་མཆུའི་ཕྱོད་ལ་གཞན་དེར་དངུལ་སློག་ཆ་བུ་རྒྱུའི་ཐག་གཅོད་བྱས་འདུག The court decided that one plaintiff had to pay restitution to the other. 2. rebate, refund ། གཞུང་ནས་ལོ་མཇུག་ཏུ་ལས་བྱེད་པ་ཁག་ཅིག་ལ་ཁྲལ་གྱི་སློག་ཆ་སྤྲོད་ཀྱི་ཡོད་པ་རེད་ At the end of year the government gives a tax rebate to some of the officials.

སློག་དངུལ་ (lɔ̄gŋüü) 1. indemnity. 2. change or money that is given back.

སློག་པ་ (lɔ̄gba) sm. སློག་གོས་.

སློག་རུལ་ (lɔ̄grüü) an old/ worn skin dress.

སློགས་ (lɔ̄ɔ) imp. of སློག.

སློང་: p. བསློངས་; f. བསློང་; imp. སློངས་ (lōŋ) 1. va. to beg, to ask for ། མི་ཚང་དེས་ཁྱིམ་མཚེས་ཀྱི་བུ་མོ་མནའ་མར་ཆུང་མར་སློང་གི་ཡོད་པ་རེད་ That household is asking for their neighbor's daughter's hand in marriage. ། ཚེས་པ་བཅོ་ལྔ་ལ་སྤྲང་པོ་མང་པོས་དངུལ་སློང་བར་ལྷ་སར་ཡོང་གི་ཡོད་པ་རེད་ Many beggars come to beg in Lhasa on the 15th of the month. 2. va. to cause or make sth. stand up/ rise ། ཚང་མ་ཀུབ་སྒྲིགས་ནས་བསློངས་པ་རེད་ (He) made everyone stand up from their seat. 3. va. to raise, to erect ། ཁོ་ཚོས་དར་ཤིང་ཞིག་སློང་གི་འདུག (They) are erecting a flag pole. 4. va. to incite, to provoke, to cause to start sth. ། དམག་འཁྲུག་ཆེན་པོ་སློང་གི་རེད་ (They) will incite a big war. ། མི་དམངས་ཁོང་ཁྲོ་བསློངས་པ་རེད་ (They) made the public angry.

སློང་རྐྱེན་ (lōŋgyen) cause/ origin/ source of a disturbance, war, etc.

སློང་བསྐུལ་ (lōŋgüü) soliciting or appealing for aid or donations; va.—བྱེད་ to solicit/ petition/ appeal for aid or donations ། དགོན་པ་རྒྱག་ཆེད་ལུང་པ་མང་པོ་ལ་ཞལ་འདེབས་སློང་བསྐུལ་བྱས་པ་རེད་ They went to many areas soliciting donations to build a monastery. 2. sm. སྐལ་སློང་.

སློང་མཁན་ (lōŋñɛn) beggar.

སློང་རྒྱག་ (lōŋ gyaà) 1. va. to beg. 2. va. to solicit/ appeal for donations.

སློང་རྒྱག་མཁན་ (lōŋgyaàñɛn) beggar.

སློང་རྔོད་ (lōŋŋöö) roasting barley in a frying pan; va.—རྒྱག.

སློང་ཆང་ (lōŋjaŋ) prenuptial "engagement" ceremony when gifts and ཆང་ are taken to ask for the hand of a bride (or groom); va.—གཏོང་.

སློང་ཆང་ཚེས་གྲངས་ (lōŋjaŋ tsēēdraŋ) astrological calculation for setting the date to do a སློང་ཆང་.

སློང་ཆང་བསུ་ཉིན་ (lōŋjaŋ sūden) sm. སློང་ཆང་.

སློང་རྟེན་ (lōŋden) gifts given at the སློང་ཆང་ ceremony.

སློང་སྣེར་ག་འཛོལ་ (lōŋder kandzöö) insistently soliciting/ begging for alms or donations.

སློང་སྣེར་མོས་མཐུན་ (lōŋder möödün) shung. a marriage mutually agreed on by both sides ། བག་མ་སློང་སྣེར་མོས་མཐུན་དང་འབྲེལ་བའི་གཉེན་སྒྲིག་གི་མཛད་སྒོ་བསྒྲུབས་པ་ The marriage ceremony was performed after the mutual agreement by both sides.

སློང་སྣེར་ཞུ་རྒྱུང་ (lōŋder shujuŋ) sm. སློང་ཆང་.

སློང་འདྲ་ (lōŋdra) a type of thick mattress.

སློང་སྣ་བྱེད་ (lōŋna ceè) sm. སློང་ཆང་གཏོང་.

སློང་ཕོར་ (lōŋbɔr) begging bowl.

སློང་འབེབས་ཞུ་ (lōŋbeb shu) shung. va. to withdraw a lawsuit and settle out of court.

སློང་མོ་ (lōŋmo) 1. soliciting for donations, begging for alms; va.—རྒྱག; —བྱེད་; —སློང་ to beg for alms, to ask for donations. 2. female beggar.

སློང་མོ་བ་ (lōŋmowa) a beggar, sb. soliciting donations.

སློང་ཡིག་ (lōŋyii) book/ letter carried by solicitors in which donations are listed (it also explains the reason for the solicitation).

སློང་རིན་ (lōŋrin) brideprice.

སློངས་ (lōŋ) imp. of སློང་.

སློད་ (lȫȫ) 1. imp. of བསླད་. 2. sm.* སློད་.

སློད་: p. and f. བསླད་; imp. of སློད་ (lȫȫ) vi. to be influenced/ corrupted by bad friends ། ངའི་ཕྲུ་གུ་དེ་གྲོགས་པོ་ངན་པས་བསླད་ནས་ཐ་མ་འཐེན་གྱི་འདུག My child was influenced by bad friends and now is smoking. 2. va. to contaminate/ pollute ། མཁའ་རླུང་རྫས་ངན་གྱིས་བསླད་སོང་ The air was polluted with bad chemicals.

སློད་ལོང་ (lȫȫloŋ) night blindness.

སློན་: p. and f. བསློན་; imp. སློན་ (lȫn) va. to combine ། དམག་སྒར་གཉིས་ཀྱི་དམག་མི་བསློན་པ་རེད་ (They) combined the soldiers of the two army garrisons.

སློབ་: p. བསླབས་; f. བསླབ་; imp. སློབས་ (lōb) 1. va. to learn, to study ། ཁོ་བོད་སྐད་སློབ་ཀྱི་ཡོད་པ་རེད་ He is learning Tibetan. 2. va. to teach, to instruct, to show ། ངས་ཁོང་ལ་མོ་ཊ་གཏོང་སྟངས་བསླབས་པ་ཡིན་ I taught him how to drive.

སློབ་སྐྱོང་ (lōbgyoŋ) educating/ bringing up/ training; va.—བྱེད་.

སློབ་ཁང་ (lōbgaŋ) classroom.

སློབ་ཁང་གི་བསྐྱར་སྦྱོང་ (lōbgaŋgi gyārjoŋ) self study/ homework done while in class.

སློབ་ཁང་གི་གྲོས་བསྡུར་ (lōbgaŋgi tro̱ödur) seminar, classroom discussion.

སློབ་ཁང་གི་སྦྱོང་ཚན་ (lōbgaŋgi jo̱ŋdzɛn) subjects to be studied in class.

སློབ་ཁྱད་ (lōbgyɛɛ̀) specialized training.

སློབ་ཁྲིད་ (lōbdriì) teaching, instructing, lecturing; va.—བྱེད་.

སློབ་ཁྲིད་ཀྱི་ཅ་གནད་ (lōbdriìgi dzānɛɛ̀) teaching program/ syllabus.

སློབ་ཁྲིད་དགེ་རྒན་ (lōbdriì ge̱gɛn) teacher.

སློབ་ཁྲིད་དངོས་སྦྱོང་ (lōbdriì ŋö̱öjoŋ) teaching using labs/ practicums/ firsthand exposure to the subject.

སློབ་ཁྲིད་བཅོས་བསྒྱུར་ (lōbdriì jö̀ögyur) teaching/ educational reform.

སློབ་ཁྲིད་འཆར་གཞི་ (lōbdriì cə̄əshi) teaching plan.

སློབ་ཁྲིད་བརྟག་དཔྱད་ཁང་ (lōbdriì dāgjɛɛ̀gaŋ) teaching research section/ institute.

སློབ་ཁྲིད་དུས་ཡུན་ (lōbdriì tṳ̄ṳyün) length/ duration of a class.

སློབ་ཁྲིད་དཔྱད་ཆས་ (lōbdriì jɛ̀ɛjɛɛ̀) teaching instruments, teaching aids.

སློབ་ཁྲིད་བྱ་རིམ་ (lōbdriì ca̱rim) the teaching process/ steps/ stages.

སློབ་ཁྲིད་བྱེད་ཐབས་ (lōbdriì ce̱ədəb) teaching method.

སློབ་ཁྲིད་བྱེད་ལོ་ (lōbdriì je̱èlo) length of service as a teacher,

སློབ་ཁྲིད་དམག་དཔོན་ (lōbdriì māgbön) drill master, instructor (in the army).

སློབ་ཁྲིད་ཅ་དོན་ (lōbdriì dzādön) principles of teaching.

སློབ་ཁྲིད་ཅ་གནད་ (lōbdriì dzānɛɛ̀) sm. སློབ་ཁྲིད་ཀྱི་ཅ་དོན་.

སློབ་ཁྲིད་ཚོགས་དུས་ (lōbdriì tsōndu) class hour, time a class starts.

སློབ་ཁྲིད་རེའུ་མིག (lōbdriì ri̱wumig) schedule of classes.

སློབ་འཁྲིད་ (lōbdriì) sm. སློབ་ཁྲིད་.

སློབ་འཁྲིད་ཡོ་བྱད་ (lōbdriì yo̱jɛɛ̀) teaching aids.

སློབ་འཁྲིད་ལས་དོན་ (lōbdriì le̱ɛ̀dön) educational administration.

སློབ་གྲྭ་ (lōbdra) school.

སློབ་གྲྭ་འགོ་ཚུགས་ (lōbdra go̱dzuù) sm. སློབ་གྲྭ་ཚུགས་.

སློབ་གྲྭ་ཆུང་བ་ (lōbdra cūŋwə) primary school.

སློབ་གྲྭ་ཆུང་འབྲིང་ (lōbdra cūŋdriŋ) primary and middle schools.

སློབ་གྲྭ་ཆེ་བ་ (lōbdra cēwa) higher level schools (university, college).

སློབ་གྲྭ་ཆེ་མོ་ (lōbdra cēmo) college, university.

སློབ་གྲྭ་ཆེན་མོ་ (lōbdra cēmo) sm. སློབ་གྲྭ་ཆེ་མོ་.

སློབ་གྲྭ་འཐེན་ (lōbdra tēn) va. to leave/ withdraw from school.

སློབ་གྲྭ་ཐོན་ (lōbdra tȫn) sm. སློབ་གྲྭ་ནས་ཐོན་.

སློབ་གྲྭ་སྤོ་ (lōbdra bō) va. to transfer schools.

སློབ་གྲྭ་འཕར་ (lōbdra pār) vi. to be promoted to a higher grade.

སློབ་གྲྭ་བ་ (lōbdrawa) students.

སློབ་གྲྭ་བ་སྡུད་ (lōbdrawa dṳ̀ṳ) va. to enroll new students.

སློབ་གྲྭ་བའི་ཚོགས་པ་ (lōbdrawɛ tsōgba) student union, student association.

སློབ་གྲྭ་བའི་ལས་འགུལ་ (lōbdrawɛ le̱ngüü) student movement.

སློབ་གྲྭ་བའི་བསྲུང་བྱ་ (lōbdrawɛ sūŋja) school rules and regulations.

སློབ་གྲྭ་བའི་ལྷན་ཚོགས་ (lōbdrawɛ lhēndzɔɔ̀) sm. སློབ་གྲྭ་བའི་ཚོགས་པ་.

སློབ་གྲྭ་འབྲིང་བ་ (lōbdra dri̱ŋwə) middle school, secondary school, high school.

སློབ་གྲྭ་འཚུགས (lōbdra tsūù) 1. vi. to have a school get started. 2. vi. to begin a semester/ academic year.

སློབ་གྲྭ་ཨ་མ་ (lōbdra āma) 1. alma mater. 2. the main school/ university.

སློབ་གྲྭའི་སྐྱིད་སྡུག (lōbdrɛ gyı̄ìduù) one's status as a member of a school ། སློབ་གྲྭའི་སྐྱིད་སྡུག་ནས་ཕུད་སོང་ He was expelled from the school's roll.

སློབ་གྲྭའི་ཁང་གཉེར་ (lōbdrɛ kāŋñer) a student who fails to graduate to the next level [Lit. the person who looks after a school] (used in a sarcastic manner).

སློབ་གྲྭའི་དགེ་བཟོ་ (lōbdrɛ ge̱so) the teachers and staff of a school.

སློབ་གྲྭའི་དུས་ཆེན་ (lōbdrɛ tṳ̀ṳjen) anniversary day of a school.

སློབ་གྲྭའི་དོན་གཉེར་ཁྲུའུ་ (lōbdrɛ tönñer trū) tib. ch. office of school affairs.

སློབ་གྲྭའི་སྨན་ཁང་ (lōbdrɛ mēngaŋ) school clinic.

སློབ་གྲྭའི་རླུང་རླབས་ (lōbdrɛ lūŋləb) student unrest, campus upheaval.

སློབ་གྲྭའི་ལམ་ལུགས་ (lōbdrɛ ləmluù) school system.

སློབ་གྲྭའི་ལོ་རིམ་ (lōbdrɛ lo̱rim) grade/ class in school.

སློབ་གྲྭར་བཅུག (lōbdraa jūù) p. of སློབ་གྲྭར་འཛུག.

སློབ་གྲྭར་འཛུག (lōbdraa ju̱ù) 1. va. to enroll (in school). 2. va. to admit a student to school ། ངའི་ཕྲུ་གུ་སློབ་གྲྭར་འཛུག་པར་ཕྱིན་ཀྱང་སློབ་གྲྭས་བཅུག་མ་བྱུང་ Even though I went to enroll my child in school, the school did not admit him.

སློབ་གྲོགས་ (lōbdrɔɔ̀) schoolmate, classmate, school friend.

སློབ་གྲོན་ (lōbdrön) school expenses; va.—གཏོང་ to pay school expenses.

སློབ་གྲོན་རོགས་དངུལ་ (lōbdrön ro̱gŋüü) scholarship, grant-in aid, fellowship.

སློབ་གླིང་ (lōbliŋ) academic speciality.

སློབ་དགེ (lōbge) school teacher.

སློབ་འགོ་བཙམས་ (lōmgo dzām) p. of སློབ་འགོ་རྩོམ་.

སློབ་འགོ་ཚུགས་ (lōmgo dzu̱ù) va. to have class/ school start (e.g. term, semester).

སློབ་རྒྱུགས་སྤྲོད་ (lōbgyuù drȫö̀) va. to take an exam.

སློབ་རྒྱུགས་ལེན་ (lōbgyuù le̱n) va. to give an exam.

སློབ་རྒྱུད་ (lōbgyüǜ) a line/ lineage of disciples.

སློབ་ཆས་ (lōbjɛɛ̀) teaching aids/ materials.

སློབ་ཆུང་ (lōbjuŋ) primary school.

སློབ་ཆུང་སློབ་གསོ་ (lōbjuŋ lōbso) primary education.

སློབ་ཆེན་ (lōbjen) abbr. of སློབ་གྲྭ་ཆེན་མོ་.

སློབ་འཛུག (lōbjuù) sm. སློབ་གྲྭར་འཛུག.

སློབ་གཉེར་ (lōbñer) studies; va.—བྱེད་ to study, do one's studies ། ང་བོད་སྐད་སློབ་གཉེར་བྱེད་སྐབས་ When I was studying Tibetan.

སློབ་གཉེར་ཁང་ (lōbñergaŋ) a place where a training program takes place, learning/ study center.

སློབ་གཉེར་བརྒྱུད་རིམ་ (lōbñer gyṳ̀ṳrim) one's educational history.

སློབ་གཉེར་ཆུད་ཟོས་ (lōbñer cṻṻsöö) neglecting one's studies; va.—གཏོང་.

སློབ་གཉེར་བ་ (lōbñerwa) 1. student. 2. disciple.

སློབ་གཉེར་རོགས་རམ་ (lōbñer ro̱ɔ̀ram) scholarship, fellowship.

སློབ་སྟངས་ (lōbdaŋ) teaching methods.

སློབ་སྟེགས་ (lōbdeg) platform / podium/ dais/ rostrum in a classroom.

སློབ་སྟོན་ (lōbdön) 1. instructing, teaching, guiding; va.—བྱེད་; —གནང་ to give instruction/ guidance/ teach ། ཕྲུ་གུས་ཕ་མའི་སློབ་སྟོན་སེམས་ལ་འཇོག་རྒྱུ་གལ་ཆེན་པོ་ཡིན་ It is important for children to keep the guidance of their parents in mind. 2.

direction (in dramatic arts).

སློབ་སྟོན་གྲོས་ཚོགས་ (lōbdön trö̤ödzoò) advisory committee.

སློབ་སྟོན་པ་ (lōbdönba) 1. one who instructs/ teaches. 2. a director. 3. political instructor (in the army).

སློབ་སྟོན་མཛད་པོ་ (lōbdön dzɛ̱ɛ̀bo) sm. སློབ་སྟོན་པ་.

སློབ་ཐབས་ (lōbdəb) sm. སློབ་སྟངས་.

སློབ་ཐོན་ (lōb tö̃n) vi. to complete one's studies/ education, to graduate.

སློབ་ཐོན་རྒྱུགས་སྤྲོད་ (lōbdön gyu̱gdröö̀) taking a final exam; va.—བྱེད་.

སློབ་ཐོན་རྒྱུགས་ཚད་ (lōbdön gyu̱gdzɛɛ̀) final/ comprehensive examination; va.—ལེན་ to give a final/ comprehensive exam; va.—སྤྲོད་ to take a final/ comprehensive exam.

སློབ་ཐོན་རྒྱུགས་ལེན་ (lōbdön gyu̱glen) giving a final exam; va.—བྱེད་.

སློབ་ཐོན་ཆེད་རྩོམ་ (lōbdön cēèdzom) graduation paper/ thesis.

སློབ་ཐོན་ཇུས་འགོད་ (lōbdön jü̱ngöö̀) graduation project.

སློབ་ཐོན་པ་ (lōbdönba) graduates.

སློབ་ཐོན་མཛད་སྒོ་ (lōbdön dzɛ̱ɛ̀go) graduation ceremony.

སློབ་ཐོན་ཟིན་ (lōbdön si̱n) sm. སློབ་ཐོན་.

སློབ་ཐོན་ལག་འཁྱེར་ (lōbdön la̱ggyer) diploma, school certificate.

སློབ་ཐོན་ལས་བགོས་ (lōbdön lɛ̱ɛ̀göö̀) job assignment on graduation.

སློབ་མཐར་འགྲོ་ (lōbdaa dro̱) vi. to graduate from school.

སློབ་འཐུས་ (lōbdüǜ) student representative/ delegate.

སློབ་དུས་ (lōbdüǜ) school semester/ term.

སློབ་དུས་སྐར་འགོད་ལམ་ལུགས་ (lōbdüǜ gārgöö̀ lə̱mluù) credit system for classes in school.

སློབ་དུས་སྐར་འགོད་ (lōbdüǜ gārgöö̀) sm. སློབ་དུས་སྐར་འགོད་ལམ་ལུགས་.

སློབ་དུས་དུས་མཇུག (lōbdüǜ tü̱njuù) the latter part of a term.

སློབ་དུས་དུས་དཀྱིལ་གྱི་ཡིག་ཚད་ (lōbdüǜ tü̱ügyiigi yigdzɛɛ̀) midterm exam; va.—ལེན་ to give a midterm exam; va.—སྤྲོད་ to take a midterm exam.

སློབ་དུས་དུས་མཇུག་གི་ཡིག་ཚད་ (lōbdüǜ tü̱njuùgi yigdzɛɛ̀) final examination.

སློབ་དེབ་ (lōbdeb) textbook.

སློབ་དོན་ཁྲུའུ་ (lōbdön trū) tib. ch. dean's office.

སློབ་དོན་འགོ་འཛིན་ (lōbdön go̱ndzin) academic dean.

སློབ་བསྡུ་གཞུང་ལས་ཁང་ (lōbdüǜ shu̱ŋlɛɛ̀gaŋ) student enrollment office.

སློབ་བསྡུ་ (lōbdu) enrolling/ recruiting students.

སློབ་སྡེ་ (lōbde) institute, academy.

སློབ་ན་ (lōbna) school age; vi.—སོན་; —ལོན་ to reach/ attain school age.

སློབ་ན་མ་སོན་གོང་གི་སློབ་གསོ་ (lōbna ma̱söngoŋgi lōbso) preschool education.

སློབ་ན་སོན་པའི་བྱིས་པ་ (lōbna sȭnbɛ ci̱ibə) children of school age.

སློབ་ན་མ་སོང་གོང་གི་སློབ་གསོ་ (lōbna masȭŋgoŋgi lōbso) preschool education.

སློབ་དཔོན་ (lōbbön) 1. teacher, master. 2. professor. 3. square ruler (right angle ruler) used in carpentry.

སློབ་དཔོན་རྒན་པ་ (lōbbön gɛ̱mba) senior/ full professor.

སློབ་དཔོན་ཆེན་པོ་ (lōbbön cēmbo) 1. great master/ teacher. 2. full professor.

སློབ་དཔོན་གཞོན་པ་ (lōbbön shö̱mba) assistant/ junior professor, lecturer.

སློབ་དཔོན་མཐོང་བ་དོན་ལྡན་ (lōbbön tōŋwa tö̱ndɛn) a title of the Dalai Lama.

སློབ་དཔྱོད་ཁང་ (lōbjööga ŋ) teaching and research section/ office.

སློབ་སྤྱི་ (lōbji) school principal.

སློབ་སྤུན་ (lōbbün) sm. སློབ་གྲོགས་.

སློབ་ཕྲུག (lōbdruù) student, pupil; va.— བྱེད་ to be a pupil.

སློབ་ཕྲུག་གི་རོགས་དངུལ་ (lōbdruùgi rɔ̱ɔ̀ŋüü) scholarship, fellowship, grant.

སློབ་ཕྲུག་གི་འཚེ་མེད་ཞི་བའི་འབྲེལ་མཐུད་ཚོགས་ཆུང་ (lōbdruùgi tsīmeè shi̱wɛ dre̱edüü tsɔ̄gjuŋ) student nonviolent coordinating committee.

སློབ་ཕྲུག་མཉམ་འབྲེལ་ཚོགས་པ་ (lōbdruù ñāmdree tsōgba) student alliance association.

སློབ་ཕྲུག་སྡུད་ (lōbdruù dü̱ü) va. to enroll new students.

སློབ་ཕྲུག་འབྲེལ་ཚོགས་ (lōbdruù dre̱edzɔɔ̀) student association/ federation.

སློབ་ཕྲུག་དེབ་བལྟ་ཁང་ (lōbdruù te̱bdagaŋ) student's reading room.

སློབ་འཕྲོས་ (lōbdröö̀) a part of one's education or studies that is left over/ still to be done.

སློབ་བུ་ (lōbbu) sm. སློབ་ཕྲུག.

སློབ་བྱ་ (lōbja) sm. བསླབ་བྱ་.

སློབ་བྱོལ་ (lōbjöö) being absent from school, cutting class, truancy; va.— བྱེད་.

སློབ་འབངས་ (lōbbaŋ) disciples, followers.

སློབ་འབྲས་ (lōbdrɛɛ̀) the result of study, academic accomplishments.

སློབ་འབྲིང་ (lōbdriŋ) sm. སློབ་གྲྭ་འབྲིང་བ་.

སློབ་འབྲིང་མཐོ་གྲས་ (lōbdriŋ tōdrɛɛ̀) sm. སློབ་འབྲིང་མཐོ་རིམ་.

སློབ་འབྲིང་མཐོ་རིམ་ (lōbdriŋ tōrim) senior high school, upper middle school.

སློབ་འབྲིང་དམའ་རིམ་ (lōbdriŋ mārim) junior high school, lower middle school.

སློབ་འབྲིང་དམའ་གྲས་ (lōbdriŋ mādrɛɛ̀) junior high school, lower middle school.

སློབ་སྦྱོང་ (lōbjoŋ) studies, studying; va.—བྱེད་ to study; vi.—ཐོན་ to finish/ complete studies, to graduate.

སློབ་སྦྱོང་ཁང་ (lōbjoŋgaŋ) learning/ study center.

སློབ་སྦྱོང་གི་ལོ་རྒྱུས་ (lōbjoŋgi lu̱gyüǜ) educational background, curriculum vitae.

སློབ་སྦྱོང་ཆད་ (lōbjoŋ cɛɛ̀) vi. to miss school, to be absent from school.

སློབ་སྦྱོང་ཐོན་ (lōbjoŋ tö̃n) see སློབ་སྦྱོང་.

སློབ་སྦྱོང་གནམ་གྲུ་ (lōbjoŋ nə̄mdru) trainer aircraft.

སློབ་སྦྱོང་བྱེད་ (lōbjoŋ ce̱è) see སློབ་སྦྱོང་.

སློབ་སྦྱོང་བྱེད་ས་ (lōbjoŋ ce̱èsa) study hall/ room.

སློབ་སྦྱོང་རོགས་དངུལ་ (lōbjoŋ rɔ̱gŋüü) educational fellowship/ stipend/ grant.

སློབ་སྦྱོང་འཛིན་གྲྭ་ (lōbjoŋ dzi̱ndra) study class (a type of detention center where suspected individuals studied Mao's thoughts and were expected to confess in detail their crimes and wrong actions).

སློབ་སྦྱོང་སླངས་འཁོར་ (lōbjoŋ lāŋgɔɔ) driver training car.

སློབ་མ་ (lōbma) 1. disciple. 2. student.

སློབ་མ་མཉམ་འབྲེལ་ཚོགས་པ་ (lōbma ña̱mdree tsɔ̄gba) federation of students.

སློབ་མ་ཚོགས་པ་ (lōbma tsɔ̄gba) student association.

སློབ་མའི་གྱོན་ཆས་ (lōbmɛ gyö̱njɛɛ̀) school uniform.

སློབ་མའི་དབང་ཡིག (lōbmɛ bāŋyii) student's identity card.

སློབ་མར་ལྟ་ཞིབ་མཁན་ (lōbmaa dāshibñɛn) proctor.

སློབ་མིང་ (lōbmiŋ) 1. student's name. 2. school name.

སློབ་གཙོ་ (lōbdzo) sm. སློབ་སྤྱི་.

སློབ་ཚན་ (lōbdzɛn) 1. lesson ¶ སློབ་ཚན་དང་པོ་ Lesson one. 2. course, class; va.—ཁྲིད་ to teach a course/ class/ lesson.

སློབ་ཚན་གྱི་རྣམ་གྲངས་ (lōbdzɛngi nāmdraŋ) school courses/ curriculum.

སློབ་ཚན་གྲ་སྒྲིག (lōbdzɛn trə̱drii) preparing for one's class/ lessons (by a teacher).

སློབ་ཚན་ཚུགས་ (lōbdzɛn tsūù) vi. to start class ¶ སློབ་ཚན་མ་ཚུགས་གོང་སློབ་ཕྲུག་རྣམས་སློབ་ཁང་དུ་འབྱོར་

དགོས་ The students have to arrive in the classroom before class starts.

སློབ་ཚིག (lōbdzii) advice, instruction.

སློབ་ཚུད་བརྡ་ཐོ་ (lōbdzüü da̱do) a notice announcing that students are being enrolled (in a school).

སློབ་ཚུལ་ (lōbdzüü) sm. སློབ་སྟངས་.

སློབ་ཚོགས་ (lōbdzɔɔ̀) study group/ club, educational or academic association/ society ¶ ཉི་འོད་ནུས་ཤུགས་སློབ་ཚོགས་ Society for solar energy.

སློབ་མཚམས་ (lōmdzam) 1. stopping school; va.—འཇོག་; —ཆད་ ¶ རིག་གནས་གསར་བརྗེའི་སྐབས་སློབ་གྲྭ་མང་པོ་སློབ་མཚམས་བཞག་པ་རེད་ During the Cultural Revolution many schools stopped functioning. 2. student strike.

སློབ་ཞུགས་རྒྱུགས་ལེན་ (lōbshuù gyu̱ùlen) school entrance exam.

སློབ་ཞོར་ (lōbshɔɔ) things done incidental to going to school ¶ ཁོས་སློབ་གྲྭའི་ཞོར་ལ་ཟ་ཁང་ལས་ཀ་བྱས་པ་རེད་ He worked in a restaurant while he was going to school.

སློབ་གཞི་ (lōbshi) teaching materials.

སློབ་བཞེས་གནང་ (lōbshe nāŋ) va. to accept/ admit students into school (h.).

སློབ་ཡུན་ (lōbyön) 1. length of schooling (of a person). 2. length of time for a class/ school/ semester.

སློབ་ཡོན་ (lōbyön) school fee, tuition; va.—སྤྲོད་ to pay school tuition.

སློབ་རན་ (lōbrɛn) reaching/ attaining school age.

སློབ་རིམ་ (lōbrim) school grade or level or class ¶ བོད་ལ་སློབ་ཆུང་སློབ་རིམ་དྲུག་ཡོད་པ་རེད་ There are six grades in primary schools in Tibet.

སློབ་རིམ་འཕར་ (lōbrim pār) vi. to get promoted (to the next grade) in school.

སློབ་རིམ་འཕར་ཚད་ (lōbrim pārdzɛɛ̀) proportion of students promoted to the next grade.

སློབ་རིམ་སྤར་ (lōbrim bār) va. to promote to next grade (in school).

སློབ་རོགས་ (lōbrɔɔ̀) helping study/ teach; va.—བྱེད་ ¶ སློབ་སྡོང་ཞན་པའི་སློབ་ཕྲུག་རྣམས་ལ་དགེ་རྒན་གྱིས་སློབ་རོགས་བྱེད་ཀྱི་ཡོད་པ་རེད་ The teacher is giving special teaching help to students who are doing poorly in their studies.

སློབ་ལོ་ (lōblo) 1. school age; vi.—ལོན་; —སོན་ to reach school age. ¶ སློབ་ལོ་ལོན་པའི་བྱིས་པ་ Children who have reached school age. 2. school/ academic year ¶ སློབ་ལོ་བཞི་པ་ Fourth year in school.

སློབ་ལོབ་འགན་ལེན་ (lōblob ge̱nlen) responsibility of the teacher to teach and the student to learn.

སློབ་ཤིང་ (lōbshiŋ) blackboard.

སློབ་ཤེས་ཅན་ (lōbsheèjɛn) scholar.

སློབ་ཤོར་ (lōbshɔɔ) 1. student who has left school (due to failing exams, lack of money, etc.). 2. vi. to inadvertently teach sth.

སློབ་ཤོར་བྱིས་པ་ (lōbshɔɔ ci̱ìbə) children who have left school (due to failing exams, lack of funds, etc.).

སློབ་བཤད་ (lōbshɛɛ̀) 1. giving advice; va.—བྱེད་. 2. va. to explain lessons (in school).

སློབ་སྲོལ་ (lōbsöö) ways of studying.

སློབ་གསར་ (lōbsar) 1. new student. 2. new class/ school.

སློབ་གསེང་ (lōbseŋ) the time between classes in school or between semesters.

སློབ་གསེང་གི་ཀློག་དེབ་ (lōbseŋgi lōgdeb) books for reading during a school break.

སློབ་གསེང་བྱེད་སྒོ་ (lōbseŋ ce̱ègo) extracurricular activities.

སློབ་གསེང་གི་སྦྱོང་ཚན་ (lōbseŋgi jo̱ndzɛn) homework.

སློབ་གསེང་གི་འཚོ་བ་ (lōbseŋgi tsōwa) extracurricular activities/ hobbies.

སློབ་གསེང་ཚོ་ཆུང་ (lōbseŋ tsōjuŋ) extracurricular activity groups.

སློབ་གསེང་ལུས་སྦྱོང་ (lōbseŋ lü̱üjoŋ) extracurricular exercise/ calisthenics/ sports.

སློབ་གསོ་ (lōbso) 1. education; va.—བྱེད་; —གཏོང་ to educate ¶ སློབ་ན་མ་སོང་གོང་གི་སློབ་གསོ་ Preschool education. 2. advice, instruction; va.—གཏོང་; —བྱེད་; —རྒྱག to give advice/ instruction ¶ ཕ་མས་ཕྲུ་གུའི་སྒྲིག་ལམ་སྐོར་སློབ་གསོ་རྒྱག་དགོས་ The parents should give their children advice concerning discipline.

སློབ་གསོ་སྐུལ་ལྕག (lōbso gǖüjaà) advising/ guiding and encouraging.

སློབ་གསོ་ཁང་ (lōbsogaŋ) ministry of education.

སློབ་གསོ་མཁས་པ་ (lōbso kɛ̄ɛba) sm. སློབ་གསོ་བ་.

སློབ་གསོ་ཆུང་རིམ་ (lōbso cūŋrim) primary education.

སློབ་གསོ་མཐོ་རིམ་ (lōbso tōrim) higher education.

སློབ་གསོ་པུའུ་ (lōbso būū) tib. ch. ministry/ bureau of education.

སློབ་གསོ་དཔེ་སྐྲུན་ཁང་ (lōbso bēdrüngaŋ) education publishing house.

སློབ་གསོ་བ་ (lōbsowa) educator.

སློབ་གསོ་འབྲིང་རིམ་ (lōbso dri̱ŋrim) middle level education, secondary education.

སློབ་གསོ་སློབ་གྲྭ་ཆེན་མོ་ (lōbso lōbdra cēmmo) institute of education, college of education.

སློབ་གསོའི་བྱེད་ཕྱོགས་ (lōbsö ce̱èjɔɔ̀) educational policy.

སློབ་གསོའི་རིག་པ་ (lōbsö ri̱gbə) pedagogy, the science of education.

སློབ་གསོའི་སེམས་ཁམས་རིག་པ་ (lōbsö sēmgam ri̱gbə) educational psychology.

སློབ་གསོས་བློ་འགུགས་ (lōbsöö lōguù) winning over by education.

སློབས་ (lōb) imp. of སློབ་.

སློམ་ (lōm) abbr. of སློ་མ་.

སློས་ (lōö) 1. imp. of སློ་. 2. va. to talk/ chat ¶ ཁོས་ལས་ཀ་བྱེད་པའི་སྐབས་ཁ་བརྡར་སློས་པ་ He chats a lot while at work.

གསག (sāà) sm. གསོག.

གསག་གཙོད་ (sāgjöö) a carpenter's tool used for engraving letters.

གསག་གསག་སྒྲུག་སྒྲུག (sāgsāg dru̱gdruù) consuming/ spending carefully so that one can gradually accumulate a surplus; va.—བྱེད་.

གསགས་ཀ་ (sāgga) sm. གསོག་ཀ་.

གསགས་ཆུ་ (sāgju) stored water supply.

གསང་: p. གསངས་; f. གསང་; imp. གསོང་ (sāŋ) 1. va. to keep a secret, to conceal ¶ འགྲོ་རྒྱུ་ཡིན་པ་གཞན་ལ་གསང་པ་རེད་ (He) kept his going a secret from the others. 2. abbr. of གསང་བ་. 3. (— + vb. + བྱེད་) to do secretly ¶ ཁོས་བོད་ལ་གསང་སྐྱོད་བྱས་སོང་ He secretly went to Tibet. 4. spaces between vital organs in the body. 5. abbr. of གསང་གཙོད་.

གསང་བཀའ་ (sāŋga) secret order.

གསང་སྐུད་ (sāŋgüü) sm. གསང་ཐག.

གསང་ཁང་ (sāŋgaŋ) 1. sm. གསང་གཙོད་. 2. secret room/ house.

གསང་ཁུང་ (sāŋguŋ) toilet hole (in outhouse).

གསང་ཁེབས་ (sāŋgeb) sanitary napkin (for menstruation).

གསང་འཁྱེར་ (sāŋgyer) smuggling; va.—བྱེད་ to smuggle.

གསང་གོས་དཀར་པོ་ (sāŋgöö) inner white dress put on statues.

གསང་གྲོས་ (sāŋdröö) secret talks/ discussions; va.—བྱེད་ to have secret talks/ discussions.

གསང་འགྲོགས་གཡེམ་སྦྱོར་ (sāŋdrɔɔ̀ yēmjɔɔ) secretly making friends and engaging in adultery.

གསང་རྒྱ་ (sāŋgya) secrecy, confidentiality; va.—བྱེད་; —སྡོམ་ to keep sth. secret; va.—སྲུང་ to keep/ maintain a secret; va.— གྲོལ་; —སྤྲོད་; —རྡོལ་ to reveal/ expose a secret; vi.—ཤོར་ to have a secret get let out/ revealed ¶ གཞུང་གིས་གནས་ཚུལ་དེའི་སྐོར་གསང་རྒྱ་བསྡམས་ཀྱང་ལས་བྱེད་པས་གསང་རྒྱ་སྲུང་ཐུབ་ཀྱི་མེད་པ་རེད་ Even though the government has made that information a secret, the cadres are unable to keep it secret.

གསང་རྒྱ་ཁྲོམ་བསྒྲགས་ (sāŋgya trōmdraà) disclosing secrets everywhere [Lit. crying out secrets in the marketplace].

གསང་རྒྱུད་ཟགས་གཤེར་སྐྱིལ་རྩི་ (sə̄ŋgyüù sagsher gūūdzi) endocrine hormone.

གསང་སྒུག (sāŋguù) waiting in hiding; va.—བྱེད་ ¶ ཉེན་རྟོགས་པས་རྐུན་མ་གསང་སྒུག་བྱས་ནས་འཛིན་བཟུང་བྱས་པ་འདུག The police waited in hiding and arrested the thief.

གསང་སྒོ (sāŋgo) secret door.

གསང་སྒོ་དཔེའུ་ (sāŋgo bēwu) secret passageway.

གསང་སྒྲུབ་ (sāŋdrub) secret meditation.

གསང་སྒྲོ་ (sāŋdro) testicles.

གསང་སྒྲོག་བྱེད་ (sāŋdrɔ̀ ceè) va. to tell sth. secretly ¶ དམག་མི་ཚོར་གོང་རིམ་གྱི་བཀའ་གསང་སྒྲོག་བྱས་འདུག The order from above was told to the soldiers secretly.

གསང་སྔགས་ (sāŋŋaà) tantra ¶ གསང་སྔགས་ཀྱི་ཆོས་ Tantric teachings/ religion.

གསང་སྔགས་ཀྱི་སྡོམ་པ་ (sāŋŋaàgi domba) tantric vows.

གསང་སྔགས་རྙིང་མ་ (sāŋŋaà ñīŋmə) tantric tradition of the Nyingma Sect.

གསང་སྔགས་ཐེག་པ་ (sāŋŋaà tēgba) Vajrayana.

གསང་སྔགས་གསར་མ་ (sāŋŋaà sārma) the tantric works that came after the second coming of Buddhism to Tibet in the 11th century.

གསང་གཅོད་ (sānjöò) toilet.

གསང་ཆ་ (sāŋja) 1. keeping secret, concealing; va.—བྱེད་. 2. secret letters/ correspondence.

གསང་ཆབ་ (sāŋjəb) h. of གཅིན་པ་.

གསང་ཆིངས་ (sə̄ŋjiŋ) secret treaty/ agreement.

གསང་ཆེན་ (sāŋjen) top secret.

གསང་ཇུས་ (sāŋjüù) scheming/ plotting secretly; va.—གཏོང་; —འགོད་ to scheme/ plot secretly.

གསང་ཉུལ་ (sə̄ŋñüü) 1. spying; va.—བྱེད་ to spy. 2. a spy.

གསང་ཏར་ (sāŋdar) secret telegram.

གསང་གཏམ་ (sāŋdam) secrets, secret/ confidential talk; va.—ཤོད་ to tell/ speak about sth. secret; vi.—ཕྱིར་གྱུར་; —ཤོར་ to inadvertently let out a secret.

གསང་གཏམ་ཕྱིར་གྱུར་ (sāŋdam ciīgyar) see གསང་གཏམ་.

གསང་རྟགས་ (sāŋdaà) secret sign, password.

གསང་བརྟོལ་ (sāŋdöö) revealing/ exposing a secret.

གསང་སྟབས་(ཀྱིས་) (sāŋdəbgi) secretly.

གསང་ཐག (sāŋdaà) secret manipulation; va.—འཐེན་ to secretly pull strings (to gain an objective), to manipulate sb. as a puppet ¶ རྒྱལ་ཁབ་ཆེ་བ་འདིས་རྒྱལ་ཁབ་ཆུང་བའི་སྲིད་གཞུང་ཞིག་ནང་གསང་ཐག་འཐེན་གྱི་ཡོད་པ་རེད་ The big country is secretly manipulating the government of the small country. [Lit. secret string]. 2. the strings in puppet theater.

གསང་ཐག་འཐེན་པའི་སྲིད་གཞུང་ (sāŋdaà tēmbɛ sīīsuŋ) puppet regime/ government.

གསང་ཐག་ཟློས་གར་ (sāŋdaà dööògar) puppet show/ theater.

གསང་ཐབས་ (sāŋdəb) secret/ covert means, secretly ¶ མཚན་མོ་གསང་ཐབས་སུ་བྲོས་པ་རེད་ (They) escaped secretly at night.

གསང་དང་མ་གསང་མི་འདུག ཞབས་རྗེས་གངས་ལ་བཞག་བཞག (sāŋdaŋ masaŋ minduù shəbjeè kaŋla shaàshaà) there is no need to hide because there is clear evidence (in one's favor on some issue) [Lit. there is no need to be secret because there are footprints on the snow].

གསང་དུ་གསོལ་ (sāŋdu sōō) va. to request to keep sth. secret (h.).

གསང་དོན་ (sāŋdön) a secret, a secret matter; va.—ཤོད་; —སྒྲོག to talk/ tell a secret; vi.—ཤོར་ to inadvertently let out a secret.

གསང་དོན་ཕྱིར་བསྒྲགས་ (sāŋdön ciīdraà) divulging/ telling a secret; va.—བྱེད་.

གསང་གནད་ (sāŋnɛɛ̀) important secrets, confidential files/ issues.

གསང་གནད་འགྲིམ་འགྲུལ་ཅུའུ་ (sāŋnɛɛ̀ drimdrüü jū) tib. ch. bureau of confidential communications.

གསང་གནད་ཡིག་ཚང་ཁང་ (sāŋnɛɛ̀ yigdzaŋgaŋ) confidential files office.

གསང་གནས་ (sāŋnɛɛ̀) 1. secret information/ news, secrets. 2. genitals.

གསང་གནོད་ (sāŋnöò) sabotage; va.—སྐྱེལ་ to sabotage.

གསང་བརྡ་ (sāŋda) 1. secret password, secret signal; va.—གཏོང་ to give or send a secret signal/ password; vi.—ཤོར་ to have a secret signal or password become known ¶ ཁོང་གིས་ང་ལ་མིག་གི་གསང་བརྡ་བཏང་ནས་སྐད་ཆ་དེ་ཚོགས་འདུའི་ཐོག་མ་ཤོད་ཟེར་བྱུང་ He sent me a secret signal with his eyes telling me not to say anything (about)that at the meeting. 2. secret message; va.—གཏོང་ to send a secret message; vi.—ཤོར་ to have a secret message become inadvertently known.

གསང་སྡོམ་ (sāŋdom) keeping sth. secret; va.—བྱེད་.

གསང་རྣམ་ (sāŋnam) secret biography.

གསང་པོ་ (sāŋbo) 1. clear ¶ མི་དེ་སྐད་གསང་པོ་འདུག He has a clear voice. 2. outspoken ¶ མི་འདི་ཁ་གསང་པོ་འདུག This man is outspoken.

གསང་སྤྱོད་ (sānjöò) toilet.

གསང་སྤྱོད་ཁ་ཤིང་ (sānjöò kəshiŋ) toilet seat/ bench.

གསང་འཕྲད་ (sāŋdrɛɛ̀) meeting secretly; va.—བྱེད་ ¶ སོ་པ་གཉིས་པོ་དེ་གསང་ཕྲད་བྱ་རྒྱུའི་ཁ་ཆད་བྱས་པ་རེད་ The two spies made an appointment to meet secretly.

གསང་འཕྲིན་ (sə̄ŋdrin) secret information/ secret message/ communication, intelligence.

གསང་འཕྲིན་ཁང་ (sə̄ŋdringaŋ) intelligence bureau.

གསང་འཕྲིན་པ་ (sə̄ŋdrinbə) intelligence agent.

གསང་བ་ (sāŋwa) secrecy, secret, clandestine, confidential; va.—བྱེད་ to keep secret/ confidential, to be secretive; vi.—ཤོར་ to have a secret get revealed ¶ གསང་བའི་ལས་འགུལ་ Secret campaign.

གསང་བ་ཁྲོམ་བསྒྲགས་ (sāŋwa trōmdraà) disclosing a secret everywhere.

གསང་བ་དམ་པོ་ (sāŋwa dombo) strict secret, strictly confidential; va.—བྱེད་.

གསང་བ་དམ་སྲུང་ (sāŋwa damsuŋ) keeping a secret; va.—བྱེད་.

གསང་བ་ཕྱིར་གྱུར་ (sāŋwa ciīgyar) disclosing a secret.

གསང་བ་ཕྱིར་ཤོར་ (sāŋwa ciīshɔɔ) sm. གསང་བ་ཕྱིར་གྱུར་.

གསང་བ་རང་མཁས་ཀྱང་ཤོད་པ་མི་མཁས་ (sāŋwa raŋkɛɛ̀gyaŋ shōòbə mikɛɛ̀) no way to keep a secret [Lit. even though one is skilled in keeping secrets, others are not skilled].

གསང་བའི་གློག་འཕྲིན་ (sāŋwɛ lɔ̄gdrin) sm. གསང་ཏར་.

གསང་བའི་བཅོས་ཐབས་ (sāŋwɛ jōòdam) secret method.

གསང་བའི་ཏང་ (sāŋwɛ dāŋ) underground/ secret party.

གསང་བའི་ཏར་ཡིག (sāŋwɛ dəryiì) sm. གསང་ཏར་.

གསང་བའི་གཏམ་ (sāŋwɛ dām) secret talk, secrets.

གསང་བའི་བདག་པོ་ (sāŋwɛ dagbo) sm. ཕྱག་ན་རྡོ་རྗེ་.

གསང་བའི་ནད (sāŋwɛ nɛɛ̀) genital diseases.

གསང་བའི་རྣམ་ཐར་ (sāŋwɛ nāmdar) sm. གསང་རྣམ་.

གསང་བའི་ཕོ་ཉ་ (sāŋwɛ pōña) secret emissary/ messenger.

གསང་བའི་མན་ངག (sāŋwɛ mennaà) secret code/ teachings.

གསང་བའི་རྩ་འཛུགས་ (sāŋwɛ dzə̄ndzuù) secret/ underground organization.

གསང་བའི་ཡིག་ཆ་ (sāŋwɛ yigjə) confidential/ secret papers or documents.

གསང་བའི་ལས་ཁུངས་ (sāŋwɛ lɛɛ̀guŋ) intelligence office/ bureau.

གསང་བའི་ལས་བྱེད་པ་ (sāŋwɛ lɛɛ̀jeba) intelligence

office/ bureau.

གསང་བའི་ཨང་ཀི་ (sāŋwɛ əŋgi) secret numbers used as a code.

གསང་བྲོས་ (sāŋdröö) secretly escaping/ fleeing; va.—བྱེད་ to escape/ flee secretly.

གསང་འབྲེལ་ (sāŋdree) secret relations; va.—བྱེད་.

གསང་སྦེད་ (sāŋbeè) secretly hiding sth.; va.—བྱེད་.

གསང་མིག་ (səŋmiì) acupuncture point.

གསང་མིང་ (səŋmiŋ) pen name, pseudonym.

གསང་མོལ་ (sāŋmöö) secret talks/ discussion.

གསང་སྙུལ་ (səŋñüü) spy, secret agent ༎ གསང་སྙུལ་གྱི་གནམ་གྲུ་ Spy plane.

གསང་སྙུལ་རུ་ཁག་ (səŋñüü ru̱gaà) intelligence wing/ unit.

གསང་ཚིག་ (səŋdzii) secret words.

གསང་ཚོགས་ (sāŋdzɔɔ̀) secret meeting/ organization.

གསང་མཚན་ (sāŋdzɛn) a new name given to a practitioner at the time of their tantric initiation.

གསང་འཚོང་ (sāŋdzoŋ) va. to sell sth. secretly.

གསང་མཛོད་ (sāŋdzöö) secret teaching given by a teacher to his pupil.

གསང་ཞིབ་ (səŋshib) secret investigation; va.—བྱེད་.

གསང་ཞིབ་པ་ (səŋshibbə) secret agent, spy, secret investigator.

གསང་ཞུ་ (səŋshu) secretly reporting sth.; va.—བྱེད་.

གསང་ཟོལ་མེད་པ་ (sāŋsöö me̱èba) direct, straightforward, without holding back.

གསང་ཡིག་ (səŋyii) a confidential/ secret letter or document.

གསང་ཡུམ་ (səŋyum) wife of an incarnate lama.

གསང་རང་མཁས་ཀྱང་ཤོད་མི་མཁས་ (sāŋ ra̱ŋkɛɛ̀gyaŋ shöö mi̱kɛɛ̀) even though one may be wise in keeping secrets, others will not and tell them.

གསང་རས་ (sāŋrɛɛ̀) sm. ཤིང་རས་.

གསང་ལམ་ (sāŋlam) 1. secret road/ path/ way. 2. vagina.

གསང་ལས་ (sāŋlɛɛ̀) 1. intelligence work; va.—བྱེད་ to do intelligence work. 2. abbr. of གསང་བའི་ལས་ཁུངས་ and གསང་བའི་ལས་བྱེད་པ་.

གསང་ཤོག་ (sāŋshoò) a kind of Tibetan paper that is very thin.

གསང་ཤོར་ (sāŋ shɔ̄ɔ) a secret that has been leaked/ revealed.

གསང་སྲུང་ (səŋsuŋ) keeping secrets; va.—བྱེད་.

གསང་སྲུང་ཨུ་ཡོན་ལྷན་ཁང་ (səŋsuŋ ūyön lhēngaŋ) security committe.

གསང་གསུམ་ (sāŋsum) shung. secrets of body, mind and speech. ༎ གསང་གསུམ་མཛད་འཕྲིན་མཐའ་དག་བསྟན་འགྲོའི་དཔལ་དུ་རྒྱས་པ་ May the secret deeds of body, mind and speech flourish for the sake of the dharma and sentient beings.

གསངས་ (sāŋ) sm. གསང་.

གསད་ (sɛ̀ɛ) f. of གསོད་.

གསན་: p. and f. **གསན་**; imp. **གསོན་** (sɛ̄n) 1. h. of ཉན་. 2. va. to understand (h.) ༎ དབྱིན་སྐད་གསན་གྱི་ཡོད་པ་རེད་ (He) understands English.

གསན་རྒྱ་ (sɛ̄ngya) sm. ཐོས་རྒྱ་.

གསན་དགོངས་ (sɛ̄n go̱ŋ) listening and thinking/ considering (h.); va.—གནང་ ༎ ཁྱེད་རང་འདིའི་སྐོར་གསན་དགོངས་གནང་དགོས་ Regarding this matter you must think and consider.

གསན་འཇོག་གནང་ (sɛ̄njɔɔ̀ nāŋ) h. of ཉན་འཇོག་གནང་.

གསན་ཐོས་ (sɛ̄ndöö) h. of གོ་ཐོས་.

གསན་དང་ (sɛ̄nda) h. of ཉན་དང་.

གསན་འདེབས་ཞུ་ (sɛ̄ndeb shu̱) 1. va. to listen to (what someone says) (h.). 2. va. to ask someone to listen ༎ གསན་འདེབས་ཞུ་ན་ཁོང་གིས་མི་གསན་ If we ask him to listen he will not listen.

གསན་ནོར་ཐེབས་ (sɛ̄nnɔɔ tēè) h. of གོ་ནོར་ཐེབས་.

གསན་ཕྱོགས་ནོར་ (sɛ̄njɔɔ̀ nɔ̱ɔ) h. of གོ་ཕྱོགས་ནོར་.

གསན་སྦྱོང་མཛད་ (sɛ̄njoŋ dzɛ̱ɛ̀) va. to study/ learn (h.).

གསན་ཚད་ (sɛ̄ndzɛɛ̀) h. of གོ་ཚད་.

གསན་འཛོལ་ (sɛ̄ndzöö) h. of གོ་འཛོལ་.

གསན་ཞུ་ (sɛ̄nshu) informing sb., letting sb. know sth.; va.—བྱེད་.

གསན་བཞེས་ (sɛ̄nshēè) 1. learning, studying (h.); va.—གནང་; —མཛད་ to learn/ study ༎ ཁོང་ཕྱི་རྒྱལ་སྐད་ཡིག་གསན་བཞེས་གནང་གི་ཡོད་པ་རེད་ He is learning a foreign language. 2. va. to listen ༎ ངས་ཞུས་པར་ཁོང་གིས་གསན་བཞེས་གནང་མ་བྱུང་ He didn't listen to what I told him.

གསན་གཟིགས་ (sɛ̄nsiì) 1. listening and looking, hearing and seeing ༎ དགེ་མཚན་དེ་དག་ཚང་མས་གསན་གཟིགས་བྱུང་བཞག All have seen or heard of these advantages. ༎ གཤམ་རིམ་ལས་བྱེད་པས་ཕྱོགས་སྡོམ་ཡིག་ཆ་ཕུལ་བ་དང་ སྙན་སེང་ཞུས་པར་ཁོང་གིས་གསན་གཟིགས་གནང་བ་རེད་ The lower officials sent up the summary report and made a verbal report and to these he listened and looked. 2. in reports this conveys: "consider this well."

གསན་རོགས་གནང་ (sɛ̄nronaŋ) h. of ཉོད་དང་.

གསན་བསམ་ (sɛ̄nsam) h. of ཐོས་བསམ་.

གསབ་ (sāb) f. of གསེབ་.

གསབ་དཀར་ (sābgar) bowl used for serving a second helping of noodles or rice (used to pour the refill into the empty first bowl).

གསབ་བསྐོ་ (sābgo) appointing a person to fill a vacancy; va.—བྱེད་.

གསབ་ཁྲིད་ (sābdrii) making-up classes (in school); va.—བྱེད་ ༎ སློབ་ཕྲུག་དེ་ན་ནས་སློབ་ཚན་འགའ་ཤས་ཆད་ཙང་དགེ་རྒན་གྱིས་གསབ་ཁྲིད་བྱས་འདུག Because the student got ill and missed several classes, the teacher made up the classes.

གསབ་རྒྱུགས་ (sābgyuù) make-up examination; va.—ལེན་ to give a make-up exam; —སྤྲོད་ to take a make-up exam.

གསབ་དངུལ་ (sābŋüü) supplementary payment/ compensation ༎ ཁོང་གཞུང་དོན་གྱི་ཆེད་དུ་རྨས་སྐྱོན་བྱུང་ཙང་སྲིད་གཞུང་ནས་གསབ་དངུལ་སྤྲད་འདུག Because he got injured doing government work, the government paid him money in compensation.

གསབ་བཅོས་ (sābjöö) editing (adding and correcting).

གསབ་ཆ་ (sābja) a supplement, compensation ༎ གཞུང་དོན་དུ་ཁོང་ལ་རྨས་སྐྱོན་བྱུང་ཙང་སྲིད་གཞུང་ནས་གསབ་ཆ་སྤྲད་འདུག He got injured doing government work so the government gave him compensation.

གསབ་ཐབས་ (sābdəb) means of giving compensation/ repaying/ supplementing/ making up ༎ རྒན་ལགས་ངའི་སློབ་ཚན་འགའ་ཤས་ཆད་སོང་བས་གསབ་ཐབས་ཡོད་དམ་ Teacher. Because I missed several classes can you give me make-up classes? ༎ ཕ་མའི་བཀའ་དྲིན་ནི་གསབ་ཐབས་མེད་པ་ཞིག་རེད་ The kindness of parents is sth. that there is no way of repaying.

གསབ་འདེབས་ (sābdeb) make-up planting (adding seeds to areas where the first seeds didn't take); va.—བྱེད་.

གསབ་འདེམས་ (sābdem) 1. by-election, runoff election; va.—བྱེད་. 2. an election to add additional members.

གསབ་སྣོན་ (sābnön) subsidy; va.—བྱེད་; —རྒྱག to subsidize.

གསབ་སྦྱོང་ (sābjoŋ) supplemental/ make-up study or classes; va.—བྱེད་.

གསབ་སྦྱོང་སློབ་གྲྭ་ (sābjoŋ lōbdra) a supplementary school to enable sb. to reach the level for attending regular school.

གསབ་ཚིག་ (sābdzii) additional/ supplementary words (usu. placed at the end of a letter/ document).

གསབ་འཛུགས་ (sābdzuù) sm. གསབ་འདེབས་.

གསའ་ (sā) snow leopard.

གསའ་མ་གཟིག་ (sāmasii) a type of snow leopard.

གསའ་གཟིག་ (sāsii) sm. གསའ་མ་གཟིག.

གསར་ (sāā) abbr. of གསར་པ་.

གསར་བཀོད་ (sārgöö) 1. va. to make a new

arrangement, to innovate, to rearrange; va.—བྱེད་ ༑ འགོ་ཁྲིད་གསར་པས་ལས་ཁུངས་ཀྱི་ལས་ཀ་བྱེད་སྟངས་སྐོར་གསར་བཀོད་འགའ་ཤས་བྱས་འདུག The new boss made several new arrangements concerning the way work is done in the office.

གསར་རྒྱང་ (sārgyaŋ) brand new ༑ མོ་ཊ་འདི་གསར་པ་གསར་རྒྱང་རེད་ This car is brand new.

གསར་སྐྱེས་ (sārgyeè) 1. newborn ༑ གསར་སྐྱེས་ཕྱུགས་ཕྲུག Newborn calves. 2. getting a new life, being reborn/ regenerated (politically) ༑ མི་སེར་གྱི་ཡུལ་དེ་རང་བཙན་ཐོབ་ནས་གསར་སྐྱེས་བྱུང་བ་རེད་ The colony was reborn after it won independence.

གསར་སྐྱེས་སྟོབས་ཤུགས་ (sārgyeè dōbshuù) new force, newly emerging/ rising power ༑ ཡུལ་དེར་དམངས་གཙོའི་ལས་འགུལ་བྱུང་བ་དེ་ནི་གསར་སྐྱེས་སྟོབས་ཤུགས་ཤིག་རེད་ The democratic movement that has occurred is a new force in that area.

གསར་སྤྲུན་ (sārdrün) sm. གསར་བསྐྲུན་.

གསར་སྤྲུན་རང་བཞིན་ (sārdrün raŋshin) creativeness.

གསར་བསྐོ་ (sārgo) appointing newly; va.—བྱེད་ to appoint newly.

གསར་བསྐྲུན་ (sārdrün) 1. building sth. new; va.—བྱེད་ ༑ ཡུལ་དེར་སློབ་གྲྭ་མང་པོ་གསར་སྐྲུན་བྱས་འདུག (They) have built many new schools in that area. 2. creating, inventing, innovating; va.—བྱེད་ ༑ ཚན་རིག་པ་ཚོས་བྱས་རྗེས་མང་པོ་གསར་སྐྲུན་བྱས་འདུག The scientists have achieved many new innovations.

གསར་བསྐྲུན་གྱི་སྤོབས་པ་ (sārdrüngi bōba) initiative, spirit of establishing sth. new.

གསར་བསྐྲུན་གྱི་རང་བཞིན་ (sārdrüngi raŋshin) creativity.

གསར་ཁང་ (sārgaŋ) abbr. of གསར་འགྱུར་ཁང་.

གསར་མཁན་ (sārñɛn) newspaper reporter.

གསར་འགོད་ (sārgöö) news report; va.—བྱེད་ to report news ༑ ཞིང་ཆ་ལྷངས་པའི་སྐོར་ཚགས་པར་ནང་གསར་འགོད་བྱས་འདུག Regarding the disturbance, it was reported in the news.

གསར་འགོད་སྙིང་བརྗོད་ (sārgöö lēŋjöö) news editorial.

གསར་འགོད་པ་ (sārgööba) newspaper reporter.

གསར་འགོད་ལྷན་ཚོགས་ (sārgöö lhɛndzɔɔ) press/ news conference.

གསར་འགྱུར་ (sɔ̄ngyur) 1. news; va.—འགོད་ to report news. 2. new changes in a situation.

གསར་འགྱུར་ཀློག་སྐོར་ (sɔ̄ngyur lɔ̄ɔgɔɔ) newspaper reading circle.

གསར་འགྱུར་བཀག་སྡོམ་ (sɔ̄ngyur gāgdom) news censorship/ blackout; va.—བྱེད་.

གསར་འགྱུར་ཁང་ (sɔ̄ngyurgaŋ) news agency, press service, newspaper office.

གསར་འགྱུར་མགོ་གཏོང་བ་ (sɔ̄ngyur kōdoŋwa) newspaper reporter.

གསར་འགྱུར་གྱི་རང་དབང་ (sɔ̄ngyurgi raŋwaŋ) freedom of the press.

གསར་འགྱུར་གྱི་ལས་དོན་ (sɔ̄ngyurgi lɛ̀ɛdön) journalism.

གསར་འགྱུར་གློག་འཕྲིན་ (sɔ̄ngyur lɔ̄ŋdrin) news broadcast; va.—གཏོང་.

གསར་འགྱུར་མཁྲིན་ཚབ་པ་ (sɔ̄ngyur drīndzɔbbɔ) press secretary, press spokesman (of an organization).

གསར་འགྱུར་འགོད་མཁན་ (sɔ̄ngyur göönɛn) reporter, correspondent, newsman.

གསར་འགྱུར་འགོད་མི་ (sɔ̄ngyur göömi) sm. གསར་འགྱུར་འགོད་མཁན་.

གསར་འགྱུར་བརྒྱུད་བསྒྲགས་ (sɔ̄ngyur gyüüdraà) relaying news broadcasts; va.—བྱེད་.

གསར་འགྱུར་དངོས་བཤུས་གློག་བརྙན་ (sɔ̄ngyur ŋööshüü lɔ̄ŋñɛn) news documentary (film).

གསར་འགྱུར་མཉམ་བསྒྲགས་ (sɔ̄ngyur ñamdraà) national news (used in Tibet to contrast with news about Tibet).

གསར་འགྱུར་མདོར་བསྡུས་ (sɔ̄ngyur dɔrdüü) news summary.

གསར་འགྱུར་པ་ (sɔ̄ngyurba) newspaper reporter.

གསར་འགྱུར་འཕར་མ་ (sɔ̄ngyur pārma) special edition of a paper/ magazine.

གསར་འགྱུར་བྱེད་པོ་ (sɔ̄ngyur ceèbo) sm. གསར་འགྱུར་འགོད་མཁན་.

གསར་འགྱུར་རྩད་ཞིབ་ (sɔ̄ngyur dzɛ̄ɛshib) news investigation.

གསར་འགྱུར་རྩོམ་སྒྲིག་མཛད་པོ་ (sɔ̄ngyur dzōmdrig dzɛ̀ɛbo) newspaper editor.

གསར་འགྱུར་འཚོལ་མཁན་ (sɔ̄ngyur tsöönɛn) sm. གསར་འགྱུར་འགོད་མཁན་.

གསར་འགྱུར་རིག་པ་ (sɔ̄ngyur rigbɔ) journalism.

གསར་འགྱུར་ལས་བྱེད་པ་ (sɔ̄ngyur lɛ̀ɛceèba) sm. གསར་འགྱུར་འགོད་མཁན་.

གསར་འགྱུར་གསལ་བསྒྲགས་ (sɔ̄ngyur sɛ̄ɛdraà) announcement in a newspaper ༑ ལས་གནས་གསར་པའི་སྐོར་གསར་འགྱུར་གསལ་བསྒྲགས་ཐོན་འདུག The announcement of the new position appeared in the newspaper.

གསར་འགྲོགས་པ་ (sār drɔgba) inconsistent, changeable, fickle.

གསར་རྒྱག (sār gyaà) constructing/ building sth. newly; va.—བྱེད་ to construct/ build anew ༑ དམག་སྒར་སོ་སོར་སྨན་ཁང་རེ་རྒྱག་བྱས་འདུག They built new hospitals in each military camp.

གསར་སྒྱུར་ (sɔ̄rgyur) reforming, changing; va.—བྱེད་.

གསར་སྒྲུབ་ (sɔ̄rdrub) creating anew; va.— བྱེད་.

གསར་སྒྲུབ་པ་ (sɔ̄rdrubbɔ) newspaper reporter.

གསར་བསྒྲིགས་ཁྱོ་ཤུག (sɔ̄rdrig kyōshug) newlyweds, newly married couple.

གསར་ངད་ (sārŋɛɛ̀) sth. that smells new (or looks brand new).

གསར་བཅོས་ (sārjöö) innovating, making changes, transforming ༑ ལག་རྩལ་གསར་བཅོས་ Technical innovations.

གསར་ཆེ་དཀའ་གསུམ་ (sār cē gā sūm) the three: new, big and difficult.

གསར་མཇལ་ (sānjɛɛ) shung. ceremony for officials when they first enter government service or when they get appointed to top positions that involve an audience with the Dalai Lama (or Regent).

གསར་བརྗེ་ (sārje) revolution; va.—བྱེད་ to make revolution ༑ ཡུལ་དེར་མི་དམངས་ཚོས་གསར་བརྗེ་བྱས་ནས་སྲིད་གཞུང་མགོ་རྡིང་བསྒྱིགས་པ་རེད་ In that area the people made a revolution and overthrew the government.

གསར་བརྗེ་མཁས་ཅན་ (sārje kɛ̄ɛjɛn) a revolutionary.

གསར་བརྗེ་ཅན་ (sārjejɛn) sm. གསར་བརྗེ་མཁས་ཅན་.

གསར་བརྗེ་ཅན་དུ་འགྱུར་ (sārjejɛndu gyur) vi. to have been revolutionized.

གསར་བརྗེ་ཆེན་པོ་ (sārje cēmbo) great revolution.

གསར་བརྗེ་པ་ (sārjeba) a revolutionary.

གསར་བརྗེ་འཕེལ་རྒྱས་ཀྱི་དུས་རིམ་སྨྲ་བ་ (sārje pēlgyɛɛgi tüürim māwa) the theory that revolution develops by stages.

གསར་བརྗེ་བ་ (sārjewa) a revolutionary.

གསར་བརྗེ་བྱ་ཡུལ་ (sārjecɔyüü) sm. གསར་བརྗེའི་ཁ་གཏད་.

གསར་བརྗེ་བྱེད་མཁན་ (sārje ceñɛn) sm. གསར་བརྗེ་པ་.

གསར་བརྗེ་ཚོགས་པ་ (sārje tsōgba) Reform Party.

གསར་བརྗེ་ལང་ (sārje laŋ) vi. to have a revolution occur/ arise ༑ ན་ཉིང་ཡུལ་དེར་གསར་བརྗེ་ལངས་འདུག Last year a revolution occurred in our country.

གསར་བརྗེའི་ཁ་གཏད་ (sārjee kāpdɛɛ̀) the object of the revolution.

གསར་བརྗེའི་དངོས་མཚོན་རིང་ལུགས་ (sārjee ŋöndzön riŋluù) revolutionary realism.

གསར་བརྗེའི་སྣོན་གཤེགས་དཔའ་བོ་ (sārjee ŋönsheg bāwo) revolutionary martyr.

གསར་བརྗེའི་འཆར་ཡན་རིང་ལུགས་ (sārjee cāryɛn riŋluù) revolutionary romanticism.

གསར་བརྗེའི་དང་ (sārjee dāŋ) revolutionary party.

གསར་བརྗེའི་དྲན་ཐོ་ (sārjee trɛndo) personal reminiscence of earlier revolutionary times.

གསར་བརྗེའི་གནས་གཞིའི་ཁུལ་ (sārjee nɛ̄ɛ̀shii kūū) revolutionary base/ area.

གསར་བརྗེའི་དཔའ་བོ་རིང་ལུགས་ (sārjee bāwo ri̲ŋluù) revolutionary heroism.

གསར་བརྗེའི་བློ་སེམས་ (sārjee drōsem) revolutionary fervor.

གསར་བརྗེའི་མི་ཆོས་རིང་ལུགས་ (sārjee mi̲jöö ri̲ŋluù) revolutionary humanitarianism.

གསར་བརྗེའི་མི་ཚེ་ལྟ་ཚུལ་ (sārjee mi̲dze dədzüü) revolutionary outlook on life.

གསར་བརྗེའི་དམག་འཁྲུག (sārjee məgdruù) revolutionary war.

གསར་བརྗེའི་བརྩོན་སེམས་ (sārjee dzōnsem) revolutionary zeal.

གསར་བརྗེའི་ཞུན་ཐབ་ (sārjee shündəb) revolutionary furnace (for tempering the character of the people like that of steel) ། གཞོན་ནུ་རྣམས་གསར་བརྗེའི་ཞུན་ཐབ་ནང་སྦྱོང་བརྡར་བྱས་པ་རེད་ The youth were trained (tempered) in the furnace of revolution.

གསར་བརྗེའི་རང་བཞིན་ (sārjee rə̲ŋshin) revolutionary character/ quality/ spirit.

གསར་བརྗེའི་རིག་པའི་གཞུང་ལུགས་ (sārjee ri̲gbɛ shu̲ŋluù) revolutionary theory.

གསར་བརྗེའི་སེམས་ཤུགས་ (sārjee sīmshuù) revolutionary enthusiasm.

གསར་བརྗེའི་སྲོལ་རྒྱུན་ (sārjee sūūgyün) revolutionary tradition.

གསར་བརྗེར་ངོ་རྒོལ་ (sārjee ŋ̲ogöö) counterrevolution; va.—བྱེད་.

གསར་བརྗེར་ངོ་རྒོལ་བ་ (sārjee ŋ̲ogööwa) counter revolutionary element, a counterrevolutionary.

གསར་བརྗེར་ངོ་ལོག (sārjee ŋ̲oloò) sm. གསར་བརྗེར་ངོ་རྒོལ་.

གསར་བརྗེར་ངོ་ལོག་པ་ (sārjee ŋ̲ologba) sm. གསར་བརྗེར་ངོ་རྒོལ་བ་.

གསར་བརྗེར་ངོ་ལོག་བྱེད་མཁན་ (sārjee ŋ̲oloò ce̲eñɛn) counterrevolutionary, counterrevolutionist.

གསར་རྙིང་ (sərñiŋ) 1. new and old, stale and fresh. 2. age, how old ། ཅ་ལག་འདི་གསར་རྙིང་རེད་ How old is this thing?

གསར་རྙིང་སྤྲོད་ (sərñiŋ drōō) va. to have the old incumbent turn over a position to the new holder.

གསར་རྙེད་ (sārñeè) discoveries ། ཚན་རིག་པ་ཚོས་གསར་རྙེད་མང་པོ་བྱུང་བ་རེད་ Scientists have made many discoveries.

གསར་རྙེད་པ་ (sārñeèba) discoverer.

གསར་གཏོད་ (sārdöö) creating, inventing, founding anew; va.—བྱེད་ ། འགྲེམས་སྟོན་ཁང་ཞིག་གསར་གཏོད་བྱས་པ་རེད་ (They) founded a new museum.

གསར་གཏོད་ཀྱི་སྙིང་སྟོབས་ (sārdöögi ñiŋdob) initiative for inventing/ creating/ innovating.

གསར་གཏོད་མདུན་སྐྱོད་ (sārdöö dü̲ŋgyöö) inventing/ creating new ways of advancing or progressing.

གསར་གཏོད་བྱེད་དབང་ (sārdöö ce̲ewaŋ) inventor's rights, patent, copyright.

གསར་གཏོད་ལྷབས་ཆེན་ (sārdöö ləbcen) a great invention/ creation.

གསར་ཐོག (sārdɔɔ) 1. while sth. is new ། གནད་དོན་གང་ཅི་གསར་ཐོག་ལ་ཐག་གཅོད་བྱ་དགོས་ Problems should be resolved when they first occur. 2. new crops.

གསར་ཐོན་ (sārdön) new products/ things ། གསར་ཐོན་བྱ་དངོས་ Newly produced things.

གསར་ཐོན་དངོས་པོ་ (sārdön ŋ̲ööbo) newly produced merchandise/ commodities.

གསར་འཐོམ་པ་ (sārtomba) a derogatory manner of addressing sb. who is new [Lit. new out of it person].

གསར་དར་ (sār ta̲r) sm. དར་སྤེལ་.

གསར་དུ་ (sārdu) newly, anew, new; va.—འཛུགས་ to establish newly/ anew.

གསར་དེབ་ (sārdeb) magazine.

གསར་བདམས་ (sārdam) newly picked/ chosen ། འཐུས་མི་གསར་བདམས་རྣམས་ The newly chosen delegates.

གསར་དོད་བྱུང་རིགས་ (sārdöö cu̲ŋrig) shung. new (customs) that have taken over ། བར་ལམ་ལམ་ངན་གསར་དོད་བྱུང་རིགས་འཕྱལ་འཕྱལ་བཅོས་སྒྲིག་དགོས་རྒྱུ་ The bad new custom that has taken over must be rectified immediately.

གསར་འདོད་ (sāndöö) penchant/ inclination for new things; va.—བྱེད་.

གསར་འདོན་ (sāndön) 1. putting or bringing out sth. new; va.—བྱེད་ ། ཁོང་ཡར་པོ་རྒྱག་རྒྱུའི་ཇུས་གཞི་གསར་འདོན་བྱས་འདུག He put forth a new plan for construction. 2. new mining/ excavating ། རི་ཁུལ་འདི་ནས་གཏེར་ཁ་མང་པོ་གསར་འདོན་བྱས་འདུག They are doing a lot of new mining from that mountain.

གསར་སྡུད་ (sārdüü) taking in sth. new (e.g., members in an organization); va.—བྱེད་.

གསར་སྣོན་ (sārnön) va. to augment/ increase anew; va.—བྱེད་.

གསར་གནས་ (sārnɛɛ̀) news ། གསར་གནས་ཕྱོགས་བསྡུས་ News summary.

གསར་པ་ (sāāba) new, fresh ། རིག་པ་གསར་པ་ A new idea.

གསར་པ་གསར་རྒྱང་ (sāāba sārgyaŋ) sm. གསར་རྒྱང་.

གསར་སྤེལ་ (sārbel) 1. spreading/ disseminating news, broadcasting news; va.—བྱེད་ ། གསར་སྤེལ་ལས་ཁངས་ News information service. 2. disseminating/ developing sth. new ། དེང་སང་སྨན་ནད་བཅོས་ཐབས་ཤིག་གསར་སྤེལ་བྱས་འདུག These days they are disseminating a new treatment for cancer.

གསར་སྤེལ་དངུལ་ཁང་ (sārbel ŋ̲ūūgaŋ) development bank.

གསར་སྲོལ་ (sārdrōō) new style/ fashion/ custom. ། དེ་རྗེས་གསར་སྲོལ་མང་དག་ཅིག་འགོ་ཚུགས་སོང་ After that, many new customs were begun.

གསར་འཕར་ (sāmbar) shung. adding anew, increasing newly ། ལོ་འདིར་ཕྱུག་རིགས་གསར་འཕར་མང་པོ་བྱུང་སོང་ This year they increased a great deal in livestock. ། མི་སེར་ཚོས་ཁྲལ་རིགས་གསར་འཕར་མང་པོ་རྒྱག་དགོས་བྱུང་ཙང་དབུལ་ཕོངས་ཆགས་པ་རེད་ Because the peasants had to fulfill many new taxes, they became poor.

གསར་འཕྲིན་ (səndrin) news.

གསར་བུ་ (sərbu) 1. new ones (students, monks, teachers, etc.). 2. inenperienced people. 3. youth.

གསར་བུ་བ་ (sərbuwa) sm. གསར་བུ་.

གསར་བྱུང་ནད་ (sārjuŋ ne̲ɛ) a new disease.

གསར་བྲིས་ (sərdrii) rewriting, writing again; va.—བྱེད་.

གསར་འབྱེད་ (sānjeè) sm. གསར་གཏོད་.

གསར་འབྱེད་དང་བཀོལ་སྤྱོད་ (sānjeè ta̲ŋ gööjöö) open and using newly; va.—བྱེད་.

གསར་འབྱོར་ (sānjɔɔ) 1. newly arrived. 2. sb. who is newly arrived.

གསར་སྦྱོང་ (sārjoŋ) 1. learning/ studying sth. new; va.—བྱེད་. 2. newly donated.

གསར་སྦྱོང་གསར་སྒྲིག (sārjoŋ sārdrig) studying and organizing sth. new; va.—བྱེད་.

གསར་སློལ་ (sārböö) breaking/ plowing up new land, reclaiming land; va.—རྒྱག; —བྱེད་.

གསར་མ་ (sārma) 1. sm. གསར་པ་. 2. the latter schools of Buddhism that spread into Tibet with the second coming of the dharma.

གསར་མ་རྙིང་ (sārma ñiŋ) sm. གསར་མིན་རྙིང་མིན་.

གསར་མ་པ་ (sārmawa) the followers of the latter schools of Buddhism that came with the second coming of dharma.

གསར་མིན་རྙིང་མིན་ (sārmin ñiŋmin) neither new or old.

གསར་མོ་ (sārmo) sm. སོ་གསར་.

གསར་རྨོས་ (sārmöö) plowing new land/ fields; va.—རྒྱག.

གསར་བཙུགས་ (sārdzuù) sm. གསར་འཛུགས་.

གསར་རྩོམ་ (sārdzom) creating, composing (literature, artistic works); va.—བྱེད་.

གསར་ཚེས་ (sārdzeè) the first day of the new month/ year.

གསར་འཛུགས་ (sārdzuù) newly establishing/ constructing; va.—བྱེད་ ¶ ཉམས་ཞིབ་ཁང་ཞིག་གསར་འཛུགས་བྱས་པ་རེད་ (They) established a new research center.

གསར་ཞུགས་ (sārshuù) a new member ¶ ལོ་འདིའི་ནང་སློབ་ཕྲུག་གསར་ཞུགས་མང་པོ་འདུག This year there are many newly joined monks.

གསར་ཞུགས་མཇལ་ཁ་ (sārshuù jɛ̱ɛga) shung. an audience for new officials/ students ¶ ལས་བྱེད་གསར་པ་རྣམས་ལ་གསར་ཞུགས་མཇལ་ཁ་དང་ དེ་མིན་རྣམས་ལ་སྤྱིབས་མཇལ་ཞིག་གནང་བ་ An audience was (specially) given to the new officials and a group audience was given to the rest of the people.

གསར་ཞུགས་ཕྱག་འབུལ་ (sārshuù cāmbüü) ceremonial audience for new members of sth.

གསར་བཞེངས་མཛད་སྒོ་ (sārsheŋ dzɛ̱ɛgo) inauguration ceremony for a new construction project.

གསར་གཟིགས་པ་ (sārsigba) newspaper audience/ readers.

གསར་བཟོ་ (sārso) making/ creating/ inventing/ building anew; va.—བྱེད་ ¶ རླངས་འཁོར་འགྲོ་ལམ་གསར་བཟོ་བྱེད་རྒྱུ་ The building of a new motorable road.

གསར་བཟོས་ (sārsöö) newly made/ manufactured/ built ¶ གསར་བཟོས་དངོས་པོ་ Newly made products.

གསར་འོངས་ (sāroŋ) sm. གསར་འགྱུར་.

གསར་ཤོག (sārshoò) newspaper.

གསར་ཤོག་རྩོམ་སྒྲིག་བྱེད་པོ་ (sārsoò dzōmdrig ce̱èbo) newspaper editor.

གསར་སྲོལ་འཛུགས་ (sārsöö dzu̱ù) va. to establish a new custom.

གསར་སློག (sārlɔɔ̀) renovating, reconditioning; va.—གཏོང་.

གསར་གསལ་ལྟར་ (sārsɛɛdar) according to a news report.

གསར་བསུའི་ཚོགས་འདུ་ (sārsü tsōndu) a meeting to welcome newcomers.

གསལ་ (sɛ̄ɛ) 1. abbr. of གསལ་པོ་. 2. vi. to be/ become visible, to be/ become clear, to be reflected (in a mirror, etc.), to show ¶ ཁོའི་གཟུགས་བརྙན་ཤེལ་སྒོའི་ནང་ལ་གསལ་བ་རེད་ His figure was reflected in the mirror. ¶ དེ་འདྲ་དེབ་ལ་གསལ་མི་འདུག Such things are not clear in the book. 3. according to, as said/ written ¶ ཚགས་ཤོག་དེའི་ནང་བཀོད་གསལ་ As was stated in that newspaper. ¶ མིང་ཐོ་ནང་གསལ་ According to the lists of names.

གསལ་བཀྲོལ་ (sɛ̄ɛdröö) a detailed/ clear explanation; va.—བྱེད་.

གསལ་སྐྱོར་རྒྱག (sɛ̄ɛgyɔɔ̀ gya̱à) va. to explain sth. clearly again.

གསལ་ཁ་གཏོད་ (sɛ̄ɛga dö̃ö) va. to clarify sth., to make sth. clear.

གསལ་ཁ་འདོན་ (sɛ̄ɛga dõn) sm. གསལ་ཁ་གཏོད་.

གསལ་ཁུང་ (sɛ̄ɛguŋ) a hole, opening.

གསལ་གྲགས་ (sɛ̄ɛdraà) well-known, famous.

གསལ་འགྲེལ་ (sɛ̄ɛdree) sm. གསལ་བཀྲོལ་.

གསལ་བསྒྲགས་ (sɛ̄ɛdraà) statement, proclamation, declaration; va.—འདོན་; —བྱེད་; —སྤེལ་ to make a proclamation/ announcement ¶ སྲིད་འཛིན་གསར་པ་འདེམས་ཐོན་བྱུས་པའི་གསལ་བསྒྲགས་སྤེལ་འདུག They made an announcement concerning the election of the new president.

གསལ་བསྒྲགས་མཛད་མཁན་ (sɛ̄ɛdraà dzɛ̱èñɛn) spokesman.

གསལ་ཆ་ (sɛ̄ɛja) 1. sm. དཀར་ཆ་. 2. clear information/ news ¶ ཕ་མ་ཚོའི་སྐོར་ལ་གསལ་ཆ་གང་ཡང་མི་འདུག Concerning (their) parents, there is no clear news at all.

གསལ་ཆ་ཅན་ (sɛ̄ɛjajɛn) clear ¶ གསལ་ཆ་ཅན་གྱི་གནས་ཚུལ་ Clear information.

གསལ་ཆ་ཐོན་ (sɛ̄ɛja tõn) vi. to have news/ information come out or become clear.

གསལ་ཆ་དྭངས་པོ་ (sɛ̄ɛja ta̱ŋbo) clear news/ information.

གསལ་མཆོག (sɛ̄ɛjɔɔ̀) sm. གསལ་ཆ་དྭངས་པོ་.

གསལ་རྗེན་ (sɛ̄ɛjen) uncamouflaged, naked; va.—དུ་འདོན་ to expose, to bring out into the open; vi.—དུ་ཐོན་ to get exposed ¶ ནོར་འཁྲུལ་རྣམས་གསལ་རྗེན་དུ་བཏོན་པ་རེད་ (They) exposed the mistakes.

གསལ་བཏབ (sɛ̄ɛdəb) p. of གསལ་འདེབས་.

གསལ་རྟོགས་ (sɛ̄ɛdɔɔ̀) thorough understanding ¶ གནས་ཚུལ་གསལ་རྟོགས་བྱུང་མ་སོང་ (They) didn't get a thorough understanding of the incident.

གསལ་སྟོན་ (sɛ̄ɛdön) a demonstration; va.—བྱེད་ to show (clearly), to demonstrate.

གསལ་བསྟན་ (sɛ̄ɛ dɛ̃n) shung. va. to show clearly.

གསལ་ཐིང་ཐིང་ (sɛ̄ɛ tĩŋdiŋ) exceptionally clear ¶ གནས་ཚུལ་གསལ་ཐིང་ཐིང་བྲིས་སོང་ (He) wrote the news exceptionally clearly.

གསལ་ཐེབས་ (sɛ̄ɛ tēb) vi. to remember sth. one has been reminded about ¶ ངའི་གནས་ཚུལ་དེའི་སྐོར་གོང་རིམ་ལ་གསལ་བཏབ་ཀྱང་གསལ་ཐེབས་མ་སོང་ I reminded the higher officials concerning this situation but they did not remember it.

གསལ་མཐོང་ (sɛ̄ɛdoŋ) 1. seeing clearly. 2. king of the nagas.

གསལ་དྭངས་ (sɛ̄ɛdaŋ) 1. good health ¶ ཁོང་ཚོ་སྐུ་ཁམས་གསལ་དྭངས་རེད་ They are all in good health. 2. clear, evident ¶ ལས་ཁུངས་ཀྱི་ཡིག་ཆ་སུས་བརྐུས་མིན་ད་ལྟ་གནས་ཚུལ་གསལ་དྭངས་བྱུང་མི་འདུག It is not now clear who stole the office's document.

གསལ་འདེབས་ (sɛ̄ndeb) 1. advising, giving guidance, suggesting; va.—ཞུ་; —བྱེད་ to advise, to guide ¶ ཚོགས་ཆུང་དེའི་གསལ་འདེབས་བཞིན་ In accordance with the advise of the committee. 2. reminding; va.—ཞུ་ ¶ ལས་ཀ་དེའི་སྐོར་ངས་གོང་རིམ་ལ་གསལ་འདེབས་ཞུས་པ་ཡིན་ I reminded all the higher officials about this work.

གསལ་བརྡ་ (sɛ̄ɛda) notice, announcement; va.—གཏོང་ to send a notice, to make an announcement.

གསལ་སྣང་ (sɛ̄ɛnaŋ) 1. clear in mind. 2. clear (sky, etc.). 3. signal of dawn (e.g., cock's crowing); va.—གཏོང་.

གསལ་པོ་ (sɛ̄ɛbo) 1. clear, clearly ¶ ངས་གསལ་པོ་ཤེས་སོང་ (I) understood it clearly. ¶ ངས་དགེ་རྒན་ལ་གནས་ཚུལ་དེ་གསལ་པོ་ཞུས་པ་ཡིན་ I reported the matter clearly to (my) teacher. 2. bright ¶ འོད་གསལ་པོ་ A bright light.

གསལ་པོ་དག་ལ་གསལ་སྐྱོར་ (sɛ̄ɛbo ta̱gla sɛ̄ɛgyɔr) sm. གསལ་པོར་གསལ་སྐྱོར་.

གསལ་པོར་སྟོན་ (sɛ̄ɛbor dõn) va. to demonstrate, to show.

གསལ་པོར་ཐོན་ (sɛ̄ɛbor tõn) vi. to reveal, to become evident, to be shown.

གསལ་པོར་བྱེད་ (sɛ̄ɛbor ce̱è) va. to make clear, to explain.

གསལ་པོར་འཕྲོ་ (sɛ̄ɛbor drō) vi. to shine brightly.

གསལ་པོར་གསལ་སྐྱོར་ (sɛ̄ɛbor sɛ̄ɛgyɔɔ) explaining again (unnecessarily) sth. that is already clear.

གསལ་བྱེད་ (sɛ̄ɛjeè) 1. consonants. 2. abbr. of གསལ་པོར་བྱེད་.

གསལ་བྱེད་ཀྱི་ཚོགས་ (sɛ̄ɛjeègi tsɔ̄ɔ̀) the alphabet.

གསལ་བྱེད་རྐྱང་པ་ (sɛ̄ɛjeè gyāŋba) a single letter of the alphabet.

གསལ་བྱེད་གཉིས་ལྡན་གྱི་སྒྲ་ (sɛ̄ɛjeè ñĩndɛngi dra̱) consonant cluster.

གསལ་བྱེད་སུམ་ཅུ་ (sɛ̄ɛjeè sūmju) the thirty consonants in the Tibetan alphabet.

གསལ་འབྱེད་ (sɛ̄ɛ je̱è) va. to distinguish, to make clear-cut, to show clearly.

གསལ་འབྱེད་ཀྱི་ཚིག (sɛ̄ɛjeègi tsĩĩ) a preposition.

གསལ་འབྱེད་ཐག་གཅོད་ (sɛ̄ɛjeè tāgjöö) a clear-cut

decision; va.—བྱེད་.

གསལ་མིག (sɛ̄ɛmii) 1. hole. 2. good vision/ eyesight.

གསལ་མིན་སྐྱོན་འགྱུར་ (sɛ̄ɛmin gyōngyur) shung. unclear and damaged ¶ རྟགས་ཐེལ་ལ་ཞིབ་འཇུག་གིས་གསལ་མིན་སྐྱོན་འགྱུར་ཐོན་ཚེ་ལམ་སེང་སྙན་སེང་ཞུ་དགོས་ You must check the seal and if you find it unclear and damaged, you should report this immediately.

གསལ་མེ་ (sɛ̄ɛme) butter lamp.

གསལ་མེད་རྙོག་འཛིང་ (sɛ̄ɛmeè ñōgdziŋ) an unclear disturbance/ disorder.

གསལ་མོ་ (sɛ̄ɛmo) sm. གསལ་པོ་.

གསལ་ཚད་ (sɛ̄ɛdzɛɛ̀) degree of clearness/ clarity.

གསལ་ཚུལ་ (sɛ̄ɛdzüü) shung. clearly mentioned ¶ ཁོས་གོང་རིམ་ལ་ཞིང་ཁ་དེ་ཁོ་ལ་བདག་པའི་སྐོར་བཀའ་གནད་ལ་གསལ་ཚུལ་ཞུས་འདུག He told the high officials that his ownership of the fields is mentioned clearly in the land tenure document.

གསལ་ཞུ་ (sɛ̄ɛshu) 1. telling clearly; va.—བྱེད་ ¶ གནས་ཚུལ་དེའི་སྐོར་ངས་འགོ་ཁྲིད་ལ་གསལ་ཞུ་བྱས་པ་ཡིན་ I told the leader clearly about that situation. 2. lamp; va.—སྦར་ to light a lamp.

གསལ་གཟིགས་ (sɛ̄ɛsii) sm. གསལ་ཞུ་.

གསལ་ལ་ (sɛ̄ɛla) a phrase used at the end of a clauses to indicate that an explanation follows ¶ ཡིག་ཆའི་ནང་དུ་འཁོད་གསལ་ལ་ What is written in the document (follows).

གསལ་ལ་མ་གསལ་ (sɛ̄ɛla ma̱sɛɛ) unclear, faint, vague.

གསལ་ལ་མི་གསལ་ (sɛ̄ɛla mi̱sɛɛ) sm. གསལ་ལ་མ་གསལ་.

གསལ་ལམ་ལམ་ (sɛ̄ɛ la̱mlam) distinctly, clearly ¶ གནས་ཚུལ་དེའི་སྐོར་ངས་གསལ་ལམ་ལམ་དྲན་གྱི་འདུག I recall this situation distinctly.

གསལ་ལེ་བ་ (sɛ̄ɛlewa) clearly, distinctly.

གསལ་ལེར་ (sɛ̄ɛlee) clearly, distinctly.

གསལ་ཤིང་ (sɛ̄ɛshiŋ) a form of ancient punishment for criminals where a wooden stick is stuck into the anus.

གསལ་ཤེས་ (sɛ̄ɛsheè) sm. གསལ་རྟོགས་.

གསལ་བཤད་ (sɛ̄ɛshɛɛ̀) explanation, clarification; va.—བྱེད་ to explain, to clarify.

གསལ་བཤད་ཀྱི་ཡི་གེ་ (sɛ̄ɛshɛɛ̀gi yigi) explanatory written guidelines/ directions, instruction notes.

གསལ་བཤད་ཀྱི་དེབ་ (sɛ̄ɛshɛɛ̀gi te̱b) instruction manual.

གསལ་སེང་ངེ་བ་ (sɛ̄ɛ sēŋŋewa) sm. གསལ་ལམ་ལམ་.

གསལ་གསལ་རྗེན་རྗེན་ (sɛ̄ɛsɛɛ je̱njen) 1. clearly, distinctly. 2. clearly coming to light, clearly uncovered/ revealed/ exposed ¶ མི་གསོད་ཀྱི་གྱོད་གཞི་དེའི་སྐོར་དེང་སང་གསལ་གསལ་རྗེན་རྗེན་དུ་ཐོན་ཞག The events of the murder case have become fully revealed these days.

གསལ་གསལ་ཐིང་ཐིང་ (sɛ̄ɛsɛɛ tīŋdiŋ) clearly, brightly.

གསལ་ལྷང་ངེ་ (sɛ̄ɛlhaŋŋe) sm. གསལ་ལམ་ལམ་.

གསལ་ལྷམ་མེ་བ་ (sɛ̄ɛ lhāmmewa) sm. གསལ་ལམ་ལམ་.

གསིག: p. **བསིགས་**; f. **བསིག**; imp. **སིགས་** (sīi) 1. va. to shake, to rattle ¶ ཁྱི་དེས་ཆུ་ནང་ནས་ཐོན་རྗེས་ལུས་པོ་བསིགས་སོང་ The dog, after it came out of the water, shook itself. 2. va.—རྒྱག to heave one's shoulders (to get a load/ pack to settle properly).

གསིག་དེབ་ (sīgdeb) the shaking that occurs when a vehicle comes to an abrupt stop; va.—བྱེད་.

གསིག་གསིག (sīgsii) shaking; va.—བྱེད་.

གསིགས་ (sīi) p. of གསིག.

གསིང་ (sīŋ) sm. གསེང་.

གསིང་ཆུ་ (sīŋju) streams that run through forests/ meadows.

གསིང་མ་ (sīŋmə) meadow, pasture, lawn.

གསིང་མ་མེ་ཏོག (sīŋmə me̱doò) flowers that grow on pasture/ meadows/ lawns.

གསིར་ (sīi) 1. va. to whirl/ swirl/ spin/ rotate ¶ བལ་ལས་འཐག་ལོ་སིར་ནས་སྐུད་འཁལ་བཞིན་འདུག The wool working women are spinning spindles to make thread. 2. va. to rotate. 3. a squeaking sound. 4. direct, straight.

གསིལ་: p. **བསིལ་**; f. **གསིལ་**; imp. **གསིལ་** (sīi) 1. va. to break into pieces, to split ¶ ཇ་རིལ་གསིལ་ནས་ Having split a round ball of tea into pieces. 2. va. to wash (h.) ¶ ཕྱག་བསིལ་བ་རེད་ (He) washed his hands. 3. va. to have one's hair cut (h.) ¶ དབུ་སྐྲ་བསིལ་བ་རེད་ He had a haircut. 4. va. to urinate. 5. va. to ring a bell.

གསིལ་ཁང་ (sīlgaŋ) shung. washroom, toilet.

གསིལ་ཉོ་ཚོང་སྒྲུབ་ (sīiño tsōŋdrub) buying miscellaneous items to sell.

གསིལ་གསིལ་བཟོ་ (sīisii so̱) sm. གསིལ་, 1.

གསུ་སེལ་ (sūbee) leucorrhoea.

གསུག (sūù) money or goods given as a bribes; va.—ཟ་ to take/ accept a bribe.

གསུང་: p. **གསུངས་**; f. **གསུང་**; imp. **གསུངས་** (sūŋ) 1. va. to say, to tell, to speak (h.) ¶ ཁོང་གིས་གསུངས་སོང་ He said it. 2. speech, teachings ¶ སངས་རྒྱས་ཀྱི་གསུང་ The oral teachings of the Buddha.

གསུང་སྐད་ (sūŋgɛɛ̀) h. of སྐད་.

གསུང་སྐད་གྲགས་ (sūŋgɛɛ̀ tra̱à) vi. to hear sb.'s voice ¶ སློབ་ཁང་ནང་ཆན་ལགས་ཀྱི་གསུང་སྐད་གྲགས་ཀྱི་འདུག (I) can hear the teacher's voice in the class.

གསུང་སྐྱོན་ (sūŋgyön) h. of སྐད་རྒྱག.

གསུང་སྐོར་སྐྱོན་ (sūŋgyɔɔ gyōn) h. of ཕོད་སྐོར་རྒྱག.

གསུང་བསྐུལ་ (sūŋgüü) the words said by the དབུ་མཛད་ to start prayers.

གསུང་ཁུངས་ (sūŋguŋ) base or foundation (of sth. said).

གསུང་མཁན་ (sūŋñɛn) h. of ཤོད་མཁན་.

གསུང་མཁས་པོ་ (sūŋ kɛ̄ɛbo) h. of ཁ་མཁས་པོ་.

གསུང་མགྲིན་ (sūŋgyen) 1. eloquent, articulate. 2. words of pleading, imploring ¶ སྐུ་མགྲིན་གསུང་མགྲིན་ ང་ལ་རོགས་གནང་རོགས་གནང་ Please help me. 3. va. to know a language (h.) ¶ ཁོང་གིས་དབྱིན་ཇིའི་གསུང་མགྲིན་གྱི་རེད་ He knows English.

གསུང་གི་ཆུ་རྒྱུན་ (sūŋgi cūgyün) continuous advice/ instruction.

གསུང་གྲོས་ (sūŋdröö) h. of གྲོས་མོལ་.

གསུང་གླིང་ (sūŋleŋ) h. of གདམ་གླིང་.

གསུང་མགུར་ (sūŋgur) h. of མགུར་.

གསུང་བགྲོས་ (sūŋdröö) h. of སྐད་ཆ་.

གསུང་འགག (sūŋgaà) h. of སྐད་འགག.

གསུང་འགྲེལ་ (sūŋdree) h. of འགྲེལ་བ་.

གསུང་རྒྱུན་ (sūŋgyün) h. of ངག་རྒྱུན་.

གསུང་བསྒྱུར་ (sūŋgyur) h. of སྐད་སྒྱུར་.

གསུང་སྒྲ་ (sūŋdra) h. of སྐད་སྒྲ་.

གསུང་སྒྲོག (sūŋdrɔɔ̀) reading out loud; va.—བྱེད་; va.—ཞུ་.

གསུང་སྒྲོས་ (sūŋdröö) sm. གསུང་གྲོས་.

གསུང་ངོ་མ་ལྡོག (sūŋ ŋo̱madɔɔ̀) h. of ངོ་མ་ལྡོག.

གསུང་བཅག་པ་ (sūŋjagba) h. of ཁ་ལ་མ་ཉན་པ་.

གསུང་ཆོས་ (sūŋjöö) religious teachings/ sermon (h.); va.—གནང་ to give religious teachings; va.— ཞུ་ to attend a religious teaching.

གསུང་ཆོས་ར་བ་ (sūŋjöö ra̱wa) a place for religious teachings.

གསུང་མཆིད་ (sūŋjii) h. of སྐད་ཆ་.

གསུང་མཆོག (sūŋjɔɔ̀) advice (h.).

གསུང་སྙན་པོ་ (sūŋ ñēmbo) h. of སྐད་སྙན་པོ་.

གསུང་བཏུས་ (sūŋdüü) quotations, excerpts (usu. a book of excerpts).

གསུང་རྟེན་ (sūŋden) religious text.

གསུང་སྟངས་ (sūŋdaŋ) h. of ཤོད་སྟངས་.

གསུང་བརྟག (sūŋdaà) divination (h.) va.—ཞུ་ to request divination; va.—གནང་ to do divination.

གསུང་ཐར་ (sūŋtar) h. of གནམ་ཐར་.

གསུང་གདངས་ (sūŋdaŋ) h. of སྐད་གདངས་.

གསུང་ནང་མ་ (sūŋ na̱ŋma) secret instructions/ teachings.

གསུང་གནང་ (sūŋnaŋ) h. of སྐད་གཏོང་.

གསུང་པར་ (sūŋbar) h. of སྐད་པར་.

གསུང་འཕྲིན་ (sūŋdrin) h. of ཕྲིན་ཡིག.

གསུང་འཕྲོས་ (sūŋdröö) 1. h. of སྐད་ཆ་. 2. conversations that were interrupted and unfinished.

གསུང་བྱོན་མ་ (sūŋjönma) a statue/ deity that has spoken.

གསུང་འབྱོན་ (sūŋjön) h. of ཁ་གྲགས་.

གསུང་བྲིས་ (sūŋdrii) sm. གསུང་འཕྲིན་.

གསུང་དབྱངས་ (sūŋyaŋ) h. of དབྱངས་.

གསུང་འབུམ་ (sūŋbum) the complete literary works of an author.

གསུང་འབུལ་ (sūŋbüü) h. of སྐད་གཏོང་.

གསུང་སྒོམ་པོ་ (sūŋ bomba) h. of སྐད་སྒོམ་པོ་.

གསུང་མོལ་ (sūŋmöö) h. of བཀའ་མོལ་.

གསུང་ཙམ་གནང་ (sūŋdzam nāŋ) h. of ལབ་ཙམ་བྱེད་.

གསུང་རྩོམ་ (sūŋdzom) writings/ works by a lama or a scholar.

གསུང་རྩོད་ (sūŋdzöö) sm. ཁ་རྩོད་.

གསུང་རྩོམ་གཅེས་བསྡུས་ (sūŋdzom jēèdüü) selected works, anthology.

གསུང་ཚུ་པོ་ (sūŋ tsübo) h. of སྐད་ཚུ་པོ་.

གསུང་རྩུལ་ (sūŋdzüü) h. of ཤོད་རྩུལ་.

གསུང་ཚོགས་ (sūŋdzɔɔ̀) collection of writings/ teachings.

གསུང་འཛེར་ (sūŋdzer) h. of སྐད་འཛེར་.

གསུང་ཟིག་པོ་ (sūŋ dzigbu) h. of སྐད་ཟིག་པོ་.

གསུང་ཞུ་ (sūŋ shu) h. of སྐད་གཏོང་.

གསུང་གཞས་ (sūŋsheɛ̀) h. of གཞས་.

གསུང་བཟང་ (sūŋsaŋ) 1. good voice. 2. prayer chant leader (umdze).

གསུང་བཟོ་དོད་པོ་ (sūŋso tööbo) h. of ཤོད་བཟོ་དོད་པོ་.

གསུང་རབ་ (sūŋrəb) Buddha's teachings.

གསུང་རབ་གླེགས་བམ་ (sūŋrəb lēgbam) religious text of Buddha's teachings.

གསུང་རིན་ཡོད་པ་མ་རེད་ (sūŋrin yöba maareè) a humble answer to sb. who thanks you (equivalent to "it is not worthy of your thanks").

གསུང་ལན་ (sūŋlɛn) h. of ལན་.

གསུང་ལུགས་ (sūŋluù) h. of ཤོད་ལུགས་.

གསུང་ལུང་ (sūŋluŋ) sm. གསུང་བརྟག.

གསུང་ཤོག (sūŋshɔɔ̀) sm. བཀའ་ཤོག.

གསུང་ཤོར་ (sūŋshɔɔ) h. of སྐད་ཤོར་.

གསུང་བཤད་ (sūŋsheɛ̀) h. of གཏམ་བཤད་.

གསུང་བཤད་སྟེགས་ཆ་ (sūŋshɛɛ̀ dinja) platform, podium for a speech.

གསུང་གསང་པོ་ (sūŋ sūŋbo) h. of སྐད་གསང་པོ་.

གསུང་སྲོལ་ (sūŋsöö) h. of ཤོད་སྲོལ་.

གསུང་གསལ་པ་ (sūŋ sēēwa) sb. who talks clearly/ lucidly.

གསུངས་ (sūŋ) p. of གསུང་.

གསུངས་གསུངས་ (sūŋsūŋ) 1. as (he) says ¶ཁོང་གི་གསུངས་གསུངས་རེད་ ལོ་ན་འདི་གར་གངས་ཧ་ཅང་མཐུག་པོ་བབས་སོང་ As he says, there was very heavy snowfall last year. 2. talk ¶ཁོང་ལས་ཁུངས་ནས་དགོང་པ་ཞུ་གི་ཡིན་ཟེར་བ་དེ་གསངས་གསུངས་མ་གཏོགས་བདེན་མདོག་མེད་ His saying that he will resign from the office is only talk, it doesn't seem true.

གསུངས་དོན་ (sūŋdön) h. of ཤོད་དོན་.

གསུད་ (süü) vi. to belch.

གསུབ་ (süb) 1. sm. སུབ་. 2. va. to bite (by a dog).

གསུམ་ (sūm) three.

གསུམ་ཀ་ (sūmga) all three ¶གསུམ་ཀ་ཕྱིན་སོང་ All three went.

གསུམ་སྐས་ (sūmgɛɛ̀) shung. ladders/ steps with three sections (e.g., in the Potala).

གསུམ་སྐོར་ (sūmgɔɔ) 1. going around sth. three times ¶ཐག་པ་འདིའི་རིང་ཐུང་གིས་ཁང་པ་འདི་ལ་གསུམ་སྐོར་འཁོར་གྱི་ཡོད་པ་རེད་ The length of the rope goes around the house three times. 2. a barter exchange of three to one ¶དེང་སང་འབྲས་དང་འབྲུ་གསུམ་སྐོར་བྱས་ནས་བརྗེ་གི་འདུག These days the exchange rate of barley for rice is three (barley for one rice). 3. yield of three times the seed sown ¶འདི་ལོའི་སྟོན་ཐོག་གསུམ་སྐོར་མ་གཏོགས་བྱུང་མ་སོང་ This year we got a yield of only three times the seed sown.

གསུམ་ཁ་ (sūmga) sm. གསུམ་ཀ་.

གསུམ་ག (sūmga) sm. གསུམ་ཁ་.

གསུམ་བརྒྱད་བུད་མེད་དུས་ཆེན་ (sūmgyɛɛ̀ püümeè tüüjen) International Women's Day (March 8th).

གསུམ་སྒྲ་ (sūmdra) sm. བྱེད་སྒྲ་.

གསུམ་སྒྲིམ་ (sūmdrim) three ply.

གསུམ་སྒྲིལ་ (sūmdrii) three of sth. tied or joined together, three ply.

གསུམ་སྒྲོན་མཉེས་དག (sūmdrön ñēèdaà) a Tibetan custom wherein a guest takes a sip of beer after which the cup is filled, and after the third sipping and refilling, the guest has to drink until the cup is empty.

གསུམ་ཅ་ (sūmja) sm. གསུམ་ཀ་.

གསུམ་ལྕོགས་ (sūmjoò) shung. holding three posts simultaneously.

གསུམ་ཆ་ (sūmja) one third ¶གསུམ་ཆ་གཉིས་ Two thirds.

གསུམ་བཅུ་ (sūmjü) thirty.

གསུམ་བཅུ་སོ་གཉིས་ (sūmjü sōñii) thirty two.

གསུམ་བཅུའི་དུས་ཆེན་ (sūmjü tüüjen) March 10th holiday (commemorating the Tibetan uprising against the Chinese in Lhasa in 1959).

གསུམ་བཅུའི་དུས་དྲན་ (sūmjü tüütren) sm. གསུམ་བཅུའི་དུས་ཆེན་.

གསུམ་ཆ་ (sūmja) a third ¶གསུམ་ཆ་གཉིས་ Two thirds.

གསུམ་གཉིས་ (sūmñii) two thirds.

གསུམ་ཐད་ནས་ (sūmtɛɛ̀nɛ) thirdly.

གསུམ་ཐོག (sūmdɔɔ̀) three story (houses, etc.).

གསུམ་ཐོག་བཞི་བརྩེགས་ (sūmdɔɔ shidzeg) piling one on top of the other; va.—རྒྱག.

གསུམ་མཐའ་ (sūmta) the three times table.

གསུམ་དུས་ (sūmtüü) abbr. of གསུམ་བཅུའི་དུས་ཆེན་.

གསུམ་འདུས་ (sūm düü) va. to combine three into one.

གསུམ་མདོ་ཁ་ (sūmdoga) crossroads where three roads meet/ join.

གསུམ་མདོ་མགོ་རུབ་ (sūmdo gorub) three people fighting together.

གསུམ་ལྡབ་ (sūmdəb) three times, triple ¶ད་རེས་ཚོང་གི་ཁེ་བཟང་གསུམ་ལྡབ་བྱུང་བཞག These days they got a business profit of triple (the capital invested).

གསུམ་པ་ (sūmba) the third ¶ཟླ་བ་གསུམ་པ་ The third month (March).

གསུམ་པར་ (sūmbar) thirdly.

གསུམ་པོ་ (sūmbo) three (together) ¶མི་གསུམ་པོ་འདི་ག་པར་ཕྱིན་སོང་ Where did the three of them go?

གསུམ་ཕྲུགས་ (sūmdruù) things that come in threes.

གསུམ་སྦྱར་པང་ལེབ་ (sūmjar bāŋleb) three ply plywood.

གསུམ་འབྲིལ་ཞབས་དག (sūmdrɛɛ shabdaà) sm. གསུམ་སྒྲོན་མཉེས་དག.

གསུམ་སྨིན་འབྲས་ (sūmmīndrɛɛ̀) triple cropping of rice.

གསུམ་སྨིན་འབྲུ་ (sūmmindru) triple cropping of grains.

གསུམ་རྩེན་ (sūmdzen) heaven, god's realm.

གསུམ་བརྩེགས་ (sūmdzaà) sm. གསུམ་བརྩེགས་.

གསུམ་བརྩེགས་ (sūmdzeg) three layers, three stacks.

གསུམ་ཚ་ (sūmdza) great great grandson.

གསུམ་ཚན་ (sūmdzɛn) sm. གསུམ་ཕྲུགས་.

གསུམ་ཚོང་ (sūmdzoŋ) sm. གསུམ་ལྡབ་.

གསུམ་ཟུར་ (sūmsur) sm. གསུམ་ཆ་.

གསུམ་རེ་གསུམ་རེ་ (sūmre sūmre) three by three, in threes ¶དམག་མི་གསུམ་རེ་གསུམ་རེ་བྱས་ནས་ཆུ་བརྒྱལ་བ་རེད་ The soldiers crossed the river in threes.

གསུམ་ཤས་ (sūmsheè) two tenant farmers jointly leasing land and thus dividing the yields three ways with the owner.

གསུམ་གསུམ་ལམ་ལུགས་ (sūmsum ləmluù) the three thirds system—a system of dividing things into three parts.

གསུམ་བསྲེས་ས་ (sūm trēèma) earth that is a mixture of three soils.

གསུར་ (sūr) burning རྩམ་པ་ and other foods to feed the spirit of sb. who has died.
གསུར་ཁོག (sūrgaà) a red clay pot in which གསུར་ is burnt (for the dead).
གསུར་དྲི་ (sūrdri) smell of གསུར་.
གསུར་བདུགས་ (sūrduù) the smell of sth. burning.
གསུར་རྩམ་ (sūrdzam) རྩམ་པ་ used as incense.
གསུས་ (sũũ) stomach, belly ༝གསུས་ཀེད་ Stomach and waist.
གསུས་ཁོག (sũũgɔɔ̀) sm. གསུས་.
གསུས་ཁྱིམ་ (sũũgyim) sm. གསུས་.
གསུས་ཁྲག (sũũdraà) 1. abdominal blood. 2. blood from the womb.
གསུས་ཁྲོད་ (sũũdröö) sm. གསུས་.
གསུས་ཕྱིབས་ (sũũjib) sm. ཀེད་དཀྲིས་.
གསུས་ལྟོ་ (sũũdo) sm. ཁྲོད་ཁོག.
གསུས་པོ་ཆེ་ (sũũboje) 1. a big stomach. 2. one of the arahats.
གསུས་འཕྱང་ (sũũjaŋ) a pot belly.
གསུས་ཏིང་ཅན་ཕྱང་ (sũŋdziŋ jɛ̄ndraŋ) sm. གསུས་འཕྱང་.
གསུས་ཤ་ (sũũsha) tripe.
གསེ་: p. གསེས་; f. གསེ་; imp. གསེས་ (sē) 1. va. to split/ cut/ chop. 2. va. to separate/ divide.
གསེག (sēg) inclined, slanted, sloped ༝ལུས་གསེག A body that slopes to one side.
གསེག་ཀ་ (sēgga) sm. གསགས་ཀ་.
གསེག་ཀ་ལི་ (sēggəli) sm. ཧོ་ཀ་ལི་.
གསེག་སྐོར་ (sēggɔɔ) turning one's body away to the side as a gesture of disappointment, etc; va.—བྱེད་.
གསེག་ཁ་ (sēgga) sm. གསེག་ཀ་.
གསེག་ཁྲོན་ (sēgdrön) an inclined/ slanting well.
གསེག་གྲི་ (sēgdri) chisel.
གསེག་གྲི་ཤུར་ཅན་ (sēgdri shūrjɛn) chisel.
གསེག་རྒྱོ་ (sēg gyo̱) sexual intercourse while lying on one's side; va.—རྒྱག.
གསེག་ངོས་ (sēgŋuoò) inclined plane/ surface.
གསེག་གཙོད་ (sēgjöö) 1. a type of carpenter's chisel. 2. cutting across at an angle; va.— རྒྱག.
གསེག་གཙོད་ཁ་གཉིས་མ་ (sērjöö kāñiìmə) double-edged.
གསེག་གཙོད་ཁ་སྦུབས་ (sēgjöö kəbub) chisel used for creating gaps between engraved letters.
གསེག་གཙོད་ཁ་རིལ་ (sēgjöökərii) a round-headed chisel for carving.
གསེག་གཙོད་ཆེ་སག (sēgjöö cēsaà) chisel for carving large letters.
གསེག་གཙོད་ཕུས་འགུགས་ (sēgjöö bũũguù) chisel for carving small gaps.
གསེག་གཙོད་སེན་གཟུགས་མ་ (sēgjöö sēnsugmə) chisel with head shaped like a fingernail.
གསེག་ཆེན་ (sēgjen) a coppersmith's tool.
གསེག་ཉལ་ (sēg ñɛ̱ɛ̱) va. to lay on a slope/ incline, to recline.
གསེག་སྙེས་ (sēgñeè) leaning/ slanting sideways; va.—རྒྱག.
གསེག་ཐིག (sēgdig) a slanting/ sloped line; va.—རྒྱག.
གསེག་མཐའ་ (sēgda) hypotenuse.
གསེག་དར་ (sēgdar) file, rasp; va.—རྒྱག to file.
གསེག་ནས་ཉལ་ (sēgnɛ ñɛ̱ɛ̱) va. to lay or recline with one's body on a slope/ incline.
གསེག་མ་ (sēgma) gravel; va.—འདིངས་ to lay gravel.
གསེག་ཚད་ (sēgdzɛɛ̀) gradient, degree of incline/ slope.
གསེག་ཟུར་ (sēgsur) angle of inclination.
གསེག་ལ་ཡོ་ (sēgla yō) vi. to lean/ slant towards a slope.
གསེག་ལམ་ (sēglam) a sloped or inclined path/ road.
གསེག་ལོན་ (sēglön) carpenter's tool.
གསེག་ཤ་ཁ་ (sēgshaga) sm. གསེག.
གསེག་སློག (sēglɔɔ̀) putting or laying at an incline or on a slope.
གསིང་ (sīŋ) sm. གསེང་.
གསེང་ (sēŋ) 1. crack, gap. 2. between ༝ལས་ཀའི་གསེང་ལ་ངས་སློབ་སྦྱོང་བྱེད་ཀྱི་ཡོད་ Between work I study.
གསེང་རྟགས་ (sēŋdaà) parenthesis.
གསེང་ཕྲག (sēŋdraà) 1. sm. གསེང་. 2. small hole.
གསེང་བར་ (sēŋbar) sm. གསེང་དབར་, 1.
གསེང་བུག (sēŋbuù) sm. གསེང་བར་, 1.
གསེང་དབར་ (sēŋbar) sm. གསེང་བར་, 1.
གསེང་དབྲག (sēŋdraà) sm. གསེང་དབར་, 1.
གསེང་རྨོས་ (sēŋmöö) plowing between furrows.
གསེང་གཡབ་ (sēŋyəb) porch, verandah.
གསེང་ལམ་ (sēŋlam) a small footpath.
གསེང་ཤོར་ (sēŋ shɔɔ̄) vi. to slip into sth. through a crack/ gap ༝ཚོང་ཁང་ནང་དུ་ཀུན་མ་གསེང་ཤོར་མི་ཡོང་བ་བྱ་དགོས་ We have to do sth. to prevent a thief from breaking in through a crack.
གསེང་གསེང་ (sēŋseŋ) 1. in your spare time ༝ཁྱེད་རང་གསེང་གསེང་ལ་ངའི་ནང་ལ་ཕེབས་རོགས་གནང་ In your spare time come visit me in my house. 2. things that are woven or knitted loosely.
གསེད་: p. བསེད་; f. གསེད་; imp. སེད་ (sēè) 1. va. card, to dress (wool, cotton, etc.). 2. va. to choose, to select. 3. va. to explain.
གསེད་བཀྲོལ་བྱེད་ (sēèdröö cɛ̀ɛ̀) sm. གསེད་འགྲོལ་.
གསེད་འགྲོལ་ (sēndröö) interpreting, explaining; va.—བྱེད་ to interpret, to explain.
གསེབ་ (sēb) 1. in, among, in the midst of ༝ནགས་ཀྱི་གསེབ་ལ་ In the forest. 2. stallion, male donkey, uncastrated camel; va.—གཏོང་ to breed animals.
གསེབ་ལྐུགས་ (sēbguù) humans and animals becoming impotent after a period of sexual inactivity.
གསེབ་དུ་ (sēbdu) sm. གསེབ་, 1.
གསེབ་ན་ (sēbna) sm. གསེབ་, 1.
གསེབ་འཚངས་ (sēbdzaŋ) shung. to avail oneself of loopholes ༝འདི་པའི་མི་སེར་གཞན་གྱིས་གསེབ་འཚངས་བྱས་པ་ཡོད་ན་ Should anyone avail himself of loopholes to take possession of the subjects of this place.
གསེབ་ལམ་ (sēblam) sm. གསེང་ལམ་.
གསེར་ (sēr) gold; va.—འདོན་ to mine gold.
གསེར་ཀོ་ (sērgo) gold painted leather hide.
གསེར་ཀོང་ (sērgoŋ) gold butter lamp.
གསེར་ཀྲམ་ (sērdram) gold coin.
གསེར་དཀར་པོ་ (sēr gārbo) white gold.
གསེར་བཀྲུ་ (sērdru) panning for gold; va.—རྒྱག.
གསེར་ཀོ་ (sēr gō) va. to dig for gold.
གསེར་སྐུ་ (sērgu) icon/ statue made of gold.
གསེར་སྐུད་ (sērgüü) gold thread.
གསེར་སྐྱ་ (sērgya) whitish gold.
གསེར་སྐྱེམས་ (sērgyem) a type of ritual offering made to propitiate the gods.
གསེར་བསྐུས་ (sērgüü) shung. gold plated.
གསེར་ཁ་ (sērga) gold mine.
གསེར་ཁབ་ (sērgəb) gold needle.
གསེར་ཁབ་མེ་བཙའ་ (sērgəb me̱dza) gold needle used for acupuncture.
གསེར་ཁྲི་ (sērdri) golden throne.
གསེར་ཁྲི་མངའ་གསོལ་ (sērdri ŋ̱a̱a̱söö) shung. the enthroning of the Dalai Lama or high lamas; va.—གནང་.
གསེར་མཁན་ (sērñɛn) sm. གསེར་བཟོ་བ་.
གསེར་མཁར་ (sērgar) palace.
གསེར་མགར་ (sērgar) sm. གསེར་བཟོ་བ་.
གསེར་གྱི་བཀའ་ (sērgi gā) king's order.
གསེར་གྱི་སྐུད་འཁྱིལ་ (sērgi gũũdrii) shung. gold rimmed.
གསེར་གྱི་འཁོར་ལོ་ (sērgi kɔɔ̄lo) 1. one of the eight auspicious symbols. 2. shung. a golden wheel symbolizing secular authority, usu. presented to the Dalai Lama at the enthronement ceremony.
གསེར་གྱི་རྒྱ་ཕིབས་ (sērgi gya̱bib) gilded roof of temples.
གསེར་གྱི་རྒྱལ་ཁབ་ཆེན་པོ་ (sērgi gyɛ̱ɛ̱gəb cēmbo) shung. the government ༝གསེར་གྱི་རྒྱལ་ཁབ་ཆེན་པོའི་བཀའ་འབྲེལ་ According to order of the

government.

གསེར་གྱི་སྒྲོམ་བུ་ (sērgi drombu) a small box made of gold.

གསེར་གྱི་འཇའ་ས་ (sērgi jaasa) shung. golden imperial edict.

གསེར་གྱི་ཉི་མ་ (sērgi ñimə) the golden sun.

གསེར་གྱི་སྙིང་པོ་ (sērgi ñīŋbu) pure gold.

གསེར་གྱི་རྟགས་མ་ (sērgi dāŋma) gold medal (in sports).

གསེར་གྱི་ཐམ་ག (sērgi tāmga) shung. golden seal.

གསེར་གྱི་དུས་སྐབས་ (sērgi tüügəb) golden age.

གསེར་གྱི་དུས་ཚོད་ (sērgi tüüdzöö) sm. གསེར་གྱི་དུས་སྐབས་.

གསེར་གྱི་ལྡེ་མིག (sērgi dimii) important key [Lit. golden key].

གསེར་གྱི་བུམ་པ་ (sērgi pumbə) golden vessel/ vase.

གསེར་གྱི་ཞུན་མར་ཁྱེར་ནས་བཙལ་ཀྱང་རྙེད་ཁག་པོ་རེད་ (sērgi shümar kyērnɛ dzɛ̄ɛ kāgbo reè) extremely rare/ good [Lit. even if one carries a golden lamp it is difficult to find].

གསེར་གྱི་ལུང་ (sērgi luŋ) shung. sm. གསེར་གྱི་འཇའ་ས་.

གསེར་གྲི་ (sērdri) scissors/ knife for cutting gold.

གསེར་གླིང་ (sērliŋ) an area with a lot of gold mines/ veins.

གསེར་འགྱུར་ (sērgyur) turning objects into gold.

གསེར་རྒྱན་ (sērgyɛn) 1. gold ornamentation on implements such as bowls; va.—རྒྱག.

གསེར་རྒྱུགས་ (sērgyuù) golden rod/ cane.

གསེར་སྒ་ (sērga) gilded saddle, gold saddle.

གསེར་ངང་ (sērŋaŋ) yellow swan.

གསེར་ངུར་ (sērŋur) golden duck/ goose.

གསེར་དངུལ་ (sērŋüü) gold and silver, precious metals in general.

གསེར་མངལ་ (sērŋɛɛ) shung. sm. ཚངས་པ་.

གསེར་ལྕུག (sērjuù) gold bar, gold ingot.

གསེར་བཅད་ (sērjɛɛ̀) thankas in with the edges of all images are painted with gold.

གསེར་ཆབ་ (sērcəb) liquid gold; va.— གཏོང་; —འབྱུག; —སྒྲོན་ to paint with liquid gold.

གསེར་ཆུ་ (sērju) sm. གསེར་ཆབ་.

གསེར་ཆོས་ (sērcöö) scripture/ text written in gold on black paper.

གསེར་མཆོག (sērjɔɔ̀) 1. the best gold. 2. name of a Buddha.

གསེར་སྦྱང་བརྡུངས་ (sērjaŋ duŋ) things made of pure gold.

གསེར་ཉ་ (sērna) goldfish.

གསེར་སྙན་ (sērñɛn) shung. 1. sm. གསེར་སྙན་རིན་པོ་ཆེ་. 2. a report sent from the Amban to the Emperor; va.—སྒྲོན་འབུལ་. 3. a report sent to a superior official; va.—སྒྲོན་.

གསེར་སྙན་དུ་འབུལ་གནང་ (sērñɛndu büünaŋ) shung. sm. གསེར་སྙན་, 2. and 3.

གསེར་སྙན་རིན་པོ་ཆེ་ (sērñɛn rimboce) shung. 1. when sending a letter to sb. of the same or higher status, an address sth. like Dear — ¶ གསེར་སྙན་ལེན་པོ་ཆེ་ ཆེད་གསོལ་ སང་ཉིན་དགོང་དྲོ་ གསོལ་སྟོན་དུ་ཕེབས་རྒྱུ་ཡོད་པ་ཞུ་ Dear Sir. Please come to dinner tomorrow. 2. way of politely referring to a higher official conveying "to his/ your ears" ¶ གུས་འབངས་འུ་ཐུག་ཐབས་ཟད་ཀྱིས་གསེར་སྙན་རིན་པོ་ཆེ་མི་གཙེར་མཐུ་མེད་བྱུང་སོང་བ་དབྱིངས་འགལ་མི་བཞེས་པ་ཞུ་ Because we subjects are desperate, do not be angry because we had no choice but to bother you.

གསེར་ཏིང་ (sērdiŋ) golden water offering bowls.

གསེར་ཏིལ་ (sērdii) gold implement used in moxabustion.

གསེར་ཊམ་ (sērdram) gold ཊམ་ཀ་ coin.

གསེར་ཏོག (sērdoò) 1. cone shaped gilded rooftop. 2. gold button on top of some official hats.

གསེར་གཏེར་ (sērder) 1. gold mine. 2. gold ore.

གསེར་སྟན་ (sērdɛn) anvil used by goldsmiths.

གསེར་སྟན་འོག་ཚ་ (sērdɛn wɔɔ̀dza) sm. གསེར་སྟན་.

གསེར་སྟིར་ (sērdir) gold tea pot.

གསེར་ཐབ་ (sērdəb) stove for smelting gold.

གསེར་ཐམ་ (sērdam) gold seal.

གསེར་ཐལ་ (sērdɛɛ) sm. གསེར་ཕྱེ་.

གསེར་ཐིགས་ (sērdig) drop of gold.

གསེར་ཐུར་ (sērdur) golden spoon.

གསེར་ཐུལ་ (sērdüü) a type of dress worn by monks in early Tibet.

གསེར་ཐེབ་ (sērdeb) shung. a kind of yellow hat (worn by monk officials and lamas).

གསེར་ཐོག (sērdɔɔ̀) gilded roof.

གསེར་ཐོད་ (sērdöö) gold head ornaments on statues.

གསེར་དམ་ (sērdam) sm. གསེར་ཐམ་.

གསེར་དེབ་ (sērdeb) shung. a book which lists the transactions of gold (in tt.).

གསེར་དོར་སྒམ་ཉར་ (sērdɔɔ gamñar) lack of judgment [Lit. throw away the gold and keep the box].

གསེར་གདུང་ (sērduŋ) a golden stupa for keeping the remains of a lama.

གསེར་མདངས་ (sērdaŋ) golden rays/ lights.

གསེར་མདུང་ (sērduŋ) golden spear.

གསེར་མདོག་ཅན་ (sērdɔjɛn) gold color.

གསེར་འདབ་ (sērdəb) gilded roof.

གསེར་འདུབ་ (sērdub) 1. sm. གསེར་ཐོག. 2. gold leaf.

གསེར་འདོན་ (sērdön) see གསེར་.

གསེར་བརྡུངས་མ་ (sērduŋma) gold that has been purified.

གསེར་རྡོ་ (sērdo) gold ore/ nugget.

གསེར་ལྡན་ (sēndɛn) 1. world. 2. Wednesday. 3. horse. 4. fire.

གསེར་ལྡན་དགའ་མ་ (sēndɛn gama) shung. sm. གསེར་ལྡན་.

གསེར་ལྡེམ་ (sēndem) shung. gold button on the hats of high officials and lamas.

གསེར་སྡོང་ (sērdoŋ) 1. sm. གསེར་གདུང་. 2. sm. དཔག་བསམ་ཤིང་.

གསེར་རྣ་ (sērna) gold earring.

གསེར་དཔོན་ (sērbön) an official in charge of gold.

གསེར་ཕག (sērbaà) gold brick.

གསེར་ཕུད་ (sērbüü) sm. གསེར་སྐྱེམས་.

གསེར་ཕོར་ (sērbɔɔ) golden bowl.

གསེར་ཕྱེ་ (sērce) gold dust.

གསེར་ཕྱེ་ལེབ་ (sēr cēleb) gold bar.

གསེར་འཕྲུ་ (sēndru) sm. གསེར་ཏོག.

གསེར་འཕྲེང་ (sērdreŋ) 1. gold rosary. 2. abbr. of ལེགས་བཤད་.'

གསེར་བུམ་བརྟག་དཔྱད་ (sērbum dāgjɛɛ̀) shung. lottery divination through shaking a golden vessel.

གསེར་བྱ་ (sērja) 1. golden bird. 2. a type of herbal medicine.

གསེར་བྱེ་མཉམ་འདྲེས་ (sērje ñamdreè) mixing good with bad [Lit. mixing golden and sand].

གསེར་བྱེ་ནག་པོ་ (sērje nagbo) datura flower (used in Tibetan medicine).

གསེར་བྱིབས་གཡོགས་ (sērjebyɔ̄ɔ̀) a stupa that is completely gold covered.

གསེར་བྲིས་ (sērdrii) writing/ painting in gold.

གསེར་འབུམ་ (sērbum) religious scriptures that are written in gold.

གསེར་སྦྱང་བརྡུངས་མ་ (sērjaŋ duŋma) sth. made of pure gold.

གསེར་སྦྱང་བཙོ་མ་ (sērjaŋ dzōma) pure gold, purified/ refined gold.

གསེར་སྦྲང་ (sērdraŋ) yellow bee/ wasp.

གསེར་སྦྲམ་ (sērdram) gold bar/ ingot.

གསེར་མིག (sēr mii) poet. fish.

གསེར་སྨར་རྐྱང་ (sēr mārgyaŋ) sm. གསེར་སྦྱང་བཙོ་མ་.

གསེར་སྨར་པོ་ (sēr mārbo) pure gold.

གསེར་སྨྱུག (sērñug) pen.

གསེར་སྨྱུག་བཟོ་གྲྭ་ (sērñug sodra) pen factory.

གསེར་བཙོ་མ་ (sēr dzōma) sm. གསེར་སྦྱང་བཙོ་མ་.

གསེར་བཙོ་སྦྱང་བྱེད་སྟངས་ (sēr dzōjaŋ ceèdaŋ) sm. གསེར་བརྩོའི་ལག་རྩལ་.

གསེར་བཙོའི་ལག་རྩལ་ (sērdzö lagdzɛɛ) the method

of purifying gold.

གསེར་ཚག་རྒྱག (sērdzaà gyaà) va. to do bas-relief style of gold work; va.—རྒྱག.

གསེར་མཛོད་ (sērdzöò) gold storage room/ treasury.

གསེར་ཞལ་ (sērshɛɛ) h. of གདོང་.

གསེར་ཞལ་རྣམ་གཉིས་ (sērshɛɛ nāmñii) husband and wife (h.).

གསེར་ཞལ་ལྷན་འཛོམས་ (sērshɛɛ lhēndzom) h. of གདོང་ཐུག་མཉམ་འཛོམས་.

གསེར་ཞུན་མ་ (sērshünma) 1. molten gold. 2. sm. གསེར་བཙོ་མ་.

གསེར་གཞི་སྦྲོ་བདགས་ (sērshi dro̱daà) a brocade woven with gold thread with the design of a dragon and peacock feathers.

གསེར་གཞི་མ་ (sēr shi̱mə) type of gold colored brocade shirt collar.

གསེར་ཟངས་ (sērsaŋ) 1. gilded; va.—གཏོང་. 2. gold and copper.

གསེར་ཟངས་རྒྱ་ཕིབས་ (sērsaŋ gya̱bib) gilded roof.

གསེར་ཟིལ་ (sērsii) 1. golden glow/ rays. 2. name of a mineral used in Tibetan medicine.

གསེར་བཟང་དྲི་མེད་ (sērsaŋ tri̱meè) 1. pure gold. 2. name of a Buddha.

གསེར་བཟོ་ (sērso) goldsmithing; va.—བྱེད་.

གསེར་བཟོ་བ་ (sērsowa) goldsmith.

གསེར་འོད་ (sērwöò) 1. sm. གསེར་ཟིལ་. 2. abbr. of མདོ་སྡེ་གསེར་འོད་དམ་པ་.

གསེར་འོད་ཆེམ་ཆེམ་ (sērwöò cēmjem) flickering golden light.

གསེར་ཡིག་ (sēryii) shung. a letter sent by the Emperor of China. 2. name of a deceased person that is written on paper burned as an offering; va.—སྲེག to burn such a paper offering. 3. gold writing.

གསེར་ཡིག་པ་ (sēryigbə) shung. 1. secretary to the Emperor of China. 2. messenger of the Emperor of China.

གསེར་ཡིག་པ་ཆེན་པོ་ (sēryigbə cēmbo) a close adjutant of Lhabsang Khan.

གསེར་ཡིག་གསེར་དམ་ (sēryig sērdam) shung. letter sent by the Emperor of China sealed with the Emperor's golden seal.

གསེར་རིལ་སྨྱུག་ཁྲིག (sērrii ñūgdrɔ̀) shung. set consisting of a holder for ink and a pen (used by the officials of the tt. government).

གསེར་རིས་ (sēèrii) picture painted with gold.

གསེར་ལས་པ་ (sēēlɛɛ̀ba) goldsmith.

གསེར་ཤོག (sēēshoò) gold leaf, gold paper.

གསེར་ས་ (sērsa) sm. གསེར་ཁ་.

གསེར་ས་ཕག (sēr sābaà) gold brick, gold bullion.

གསེར་ས་འོག་ལ་ཡོད་ཀྱང་འོད་ནམ་མཁའ་ལ་འཆར་ (sēr sāwɔ̄la yö̱ògyaŋ wö̱ò na̱mgala cār) the fame of one's knowledge/ accomplishments will spread by itself [Lit. even though the gold is under the earth its light shines in the sky].

གསེར་ས་ལེ་སྦྲམ་ (sērsa le̱dram) pure natural gold.

གསེར་སོ་ (sērso) gold tooth.

གསེར་སྲང་ (sērsaŋ) a སྲང་ of gold.

གསེར་སྲབ་ (sērdrəb) gold bridle.

གསེར་སློང་ (sērloŋ) begging for gold.

གསེས་ (sēè) 1. p. of གསེ་. 2. see ནང་གསེས་.

གསེས་འགྲེམས་ (sēè dre̱m) shung. va. to distribute ¶ སེམས་ཅན་རྣམས་མི་སྡེ་དགོན་རྣམས་ལ་གསེས་འགྲེམས་ཐོག The animals were distributed to subjects and to monasteries.

གསོ་: p. གསོས་; f. གསོ་; imp. གསོས་ (sō) 1. vi. to heal ¶ རྨ་ཁ་གསོ་གི་འདུག The wound is healing. 2. va. to feed, to rear, to nourish ¶ ཉ་རིགས་མང་པོ་གསོ་གི་ཡོད་པ་རེད་ (They) rear many species of fish. 3. vi. to regain (consciousness) ¶ སྐར་མ་འགའ་ཤས་སོང་ནས་དྲན་པ་གསོས་པ་རེད་ (He) regained consciousness after several minutes. 4. see ཞིག་གསོ་. 5. abbr. for གསོ་མ་.

གསོ་སྐུད་འཁེལ་ (sōgüù kēē) va. to spin flax/ jute into thread.

གསོ་སྐྱི་ (sōgyeè) gunnysack.

གསོ་སྐྱིད་ལེན་པོ་ (sōgyeè le̱nbo) animals that get fat easily.

གསོ་སྐྱོང་ (sōgyoŋ) 1. rearing, fostering, bringing up, caring for; va.—བྱེད་ ¶ སྲིད་གཞུང་ནས་དྭ་ཕྲུག་ཚང་མ་གསོ་སྐྱོང་བྱེད་ཀྱི་ཡོད་པ་རེད་ The government is caring for all the orphans. 2. training; va.—བྱེད་ to train ¶ བཟོ་ལས་ལག་རྩལ་པ་གསོ་སྐྱོང་བྱེད་ཀྱི་ཡོད་པ་རེད་ (They) are training mechanical technicians.

གསོ་སྐྱོང་མ་ (sōgyoŋma) child care worker, nanny.

གསོ་བསྐྲུན་ (sōdrün) renovating/ reconstructing buildings; va.—བྱེད་.

གསོ་བསྐྲུན་ཨུ་ཡོན་ལྷན་ཁང་ (sōdrün ūyün lhēngaŋ) building committee.

གསོ་མཁན་ (sōgɛn) provider, bread earner. 2. sm. གསོ་བྱེད་.

གསོ་སྒྲིག་ཁང་ (sōdriggaŋ) repair and installation factory/ workshop.

གསོ་བཅོལ་ (sōjöò) temporarily leaving a child with sb. to take care of them; va.—བྱེད་ ¶ གུང་སེང་དུ་འགྲོ་ཤུལ་ཕྲུ་གུ་སྤུན་མཆེད་ལ་གསོ་བཅོལ་བྱས་པ་ཡིན་ While I went on vacation I left my children with a relative (to look after).

གསོ་བཅོལ་ཁང་ (sōjöògaŋ) nursery (for young children).

གསོ་བཅོས་ (sōjöò) medical treatment.

གསོ་ཆག (sōjaà) fodder ¶ གསོ་ཆག་ལས་སྒྱུར་བཟོ་གྲྭ་ A fodder processing plant.

གསོ་ཉར་ (sōñar) rearing, keeping, raising (usu. animals, livestock); va.—བྱེད་.

གསོ་རྟེན་ (sōden) money or things paid for the subsistence/ upkeep of sb. (usu. one's illegitimate child).

གསོ་ཐག་བཟོ་གྲྭ་ (sōdaà so̱dra) flax mill.

གསོ་ཐབས་ (sōtəb) 1. means/ method of rearing, nourishing, fostering. 2. means/ methods of healing.

གསོ་དཔྱད་ (sōjɛɛ̀) science of medicine, medical treatment, medical diagnosis.

གསོ་དཔྱད་པ་ (sōjɛɛ̀ba) physician, doctor.

གསོ་སྤེལ་ (sōbel) breeding, raising; va.—བྱེད་ to breed, to raise (animals).

གསོ་སྤྱད་ (sōjɛɛ̀) medical tools.

གསོ་ཕད་ (sōpɛɛ̀) gunny bag/ sack.

གསོ་བ་པོ་ (sōwabo) sm. གསོ་མཁན་.

གསོ་བ་རིག་པ་ (sōwa ri̱gbə) the science of Tibetan medicine.

གསོ་འབྲས་ (sōdrɛɛ̀) jute seed.

གསོ་སྦྱོང་ (sōjoŋ) 1. gelong's confessional assembly (that meets once a month on the 15th). 2. raising and training (usu. for sports); va.—བྱེད་ ¶ སྲིད་གཞུང་ནས་ལུས་རྩལ་པ་ཁག་ཅིག་གསོ་སྦྱོང་བྱས་པ་རེད་ The government cared for and trained a group of athletes (conveys they housed and fed them while giving them training).

གསོ་སྦྱོང་ཐེབས་རྩ་ (sōjoŋ tēbdza) shung. a trust fund for monk's གསོ་སྦྱོང་.

གསོ་མ་ (sōma) 1. jute, flax. 2. nanny.

གསོ་མ་སྔོན་པོ་ (sōma ŋō̃mbo) a type of greenish jute/ flax.

གསོ་མ་གསེར་པོ་ (sōmo sērbo) a type of yellowish jute/ flax.

གསོ་སྨན་ (sōmɛn) medicine.

གསོ་ཚགས་ (sōdzaà) sm. གསོ་ཉར་.

གསོ་རྩོལ་ (sōdzüù) sm. གསོ་ཐབས་.

གསོ་ར་ (sōra) any enclosed place where animals/ plants are raised ¶ བྱ་དེ་གསོ་ར་ A poultry farm.

གསོ་རས་ (sōrɛɛ̀) cloth made of jute/ flax.

གསོ་རིག (sōrig) abbr. of གསོ་བ་རིག་པ་.

གསོ་རིག་པ་ (sō ri̱gbə) doctor.

གསོ་རིག་ཚན་ཁག (sōrig tsēngaà) medical department.

གསོ་རིག་འཛིན་པ་ (sōrig dzi̱mbə) shung. an imperial physician.

གསོ་རིག་སློབ་གྲྭ་ཆེན་མོ་ (sōrig lōbdra cēmmo)

medical college.

གསོ་རོགས་ (sōroò) sm. གསོ་སྐྱོང་.

གསོ་རླུང་ (sōluŋ) oxygen.

གསོག: p. བསགས་; f. བསག; imp. སོག or གསོགས་ (sɔ̄ɔ̀) va. to accumulate, to store, to save up ¶ ནོར་མང་པོ་བསགས་ཡོད་པ་རེད་ (They) have accumulated much wealth. ¶ ཟླ་རེའི་ཕོགས་ཐོབ་ནས་བརྒྱ་ཟུར་ཁ་ཤས་བསོག་ཐུབ་ཀྱི་ཡོད་པ་རེད་ (They) are able to save a few percent of their monthly salary.

གསོག་ཁྲ་ (sɔ̄gdra) inventory of things accumulated.

གསོག་གྲུན་ (sɔ̄gdrün) sm. གསོག་འཇོག.

གསོག་སྒྲུབ་ (sɔ̄ɔ̀drub) sm. གསོག་འཇོག.

གསོག་དངུལ་ (sɔ̄ɔ̀ŋüü) 1. a deposit (in a bank). 2. money taken from salary and put in a bank for a retirement fund.

གསོག་ཆས་ (sɔ̄gjɛɛ̀) condensing apparatus.

གསོག་འཇོག (sɔ̄njɔɔ̀) 1. saving, accumulating, stockpiling, setting aside as a reserve; va.—བྱེད་.

གསོག་འཇོག་མ་དངུལ་ (sɔ̄njɔɔ̀ ma̲ŋüü) reserve funds.

གསོག་ཉར་ (sɔ̄gñar) sm. གསོག་འཇོག.

གསོག་ཉར་ཁང་ (sɔ̄gñargaŋ) storehouse.

གསོག་ལྡང་ (sɔ̄gdaŋ) dormant/ latent diseases and diseases that manifest themselves.

གསོག་ལྡང་ཞི་གསུམ་ (sɔ̄ɔ̀ da̲ŋ shi̲ sūm) the three: diseases that first remain latent, then manifest themselves, and then get cured.

གསོག་པོ་ (sɔ̄gbo) soft, spongy.

གསོག་འཕྱུག (sɔ̄ŋjaà) sweeping up and accumulating; va.—བྱེད་ ¶ གངས་གསོག་འཕྱུག་བྱས་ནས་ཁ་བའི་གྱང་བརྩིགས་བྱས་པ་རེད་ Sweeping up and accumulating snow, (they) built a wall of snow.

གསོག་སྒྲུབ་ (sɔ̄gdrub) gathering/ collecting together; va.—བྱེད་.

གསོག་འབྲུ་ (sɔ̄ŋdru) reserve grain.

གསོག་བརྫུས་ (sɔ̄gdzüù) false, fake.

གསོག་རུན་ (sɔ̄grün) sm. གསོག་རུམ་.

གསོག་རུམ་ (sɔ̄grum) sm. གསོག་སྒྲུབ་.

གསོགས་ (sɔ̄ɔ̀) 1. sm. བསག. 2. imp. of གསོག.

གསོང་ (sōŋ) 1. abbr. of གསོང་པོ་. 2. imp. of གསང་.

གསོག་ཁང་ (sɔ̄ɔ̀gaŋ) storeroom.

གསོག་ལྡོང་ (sɔ̄gdoŋ) sewer, water drain.

གསོང་པོ་ (sōŋbo) straightforward, honest, sincere.

གསོད་: p. བསད་; f. གསད་; imp. སོད་ (sȫö̀) 1. va. to kill ¶ ཁོས་སྟག་གཅིག་བསད་པ་རེད་ He killed a tiger. 2. va. to extinguish, to put/ turn off ¶ མེ་དེ་ལམ་སེང་བསད་པ་རེད་ (They) extinguished the fire right away. ¶ གློག་གསོད་ཀྱི་ཡིན་ (I) am going to turn off the light.

གསོད་གཅོད་ (sȫö̀jöö̀) 1. killing, murdering; va.—བྱེད་. 2. term used for the number of head of livestock nomad households have to kill (or sell) to meet their household stocking limit.

གསོད་རྟགས་ (sȫö̀daà) 1. mark/ sign that is put on a person who is to be executed. 2. name for an ancient spear-like weapon.

གསོད་བརྡུང་བཀོལ་གསུམ་ (sȫö̀ du̲ŋ gȫȫsum) the three: killing, beating and putting into servitude.

གསོད་བརྡུང་བཅོམ་གསུམ་ (sȫö̀ du̲ŋ jōmsum) the three: killing, beating and robbing.

གསོད་བརྡུང་མནར་གཅོད་ (sȫö̀duŋ nārjöö̀) killing, beating and oppressing/ exploiting.

གསོད་པ་ལག་པ་འཇམ་ལོས་ (sȫö̀ba la̲gba ja̲mlöö̀) doing things gently [Lit. even when killing there is a way of killing gently].

གསོད་དཔུང་གྲ་སྡེབས་ (sȫö̀buŋ tra̲deb) shung. a killing by a mass of people.

གསོད་སྐྱེད་ (sȫö̀jɛɛ̀) a weapon used for killing.

གསོད་ར་ (sȫö̀ra) sm. གསོད་ས་.

གསོད་རེས་གཏོང་ (sȫö̀reè dōŋ) va. to kill one another.

གསོད་གཞོམ་ (sȫö̀shom) planning/ plotting to kill; va.—བྱེད་.

གསོད་ས་ (sȫö̀sa) place of execution, place where sth./ sb. is killed.

གསོད་གསོན་འཕྲོག་སྟེར་ (sȫö̀sön trɔ̄ɔ̀der) having complete power over sb's. life and property.

གསོན་ (sȫn) 1. imp. of གསན་. 2. vi. to survive ¶ འདི་ལོ་ཕྱུགས་ཕྲུག་མགོ་གྲངས་ཁྲི་ཅིག་གསོན་པ་རེད་ This year ten thousand calves survived.

གསོན་སྐྱུར་ (sȫngyur) shung. an ancient law that executes criminals by having them thrown off a cliff or into a river bound up.

གསོན་གྱེས་ཤི་བྲལ་ (sȫngyeè shī̄drɛɛ) parting forever.

གསོན་འགྱུར་ (sȫngyur) surviving.

གསོན་འགྱེད་ (sȫngyee) shung. alms given for the well-being of a person who is alive.

གསོན་ངོགས་ (sȫnŋɔ̲ɔ̀) alive.

གསོན་བསྔོ་ (sȫnŋo) shung. dedication made while a person is alive.

གསོན་ཉམས་ལྡན་པ་ (sȫnñam dɛ̲mba) sm. གསོན་ཉམས་དོད་པོ་.

གསོན་རྗེན་ (sȫnjen) firsthand knowledge, seeing with one's own eyes ¶ ཁོས་རྐུ་མ་བརྐུས་པ་ངས་གསོན་རྗེན་དུ་མཐོང་བྱུང་ I saw him steal with my own eyes.

གསོན་ཉམས་དོད་པོ་ (sȫnñam tö̲ö̀bo) lively, vivacious, vivid, expressive ¶ རྣམ་འགྱུར་གསོན་ཉམས་དོད་པོ་ A lively expression.

གསོན་ཉམས་ལྡན་པ་ (sȫnñam dɛ̲mba) sm. གསོན་ཉམས་དོད་པོ་.

གསོན་སྡོང་ (sȫndoŋ) 1. shung. compensation made to people who prove the accused intended to commit murder (although they are still alive). 2. compensation/ payment for injury.

གསོན་ཐང་ (sȫndaŋ) rate/ amount of གསོན་སྡོང་.

གསོན་ཐབས་ (sȫndəb) means of surviving; va.—བྱེད་ to do things to survive ¶ ཡུལ་དེ་རར་མུ་གེ་བྱུང་སྐབས་མི་མང་པོས་སྤོ་ཚད་བཟས་ནས་རང་ཉིད་གསོན་ཐབས་བྱས་པ་རེད་ When there was a famine in that area many people ate wild plants to survive.

གསོན་དུར་དུ་འཇུག (sȫndurdu ju̲ù) va. to bury/ entomb alive.

གསོན་འདྲེ་ (sȫndre) living people who cause evil like ghosts.

གསོན་འདྲེ་མ་ (sȫndrema) a female གསོན་འདྲེ་.

གསོན་གནས་ (sȫnnɛɛ̀) a survivor.

གསོན་པ་ (sȫmba) live ¶ ཉ་གསོན་པ་ Live fish.

གསོན་པ་ཟ་ (sȫmba sa̲) 1. va. to lie blatantly [Lit. to eat alive]. 2. va. to eat sth. that is still alive.

གསོན་པོ་ (sȫmbo) 1. live, alive ¶ ཉ་གསོན་པོ་ Live fish. 2. firsthand information, true, real ¶ ངས་ཞུས་པའི་སྐད་ཆ་འདི་གསོན་པོ་རང་ཡིན་ What I have said is really true (I have firsthand knowledge).

གསོན་པོར་འཛིན་ (sȫmbor dzi̲n) va. to capture alive.

གསོན་པོར་ལུས་ (sȫmbor lü̲ù) vi. to survive ¶ ས་གཡོས་ཆེན་པོ་དེ་བྱུང་རྗེས་མི་གསོན་པོར་ལུས་པ་ཉུང་ཤས་ལས་མི་འདུག After the earthquake there were only few who survived.

གསོན་དཔེ་ (sȫnbe) a live/ living model.

གསོན་ཕྱགས་ (sȫnbe) skinning sth. while it is alive/ living; va.—བཤུ་ to skin sth. while it is alive.

གསོན་བྲལ་ (sȫndrɛɛ) separating while still alive; va.—བྱེད་.

གསོན་སྦས་ (sȫnbɛɛ̀) sm. གསོན་སྦེད་.

གསོན་སྦྱང་ (sȫnjaŋ) clearing/ washing away one's sins while still alive; va.—བྱེད་.

གསོན་སྦེད་ (sȫnbɛɛ̀) burying alive; va.—བྱེད་; —གཏོང་.

གསོན་ཚད་ (sȫndzɛɛ̀) survival rate ¶ གསོན་ཚད་བརྒྱ་ཆ་བརྒྱད་བཅུ་ཡན་ལོན་རྒྱུ་རེད་ The survival rate will exceed 80%.

གསོན་བཟུང་ (sȫnsuŋ) capturing/ catching alive; va.—བྱེད་.

གསོན་བཟུང་དམག་སྒར་ (sȫnsuŋ māàgar) prisoner of war camp.

གསོན་རེ་ (sȫnre) the hope of surviving death ¶ ཁོ་ཚོ་གསོན་རེ་བྲལ་སོང་ They have no hope of surviving.

གསོན་ལམ་ (sȫnlam) means/ ways of surviving; va.—འཚོལ་ to search for means/ ways to survive.

གསོན་ལུས་ (sōnlüü) abbr. of གསོན་པོར་ལུས་.

གསོན་ཤུགས་ (sōnshuù) vigor, vitality (in growing/ living).

གསོན་གཤིན་ (sōnshin) alive and dead.

གསོན་གསོན་རྗེན་རྗེན་ (sōnsön jenjen) abbr. of གསོན་རྗེན་.

གསོབ་: p. བསབས་; f. གསོབ་; imp. སོབས་ (sōb) 1. va. to repay from gratitude, to repay kindness ¶ རང་གི་ཕ་མའི་བཀའ་དྲིན་གསོབ་ཕྱིར་ནད་གཡོག་གང་ཐུབ་ཞུས་པ་ཡིན་ I repaid the kindness of my parents by helping them as best as I could when they were sick. 2. an effigy. 3. vi. to become soft ¶ དེང་སང་ལུས་རྩལ་མ་བྱས་ཙང་གཟུགས་པོ་གསོབ་བཞག These days, because I don't exercise, I have become soft. 4. va. to supplement, to make up for ¶ དམག་གསར་བསྡུས་ནས་དམག་མི་འདས་པ་གྲོངས་སོང་བའི་གྲངས་ཀ་བསབས་པ་རེད་ (They) supplemented the soldiers that died by recruiting new ones.

གསོབ་རྒྱོང་ (sōbgyoŋ) stuffing the skin of animals; va.—བྱེད་.

གསོབ་པོ་ (sōbbo) sm. སོབ་སོབ་.

གསོབ་ཕྱུར་ (sōbjur) a type of dried cheese that is soft.

གསོབ་འབུ་ (sōmbu) spider beetle.

གསོབ་སྨན་ (sōbmɛn) soft medical pills/ capsules.

གསོབ་ཚིག (sōbdzii) lies.

གསོམ་ (sōm) members of the pine tree family.

གསོམ་ནག (sōmnaà) black pine.

གསོམ་ཤིང་ (sōmshiŋ) pine tree.

གསོར་ (sɔ̄ɔ̄) 1. drill, awl. 2. va. to swing and hit with a sword.

གསོར་: p. and f. བསར་; imp. གསོར་ (sɔ̄ɔ̄) va. to prepare, to make ready ¶ སང་ཉིན་དགོས་པའི་ཅ་ལག་ཚང་མ་བསར་ཡོད་ I have prepared all the things we need for tomorrow.

གསོར་ཁ་ (sɔ̄rga) drill, awl; va.—རྒྱག to drill/ bore holes.

གསོར་ཁྲོན་ (sɔ̄rdrün) a well that has been drilled.

གསོར་མགོ་ (sɔ̄ŋgo) the head of a drill.

གསོར་མགོ་གཙུས་རིལ་ཅན་ (sɔ̄ngo jüüriijɛn) drilling head/ bit.

གསོར་སྒྲོམ་ (sɔ̄rdrom) drilling platform/ tower/ stand.

གསོར་སྟེགས་ (sɔ̄rdeg) drilling platform/ tower/ stand.

གསོར་ཐེམ་ (sɔ̄ndem) scouring rush.

གསོར་འབིགས་ (sɔ̄mbig) a drill (for wells); va.—རྒྱག to drill a well.

གསོར་འབིགས་འཁྲུལ་འཁོར་ (sɔ̄mbig trüügɔɔ) drilling machine.

གསོར་འབིགས་བརྟག་ཞིབ་འཁྲུལ་འཁོར་ (sɔ̄mbig dəgshib trüügɔɔ) surveying machines to determine where to drill.

གསོར་འབིགས་བཟོ་པ་ (sɔ̄mbig soba) drilling worker.

གསོར་འབིགས་ཡོ་བྱད་ (sɔ̄mbig yojɛɛ̀) drilling tools/ equipment.

གསོར་འབིགས་ལས་རིགས་ (sɔ̄mbig lɛ̀ɛrii) drilling profession/ occupation.

གསོར་ལེན་ (sɔ̄rlen) sm. བརྗེ་ལེན་.

གསོར་ཤུབས་ (sɔ̄ɔshub) pipes (used in drilling).

གསོལ་ (sȫȫ) 1. va. to inform, to tell (h.) ¶ རྒྱལ་པོར་ལོ་རྒྱུས་རྣམས་གསོལ་བ་རེད་ (He) informed the king of the history. 2. va. to put on, to dress (h.) ¶ ཁོང་ལ་ན་བཟའ་གསོལ་བ་རེད་ (They) put clothes on him. 3. va. to take, to eat/ drink (h.) ¶ གསོལ་ཇ་གསོལ་གྱི་འདུག (He) is drinking tea. 4. term that makes honorifics, e.g. སྨན་ becomes གསོལ་སྨན་. 5. trance ¶ ཟླ་གསོལ་ The monthly trance.

གསོལ་ཀྲུམ་ (sȫȫdrum) h. of ཤ་.

གསོལ་ཀྲུམ་སྐམ་པོ་ (sȫȫdrum gāmbo) h. of ཤ་སྐམ་པོ་.

གསོལ་དཀྲུམ་ (sȫȫdrum) sm. གསོལ་ཀྲུམ་.

གསོལ་བསྐངས་ (sȫȫgaŋ) shung. the first offering of fried dough to the Dalai Lama during the New Year Ceremony in the Potala.

གསོལ་ཁ་ (sȫȫga) prayer/ rite to a protective deity; va.—གཏོང་.

གསོལ་ཁ་ཁང་ (sȫȫga kāŋ) sm. མགོན་ཁང་.

གསོལ་ཁ་བ་ (sȫȫgawa) person who does གསོལ་ཁ་.

གསོལ་ཁང་ (sȫȫgaŋ) 1. h. of ཐབ་ཚང་. 2. canteen, banquet hall.

གསོལ་ཁང་ཆུང་བ་ (sȫȫgaŋ cūŋwa) snack counter.

གསོལ་སྒྲོད་ (sȫȫdröö) h. of སྒྲོད་ཁོག.

གསོལ་སྒྲོད་བཀྲེས་ (sȫȫdröö drēe) h. of སྒྲོད་ཁོག་ལྟོགས་.

གསོལ་སྒྲོད་བཅོམ་ (sȫȫdröö jōm) sm. གསོལ་སྒྲོད་བཀྲེས་.

གསོལ་མགྲོན་ཁང་ (sȫȫdröngaŋ) hotel ¶ ལྷ་ས་གསོལ་མགྲོན་ཁང་ The Lhasa Hotel.

གསོལ་འགོ་ (sȫngo) shung. the one who goes at the head of the New Year's official horse procession.

གསོལ་སྐྱོ་ (sȫȫgyo) h. of སྐྱོ་.

གསོལ་ངན་ (sȫȫŋɛn) poisonous food.

གསོལ་ཅོག (sȫȫjoò) sm. གསོལ་ལྕོག.

གསོལ་ལྕོག (sȫȫjoò) h. of ལྕོག་ཙེ་.

གསོལ་ཆང་ (sȫȫjaŋ) sm. མཆོད་ཆང་.

གསོལ་ཆས་ (sȫȫjɛɛ̀) h. of ལྟོ་ཆས་.

གསོལ་ཆེན་ (sȫȫjen) shung. abbr. of གསོལ་དཔོན་ཆེན་མོ་.

གསོལ་མཆོད་ (sȫȫjöö) 1. sm. གསོལ་ཁ་. 2. Chinese funeral rite.

གསོལ་ཇ་ (sȫȫja) h. of ཇ་.

གསོལ་ཇ་བཞེས་རྟོག (sȫȫja sheedoò) tea and snacks/ cookies (h.).

གསོལ་ལྡིར་ (sȫȫdir) h. of ཁོག་ལྡིར་.

གསོལ་སྟོན་ (sȫȫdɛn) banquet, feast, reception at which food is served (h.); va.—བཤམས་; —གཏོང་; —འབུལ་ to give a banquet/ feast, to have a reception.

གསོལ་སྟོན་ཁང་ (sȫȫdöngaŋ) banquet hall.

གསོལ་ཐང་ (sȫȫdaŋ) 1. h. of ཇ་ཐང་. 2. arc. གསོལ་ཡོགས་.

གསོལ་ཐབ་ (sȫȫdəb) h. of ཐབ་ཚང་.

གསོལ་ཐབ་པ་ (sȫȫdəbbə) shung. a person who works in the Dalai Lama's kitchen.

གསོལ་དམ་ (sȫȫdam) h. of ཇ་དམ་.

གསོལ་དྭངས་ (sȫȫdaŋ) sm. གསོལ་ཐང་.

གསོལ་དོད་ (sȫȫdöö) h. of ལྟོ་དོད་.

གསོལ་དོན་ (sȫȫdön) a request (h.).

གསོལ་དོན་སྨིན་སྒྲུབ་ (sȫȫdön mīndrub) shung. receiving what one requested.

གསོལ་མདོང་ (sȫȫdoŋ) h. of མདོང་མོ་.

གསོལ་འདེབས་ (sȫȫndeb) 1. prayers asking for sth.; va.—བྱེད་; —སྐྱོར་ to pray for ¶ ལམ་བར་དུ་གེགས་བར་མི་ཡོང་བའི་ཆེད་དུ་ལྷའི་མདུན་དུ་གསོལ་འདེབས་སྐྱོར་བ་རེད་ He prayed to the deity asking that no obstacles arise on the road. 2. va. to request/ appeal; va.—བྱེད་ ¶ ཁོ་ཚོས་བླ་མ་གསོལ་འདེབས་ཞུས་པ་ལྟར་ In accordance with their request to the lama.

གསོལ་འདྲེན་ (sȫȫ drɛn) va. to serve food (h.).

གསོལ་སྡེད་ (sȫȫdeè) h. of སྡེད་ཙེ་.

གསོལ་སྣ་ (sȫȫna) h. of ཟས་སྣ་.

གསོལ་སྣོད་ (sȫȫnöö) h. of ལྟོ་སྣོད་.

གསོལ་དཔོན་ (sȫȫbön) 1. a lama's servant/ attendant. 2. attendant/ steward in charge of food.

གསོལ་དཔོན་ཆེན་མོ་ (sȫȫbön cēmmo) shung. chief attendant of a high lama whose duty is to serve food.

གསོལ་དཔོན་མཁན་པོ་ (sȫȫbön kēmbo) shung. the monk (official) in charge of the preparation and serving of food for the Dalai Lama.

གསོལ་ཕད་ (sȫȫbɛɛ̀) h. of ལྟོ་ཕད་.

གསོལ་ཕོགས་ (sȫȫbɔɔ̀) h. of ཕོགས་.

གསོལ་ཕྱུགས་ཁང་ (sȫȫjuùgaŋ) cow shed/ stables.

གསོལ་འཕྲིན་ (sȫȫdrin) sm. ཕྲིན་བཅོལ་.

གསོལ་འཕྲོ་ (sȫȫdro) 1. leftover food. 2. used clothing.

གསོལ་བ་ (sȫȫwa) 1. h. of ཟློགས་. 2. h. of ལྟོ་ཆས་.

གསོལ་བ་འདེབས་ (sȫȫwa deb) sm. གསོལ་འདེབས་.

གསོལ་བ་འདེབས་རྟེན་ (sööwa debden) things offered to deities and lamas asking them to grant a favor.
གསོལ་བ་ཕུར་ཚུགས་ (sööwa pūrdzuù) praying wholeheartedly for sth.; va.—སུ་འདེབས་.
གསོལ་བ་སྨོན་ལམ་ (sööwa mönlam) sm. གསོལ་འདེབས་.
གསོལ་བ་འཚལ་ (sööwa) va. to eat food.
གསོལ་བ་བཞེས་ (sööwa sheè) h. of ཐུགས་ཟ་; ལྟོ་ཟ་.
གསོལ་བ་གཡོ་ (sööwa yō) h. of ཐུགས་གཡོ་.
གསོལ་འབྲས་དོད་ (söndrɛɛ̀ töö) ceremonial offering of money in place of གྲོ་མ་འབྲས་སིལ་.
གསོལ་མ་ (sööma) a kind of twisted fried pastry.
གསོལ་མར་ (söömar) h. of མར་.
གསོལ་སྨན་ (söömɛn) h. of སྨན་.
གསོལ་རྫམ་ (söödzam) h. of རྫམ་པ་.
གསོལ་སྒྲུལ་ (söö) sm. གསོལ་རས་སྒྲུལ་.
གསོལ་ཚིགས་ (söödzii) h. of ཁ་ལག.
གསོལ་ཚིགས་བཀྱག (söödzii gyāà) h. of ཁ་ལག་འདྲེན་.
གསོལ་ཚིགས་རྒྱས་པ་ (söödzii) dinner, banquet (h.).
གསོལ་ཚིགས་གནང་ (söödzii nāŋ) h. of ཁ་ལག་ཟ་.
གསོལ་ཚིགས་འབུལ་ (söödzii büü) sm. གསོལ་ཚིགས་བཀྱག.
གསོལ་ཚིགས་ཞུ་ (söödzii shu) h. of ཁ་ལག་འདྲེན་.
གསོལ་ཞག (sööshaà) h. of ཞག.
གསོལ་ཞལ་ (sööshɛɛ) h. of ཕོར་པ་.
གསོལ་ཞབས་ (sööshəb) shung. tea servers at government meetings in tt.
གསོལ་ཞིབ་ (sööshib) h. of རྫམ་པ་.
གསོལ་ཞོ་ (sööshо) h. of ཞོ་.
གསོལ་བཞེས་ཕེབས་ (sööshee pēb) shung. tea served at a ceremony (h.).
གསོལ་ཟས་ (söösɛɛ̀) h. of ལྟོ་ཆས་.
གསོལ་གཟིམ་ (söösim) shung. abbr. of གསོལ་དཔོན་མཁན་པོ་ and གཟིམ་དཔོན་མཁན་པོ་.
གསོལ་གཟིམ་ཆོས་གསུམ་ (söösim cöösum) shung. abbr. of གསོལ་དཔོན་མཁན་པོ་, མཆོད་དཔོན་མཁན་པོ་, གཟིམ་དཔོན་མཁན་པོ་ (the heads of the Dalai Lama's household).
གསོལ་འོ་ (söö wo) h. of འོ་མ་.
གསོལ་རས་ (söörɛɛ̀) 1. giving sth. (h.); va.—གནང་ to give, to bestow; va.—ཞུ་ to ask for sth. ¶ཁོ་ལ་ཕྱག་དཔེ་ཞིག་གསོལ་རས་གནང་སོང་ He gave him a book. 2. gift, present, tip; va.—གནང་ to give a gift, to tip ¶ཁོང་ཚོས་གསོལ་རས་ཆེན་པོ་གནང་བ་རེད་ (They) gave big gifts. 3. napkin.
གསོལ་རས་གནང་སྦྱིན་ (söörɛɛ̀ nəŋjin) gift, prize, reward.
གསོལ་རས་སྤམ་མདོ་ (söörɛɛ̀ bāmdo) shung. generous gift.
གསོལ་གསོལ་མཆོད་མཆོད་ (söösöö cööjöö) worshiping (deities).
གསོལ་ལྷག (söölhaà) h. of ཟས་ལྷག.
གསོས་ (söö) p. of གསོ་.
གསོས་སྐྱོར་ (söögyɔɔ) repairing, renovating, restoring; va.—བྱེད་.
གསོས་སྒྲོན་ (söödrön) restoring to good health.
གསོས་ཆུ་ (sööju) water for irrigating fields; va.—གཏོང་.
གསོས་ཐང་ (söödaŋ) rate of reparation/ restitution for injury.
གསོས་ཕྲུག (söödruù) a child one takes in an raises, usually after its paretns die. This is therefore slightly different from a consciously adopted child.
གསོས་བུ་ (sööbu) sm. གསོས་ཕྲུག.
གསོས་མ་ (sööma) medical treatment, cure; va.—འདེབས་ to treat medically.
གསོས་རིལ་རིལ་ (söö riirii) alert, perky (after being ill or limp).
བསག (sāà) f. of གསོག.
བསགས་ (sāà) p. of གསོག.
བསགས་གྲངས་ (sāàdraŋ) amount of sth. stored.
བསགས་དངུལ་ (sāàŋüü) amassed/ stored money.
བསགས་དངོས་ (sāàŋöö) amassed/ stored goods.
བསགས་ཆུ་ (sāàju) water that has been stored/ collected (e.g., in a reservoir); va.—གཏོང་; —འདྲེན་ to irrigate with such water.
བསགས་རྡུལ་ (sāàdüü) subatomic particles.
བསགས་པའི་རྡུལ་ཕྲ་རབ་ (sāgbɛ düü trārəb) sm. བསགས་རྡུལ་.
བསགས་པའི་ལས་ (sāgbɛ lɛɛ̀) accumulated karma.
བསགས་འབོར་ (sāàbɔɔ) amount in reserve, amount collected/ amassed.
བསགས་སྦྱང་ (sāgjaŋ) accumulating good karma and removing bad karma.
བསང་: p. **བསངས་**; f. **བསང་**; imp. **སོངས་** (sāŋ) 1. vi. to clear away, to clear up ¶དུ་བ་དེ་བསངས་སོང་ The smoke cleared away. 2. vi. to come out of or get over (grief, hardship, sorrow) ¶དེང་སང་ཁོང་ཕ་མ་གྲོངས་པའི་སྡུག་བསྔལ་བསངས་བཞག These days he has gotten over the suffering of his parents dying. 3. incense; va.—གཏོང་ to burn incense, to make an offering of incense. 4. va. to cleanse/ purify ¶ཁོང་གིས་ཕྱག་འཚལ་སྐོར་སྐྱོང་བྱས་ནས་སྡིག་པ་བསངས་འདུག He did many religious acts and cleansed his sins.
བསང་ཁུང་ (sāŋguŋ) an incense burner that is cone shaped.
བསང་ཆུ་ (sāŋju) 1. water sprinkled on incense to prevent it from catching fire. 2. water used in religious vases.
བསང་མཆོད་ (sāŋjöö) incense burning ritual.
བསང་གཏོར་ (sāŋdɔɔ) 1. sprinkling water to cool sth. off. 2. blessed/ holy water that is used to cleanse misdeeds. 3. abbr. of བསང་ and གཏོར་མ་.
བསང་རྫམ་ (sāŋdzam) རྫམ་མ་ tossed on incense (during rites).
བསང་གསུར་ (sāŋsur) abbr. of བསང་ and གསུར་.
བསངས་ (sāŋ) 1. p. of བསང་. 2. sm. བསང་, 3.
བསངས་ཁུག (sāŋguù) incense bag.
བསངས་ཁུང་ (sāŋguŋ) incense burner.
བསངས་མཆོད་ (sāŋjöö) sm. བསང་གསོལ་.
བསངས་གཏོང་ (sāŋ dōŋ) va. to burn incense, to make an incense offering.
བསངས་དུད་ (sāŋdüü) smoke from incense.
བསངས་བདུག (sāŋ dug) 1. va. to put incense on hot embers/ coals. 2. putting incense on hot embers/ coals to create the smell of incense; va.— བྱེད་.
བསངས་ཕོར་ (sāŋbɔɔ) bowl used for burning incense.
བསངས་ཤིང་ (sāŋshiŋ) plants/ trees/ bushes used for incense.
བསངས་གསོལ་ (sāŋsöö) religious ceremony that involves burning incense; va.— བྱེད་.
བསད་ (sɛɛ̀) p. of གསོད་.
བསད་སྐྱོན་ (sɛɛ̀gyön) 1. sm. བསད་རྨས་. 2. killing, murdering; va.—གཏོང་.
བསད་མཁན་ (sɛɛ̀ñɛn) 1. killer, murder. 2. butcher.
བསད་སྟོང་གི་ཞལ་ཕྱི་ (sɛɛ̀) shung. compensation made to the family of the person killed by the killer.
བསད་ཆེས་རྡུང་ཆུང་ (sɛɛ̀) a difficult decision [Lit. killing is too harsh and beating is too lenient].
བསད་སྤར་ (sɛɛ̀) on-off switch.
བསད་རྨས་ (sɛɛ̀mɛɛ̀) killed and wounded (in war/ battle), casualties.
བསད་རྨས་གཏོང་ཤུགས་ (sɛɛ̀mɛɛ̀ dōŋshuù) the power to kill and wound/ maim.
བསད་བཟུང་ (sɛɛ̀suŋ) killed and captured ¶མན་ཇུ་དམགས་ཀྱང་བསད་བཟུང་མང་ཙམ་ཐུབ་པ་རེད་ They were able to kill and capture many Manchu soldiers.
བསད་ལན་ (sɛɛ̀lɛn) taking revenge/ retribution; va.—བྱེད་.
བསད་ཤ་ (sɛɛ̀sha) meat of animals that have been slaughtered.
བསབ་ (səb) f. of གསོབ་.
བསབས་ (səb) p. of གསོབ་.
བསམ་: p. **བསམས་**; f. **བསམ་**; imp. **སོམས་** (sām) va. to think ¶ཁོང་གུང་སེང་དུ་འགྲོ་དགོས་བསམ་ནས་དགོང་པ་ཞུས་པ་རེད་ He thought he should go on vacation

so he took leave.

བསམ་གྱིས་མི་ཁྱབ་པ་ (sāmgi migyəbbə) unthinkable, inconceivable, incomprehensible, beyond one's imagination.

བསམ་གྲུབ་ (sə̄mdrub) 1. name of a person. 2. vi. to have one's wish fulfilled.

བསམ་གྲོས་ (sāmdröö̀) opinions/ views (expressed in a discussion) ¶ བསམ་གྲོས་མི་མཐུན་པ་ཁག་གཉིས་བྱུང་ Two groups arose with views that weren't in agreement.

བསམ་གྲོས་གཅིག་མཐུན་ (sāmdröö̀ jīgdün) unity in thinking/ views/ opinions.

བསམ་གྲོས་མཐུན་ (sāmdröö̀ tü̃n) agreement in thoughts/ views/ opinions.

བསམ་གྲོས་ལེགས་བསྡུར་ (sāmdröö̀ legdur) a thorough/ meticulous discussion.

བསམ་རྒྱ་ (sāmgya) sm. བློ་རྒྱ་.

བསམ་རྒྱུ་དྲན་རྒྱུ་མེད་པ་ (sə̄mgyu trengyu meèba) 1. being unconscious/ unable to think or speak (as in a coma) ¶ མི་དེ་མགོ་བརྡབས་ནས་བསམ་རྒྱུ་དྲན་རྒྱུ་མེད་པ་ཆགས་བཞག After that man banged his head he became unconscious. 2. not knowing how to handle sth. or what to do about sth. ¶ དོན་དག་འདི་རྙོག་དྲ་ཚ་ཐག་ཆོད་ནས་ང་བསམ་རྒྱུ་དྲན་རྒྱུ་མེད་པ་ཆགས་སོང་ This issue is too complicated so I don't know what to do about it. 3. sb. who is stupid.

བསམ་ངན་ (sāmŋɛn) evil/ malicious ideas or thoughts; va.—བྱེད་ to do sth. bad/ evil.

བསམ་ངན་ཁོག་བཅུག (sāmŋɛn kɔ̄gjuù) holding on to evil/ bad thoughts; va.—བྱེད་ ¶ ཁོང་བསམ་ངན་ཁོག་བཅུག་བྱས་ནས་ཟམ་པ་ལ་མེ་རྒྱག་རྒྱུའི་གོ་སྐབས་བཙོལ་བ་རེད་ He held evil thoughts and searched for an opportunity to burn down the bridge.

བསམ་ངན་ཁོག་འཇུག (sāmŋɛn kɔ̄gjuù) sm. བསམ་ངན་ཁོག་བཅུག.

བསམ་ངན་ཁོག་བཅངས་ (sāmŋɛn kɔ̄gjaŋ) sm. བསམ་ངན་ཁོག་བཅུག.

བསམ་ངན་ཅན་ (sāmŋɛnjɛn) malicious, evil, bad, spiteful.

བསམ་ངན་གདུག་རྩུབ་ (sāmŋɛn dugdzub) evil, cruel.

བསམ་ངན་སྤྱོད་ངན་ (sāmŋɛn jö̃ö̀ŋɛn) evil in thought and deed.

བསམ་ངན་ཕུགས་བཅུག (sāmŋɛn pūgjuù) harboring evil/ malicious intentions.

བསམ་ངན་ཕུང་སྤྱོར་ (sāmŋɛn pūŋjɔɔ) evil sm. བསམ་ངན་ཕུགས་བཅུག.

བསམ་ངན་སྤྱོར་རྩུབ་ (sāmŋɛn jɔɔdzub) evil thoughts and cruel/ harsh actions.

བསམ་ངན་མ་ཎི་འདྲེན་པ་ལས་ སེམས་བཟང་གླུ་རྒྱང་ལེན་པ་དགའ་ (sāmŋɛn mani trembalɛ sēmsaŋ lūjuŋ lemba ga) it is better to be a kind layman than an evil religious practitioner [Lit. it is better to be a kind person who sings songs than to be an evil person who recites prayers].

བསམ་འཆར་ (sāmjar) 1. opinion, suggestion; va.—འདོན་; —ཤོད་; —གཏོང་ —འབུལ་ ¶ མང་ཚོགས་ཀྱི་བསམ་འཆར་ Public opinion. ¶ ཁོང་ཚོས་ཚོགས་འདུའི་ཐོག་ལས་ཀའི་བྱེད་སྟངས་ལེགས་བཅོས་གཏོང་ཕྱོགས་ཀྱི་བསམ་འཆར་མང་པོ་བཤད་འདུག At the meeting they made many suggestions about improving the way work is done. 2. criticism; va.—འདོན་; —ཤོད་; —གཏོང་ ¶ ངས་ལས་ཀ་ཡག་པོ་བྱེད་མི་འདུག་ཟེར་ཁོས་ང་ལ་བསམ་འཆར་བཏང་བྱུང་ He criticized me saying I am not doing good work.

བསམ་འཆར་སྟོན་སྒམ་ (sāmjar dõngam) suggestion box.

བསམ་འཆར་འབྲི་དེབ་ (sāmjar drideb) suggestion book.

བསམ་ཇུས་ (sāmjüù) strategy, tactic, scheme, plan, idea; va.—འདོན་ to bring forth a strategy/ tactic/ scheme/ plan, to give an idea.

བསམ་ལྗོངས་ (sāmjoŋ) abbr. of བསམ་གྲུབ་ལྗོང་ཁར་.

བསམ་བརྗོད་ (sāmjöö̀) abbr. thought/ thinking and speech.

བསམ་བརྗོད་ལས་འདས་པ་ (sāmjöö̀lɛ dɛɛ̀ba) beyond expectations, beyond imagination.

བསམ་གཏན་ (sāmdɛn) meditation, contemplation; va.—བཞུགས་ to meditate, to contemplate.

བསམ་བཏང་དྲན་སྐྱེས་ (sāmdaŋ trɛngyeè) shung. having new thoughts, changing one's mind ¶ གན་རྒྱ་འདི་བཞག་རྗེས་མ་འོང་པར་བསམ་བཏང་དྲན་སྐྱེད་བྱེད་མི་ཆོག After signing this agreement it is not permitted to change one's mind (about it) in the future.

བསམ་བཏང་དྲན་གསལ་ (sāmdaŋ trɛnsɛɛ) sm. བསམ་བཏང་དྲན་སྐྱེད་.

བསམ་སྣང་ (sāmdoŋ) illusion, illusory thoughts.

བསམ་ཐག (sāmdaà) from the bottom of one's heart.

བསམ་ཐོག་དོན་འཁེལ་ (sāmdɔɔ̀ tõngee) getting what one wishes/ desires, putting into practice what one thinks.

བསམ་མཐུན་ (sāmdün) in agreement, of the same opinion/ thinking.

བསམ་དོན་ (sāmdön) desire, wish, goal, hope; vi.—འགྲུབ་ to fulfill one's desire/ wishes, to achieve one's goal/ hope.

བསམ་དོན་ལྷུན་གྲུབ་ (sāmdön lhūndrub) sm. བསམ་ཐོག་དོན་འཁེལ་.

བསམ་འདས་ (sāmdɛɛ̀) abbr. of བསམ་བརྗོད་ལས་འདས་པ་.

བསམ་འདུན་ (sə̄mdün) hope, wish; va.—འདོན་ to put forth/ express a wish or hope ¶ འཐུས་མི་ཚོས་གཞུང་གིས་ཞིང་ལས་ཡར་རྒྱས་གཏོང་རྒྱུར་འགྲོ་སོང་འཕར་སྣོན་གཏོང་དགོས་པའི་བསམ་འདུན་བཏོན་པ་རེད་ The delegates expressed the wish that the government should increase expenditures to improve agriculture.

བསམ་སྡིང་ (sə̄mdiŋ) name of monastery.

བསམ་ནག་སྦྱོར་རྩུབ་ (sāmnaà jɔɔdzub) sm. བསམ་གནག་སྦྱོར་རྩུབ་.

བསམ་ནག་ཚ་པོ་ (sāmnaà tsābo) sm. བསམ་གནག་ཚ་པོ་.

བསམ་ནོར་ (sāmnɔɔ) thinking/ misunderstanding incorrectly; vi.—ཤོར་ to think/ understand incorrectly.

བསམ་གནག (sāmnaà) 1. va. to tease (usu. girls) ¶ མི་དེས་ང་ལ་བསམ་གནག་བྱས་ནས་ཤ་ཙུས་བརྒྱབ་བྱུང་ That man teased me by pinching my arm. 2. doing malicious/ spiteful things; va.—བྱེད་ ¶ ཁོས་ང་ལ་བསམ་གནག་བྱས་ནས་ངའི་སློབ་དེབ་སྦས་བཞག He was spiteful and hid my textbook.

བསམ་གནག་སྦྱོར་རྩུབ་ (sāmnaà jɔɔdzub) sm. བསམ་ངན་སྦྱོར་རྩུབ་.

བསམ་གནག་ཚ་པོ་ (sāmnaà tsābo) malicious/ vindictive/ mean.

བསམ་མནོ་ (sāmno) sm. བསམ་བློ་.

བསམ་པ་ (sāmba) thoughts, ideas; vi.—འཁོར་ to get an idea/ thought, to have a thought come to mind.

བསམ་པ་དཀར་པོ་ (sāmba gārbo) kind hearted, good-willed, good-intentioned.

བསམ་པ་ཁུག (sāmba kūù) sm. སེམས་ཁུག.

བསམ་པ་འཁོར་ (sāmba kɔ̄ɔ̄) see སེམས་པ་.

བསམ་པ་འགུག (sāmba guù) sm. སེམས་ཁུག.

བསམ་པ་གྲུ་གཅིག (sāmba trujig) with one mind, with single purpose ¶ བོད་མི་ཚང་མ་བསམ་པ་གྲུ་གཅིག་ལྷ་བུའི་བསྟུན་སྒྲིལ་བྱེད་དགོས་ All the Tibetans should unite with a single purpose.

བསམ་པ་གྲུ་ནང་དུ་ཚུད་པ་ (sāmba tru naŋdu tsü̃ùbə) sm. བསམ་པ་གྲུ་གཅིག.

བསམ་པ་རྒྱ་ཆེ་བ་ (sāmba gyajewa) broadminded.

བསམ་པ་ངན་པོ་ (sāmba ŋəmbo) sm. བསམ་ངན་.

བསམ་པ་གཏད་ (sāmba dɛɛ̀) p. of བསལ་པ་གཏོད་.

བསལ་པ་གཏོད་ (sāmba dõò) va. to put one's hope in sb., to be the source of fulfilling one's hopes/ needs/ aspirations ¶ མི་དམངས་ཀྱིས་སྲིད་གཞུང་ལ་བསམ་པ་གཏོད་ཀྱི་ཡོད་པ་རེད་ The people consider the government as the one that fulfills their hopes and needs.

བསམ་པ་རྣམ་དག (sāmba nāmdaà) sincere, genuine (in thought), pure in intention.

བསམ་པ་རྫོགས་ (sāmba dzɔ̀ɔ) vi. to be satisfied/ content/ fulfilled.

བསམ་པ་ཟོལ་མེད་ (sāmba söömeè) sincere/ genuine in thought ¶ ངས་ཁོང་ལ་བསམ་པ་ཟོལ་མེད་ཀྱི་བསམ་འཆར་བཤད་པར་ཁོང་ལངས་སོང་ I gave him a sincere suggestion but he got angry.

བསམ་པ་ལོག (sāmba lɔ̀ɔ) vi. to change one's mind, to have a change of heart/ views ¶ ཁོང་རང་གི་རྒྱལ་ཁབ་ལ་བསམ་པ་ལོག་ནས་གསང་བའི་ཚོགས་པར་འཛུལ་འདུག He changed his view about the government and joined a secret organization.

བསམ་པའི་བཀོད་པ་ (sāmbɛ gö̃öba) imagination, mental vision.

བསམ་པའི་བཀོད་ཤུགས་ (sāmbɛ gö̃öshuù) power of imagination.

བསམ་པའི་འཁོར་ཕྱོགས་ (sāmbɛ kōrjɔ̀ɔ) current/ trend of thinking ¶ ཡུལ་དེའི་མི་མང་ཆེ་བའི་བསམ་པའི་འཁོར་ཕྱོགས་དེ་མ་རྩ་རིང་ལུགས་རེད་འདུག The current trend of thinking of most people in that area is capitalism.

བསམ་པའི་ཁྱད་ (sāmbɛ kyɛ̀ɛ) sm. བསམ་པའི་མཚོན་བྱེད་.

བསམ་པའི་འཁྱེར་ཕྱོགས་ (sāmbɛ kyērjɔ̀ɔ) sm. བསམ་པའི་འཁྱེར་སོ་.

བསམ་པའི་འཁྱེར་སོ་ (sāmbɛ kyērso) attitude, mental outlook.

བསམ་པའི་གོ་མཚོན་ (sāmbɛ kodzön) ideological weapons.

བསམ་པའི་རྒྱགས་ཕྱེ་ (sāmbɛ gyagje) spiritual food, ideological food.

བསམ་པའི་བསྒྱུར་བཅོས་ (sāmbɛ gyurjöö) ideological reform.

བསམ་པའི་ངལ་རྩོལ་ (sāmbɛ ŋɛɛdzöö) mental work.

བསམ་པའི་མངོན་ཕྱོགས་ (sāmbɛ ŋönjɔ̀ɔ) mental inclination.

བསམ་པའི་འཆར་སྒོ་ (sāmbɛ cārgo) suggestion.

བསམ་པའི་འཇིག་རྟེན་ (sāmbɛ jigden) spiritual world.

བསམ་པའི་གཏིང་ (sāmbɛ diŋ) the innermost thoughts, bottom of one's heart.

བསམ་པའི་མདུད་པ་ (sāmbɛ düübə) mental knot.

བསམ་པའི་འདུ་ཤེས་ (sāmbɛ dusheè) ideology.

བསམ་པའི་དོག་ཁྲེས་ (sāmbɛ dogdreè) mental burden.

བསམ་པའི་ནུས་པ་ (sāmbɛ nüübə) mental power/ energy.

བསམ་པའི་རྣམ་པ་ (sāmbɛ nāmba) ideological form.

བསམ་པའི་དཔལ་ཡོན་ (sāmbɛ pɛ̄ɛyön) spiritual civilization.

བསམ་པའི་ཕུགས་ (sāmbɛ pūù) future goal/ aim; va.—བཅོལ་ to hold sth. as a future goal/ aim ¶ ངའི་བུ་ཆེན་པ་འདི་བསམ་པའི་ཕུགས་བཅོལ་ས་ཡིན་ My oldest son is my future hope.

བསམ་པའི་བྱ་བ་ (sāmbɛ cawa) ideological function, mental activity.

བསམ་པའི་མཚོན་བྱེད་ (sāmbɛ tsönjeè) symbol of (one's) thought ¶ ལག་རྟགས་འདི་ཆུང་ཆུང་ཡིན་ཡང་ངའི་བསམ་པའི་མཚོན་བྱེད་ཡིན་ This gift is small but it is a symbol of my thought.

བསམ་པའི་འཚོ་བ་ (sāmbɛ tsōwa) spiritual life.

བསམ་པའི་ཞིབ་ཀྱིས་མིང་བ་ (sāmbɛ shibgi miŋwə) beyond expectations, beyond imagination.

བསམ་པའི་ཡུལ་ལས་འགོངས་པ་ (sāmbɛ yüülɛ goŋba) shung. sm. བསམ་པའི་ཡུལ་ལས་འདས་པ་.

བསམ་པའི་རླབས་རྒྱུན་ (sāmbɛ lābgyün) trend of thought/ thinking.

བསམ་པའི་ལས་ཀ་ (sāmbɛ lɛ̀ɛga) ideological/ intellectual work.

བསམ་ཕུགས་ (sāmpuù) goal, aim, future plan; va.—བཅོལ་ to hold as a goal/ future aim/ hope.

བསམ་ཕོད་ (sām pöö) va. to dare to think ¶ མི་དེ་ལས་ཀ་དེ་འདྲ་བྱེད་རྒྱ་ལྟ་བཞག་བསམ་ཕོད་ཀྱི་མ་རེད་ Let alone doing that, he won't even dare think about it.

བསམ་ཕྱོགས་ (sāmjɔ̀ɔ) way of thinking about sth., inclination, attitude.

བསམ་ཕྱོགས་མཐུན་པ་ (sāmjɔ̀ tũmbə) having harmonious/ agreeable thoughts or opinions.

བསམ་བྱ་ (sāmja) thoughts ¶ ངའི་བསམ་བྱའི་དེབ་ The book I was thinking about.

བསམ་བློ་ (sāmlo) thought, idea; va.—གཏོང་ to think, to think about/ over, to consider; vi.—འཁོར་ to get an idea, to come to mind ¶ བསམ་བློའི་མ་ལག Ideological system. ¶ བསམ་བློ་ཡང་དག་པ་ Correct ideas.

བསམ་བློ་དཀྲུགས་ (sāmlo drūù) va. to disturb/ upset sb.'s thinking.

བསམ་བློ་ཀུན་སྤྱོད་ (sāmlo gũnjöö) moral education.

བསམ་བློ་ཁུག (sāmlo kūù) sm. སེམས་ཁུག.

བསམ་བློ་འཁོར་པོ་ (sāmlo kɔ̄ɔbo) thoughtful (person).

བསམ་བློ་འཁྱེར་སྟངས་ (sāmlo kyērdaŋ) the way of thinking, attitude.

བསམ་བློ་འཁྲུག་པོ་ (sāmlo trūgbu) ideologically active, active in thinking.

བསམ་བློ་འགུག (sāmlo guù) va. to persuade others to one's point of view.

བསམ་བློ་འགྱུར་ (sāmlo gyur) vi. to be or get changed in one's views/ ideas/ thoughts ¶ ཁོང་བོད་ལ་འགྲོ་རྒྱུའི་བསམ་བློ་འགྱུར་བཞག He has changed his mind about going to Tibet.

བསམ་བློ་རྒྱ་ཆེན་པོ་ (sāmlo gya cēmbo) broadminded/ thoughtful person.

བསམ་བློ་སྒྱུར་ (sāmlo gyur) va. to change one's mind ¶ ང་བོད་ལ་འགྲོ་རྒྱུའི་བསམ་བློ་བསྒྱུར་བ་ཡིན་ I changed my mind about going to Tibet.

བསམ་བློ་བསྒྱུར་བཀོད་ (sāmlo gyurgöö) ideological remolding/ brainwashing.

བསམ་བློ་སྔོན་ལ་བཏང་ན་མཁས་པ་དང་འགྱོད་པ་རྗེས་ལ་སྐྱེ་བ་བླུན་པོ་ཡིན་ (sāmlo ŋõnla dāŋna kɛ̄ɛbadaŋ gyööba jeela gyēba lũmbo min) thinking beforehand is a wise man, regretting afterwards is a foolish man.

བསམ་བློ་སྔ་གཏོང་མཁས་པ་ཡིན་ འགྱོད་པ་ཕྱིས་ན་ཕན་པ་ཡིན་ (sāmlo ŋādoŋ kɛ̄ɛbayin gyööba cĩinə pēmba yin) sm. བསམ་བློ་སྔོན་ལ་བཏང་ན་མཁས་པ་དང་འགྱོད་པ་རྗེས་ལ་སྐྱེ་བ་བླུན་པོ་ཡིན་.

བསམ་བློ་བཅོས་བསྒྱུར་ (sāmlo jöögyur) ideological reform.

བསམ་བློ་གཏོང་ས་ (sāmlo dōŋsa) object of thinking ¶ ཕ་མའི་བསམ་བློ་གཏོང་ས་གཙོ་བོ་དེ་ཕྲུ་གུའི་སློབ་སྦྱོང་རེད་ The main object of the parent's thinking was the education of their children.

བསམ་བློ་སྟོང་པ་ (sāmlo dōŋba) idle thoughts, empty thoughts.

བསམ་བློ་ལྡུམ་ལྡུམ་ (sāmlo dumdum) shortsighted (in thinking).

བསམ་བློ་དྲུག་གསུམ་བཅོ་བརྒྱད་གཏོང་ (sāmlo trugsum jobgyɛɛ̀ dōŋ) va. to think very carefully and many times.

བསམ་བློ་ཕྱོགས་ (sāmlo cɔ̄ɔ) vi. to have one's thought shift/ change towards sth. ¶ ཁོང་དམངས་གཙོ་ལམ་ལུགས་ཐོག་བསམ་བློ་ཕྱོགས་བཞག His thoughts have shifted towards democracy.

བསམ་བློ་བ་ (sāmlowa) a thinker, a thoughtful person.

བསམ་བློ་མེད་པ་ (sāmlo meèba) sb. or some action that is not thoughtful.

བསམ་བློ་མོས་ (sāmlo möö) vi. to agree to have the same thoughts ¶ དེ་རིང་གླིང་ཁར་འགྲོ་རྒྱུར་ནང་མི་ཚང་མ་བསམ་བློ་མོས་སོང་ Today all the family members agreed to go for a picnic.

བསམ་བློ་སོས་པོ་ (sāmlo sööbo) fresh/ new ideas not said before ¶ ཚོགས་འདུའི་ཐོག་བསམ་བློ་སོས་པ་ཤོད་དགོས་པ་ལས་སྐད་ཆ་རྙིང་པ་ཤོད་མི་དགོས་ At the meeting one must say new things not old things said before (usu. refers to confessing one's crimes/ mistakes).

བསམ་བློ་གསལ་བཟོ་ (sāmlo sɛ̄ɛso) clearing up people's thinking/ thoughts; va.—བྱེད་.

བསམ་བློའི་འཁོར་དུ་འཛུག (sāmlö kɔ̄ɔdu juù) vi. to make think about sth.

བསམ་བློའི་འཁོར་དུ་ཚུད་ (sāmlö kɔ̄ɔ̄du tsüü) sm. བསམ་བློའི་འཁོར་དུ་འཛུག.

བསམ་བློའི་ཁུར་ (sāmlö kūr) mental burden.

བསམ་བློའི་འཁྱེར་སོ་ (sāmlö kyērso) attitude, mental outlook, ideological style.

བསམ་བློའི་གོ་རྟོགས་ (sāmlö kodɔɔ̀) understanding, comprehension.

བསམ་བློའི་རྒྱབ་རྟེན་ (sāmlö gyabden) mental support.

བསམ་བློའི་ཆུ་ཚད་ (sāmlö cūdzɛɛ̀) ideological level/ standard, level of thinking.

བསམ་བློའི་གཏོང་ཕྱོགས་ (sāmlö dōŋjɔɔ̀) way of thinking.

བསམ་བློའི་ཐོག་གི་གྲ་སྒྲིག (sāmlö tɔ̄ɔ̀gi tradrii) mental preparation.

བསམ་བློའི་ཐོག་གི་གདོང་གཏུག (sāmlö tɔ̄ɔ̀gi doŋduù) confrontation of ideas.

བསམ་བློའི་འཐབ་ཕྱོགས་ (sāmlö tābjɔɔ̀) ideological front.

བསམ་བློའི་འཐབ་རྩོད་ (sāmlö tābdzöö) mental struggle, ideological struggle.

བསམ་བློའི་འདུ་ཤེས་ (sāmlö dusheè) ideology.

བསམ་བློའི་སྤྱོད་ཚུལ་ (sāmlö jöödzüü) sm. བསམ་བློའི་འཁྱེར་སོ་.

བསམ་བློའི་ཕྱོགས་ལྷུང་ (sāmlö cɔ̄ɔ̀lhuŋ) ideological trend.

བསམ་བློའི་མ་ལག (sāmlö malaà) ideological system.

བསམ་བློའི་བརྩེ་དུང་ (sāmlö dzēduŋ) ideological sentiment/ love.

བསམ་བློའི་མཚོན་ཆ་ (sāmlö tsōnja) ideological weapon.

བསམ་བློའི་རང་བཞིན་ (sāmlö raŋshin) ideological character.

བསམ་བློའི་ལམ་ཕྱོགས་ (sāmlö lamjɔɔ̀) ideological line.

བསམ་བློའི་ལས་ཀ་ (sāmlö lɛ̄ɛ̀ga) ideological work; va.—བྱེད་ ¶ ངས་ཁོང་ལ་བསམ་བློའི་ལས་ཀ་བྱས་པའི་རྗེས་ལ་ཁོང་ཡར་རྒྱས་ཞེ་དྲག་ཕྱིན་སོང་ He improved greatly (usu. political views) after I did ideological work with him.

བསམ་སྦྱོར་ (sāmjɔɔ) thought and deed/ acts ¶ བསམ་སྦྱོར་ངན་པ་མ་བྱེད་. Don't think and do bad things.

བསམ་སྦྱོར་གཉིས་ལྡན་ (sāmjɔɔ ñīidɛn) both thinking and acting, both thought and deed.

བསམ་སྦྱོར་གཉིས་ནག (sāmjɔɔ ñīinaà) evil in thought and deed.

བསམ་མེད་ (sāmmeè) thoughtless, stupid.

བསམ་མེད་འདོད་མེད་ (sāmmeè domeè) thoughtless, unaware.

བསམ་མེད་དྲན་མེད་ (sāmmeè trɛnmeè) 1. sm. བསམ་རྒྱུ་དྲན་རྒྱུ་མེད་པ་. 2. insensitive, uncaring.

བསམ་ཚུལ་ (sāmdzüü) opinion, notion, impression; va.—ཕོད་; va.—ཞུ་ to express one's opinion/ idea/ suggestion ¶ བསམ་ཚུལ་འབྲི་དེབ་ Suggestion/ comment book.

བསམ་ཚུལ་འཛོལ་མེད་ (sāmdzüü dzöömeè) correct opinion/ impression/ understanding/ opinion.

བསམ་ཚོད་ (sāmdzöö) approximation, estimation, speculation; va.—བྱེད་ ¶ ངའི་བསམ་ཚུལ་བྱས་ན་བཟོ་གྲྭ་འདིར་བཟོ་པ་ཆིག་སྟོང་ཙམ་ཡོད་པ་འདྲ་ If I estimate, that factory has about 1,000 workers.

བསམ་ཚོད་དཀའ་བ་ (sāmdzöö gāwa) 1. hard to estimate. 2. hard to imagine, unimaginable.

བསམ་འཛིན་ (sāmdzin) anger ¶ ངས་ཁྱེད་རང་ལ་བསམ་འཆར་ཞུས་པ་དེར་བསམ་འཛིན་མ་གནང་རོགས་གནང་ Please don't be angry about my criticizing you.

བསམ་རྫོགས་ (sāmdzɔɔ̀) abbr. of བསམ་པ་རྫོགས་.

བསམ་ཞིབ་ (sōmshib) thinking, considering, looking into carefully or in detail; va.—བྱེད་ ¶ གནས་ཚུལ་དེ་སྐོར་བསམ་ཞིབ་བྱས་ཆོག I will look into that matter in detail.

བསམ་གཞིགས་ (sōmshii) sm. བསམ་ཞིབ་.

བསམ་གཞིགས་ལེགས་བཏང་ (sōmshig legdaŋ) thinking carefully; va.—བྱེད་ ¶ གནད་དོན་འདི་སྐོར་བསམ་གཞིགས་ལེགས་བཏང་བྱ་དགོས་ Regarding this matter, one must think carefully.

བསམ་བཞིན་དུ་ (sāmshindu) consciously, on purpose, intentionally, deliberately ¶ ལས་ཀ་འདི་ངས་བསམ་བཞིན་དུ་བྱས་པ་མིན་ I didn't do that act on purpose.

བསམ་ཡས་ (sāmyɛɛ̀) 1. Samye (the first monastery in Tibet). 2. abbr. of བསམ་ཡུལ་ལས་འདས་པ་.

བསམ་ཡས་མི་འགྱུར་ལྷུན་གྱིས་གྲུབ་པའི་གཙུག་ལག་ཁང་ (sāmyɛɛ̀ mingyur lhūngi drubɛ dzūglagaŋ) shung. sm. བསམ་ཡས་གཙུག་ལག་ཁང་.

བསམ་ཡས་གཙུག་ལག་ཁང་ (sāmyɛɛ̀ dzūglagaŋ) Samye, the first Buddhist monastery in Tibet.

བསམ་ཡུལ་དུ་མི་ཤོང་ (sāmyüüdu mishoŋ) sm. བསམ་ཡུལ་ལས་འདས་པ་.

བསམ་ཡུལ་ལས་འདས་པ་ (sāmyüülɛ dɛɛ̀ba) beyond imagination/ comprehension, inconceivable.

བསམ་ཡོད་ (sāmyöö) thoughtful.

བསམ་ལམ་ (sāmlam) one's train of thought, the direction of one's thinking.

བསམ་ཤེས་ (sāmsheè) 1. giving consideration, being considerate, making an allowance; va.—བྱེད་ ¶ སྲིད་དོན་བཙོན་པར་གཞུང་ནས་བསམ་ཤེས་བྱས་ཏེ་ལྟོ་ཆས་དྲག་པ་སྤྲོད་ཀྱི་ཡོད་པ་རེད་ They are giving consideration to the political prisoners and giving them better food. 2. considerate, thoughtful, understanding ¶ ཁོང་བསམ་ཤེས་ཡོད་པའི་མི་རེད་ He is a considerate man.

བསམ་ཤེས་ཅན་ (sāmsheèjɛn) sm. བསམ་ཤེས་, 2.

བསམ་ཤེས་སྐྱེད་ (sāmsheè ñeè) vi. to become thoughtful (usu. used for young adults) ¶ ཕྲུ་གུ་དེ་ལོ་བཅོ་ལྔ་སླེབས་དུས་གཞི་ནས་བསམ་ཤེས་སྐྱེད་སོང་ When that child reached the age of fifteen, only then did he become thoughtful.

བསམ་ཤེས་མེད་པ་ (sāmsheè meèba) thoughtless, inconsiderate.

བསམ་ཤེས་ཡག་པོ་ (sāmsheè yagbo) thoughtful, considerate, understanding.

བསམ་ཤོག (sāmshoò) a letter in which one's feeling and thoughts are written.

བསམ་བསམ་མེད་པ་ (sāmsam meèba) unexpected.

བསམ་བསེའུ་ (sāmsewu) gonads.

བསམ་བསེའུའི་གསང་ (sāmsewü sāŋ) a point on the gonads where moxabustion is applied.

བསམས་ (sām) p. of སེམས་ and བསམ་.

བསར་ (sār) sm. གྲ་སྒྲིག.

བསལ་ (sɛ̄ɛ̀) 1. p. of སེལ་. 2. division (in math).

བསལ་སྤྱོད་ (sɛ̄ɛ̀jöö) thoughts and actions/ deeds, thinking and doing.

བསལ་ཚགས་ (sɛ̄ɛ̀jaà) strainer (for tea).

བསེ་ལི་སྦྲིད་གོག (sīli bɛ̄ɛ̀gɔɔ) sm. བསེ་ལི་སྦྲད་གོག.

བསེ་ལི་སྦྲད་གོག (sīli bɛ̄ɛ̀gɔɔ) dung beetle.

བསིག (sii) f. of གསིག.

བསིགས་ (sii) p. of གསིག.

བསིང་: p. **བསིངས་**; f. **སིངས་**; imp. **བསིང་** (sīŋ) sm. འཚགས་.

བསིང་སྙུར་ (sīŋgyur) the final brew (addition of water) in ཆང་ (which is considered the most inferior since it is very weak in alcoholic content).

བསིངས་ (sīŋ) p. of བསིང་.

བསིངས་ཁུ་ (sīŋgu) sm. བསིང་སྙུར་.

བསིངས་སྙིགས་ (sīŋñig) residue/ dregs of chang.

བསིངས་བདུང་ (sīŋduŋ) sm. བསིངས་སྙུར་.

བསིངས་པོ་ (sīŋbu) sm. བསིང་སྙུར་.

བསིར་ (sii) va. to shoot/ fire (a gun, arrow).

བསིལ་ (sii) 1. va. to wash (h.) ¶ ཕྱག་བསིལ་གྱི་འདུག (He) is washing his hands. 2. va. to take off (clothes) ¶ མནའ་བཟའ་བསིལ་པ་རེད་ (He) took off his clothes. 3. vi. to get/ feel cold ¶ སྐུ་བསིལ་གྱི་མི་འདུག་གམ་ Aren't you cold? 4. abbr. of བསིལ་བུ་. 5. p. of གསིལ་.

བསིལ་སྐམ་ (siigam) letting sth. dry in the breeze; va.—གཏོང་.

བསིལ་ཁང་ (siigaŋ) summer house/ cottage.

བསིལ་ཁུག (sii güù) vi. to start to be cool/ cold (weather) ¶ དེང་སང་སྟོན་མཇུག་ལ་སླེབས་ཙང་གནམ་

ག་ཤིས་བསིལ་ཁུག་བཞག These days late fall has arrived and the weather has turned cold.

བསིལ་གོས་ (sīigöö̀) thin/ light summer clothes.

བསིལ་གྲིབ་ (sīidrib) shade ¶ བསིལ་གྲིབ་དུ་ངལ་གསོ་རྒྱག་གི་འདུག (He) is resting in the shade.

བསིལ་འགུགས་ (sīinguù) sm. བསིལ་ཁུག.

བསིལ་ངད་ (sīiŋɛɛ̀) coolness, coldness.

བསིལ་ངད་ཅན་ (sīiŋɛɛ̀jɛn) cool, cold.

བསིལ་ཆང་ (sīijaŋ) cold ཆང་.

བསིལ་ཆབ་ (sīijəb) cold/ cool water.

བསིལ་ལྗོངས་ (sīijoŋ) Tibet.

བསིལ་སྡན་ (sīidɛn) bamboo/ straw mat. (used in the summer because it is cool).

བསིལ་དུགས་ (sīidüù) traditional medical treatment that applies cold stones or metal (compresses) on the body.

བསིལ་དྲོད་ (sīidrüü) cool and warm; temperature ¶ བསིལ་དྲོད་བསྟོམས་པོ་ Moderate temperature/ climate.

བསིལ་གདུགས་ (sīiduù) parasol, umbrella (for sun).

བསིལ་ལྡན་ (sīidɛn) 1. cool, cold. 2. poet. moon.

བསིལ་ལྡན་ར་བསྐོར་ (sīidɛn ra̲gɔɔ) Tibet.

བསིལ་ལྡན་ས་ལའི་སྨན་ལྗོངས་ (sīidɛn sālɛ mēnjoŋ) Tibet.

བསིལ་ལྡན་ར་བ་དཀར་པོ་ (sīidɛn ra̲wa gārbo) shung. the land surrounded by snow mountains, Tibet.

བསིལ་པོ་ (sīibu) cool; vi.—ཆགས་ to become cool/ cold; va.—བྱེད་ to make oneself cool ¶ བསིལ་པོ་བྱས་ན་ན་ཚ་ཡོང་རྒྱུའི་ཉེན་ཁ་ཡོད་ If you let yourself get cold, there is a danger you will get sick.

བསིལ་བ་ (sīiwə) cool/ cold; cooler/ colder ¶ དྭངས་ཤིང་བསིལ་བའི་གཙང་པོ་ A clear and cool river.

བསིལ་བ་ཐོབ་ (sīiwa tōb) vi. to achieve liberation/ nirvana.

བསིལ་བབ་ (sīi bə̲b) sm. བསིལ་ཁུག.

བསིལ་བའི་དངོས་པོ་ (sīiwɛ ŋöōbo) things that are inherently cold. 2. nirvana.

བསིལ་བའི་རླུང་ཚོམ་ (sīiwɛ lūŋdzom) cold/ cool air mass.

བསིལ་བུ་ (sīibu) cool, cold.

བསིལ་སྦྱིན་མགོ་སྨན་ (sīijin go̲mɛn) a traditional medicine for headaches and other minor ailments.

བསིལ་མོ་ (sīimu) sm. བསིལ་བ་.

བསིལ་སྨན་ (sīimɛn) traditional medicine for colds/ fever.

བསིལ་ཞིང་མངར་བ་ (sīishiŋ ŋāāwa) sweet and cool/ refreshing.

བསིལ་ཞྭ་ (sīisha) summer hat.

བསིལ་ཟེར་ (sīiser) sm. བསིལ་འོད་.

བསིལ་འོད་ (sīiwöö) a cool light.

བསིལ་གཡབ་ (sīiyəb) a fan; va.—གཡུག་ to fan.

བསིལ་རི་ (sīiri) sm. གངས་རི་.

བསིལ་རིའི་ཁོར་ཡུག (sīirii kɔ̄ɔyuù) shung. sm. བསིལ་ལྡན་ར་བ་དཀར་པོ་.

བསིལ་རླུང་ (sīiluŋ) cool air or breeze.

བསིལ་རླུང་གི་སྒྲིག་ཆས་ (sīiluŋgi drigjɛɛ̀) air-cooling system, air-conditioner.

བསིལ་ལམ་ (sīilam) a cool road, i.e., a tree lined road.

བསིལ་ས་ (sīisə) a cool place.

བསིལ་བསིལ་ (sīisii) cool, cold.

བསུ་: p. **བསུས་**; f. **བསུ་**; imp. **བསུས་** (sū) va. to receive, to welcome ¶ ཁོ་ཚོ་གནམ་ཐང་དུ་བསུས་པ་རེད་ (They) welcomed (them) at the airport. ¶ ཁོས་འགྲུལ་པ་ཚོ་ནང་ལ་བསུས་པ་རེད་ He welcomed the travelers at his house.

བསུ་སྐྱེལ་བྱེད་ (sūgyee ce̲è) va. to welcome and to see off.

བསུ་གོས་ (sūgöö̀) clothes made for the in-marrying bride or bridegroom to "welcome" them.

བསུ་ཆང་ (sūjaŋ) custom of going to receive/ welcome visitors with ཆང་; va.—འདྲེན་.

བསུ་བ་ (sūwə) sm. བསུ་མ་.

བསུ་རྟ་ (sūda) a horse sent to receive sb.

བསུ་བིལ་ (sūbee) sm. གསུ་བིལ་.

བསུ་འབྱོར་ (sūjɔɔ) arriving/ coming to welcome sb. ¶ ང་གནམ་ཐང་སླེབས་སྐབས་ནང་མི་བསུ་འབྱོར་བྱུང་ When I came to the airport, my family came to welcome me.

བསུ་མ་ (sūmə) welcoming/ receiving/ meeting guests; va.—བྱེད་ ¶ ཁོང་གནམ་ཐང་དུ་སྐུ་མགྲོན་བསུ་མ་བྱེད་པར་ཕྱིན་སོང་ He went to receive the guests at the airport.

བསུ་མི་ (sūmi) sb. who goes to receive/ meet/ welcome a visitor or guest ¶ གནམ་ཐང་དུ་བསུ་མི་ཞིག་བཏང་འདུག (They) sent someone to the airport to receive (him).

བསུ་ལེན་ (sūlen) 1. sm. བསུ་མ་. 2. receiving/ taking an in-marrying bride; va.—བྱེད་.

བསུང་ (sūŋ) fragrant, sweet smelling.

བསུང་ཞིམ་ (sūŋshim) sm. བསུང་.

བསུན་ (sūn) sm. སུན་.

བསུན་པོ་ (sūnbu) sm. སུན་པོ་.

བསུབ་ (sūb) f. of སུབ་.

བསུབ་འགྱིག (sūbgyig) rubber eraser.

བསུབས་ (sūb) p. of སུབ་.

བསུམ་ (sūm) f. of སུམ་.

བསུམས་ (sūm) p. of སུམ་.

བསུར་གདོང་ (sūrdoŋ) sm. གསུར་གདོང་.

བསུས་ (sūù) p. of བསུ་.

བསེ་ (sē) sm. བསེ་རུ་.

བསེ་ཀོ་ (sēgo) 1. rhinoceros hide. 2. varnished/ lacquered hide.

བསེ་སྒ་ (sēga) a saddle that is covered with hide.

བསེ་སྒམ་ (sēgam) wooden box covered with hide that has been varnished/ lacquered.

བསེ་ཐེབ་ (sēdeb) shung. a lacquered hat worn by monk officials.

བསེ་ཐེབས་ (sēdeb) shung. sm. བསེ་ཐེབ་.

བསེ་དོང་ (sēdoŋ) lacquered arrow quiver.

བསེ་དྲི་ (sēdri) body odor (foul smelling); vi.—འདྲོ་; —ཁ་ to smell of body odor.

བསེ་པོ་ (sēwo) dung beetle.

བསེ་འབག (sēbaà) mask made of lacquered/ varnished cloth.

བསེ་སྦུར་ (sēbur) dung beetle.

བསེ་མོག (sēmɔɔ̀) syphilis.

བསེ་ཡབ་ (sēyəb) papaya.

བསེ་རུ་ (sēru) 1. rhinoceros. 2. rhinocerous horn.

བསེ་རག (sēraà) a type of ཡི་དྭགས་.

བསེ་རུ་དཀར་པོ་ (sērru gārbo) 1. white rhinoceros. 2. horn of the white rhinoceros.

བསེ་རུ་ནག་པོ་ (sērru na̲gbo) 1. black rhinoceros. 2. horn of the black rhinoceros.

བསེ་རུའི་རྭ་ (sērrü ra̲) rhinoceros horn.

བསེ་ལི་སྦུར་གོག (sēle bu̲gɔɔ̀) sm. བསི་ལི་སྦྲད་གོག.

བསེ་ཤིང་ (sēshiŋ) a tree from which lacquer is produced.

བསེ་ཤིང་དུག (sēshiŋ du̲ù) a harmful substance given off by the བསེ་ཤིང་.

བསེགས་ (sēg) sm. གསེག.

བསེད་ (sēè) p. of གསེད་.

བསེད་བལ་ (sɛ̄ɛ̀pɛɛ) wool that has been carded.

བསེན་ཐོར་ (sēndɔɔ) type of pimple infants get.

བསེན་མོ་ (sēnmo) demoness.

བསེའི་སྒྲོམ་བུ་ (sēē dro̲mbu) a small box covered with lacquered hide.

བསེར་བུ་ (sērbu) poet. wind.

བསེར་མ་ (sērma) sm. བསེར་བུ་.

བསེར་འཚུབ་ (sērdzub) sm. རླུང་འཚུབ་.

བསེལ་ (sēē) va. to protect, to escort.

བསོ་ (sō) sm. གསོ་.

བསོ་སྒྲ་ (sōdra) yelling at deities when doing propitiation rites.

བསོ་བདེ་ (sōde) sm. བསོད་བདེ་.

བསོག (sɔ̄ɔ̀) f. of གསོག.

བསོགས་ (sɔ̄ɔ̀) p. of གསོག.

བསོངས་ (sōŋ) sm. བསང་.

བསོད་སྐམ་ (söögam) abbr. of བསོད་བདེ་སྐམ་པོ་.

བསོད་སྐམ་པ་ (sȫȫgamba) unfortunate/ unlucky person.

བསོད་སྐལ་ (sȫȫgɛɛ) one's karmic share of merit.

བསོད་ཉམས་པ་ (sȫȫñamba) 1. down on one's luck, having one's luck decrease. 2. in poor health, weakly.

བསོད་སྙོམས་ (sȫȫñom) alms; va.—སློང་; —རྒྱག; —བྱེད་; —ཞུ་ to ask for alms (monks); va.—འབུལ་ to give alms to monks.

བསོད་བཏགས་ (sȫȫdaà) an inferior type of ceremonial scarf.

བསོད་བདེ་ (sȫȫde) 1. sm. བསོད་ནམས་. 2. luck.

བསོད་བདེ་སྐམ་ (sȫȫde gām) vi. to have/ get bad luck.

བསོད་བདེ་སྐམ་པོ་ (sȫȫde gāmbo) unlucky.

བསོད་བདེ་ཆེན་པོ་ (sȫȫde cēmbo) lucky, fortunate.

བསོད་ནམས་ (sȫȫnam) 1. good merit; vi.—ཉམས་ to have one's merit decrease/ diminish ¶ བསོད་ནམས་མེད་པའི་མི་ A person without good merit. ¶ ལྷ་ཁང་ནང་ལ་ཐ་མག་འཐེན་ན་བསོད་ནམས་ཉམས་ཀྱི་རེད་ If (one) smokes in the temple (one's) good merit will decrease. 2. a person's name.

བསོད་ནམས་ཀྱི་འབྲས་བུ་ (sȫȫnamgi drɛ̱ɛ̀bu) the fruit of one's good merits.

བསོད་ནམས་ཀྱི་འཇུ་མེད་ (sȫȫnamgi jumeè) (+ neg.) vi. to be unlucky.

བསོད་ནམས་རྒྱ་མཚོ་ (sȫȫnam gya̱dzo) name of the third Dalai Lama.

བསོད་ནམས་ཅན་ (sȫȫnamjɛn) a person with accumulated good merit.

བསོད་ནམས་དཔལ་འཛོམས་ (sȫȫnam bɛ̄ndzom) coriander.

བསོད་ནམས་ཆུང་ཆུང་ (sȫȫnam cūŋjuŋ) unfortunate, unlucky.

བསོད་ནམས་ཆེན་པོ་ (sȫȫnam cēmbo) sm. བསོད་བདེ་ཆེན་པོ་.

བསོད་ནམས་མེད་པའི་གཏུན་ཁུང་ལ་ ཚིལ་ལུ་བརྡུངས་ཀྱང་ཞག་མི་འགོས་ (sȫȫnam me̱èbɛ dūŋgyoŋla tsīīlu du̱ŋgyaŋ sha̱à mi̱gȫȫ) without good merit one can never be rich/ fortunate [Lit. even though one smashes fat into a meritless mortar it will not become shiny with greese].

བསོད་ནམས་དམན་པ་ (sȫȫnam mɛ̄mba) sm. བསོད་ནམས་ཆུང་ཆུང་.

བསོད་པ་ (sȫȫba) especially good ¶ འབྲས་དཀོན་པའི་ལུང་པར་འབྲས་དེ་ཟས་བསོད་པར་བརྩི་གི་ཡོད་པ་རེད་ (It) is considered especially good to eat rice in areas where rice is scarce.

བསོད་ཞན་པོ་ (sȫȫ shɛ̱mbo) 1. demerits, negative merit. 2. bad tasting.

བསོད་ཟད་ (sȫȫ sɛ̱ɛ̀) vi. to exhaust one's accumulated good merits.

བསོས་ (sȫȫ) p. of གསོ་.

བསྭ་སྲ་ (sādra) sm. བསོ་སྲ་.

བསྲ་བརྟན་ (drāden) sm. སྲ་བརྟན་.

བསྲང་ (sāŋ) f. of སྲོང་.

བསྲང་པོ་ (sāŋbo) sm. སྲང་པོ་.

བསྲངས་ (sāŋ) p. of སྲོང་.

བསྲན་ (drɛ̄n) p. of སྲན་.

བསྲན་མ་བསྲན་ (drɛ̄nma drɛ̄n) va. to tolerate.

བསྲན་གཟུགས་ (drɛ̄nsug) tolerance, patience.

བསྲབ་ (drə̄b) f. of སྲབ་.

བསྲབས་ (drə̄b) p. of སྲབ་.

བསྲལ་ (drɛ̄ɛ) arc. va. to concentrate (e.g., on work, etc.).

བསྲལ་ཆེ་བ་ (drɛ̄ɛcewa) diligent.

བསྲི་ (drī) f. of སྲི་.

བསྲི་ཚགས་ (sīdzaà) thrifty, economizing; va.—བྱེད་ to economize, to be thrifty ¶ འགྲོ་སོང་གཏོང་དུས་བསྲི་ཚགས་བྱེད་དགོས་ One must economize when expending expenditures.

བསྲི་ཚགས་གྲོན་ཆུང་ (sīdzaà drö̱njuŋ) being thrifty, economizing.

བསྲིང་ (sīŋ) f. of སྲིང་.

བསྲིང་སྡུད་ (sīŋ dǖn) expansion and contraction, elasticity.

བསྲིངས་ (sīŋ) p. of སྲིང་.

བསྲིངས་འབྱོར་ (sīŋ jɔ̱ɔ̱) sending and getting/ receiving.

བསྲིངས་མིག (sīŋmiì) farsighted.

བསྲིས་ (sīì) p. of སྲི་.

བསྲུང་ (sūŋ) f. of སྲུང་.

བསྲུང་བྱ་ (sūŋja) regulation, rules, codes, conventions.

བསྲུངས་ (sūŋ) p. of སྲུང་.

བསྲན་མ་འཁྱོལ་ (sɛ̄nma kyȫȫ) unbearable, intolerable.

བསྲུན་པ་ (sǖn) sm. སྲུན་པ་.

བསྲུན་པོ་ (sǖnbu) sm. སྲུན་པ་.

བསྲུན་མོ་ (sǖnmo) sm. བསྲུན་པ་.

བསྲུབ་ (sūb) f. of སྲུབ་.

བསྲུབས་ (sūb) p. of སྲུབ་.

བསྲུབས་མ་ (sūbmə) churned butter tea.

བསྲུལ་ (sǖǖ) p. and f. of སྲུལ་.

བསྲེ་ (drē) f. of སྲེ་.

བསྲེ་བོ་ (drēwo) 1. multicolored. 2. maroon.

བསྲེག (sēè) f. of སྲེག.

བསྲེག་བྱ་ (sēgja) fuel, firewood.

བསྲེག་བླུགས་ (sēgluù) sm. སྦྱིན་བསྲེག.

བསྲེག་སྦྱོར་ (sēgjɔɔ) cremation.

བསྲེག་རྫས་ (sēgdzɛɛ̀) 1. things that are burned in a སྦྱིན་བསྲེག rite. 2. fuel, gasoline, petrol.

བསྲེགས་ (sēè) p. of སྲེག.

བསྲེགས་ཁང་ (sēggaŋ) crematory.

བསྲེགས་བཅད་བརྡར་ (sēgjɛɛ̀ da̱r) sm. བསྲེགས་བཅད་བརྡར་གསུམ་.

བསྲེགས་བཅད་བརྡར་གསུམ་ (sēgjɛɛ̀ da̱rsum) looking into a matter carefully or in great detail; va.—བྱེད་ ¶ གྱོད་དོན་འདིའི་སྐོར་ཁྲིམས་ཁང་ནས་བསྲེགས་བཅད་བརྡར་གསུམ་བྱས་ནས་ཐག་བཅད་འདུག Concerning this case, the court investigated it carefully and issued a decision. [Lit. the three: burn, cut and sharpen].

བསྲེགས་ཐམ་ (drēgdam) brand, branding iron; va.—རྒྱག.

བསྲེགས་ཚ་ (sēgdza) welding; va.—རྒྱག.

བསྲེགས་རྫས་ (sēgdzɛɛ̀) sm. བསྲེག་རྫས་.

བསྲེགས་བརླག (sēglaà) demolishing by burning down; va.—གཏོང་ to destroy, to demolish, to burn down.

བསྲེགས་གསོད་འཕྲོག་གསུམ་ (sēg sȫȫ trɔ̄ɔ̀sum) the three: burning, killing and looting.

བསྲེགས་གསོད་བཅོམ་འཕྲོག (sēg sȫȫ jōm trɔ̄ɔ̀) sm. བསྲེགས་གསོད་འཕྲོག་གསུམ་.

བསྲེལ་ (drēē) f. and p. སྲེལ་.

བསྲེས་ (drēè) p. of སྲེ་.

བསྲེས་དཀྲུགས་ (drēèdruù) mixed up, out of order; va.—བྱེད་.

བསྲེས་འགྱིག (drēègyig) vulcanized rubber.

བསྲེས་ལྕགས་ (drēèjaà) alloyed steel.

བསྲེས་ལྷད་ (drēèlhɛɛ̀) adulterating (mixing something inferior with the original); va.—གཏོང་.

བསྲེས་བསྲེས་གཏོང་ (drēèdreè dōŋ) va. to mix together.

བསྲོ་ (drō) f. of སྲོ་.

བསྲོ་ཁང་ (drōgaŋ) sm. སྲོ་ཁང་.

བསྲོ་སྡེགས་ (drōdeg) drying rack.

བསྲོ་སྤྱད་ (drōjɛɛ̀) utensils used in a བསྲོ་ཁང་.

བསྲོས་ (drȫȫ) p. of སྲོ་.

བསྲོས་མ་ (drȫȫma) a type of fried pastry.

བསླ་ (lā) f. of སླ་.

བསླང་ (lāŋ) f. of སློང་.

བསླངས་གཟུགས་ (lāŋsuù) cube.

བསླངས་ (lāŋ) p. of སློང་.

བསླད་ (lɛ̄ɛ̀) p. and f. of སློད་.

བསླད་སྐྱོན་ (lɛ̄ɛ̀gyön) corrupted, spoiled; va.—བྱེད་; —གཏོང་; —རྒྱག to corrupt; —ཐེབས་ to get corrupted ¶ ཁོས་འགག་སྒོའི་ལས་བྱེད་པ་ཛན་པ་མང་པོ་སྤྲད་དེ་བསླད་སྐྱོན་བཏང་ནས་ལྐོག་ཚོང་བརྒྱབ་པ་རེད་ He corrupted the customs official with many gifts and smuggled in goods.

བསླན་ (lɛ̄n) p. and f. of སློན་.

བསླབ་ (lāb) f. of སློབ་.

བསླབ་སྐྱོན་ཡོད་རིགས་ (lābgyön yö̱ö̱rii) shung. monks who have lost their celibacy ¶ གྲྭ་སར་བསླབ་སྐྱོན་ཡོད་རིགས་རང་མཚང་ངོས་བླངས་ཀྱིས་སྒྲིག་འཛིན་ཞུ་དགོས་ Monks who have lost their celibacy must confess and withdraw from the monastic order.

བསླབ་ཁྲིམས་ (lābdrim) shung. monk's vows.

བསླབ་གྲྭ་ (lābdra) school.

བསླབ་རྒན་ (lābgɛn) abbr. of བསླབ་པ་རྒན་པ་.

བསླབ་གཅུན་ (lābjün) disciplining; va.—བྱེད་.

བསླབ་གཉེར་ (lābñer) sm. སློབ་གཉེར་

བསླབ་སྟོན་ (lābdön) sm. སློབ་སྟོན་.

བསླབ་དོན་ (lābdön) the subject that one is teaching and studying.

བསླབ་སྡོམ་ (lābdom) vows taken by monks and nuns.

བསླབ་གནས་ (lābnɛɛ̀) degree, diploma.

བསླབ་པ་ (lābba) vows.

བསླབ་པ་རྒན་པ་ (lābba gɛ̱mba) seniority ¶ ལས་བྱེད་པ་བསླབ་པ་རྒན་པ་རྣམས་ལ་གླ་ཕོགས་མཐོ་པོ་སྤྲད་འདུག The cadres with seniority were given high salary.

བསླབ་པ་རྒན་གཞོན་ (lābba gɛ̱nshön) seniority ¶ ལས་བྱེད་པ་བསླབ་པ་རྒན་གཞོན་ལ་གཞིགས་པའི་གླ་ཕོགས་སྤྲོད་ཀྱི་ཡོད་པ་རེད་ The officials are given salary on the basis of their seniority.

བསླབ་པ་མཐོ་པོ་ (lābba tōbo) sm. བསླབ་པ་རྒན་པ་.

བསླབ་པ་དོན་གཉེར་ (lābba tö̱nñer) seeking knowledge; va.—བྱེད་ to seek knowledge, to pursue one's studies.

བསླབ་པ་འབུལ་ (lābba pü̱ü̱) va. to give up/ return one's vows (for monks and nuns).

བསླབ་པ་གཞོན་པ་ (lābba sho̱mba) those without seniority.

བསླབ་པ་སློབ་གཉེར་ (lābba lōbñer) study and training.

བསླབ་ཕྲུག (lābdruù) student.

བསླབ་བྱ་ (lābja) advice, instruction; va.—རྒྱག; —བྱེད་ to give advice, to instruct; vi.—ཐོབ་ to receive advice; va.—ལེན་ to draw a lesson ¶ ཕ་མས་ཕྲུ་གུར་སློབ་སྦྱོང་ཡག་པོ་བྱེད་དགོས་པའི་བསླབ་བྱ་བརྒྱབ་པ་རེད་ The parents advised their children they should study well. ¶ དེ་སྔའི་ཕམ་ཉེས་ནས་བསླབ་བྱ་བླངས་ནས་རྗེས་སུ་གཟབ་གཟབ་བྱེད་དགོས་ You should learn from the past defeat and in the future be careful.

བསླབ་གཙང་ (lābdzaŋ) shung. pure vows (vows that have been kept).

བསླབ་ཚིག (lābdzii̇) sm. བསླབ་བྱ་.

བསླབ་ཚིགས་ (lābdzii̇) the stages in the vows of monks.

བསླབ་གཞི་ (lābshi) 1. teaching materials. 2. teaching plan.

བསླབ་ཡར་ (lābyaa) sm. བསླབ་བྱ་.

བསླབ་ཡར་བརྒྱ་ལས་སྣ་སུན་གཅིག་དགའ་ (lābyaa gyalɛ nāsünjig ga̱) meeting with a single rebuff is worth more than a hundred pieces of advice.

བསླབ་རིགས་ (lābrii̇) sm. བསླབ་བྱ་.

བསླབ་པ་ཤེས་ཅན་ (lābba shēėjɛn) sm. ཤེས་རབ་ཅན་.

བསླབས་ (lāb) p. of སློབ་.

བསླས་ (lɛɛ̀) p. of སླ་.

བསླས་མ་ (lɛɛ̀ma) things that are knitted.

བསླུ་ (lū) f. of སླུ་.

བསླུ་ཁྲིད་ (lūdrii̇) sm. སླུ་འཁྲིད་.

བསླུ་ཉོ་ (lūño) deceiving/ tricking and buying; va.—བྱེད་.

བསླུ་ཐབས་ (lūdəb) method/ plan for tricking.

བསླུ་རྡོ་ (lūdo) sm. སླུ་རྡོ་.

བསླུ་འདྲིད་ (lūdrii̇) sm. སླུ་འཁྲིད་.

བསླུ་མིད་ (lūmeė) sm. སླུ་མིད་.

བསླུ་ཚིག (lūdzii̇) false/ lying/ deceitful words.

བསླུ་ཟས་ (lūsɛɛ̀) bait (to trick sb.).

བསླུ་ཡོན་ (lūyün) sm. སླུ་ཡོན་.

བསླུགས་ (lūù) va. to tear down sth.

བསླུས་ (lṻù) p. of སླུ་.

བསླུས་ཚོང་ (lö̈ödzoŋ) deceiving/ tricking and selling; va.—བྱེད་ ¶ ལོ་ཆུང་བུ་མོ་བསླུས་ཚོང་བྱས་སོང་ (They) deceived the young girls and sold them.

བསླུས་གསོད་ (lṻüsö̈ö) killing by trickery, luring and then killing.

བསློག (lɔ̄ɔ̀) f. of སློག.

བསློགས་ (lɔ̄ɔ̀) p. of སློག.

ཧ

ཧ་ (hā) the letter ཧ་ (used in alphabetical numbering).

ཧ་གོ་ (hā ko) vi. to know, to understand ¶ལམ་ག་འདྲ་ཞིག་ཏུ་འགྲོ་དགོས་རྒྱུ་ཧ་གོ་བ་རེད་ (He) knew what road to take.

ཧ་གོ་དེ་གོ་མེད་པ་ (hāgo tego meèba) unknowingly ¶ཧ་གོ་དེ་གོ་མེད་པར་ནོར་འཁྲུལ་ཤོར་བཞག I unknowingly made a mistake.

ཧ་གོ་དོན་རྟོགས་ (hāgo tõndoò) knowing/ understanding sth. exactly or clearly. ¶ཁྱེད་རང་ག་འདྲ་ཡིན་མིན་ཧ་གོ་དོན་རྟོགས་རེད་ Everyone knows clearly what kind of person you are.

ཧ་གོ་ལ་མ་གོ་ (hāgola mago) not understanding things too clearly, unsure, uncertain ¶མིའི་དྲི་བ་ལ་ཧ་གོ་ལ་མ་གོ་ལ་ལན་རྒྱག་རྒྱུ་མེད་ You shouldn't answer questions you don't understand clearly.

ཧ་གོད་ (hāgöò) laughing loudly; va.—དགོད་; —བྱེད་.

ཧ་རྒྱག (hā gyaà) va. to breath on sth. to fog it (e.g., glasses).

ཧ་རྒྱུགས་ལེན་ (hāgyuù len) va. to test sb's breath for drinking or smoking.

ཧ་བྲ་ (hādra) sound of laughter.

ཧ་ཅང་ (hājaŋ) very ¶ཁང་པ་འདི་ཧ་ཅང་ཆེན་པོ་རེད་ This house is very big.

ཧ་ཅང་མང་ན་ཧམ་པ་འགྱུར་ (hājaŋ maŋna hāmba gyur) if one does sth. too much it becomes bad.

ཧ་ཅང་བཙུན་མོ་ (hājaŋ dzũnmo) an evil queen in the Tibetan opera Drowasangmo.

ཧ་ཆ་ (hāja) jeering, mocking, ridiculing; va.—རྒྱག.

ཧ་གཉིད་སད་ (hāñiì sɛ̀ɛ) 1. vi. to come to one's senses, to come to know the situation ¶དེང་སང་ཞིང་པ་ཚང་མ་ཧ་གཉིད་སད་ནས་དམངས་གཙོ་དོན་གཉེར་བྱེད་ཀྱི་ཡོད་པ་རེད་ These days all the peasants have come to their senses and are striving for democracy. 2. sm. བསམ་ཤེས་སྐྱེད་.

ཧ་བདབ་ (hā dəb) sm. ཧ་རྒྱག.

ཧ་མཐོ་ན་ (hā tōna) at most ¶ང་རེས་ང་ནོར་འཁྲུལ་ཤོར་བ་དེས་ཧ་མཐོ་ན་ངའི་ལས་ཀ་ཤོར་གྱི་རེད་ At most my mistakes will cause me to lose my job.

ཧ་དང་ཕུགས་ཤེས་ (hādaŋ pūg shēè) va. to know the origin of sth. in detail.

ཧ་ནེ་ཧོན་ནེ་ (hāne hõnne) sm. འཐམ་མེ་འཐོམ་མེ་.

ཧ་ནེ་ (hāne) Hanoi.

ཧ་ནོས་ (hānöò) sm. ཧ་ནེ་.

ཧ་པ་ (hāba) 1. sb. who tricks/ deceives. 2. person who does business without capital. 3. sb. with heavy debts.

ཧ་པ་བུ་ལོན་ལེན་ཤོར་དང་ སྡིག་ཆེན་དམྱལ་བར་འགྲོ་ཤོར་ (hāba pulön lenshɔɔdaŋ digjen ñɛ̃ɛ̃war droshɔɔ) sb. who doesn't worry about future risks/ consequences [Lit. the heavy debtor casually taking more loans, the great sinner casually goes to hell].

ཧ་ཕེ་ཧོ་ཕེ་ (hābe hōbe) sm. ཧ་བེ་ཧོ་བེ་.

ཧ་ཕྲུག (hādruù) a small aluminum pot.

ཧ་བེ་ཧོ་བེ་ (hābe hōbe) hurriedly, quickly, hastily, in a rush, carelessly ¶ཧ་བེ་ཧོ་པེ་ལངས་ནས་ཕྱིན་པ་རེད་ (He) got up hurriedly and went.

ཧ་སྦྲིད་ (hədriì) sneezing; vi.—རྒྱག.

ཧ་མི་ས་གཤོང་ (hāmi sāshoŋ) the Hami Basin.

ཧ་འཛོང་ (hādzoŋ) buying on; va.—རྒྱག.

ཧ་ཝ་ན་ (hāwana) Havana.

ཧ་ཤུ་ཧུ་འཁྱུགས་ (hāshu hūgyaà) 1. a person who cannot bear (cold, heat, pain, etc.). 2. inconsistently, haphazardly; va.—བྱེད་ ¶ལས་ཀ་ཉིན་མ་གཅིག་ནང་བཞིན་རྒྱུན་བསྲིངས་དགོས་པ་ལས་ཧ་ཤུ་ཧུ་འཁྱུགས་བྱ་རྒྱུ་མེད་ One should not work inconsistently each day.

ཧ་ཡང་ (hāyaŋ) 1. aluminum. 2. aluminum pot.

ཧ་ཡང་དངུལ་སྒོར་ (hāyaŋ ŋũũgɔɔ) aluminum coin.

ཧ་ཡང་ལེབ་མོ་ (hāyaŋ lebmo) aluminum plank.

ཧ་ཡང་སྲབ་མོ་ (hāyaŋ drābmo) aluminum foil.

ཧ་ཡང་ཧ་ (hāyaŋha) counterfeit money.

ཧ་ཡོ་ (həyo) a sigh.

ཧ་རི་ཙན་དན་ (həri dzɛ̃ndɛn) white sandalwood.

ཧ་རི་ཧུ་རི་ (həri hūri) doing things hurriedly, not doing things carefully/ diligently, doing carelessly; va.—བྱེད་ ¶ཁོས་ལས་ཀ་ཧ་རི་ཧུ་རི་བྱས་ཙང་ཡག་པོ་མ་བྱུང་བ་རེད་ Because he worked hurriedly the outcome was not good.

ཧ་རི་ཧུ་རི་ཚ་པོ་ (həri hūri tsābo) sb. who does things hurriedly/ carelessly.

ཧ་རུབ་འབད་རུབ་ (həru bɛ̀ɛru) sm. ཧ་རུབ་སྦར་རུབ་.

ཧ་རུབ་སྦར་རུབ་ (həru baru) doing things diligently/ quickly/ energetically/ efficiently, working together with full effort; va.—བྱེད་ ¶ཚང་མས་ཧ་རུབ་སྦར་རུབ་བྱས་ན་ལས་ཀ་མགྱོགས་པོ་ཚར་གྱི་རེད་ If everyone works together energetically, the work will be completed quickly.

ཧ་རེ་བ་ (hārewa) staring at sth; va.—བལྟ་ to stare.

ཧ་རེ་ལོང་བ་ (hāre loŋwa) a blind person whose eyes seems normal.

ཧ་རེ་ཧུ་རེ་ (hāre hūre) sm. ཧ་རི་ཧུ་རི་.

ཧ་ལྷངས་ (hālaŋ) breath/ breathing causing sth. to fog up; va.—རྒྱག to breathe on sth. to fog it up; vi.—ཤོག to get fogged up with breath.

ཧ་ལ་གནས་ (hālanɛ̀ɛ) Ganesh (the Hindu god).

ཧ་ལ་ཤོར་ (hāla shɔ̄ɔ) vi. to lose money when sb. gives items to another to sell and that person never repays them.

ཧ་ལཱ་ཧ་ལ་ (hālahala) one of the five emanations of Avaloketisvara.

ཧ་ལམ་ (hālam) more or less, approximately, roughly, almost ¶འདི་གཉིས་ཧ་ལམ་གཅིག་པ་རེད་ These two are more or less the same.

ཧ་ལམ་འདྲ་བ་ (hālam drawa) almost the same.

ཧ་ལས་ (hā lɛ̀ɛ) vi. to be amazed, to be surprised, to be shocked/ astonished ¶ཁོ་བྲོས་བྱོལ་དུ་ཕྱིན་པ་དེ་ང་ཧ་ལས་བྱུང་ His fleeing amazed me. ¶ཧ་ལས་རྒྱུ་ག་རེ་ཡོད་པ་རེད་ What is there to be amazed about?

ཧ་ལས་རྒྱུ་ཅི་ཡོད་ (hā lɛ̀ɛgyu jĩyöò) what is there to be amazed about?

ཧ་ལས་པོ་ (hā lɛ̀ɛbo) surprising, amazing, astonishing ¶མཁས་པ་དེའི་རྩོམ་ཡིག་དེ་ཧ་ལས་པོ་གཞི་མི་འདུག That expert's article is not so amazing (i.e., good).

ཧ་ལས་ལས་ (hā lɛ̀ɛlɛ̀ɛ) exceedingly astonished/ surprised; va.—བྱེད་ ¶གསར་འགྱུར་དེ་གོ་མ་ཐག་མི་ཚང་མ་ཧ་ལས་ལས་བྱས་སོང་ After hearing the news, they all were exceedingly astonished.

ཧ་ལས་ཧོན་འཐོར་ (hālɛ̀ɛ hõndɔr) surprised, shocked ¶ས་ཡོམ་ཆེན་པོ་བརྒྱབ་པའི་གནས་ཚུལ་ཐོས་སྐབས་ཚང་མ་ཧ་ལས་ཧོན་འཐོར་སོང་ When (they) heard the news of the earthquake everyone was shocked.

ཧ་ལི་ (hāle) ch. li (Chinese distance measure equal to half a kilometer).

ཧ་ལི་ཧོ་ལི་ (hāle hōle) sm. ཧ་རི་ཧུ་རི་.

ཧ་ལེན་ (hā len) 1. va. to borrow money when one has no means for repaying it. 2. va. to buy sth. on credit with the idea of selling it and repaying the loan ¶དངུལ་མ་ལྷང་ཙང་ཚོང་ཟོག་ཁག་ཅིག་ཧ་ལྷངས་པ་ཡིན་ Because I was short of cash, I took the goods for sale on credit.

ཧ་ལོ་ (hālo) a plant of the genus althea (used in Tibetan medicine).

ཧ་ལོ་དཀར་པོའི་མེ་ཏོག (hālo gārbö medoò) white high mallow (used in Tibetan medicine).

ཧ་ལོ་དཀར་དམར་ (hālo gārmar) a plant of the genus althea (used in Tibetan medicine).

ཧ་ལོ་མེ་ཏོག (hālo medoò) flower of althaea rosea (used in Tibetan medicine).

ཧ་ལོ་དམར་པོ་ (hālo mārbo) red flower of althea rosea (used in Tibetan medicine).

ཧ་ལོག (hā lɔ̀ɔ) 1. vi. to be insolvent/ bankrupt ། མ་རྩ་བརྡབས་ནས་ཧ་ལོག་པ་རེད་ Having lost his capital, he became bankrupt. 2. vi. to have sth. not work out well ། ཁོས་བཟོ་གྲྭའི་འགོ་ཁྲིད་དུ་རྒྱུའི་ཐབས་ཤེས་མང་པོ་བྱས་ཀྱང་མཐའ་མ་ཧ་ལོག་པ་རེད་ He did lots of things to become the head of the factory but in the end it didn't work out.

ཧ་ཤང་ (hāshaŋ) ch. monk.

ཧ་ཤིག (hāshiì) ch. talcum.

ཧ་སག (hāsaà) Kazakh.

ཧ་སོང་གཏོང་ (hāsoŋ dōŋ) 1. exaggerating; va.—གཏོང་; —ཤོད་ ། མི་དེས་ཁོ་པའི་ལོ་རྒྱུས་ཤོད་དུས་ཧ་སོང་ཆེན་པོ་ཤོད་ཀྱི་འདུག He exaggerates when talking about his history. 2. discrepancy/ difference in an accounting or in talk ། ལོ་འཁོར་གྱི་ཡོང་སོང་རྩིས་ཁྲར་ཧ་སོང་ཆེན་པོ་འདུག There was a large discrepancy in the year end accounting between income and expenditures.

ཧ་སོང་ཆེན་པོ་ (hāsoŋ cēmbo) sm. ཧ་སོང་ཚ་པོ་.

ཧ་སོང་ཚ་པོ་ (hāsoŋ tsābo) sb. who exaggerates a lot.

ཧ་ཧ་ (hāha) sound of laughter.

ཧ་ཧ་ཧེ་ཧེ་ (hāha hēhe) Ha! ha! he! he! (sound of laughter).

ཧ་ཧར་གོད་པ་ (hāhar gö̱öba) va. to laugh loudly.

ཧག་སྒྲ་ (hāgdra) sound made to clear one's throat; va.—རྒྱག; —སྒྲོག.

ཧང་ (hāŋ) 1. vi. to be shattered (emotionally/ mentally). 2. sm. དབུགས་ཧལ་.

ཧང་ཀྲའོ་ (hāŋdrao) Hangzhou.

ཧང་ག་རི་ (hāŋgari) Hungary.

ཧང་གོག (hāŋgɔ̀ɔ) boots, shoes.

ཧང་འགྲོས་ (hāŋdröö) walking pompously; va.—བྱེད་.

ཧང་རྒྱ་ (hāŋgya) putting up an ostentatious/ grandiose front when one really does not have the income to afford it; va.—བྱེད་.

ཧང་རྒྱ་ཚ་པོ་ (hāŋgya tsābo) sb. who is ཧང་རྒྱ་.

ཧང་རྒྱག (hāŋgyaà) sm. ཧོལ་རྒྱག.

ཧང་རྒྱག་ཚ་པོ་ (hāŋgyaà tsābo) 1. sm. ཧོལ་རྒྱག་ཚ་པོ་. 2. sb. who exaggerates a lot.

ཧང་དི་ (hāŋdi) shung. ch. Emperor of China ། ཆེ་རིང་གནམ་གྱི་ཤེ་མོང་གི་དཔལ་ཡོངས་ཀྱི་བདག་པོ་ཧང་དིའི་བཀའ་ (by) the order of His Majesty the Emperor, who reigns by the mandate of heaven.

ཧང་གདམ་ (hāŋdam) exaggeration in talk; va.—ཤོད་ ། མི་དེས་ལོ་རྒྱུས་ཤོད་སྐབས་ཧང་གདམ་ཤོད་ཀྱི་འདུག That person is exaggerating when telling his life story.

ཧང་བུག (hāŋbuù) 1. gaps, holes ། ལྕགས་རི་ལ་ཧང་བུག་མང་པོ་འདུག There are many holes in the fence. 2. error, mistake ། ངས་བྱས་པའི་ལས་ཀ་འདིར་ཧང་བུག་ཡོད་མེད་གཟིགས་རོགས་གནང་ Please check if there are any errors in my work.

ཧང་བུབ་ (hāŋbub) sm. ཧང་བུག.

ཧང་ཚང་ (hāndzaŋ) sm. ཧང་བུག, 2.

ཧང་ཚིག (hāŋdziì) talking without thinking; va.—ཤོད་.

ཧང་ཚེར་ནག་པོ་ (hāŋdzer nagbo) black mica.

ཧང་ཟོམ་ (hāŋsom) 1. sm. ཧ་སོང་. 2. error in calculating/ accounting.

ཧང་གཡེང་ (hāŋyeŋ) sm. ཧོལ་རྒྱུགས་.

ཧང་རལ་ (hāŋrɛɛ) rashness, impulsiveness.

ཧང་རལ་ཚ་པོ་ (hāŋrɛɛ tsābo) sb. who is extremely rash/ impulsive.

ཧང་ལུ་ (hāŋlu) ch. a state of stupor.

ཧང་ཤེད་ (hāŋsheè) sm. ཧང་རལ་.

ཧང་སང་ (hāŋsaŋ) sm. ཧ་ལས་.

ཧང་སང་སང་ (hāŋ sāŋsaŋ) sm. ཧ་ལས་ལས་.

ཧང་ཧང་ (hāŋhaŋ) emotionally shattered, feeling sad and empty.

ཧད་ (hɛ̄ɛ̀) 1. a town in Bhutan. 2. suddenly. 3. ch. slipper. 4. vi. to be stupified, stunned, astonished.

ཧད་ཀྱིས་ (hɛ̄ɛ̀gi) sm. ཧད་དེ་ཁ་ལ་.

ཧད་ཐང་མེ་ཏོག (hɛ̄ɛ̀daŋ me̱doò) ch.tib. flowering crabapple tree.

ཧད་དུ་འཇུག (hɛ̄ɛ̀du ju̱ù) va. to cause sb. to be shocked/ astonished/ stunned.

ཧད་དེ་ (hɛ̄ɛ̀de) sm. ཧད་དེ་ཁ་ལ་.

ཧད་དེ་ཁ་ལ་ (hɛ̄ɛ̀de kāla) suddenly ། དེ་རིང་ངའི་གྲོགས་པོ་ཧད་དེ་ཁ་ལ་སླེབས་བྱུང་ Today my friend suddenly arrived.

ཧད་པོར་ (hɛ̄ɛ̀bor) sm. ཧད་དེ་ཁ་ལ་.

ཧད་ཤོར་ཤོར་ (hɛ̄ɛ̀ shɔ̄ɔshɔɔ) surprised, shocked.

ཧད་སད་རྒྱག (hɛ̄ɛ̀sɛɛ̀ gya̱à) vi. to suddenly wake up because of a bad dream.

ཧད་ཧད་ (hɛ̄ɛ̀hɛɛ̀) ha, ha (the sound of laughing).

ཧན་ (hān) 1. mong. khan. 2. ch. Han (Chinese).

ཧན་རྒྱལ་རབས་ (hān gyɛ̱ɛrəb) Han Dynasty.

ཧན་པའོ་ (hēmbao) Hamburg.

ཧན་མི་རིགས་ (he̱nrii) Han people/ race/ nationality.

ཧན་ནེ་ཧོན་ནེ་ (hēnne hõnne) sm. ཧ་ནེ་ཧོན་ནེ་.

ཧན་ཧྲུའུ་གྲངས་ཀ་ (hēnhru dra̱ŋga) a function (in math).

ཧབ་ (hāb) 1. suddenly, unexpectedly. 2. eng. half. 3. short pants.

ཧབ་དགོད་ (hābgöö) jeering/ mocking and laughing at the same time.

ཧབ་རྒྱུག (hābgyuù) going suddenly; va.—བྱེད་ to go suddenly.

ཧབ་སྒྲ་ (hābdra) sound made when one gulps down one's food.

ཧབ་ཆ་ (hābja) sm. ཧ་ཆ་.

ཧབ་ཆི་ (hābji) sneezing; vi.—རྒྱག; —ཤོར་.

ཧབ་ཐོབ་ (hābdob) grabbing/ scrambling/ rushing (for sth.); va.—རྒྱག ། གསེར་མཐོང་པ་ད་ག་ཁོ་ཚོས་ཧབ་ཐོབ་བརྒྱབ་པ་རེད་ As soon as they saw the gold they (all) scrambled to grab it.

ཧབ་འཐུང་ (hābduŋ) gulping down a drink; va.—རྒྱག.

ཧབ་པན་ (hābben) eng. short/ half pants.

ཧབ་པེ་ཧོབ་པེ་ (hābbe hōbbe) sm. ཧ་པེ་ཧོབ་པེ་.

ཧབ་བྲིད་ (hābdriì) sm. ཧབ་སྦྲིད་.

ཧབ་སྦྲིད་ (hābdriì) sm. ཧབ་ཆི་.

ཧབ་ཚེམ་ (hābdzem) sewing with long stitches; va.—རྒྱག.

ཧབ་འཚོང་ (hābdzoŋ) a sale of merchandise where there is a lot of pushing and shoving to get at the goods (e.g., goods sold off a truck or piled on the street); va.—རྒྱག.

ཧབ་ཟ་ (hābsa) gulping/ gobbling down food; va.—བྱེད་.

ཧབ་ཤ་ (hābsha) sm. ཧབ་ཐོབ་.

ཧབ་གཤགས་ (hābshaà) arguing in a disorderly manner; va.—རྒྱག.

ཧབ་བཤགས་ (hābshaà) breaking sth. such as a stone into two pieces; va.—གཏོང་.

ཧབ་སད་ (hābsɛɛ̀) waking up with a startle; vi.—རྒྱག.

ཧབ་ཧབ་ (hābhəb) having strong attachment to things/ foods.

ཧབ་ཧོབ་ (hābhob) abbr. of ཧ་པེ་ཧོབ་པེ་.

ཧམ་ (hām) abbr. of ཧམ་པ་.

ཧམ་བསྐྱོད་ (hāmgyöö) sm. ཐལ་སྐྱོད་.

ཧམ་ཁྱེར་ (hāgyer) sm. ཧམ་ལེན་.

ཧམ་འཁྱེར་ (hāmgyer) sm. ཧམ་ཁྱེར་.

ཧམ་ཅན་ (hāmjɛn) person who is shameless/ deceitful.

ཧམ་བཅོས་ (hāmjöö) tampering, altering; va.—བྱེད་.

ཧམ་ཆེན་ (hāmjen) sb. who is shameless/ brazen.

ཧམ་ཉམས་ (hāmñam) appearance of being ཧམ་ཆེན་.

ཧམ་གཉེར་ (hāmñer) brazenly/ shamelessly managing sth.(for one's own benefit) ། མི་དེས་ཚོགས་པར་དབང་བའི་ཟ་ཁང་དེ་ཁོ་པ་མི་སྒེར་གྱིས་ཧམ་གཉེར་བྱས་པ་རེད་ That person brazenly ran the restaurant that belonged to the association for his own benefit.

ཧམ་བསྙོན་ (hāmñön) brazenly/ shamelessly

blaming; va.—བྱེད་; —འཛུགས་.

ཧམ་བསྟོད་ (hāmdöö) praising in an excessive/ exaggerated manner; va.—བྱེད་.

ཧམ་ཐལ་ (hāmdɛɛ) excessively brazen/ arrogant.

ཧམ་དྲི་ (hāmdri) 1. moldy/ musty smell; —ཁ་ to smell of mold; va.—རྒྱག to get moldy. 2. the smell of sth. going stale/ rotten.

ཧམ་བདག (hāmdaà) taking possession of things greedily/ avariciously/ shamelessly ¶ མི་ངན་འདིས་གཞན་ནོར་ལ་ཧམ་བདག་བྱེད་པ་རེད་ The evil person is avariciously taking possession of things that belong to other people.

ཧམ་འདོད་ (hāmdöö) wanting/ desiring/ coveting things one isn't entitled to; va.—བྱེད་.

ཧམ་འདོད་ངོམས་མེད་ (hāmdöö n̲ommeè) sm. ཧམ་འདོད་ཚ་པོ་.

ཧམ་འདོད་ཆེན་པོ་ (hāmdöö cēmbo) sm. ཧམ་འདོད་ཚ་པོ་.

ཧམ་འདོད་ཚ་པོ་ (hāmdöö tsābo) a person who covet and desires what others have, excessively greedy.

ཧམ་འདོད་ཡིད་འཕྲུལ་ (hāmdöö y̲indrüü) blinded by greed, obsessed with the desire for gain; va.—བྱེད་.

ཧམ་སྡོད་ (hāmdöö) occupying a place brazenly/ shamelessly; va.—བྱེད་.

ཧམ་གནོན་ (hāmnön) shamelessly/ brazenly bullying and oppressing; va.—བྱེད་.

ཧམ་པ་ (hāmba) brazen or shameless exaggerating/ lying/ asserting; va.—ཤོད་. 2. greed. 3. sm. ཧམ་སྤུ་.

ཧམ་པ་ཅན་ (h̲əmbujɛn) sm. ཧམ་ཅན་.

ཧམ་པ་དཔའ་ཐལ་ (hāmba bāādɛɛ) shung. excessive audacity ¶ ཧམ་པ་དཔའ་ཐལ་ཞུ་བབས་ལ་གཞིགས་ན་ཉེས་པ་ཞིག་རང་ཐོབ་རྒྱུ་ When you consider his excessive audacity he deserves punishment.

ཧམ་པ་ཚ་པོ་ (hāmba tsābo) 1. shameless, audacious, brazen. 2. greedy.

ཧམ་པ་འཛུགས་ (hāmba dzu̲ù) va. to brazenly/ shamelessly blame sb.

ཧམ་པ་རི་ཙམ་བཤད་ན་བདེན་པ་གཡག་ཙམ་ཐོབ་ (hāmba r̲idzam shɛ̄ɛna d̲emba yāgdzam tōb) if one shamelessly exaggerates a great deal some of what one says will be believed [Lit. if one exaggerates as much as a mountain, one will get a truth as much as a yak].

ཧམ་པ་ཤོད་ (hāmba shöö) see ཧམ་པ་.

ཧམ་པས་འཁྱེར་ (hāmbɛ kyēr) sm. ཧམ་འཁྱེར་.

ཧམ་སྤུ་ (həmbu) moldy, musty; vi.—རྒྱག to be/ get moldy, musty.

ཧམ་སྤྱོད་ (hāmjöö) brazen/ shameless behavior.

ཧམ་ཕོད་ཅན་ (hāmbööjɛn) sm. ཧམ་པ་ཚ་པོ་.

ཧམ་འཕྲོག་བྱེད་ (hāmdrɔɔ c̲eè) brazenly/ audaciously/ shamelessly stealing; va.—བྱེད་.

ཧམ་བུ་ (hāmbu) one mouthful ¶ ཇ་ཧམ་བུ་གང་ One mouthful of tea.

ཧམ་སྨྱོན་ (hāmñön) belligerently crazy.

ཧམ་སྨྱོན་གདུམ་སྤྱོད་ (hāmñön dūmjöö) mad belligerent behavior.

ཧམ་བཙན་ (hāmdzɛn) ruling by force, brazenly/ shamelessly using force; va.—བྱེད་.

ཧམ་རྩོད་ (hāmdzöö) shamelessly arguing for sth. out of greed/ avarice.

ཧམ་འཛིན་ (hāmdzin) brazenly/ shamelessly controlling or monopolizing; va.—བྱེད་.

ཧམ་འཛུལ་ (hāmdzüü) brazenly/ shamelessly invading; va.—བྱེད་.

ཧམ་རྫུན་ (hāmdzün) shameless/ brazen lies.

ཧམ་ཞུ་བྱེད་ (hāmshu c̲e̲è) shung. sm. ཧམ་པ་ཤོད་.

ཧམ་ཟ་ (hāmsa) shameless/ brazen corruption or embezzling.

ཧམ་ཟོས་ (hāmsöö) sm. ཧམ་ཟ་.

ཧམ་གཟུང་ (hāmsuŋ) sm. ཧམ་འཛིན་.

ཧམ་བཟུང་ (hāmsuŋ) sm. ཧམ་འཛིན་.

ཧམ་ཡུ་ (hāmyu) sm. ལྷམ་ཡུ་.

ཧམ་ཡུས་ (hāmyüü) excessively praising oneself; va.—ཤོད་.

ཧམ་རེ་ (hāmre) abbr. of ཧམ་པའི་རེ་བ་.

ཧམ་ལུ་ (hāmlu) children's shoes/ boots.

ཧམ་ལེན་ (hāmlen) taking away by force; va.—བྱེད་ ¶ མི་དམངས་ཀྱི་རྒྱུ་ནོར་ཧམ་ལེན་བྱེད་མི་ཆོག (One) can't take the people's wealth and property by force.

ཧམ་ཤེད་ (hāmsheè) brazen, shameless; va.—བྱེད་.

ཧམ་ཤེད་གང་འདོད་ (hāmsheè k̲aŋdöö) brazen/ shameless greed, using whatever force/ means one needs to get one's way.

ཧམ་བཤད་ (hāmshɛ̀ɛ) brazen/ shameless talk or lies; va.—བྱེད་.

ཧམ་བཤད་མགོ་སྐོར་ (hāmshɛ̀ɛ gogɔɔ) swindling/ tricking by brazen talk, conning.

ཧམ་སེམས་ (hāmsem) greedily ambitious/ scheming, shamelessly avaricious.

ཧམ་སེམས་ཅན་ (hāmsemjɛn) greedy, scheming, shamelessly ambitious.

ཧམ་སེམས་ཆེན་པོ་ (hāmsem cēmbo) shamelessly greedy, overly ambitious.

ཧམ་སོང་ (hāmsoŋ) exaggeration, exaggerating ¶ གནས་ཚུལ་འདི་ཧམ་སོང་མི་འདུག This news is no exaggeration.

ཧའི་སིན་ (hɛ̄sin) ch. sea slug.

ཧའི་ (hē) exclamation of wonderment.

ཧའི་ཀྲུའུ་ (hɛ̄dru) Haichow.

ཧའི་ཀྲི་ (hɛ̄dre) ch. sea blubber.

ཧའི་ཏའི་ (hɛ̄de) ch. kelp.

ཧའོ་སྨི་ (hāomi) ch. millimeter.

ཧའི་ནན་ (hēnɛn) Hainan (Island).

ཧའི་མན་ (hɛ̄mɛn) ch. sponge.

ཧའི་ལུན་ཅན་ (hɛ̄lünjɛn) Amur River.

ཧའི་ཧྲེན་ (hɛ̄drɛn) sm. ཧའི་སིན་.

ཧའི་ཨོའུ་ (hɛ̄wo) ch. gull.

ཧའོ་མི་ (hāomi) millimeter.

ཧའོ་ལན་ (hāolɛn) Holland.

ཧའོ་ཧྲེང་ (hāodreŋ) ch. milliliter.

ཧར་ (hār) 1. suddenly, at once, abruptly ¶ ཧར་ར་ལངས་ནས་ཕྱིན་པ་རེད་ (He) got up suddenly and went. 2. abbr. of ཧར་པོ་. 3. exaggerating, overstating; va.—ཤོད་.

ཧར་བཀྲ་བ་ (hārdrawa) sm. ཧར་པོ་.

ཧར་གོང་རྒྱག (hārgoŋ gy̲aà) excessively pricing an item with the idea of bargaining lower; va.—རྒྱག.

ཧར་རྒྱུག (hār gyu̲ù) suddenly running; va.—བྱེད་.

ཧར་སྒོམ་ (hārgom) meditating with one's eyes open; va.—བྱེད་.

ཧར་སྒྲ་ (hārdra) 1. sound of snoring; va.—རྒྱག. 2. panting/ gasping sound.

ཧར་སྒྲ་ཚ་པོ་ (hārdra tsābo) sb. who snores loudly.

ཧར་ཅན་ (hārjɛn) sm. ཧམ་པ་ཅན་.

ཧར་ཆེན་ (hārjen) person who exaggerates/ overstates greatly.

ཧར་དེ་ (hārde) suddenly.

ཧར་གདམ་ (hārdam) exaggerating, overstating; va.—ཤོད་.

ཧར་ཐོན་ (hārdön) suddenly leaving/ departing; va.—བྱེད་.

ཧར་འདོན་ (hārdön) 1. va. to make a hole/ opening in sth. 2. sm. ཧར་ཐོན་.

ཧར་པ་ (hārba) sm. ཧམ་པ་ཅན་. 2. space between two walls/ houses.

ཧར་པིང་ (hārbiŋ) sm. ཧར་པིན་.

ཧར་པིན་ (hārbin) Harbin.

ཧར་པོ་ (hārbo) 1. flashy, gaudy, bright. 2. sb. who is showoffish. 3. staring at.

ཧར་བར་མི་ཤོང་ (hārbar m̲ishoŋ) a large gap/ crack (the size of a person).

ཧར་མིག (hərm iì) hole (in a wall/ fence).

ཧར་ཚ་པོ་ (hār tsābo) sb. who exaggerates/ boasts/ overstates.

ཧར་ལངས་ (hārlaŋ) getting up/ rising up suddenly; va.—བྱེད་.

ཧར་བཤད་ (hārshɛ̀ɛ) boasting, exaggerating; va.—

བྱེད་.

ཧར་ཧར་ཧོད་རྒྱུག (hārhar hȍȍgyuù) acting rashly/ hastily, taking reckless action; va.—བྱེད་.

ཧར་ཧུར་ (hārhur) sm. ཧ་རེ་ཧུ་རེ་.

ཧར་ཧོར་ (hārhor) thoughtless, unplanned, hasty ¶ ཧར་ཧོར་བྱས་པའི་ལས་ཀ་ Work done in a hasty manner.

ཧལ་ (hɛ̄ɛ) vi. to pant/ gasp, to be short of breath.

ཧལ་ལི་བ་ (hɛ̄ɛlewa) panting, gasping for breath.

ཧལ་ལི་ཧལ་ལི་ (hɛ̄ɛle hɛ̄ɛle) sm. ཧལ་ལི་ཧོལ་ལི་.

ཧལ་ལི་ཧོལ་ལི་ (hɛ̄ɛle hȍȍle) sm. ཧ་རེ་ཧུ་རེ་.

ཧལ་ཤ་ (hɛ̄ɛsha) panting, gasping; vi.—ཐོན་ to pant/ gasp.

ཧལ་ཧལ་ (hɛ̄ɛhɛɛ) sm. ཧལ་ཤ་.

ཧལ་ཧོལ་ (hɛ̄ɛhöö) abbr. of ཧལ་ལི་ཧོལ་ལི་.

ཧས་ (hɛ̄ɛ̀) sm. ཧལ་. 2. slipper.

ཧས་འདེབས་ (hɛ̄ɛ̀ndeb) sm. དབུགས་ཧལ་.

ཧི་ཀ་ (hīgə) hiccup.

ཧི་མ་ལ་ཡ་ (hīmlaya) Himalayan Mountains.

ཧི་མ་ལ་ཡའི་རི་རྒྱུད་ (himalayɛ rigyüù) the Himalayan Mountain Range.

ཧིཊ་ལར་ (hīdlar) Hitler.

ཧིན་སྒྲ་ (hīndra) a "hən" sounding exclamation made when people are very disappointed.

ཧིན་སྒོར་ (hīngɔɔ) rupee (Indian).

ཧིན་དི་ (hīndi) Hindi.

ཧིན་དུ་ (hīndu) 1. Hindu, Indian. 2. India.

ཧིན་དུ་རྒྱ་མཚོ་ (hīndu gyadzo) Indian Ocean.

ཧིན་དུ་ཙི་ན་ (hīndu dzīnə) Indo-China.

ཧིན་དུ་སི་ཏན་སི་ཊཱན་ཌཊ་ (hīndusidɛn sīdrɛndar) Hindustan Standard (newspaper).

ཧིན་དྷུ་ (hīndu) Hindu.

ཧིན་དུ་ཉི་ཤི་ཡ་ (hīndu ñishiya) Indonesia.

ཧིན་དུ་དབྱང་རྒྱ་མཚོ་ཆེན་པོ་ (hīnduyaŋ gyadzo cēmmo) the Indian Ocean.

ཧིན་དུའི་ཆོས་ལུགས་ (hīndü cȍȍluù) Hinduism.

ཧིན་བོད་ (hīnbȍȍ) India and Tibet, Indo-Tibetan.

ཧིན་དམག (hīnmaà) Indian soldiers/ troops.

ཧིན་གཞུང་ (hīnshuŋ) Indian Government.

ཧིཛ་བུ་ལ་ (hīzbula) Hezbollah.

ཧེར་ཤིན་ཅི་ (hīnshinji) Helsinki.

ཧུ་ཀྲི་མིན་ (hūdrimin) Ho Chi-minh.

ཧུ་ཁྱུ་ (hūgyu) a sigh.

ཧུ་སྒྲ་ (hūdra) a sighing sound.

ཧུ་ཅིན་ (hūjin) ch. a Chinese two stringed instrument played with a bow.

ཧུ་ཆིན་ (hūjin) sm. ཧུ་ཅིན་.

ཧུ་ཐུག་ཐུ་ (hūtugdu) mong. Hutuktu (title of the highest ranking lamas).

ཧུ་རུ་རུ་ (hūruru) sm. ཧུ་ལུ་. 2. sound of wind.

ཧུ་རེ་བ་ (hūrewa) staring.

ཧུར་རེར་ལྟ་ (hārre dā) va. to stare.

ཧུ་ལུ་ (hūlu) slurping manner of eating soup/ noodles.

ཧུ་ཤུར་ཤུར་ (hū shūūshuu) sm. ཧུ་ཤོར་ཤོར་.

ཧུ་ཤོར་ཤོར་ (hū shɔ̄ɔshɔɔ) expressing or showing anger and shock/ surprise.

ཧུ་ཧུ་ (hūhu) sm. ཧུ་ལུ་.

ཧུང་ཀྲ་ཅི་གནམ་གྲུ་ (hūŋdraji nāmdru) ch.tib. bomber plane.

ཧུང་ཁྲང་ (hūŋdraŋ) ch. Red Square (Moscow).

ཧུང་ག་རི་ (hūŋgari) Hungary.

ཧུང་སྒྲ་ (hūŋdra) the sound "hung" (of artillery firing).

ཧུང་མེ་སུའུ་ (hūŋmesu) ch. erythromycin.

ཧུང་ཝོའི་ཤེན་ (hūŋwoshɛn) ch. infrared rays.

ཧུད་ (hȕȕ) ch. committee, society, association, meeting.

ཧུན་ཧྲ་ (hūnha) Hue (Vietnam).

ཧུབ་ (hūb) mouthful/ gulp (of drink); va.—རྒྱག to drink by gulping mouthfuls ¶ ཆང་ཧུབ་གང་ A mouthful of beer. 2. a drag/ puff on a cigarette.

ཧུབ་སྐོར་ (hūbgɔɔ) sharing/ passing around the same bowl to drink; va.—རྒྱག.

ཧུབ་འདེབས་ (hūmdeb) sm. ཧུབ་རྒྱག.

ཧུབ་རེས་ (hūbreè) sm. ཧུབ་སྐོར་.

ཧུབ་ལོག (hūblɔɔ̀) gulping down a liquid quickly; va.—རྒྱག.

ཧུའ་ཧྲིན་ (hūhrin) ch. peanut.

ཧུའང་ཕུའུ་ཅང་ (hūaŋ pū jāŋ) ch. Yellow River.

ཧུའང་ཧྭ་ཚལ་ (hūaŋ hādzɛɛ) ch. day lilly.

ཧུའི་ (hūwe) Hui nationality (Chinese Muslim).

ཧུའུ་ (hūū) ch. kettle, pot (made of metal).

ཧུའུ་ཆིན་ (hūūjin) sm. ཧུ་ཆིན་.

ཧུའུ་ཀྲི་མིང་ (hūūdrimiŋ) sm. ཧུ་ཀྲི་མིན་.

ཧུའུ་ནན་ (hūūnɛn) Hunan (Province).

ཧུའུ་པེ་ (hūūbe) Hubei (Province).

ཧུའུ་རི་ཙེ་ (hūūridze) ch. a type of winter hat with earflaps.

ཧུའུ་ཧོ་ཧའོ་ཐེ་ (hūūhot) Huhot (capital of Inner Mongolia).

ཧུའེ་ (hūwe) sm. ཧུད་.

ཧུའེ་ཀྲང་ (hūwedraŋ) ch. head of a ཧུའེ་.

ཧུའེ་ཧྥུང་དངུལ་ཁང་ (hūūfuŋ ŋūūgaŋ) ch.tib. Hong Kong and Shanghai Bank.

ཧུའོ་ཁྲེ་ (hūwodre) ch. train.

ཧུའོ་ཁྲིའི་ (hūwodre) sm. ཧུའོ་ཁྲེ་.

ཧུའོ་ཇན་ཐུང་ (hūwo jenduŋ) ch. rocket launcher.

ཧུར་སྐྱིད་ (hūrgyeè) sm. ཧུར་ཐག.

ཧུར་སྐྱིད་འབད་བརྩོན་ (hūrgyɛɛ̀ bɛ̀ɛdzön) sm. ཧུར་ཐག་འབད་ཐག.

ཧུར་བསྐྱིད་ (hūrgyeè) sm. ཧུར་བསྐྱེད་.

ཧུར་ཐག (hūrdaà) diligence, conscientiousness, hard work; va.—བྱེད་ to do sth. diligently/ conscientiously/ energetically, to work hard.

ཧུར་ཐག་གིས་ (hūrdaàgi) diligently, conscientiously, energetically, via hard work.

ཧུར་ཐག་འབད་ཐག (hūrdaà bɛ̀ɛdaà) sm. ཧུར་ཐག.

ཧུར་འདུམས་ (hūrdum) sm. ཧོལ་རྒྱུག.

ཧུར་པོ་ (hūrbu) hard working energetic/ diligent (with respect to work); va.—བྱེད་ to do sth. energetically/ diligently, to work hard ¶ ཁོ་ལས་ཀའི་ཐོག་ལ་ཧུར་པོ་ཞེ་དྲག་འདུག He is very energetic about work.

ཧུར་བག་ཅན་ (hūrbaàjɛn) sm. ཧུར་པོ་.

ཧུར་འབུངས་ཞེ་བསྐྱེད་ (hūrbuŋ shegyeè) sm. ཧུར་ཐག.

ཧུར་བརྩོན་ (hūrdzön) sm. ཧུར་ཐག.

ཧུར་བརྩོན་གྱིས་ (hūrdzöngi) sm. ཧུར་ཐག་གིས་.

ཧུར་བརྩོན་གྲོན་ཆུང་ (hūrdzön drȫnjuŋ) working energetically and economically; va.—བྱེད་.

ཧུར་བརྩོན་ཅན་ (hūrdzünjɛn) an activist ¶ ཧུར་བརྩོན་ཅན་བཟོ་པ་ An activist worker.

ཧུར་བརྩོན་ཆེན་པོ་ (hūrdzün vcēmbo) energetic, diligent, conscientious, hardworking.

ཧུར་བརྩོན་པ་ (hurdzümba) sm. ཧུར་བརྩོན་ཅན་.

ཧུར་བརྩོན་རང་བཞིན་ (hūrdzün rəŋshin) activist nature/ character.

ཧུར་རེ་ (hūrre) sm. ཧུར་རེ་བ་.

ཧུར་རེར་བལྟ་ (hūrre dā) va. to stare.

ཧུར་ལེན་ (hūrlen) sm. ལྷུར་ལེན་.

ཧུར་སེམས་ (hūrsem) enthusiasm to be diligent/ hard working.

ཧུར་སེམས་ཆེན་པོ་ (hūrsem cēmbo) sm. ཧུར་བརྩོན་ཆེན་པོ་.

ཧུར་བསྲིས་ཁྱིམ་སྐྱོང་ (hūrsiì kyīmgyoŋ) industrious and thrifty in maintaining a household; va.—བྱེད་.

ཧུར་བསྲིས་རྒྱལ་འཛུགས་ (hūrsiì gyɛɛdzuù) building a country through hard work/ thrift; va.—བྱེད་.

ཧུར་ཧུར་ (hūrhur) 1. sound made by the flapping of bird wings and by gun fire. 2. starring.

ཧུར་ཧུར་དུ་རྒྱག (hūrhurdu gyaà) the sound of strong wind, the sound of a slingshot being whirled.

ཧུས་ཧུས་ (hȕȕhȕȕ) Hui nationality (Chinese Muslims).

ཧེ་ (hē) sound of laughter (he, he).

ཧེ་པན་ (hēbɛn) ch. blackboard.

ཧེ་བག (hēbaà) difference ¶ འདི་གཉིས་ཧེ་བག་འདུག་གས་ Is there a difference between these two?

ཧེ་བག་གཏོང་ (hēbaà dōŋ) va. to misrepresent an accounting ¶ རྩིས་པ་དེས་རྩིས་ཁྲར་ཧེ་བག་བཏང་ཙང་

ལས་ཁུངས་ནས་ཕུད་འདུག The accountant misrepresented the accounts and was fired.

ཧེ་བག་ཤོད་ (hēbaà shöö) va. to say sth. differently than is, to misrepresent/ lie.

ཧེ་བག་ཤོར་ (hēbaà shōō) vi. to unintentionally have a difference (usu. in accounts).

ཧེ་ཡི་མཚོན་ཆ་ (hēyi tsōnja) ch.tib. atomic/ nuclear weapon.

ཧེ་རུ་ཀ་ (hēruga) sm. བདེ་མཆོག.

ཧེ་སོང་གདོང་ (hēsoŋ dōŋ) sm. ཧ་སོང་གདོང་.

ཧེག་ཊར་ (hēgdar) eng. hectare.

ཧེབ་ལངས་ (hēb laŋ) vi. to keep up with the Jones ¶ ལས་བྱེད་པ་གཅིག་གིས་བརྙན་འཕྲིན་ཉོས་ཙང་ལས་བྱེད་ཚང་མར་ཧེབ་ལངས་ནས་བརྙན་འཕྲིན་ཉོས་འདུག Because one official bought a T.V., all bought televisions to "keep up with the Jones."

ཧེའི་ནན་ (hēnɛn) Henan (Province).

ཧེའི་ལུང་ཅང་ (hēluŋjaŋ) sm. ཧེ་ལུང་ཅང་.

ཧེའི་སིན་ (hēsin) ch. sea slug.

ཧོ་ (hō) ch. nuclear, atomic ¶ ཧོའི་ཚོད་ལྟ་ Nuclear test.

ཧོ་ཁྲིའི་ (hōdre) ch. train ¶ ཧོ་ཁྲིའི་བབས་ཚུགས་ Railway station.

ཧོ་གློག་ཁང་ (hōlɔɔgaŋ) ch.tib. nuclear generator plant.

ཧོ་སྒྲ་ཀུ་སྒྲ་ (hōdra gūdra) a sound/ cry/ yell made to frighten people.

ཧོ་ཐུད་ (hōdüü) ch. ham.

ཧོ་ཐོག་ཐུ་ (hōtɔgdu) sm. ཧུ་ཐུག་ཐུ་.

ཧོ་དན་ (hōdɛn) Khotan.

ཧོ་ནན་ (hōnɛn) Henan (Province).

ཧོ་པེ་ (hōbɛ) Hebei (Province).

ཧོ་འབར་གས་ (hō bargɛɛ̀) ch.tib. nuclear explosion.

ཧོ་མེ་སུའུ་ (hōmesu) ch. streptomycin.

ཧོ་ཙི་ (hōdzi) ch. nuclear, atomic.

ཧོ་དམག (hōmaà) ch.tib. nuclear war.

ཧོ་དམག་གྲབས་ཆོད་འཛིན་ (hō mɔgdrəb tsōndzin) ch.tib. nuclear disarmament.

ཧོ་མཚོན་ཆ་ (hō tsōnja) ch.tib. atomic/ nuclear weapons.

ཧོ་མཚོན་ཆའི་ཐྲིགས་མོ་ (hō tsōnjɛ digmo) ch.tib. nuclear blackmail; va.—བྱེད་.

ཧོ་ཤོད་ (hōshod) Qoshot Mongols.

ཧོ་ལན་ (hōlɛn) Holland.

ཧོ་ལུའུ་ཞའོ་ཧྥུ་ (hōlu shafu) ch. Krushchev.

ཧོ་ཧོ་ (hōho) sound of laughter (ho, ho).

ཧོག་པིན་ (hōgbin) ch. frying pan.

ཧོག་སེ་ (hōgse) rayon.

ཧོང་ཀོང་ (hōŋgoŋ) Hong Kong.

ཧོང་དུ་ར་སི་ (hōŋdurasi) Honduras.

ཧོང་ཡུས་ (hōŋyüü) ch. yellow croaker fish.

ཧོང་ལེན་ (hōŋlen) ch. Coptis chinensis.

ཧོང་ཧའི་རྒྱ་མཚོ་ (hōŋhɛ gyadzo) ch.tib. Yellow Sea.

ཧོད་རྒྱུག (höögyuù) 1. careless, hurriedly, irresponsibly; va.—བྱེད་; —སྤྱོད་ ¶ ལས་འགན་ལ་ཧོད་རྒྱུག་བྱས་ནས་ནོར་འཁྲུལ་ཤོར་བ་རེད་ (They) worked carelessly and made mistakes. 2. acting rashly, leaping in without thinking; va.—བྱེད་.

ཧོད་རྒྱུག་ཚ་པོ་ (höögyuù tsābo) 1. sb. who does things carelessly/ hurriedly. 2. sb. who does things rashly without thinking them through.

ཧོད་རྒྱུགས་ (höögyuù) sm. ཧོད་རྒྱུག.

ཧོན་ (hōn) sm. ཧོན་ནད་.

ཧོན་གོད་ (hōngöö) sm. ཧོན་ནད་.

ཧོན་སྡོར་ (hōndɔr) sm. ཧོན་ཐོར་.

ཧོན་ཐོར་ (hōndɔr) vi. to be shocked/ astonished/ surprised/ stunned ¶ སྐད་ཆ་འདི་གོ་དུས་ཧོན་ཐོར་ནས་ལན་རྒྱག་ཐུབ་མ་བྱུང་ When (I) heard the (talk) I was so shocked that I was unable to answer.

ཧོན་ཐོར་ཐོར་ (hōn tōrdɔr) sm. ཧོན་ཐོར་.

ཧོན་ཐོར་ལྷ་ཆད་ (hōndɔr lājɛɛ̀) being shocked/ astonished and frightened.

ཧོན་འཐོར་ (hōndɔr) sm. ཧོན་ཐོར་.

ཧོན་ནད་ (hōnnɛɛ̀) rinderpest.

ཧོབ་ (hōb) sudden, suddenly.

ཧོབ་དེ་ (hōbde) sm. ཧོབ་དེ་ཁ་ལ་.

ཧོབ་དེ་ཁ་ལ་ (hōbde kāla) suddenly ¶ ཁ་སང་ཁོ་ཧོབ་དེ་ཁ་ལ་བྲོས་ཕྱིན་འདུག Yesterday he suddenly fled.

ཧོབ་ཚོད་ (hōbdzöö) guess/ approximation; va.—བྱེད་ to approximate/ guess ¶ བཟོ་པ་ཆིག་སྟོང་ཙམ་ཡོད་པ་རེད་ If I make an approximation, there are about 1,000 workers in this factory.

ཧོབ་ལངས་ (hōblaŋ) getting up suddenly; va.—རྒྱག.

ཧོབ་ཧོབ་ལ་ (hōb hōbla) sm. ཧོབ་དེ་ཁ་ལ་.

ཧོམ་ (hōm) a kind of exorcism ritual.

ཧོམ་ཆང་ (hōmjaŋ) shung. ཆང་ used in the performance of exorcism rites.

ཧོམ་སྦར་ (hōm bār) va. to light the fire for an exorcism. ritual.

ཧོམ་སླང་ (hōmlaŋ) shung. a frying pan used in the performance of exorcism rites.

ཧོམ་ཤིང་ (hōmshiŋ) wood used in the ཧོམ་ exorcism rite.

ཧོམ་སྲེག (hōmseg) sm. ཧོམ་སྦར་.

ཧོའང་ཀོའ་ (hōaŋgo) ch. cucumber.

ཧའོ་ (hō) 1/10 of a meter.

ཧའོ་ཚོད་ལྟ་ (hǒ tsööda) ch.tib. nuclear test.

ཧའོ་ཅིན་ (hōjin) sm. ཧོ་ཅིན་.

ཧོར་ (hōr) 1. Mongolia, Mongolian. 2. name of the nomads living in Northern Tibet.

ཧོར་གོང་ (hōrgoŋ) space, gaps.

ཧོར་ཁ་ (hōrga) water pipe (for smoking); va.—འཐེན་ to smoke a water pipe.

ཧོར་ཁོང་ (hōrgoŋ) sm. ཧོར་གོང་.

ཧོར་ཁོངས་ (hōrgoŋ) 1. sm. ཧོར་གོང་. 2. places/ areas which belong to the Mongols.

ཧོར་གོས་ (hōrgöö) 1. Mongolian clothing. 2. brocade made during the Yuan Dynasty.

ཧོར་གླིང་ (hōrliŋ) two groups in the Gesar epic.

ཧོར་གླུ་ (hōrlu) Mongolian songs.

ཧོར་སྒྲ་ (hōrdra) sm. ཧ་ར་སྒྲ་.

ཧོར་ཆས་ (hōrjɛɛ̀) shung. Mongolian dress.

ཧོར་ཇུས་ (hōrjüü) a type of brocade made during the Yuan Dynasty.

ཧོར་དིང་ (hōrdiŋ) water offering bowls made in Mongolian.

ཧོར་ཐང་འཐེན་ (hōrdaŋ tēn) vi. to be/ get very tired from doing sth.

ཧོར་དུད་ (hōrdüü) nomad household/ families in the Hor areas of northern Tibet.

ཧོར་འདྲ་ (hōndra) shung. petty officials.

ཧོར་འདྲ་ཟ་ཁང་གི་ཞལ་ཕྱི་ (hōndra sagaŋgi shɛɛje) shung. a tax requiring giving food and accommodations to ཧོར་འདྲ་.

ཧོར་པ་ (hōrba) 1. a person from northern Tibet. 2. Mongolian.

ཧོར་སྤྱི་ (hōrji) shung. Tibetan governor in charge of northern Tibet.

ཧོར་སྦུབ་ (hōrbub) Mongolian cymbal.

ཧོར་ཚོ་པ་ (hōr tsōba) the nomad tribes of northern Tibet.

ཧོར་ཟླ་ (hōnda) a Mongolian system of lunar months/ years.

ཧོར་ཡིག (hōryiì) Mongolian script.

ཧོར་ཡིག་གསར་པ་ (hōryiì sāāba) the new Mongolian script introduced during the time of Kublai Khan by Phakspa.

ཧོར་ཡུལ་ (hōryüü) sm. ཧོར་.

ཧོར་རིགས་ (hōrriì) 1. Mongolians. 2. nomadic people of northern Tibet.

ཧོར་ལུགས་ (hōrluù) shung. Mongolian tradition/ custom.

ཧོལ་སྐྱོད་ (höögyöö) going/ advancing rashly, going/ advancing without thought and investigation.

ཧོལ་འགྲོས་ (höödröö) sm. ཧང་འགྲོས་.

ཧོལ་རྒྱུག (höögyuù) thoughtless/ rash behavior ¶ ཁོའི་སྐད་ཆ་ཤོད་སྟངས་ཧོལ་རྒྱུག་ཚ་ཐག་ཆོད་བཞག His manner of talking is too rash.

ཧོལ་རྒྱུག་དོན་གཅོད་ (höögyuù tönjöö) doing things rashly/ carelessly.

ཧོལ་རྒྱུག་ཚ་པོ་ (hōōgyuù tsābo) sb. who does things rashly/ carelessly.

ཧོལ་རྒྱུག་བླ་བཅོས་ (hōōgyuù lājöö) acting rashly and carelessly.

ཧོལ་རྒྱུགས་ (hōōgyuù) sm. ཧོལ་རྒྱུག.

ཧོལ་སྤྱོད་ (hōōjöö) sm. ཧོལ་རྒྱུག.

ཧོལ་སྤྱོད་ཚ་པོ་ (hōōjöö tsābo) sm. ཧོལ་རྒྱུག་ཚ་པོ་.

ཧོས་རིགས་ (hōōrii) ch.tib. Hui (the Chinese Muslim ethnic group).

ཧྭ་ཀང་ཡན་ (hāgaŋyɛn) ch. granite.

ཧྭ་ཀྲུང་ (hādruŋ) ch. Central China.

ཧྭ་ཆོན་རྒྱག (hājön gyaà) a drinking game.

ཧྭ་ཏུང་ (hāduŋ) ch. East China.

ཧྭ་ཐུང་ (hāduŋ) ch. telephone (receiver).

ཧྭ་ནན་ (hānɛn) ch. South China.

ཧྭ་པེ་ (hābe) ch. North China.

ཧྭ་ཞང་ཅི་ (hāshaŋji) ch. glider.

ཧྭ་ཤང་ (hāshaŋ) Chinese Buddhist monk.

ཧྭ་ཤིན་ཀྲོན་ (hāshindrön) sm. ཧྭ་ཧྲིང་ཏུན་.

ཧྭ་ས་ (hāsa) sm. ཧྭ་ཧྲིང་ཏུན་.

ཧྭ་ཧྲིང་ཏུན་ (hādreŋdün) ch. Washington.

ཧྭགས་ (haà) ch. sugar.

ཧྭགས་ཀྱི་ལ་དུ་ (hāgi lədu) ch. a cookie made of brown sugar and honey.

ཧྭང་དི་ (hāŋdi) ch. emperor.

ཧྥ་གོ་ (fāgo) ch. France.

ཧྥ་དན་ཅི་ (fādenji) ch. gasoline generator.

ཧྥ་རན་སི་ (fārɛnsi) sm. ཧྥ་གོ་.

ཧྥ་ལན་ཤི་ (fālɛnshi) sm. ཧྥ་གོ་.

ཧྥ་ཤི་སི་ (fāshisi) fascism, fascist.

ཧྥ་ཤི་སིའི་རིང་ལུགས་ (fāshisii riŋluù) ch.tib. fascism.

ཧྥང་ཁྲིང་ཧྲི་ (fāŋ trēŋhri) ch. mathematical equation.

ཧྥང་ཧྲེ་ཞིང་ (fāŋhreshiŋ) ch. radioactive ¶ ཧྥང་ཧྲེ་ཞིང་ཐུང་ཝེ་སུའུ་ Radioactive isotope.

ཧྥན་ཆེ་ (fānje) ch. tomato.

ཧྥན་པུའུ་ (fānbu) ch. canvas.

ཧྥན་ཡིང་དུའི་ (fāyiŋdu) ch. atomic reactor.

ཧྥན་ཧྲི་ལིན་ (fānhrilin) ch. vaseline.

ཧྥི་ཀྲོའུ་གླིང་ (fīdraoliŋ) ch.tib. African continent.

ཧྥི་ལིའི་པིན་ (fīlibin) Philippines.

ཧྥིན་ལན་ (fīnlɛn) Finland.

ཧྥུ་ (fū) ch. deputy, vice- ¶ ཧྥུ་ཙུང་ལི་ Vice premier. ¶ ཧྥུ་ཀྲུའུ་རེན་ Deputy director.

ཧྥུ་ཅན་ (fūjɛn) Fukien (Province).

ཧྥུ་ཇན་ (fūjɛn) sm. ཧྥུ་ཅན་.

ཧྥུ་དའོ་ཡོན་ (fūdaoyön) ch. coach, tutor, guide, counselor.

ཧྥུ་ཐེ་ (fūde) ch. sm. ཧྥུ་ཐའི་.

ཧྥུ་ཐའི་ (fūdee) ch. volt.

ཧྥུ་ཙུང་ལི་ (fū dzūŋli) vice-premier.

ཧྥུ་ཨར་ཅང་ (fū ārjaŋ) ch. Volga River.

ཧྥུན་ཙི་ (fūndzi) ch. molecule.

ཧྥུའུ་ཇི་འཛན་ (fū jian) sm. ཧྥུ་ཅན་.

ཧྥེ་གླིང་ (fēliŋ) ch.tib. Africa ¶ ཧྥེ་ལིང་ལྷོ་ནུབ་ Southwest Africa.

ཧྥེང་ཆིན་ (fēŋjiŋ) ch. organ (musical instrument).

ཧྥེན་ (fēn) ch. centimeter.

ཧྱང་ (hyāŋ) vi. to float.

ཧྱང་ཧྱང་ (hyāŋhyaŋ) not heavy, light.

ངངེ་ཧྱིང་ངེ་ (hyāŋŋe hyīŋŋe) sm. ཡང་ངེ་ཡིང་ངེ་.

ཧྱང་ངེ་ཧྱེང་ངེ་ (hyāŋŋe hyēŋŋe) sm. ཡང་ངེ་ཡིང་ངེ་.

ཧྱང་ཟམ་ (hyāŋsam) floating bridge.

ཧྱབ་ (hyəb) 1. va. to skim sth. off the top (usu. coagulated butter from a cup of tea). 2. sm. གཡབ་.

ཧྱབ་ཧྱབ་བྱེད་ (hyəbhyəb ceè) 1. sm. ཧྱབ་. 2. va. to do carelessly/ thoughtlessly.

ཧྱབ་ཏེ་ཁ་ལ་ (hyəde kāla) lightly, agilely ¶ ཁོང་གིས་རྟ་ཧྱབ་ཏེ་ཁ་ལ་བཞོན་པ་རེད་ He mounted the horse agilely.

ཧྲ་ཆགས་ (hrā caà) vi. to become hard.

ཧྲ་དག་དག (hrā dāgdaà) good, well, solid; va.—བྱེད་ ¶ ཁོས་ལས་ཀ་ཧྲ་དག་དག་བྱས་པ་རེད་ He did the work well. ¶ དེང་སང་ནད་པ་དེ་གཟུགས་པོ་ཧྲ་དག་དག་ཆགས་བཞག These days the patient had become well. ¶ དེང་སང་ཁོང་ཚོས་ཚོང་བརྒྱབ་ནས་མི་ཚང་ཧྲ་དག་དག་ཆགས་བཞག These days they did business and their household has become well off.

ཧྲ་ཐང་ཐང་ (hrā tāŋdaŋ) sm. ཧྲ་དག་དག.

ཧྲ་ཐི་ཨར་ལ་པྱི་ (hrādi ārlabe) Saudi Arabia.

ཧྲ་ཐི་ཨ་ལ་པོ་ (hrāde ālabo) sm. ཧྲ་ཐི་ཨར་ལ་པྱི་.

ཧྲ་མུན་ (hrāmün) Amoy.

ཧྲ་མེན་ (hrāmen) sm. ཧྲ་མུན་.

ཧྲ་ཝུན་ (hrāwün) ch. chauvinism.

ཧྲ་ལེ་ཧྲི་ལེ་ (hrāle hrīle) small round items.

ཧྲ་ལི་ཧྲི་ལི་ (hrāli hrīle) sm. ཧྲ་ལེ་ཧྲི་ལེ་.

ཧྲ་ཧོང་གོང་མ་ (hrāhoŋ koŋma) ch.tib. czar ¶ ཧྲ་ཧོང་གོང་མའི་ལམ་ལུགས་ Czarism.

ཧྲ་ཧྥ་ (hrāfa) ch. sofa ¶ ཤུབ་ཀུག་ཧྲ་ཧྥ་ Sofa.

ཧྲ་ཨ་ (hrāa) shah.

ཧྲག (hraà) abbr. of ཧྲག་ཧྲག.

ཧྲག་གི་ཧྲུག་གི་ (hrāggi hrūggi) bits and pieces; va.—གཏོང་; —བཟོ་ to break into bits and pieces.

ཧྲག་སྒྲུག (hrāgdruù) selecting the best; va.—བྱེད་; —རྒྱག to select the best, to pick the highest quality.

ཧྲག་བསྡུས་ (hrāgdüü) shung. selecting/ collecting those of high quality or the better ones; va.—བྱེད་ ¶ ཚོགས་འདུ་ཧྲག་བསྡུས་ The (Tibetan) Abbreviated Assembly.

ཧྲག་བསྡུས་རྒྱས་པ་ (hrāgdüü gyeeba) shung. an intermediate size national assembly in tt. that was smaller than the full assembly but larger than the abbreviated assembly.

ཧྲག་པ་ (hrāgba) the best, high quality ¶ མི་རྟ་ཧྲག་པ་ Men and horses of high quality.

ཧྲག་པོ་ (hrāgbo) sm. ཧྲག་ཧྲག.

ཧྲག་དམག (hrāgmaà) the best troops.

ཧྲག་ཤོབ་ (hrāgshob) giving/ paying money right away in gambling (i.e., not allowing losses to become a debt) ¶ དེ་རིང་ཅེད་མོ་རྩེ་དུས་དངུལ་ཧྲག་ཤོབ་པ་སྤྲོད་ལེན་བྱེད་དགོས་ Lets gamble today, but we should pay (if one loses) right away.

ཧྲག་ཧྲག (hrāghraà) 1. high quality ¶ དམག་དཔུང་མང་བ་ལས་ཉུང་ཉུང་ཧྲག་ཧྲག་ཅིག་ཡོད་ན་དགའ་ In terms of troops, it is better to have a smaller number of high quality ones than more quantity. 2. for people: high quality, capable ¶ མི་ཧྲག་ཧྲག་བརྒྱད་ Eight capable men. 3. (usu. when gambling) in cash (not on credit) ¶ ང་ཚོ་མ་ཚང་རྒྱག་དུས་དངུལ་ཧྲག་ཧྲག་སྤྲོད་རེས་གཏོང་གི་ཡོད་ When we play mahjong we play with cash (no chips or IOU). 4. in a large piece ¶ མེ་ཤིང་འདི་ཚོ་ཧྲག་ཧྲག་གཤགས་དགོས་ You must cut (split) the firewood in large pieces. 5. stiff (for cloth, leather, etc.).

ཧྲག་ཧྲུག (hrəghrug) abbr. of ཧྲག་གི་ཧྲུག་གི་.

ཧྲགས་ (hrāà) stiff (for cloth, leather, etc.).

ཧྲགས་བསྡུས་ (hrəgdüü) sm. ཧྲག་བསྡུས་.

ཧྲང་ (hrāŋ) 1. vi. to coagulate ¶ ཁྲག་ཧྲང་བཞག The blood coagulated. 2. stiff (due to freezing, rigamortis, etc.) ¶ མཛུབ་གུ་ཧྲང་ནས་འགུལ་སྐྱོད་གཏོང་མ་ཐུབ་པ་རེད་ (He) was unable to move his fingers because they were frozen stiff. 3. vi. to be get/ spoiled ¶ དེང་སང་ཕ་མ་འཁྲིས་ལ་མེད་ཙང་ཕྲུ་གུ་དེ་ཧྲང་བཞག These days the child has become spoiled because he is not near his parents.

ཧྲང་ཀྱེ་ (hrāŋgye) sm. ཧྲང་.

ཧྲང་གོང་ (hrāŋgoŋ) sm. ཧྲང་.

ཧྲང་རྒྱལ་རབས་ (hrāŋ gyeerəb) Shang Dynasty.

ཧྲང་ངེ་བ་ (hrāŋŋewa) alone, solitary.

ཧྲང་ཅང་ (hrāŋjaŋ) ch. general, admiral.

ཧྲང་ཏོ་ (hrāŋdo) sm. ཧྲང་ཀྱེ་.

ཧྲང་པོ་ (hrāŋbo) sm. ཧྲང་ཀྱེ་.

ཧྲང་མའོ་ (hrāŋmo) ch. 1. cap worn by Chinese feudal officials. 2. traveling hat worn by Tibetan lay officials.

ཧྲང་ཝེ་ (hrāŋwe) ch. captain (in army and air force), lieutenant (in navy).

ཧྲང་ཞའོ་ (hrāŋshao) ch. colonel (in army and air force), captain (in navy).

ཧྲང་ཧྲང་ (hrāŋhraŋ) 1. single, alone (without spouse

or others in household); vi.—ཆགས་ to become single, to become alone ། ཁོ་ཧྲང་ཧྲང་རེད་ He is (lives) alone.

ཧྲང་ཧྲད་ (hrāŋhrɛ) Shanghai.

ཧྲང་ཧྲུའུ་ (hrāŋhru) ch. a minister (in the Ming and Qing Dynasties).

ཧྲངས་ (hrāŋ) sm. ཧྲང་.

ཧྲངས་ཧྲོ་ (hrāŋdo) sm. ཧྲང་ཧྲོ་.

ཧྲད་ (hrɛ̄ɛ̀) va. to scratch ། གཟུགས་པོར་ཟ་འཕྲུག་ལངས་ནས་ཧྲད་དགོས་ཀྱི་འདུག (I) have to scratch because my body itches.

ཧྲད་ཧྲད་ (hrɛ̄ɛ̀hrɛɛ̀) scratching; va.—གཏོང་.

ཧྲན་ཀན་ཉིང་ (hrɛ̄ngɛnñiŋ) abbr. of Shanxi-Gansu-Ningxia.

ཧྲན་ཏུང་ (hrɛ̄nduŋ) Shandong (Province).

ཧྲན་ཙེ་ (hrɛ̄ndze) ch. fan.

ཧྲན་ཞི་ (hrɛ̄nshi) Shanxi (Province).

ཧྲན་ཤིས་ (hrɛ̄nshii) sm. ཧྲན་ཞིས་.

ཧྲབ་ཧྲིབ་ (hrəbhrib) sm. རབ་བི་རི་བི་.

ཧྲམ་མེ་ཧྲོམ་མེ་ (hrāmme hrōmme) aches and pains ། དེ་རིང་ཉིན་གང་ངལ་རྩོལ་བྱས་རྗེས་གཟུགས་པོ་ཧྲམ་མེ་ཧྲོམ་མེ་ཆགས་བཞག Having done hard work all day long my body is full of aches and pains.

ཧྲའན་ཀན་ཉིང་ (hrāngɛnñiŋ) sm. ཧྲན་ཀན་ཉིང་.

ཧྲའན་ཞི་ (hrānshi) sm. ཧྲན་ཞི་.

ཧྲའོ་ཅང་ (hrāojaŋ) ch. major general, rear admiral.

ཧྲའོ་ཝེ་ (hrāowe) ch. second lieutenant, ensign.

ཧྲའོ་ཞའོ་ (hrāoshao) ch. major, lieutenant, commander.

ཧྲལ་ཐུག (hrɛ̄ɛ̄duù) broth made of pounded barley or wheat.

ཧྲལ་པོ་ (hrɛ̄ɛ̄bo) 1. lose in weave. 2. torn, tattered, shabby, in tatters; va.—བཟོ་ ། གོས་དྲབ་ལོག་ཧྲལ་པོ་ཞིག་གྱོན་འདུག He is wearing tattered clothes. 3. widely spaced stitches. 4. sm. གཤིས་ཀ་རྩིང་པོ་.

ཧྲལ་བ་ (hrɛ̄ɛ̄wa) sm. ཧྲལ་པོ་.

ཧྲལ་ལི་ཧྲུལ་ལི་ (hrɛ̄ɛ̄le hrū̃ūle) tattered (for clothes).

ཧྲལ་ཧྲལ་ (hrɛ̄ɛ̄hrɛɛ) 1. wide gaps, widely spaced ། ཡི་གེ་ཧྲལ་ཧྲལ་ Letters with wide spaces between them. 2. granular, coarsely grounded. 3. torn, tattered.

ཧྲལ་ཧྲུལ་ (hrɛ̄ɛ̄hrüü) sm. ཧྲལ་པོ་, 2.

ཧྲལ་ཧྲིལ་ (hrɛ̄ɛ̄hrii) sm. ཧྲ་ལི་ཧྲི་ལི་.

ཧྲི་ (hrī) ch. division (in army) ། ཧྲི་དང་པོ་ The first division.

ཧྲི་ (hrī) ch. sm. ཧྲི་.

ཧྲི་ཀྲང་ (hrīdraŋ) ch. 1. division commander.

ཧྲི་ཁག (hrīgaà) ch.tib. divisions (in army).

ཧྲི་ཐན་སོན་ (hrītɛnsön) ch. carbolic acid.

ཧྲི་ཏོན་ (hrīdön) ch. division and company (in army).

ཧྲི་ཕུའུ་ (hrību) ch. division headquarters (in army).

ཧྲི་དཔོན་ (hrībün) ch.tib. division commander (in army).

ཧྲི་མོ་ (hrīmu) ch. graphite.

ཧྲི་ཝུའུ་ཀྲང་ (hrīwudraŋ) ch. head of an office, business manager.

ཧྲི་ལ་ (hrīla) ch. paraffin wax.

ཧྲི་ཤོག (hrīshoò) sm. ཧྲི་ཁག.

ཧྲི་ཨུ་ (hrī ū) ch. municipal party committee.

ཧྲིག (hrīi) va. to cut.

ཧྲིག་གེ་ (hrīgge) staring wide-eyed, glaring.

ཧྲིག་ཧྲིག (hrīghrig) 1. sm. ཧྲིག་གེ་. 2. moving eyes (back and forth); va.—བྱེད་.

ཧྲིང་ཡང་ (hrīŋyaŋ) Shenyang.

ཧྲིངས་ (hrīŋ) sm. ཧྲང་.

ཧྲིན་ཡང་ (hrīnyaŋ) sm. ཧྲིན་ཡང་.

ཧྲིབ་ཀྱིས་ (hrībgyii) sm. ཧྲིབ་ཙམ་གཅིག་ལ་.

ཧྲིབ་ཙ་ (hrībdza) sm. ཧྲིབ་ཙམ་.

ཧྲིབ་ཙམ་ (hrībdzam) sm. for a very short/ brief time ། ཁོ་འདིར་ཧྲིབ་ཙམ་བསྡད་སོང་ He stayed here for a brief time.

ཧྲིབ་ཙམ་གྱིས་ (hrībdzamgi) sm. ཧྲིབ་ཙམ་གཅིག་ལ་.

ཧྲིབ་ཙམ་གཅིག་ལ་ (hrībdzam jīglə) quickly ། ཁོ་ཐ་མག་ཉོ་བར་ཕྱིན་ནས་ཧྲིབ་ཙམ་གཅིག་ལ་སླེབས་བྱུང་ He returned quickly from going to buy cigarettes.

ཧྲིབ་རྫེ་ (hrībdze) sm. གཡོ་རྫུན་མགོ་སྐོར་.

ཧྲིབ་ཧྲིབ་ (hrībhrib) dim, hazy, blurred, unclear visually; va.—བྱེད་ to see unclearly.

ཧྲིལ་ (hrīi) whole, full, entire.

ཧྲིལ་གྲངས་ (hrīidraŋ) whole number (in math).

ཧྲིལ་གྲངས་པོ་ (hrīidraŋ pō) sm. ཧྲིལ་ནོར་གྲངས་.

ཧྲིལ་ནོར་གྲངས་ (hrīi nərdraŋ) positive integer.

ཧྲིལ་པོ་ (hrīibu) 1. whole, full, entire ། ལོ་ཧྲིལ་པོ་ཞིག A whole year. 2. round; va.—བཟོ་; —དྲིལ་ to make round ། འཛམ་གླིང་གི་བཟོ་དབྱིབས་ཧྲིལ་པོ་རེད་ The shape of the world is round.

ཧྲིལ་བ་ (hrīiwə) sm. ཧྲིལ་པོ་.

ཧྲིལ་འཛིན་ (hrīndzin) total eclipse (of moon and sun); va.—བྱེད་.

ཧྲིལ་ལེ་བ་ (hrīilewa) completely, entirely ། ལས་ཀ་ཚང་མ་ཧྲིལ་ལེ་བར་ཚར་སོང་ All the work was completely finished. ། ཁང་པ་འདི་རྒྱག་པར་ཨ་སྒོར་འབུམ་ལྔ་ཧྲིལ་ལེ་བར་འགྲོ་གི་རེད་ To build this house it will cost a total of $500,000 (USD).

ཧྲིལ་ཧྲིལ་ (hrīihrii) sm. ཧྲིལ་པོ་.

ཧྲུ་ཅི་ (hruji) sm. ཧྲུའུ་ཅི་.

ཧྲུག་གེ་ (hrūùge) 1. the crunching sound (of sb. eating).

ཧྲུག་གེ་ཆག་པ་ (hrugge cāgba) sm. ཧྲུག་ཆག.

ཧྲུག་བཅག (hrūgjaà) breaking into two pieces; va.—གཏོང་.

ཧྲུག་ཆག་ཐེབས་ (hrūgjaà tēè) vi. to get broken into two pieces (usu. wood).

ཧྲུག་ཆད་ཐེབས་ (hrūgjɛɛ̀ tēè) vi. to get broken/ cut into two pieces (usu. rope).

ཧྲུག་པ་ (hrūgbə) sm. ཧྲུག་ཧྲུག.

ཧྲུག་པོ་ (hrūgbu) sm. ཧྲུག་ཧྲུག.

ཧྲུག་མ་ (hrūgma) sm. ཧྲུག་ཧྲུག.

ཧྲུག་ཧྲུག (hrūghrug) 1. small pieces; va.—རྡོག to pound into small pieces; va.—བཟོ་ to make into small pieces; vi.—ཆགས་ to break/ crumble into small pieces. 2. sm. ཧྲུག་གེ་.

ཧྲུད་ཧྲུད་པོ་ (hrūùhrüübo) 1. coarse, rough. 2. tasteless.

ཧྲུབ་པ་ (hrūbbə) sm. ཧྲུག་ཧྲུག.

ཧྲུབ་ཧྲུབ་ (hrūbhrub) sm. ཧྲུག་ཧྲུག.

ཧྲུའི་ཅིན་ (hrūjin) ch. crystal.

ཧྲུའི་ཤན་ (hrūshɛn) ch. narcissus plant.

ཧྲུའི་ཙའོ་ཙི་ (hrūjadzi) sm. ཧྲུའི་ཙོ་ཙི་.

ཧྲུའུ་ཅི་ (hrūūji) ch. secretary ། ཏང་གི་ཕུའུ་ཧྲུའུ་ཅི་ Party branch secretary.

ཧྲུའུ་ཅི་ཁྲུའུ་ (hrūūji trūwu) ch. secretariat.

ཧྲུའུ་ཅོ་ཙེ་ (hrūjodze) a type of soup with dumplings.

ཧྲུའུ་ཡན་ (hrūyɛn) ch. water pipe.

ཧྲུའུ་ཡན་ཚལ་ (hrūūyɛndzɛɛ) ch.tib. pickled vegetables.

ཧྲུའུ་ལགས་ (hrūūlaà) maternal aunt.

ཧྲུའི་དབྱང་སོན་ (hrūūyaŋsön) ch. salicylic acid.

ཧྲུའི་ཡན་ (hrūyɛn) sm. ཧྲུའུ་ཡན་.

ཧྲུའོ་ཧྲི་ (hruhri) ch. M.A. or M.S. degree.

ཧྲུལ་ (hrūū) abbr. of ཧྲུལ་པོ་.

ཧྲུལ་སྐྱོན་ (hrūūgyön) dilapidated, crumbled, tattered.

ཧྲུལ་པོ་ (hrūūbu) tattered ། ཉལ་ཆས་ཧྲུལ་པོ་ཞིག་ལས་མེད་པ་རེད་ There was only one tattered bedding.

ཧྲུལ་བ་ (hrūūwa) sm. ཧྲུལ་པོ་.

ཧྲུལ་བུ་ (hūūbu) sm. ཧྲུལ་པོ་.

ཧྲེ་ (hrē) ch. 1. commune. 2. sm. ཧྲི་.

ཧྲེ་ཀྲང་ (hrēdraŋ) ch. head of a commune.

ཧྲེ་ནང་དག་ཐེར་ (hrēnaŋ tagder) ch.tib. commune rectification, checking up on communes; va.—བྱེད་.

ཧྲེ་ཡོན་ (hrēyün) ch. commune member.

ཧྲེ་ཡོན་འཐུས་མིའི་ཚོགས་ཆེན་ (hrēyön tūūmii tsōgjen) ch.tib. meeting of commune representatives.

ཧྲེ་ཡོན་ཚོགས་ཆེན་ (hrēyön tsōgjen) ch.tib. general meeting of commune members.

ཧྲེ་ཧྲི་གླད་ཀོར་འོག (hrēhri lɛ̄ɛ̀gɔɔ wɔ̄ɔ̀) ch.tib. degrees celsius below zero.

ཧྲེ་ཧྲི་དྲོ་གྲང་ཚད་གཞི་ (hrēhri tsɛ̄ɛshi) sm. ཧྲེ་ཧྲི་དྲོད་རྟགས་.

ཧྲེ་ཧྲི་དྲོད་རྟགས་ (hrēhri trö̱ödaà) ch.tib. celsius temperature scale, centigrade temperature scale.

ཧྲེ་ཧྲིའི་དྲོད་ཚད་ (hrēhrii trö̱ödzɛɛ̀ ch.tib. degrees of celsius, centigrade.

ཧྲེ་ཧྲིའི་དྲོད་ཚད་དཔྱད་ཆས་ (hrēhrii trö̱ödzɛɛ̀) ch.tib. centigrade thermometer, celsius thermometer.

ཧྲེང་ (hrēŋ) 1. alone, single ¶ མི་ཧྲེང་ A single person alone (without a family). 2. chisel. 3. ch. a province. 4. ch. 1 liter.

ཧྲེང་ཀྲང་ (hrēŋjaŋ) ch. governor of a province.

ཧྲེང་ངེ་ (hrēŋŋè) sm. ཧྲང་ངེ་.

ཧྲེང་པོ་ (hrēŋbu) 1. sm. ཧྲང་ཧྲང་. 2. sm. ཧྲེང་, 1.

ཧྲེང་ཚེ་ (hrēŋdze) ch. liter.

ཧྲེང་ཧྲེང་ (hrēŋhreŋ) sm. ཧྲང་ཧྲང་.

ཧྲེང་ཨུ་ (hrēŋ ü) ch. provincial committee.

ཧྲེན་ཡང་ (hrēnyaŋ) sm. ཧྲེང་ཡང་.

ཧྲེང་ཨུའི་ཧྲུའུ་ཅི་ (hrēŋ ü hrūji) ch. secretary of provincial party committee.

ཧྲེམ་པོ་ (hrēmbo) hardened, stiff.

ཧྲེའན་ཤིས་ (hrēnshiì) Shanxi (Province).

ཧྲེས་གཉེར་ཁེ་ལས་ (hrɛ̄ɛ ñēr kēlɛɛ̀) ch.tib. commune-managed enterprise/ business.

ཧྲེས་གཉེར་བཟོ་ལས་ (hrēèñer so̱kɛɛ̀) ch.tib. commune-managed factory.

ཧྲོག (hrɔ̄ɔ̀) the upper and lower pieces of wood in a carpet weaving loom.

ཧྲོག་པ་ (hrōgba) granulated ¶ ཅི་ནི་ཧྲོག་པ་ Granulated sugar.

ཧྲོག་པོ་ (hrōgbo) sm. ཧྲོག་པ་.

ཧྲོག་ཧྲོག (hrōghrog) sm. ཧྲོག་པ་.

ཧྲོད་ལོང་ (hrōòloŋ) sm. སྲོད་ལོང་.

ཧྲོབ་བསྡུས་ (hrōɔ̄düù) sm. ཧྲོབ་སྡུད་.

ཧྲོབ་པོ་ (hrōbbo) sm. ཧྲོག་པ་.

ཧྲོབ་ཙམ་ (hrōbdzam) sm. རོབ་ཙམ་.

ཧྲོབ་སྲང་ (hrōbsaŋ) a type of weighing scale.

ཧྲོབ་ཧྲོབ་ (hrōbdrob) sm. ཧྲོག་ཧྲོག.

ཧྲོའུ་དབྱིན་ཅི་ hrūyinji) ch. radio, wireless set.

ཧྲོའུ་དབྱིན་བཅའ་ཚུགས་ (hrōjin ba̱ndzu) ch.tib. radio station.

ཧྲོའུ་ཧྭ་ཧྲི་ (hro fāhri) ch. message center.

ཧྲོའུ་ཧྭང་ཆིན་ (hrōfuŋòin) ch. accordion.

ལྷ་ (lhā) 1. god, deity ¶ རི་འདིའི་སྟེང་ལ་ལྷ་མང་པོ་གནས་ཡོད་པ་རེད་ Many gods dwell on this mountain. 2. abbr. for Lhasa. 3. abbr. ལྷ་ལྕམ་.

ལྷ་ཀླུ་ (lhəlu) 1. name of an aristocratic family. 2. abbr. gods and nāgas.

ལྷ་སྐལ་ (lhəgɛɛ) 1. deities who have an obligation to liberate the sentient beings in certain places, e.g., Avaloketisvara in Tibet. 2. the deities drawn in a tanka commissioned on behalf of someone who has died. 3. one's share of statues.

ལྷ་སྐལ་ཆོས་སྐལ་ (lhəgɛɛ cöögɛɛ) shares of statues and scriptures.

ལྷ་སྐུ་ (lhəgu) 1. icon/ statue of deities. 2. abbr. of ལྷ་ལྕམ་སྐུ་ཞབས་.

ལྷ་སྐུ་ཡལ་ (lhāgu yɛɛ̀) vi. to lose one's trance (shamans) [Lit. the god's body vanishes].

ལྷ་སྐྱོང་ (lhāgyoŋ) shung. the Chinese Emperor Qianlong.

ལྷ་ཁང་ (lhagaŋ) temple, chapel, shrine.

ལྷ་ཁང་པ་ (lhā kāŋba) caretaker of a ལྷ་ཁང་.

ལྷ་ཁང་སྲུང་བ་ (lhāgaŋ sūŋwə) sm. ལྷ་ཁང་པ་.

ལྷ་ཁུལ་ (lhəgüü) 1. the Lhasa area. 2. the realm of the gods.

ལྷ་གོག་འདྲེ་ཞུགས་ (lhāgɔɔ̀ dre̱shuù) 1. a good person being influenced by an evil man. 2. an oracle who goes into a trance being possessed by an evil spirit instead of a deity.

ལྷ་གྲོ་ (lhādro) sm. ལྷ་འཁུ་.

ལྷ་གྲོ་མི་འཁོན་ (lhādro mi̱gön) widespread indignation and discontentment [Lit. the wrath of god and the hatred of men].

ལྷ་མཁར་ (lhāgar) temple for local deities such as ཡུལ་ལྷ་.

ལྷ་འཁུ་ (lhā kū) 1. vi. to get angry (for a god/ deity). 2. va. to cause harm (by a god).

ལྷ་འཁོན་ (lhāgön) sm. ལྷ་འཁུ་.

ལྷ་འཁྲུག (lhādruù) fighting/ quarelling among the gods.

ལྷ་འཁྲོལ་ (lhādröö) asking a god (for permission to leave one's natal house and go as a bride or groom); va.—ཞུ་.

ལྷ་གོས་ (lāgöö) 1. white ceremonial scarf. 2. garments worn by gods/ deities.

ལྷ་དགོངས་དྭངས་ཐབས་ (lhāgoŋ ta̱ŋdəb) trying to do sth. to make a lama or superior's anger subside (apologize); va.—བྱེད་.

ལྷ་དགོངས་དྭངས་གསལ་ (lhāgoŋ ta̱nsɛɛ) to to have a lama or superior's anger subside/ end.

ལྷ་རྒྱ་རི་ (lhəgyəri) name of an old aristocratic family in Tibet.

ལྷ་རྒྱལ་ (lhāgyɛɛ) 1. a male's name. 2. va.—འཐེན་ to toss རྩམ་པ་ into the air while yelling "May the gods be victorious" as an offering to the gods.

ལྷ་རྒྱལ་ཁང་ (lhāgyɛɛgaŋ) house of worship.

ལྷ་སྒྲུང་ (lhādruŋ) myth, fable (about gods).

ལྷ་སྒྲུང་རིག་པ་ (lhādruŋ ri̱gbə) mythology.

ལྷ་ང་ (lhāŋa) kneecap.

ལྷ་ངམ་ཕུན་གསུམ་ (lhāŋam pūnsu) the three districts in S.W. Tibet that belong to the Panchen Lama: ལྷ་རྩེ་; ངམ་རིང་; ཕུན་ཚོགས་གླིང་.

ལྷ་རྔ་ (lhāŋa) god's drum.

ལྷ་ཅིག (lhājig) sm. ལྷ་གཅིག.

ལྷ་གཅིག (lājig) 1. princess. 2. savior, redeemer, monotheistic god.

ལྷ་གཅིག་རྒྱ་བཟའ་ (lhājig gya̱sa) Chinese wife of King Srongtsen Gampo.

ལྷ་གཅིག་ཆོས་ལུགས་ (lhājig cööluù) monotheism.

ལྷ་ལྕམ་ (lhajam) title for wives of tt. government officials.

ལྷ་ལྕམ་སྐུ་ཞབས་ (lhājam gūshəb) term of address for ལྷ་ལྕམ་.

ལྷ་ལྕམ་ཁང་ (lhājamgaŋ) a room set aside for ལྷ་ལྕམ་ at large parties.

ལྷ་ལྕམ་གྱི་ཆས་ (lhājamgi cɛɛ̀) special dress and ornaments worn by ལྷ་ལྕམ་.

ལྷ་ལྕམ་ཆེན་མོ་ (lhajam cēmmo) title for wives of the highest tt. government officials.

ལྷ་ཆས་ (lhājɛɛ̀) 1. garments worn by oracles/ shamans who go into trance. 2. garments put on religious statues.

ལྷ་ཆུ་ (lhəju) 1. a holy spring. 2. the Ganges River.

ལྷ་ཆུ་ལྷ་སྨན་ (lhəju lhāmɛn) medicine consisting of water from a ལྷ་ཆུ་.

ལྷ་ཆོས་ (lhājöö) 1. Buddhism. 2. virtuous deeds.

ལྷ་མཆོད་ཀླུ་མཆོད་ (lhājöö lūjöö) worshipping/ propitiating/ appeasing gods and nagas.

ལྷ་ཆོས་དགེ་བ་བཅུ་ (lhājöö ge̱wa jū) code of ten virtuous deeds people should follow.

ལྷ་མཆོད་མོ་རྒྱག (lhājöö mo̱gyaà) doing propitiation offerings to gods and doing divination.

ལྷ་མཇལ་ (lhājɛɛ) sm. མཆོད་མཇལ་.

ལྷ་རྗེ་ (lhāje) a title for traditional Tibetan doctors.

ལྷ་ཉིད་ (lhāñiì) 1. the god itself. 2. you the god.

ལྷ་ཉིན་དཀར་པོ་ (lhāñiì gārbo) an auspicious day.

ལྷ་གཉེར་ (lhāñer) 1. shung. abbr. of ལྷ་ས་གཉེར་ཚང་ལས་ཁུངས་. 2. shung. the official in charge of the ལྷ་གཉེར་ office. 3. a monk in charge of a temple/ chapel, monk caretaker of a temple/ chapel.

ལྷ་གཉེར་ལས་ཁུངས་ (lhāñer lɛ̱ɛ̀guŋ) abbr. of ལྷ་ས་གཉེར་ཚང་ལས་ཁུངས་.

ལྷ་རྟ་ (lhāda) horse of the deities (a horse that is set aside as an offering and not ridden).

ལྷ་རྟེན་ (lhāden) sm. ལྷ་མཁར་.

ལྷ་སྟིམ་ (lhā dīm) visualizing a meditative deity in meditation and having the deity submerge into oneself.

ལྷ་དོ་ (lhādo) sm. ལྷ་བཙུགས་.

ལྷ་ཐོ་ཐོ་རི་གཉན་བཙན་ (lhā tōtori ñɛndzɛn) the 28th of the ancient Tibetan Kings.

ལྷ་ཐོར་ (lhātɔɔ) smallpox; vi.—ཐོན་ to get smallpox.

ལྷ་མཐོང་འདྲེ་མཐོང་ (lhādoŋ dr̲edoŋ) person whose comments cannot be taken seriously [Lit. see god, see demon].

ལྷ་བདུད་ (lhā dü̲ü̲) gods and demons.

ལྷ་མདུན་ལ་བཞག ཕྱག་རྒྱབ་ལ་བཙལ་ (lhā dü̲nla shaà cāà gyə̲blə dzɛɛ) asking the wrong person for a favor [Lit. leaving the statue in the front and prostrating at the back].

ལྷ་འདེགས་ (lhāndeg) a weighing scale.

ལྷ་འདོགས་ (lhādɔ̀ɔ) a prayer flag which matches the birth sign of a new bride that is put on the roof of the house into which she marries.

ལྷ་འདྲེ་ (lhāndre) spirits, gods and ghost/ demons.

ལྷ་འདྲེ་ཁོག་ཞུགས་ཀྱི་རྟེན་ཁོག (lhāndre kōgshuùgi dēngɔɔ̀) medium, oracle, shaman (a person into whose body gods enter and speak).

ལྷ་འདྲེ་གདོན་བགེགས་ (lhāndre dö̲ngeg) demons and monsters.

ལྷ་འདྲེ་མི་གསུམ་ (lhāndre mi̲sum) the three: gods, demons and men.

ལྷ་འདྲེའི་ཁོག་རྟེན་བུད་མེད་ (lhāndre kōgden pü̲ü̲meè) a female medium/ oracle/ shaman.

ལྷ་འདྲེན་ (lhā dre̲n) shung. transporting things to Lhasa.

ལྷ་རྡོ་དཀར་པོ་ (lhādo gārbo) white stones picked up as symbols of good luck on the 29th of the 12th lunar month.

ལྷ་རྡོ་སློང་ (lhādo lōŋ) va. to pile up stones near the door to indicate that mourning is going on inside.

ལྷ་ལྡན་ (lhādɛn) shung. Lhasa.

ལྷ་ལྡན་རྒྱལ་ཁབ་ (lhādɛn gyɛɛ̲gəb) shung. Lhasa (the seat of the Tibetan government).

ལྷ་ལྡན་གཙུག་ལག་ཁང་ (lhādɛn dzūglagaŋ) the Lhasa Cathedral/Temple (in which the Jokang is located).

ལྷ་སྡེ་མི་སྡེ་ (lhāde mi̲de) shung. 1. monks and lay people. 2. serfs/ subjects on aristocratic and the monastic estates.

ལྷ་སྡོད་ (lhādöö) shung. living/ residing in Lhasa ¶ ལྷ་སྡོད་སྐུ་ཚབ་ The representative living in Lhasa.

ལྷ་གནས་ (lhānɛɛ̀) the abode of the gods.

ལྷ་པ་ (lhāba) sm. ལྷ་ཕེབས་མཁན་.

ལྷ་ཕེབས་ (lhā pēè) va. to have a god enter a medium who is in trance ¶ ལྷ་ཕེབས་མཁན་དེ་ལ་དེང་སང་ལྷ་ཕེབས་ཀྱི་མི་འདུག The god is not entering into that medium these days.

ལྷ་ཕེབས་མཁན་ (lhāpeèñɛn) medium/ oracle/ shaman into whom a god enters to speak.

ལྷ་ཕྱག (lhājaà) prostrating before gods.

ལྷ་ཕྲུག (lhədruù) children of gods and deities.

ལྷ་བ་ (lhāwa) cartilage bone.

ལྷ་བབ་ (lhābəb) 1. a Buddha/ god coming back to this world. 2. sm. ལྷ་ཕེབས་.

ལྷ་བབ་དུས་ཆེན་ (lhābəb dü̲ü̲jen) religious festival commemorating the Buddha coming back to this world.

ལྷ་བུ་ (lhəbu) sm. ལྷ་ཕྲུག.

ལྷ་བྲིས་ (lhədriì) religious artist, painter of tankas.

ལྷ་བྲིས་པ་ (lhəbribə) sm. ལྷ་བྲིས་.

ལྷ་བླ་ (lhāla) sm. ལྷ་བླ་མ་.

ལྷ་བླ་མ་ (lhā lāma)1. abbr. gods and lamas. 2. a king who has become a monk.

ལྷ་དབང་ (lhāwaŋ) 1. religious authority, theocratic power, rule by divine right. 2. power/ authority of the gods. 3. person's name.

ལྷ་དབང་བརྒྱ་བྱིན་ (lhāwaŋ gya̲jin) king of gods.

ལྷ་འབག (lhāmbaà) masks of deities (used in religious dances).

ལྷ་འབངས་ (lhābaŋ) 1. king's subjects. 2. monastic serfs/ subjects.

ལྷ་འབུལ་ (lhā bü̲ü̲) shung. va. to send/ deliver to Lhasa ¶ འཕྲལ་དུ་ལྷ་འབུལ་ཞུ་དགོས་ This must be delivered to Lhasa immediately.

ལྷ་འབེབས་ (lhāmbeb) sm. ལྷ་ཕེབས་.

ལྷ་འབོད་ཀླུ་སྐྱོང་ (lhāmböö lūgyoŋ) sm. ལྷ་འབོད་ཀླུ་འབོད་.

ལྷ་འབོད་ཀླུ་འབོད་ (lhāmböö lūmböö) seeking help everywhere/ desperately [Lit. calling to the deities and calling to the nāgas].

ལྷ་འབྱོར་ (lhānjɔɔ) arriving in India.

ལྷ་འབྲི་ (lhā dri̲) va. to draw/ paint religious scenes (gods and deities).

ལྷ་འབྲུམ་ (lhəndrum) 1. smallpox; vi.— ན་; —ཐོན་ to get/ have smallpox. 2. smallpox vaccination; va.—འཛུགས་ to vaccinate with smallpox.

ལྷ་འབྲུམ་གྱི་སྨན་ (lhəndrumgi mɛ̄n) smallpox vaccine.

ལྷ་མ་ (lhāma) female medium/ oracle/ shaman.

ལྷ་མ་ཡིན་ (lhāmayin) asura, demigods.

ལྷ་མང་ཆོས་ལུགས་ (lhāmaŋ cöölùù) polytheism.

ལྷ་མི་ (lhāmi) gods/ deities and humans.

ལྷ་མི་ཀུན་ (lhāmigün) everyone ¶ ལྷ་མི་ཀུན་ཤེས་ Known by all. [Lit. gods/ deities, men, all].

ལྷ་མིན་ (lhāmin) sm. ལྷ་མ་ཡིན་.

ལྷ་མིན་དབང་པོ་ (lhāmin wāŋbo) king of demigods.

ལྷ་མིན་འདྲེ་མིན་ (lhāmin dre̲min) neither god nor demon.

ལྷ་མིའི་འདྲེན་མཆོག (lhāmii dre̲njɔɔ̀) sm. ལྷ་མིའི་རྣམ་འདྲེན་.

ལྷ་མིའི་རྣམ་འདྲེན་ (lhāmii nāmdren) a term that refers to the Dalai Lama and other high lamas when writing a petition [Lit. liberator of gods and humans].

ལྷ་མེད་སྨྲ་བ་ (lhāmeè māwa) atheism.

ལྷ་མེད་སྨྲ་བ་པོ་ (lhāmeè māwabo) atheist.

ལྷ་མོ་ (lhāmo) 1. goddess. 2. Tibetan folk opera; va.—འཁྲབ་ to perform the Tibetan folk opera.

ལྷ་མོ་དཔལ་ཆེན་མོ་ (lhāmo bɛ̄ɛ cēmmo) sm. དཔལ་ལྡན་ལྷ་མོ་.

ལྷ་མོའི་ཆས་ (lhāmö cɛ̄ɛ̀) Tibetan opera costumes.

ལྷ་མོ་བ་ (lhāmowa) performers in Tibetan folk opera.

ལྷ་མོའི་སྐར་ཚོམ་ (lhāmö gārdzom) the constellation Andromeda.

ལྷ་མོའི་རྟེན་ཁང་ (lhāmö dēngaŋ) a temple dedicated to the worship of a goddess.

ལྷ་མོའི་འདོན་ (lhāmö dö̲n) the beginning of a Tibetan opera.

ལྷ་མོའི་བླ་མཚོ་ (lhāmö lādzo) a sacred lake in southern Tibet where prophetic visions can be seen.

ལྷ་མོའི་གཞུང་ (lhāmö shu̲ŋ) the story of a Tibetan opera.

ལྷ་དམག (lhāmaà) war of the gods/ deities.

ལྷ་སྨན་པ་ (lhāmɛmba) a high title for Tibetan doctors, title of the Dalai Lama's doctor.

ལྷ་བཙུགས་ (lhədzuù) a cairn or small building on a mountain pass for propitiating the gods.

ལྷ་བཙུན་ (lhādzün) 1. monks. 2. a king who became a monk.

ལྷ་ཚངས་པ་ (lhā tsāŋba) Brahma.

ལྷ་རྩུགས་ (lhədzuù) sm. ལྷ་མཁར་.

ལྷ་ཚོགས་ (lhādzɔɔ̀) gathering of gods/ deities.

ལྷ་ཚོང་ (lhādzoŋ) a Lhasa trader.

ལྷ་འཛུགས་ (lhāndzuù) sm. ལྷ་བཙུགས་.

ལྷ་རྫས་མེ་ཏོག (lhāndzɛɛ̀ me̲dog) a type of flower put in letters as an auspicious symbol.

ལྷ་ཞལ་ (lhāshɛɛ) the face of a statue/ god.

ལྷ་ཞིབ་ (lhāshib) checking or investigating an oracle/ shaman.

ལྷ་ཞོ་ (lhāsho) a ཞོ་ unit of weight (in accordance with Lhasa's wight standard).

ལྷ་ཞོལ་ (lhāshöö) 1. the ཞོལ་ area of Lhasa. 2. Lhasa and the ཞོལ་ area.

ལྷ་ཞོལ་གཉིས་ (lhāshöö ñii) the two: Lhasa and the

ཞོལ་ area.

ལྷ་བཞེངས་པ་ལས་བཞུགས་པ་དགའ་ (lhāshɛŋbalɛ shugba ga) it is better to remain calm than to fight or quarrel [Lit. it is better for the statue to sit down than to stand up].

ལྷ་བཟང་ཧན་ (lhāpsaŋ hān) Lhasang khan (Mongol king of Tibet in early 18th century).

ལྷ་བཟོ་བ་ (lhāsowa) makers of statues/ images.

ལྷ་ཡི་བདུད་རྩི་ (lhāyi düüdzi) 1. god's nector. 2. slang for sperm/ sexual intercourse ༑ང་ལ་ལྷ་ཡི་བདུད་རྩི་གནང་རོགས་གནང་ Please have sexual intercourse with me (please give me some god's nectar).

ལྷ་ཡུམ་ (lhāyum) title for the mother of high officials and lamas.

ལྷ་ཡུམ་ཆེན་མོ་ (lhāyum cēmmo) title of the mother of the Dalai Lama.

ལྷ་ཡུལ་ (lhāyüü) the abode of the gods, heaven, paradise.

ལྷ་ཡོད་ (lhāyöö) existing/ present in Lhasa ༑ལྷ་ཡོད་འཐུས་མི་ Delegates present in Lhasa.

ལྷ་ཡོད་པར་སྨྲ་བ་ (lhāyööbar māwa) theism.

ལྷ་ཡོད་སྨྲ་བ་ (lhāyöö māwa) sm. ལྷ་ཡོད་པར་སྨྲ་བ་.

ལྷ་གཡག་ (lhāyaà) a yak that has been set aside and not killed as propitiation for a god.

ལྷ་གཡོག་ (lhāyɔ̀ɔ̀) a person who serves an oracle/ shaman when they go into trance; va.—ཞུ་.

ལྷ་རབ་ལ་ (lhārəbla) the best ༑ལྷ་རབ་ལ་ལོ་གསུམ་བཞུགས་རོགས་ དེ་མ་བྱུང་ན་ལོ་གཅིག་བཞུགས་རོགས་ The best is if you stay three years. If this isn't possible, please stay one year.

ལྷ་རབ་བྱུང་ན་ (lhārəb cuŋna) sm. ལྷ་རབ་ལ་.

ལྷ་རམས་པ་ (lhāramba) the highest geshe degree.

ལྷ་རས་ (lhārɛɛ̀) h. of ཁ་བཏགས་.

ལྷ་རི་ཙན་དན་ (lhāri dzɛ̄ndɛn) white sandalwood.

ལྷ་རིག་ (lhārig) the study of theology.

ལྷ་རིས་ (lhāriì) 1. royal lineage. 2. sm. ལྷ་སྲས་. 3. arc. religious subjects.

ལྷ་རེག་ (lhāreg) h. of ཁ་བཏགས་.

ལྷ་ལ་སྨད་པོ་ (lhāla mɛ̄ɛ̀bo) sb. who insults/ demeans the gods.

ལྷ་ལམ་ (lhālam) sky; vi.—འཁེངས་ the sky being filled with sth. (like clouds/ smoke).

ལྷ་ལུག་ (lhəlug) a sheep whose life has been spared as propitiation of a god.

ལྷ་ལུང་ (lhəluŋ) 1. a god's prophecy. 2. heaven, the god's realm. 3. name of an area in Tsang.

ལྷ་ཤིང་ (lhāshiŋ) tree in which a deity reside.

ལྷ་ཤིང་ཤུག་པ་ (lhāshiŋ shūgbə) 1. sm. ཤུག་པ་. 2. a juniper tree in which a god resides.

ལྷ་ཤུག་ (lhāshug) the root of Dahurian angelica (used in Tibetan medicine).

ལྷ་གསོལ་ཀླུ་གསོལ་ (lhāshöö lūsöö) flattering; va.—བྱེད་ [Lit. worshipping gods, worshipping nāga].

ལྷ་བཤད་འདྲེ་བཤད་ (lhāshɛɛ̀ dreshɛɛ̀) unreliable/ untrustworthy talk [Lit. talking of gods and talking of demons].

ལྷ་བསོས་ (lhāshöö) torma offerings to deities and gods.

ལྷ་ས་ (lhāsa) Lhasa.

ལྷ་ས་སྐྱིད་ཆུ་ (lhāsa gyīìju) Lhasa's Kyichu River.

ལྷ་ས་དགོང་དྲོའི་ཚགས་པར་ (lhāsa goŋdrö tsāgbar) Lhasa Evening Newspaper.

ལྷ་ས་འགྲིམས་འགྲུལ་ཚོང་ལས་ཁང་ (lhāsa dremdrüü tsōŋlɛɛ̀gaŋ) Lhasa Travel Company.

ལྷ་ས་གཉེར་ཚང་ལས་ཁུངས་ (lhāsa ñērdzaŋ lɛɛ̀guŋ) shung. an office of tt. government that was in charge of offerings and supplies.

ལྷ་ས་བ་ (lhɛ̄ɛ̄saà) people from Lhasa.

ལྷ་ས་ཚོ་པ་ (lhāsa tsōba) shung. person in charge of the corvee transport system in Lhasa.

ལྷ་ས་རླུང་འཕྲིན་ (lhāsa lūŋdrin) Lhasa Radio.

ལྷ་ས་གཟུགས་མཐོང་བརྙན་འཕྲིན་ (lhāsa sugdoŋ ñɛ̄ndrin) Lhasa TV.

ལྷ་ས་ཧོ་ལི་ཌེ་ཨིན་མགྲོན་ཁང་ (lhāsa hōlidein dröngaŋ) Holiday Inn, Lhasa.

ལྷ་སའི་ཇོ་བོ་ (lhāsɛɛ jowo) the statue of the Buddha in the Jokang chapel (in Lhasa's cathedral).

ལྷ་སའི་གསར་བརྗེའི་གྱེན་ལོག་ (lhāsɛ sārjee gyenlɔg) Lhasa Revolutionary Rebels (a Lhasa Red Guard Organization).

ལྷ་སང་ཉ་ག་ (lhāsaŋ ñaga) a type weighing scale.

ལྷ་སྲས་ (lhāsɛɛ̀) name given to the sons of high ranking government officials.

ལྷ་སྲིན་ (lhāsin) sm. ལྷ་འདྲེ་.

ལྷ་སྲུང་ (lhāsuŋ) protective deities.

ལྷ་སྲུང་རྒྱུད་སྐུལ་ (lhəsuŋ gyüügüü) asking/ requesting sth. from a protective deity.

ལྷ་གསོལ་ (lhāsöö) religious offerings to gods/ deities; va.—གཏོང་.

ལྷ་གསོལ་ཀླུ་གསོལ་ (lhāsöö lūsöö) 1. sm. ལྷ་མཆོད་ཀླུ་མཆོད་. 2. flattering, bribing.

ལྷ་གསོལ་འདྲེ་བརྡུང་ (lhāsöö dreduŋ) flattering one's superiors and abusing one's inferiors [Lit. worship the gods and beat the demons].

ལྷ་གསོལ་གཞིས་སྐོར་ (lhāsöö shiìgɔɔ) shung. the first vacation of new lay officials when (in theory) they make a tour of their estate(s).

ལྷ་གསོལ་ལོ་ (lhāsöölo) a phrase meaning "offerings to the deities" that is shouted when reaching the top of a mountain pass where the prayer flags are located.

ལྷ་བསངས་ (lhāpsaŋ) burning incense as a ritual offering; va.—གཏོང་.

ལྷ་བསངས་ཁང་ (lhāpsaŋgaŋ) shung. a room in which incense burning ceremonies are held.

ལྷ་ལྷམ་ (lhālham) shoes of gods.

ལྷག་ (lhāà) more than, exceeding ༑རྒྱ་གར་དུ་གྲུ་ཁ་ཆུང་རིགས་ ༡༤༠ ལྷག་ཙམ་ཡོད་པ་རེད་ There are more than one hundred and forty small ports in India. 2. sm. ལྷག་པ་. 3. vi. to be left over, to be remaining ༑གྲོན་དངུལ་བཏང་ནས་སྒོར་སུམ་བརྒྱ་ལྷག་བཞག After paying the expenses, 300 dollars remained.

ལྷགས་སྐྱོན་ (lhāggyön) an error of sth. being too much.

ལྷགས་སྐྱོར་ (lhāggyɔɔ) protecting (one's eyes) from the wind; va.—བྱེད་.

ལྷག་འགྲོལ་ (lhāgdröö) sm. ལྷག་འཕྲོས་.

ལྷག་གེ་བ་ (lhaàgewa) shinning brightly.

ལྷག་གི་ལྷུག་གི་ (lhāgi lhuùgi) baggy, loose.

ལྷག་གྲངས་ (lhāgdraŋ) remainder, balance (in math).

ལྷག་བཅས་ (lhāgjɛɛ̀) remainder, excess, leftover, surplus; vi.—གྲུབ་ to over fulfill, to obtain an excess/ surplus.

ལྷག་ཆད་ (lhāgjɛɛ̀) having extra inclusion and omissions, having too many and too few of sth. ༑ཁོས་ཡི་གེ་བཤུ་སྐབས་ལྷག་ཆད་མང་པོ་བཏང་འདུག When he copied the letter, he added many words and omitted many.

ལྷག་ཆད་ནོར་གསུམ་ (lhāgjɛɛ̀ nɔɔ sūm) the three: adding extra, omitting/ leaving out, and making mistakes ༑རྩིས་ཁྲ་འདིར་ལྷག་ཆད་ནོར་གསུམ་གང་ཡང་མི་འདུག There are no errors, additions or omissions in this accounting.

ལྷག་ཆད་མེད་པ་ (lhāgjɛɛ̀ meèba) not short of or in excess, exactly right.

ལྷག་ཅེ་བ་ (lhāgjewa) excess, surplus.

ལྷག་མཆོད་ (lhāgjöö) the party given after the main party when the leftover supplies are used.

ལྷག་དུ་ (lhagdu) sm. ལྷག་པར་དུ་.

ལྷག་ཐོན་ (lhāg tön) 1. vi. to have an excess of sth. 2. va. to stand out from the rest.

ལྷག་འཐེན་ཆད་གསབ་ (lhāgden cɛ̄ɛ̀səb) taking from excess/ surplus to make up a deficit.

ལྷག་དོན་ (lhāgdön) moreover, furthermore ༑ཁོང་བོད་ལ་ཕེབས་པ་མ་ཟད་ ལྷག་དོན་ལྷ་སར་ཡུན་རིང་བཞུགས་འདུག Not only did he go to Tibet, but furthermore, he lived in Lhasa for a long time.

ལྷག་དོན་དུ་ (lhāgdöndu) sm. ལྷག་དོན་.

ལྷག་གནས་ (lhāgnɛɛ̀) 1. preparation. 2. consecration.

ལྷག་པ་ (lhāgba) 1. Wednesday (usu. གཟའ་ + —). 2. the planet Mercury. 3. sm. ལྷག. 4. sm. ལྷགས་པ་.

ལྷག་པའི་བསམ་པ་རྣམ་པར་དག་པ་ (lhāgbɛ sāmba nāmbar tagba) shung. sm. ལྷག་བསམ་རྣམ་དག.

ལྷག་པར་ (lhāgbar) particularly, extremely ། ལྷག་པར་ཡག་པོ་ Particularly good.

ལྷག་པར་དུ་ (lhāgbardu) sm. ལྷག་དོན་.

ལྷག་པོ་ (lhāgbo) leftover, remainder, extra.

ལྷག་ཕྱོགས་ (lhāgjɔɔ̀) sm. ལྷགས་ཕྱོགས་.

ལྷག་འཕྲོ་ (lhāgdro) sm. ལྷག་འཕྲོས་.

ལྷག་འཕྲོའི་འབོར་གྲངས་ (lhāgdrö bɔrdraŋ) the amount of surplus/ leftover.

ལྷག་འཕྲོས་ (lhāgdruoò) surplus, remnant, remainder, leftover ། དམག་དཔུང་ལྷག་འཕྲོས་ The remaining troops.

ལྷག་བློ་ཟབ་དཀྱིལ་ (lhāglo sabgyee) shung. sm. ལྷག་བསམ་རྣམ་དག.

ལྷག་མ་ (lhāàma) 1. surplus, excess, leftover, remainder ། ངལ་རྩོལ་ལྷག་མ་ Surplus labor. ། རིན་ཐང་ལྷག་མ་ Surplus value. 2. (— + འགྱུར་) vi. to be left behind ། མཁས་པ་ཆེན་པོ་དེ་མིང་གི་ལྷག་མར་གྱུར་པ་རེད་ All that is left behind of that great scholar was his name.

ལྷག་མ་འཇོག (lhāàma jɔ̀ɔ) va. to leave a leftover.

ལྷག་མ་ལུས་ (lhāàma lɛ̀ɛ) vi. to have a leftover/ surplus.

ལྷག་མ་ལུས་ (lhāàma lṳ̀ṳ) sm. ལྷག་མ་ལུས་.

ལྷག་མ་ལྷག (lhāàma lhāà) sm. ལྷག་མ་ལུས་.

ལྷག་མེད་ (lhāàmeè) without remainder/ leftover.

ལྷག་ཙམ་ (lhāgdzam) a little over, a little more ། ལོ་གཅིག་ལྷག་ཙམ་གྱི་རྗེས་སུ་ A little over a year later.

ལྷག་ཚད་ (lhāgdzɛɛ̀) sm. ལྷག་མ་.

ལྷག་རོ་ (lhāgro) sm. ལྷག་མ་.

ལྷག་རོ་དོན་མེད་ (lhāgro tönmeè) superfluous, not needed/ useful.

ལྷག་ལུས་ (lhāglüù) sm. ལྷག་འཕྲོས་.

ལྷག་ལུས་མེད་པ་ (lhāglüù meèba) nothing leftover.

ལྷག་ལེན་ཆད་གསབ་ (lhāglen cɛ̀ɛsəb) taking out excesses and adding to make up deficits/ shortages.

ལྷག་སེམས་ (lhāgsem) sm. ལྷག་བསམ་.

ལྷག་བསམ་ (lhāgsam) 1. sincere, genuine ། ལྷག་བསམ་དགོངས་འཆར་ Sincere suggestion. 2. loyal, faithful ། རྒྱལ་ཁབ་ལ་ལྷག་བསམ་དགོས་པ་རེད་ One should be loyal to the country.

ལྷག་བསམ་དག་པ་ (lhāgsam tagba) sm. ལྷག་བསམ་རྣམ་དག.

ལྷག་བསམ་རྣམ་དག (lhāgsam nāmdaà) 1. sincere, genuine ། ཡོ་ནན་མི་དམངས་ཀྱིས་ལྷག་བསམ་རྣམ་དག་གི་སྒོ་ནས་ཐུགས་རྗེ་ཆེ་ཞུ་གི་ཡིན་ The Vietnamese people sincerely thank (you). 2. loyal, faithful (e.g., to a country).

ལྷག་བསམ་རྣམ་པར་དག་པ་ (lhāgsam nāmbar tagba) sm. ལྷག་བསམ་རྣམ་དག.

ལྷག་བསམ་ཟོལ་མེད་ (lhāgsam sö̀ö̀meè) sm. ལྷག་བསམ་རྣམ་དག.

ལྷག་བསམ་ཟོལ་བྲལ་ (lhāgsam sö̀ö̀drɛɛ) shung. sm. ལྷག་བསམ་རྣམ་དག.

ལྷག་བསམ་བཟང་པོ་ (lhāgsam saŋbo) sm. ལྷག་བསམ་རྣམ་དག.

ལྷག་ལྷག་ཤུལ་ཤུལ་ (lhāglaà shṹṹshüü) leftover, remainder.

ལྷག་ལྷག་ལྷུག་ལྷུག (lhāglaà lhūglhuù) a lot remaining/ leftover.

ལྷག་ལྷུག (lhāglhug) abbr. of ལྷག་ལྷག་ལྷུག་ལྷུག.

ལྷག་ཧྲུལ་ (lhāghrüü) a worthless/ useless remnant, junk.

ལྷགས་ (lhāà) 1. abbr. of ལྷགས་པ་. 2. to arrive, to come ། མི་དེ་མདུན་དུ་ལྷགས་ནས་ The man arrived in his presence. 3. vi. to be left over (with གནས་ཚུལ་ conveys a problem) ། རྩིས་པ་དེ་རྩིས་ཁྲའི་ཐོག་གནས་ཚུལ་ལྷགས་འདུག There is a problem with the accountant's accounting.

ལྷགས་སྐྱོབ་ (lhāggyob) sth. to protect against the wind.

ལྷགས་སྐྱོར་ (lhāggyɔɔ) a wall to break the wind; va.—གཏོང་.

ལྷགས་བསྐྱོད་ (lhāggyöö) shung. va. to arrive ། དབྱིན་ཇིའི་འགོ་དམག་བོད་ལ་ལྷགས་བསྐྱོད་སྐབས་ When the British army arrived in Tibet.

ལྷགས་སྣང་ (lhāggaŋ) sm. ལྷགས་ངར་.

ལྷགས་ངར་ (lhāgŋar) cold wind.

ལྷགས་ཆར་ (lhāgjar) wind and rain.

ལྷགས་པ་ (lhāgba) 1. wind; vi.—རྒྱག to be windy, to blow (wind); vi.—འཇགས་ to subside (wind); vi.—ལང་ to start blowing (wind).

ལྷགས་པ་སྒོར་འཚུབ་ (lhāgba gɔ̄ɔ̄dzub) sm. རླུང་སྒོར་འཚུབ་.

ལྷགས་པ་ཚ་པོ་ (lhāgba tsābo) windy.

ལྷགས་པའི་འགྲོ་ཕྱོགས་ (lhāgbɛ drojɔɔ̀) sm. དུས་ཀྱི་འཁོར་ཕྱོགས་.

ལྷགས་པར་འཕྱར་ (lhāgbar cār) va. to winnow by the wind.

ལྷགས་ཕྱོགས་ (lhāgjɔɔ̀) direction of the wind.

ལྷགས་འཕྱར་གཏོང་ (lhāgjar dōŋ) sm. ལྷགས་པར་འཕྱར་.

ལྷགས་འབྱོར་ (lhāg jɔ̀ɔ) va. to arrive, to come ། མི་དེ་ལྷ་སར་ལྷགས་འབྱོར་བྱུང་རྗེས་སྦྱར་ཆོག་མང་པོ་སྦྱར་འདུག After that person came to Lhasa, he put up many wall posters.

ལྷགས་འཚུབ་ (lhāgdzub) whirlwind; vi.—རྒྱག to blow in the form of a whirlwind.

ལྷགས་རླུང་ (lhəgluŋ) sm. ལྷགས་པ་.

ལྷགས་སིར་ (lhāgsir) cool wind.

ལྷགས་བསིལ་ (lhāgsii) sm. ལྷགས་སིར་.

ལྷང་ངེ་ (lhāŋŋe) clear, distinct.

ལྷང་ཙམ་ (lhāŋdzam) briefly, a little ། ཁྱེད་རང་དགོངས་པ་ཞུ་དགོས་ཡོད་ན་འགོ་ཁྲིད་ལ་ལྷང་ཙམ་ཞུ་དགོས་ If you want to take a leave of absence, you should briefly tell the boss.

ལྷང་ཚེར་ (lhāŋdzer) mica.

ལྷང་འོག་བུ་རོག་མིག (lhāŋ wɔ̀ɔ caroò mi̱i) two points in the knee used for acupuncture.

ལྷང་ལྷང་ (lhāŋlhaŋ) clear, distinct.

ལྷངས་ (lhāŋ) hotness, heat (from liquid/ fire).

ལྷད་ (lhɛ̀ɛ) 1. dilutant, alloy, adulterant; va.—གཏོང་; —ཞུགས་ to dilute, to water down, to alloy, to adulterate ། འོ་མར་ཆུ་ཡི་ལྷད་ཞུགས་བཞག The milk was watered down. 2. vi.—འདྲེ་ to get adulterated །ཁོའི་ལྟ་བ་ལ་དམར་པོའི་ལྷད་འདྲེས་བཞག His views have been adulterated (influenced) by communism.

ལྷད་སྐྱོན་ (lhɛ̀ɛgyön) impurity, adulterant.

ལྷད་སྐྱོན་མེད་པ་ (lhɛ̀ɛgyön meèba) without impurity, pure.

ལྷད་ཅན་ (lhɛ̀ɛjɛn) diluted, alloyed, adulterated.

ལྷད་བཙོས་ (lhɛ̀ɛjöö) tampering, altering, adulterating; va.—བྱེད་.

ལྷད་གཏོང་ (lhɛ̀ɛ dōŋ) see ལྷད་.

ལྷད་དེ་ལྷོད་དེ་ (lhɛ̀ɛde lhö̃ö̃de) loose, loosely (tied).

ལྷད་མ་ (lhɛ̀ɛma) braids; va.—རྒྱག to braid.

ལྷད་མེད་ (lhɛ̀ɛmeè) genuine, pure, unadulterated.

ལྷད་མེད་གད་གཙང་ (lhɛ̀ɛmeè kɛ̀ɛdzaŋ) shung. unmixed, pure.

ལྷད་མེད་རྣམ་དག (lhɛ̀ɛmeè nāmdaà) sincere, genuine.

ལྷད་མེད་པ་ (lhɛ̀ɛmeèba) sm. ལྷད་མེད་.

ལྷད་རྫས་ (lhɛ̀ɛdzɛɛ̀) adulterant, impure substance.

ལྷད་བཞུགས་ (lhɛ̀ɛshuù) see ལྷད་.

ལྷད་ཟན་ (lhɛ̀ɛsɛn) inferior རྩམ་པ་ (barley mixed with other grains).

ལྷད་ཡོད་པ་ (lhɛ̀ɛ yö̀öba) impure, diluted.

ལྷན་ (lhɛn) 1. together ། ཁོང་ཚོ་གསོལ་སྟོན་དུ་ལྷན་ཞིབས་གནང་བ་རེད་ They went together to the party. 2. abbr. of ལྷན་པ་.

ལྷན་སྐྱེས་ (lhɛngyeè) hereditary, innate ། ལྷན་སྐྱེས་ནད་ Hereditary disease.

ལྷན་སྐྱེས་ཀྱི་ཡོན་དན་ (lhɛngyeègi yö̀ndɛn) innate/ inborn knowledge.

ལྷན་སྐྱེས་སྲིན་འབུ་འབྲུག་པ་ (lhɛ̄ngyeè sīmbu trūgbə) AIDS.

ལྷན་ཁང་ (lhɛ̄ngaŋ) committee.

ལྷན་འཁྲབ་ (lhɛ̄ndrəb) joint performance/ festival (theater).

ལྷན་གླན་ (lhɛ̄n lɛ̄n) va. to patch up sth.

ལྷན་རྒྱས་ (lhɛ̄ngyɛɛ̀) 1. together (h.) ¶ཁོང་ལྷན་རྒྱས་ Together with him. 2. council, committee ¶ལྷན་རྒྱས་ཚོགས་པ་དང་སྙན་སེང་ཞུ་རྒྱུ་ཡིན་ As soon as the council is convened, (I) will submit the report.

ལྷན་རྒྱས་གྲོལ་ (lhɛ̄ngyɛɛ̀ tröö) vi. to be over/ let out/ adjourned ¶ད་ལས་ཁུངས་ལྷན་རྒྱས་གྲོལ་སོང་ སྙན་ཞུ་འབུལ་ས་མི་འདུག Now the office has let out so there is no place to submit a report.

ལྷན་རྒྱས་གྲོས་ཚོགས་ (lhɛ̄ngyɛɛ̀ tröödzoò) plenary session/ meeting.

ལྷན་རྒྱས་འཚོག (lhɛ̄ngyɛɛ̀ tsɔ̄ɔ̀) va. to assemble/ gather together.

ལྷན་རྒྱས་འཛོམ་ (lhɛ̄ngyɛɛ̀ dzom) sm. ལྷན་རྒྱས་འཚོག.

ལྷན་རྒྱས་བཞུགས་ (lhɛ̄ngyɛɛ̀ shuù) 1. va. to sit together (h.). 2. va. to cohabit (h.).

ལྷན་སྒྲུབ་ (lhɛ̄ndrub) joint effort; va.—བྱེད་ to make a joint effort.

ལྷན་ཅིག (lhɛ̄njig) together (h.).

ལྷན་ཅིག་སྐྱེས་པ་ (lhɛ̄njig gyēèba) 1. sm. ལྷན་སྐྱེས་. 2. multiple births (twins, triplets, etc.).

ལྷན་ཅིག་ཏུ་ (lhɛ̄njigdu) together (h.).

ལྷན་ཅིག་པ་ (lhɛ̄njigbə) togetherness.

ལྷན་གཅིག (lhɛ̄njig) sm. ལྷན་ཅིག.

ལྷན་བཅར (lhɛ̄njar) going together with sb., accompanying someone (h.).

ལྷན་ཐབས་ (lhɛ̄ndəb) supplementary, additional.

ལྷན་ཐོག (lɛ̄ndɔɔ̀) shung. time when the heads of an office are all present ¶གནས་ཚུལ་དེའི་སྐོར་ངས་ལྷན་ཐོག་སྙན་སེང་ཞུས་པ་ཡིན་ Concerning this information, I made a report when the heads were present.

ལྷན་དུ་ (lhɛ̄ndu) sm. ལྷན་གཅིག་ཏུ་.

ལྷན་ནེ་ (lhɛ̄nne) sm. ལྷང་ངེ་.

ལྷན་ནེ་བ་ (lhɛ̄nnewa) sm. ལྷན་ནེ་.

ལྷན་པ་ (lhɛ̄mba) a patch; va.—རྒྱག; —གླན་ to patch up sth.

ལྷན་པ་ཆུ་ལ་བཙོས་པ་བཞིན་ (lhɛ̄mba cūlə dzōòbəshin) sth. that has no effect or is pointless [Lit. boiling a patch in water].

ལྷན་ཕེབས་མི་སྣ་ (lhɛ̄n pēè minə) entourage, party accompanying sb. (h.) ¶སྲིད་འཛིན་དང་ལྷན་ཕེབས་མི་སྣ་ The president and his party.

ལྷན་པོག (lhɛ̄nbɔɔ̀) shung. sth. that is patched.

ལྷན་མོལ་ (lhɛ̄nmöö) discussion, talk (h.); —བྱེད་; —གནང་.

ལྷན་ཚོགས་ (lhɛ̄ndzɔɔ̀) society, association, council.

ལྷན་འཛོམས་ (lhɛ̄ndzom) h. of མཉམ་འཛོམས་.

ལྷན་འཛོམས་འཁྲབ་སྟོན་ (lhɛ̄ndzom trəbdön) h. of མཉམ་འཛོམས་འཁྲབ་སྟོན་.

ལྷན་འཛོམས་གྲོས་མོལ་ (lhɛ̄ndzom tröömöö) h. of མཉམ་འཛོམས་གྲོས་མོལ་.

ལྷན་འཛོམས་གྲོས་ཚོགས་ (lhɛ̄ndzom tröödzɔɔ̀) sm. ལྷན་འཛོམས་ཚོགས་ཆེན་.

ལྷན་འཛོམས་འདྲི་གཅོད་ (lhɛ̄ndzom drijöö) h. of མཉམ་འཛོམས་འདྲི་གཅོད་.

ལྷན་འཛོམས་ནན་དཔྱད་ (lhɛ̄ndzom nɛ̄ɛ̀jɛɛ̀) h. of མཉམ་འཛོམས་ནན་དཔྱད་.

ལྷན་འཛོམས་ཚོགས་ཆེན་ (lhɛ̄ndzom tsōgjen) (plenary/ full) meeting conference; va.—བྱེད་; —འཚོག.

ལྷན་བཞུགས་ (lhɛ̄nshuù) h. of མཉམ་སྡོད་.

ལྷན་ས་ (lhɛ̄nsa) shung. sm. ལྷན་རྒྱས་.

ལྷབ་བེ་ལྷུབ་བེ་ (lhəbbe lhūbbe) flapping, fluttering.

ལྷབ་ལྷབ་ (lhəbləb) 1. a straightforward/ frank person. 2. sm. ལྷབ་ལྷུབ་.

ལྷབ་ལྷབ་དུ་གཡོ་ (lhəbləbdu yō) vi. to be waving/ fluttering.

ལྷབ་ལྷབ་བྱེད་ (lhəbləb cēè) sm. ལྷབ་ལྷབ་དུ་གཡོ་.

ལྷབ་ལྷུབ་ (ləblub) abbr. of ལྷབ་བེ་ལྷུབ་བེ་.

ལྷབ་ལྷེབ་དུ་འབབ་ (lhəblhebdu bəb) vi. to fall softly (e.g., snowflakes).

ལྷབ་ལྷོབ་ (lhəblob) sm. ལྷབ་ལྷུབ་.

ལྷབས་སེ་ལྷབ་ (lhəbse lhəb) sm. ལྷབ་ལྷུབ་.

ལྷམ་ (lhām) boots, shoes; va.—གྱོན་ to put on or wear boots/ shoes; va.—ཕུད་ to take off boots/ shoes.

ལྷམ་ཀོ་ (lhāmgo) leather for making a boot/ shoe.

ལྷམ་ཀྲད་ (lhāmdrɛɛ̀) heel (of a boot, shoe).

ལྷམ་ཁོག (lhāmgɔɔ̀) sm. ལྷམ་གོག.

ལྷམ་གོག (lhāmgɔɔ̀) shoe, boot.

ལྷམ་གོག་སྣ་ཁུག (lhāmgɔɔ̀ nāguù) toe of a shoe/ boot.

ལྷམ་གོག་ཡུ་རིང་ (lhāmgɔɔ̀ yuriŋ) long boots.

ལྷམ་གྱི་ཆེད་དུ་ རྐང་པ་གཞོག (lhāmgi cēèdu gāŋba shɔɔ̀) sm. ལྷམ་བསྟུན་རྐང་གཞོག.

ལྷམ་མགོ་ (lhāmgo) 1. front part of shoe/ boot. 2. boot, shoe.

ལྷམ་སྒྲོ་གུ་ཅན་ (lhāmdro kujɛn) shoes and boots that have laces or boot straps.

ལྷམ་སྒྲོག (lhāmdrɔɔ̀) shoelace, bootstrap; va.—འགྲོལ་ to undo/ untie shoelaces or bootstrap; va.—འཆིང་ to tie shoelaces or bootstrap.

ལྷམ་ལྕགས་ (lhāmjaà) heel taps/ lifts.

ལྷམ་ཆུང་ (lhāmjuŋ) under political surveillance/ suspicion; va.—གཡོགས་ to place sb. under political surveillance.

ལྷམ་འཇའ་ཆེན་སྔོན་པོ་ (lhām jaajen ŋōmbo) a type of boot worn by the high tt. officials.

ལྷམ་ཏ་ཟེན་མ་ (lhāmda sömma) woolen boots worn by the wives of tt. officials.

ལྷམ་རྟིང་མཐོ་ (lhām diŋdo) high heel shoes.

ལྷམ་བསྟུན་རྐང་གཞོག (lhāmdün gāŋshɔɔ̀) stretch the facts to fit a preconceived idea [Lit. whittle the feet to fit the shoe].

ལྷམ་ཐག (lhāmdaà) sm. ལྷམ་སྒྲོག.

ལྷམ་མཐིལ་ (lhāmdii) sole of boots/ shoes; va.—འདེབས་; —རྒྱག.

ལྷམ་དོག (lhāmdɔɔ̀) sm. ལྷམ་ཀྲད་.

ལྷམ་འདེབས་ (lhām deb) va. to put soles on shoes.

ལྷམ་སྣ་བསྒྱུར་ (lhāmna gyur) va. to leave, to depart.

ལྷམ་སྣུ་ (lhāmbu) woolen (flannel) material for making boots.

ལྷམ་སྣུ་མ་ (lhām būmə) boots made from woolen flannel material.

ལྷམ་བུ་ཆུ་གཤེར་ (lhāmbu cūsher) ladybeetle, ladybug.

ལྷམ་བུ་གཤེར་ (lhāmbusher) abbr. of ལྷམ་བུ་ཆུ་གཤེར་.

ལྷམ་འབོལ་ (lhāmböö) cloth boots/ shoes.

ལྷམ་མེ་ (lhāmme) shining, illuminated; va.—འཕྲོ་ to be shining/ illuminated.

ལྷམ་མེ་ལྷན་ནེ་ལྷང་ངེ་ (lhāmme lhɛ̄nne lhāŋŋe) a majestic appearance (normally in reference to icons and statues).

ལྷམ་མེར་ (lhāmer) sm. ལྷང་ངེར་.

ལྷམ་ཟེན་ (lhāmsön) woolen boots.

ལྷམ་ཟེམ་པ་ (lhāmsömba) sm. ལྷམ་ཟེན་.

ལྷམ་གཟེར་རྒྱག (lhāmsee gyaà) va. to nail the sole of boots/ shoes.

ལྷམ་བཟོ་ (lhāmso) shoemaking, cobbling.

ལྷམ་བཟོ་བ་ (lhāmsɔɔ̀) cobbler, shoemaker.

ལྷམ་ཡུ་ (lhāmyu) leg of boots.

ལྷམ་ཡུ་རིང་ (lhām yuriŋ) sm. ལྷམ་གོག་ཡུ་རིང་.

ལྷམ་རལ་གོས་རལ་ (lhāmrɛɛ kööɾɛɛ) clothing in tatters/ in rags.

ལྷམ་རལ་གོས་ཧྲུལ་ (lhāmrɛɛ kööhrüü) sm. ལྷམ་རལ་གོས་རལ་.

ལྷམ་ཤ་སུམ་མ་ (lhāmsha sūmmə) a type of leather boot worn by monks.

ལྷམ་ཤོལ་ (lhāmshöö) a type of pointed leather shoe.

ལྷམ་ལྷམ་ (lhāmlham) twinkling, shining (of light).

ལྷའི་སྐད་ (lhēgɛɛ̀) Sanskrit.

ལྷའི་གོན་རྒྱག (lhēgön gyaà) va. to wear one's dress untied (with one's arms not in the sleeves).

ལྷའི་འཇིག་རྟེན་ (lhɛ̄ jigden) abode of the gods.

ལྷའི་ཐོ་ཡོར་ (lhɛ̄ tōyɔr) sm. ལྷ་མཁར་.

ལྷའི་གནས་ (lhɛ̄nɛɛ̀) 1. sky. 2. Mount Mehru. 3. abode of the gods, heaven.

ལྷའི་དབང་པོ་ (lhɛ̄ wāŋbo) the creator, Brahama, the lord of the gods.

ལྷའི་རིག་པ་ (lhɛ̄ rigbə) sm. ལྷ་རིག.

ལྷའི་ས་ (lhɛ̄ sā) 1. Lhasa. 2. realm of the gods.

ལྷར་གཡར་འདྲེར་བསྐྱིས་ (lhār yāā dre gyīi) borrowing from everywhere [Lit. to borrow from the gods, borrow from the demons].

ལྷས་ (lhɛ̄ɛ̀) fenced enclosure/ pen/ corral, a place where livestock are kept.

ལྷས་མ་ (lhɛ̄ɛ̀ma) sm. ལྷད་མ་.

ལྷས་མལ་ (lhɛ̄ɛ̀mɛɛ) shung. sm. ལྷས་ར་.

ལྷས་ར་ (lhɛ̄ɛ̀ra) stable, pen, corral.

ལྷས་ལུད་ (lhɛ̄ɛ̀lüü) manure gathered from a corral/ pen.

ལྷིང་ཆགས་ (lhīŋ cāà) vi. to be serene/ calm/ peaceful.

ལྷིང་ཆགས་པོ་ (lhīŋ cāgbo) tranquil, peaceful, calm, quiet.

ལྷིང་འཇགས་ (lhīŋjaà) calm, peaceful, tranquil; va.—སུ་གཏོང་; —འཇུག to calm, to make peaceful/ tranquil, to pacify.

ལྷིང་འཇགས་འཁོར་ཕེབས་ (lhīŋjaà kōōbeb) sm. ལྷིང་འཇགས་.

ལྷིང་འཇགས་པོ་ (lhīŋ jagbo) sm. ལྷིང་ཆགས་པོ་.

ལྷིང་འཇགས་སུ་འཇུག (lhīŋjaàsu juù) see ལྷིང་འཇགས་.

ལྷིང་ནན་ (lhīŋnɛn) abbr. of ལྷིང་པོ་ and ནན་པོ་.

ལྷིང་པོ་ (lhīŋbu) calm, peaceful, tranquil; vi.—ཆགས་ to become peaceful/ calm/ tranquil; va.—བཟོ་ to make peaceful/ calm/ tranquil.

ལྷུ་ (lhū) parts/ pieces of machines.

ལྷུ་ཀང་ (lhūgaŋ) sm. ལྷུ་.

ལྷུ་འགྲིག (lhū drig) vi. to have things fit together well.

ལྷུ་སྒྲིག (lhūdrig) assembling, putting together, installing, erecting; va.—བྱེད་ to assemble, to put together, to install, to erect ། ལས་སྣོན་དང་ལྷུ་སྒྲིག་བྱས་རྗེས་ After processing and assembling.

ལྷུ་སྒྲིག་འཁོར་ཁང་ (lhūdrig kɔ̄ɔgaŋ) assembly shop.

ལྷུ་སྒྲིག་བཟོ་གྲྭ་ (lhūdrig sodra) assembly plant.

ལྷུ་སྒྲིག་བཟོ་པ་ (lhūdrig soba) mechanic, assembler, installer.

ལྷུ་སྒྲིག་རུ་ཁག (lhūdrig rugaà) assembly team.

ལྷུ་སྒྲིག་ལས་རིམ་ (lhūdrig lɛ̀ɛrim) sm. ལྷུ་ལག་སྒྲིག་རིམ་.

ལྷུ་ཆ་ (lhūja) parts of machines.

ལྷུ་ཆུང་ (lhūjuŋ) small parts (of machines).

ལྷུ་ཆེན་ (lhūjen) big parts (of machines).

ལྷུ་གཏོར་ (lhū dɔ̄ɔ) va. to break up, to disintegrate, to demolish sth.

ལྷུ་ཕྲག (lhūdraà) space between joints/ parts/ pieces.

ལྷུ་ཕྲལ་ (lhū trɛ̄ɛ) va. to dismantle, to take apart.

ལྷུ་བུད་ (lhū büü) vi. to have something come loose/ apart.

ལྷུ་འབྲལ་ (lhū drɛɛ) vi. to become dismantled, to come apart.

ལྷུ་ཚིགས་ (lhūdzii) 1. joints (of the hands and legs). 2. parts/ components of a job or task.

ལྷུ་མཚམས་ (lhūndzam) sm. ལྷུ་ཚིགས་.

ལྷུ་ཡངས་པོ་ (lhū yaŋbo) easygoing, relaxed, not strict.

ལྷུ་རུས་ (lhūrüü) sm. ལྷུ་ཚིགས་, 1.

ལྷུ་ལག (lhūlaà) parts of a machine; va.—སྒྲིག to assemble, to install, to put together parts of sth.; vi.—བུད་; —འབྲལ་ to have the parts of sth. come apart ། འཕྲུལ་འཁོར་གསར་པའི་ལྷུ་ལག་དགུ་བརྒྱ་ལྷག་ཙམ་ཡོད་པ་རེད་ There are over nine hundred parts to the new machines.

ལྷུ་ལག་ཀུང་སི་ (lhūlaà gūŋsi) tib. ch. components/ parts company.

ལྷུ་ལག་སྒྲིག་རིམ་ (lhūlaà drigrim) assembly line.

ལྷུ་ལག་རགས་བཟོ་ (lhūlaà ragso) prefabricated components/ parts.

ལྷུ་བཤིག (lhū shīi) va. to disassemble, to take apart.

ལྷུག (lhūù) abbr. of ལྷུག་ལྷུག.

ལྷུག་གེ་བ་ (lhūùgewa) things that hang down loosely (e.g., pot belly, unbelted dress).

ལྷུག་གླེང་ (lhūgleŋ) abbr. of ལྷུག་པོར་གླེང་བ་.

ལྷུག་དུ་གཏོང་ (lhūgdu dōŋ) va. to loosen, to slacken.

ལྷུག་པ་ (lhūgba) 1. prose (in writing). 2. loose.

ལྷུག་པར་བཤད་ (lhūgbar shɛ̄ɛ) 1. prose. 2. sm. ལྷུག་པར་གླེང་.

ལྷུག་པོ་ (lhūgbo) 1. lavish, abundant ། ཁོས་དངུལ་ལྷུག་པོ་བཏང་བ་རེད་ He spent money lavishly. 2. loose, easy, natural, free ། ཁོས་ང་ཚོ་དང་སྐད་ཆ་ལྷུག་པོ་བཤད་པ་རེད་ He spoke naturally with us. ། ཕྱུ་པ་ལྷུག་པོ་ཞིག་དགོས་ (I) need a loose dress.

ལྷུག་པོར་གླེང་ (lhūgbor lēŋ) va. to tell without reservations,to tell as one remembers/ knows.

ལྷུག་པོར་ཤོད་ (lhūgbor shȫö) sm. ལྷུག་པོར་གླེང་.

ལྷུག་མ་ (lhūgmə) prose.

ལྷུག་སྤྲོལ་ (lhūgdzöö) phrase usually used when writing letters to convey: please write often.

ལྷུག་ཚིག (lhūgdzii) sm. ལྷུག་མ་.

ལྷུག་ཡངས་པོ་ (lhūg yaŋbo) sm. ལྷུ་ཡངས་པོ་.

ལྷུག་ཤིག་གེ་བ་ (lhūgshiìgewa) sm. ལྷུག་གེ་བ་.

ལྷུག་བཤད་ (lhūgshɛ̄ɛ) abbr. of ལྷུག་པོར་ཤོད་.

ལྷུག་ལྷུག (lhūglhuù) loose, easygoing, not strict, relaxed; va.—བཟོ་ to loosen; va.—བྱེད་ to act relaxed/ at ease; vi.—ཆགས་ to become loose, to become easygoing/ relaxed/ not strict ། ཕྱུ་པ་ལྷུག་ལྷུག་ཅིག་ཉོས་པ་ཡིན་ I bought a loose dress. ། འགོ་ཁྲིད་གསར་པ་སླེབས་ནས་ལས་ཁུངས་ཀྱི་སྒྲིག་ལམ་ལྷུག་ལྷུག་རེད་བཞག Since the new head arrived, the office's discipline is easygoing.

ལྷུགས་པ་ (lhūgba) sm. ལྷུག་པ་.

ལྷུགས་ཚིག (lhūgdzii) sm. ལྷུག་ཚིག.

ལྷུགས་ལྷུགས་ (lhūglhuù) sm. ལྷུག་ལྷུག.

ལྷུང་ : p. ལྷུངས་; f. ལྷུང་ (lhūŋ) vi. to fall ། ཤ་དེ་ཆུ་ལ་ལྷུང་བཞག The meat fell in the water.

ལྷུང་སྐྱོན་ (lhūŋgyön) accident involving falling over sth. ། གནམ་གྲུ་ལྷུང་སྐྱོན་བྱུང་ནས་འགྲུལ་པ་ཚང་མ་འཆི་སྐྱོན་བྱུང་འདུག The plane crashed and all the travelers were killed.

ལྷུང་ཉེ་ (lhūŋñe) about to fall.

ལྷུང་མ་ (lhūgmə) loose, hanging down.

ལྷུང་བཟེད་ (lhūŋseè) alms bowl (carried by monks).

ལྷུང་ལྷུང་ (lhūŋlhuŋ) descriptive term for the slow flow of a river; vi.—འབབ་ to flow slowly (river).

ལྷུངས་ (lhūŋ) p. of ལྷུང་.

ལྷུན་གྲུབ་ (lhūndrub) 1. natural, occurring naturally ། ལྷུན་གྲུབ་ཀྱི་ནགས་ཚལ་ A natural forest. 2. person's name.

ལྷུན་གྲུབ་མཛེས་སྡུག (lhūndrub dzeèduù) natural beauty.

ལྷུན་གྲུབ་རྫོང་ (lhūndrub dzoŋ) a district just north of Lhasa.

ལྷུན་ཆགས་ (lhūnjaà) grand, majestic.

ལྷུན་ཆེ་བ་ (lhūnjewa) sm. ལྷུན་ཆགས་.

ལྷུན་སྟུག (lhūnduù) 1. tall and majestic (for mountains). 2. sm. ལྷུན་མཐུག་པོ་.

ལྷུན་མཐུག་པོ་ (lhūn tūgbo) thick (usu. for forests).

ལྷུན་སྡུག (lhūnduù) sm. ལྷུན་སྟུག.

ལྷུན་པོ་ (lhūmbu) Mt. Mehru.

ལྷུན་པོ་བརྩེགས་པ་ (lhūmbo dzēgba) tall, high, majestic, grand (for mountains).

ལྷུན་པོར་སྦྲང་མས་གཤོག་རྒྱག (lhūnbɔr draŋmɛ shōggyaà) futile action, sb. weak attacking sb. very strong [Lit. a fly beating his wings against Mt. Mehru].

ལྷུན་རྩེ་རྫོང་ (lhūndze dzoŋ) a district in southern Tibet.

ལྷུབ་ (lhūb) flapping, fluttering.

ལྷུབ་གོན་རྒྱག (lhūbgön gyaà) sm. ལྷའི་གོན་རྒྱག.

ལྷུམས་ (lhūm) h. of མངལ་.

ལྷུམས་ཀྱི་རྒྱ་ལས་གྲོལ་ (lūmgi gyalɛ tröö) vi. to give birth.

ལྷུམས་འཇུག (lhūmjuù) h. of མངལ་འཇུག.

ལྷུམས་སུ་ཞུགས་ (lhūmsu shuù) h. of མངལ་དུ་ཞུགས་.

ལྷུར་པོ་ (lhūrbu) sm. ཧུར་པོ་.

ལྷུར་བརྩོན་ (lhūrdzön) sm. ཧུར་བརྩོན་.

ལྷུར་བཞེས་ (lhūr sheè) h. of ལྷུར་ལེན་.

ལྷུར་ལེན་ (lhūrlen) taking responsibility; va.—བྱེད་ ¶ ལས་འགན་ལྷུར་ལེན་བྱེད་དགོས་པའི་བྱེད་ཕྱོགས་ The policy of needing to take responsibility.

ལྷུས་ཐིངས་ (lhūù tīŋ) sm. ཚོད་ཐིག་པ་.

ལྷེ་པ་ (lhēba) slice/ sliver/ piece of sth. flat ¶ རས་ལྷེ་པ་ཞིག A piece of cloth.

ལྷེན་ (lhēn) cartilage in the middle of the chest.

ལྷེན་རུས་ (lhēnrüù) sm. ལྷེན་.

ལྷེབ་ (lhēb) 1. sm. ལྷེ་པ་. 2. a sickness of horses and mules.

ལྷེབ་ཐུག (lhēbduù) a traditional soup containing flat pieces of dough.

ལྷེབ་པེ་ (lhēbbe) flat.

ལྷེབ་འདྲེག (lhēbdreè) cutting sth. (like meat) into slices; va.—རྒྱག.

ལྷེབ་ཙམ་ལྷེབ་ཙམ་ (lhēbdzam lhēbdzam) 1. slow/ shallow breathing. 2. flapping, fluttering. 3. small pieces.

ལྷེབ་འཛར་ཅན་ (lhēbdzarjɛn) sth. with tassels.

ལྷེབ་ལྷེབ་ (lhēblheb) sm. ལྷེབ་ཙམ་ལྷེབ་ཙམ་.

ལྷེམ་ལྷེམ་ (lhēmlhem) 1. sm. ལྷེབ་ཙམ་ལྷེབ་ཙམ་. 2. shining.

ལྷོ་ (lhō) south.

ལྷོ་ཀོ་རི་ཡ་ (lhō gōriyə) South Korea.

ལྷོ་སྐད་བྱང་སྐད་ (lhōgɛè jaŋgɛè) mixed speech/ dialects/ languages [Lit. southern language, northern language].

ལྷོ་ཁ་ (lhōga) province just southeast of Lhasa.

ལྷོ་ཁ་སྤྱི་ཁྱབ་ (lhōga jīgyəb) shung. governor of Lhoka province.

ལྷོ་ཁ་ས་ཁུལ་ (lhōga sōgüü) area/ region of Lhoka.

ལྷོ་ཁ་བ་ (lhogawa) person from Lhoka.

ལྷོ་ཁུལ་ (lhōgüü) sm. ལྷོ་ཁ་ས་ཁུལ་.

ལྷོ་ཁྲའོ་ཞན་ (lhō trāwoshɛn) tib. ch. South Korea.

ལྷོ་རྒྱུད་ (lhōgyüù) sm. ལྷོ་ངོས་.

ལྷོ་སྒོ་ (lhōgo) a door facing south.

ལྷོ་ངོས་ (lhōŋöò) south, southern direction.

ལྷོ་བལྟ་ (lhō dā) 1. va. to look to the south. 2. southward ¶ ཁང་པ་དེའི་སྒོ་ལྷོ་བལྟ་རེད་བཞག This house's door is facing south.

ལྷོ་སྟོད་ (lhōdöò) southeast.

ལྷོ་མཐའ་ (lhōta) sm. ལྷོ་སྣེ་.

ལྷོ་འདུལ་བྱང་འཐབ་ (lhōndüü caŋdəb) fighting everywhere, campaigning all across the country [Lit. vanquishing the south and battling the north].

ལྷོ་ནུབ་ (lhūnub) southwest.

ལྷོ་སྣམ་ (lhōnam) shung. a woolen material made in southern Tibet.

ལྷོ་སྣེ་ (lhōne) South Pole.

ལྷོ་སྣེ་གླིང་ (lhōne lïŋ) Antarctica.

ལྷོ་པ་ (lhōba) 1. southerner. 2. Sikkimese, Bhutanese.

ལྷོ་སྤྱི་ (lhōji) shung. abbr. of ལྷོ་ཁ་སྤྱི་ཁྱབ་.

ལྷོ་སྤྲིན་ (lhōdrin) southern clouds.

ལྷོ་ཕྱོགས་ (lhōjɔɔ̀) sm. ལྷོ་ངོས་.

ལྷོ་ཕྱོགས་མཚོ་འགྲམ་ས་ཁུལ་ (lhōjɔɔ̀ tsōndram sōgüü) southern coastal areas.

ལྷོ་བུན་ (lhōbün) fog.

ལྷོ་བུར་ (lhōbur) sm. ལྷོ་བུན་.

ལྷོ་བྱང་ (lōjaŋ) north-south, south and north.

ལྷོ་བྱང་དཀྱིལ་ཐིག (lhōjaŋ gyïïdig) meridian line.

ལྷོ་བྱང་ཨ་མེ་རི་ཀ་མཉམ་འབྲེལ་ (lhōjaŋ āmerika ñāmdree) Pan-American Union.

ལྷོ་བྲག (lhōbraà) area in southeast Tibet.

ལྷོ་འབྲས་ (lhō drɛ̱ɛ̀) rice produced in India/ Bhutan.

ལྷོ་འབྲུག་པ་ (lhō drugba) Bhutanese.

ལྷོ་མ་ (lhōma) southern ¶ ལམ་ལྷོ་མ་ Southern road/ route.

ལྷོ་མིན་བྱང་མིན་ (lhōmin caŋmin) sm. གང་ཡིན་འདི་ཡིན་མེད་པ་.

ལྷོ་མོན་ (lhōmön) Monpa ethnic area in southeastern Tibet.

ལྷོ་སྨད་ (lhōmɛɛ̀) lower part of a southern (valley).

ལྷོ་ཚོང་ (lhōdzoŋ) trading in the southern part of Tibet; va.—རྒྱག.

ལྷོ་ཚོང་བྱང་སྐྱེལ་ (lhōdzoŋ caŋgyee) trading goods from the south to the north.

ལྷོ་ཟས་ (lhōsɛɛ̀) foodstuffs from the south of Tibet.

ལྷོ་ཡུལ་ (lhōyüü) places in the south, southern area.

ལྷོ་ཡོ་ནན་ (lhō yonɛn) South Vietnam.

ལྷོ་ཤར་ (lhōshar) southeast.

ལྷོ་ཤར་ཨེ་ཤེ་ཡའི་དམག་དོན་མཐུན་ཚོགས་ (lhōshar ēshiyɛ māgdön tǖndzoò) Southeast Asian Treaty Organization (SEATO).

ལྷོ་ཤར་ཨེ་ཤེ་ཡའི་མཐུན་ཚོགས་རྒྱལ་ཁབ་ (lhōshar ēshiyɛ tǖndzoò gyɛɛgəb) Alliance of Southeast Asian Nations (ASEAN).

ལྷོ་ཤིང་ (lhōshiŋ) Chinese cassia tree.

ལྷོ་ཤོག (lhōshoò) paper produced in southern Tibet.

ལྷོ་ལྷོ་ (lhōlho) exactly south ¶ ཁོང་གི་ཁང་པ་དེ་ཁ་ལྷོ་ལྷོ་ལ་བཞེངས་ནས་བརྒྱབ་བཞག His house was built exactly (facing) south.

ལྷོ་ལྷོ་རྒྱང་ (lhō lhōgyaŋ) sm. ལྷོ་ལྷོ་.

ལྷོ་ཨ་མེ་རི་ཀ་ (lhō āmerigə) South America.

ལྷོག (lhɔɔ̀) va. to recoup, to get back (what was lost in a wager).

ལྷོག་པ་ (lhōgba) an illness.

ལྷོག་ལྷོག (lhōglhɔɔ̀) sm. ལོང་ལོང་.

ལྷོགས་ (lhɔɔ̀) sm. ལྷོག.

ལྷོང་: p. ལྷོངས་; f. ལྷོང་ (lhōŋ) 1. vi. to reach the ear of a superior ¶ གནས་ཚུལ་དེ་རྒྱལ་པོའི་སྙན་དུ་ལྷོངས་བཞག The matter has reached the ear of the king. 2. vi. to erect/ stand up ¶ དར་ཆེན་དེ་མི་མང་པོས་ཡར་ལྷོངས་ཐུབ་སོང་ Many people were able to erect the big flag pole. 3. see ལམ་དུ་ལྷོངས་.

ལྷོང་ལྷོང་ (lhōŋlhoŋ) 1. crowded, packed, buzzing (with people).

ལྷོངས་ (lhōŋ) 1. p. of ལྷོང་. 2. incidental.

ལྷོད་ (lhȫò) 1. abbr. of ལྷོད་པོ་ and ལྷོད་ལྷོད་. 2. sm. གློད་.

ལྷོད་བཀྲོལ་ (lhȫòdröö) releasing, letting loose/ free (e.g. prisoners); va.—གཏོང་ to release, to let loose/ free.

ལྷོད་མཇལ་ (lhȫòjɛɛ) meeting leisurely; va.—བྱེད་.

ལྷོད་འཇགས་ (lhȫòjaà) 1. calmness, tranquility. 2. pacification of a disturbance, making calm/ tranquil; va.—གཏོང་ ¶ ལུང་པ་དེའི་ཟིང་ཆ་ལྷོད་འཇགས་བཏང་འདུག (They) pacified the disturbance in this area.

ལྷོད་འཇགས་སྨན་ (lhȫòjaà mɛ̄n) sedative, tranquilizer.

ལྷོད་འཇགས་སུ་འགྲོ་ (lhȫòjaàsu dro) 1. vi. to become calm/ tranquil/ relaxed. 2. vi. to get pacified.

ལྷོད་འཇོག (lhȫò jɔɔ̀) shung. va. to treat/ leave sth. complacently ¶ ལས་དོན་གལ་ཆེའི་རིགས་ལྷོད་འཇོག་བྱས་ན་མི་འགྲིགས་ One must not treat important tasks complacently.

ལྷོད་བརྟན་ (lhȫòdɛn) sm. ལྷོད་བསྡེང་.

ལྷོད་དལ་ (lhȫòdɛɛ) leisurely, relaxed.

ལྷོད་དུ་འགྲོ་ (lhȫòdu dro) 1. sm. ལྷོད་འཇགས་སུ་འགྲོ་. 2. vi. to become easygoing/ not strict.

ལྷོད་དུ་ཕྱིན་ (lhȫòdu cïn) p. of ལྷོད་དུ་འགྲོ་.

ལྷོད་བདེ་ (lhȫòde) sm. ལྷོད་དལ་.

ལྷོད་པོ་ (lhȫòbo) 1. loose. 2. at ease, relaxed, taking it easy; va.—བྱེད་ ¶ དེང་སང་ང་རྒན་ཡོལ་བྱས་ཏེ་ལྷོད་པོ་བྱས་ནས་བསྡད་ཡོད་ These days I am retired and taking it easy.

ལྷོད་བབ་ (lhȫòbəb) vi. to be at ease/ calm/ relaxed/ at leisure.

ལྷོད་མེད་ (lhȫòmeè) untiring, without rest/ leisure ¶ ཁྲའོ་ཞན་གཅིག་སྒྱུར་དངོས་སུ་འགྲུབ་ཆེད་འབད་བརྩོན་ལྷོད་མེད་བྱས་པ་རེད་ (They) have acted with untiring diligence for the unity of Korea.

ལྷོད་ཙམ་བྱེད་ (lhȫòdzam ceè) 1. va. to take a short break. 2. va. to make sth. more easygoing/ relaxed/ not strict.

ལྷོད་ཞིབ་ (lhȫö̀shib) leisurely and in detail ¶ ཁོང་ཚོས་ཀའ་མོལ་ལྷོད་ཞིབ་མཛད་སོང་ They had a leisurely and detailed conversation.

ལྷོད་ཡངས་ (lhȫö̀yaŋ) 1. complacent, taking things too lightly; va.—བྱེད་; —གཏོང་ ¶ སློབ་སྦྱོང་ལ་ལྷོད་ཡངས་བྱས་ན་ཡར་རྒྱས་ཡོང་གི་མ་རེད་ If one is complacent about one's studies one will not improve. 2. lenient; va.—བྱེད་; —གཏོང་ ¶ གཞུང་གིས་སྲིད་དོན་བཙོན་པར་དོ་དམ་ལྷོད་ཡངས་སུ་གཏོང་གི་ཡོད་པ་རེད་ The government made its policy toward prisoners more lenient.

ལྷོད་ཡངས་ཤོར་ (lhȫö̀yaŋ shɔ̄ɔ̄) 1. vi. to take a matter too lightly, to be careless/ negligent. 2. vi. to be too lenient.

ལྷོད་ཡེངས་ (lhȫö̀yeŋ) sm. ལྷོད་ཡངས་, 1.

ལྷོད་གཡེང་ (lhȫö̀yeŋ) sm. ལྷོད་ཡངས་, 1.

ལྷོད་གཡེང་སྣང་མེད་ (lhȫö̀yeŋ nāŋmeè) complacent, inattentive, careless. 2. taking maters lightly.

ལྷོད་བསླིང་ (lhȫö̀liŋ) calm, peaceful.

ལྷོད་ཤིག་ཤིག (lhȫö̀ shīgshiì) sm. ལྷོད་དལ་.

ལྷོད་ལྷོད་ (lhȫö̀lhöö̀) sm. ལྷོད་པོ་.

ལྷོད་ལྷོད་གནས་ (lhȫö̀lhöö̀ nɛ̄ɛ̀) vi. to be at ease/ at leisure/ relaxed.

ལྷོན་ (lhȫn) sm. ལྷོང་.

ལྷོའི་འཕྲེད་ཐིག (lhȫ trēŋdig) southern latitude.

ལྷོའི་ཁུར་མ་ (lhȫ wu̲rmə) fog.

ཨ

ཨ་ (ā) 1. the letter "a" (used in alphabetical ordering). 2. a polite imperative particle ། སློབ་སྦྱོང་ཡག་པོ་བྱེད་ཨ་ (You) study well. 3. (— + ཡིན་/ ཡོང་/ ཡོད་) express doubt that sth. exists or will happen ། ཁོ་དེ་རིང་སླེབས་ཨ་ཡོང་ (I) don't think he will come today. ། འདི་ཁོང་གི་དེབ་ཨ་ཡིན་ (I) don't think this is his book. ། ཁོ་དེ་རིང་སློབ་གྲྭར་ཨ་ཡོད་ (I) don't think he is at school today. 4. abbr. for ཨ་མི་རི་ཀ་. 5. exclamation: Oh! ། ཨ་ཡ་མཚར་ Oh, how strange.

ཨ་ཀ་མ་ (āgama) sm. སེར་ག་མ་.

ཨ་ཀ་རུ་ (āgaru) sm. ཨ་ག་རུ་.

ཨ་ཀི་ (āge) monkey.

ཨ་ཀོར་ (āgɔɔ) woman's earings.

ཨ་ཀྱང་ (āgyaŋ) a phrase conveying: it was only a joke ། ཨ་ཀྱང་ ངས་སྐྱ་རྩེད་ཞུས་པ་ཡིན་ Its only a joke. I was just kidding.

ཨ་ཀྱུ་ (əgyu) a small hook.

ཨ་ཀྱོག་པ་ཀྱོག (āgyoò bāgyoò) bend, zig zag, not straight.

ཨ་ཀྲད་ (ādreè) wornout soles (of shoes).

ཨ་ཀྲི་ལན་ཀྲིག (ādre lendrig) Atlantic.

ཨ་ཀྲོང་ (ādroŋ) Artemisia capillaris.

ཨ་སྐྱ་ (āgya) lay person.

ཨ་ཁ་ (ā kā) expression of regret/ pity: oh, what a shame/ pity!

ཨ་ཁ་ཁ་ (ā kāga) sm. ཨ་ཁ་.

ཨ་ཁ་ཁ་ཁ་ (ā kāgaga) sm. ཨ་ཁ་.

ཨ་ཁ་མ་ (āgama) a reference to a person or thing that is useless/ worthless.

ཨ་ཁུ་ (əgu) paternal uncle, any paternal male relative of the first ascending generation.

ཨ་ཁུ་སྡོམ་ཐག (əgu domdaà) spider.

ཨ་ཁུ་བསྟན་པ་ (əgu dēmba) a famous Tibetan folk literature trickster.

ཨ་ཁུ་ལྷ་ཤིང་ཤུག་པ་ (əgu lhāshiŋ shūgbə) the tree erected in the middle of the stage when performing Tibetan opera.

ཨ་ཁྱད་མཚར་ (ā kyēndzaa) oh, that is so strange/ wierd.

ཨ་ཁྲ་སྦ་ཁྲ་ (ādra badra) a type of crisscross design.

ཨ་ག་མ་ (āgama) sm. ཨ་ཁ་མ་.

ཨ་ག་རུ་ (āgaru) agalloch eaglewood.

ཨ་ག་རུ་ནག་པོ་ (āgaru nagbo) black ཨ་ག་རུ་.

ཨ་གར་ (āgar) abbr. of ཨ་ག་རུ་.

ཨ་གྲང་ད་གྲང་ (ādraŋ tadraŋ) sm. ཨ་རང་ད་རང་.

ཨ་གྲོ་ (ādro) a high quality wheat.

ཨ་དགོས་ཆུང་ (ā göòjuŋ) without means/ methods of overcoming sth.

ཨ་མགོ་ (āŋgo) the water channel/ way for a water mill.

ཨ་འགོག་ཁྲའོ་རོགས་ (āgɔɔ̀ trāworoò) resist the U.S., help Korea (political slogan).

ཨ་སྒོར་ (āgɔɔ) 1. woman's ear ornament. 2. U.S. dollar.

ཨ་སྒོར་ཁུལ་ (āgɔɔ kǖü) area where U.S. dollars are used.

ཨ་རྒྱ་ (āgya) sm. གཅེན་པོ་.

ཨ་རྒྱལ་ཡང་རྒྱལ་ (āgyεε yaŋgyεε) one victory on top of another.

ཨ་སྔོན་ (āŋön) sm. གནམ་.

ཨ་སྔོན་མཐོངས་ (āŋön tōŋ) sm. གནམ་.

ཨ་ཅག (ājaà) 1. older sister; older female relative of the same generation. 2. polite way of addressing a woman.

ཨ་ཅང་ཅང་ (ā jāŋjaŋ) of course, no need to say, certainly, surely, definitely.

ཨ་ཅང་ཆེ་ (ājanje) sm. ཨ་ཅང་ཅང་.

ཨ་ཅང་བརྗོད་མེད་ (ājaŋ jöömeè) sm. ཨ་ཅང་ཅང་.

ཨ་ཅུག (əjuù) shin bone of sheep (used as in child's game).

ཨ་ཅེ་ (āje) 1. wife. 2. woman.

ཨ་ཅེ་རྒྱ་བཟའ་ (āje gyasa) the Chinese wife of King Srontsen Gampo.

ཨ་ཅེ་ལྷ་མོ་ (āje lhāmo) Tibetan opera; Tibetan opera troupe.

ཨ་ཅེའི་ཕྱུ་པ་ (ājee cūbə) women's dress.

ཨ་ཅོར་ (ājɔɔ) mong. towel.

ཨ་ལྕི་ (əji) arc. father's mother.

ཨ་ལྕོག (ājɔɔ̀) ears.

ཨ་ཆད་ཨུ་ཐུག (ājεὲ ūduù) sm. འ་ཆད་ཨུ་ཐུག.

ཨ་ཆུ་ (əcu) exclamation of feeling cold.

ཨ་ཆུ་ཟེར་བ་ (əju serwa) one of eight cold hells.

ཨ་ཆུང་ (ājuŋ) sm. འ་ཆུང་.

ཨ་ཆུ་ཆུ་ (ā cūju) sm. ཨ་ཆུ་.

ཨ་ཆུག (əjuù) sheep's shin bone used in Tibetan children's game.

ཨ་ཆེ་ (āje) sm. ཨ་ཅེ་.

ཨ་ཆེ་ལྷ་མོ་ (āje lhāmo) Tibetan folk opera.

ཨ་ཆེན་ཐང་ (ājen tāŋ) large field.

ཨ་ཆོར་ (ājɔɔ) sm. ཨ་ཅོར་.

ཨ་མཆོག (āmjɔɔ̀) ear.

ཨ་མཆོག་གྲོང་གྲོང་ (āmjɔɔ̀ drōŋdroŋ) 1. ears standing erectly. 2. hoping for sth.; va.—བྱེད་ to hope for sth.

ཨ་མཆོག་བཀོག་ནས་རྐུབ་ལ་ལྷན་པ་ (āmjɔɔ̀ gɔgnε gūbla lhεmba) doing things that help one aspect but hurt another. [Lit. to pluck off one's ear to patch up one's buttocks].

ཨ་མཆོག་གི་ཨེ་ཁུང་ (āmjɔɔ̀gi ēguŋ) hole in the ear (for placing an earing).

ཨ་མཆོག་སྔོག (āmjɔɔ̀ ŋɔ̀ɔ̀) va. to clean one's ears.

ཨ་མཆོག་སྔོག་ཡག (āmjɔɔ̀ ŋɔ̀ɔ̀yaà) a piece of wood used for cleaning one's ears, an ear pick.

ཨ་མཆོག་ལྟབ་རྗེས་རྒྱག (āmjɔɔ̀ dābdeè gyaà) 1. va. to be sick of hearing sth. and pay no heed. 2. va. to give up hope [Lit. to fold up one's ears].

ཨ་མཆོག་དམར་པོ་ (āmjɔɔ̀ māābo) ears turning red because of shyness/ embarrassment; vi.—ཆགས་ to be embarrassed.

ཨ་མཆོག་རྨ་ཁའི་ལྷན་པ་ (āmjɔɔ̀ māgü lhεmba) sm. ཨ་མཆོག་བཀོག་ནས་རྐུབ་ལ་ལྷན་པ་.

ཨ་མཆོག་ཚ་པོ་ (āmjɔɔ̀ tsābo) very loud, noisy.

ཨ་མཆོག་འོན་ (āmjɔɔ̀ wön) vi. to be/ become deaf.

ཨ་མཆོག་འོན་པོ་ (āmjɔɔ̀ wömbo) deaf.

ཨ་མཆོག་སངས་པོ་ (āmjɔɔ̀ sāŋbo) 1. well informed. 2. having good hearing.

ཨ་མཆོད་ (āmjöö) monks who perform religious services in people's homes.

ཨ་ཇོ་ (ājo) elder brother; elder male relative of the same generation.

ཨ་འཇོག (āmjɔɔ̀) saddle rug.

ཨ་ཉན་ (āñεn) sm. ཤག་ཉན་.

ཨ་ཉོག (āñoò) sm. ཕྱུ་གུ་.

ཨ་མཉམ་ད་མཉམ་ (āñam tañam) even in size/ balance.

ཨ་ད་ (āda) ch. father.

ཨ་ཏི་ཤ་ (ādisha) Atisha.

ཨ་ཏིག་ཡང་ཏིག (ādig yaŋdig) real, essential, final (price) ། ཁྱེད་རང་ལ་བསམ་འཆར་ཨ་ཏིག་ཡང་ཏིག་ག་རེ་གསུང་རྒྱུ་ཡོད་ What is your real opinion? ། རིན་གོང་ཨ་ཏིག་ཡང་ཏིག་གསུངས་དང་ Tell me what is your final price?

ཨ་ཏོ་ (ādo) sm. ཕལ་ཆེར་.

ཨ་ལྟས་ (ādεὲ) handcuffs; va.—རྒྱག to handcuff.

ཨ་སྟོང་ (ādoŋ) yawning; vi.—རྒྱག to yawn.

ཨ་བརྟན་ (ādεn) 1. sm. བརྟན་བརྟན་. 2. the north star.

ཨ་ཐོད་ (ādöö) skull.

ཨ་ཐོད་རི་མོ་ (ādöö rimu) merit, good fortune.

ཨ་འཐས་ (ādεὲ) insisting ། ཁྱེད་རང་ཞིབས་འདོད་ཡོད་ན་ ལྟད་མོར་མཉམ་དུ་ཞིབས་ད་ ཡིན་ན་ཡང་ངས་ཨ་འཐས་ཞུ་

གི་མིན་ If you want to go lets go to the show together, but I am not insisting.

ཨ་དང་ (ādaŋ) physically strong.

ཨ་དར་ (ādaa) term of address for men in Kongpo.

ཨ་དི་ཡང་དི་ (ədi yəŋdi) 1. the best. 2. the final price.

ཨ་དོན་ (ādön) emptiness, void, nothingness.

ཨ་དྲུང་ (ədruŋ) shung. a government messenger (on horseback).

ཨ་དྲུང་རྟ་གཞོན་ (ədruŋ dāshön) shung. sm. ཨ་དྲུང་.

ཨ་དྲུང་རྟ་ཤད་ (ədruŋ dāshɛ̀ɛ) shung. sm. ཨ་དྲུང་རྟ་བཞོན་.

ཨ་མདོ་ (āmdo) Amdo (traditionally the northeastern part of Tibet, now divided between Qinghai, Gansu and Sichuan provinces).

ཨ་མདོ་མགོ་རིལ་ (āmdo gorii) a type of needle made in Amdo.

ཨ་མདོའི་སྐད་ (āmdö gɛ̀ɛ) Amdo dialect.

ཨ་འདྲ་མ་འདྲ་ (ādra madra) same, similar, alike.

ཨ་རྡིང་མགོ་རྡིང་ (ārdiŋ godiŋ) sommersaulting; va.—སློག to sommersault.

ཨ་རྡོ་ (ārdo) cobblestone.

ཨ་སྡུག་ནང་གི་ཡང་སྡུག (əduù naŋgi yaŋduù) the worst of the worst.

ཨ་ན་ (āna) anna (a kind of Indian currency).

ཨ་ན་མ་ན་ (āna mana) 1. persisting, insisting; va.—བྱེད་ ༎ ཁོང་གིས་ཨ་ན་མ་ན་བྱས་ནས་ང་ཐུགས་སྒྲོར་སྐད་བཏང་བྱུང་ He insistingly invited me to the party. 2. similar looking, alike ༎ གཅེན་གཅུང་གཉིས་གཟུགས་པོ་ཆེ་ཆུང་ཨ་ན་མ་ན་རེད་བཞག The younger and older brothers are similar in size.

ཨ་ན་ཨུ་ཚུགས་ (āna ūdzuù) sm. ཨ་ན་མ་ན་, 1.

ཨ་ན་ཨ་ར་ (āna āra) pain.

ཨ་ནན་ (ānɛn) a nickname given to the youngest child.

ཨ་ནན་མ་ནན་ (ānɛn manɛn) being exceedingly careful/ diligent.

ཨ་ནི་ (əni) and then.

ཨ་ནེ་ (əni) nun; va.—བྱེད་ to become a nun; va.—བཟོ་ to make sb. a nun.

ཨ་ནེ་ལོག (əni lɔ̀ɔ) vi. to lose one's vows (for a nun usually as a result of sexual intercourse).

ཨ་ནེ་ལོག་འཁྱོག (əni lɔgyɔ̀ɔ) nuns who go back to secular life.

ཨ་ནེ་ཨ་རྒྱང་ (əni āgyaŋ) sb. who has nothing (slang) ༎ མནའ་མ་འདི་མི་ཚང་དེ་ར་སླེབས་དུས་ཨ་ནེ་ཨ་རྒྱང་རེད་ When the bride arrived at the household (into which she was marrying) she had nothing at all. [Lit. a true nun].

ཨ་ནེ་སློག (əni lɔ̄ɔ) va. to do sth. to make a nun lose her vows.

ཨ་ནེའི་དགོན་པ་ (ənii gömba) nunnery.

ཨ་ནེའི་དབུ་མཛད་ (ənii ūmdzɛ̀ɛ) nun who leads/ conducts collective prayer assemblies.

ཨ་ནུ་ (ānu) 1. child, youth, kid. 2. few, little, small. 3. younger brother.

ཨ་ནེ་ (əne) 1. paternal aunt, female relative of the first ascending generation patrilaterally. 2. nun.

ཨ་ནེ་ལགས་ (ənelaà) term of address for nuns/ paternal aunt.

ཨ་པ་ (āba) sm. ཨ་པ་ལ་.

ཨ་པ་ལ་ (ābala) wow! ༎ ཨ་པ་ལ་ དེ་འདྲའི་ཁང་པ་དེ་ཆེ་བ་ལ་ཨང་ Wow! The building is so big.

ཨ་པོ་ (ābo) 1. older relatives. 2. abbr. of ཨ་པོ་ཧོར་. 3. household. 4. sm. ཨ་པ་. 5. term of address for nomad and Khampa men.

ཨ་པོ་ཧོར་ (ābohɔɔ) a name for the nomads of northern Tibet.

ཨ་ཕ་ (āba) father.

ཨ་ཕ་སྟག་དང་ཨ་མ་གཟིག (āba dāàdaŋ āma sii) having very powerful backers/ supporters [Lit. father is a tiger and mother is a leopard].

ཨ་ཕའི་རོ་ (ābɛro) a slang swear word [Lit. the corpse of your father].

ཨ་ཕེམ་སྐྱ་གོག (ābim gyāgɔ̀ɔ) ཐུད་ made without butter.

ཨ་ཕེ་རི་ཀ་ (ābe rigə) Africa ༎ གླིང་ཆེན་ཨ་ཕེ་རི་ཀ་ The African continent.

ཨ་ཕེ་རི་ཀའི་ཡུལ་ཁག་ཅིག་སྒྲིལ་གྱི་སྒྲིག་འཛུགས་ (ābe rigɛ yüügaà cīgdriigi drigdzuù) Organization of African Unity.

ཨ་ཕེ་རི་ཁ་ (ābe rigə) sm. ཨ་ཕེ་རི་ཀ་.

ཨ་ཕོ་ (āpo) sm. ཨ་པོ་, 5.

ཨ་ཕོ་རྒྱ་བོ་ (ābo gyawo) a type of barley.

ཨ་ཕོ་ང་ཡིན་ (ābo ŋəyin) considering oneself first/ best.

ཨ་ཕོ་ཧོར་ (ābohɔɔ) sm. ཨ་པོ་ཧོར་.

ཨ་ཕྱི་ (əji) 1. sm. ཨ་ཕྱི་མ་. 2. an old woman.

ཨ་ཕྱི་མ་ (əjimə) 1. maternal or paternal grandmother. 2. a protective female deity of Drigung.

ཨ་ཕྱུག་ཚག་པ་ (əjuù tsāgba) grasshopper.

ཨ་ཕྲེང་ (ādreŋ) the vowels in Tibetan.

ཨ་ཕྲུག (əbdruù) young men accompanying sb. on a trip (a kind of bodyguard) ༎ ཚོང་པ་དེ་རྒྱ་གར་ལ་འགྲོ་དུས་ཨ་ཕྲུག་གསུམ་ཁྲིད་བཞག The trader took three young men to accompanying him when he went to India.

ཨ་ཕྲུམ་ (ədrum) cartilage.

ཨ་བ་རི་ (āwari) using the word "pity" in a disdainful manner.

ཨ་བ་ལོ་ཀི་ཏ་ (āwa lokida) Avaloketisvara.

ཨ་བོ་ (ābo) sm. ཨ་པོ་.

ཨ་བོ་ཙམ་ (ābodzam) so so, not bad.

ཨ་བྲ་ (ābdra) pika, vole.

ཨ་བྲས་བསགས་པ་ མཛོ་མོའི་ཁ་ཟས་ (ābrɛ sāgba dzomö kāsɛɛ̀) sb. making use of the things another has accumulated [Lit. the dzo eats what the pika has stored up].

ཨ་བྷི་ཁ་ (ābhigə) fritillaria thunbergii.

ཨ་འབྱོར་ (āmjɔɔ) a pilgrim who travels carrying a long staff.

ཨ་འབྱོར་ལ་ཡ་ང་རྟོག་ཁྲིས་ལ་ཤ་ཚ་ (āmjɔɔ lə yaŋa dogdreèla shādza) envying sb.'s wealth/ possessions but disliking their condition/ looks [Lit. looking down on the pilgrim but envying his pack].

ཨ་བྲ་ (ābra) pika, vole.

ཨ་སྦྱར་ (ājɔɔ) tea with རྩམ་པ་ and butter mixed in.

ཨ་མ་ (āma) 1. mother. 2. main, principal ༎ བཟོ་གྲྭ་ཨ་མ་ The main factory.

ཨ་མ་རྒྱུགས་མཁན་ (āma gyuùñɛn) (with regard to taxes) the main one who pays taxes.

ཨ་མ་དངོས་གནས་ (āma ŋö̀önɛɛ̀) biological mother, real mother.

ཨ་མ་མ་ (āmama) wow (so big, so much).

ཨ་མ་མ་གཡར་ (āma mayaa) stepmother.

ཨ་མ་ཚད་རྡོ་ (āma tsɛɛ̀do) a large stone or pile of stones used in fields as a marker.

ཨ་མ་ལོ་ (āmalo) an expression of surprise such as "wow".

ཨ་མའོ་ (āmo) sm. ཨ་མ་ལོ་ ༎ ཨ་མའོ་ དེ་འདྲའི་མི་མང་བ་ལ་ཨང་ Wow! So many people.

ཨ་མི་དྷ་བྷ་ (āmidabha) Amitabha (Buddha).

ཨ་མའི་བུ་ (āmɛ pu) a real man.

ཨ་མའི་རོ་ (āmɛ ro) slang swear word [Lit. the corpse of your mother].

ཨ་མའི་ཨོ་ལོ་ (āmɛ ōlo) sm. ཨ་མའི་བུ་.

ཨ་མི་རི་ཀ་ (āmirigə) America.

ཨ་མེ་རི་ཀ་ (āmerigə) sm. ཨ་མི་རི་ཀ་.

ཨ་མེ་རི་ཀ་གླིང་ལྷོ་མ་ (āmerigə lī̃ŋ lhōma) South America.

ཨ་མེ་རི་ཀའི་ཁྲིམས་རྩོད་པའི་མཐུན་ཚོགས་ (āmerigɛ trīmdzööbɛ tũ̄ndzɔ̀ɔ) American Bar Association (ABA).

ཨ་མེ་རི་ཀའི་ཁྲིམས་རྩོད་རོགས་སྐྱོར་ཚོགས་པ་ (āmerigɛ trīmdzöö̀ rɔggyɔɔ tsɔ̄gba) Legal Aid Society (U.S.A.).

ཨ་མེ་རི་ཀའི་གྲུ་དམག་དཔུང་སྡེ་ (āmerigɛ trumaà būŋde) United States Marine Corps.

ཨ་མི་རི་ཀའི་གྲོས་ཚོགས་ཀྱི་སྔོན་རྩིས་ལས་དོན་ཁང་ (āmerigɛ trö̱ödzɔɔ̀gi ŋöndzii̇ lɛ̱ɛ̀döngaŋ) Congressional Budget Office (U.S.A.).

ཨ་མི་རི་ཀའི་བགྲེས་ཡོལ་མི་དམངས་མཐུན་ཚོགས་ (āmerigɛ dre̱èyöö mi̱maŋ tǖndzɔɔ̀) American Association of Retired Persons (AARP).

ཨ་མི་རི་ཀའི་རྒྱལ་ནང་ས་ཞིབ་ལས་ཁུངས་ (āmerigɛ gyɛ̱ɛ̱naŋ sɔ̄shib lɛ̱ɛ̀guŋ) Department of the Interior (U.S.A.).

ཨ་མི་རི་ཀའི་རྒྱལ་ཡོངས་གྲོང་ཁྱེར་ཁག་གི་མནའ་འབྲེལ་ (āmerigɛ gyɛ̱ɛ̱yoŋ tro̱ŋgyer kāàgi nāndree) National Urban League.

ཨ་མི་རི་ཀའི་རྒྱལ་ཡོངས་གྲོས་ཚོགས་ (āmerigɛ gyɛ̱ɛ̱yoŋ trö̱ödzɔɔ̀) United States Congress.

ཨ་མི་རི་ཀའི་རྒྱལ་ཡོངས་རི་སྐྱེས་སྲོག་ཆགས་ཀྱི་མཐུན་ཚོགས་ (āmerigɛ gyɛ̱ɛ̱yoŋ rrigyeè sɔ̄gjaàgi tǖndzɔɔ̀) National Wildlife Federation (U.S.A.).

ཨ་མི་རི་ཀའི་རྒྱལ་སྒྲིང་ལུང་འཕྲིན་ཁང་ (āmerigɛ gyɛ̱ɛ̱siŋ lǖŋdringaŋ) Voice of America (VOA).

ཨ་མི་རི་ཀའི་རྒྱལ་སྲུང་སྤུའུ་ (āmerigɛ gyɛ̱ɛ̱suŋbu) the Pentagon (U.S.A.).

ཨ་མི་རི་ཀའི་དྲིལ་བསྒྲགས་ལས་དོན་ཁང་ (āmerigɛ tri̱idraà lɛ̱ɛ̀döngaŋ) United States Information Agency (USIA).

ཨ་མི་རི་ཀའི་གནའ་བོའི་མི་བརྒྱུད་གནད་དོན་སྐོར་གྱི་ལས་ཁང་ (āmerigɛ nāwö mi̱gyüü nɛ̄ɛ̀döŋgɔɔgi lɛ̱ɛ̀gaŋ) Bureau of Indian Affairs (BIA, U.S.A.).

ཨ་མི་རི་ཀའི་སྤྱི་དམངས་རང་དབང་སྲུང་སྐྱོབ་ཀྱི་མཐུན་ཚོགས་ (āmerigɛ jīmaŋ ra̱ŋwaŋ sǖŋgyobgi tǖndzɔɔ̀ American Civil Liberties Union (ACLU).

ཨ་མི་རི་ཀའི་བོད་དོན་རྒྱབ་སྐྱོར་ཚོགས་པ་ (āmerigɛ pö̱ödön gyɔ̱bgyɔɔ tsɔ̄gba) U.S. Tibet Committee.

ཨ་མི་རི་ཀའི་དབུས་སྤྱི་ཁྱབ་ཁྲིམས་འཛིན་པ་ (āmerigɛ ǖü jīgyɔb trīmdzimbɔ) Attorney General (U.S.A.).

ཨ་མི་རི་ཀའི་དབུས་འཕྲོད་བསྟེན་སྤྱི་ཁྱབ་ (āmerigɛ ǖü trö̱öden jīgyɔb) Surgeon General (U.S.A.).

ཨ་མི་རི་ཀའི་དབུས་གསང་བའི་ལས་ཁང་ (āmerigɛ ǖü sāŋwɛ lɛ̱ɛ̀gaŋ) Central Intelligence Agency (CIA, U.S.A.).

ཨ་མི་རི་ཀའི་དམག་ཞབས་ཟུར་པའི་བདེ་དོན་ལས་ཁང་ (āmerigɛ māgshɔb su̱rbɛ de̱dön lɛ̱ɛ̀gaŋ) Veterans Administration (VA, U.S.A.).

ཨ་མི་རི་ཀའི་སྨན་པའི་མཐུན་ཚོགས་ (āmerigɛ mēmbɛ tǖndzɔɔ̀) American Medical Association (AMA).

ཨ་མི་རི་ཀའི་ཚན་རིག་ཡར་རྒྱས་ཀྱི་མཐུན་ཚོགས་ (āmerigɛ tsēnrii̇ ya̱rgyɛɛ̀gi tǖndzɔɔ̀) American Association for the Advancement of Science (AAAS).

ཨ་མི་རི་ཀའི་མཚོ་སྲུང་དཔུང་སྡེ་ (āmerigɛ tsōsuŋ bǖŋde) United States Coast Guard.

ཨ་མི་རི་ཀའི་ཞི་བདེ་ཞིབ་འཇུག་ཁང་ (āmerigɛ shi̱de shīmjuùgaŋ) United States Institute for Peace.

ཨ་མི་རི་ཀའི་བཟའ་འབྲུ་དང་སྨན་རྫས་འཛིན་སྐྱོང་ལས་ཁང་ (ɔ̄merigɛ sa̱ndrudaŋ mēndzɛɛ̀ dzi̱ngyoŋ lɛ̱ɛ̀gaŋ) Food and Drug Aministration (FDA, U.S.A.).

ཨ་མི་རི་ཀའི་ཡིག་ཟམ་ལས་དོན་ཁང་ (ɔ̄merigɛ yigsam lɛ̱ɛ̀döngaŋ) United States Postal Service.

ཨ་མི་རི་ཀར་ཆེད་གཉེར་ཅན་གྱི་ལས་འཆར་ (āmerigɛ cēèñerjɛngi lɛ̱ɛ̀jar) "Contract with America."

ཨ་མེས་ (āmeè) grandfather.

ཨ་མོ་ནིག (āmonig) sm. ཕྱལ་ཇོ་.

ཨ་མོང་ (āmoŋ) sm. ཇ་མོང་.

ཨ་མྲ་ (ām) mango ¶ཨ་མྲའི་སྡོང་པོ་ Mango tree.

ཨ་མྲིད་སྦ་ཛར་པ་ཏྲི་རི་ཀ (āmdriddza bādirigɔ) Amrita Bazar Patrika (an Indian Newspaper).

ཨ་ཙ་མ་ (ādzama) an expression of sorrow: too bad ¶ཨ་ཙ་མ་ ལས་ཀ་འདི་ཡག་པོ་བྱུང་མ་སོང་ Too bad, this work didn't turn out well.

ཨ་ཙ་ར་ (ādzara) skt. acharya: a title for scholars.

ཨ་ཙ་ཙ་ (ā dzādza) sm. ཨ་ཚ་.

ཨ་ཙི་ (ɔ̄dzi) an exclamation of shock, surprise and dismay: oh.

ཨ་ཙི་ཙི་ (ɔ̄ dzīdzi) sm. ཨ་ཙི་.

ཨ་ཙུག་ (ɔ̄dzuù) how? ¶ད་རེས་ཀྱི་ཚོང་དེ་ལམ་འགྲོ་ཆེ་ལོས་ཨ་ཙུག་ཡོང་ How will the business do this time?

ཨ་ཙེ་ (ādze) sm. ཨ་ཙི་.

ཨ་ཚ་ (ādza) expression used for pain: ouch.

ཨ་ཚ་ཚ་ (ā tsādza) sm. ཨ་ཚ་

ཨ་ཚག་ཚག་པ་ (ādzaà tsāgba) grasshopper.

ཨ་མཚར་པོ་ (ā tsārbo) sm. ཨ་མཚན་པོ་.

ཨ་ཝ་ (āwa) h. of ཕྲུ་གུ་.

ཨ་ཝ་སྲས་ (āwa sɛ̄ɛ̀) h. of བུ་.

ཨ་ཝ་སྲས་མོ་ (āwa sɛ̄ɛ̀mo) h. of བུ་མོ་.

ཨ་ཞང་ (āshaŋ) maternal uncle, male relative of first ascending generation matrilaterally.

ཨ་ཞིམ་ (āshim) tasty.

ཨ་ཞེ་ (āshe) female head of a household.

ཨ་ཟེང་སྟག་སེང་ (āsiŋ dāgseŋ) the stuffed lion and tiger displayed during Monlam.

ཨ་འུ་ (āwu) sm. ཨ་འོ་.

ཨ་འུ་ཙི་ (āwodzi) not too bad, so-so.

ཨ་འོ་ (āwo) expression of doubt: oh my ¶ཨ་འོ་ ད་རེས་ན་ཚ་འདི་དྲག་ཨེ་ཡོང་ Oh my, this time I doubt the sickness will get better.

ཨ་འུ་སི་ཀ་ (āwo sīgɔ) a rake.

ཨ་ཡ་ (āya) 1. one of a pair. 2. an expression of frustration/ regret.

ཨ་ཡ་མཚན་ (ā ya̱mdzɛn) sm. ཡ་མཚན་.

ཨ་ཡ་ཡ་ (ā ya̱ya) sm. ཨ་ཡ་, 2.

ཨ་ཡག་དགོས་ན་ཨ་ཚ་སྒོམ་ (āyaà gö̱öna ādza go̱m) if one wants to look good, one must also bear the pain (e.g., by plucking out facial hair).

ཨ་ཡས་ (āyɛɛ̀) sm. ཨ་ཡི་.

ཨ་ཡུ་ (ɔ̄yu) hornless cattle.

ཨ་ཡོ་ (āyo) 1. sm. ཨ་ཡ་. 2. puppy.

ཨ་ཡོང་མགོ་དཀར་ (āyoŋ go̱gar) sm. ཨི་ཡོང་མགོ་དཀར་.

ཨ་ཡོད་ (āyöö̀) probably does not have/ is not ¶ཁོང་ལ་དངུལ་ཨ་ཡོད་ He probably does not have money.

ཨ་ཡོད་ད་ཡོད་ (āyöö̀ ta̱yöö̀) sm. ཨ་ཡོད་ནང་གི་ད་ཡོད་.

ཨ་ཡོད་ནང་གི་ད་ཡོད་ (āyö na̱ŋgi ta̱yöö̀) the very best, the best of the best ¶མི་དེ་ང་ཚོའི་ལས་ཁུངས་ནང་གི་ཨ་ཡོད་ནང་གི་ད་ཡོད་དེ་ཡིན་ That person is the best in our office.

ཨ་ཡོད་ནང་གི་ད་ཡོད་ སྔོང་ངའི་ནང་གི་སེར་རིལ་ (āyö na̱ŋgi ta̱yöö̀ go̱ŋŋɛ na̱ŋgi sērrii) sm. ཨ་ཡོད་ནང་གི་ད་ཡོད་.

ཨ་གཡོག་ནང་གི་ཡང་གཡོག (āyɔɔ̀ na̱ŋgi ya̱ŋyɔɔ̀) servant's servant.

ཨ་ར་ (āra) 1. sm. ཨ་ར་ར་. 2. moustache, beard; va.—འཐོག to pluck one's moustache/ beard. 3. name of a ཁང་ཚན་ in Sera Monastery.

ཨ་ར་དཀར་པོ་ (āra gāàbo) 1. white beard/ moustache. 2. sm. ཧག་ཆེན་.

ཨ་ར་པ་ཙ་ (āra bādza) prayer/ incantation for Manjushri.

ཨ་ར་མ་བཏན་ (āra ma̱dɛn) unable to cope with/ tolerate ¶བྱང་ལ་གནམ་གཤིས་གྲང་མོ་ཡོད་ཙང་ཨ་ར་མ་བཏན་པར་ལོག་དགོས་བྱུང་ Because the weather was so cold in the North I couldn't cope and had to leave.

ཨ་ར་འཛོབ་འཛོབ་ (āra dzo̱bdzob) thick bearded.

ཨ་ར་ར་ (ārara) a cry of pain.

ཨ་ར་སོབ་སོབ་ (āra sōbsob) sm. ཨ་ར་འཛོབ་འཛོབ་.

ཨ་ར་ཡུ་རུ་ (āra yūru) sm. ཨ་ར་ར་.

ཨ་རག (āraà) liquor ¶ཨ་རག་གར་པོ་ Strong/ potent liquor.

ཨ་རག་ཅིའུ་ཅིང་ (āraà jīwujiŋ) tib. ch. ethyl alchol.

ཨ་རག་ཤང་པིན་ (āraà sha̱ŋbin) tib. ch. champagne.

ཨ་རང་སྒང་རང་ (āraŋ ga̱nraŋ) sm. ཨ་རང་ད་རང་.

ཨ་རང་ད་རང་ (āraŋ ta̱raŋ) 1. real, authentic. 2. (with དགུན་) coldest part of winter.

ཨ་རབ་ (ārɔb) Arab.

ཨ་རབ་དམངས་གཙོ་སྤྱི་མཐུན་རྒྱལ་ཁབ་ (ārab māŋdzo jīdün gyɛ̱ɛ̱gɔb) United Arab Republic.

ཨ་རི་ (ɔ̄ri) abbr. of ཨ་མི་རི་ཀ་.

ཨ་རི་དབུས་འཕྲོད་བསྟེན་དང་སྤྱི་དམངས་བདེ་དོན་ལས་ཁང་ (ɔ̄ri ǖü trö̱ödendaŋ jīmaŋ de̱dön lɛ̱ɛ̀guŋ) Department of Health and Human Services

(HHS, in U.S.A.).

ཨ་རི་མང་སྤྱི་གཅིག་སྒྲིལ་ (əri maŋde jīgdrii) United States of America.

ཨ་རི་དམག་ཞབས་འི་སྒྲིག་འཛུགས་ (əri māgshəbbɛ drigdzuù) American Legion.

ཨ་རི་གསང་འཛིན་ལས་ཁངས་ (əri sōŋdrin lɛ̀ɛguŋ) Central Intelligence Agency (CIA).

ཨ་རིའི་ཁྲིམས་རྩོད་པའི་བོད་དོན་རྒྱབ་སྐྱོར་ཚོགས་པ་ (ərii trīmdzööbɛ pöödön gyəbgyɔɔ tsōgba) U.S. Committee of Lawyers for Tibet.

ཨ་རིའི་གྲོས་ཚོགས་ཀྱི་རྒྱལ་ཡོངས་དཔེ་མཛོད་ (ərii tröödzɔɔgi gyɛɛyoŋ bēndzöö) Library of Congress.

ཨ་རིའི་གྲོས་ཚོགས་ཀྱི་ཉམས་ཞིབ་ལས་དོན་ཁང་ (ərii tröödzɔɔgi ñamshib lɛ̀ɛdöngaŋ) Congressional Research Service (U.S.A.).

ཨ་རིའི་གྲོས་ཚོགས་གོང་མ་ (ərii tröödzɔɔ koŋma) United States Senate.

ཨ་རིའི་གྲོས་ཚོགས་འོག་མ་ (ərii tröödzɔɔ wɔ̄ma) U.S. House of Representatives.

ཨ་རིའི་རྒྱལ་ཕྱིན་མཉམ་འབྲེལ་གྱི་བྲ་སྒྲིག་ལས་ཁངས་ (ərii gyɛɛdrɛn ñamdreegi trədrig lɛ̀ɛguŋ) Federal Reserve System (in U.S.A.).

ཨ་རིའི་རྒྱལ་ཚོགས་ (ərii gyɛɛdzɔɔ) U.S. Congress.

ཨ་རིའི་རྒྱལ་ཡོངས་མཁའ་འགྲུལ་དང་མཁའ་དབྱིངས་ལས་དོན་ཁང་ (ərii gyɛɛyoŋ kāndrüüdaŋ kāyiŋ lɛ̀ɛdöngaŋ) National Aeronautics and Space Administration (NASA).

ཨ་རིའི་རྒྱལ་ཡོངས་འཁྱག་བཞུད་དབྱུག་རྩེད་མཐུན་ཚོགས་ (ərii gyɛɛyoŋ kyāgshüü yūgdzeè tűndzɔɔ) National Hockey League.

ཨ་རིའི་རྒྱལ་ཡོངས་ཉམས་ཞིབ་གསར་ཤོག (ərii gyɛɛyoŋ ñamshib sārshoò) National Enquirer newspaper.

ཨ་རིའི་རྒྱལ་ཡོངས་ནང་ཁྲལ་བསྡུ་ལས་ཁང་ (ərii gyɛɛyoŋ naŋ trɛ̄ɛdüü lɛ̀ɛgaŋ) Internal Revenue Service (U.S.A.).

ཨ་རིའི་རྒྱལ་ཡོངས་མི་དམངས་རླུང་འཕྲིན་ཁང་ (ərii gyɛɛyoŋ mimaŋ lūŋdringaŋ) National Public Radio (NPR).

ཨ་རིའི་རྒྱལ་ཡོངས་མི་རིགས་ནག་པོའི་བདེ་དོན་གོང་འཕེལ་གྱི་སྒྲིག་འཛུགས་ (ərii gyɛɛyoŋ mirii nagbö dedön koŋbelgi drigdzuù) National Association for the Advancement of Colored People (NAACP).

ཨ་རིའི་རྒྱལ་ཡོངས་དམངས་གཙོ་དར་སྤེལ་ཐེབས་རྩ་ཁང་ (ərii gyɛɛyoŋ māŋdzo tarbel tēbdzagaŋ) National Endowment for Democracy.

ཨ་རིའི་རྒྱལ་ཡོངས་མེ་མདའི་མཐུན་ཚོགས་ (ərii gyɛɛyoŋ mendɛ tűndzɔɔ) National Rifle Association (NRA).

ཨ་རིའི་རྒྱལ་ཡོངས་ལག་རྩེད་སྦོ་ལོའི་མཐུན་ཚོགས་ (ərii gyɛɛyoŋ lagdzeè bōlö tűndzɔɔ) National Basketball Association (NBA).

ཨ་རིའི་རྒྱལ་ཡོངས་ཤེས་ཡོན་སློབ་གསོའི་མཐུན་ཚོགས་ (ərii gyɛɛyoŋ shēèyön lōbsö tűndzɔɔ) National Education Association (NEA).

ཨ་རིའི་རྒྱལ་ཡོངས་ཨོག་དོམ་སྦོ་ལོའི་མཐུན་ཚོགས་ (ərii gyɛɛyoŋ ōgdom bōlö tűndzɔɔ) National Football League (NFL).

ཨ་རིའི་རྒྱལ་སྲུང་ལྷན་ཁང་ (ərii gyɛɛsuŋ lhɛ̄ngaŋ) National Security Council (U.S.A.).

ཨ་རིའི་སྒྲ་སྐད་ (ərii drəgeɛ̀) Voice of America.

ཨ་རིའི་མངའ་སྡེ་ནང་ཁུལ་གྱི་ཚོང་ལས་འགན་འཛིན་ལྷན་ཁང་ (ərii ŋade nəŋgüügi tsōŋlɛɛ̀ gendzin lhɛ̄ngaŋ) Interstate Commerce Commission (U.S.A.).

ཨ་རིའི་ནག་ཉེས་ལ་ཞུ་གཏུགས་ཀྱི་ཁྲིམས་ཁང་ (ərii nagñeèla shuduùgi trīmgaŋ) United States Courts of Appeal.

ཨ་རིའི་དབུས་གཞུང་གི་བཀར་འཇུག་འགན་འཛིན་ལྷན་ཚོགས་ (ərii üüshuŋgi gānjuù gendzin lhɛ̄ndzoò) Federal Reserve Board (U.S.A.).

ཨ་རིའི་དབུས་གཞུང་གི་དངུལ་ཁང་འཛིན་སྐྱོང་ཁང་ (ərii üüshuŋgi ŋüügaŋ dzingyoŋgaŋ) Federal Reserve System (U.S.A.).

ཨ་རིའི་དབུས་གཞུང་གི་འཛིན་ཆས་ཉོ་སྒྲུབ་དང་བདག་འཛིན་ལས་ཁང་ (ərii üüshuŋgi dzinjɛɛ̀ ñodrubdaŋ dāŋdzin lɛ̀ɛgaŋ) General Services Administration (GSA, U.S.A.).

ཨ་རིའི་སྦྱིན་གཏོང་ཐབས་འཚོལ་སྒྲིག་འཛུགས་ (ərii jindoŋ tābdzöö drigdzuù) United Way (U.S.A.).

ཨ་རིའི་དམག་ཞབས་པའི་སྒྲིག་འཛུགས་ (ərii māgshəbbɛ drigdzuù) American Legion.

ཨ་རིའི་བཟའ་འབྲུ་དང་སྨན་རྫས་འཛིན་སྐྱོང་ལས་ཁང་ (ərii sandrudaŋ mɛ̄ndzɛɛ̀ dzingyoŋ lɛ̀ɛgaŋ) Food and Drug Aministration (FDA, U.S.A.).

ཨ་རིའི་རླང་འཁོར་འཕྲུལ་ལས་པའི་མཉམ་འབྲེལ་ (ərii lāŋgɔɔ trüülɛɛ̀bɛ ñāmdree) United Auto Workers (UAW, U.S.A.).

ཨ་རིའི་ལས་རྩོལ་དང་བཟོ་ལས་མཉམ་སྦྲེལ་སྒྲིག་འཛུགས་ (ərii lɛ̀ɛdzöödaŋ solɛɛ̀ ñāmdree drigdzuù) American Federation of Labor and Congress of Industrial Organizations (AFL-CIO).

ཨ་རིའི་ཨོ་ལིམ་པིག་རྩེད་རིགས་འགན་འཛིན་ཚོགས་ཆུང་ (ərii ōlembig dzēèrig gendzin tsōgjuŋ) United States Olympic Committee.

ཨ་རིལ་ (ərii) having money, well off.

ཨ་རིལ་མཁས་རིལ་ (ərii kɛ̄ɛrii) kidney.

ཨ་རུ་ (əru) 1. a milking utensil made of a yak horn. 2. Myrobulan (Terminalia Chebula).

ཨ་རུ་སྡེར་ཐོན་ (əru derdön) shung. ferreting out, exposing.

ཨ་རེ་ (āre) extremely, very །བུ་མོ་དེ་ཨ་རེ་མཛེས་པོ་འདུག That girl is extremely beautiful.

ཨ་རོ་ (āro) sm. ཨ་ར་.

ཨ་རོགས་ (āroò) an expression of greeting to a friend.

ཨ་ལ་པ་ལ་ (āla bāla) 1. mediocre, common, inferior. 2. slipshod, careless (for work).

ཨ་ལ་པོ་ (ālabo) Arabia.

ཨ་ལ་པོའི་ཨང་ཀི་ (ālabö āŋgi) Arabic numerals.

ཨ་ལ་བ་ལ་ (āla bala) sm. ཨ་ལ་པ་ལ་.

ཨ་ལ་ལ་ (ālala) of course, without doubt, by all means.

ཨ་ལ་ཨོམ་བསྒྲིལ་ (āla ōmdrii) all together །དེ་རིང་གི་ཁེ་བཟང་ཨ་ལ་ཨོམ་བསྒྲིལ་སྒོར་བརྒྱ་བྱུང་བཞག Today, all together, the profit was 100 dollars.

ཨ་ལགས་ (ālaà) surrendering/ giving in/ yielding ། ཨབ་དང་ཚད་སྐབས་མི་ཁོ་འདྲ་པོ་ལ་ཨ་ལགས་ཞུ་གི་མ་རེད་ When wrestling, I will not yield to sb. like him.

ཨ་ལན་ (ālɛn) response, answer; va.—འདེབས་; —རྒྱག་ to respond, to answer (verbally) །ངས་ཁོང་ལ་སྐད་ཆ་དྲིས་པར་ཨ་ལན་བསྒྲིགས་མ་བྱུང་ I asked him sth. but he didn't respond.

ཨ་ལའི་ (ālɛ) an expression of suddenly remembering or of surprise: oh!

ཨ་ལའི་བློའི་ལས་སེ་ (ālɛ lōlüs) 1. scarcastic expression conveying disbelief. 2. sm. ཨ་ལའི་.

ཨ་ལས་ (ālɛɛ̀) 1. an expression of disapproval used before a sentence །ཨ་ལས་འདི་འདྲ་གསུང་རྒྱུ་ཡོད་པ་མ་རེད་ You should not have said that. 2. sm. ཨ་ལའི་.

ཨ་ལས་པད་གོག (ālɛɛ̀ bɛ̄ɛ̀gɔɔ) a doll.

ཨ་ལས་ལ་མོ་ (ālɛɛ̀ lamo) a meaningless phrase used in Tibetan songs to carry a tune.

ཨ་ལུ་ (ālu) children.

ཨ་ལུང་ (āluŋ) sm. ཨ་ལོང་.

ཨ་ལེ་ (āle) 1. sm. ཨ་ལའི་. 2. phrase conveying: shame on you. 3. clitorus.

ཨ་ལེ་པེ་ཀོ་ (āle bēgo) doll.

ཨ་ལེའི་ (ālee) 1. first །ཨ་ལེའི་ང་ཁོང་ལ་སྐད་ཆ་ཤོད་དགོས་ཡོད་ First, I have to talk to him.

ཨ་ལོ་ཀྱོག་ལོ་ (ālo gyɔ̄ɔlo) expression of disapproval/ dislike.

ཨ་ལོག (ālɔɔ̀) 1. turning over, rolling over, va.—རྒྱག to turn over; vi.—ཐེབས་ to be/ get turned over ། རས་སྐམ་བཞག་པ་དེ་ཨ་ལོག་རྒྱབས་དང་ Turn over the cloth that is drying. 2. sm. སྒྲི་མ་.

ཨ་ལོག་ཐེབས་ (ālɔɔ tēb) 1. vi. to improve greatly in wealth །མི་ཚང་དེས་ཚོང་བརྒྱབ་ནས་ལོ་གཅིག་ནང་ཨ་ལོག་ཐེབས་བཞག That family did business and in one year improved greatly in wealth. 2. see ཨ་ལོག ། ཆར་མ་ཨ་ལོག་ཐེབས་མི་འདུག The unthreshed grain has not been turned well.

ཨ་ལོང་ (āloŋ) 1. earring. 2. any circular band of metal. 3. interuterine birth control device (IUD).

ཨ་ལོང་ཁ་ཟ་ (āloŋ kāsa) anus.

ཨ་ལོང་སྒོར་མོ་ (āloŋ gɔ̱ɔmo) sm. ཨ་ལོང་.

ཨ་ལོང་མེ་ལོང་ (āloŋ me̱loŋ) flat/ even (fields or pastures).

ཨ་ལོང་ཡང་ལོང་ (āloŋ ya̱ŋloŋ) 1. a chain of linked rings. 2. repeatedly saying things over again.

ཨ་ཤག (āshaà) buddy, friend.

ཨ་ཤིང་ (əshiŋ) door bolt/ bar; va.—རྒྱག to bolt the door.

ཨ་ཤེ་ (āshe) a high quality ceremonial scarf.

ཨ་ཤོམ་ (āshom) 1. corn. 2. food made of roasted corn.

ཨ་སམ་ (āsam) Assam.

ཨ་སི་ཕི་ལིང་ (āsibiliŋ) aspirin.

ཨ་སུ་ར་ (āsura) skt. a demigod.

ཨ་སུ་འཁར་ (āsu kār) vi. to be in a difficult/ troublesome situation ། ཁོ་དེང་སང་ལས་ཁུངས་ནང་རྩིས་ཁྲའི་སྐོར་ཨ་སུ་འཁར་བརྡུད་བཞག Nowadays he is in a troublesome situation in his office over his accounts.

ཨ་སུ་མུ་ (āsumu) Assam.

ཨ་སོབ་ (āsob) hairy in the face ། ཁྱི་ཨ་སོབ་ Lhasa Apso (dog).

ཨ་སྲུ་ (əsu) maternal aunt; female relatice of the first generation matrilaterally.

ཨ་ལེ་པད་ཀོག (āle bɛ̄ɛ̀gɔɔ̀) a doll.

ཨ་ལྡོག་རྒྱག (ālɔɔ̀ gya̱à) sm. ཨ་ལོག་རྒྱག.

ཨ་གསར་ (āsar) fickle; va.—བྱེད་ to act in a fickle way.

ཨ་གསར་ཅན་ (ā sārjɛn) sm. ཨ་གསར་ཚ་པོ་.

ཨ་གསར་ཅན་ལ་ཕྱི་ཐག་ཐུང་ (ā sārjɛnla ci̱daà tūŋ) fickle and changeable.

ཨ་གསར་ཏ་ལས་མགྱོགས་པ་ གཞུག་གུ་ལུག་ལས་ཐུང་བ་ (ā sār dālɛ gyɔ̱gba shu̱gu lu̱ùlɛ tūŋwə) sm. ཨ་གསར་ཅན་ལ་ཕྱི་ཐག་ཐུང་.

ཨ་གསར་ཚ་པོ་ (āsar tsābo) fickle.

ཨ་ཧ་ (āha) sound of laughter: ha ha.

ཨ་ཧ་ཧ་ (ā hāha) sound of laughter: ha ha.

ཨ་ཧུང་ (āhuŋ) imam, Muslim clergy.

ཨ་ཧྲང་ད་ཧྲང་ (āhraŋ dāhraŋ) extremely cold weather.

ཨ་ཧྲུག་ཅ་ཧྲུག (əhru jəhru) best in quality.

ཨཱ་ལས་ (ālɛɛ̀) sm. ཨ་ལས་.

ཨཱ་ལི་བཞི་ (āli shi̱) the four vowels.

ཨཱ་ཙརྻ་ (ādzarya) sm. ཨ་ཙ་ར་.

ཨ་ཕྲི་གླིང་ (āfiliŋ) African continent.

ཨ་ཕྲི་རི་ཁ་གླིང་ (āfirigə lǐŋ) Africa, African continent.

ཨ་ཧྥུ་ཧན་ (āfuhɛn) Afghanistan.

ཨག (āà) vi. to fall/ drop.

ཨག་ཚོམ་ (āgdom) goatee, beard.

ཨག་ཟ་ (āgsa) sm. ཁ་ཚོམ་ཟ་.

ཨག་ཟེར་ (āg se̱r) va. to scold ། སློབ་གྲྭར་མ་ཕྱིན་ན་ཨ་མ་ལགས་ཀྱིས་ཨག་ཟེར་གྱི་རེད་ If I don't go to school (your) mother will scold you.

ཨག་ལིག (āglig) Poria cocus (an edible fungus used in Tibetan medicine).

ཨག་ཤོག (āgshoò) shung. a type of paper collected as a tax.

ཨང་ (āŋ) 1. rank, position ། ཁོང་ལ་ལྷིད་འདེགས་ཀྱི་ཨང་དང་པོ་རག་པ་རེད་ He got first place in weightlifting. 2. used after verbs to convey sth. like "okay" ། ཁ་ལག་ཟོ་ཨང་ Eat your food, okay.

ཨང་ཀ་ (āŋga) sm. ཨང་ཀི་.

ཨང་ཀ་རྡིང་ཀ་ཀྱག (āŋga dǐŋgə gyāà) a game where each participant stands on one leg and tries to push the other off balance so that he lands on both feet.

ཨང་ཀི་ (āŋgi) number ། ཁང་པ་ཨང་ཀི་དང་པོ་ House (or room) number one.

ཨང་ཀི་དང་པོ་ (āŋgi ta̱ŋbo) 1. number one. 2. the first, the best.

ཨང་ཀི་ལོན་ (əŋgi lö̱n) vi. to pass an exam, to reach the required number to pass (an exam).

ཨང་གོང་ (āŋgoŋ) the second word Tibetans teach babies to get them talking.

ཨང་གི་ (āŋgi) sm.* ཨང་ཀི་.

ཨང་གྲངས་ (āŋdraŋ) number, numeral ། ཁྱེད་རང་གི་ཁ་པར་ཨང་གྲངས་ག་རེ་རེད་ What is your telephone number?

ཨང་གྲངས་འགོད་ (āŋdraŋ gö̱ö̀) va. to register (to get a number) ། སྨན་ཁང་ལ་འགྲོ་དུས་ཨང་གྲངས་འགོད་དགོས་ཀྱི་འདུག One has to register to go to the hospital.

ཨང་གྲངས་སྒྲིག (āŋdraŋ dri̱g) va. to order/ arrange by number, to set in numerical order.

ཨང་གྲངས་འབོད་ (āŋdraŋ bö̱ö̀) 1. va. to call a number.

ཨང་ཅོ་ལི་ (āŋcole) the whelping/ crying sound when a dog is beaten.

ཨང་ཉན་བྱེད་ (āŋñɛn ce̱è) va. to eagerly await/ expect sth. to come ། ཁོང་གིས་ནང་ནས་ཡི་གེ་འབྱོར་རྒྱུ་ཉིན་ལྟར་ཨང་ཉན་བྱེད་ཀྱི་འདུག Every day he is eagerly awaiting receiving a letter from home.

ཨང་གཉིས་པ་ (āŋ ñi̱ibə) 1. number two, second. 2. runner up.

ཨང་ཏར་ (āŋdar) telegram in code.

ཨང་རྟགས་ (āŋdaà) registering, giving a number; va.—རྒྱག; —འགོད་ ། ཡིག་ཆ་རེ་རེ་ལ་ཨང་རྟགས་རྒྱག་དགོས་ Each document must be given a number.

ཨང་ཐོ་ (āŋdo) a register/ list with numbers; va.—འགོད་.

ཨང་དང་ (āŋdaŋ) sm. ཨང་དང་པོ་.

ཨང་དང་པོ་ (āŋ ta̱ŋbo) sm. ཨང་གི་དང་པོ་.

ཨང་གནས་ (āŋnɛɛ̀) 1. a place in the decimal system. 2. the numeral place sb. finishes in a contest.

ཨང་རྩིས་ (əŋdzii) arithmetic; va.—རྒྱག to do arithmetic, to calculate.

ཨང་ཚད་ (āŋdzɛɛ̀) a numerical standard/ mark/ number; vi.—ལོན་ to reach a numerical standard/ mark/ number, to pass an exam.

ཨང་ཚབ་ (āŋdzəb) algebra.

ཨང་འཛིན་ (əŋdzin) license, certificate ། འཁོར་ལོའི་ཨང་འཛིན་ Automobile license.

ཨང་ཡིག (əŋyii) 1. numerical code (in place of letters). 2. digit.

ཨང་ལན་ (āŋlɛn) responding, answering; vi.—སློག to respond/ answer.

ཨང་ཤོག (āŋshoò) slip, ticket, coupon (numbered piece of paper).

ཨང་སི་ (āŋsi) eng. ounce.

ཨང་གསར་ (āŋsar) alert, ready to do/ go; va.—བྱེད་ ། ང་ཚོ་གྲ་སྒྲིག་ཨང་གསར་བྱས་ཡོད་ We are alert and prepared.

ཨང་གསར་ཕྲེ་ལེན་ (āŋsar we̱len) sm. ཨང་གསར་.

ཨན་ (ān) the first vertebra. 2. abbr. of ཨན་གདད་.

ཨན་ཏར་ (āndar) sm. ཨན་རྡར་.

ཨན་དི་སི་ (āndisi) Andes.

ཨན་གདད་ (āndɛɛ̀) wooden shackle/ fetter for the legs.

ཨན་སྡོང་ (āndoŋ) sm. ཨན་, 1.

ཨན་ད་རྙིལ་ (āndañii) sapphire.

ཨན་ཏར་ (āndaa) sm. ཨན་རྡར་.

ཨན་དར་ (āndaa) sm. ཨན་རྡར་.

ཨན་རྡར་ (āndaa) chopping block/ board/ stand.

ཨན་པང་ (ānbaŋ) sm. འང་པན་.

ཨན་པེ་ (ānbe) amphere.

ཨན་པེ་འཇལ་ཆས་ (ānbe je̱ɛjɛɛ̀) eng.tib. ampheremeter.

ཨན་ཚིགས་ (əndzii) sm. ཨན་སྡོང་.

ཨན་ཧུའི་ཞིང་ཆེན་ (ānhwi shi̱njen) Anhui Province.

ཨབ་ (əb) 1. vi. to be numb from cold. 2. sm. ཨབ་བཏབ་.

ཨབ་ཅོར་ (əbjɔɔ) pilgrims who beg on their journey.

ཨབ་ཅོར་ལ་ཡང་བ་མ་རེད་ རྫོག་ཁྲིམས་ལ་ཤ་ཆ་བ་རེད་

(əbjɔɔla yaŋawa mareè dogdreèla shādzawa reè) being concerned not about the person but his wealth [Lit. not compassionate to the pilgrim but concerned about his baggage].

ཨབ་དང་ (əbdaŋ) wrestling; va.—འཆང་; —དཀོར་; —ཙད་ to wrestle.

ཨབ་བདབ་ (əbdəb) va. to embezzle ¶ མི་དེས་གཞུང་གིས་དངུལ་མང་པོ་ཨབ་བདབ་བཞག That person has embezzled a lot of government money.

ཨབ་ཡག (əbyaà) a wooden brush that sweeps the grinding wheel in a water mill.

ཨབ་ར་ (ābra) sm. ཨ་བྲ་.

ཨབ་རས་ཐང་ཁུག་བརྟོལ་ བྱི་བར་ཡ་ལས་ཁེལ་ (ābrɛ tāŋgu dȫȫ ciwar yala kēē) blaming the worng person [Lit. the pika tore up the skin bag and the mouse was blamed].

ཨབ་རིལ་ (əbrii) a family or person who has solid resources.

ཨབ་སོག (əbsɔɔ̀) 1. a type of small hairy dog (e.g., Lhasa apso). 2. face hairy (eg., sb. with a bushy beard).

ཨམ་ (ām) abbr. of ཨ་མཆོག.

ཨམ་གྲོང་ (āmdroŋ) sm. ཨ་མཆོག་གྲོང་གྲོང་.

ཨམ་སྐྲ་ (āmdra) hair in the ear.

ཨམ་ཁྲལ་ (āmdrɛɛ) shung. a tax on animals calculated by counting the number of animal ears.

ཨམ་གུག (āmguù) bent/ drooping ears.

ཨམ་གྲི་ (əmdri) dagger.

ཨམ་ཅོག (āmjoò) ear.

ཨམ་ཆས་ (āmjɛɛ̀) Amdo-style dress.

ཨམ་ཆི་ (əmji) sm. ཨེམ་ཆི་.

ཨམ་ཆོག (āmjoò) sm. རྣ་བ་.

ཨམ་མཆོག (āmjɔɔ̀) sm. ཨམ་ཆོག.

ཨམ་བསྙལ་ (āmñɛɛ) 1. dogs with drooping ears. 2. a hopeless situation.

ཨམ་ཐང་ (āmdaŋ) young and strong.

ཨམ་ཐེར་ར་ (āmtera) person with large ears.

ཨམ་དུམ་ (āmdum) small ears.

ཨམ་གནོན་ (āmnön) a piece of woolen material used inside the Tibetan woolen boot.

ཨམ་པག (āmbaà sm. ཨམ་ཕྲག.

ཨམ་ཕོའི་ཆས་ (āmbö cɛ̄ɛ̀) Amdo-style male dress.

ཨམ་ཕྲག (āmdraà) pouch or pocket (formed by the fold of a dress).

ཨམ་ཕྲག་ལག་རྒྱུས་ (āmdraà laggyüǜ) sb. on the inside knows best what is going on there ¶ ཨམ་ཕྲག་ལག་རྒྱུས་ཀྱི་དཔེ་ལྟར་ང་ཚོའི་ལས་ཁུངས་ཀྱི་གནས་ཚུལ་ངས་མ་ཤེས་པ་མེད་ Like the proverb 'the hand knows what is in the pocket' there is nothing about the affairs of the office that I do not know. [Lit. what is in the pocket is known to the hand].

ཨམ་ཕྲག་ལ་གང་ཡོད་རྫོག་མགོའི་རྒྱུས་ཡོད་རེད་ (āmdraàla kaŋyöȍ dzoggö gyüǜ yɔɔ̀reè) sm. ཨམ་ཕྲག་ལག་རྒྱུས་.

ཨམ་བན་ (āmbɛb) Amban (Chinese Imperial Commissioner).

ཨམ་བན་ཆེན་མོ་ (āmbɛn cēmmo) sm. ཨམ་བན་.

ཨམ་འབྱར་ (āmjar) sb. with flattened ears.

ཨམ་མྱེས་རྨ་ཆེན་གངས་རི་ (āmñeè mājen kəŋri) Amnye Machen Range (in Qinghai).

ཨམ་གཙིགས་ཁོག་བཅུག (əmdziì kɔ̄gjuù) hatred and anger one keeps inside; va.—བྱེད་.

ཨམ་གཙིགས་སྡོམ་ (əmdziì dom) 1. va. to make a face to scare sb. by putting one's upper teeth over one's lower lip. 2. va. to grit teeth ¶ མི་འདི་རྐང་པ་ལ་མེ་མདའ་ཐེབས་ན་ཡང་ཨམ་གཙིགས་བསྡམས་ནས་ཕྱིན་སོང་ Even though this man was shot in the foot he gritted his teeth in pain and left.

ཨམ་ཙ་ (āmdza) near the ears.

ཨམ་ཙེ་དབྱུགས་ (āmdzi yūù) va. to eat ¶ ཁོས་ཨམ་ཙེ་དབྱུག་གི་འདུག He is eating sth.

ཨམ་རལ་ (āmrɛɛ) torn ears (from earings).

ཨམ་ལུག (āmluù) drooping ears.

ཨམ་ཧྲག (āmhraà) sm. ཨམ་ཕྲག.

ཨའི་ཀྲིན་ (ɛ̄drin) eng. iodine.

ཨའུ་ (əwu) 1. grandmother. 2. an expression of worriedness or uncertainty ¶ ཨའུ་ ཁོ་སླེབས་ཤེ་ཡོང་ Oh! Maybe he will not come.

ཨའུ་ནེ་ཙོ་ (əwu nedzo) parrot.

ཨའུ་ཙི་ (ēwudzi) sm. ཨ་བོ་ཙམ་.

ཨའུ་བཞི་དཀའ་ (ēwu shiga) farm implement used for gathering grain ears.

ཨའི་ཅི་ (ēji) Egypt.

ཨའི་ཙེ་ (ēdze) the disease AIDS.

ཨའོ་གླིང་ (āoliŋ) sm. ཨའོ་ད་ལི་ཡ་གླིང་.

ཨའོ་ད་ལི་ཡ་གླིང་ (āodaliya lı̄ŋ) Australian continent.

ཨའོ་ད་ལི་ཡའ་ (āodaliya) ch. Australia.

ཨའོ་མན་ (āomɛn) sm. ཨའོ་མུན་.

ཨའོ་མུན་ (āomün) Macao.

ཨའོ་མུན་པ་ (āomünba) person from Macao.

ཨའོ་ཙམ་ (āodzam) so-so.

ཨར་ཀ་ (ārga) a kind of material used in making roofs.

ཨར་ཀ་གཅོག (ārga jōò) va. to pound/ flatten the floor with ཨར་ཀ་ to put a finish on it.

ཨར་ཀོང་ (ārgoŋ) shung. a white hat worn by officials of the traditional Tibetan Government.

ཨར་ཀྱེ་ (ārgye) an alcoholic, sb. who drinks all the time.

ཨར་སྐྱ་ (ārgya) white myrobalan.

ཨར་སྐོན་ (ārgön) sm. ཨར་ཀོང་.

ཨར་ཁང་ (ārgaŋ) tavern, beer hall, bar. 2. restaurant (that serves alcohol).

ཨར་ཁྲལ་ (ārdrɛɛ) shung. taxes imposed on building houses.

ཨར་ཁྲིམས་སྡོམ་ (ārdrim dom) va. to pass a law against construction/ building.

ཨར་ག (ārga) sm. ཨར་ཀ་.

ཨར་གོང་ (ārgoŋ) quartz.

ཨར་རྒྱག་གི་འུ་ལག (ārgyaàgi wulaà) shung. corvee labor for building/ construction.

ཨར་རྒྱག་བྱེད་སྒོ་ (ārgyaà ceègo) building construction work.

ཨར་རྒྱག་ལས་གྲྭ་ (ārgyaà lɛɛ̀dra) construction/ building site.

ཨར་རྒྱག་ས་ཡུལ་ (ārgyaà səyüü) construction/ building site.

ཨར་རྒྱབ་པ་ (ārgyaàba) building supervisor.

ཨར་ཅལ་ (ārjɛɛ) sm. ཨར་འདམ་ཞལ་བ་.

ཨར་ཆོར་ (ārjɔɔ) sm. ཨ་ཅོར་.

ཨར་ཇག (ārjaà) robbers, bandits.

ཨར་འཇགས་ (ārjaà) 1. vi. to have a situation get calmed down. 2. ཐྲིལ་བ་འཇགས་.

ཨར་གདད་བྱེད་ (ārdɛɛ̀ ceè) va. to do sth. carefully/ meticulously.

ཨར་སྟོན་གཏོང་ (ārdön dōŋ) va. to reward construction workers with food and drinks (at a party).

ཨར་བརྟེན་ (ārden) vi. to endure/ bear ¶ མགོ་ན་ནས་ཨར་བརྟེན་གྱི་མི་འདུག (I) cannot endure the headache.

ཨར་ཐའི་རི་བོ་ (ārde riwo) Altai Mts.

ཨར་འཐུང་རྒྱག (ārduŋ gyaà) va. to drink alcohol together.

ཨར་དམ་ (ārdam) wine/ liquor bottle.

ཨར་འདམ་ (ārdam) cement, concrete; va.—བླུག to lay concrete.

ཨར་འདམ་གྲུ་གཟིང་ (ārdam trusiŋ) concrete boat.

ཨར་འདམ་ལྕགས་རྩིབས་མ་ (ārdam jāgdzibmə) reinforced concrete.

ཨར་འདམ་སྦུ་གུ་བཟོ་གྲྭ་ (ārdam bugu sodra) cement pipe factory.

ཨར་འདམ་ཞལ་བ་ (ārdam shɛɛwa) concrete floor; va.—འདིང་ to lay a concrete floor. 2. concrete wall; va.—རྒྱག.

ཨར་འདམ་བཟོ་གྲྭ་ (ārdam sodra) cement factory.

ཨར་འདམ་བསྲེས་བྱེད་འཁྲུལ་འཁོར་ (ārdam sēèjeè trǖǖgɔɔ) cement mixing machine.

ཨར་པ་ (ārba) 1. drunkard, wino. 2. bandit.

ཨར་པ་ཉི་ཡ་ (ārbañiyə) Albania.

ཨར་པོ་ (ārbo) construction, building; va.—རྒྱག to construct, to build ༁ དེང་སང་གྲོང་ཁྱེར་ནང་ཨར་པོ་མང་པོ་བརྒྱབ་འདུག These days they are doing a lot of construction in the city.

ཨར་པོ་རྒྱག (ārbo gyuù) va. to do construction work/ building.

ཨར་པོ་བ་ (ārbowa) sm. ཨར་ལས་བཟོ་པ་.

ཨར་པོའི་ལས་ཁུངས་ (āwbö lɛ̀ɛguŋ) shung. office in charge of building and construction.

ཨར་པོའི་དོ་དམ་ (ārbö todam) shung. person in charge of construction during the tt. (head of the ཨར་པོའི་ལས་ཁུངས་).

ཨར་བཙུན་ (ārdzün) monks who drink alcohol.

ཨར་ཚོས་ (ārdzöö) beige, tan, camel-colored.

ཨར་རྫུས་ (ārdzüü) false beard.

ཨར་ཞལ་ (ārshɛɛ) abbr. of ཨར་ཀའི་ཞལ་པ་.

ཨར་ཞྭ་ (ārsha) a hat worn by the nomads.

ཨར་གཞས་ (ārshɛ̀ɛ) work songs sung by construction workers.

ཨར་ལན་ (ārlɛn) Ireland.

ཨར་ལས་ (ārlɛ̀ɛ) construction, building work; va.—བྱེད་ to construct, to build.

ཨར་ལས་རྒྱུ་ཆ་ (ārlɛ̀ɛ gyuja) building materials.

ཨར་ལས་དགེ་རྒན་ (ārlɛ̀ɛ) master builder.

ཨར་ལས་དགེ་རྒན་སྤྱི་ཁྱབ་ (ārlɛɛ̀ gegɛn jīgyəb) chief engineer, chief of building site operation.

ཨར་ལས་འཆར་འགོད་པ་ (ārlɛɛ̀ cārgööba) engineer.

ཨར་ལས་པ་ (ārlɛɛ̀ba) sm. ཨར་ལས་བཟོ་པ་.

ཨར་ལས་བཟོ་པ་ (ārlɛɛ̀ soba) construction workers.

ཨར་ལས་ལག་རྩལ་ (ārlɛɛ̀ lagdzɛɛ) civil engineering.

ཨར་ལས་ཡོ་ཆས་ (ārlɛɛ yojɛɛ̀) construction/ building materials.

ཨར་ས་ (ārsa) cement.

ཨར་ཨུར་ (ārur) abbr. of ཨ་ར་ཨུར་ཏུ་.

ཨལ་ཇི་རི་ཡ་ (ɛ̄jiriyə) Algeria.

ཨལ་སྟོང་ (ēdoŋ) sm. ཨ་སྟོང་.

ཨལ་ཐན་ཧན་ (ɛ̄l tēnhan) shung. Altyn Khan: the Mongolian chief (1507-1581) who invited the 3rd Dalai Lama and helped spread Buddhism to Mongolia.

ཨས་གོར་ (ɛɛ̀gɔɔ) sm. ཨ་གོར་.

ཨས་སྒོར་ (ɛ̀ɛgɔɔ) sm. ཨ་གོར་.

ཨས་སི་པི་ལིན་ (ɛ̀ɛsi bīlin) eng. aspirin.

ཨ་སི་ཊེ་རེ་ཡར་ (āsedereya) Australia.

ཨི་ཀ་ (īgə) sm. ཨིག་ཀ་.

ཨི་ཁུང་ (īguŋ) hole; va.—འབིགས་ to drill/ bore a hole.

ཨི་ཁུང་དབྱིབས་གཟུགས་ (īguŋ yībsuù) shape of a hole.

ཨི་ཊ་ལི་ (īdali) Italy.

ཨི་ཐི་ཡོ་པི་ཡ་ (īdiobiya) Ethiopia.

ཨི་ལྡན་གྱི་རྣམ་དབྱེ་ (īdɛngi nāmje) sm. འབྲེལ་སྒྲ་དང་བྱེད་སྒྲ་.

ཨི་ཙི་ལུ་གུ་ (īdzi lugu) tickling, ticklish; va.—གསོག to tickle sb. 2. vi.—ཟ་ to be/ feel ticklish.

ཨི་རན་ (īrɛn) Iran.

ཨི་རིས་འཐག་འཐག (īriì tāgdaà) the sound of Tibetan weaving on a loom.

ཨི་སི་ཀུལ་ (īsigüü) eng. school.

ཨི་སི་པི་རིང་ (īsibiriŋ) eng. spring, coil.

ཨི་སི་སྤི་རི་ (īsi biri) eng. spirit (used for starting pressure lamps).

ཨི་སི་ལ་མུ་ (īsilamu) Islam.

ཨི་སི་རལ་ (īserɛɛ) Israel.

ཨིག་ཀ་ (īggə) hiccups; vi.—རྒྱག to have hiccups.

ཨིག་སྒྲ་ (īgdra) sound of hiccups.

ཨིགས་པ་ (īgbə) sm. ཨིག་ཀ་.

ཨིག་བུ་ (īgbu) sm. ཨིག་ཀ་.

ཨིང་ཇི་ (īŋji) Britain, British.

ཨིང་ལན་ (īŋlɛn) England.

ཨིང་ལན་ཊ་ (īŋlɛnda) England.

ཨིན་དུ་ནི་ཤ་ཡ་ (īndu nishyə) Indonesia.

ཨིན་དྲ་ནི་ལ་ (īndra nilə) sapphire.

ཨིན་ཌོ་ནི་ཤི་ཡ་ (īndo niya) Indonesia.

ཨིནྡྲ་ནཱི་ལ་ (īndrañi) sapphire.

ཨིནྡྲ་ནི་ལ་ (īndrañi) sapphire.

ཨིས་ (yiì) ch. beer.

ཨུ་ (ū) abbr. ch. committee, council, commission.

ཨུ་ཐུག (ūduù) sm. ཏུ་ཐུག.

ཨུ་ནན་ (ūnün) sm. ཨུ་ཚུགས་ཆེ་པོ་.

ཨུ་ལུག་དགུ་ལུག (ūluù guluù) full (with drinks).

ཨུ་མའི་མངལ་ཁྲག (ūmɛ ŋɛ̀ɛdraà) sm. ཐུག་ཞེན་.

ཨུ་མའི་བདག་པོ་ (ūmɛ dagbo) Shiva (a Hindu god).

ཨུ་མུ་སུ་ (ūmusu) sm. ཨོ་མོ་སུ་ལུ་.

ཨུ་མུ་སུ་ཞྭ་མོ་ (ūmusu shamo) woollen knit cap/ hat.

ཨུ་མུ་སུ་ལུ་ (ūmu sūlu) sm. ཨོ་མོ་སུ་ལུ་.

ཨུ་བཙུགས་ (ūdzuù) sm. ཨུ་ཚུགས་.

ཨུ་ཙ་དིང་ག (ūdz dīŋgə) hopping; va.—རྒྱག.

ཨུ་ཚུགས་ (ūdzuù) insisting; va.—བྱེད་; —རྒྱག to insist ༁ ཁོང་གིས་ང་ནང་ལ་ཤོག་ཟེར་ཨུ་ཚུགས་རྒྱག་གི་འདུག He is insisting saying, "Come to my house".

ཨུ་ཚུགས་མཐར་སྐྱེལ་ (ūdzuù tārgyee) sm. ཨུ་ཚུགས་.

ཨུ་ཚུགས་ཆེ་པོ་ (ūdzuù tsābo) sb. who is very insistent.

ཨུ་ཟུར་ཁ་ (ū surga) a point in the shoulder for doing moxabustion.

ཨུ་ཡོ་ (ūyo) puppy.

ཨུ་ཡོན་ (ūyün) ch. committee member.

ཨུ་ཡོན་ཀྲང་ (ūyündraŋ) ch. chairman of a committee.

ཨུ་ཡོན་ཀྲང་གཞོན་པ་ (ūyündraŋ shomba) ch.tib. vice chairman of a committee.

ཨུ་ཡོན་ལྷན་ཁང་ (ūyün lhɛ̄ngaŋ) committee, commission, council.

ཨུ་རུ་སུ་ (ūrusu) Russia.

ཨུ་རུ་སུ་གོང་མའི་རྒྱལ་ཁབ་ (ūrusu koŋmɛ gyɛɛgəb) Czarist Russian state.

ཨུ་རུ་སུ་རྒྱ་གསེར་ (ūrusu gyaser) Russian brocade.

ཨུ་རུ་སུའི་སྐད་ (ūrusü gɛ̄ɛ̀) the Russian language.

ཨུ་རུས་མུ་རུས་ (ūrüù murüù) doing diligently; va.—བྱེད་ ༁ ཁོང་གིས་ཨུ་རུས་མུ་རུས་བྱས་ནས་ལས་འགན་དེ་བསྒྲུབས་སོང་ He worked diligently and accomplished his task.

ཨུ་ལུ་ (ūlu) pot, vessel (liquids).

ཨུ་སུ་ (ūsu) socks.

ཨུ་སུ་གུ་དུང་ (ūsu kuduŋ) knit underwear.

ཨུ་སུ་སྟོད་ཐུང་ (ūsu dȫöduŋ) knit sweater.

ཨུ་སུ་ཞྭ་མོ་ (ūsu shamo) sm. ཨུ་མུ་སུ་ཞྭ་མོ་.

ཨུ་ཧན་ (ūhɛn) Wuhan.

ཨུ་ཧུ་ལགས་ (ūhulaà) word expressing sadness/ sorrow/ regret.

ཨུ་ཧུ་ཧུ་ (ūhuhu) sound made when a person is disappointed or regretting.

ཨུང་གུ་ (ūŋgu) oil lamp.

ཨུང་དིའི་ (ūŋdii) sm. ཝོང་ཏི་.

ཨུད་ (ūù) ch. abbr. of ཨུ་ཡོན་ལྷན་ཁང་.

ཨུར་ (ūr) sm. དབུར་.

ཨུར་གེར་ཏུ་ (ūrgerda) mong. a person in charge of loading yaks.

ཨུར་ཆག (ūrjaà) polishing; va.—རྒྱག.

ཨུར་དི་ (ūrdi) sm. དབུར་དི་.

ཨུར་ཤིང་ (ūrshiŋ) wood for polishing wooden bowls.

ཨེ་ (ē) particle conveying probably not ༁ མོ་ནང་ལ་ཨེ་ཡོད་ She is probably not at home.

ཨེ་ཀར་ (ēgar) eng. acre.

ཨེ་གོར་ (ēgɔr) long female earing.

ཨེ་ཁང་ (ēgaŋ) shung. an office in the tt. where letters and documents were copied.

ཨེ་ཁུང་ (īguŋ) sm. ཨི་ཁུང་.

ཨེ་ལིང་ (ēliŋ) Asia.

ཨེ་འགྲོ་རྒྱ་སྐད་ མི་འགྲོ་སོག་སྐད་ (ēndro gyagɛɛ̀ mindro söggɛɛ̀) sm. འགྲོ་ཆོད་བལྟ་.

ཨེ་ཆུང་བ་ (ījuŋwə) little finger, pinky.

ཨེ་ཐུབ་ལྟ་ (ētub dā) va. to see if one can do sth. or not.

ཨེ་དྲུང་ (ēdruŋ) shung. clerk in ཨེ་ཁང་.

ཨེ་ནི་ (ēni) sm. ཨ་ནི་.

ཨེ་པ་ (ēba) shung. a person trained for copying government documents who works in the ཨེ་ཁང་.

ཨེ་པ་ཡོན་བདག (ēba yöndaà) shung. head/ chief of ཨེ་ཁང་.

ཨེ་པི་གསར་སྤེལ་ལས་ཁང་ (ēbi sārbel lɛ̀ɛgaŋ) Association Press (AP).

ཨེ་ཕྲུག (īdruù) shung. name of young boys recruited as a tax to be trained for copying government documents (in ཨེ་ཁང་).

ཨེ་བྲིས་ (ēdrii) a type of caligraphy used by government clerks/ copyists.

ཨེ་མ་ (ēma) sm. གཡེར་མ་.

ཨེ་མ་ཁྲ་སི་ (ēmadrasi) a low quality gem.

ཨེ་ཡིན་ (ēyin) probably (it) is not.

ཨེ་ཡོང་ (ēyoŋ) probably it is not/ will not ༈ང་འདིར་སྡོད་ནྲོས་བཙོད་ཨེ་ཡོང་ I probably won't dare to stay here.

ཨེ་ཡོང་མགོ་དཀར་ (ēyoŋ gogar) becoming old without getting a suitable partner.

ཨེ་རིས་ (ērii) sm. ཨེ་བྲིས་.

ཨེ་ཤི་ཡ་ (ēshiya) Asia.

ཨེ་ཤི་ཡ་ལྟ་རྟོག་ཚོགས་པ་ (ēshiya dādoò tsɔ̄gba) Asia Watch.

ཨེ་ཤི་ཡ་དང་ཞི་བདེ་རྒྱ་མཚོའི་དཔལ་འབྱོར་མཉམ་སྦྲེལ་མཐུན་ཚོགས་ (ēshiyadaŋ shide gyatsö pɛ̄njɔɔ ñamdree tǖndzɔɔ̀) Asia-Pacific Economic Council (APEC).

ཨེ་ཤི་ཡ་ཚོགས་པ་ (ēshiya tsɔ̄gba) Asia Society.

ཨེ་ཤི་ཡ་ཡར་རྒྱས་ཀྱི་དངུལ་ཁང་ (ēshiya yargyɛɛ̀gi ŋṻügaŋ) Asian Development Bank.

ཨེ་ཤི་ཡ་ཤར་རྒྱུད་ (ēshiya shārgyüü) Far East.

ཨེ་ཤི་ཡའི་རང་དབང་རླུང་འཕྲིན་ (ēshiya raŋwaŋ lūŋdrin) Radio Free Asia.

ཨེ་གསང་ (ēsaŋ) vagina.

ཨེ་ཨེན་སི་ཞེས་པའི་ཨ་ཕི་རི་ཀའི་ཚབ་སྲིད་ཚོགས་པ་ (ē ēnsi sheèbɛ ābi rige cə̄bsiì tsɔ̄gba) African National Congress (ANC).

ཨེང་ཀེ་སི་ (ēŋgesi) Engels.

ཨེན་ (ēn) few, a little bit, not many.

ཨེན་ཅིག (ēnjig) sm. ཨེན་.

ཨེན་ཅུང་ (ēnjuŋ) sm. དཀོན་ཅུང་.

ཨེན་ཙམ་ (ēndzam) sm. ཨེན་.

ཨེན་ཙམ་མིན་ན་ (ēndzam minnə) sm. ཧྲག་ཙམ་མ་གཏོགས་.

ཨེབ་རོ་ཨེ་ཤན་ (ēbro ēshɛn) Afro-Asian.

ཨེབ་གསར་ (ēbsar) sm. ཨ་གསར་.

ཨེམ་ཆི་ (ēmji) mong. physician, doctor; va.—བསྟེན་ to consult a doctor; va.—བྱེད་ to act/ work as a doctor.

ཨེམ་ཆིའི་ལས་རོགས་ (ēmjii lɛ̀ɛrɔɔ̀) physician's assistant, paramedic.

ཨེམ་རྗེ་ (ēmje) sm. ཨེམ་ཆི་.

ཨེམ་ཏི་ཝི་ཞེས་པའི་རོལ་གཞས་ཀྱི་བརྙན་འཕྲིན་ (ēmdiwi sheèbɛ cööshɛɛ̀gi ñɛ̄ndrin) MTV.

ཨེར་ཀ་ (ērga) eng. ace (in playing cards).

ཨེར་ཀོག་གཞུ་ (ērgɔɔ̀ shu) va. to hit with one's finger (by flicking one's finger).

ཨེར་ཁ་ (ērga) small bells.

ཨེར་དེ་ནི་ (ērdeni) title for the Panchen Lama of Tibet originally given by the Kangxi Emperor to the 5th Panchen Lama.

ཨེར་ཕྲུག (ērdruù) small bells usually placed on dog's collars.

ཨོ་རྒྱན་པད་མ་ (ōrgyɛn bɛ̀ɛma) Padmasambava.

ཨོ་རྒྱན་རིན་པོ་ཆེ་ (ōrgyɛn rimboje) sm. ཨོ་རྒྱན་པད་མ་.

ཨོ་མོ་སུ་ (ōmosu) socks.

ཨོ་མོ་སུ་ལུ་ (ōmo sūlu) sm. ཨོ་མོ་སུ་.

ཨོ་ཙི་ (ōdzi) so so.

ཨོ་ཚོད་ (ōdzöö̀) guessing, surmising, conjecturing; va.—བྱེད་ ༈ལས་ཀ་བྱེད་སྟངས་མ་ཤེས་ན་འགོ་ཁྲིད་ལ་སྐད་ཆ་འདྲི་དགོས་པ་ལས་ཨོ་ཚོད་བྱ་རྒྱུ་མེད་ If you don't know how to do the work, you must ask the leader rather than guess.

ཨོ་ཚོད་ཚོད་ (ō tsöö̀dzöö̀) sm. ཨོ་ཚོད་ཚོད་ཚ་པོ་.

ཨོ་ཚོད་ཚོད་ཚ་པོ་ (ō tsȫö̀dzöö̀ tsābo) 1. a person who does things without really knowing but guesses/ conjectures/ surmises. 2. unreliable, undependable ༈ཁ་ས་ཁྱེད་རང་ཕེབས་རྒྱུ་གཏན་གཏན་གནང་ཡང་ཕེབས་མ་བྱུང་ ཁྱེད་རང་ཨོ་ཚོད་ཚོད་ཚ་པོ་འདུག You were to come yesterday but you didn't so you are very unreliable.

ཨོ་ཟོབ་ (ōsob) pretending to know; va.—བྱེད་.

ཨོ་འོའི་ (ōwo) exclamation conveying doubts.

ཨོ་ཡོ་ (ōyo) sm. ཨུ་ཡོ་.

ཨོ་རོང་ཇུན་གར་ (ōroŋ jüngar) shung. Dzungar (a Mongol tribe).

ཨོ་ལིན་ཕིག་ལུས་རྩལ་འགྲན་ཚོགས་ (lōlinbiì lṳ̈üdzɛɛ drḛndzɔɔ̀) eng.tib. Olympic Games.

ཨོ་ལོ་ (ōlo) 1. boy. 2. tea servers in the Monlam Prayer Festival.

ཨོ་ཤེ་ (ōshe) an exclamation made when begging or pleading: please.

ཨོ་ཤེས་ (ōsheè) sm. ཨོ་ཤེ་.

ཨོ་སུན་ (ōsün) ch. a kind of vegetable.

ཨོ་སོར་ (ōsɔɔ) ch. wrench.

ཨོཾ་ (ōm) the mantra "om".

ཨོག་ཀོར་ (ōggɔɔ) sm. ཨོག་སྐོར་.

ཨོག་སྐོར་ (ōggɔɔ) front of the neck.

ཨོག་རྒྱ་ (ōggya) sm. ཨོག་ཚོམ་.

ཨོག་སྒྲོག (ōgdrɔɔ̀) 1. hat strap. 2. stitching under the sleeve to the hem of a garment.

ཨོག་འཇོལ་ (ōŋjöö) the flabby skin under the neck of ox/ cows/ etc.

ཨོག་དི་ (ōgdi) an infection under the neck of a horse.

ཨོག་སྡེགས་ (ōgdeg) a support put under the chin when meditating (to keep the head up); va.—རྒྱག.

ཨོག་དོང་ (ɔ̄gdoŋ) larynx, windpipe.

ཨོག་དོམ་ (ɔ̄gdom) a red tassle (indicating rank) hung around the neck of the horses of tt. officials.

ཨོག་མདུད་ཐེབས་ (ɔ̄gdüǜ tēb) vi. to have (sweat) pouring down on the cheeks.

ཨོག་རྡོག (ɔ̄gdɔɔ̀) adam's apple.

ཨོག་བལ་ (ɔ̄gbɛɛ) shung. wool from the throat area of sheep.

ཨོག་མ་ (ɔ̄gna) the chin.

ཨོག་ཚར་ (ɔ̄gdzar) sm. ཨོག་ཚོམ་.

ཨོག་ཚོམ་ (ɔ̄gdzom) goatee, chin beard.

ཨོག་འཛུམ་ (ɔ̄gdzum) wrinkle under the lower lip caused by smiling.

ཨོག་ཞོལ་ (ɔ̄gshöö) sm. ཨོག་འཇོལ་.

ཨོག་རིལ་ (ɔ̄grii) sm. ཨོང་རིལ་.

ཨོག་ལིན་ (ɔ̄glen) ch. violin.

ཨོག་ལིན་འབྲིང་པ་ (ɔ̄glen drḭŋwə) viola.

ཨོང་ (ōŋ) sm. ཀུབ་.

ཨོང་བཀྱག (ōŋgyaà) chair.

ཨོང་གོང་ (ōŋgoŋ) rear end, ass.

ཨོང་དི་ (ōŋdi) baby donkey.

ཨོང་དུ་ (ōŋdu) woman's underwear.

ཨོང་སྡེགས་ (ōŋdeg) chair.

ཨོང་ཐག (ōŋdaà) the woolen strap placed under the tail of yaks to keep the saddle from moving forward.

ཨོང་དོ་ (ōŋdo) sm. ཀུབ་.

ཨོང་པ་ (ōŋwa) dry cow dung.

ཨོང་རས་ (ōŋrɛɛ̀) sm. ཨང་རག.

ཨོང་རིལ་ (ōŋrii) dung (horses, donkeys and mules).

ཨོང་ཤ་ (ōŋsha) buttocks.

ཨོམ་ (ōm) 1. long poles for erecting prayer flags; va.—རྒྱག to erect a large prayer flag; to pile up poles in a tepee shape.

ཨོམ་རྡོར་ (ōmdɔɔ) sm. ཨོམ་དོར་.

ཨོམ་དོར་ (ōmdɔɔ) the boss, the man in charge.

ཨོམ་པོ་ (ōmbo) sm. དཔོན་པོ་.

ཨོམ་རྒུགས་ (ōmdzuù) taking a rest by putting one's chin on a walking stick; va.—བྱེད་.

ཨོམ་ཤིང་ (ōmshiŋ) sm. ཨོམ་.

ཨོའུ་གླིང་ (ōōliŋ) ch.tib. European continent.

ཨོའི་རིས་ (ōōrii) sm. ཨོང་རིལ་.

ཨོའི་ལགས་ (ōōlaà) h. of གཅུང་པོ་; གཅུང་མོ་ and younger relatives of either gender.

ཨོའོ་ལིན་པེ་ཁེ་ལུས་རྩལ་ཚོགས་པ་ (ōōlenbeke lṳ̈ǜdzɛɛ tsɔ̄gba) the Olympic Games.

ཨོར་ (ɔ̄r) sm. དཔོར་.

ཨོར་ཁང་ (ɔ̄rguŋ) sm. ཕྱི་ཁ་.

ཨོར་ཆུ་ (ōrju) sm. དབར་ཆུ་.

ཨོར་གདུམ་ཚ་པོ་ (ōrdum tsābo) sm. ཨུ་ཚུགས་ཚ་པོ་.

ཨོར་དོམ་སྦོ་ལོ་ (ɔ̄rdom bōlo) football (American style).

ཨོར་འདོམ་ (ɔ̄rdom) sm. རང་ཤེད་.

ཨོར་འདོམ་སྦོ་ལོ་ (ɔ̄rdom bōlo) football (American style) ༑ ཨ་མི་རི་ཀའི་ཨོར་འདོམ་སྦོ་ལོའི་མཐུན་ཚོགས་ American Football League (AFL).

ཨོར་འདོམ་སྦོ་ལོ་ཚོགས་པ་ (ɔ̄rdom bōlo tsɔ̄gba) American Football Conference (AFC).

ཨོར་པ་ (ɔ̄rba) sm. ཕྱི་ཆུ་.

ཨོར་པོ་ (ɔ̄rbo) sm. དཔོར་པོ་.

ཨོར་སྦོག (ɔ̄rbɔɔ̀) shung. the shoulder padding worn by the monks in charge of monastic discipline and dobdos.

ཨོལ་སྐོ་ (ȫȫgo) chin.

ཨོལ་གྲོང་ (ȫȫdroŋ) windpipe.

ཨོལ་ཁུང་ (ȫȫguŋ) drain.

ཨོལ་གོང་ (ȫȫgoŋ) front of the neck.

ཨོལ་སྐོའི་ཚ་ནད་ (ȫȫgö tsānɛɛ̀) laryngitis.

ཨོལ་ཅོག (ȫȫjoò) windpipe.

ཨོལ་མདུད་ (ȫȫdüǜ) adam's apple.

ཨོལ་བ་ (ȫȫwa) sm. ཨོལ་གོང་.

ཨོྒྱན་ (ōrgyɛn) abbr. of ཨོ་རྒྱན་.